1 Stock, 100 Soups

1 Stock, 100 Soups

Linda Doeser

LOVE FOOD

First published in 2009
Love Food ® is an imprint of Parragon Books Ltd

Parragon
Queen Street House
4 Queen Street
Bath BA1 1HE, UK

ISBN: 978-1-4075-7494-3

Printed in China

Written by Linda Doeser
Internal design by Simon Levy
Photography by Mike Cooper
Home economy by Lincoln Jefferson

Notes for the Reader
This book uses imperial, metric, and US cup measurements. Follow the same units of measurement throughout; do not mix imperial and metric. All spoon measurements are level: teaspoons are assumed to be 5 ml, and tablespoons are assumed to be 15 ml. Unless otherwise stated, milk is assumed to be whole, eggs and individual vegetables such as potatoes are medium, and pepper is freshly ground black pepper.

The times given are an approximate guide only. Preparation times differ according to the techniques used by different people and the cooking times may also vary from those given as a result of the type of oven used. Optional ingredients, variations, or serving suggestions have not been included in the calculations.

Recipes using raw or very lightly cooked eggs should be avoided by infants, the elderly, pregnant women, convalescents, and anyone with a chronic condition. Pregnant and breastfeeding women are advised to avoid eating peanuts and peanut products. People with nut allergies should be aware that some of the prepared ingredients used in the recipes in this book may contain nuts. Always check the packaging before use.

Contents

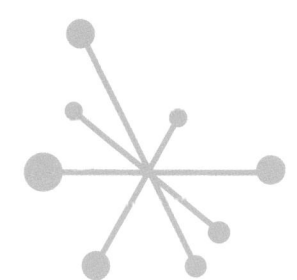

6 Introduction

12 Hearty

58 Tasty

100 Stylish

134 Cool

172 World Classics

222 Index

Introduction

It must have been a great, if unsung, moment in the history of civilization when one of our enterprising prehistoric ancestors first put some roots and aromatics into a pot of water and heated it over a fire. Although today's cooking methods are somewhat less primitive and ingredients are more sophisticated and varied, soup remains one of the easiest dishes to prepare, while still being tasty, nourishing, versatile, easy to digest, and the ultimate comfort food.

Soups may be served hot or chilled, they can be a first course or a meal-in-a bowl, they may be hearty and rustic, elegant and subtle, thick and creamy, or delicate and clear, and can incorporate almost every imaginable ingredient from meat and poultry to vegetables and fruit and from cheese and eggs to fish and shellfish. Virtually every cuisine in the world features at least one—and usually many—soup recipes based on local ingredients and preferences.

The hundred recipes in this book celebrate the immense versatility of soup. Whatever your taste and whatever the occasion, you are sure to find a recipe to suit you. If you're looking for a first course for a dinner party, try Stylish Soups with its collection of clear broths and special flavors or, if it's summer time, Cool Soups with both familiar and unusual chilled delights.

Hearty Soups offers a profusion of great ideas for economical yet satisfying family meals, while Tasty Soups are perfect winter warmers and restoratives for anyone feeling under the weather. For an international flavor, turn to World Classics, which features recipes as varied as a simple yet delicious Greek egg and lemon soup, an unusual sweet and sour onion soup from Iran, Thailand's spicy signature dish Tom Yam Goong, and a bacon and split pea soup from England. All of the recipes are easy to follow, many of them are surprisingly quick to prepare, all of them taste fabulous, and, best of all, they are all based on one basic vegetable stock (see page 10).

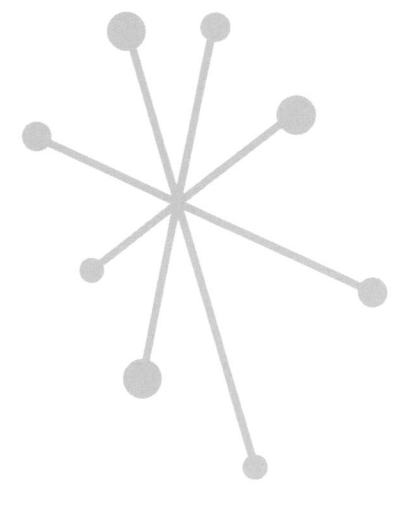

Making and adapting stock

Obviously, any soup can be made using water as the basic liquid and a few fairly unusual recipes always are. However, as a general rule, the flavor is enriched and intensified with a good-quality stock, which also adds to the nutritional value and helps give "eye appeal." Stock can be made from many different ingredients, and restaurant kitchens will have at least a basic collection of chicken, beef, and possibly other meat, fish, shellfish, and vegetable stocks at hand. This would be demanding for even the most enthusiastic home cook, and as most of us are preparing only family meals, an entire freezer would have to be allocated to their storage.

Vegetable stock has been chosen as the basis of the soups in this book for a variety of reasons. It is relatively unusual for any soup, whether featuring chicken, meat, fish, mushrooms, sausages, or whatever, not to include some vegetables, so it will always go well with other ingredients. Of course, some of the best-loved soups are, in any case, vegetable broths. While it is flavorful, it is not so strong that it will overpower other delicate ingredients. It is acceptable to both meat eaters and vegetarians. Finally, it is easier, more economical, and quicker to make a tasty vegetable stock than any other type.

The basic recipe is for what is known as a light stock, meaning its color not its flavor, and it is suitable for all the soups in the book (and many others). The ingredients are widely available and inexpensive, but you can substitute other vegetables if you particularly dislike one ingredient, you have others at hand or you want to enhance the flavor of a special soup for a particular occasion. All members of the onion family can be used, as well as those suggested. Both fresh and dried mushrooms will add an earthy flavor that some people relish, while others appreciate the sweetness imparted by corn. However, some vegetables should be used with caution. Any members of the cabbage family, including Brussels sprouts and kohlrabi, are likely to overpower other flavors. Fennel has a distinctive aniseed flavor that won't go with everything but works well with fish and shellfish soups.

Leftover cooked vegetables have neither the flavor nor the nutritional content for making a good stock, but you can make beneficial use of some trimmings. Once again, beware of the cabbage family and avoid onion skins, which can make the stock bitter; however, the outer leaves of lettuce, broccoli, and cauliflower, mushroom stems, chard stems, and trimmings from asparagus spears and green beans will all add extra flavor—and at no extra cost. Sometimes the water in which vegetables have been cooked can be substituted for some of the water in the recipe—that from cooking asparagus, broccoli, cauliflower, chard, corn cobs, and green beans, for example.

The basic recipe can easily be adapted to make a brown stock, which has a deeper flavor and color and is especially suitable for meat soups. Substitute 2–3 large tomatoes for the potato, parsnips, and turnip. Cook the onion, leeks, celery, and carrots over very low heat, stirring occasionally, for about 30 minutes, until they are a rich golden brown. Meanwhile, broil the halved tomatoes until they are golden brown. Add the tomatoes in step 2 with the herbs.

Whatever vegetables you use for the stock and however you cook it, it is advisable not to season it with salt during cooking. As the stock becomes more concentrated, it can become unpleasantly salty. There is an even greater risk of this if you concentrate the stock even more later. Adding salt is best left until you make the soup. This also applies to the addition of spices.

For clarifying stock to make jewel-clear broths, see Jellied Vegetable Consommé (page 165).

Because stock can be stored in the freezer for up to 3 months, it is worth making a large batch. Freeze it in measured quantities, such as 2 cups, so it is easy to remove the amount you need to use for a particular soup.

So as the temperature drops outside in those long winter months, delicious and nutritious soups can be quickly and easily created for instant warmth. Whether you are entertaining guests, feeding the family, or need something tasty to serve at an impromptu gathering, soup wins every time—your only problem will be choosing which one to serve!

Basic Vegetable Stock

This is the recipe that all 100 variations of soup in the book are based on. For each recipe the basic stock is highlighted (✳) for easy reference, so then all you have to do is follow the easy steps each time and a world of delicious and delectable soups will await you.

Makes 4 cups

- ✳ 2 tbsp sunflower oil
- ✳ 1 onion, finely chopped
- ✳ 2 leeks, thinly sliced
- ✳ 2 celery stalks, finely chopped
- ✳ 1 large potato, diced
- ✳ 2 carrots, thinly sliced
- ✳ 2 small parsnips, thinly sliced
- ✳ 1 small turnip, thinly sliced
- ✳ 2 bay leaves
- ✳ 6 fresh parsley sprigs
- ✳ ⅔ cup dry white wine
- ✳ 4 cups water

1. Heat the oil in a large pan. Add the onion, leeks, celery, and potato and cook over a low heat, stirring frequently, for about 8 minutes, until softened and just beginning to color.

2. Add the carrots, parsnips, turnip, bay leaves, parsley sprigs, and white wine, stir well, and cook for 2 minutes, until the alcohol has evaporated. Increase the heat to medium, pour in the water, and bring to a boil. Reduce the heat, cover, and simmer for 1 hour.

3. Remove the pan from the heat and strain the basic vegetable stock into a bowl through a fine strainer, pressing the vegetables with the back of a ladle to extract as much liquid as possible; do not press the vegetables through the strainer. Strain again and let cool completely, then cover with plastic wrap, and store in the refrigerator for up to 2 days. Alternatively, freeze for up to 3 months.

Hearty

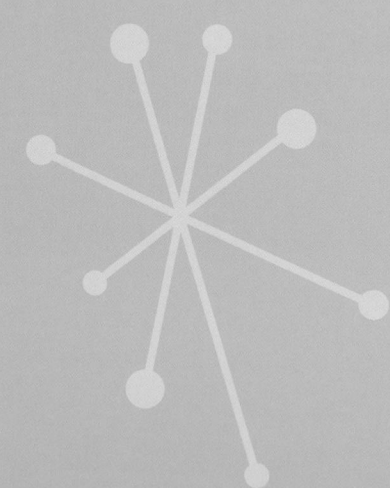

Summer Tomato Soup

1. Heat the olive oil in a large, heavy pan. Add the onion, scallions, garlic, and celery and cook over low heat, stirring occasionally, for 5 minutes, until softened. Add the tomatoes, cover, and simmer, stirring occasionally, for 50 minutes, until thickened.

2. Remove the pan from the heat and let cool slightly. Transfer the mixture to a food processor or blender, in batches if necessary, and process to a smooth puree, then pass the puree through a strainer into a clean pan.

3. Add the basic vegetable stock and bring to a boil, stirring constantly. Season to taste with cayenne, salt, and pepper, add the pasta, and bring back to a boil. Boil over medium heat for 8–10 minutes, until the pasta is tender, but still firm to the bite.

4. Meanwhile, make the garnish. Melt the butter in a small skillet. Add the parsley sprigs, in batches, and cook for a few seconds, then turn and cook for a few seconds more. Remove from the skillet and drain on paper towels.

5. Taste the soup and adjust the seasoning, if necessary. Ladle into warmed bowls, sprinkle with the fried parsley, and serve immediately.

Serves 6

3 tbsp olive oil

1 large onion, finely chopped

4 scallions, finely chopped

3 garlic cloves, finely chopped

2 celery stalks, finely chopped

1 lb 12 oz/800 g tomatoes, peeled and chopped

* 3 cups basic vegetable stock

pinch of cayenne pepper

¾ cup stellette or other small pasta shapes

salt and pepper

To garnish

6 tbsp sweet butter

12 fresh flat-leaf parsley sprigs

Tomato & White Bean Soup

Serves 6

- 3 tbsp olive oil
- 1⅔ cups chopped red onions
- 1 celery stalk with leaves, chopped
- 1 red bell pepper, seeded and chopped
- 2 garlic cloves, finely chopped
- 4 cups peeled and chopped plum tomatoes
- * 5⅔ cups basic vegetable stock
- 2 tbsp tomato paste
- 1 tsp sugar
- 1 tbsp sweet paprika
- 1 tbsp butter
- 1 tbsp all-purpose flour
- 14 oz/400 g canned cannellini beans, drained and rinsed
- salt and pepper
- 3 tbsp chopped fresh flat-leaf parsley, to garnish

1. Heat the olive oil in a large pan. Add the onions, celery, bell pepper, and garlic and cook over low heat, stirring occasionally, for 5 minutes, until softened.

2. Increase the heat to medium, add the tomatoes, and cook, stirring occasionally, for 5 minutes more, then pour in the basic vegetable stock. Stir in the tomato paste, sugar, and sweet paprika and season to taste with salt and pepper. Bring to a boil, reduce the heat, and simmer for 15 minutes.

3. Meanwhile, mash together the butter and flour to a paste in a small bowl with a fork. Stir the paste, in small pieces at a time, into the soup. Make sure each piece is fully incorporated before adding the next.

4. Add the beans, stir well, and simmer for another 5 minutes, until heated through. Sprinkle with the parsley and serve immediately.

3

Barley, Lentil & Onion Soup

1. Put the barley into a large pan, pour in the water, and bring to a boil. Reduce the heat, cover, and simmer gently, stirring frequently, for about 30 minutes, until all the liquid has been absorbed.

2. Add the basic vegetable stock, onions, lentils, ginger, and cumin and bring to a boil over medium heat. Reduce the heat, cover, and simmer, stirring occasionally, for 1½ hours, adding a little more stock if necessary.

3. Meanwhile, make the garnish. Spread out the onions on a thick layer of paper towels and cover with another thick layer. Let dry out for 30 minutes. Heat the oil in a skillet. Add the onions and cook over low heat, stirring constantly, for about 20 minutes, until well browned. Add the garlic and cook, stirring constantly, for 5 minutes more. Remove the onions with a slotted spoon and drain well on paper towels.

4. Season the soup to taste with salt and pepper, stir in the lemon juice and cilantro, and simmer for another 5 minutes. Serve immediately, garnished with the browned onions.

Serves 6

2 tbsp pearl barley
⅔ cup water
* 7½ cups basic vegetable stock
1 lb 2 oz/500 g onions, thinly sliced into rings
⅔ cup Puy lentils
½ tsp ground ginger
1 tsp ground cumin
3 tablespoons lemon juice
2 tbsp chopped fresh cilantro
salt and pepper

To garnish

2 onions, halved and thinly sliced
5 tbsp vegetable oil
2 garlic cloves, finely chopped

Green Vegetable Soup

1. Pour the basic vegetable stock into a pan and bring to a boil. Meanwhile, heat the oil in a large pan. Add the leeks and cook over low heat, stirring occasionally, for 5 minutes, until softened, then remove the pan from the heat.

2. Stir in the flour until fully incorporated, then gradually stir in the hot stock, a little at a time. Season with salt and pepper and add the thyme and fennel seeds.

3. Return the pan to the heat and bring to a boil, stirring constantly. Add the lettuce, spinach, peas, watercress, and mint and bring back to a boil. Boil, stirring constantly, for 3–4 minutes, then reduce the heat, cover, and simmer gently for 30 minutes.

4. Remove the soup from the heat and let cool slightly. Ladle it into a food processor or blender, in batches if necessary, and process to a smooth puree. Return the soup to the rinsed-out pan and reheat, stirring occasionally. When it is piping hot, ladle into warmed bowls, sprinkle with the parsley, and serve with garlic and herb bread.

Serves 6

- generous 6¾ cups basic vegetable stock
- 3 tablespoons olive oil
- 2 leeks, white parts only, chopped
- 2 tbsp all-purpose flour
- 1 tsp dried thyme
- ½ tsp fennel seeds
- 1 Boston lettuce, coarsely chopped
- 1 lb 2 oz/500 g spinach, coarse stalks removed
- 2½ cups shelled fresh or frozen peas
- 1 bunch of watercress or arugula
- 4 tbsp chopped fresh mint
- salt and pepper
- 2 tbsp chopped fresh parsley, to garnish
- garlic and herb bread, to serve

5

Squash & Lentil Soup

1. Heat the oil in a large pan. Add the onions and garlic and cook over low heat, stirring occasionally, for 5 minutes, until softened. Add the cumin, cinnamon, nutmeg, ginger, and coriander and cook, stirring constantly, for 1 minute.

2. Stir in the butternut squash and lentils and cook, stirring constantly for 2 minutes, then pour in the basic vegetable stock, and bring to a boil over medium heat. Reduce the heat and simmer, stirring occasionally, for 50–60 minutes, until the vegetables are tender.

3. Remove from the heat and let cool slightly, then ladle into a food processor or blender, in batches if necessary, and process to a smooth puree.

4. Return the soup to the rinsed-out pan, stir in the lemon juice, season to taste with salt and pepper, and reheat gently. Ladle into warmed bowls, top with a swirl of crème fraîche, and serve.

Serves 6

3 tbsp olive oil

2 large onions, chopped

2 garlic cloves, chopped

2 tsp ground cumin

1 tsp ground cinnamon

½ tsp freshly grated nutmeg

½ tsp ground ginger

½ tsp ground coriander

2 lb 4 oz/1 kg butternut squash or pumpkin, seeded, and cut into small chunks

1½ cups red or yellow lentils

* 7½ cups basic vegetable stock

3 tbsp lemon juice

salt and pepper

crème fraîche or strained plain yogurt, to garnish

Ribollita

1. Put half the beans into a food processor and process briefly to a coarse puree. Scrape into a bowl and set aside.

2. Heat the oil in a large pan. Add the onion, leek, garlic, carrots, and celery and cook over low heat, stirring occasionally, for 8–10 minutes. Add the potatoes and zucchini and cook, stirring constantly, for 2 minutes.

3. Add the tomatoes, tomato paste, and dried chile, if using, and cook, stirring constantly, for 3 minutes, then stir in the bean puree. Cook, stirring constantly, for 2 minutes more.

4. Pour in the basic vegetable stock and add the black cabbage and savoy cabbage. Bring to a boil, reduce the heat, and simmer for 2 hours.

5. Meanwhile, preheat the broiler. Rub the bread with the halved garlic cloves and toast on both sides.

6. Stir the whole beans into the soup and heat through gently for 10 minutes. Season with salt and pepper. Put the garlic-flavored bread in the base of warmed soup bowls and ladle the soup over it. Drizzle with a little oil and serve immediately.

Serves 6

14 oz/400 g canned cannellini beans, drained and rinsed

3 tbsp olive oil, plus extra for drizzling

1 Bermuda onion, chopped

1 leek, chopped

4 garlic cloves, finely chopped

2 carrots, diced

2 celery stalks, chopped

2 potatoes, diced

2 zucchini, diced

2 large tomatoes, peeled, seeded, and chopped

1 tsp sun-dried tomato paste

1 dried chile, crushed (optional)

* 7½ cups basic vegetable stock

2½ cups shredded black cabbage, kale, or Swiss chard

2½ cups shredded savoy cabbage

6 slices of ciabatta

2 garlic cloves, halved

salt and pepper

7

Bacon & Potato Soup

1. Heat the olive oil in a large pan. Add the bacon, onions, and garlic and cook over medium heat, stirring frequently, for 5–7 minutes, until the bacon is crisp and the onions are lightly browned.
2. Pour in the basic vegetable stock and add the potatoes, cabbage, Worcestershire sauce, and mustard, season with pepper to taste, and mix well. Bring to a boil, then reduce the heat and simmer, stirring occasionally, for 30 minutes.
3. Remove the pan from the heat and let cool slightly, then transfer 2½ cups to a food processor or blender. Process briefly to a coarse puree and return to the pan. Stir well and return the soup to the heat. Cook, stirring frequently, for 5–10 minutes, until heated through. Season with salt to taste, stir in the parsley, and ladle into warmed bowls. Serve immediately with crusty rolls.

Serves 6

2 tbsp olive oil
1 cup chopped lean bacon
2 onions, chopped
2 garlic cloves, finely chopped
* 7½ cups basic vegetable stock
2⅓ cups diced potatoes
3 cups shredded savoy cabbage
1 teaspoon Worcestershire or Tabasco sauce
1 tsp Dijon mustard
3 tbsp finely chopped fresh flat-leaf parsley
salt and pepper
crusty rolls, to serve

Pork Soup with Bulgur Wheat

1. Heat the oil in a large pan. Add the pork, onions, and garlic, if using, and cook over medium heat, stirring occasionally, for 8 minutes, until the meat is lightly browned.

2. Pour in the wine and cook, stirring constantly, for 2 minutes, until the alcohol has evaporated, then pour in the basic vegetable stock. Reduce the heat, cover, and simmer for 15 minutes.

3. Add the bulgur wheat, season with salt and pepper, and cook for 15 minutes more, until the meat and wheat are tender and the soup has thickened.

4. Stir in the lemon juice. Taste and adjust the seasoning, if necessary. Serve the soup immediately, sprinkled with a little cayenne pepper and accompanied by soda bread and butter.

Serves 4–6

5 tablespoons olive oil
1 lb 2 oz/500 g boneless pork, diced
2 onions, chopped
2 garlic cloves, finely chopped (optional)
½ cup white wine
* 6¼ cups basic vegetable stock
generous 1 cup bulgur wheat
3 tablespoons lemon juice
pinch of cayenne pepper
salt and pepper
soda bread and butter, to serve

9

Salt Pork & Lentil Soup

Serves 6–8

- 8 oz/225 g salt pork, diced
- 2 tbsp olive oil
- 1 onion, chopped
- 3 garlic cloves, finely chopped
- 4 potatoes, diced
- 2¼ cups red lentils
- * 8¾ cups basic vegetable stock
- 1 bouquet garni (1 bay leaf, 1 fresh thyme sprig, and 3 fresh parsley sprigs, tied together)
- salt and pepper
- crusty bread, to serve

1. Put the salt pork into a large pan and cook over medium heat, stirring frequently, for 8–10 minutes, until it has released most of its fat and is browned all over. Remove from the pan with a slotted spoon and drain on paper towels. Set aside.

2. Add the oil to the pan and heat. Add the onion, garlic, and potatoes and cook over low heat, stirring occasionally, for 5 minutes, until the onion has softened. Stir in the lentils and cook, stirring constantly, for 5 minutes,.

3. Pour in the basic vegetable stock, increase the heat to medium, add the bouquet garni, and bring to a boil, stirring constantly. Reduce the heat, cover, and simmer for 1½–2 hours, until the lentils are very soft. Stir in the salt pork, season with salt and pepper, if necessary, and cook, stirring occasionally, for another 10 minutes, until heated through.

4. Remove the pan from the heat. Remove and discard the bouquet garni. Pour the soup into a warmed tureen and serve immediately with crusty bread.

10

Mixed Vegetable Soup with Lamb Meatballs

1. Put the onions, celeriac, rutabaga, carrots, potatoes, bell peppers, tomatoes, peas, and lemon slices into a large pan, pour in the basic vegetable stock, and season with salt and pepper. Bring to a boil, then reduce the heat, cover, and simmer for 25–30 minutes.

2. Meanwhile, make the meatballs. Combine the lamb, parsley, and rice in a bowl, kneading well until thoroughly mixed. Season with salt and pepper. Break off pieces of the mixture, about the size of golf balls, and shape them into balls between the palms of your hand. Dust with flour, shaking off the excess.

3. Add the meatballs to the soup, re-cover the pan, and cook, stirring occasionally, for 40–45 minutes more. Serve immediately.

Serves 6

2 onions, finely chopped

1 small celeriac, diced

½ rutabaga, diced

3 carrots, diced

2 potatoes, diced

2 red bell peppers, seeded and diced

4 tomatoes, peeled, seeded, and chopped

1 cup shelled fresh or frozen peas

1 lemon, sliced

* generous 6¾ cups basic vegetable stock

salt and pepper

Lamb meatballs

12 oz/350 g ground lamb

3 tbsp chopped fresh flat-leaf parsley

⅓ cup medium-grain rice

all-purpose flour, for dusting

salt and pepper

Beef Noodle Soup

Serves 6

- ¼ cup dried Chinese mushrooms or porcini mushrooms
- 3 tbsp corn oil
- 1 lb 2 oz/500 g lean beef, such as tenderloin or sirloin, cut into thin strips
- 3 medium carrots, cut into julienne strips
- 10 scallions, finely shredded
- 2 garlic cloves, finely chopped
- 1 tbsp finely chopped fresh ginger
- * 7½ cups basic vegetable stock
- 4 tbsp dark soy sauce
- 1 tbsp hoisin sauce
- 6 tbsp Chinese rice wine or dry sherry
- 5 oz/140 g egg noodles
- 1⅔ cups shredded spinach leaves
- pepper

1. Put the dried mushrooms into a bowl, pour in boiling water to cover, and let soak for 20 minutes. If using Chinese mushrooms, drain and rinse. If using porcini, drain, reserving the soaking water. Strain the soaking water through a fine strainer or coffee filter paper into a bowl.

2. Heat the oil in a large pan. Add the strips of beef and cook, stirring constantly, until browned all over. Remove with a slotted spoon and drain on paper towels.

3. Add the carrots, scallions, garlic, and ginger to the pan and cook, stirring constantly, for 5 minutes. Return the beef to the pan, pour in the basic vegetable stock, and add the soy sauce, hoisin sauce, and rice wine. Add the mushrooms and porcini soaking water, if using. Season with pepper and bring to a boil over medium heat, then reduce the heat and simmer for 15 minutes.

4. Add the noodles and spinach to the pan, stir well, and simmer for another 7–8 minutes. Taste and add more pepper or soy sauce, if necessary. Serve immediately.

Split Pea & Sausage Soup

Serves 6

- 6 oz/175 g boneless side of pork, cut into cubes
- 8¾ cups basic vegetable stock
- 1 onion, chopped
- 4 leeks, chopped
- 3 carrots, chopped
- 3 celery stalks, chopped
- 1 tart apple, peeled, cored, and chopped
- 1⅔ cups split peas, soaked overnight in cold water to cover, drained and rinsed
- 1 bouquet garni (2 fresh parsley sprigs, 1 fresh thyme sprig, and 1 fresh mint sprig)
- 1 tbsp molasses
- 4 bockwurst, Wienerwurst, or frankfurters, cut into 1-inch/2.5-cm lengths
- 2 tbsp butter
- salt and pepper
- crusty rye bread, to serve

1. Put the pork into a large pan and pour in the basic vegetable stock. Add the onion, leeks, carrots, celery, apple, peas, bouquet garni, and molasses and bring to a boil. Using a skimmer or slotted spoon, skim off any foam that rises to the surface, then reduce the heat, cover, and simmer, stirring occasionally, for 2 hours.

2. Season the soup to taste with salt and pepper and remove and discard the bouquet garni. Stir in the sausages and butter and simmer for another 5 minutes. Serve immediately with rye bread.

13

Sauerkraut & Sausage Soup

Serves 6

2 tbsp butter

1 tbsp all-purpose flour

1 tbsp sweet paprika

* 8¾ cups basic vegetable stock

1 lb 7 oz/650 g sauerkraut, drained

1 lb 2 oz/500 g smoked pork sausages, cut into 1-inch/2.5-cm slices

⅔ cup sour cream

salt and pepper

Dumplings

¾ cup white bread flour, plus extra for dusting

pinch of salt

1 extra large egg

1. Melt the butter in a large pan over low heat. Add the all-purpose flour and paprika and cook, stirring constantly, for 2 minutes, then remove the pan from the heat. Gradually stir in the basic vegetable stock, a little at a time, until fully incorporated and the mixture is smooth.
2. Return the pan to medium heat and bring to a boil, stirring constantly. Add the sauerkraut and sausages and season with salt and pepper. Reduce the heat, cover, and simmer for 30 minutes.
3. Meanwhile, make the dumplings. Sift together the flour and salt into a bowl. Beat the egg in another bowl, then gradually beat in the dry ingredients, a little at a time. Turn out onto a floured surface and knead until smooth. Cover and let rest for 15 minutes.
4. Divide the dough into 6 pieces and roll into sausage shapes. Flour your hands, pinch off pieces of the dough, and add to the soup. Re-cover the pan and simmer for 5 minutes more. Remove the pan from the heat, stir in the sour cream, and serve immediately.

Chicken & Lentil Soup

1. Heat the oil in a large pan. Add the onion, leeks, carrots, celery, and mushrooms and cook over low heat, stirring occasionally, for 5–7 minutes, until softened but not colored.

2. Increase the heat to medium, pour in the wine, and cook for 2–3 minutes, until the alcohol has evaporated, then pour in the basic vegetable stock. Bring to a boil, add the bay leaf and herbs, reduce the heat, cover, and simmer for 30 minutes.

3. Add the lentils, re-cover the pan, and simmer, stirring occasionally, for 40 minutes more, until they are tender.

4. Stir in the chicken, season to taste with salt and pepper, and simmer for another 5–10 minutes, until heated through. Serve immediately.

Serves 6

3 tbsp olive oil
1 large onion, chopped
2 leeks, chopped
2 carrots, chopped
2 celery stalks, chopped
scant 2½ cups chopped white mushrooms
4 tbsp dry white wine
* 5 cups basic vegetable stock
1 bay leaf
2 tsp dried mixed herbs
¾ cup Puy lentils
scant 2½ cups diced cooked chicken
salt and pepper

15

Chicken Soup with Matzo Balls

1. First, make the matzo balls. Melt 1 tbsp of the butter in a small skillet. Add the grated onion and cook over low heat, stirring occasionally, for 5 minutes, until softened. Remove from the heat and let cool.

2. Beat the remaining butter in a bowl until fluffy, then gradually beat in the egg and egg yolk. Add the parsley and onion, season with salt and pepper, and mix well, then beat in the water. Mix in the matzo crumbs until thoroughly incorporated. Cover and let rest in the refrigerator for 30 minutes.

3. Meanwhile, put the chicken into a large pan and pour in the basic vegetable stock. Bring to a boil over a medium–low heat, skimming off the foam that rises to the surface. Simmer for 15 minutes.

4. Add the chopped onion, celery, carrots, tomatoes, and parsley and season with salt and pepper. Reduce the heat, cover, and simmer for 50–60 minutes, until the chicken is cooked through and tender. Meanwhile, shape the matzo mixture into 18 balls.

5. Strain the soup into a clean pan, reserving the chicken quarters. Remove and discard the skin and bones and cut the meat into bite-size pieces. Add the chicken, vermicelli, and matzo balls to the pan, cover, and simmer gently for 20–30 minutes. Serve immediately.

Serves 6

2 chicken quarters
* 11¼ cups basic vegetable stock
2 onions, chopped
2 celery stalks, chopped
2 carrots, chopped
2 tomatoes, peeled and chopped
2 fresh parsley sprigs
2 oz/55 g vermicelli
salt and pepper

Matzo balls
4 tbsp butter
½ onion, grated
1 egg
1 egg yolk
1 tbsp finely chopped fresh parsley
1 tbsp water
2 cups crushed matzo crackers
salt and pepper

Chicken & Almond Soup

1. Melt the butter in a pan. Add the leeks and ginger and cook over low heat, stirring occasionally, for 5 minutes, until softened. Add the chicken, carrots, peas, chiles, and ground almonds and cook, stirring constantly, for 10 minutes.

2. Stir in the cilantro, remove from the heat, and let cool slightly. Spoon the chicken mixture into a food processor and process until very finely chopped. Add the basic vegetable stock and process to a puree.

3. Return the mixture to the pan, season with salt and pepper, and bring to a boil. Reduce the heat to very low and gradually stir in the cream; do not let the soup boil. Simmer, stirring frequently, for 2 minutes. Ladle into warmed bowls, sprinkle with chopped cilantro and ground almonds, and serve.

Serves 6

½ cup butter

2 leeks, chopped

1½ tbsp finely chopped fresh ginger

6 oz/175 g skinless, boneless chicken, diced

2 carrots, chopped

¾ cup shelled fresh or frozen peas

2 green chiles, seeded and chopped

1¼ cups ground almonds, plus extra to decorate

1 tbsp chopped fresh cilantro, plus extra to garnish

* generous 3 cups basic vegetable stock

1½ cups light cream

salt and pepper

17

Chicken Soup with Leeks & Rice

1. Heat the oil in a pan. Add the leeks and cook over low heat, stirring occasionally, for 5 minutes, until softened. Add the chicken, increase the heat to medium, and cook, stirring frequently, for 2 minutes. Add the rice and cook, stirring constantly, for 2 minutes more.

2. Pour in the basic vegetable stock, add the Worcestershire sauce and chives, and bring to a boil. Reduce the heat, cover, and simmer for 20–25 minutes.

3. Meanwhile, preheat the broiler. Broil the bacon for 2–4 minutes on each side, until crisp. Remove and let cool, then crumble.

4. Season the soup to taste with salt and pepper and stir in the parsley. Ladle into warmed bowls, sprinkle with the crumbled bacon, and serve.

Serves 6

2 tbsp olive oil

3 leeks, chopped

6 skinless, boneless chicken thighs, diced

generous ¼ cup long-grain rice

* 5⅔ cups basic vegetable stock

dash of Worcestershire sauce

6 fresh chives, chopped

6 thin bacon slices

2 tbsp chopped fresh flat-leaf parsley

salt and pepper

18

Fish Soup with Semolina & Dill Dumplings

1. Put the chorizo into a heavy pan and cook over medium–low heat, stirring frequently, for 5 minutes until lightly browned. Add the fish and cook, occasionally stirring gently, for 2 minutes.

2. Sprinkle in the paprika and cayenne, pour in the basic vegetable stock, and bring to a boil. Reduce the heat, cover, and simmer for 10 minutes.

3. Add the potatoes, tomatoes, and parsley, stir gently, re-cover the pan, and simmer for 10 minutes.

4. Meanwhile, make the semolina and dill dumplings. Combine the semolina, salt, and dill in a bowl. Lightly beat together the egg and milk in another bowl, then stir into the dry ingredients until thoroughly combined. Cover and let rest in the refrigerator for 10 minutes.

5. Scoop up tablespoonfuls of the dumpling mixture and add them to the soup. Season to taste with salt and pepper. Re-cover the pan and simmer for another 10 minutes. Serve immediately.

Serves 6

¾ cup diced chorizo

1 lb 2 oz/500 g white fish fillets, skinned and diced

1 tbsp sweet paprika

pinch of cayenne pepper

* 6¼ cups basic vegetable stock

4 potatoes, diced

4 tomatoes, peeled and diced

1 tbsp chopped fresh flat-leaf parsley

salt and pepper

Semolina and dill dumplings

½ cup fine semolina

pinch of salt

1 tbsp chopped fresh dill

1 egg

3 tbsp milk

19

Fish & Sweet Potato Soup

Serves 6

- 12 oz/350 g white fish fillet, skinned
- scant 1 cup diced sweet potato
- 1 onion, chopped
- 2 carrots, diced
- ½ tsp ground cinnamon
- * 7½ cups basic vegetable stock
- 14 oz/400 g clams
- ⅔ cup dry white wine
- 1 cup light cream
- salt and pepper
- chopped fresh flat-leaf parsley, to garnish
- extra virgin olive oil, for drizzling

1. Put the fish, sweet potato, onion, carrots, and cinnamon into a pan, pour in 4 cups of the basic vegetable stock, and bring to a boil. Reduce the heat, cover, and simmer for 30 minutes.

2. Meanwhile, scrub the clams under cold running water and remove any with broken shells or that do not shut immediately when sharply tapped. Put them into a pan, pour in the wine, cover, and cook over high heat, shaking the pan occasionally, for 3–5 minutes, until the clams have opened. Remove from the heat and lift out the clams with a slotted spoon, reserving the cooking liquid. Discard any clams that remain shut. Strain the cooking liquid through a fine strainer into a bowl.

3. Remove the pan of fish and vegetables from the heat and let cool slightly, then ladle the mixture into a food processor, in batches if necessary, and process until smooth.

4. Return the soup to the pan, add the remaining stock and the reserved cooking liquid, and bring back to a boil. Reduce the heat and gradually stir in the cream; do not let the soup boil. Add the clams, season to taste with salt and pepper, and simmer, stirring frequently, for 2 minutes, until heated through. Garnish with parsley, drizzle with olive oil, and serve immediately.

20

Clam & Pasta Soup

1. Heat the oil in a large pan. Add the onion and garlic and cook over low heat, stirring occasionally, for 5 minutes, until softened. Add the tomatoes, tomato paste, sugar, oregano, and basic vegetable stock and season with salt and pepper. Mix well and bring to a boil, then reduce the heat, cover, and simmer, stirring occasionally, for 10 minutes.

2. Meanwhile, scrub the clams under cold running water and discard any with broken shells or that do not shut immediately when sharply tapped. Put the clams into a pan, pour in the wine, cover, and cook over high heat, shaking the pan occasionally, for 3–5 minutes, until the clams have opened. Remove from the heat and lift out the clams with a slotted spoon, reserving the cooking liquid. Discard any clams that remain shut and remove the remainder from the half shells. Strain the reserved cooking liquid through a fine strainer into a bowl.

3. Add the pasta to the soup and simmer, uncovered, for 10 minutes. Add the clams and the reserved cooking liquid, stir well, and heat gently for 4–5 minutes; do not let the soup come back to a boil. If the soup is very thick, add a little hot water or stock. Taste and adjust the seasoning, if necessary, stir in the parsley, and serve immediately.

Serves 6

- 3 tbsp olive oil
- 1 Bermuda onion, finely chopped
- 3 garlic cloves, finely chopped
- 1 lb 5 oz/600 g canned chopped tomatoes
- 2 tbsp tomato paste
- 2 tsp sugar
- 1 tsp dried oregano
- * 4 cups basic vegetable stock
- 1 lb 2 oz/500 g clams
- ¾ cup dry white wine
- ¾ cup conchigliette or other small pasta shapes
- 3 tbsp chopped fresh flat-leaf parsley
- salt and pepper

21

Quick Sea Scallop Soup with Pasta

Serves 6

- 1 lb 2 oz/500 g shelled sea scallops
- 1½ cups milk
- generous 6¾ cups basic vegetable stock
- generous 1 cup frozen baby peas
- 6 oz/175 g taglialini
- 5 tbsp butter
- 2 scallions, finely chopped
- ¾ cup dry white wine
- 3 slices of prosciutto, cut into thin strips
- salt and pepper
- chopped fresh flat-leaf parsley, to garnish

1. Slice the sea scallops in half horizontally and season with salt and pepper.
2. Pour the milk and basic vegetable stock into a pan, add a pinch of salt, and bring to a boil. Add the peas and pasta, bring back to a boil, and cook for 8–10 minutes, until the taglialini is tender but still firm to the bite.
3. Meanwhile, melt the butter in a skillet. Add the scallions and cook over low heat, stirring occasionally, for 3 minutes. Add the sea scallops and cook for 45 seconds on each side. Pour in the wine, add the prosciutto, and cook for 2–3 minutes.
4. Stir the sea scallop mixture into the soup, taste, and adjust the seasoning, if necessary, and garnish with the parsley. Serve immediately.

22

Mediterranean Fish Soup with Garlic Mayonnaise

1. Cut out and discard the gills of any reserved fish heads. Cut the fish fillets into chunks. Put the fish bones, heads, and trimmings into a pan, pour in the wine vinegar, half the lemon juice, and the basic vegetable stock, add the herbes de Provence and bay leaves, and bring to a boil. Season with salt, reduce the heat, and simmer for 30 minutes.

2. Meanwhile, make the garlic mayonnaise. Pound the garlic with a pinch of salt in a mortar with a pestle. Transfer to a bowl, add the egg yolks, and whisk briefly with an electric mixer until creamy. Combine the oils in a pitcher and, whisking constantly, gradually add them to the egg mixture. When about half the oil has been incorporated, add the remainder in a thin, steady stream, whisking constantly. Stir in lemon juice to thin to the desired consistency. Transfer the mayonnaise to a sauce boat, cover, and set aside.

3. Strain the cooking liquid into a bowl and discard the contents of the strainer. Measure the cooking liquid and make up to 7½ cups with water, if necessary. Return it to the pan.

4. Beat the egg yolks with the remaining lemon juice in a bowl and stir it into the pan. Add the pieces of fish, stir gently to mix, and cook over low heat for 7–8 minutes, until the fish is tender and the soup has thickened. Do not let the soup boil.

5. Remove the pan from the heat and pour the soup into a warmed tureen. Serve immediately, handing the garlic mayonnaise separately and accompanied by toasted bread.

Serves 6

- 4 lb 8 oz/2 kg mixed white fish, such as gurnard, red snapper, grouper, and haddock, filleted, with bones, heads, and trimmings reserved
- 2 tbsp white wine vinegar
- 2 tbsp lemon juice
- * 7½ cups basic vegetable stock
- 2 tsp herbes de Provence
- 2 bay leaves
- 4 egg yolks
- salt and pepper
- toasted country bread, to serve

Garlic mayonnaise

- 4 garlic cloves
- 2 egg yolks
- ½ cup extra virgin olive oil
- ½ cup sunflower or safflower oil
- 1–2 tbsp lemon juice
- salt

Tasty

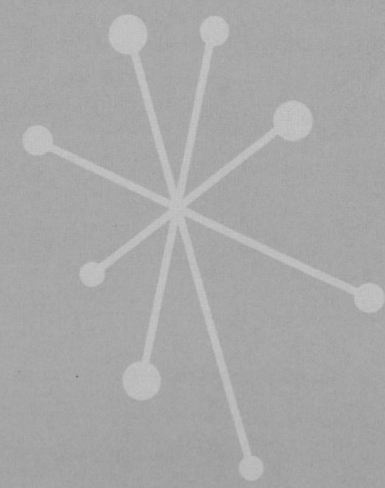

23

Carrot & Parsnip Soup

1. Put the carrots, parsnips, shallots, and chervil into a pan, pour in the basic vegetable stock, and season with salt and pepper. Bring to a boil, reduce the heat, and simmer for 20–25 minutes, until the vegetables are tender.

2. Remove the pan from the heat and let cool slightly. Remove and discard the chervil, then transfer to a food processor or blender, in batches if necessary, and process to a puree.

3. Return the soup to the rinsed-out pan and reheat gently. Ladle into warmed bowls, swirl about 1 tablespoon cream on the top of each, and serve.

Serves 6

1¾ cups chopped carrots
1¾ cups chopped parsnips
4 shallots, chopped
4 fresh chervil sprigs
* 3¾ cups basic vegetable stock
salt and pepper
heavy cream, to garnish

24

Carrot & Cilantro Soup

1. Heat the oil in a large pan. Add the onion and cook over low heat, stirring occasionally, for 5 minutes, until softened.
2. Add the potato and celery and cook, stirring occasionally, for another 5 minutes, then add the carrots, and cook, stirring occasionally, for 5 minutes more. Cover the pan, reduce the heat to very low, and cook, shaking the pan occasionally, for 10 minutes.
3. Pour in the basic vegetable stock and bring to a boil, then cover, and simmer for 10 minutes, until the vegetables are tender.
4. Meanwhile, melt the butter in a skillet. Add the coriander seeds and cook, stirring constantly, for 1 minute. Add the chopped cilantro and cook, stirring constantly, for 1 minute, then remove from the heat.
5. Remove the soup from the heat and let cool slightly. Transfer to a food processor or blender, in batches if necessary, and process to a puree. Return the soup to the rinsed-out pan, stir in the cilantro mixture and milk and season to taste with salt and pepper. Reheat gently, then serve, sprinkled with chopped cilantro.

Serves 6

3 tbsp olive oil
1 red onion, chopped
1 large potato, chopped
1 celery stalk, chopped
2¾ cups chopped carrots
* 4 cups basic vegetable stock
1 tbsp butter
2 tsp coriander seeds, crushed
1½ tbsp chopped fresh cilantro, plus extra to garnish
1 cup milk
salt and pepper

25

Cream of Tomato Soup

Serves 6

4 tbsp butter

1 onion, chopped

2 lb 4 oz/1 kg ripe tomatoes, peeled, seeded, and chopped

1 bay leaf

4 fresh basil sprigs

4 fresh parsley sprigs

7½ cups basic vegetable stock

1 tbsp ketchup

¾ cup heavy cream

salt and pepper

fresh basil leaves, to garnish

Croutons

2 slices day-old bread, crusts removed

2 tbsp olive oil

1. Melt the butter in a large pan. Add the onion and cook over low heat, stirring occasionally, for 5 minutes, until softened. Add the tomatoes, bay leaf, basil, and parsley, season with salt and pepper, and simmer, stirring occasionally, for 15 minutes, until the tomatoes have cooked down and most of the liquid has evaporated.

2. Increase the heat to medium, pour in the basic vegetable stock, and bring to a boil. Reduce the heat, cover, and simmer for 25 minutes.

3. Meanwhile, make the croutons. Cut the bread into ¼-inch/5-mm squares. Heat the oil in a skillet. Add the bread squares and cook, turning and tossing frequently, until golden brown all over. Remove with a slotted spoon and drain on paper towels.

4. Remove the soup from the heat and let cool slightly. Remove and discard the herbs and stir the ketchup into the soup. Transfer the soup to a food processor or blender, in batches if necessary, and process to a puree. If any tomato seeds remain, pass the puree through a fine strainer.

5. Return the soup to the rinsed-out pan and reheat. Stir in the cream and heat gently for 1–2 minutes more, until the soup is hot. Taste and adjust the seasoning, if necessary, and ladle into warmed bowls. Tear the basil leaves and sprinkle them over the soup, add the croutons, and serve immediately.

26

Tomato & Parsnip Soup

Serves 6

- 2 tbsp butter
- 2 onions, chopped
- 1 garlic clove, finely chopped
- 2¾ cups chopped parsnips
- 3 tbsp all-purpose flour
- ½ tsp dried thyme
- * 4 cups basic vegetable stock
- ⅔ cup milk
- 1 bay leaf
- 14 oz/400 g canned chopped tomatoes
- salt and pepper
- snipped fresh chives, to garnish

1. Melt the butter in a pan. Add the onions and garlic and cook over low heat, stirring occasionally, for 5 minutes, until softened. Add the parsnips and cook, stirring occasionally, for 5 minutes more.

2. Sprinkle in the flour and thyme, season with salt and pepper, and cook, stirring constantly, for 2 minutes. Remove the pan from the heat. Gradually stir in the basic vegetable stock, a little at a time, then stir in the milk and add the bay leaf and tomatoes.

3. Return the pan to medium heat and bring to a boil, stirring constantly. Reduce the heat, cover, and simmer for 45 minutes, until the parsnips are tender.

4. Remove the pan from the heat and let cool slightly. Remove and discard the bay leaf. Transfer the soup to a food processor or blender, in batches if necessary, and process to a puree.

5. Return the soup to the rinsed-out pan and reheat gently, stirring occasionally. Taste and adjust the seasoning, if necessary. Ladle into warmed bowls, garnish with snipped chives, and serve immediately.

27

Mushroom Soup

Serves 6

- 5 oz/140 g ciabatta or other rustic bread, crusts removed
- 4 tbsp butter
- 1 small onion, chopped
- 8½ cups coarsely chopped portobello mushrooms
- 1 garlic clove, finely chopped
- ½ tsp dried thyme
- ⅔ cup red wine or Madeira
- 4 cups basic vegetable stock
- salt and pepper

1. Tear the bread into pieces and put it into a bowl. Pour in cold water to cover and let soak for 10 minutes, then drain, and squeeze out.

2. Meanwhile, melt the butter in a large pan. Add the onion and cook over low heat, stirring occasionally, for 8–10 minutes, until golden. Add the mushrooms and garlic and cook, stirring frequently, for 5–7 minutes, until they have released their liquid.

3. Add the bread and thyme and pour in the wine. Cook for 2 minutes, until the alcohol has evaporated, then pour in the basic vegetable stock and bring to a boil over medium heat. Reduce the heat, cover, and simmer for 20–25 minutes.

4. Remove the pan from the heat and let cool slightly. Transfer the soup to a food processor or blender, in batches if necessary, and process to a puree.

5. Return the soup to the rinsed-out pan, season to taste with salt and pepper, and reheat gently, stirring occasionally. Ladle into warmed bowls and serve.

28

Mushroom & Ginger Soup

1. Heat the oil in a pan. Add the shallots and ginger and cook over low heat, stirring occasionally, for 5 minutes, until softened. Add the mushrooms and cook, stirring frequently, for 5–7 minutes, until they have released their liquid.

2. Pour in the basic vegetable stock and bring to a boil. Reduce the heat and simmer for 10 minutes.

3. Remove the pan from the heat and let cool slightly. Transfer the soup to a food processor or blender, in batches if necessary, and process to a puree.

4. Return to the rinsed out-pan, stir in the sour cream, season to taste with salt and pepper, and reheat gently, stirring occasionally. Ladle into warmed bowls, sprinkle with the parsley, and serve immediately.

Serves 6

3 tbsp olive oil

4 shallots, chopped

1 tbsp finely chopped fresh ginger

2 lb 4 oz/1 kg cremini mushrooms, coarsely chopped

* 4 cups basic vegetable stock

⅔ cup sour cream

2 tbsp chopped fresh flat-leaf parsley, to garnish

salt and pepper

29

Red Bell Pepper Soup

Serves 6

2 red bell peppers
5⅔ cups basic vegetable stock
1 Bermuda onion, finely chopped
2 carrots, chopped
¾ cup peeled, seeded, and chopped cucumber
scant 1 cup cauliflower florets
1 extra large egg yolk
6 tbsp heavy cream
3 tbsp dry sherry
salt and pepper

1. Preheat the broiler. Put the bell peppers on a cookie sheet and broil, turning frequently, for 10 minutes, until blistered and charred. Remove with tongs, put them into a plastic bag, seal the top, and let stand until cool enough to handle. Peel, halve, and seed them, then chop the flesh.

2. Meanwhile, pour the basic vegetable stock into a pan and bring to a boil. Add the bell peppers, onion, carrots, cucumber, and cauliflower and bring back to a boil. Reduce the heat, cover, and simmer for 20 minutes.

3. Remove the pan from the heat and let cool slightly. Transfer the soup to a food processor blender, in batches if necessary, and process to a puree.

4. Return the soup to the rinsed-out pan. Beat together the egg yolk and cream in a bowl and stir into the soup, season to taste with salt and pepper, and reheat gently, stirring occasionally; do not let the soup boil. Stir in the sherry, ladle into warmed bowls, and serve immediately.

30

Cauliflower & Coconut Soup

1. Pour the basic vegetable stock into a pan and add the lemongrass, lime rind, and galangal. Pound 1 garlic clove with the cilantro roots in a mortar with a pestle and add to the pan. Bring to a boil, then reduce the heat, cover, and simmer for 40 minutes. Meanwhile, finely chop the remaining garlic.

2. Remove the pan from the heat and strain the stock into a bowl. Discard the contents of the strainer.

3. Heat the oil in a pan. Add the scallions, chiles, and chopped garlic and cook over low heat, stirring occasionally, for 5 minutes. Add the cauliflower and cook, stirring frequently, for 6–8 minutes, until just beginning to color.

4. Add the strained stock, coconut milk, Thai fish sauce, if using, and chopped cilantro and bring to a boil over medium heat. Stir well, reduce the heat, cover, and simmer for 25–30 minutes. Season to taste with salt and pepper and stir in the lime juice. Ladle into warmed bowls, garnish with cilantro and browned onions, and serve immediately.

Serves 6

- 5⅔ cups basic vegetable stock
- 2 lemongrass stalks, bruised
- coarsely grated rind of 1 lime
- 6 slices of galangal or fresh ginger
- 2 garlic cloves
- 6 cilantro roots
- 3 tbsp peanut oil
- 6 scallions, thinly sliced
- 1 green chile, seeded and chopped
- 1 red Thai chile, seeded and thinly sliced
- 1 large cauliflower, cut into small florets
- 1¾ cups canned coconut milk
- 2 tbsp Thai fish sauce (optional)
- 2 tbsp chopped fresh cilantro, plus extra to garnish
- 1 tbsp lime juice
- salt and pepper
- browned onions, to garnish (see page 19)

Jerusalem Artichoke Soup

1. Fill a bowl with water and stir in the lemon juice. Peel the artichokes and cut into chunks, then immediately drop them into the bowl of acidulated water to prevent discoloration.
2. Heat the butter with the oil in a large pan. Add the onion and cook over low heat, stirring occasionally, for 5 minutes, until softened. Drain the artichokes, add them to the pan, and stir well. Cover and cook, stirring occasionally, for 15 minutes.
3. Pour in the basic vegetable stock and milk, increase the heat to medium, and bring to a boil. Reduce the heat, re-cover the pan, and simmer for 20 minutes, until the artichokes are soft.
4. Remove the pan from the heat and let cool slightly. Add the chives and transfer the soup to a food processor or blender, in batches if necessary, and process to a puree.
5. Pour the soup back into the rinsed-out pan, stir in the cream, and season with salt and pepper. Reheat gently, stirring occasionally, but do not let the soup boil. Ladle into warmed bowls, garnish with croutons, drizzle over the oil, and serve immediately.

Serves 6

1 tbsp lemon juice
1 lb 9 oz/700 g Jerusalem artichokes
4 tbsp butter
1 tbsp sunflower oil
1 large onion, chopped
* 5⅔ cups basic vegetable stock
¾ cup milk
1 tbsp snipped fresh chives
scant ½ cup heavy cream
salt and pepper
croutons, to garnish (see page 65)
extra virgin olive oil, for drizzling

32

Goulash Soup

1. Heat the oil in a large pan. Add the onion, garlic, and carrots and cook over low heat, stirring occasionally, for 8–10 minutes, until lightly colored. Add the cabbage and bell pepper and cook, stirring frequently, for 3–4 minutes.

2. Sprinkle in the flour and paprika and cook, stirring constantly, for 1 minute. Gradually stir in the basic vegetable stock, a little at a time. Increase the heat to medium and bring to a boil, stirring constantly. Season with salt, reduce the heat, cover, and simmer for 30 minutes.

3. Add the potatoes and bring back to a boil, then reduce the heat, re-cover the pan, and simmer for another 20–30 minutes, until the potatoes are soft but not falling apart.

4. Taste and adjust the seasoning and add the sugar, if necessary. Ladle the soup into warmed bowls, swirl a little crème fraîche on top of each, and serve immediately.

Serves 6

2 tbsp olive oil

1 large onion, chopped

2 garlic cloves, finely chopped

3–4 carrots, thinly sliced

½ savoy cabbage, cored and shredded

1 small red bell pepper, seeded and chopped

1 tbsp all-purpose flour

2 tbsp sweet paprika

4 cups basic vegetable stock

2 potatoes, cut into chunks

1–2 teaspoons sugar (optional)

salt and pepper

crème fraîche, to garnish

33

Bacon & Pumpkin Soup

1. Heat the oil in a large pan. Add the onions and cook over low heat, stirring occasionally, for 5 minutes, until softened.

2. Add the pumpkin, bacon, and nutmeg, stir well, then cover and simmer, stirring occasionally, for 5–8 minutes.

3. Pour in the basic vegetable stock, increase the heat to medium, and bring to a boil. Reduce the heat and simmer for 10–15 minutes.

4. Meanwhile, make the bacon croutons. Heat the oil in a skillet. Add the bacon and fry for 4–6 minutes on each side, until crisp and all the fat has been released. Meanwhile, cut the bread into ½-inch/1-cm squares. Remove the bacon from the skillet and drain on paper towels. Add the bread squares and cook, turning and tossing until golden brown all over. Remove from the pan and drain on paper towels.

5. Remove the pan from the heat and let cool slightly. Transfer the soup to a food processor or blender, in batches, if necessary, and process until smooth. Return to the rinsed-out pan, season to taste with salt and pepper, and reheat gently, stirring occasionally.

6. Remove the soup from the heat and ladle into warmed bowls. Sprinkle with the croutons, crumble the bacon over the bowls, and serve immediately.

Serves 6

2 tbsp olive oil

2 onions, chopped

1 lb 5 oz/600 g canned unsweetened pumpkin

generous 1 cup diced smoked bacon

pinch of grated nutmeg

5 cups basic vegetable stock

salt and pepper

Bacon croutons

2 tbsp sunflower oil

4 slices smoked bacon

2 slices day-old bread, crusts removed

34

Lentil Soup with Ham

1. Heat the oil in a large pan. Add the onion, garlic, celery, carrot, and potato and cook over low heat, stirring occasionally, for 5–7 minutes, until softened. Add the ham and cook, stirring occasionally, for another 3 minutes. Remove from the pan with a slotted spoon and set aside.
2. Add the lentils, basic vegetable stock, bay leaf, and parsley sprigs to the pan, increase the heat to medium, and bring to a boil. Reduce the heat and simmer, stirring occasionally, for 30 minutes.
3. Add the tomatoes and return the vegetables and ham to the pan. Stir well and simmer for 25–30 minutes more.
4. Remove and discard the bay leaf and parsley. Stir in the paprika and vinegar, season to taste with salt and pepper, and heat through for 2–3 minutes. Ladle into a warmed tureen or individual bowls and serve immediately.

Serves 6

3 tbsp olive oil
1 Bermuda onion, chopped
3 garlic cloves, chopped
2 celery stalks, chopped
1 carrot, chopped
1 potato chopped
1 cup chopped smoked ham
2 cups green or brown lentils
13 cups basic vegetable stock
1 bay leaf
4 fresh parsley sprigs
4 tomatoes, peeled and chopped
1½ teaspoons sweet paprika
4 tablespoons sherry vinegar
salt and pepper

35

Lamb & Vegetable Broth

1. Put the lamb into a large pan, pour in the basic vegetable stock, and bring to a boil over medium–low heat, skimming off the foam that rises to the surface.
2. Add the onion, barley, peas, and thyme sprig and bring back to a boil. Reduce the heat, cover, and simmer for 1 hour.
3. Increase the heat to medium, add the leeks, rutabaga, carrots, and cabbage, season with salt and pepper, and bring back to a boil. Stir, reduce the heat, cover, and simmer for 30 minutes, until the meat and vegetables are tender.
4. Skim off any fat from the surface of the soup and taste and adjust the seasoning, if necessary. Ladle into warmed bowls, sprinkle with parsley, and serve immediately.

Serves 6

2 lb 4 oz/1 kg boneless lamb, cut into cubes

* 7½ cups basic vegetable stock

1 onion, chopped

¼ cup pearl barley

⅓ cup dried green peas, soaked overnight in water to cover, and drained

1 fresh thyme sprig

2 leeks, chopped

1 rutabaga or turnip, chopped

2 carrots, chopped

½ savoy cabbage, cored and shredded

2 tbsp chopped fresh flat-leaf parsley, to garnish

salt and pepper

36

Lamb & Eggplant Soup

1. Preheat the oven to 400°F/200°C. Prick the eggplants in several places with a fork and put them on a cookie sheet. Bake, turning once or twice, for 50–60 minutes, until soft, then remove from the oven and let cool.

2. Meanwhile, heat the oil in a large pan. Add the lamb and cook over medium heat, turning frequently, for 8–10 minutes, until lightly browned all over. Add the basic vegetable stock and onion and bring to a boil. Reduce the heat and simmer for 1½ hours.

3. Remove the lamb from the pan with a slotted spoon and let cool slightly. Add the potatoes, cinnamon, coriander, and cumin to the pan, stir well, and bring back to a boil. Reduce the heat and simmer for 20–25 minutes, until the potatoes have softened.

4. Meanwhile, cut the meat off the bones and chop into bite-size pieces. Peel the eggplants and coarsely chop the flesh.

5. Remove the pan from the heat and let cool slightly. Remove and discard the cinnamon stick. Ladle the soup into a food processor or blender, in batches if necessary, add the eggplants, and process to a puree.

6. Return the puree to the rinsed-out pan, add the lamb and parsley, season to taste with salt and pepper, and reheat gently, stirring occasionally. Garnish with lemon slices and serve with rye bread.

Serves 6

2 eggplants
2 tbsp olive oil
4 lb/1.8 kg lamb shanks or shoulder of lamb
* 11¼ cups basic vegetable stock
1 large onion, chopped
2 potatoes, cut into chunks
1 cinnamon stick
½ tsp ground coriander
½ tsp ground cumin
3 tbsp chopped fresh flat-leaf parsley
salt and pepper
lemon slices, halved, to garnish
rye bread, to serve

37

Lamb & Lemon Soup

Serves 6

½ cup all-purpose flour
1 lb 2 oz/500 g boneless leg of lamb, cut into cubes
3 tbsp olive oil
5 cups basic vegetable stock
2 carrots, cut into chunks
2 onions, cut into quarters
1 tsp cayenne pepper
3 egg yolks
2 tbsp lemon juice
salt and pepper
flatbreads, to serve

To garnish

4 tablespoons butter
½ tsp ground cinnamon
2 tsp sweet or hot paprika
3 tbsp chopped fresh mint

1. Put the flour into a plastic bag and season with salt and pepper. Add the cubes of lamb, a few at a time, seal the bag, and shake to coat. Shake off any excess.
2. Heat the oil in a large pan. Add the lamb and cook over medium heat, stirring frequently, for 8–10 minutes, until lightly browned all over. Pour in the basic vegetable stock and bring to a boil, skimming off the foam that rises to the surface.
3. Add the carrots, onions, and cayenne pepper, season with salt and pepper, and bring back to a boil. Reduce the heat, cover, and simmer for 1½–2 hours, until the meat is tender.
4. For the garnish, melt the butter in a pan over very low heat or in a microwave-safe bowl in the microwave. Remove from the heat and stir in the cinnamon and paprika.
5. Beat the egg yolks with the lemon juice in a bowl. Remove the pan from the heat and whisk a ladleful of the hot soup into the egg mixture, then add it to the pan. Return the pan to very low heat and heat through, gently rotating the pan, for 1–2 minutes; do not let the soup boil.
6. Ladle the soup into a warm tureen, spoon the spiced melted butter over the top, sprinkle with the mint, and serve immediately, accompanied by flatbreads.

38

Cream of Chicken Soup

1. Put the chicken into a large pan, pour in the basic vegetable stock, add the bouquet garni, and season with salt and pepper. Bring to a boil over medium heat, skimming off the foam that rises to the surface. Reduce the heat, cover, and simmer for 1–1¼ hours, until the chicken is tender.

2. Remove the chicken from the pan and let cool. Strain the stock into a bowl and let cool, then either chill in the refrigerator overnight or in the freezer for 30 minutes.

3. Meanwhile, mash the butter into the flour in a small bowl to make a paste.

4. Remove and discard the chicken skin, cut the meat off the bones, and chop coarsely. Remove any fat that has solidified on the surface of the stock. Put the chicken and stock into a food processor, in batches if necessary, and process to a smooth puree.

5. Transfer the puree to the rinsed-out pan and heat gently. Gradually whisk in the butter-and-flour mixture, in small pieces at a time, making sure each piece has been fully incorporated before adding the next. Bring to a boil, stirring constantly, then reduce the heat, and simmer for 5 minutes. Taste and adjust the seasoning, if necessary, and stir in the cream. Serve immediately, garnished with croutons.

Serves 6

1 chicken, about 3 lb/1.3 kg

* 6¾ cups basic vegetable stock

1 bouquet garni (3 fresh parsley sprigs, 2 fresh thyme sprigs, 1 fresh tarragon sprig, and 1 bay leaf, tied together)

1 tbsp butter, softened

2 tbsp all-purpose flour

4 tbsp heavy cream

salt and pepper

croutons, to garnish (see page 65)

39

Cream of Clam Soup

1. Melt the butter in a pan. Add the onion and garlic and cook over low heat, stirring occasionally, for 5 minutes, until softened.

2. Stir in the flour and cook, stirring constantly, for 1 minute, then remove the pan from the heat. Gradually stir in the basic vegetable stock, a little at a time, then stir in the wine.

3. Return the pan to medium heat, add the bay leaf and parsley sprigs, season with salt and pepper, and bring to a boil, stirring constantly. Reduce the heat, cover, and simmer for 15 minutes.

4. Meanwhile, drain the clams, reserving the juices. Finely chop the clams.

5. Add the clams and the reserved juices to the pan, bring back to a boil, and simmer for 5 minutes more.

6. Remove and discard the bay leaf and parsley sprigs. Gradually stir in the cream and heat through gently; do not let the soup boil. Taste and adjust the seasoning, if necessary, and ladle into warmed bowls. Sprinkle with the chopped parsley and serve immediately with whole wheat bread.

Serves 6

3 tbsp butter
1 large onion, finely chopped
2 garlic cloves, finely chopped
1 tbsp all-purpose flour
* 1¾ cups basic vegetable stock
½ cup medium-dry white wine
1 bay leaf
6 fresh parsley sprigs
1 lb 7 oz/650 g bottled or canned clams
generous 1 cup light cream
salt and pepper
3 tbsp chopped fresh flat-leaf parsley, to garnish
whole wheat bread, to serve

40

Cajun Crab & Corn Chowder

1. Melt the butter in a large pan. Add the onion, garlic, celery, and carrot and cook over low heat, stirring occasionally, for 5 minutes, until softened.

2. Increase the heat to medium, pour in the wine, and cook for 2 minutes, until the alcohol has evaporated. Pour in the basic vegetable stock and bring to a boil, then add the corn, cayenne, and mixed herbs. Bring back to a boil, reduce the heat, and simmer for 15 minutes.

3. Add the cream and simmer gently over very low heat for 10–15 minutes more; do not let the soup boil.

4. Gradually add the crème fraîche, whisking constantly with a balloon whisk, then stir in the dill and crabmeat, and season to taste with salt and pepper. Heat gently for 3–4 minutes, then serve with whole wheat rolls.

Serves 6

3 tbsp butter
1 onion, finely chopped
2 garlic cloves, finely chopped
2 celery stalks finely chopped
1 small carrot, finely chopped
¾ cup medium-dry white wine
* 2¼ cups basic vegetable stock
1½ cups frozen corn kernels
pinch of cayenne pepper
½ tsp dried mixed herbs
1½ cups heavy cream
¾ cup crème fraîche
1 tbsp chopped fresh dill
8 oz/225 g white crabmeat
salt and pepper
whole wheat rolls, to serve

Fish & Corn Soup

1. Put the fish fillets into a heatproof dish that will fit into a steamer and sprinkle with the wine. Put the slices of ginger in a garlic crusher and squeeze out the juice over the fish. You may have to do this in batches. Let marinate for 15 minutes.

2. Pour the basic vegetable stock into a pan and bring to a boil. Put the dish of fish into the steamer and set it over the pan. Cover and steam for 8–10 minutes, until the flesh flakes easily. Remove the steamer and set the dish of fish aside.

3. Add the corn to the stock and bring back to a boil, then stir in the sesame oil and season with salt. Reduce the heat and simmer for 10 minutes.

4. Meanwhile, mash the fish fillets with a fork. Mix the cornstarch to a paste with the water.

5. Add the cornstarch paste to the soup and cook, stirring constantly, until thickened. Add the fish and cook for 2–3 minutes, or until heated through.

6. Taste and adjust the seasoning, if necessary, then ladle into warmed bowls. Sprinkle with the scallions and serve immediately.

Serves 6

1 lb 7 oz/650 g sea bass or porgy fillets, skinned

2 tsp Chinese rice wine or dry sherry

¾-inch/2-cm piece of fresh ginger, thinly sliced

* 5⅔ cups basic vegetable stock

2 cups frozen corn kernels

1 tsp sesame oil

2½ tsp cornstarch

3 tbsp water

2 scallions, chopped

salt

Carrot & Mussel Soup

1. Reserve 3 carrots and slice the remainder. Melt 4 tablespoons of the butter in a large pan. Add the sliced carrots and half the sugar and cook over low heat, stirring occasionally, for 5 minutes. Increase the heat to medium, pour in the basic vegetable stock, season with salt, and bring to a boil. Reduce the heat, cover, and simmer, stirring occasionally, for 25 minutes.

2. Meanwhile, finely chop the reserved carrots. Melt the remaining butter in a small pan. Add the carrots and the remaining sugar and cook over low heat, stirring occasionally, for 10 minutes, then remove from the heat.

3. Scrub the mussels under cold running water and pull off the "beards." Discard any with broken shells or that do not shut immediately when sharply tapped. Put them into a pan, pour in the wine, and add the garlic. Cover and cook over high heat, shaking the pan occasionally, for 4–5 minutes, until they open. Remove the pan from the heat and lift out the mussels. Discard any that remain shut. Remove the mussels from the half shell. Strain the cooking liquid through a cheesecloth-lined strainer into a bowl. Remove the pan of carrots from the heat and let cool slightly, then ladle into a food processor, add the mussels cooking liquid, and process. Return the soup to the rinsed-out pan, season to taste, and reheat gently for 3–4 minutes. Ladle into a warmed tureen, gently stir in the mussels, sprinkle with the parsley, and serve with whole wheat rolls.

Serves 6

2 lb 4 oz/1 kg carrots

7 tbsp butter

1 tsp sugar

* 5⅔ cups basic vegetable stock

48 mussels

1¼ cups dry white wine

1 garlic clove, coarsely chopped

salt and pepper

2 tbsp chopped fresh flat-leaf parsley, to garnish

whole wheat rolls, to serve

Stylish

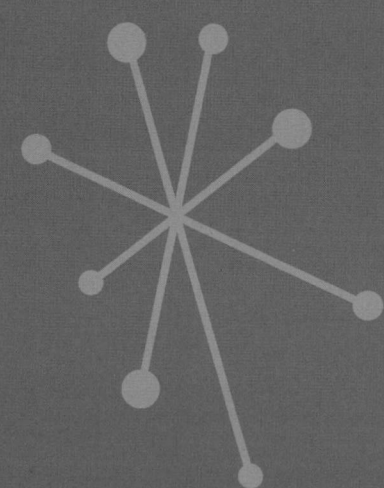

43

Asparagus Soup

1. Trim off and reserve the woody ends of the asparagus, leaving the spears 2¾–3½ inches/7–8 cm long. Pour the basic vegetable stock into a pan, add the woody asparagus ends, and bring to a boil. Reduce the heat and simmer for 15 minutes. Meanwhile, cut the remaining asparagus into 1-inch/2.5 cm lengths.

2. Bring a pan of lightly salted water to a boil. Add half the asparagus tips and simmer for 7–10 minutes, until tender. Remove from the heat, drain, and reserve. Remove the basic vegetable stock from the heat and strain into a bowl. Discard the woody asparagus ends.

3. Melt 3 tablespoons of the butter in a large pan, add the leeks and remaining asparagus, and cook over low heat, stirring occasionally, for 5 minutes. Pour in the stock, season with salt and pepper, and bring to a boil over medium heat. Reduce the heat, cover, and simmer for 10–15 minutes, until the asparagus is tender. Remove the pan from the heat and let cool slightly. Ladle the soup into a food processor or blender, in batches if necessary, and process to a smooth puree.

4. Melt the remaining butter in a pan. Stir in the flour and cook, stirring constantly, for 1 minute. Stir in the puree and bring to a boil, stirring constantly. Add the milk and cook, stirring, for a few minutes more, then stir in the cream and reserved asparagus tips. Ladle the soup into warmed bowls, top each with a teaspoonful of caviar, and serve immediately.

Serves 6

1 lb 2 oz/500 g asparagus spears

* 4 cups basic vegetable stock

5 tbsp butter

1½ cups thinly sliced leeks

¼ cup all-purpose flour

⅔ cup milk

6 tbsp heavy cream

salt and pepper

6 tsp caviar or keta (salmon roe), to garnish

Avocado Soup

1. Halve the avocados lengthwise and gently twist the halves apart. Remove and discard the pits and scoop out the flesh. Chop into small pieces, put them into a bowl, sprinkle with the lemon juice, and toss well to coat. Melt the butter in a pan. Add the shallots and cook over low heat, stirring occasionally, for 5 minutes, until softened. Stir in the flour and cook, stirring constantly, for 1 minute.

2. Remove the pan from the heat and gradually stir in the basic vegetable stock. Return the pan to medium heat and bring to a boil, stirring constantly. Add the avocados, reduce the heat, cover, and simmer for 15 minutes.

3. Meanwhile, preheat the broiler. Make the guacamole croutes. Toast the bread on one side under the broiler. Turn the slices over, brush with the oil, and toast. Remove from the heat. Scoop out the avocado flesh into a bowl and mash with the lime juice and chili sauce, to taste, and season. Divide the avocado mixture among the croutes and set aside.

4. Remove the soup from the heat and push it through a strainer set over a bowl, pressing the vegetables with the back of the ladle. Return the soup to the rinsed-out pan, stir in the cream, season to taste, and reheat gently; do not let the soup boil.

5. Ladle the soup into warmed bowls, float the lime slices on top, add the oil, and serve immediately, passing around the guacamole croutes separately.

Serves 6

3 ripe avocados
2 tbsp lemon juice
6 tbsp butter
6 shallots, chopped
1½ tbsp all-purpose flour
* 3¾ cups basic vegetable stock
¾ cup light cream
1 lime, thinly sliced
salt and pepper
extra virgin olive oil, for drizzling

Guacamole croutes

6 thin slices of day-old baguette
olive oil, for brushing
½ large ripe avocado, pitted and brushed with lime juice
juice of 1 lime
¼–¾ tsp chili or Tabasco sauce
salt and pepper

45

Broccoli & Roquefort Soup

1. Melt the butter in a large pan. Add the onions and potato and stir well. Cover and cook over low heat for 7 minutes. Add the broccoli and stir well, then re-cover the pan, and cook for 5 minutes more.
2. Increase the heat to medium, pour in the basic vegetable stock, and bring to a boil. Reduce the heat, season with salt and pepper, re-cover, and simmer for 15–20 minutes, until the vegetables are tender.
3. Remove the pan from the heat, strain into a bowl, reserving the vegetables, and let cool slightly. Put the vegetables into a food processor, add 1 ladleful of the stock, and process to a smooth puree. With the motor running, gradually add the remaining stock.
4. Return the soup to the rinsed-out pan and reheat gently until very hot but not boiling. Remove from the heat and stir in the cheese until melted and thoroughly combined. Stir in the mace and taste and adjust the seasoning, if necessary. Ladle into warmed bowls, sprinkle with the croutons, and serve immediately.

Serves 6

3 tbsp butter
2 white onions, chopped
1 large potato, chopped
1 lb 10 oz/750 g broccoli, cut into small florets
* 6¾ cups basic vegetable stock
5½ oz/150 g Roquefort cheese, diced
pinch of ground mace
salt and pepper
croutons, to garnish (see page 65)

46

Spicy Cucumber Soup

1. Pour the basic vegetable stock into a pan, add the lemongrass, 2 tablespoons of the lime juice, and the cilantro sprigs and bring to a boil over medium heat. Reduce the heat, cover, and simmer for 25 minutes.

2. Remove the pan from the heat and strain the stock into a clean pan. Stir in the remaining lime juice and the cucumber and season to taste with salt and pepper.

3. Bring back to a boil, stirring constantly, then reduce the heat, and simmer for 5 minutes.

4. Remove the pan from the heat, taste, and adjust the seasoning, if necessary, and ladle into individual bowls. Divide the scallions, chiles, and cilantro among the bowls and serve immediately.

Serves 6

* 5 cups basic vegetable stock
2 tbsp chopped lemongrass
3½ tbsp lime juice
16 fresh cilantro sprigs
6 oz/175 g cucumber, peeled and cut into julienne strips
salt and pepper

To garnish
3 scallions, thinly sliced
3 green chiles, seeded and finely chopped
2 tbsp chopped fresh cilantro

47

Vegetable Broth

1. Pour the basic vegetable stock into a pan and bring to a boil over medium heat. Add the corn cobs and carrots and cook for 3 minutes, then add the snow peas, mushrooms, and Chinese cabbage, and cook for another 2 minutes.

2. Add the Chinese chives and soy sauce and season to taste with salt, if necessary (soy sauce is very salty), and pepper. Simmer for 2–3 minutes more, then ladle into warmed bowls, garnish with the scallions, and serve immediately.

Serves 6

- 4 cups basic vegetable stock
- ¾ cup baby corn cobs, thinly sliced diagonally
- ⅓ cup baby carrots, thinly sliced diagonally
- 1 cup snow peas or green beans, sliced diagonally
- 1¼ cups thinly sliced cremini mushrooms
- 3 oz/85 g Chinese cabbage or spinach, shredded
- 1 tbsp chopped Chinese chives
- 2 tbsp light soy sauce
- salt and pepper
- thinly sliced scallions, to garnish

Vegetable Soup with Semolina Dumplings

1. First, make the dumplings. Pour the milk into a pan and add the water, sugar, nutmeg, and a pinch of salt. Bring to a boil over medium heat, then reduce the heat, and sprinkle the semolina over the surface of the liquid. Simmer, stirring constantly, until thickened, then remove the pan from the heat and let cool for 15 minutes. Stir in the beaten egg until thoroughly combined, then cover, and chill in the refrigerator for 30 minutes.

2. To make the soup, blanch the turnips and carrots in a pan of boiling water for 3 minutes, then drain. Melt the butter in a large pan, add the turnips and carrots, and cook over low heat, stirring frequently, for 5 minutes.

3. Sprinkle the sugar over the vegetables, increase the heat to medium, and cook, stirring constantly, until they begin to caramelize. Pour in the basic vegetable stock, season with salt and pepper, and bring to a boil, then reduce the heat, and simmer for 20 minutes.

4. Meanwhile, flour your hands and shape the semolina mixture into small balls. About 7–10 minutes before the end of the cooking time, add the dumplings to the soup and simmer until they have risen to the surface.

5. Taste and adjust the seasoning, if necessary, and ladle the soup into warmed bowls. Sprinkle with the parsley and serve immediately.

Serves 6

⅓ cup diced turnip
scant 1 cup diced carrots
4 tbsp butter
1½ tsp sugar
7½ cups basic vegetable stock
salt and pepper
3 tbsp chopped fresh flat-leaf parsley, to garnish

Dumplings
5 tbsp milk
⅔ cup water
1 tsp sugar
pinch of grated nutmeg
¾ cup semolina
1 extra large egg, lightly beaten
all-purpose flour, for dusting
salt

49

Curried Vegetable Soup

Serves 6

- 3 tbsp butter
- 2 onions, chopped
- 2 garlic cloves, finely chopped
- 1½ tsp ground cumin
- 1 tsp ground coriander
- 1 sweet potato, chopped
- 2 carrots, chopped
- 3 parsnips chopped
- 1 tbsp curry paste
- * 3 cups basic vegetable stock
- 3 cups milk
- 1 tsp lime juice
- 6 tbsp sour cream
- salt and pepper
- naan, to serve

To garnish

- 4-inch/10-cm piece fresh ginger
- 2 tbsp peanut oil

1. Melt the butter in a large pan. Add the onions and garlic and cook over low heat, stirring occasionally, for 8–10 minutes, until lightly browned. Stir in the cumin and coriander and cook, stirring constantly, for 2 minutes. Add the sweet potato, carrots, and parsnips and cook, stirring frequently, for 5 minutes, then stir in the curry paste, and mix well. Increase the heat to medium, pour in the basic vegetable stock, and bring to a boil, stirring occasionally. Reduce the heat, cover, and simmer for 20–25 minutes, until the vegetables are tender.
2. Meanwhile, make the garnish. Cut the ginger in half and then into thin julienne strips. Heat the oil in a small skillet over high heat. Reduce the heat, add the ginger, and cook, stirring and twisting constantly, for 1 minute. Remove with a slotted spoon and drain on paper towels.
3. Remove the pan of soup from the heat and let cool slightly. Ladle the soup into a food processor or blender, in batches if necessary, and process to a puree.
4. Return the soup to the rinsed-out pan and stir in the milk. Cook, stirring occasionally, for 5 minutes. Stir in the lime juice and 3 tablespoons of the sour cream and season to taste with salt and pepper.
5. Ladle the soup into warmed bowls, add a swirl of the remaining sour cream, and garnish with the fried ginger. Serve immediately with naan.

50

Mexican Tomato & Vermicelli Soup

Serves 6

- 1 Bermuda onion, chopped
- 2 garlic cloves, chopped
- 1–2 red Serrano chiles, seeded and chopped
- 2½ cups peeled, seeded, and chopped tomatoes
- 3 tbsp corn oil
- 3 oz/85 g vermicelli
- 6¾ cups basic vegetable stock
- 1 tbsp ketchup
- 1 tbsp tomato paste
- 1 tbsp chopped fresh cilantro
- salt and pepper
- finely shredded lime rind, to garnish

1. Put the onion, garlic, chiles, and tomatoes into a food processor and process to a smooth puree.
2. Heat the oil in a heavy skillet. Add the vermicelli and stir-fry over low heat for a few minutes, until golden brown. Remove from the skillet and drain on paper towels.
3. Add the vegetable puree to the skillet and cook, stirring constantly, for 6–8 minutes, until thickened. Remove the skillet from the heat.
4. Spoon the vegetable puree into a large pan, pour in the basic vegetable stock, stir in the ketchup and tomato paste, and add the vermicelli and cilantro. Season to taste with salt and pepper and bring to a boil. Reduce the heat, cover, and simmer for 5 minutes, or until the vermicelli is tender.
5. Ladle the soup into warmed bowls, sprinkle with the shreds of lime rind, and serve immediately.

51

Shiitake Mushroom Soup with Egg

1. Pour the basic vegetable stock into a pan, add the kombu, and bring just to a boil over low heat. Immediately remove the kombu. Add the bonito flakes and bring to a boil, then remove the pan from the heat and let the bonito flakes settle. Strain the stock through a cheesecloth-lined strainer into a clean pan.

2. Meanwhile, cut off and discard the mushroom stems and thinly slice the caps.

3. Bring the basic vegetable stock to a boil. Reduce the heat, add the mushrooms, and simmer for 2–3 minutes, until just tender but still firm to the bite. Stir in the Japanese soy sauce and sake and season to taste with salt.

4. Increase the heat to medium–low. Gradually pour in the eggs, moving the bowl continuously around the pan so that they are evenly distributed and set immediately. Simmer for about 15 seconds, then remove the pan from the heat.

5. Break up the "omelet" and divide it and the soup among individual bowls. Garnish with the scallions and serve immediately.

Serves 6

- 3¾ cups basic vegetable stock
- ¼ oz/10 g kombu seaweed
- ½ oz/10 g bonito flakes
- 6 shiitake mushrooms
- 1 tbsp Japanese soy sauce
- 2 tsp sake or dry white wine
- 2 extra large eggs, lightly beaten
- salt
- scallions, thinly sliced, to garnish

52

Egg Flower Soup

1. Pour the basic vegetable stock into a pan and stir in the rice wine, soy sauce, and sesame oil. Put the slices of ginger into a garlic crusher and squeeze out the juice into the pan. Add the Chinese cabbage leaves and bring to a boil, then reduce the heat, and simmer for 3–4 minutes.

2. Increase the heat to medium–low. Gradually pour the eggs into the center of the soup in a steady stream. Simmer for 2 seconds, then stir to break the eggs into filaments. Season to taste, ladle into warmed bowls, and serve.

Serves 6

- 4 cups basic vegetable stock
- 3 tbsp Chinese rice wine or dry sherry
- 3 tbsp light soy sauce
- 1 tsp sesame oil
- ½-inch/1-cm piece fresh ginger, thinly sliced
- 6 Chinese cabbage leaves or bok choy, shredded
- 2 eggs, beaten
- salt and pepper

53

Garlic Soup

1. Crush the garlic cloves with the flat side of a heavy knife blade, then peel off and discard the skins. Put the garlic cloves into a pan and add the bay leaf, cloves, peppercorns, saffron, parsley sprigs, chervil sprigs, thyme sprigs, sage leaves, and olive oil.

2. Pour in the basic vegetable stock and bring to a boil, then reduce the heat, cover, and simmer for 40 minutes.

3. Remove the pan from the heat and strain the soup into a warmed tureen. Season to taste with salt and pepper, sprinkle with the parsley, and serve with whole wheat rolls, passing around the Parmesan separately.

Serves 6

2 garlic bulbs, separated into cloves
1 bay leaf
3 cloves
3 black peppercorns
½ tsp saffron threads
2 fresh flat-leaf parsley sprigs
2 fresh chervil sprigs
4 fresh thyme sprigs
16 fresh sage leaves
1½ tbsp olive oil
* 7½ cups basic vegetable stock
2 tbsp chopped fresh flat-leaf parsley, to garnish
salt and pepper

To serve
whole wheat rolls
thinly shaved Parmesan cheese

54

Hot & Sour Soup

1. Pour the basic vegetable stock into a pan and add the lime leaves, lemongrass, half the chiles, half the scallions, and the garlic. Bring to a boil, then reduce the heat and simmer for 30 minutes.

2. Remove the pan from the heat and strain the soup into a clean pan. Discard the contents of the strainer.

3. Return the soup to the heat, stir in the lime juice, sugar, cilantro, and remaining chiles and scallions, and season to taste with salt. Bring back to a boil, then reduce the heat, and simmer for 5 minutes. Add the tofu and carrots and simmer for another 4–5 minutes. Serve immediately.

Serves 6

- 5⅔ cups basic vegetable stock
- 6 fresh or dried kaffir lime leaves
- 3 lemongrass stalks, cut into 1½-inch/4-cm lengths
- 3 fresh red chiles, seeded and sliced
- 6 scallions, thinly sliced
- 3 garlic cloves, thinly sliced
- 6 tbsp lime juice
- 2 tsp sugar
- 2 tbsp chopped fresh cilantro
- 12 oz/350 g firm tofu, thinly sliced
- 2 carrots, thinly sliced
- salt

55

Pork Rib Soup with Pickled Mustard Greens

1. Heat the oil in a small skillet or wok. Add the garlic and stir-fry for a few minutes, until golden. Transfer to a plate and set aside.
2. Pour the basic vegetable stock into a pan and bring to a boil over medium heat. Add the spareribs and bring back to a boil, then reduce the heat, cover, and simmer for 15 minutes, until tender.
3. Meanwhile, put the cellophane noodles into a bowl, pour in hot water to cover, and let soak for 10 minutes, until softened. Drain well.
4. Add the noodles and pickled greens to the soup and bring back to a boil. Stir in the Thai fish sauce and sugar, season to taste with pepper, and ladle into warmed bowls. Garnish with the garlic slices and red and green chiles and serve immediately.

Serves 6

1 tbsp peanut oil

3 garlic cloves, thinly sliced

* 5 cups basic vegetable stock

1 lb 2 oz/500 g pork finger spareribs

3 oz/85 g cellophane noodles

10 oz/280 g canned Thai pickled mustard greens or Chinese snow pickles, well-rinsed and coarsely chopped

2 tbsp Thai fish sauce

½ tsp sugar

pepper

1 red and 1 green chile, seeded and thinly sliced, to garnish

56

Chicken Noodle Soup

1. Bring a pan of water to a boil. Add the noodles and cook according to the instructions on the package. Drain, refresh under cold running water, and let stand in a bowl of water.

2. Heat the oil in a large pan. Add the scallions and bacon and cook over low heat, stirring occasionally, for 5 minutes, until the scallions have softened and the bacon is beginning to color.

3. Add the tarragon and chicken, increase the heat to medium, and cook, stirring frequently, for about 8 minutes, until the chicken is golden brown all over.

4. Pour in the wine and cook for 2 minutes, until the alcohol has evaporated, then pour enough of the basic vegetable stock just to cover the meat. Reduce the heat, cover, and simmer for 20–30 minutes, until the chicken is tender.

5. Pour in the remaining stock, season with salt and pepper, and bring to a boil. Add the noodles and heat through briefly. Ladle the soup into warmed bowls and serve immediately with crusty bread, passing around the Parmesan separately.

Serves 6

6 oz/175 g egg noodles
2 tbsp olive oil
1 cup chopped scallions
4 bacon slices, chopped
2 tsp chopped fresh tarragon
6 skinless boneless chicken thighs, diced
⅔ cup dry white wine
5 cups basic vegetable stock
salt and pepper

To serve

grated Parmesan cheese
crusty bread

57

Crab & Noodle Soup

1. Bring a pan of water to a boil. Add the noodles and cook according to the instructions on the package. Drain, refresh under cold running water, and let stand in a bowl of water.

2. Heat the oil in a large pan. Add the shallots, carrots, and celery and cook over low heat, stirring occasionally, for 5 minutes, until softened.

3. Increase the heat to medium, pour in the vermouth, and cook for 2 minutes, until the alcohol has evaporated. Pour in the basic vegetable stock and bring to a boil, then reduce the heat and simmer for 10 minutes.

4. Meanwhile, flake the crabmeat and remove any pieces of shell or cartilage. Drain the noodles and add them to the pan. Add the crab and stir in the anchovy essence and lemon juice. Season to taste with salt and pepper. Simmer for a few minutes more to heat through, then ladle the soup into warmed bowls, garnish with the chopped parsley, and serve immediately.

Serves 6

5 oz/150 g egg noodles
3 tbsp peanut oil
4 shallots, chopped
2 carrots, chopped
2 celery stalks, chopped
6 tbsp dry vermouth
* 7½ cups basic vegetable stock
6 oz/175 g white crabmeat, thawed if frozen
a few drops of anchovy essence
1 tbsp lemon juice
salt and pepper
chopped fresh flat-leaf parsley, to garnish

Shrimp Bisque

1. Melt the butter in a large pan. Add the onion, carrots, celery, and bay leaves and cook over low heat, stirring occasionally, for 8–10 minutes, until golden brown. Increase the heat to medium, add the shrimp, and cook, stirring occasionally, for 4–5 minutes, until they change color.

2. Pour in the brandy and wine and cook for 4–5 minutes more, until the alcohol has evaporated and the shrimp are cooked. Remove the shrimp with a slotted spoon and let cool slightly.

3. Add the tomatoes, tomato paste, parsley, and basic vegetable stock to the pan and bring to a boil. Meanwhile, peel the shrimp, reserving the shells. Add the shells to the pan, reduce the heat, and simmer for 30 minutes. Devein the shrimp by cutting a slit along their backs with a sharp knife and removing the black vein with the point of the knife. Chop the shrimp.

4. Remove the soup from the heat, add the chopped shrimp, and let cool slightly. Ladle the soup into a food processor, in batches if necessary, and process. Pour the soup through a strainer into the rinsed-out pan, pressing the contents of the strainer with the back of a ladle to extract the liquid. Bring the soup back to a boil, then reduce the heat, and stir in the cream, lemon juice, and cayenne. Taste and adjust the seasoning, if necessary, and heat for 1–2 minutes more; do not let the soup boil. Ladle into warmed bowls, decorate with the heavy cream, and add some cayenne. Serve with crusty bread.

Serves 6

6 tbsp butter
1 small onion, chopped
2 small carrots, chopped
1 celery stalk, chopped
2 bay leaves
1 lb 7 oz/650 g unpeeled shrimp
3 tbsp brandy
scant ½ cup dry white wine
1 lb 7 oz/650 g tomatoes, chopped
1½ tsp tomato paste
2 fresh parsley sprigs
* 11¼ cups basic vegetable stock
6 tbsp heavy cream, plus extra to decorate
1 tbsp lemon juice
pinch of cayenne pepper or dash of Tabasco sauce, plus extra to decorate
salt and pepper
crusty bread, to serve

Cool

59

Al Fresco Avocado Soup

1. Halve the avocados lengthwise and gently twist the halves apart. Remove and discard the pits and, using a teaspoon, scoop out the flesh.

2. Put the avocado flesh, lemon juice, basic vegetable stock, shallot, and chili and garlic sauce into a food processor or blender and process to a smooth puree. Scrape into a bowl and whisk in the cream with a balloon whisk. Season to taste with salt and pepper.

3. Cover tightly with plastic wrap and chill in the refrigerator for at least 3 hours. To serve, stir the soup and taste and adjust the seasoning, if necessary. Ladle into individual bowls, garnish with watercress sprigs, and serve immediately.

Serves 6

2 avocados
1 tbsp lemon juice
* 4 cups basic vegetable stock
1 shallot, chopped
dash of chili and garlic sauce
⅔ cup heavy cream
salt and pepper
watercress sprigs, to garnish

60

Fava Bean Soup

1. Pour the basic vegetable stock into a pan and bring to a boil. Reduce the heat to a simmer, add the beans, and cook for about 7 minutes, until just tender.

2. Remove the pan from the heat and let cool slightly. Ladle into a food processor or blender, in batches if necessary, and process to a puree. Strain the puree into a bowl to remove the skins.

3. Stir in the lemon juice and summer savory and season to taste with salt and pepper. Let cool completely, then cover with plastic wrap and chill in the refrigerator for at least 3 hours.

4. To serve, stir the soup and taste and adjust the seasoning, if necessary. Ladle into bowls and garnish with the yogurt and fresh mint leaves.

Serves 6

- 3¾ cups basic vegetable stock
- 4⅔ cups shelled young fava beans
- 3 tbsp lemon juice
- 2 tbsp chopped fresh summer savory
- 6 tbsp strained plain yogurt, chilled
- salt and pepper
- fresh mint leaves or marjoram flowers, to garnish

61

Cucumber & Mint Soup

1. Pour the basic vegetable stock into a large pan, add the scallions, and bring to a boil. Reduce the heat and simmer for 10 minutes. Reserve a little of the diced cucumber for the garnish and add the remainder and the mint sprigs to the pan. Simmer for another 20 minutes. Remove the pan from the heat and let cool slightly.

2. Remove and discard the mint sprigs. Ladle the soup into a food processor or blender, in batches if necessary, and process to a puree. Return the soup to the rinsed-out pan and reheat gently.

3. Mix the cornstarch to a paste with the water in a bowl. Stir the paste into the pan and bring to a boil, stirring constantly. Simmer, stirring constantly, for a few minutes, until thickened.

4. Stir in the cream and season to taste with salt and pepper. Remove the pan from the heat and stir in a few drops of food coloring, if using, to give the soup an attractive pale green color.

5. Ladle into bowls, garnish with the reserved cucumber and fresh mint leaves, and drizzle over the oil. Serve with warm pita bread.

Serves 6

* 5⅔ cups basic vegetable stock
* 6 scallions, chopped
* 2 cucumbers, peeled, seeded, and diced
* 3 fresh mint sprigs
* 1½ tbsp cornstarch
* 3 tbsp water
* 5 tbsp heavy cream
* green food coloring (optional)
* salt and pepper
* fresh mint leaves, to garnish
* extra virgin olive oil, for drizzling
* warm pita bread, to serve

Curried Cucumber Soup

Serves 6

½ cup crème fraîche
1½ cups plain yogurt
1–1½ tsp curry powder
pinch of cayenne pepper
1 white onion, grated
2 cucumbers, peeled, seeded, and diced
4 tbsp finely chopped fresh cilantro
* 1¼ cups basic vegetable stock
salt and pepper
fresh cilantro sprigs, to garnish
garlic naan, to serve

1. Whisk together the crème fraîche, 1 cup of the yogurt, the curry powder, and cayenne pepper in a bowl until thoroughly combined.
2. Stir in the onion, cucumbers, cilantro, and basic vegetable stock and season to taste with salt and pepper. Cover with plastic wrap and chill in the refrigerator for at least 3 hours. Chill the remaining yogurt.
3. To serve, stir the soup and taste and adjust the seasoning, if necessary. Ladle into bowls, garnish with the remaining yogurt and fresh cilantro sprigs, and serve with garlic naan.

63

Pea Soup

1. Pour the basic vegetable stock into a pan, add the onion and garlic, and bring to a boil over medium heat. Reduce the heat and simmer for 15 minutes.

2. Increase the heat to medium, add the peas, mint, lavender, if using, and sugar, and bring back to a boil. Reduce the heat and simmer for another 5–7 minutes.

3. Remove the pan from the heat and let cool completely. Remove and discard the herb sprigs. Ladle the soup into a food processor or blender, in batches if necessary, and process to a smooth puree.

4. Transfer to a bowl and stir in the lemon juice and sour cream. Season to taste with salt and pepper, cover with plastic wrap, and chill in the refrigerator for at least 3 hours. To serve, stir well, taste and adjust the seasoning, if necessary, and ladle into bowls.

Serves 6

- 3¾ cups basic vegetable stock
- 1 Bermuda onion, finely chopped
- 2 garlic cloves, finely chopped
- 3 cups frozen baby peas
- 2 fresh mint sprigs
- 1 fresh lavender sprig (optional)
- ½ tsp sugar
- 1 tbsp lemon juice
- 1 cup sour cream or plain yogurt
- salt and pepper

64

Asparagus Soup

Serves 6

2¼ lb/1 kg asparagus, trimmed
4 tbsp butter
6 scallions, chopped
3 tbsp all-purpose flour
6¼ cups basic vegetable stock
½ cup crème fraîche
1 tsp finely grated lemon rind
salt and pepper

To serve
grated Parmesan cheese
melba toast

1. Cut off the tips of the asparagus and set aside. Cut the remaining spears into ½-inch/1-cm lengths.

2. Melt the butter in a large pan. Add the scallions and cook over low heat, stirring occasionally, for 5 minutes. Add the pieces of asparagus spears and cook, stirring occasionally, for another 5 minutes.

3. Stir in the flour and cook, stirring constantly, for 2 minutes. Remove the pan from the heat and gradually stir in the basic vegetable stock. Return the pan to medium heat and bring to a boil, stirring constantly. Reduce the heat, season with salt and pepper, and simmer for 35–40 minutes.

4. Meanwhile, bring a pan of water to a boil. Add the asparagus tips and cook for 5–8 minutes, until tender. Drain and cut in half.

5. Remove the soup from the heat and let cool slightly. Ladle it into a food processor or blender, in batches if necessary, and process to a smooth puree. Pour the soup into a bowl and stir in the crème fraîche, lemon rind, and asparagus tips. Let cool completely, then cover with plastic wrap, and chill in the refrigerator for at least 3 hours.

6. To serve, stir the soup and taste and adjust the seasoning, if necessary. Ladle into bowls, add the Parmesan, and serve with melba toast.

Carrot & Orange Soup

1. Melt the butter in a large pan. Add the shallots and carrots and cook over low heat, stirring occasionally, for 5–8 minutes, until softened.
2. Pour in the stock, increase the heat to medium, and bring to a boil. Season with salt and pepper, reduce the heat, cover, and simmer for 1 hour.
3. Remove the pan from the heat and let cool slightly. Ladle the soup into a food processor or blender, in batches if necessary, and process to a smooth puree.
4. Transfer the soup to a bowl and stir in the orange juice and orange rind. Let cool completely, then cover with plastic wrap and chill in the refrigerator for at least 3 hours.
5. To serve, stir in the cream, taste and adjust the seasoning, if necessary, and ladle into bowls.

Serves 6

3 tbsp butter
4 shallots, chopped
1 lb 5 oz/600 g baby carrots, sliced
* 4 cups basic vegetable stock
1½ cups orange juice
grated rind of 1 orange
⅔ cup light cream, chilled
salt and pepper

Beet & Egg Soup

1. Put the beets and lemons into a large pan, pour in the basic vegetable stock, and bring to a boil. Reduce the heat and simmer for 20 minutes.

2. Remove the pan from the heat and let cool slightly. Ladle the soup into a food processor or blender, in batches if necessary, and process to a puree. Pass the soup through a strainer into a bowl to remove any membrane or fibers. Let cool completely.

3. Meanwhile, put the eggs, honey, and a pinch of salt into a food processor blender and process until thoroughly combined. Gradually add the mixture to the soup, stirring constantly.

4. Cover with plastic wrap and chill in the refrigerator for at least 3 hours. To serve, stir the soup and taste and adjust the seasoning, if necessary. Ladle into bowls, garnish with the sour cream and snipped chives, and drizzle over the honey. Serve.

Serves 6

1 lb 7 oz/650 g cooked beets, peeled and chopped

2 lemons, peeled, seeded, and chopped

* 5⅔ cups basic vegetable stock

3 extra large eggs

1½ tbsp honey, plus extra for drizzling

salt

To garnish

sour cream, chilled

snipped fresh chives

67

Vichyssoise

1. Melt the butter in a large pan. Add the leeks and onions and stir well. Cover and cook over low heat, stirring occasionally, for 8–10 minutes, until very soft but not colored.

2. Increase the heat to medium, add the potatoes, pour in the basic vegetable stock, and bring to a boil. Reduce the heat, cover, and simmer for 25 minutes. Stir in the cream, season with salt and pepper, and cook for 5 minutes more; do not let the soup boil.

3. Remove the pan from the heat and let cool slightly. Ladle the soup into a food processor or blender, in batches if necessary, and process to a smooth puree.

4. Pour the soup into a bowl and let cool completely. Cover with plastic wrap and chill in the refrigerator for at least 3 hours.

5. To serve, stir the soup and taste and adjust the seasoning, if necessary. Ladle into bowls, garnish with the snipped chives, and serve immediately.

Serves 6

3 tbsp butter

1 lb 4 oz/550 g leeks, finely chopped

1½ onions, chopped

8 oz/225 g potatoes, thickly sliced

* 5⅔ cups basic vegetable stock

1½ cups heavy cream

salt and pepper

snipped fresh chives, to garnish

68

Leek, Potato & Pear Soup

Serves 6

- 5⅔ cups basic vegetable stock
- pinch of saffron strands, lightly crushed
- 3 tbsp butter
- 3 cups thinly sliced leeks
- ⅔ cup diced potatoes
- 3 ripe pears, peeled, cored, and chopped
- salt and pepper

To garnish

- crème fraîche, chilled
- watercress sprigs

1. Measure 3 tablespoons of the basic vegetable stock into a small bowl, stir in the saffron, and set aside.
2. Melt the butter in a large pan. Add the leeks and potatoes and cook over low heat, stirring occasionally, for 5 minutes, until the leeks have softened.
3. Increase the heat to medium, add the pears, pour in the remaining stock and the saffron mixture, and bring to a boil, stirring frequently. Reduce the heat, cover, and simmer for 20–25 minutes, until the vegetables and pears are tender.
4. Remove the pan from the heat and let cool slightly. Ladle the soup into a food processor or blender, in batches if necessary, and process to a smooth puree.
5. Pour the soup into a bowl, season to taste with salt and pepper, and let cool completely. Cover with plastic wrap and chill in the refrigerator for at least 3 hours.
6. To serve, stir the soup and taste and adjust the seasoning, if necessary. Ladle into bowls, top each with a spoonful of crème fraîche and a sprig of watercress, and serve immediately.

69

Apple & Fennel Soup

Serves 6

- 2 tbsp butter
- 1 small onion, chopped
- 1 small garlic clove, finely chopped
- 1 large fennel bulb, fronds reserved, diced
- 2 potatoes, diced
- 1¼ cups hard cider
- 1 star anise
- 1 bouquet garni (3 fresh parsley sprigs, 2 fresh thyme sprigs, and 1 bay leaf, tied together)
- 2 tbsp lemon juice
- 1¼ cups basic vegetable stock
- 1 cup crème fraîche or strained plain yogurt, chilled
- 6 lemon slices
- salt and pepper

1. Melt the butter in a large pan. Add the onion and garlic and cook over low heat, stirring occasionally, for 5 minutes, until softened. Add the fennel and potatoes and cook, stirring occasionally, for another 8–10 minutes.

2. Gradually pour in the hard cider, being careful because it will foam, and cook for 2 minutes, until the alcohol has evaporated. Increase the heat to medium, add the star anise, bouquet garni, lemon juice, and basic vegetable stock, and bring to a boil. Season to taste with salt and pepper, reduce the heat, and simmer for 20–25 minutes, until the vegetables are tender.

3. Remove the pan from the heat and let cool slightly. Remove and discard the star anise and bouquet garni. Ladle the soup into a food processor or blender, in batches if necessary, and process to a smooth puree.

4. Transfer the soup to a bowl and let cool completely. Cover with plastic wrap and chill in the refrigerator for at least 3 hours.

5. Chop the reserved fennel fronds. To serve, stir in the crème fraîche and taste and adjust the seasoning, if necessary. Ladle into bowls, garnish each with a lemon slice and fennel fronds, and serve immediately.

70

Apple Soup

Serves 6

- 2¼ lb/1 kg apples
- 2 tbsp lemon juice
- 5 tbsp butter
- 2 leeks, sliced
- 2 potatoes, diced
- * 6¼ cups basic vegetable stock
- ⅔ cup heavy cream
- pinch of grated nutmeg
- salt and pepper

1. Reserve 2 of the apples and peel, core, and dice the remainder. Put the diced apple into a bowl, add the lemon juice, and toss well to prevent discoloration.

2. Melt 3 tablespoons of the butter in a large pan. Add the leeks and stir well, then cover and cook over low heat, stirring occasionally, for 8–10 minutes, until softened. Add the diced apple and cook, stirring occasionally, for another 5 minutes. Add the potatoes and cook, stirring occasionally, for an additional 5 minutes. Increase the heat to medium, pour in the basic vegetable stock, and bring to a boil. Reduce the heat, cover, and simmer for 45–50 minutes, until the leeks and apples are soft.

3. Remove the pan from the heat and let cool slightly. Ladle the soup into a food processor or blender, in batches if necessary, and process to a smooth puree. Transfer to a bowl, stir in the cream and nutmeg, season to taste with salt and pepper, and let cool completely. Cover with plastic wrap and chill for at least 3 hours.

4. To serve, peel, core, and dice the reserved apples. Melt the remaining butter in a skillet. Add the diced apples and cook over low heat, stirring occasionally, for 5 minutes, until lightly colored and softened but not disintegrating. Remove with a slotted spoon and drain on paper towels. Stir the soup and taste and adjust the seasoning, if necessary. Ladle into bowls, garnish with the fried apples, and serve immediately.

71

Roasted Red Bell Pepper Soup with Garlic Croutons

Serves 6

3 red bell peppers

3 tbsp olive oil

1 Bermuda onion, chopped

3 garlic cloves, finely chopped

2¼ lb/1 kg ripe tomatoes, peeled, seeded, and coarsely chopped

6 tbsp red wine

1 tsp sugar

* 4 cups basic vegetable stock

salt and pepper

chili oil, for drizzling

Garlic croutons

3 tbsp olive oil

2 garlic cloves, chopped

3 slices of day-old bread, crusts removed, cut into ¼-inch/5-mm dice

1. Preheat the broiler. Put the bell peppers on a cookie sheet and broil, turning frequently, for 10 minutes, until the skins are charred. Remove with tongs, put them into a plastic bag, tie the top, and let stand until cool enough to handle. Peel off the skins, halve, and seed, then coarsely chop the flesh.

2. Heat the oil in a large pan. Add the onion and garlic and cook over low heat, stirring occasionally, for 5 minutes, until softened. Add the bell peppers and tomatoes, stir well, cover, and cook, stirring occasionally, for 8–10 minutes, until pulpy. Increase the heat to medium, pour in the wine, and cook for 2 minutes, until the alcohol has evaporated. Stir in the sugar, pour in the basic vegetable stock, and bring to a boil. Season, reduce the heat, and simmer for 30 minutes.

3. Remove the pan from the heat and let cool slightly. Ladle the soup into a food processor or blender, and process to a smooth puree. Transfer to a bowl and let cool completely, then cover with plastic wrap, and chill in the refrigerator for at least 3 hours.

4. To make the garlic croutons, heat the oil in a skillet. Add the garlic and stir-fry over low heat for about 2 minutes. Remove and discard the garlic, add the diced bread, and cook, stirring and tossing frequently, until golden brown.

5. To serve, stir the soup and taste and adjust the seasoning, if necessary. Ladle into bowls, sprinkle with the garlic croutons, drizzle with the chili oil, and serve immediately.

72

Quick-and-Easy Chickpea Soup with Sesame Paste

1. Heat a heavy skillet. Add the coriander and cumin seeds and cook over low heat, stirring constantly, for a few minutes, until they give off their aroma. Remove from the heat, tip the seeds into a mortar, and pound with a pestle until ground.

2. Pour the basic vegetable stock into a food processor or blender, add the sesame paste, lemon juice, garlic, and roasted spices and process until thoroughly combined. Pour into a bowl, stir in the mint, and season to taste with salt and pepper. Cover with plastic wrap and chill for 1 hour.

3. To serve, stir the soup and taste and adjust the seasoning. Stir in the chickpeas, ladle into bowls, garnish with the chopped cilantro, and drizzle with the oil. Serve immediately with warm pita bread.

Serves 6

½ tsp coriander seeds

1 tsp cumin seeds

* 2½ cups basic vegetable stock

2 cups sesame paste

1½ cups lemon juice

2 garlic cloves, finely chopped

1 tbsp chopped fresh mint

7 oz/200 g canned chickpeas, drained and rinsed

salt and pepper

chopped fresh cilantro, to garnish

extra virgin olive oil, for drizzling

warm pita bread, to serve

73

Jellied Vegetable Consommé

Serves 6

- 1 tbsp olive oil
- 1 small onion, finely chopped
- 1 leek, thinly sliced
- 2 tomatoes, halved crosswise
- 8 oz/225 g cremini mushrooms, sliced
- 6¾ cups basic vegetable stock
- 2 tsp yeast extract
- 2 egg whites
- 1 envelope (½ oz/15 g) powdered gelatin
- ¾ cup Madeira or medium sherry
- salt and pepper
- chopped fresh flat-leaf parsley, to garnish

1. Heat the oil in a large pan. Add the onion and leek, stir well, cover, and cook over low heat, stirring occasionally, for 30 minutes. Add the tomatoes and mushrooms and cook for 5 minutes, then pour in the basic vegetable stock and bring to a boil. Cover and simmer for 1 hour.

2. Remove the pan from the heat, strain the stock into a bowl, pressing the vegetables with the back of a ladle to extract the liquid, stir in the yeast extract, and let cool completely. Discard the contents of the strainer.

3. Return the cooled stock to a clean pan and whisk in the egg whites. Bring to a boil over medium-low heat. When the egg white floats on the surface, reduce the heat and simmer for 1 minute. Remove from the heat and strain the stock through a cheesecloth-lined strainer into a bowl. Let cool. Pour ⅔ cup of the cooled stock into a pan, sprinkle the gelatin over the surface, and let stand for 5 minutes. (If using vegetarian gelatin, follow the package instructions.) Add 5 cups of the remaining stock and simmer over low heat, gently stirring occasionally, for 5 minutes, until the gelatin has dissolved completely. Remove the pan from the heat and let cool.

4. Stir the Madeira into the consommé and season to taste with salt and pepper. Pour into a bowl and chill in the refrigerator for 4 hours, until set. Chop the jellied consommé and spoon into individual bowls. Sprinkle with the parsley and serve immediately.

74

Cucumber & Shrimp Soup

1. Pour the basic vegetable stock into a pan. Add the cucumber, scallions, and dill and bring to a boil. Reduce the heat and simmer for 20–25 minutes, until the vegetables are tender.

2. Remove the pan from the heat and let cool slightly. Ladle the soup into a food processor or blender, in batches if necessary, and process to a smooth puree.

3. Return the soup to the rinsed-out pan and reheat gently. Meanwhile, stir the cornstarch to a paste with the water in a bowl. Stir the paste into the soup and bring to a boil, stirring constantly. Reduce the heat and simmer for 3 minutes, then remove from the heat, season to taste with salt and pepper, pour into a bowl, and let cool completely.

4. Stir in a few drops of green food coloring, if using, and add the shrimp. Cover with plastic wrap and chill in the refrigerator for at least 3 hours.

5. Stir the soup and taste and adjust the seasoning, if necessary. Ladle into bowls, swirl in the cream, and serve immediately.

Serves 6

- 5⅔ cups basic vegetable stock
- 2 cucumbers, peeled, halved lengthwise, seeded, and sliced
- 10 scallions, chopped
- 1 tbsp chopped fresh dill
- 5 tbsp cornstarch
- 5 tbsp water
- green food coloring (optional)
- 3 oz/85 g peeled cooked shrimp
- 6 tbsp light cream, chilled, to garnish
- salt and pepper

75

Tomato & Smoked Shellfish Soup

1. Pour the basic vegetable stock into a bowl. Add the tomatoes, cucumber, shallot, vinegar, sugar, mustard, Tabasco sauce, and smoked shellfish and stir well. Season to taste with salt and pepper, cover with plastic wrap, and chill for at least 2 hours.

2. To serve, stir the soup and taste and adjust the seasoning, if necessary. Ladle into bowls, sprinkle with croutons, and serve.

Serves 6

- 3 cups basic vegetable stock
- 6 ripe tomatoes, peeled, seeded, and chopped
- 1 cucumber, peeled, halved lengthwise, seeded, and chopped
- 1 shallot, chopped
- 3 tbsp sherry vinegar
- 1 tsp sugar
- 1½ tsp Dijon mustard
- ¼ tsp Tabasco sauce or pinch of cayenne pepper
- 1 lb 2 oz/500 g smoked oysters or smoked mussels
- salt and pepper
- croutons, to serve (see page 65)

Mussel Soup

Serves 6

- 36 live mussels
- ⅔ cup basic vegetable stock
- 1¼ cups dry white wine
- ¼ onion, finely chopped
- ½ celery stalk, finely chopped
- 5 tbsp chopped fresh flat-leaf parsley
- 2½ cups heavy cream
- pinch of cayenne pepper or dash of Tabasco sauce
- salt and pepper
- garlic and herb bread, to serve

1. Scrub the mussels under cold running water and pull off the "beards." Discard any with broken shells or that do not shut immediately when sharply tapped. Put them into a large pan, pour in the basic vegetable stock and wine, and add the onion, celery, and parsley. Cover and bring to a boil over high heat. Cook, shaking the pan occasionally, for 3–5 minutes, until the shells have opened.

2. Remove the pan from the heat and lift out the mussels with a slotted spoon. Discard any that remain shut, shell the remainder, and set aside for another dish.

3. Strain the soup into a clean pan and discard the contents of the strainer. Stir in the cream and cayenne, season to taste with salt and pepper, and let cool completely. Cover with plastic wrap and chill for at least 3 hours.

4. To serve, stir the soup and taste and adjust the seasoning, if necessary. Ladle into bowls and serve immediately with garlic and herb bread.

World Classics

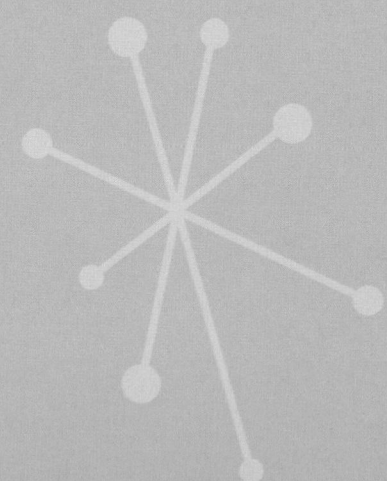

77

Borscht—Russia

1. Peel and coarsely grate 4 of the beets. Melt the butter in a large pan. Add the onions and cook over low heat, stirring occasionally, for 5 minutes, until softened. Add the grated beets, carrots, and celery and cook, stirring occasionally, for another 5 minutes.

2. Increase the heat to medium, add the tomatoes, vinegar, sugar, garlic, and bouquet garni, season with salt and pepper, and stir well, then pour in the basic vegetable stock and bring to a boil. Reduce the heat, cover, and simmer for 1¼ hours.

3. Meanwhile, peel and grate the remaining beet. Add it and any juices to the pan and simmer for another 10 minutes. Remove the pan from the heat and let stand for 10 minutes.

4. Remove and discard the bouquet garni. Ladle the soup into warmed bowls and top each with a spoonful of sour cream, sprinkle with chopped dill, and serve immediately with rye bread.

Serves 6

5 beets, about 2¼ lb/1 kg
5 tbsp butter
2 onions, thinly sliced
3 carrots, thinly sliced
3 celery stalks, thinly sliced
6 tomatoes, peeled, seeded, and chopped
1 tbsp red wine vinegar
1 tbsp sugar
2 garlic cloves, finely chopped
1 bouquet garni (3 fresh parsley sprigs, 2 fresh thyme sprigs, and 1 bay leaf, tied together)
* 5⅔ cups basic vegetable stock
salt and pepper
rye bread, to serve

To garnish
sour cream
chopped fresh dill

French Onion Soup

Serves 6

1 tbsp olive oil

2 tbsp butter

4–5 onions, about 1 lb 7 oz/650 g, thinly sliced

3 garlic cloves, finely chopped

1 tsp sugar

* 8¾ cups basic vegetable stock

2 tbsp all-purpose flour

⅔ cup dry white vermouth

3 tbsp brandy

salt and pepper

Cheese croutes

6 slices of French bread

1 garlic clove, halved

2 cups grated Gruyère cheese

1. Heat the oil with the butter in a large pan. Add the onions, stir well, cover, and cook over very low heat, stirring occasionally, for 15 minutes. Uncover the pan, increase the heat to medium, stir in the garlic, sugar, and 1 teaspoon of salt, and cook, stirring frequently, for 30–40 minutes, until the onions are deep golden brown.

2. Meanwhile, bring the basic vegetable stock to a boil in another pan. Sprinkle the flour over the onions and cook, stirring constantly, for 3 minutes. Stir in the vermouth and cook, stirring constantly, for 2 minutes, until the alcohol has evaporated, then gradually stir in the hot stock and bring to a boil. Skim off any foam that rises to the surface, reduce the heat, cover, and simmer for 40 minutes.

3. Meanwhile, make the cheese croutes. Preheat the broiler. Toast the slices of bread on both sides. Rub each slice with the garlic clove, then top with the cheese and broil for a few minutes, until melted.

4. Stir in the brandy, remove the pan from the heat, and taste and adjust the seasoning. Ladle into warmed bowls, top each with a cheese croute, and serve immediately.

Bouillabaisse—France

1. Cut the large fish into 3–4 pieces. Leave the small ones whole. Scrub the mussels under cold running water and pull of the "beards." Discard any with broken shells or that do not shut immediately when sharply tapped. Pour the basic vegetable stock into a pan and bring to a boil. Put the saffron into a bowl, pour in hot water to cover, and let soak.

2. Put the onions, leeks, celery, fennel, tomatoes, garlic, orange rind, chile, thyme sprig, bay leaves, peppercorns, and cloves into a large pan. Put the firm-fleshed fish, such as monkfish, on top, pour in half the olive oil, and season with salt. Pour in the stock, bring back to a boil, cover, and simmer for 8 minutes.

3. Add the softer fish, the remaining olive oil, and the saffron with its soaking water. Cover and simmer for another 4 minutes. Add the mussels and langoustines, cover, and cook for 4 minutes more, until the mussels have opened and all the fish is cooked. Discard any mussels that remain closed.

4. Carefully transfer the fish, shellfish, and vegetables to a warm serving dish. Strain the broth into a warmed tureen and taste and adjust the seasoning, if necessary. Serve the fish and broth immediately.

Serves 8

5 lb/2.25 kg mixed fish, such as monkfish, red snapper, and whiting
1 lb/450 g mussels
* 15 cups basic vegetable stock
½ tsp saffron threads
2 onions, chopped
2 leeks, white parts only, chopped
3 celery stalks, chopped
1 fennel bulb, sliced
2 large tomatoes, peeled and chopped
4 garlic cloves, finely chopped
1 strip of thinly pared orange rind
1 red chile, seeded and chopped
1 fresh thyme sprig
2 bay leaves
8 black peppercorns
2 cloves
1 cup olive oil
1 lb/450 g cooked langoustines
salt and pepper

80

Bauernsuppe—Germany

Serves 6

4 tbsp butter

2¼ lb/1 kg stewing steak, trimmed of fat and cut into ¾-inch/2-cm cubes

11¼ cups basic vegetable stock

2 onions, chopped

1 garlic clove, finely chopped

1 tsp paprika

4 tbsp all-purpose flour

1 bouquet garni (3 fresh parsley sprigs, 2 fresh thyme sprigs, and 1 bay leaf, tied together)

3 potatoes, diced

salt

To garnish

2 tsp chopped fresh dill

½ cup grated Gruyère cheese

1. Melt the butter in a large pan. Add the meat and cook over medium heat, stirring frequently, for 8–10 minutes, until lightly browned all over. Meanwhile, bring the basic vegetable stock to a boil in another pan.

2. Add the onions to the meat, reduce the heat, and cook, stirring frequently, for 5 minutes, until softened. Add the garlic and cook for another 2 minutes. Stir in the paprika and flour and cook, stirring constantly, for 3–4 minutes. Gradually stir in the hot basic vegetable stock and bring to a boil. Add the bouquet garni, season with salt, cover, and simmer, stirring occasionally, for 1 hour.

3. Add the potatoes to the soup, re-cover the pan, and simmer for another 45 minutes, until the meat and vegetables are tender.

4. Remove the pan from the heat and taste and adjust the seasoning, if necessary. Remove and discard the bouquet garni. Ladle the soup into warmed bowls, sprinkle with the dill and grated cheese, and serve immediately.

81

Minestrone—Italy

Serves 6

- 2 tbsp olive oil
- 1 Bermuda onion, chopped
- 2 garlic cloves, finely chopped
- 2 celery stalks, chopped
- 4 slices of bacon, diced
- ½ small white cabbage, cored and shredded
- ⅔ cup red wine
- 7½ cups basic vegetable stock
- ⅓ cup dried cannellini beans, soaked overnight in cold water to cover, and drained
- 4 plum tomatoes, peeled, seeded, and chopped
- 2 tbsp tomato paste
- 2 tsp sugar
- 2 carrots, diced
- ½ cup fresh shelled peas
- 2 oz/55 g green beans, cut into short lengths
- ½ cup ziti pasta
- 2 tbsp chopped fresh mixed herbs
- salt and pepper
- grated Parmesan cheese, to serve

1. Heat the oil in a large pan. Add the onion, garlic, celery, and bacon, and cook over low heat, stirring occasionally, for 5–7 minutes, until the onion has softened and the bacon is crisp. Stir in the cabbage and cook, stirring frequently, for another 5 minutes.

2. Increase the heat to medium, pour in the wine, and cook for about 2 minutes, until the alcohol has evaporated, then pour in the basic vegetable stock. Add the cannellini beans and bring to a boil, then lower the heat, cover, and simmer for 2½ hours.

3. Add the tomatoes, tomato paste, sugar, carrots, peas, green beans, pasta, and herbs and season to taste with salt and pepper. Simmer for 20–25 minutes, until the pasta is cooked and the vegetables are tender.

4. Ladle the soup into warmed bowls and serve immediately, passing around the grated cheese separately.

82

Fabada—Spain

1. Bring the basic vegetable stock to a boil in a large pan. Add the beans, onion, and garlic and bring back to a boil, then reduce the heat, cover, and simmer for 1 hour, until the beans are tender.

2. Meanwhile, put the saffron into a small bowl, add water to cover, and let soak.

3. Add the sausages, bacon, ham, thyme, and saffron with its soaking water to the pan, season to taste with salt and pepper, and mix well. Re-cover and simmer the soup for another 30–35 minutes. Ladle into warmed bowls and serve immediately.

Serves 6

- 7½ cups basic vegetable stock
- 1¼ cups dried lima beans, soaked overnight in cold water to cover, and drained
- 1¼ cups dried large white kidney beans (fabes de la granja) or cannellini beans, soaked overnight in water to cover, and drained
- 1 Bermuda onion, chopped
- 2 garlic cloves, finely chopped
- pinch of saffron threads
- 4 oz/125 g morcilla or other blood sausage, sliced
- 2 chorizo sausages, sliced
- 4 slices of bacon, diced
- ⅓ cup diced smoked ham
- pinch of dried thyme
- salt and pepper

83

Caldo Verde—Portugal

Serves 6

- 3 tbsp olive oil, plus extra for drizzling
- 1 Bermuda onion, finely chopped
- 2 garlic cloves, finely chopped
- 3¼ cups diced potatoes
- 6¾ cups basic vegetable stock
- 4½ oz/125 g chorizo or other spicy sausage, thinly sliced
- 5 cups finely shredded kale or savoy cabbage
- salt and pepper

1. Heat 2 tablespoons of the olive oil in a large pan. Add the onion and garlic and cook over low heat, stirring occasionally, for 5 minutes, until softened. Add the potatoes and cook, stirring constantly, for 3 minutes more.

2. Increase the heat to medium, pour in the basic vegetable stock, and bring to a boil. Reduce the heat, cover, and cook for 10 minutes.

3. Meanwhile, heat the remaining olive oil in a skillet. Add the sausage slices and cook over low heat, turning occasionally, for a few minutes, until the fat runs. Remove with a slotted spoon and drain on paper towels.

4. Remove the pan of soup from the heat and mash the potatoes with a potato masher. Return to the heat, add the kale, and bring back to a boil. Reduce the heat and simmer for 5–6 minutes, until tender.

5. Remove the pan from the heat and mash the potatoes again to incorporate. Stir in the sausage slices, season to taste with salt and pepper, and ladle into warmed bowls. Drizzle each with a little olive oil and serve immediately.

84

London Particular—England

Serves 6

8 thick slices of bacon
2 tbsp butter
2 onions, chopped
2 carrots, chopped
2 celery stalks, chopped
generous ½ cup yellow split peas, soaked in cold water for 1–2 hours, and drained
* 7½ cups basic vegetable stock
salt and pepper
croutons, to garnish (see page 65)

1. Dice 6 slices of the bacon. Melt the butter in a pan. Add the diced bacon and cook over low heat, stirring frequently, for 4–5 minutes. Add the onions, carrots, and celery and cook, stirring frequently, for another 5 minutes.

2. Increase the heat to medium, add the peas, pour in the basic vegetable stock, and bring to a boil. Reduce the heat, cover, and simmer for 1 hour.

3. Meanwhile, preheat the broiler. Broil the remaining bacon for 2–4 minutes on each side, until crisp, then remove from the heat. Let cool slightly, then crumble.

4. Remove the soup from the heat and season to taste with salt and pepper. Ladle into warmed bowls, garnish with the crumbled bacon and the croutons, and serve immediately.

85

Cullen Skink—Scotland

Serves 6

- 1 lb 2 oz/500 g smoked white fish (traditionally smoked haddock)
- 1 large onion, chopped
- 4 fresh parsley sprigs
- * 5⅔ cups basic vegetable stock
- 1 lb 10 oz/750 g potatoes, cut into chunks
- 4 tbsp butter
- 3¾ cups milk
- salt and pepper
- chopped fresh flat-leaf parsley, to garnish
- crusty bread, to serve

1. Put the fish, onion, and parsley into a large pan, pour in the basic vegetable stock, and bring to a boil, skimming off the foam that rises to the surface. Reduce the heat, cover, and simmer for 10 minutes, until the flesh flakes easily.
2. Remove the pan from the heat and lift out the fish with a slotted spatula. Remove and discard the skin and bones and flake the flesh. Strain the basic vegetable stock into a clean pan.
3. Return the pan to the heat, add the potatoes, and bring back to a boil. Reduce the heat and simmer for 20–30 minutes, until tender.
4. Remove the pan from the heat. Using a slotted spoon, transfer the potatoes to a bowl, add the butter, and mash until smooth.
5. Return the pan to the heat, add the milk, and bring to a boil. Whisk in the mashed potatoes, a little at a time, until thoroughly incorporated. Gently stir in the fish and season to taste with salt and pepper. Ladle into warmed bowls, sprinkle with chopped parsley, and serve immediately with crusty bread.

86

Mussel Soup—Ireland

1. Scrub the mussels under cold running water and pull of the "beards." Discard any with broken shells or that do not shut when sharply tapped. Sprinkle the onion, parsley, and bay leaves over the bottom of a large pan, put the mussels on top, season with pepper, and pour in the hard cider. Cover, bring to a boil over high heat, and cook, shaking the pan occasionally, for 4–5 minutes, until the mussels have opened. Remove the pan from the heat and lift out the mussels. Discard any that remain shut. Remove the mussels from the shells and set aside. Strain the cooking liquid into a bowl.

2. Melt the butter in a large pan. Add the celery and leeks and cook over low heat, stirring occasionally, for 8 minutes, until lightly browned. Meanwhile, pour the milk into another pan and bring just to a boil, then remove from the heat.

3. Sprinkle the flour over the vegetables and cook, stirring constantly, for 2 minutes. Increase the heat to medium and gradually stir in the milk, a little at a time, then stir in the basic vegetable stock. Bring to a boil, stirring constantly, then reduce the heat, and simmer for 15 minutes.

4. Remove the pan from the heat and strain the soup into a bowl. Return to the rinsed-out pan, add the reserved cooking liquid, the nutmeg, fennel seeds, and mussels, and season to taste with salt and pepper. Return to the heat and stir in the cream. Reheat gently for a few minutes but do not let the soup boil. Ladle into warmed bowls and serve with whole wheat bread.

Serves 6

48 mussels
1 onion, finely chopped
2 tbsp chopped fresh flat-leaf parsley
2 bay leaves
generous 1 cup hard cider
4 tbsp butter
2 celery stalks, chopped
2 leeks, thinly sliced
2½ cups milk
⅓ cup all-purpose flour
* 2½ cups basic vegetable stock
pinch of grated nutmeg
½ tsp fennel seeds
1 cup heavy cream
salt and pepper
whole wheat bread, to serve

87

Avgolemono—Greece

1. Pour the basic vegetable stock into a large pan and bring to a boil. Add the rice, bring back to a boil, then reduce the heat, and simmer for 15 minutes, until the rice is tender.

2. Meanwhile, beat the eggs in a bowl and gradually beat in the lemon juice. Gradually beat in a ladleful of the hot soup, then add the mixture to the pan. Cook over low heat, rotating the pan occasionally to distribute the egg and lemon sauce evenly, for 2–3 minutes.

3. Remove from the heat, season the soup to taste with pepper, and ladle into warmed bowls. Sprinkle with parsley and serve immediately.

Serves 6

* 7½ cups basic vegetable stock
* generous ½ cup long-grain rice
* 4 eggs
* ½ cup lemon juice
* pepper
* chopped fresh flat-leaf parsley, to garnish

88

Harira—North Africa

1 Heat the olive oil in a large pan. Add the lamb and cook over medium heat, stirring frequently, for 8–10 minutes, until lightly browned all over. Reduce the heat, add the onion, and cook, stirring frequently, for 5 minutes, until softened.

2 Increase the heat to medium, add the chickpeas, pour in the basic vegetable stock, and bring to a boil. Reduce the heat, cover, and simmer for 2 hours.

3 Stir in the lentils, tomatoes, bell pepper, tomato paste, sugar, cinnamon, turmeric, ginger, cilantro, and parsley and simmer for another 15 minutes. Add the rice and simmer for an additional 15 minutes, until the rice is cooked and the lentils are tender.

4 Season to taste with salt and pepper and remove the pan from the heat. Ladle the soup into warmed bowls, sprinkle with a little chopped cilantro, and serve immediately.

Serves 6

2 tbsp olive oil

8 oz/225 g boneless lean lamb, cut into cubes

1 onion, chopped

½ cup dried chickpeas, soaked overnight in water to cover, and drained

6¾ cups basic vegetable stock

½ cup red or yellow lentils

2 large tomatoes, peeled, seeded, and diced

1 red bell pepper, seeded and diced

1 tbsp tomato paste

1 tsp sugar

1 tsp ground cinnamon

½ tsp ground turmeric

½ tsp ground ginger

1 tbsp chopped fresh cilantro, plus extra to garnish

1 tbsp chopped fresh flat-leaf parsley

scant ⅓ cup long-grain rice

salt and pepper

89

Eshkaneh—Iran

1. Melt the butter in a large pan. Add the onions and cook over low heat, stirring occasionally, for 7–8 minutes, until just beginning to color.

2. Sprinkle in the flour and cook, stirring constantly, for 2 minutes. Remove the pan from the heat and gradually stir in the basic vegetable stock, a little at a time. Return the pan to medium heat and bring to a boil, stirring constantly. Add the turmeric, lemon juice, sugar, and cilantro and season generously with salt and pepper. Reduce the heat, cover, and simmer for 10 minutes.

3. Lightly beat the egg in a bowl. Whisk it into the soup and remove the pan from the heat. Ladle into warmed bowls and serve immediately with warm flat bread.

Serves 6

4 tbsp butter
4 onions, thinly sliced
2 tbsp all-purpose flour
5 cups basic vegetable stock
1 tsp ground turmeric
½ cup lemon juice
1 tbsp superfine sugar
1 tbsp chopped fresh cilantro
1 egg
salt and pepper
warm flat bread, to serve

90

Wonton Soup—China

Serves 6

- 6 oz/175 g pork or chicken, ground
- 2 oz/55 g peeled shrimp, ground
- 1 finely chopped scallion
- 1 tsp finely chopped fresh ginger
- 1 tsp sugar
- 1 tbsp Chinese rice wine or dry sherry
- 2 tbsp light soy sauce
- 24 store-bought wonton wrappers
- 3¾ cups basic vegetable stock
- snipped fresh chives, to garnish

1. Combine the pork, shrimp, scallion, ginger, sugar, rice wine, and half the soy sauce in a bowl until thoroughly mixed. Cover and let marinate for 20 minutes.
2. Put 1 tsp of the mixture in the center of each wonton wrapper. Dampen the edges, fold corner to corner into a triangle, and press to seal, then seal the bottom corners together.
3. Bring the basic vegetable stock to a boil in a large pan. Add the wontons and cook for 5 minutes. Stir in the remaining soy sauce and remove from the heat. Ladle the soup and wontons into warmed bowls, sprinkle with snipped chives, and serve immediately.

91

Three Delicacy Soup—China

1. Combine the chicken and shrimp in a bowl. Mix the cornstarch to a paste with the water in another bowl and add to the mixture, together with the egg white and a pinch of salt, stirring well to coat.

2. Bring the basic vegetable stock to a boil in a pan over medium heat. Add the chicken mixture and the ham and bring back to a boil. Reduce the heat and simmer for 1 minute. Taste and adjust the seasoning, if necessary, and remove from the heat. Ladle into warmed bowls, garnish with scallions, and serve immediately.

Serves 6

6 oz/175 g skinless boneless chicken breast portion, very thinly sliced into strips

6 oz/175 g peeled shrimp, halved if large

1 tsp cornstarch

2 tsp water

1 medium egg white, lightly beaten

* 4 cups basic vegetable stock

6 oz/175 g honey-roast ham, very thinly sliced into strips

salt

chopped scallions or snipped fresh chives, to garnish

92

Seaweed Soup with Miso—Japan

1. Heat the oil in a pan. Add the onion and garlic and cook over low heat, stirring occasionally, for 5 minutes, until softened. Meanwhile, pour the basic vegetable stock into another pan and bring to a boil.

2. Stir the miso paste, tomato paste, ginger, and coriander into the onion mixture, mixing well, then add the carrots, and cook, stirring frequently, for 5 minutes. If the mixture looks as if it might scorch, stir in 1–2 tablespoons of the hot stock.

3. Add the yaki-nori to the stock, then stir in the onion mixture, and simmer gently for 10 minutes. Ladle into warmed bowls and serve immediately, garnished with snipped chives.

Serves 6

1 tbsp sunflower oil

1 large onion, thinly sliced

2 garlic cloves, finely chopped

* 7½ cups basic vegetable stock

1½ tbsp red miso paste

1 tbsp tomato paste

1 tsp ground ginger

1 tsp ground coriander

2 carrots, thinly sliced

3 sheets yaki-nori seaweed (seasoned and toasted nori seaweed), torn into shreds

snipped fresh chives, to garnish

93

Crab Soup—Vietnam

Serves 6

6 dried shiitake mushrooms
1½ cups hot water
5 scallions
12 oz/350 g asparagus spears, trimmed
1 lb 10 oz/750 g white crabmeat, thawed if frozen
2 tbsp peanut oil
3 garlic cloves, finely chopped
* 7½ cups basic vegetable stock
1–2 tbsp Thai fish sauce
3 tbsp chopped fresh cilantro

1. Put the mushrooms into a bowl, pour in the water, and let soak for 20 minutes. Meanwhile, chop the white parts of the scallions and thinly slice the green parts diagonally. Slice the asparagus diagonally into ¾-inch/2-cm pieces. Pick over the crabmeat and remove any pieces of shell and cartilage.

2. Drain the mushrooms, reserving the soaking liquid, and squeeze gently to remove the excess liquid. Remove and discard the stalks and thinly slice the caps. Strain the soaking liquid through a cheesecloth-lined strainer.

3. Heat the oil in a large pan. Add the chopped scallions and garlic and stir-fry over medium heat for 2 minutes. Pour in the basic vegetable stock and reserved soaking liquid, add the mushrooms, and bring to a boil.

4. Stir in 1 tablespoon of the Thai fish sauce, add the sliced scallions and asparagus pieces, and bring back to a boil. Reduce the heat and simmer for 5 minutes, then gently stir in the crabmeat and cilantro. Simmer for another 3–4 minutes to heat through.

5. Remove the pan from the heat, taste, and stir in more fish sauce, if necessary. Ladle into warmed bowls and serve immediately.

94

Laksa—Malaysia

1. Peel the shrimp, reserving the heads and shells. Devein the shrimp by cutting a slit along their backs with a sharp knife and removing the black thread with the point of the knife. Rinse the heads and shells. Heat 1 tablespoon of the oil in a pan. Add the shrimp heads and shells and stir-fry over medium heat for 2–3 minutes, until lightly colored, then pour in the basic vegetable stock and bring to a boil. Reduce the heat and simmer for 15 minutes. Strain the stock into a bowl and discard the shrimp shells.

2. Combine the curry paste and ground nuts in a bowl. Heat the remaining oil in a pan. Add the curry paste and cook over low heat, stirring frequently, for 4–5 minutes. Increase the heat to medium, pour in the basic vegetable stock, and bring to a boil, then reduce the heat, cover, and simmer for 20 minutes.

3. Meanwhile, put the noodles into a bowl, pour in boiling water to cover, and let soak for 5 minutes, then drain. Blanch the bean sprouts in boiling salted water for a few minutes, then drain. Whisk the coconut milk into the pan and simmer for 2 minutes, then add the shrimp, squid, and sugar, and season to taste with salt. Simmer for 5 minutes, until the shrimp and squid are tender, then remove from the heat. Divide the noodles and bean sprouts among warmed bowls and ladle the soup over them. Garnish with chopped cilantro, cucumber strips, and scallions, and serve immediately.

Serves 6

12 oz/350 g large shrimp

6 tbsp peanut oil

5⅔ cups basic vegetable stock

2 tbsp Panang curry paste (very hot) or red curry paste (hot)

¼ cup candlenuts or cashew nuts, ground

9 oz/250 g rice noodles

3 cups bean sprouts

2½ cups canned coconut milk

6 oz/175 g prepared squid, scored and cut into small diamonds

1 tbsp brown sugar

salt

To garnish

fresh cilantro sprigs

julienne strips of cucumber

chopped scallions

Tom Yam Goong—Thailand

1. Peel the shrimp, reserving the heads and shells. Devein the shrimp by cutting a slit along their backs with a sharp knife and removing the black thread with the point of the knife. Rinse the heads and shells.

2. Pour the basic vegetable stock into a pan, add the shrimp heads and tails, lemongrass, kaffir lime leaves, and a pinch of salt, and bring to a boil. Reduce the heat and simmer for 10 minutes. Remove the pan from the heat and strain into a clean pan.

3. Return the pan to the heat, add the green chiles, and bring back to a boil, then reduce the heat and simmer for another 10 minutes. Stir in the Thai fish sauce and shrimp and simmer for 5 minutes. Add the scallions, lime juice, and red chiles, and heat through for 1–2 minutes.

4. Remove the pan from the heat and taste and adjust the seasoning with more lime juice, fish sauce, or salt, if necessary. Ladle into warmed bowls, sprinkle with the cilantro, and serve immediately with the lime wedges.

Serves 6

1 lb 2 oz/500 g large shrimp
6¾ cups stock
3 lemongrass stalks bruised
6 kaffir lime leaves, torn
3 green chiles, seeded and thinly sliced
3 tbsp Thai fish sauce
3 scallions, chopped
2 tbsp lime juice
2 red chiles, seeded and thinly sliced
1 tbsp chopped fresh cilantro
salt
lime wedges, to serve

96

Chicken Soup with Ginger & Coconut Milk—Thailand

1. Put the chicken, rice, lemongrass, garlic, chiles, lime leaves, ginger, and cilantro into a pan, pour in the basic vegetable stock and coconut milk, and bring to a boil over medium heat, stirring occasionally. Reduce the heat, cover, and simmer for 1 hour.

2. Remove the pan from the heat and let cool slightly. Remove and discard the lemongrass and kaffir lime leaves. Ladle the soup into a food processor or blender, in batches if necessary, and process to a puree.

3. Return the soup to the rinsed-out pan, season to taste with salt, and add the scallions, corn cobs, and mushrooms. Bring back to a boil, then reduce the heat, and simmer for 5 minutes.

4. Remove the pan from the heat. Ladle the soup into warmed bowls, garnish with chopped cilantro and chile, and serve immediately.

Serves 6

14 oz/400g skinless, boneless chicken breast portions, cut into strips

½ cup Thai fragrant rice

1 lemongrass stalk, bruised

4 garlic cloves, coarsely chopped

2 green chiles, seeded and sliced

4 kaffir lime leaves, torn

1-inch/2.5-cm piece fresh ginger, chopped

4 tbsp chopped fresh cilantro, plus extra to garnish

* 6¾ cups basic vegetable stock

1¾ cups canned coconut milk

4 scallions, thinly sliced

1 cup baby corn cobs

4 oz/115 g white mushrooms, halved

salt

chopped red chile, to garnish

97

Manhattan Clam Chowder—United States

1. Heat the oil in a pan. Add the salt pork and cook over medium heat, stirring frequently, for 6–8 minutes, until golden brown. Remove with a slotted spoon.

2. Add the onion and celery to the pan, reduce the heat to low, and cook, stirring occasionally, for 5 minutes, until softened. Increase the heat to medium, add the tomatoes, potatoes, thyme, and parsley, return the pork to the pan, season with salt and pepper, and pour in the tomato juice and basic vegetable stock. Bring to a boil, stirring constantly, then reduce the heat, cover, and simmer for 15–20 minutes, until the potatoes are just tender.

3. Meanwhile, scrub the clams under cold running water. Discard any with broken shells or that do not shut when sharply tapped. Put them into a pan, pour in the wine, cover, and cook over high heat, shaking the pan occasionally, for 4–5 minutes, until the shells have opened.

4. Remove the clams with a slotted spoon and let cool slightly. Discard any clams that remain shut. Strain the cooking liquid through a cheesecloth-lined strainer into the soup. Remove the clams from the shells.

5. Add the clams to the soup and heat through, stirring constantly, for 2–3 minutes. Remove from the heat and taste and adjust the seasoning, if necessary. Ladle into warmed bowls and serve immediately with crusty bread.

Serves 6

1 tsp sunflower oil
4 oz/115 g salt pork or unsmoked bacon, diced
1 onion, finely chopped
2 celery stalks, chopped
4 tomatoes, peeled, seeded, and chopped
3 potatoes, diced
pinch of dried thyme
3 tbsp chopped fresh parsley
⅔ cup tomato juice
* 2½ cups basic vegetable stock
36 quahog or littleneck clams
⅔ cups dry white wine
salt and pepper
crusty bread, to serve

Chicken & Corn Soup—United States

1. Remove the skin from the chicken, cut the meat off the bones, and cut into small pieces. Put the saffron into a bowl, pour in hot water to cover, and let soak.

2. Heat the oil in a pan. Add the onions and celery and cook over low heat, stirring occasionally, for 5 minutes, until softened. Increase the heat to medium, pour in the basic vegetable stock, add the peppercorns and mace, and bring to a boil. Reduce the heat and simmer for 25 minutes.

3. Increase the heat to medium, add the chicken, noodles, corn, sage, parsley, and saffron with its soaking water, season to taste with salt and pepper, and bring back to a boil. Reduce the heat and simmer for another 20 minutes.

4. Remove the pan from the heat, taste and adjust the seasoning, if necessary, ladle into warmed bowls, and serve immediately.

Serves 6

- 1 roasted chicken, about 3 lb/1.3 kg
- ½ tsp saffron threads
- 3 tbsp corn oil
- 2 onions, thinly sliced
- 3 celery stalks, sliced
- * 7½ cups basic vegetable stock
- 8 black peppercorns
- 1 mace blade
- 4 oz/115 g egg noodles
- 2⅓ cups frozen corn
- pinch of dried sage
- 2 tbsp chopped fresh flat-leaf parsley
- salt and pepper

99

Jamaican Pepper Pot—Caribbean

Serves 6

- 8 oz/225 g stewing steak, diced
- 8 oz/225 g salt pork, diced
- 8 oz/225 g callaloo or spinach, coarse stalks removed, finely chopped
- * 12½ cups basic vegetable stock
- 8 oz/225 g fresh or frozen okra
- 1 tbsp lemon juice
- 8 oz/225 g sweet potato, sliced
- 8 oz/225 g christophine (chayote), peeled and thinly sliced
- 1 green chile, seeded and sliced
- 3 cups canned coconut milk
- 2 scallions, finely chopped
- salt and pepper

Plantain chips

- 2 plantains
- ice water
- ground cinnamon, for dusting
- vegetable oil, for deep-frying

1. Put the steak, pork, and callaloo into a large pan, pour in the basic vegetable stock, and bring to a boil over medium heat. Reduce the heat and simmer for 2–2¼ hours, until the meat is tender. Meanwhile, cut off the stems of fresh okra, if using, being careful not to pierce the pods. Dip the cut ends into salt and let drain in a colander for 30 minutes. Rinse well in water mixed with the lemon juice. If using frozen okra, rinse in water mixed with the lemon juice.

2. Make the plantain chips. Using a sharp knife, cut through the plantain skins along the ridges and peel off. Cut the flesh into wafer-thin slices with a mandoline or very sharp knife, put into a bowl of ice water, and let soak for 30 minutes. Heat the oil in a deep-fryer to 360–375°F/180–190°C, or until a cube of day-old bread browns in 30 seconds. Drain the plantain slices and pat dry with a dish towel. Dust with the cinnamon, add to the hot oil, in batches if necessary, and cook until golden brown. Remove with a slotted spoon and drain on paper towels.

3. Add the okra, sweet potato, christophine, chile, coconut milk, and scallions to the pan with the stock, season with salt and pepper, and bring back to a boil. Simmer for 35–40 minutes, until all the vegetables are tender and the soup has thickened. Remove the pan from the heat and taste and adjust the seasoning, if necessary. Ladle into warmed bowls and serve immediately, passing around the plantain chips separately.

100

Black Bean Soup—Caribbean

Serves 6

- 3 tbsp corn oil
- 1 large onion, chopped
- 2 celery stalks, chopped
- 2 garlic cloves, chopped
- 2½ cups dried black beans or black-eyed peas, soaked overnight in cold water to cover, and drained
- * 11¼ cups basic vegetable stock
- ¾ tsp cayenne pepper
- 5 tbsp lemon juice
- 2 tbsp red wine vinegar
- 2 tbsp dry sherry
- 4 hard-cooked eggs, coarsely chopped
- salt and pepper
- chopped celery leaves, to garnish
- grated cheddar cheese, to serve

1. Heat the oil in a large pan. Add the onion, celery, and garlic and cook over low heat, stirring occasionally, for 6–8 minutes, until softened.

2. Increase the heat to medium, add the beans, pour in the basic vegetable stock, and bring to a boil. Reduce the heat, cover, and simmer for 2–2½ hours, until the beans are tender.

3. Remove the pan from the heat and let cool slightly. Ladle all or half the soup, depending on the texture you require, into a food processor or blender, in batches if necessary, and process to a puree.

4. Return the soup to the pan and bring just to a boil. If it is very thick, add a little more stock or water. Stir in the cayenne, lemon juice, vinegar, sherry, and hard-cooked eggs and season to taste with salt and pepper. Reduce the heat and simmer, stirring constantly, for 10 minutes.

5. Remove the pan from the heat and ladle the soup into warmed bowls. Garnish with celery leaves and serve immediately, passing around the grated cheese separately.

almonds: chicken & almond soup 44
apples
apple & fennel soup 156
apple soup 159
split pea and sausage soup 37
see also cider
arugula: green vegetable soup 20
asparagus
asparagus soup 102
asparagus soup (chilled) 147
crab soup 206
avgolemono 194
avocados
al fresco avocado soup 136
avocado soup 104

bacon
bacon & potato soup 26
bacon & pumpkin soup 80
chicken noodle soup 128
chicken soup with leeks & rice 46
fabada 185
London particular 188
Manhattan clam chowder 215
minestrone 182
bauernsuppe 180
bean sprouts: laksa 209
beef
bauernsuppe 180
beef noodle soup 34
Jamaican pepper pot 218
beets
beet & egg soup 150
borscht 174
bell peppers
goulash soup 78
harira 197
mixed vegetable soup with lamb meatballs 32
red bell pepper soup 72
roasted red bell pepper soup with garlic croutons 160
tomato & white bean soup 16
black bean soup 221
bok choy: egg flower soup 120
borscht 174
bouillabaisse 179
bread
mushroom soup 68
ribollita 25
broccoli & Roquefort soup 107
bulgur wheat: pork soup with bulgur wheat 28

cabbage
bacon & potato soup 26
caldo verde 186
goulash soup 78
lamb & vegetable broth 84
minestrone 182
ribollita 25
caldo verde 186
callaloo: Jamaican pepper pot 218
cannellini beans
minestrone 182
ribollita 25
tomato & white bean soup 16
carrots
beef noodle soup 34
borscht 174
Cajun crab & corn chowder 95
carrot & cilantro soup 62
carrot & mussel soup 98
carrot & orange soup 148
carrot & parsnip soup 60
chicken & almond soup 44
chicken & lentil soup 40
chicken soup with matzo balls 43
crab & noodle soup 131
curried vegetable soup 114
fish & sweet potato soup 50
goulash soup 78
hot & sour soup 125
lamb & lemon soup 89
lamb & vegetable broth 84
lentil soup with ham 83
London particular 188
minestrone 182
mixed vegetable soup with lamb meatballs 32
red bell pepper soup 72
ribollita 25
seaweed soup with miso 204
shrimp bisque 132
split pea and sausage soup 37
vegetable broth 110
vegetable soup with semolina dumplings 113
cashew nuts: laksa 209
cauliflower
cauliflower & coconut soup 74
red bell pepper soup 72
caviar: asparagus soup 102
celeriac: mixed vegetable soup with lamb meatballs 32
celery
black bean soup 221
borscht 174
bouillabaisse 179
Cajun crab & corn chowder 95
carrot & cilantro soup 62
chicken & corn soup 216
chicken & lentil soup 40
chicken soup with matzo balls 43
crab & noodle soup 131
lentil soup with ham 83
London particular 188
Manhattan clam chowder 215
minestrone 182
mussel soup (Irish) 192
ribollita 25
shrimp bisque 132
split pea and sausage soup 37
summer tomato soup 14
tomato & white bean soup 16
cheese
bauernsuppe 180
broccoli & Roquefort soup 107
chicken
chicken & almond soup 44
chicken & corn soup 216
chicken & lentil soup 40
chicken noodle soup 128
chicken soup with ginger & coconut milk 212
chicken soup with leeks & rice 46
chicken soup with matzo balls 43
cream of chicken soup 90
three delicacy soup 203
wonton soup 200
chickpeas
harira 197
quick-and-easy chickpea soup with sesame paste 162
chiles
bouillabaisse 179
cauliflower & coconut soup 74
chicken & almond soup 44
chicken soup with ginger & coconut milk 212
hot & sour soup 125
Jamaican pepper pot 218
Mexican tomato & vermicelli soup 116
ribollita 25
spicy cucumber soup 108
tom yam goong 210
Chinese cabbage
egg flower soup 120
vegetable broth 110
chorizo
caldo verde 186
fabada 185
fish soup with semolina & dill dumplings 49
christophine: Jamaican pepper pepper potpot 218
cider
apple & fennel soup 156
mussel soup (Irish) 192
cilantro
barley, lentil & onion soup 19
carrot & cilantro soup 62
cauliflower & coconut soup 74
chicken & almond soup 44
chicken soup with ginger & coconut milk 212
crab soup 206
curried cucumber soup 142
eshkaneh 198
harira 197
hot & sour soup 125
Mexican tomato & vermicelli soup 116
spicy cucumber soup 108
tom yam goong 210
clams
clam & pasta soup 52
cream of clam soup 92
fish & sweet potato soup 50
Manhattan clam chowder 215
coconut milk
cauliflower & coconut soup 74
chicken soup with ginger & coconut milk 212
Jamaican pepper pot 218
laksa 209
corn
Cajun crab & corn chowder 95
chicken & corn soup 216
chicken soup with ginger & coconut milk 212
fish & corn soup 96
vegetable broth 110
crabmeat
Cajun crab & corn chowder 95
crab & noodle soup 131
crab soup 206
cream
al fresco avocado soup 136
apple soup 159
asparagus soup 102
avocado soup 104
Cajun crab & corn chowder 95
carrot & orange soup 148
chicken & almond soup 44
cream of chicken soup 90
cream of clam soup 92
cream of tomato soup 65
cucumber & mint soup 141
cucumber & shrimp soup 166
fish & sweet potato soup 50
Jerusalem artichoke soup 77
mussel soup 171
mussel soup (Irish) 192
red bell pepper soup 72
shrimp bisque 132
vichyssoise 153
see also crème fraîche; sour cream
crème fraîche
apple & fennel soup 156
asparagus soup (chilled) 147
Cajun crab & corn chowder 95
curried cucumber soup 142
croutons 65
garlic croutons 160
guacamole croutes 104
cucumbers
cucumber & mint soup 141
cucumber & shrimp soup 166
curried cucumber soup 142
red bell pepper soup 72
spicy cucumber soup 108
tomato & smoked shellfish soup 168
cullen skink 191
curry powder/paste
curried cucumber soup 142
curried vegetable soup 114
laksa 209

dill
bauernsuppe 180
Cajun crab & corn chowder 95
cucumber & shrimp soup 166
fish soup with semolina & dill dumplings 49

eggplants: lamb & eggplant soup 86
eggs
avgolemono 194
beet & egg soup 150
black bean soup 221
egg flower soup 120

Barnabas .... Acts 13:1–3 882
Bartholomew .... Matthew 10:1–4 784
Acts 1:13 871
Belshazzar .... Daniel 5:1–30 715
Benjamin .... Genesis 42:4 33
Genesis 43:1—44:34 36
Boaz .... Ruth 2—4 213
Caiaphas .... John 18:12–14 867
Cain and Abel .... Genesis 4 3
Caleb .... Numbers 13:1—14:32 115
Cornelius .... Acts 10 879
Cyrus .... Ezra 1:1–4 378
Daniel .... Daniel 1—6 711
David .... 1 Samuel 16—17 228
2 Samuel 1—6 242
2 Samuel 11—12 249
1 Kings 1:28—2:12 265
Deborah .... Judges 4 194
Eli .... 1 Samuel 3 218
Elijah .... 1 Kings 18:16—19:18 286
2 Kings 2:11–12 293
Elisha .... 2 Kings 4:1–7 294
Luke 4:24–27 825
Elizabeth .... Luke 1:5–25,57–66 821
Esau .... Genesis 25:29–34 18
Malachi 1:2–3 772
Esther .... Esther 5—8 405
Ezekiel .... Ezekiel 2:9—3:3 670
Felix .... Acts 24 892
Gabriel .... Daniel 8:15–26 719
Luke 1:26–38 821
Gideon .... Judges 6—7 196
Goliath .... 1 Samuel 17:4–51 229
Hagar .... Genesis 16:3 10
Genesis 21:9–21 14
Hannah .... 1 Samuel 1:1—2:21 216
Herod .... Matthew 2:3–16 777
Hezekiah .... 2 Kings 20:1–21 292
Hosea .... Hosea 1–3 724
Isaac .... Genesis 24—27 16
Isaiah .... 2 Kings 19—20 287
Ishmael .... Genesis 16:15–16 11
Genesis 21:9–21 14
Jacob .... Genesis 27—33 19
James .... Matthew 13:55 788
John 7:2–5 856
Jeremiah .... Jeremiah 26 633
Jeremiah 32 639
Jeremiah 36:1—40:6 643
Jesus .... Luke 2:1–20 823
Luke 2:41–52 823
Mark 15:33–41 819
Matthew 28 803
Job .... Job 1:1—2:13 409
Job 42:7–17 455
John .... John 19:26–27 869
Acts 4:1–31 873

Kindness	Psalm 103:8–12	484
	Micah 6:8	752
	1 John 3:11–24	977
Living What You Believe	Zechariah 7:2–14	767
	Matthew 6:1–24	780
	James 1:22–27	967
Loneliness	1 Kings 19:1–18	287
	Psalm 41	454
	Matthew 26:36–46	800
Lord's Supper	Luke 22:7–23	845
	John 13	863
	1 Corinthians 11:17–34	916
Love	Mark 12:28–34	815
	1 Corinthians 13	917
	1 John 4:7–21	978
Peace	John 14:25–27	864
	Ephesians 2:14–18	934
	Philippians 4:4–9	939
Poor	Amos 5:11–15	740
	Matthew 25:31–46	799
	James 2:1–13	967
Salvation	Psalm 62	493
	Luke 19:1–10	842
	Ephesians 2:1–10	933
Swearing	Exodus 20:7	14
	Ephesians 4:29–32	935
	James 3:1–12	968
Suffering	Psalm 77	471
	Isaiah 53	594
	1 Peter 4:12–19	972
Worry	Luke 12:22–34	836
	Philippians 4:4–9	939
	Hebrews 13:5–6	966

3. Read About a Person at a Time.

You can read about people in the Bible. In your notebook, write down the name of the person you want to read about. Read the story about that person. Write down one thing you learned. Here is a list of people from the Bible. Get to know them as you read about them.

PERSON(S)	WHERE TO FIND THEM	PAGE
Aaron	Exodus 4:14–17, 27–31	44
	Exodus 32:1–24	66
	Leviticus 8:1–36	80
	Numbers 20:1–12	121
Abraham	Genesis 11:26–29	8
	Genesis 12:10–20	8
	Genesis 18:1–33	12
	Genesis 21:1–3	14
	Genesis 22:1–18	15
Adam and Eve	Genesis 2:21—3:19	2
Agrippa	Acts 25:22—26:3	894
Amos	Amos 1—9	737
Ananias and Sapphira	Acts 5:1–10	874
Andrew	John 1:40–42	850
Anna	Luke 2:36–38	823
Balaam	Numbers 22:4–35	123
Bathsheba	2 Samuel 11:3—12:24	249

Creation	Genesis 1—2	1
	Psalm 8	438
	Colossians 1:15–17	940
Death	Psalm 116:15–16	492
	John 12:23–26	862
	Romans 6:1–23	901
Divorce	Malachi 2:13–16	773
	Matthew 19:1–12	792
	1 Corinthians 7:10–16	913
Eternal Life	Job 19:25–27	420
	Matthew 19:16–30	793
	John 3:1–21	851
Faith	Proverbs 3:5–6	508
	Romans 5:1–11	901
	Hebrews 11	964
Following Jesus	Luke 14:25–34	838
	John 15:1–17	865
	John 21:15–19	870
Freedom	John 8:31–41	858
	Romans 8:1–17	902
	Galatians 4:21—5:26	931
Friendship	Ecclesiastes 4:9–12	535
	John 14:23—15:17	864
	Colossians 3:12–17	941
Getting Even	Matthew 5:38–47	780
	Romans 12:17–21	907
	1 Peter 3:8–14	971
Giving	Deuteronomy 15:7–11	152
	Malachi 3:10–12	773
	Matthew 6:1–4	780
Grace	Micah 7:18–20	753
	Luke 15:11–31	839
	Ephesians 2:1–10	933
Greed	1 Kings 21:1–22	289
	Luke 12:13–21	836
	1 Timothy 6:3–10	950
Happiness	Isaiah 52:7–10	593
	Matthew 5:1–12	779
	Philippians 4:4–9	939
Heaven	Isaiah 65:17–25	604
	Matthew 6:19–24	781
	Matthew 25:31–46	799
Holy Spirit	John 14:15–31	864
	Acts 2	871
	Romans 8:1–17	902
Hope	Psalm 130	499
	Romans 5:1–11	901
	1 Peter 1:3–9	970
Jesus Paid for Your Sins	Isaiah 53:1–12	594
	2 Corinthians 5:14–21	923
	1 Peter 2:22–25	971
Jesus' Second Coming	Matthew 24	797
	John 14:1–4	864
	1 Thessalonians 4:13—5:11	944
Joy	Isaiah 52:7–10	593
	Luke 15	839
	1 Peter 4:12–19	972

The Good Samaritan Helps	Luke 10:25–37	833
Do Not Worry	Luke 12:22–34	836
A Sheep Is Lost	Luke 15:1–7	839
A Coin Is Lost	Luke 15:8–10	839
A Son Runs Away	Luke 15:11–32	839
Jesus Heals Ten Men	Luke 17:11–19	841
Jesus Raises Lazarus	John 11:1–46	860
Jesus Blesses the Children	Mark 10:13–16	813
A Young Man Comes to Jesus	Mark 10:17–31	813
Zacchaeus Climbs a Tree	Luke 19:1–10	842
Jesus Enters Jerusalem	Luke 19:28–44	843
Jesus Eats the Last Supper	Matthew 26:17–30	800
Jesus Prays in the Garden	Matthew 26:36–56	800
Peter Denies Jesus	Matthew 26:69–75	801
Jesus Is on Trial	Matthew 27:1–30	801
Jesus Dies on the Cross	Matthew 27:31–56	802
Jesus Is Buried	Matthew 27:57–66	803
Jesus Comes Back to Life	Luke 24:1–12	848
Jesus Talks to Two Men	Luke 24:13–35	848
Jesus Appears to His Disciples	Luke 24:36–53	849
Jesus Goes to Heaven	Acts 1:4–11	871
The Holy Spirit Comes	Acts 1:12—2:47	871
Saul Begins to Follow Jesus	Acts 9:1–19	878
Peter Escapes From Prison	Acts 12:1–17	881
Paul and Silas Sing in Prison	Acts 16:16–40	885
The Lamb Is Worshiped	Revelation 5	984
The New Jerusalem Comes	Revelation 21:1—22:6	994
Jesus Is Coming Again	Revelation 22:7–21	995

2. Read a Subject at a Time.

You might want to find out what the Bible says about one special subject. You could read about "Children" or about "Following Jesus." Read about a subject. Write down in your notebook what you think about the subject. Look up the word in a Bible dictionary to learn more. Here are some subjects you may want to read about.

SUBJECT	WHERE TO FIND IT	PAGE
Anger	Psalm 4:4	437
	Proverbs 16:32	519
	Matthew 5:21–26	803
Baptism	Matthew 3:1–12	778
	Matthew 28:16–20	803
	Romans 6:1–5	901
Being Right With God	Genesis 15:1–6	10
	Romans 3:21–31	900
	Galatians 2:15–21	930
Being Sorry for Your Sins	Ezekiel 18:30–32	681
	Matthew 4:12–17	779
	Acts 2:37–41	872
Bible Reading	Nehemiah 8:1–6	394
	2 Timothy 3:14–17	953
	James 1:19–27	967
Children	Psalm 78:1–7	472
	Mark 10:13–16	813
	Ephesians 6:1–4	936
Correction	Proverbs 3:11–12	508
	Proverbs 13:24	516
	Hebrews 12:1–13	965

Jacob and Esau Are Brothers	Genesis 25:19–34	18
Jacob Gets the Blessing	Genesis 27:1–40	19
Jacob Has a Dream	Genesis 28:10–22	21
Jacob Marries Two Wives	Genesis 29:14–30	22
Joseph Goes to Egypt	Genesis 37:12–36	29
Pharaoh Has Two Dreams	Genesis 41	32
Joseph's Brothers Go to Egypt	Genesis 42—45	33
Moses Is Born	Exodus 1:8—2:10	42
God Calls Moses	Exodus 3:1–15	43
God Sends Ten Plagues	Exodus 7:14—11:10	46
The Israelites Celebrate Passover	Exodus 12	50
The Israelites Cross the Sea	Exodus 13:17—14:31	51
God Gives Water	Exodus 15:22–27; 17:1–7	53
God Gives Food	Exodus 16	53
God Gives His Laws to Moses	Exodus 19:1—20:21	56
The People Worship a Golden Calf	Exodus 32	66
Spies Explore thePromised Land	Numbers 13:1—14:12	115
A Donkey Talks	Numbers 22:1–35	123
Jericho's Walls Fall Down	Joshua 5:13—6:27	173
Gideon Tests God	Judges 6	196
Gideon Wins the War	Judges 7	198
Samson Is Tricked by Delilah	Judges 16	206
God Blesses Ruth	Ruth 1—4	213
The Lord Calls Samuel	1 Samuel 3	218
David Fights Goliath	1 Samuel 17	229
David and Jonathan Are Friends	1 Samuel 20	232
Solomon Is a Wise Ruler	1 Kings 3:16–28	268
Elijah Is Fed by Birds	1 Kings 17:1–6	284
Elijah Worships God	1 Kings 18:16–46	286
Elijah Goes to Heaven	2 Kings 2:1–12	292
God Heals Naaman	2 Kings 5	296
A Fish Swallows Jonah	Jonah 1—4	746
God Protects Three Men in a Fire	Daniel 3	713
Daniel Is Safe From the Lions	Daniel 6	717
Esther Saves Her People	Esther 2:5–18; 3:12—5:8; 7:1–10	403
A Savior Will Be Born	Luke 1:26–38	821
Jesus Is Born	Luke 2:1–7	822
The Shepherds Worship Jesus	Luke 2:8–20	823
The Wise Men Visit Jesus	Matthew 2:1–12	777
Jesus' Family Escapes	Matthew 2:13–23	778
Baby Jesus Is Taken to the Temple	Luke 2:22–40	823
The Boy Jesus Visits the Temple	Luke 2:41–52	823
Jesus Is Baptized	John 1:29–34	850
Satan Tempts Jesus	Luke 4:1–13	825
Jesus Calls His Disciples	John 1:35–51	850
Water Becomes Wine	John 2:1–11	851
A Man Comes Through the Roof	Luke 5:17–26	826
Jesus Teaches Nicodemus	John 3:1–21	851
Jesus Talks to a Woman at a Well	John 4:4–42	852
A Soldier Has Great Faith	Luke 7:1–10	828
Jesus Calms a Storm	Mark 4:35–41	807
A Dead Girl Lives Again	Mark 5:21–24, 35–43	807
A Sick Woman Is Healed	Mark 5:25–34	808
John the Baptist Is Killed	Mark 6:14–29	808
Jesus Feeds Five Thousand People	Mark 6:30–44	809
Jesus Walks on Water	Mark 6:45–56	809
Jesus Heals a Boy	Luke 9:37–43	832
Jesus Heals a Man Born Blind	John 9:1–34	850

3 Ways to Read the Bible

Why should you read the Bible?

A man builds a big boat to get away from a flood. A slave becomes a ruler. Angels visit common people. A man walks on the water. A blind person sees again. A man chooses to die for his people. All of these stories are in the Bible. The Bible also tells us about Adam and Eve and how the world began. You can read about Abraham and Isaac and God's words to them. You will find out about Peter and Paul and how the church began. All these things are in this book.

The Bible is more than just a big book of stories, however. The Bible tells you how to live as God's child. The Bible tells you God's words of love. You will get to know God better as you read the Bible. As you get to know him better, you will see how much God loves you. Your love for him will grow too.

How should you begin?

Take some time every day. Make it the same time every day, if you can. Find a quiet and comfortable place.

Ask the Holy Spirit to help you as you read. He knows that you want to read the Bible. He knows that you want to learn.

Don't worry if you don't understand everything you read the first time. You may have to read the same verse many times. You may find words you do not know. In the back of the Bible is a dictionary. It will tell you what the words mean.

You might want to ask your mom or dad or another grownup to help you understand a verse or story.

Use a notebook. Write down special things you learn.

Pick out a plan for your reading. You can choose a plan from the ideas on the next few pages. The plan will help you as you read. When you are finished, try another plan!

1. Read a Story at a Time.

You can read one story at a time. You don't have to read all the stories. You could pick out a story from the list that sounds interesting. When you read a story from the Bible, ask yourself these questions:

Who are the people in the story?
What happens in the story?
What can I learn from this story?

Use your notebook. Write down the name of the story. Write down your answers to the questions. Here are some Bible stories you may want to read. If you know where the book of the Bible is found, you can find the story that way. Or you may go to the page number listed.

STORY	WHERE TO FIND IT	PAGE
The World Begins	Genesis 1:1—2:3	1
God Creates People	Genesis 2:4–25	2
A Flood Destroys the World	Genesis 6:9—9:17	4
People Build a Tower	Genesis 11:1–9	7
God Calls Abraham	Genesis 12:1–9; 17:1–8	8
God Destroys Two Cities	Genesis 19:1–29	12
Isaac Is Born	Genesis 21:1–7	14
God Tests Abraham	Genesis 22:1–19	15
Isaac Marries Rebekah	Genesis 24	16

Matthew 17:21	But that kind does not go out except by prayer and fasting.
Matthew 18:11	The Son of Man came to save what was lost.
Matthew 23:14	How terrible for you, teachers of the law and Pharisees! You pretenders! You take over the houses of widows. You say long prayers to show off. So God will punish you much more.
Mark 7:16	Everyone who has ears to hear should listen.
Mark 9:44	In hell,/ "the worms do not die./ The fire is not put out."
Mark 9:46	In hell,/ "the worms do not die./ The fire is not put out."
Mark 11:26	But if you do not forgive, your Father who is in heaven will not forgive your sins either.
Mark 15:28	Scripture came true. It says, "And he was counted among those who disobey the law."
Luke 17:36	Two men will be in the field. One will be taken and the other left.
Luke 23:17	It was Pilate's duty to let one prisoner go free for them at the Feast.
John 5:4	From time to time an angel of the Lord would come down. The angel would stir up the waters. The first disabled person to go into the pool after it was stirred would be healed.
Acts 8:37	Philip said, "If you believe with all your heart, you can." The official answered, "I believe that Jesus Christ is the Son of God."
Acts 15:34	But Silas decided to remain there.
Acts 24:7	But Lysias, the commander, came. By using a lot of force, he took Paul from our hands.
Acts 28:29	After he said that, the Jews left. They were arguing strongly among themselves.
Romans 16:24	May the grace of our Lord Jesus Christ be with all of you. Amen.

What Is Our Prayer for You?

The Lord has blessed the *New International Version* in a wonderful way. He has used it to help millions of its readers. Many have put their faith in Jesus after reading it. Many others have become stronger believers because they have read it.

We hope and pray that the *New International Reader's Version* will help you in the same way. If that happens, we will give God all of the glory.

A Word About the New International Reader's Version

God has always spoken so people would know what he meant. When God first gave the Bible to his people, he used their languages. They could understand what they read. God wants us to understand the Bible today too. So we have worked hard to make the *New International Reader's Version* easy to read and understand.

What Is the New International Reader's Version?

The *New International Reader's Version* (NIrV) is a new Bible translation based on the *New International Version* (NIV). The NIV Committee on Bible Translation (CBT) didn't produce the NIrV. But several members of CBT worked hard to make the NIrV possible. The NIV is easy to understand and very clear. More people read the NIV than any other English Bible. We made the NIrV even easier to read and understand. We used the words of the NIV when we could. Sometimes we used shorter words. We explained words that might be hard to understand. We made the sentences shorter.

We also did some other things to make the NIrV a helpful Bible version for you. For example, sometimes a Bible verse quotes from another place in the Bible. When that happens, we put the other Bible book's name, chapter and verse right there.

We separated each chapter into shorter sections. We gave a title to almost every chapter. Sometimes we even gave a title to the shorter sections. That will help you understand what each chapter or section is all about.

Sometimes the writers of the Bible used more than one name for the same person or place. For example, in the New Testament the Sea of Galilee is also called the Sea of Gennesaret and the Sea of Tiberias. But in the NIrV we decided to call it the Sea of Galilee everywhere it appears in the New Testament. We did it because that is its most familiar name.

We also wanted to help our readers learn the names of people and places even in verses where those names don't actually appear. For example, when we knew that "the River" meant "the Euphrates River," we used those words even in verses where only the words "the River" are found. When we knew that the name of "Pharaoh" in a certain verse was "Hophra," we wrote his name in that verse. We did all of those things because we wanted to make the NIrV as clear as possible.

Is the NIrV an Accurate Bible?

At the time the Bible was written, God's people used the Hebrew and Greek languages. So the first writers of the Bible used those languages. We wanted the NIrV to say just what the first writers of the Bible said. So we kept checking what the Hebrew and Greek said.

We used the best and oldest copies of the Hebrew and Greek. Some of the first English Bibles could not use those copies because they had not yet been found. But today we can check copies that are closer in time to the ones the first Bible writers wrote. We wanted to make sure we were giving you the actual Word of God.

There are two places in the NIrV where some verse are marked with long lines. We don't know whether the first writers of the Bible wrote those verses. They may have been added later on. You will find the long lines at Mark 16:9–20 and John 7:53—8:1.

Verses That Were Not Found in Earliest Greek New Testaments

Later copies of the Greek New Testament added several verses that the earlier ones don't have. An example is Mark 9:44. That verse is not in the oldest Greek New Testaments. So we put the number 43/44 right before Mark 9:43. The verse for Mark 9:44 is listed below.

Contents

A Word About the New International Reader's Version vi
3 Ways to Read the Bible viii

The Old Testament

Genesis 1
Exodus 42
Leviticus 75
Numbers 101
Deuteronomy 139
Joshua 170
Judges 192
Ruth 213
1 Samuel 216
2 Samuel 242
1 Kings 265
2 Kings 292
1 Chronicles 319
2 Chronicles 348
Ezra 378
Nehemiah 388
Esther 402
Job 409
Psalms 436
Proverbs 507
Ecclesiastes 533
Song of Songs 541
Isaiah 546
Jeremiah 607
Lamentations 663
Ezekiel 669
Daniel 711
Hosea 724
Joel 733
Amos 737
Obadiah 744
Jonah 746
Micah 748
Nahum 754
Habakkuk 757
Zephaniah 760
Haggai 763
Zechariah 765
Malachi 772

The New Testament

Matthew 777
Mark 804
Luke 821
John 850
Acts 871
Romans 898
1 Corinthians 910
2 Corinthians 921
Galatians 929
Ephesians 933
Philippians 937
Colossians 940
1 Thessalonians 943
2 Thessalonians 946
1 Timothy 948
2 Timothy 952
Titus 955
Philemon 957
Hebrews 958
James 967
1 Peter 970
2 Peter 974
1 John 976
2 John 979
3 John 980
Jude 981
Revelation 982

Dictionary 996
About the Bible 1001
Life in New Testament Times 1003
The ABCs of Salvation 1006

zonderkidz
The children's group of Zondervan

MCP
Mission City Press

Children's Bible, Beginner's Bible Edition, New International Reader's Version

Published by Zondervan
Grand Rapids, Michigan 49530

www.zondervan.com

Library of Congress Catalog Card Number 2005921219

Printed in the United States of America

08 09 10 /DCI/ 9 8 7 6 5 4 3

You will be pleased to know that a portion of the purchase price of your new NIrV Bible has been provided to International Bible Society to help spread the gospel of Jesus Christ around the world!

Holy Bible

The Beginner's Bible™

zonderkidz

Holy Bible

The Beginner's Bible™

My name is Ruth.

I am 9 years old.

I got this book for A New Bible.

The Beginner's Bible™

To
Harris Edward
From
Noah's Place Preschool
Date
June 4th 2009

Call Fritsch First!

OVER 55 MILLION CARDS IN STOCK!

FACTORY SETS

1992 Topps
April Delivery - **$31.75** ppd

1992 Fleer
April Delivery - **$28.75** ppd

1992 Score
April Delivery - **$29.00** ppd

1992 Upper Deck
September Delivery - **$47.50** ppd

JUST A SAMPLE OF SETS AVAILABLE FROM OUR VAST INVENTORY!

(All sets are in NrMT-MT condition) See shipping and insurance table. NOTE: All prices subject to change without notice.

BASEBALL SETS

1991 Topps Traded (132) $14.50
1991 Fleer Update (132) 13.95
1991 Score Traded (110) 13.75
1991 Score Rookies (40) 8.75
1991 Donruss Rookies (56) 9.95
1991 Bowman Wax (504) 15.95
1991 Conlon Collection (330) 26.95
1991 Topps (792) Factory 29.75
1991 Fleer (720) Factory 24.50
1991 Score (900) Factory 34.50
1991 Upper Deck (800) Factory 44.50
1991 Bowman (660) Factory 24.95
1991 O-Pee-Chee (792) Factory 36.75
1990 Upper Deck (800) Factory 49.75
1990 Upper Deck High Number Series (701-800) Factory 14.50
1990 Topps Traded (132) 13.75
1990 Fleer Update (132) 14.25
1990 Score Traded (110) 22.00
1990 Donruss Rookie (56) 10.95
1990 Topps (792) Factory 28.75
1990 Fleer (660) Factory 24.75
1990 Score Factory (714) 62.75
1989 Topps (792) Factory 27.50
1989 Topps (792) 25.50
1989 Fleer (660) 31.50
1989 Score (660) 27.50
1989 Donruss (660) Factory 37.50
1989 Bowman (484) Factory 32.95
1989 Topps Traded (132) 15.00
1989 Fleer Update (132) 20.00
1989 Score Traded (110) 14.00
1989 Donruss Traded (56) 25.00
1989 Donruss Rookies (56) 21.95
1989 Topps Glossy (792) 195.00
1989 Bowman Glossy (484) 169.95
1989 Bowman Wax Box (468) 12.00
1988 Topps (792) 35.00
1988 Fleer (660) Factory 50.00
1988 Score (660) Factory 27.50
1988 Donruss (660) Factory 32.50
1988 Topps Traded (132) 32.50
1988 Fleer Update (132) 14.50

BASEBALL SETS

1988 Fleer Glossy Update (132) $22.95
1988 Score Traded (110) 75.00
1988 Donruss Rookies (56) 14.95
1988 Donruss Best 24.95
1988 Fleer Glossy (660) 44.95
1988 Topps Glossy (792) 135.00
1987 Topps (792) 53.50
1987 Fleer (660) Factory 135.00
1987 Sportflics (200 plus trivia) 42.50
1987 Sportflics Rookies #2 (25 plus trivia) 17.00
1987 Fleer Glossy (660 in collectors tin) 89.95
1987 Topps Glossy (792) 125.00
1987 Topps Traded (132) 17.50
1987 Fleer Update (132) 20.00
1987 Fleer Glossy Update (132 plus tin) 19.95
1987 Donruss Opening Day (272) 25.00
1987 Donruss Rookies (56) 22.95
1986 Topps (792) 60.00
1986 Topps Traded (132) 39.00
1986 Fleer (660) 150.00
1986 Fleer Update (132) 40.00
1986 Donruss (660) 250.00
1986 Sportflics (200) 48.00
1986 SF Decade Greats (75) 24.75
1986 SF Rookies (50) 25.00
1985 Topps (792) 125.00
1985 Topps Traded (132) 27.00
1985 Fleer (660) 175.00
1985 Fleer Traded (132) 27.50
1985 Donruss (660) 190.00
1984 Topps (792) lacking Mattingly 100.00
1984 Topps Traded (132) 125.00
1984 Fleer (660) 220.00
1984 Fleer Update (132) 750.00
1984 Donruss (660) 500.00
1983 Topps (792) 190.00
1983 Topps Traded (132) 130.00
1983 Fleer (660) 130.00
1983 Donruss (660) 160.00
1982 Topps Traded (132) 175.00
1982 Fleer (660) 85.00
1982 Donruss (660) 85.00

BASEBALL SETS

1981 Topps (726) $130.00
1981 Topps Traded (132) 37.50
1981 Fleer (660) 62.50
1981 Donruss (605) 65.00
1980 Topps (726) 325.00
1979 Topps (726) (Wills-Blue Jays) 225.00
1978 Topps (726) 275.00
1977 Topps (660) 375.00
1976 Topps (660) 400.00
1975 Topps (660) 725.00
1974 Topps (660) 550.00
1973 Topps (660) 1,100.00

FOOTBALL SETS

1991 Topps (660) $29.95
1991 Topps Update (132) 15.50
1991 Topps Stadium Club (432) 95.00
1991 Bowman (561) 26.95
1991 Action Packed (291) 124.95
1991 Action Packed (84) 40.00
1991 Upper Deck Foil Box (432) 39.95
1991 Score (690) 24.95
1991 Socre Traded (110) 16.00
1991 Fleer (432) 23.95
1991 Stars N' Stripes (140) 18.25
1991 Pro Line Box (432) 31.95
1991 Pro Set Box (540) 19.95
1991 Star Pics (112) 19.95
1991 Classic Draft (50) 18.25
1990 Topps (528) Factory 23.95
1990 Topps Update (132) 14.50
1990 Score (665) Factory 22.95
1990 Score Supplement (110) 115.00
1990 Score Young Superstars (40) 20.00
1990 CFL I (220) 47.00
1990 Score Unopened Box Series 1 (576) 12.75
Series 2 (576) 12.75
1990 Pro Set Unopened Box Series 1 (540) 13.00
Series 2 (540) 13.50
1989 Topps (396) 24.50
1989 Topps Football Update (132) 12.95
1989 Score (330) 195.00
1989 Score Football Supplement (110 plus 10 trivia) 30.95

FOOTBALL SETS

1989 Pro Set Unopened Box 1st Series (540) $29.50
1988 Topps (396) 35.00
1987 Topps (396) 60.00
1986 Topps (396) 95.00
1985 Topps (396) 85.00
1985 Topps USFL (132) 105.00
1984 Topps (396) 155.00
1984 Topps USFL (132) 550.00
1983 Topps (396) 65.00
1982 Topps (528) 115.00
1981 Topps (528) 250.00
1980 Topps (528) 100.00
1979 Topps (528) 125.00
1977 Topps (528) 275.00
1976 Topps (528) 400.00
1975 Topps (528) 275.00
1974 Topps (528) 300.00
1973 Topps (528) 425.00
1972 Topps (351) 1,325.00
1971 Topps (263) 475.00
1970 Topps (263) 450.00
1970 Topps Super (35) 200.00
1968 Topps (219) 475.00

BASKETBALL SETS

1991-92 Fleer (240) $16.50
1991-92 Hoops #1 Box (540) 16.95
1991-92 Star Pics (70) 18.95
1990-91 Fleer (198) 18.50
1990-91 Fleer Update (100) 22.00
1990-91 Hoops Unopened Box
Series I (540) 18.00
Series II (540) 19.00
1990 Star Pics (70) 54.95
1989-90 Fleer Basketball (168) 42.50
1988-89 Fleer (132) 100.00
1988-89 Fleer NBA Sticker Cards (11) 15.00
1987-88 Fleer (132) 245.00
1987-88 Fleer NBA Sticker Cards (11) 25.00
1986-87 Fleer (132) 850.00
1986-87 Fleer NBA Sticker Cards (11) 75.00
1981-82 Topps (198) 135.00
1980-81 Topps (88) Bird & Johnson Same Cards 450.00

BASKETBALL SETS

1980-81 Topps (88) 225.00
1979-80 Topps (132) 85.00
1978-79 Topps (132) 95.00
1977-78 Topps (132) 105.00
1976-77 Topps (144) 155.00
1975-76 Topps (330) 600.00
1974-75 Topps (264) 275.00
1973-74 Topps (264) 300.00
1972-73 Topps (264) 700.00
1971-72 Topps (233) 750.00
1970-71 Topps (175) (short set lacking 21 commons & Havlicek) 1,000.00

HOCKEY SETS

1991-92 Topps (528) $28.25
1991-92 Bowman (429) 26.25
1991-92 Score Update (110) 14.75
1991-92 Upper Deck Unopened Box (432) 32.25
1991-92 Score USA (440) 23.95
1991-92 Score Canada (660) 35.95
1990-91 Topps (396) 15.95
1990-91 Score-USA (445) 52.50
1990-91 Bowman (264) 17.75
1990-91 Pro Set Unopened Box
Series I (540) 11.95
Series II (540) 14.95
1990-91 Upper Deck Unopened Box (432) 89.95
1990-91 O-Pee-Chee (528) 25.75
1989-90 O-Pee-Chee (330) 25.00
1989-90 Topps Hockey (198) 42.50
1989-90 Topps Hockey Sticker Cards (33) 10.00
1984-85 Topps (165) 62.50
1981-82 Topps (198) 110.00
1980-81 Topps (264) 225.00
1978-79 Topps (264) 75.00
1977-78 Topps (265) 100.00
1976-77 Topps (264) 110.00
1975-76 Topps (330) 275.00
1974-75 Topps (264) 200.00
1973-74 Topps (198) 225.00
1972-73 Topps (176) 400.00
1971-72 Topps (132) 425.00
1968-69 Topps (132) 600.00

RARE REPRINT SETS!

1909-11 T206 Complete Set, 532 cards. ($150,000.00 original value) ... $49.95
1911 T205 Complete Set, 208 cards. ($60,000.00 original value) 33.95
1951 Bowman Complete Set, 324 cards. ($16,000.00 original value) 49.95
1933 Goudy Complete Set, 240 cards. ($50,000.00 original value) 40.95
1938 Horrors Of War, 228 cards. (with a special collectors box) 42.95

NEED SINGLE CARDS?

If you need single cards from 1880 to 1980, any sport, please write (send SASE) or call for a **"New Concept"** form which makes over 8 million single cards available to you! Also available is our "ONE-OF-A-KIND" catalog that contains over 75 pages of individually graded and priced single cards. If you have an interest in 1950s Bowman and Topps singles, our "ONE-OF-A-KIND" catalog presents four different grades for each of the 1954-55 Bowman and 1955-57 Topps' single cards. Relive the history of sports with a simple purchase. CALL OR WRITE TODAY!

WE ARE BUYING!

All cards and collectibles issued prior to 1955! Before you sell, see us! We have over 45 years of card collecting experience with a reputation beyond repute. Our experience and knowledge gives us the edge. WE BUY CARDS AT A HIGHER PRICE THAN ANYONE! With a mailing list of over 95,000 active collectors we have the exposure and leverage and can pay the higher prices. All purchases are strictly confidential. Items on consignment are accepted, you may call us for details. We pay the shipping both ways if we do not buy your collection. CALL US TODAY!

Call for our FREE CATALOG - A must for the novice as well as the serious collector!

FREE 128-PAGE CATALOG!!

Subscribe today and receive the largest catalog we've ever put together! This 128 page issue is jam-packed with baseball, football, basketball, and hockey cards from the 1960s to 1992, sets and singles. Also included are magazines and hobby supplies, plus much more! If you need single cards from 1880 to 1980 - any sport - browse through our 76-page "One-of-a-Kind" section or use the "New Concept" form, which makes over 8 million cards available to you!

Simply send your name and address to receive our biggest catalog ever! Canada residents send $2.00 (shipped 1st class).

SHIPPING AND INSURANCE TABLE

$.01 TO $25.00 .... add $4.50
$25.01 to $50.00 .... add 5.50
$50.01 and over .... add 6.50

MasterCard VISA

All prices subject to change. Call to verify prices.

CHECK POLICY:
All personal checks will be held 15 working days for clearance. For faster service, please send postal money orders.

CANADA CUSTOMERS:
Please send postal money order in U.S. Funds only and an additional $7.00 per set for sets over 250 cards, $3.50 per set for sets under 250 cards for shipping your sets.

Fritsch

LARRY FRITSCH CARDS, INC.
735 OLD WAUSAU RD.
P.O. BOX 863, DEPT. 902
STEVENS POINT, WI 54481

(715) 344-8687
FAX #(715) 344-1778

See our inside back cover ad for other items we have in stock.

ALASKA, HAWAII, PUERTO RICO, FPO & P.O. CUSTOMERS:
Add an additional $5.00 per set for sets over 250 cards and $3.00 per set for sets under 250 cards for shipping your set (if you have a P.O. Box and want your order shipped via UPS, please include your UPS shipping address.)

WITH OVER 50 MILLION CARDS IN STOCK ... WE HAVE AMERICA'S MOST COMPLETE STOCK OF SPORTS TRADING CARDS. Full money back guarantee if you are not completely satisfied with our service and products. YOU, the customers are always NO. 1 to us!

To receive Super Service it is necessary to send a POSTAL MONEY ORDER with your order. (All personal checks are held 15 days for clearance.) (Charge orders add 5% to total.) Minimum charge order $20.00. WI residents add 5.5% sales tax.

Sixth Edition — 1992

Sports Collectors Digest Voice for the Hobby

Baseball Card Price Guide

Jeff Kurowski, Editor

Library of Congress Catalog Number: 87-80033
ISBN: 0-87341-182-X

Krause Publications Inc.
700 E. State St.
Iola, Wis. 54990

Printed in the United States of America

ACKNOWLEDGEMENTS

Dozens of individuals have made countless valuable contributions which have been incorporated into the *Sports Collectors Digest Baseball Card Price Guide* While all cannot be acknowledged, special appreciation is extended to the following principal contributors who have exhibited a special dedication by creating, revising or verifying listings and technical data, reviewing market valuations or loaning cards for photography.

Johnny Adams, Jr.
Ken Agona
(Sports Cards Plus)
Gary Agostino
Lisa Albano
Dan Albaugh
Mark Anker
Steve Applebaum
Bill Ballew
John Beisiegel
Karen Bell
Cathy Black
Mike Bodner
Bill Bossert
(Mid-Atlantic Coin Exchange)
Brian Boston
Mike Boyd
Jon Brecka
John Brigandi
(Brigandi Coin Co.)
Lou Brown
Dan Bruner
(The Card King)
Greg Bussineau
(Superior Sports Cards)
Billy Caldwell
(Packman)
Len Caprisecca
Tony Carrafiell
(Delco Sports Cards)
Lee Champion
Dwight Chapin
Chriss Christiansen
Shane Cohen
(Grand Slam Sports Collectibles)
Rich Cole
Charles Conlon
Eric Cooper
(All Star Cards)
Bryan Couling
Clyde Cripe
Jim Cumpton
Robert Curtiss
Tom Daniels
(T&J Sports Cards)
Tom Day
Dick DeCourcy
Ken Degnan
(Georgia Music & Sports)
Mike Del Gado
(All American Sportscards)
Larry Dluhy
(Texas Trading Cards)
John Dorsey
Curtis Earl
Steve Ellingboe
Mark Elliott
Joe Esposito
(B&E Collectibles)
Doak Ewing
Shirley Eross
(Hobbyrama Sports By Eross)
David Festberg
(Baseball and Hobby Shop)
Jay Finglass
Nick Flaviano
Jeff Fritsch
Larry Fritsch
Richard Galasso
Tom Galic
Tony Galovich
(American Card Exchange)
Frank Giffune
Richard Gilkeson
Dick Goddard
Jack Goodman
Bill Goodwin
(St. Louis Baseball Cards)
Audre Gold
(Au Sports Memorabilia)
Mike Gordon
Howard Gordon
Bob Gray
Paul Green
Wayne Grove
(First Base)
Gerry Guenther
Don Guilbert
Tom Guilfoile
David, Joel & Walter Hall
(Hall's Nostalgia)
Gary Hamilton
Tom Harbin
Don Harrison
Rick Hawksley
Herbert Hecht
Bill Henderson
Gregg Hitesman
Jack Horkan
Jim Horne
Ron Hosmer
Marvin Huck
Robert Jacobsen
Donn Jennings
Scott Jensen
Jim Johnston
Stewart Jones
Larry Jordon
Judy Kay
(Kay's Baseball Cards)
Allan Kaye
Michael Kee[illegible]
Mark Kemmerle
Rick Keplinger
Kit Kiefer
John King
John Kittleson
(Sports Collectibles)
Bob Koehler
David Kohler
John Kurowski
Steve Lacasse
Lee Lasseigne
Mark K. Larson
William Lawrence
Morley Leeking
Don Lepore
Rod Lethbridge
Paul Lewicki
Neil Lewis
Howie Levy
(Blue Chip Sportscard)
Rob Lifson
Ken & Norman Liss
Jeff Litteral
Mark MacRae
Ken Magee
Paul Marchant
Bill Mastro
Jay McCracken
Tony McLaughlin
Don McPherson
John Mehlin
Bill Mendel
Blake Meyer
(Lone Star Sportcard Co.)
Dick Millerd
Minnesota Sports Collectibles
Keith Mitchell
J.A. Monaco
Joe Morano
Brian Morris
Mike Mowery
Peter Muldavin
Mark Murphy
(The Baseball Card "Kid")
Vincent Murray
David Musser
(D.M.B.'s Baseball Cards)
Frank Nagy
Chuck Nobriga
Mark Nochta
Wayne Nochta
Keith Olbermann
Joe Pasternack
(Card Collectors Co.)
Marty Perry
Tom Pfirrman
(Baseball Card Corner)
Dan Piepenbrok
(Uneeda Hobbie)
[illegible] Pietruska
(Pro Sports Investments)
Paul Pollard
Ed Ransom
Fred Rapoport
(Yesterday's Heroes)
Tom Reid
Bob Richardson
Gavin Riley
Ron Ritzler
Mike Rodell
Mike Rogers
Chris Ronan
Rocky Rosato
Alan Rosen
John Rumierz
Bob Rund
Jon Sands
(Howard's Coin Shop)
Kevin Savage
(The Sports Gallery)
Stephen Schauer
Dave Schwartz
(Dave's Sportscards)
Robert Scott
Corey Shanus
Dan Shedrick
Max Silberman
Barry Sloate
Joe Smith
Mark Soltan
John Spalding
Kevin Spears
Gene Speranza
David Spivack
Don Steinbach
Dan Stickney
Larry Stone
Doug Stultz
Joe Szeremet
Erik Teller
K.J. Terplak
Dick Tinsley
Bud Tompkins
(Minnesota Connection)
Scott Torrey
Rich Unruh
Jack Urban
Joe Valle
(Cardboard Dreams)
Pete Waldman
Eric Waller
Gary Walter
Ken Weimer
Dale Weselowski
E.C. Wharton-Tigar
Chris Williams
Charles Williamson
Kit Young
Ted Zanidakis

ROOKIE/FIRST CARD DESIGNATIONS

A player's name in italic type indicates a rookie card. An (FC) designation indicates a player's first card for that particular company. FCs will be found in 1981-90 Donruss, Fleer, Score and Topps sets. They will also be located in the Donruss Rookies, Fleer Update, Topps Traded and Score Traded sets.

BASEBALL CARD HISTORY

In 1887 — over 100 years ago — the first nationally distributed baseball cards were issued by Goodwin & Co. of New York City. The 1½" x 2½" cards featured posed studio photographs glued to stiff cardboard. They were inserted into cigarette packages with such exotic brand names as Old Judge, Gypsy Queen and Dog's Head. Poses were formal, with artificial backgrounds and bare-handed players fielding balls suspended on strings to simulate action.

Then, as now, baseball cards were intended to stimulate product sales. What could be more American than using the diamond heroes of the national pastime to gain an edge on the competition? It is a tradition that has continued virtually unbroken for a century.

Following Goodwin's lead a year later, competitors began issuing baseball cards with their cigarettes, using full-color lithography to bring to life painted portraits of the era's top players.

After a few short years of intense competition, the cigarette industry's leading firms formed a monopoly and cornered the market. By the mid-1980s there was little competition, and no reason to issue baseball cards. The first great period of baseball card issues came to an end.

The importing of Turkish tobaccos in the years just prior to 1910 created a revolution in American smoking habits. With dozens of new firms entering the market, the idea of using baseball cards to boost sales was revived.

In the years from 1909-1912, dozens of different sets of cards were produced to be given away in cigarette packages. There was a greater than ever variety in sizes, shapes and designs, from the extremely popular 1½" x 2⅝" color lithographed set of 500+ players which collectors call T206, to the large (5" x 8") Turkey Red brand cards. There were double folders, featuring two players on the same card, and triple folders, which had two player portraits and an action scene. Gold ink and embossed designs were also tried to make competing companies' cards attractive and popular.

It was this era that saw the issue of the king of baseball cards, the T206 Honus Wagner card, worth $400,000.

The zeal with which America's youngsters pursued their fathers, uncles, and neighbors for cigarette cards in the years just prior to World War I convinced the nation's confectioners that baseball cards could also be used to boost candy sales.

While baseball cards had been produced by candy companies on a limited basis as far back as the 1880s, by the early 1920s the concept was being widely used in the industry. The highly competitive caramel business was a major force in this new marketing strategy, offering a baseball card in each package of candy. Not to be outdone, Cracker Jack began including baseball cards in each box. The 1914-1915 Cracker Jack cards are important because they were the most popular of the candy cards to include players from a short-lived third major league, the Federal League.

Generally, candy cards of the era were not as colorful or well-printed as the earlier tobacco cards, due to the shortage of paper and ink-making ingredients caused by World War I.

The association of bubble gum and baseball cards is a phenomenon of only the past half-century. In the early 1930s techniques were developed using rubber tree products to give the elasticity necessary for blowing bubbles.

During this era the standard method of selling a slab of bubble gum and a baseball card in a colorfully wax-wrapped 1-cent package was developed. Bubble gum — and baseball card — production in this era was centered in Massachusetts, where National Chicle Co. (Cambridge) and Goudey Gum Co. (Boston) were headquartered.

Most bubble gum cards produced in the early 1930s featured a roughly square (about 2½") format, with players depicted in colorful paintings. For the first time, considerable attention was paid to the backs of the cards, where biographical details, career highlights and past season statistics were presented.

In 1939, a new company entered the baseball card market — Gum Inc., of Philadelphia. Its "Play Ball" gum was the major supplier of baseball cards until 1941, when World War II caused a shortage of the materials necessary both for the production of bubble gum and the printing of baseball cards.

Three years after the end of World War II baseball cards returned on a national scale, with two companies competing for the bubble gum market. In Philadelphia, the former Gum Inc. reappeared on the market as Bowman Gum Inc.

Bowman's first baseball card set appeared in 1948, very similar in format to the cards which had existed prior to the war, black-and-white player photos on nearly square (2" x 2½") cardboard. The 1948 Bowman effort was modest, with only 48 cards. The following year, color was added to the photos. For 1950, Bowman replaced the retouched photos with original color paintings of players, many of which were repeated a year later in the 1951 issue. Also new for 1951 was a larger card size, 2" x 3⅛".

Bowman had little national competition in this era. In 1948-1949, Leaf Gum in Chicago produced a 98-card set that is the only bubble gum issue of the era to include a Joe DiMaggio card.

While Bowman dominated the post-war era through 1951, in that year Topps began production of its first baseball cards, issuing three different small sets of cards and serving warning that it was going to become a major force in the baseball card field.

In 1952, Brooklyn-based Topps entered the baseball card market in a big way. Not only was its 407-card set the largest single-year issue ever produced, but its 2⅝" x 3¾" format was the largest-sized baseball card ever offered for over-the-counter sale. Other innovations in Topps' premiere issue for 1952 included the first-ever use of team logos in card design, and on the back of the card, the first use of line statistics to document the player's previous year and career performance. By contrast, Bowman's set for 1952 remained in the smaller format, had 72 fewer cards and showed little change in design from 1951.

Just as clearly as Topps won the 1952 baseball card battle, Bowman came back in 1953 with what is often considered the finest baseball card set ever produced. For the first time ever, actual color photographs were reproduced on baseball cards in Bowman's 160-card set. To allow the full impact of the new technology, there were no other design elements on the front of the card and Bowman adopted a larger format, 2½" x 3¾".

And so the competition went for five years, with each

THE BUYING MACHINE

MAJOR PURCHASES:

FIND I - Purchaser of over $400,000 worth of Gem-Mint high-number series of 1952 Topps cards.
FIND II - Purchaser of over $400,000 worth of 1954 & 1955 Topps and Bowan unopened boxes in Paris, Tennessee.
FIND III - Purchaser of over $125,000 worth of rare vintage World Series press pins.
FIND IV - Purchaser of the Kansas City Bowman Find of over $125,000 in catalog value.
FIND V - Purchaser of $385,000 Topps Bowmans in the ABC Collectables Find in Moline, Illinois.
FIND VI - Purchaser of $400,000 of the Hit King Marketing 500 Homerun print and baseball buyout.
FIND VII - Purchaser of Manny's Baseball Land over $400,000 worth of yearbooks, World Series & All-Star programs in the original boxes.
FIND VIII - Purchaser of Baseball Cards Unlimited. Over $250,000 worth of unopened cases and new sets.
FIND IX - Purchaser of over $500,000 worth of Mint Topps sets, Quincy, IL.
FIND X - Purchaser of Bob Lemke Collection.

Purchaser of over $11 Million in old cards in the past three years.
New cards sales not included.

PRESS CREDENTIALS:

July 1, 1988 Sports Illustrated
8-page spread

Appeared in ABC's
Good Morning America

Feature stories in such fine National magazines is Sports Illustrated, Sport Magazine, February, 1989. Money Magazine, Forbes Magazine, New York Magazine, Baseball Today, A.C. Delco's In Tune Magazine, Northwest Airlines Magazine, Globe, and in addition, major daily newspapers such as New York Times, New York Post, Philadelphia Times, New York Daily News, New Jersey's Bergen Record, St. Petersburg Times, L.A. Times, USA Today, Honolulu Advertiser, Sar Ledger, Patterson News, Archie Comics, Japanese (Mono) and mentioned in hundreds of other baseball card related articles across the country.

Has appeared on National Television shows as, Good Morning America, CBS Sports, ESPN, NBC's Game of the Week, ABC Nightline, FNN CBS News Network, Rob Michaud's Sports Talk, Home Shopping Network, CNBC, Channel 5's Good Day New York, NBC's Sunday A.M., and major radio shows on such stations as The Art Rust Show, WABC, WFAN, WCBS and WNBC affiliates.

NEW BOOK

Available at book stores nation wide.

ALAN ROSEN - MR MINT
70-I Chestnut Ridge Rd.
Montvale, NJ 07645
FAX 201-307-1653
201-307-0700
SCD's Largest Advertiser

MasterCard VISA SCA INTERNATIONAL Krause Publications 5 YEAR CUSTOMER SERVICE AWARD

company trying to gain an edge by signing players to exclusive contracts and creating new and exciting card designs each year. Gradually, Topps became the dominant force in the baseball card market. In late 1955, Bowman admitted defeat and the company was sold to Topps.

Baseball cards entered a new era in 1957. After years of intense competition, Topps enjoyed a virtual monopoly that was rarely seriously challenged in the next 25 years. One such challenge in the opening years of the 1960s came from Post cereal, which from 1961-1963 issued 200-card sets on the backs of its cereal boxes.

In 1957, Topps' baseball cards were issued in a new size — 2½" x 3½" — that would become the industry-wide standard that prevails to this day. It was also the year that Topps first used full-color photographs for its cards, rather than paintings or retouched black-and-white photos. Another innovation in the 1957 set was the introduction of complete major/and or minor league statistics on the card backs. This feature quickly became a favorite with youngsters and provided fuel for endless schoolyard debates about whether one player was better than another.

In the ensuing five years, major league baseball underwent monumental changes. In 1958, the Giants and Dodgers left New York for California. In 1961-1962 expansion came to the major leagues, with new teams springing up from coast to coast and border to border.

The Topps baseball cards of the era preserve those days when modern baseball was in its formative stages.

In 1963, for the first time in seven years, it looked as if there might once again be two baseball card issues to choose from. After three years of issuing "old-timers" card sets, Fleer issued a 66-card set of current players. Topps took Fleer to court, where the validity of Topps' exclusive contracts with baseball players to appear on bubble gum cards was upheld. It was the last major challenge to Topps for nearly 20 years.

The 1960s offered baseball card collecting at its traditional finest. Youngsters would wait and worry through the long winter, watching candy store shelves for the first appearance of the brightly colored 5-cent card packs in the spring. A cry of "They're in!" could empty a playground in seconds as youngters rushed to the corner store to see what design innovations Topps had come up with for the new year. Then, periodically during the summer, new series would be released, offering a new challenge to complete. As the seasons wore down, fewer and fewer stores carried the final few series, and it became a real struggle to complete the "high numbers" from a given year's set. But it was all part of the fun of buying baseball cards in the 1960s.

The early 1970s brought some important changes to the baseball card scene. The decade's first two Topps issues were stunning in that the traditional white border was dropped in favor of gray in 1970, and black in 1971. In 1972, Topps' card design was absolutely psychedelic, with brightly colored frames around the player photos, and comic book typography popping out all over. The design for the 1973 cards was more traditional, but the photos were not. Instead of close-up portraits or posed "action" shots, many cards in the 1973 Topps set featured actual game action photos. Unfortunately, too many of those photos made it hard to tell which player was which, and the set was roundly panned by collectors.

But most significantly, 1973 marked the last year in which baseball cards were issued by series through the course of the summer. On the positive side, this eliminated the traditional scarce "high numbers" produced toward the end of the season. On the negative side, it meant players who had been traded in the pre-season could no longer be shown in their correct uniforms, and outstanding new players had to wait a full year before their rookie cards would debut.

This marketing change made a significant impact on the hobby and helped spur a tremendous growth period in the late 1970s. By offering all of the cards at once, Topps made it easy for baseball card dealers to offer complete sets early in the year. Previously, collectors had to either assemble their sets by buying packs of cards, or wait until all series had been issued to buy a set from a dealer. It was in this era that many of today's top baseball card dealers got their start or made the switch to baseball cards a full-time business.

During this era, the first significant national competition to Topps' baseball card monopoly in many years was introduced. Hostess, a bakery products company, began distributing baseball cards printed on the bottoms of packages of its snack cakes, while the Kellogg's company distributed simulated 3-D cards in boxes of its cereals. The eagerness with which collectors gobbled up these issues showed that the hobby was ready for a period of unprecedented growth.

The baseball card hobby literally boomed in 1981. A federal court broke Topps' monopoly on the issue of baseball cards with bubble gum, and Fleer, from Philadelphia, and Donruss, of Memphis, entered the field as the first meaningful competition in nearly 20 years.

That same year also marked a beginning of the resurgence in the number of regional baseball card issues. Over the next few years, dozens of such sets came onto the market, helping to boost sales of everything from snack cakes to soda pop and police public relations. By 1984, more than half of the teams in the major leagues were issuing some type of baseball cards on a regional basis. The hobby had not enjoyed such diversity of issues since the mid-1950s.

While yet another court decision cost Fleer and Donruss the right to sell their baseball cards with bubble gum, both companies remained in the market and gained strength.

Topps' major contribution in this era was the introduction of annual "Traded" sets which offered cards of the year's new rookies as well as cards of traded players in their correct uniforms.

The mid-1980s showed continued strong growth in the number of active baseball card collectors, as well as the number of new baseball card issues. Topps, still the industry's leader, expanded the number and variety of its baseball issues with many different test issues and on-going speciality sets, including oversize cards, 3-D plastic cards, metal "cards" and much more.

After three years of over-production of its baseball card sets, Donruss, in 1984, significantly limited the number of cards printed, creating a situation in which demand exceeded supply, causing the value of Donruss cards to rise above Topps for the first time.

In 1984, Fleer followed Topps' lead and produced a season's-end "Update" set. Because the quantity of sets printed was extremely limited, and because it contains many of today's hottest young players, the 1984 Fleer Update set has become the most valuable baseball card issue produced in recent times.

In 1986, a fourth company joined the baseball card wars. Called "Sportflics," the cards were produced by a subsidiary of the Wrigley Gum Co., and featured three different photos on each card in a simulated 3-D effect. For 1987, a fourth national baseball card set, called Score, entered the scene. A fifth national baseball card set, Upper Deck, was created in 1989.

HOW TO USE THIS CATALOG

This catalog has been uniquely designed to serve the needs of beginning and advanced collectors. It provides

a comprehensive guide to more than 100 years of baseball card issues, arranged so that even the most novice collector can consult it with confidence and ease.

The following explanations summarize the general practices used in preparing this catalog's listings. However, because of specialized requirements which may vary from card set to card set, these must not be considered ironclad. Where these standards have been set aside, appropriate notations are incorporated.

ARRANGEMENT

Because the most important feature in identifying, and pricing, a baseball card is its set of origin, this catalog has been alphabetically arranged according to the name by which the set is most popularly known to collectors.

Those sets that were issued for more than one year are then listed chronologically, from earliest to most recent.

Within each set, the cards are listed by their designated card number, or in the absence of card numbers, alphabetically according to the last name of the player pictured.

IDENTIFICATION

While most modern baseball cards are well identified on front, back or both, as to date and issue, such has not always been the case. In general, the back of the card is more useful in identifying the set of origin than the front. The issuer or sponsor's name will usually appear on the back since, after all, baseball cards were first issued as a promotional item to stimulate sales of other products. As often as not, that issuer's name is the name by which the set is known to collectors and under which it will be found listed in this catalog.

Virtually every set listed in this catalog is accompanied by a photograph of a representative card. If all else fails, a comparison of an unknown card with the photos in this book will usually produce a match.

As a special feature, each set listed in this catalog has been cross-indexed by its date of issue. This will allow identification in some difficult cases because a baseball card's general age, if not specific year of issue, can usually be fixed by studying the biographical or statistical information on the back of the card. The last year mentioned in either the biography or stats is usually the year which preceded the year of issue.

PHOTOGRAPHS

A photograph on the front and back of at least one representative card from virtually every set listed in this catalog has been incorporated into the listings to aid in identification.

Photographs have been printed in reduced size. The actual size of cards in each set is given in the introductory text preceding its listing.

DATING

The dating of baseball cards by year of issue on the front or back of the card itself is a relatively new phenomenon. In most cases, to accurately determine a date of issue for an unidentified card, it must be studied for clues. As mentioned, the biography, career summary or statistics on the back of the card are the best way to pinpoint a year of issue. In most cases, the year of issue will be the year after the last season mentioned on the card.

Luckily for today's collector, earlier generations have done much of the research in determining year of issue for those cards which bear no clues. The painstaking task of matching players' listed and/or pictured team against their career records often allowed an issue date to be determined.

In some cases, particular cards sets were issued over a period of more than one calendar year, but since they are collected together as a single set, their specific year of issue is not important. Such sets will be listed with their complete known range of issue years.

NUMBERING

While many baseball card issues as far back as the 1880s have contained card numbers assigned by the issuer, to facilitate the collecting of a compete set, the practice has by no means been universal. Even today, not every set bears card numbers.

Logically, those baseball cards which were numbered by their manufacturer are presented in that numerical order within the listings of this catalog. The many unnumbered issues, however, have been assigned *Sports Collectors Digest Baseball Card Price Guide* numbers to facilitate their universal identification within the hobby, especially when buying and selling by mail. In all cases, numbers which have been assigned, or which otherwise do not appear on the card through error or by design, are shown in this catalog within parentheses. In virtually all cases, unless a more natural system suggested itself by the unique nature of a particular set, the assignment of *Sports Collectors Digest Baseball Card Price Guide* numbers by the cataloging staff has been done by alphabetical arrangement of the player's last names or the card's principal title.

Significant collectible variations of any particular card are noted within the listings by the application of a suffix letter within parentheses. In instances of variations, the suffix "a" is assigned to the variation which was created first.

NAMES

The identification of a player by full name on the front of his baseball card has been a common practice only since the 1920s. Prior to that, the player's last name and team were the usual information found on the card front.

As a standard practice, the listings in the *Sports Collectors Digest Baseball Card Price Guide* present the player's name exactly as it appears on the front of the card, if his full name is given there. If the player's full name only appears on the back, rather than the front of the card, the listing corresponds to that designation.

In cases where only the player's last name is given on the card, the cataloging staff has included the first name by which he was most often known for ease of

identification.

Cards which contain misspelled first or last names, or even wrong initials, will have included in their listings the incorrect information, with a correction accompanying in parentheses. This extends, also, to cases where the name on the card does not correspond to the player actually pictured.

GRADING

It is necessary that some sort of card grading standard be used so that buyer and seller (especially when dealing by mail) may reach an informed agreement on the value of a card. Each card set's listings are priced in the three grades of preservation in which those cards are most commonly encountered in the daily buying and selling of the hobby marketplace.

Older cards are listed in grades of Near Mint (NR MT), Excellent (EX) and Very Good (VG), reflecting the basic fact that few cards were able to survive for 25, 50 or even 100 years in close semblance to the condition of their issue. The pricing of cards in these three conditions will allow readers to accurately price cards which fall in intermediate grades, such as EX-MT, or VG-EX.

More recent issues, which have been preserved in top condition in considerable number, are listed in the grades of Mint (MT), Near Mint and Excellent, reflective of the fact that there exists in the current market little or no demand for cards of the recent past in grades below Excellent.

In general, although grades below Very Good are not priced in this catalog, close approximations of low-grade card values may figure on the following formula: Good condition cards are valued at about 50% of VG price, with Fair cards priced about 50% of Good. Cards in Poor condition have no market value except in the cases of the rarest and most expensive cards. In such cases, value has to be negotiated individually.

For the benefit of the reader, we present herewith the grading guide which was orginally formulated by *Baseball Cards* magazine and *Sports Collectors Digest* in 1981, and has been continually refined since that time. These grading definitions have been used in the pricing of cards in this) catalog, but they are by no means a universally accepted grading standard. The potential buyer of a baseball card should keep that in mind when encountering cards of nominally the same grade, but at a price which differs widely from that quoted in this book. Ultimately, the collector himself must formulate his own personal grading standards in deciding whether cards available for purchase meet the needs of his own collection.

No collector or dealer is required to adhere to the grading standards presented herewith — or to any other published grading standards — but all are invited to do so. The editors of the *Sports Collectors Digest Baseball Card Price Guide* are eager to work toward the development of a standardized system of card grading that will be consistent with the realities of the hobby marketplace. Contact the editors.

Mint (MT): A perfect card. Well-centered, with parallel borders which appear equal to the naked eye. Four sharp, square corners. No creases, edge dents, surface scratches, paper flaws, loss of luster, yellowing or fading, regardless of age. No imperfectly printed card — out of register, badly cut or ink flawed — or card stained by contact with gum, wax or other substances can be considered truly Mint, even if new out of the pack.

Near Mint (NR MT): A nearly perfect card. At first glance, a Near Mint card appears perfect; upon closer examination, however, a minor flaw will be discovered. On well-centered cards, three of the four corners must be perfectly sharp; only one corner shows a minor imperfection upon close inspection. A slightly off-center card with one or more borders being noticeably unequal — but still present — would also fit this grade.

Excellent (EX): Corners are still fairly sharp with only moderate wear. Card borders may be off center. No creases. May have very minor gum, wax or product stains, front or back. Surfaces may show slight loss of luster from rubbing across other cards.

Very Good (VG): Shows obvious handling. Corners rounded and/or perhaps showing minor creases. Other minor creases may be visible. Surfaces may exhibit loss of luster, but all printing is intact. May show major gum, wax or other packaging stains. No major creases, tape marks or extraneous markings or writing. Exhibit honest wear.

Good (G): A well-worn card, but exhibits no intentional damage or abuse. May have major or multiple creases. Corners rounded well beyond the border.

Fair (F): Shows excessive wear, along with damage or abuse. Will show all the wear characteristics of a Good card, along with such damage as thumb tack holes in or near margins, evidence of having been taped or pasted, perhaps small tears around the edges, or creases so heavy as to break the cardboard. Backs may show minor added pen or pencil writing, or be missing small bits of paper. Still, a basically complete card.

Poor: A card that has been tortured to death. Corners or other areas may be torn off. Card may have been trimmed, show holes from paper punch or have been used for BB gun practice. Front may have extraneous pen or pencil writing, or other defacement. Major portions of front or back design may be missing. Not a pretty sight.

In addition to these seven widely-used terms, collectors will often encounter intermediate grades, such as VG-EX (Very Good to Excellent), EX-MT (Excellent to Mint), or NR MT-MT (Near Mint to Mint). Persons who describe a card with such grades are usually trying to convey that the card has all the characteristics of the lower grade, with enough of the higher grade to merit mention. Such cards are usually priced at a point midway between the two grades.

VALUATIONS

Values quoted in this book represent the current retail market and are compiled from recommendations provided and verified through the author's daily involvement in the publication of the hobby's leading advertising periodicals, as well as the input of specialized consultants.

It should be stressed, however, that this book is intended to serve only as an aid in evaluating cards; actual market conditions are constantly changing. This is especially true of the cards of current players, whose on-field performance during the course of a season can greatly affect the value of their cards — upwards or downwards.

Publication of this catalog is not intended as a solicitation to buy or sell the listed cards by the editors, publishers or contributors.

Again, the values here are retail prices — what a collector can expect to pay when buying a card from a dealer. The wholesale price, that which a collector can expect to receive from a dealer when selling cards, will be significantly lower. Most dealers operate on a 100% mark-up, generally paying about 50% of a card's retail

BARRY COLLA PHOTOGRAPHY
THE COLLA COLLECTION
1992

THE COLLA COLLECTION

CONTINUES IN 1992 WITH

LIMITED EDITION BASEBALL CARD SETS

- LIMITED EDITION AND NUMBERED
- EACH SET COMES IN A COLLECTORS' BOX
- FREE LIMITED PROMO CARDS
- EACH SET HAS 12 CARDS
- PRINTED WITH A DIAMOND VIEW™ PROCESS
- RECEIVE 1 ALLOCATION RIGHT IN EACH SET FOR THE

PREMIER LIMITED EDITION COLLA ROOKIE SET

PRICING

- PRICE PER SET WITH COLLECTORS' BOX . . . . $ 10.00
- DIE CUT DISPLAY BOX . . . . $ 10.00
  This is different from the collectors' box. The die cut display box holds 24 collectors' boxes and sets. There is a large photo baseball card on the bottom of the box.
- SET WITH COLLECTORS' BOX AND DIE CUT BOX . . . . . . $ 18.00
- DIE CUT DISPLAY BOX WITH 24 SETS AND COLLECTORS' BOXES AND SIX ***FREE*** PROMO CARDS . . . . $ 165.00
- ½ CASE, 4 DIE CUT DISPLAY BOXES WITH 96 SETS AND 28 ***FREE*** PROMO CARDS . . . . $ 585.00
- FULL CASE, 8 DIE CUT DISPLAY BOXES WITH 192 SETS AND 70 ***FREE*** PROMO CARDS $1099.00

FIRST TWO PLAYERS ISSUED IN 1992 WILL BE FRANK THOMAS AND JEFF BAGWELL

WIN! One of 200 numbered and autographed baseball cards of the player featured in each limited edition set (photos different from those in set). Randomly packed throughout the sets issued.* All sets are factory sealed.

*OFFICIAL RULES — Win instantly. Open box to see if you are an instant winner of one of 200 autographed baseball cards. Odds of winning are no less than 1:12,250 (for Thomas and Bagwell cards). NO PURCHASE NECESSARY. For an opportunity to win without purchase or for a copy of the official rules, print your name and complete address on a 3x5" card and send by first class mail to Barry Colla Photography, P.O. Box 2476, Santa Clara, CA 95055. Requests must be received by 3/31/92. Only instant winners will be notified. Open to U.S. residents. Void where prohibited.

COLLA CLUB CARDS

- Receive a 24 card *COLLA COLLECTION* limited edition numbered set in a collectors' box. This set will include the Top Stars and events of the 1992 season. Value $15.00.
- Special Promo card for club members only for every *COLLA COLLECTION* player set in 1992. Value $18.00. Expected release date. October, 1992.
- JOIN NOW! Sets will be limited! Retail value $33.00.
- MEMBERSHIP FEE $12.00 plus $3.00 postage.

GENUINE MERCHANDISE

MAJOR LEAGUE BASEBALL PLAYERS MLB © 1992 MLBPA

THE COLLA COLLECTION

Barry Colla Photography has issued other player sets with the first card of each limited edition set numbered to insure the investment potential. All sets have 12 cards and a limited number of Promo cards. ALL COLLA LIMITED EDITION SETS ARE LISTED IN THE ANNUAL BECKETT GUIDE.

PLAYER	Price per Set	Price per Promo Card
CLARK	$ 25.00	$ 4.50
GRIFFEY JR.	$ 20.00	$ 3.75
MATTINGLY	$ 15.00	$ 3.25
CANSECO	$ 12.00	$ 3.25
MAAS	$ 10.00	$ 3.00
SANDBERG	$ 10.00	$ 3.00
STRAWBERRY	$ 10.00	$ 3.00
JUSTICE	$ 10.00	$ 3.00
GOODEN	$ 10.00	$ 3.00
ALOMAR	$ 10.00	$ 3.00
CARTER	$ 10.00	$ 3.00
BONDS	$ 10.00	$ 3.00
ALL OF ABOVE	$109.00	$31.00

PREMIER LIMITED EDITION COLLA ROOKIE SET

ALLOCATION RIGHTS

The *PREMIER LIMITED EDITION COLLA ROOKIE SET* will be issued at the end of the baseball season. This FIRST EVER ROOKIE SET will include the top 25 Rookies of the 1992 season. This set is expected to be sold out at release time. We want to thank the supporters of *THE COLLA COLLECTION*. In every individual player set issued you will receive a right to purchase the *COLLA ROOKIE SET*. Buy 1 set and you can purchase 1 *ROOKIE SET*. All sets will be numbered and in a collectors' box.

New 96 page catalog free with every order.

VISA MasterCard AMERICAN EXPRESS

FOUNDING MEMBERS SCA Sports Collectables Association International

CARD COLLECTOR'S CO.

A division of Nostalgia, Inc.

105 West 77th Street, New York, NY 10024
(212) 873-6999

Visit our store, open 7 days 12-7 p.m.

CALL TOLL FREE FOR ORDERS ONLY 1-800-822-0028
FAX: (212) 787-2279

NASDAM

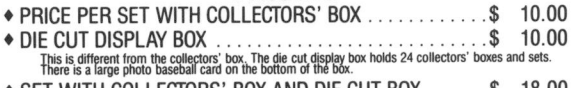

POSTAGE AND HANDLING CHARGE
$3.50 Per Order
New York State Residents Please Add Sales Tax

value. On some high-demand cards, dealers will pay up to 75% or even 100% or more of retail value, anticipating continued price increases. Conversely, for may low-demand cards, such as common player's cards of recent years, dealers may pay 25% or even less of retail.

It should also be noted that with several hundred thousand valuations quoted in this book, there are bound to be a few compilations or typographical errors which will creep into the final product, a fact readers should remember if they encounter a listing at a fraction of, or several times, the card's actual current retail price. The editors welcome the correction of any such errors discovered. Write: *Sports Collectors Digest Baseball Card Price Guide*, 700 E. State St., Iola, Wis. 54990.

SETS

Collectors may note that the complete set prices for newer issues quoted in these listings are usually significantly lower than the total of the value of the individual cards which comprise the set.

This reflects two factors in the baseball card market. First, a seller is often willing to take a lower composite price for a complete set as a "volume discount" and to avoid inventorying a large number of common player or other lower-demand cards.

Second, to a degree, the value of common cards can be said to be inflated as a result of having a built-in overhead charge to justify the dealer's time in sorting cards, carrying them in stock and filling orders. This accounts for the fact that even brand new baseball cards, which cost the dealer around 1 cent each when bought in bulk, carry individual price tags of 3 cents or higher.

ERRORS/VARIATIONS

It is often hard for the beginning collector to understand that an error on a baseball card, in and of itself, does not usually add premium value to that card. It is usually only when the correcting of an error in the subsequent printing creates a variation that premium value attaches to an error.

Minor errors, such as wrong stats or personal data, create a variation that premium value attaches to an error. Misspellings, inconsistencies, etc. — usually affecting the back of the card — are very common, especially in recent years. Unless a corrected variation was also printed, these errors are not noted in the listings of this book because they are not generally perceived by collectors to have premium value.

On the other hand, major effort has been expended to include the most complete listings ever for collectible variation cards. Many scarce and valuable variations — dozens of them never before cataloged — are included in these listings because they are widely collected and often have significant premium value.

COUNTERFEITS/REPRINTS

As the value of baseball cards has risen in the past 10-20 years, certains cards and sets have become too expensive for the average collector to obtain. This, along with changes in the technology of color printing, has given rise to increasing numbers of counterfeit and reprint cards.

While both terms describe essentially the same thing — a modern copy which attempts to duplicate as closely as possible an original baseball card — there are differences which are important to the collector.

Generally, a counterfeit is made with the intention of deceiving somebody into believing it is genuine, and thus paying large amounts of money for it. The counterfeiter takes every pain to try to make his fakes look as authentic as possible. In recent years, the 1963 Pete Rose, 1984 Donruss Don Mattingly and more than 30 superstar cards of the late 1960s-early 1980s have been counterfeited — all were quickly detected because of the differences in quality of cardboard on which they were printed.

A reprint, on the other hand, while it may have been made to look as close as possible to an original card, is made with the intention of allowing collectors to buy them as substitutes for cards they may never be otherwise able to afford. The big difference is that a reprint is generally marked as such, usually on the back of the card. In other cases, like the Topps 1952 reprint set, the replicas are printed in a size markedly different from the originals.

Collectors should be aware, however, that unscrupulous persons will sometimes cut off or otherwise obliterate the distinguishing word — "Reprint," "Copy," — or modern copyright date on the back of a reprint card in an attempt to pass it as genuine.

A collector's best defense against reprints and counterfeits is to acquire a knowledge of the look and feel of genuine baseball cards of various eras and issues.

UNLISTED CARDS

Readers who have cards or sets which are not covered in this edition are invited to correspond with the editor for purposes of adding to the compilation work now in progress. Address: *Sports Collectors Digest Baseball Card Price Guide*, 700 E. State St., Iola, Wis. 54990.

Contributors will be acknowledged in future editions.

COLLECTORS ISSUES

There exists within the hobby a great body of cards which do not fall under the scope of this catalog by virtue of their nature of having been issued solely for the collector market. Known as "collector issues," these cards and sets are distinguished from "legitimate" issues in not having been created as a sales promotional item for another product or service — bubble gum, soda, snack cakes, dog food, cigarettes, gasoline, etc.

By their nature, and principally because the person issuing them is always free to print and distribute more of the same if they should ever attain any real value, collector issues are generally regarded by collectors as having little or no premium value.

NEW ISSUES

Because new baseball cards are being issued all the time, the cataloging of them remains an on-going challenge. The editor will attempt to keep abreast of new issues so that they may be added to future editions of this book.

Readers are invited to submit news of new issues, especially limited-edition or regionally issued cards to the editors. Address: *Sports Collectors Digest Baseball Card Price Guide*, 700 E. State St., Iola, Wis. 54990.

BILL HENDERSON'S CARDS

"King of the Commons"

"ALWAYS BUYING"
Call or Write for Quote

2320 Ruger Ave. - KG
Janesville, Wisconsin 53545
1-608-755-0922

"ALWAYS BUYING"
Call or Write for Quote

	EX/MT TO MINT CONDITION			EX/MT TO MINT CONDITION		EX/MT TO MINT CONDITION GROUP LOTS FOR SALE MY CHOICE OF CARDS					VG + TO EX CONDITION		
	Hi # or Semi Hi Scarce Series	Price Per Common Card	Common Each	Other Series	Price Per Common Card	50. Diff.	100 Diff.	200 Asst.	300 Asst.	500 Asst.	50 Different	100 Different	200 Different
1948 Bowman	(37-48)	$30.00	20.00										
1949 Bowman	(145-240)	80.00	16.00			720.					480.		
1950-51 Bowman	50 (1-72); 51 (253-324)	60.00	16.00	51 (2-36)	25.00	720.					480.		
1952 Topps	(311-407)	P.O.R.	30.00	(2-80)	60.00	1350.					900.		
1952 Bowman	(217-252)	30.00	16.00	(2-36)	20.00	720.					480.		
1953 Topps	(220-280)	80.00	20.00	(2-165)	30.00	900.					600.		
1953 Bowman	(129-160)	40.00	30.00	(113-128)	50.00	1350.					900.		
1954 Topps			14.00	(51-75)	30.00	630.					420.		
1954 Bowman			9.00	(129-224)	13.00	400.	750.				270.		
1955 Topps	(161-210)	28.00	8.00	(151-160)	18.00	360.					240.		
1955 Bowman	(225-320)	15.-25. Umps	7.00	(2-96)	8.00	320.	600.				210.	400.	
1956 Topps	(261-340)	12.00	9.00	(181-260)	15.00	400.					270.	530.	
1957 Topps	(265-352)	20.00	6.00	(1-88)	7.50	270.	500.				180.	350.	
1958 Topps	(111-198)	5.00	4.00	(1-110)	7.50	190.	370.	720.	1020.		120.	230.	
1959 Topps	(507-572)	15.00	3.50	(1-110)	6.00	165.	320.	620.	900.		90.	175.	385.
1960 Topps	(441-506) 4.50 (507-572)	15.00	2.50	(287-440)	3.00	115.	220.	430.	635.	1000.	75.	140.	270.
1961 Topps	(447-522) 4.00 (523-589)	30.00	2.50	(371-446)	3.50	115.	220.	430.	635.	1000.	60.	110.	210.
1962 Topps	(371-522) 4.50 (523-590)	15.00	2.50	(284-370)	3.00	115.	220.				60.	110.	210.
1963 Topps	(447-522) 12.00 (523-573)	8.00	2.00	(284-446)	3.50	90.	175.				60.	110.	
1964 Topps	(523-587)	8.50	2.00	(371-522)	4.00	90.	175.	*340.			60.	110.	210.
1965 Topps	(447-522) 5.00 (523-598)	6.00	1.75	(284-446)	3.00	85.	160.				52.	100.	190.
1966 Topps	(447-522) 5.00 (523-598)	15.00	1.50	(371-446)	3.50	65.	125.	*240.			45.	85.	160.
1967 Topps	(458-533) 6.00 (*534-609)	20.00	1.50	(371-457)	2.50	65.	125.	*240.			45.	85.	160.
1968 Topps	(534-598)	3.00	1.50	(458-533)	2.50	60.	115.	*220.			37.	70.	130.
1969 Topps	(589-664)	2.00	1.25	(219-327)	2.00	60.	115.	*220.			30.	55.	105.
1970 Topps	(547-633) 2.50 (634-720)	5.00	.85	(460-546)	1.50	40.	75.	*145.	190.	360.	20.	38.	70.
1971 Topps	(524-643) 3.00 (644-752)	6.00	.85	(394-523)	1.50	40.	75.	*145.	190.	360.	20.	38.	70.
1972 Topps	(526-656) 2.50 (657-787)	6.00	.60	(395-525)	1.00	28.	54.	*105.	*150.	215.	15.	28.	50.
1973 Topps	(529-660)	2.50	.45	(397-528)	1.00	22.	42.	*80.	*115.	*190.	12.	22.	40.
1974 Topps			.40			18.	35.	*68.	*100.	*170.		22.	40.
1975 Topps	(8-132)	.50	.40			18.	35.	*68.	*100.			22.	40.
1976-77 Topps & 84 Donruss			.25				23.	*44.	*65.	*100.		15.	28.
1978-1980 Topps			.15				13.	*25.	*38.	*65.		8.	15.
1981 thru 1991 Topps, Fleer, or Donruss except those listed separately (specify year & co.)			.10				9. Per Yr.	*17. Per Yr.	*26. Per Yr.	*40. Per Yr.			
1985-86 Donruss, 1984-86 Fleer			.15				13.	*25.	*38.	*65.			

Krause Publications 5 YEAR CUSTOMER SERVICE AWARD

* Group Lots are all different

SPECIAL IN VG + to EX CONDITION - POSTPAID
Equal Distribution of Each Year

250	1958-62	$325.00
500	1958-62	620.00
250	1960-69	230.00
500	1960-69	425.00
1000	1960-69	800.00
250	1970-79	60.00
500	1970-79	110.00
1000	1970-79	200.00
250	1980-84	15.00
500	1980-84	28.00
1000	1980-84	55.00

Special 1 Different from each year 1949-80 EX/MT - $150.00, VG-EX $110.00
Special 100 Different from each year 1956-80 EX/MT - $3000.00, VG-EX $2100.00
Special 10 Different from each year 1956-80 EX/MT - $310.00, VG-EX $220.00

All lot groups are my choice only.

All assorted lots will contain as many different as possible.
Please list alternates whenever possible.
Send your want list and I will fill them at the above price for commons./ High numbers, specials, scarce series, and stars are priced at current Beckett.
You can use your Master Card or VISA to charge your purchase.
Minimum order $7.50 - Postage and handling .50 per 100 cards (minimum $1.75)

SETS AVAILABLE
Topps 1988, 1979, 1990, 1991
$20.95 ea. + 2.50 UPS
6 for 20.95 + 9.00 UPS
18 for 20.25 ea. + 20.00 UPS
54 for 19.75 ea. + 60.00 UPS
MIX OR MATCH

ANY CARD NOT LISTED ON PRICE SHEET IS PRICED AT CURRENT BECKETT MONTHLY HIGH COLUMN

Table of Contents

Title Page 2
Acknowledgements 3
Rookie/First Card Designations 4
Baseball Card History 4
How To Use This Catalog 8
Table of Contents 16
Rookie Checklist/Features 693

A

1989 Ames 20/20 Club 24
1990 Ames All-Stars 24

B

1948 Babe Ruth Story 24
1987 Baseball Super Stars Discs 26
1988 Baseball Superstars Discs 26
1959 Bazooka 28
1960 Bazooka 28
1961 Bazooka 29
1962 Bazooka 29
1963 Bazooka 30
1963 Bazooka All-Time Greats 30
1964 Bazooka 31
1964 Bazooka Stamps 31
1965 Bazooka 32
1966 Bazooka 32
1967 Bazooka 33
1968 Bazooka 34
1969-70 Bazooka 34
1971 Bazooka Unnumbered Set 35
1971 Bazooka Numbered Set 35
1988 Bazooka 35
1989 Bazooka 36
1990 Bazooka 36
1991 Bazooka 37
1951 Berk Ross 37
1952 Berk Ross 37
1986 Big League Chew 38
1987 Boardwalk and Baseball 38
1987 Bohemian Hearth Bread Padres 39
1948 Bowman 39
1949 Bowman 40
1949 Bowman Pacific Coast League 41
1950 Bowman 42
1951 Bowman 43
1952 Bowman 45
1953 Bowman Color 47
1953 Bowman Black & White 48
1954 Bowman 49
1955 Bowman 51
1989 Bowman 53
1990 Bowman 56
1991 Bowman 59
1977 Burger King Yankees 63
1978 Burger King Astros 63
1978 Burger King Rangers 64
1978 Burger King Tigers 64
1978 Burger King Yankees 65
1979 Burger King Phillies 65
1979 Burger King Yankees 65
1980 Burger King Phillies 66
1980 Burger King Pitch, Hit & Run 66
1982 Burger King Braves 66
1982 Burger King Indians 67
1986 Burger King 67
1987 Burger King 67

C

1989 Cap'n Crunch 68
1984 Cereal Series 68
1987 Champion Phillies 68
1988 Chef Boyardee 69
1985 Circle K 69
1987 Classic Baseball 70
1987 Classic Baseball Travel Edition 71
1988 Classic Baseball Travel Edition-Red 71
1988 Classic Baseball Travel Edition-Blue 72
1989 Classic Baseball 72
1989 Classic Update 73
1990 Classic Baseball 74
1990 Classic Baseball Series II 75
1990 Classic Series III 75
1990 Classic ffl1 Draft Picks 76
1991 Classic 76
1991 Classic Series II 77
1991 Classic Collector's Edition 78
1991 Classic Draft Picks 79
1989 Cleveland Indians Team Set 80
1981 Coca-Cola 80
1982 Coca-Cola/Brigham's Red Sox 81
1982 Coca-Cola Reds 81
1985 Coca-Cola White Sox 82
1986 Coca-Cola White Sox 82
1987 Coca-Cola Tigers 83
1987 Coca-Cola White Sox 83
1988 Coca-Cola Padres 83
1988 Coca-Cola White Sox 84
1989 Coca-Cola Padres 84
1989 Coca-Cola White Sox 85
1990 Coca-Cola Garry Templeton 85
1990 Coca-Cola White Sox 85
1982 Cracker Jack 86
1976 Crane Potato Chips 86

D

1954 Dan-Dee Potato Chips 87
1987 David Berg Hot Dogs Cubs 87
1988 David Berg Hot Dogs Cubs 87
1988 Domino's Pizza Tigers 88
1981 Donruss 88
1982 Donruss 92
1983 Donruss 96
1983 Donruss Action All-Stars 100
1983 Donruss Hall of Fame Heroes 101
1984 Donruss 101
1984 Donruss Action All-Stars 106
1984 Donruss Champions 106
1985 Donruss 107
1985 Donruss Action All-Stars 111
1985 Donruss Box Panels 111
1985 Donruss Diamond Kings Supers 112
1985 Donruss Highlights 112
1985 Donruss Sluggers of the Hall of Fame 113
1986 Donruss 113
1986 Donruss All-Stars 117
1986 Donruss Box Panels 118
1986 Donruss Diamond Kings Supers 118
1986 Donruss Highlights 118
1986 Donruss Pop-Ups 119
1986 Donruss Rookies 119
1987 Donruss 120
1987 Donruss All-Stars 124
1987 Donruss Box Panels 124
1987 Donruss Diamond Kings Supers 125
1987 Donruss Highlights 125
1987 Donruss Opening Day 126
1987 Donruss Pop-Ups 128
1987 Donruss Rookies 128
1988 Donruss 129
1988 Donruss All-Stars 133
1988 Donruss Baseball's Best 133
1988 Donruss Boston Team Book 135
1988 Donruss Chicago Cubs Team Book 136
1988 Donruss Diamond Kings Supers 136
1988 Donruss MVP 136
1988 Donruss New York Mets Team Book 137
1988 Donruss New York Yankees Team Book 137
1988 Donruss Oakland Team Book 138
1988 Donruss Pop-Ups 138
1988 Donruss Rookies 138
1989 Donruss 139
1989 Donruss Grand Slammers 143
1989 Donruss Traded 143
1989 Donruss Rookies 144
1989 Donruss Pop-Ups 144
1989 Donruss All-Stars 145
1989 Donruss MVP 145
1989 Donruss Baseball's Best 146
1990 Donruss MVP 148
1990 Donruss 148
1990 Donruss A.L. Best 152
1990 Donruss Diamond Kings Supers 153
1990 Donruss N.L. Best 154
1990 Donruss Rookies 155
1990 Donruss Grand Slammers 155
1991 Donruss 155
1991 Donruss Highlights 160
1991 Donruss Rookies 160
1991 Donruss Grand Slammers 161
1991 Donruss Studio 161
1992 Donruss 163
1986 Dorman's Cheese 165
1950 Drake's 166
1981 Drake's 166
1982 Drake's 166
1983 Drake's 167
1984 Drake's 167
1985 Drake's 168
1986 Drake's 168
1987 Drake's 169
1988 Drake's 169

E

1966 East Hill Pirates 170
1947-66 Exhibit Supply Co. 170
1962 Exhibit—Statistic Backs 172
1963 Exhibit—Statistic Backs 173

F

1988 Fantastic Sam's 173
1987 Farmland Dairies Mets 174
1988 Farmland Dairies Mets 174
1959 Fleer Ted Williams 174
1960 Fleer 175
1961-62 Fleer 176
1963 Fleer 177
1981 Fleer 177
1981 Fleer Star Stickers 182
1982 Fleer 183
1983 Fleer 187
1984 Fleer 191
1984 Fleer Update 195
1985 Fleer 196
1985 Fleer Limited Edition 199
1985 Fleer Update 200
1986 Fleer 201
1986 Fleer All Star Team 205
1986 Fleer Baseball's Best 205
1986 Fleer Box Panels 206
1986 Fleer Future Hall of Famers 206
1986 Fleer League Leaders 206
1986 Fleer Limited Edition 207
1986 Fleer Mini 207
1986 Fleer Star Stickers 208
1986 Fleer Star Stickers Box Panel 209
1986 Fleer Update 209
1987 Fleer 210
1987 Fleer All Star Team 214
1987 Fleer Award Winner 215
1987 Fleer Baseball All Stars 215
1987 Fleer Baseball's Best 216
1987 Fleer Baseball's Exciting Stars 216
1987 Fleer Baseball's Game Winners 217
1987 Fleer Baseball's Hottest Stars 217
1987 Fleer Box Panels 218
1987 Fleer '86 World Series 218
1987 Fleer Headliners 219
1987 Fleer League Leaders 219
1987 Fleer Limited Edition 219
1987 Fleer Mini 220
1987 Fleer Record Setters 220
1987 Fleer Star Stickers 221
1987 Fleer Star Stickers Box Panels 222
1987 Fleer Update 222
1988 Fleer 223
1988 Fleer All Star Team 227
1988 Fleer Award Winners 228
1988 Fleer Baseball All Stars 228
1988 Fleer Baseball MVP 229
1988 Fleer Baseball's Best 229
1988 Fleer Baseball's Best Box Panels 230
1988 Fleer Baseball's Exciting Stars 230
1988 Fleer Baseball's Hottest Stars 230
1988 Fleer Box Panels 231
1988 Fleer '87 World Series 231
1988 Fleer Headliners 232
1988 Fleer League Leaders 232
1988 Fleer Mini 232
1988 Fleer Record Setters 233
1988 Fleer Star Stickers 234
1988 Fleer Star Stickers Box Panels 235
1988 Fleer Superstars 235

1988 Fleer Update 236
1989 Fleer 237
1989 Fleer All Star Team 241
1989 Fleer Baseball All Stars 241
1989 Fleer Update 241
1989 Fleer Baseball MVP 242
1989 Fleer Baseball's Exciting Stars 243
1989 Fleer Heroes of Baseball 243
1989 Fleer League Leaders 244
1989 Fleer Superstars 244
1989 Fleer Box Panels 245
1989 Fleer For The Record 245
1989 Fleer '88 World Series 245
1990 Fleer 246
1990 Fleer All-Star Team 250
1990 Fleer Award Winners 250
1990 Fleer Baseball All Stars 250
1990 Fleer Baseball MVP 251
1990 Fleer Box Panels 251
1990 Fleer '89 World Series 252
1990 Fleer League Leaders 252
1990 Fleer League Standouts 253
1990 Fleer Update 253
1991 Fleer 254
1991 Fleer All Stars 258
1991 Fleer Box Panels 258
1991 Fleer '90 World Series 259
1991 Fleer Pro Vision 259
1991 Fleer Update 259
1991 Fleer Ultra 260
1991 Fleer Ultra Update 263
1992 Fleer 264
1991 Front Row Draft Picks 268

G

1953 Glendale Hot Dogs Tigers 268
1961 Golden Press 268

H

1989 Hill's Team MVP's 269
1990 Hill's Hit Men 269
1958 Hire's Root Beer Test Set 270
1958 Hire's Root Beer 270
1959 Home Run Derby 271
1975 Hostess 271
1975 Hostess Twinkie 272
1976 Hostess 273
1976 Hostess Twinkie 274
1977 Hostess 275
1977 Hostess Twinkie 276
1978 Hostess 277
1979 Hostess 278
1985 Hostess Braves 279
1987 Hostess Stickers 280
1988 Hostess Potato Chips Expos 281
1982 Hygrade Meats Expos 281

J

1984 Jarvis Press Rangers 282
1986 Jays Potato Chips 282
1962 Jell-O 282
1963 Jell-O 284
1986 Jiffy Pop 285
1987 Jiffy Pop 285
1988 Jiffy Pop 286
1991 Jimmy Dean 286
1953 Johnston's Cookies Braves 286
1954 Johnston's Cookies Braves 287
1955 Johnston's Cookies Braves 287

K

1982 K-Mart 288
1987 K-Mart 288
1988 K-Mart 289
1989 K-Mart 289
1990 K-Mart 290
1955 Kahn's Wieners Reds 290
1956 Kahn's Wieners Reds 290
1957 Kahn's Wieners 291
1958 Kahn's Wieners 291
1959 Kahn's Wieners 291
1960 Kahn's Wieners 292
1961 Kahn's Wieners 292
1962 Kahn's Wieners 293
1963 Kahn's Wieners 293
1964 Kahn's Wieners 294
1965 Kahn's Wieners 294
1966 Kahn's Wieners 295
1967 Kahn's Wieners 295
1968 Kahn's Wieners 296
1969 Kahn's Wieners 296
1987 Kahn's Wieners Reds 297
1988 Kahn's Wieners Mets 297
1988 Kahn's Wieners Reds 298
1989 Kahn's-Hillshire Farms 299
1989 Kahn's Wieners Mets 299
1989 Kahn's Wieners Reds 299
1990 Kahn's Wieners Mets 299
1990 Kahn's Wieners Reds 300
1991 Kahn's Wieners Reds 300
1986 Kas Potato Chips Cardinals 300
1986 Kay Bee 300
1987 Kay Bee 301
1988 Kay Bee Superstars of Baseball 301
1988 Kay Bee Team Leaders 302
1989 Kay Bee Superstars 302
1970 Kellogg's 303
1971 Kellogg's 303
1972 Kellogg's 304
1972 Kellogg's All-Time Greats 305
1973 Kellogg's 305
1974 Kellogg's 306
1975 Kellogg's 306
1976 Kellogg's 307
1977 Kellogg's 307
1978 Kellogg's 308
1979 Kellogg's 308
1980 Kellogg's 309
1981 Kellogg's 309
1982 Kellogg's 310
1983 Kellogg's 310
1988 King-B 311
1989 King-B 312
1986 Kitty Clover Potato Chips Royals 312
1987 Kraft 312

L

1960 Lake to Lake Dairy Braves 313
1948-49 Leaf 313
1960 Leaf 314
1990 Leaf 315
1991 Leaf Series I 318
1991 Leaf Gold Rookies 320
1986 Lite Beer Astros 320
1986 Lite Beer Rangers 321

M

1987 M&M's 321
1989 Marathon Cubs 322
1989 Marathon Tigers 322
1990 Marathon Cubs 322
1988 Master Bread Twins 323
1986 Meadow Gold—Set of 16 323
1986 Meadow Gold—Set of 20 323
1986 Meadow Gold Milk 324
1971 Milk Duds 324
1984 Milton Bradley 325
1991 Mootown Snackers 325

N

1969 Nabisco Team Flakes 325
1986 National Photo Royals 326
1984 Nestle Dream Team 326
1987 Nestle 326
1988 Nestle 327
1954 N.Y. Journal-American 327
1986 N.Y. Mets Super Fan Club 328
1960 Nu-Card Baseball Hi-Lites 328
1961 Nu-Card Baseball Scoops 329

O

1991 O-Pee-Chee Premier 330
1986 Oh Henry! Indians 331

P

1988 Pacific Trading Cards Baseball Legends 331
1989 Pacific Trading Cards Baseball Legends II 332
1990 Pacific Trading Cards Baseball Legends III 332
1963 Pepsi-Cola Colt .45's 334
1988 Pepsi Cola/Kroger Tigers 334
1990 Pepsi-Cola Red Sox 335
1991 Pepsi-Cola Red Sox 335
1985 Performance Printing Rangers 335
1986 Performance Printing Rangers 336
1961 Peters Meats Twins 336
1960 Post Cereal 337
1961 Post Cereal 337
1962 Post Cereal 339
1962 Post Cereal Canadian 341
1963 Post Cereal 342
1990 Post 344
1991 Post 344

Q

1986 Quaker Oats 345

R

1984 Ralston Purina 345
1987 Ralston Purina 345
1989 Ralston Purina 345
1954 Red Heart Dog Food 346
1982 Red Lobster Cubs 347
1952 Red Man Tobacco 347
1953 Red Man Tobacco 348
1954 Red Man Tobacco 348
1955 Red Man Tobacco 349
1988 Revco 349
1988 Rite Aid 350
1955 Rodeo Meats Athletics 351
1956 Rodeo Meats Athletics 351
1970 Rold Gold Pretzels 351
1950-52 Royal Desserts 351
1952 Royal Desserts 352

S

1988 Score 352
1988 Score Box Panels 356
1988 Score Traded 357
1988 Score Young Superstar 358
1988 Score Young Superstar Series II 358
1989 Score 359
1989 Score Traded 363
1989 Score Young Superstar Series I 363
1989 Score Young Superstar Series II 364
1989 Score Rising Star 364
1989 Score Superstar 365
1989 Score Yankees 366
1990 Score 366
1990 Score Rising Stars 371
1990 Score Superstar 371
1990 Score Traded 372
1991 Score 373
1991 Score Rising Star 378
1991 Score Superstar 379
1991 Score Rookies 380
1991 Score Traded 380
1992 Score 381
1989 Scoremasters 384
1985 7-11 Twins 384
1984 7-Up Cubs 384
1985 7-Up Cubs 385
1986 Sportflics 385
1986 Sportflics Decade Greats 387
1986 Sportflics Rookies 388
1987 Sportflics 388
1987 Sportflics Rookie Discs 390
1987 Sportflics Rookie Prospects 390
1987 Sportflics Rookies 390
1987 Sportflics Superstar Discs 391
1987 Sportflics Team Preview 391
1988 Sportflics 392
1988 Sportflics Gamewinners 393
1989 Sportflics 394
1990 Sportflics 395

T

1948 Topps Magic Photos 397
1951 Topps Blue Backs 397
1951 Topps Red Backs 397
1951 Topps Connie Mack All-Stars 398
1951 Topps Current All-Stars 398
1951 Topps Teams 399
1952 Topps 399
1953 Topps 401
1954 Topps 403
1955 Topps 405
1955 Topps Double Headers 406
1956 Topps 407
1956 Topps Hocus Focus Large 410
1956 Topps Pins 410
1957 Topps 411
1958 Topps 413
1959 Topps 417
1960 Topps 420
1960 Topps Baseball Tattoos 424
1961 Topps 425

1961 Topps Dice Game 429
1961 Topps Magic Rub Offs 429
1961 Topps Stamps 429
1962 Topps 431
1962 Topps Baseball Bucks 435
1962 Topps Stamps 436
1963 Topps 437
1963 Topps Peel-Offs 441
1964 Topps 441
1964 Topps Coins 445
1964 Topps Giants 446
1964 Topps Photo Tatoos 447
1964 Topps Stand-Ups 448
1965 Topps 448
1965 Topps Embossed 452
1965 Topps Transfers 453
1966 Topps 454
1966 Topps Rub-Offs 458
1967 Topps 458
1967 Topps Pin-Ups 463
1967 Topps Giant Stand-Ups 463
1967 Topps Stickers Pirates 463
1967 Topps Stickers Red Sox 464
1968 Topps 464
1968 Topps Action All-Star Stickers 468
1968 Topps Discs 469
1968 Topps Game 469
1968 Topps Plaks 469
1968 Topps Posters 470
1968 Topps 3-D 470
1969 Topps 470
1969 Topps Decals 475
1969 Topps Deckle Edge 476
1969 Topps 4-on-1 Mini Stickers 476
1969 Topps Stamps 477
1969 Topps Super 477
1969 Topps Team Posters 478
1970 Topps 479
1970 Topps Candy Lids 484
1970 Topps Posters 484
1970-71 Topps Scratch-Offs 484
1970 Topps Story Booklets 485
1970 Topps Super 485
1971 Topps 486
1971 Topps Baseball Tattoos 486
1971 Topps Coins 491
1971 Topps Greatest Moments 492
1971 Topps Super 493
1972 Topps 493
1972 Topps Cloth Stickers 498
1972 Topps Posters 499
1973 Topps 499
1973 Topps Candy Lids 504
1973 Topps Comics 504
1973 Topps Pin-Ups 505
1973 Topps Team Checklists 505
1974 Topps 505
1974 Topps Deckle Edge 510
1974 Topps Puzzles 510
1974 Topps Stamps 511
1974 Topps Team Checklists 512
1974 Topps Traded 512
1975 Topps 512
1976 Topps 517
1976 Topps Traded 521
1977 Topps 521
1977 Topps Cloth Stickers 525
1978 Topps 526
1979 Topps 530
1979 Topps Comics 535
1980 Topps 535
1980 Topps Superstar 5x7 Photos 540
1981 Topps 540
1981 Topps Home Team 5x7 Photos 545
1981 Topps National 5x7 Photos 545
1981 Topps Scratch-Offs 546
1981 Topps Stickers 547
1981 Topps Traded 548
1982 Topps 549
1982 Topps Insert Stickers 554
1982 Topps Stickers 555
1982 Topps Traded 556
1983 Topps 557
1983 Topps All-Star Glossy Set of 40 562
1983 Topps Foldouts 563
1983 Topps Stickers 563
1983 Topps Stickers Boxes 565
1983 Topps Traded 565
1984 Topps 566
1984 Topps All-Star Glossy Set of 22 571
1984 Topps All-Star Glossy Set of 40 572
1984 Topps Gallery of Immortals 572
1984 Topps Rub Downs 573
1984 Topps Stickers 573
1984 Topps Stickers Boxes 576
1984 Topps Super 576
1984 Topps Traded 576
1985 Topps 577
1985 Topps All-Star Glossy Set of 22 582
1985 Topps All-Star Glossy Set of 40 582
1985 Topps All-Time Record Holders 583
1985 Topps Rub Downs 618
1985 Topps Gallery of Champions 583
1985 Topps Rub Downs 584
1985 Topps Stickers 584
1985 Topps Super 587
1985 Topps 3-D 587
1985 Topps Traded 588
1986 Topps 589
1986 Topps All-Star Glossy Set of 22 593
1986 Topps All-Star Glossy Set of 60 594
1986 Topps Box Panels 594
1986 Topps Gallery of Champions 595
1986 Topps Mini League Leaders 595
1986 Topps Stickers 596
1986 Topps Super 598
1986 Topps Super Star 598
1986 Topps Tattoos 599
1986 Topps Traded 599
1986 Topps 3-D 600
1987 Topps 601
1987 Topps All-Star Glossy Set of 22 606
1987 Topps All-Star Glossy Set of 60 606
1987 Topps Baseball Highlights 606
1987 Topps Box Panels 607
1987 Topps Coins 607
1987 Topps Gallery of Champions 608
1987 Topps Glossy Rookies 608
1987 Topps Mini League Leaders 609
1987 Topps Stickers 609
1987 Topps Traded 611
1988 Topps 612
1988 Topps All-Star Glossy Set of 22 617
1988 Topps All-Star Glossy Set of 60 617
1988 Topps American Baseball 618
1988 Topps Big Baseball 619
1988 Topps Box Panels 621
1988 Topps Coins 621
1988 Topps Gallery of Champions 622
1988 Topps Glossy Rookies 622
1988 Topps Mini League Leaders 623
1988 Topps Stickercards 623
1988 Topps Stickers 623
1988 Topps Traded 624
1989 Topps 627
1989 Topps All-Star Glossy Set of 22 633
1989 Topps All-Star Glossy Set of 60 633
1989 Topps American Baseball 638
1989 Topps Big Baseball 634
1989 Topps Box Panels 636
1989 Topps Major League Debut 636
1989 Topps Mini League Leaders 637
1989 Topps Traded 632
1990 Topps 639
1990 Topps All-Star Glossy Set of 22 643
1990 Topps All-Star Glossy Set of 60 644
1990 Topps Big Baseball 644
1990 Topps Box Panels 646
1990 Topps Traded 647
1991 Topps 648
1991 Topps Box Panels 652
1991 Topps Major League Debut 653
1991 Topps Stadium Club 654
1991 Topps Traded 657
1992 Topps 658
1987 Toys "R" Us 663
1988 Toys "R" Us Rookies 663
1989 Toys "R" Us Rookies 664
1990 Toys "R" Us Rookies 664
1969 Transogram 665
1970 Transogram 665
1970 Transogram Mets 666
1983 True Value White Sox 666
1984 True Value White Sox 666
1986 True Value 667

U

1989 Upper Deck 667
1990 Upper Deck 672
1991 Upper Deck 678
1991 Upper Deck Final Edition 683
1991 Upper Deck Silver Sluggers 683
1991 Upper Deck Heroes of Baseball 684
1992 Upper Deck 684

V

1989 Very Fine Pirates 688

W

1950-56 W576 Callahan Hall of Fame 689
1985 Wendy's Tigers 690
1954 Wilson Franks 690
1988 Woolworth 690
1989 Woolworth 691
1990 Woolworth 691

Z

1982 Zellers Expos 692

FOUR "C'S"

COLLECTORS WORLD

520 Army Post Rd. #23
Des Moines, Iowa 50315
515-287-2258

Baseball,
Football,
Basketball,
Hockey Cards,
Comics,
Beer
Steins,
Supplies
and
Collectibles

(OWNERS)

Wayne and Ruth Hugen

Card Company Addresses

Bowman Co.: See Topps
Classic Games Inc.: 6488 E. Spring St., #203, Douglasville, Ga. 30134
Donruss-Leaf: 2355 Waukegan Road, Bannockburn, Ill. 60015
Fleer Corp.: 10th and Somerville, Philadelphia, Pa. 19141
O-Pee-Chee Co.: P.O. Box 6306, London, Ontario, Canada N5W 5S1
Pacific Trading Cards: 18424 Highway 99, Lynnwood, Wash. 98037
Score: c/o Major League Marketing, 25 Ford Road, Westport, Conn. 06880
Swell: Philadelphia Chewing Gum Corp., Havertown, Pa. 19083-2198
Topps Gum Co.: 254 36th St., Brooklyn, N.Y. 11232
Upper Deck Co.: 23705 Via del Rio, Yorba Linda, Calif. 92686

Major League Baseball Team Addresses

American League

Baltimore Orioles, Memorial Stadium, Baltimore, Md. 21218
Boston Red Sox, Fenway Park, Boston, Mass. 02215
California Angels, P.O. Box 2000, Anaheim Stadium, Anaheim, Calif. 92803
Chicago White Sox, 324 West 35th St., Comiskey Park, Chicago, Ill. 60616
Cleveland Indians, Municipal Stadium, Cleveland, Ohio 44114
Detroit Tigers, Tiger Stadium, Detroit, Mich. 48216
Kansas City Royals, P.O. Box 1969, Royals Stadium, Kansas City, Mo. 64141
Milwaukee Brewers, Milwaukee County Stadium, Milwaukee, Wis. 53214
Minnesota Twins, 501 Chicago Ave. South, Hubert H. Humphrey Metrodome, Minneapolis, Minn. 55415
New York Yankees, Yankee Stadium, Bronx, N.Y. 10451
Oakland Athletics, Oakland-Alameda County Coliseum, Oakland, Calif. 94621
Seattle Mariners, P.O. Box 4100, The Kingdome, Seattle, Wash. 98104
Texas Rangers, P.O. Box 1111, Arlington Stadium, Arlington, Texas 76010
Toronto Blue Jays, The SkyDome, 300 The Esplanade West, Suite #3200, Toronto, Ontario, Canada M5V 3B3

National League

Atlanta Braves, P.O. Box 4064, Atlanta-Fulton County Stadium, Atlanta, Ga. 30312
Chicago Cubs, 1060 West Addison St., Wrigley Field, Chicago, Ill. 60613
Cincinnati Reds, 100 Riverfront Stadium, Cincinnati, Ohio 45202
Houston Astros, P.O. Box 288, The Astrodome, Houston, Texas 77001
Los Angeles Dodgers, 1000 Elysian Park Ave., Dodger Stadium, Los Angeles, Calif. 90012
Montreal Expos, P.O. Box 500, Station M, Olympic Stadium, Montreal, Quebec, Canada, H1V 3P2
New York Mets, William A. Shea Stadium, Flushing, N.Y. 11368
Philadelphia Phillies, Box 7575, Veterans Stadium, Philadelphia, Pa. 19101
Pittsburgh Pirates, P.O. Box 7000, Three Rivers Stadium, Pittsburgh, Pa. 15212
St. Louis Cardinals, 250 Stadium Plaza, Busch Stadium, St. Louis, Mo. 63102
San Diego Padres, 9449 Friars Road, San Diego — Jack Murphy Stadium, San Diego, Calif. 92108
San Francisco Giants, Candlestick Park, San Francisco, Calif. 94124

A

1989 Ames 20/20 Club

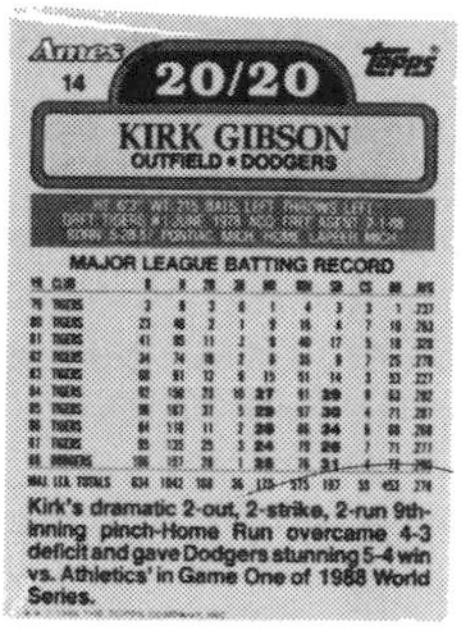

This 33-card set was produced by Topps for the Ames toy store chain. As its name implies, the special boxed set highlights members of the 20/20 club, players who have recorded 20 home runs and 20 stolen bases in the same season. The glossy cards feature action or posed photos on the front with the player's name at the top and "Ames 20/20 Club" along the bottom. The Topps logo appears in the upper right corner.

		MT	NR MT	EX
Complete Set:		4.00	3.00	1.50
Common Player:		.09	.07	.04
1	Jesse Barfield	.09	.07	.04
2	Kevin Bass	.09	.07	.04
3	Don Baylor	.09	.07	.04
4	George Bell	.12	.09	.05
5	Barry Bonds	.40	.30	.15
6	Phil Bradley	.09	.07	.04
7	Ellis Burks	.20	.15	.08
8	Jose Canseco	.70	.50	.30
9	Joe Carter	.20	.15	.08
10	Kal Daniels	.09	.07	.04
11	Eric Davis	.20	.15	.08
12	Mike Davis	.09	.07	.04
13	Andre Dawson	.12	.09	.05
14	Kirk Gibson	.09	.07	.04
15	Pedro Guerrero	.12	.09	.05
16	Rickey Henderson	.50	.40	.20
17	Bo Jackson	.60	.45	.25
18	Howard Johnson	.20	.15	.08
19	Jeffrey Leonard	.09	.07	.04
20	Kevin McReynolds	.12	.09	.05
21	Dale Murphy	.09	.07	.04
22	Dwayne Murphy	.09	.07	.04
23	Dave Parker	.12	.09	.05
24	Kirby Puckett	.50	.40	.20
25	Juan Samuel	.09	.07	.04
26	Ryne Sandberg	.20	.15	.08
27	Mike Schmidt	.80	.60	.30
28	Darryl Strawberry	.25	.20	.10
29	Alan Trammell	.09	.07	.04
30	Andy Van Slyke	.09	.07	.04
31	Devon White	.09	.07	.04
32	Dave Winfield	.12	.09	.05
33	Robin Yount	.30	.25	.12

1990 Ames All-Stars

This 33-card set was the second consecutive issue produced by Topps for the Ames toy store chain. The cards measure 2-1/2" by 3-1/2" in size and feature baseball's top active hitters. Both the Ames and Topps logos appear on the cards.

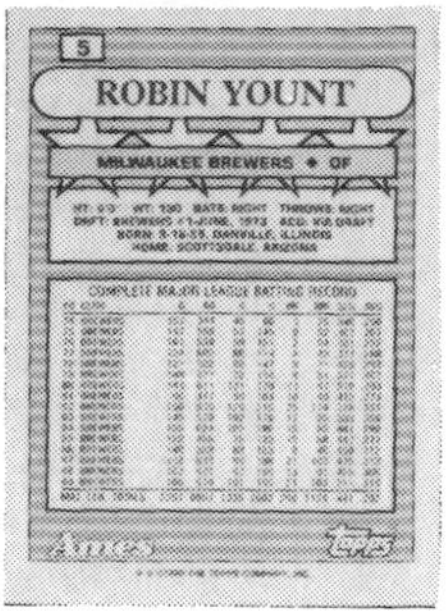

		MT	NR MT	EX
Complete Set:		4.00	3.00	1.50
Common Player:		.08	.06	.03
1	Dave Winfield	.12	.09	.05
2	George Brett	.25	.20	.10
3	Jim Rice	.12	.09	.05
4	Dwight Evans	.12	.09	.05
5	Robin Yount	.25	.20	.10
6	Dave Parker	.10	.08	.04
7	Eddie Murray	.20	.15	.08
8	Keith Hernandez	.08	.06	.03
9	Andre Dawson	.20	.15	.08
10	Fred Lynn	.08	.06	.03
11	Dale Murphy	.15	.11	.06
12	Jack Clark	.08	.06	.03
13	Rickey Henderson	.50	.40	.20
14	Paul Molitor	.10	.08	.04
15	Cal Ripken	.25	.20	.10
16	Wade Boggs	.25	.20	.10
17	Tim Raines	.10	.08	.04
18	Don Mattingly	.40	.30	.15
19	Kent Hrbek	.08	.06	.03
20	Kirk Gibson	.10	.08	.04
21	Julio Franco	.12	.09	.05
22	George Bell	.12	.09	.05
23	Darryl Strawberry	.30	.25	.12
24	Kirby Puckett	.25	.20	.10
25	Juan Samuel	.08	.06	.03
26	Alvin Davis	.08	.06	.03
27	Joe Carter	.15	.11	.06
28	Eric Davis	.20	.15	.08
29	Jose Canseco	.50	.40	.20
30	Wally Joyner	.12	.09	.05
31	Will Clark	.50	.40	.20
32	Ruben Sierra	.25	.20	.10
33	Danny Tartabull	.15	.11	.06

B

1948 Babe Ruth Story

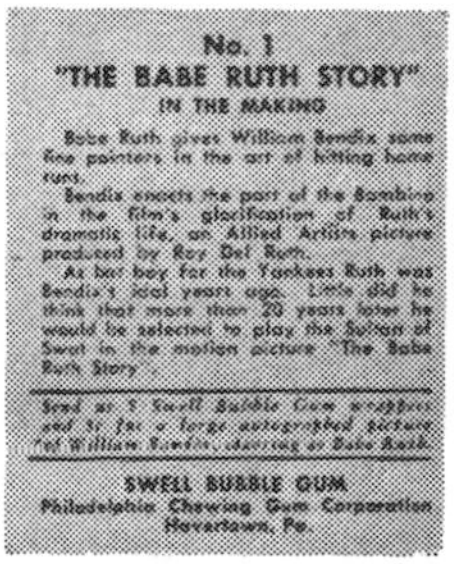

The Philadelphia Gum Co., in 1948, created a card set about the movie "The Babe Ruth Story", which starred William Bendix and Claire Trevor. The set,

whose American Card Catalog designation is R421, contains 28 black and white, numbered cards which measure 2" by 2-1/2". The Babe Ruth Story set was originally intended to consist of sixteen cards. Twelve additional cards (#'s 17-28) were added when Ruth died before the release of the film. The card backs include a offer for an autographed photo of William Bendix, starring as the Babe, for five Swell Bubble Gum wrappers and five cents.

		NR MT	EX	VG
Complete Set:		1200.00	600.00	360.00
Common Player: 1-16		13.00	6.50	4.00
Common Player: 17-28		40.00	20.00	12.00
1	"The Babe Ruth Story" In The Making	75.00	38.00	23.00
2	Bat Boy Becomes the Babe... William Bendix	13.00	6.50	4.00
3	Claire Hodgson...Claire Trevor	13.00	6.50	4.00
4	Babe Ruth and Claire Hodgson	13.00	6.50	4.00
5	Brother Matthias...Charles Bickford	13.00	6.50	4.00
6	Phil Conrad...Sam Levene	13.00	6.50	4.00
7	Night Club Singer...Gertrude Niesen	13.00	6.50	4.00
8	Baseball's Famous Deal...Jack Dunn (William Frawley)	13.00	6.50	4.00
9	Mr. & Mrs. Babe Ruth	13.00	6.50	4.00
10	Babe Ruth, Claire Ruth, and Brother Matthias	13.00	6.50	4.00
11	Babe Ruth and Miller Huggins (Fred Lightner)	13.00	6.50	4.00
12	Babe Ruth At Bed Of Ill Boy Johnny Sylvester (Gregory Marshall)	13.00	6.50	4.00
13	Sylvester Family Listening To Game	13.00	6.50	4.00
14	"When A Feller Needs a Friend" (With Dog At Police Station)	13.00	6.50	4.00
15	Dramatic Home Run	13.00	6.50	4.00
16	The Homer That Set the Record (#60)	13.00	6.50	4.00
17	"The Slap That Started Baseball's Famous Career"	40.00	20.00	12.00
18	The Babe Plays Santa Claus	40.00	20.00	12.00
19	Meeting Of Owner And Manager	40.00	20.00	12.00
20	"Broken Window Paid Off"	40.00	20.00	12.00
21	Babe In A Crowd Of Autograph Collectors	40.00	20.00	12.00
22	Charley Grimm And William Bendix	40.00	20.00	12.00
23	Ted Lyons And William Bendix	50.00	25.00	15.00
24	Lefty Gomez, William Bendix, And Bucky Harris	50.00	25.00	15.00
25	Babe Ruth and William Bendix	115.00	57.00	34.00
26	Babe Ruth And William Bendix	115.00	57.00	34.00
27	Babe Ruth And Claire Trevor	115.00	57.00	34.00
28	William Bendix, Babe Ruth, And Claire Trevor	115.00	57.00	34.00

1987 Baseball Super Stars Discs

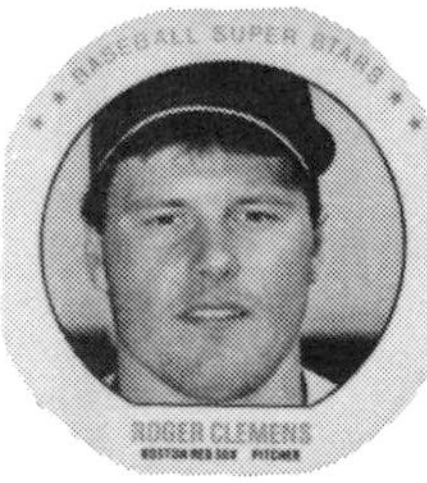

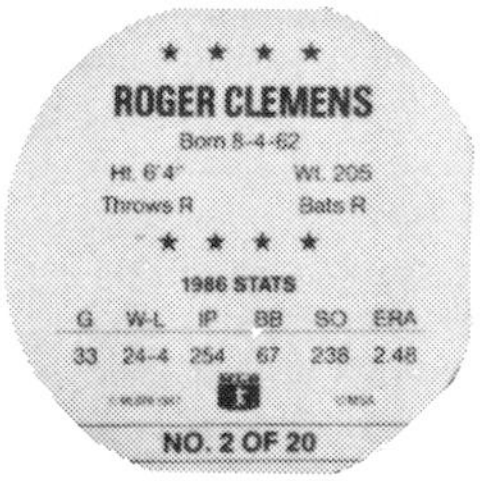

Produced by Mike Schecter and Associates, the "Baseball Super Stars" disc set was released as part of a promotion for various brands of iced tea mixes in many parts of the country. Among the brands participating in the promotion were Acme, Alpha Beta, Bustelo, Key, King Kullen, Lady Lee, Our Own and Weis. The discs were issued in three-part folding panels with each disc measuring 2-1/2" in diameter. The disc fronts feature a full-color photo inside a bright yellow border. Two player discs were included in each panel along with a coupon disc offering either an uncut press sheet of the set or a facsimile autographed ball.

		MT	NR MT	EX
Complete Panel Set:		10.00	7.50	4.00
Complete Singles Set:		5.00	3.75	2.00
Common Panel:		.25	.20	.10
Common Single Player:		.05	.04	.02
	Panel	1.00	.70	.40
1	Darryl Strawberry	.20	.15	.08
2	Roger Clemens	.50	.40	.20
	Panel	.35	.25	.14
3	Ron Darling	.05	.04	.02
4	Keith Hernandez	.10	.08	.04
	Panel	1.00	.70	.40
5	Tony Pena	.05	.04	.02
6	Don Mattingly	.70	.50	.30
	Panel	1.00	.70	.40
7	Eric Davis	.35	.25	.14
8	Gary Carter	.08	.06	.03
	Panel	.80	.60	.30
9	Dave Winfield	.12	.09	.05
10	Wally Joyner	.20	.15	.08
	Panel	.50	.40	.20
11	Mike Schmidt	.25	.20	.10
12	Robby Thompson	.05	.04	.02
	Panel	1.00	.70	.40
13	Wade Boggs	.35	.25	.14
14	Cal Ripken Jr.	.40	.30	.15
	Panel	1.00	.70	.40
15	Dale Murphy	.15	.11	.06
16	Tony Gwynn	.15	.11	.06
	Panel	1.75	1.25	.70
17	Jose Canseco	.70	.50	.30
18	Rickey Henderson	.30	.25	.12
	Panel	.25	.20	.10
19	Lance Parrish	.08	.06	.03
20	Dave Righetti	.08	.06	.03

1988 Baseball Superstars Discs

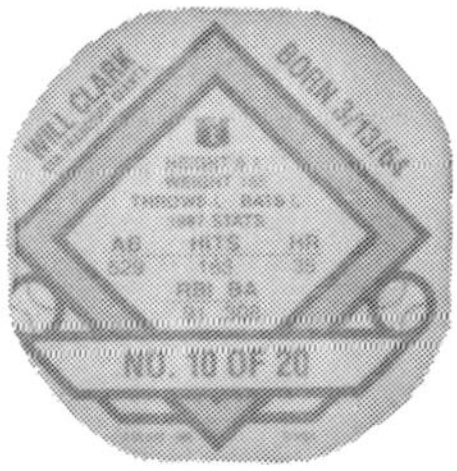

The "Second Annual Collector's Edition" of Baseball Super Stars Discs is very similar to the 1987 issue. A set of 20 discs (2-1/2" diameter) featuring full-color baseball player photos was inserted in specially marked cannisters of iced tea and fruit drinks. Each triple-fold insert consists of 2 player discs and one redemption card. Player discs are bright blue, yellow, red and green with a diamond design framing the player closeup. The player name appears upper left, the set logo appears upper right. Personalized disc series were issued for Tetley, Weis, Key Food and A&P supermarkets (untitled series were also sold at Lucky, Skaggs, Alpha Beta, Acme King Kullen, Laneco and Krasdale stores). The series name (i.e. Weis Winners) is printed below the player photo.

LINEUP

Sport Card Inventory and Value System ™

Software for your IBM® or compatible PC

Baseball, Football, Basketball & Hockey!

$39.95 Complete LINEUP software with one free data option

$9.95 Each for additional optional groups of data:

Baseball: 1990–present, 85–89, 80–84, 70–79, 60–69 or 48–59;
Football: 1990–present, 80–89, 70–79, 60–69 or 48–59;
Basketball: 90–pres, 80–89, 48–79;
Hockey: 90–pres, 80–89, 70–79, 51–69.

Washinton State residents add 8.2% sales tax.

Mail Orders: Add $2.25 per order Postage/Handling.

Demo disks are free (but add P/H)

Rebate:
If you already own another commercial package you are not satisfied with, we willl rebate you $25 with your purchase of LINEUP. Call for details. Offer is limited to new LINEUP purchases from ECSC and expires 6/30/92.

- Contains data for ALL cards for all major brands of Baseball, Football, Basketball & Hockey Cards since 1948 (regular issue and traded/update sets). No need to spend hours entering data – it's already there.
- Data fields include player name, value & quantity for 3 different conditions, Team, Rookie Flag & a Special Card Flag; all fields except quantity and Special Flag are already entered for you (including common player names). Even contains the full name of ALL players on multi-player cards! Also has data for the complete set, a typical common, and room for your own needs (e.g. unopened wax, cases, etc.). All data fields can be easily changed.
- New buy/sell feature tracks your investments. With this feature you are NOT locked into preset conditions.
- You can change card values yourself or order a value update program from us whenever you wish. We update values monthly and the cost is $5+P/H. Subscriptions are available. Updates always include data for newly released sets and the latest version of the program free. Updates are NOT incremental – they include new values for ALL cards!
- The data files DO NOT grow as you add cards to your inventory! Adding cards DOES NOT increase search times!
- Simple to use menu driven system with on-line help and documentation. Many actions (e.g. increase quantity by 1) can be accomplished with a single key stroke! Optionally uses the mouse if you have one.
- Contains many useful reports including: what-you-need to complete a set; Rookie lists; Premium lists; Inventory Reports (great for insurance); Sorts by player name, value, card # or quantity; find all cards for a particular player; separate premiums from common cards; etc. All reports can be sent to the screen, printer or ASCII file.
- You may define your own custom sets (e.g. minor league, Star Trek, etc.).

Performance: LINEUP is extremely fast because it is a custom program. It does not have the overhead of a typical database system written in languages such as dBase.

Mature Product: LINEUP has been on the market for over 4 years (with continuous improvement), and has thousands of satisfied users. LINEUP was written by card collecting computer professionals who specialize in custom database applications.

Computer/Cards Mix: The program is maintained by the computer people at Compusoft. The values are established by the card people at ECSC. This mix gives you the best of both worlds.

Absolutely Guaranteed: If LINEUP fails to meet your expectations we will refund your money. Our current satisfaction rate is better than 99.9%.

Value Updates: Optional but offered monthly.

Unique Menu Design: LINEUP's easy to use menu system is unique to the software industry and has been the subject of hundreds of praise letters from our customers. Many features can be accomplished with a single keystroke (or mouse click)!

Statistics: LINEUP provides some interesting stats that you never see in price guides or magazines. Critical information for investors!

The Standard: LINEUP has received very favorable reviews by many PC and Hobby publications, and is the standard by which others are measured.

Look for LINEUP at your local Hobby or Software store, or order direct.

New Version !!! LINEUP continues to improve as promised. Version 4.0 now adds the following features: Team; Card Variation/Error Flag; Full Name of ALL players on a multi-player card; Buy/sell investment tracking; More report options; and much more! Current LINEUP customers can convert FREE with your next Value Update! LINEUP – Remaining the best!

When considering software to track your collection be careful – there's a lot of junk on the market. LINEUP is the leader – not because of slick marketing, but because it is a quality product filled with features that card collectors need. We do card collecting software, not games! A major reason for LINEUP's success is user input. There are many features that are a result of user suggestions; we couldn't have thought of everything ourselves. LINEUP is superior to what it was last year and inferior to next year – we are constantly improving. Many programs have come and gone in the past few years, but we're in it for the long haul. Our price is more than fair and there is no better program at any price. Why settle for an inferior product or clone when you can get the real thing? And it is absolutely guaranteed! Compare and you will see that LINEUP is the Hobby's most powerful tool. We gladly challenge any other program to participate in a jointly prepared product comparison.

PC System Requirements:
- IBM PC or compatible;
- DOS 2.1 or greater;
- 320K RAM Minimum
- 5.25" or 3.5" disk (specifiy when ordering)

CompuServe [73520, 1372]

Emerald City Sports Cards
8046 S. 114th St. Dept. APG (206) 772-4266
Seattle, WA 98178 (800) 222-1233

VISA MasterCard AMERICAN EXPRESS Krause Publications

		MT	NR MT	EX
Complete Panel Set:		9.00	6.75	3.50
Complete Singles Set:		4.00	3.00	1.50
Common Panel:		.60	.45	.25
Common Single Player:		.05	.04	.02
	Panel	1.00	.70	.40
1	Wade Boggs	.35	.25	.14
2	Ellis Burks	.20	.15	.08
	Panel	1.00	.70	.40
3	Don Mattingly	.50	.40	.20
4	Mark McGwire	.25	.20	.10
	Panel	.70	.50	.30
5	Matt Nokes	.10	.08	.04
6	Kirby Puckett	.30	.25	.12
	Panel	.80	.60	.30
7	Billy Ripken	.05	.04	.02
8	Kevin Seitzer	.15	.11	.06
	Panel	.90	.70	.35
9	Roger Clemens	.30	.25	.12
10	Will Clark	.50	.40	.20
	Panel	.80	.60	.30
11	Vince Coleman	.10	.08	.04
12	Eric Davis	.30	.25	.12
	Panel	.70	.50	.30
13	Dave Magadan	.05	.04	.02
14	Dale Murphy	.15	.11	.06
	Panel	.80	.60	.30
15	Benito Santiago	.15	.11	.06
16	Mike Schmidt	.30	.25	.12
	Panel	.60	.45	.25
17	Darryl Strawberry	.20	.15	.08
18	Steve Bedrosian	.05	.04	.02
	Panel	.80	.60	.30
19	Dwight Gooden	.20	.15	.08
20	Fernando Valenzuela	.08	.06	.03

1959 Bazooka

The 1959 Bazooka set, consisting of 23 full-color, unnumbered cards, was issued on boxes of Bazooka one-cent bubble gum. The individually wrapped pieces of Bazooka gum were produced by Topps Chewing Gum. The blank-backed cards measure 2-13/16" by 4-15/16" Nine cards were first issued, with 14 being added to the set later. The nine more plentiful cards are #'s 1, 5, 8, 9, 14, 15, 16, 17 and 22. Complete boxes would command 75 percent over the prices in the checklist that follows.

		NR MT	EX	VG
Complete Set:		8500.00	4250.00	2550.
Common Player:		125.00	62.00	37.00
(1a)	Hank Aaron (name in white)	650.00	325.00	195.00
(1b)	Hank Aaron (name in yellow)	650.00	325.00	195.00
(2)	Richie Ashburn	400.00	200.00	120.00
(3)	Ernie Banks	650.00	325.00	195.00
(4)	Ken Boyer	300.00	150.00	90.00
(5)	Orlando Cepeda	200.00	100.00	60.00
(6)	Bob Cerv	200.00	100.00	60.00
(7)	Rocco Colavito	500.00	250.00	150.00
(8)	Del Crandall	125.00	62.00	37.00
(9)	Jim Davenport	125.00	62.00	37.00
(10)	Don Drysdale	650.00	325.00	210.00
(11)	Nellie Fox	350.00	175.00	105.00
(12)	Jackie Jensen	250.00	125.00	75.00
(13)	Harvey Kuenn	250.00	125.00	75.00
(14)	Mickey Mantle	2000.00	1000.00	600.00
(15)	Willie Mays	500.00	250.00	150.00
(16)	Bill Mazeroski	150.00	75.00	45.00
(17)	Roy McMillan	125.00	62.00	37.00
(18)	Billy Pierce	200.00	100.00	60.00
(19)	Roy Sievers	200.00	100.00	60.00
(20)	Duke Snider	800.00	400.00	250.00
(21)	Gus Triandos	200.00	100.00	60.00
(22)	Bob Turley	125.00	62.00	37.00
(23)	Vic Wertz	200.00	100.00	60.00

1960 Bazooka

Three-card panels were found on the bottoms of Bazooka bubble gum boxes in 1960. The blank-backed set is comprised of 36 cards with the card number located at the bottom of each full-color card. The individual cards measure 1-13/16" by 2-3/4"; the panels measure 2-3/4" by 5-1/2" in size. Prices, in the checklist that follows, are given for complete panels and individual cards.

		NR MT	EX	VG
Complete Panel Set:		1750.00	875.00	525.00
Complete Singles Set:		1200.00	600.00	360.00
Common Panel:		75.00	37.00	22.00
Common Single Player:		5.00	2.50	1.50
	Panel	100.00	50.00	30.00
1	Ernie Banks	50.00	25.00	15.00
2	Bud Daley	5.00	2.50	1.50
3	Wally Moon	5.00	2.50	1.50
	Panel	150.00	75.00	45.00
4	Hank Aaron	80.00	40.00	25.00
5	Milt Pappas	10.00	5.00	3.00
6	Dick Stuart	10.00	5.00	3.00
	Panel	200.00	100.00	60.00
7	Bob Clemente	100.00	50.00	30.00
8	Yogi Berra	50.00	25.00	15.00
9	Ken Boyer	12.00	6.00	3.50
	Panel	75.00	38.00	23.00
10	Orlando Cepeda	15.00	7.50	4.50
11	Gus Triandos	10.00	5.00	3.00
12	Frank Malzone	10.00	5.00	3.00
	Panel	80.00	40.00	25.00
13	Willie Mays	60.00	30.00	18.00
14	Camilo Pascual	5.00	2.50	1.50
15	Bob Cerv	5.00	2.50	1.50
	Panel	100.00	50.00	30.00
16	Vic Power	5.00	2.50	1.50
17	Larry Sherry	5.00	2.50	1.50
18	Al Kaline	50.00	25.00	15.00
	Panel	110.00	55.00	33.00
19	Warren Spahn	40.00	20.00	12.50
20	Harmon Killebrew	30.00	15.00	9.00
21	Jackie Jensen	12.00	6.00	3.50
	Panel	115.00	57.00	34.00
22	Luis Aparicio	25.00	12.50	7.50
23	Gil Hodges	30.00	15.00	9.00
24	Richie Ashburn	30.00	15.00	9.00
	Panel	110.00	55.00	33.00
25	Nellie Fox	30.00	15.00	9.00
26	Robin Roberts	30.00	15.00	9.00
27	Joe Cunningham	5.00	2.50	1.50
	Panel	110.00	55.00	33.00
28	Early Wynn	25.00	12.50	7.50
29	Frank Robinson	50.00	25.00	15.00
30	Rocky Colavito	15.00	7.50	4.50
	Panel	450.00	225.00	135.00

		NR MT	EX	VG
31	Mickey Mantle	300.00	150.00	90.00
32	Glen Hobbie	5.00	2.50	1.50
33	Roy McMillan	5.00	2.50	1.50
	Panel	75.00	37.00	22.00
34	Harvey Kuenn	12.00	6.00	3.50
35	Johnny Antonelli	5.00	2.50	1.50
36	Del Crandall	10.00	5.00	3.00

1961 Bazooka

Similar in design to the 1960 Bazooka set, the 1961 edition consists of 36 cards issued in panels of three on the bottom of Bazooka bubble gum boxes. The full-color cards, which measure 1-13/16" by 2-3/4" individually and 2-3/4" by 5-1/2" as panels, are numbered 1 through 36. The backs are blank.

		NR MT	EX	VG
Complete Panel Set:		1500.00	750.00	450.00
Complete Singles Set:		800.00	400.00	240.00
Common Panel:		60.00	30.00	18.00
Common Single Player:		5.00	2.50	1.50
	Panel	450.00	225.00	135.00
1	Art Mahaffey	10.00	5.00	3.00
2	Mickey Mantle	300.00	150.00	90.00
3	Ron Santo	12.00	6.00	3.50
	Panel	80.00	40.00	24.00
4	Bud Daley	5.00	2.50	1.50
5	Roger Maris	80.00	40.00	24.00
6	Eddie Yost	5.00	2.50	1.50
	Panel	65.00	32.00	19.50
7	Minnie Minoso	12.00	6.00	3.50
8	Dick Groat	12.00	6.00	3.50
9	Frank Malzone	10.00	5.00	3.00
	Panel	80.00	40.00	24.00
10	Dick Donovan	5.00	2.50	1.50
11	Ed Mathews	30.00	15.00	9.00
12	Jim Lemon	5.00	2.50	1.50
	Panel	60.00	30.00	18.00
13	Chuck Estrada	5.00	2.50	1.50
14	Ken Boyer	12.00	6.00	3.50
15	Harvey Kuenn	12.00	6.00	3.50
	Panel	60.00	30.00	18.00
16	Ernie Broglio	5.00	2.50	1.50
17	Rocky Colavito	15.00	7.50	4.50
18	Ted Kluszewski	15.00	7.50	4.50
	Panel	300.00	150.00	90.00
19	Ernie Banks	75.00	38.00	23.00
20	Al Kaline	75.00	38.00	23.00
21	Ed Bailey	5.00	2.50	1.50
	Panel	75.00	37.00	22.00
22	Jim Perry	5.00	2.50	1.50
23	Willie Mays	80.00	40.00	24.00
24	Bill Mazeroski	12.00	6.00	3.50
	Panel	80.00	40.00	24.00
25	Gus Triandos	5.00	2.50	1.50
26	Don Drysdale	25.00	12.50	7.50
27	Frank Herrera	10.00	5.00	3.00
	Panel	80.00	40.00	24.00
28	Earl Battey	5.00	2.50	1.50
29	Warren Spahn	35.00	17.50	10.50
30	Gene Woodling	10.00	5.00	3.00
	Panel	60.00	30.00	18.00
31	Frank Robinson	35.00	17.50	10.50
32	Pete Runnels	10.00	5.00	3.00
33	Woodie Held	5.00	2.50	1.50
	Panel	65.00	32.00	19.50
34	Norm Larker	5.00	2.50	1.50
35	Luis Aparicio	20.00	10.00	6.00
36	Bill Tuttle	5.00	2.50	1.50

1962 Bazooka

In 1962, Bazooka increased the size of its set to 45 full-color cards. The set is unnumbered and was issued in panels of three on the bottoms of bubble gum boxes. The individual cards measure 1-13/16" by 2-3/4" in size, whereas the panels are 2-3/4" by 5-1/2". In the checklist that follows the cards have been numbered by panel using the name of the player who appears on the left side of the panel. Panel #'s 1-3, 31-33 and 43-45 were issued in much shorter supply and command a higher price.

		NR MT	EX	VG
Complete Panel Set:		3500.00	1750.00	1050.
Complete Singles Set:		1800.00	900.00	540.00
Common Panel:		30.00	15.00	9.00
Common Single Player:		8.00	4.00	2.50
	Panel	1200.00	600.00	360.00
(1)	Bob Allison	150.00	75.00	45.00
(2)	Ed Mathews	350.00	175.00	105.00
(3)	Vada Pinson	150.00	75.00	45.00
	Panel	50.00	25.00	15.00
(4)	Earl Battey	8.00	4.00	2.50
(5)	Warren Spahn	30.00	15.00	9.00
(6)	Lee Thomas	8.00	4.00	2.50
	Panel	40.00	20.00	12.00
(7)	Orlando Cepeda	15.00	7.50	4.50
(8)	Woodie Held	8.00	4.00	2.50
(9)	Bob Aspromonte	8.00	4.00	2.50
	Panel	100.00	50.00	30.00
(10)	Dick Howser	10.00	5.00	3.00
(11)	Bob Clemente	50.00	25.00	15.00
(12)	Al Kaline	30.00	15.00	9.00
	Panel	100.00	50.00	30.00
(13)	Joey Jay	8.00	4.00	2.50
(14)	Roger Maris	40.00	20.00	12.00
(15)	Frank Howard	15.00	7.50	4.50
	Panel	70.00	35.00	21.00
(16)	Sandy Koufax	50.00	25.00	15.00
(17)	Jim Gentile	8.00	4.00	2.50
(18)	Johnny Callison	10.00	5.00	3.00
	Panel	30.00	15.00	9.00
(19)	Jim Landis	8.00	4.00	2.50
(20)	Ken Boyer	12.00	6.00	3.50
(21)	Chuck Schilling	8.00	4.00	2.50
	Panel	500.00	250.00	150.00
(22)	Art Mahaffey	10.00	5.00	3.00
(23)	Mickey Mantle	200.00	100.00	60.00
(24)	Dick Stuart	10.00	5.00	3.00
	Panel	100.00	50.00	30.00
(25)	Ken McBride	8.00	4.00	2.50
(26)	Frank Robinson	35.00	17.50	10.50
(27)	Gil Hodges	25.00	12.50	7.50
	Panel	100.00	50.00	30.00
(28)	Milt Pappas	10.00	5.00	3.00
(29)	Hank Aaron	70.00	35.00	21.00
(30)	Luis Aparicio	20.00	10.00	6.00
	Panel	1200.00	600.00	360.00
(31)	Johnny Romano	150.00	75.00	45.00
(32)	Ernie Banks	500.00	250.00	150.00
(33)	Norm Siebern	150.00	75.00	45.00

		NR MT	EX	VG
	Panel	40.00	20.00	12.00
(34)	Ron Santo	12.00	6.00	3.50
(35)	Norm Cash	10.00	5.00	3.00
(36)	Jim Piersall	10.00	5.00	3.00
	Panel	70.00	35.00	21.00
(37)	Don Schwall	8.00	4.00	2.50
(38)	Willie Mays	50.00	25.00	15.00
(39)	Norm Larker	8.00	4.00	2.50
	Panel	70.00	35.00	21.00
(40)	Bill White	10.00	5.00	3.00
(41)	Whitey Ford	30.00	15.00	9.00
(42)	Rocky Colavito	15.00	7.50	4.50
	Panel	1200.00	600.00	360.00
(43)	Don Zimmer	200.00	100.00	60.00
(44)	Harmon Killebrew	300.00	150.00	90.00
(45)	Gene Woodling	150.00	75.00	45.00

1963 Bazooka

The 1963 Bazooka issue reverted back to a 12-panel, 36-card set, but saw a change in the size of the cards. Individual cards measure 1-9/16" by 2-1/2", while panels are 2-1/2" by 4-11/16" in size. The card design was altered also, with the player's name, team and position situated in a white oval space at the bottom of the card. The full-color, blank-backed set is numbered 1-36. Five Bazooka All-Time Greats cards were inserted in each box of bubble gum.

		NR MT	EX	VG
Complete Panel Set:		1500.00	750.00	450.00
Complete Singles Set:		800.00	400.00	240.00
Common Panel:		30.00	15.00	9.00
Common Single Player:		5.00	2.50	1.50
	Panel	400.00	200.00	120.00
1	Mickey Mantle (batting righty)	300.00	150.00	90.00
2	Bob Rodgers	5.00	2.50	1.50
3	Ernie Banks	40.00	20.00	12.50
	Panel	50.00	25.00	15.00
4	Norm Siebern	5.00	2.50	1.50
5	Warren Spahn (portrait)	30.00	15.00	9.00
6	Bill Mazeroski	10.00	5.00	3.00
	Panel	115.00	57.00	34.00
7	Harmon Killebrew (batting)	30.00	15.00	9.00
8	Dick Farrell (portrait)	5.00	2.50	1.50
9	Hank Aaron (glove in front)	60.00	30.00	17.50
	Panel	150.00	75.00	45.00
10	Dick Donovan	5.00	2.50	1.50
11	Jim Gentile (batting)	5.00	2.50	1.50
12	Willie Mays (bat in front)	75.00	38.00	23.00
	Panel	70.00	35.00	21.00
13	Camilo Pascual (hands at waist)	5.00	2.50	1.50
14	Bob Clemente (portrait)	50.00	25.00	15.00
15	Johnny Callison (wearing pinstripe uniform)	8.00	4.00	2.50
	Panel	200.00	100.00	60.00
16	Carl Yastrzemski (kneeling)	100.00	50.00	30.00
17	Don Drysdale	70.00	35.00	20.00
18	Johnny Romano (portrait)	5.00	2.50	1.50
	Panel	30.00	15.00	9.00
19	Al Jackson	8.00	4.00	2.50
20	Ralph Terry	8.00	4.00	2.50
21	Bill Monbouquette	5.00	2.50	1.50
	Panel	95.00	47.00	28.00
22	Orlando Cepeda	15.00	7.50	4.50
23	Stan Musial	50.00	25.00	15.00
24	Floyd Robinson (no pinstripes on uniform)	5.00	2.50	1.50
	Panel	30.00	15.00	9.00
25	Chuck Hinton (batting)	5.00	2.50	1.50
26	Bob Purkey	5.00	2.50	1.50
27	Ken Hubbs	12.00	6.00	3.50
	Panel	60.00	30.00	18.00
28	Bill White	8.00	4.00	2.50
29	Ray Herbert	5.00	2.50	1.50
30	Brooks Robinson (glove in front)	35.00	17.50	10.50
	Panel	60.00	30.00	18.00
31	Frank Robinson (batting, uniforn number doesn't show)	50.00	25.00	15.00
32	Lee Thomas	5.00	2.50	1.50
33	Rocky Colavito (Detroit)	10.00	5.00	3.00
	Panel	60.00	30.00	18.00
34	Al Kaline (kneeling)	35.00	17.50	10.50
35	Art Mahaffey	5.00	2.50	1.50
36	Tommy Davis (batting follow-thru)	8.00	4.00	2.50

1963 Bazooka All-Time Greats

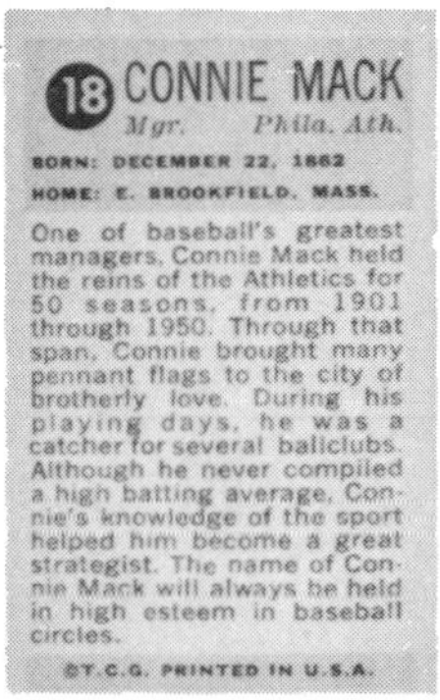

Consisting of 41 cards, the Bazooka All-Time Greats set was issued as inserts (5 per box) in boxes of Bazooka bubble gum. A black and white head-shot of the player is placed inside a gold plaque within a white border. The card backs have black print on white and white and yellow and contain a brief biography of the player. The numbered cards measure 1-9/16" by 2-1/2" in size. The cards can be found with silver fronts instead of gold. The silver are worth double the values listed in the following checklist.

		NR MT	EX	VG
Complete Set:		250.00	125.00	75.00
Common Player:		3.00	1.50	.90
1	Joe Tinker	3.50	1.75	1.00
2	Harry Heilmann	3.00	1.50	.90
3	Jack Chesbro	3.00	1.50	.90
4	Christy Mathewson	5.00	2.50	1.50
5	Herb Pennock	3.00	1.50	.90
6	Cy Young	6.00	3.00	1.75
7	Big Ed Walsh	3.00	1.50	.90
8	Nap Lajoie	3.50	1.75	1.00
9	Eddie Plank	3.00	1.50	.90
10	Honus Wagner	8.00	4.00	2.50
11	Chief Bender	3.00	1.50	.90
12	Walter Johnson	8.00	4.00	2.50
13	Three-Fingered Brown	3.00	1.50	.90
14	Rabbit Maranville	3.00	1.50	.90
15	Lou Gehrig	40.00	20.00	12.00
16	Ban Johnson	3.00	1.50	.90
17	Babe Ruth	55.00	27.00	16.50
18	Connie Mack	5.00	2.50	1.50
19	Hank Greenberg	3.50	1.75	1.00
20	John McGraw	3.50	1.75	1.00
21	Johnny Evers	3.00	1.50	.90
22	Al Simmons	3.00	1.50	.90
23	Jimmy Collins	3.00	1.50	.90
24	Tris Speaker	3.50	1.75	1.00
25	Frank Chance	3.00	1.50	.90
26	Fred Clarke	3.00	1.50	.90
27	Wilbert Robinson	3.00	1.50	.90
28	Dazzy Vance	3.00	1.50	.90
29	Pete Alexander	3.50	1.75	1.00
30	Judge Landis	3.00	1.50	.90
31	Wee Willie Keeler	3.00	1.50	.90
32	Rogers Hornsby	5.00	2.50	1.50

		NR MT	EX	VG
33	Hugh Duffy	3.00	1.50	.90
34	Mickey Cochrane	3.50	1.75	1.00
35	Ty Cobb	40.00	20.00	12.00
36	Mel Ott	3.50	1.75	1.00
37	Clark Griffith	3.00	1.50	.90
38	Ted Lyons	3.00	1.50	.90
39	Cap Anson	3.50	1.75	1.00
40	Bill Dickey	3.50	1.75	1.00
41	Eddie Collins	3.50	1.75	1.00

1964 Bazooka

The 1964 Bazooka set is identical in design and size to the previous year's effort. However, different photographs were used from year to year by Topps, issuer of Bazooka bubble gum. The 1964 set consists of 36 full-color, blank-backed cards numbered 1 through 36. Individual cards measure 1-9/16" by 2-1/2"; three-card panels measure 2-1/2" by 4-11/16". Sheets of ten full-color baseball stamps were inserted in each box of bubble gum.

	NR MT	EX	VG
Complete Panel Set:	1500.00	750.00	450.00
Complete Singles Set:	750.00	375.00	225.00
Common Panel:	30.00	15.00	9.00
Common Single Player:	5.00	2.50	1.50

		NR MT	EX	VG
	Panel	250.00	125.00	75.00
1	Mickey Mantle (portrait)	200.00	100.00	60.00
2	Dick Groat	8.00	4.00	2.50
3	Steve Barber	5.00	2.50	1.50
	Panel	40.00	20.00	12.00
4	Ken McBride	5.00	2.50	1.50
5	Warren Spahn (head to waist shot)	30.00	15.00	9.00
6	Bob Friend	6.00	3.00	1.75
	Panel	115.00	57.00	34.00
7	Harmon Killebrew (portrait)	30.00	15.00	9.00
8	Dick Farrell (hands above head)	5.00	2.50	1.50
9	Hank Aaron (glove to left)	70.00	35.00	20.00
	Panel	70.00	35.00	21.00
10	Rich Rollins	5.00	2.50	1.50
11	Jim Gentile (portrait)	5.00	2.50	1.50
12	Willie Mays (looking to left)	50.00	25.00	15.00
	Panel	70.00	35.00	21.00
13	Camilo Pascual (pitching follow-thru)	5.00	2.50	1.50
14	Bob Clemente (throwing)	50.00	25.00	15.00
15	Johnny Callison (batting, screen showing)	8.00	4.00	2.50
	Panel	75.00	37.00	22.00
16	Carl Yastrzemski (batting)	50.00	25.00	15.00
17	Billy Williams (kneeling)	30.00	15.00	9.00
18	Johnny Romano (batting)	5.00	2.50	1.50
	Panel	55.00	27.00	16.50
19	Jim Maloney	5.00	2.50	1.50
20	Norm Cash	8.00	4.00	2.50
21	Willie McCovey	30.00	15.00	9.00
	Panel	30.00	15.00	9.00
22	Jim Fregosi (batting)	6.00	3.00	1.75
23	George Altman	5.00	2.50	1.50
24	Floyd Robinson (wearing pinstripe uniform)	5.00	2.50	1.50
	Panel	30.00	15.00	9.00
25	Chuck Hinton (portrait)	5.00	2.50	1.50
26	Ron Hunt (batting)	8.00	4.00	2.50
27	Gary Peters (pitching)	5.00	2.50	1.50
	Panel	60.00	30.00	18.00
28	Dick Ellsworth	5.00	2.50	1.50
29	Elston Howard (holding bat)	12.00	6.00	3.50
30	Brooks Robinson (kneeling with glove)	30.00	15.00	9.00
	Panel	110.00	55.00	33.00
31	Frank Robinson (uniforn number shows)	40.00	20.00	12.00
32	Sandy Koufax (glove in front)	50.00	25.00	15.00
33	Rocky Colavito (Kansas City)	10.00	5.00	3.00
	Panel	65.00	32.00	19.50
34	Al Kaline (holding two bats)	30.00	15.00	9.00
35	Ken Boyer (head to waist shot)	10.00	5.00	3.00
36	Tommy Davis (batting)	8.00	4.00	2.50

1964 Bazooka Stamps

Occasionally mislabeled "Topps Stamps," the 1964 Bazooka Stamps set was produced by Topps, but was found only in boxes of 1¢ Bazooka bubble gum. Issued in sheets of ten, 100 color stamps make up the set. Each stamp measures 1" by 1-1/2" in size. While the stamps are not individually numbered, the sheets are numbered one through ten. The stamps are commonly found as complete sheets of ten and are priced in that fashion in the checklist that follows.

	NR MT	EX	VG
Complete Sheet Set:	500.00	250.00	150.00
Common Sheet:	25.00	12.50	7.50

		NR MT	EX	VG
1	Max Alvis, Ed Charles, Dick Ellsworth, Jimmie Hall, Frank Malzone, Milt Pappas, Vada Pinson, Tony Taylor, Pete Ward, Bill White	25.00	12.50	7.50
2	Bob Aspromonte, Larry Jackson, Willie Mays, Al McBean, Bill Monbouquette, Bobby Richardson, Floyd Robinson, Frank Robinson, Norm Siebern, Don Zimmer	40.00	20.00	12.00
3	Ernie Banks, Bob Clemente, Curt Flood, Jesse Gonder, Woody Held, Don Lock, Dave Nicholson, Joe Pepitone, Brooks Robinson, Carl Yastrzemski	60.00	30.00	18.00
4	Hank Aguirre, Jim Grant, Harmon Killebrew, Jim Maloney, Juan Marichal, Bill Mazeroski, Juan Pizarro, Boog Powell, Ed Roebuck, Ron Santo	40.00	20.00	12.00
5	Jim Bouton, Norm Cash, Orlando Cepeda, Tommy Harper, Chuck Hinton, Albie Pearson, Ron Perranoski, Dick Radatz, Johnny Romano, Carl Willey	30.00	15.00	9.00
6	Steve Barber, Jim Fregosi, Tony Gonzalez, Mickey Mantle, Jim O'Toole, Gary Peters, Rich Rollins, Warren Spahn, Dick Stuart, Joe Torre	125.00	62.00	37.00
7	Felipe Alou, George Altman, Ken Boyer, Rocky Colavito, Jim Davenport, Tommy Davis, Bill Freehan, Bob Friend, Ken Johnson, Billy Moran	30.00	15.00	9.00
8	Earl Battey, Ernie Broglio, Johnny Callison, Donn Clendenon, Don Drysdale, Jim Gentile, Elston Howard, Claude Osteen, Billy Williams, Hal Woodeshick	35.00	17.50	10.50
9	Hank Aaron, Jack Baldschun, Wayne Causey, Moe Drabowsky, Dick Groat, Frank Howard, Al Jackson, Jerry Lumpe, Ken McBride, Rusty Staub	40.00	20.00	12.00
10	Ray Culp, Vic Davalillo, Dick Farrell, Ron Hunt, Al Kaline, Sandy Koufax, Ed Mathews, Willie McCovey, Camilo Pascual, Lee Thomas	50.00	25.00	15.00

1965 Bazooka

The 1965 Bazooka set is identical to the 1963 and 1964 sets. Different players were added each year and different photographs were used for those players being included again. Individual cards cut from the boxes measure 1-9/16" by 2-1/2". Complete three-card panels measure 2-1/2" by 4-11/16". Thirty-six full-color, blank-backed, numbered cards comprise the set. Prices are given for individual cards and complete panels in the checklist that follows.

		NR MT	EX	VG
Complete Panel Set:		1300.00	650.00	390.00
Complete Singles Set:		700.00	350.00	210.00
Common Panel:		25.00	12.50	7.50
Common Single Player:		5.00	2.50	1.50
	Panel	225.00	115.00	70.00
1	Mickey Mantle (batting lefty)	200.00	100.00	60.00
2	Larry Jackson	5.00	2.50	1.50
3	Chuck Hinton	5.00	2.50	1.50
	Panel	30.00	15.00	9.00
4	Tony Oliva	10.00	5.00	3.00
5	Dean Chance	5.00	2.50	1.50
6	Jim O'Toole	5.00	2.50	1.50
	Panel	110.00	55.00	33.00
7	Harmon Killebrew (bat on shoulder)	25.00	12.50	7.50
8	Pete Ward	5.00	2.50	1.50
9	Hank Aaron (batting)	50.00	25.00	15.00
	Panel	80.00	40.00	24.00
10	Dick Radatz	5.00	2.50	1.50
11	Boog Powell	10.00	5.00	3.00
12	Willie Mays (looking down)	40.00	20.00	12.00
	Panel	65.00	32.00	19.50
13	Bob Veale	5.00	2.50	1.50
14	Bob Clemente (batting)	40.00	20.00	12.00
15	Johnny Callison (batting, no screen in background)	8.00	4.00	2.50
	Panel	45.00	22.00	13.50
16	Joe Torre	8.00	4.00	2.50
17	Billy Williams (batting)	20.00	10.00	6.00
18	Bob Chance	5.00	2.50	1.50
	Panel	30.00	15.00	9.00
19	Bob Aspromonte	5.00	2.50	1.50
20	Joe Christopher	5.00	2.50	1.50
21	Jim Bunning	12.00	6.00	3.50
	Panel	80.00	40.00	24.00
22	Jim Fregosi (portrait)	8.00	4.00	2.50
23	Bob Gibson	25.00	12.50	7.50
24	Juan Marichal	20.00	10.00	6.00
	Panel	25.00	12.50	7.50
25	Dave Wickersham	5.00	2.50	1.50
26	Ron Hunt (throwing)	8.00	4.00	2.50
27	Gary Peters (portrait)	5.00	2.50	1.50
	Panel	80.00	40.00	24.00
28	Ron Santo	10.00	5.00	3.00
29	Elston Howard (with glove)	12.00	6.00	3.50
30	Brooks Robinson (portrait)	30.00	15.00	9.00
	Panel	110.00	55.00	33.00
31	Frank Robinson (portrait)	35.00	17.50	10.50
32	Sandy Koufax (hands over head)	40.00	20.00	12.00
33	Rocky Colavito (Cleveland)	10.00	5.00	3.00
	Panel	60.00	30.00	18.00
34	Al Kaline (portrait)	30.00	15.00	9.00
35	Ken Boyer (portrait)	10.00	5.00	3.00
36	Tommy Davis (fielding)	8.00	4.00	2.50

1966 Bazooka

The 1966 Bazooka set was increased to 48 cards. Issued in panels of three on the bottoms of boxes of bubble gum, the full-color cards are blank-backed and numbered. Individual cards measure 1-9/16" by 2-1/2", whereas panels measure 2-1/2" by 4-11/16".

		NR MT	EX	VG
Complete Panel Set:		1750.00	875.00	525.00
Complete Singles Set:		1000.00	500.00	300.00
Common Panel:		25.00	12.50	7.50
Common Single Player:		5.00	2.50	1.50
	Panel	65.00	32.00	19.50
1	Sandy Koufax	50.00	25.00	15.00
2	Willie Horton	6.00	3.00	1.75
3	Frank Howard	8.00	4.00	2.50
	Panel	50.00	25.00	15.00
4	Richie Allen	10.00	5.00	3.00
5	Mel Stottlemyre	8.00	4.00	2.50
6	Tony Conigliaro	15.00	7.50	4.50
	Panel	275.00	137.00	82.00
7	Mickey Mantle	200.00	100.00	60.00
8	Leon Wagner	5.00	2.50	1.50
9	Ed Kranepool	6.00	3.00	1.75
	Panel	70.00	35.00	21.00
10	Juan Marichal	20.00	10.00	6.00
11	Harmon Killebrew	25.00	12.50	7.50
12	Johnny Callison	6.00	3.00	1.75
	Panel	55.00	27.00	16.50
13	Roy McMillan	5.00	2.50	1.50
14	Willie McCovey	25.00	12.50	7.50
15	Rocky Colavito	10.00	5.00	3.00
	Panel	65.00	32.00	19.50
16	Willie Mays	50.00	25.00	15.00
17	Sam McDowell	8.00	4.00	2.50
18	Vern Law	6.00	3.00	1.75
	Panel	55.00	27.00	16.50
19	Jim Fregosi	6.00	3.00	1.75
20	Ron Fairly	6.00	3.00	1.75
21	Bob Gibson	25.00	12.50	7.50
	Panel	70.00	35.00	21.00
22	Carl Yastrzemski	50.00	25.00	15.00
23	Bill White	8.00	4.00	2.50
24	Bob Aspromonte	5.00	2.50	1.50
	Panel	55.00	27.00	16.50
25	Dean Chance (California)	5.00	2.50	1.50
26	Bob Clemente	50.00	25.00	15.00
27	Tony Cloninger	5.00	2.50	1.50
	Panel	70.00	35.00	21.00
28	Curt Blefary	5.00	2.50	1.50
29	Milt Pappas	5.00	2.50	1.50
30	Hank Aaron	55.00	27.00	16.50
	Panel	60.00	30.00	18.00
31	Jim Bunning	12.00	6.00	3.50
32	Frank Robinson (portrait)	30.00	15.00	9.00
33	Bill Skowron	8.00	4.00	2.50
	Panel	60.00	30.00	18.00
34	Brooks Robinson	30.00	15.00	9.00
35	Jim Wynn	6.00	3.00	1.75
36	Joe Torre	8.00	4.00	2.50
	Panel	160.00	80.00	48.00
37	Jim Grant	5.00	2.50	1.50
38	Pete Rose	110.00	55.00	33.00

		NR MT	EX	VG
39	Ron Santo	10.00	5.00	3.00
	Panel	60.00	30.00	18.00
40	Tom Tresh	8.00	4.00	2.50
41	Tony Oliva	10.00	5.00	3.00
42	Don Drysdale	25.00	12.50	7.50
	Panel	25.00	12.50	7.50
43	Pete Richert	5.00	2.50	1.50
44	Bert Campaneris	8.00	4.00	2.50
45	Jim Maloney	5.00	2.50	1.50
	Panel	70.00	35.00	21.00
46	Al Kaline	30.00	15.00	9.00
47	Eddie Fisher	5.00	2.50	1.50
48	Billy Williams	20.00	10.00	6.00

1967 Bazooka

The 1967 Bazooka set is identical in design to the Bazooka sets of 1964-1966. Issued in panels of three on the bottoms of bubble gum boxes, the set is made up of 48 full-color, blank-backed, numbered cards. Individual cards measure 1-9/16" by 2-1/2"; complete panels measure 2-1/2" by 4-11/16" in size.

	NR MT	EX	VG
Complete Panel Set:	1600.00	800.00	480.00
Complete Singles Set:	900.00	450.00	270.00
Common Panel:	25.00	12.50	7.50
Common Single Player:	5.00	2.50	1.50

		NR MT	EX	VG
	Panel	25.00	12.50	7.50
1	Rick Reichardt	5.00	2.50	1.50
2	Tommy Agee	5.00	2.50	1.50
3	Frank Howard	8.00	4.00	2.50
	Panel	35.00	17.50	10.50
4	Richie Allen	10.00	5.00	3.00
5	Mel Stottlemyre	8.00	4.00	2.50
6	Tony Conigliaro	15.00	7.50	4.50
	Panel	250.00	125.00	75.00
7	Mickey Mantle	200.00	100.00	60.00
8	Leon Wagner	5.00	2.50	1.50
9	Gary Peters	5.00	2.50	1.50
	Panel	80.00	40.00	24.00
10	Juan Marichal	20.00	10.00	6.00
11	Harmon Killebrew	25.00	12.50	7.50
12	Johnny Callison	6.00	3.00	1.75
	Panel	50.00	25.00	15.00
13	Denny McLain	12.00	6.00	3.50
14	Willie McCovey	25.00	12.50	7.50
15	Rocky Colavito	10.00	5.00	3.00
	Panel	65.00	32.00	19.50
16	Willie Mays	40.00	20.00	12.00
17	Sam McDowell	6.00	3.00	1.75
18	Jim Kaat	12.00	6.00	3.50
	Panel	50.00	25.00	15.00
19	Jim Fregosi	6.00	3.00	1.75
20	Ron Fairly	6.00	3.00	1.75
21	Bob Gibson	25.00	12.50	7.50
	Panel	80.00	40.00	24.00
22	Carl Yastrzemski	40.00	20.00	12.00
23	Bill White	6.00	3.00	1.75
24	Bob Aspromonte	5.00	2.50	1.50
	Panel	60.00	30.00	18.00
25	Dean Chance (Minnesota)	5.00	2.50	1.50
26	Bob Clemente	40.00	20.00	12.00
27	Tony Cloninger	5.00	2.50	1.50
	Panel	80.00	40.00	24.00
28	Curt Blefary	5.00	2.50	1.50
29	Phil Regan	5.00	2.50	1.50
30	Hank Aaron	50.00	25.00	15.00
	Panel	60.00	30.00	18.00
31	Jim Bunning	12.00	6.00	3.50
32	Frank Robinson (batting)	25.00	12.50	7.50
33	Ken Boyer	10.00	5.00	3.00
	Panel	60.00	30.00	18.00
34	Brooks Robinson	30.00	15.00	9.00
35	Jim Wynn	6.00	3.00	1.75
36	Joe Torre	8.00	4.00	2.50
	Panel	160.00	80.00	48.00
37	Tommy Davis	6.00	3.00	1.75
38	Pete Rose	90.00	45.00	27.00
39	Ron Santo	10.00	5.00	3.00
	Panel	60.00	30.00	18.00
40	Tom Tresh	8.00	4.00	2.50
41	Tony Oliva	10.00	5.00	3.00
42	Don Drysdale	25.00	12.50	7.50
	Panel	25.00	12.50	7.50
43	Pete Richert	5.00	2.50	1.50
44	Bert Campaneris	6.00	3.00	1.75
45	Jim Maloney	5.00	2.50	1.50
	Panel	80.00	40.00	24.00
46	Al Kaline	30.00	15.00	9.00
47	Matty Alou	6.00	3.00	1.75
48	Billy Williams	20.00	10.00	6.00

1968 Bazooka

The design of the 1968 Bazooka set is radically different from previous years. The player cards are situated on the sides of the boxes with the box back containing "Tipps From The Topps." Four unnumbered player cards, measuring 1-1/4" by 3-1/8", are featured on each box. The box back includes a small player photo plus illustrated tips on various aspects of the game of baseball. The boxes are numbered 1-15 on the top panels. There are 56 different player cards in the set, with four of the cards (Agee, Drysdale, Rose, Santo) being used twice to round out the set of fifteen boxes.

	NR MT	EX	VG
Complete Box Set:	3300.00	1650.00	990.00
Complete Singles Set:	2000.00	1000.00	600.00
Common Box:	120.00	60.00	36.00
Common Single Player:	5.00	2.50	1.50

		NR MT	EX	VG
	Box	200.00	100.00	60.00
	Maury Wills (Bunting)	20.00	10.00	6.00
(1)	Clete Boyer	9.00	4.50	2.75
(2)	Paul Casanova	7.00	3.50	2.00
(3)	Al Kaline	30.00	15.00	9.00
(4)	Tom Seaver	70.00	35.00	21.00
	Box	150.00	75.00	45.00
2	Carl Yastrzemski (Batting)	50.00	25.00	15.00
(5)	Matty Alou	9.00	4.50	2.75
(6)	Bill Freehan	9.00	4.50	2.75
(7)	Jim Hunter	20.00	10.00	6.00
(8)	Jim Lefebvre	7.00	3.50	2.00
	Box	120.00	60.00	36.00
3	Bert Campaneris (Stealing bases)	20.00	10.00	6.00
(9)	Bobby Knoop	7.00	3.50	2.00
(10)	Tim McCarver	12.00	6.00	3.50
(11)	Frank Robinson	25.00	12.50	7.50
(12)	Bob Veale	7.00	3.50	2.00

		NR MT	EX	VG
	Box	90.00	45.00	27.00
4	Maury Wills (Sliding)	20.00	10.00	6.00
(13)	Joe Azcue	7.00	3.50	2.00
(14)	Tony Conigliaro	15.00	7.50	4.50
(15)	Ken Holtzman	9.00	4.50	2.75
(16)	Bill White	9.00	4.50	2.75
	Box	150.00	75.00	45.00
5	Julian Javier (The Double Play)	20.00	10.00	6.00
(17)	Hank Aaron	50.00	25.00	15.00
(18)	Juan Marichal	20.00	10.00	6.00
(19)	Joe Pepitone	12.00	6.00	3.50
(20)	Rico Petrocelli	9.00	4.50	2.75
	Box	200.00	100.00	60.00
6	Orlando Cepeda (Playing 1st Base)	25.00	12.50	7.50
(21)	Tommie Agee	5.00	2.50	1.50
(22)	Don Drysdale	10.00	5.00	3.00
(23)	Pete Rose	70.00	35.00	21.00
(24)	Ron Santo	5.00	2.50	1.50
	Box	120.00	60.00	36.00
7	Bill Mazeroski (Playing 2nd Base)	20.00	10.00	6.00
(25)	Jim Bunning	12.00	6.00	3.50
(26)	Frank Howard	12.00	6.00	3.50
(27)	John Roseboro	9.00	4.50	2.75
(28)	George Scott	9.00	4.50	2.75
	Box	150.00	75.00	45.00
8	Brooks Robinson (Playing 3rd Base)	50.00	25.00	15.00
(29)	Tony Gonzalez	7.00	3.50	2.00
(30)	Willie Horton	9.00	4.50	2.75
(31)	Harmon Killebrew	25.00	12.50	7.50
(32)	Jim McGlothlin	7.00	3.50	2.00
	Box	120.00	60.00	36.00
9	Jim Fregosi (Playing Shortstop)	20.00	10.00	6.00
(33)	Max Alvis	7.00	3.50	2.00
(34)	Bob Gibson	20.00	10.00	6.00
(35)	Tony Oliva	12.00	6.00	3.50
(36)	Vada Pinson	12.00	6.00	3.50
	Box	120.00	60.00	36.00
10	Joe Torre (Catching)	25.00	12.50	7.50
(37)	Dean Chance	7.00	3.50	2.00
(38)	Tommy Davis	9.00	4.50	2.75
(39)	Ferguson Jenkins	15.00	7.50	4.50
(40)	Rick Monday	9.00	4.50	2.75
	Box	300.00	150.00	90.00
11	Jim Lonborg (Pitching)	25.00	12.50	7.50
(41)	Curt Flood	9.00	4.50	2.75
(42)	Joel Horlen	7.00	3.50	2.00
(43)	Mickey Mantle	150.00	75.00	45.00
(44)	Jim Wynn	7.00	3.50	2.00
	Box	150.00	75.00	45.00
12	Mike McCormick (Fielding the Pitcher's Position)	20.00	10.00	6.00
(45)	Bob Clemente	40.00	20.00	12.00
(46)	Al Downing	9.00	4.50	2.75
(47)	Don Mincher	7.00	3.50	2.00
(48)	Tony Perez	15.00	7.50	4.50
	Box	200.00	100.00	60.00
13	Frank Crosetti (Coaching)	35.00	17.50	10.50
(49)	Rod Carew	40.00	20.00	12.00
(50)	Willie McCovey	25.00	12.50	7.50
(51)	Ron Swoboda	7.00	3.50	2.00
(52)	Earl Wilson	7.00	3.50	2.00
	Box	150.00	75.00	45.00
14	Willie Mays (Playing the Outfield)	50.00	25.00	15.00
(53)	Richie Allen	12.00	6.00	3.50
(54)	Gary Peters	7.00	3.50	2.00
(55)	Rusty Staub	10.00	5.00	3.00
(56)	Billy Williams	20.00	10.00	6.00
	Box	200.00	100.00	60.00
15	Lou Brock (Base Running)	40.00	20.00	12.00
(57)	Tommie Agee	5.00	2.50	1.50
(58)	Don Drysdale	10.00	5.00	3.00
(59)	Pete Rose	70.00	35.00	21.00
(60)	Ron Santo	5.00	2.50	1.50

1969 Bazooka

Issued over a two-year span, the 1969-70 Bazooka set utilized the box bottom and sides. The box bottom, entitled "Baseball Extra," features an historic event in baseball. The bottom panels are numbered 1 through 12. Two "All-Time Great" cards were located on each side of the box. These cards are not numbered and have no distinct borders. Individual cards measure 1-1/4" by 3-1/8"; the "Baseball Extra" panels measure 3" by 6-1/4". The prices in the checklist that follows are for complete boxes only. Cards/panels cut from the boxes have a greatly reduced value - 25 per cent of the complete box prices for all cut pieces.

		NR MT	EX	VG
Complete Box Set:		250.00	125.00	75.00
Common Box:		15.00	7.50	4.50
1	No-Hit Duel By Toney And Vaughn (Mordecai Brown, Ty Cobb, Willie Keeler, Eddie Plank)	18.00	9.00	5.50
2	Alexander Conquers Yanks (Rogers Hornsby, Ban Johnson, Walter Johnson, Al Simmons)	15.00	7.50	4.50
3	Yanks Lazzeri Sets A.L. Hit Record (Hugh Duffy, Lou Gehrig, Tris Speaker, Joe Tinker)	18.00	9.00	5.50
4	Home Run Almost Hit Out Of Stadium (Grover Alexander, Chief Bender, Christy Mathewson, Cy Young)	15.00	7.50	4.50
5	Four Consecutive Homers By Gehrig (Frank Chance, Mickey Cochrane, John McGraw, Babe Ruth)	30.00	15.00	9.00
6	No-Hit Game By Walter Johnson (Johnny Evers, Walter Johnson, John McGraw, Cy Young)	15.00	7.50	4.50
7	Twelve RBI's By Bottomley (Ty Cobb, Eddie Collins, Johnny Evers, Lou Gehrig)	20.00	10.00	6.00
8	Ty Ties Record (Mickey Cochrane, Eddie Collins, Met Ott, Honus Wagner)	15.00	7.50	4.50
9	Babe Ruth Hits Three Homers In Game (Cap Anson, Jack Chesbro, Al Simmons, Tris Speaker)	25.00	12.50	7.50
10	Calls Shot In Series Game (Nap Lajoie, Connie Mack, Rabbit Maranville, Ed Walsh)	25.00	12.50	7.50
11	Ruth's 60th Homer Sets New Record (Frank Chance, Nap Lajoie, Mel Ott, Joe Tinker)	25.00	12.50	7.50
12	Double Shutout By Ed Reulbach (Rogers Hornsby, Rabbit Maranville, Christy Mathewson, Honus Wagner)	15.00	7.50	4.50

1971 Bazooka Unnumbered Set

This Bazooka set was issued in 1971, consisting of 36 full-color, blank-backed, unnumbered cards. Issued in panels of three on the bottoms of Bazooka bubble gum boxes, individual cards measure 2" by 2-5/8" whereas complete panels measure 2-5/8" by 5-5/16". In the checklist that follows, the cards have been numbered by panel using the name of the player who appears on the left portion of the panel.

		NR MT	EX	VG
Complete Panel Set:		375.00	187.00	112.00
Complete Singles Set:		225.00	112.00	67.00
Common Panel:		10.00	5.00	3.00
Common Single Player:		1.50	.70	.45
1	Panel	30.00	15.00	9.00
(1)	Tommie Agee	1.50	.70	.45
(2)	Harmon Killebrew	7.00	3.50	2.00
2	Panel	40.00	20.00	12.00
(3)	Reggie Jackson	20.00	10.00	6.00
3	Panel	25.00	12.50	7.50
(4)	Bert Campaneris	1.50	.70	.45
4	Panel	25.00	12.50	7.50
(5)	Pete Rose	25.00	12.50	7.50
5	Panel	15.00	7.50	4.50
(6)	Orlando Cepeda	3.00	1.50	.90
6	Panel	30.00	15.00	9.00
(7)	Rico Carty	2.00	1.00	.60
7	Panel	15.00	7.50	4.50
(8)	Johnny Bench	20.00	10.00	6.00
8	Panel	30.00	15.00	9.00
(9)	Tommy Harper	1.50	.70	.45
9	Panel	15.00	7.50	4.50
(10)	Bill Freehan	2.00	1.00	.60
10	Panel	10.00	5.00	3.00
(11)	Roberto Clemente	20.00	10.00	6.00
11	Panel	30.00	15.00	9.00
(12)	Claude Osteen	1.50	.70	.45
12	Panel	15.00	7.50	4.50
(13)	Jim Fregosi	2.00	1.00	.60
(14)	Billy Williams	6.00	3.00	1.75
(15)	Dave McNally	1.50	.70	.45
(16)	Randy Hundley	1.50	.70	.45
(17)	Willie Mays	20.00	10.00	4.50
(18)	Jim Hunter	6.00	3.00	1.75
(19)	Juan Marichal	6.00	3.00	1.75
(20)	Frank Howard	3.00	1.50	.90
(21)	Bill Melton	1.50	.70	.45
(22)	Willie McCovey	7.00	3.50	2.00
(23)	Carl Yastrzemski	12.00	6.00	3.50
(24)	Clyde Wright	1.50	.70	.45
(25)	Jim Merritt	1.50	.70	.45
(26)	Luis Aparicio	6.00	3.00	1.75
(27)	Bobby Murcer	3.00	1.50	.90
(28)	Rico Petrocelli	2.00	1.00	.60
(29)	Sam McDowell	2.00	1.00	.60
(30)	Clarence Gaston	1.50	.70	.45
(31)	Brooks Robinson	6.50	3.25	2.00
(32)	Hank Aaron	20.00	10.00	4.50
(33)	Larry Dierker	1.50	.70	.45
(34)	Rusty Staub	2.00	1.00	.60
(35)	Bob Gibson	7.00	3.50	2.00
(36)	Amos Otis	1.50	.70	.45

A player's name in *italic* indicates a rookie card. An (FC) indicates a player's first card for that particular card company.

1971 Bazooka Numbered Set

The 1971 Bazooka numbered set is a proof set produced by the company after the unnumbered set was released. The set is comprised of 48 cards as opposed to the 36 cards which make up the unnumbered set. Issued in panels of three, the nine cards not found in the unnumbered set are #'s 1-3, 13-15 and 43-45. All other cards are identical to those found in the unnumbered set. The cards, which measure 2" by 2-5/8", contain full-color photos and are blank-backed.

		NR MT	EX	VG
Complete Panel Set:		1000.00	500.00	300.00
Complete Singles Set:		550.00	275.00	165.00
Common Panel:		10.00	5.00	3.00
Common Single Player:		2.00	1.00	.60
	Panel	150.00	75.00	45.00
1	Tim McCarver	15.00	7.50	4.50
2	Frank Robinson	45.00	23.00	13.50
3	Bill Mazeroski	15.00	7.50	4.50
	Panel	45.00	22.00	13.50
4	Willie McCovey	12.00	6.00	3.50
5	Carl Yastrzemski	20.00	10.00	6.00
6	Clyde Wright	2.00	1.00	.60
	Panel	20.00	10.00	6.00
7	Jim Merritt	2.00	1.00	.60
8	Luis Aparicio	9.00	4.50	2.75
9	Bobby Murcer	5.00	2.50	1.50
	Panel	10.00	5.00	3.00
10	Rico Petrocelli	3.00	1.50	.90
11	Sam McDowell	3.00	1.50	.90
12	Clarence Gaston	2.00	1.00	.60
	Panel	150.00	75.00	45.00
13	Ferguson Jenkins	20.00	10.00	6.00
14	Al Kaline	45.00	23.00	13.50
15	Ken Harrelson	15.00	7.50	4.50
	Panel	45.00	22.00	13.50
16	Tommie Agee	2.00	1.00	.60
17	Harmon Killebrew	12.00	6.00	3.50
18	Reggie Jackson	20.00	10.00	6.00
	Panel	20.00	10.00	6.00
19	Juan Marichal	9.00	4.50	2.75
20	Frank Howard	5.00	2.50	1.50
21	Bill Melton	2.00	1.00	.60
	Panel	55.00	27.00	16.50
22	Brooks Robinson	15.00	7.50	4.50
23	Hank Aaron	30.00	15.00	9.00
24	Larry Dierker	2.00	1.00	.60
	Panel	20.00	10.00	6.00
25	Jim Fregosi	3.00	1.50	.90
26	Billy Williams	10.00	5.00	3.00
27	Dave McNally	2.00	1.00	.60
	Panel	30.00	15.00	9.00
28	Rico Carty	3.00	1.50	.90
29	Johnny Bench	18.00	9.00	5.50
30	Tommy Harper	2.00	1.00	.60
	Panel	60.00	30.00	18.00
31	Bert Campaneris	2.00	1.00	.60
32	Pete Rose	35.00	17.50	10.50
33	Orlando Cepeda	6.00	3.00	1.75
	Panel	45.00	22.00	13.50
34	Maury Wills	6.00	3.00	1.75
35	Tom Seaver	20.00	10.00	6.00
36	Tony Oliva	6.00	3.00	1.75
	Panel	30.00	15.00	9.00
37	Bill Freehan	3.00	1.50	.90
38	Roberto Clemente	25.00	12.50	7.50
39	Claude Osteen	2.00	1.00	.60
	Panel	20.00	10.00	6.00
40	Rusty Staub	3.00	1.50	.90
41	Bob Gibson	10.00	5.00	3.00
42	Amos Otis	2.00	1.00	.60
	Panel	125.00	62.00	37.00
43	Jim Wynn	10.00	5.00	3.00
44	Rich Allen	18.00	9.00	5.50
45	Tony Conigliaro	10.00	5.00	3.00
	Panel	40.00	20.00	12.00
46	Randy Hundley	2.00	1.00	.60
47	Willie Mays	30.00	15.00	9.00
48	Jim Hunter	9.00	4.50	2.75

1988 Bazooka

This 22-card set from Topps marks the first Bazooka issue since 1971. Full-color player photos are bordered in white, with the player name printed on a red, white and blue bubble gum box in the lower right corner. Flip sides are also red, white and blue,

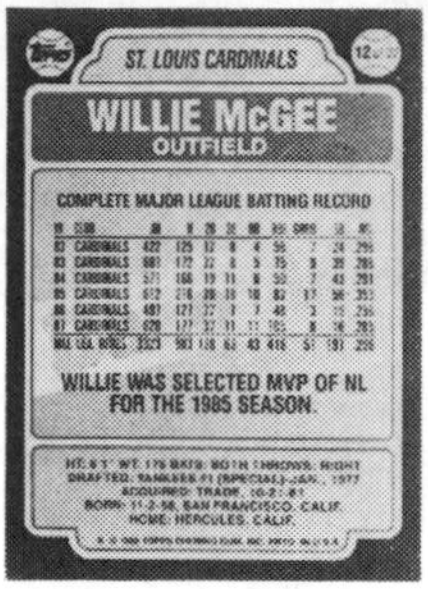

printed vertically. A large, but faint, Bazooka logo backs the Topps baseball logo, team name, card number, player's name and position, followed by batting records, personal information and brief career highlights. Cards were sold inside specially marked 59¢ and 79¢ Bazooka gum and candy boxes, one card per box.

		MT	NR MT	EX
Complete Set:		8.00	6.00	3.25
Common Player:		.20	.15	.08
1	George Bell	.25	.20	.10
2	Wade Boggs	.70	.50	.30
3	Jose Canseco	1.00	.70	.40
4	Roger Clemens	.60	.45	.25
5	Vince Coleman	.20	.15	.08
6	Eric Davis	.30	.25	.12
7	Tony Fernandez	.20	.15	.08
8	Dwight Gooden	.60	.45	.25
9	Tony Gwynn	.40	.30	.15
10	Wally Joyner	.40	.30	.15
11	Don Mattingly	1.50	1.25	.60
12	Willie McGee	.20	.15	.08
13	Mark McGwire	.40	.30	.15
14	Kirby Puckett	.50	.40	.20
15	Tim Raines	.30	.25	.12
16	Dave Righetti	.20	.15	.08
17	Cal Ripken	.50	.40	.20
18	Juan Samuel	.20	.15	.08
19	Ryne Sandberg	.50	.40	.20
20	Benny Santiago	.20	.15	.08
21	Darryl Strawberry	.60	.45	.25
22	Todd Worrell	.20	.15	.08

1989 Bazooka

This 22-card set marks the second consecutive year Bazooka has issued following a 17-year absence. Full color action and posed player shots are bordered by a white frame. Other features of this standard-size includes a "Shining Stars" logo across the top, a yellow stripe enclosing the player's name at the bottom, and the Topps/Bazooka logo in the bottom right corner. Flip sides are printed in red and blue, and contain a large but faint Bazooka logo, the Topps baseball logo, card number, team name, player's name and position, followed by batting or pitching records, personal information and brief highlights. Topps produced this 22-card set in 1989 to be included (one card per box) in specially-marked boxes of its Bazooka brand bubblegum. The player photos have the words "Shining Star" along the top, while the player's name appears along the bottom of the card, along with the Topps Bazooka logo in the lower right corner. The cards are numbered alphabetically.

		MT	NR MT	EX
Complete Set:		5.00	3.75	2.00
Common Player:		.15	.11	.06
1	Tim Belcher	.15	.11	.06
2	Damon Berryhill	.15	.11	.06
3	Wade Boggs	.60	.45	.25
4	Jay Buhner	.15	.11	.06
5	Jose Canseco	.80	.60	.30
6	Vince Coleman	.15	.11	.06
7	Cecil Espy	.15	.11	.06
8	Dave Gallagher	.15	.11	.06
9	Ron Gant	.35	.25	.14
10	Kirk Gibson	.15	.11	.06
11	Paul Gibson	.15	.11	.06
12	Mark Grace	.60	.45	.25
13	Tony Gwynn	.35	.25	.14
14	Rickey Henderson	.40	.30	.15
15	Orel Hershiser	.25	.20	.10
16	Gregg Jefferies	.50	.40	.20
17	Ricky Jordan	.25	.20	.10
18	Chris Sabo	.15	.11	.06
19	Gary Sheffield	.50	.40	.20
20	Darryl Strawberry	.50	.40	.20
21	Frank Viola	.20	.15	.08
22	Walt Weiss	.15	.11	.06

1990 Bazooka

For the second consecutive year, Bazooka entitled its set "Shining Stars." Full color action and posed player shots are featured on the card fronts. The flip sides feature player statistics in a style much like the cards from the previous two Bazooka issues. Unlike the past two releases, the cards are not numbered alphabetically. The cards measure 2-1/2" by 3-1/2" in size and 22 cards complete the set.

		MT	NR MT	EX
Complete Set:		7.00	5.25	2.75
Common Player:		.15	.11	.06
1	Kevin Mitchell	.30	.25	.12
2	Robin Yount	.20	.15	.08
3	Mark Davis	.15	.11	.06
4	Bret Saberhagen	.15	.11	.06
5	Fred McGriff	.20	.15	.08
6	Tony Gwynn	.20	.15	.08
7	Kirby Puckett	.30	.25	.12
8	Vince Coleman	.15	.11	.06
9	Rickey Henderson	.40	.30	.15
10	Ben McDonald	.50	.40	.20
11	Gregg Olson	.20	.15	.08
12	Todd Zeile	.30	.25	.12
13	Carlos Martinez	.20	.15	.08
14	Gregg Jefferies	.40	.30	.15

		MT	NR MT	EX
15	Craig Worthington	.15	.11	.06
16	Gary Sheffield	.40	.30	.15
17	Greg Briley	.15	.11	.06
18	Ken Griffey,Jr.	2.00	1.50	.80
19	Jerome Walton	.20	.15	.08
20	Bob Geren	.15	.11	.06
21	Tom Gordon	.20	.15	.08
22	Jim Abbott	.20	.15	.08

1991 Bazooka

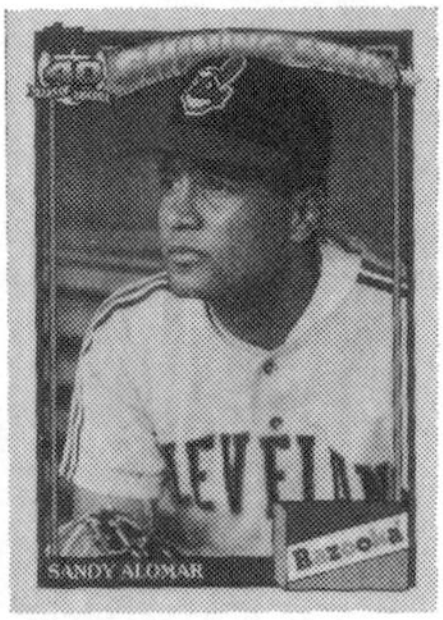

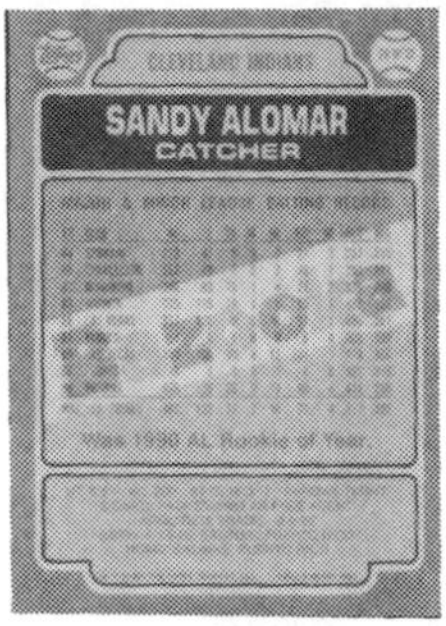

For the third consecutive year Bazooka entitled its set "Shining Stars." The cards are styled like the 1990 issue, but include the Topps "40th Anniversary" logo. The 1991 issue is considered much scarcer than the previous releases. The cards measure 2-1/2" by 3-1/2" in size and 22 cards complete the set.

		MT	NR MT	EX
Complete Set:		15.00	11.00	6.00
Common Player:		.30	.25	.12
1	Barry Bonds	.50	.40	.20
2	Rickey Henderson	.50	.40	.20
3	Bob Welch	.30	.25	.12
4	Doug Drabek	.40	.30	.15
5	Alex Fernandez	.80	.60	.30
6	Jose Offerman	.60	.45	.25
7	Frank Thomas	3.00	2.25	1.25
8	Cecil Fielder	.60	.45	.25
9	Ryne Sandberg	.60	.45	.25
10	George Brett	.40	.30	.15
11	Willie McGee	.30	.25	.12
12	Vince Coleman	.30	.25	.12
13	Hal Morris	.60	.45	.25
14	Delino DeShields	.50	.40	.20
15	Robin Ventura	.70	.50	.30
16	Jeff Huson	.30	.25	.12
17	Felix Jose	.50	.40	.20
18	Dave Justice	.60	.45	.25
19	Larry Walker	.35	.25	.14
20	Sandy Alomar, Jr.	.40	.30	.15
21	Kevin Appier	.30	.25	.12
22	Scott Radinsky	.30	.25	.12

1951 Berk Ross

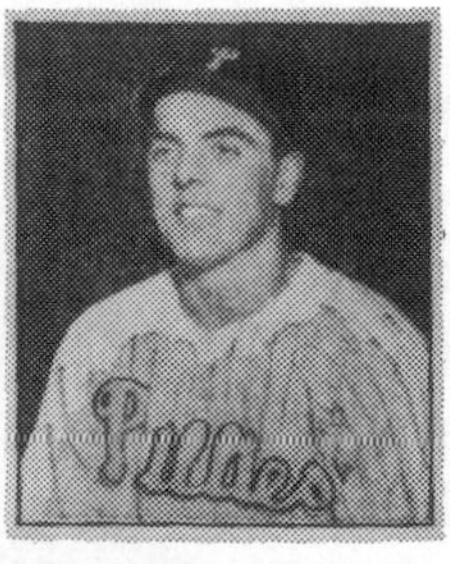

Entitled "Hit Parade of Champions," the 1951 Berk Ross set features 72 stars of various sports. The cards, which measure 2-1/16" by 2-1/2" and have tinted color photographs, were issued in boxes containing two-card panels. The issue is divided into four subsets with the first ten players of each series being baseball players. Only the baseball players are listed in the checklist that follows. Complete panels are valued 50 per cent higher than the sum of the individual cards.

		NR MT	EX	VG
Complete Set:		1200.00	600.00	360.00
Common Player:		12.00	6.00	3.50
1-1	Al Rosen	20.00	10.00	6.00
1-2	Bob Lemon	20.00	10.00	6.00
1-3	Phil Rizzuto	50.00	25.00	15.00
1-4	Hank Bauer	30.00	15.00	9.00
1-5	Billy Johnson	13.00	6.50	4.00
1-6	Jerry Coleman	13.00	6.50	4.00
1-7	Johnny Mize	30.00	15.00	7.50
1-8	Dom DiMaggio	30.00	15.00	9.00
1-9	Richie Ashburn	15.00	7.50	4.50
1-10	Del Ennis	13.00	6.50	4.00
2-1	Stan Musial	300.00	150.00	90.00
2-2	Warren Spahn	30.00	15.00	9.00
2-3	Tommy Henrich	15.00	7.50	4.50
2-4	Larry "Yogi" Berra	225.00	112.00	67.00
2-5	Joe DiMaggio	400.00	200.00	120.00
2-6	Bobby Brown	15.00	7.50	4.50
2-7	Granville Hamner	12.00	6.00	3.50
2-8	Willie Jones	12.00	6.00	3.50
2-9	Stanley Lopata	12.00	6.00	3.50
2-10	Mike Goliat	12.00	6.00	3.50
3-1	Ralph Kiner	30.00	15.00	9.00
3-2	Billy Goodman	12.00	6.00	3.50
3-3	Allie Reynolds	15.00	7.50	4.50
3-4	Vic Raschi	15.00	7.50	4.50
3-5	Joe Page	13.00	6.50	4.00
3-6	Eddie Lopat	15.00	7.50	4.50
3-7	Andy Seminick	12.00	6.00	3.50
3-8	Dick Sisler	12.00	6.00	3.50
3-9	Eddie Waitkus	12.00	6.00	3.50
3-10	Ken Heintzelman	12.00	6.00	3.50
4-1	Gene Woodling	15.00	7.50	4.50
4-2	Cliff Mapes	13.00	6.50	4.00
4-3	Fred Sanford	13.00	6.50	4.00
4-4	Tommy Bryne	13.00	6.50	4.00
4-5	Eddie (Whitey) Ford	125.00	62.00	37.00
4-6	Jim Konstanty	13.00	6.50	4.00
4-7	Russ Meyer	12.00	6.00	3.50
4-8	Robin Roberts	30.00	15.00	9.00
4-9	Curt Simmons	13.00	6.50	4.00
4-10	Sam Jethroe	30.00	15.00	9.00

1952 Berk Ross

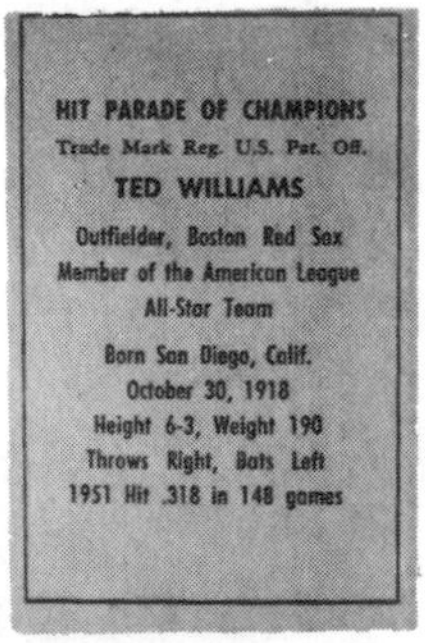

Although the card size is different (2" by 3"), the style of the fronts and backs of the 1952 Berk Ross set is similar to the previous year's effort. Seventy-two unnumbered cards make up the set. Rizzuto is included twice in the set and the Blackwell and Fox cards have transposed backs. The cards were issued individually rather than as two-card panels like in 1951.

	NR MT	EX	VG
Complete Set:	4250.00	2125.00	1275.
Common Player:	12.00	6.00	3.50

		NR MT	EX	VG
(1)	Richie Ashburn	30.00	15.00	9.00
(2)	Hank Bauer	18.00	9.00	5.50
(3)	Larry "Yogi" Berra	100.00	50.00	30.00
(4)	Ewell Blackwell (photo actually Nelson Fox)	18.00	9.00	5.50
(5)	Bobby Brown	18.00	9.00	5.50
(6)	Jim Busby	12.00	6.00	3.50
(7)	Roy Campanella	125.00	56.00	35.00
(8)	Chico Carrasquel	12.00	6.00	3.50
(9)	Jerry Coleman	15.00	7.50	4.50
(10)	Joe Collins	15.00	7.50	4.50
(11)	Alvin Dark	15.00	7.50	4.50
(12)	Dom DiMaggio	18.00	9.00	5.50
(13)	Joe DiMaggio	700.00	350.00	200.00
(14)	Larry Doby	18.00	9.00	5.50
(15)	Bobby Doerr	35.00	17.50	10.50
(16)	Bob Elliot (Elliott)	12.00	6.00	3.50
(17)	Del Ennis	12.00	6.00	3.50
(18)	Ferris Fain	12.00	6.00	3.50
(19)	Bob Feller	75.00	38.00	23.00
(20)	Nelson Fox (photo actually Ewell Blackwell)	18.00	9.00	5.50
(21)	Ned Garver	12.00	6.00	3.50
(22)	Clint Hartung	12.00	6.00	3.50
(23)	Jim Hearn	12.00	6.00	3.50
(24)	Gil Hodges	50.00	30.00	15.00
(25)	Monte Irvin	30.00	15.00	9.00
(26)	Larry Jansen	12.00	6.00	3.50
(27)	George Kell	25.00	12.50	7.50
(28)	Sheldon Jones	12.00	6.00	3.50
(29)	Monte Kennedy	12.00	6.00	3.50
(30)	Ralph Kiner	40.00	20.00	12.00
(31)	Dave Koslo	12.00	6.00	3.50
(32)	Bob Kuzava	15.00	7.50	4.50
(33)	Bob Lemon	30.00	15.00	9.00
(34)	Whitey Lockman	12.00	6.00	3.50
(35)	Eddie Lopat	18.00	9.00	5.50
(36)	Sal Maglie	15.00	7.50	4.50
(37)	Mickey Mantle	1200.00	600.00	360.00
(38)	Billy Martin	50.00	30.00	15.00
(39)	Willie Mays	500.00	250.00	150.00
(40)	Gil McDougal (McDougald)	18.00	9.00	5.50
(41)	Orestes Minoso	15.00	7.50	4.50
(42)	Johnny Mize	40.00	20.00	12.00
(43)	Tom Morgan	15.00	7.50	4.50
(44)	Don Mueller	12.00	6.00	3.50
(45)	Stan Musial	400.00	200.00	120.00
(46)	Don Newcombe	18.00	9.00	5.50
(47)	Ray Noble	12.00	6.00	3.50
(48)	Joe Ostrowski	15.00	7.50	4.50
(49)	Mel Parnell	12.00	6.00	3.50
(50)	Vic Raschi	18.00	9.00	5.50
(51)	Pee Wee Reese	65.00	33.00	20.00
(52)	Allie Reynolds	18.00	9.00	5.50
(53)	Bill Rigney	12.00	6.00	3.50
(54)	Phil Rizzuto (bunting)	55.00	28.00	16.50
(55)	Phil Rizzuto (swinging)	55.00	28.00	16.50
(56)	Robin Roberts	30.00	15.00	9.00
(57)	Eddie Robinson	12.00	6.00	3.50
(58)	Jackie Robinson	200.00	100.00	60.00
(59)	Elwin "Preacher" Roe	15.00	7.50	4.50
(60)	Johnny Sain	15.00	7.50	4.50
(61)	Albert "Red" Schoendienst	30.00	15.00	9.00
(62)	Duke Snider	125.00	56.00	35.00
(63)	George Spencer	12.00	6.00	3.50
(64)	Eddie Stanky	15.00	7.50	4.50
(65)	Henry Thompson	12.00	6.00	3.50
(66)	Bobby Thomson	18.00	9.00	5.50
(67)	Vic Wertz	12.00	6.00	3.50
(68)	Waldon Westlake	12.00	6.00	3.50
(69)	Wes Westrum	12.00	6.00	3.50
(70)	Ted Williams	400.00	200.00	120.00
(71)	Gene Woodling	18.00	9.00	5.50
(72)	Gus Zernial	12.00	6.00	3.50

1986 Big League Chew

The 1986 Big Leauge Chew set consists of 12 cards featuring the players who have hit 500 or more career home runs. The cards, which measure 2-1/2" by 3-1/2", were inserted in specially marked packages of Big League Chew, the shredded bubble gum developed by former major leaguer Jim Bouton. The set is entitled "Home Run Legends" and was

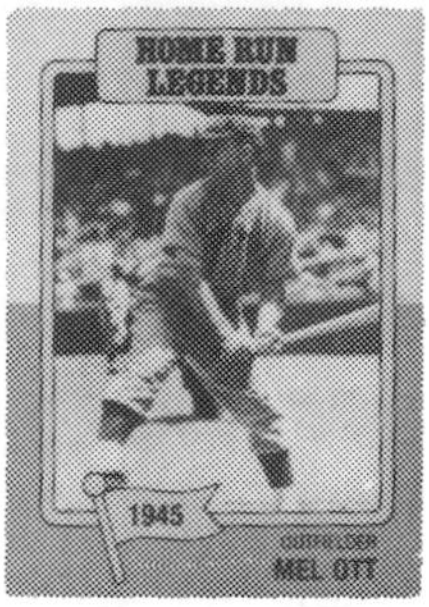

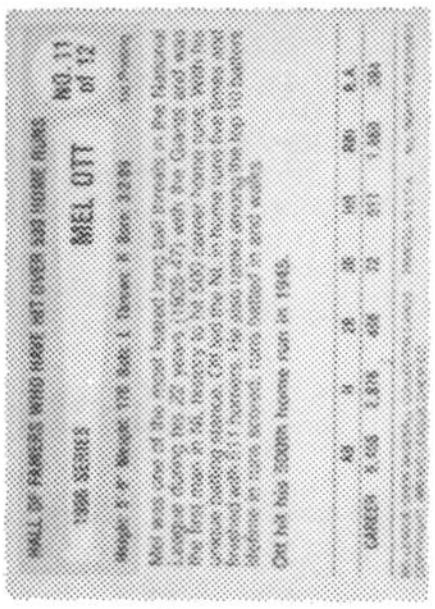

available through a write-in offer on the package. Recent-day players in the set are shown in color photos, while the older sluggers are pictured in black and white.

	MT	NR MT	EX
Complete Set:	6.00	4.50	2.50
Common Player:	.40	.30	.15

		MT	NR MT	EX
1	Hank Aaron	.60	.45	.25
2	Babe Ruth	1.00	.70	.40
3	Willie Mays	.60	.45	.25
4	Frank Robinson	.40	.30	.15
5	Harmon Killebrew	.40	.30	.15
6	Mickey Mantle	1.25	.90	.50
7	Jimmie Foxx	.40	.30	.15
8	Ted Williams	.70	.50	.30
9	Ernie Banks	.40	.30	.15
10	Eddie Mathews	.40	.30	.15
11	Mel Ott	.40	.30	.15
12	500-HR Group Card	.50	.40	.20

1987 Boardwalk And Baseball

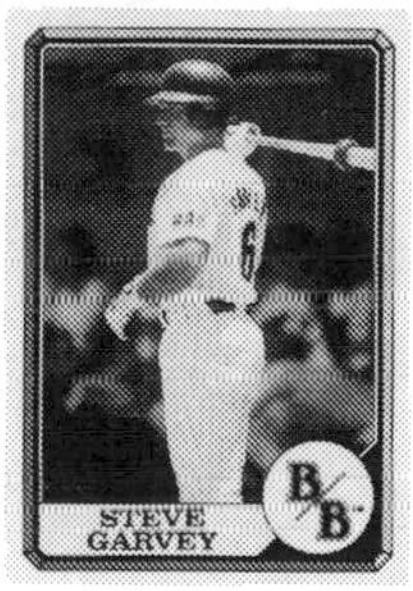

The 33-card "Top Run Makers" set was produced by Topps for distribution by the recreation amusement park "Boardwalk and Baseball," located near Orlando, Fla. The cards, which measure 2-1/2" by 3-1/2", feature fronts which contain full-color player photos and the park's logo (B/B). The card backs are printed in black and pink on white stock and offer personal data and career statistics. The set was issued in a specially designed box.

	MT	NR MT	EX
Complete Set:	6.00	4.50	2.50
Common Player:	.09	.07	.04

		MT	NR MT	EX
1	Mike Schmidt	.50	.40	.20
2	Eddie Murray	.35	.25	.14
3	Dale Murphy	.40	.30	.15
4	Dave Winfield	.30	.25	.12
5	Jim Rice	.30	.25	.12
6	Cecil Cooper	.12	.09	.05
7	Dwight Evans	.15	.11	.06
8	Rickey Henderson	.40	.30	.15
9	Robin Yount	.35	.25	.14
10	Andre Dawson	.25	.20	.10

		MT	NR MT	EX
11	Gary Carter	.35	.25	.14
12	Keith Hernandez	.30	.25	.12
13	George Brett	.40	.30	.15
14	Bill Buckner	.09	.07	.04
15	Tony Armas	.09	.07	.04
16	Harold Baines	.15	.11	.06
17	Don Baylor	.12	.09	.05
18	Steve Garvey	.35	.25	.14
19	Lance Parrish	.20	.15	.08
20	Dave Parker	.15	.11	.06
21	Buddy Bell	.09	.07	.04
22	Cal Ripken	.60	.45	.25
23	Bob Horner	.12	.09	.05
24	Tim Raines	.30	.25	.12
25	Jack Clark	.15	.11	.06
26	Leon Durham	.09	.07	.04
27	Pedro Guerrero	.15	.11	.06
28	Kent Hrbek	.15	.11	.06
29	Kirk Gibson	.20	.15	.08
30	Ryne Sandberg	.60	.45	.25
31	Wade Boggs	.70	.50	.30
32	Don Mattingly	1.00	.70	.40
33	Darryl Strawberry	.60	.45	.25

1987 Bohemian Hearth Bread Padres

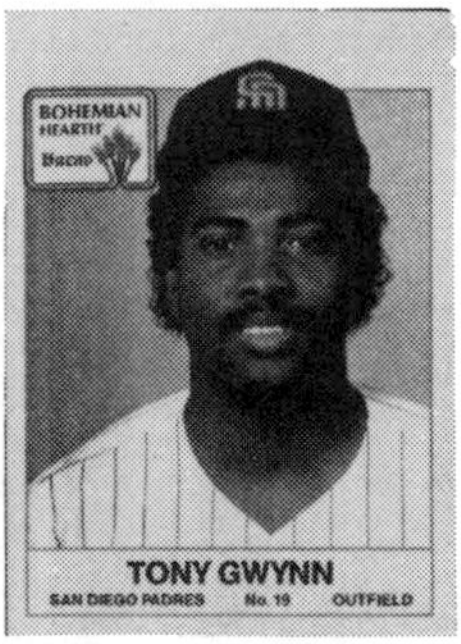

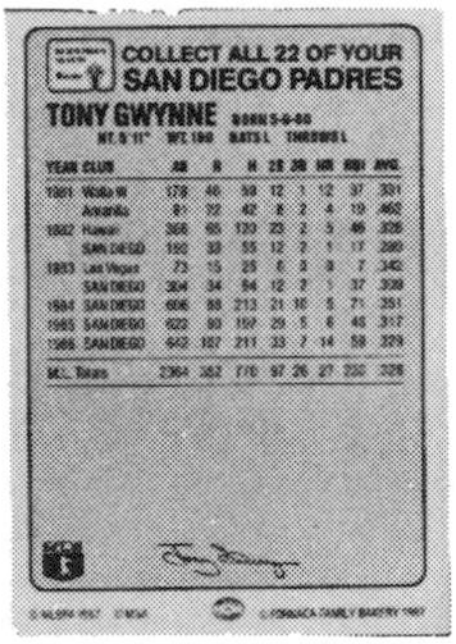

Bohemian Hearth Bread Company of San Diego issued a 22-card set highlighting the San Diego Padres. Produced in conjunction with Mike Schechter Associates, the cards are the standard 2-1/2" by 3-1/2" size. The card fronts contain a full-color photo encompassed by a yellow border. The Bohemian Hearth Bread logo is located in the upper left corner of the card. The card backs are printed in light brown ink on a cream color card stock and carry player personal and statistical information.

		MT	NR MT	EX
Complete Set:		50.00	37.50	20.00
Common Player:		.50	.40	.20
1	Garry Templeton	1.25	.90	.50
4	Jose Cora	.60	.45	.25
5	Randy Ready	.50	.40	.20
6	Steve Garvey	5.00	3.75	2.00
7	Kevin Mitchell	6.00	4.50	2.50
8	John Kruk	4.00	3.00	1.50
9	Benito Santiago	8.00	6.00	3.25
10	Larry Bowa	1.00	.70	.40
11	Tim Flannery	.50	.40	.20
14	Carmelo Martinez	.50	.40	.20
16	Marvell Wynne	.50	.40	.20
19	Tony Gwynn	12.00	9.00	4.75
21	James Steels	.50	.40	.20
22	Stan Jefferson	1.00	.70	.40
30	Eric Show	1.00	.70	.40
31	Ed Whitson	1.00	.70	.40
34	Storm Davis	1.00	.70	.40
37	Craig Lefferts	.80	.60	.30
40	Andy Hawkins	1.00	.70	.40
41	Lance McCullers	.50	.40	.20
43	Dave Dravecky	2.00	1.50	.80
54	Rich Gossage	2.25	1.75	.90

1948 Bowman

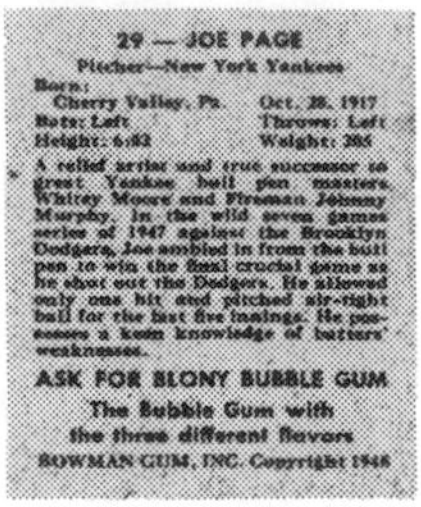

Bowman Gum Co.'s premiere set was produced in 1948, making it one of the first major issues of the post-war period. Forty-eight black and white cards comprise the set, with each card measuring 2-1/16" by 2-1/2" in size. The card backs, printed in black ink on grey stock, include the card number and the player's name, team, position, and a short biography. Twelve cards (#'s 7, 8, 13, 16, 20, 22, 24, 26, 29, 30 and 34) were printed in short supply when they were removed from the 36-card printing sheet to make room for the set's high numbers (#'s 37-48). These 24 cards command a higher price than the remaining cards in the set.

		NR MT	EX	VG
Complete Set:		3000.00	1500.00	900.00
Common Player: 1-36		18.00	9.00	5.50
Common Player: 37-48		25.00	12.50	7.50
1	Bob Elliott	90.00	25.00	12.00
2	Ewell (The Whip) Blackwell	25.00	12.50	7.50
3	Ralph Kiner	125.00	60.00	40.00
4	Johnny Mize	100.00	50.00	30.00
5	Bob Feller	200.00	100.00	60.00
6	*Larry (Yogi) Berra*	450.00	225.00	135.00
7	Pete (Pistol Pete) Reiser	40.00	20.00	12.00
8	Phil (Scooter) Rizzuto	225.00	112.00	67.00
9	Walker Cooper	18.00	9.00	5.50
10	Buddy Rosar	18.00	9.00	5.50
11	Johnny Lindell	18.00	9.00	5.50
12	Johnny Sain	25.00	12.50	7.50
13	Willard Marshall	30.00	15.00	9.00
14	Allie Reynolds	30.00	15.00	9.00
15	Eddie Joost	18.00	9.00	5.50
16	Jack Lohrke	30.00	15.00	9.00
17	Enos (Country) Slaughter	100.00	50.00	30.00
18	Warren Spahn	250.00	125.00	75.00
19	Tommy (The Clutch) Henrich	25.00	12.50	7.50
20	Buddy Kerr	30.00	15.00	9.00
21	Ferris Fain	15.00	7.50	4.50
22	Floyd (Bill) Bevins (Bevens)	40.00	20.00	12.00
23	Larry Jansen	18.00	9.00	5.50
24	Emil (Dutch) Leonard	30.00	15.00	9.00
25	Barney McCoskey (McCosky)	18.00	9.00	5.50
26	Frank Shea	40.00	20.00	12.00
27	Sid Gordon	18.00	9.00	5.50
28	Emil (The Antelope) Verban	30.00	15.00	9.00
29	Joe Page	45.00	23.00	13.50
30	"Whitey" Lockman	40.00	20.00	12.00
31	Bill McCahan	18.00	9.00	5.50
32	Bill Rigney	15.00	7.50	4.50
33	Bill (The Bull) Johnson	18.00	9.00	5.50
34	Sheldon (Available) Jones	30.00	15.00	9.00
35	George (Snuffy) Stirnweiss	18.00	9.00	5.50
36	Stan Musial	750.00	375.00	225.00
37	Clint Hartung	25.00	12.50	7.50
38	Al "Red" Schoendienst	125.00	60.00	35.00
39	Augie Galan	25.00	12.50	7.50
40	Marty Marion	70.00	35.00	21.00
41	Rex Barney	25.00	12.50	7.50
42	Ray Poat	25.00	12.50	7.50
43	Bruce Edwards	25.00	12.50	7.50
44	Johnny Wyrostek	25.00	12.50	7.50
45	Hank Sauer	25.00	12.50	7.50
46	Herman Wehmeier	25.00	12.50	7.50
47	Bobby Thomson	75.00	38.00	23.00
48	George "Dave" Koslo	60.00	10.00	6.00

1949 Bowman

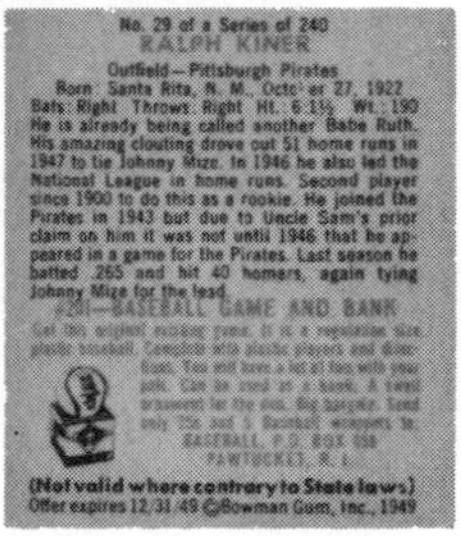

In 1949, Bowman increased the size of its issue to 240 numbered cards. The cards, which measure 2-1/16" by 2-1/2", are black and white photos overprinted with various pastel colors. Beginning with card #109 in the set, Bowman inserted the player's names on the card fronts. Twelve cards (#'s 4, 78, 83, 85, 88, 98, 109, 124, 127, 132 and 143), which were produced in the first four series of printings, were reprinted in the seventh series with either a card front or back modification. These variations are noted in the checklist that follows. Card #'s 1-3 and 5-73 can be found with either white or grey backs. The complete set of value in the following checklist does not include the higher priced variation cards.

	NR MT	EX	VG
Complete Set:	15200.00	7600.00	4560.
Common Player: 1-36	15.00	7.50	4.50
Common Player: 37-73	18.00	9.00	5.50
Common Player: 74-144	15.00	7.50	4.50
Common Player: 145-240	70.00	35.00	21.00

		NR MT	EX	VG
1	Vernon Bickford	100.00	30.00	15.00
2	Carroll "Whitey" Lockman	18.00	9.00	5.50
3	Bob Porterfield	18.00	9.00	5.50
4a	Jerry Priddy (no name on front)	18.00	9.00	5.50
4b	Jerry Priddy (name on front)	40.00	20.00	12.00
5	Hank Sauer	15.00	7.50	4.50
6	Phil Cavarretta	20.00	10.00	6.00
7	Joe Dobson	15.00	7.50	4.50
8	Murry Dickson	15.00	7.50	4.50
9	Ferris Fain	18.00	9.00	5.50
10	Ted Gray	15.00	7.50	4.50
11	Lou Boudreau	60.00	30.00	18.00
12	Cass Michaels	15.00	7.50	4.50
13	Bob Chesnes	15.00	7.50	4.50
14	*Curt Simmons*	25.00	12.50	7.50
15	Ned Garver	15.00	7.50	4.50
16	Al Kozar	15.00	7.50	4.50
17	Earl Torgeson	15.00	7.50	4.50
18	Bobby Thomson	30.00	15.00	9.00
19	*Bobby Brown*	50.00	25.00	15.00
20	Gene Hermanski	18.00	9.00	5.50
21	Frank Baumholtz	15.00	7.50	4.50
22	Harry "P-Nuts" Lowrey	15.00	7.50	4.50
23	Bobby Doerr	70.00	35.00	21.00
24	Stan Musial	500.00	250.00	150.00
25	Carl Scheib	15.00	7.50	4.50
26	George Kell	60.00	30.00	18.00
27	Bob Feller	150.00	75.00	45.00
28	Don Kolloway	15.00	7.50	4.50
29	Ralph Kiner	80.00	40.00	25.00
30	Andy Seminick	15.00	7.50	4.50
31	Dick Kokos	15.00	7.50	4.50
32	Eddie Yost	15.00	7.50	4.50
33	Warren Spahn	150.00	75.00	45.00
34	Dave Koslo	15.00	7.50	4.50
35	Vic Raschi	20.00	10.00	6.00
36	Harold "Peewee" Reese	175.00	87.00	52.00
37	John Wyrostek	18.00	9.00	5.50
38	Emil "The Antelope" Verban	18.00	9.00	5.50
39	Bill Goodman	18.00	9.00	5.50
40	George "Red" Munger	18.00	9.00	5.50
41	Lou Brissie	18.00	9.00	5.50
42	Walter "Hoot" Evers	18.00	9.00	5.50
43	Dale Mitchell	18.00	9.00	5.50
44	Dave Philley	18.00	9.00	5.50

		NR MT	EX	VG
45	Wally Westlake	18.00	9.00	5.50
46	*Robin Roberts*	250.00	125.00	70.00
47	Johnny Sain	18.00	9.00	5.50
48	Willard Marshall	18.00	9.00	5.50
49	Frank Shea	18.00	9.00	5.50
50	Jackie Robinson	700.00	350.00	200.00
51	Herman Wehmeier	18.00	9.00	5.50
52	Johnny Schmitz	18.00	9.00	5.50
53	Jack Kramer	18.00	9.00	5.50
54	Marty "Slats" Marion	16.00	8.00	4.75
55	Eddie Joost	18.00	9.00	5.50
56	Pat Mullin	18.00	9.00	5.50
57	Gene Bearden	18.00	9.00	5.50
58	Bob Elliott	18.00	9.00	5.50
59	Jack "Lucky" Lohrke	18.00	9.00	5.50
60	Larry "Yogi" Berra	300.00	150.00	90.00
61	Rex Barney	16.00	8.00	4.75
62	Grady Hatton	18.00	9.00	5.50
63	Andy Pafko	16.00	8.00	4.75
64	Dom "The Little Professor" DiMaggio	25.00	12.50	7.50
65	Enos "Country" Slaughter	75.00	37.00	23.00
66	Elmer Valo	18.00	9.00	5.50
67	Alvin Dark	25.00	12.50	7.50
68	Sheldon "Available" Jones	18.00	9.00	5.50
69	Tommy "The Clutch" Henrich	25.00	12.50	7.50
70	Carl Furillo	50.00	25.00	15.00
71	Vern "Junior" Stephens	18.00	9.00	5.50
72	Tommy Holmes	16.00	8.00	4.75
73	Billy Cox	16.00	8.00	4.75
74	Tom McBride	15.00	7.50	4.50
75	Eddie Mayo	15.00	7.50	4.50
76	Bill Nicholson	15.00	7.50	4.50
77	Ernie (Jumbo and Tiny) Bonham	15.00	7.50	4.50
78a	Sam Zoldak (no name on front)	18.00	9.00	5.50
78b	Sam Zoldak (name on front)	40.00	20.00	12.00
79	Ron Northey	15.00	7.50	4.50
80	Bill McCahan	15.00	7.50	4.50
81	Virgil "Red" Stallcup	15.00	7.50	4.50
82	Joe Page	16.00	8.00	4.75
83a	Bob Scheffing (no name on front)	18.00	9.00	5.50
83b	Bob Scheffing (name on front)	40.00	20.00	12.00
84	*Roy Campanella*	600.00	300.00	175.00
85a	Johnny "Big John" Mize (no name on front)	75.00	37.00	23.00
85b	Johnny "Big John" Mize (name on front)	125.00	62.00	37.00
86	Johnny Pesky	18.00	9.00	5.50
87	Randy Gumpert	15.00	7.50	4.50
88a	Bill Salkeld (no name on front)	18.00	9.00	5.50
88b	Bill Salkeld (name on front)	40.00	20.00	12.00
89	Mizell "Whitey" Platt	15.00	7.50	4.50
90	Gil Coan	15.00	7.50	4.50
91	Dick Wakefield	15.00	7.50	4.50
92	Willie "Puddin-Head" Jones	15.00	7.50	4.50
93	Ed Stevens	15.00	7.50	4.50
94	James "Mickey" Vernon	18.00	9.00	5.50
95	Howie Pollett	15.00	7.50	4.50
96	Taft Wright	15.00	7.50	4.50
97	Danny Litwhiler	15.00	7.50	4.50
98a	Phil Rizzuto (no name on front)	90.00	45.00	25.00
98b	Phil Rizzuto (name on front)	200.00	100.00	60.00
99	Frank Gustine	15.00	7.50	4.50
100	Gil Hodges	200.00	100.00	60.00
101	Sid Gordon	15.00	7.50	4.50
102	Stan Spence	15.00	7.50	4.50
103	Joe Tipton	15.00	7.50	4.50
104	Ed Stanky	18.00	9.00	5.50
105	Bill Kennedy	15.00	7.50	4.50
106	Jake Early	15.00	7.50	4.50
107	Eddie Lake	15.00	7.50	4.50
108	Ken Heintzelman	15.00	7.50	4.50
109a	Ed Fitzgerald (Fitz Gerald) (script name on back)	18.00	9.00	5.50
109b	Ed Fitzgerald (Fitz Gerald) (printed name on back)	40.00	20.00	12.00
110	Early Wynn	125.00	62.00	37.00
111	Al "Red" Schoendienst	75.00	37.00	23.00
112	Sam Chapman	15.00	7.50	4.50
113	Ray Lamanno	15.00	7.50	4.50
114	Allie Reynolds	30.00	15.00	9.00
115	Emil "Dutch" Leonard	15.00	7.50	4.50
116	Joe Hatten	18.00	9.00	5.50
117	Walker Cooper	15.00	7.50	4.50
118	Sam Mele	15.00	7.50	4.50
119	Floyd Baker	15.00	7.50	4.50
120	Cliff Fannin	15.00	7.50	4.50
121	Mark Christman	15.00	7.50	4.50
122	George Vico	15.00	7.50	4.50
123	Johnny Blatnick	15.00	7.50	4.50
124a	Danny Murtaugh (script name on back)	18.00	9.00	5.50

		NR MT	EX	VG
122	George Vico	12.00	6.00	3.50
123	Johnny Blatnick	12.00	6.00	3.50
124a	Danny Murtaugh (script name on back)	15.00	7.50	4.50
124b	Danny Murtaugh (printed name on back)	40.00	20.00	12.00
125	Ken Keltner	15.00	7.50	4.50
126a	Al Brazle (script name on back)	15.00	7.50	4.50
126b	Al Brazle (printed name on back)	40.00	20.00	12.00
127a	Henry "Heeney" Majeski (script name on back)	15.00	7.50	4.50
127b	Henry "Heeney" Majeski (printed name on back)	40.00	20.00	12.00
128	Johnny Vander Meer	16.00	8.00	4.75
129	Bill "The Bull" Johnson	16.00	8.00	4.75
130	Harry "The Hat" Walker	15.00	7.50	4.50
131	Paul Lehner	12.00	6.00	3.50
132a	Al Evans (script name on back)	15.00	7.50	4.50
132b	Al Evans (printed name on back)	40.00	20.00	12.00
133	Aaron Robinson	12.00	6.00	3.50
134	Hank Borowy	12.00	6.00	3.50
135	Stan Rojek	12.00	6.00	3.50
136	Henry "Hank" Edwards	12.00	6.00	3.50
137	Ted Wilks	12.00	6.00	3.50
138	Warren "Buddy" Rosar	12.00	6.00	3.50
139	Hank "Bow-Wow" Arft	12.00	6.00	3.50
140	Rae Scarborough (Ray)	12.00	6.00	3.50
141	Ulysses "Tony" Lupien	12.00	6.00	3.50
142	Eddie Waitkus	12.00	6.00	3.50
143a	Bob Dillinger (script name on back)	15.00	7.50	4.50
143b	Bob Dillinger (printed name on back)	40.00	20.00	12.00
144	Milton "Mickey" Haefner	12.00	6.00	3.50
145	Sylvester "Blix" Donnelly	70.00	35.00	21.00
146	Myron "Mike" McCormick	55.00	27.00	16.50
147	Elmer "Bert" Singleton	70.00	35.00	21.00
148	Bob Swift	70.00	35.00	21.00
149	Roy Partee	55.00	27.00	16.50
150	Alfred "Allie" Clark	70.00	35.00	21.00
151	Maurice "Mickey" Harris	70.00	35.00	21.00
152	Clarence Maddern	70.00	35.00	21.00
153	Phil Masi	70.00	35.00	21.00
154	Clint Hartung	70.00	35.00	21.00
155	Fermin "Mickey" Guerra	70.00	35.00	21.00
156	Al "Zeke" Zarilla	70.00	35.00	21.00
157	Walt Masterson	70.00	35.00	21.00
158	Harry "The Cat" Brecheen	70.00	35.00	21.00
159	Glen Moulder	70.00	35.00	21.00
160	Jim Blackburn	70.00	35.00	21.00
161	John "Jocko" Thompson	70.00	35.00	21.00
162	Elwin "Preacher" Roe	125.00	56.00	35.00
163	Clyde McCullough	70.00	35.00	21.00
164	Vic Wertz	55.00	27.00	16.50
165	George "Snuffy" Stirnweiss	70.00	35.00	21.00
166	Mike Tresh	70.00	35.00	21.00
167	Boris "Babe" Martin	70.00	35.00	21.00
168	Doyle Lade	70.00	35.00	21.00
169	Jeff Heath	70.00	35.00	21.00
170	Bill Rigney	55.00	27.00	16.50
171	Dick Fowler	70.00	35.00	21.00
172	Eddie Pellagrini	70.00	35.00	21.00
173	Eddie Stewart	70.00	35.00	21.00
174	Terry Moore	55.00	27.00	16.50
175	Luke Appling	125.00	62.00	37.00
176	Ken Raffensberger	70.00	35.00	21.00
177	Stan Lopata	70.00	35.00	21.00
178	Tommy Brown	55.00	27.00	16.50
179	Hugh Casey	55.00	27.00	16.50
180	Connie Berry	70.00	35.00	21.00
181	Gus Niarhos	70.00	35.00	21.00
182	Hal Peck	70.00	35.00	21.00
183	Lou Stringer	70.00	35.00	21.00
184	Bob Chipman	70.00	35.00	21.00
185	Pete Reiser	55.00	27.00	16.50
186	John "Buddy" Kerr	70.00	35.00	21.00
187	Phil Marchildon	70.00	35.00	21.00
188	Karl Drews	70.00	35.00	21.00
189	Earl Wooten	70.00	35.00	21.00
190	Jim Hearn	70.00	35.00	21.00
191	Joe Haynes	70.00	35.00	21.00
192	Harry Gumbert	70.00	35.00	21.00
193	Ken Trinkle	70.00	35.00	21.00
194	Ralph Branca	100.00	45.00	27.00
195	Eddie Bockman	70.00	35.00	21.00
196	Fred Hutchinson	55.00	27.00	16.50
197	Johnny Lindell	70.00	35.00	21.00
198	Steve Gromek	70.00	35.00	21.00
199	Cecil "Tex" Hughson	70.00	35.00	21.00
200	Jess Dobernic	70.00	35.00	21.00

		NR MT	EX	VG
201	Sibby Sisti	70.00	35.00	21.00
202	Larry Jansen	70.00	35.00	21.00
203	Barney McCosky	70.00	35.00	21.00
204	Bob Savage	70.00	35.00	21.00
205	Dick Sisler	70.00	35.00	21.00
206	Bruce Edwards	55.00	27.00	16.50
207	Johnny "Hippity" Hopp	70.00	35.00	21.00
208	Paul "Dizzy" Trout	55.00	27.00	16.50
209	Charlie "King Kong" Keller	100.00	50.00	30.00
210	Joe "Flash" Gordon	55.00	27.00	16.50
211	Dave "Boo" Ferris	70.00	35.00	21.00
212	Ralph Hamner	70.00	35.00	21.00
213	Charles "Red" Barrett	70.00	35.00	21.00
214	*Richie Ashburn*	500.00	250.00	150.00
215	Kirby Higbe	70.00	35.00	21.00
216	Lynwood "Schoolboy" Rowe	70.00	35.00	21.00
217	Marino Pieretti	70.00	35.00	21.00
218	Dick Kryhoski	70.00	35.00	21.00
219	Virgil "Fire" Trucks	55.00	27.00	16.50
220	Johnny McCarthy	70.00	35.00	21.00
221	Bob Muncrief	70.00	35.00	21.00
222	Alex Kellner	70.00	35.00	21.00
223	Bob Hoffman (Hofman)	70.00	35.00	21.00
224	*Leroy "Satchel" Paige*	1200.00	600.00	350.00
225	*Gerry Coleman*	100.00	50.00	30.00
226	Edwin "Duke" Snider	1000.00	500.00	300.00
227	Fritz Ostermueller	70.00	35.00	21.00
228	Jackie Mayo	70.00	35.00	21.00
229	Ed Lopat	125.00	60.00	40.00
230	Augie Galan	70.00	35.00	21.00
231	Earl Johnson	70.00	35.00	21.00
232	George McQuinn	70.00	35.00	21.00
233	*Larry Doby*	150.00	75.00	45.00
234	Truett "Rip" Sewell	55.00	27.00	16.50
235	Jim Russell	70.00	35.00	21.00
236	Fred Sanford	70.00	35.00	21.00
237	Monte Kennedy	70.00	35.00	21.00
238	Bob Lemon	225.00	112.00	67.00
239	Frank McCormick	70.00	35.00	21.00
240	Norman "Babe" Young (photo actually Bobby Young)	150.00	75.00	45.00

1949 Bowman Pacific Coast League

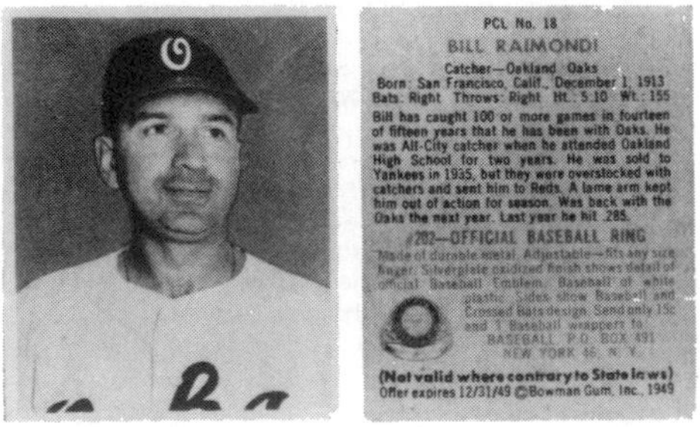

One of the scarcest issues of the post-war period, the 1949 Bowman PCL set was issued only on the West Coast. Like the 1949 Bowman regular issue, the cards contain black and white photos overprinted with various pastel colors. Thirty-six cards, which measure 2-1/16" by 2-1/2", make up the set. It is believed that the cards may have been issued only in sheets and not sold in gum packs.

		NR MT	EX	VG
Complete Set:		5500.00	2750.00	1650.
Common Player:		150.00	75.00	45.00
1	Lee Anthony	150.00	75.00	45.00
2	George Metkovich	150.00	75.00	45.00
3	Ralph Hodgin	150.00	75.00	45.00
4	George Woods	150.00	75.00	45.00
5	Xavier Rescigno	150.00	75.00	45.00
6	Mickey Grasso	150.00	75.00	45.00
7	Johnny Rucker	150.00	75.00	45.00
8	Jack Brewer	150.00	75.00	45.00

		NR MT	EX	VG
13	John Jensen	150.00	75.00	45.00
14	Joyner White	150.00	75.00	45.00
15	Harvey Storey	150.00	75.00	45.00
16	Dick Lajeski	150.00	75.00	45.00
17	Albie Glossop	150.00	75.00	45.00
18	Bill Raimondi	150.00	75.00	45.00
19	Ken Holcombe	150.00	75.00	45.00
20	Don Ross	150.00	75.00	45.00
21	Pete Coscarart	150.00	75.00	45.00
22	Tony York	150.00	75.00	45.00
23	Jake Mooty	150.00	75.00	45.00
24	Charles Adams	150.00	75.00	45.00
25	Les Scarsella	150.00	75.00	45.00
26	Joe Marty	150.00	75.00	45.00
27	Frank Kelleher	150.00	75.00	45.00
28	Lee Handley	150.00	75.00	45.00
29	Herman Besse	150.00	75.00	45.00
30	John Lazor	150.00	75.00	45.00
31	Eddie Malone	150.00	75.00	45.00
32	Maurice Van Robays	150.00	75.00	45.00
33	Jim Tabor	150.00	75.00	45.00
34	Gene Handley	150.00	75.00	45.00
35	Tom Seats	150.00	75.00	45.00
36	Ora Burnett	150.00	75.00	45.00

1950 Bowman

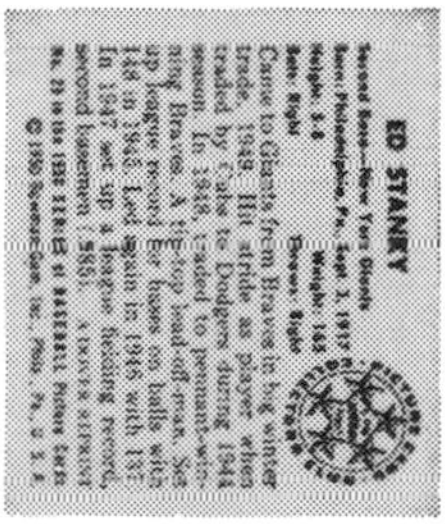

The quality of the 1950 Bowman issue showed a marked improvement over the company's previous efforts. The cards are beautiful color art reproductions of actual photographs and measure 2-1/16" by 2-1/2" in size. The card backs include the same type of information as found in the previous year's issue but are designed in a horizontal format. Cards found in the first two series of the set (#'s 1-72) are the scarcest in the issue. The backs of the final 72 cards in the set (#'s 181-252) can be found with or without the copyright line at the bottom of the card, the "without" version being the less common.

	NR MT	EX	VG
Complete Set:	9000.00	4500.00	2700.
Common Player: 1-72	50.00	25.00	15.00
Common Player: 73-252	16.00	8.00	4.75

		NR MT	EX	VG
1	Mel Parnell	200.00	25.00	8.00
2	Vern Stephens	50.00	25.00	15.00
3	Dom DiMaggio	60.00	30.00	18.00
4	Gus Zernial	50.00	25.00	15.00
5	Bob Kuzava	50.00	25.00	15.00
6	Bob Feller	150.00	75.00	45.00
7	Jim Hegan	50.00	25.00	15.00
8	George Kell	80.00	40.00	25.00
9	Vic Wertz	50.00	25.00	15.00
10	Tommy Henrich	50.00	25.00	15.00
11	Phil Rizzuto	150.00	75.00	45.00
12	Joe Page	50.00	25.00	15.00
13	Ferris Fain	50.00	25.00	15.00
14	Alex Kellner	50.00	25.00	15.00
15	Al Kozar	50.00	25.00	15.00
16	*Roy Sievers*	50.00	25.00	15.00
17	Sid Hudson	50.00	25.00	15.00
18	Eddie Robinson	50.00	25.00	15.00
19	Warren Spahn	150.00	75.00	45.00
20	Bob Elliott	50.00	25.00	15.00
21	Harold Reese	150.00	60.00	38.00
22	Jackie Robinson	600.00	300.00	175.00
23	*Don Newcombe*	125.00	67.00	37.00
24	Johnny Schmitz	50.00	25.00	15.00
25	Hank Sauer	50.00	25.00	15.00
26	Grady Hatton	50.00	25.00	15.00
27	Herman Wehmeier	50.00	25.00	15.00
28	Bobby Thomson	60.00	30.00	18.00
29	Ed Stanky	50.00	25.00	15.00
30	Eddie Waitkus	50.00	25.00	15.00
31	Del Ennis	50.00	25.00	15.00
32	Robin Roberts	125.00	62.00	37.00
33	Ralph Kiner	125.00	62.00	37.00
34	Murry Dickson	50.00	25.00	15.00
35	Enos Slaughter	100.00	50.00	30.00
36	Eddie Kazak	50.00	25.00	15.00
37	Luke Appling	60.00	30.00	18.00
38	Bill Wight	50.00	25.00	15.00
39	Larry Doby	60.00	30.00	18.00
40	Bob Lemon	100.00	50.00	30.00
41	Walter "Hoot" Evers	50.00	25.00	15.00
42	Art Houtteman	50.00	25.00	15.00
43	Bobby Doerr	80.00	40.00	25.00
44	Joe Dobson	50.00	25.00	15.00
45	Al "Zeke" Zarilla	50.00	25.00	15.00
46	Larry "Yogi" Berra	350.00	175.00	100.00
47	Jerry Coleman	35.00	17.50	10.50
48	Leland "Lou" Brissie	50.00	25.00	15.00
49	Elmer Valo	50.00	25.00	15.00
50	Dick Kokos	50.00	25.00	15.00
51	Ned Garver	50.00	25.00	15.00
52	Sam Mele	50.00	25.00	15.00
53	Clyde Vollmer	50.00	25.00	15.00
54	Gil Coan	50.00	25.00	15.00
55	John "Buddy" Kerr	50.00	25.00	15.00
56	*Del Crandell (Crandall)*	50.00	25.00	15.00
57	Vernon Bickford	50.00	25.00	15.00
58	Carl Furillo	45.00	23.00	13.50
59	Ralph Branca	45.00	23.00	13.50
60	Andy Pafko	22.00	11.00	6.50
61	Bob Rush	50.00	25.00	15.00
62	Ted Kluszewski	70.00	35.00	21.00
63	Ewell Blackwell	22.00	11.00	6.50
64	Alvin Dark	45.00	23.00	13.50
65	Dave Koslo	50.00	25.00	15.00
66	Larry Jansen	50.00	25.00	15.00
67	Willie Jones	50.00	25.00	15.00
68	Curt Simmons	50.00	25.00	15.00
69	Wally Westlake	50.00	25.00	15.00
70	Bob Chesnes	50.00	25.00	15.00
71	Al Schoendienst	90.00	45.00	27.00
72	Howie Pollet	50.00	25.00	15.00
73	Willard Marshall	16.00	8.00	4.75
74	*Johnny Antonelli*	16.00	8.00	4.75
75	Roy Campanella	300.00	150.00	90.00
76	Rex Barney	16.00	8.00	4.75
77	Edwin "Duke" Snider	275.00	137.00	80.00
78	Mickey Owen	16.00	8.00	4.75
79	Johnny Vander Meer	16.00	8.00	4.75
80	Howard Fox	16.00	8.00	4.75
81	Ron Northey	16.00	8.00	4.75
82	Carroll Lockman	16.00	8.00	4.75
83	Sheldon Jones	16.00	8.00	4.75
84	Richie Ashburn	75.00	38.00	23.00
85	Ken Heintzelman	16.00	8.00	4.75
86	Stan Rojek	16.00	8.00	4.75
87	Bill Werle	16.00	8.00	4.75
88	Marty Marion	16.00	8.00	4.75
89	George Munger	16.00	8.00	4.75
90	Harry Brecheen	16.00	8.00	4.75
91	Cass Michaels	16.00	8.00	4.75
92	Hank Majeski	16.00	8.00	4.75
93	Gene Bearden	16.00	8.00	4.75
94	Lou Boudreau	50.00	25.00	15.00
95	Aaron Robinson	16.00	8.00	4.75
96	Virgil "Fire" Trucks	16.00	8.00	4.75
97	Maurice McDermott	16.00	8.00	4.75
98	Ted Williams	650.00	325.00	200.00
99	Billy Goodman	16.00	8.00	4.75
100	Vic Raschi	20.00	10.00	6.00
101	Bobby Brown	20.00	10.00	6.00
102	Billy Johnson	16.00	8.00	4.75
103	Eddie Joost	16.00	8.00	4.75
104	Sam Chapman	16.00	8.00	4.75
105	Bob Dillinger	16.00	8.00	4.75
106	Cliff Fannin	16.00	8.00	4.75
107	Sam Dente	16.00	8.00	4.75
108	Rae Scarborough (Ray)	16.00	8.00	4.75
109	Sid Gordon	16.00	8.00	4.75
110	Tommy Holmes	16.00	8.00	4.75
111	Walker Cooper	16.00	8.00	4.75
112	Gil Hodges	80.00	40.00	24.00
113	Gene Hermanski	16.00	8.00	4.75

		NR MT	EX	VG
114	Wayne Terwilliger	16.00	8.00	4.75
115	Roy Smalley	16.00	8.00	4.75
116	Virgil "Red" Stallcup	16.00	8.00	4.75
117	Bill Rigney	16.00	8.00	4.75
118	Clint Hartung	16.00	8.00	4.75
119	Dick Sisler	16.00	8.00	4.75
120	John Thompson	16.00	8.00	4.75
121	Andy Seminick	16.00	8.00	4.75
122	Johnny Hopp	16.00	8.00	4.75
123	Dino Restelli	16.00	8.00	4.75
124	Clyde McCullough	16.00	8.00	4.75
125	Del Rice	16.00	8.00	4.75
126	Al Brazle	16.00	8.00	4.75
127	Dave Philley	16.00	8.00	4.75
128	Phil Masi	16.00	8.00	4.75
129	Joe "Flash" Gordon	16.00	8.00	4.75
130	Dale Mitchell	16.00	8.00	4.75
131	Steve Gromek	16.00	8.00	4.75
132	James Vernon	16.00	8.00	4.75
133	Don Kolloway	16.00	8.00	4.75
134	Paul "Dizzy" Trout	16.00	8.00	4.75
135	Pat Mullin	16.00	8.00	4.75
136	Warren Rosar	16.00	8.00	4.75
137	Johnny Pesky	16.00	8.00	4.75
138	Allie Reynolds	45.00	23.00	13.50
139	Johnny Mize	60.00	30.00	18.00
140	Pete Suder	16.00	8.00	4.75
141	Joe Coleman	16.00	8.00	4.75
142	*Sherman Lollar*	16.00	8.00	4.75
143	Eddie Stewart	16.00	8.00	4.75
144	Al Evans	16.00	8.00	4.75
145	Jack Graham	16.00	8.00	4.75
146	Floyd Baker	16.00	8.00	4.75
147	*Mike Garcia*	16.00	8.00	4.75
148	Early Wynn	60.00	30.00	18.00
149	Bob Swift	16.00	8.00	4.75
150	George Vico	16.00	8.00	4.75
151	Fred Hutchinson	16.00	8.00	4.75
152	Ellis Kinder	16.00	8.00	4.75
153	Walt Masterson	16.00	8.00	4.75
154	Gus Niarhos	16.00	8.00	4.75
155	Frank "Spec" Shea	16.00	8.00	4.75
156	Fred Sanford	16.00	8.00	4.75
157	Mike Guerra	16.00	8.00	4.75
158	Paul Lehner	16.00	8.00	4.75
159	Joe Tipton	16.00	8.00	4.75
160	Mickey Harris	16.00	8.00	4.75
161	Sherry Robertson	16.00	8.00	4.75
162	Eddie Yost	16.00	8.00	4.75
163	Earl Torgeson	16.00	8.00	4.75
164	Sibby Sisti	16.00	8.00	4.75
165	Bruce Edwards	16.00	8.00	4.75
166	Joe Hatten	16.00	8.00	4.75
167	Elwin Roe	45.00	23.00	13.50
168	Bob Scheffing	16.00	8.00	4.75
169	Hank Edwards	16.00	8.00	4.75
170	Emil Leonard	16.00	8.00	4.75
171	Harry Gumbert	16.00	8.00	4.75
172	Harry Lowrey	16.00	8.00	4.75
173	Lloyd Merriman	16.00	8.00	4.75
174	Henry Thompson	16.00	8.00	4.75
175	Monte Kennedy	16.00	8.00	4.75
176	Sylvester Donnelly	16.00	8.00	4.75
177	Hank Borowy	16.00	8.00	4.75
178	Eddy Fitzgerald (Fitz Gerald)	16.00	8.00	4.75
179	Charles Diering	16.00	8.00	4.75
180	Harry Walker	16.00	8.00	4.75
181	Marino Pieretti	16.00	8.00	4.75
182	Sam Zoldak	16.00	8.00	4.75
183	Mickey Haefner	16.00	8.00	4.75
184	Randy Gumpert	16.00	8.00	4.75
185	Howie Judson	16.00	8.00	4.75
186	Ken Keltner	16.00	8.00	4.75
187	Lou Stringer	16.00	8.00	4.75
188	Earl Johnson	16.00	8.00	4.75
189	Owen Friend	16.00	8.00	4.75
190	Ken Wood	16.00	8.00	4.75
191	Dick Starr	16.00	8.00	4.75
192	Bob Chipman	16.00	8.00	4.75
193	Harold "Pete" Reiser	16.00	8.00	4.75
194	Billy Cox	16.00	8.00	4.75
195	Phil Cavaretta (Cavarretta)	16.00	8.00	4.75
196	Doyle Lade	16.00	8.00	4.75
197	Johnny Wyrostek	16.00	8.00	4.75
198	Danny Litwhiler	16.00	8.00	4.75
199	Jack Kramer	16.00	8.00	4.75
200	Kirby Higbe	16.00	8.00	4.75
201	Pete Castiglione	16.00	8.00	4.75
202	Cliff Chambers	16.00	8.00	4.75
203	Danny Murtaugh	16.00	8.00	4.75
204	Granville Hamner	16.00	8.00	4.75
205	Mike Goliat	16.00	8.00	4.75
206	Stan Lopata	16.00	8.00	4.75
207	Max Lanier	16.00	8.00	4.75
208	Jim Hearn	16.00	8.00	4.75
209	Johnny Lindell	16.00	8.00	4.75
210	Ted Gray	16.00	8.00	4.75
211	Charlie Keller	16.00	8.00	4.75
212	Gerry Priddy	16.00	8.00	4.75
213	Carl Scheib	16.00	8.00	4.75
214	Dick Fowler	16.00	8.00	4.75
215	Ed Lopat	20.00	10.00	6.00
216	Bob Porterfield	16.00	8.00	4.75
217	Casey Stengel	125.00	67.00	37.00
218	Cliff Mapes	16.00	8.00	4.75
219	*Hank Bauer*	70.00	35.00	20.00
220	Leo Durocher	50.00	25.00	15.00
221	Don Mueller	16.00	8.00	4.75
222	Bobby Morgan	16.00	8.00	4.75
223	Jimmy Russell	16.00	8.00	4.75
224	Jack Banta	16.00	8.00	4.75
225	Eddie Sawyer	16.00	8.00	4.75
226	Jim Konstanty	16.00	8.00	4.75
227	Bob Miller	16.00	8.00	4.75
228	Bill Nicholson	16.00	8.00	4.75
229	Frank Frisch	45.00	23.00	13.50
230	Bill Serena	16.00	8.00	4.75
231	Preston Ward	16.00	8.00	4.75
232	*Al "Flip" Rosen*	50.00	25.00	15.00
233	Allie Clark	16.00	8.00	4.75
234	*Bobby Shantz*	25.00	12.50	7.50
235	Harold Gilbert	16.00	8.00	4.75
236	Bob Cain	16.00	8.00	4.75
237	Bill Salkeld	16.00	8.00	4.75
238	Vernal Jones	16.00	8.00	4.75
239	Bill Howerton	16.00	8.00	4.75
240	Eddie Lake	16.00	8.00	4.75
241	Neil Berry	16.00	8.00	4.75
242	Dick Kryhoski	16.00	8.00	4.75
243	Johnny Groth	16.00	8.00	4.75
244	Dale Coogan	16.00	8.00	4.75
245	Al Papai	16.00	8.00	4.75
246	*Walt Dropo*	25.00	12.50	7.50
247	Irv Noren	16.00	8.00	4.75
248	*Sam Jethroe*	16.00	8.00	4.75
249	George Stirnweiss	16.00	8.00	4.75
250	Ray Coleman	16.00	8.00	4.75
251	John Lester Moss	16.00	8.00	4.75
252	Billy DeMars	100.00	50.00	30.00

1951 Bowman

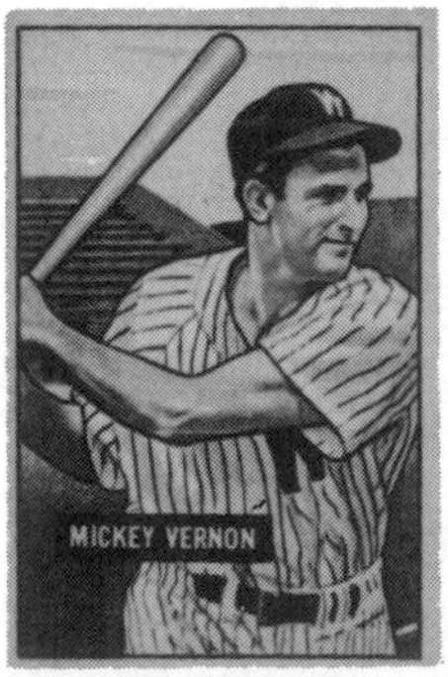

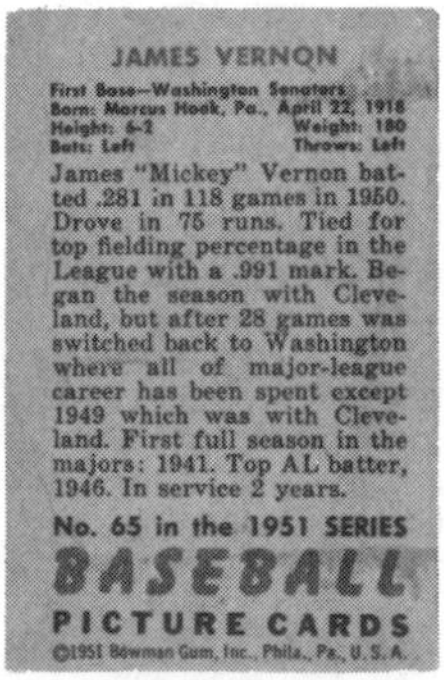

In 1951, Bowman increased the numbers of cards in its set for the third consecutive year when it issued 324 cards. The cards are, like 1950, color art reproductions of actual photographs but now measured 2-1/16" by 3-1/8" in size. The player's name is situated in a small, black box on the card front. Several of the card fronts are enlargements of the 1950 version. The high-numbered series of the set (#'s 253-324), which includes the rookie cards of Mantle and Mays, are the scarcest of the issue.

	NR MT	EX	VG
Complete Set:	17000.00	8500.00	5350.
Common Player: 1-36	20.00	10.00	6.00
Common Player: 37-252	14.00	7.00	4.25
Common Player: 253-324	60.00	30.00	18.00

		NR MT	EX	VG
Common Player: 1-36		15.00	7.50	4.50
Common Player: 37-252		12.00	6.00	3.50
Common Player: 253-324		50.00	25.00	15.00
1	*Ed Ford*	1200.00	500.00	275.00
2	Larry "Yogi" Berra	400.00	200.00	120.00
3	Robin Roberts	70.00	35.00	20.00
4	Del Ennis	15.00	7.50	4.50
5	Dale Mitchell	15.00	7.50	4.50
6	Don Newcombe	35.00	17.50	10.50
7	Gil Hodges	80.00	40.00	25.00
8	Paul Lehner	15.00	7.50	4.50
9	Sam Chapman	15.00	7.50	4.50
10	Al "Red" Schoendienst	70.00	35.00	21.00
11	George "Red" Munger	15.00	7.50	4.50
12	Hank Majeski	15.00	7.50	4.50
13	Ed Stanky	15.00	7.50	4.50
14	Alvin Dark	18.00	9.00	5.50
15	Johnny Pesky	15.00	7.50	4.50
16	Maurice McDermott	15.00	7.50	4.50
17	Pete Castiglione	15.00	7.50	4.50
18	Gil Coan	15.00	7.50	4.50
19	Sid Gordon	15.00	7.50	4.50
20	Del Crandall	15.00	7.50	4.50
21	George "Snuffy" Stirnweiss	15.00	7.50	4.50
22	Hank Sauer	15.00	7.50	4.50
23	Walter "Hoot" Evers	15.00	7.50	4.50
24	Ewell Blackwell	15.00	7.50	4.50
25	Vic Raschi	30.00	15.00	9.00
26	Phil Rizzuto	75.00	38.00	23.00
27	Jim Konstanty	15.00	7.50	4.50
28	Eddie Waitkus	15.00	7.50	4.50
29	Allie Clark	15.00	7.50	4.50
30	Bob Feller	125.00	62.00	37.00
31	Roy Campanella	225.00	100.00	60.00
32	Duke Snider	250.00	125.00	75.00
33	Bob Hooper	15.00	7.50	4.50
34	Marty Marion	15.00	7.50	4.50
35	Al Zarilla	15.00	7.50	4.50
36	Joe Dobson	15.00	7.50	4.50
37	Whitey Lockman	12.00	6.00	3.50
38	Al Evans	12.00	6.00	3.50
39	Ray Scarborough	12.00	6.00	3.50
40	*Dave "Gus" Bell*	15.00	7.50	4.50
41	Eddie Yost	15.00	7.50	4.50
42	Vern Bickford	12.00	6.00	3.50
43	Billy DeMars	12.00	6.00	3.50
44	Roy Smalley	12.00	6.00	3.50
45	Art Houtteman	12.00	6.00	3.50
46	George Kell	50.00	25.00	15.00
47	Grady Hatton	12.00	6.00	3.50
48	Ken Raffensberger	12.00	6.00	3.50
49	Jerry Coleman	15.00	7.50	4.50
50	Johnny Mize	50.00	25.00	15.00
51	Andy Seminick	12.00	6.00	3.50
52	Dick Sisler	12.00	6.00	3.50
53	Bob Lemon	40.00	20.00	12.00
54	Ray Boone	15.00	7.50	4.50
55	Gene Hermanski	15.00	7.50	4.50
56	Ralph Branca	30.00	15.00	9.00
57	Alex Kellner	12.00	6.00	3.50
58	Enos Slaughter	50.00	25.00	15.00
59	Randy Gumpert	12.00	6.00	3.50
60	Alfonso Carrasquel	12.00	6.00	3.50
61	Jim Hearn	12.00	6.00	3.50
62	Lou Boudreau	40.00	20.00	12.00
63	Bob Dillinger	12.00	6.00	3.50
64	Bill Werle	12.00	6.00	3.50
65	Mickey Vernon	15.00	7.50	4.50
66	Bob Elliott	12.00	6.00	3.50
67	Roy Sievers	15.00	7.50	4.50
68	Dick Kokos	12.00	6.00	3.50
69	Johnny Schmitz	12.00	6.00	3.50
70	Ron Northey	12.00	6.00	3.50
71	Jerry Priddy	12.00	6.00	3.50
72	Lloyd Merriman	12.00	6.00	3.50
73	Tommy Byrne	15.00	7.50	4.50
74	Billy Johnson	15.00	7.50	4.50
75	Russ Meyer	12.00	6.00	3.50
76	Stan Lopata	12.00	6.00	3.50
77	Mike Goliat	12.00	6.00	3.50
78	Early Wynn	50.00	25.00	15.00
79	Jim Hegan	12.00	6.00	3.50
80	Harold "Peewee" Reese	125.00	62.00	37.00
81	Carl Furillo	40.00	20.00	12.00
82	Joe Tipton	12.00	6.00	3.50
83	Carl Scheib	12.00	6.00	3.50
84	Barney McCosky	12.00	6.00	3.50
85	Eddie Kazak	12.00	6.00	3.50
86	Harry Brecheen	15.00	7.50	4.50
87	Floyd Baker	12.00	6.00	3.50
88	Eddie Robinson	12.00	6.00	3.50

		NR MT	EX	VG
89	Henry Thompson	12.00	6.00	3.50
90	Dave Koslo	12.00	6.00	3.50
91	Clyde Vollmer	12.00	6.00	3.50
92	Vern "Junior" Stephens	15.00	7.50	4.50
93	Danny O'Connell	12.00	6.00	3.50
94	Clyde McCullough	12.00	6.00	3.50
95	Sherry Robertson	12.00	6.00	3.50
96	Sandalio Consuegra	12.00	6.00	3.50
97	Bob Kuzava	12.00	6.00	3.50
98	Willard Marshall	12.00	6.00	3.50
99	Earl Torgeson	12.00	6.00	3.50
100	Sherman Lollar	15.00	7.50	4.50
101	Owen Friend	12.00	6.00	3.50
102	Emil "Dutch" Leonard	12.00	6.00	3.50
103	Andy Pafko	15.00	7.50	4.50
104	Virgil "Fire" Trucks	15.00	7.50	4.50
105	Don Kolloway	12.00	6.00	3.50
106	Pat Mullin	12.00	6.00	3.50
107	Johnny Wyrostek	12.00	6.00	3.50
108	Virgil Stallcup	12.00	6.00	3.50
109	Allie Reynolds	40.00	20.00	12.00
110	Bobby Brown	40.00	20.00	12.00
111	Curt Simmons	15.00	7.50	4.50
112	Willie Jones	12.00	6.00	3.50
113	Bill "Swish" Nicholson	12.00	6.00	3.50
114	Sam Zoldak	12.00	6.00	3.50
115	Steve Gromek	12.00	6.00	3.50
116	Bruce Edwards	15.00	7.50	4.50
117	Eddie Miksis	15.00	7.50	4.50
118	Preacher Roe	40.00	20.00	12.00
119	Eddie Joost	12.00	6.00	3.50
120	Joe Coleman	12.00	6.00	3.50
121	Gerry Staley	12.00	6.00	3.50
122	Joe Garagiola	125.00	67.00	37.00
123	Howie Judson	12.00	6.00	3.50
124	Gus Niarhos	12.00	6.00	3.50
125	Bill Rigney	15.00	7.50	4.50
126	Bobby Thomson	30.00	15.00	9.00
127	Sal Maglie	40.00	20.00	12.00
128	Ellis Kinder	12.00	6.00	3.50
129	Matt Batts	12.00	6.00	3.50
130	Tom Saffell	12.00	6.00	3.50
131	Cliff Chambers	12.00	6.00	3.50
132	Cass Michaels	12.00	6.00	3.50
133	Sam Dente	12.00	6.00	3.50
134	Warren Spahn	100.00	50.00	30.00
135	Walker Cooper	12.00	6.00	3.50
136	Ray Coleman	12.00	6.00	3.50
137	Dick Starr	12.00	6.00	3.50
138	Phil Cavarretta	15.00	7.50	4.50
139	Doyle Lade	12.00	6.00	3.50
140	Eddie Lake	12.00	6.00	3.50
141	Fred Hutchinson	15.00	7.50	4.50
142	Aaron Robinson	12.00	6.00	3.50
143	Ted Kluszewski	40.00	20.00	12.00
144	Herman Wehmeier	12.00	6.00	3.50
145	Fred Sanford	15.00	7.50	4.50
146	Johnny Hopp	15.00	7.50	4.50
147	Ken Heintzelman	12.00	6.00	3.50
148	Granny Hamner	12.00	6.00	3.50
149	Emory "Bubba" Church	12.00	6.00	3.50
150	Mike Garcia	15.00	7.50	4.50
151	Larry Doby	20.00	10.00	6.00
152	Cal Abrams	15.00	7.50	4.50
153	Rex Barney	15.00	7.50	4.50
154	Pete Suder	12.00	6.00	3.50
155	Lou Brissie	12.00	6.00	3.50
156	Del Rice	12.00	6.00	3.50
157	Al Brazle	12.00	6.00	3.50
158	Chuck Diering	12.00	6.00	3.50
159	Eddie Stewart	12.00	6.00	3.50
160	Phil Masi	12.00	6.00	3.50
161	Wes Westrum	15.00	7.50	4.50
162	Larry Jansen	12.00	6.00	3.50
163	Monte Kennedy	12.00	6.00	3.50
164	Bill Wight	12.00	6.00	3.50
165	Ted Williams	550.00	275.00	165.00
166	Stan Rojek	12.00	6.00	3.50
167	Murry Dickson	12.00	6.00	3.50
168	Sam Mele	12.00	6.00	3.50
169	Sid Hudson	12.00	6.00	3.50
170	Sibby Sisti	12.00	6.00	3.50
171	Buddy Kerr	12.00	6.00	3.50
172	Ned Garver	12.00	6.00	3.50
173	Hank Arft	12.00	6.00	3.50
174	Mickey Owen	12.00	6.00	3.50
175	Wayne Terwilliger	12.00	6.00	3.50
176	Vic Wertz	15.00	7.50	4.50
177	Charlie Keller	15.00	7.50	4.50
178	Ted Gray	12.00	6.00	3.50
179	Danny Litwhiler	12.00	6.00	3.50

		NR MT	EX	VG
184	Eddie Sawyer	14.00	7.00	4.25
185	Jimmy Bloodworth	14.00	7.00	4.25
186	Richie Ashburn	60.00	30.00	18.00
187	Al "Flip" Rosen	25.00	12.50	7.50
188	*Roberto Avila*	20.00	10.00	6.00
189	Erv Palica	20.00	10.00	6.00
190	Joe Hatten	20.00	10.00	6.00
191	Billy Hitchcock	14.00	7.00	4.25
192	Hank Wyse	14.00	7.00	4.25
193	Ted Wilks	14.00	7.00	4.25
194	Harry "Peanuts" Lowrey	14.00	7.00	4.25
195	Paul Richards	30.00	15.00	9.00
196	Bill Pierce	20.00	10.00	6.00
197	Bob Cain	14.00	7.00	4.25
198	*Monte Irvin*	100.00	50.00	30.00
199	Sheldon Jones	14.00	7.00	4.25
200	Jack Kramer	14.00	7.00	4.25
201	Steve O'Neill	14.00	7.00	4.25
202	Mike Guerra	14.00	7.00	4.25
203	*Vernon Law*	20.00	10.00	6.00
204	Vic Lombardi	14.00	7.00	4.25
205	Mickey Grasso	14.00	7.00	4.25
206	Conrado Marrero	14.00	7.00	4.25
207	Billy Southworth	14.00	7.00	4.25
208	Blix Donnelly	14.00	7.00	4.25
209	Ken Wood	14.00	7.00	4.25
210	Les Moss	14.00	7.00	4.25
211	Hal Jeffcoat	14.00	7.00	4.25
212	Bob Rush	14.00	7.00	4.25
213	Neil Berry	14.00	7.00	4.25
214	Bob Swift	14.00	7.00	4.25
215	Kent Peterson	14.00	7.00	4.25
216	Connie Ryan	14.00	7.00	4.25
217	Joe Page	20.00	10.00	6.00
218	Ed Lopat	20.00	10.00	6.00
219	Gene Woodling	40.00	20.00	12.00
220	Bob Miller	14.00	7.00	4.25
221	Dick Whitman	14.00	7.00	4.25
222	Thurman Tucker	14.00	7.00	4.25
223	Johnny Vander Meer	20.00	10.00	6.00
224	Billy Cox	20.00	10.00	6.00
225	Dan Bankhead	20.00	10.00	6.00
226	Jimmy Dykes	20.00	10.00	6.00
227	Bobby Schantz (Shantz)	20.00	10.00	6.00
228	Cloyd Boyer	14.00	7.00	4.25
229	Bill Howerton	14.00	7.00	4.25
230	Max Lanier	14.00	7.00	4.25
231	Luis Aloma	14.00	7.00	4.25
232	Nelson Fox	110.00	55.00	33.00
233	Leo Durocher	60.00	30.00	18.00
234	Clint Hartung	14.00	7.00	4.25
235	Jack "Lucky" Lohrke	14.00	7.00	4.25
236	Warren "Buddy" Rosar	14.00	7.00	4.25
237	Billy Goodman	14.00	7.00	4.25
238	Pete Reiser	20.00	10.00	6.00
239	Bill MacDonald	14.00	7.00	4.25
240	Joe Haynes	14.00	7.00	4.25
241	Irv Noren	14.00	7.00	4.25
242	Sam Jethroe	20.00	10.00	6.00
243	John Antonelli	20.00	10.00	6.00
244	Cliff Fannin	14.00	7.00	4.25
245	John Berardino	20.00	10.00	6.00
246	Bill Serena	14.00	7.00	4.25
247	Bob Ramazotti	14.00	7.00	4.25
248	*Johnny Klippstein*	20.00	10.00	6.00
249	Johnny Groth	14.00	7.00	4.25
250	Hank Borowy	14.00	7.00	4.25
251	Willard Ramsdell	14.00	7.00	4.25
252	Homer "Dixie" Howell	14.00	7.00	4.25
253	*Mickey Mantle*	5000.00	2500.00	1500.
254	*Jackie Jensen*	70.00	35.00	21.00
255	Milo Candini	60.00	30.00	18.00
256	Ken Silvestri	60.00	30.00	18.00
257	Birdie Tebbetts	60.00	30.00	18.00
258	*Luke Easter*	60.00	30.00	18.00
259	Charlie Dressen	60.00	30.00	18.00
260	Carl Erskine	90.00	45.00	27.00
261	Wally Moses	60.00	30.00	18.00
262	Gus Zernial	60.00	30.00	18.00
263	Howie Pollett (Pollet)	60.00	30.00	18.00
264	Don Richmond	60.00	30.00	18.00
265	Steve Bilko	60.00	30.00	18.00
266	Harry Dorish	60.00	30.00	18.00
267	Ken Holcombe	60.00	30.00	18.00
268	Don Mueller	60.00	30.00	18.00
269	Ray Noble	60.00	30.00	18.00
270	Willard Nixon	60.00	30.00	18.00
271	Tommy Wright	60.00	30.00	18.00
272	Billy Meyer	60.00	30.00	18.00
273	Danny Murtaugh	60.00	30.00	18.00
274	George Metkovich	60.00	30.00	18.00
275	Bucky Harris	60.00	30.00	18.00
276	Frank Quinn	60.00	30.00	18.00
277	Roy Hartsfield	60.00	30.00	18.00
278	Norman Roy	60.00	30.00	18.00
279	Jim Delsing	60.00	30.00	18.00
280	Frank Overmire	60.00	30.00	18.00
281	Al Widmar	60.00	30.00	18.00
282	Frank Frisch	80.00	40.00	25.00
283	Walt Dubiel	60.00	30.00	18.00
284	Gene Bearden	60.00	30.00	18.00
285	Johnny Lipon	60.00	30.00	18.00
286	Bob Usher	60.00	30.00	18.00
287	Jim Blackburn	60.00	30.00	18.00
288	Bobby Adams	60.00	30.00	18.00
289	Cliff Mapes	60.00	30.00	18.00
290	Bill Dickey	175.00	70.00	44.00
291	Tommy Henrich	70.00	35.00	20.00
292	Eddie Pellagrini	60.00	30.00	18.00
293	Ken Johnson	60.00	30.00	18.00
294	Jocko Thompson	60.00	30.00	18.00
295	Al Lopez	90.00	45.00	25.00
296	Bob Kennedy	60.00	30.00	18.00
297	Dave Philley	60.00	30.00	18.00
298	Joe Astroth	60.00	30.00	18.00
299	Clyde King	60.00	30.00	18.00
300	Hal Rice	60.00	30.00	18.00
301	Tommy Glaviano	60.00	30.00	18.00
302	Jim Busby	60.00	30.00	18.00
303	Marv Rotblatt	60.00	30.00	18.00
304	Allen Gettel	60.00	30.00	18.00
305	*Willie Mays*	2000.00	1000.00	600.00
306	*Jim Piersall*	90.00	45.00	27.00
307	Walt Masterson	60.00	30.00	18.00
308	Ted Beard	60.00	30.00	18.00
309	Mel Queen	60.00	30.00	18.00
310	Erv Dusak	60.00	30.00	18.00
311	Mickey Harris	60.00	30.00	18.00
312	Gene Mauch	60.00	30.00	18.00
313	Ray Mueller	60.00	30.00	18.00
314	Johnny Sain	60.00	30.00	18.00
315	Zack Taylor	60.00	30.00	18.00
316	Duane Pillette	60.00	30.00	18.00
317	*Forrest Burgess*	70.00	35.00	20.00
318	Warren Hacker	60.00	30.00	18.00
319	Red Rolfe	60.00	30.00	18.00
320	Hal White	60.00	30.00	18.00
321	Earl Johnson	60.00	30.00	18.00
322	Luke Sewell	60.00	30.00	18.00
323	*Joe Adcock*	90.00	45.00	27.00
324	Johnny Pramesa	90.00	20.00	12.00

1952 Bowman

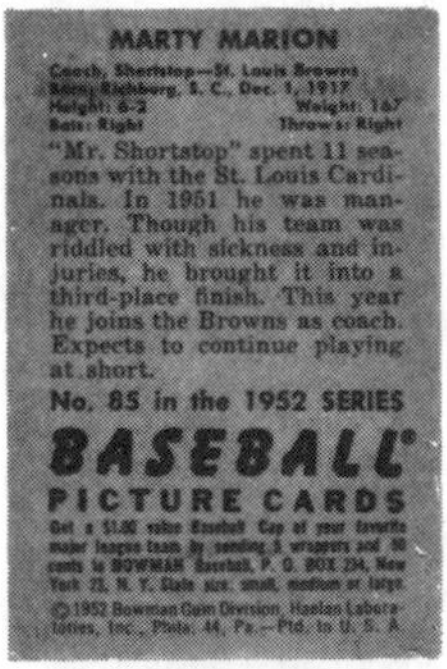

Bowman reverted back to a 252-card set in 1952, but retained the card size (2-1/16" by 3-1/8") employed the preceding year. The cards, which are color art reproductions of actual photographs, feature a facsimile autograph on the fronts. Artwork for 15 cards that were never issued was uncovered several years ago and a set featuring those cards was subsequently made available to the collecting public.

	NR MT	EX	VG
Complete Set:	8500.00	4250.00	2750.
Common Player: 1-36	18.00	9.00	5.50
Common Player: 37-216	18.00	9.00	5.50
Common Player: 217-252	30.00	15.00	9.00

		NR MT	EX	VG
Common Player: 1-36		12.00	6.00	3.50
Common Player: 37-216		12.00	6.00	3.50
Common Player: 217-252		20.00	10.00	6.00
1	Larry "Yogi" Berra	550.00	200.00	75.00
2	Bobby Thomson	30.00	10.00	6.00
3	Fred Hutchinson	14.00	7.00	4.25
4	Robin Roberts	50.00	25.00	15.00
5	*Orestes Minoso*	75.00	38.00	23.00
6	Virgil "Red" Stallcup	12.00	6.00	3.50
7	Mike Garcia	14.00	7.00	4.25
8	Harold "Pee Wee" Reese	120.00	60.00	35.00
9	Vern Stephens	12.00	6.00	3.50
10	Bob Hooper	12.00	6.00	3.50
11	Ralph Kiner	50.00	25.00	15.00
12	Max Surkont	12.00	6.00	3.50
13	Cliff Mapes	12.00	6.00	3.50
14	Cliff Chambers	12.00	6.00	3.50
15	Sam Mele	12.00	6.00	3.50
16	Omar Lown	12.00	6.00	3.50
17	Ed Lopat	25.00	12.50	7.50
18	Don Mueller	12.00	6.00	3.50
19	Bob Cain	12.00	6.00	3.50
20	Willie Jones	12.00	6.00	3.50
21	Nelson Fox	50.00	25.00	15.00
22	Willard Ramsdell	12.00	6.00	3.50
23	Bob Lemon	35.00	17.50	10.50
24	Carl Furillo	20.00	10.00	6.00
25	Maurice McDermott	12.00	6.00	3.50
26	Eddie Joost	12.00	6.00	3.50
27	Joe Garagiola	80.00	40.00	25.00
28	Roy Hartsfield	12.00	6.00	3.50
29	Ned Garver	12.00	6.00	3.50
30	Al "Red" Schoendienst	60.00	30.00	18.00
31	Eddie Yost	12.00	6.00	3.50
32	Eddie Miksis	12.00	6.00	3.50
33	*Gil McDougald*	50.00	25.00	15.00
34	Al Dark	16.00	8.00	4.75
35	Gran Hamner	12.00	6.00	3.50
36	Cass Michaels	12.00	6.00	3.50
37	Vic Raschi	18.00	9.00	5.50
38	Whitey Lockman	12.00	6.00	3.50
39	Vic Wertz	12.00	6.00	3.50
40	Emory Church	12.00	6.00	3.50
41	Chico Carrasquel	12.00	6.00	3.50
42	Johnny Wyrostek	12.00	6.00	3.50
43	Bob Feller	90.00	45.00	27.00
44	Roy Campanella	175.00	87.00	52.00
45	Johnny Pesky	12.00	6.00	3.50
46	Carl Scheib	12.00	6.00	3.50
47	Pete Castiglione	12.00	6.00	3.50
48	Vern Bickford	12.00	6.00	3.50
49	Jim Hearn	12.00	6.00	3.50
50	Gerry Staley	12.00	6.00	3.50
51	Gil Coan	12.00	6.00	3.50
52	Phil Rizzuto	80.00	40.00	25.00
53	Richie Ashburn	50.00	25.00	15.00
54	Billy Pierce	12.00	6.00	3.50
55	Ken Raffensberger	12.00	6.00	3.50
56	Clyde King	12.00	6.00	3.50
57	Clyde Vollmer	12.00	6.00	3.50
58	Hank Majeski	12.00	6.00	3.50
59	Murray Dickson (Murry)	12.00	6.00	3.50
60	Sid Gordon	12.00	6.00	3.50
61	Tommy Byrne	12.00	6.00	3.50
62	Joe Presko	12.00	6.00	3.50
63	Irv Noren	12.00	6.00	3.50
64	Roy Smalley	12.00	6.00	3.50
65	Hank Bauer	20.00	10.00	6.00
66	Sal Maglie	20.00	10.00	6.00
67	Johnny Groth	12.00	6.00	3.50
68	Jim Busby	12.00	6.00	3.50
69	Joe Adcock	20.00	10.00	6.00
70	Carl Erskine	20.00	10.00	6.00
71	Vernon Law	12.00	6.00	3.50
72	Earl Torgeson	12.00	6.00	3.50
73	Jerry Coleman	18.00	9.00	5.50
74	Wes Westrum	12.00	6.00	3.50
75	George Kell	40.00	20.00	12.00
76	Del Ennis	12.00	6.00	3.50
77	Eddie Robinson	12.00	6.00	3.50
78	Lloyd Merriman	12.00	6.00	3.50
79	Lou Brissie	12.00	6.00	3.50
80	Gil Hodges	60.00	30.00	15.00
81	Billy Goodman	12.00	6.00	3.50
82	Gus Zernial	12.00	6.00	3.50
83	Howie Pollet	12.00	6.00	3.50
84	Sam Jethroe	12.00	6.00	3.50
85	Marty Marion	12.00	6.00	3.50
86	Cal Abrams	12.00	6.00	3.50
87	Mickey Vernon	12.00	6.00	3.50

		NR MT	EX	VG
88	Bruce Edwards	12.00	6.00	3.50
89	Billy Hitchcock	12.00	6.00	3.50
90	Larry Jansen	12.00	6.00	3.50
91	Don Kolloway	12.00	6.00	3.50
92	Eddie Waitkus	12.00	6.00	3.50
93	Paul Richards	12.00	6.00	3.50
94	Luke Sewell	12.00	6.00	3.50
95	Luke Easter	12.00	6.00	3.50
96	Ralph Branca	18.00	9.00	5.50
97	Willard Marshall	12.00	6.00	3.50
98	Jimmy Dykes	12.00	6.00	3.50
99	Clyde McCullough	12.00	6.00	3.50
100	Sibby Sisti	12.00	6.00	3.50
101	Mickey Mantle	2000.00	1000.00	600.00
102	Peanuts Lowrey	12.00	6.00	3.50
103	Joe Haynes	12.00	6.00	3.50
104	Hal Jeffcoat	12.00	6.00	3.50
105	Bobby Brown	18.00	9.00	5.50
106	Randy Gumpert	12.00	6.00	3.50
107	Del Rice	12.00	6.00	3.50
108	George Metkovich	12.00	6.00	3.50
109	Tom Morgan	15.00	7.50	4.50
110	Max Lanier	12.00	6.00	3.50
111	Walter "Hoot" Evers	12.00	6.00	3.50
112	Forrest "Smokey" Burgess	12.00	6.00	3.50
113	Al Zarilla	12.00	6.00	3.50
114	Frank Hiller	12.00	6.00	3.50
115	Larry Doby	20.00	10.00	6.00
116	Duke Snider	175.00	87.00	52.00
117	Bill Wight	12.00	6.00	3.50
118	Ray Murray	12.00	6.00	3.50
119	Bill Howerton	12.00	6.00	3.50
120	Chet Nichols	12.00	6.00	3.50
121	Al Corwin	12.00	6.00	3.50
122	Billy Johnson	12.00	6.00	3.50
123	Sid Hudson	12.00	6.00	3.50
124	George Tebbetts	12.00	6.00	3.50
125	Howie Fox	12.00	6.00	3.50
126	Phil Cavarretta	12.00	6.00	3.50
127	Dick Sisler	12.00	6.00	3.50
128	Don Newcombe	30.00	15.00	9.00
129	Gus Niarhos	12.00	6.00	3.50
130	Allie Clark	12.00	6.00	3.50
131	Bob Swift	12.00	6.00	3.50
132	Dave Cole	12.00	6.00	3.50
133	Dick Kryhoski	12.00	6.00	3.50
134	Al Brazle	12.00	6.00	3.50
135	Mickey Harris	12.00	6.00	3.50
136	Gene Hermanski	12.00	6.00	3.50
137	Stan Rojek	12.00	6.00	3.50
138	Ted Wilks	12.00	6.00	3.50
139	Jerry Priddy	12.00	6.00	3.50
140	Ray Scarborough	12.00	6.00	3.50
141	Hank Edwards	12.00	6.00	3.50
142	Early Wynn	40.00	20.00	12.00
143	Sandalio Consuegra	12.00	6.00	3.50
144	Joe Hatten	12.00	6.00	3.50
145	Johnny Mize	50.00	30.00	15.00
146	Leo Durocher	35.00	17.50	10.50
147	Marlin Stuart	12.00	6.00	3.50
148	Ken Heintzelman	12.00	6.00	3.50
149	Howie Judson	12.00	6.00	3.50
150	Herman Wehmeier	12.00	6.00	3.50
151	Al "Flip" Rosen	20.00	10.00	6.00
152	Billy Cox	12.00	6.00	3.50
153	Fred Hatfield	12.00	6.00	3.50
154	Ferris Fain	12.00	6.00	3.50
155	Billy Meyer	12.00	6.00	3.50
156	Warren Spahn	80.00	40.00	24.00
157	Jim Delsing	12.00	6.00	3.50
158	Bucky Harris	30.00	15.00	9.00
159	Dutch Leonard	12.00	6.00	3.50
160	Eddie Stanky	12.00	6.00	3.50
161	Jackie Jensen	25.00	12.50	7.50
162	Monte Irvin	50.00	25.00	15.00
163	Johnny Lipon	12.00	6.00	3.50
164	Connie Ryan	12.00	6.00	3.50
165	Saul Rogovin	12.00	6.00	3.50
166	Bobby Adams	12.00	6.00	3.50
167	Bob Avila	12.00	6.00	3.50
168	Preacher Roe	25.00	12.50	7.50
169	Walt Dropo	12.00	6.00	3.50
170	Joe Astroth	12.00	6.00	3.50
171	Mel Queen	12.00	6.00	3.50
172	Ebba St. Claire	12.00	6.00	3.50
173	Gene Bearden	12.00	6.00	3.50
174	Mickey Grasso	12.00	6.00	3.50
175	Ransom Jackson	12.00	6.00	3.50
176	Harry Brecheen	12.00	6.00	3.50
177	Gene Woodling	20.00	10.00	6.00
178	Dave Williams	12.00	6.00	3.50

		NR MT	EX	VG
179	Pete Suder	12.00	6.00	3.50
180	Eddie Fitzgerald (Fitz Gerald)	12.00	6.00	3.50
181	Joe Collins	15.00	7.50	4.50
182	Dave Koslo	12.00	6.00	3.50
183	Pat Mullin	12.00	6.00	3.50
184	Curt Simmons	12.00	6.00	3.50
185	Eddie Stewart	12.00	6.00	3.50
186	Frank Smith	12.00	6.00	3.50
187	Jim Hegan	12.00	6.00	3.50
188	Charlie Dressen	15.00	7.50	4.50
189	Jim Piersall	18.00	9.00	5.50
190	Dick Fowler	12.00	6.00	3.50
191	*Bob Friend*	15.00	7.50	4.50
192	John Cusick	12.00	6.00	3.50
193	Bobby Young	12.00	6.00	3.50
194	Bob Porterfield	12.00	6.00	3.50
195	Frank Baumholtz	12.00	6.00	3.50
196	Stan Musial	450.00	225.00	135.00
197	Charlie Silvera	15.00	7.50	4.50
198	Chuck Diering	12.00	6.00	3.50
199	Ted Gray	12.00	6.00	3.50
200	Ken Silvestri	12.00	6.00	3.50
201	Ray Coleman	12.00	6.00	3.50
202	Harry Perkowski	12.00	6.00	3.50
203	Steve Gromek	12.00	6.00	3.50
204	Andy Pafko	12.00	6.00	3.50
205	Walt Masterson	12.00	6.00	3.50
206	Elmer Valo	12.00	6.00	3.50
207	George Strickland	12.00	6.00	3.50
208	Walker Cooper	12.00	6.00	3.50
209	Dick Littlefield	12.00	6.00	3.50
210	Archie Wilson	12.00	6.00	3.50
211	Paul Minner	12.00	6.00	3.50
212	Solly Hemus	12.00	6.00	3.50
213	Monte Kennedy	12.00	6.00	3.50
214	Ray Boone	12.00	6.00	3.50
215	Sheldon Jones	12.00	6.00	3.50
216	Matt Batts	12.00	6.00	3.50
217	Casey Stengel	125.00	67.00	37.00
218	Willie Mays	900.00	450.00	275.00
219	Neil Berry	25.00	12.50	7.50
220	Russ Meyer	25.00	12.50	7.50
221	Lou Kretlow	25.00	12.50	7.50
222	Homer "Dixie" Howell	25.00	12.50	7.50
223	Harry Simpson	25.00	12.50	7.50
224	Johnny Schmitz	27.00	13.50	8.00
225	Del Wilber	25.00	12.50	7.50
226	Alex Kellner	25.00	12.50	7.50
227	Clyde Sukeforth	25.00	12.50	7.50
228	Bob Chipman	25.00	12.50	7.50
229	Hank Arft	25.00	12.50	7.50
230	Frank Shea	25.00	12.50	7.50
231	Dee Fondy	25.00	12.50	7.50
232	Enos Slaughter	75.00	38.00	23.00
233	Bob Kuzava	32.00	16.00	9.50
234	Fred Fitzsimmons	25.00	12.50	7.50
235	Steve Souchock	25.00	12.50	7.50
236	Tommy Brown	25.00	12.50	7.50
237	Sherman Lollar	27.00	13.50	8.00
238	*Roy McMillan*	27.00	13.50	8.00
239	Dale Mitchell	25.00	12.50	7.50
240	*Billy Loes*	35.00	17.50	10.50
241	Mel Parnell	27.00	13.50	8.00
242	Everett Kell	25.00	12.50	7.50
243	George "Red" Munger	25.00	12.50	7.50
244	*Lew Burdette*	60.00	30.00	18.00
245	George Schmees	25.00	12.50	7.50
246	Jerry Snyder	25.00	12.50	7.50
247	John Pramesa	25.00	12.50	7.50
248	Bill Werle	25.00	12.50	7.50
249	Henry Thompson	25.00	12.50	7.50
250	Ivan Delock	25.00	12.50	7.50
251	Jack Lohrke	32.00	12.50	7.50
252	Frank Crosetti	125.00	30.00	15.00

1953 Bowman Color

The first set of current major league players featuring actual color photographs, the 160-card 1953 Bowman Color set remains one of the most popular issues of the post-war era. The set is greatly appreciated for its uncluttered look; card fronts that contain no names, teams or facsimile autographs. Bowman increased the size of their cards to a 2-1/2" by 3-3/4" size in order to better compete with Topps Chewing Gum. Bowman copied an idea from the 1952 Topps set and developed card backs that gave player

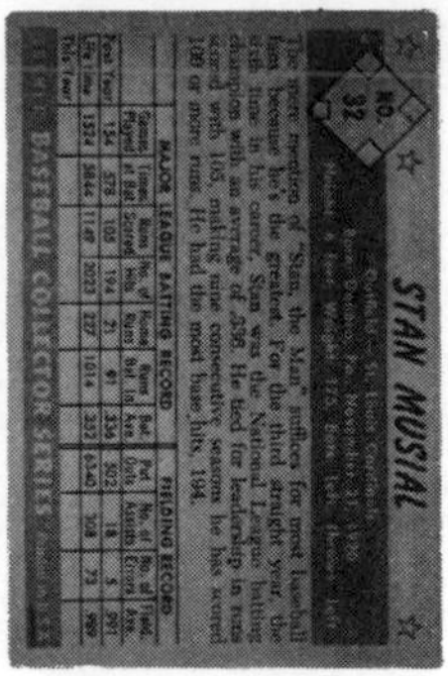

career and previous year statistics. The high-numbered cards (#'s 113-160) are the scarcest of the set, with #'s 113-128 being exceptionally difficult to find.

		NR MT	EX	VG
Complete Set:		10000.00	5000.00	3000.
Common Player: 1-112		25.00	12.50	7.50
Common Player: 113-128		35.00	17.50	10.50
Common Player: 129-160		35.00	17.50	10.50
1	Davey Williams	90.00	15.00	9.00
2	Vic Wertz	25.00	12.50	7.50
3	Sam Jethroe	25.00	12.50	7.50
4	Art Houtteman	25.00	12.50	7.50
5	Sid Gordon	25.00	12.50	7.50
6	Joe Ginsberg	25.00	12.50	7.50
7	Harry Chiti	25.00	12.50	7.50
8	Al Rosen	40.00	20.00	12.00
9	Phil Rizzuto	90.00	45.00	27.00
10	Richie Ashburn	75.00	38.00	23.00
11	Bobby Shantz	25.00	12.50	7.50
12	Carl Erskine	50.00	30.00	15.00
13	Gus Zernial	25.00	12.50	7.50
14	Billy Loes	25.00	12.50	7.50
15	Jim Busby	25.00	12.50	7.50
16	Bob Friend	25.00	12.50	7.50
17	Gerry Staley	25.00	12.50	7.50
18	Nelson Fox	60.00	30.00	18.00
19	Al Dark	30.00	15.00	9.00
20	Don Lenhardt	25.00	12.50	7.50
21	Joe Garagiola	60.00	30.00	18.00
22	Bob Porterfield	25.00	12.50	7.50
23	Herman Wehmeier	25.00	12.50	7.50
24	Jackie Jensen	35.00	17.50	10.50
25	Walter "Hoot" Evers	25.00	12.50	7.50
26	Roy McMillan	25.00	12.50	7.50
27	Vic Raschi	40.00	20.00	12.00
28	Forrest "Smoky" Burgess	25.00	12.50	7.50
29	Roberto Avila	25.00	12.50	7.50
30	Phil Cavarretta	25.00	12.50	7.50
31	Jimmy Dykes	25.00	12.50	7.50
32	Stan Musial	400.00	160.00	100.00
33	Harold "Peewee" Reese	300.00	150.00	90.00
34	Gil Coan	25.00	12.50	7.50
35	Maury McDermott	25.00	12.50	7.50
36	Orestes Minoso	50.00	30.00	15.00
37	Jim Wilson	25.00	12.50	7.50
38	Harry Byrd	25.00	12.50	7.50
39	Paul Richards	25.00	12.50	7.50
40	Larry Doby	35.00	17.50	10.50
41	Sammy White	25.00	12.50	7.50
42	Tommy Brown	25.00	12.50	7.50
43	Mike Garcia	25.00	12.50	7.50
44	Hank Bauer, Yogi Berra, Mickey Mantle	350.00	175.00	105.00
45	Walt Dropo	25.00	12.50	7.50
46	Roy Campanella	250.00	125.00	75.00
47	Ned Garver	25.00	12.50	7.50
48	Hank Sauer	25.00	12.50	7.50
49	Eddie Stanky	25.00	12.50	7.50
50	Lou Kretlow	25.00	12.50	7.50
51	Monte Irvin	50.00	25.00	15.00
52	Marty Marion	25.00	12.50	7.50
53	Del Rice	25.00	12.50	7.50
54	Chico Carrasquel	25.00	12.50	7.50
55	Leo Durocher	50.00	30.00	15.00
56	Bob Cain	25.00	12.50	7.50
57	Lou Boudreau	50.00	25.00	15.00
58	Willard Marshall	25.00	12.50	7.50
59	Mickey Mantle	1300.00	650.00	375.00

		NR MT	EX	VG
70	Clint Courtney	30.00	15.00	9.00
71	Paul Minner	30.00	15.00	9.00
72	Ted Gray	30.00	15.00	9.00
73	Billy Pierce	30.00	15.00	9.00
74	Don Mueller	30.00	15.00	9.00
75	Saul Rogovin	30.00	15.00	9.00
76	Jim Hearn	30.00	15.00	9.00
77	Mickey Grasso	30.00	15.00	9.00
78	Carl Furillo	40.00	20.00	12.00
79	Ray Boone	30.00	15.00	9.00
80	Ralph Kiner	80.00	40.00	25.00
81	Enos Slaughter	70.00	35.00	21.00
82	Joe Astroth	30.00	15.00	9.00
83	Jack Daniels	30.00	15.00	9.00
84	Hank Bauer	50.00	25.00	15.00
85	Solly Hemus	30.00	15.00	9.00
86	Harry Simpson	30.00	15.00	9.00
87	Harry Perkowski	30.00	15.00	9.00
88	Joe Dobson	30.00	15.00	9.00
89	Sandalio Consuegra	30.00	15.00	9.00
90	Joe Nuxhall	30.00	15.00	9.00
91	Steve Souchock	30.00	15.00	9.00
92	Gil Hodges	100.00	45.00	27.00
93	Billy Martin, Phil Rizzuto	200.00	100.00	60.00
94	Bob Addis	30.00	15.00	9.00
95	Wally Moses	30.00	15.00	9.00
96	Sal Maglie	40.00	20.00	12.00
97	Eddie Mathews	150.00	75.00	45.00
98	Hector Rodriquez	30.00	15.00	9.00
99	Warren Spahn	125.00	62.00	37.00
100	Bill Wight	30.00	15.00	9.00
101	Al "Red" Schoendienst	80.00	40.00	25.00
102	Jim Hegan	30.00	15.00	9.00
103	Del Ennis	30.00	15.00	9.00
104	Luke Easter	30.00	15.00	9.00
105	Eddie Joost	30.00	15.00	9.00
106	Ken Raffensberger	30.00	15.00	9.00
107	Alex Kellner	30.00	15.00	9.00
108	Bobby Adams	30.00	15.00	9.00
109	Ken Wood	30.00	15.00	9.00
110	Bob Rush	30.00	15.00	9.00
111	Jim Dyck	30.00	15.00	9.00
112	Toby Atwell	30.00	15.00	9.00
113	Karl Drews	40.00	20.00	12.00
114	Bob Feller	250.00	125.00	75.00
115	Cloyd Boyer	40.00	20.00	12.00
116	Eddie Yost	40.00	20.00	12.00
117	Duke Snider	475.00	237.00	152.00
118	Billy Martin	300.00	150.00	90.00
119	Dale Mitchell	40.00	20.00	12.00
120	Marlin Stuart	40.00	20.00	12.00
121	Yogi Berra	500.00	250.00	150.00
122	Bill Serena	40.00	20.00	12.00
123	Johnny Lipon	40.00	20.00	12.00
124	Charlie Dressen	45.00	23.00	13.50
125	Fred Hatfield	40.00	20.00	12.00
126	Al Corwin	40.00	20.00	12.00
127	Dick Kryhoski	40.00	20.00	12.00
128	Whitey Lockman	40.00	20.00	12.00
129	Russ Meyer	50.00	25.00	15.00
130	Cass Michaels	40.00	20.00	12.00
131	Connie Ryan	40.00	20.00	12.00
132	Fred Hutchinson	50.00	25.00	15.00
133	Willie Jones	40.00	20.00	12.00
134	Johnny Pesky	50.00	25.00	15.00
135	Bobby Morgan	50.00	25.00	15.00
136	Jim Brideweser	40.00	20.00	12.00
137	Sam Dente	40.00	20.00	12.00
138	Bubba Church	40.00	20.00	12.00
139	Pete Runnels	50.00	25.00	15.00
140	Alpha Brazle	40.00	20.00	12.00
141	Frank "Spec" Shea	40.00	20.00	12.00
142	Larry Miggins	40.00	20.00	12.00
143	Al Lopez	60.00	30.00	18.00
144	Warren Hacker	40.00	20.00	12.00
145	George Shuba	50.00	25.00	15.00
146	Early Wynn	125.00	62.00	40.00
147	Clem Koshorek	40.00	20.00	12.00
148	Billy Goodman	40.00	20.00	12.00
149	Al Corwin	40.00	20.00	12.00
150	Carl Scheib	40.00	20.00	12.00
151	Joe Adcock	40.00	20.00	12.00
152	Clyde Vollmer	40.00	20.00	12.00
153	Ed "Whitey" Ford	400.00	200.00	125.00
154	Omar "Turk" Lown	40.00	20.00	12.00
155	Allie Clark	40.00	20.00	12.00
156	Max Surkont	40.00	20.00	12.00
157	Sherman Lollar	50.00	25.00	15.00
158	Howard Fox	40.00	20.00	12.00
159	Mickey Vernon (Photo actually Floyd Baker)	40.00	17.50	10.50
160	Cal Abrams	90.00	30.00	15.00

1953 Bowman Black & White

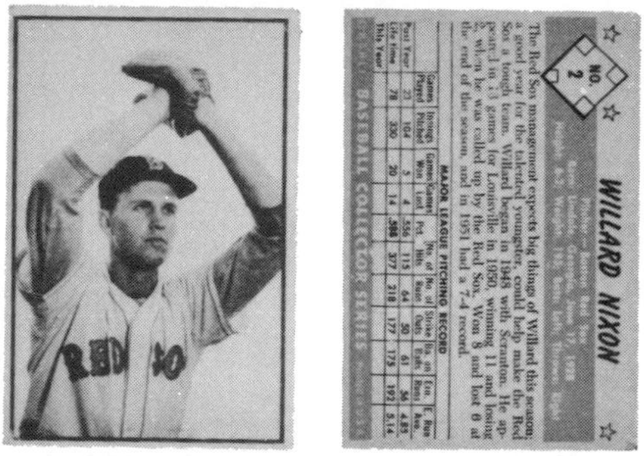

The 1953 Bowman Black and White set is similar in all respects to the 1953 Bowman Color set, except that it lacks color. Purportedly, high costs in producing the color series forced Bowman to issue the set in black and white. Sixty-four cards, which measure 2-1/2" by 3-3/4", comprise the set.

		NR MT	EX	VG
Complete Set:		2300.00	1150.00	500.00
Common Player:		30.00	15.00	9.00
1	Gus Bell	125.00	55.00	35.00
2	Willard Nixon	32.00	11.00	6.50
3	Bill Rigney	32.00	16.00	9.50
4	Pat Mullin	30.00	15.00	9.00
5	Dee Fondy	30.00	15.00	9.00
6	Ray Murray	30.00	15.00	9.00
7	Andy Seminick	30.00	15.00	9.00
8	Pete Suder	30.00	15.00	9.00
9	Walt Masterson	30.00	15.00	9.00
10	Dick Sisler	30.00	15.00	9.00
11	Dick Gernert	30.00	15.00	9.00
12	Randy Jackson	30.00	15.00	9.00
13	Joe Tipton	30.00	15.00	9.00
14	Bill Nicholson	30.00	15.00	9.00
15	Johnny Mize	110.00	50.00	28.00
16	Stu Miller	30.00	15.00	9.00
17	Virgil Trucks	32.00	16.00	9.50
18	Billy Hoeft	30.00	15.00	9.00
19	Paul LaPalme	30.00	15.00	9.00
20	Eddie Robinson	30.00	15.00	9.00
21	Clarence "Bud" Podbielan	30.00	15.00	9.00
22	Matt Batts	30.00	15.00	9.00
23	Wilmer Mizell	30.00	15.00	9.00
24	Del Wilber	30.00	15.00	9.00
25	John Sain	60.00	30.00	18.00
26	Preacher Roe	60.00	30.00	18.00
27	Bob Lemon	110.00	55.00	33.00
28	Hoyt Wilhelm	110.00	55.00	33.00
29	Sid Hudson	30.00	15.00	9.00
30	Walker Cooper	30.00	15.00	9.00
31	Gene Woodling	40.00	20.00	12.00
32	Rocky Bridges	30.00	15.00	9.00
33	Bob Kuzava	32.00	16.00	9.50
34	Ebba St. Clair (St. Claire)	30.00	15.00	9.00
35	Johnny Wyrostek	30.00	15.00	9.00
36	Jim Piersall	50.00	25.00	15.00
37	Hal Jeffcoat	30.00	15.00	9.00
38	Dave Cole	30.00	15.00	9.00
39	Casey Stengel	300.00	150.00	90.00
40	Larry Jansen	30.00	15.00	9.00
41	Bob Ramazotti	30.00	15.00	9.00
42	Howie Judson	30.00	15.00	9.00
43	Hal Bevan	30.00	15.00	9.00
44	Jim Delsing	30.00	15.00	9.00
45	Irv Noren	32.00	16.00	9.50
46	Bucky Harris	70.00	35.00	21.00
47	Jack Lohrke	30.00	15.00	9.00
48	Steve Ridzik	30.00	15.00	9.00
49	Floyd Baker	30.00	15.00	9.00
50	Emil "Dutch" Leonard	30.00	15.00	9.00
51	Lou Burdette	50.00	25.00	15.00

		NR MT	EX	VG
52	Ralph Branca	40.00	20.00	12.00
53	Morris Martin	30.00	15.00	9.00
54	Bill Miller	32.00	16.00	9.50
55	Don Johnson	30.00	15.00	9.00
56	Roy Smalley	30.00	15.00	9.00
57	Andy Pafko	30.00	15.00	9.00
58	Jim Konstanty	30.00	15.00	9.00
59	Duane Pillette	30.00	15.00	9.00
60	Billy Cox	30.00	15.00	9.00
61	Tom Gorman	32.00	16.00	9.50
62	Keith Thomas	30.00	15.00	9.00
63	Steve Gromek	32.00	16.00	9.50
64	Andy Hansen	45.00	13.50	6.50
81	Joe Black	50.00	25.00	15.00

1954 Bowman

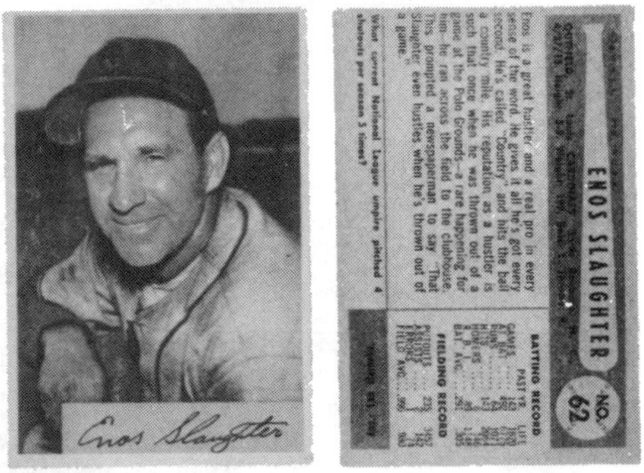

Bowman's 1954 set consists of 224 full-color cards that measure 2-1/2" by 3-3/4". It is believed that contractual problems caused the pulling of card #66 (Ted Williams) from the set, creating one of the most sought-after scarcities of the post-war era. The Williams card was replaced by Jim Piersall (who is also #210) in subsequent print runs. The set contains over 40 variations, most involving statistical errors on the card backs that were corrected. Neither variation carries a premium value as both varieties appear to have been printed in equal amounts. The complete set price that follows does not include all variations or #66 Williams.

	NR MT	EX	VG
Complete Set:	4000.00	2000.00	1200.
Common Player: 1-112	8.00	4.00	2.50
Common Player:113-224	5.00	3.00	

		NR MT	EX	VG
1	Phil Rizzuto	150.00	50.00	21.00
2	Jack Jensen	15.00	7.50	4.50
3	Marion Fricano	8.00	4.00	2.50
4	Bob Hooper	8.00	4.00	2.50
5	William Hunter	8.00	4.00	2.50
6	Nelson Fox	20.00	10.00	6.00
7	Walter Dropo	8.00	4.00	2.50
8	James F. Busby	8.00	4.00	2.50
9	Dave Williams	8.00	4.00	2.50
10	Carl Daniel Erskine	12.00	6.00	3.50
11	Sid Gordon	8.00	4.00	2.50
12a	Roy McMillan (551/1290 At Bat)	8.00	4.00	2.50
12b	Roy McMillan (557/1296 At Bat)	8.00	4.00	2.50
13	Paul Minner	8.00	4.00	2.50
14	Gerald Staley	8.00	4.00	2.50
15	Richie Ashburn	30.00	15.00	9.00
16	Jim Wilson	8.00	4.00	2.50
17	Tom Gorman	8.00	4.00	2.50
18	Walter "Hoot" Evers	8.00	4.00	2.50
19	Bobby Shantz	8.00	4.00	2.50
20	Artie Houtteman	8.00	4.00	2.50
21	Victor Wertz	8.00	4.00	2.50
22a	Sam Mele (213/1661 Putouts)	8.00	4.00	2.50
22b	Sam Mele (217/1665 Putouts)	8.00	4.00	2.50
23	*Harvey Kuenn*	25.00	12.50	7.50
24	Bob Porterfield	8.00	4.00	2.50
25a	Wes Westrum (1.000/.987 Field Avg.)	8.00	4.00	2.50
25b	Wes Westrum (.982/.986 Field Avg.)	8.00	4.00	2.50
26a	Billy Cox (1.000/.960 Field Avg.)	8.00	4.00	2.50
26b	Billy Cox (.972/.960 Field Avg.)	8.00	4.00	2.50
27	Richard Roy Cole	8.00	4.00	2.50
28a	Jim Greengrass (Birthplace Addison, N.J.)	8.00	4.00	2.50
28b	Jim Greengrass (Birthplace Addison, N.Y.)	8.00	4.00	2.50
29	Johnny Klippstein	8.00	4.00	2.50
30	Delbert Rice Jr.	8.00	4.00	2.50
31	"Smoky" Burgess	8.00	4.00	2.50
32	Del Crandall	8.00	4.00	2.50
33a	Victor Raschi (no traded line)	12.00	6.00	3.50
33b	Victor Raschi (with traded line)	25.00	12.50	7.50
34	Sammy White	8.00	4.00	2.50
35a	Eddie Joost (quiz answer is 8)	8.00	4.00	2.50
35b	Eddie Joost (quiz answer is 33)	8.00	4.00	2.50
36	George Strickland	8.00	4.00	2.50
37	Dick Kokos	8.00	4.00	2.50
38a	Orestes Minoso (.895/.961 Field Avg.)	8.00	4.00	2.50
38b	Orestes Minoso (.963/.963 Field Avg.)	8.00	4.00	2.50
39	Ned Garver	8.00	4.00	2.50
40	Gil Coan	8.00	4.00	2.50
41a	Alvin Dark (.986/.960 Field Avg.)	8.00	4.00	2.50
41b	Alvin Dark (.968/.960 Field Avg.)	8.00	4.00	2.50
42	Billy Loes	8.00	4.00	2.50
43a	Robert B. Friend (20 shutouts in quiz question)	8.00	4.00	2.50
43b	Robert B. Friend (16 shutouts in quiz question)	8.00	4.00	2.50
44	Harry Perkowski	8.00	4.00	2.50
45	Ralph Kiner	40.00	20.00	12.00
46	Eldon Repulski	8.00	4.00	2.50
47a	Granville Hamner (.970/.953 Field Avg.)	8.00	4.00	2.50
47b	Granville Hamner (.953/.951 Field Avg.)	8.00	4.00	2.50
48	Jack Dittmer	8.00	4.00	2.50
49	Harry Byrd	8.00	4.00	2.50
50	George Kell	25.00	12.50	7.50
51	Alex Kellner	8.00	4.00	2.50
52	Myron N. Ginsberg	8.00	4.00	2.50
53a	Don Lenhardt (.969/.984 Field Avg.)	8.00	4.00	2.50
53b	Don Lenhardt (.966/.983 Field Avg.)	8.00	4.00	2.50
54	Alfonso Carrasquel	8.00	4.00	2.50
55	Jim Delsing	8.00	4.00	2.50
56	Maurice M. McDermott	8.00	4.00	2.50
57	Hoyt Wilhelm	25.00	12.50	7.50
58	"Pee Wee" Reese	60.00	30.00	18.00
59	Robert D. Schultz	8.00	4.00	2.50
60	Fred Baczewski	8.00	4.00	2.50
61a	Eddie Miksis (.954/.962 Field Avg.)	8.00	4.00	2.50
61b	Eddie Miksis (.954/.961 Field Avg.)	8.00	4.00	2.50
62	Enos Slaughter	40.00	20.00	12.00
63	Earl Torgeson	8.00	4.00	2.50
64	Ed Mathews	60.00	30.00	18.00
65	Mickey Mantle	800.00	400.00	250.00
66a	Ted Williams	3000.00	1500.00	900.00
66b	Jimmy Piersall	90.00	45.00	27.00
67a	Carl Scheib (.306 Pct. with two lines under bio)	8.00	4.00	2.50
67b	Carl Scheib (.306 Pct. with one line under bio)	8.00	4.00	2.50
67c	Carl Scheib (.300 Pct.)	8.00	4.00	2.50
68	Bob Avila	8.00	4.00	2.50
69	Clinton Courtney	8.00	4.00	2.50
70	Willard Marshall	8.00	4.00	2.50
71	Ted Gray	8.00	4.00	2.50
72	Ed Yost	8.00	4.00	2.50
73	Don Mueller	8.00	4.00	2.50
74	James Gilliam	15.00	7.50	4.50
75	Max Surkont	8.00	4.00	2.50
76	Joe Nuxhall	8.00	4.00	2.50
77	Bob Rush	8.00	4.00	2.50
78	Sal A. Yvars	8.00	4.00	2.50
79	Curt Simmons	8.00	4.00	2.50
80a	John Logan (106 Runs)	8.00	4.00	2.50
80b	John Logan (100 Runs)	8.00	4.00	2.50
81a	Jerry Coleman (1.000/.975 Field Avg.)	8.00	4.00	2.50
81b	Jerry Coleman (.952/.975 Field Avg.)	8.00	4.00	2.50
82a	Bill Goodman (.965/.986 Field Avg.)	8.00	4.00	2.50
82b	Bill Goodman (.972/.985 Field Avg.)	8.00	4.00	2.50
83	Ray Murray	8.00	4.00	2.50

		NR MT	EX	VG
80b	John Logan (100 Runs)	6.00	3.00	1.75
81a	Jerry Coleman (1.000/.975 Field Avg.)	8.00	4.00	2.50
81b	Jerry Coleman (.952/.975 Field Avg.)	8.00	4.00	2.50
82a	Bill Goodman (.965/.986 Field Avg.)	6.00	3.00	1.75
82b	Bill Goodman (.972/.985 Field Avg.)	6.00	3.00	1.75
83	Ray Murray	6.00	3.00	1.75
84	Larry Doby	8.00	4.00	2.50
85a	Jim Dyck (.926/.956 Field Avg.)	6.00	3.00	1.75
85b	Jim Dyck (.947/.960 Field Avg.)	6.00	3.00	1.75
86	Harry Dorish	6.00	3.00	1.75
87	Don Lund	6.00	3.00	1.75
88	Tommy Umphlett	6.00	3.00	1.75
89	Willie May (Mays)	350.00	175.00	105.00
90	Roy Campanella	150.00	60.00	38.00
91	Cal Abrams	6.00	3.00	1.75
92	Kenneth David Raffensberger	6.00	3.00	1.75
93a	Bill Serena (.983/.966 Field Avg.)	6.00	3.00	1.75
93b	Bill Serena (.977/.966 Field Avg.)	6.00	3.00	1.75
94a	Solly Hemus (476/1343 Assists)	6.00	3.00	1.75
94b	Solly Hemus (477/1343 Assists)	6.00	3.00	1.75
95	Robin Roberts	30.00	15.00	9.00
96	Joe Adcock	6.00	3.00	1.75
97	Gil McDougald	15.00	7.50	4.50
98	Ellis Kinder	6.00	3.00	1.75
99a	Peter Suder (.985/.974 Field Avg.)	6.00	3.00	1.75
99b	Peter Suder (.978/.974 Field Avg.)	6.00	3.00	1.75
100	Mike Garcia	6.00	3.00	1.75
101	*Don James Larsen*	30.00	15.00	9.00
102	Bill Pierce	6.00	3.00	1.75
103a	Stephen Souchock (144/1192 Putouts)	6.00	3.00	1.75
103b	Stephen Souchock (147/1195 Putouts)	6.00	3.00	1.75
104	Frank Spec Shea	6.00	3.00	1.75
105a	Sal Maglie (quiz answer is 8)	6.00	3.00	1.75
105b	Sal Maglie (quiz answer is 1904)	6.00	3.00	1.75
106	"Clem" Labine	6.00	3.00	1.75
107	Paul E. LaPalme	6.00	3.00	1.75
108	Bobby Adams	6.00	3.00	1.75
109	Roy Smalley	6.00	3.00	1.75
110	Al Schoendienst	35.00	17.50	10.50
111	Murry Monroe Dickson	6.00	3.00	1.75
112	Andy Pafko	6.00	3.00	1.75
113	Allie Reynolds	12.00	6.00	3.50
114	Willard Nixon	10.00	5.00	3.00
115	Don Bollweg	10.00	5.00	3.00
116	Luscious Luke Easter	10.00	5.00	3.00
117	Dick Kryhoski	10.00	5.00	3.00
118	Robert R. Boyd	10.00	5.00	3.00
119	Fred Hatfield	10.00	5.00	3.00
120	Mel Hoderlein	10.00	5.00	3.00
121	Ray Katt	10.00	5.00	3.00
122	Carl Furillo	15.00	7.50	4.50
123	Toby Atwell	10.00	5.00	3.00
124a	Gus Bell (15/27 Errors)	10.00	5.00	3.00
124b	Gus Bell (11/26 Errors)	10.00	5.00	3.00
125	Warren Hacker	10.00	5.00	3.00
126	Cliff Chambers	10.00	5.00	3.00
127	Del Ennis	10.00	5.00	3.00
128	Ebba St Claire	10.00	5.00	3.00
129	Hank Bauer	20.00	10.00	6.00
130	Milt Bolling	10.00	5.00	3.00
131	Joe Astroth	10.00	5.00	3.00
132	Bob Feller	80.00	40.00	25.00
133	Duane Pillette	10.00	5.00	3.00
134	Luis Aloma	10.00	5.00	3.00
135	Johnny Pesky	10.00	5.00	3.00
136	Clyde Vollmer	10.00	5.00	3.00
137	Elmer N. Corwin Jr.	10.00	5.00	3.00
138a	Gil Hodges (.993/.991 Field Avg.)	50.00	25.00	15.00
138b	Gil Hodges (.992/.991 Field Avg.)	55.00	28.00	16.50
139a	Preston Ward (.961/.992 Field Avg.)	10.00	5.00	3.00
139b	Preston Ward (.990/.992 Field Avg.)	10.00	5.00	3.00
140a	Saul Rogovin (7-12 Won/Lost with 2 Strikeouts)	10.00	5.00	3.00
140b	Saul Rogovin (7-12 Won/Lost with 62 Strikeouts)	10.00	5.00	3.00
140c	Saul Rogovin (8-12 Won/Lost)	10.00	5.00	3.00
141	Joe Garagiola	45.00	23.00	13.50
142	Al Brazle	10.00	5.00	3.00
143	Puddin Head Jones	10.00	5.00	3.00
144	Ernie Johnson	10.00	5.00	3.00
145a	Billy Martin (.985/.983 Field Avg.)	50.00	25.00	15.00
145b	Billy Martin (.983/.982 Field Avg.)	60.00	30.00	18.00
146	Dick Gernert	10.00	5.00	3.00
147	Joe DeMaestri	10.00	5.00	3.00
148	Dale Mitchell	10.00	5.00	3.00
149	Bob Young	10.00	5.00	3.00
150	Cass Michaels	10.00	5.00	3.00
151	Patrick J. Mullin	10.00	5.00	3.00
152	Mickey Vernon	10.00	5.00	3.00
153a	Whitey Lockman (100/331 Assists)	10.00	5.00	3.00
153b	Whitey Lockman (102/333 Assists)	10.00	5.00	3.00
154	Don Newcombe	20.00	10.00	6.00
155	*Frank J. Thomas*	10.00	5.00	3.00
156a	Everett Lamar Bridges (320/467 Assists)	10.00	5.00	3.00
156b	Everett Lamar Bridges (328/475 Assists)	10.00	5.00	3.00
157	Omar Lown	10.00	5.00	3.00
158	Stu Miller	10.00	5.00	3.00
159	John Lindell	10.00	5.00	3.00
160	Danny O'Connell	10.00	5.00	3.00
161	Yogi Berra	135.00	67.00	40.00
162	Ted Lepcio	10.00	5.00	3.00
163a	Dave Philley (152 Games with no traded line)	10.00	5.00	3.00
163b	Dave Philley (152 Games with traded line)	25.00	12.50	7.50
163c	Dave Philley (157 Games with traded line)	10.00	5.00	3.00
164	Early "Gus" Wynn	35.00	17.50	10.50
165	Johnny Groth	10.00	5.00	3.00
166	Sandalio Consuegra	10.00	5.00	3.00
167	Bill Hoeft	10.00	5.00	3.00
168	Edward Fitzgerald (Fitz Gerald)	10.00	5.00	3.00
169	Larry Jansen	10.00	5.00	3.00
170	Edwin D. Snider	150.00	75.00	45.00
171	Carlos Bernier	10.00	5.00	3.00
172	Andy Seminick	10.00	5.00	3.00
173	Dee V. Fondy Jr.	10.00	5.00	3.00
174a	Peter Paul Castiglione (.966/.959 Field Avg.)	10.00	5.00	3.00
174b	Peter Paul Castiglione (.970/.959 Field Avg.)	10.00	5.00	3.00
175	Melvin E. Clark	10.00	5.00	3.00
176	Vernon Bickford	10.00	5.00	3.00
177	Edward Ford	80.00	40.00	25.00
178	Del Wilber	10.00	5.00	3.00
179a	Morris Martin (44 ERA)	10.00	5.00	3.00
179b	Morris Martin (4.44 ERA)	10.00	5.00	3.00
180	Joe Tipton	10.00	5.00	3.00
181	Lester Moss	10.00	5.00	3.00
182	Sherman Lollar	10.00	5.00	3.00
183	Matt Batts	10.00	5.00	3.00
184	Mickey Grasso	10.00	5.00	3.00
185a	*Daryl Spencer* (.941/.944 Field Avg.)	10.00	5.00	3.00
185b	*Daryl Spencer* (.933/.936 Field Avg.)	10.00	5.00	3.00
186	Russell Meyer	10.00	5.00	3.00
187	Verne Law (Vern)	10.00	5.00	3.00
188	Frank Smith	10.00	5.00	3.00
189	Ransom Jackson	10.00	5.00	3.00
190	Joe Presko	10.00	5.00	3.00
191	Karl A. Drews	10.00	5.00	3.00
192	Selva L. Burdette	10.00	5.00	3.00
193	Eddie Robinson	12.00	6.00	3.50
194	Sid Hudson	10.00	5.00	3.00
195	Bob Cain	10.00	5.00	3.00
196	Bob Lemon	35.00	17.50	10.50
197	Lou Kretlow	10.00	5.00	3.00
198	Virgil Trucks	10.00	5.00	3.00
199	Steve Gromek	10.00	5.00	3.00
200	C. Marrero	10.00	5.00	3.00
201	Bob Thomson	10.00	5.00	3.00
202	George Shuba	10.00	5.00	3.00
203	Vic Janowicz	10.00	5.00	3.00
204	Jack Collum	10.00	5.00	3.00
205	Hal Jeffcoat	10.00	5.00	3.00
206	Steve Bilko	10.00	5.00	3.00
207	Stan Lopata	10.00	5.00	3.00
208	Johnny Antonelli	10.00	5.00	3.00
209	Gene Woodling (photo reversed)	12.00	6.00	3.50
210	Jimmy Piersall	12.00	6.00	3.50
211	Alfred James Robertson Jr.	10.00	5.00	3.00
212a	Owen L. Friend (.964/.957 Field Avg.)	10.00	5.00	3.00

		NR MT	EX	VG
212b	Owen L. Friend (.967/.958 Field Avg.)	10.00	5.00	3.00
213	Dick Littlefield	10.00	5.00	3.00
214	Ferris Fain	10.00	5.00	3.00
215	Johnny Bucha	10.00	5.00	3.00
216a	Jerry Snyder (.988/.988 Field Avg.)	10.00	5.00	3.00
216b	Jerry Snyder (.968/.968 Field Avg.)	10.00	5.00	3.00
217a	Henry Thompson (.956/.951 Field Avg.)	10.00	5.00	3.00
217b	Henry Thompson (.958/.952 Field Avg.)	10.00	5.00	3.00
218	Preacher Roe	12.00	6.00	3.50
219	Hal Rice	10.00	5.00	3.00
220	Hobie Landrith	10.00	5.00	3.00
221	Frank Baumholtz	10.00	5.00	3.00
222	Memo Luna	10.00	5.00	3.00
223	Steve Ridzik	10.00	5.00	3.00
224	William Bruton	30.00	9.00	4.00

1955 Bowman

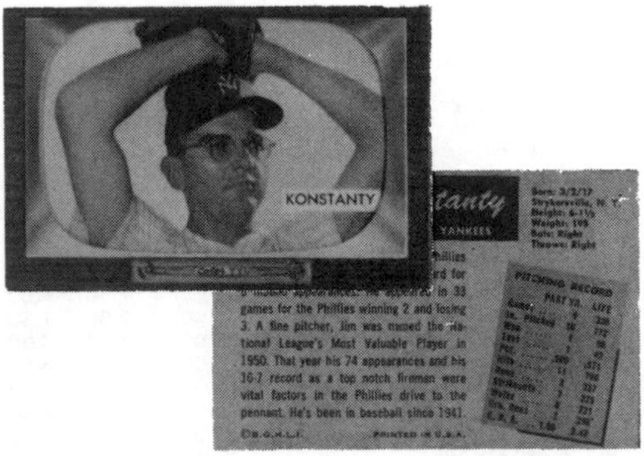

Bowman produced its final baseball card set in 1955, a popular issue which has player photographs placed inside a television set design. The set consists of 320 cards that measure 2-1/2" by 3-3/4" in size. The high-numbered cards (#'s 225-320) are scarcest in the set and include 31 umpire cards.

	NR MT	EX	VG
Complete Set:	4500.00	2300.00	1350.
Common Player: 1-224	4.00	2.00	1.25
Common Player: 225-320	15.00	7.50	4.50

		NR MT	EX	VG
1	Hoyt Wilhelm	100.00	20.00	12.00
2	Al Dark	8.00	4.00	2.00
3	Joe Coleman	4.00	2.00	1.25
4	Eddie Waitkus	4.00	2.00	1.25
5	Jim Robertson	4.00	2.00	1.25
6	Pete Suder	4.00	2.00	1.25
7	Gene Baker	4.00	2.00	1.25
8	Warren Hacker	4.00	2.00	1.25
9	Gil McDougald	12.00	6.00	3.50
10	Phil Rizzuto	40.00	20.00	12.00
11	Billy Bruton	4.00	2.00	1.25
12	Andy Pafko	6.00	3.00	1.75
13	Clyde Vollmer	4.00	2.00	1.25
14	Gus Keriazakos	4.00	2.00	1.25
15	*Frank Sullivan*	6.00	3.00	1.75
16	Jim Piersall	7.00	3.50	2.00
17	Del Ennis	6.00	3.00	1.75
18	Stan Lopata	4.00	2.00	1.25
19	Bobby Avila	4.00	2.00	1.25
20	Al Smith	4.00	2.00	1.25
21	Don Hoak	7.00	3.50	2.00
22	Roy Campanella	100.00	50.00	30.00
23	Al Kaline	125.00	62.00	37.00
24	Al Aber	4.00	2.00	1.25
25	Orestes "Minnie" Minoso	15.00	7.50	4.50
26	Virgil Trucks	6.00	3.00	1.75
27	Preston Ward	4.00	2.00	1.25
28	Dick Cole	4.00	2.00	1.25
29	Al "Red" Schoendienst	30.00	15.00	10.50
30	Bill Sarni	4.00	2.00	1.25
31	Johnny Temple	4.00	2.00	1.25
32	Wally Post	4.00	2.00	1.25
33	Nelson Fox	18.00	9.00	5.50
34	Clint Courtney	4.00	2.00	1.25
35	Bill Tuttle	4.00	2.00	1.25
36	Wayne Belardi	4.00	2.00	1.25
37	Harold "Pee Wee" Reese	60.00	30.00	18.00
38	Early Wynn	20.00	10.00	6.00
39	Bob Darnell	6.00	3.00	1.75
40	Vic Wertz	6.00	3.00	1.75
41	Mel Clark	4.00	2.00	1.25
42	Bob Greenwood	4.00	2.00	1.25
43	Bob Buhl	6.00	3.00	1.75
44	Danny O'Connell	4.00	2.00	1.25
45	Tom Umphlett	4.00	2.00	1.25
46	Mickey Vernon	6.00	3.00	1.75
47	Sammy White	4.00	2.00	1.25
48a	Milt Bolling (Frank Bolling back)	6.00	3.00	1.75
48b	Milt Bolling (Milt Bolling back)	15.00	7.50	4.50
49	Jim Greengrass	4.00	2.00	1.25
50	Hobie Landrith	4.00	2.00	1.25
51	Elvin Tappe	4.00	2.00	1.25
52	Hal Rice	4.00	2.00	1.25
53	Alex Kellner	4.00	2.00	1.25
54	Don Bollweg	4.00	2.00	1.25
55	Cal Abrams	4.00	2.00	1.25
56	Billy Cox	4.00	2.00	1.25
57	Bob Friend	6.00	3.00	1.75
58	Frank Thomas	4.00	2.00	1.25
59	Ed "Whitey" Ford	70.00	35.00	20.00
60	Enos Slaughter	25.00	12.50	7.50
61	Paul LaPalme	4.00	2.00	1.25
62	Royce Lint	4.00	2.00	1.25
63	Irv Noren	8.00	4.00	2.50
64	Curt Simmons	6.00	3.00	1.75
65	*Don Zimmer*	25.00	12.50	7.50
66	George Shuba	6.00	3.00	1.75
67	Don Larsen	15.00	7.50	4.50
68	*Elston Howard*	40.00	20.00	12.00
69	Bill Hunter	8.00	4.00	2.50
70	Lou Burdette	7.00	3.50	2.00
71	Dave Jolly	4.00	2.00	1.25
72	Chet Nichols	4.00	2.00	1.25
73	Eddie Yost	4.00	2.00	1.25
74	Jerry Snyder	4.00	2.00	1.25
75	Brooks Lawrence	4.00	2.00	1.25
76	Tom Poholsky	4.00	2.00	1.25
77	Jim McDonald	4.00	2.00	1.25
78	Gil Coan	4.00	2.00	1.25
79	Willie Miranda	4.00	2.00	1.25
80	Lou Limmer	4.00	2.00	1.25
81	Bob Morgan	4.00	2.00	1.25
82	Lee Walls	4.00	2.00	1.25
83	Max Surkont	4.00	2.00	1.25
84	George Freese	4.00	2.00	1.25
85	Cass Michaels	4.00	2.00	1.25
86	Ted Gray	4.00	2.00	1.25
87	Randy Jackson	4.00	2.00	1.25
88	Steve Bilko	4.00	2.00	1.25
89	Lou Boudreau	20.00	10.00	6.00
90	Art Ditmar	4.00	2.00	1.25
91	Dick Marlowe	4.00	2.00	1.25
92	George Zuverink	4.00	2.00	1.25
93	Andy Seminick	4.00	2.00	1.25
94	Hank Thompson	4.00	2.00	1.25
95	Sal Maglie	12.00	6.00	3.50
96	Ray Narleski	4.00	2.00	1.25
97	John Podres	15.00	7.50	4.50
98	James "Junior" Gilliam	12.00	6.00	3.50
99	Jerry Coleman	8.00	4.00	2.50
100	Tom Morgan	8.00	4.00	2.50
101a	Don Johnson (Ernie Johnson (Braves) on front)	6.00	3.00	1.75
101b	Don Johnson (Don Johnson (Orioles) on front)	15.00	7.50	4.50
102	Bobby Thomson	12.00	6.00	3.50
103	Eddie Mathews	45.00	23.00	13.50
104	Bob Porterfield	4.00	2.00	1.25
105	Johnny Schmitz	4.00	2.00	1.25
106	Del Rice	4.00	2.00	1.25
107	Solly Hemus	4.00	2.00	1.25
108	Lou Kretlow	4.00	2.00	1.25
109	Vern Stephens	4.00	2.00	1.25
110	Bob Miller	4.00	2.00	1.25
111	Steve Ridzik	4.00	2.00	1.25
112	Gran Hamner	4.00	2.00	1.25
113	Bob Hall	4.00	2.00	1.25
114	Vic Janowicz	4.00	2.00	1.25
115	Roger Bowman	4.00	2.00	1.25
116	Sandalio Consuegra	4.00	2.00	1.25
117	Johnny Groth	4.00	2.00	1.25
118	Bobby Adams	4.00	2.00	1.25
119	Joe Astroth	4.00	2.00	1.25
120	Ed Burtschy	4.00	2.00	1.25
121	Rufus Crawford	4.00	2.00	1.25
122	Al Corwin	4.00	2.00	1.25

No.	Player	NR MT	EX	VG
132a	Harvey Kueen (incorrect spelling on back)	7.00	3.50	2.00
132b	Harvey Kuenn (correct spelling on back)	30.00	15.00	9.00
133	Charles King	7.00	3.50	2.00
134	Bob Feller	55.00	28.00	16.50
135	Lloyd Merriman	7.00	3.50	2.00
136	Rocky Bridges	7.00	3.50	2.00
137	Bob Talbot	7.00	3.50	2.00
138	Davey Williams	7.00	3.50	2.00
139	Billy & Bobby Shantz	7.00	3.50	2.00
140	Bobby Shantz	8.00	4.00	2.50
141	Wes Westrum	8.00	4.00	2.50
142	Rudy Regalado	7.00	3.50	2.00
143	Don Newcombe	25.00	12.50	7.50
144	Art Houtteman	7.00	3.50	2.00
145	Bob Nieman	7.00	3.50	2.00
146	Don Liddle	7.00	3.50	2.00
147	Sam Mele	7.00	3.50	2.00
148	Bob Chakales	7.00	3.50	2.00
149	Cloyd Boyer	7.00	3.50	2.00
150	Bill Klaus	7.00	3.50	2.00
151	Jim Brideweser	7.00	3.50	2.00
152	Johnny Klippstein	7.00	3.50	2.00
153	Eddie Robinson	8.00	4.00	2.50
154	*Frank Lary*	7.00	3.50	2.00
155	Gerry Staley	7.00	3.50	2.00
156	Jim Hughes	8.00	4.00	2.50
157a	Ernie Johnson (Don Johnson (Orioles) picture on front)	8.00	4.00	2.50
157b	Ernie Johnson (Ernie Johnson (Braves) picture on front)	18.00	9.00	5.50
158	Gil Hodges	40.00	20.00	12.00
159	Harry Byrd	7.00	3.50	2.00
160	Bill Skowron	25.00	12.50	7.50
161	Matt Batts	7.00	3.50	2.00
162	Charlie Maxwell	7.00	3.50	2.00
163	Sid Gordon	7.00	3.50	2.00
164	Toby Atwell	7.00	3.50	2.00
165	Maurice McDermott	7.00	3.50	2.00
166	Jim Busby	7.00	3.50	2.00
167	Bob Grim	8.00	4.00	2.50
168	Larry "Yogi" Berra	80.00	40.00	25.00
169	Carl Furillo	25.00	12.50	7.50
170	Carl Erskine	15.00	7.50	4.50
171	Robin Roberts	30.00	15.00	9.00
172	Willie Jones	7.00	3.50	2.00
173	Al "Chico" Carrasquel	7.00	3.50	2.00
174	Sherman Lollar	8.00	4.00	2.50
175	Wilmer Shantz	7.00	3.50	2.00
176	Joe DeMaestri	7.00	3.50	2.00
177	Willard Nixon	7.00	3.50	2.00
178	Tom Brewer	7.00	3.50	2.00
179	Hank Aaron	225.00	112.00	67.00
180	Johnny Logan	7.00	3.50	2.00
181	Eddie Miksis	7.00	3.50	2.00
182	Bob Rush	7.00	3.50	2.00
183	Ray Katt	7.00	3.50	2.00
184	Willie Mays	225.00	112.00	67.00
185	Vic Raschi	8.00	4.00	2.50
186	Alex Grammas	7.00	3.50	2.00
187	Fred Hatfield	7.00	3.50	2.00
188	Ned Garver	7.00	3.50	2.00
189	Jack Collum	7.00	3.50	2.00
190	Fred Baczewski	7.00	3.50	2.00
191	Bob Lemon	25.00	12.50	7.50
192	George Strickland	7.00	3.50	2.00
193	Howie Judson	7.00	3.50	2.00
194	Joe Nuxhall	8.00	4.00	2.50
195a	Erv Palica (no traded line on back)	7.00	3.50	2.00
195b	Erv Palica (traded line on back)	25.00	12.50	7.50
196	Russ Meyer	8.00	4.00	2.50
197	Ralph Kiner	30.00	15.00	9.00
198	Dave Pope	7.00	3.50	2.00
199	Vernon Law	8.00	4.00	2.50
200	Dick Littlefield	7.00	3.50	2.00
201	Allie Reynolds	25.00	12.50	7.50
202	Mickey Mantle	375.00	175.00	100.00
203	Steve Gromek	7.00	3.50	2.00
204a	*Frank Bolling* (Milt Bolling back)	8.00	4.00	2.50
204b	*Frank Bolling* (Frank Bolling back)	20.00	10.00	6.00
205	Eldon "Rip" Repulski	7.00	3.50	2.00
206	Ralph Beard	7.00	3.50	2.00
207	Frank Shea	7.00	3.50	2.00
208	Eddy Fitzgerald (Fitz Gerald)	7.00	3.50	2.00
209	Forrest "Smoky" Burgess	8.00	4.00	2.50
210	Earl Torgeson	7.00	3.50	2.00
211	John "Sonny" Dixon	7.00	3.50	2.00
212	Jack Dittmer	7.00	3.50	2.00

No.	Player	NR MT	EX	VG
213	George Kell	25.00	12.50	7.50
214	Billy Pierce	8.00	4.00	2.50
215	Bob Kuzava	7.00	3.50	2.00
216	Preacher Roe	8.00	4.00	2.50
217	Del Crandall	8.00	4.00	2.50
218	Joe Adcock	8.00	4.00	2.50
219	Whitey Lockman	7.00	3.50	2.00
220	Jim Hearn	7.00	3.50	2.00
221	Hector "Skinny" Brown	7.00	3.50	2.00
222	Russ Kemmerer	7.00	3.50	2.00
223	Hal Jeffcoat	7.00	3.50	2.00
224	Dee Fondy	7.00	3.50	2.00
225	Paul Richards	16.00	8.00	4.75
226	W.F. McKinley (umpire)	25.00	12.50	7.50
227	Frank Baumholtz	15.00	7.50	4.50
228	John M. Phillips	15.00	7.50	4.50
229	Jim Brosnan	16.00	8.00	4.75
230	Al Brazle	15.00	7.50	4.50
231	Jim Konstanty	25.00	12.50	7.50
232	Birdie Tebbetts	15.00	7.50	4.50
233	Bill Serena	15.00	7.50	4.50
234	Dick Bartell	15.00	7.50	4.50
235	J.A. Paparella (umpire)	25.00	12.50	7.50
236	Murray Dickson (Murry)	15.00	7.50	4.50
237	Johnny Wyrostek	15.00	7.50	4.50
238	Eddie Stanky	16.00	8.00	4.75
239	Edwin A. Rommel (umpire)	25.00	12.50	7.50
240	Billy Loes	16.00	8.00	4.75
241	John Pesky	16.00	8.00	4.75
242	Ernie Banks	350.00	175.00	100.00
243	Gus Bell	16.00	8.00	4.75
244	Duane Pillette	15.00	7.50	4.50
245	Bill Miller	15.00	7.50	4.50
246	Hank Bauer	30.00	15.00	9.00
247	Dutch Leonard	15.00	7.50	4.50
248	Harry Dorish	15.00	7.50	4.50
249	Billy Gardner	15.00	7.50	4.50
250	Larry Napp (umpire)	25.00	12.50	7.50
251	Stan Jok	15.00	7.50	4.50
252	Roy Smalley	15.00	7.50	4.50
253	Jim Wilson	15.00	7.50	4.50
254	Bennett Flowers	15.00	7.50	4.50
255	Pete Runnels	16.00	8.00	4.75
256	Owen Friend	15.00	7.50	4.50
257	Tom Alston	15.00	7.50	4.50
258	John W. Stevens (umpire)	25.00	12.50	7.50
259	*Don Mossi*	25.00	12.50	7.50
260	Edwin H. Hurley (umpire)	25.00	12.50	7.50
261	Walt Moryn	16.00	8.00	4.75
262	Jim Lemon	16.00	8.00	4.75
263	Eddie Joost	15.00	7.50	4.50
264	Bill Henry	15.00	7.50	4.50
265	Albert J. Barlick (umpire)	80.00	40.00	25.00
266	Mike Fornieles	15.00	7.50	4.50
267	George (Jim) Honochick (umpire)	60.00	30.00	18.00
268	Roy Lee Hawes	15.00	7.50	4.50
269	Joe Amalfitano	15.00	7.50	4.50
270	Chico Fernandez	16.00	8.00	4.75
271	Bob Hooper	15.00	7.50	4.50
272	John Flaherty (umpire)	25.00	12.50	7.50
273	Emory "Bubba" Church	15.00	7.50	4.50
274	Jim Delsing	15.00	7.50	4.50
275	William T. Grieve (umpire)	25.00	12.50	7.50
276	Ivan Delock	15.00	7.50	4.50
277	Ed Runge (umpire)	25.00	12.50	7.50
278	*Charles Neal*	25.00	12.50	7.50
279	Hank Soar (umpire)	25.00	12.50	7.50
280	Clyde McCullough	15.00	7.50	4.50
281	Charles Berry (umpire)	25.00	12.50	7.50
282	Phil Cavarretta	16.00	8.00	4.75
283	Nestor Chylak (umpire)	25.00	12.50	7.50
284	William A. Jackowski (umpire)	25.00	12.50	7.50
285	Walt Dropo	16.00	8.00	4.75
286	Frank E. Secory (umpire)	25.00	12.50	7.50
287	Ron Mrozinski	15.00	7.50	4.50
288	Dick Smith	15.00	7.50	4.50
289	Arthur J. Gore (umpire)	25.00	12.50	7.50
290	Hershell Freeman	15.00	7.50	4.50
291	Frank Dascoli (umpire)	25.00	12.50	7.50
292	Marv Blaylock	15.00	7.50	4.50
293	Thomas D. Gorman (umpire)	25.00	12.50	7.50
294	Wally Moses	15.00	7.50	4.50
295	E. Lee Ballanfant (umpire)	25.00	12.50	7.50
296	*Bill Virdon*	30.00	15.00	9.00
297	L.R. "Dusty" Boggess (umpire)	25.00	12.50	7.50
298	Charlie Grimm	25.00	12.50	7.50
299	Lonnie Warneke (umpire)	25.00	12.50	7.50
300	Tommy Byrne	14.00	7.00	4.25
301	William R. Engeln (umpire)	25.00	12.50	7.50
302	*Frank Malzone*	25.00	12.50	7.50

		NR MT	EX	VG
295	E. Lee Ballanfant (umpire)	15.00	7.50	4.50
296	*Bill Virdon*	30.00	15.00	9.00
297	L.R. "Dusty" Boggess (umpire)	15.00	7.50	4.50
298	Charlie Grimm	15.00	7.50	4.50
299	Lonnie Warneke (umpire)	15.00	7.50	4.50
300	Tommy Byrne	14.00	7.00	4.25
301	William R. Engeln (umpire)	15.00	7.50	4.50
302	*Frank Malzone*	25.00	12.50	7.50
303	J.B. "Jocko" Conlan (umpire)	90.00	45.00	30.00
304	Harry Chiti	15.00	7.50	4.50
305	Frank Umont (umpire)	25.00	12.50	7.50
306	Bob Cerv	25.00	12.50	7.50
307	R.A. "Babe" Pinelli (umpire)	25.00	12.50	7.50
308	Al Lopez	40.00	20.00	12.00
309	Hal H. Dixon (umpire)	25.00	12.50	7.50
310	Ken Lehman	16.00	8.00	4.75
311	Lawrence J. Goetz (umpire)	25.00	12.50	7.50
312	Bill Wight	15.00	7.50	4.50
313	A.J. Donatelli (umpire)	25.00	12.50	7.50
314	Dale Mitchell	15.00	7.50	4.50
315	Cal Hubbard (umpire)	90.00	45.00	27.00
316	Marion Fricano	15.00	7.50	4.50
317	Wm. R. Summers (umpire)	25.00	12.50	7.50
318	Sid Hudson	15.00	7.50	4.50
319	Albert B. Schroll	25.00	12.50	7.50
320	George D. Susce, Jr.	60.00	30.00	18.00

1989 Bowman

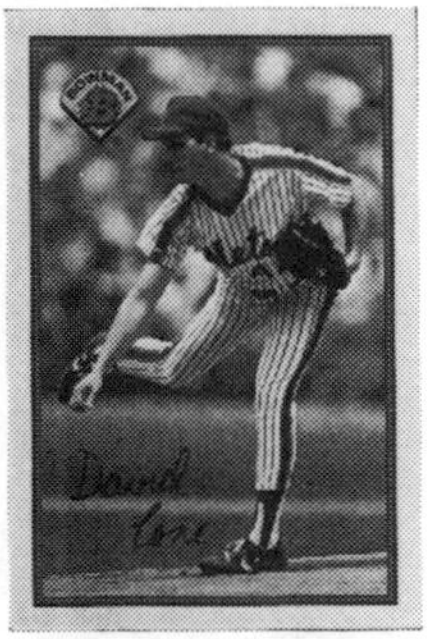

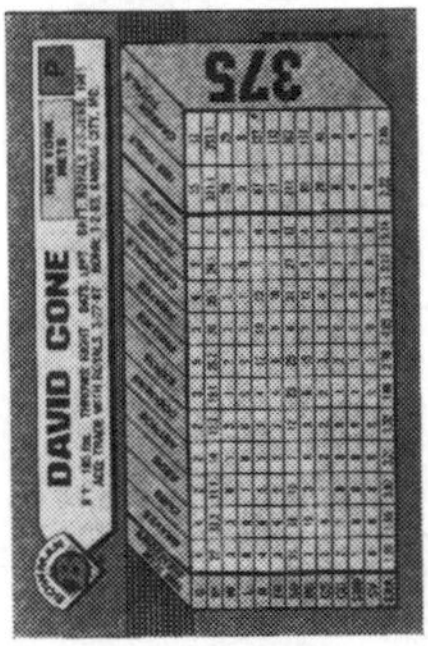

Topps, which purchased the Bowman Co. back in 1955, revived the Bowman name in 1989, issuing a 484-card set modeled after the 1953 Bowman cards. The cards are 2-1/2" by 3-3/4", slightly larger than a current standard-sized card. The fronts contain a full-color player photo, with facsimile autograph on the bottom and the Bowman logo in an upper corner. The unique card backs include a breakdown of the player's stats against each team in his league. A series of "Hot Rookie Stars" highlight the set. The cards were distributed in both wax packs and rack packs. Each pack included a special reproduction of a classic Bowman card with a sweepstakes on the back. The special cards said "reprint" on the front.

	MT	NR MT	EX
Complete Set:	20.00	15.00	8.00
Common Player:	.03	.02	.01

		MT	NR MT	EX
1	Oswald Peraza	.05	.04	.02
2	Brian Holton	.05	.04	.02
3	Jose Bautista	.05	.04	.02
4	Pete Harnisch	.10	.08	.04
5	Dave Schmidt	.03	.02	.01
6	Gregg Olson	.30	.25	.12
7	Jeff Ballard	.10	.08	.04
8	Bob Melvin	.03	.02	.01
9	Cal Ripken	.20	.15	.08
10	Randy Milligan	.08	.06	.03
11	Juan Bell	.15	.11	.06
12	Billy Ripken	.05	.04	.02
13	Jim Traber	.03	.02	.01
14	Pete Stanicek	.03	.02	.01
15	Steve Finley	.20	.15	.08
16	Larry Sheets	.03	.02	.01
17	Phil Bradley	.05	.04	.02
18	Brady Anderson	.10	.08	.04
19	Lee Smith	.03	.02	.01
20	Tom Fischer	.15	.11	.06
21	Mike Boddicker	.03	.02	.01
22	Rob Murphy	.03	.02	.01
23	Wes Gardner	.03	.02	.01
24	John Dopson	.10	.08	.04
25	Bob Stanley	.03	.02	.01
26	Roger Clemens	.20	.15	.08
27	Rich Gedman	.03	.02	.01
28	Marty Barrett	.03	.02	.01
29	Luis Rivera	.03	.02	.01
30	Jody Reed	.05	.04	.02
31	Nick Esasky	.05	.04	.02
32	Wade Boggs	.40	.30	.15
33	Jim Rice	.10	.08	.04
34	Mike Greenwell	.30	.25	.12
35	Dwight Evans	.15	.11	.06
36	Ellis Burks	.25	.20	.10
37	Chuck Finley	.05	.04	.02
38	Kirk McCaskill	.05	.04	.02
39	Jim Abbott	.60	.45	.25
40	Bryan Harvey	.05	.04	.02
41	Bert Blyleven	.08	.06	.03
42	Mike Witt	.03	.02	.01
43	Bob McClure	.03	.02	.01
44	Bill Schroeder	.03	.02	.01
45	Lance Parrish	.05	.04	.02
46	Dick Schofield	.03	.02	.01
47	Wally Joyner	.10	.08	.04
48	Jack Howell	.03	.02	.01
49	Johnny Ray	.03	.02	.01
50	Chili Davis	.05	.04	.02
51	Tony Armas	.03	.02	.01
52	Claudell Washington	.03	.02	.01
53	Brian Downing	.03	.02	.01
54	Devon White	.10	.08	.04
55	Bobby Thigpen	.08	.06	.03
56	Bill Long	.03	.02	.01
57	Jerry Reuss	.03	.02	.01
58	Shawn Hillegas	.03	.02	.01
59	Melido Perez	.05	.04	.02
60	Jeff Bittiger	.05	.04	.02
61	Jack McDowell	.03	.02	.01
62	Carlton Fisk	.10	.08	.04
63	Steve Lyons	.03	.02	.01
64	Ozzie Guillen	.05	.04	.02
65	Robin Ventura	1.25	.90	.50
66	Fred Manrique	.03	.02	.01
67	Dan Pasqua	.03	.02	.01
68	Ivan Calderon	.03	.02	.01
69	Ron Kittle	.03	.02	.01
70	Daryl Boston	.03	.02	.01
71	Dave Gallagher	.05	.04	.02
72	Harold Baines	.08	.06	.03
73	Charles Nagy	.20	.15	.08
74	John Farrell	.03	.02	.01
75	Kevin Wickander	.25	.20	.10
76	Greg Swindell	.15	.11	.06
77	Mike Walker	.15	.11	.06
78	Doug Jones	.05	.04	.02
79	Rich Yett	.03	.02	.01
80	Tom Candiotti	.03	.02	.01
81	Jesse Orosco	.03	.02	.01
82	Bud Black	.03	.02	.01
83	Andy Allanson	.03	.02	.01
84	Pete O'Brien	.05	.04	.02
85	Jerry Browne	.05	.04	.02
86	Brook Jacoby	.03	.02	.01
87	Mark Lewis	.70	.50	.30
88	Luis Aguayo	.03	.02	.01
89	Cory Snyder	.05	.04	.02
90	Oddibe McDowell	.05	.04	.02
91	Joe Carter	.15	.11	.06
92	Frank Tanana	.03	.02	.01
93	Jack Morris	.03	.02	.01
94	Doyle Alexander	.03	.02	.01
95	Steve Searcy	.08	.06	.03
96	Randy Bockus	.05	.04	.02
97	Jeff Robinson	.05	.04	.02
98	Mike Henneman	.05	.04	.02
99	Paul Gibson	.03	.02	.01
100	Frank Williams	.03	.02	.01
101	Matt Nokes	.05	.04	.02
102	Rico Brogna	.15	.11	.06
103	Lou Whitaker	.08	.06	.03
104	Al Pedrique	.03	.02	.01
105	Alan Trammell	.05	.04	.02
106	Chris Brown	.03	.02	.01
107	Pat Sheridan	.03	.02	.01
108	Gary Pettis	.03	.02	.01
109	Keith Moreland	.03	.02	.01
110	Mel Stottlemyre, Jr.	.15	.11	.06

		MT	NR MT	EX
111	Bret Saberhagen	.10	.08	.04
112	Floyd Bannister	.03	.02	.01
113	Jeff Montgomery	.05	.04	.02
114	Steve Farr	.05	.04	.02
115	Tom Gordon	.40	.30	.15
116	Charlie Leibrandt	.03	.02	.01
117	Mark Gubicza	.08	.06	.03
118	Mike MacFarlane	.03	.02	.01
119	Bob Boone	.05	.04	.02
120	Kurt Stillwell	.05	.04	.02
121	George Brett	.15	.11	.06
122	Frank White	.05	.04	.02
123	Kevin Seitzer	.08	.06	.03
124	Willie Wilson	.03	.02	.01
125	Pat Tabler	.03	.02	.01
126	Bo Jackson	1.00	.70	.40
127	Hugh Walker	.20	.15	.08
128	Danny Tartabull	.05	.04	.02
129	Teddy Higuera	.08	.06	.03
130	Don August	.03	.02	.01
131	Juan Nieves	.03	.02	.01
132	Mike Birkbeck	.03	.02	.01
133	Dan Plesac	.05	.04	.02
134	Chris Bosio	.05	.04	.02
135	Bill Wegman	.03	.02	.01
136	Chuck Crim	.03	.02	.01
137	B.J. Surhoff	.05	.04	.02
138	Joey Meyer	.03	.02	.01
139	Dale Sveum	.03	.02	.01
140	Paul Molitor	.08	.06	.03
141	Jim Gantner	.03	.02	.01
142	Gary Sheffield	1.00	.70	.40
143	Greg Brock	.03	.02	.01
144	Robin Yount	.25	.20	.10
145	Glenn Braggs	.03	.02	.01
146	Rob Deer	.03	.02	.01
147	Fred Toliver	.03	.02	.01
148	Jeff Reardon	.03	.02	.01
149	Allan Anderson	.05	.04	.02
150	Frank Viola	.15	.11	.06
151	Shane Rawley	.03	.02	.01
152	Juan Berenguer	.03	.02	.01
153	Johnny Ard	.20	.15	.08
154	Tim Laudner	.03	.02	.01
155	Brian Harper	.03	.02	.01
156	Al Newman	.03	.02	.01
157	Kent Hrbek	.08	.06	.03
158	Gary Gaetti	.08	.06	.03
159	Wally Backman	.03	.02	.01
160	Gene Larkin	.03	.02	.01
161	Greg Gagne	.03	.02	.01
162	Kirby Puckett	.35	.25	.14
163	Danny Gladden	.03	.02	.01
164	Randy Bush	.03	.02	.01
165	Dave LaPoint	.03	.02	.01
166	Andy Hawkins	.03	.02	.01
167	Dave Righetti	.05	.04	.02
168	Lance McCullers	.03	.02	.01
169	Jimmy Jones	.03	.02	.01
170	Al Leiter	.03	.02	.01
171	John Candelaria	.03	.02	.01
172	Don Slaught	.03	.02	.01
173	Jamie Quirk	.03	.02	.01
174	Rafael Santana	.03	.02	.01
175	Mike Pagliarulo	.03	.02	.01
176	Don Mattingly	.40	.30	.15
177	Ken Phelps	.03	.02	.01
178	Steve Sax	.08	.06	.03
179	Dave Winfield	.20	.15	.08
180	Stan Jefferson	.03	.02	.01
181	Rickey Henderson	.40	.30	.15
182	Bob Brower	.03	.02	.01
183	Roberto Kelly	.10	.08	.04
184	Curt Young	.03	.02	.01
185	Gene Nelson	.03	.02	.01
186	Bob Welch	.03	.02	.01
187	Rick Honeycutt	.03	.02	.01
188	Dave Stewart	.08	.06	.03
189	Mike Moore	.08	.06	.03
190	Dennis Eckersley	.08	.06	.03
191	Eric Plunk	.03	.02	.01
192	Storm Davis	.03	.02	.01
193	Terry Steinbach	.10	.08	.04
194	Ron Hassey	.03	.02	.01
195	Stan Royer	.15	.11	.06
196	Walt Weiss	.15	.11	.06
197	Mark McGwire	.40	.30	.15
198	Carney Lansford	.08	.06	.03
199	Glenn Hubbard	.03	.02	.01
200	Dave Henderson	.05	.04	.02
201	Jose Canseco	.60	.45	.25

		MT	NR MT	EX
202	Dave Parker	.05	.04	.02
203	Scott Bankhead	.05	.04	.02
204	Tom Niedenfuer	.03	.02	.01
205	Mark Langston	.15	.11	.06
206	Erik Hanson	.50	.40	.20
207	Mike Jackson	.03	.02	.01
208	Dave Valle	.03	.02	.01
209	Scott Bradley	.03	.02	.01
210	Harold Reynolds	.08	.06	.03
211	Tino Martinez	1.25	.90	.50
212	Rich Renteria	.03	.02	.01
213	Rey Quinones	.03	.02	.01
214	Jim Presley	.03	.02	.01
215	Alvin Davis	.10	.08	.04
216	Edgar Martinez	.03	.02	.01
217	Darnell Coles	.03	.02	.01
218	Jeffrey Leonard	.08	.06	.04
219	Jay Buhner	.03	.02	.01
220	Ken Griffey, Jr.	5.00	3.75	2.00
221	Drew Hall	.03	.02	.01
222	Bobby Witt	.03	.02	.01
223	Jamie Moyer	.03	.02	.01
224	Charlie Hough	.03	.02	.01
225	Nolan Ryan	.70	.50	.30
226	Jeff Russell	.05	.04	.02
227	Jim Sundberg	.03	.02	.01
228	Julio Franco	.15	.11	.06
229	Buddy Bell	.03	.02	.01
230	Scott Fletcher	.03	.02	.01
231	Jeff Kunkel	.03	.02	.01
232	Steve Buechele	.03	.02	.01
233	Monty Fariss	.25	.20	.10
234	Rick Leach	.03	.02	.01
235	Ruben Sierra	.40	.30	.15
236	Cecil Espy	.05	.04	.02
237	Rafael Palmeiro	.10	.08	.04
238	Pete Incaviglia	.03	.02	.01
239	Dave Steib	.05	.04	.02
240	Jeff Musselman	.03	.02	.01
241	Mike Flanagan	.03	.02	.01
242	Todd Stottlemyre	.05	.04	.02
243	Jimmy Key	.05	.04	.02
244	Tony Castillo	.10	.08	.04
245	Alex Sanchez	.05	.04	.02
246	Tom Henke	.03	.02	.01
247	John Cerutti	.03	.02	.01
248	Ernie Whitt	.03	.02	.01
249	Bob Brenly	.03	.02	.01
250	Rance Mulliniks	.03	.02	.01
251	Kelly Gruber	.10	.08	.04
252	Ed Sprague	.20	.15	.08
253	Fred McGriff	.50	.40	.20
254	Tony Fernandez	.08	.06	.03
255	Tom Lawless	.03	.02	.01
256	George Bell	.10	.08	.04
257	Jesse Barfield	.05	.04	.02
258	Sandy Alomar	.20	.15	.08
259	Ken Griffey	1.00	.70	.40
260	Cal Ripken, Sr.	.15	.11	.06
261	Mel Stottlemyre	.15	.11	.06
262	Zane Smith	.03	.02	.01
263	Charlie Puleo	.03	.02	.01
264	Derek Lilliquist	.15	.11	.06
265	Paul Assenmacher	.03	.02	.01
266	John Smoltz	.60	.45	.25
267	Tom Glavine	.10	.08	.04
268	Steve Avery	1.00	.70	.40
269	Pete Smith	.05	.04	.02
270	Jody Davis	.03	.02	.01
271	Bruce Benedict	.03	.02	.01
272	Andres Thomas	.03	.02	.01
273	Gerald Perry	.05	.04	.02
274	Ron Gant	.05	.04	.02
275	Darrell Evans	.03	.02	.01
276	Dale Murphy	.08	.06	.03
277	Dion James	.03	.02	.01
278	Lonnie Smith	.08	.06	.03
279	Geronimo Berroa	.05	.04	.02
280	Steve Wilson	.20	.15	.08
281	Rick Suctcliffe	.05	.04	.02
282	Kevin Coffman	.03	.02	.01
283	Mitch Williams	.10	.08	.04
284	Greg Maddux	.05	.04	.02
285	Paul Kilgus	.03	.02	.01
286	Mike Harkey	.10	.08	.04
287	Lloyd McClendon	.05	.04	.02
288	Damon Berryhill	.05	.04	.02
289	Ty Griffin	.20	.15	.08
290	Ryne Sandberg	.15	.11	.06
291	Mark Grace	.60	.45	.25
292	Curt Wilkerson	.03	.02	.01

		MT	NR MT	EX
293	Vance Law	.03	.02	.01
294	Shawon Dunston	.08	.06	.04
295	Jerome Walton	.50	.40	.20
296	Mitch Webster	.03	.02	.01
297	Dwight Smith	.20	.15	.08
298	Andre Dawson	.15	.11	.06
299	Jeff Sellers	.03	.02	.01
300	Jose Rijo	.05	.04	.02
301	John Franco	.05	.04	.02
302	Rick Mahler	.03	.02	.01
303	Ron Robinson	.03	.02	.01
304	Danny Jackson	.03	.02	.01
305	Rob Dibble	.08	.06	.04
306	Tom Browning	.03	.02	.01
307	Bo Diaz	.03	.02	.01
308	Manny Trillo	.03	.02	.01
309	Chris Sabo	.15	.11	.06
310	Ron Oester	.03	.02	.01
311	Barry Larkin	.15	.11	.06
312	Todd Benzinger	.05	.04	.02
313	Paul O'Neil	.05	.04	.02
314	Kal Daniels	.05	.04	.02
315	Joel Youngblood	.03	.02	.01
316	Eric Davis	.25	.20	.10
317	Dave Smith	.05	.04	.03
318	Mark Portugal	.03	.02	.01
319	Brian Meyer	.03	.02	.01
320	Jim Deshaies	.05	.04	.02
321	Juan Agosto	.03	.02	.01
322	Mike Scott	.10	.08	.04
323	Rick Rhoden	.03	.02	.01
324	Jim Clancy	.03	.02	.01
325	Larry Andersen	.03	.02	.01
326	Alex Trevino	.03	.02	.01
327	Alan Ashby	.03	.02	.01
328	Craig Reynolds	.03	.02	.01
329	Bill Doran	.03	.02	.01
330	Rafael Ramirez	.03	.02	.01
331	Glenn Davis	.10	.08	.04
332	Willie Ansley	.25	.20	.10
333	Gerald Young	.03	.02	.01
334	Cameron Drew	.10	.08	.04
335	Jay Howell	.05	.04	.03
336	Tim Belcher	.05	.04	.03
337	Fernando Valenzuela	.05	.04	.03
338	Ricky Horton	.03	.02	.01
339	Tim Leary	.03	.02	.01
340	Bill Bene	.15	.11	.06
341	Orel Hershiser	.20	.15	.08
342	Mike Scioscia	.05	.04	.02
343	Rick Dempsey	.03	.02	.01
344	Willie Randolph	.03	.02	.01
345	Alfredo Griffin	.03	.02	.01
346	Eddie Murray	.08	.06	.03
347	Mickey Hatcher	.03	.02	.01
348	Mike Sharperson	.03	.02	.01
349	John Shelby	.03	.02	.01
350	Mike Marshall	.03	.02	.01
351	Kirk Gibson	.05	.04	.02
352	Mike Davis	.03	.02	.01
353	Bryn Smith	.03	.02	.01
354	Pascual Perez	.03	.02	.01
355	Kevin Gross	.03	.02	.01
356	Andy McGaffigan	.03	.02	.01
357	Brian Holman	.05	.04	.02
358	Dave Wainhouse	.20	.15	.08
359	Denny Martinez	.03	.02	.01
360	Tim Burke	.03	.02	.01
361	Nelson Santovenia	.08	.06	.04
362	Tim Wallach	.05	.04	.02
363	Spike Owen	.03	.02	.01
364	Rex Hudler	.03	.02	.01
365	Andres Galarraga	.08	.06	.03
366	Otis Nixon	.03	.02	.01
367	Hubie Brooks	.03	.02	.01
368	Mike Aldrete	.03	.02	.01
369	Rock Raines	.08	.06	.03
370	Dave Martinez	.03	.02	.01
371	Bob Ojeda	.03	.02	.01
372	Ron Darling	.05	.04	.02
373	Wally Whitehurst	.20	.15	.08
374	Randy Myers	.05	.04	.02
375	David Cone	.05	.04	.02
376	Doc Gooden	.25	.20	.10
377	Sid Fernandez	.05	.04	.02
378	Dave Proctor	.20	.15	.08
379	Gary Carter	.03	.02	.01
380	Keith Miller	.05	.04	.02
381	Gregg Jefferies	.60	.45	.25
382	Tim Teufel	.03	.02	.01
383	Kevin Elster	.03	.02	.01

		MT	NR MT	EX
384	Dave Magadan	.03	.02	.01
385	Keith Hernandez	.05	.04	.02
386	Mookie Wilson	.05	.04	.02
387	Darryl Strawberry	.40	.30	.15
388	Kevin McReynolds	.10	.08	.04
389	Mark Carreon	.05	.04	.02
390	Jeff Parrett	.05	.04	.02
391	Mike Maddux	.03	.02	.01
392	Don Carman	.03	.02	.01
393	Bruce Ruffin	.03	.02	.01
394	Ken Howell	.03	.02	.01
395	Steve Bedrosian	.05	.04	.02
396	Floyd Youmans	.03	.02	.01
397	Larry McWilliams	.03	.02	.01
398	Pat Combs	.25	.20	.10
399	Steve Lake	.03	.02	.01
400	Dickie Thon	.03	.02	.01
401	Ricky Jordan	.35	.25	.14
402	Mike Schmidt	.60	.45	.25
403	Tom Herr	.03	.02	.01
404	Chris James	.03	.02	.01
405	Juan Samuel	.08	.06	.03
406	Von Hayes	.08	.06	.03
407	Ron Jones	.15	.11	.06
408	Curt Ford	.03	.02	.01
409	Bob Walk	.03	.02	.01
410	Jeff Robinson	.03	.02	.01
411	Jim Gott	.03	.02	.01
412	Scott Medvin	.03	.02	.01
413	John Smiley	.03	.02	.01
414	Bob Kipper	.03	.02	.01
415	Brian Fisher	.03	.02	.01
416	Doug Drabek	.03	.02	.01
417	Mike Lavalliere	.03	.02	.01
418	Ken Oberkfell	.03	.02	.01
419	Sid Bream	.03	.02	.01
420	Austin Manahan	.20	.15	.08
421	Jose Lind	.03	.02	.01
422	Bobby Bonilla	.30	.25	.12
423	Glenn Wilson	.03	.02	.01
424	Andy Van Slyke	.10	.08	.04
425	Gary Redus	.03	.02	.01
426	Barry Bonds	.30	.25	.12
427	Don Heinkel	.03	.02	.01
428	Ken Dayley	.03	.02	.01
429	Todd Worrell	.05	.04	.02
430	Brad DuVall	.20	.15	.08
431	Jose DeLeon	.03	.02	.01
432	Joe Magrane	.10	.08	.04
433	John Ericks	.20	.15	.08
434	Frank DiPino	.03	.02	.01
435	Tony Pena	.05	.04	.02
436	Ozzie Smith	.08	.06	.03
437	Terry Pendleton	.03	.02	.01
438	Jose Oquendo	.03	.02	.01
439	Tim Jones	.05	.04	.02
440	Pedro Guerrero	.10	.08	.04
441	Milt Thompson	.03	.02	.01
442	Willie McGee	.05	.04	.02
443	Vince Coleman	.05	.04	.02
444	Tom Brunansky	.05	.04	.02
445	Walt Terrell	.03	.02	.01
446	Eric Show	.03	.02	.01
447	Mark Davis	.10	.08	.04
448	Andy Benes	.50	.40	.20
449	Eddie Whitson	.03	.02	.01
450	Dennis Rasmussen	.03	.02	.01
451	Bruce Hurst	.03	.02	.01
452	Pat Clements	.03	.02	.01
453	Benito Santiago	.10	.08	.04
454	Sandy Alomar, Jr.	.50	.40	.20
455	Garry Templeton	.03	.02	.01
456	Jack Clark	.05	.04	.02
457	Tim Flannery	.03	.02	.01
458	Roberto Alomar	.80	.60	.30
459	Camelo Martinez	.03	.02	.01
460	John Kruk	.03	.02	.01
461	Tony Gwynn	.20	.15	.08
462	Jerald Clark	.05	.04	.02
463	Don Robinson	.03	.02	.01
464	Craig Lefferts	.03	.02	.01
465	Kelly Downs	.03	.02	.01
466	Rick Rueschel	.05	.04	.02
467	Scott Garrelts	.03	.02	.01
468	Wil Tejada	.03	.02	.01
469	Kirt Manwaring	.10	.08	.04
470	Terry Kennedy	.03	.02	.01
471	Jose Uribe	.03	.02	.01
472	Royce Clayton	.50	.40	.20
473	Robby Thompson	.05	.04	.02
474	Kevin Mitchell	.80	.60	.30

		MT	NR MT	EX
475	Ernie Riles	.03	.02	.01
476	Will Clark	.80	.60	.30
477	Donnell Nixon	.03	.02	.01
478	Candy Maldonado	.03	.02	.01
479	Tracy Jones	.03	.02	.01
480	Brett Butler	.05	.04	.02
481	Checklist	.05	.04	.02
482	Checklist	.05	.04	.02
483	Checklist	.05	.04	.02
484	Checklist	.05	.04	.02

1990 Bowman

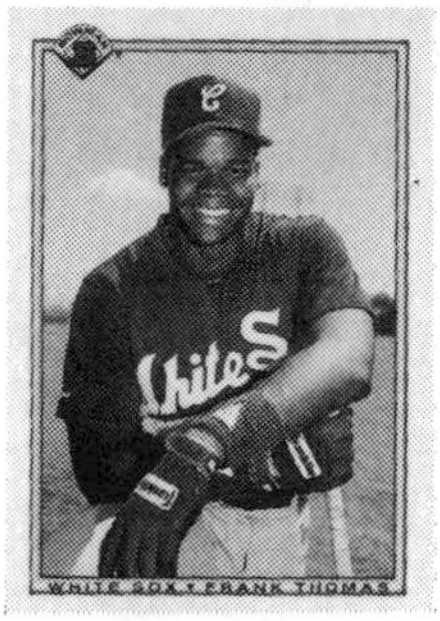

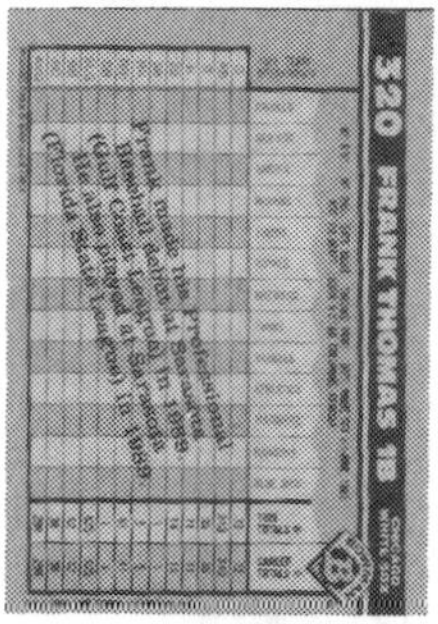

Bowman followed up its 1989 release with 528-card set in 1990. The 1990 cards follow the classic Bowman style featuring a full color photo bordered in white. The Bowman logo appears in the upper left corner. The player's team nickname and name appear on the bottom border of the card photo. Unlike the 1989 set, the 1990 cards measure 2-1/2" by 3-1/2" in size. The card backs are horizontal and display the player's statistics against the teams in his respective league. Included in the set are special insert cards that feature a reproduction of a painting of a modern-day superstar done in the style of the 1951 Bowman cards. The paintings were produced for Bowman by artist Craig Pursley. The card backs contain a sweepstakes offer with a chance to win a complete set of 11 lithographs made from these paintings.

		MT	NR MT	EX
Complete Set:		20.00	15.00	8.00
Common Player:		.05	.04	.02
1	Tommy Greene	.25	.20	.10
2	Tom Glavine	.06	.05	.02
3	Andy Nezelek	.08	.06	.03
4	Mike Stanton	.20	.15	.08
5	Rick Lueken	.08	.06	.03
6	Kent Mercker	.25	.20	.10
7	Derek Lilliquist	.06	.05	.02
8	Charlie Liebrandt	.05	.04	.02
9	Steve Avery	.60	.45	.25
10	John Smoltz	.15	.11	.06
11	Mark Lemke	.08	.06	.03
12	Lonnie Smith	.06	.05	.02
13	Oddibe McDowell	.05	.04	.02
14	Tyler Houston	.30	.25	.12
15	Jeff Blauser	.05	.04	.02
16	Ernie Whitt	.05	.04	.02
17	Alexis Infante	.10	.08	.04
18	Jim Presley	.06	.05	.02
19	Dale Murphy	.10	.08	.04
20	Nick Esasky	.06	.05	.02
21	Rick Sutcliffe	.06	.05	.02
22	Mike Bielecki	.06	.05	.02
23	Steve Wilson	.10	.08	.04
24	Kevin Blankenship	.10	.08	.04
25	Mitch Williams	.10	.08	.04
26	Dean Wilkins	.10	.08	.04
27	Greg Maddux	.12	.09	.05
28	Mike Harkey	.20	.15	.08
29	Mark Grace	.20	.15	.08
30	Ryne Sandberg	.40	.30	.15
31	Greg Smith	.20	.15	.08
32	Dwight Smith	.15	.11	.06
33	Damon Berryhill	.05	.04	.02
34	Earl Cunningham	.30	.25	.12
35	Jerome Walton	.25	.20	.10
36	Lloyd McClendon	.05	.04	.02
37	Ty Griffin	.20	.15	.08
38	Shawon Dunston	.10	.08	.04
39	Andre Dawson	.10	.08	.04
40	Luis Salazar	.05	.04	.02
41	Tim Layana	.20	.15	.08
42	Rob Dibble	.10	.08	.04
43	Tom Browning	.05	.04	.02
44	Danny Jackson	.05	.04	.02
45	Jose Rijo	.06	.05	.02
46	Scott Scudder	.20	.15	.08
47	Randy Myers	.06	.05	.02
48	Brian Lane	.15	.11	.06
49	Paul O'Neill	.05	.04	.02
50	Barry Larkin	.10	.08	.04
51	Reggie Jefferson	.40	.30	.15
52	Jeff Branson	.20	.15	.08
53	Chris Sabo	.08	.06	.03
54	Joe Oliver	.10	.08	.04
55	Todd Benzinger	.05	.04	.02
56	Rolando Roomes	.05	.04	.02
57	Hal Morris	.30	.25	.12
58	Eric Davis	.15	.11	.06
59	Scott Bryant	.20	.15	.08
60	Ken Griffey	.06	.05	.02
61	Darryl Kile	.15	.11	.06
62	Dave Smith	.05	.04	.02
63	Mark Portugal	.05	.04	.02
64	Jeff Juden	.35	.25	.14
65	Bill Guullickson	.05	.04	.02
66	Danny Darwin	.05	.04	.02
67	Larry Andersen	.05	.04	.02
68	Jose Cano	.10	.08	.04
69	Dan Schatzeder	.05	.04	.02
70	Jim Deshaies	.05	.04	.02
71	Mike Scott	.06	.05	.02
72	Gerald Young	.05	.04	.02
73	Ken Caminiti	.05	.04	.02
74	Ken Oberkfell	.05	.04	.02
75	Dave Rhode	.20	.15	.08
76	Bill Doran	.06	.05	.02
77	Andujar Cedeno	.20	.15	.08
78	Craig Biggio	.08	.06	.03
79	Karl Rhodes	.15	.11	.06
80	Glenn Davis	.10	.08	.04
81	Eric Anthony	.30	.25	.12
82	John Wetteland	.20	.15	.08
83	Jay Howell	.06	.05	.02
84	Orel Hershiser	.10	.08	.04
85	Tim Belcher	.08	.06	.03
86	Kiki Jones	.25	.20	.10
87	Mike Hartley	.20	.15	.08
88	Ramon Martinez	.60	.45	.25
89	Mike Scioscia	.06	.05	.02
90	Willie Randolph	.06	.05	.02
91	Juan Samuel	.06	.05	.02
92	Jose Offerman	.30	.25	.12
93	Dave Hansen	.30	.25	.12
94	Jeff Hamilton	.05	.04	.02
95	Alfredo Griffin	.05	.04	.02
96	Tom Goodwin	.35	.25	.14
97	Kirk Gibson	.06	.05	.02
98	Jose Vizcaino	.20	.15	.08
99	Kal Daniels	.06	.05	.02
100	Hubie Brooks	.06	.05	.02
101	Eddie Murray	.08	.06	.03
102	Dennis Boyd	.05	.04	.02
103	Tim Burke	.06	.05	.02
104	Bill Sampen	.20	.15	.08
105	Brett Gideon	.06	.05	.02
106	Mark Gardner	.20	.15	.08
107	Howard Farmer	.15	.11	.06
108	Mel Rojas	.15	.11	.06
109	Kevin Gross	.05	.04	.02
110	Dave Schmidt	.05	.04	.02
111	Denny Martinez	.06	.05	.02
112	Jerry Goff	.10	.08	.04
113	Andres Galarraga	.08	.06	.03
114	Tim Welch	.12	.09	.05
115	Marquis Grissom	.40	.30	.15
116	Spike Owen	.05	.04	.02
117	Larry Walker	.30	.25	.12
118	Rock Raines	.08	.06	.03
119	Delino DeShields	.40	.30	.15
120	Tom Foley	.05	.04	.02
121	Dave Martinez	.05	.04	.02
122	Frank Viola	.10	.08	.04
123	Julio Valera	.15	.11	.06
124	Alejandro Pena	.05	.04	.02
125	David Cone	.08	.06	.03
126	Doc Gooden	.20	.15	.08

		MT	NR MT	EX
127	Kevin Brown	.20	.15	.08
128	John Franco	.08	.06	.03
129	Terry Bross	.25	.20	.10
130	Blaine Beatty	.20	.15	.08
131	Sid Fernandez	.08	.06	.03
132	Mike Marshall	.05	.04	.02
133	Howard Johnson	.10	.08	.04
134	Jaime Roseboro	.20	.15	.08
135	Alan Zinter	.20	.15	.08
136	Keith Miller	.06	.05	.02
137	Kevin Elster	.05	.04	.02
138	Kevin McReynolds	.06	.05	.02
139	Barry Lyons	.05	.04	.02
140	Gregg Jefferies	.25	.20	.10
141	Darryl Strawberry	.25	.20	.10
142	Todd Hundley	.25	.20	.10
143	Scott Service	.15	.11	.06
144	Chuck Malone	.15	.11	.06
145	Steve Ontiveros	.05	.04	.02
146	Roger McDowell	.06	.05	.02
147	Ken Howell	.05	.04	.02
148	Pat Combs	.15	.11	.06
149	Jeff Parrett	.05	.04	.02
150	Chuck McElroy	.15	.11	.06
151	Jason Grimsley	.15	.11	.06
152	Len Dykstra	.08	.06	.03
153	Mickey Morandini	.15	.11	.06
154	John Kruk	.05	.04	.02
155	Dickie Thon	.05	.04	.02
156	Ricky Jordan	.10	.08	.04
157	Jeff Jackson	.10	.08	.04
158	Darren Daulton	.05	.04	.02
159	Tom Herr	.05	.04	.02
160	Von Hayes	.06	.05	.02
161	Dave Hollins	.35	.25	.14
162	Carmelo Martinez	.05	.04	.02
163	Bob Walk	.05	.04	.02
164	Doug Drabek	.08	.06	.03
165	Walt Terrell	.05	.04	.02
166	Bill Landrum	.05	.04	.02
167	Scott Ruskin	.08	.06	.03
168	Bob Patterson	.05	.04	.02
169	Bobby Bonilla	.10	.08	.04
170	Jose Lind	.05	.04	.02
171	Andy Van Slyke	.08	.06	.03
172	Mike LaValliere	.05	.04	.02
173	Willie Greene	.20	.15	.08
174	Jay Bell	.06	.05	.02
175	Sid Bream	.05	.04	.02
176	Tom Prince	.05	.04	.02
177	Wally Backman	.05	.04	.02
178	Moises Alou	.25	.20	.10
179	Steve Carter	.08	.06	.03
180	Gary Redus	.05	.04	.02
181	Barry Bonds	.10	.08	.04
182	Don Slaught	.05	.04	.02
183	Joe Magrane	.06	.05	.02
184	Bryn Smith	.05	.04	.02
185	Todd Worrell	.06	.05	.02
186	Jose Deleon	.05	.04	.02
187	Frank DiPino	.05	.04	.02
188	John Tudor	.05	.04	.02
189	Howard Hilton	.10	.08	.04
190	John Ericks	.10	.08	.04
191	Ken Dayley	.05	.04	.02
192	Ray Lankford	.80	.60	.30
193	Todd Zeile	.80	.60	.30
194	Willie McGee	.06	.05	.02
195	Ozzie Smith	.06	.05	.02
196	Milt Thompson	.05	.04	.02
197	Terry Pendleton	.05	.04	.02
198	Vince Coleman	.06	.05	.02
199	Paul Coleman	.25	.20	.10
200	Jose Oquendo	.05	.04	.02
201	Pedro Guerrero	.06	.05	.02
202	Tom Brunansky	.06	.05	.02
203	Roger Smithberg	.10	.08	.04
204	Eddie Whitson	.05	.04	.02
205	Dennis Rasmussen	.05	.04	.02
206	Craig Lefferts	.05	.04	.02
207	Andy Benes	.15	.11	.06
208	Bruce Hurst	.06	.05	.02
209	Eric Show	.05	.04	.02
210	Rafael Valdez	.10	.08	.04
211	Joey Cora	.05	.04	.02
212	Thomas Howard	.20	.15	.08
213	Rob Nelson	.05	.04	.02
214	Jack Clark	.06	.05	.02
215	Garry Templeton	.05	.04	.02
216	Fred Lynn	.05	.04	.02
217	Tony Gwynn	.08	.06	.03

		MT	NR MT	EX
218	Benny Santiago	.08	.06	.03
219	Mike Pagliarulo	.05	.04	.02
220	Joe Carter	.08	.06	.03
221	Roberto Alomar	.08	.06	.03
222	Bip Roberts	.05	.04	.02
223	Rick Reuschel	.05	.04	.02
224	Russ Swan	.20	.15	.08
225	Eric Gunderson	.20	.15	.08
226	Steve Bedrosian	.05	.04	.02
227	Mike Remlinger	.40	.30	.15
228	Scott Garrelts	.05	.04	.02
229	Ernie Camacho	.05	.04	.02
230	Andres Santana	.25	.20	.10
231	Will Clark	.35	.25	.14
232	Kevin Mitchell	.25	.20	.10
233	Robby Thompson	.05	.04	.02
234	Bill Bathe	.06	.05	.02
235	Tony Perezchica	.08	.06	.03
236	Gary Carter	.05	.04	.02
237	Brett Butler	.05	.04	.02
238	Matt Williams	.15	.11	.06
239	Ernie Riles	.05	.04	.02
240	Kevin Bass	.05	.04	.02
241	Terry Kennedy	.05	.04	.02
242	Steve Hosey	.30	.25	.12
243	Ben McDonald	1.00	.70	.40
244	Jeff Ballard	.05	.04	.02
245	Joe Price	.05	.04	.02
246	Curt Schilling	.05	.04	.02
247	Pete Harnisch	.06	.05	.02
248	Mark Williamson	.05	.04	.02
249	Gregg Olson	.15	.11	.06
250	Chris Myers	.15	.11	.06
251	David Segui	.40	.30	.15
252	Joe Orsulak	.05	.04	.02
253	Craig Worthington	.05	.04	.02
254	Mickey Tettleton	.06	.05	.02
255	Cal Ripken	.08	.06	.03
256	Billy Ripken	.05	.04	.02
257	Randy Milligan	.06	.05	.02
258	Brady Anderson	.05	.04	.02
259	Chris Hoiles	.20	.15	.08
260	Mike Devereaux	.05	.04	.02
261	Phil Bradley	.05	.04	.02
262	Leo Gomez	.30	.25	.12
263	Lee Smith	.06	.05	.02
264	Mike Rochford	.06	.05	.02
265	Jeff Reardon	.06	.05	.02
266	Wes Gardner	.05	.04	.02
267	Mike Boddicker	.05	.04	.02
268	Roger Clemens	.25	.20	.10
269	Rob Murphy	.05	.04	.02
270	Mickey Pina	.25	.20	.10
271	Tony Pena	.06	.05	.02
272	Jody Reed	.06	.05	.02
273	Kevin Romine	.05	.04	.02
274	Mike Greenwell	.08	.06	.03
275	Maurice Vaughn	.80	.60	.30
276	Danny Heep	.05	.04	.02
277	Scott Cooper	.25	.20	.10
278	Greg Blosser	.25	.20	.10
279	Dwight Evans	.06	.05	.02
280	Ellis Burks	.08	.06	.03
281	Wade Boggs	.10	.08	.04
282	Marty Barrett	.05	.04	.02
283	Kirk McCaskill	.06	.05	.02
284	Mark Langston	.06	.05	.02
285	Bert Blyleven	.06	.05	.02
286	Mike Fetters	.08	.06	.03
287	Kyle Abbott	.20	.15	.08
288	Jim Abbott	.10	.08	.04
289	Chuck Finley	.06	.05	.02
290	Gary DiSarcina	.15	.11	.06
291	Dick Schofield	.05	.04	.02
292	Devon White	.06	.05	.02
293	Bobby Rose	.15	.11	.06
294	Brian Downing	.05	.04	.02
295	Lance Parrish	.06	.05	.02
296	Jack Howell	.05	.04	.02
297	Claudell Washington	.05	.04	.02
298	John Orton	.06	.05	.02
299	Wally Joyner	.08	.06	.03
300	Lee Stevens	.30	.25	.12
301	Chili Davis	.05	.04	.02
302	Johnny Ray	.05	.04	.02
303	Greg Hibbard	.15	.11	.06
304	Eric King	.06	.05	.02
305	Jack McDowell	.08	.06	.03
306	Bobby Thigpen	.08	.06	.03
307	Adam Peterson	.05	.04	.02
308	Scott Radinsky	.20	.15	.08

		MT	NR MT	EX
309	Wayne Edwards	.06	.05	.02
310	Melido Perez	.06	.05	.02
311	Robin Ventura	.50	.40	.20
312	Sammy Sosa	.30	.25	.12
313	Dan Pasqua	.05	.04	.02
314	Carlton Fisk	.08	.06	.03
315	Ozzie Guillen	.08	.06	.03
316	Ivan Calderon	.08	.06	.03
317	Daryl Boston	.05	.04	.02
318	Craig Grebeck	.15	.11	.06
319	Scott Fletcher	.05	.04	.02
320	Frank Thomas	4.00	3.00	1.50
321	Steve Lyons	.05	.04	.02
322	Carlos Martinez	.10	.08	.04
323	Joe Skalski	.08	.06	.03
324	Tom Candiotti	.05	.04	.02
325	Greg Swindell	.06	.05	.02
326	Steve Olin	.15	.11	.06
327	Kevin Wickander	.08	.06	.03
328	Doug Jones	.06	.05	.02
329	Jeff Shaw	.10	.08	.04
330	Kevin Bearse	.10	.08	.04
331	Dion James	.05	.04	.02
332	Jerry Browne	.06	.05	.02
333	Joey Belle	.40	.30	.15
334	Felix Fermin	.05	.04	.02
335	Candy Maldonado	.06	.05	.02
336	Cory Snyder	.06	.05	.02
337	Sandy Alomar	.30	.25	.12
338	Mark Lewis	.12	.09	.05
339	Carlos Baerga	.40	.30	.15
340	Chris James	.05	.04	.02
341	Brook Jacoby	.06	.05	.02
342	Keith Hernandez	.06	.05	.02
343	Frank Tanana	.05	.04	.02
344	Scott Aldred	.15	.11	.06
345	Mike Henneman	.06	.05	.02
346	Steve Wapnick	.15	.11	.06
347	Greg Gohr	.15	.11	.06
348	Eric Stone	.15	.11	.06
349	Brian DuBois	.10	.08	.04
350	Kevin Ritz	.10	.08	.04
351	Rico Brogna	.10	.08	.04
352	Mike Heath	.05	.04	.02
353	Alan Trammell	.08	.06	.03
354	Chet Lemon	.06	.05	.02
355	Dave Bergman	.05	.04	.02
356	Lou Whitaker	.08	.06	.03
357	Cecil Fielder	.40	.30	.15
358	Milt Cuyler	.20	.15	.08
359	Tony Phillips	.06	.05	.02
360	Travis Fryman	1.25	.90	.50
361	Ed Romero	.05	.04	.02
362	Lloyd Moseby	.06	.05	.02
363	Mark Gubicza	.08	.06	.03
364	Bret Saberhagen	.10	.08	.04
365	Tom Gordon	.15	.11	.06
366	Steve Farr	.05	.04	.02
367	Kevin Appier	.30	.25	.12
368	Storm Davis	.05	.04	.02
369	Mark Davis	.05	.04	.02
370	Jeff Montgomery	.06	.05	.02
371	Frank White	.06	.05	.02
372	Brent Mayne	.20	.15	.08
373	Bob Boone	.06	.05	.02
374	Jim Eisenreich	.05	.04	.02
375	Danny Tartabull	.08	.06	.03
376	Kurt Stillwell	.05	.04	.02
377	Bill Pecota	.05	.04	.02
378	Bo Jackson	.80	.60	.30
379	Bob Hamelin	.20	.15	.08
380	Kevin Seitzer	.08	.06	.03
381	Rey Palacios	.05	.04	.02
382	George Brett	.12	.09	.05
383	Gerald Perry	.05	.04	.02
384	Teddy Higuera	.08	.06	.03
385	Tom Filer	.05	.04	.02
386	Dan Plesac	.06	.05	.02
387	Cal Eldred	.20	.15	.08
388	Jaime Navarro	.06	.05	.02
389	Chris Bosio	.05	.04	.02
390	Randy Veres	.05	.04	.02
391	Gary Sheffield	.20	.15	.08
392	George Canale	.10	.08	.04
393	B.J. Surhoff	.06	.05	.02
394	Tim McIntosh	.15	.11	.06
395	Greg Brock	.05	.04	.02
396	Greg Vaughn	.50	.40	.20
397	Darryl Hamilton	.10	.08	.04
398	Dave Parker	.10	.08	.04
399	Paul Molitor	.08	.06	.03

		MT	NR MT	EX
400	Jim Gantner	.05	.04	.02
401	Rob Deer	.05	.04	.02
402	Billy Spiers	.15	.11	.06
403	Glenn Braggs	.06	.05	.02
404	Robin Yount	.15	.11	.06
405	Rick Aguilera	.05	.04	.02
406	Johnny Ard	.15	.11	.06
407	Kevin Tapani	.25	.20	.10
408	Park Pittman	.20	.15	.08
409	Allan Anderson	.05	.04	.02
410	Juan Berenguer	.05	.04	.02
411	Willie Banks	.40	.30	.15
412	Rich Yett	.05	.04	.02
413	Dave West	.08	.06	.03
414	Greg Gagne	.05	.04	.02
415	Chuck Knoblauch	.50	.40	.20
416	Randy Bush	.05	.04	.02
417	Gary Gaetti	.08	.06	.03
418	Kent Hrbek	.08	.06	.03
419	Al Newman	.05	.04	.02
420	Danny Gladden	.05	.04	.02
421	Paul Sorrento	.15	.11	.06
422	Derek Parks	.25	.20	.10
423	Scott Leius	.20	.15	.08
424	Kirby Puckett	.20	.15	.08
425	Willie Smith	.20	.15	.08
426	Dave Righetti	.08	.06	.02
427	Jeff Robinson	.05	.04	.02
428	Alan Mills	.20	.15	.08
429	Tim Leary	.05	.04	.02
430	Pascual Perez	.05	.04	.02
431	Alvaro Espinoza	.05	.04	.02
432	Dave Winfield	.12	.09	.05
433	Jesse Barfield	.06	.05	.02
434	Randy Velarde	.05	.04	.02
435	Rick Cerone	.05	.04	.02
436	Steve Balboni	.05	.04	.02
437	Mel Hall	.05	.04	.02
438	Bob Geren	.06	.05	.02
439	Bernie Williams	.40	.30	.15
440	Kevin Maas	1.25	.90	.50
441	Mike Blowers	.15	.11	.06
442	Steve Sax	.08	.06	.03
443	Don Mattingly	.35	.25	.14
444	Roberto Kelly	.08	.06	.03
445	Mike Moore	.06	.05	.02
446	Reggie Harris	.15	.11	.06
447	Scott Sanderson	.05	.04	.02
448	Dave Otto	.05	.04	.02
449	Dave Stewart	.08	.06	.03
450	Rick Honeycutt	.05	.04	.02
451	Dennis Eckersley	.08	.06	.03
452	Carney Lansford	.06	.05	.02
453	Scott Hemond	.15	.11	.06
454	Mark McGwire	.20	.15	.08
455	Felix Jose	.15	.11	.06
456	Terry Steinbach	.06	.05	.02
457	Rickey Henderson	.25	.20	.10
458	Dave Henderson	.06	.05	.02
459	Mike Gallego	.05	.04	.02
460	Jose Canseco	.50	.40	.20
461	Walt Weiss	.06	.05	.02
462	Ken Phelps	.05	.04	.02
463	Darren Lewis	.40	.30	.15
464	Ron Hassey	.05	.04	.02
465	Roger Salkeld	.30	.25	.12
466	Scott Bankhead	.06	.05	.02
467	Keith Comstock	.05	.04	.02
468	Randy Johnson	.10	.08	.04
469	Erik Hanson	.10	.08	.04
470	Mike Schooler	.06	.05	.04
471	Gary Eave	.15	.11	.06
472	Jeffrey Leonard	.06	.05	.02
473	Dave Valle	.05	.04	.02
474	Omar Vizquel	.05	.04	.02
475	Pete O'Brien	.05	.04	.02
476	Henry Cotto	.05	.04	.02
477	Jay Buhner	.06	.05	.02
478	Harold Reynolds	.06	.05	.02
479	Alvin Davis	.08	.06	.03
480	Darnell Coles	.05	.04	.02
481	Ken Griffey, Jr.	2.50	2.00	1.00
482	Greg Briley	.12	.09	.05
483	Scott Bradley	.05	.04	.02
484	Tino Martinez	.40	.30	.15
485	Jeff Russell	.06	.05	.02
486	Nolan Ryan	.40	.30	.15
487	Robb Nen	.20	.15	.08
488	Kevin Brown	.06	.05	.02
489	Brian Bohanon	.20	.15	.08
490	Ruben Sierra	.15	.11	.06

		MT	NR MT	EX
491	Pete Incaviglia	.06	.05	.02
492	Juan Gonzalez	2.00	1.50	.80
493	Steve Buechele	.05	.04	.02
494	Scott Coolbaugh	.15	.11	.06
495	Geno Petralli	.05	.04	.02
496	Rafael Palmeiro	.08	.06	.03
497	Julio Franco	.08	.06	.03
498	Gary Pettis	.05	.04	.02
499	Donald Harris	.20	.15	.08
500	Monty Fariss	.20	.15	.08
501	Harold Baines	.08	.06	.03
502	Cecil Espy	.05	.04	.02
503	Jack Daugherty	.08	.06	.03
504	Willie Blair	.15	.11	.06
505	Dave Steib	.06	.05	.02
506	Tom Henke	.06	.05	.02
507	John Cerutti	.05	.04	.02
508	Paul Kilgus	.05	.04	.02
509	Jimmy Key	.06	.05	.02
510	John Olerud	1.00	.70	.40
511	Ed Sprague	.20	.15	.08
512	Manny Lee	.05	.04	.02
513	Fred McGriff	.08	.06	.03
514	Glenallen Hill	.10	.08	.04
515	George Bell	.08	.06	.03
516	Mookie Wilson	.06	.05	.02
517	Luis Sojo	.15	.11	.06
518	Nelson Liriano	.05	.04	.02
519	Kelly Gruber	.08	.06	.03
520	Greg Myers	.06	.05	.02
521	Pat Borders	.06	.05	.02
522	Junior Felix	.25	.20	.10
523	Eddie Zosky	.25	.20	.10
524	Tony Fernandez	.06	.05	.02
525	Checklist	.05	.04	.02
526	Checklist	.05	.04	.02
527	Checklist	.05	.04	.02
528	Checklist	.05	.04	.02

1991 Bowman

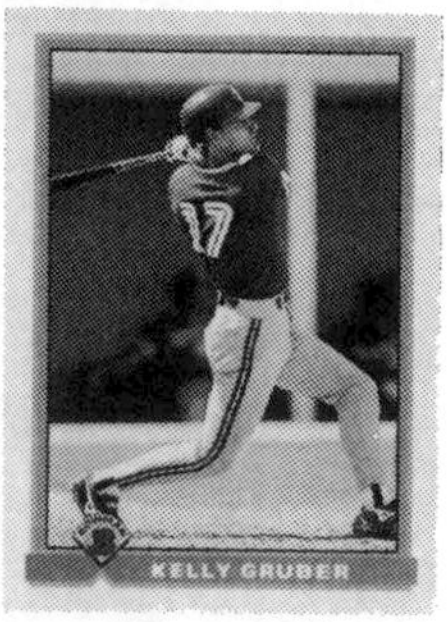

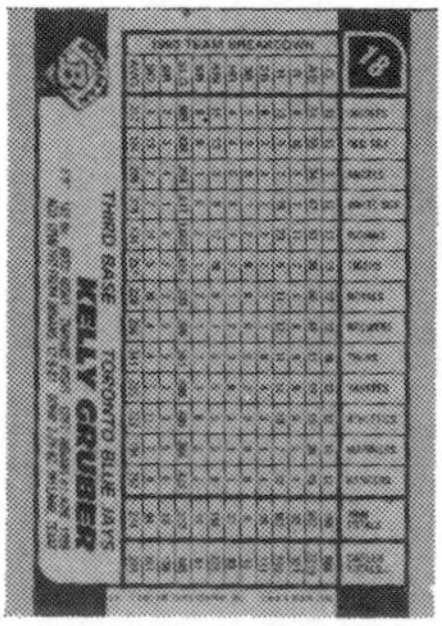

The 1991 Bowman set features 704 cards compared to 528 cards in the 1990 issue. The cards feature the 1953 Bowman style. Special Rod Carew cards, slugger cards and foil cards are included. The set is numbered by teams. Like the 1989 and 1990 issues, the card backs feature a breakdown of performance against each other team in the league.

	MT	NR MT	EX
Complete Set:	20.00	15.00	8.00
Common Player:	.05	.04	.02

		MT	NR MT	EX
1	Rod Carew-I	.15	.11	.06
2	Rod Carew-II	.15	.11	.06
3	Rod Carew-III	.15	.11	.06
4	Rod Carew-IV	.15	.11	.06
5	Rod Carew-V	.15	.11	.06
6	Willie Fraser	.05	.04	.02
7	John Olerud	.10	.08	.04
8	William Suero	.15	.11	.06
9	Roberto Alomar	.10	.08	.04
10	Todd Stottlemyre	.06	.05	.02
11	Joe Carter	.10	.08	.04
12	Steve Karsay	.20	.15	.08
13	Mark Whiten	.20	.15	.08
14	Pat Borders	.05	.04	.02
15	Mike Timlin	.15	.11	.06
16	Tom Henke	.06	.05	.02
17	Eddie Zosky	.08	.06	.03
18	Kelly Gruber	.08	.06	.03
19	Jimmy Key	.06	.05	.02
20	Jerry Schunk	.12	.09	.05
21	Manny Lee	.05	.04	.02
22	Dave Steib	.08	.06	.03
23	Pat Hentgen	.12	.09	.05
24	Glenallen Hill	.08	.06	.03
25	Rene Gonzales	.05	.04	.02
26	Ed Sprague	.10	.08	.04
27	Ken Dayley	.05	.04	.02
28	Pat Tabler	.05	.04	.02
29	Denis Boucher	.12	.09	.05
30	Devon White	.08	.06	.03
31	Dante Bichette	.05	.04	.02
32	Paul Molitor	.08	.06	.03
33	Greg Vaughn	.08	.06	.03
34	Dan Plesac	.05	.04	.02
35	Chris George	.12	.09	.05
36	Tim McIntosh	.08	.06	.03
37	Franklin Stubbs	.05	.04	.02
38	Bo Dodson	.15	.11	.06
39	Ron Robinson	.05	.04	.02
40	Ed Nunez	.05	.04	.02
41	Greg Brock	.05	.04	.02
42	Jaime Navarro	.06	.05	.02
43	Chris Bosio	.05	.05	.02
44	B.J. Surhoff	.06	.05	.02
45	Chris Johnson	.12	.09	.05
46	Willie Randolph	.06	.05	.02
47	Narciso Elvira	.10	.08	.04
48	Jim Gantner	.05	.04	.02
49	Kevin Brown	.05	.04	.02
50	Julio Machado	.05	.04	.02
51	Chuck Crim	.05	.04	.02
52	Gary Sheffield	.08	.06	.03
53	Angel Miranda	.12	.09	.05
54	Teddy Higuera	.06	.05	.02
55	Robin Yount	.10	.08	.04
56	Cal Eldred	.12	.09	.05
57	Sandy Alomar	.08	.06	.03
58	Greg Swindell	.06	.05	.02
59	Brook Jacoby	.06	.05	.02
60	Efrain Valdez	.08	.06	.03
61	Ever Magallanes	.12	.09	.05
62	Tom Candiotti	.05	.04	.02
63	Eric King	.05	.04	.02
64	Alex Cole	.05	.04	.02
65	Charles Nagy	.08	.06	.03
66	Mitch Webster	.05	.04	.02
67	Chris James	.05	.04	.02
68	Jim Thome	.30	.25	.12
69	Carlos Baerga	.06	.05	.02
70	Mark Lewis	.08	.06	.03
71	Jerry Browne	.05	.04	.02
72	Jesse Orosco	.05	.04	.02
73	Mike Huff	.06	.05	.02
74	Jose Escobar	.12	.09	.05
75	Jeff Manto	.06	.05	.02
76	Turner Ward	.10	.08	.04
77	Doug Jones	.05	.04	.02
78	Bruce Egloff	.12	.09	.05
79	Tim Costo	.20	.15	.08
80	Beau Allred	.06	.05	.02
81	Albert Belle	.20	.15	.08
82	John Farrell	.05	.04	.02
83	Glenn Davis	.08	.06	.03
84	Joe Orsulak	.05	.04	.02
85	Mark Williamson	.05	.04	.02
86	Ben McDonald	.15	.11	.06
87	Billy Ripken	.05	.04	.02
88	Leo Gomez	.08	.06	.03
89	Bob Melvin	.05	.04	.02
90	Jeff Robinson	.05	.04	.02
91	Jose Mesa	.05	.04	.02
92	Gregg Olson	.08	.06	.03
93	Mike Devereaux	.06	.05	.02
94	Luis Mercedes	.20	.15	.08
95	Arthur Rhodes	.20	.15	.08
96	Juan Bell	.05	.04	.02
97	Mike Mussina	.25	.20	.10
98	Jeff Ballard	.05	.04	.02
99	Chris Hoiles	.08	.06	.03
100	Brady Anderson	.05	.04	.02
101	Bob Milacki	.05	.04	.02
102	David Segui	.06	.05	.02
103	Dwight Evans	.06	.05	.02
104	Cal Ripken	.12	.09	.05
105	Mike Linskey	.12	.09	.05
106	Jeff Tackett	.12	.09	.05

		MT	NR MT	EX
107	Jeff Reardon	.08	.06	.03
108	Dana Kiecker	.05	.04	.02
109	Ellis Burks	.08	.06	.03
110	Dave Owen	.12	.09	.05
111	Danny Darwin	.05	.04	.02
112	Mo Vaughn	.20	.15	.08
113	Jeff McNeely	.25	.20	.10
114	Tom Bolton	.05	.04	.02
115	Greg Blosser	.12	.09	.05
116	Mike Greenwell	.10	.08	.04
117	Phil Plantier	.80	.60	.30
118	Roger Clemens	.15	.11	.06
119	John Marzano	.05	.04	.02
120	Jody Reed	.06	.05	.02
121	Scott Taylor	.12	.09	.05
122	Jack Clark	.06	.05	.02
123	Derek Livernois	.12	.09	.05
124	Tony Pena	.05	.04	.02
125	Tom Brunansky	.05	.04	.02
126	Carlos Quintana	.05	.04	.02
127	Tim Naehring	.10	.08	.04
128	Matt Young	.05	.04	.02
129	Wade Boggs	.15	.11	.06
130	Kevin Morton	.15	.11	.06
131	Pete Incaviglia	.05	.04	.02
132	Rob Deer	.05	.04	.02
133	Bill Gullickson	.05	.04	.02
134	Rico Brogna	.12	.09	.05
135	Lloyd Moseby	.05	.04	.02
136	Cecil Fielder	.15	.11	.06
137	Tony Phillips	.05	.04	.02
138	Mark Leiter	.05	.04	.02
139	John Cerutti	.05	.04	.02
140	Mickey Tettleton	.06	.05	.02
141	Milt Cuyler	.10	.08	.04
142	Greg Gohr	.10	.08	.04
143	Tony Bernazard	.05	.04	.02
144	Dan Gakeler	.12	.09	.05
145	Travis Fryman	.20	.15	.08
146	Dan Petry	.05	.04	.02
147	Scott Aldred	.08	.06	.03
148	John DeSilva	.12	.09	.05
149	Rusty Meacham	.12	.09	.05
150	Lou Whitaker	.06	.05	.02
151	Dave Haas	.06	.05	.02
152	Luis de los Santos	.05	.04	.02
153	Ivan Cruz	.12	.09	.05
154	Alan Trammell	.08	.06	.03
155	Pat Kelly	.35	.25	.14
156	Carl Everett	.35	.25	.14
157	Greg Cadaret	.05	.04	.02
158	Kevin Maas	.15	.11	.06
159	Jeff Johnson	.15	.11	.06
160	Willie Smith	.15	.11	.06
161	Gerald Williams	.20	.15	.08
162	Mike Humphreys	.15	.11	.06
163	Alvaro Espinoza	.05	.04	.02
164	Matt Nokes	.05	.04	.02
165	Wade Taylor	.12	.09	.05
166	Roberto Kelly	.08	.06	.03
167	John Habyan	.05	.04	.02
168	Steve Farr	.05	.04	.02
169	Jesse Barfield	.05	.04	.02
170	Steve Sax	.06	.05	.02
171	Jim Leyritz	.05	.04	.02
172	Robert Eenhoorn	.15	.11	.06
173	Bernie Williams	.15	.11	.06
174	Scott Lusader	.05	.04	.02
175	Torey Lovullo	.08	.06	.03
176	Chuck Cary	.05	.04	.02
177	Scott Sanderson	.05	.04	.02
178	Don Mattingly	.15	.11	.06
179	Mel Hall	.06	.05	.02
180	Juan Gonzalez	.30	.25	.12
181	Hensley Meulens	.08	.06	.03
182	Jose Offerman	.15	.11	.06
183	Jeff Bagwell (Foil)	2.00	1.50	.80
184	Jeff Conine	.20	.15	.08
185	Henry Rodriguez (Foil)	.25	.20	.10
186	Jimmie Reese (Foil)	.15	.11	.06
187	Kyle Abbott	.10	.08	.04
188	Lance Parrish	.06	.05	.02
189	Rafael Montalvo	.12	.09	.05
190	Floyd Bannister	.05	.04	.02
191	Dick Schofield	.05	.04	.02
192	Scott Lewis	.12	.09	.05
193	Jeff Robinson	.05	.04	.02
194	Kent Anderson	.05	.04	.02
195	Wally Joyner	.10	.08	.04
196	Chuck Finley	.08	.06	.03
197	Luis Sojo	.05	.04	.02

		MT	NR MT	EX
198	Jeff Richardson	.08	.06	.03
199	Dave Parker	.08	.06	.03
200	Jim Abbott	.08	.06	.03
201	Junior Felix	.06	.05	.02
202	Mark Langston	.08	.06	.03
203	Tim Salmon	.20	.15	.08
204	Cliff Young	.08	.06	.03
205	Scott Bailes	.05	.04	.02
206	Bobby Rose	.06	.05	.02
207	Gary Gaetti	.06	.05	.02
208	Ruben Amaro	.12	.09	.05
209	Luis Polonia	.06	.05	.02
210	Dave Winfield	.10	.08	.04
211	Bryan Harvey	.06	.05	.02
212	Mike Moore	.05	.04	.02
213	Rickey Henderson	.15	.11	.06
214	Steve Chitren	.15	.11	.06
215	Bob Welch	.06	.05	.02
216	Terry Steinbach	.06	.05	.02
217	Ernie Riles	.05	.04	.02
218	Todd Van Poppel	1.25	.90	.50
219	Mike Gallego	.05	.04	.02
220	Curt Young	.05	.04	.02
221	Todd Burns	.05	.04	.02
222	Vance Law	.05	.04	.02
223	Eric Show	.05	.04	.02
224	Don Peters	.15	.11	.06
225	Dave Stewart	.10	.08	.04
226	Dave Henderson	.06	.05	.02
227	Jose Canseco	.20	.15	.08
228	Walt Weiss	.06	.05	.02
229	Dann Howitt	.06	.05	.02
230	Willie Wilson	.05	.04	.02
231	Harold Baines	.06	.05	.02
232	Scott Hemond	.06	.05	.02
233	Joe Slusarski	.12	.09	.05
234	Mark McGwire	.10	.08	.04
235	Kirk Dressendorfer	.30	.25	.12
236	Craig Paquette	.15	.11	.06
237	Dennis Eckersley	.10	.08	.04
238	Dana Allison	.12	.09	.05
239	Scott Bradley	.05	.04	.02
240	Brian Holman	.06	.05	.02
241	Mike Schooler	.06	.05	.02
242	Rich Delucia	.12	.09	.05
243	Edgar Martinez	.08	.06	.03
244	Henry Cotto	.05	.04	.02
245	Omar Vizquel	.05	.04	.02
246	Ken Griffey, Jr.	1.00	.70	.40
247	Jay Buhner	.06	.05	.02
248	Bill Krueger	.05	.04	.02
249	Dave Fleming	.12	.09	.05
250	Patrick Lennon	.15	.11	.06
251	Dave Valle	.05	.04	.02
252	Harold Reynolds	.06	.05	.02
253	Randy Johnson	.08	.06	.03
254	Scott Bankhead	.06	.05	.02
255	Ken Griffey	.08	.06	.03
256	Greg Briley	.05	.04	.02
257	Tino Martinez	.12	.09	.05
258	Alvin Davis	.06	.05	.02
259	Pete O'Brien	.05	.04	.02
260	Erik Hanson	.08	.06	.03
261	Bret Boone	.15	.11	.06
262	Roger Salkeld	.15	.11	.06
263	Dave Burba	.08	.06	.03
264	Kerry Woodson	.12	.09	.05
265	Julio Franco	.08	.06	.03
266	Dan Peltier	.20	.15	.08
267	Jeff Russell	.05	.04	.02
268	Steve Buechele	.06	.05	.02
269	Donald Harris	.12	.09	.05
270	Robb Nen	.10	.08	.04
271	Rich Gossage	.06	.05	.02
272	Ivan Rodriguez	2.00	1.50	.80
273	Jeff Huson	.06	.05	.02
274	Kevin Brown	.06	.05	.02
275	Dan Smith	.15	.11	.06
276	Gary Pettis	.05	.04	.02
277	Jack Daugherty	.05	.04	.02
278	Mike Jeffcoat	.05	.04	.02
279	Brad Arnsbarg	.06	.05	.02
280	Nolan Ryan	.25	.20	.10
281	Eric McCray	.12	.09	.05
282	Scott Chiamparino	.08	.06	.03
283	Ruben Sierra	.15	.11	.06
284	Geno Petralli	.05	.04	.02
285	Monty Fariss	.08	.06	.03
286	Rafael Palmeiro	.08	.06	.03
287	Bobb Witt	.06	.05	.02
288	Dean Palmer	.25	.20	.10

		MT	NR MT	EX
289	Tony Scruggs	.12	.09	.05
290	Kenny Rogers	.05	.04	.02
291	Bret Saberhagen	.08	.06	.03
292	Brian McRae	.40	.30	.15
293	Storm Davis	.05	.04	.02
294	Danny Tartabull	.08	.06	.03
295	David Howard	.12	.09	.05
296	Mike Boddicker	.06	.05	.02
297	Joel Johnston	.12	.09	.05
298	Tim Spehr	.15	.11	.06
299	Hector Wagner	.12	.09	.05
300	George Brett	.12	.09	.05
301	Mike Macfarlane	.06	.05	.02
302	Kirk Gibson	.06	.05	.02
303	Harvey Pulliam	.15	.11	.06
304	Jim Eisenreich	.05	.04	.02
305	Kevin Seitzer	.06	.05	.02
306	Mark Davis	.05	.04	.02
307	Kurt Stillwell	.05	.04	.02
308	Jeff Montgomery	.06	.05	.02
309	Kevin Appier	.06	.05	.02
310	Bob Hamelin	.10	.08	.04
311	Tom Gordon	.06	.05	.02
312	Kerwin Moore	.12	.09	.05
313	Hugh Walker	.12	.09	.05
314	Terry Shumpert	.05	.04	.02
315	Warren Cromartie	.05	.04	.02
316	Gary Thurman	.05	.04	.02
317	Steve Bedrosian	.05	.04	.02
318	Danny Gladden	.05	.04	.02
319	Jack Morris	.08	.06	.03
320	Kirby Puckett	.15	.11	.06
321	Kent Hrbek	.08	.06	.03
322	Kevin Tapani	.08	.06	.03
323	Denny Neagle	.25	.20	.10
324	Rich Garces	.12	.09	.05
325	Larry Casian	.10	.08	.04
326	Shane Mack	.08	.06	.03
327	Allan Anderson	.05	.04	.02
328	Junior Ortiz	.05	.04	.02
329	Paul Abbott	.10	.08	.04
330	Chuck Knoblauch	.20	.15	.08
331	Chili Davis	.08	.06	.03
332	Todd Ritchie	.12	.09	.05
333	Brian Harper	.06	.05	.02
334	Rick Aguilera	.06	.05	.02
335	Scott Erickson	.60	.45	.25
336	Pedro Munoz	.20	.15	.08
337	Scott Leuis	.10	.08	.04
338	Greg Gagne	.05	.04	.02
339	Mike Pagliarulo	.05	.04	.02
340	Terry Leach	.05	.04	.02
341	Willie Banks	.10	.08	.04
342	Bobby Thigpen	.06	.05	.02
343	Roberto Hernandez	.15	.11	.06
344	Melido Perez	.05	.04	.02
345	Carlton Fisk	.10	.08	.04
346	Norberto Martin	.12	.09	.05
347	Johnny Ruffin	.12	.09	.05
348	Jeff Carter	.12	.09	.05
349	Lance Johnson	.05	.04	.02
350	Sammy Sosa	.10	.08	.04
351	Alex Fernandez	.20	.15	.08
352	Jack McDowell	.10	.08	.04
353	Bob Wickman	.15	.11	.06
354	Wilson Alvarez	.15	.11	.06
355	Charlie Hough	.05	.04	.02
356	Ozzie Guillen	.06	.05	.02
357	Cory Snyder	.05	.04	.02
358	Robin Ventura	.15	.11	.06
359	Scott Fletcher	.05	.04	.02
360	Cesar Bernhardt	.12	.09	.05
361	Dan Pasqua	.05	.04	.02
362	Rock Raines	.08	.06	.03
363	Brian Drahman	.12	.09	.05
364	Wayne Edwards	.05	.04	.02
365	Scott Radinsky	.06	.05	.02
366	Frank Thomas	1.00	.70	.40
367	Cecil Fielder (AL Slugger)	.10	.08	.04
368	Julio Franco (AL Slugger)	.10	.08	.04
369	Kelly Gruber (AL Slugger)	.08	.06	.03
370	Alan Trammell (AL Slugger)	.08	.06	.03
371	Rickey Henderson (AL Slugger)	.10	.08	.04
372	Jose Canseco (AL Slugger)	.15	.11	.06
373	Ellis Burks (AL Slugger)	.08	.06	.03
374	Lance Parrish (AL Slugger)	.06	.05	.02
375	Dave Parker (AL Slugger)	.08	.06	.03
376	Eddie Murray (NL Slugger)	.08	.06	.03
377	Ryne Sandberg (NL Slugger)	.12	.09	.05
378	Matt Williams (NL Slugger)	.08	.06	.03
379	Barry Larkin (NL Slugger)	.08	.06	.03

		MT	NR MT	EX
380	Barry Bonds (NL Slugger)	.10	.08	.04
381	Bobby Bonilla (NL Slugger)	.10	.08	.04
382	Darryl Strawberry (NL Slugger)	.10	.08	.04
383	Benny Santiago (NL Slugger)	.06	.05	.02
384	Don Robinson (NL Slugger)	.05	.04	.02
385	Paul Coleman	.10	.08	.04
386	Milt Thompson	.05	.04	.02
387	Lee Smith	.06	.05	.02
388	Ray Lankford	.15	.11	.06
389	Tom Pagnozzi	.06	.05	.02
390	Ken Hill	.06	.05	.02
391	Jamie Moyer	.05	.04	.02
392	Greg Carmona	.12	.09	.05
393	John Ericks	.10	.08	.04
394	Bob Tewksbury	.05	.04	.02
395	Jose Oquendo	.05	.04	.02
396	Rheal Cormier	.30	.25	.12
397	Mike Milchin	.12	.09	.05
398	Ozzie Smith	.10	.08	.04
399	Aaron Holbert	.15	.11	.06
400	Jose DeLeon	.05	.04	.02
401	Felix Jose	.12	.09	.05
402	Juan Agosto	.05	.04	.02
403	Pedro Guerrero	.08	.06	.03
404	Todd Zeile	.08	.06	.03
405	Gerald Perry	.05	.04	.02
406	Donovan Osborne	.12	.09	.05
407	Bryn Smith	.05	.04	.02
408	Bernard Gilkey	.15	.11	.06
409	Rex Hudler	.05	.04	.02
410	Thomson/Branca (Foil)	.10	.08	.04
411	Lance Dickson	.15	.11	.06
412	Danny Jackson	.05	.04	.02
413	Jerome Walton	.06	.05	.02
414	Sean Cheetham	.12	.09	.05
415	Joe Girardi	.05	.04	.02
416	Ryne Sandberg	.15	.11	.06
417	Mike Harkey	.06	.05	.02
418	George Bell	.08	.06	.03
419	Rick Wilkins	.20	.15	.08
420	Earl Cunningham	.06	.05	.02
421	Heathcliff Slocumb	.12	.09	.05
422	Mike Bielecki	.05	.04	.02
423	Jessie Hollins	.12	.09	.05
424	Shawon Dunston	.06	.05	.02
425	Dave Smith	.05	.04	.02
426	Greg Maddux	.08	.06	.03
427	Jose Vizcaino	.05	.04	.02
428	Luis Salazar	.05	.04	.02
429	Andre Dawson	.10	.08	.04
430	Rick Sutcliffe	.05	.04	.02
431	Paul Assenmacher	.05	.04	.02
432	Erik Pappas	.12	.09	.05
433	Mark Grace	.08	.06	.03
434	Denny Martinez	.06	.05	.02
435	Marquis Grissom	.10	.08	.04
436	Wilfredo Cordero	.30	.25	.12
437	Tim Wallach	.06	.05	.02
438	Brian Barnes	.15	.11	.06
439	Barry Jones	.05	.04	.02
440	Ivan Calderon	.08	.06	.03
441	Stan Spencer	.12	.09	.05
442	Larry Walker	.08	.06	.03
443	Chris Haney	.12	.09	.05
444	Hector Rivera	.12	.09	.05
445	Delino DeShields	.12	.09	.05
446	Andres Galarraga	.06	.05	.02
447	Gilberto Reyes	.06	.05	.02
448	Willie Greene	.10	.08	.04
449	Greg Colbrunn	.12	.09	.05
450	Rondell White	.30	.25	.12
451	Steve Frey	.06	.05	.02
452	Shane Andrews	.15	.11	.06
453	Mike Fitzgerald	.05	.04	.02
454	Spike Owen	.05	.04	.02
455	Dave Martinez	.05	.04	.02
456	Dennis Boyd	.05	.04	.02
457	Eric Bullock	.06	.05	.02
458	Reid Cornelius	.15	.11	.06
459	Chris Nabholz	.15	.11	.06
460	David Cone	.08	.06	.03
461	Hubie Brooks	.06	.05	.02
462	Sid Fernandez	.06	.05	.02
463	Doug Simons	.10	.08	.04
464	Howard Johnson	.10	.08	.04
465	Chris Donnels	.15	.11	.06
466	Anthony Young	.15	.11	.06
467	Todd Hundley	.12	.09	.05
468	Rick Cerone	.05	.04	.02
469	Kevin Elster	.05	.04	.02
470	Wally Whitehurst	.06	.05	.02

		MT	NR MT	EX
471	Vince Coleman	.08	.06	.03
472	Doc Gooden	.08	.06	.03
473	Charlie O'Brien	.05	.04	.02
474	Jeromy Burnitz	.40	.30	.15
475	John Franco	.08	.06	.03
476	Daryl Boston	.05	.04	.02
477	Frank Viola	.08	.06	.03
478	D.J. Dozier	.10	.08	.04
479	Kevin McReynolds	.06	.05	.02
480	Tom Herr	.05	.04	.02
481	Gregg Jefferies	.08	.06	.03
482	Pete Schourek	.12	.09	.05
483	Ron Darling	.06	.05	.02
484	Dave Magadan	.06	.05	.02
485	Andy Ashby	.10	.08	.04
486	Dale Murphy	.08	.06	.03
487	Von Hayes	.06	.05	.02
488	Kim Batiste	.08	.06	.03
489	Tony Longmire	.15	.11	.06
490	Wally Backman	.05	.04	.02
491	Jeff Jackson	.08	.06	.03
492	Mickey Morandini	.08	.06	.03
493	Darrel Akerfelds	.05	.04	.02
494	Ricky Jordan	.06	.05	.02
495	Randy Ready	.05	.04	.02
496	Darrin Fletcher	.06	.05	.02
497	Chuck Malone	.05	.04	.02
498	Pat Combs	.06	.05	.02
499	Dickie Thon	.05	.04	.02
500	Roger McDowell	.06	.05	.02
501	Len Dykstra	.06	.05	.02
502	Joe Boever	.05	.04	.02
503	John Kruk	.06	.05	.02
504	Terry Mulholland	.06	.05	.02
505	Wes Chamberlain	.35	.25	.14
506	Mike Lieberthal	.15	.11	.06
507	Darren Daulton	.06	.05	.02
508	Charlie Hayes	.06	.05	.02
509	John Smiley	.06	.05	.02
510	Gary Varsho	.05	.04	.02
511	Curt Wilkerson	.05	.04	.02
512	Orlando Merced	.25	.20	.10
513	Barry Bonds	.12	.09	.05
514	Mike Lavalliere	.05	.04	.02
515	Doug Drabek	.06	.05	.02
516	Gary Redus	.05	.04	.02
517	William Pennyfeather	.15	.11	.06
518	Randy Tomlin	.06	.05	.02
519	Mike Zimmerman	.12	.09	.05
520	Jeff King	.06	.05	.02
521	Kurt Miller	.15	.11	.06
522	Jay Bell	.06	.05	.02
523	Bill Landrum	.05	.04	.02
524	Zane Smith	.05	.04	.02
525	Bobby Bonilla	.10	.08	.04
526	Bob Walk	.05	.04	.02
527	Austin Manahan	.08	.06	.03
528	Joe Ausanio	.12	.09	.05
529	Andy Van Slyke	.08	.06	.03
530	Jose Lind	.05	.04	.02
531	Carlos Garcia	.12	.09	.05
532	Don Slaught	.05	.04	.02
533	Colin Powell (Foil)	.25	.20	.10
534	Frank Bolick (Foil)	.25	.20	.10
535	Gary Scott (Foil)	.30	.25	.12
536	Nikco Riesgo (Foil)	.30	.25	.12
537	Reggie Sanders	.35	.25	.14
538	Tim Howard (Foil)	.25	.20	.10
539	Ryan Bowen	.15	.11	.06
540	Eric Anthony	.08	.06	.03
541	Jim Deshaies	.05	.04	.02
542	Tom Nevers	.12	.09	.05
543	Ken Caminiti	.05	.04	.02
544	Karl Rhodes	.12	.09	.05
545	Xavier Hernandez	.08	.06	.03
546	Mike Scott	.06	.05	.02
547	Jeff Juden	.15	.11	.06
548	Darryl Kile	.08	.06	.03
549	Willie Ansley	.10	.08	.04
550	Luis Gonzalez	.35	.25	.14
551	Mike Simms	.15	.11	.06
552	Mark Portugal	.05	.04	.02
553	Jimmy Jones	.05	.04	.02
554	Jim Clancy	.05	.04	.02
555	Pete Harnisch	.06	.05	.02
556	Craig Biggio	.08	.06	.03
557	Eric Yelding	.05	.04	.02
558	Dave Rohde	.06	.05	.02
559	Casey Candaele	.05	.04	.02
560	Curt Schilling	.05	.04	.02
561	Steve Finley	.06	.05	.02
562	Javier Ortiz	.08	.06	.03
563	Andujar Cedeno	.20	.15	.08
564	Rafael Ramirez	.05	.04	.02
565	Kenny Lofton	.30	.25	.12
566	Steve Avery	.15	.11	.06
567	Lonnie Smith	.05	.04	.02
568	Kent Mercker	.06	.05	.02
569	Chipper Jones	.25	.20	.10
570	Terry Pendleton	.06	.05	.02
571	Otis Nixon	.05	.04	.02
572	Juan Berenguer	.05	.04	.02
573	Charlie Leibrandt	.05	.04	.02
574	David Justice	.30	.25	.12
575	Keith Mitchell	.25	.20	.10
576	Tom Glavine	.08	.06	.03
577	Greg Olson	.05	.04	.02
578	Rafael Belliard	.05	.04	.02
579	Ben Rivera	.10	.08	.04
580	John Smoltz	.06	.05	.02
581	Tyler Houston	.05	.04	.02
582	Mark Wohlers	.40	.30	.15
583	Ron Gant	.10	.08	.04
584	Ramon Caraballo	.10	.08	.04
585	Sid Bream	.05	.04	.02
586	Jeff Treadway	.05	.04	.02
587	Javier Lopez	.12	.09	.05
588	Deion Sanders	.08	.06	.03
589	Mike Heath	.05	.04	.02
590	Ryan Klesko	.60	.45	.25
591	Bob Ojeda	.05	.04	.02
592	Alfredo Griffin	.05	.04	.02
593	Raul Mondesi	.20	.15	.08
594	Greg Smith	.05	.04	.02
595	Orel Hershiser	.08	.06	.03
596	Juan Samuel	.06	.05	.02
597	Brett Butler	.06	.05	.02
598	Gary Carter	.06	.05	.02
599	Stan Javier	.05	.04	.02
600	Kal Daniels	.08	.06	.03
601	Jamie McAndrew	.15	.11	.06
602	Mike Sharperson	.05	.04	.02
603	Jay Howell	.05	.04	.02
604	Eric Karros	.30	.25	.12
605	Tim Belcher	.06	.05	.02
606	Dan Opperman	.12	.09	.05
607	Lenny Harris	.05	.04	.02
608	Tom Goodwin	.10	.08	.04
609	Darryl Strawberry	.15	.11	.06
610	Ramon Martinez	.12	.09	.05
611	Kevin Gross	.05	.04	.02
612	Zakary Shinall	.12	.09	.05
613	Mike Scioscia	.05	.04	.02
614	Eddie Murray	.08	.06	.03
615	Ronnie Walden	.15	.11	.06
616	Will Clark	.20	.15	.08
617	Adam Hyzdu	.15	.11	.06
618	Matt Williams	.08	.06	.03
619	Don Robinson	.05	.04	.02
620	Jeff Brantley	.05	.04	.02
621	Greg Litton	.05	.04	.02
622	Steve Decker	.25	.20	.10
623	Robby Thompson	.06	.05	.02
624	Mark Leonard	.12	.09	.05
625	Kevin Bass	.05	.04	.02
626	Scott Garrelts	.05	.04	.02
627	Jose Uribe	.05	.04	.02
628	Eric Gunderson	.08	.06	.03
629	Steve Hosey	.08	.06	.03
630	Trevor Wilson	.06	.05	.02
631	Terry Kennedy	.05	.04	.02
632	Dave Righetti	.06	.05	.02
633	Kelly Downs	.05	.04	.02
634	Johnny Ard	.08	.06	.03
635	Eric Christopherson	.12	.09	.05
636	Kevin Mitchell	.10	.08	.04
637	John Burkett	.05	.04	.02
638	Kevin Rogers	.12	.09	.05
639	Bud Black	.05	.04	.02
640	Willie McGee	.06	.05	.02
641	Royce Clayton	.15	.11	.06
642	Tony Fernandez	.06	.05	.02
643	Ricky Bones	.12	.09	.05
644	Thomas Howard	.06	.05	.02
645	Dave Staton	.15	.11	.06
646	Jim Presley	.05	.04	.02
647	Tony Gwynn	.10	.08	.04
648	Marty Barrett	.05	.04	.02
649	Scott Coolbaugh	.06	.05	.02
650	Craig Lefferts	.05	.04	.02
651	Eddie Whitson	.05	.04	.02
652	Oscar Azocar	.05	.04	.02

		MT	NR MT	EX
653	Wes Gardner	.05	.04	.02
654	Bip Roberts	.06	.05	.02
655	Robbie Beckett	.15	.11	.06
656	Benny Santiago	.06	.05	.02
657	Greg W. Harris	.05	.04	.02
658	Jerald Clark	.06	.05	.02
659	Fred McGriff	.10	.08	.04
660	Larry Andersen	.05	.04	.02
661	Bruce Hurst	.06	.05	.02
662	Steve Martin	.12	.09	.05
663	Rafael Valdez	.06	.05	.02
664	Paul Faries	.06	.05	.02
665	Andy Benes	.08	.06	.03
666	Randy Myers	.06	.05	.02
667	Rob Dibble	.08	.06	.03
668	Glenn Sutko	.12	.09	.05
669	Glenn Braggs	.05	.04	.02
670	Billy Hatcher	.05	.04	.02
671	Joe Oliver	.05	.04	.02
672	Freddie Benavides	.12	.09	.05
673	Barry Larkin	.08	.06	.03
674	Chris Sabo	.08	.06	.03
675	Mariano Duncan	.05	.04	.02
676	Chris Jones	.15	.11	.06
677	Gino Minutelli	.12	.09	.05
678	Reggie Jefferson	.12	.09	.05
679	Jack Armstrong	.06	.05	.02
680	Chris Hammond	.06	.05	.02
681	Jose Rijo	.08	.06	.03
682	Bill Doran	.05	.04	.02
683	Terry Lee	.06	.05	.02
684	Tom Browning	.06	.05	.02
685	Paul O'Neill	.08	.06	.03
686	Eric Davis	.10	.08	.04
687	Dan Wilson	.15	.11	.06
688	Ted Power	.05	.04	.02
689	Tim Layana	.05	.04	.02
690	Norm Charlton	.06	.05	.02
691	Hal Morris	.10	.08	.04
692	Rickey Henderson (Foil)	.20	.15	.08
693	Sam Militello (Foil)	.20	.15	.08
694	Matt Mieske (Foil)	.60	.45	.25
695	Paul Russo (Foil)	.25	.20	.10
696	Domingo Mota (Foil)	.25	.20	.10
697	Todd Guggiana (Foil)	.20	.15	.08
698	Marc Newfield	.40	.30	.15
699	Checklist	.05	.04	.02
700	Checklist	.05	.04	.02
701	Checklist	.05	.04	.02
702	Checklist	.05	.04	.02
703	Checklist	.05	.04	.02
704	Checklist	.05	.04	.02

1977 Burger King Yankees

The first Topps-produced set for Burger King restaurants was issued in the New York area in 1977 and featured the A.L. champion New York Yankees. Twenty-two players plus an unnumbered checklist were issued at the beginning of the promotion with card #23 (Lou Piniella) being added to the set at a later date. The Piniella card was issued in limited quantities. The cards, numbered 1 through 23, are 2-1/2" by 3-1/2" in size and have fronts identical to the regular 1977 Topps set except for the following numbers: 2, 6, 7, 13, 14, 15, 17, 20 and 21. These cards feature different poses or major picture-cropping variations. It should be noted that very minor cropping variations between the regular Topps sets and the Burger King issues exist throughout the years the sets were produced.

		NR MT	EX	VG
Complete Set:		45.00	22.00	13.50
Common Player:		.30	.15	.09
1	Yankees Team (Billy Martin)	1.00	.50	.30
2	Thurman Munson	7.00	3.50	2.00
3	Fran Healy	.30	.15	.09
4	Jim Hunter	2.00	1.00	.60
5	Ed Figueroa	.30	.15	.09
6	Don Gullett	.70	.35	.20
7	Mike Torrez	.70	.35	.20
8	Ken Holtzman	.50	.25	.15
9	Dick Tidrow	.30	.15	.09
10	Sparky Lyle	.50	.25	.15
11	Ron Guidry	1.00	.50	.30
12	Chris Chambliss	.50	.25	.15
13	Willie Randolph	1.00	.50	.30
14	Bucky Dent	1.00	.50	.30
15	Graig Nettles	1.00	.50	.30
16	Fred Stanley	.30	.15	.09
17	Reggie Jackson	8.00	4.00	2.50
18	Mickey Rivers	.50	.25	.15
19	Roy White	.50	.25	.15
20	Jim Wynn	.70	.35	.20
21	Paul Blair	.70	.35	.20
22	Carlos May	.30	.15	.09
23	Lou Piniella	25.00	12.50	7.50
----	Checklist	.10	.05	.03

1978 Burger King Astros

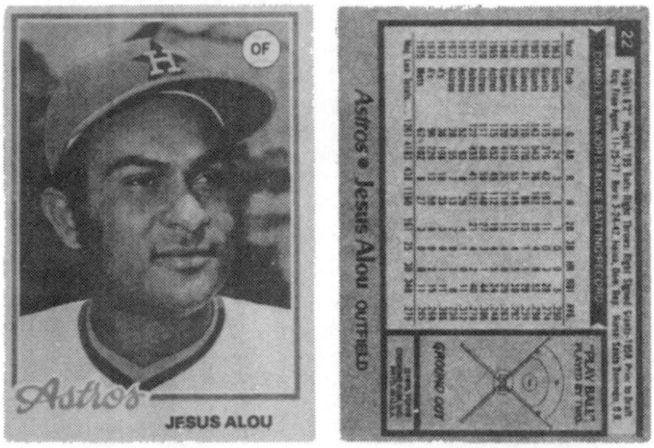

Burger King restaurants in the Houston area distributed a Topps-produced 23-card set showcasing the Astros in 1978. The cards are standard size (2-1/2" by 3-1/2") and are numbered 1 through 22. The checklist card is unnumbered. The card fronts are identical to the regular 1978 Topps set with the exception of card numbers 21 and 22, which have different poses. Although not noted in the following checklist, it should be remembered that very minor picture-cropping variations between the regular Topps issues and the 1977-1980 Burger King sets do exist.

		NR MT	EX	VG
Complete Set:		12.00	6.00	3.50
Common Player:		.35	.20	.11
1	Bill Virdon	.50	.25	.15
2	Joe Ferguson	.35	.20	.11
3	Ed Herrmann	.35	.20	.11
4	J.R. Richard	.60	.30	.20
5	Joe Niekro	.60	.30	.20
6	Floyd Bannister	.70	.35	.20
7	Joaquin Andujar	.60	.30	.20
8	Ken Forsch	.40	.20	.12
9	Mark Lemongello	.35	.20	.11
10	Joe Sambito	.40	.20	.12
11	Gene Pentz	.35	.20	.11

		NR MT	EX	VG
12	Bob Watson	.40	.20	.12
13	Julio Gonzalez	.35	.20	.11
14	Enos Cabell	.40	.20	.12
15	Roger Metzger	.35	.20	.11
16	Art Howe	.60	.30	.20
17	Jose Cruz	.80	.40	.25
18	Cesar Cedeno	.80	.40	.25
19	Terry Puhl	.40	.20	.12
20	Wilbur Howard	.35	.20	.11
21	Dave Bergman	.60	.30	.20
22	Jesus Alou	.60	.30	.20
----	Checklist	.04	.02	.01

1978 Burger King Rangers

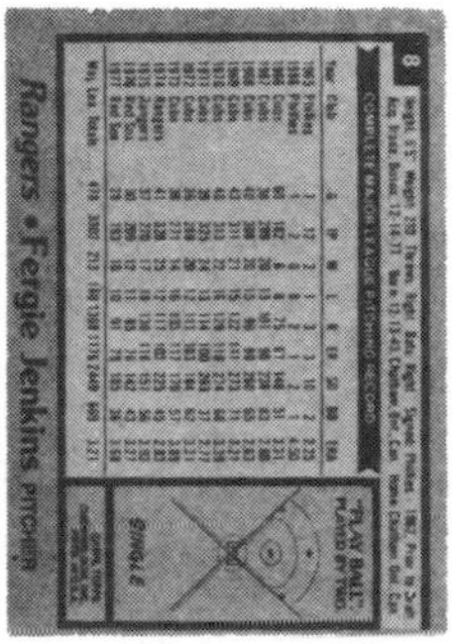

Issued by Burger King restaurants in the Dallas-Fort Worth area, this 23-card Topps-produced set features the Texas Rangers. The cards are standard size (2-1/2" by 3-1/2") and are identical in style to the regular 1978 Topps set with the following exceptions: #'s 5, 8, 10, 12, 17, 21 and 22. An unnumbered checklist card was included with the set.

		NR MT	EX	VG
Complete Set:		12.00	6.00	3.50
Common Player:		.35	.20	.11
1	Billy Hunter	.35	.20	.11
2	Jim Sundberg	.50	.25	.15
3	John Ellis	.35	.20	.11
4	Doyle Alexander	.50	.25	.15
5	Jon Matlack	.60	.30	.20
6	Dock Ellis	.35	.20	.11
7	George Medich	.35	.20	.11
8	Fergie Jenkins	1.75	.90	.50
9	Len Barker	.35	.20	.11
10	Reggie Cleveland	.60	.30	.20
11	Mike Hargrove	.40	.20	.12
12	Bump Wills	.60	.30	.20
13	Toby Harrah	.50	.25	.15
14	Bert Campaneris	.50	.25	.15
15	Sandy Alomar	.35	.20	.11
16	Kurt Bevacqua	.35	.20	.11
17	Al Oliver	1.00	.50	.30
18	Juan Beniquez	.35	.20	.11
19	Claudell Washington	.50	.25	.15
20	Richie Zisk	.40	.20	.12
21	John Lowenstein	.60	.30	.20
22	Bobby Thompson	.60	.30	.20
----	Checklist	.04	.02	.01

1978 Burger King Tigers

Rookie cards of Morris, Trammell and Whitaker make the Topps-produced 1978 Burger King Detroit Tigers issue the most popular of the BK sets. Twenty-two player cards and an unnumbered checklist make up the set which was issued in the Detroit area. The cards measure 2-1/2" by 3-1/2", and are identical to the regular 1978 Topps issue with the following exceptions - card #'s 6, 7, 8, 13, 15 and 16. Collectors are reminded that numerous minor picture-cropping variations between the regular Topps issues and the Burger King sets appear from the 1977 through 1980. These minor variations are not noted in the following checklist.

A player's name in *italic* indicates a rookie card. An (FC) indicates a player's first card for that particular card company.

		NR MT	EX	VG
Complete Set:		65.00	32.00	19.50
Common Player:		.40	.20	.12
1	Ralph Houk	.40	.20	.12
2	Milt May	.40	.20	.12
3	John Wockenfuss	.40	.20	.12
4	Mark Fidrych	1.00	.50	.30
5	Dave Rozema	.40	.20	.12
6	Jack Billingham	.40	.20	.12
7	Jim Slaton	.40	.20	.12
8	Jack Morris	15.00	7.50	4.50
9	John Hiller	.50	.25	.15
10	Steve Foucault	.40	.20	.12
11	Milt Wilcox	.40	.20	.12
12	Jason Thompson	.50	.25	.15
13	Lou Whitaker	15.00	7.50	4.50
14	Aurelio Rodriguez	.40	.20	.12
15	Alan Trammell	20.00	10.00	6.00
16	Steve Dillard	.40	.20	.12
17	Phil Mankowski	.40	.20	.12
18	Steve Kemp	.50	.25	.15
19	Ron LeFlore	.50	.25	.15
20	Tim Corcoran	.40	.20	.12
21	Mickey Stanley	.40	.20	.12
22	Rusty Staub	1.00	.50	.30
---)	Checklist	.10	.05	.03

1978 Burger King Yankees

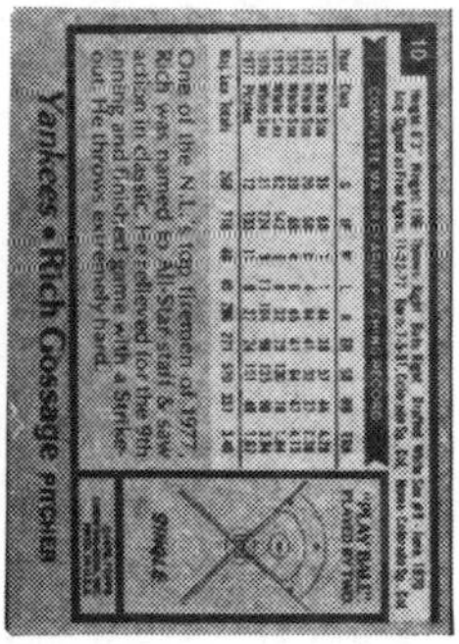

Produced by Topps for Burger King outlets in the New York area for the second year in a row, the 1978 Yankees set contains 22 cards plus an unnumbered checklist. The cards are numbered 1 through 22 and are the standard size of 2-1/2" by 3-1/2". The cards feature the same pictures found in the regular 1978 Topps set except for numbers 10, 11 and 16. Only those variations containing different poses or major picture-cropping differences are noted. Numerous minor picture-cropping variations, that are very

Here's your repli-card . . .

The 1933 DeLong set is one of the classic baseball card sets of all time. Issued by the DeLong Gum Company of Boston, Mass., the DeLongs were among the first issues to be sold with gum.

The photos in the 24-card set positioned players in the middle of a miniature stadium setting so that they appear to be giant in size.

If Frank Thomas of the Chicago White Sox had been playing in 1933 here's what his card in the DeLong set might have looked like.

We hope you enjoy it. It's yours free for reading the Sixth Edition of the Sports Collectors Digest Baseball Card Price Guide annual.

Sports Collectors Digest SIXTH EDITION 1992
BASEBALL CARD price guide
700 E. State St., Iola, WI 54990-0001

Return this postcard for a

FREE ISSUE!

Your choice of Sports Card Price Guide or Baseball Card News!

CHECK ONE: Please send an issue of

☐ **Sports Card Price Guide**

☐ **Baseball Card News**

...to the following address:

Name ____________________

Address ____________________

City ____________________

State __________ Zip __________

Complete information above and drop in mail.

No. 1. FIELDING AT FIRST.

The first baseman has one of the busiest jobs on the baseball diamond. He must not only catch the throws from the infielders, but be in position to cut-off throws from the outfield. He must also be a good glove man, to field the "hot shots" that are hit his way. When the ball is bunted, it is important for the first baseman to get to the ball as quickly as possible.

By Kit Kiefer
Editor, *Baseball Cards* magazine

This repli-card of a 1933 DeLong baseball card is a special insert in the Sixth Edition of the SCD Baseball Card Price Guide annual.

The SCD PRICE GUIDE annual is the best way to evaluate your collection.

 KRAUSE PUBLICATIONS Iola, Wis.

Krause Publications
700 E. State St., Iola, WI 54990

1933 DeLong

If you collect DeLong cards, or other pre-War issues, we refer you to the **Standard Catalog of Baseball Cards**, another fine reference book from Krause Publications. Listing virtually every baseball card produced since 1886, the **Standard Catalog of Baseball Cards** is the hobby's ultimate catalog and price guide for the more advanced collector and investor.

Serving the sports collector since 1981!

NO POSTAGE
NECESSARY
IF MAILED
IN THE
UNITED STATES

BUSINESS REPLY MAIL
FIRST CLASS MAIL PERMIT NO.12 IOLA, WI

POSTAGE WILL BE PAID BY ADDRESSEE

KRAUSE PUBLICATIONS
SPORTS CIRCULATION DEPT
700 E STATE ST
IOLA WI 54945-9989

insignificant in nature, exist between the regular Topps sets and the Burger King issues of 1977-1980.

		NR MT	EX	VG
Complete Set:		10.00	5.00	3.00
Common Player:		.30	.15	.09
1	Billy Martin	.80	.40	.25
2	Thurman Munson	3.00	1.50	.90
3	Cliff Johnson	.30	.15	.09
4	Ron Guidry	1.00	.50	.30
5	Ed Figueroa	.30	.15	.09
6	Dick Tidrow	.30	.15	.09
7	Jim Hunter	1.00	.50	.30
8	Don Gullett	.30	.15	.09
9	Sparky Lyle	.50	.25	.15
10	Rich Gossage	1.00	.50	.30
11	Rawly Eastwick	.70	.35	.20
12	Chris Chambliss	.50	.25	.15
13	Willie Randolph	.50	.25	.15
14	Graig Nettles	.80	.40	.25
15	Bucky Dent	.50	.25	.15
16	Jim Spencer	.70	.35	.20
17	Fred Stanley	.30	.15	.09
18	Lou Piniella	.80	.40	.25
19	Roy White	.50	.25	.15
20	Mickey Rivers	.50	.25	.15
21	Reggie Jackson	4.00	2.00	1.25
22	Paul Blair	.30	.15	.09
----	Checklist	.04	.02	.01

1979 Burger King Phillies

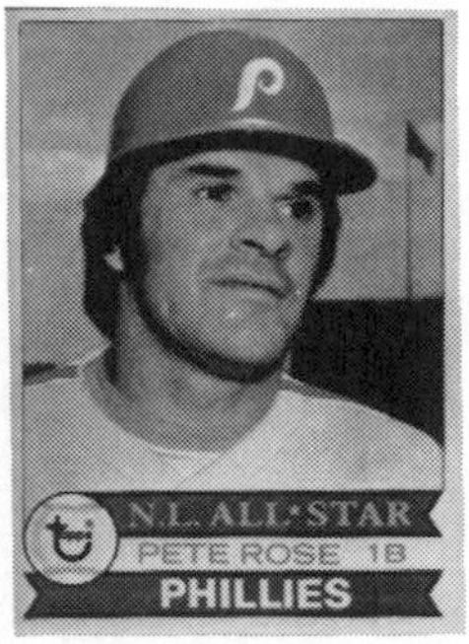

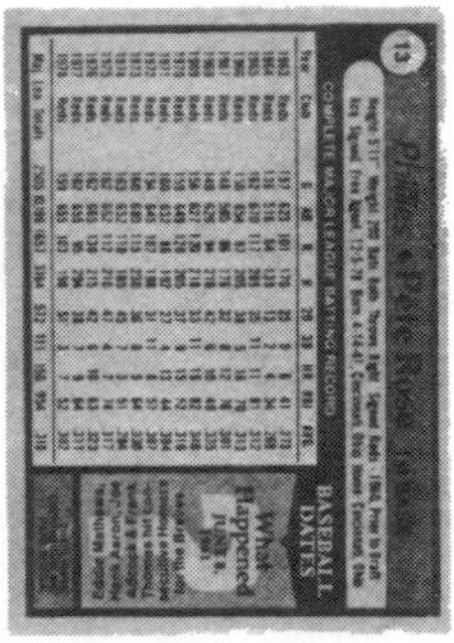

Twenty-two Philadelphia Phillies players are featured in the 1979 Burger King issue given out in the Philadelphia area. The Topps-produced set, whose cards measure 2-1/2" by 3-1/2", also includes an unnumbered checklist. The cards are identical to the regular 1979 Topps set except in seven instances. Card numbers 1, 11, 12, 13, 14, 17 and 22 have different poses. Very minor picture-cropping variations between the regular Topps issues and the Burger King sets can be found throughout the four years the cards were produced, but only those variations featuring major changes are noted in the following checklist.

		NR MT	EX	VG
Complete Set:		10.00	5.00	3.00
Common Player:		.20	.10	.06
1	Danny Ozark	.60	.30	.20
2	Bob Boone	.60	.30	.20
3	Tim McCarver	.60	.30	.20
4	Steve Carlton	3.00	1.50	.90
5	Larry Christenson	.20	.10	.06
6	Dick Ruthven	.20	.10	.06
7	Ron Reed	.20	.10	.06
8	Randy Lerch	.20	.10	.06
9	Warren Brusstar	.20	.10	.06
10	Tug McGraw	.40	.20	.12
11	Nino Espinosa	.60	.30	.20
12	Doug Bird	.20	.10	.06
13	Pete Rose	4.00	1.25	.90
14	Manny Trillo	.60	.30	.20
15	Larry Bowa	.50	.25	.15
16	Mike Schmidt	4.00	2.00	1.25
17	Pete Mackanin	.60	.30	.20
18	Jose Cardenal	.20	.10	.06
19	Greg Luzinski	.40	.20	.12
20	Garry Maddox	.30	.15	.09
21	Bake McBride	.20	.10	.06
22	Greg Gross	.20	.10	.06
----	Checklist	.04	.02	.01

1979 Burger King Yankees

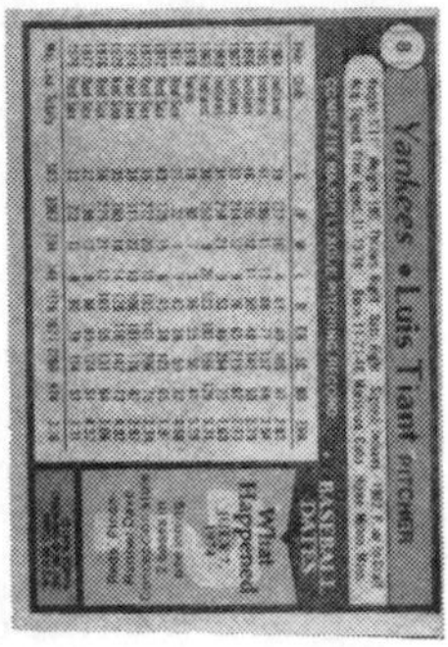

The New York Yankees were featured in a Topps-produced Burger King set for the third consecutive year in 1979. Once again, 22 numbered player cards and an unnumbered checklist made up the set. The cards, which measure 2-1/2" by 3-1/2", are identical to the 1979 Topps regular set except for card numbers 4, 8, 9 and 22 which included new poses. Only different poses or major picture-cropping variations between the regular Topps set and the Burger King issue are recognized in the checklist that follows. Numerous minor picture cropping variations between the regular Topps issue and the Burger King sets of 1977-1980 exist.

		NR MT	EX	VG
Complete Set:		10.00	5.00	3.00
Common Player:		.30	.15	.09
1	Yankees Team (Bob Lemon)	.50	.25	.15
2	Thurman Munson	2.00	1.00	.60
3	Cliff Johnson	.30	.15	.09
4	Ron Guidry	1.00	.50	.30
5	Jay Johnstone	.40	.20	.12
6	Jim Hunter	.90	.45	.25
7	Jim Beattie	.30	.15	.09
8	Luis Tiant	.80	.40	.25
9	Tommy John	1.00	.50	.30
10	Rich Gossage	.90	.45	.25
11	Ed Figueroa	.30	.15	.09
12	Chris Chambliss	.50	.25	.15
13	Willie Randolph	.50	.25	.15
14	Bucky Dent	.50	.25	.15
15	Graig Nettles	.70	.35	.20
16	Fred Stanley	.30	.15	.09
17	Jim Spencer	.30	.15	.09
18	Lou Piniella	.70	.35	.20
19	Roy White	.50	.25	.15
20	Mickey Rivers	.50	.25	.15
21	Reggie Jackson	3.00	1.50	.90
22	Juan Beniquez	.30	.15	.09
----	Checklist	.04	.02	.01

Definitions for grading conditions are located in the introduction section at the front of this book.

1980 Burger King Phillies

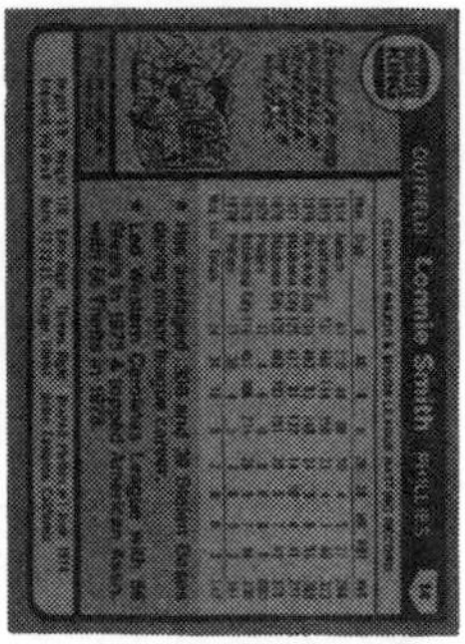

Philadelphia-area Burger King outlets issued a 23-card set featuring the Phillies for the second in a row in 1980. The Topps-produced set, whose cards measure 2-1/2" by 3-1/2", contains 22 player cards and an unnumbered checklist. The card fronts are identical in design to the regular 1980 Topps sets with the following exceptions - card numbers 1, 3, 8, 14 and 22 feature new poses. Collectors should note that very minor picture-cropping variations between the regular Topps issues and the Burger King sets exist in all years. Those minor differences are not noted in the checklist that follows. The 1980 Burger King sets were the first to include the Burger King logo on the card backs.

		NR MT	EX	VG
Complete Set:		8.00	4.00	2.50
Common Player:		.15	.08	.05
1	Dallas Green	.50	.25	.15
2	Bob Boone	.25	.13	.08
3	Keith Moreland	.60	.30	.20
4	Pete Rose	3.00	1.50	.90
5	Manny Trillo	.20	.10	.06
6	Mike Schmidt	3.00	1.50	.90
7	Larry Bowa	.40	.20	.12
8	John Vukovich	.50	.25	.15
9	Bake McBride	.15	.08	.05
10	Garry Maddox	.20	.10	.06
11	Greg Luzinski	.30	.15	.09
12	Greg Gross	.15	.08	.05
13	Del Unser	.15	.08	.05
14	Lonnie Smith	.50	.25	.15
15	Steve Carlton	1.75	.90	.50
16	Larry Christenson	.15	.08	.05
17	Nino Espinosa	.15	.08	.05
18	Randy Lerch	.15	.08	.05
19	Dick Ruthven	.15	.08	.05
20	Tug McGraw	.30	.15	.09
21	Ron Reed	.15	.08	.05
22	Kevin Saucier	.50	.25	.15
----	Checklist	.04	.02	.01

1980 Burger King Pitch, Hit & Run

In 1980, Burger King issued, in conjunction with its "Pitch, Hit & Run" promotion, a Topps-produced 34-card set featuring pitchers (card #'s 1-11), hitters (#'s 12-22), and base stealers (#'s 23-33). The card fronts, which carry the Burger King logo, are identical in nature to the regular 1980 Topps set except for numbers 1, 4, 5, 7, 9, 10, 16, 17, 18, 22, 23, 27, 28, 29 and 30, which feature different poses. The cards, which are numbered 1 through 33, measure 2-1/2" by 3-1/2" in size. An unnumbered checklist was included with the set.

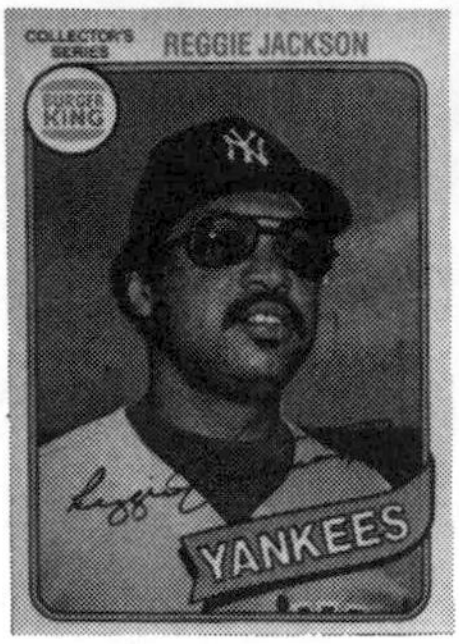

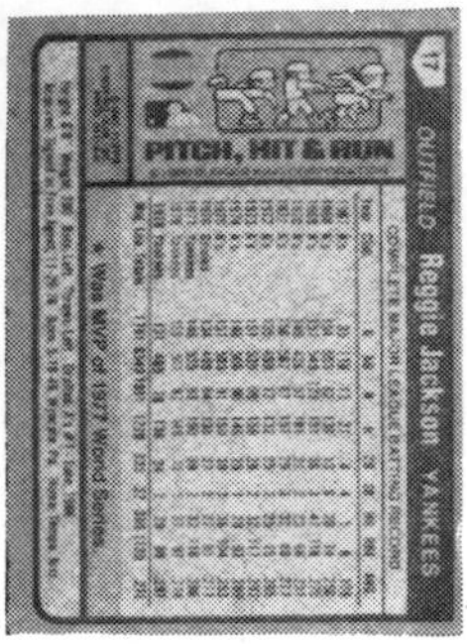

		NR MT	EX	VG
Complete Set:		25.00	12.50	7.50
Common Player:		.20	.10	.06
1	Vida Blue	.50	.25	.15
2	Steve Carlton	1.00	.50	.30
3	Rollie Fingers	.30	.15	.09
4	Ron Guidry	.70	.35	.20
5	Jerry Koosman	.40	.20	.12
6	Phil Niekro	.40	.20	.12
7	Jim Palmer	1.50	.70	.45
8	J.R. Richard	.20	.10	.06
9	Nolan Ryan	8.00	4.00	2.50
10	Tom Seaver	1.50	.70	.45
11	Bruce Sutter	.25	.13	.08
12	Don Baylor	.25	.13	.08
13	George Brett	1.50	.70	.45
14	Rod Carew	.90	.45	.25
15	George Foster	.25	.13	.08
16	Keith Hernandez	.90	.45	.25
17	Reggie Jackson	2.25	1.25	.70
18	Fred Lynn	.70	.35	.20
19	Dave Parker	.40	.20	.12
20	Jim Rice	.80	.40	.25
21	Pete Rose	2.50	1.25	.70
22	Dave Winfield	1.50	.70	.45
23	Bobby Bonds	.40	.20	.12
24	Enos Cabell	.20	.10	.06
25	Cesar Cedeno	.20	.10	.06
26	Julio Cruz	.20	.10	.06
27	Ron LeFlore	.40	.20	.12
28	Dave Lopes	.40	.20	.12
29	Omar Moreno	.40	.20	.12
30	Joe Morgan	1.00	.50	.30
31	Bill North	.20	.10	.06
32	Frank Taveras	.20	.10	.06
33	Willie Wilson	.25	.13	.08
----	Checklist	.04	.02	.01

1982 Burger King Braves

A set consisting of 27 "Collector Lids" featuring the Atlanta Braves was issued by Burger King restaurants in 1982. The lids, which measure 3-5/8" in diameter, were placed on a special Coca-Cola cup which listed the scores of the Braves' season-opening 13-game win streak. A black and white photo plus the player's name, position, height, weight, and 1981 statistics

are found on the lid front. The unnumbered, blank-backed lids also contain logos for Burger King, Coca-Cola, and the Major League Baseball Players Association.

		MT	NR MT	EX
Complete Set:		40.00	30.00	16.00
Common Player:		1.00	.70	.40
(1)	Steve Bedrosian	2.50	2.00	1.00
(2)	Bruce Benedict	1.00	.70	.40
(3)	Tommy Boggs	1.00	.70	.40
(4)	Brett Butler	2.50	2.00	1.00
(5)	Rick Camp	1.00	.70	.40
(6)	Chris Chambliss	1.25	.90	.50
(7)	Ken Dayley	1.00	.70	.40
(8)	Gene Garber	1.00	.70	.40
(9)	Preston Hanna	1.00	.70	.40
(10)	Terry Harper	1.00	.70	.40
(11)	Bob Horner	2.00	1.50	.80
(12)	Al Hrabosky	1.25	.90	.50
(13)	Glenn Hubbard	1.00	.70	.40
(14)	Randy Johnson	1.00	.70	.40
(15)	Rufino Linares	1.00	.70	.40
(16)	Rick Mahler	1.50	1.25	.60
(17)	Larry McWilliams	1.00	.70	.40
(18)	Dale Murphy	12.00	9.00	4.75
(19)	Phil Niekro	5.00	3.75	2.00
(20)	Biff Pocoroba	1.00	.70	.40
(21)	Rafael Ramirez	1.00	.70	.40
(22)	Jerry Royster	1.00	.70	.40
(23)	Ken Smith	1.00	.70	.40
(24)	Bob Walk	1.00	.70	.40
(25)	Claudell Washington	1.25	.90	.50
(26)	Bob Watson	1.00	.70	.40
(27)	Larry Whisenton	1.00	.70	.40

1982 Burger King Indians

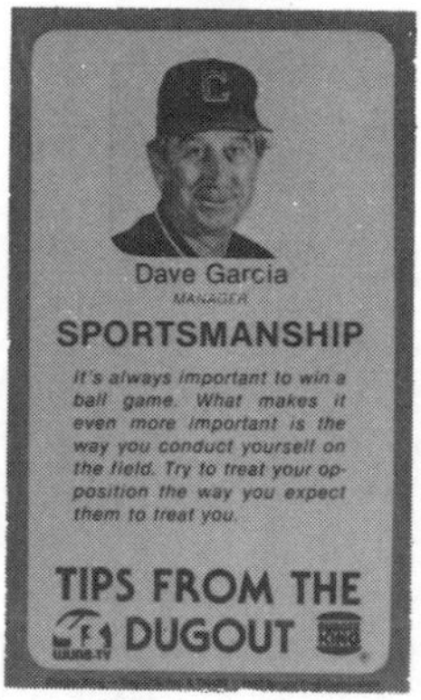
Dave Garcia
MANAGER
SPORTSMANSHIP
It's always important to win a ball game. What makes it even more important is the way you conduct yourself on the field. Try to treat your opposition the way you expect them to treat you.
TIPS FROM THE DUGOUT

The 1982 Burger King Indians set was sponsored by WUAB-TV and Burger Kings in the Cleveland vicinity. The cards' green borders encompass a large yellow area which contains a black and white photo plus a baseball tip. Manager Dave Garcia and his four coaches provide the baseball hints. The cards, which measure 3" x 5", are unnumbered and blank-backed.

		MT	NR MT	EX
Complete Set:		8.00	6.00	3.25
Common Player:		.70	.50	.30
(1)	Dave Garcia (Be In The Game)	.70	.50	.30
(2)	Dave Garcia (Sportsmanship)	.70	.50	.30
(3)	Johnny Goryl (Rounding The Bases)	.70	.50	.30
(4)	Johnny Goryl (3rd Base Running)	.70	.50	.30
(5)	Tom McCraw (Follow Thru)	.70	.50	.30
(6)	Tom McCraw (Selecting A Bat)	.70	.50	.30
(7)	Tom McCraw (Watch The Ball)	.70	.50	.30
(8)	Mel Queen (Master One Pitch)	.70	.50	.30
(9)	Mel Queen (Warm Up)	.70	.50	.30
(10)	Dennis Sommers (Get Down On A Ground Ball)	.70	.50	.30
(11)	Dennis Sommers (Protect Your Fingers)	.70	.50	.30
(12)	Dennis Sommers (Tagging First Base)	.70	.50	.30

1986 Burger King

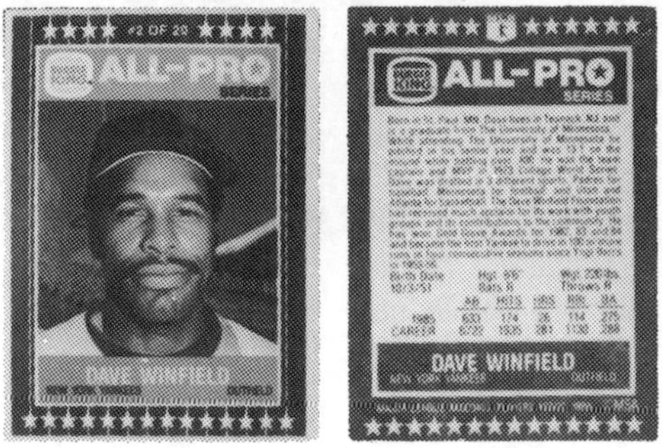

Burger King restaurants in the Pennsylvania and New Jersey areas issued a 20-card set entitled "All-Pro Series". The cards were issued with the purchase of a Whopper sandwich and came in folded panels of two cards each, along with a coupon card. The card fronts feature a color photo and contain the player's name, team and position plus the Burger King logo. Due to a licensing problem, the team insignias on the players' caps were airbrushed away. The card backs feature black print on white stock and contain brief biographical and statistical information.

		MT	NR MT	EX
Complete Panel Set		9.00	6.75	3.50
Complete Singles Set		6.00	4.50	2.50
Common Panel		.75	.60	.30
Common Single Player		.10	.08	.04
	Panel	.70	.50	.30
1	Tony Pena	.10	.08	.04
2	Dave Winfield	.20	.15	.08
	Panel	2.00	1.50	.80
3	Fernando Valenzuela	.20	.15	.08
4	Pete Rose	.50	.40	.20
	Panel	1.50	1.25	.60
5	Mike Schmidt	1.00	.70	.40
6	Steve Carlton	.30	.25	.12
	Panel	.70	.50	.30
7	Glenn Wilson	.10	.08	.04
8	Jim Rice	.20	.15	.08
	Panel	2.50	2.00	1.00
9	Wade Boggs	.80	.60	.30
10	Juan Samuel	.10	.08	.04
	Panel	1.50	1.25	.60
11	Dale Murphy	.40	.30	.15
12	Reggie Jackson	.30	.25	.12
	Panel	1.25	.90	.50
13	Kirk Gibson	.20	.15	.08
14	Eddie Murray	.30	.25	.12
	Panel	1.00	.70	.40
15	Cal Ripken, Jr.	.30	.25	.12
16	Willie McGee	.10	.08	.04
	Panel	1.75	1.25	.70
17	Dwight Gooden	.50	.40	.20
18	Steve Garvey	.25	.20	.10
	Panel	3.00	2.25	1.25
19	Don Mattingly	1.50	1.25	.60
20	George Brett	.40	.30	.15

1987 Burger King

The 1987 Burger King "All-Pro 2nd Edition Series" set was part of a giveaway promotion at participating Burger King restaurants. The set is comprised of 20 players on ten different panels. The cards measure 2-1/2" by 3-1/2" each with a three-card panel (includes a coupon card) measuring 7-5/8" by 3-1/2". The card fronts feature a full-color photo and

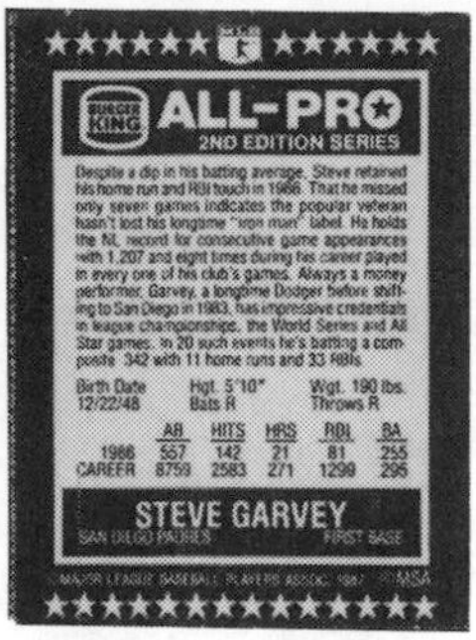

the Burger King logo surrounded by a blue stars-and-stripes border. The backs contain black print on white stock and carry a brief player biography and 1986 career statistics. The set was produced by Mike Schecter Associates and, as with many MSA issues, all team insignias were airbrushed away.

		MT	NR MT	EX
Complete Panel Set:		8.00	6.00	3.25
Complete Singles Set:		4.00	3.00	1.50
Common Panel:		.25	.20	.10
Common Single Player:		.05	.04	.02
	Panel	1.25	.90	.50
1	Wade Boggs	.40	.30	.15
2	Gary Carter	.15	.11	.06
	Panel	1.00	.70	.40
3	Will Clark	.50	.40	.20
4	Roger Clemens	.20	.15	.08
	Panel	.50	.40	.20
5	Steve Garvey	.15	.11	.06
6	Ron Darling	.08	.06	.03
	Panel	.25	.20	.10
7	Pedro Guerrero	.08	.06	.03
8	Von Hayes	.05	.04	.02
	Panel	.60	.45	.25
9	Rickey Henderson	.25	.20	.10
10	Keith Hernandez	.12	.09	.05
	Panel	.60	.45	.25
11	Wally Joyner	.20	.15	.08
12	Mike Krukow	.05	.04	.02
	Panel	1.75	1.25	.70
13	Don Mattingly	8.00	6.00	3.25
14	Ozzie Smith	.08	.06	.03
	Panel	.50	.40	.20
15	Tony Pena	.05	.04	.02
16	Jim Rice	.15	.11	.06
	Panel	.80	.60	.30
17	Ryne Sandberg	.25	.20	.10
18	Mike Schmidt	.40	.30	.15
	Panel	.80	.60	.30
19	Darryl Strawberry	.12	.09	.05
20	Fernando Valenzuela	.20	.15	.08

C

1989 Cap'n Crunch

This 22-card set was produced by Topps for Cap'n Crunch cereal boxes. Two cards and a stick of gum were included in each cereal box while the offer was active. The fronts of these 2-1/2" by 3-1/2" cards feature red, white and blue borders. The card backs are horizontal and feature lifetime statistics. The set was not offered in any complete set deal.

	MT	NR MT	EX
Complete Set:	15.00	11.00	6.00
Common Player:	.50	.40	.20

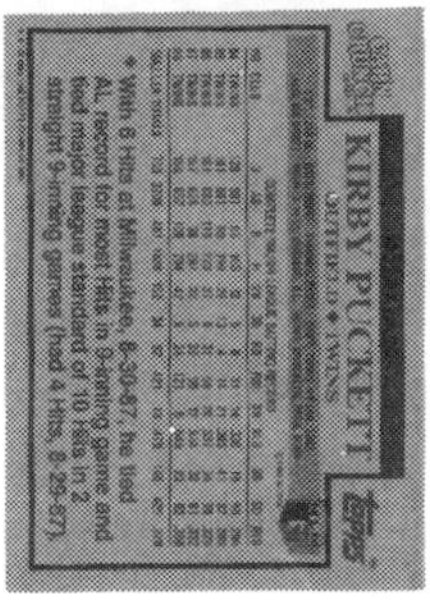

1	Jose Canseco	1.00	.70	.40
2	Kirk Gibson	.50	.40	.20
3	Orel Hershiser	.60	.45	.35
4	Frank Viola	.70	.50	.30
5	Tony Gwynn	.60	.45	.35
6	Cal Ripken	.70	.50	.30
7	Darryl Strawberry	.80	.60	.30
8	Don Mattingly	.80	.60	.30
9	George Brett	.70	.50	.30
10	Andre Dawson	.60	.45	.25
11	Dale Murphy	.50	.40	.20
12	Alan Trammell	.50	.40	.20
13	Eric Davis	.80	.60	.30
14	Jack Clark	.50	.40	.20
15	Eddie Murray	.50	.40	.20
16	Mike Schmidt	1.00	.70	.40
17	Dwight Gooden	.80	.60	.30
18	Roger Clemens	1.00	.70	.40
19	Will Clark	1.00	.70	.40
20	Kirby Puckett	.70	.50	.30
21	Robin Yount	.60	.45	.25
22	Mark McGwire	.60	.45	.25

1984 Cereal Series

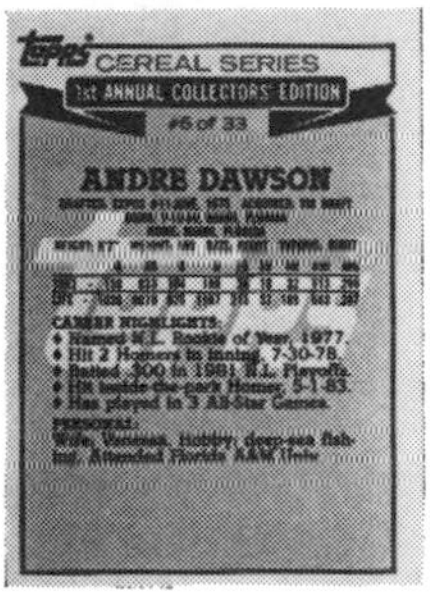

The Topps-produced 1984 Cereal Series set is identical to the Ralston Purina set from the same year in nearly all aspects. On the card fronts the words "Ralston Purina Company" were replaced by "Cereal Series" and Topps logos were substituted for Ralston checkerboard logos. The set is comprised of 33 cards, each measuring 2-1/2" by 3-1/2." The cards were inserted in unmarked boxes of Chex brand cereals.

		MT	NR MT	EX
Complete Set		13.00	9.75	5.25
Common Player		.20	.15	.08
1	Eddie Murray	.50	.40	.20
2	Ozzie Smith	.30	.25	.12
3	Ted Simmons	.20	.15	.08
4	Pete Rose	1.00	.70	.40
5	Greg Luzinski	.20	.15	.08
6	Andre Dawson	.50	.40	.20
7	Dave Winfield	.50	.40	.20
8	Tom Seaver	.50	.40	.20
9	Jim Rice	.50	.40	.20

		MT	NR MT	EX
10	Fernando Valenzuela	.40	.30	.15
11	Wade Boggs	1.00	.70	.40
12	Dale Murphy	.70	.50	.30
13	George Brett	.70	.50	.30
14	Nolan Ryan	2.00	1.50	.80
15	Rickey Henderson	.80	.60	.30
16	Steve Carlton	.50	.40	.20
17	Rod Carew	.60	.45	.25
18	Steve Garvey	.50	.40	.20
19	Reggie Jackson	.60	.45	.25
20	Dave Concepcion	.20	.15	.08
21	Robin Yount	.60	.45	.25
22	Mike Schmidt	1.00	.70	.40
23	Jim Palmer	1.00	.70	.40
24	Bruce Sutter	.20	.15	.08
25	Dan Quisenberry	.20	.15	.08
26	Bill Madlock	.20	.15	.08
27	Cecil Cooper	.20	.15	.08
28	Gary Carter	.30	.25	.12
29	Fred Lynn	.30	.25	.12
30	Pedro Guerrero	.30	.25	.12
31	Ron Guidry	.30	.25	.12
32	Keith Hernandez	.40	.30	.15
33	Carlton Fisk	.30	.25	.12

1987 Champion Phillies

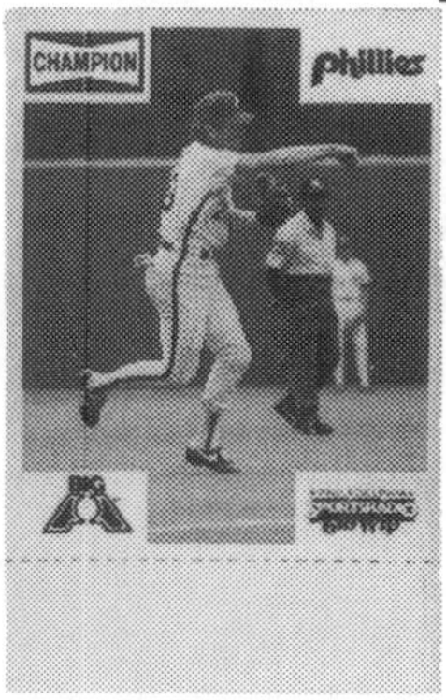

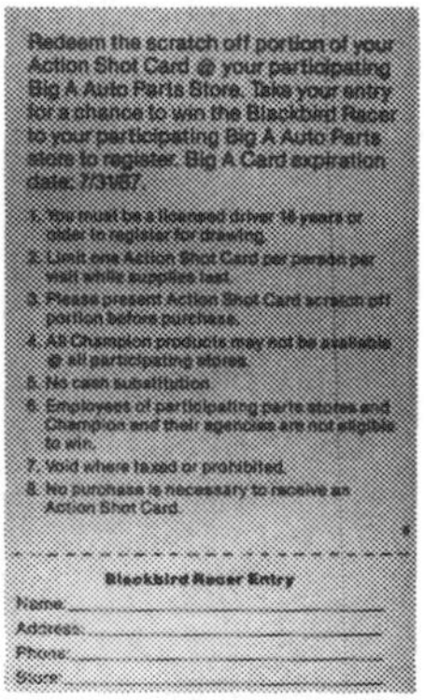

This four card set is interesting in that the players are not identified on the card fronts or backs. The full-color cards, which measure 2-3/4" by 4-5/16", were produced by the Champion Spark Plug Co. as part of a contest held at participating Big A, Car Quest and Pep Boys auto parts stores. Entrants were advised to return the scratch-off coupon portion of the card for a chance to win a Blackbird Racer. Each card contains a scratch-off portion which may have contained an instant prize. Each card can be found with either a Big A, Car Quest or Pep Boys logo in the lower left corner on the card front. The contest was also sponsored in part by the Philadelphia Phillies and radio station WIP.

		MT	NR MT	EX
Complete Set:		20.00	15.00	8.00
Common Player:		1.00	.70	.40
(1)	Von Hayes (glove on knee)	3.00	2.25	1.25
(2)	Steve Jeltz (#30 on uniform)	1.00	.70	.40
(3)	Juan Samuel (laying on base)	4.00	3.00	1.50
(4)	Mike Schmidt (making throw)	12.00	9.00	4.75

1988 Chef Boyardee

This uncut sheet of 24 cards highlights 12 American and 12 National League players. Full-color player closeup photos are printed beneath a red, white and blue "1988 1st Annual Collector's Edition" header. The player name, team and position appear beneath his photo. Card backs are printed in blue ink on a red background and include biographical information, stats and career highlights including acquisition date and draft date/choice number. The set was produced by American Home Food Products

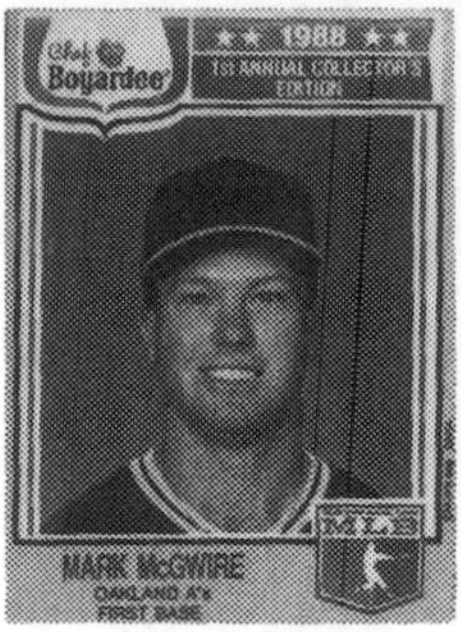

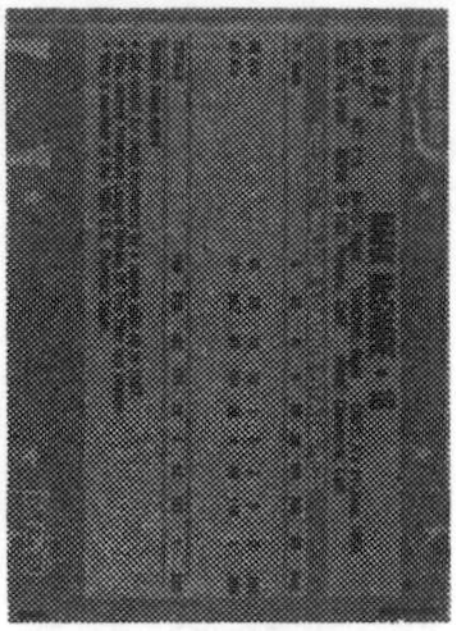

for exclusive distribution via a mail-in offer involving proofs of purchase from the company's Chef Boyardee products.

		MT	NR MT	EX
Complete Uncut Sheet:		25.00	18.50	10.00
Complete Singles Set:		20.00	15.00	8.00
Common Single Player:		.50	.40	.20
1	Mark McGwire	1.50	1.25	.60
2	Eric Davis	1.00	.70	.40
3	Jack Morris	.50	.40	.20
4	George Bell	.75	.60	.30
5	Ozzie Smith	.50	.40	.20
6	Tony Gwynn	1.00	.70	.40
7	Cal Ripken, Jr.	1.50	1.25	.60
8	Todd Worrell	.50	.40	.20
9	Larry Parrish	.50	.40	.20
10	Gary Carter	.70	.50	.30
11	Ryne Sandberg	1.50	1.25	.60
12	Keith Hernandez	.60	.45	.25
13	Kirby Puckett	1.25	.90	.50
14	Mike Schmidt	1.75	1.25	.70
15	Frank Viola	.50	.40	.20
16	Don Mattingly	2.00	1.50	.80
17	Dale Murphy	.50	.40	.20
18a	Andre Dawson (1987 team is Expos)	.75	.60	.30
18b	Andre Dawson (1987 team is Cubs)	.75	.60	.30
19	Mike Scott	.50	.40	.20
20	Rickey Henderson	1.25	.90	.50
21	Jim Rice	.75	.60	.30
22	Wade Boggs	1.25	.90	.50
23	Roger Clemens	1.75	1.25	.70
24	Fernando Valenzuela	.75	.60	.30

1985 Circle K

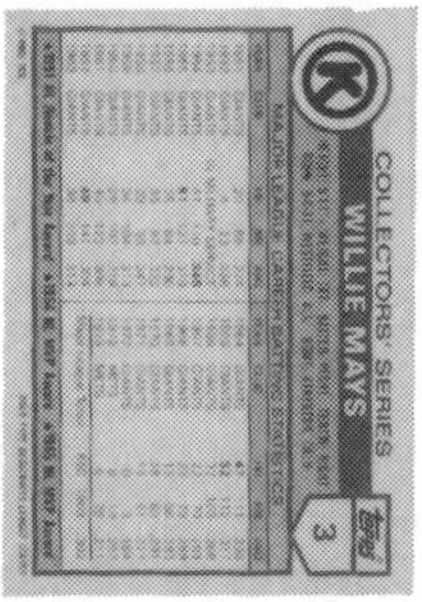

Produced by Topps for Circle K stores, this 33-card set is entitled "Baseball All Time Home Run Kings". The cards, which measure 2-1/2" by 3-1/2", are numbered on the back according to the player's position on the all-time career home run list. Joe DiMaggio, who ranked 31st, was not included in the set. The set is skip-numbered from 30 to 32. The glossy card fronts contain the player's name in the lower left corner and feature a color photo, although black and white photos were utilized for a few of the homer kings who played before 1960. The card backs

have blue and red print on white stock and contain the player's career batting statistics. The set was issued with a specially designed box.

		MT	NR MT	EX
Complete Set:		8.00	6.00	3.25
Common Player:		.15	.11	.06
1	Hank Aaron	.60	.45	.25
2	Babe Ruth	2.00	1.50	.80
3	Willie Mays	.60	.45	.25
4	Frank Robinson	.25	.20	.10
5	Harmon Killebrew	.25	.20	.10
6	Mickey Mantle	2.00	1.50	.80
7	Jimmie Foxx	.25	.20	.10
8	Willie McCovey	.25	.20	.10
9	Ted Williams	.70	.50	.30
10	Ernie Banks	.35	.25	.14
11	Eddie Mathews	.25	.20	.10
12	Mel Ott	.20	.15	.08
13	Reggie Jackson	.40	.30	.15
14	Lou Gehrig	1.00	.70	.40
15	Stan Musial	.60	.45	.25
16	Willie Stargell	.20	.15	.08
17	Carl Yastrzemski	.50	.40	.20
18	Billy Williams	.20	.15	.08
19	Mike Schmidt	.40	.30	.15
20	Duke Snider	.40	.30	.15
21	Al Kaline	.25	.20	.10
22	Johnny Bench	.35	.25	.14
23	Frank Howard	.15	.11	.06
24	Orlando Cepeda	.15	.11	.06
25	Norm Cash	.15	.11	.06
26	Dave Kingman	.15	.11	.06
27	Rocky Colavito	.15	.11	.06
28	Tony Perez	.15	.11	.06
29	Gil Hodges	.20	.15	.08
30	Ralph Kiner	.20	.15	.08
32	Johnny Mize	.20	.15	.08
33	Yogi Berra	.35	.25	.14
34	Lee May	.15	.11	.06

1987 Classic Major League Baseball Game

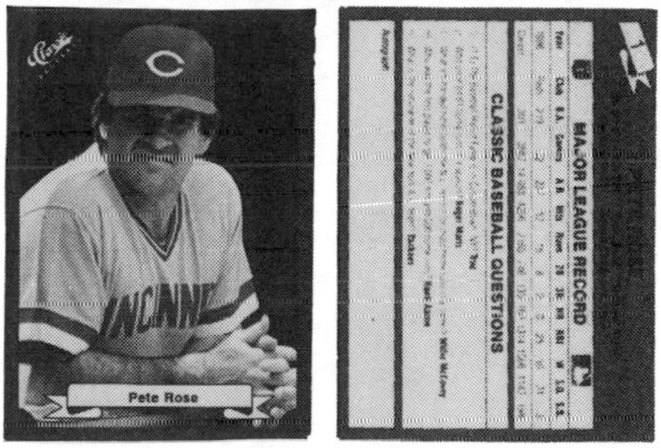

The "Classic Major League Baseball Board Game" set consists of 100 full-color cards which were used to play the game. Game participants were required to answer trivia questions found on the backs of the cards. The attractive cards measure 2 1/2" by 3 1/2" and are printed on glossy card stock. The card backs carry the player's career statistics besides the Classic Baseball Questions. The game was produced by Game Time, Ltd. of Marietta, Ga., and sold for $19.95 in most retail outlets.

		MT	NR MT	EX
Complete Set:		225.00	175.00	90.00
Common Player:		.10	.08	.04
1	Pete Rose	3.00	2.25	1.25
2	Len Dykstra	2.00	1.50	.80
3	Darryl Strawberry	5.00	3.75	2.00
4	Keith Hernandez	.40	.30	.15
5	Gary Carter	.50	.40	.20
6	Wally Joyner	1.00	.70	.40
7	Andres Thomas	.15	.11	.06
8	Pat Dodson	.15	.11	.06
9	Kirk Gibson	.30	.25	.12
10	Don Mattingly	4.00	3.00	1.50
11	Dave Winfield	.50	.40	.20
12	Rickey Henderson	8.00	6.00	3.25
13	Dan Pasqua	.15	.11	.06
14	Don Baylor	.15	.11	.06
15	Bo Jackson	100.00	75.00	32.00
16	Pete Incaviglia	.30	.25	.12
17	Kevin Bass	.10	.08	.04
18	Barry Larkin	1.00	.70	.40
19	Dave Magadan	1.00	.70	.40
20	Steve Sax	.20	.15	.08
21	Eric Davis	1.25	.90	.50
22	Mike Pagliarulo	.15	.11	.06
23	Fred Lynn	.20	.15	.08
24	Reggie Jackson	1.00	.70	.40
25	Larry Parrish	.10	.08	.04
26	Tony Gwynn	2.00	1.50	.80
27	Steve Garvey	.40	.30	.15
28	Glenn Davis	.20	.15	.08
29	Tim Raines	.40	.30	.15
30	Vince Coleman	.20	.15	.08
31	Willie McGee	.15	.11	.06
32	Ozzie Smith	.80	.60	.30
33	Dave Parker	.20	.15	.08
34	Tony Pena	.10	.08	.04
35	Ryne Sandberg	8.00	6.00	3.25
36	Brett Butler	.10	.08	.04
37	Dale Murphy	.50	.40	.20
38	Bob Horner	.15	.11	.06
39	Pedro Guerrero	.25	.20	.10
40	Brook Jacoby	.15	.11	.06
41	Carlton Fisk	.20	.15	.08
42	Harold Baines	.15	.11	.06
43	Rob Deer	.10	.08	.04
44	Robin Yount	2.00	1.50	.80
45	Paul Molitor	.20	.15	.08
46	Jose Canseco	40.00	30.00	15.00
47	George Brett	1.00	.70	.40
48	Jim Presley	.15	.11	.06
49	Rich Gedman	.10	.08	.04
50	Lance Parrish	.20	.15	.08
51	Eddie Murray	.50	.40	.20
52	Cal Ripken, Jr.	4.00	3.00	1.50
53	Kent Hrbek	.25	.20	.10
54	Gary Gaetti	.20	.15	.08
55	Kirby Puckett	3.00	2.25	1.25
56	George Bell	.40	.30	.15
57	Tony Fernandez	.20	.15	.08
58	Jesse Barfield	.15	.11	.06
59	Jim Rice	.40	.30	.15
60	Wade Boggs	1.75	1.25	.70
61	Marty Barrett	.10	.08	.04
62	Mike Schmidt	5.00	3.75	2.00
63	Von Hayes	.15	.11	.06
64	Jeff Leonard	.10	.08	.04
65	Chris Brown	.15	.11	.06
66	Dave Smith	.10	.08	.04
67	Mike Krukow	.10	.08	.04
68	Ron Guidry	.20	.15	.08
69	Rob Woodward	.15	.11	.06
70	Rob Murphy	.15	.11	.06
71	Andres Galarraga	.25	.20	.10
72	Dwight Gooden	1.25	.90	.50
73	Bob Ojeda	.10	.08	.04
74	Sid Fernandez	.15	.11	.06
75	Jesse Orosco	.10	.08	.04
76	Roger McDowell	.15	.11	.06
77	John Tutor (Tudor)	.15	.11	.06
78	Tom Browning	.15	.11	.06
79	Rick Aguilera	.10	.08	.04
80	Lance McCullers	.15	.11	.06
81	Mike Scott	.20	.15	.08
82	Nolan Ryan	10.00	7.50	4.00
83	Bruce Hurst	.15	.11	.06
84	Roger Clemens	2.00	1.50	.80
85	Oil Can Boyd	.10	.08	.04
86	Dave Righetti	.20	.15	.08
87	Dennis Rasmussen	.10	.08	.04
88	Bret Saberhagan (Saberhagen)	.35	.25	.14
89	Mark Langston	.35	.25	.14
90	Jack Morris	.15	.11	.06
91	Fernando Valenzuela	.25	.20	.10
92	Orel Hershiser	.35	.25	.14
93	Rick Honeycutt	.10	.08	.04
94	Jeff Reardon	.15	.11	.06
95	John Habyan	.10	.08	.04
96	Goose Gossage	.15	.11	.06
97	Todd Worrell	.20	.15	.08

		MT	NR MT	EX
98	Floyd Youmans	.10	.08	.04
99	Don Aase	.10	.08	.04
100	John Franco	.15	.11	.06

1987 Classic Baseball Travel Edition

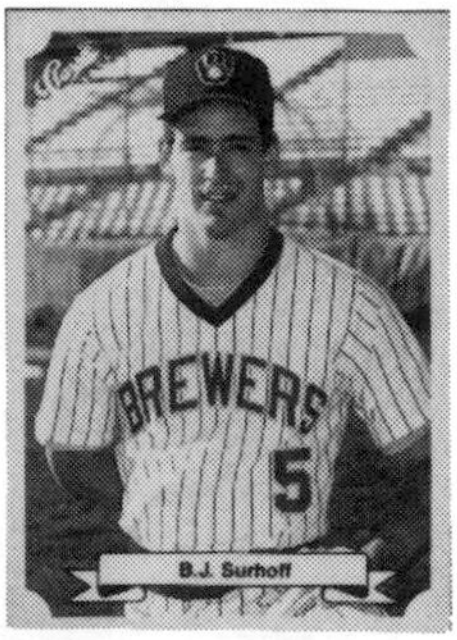

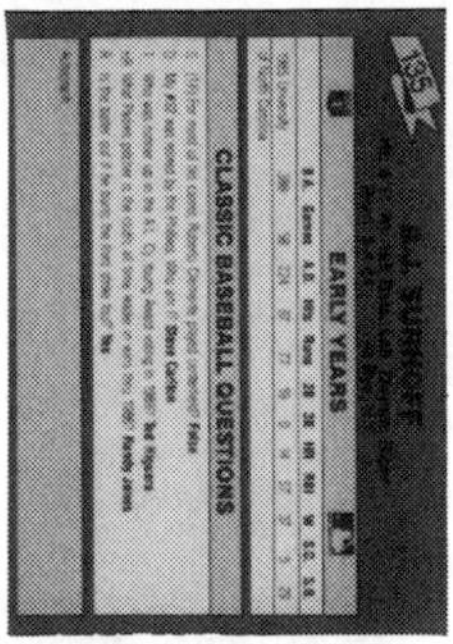

Game Time, Ltd. of Marietta, Ga., issued as an update to their Classic Baseball Board Game a 50-card set entitled "Travel Edition." The cards measure 2-1/2" by 3-1/2" and feature the same outstanding quality characteristic of the first release. Numbered from 101 to 150, the "Travel Edition" is an extension of the original set. Besides updating player trades and showcasing rookies, the set offers several highlights from the 1987 season, including Andre Dawson's beaning. All new trivia questions are contained on the card backs.

		MT	NR MT	EX
Complete Set:		30.00	22.00	12.00
Common Player:		.08	.06	.03
101	Mike Schmidt	2.00	1.50	.80
102	Eric Davis	1.00	.70	.40
103	Pete Rose	1.00	.70	.40
104	Don Mattingly	2.00	1.50	.80
105	Wade Boggs	1.50	1.25	.60
106	Dale Murphy	.40	.30	.15
107	Glenn Davis	.20	.15	.08
108	Wally Joyner	2.00	1.50	.80
109	Bo Jackson	5.00	3.75	2.00
110	Cory Snyder	.20	.15	.08
111	Jim Lindeman	.15	.11	.06
112	Kirby Puckett	1.00	.70	.40
113	Barry Bonds	4.00	3.00	1.50
114	Roger Clemens	1.00	.70	.40
115	Oddibe McDowell	.08	.06	.03
116	Bret Saberhagen	.30	.25	.12
117	Joe Magrane	.30	.25	.12
118	Scott Fletcher	.08	.06	.03
119	Mark McLemore	.08	.06	.03
120	Who Me? (Joe Niekro)	.25	.20	.10
121	Mark McGwire	2.00	1.50	.80
122	Darryl Strawberry	1.50	1.25	.60
123	Mike Scott	.20	.15	.08
124	Andre Dawson	.50	.40	.20
125	Jose Canseco	5.00	3.75	2.00
126	Kevin McReynolds	.25	.20	.10
127	Joe Carter	1.00	.70	.40
128	Casey Candaele	.08	.06	.03
129	Matt Nokes	.30	.25	.12
130	Kal Daniels	.50	.40	.20
131	Pete Incaviglia	.50	.40	.20
132	Benito Santiago	1.00	.70	.40
133	Barry Larkin	1.00	.70	.40
134	Gary Pettis	.08	.06	.03
135	B.J. Surhoff	.60	.45	.25
136	Juan Nieves	.15	.11	.06
137	Jim Deshaies	.15	.11	.06
138	Pete O'Brien	.15	.11	.06
139	Kevin Seitzer	.30	.25	.12
140	Devon White	.50	.40	.20
141	Rob Deer	.08	.06	.03
142	Kurt Stillwell	.25	.20	.10
143	Edwin Correa	.08	.06	.03
144	Dion James	.08	.06	.03
145	Danny Tartabull	.60	.45	.25
146	Jerry Browne	.08	.06	.03
147	Ted Higuera	.15	.11	.06
148	Jack Clark	.20	.15	.08
149	Ruben Sierra	2.00	1.50	.80
150	McGwire/Davis (Eric Davis, Mark McGwire)	1.50	1.25	.60

1988 Classic Baseball Travel Edition - Blue

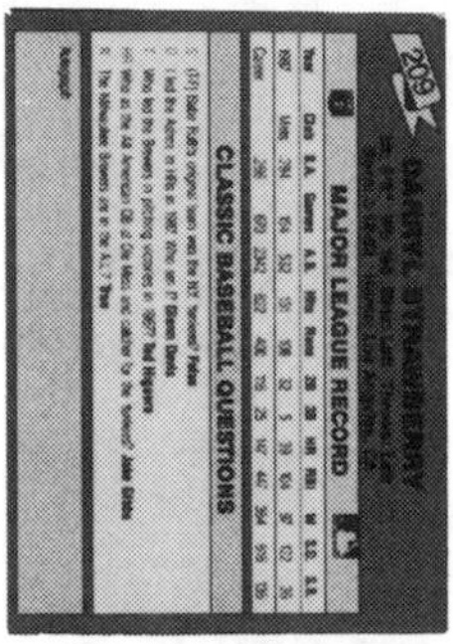

This 50-card set, numbered 201-250, was produced for use with the travel edition of Game Time's Classic Baseball Board Game. Two cards in the set feature two players: Davis/Murphy and McGwire/Mattingly. A follow-up to the first edition in 1987, the 1988 Blue was designed for use with the 1988 Red Series (151-200). Blue Series card fronts have blue borders, a yellow classic logo in the upper left corner and a black and beige player name banner beneath the photo. The card backs are printed in blue on white and include the player name, personal info, major league records, a baseball question and space for the player autograph. Classic card series are sold via hobby dealers and retail toy stores nationwide. Game Time Ltd., the set's producer, was purchased by Scoreboard of Cherry Hill, N.J. in 1988.

		MT	NR MT	EX
Complete Set:		20.00	15.00	8.00
Common Player:		.15	.11	.06
201	Davis/Murphy (Eric Davis, Dale Murphy)	.40	.30	.15
202	B.J. Surhoff	.15	.11	.06
203	John Kruk	.20	.15	.08
204	Sam Horn	.15	.11	.06
205	Jack Clark	.25	.20	.10
206	Wally Joyner	.40	.30	.15
207	Matt Nokes	.30	.25	.12
208	Bo Jackson	4.00	3.00	1.50
209	Darryl Strawberry	1.00	.70	.40
210	Ozzie Smith	.25	.20	.10
211	Don Mattingly	1.00	.70	.40
212	Mark McGwire	1.00	.70	.40
213	Eric Davis	.70	.50	.30
214	Wade Boggs	1.50	1.25	.60
215	Dale Murphy	.30	.25	.12
216	Andre Dawson	.30	.25	.12
217	Roger Clemens	1.00	.70	.40
218	Kevin Seitzer	.30	.25	.12
219	Benito Santiago	.30	.25	.12
220	Tony Gwynn	.80	.60	.30
221	Mike Scott	.20	.15	.08
222	Steve Bedrosian	.15	.11	.06
223	Vince Coleman	.25	.20	.10
224	Rick Sutcliffe	.15	.11	.06
225	Will Clark	7.00	5.25	2.75
226	Pete Rose	1.50	1.25	.60
227	Mike Greenwell	.70	.50	.30
228	Ken Caminiti	.15	.11	.06
229	Ellis Burks	1.00	.70	.40
230	Dave Magadan	.15	.11	.06

		MT	NR MT	EX
231	Alan Trammell	.30	.25	.12
232	Paul Molitor	.25	.20	.10
233	Gary Gaetti	.25	.20	.10
234	Rickey Henderson	1.25	.90	.50
235	Danny Tartabull	.60	.45	.25
236	Bobby Bonilla	1.00	.70	.40
237	Mike Dunne	.20	.15	.08
238	Al Leiter	.15	.11	.06
239	John Farrell	.15	.11	.06
240	Joe Magrane	.15	.11	.06
241	Mike Henneman	.15	.11	.06
242	George Bell	.40	.30	.15
243	Gregg Jefferies	1.25	.90	.50
244	Jay Buhner	.40	.30	.15
245	Todd Benzinger	.30	.25	.12
246	Matt Williams	2.00	1.50	.80
247	McGwire/Mattingly (Don Mattingly, Mark McGwire) (no card number on back)	1.00	.70	.40
248	George Brett	.60	.45	.25
249	Jimmy Key	.20	.15	.08
250	Mark Langston	.20	.15	.08

1988 Classic Baseball Travel Edition - Red

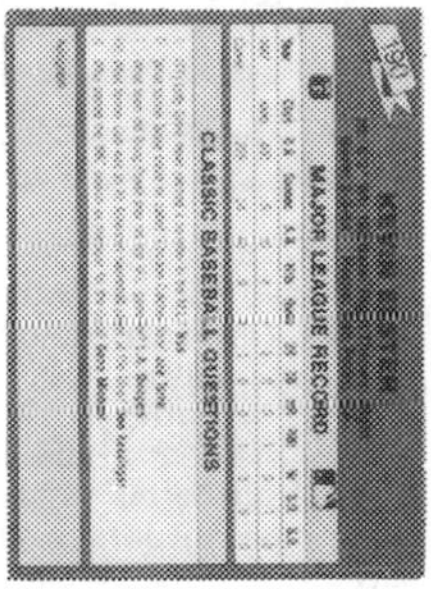

	MT	NR MT	EX
Complete Set:	10.00	7.50	4.00
Common Player:	.08	.06	.03

		MT	NR MT	EX
151	McGwire/Mattingly (Don Mattingly, Mark McGwire)	1.50	1.25	.60
152	Don Mattingly	2.00	1.50	.80
153	Mark McGwire	1.00	.70	.40
154	Eric Davis	1.00	.70	.40
155	Wade Boggs	1.50	1.25	.60
156	Dale Murphy	.70	.50	.30
157	Andre Dawson	.30	.25	.12
158	Roger Clemens	.70	.50	.30
159	Kevin Seitzer	.30	.25	.12
160	Benito Santigo	.30	.25	.12
161	Kal Daniels	.25	.20	.10
162	John Kruk	.15	.11	.06
163	Billy Ripkin (Ripken)	.08	.06	.03
164	Kirby Puckett	.50	.40	.20
165	Jose Canseco	2.50	2.00	1.00
166	Matt Nokes	.20	.15	.08
167	Mike Schmidt	.70	.50	.30
168	Tim Raines	.50	.40	.20
169	Ryne Sandberg	.60	.45	.25
170	Dave Winfield	.40	.30	.15
171	Dwight Gooden	.70	.50	.30
172	Bret Saberhagen	.25	.20	.10
173	Willie McGee	.20	.15	.08
174	Jack Morris	.20	.15	.08
175	Jeff Leonard	.08	.06	.03
176	Cal Ripkin, Jr. (Ripkin)	.60	.45	.25
177	Pete Incaviglia	.20	.15	.08
178	Devon White	.25	.20	.10
179	Nolan Ryan	.50	.40	.20
180	Ruben Sierra	.30	.25	.12
181	Todd Worrell	.20	.15	.08
182	Glenn Davis	.25	.20	.10
183	Frank Viola	.25	.20	.10
184	Cory Snyder	.15	.11	.06
185	Tracy Jones	.20	.15	.08
186	Terry Steinbach	.15	.11	.06
187	Julio Franco	.15	.11	.06
188	Larry Sheets	.08	.06	.03
189	John Marzano	.08	.06	.03
190	Kevin Elster	.20	.15	.08
191	Vince Palacios (Vicente)	.15	.11	.06
192	Kent Hrbek	.30	.25	.12
193	Eric Bell	.08	.06	.03
194	Kelly Downs	.15	.11	.06
195	Jose Lind	.20	.15	.08
196	Dave Stewart	.30	.25	.12
197	McGwire/Canseco (Jose Canseco, Mark McGwire) (no card number on back)	2.00	1.50	.80
198	Phil Niekro (Indians)	.30	.25	.12
199	Phil Niekro (Blue Jays)	.30	.25	.12
200	Phil Niekro (Braves)	.30	.25	.12

1989 Classic Baseball

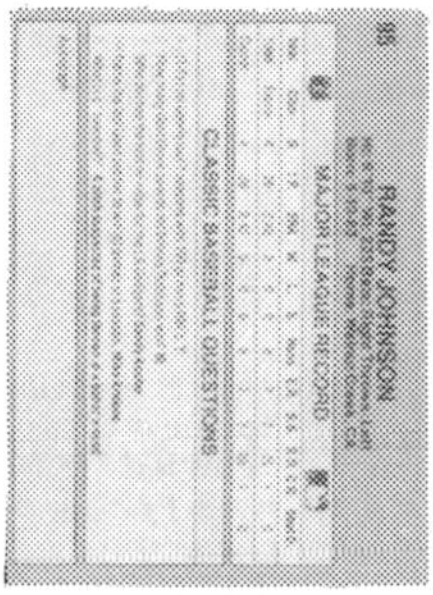

This 100-card set was released by The Score Board to accompany trivia board games. Cards numbered 1-100 correlate with the 1989 Classic Baseball Game, while cards numbered 101-150 belong to the 1989 Classic Travel Series No. 1. The card fronts display full-color photos with the Classic Baseball logo in the upper left corner. The player's name appears beneath the photo. The flip side includes the card number in the upper left, personal information, and the player's major league record in a boxed area. Another boxed area below the record presents five trivia questions. The lower border of the flip side provides an autograph space. The Classic card series was sold by retail stores and hobby dealers nationwide.

	MT	NR MT	EX
Complete Set:	25.00	20.00	10.00
Common Player:	.08	.06	.03

		MT	NR MT	EX
1	Orel Hershiser	.30	.25	.12
2	Wade Boggs	.60	.45	.25
3	Jose Canseco	1.50	1.25	.60
4	Mark McGwire	.40	.30	.15
5	Don Mattingly	.60	.45	.25
6	Gregg Jefferies	1.00	.70	.40
7	Dwight Gooden	.60	.45	.25
8	Darryl Strawberry	.40	.30	.15
9	Eric Davis	.40	.30	.15
10	Joey Meyer	.08	.06	.03
11	Joe Carter	.15	.11	.06
12	Paul Molitor	.15	.11	.06
13	Mark Grace	1.00	.70	.40
14	Kurt Stillwell	.08	.06	.03
15	Kirby Puckett	.60	.45	.25
16	Keith Miller	.08	.06	.03
17	Glenn Davis	.15	.11	.06
18	Will Clark	1.50	1.25	.60
19	Cory Snyder	.15	.11	.06
20	Jose Lind	.08	.06	.03
21	Andres Thomas	.08	.06	.03
22	Dave Smith	.08	.06	.03
23	Mike Scott	.15	.11	.06
24	Kevin McReynolds	.20	.15	.08
25	B.J. Surhoff	.20	.15	.08
26	Mackey Sasser	.08	.06	.03
27	Chad Kreuter	.20	.15	.08
28	Hal Morris	1.00	.70	.40
29	Wally Joyner	.20	.15	.08
30	Tony Gwynn	.40	.30	.15

		MT	NR MT	EX
31	Kevin Mitchell	1.00	.70	.40
32	Dave Winfield	.25	.20	.10
33	Billy Bean	.08	.06	.03
34	Steve Bedrosian	.08	.06	.03
35	Ron Gant	.70	.50	.30
36	Len Dykstra	.20	.15	.08
37	Andre Dawson	.20	.15	.08
38	Brett Butler	.20	.15	.08
39	Rob Deer	.08	.06	.03
40	Tommy John	.08	.06	.03
41	Gary Gaetti	.20	.15	.08
42	Tim Raines	.20	.15	.08
43	George Bell	.20	.15	.08
44	Dwight Evans	.20	.15	.08
45	Denny Martinez	.08	.06	.03
46	Andres Galarraga	.20	.15	.08
47	George Brett	.40	.30	.15
48	Mike Schmidt	1.25	.90	.50
49	Dave Steib	.20	.15	.08
50	Rickey Henderson	.70	.50	.30
51	Craig Biggio	.80	.60	.30
52	Mark Lemke	.25	.20	.10
53	Chris Sabo	.60	.45	.25
54	Jeff Treadway	.15	.11	.06
55	Kent Hrbek	.15	.11	.06
56	Cal Ripken, Jr.	1.00	.70	.40
57	Tim Belcher	.15	.11	.06
58	Ozzie Smith	.40	.30	.15
59	Keith Hernandez	.20	.15	.08
60	Pedro Guerrero	.20	.15	.08
61	Greg Swindell	.25	.20	.10
62	Bret Saberhagen	.40	.30	.15
63	John Tudor	.08	.06	.03
64	Gary Carter	.15	.11	.06
65	Kevin Seitzer	.20	.15	.08
66	Jesse Barfield	.20	.15	.08
67	Luis Medina	.20	.15	.08
68	Walt Weiss	.35	.25	.14
69	Terry Steinbach	.30	.25	.12
70	Barry Larkin	.30	.25	.12
71	Pete Rose	.80	.60	.30
72	Luis Salazar	.08	.06	.03
73	Benito Santiago	.40	.30	.15
74	Kal Daniels	.20	.15	.08
75	Kevin Elster	.08	.06	.03
76	Rob Dibble	.50	.40	.20
77	Bobby Witt	.50	.40	.20
78	Steve Searcy	.25	.20	.10
79	Sandy Alomar	1.00	.70	.40
80	Chili Davis	.20	.15	.08
81	Alvin Davis	.20	.15	.08
82	Charlie Leibrandt	.08	.06	.03
83	Robin Yount	.80	.60	.30
84	Mark Carreon	.25	.20	.10
85	Pascual Perez	.08	.06	.03
86	Dennis Rasmussen	.08	.06	.03
87	Ernie Riles	.08	.06	.03
88	Melido Perez	.20	.15	.08
89	Doug Jones	.08	.06	.03
90	Dennis Eckersley	.15	.11	.06
91	Bob Welch	.15	.11	.06
92	Bob Milacki	.15	.11	.06
93	Jeff Robinson	.15	.11	.06
94	Mike Henneman	.15	.11	.06
95	Randy Johnson	.40	.30	.15
96	Ron Jones	.15	.11	.06
97	Jack Armstrong	.25	.20	.10
98	Willie McGee	.08	.06	.03
99	Ryne Sandberg	.80	.60	.30
100	David Cone / Danny Jackson	.70	.50	.25
101	Gary Sheffield	2.00	1.50	.80
102	Wade Boggs	.60	.45	.25
103	Jose Canseco	1.25	.90	.50
104	Mark McGwire	.80	.60	.30
105	Orel Hershiser	.30	.25	.12
106	Don Mattingly	1.25	.90	.50
107	Dwight Gooden	.70	.50	.30
108	Darryl Strawberry	.40	.30	.15
109	Eric Davis	.40	.30	.15
110	Bam Bam Meulens	.40	.30	.15
111	Andy Van Slyke	.20	.15	.08
112	Al Leiter	.08	.06	.03
113	Matt Nokes	.15	.11	.06
114	Mike Krukow	.08	.06	.03
115	Tony Fernandez	.25	.20	.10
116	Fred McGriff	.30	.25	.12
117	Barry Bonds	.60	.45	.25
118	Gerald Perry	.08	.06	.03
119	Roger Clemens	.50	.40	.20
120	Kirk Gibson	.12	.09	.05
121	Greg Maddux	.30	.25	.12
122	Bo Jackson	1.25	.90	.50
123	Danny Jackson	.08	.06	.03
124	Dale Murphy	.20	.15	.08
125	David Cone	.35	.25	.14
126	Tom Browning	.15	.11	.06
127	Roberto Alomar	.50	.40	.20
128	Alan Trammell	.15	.11	.06
129	Rickey Jordan	.20	.15	.08
130	Ramon Martinez	1.00	.70	.40
131	Ken Griffey, Jr.	5.00	3.75	2.00
132	Gregg Olson	.50	.40	.20
133	Carlos Quintana	.35	.25	.14
134	Dave West	.30	.25	.12
135	Cameron Drew	.15	.11	.06
136	Ted Higuera	.25	.20	.20
137	Sil Campusano	.20	.15	.08
138	Mark Gubicza	.20	.15	.08
139	Mike Boddicker	.08	.06	.03
140	Paul Gibson	.08	.06	.03
141	Jose Rijo	.30	.25	.12
142	John Costello	.08	.06	.03
143	Cecil Espy	.08	.06	.03
144	Frank Viola	.25	.20	.10
145	Erik Hanson	.30	.25	.12
146	Juan Samuel	.08	.06	.03
147	Harold Reynolds	.15	.11	.06
148	Joe Magrane	.15	.11	.06
149	Mike Greenwell	.30	.25	.12
150	Darryl Strawberry / Will Clark	1.00	.70	.40

1989 Classic Update

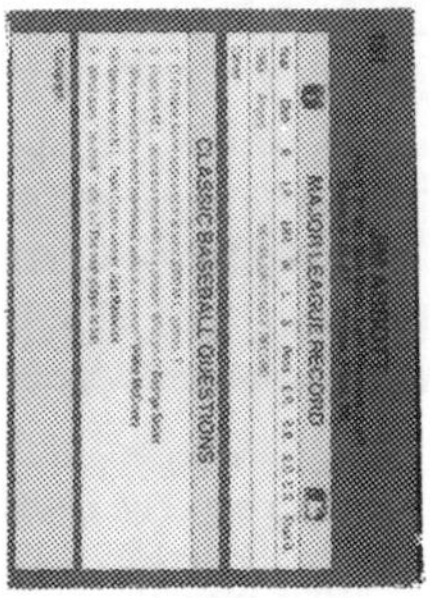

Numbered from 151-200, this 50-card set features rookies and traded players with their new teams. The cards are purple and gray and were sold as part of a board game with baseball trivia questions.

		MT	NR MT	EX
Complete Set:		15.00	11.00	6.00
Common Player:		.05	.04	.02
151	Jim Abbott	.50	.40	.20
152	Ellis Burks	.30	.25	.12
153	Mike Schmidt	1.00	.70	.30
154	Gregg Jefferies	.50	.40	.20
155	Mark Grace	.30	.25	.12
156	Jerome Walton	.40	.30	.15
157	Bo Jackson	1.00	.70	.40
158	Jack Clark	.05	.04	.02
159	Tom Glavine	.10	.08	.04
160	Eddie Murray	.10	.08	.04
161	John Dopson	.05	.04	.02
162	Ruben Sierra	.40	.30	.15
163	Rafael Palmeiro	.40	.30	.15
164	Nolan Ryan	1.00	.70	.30
165	Barry Larkin	.20	.15	.08
166	Tommy Herr	.05	.04	.02
167	Roberto Kelly	.25	.20	.10
168	Glenn Davis	.10	.08	.04
169	Glenn Braggs	.05	.04	.02
170	Juan Bell	.20	.15	.08
171	Todd Burns	.05	.04	.02
172	Derek Lilliquist	.10	.08	.04
173	Orel Hershiser	.20	.15	.08
174	John Smoltz	.40	.30	.15
175	Ozzie Guillen / Ellis Burks	.30	.25	.12
176	Kirby Puckett	.50	.40	.20
177	Robin Ventura	1.50	1.25	.60
178	Allan Anderson	.05	.04	.02

		MT	NR MT	EX
179	Steve Sax	.05	.04	.02
180	Will Clark	1.00	.70	.40
181	Mike Devereaux	.05	.04	.02
182	Tom Gordon	.40	.30	.15
183	Rob Murphy	.05	.04	.02
184	Pete O'Brien	.05	.04	.02
185	Cris Carpenter	.10	.08	.04
186	Tom Brunansky	.05	.04	.02
187	Bob Boone	.05	.04	.02
188	Lou Whitaker	.05	.04	.02
189	Dwight Gooden	.40	.30	.15
190	Mark McGwire	.40	.30	.15
191	John Smiley	.05	.04	.02
192	Tommy Gregg	.05	.04	.02
193	Ken Griffey, Jr.	4.00	3.00	1.50
194	Bruce Hurst	.05	.04	.02
195	Greg Swindell	.20	.15	.08
196	Nelson Liriano	.05	.04	.02
197	Randy Myers	.05	.04	.02
198	Kevin Mitchell	.70	.50	.30
199	Dante Bichette	.10	.08	.04
200	Deion Sanders	.40	.30	.15

1990 Classic Baseball

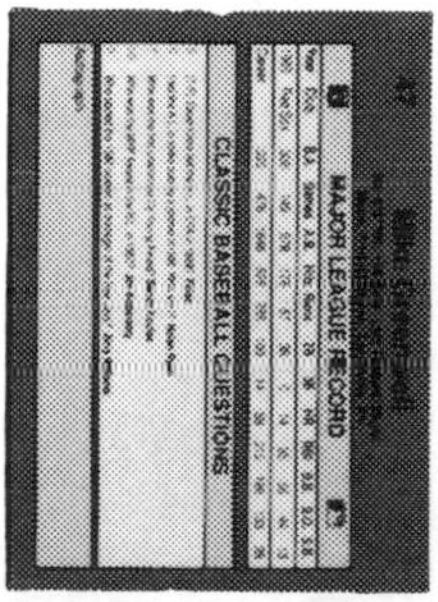

Classic Baseball returned in 1990 with another 150-card set. The cards were again sold as part of a baseball trivia game, and each game included a box designed to store all the cards in the set.

		MT	NR MT	EX
Complete Set:		20.00	15.00	7.50
Common Player:		.05	.04	.02
1	Nolan Ryan	2.00	1.50	.80
2	Bo Jackson	.80	.60	.30
3	Gregg Olson	.30	.25	.12
4	Tom Gordon	.50	.40	.20
5	Robin Ventura	.80	.60	.30
6	Will Clark	.50	.40	.20
7	Ruben Sierra	.30	.25	.12
8	Mark Grace	.30	.25	.12
9	Luis de los Santos	.05	.04	.02
10	Bernie Williams	.40	.30	.15
11	Eric Davis	.10	.08	.04
12	Carney Lansford	.05	.04	.02
13	John Smoltz	.10	.08	.04
14	Gary Sheffield	.40	.30	.15
15	Kent Merker	.40	.30	.15
16	Don Mattingly	.50	.40	.20
17	Tony Gwynn	.15	.11	.06
18	Ozzie Smith	.05	.04	.02
19	Fred McGriff	.25	.20	.10
20	Ken Griffey, Jr.	2.00	1.50	.80
21a	Deion Sanders ("Prime Time")	8.00	6.00	3.25
21b	Deion Sanders (Deion "Prime Time" Sanders)	1.50	1.25	.60
22	Jose Canseco	.50	.40	.20
23	Mitch Williams	.20	.15	.08
24	Cal Ripken, Jr.	.10	.08	.04
25	Bob Geren	.20	.15	.08
26	Wade Boggs	.15	.11	.06
27	Ryne Sandberg	.35	.25	.14
28	Kirby Puckett	.25	.20	.10
29	Mike Scott	.05	.04	.02
30	Dwight Smith	.20	.15	.08
31	Craig Worthington	.10	.08	.04
32	Ricky Jordan	.15	.11	.06

		MT	NR MT	EX
33	Darryl Strawberry	.10	.08	.04
34	Jerome Walton	.70	.50	.30
35	John Olerud	1.25	.90	.50
36	Tom Glavine	.05	.04	.02
37	Rickey Henderson	.40	.30	.15
38	Rolando Roomes	.10	.08	.04
39	Mickey Tettleton	.10	.08	.04
40	Jim Abbott	.50	.40	.20
41	Dave Righetti	.05	.04	.02
42	Mike LaValliere	.05	.04	.02
43	Rob Dibble	.25	.20	.10
44	Pete Harnisch	.10	.08	.04
45	Jose Offerman	1.50	1.25	.60
46	Walt Weiss	.05	.04	.02
47	Mike Greenwell	.25	.20	.10
48	Barry Larkin	.10	.08	.04
49	Dave Gallagher	.05	.04	.02
50	Junior Felix	.25	.20	.10
51	Roger Clemens	.20	.15	.08
52	Lonnie Smith	.05	.04	.02
53	Jerry Browne	.05	.04	.02
54	Greg Briley	.25	.20	.10
55	Delino Desheilds	.80	.60	.30
56	Carmelo Martinez	.05	.04	.02
57	Craig Biggio	.20	.15	.08
58	Dwight Gooden	.15	.11	.06
59a	Bo Jackson, Ruben Sierra, Mark McGwire (Bo, Ruben, Mark)	4.00	3.00	1.50
59b	Bo Jackson, Ruben Sierra, Mark McGwire (A.L. Fence Busters)	.60	.45	.25
60	Greg Vaughn	.70	.50	.30
61	Roberto Alomar	.10	.08	.04
62	Steve Bedrosian	.05	.04	.02
63	Devon White	.05	.04	.02
64	Kevin Mitchell	.40	.30	.15
65	Marquis Grissom	.70	.50	.30
66	Brian Holman	.05	.04	.02
67	Julio Franco	.10	.08	.04
68	Dave West	.10	.08	.04
69	Harold Baines	.10	.08	.04
70	Eric Anthony	.70	.50	.30
71	Glenn Davis	.05	.04	.02
72	Mark Langston	.15	.11	.06
73	Matt Williams	.25	.20	.10
74	Rafael Palmeiro	.05	.04	.02
75	Pete Rose, Jr.	.40	.30	.15
76	Ramon Martinez	.50	.40	.20
77	Dwight Evans	.10	.08	.04
78	Mackey Sasser	.05	.04	.02
79	Mike Schooler	.05	.04	.02
80	Dennis Cook	.10	.08	.04
81	Orel Hershiser	.20	.15	.08
82	Barry Bonds	.30	.25	.12
83	Geronimo Berroa	.10	.08	.04
84	George Bell	.10	.08	.04
85	Andre Dawson	.10	.08	.04
86	John Franco	.05	.04	.02
87a	Will Clark, Tony Gwynn (Clark/Gwynn)	3.00	2.25	1.25
87b	Will Clark, Tony Gwynn (N.L. Hit Kings)	.40	.30	.15
88	Glenallen Hill	.35	.25	.14
89	Jeff Ballard	.10	.08	.04
90	Todd Zeile	1.25	.90	.50
91	Frank Viola	.15	.11	.06
92	Ozzie Guillen	.10	.08	.04
93	Jeff Leonard	.05	.04	.02
94	Dave Smith	.05	.04	.02
95	Dave Parker	.10	.08	.04
96	Jose Gonzalez	.20	.15	.08
97	Dave Steib	.05	.04	.02
98	Charlie Hayes	.15	.11	.06
99	Jesse Barfield	.05	.04	.02
100	Joey Belle	.60	.45	.25
101	Jeff Reardon	.05	.04	.02
102	Bruce Hurst	.05	.04	.02
103	Luis Medina	.05	.04	.02
104	Mike Moore	.10	.08	.04
105	Vince Coleman	.10	.08	.04
106	Alan Trammell	.10	.08	.04
107	Randy Myers	.05	.04	.02
108	Frank Tanana	.05	.04	.02
109	Craig Lefferts	.05	.04	.02
110	John Wetteland	.20	.15	.08
111	Chris Gwynn	.10	.08	.04
112	Mark Carreon	.10	.08	.04
113	Von Hayes	.05	.04	.02
114	Doug Jones	.05	.04	.02
115	Andres Galarraga	.10	.08	.04
116	Carlton Fisk	.10	.08	.04
117	Paul O'Neill	.05	.04	.02

		MT	NR MT	EX
118	Tim Raines	.10	.08	.04
119	Tom Brunansky	.05	.04	.02
120	Andy Benes	.35	.25	.14
121	Mark Portugal	.05	.04	.02
122	Willie Randolph	.05	.04	.02
123	Jeff Blauser	.05	.04	.02
124	Don August	.05	.04	.02
125	Chuck Cary	.05	.04	.02
126	John Smiley	.05	.04	.02
127	Terry Mullholland	.05	.04	.02
128	Harold Reynolds	.05	.04	.02
129	Hubie Brooks	.05	.04	.02
130	Ben McDonald	1.00	.70	.40
131	Kevin Ritz	.20	.15	.08
132	Luis Quinones	.05	.04	.02
133	Bam Bam Meulens	.20	.15	.08
134	Bill Spiers	.20	.15	.08
135	Andy Hawkins	.05	.04	.02
136	Alvin Davis	.10	.08	.04
137	Lee Smith	.05	.04	.02
138	Joe Carter	.10	.08	.04
139	Bret Saberhagen	.10	.08	.04
140	Sammy Sosa	.30	.25	.12
141	Matt Nokes	.05	.04	.02
142	Bert Blyleven	.10	.08	.04
143	Bobby Bonilla	.35	.25	.14
144	Howard Johnson	.10	.08	.04
145	Joe Magrane	.05	.04	.02
146	Pedro Guerrero	.10	.08	.04
147	Robin Yount	.35	.25	.14
148	Dan Gladden	.05	.04	.02
149	Steve Sax	.10	.08	.04
150a	Will Clark, Kevin Mitchell (Clark/Mitchell)	3.00	2.25	1.25
150b	Will Clark, Kevin Mitchell (Bay Bombers)	.50	.40	.20

		MT	NR MT	EX
14	Mark Davis	.05	.04	.02
15	Storm Davis	.05	.04	.02
16	Larry Walker	.10	.08	.04
17	Brian DuBois	.10	.08	.04
18	Len Dykstra	.10	.08	.04
19	John Franco	.10	.08	.04
20	Kirk Gibson	.05	.04	.02
21	Juan Gonzalez	2.00	1.50	.80
22	Tommy Greene	.30	.25	.12
23	Kent Hrbek	.05	.04	.02
24	Mike Huff	.30	.25	.12
25	Bo Jackson	1.50	1.25	.60
26	Nolan Knows Bo	3.00	2.25	1.25
27	Roberto Kelly	.05	.04	.02
28	Mark Langston	.10	.08	.04
29	Ray Lankford	.80	.60	.30
30	Kevin Maas	1.50	1.25	.60
31	Julio Machado	.15	.11	.06
32	Greg Maddux	.05	.04	.02
33	Mark McGwire	.15	.11	.06
34	Paul Molitor	.05	.04	.02
35	Hal Morris	.60	.45	.25
36	Dale Murphy	.05	.04	.02
37	Eddie Murray	.05	.04	.02
38	Jaime Navarro	.10	.08	.04
39	Dean Palmer	.50	.40	.20
40	Derek Parks	.30	.25	.12
41	Bobby Rose	.20	.15	.08
42	Wally Joyner	.05	.04	.02
43	Chris Sabo	.05	.04	.02
44	Benito Santiago	.05	.04	.02
45	Mike Stanton	.10	.08	.04
46	Terry Steinbach	.05	.04	.02
47	Dave Stewart	.10	.08	.04
48	Greg Swindell	.05	.04	.02
49	Jose Vizcaino	.15	.11	.06
50	"Royal Flush"	.25	.20	.10

1990 Classic Series II

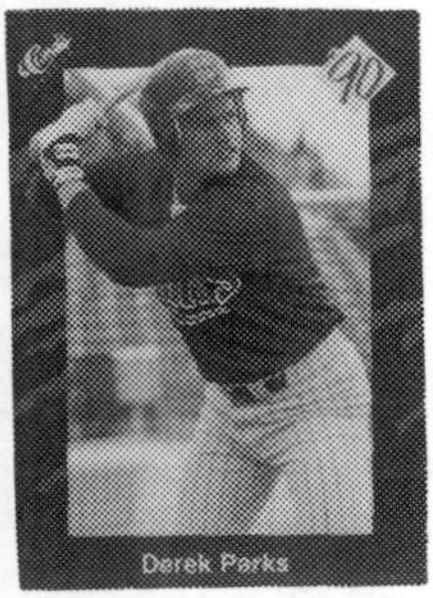

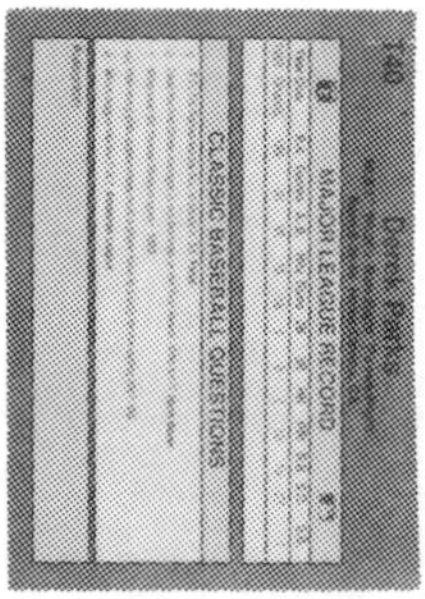

Like in previous years, Classic released a 50-card second series set for use with its baseball trivia game. Unlike the 1989 update set, the 1990 Classic Series II set is numbered 1-50 with a "T" designation accompanying the card number. The cards measure 2-1/2" by 3-1/2" and are designed after the original 1990 Classic cards. Series II cards have pink borders with a blue design, while the cards from the regular issue feature the opposite color combination. The cards are issued in a complete Series II set form.

		MT	NR MT	EX
Complete Set:		12.00	9.00	4.75
Common Player:		.05	.04	.02
1	Gregg Jefferies	.25	.20	.10
2	Steve Adkins	.30	.25	.12
3	Sandy Alomar, Jr.	.25	.20	.10
4	Steve Avery	.30	.25	.12
5	Mike Blowers	.20	.15	.08
6	George Brett	.05	.04	.02
7	Tom Browning	.05	.04	.02
8	Ellis Burks	.10	.08	.04
9	Joe Carter	.10	.08	.04
10	Jerald Clark	.10	.08	.04
11	"Hot Corners"	.40	.30	.15
12	Pat Combs	.25	.20	.10
13	Scott Cooper	.25	.20	.10

1990 Classic Series III

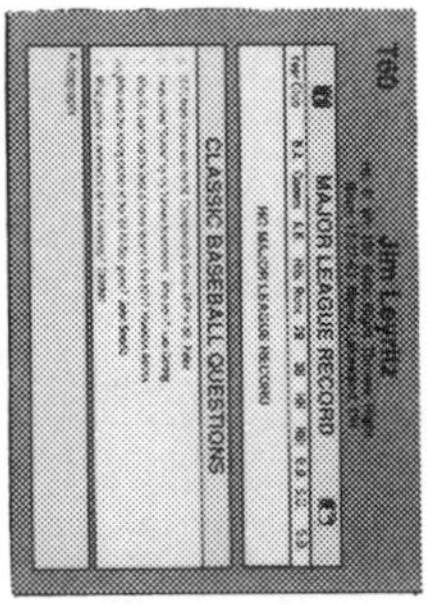

Classic's third series of 1990, features the same style as the previous two releases. The only major difference is the border color. Series 3 features yellow borders with blue accent. 100 trivia playing cards are included in series 3. the cards are numbered 1T-100T. No card 51T or 57T exist. Two cards in the set are unnumbered. Like all other Classic issues, the cards are designed for use with the trivia board game.

		MT	NR MT	EX
Complete Set:		13.00	9.75	5.25
Common Player:		.05	.04	.02
1	Ken Griffey Jr.	1.50	1.25	.60
2	John Tudor	.05	.04	.02
3	John Kruk	.05	.04	.02
4	Mark Gardner	.15	.11	.06
5	Scott Radinsky	.20	.15	.08
6	John Burkett	.20	.15	.08
7	Will Clark	.40	.30	.15
8	Gary Carter	.05	.04	.02
9	Ted Higuera	.05	.04	.02
10	Dave Parker	.10	.08	.04
11	Dante Bichette	.05	.04	.02
12	Don Mattingly	.35	.25	.14
13	Greg Harris	.05	.04	.02
14	David Hollins	.10	.08	.04

		MT	NR MT	EX
15	Matt Nokes	.05	.04	.02
16	Kevin Tapani	.15	.11	.06
17	Shane Mack	.05	.04	.02
18	Randy Myers	.05	.04	.02
19	Greg Olson	.15	.11	.06
20	Shawn Abner	.05	.04	.02
21	Jim Presley	.05	.04	.02
22	Randy Johnson	.05	.04	.02
23	Edgar Martinez	.05	.04	.02
24	Scott Coolbaugh	.15	.11	.06
25	Jeff Treadway	.05	.04	.02
26	Joe Klink	.05	.04	.02
27	Rickey Henderson	.30	.25	.12
28	Sam Horn	.05	.04	.02
29	Kurt Stillwell	.05	.04	.02
30	Andy Van Slyke	.05	.04	.02
31	Willie Banks	.40	.30	.15
32	Jose Canseco	.40	.30	.15
33	Felix Jose	.10	.08	.04
34	Candy Maldonado	.05	.04	.02
35	Carlos Baerga	.30	.25	.12
36	Keith Hernandez	.05	.04	.02
37	Frank Viola	.05	.04	.02
38	Pete O'Brien	.05	.04	.02
39	Pat Borders	.05	.04	.02
40	Mike Heath	.05	.04	.02
41	Kevin Brown	.10	.08	.04
42	Chris Bosio	.05	.04	.02
43	Shawn Boskie	.25	.20	.10
44	Carlos Quintana	.05	.04	.02
45	Juan Samuel	.05	.04	.02
46	Tim Layana	.15	.11	.06
47	Mike Harkey	.10	.08	.04
48	Gerald Perry	.05	.04	.02
49	Mike Witt	.05	.04	.02
50	Joe Orsulak	.05	.04	.02
52	Willie Blair	.10	.08	.04
53	Gene Larkin	.05	.04	.02
54	Jody Reed	.05	.04	.02
55	Jeff Reardon	.05	.04	.02
56	Kevin McReynolds	.05	.04	.02
58	Eric Yelding	.05	.04	.02
59	Fred Lynn	.05	.04	.02
60	Jim Leyritz	.20	.15	.08
61	John Orton	.05	.04	.02
62	Mike Lieberthal	.50	.40	.20
63	Mike Hartley	.10	.08	.04
64	Kal Daniels	.05	.04	.02
65	Terry Shumpert	.20	.15	.08
66	Sil Campusano	.05	.04	.02
67	Tony Pena	.05	.04	.02
68	Barry Bonds	.25	.20	.10
69	Oddibe McDowell	.05	.04	.02
70	Kelly Gruber	.10	.08	.04
71	Willie Randolph	.05	.04	.02
72	Rick Parker	.15	.11	.06
73	Bobby Bonilla	.10	.08	.04
74	Jack Armstrong	.10	.08	.04
75	Hubie Brooks	.05	.04	.02
76	Sandy Alomar, Jr.	.15	.11	.06
77	Ruben Sierra	.10	.08	.04
78	Erik Hanson	.08	.06	.03
79	Tony Phillips	.05	.04	.02
80	Rondell White	.25	.20	.10
81	Bobby Thigpen	.08	.06	.03
82	Ron Walden	.20	.15	.08
83	Don Peters	.30	.25	.12
84	#6 (Nolan Ryan)	1.00	.70	.40
85	Lance Dickson	.20	.15	.08
86	Ryne Sandberg	.10	.08	.04
87	Eric Christopherson	.20	.15	.08
88	Shane Andrews	.25	.20	.10
89	Marc Newfield	1.00	.70	.40
90	Adam Hyzdu	.25	.20	.10
91	"Texas Heat" (Nolan Ryan, Reid Ryan)	2.00	1.50	.80
92	Chipper Jones	.50	.40	.20
93	Frank Thomas	3.00	2.25	1.25
94	Cecil Fielder	.40	.30	.15
95	Delino DeShields	.30	.25	.12
96	John Olerud	.80	.60	.30
97	Dave Justice	1.50	1.25	.60
98	Joe Oliver	.10	.08	.04
99	Alex Fernandez	.60	.45	.25
100	Todd Hundley	.20	.15	.08
----	Mike Marshall (Game Instructions On Back)	.05	.04	.02
----	4 in 1 (Frank Viola)	.30	.25	.12
----	4 in 1 ("Texas Heat")	.30	.25	.12
----	4 in 1 (Chipper Jones)	.30	.25	.12
----	4 in 1 (Don Mattingly)	.30	.25	.12

1990 Classic #1 Draft Picks

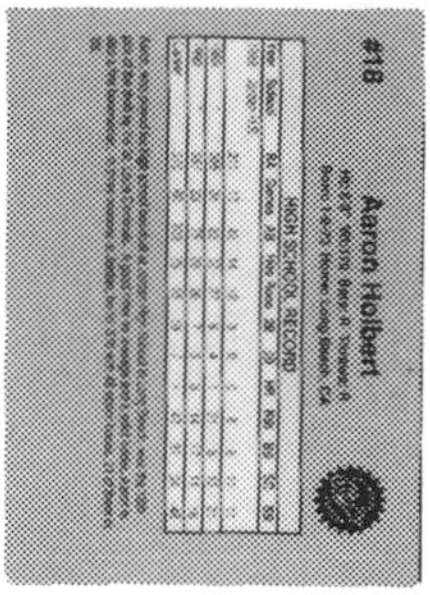

Todd Van Poppel and Alex Fernandez head up the 24- 1990 first round draft picks featured in this 25-card set. The set is limited with only 150,000 sets released to the hobby. A letter of authenticity accompanies each individually numbered set. Unlike other Classic issues, this set is not designed for use with the trivia board game.

		MT	NR MT	EX
	Complete Set:	16.00	12.00	6.50
	Common Player:	.20	.15	.08
1	Chipper Jones	.40	.30	.15
3	Mike Lieberthal	.35	.25	.14
4	Alex Fernandez	1.00	.70	.40
5	Kurt Miller	.30	.25	.12
6	Marc Newfield	1.00	.70	.40
7	Dan Wilson	.50	.40	.20
8	Tim Costo	.80	.60	.30
9	Ron Walden	.25	.20	.10
10	Carl Everett	.25	.20	.10
11	Shane Andrews	.20	.15	.08
12	Todd Ritchie	.25	.20	.10
13	Donovan Osborne	.20	.15	.08
14	Todd Van Poppel	3.00	2.25	1.25
15	Adam Hyzdu	.20	.15	.08
16	Dan Smith	.20	.15	.08
17	Jeromy Burnitz	1.00	.70	.40
18	Aaron Holbert	.25	.20	.10
19	Eric Christopherson	.20	.15	.08
20	Mike Mussina	.50	.40	.20
21	Tom Nevers	.20	.15	.08
23	Lance Dickson	.30	.25	.12
24	Rondell White	.20	.15	.08
25	Robbie Beckett	.20	.15	.08
26	Don Peters	.20	.15	.08
----	Future Stars-Checklist (Chipper Jones/ Rondell White)	.35	.25	.14

1991 Classic

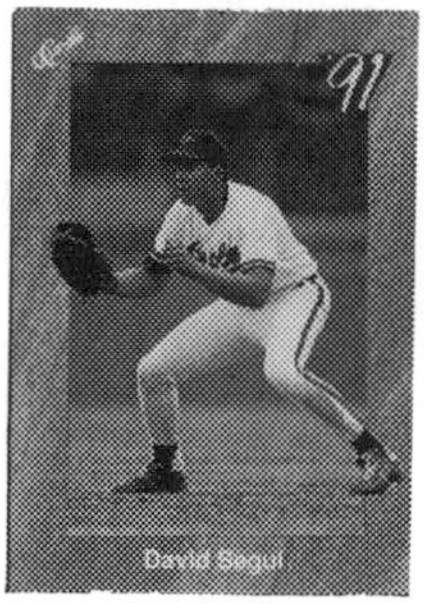

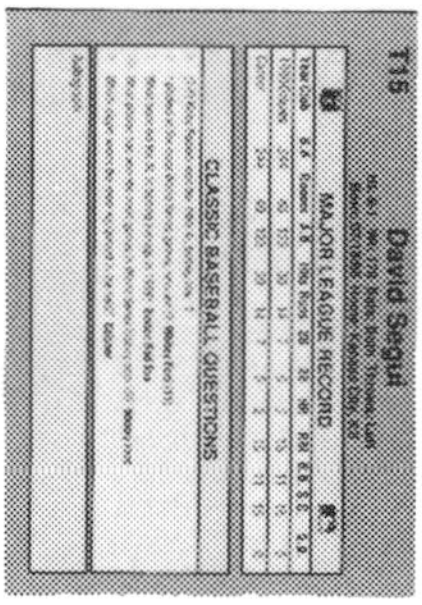

Top rookies and draft picks highlight this 99-card set from Classic. The cards come along with a boardgame and accessories designed for trivia game

use. The card fronts feature fading blue borders with a touch of red. A "4-in-1" micro-player piece is included with each game set.

		MT	NR MT	EX
Complete Set:		12.00	9.00	4.75
Common Player:		.08	.06	.03
1	Ron Gant	.08	.06	.03
2	Dave Justice	.35	.25	.14
3	Leo Gomez	.30	.25	.12
4	Chris Hoiles	.20	.15	.08
5	Ben McDonald	.30	.25	.12
6	David Segui	.25	.20	.10
7	Anthony Telford	.25	.20	.10
8	Mike Mussina	.35	.25	.14
9	Wade Boggs	.10	.08	.04
10	Roger Clemens	.12	.09	.05
11	Tim Naehring	.40	.30	.15
12	Phil Plantier	.60	.45	.25
13	Maurice Vaughn	.50	.40	.20
14	Lee Stevens	.20	.15	.08
15	Mark Grace	.08	.06	.03
16	Derrick May	.60	.45	.25
17	Ryne Sandberg	.15	.11	.06
18	Matt Stark	.30	.25	.12
19	Frank Thomas	1.25	.90	.50
20	Bobby Thigpen	.08	.06	.03
21	Reggie Jefferson	.40	.30	.15
22	Rob Dibble	.08	.06	.03
23	Hal Morris	.12	.09	.05
24	Chris Sabo	.08	.06	.03
25	Eric Davis	.10	.08	.04
26	Alex Cole	.20	.15	.08
27	Mark Lewis	.20	.15	.08
28	Tim Costo	.40	.30	.15
29	Sandy Alomar,Jr.	.15	.11	.06
30	Travis Fryman	.50	.40	.20
31	Cecil Fielder	.15	.11	.06
32	Milt Cuyler	.15	.11	.06
33	Andujar Cedeno	.50	.40	.20
34	Danny Darwin	.08	.06	.03
35	Randy Henis	.20	.15	.08
36	George Brett	.10	.08	.04
37	Jeff Conine	.60	.45	.25
38	Bo Jackson	.40	.30	.15
39	Brian McRae	.40	.30	.15
40	Brent Mayne	.20	.15	.08
41	Eddie Murray	.08	.06	.03
42	Ramon Martinez	.12	.09	.05
43	Jim Neidlinger	.15	.11	.06
44	Jim Poole	.30	.25	.12
45	Darryl Strawberry	.12	.09	.05
46	Tim McIntosh	.20	.15	.08
47	Randy Veres	.08	.06	.03
48	Kirby Puckett	.10	.08	.04
49	Todd Ritchie	.20	.15	.08
50	Rich Garces	.20	.15	.08
51	Moises Alou	.12	.09	.05
52	Delino DeShields	.15	.11	.06
53	Oscar Azocar	.25	.20	.10
54	Kevin Maas	.25	.20	.10
55	Alan Mills	.15	.11	.06
56	Don Mattingly	.15	.11	.06
57	Hensley Muelens	.10	.08	.04
58	John Franco	.08	.06	.03
59	Chris Jelic	.30	.25	.12
60	Dave Magadan	.08	.06	.03
61	Jeromy Burnitz	.35	.25	.14
62	Reggie Harris	.30	.25	.12
63	Rickey Henderson	.20	.15	.08
64	Mark McGwire	.15	.11	.06
65	Willie McGee	.08	.06	.03
66	Todd Van Poppel	2.00	1.50	.80
67	Bob Welch	.08	.06	.03
68	"Future Aces"	3.00	2.25	1.25
69	Chuck Finley	.08	.06	.03
70	Lenny Dykstra	.08	.06	.03
71	Mickey Morandini	.20	.15	.08
72	Wes Chamberlain	.40	.30	.15
73	Dale Murphy	.08	.06	.03
74	Barry Bonds	.15	.11	.06
75	Doug Drabek	.08	.06	.03
76	Randy Tomlin	.20	.15	.08
77	Rod Brewer	.12	.09	.05
78	Bernard Gilkey	.35	.25	.14
79	Vince Coleman	.08	.06	.03
80	Roberto Alomar	.08	.06	.03
81	Joe Carter	.08	.06	.03
82	Kevin Mitchell	.10	.08	.04
83	Rafael Novoa	.20	.15	.08
84	Matt Williams	.10	.08	.04
85	Steve Decker	.35	.25	.12
86	Mike Benjamin	.15	.11	.06
87	Jose Rijo	.08	.06	.03
88	Ken Griffey,Jr.	1.25	.90	.50
89	Tino Martinez	.30	.25	.12
90	Scott Chiamparino	.25	.20	.10
91	Rafael Palmeiro	.08	.06	.03
92	Nolan Ryan	.35	.25	.14
93	Bobby Witt	.08	.06	.03
94	Juan Gonzalez	1.00	.70	.40
95	Fred McGriff	.08	.06	.03
96	Dave Steib	.08	.06	.03
97	Ed Sprague	.30	.25	.12
98	John Olerud	.25	.20	.10
99	Strawberry and Gooden	.10	.08	.04

1991 Classic Series II

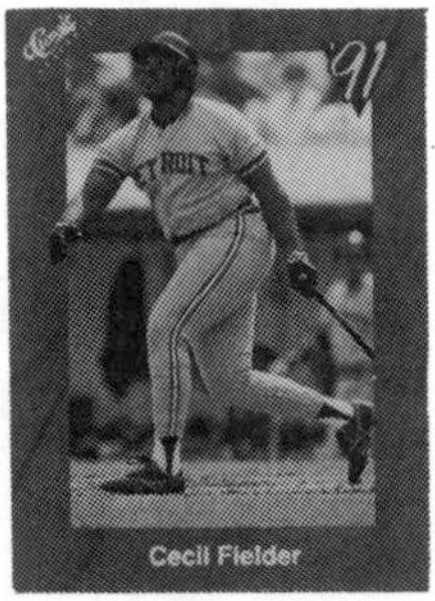

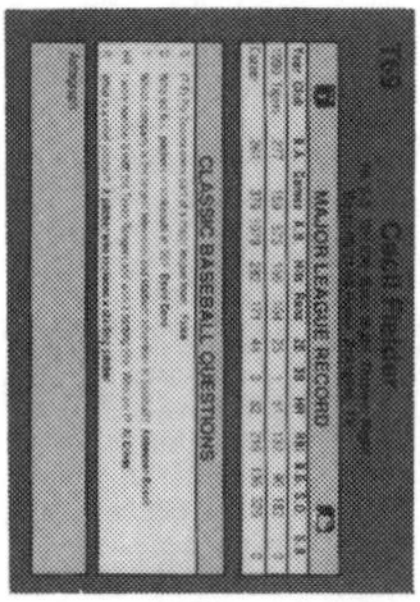

Classic released a 100-card second series in 1991 compared to a 50-card second series in 1990. The cards feature the same style as the first Classic series of 1991 with the exception of the border color. The first series featured blue borders, while Series II features maroon borders. The cards are designed for trivia game use. Series II includes several players with new teams and top rookies. Special Four-In-One, 300 Game Winner and Strikout Kings cards are included with each set.

		MT	NR MT	EX
Complete Set:		10.00	7.50	4.00
Common Player:		.08	.06	.03
1	Ken Griffey, Jr.	.80	.60	.30
2	Wilfredo Cordero	.25	.20	.10
3	Cal Ripken, Jr.	.15	.11	.06
4	D.J. Dozier	.15	.11	.06
5	Darrin Fletcher	.08	.06	.03
6	Glenn Davis	.10	.08	.04
7	Alex Fernandez	.20	.15	.08
8	Cory Snyder	.08	.06	.03
9	Tim Raines	.10	.08	.04
10	Greg Swindell	.10	.08	.04
11	Mark Lewis	.25	.20	.10
12	Rico Brogna	.20	.15	.08
13	Gary Sheffield	.10	.08	.04
14	Paul Molitor	.10	.08	.04
15	Kent Hrbek	.08	.04	.02
16	Scott Erickson	.40	.30	.15
17	Steve Sax	.08	.06	.03
18	Dennis Eckersley	.08	.06	.03
19	Jose Canseco	.25	.20	.10
20	Kirk Dressendorfer	.40	.30	.15
21	Ken Griffey,Sr.	.08	.06	.03
22	Erik Hanson	.10	.08	.04
23	Dan Peltier	.15	.11	.06
24	John Olerud	.10	.08	.04
25	Eddie Zosky	.15	.11	.06
26	Steve Avery	.20	.15	.08
27	John Smoltz	.10	.08	.04
28	Frank Thomas	.60	.45	.25
29	Jerome Walton	.08	.06	.03
30	George Bell	.08	.06	.03
31	Jose Rijo	.08	.06	.03
32	Randy Myers	.08	.06	.03
33	Barry Larkin	.10	.08	.04
34	Eric Anthony	.08	.06	.03

		MT	NR MT	EX
35	Dave Hansen	.08	.06	.03
36	Eric Karros	.20	.15	.08
37	Jose Offerman	.15	.11	.06
38	Marquis Grissom	.10	.08	.04
39	Dwight Gooden	.10	.08	.04
40	Gregg Jefferies	.10	.08	.04
41	Pat Combs	.08	.06	.03
42	Todd Zeile	.10	.08	.04
43	Benito Santiago	.08	.06	.03
44	Dave Staton	.10	.08	.04
45	Tony Fernandez	.08	.06	.03
46	Fred McGriff	.10	.08	.04
47	Jeff Brantley	.08	.06	.03
48	Junior Felix	.08	.06	.03
49	Jack Morris	.10	.08	.04
50	Chris George	.10	.08	.04
51	Henry Rodriguez	.25	.20	.10
52	Paul Marak	.10	.08	.04
53	Ryan Klesko	.60	.45	.25
54	Darren Lewis	.15	.11	.06
55	Lance Dickson	.15	.11	.06
56	Anthony Young	.25	.20	.10
57	Willie Banks	.10	.08	.04
58	Mike Bordick	.10	.08	.04
59	Roger Salkeld	.20	.15	.08
60	Steve Karsay	.20	.15	.08
61	Bernie Williams	.20	.15	.08
62	Mickey Tettleton	.08	.06	.03
63	Dave Justice	.20	.15	.08
64	Steve Decker	.20	.15	.08
65	Roger Clemens	.15	.11	.06
66	Phil Plantier	.60	.45	.25
67	Ryne Sandberg	.15	.11	.06
68	Sandy Alomar,Jr.	.10	.08	.04
69	Cecil Fielder	.15	.11	.06
70	George Brett	.10	.08	.04
71	Delino DeShields	.10	.08	.04
72	Dave Magadan	.08	.06	.03
73	Darryl Strawberry	.08	.06	.03
74	Juan Gonzalez	.35	.25	.14
75	Rickey Henderson	.10	.08	.04
76	Willie McGee	.08	.06	.03
77	Todd Van Poppel	1.00	.70	.40
78	Barry Bonds	.10	.08	.04
79	Doug Drabek	.08	.06	.03
80	Ryan-300 Game Winner	.35	.25	.14
81	Roberto Alomar	.10	.08	.04
82	Ivan Rodriguez	.80	.60	.30
83	Dan Opperman	.20	.15	.08
84	Jeff Bagwell	1.50	1.25	.60
85	Braulio Castillo	.15	.11	.06
86	Doug Simons	.10	.08	.04
87	Wade Taylor	.15	.11	.06
88	Gary Scott	.40	.30	.15
89	Dave Stewart	.08	.06	.03
90	Mike Simms	.15	.11	.06
91	Luis Gonzalez	.30	.25	.12
92	Bobby Bonilla	.10	.08	.04
93	Tony Gwynn	.10	.08	.04
94	Will Clark	.15	.11	.06
95	Rich Rowland	.10	.08	.04
96	Alan Trammell	.08	.06	.03
97	Strikeout Kings	.40	.30	.15
98	Joe Carter	.08	.06	.03
99	Jack Clark	.08	.06	.03
100	Four-In-One	.25	.20	.10

1991 Classic Collector's Edition

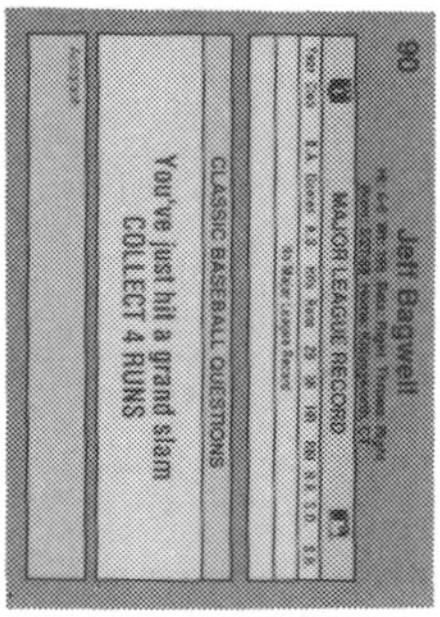

The Classic Collector's edition made its debut in 1991. This package includes a board game, trivia baseball cards, a baseball tips booklet and a certificate of authenticity. It is all packaged in an attractive collector's edition box. Each box is individually and sequentially numbered on the outside. This issue was limited with only 100,000 available. The card set features 200 trivia baseball cards. Mickey Morandini's card features a photo of Darren Daulton.

		MT	NR MT	EX
Complete Set:		35.00	27.00	15.00
Common Player:		.08	.06	.03
1	Frank Viola	.10	.08	.04
2	Tim Wallach	.08	.06	.03
3	Lou Whitaker	.08	.06	.03
4	Brett Butler	.10	.08	.04
5	Jim Abbott	.10	.08	.04
6	Jack Armstrong	.08	.06	.03
7	Craig Biggio	.10	.08	.04
8	Brian Barnes	.20	.15	.08
9	Dennis "Oil Can" Boyd	.08	.06	.03
10	Tom Browning	.10	.08	.04
11	Tom Brunansky	.08	.06	.03
12	Ellis Burks	.10	.08	.04
13	Harold Baines	.10	.08	.04
14	Kal Daniels	.10	.08	.04
15	Mark Davis	.08	.06	.03
16	Storm Davis	.08	.06	.03
17	Tom Glavine	.12	.09	.05
18	Mike Greenwell	.10	.08	.04
19	Kelly Gruber	.12	.09	.05
20	Mark Gubicza	.08	.06	.03
21	Pedro Guerrero	.10	.08	.04
22	Mike Harkey	.10	.08	.04
23	Orel Hershiser	.10	.08	.04
24	Ted Higuera	.10	.08	.04
25	Von Hayes	.08	.06	.03
26	Andre Dawson	.15	.11	.06
27	Shawon Dunston	.10	.08	.04
28	Roberto Kelly	.10	.08	.04
29	Joe Magrane	.08	.06	.03
30	Dennis Martinez	.10	.08	.04
31	Kevin McReynolds	.10	.08	.04
32	Matt Nokes	.08	.06	.03
33	Dan Plesac	.08	.06	.03
34	Dave Parker	.10	.08	.04
35	Randy Johnson	.10	.08	.04
36	Bret Saberhagen	.10	.08	.04
37	Mackey Sasser	.08	.06	.03
38	Mike Scott	.08	.06	.03
39	Ozzie Smith	.15	.11	.06
40	Kevin Seitzer	.08	.06	.03
41	Ruben Sierra	.25	.20	.10
42	Kevin Tapani	.10	.08	.04
43	Danny Tartabull	.20	.15	.08
44	Robby Thompson	.08	.06	.03
45	Andy Van Slyke	.12	.09	.05
46	Greg Vaughn	.15	.11	.06
47	Harold Reynolds	.10	.08	.04
48	Will Clark	.40	.30	.15
49	Gary Gaetti	.10	.08	.04
50	Joe Grahe	.15	.11	.06
51	Carlton Fisk	.20	.15	.08
52	Robin Ventura	.30	.25	.12
53	Ozzie Guillen	.12	.09	.05
54	Tom Candiotti	.08	.06	.03
55	Doug Jones	.08	.06	.03
56	Eric King	.08	.06	.03
57	Kirk Gibson	.12	.09	.05
58	Tim Costo	.40	.30	.15
59	Robin Yount	.25	.20	.10
60	Sammy Sosa	.20	.15	.08
61	Jesse Barfield	.10	.08	.04
62	Marc Newfield	1.00	.70	.40
63	Jimmy Key	.10	.08	.04
64	Felix Jose	.30	.25	.12
65	Mark Whiten	.50	.40	.20
66	Tommy Greene	.15	.11	.06
67	Kent Mercker	.10	.08	.04
68	Greg Maddux	.12	.09	.05
69	Danny Jackson	.08	.06	.03
70	Reggie Sanders	1.00	.70	.40
71	Eric Yelding	.08	.06	.03
72	Karl Rhodes	.40	.30	.15
73	Fernando Valenzuela	.10	.08	.04
74	Chris Nabholz	.12	.09	.05
75	Andres Galarraga	.10	.08	.04
76	Howard Johnson	.20	.15	.08
77	Hubie Brooks	.10	.08	.04

		MT	NR MT	EX
78	Terry Mulholland	.10	.08	.04
79	Paul Molitor	.15	.11	.06
80	Roger McDowell	.08	.06	.03
81	Darren Daulton	.08	.06	.03
82	Zane Smith	.08	.06	.03
83	Ray Lankford	.50	.40	.20
84	Bruce Hurst	.10	.08	.04
85	Andy Benes	.25	.20	.10
86	John Burkett	.08	.06	.03
87	Dave Righetti	.15	.11	.06
88	Steve Karsay	.40	.30	.15
89	D.J. Dozier	.40	.30	.15
90	Jeff Bagwell	2.00	1.50	.80
91	Joe Carter	.20	.15	.08
92	Wes Chamberlain	.60	.45	.25
93	Vince Coleman	.15	.11	.06
94	Pat Combs	.10	.08	.04
95	Jerome Walton	.15	.11	.06
96	Jeff Conine	.40	.30	.15
97	Alan Trammell	.15	.11	.06
98	Don Mattingly	.30	.25	.12
99	Ramon Martinez	.40	.30	.15
100	Dave Magadan	.12	.09	.05
101	Greg Swindell	.12	.09	.05
102	Dave Stewart	.15	.11	.06
103	Gary Sheffield	.20	.15	.08
104	George Bell	.15	.11	.06
105	Mark Grace	.25	.20	.10
106	Steve Sax	.10	.08	.04
107	Ryne Sandberg	.50	.40	.20
108	Chris Sabo	.15	.11	.06
109	Jose Rijo	.10	.08	.04
110	Cal Ripken, Jr.	.80	.60	.30
111	Kirby Puckett	.40	.30	.15
112	Eddie Murray	.15	.11	.06
113	Roberto Alomar	.30	.25	.12
114	Randy Myers	.10	.08	.04
115	Rafael Palmeiro	.25	.20	.10
116	John Olerud	.25	.20	.10
117	Gregg Jefferies	.20	.15	.08
118	Kent Hrbek	.10	.08	.04
119	Marquis Grissom	.25	.20	.10
120	Ken Griffey, Jr.	1.50	1.25	.60
121	Dwight Gooden	.35	.25	.14
122	Juan Gonzalez	.80	.60	.30
123	Ron Gant	.20	.15	.08
124	Travis Fryman	.80	.60	.30
125	John Franco	.12	.09	.05
126	Dennis Eckersley	.15	.11	.06
127	Cecil Fielder	.30	.25	.12
128	Phil Plantier	1.00	.70	.40
129	Kevin Mitchell	.30	.25	.12
130	Kevin Maas	.40	.30	.15
131	Mark McGwire	.30	.25	.12
132	Ben McDonald	.30	.25	.12
133	Lenny Dykstra	.12	.09	.05
134	Delino DeShields	.20	.15	.08
135	Jose Canseco	.60	.45	.25
136	Eric Davis	.20	.15	.08
137	George Brett	.20	.15	.08
138	Steve Avery	.30	.25	.12
139	Eric Anthony	.10	.08	.04
140	Bobby Thigpen	.12	.09	.05
141	Ken Griffey, Sr.	.10	.08	.04
142	Barry Larkin	.20	.15	.08
143	Jeff Brantley	.08	.06	.03
144	Bobby Bonilla	.30	.25	.12
145	Jose Offerman	.30	.25	.12
146	Mike Mussina	.30	.25	.12
147	Erik Hanson	.15	.11	.06
148	Dale Murphy	.15	.11	.06
149	Roger Clemens	.50	.40	.20
150	Tino Martinez	.50	.40	.20
151	Todd Van Poppel	2.00	1.50	.80
152	Maurice Vaughn	1.00	.70	.40
153	Derrick May	.40	.30	.15
154	Jack Clark	.15	.11	.06
155	Dave Hansen	.12	.09	.05
156	Tony Gwynn	.25	.20	.10
157	Brian McRae	.70	.50	.30
158	Matt Williams	.20	.15	.08
159	Kirk Dressendorfer	1.00	.70	.40
160	Scott Erickson	1.50	1.25	.60
161	Tony Fernandez	.12	.09	.05
162	Willie McGee	.12	.09	.05
163	Fred McGriff	.20	.15	.08
164	Leo Gomez	.30	.25	.12
165	Bernard Gilkey	.30	.25	.12
166	Bobby Witt	.10	.08	.04
167	Doug Drabek	.15	.11	.06
168	Rob Dibble	.15	.11	.06
169	Glenn Davis	.15	.11	.06
170	Danny Darwin	.08	.06	.03
171	Eric Karros	.70	.50	.30
172	Eddie Zosky	.30	.25	.12
173	Todd Zeile	.25	.20	.10
174	Tim Raines	.15	.11	.06
175	Benito Santiago	.15	.11	.06
176	Dan Peltier	.35	.25	.14
177	Darryl Strawberry	.40	.30	.15
178	Hal Morris	.30	.25	.12
179	Hensley Meulens	.20	.15	.08
180	John Smoltz	.15	.11	.06
181	Frank Thomas	2.50	2.00	1.00
182	Dave Staton	.35	.25	.12
183	Scott Chiamparino	.12	.09	.05
184	Alex Fernandez	.30	.25	.12
185	Mark Lewis	.50	.40	.20
186	Bo Jackson	1.25	.90	.50
187	Mickey Morandini	.30	.25	.12
188	Cory Snyder	.08	.06	.03
189	Rickey Henderson	.60	.45	.25
190	Junior Felix	.12	.09	.05
191	Milt Cuyler	.25	.20	.10
192	Wade Boggs	.30	.25	.12
193	"Justice Prevails"	2.50	2.00	1.00
194	Sandy Alomar, Jr.	.25	.20	.10
195	Barry Bonds	.40	.30	.15
196	Nolan Ryan	1.25	.90	.50
197	Rico Brogna	.35	.25	.14
198	Steve Decker	.30	.25	.12
199	Bob Welch	.10	.08	.04
200	Andujar Cedeno	.50	.40	.20

1991 Classic #1 Draft Picks

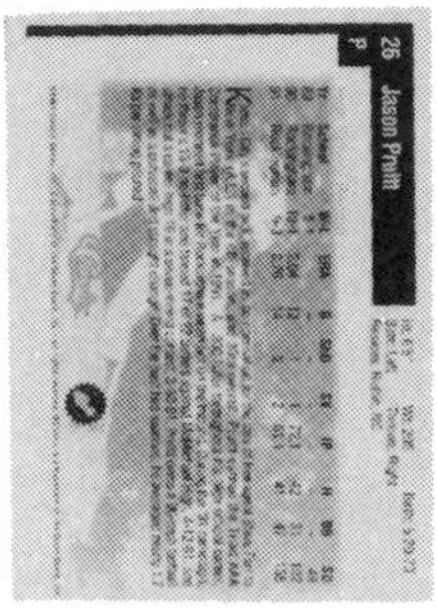

After releasing a 26-card draft pick set in 1990, Classic returned with a 50-card issue for 1991. Only 330,000 hobby sets were produced. The card fronts feature gray and maroon borders surrounding full-color photos and the Classic logo in the upper left corner. A special bonus card of Frankie Rodriguez is also included with the set. Each set also includes a certificate of authenticity.

	MT	NR MT	EX
Complete Set:	18.00	13.50	7.25
Common Player:	.30	.25	.12

		MT	NR MT	EX
1	Brien Taylor	3.00	2.25	1.25
2	Mike Kelly	2.50	2.00	1.00
3	David McCarty	1.50	1.25	.60
4	Dmitri Young	1.50	1.25	.60
5	Joe Vitiello	1.50	1.25	.60
6	Mark Smith	.80	.60	.30
7	Tyler Green	.80	.60	.30
8	Shawn Estes	.50	.40	.20
9	Doug Glanville	.80	.60	.30
10	Manny Ramirez	.60	.45	.25
11	Cliff Floyd	.50	.40	.20
12	Tyrone Hill	.80	.60	.30
13	Eduardo Perez	1.00	.70	.40
14	Al Shirley	.70	.50	.30
15	Benji Gil	.35	.25	.14
16	Calvin Reese	.35	.25	.14
17	Allen Watson	.35	.25	.14
18	Brian Barber	.35	.25	.14
19	Aaron Sele	.50	.40	.20

		MT	NR MT	EX
20	John Farrell	.35	.25	.14
21	Scott Ruffcorn	.40	.30	.15
22	Brent Gates	.40	.30	.15
23	Scott Stahoviak	.50	.40	.20
24	Tom McKinnon	.30	.25	.12
25	Shawn Livsey	.30	.25	.12
26	Jason Pruitt	.30	.25	.12
27	Greg Anthony	.35	.25	.14
28	Justin Thompson	.35	.25	.14
29	Steve Whitaker	.35	.25	.14
30	Jorge Fabregas	.60	.45	.25
31	Jeff Ware	.35	.25	.12
32	Bobby Jones	.60	.45	.25
33	J.J. Johnson	.40	.30	.15
34	Mike Rossiter	.30	.25	.12
35	Dan Chowlowsky	.30	.25	.12
36	Jimmy Gonzalez	.30	.25	.12
37	Trevor Miller	.30	.25	.12
38	Scott Hatteberg	.30	.25	.12
39	Mike Groppuso	.40	.30	.15
40	Ryan Long	.30	.25	.12
41	Eddie Williams	.30	.25	.14
42	Mike Durant	.30	.25	.14
43	Buck McNabb	.30	.25	.14
44	Jimmy Lewis	.30	.25	.14
45	Eddie Ramos	.30	.25	.14
46	Terry Horn	.30	.25	.14
47	Jon Barnes	.30	.25	.14
48	Shawn Curran	.30	.25	.14
49	Tommy Adams	.50	.40	.20
50	Trevor Mallory	.30	.25	.12
---	Frankie Rodriguez (Bonus Card)	1.75	1.25	.70

1989 Cleveland Indians Team Set

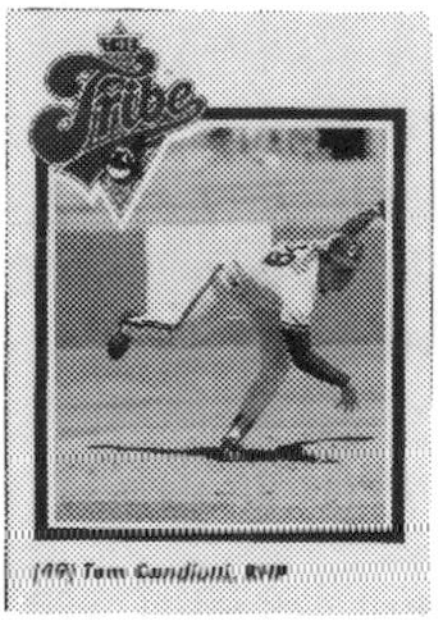

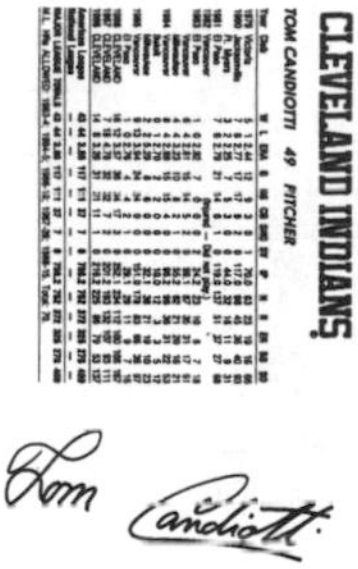

The Cleveland Indians released this oversized (2-3/4" by 4-1/2") 28-card set in 1989. The cards feature a full-color player photo on the front with the "Tribe" logo in the upper left corner. Card backs include major and minor league statistics and a facsimile autograph.

		MT	NR MT	EX
Complete Set:		5.00	3.75	2.00
Common Player:		.20	.15	.08
(1)	Doc Edwards	.20	.15	.08
(2)	Joel Skinner	.20	.15	.08
(3)	Andy Allanson	.20	.15	.08
(4)	Tom Candiotti	.20	.15	.08
(5)	Doug Jones	.20	.15	.08
(6)	Keith Atherton	.20	.15	.08
(7)	Rich Yett	.20	.15	.08
(8)	John Farrell	.20	.15	.08
(9)	Rod Nichols	.20	.15	.08
(10)	Joe Skalski	.30	.25	.12
(11)	Pete O'Brien	.30	.25	.12
(12)	Jerry Browne	.30	.25	.12
(13)	Brook Jacoby	.30	.25	.12
(14)	Felix Fermin	.20	.15	.08
(15)	Bud Black	.20	.15	.08
(16)	Brad Havens	.20	.15	.08
(17)	Greg Swindell	.40	.30	.15
(18)	Scott Bailes	.20	.15	.08
(19)	Jesse Orosco	.20	.15	.08
(20)	Oddibe McDowell	.30	.25	.12
(21)	Joe Carter	.50	.40	.20
(22)	Cory Snyder	.25	.20	.10
(23)	Louie Medina	.20	.15	.08
(24)	Dave Clark	.20	.15	.08
(25)	Brad Komminsk	.20	.15	.08
(26)	Luis Aguayo	.20	.15	.08
(27)	Pat Keedy	.20	.15	.08
(28)	Tribe Coaches	.20	.15	.08

1981 Coca-Cola

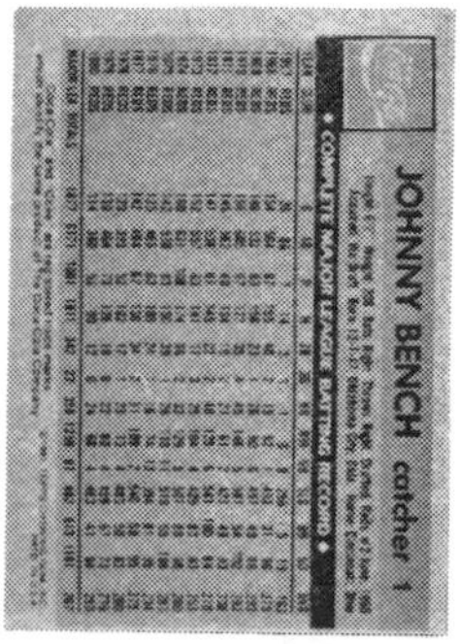

In 1981, Topps produced for Coca-Cola 12-card sets for 11 various American and National League teams. The sets include 11 player cards and one unnumbered header card. The card fronts, which measure 2-1/2" by 3-1/2", are identical in style to the 1981 Topps regular issue save for the Coca-Cola logo. The backs differ only from the '81 Topps regular set in that they are numbered 1-11 and carry the Coca-Cola trademark and copyright line. The backs of the header cards contain an offer for 132-card uncut sheets of 1981 Topps baseball cards.

		MT	NR MT	EX
Complete Set:		35.00	27.00	15.00
Common Player:		.06	.05	.02
1	Tom Burgmeier	.06	.05	.02
2	Dennis Eckersley	.15	.11	.06
3	Dwight Evans	.60	.45	.25
4	Bob Stanley	.10	.08	.04
5	Glenn Hoffman	.06	.05	.02
6	Carney Lansford	.20	.15	.08
7	Frank Tanana	.10	.08	.04
8	Tony Perez	.20	.15	.08
9	Jim Rice	.80	.60	.30
10	Dave Stapleton	.06	.05	.02
11	Carl Yastrzemski	2.00	1.50	.80
---	Header Card	.03	.02	.01
1	Tim Blackwell	.06	.05	.02
2	Bill Buckner	.15	.11	.06
3	Ivan DeJesus	.06	.05	.02
4	Leon Durham	.15	.11	.06
5	Steve Henderson	.06	.05	.02
6	Mike Krukow	.10	.08	.04
7	Ken Reitz	.06	.05	.02
8	Rick Reuschel	.15	.11	.06
9	Scot Thompson	.06	.05	.02
10	Dick Tidrow	.06	.05	.02
11	Mike Tyson	.06	.05	.02
---	Header Card	.03	.02	.01
1	Britt Burns	.10	.08	.04
2	Todd Cruz	.06	.05	.02
3	Rich Dotson	.20	.15	.08
4	Jim Essian	.06	.05	.02
5	Ed Farmer	.06	.05	.02
6	Lamar Johnson	.06	.05	.02
7	Ron LeFlore	.10	.08	.04
8	Chet Lemon	.10	.08	.04
9	Bob Molinaro	.06	.05	.02
10	Jim Morrison	.06	.05	.02
11	Wayne Nordhagen	.06	.05	.02
---	Header Card	.03	.02	.01
1	Johnny Bench	2.00	1.50	.80
2	Dave Collins	.10	.08	.04
3	Dave Concepcion	.15	.11	.06
4	Dan Driessen	.10	.08	.04

		MT	NR MT	EX
5	George Foster	.25	.20	.10
6	Ken Griffey	.15	.11	.06
7	Tom Hume	.06	.05	.02
8	Ray Knight	.10	.08	.04
9	Ron Oester	.06	.05	.02
10	Tom Seaver	1.25	.90	.50
11	Mario Soto	.10	.08	.04
---	Header Card	.03	.02	.01
1	Champ Summers	.06	.05	.02
2	Al Cowens	.06	.05	.02
3	Rich Hebner	.06	.05	.02
4	Steve Kemp	.10	.08	.04
5	Aurelio Lopez	.06	.05	.02
6	Jack Morris	.35	.25	.14
7	Lance Parrish	.35	.25	.14
8	Johnny Wockenfuss	.06	.05	.02
9	Alan Trammell	1.00	.70	.40
10	Lou Whitaker	1.00	.70	.40
11	Kirk Gibson	1.00	.70	.40
---	Header Card	.03	.02	.01
1	Alan Ashby	.06	.05	.02
2	Cesar Cedeno	.15	.11	.06
3	Jose Cruz	.15	.11	.06
4	Art Howe	.06	.05	.02
5	Rafael Landestoy	.06	.05	.02
6	Joe Niekro	.15	.11	.06
7	Terry Puhl	.06	.05	.02
8	J.R. Richard	.15	.11	.06
9	Nolan Ryan	8.00	6.00	3.25
10	Joe Sambito	.06	.05	.02
11	Don Sutton	.35	.25	.14
---	Header Card	.03	.02	.01
1	Willie Aikens	.06	.05	.02
2	George Brett	1.50	1.25	.60
3	Larry Gura	.06	.05	.02
4	Dennis Leonard	.06	.05	.02
5	Hal McRae	.15	.11	.06
6	Amos Otis	.10	.08	.04
7	Dan Quisenberry	.15	.11	.06
8	U.L. Washington	.06	.05	.02
9	John Wathan	.10	.08	.04
10	Frank White	.10	.08	.04
11	Willie Wilson	.15	.11	.06
---	Header Card	.03	.02	.01
1	Neil Allen	.06	.05	.02
2	Doug Flynn	.06	.05	.02
3	Dave Kingman	.15	.11	.06
4	Randy Jones	.06	.05	.02
5	Pat Zachry	.06	.05	.02
6	Lee Mazzilli	.10	.08	.04
7	Rusty Staub	.15	.11	.06
8	Craig Swan	.06	.05	.02
9	Frank Taveras	.06	.05	.02
10	Alex Trevino	.06	.05	.02
11	Joel Youngblood	.06	.05	.02
---	Header Card	.03	.02	.01
1	Bob Boone	.30	.25	.12
2	Larry Bowa	.15	.11	.06
3	Steve Carlton	1.00	.70	.40
4	Greg Luzinski	.15	.11	.06
5	Garry Maddox	.10	.08	.04
6	Bake McBride	.06	.05	.02
7	Tug McGraw	.15	.11	.06
8	Pete Rose	2.00	1.50	.80
9	Mike Schmidt	2.25	1.75	.90
10	Lonnie Smith	.15	.11	.06
11	Manny Trillo	.06	.05	.02
---	Header Card	.03	.02	.01
1	Jim Bibby	.06	.05	.02
2	John Candelaria	.10	.08	.04
3	Mike Easler	.10	.08	.04
4	Tim Foli	.06	.05	.02
5	Phil Garner	.06	.05	.02
6	Bill Madlock	.15	.11	.06
7	Omar Moreno	.06	.05	.02
8	Ed Ott	.06	.05	.02
9	Dave Parker	.35	.25	.14
10	Willie Stargell	1.00	.70	.40
11	Kent Tekulve	.10	.08	.04
---	Header Card	.03	.02	.01
1	Bob Forsch	.10	.08	.04
2	George Hendrick	.10	.08	.04
3	Keith Hernandez	.50	.40	.20
4	Tom Herr	.15	.11	.06
5	Sixto Lezcano	.06	.05	.02
6	Ken Oberkfell	.06	.05	.02
7	Darrell Porter	.10	.08	.04
8	Tony Scott	.06	.05	.02
9	Lary Sorensen	.06	.05	.02
10	Bruce Sutter	.15	.11	.06
11	Garry Templeton	.10	.08	.04

		MT	NR MT	EX
---	Header Card	.03	.02	.01

1982 Coca-Cola/Brigham's Red Sox

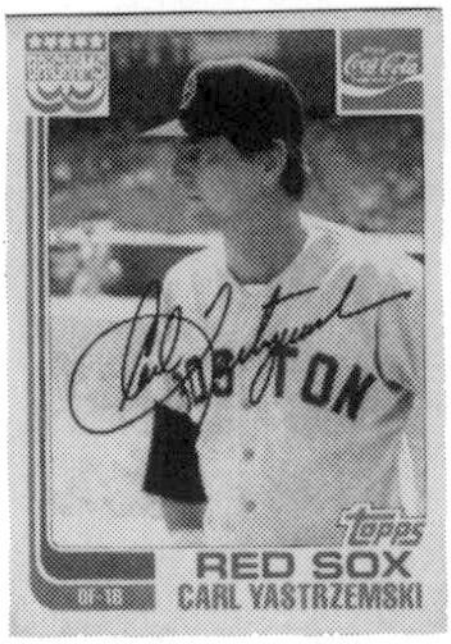

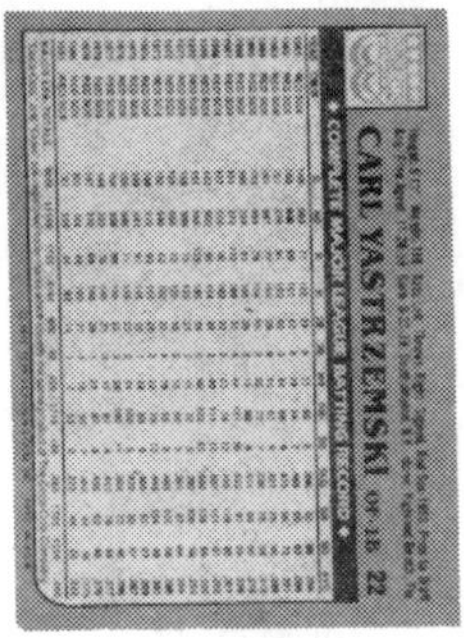

Coca-Cola, in conjunction with Brigham's Ice Cream stores, issued a 23-card set in the Boston area featuring Red Sox players. The Topps-produced cards, which measure 2-1/2" by 3-1/2", are identical in style to the regular 1982 Topps set but contain the Coca-Cola and Brigham's logos in the corners. The cards were distributed in three-card cello packs, including an unnumbered header card.

		MT	NR MT	EX
Complete Set:		8.00	6.00	3.25
Common Player:		.08	.06	.03
1	Gary Allenson	.08	.06	.03
2	Tom Burgmeier	.08	.06	.03
3	Mark Clear	.15	.11	.06
4	Steve Crawford	.08	.06	.03
5	Dennis Eckersley	1.00	.70	.40
6	Dwight Evans	.80	.60	.30
7	Rich Gedman	.30	.25	.12
8	Garry Hancock	.08	.06	.03
9	Glen Hoffman (Glenn)	.08	.06	.03
10	Carney Lansford	.20	.15	.08
11	Rick Miller	.08	.06	.03
12	Reid Nichols	.08	.06	.03
13	Bob Ojeda	.20	.15	.08
14	Tony Perez	.30	.25	.12
15	Chuck Rainey	.08	.06	.03
16	Jerry Remy	.08	.06	.03
17	Jim Rice	.80	.60	.30
18	Bob Stanley	.15	.11	.06
19	Dave Stapleton	.08	.06	.03
20	Mike Torrez	.08	.06	.03
21	John Tudor	.30	.25	.12
22	Carl Yastrzemski	3.00	2.25	1.25
---	Header Card	.05	.04	.02

1982 Coca-Cola Reds

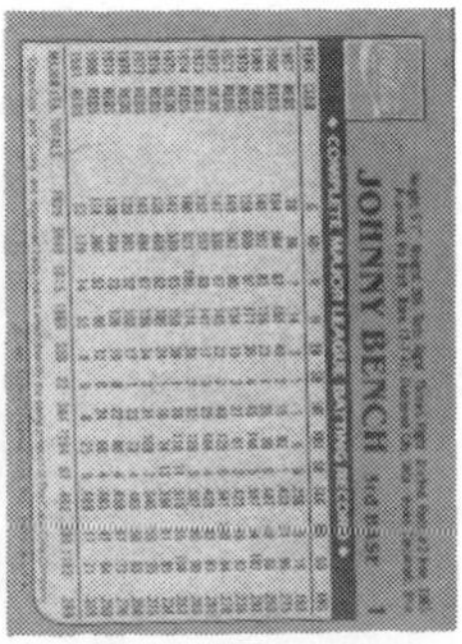

Produced by Topps for Coca-Cola, the set consists

of 23 cards featuring the Cincinnati Reds and was distributed in the Cincinnati area. The cards, which are 2-1/2" by 3-1/2" in size, are identical in design to the regular 1982 Topps set but have a Coca-Cola logo on the front and red backs. An unnumbered header card is included in the set.

		MT	NR MT	EX
Complete Set:		9.00	6.75	3.50
Common Player:		.08	.06	.03
1	Johnny Bench	3.00	2.25	1.25
2	Bruce Berenyi	.08	.06	.03
3	Larry Biittner	.08	.06	.03
4	Cesar Cedeno	.15	.11	.06
5	Dave Concepcion	.25	.20	.10
6	Dan Driessen	.15	.11	.06
7	Greg Harris	.08	.06	.03
8	Paul Householder	.08	.06	.03
9	Tom Hume	.08	.06	.03
10	Clint Hurdle	.08	.06	.03
11	Jim Kern	.08	.06	.03
12	Wayne Krenchicki	.08	.06	.03
13	Rafael Landestoy	.08	.06	.03
14	Charlie Leibrandt	.15	.11	.06
15	Mike O'Berry	.08	.06	.03
16	Ron Oester	.08	.06	.03
17	Frank Pastore	.08	.06	.03
18	Joe Price	.08	.06	.03
19	Tom Seaver	3.00	2.25	1.25
20	Mario Soto	.15	.11	.06
21	Alex Trevino	.08	.06	.03
22	Mike Vail	.08	.06	.03
----	Header Card	.04	.03	.02

1985 Coca-Cola White Sox

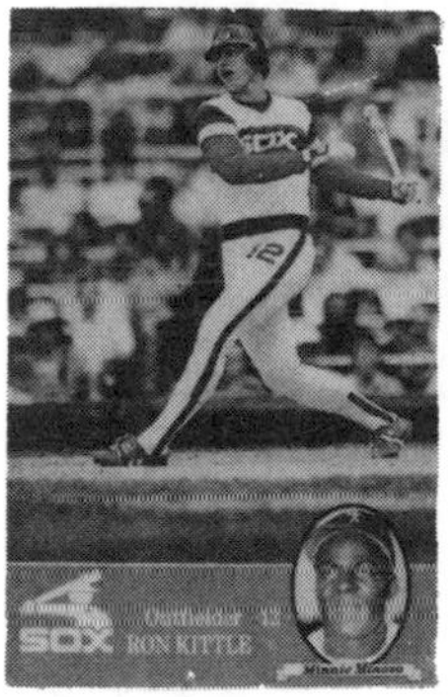

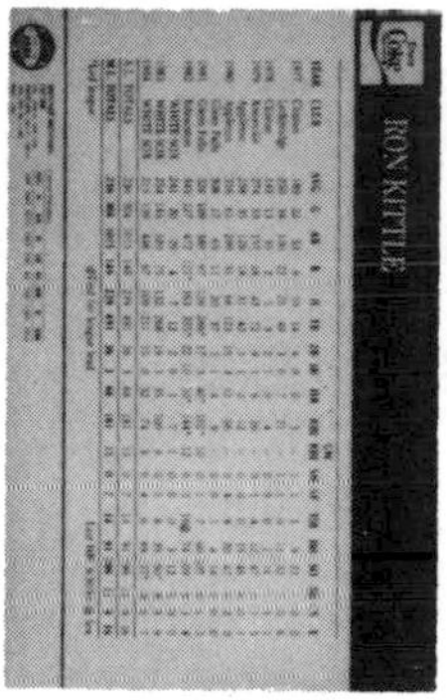

Featuring past and present White Sox players, the cards in this set were given out on Tuesday night home games. The cards, which measure 2-5/8" by 4-1/8", contain a color photo of a current Sox member. A red box at the bottom of the card carries the team logo, the player's name, uniform number and position, plus a small oval portrait of a past Sox player. The card backs contain the Coca-Cola logo and the lifetime hitting or pitching statistics for the current and past player. The set is numbered in the checklist that follows by the player's uniform number with the last three cards being unnumbered. Complete sets were available through a fan club offer found in White Sox programs.

		MT	NR MT	EX
Complete Set:		14.00	10.50	5.50
Common Player:		.25	.20	.10
	Oscar Gamble (Zeke Bonura)	.25	.20	.10
1	Scott Fletcher (Luke Appling)	.40	.30	.15
3	Harold Baines (Bill Melton)	.80	.60	.30
5	Luis Salazar (Chico Carrasquel)	.25	.20	.10
7	Marc Hill (Sherm Lollar)	.25	.20	.10
8	Daryl Boston (Jim Landis)	.25	.20	.10
10	Tony LaRussa (Al Lopez)	.40	.30	.15
12	Julio Cruz (Nellie Fox)	.40	.30	.15
13	Ozzie Guillen (Luis Aparicio)	1.50	1.25	.60
17	Jerry Hairston (Smoky Burgess)	.25	.20	.10
20	Joe DeSa (Carlos May)	.25	.20	.10
22	Joel Skinner (J.C. Martin)	.25	.20	.10
23	Rudy Law (Bill Skowron)	.25	.20	.10
24	Floyd Bannister (Red Faber)	.35	.25	.14
29	Greg Walker (Dick Allen)	.70	.50	.30
30	Gene Nelson (Early Wynn)	.35	.25	.14
32	Tim Hulett (Pete Ward)	.25	.20	.10
34	Richard Dotson (Ed Walsh)	.35	.25	.14
37	Dan Spillner (Thornton Lee)	.25	.20	.10
40	Britt Burns (Gary Peters)	.25	.20	.10
41	Tom Seaver (Ted Lyons)	1.50	1.25	.60
42	Ron Kittle (Minnie Minoso)	.40	.30	.15
43	Bob James (Hoyt Wilhelm)	.40	.30	.15
44	Tom Paciorek (Eddie Collins)	.35	.25	.14
46	Tim Lollar (Billy Pierce)	.25	.20	.10
50	Juan Agosto (Wilbur Wood)	.25	.20	.10
72	Carlton Fisk (Ray Schalk)	1.50	1.25	.60
----	Comiskey Park	.50	.40	.20
----	Ribbie and Roobarb (mascots)	.25	.20	.10
----	Nancy Faust (organist)	.25	.20	.10

1986 Coca-Cola White Sox

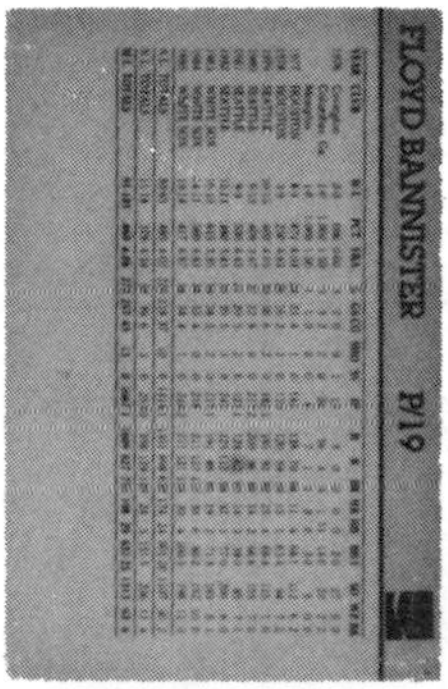

For the second year in a row, Coca-Cola, in conjunction with the Chicago White Sox, issued a 30-card set. As in 1985, cards were given out at the park on Tuesday night games. Full sets were again available through a fan club offer found in the White Sox program. The cards, which measure 2-5/8" by 4-1/8", feature 25 players plus other White Sox personnel. The card fronts feature a color photo (an action shot in most instances) and a white bar at the bottom. A black and white bat with "SOX" shown on the barrel is located within the white bar, along with the player's name, position and uniform number. The white and grey backs with black print include the Coca-Cola trademark. Lifetime statistics are shown on all player cards, but there is no personal information such as height, weight or age. The non-player cards are blank-backed save for the name and logo at the top. The cards in the checklist that follows are numbered by the players' uniform numbers, with the last five cards of the set being unnumbered.

		MT	NR MT	EX
Complete Set:		15.00	11.00	6.00
Common Player:		.25	.20	.10
1	Wayne Tolleson	.25	.20	.10
3	Harold Baines	.80	.60	.30
7	Marc Hill	.25	.20	.10
8	Daryl Boston	.25	.20	.10
12	Julio Cruz	.25	.20	.10
13	Ozzie Guillen	.80	.60	.30
17	Jerry Hairston	.25	.20	.10
19	Floyd Bannister	.35	.25	.14
20	Reid Nichols	.25	.20	.10
22	Joel Skinner	.25	.20	.10
24	Dave Schmidt	.25	.20	.10
26	Bobby Bonilla	2.50	2.00	1.00
29	Greg Walker	.40	.30	.15
30	Gene Nelson	.25	.20	.10
32	Tim Hulett	.25	.20	.10
33	Neil Allen	.25	.20	.10
34	Richard Dotson	.35	.25	.14

		MT	NR MT	EX
40	Joe Cowley	.25	.20	.10
41	Tom Seaver	1.25	.90	.50
42	Ron Kittle	.35	.25	.14
43	Bob James	.25	.20	.10
44	John Cangelosi	.35	.25	.14
50	Juan Agosto	.25	.20	.10
52	Joel Davis	.25	.20	.10
72	Carlton Fisk	1.25	.90	.50
----	Ribbie & Roobarb (mascots)	.25	.20	.10
----	Nancy Faust (organist)	.25	.20	.10
----	Ken "Hawk" Harrelson	.30	.25	.12
----	Tony LaRussa	.30	.25	.12
----	Minnie Minoso	.30	.25	.12

1987 Coca-Cola Tigers

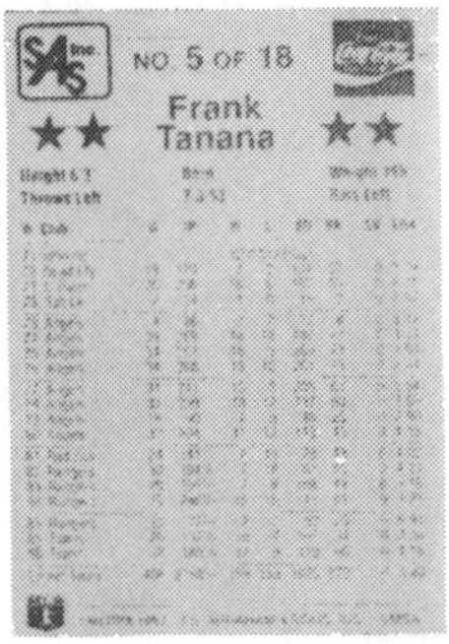

Coca-Cola and S. Abraham & Sons, Inc. issued a set of 18 baseball cards featuring members of the Detroit Tigers. The set is comprised of six four-part folding panels. Each panel includes three player cards (each 2-1/2" by 3-1/2") and one team logo card. A bright yellow border surrounds the full-color photo. The backs are designed on a vertical format and contain personal data and career statistics. The set was produced by Mike Schecter and Associates.

		MT	NR MT	EX
Complete Set:		6.00	4.50	2.50
Complete Singles Set:		2.00	1.50	.80
Common Panel:		.60	.45	.25
Common Single Player:		.05	.04	.02
	Panel	1.25	.90	.50
1	Kirk Gibson	.50	.40	.20
2	Larry Herndon	.08	.06	.03
3	Walt Terrell	.10	.08	.04
	Panel	1.25	.90	.50
4	Alan Trammell	.50	.40	.20
5	Frank Tanana	.10	.08	.04
6	Pat Sheridan	.05	.04	.02
	Panel	.90	.70	.35
7	Jack Morris	.30	.25	.12
8	Mike Heath	.05	.04	.02
9	Dave Bergman	.05	.04	.02
	Panel	.60	.45	.25
10	Chet Lemon	.10	.08	.04
11	Dwight Lowry	.08	.06	.03
12	Dan Petry	.10	.08	.04
	Panel	.80	.60	.30
13	Darrell Evans	.20	.15	.08
14	Darnell Coles	.10	.08	.04
15	Willie Hernandez	.10	.08	.04
	Panel	1.00	.70	.40
16	Lou Whitaker	.30	.25	.12
17	Tom Brookens	.05	.04	.02
18	John Grubb	.05	.04	.02

1987 Coca-Cola White Sox

The Chicago White Sox Fan Club, in conjunction with Coca-Cola, offered members a set of 30 trading cards. For the $10 membership fee, fans received the set plus additional fan club gifts and privileges. The cards, which measure 2-5/8" by 4", feature full-color

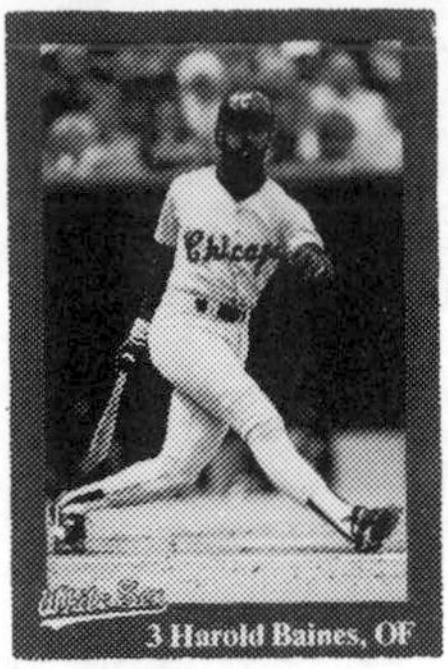

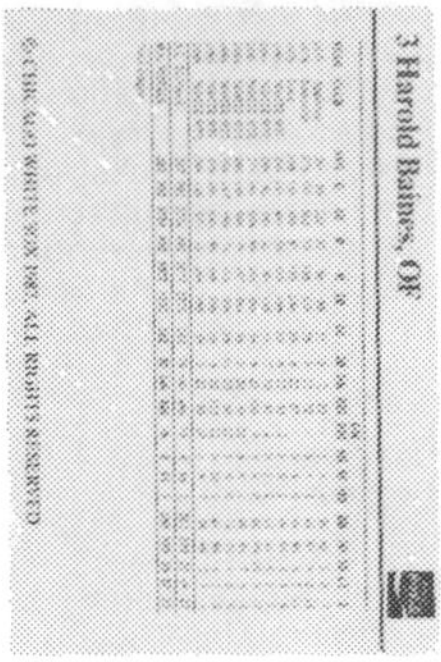

photos inside a blue and red border. The backs include the player's name, position, uniform number and statistics. The Coca-Cola logo is also included on the card backs.

		MT	NR MT	EX
Complete Set:		12.00	9.00	4.75
Common Player:		.25	.20	.10
1	Jerry Royster	.25	.20	.10
3	Harold Baines	.60	.45	.25
5	Ron Karkovice	.30	.25	.12
8	Daryl Boston	.25	.20	.10
10	Fred Manrique	.30	.25	.12
12	Steve Lyons	.25	.20	.10
13	Ozzie Guillen	.60	.45	.25
14	Russ Morman	.30	.25	.12
15	Donnie Hill	.25	.20	.10
16	Jim Fregosi	.30	.25	.12
17	Jerry Hairston	.25	.20	.10
19	Floyd Bannister	.35	.25	.14
21	Gary Redus	.25	.20	.10
22	Ivan Calderon	.60	.45	.25
25	Ron Hassey	.25	.20	.10
26	Jose DeLeon	.30	.25	.12
29	Greg Walker	.30	.25	.14
32	Tim Hulett	.25	.20	.10
33	Neil Allen	.25	.20	.10
34	Rich Dotson	.35	.25	.14
36	Ray Searage	.25	.20	.10
37	Bobby Thigpen	.60	.45	.25
40	Jim Winn	.25	.20	.10
43	Bob James	.25	.20	.10
50	Joel McKeon	.25	.20	.10
52	Joel Davis	.25	.20	.10
72	Carlton Fisk	.80	.60	.30
----	Ribbie & Roobarb (mascots)	.25	.20	.10
----	Nancy Faust (organist)	.25	.20	.10
----	Minnie Minoso	.30	.25	.12

1988 Coca-Cola Padres

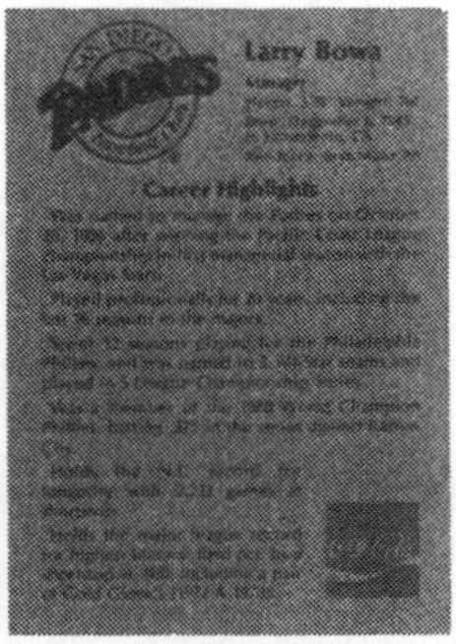

A 20-card team set sponsored by Coca-Cola was designed as part of the San Diego Padres Junior Fan Club promotion for 1988. This set was distributed as a nine-card starter sheet, with 11 additional single cards handed out during the team's home games. The standard-size cards feature full-color player

photos framed by a black and orange border. The player's name is printed above the photo; uniform number and position appear lower right. A large Padres logo curves upward from the lower left corner. Card backs are brown on white and include the Padres logo upper left opposite the player's name and personal information. Career highlights and 1987 stats appear in the center of the card back above the Coca-Cola and Junior Padres Fan Club logos.

		MT	NR MT	EX
Complete Set:		35.00	25.00	13.00
Common Player:		.50	.40	.20
	Panel			
1	Garry Templeton	.75	.60	.30
5	Randy Ready	.50	.40	.20
10	Larry Bowa	.75	.60	.30
11	Tim Flannery	.50	.40	.20
35	Chris Brown	.75	.60	.30
45	Jimmy Jones	1.00	.70	.40
48	Mark Davis	.50	.40	.20
55	Mark Grant	.50	.40	.20
---	20th Anniversary Logo Card	.10	.08	.04
	Singles			
7	Keith Moreland	1.00	.70	.40
8	John Kruk	2.25	1.75	.90
9	Benito Santiago	3.25	2.50	1.25
14	Carmelo Martinez	1.00	.70	.40
15	Jack McKeon	1.00	.70	.40
19	Tony Gwynn	10.00	7.50	4.00
22	Stan Jefferson	1.00	.70	.40
27	Mark Parent	2.00	1.50	.80
30	Eric Show	1.50	1.25	.60
31	Ed Whitson	1.00	.70	.40
41	Lance McCullers	1.25	.90	.50
51	Greg Booker	1.00	.70	.40

1988 Coca-Cola White Sox

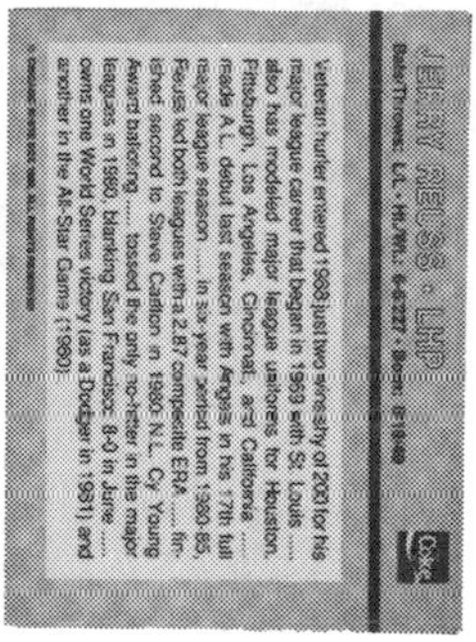

Part of a fan club membership package, this unnumbered 30-card set features full-color photos of 27 players, the team mascot, team organist and Comiskey Park. Cards have a bright red border, with the team logo in the lower left corner of the photo. A large player name fills the bottom border. Card backs are printed in black on grey and white and include player name, personal info and career summary. The set was included in the $10 membership package, with a portion of the cost going to the ChiSox Kids Charity.

		MT	NR MT	EX
Complete Set:		8.00	6.00	3.25
Common Player:		.20	.15	.08
(1)	Harold Baines	.50	.40	.20
(2)	Daryl Boston	.20	.15	.08
(3)	Ivan Calderon	.40	.30	.15
(4)	John Davis	.20	.15	.08
(5)	Jim Fregosi	.25	.20	.10
(6)	Carlton Fisk	.60	.45	.25
(7)	Ozzie Guillen	.40	.30	.15
(8)	Donnie Hill	.20	.15	.08
(9)	Rick Horton	.20	.15	.08
(10)	Lance Johnson	.30	.25	.12
(11)	Dave LaPoint	.20	.15	.08
(12)	Bill Long	.25	.20	.10
(13)	Steve Lyons	.20	.15	.08
(14)	Jack McDowell	.70	.50	.30
(15)	Fred Manrique	.20	.15	.08
(16)	Minnie Minoso	.25	.20	.10
(17)	Dan Pasqua	.30	.25	.12
(18)	John Pawlowski	.25	.20	.10
(19)	Melido Perez	.40	.30	.15
(20)	Billy Pierce	.25	.20	.10
(21)	Gary Redus	.20	.15	.08
(22)	Jerry Reuss	.25	.20	.10
(23)	Mark Salas	.20	.15	.08
(24)	Jose Segura	.30	.25	.12
(25)	Bobby Thigpen	.35	.25	.14
(26)	Greg Walker	.30	.25	.12
(27)	Kenny Williams	.30	.25	.12
(28)	Nancy Faust (organist)	.20	.15	.08
(29)	Ribbie & Roobarb (mascots)	.20	.15	.08
(30)	Comiskey Park	.40	.30	.15

1989 Coca-Cola Padres

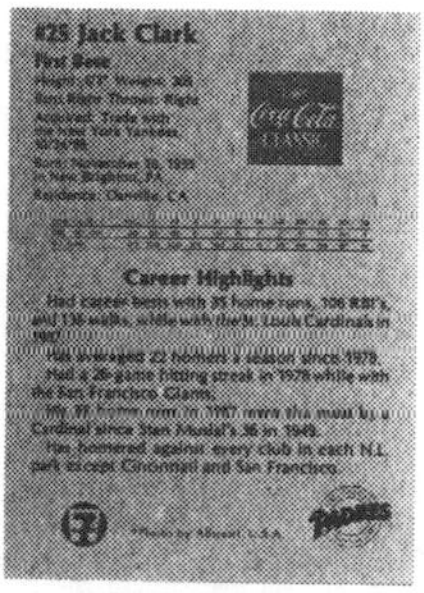

This 20-card set is part of the Junior Padres Fan Club membership package. Members receive a 9-card starter set printed on one large perforated sheet. Additional cards are distributed to kids at specially designated games (free admission for kids). Card fronts feature an orange-and-brown double border, with a bright orange Padres logo printed lower left. Player uniform number and position are printed diagonally across the upper right corner, with the player's name in large block letters along the bottom border.

		MT	NR MT	EX
Complete Set:		30.00	22.00	12.00
Common Player:		.50	.40	.30
	Panel			
1	Garry Templeton	.70	.50	.30
5	Randy Ready	.50	.40	.20
12	Roberto Alomar	1.00	.70	.40
14	Carmelo Martinez	.50	.40	.20
15	Jack McKeon	.50	.40	.20
30	Eric Show	.50	.40	.20
31	Ed Whitson	.50	.40	.20
43	Dennis Rasmussen	.50	.40	.20
---	Logo Card	.10	.08	.04
	Singles			
6	Luis Salazar	1.00	.70	.40
9	Benito Santiago	3.00	2.25	1.25
10	Leon Roberts	1.00	.70	.40
11	Tim Flannery	1.00	.70	.40
18	Chris James	2.00	1.50	.80
19	Tony Gwynn	8.00	6.00	3.25
25	Jack Clark	3.00	2.25	1.25
27	Mark Parent	2.00	1.50	.80
35	Walt Terrell	1.00	.70	.40
47	Bruce Hurst	2.00	1.50	.80
48	Mark Davis	3.00	2.25	1.25
55	Mark Grant	1.00	.70	.30

NOTE: A card number in parentheses ( ) indicates the set is unnumbered.

1989 Coca-Cola White Sox

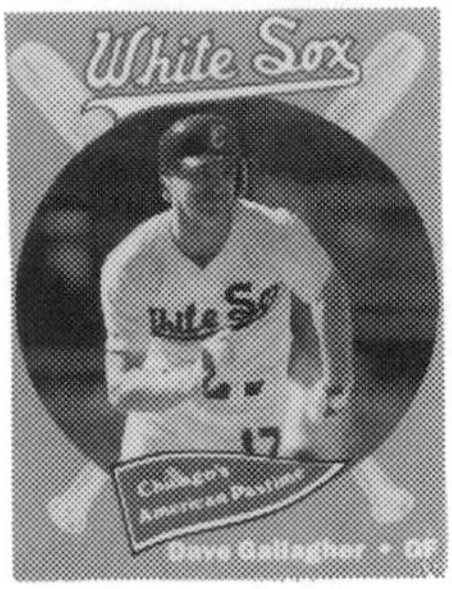

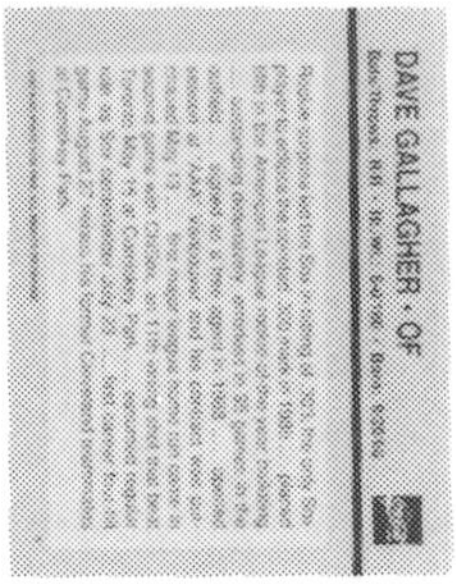

For the fifth straight year, Coca-Cola sponsored a set of cards featuring the Chicago White Sox. The 30-card set was distributed to fans attending a special promotional day at Comiskey Park and was also available by mail to members of the ChiSox fan club. The fronts of the cards feature a red, white and blue color scheme and include a pair of crossed bats. "White Sox" appears along the top, while the name and position are in the lower right, and a pennant proclaiming "Chicago's American Pastime" is just below the photo. The horizontal backs include player biographies, other data, special facts about Comiskey Park and the Coca-Cola logo.

		MT	NR MT	EX
Complete Set:		7.00	5.25	2.75
Common Player:		.20	.15	.08
1	New Comiskey Park, 1991	.40	.30	.15
2	Comiskey Park	.40	.30	.15
3	Jeff Torborg	.20	.15	.08
4	Coaching Staff	.20	.15	.08
5	Harold Baines	.50	.40	.20
6	Daryl Boston	.20	.15	.08
7	Ivan Calderon	.30	.25	.12
8	Carlton Fisk	.40	.30	.15
9	Dave Gallagher	.30	.25	.12
10	Ozzie Guillen	.30	.25	.12
11	Shawn Hillegas	.20	.15	.08
12	Barry Jones	.20	.15	.08
13	Ron Karkovice	.20	.15	.08
14	Eric King	.20	.15	.08
15	Ron Kittle	.30	.25	.12
16	Bill Long	.20	.15	.08
17	Steve Lyons	.20	.15	.08
18	Donn Pall	.20	.15	.08
19	Dan Pasqua	.30	.25	.12
20	Ken Patterson	.20	.15	.08
21	Melido Perez	.30	.25	.12
22	Jerry Reuss	.25	.20	.10
23	Billy Jo Robidoux	.20	.15	.08
24	Steve Rosenberg	.20	.15	.08
25	Jeff Schaefer	.25	.20	.10
26	Bobby Thigpen	.35	.25	.14
27	Greg Walker	.25	.20	.10
28	Eddie Williams	.25	.20	.10
29	Nancy Faust, organist	.20	.15	.08
30	Minnie Minoso	.20	.15	.08

1990 Coca-Cola-Garry Templeton

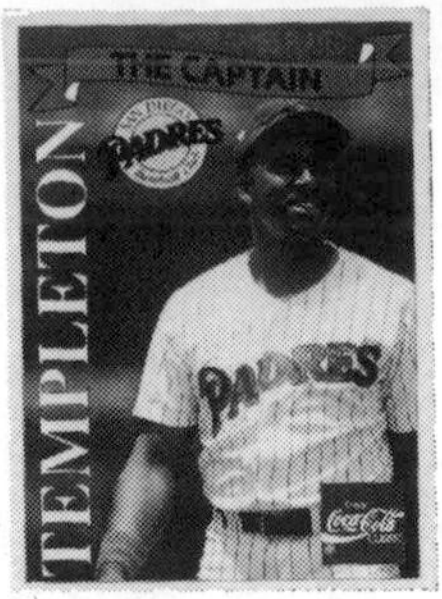

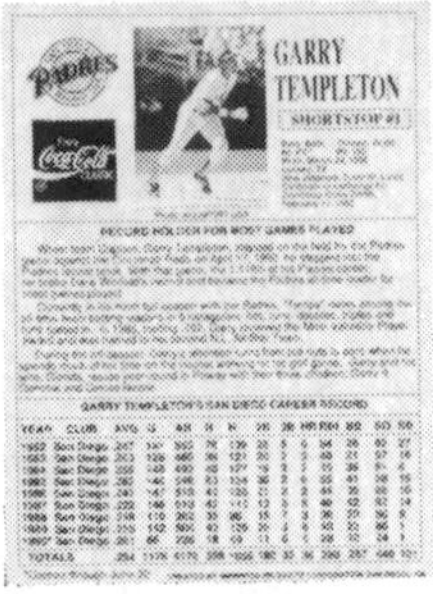

Coca-Cola, Vons stores and the San Diego Padres joined forces to release this special pin/baseball card collectible in honor of Garry Templeton becoming the club's all-time leader in games played. The card front features a full-color photo of Templeton and displays "Most Games Played" and "The Captain" in orange at the top of the photo. "Templeton" appears vertically in white along the left border. The Coca- Cola and Padre logos also appear on the card front. The bottom of the card features a perforated edge where the pin is attached as an extension of the card. The card back is printed in black and white and displays biographical information, career highlights and career statistics. The card was created by Imprinted Products Corporation of San Diego.

	MT	NR MT	EX
Complete Set:	1.50	1.25	.60
(1) Most Games Played card (Garry Templeton)	.50	.40	.20
(2) Most Games Played Pin (Garry Templeton)	1.00	.70	.40

1990 Coca-Cola White Sox

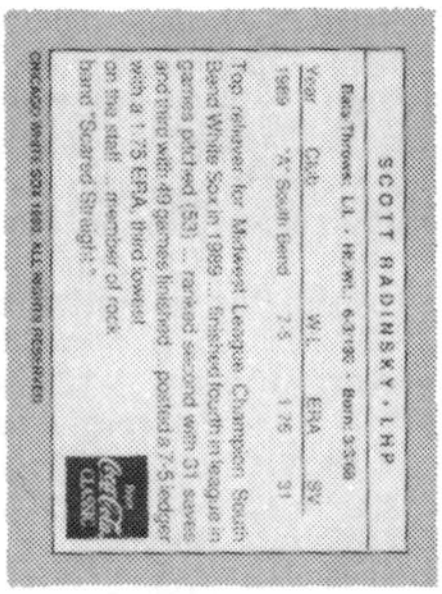

An attractive "Comiskey Park 1910-1990" logo is featured on the front of each of the 30 cards in this set. The card fronts feature full-color photos with a thin white inner border. The cards are numbered according to uniform number, with the exception of four special cards including Top Prospect Frank Thomas. The horizontal card backs feature black print on white and gray stock. 1989 statistics and career highlights are provided. The set was made available nationally through hobby dealers. The 1990 set marks the sixth straight year that Coca-Cola sponsored a White Sox set.

		MT	NR MT	EX
Complete Set:		10.00	7.50	4.00
Common Player:		.15	.11	.06
1	Lance Johnson	.20	.15	.08
7	Scott Fletcher	.15	.11	.06
10	Jeff Torborg	.15	.11	.06
12	Steve Lyons	.15	.11	.06
13	Ozzie Guillen	.25	.20	.10
14	Craig Grebeck	.20	.15	.08
17	Dave Gallagher	.15	.11	.06
20	Ron Karkovice	.15	.11	.06
22	Ivan Calderon	.25	.20	.10
23	Robin Ventura	.60	.45	.25
24	Carlos Martinez	.20	.15	.08
25	Sammy Sosa	.30	.25	.12

		MT	NR MT	EX
27	Greg Hibbard	.20	.15	.08
29	Jack McDowell	.35	.25	.14
30	Donn Pall	.15	.11	.06
31	Scott Radinsky	.25	.20	.10
33	Melido Perez	.15	.11	.06
34	Ken Patterson	.15	.11	.06
36	Eric King	.15	.11	.06
37	Bobby Thigpen	.35	.25	.14
42	Ron Kittle	.20	.15	.08
44	Dan Pasqua	.20	.15	.08
45	Wayne Edwards	.15	.11	.06
50	Barry Jones	.15	.11	.06
52	Jerry Kutzler	.15	.11	.06
72	Carlton Fisk	.35	.25	.14
----	Top Prospect (Frank Thomas)	3.00	2.25	1.25
----	Coaches	.15	.11	.06
----	Captains-Guillen, Fisk	.20	.15	.08
----	Rookies	.20	.15	.08

1982 Cracker Jack

The Topps-produced 1982 Cracker Jack set was issued to promote the first "Old Timers Baseball Classic," held in Washington, D.C. Sixteen cards comprise the set which was issued in two sheets of eight cards, plus an advertising card located in the center. The individual cards are 2-1/2" by 3-1/2" in size with the complete sheets measuring 7-1/2" by 10-1/2". Card #'s 1-8 feature American League players with #'s 9-16 being former National League stars. The card fronts feature a full-color photo inside a Cracker Jack border. The backs contain the Cracker Jack logo plus a short player biography and his lifetime pitching or batting record. Complete sheets were available through a write-in offer.

		MT	NR MT	EX
Complete Panel Set:		10.00	7.50	4.00
Complete Singles Set:		4.00	3.00	1.50
Common Single Player:		.05	.04	.02
	Panel	5.00	3.75	2.00
1	Larry Doby	.05	.04	.02
2	Bob Feller	.10	.08	.04
3	Whitey Ford	.10	.08	.04
4	Al Kaline	.10	.08	.04
5	Harmon Killebrew	.10	.08	.04
6	Mickey Mantle	2.50	2.00	1.00
7	Tony Oliva	.05	.04	.02
8	Brooks Robinson	.10	.08	.04
	Panel	4.00	3.00	1.50
9	Hank Aaron	1.25	.90	.50
10	Ernie Banks	.10	.08	.04
11	Ralph Kiner	.10	.08	.04
12	Eddie Mathews	.10	.08	.04
13	Willie Mays	1.00	.70	.40
14	Robin Roberts	.10	.08	.04
15	Duke Snider	.10	.08	.04
16	Warren Spahn	.10	.08	.04
----	Advertising Card	.02	.02	.01

A player's name in *italic* type indicates a rookie card. An (FC) indicates a player's first card for that particular card company.

1976 Crane Potato Chips

This unnumbered 70-card set of player discs was issued with Crane Potato Chips in 1976. The front of the discs are designed to look like a baseball with the player's portrait in the center and his name, position and team beneath.

		NR MT	EX	VG
Complete Set:		30.00	15.00	9.00
Common Player:		.10	.05	.03
(1)	Henry Aaron	2.25	1.25	.70
(2)	Johnny Bench	1.25	.60	.40
(3)	Vida Blue	.12	.06	.04
(4)	Larry Bowa	.12	.06	.04
(5)	Lou Brock	.60	.30	.20
(6)	Jeff Burroughs	.10	.05	.03
(7)	John Candelaria	.12	.06	.04
(8)	Jose Cardenal	.10	.05	.03
(9)	Rod Carew	1.25	.60	.40
(10)	Steve Carlton	1.25	.60	.40
(11)	Dave Cash	.10	.05	.03
(12)	Cesar Cedeno	.12	.06	.04
(13)	Ron Cey	.12	.06	.04
(14)	Carlton Fisk	.60	.30	.20
(15)	Tito Fuentes	.10	.05	.03
(16)	Steve Garvey	.70	.35	.20
(17)	Ken Griffey	.12	.06	.04
(18)	Don Gullett	.10	.05	.03
(19)	Willie Horton	.10	.05	.03
(20)	Al Hrabosky	.10	.05	.03
(21)	Catfish Hunter	.50	.25	.15
(22)	Reggie Jackson	1.75	.90	.50
(23)	Randy Jones	.10	.05	.03
(24)	Jim Kaat	.15	.08	.05
(25)	Don Kessinger	.10	.05	.03
(26)	Dave Kingman	.15	.08	.05
(27)	Jerry Koosman	.12	.06	.04
(28)	Mickey Lolich	.15	.08	.05
(29)	Greg Luzinski	.15	.08	.05
(30)	Fred Lynn	.20	.10	.06
(31)	Bill Madlock	.15	.08	.05
(32)	Carlos May	.10	.05	.03
(33)	John Mayberry	.10	.05	.03
(34)	Bake McBride	.10	.05	.03
(35)	Doc Medich	.10	.05	.03
(36)	Andy Messersmith	.10	.05	.03
(37)	Rick Monday	.12	.06	.04
(38)	John Montefusco	.10	.05	.03
(39)	Jerry Morales	.10	.05	.03
(40)	Joe Morgan	.60	.30	.20
(41)	Thurman Munson	.60	.30	.20
(42)	Bobby Murcer	.12	.06	.04
(43)	Al Oliver	.15	.08	.05
(44)	Jim Palmer	.60	.30	.20
(45)	Dave Parker	.20	.10	.06
(46)	Tony Perez	.20	.10	.06
(47)	Jerry Reuss	.12	.06	.04
(48)	Brooks Robinson	.70	.35	.20
(49)	Frank Robinson	.70	.35	.20
(50)	Steve Rogers	.10	.05	.03
(51)	Pete Rose	2.25	1.25	.70
(52)	Nolan Ryan	2.25	1.25	.70
(53)	Manny Sanguillen	.10	.05	.03
(54)	Mike Schmidt	1.75	.90	.50
(55)	Tom Seaver	1.75	.90	.50
(56)	Ted Simmons	.15	.08	.05
(57)	Reggie Smith	.12	.06	.04
(58)	Willie Stargell	.60	.30	.20

		NR MT	EX	VG
(59)	Rusty Staub	.15	.08	.05
(60)	Rennie Stennett	.10	.05	.03
(61)	Don Sutton	.20	.10	.06
(62)	Andy Thornton	.12	.06	.04
(63)	Luis Tiant	.15	.08	.05
(64)	Joe Torre	.12	.06	.04
(65)	Mike Tyson	.10	.05	.03
(66)	Bob Watson	.10	.05	.03
(67)	Wilbur Wood	.10	.05	.03
(68)	Jimmy Wynn	.10	.05	.03
(69)	Carl Yastrzemski	1.75	.90	.50
(70)	Richie Zisk	.10	.05	.03

D

1954 Dan-Dee Potato Chips

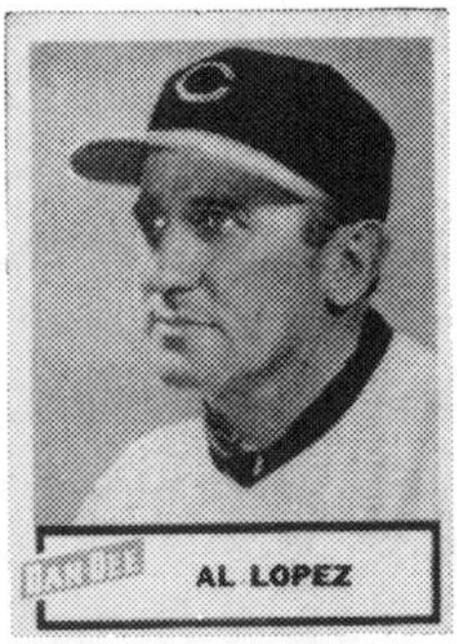

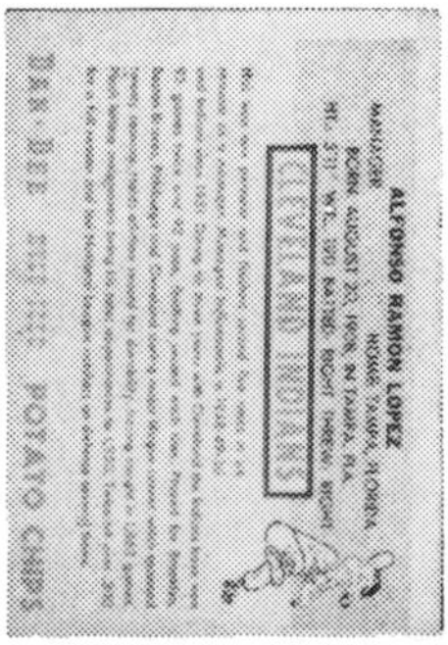

Issued in bags of potato chips, the cards in this 29-card set are commonly found with grease stains despite their waxed surface. The unnumbered cards, which measure 2-1/2" by 3-5/8", feature full-color photos. The card backs contain player statistical and biographical information. The set consists mostly of players from the Indians and Pirates. Photos of the Yankees players were also used for the Briggs Meats and Stahl-Meyer Franks sets. Cooper and Smith are the scarcest cards in the set.

		NR MT	EX	VG
Complete Set		4500.00	2250.00	1350.
Common Player		60.00	30.00	18.00
(1)	Bob Avila	60.00	30.00	18.00
(2)	Hank Bauer	80.00	40.00	24.00
(3)	Walker Cooper	350.00	175.00	105.00
(4)	Larry Doby	90.00	45.00	27.00
(5)	Luke Easter	60.00	30.00	18.00
(6)	Bob Feller	200.00	100.00	60.00
(7)	Bob Friend	60.00	30.00	18.00
(8)	Mike Garcia	60.00	30.00	18.00
(9)	Sid Gordon	60.00	30.00	18.00
(10)	Jim Hegan	60.00	30.00	18.00
(11)	Gil Hodges	150.00	75.00	45.00
(12)	Art Houtteman	60.00	30.00	18.00
(13)	Monte Irvin	100.00	50.00	30.00
(14)	Paul LaPalm (LaPalme)	60.00	30.00	18.00
(15)	Bob Lemon	110.00	55.00	33.00
(16)	Al Lopez	90.00	45.00	27.00
(17)	Mickey Mantle	1500.00	750.00	450.00
(18)	Dale Mitchell	60.00	30.00	18.00
(19)	Phil Rizzuto	125.00	62.00	37.00
(20)	Curtis Roberts	60.00	30.00	18.00
(21)	Al Rosen	80.00	40.00	24.00
(22)	Red Schoendienst	110.00	55.00	33.00
(23)	Paul Smith	450.00	225.00	135.00
(24)	Duke Snider	225.00	112.00	67.00
(25)	George Strickland	60.00	30.00	18.00
(26)	Max Surkont	60.00	30.00	18.00
(27)	Frank Thomas	125.00	62.00	37.00
(28)	Wally Westlake	60.00	30.00	18.00
(29)	Early Wynn	110.00	55.00	33.00

1987 David Berg Hot Dogs Cubs

Changing sponsors from Gatorade to David Berg Pure Beef Hot Dogs, the Chicago Cubs handed out a 26-card set of baseball cards to fans attending the July 29th game at Wrigley Field. The cards are printed in full-color on white stock and measure 2-7/8" by 4-1/4" in size. The set is numbered by the players' uniform numbers. The card backs contain player personal and statistical information, plus a full-color picture of a David Berg hot dog in a bun with all the garnishings. The set marked the sixth consecutive year the Cubs held a baseball card giveaway promotion.

		MT	NR MT	EX
Complete Set:		9.00	6.75	3.50
Common Player:		.15	.11	.06
1	Dave Martinez	.50	.40	.20
4	Gene Michael	.15	.11	.06
6	Keith Moreland	.30	.25	.12
7	Jody Davis	.30	.25	.12
8	Andre Dawson	1.00	.70	.40
10	Leon Durham	.30	.25	.12
11	Jim Sundberg	.15	.11	.06
12	Shawon Dunston	.60	.45	.25
19	Manny Trillo	.15	.11	.06
20	Bob Dernier	.15	.11	.06
21	Scott Sanderson	.15	.11	.06
22	Jerry Mumphrey	.15	.11	.06
23	Ryne Sandberg	2.00	1.50	.80
24	Brian Dayett	.15	.11	.06
29	Chico Walker	.15	.11	.06
31	Greg Maddux	.70	.50	.30
33	Frank DiPino	.15	.11	.06
34	Steve Trout	.20	.15	.08
36	Gary Matthews	.20	.15	.08
37	Ed Lynch	.15	.11	.06
39	Ron Davis	.15	.11	.06
40	Rick Sutcliffe	.40	.30	.15
46	Lee Smith	.30	.25	.12
47	Dickie Noles	.15	.11	.06
49	Jamie Moyer	.20	.15	.08
----	The Coaching Staff (Johnny Oates, Jim Snyder, Herm Starrette, John Vukovich, Billy Williams)	.15	.11	.06

1988 David Berg Hot Dogs Cubs

This oversized (2-7/8" by 4-1/2") set of 26 cards was distributed to fans at Wrigley Field on August 24th. The set includes cards for the manager and coaching staff, as well as players. Full-color action photos are framed in red and blue on a white background. The backs feature small black and white player close-ups, colorful team logos, statistics and sponsor logos (David Berg Hot Dogs and Venture Store Restaurants). The numbers in the following checklist refer to players' uniforms.

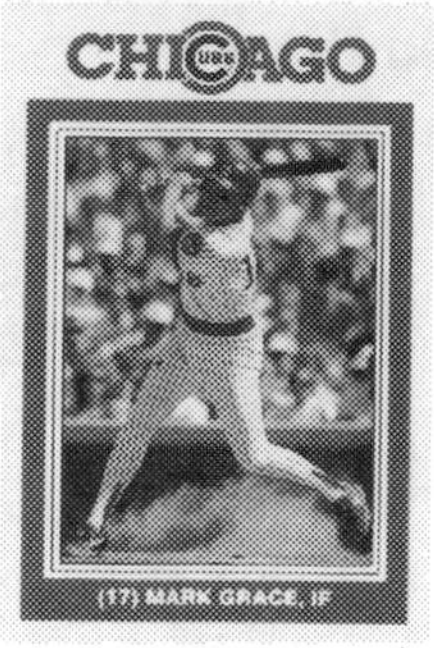

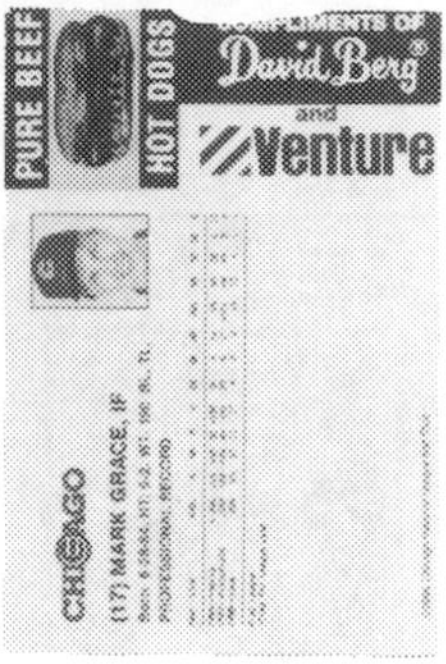

	MT	NR MT	EX
Complete Set:	10.00	7.50	4.00
Common Player:	.15	.11	.06

2	Vance Law	.15	.11	.06
4	Don Zimmer	.15	.11	.06
7	Jody Davis	.30	.25	.12
8	Andre Dawson	1.00	.70	.40
9	Damon Berryhill	.50	.40	.20
12	Shawon Dunston	.60	.45	.25
17	Mark Grace	2.00	1.50	.80
18	Angel Salazar	.15	.11	.06
19	Manny Trillo	.15	.11	.06
21	Scott Sanderson	.15	.11	.06
22	Jerry Mumphrey	.15	.11	.06
23	Ryne Sandberg	2.00	1.50	.80
24	Gary Varsho	.40	.30	.15
25	Rafael Palmeiro	1.25	.90	.50
28	Mitch Webster	.15	.11	.06
30	Darrin Jackson	.40	.30	.15
31	Greg Maddux	.70	.50	.30
32	Calvin Schiraldi	.20	.15	.08
33	Frank DiPino	.15	.11	.06
37	Pat Perry	.15	.11	.06
40	Rick Sutcliffe	.40	.30	.15
41	Jeff Pico	.25	.20	.10
45	Al Nipper	.15	.11	.06
49	Jamie Moyer	.20	.15	.08
50	Les Lancaster	.15	.11	.06
54	Rich Gossage	.70	.50	.30
---	Joe Altobelli, Chuck Cottier, Larry Cox, Jose Martinez, Dick Pole	.15	.11	.06

1988 Domino's Pizza Tigers

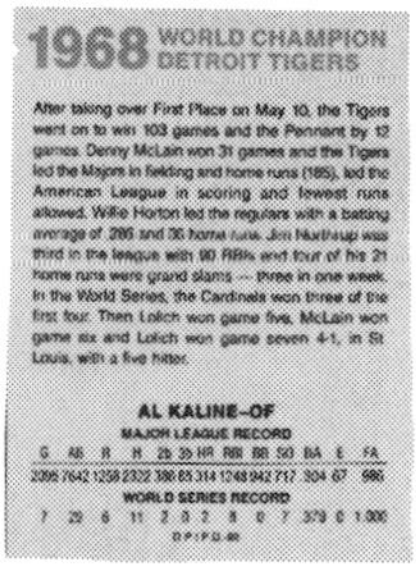

Domino's Pizza produced a 28-card set commemorating the 20th anniversary of the 1968 World Champion Detroit Tigers. The cards were given away at an Old Timers Game at Tiger Stadium in 1988. The cards, which measure 2-1/2" by 3-1/2", feature black and white photos semi-surrounded by a two-stripe band. The stripes on the card's left side are the same color (red and light blue) as the Domino's Pizza logo in the upper corner. The stripes on the card's right side match the colors of the Tigers logo (red and dark blue). The backs of all the cards (except for Ernie Harwell) contain a brief summary of the Tigers' 1968 season. Located at the bottom on the card backs are the players' major league records through 1968 plus their 1968 World Series statistics.

	MT	NR MT	EX
Complete Set:	9.00	6.75	3.50
Common Player:	.20	.15	.08

(1)	Gates Brown	.30	.25	.12
(2)	Norm Cash	.90	.70	.35
(3)	Wayne Comer	.20	.15	.08
(4)	Pat Dobson	.20	.15	.08
(5)	Bill Freehan	.60	.45	.25
(6)	John Hiller	.30	.25	.12
(7)	Ernie Harwell (announcer)	.30	.25	.12
(8)	Willie Horton	.60	.45	.25
(9)	Al Kaline	1.50	1.25	.60
(10)	Fred Lasher	.20	.15	.08
(11)	Mickey Lolich	.90	.70	.35
(12)	Tom Matchick	.20	.15	.08
(13)	Ed Mathews	1.00	.70	.40
(14)	Dick McAuliff (McAuliffe)	.40	.30	.15
(15)	Denny McLain	.80	.60	.30
(16)	Don McMahon	.20	.15	.08
(17)	Jim Northrup	.40	.30	.15
(18)	Ray Oyler	.20	.15	.08
(19)	Daryl Patterson	.20	.15	.08
(20)	Jim Price	.20	.15	.08
(21)	Joe Sparma	.20	.15	.08
(22)	Mickey Stanley	.40	.30	.15
(23)	Dick Tracewski	.20	.15	.08
(24)	Jon Warden	.20	.15	.08
(25)	Don Wert	.20	.15	.08
(26)	Earl Wilson	.20	.15	.08
(27)	Header Card	.20	.15	.08
(28)	Coupon Card	.20	.15	.08

1981 Donruss

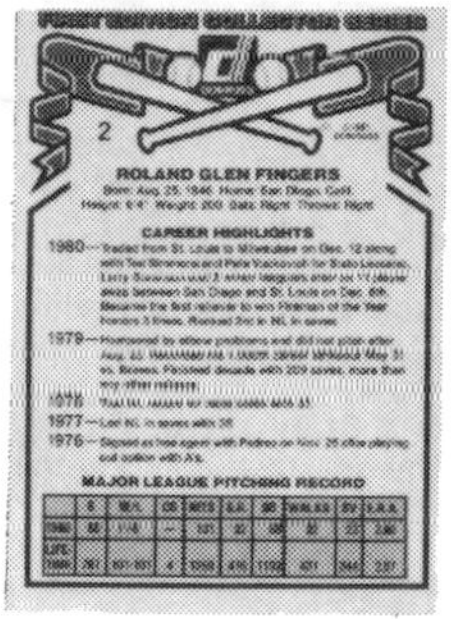

The Donruss Co. of Memphis, Tenn., produced its premiere baseball card issue in 1981 with a set that consisted of 600 numbered cards and five unnumbered checklists. The cards, which measure 2-1/2" by 3-1/2", are printed on thin stock. The card fronts contain the Donruss logo plus the year of issue. The card backs are designed on a vertical format and have black print on red and white. The set, entitled "First Edition Collector Series," contains nearly 40 variations, those being first-printing errors that were corrected in a subsequent print run. The cards were issued in gum wax packs, with hobby dealer sales being coordinated by TCMA of Amawalk, N.Y. The complete set price does not include the higher priced variations.

	MT	NR MT	EX
Complete Set:	55.00	40.00	22.00
Common Player:	.06	.05	.02

1	Ozzie Smith	2.00	1.50	.80
2	Rollie Fingers	.50	.40	.20
3	Rick Wise	.08	.06	.03
4	Gene Richards	.06	.05	.02
5	Alan Trammell	.40	.30	.15
6	Tom Brookens	.08	.06	.03

		MT	NR MT	EX
7a	Duffy Dyer (1980 Avg. .185)	1.00	.70	.40
7b	Duffy Dyer (1980 Avg. 185)	.10	.08	.04
8	Mark Fidrych	.08	.06	.03
9	Dave Rozema	.06	.05	.02
10	Ricky Peters	.06	.05	.02
11	Mike Schmidt	2.50	2.00	1.00
12	Willie Stargell	.40	.30	.15
13	Tim Foli	.06	.05	.02
14	Manny Sanguillen	.06	.05	.02
15	Grant Jackson	.06	.05	.02
16	Eddie Solomon	.06	.05	.02
17	Omar Moreno	.06	.05	.02
18	Joe Morgan	.60	.45	.25
19	Rafael Landestoy	.06	.05	.02
20	Bruce Bochy	.06	.05	.02
21	Joe Sambito	.06	.05	.02
22	Manny Trillo	.08	.06	.03
23a	*Dave Smith* (incomplete box around stats)	1.00	.70	.40
23b	*Dave Smith* (complete box around stats)	.30	.25	.12
24	Terry Puhl	.06	.05	.02
25	Bump Wills	.06	.05	.02
26a	John Ellis (Danny Walton photo - with bat)	1.25	.90	.50
26b	John Ellis (John Ellis photo - with glove)	.10	.08	.04
27	Jim Kern	.06	.05	.02
28	Richie Zisk	.08	.06	.03
29	John Mayberry	.08	.06	.03
30	Bob Davis	.06	.05	.02
31	Jackson Todd	.06	.05	.02
32	Al Woods	.06	.05	.02
33	Steve Carlton	1.00	.70	.40
34	Lee Mazzilli	.08	.06	.03
35	John Stearns	.06	.05	.02
36	Roy Jackson	.06	.05	.02
37	Mike Scott	.70	.50	.30
38	Lamar Johnson	.06	.05	.02
39	Kevin Bell	.06	.05	.02
40	Ed Farmer	.06	.05	.02
41	Ross Baumgarten	.06	.05	.02
42	Leo Sutherland	.06	.05	.02
43	Dan Meyer	.06	.05	.02
44	Ron Reed	.06	.05	.02
45	Mario Mendoza	.06	.05	.02
46	Rick Honeycutt	.06	.05	.02
47	Glenn Abbott	.06	.05	.02
48	Leon Roberts	.06	.05	.02
49	Rod Carew	1.25	.90	.50
50	Bert Campaneris	.10	.08	.04
51a	Tom Donahue (incorrect spelling)	1.00	.70	.40
51b	Tom Donohue (Donohue on front)	.10	.08	.04
52	Dave Frost	.06	.05	.02
53	Ed Halicki	.06	.05	.02
54	Dan Ford	.06	.05	.02
55	Garry Maddox	.10	.08	.04
56a	Steve Garvey ("Surpassed 25 HR..." on back)	1.75	1.25	.70
56b	Steve Garvey ("Surpassed 21 HR..." on back)	.60	.45	.25
57	Bill Russell	.08	.06	.03
58	Don Sutton	.30	.25	.12
59	Reggie Smith	.10	.08	.04
60	Rick Monday	.10	.08	.04
61	Ray Knight	.10	.08	.04
62	Johnny Bench	1.25	.90	.50
63	Mario Soto	.08	.06	.03
64	Doug Bair	.06	.05	.02
65	George Foster	.20	.15	.08
66	Jeff Burroughs	.08	.06	.03
67	Keith Hernandez	.40	.30	.15
68	Tom Herr	.10	.08	.04
69	Bob Forsch	.08	.06	.03
70	John Fulgham	.06	.05	.02
71a	Bobby Bonds (lifetime HR 986)	1.00	.70	.40
71b	Bobby Bonds (lifetime HR 326)	.15	.11	.06
72a	Rennie Stennett ("...breaking broke leg..." on back)	1.00	.70	.40
72b	Rennie Stennett ("...breaking leg..." on back)	.10	.08	.04
73	Joe Strain	.06	.05	.02
74	Ed Whitson	.06	.05	.02
75	Tom Griffin	.06	.05	.02
76	Bill North	.06	.05	.02
77	Gene Garber	.06	.05	.02
78	Mike Hargrove	.06	.05	.02
79	Dave Rosello	.06	.05	.02
80	Ron Hassey	.06	.05	.02
81	Sid Monge	.06	.05	.02
82a	*Joe Charboneau* ("For some reason, Phillies..." on back)	1.00	.70	.40
82b	*Joe Charboneau* ("Phillies..." on back)	.12	.09	.05
83	Cecil Cooper	.15	.11	.06
84	Sal Bando	.10	.08	.04
85	Moose Haas	.06	.05	.02
86	Mike Caldwell	.06	.05	.02
87a	Larry Hisle ("...Twins with 28 RBI." on back)	1.00	.70	.40
87b	Larry Hisle ("...Twins with 28 HR" on back)	.10	.08	.04
88	Luis Gomez	.06	.05	.02
89	Larry Parrish	.10	.08	.04
90	Gary Carter	.50	.40	.20
91	*Bill Gullickson*	.15	.11	.06
92	Fred Norman	.06	.05	.02
93	Tommy Hutton	.06	.05	.02
94	Carl Yastrzemski	1.00	.70	.40
95	Glenn Hoffman	.06	.05	.02
96	Dennis Eckersley	.50	.40	.20
97a	Tom Burgmeier (Throws: Right)	1.00	.70	.40
97b	Tom Burgmeier (Throws: Left)	.10	.08	.04
98	Win Remmerswaal	.06	.05	.02
99	Bob Horner	.12	.09	.05
100	George Brett	2.00	1.50	.80
101	Dave Chalk	.06	.05	.02
102	Dennis Leonard	.08	.06	.03
103	Renie Martin	.06	.05	.02
104	Amos Otis	.08	.06	.03
105	Graig Nettles	.15	.11	.06
106	Eric Soderholm	.06	.05	.02
107	Tommy John	.20	.15	.08
108	Tom Underwood	.06	.05	.02
109	Lou Piniella	.12	.09	.05
110	Mickey Klutts	.06	.05	.02
111	Bobby Murcer	.10	.08	.04
112	Eddie Murray	2.00	1.50	.80
113	Rick Dempsey	.08	.06	.03
114	Scott McGregor	.08	.06	.03
115	Ken Singleton	.10	.08	.04
116	Gary Roenicke	.06	.05	.02
117	Dave Revering	.06	.05	.02
118	Mike Norris	.06	.05	.02
119	Rickey Henderson	25.00	20.00	10.00
120	Mike Heath	.06	.05	.02
121	Dave Cash	.06	.05	.02
122	Randy Jones	.08	.06	.03
123	Eric Rasmussen	.06	.05	.02
124	Jerry Mumphrey	.06	.05	.02
125	Richie Hebner	.06	.05	.02
126	Mark Wagner	.06	.05	.02
127	Jack Morris	.30	.25	.12
128	Dan Petry	.08	.06	.03
129	Bruce Robbins	.06	.05	.02
130	Champ Summers	.06	.05	.02
131a	Pete Rose ("...see card 251." on back)	2.25	1.75	.90
131b	Pete Rose ("...see card 371." on back)	1.25	.90	.50
132	Willie Stargell	.40	.30	.15
133	Ed Ott	.06	.05	.02
134	Jim Bibby	.06	.05	.02
135	Bert Blyleven	.12	.09	.05
136	Dave Parker	.30	.25	.12
137	Bill Robinson	.06	.05	.02
138	Enos Cabell	.06	.05	.02
139	Dave Bergman	.06	.05	.02
140	J R Richard	.10	.08	.04
141	Ken Forsch	.06	.05	.02
142	Larry Bowa	.15	.11	.06
143	Frank LaCorte (photo actually Randy Niemann)	.06	.05	.02
144	Dennis Walling	.06	.05	.02
145	Buddy Bell	.12	.09	.05
146	Ferguson Jenkins	.50	.40	.30
147	Danny Darwin	.06	.05	.02
148	John Grubb	.06	.05	.02
149	Alfredo Griffin	.08	.06	.03
150	Jerry Garvin	.06	.05	.02
151	*Paul Mirabella*(FC)	.10	.08	.04
152	Rick Bosetti	.06	.05	.02
153	Dick Ruthven	.06	.05	.02
154	Frank Taveras	.06	.05	.02
155	Craig Swan	.06	.05	.02
156	*Jeff Reardon*	3.00	2.25	1.25
157	Steve Henderson	.06	.05	.02
158	Jim Morrison	.06	.05	.02
159	Glenn Borgmann	.06	.05	.02
160	*Lamarr Hoyt (LaMarr)*	.10	.08	.04
161	Rich Wortham	.06	.05	.02
162	Thad Bosley	.06	.05	.02
163	Julio Cruz	.06	.05	.02

		MT	NR MT	EX
164a	Del Unser (no 3B in stat heads)	1.00	.70	.40
164b	Del Unser (3B in stat heads)	.10	.08	.04
165	Jim Anderson	.06	.05	.02
166	Jim Beattie	.06	.05	.02
167	Shane Rawley	.10	.08	.04
168	Joe Simpson	.06	.05	.02
169	Rod Carew	1.50	1.25	.60
170	Fred Patek	.06	.05	.02
171	Frank Tanana	.10	.08	.04
172	Alfredo Martinez	.06	.05	.02
173	Chris Knapp	.06	.05	.02
174	Joe Rudi	.10	.08	.04
175	Greg Luzinski	.15	.11	.06
176	Steve Garvey	.50	.40	.20
177	Joe Ferguson	.06	.05	.02
178	Bob Welch	.60	.45	.25
179	Dusty Baker	.10	.08	.04
180	Rudy Law	.06	.05	.02
181	Dave Concepcion	.15	.11	.06
182	Johnny Bench	1.00	.70	.40
183	Mike LaCoss	.06	.05	.02
184	Ken Griffey	.12	.09	.05
185	Dave Collins	.08	.06	.03
186	Brian Asselstine	.06	.05	.02
187	Garry Templeton	.10	.08	.04
188	Mike Phillips	.06	.05	.02
189	Pete Vukovich	.08	.06	.03
190	John Urrea	.06	.05	.02
191	Tony Scott	.06	.05	.02
192	Darrell Evans	.12	.09	.05
193	Milt May	.06	.05	.02
194	Bob Knepper	.08	.06	.03
195	Randy Moffitt	.06	.05	.02
196	Larry Herndon	.08	.06	.03
197	Rick Camp	.06	.05	.02
198	Andre Thornton	.10	.08	.04
199	Tom Veryzer	.06	.05	.02
200	Gary Alexander	.06	.05	.02
201	Rick Waits	.06	.05	.02
202	Rick Manning	.06	.05	.02
203	Paul Molitor	.20	.15	.08
204	Jim Gantner	.08	.06	.03
205	Paul Mitchell	.06	.05	.02
206	Reggie Cleveland	.06	.05	.02
207	Sixto Lezcano	.06	.05	.02
208	Bruce Benedict	.06	.05	.02
209	Rodney Scott	.06	.05	.02
210	John Tamargo	.06	.05	.02
211	Bill Lee	.08	.06	.03
212	Andre Dawson	.80	.60	.30
213	Rowland Office	.06	.05	.02
214	Carl Yastrzemski	1.25	.90	.50
215	Jerry Remy	.06	.05	.02
216	Mike Torrez	.08	.06	.03
217	Skip Lockwood	.06	.05	.02
218	Fred Lynn	.20	.15	.08
219	Chris Chambliss	.08	.06	.03
220	Willie Aikens	.06	.05	.02
221	John Wathan	.08	.06	.03
222	Dan Quisenberry	.15	.11	.06
223	Willie Wilson	.15	.11	.06
224	Clint Hurdle	.06	.05	.02
225	Bob Watson	.08	.06	.03
226	Jim Spencer	.06	.05	.02
227	Ron Guidry	.25	.20	.10
228	Reggie Jackson	1.25	.90	.50
229	Oscar Gamble	.08	.06	.03
230	Jeff Cox	.06	.05	.02
231	Luis Tiant	.12	.09	.05
232	Rich Dauer	.06	.05	.02
233	Dan Graham	.06	.05	.02
234	Mike Flanagan	.10	.08	.04
235	John Lowenstein	.06	.05	.02
236	Benny Ayala	.06	.05	.02
237	Wayne Gross	.06	.05	.02
238	Rick Langford	.06	.05	.02
239	Tony Armas	.10	.08	.04
240a	Bob Lacy (incorrect spelling)	1.00	.70	.40
240b	Bob Lacey (correct spelling)	.10	.08	.04
241	Gene Tenace	.08	.06	.03
242	Bob Shirley	.06	.05	.02
243	Gary Lucas	.08	.06	.03
244	Jerry Turner	.06	.05	.02
245	John Wockenfuss	.06	.05	.02
246	Stan Papi	.06	.05	.02
247	Milt Wilcox	.06	.05	.02
248	Dan Schatzeder	.06	.05	.02
249	Steve Kemp	.08	.06	.03
250	Jim Lentine	.06	.05	.02
251	Pete Rose	1.00	.70	.40
252	Bill Madlock	.12	.09	.05

		MT	NR MT	EX
253	Dale Berra	.06	.05	.02
254	Kent Tekulve	.08	.06	.03
255	Enrique Romo	.06	.05	.02
256	Mike Easler	.08	.06	.03
257	Chuck Tanner	.06	.05	.02
258	Art Howe	.06	.05	.02
259	Alan Ashby	.06	.05	.02
260	Nolan Ryan	6.00	4.50	2.50
261a	Vern Ruhle (Ken Forsch photo - head shot)	1.25	.90	.50
261b	Vern Ruhle (Vern Ruhle photo - waist to head shot)	.10	.08	.04
262	Bob Boone	.10	.08	.04
263	Cesar Cedeno	.12	.09	.05
264	Jeff Leonard	.12	.09	.05
265	Pat Putnam	.06	.05	.02
266	Jon Matlack	.08	.06	.03
267	Dave Rajsich	.06	.05	.02
268	Billy Sample	.06	.05	.02
269	*Damaso Garcia*	.10	.08	.04
270	Tom Buskey	.06	.05	.02
271	Joey McLaughlin	.06	.05	.02
272	Barry Bonnell	.06	.05	.02
273	Tug McGraw	.10	.08	.04
274	Mike Jorgensen	.06	.05	.02
275	Pat Zachry	.06	.05	.02
276	Neil Allen	.08	.06	.03
277	Joel Youngblood	.06	.05	.02
278	Greg Pryor	.06	.05	.02
279	*Britt Burns*	.10	.08	.04
280	*Rich Dotson*	.25	.20	.10
281	Chet Lemon	.08	.06	.03
282	Rusty Kuntz	.06	.05	.02
283	Ted Cox	.06	.05	.02
284	Sparky Lyle	.10	.08	.04
285	Larry Cox	.06	.05	.02
286	Floyd Bannister	.10	.08	.04
287	Byron McLaughlin	.06	.05	.02
288	Rodney Craig	.06	.05	.02
289	Bobby Grich	.10	.08	.04
290	Dickie Thon	.08	.06	.03
291	Mark Clear	.06	.05	.02
292	Dave Lemanczyk	.06	.05	.02
293	Jason Thompson	.06	.05	.02
294	Rick Miller	.06	.05	.02
295	Lonnie Smith	.08	.06	.03
296	Ron Cey	.12	.09	.05
297	Steve Yeager	.06	.05	.02
298	Bobby Castillo	.06	.05	.02
299	Manny Mota	.08	.06	.03
300	Jay Johnstone	.08	.06	.03
301	Dan Driessen	.08	.06	.03
302	Joe Nolan	.06	.05	.02
303	Paul Householder	.06	.05	.02
304	Harry Spilman	.06	.05	.02
305	Cesar Geronimo	.06	.05	.02
306a	Gary Mathews (Mathews on front)	1.25	.90	.50
306b	Gary Matthews (Matthews on front)	.10	.08	.04
307	Ken Reitz	.06	.05	.02
308	Ted Simmons	.12	.09	.05
309	John Littlefield	.06	.05	.02
310	George Frazier	.06	.05	.02
311	Dane Iorg	.06	.05	.02
312	Mike Ivie	.06	.05	.02
313	Dennis Littlejohn	.06	.05	.02
314	Gary LaVelle (Lavelle)	.06	.05	.02
315	Jack Clark	.25	.20	.10
316	Jim Wohlford	.06	.05	.02
317	Rick Matula	.06	.05	.02
318	Toby Harrah	.08	.06	.03
319a	Dwane Kuiper (Dwane on front)	1.00	.70	.40
319b	Duane Kuiper (Duane on front)	.10	.08	.04
320	Len Barker	.08	.06	.03
321	Victor Cruz	.06	.05	.02
322	Dell Alston	.06	.05	.02
323	Robin Yount	1.25	.90	.50
324	Charlie Moore	.06	.05	.02
325	Lary Sorensen	.06	.05	.02
326a	Gorman Thomas ("...30-HR mark 4th..." on back)	1.25	.90	.50
326b	Gorman Thomas ("...30-HR mark 3rd..." on back)	.10	.08	.04
327	Bob Rodgers	.08	.06	.03
328	Phil Niekro	.30	.25	.12
329	Chris Speier	.06	.05	.02
330a	Steve Rodgers (Rodgers on front)	1.00	.70	.40
330b	Steve Rogers (Rogers on front)	.10	.08	.04
331	Woodie Fryman	.08	.06	.03
332	Warren Cromartie	.06	.05	.02

		MT	NR MT	EX
333	Jerry White	.06	.05	.02
334	Tony Perez	.20	.15	.08
335	Carlton Fisk	.70	.50	.30
336	Dick Drago	.06	.05	.02
337	Steve Renko	.06	.05	.02
338	Jim Rice	.50	.40	.20
339	Jerry Royster	.06	.05	.02
340	Frank White	.10	.08	.04
341	Jamie Quirk	.06	.05	.02
342a	Paul Spittorff (Spittorff on front)	1.00	.70	.40
342b	Paul Splittorff (Splittorff on front)	.08	.06	.03
343	Marty Pattin	.06	.05	.02
344	Pete LaCock	.06	.05	.02
345	Willie Randolph	.10	.08	.04
346	Rick Cerone	.06	.05	.02
347	Rich Gossage	.20	.15	.08
348	Reggie Jackson	1.50	1.25	.60
349	Ruppert Jones	.06	.05	.02
350	Dave McKay	.06	.05	.02
351	Yogi Berra	.15	.11	.06
352	Doug Decinces (DeCinces)	.10	.08	.04
353	Jim Palmer	1.00	.70	.40
354	Tippy Martinez	.06	.05	.02
355	Al Bumbry	.08	.06	.03
356	Earl Weaver	.10	.08	.04
357a	Bob Picciolo (Bob on front)	1.00	.70	.40
357b	Rob Picciolo (Rob on front)	.10	.08	.04
358	Matt Keough	.06	.05	.02
359	Dwayne Murphy	.08	.06	.03
360	Brian Kingman	.06	.05	.02
361	Bill Fahey	.06	.05	.02
362	Steve Mura	.06	.05	.02
363	Dennis Kinney	.06	.05	.02
364	Dave Winfield	1.00	.70	.40
365	Lou Whitaker	.40	.30	.15
366	Lance Parrish	.35	.25	.14
367	Tim Corcoran	.06	.05	.02
368	Pat Underwood	.06	.05	.02
369	Al Cowens	.06	.05	.02
370	Sparky Anderson	.10	.08	.04
371	Pete Rose	1.00	.70	.40
372	Phil Garner	.08	.06	.03
373	Steve Nicosia	.06	.05	.02
374	John Candelaria	.10	.08	.04
375	Don Robinson	.08	.06	.03
376	Lee Lacy	.06	.05	.02
377	John Milner	.06	.05	.02
378	Craig Reynolds	.06	.05	.02
379a	Luis Pujois (Pujois on front)	1.00	.70	.40
379b	Luis Pujols (Pujols on front)	.10	.08	.04
380	Joe Niekro	.12	.09	.05
381	Joaquin Andujar	.10	.08	.04
382	*Keith Moreland*	.35	.25	.14
383	Jose Cruz	.12	.09	.05
384	Bill Virdon	.06	.05	.02
385	Jim Sundberg	.08	.06	.03
386	Doc Medich	.06	.05	.02
387	Al Oliver	.15	.11	.06
388	Jim Norris	.06	.05	.02
389	Bob Bailor	.06	.05	.02
390	Ernie Whitt	.08	.06	.03
391	Otto Velez	.06	.05	.02
392	Roy Howell	.06	.05	.02
393	*Bob Walk*	.35	.25	.14
394	Doug Flynn	.06	.05	.02
395	Pete Falcone	.06	.05	.02
396	Tom Hausman	.06	.05	.02
397	Elliott Maddox	.06	.05	.02
398	Mike Squires	.06	.05	.02
399	Marvis Foley	.06	.05	.02
400	Steve Trout	.06	.05	.02
401	Wayne Nordhagen	.06	.05	.02
402	Tony Larussa (LaRussa)	.08	.06	.03
403	Bruce Bochte	.06	.05	.02
404	Bake McBride	.06	.05	.02
405	Jerry Narron	.06	.05	.02
406	Rob Dressler	.06	.05	.02
407	Dave Heaverlo	.06	.05	.02
408	Tom Paciorek	.06	.05	.02
409	Carney Lansford	.10	.08	.04
410	Brian Downing	.10	.08	.04
411	Don Aase	.06	.05	.02
412	Jim Barr	.06	.05	.02
413	Don Baylor	.12	.09	.05
414	Jim Fregosi	.08	.06	.03
415	Dallas Green	.08	.06	.03
416	Dave Lopes	.10	.08	.04
417	Jerry Reuss	.10	.08	.04
418	Rick Sutcliffe	.20	.15	.08
419	Derrel Thomas	.06	.05	.02
420	Tommy LaSorda (Lasorda)	.10	.08	.04

		MT	NR MT	EX
421	*Charlie Leibrandt*	.40	.30	.15
422	Tom Seaver	1.50	1.25	.60
423	Ron Oester	.06	.05	.02
424	Junior Kennedy	.06	.05	.02
425	Tom Seaver	1.50	1.25	.60
426	Bobby Cox	.06	.05	.02
427	*Leon Durham*	.20	.15	.08
428	Terry Kennedy	.08	.06	.03
429	Silvio Martinez	.06	.05	.02
430	George Hendrick	.08	.06	.03
431	Red Schoendienst	.08	.06	.03
432	John LeMaster	.06	.05	.02
433	Vida Blue	.12	.09	.05
434	John Montefusco	.08	.06	.03
435	Terry Whitfield	.06	.05	.02
436	Dave Bristol	.06	.05	.02
437	Dale Murphy	.90	.70	.35
438	Jerry Dybzinski	.06	.05	.02
439	Jorge Orta	.06	.05	.02
440	Wayne Garland	.06	.05	.02
441	Miguel Dilone	.06	.05	.02
442	Dave Garcia	.06	.05	.02
443	Don Money	.06	.05	.02
444a	Buck Martinez (photo reversed)	1.00	.70	.40
444b	Buck Martinez (photo correct)	.10	.08	.04
445	Jerry Augustine	.06	.05	.02
446	Ben Oglivie	.08	.06	.03
447	Jim Slaton	.06	.05	.02
448	Doyle Alexander	.10	.08	.04
449	Tony Bernazard	.06	.05	.02
450	Scott Sanderson	.06	.05	.02
451	Dave Palmer	.06	.05	.02
452	Stan Bahnsen	.06	.05	.02
453	Dick Williams	.06	.05	.02
454	Rick Burleson	.08	.06	.03
455	Gary Allenson	.06	.05	.02
456	Bob Stanley	.06	.05	.02
457a	*John Tudor* (lifetime W/L 9.7)	1.50	1.25	.60
457b	*John Tudor* (lifetime W/L 9-7)	1.00	.70	.40
458	Dwight Evans	.15	.11	.06
459	Glenn Hubbard	.08	.06	.03
460	U L Washington	.06	.05	.02
461	Larry Gura	.06	.05	.02
462	Rich Gale	.06	.05	.02
463	Hal McRae	.10	.08	.04
464	Jim Frey	.06	.05	.02
465	Bucky Dent	.10	.08	.04
466	Dennis Werth	.06	.05	.02
467	Ron Davis	.08	.06	.03
468	Reggie Jackson	1.50	1.25	.60
469	Bobby Brown	.06	.05	.02
470	*Mike Davis*	.20	.15	.08
471	Gaylord Perry	.50	.40	.20
472	Mark Belanger	.08	.06	.03
473	Jim Palmer	.80	.60	.30
474	Sammy Stewart	.06	.05	.02
475	Tim Stoddard	.06	.05	.02
476	Steve Stone	.08	.06	.03
477	Jeff Newman	.06	.05	.02
478	Steve McCatty	.06	.05	.02
479	Billy Martin	.12	.09	.05
480	Mitchell Page	.06	.05	.02
481	Cy Young 1980 (Steve Carlton)	.40	.30	.15
482	Bill Buckner	.12	.09	.05
483a	Ivan DeJesus (lifetime hits 702)	1.00	.70	.40
483b	Ivan DeJesus (lifetime hits 642)	.10	.08	.04
484	Cliff Johnson	.06	.05	.02
485	Lenny Randle	.06	.05	.02
486	Larry Milbourne	.06	.05	.02
487	Roy Smalley	.06	.05	.02
488	John Castino	.06	.05	.02
489	Ron Jackson	.06	.05	.02
490a	Dave Roberts (1980 highlights begins "Showed pop...")	1.00	.70	.40
490b	Dave Roberts (1980 highlights begins "Declared himself...")	.10	.08	.04
491	MVP (George Brett)	1.00	.70	.40
492	Mike Cubbage	.06	.05	.02
493	Rob Wilfong	.06	.05	.02
494	Danny Goodwin	.06	.05	.02
495	Jose Morales	.06	.05	.02
496	Mickey Rivers	.08	.06	.03
497	Mike Edwards	.06	.05	.02
498	Mike Sadek	.06	.05	.02
499	Lenn Sakata	.06	.05	.02
500	Gene Michael	.06	.05	.02
501	Dave Roberts	.06	.05	.02
502	Steve Dillard	.06	.05	.02
503	Jim Essian	.06	.05	.02
504	Rance Mulliniks	.06	.05	.02
505	Darrell Porter	.08	.06	.03

		MT	NR MT	EX
506	Joe Torre	.08	.06	.03
507	Terry Crowley	.06	.05	.02
508	Bill Travers	.06	.05	.02
509	Nelson Norman	.06	.05	.02
510	Bob McClure	.06	.05	.02
511	*Steve Howe*	.10	.08	.04
512	Dave Rader	.06	.05	.02
513	Mick Kelleher	.06	.05	.02
514	Kiko Garcia	.06	.05	.02
515	Larry Biittner	.06	.05	.02
516a	Willie Norwood (1980 highlights begins "Spent most...")	1.00	.70	.40
516b	Willie Norwood (1980 highlights begins "Traded to...")	.10	.08	.04
517	Bo Diaz	.08	.06	.03
518	Juan Beniquez	.06	.05	.02
519	Scot Thompson	.06	.05	.02
520	Jim Tracy	.06	.05	.02
521	Carlos Lezcano	.06	.05	.02
522	Joe Amalfitano	.06	.05	.02
523	Preston Hanna	.06	.05	.02
524a	Ray Burris (1980 highlights begins "Went on...")	1.00	.70	.40
524b	Ray Burris (1980 highlights begins "Drafted by...")	.10	.08	.04
525	Broderick Perkins	.06	.05	.02
526	Mickey Hatcher	.08	.06	.03
527	John Goryl	.06	.05	.02
528	Dick Davis	.06	.05	.02
529	Butch Wynegar	.06	.05	.02
530	Sal Butera	.06	.05	.02
531	Jerry Koosman	.10	.08	.04
532a	Jeff Zahn (Geoff) (1980 highlights begins "Was 2nd in...")	1.00	.70	.40
532b	Jeff Zahn (Geoff) (1980 highlights begins "Signed a 3 year...")	.10	.08	.04
533	Dennis Martinez	.08	.06	.03
534	Gary Thomasson	.06	.05	.02
535	Steve Macko	.06	.05	.02
536	Jim Kaat	.15	.11	.06
537	Best Hitters (George Brett, Rod Carew)	1.50	1.25	.60
538	*Tim Raines*	7.00	5.25	2.75
539	Keith Smith	.06	.05	.02
540	Ken Macha	.06	.05	.02
541	Burt Hooton	.08	.06	.03
542	Butch Hobson	.06	.05	.02
543	Bill Stein	.06	.05	.02
544	Dave Stapleton	.06	.05	.02
545	Bob Pate	.06	.05	.02
546	Doug Corbett	.06	.05	.02
547	Darrell Jackson	.06	.05	.02
548	Pete Redfern	.06	.05	.02
549	Roger Erickson	.06	.05	.02
550	Al Hrabosky	.08	.06	.03
551	Dick Tidrow	.06	.05	.02
552	Dave Ford	.06	.05	.02
553	Dave Kingman	.15	.11	.06
554a	Mike Vail (1980 highlights begins "After...")	1.00	.70	.40
554b	Mike Vail (1980 highlights begins "Traded...")	.10	.08	.04
555a	Jerry Martin (1980 highlights begins "Overcame...")	1.00	.70	.40
555b	Jerry Martin (1980 highlights begins "Traded...")	.10	.08	.04
556a	Jesus Figueroa (1980 highlights begins "Had...")	1.00	.70	.40
556b	Jesus Figueroa (1980 highlights begins "Traded...")	.10	.08	.04
557	Don Stanhouse	.06	.05	.02
558	Barry Foote	.06	.05	.02
559	Tim Blackwell	.06	.05	.02
560	Bruce Sutter	.15	.11	.06
561	Rick Reuschel	.10	.08	.04
562	Lynn McGlothen	.06	.05	.02
563a	Bob Owchinko (1980 highlights begins "Traded...")	1.00	.70	.40
563b	Bob Owchinko (1980 highlights begins "Involved...")	.10	.08	.04
564	John Verhoeven	.06	.05	.02
565	Ken Landreaux	.06	.05	.02
566a	Glen Adams (Glen on front)	1.00	.70	.40
566b	Glenn Adams (Glenn on front)	.10	.08	.04
567	Hosken Powell	.06	.05	.02
568	Dick Noles	.06	.05	.02
569	*Danny Ainge*	.25	.20	.10
570	Bobby Mattick	.06	.05	.02
571	Joe LeFebvre (Lefebvre)	.06	.05	.02
572	Bobby Clark	.06	.05	.02
573	Dennis Lamp	.06	.05	.02

		MT	NR MT	EX
574	Randy Lerch	.06	.05	.02
575	*Mookie Wilson*	.60	.45	.25
576	Ron LeFlore	.08	.06	.03
577	Jim Dwyer	.06	.05	.02
578	Bill Castro	.06	.05	.02
579	Greg Minton	.06	.05	.02
580	Mark Littell	.06	.05	.02
581	Andy Hassler	.06	.05	.02
582	Dave Stieb	.60	.45	.25
583	Ken Oberkfell	.06	.05	.02
584	Larry Bradford	.06	.05	.02
585	Fred Stanley	.06	.05	.02
586	Bill Caudill	.06	.05	.02
587	Doug Capilla	.06	.05	.02
588	George Riley	.06	.05	.02
589	Willie Hernandez	.10	.08	.04
590	MVP (Mike Schmidt)	1.00	.70	.40
591	Cy Young 1980 (Steve Stone)	.08	.06	.03
592	Rick Sofield	.06	.05	.02
593	Bombo Rivera	.06	.05	.02
594	Gary Ward	.08	.06	.03
595a	Dave Edwards (1980 highlights begins "Sidelined...")	1.00	.70	.40
595b	Dave Edwards (1980 highlights begins "Traded...")	.10	.08	.04
596	Mike Proly	.06	.05	.02
597	Tommy Boggs	.06	.05	.02
598	Greg Gross	.06	.05	.02
599	Elias Sosa	.06	.05	.02
600	Pat Kelly	.06	.05	.02
---a	Checklist 1-120 (51 Tom Donohue)	2.00	1.50	.80
---b	Checklist 1-120 (51 Tom Donahue)	.10	.08	.04
-----	Checklist 121-240	.06	.05	.02
---a	Checklist 241-360 (306 Gary Mathews)	.70	.50	.30
---b	Checklist 241-360 (306 Gary Matthews)	.10	.08	.04
---a	Checklist 361-480 (379 Luis Pujois)	.70	.50	.30
---b	Checklist 361-480 (379 Luis Pujols)	.10	.08	.04
---a	Checklist 481-600 (566 Glen Adams)	.70	.50	.30
---b	Checklist 481-600 (566 Glenn Adams)	.10	.08	.04

1982 Donruss

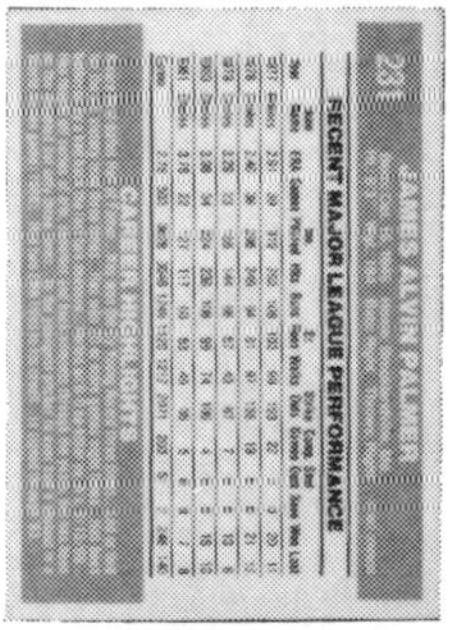

Using card stock thicker than the previous year, Donruss issued a 660-card set which includes 653 numbered cards and seven unnumbered checklists. The cards, which measure 2-1/2" by 3-1/2", were sold with puzzle pieces rather than gum as a result of a lawsuit by Topps. The puzzle pieces (three pieces on one card per pack) feature Babe Ruth. The first 26 cards of the set, entitled Diamond Kings, showcase the artwork of Dick Perez of Perez-Steele Galleries. The card fronts display the Donruss logo and the year of issue. The card backs have black and blue ink on white stock and include the player's career highlights. The complete set price does not include the higher priced variations.

	MT	NR MT	EX
Complete Set:	70.00	52.00	27.00
Common Player:	.06	.05	.02

		MT	NR MT	EX
1	Pete Rose (DK)	1.50	1.25	.60
2	Gary Carter (DK)	.50	.40	.20
3	Steve Garvey (DK)	.50	.40	.20
4	Vida Blue (DK)	.12	.09	.05
5a	Alan Trammel (DK) (name incorrect)	1.50	1.25	.60
5b	Alan Trammell (DK) (name correct)	.40	.30	.15
6	Len Barker (DK)	.08	.06	.03
7	Dwight Evans (DK)	.15	.11	.06
8	Rod Carew (DK)	.60	.45	.25
9	George Hendrick (DK)	.08	.06	.03
10	Phil Niekro (DK)	.30	.25	.12
11	Richie Zisk (DK)	.08	.06	.03
12	Dave Parker (DK)	.30	.25	.12
13	Nolan Ryan (DK)	2.50	2.00	1.00
14	Ivan DeJesus (DK)	.08	.06	.03
15	George Brett (DK)	.70	.50	.30
16	Tom Seaver (DK)	.50	.40	.20
17	Dave Kingman (DK)	.15	.11	.06
18	Dave Winfield (DK)	.50	.40	.20
19	Mike Norris (DK)	.08	.06	.03
20	Carlton Fisk (DK)	.50	.40	.20
21	Ozzie Smith (DK)	.20	.15	.08
22	Roy Smalley (DK)	.08	.06	.03
23	Buddy Bell (DK)	.12	.09	.05
24	Ken Singleton (DK)	.10	.08	.04
25	John Mayberry (DK)	.08	.06	.03
26	Gorman Thomas (DK)	.10	.08	.04
27	Earl Weaver	.10	.08	.04
28	Rollie Fingers	.20	.15	.08
29	Sparky Anderson	.10	.08	.04
30	Dennis Eckersley	.12	.09	.05
31	Dave Winfield	.80	.60	.30
32	Burt Hooton	.08	.06	.03
33	Rick Waits	.06	.05	.02
34	George Brett	1.25	.90	.50
35	Steve McCatty	.06	.05	.02
36	Steve Rogers	.08	.06	.03
37	Bill Stein	.06	.05	.02
38	Steve Renko	.06	.05	.02
39	Mike Squires	.06	.05	.02
40	George Hendrick	.08	.06	.03
41	Bob Knepper	.08	.06	.03
42	Steve Carlton	1.00	.70	.40
43	Larry Biittner	.06	.05	.02
44	Chris Welsh	.06	.05	.02
45	Steve Nicosia	.06	.05	.02
46	Jack Clark	.25	.20	.10
47	Chris Chambliss	.08	.06	.03
48	Ivan DeJesus	.06	.05	.02
49	Lee Mazzilli	.08	.06	.03
50	Julio Cruz	.06	.05	.02
51	Pete Redfern	.06	.05	.02
52	Dave Stieb	.12	.09	.05
53	Doug Corbett	.06	.05	.02
54	*Jorge Bell*(FC)	9.00	6.75	3.50
55	Joe Simpson	.06	.05	.02
56	Rusty Staub	.10	.08	.04
57	Hector Cruz	.06	.05	.02
58	Claudell Washington(FC)	.10	.08	.04
59	Enrique Romo	.06	.05	.02
60	Gary Lavelle	.06	.05	.02
61	Tim Flannery	.06	.05	.02
62	Joe Nolan	.06	.05	.02
63	Larry Bowa	.15	.11	.06
64	Sixto Lezcano	.06	.05	.02
65	Joe Sambito	.06	.05	.02
66	Bruce Kison	.06	.05	.02
67	Wayne Nordhagen	.06	.05	.02
68	Woodie Fryman	.08	.06	.03
69	Billy Sample	.06	.05	.02
70	Amos Otis	.08	.06	.03
71	Matt Keough	.06	.05	.02
72	Toby Harrah	.08	.06	.03
73	*Dave Righetti*(FC)	2.00	1.50	.80
74	Carl Yastrzemski	1.00	.70	.40
75	Bob Welch	.12	.09	.05
76a	Alan Trammel (name incorrect)	2.00	1.50	.80
76b	Alan Trammell (name correct)	.60	.45	.25
77	Rick Dempsey	.08	.06	.03
78	Paul Molitor	.20	.15	.08
79	Dennis Martinez	.08	.06	.03
80	Jim Slaton	.06	.05	.02
81	Champ Summers	.06	.05	.02
82	Carney Lansford	.08	.06	.03
83	Barry Foote	.06	.05	.02
84	Steve Garvey	.50	.40	.20
85	Rick Manning	.06	.05	.02
86	John Wathan	.08	.06	.03
87	Brian Kingman	.06	.05	.02
88	Andre Dawson	1.00	.70	.40
89	Jim Kern	.06	.05	.02
90	Bobby Grich	.10	.08	.04
91	Bob Forsch	.08	.06	.03
92	Art Howe	.06	.05	.02
93	Marty Bystrom	.06	.05	.02
94	Ozzie Smith	.80	.60	.30
95	Dave Parker	.30	.25	.12
96	Doyle Alexander	.10	.08	.04
97	Al Hrabosky	.08	.06	.03
98	Frank Taveras	.06	.05	.02
99	Tim Blackwell	.06	.05	.02
100	Floyd Bannister	.10	.08	.04
101	Alfredo Griffin	.08	.06	.03
102	Dave Engle	.06	.05	.02
103	Mario Soto	.08	.06	.03
104	Ross Baumgarten	.06	.05	.02
105	Ken Singleton	.10	.08	.04
106	Ted Simmons	.12	.09	.05
107	Jack Morris	.30	.25	.12
108	Bob Watson	.08	.06	.03
109	Dwight Evans	.15	.11	.06
110	Tom Lasorda	.10	.08	.04
111	Bert Blyleven	.12	.09	.05
112	Dan Quisenberry	.15	.11	.06
113	Rickey Henderson	5.00	3.75	2.00
114	Gary Carter	.35	.25	.14
115	Brian Downing	.10	.08	.04
116	Al Oliver	.15	.11	.06
117	LaMarr Hoyt	.06	.05	.02
118	Cesar Cedeno	.12	.09	.05
119	Keith Moreland	.10	.08	.04
120	Bob Shirley	.06	.05	.02
121	Terry Kennedy	.08	.06	.03
122	Frank Pastore	.06	.05	.02
123	Gene Garber	.06	.05	.02
124	Tony Pena(FC)	.25	.20	.10
125	Allen Ripley	.06	.05	.02
126	Randy Martz	.06	.05	.02
127	Richie Zisk	.08	.06	.03
128	Mike Scott	.15	.11	.06
129	Lloyd Moseby(FC)	.20	.15	.08
130	Rob Wilfong	.06	.05	.02
131	Tim Stoddard	.06	.05	.02
132	Gorman Thomas	.10	.08	.04
133	Dan Petry	.08	.06	.03
134	Bob Stanley	.06	.05	.02
135	Lou Piniella	.12	.09	.05
136	Pedro Guerrero(FC)	.70	.50	.30
137	Len Barker	.08	.06	.03
138	Richard Gale	.06	.05	.02
139	Wayne Gross	.06	.05	.02
140	*Tim Wallach*(FC)	2.00	1.50	.80
141	Gene Mauch	.08	.06	.03
142	Doc Medich	.06	.05	.02
143	Tony Bernazard	.06	.05	.02
144	Bill Virdon	.06	.05	.02
145	John Littlefield	.06	.05	.02
146	Dave Bergman	.06	.05	.02
147	Dick Davis	.06	.05	.02
148	Tom Seaver	.60	.45	.25
149	Matt Sinatro	.06	.05	.02
150	Chuck Tanner	.06	.05	.02
151	Leon Durham	.08	.06	.03
152	Gene Tenace	.08	.06	.03
153	Al Bumbry	.08	.06	.03
154	Mark Brouhard	.06	.05	.02
155	Rick Peters	.06	.05	.02
156	Jerry Remy	.06	.05	.02
157	Rick Reuschel	.10	.08	.04
158	Steve Howe	.08	.06	.03
159	Alan Bannister	.06	.05	.02
160	U L Washington	.06	.05	.02
161	Rick Langford	.06	.05	.02
162	Bill Gullickson	.08	.06	.03
163	Mark Wagner	.06	.05	.02
164	Geoff Zahn	.06	.05	.02
165	Ron LeFlore	.08	.06	.03
166	Dane Iorg	.06	.05	.02
167	Joe Niekro	.12	.09	.05
168	Pete Rose	1.00	.70	.40
169	Dave Collins	.08	.06	.03
170	Rick Wise	.08	.06	.03
171	Jim Bibby	.06	.05	.02
172	Larry Herndon	.08	.06	.03
173	Bob Horner	.12	.09	.05
174	Steve Dillard	.06	.05	.02
175	Mookie Wilson	.12	.09	.05
176	Dan Meyer	.06	.05	.02
177	Fernando Arroyo	.06	.05	.02
178	Jackson Todd	.06	.05	.02

		MT	NR MT	EX
179	Darrell Jackson	.06	.05	.02
180	Al Woods	.06	.05	.02
181	Jim Anderson	.06	.05	.02
182	Dave Kingman	.15	.11	.06
183	Steve Henderson	.06	.05	.02
184	Brian Asselstine	.06	.05	.02
185	Rod Scurry	.06	.05	.02
186	Fred Breining	.06	.05	.02
187	Danny Boone	.06	.05	.02
188	Junior Kennedy	.06	.05	.02
189	Sparky Lyle	.10	.08	.04
190	Whitey Herzog	.08	.06	.03
191	Dave Smith	.10	.08	.04
192	Ed Ott	.06	.05	.02
193	Greg Luzinski	.15	.11	.06
194	Bill Lee	.08	.06	.03
195	Don Zimmer	.06	.05	.02
196	Hal McRae	.12	.09	.05
197	Mike Norris	.06	.05	.02
198	Duane Kuiper	.06	.05	.02
199	Rick Cerone	.06	.05	.02
200	Jim Rice	.40	.30	.15
201	Steve Yeager	.06	.05	.02
202	Tom Brookens	.06	.05	.02
203	Jose Morales	.06	.05	.02
204	Roy Howell	.06	.05	.02
205	Tippy Martinez	.06	.05	.02
206	Moose Haas	.06	.05	.02
207	Al Cowens	.06	.05	.02
208	Dave Stapleton	.06	.05	.02
209	Bucky Dent	.10	.08	.04
210	Ron Cey	.12	.09	.05
211	Jorge Orta	.06	.05	.02
212	Jamie Quirk	.06	.05	.02
213	Jeff Jones	.06	.05	.02
214	Tim Raines	1.00	.70	.40
215	Jon Matlack	.08	.06	.03
216	Rod Carew	1.00	.70	.40
217	Jim Kaat	.15	.11	.06
218	Joe Pittman	.06	.05	.02
219	Larry Christenson	.06	.05	.02
220	Juan Bonilla	.06	.05	.02
221	Mike Easler	.08	.06	.03
222	Vida Blue	.12	.09	.05
223	Rick Camp	.06	.05	.02
224	Mike Jorgensen	.06	.05	.02
225	*Jody Davis*(FC)	.30	.25	.12
226	Mike Parrott	.06	.05	.02
227	Jim Clancy	.08	.06	.03
228	Hosken Powell	.06	.05	.02
229	Tom Hume	.06	.05	.02
230	Britt Burns	.06	.05	.02
231	Jim Palmer	.70	.50	.30
232	Bob Rodgers	.08	.06	.03
233	Milt Wilcox	.06	.05	.02
234	Dave Revering	.06	.05	.02
235	Mike Torrez	.08	.06	.03
236	Robert Castillo	.06	.05	.02
237	*Von Hayes*(FC)	1.00	.70	.40
238	Renie Martin	.06	.05	.02
239	Dwayne Murphy	.08	.06	.03
240	Rodney Scott	.06	.05	.02
241	Fred Patek	.06	.05	.02
242	Mickey Rivers	.08	.06	.03
243	Steve Trout	.06	.05	.02
244	Jose Cruz	.12	.09	.05
245	Manny Trillo	.08	.06	.03
246	Lary Sorensen	.06	.05	.02
247	Dave Edwards	.06	.05	.02
248	Dan Driessen	.08	.06	.03
249	Tommy Boggs	.06	.05	.02
250	Dale Berra	.06	.05	.02
251	Ed Whitson	.06	.05	.02
252	*Lee Smith*(FC)	1.25	.90	.50
253	Tom Paciorek	.06	.05	.02
254	Pat Zachry	.06	.05	.02
255	Luis Leal	.06	.05	.02
256	John Castino	.06	.05	.02
257	Rich Dauer	.06	.05	.02
258	Cecil Cooper	.15	.11	.06
259	Dave Rozema	.06	.05	.02
260	John Tudor	.15	.11	.06
261	Jerry Mumphrey	.06	.05	.02
262	Jay Johnstone	.08	.06	.03
263	Bo Diaz	.08	.06	.03
264	Dennis Leonard	.08	.06	.03
265	Jim Spencer	.06	.05	.02
266	John Milner	.06	.05	.02
267	Don Aase	.06	.05	.02
268	Jim Sundberg	.08	.06	.03
269	Lamar Johnson	.06	.05	.02

		MT	NR MT	EX
270	Frank LaCorte	.06	.05	.02
271	Barry Evans	.06	.05	.02
272	Enos Cabell	.06	.05	.02
273	Del Unser	.06	.05	.02
274	George Foster	.20	.15	.08
275	*Brett Butler*(FC)	2.50	2.00	1.00
276	Lee Lacy	.06	.05	.02
277	Ken Reitz	.06	.05	.02
278	Keith Hernandez	.40	.30	.15
279	Doug DeCinces	.10	.08	.04
280	Charlie Moore	.06	.05	.02
281	Lance Parrish	.35	.25	.14
282	Ralph Houk	.08	.06	.03
283	Rich Gossage	.20	.15	.08
284	Jerry Reuss	.10	.08	.04
285	Mike Stanton	.06	.05	.02
286	Frank White	.10	.08	.04
287	Bob Owchinko	.06	.05	.02
288	Scott Sanderson	.06	.05	.02
289	Bump Wills	.06	.05	.02
290	Dave Frost	.06	.05	.02
291	Chet Lemon	.08	.06	.03
292	Tito Landrum	.06	.05	.02
293	Vern Ruhle	.06	.05	.02
294	Mike Schmidt	2.50	2.00	1.00
295	Sam Mejias	.06	.05	.02
296	Gary Lucas	.06	.05	.02
297	John Candelaria	.10	.08	.04
298	Jerry Martin	.06	.05	.02
299	Dale Murphy	.90	.70	.35
300	Mike Lum	.06	.05	.02
301	Tom Hausman	.06	.05	.02
302	Glenn Abbott	.06	.05	.02
303	Roger Erickson	.06	.05	.02
304	Otto Velez	.06	.05	.02
305	Danny Goodwin	.06	.05	.02
306	John Mayberry	.08	.06	.03
307	Lenny Randle	.06	.05	.02
308	Bob Bailor	.06	.05	.02
309	Jerry Morales	.06	.05	.02
310	Rufino Linares	.06	.05	.02
311	Kent Tekulve	.08	.06	.03
312	Joe Morgan	.50	.40	.20
313	John Urrea	.06	.05	.02
314	Paul Householder	.06	.05	.02
315	Garry Maddox	.10	.08	.04
316	Mike Ramsey	.06	.05	.02
317	Alan Ashby	.06	.05	.02
318	Bob Clark	.06	.05	.02
319	Tony LaRussa	.08	.06	.03
320	Charlie Lea	.08	.06	.03
321	Danny Darwin	.06	.05	.02
322	Cesar Geronimo	.06	.05	.02
323	Tom Underwood	.06	.05	.02
324	Andre Thornton	.10	.08	.04
325	Rudy May	.06	.05	.02
326	Frank Tanana	.10	.08	.04
327	Davey Lopes	.10	.08	.04
328	Richie Hebner	.06	.05	.02
329	Mike Flanagan	.10	.08	.04
330	Mike Caldwell	.06	.05	.02
331	Scott McGregor	.08	.06	.03
332	Jerry Augustine	.06	.05	.02
333	Stan Papi	.06	.05	.02
334	Rick Miller	.06	.05	.02
335	Graig Nettles	.15	.11	.06
336	Dusty Baker	.10	.08	.04
337	Dave Garcia	.06	.05	.02
338	Larry Gura	.06	.05	.02
339	Cliff Johnson	.06	.05	.02
340	Warren Cromartie	.06	.05	.02
341	Steve Comer	.06	.05	.02
342	Rick Burleson	.08	.06	.03
343	John Martin	.06	.05	.02
344	Craig Reynolds	.06	.05	.02
345	Mike Proly	.06	.05	.02
346	Ruppert Jones	.06	.05	.02
347	Omar Moreno	.06	.05	.02
348	Greg Minton	.06	.05	.02
349	*Rick Mahler*(FC)	.25	.20	.10
350	Alex Trevino	.06	.05	.02
351	Mike Krukow	.08	.06	.03
352a	Shane Rawley (Jim Anderson photo — shaking hands)	1.25	.90	.50
352b	Shane Rawley (correct photo - kneeling)	.15	.11	.06
353	Garth Iorg	.06	.05	.02
354	Pete Mackanin	.06	.05	.02
355	Paul Moskau	.06	.05	.02
356	Richard Dotson	.10	.08	.04
357	Steve Stone	.08	.06	.03

		MT	NR MT	EX
358	Larry Hisle	.08	.06	.03
359	Aurelio Lopez	.06	.05	.02
360	Oscar Gamble	.08	.06	.03
361	Tom Burgmeier	.06	.05	.02
362	Terry Forster	.08	.06	.03
363	Joe Charboneau	.08	.06	.03
364	Ken Brett	.08	.06	.03
365	Tony Armas	.10	.08	.04
366	Chris Speier	.06	.05	.02
367	Fred Lynn	.20	.15	.08
368	Buddy Bell	.12	.09	.05
369	Jim Essian	.06	.05	.02
370	Terry Puhl	.06	.05	.02
371	Greg Gross	.06	.05	.02
372	Bruce Sutter	.15	.11	.06
373	Joe Lefebvre	.06	.05	.02
374	Ray Knight	.10	.08	.04
375	Bruce Benedict	.06	.05	.02
376	Tim Foli	.06	.05	.02
377	Al Holland	.06	.05	.02
378	Ken Kravec	.06	.05	.02
379	Jeff Burroughs	.08	.06	.03
380	Pete Falcone	.06	.05	.02
381	Ernie Whitt	.08	.06	.03
382	Brad Havens	.06	.05	.02
383	Terry Crowley	.06	.05	.02
384	Don Money	.06	.05	.02
385	Dan Schatzeder	.06	.05	.02
386	Gary Allenson	.06	.05	.02
387	Yogi Berra	.15	.11	.06
388	Ken Landreaux	.06	.05	.02
389	Mike Hargrove	.06	.05	.02
390	Darryl Motley	.06	.05	.02
391	Dave McKay	.06	.05	.02
392	Stan Bahnsen	.06	.05	.02
393	Ken Forsch	.06	.05	.02
394	Mario Mendoza	.06	.05	.02
395	Jim Morrison	.06	.05	.02
396	Mike Ivie	.06	.05	.02
397	Broderick Perkins	.06	.05	.02
398	Darrell Evans	.15	.11	.06
399	Ron Reed	.06	.05	.02
400	Johnny Bench	.60	.45	.25
401	*Steve Bedrosian*(FC)	.80	.60	.30
402	Bill Robinson	.06	.05	.02
403	Bill Buckner	.12	.09	.05
404	Ken Oberkfell	.06	.05	.02
405	*Cal Ripken, Jr.*(FC)	50.00	37.00	20.00
406	Jim Gantner	.08	.06	.03
407	Kirk Gibson(FC)	1.50	1.25	.60
408	Tony Perez	.20	.15	.08
409	Tommy John	.20	.15	.08
410	*Dave Stewart*(FC)	6.00	4.50	2.50
411	Dan Spillner	.06	.05	.02
412	Willie Aikens	.06	.05	.02
413	Mike Heath	.06	.05	.02
414	Ray Burris	.06	.05	.02
415	Leon Roberts	.06	.05	.02
416	*Mike Witt*(FC)	.35	.25	.14
417	Bobby Molinaro	.06	.05	.02
418	Steve Braun	.06	.05	.02
419	Nolan Ryan	5.00	3.75	2.00
420	Tug McGraw	.12	.09	.05
421	Dave Concepcion	.12	.09	.05
422a	Juan Eichelberger (Gary Lucas photo — white player)	1.25	.90	.50
422b	Juan Eichelberger (correct photo - black player)	.08	.06	.03
423	Rick Rhoden	.10	.08	.04
424	Frank Robinson	.12	.09	.05
425	Eddie Miller	.06	.05	.02
426	Bill Caudill	.06	.05	.02
427	Doug Flynn	.06	.05	.02
428	Larry Anderson (Andersen)	.06	.05	.02
429	Al Williams	.06	.05	.02
430	Jerry Garvin	.06	.05	.02
431	Glenn Adams	.06	.05	.02
432	Barry Bonnell	.06	.05	.02
433	Jerry Narron	.06	.05	.02
434	John Stearns	.06	.05	.02
435	Mike Tyson	.06	.05	.02
436	Glenn Hubbard	.08	.06	.03
437	Eddie Solomon	.06	.05	.02
438	Jeff Leonard	.10	.08	.04
439	Randy Bass	.06	.05	.02
440	Mike LaCoss	.06	.05	.02
441	Gary Matthews	.10	.08	.04
442	Mark Littell	.06	.05	.02
443	Don Sutton	.30	.25	.12
444	John Harris	.06	.05	.02
445	Vada Pinson	.08	.06	.03
446	Elias Sosa	.06	.05	.02
447	Charlie Hough	.10	.08	.04
448	Willie Wilson	.15	.11	.06
449	Fred Stanley	.06	.05	.02
450	Tom Veryzer	.06	.05	.02
451	Ron Davis	.06	.05	.02
452	Mark Clear	.06	.05	.02
453	Bill Russell	.08	.06	.03
454	Lou Whitaker	.40	.30	.15
455	Dan Graham	.06	.05	.02
456	Reggie Cleveland	.06	.05	.02
457	Sammy Stewart	.06	.05	.02
458	Pete Vuckovich	.08	.06	.03
459	John Wockenfuss	.06	.05	.02
460	Glenn Hoffman	.06	.05	.02
461	Willie Randolph	.10	.08	.04
462	Fernando Valenzuela(FC)	.80	.60	.30
463	Ron Hassey	.06	.05	.02
464	Paul Splittorff	.06	.05	.02
465	Rob Picciolo	.06	.05	.02
466	Larry Parrish	.10	.08	.04
467	Johnny Grubb	.06	.05	.02
468	Dan Ford	.06	.05	.02
469	Silvio Martinez	.06	.05	.02
470	Kiko Garcia	.06	.05	.02
471	Bob Boone	.10	.08	.04
472	Luis Salazar	.08	.06	.03
473	Randy Niemann	.06	.05	.02
474	Tom Griffin	.06	.05	.02
475	Phil Niekro	.30	.25	.12
476	Hubie Brooks(FC)	.25	.20	.10
477	Dick Tidrow	.06	.05	.02
478	Jim Beattie	.06	.05	.02
479	Damaso Garcia	.06	.05	.02
480	Mickey Hatcher	.08	.06	.03
481	Joe Price	.06	.05	.02
482	Ed Farmer	.06	.05	.02
483	Eddie Murray	1.00	.70	.40
484	Ben Oglivie	.08	.06	.03
485	Kevin Saucier	.06	.05	.02
486	Bobby Murcer	.10	.08	.04
487	Bill Campbell	.06	.05	.02
488	Reggie Smith	.10	.08	.04
489	Wayne Garland	.06	.05	.02
490	Jim Wright	.06	.05	.02
491	Billy Martin	.12	.09	.05
492	Jim Fanning	.06	.05	.02
493	Don Baylor	.12	.09	.05
494	Rick Honeycutt	.06	.05	.02
495	Carlton Fisk	.80	.60	.30
496	Denny Walling	.06	.05	.02
497	Bake McBride	.06	.05	.02
498	Darrell Porter	.08	.06	.03
499	Gene Richards	.06	.05	.02
500	Ron Oester	.06	.05	.02
501	*Ken Dayley*(FC)	.20	.15	.08
502	Jason Thompson	.06	.05	.02
503	Milt May	.06	.05	.02
504	Doug Bird	.06	.05	.02
505	Bruce Bochte	.06	.05	.02
506	Neil Allen	.06	.05	.02
507	Joey McLaughlin	.06	.05	.02
508	Butch Wynegar	.06	.05	.02
509	Gary Roenicke	.06	.05	.02
510	Robin Yount	1.50	1.25	.60
511	Dave Tobik	.06	.05	.02
512	*Rich Gedman*(FC)	.25	.20	.10
513	*Gene Nelson*(FC)	.12	.09	.05
514	Rick Monday	.10	.08	.04
515	Miguel Dilone	.06	.05	.02
516	Clint Hurdle	.06	.05	.02
517	Jeff Newman	.06	.05	.02
518	Grant Jackson	.06	.05	.02
519	Andy Hassler	.06	.05	.02
520	Pat Putnam	.06	.05	.02
521	Greg Pryor	.06	.05	.02
522	Tony Scott	.06	.05	.02
523	Steve Mura	.06	.05	.02
524	Johnnie LeMaster	.06	.05	.02
525	Dick Ruthven	.06	.05	.02
526	John McNamara	.06	.05	.02
527	Larry McWilliams	.06	.05	.02
528	*Johnny Ray*(FC)	.30	.25	.12
529	*Pat Tabler*(FC)	.40	.30	.15
530	Tom Herr	.10	.08	.04
531a	San Diego Chicken (trademark symbol on front)	1.25	.90	.50
531b	San Diego Chicken (no trademark symbol)	.80	.60	.30
532	Sal Butera	.06	.05	.02
533	Mike Griffin	.06	.05	.02

		MT	NR MT	EX
534	Kelvin Moore	.06	.05	.02
535	Reggie Jackson	.80	.60	.30
536	Ed Romero	.06	.05	.02
537	Derrel Thomas	.06	.05	.02
538	Mike O'Berry	.06	.05	.02
539	Jack O'Connor	.06	.05	.02
540	*Bob Ojeda*(FC)	.50	.40	.20
541	Roy Lee Jackson	.06	.05	.02
542	Lynn Jones	.06	.05	.02
543	Gaylord Perry	.40	.30	.15
544a	Phil Garner (photo reversed)	1.25	.90	.50
544b	Phil Garner (photo correct)	.10	.08	.04
545	Garry Templeton	.10	.08	.04
546	Rafael Ramirez(FC)	.10	.08	.04
547	Jeff Reardon	.20	.15	.08
548	Ron Guidry	.25	.20	.10
549	*Tim Laudner*(FC)	.25	.20	.10
550	John Henry Johnson	.06	.05	.02
551	Chris Bando	.06	.05	.02
552	Bobby Brown	.06	.05	.02
553	Larry Bradford	.06	.05	.02
554	*Scott Fletcher*(FC)	.30	.25	.12
555	Jerry Royster	.06	.05	.02
556	Shooty Babbitt	.06	.05	.02
557	*Kent Hrbek*(FC)	3.00	2.25	1.25
558	Yankee Winners (Ron Guidry, Tommy John)	.15	.11	.06
559	Mark Bomback	.06	.05	.02
560	Julio Valdez	.06	.05	.02
561	Buck Martinez	.06	.05	.02
562	*Mike Marshall*(FC)	.50	.40	.20
563	Rennie Stennett	.06	.05	.02
564	Steve Crawford	.06	.05	.02
565	Bob Babcock	.06	.05	.02
566	Johnny Podres	.08	.06	.03
567	Paul Serna	.06	.05	.02
568	Harold Baines(FC)	1.25	.90	.50
569	Dave LaRoche	.06	.05	.02
570	Lee May	.08	.06	.03
571	Gary Ward(FC)	.10	.08	.04
572	John Denny	.06	.05	.02
573	Roy Smalley	.06	.05	.02
574	*Bob Brenly*(FC)	.20	.15	.08
575	Bronx Bombers (Reggie Jackson, Dave Winfield)	.40	.30	.15
576	Luis Pujols	.06	.05	.02
577	Butch Hobson	.06	.05	.02
578	Harvey Kuenn	.08	.06	.03
579	Cal Ripken, Sr.	.08	.06	.03
580	Juan Berenguer	.08	.06	.03
581	Benny Ayala	.06	.05	.02
582	Vance Law(FC)	.15	.11	.06
583	*Rick Leach*(FC)	.12	.09	.05
584	George Frazier	.06	.05	.02
585	Phillies Finest (Pete Rose, Mike Schmidt)	.70	.50	.30
586	Joe Rudi	.10	.08	.04
587	Juan Beniquez	.06	.05	.02
588	*Luis DeLeon*(FC)	.08	.06	.03
589	Craig Swan	.06	.05	.02
590	Dave Chalk	.06	.05	.02
591	Billy Gardner	.06	.05	.02
592	Sal Bando	.08	.06	.03
593	Bert Campaneris	.10	.08	.04
594	Steve Kemp	.08	.06	.03
595a	Randy Lerch (Braves)	1.25	.90	.50
595b	Randy Lerch (Brewers)	.08	.06	.03
596	Bryan Clark	.06	.05	.02
597	Dave Ford	.06	.05	.02
598	Mike Scioscia(FC)	.20	.15	.08
599	John Lowenstein	.06	.05	.02
600	Rene Lachmann (Lachemann)	.06	.05	.02
601	Mick Kelleher	.06	.05	.02
602	Ron Jackson	.06	.05	.02
603	Jerry Koosman	.10	.08	.04
604	Dave Goltz	.08	.06	.03
605	Ellis Valentine	.06	.05	.02
606	Lonnie Smith	.08	.06	.03
607	Joaquin Andujar	.08	.06	.03
608	Garry Hancock	.06	.05	.02
609	Jerry Turner	.06	.05	.02
610	Bob Bonner	.06	.05	.02
611	Jim Dwyer	.06	.05	.02
612	Terry Bulling	.06	.05	.02
613	Joel Youngblood	.06	.05	.02
614	Larry Milbourne	.06	.05	.02
615	Phil Roof (Gene)	.06	.05	.02
616	Keith Drumright	.06	.05	.02
617	Dave Rosello	.06	.05	.02
618	Rickey Keeton	.06	.05	.02
619	Dennis Lamp	.06	.05	.02

		MT	NR MT	EX
620	Sid Monge	.06	.05	.02
621	Jerry White	.06	.05	.02
622	*Luis Aguayo*(FC)	.10	.08	.04
623	Jamie Easterly	.06	.05	.02
624	*Steve Sax*(FC)	4.00	3.00	1.50
625	Dave Roberts	.06	.05	.02
626	Rick Bosetti	.06	.05	.02
627	*Terry Francona*(FC)	.10	.08	.04
628	Pride of the Reds (Johnny Bench, Tom Seaver)	.35	.25	.14
629	Paul Mirabella	.06	.05	.02
630	Rance Mulliniks	.06	.05	.02
631	Kevin Hickey	.06	.05	.02
632	Reid Nichols	.06	.05	.02
633	Dave Geisel	.06	.05	.02
634	Ken Griffey	.12	.09	.05
635	Bob Lemon	.10	.08	.04
636	Orlando Sanchez	.06	.05	.02
637	Bill Almon	.06	.05	.02
638	Danny Ainge	.12	.09	.05
639	Willie Stargell	.40	.30	.15
640	Bob Sykes	.06	.05	.02
641	Ed Lynch	.06	.05	.02
642	John Ellis	.06	.05	.02
643	Fergie Jenkins	.15	.11	.06
644	Lenn Sakata	.06	.05	.02
645	Julio Gonzales	.06	.05	.02
646	Jesse Orosco(FC)	.15	.11	.06
647	Jerry Dybzinski	.06	.05	.02
648	Tommy Davis	.08	.06	.03
649	Ron Gardenhire	.06	.05	.02
650	Felipe Alou	.08	.06	.03
651	Harvey Haddix	.08	.06	.03
652	Willie Upshaw(FC)	.15	.11	.06
653	Bill Madlock	.12	.09	.05
---a	Checklist 1-26 DK (5 Trammel)	.70	.50	.30
---b	Checklist 1-26 DK (5 Trammell)	.08	.06	.03
----	Checklist 27-130	.06	.05	.02
----	Checklist 131-234	.06	.05	.02
----	Checklist 235-338	.06	.05	.02
----	Checklist 339-442	.06	.05	.02
----	Checklist 443-544	.06	.05	.02
----	Checklist 545-653	.06	.05	.02

1983 Donruss

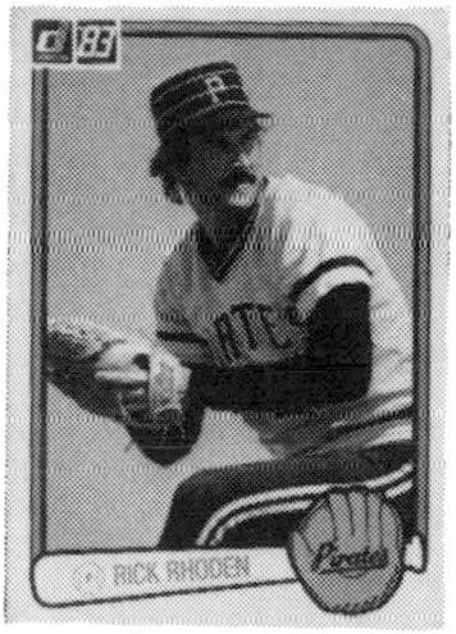

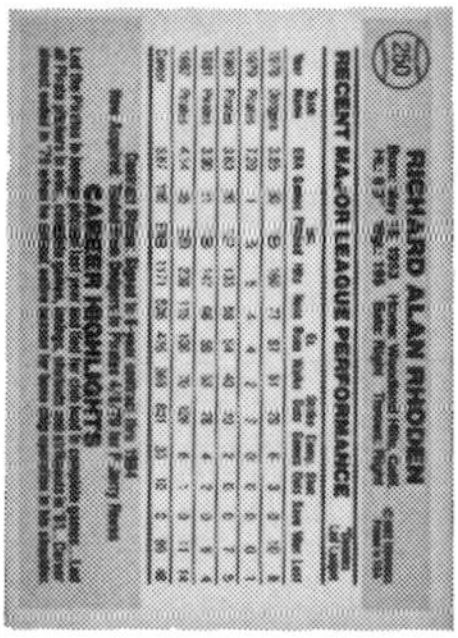

The 1983 Donruss set consists of 653 numbered cards plus seven unnumbered checklists. The cards, which measure 2-1/2" by 3-1/2", were issued with puzzle pieces (three pieces on one card per pack) that feature Ty Cobb. The first 26 cards in the set were once again the Diamond Kings series. The card fronts display the Donruss logo and the year of issue. The card backs have black print on yellow and white and include statistics, career highlights, and the player's contract status. (DK) in the checklist that follows indicates cards which belong to the Diamond Kings series.

		MT	NR MT	EX
Complete Set:		110.00	82.00	44.00
Common Player:		.06	.05	.02
1	Fernando Valenzuela (DK)	.40	.30	.15
2	Rollie Fingers (DK)	.20	.15	.08
3	Reggie Jackson (DK)	.60	.45	.25
4	Jim Palmer (DK)	.40	.30	.15

		MT	NR MT	EX
5	Jack Morris (DK)	.30	.25	.12
6	George Foster (DK)	.20	.15	.08
7	Jim Sundberg (DK)	.08	.06	.03
8	Willie Stargell (DK)	.40	.30	.15
9	Dave Stieb (DK)	.12	.09	.05
10	Joe Niekro (DK)	.12	.09	.05
11	Rickey Henderson (DK)	2.00	1.50	.80
12	Dale Murphy (DK)	.80	.60	.30
13	Toby Harrah (DK)	.08	.06	.03
14	Bill Buckner (DK)	.12	.09	.05
15	Willie Wilson (DK)	.15	.11	.06
16	Steve Carlton (DK)	.40	.30	.15
17	Ron Guidry (DK)	.25	.20	.10
18	Steve Rogers (DK)	.08	.06	.03
19	Kent Hrbek (DK)	.40	.30	.15
20	Keith Hernandez (DK)	.40	.30	.15
21	Floyd Bannister (DK)	.10	.08	.04
22	Johnny Bench (DK)	.40	.30	.15
23	Britt Burns (DK)	.08	.06	.03
24	Joe Morgan (DK)	.30	.25	.12
25	Carl Yastrzemski (DK)	.80	.60	.30
26	Terry Kennedy (DK)	.08	.06	.03
27	Gary Roenicke	.06	.05	.02
28	Dwight Bernard	.06	.05	.02
29	Pat Underwood	.06	.05	.02
30	Gary Allenson	.06	.05	.02
31	Ron Guidry	.25	.20	.10
32	Burt Hooton	.08	.06	.03
33	Chris Bando	.06	.05	.02
34	Vida Blue	.12	.09	.05
35	Rickey Henderson	5.00	3.75	2.00
36	Ray Burris	.06	.05	.02
37	John Butcher	.06	.05	.02
38	Don Aase	.06	.05	.02
39	Jerry Koosman	.10	.08	.04
40	Bruce Sutter	.15	.11	.06
41	Jose Cruz	.12	.09	.05
42	Pete Rose	1.00	.70	.40
43	Cesar Cedeno	.12	.09	.05
44	Floyd Chiffer	.06	.05	.02
45	Larry McWilliams	.06	.05	.02
46	Alan Fowlkes	.06	.05	.02
47	Dale Murphy	.70	.50	.30
48	Doug Bird	.06	.05	.02
49	Hubie Brooks	.12	.09	.05
50	Floyd Bannister	.10	.08	.04
51	Jack O'Connor	.06	.05	.02
52	Steve Senteney	.06	.05	.02
53	*Gary Gaetti*(FC)	2.00	1.50	.80
54	Damaso Garcia	.06	.05	.02
55	Gene Nelson	.06	.05	.02
56	Mookie Wilson	.10	.08	.04
57	Allen Ripley	.06	.05	.02
58	Bob Horner	.12	.09	.05
59	Tony Pena	.10	.08	.04
60	Gary Lavelle	.06	.05	.02
61	Tim Lollar	.06	.05	.02
62	Frank Pastore	.06	.05	.02
63	Garry Maddox	.10	.08	.04
64	Bob Forsch	.08	.06	.03
65	Harry Spilman	.06	.05	.02
66	Geoff Zahn	.06	.05	.02
67	Salome Barojas	.06	.05	.02
68	David Palmer	.06	.05	.02
69	Charlie Hough	.10	.08	.04
70	Dan Quisenberry	.15	.11	.06
71	Tony Armas	.10	.08	.04
72	Rick Sutcliffe	.12	.09	.05
73	Steve Balboni(FC)	.15	.11	.06
74	Jerry Remy	.06	.05	.02
75	Mike Scioscia	.08	.06	.03
76	John Wockenfuss	.06	.05	.02
77	Jim Palmer	.80	.60	.30
78	Rollie Fingers	.20	.15	.08
79	Joe Nolan	.06	.05	.02
80	Pete Vuckovich	.08	.06	.03
81	Rick Leach	.06	.05	.02
82	Rick Miller	.06	.05	.02
83	Graig Nettles	.15	.11	.06
84	Ron Cey	.12	.09	.05
85	Miguel Dilone	.06	.05	.02
86	John Wathan	.08	.06	.03
87	Kelvin Moore	.06	.05	.02
88a	Byrn Smith (first name incorrect)	.70	.50	.30
88b	Bryn Smith (first name correct)	.08	.06	.03
89	Dave Hostetler	.06	.05	.02
90	Rod Carew	1.00	.70	.40
91	Lonnie Smith	.08	.06	.03
92	Bob Knepper	.08	.06	.03
93	Marty Bystrom	.06	.05	.02
94	Chris Welsh	.06	.05	.02

		MT	NR MT	EX
95	Jason Thompson	.06	.05	.02
96	Tom O'Malley	.06	.05	.02
97	Phil Niekro	.30	.25	.12
98	Neil Allen	.06	.05	.02
99	Bill Buckner	.12	.09	.05
100	*Ed VandeBerg (Vande Berg)*(FC)	.10	.08	.04
101	Jim Clancy	.08	.06	.03
102	Robert Castillo	.06	.05	.02
103	Bruce Berenyi	.06	.05	.02
104	Carlton Fisk	.70	.50	.30
105	Mike Flanagan	.10	.08	.04
106	Cecil Cooper	.15	.11	.06
107	Jack Morris	.30	.25	.12
108	Mike Morgan(FC)	.12	.09	.05
109	Luis Aponte	.06	.05	.02
110	Pedro Guerrero	.25	.20	.10
111	Len Barker	.08	.06	.03
112	Willie Wilson	.15	.11	.06
113	Dave Beard	.06	.05	.02
114	Mike Gates	.06	.05	.02
115	Reggie Jackson	.70	.50	.30
116	George Wright	.06	.05	.02
117	Vance Law	.08	.06	.03
118	Nolan Ryan	5.00	3.75	2.00
119	Mike Krukow	.08	.06	.03
120	Ozzie Smith	.20	.15	.08
121	Broderick Perkins	.06	.05	.02
122	Tom Seaver	1.00	.70	.40
123	Chris Chambliss	.08	.06	.03
124	Chuck Tanner	.06	.05	.02
125	Johnnie LeMaster	.06	.05	.02
126	*Mel Hall*(FC)	1.00	.70	.40
127	Bruce Bochte	.06	.05	.02
128	*Charlie Puleo*(FC)	.12	.09	.05
129	Luis Leal	.06	.05	.02
130	John Pacella	.06	.05	.02
131	Glenn Gulliver	.06	.05	.02
132	Don Money	.06	.05	.02
133	Dave Rozema	.06	.05	.02
134	Bruce Hurst(FC)	.25	.20	.10
135	Rudy May	.06	.05	.02
136	Tom LaSorda (Lasorda)	.10	.08	.04
137	Dan Spillner (photo actually Ed Whitson)	.06	.05	.02
138	Jerry Martin	.06	.05	.02
139	Mike Norris	.06	.05	.02
140	Al Oliver	.15	.11	.06
141	Daryl Sconiers	.06	.05	.02
142	Lamar Johnson	.06	.05	.02
143	Harold Baines	.15	.11	.06
144	Alan Ashby	.06	.05	.02
145	Garry Templeton	.10	.08	.04
146	Al Holland	.06	.05	.02
147	Bo Diaz	.08	.06	.03
148	Dave Concepcion	.12	.09	.05
149	Rick Camp	.06	.05	.02
150	Jim Morrison	.06	.05	.02
151	Randy Martz	.06	.05	.02
152	Keith Hernandez	.40	.30	.15
153	John Lowenstein	.06	.05	.02
154	Mike Caldwell	.06	.05	.02
155	Milt Wilcox	.06	.05	.02
156	Rich Gedman	.08	.06	.03
157	Rich Gossage	.20	.15	.08
158	Jerry Reuss	.10	.08	.04
159	Ron Hassey	.06	.05	.02
160	Larry Gura	.06	.05	.02
161	Dwayne Murphy	.08	.06	.03
162	Woodie Fryman	.08	.06	.03
163	Steve Comer	.06	.05	.02
164	Ken Forsch	.06	.05	.02
165	Dennis Lamp	.06	.05	.02
166	David Green	.06	.05	.02
167	Terry Puhl	.06	.05	.02
168	Mike Schmidt	2.00	1.50	.80
169	*Eddie Milner*(FC)	.10	.08	.04
170	John Curtis	.06	.05	.02
171	Don Robinson	.08	.06	.03
172	Richard Gale	.06	.05	.02
173	Steve Bedrosian	.12	.09	.05
174	Willie Hernandez	.08	.06	.03
175	Ron Gardenhire	.06	.05	.02
176	Jim Beattie	.06	.05	.02
177	Tim Laudner	.08	.06	.03
178	Buck Martinez	.06	.05	.02
179	Kent Hrbek	.80	.60	.30
180	Alfredo Griffin	.08	.06	.03
181	Larry Andersen	.06	.05	.02
182	Pete Falcone	.06	.05	.02
183	Jody Davis	.10	.08	.04

		MT	NR MT	EX
184	Glenn Hubbard	.08	.06	.03
185	Dale Berra	.06	.05	.02
186	Greg Minton	.06	.05	.02
187	Gary Lucas	.06	.05	.02
188	Dave Van Gorder	.06	.05	.02
189	Bob Dernier(FC)	.10	.08	.04
190	*Willie McGee*(FC)	4.00	3.00	1.50
191	Dickie Thon	.08	.06	.03
192	Bob Boone	.10	.08	.04
193	Britt Burns	.06	.05	.02
194	Jeff Reardon	.12	.09	.05
195	Jon Matlack	.08	.06	.03
196	*Don Slaught*(FC)	.20	.15	.08
197	Fred Stanley	.06	.05	.02
198	Rick Manning	.06	.05	.02
199	Dave Righetti	.25	.20	.10
200	Dave Stapleton	.06	.05	.02
201	Steve Yeager	.06	.05	.02
202	Enos Cabell	.06	.05	.02
203	Sammy Stewart	.06	.05	.02
204	Moose Haas	.06	.05	.02
205	Lenn Sakata	.06	.05	.02
206	Charlie Moore	.06	.05	.02
207	Alan Trammell	.40	.30	.15
208	Jim Rice	.40	.30	.15
209	Roy Smalley	.06	.05	.02
210	Bill Russell	.08	.06	.03
211	Andre Thornton	.10	.08	.04
212	Willie Aikens	.06	.05	.02
213	Dave McKay	.06	.05	.02
214	Tim Blackwell	.06	.05	.02
215	Buddy Bell	.12	.09	.05
216	Doug DeCinces	.10	.08	.04
217	Tom Herr	.10	.08	.04
218	Frank LaCorte	.06	.05	.02
219	Steve Carlton	.70	.50	.30
220	Terry Kennedy	.08	.06	.03
221	Mike Easler	.08	.06	.03
222	Jack Clark	.25	.20	.10
223	Gene Garber	.06	.05	.02
224	Scott Holman	.06	.05	.02
225	Mike Proly	.06	.05	.02
226	Terry Bulling	.06	.05	.02
227	Jerry Garvin	.06	.05	.02
228	Ron Davis	.06	.05	.02
229	Tom Hume	.06	.05	.02
230	Marc Hill	.06	.05	.02
231	Dennis Martinez	.08	.06	.03
232	Jim Gantner	.08	.06	.03
233	Larry Pashnick	.06	.05	.02
234	Dave Collins	.08	.06	.03
235	Tom Burgmeier	.06	.05	.02
236	Ken Landreaux	.06	.05	.02
237	John Denny	.06	.05	.02
238	Hal McRae	.12	.09	.05
239	Matt Keough	.06	.05	.02
240	Doug Flynn	.06	.05	.02
241	Fred Lynn	.20	.15	.08
242	Billy Sample	.06	.05	.02
243	Tom Paciorek	.06	.05	.02
244	Joe Sambito	.06	.05	.02
245	Sid Monge	.06	.05	.02
246	Ken Oberkfell	.06	.05	.02
247	Joe Pittman (photo actually Juan Eichelberger)	.06	.05	.02
248	Mario Soto	.08	.06	.03
249	Claudell Washington	.08	.06	.03
250	Rick Rhoden	.10	.08	.04
251	Darrell Evans	.15	.11	.06
252	Steve Henderson	.06	.05	.02
253	Manny Castillo	.06	.05	.02
254	Craig Swan	.06	.05	.02
255	Joey McLaughlin	.06	.05	.02
256	Pete Redfern	.06	.05	.02
257	Ken Singleton	.10	.08	.04
258	Robin Yount	.80	.60	.30
259	Elias Sosa	.06	.05	.02
260	Bob Ojeda	.12	.09	.05
261	Bobby Murcer	.10	.08	.04
262	*Candy Maldonado*(FC)	1.00	.70	.40
263	Rick Waits	.06	.05	.02
264	Greg Pryor	.06	.05	.02
265	Bob Owchinko	.06	.05	.02
266	Chris Speier	.06	.05	.02
267	Bruce Kison	.06	.05	.02
268	Mark Wagner	.06	.05	.02
269	Steve Kemp	.10	.08	.04
270	Phil Garner	.08	.06	.03
271	Gene Richards	.06	.05	.02
272	Renie Martin	.06	.05	.02
273	Dave Roberts	.06	.05	.02

		MT	NR MT	EX
274	Dan Driessen	.08	.06	.03
275	Rufino Linares	.06	.05	.02
276	Lee Lacy	.06	.05	.02
277	*Ryne Sandberg*(FC)	35.00	27.00	15.00
278	Darrell Porter	.08	.06	.03
279	Cal Ripken	12.00	9.00	4.75
280	Jamie Easterly	.06	.05	.02
281	Bill Fahey	.06	.05	.02
282	Glenn Hoffman	.06	.05	.02
283	Willie Randolph	.10	.08	.04
284	Fernando Valenzuela	.30	.25	.12
285	Alan Bannister	.06	.05	.02
286	Paul Splittorff	.06	.05	.02
287	Joe Rudi	.10	.08	.04
288	Bill Gullickson	.06	.05	.02
289	Danny Darwin	.06	.05	.02
290	Andy Hassler	.06	.05	.02
291	Ernesto Escarrega	.06	.05	.02
292	Steve Mura	.06	.05	.02
293	Tony Scott	.06	.05	.02
294	Manny Trillo	.08	.06	.03
295	Greg Harris(FC)	.08	.06	.03
296	Luis DeLeon	.06	.05	.02
297	Kent Tekulve	.08	.06	.03
298	Atlee Hammaker(FC)	.12	.09	.05
299	Bruce Benedict	.06	.05	.02
300	Fergie Jenkins	.15	.11	.06
301	Dave Kingman	.15	.11	.06
302	Bill Caudill	.06	.05	.02
303	John Castino	.06	.05	.02
304	Ernie Whitt	.08	.06	.03
305	Randy Johnson	.06	.05	.02
306	Garth Iorg	.06	.05	.02
307	Gaylord Perry	.40	.30	.15
308	Ed Lynch	.06	.05	.02
309	Keith Moreland	.08	.06	.03
310	Rafael Ramirez	.06	.05	.02
311	Bill Madlock	.12	.09	.05
312	Milt May	.06	.05	.02
313	John Montefusco	.06	.05	.02
314	Wayne Krenchicki	.06	.05	.02
315	George Vukovich	.06	.05	.02
316	Joaquin Andujar	.08	.06	.03
317	Craig Reynolds	.06	.05	.02
318	Rick Burleson	.08	.06	.03
319	Richard Dotson	.10	.08	.04
320	Steve Rogers	.08	.06	.03
321	Dave Schmidt(FC)	.10	.08	.04
322	*Bud Black*(FC)	.20	.15	.08
323	Jeff Burroughs	.08	.06	.03
324	Von Hayes	.15	.11	.06
325	Butch Wynegar	.06	.05	.02
326	Carl Yastrzemski	.80	.60	.30
327	Ron Roenicke	.06	.05	.02
328	*Howard Johnson*(FC)	12.00	9.00	4.75
329	Rick Dempsey	.08	.06	.03
330a	Jim Slaton (one yellow box on back)	.70	.50	.30
330b	Jim Slaton (two yellow boxes on back)	.08	.06	.03
331	Benny Ayala	.06	.05	.02
332	Ted Simmons	.12	.09	.05
333	Lou Whitaker	.40	.30	.15
334	Chuck Rainey	.06	.05	.02
335	Lou Piniella	.12	.09	.05
336	Steve Sax	.30	.25	.12
337	Toby Harrah	.08	.06	.03
338	George Brett	1.00	.70	.40
339	Davey Lopes	.10	.08	.04
340	Gary Carter	.40	.30	.15
341	John Grubb	.06	.05	.02
342	Tim Foli	.06	.05	.02
343	Jim Kaat	.15	.11	.06
344	Mike LaCoss	.06	.05	.02
345	Larry Christenson	.06	.05	.02
346	Juan Bonilla	.06	.05	.02
347	Omar Moreno	.06	.05	.02
348	Charles Davis(FC)	.20	.15	.08
349	Tommy Boggs	.06	.05	.02
350	Rusty Staub	.10	.08	.04
351	Bump Wills	.06	.05	.02
352	Rick Sweet	.06	.05	.02
353	*Jim Gott*(FC)	.20	.15	.08
354	Terry Felton	.06	.05	.02
355	Jim Kern	.06	.05	.02
356	Bill Almon	.06	.05	.02
357	Tippy Martinez	.06	.05	.02
358	Roy Howell	.06	.05	.02
359	Dan Petry	.08	.06	.03
360	Jerry Mumphrey	.06	.05	.02
361	Mark Clear	.06	.05	.02

		MT	NR MT	EX
362	Mike Marshall	.20	.15	.08
363	Lary Sorensen	.06	.05	.02
364	Amos Otis	.08	.06	.03
365	Rick Langford	.06	.05	.02
366	Brad Mills	.06	.05	.02
367	Brian Downing	.10	.08	.04
368	Mike Richardt	.06	.05	.02
369	Aurelio Rodriguez	.08	.06	.03
370	Dave Smith	.08	.06	.03
371	Tug McGraw	.12	.09	.05
372	Doug Bair	.06	.05	.02
373	Ruppert Jones	.06	.05	.02
374	Alex Trevino	.06	.05	.02
375	Ken Dayley	.06	.05	.02
376	Rod Scurry	.06	.05	.02
377	Bob Brenly(FC)	.08	.06	.03
378	Scot Thompson	.06	.05	.02
379	Julio Cruz	.06	.05	.02
380	John Stearns	.06	.05	.02
381	Dale Murray	.06	.05	.02
382	*Frank Viola*(FC)	6.00	4.50	2.50
383	Al Bumbry	.08	.06	.03
384	Ben Oglivie	.08	.06	.03
385	Dave Tobik	.06	.05	.02
386	Bob Stanley	.06	.05	.02
387	Andre Robertson	.06	.05	.02
388	Jorge Orta	.06	.05	.02
389	Ed Whitson	.06	.05	.02
390	Don Hood	.06	.05	.02
391	Tom Underwood	.06	.05	.02
392	Tim Wallach	.20	.15	.08
393	Steve Renko	.06	.05	.02
394	Mickey Rivers	.08	.06	.03
395	Greg Luzinski	.12	.09	.05
396	Art Howe	.06	.05	.02
397	Alan Wiggins	.06	.05	.02
398	Jim Barr	.06	.05	.02
399	Ivan DeJesus	.06	.05	.02
400	*Tom Lawless*(FC)	.08	.06	.03
401	Bob Walk	.08	.06	.03
402	Jimmy Smith	.06	.05	.02
403	Lee Smith	.15	.11	.06
404	George Hendrick	.08	.06	.03
405	Eddie Murray	.80	.60	.30
406	Marshall Edwards	.06	.05	.02
407	Lance Parrish	.35	.25	.14
408	Carney Lansford	.08	.06	.03
409	Dave Winfield	.40	.30	.15
410	Bob Welch	.12	.09	.05
411	Larry Milbourne	.06	.05	.02
412	Dennis Leonard	.08	.06	.03
413	Dan Meyer	.06	.05	.02
414	Charlie Lea	.06	.05	.02
415	Rick Honeycutt	.06	.05	.02
416	Mike Witt	.15	.11	.06
417	Steve Trout	.06	.05	.02
418	Glenn Brummer	.06	.05	.02
419	Denny Walling	.06	.05	.02
420	Gary Matthews	.10	.08	.04
421	Charlie Liebrandt (Leibrandt)	.08	.06	.03
422	Juan Eichelberger	.06	.05	.02
423	*Matt Guante (Cecilio)*(FC)	.15	.11	.06
424	Bill Laskey	.06	.05	.02
425	Jerry Royster	.06	.05	.02
426	Dickie Noles	.06	.05	.02
427	George Foster	.15	.11	.06
428	*Mike Moore*(FC)	1.00	.70	.40
429	Gary Ward	.08	.06	.03
430	Barry Bonnell	.06	.05	.02
431	Ron Washington	.06	.05	.02
432	Rance Mulliniks	.06	.05	.02
433	Mike Stanton	.06	.05	.02
434	Jesse Orosco	.10	.08	.04
435	Larry Bowa	.12	.09	.05
436	Biff Pocoroba	.06	.05	.02
437	Johnny Ray	.12	.09	.05
438	Joe Morgan	.40	.30	.15
439	*Eric Show*(FC)	.30	.25	.12
440	Larry Biittner	.06	.05	.02
441	Greg Gross	.06	.05	.02
442	Gene Tenace	.08	.06	.03
443	Danny Heep	.06	.05	.02
444	Bobby Clark	.06	.05	.02
445	Kevin Hickey	.06	.05	.02
446	Scott Sanderson	.06	.05	.02
447	Frank Tanana	.10	.08	.04
448	Cesar Geronimo	.06	.05	.02
449	Jimmy Sexton	.06	.05	.02
450	Mike Hargrove	.06	.05	.02
451	Doyle Alexander	.10	.08	.04
452	Dwight Evans	.15	.11	.06
453	Terry Forster	.08	.06	.03
454	Tom Brookens	.06	.05	.02
455	Rich Dauer	.06	.05	.02
456	Rob Picciolo	.06	.05	.02
457	Terry Crowley	.06	.05	.02
458	Ned Yost	.06	.05	.02
459	Kirk Gibson	.40	.30	.15
460	Reid Nichols	.06	.05	.02
461	Oscar Gamble	.08	.06	.03
462	Dusty Baker	.10	.08	.04
463	Jack Perconte	.06	.05	.02
464	Frank White	.10	.08	.04
465	Mickey Klutts	.06	.05	.02
466	Warren Cromartie	.06	.05	.02
467	Larry Parrish	.10	.08	.04
468	Bobby Grich	.10	.08	.04
469	Dane Iorg	.06	.05	.02
470	Joe Niekro	.12	.09	.05
471	Ed Farmer	.06	.05	.02
472	Tim Flannery	.06	.05	.02
473	Dave Parker	.30	.25	.12
474	Jeff Leonard	.10	.08	.04
475	Al Hrabosky	.08	.06	.03
476	Ron Hodges	.06	.05	.02
477	Leon Durham	.08	.06	.03
478	Jim Essian	.06	.05	.02
479	Roy Lee Jackson	.06	.05	.02
480	Brad Havens	.06	.05	.02
481	Joe Price	.06	.05	.02
482	Tony Bernazard	.06	.05	.02
483	Scott McGregor	.08	.06	.03
484	Paul Molitor	.20	.15	.08
485	Mike Ivie	.06	.05	.02
486	Ken Griffey	.12	.09	.05
487	Dennis Eckersley	.12	.09	.05
488	Steve Garvey	.40	.30	.15
489	Mike Fischlin	.06	.05	.02
490	U.L. Washington	.06	.05	.02
491	Steve McCatty	.06	.05	.02
492	Roy Johnson	.06	.05	.02
493	Don Baylor	.12	.09	.05
494	Bobby Johnson	.06	.05	.02
495	Mike Squires	.06	.05	.02
496	Bert Roberge	.06	.05	.02
497	Dick Ruthven	.06	.05	.02
498	Tito Landrum	.06	.05	.02
499	Sixto Lezcano	.06	.05	.02
500	Johnny Bench	.70	.50	.30
501	Larry Whisenton	.06	.05	.02
502	Manny Sarmiento	.06	.05	.02
503	Fred Breining	.06	.05	.02
504	Bill Campbell	.06	.05	.02
505	Todd Cruz	.06	.05	.02
506	Bob Bailor	.06	.05	.02
507	Dave Stieb	.12	.09	.05
508	Al Williams	.06	.05	.02
509	Dan Ford	.06	.05	.02
510	Gorman Thomas	.10	.08	.04
511	Chet Lemon	.08	.06	.03
512	Mike Torrez	.08	.06	.03
513	Shane Rawley	.10	.08	.04
514	Mark Belanger	.08	.06	.03
515	Rodney Craig	.06	.05	.02
516	Onix Concepcion	.06	.05	.02
517	Mike Heath	.06	.05	.02
518	Andre Dawson	.70	.50	.30
519	Luis Sanchez	.06	.05	.02
520	Terry Bogener	.06	.05	.02
521	Rudy Law	.06	.05	.02
522	Ray Knight	.10	.08	.04
523	Joe Lefebvre	.06	.05	.02
524	Jim Wohlford	.06	.05	.02
525	*Julio Franco*(FC)	8.00	6.00	3.25
526	Ron Oester	.06	.05	.02
527	Rick Mahler	.08	.06	.03
528	Steve Nicosia	.06	.05	.02
529	Junior Kennedy	.06	.05	.02
530a	Whitey Herzog (one yellow box on back)	.70	.50	.30
530b	Whitey Herzog (two yellow boxes on back)	.10	.08	.04
531a	Don Sutton (blue frame around photo)	1.00	.70	.40
531b	Don Sutton (green frame around photo)	.30	.25	.12
532	Mark Brouhard	.06	.05	.02
533a	Sparky Anderson (one yellow box on back)	.70	.50	.30
533b	Sparky Anderson (two yellow boxes on back)	.10	.08	.04
534	Roger LaFrancois	.06	.05	.02

		MT	NR MT	EX
535	George Frazier	.06	.05	.02
536	Tom Niedenfuer	.08	.06	.03
537	Ed Glynn	.06	.05	.02
538	Lee May	.08	.06	.03
539	Bob Kearney	.06	.05	.02
540	Tim Raines	.35	.25	.14
541	Paul Mirabella	.06	.05	.02
542	Luis Tiant	.12	.09	.05
543	Ron LeFlore	.08	.06	.03
544	*Dave LaPoint*(FC)	.30	.25	.12
545	Randy Moffitt	.06	.05	.02
546	Luis Aguayo	.06	.05	.02
547	Brad Lesley	.06	.05	.02
548	Luis Salazar	.06	.05	.02
549	John Candelaria	.10	.08	.04
550	Dave Bergman	.06	.05	.02
551	Bob Watson	.08	.06	.03
552	Pat Tabler	.10	.08	.04
553	Brent Gaff	.06	.05	.02
554	Al Cowens	.06	.05	.02
555	Tom Brunansky(FC)	.25	.20	.10
556	Lloyd Moseby	.12	.09	.05
557a	Pascual Perez (Twins)(FC)	.90	.70	.35
557b	Pascual Perez (Braves)(FC)	.15	.11	.06
558	Willie Upshaw	.08	.06	.03
559	Richie Zisk	.08	.06	.03
560	Pat Zachry	.06	.05	.02
561	Jay Johnstone	.08	.06	.03
562	Carlos Diaz	.06	.05	.02
563	John Tudor	.10	.08	.04
564	Frank Robinson	.12	.09	.05
565	Dave Edwards	.06	.05	.02
566	Paul Householder	.06	.05	.02
567	Ron Reed	.06	.05	.02
568	Mike Ramsey	.06	.05	.02
569	Kiko Garcia	.06	.05	.02
570	Tommy John	.20	.15	.08
571	Tony LaRussa	.08	.06	.03
572	Joel Youngblood	.06	.05	.02
573	*Wayne Tolleson*(FC)	.12	.09	.05
574	Keith Creel	.06	.05	.02
575	Billy Martin	.12	.09	.05
576	Jerry Dybzinski	.06	.05	.02
577	Rick Cerone	.06	.05	.02
578	Tony Perez	.20	.15	.08
579	*Greg Brock*(FC)	.35	.25	.14
580	*Glen Wilson (Glenn)*(FC)	.35	.25	.14
581	Tim Stoddard	.06	.05	.02
582	Bob McClure	.06	.05	.02
583	Jim Dwyer	.06	.05	.02
584	Ed Romero	.06	.05	.02
585	Larry Herndon	.08	.06	.03
586	*Wade Boggs*(FC)	20.00	15.00	8.00
587	Jay Howell(FC)	.15	.11	.06
588	Dave Stewart	1.00	.70	.40
589	Bert Blyleven	.12	.09	.05
590	Dick Howser	.06	.05	.02
591	Wayne Gross	.06	.05	.02
592	Terry Francona	.06	.05	.02
593	Don Werner	.06	.05	.02
594	Bill Stein	.06	.05	.02
595	Jesse Barfield(FC)	.70	.50	.30
596	Bobby Molinaro	.06	.05	.02
597	Mike Vail	.06	.05	.02
598	*Tony Gwynn*(FC)	20.00	15.00	8.00
599	Gary Rajsich	.06	.05	.02
600	Jerry Ujdur	.06	.05	.02
601	Cliff Johnson	.06	.05	.02
602	Jerry White	.06	.05	.02
603	Bryan Clark	.06	.05	.02
604	Joe Ferguson	.06	.05	.02
605	Guy Sularz	.06	.05	.02
606a	Ozzie Virgil (green frame around photo)(FC)	.90	.70	.35
606b	Ozzie Virgil (orange frame around photo)(FC)	.08	.06	.03
607	Terry Harper(FC)	.06	.05	.02
608	Harvey Kuenn	.08	.06	.03
609	Jim Sundberg	.08	.06	.03
610	Willie Stargell	.40	.30	.15
611	Reggie Smith	.10	.08	.04
612	Rob Wilfong	.06	.05	.02
613	Niekro Brothers (Joe Niekro, Phil Niekro)	.15	.11	.06
614	Lee Elia	.06	.05	.02
615	Mickey Hatcher	.08	.06	.03
616	Jerry Hairston	.06	.05	.02
617	John Martin	.06	.05	.02
618	Wally Backman(FC)	.15	.11	.06
619	*Storm Davis*(FC)	.40	.30	.15
620	Alan Knicely	.06	.05	.02

		MT	NR MT	EX
621	John Stuper	.06	.05	.02
622	Matt Sinatro	.06	.05	.02
623	*Gene Petralli*(FC)	.15	.11	.06
624	Duane Walker	.06	.05	.02
625	Dick Williams	.06	.05	.02
626	Pat Corrales	.06	.05	.02
627	Vern Ruhle	.06	.05	.02
628	Joe Torre	.08	.06	.03
629	Anthony Johnson	.06	.05	.02
630	Steve Howe	.08	.06	.03
631	Gary Woods	.06	.05	.02
632	Lamarr Hoyt (LaMarr)	.06	.05	.02
633	Steve Swisher	.06	.05	.02
634	Terry Leach(FC)	.12	.09	.05
635	Jeff Newman	.06	.05	.02
636	Brett Butler	.10	.08	.04
637	Gary Gray	.06	.05	.02
638	Lee Mazzilli	.08	.06	.03
639a	Ron Jackson (A's)	10.00	7.50	4.00
639b	Ron Jackson (Angels - green frame around photo)	.90	.70	.35
639c	Ron Jackson (Angels - red frame around photo)	.20	.15	.08
640	Juan Beniquez	.06	.05	.02
641	Dave Rucker	.06	.05	.02
642	Luis Pujols	.06	.05	.02
643	Rick Monday	.10	.08	.04
644	Hosken Powell	.06	.05	.02
645	San Diego Chicken	.20	.15	.08
646	Dave Engle	.06	.05	.02
647	Dick Davis	.06	.05	.02
648	MVP's (Vida Blue, Joe Morgan, Frank Robinson)	.15	.11	.06
649	Al Chambers	.06	.05	.02
650	Jesus Vega	.06	.05	.02
651	Jeff Jones	.06	.05	.02
652	Marvis Foley	.06	.05	.02
653	Ty Cobb Puzzle	.06	.05	.02
---a	Dick Perez/DK Checklist (no word "Checklist" on back)	.70	.50	.30
---b	Dick Perez/DK Checklist (word "Checklist" on back)	.08	.06	.03
——	Checklist 27-130	.06	.05	.02
——	Checklist 131-234	.06	.05	.02
——	Checklist 235-338	.06	.05	.02
——	Checklist 339-442	.06	.05	.02
——	Checklist 443-546	.06	.05	.02
——	Checklist 547-653	.06	.05	.02

1983 Donruss Action All-Stars

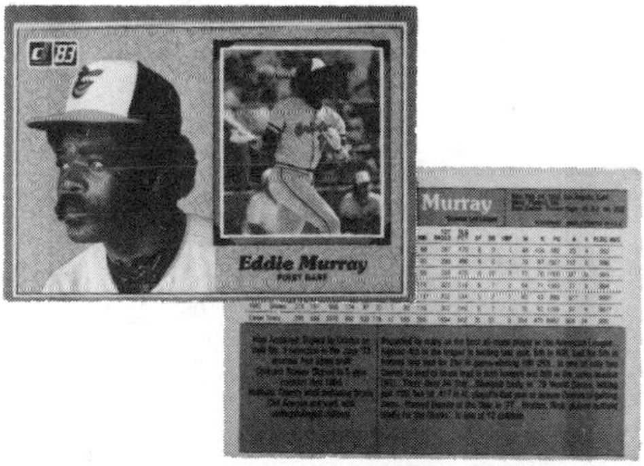

The cards in this 60-card set are designed on a horizontal format and contain a large close-up photo of the player on the left and a smaller action photo on the right. The cards, which measure 3-1/2" by 5", have deep red borders and contain the Donruss logo and the year of issue. The card backs have black print on red and white and contain various statistical and biographical information. The cards were sold with puzzle pieces (three pieces on one card per pack) that feature Mickey Mantle.

	MT	NR MT	EX
Complete Set:	9.00	6.75	3.50
Common Player:	.10	.08	.04

1	Eddie Murray	.30	.25	.12
2	Dwight Evans	.15	.11	.06
3a	Reggie Jackson (red covers part of statistics on back)	.60	.45	.25
3b	Reggie Jackson (red does not cover any statistics on back)	.60	.45	.25
4	Greg Luzinski	.12	.09	.05
5	Larry Herndon	.10	.08	.04
6	Al Oliver	.12	.09	.05
7	Bill Buckner	.10	.08	.04
8	Jason Thompson	.10	.08	.04
9	Andre Dawson	.20	.15	.08
10	Greg Minton	.10	.08	.04
11	Terry Kennedy	.10	.08	.04
12	Phil Niekro	.20	.15	.08
13	Willie Wilson	.12	.09	.05
14	Johnny Bench	.60	.45	.25
15	Ron Guidry	.15	.11	.06
16	Hal McRae	.10	.08	.04
17	Damaso Garcia	.10	.08	.04
18	Gary Ward	.10	.08	.04
19	Cecil Cooper	.12	.09	.05
20	Keith Hernandez	.25	.20	.10
21	Ron Cey	.12	.09	.05
22	Rickey Henderson	1.00	.70	.40
23	Nolan Ryan	2.50	2.00	1.00
24	Steve Carlton	.30	.25	.12
25	John Stearns	.10	.08	.04
26	Jim Sundberg	.10	.08	.04
27	Joaquin Andujar	.10	.08	.04
28	Gaylord Perry	.15	.11	.06
29	Jack Clark	.15	.11	.06
30	Bill Madlock	.12	.09	.05
31	Pete Rose	.60	.45	.25
32	Mookie Wilson	.10	.08	.04
33	Rollie Fingers	.15	.11	.06
34	Lonnie Smith	.10	.08	.04
35	Tony Pena	.10	.08	.04
36	Dave Winfield	.30	.25	.12
37	Tim Lollar	.10	.08	.04
38	Rod Carew	.60	.45	.25
39	Toby Harrah	.10	.08	.04
40	Buddy Bell	.10	.08	.04
41	Bruce Sutter	.12	.09	.05
42	George Brett	.70	.50	.30
43	Carlton Fisk	.60	.45	.25
44	Carl Yastrzemski	.70	.50	.30
45	Dale Murphy	.25	.20	.10
46	Bob Horner	.12	.09	.05
47	Dave Concepcion	.12	.09	.05
48	Dave Stieb	.12	.09	.05
49	Kent Hrbek	.20	.15	.08
50	Lance Parrish	.15	.11	.06
51	Joe Niekro	.12	.09	.05
52	Cal Ripken Jr.	.80	.60	.30
53	Fernando Valenzuela	.12	.09	.05
54	Rickie Zisk	.10	.08	.04
55	Leon Durham	.10	.08	.04
56	Robin Yount	.70	.50	.30
57	Mike Schmidt	1.25	.90	.50
58	Gary Carter	.15	.11	.06
59	Fred Lynn	.15	.11	.06
60	Checklist	.10	.08	.04

1983 Donruss Hall Of Fame Heroes

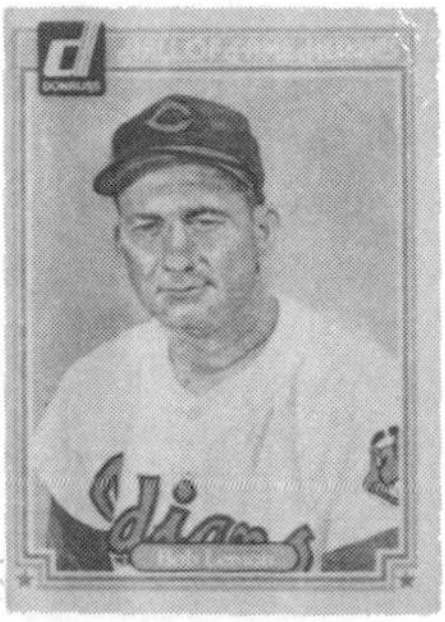

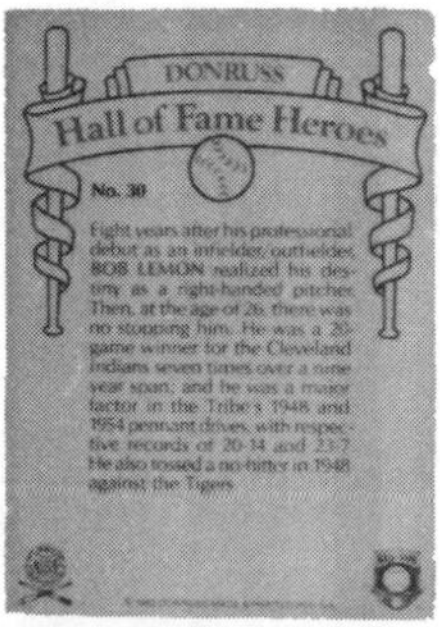

The artwork of Dick Perez is featured in the 44-card Donruss Hall of Fame Heroes set issued in 1983. The standard-size cards (2-1/2" by 3-1/2") were available in wax packs that contained eight cards plus a Mickey Mantle puzzle piece card (three pieces on one card per pack). The backs, which display red and blue print on white stock, contain a short player biograpical sketch derived from the Hall of Fame yearbook. The numbered set consists of 44 player cards, a Mantle puzzle card, and a checklist.

		MT	NR MT	EX
Complete Set:		8.00	6.00	3.25
Common Player:		.05	.04	.02
1	Ty Cobb	.70	.50	.30
2	Walter Johnson	.15	.11	.06
3	Christy Mathewson	.15	.11	.06
4	Josh Gibson	.10	.08	.04
5	Honus Wagner	.15	.11	.06
6	Jackie Robinson	.50	.40	.20
7	Mickey Mantle	1.00	.70	.40
8	Luke Appling	.05	.04	.02
9	Ted Williams	.70	.50	.30
10	Johnny Mize	.15	.11	.06
11	Satchel Paige	.15	.11	.06
12	Lou Boudreau	.15	.11	.06
13	Jimmie Foxx	.15	.11	.06
14	Duke Snider	.70	.50	.30
15	Monte Irvin	.15	.11	.06
16	Hank Greenberg	.15	.11	.06
17	Roberto Clemente	.50	.40	.20
18	Al Kaline	.50	.40	.20
19	Frank Robinson	.50	.40	.20
20	Joe Cronin	.09	.07	.04
21	Burleigh Grimes	.05	.04	.02
22	The Waner Brothers (Lloyd Waner, Paul Waner)	.09	.07	.04
23	Grover Alexander	.09	.07	.04
24	Yogi Berra	.50	.40	.20
25	James Bell	.05	.04	.02
26	Bill Dickey	.09	.07	.04
27	Cy Young	.15	.11	.06
28	Charlie Gehringer	.09	.07	.04
29	Dizzy Dean	.15	.11	.06
30	Bob Lemon	.15	.11	.06
31	Red Ruffing	.05	.04	.02
32	Stan Musial	.70	.50	.30
33	Carl Hubbell	.15	.11	.06
34	Hank Aaron	.70	.50	.30
35	John McGraw	.09	.07	.04
36	Bob Feller	.50	.40	.20
37	Casey Stengel	.15	.11	.06
38	Ralph Kiner	.15	.11	.06
39	Roy Campanella	.15	.11	.06
40	Mel Ott	.09	.07	.04
41	Robin Roberts	.15	.11	.06
42	Early Wynn	.15	.11	.06
43	Mickey Mantle Puzzle Card	.09	.07	.04
----	Checklist	.09	.07	.04

1984 Donruss

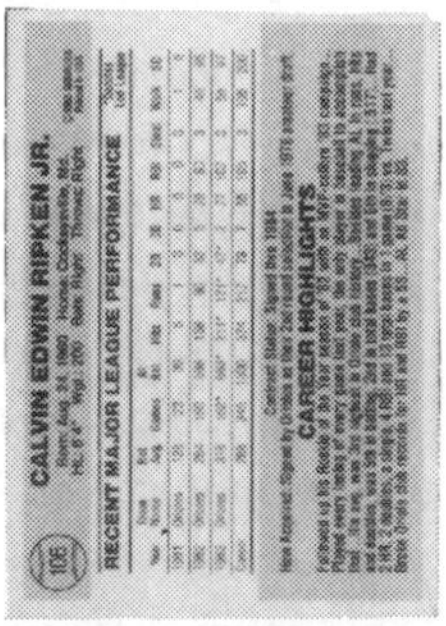

The 1984 Donruss set consists of 651 numbered cards, seven unnumbered checklists and two "Living Legends" cards (designated A and B). The A and B cards were issued only in wax packs and not available to hobby dealers purchasing vending sets. The card fronts differ in style from the previous years, however

the Donruss logo and year of issue are still included. The card backs have black print on green and white and are identical in format to the preceding year. The standard-size cards (2-1/2" by 3-1/2") were issued with a 63-piece puzzle of Duke Snider. A limited print run of the issue by Donruss has caused the set to escalate in price in recent years. The complete set price in the checklist that follows does not include the higher priced variations. Cards marked with (DK) or (RR) in the checklist refer to the Diamond Kings and Rated Rookies subsets.

		MT	NR MT	EX
Complete Set:		400.00	300.00	150.00
Common Player:		.12	.09	.05
1a	Robin Yount (DK) (Perez-Steel on back)	.80	.60	.30
1b	Robin Yount (DK) (Perez-Steele on back)	2.00	1.50	.80
2a	Dave Concepcion (DK) (Perez-Steel on back)	.30	.25	.12
2b	Dave Concepcion (DK) (Perez-Steele on back)	.60	.45	.25
3a	Dwayne Murphy (DK) (Perez-Steel on back)	.25	.20	.10
3b	Dwayne Murphy (DK) (Perez-Steele on back)	.60	.45	.25
4a	John Castino (DK) (Perez-Steel on back)	.20	.15	.08
4b	John Castino (DK) (Perez-Steele on back)	.60	.45	.25
5a	Leon Durham (DK) (Perez-Steel on back)	.25	.20	.10
5b	Leon Durham (DK) (Perez-Steele on back)	.60	.45	.25
6a	Rusty Staub (DK) (Perez-Steel on back)	.30	.25	.12
6b	Rusty Staub (DK) (Perez-Steele on back)	.60	.45	.25
7a	Jack Clark (DK) (Perez-Steel on back)	.40	.30	.15
7b	Jack Clark (DK) (Perez-Steele on back)	.80	.60	.30
8a	Dave Dravecky (DK) (Perez-Steel on back)	.25	.20	.10
8b	Dave Dravecky (DK) (Perez-Steele on back)	.60	.45	.25
9a	Al Oliver (DK) (Perez-Steel on back)	.35	.25	.14
9b	Al Oliver (DK) (Perez-Steele on back)	.70	.50	.30
10a	Dave Righetti (DK) (Perez-Steel on back)	.40	.30	.15
10b	Dave Righetti (DK) (Perez-Steele on back)	.80	.60	.30
11a	Hal McRae (DK) (Perez-Steel on back)	.30	.25	.12
11b	Hal McRae (DK) (Perez-Steele on back)	.60	.45	.25
12a	Ray Knight (DK) (Perez-Steel on back)	.25	.20	.10
12b	Ray Knight (DK) (Perez-Steele on back)	.60	.45	.25
13a	Bruce Sutter (DK) (Perez-Steel on back)	.35	.25	.14
13b	Bruce Sutter (DK) (Perez-Steele on back)	.70	.50	.30
14a	Bob Horner (DK) (Perez-Steel on back)	.40	.30	.15
14b	Bob Horner (DK) (Perez-Steele on back)	.80	.60	.30
15a	Lance Parrish (DK) (Perez-Steel on back)	.60	.45	.25
15b	Lance Parrish (DK) (Perez-Steele on back)	1.25	.90	.50
16a	Matt Young (DK) (Perez-Steel on back)	.25	.20	.10
16b	Matt Young (DK) (Perez-Steele on back)	.60	.45	.25
17a	Fred Lynn (DK) (Perez-Steel on back)	.35	.25	.14
17b	Fred Lynn (DK) (Perez-Steele on back)	.70	.50	.30
18a	Ron Kittle (DK) (Perez-Steel on back)(FC)	.35	.25	.14
18b	Ron Kittle (DK) (Perez-Steele on back)(FC)	.70	.50	.30
19a	Jim Clancy (DK) (Perez-Steel on back)	.25	.20	.10
19b	Jim Clancy (DK) (Perez-Steele on back)	.60	.45	.25
20a	Bill Madlock (DK) (Perez-Steele on back)	.30	.25	.12
20b	Bill Madlock (DK) (Perez-Steele on back)	.60	.45	.25
21a	Larry Parrish (DK) (Perez-Steel on back)	.30	.25	.12
21b	Larry Parrish (DK) (Perez-Steele on back)	.60	.45	.25
22a	Eddie Murray (DK) (Perez-Steel on back)	1.25	.90	.50
22b	Eddie Murray (DK) (Perez-Steele on back)	2.50	2.00	1.00
23a	Mike Schmidt (DK) (Perez-Steel on back)	1.25	.90	.50
23b	Mike Schmidt (DK) (Perez-Steele on back)	2.50	2.00	1.00
24a	Pedro Guerrero (DK) (Perez-Steel on back)	.50	.40	.20
24b	Pedro Guerrero (DK) (Perez-Steele on back)	1.00	.70	.40
25a	Andre Thornton (DK) (Perez-Steel on back)	.30	.25	.12
25b	Andre Thornton (DK) (Perez-Steele on back)	.60	.45	.25
26a	Wade Boggs (DK) (Perez-Steel on back)	3.00	2.25	1.25
26b	Wade Boggs (DK) (Perez-Steele on back)	4.00	3.00	1.50
27	*Joel Skinner (RR)*(FC)	.20	.15	.08
28	Tom Dunbar (RR)	.12	.09	.05
29a	Mike Stenhouse (RR) (no number on back)	.15	.11	.06
29b	Mike Stenhouse (RR) (29 on back)	4.00	3.00	1.50
30a	*Ron Darling* (no number on back)(FC)	5.00	3.75	2.00
30b	*Ron Darling* (30 on back)(FC)	10.00	7.50	4.00
31	*Dion James (RR)*(FC)	.40	.30	.15
32	*Tony Fernandez (RR)*(FC)	8.00	6.00	3.25
33	Angel Salazar (RR)	.12	.09	.05
34	*Kevin McReynolds (RR)*(FC)	10.00	7.50	4.00
35	*Dick Schofield (RR)*(FC)	.40	.30	.15
36	*Brad Komminsk (RR)*(FC)	.15	.11	.06
37	*Tim Teufel (RR)*(FC)	.30	.25	.12
38	Doug Frobel (RR)	.12	.09	.05
39	*Greg Gagne (RR)*(FC)	.60	.45	.25
40	Mike Fuentes (RR)	.12	.09	.05
41	*Joe Carter (RR)*(FC)	30.00	22.00	12.00
42	Mike Brown (RR)	.12	.09	.05
43	Mike Jeffcoat (RR)	.12	.09	.05
44	*Sid Fernandez (RR)*(FC)	5.00	3.75	2.00
45	Brian Dayett (RR)	.12	.09	.05
46	Chris Smith (RR)	.12	.09	.05
47	Eddie Murray	4.00	3.00	1.50
48	Robin Yount	4.00	3.00	1.50
49	Lance Parrish	.50	.40	.20
50	Jim Rice	.90	.70	.35
51	Dave Winfield	2.00	1.50	.80
52	Fernando Valenzuela	.70	.50	.30
53	George Brett	4.00	3.00	1.50
54	Rickey Henderson	15.00	11.00	6.00
55	Gary Carter	.80	.60	.30
56	Buddy Bell	.20	.15	.08
57	Reggie Jackson	3.00	2.25	1.25
58	Harold Baines	.25	.20	.10
59	Ozzie Smith	2.00	1.50	.80
60	Nolan Ryan	15.00	11.00	6.00
61	Pete Rose	3.00	2.25	1.25
62	Ron Oester	.12	.09	.05
63	Steve Garvey	.90	.70	.35
64	Jason Thompson	.12	.09	.05
65	Jack Clark	.35	.25	.14
66	Dale Murphy	2.00	1.50	.80
67	Leon Durham	.12	.09	.05
68	*Darryl Strawberry*(FC)	70.00	52.00	27.00
69	Richie Zisk	.12	.09	.05
70	Kent Hrbek	.60	.45	.25
71	Dave Stieb	.25	.20	.10
72	Ken Schrom	.12	.09	.05
73	George Bell	2.00	1.50	.80
74	John Moses	.15	.11	.06
75	Ed Lynch	.12	.09	.05
76	Chuck Rainey	.12	.09	.05
77	Biff Pocoroba	.12	.09	.05
78	Cecilio Guante	.12	.09	.05
79	Jim Barr	.12	.09	.05
80	Kurt Bevacqua	.12	.09	.05
81	Tom Foley	.12	.09	.05
82	Joe Lefebvre	.12	.09	.05

		MT	NR MT	EX
83	*Andy Van Slyke*(FC)	8.00	6.00	3.25
84	Bob Lillis	.12	.09	.05
85	Rick Adams	.12	.09	.05
86	Jerry Hairston	.12	.09	.05
87	Bob James	.12	.09	.05
88	Joe Altobelli	.12	.09	.05
89	Ed Romero	.12	.09	.05
90	John Grubb	.12	.09	.05
91	John Henry Johnson	.12	.09	.05
92	Juan Espino	.12	.09	.05
93	Candy Maldonado	.20	.15	.08
94	Andre Thornton	.20	.15	.08
95	Onix Concepcion	.12	.09	.05
96	*Don Hill*(FC)	.20	.15	.08
97	Andre Dawson	3.00	2.25	1.25
98	Frank Tanana	.15	.11	.06
99	*Curt Wilkerson*(FC)	.15	.11	.06
100	Larry Gura	.12	.09	.05
101	Dwayne Murphy	.12	.09	.05
102	Tom Brennan	.12	.09	.05
103	Dave Righetti	.40	.30	.15
104	Steve Sax	.30	.25	.12
105	Dan Petry	.12	.09	.05
106	Cal Ripken	15.00	11.00	6.00
107	Paul Molitor	.70	.50	.30
108	Fred Lynn	.35	.25	.14
109	Neil Allen	.12	.09	.05
110	Joe Niekro	.20	.15	.08
111	Steve Carlton	2.00	1.50	.80
112	Terry Kennedy	.15	.11	.06
113	Bill Madlock	.20	.15	.08
114	Chili Davis	.15	.11	.06
115	Jim Gantner	.12	.09	.05
116	Tom Seaver	4.00	3.00	1.50
117	Bill Buckner	.20	.15	.08
118	Bill Caudill	.12	.09	.05
119	Jim Clancy	.15	.11	.06
120	John Castino	.12	.09	.05
121	Dave Concepcion	.20	.15	.08
122	Greg Luzinski	.20	.15	.08
123	Mike Boddicker(FC)	.20	.15	.08
124	Pete Ladd	.12	.09	.05
125	Juan Berenguer	.12	.09	.05
126	John Montefusco	.12	.09	.05
127	Ed Jurak	.12	.09	.05
128	Tom Niedenfuer	.12	.09	.05
129	Bert Blyleven	.30	.25	.12
130	Bud Black	.12	.09	.05
131	Gorman Heimueller	.12	.09	.05
132	Dan Schatzeder	.12	.09	.05
133	Ron Jackson	.12	.09	.05
134	*Tom Henke*(FC)	1.25	.90	.50
135	Kevin Hickey	.12	.09	.05
136	Mike Scott	.30	.25	.12
137	Bo Diaz	.12	.09	.05
138	Glenn Brummer	.12	.09	.05
139	Sid Monge	.12	.09	.05
140	Rich Gale	.12	.09	.05
141	Brett Butler	.15	.11	.06
142	Brian Harper	.80	.60	.30
143	John Rabb	.12	.09	.05
144	Gary Woods	.12	.09	.05
145	Pat Putnam	.12	.09	.05
146	*Jim Acker*(FC)	.15	.11	.06
147	Mickey Hatcher	.12	.09	.05
148	Todd Cruz	.12	.09	.05
149	Tom Tellmann	.12	.09	.05
150	John Wockenfuss	.12	.09	.05
151	Wade Boggs	12.00	9.00	4.75
152	Don Baylor	.20	.15	.08
153	Bob Welch	.20	.15	.08
154	Alan Bannister	.12	.09	.05
155	Willie Aikens	.12	.09	.05
156	Jeff Burroughs	.12	.09	.05
157	Bryan Little	.12	.09	.05
158	Bob Boone	.15	.11	.06
159	Dave Hostetler	.12	.09	.05
160	Jerry Dybzinski	.12	.09	.05
161	Mike Madden	.12	.09	.05
162	Luis DeLeon	.12	.09	.05
163	Willie Hernandez	.15	.11	.06
164	Frank Pastore	.12	.09	.05
165	Rick Camp	.12	.09	.05
166	Lee Mazzilli	.12	.09	.05
167	Scot Thompson	.12	.09	.05
168	Bob Forsch	.12	.09	.05
169	Mike Flanagan	.15	.11	.06
170	Rick Manning	.12	.09	.05
171	Chet Lemon	.12	.09	.05
172	Jerry Remy	.12	.09	.05
173	Ron Guidry	.35	.25	.14

		MT	NR MT	EX
174	Pedro Guerrero	.50	.40	.20
175	Willie Wilson	.25	.20	.10
176	Carney Lansford	.20	.15	.08
177	Al Oliver	.30	.25	.12
178	Jim Sundberg	.12	.09	.05
179	Bobby Grich	.20	.15	.08
180	Richard Dotson	.20	.15	.08
181	Joaquin Andujar	.12	.09	.05
182	Jose Cruz	.20	.15	.08
183	Mike Schmidt	12.00	9.00	4.75
184	*Gary Redus*(FC)	.30	.25	.12
185	Garry Templeton	.15	.11	.06
186	Tony Pena	.20	.15	.08
187	Greg Minton	.12	.09	.05
188	Phil Niekro	.50	.40	.20
189	Ferguson Jenkins	.30	.25	.12
190	Mookie Wilson	.15	.11	.06
191	Jim Beattie	.12	.09	.05
192	Gary Ward	.12	.09	.05
193	Jesse Barfield	.40	.30	.15
194	Pete Filson	.12	.09	.05
195	Roy Lee Jackson	.12	.09	.05
196	Rick Sweet	.12	.09	.05
197	Jesse Orosco	.15	.11	.06
198	*Steve Lake*(FC)	.12	.09	.05
199	Ken Dayley	.12	.09	.05
200	Manny Sarmiento	.12	.09	.05
201	Mark Davis(FC)	.25	.20	.10
202	Tim Flannery	.12	.09	.05
203	Bill Scherrer	.12	.09	.05
204	Al Holland	.12	.09	.05
205	David Von Ohlen	.12	.09	.05
206	Mike LaCoss	.12	.09	.05
207	Juan Beniquez	.12	.09	.05
208	*Juan Agosto*(FC)	.20	.15	.08
209	Bobby Ramos	.12	.09	.05
210	Al Bumbry	.12	.09	.05
211	Mark Brouhard	.12	.09	.05
212	Howard Bailey	.12	.09	.05
213	Bruce Hurst	.20	.15	.08
214	Bob Shirley	.12	.09	.05
215	Pat Zachry	.12	.09	.05
216	Julio Franco	4.00	3.00	1.50
217	Mike Armstrong	.12	.09	.05
218	Dave Beard	.12	.09	.05
219	Steve Rogers	.12	.09	.05
220	John Butcher	.12	.09	.05
221	*Mike Smithson*(FC)	.20	.15	.08
222	Frank White	.20	.15	.08
223	Mike Heath	.12	.09	.05
224	Chris Bando	.12	.09	.05
225	Roy Smalley	.12	.09	.05
226	Dusty Baker	.20	.15	.08
227	Lou Whitaker	.60	.45	.25
228	John Lowenstein	.12	.09	.05
229	Ben Oglivie	.12	.09	.05
230	Doug DeCinces	.15	.11	.06
231	Lonnie Smith	.12	.09	.05
232	Ray Knight	.15	.11	.06
233	Gary Matthews	.20	.15	.08
234	Juan Bonilla	.12	.09	.05
235	Rod Scurry	.12	.09	.05
236	Atlee Hammaker	.12	.09	.05
237	Mike Caldwell	.12	.09	.05
238	Keith Hernandez	.80	.60	.30
239	Larry Bowa	.25	.20	.10
240	Tony Bernazard	.12	.09	.05
241	Damaso Garcia	.12	.09	.05
242	Tom Brunansky	.35	.25	.14
243	Dan Driessen	.12	.09	.05
244	Ron Kittle(FC)	.30	.25	.12
245	Tim Stoddard	.12	.09	.05
246	Bob Gibson	.12	.09	.05
247	Marty Castillo	.12	.09	.05
248	*Don Mattingly*(FC)	80.00	60.00	30.00
249	Jeff Newman	.12	.09	.05
250	*Alejandro Pena*(FC)	.40	.30	.15
251	Toby Harrah	.12	.09	.05
252	Cesar Geronimo	.12	.09	.05
253	Tom Underwood	.12	.09	.05
254	Doug Flynn	.12	.09	.05
255	Andy Hassler	.12	.09	.05
256	Odell Jones	.12	.09	.05
257	Rudy Law	.12	.09	.05
258	Harry Spilman	.12	.09	.05
259	Marty Bystrom	.12	.09	.05
260	Dave Rucker	.12	.09	.05
261	Ruppert Jones	.12	.09	.05
262	Jeff Jones	.12	.09	.05
263	*Gerald Perry*(FC)	1.00	.70	.40
264	Gene Tenace	.12	.09	.05

		MT	NR MT	EX
265	Brad Wellman	.12	.09	.05
266	Dickie Noles	.12	.09	.05
267	Jamie Allen	.12	.09	.05
268	Jim Gott	.15	.11	.06
269	Ron Davis	.12	.09	.05
270	Benny Ayala	.12	.09	.05
271	Ned Yost	.12	.09	.05
272	Dave Rozema	.12	.09	.05
273	Dave Stapleton	.12	.09	.05
274	Lou Piniella	.20	.15	.08
275	Jose Morales	.12	.09	.05
276	Brod Perkins	.12	.09	.05
277	Butch Davis	.12	.09	.05
278	*Tony Phillips*(FC)	.20	.15	.08
279	Jeff Reardon	.25	.20	.10
280	Ken Forsch	.12	.09	.05
281	*Pete O'Brien*(FC)	1.00	.70	.40
282	Tom Paciorek	.12	.09	.05
283	Frank LaCorte	.12	.09	.05
284	Tim Lollar	.12	.09	.05
285	Greg Gross	.12	.09	.05
286	Alex Trevino	.12	.09	.05
287	Gene Garber	.12	.09	.05
288	Dave Parker	.50	.40	.20
289	Lee Smith	.20	.15	.08
290	Dave LaPoint	.15	.11	.06
291	*John Shelby*(FC)	.25	.20	.10
292	Charlie Moore	.12	.09	.05
293	Alan Trammell	.60	.45	.25
294	Tony Armas	.20	.15	.08
295	Shane Rawley	.20	.15	.08
296	Greg Brock	.15	.11	.06
297	Hal McRae	.20	.15	.08
298	Mike Davis	.12	.09	.05
299	Tim Raines	.80	.60	.30
300	Bucky Dent	.15	.11	.06
301	Tommy John	.35	.25	.14
302	Carlton Fisk	2.00	1.50	.80
303	Darrell Porter	.12	.09	.05
304	Dickie Thon	.12	.09	.05
305	Garry Maddox	.12	.09	.05
306	Cesar Cedeno	.20	.15	.08
307	Gary Lucas	.12	.09	.05
308	Johnny Ray	.20	.15	.08
309	Andy McGaffigan	.12	.09	.05
310	Claudell Washington	.12	.09	.05
311	Ryne Sandberg	20.00	15.00	7.50
312	George Foster	.30	.25	.12
313	*Spike Owen*(FC)	.70	.50	.30
314	Gary Gaetti	.90	.70	.35
315	Willie Upshaw	.12	.09	.05
316	Al Williams	.12	.09	.05
317	Jorge Orta	.12	.09	.05
318	Orlando Mercado	.12	.09	.05
319	*Junior Ortiz*(FC)	.12	.09	.05
320	Mike Proly	.12	.09	.05
321	Randy Johnson	.12	.09	.05
322	Jim Morrison	.12	.09	.05
323	Max Venable	.12	.09	.05
324	Tony Gwynn	12.00	9.00	4.75
325	Duane Walker	.12	.09	.05
326	Ozzie Virgil	.12	.09	.05
327	Jeff Lahti	.12	.09	.05
328	*Bill Dawley*(FC)	.12	.09	.05
329	Rob Wilfong	.12	.09	.05
330	Marc Hill	.12	.09	.05
331	Ray Burris	.12	.09	.05
332	Allan Ramirez	.12	.09	.05
333	Chuck Porter	.12	.09	.05
334	Wayne Krenchicki	.12	.09	.05
335	Gary Allenson	.12	.09	.05
336	*Bob Meacham*(FC)	.20	.15	.08
337	Joe Beckwith	.12	.09	.05
338	Rick Sutcliffe	.25	.20	.10
339	*Mark Huismann*(FC)	.15	.11	.06
340	*Tim Conroy*(FC)	.15	.11	.06
341	Scott Sanderson	.12	.09	.05
342	Larry Biittner	.12	.09	.05
343	Dave Stewart	2.00	1.50	.80
344	Darryl Motley	.12	.09	.05
345	*Chris Codiroli*(FC)	.12	.09	.05
346	Rick Behenna	.12	.09	.05
347	Andre Robertson	.12	.09	.05
348	Mike Marshall	.25	.20	.10
349	Larry Herndon	.12	.09	.05
350	Rich Dauer	.12	.09	.05
351	Cecil Cooper	.25	.20	.10
352	Rod Carew	3.00	2.25	1.25
353	Willie McGee	.40	.30	.15
354	Phil Garner	.12	.09	.05
355	Joe Morgan	.60	.45	.25
356	Luis Salazar	.12	.09	.05
357	John Candelaria	.20	.15	.08
358	Bill Laskey	.12	.09	.05
359	Bob McClure	.12	.09	.05
360	Dave Kingman	.30	.25	.12
361	Ron Cey	.20	.15	.08
362	*Matt Young*(FC)	.20	.15	.08
363	Lloyd Moseby	.20	.15	.08
364	Frank Viola	2.00	1.50	.80
365	Eddie Milner	.12	.09	.05
366	Floyd Bannister	.20	.15	.08
367	Dan Ford	.12	.09	.05
368	Moose Haas	.12	.09	.05
369	Doug Bair	.12	.09	.05
370	*Ray Fontenot*(FC)	.12	.09	.05
371	Luis Aponte	.12	.09	.05
372	Jack Fimple	.12	.09	.05
373	*Neal Heaton*(FC)	.20	.15	.08
374	Greg Pryor	.12	.09	.05
375	Wayne Gross	.12	.09	.05
376	Charlie Lea	.12	.09	.05
377	Steve Lubratich	.12	.09	.05
378	Jon Matlack	.12	.09	.05
379	Julio Cruz	.12	.09	.05
380	John Mizerock	.12	.09	.05
381	*Kevin Gross*(FC)	.50	.40	.20
382	Mike Ramsey	.12	.09	.05
383	Doug Gwosdz	.12	.09	.05
384	Kelly Paris	.12	.09	.05
385	Pete Falcone	.12	.09	.05
386	Milt May	.12	.09	.05
387	Fred Breining	.12	.09	.05
388	*Craig Lefferts*(FC)	.25	.20	.10
389	Steve Henderson	.12	.09	.05
390	Randy Moffitt	.12	.09	.05
391	Ron Washington	.12	.09	.05
392	Gary Roenicke	.12	.09	.05
393	*Tom Candiotti*(FC)	.30	.25	.12
394	Larry Pashnick	.12	.09	.05
395	Dwight Evans	.30	.25	.12
396	Goose Gossage	.40	.30	.15
397	Derrel Thomas	.12	.09	.05
398	Juan Eichelberger	.12	.09	.05
399	Leon Roberts	.12	.09	.05
400	Davey Lopes	.15	.11	.06
401	Bill Gullickson	.12	.09	.05
402	Geoff Zahn	.12	.09	.05
403	Billy Sample	.12	.09	.05
404	Mike Squires	.12	.09	.05
405	Craig Reynolds	.12	.09	.05
406	Eric Show	.15	.11	.06
407	John Denny	.12	.09	.05
408	Dann Bilardello	.12	.09	.05
409	Bruce Benedict	.12	.09	.05
410	Kent Tekulve	.12	.09	.05
411	Mel Hall	.20	.15	.08
412	John Stuper	.12	.09	.05
413	Rick Dempsey	.12	.09	.05
414	Don Sutton	.50	.40	.20
415	Jack Morris	.50	.40	.20
416	John Tudor	.20	.15	.08
417	Willie Randolph	.20	.15	.08
418	Jerry Reuss	.15	.11	.06
419	Don Slaught	.12	.09	.05
420	Steve McCatty	.12	.09	.05
421	Tim Wallach	.25	.20	.10
422	Larry Parrish	.20	.15	.08
423	Brian Downing	.20	.15	.08
424	Britt Burns	.12	.09	.05
425	David Green	.12	.09	.05
426	Jerry Mumphrey	.12	.09	.05
427	Ivan DeJesus	.12	.09	.05
428	Mario Soto	.12	.09	.05
429	Gene Richards	.12	.09	.05
430	Dale Berra	.12	.09	.05
431	Darrell Evans	.25	.20	.10
432	Glenn Hubbard	.12	.09	.05
433	Jody Davis	.15	.11	.06
434	Danny Heep	.12	.09	.05
435	*Ed Nunez*(FC)	.20	.15	.08
436	Bobby Castillo	.12	.09	.05
437	Ernie Whitt	.12	.09	.05
438	Scott Ullger	.12	.09	.05
439	Doyle Alexander	.15	.11	.06
440	Domingo Ramos	.12	.09	.05
441	Craig Swan	.12	.09	.05
442	Warren Brusstar	.12	.09	.05
443	Len Barker	.12	.09	.05
444	Mike Easler	.12	.09	.05
445	Renie Martin	.12	.09	.05
446	*Dennis Rasmussen*(FC)	.70	.50	.30

		MT	NR MT	EX
447	Ted Power(FC)	.15	.11	.06
448	*Charlie Hudson*(FC)	.25	.20	.10
449	*Danny Cox*(FC)	.70	.50	.30
450	Kevin Bass(FC)	.30	.25	.12
451	Daryl Sconiers	.12	.09	.05
452	Scott Fletcher	.12	.09	.05
453	Bryn Smith	.12	.09	.05
454	Jim Dwyer	.12	.09	.05
455	Rob Picciolo	.12	.09	.05
456	Enos Cabell	.12	.09	.05
457	*Dennis "Oil Can" Boyd*(FC)	1.25	.90	.50
458	Butch Wynegar	.12	.09	.05
459	Burt Hooton	.12	.09	.05
460	Ron Hassey	.12	.09	.05
461	*Danny Jackson*(FC)	1.75	1.25	.70
462	Bob Kearney	.12	.09	.05
463	Terry Francona	.12	.09	.05
464	Wayne Tolleson	.12	.09	.05
465	Mickey Rivers	.12	.09	.05
466	John Wathan	.12	.09	.05
467	Bill Almon	.12	.09	.05
468	George Vukovich	.12	.09	.05
469	Steve Kemp	.15	.11	.06
470	Ken Landreaux	.12	.09	.05
471	Milt Wilcox	.12	.09	.05
472	Tippy Martinez	.12	.09	.05
473	Ted Simmons	.20	.15	.08
474	Tim Foli	.12	.09	.05
475	George Hendrick	.12	.09	.05
476	Terry Puhl	.12	.09	.05
477	Von Hayes	.25	.20	.10
478	Bobby Brown	.12	.09	.05
479	Lee Lacy	.12	.09	.05
480	Joel Youngblood	.12	.09	.05
481	Jim Slaton	.12	.09	.05
482	*Mike Fitzgerald*(FC)	.20	.15	.08
483	Keith Moreland	.12	.09	.05
484	Ron Roenicke	.12	.09	.05
485	Luis Leal	.12	.09	.05
486	Bryan Oelkers	.12	.09	.05
487	Bruce Berenyi	.12	.09	.05
488	LaMarr Hoyt	.12	.09	.05
489	Joe Nolan	.12	.09	.05
490	Marshall Edwards	.12	.09	.05
491	*Mike Laga*(FC)	.12	.09	.05
492	Rick Cerone	.12	.09	.05
493	Mike Miller (Rick)	.12	.09	.05
494	Rick Honeycutt	.12	.09	.05
495	Mike Hargrove	.12	.09	.05
496	Joe Simpson	.12	.09	.05
497	*Keith Atherton*(FC)	.25	.20	.10
498	Chris Welsh	.12	.09	.05
499	Bruce Kison	.12	.09	.05
500	Bob Johnson	.12	.09	.05
501	Jerry Koosman	.15	.11	.06
502	Frank DiPino	.12	.09	.05
503	Tony Perez	.40	.30	.15
504	Ken Oberkfell	.12	.09	.05
505	*Mark Thurmond*(FC)	.12	.09	.05
506	Joe Price	.12	.09	.05
507	Pascual Perez	.15	.11	.06
508	*Marvell Wynne*(FC)	.25	.20	.10
509	Mike Krukow	.12	.09	.05
510	Dick Ruthven	.12	.09	.05
511	Al Cowens	.12	.09	.05
512	Cliff Johnson	.12	.09	.05
513	*Randy Bush*(FC)	.20	.15	.08
514	Sammy Stewart	.12	.09	.05
515	*Bill Schroeder*(FC)	.25	.20	.10
516	Aurelio Lopez	.12	.09	.05
517	Mike Brown	.12	.09	.05
518	Graig Nettles	.35	.25	.14
519	Dave Sax	.12	.09	.05
520	Gerry Willard	.12	.09	.05
521	Paul Splittorff	.12	.09	.05
522	Tom Burgmeier	.12	.09	.05
523	Chris Speier	.12	.09	.05
524	Bobby Clark	.12	.09	.05
525	George Wright	.12	.09	.05
526	Dennis Lamp	.12	.09	.05
527	Tony Scott	.12	.09	.05
528	Ed Whitson	.12	.09	.05
529	Ron Reed	.12	.09	.05
530	Charlie Puleo	.12	.09	.05
531	Jerry Royster	.12	.09	.05
532	Don Robinson	.12	.09	.05
533	Steve Trout	.12	.09	.05
534	Bruce Sutter	.30	.25	.12
535	Bob Horner	.20	.15	.08
536	Pat Tabler	.15	.11	.06
537	Chris Chambliss	.12	.09	.05
538	Bob Ojeda	.15	.11	.06
539	Alan Ashby	.12	.09	.05
540	Jay Johnstone	.12	.09	.05
541	Bob Dernier	.12	.09	.05
542	*Brook Jacoby*(FC)	3.00	2.25	1.25
543	U.L. Washington	.12	.09	.05
544	Danny Darwin	.12	.09	.05
545	Kiko Garcia	.12	.09	.05
546	Vance Law	.12	.09	.05
547	Tug McGraw	.20	.15	.08
548	Dave Smith	.12	.09	.05
549	Len Matuszek	.12	.09	.05
550	Tom Hume	.12	.09	.05
551	Dave Dravecky	.15	.11	.06
552	Rick Rhoden	.15	.11	.06
553	Duane Kuiper	.12	.09	.05
554	Rusty Staub	.20	.15	.08
555	Bill Campbell	.12	.09	.05
556	Mike Torrez	.12	.09	.05
557	Dave Henderson(FC)	.25	.20	.10
558	Len Whitehouse	.12	.09	.05
559	Barry Bonnell	.12	.09	.05
560	Rick Lysander	.12	.09	.05
561	Garth Iorg	.12	.09	.05
562	Bryan Clark	.12	.09	.05
563	Brian Giles	.12	.09	.05
564	Vern Ruhle	.12	.09	.05
565	Steve Bedrosian	.20	.15	.08
566	Larry McWilliams	.12	.09	.05
567	Jeff Leonard	.15	.11	.06
568	Alan Wiggins	.12	.09	.05
569	*Jeff Russell*(FC)	.25	.20	.10
570	Salome Barojas	.12	.09	.05
571	Dane Iorg	.12	.09	.05
572	Bob Knepper	.15	.11	.06
573	Gary Lavelle	.12	.09	.05
574	Gorman Thomas	.15	.11	.06
575	Manny Trillo	.12	.09	.05
576	Jim Palmer	2.00	1.50	.80
577	Dale Murray	.12	.09	.05
578	Tom Brookens	.12	.09	.05
579	Rich Gedman	.15	.11	.06
580	*Bill Doran*(FC)	1.25	.90	.50
581	Steve Yeager	.12	.09	.05
582	Dan Spillner	.12	.09	.05
583	Dan Quisenberry	.15	.11	.06
584	Rance Mulliniks	.12	.09	.05
585	Storm Davis	.15	.11	.06
586	Dave Schmidt	.12	.09	.05
587	Bill Russell	.12	.09	.05
588	*Pat Sheridan*(FC)	.20	.15	.08
589	Rafael Ramirez	.12	.09	.05
590	Bud Anderson	.12	.09	.05
591	George Frazier	.12	.09	.05
592	*Lee Tunnell*(FC)	.12	.09	.05
593	Kirk Gibson	.60	.45	.25
594	Scott McGregor	.12	.09	.05
595	Bob Bailor	.12	.09	.05
596	Tom Herr	.20	.15	.08
597	Luis Sanchez	.12	.09	.05
598	Dave Engle	.12	.09	.05
599	*Craig McMurtry*(FC)	.15	.11	.06
600	Carlos Diaz	.12	.09	.05
601	Tom O'Malley	.12	.09	.05
602	*Nick Esasky*(FC)	.70	.50	.30
603	Ron Hodges	.12	.09	.05
604	Ed Vande Berg	.12	.09	.05
605	Alfredo Griffin	.12	.09	.05
606	Glenn Hoffman	.12	.09	.05
607	Hubie Brooks	.20	.15	.08
608	Richard Barnes (photo actually Neal Heaton)	.12	.09	.05
609	*Greg Walker*(FC)	.40	.30	.15
610	Ken Singleton	.20	.15	.08
611	Mark Clear	.12	.09	.05
612	Buck Martinez	.12	.09	.05
613	Ken Griffey	.15	.11	.06
614	Reid Nichols	.12	.09	.05
615	*Doug Sisk*(FC)	.12	.09	.05
616	Bob Brenly	.12	.09	.05
617	Joey McLaughlin	.12	.09	.05
618	Glenn Wilson	.12	.09	.05
619	Bob Stoddard	.12	.09	.05
620	Len Sakata (Lenn)	.12	.09	.05
621	*Mike Young*(FC)	.25	.20	.10
622	John Stefero	.12	.09	.05
623	*Carmelo Martinez*(FC)	.30	.25	.12
624	Dave Bergman	.12	.09	.05
625	Runnin' Reds (David Green, Willie McGee, Lonnie Smith, Ozzie Smith)	.30	.25	.12
626	Rudy May	.12	.09	.05

		MT	NR MT	EX
627	Matt Keough	.12	.09	.05
628	*Jose DeLeon*(FC)	.80	.60	.30
629	Jim Essian	.12	.09	.05
630	*Darnell Coles*(FC)	.35	.25	.14
631	Mike Warren	.12	.09	.05
632	Del Crandall	.12	.09	.05
633	Dennis Martinez	.12	.09	.05
634	Mike Moore	.12	.09	.05
635	Lary Sorensen	.12	.09	.05
636	Ricky Nelson	.12	.09	.05
637	Omar Moreno	.12	.09	.05
638	Charlie Hough	.15	.11	.06
639	Dennis Eckersley	.25	.20	.10
640	*Walt Terrell*(FC)	.40	.30	.15
641	Denny Walling	.12	.09	.05
642	*Dave Anderson*(FC)	.20	.15	.08
643	*Jose Oquendo*(FC)	.25	.20	.10
644	Bob Stanley	.12	.09	.05
645	Dave Geisel	.12	.09	.05
646	*Scott Garrelts*(FC)	.70	.50	.30
647	*Gary Pettis*(FC)	.40	.30	.15
648	Duke Snider Puzzle Card	.12	.09	.05
649	Johnnie LeMaster	.12	.09	.05
650	Dave Collins	.12	.09	.05
651	San Diego Chicken	.25	.20	.10
---a	Checklist 1-26 DK (Perez-Steel on back)	.12	.09	.05
---b	Checklist 1-26 DK (Perez-Steele on back)	.40	.30	.15
----	Checklist 27-130	.12	.09	.05
----	Checklist 131-234	.12	.09	.05
----	Checklist 235-338	.12	.09	.05
----	Checklist 339-442	.12	.09	.05
----	Checklist 443-546	.12	.09	.05
----	Checklist 547-651	.12	.09	.05
---A	Living Legends (Rollie Fingers, Gaylord Perry)	3.50	2.75	1.50
---B	Living Legends (Johnny Bench, Carl Yastrzemski)	7.00	5.25	2.75

1984 Donruss Action All-Stars

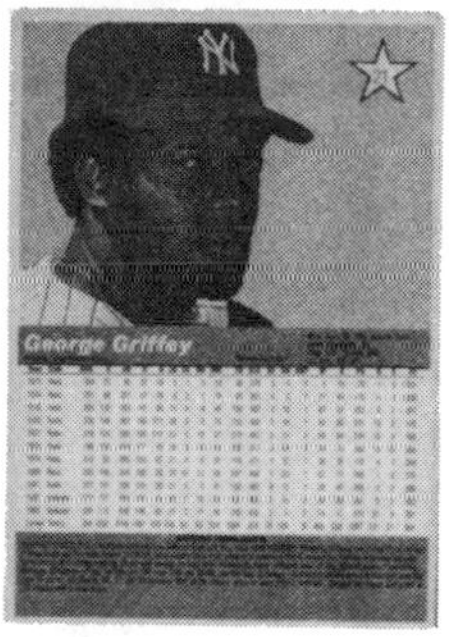

Full-color photos on the card fronts and backs make the 1984 Donruss Action All-Stars set somewhat unusual. The fronts contain a large action photo plus the Donruss logo and year of issue inside a deep red border. The top half of the card backs feature a close-up photo with the bottom portion containing biographical and statistical information. The cards, which measure 3-1/2" by 5", were sold with Ted Williams puzzle pieces.

		MT	NR MT	EX
Complete Set:		9.00	6.75	3.50
Common Player:		.09	.07	.04
1	Gary Lavelle	.09	.07	.04
2	Willie McGee	.15	.11	.06
3	Tony Pena	.09	.07	.04
4	Lou Whitaker	.15	.11	.06
5	Robin Yount	.35	.25	.14
6	Doug DeCinces	.09	.07	.04
7	John Castino	.09	.07	.04
8	Terry Kennedy	.09	.07	.04
9	Rickey Henderson	.50	.40	.20
10	Bob Horner	.12	.09	.05
11	Harold Baines	.15	.11	.06
12	Buddy Bell	.09	.07	.04
13	Fernando Valenzuela	.12	.09	.05
14	Nolan Ryan	2.00	1.50	.80
15	Andre Thornton	.09	.07	.04
16	Gary Redus	.09	.07	.04
17	Pedro Guerrero	.15	.11	.06
18	Andre Dawson	.20	.15	.08
19	Dave Stieb	.12	.09	.05
20	Cal Ripken	.60	.45	.25
21	Ken Griffey	.12	.09	.05
22	Wade Boggs	.70	.50	.30
23	Keith Hernandez	.25	.20	.10
24	Steve Carlton	.30	.25	.12
25	Hal McRae	.12	.09	.05
26	John Lowenstein	.09	.07	.04
27	Fred Lynn	.15	.11	.06
28	Bill Buckner	.09	.07	.04
29	Chris Chambliss	.09	.07	.04
30	Richie Zisk	.09	.07	.04
31	Jack Clark	.15	.11	.06
32	George Hendrick	.09	.07	.04
33	Bill Madlock	.12	.09	.05
34	Lance Parrish	.15	.11	.06
35	Paul Molitor	.15	.11	.06
36	Reggie Jackson	.35	.25	.14
37	Kent Hrbek	.20	.15	.08
38	Steve Garvey	.20	.15	.08
39	Carney Lansford	.09	.07	.04
40	Dale Murphy	.30	.25	.12
41	Greg Luzinski	.12	.09	.05
42	Larry Parrish	.09	.07	.04
43	Ryne Sandberg	.60	.45	.25
44	Dickie Thon	.09	.07	.04
45	Bert Blyleven	.12	.09	.05
46	Ron Oester	.09	.07	.04
47	Dusty Baker	.09	.07	.04
48	Steve Rogers	.09	.07	.04
49	Jim Clancy	.09	.07	.04
50	Eddie Murray	.15	.11	.06
51	Ron Guidry	.15	.11	.06
52	Jim Rice	.15	.11	.06
53	Tom Seaver	.30	.25	.12
54	Pete Rose	.30	.25	.12
55	George Brett	.40	.30	.15
56	Dan Quisenberry	.09	.07	.04
57	Mike Schmidt	.60	.45	.25
58	Ted Simmons	.12	.09	.05
59	Dave Righetti	.15	.11	.06
60	Checklist	.09	.07	.04

1984 Donruss Champions

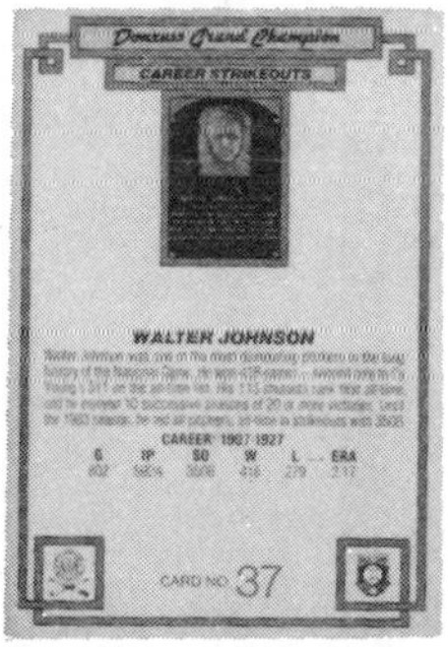

The 60-card Donruss Champions set includes ten Hall of Famers, forty-nine current players and one numbered checklist. The ten Hall of Famers' cards (called Grand Champions) feature the artwork of Dick Perez, while cards of the current players (called Champions) are color photos. The cards measure 3-1/2" by 5". The Grand Champions represent hallmarks of excellence in various statistical categories, while the Champions are the leaders among active players in each category. The ten Grand Champion cards are #'s 1, 8, 14, 20, 26, 31, 37, 43, 50 and 55. The cards were issued with Duke Snider puzzle pieces.

		MT	NR MT	EX
Complete Set:		7.00	5.25	275.00
Common Player:		.07	.05	.03
1	Babe Ruth	1.00	.70	.40
2	George Foster	.10	.08	.04
3	Dave Kingman	.10	.08	.04
4	Jim Rice	.10	.08	.04
5	Gorman Thomas	.10	.08	.04
6	Ben Oglivie	.07	.05	.03
7	Jeff Burroughs	.07	.05	.03
8	Hank Aaron	.35	.25	.14
9	Reggie Jackson	.30	.25	.12
10	Carl Yastrzemski	.50	.40	.20
11	Mike Schmidt	.50	.40	.20
12	Graig Nettles	.14	.11	.06
13	Greg Luzinski	.10	.08	.04
14	Ted Williams	1.00	.70	.40
15	George Brett	.35	.25	.14
16	Wade Boggs	.50	.40	.20
17	Hal McRae	.10	.08	.04
18	Bill Buckner	.10	.08	.04
19	Eddie Murray	.10	.08	.04
20	Rogers Hornsby	.14	.11	.06
21	Rod Carew	.20	.15	.08
22	Bill Madlock	.10	.08	.04
23	Lonnie Smith	.07	.05	.03
24	Cecil Cooper	.10	.08	.04
25	Ken Griffey	.10	.08	.04
26	Ty Cobb	.40	.30	.15
27	Pete Rose	.40	.30	.15
28	Rusty Staub	.10	.08	.04
29	Tony Perez	.10	.08	.04
30	Al Oliver	.10	.08	.04
31	Cy Young	.14	.11	.06
32	Gaylord Perry	.14	.11	.06
33	Ferguson Jenkins	.10	.08	.04
34	Phil Niekro	.14	.11	.06
35	Jim Palmer	.30	.25	.12
36	Tommy John	.10	.08	.04
37	Walter Johnson	.20	.15	.08
38	Steve Carlton	.25	.20	.10
39	Nolan Ryan	.50	.40	.20
40	Tom Seaver	.25	.20	.10
41	Don Sutton	.14	.11	.06
42	Bert Blyleven	.10	.08	.04
43	Frank Robinson	.35	.25	.14
44	Joe Morgan	.25	.20	.10
45	Rollie Fingers	.14	.11	.06
46	Keith Hernandez	.10	.08	.04
47	Robin Yount	.50	.40	.20
48	Cal Ripken	.25	.20	.10
49	Dale Murphy	.35	.25	.14
50	Mickey Mantle	1.00	.70	.40
51	Johnny Bench	.50	.40	.20
52	Carlton Fisk	.30	.25	.12
53	Tug McGraw	.10	.08	.04
54	Paul Molitor	.10	.08	.04
55	Carl Hubbell	.14	.11	.06
56	Steve Garvey	.15	.11	.06
57	Dave Parker	.14	.11	.06
58	Gary Carter	.15	.11	.06
59	Fred Lynn	.14	.11	.06
60	Checklist	.10	.08	.04

1985 Donruss

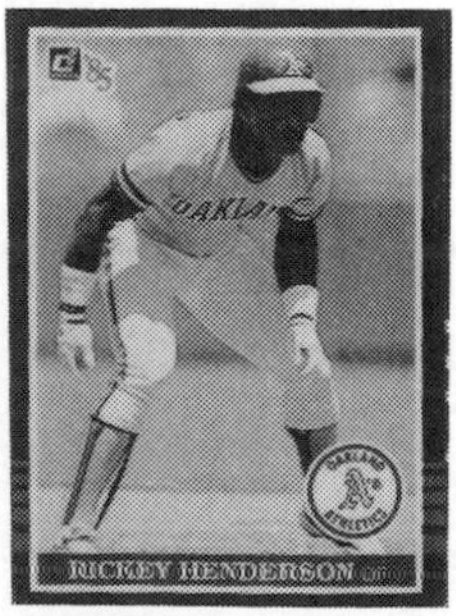

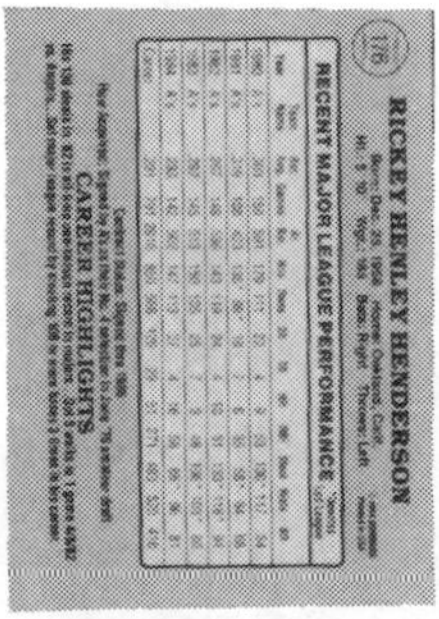

The black-bordered 1985 Donruss set includes 653 numbered cards and seven unnumbered checklists. Displaying the artwork of Dick Perez for the fourth consecutive year, card #'s 1-26 feature the Diamond Kings series. Donruss, realizing the hobby craze over rookie cards, included a Rated Rookies subset (card #'s 27-46). The cards, which are the standard size of 2-1/2" by 3-1/2", were issued with a Lou Gehrig puzzle. The backs of the cards have black print on yellow and white. The complete set price does not include the higher priced variations. (DK) and (RR) refer to the Diamond Kings and Rated Rookies subsets.

		MT	NR MT	EX
Complete Set:		175.00	125.00	70.00
Common Player:		.08	.06	.03
1	Ryne Sandberg (DK)	2.00	1.50	.80
2	Doug DeCinces (DK)	.10	.08	.04
3	Rich Dotson (DK)	.12	.09	.05
4	Bert Blyleven (DK)	.15	.11	.06
5	Lou Whitaker (DK)	.30	.25	.12
6	Dan Quisenberry (DK)	.15	.11	.06
7	Don Mattingly (DK)	4.00	3.00	1.50
8	Carney Lansford (DK)	.10	.08	.04
9	Frank Tanana (DK)	.12	.09	.05
10	Willie Upshaw (DK)	.10	.08	.04
11	Claudell Washington (DK)	.10	.08	.04
12	Mike Marshall (DK)	.20	.15	.08
13	Joaquin Andujar (DK)	.10	.08	.04
14	Cal Ripken, Jr. (DK)	1.00	.70	.40
15	Jim Rice (DK)	.50	.40	.20
16	Don Sutton (DK)	.30	.25	.12
17	Frank Viola (DK)	.15	.11	.06
18	Alvin Davis (DK)(FC)	.60	.45	.25
19	Mario Soto (DK)	.10	.08	.04
20	Jose Cruz (DK)	.12	.09	.05
21	Charlie Lea (DK)	.10	.08	.04
22	Jesse Orosco (DK)	.10	.08	.04
23	Juan Samuel (DK)(FC)	.40	.30	.15
24	Tony Pena (DK)	.12	.09	.05
25	Tony Gwynn (DK)	.50	.40	.20
26	Bob Brenly (DK)	.10	.08	.04
27	*Danny Tartabull (RR)*(FC)	8.00	6.00	3.25
28	*Mike Bielecki (RR)*(FC)	.15	.11	.06
29	*Steve Lyons (RR)*(FC)	.20	.15	.08
30	*Jeff Reed (RR)*(FC)	.15	.11	.06
31	Tony Brewer (RR)	.08	.06	.03
32	*John Morris (RR)*(FC)	.15	.11	.06
33	*Daryl Boston (RR)*(FC)	.25	.20	.10
34	Alfonso Pulido (RR)	.08	.06	.03
35	*Steve Kiefer (RR)*(FC)	.10	.08	.04
36	*Larry Sheets (RR)*(FC)	.50	.40	.20
37	*Scott Bradley (RR)*(FC)	.25	.20	.10
38	*Calvin Schiraldi (RR)*(FC)	.20	.15	.08
39	*Shawon Dunston (RR)*(FC)	5.00	3.75	2.00
40	Charlie Mitchell (RR)	.08	.06	.03
41	*Billy Hatcher (RR)*(FC)	1.25	.90	.50
42	Russ Stephans (RR)	.08	.06	.03
43	Alejandro Sanchez (RR)	.08	.06	.03
44	*Steve Jeltz (RR)*(FC)	.15	.11	.06
45	*Jim Traber (RR)*(FC)	.30	.25	.12
46	Doug Loman (RR)	.08	.06	.03
47	Eddie Murray	1.00	.70	.40
48	Robin Yount	1.25	.90	.50
49	Lance Parrish	.30	.25	.12
50	Jim Rice	.50	.40	.20
51	Dave Winfield	.70	.50	.30
52	Fernando Valenzuela	.35	.25	.14
53	George Brett	.70	.50	.30
54	Dave Kingman	.15	.11	.06
55	Gary Carter	.40	.30	.15
56	Buddy Bell	.12	.09	.05
57	Reggie Jackson	.60	.45	.25
58	Harold Baines	.20	.15	.08
59	Ozzie Smith	.20	.15	.08
60	Nolan Ryan	4.00	3.00	1.50
61	Mike Schmidt	3.00	2.25	1.25
62	Dave Parker	.35	.25	.14
63	Tony Gwynn	2.00	1.50	.80
64	Tony Pena	.12	.09	.05
65	Jack Clark	.25	.20	.10
66	Dale Murphy	.80	.60	.30
67	Ryne Sandberg	6.00	4.50	2.50
68	Keith Hernandez	.40	.30	.15
69	*Alvin Davis*(FC)	3.00	2.25	1.25
70	Kent Hrbek	.30	.25	.12
71	Willie Upshaw	.10	.08	.04
72	Dave Engle	.08	.06	.03
73	Alfredo Griffin	.10	.08	.04
74a	Jack Perconte (last line of highlights begins "Batted .346...")	.10	.08	.04
74b	Jack Perconte (last line of highlights begins "Led the...")	1.25	.90	.50

		MT	NR MT	EX
75	Jesse Orosco	.10	.08	.04
76	Jody Davis	.12	.09	.05
77	Bob Horner	.12	.09	.05
78	Larry McWilliams	.08	.06	.03
79	Joel Youngblood	.08	.06	.03
80	Alan Wiggins	.08	.06	.03
81	Ron Oester	.08	.06	.03
82	Ozzie Virgil	.08	.06	.03
83	*Ricky Horton*(FC)	.35	.25	.14
84	Bill Doran	.12	.09	.05
85	Rod Carew	1.00	.70	.40
86	LaMarr Hoyt	.08	.06	.03
87	Tim Wallach	.15	.11	.06
88	Mike Flanagan	.12	.09	.05
89	Jim Sundberg	.10	.08	.04
90	Chet Lemon	.10	.08	.04
91	Bob Stanley	.08	.06	.03
92	Willie Randolph	.12	.09	.05
93	Bill Russell	.10	.08	.04
94	Julio Franco	.15	.11	.06
95	Dan Quisenberry	.12	.09	.05
96	Bill Caudill	.08	.06	.03
97	Bill Gullickson	.08	.06	.03
98	Danny Darwin	.08	.06	.03
99	Curtis Wilkerson	.08	.06	.03
100	Bud Black	.08	.06	.03
101	Tony Phillips	.08	.06	.03
102	Tony Bernazard	.08	.06	.03
103	Jay Howell	.10	.08	.04
104	Burt Hooton	.10	.08	.04
105	Milt Wilcox	.08	.06	.03
106	Rich Dauer	.08	.06	.03
107	Don Sutton	.35	.25	.14
108	Mike Witt	.15	.11	.06
109	Bruce Sutter	.15	.11	.06
110	Enos Cabell	.08	.06	.03
111	John Denny	.08	.06	.03
112	Dave Dravecky	.10	.08	.04
113	Marvell Wynne	.08	.06	.03
114	Johnnie LeMaster	.08	.06	.03
115	Chuck Porter	.08	.06	.03
116	John Gibbons	.08	.06	.03
117	Keith Moreland	.10	.08	.04
118	Darnell Coles	.12	.09	.05
119	Dennis Lamp	.08	.06	.03
120	Ron Davis	.08	.06	.03
121	Nick Esasky	.10	.08	.04
122	Vance Law	.10	.08	.04
123	Gary Roenicke	.08	.06	.03
124	Bill Schroeder	.08	.06	.03
125	Dave Rozema	.08	.06	.03
126	Bobby Meacham	.08	.06	.03
127	Marty Barrett(FC)	.25	.20	.10
128	*R.J. Reynolds*(FC)	.30	.25	.12
129	Ernie Camacho	.08	.06	.03
130	Jorge Orta	.08	.06	.03
131	Lary Sorensen	.08	.06	.03
132	Terry Francona	.08	.06	.03
133	Fred Lynn	.25	.20	.10
134	Bobby Jones	.08	.06	.03
135	Jerry Hairston	.08	.06	.03
136	Kevin Bass	.12	.09	.05
137	Garry Maddox	.08	.06	.03
138	Dave LaPoint	.10	.08	.04
139	Kevin McReynolds	1.00	.70	.40
140	Wayne Krenchicki	.08	.06	.03
141	Rafael Ramirez	.08	.06	.03
142	Rod Scurry	.08	.06	.03
143	Greg Minton	.08	.06	.03
144	Tim Stoddard	.08	.06	.03
145	Steve Henderson	.08	.06	.03
146	George Bell	.70	.50	.30
147	Dave Meier	.08	.06	.03
148	Sammy Stewart	.08	.06	.03
149	Mark Brouhard	.08	.06	.03
150	Larry Herndon	.10	.08	.04
151	Oil Can Boyd	.10	.08	.04
152	Brian Dayett	.08	.06	.03
153	Tom Niedenfuer	.10	.08	.04
154	Brook Jacoby	.15	.11	.06
155	Onix Concepcion	.08	.06	.03
156	Tim Conroy	.08	.06	.03
157	*Joe Hesketh*(FC)	.15	.11	.06
158	Brian Downing	.12	.09	.05
159	Tommy Dunbar	.08	.06	.03
160	Marc Hill	.08	.06	.03
161	Phil Garner	.10	.08	.04
162	Jerry Davis	.08	.06	.03
163	Bill Campbell	.08	.06	.03
164	*John Franco*(FC)	2.00	1.50	.80
165	Len Barker	.10	.08	.04
166	*Benny Distefano*(FC)	.10	.08	.04

		MT	NR MT	EX
167	George Frazier	.08	.06	.03
168	Tito Landrum	.08	.06	.03
169	Cal Ripken	5.00	3.75	2.00
170	Cecil Cooper	.15	.11	.06
171	Alan Trammell	.40	.30	.15
172	Wade Boggs	5.00	3.75	2.00
173	Don Baylor	.15	.11	.06
174	Pedro Guerrero	.30	.25	.12
175	Frank White	.12	.09	.05
176	Rickey Henderson	5.00	3.75	2.00
177	Charlie Lea	.08	.06	.03
178	Pete O'Brien	.20	.15	.08
179	Doug DeCinces	.12	.09	.05
180	Ron Kittle	.12	.09	.05
181	George Hendrick	.10	.08	.04
182	Joe Niekro	.12	.09	.05
183	Juan Samuel(FC)	.60	.45	.25
184	Mario Soto	.10	.08	.04
185	Goose Gossage	.25	.20	.10
186	Johnny Ray	.15	.11	.06
187	Bob Brenly	.08	.06	.03
188	Craig McMurtry	.08	.06	.03
189	Leon Durham	.10	.08	.04
190	*Dwight Gooden*(FC)	15.00	11.00	6.00
191	Barry Bonnell	.08	.06	.03
192	Tim Teufel	.12	.09	.05
193	Dave Stieb	.15	.11	.06
194	Mickey Hatcher	.08	.06	.03
195	Jesse Barfield	.25	.20	.10
196	Al Cowens	.08	.06	.03
197	Hubie Brooks	.12	.09	.05
198	Steve Trout	.08	.06	.03
199	Glenn Hubbard	.08	.06	.03
200	Bill Madlock	.15	.11	.06
201	*Jeff Robinson*(FC)	.35	.25	.14
202	Eric Show	.10	.08	.04
203	Dave Concepcion	.15	.11	.06
204	Ivan DeJesus	.08	.06	.03
205	Neil Allen	.08	.06	.03
206	Jerry Mumphrey	.08	.06	.03
207	Mike Brown	.08	.06	.03
208	Carlton Fisk	.40	.30	.15
209	Bryn Smith	.08	.06	.03
210	Tippy Martinez	.08	.06	.03
211	Dion James	.10	.08	.04
212	Willie Hernandez	.10	.08	.04
213	Mike Easler	.10	.08	.04
214	Ron Guidry	.30	.25	.12
215	Rick Honeycutt	.08	.06	.03
216	Brett Butler	.12	.09	.05
217	Larry Gura	.08	.06	.03
218	Ray Burris	.08	.06	.03
219	Steve Rogers	.10	.08	.04
220	Frank Tanana	.12	.09	.05
221	Ned Yost	.08	.06	.03
222	*Bret Saberhagen*	8.00	6.00	3.25
223	Mike Davis	.10	.08	.04
224	Bert Blyleven	.15	.11	.06
225	Steve Kemp	.10	.08	.04
226	Jerry Reuss	.10	.08	.04
227	Darrell Evans	.15	.11	.06
228	Wayne Gross	.08	.06	.03
229	Jim Gantner	.10	.08	.04
230	Bob Boone	.10	.08	.04
231	Lonnie Smith	.10	.08	.04
232	Frank DiPino	.08	.06	.03
233	Jerry Koosman	.12	.09	.05
234	Graig Nettles	.20	.15	.08
235	John Tudor	.12	.09	.05
236	John Rabb	.08	.06	.03
237	Rick Manning	.08	.06	.03
238	Mike Fitzgerald	.08	.06	.03
239	Gary Matthews	.12	.09	.05
240	*Jim Presley*(FC)	.50	.40	.20
241	Dave Collins	.10	.08	.04
242	Gary Gaetti	.30	.25	.12
243	Dann Bilardello	.08	.06	.03
244	Rudy Law	.08	.06	.03
245	John Lowenstein	.08	.06	.03
246	Tom Tellmann	.08	.06	.03
247	Howard Johnson	1.75	1.25	.70
248	Ray Fontenot	.08	.06	.03
249	Tony Armas	.12	.09	.05
250	Candy Maldonado	.12	.09	.05
251	*Mike Jeffcoat*(FC)	.10	.08	.04
252	Dane Iorg	.08	.06	.03
253	Bruce Bochte	.08	.06	.03
254	Pete Rose	1.25	.90	.50
255	Don Aase	.08	.06	.03
256	George Wright	.08	.06	.03
257	Britt Burns	.08	.06	.03

		MT	NR MT	EX
258	Mike Scott	.20	.15	.08
259	Len Matuszek	.08	.06	.03
260	Dave Rucker	.08	.06	.03
261	Craig Lefferts	.10	.08	.04
262	*Jay Tibbs*(FC)	.20	.15	.08
263	Bruce Benedict	.08	.06	.03
264	Don Robinson	.10	.08	.04
265	Gary Lavelle	.08	.06	.03
266	Scott Sanderson	.08	.06	.03
267	Matt Young	.08	.06	.03
268	Ernie Whitt	.10	.08	.04
269	Houston Jimenez	.08	.06	.03
270	*Ken Dixon*(FC)	.12	.09	.05
271	Peter Ladd	.08	.06	.03
272	Juan Berenguer	.08	.06	.03
273	*Roger Clemens*(FC)	35.00	27.00	15.00
274	Rick Cerone	.08	.06	.03
275	Dave Anderson	.08	.06	.03
276	George Vukovich	.08	.06	.03
277	Greg Pryor	.08	.06	.03
278	Mike Warren	.08	.06	.03
279	Bob James	.08	.06	.03
280	Bobby Grich	.12	.09	.05
281	*Mike Mason*(FC)	.12	.09	.05
282	Ron Reed	.08	.06	.03
283	Alan Ashby	.08	.06	.03
284	Mark Thurmond	.08	.06	.03
285	Joe Lefebvre	.08	.06	.03
286	Ted Power	.08	.06	.03
287	Chris Chambliss	.10	.08	.04
288	Lee Tunnell	.08	.06	.03
289	Rich Bordi	.08	.06	.03
290	Glenn Brummer	.08	.06	.03
291	Mike Boddicker	.12	.09	.05
292	Rollie Fingers	.25	.20	.10
293	Lou Whitaker	.40	.30	.15
294	Dwight Evans	.15	.11	.06
295	Don Mattingly	12.00	9.00	4.75
296	Mike Marshall	.15	.11	.06
297	Willie Wilson	.15	.11	.06
298	Mike Heath	.08	.06	.03
299	Tim Raines	.50	.40	.20
300	Larry Parrish	.12	.09	.05
301	Geoff Zahn	.08	.06	.03
302	Rich Dotson	.12	.09	.05
303	David Green	.08	.06	.03
304	Jose Cruz	.12	.09	.05
305	Steve Carlton	.50	.40	.20
306	Gary Redus	.10	.08	.04
307	Steve Garvey	.50	.40	.20
308	Jose DeLeon	.10	.08	.04
309	Randy Lerch	.08	.06	.03
310	Claudell Washington	.10	.08	.04
311	Lee Smith	.12	.09	.05
312	Darryl Strawberry	12.00	9.00	4.75
313	Jim Beattie	.08	.06	.03
314	John Butcher	.08	.06	.03
315	Damaso Garcia	.10	.08	.04
316	Mike Smithson	.08	.06	.03
317	Luis Leal	.08	.06	.03
318	Ken Phelps(FC)	.25	.20	.10
319	Wally Backman	.10	.08	.04
320	Ron Cey	.12	.09	.05
321	Brad Komminsk	.08	.06	.03
322	Jason Thompson	.08	.06	.03
323	*Frank Williams*(FC)	.20	.15	.08
324	Tim Lollar	.08	.06	.03
325	*Eric Davis*(FC)	15.00	11.00	6.00
326	Von Hayes	.12	.09	.05
327	Andy Van Slyke	.40	.30	.15
328	Craig Reynolds	.08	.06	.03
329	Dick Schofield	.10	.08	.04
330	Scott Fletcher	.10	.08	.04
331	Jeff Reardon	.15	.11	.06
332	Rick Dempsey	.10	.08	.04
333	Ben Oglivie	.10	.08	.04
334	Dan Petry	.10	.08	.04
335	Jackie Gutierrez	.08	.06	.03
336	Dave Righetti	.25	.20	.10
337	Alejandro Pena	.10	.08	.04
338	Mel Hall	.10	.08	.04
339	Pat Sheridan	.08	.06	.03
340	Keith Atherton	.08	.06	.03
341	David Palmer	.08	.06	.03
342	Gary Ward	.10	.08	.04
343	Dave Stewart	.15	.11	.06
344	*Mark Gubicza*(FC)	2.00	1.50	.80
345	Carney Lansford	.12	.09	.05
346	Jerry Willard	.08	.06	.03
347	Ken Griffey	.12	.09	.05
348	*Franklin Stubbs*(FC)	.60	.45	.25

		MT	NR MT	EX
349	Aurelio Lopez	.08	.06	.03
350	Al Bumbry	.10	.08	.04
351	Charlie Moore	.08	.06	.03
352	Luis Sanchez	.08	.06	.03
353	Darrell Porter	.10	.08	.04
354	Bill Dawley	.08	.06	.03
355	Charlie Hudson	.10	.08	.04
356	Garry Templeton	.10	.08	.04
357	Cecilio Guante	.08	.06	.03
358	Jeff Leonard	.12	.09	.05
359	Paul Molitor	.20	.15	.08
360	Ron Gardenhire	.08	.06	.03
361	Larry Bowa	.12	.09	.05
362	Bob Kearney	.08	.06	.03
363	Garth Iorg	.08	.06	.03
364	Tom Brunansky	.15	.11	.06
365	Brad Gulden	.08	.06	.03
366	Greg Walker	.12	.09	.05
367	Mike Young	.10	.08	.04
368	Rick Waits	.08	.06	.03
369	Doug Bair	.08	.06	.03
370	Bob Shirley	.08	.06	.03
371	Bob Ojeda	.12	.09	.05
372	Bob Welch	.15	.11	.06
373	Neal Heaton	.08	.06	.03
374	Danny Jackson (photo actually Steve Farr)	.80	.60	.30
375	Donnie Hill	.08	.06	.03
376	Mike Stenhouse	.08	.06	.03
377	Bruce Kison	.08	.06	.03
378	Wayne Tolleson	.08	.06	.03
379	Floyd Bannister	.12	.09	.05
380	Vern Ruhle	.08	.06	.03
381	Tim Corcoran	.08	.06	.03
382	Kurt Kepshire	.08	.06	.03
383	Bobby Brown	.08	.06	.03
384	Dave Van Gorder	.08	.06	.03
385	Rick Mahler	.08	.06	.03
386	Lee Mazzilli	.10	.08	.04
387	Bill Laskey	.08	.06	.03
388	Thad Bosley	.08	.06	.03
389	Al Chambers	.08	.06	.03
390	Tony Fernandez	.70	.50	.30
391	Ron Washington	.08	.06	.03
392	Bill Swaggerty	.08	.06	.03
393	Bob Gibson	.08	.06	.03
394	Marty Castillo	.08	.06	.03
395	Steve Crawford	.08	.06	.03
396	Clay Christiansen	.08	.06	.03
397	Bob Bailor	.08	.06	.03
398	Mike Hargrove	.08	.06	.03
399	Charlie Leibrandt	.10	.08	.04
400	Tom Burgmeier	.08	.06	.03
401	Razor Shines	.08	.06	.03
402	Rob Wilfong	.08	.06	.03
403	Tom Henke	.12	.09	.05
404	Al Jones	.08	.06	.03
405	Mike LaCoss	.08	.06	.03
406	Luis DeLeon	.08	.06	.03
407	Greg Gross	.08	.06	.03
408	Tom Hume	.08	.06	.03
409	Rick Camp	.08	.06	.03
410	Milt May	.08	.06	.03
411	*Henry Cotto*(FC)	.20	.15	.08
412	Dave Von Ohlen	.08	.06	.03
413	Scott McGregor	.10	.08	.04
414	Ted Simmons	.15	.11	.06
415	Jack Morris	.30	.25	.12
416	Bill Buckner	.15	.11	.06
417	Butch Wynegar	.08	.06	.03
418	Steve Sax	.25	.20	.10
419	Steve Balboni	.10	.08	.04
420	Dwayne Murphy	.10	.08	.04
421	Andre Dawson	.70	.50	.30
422	Charlie Hough	.10	.08	.04
423	Tommy John	.25	.20	.10
424a	Tom Seaver (Floyd Bannister photo — throwing left)	1.00	.70	.40
424b	Tom Seaver (correct photo - throwing right)	15.00	11.00	6.00
425	Tom Herr	.12	.09	.05
426	Terry Puhl	.08	.06	.03
427	Al Holland	.08	.06	.03
428	Eddie Milner	.08	.06	.03
429	Terry Kennedy	.10	.08	.04
430	John Candelaria	.12	.09	.05
431	Manny Trillo	.10	.08	.04
432	Ken Oberkfell	.08	.06	.03
433	Rick Sutcliffe	.15	.11	.06
434	Ron Darling	.70	.50	.30
435	Spike Owen	.10	.08	.04

		MT	NR MT	EX
436	Frank Viola	.25	.20	.10
437	Lloyd Moseby	.12	.09	.05
438	*Kirby Puckett*(FC)	25.00	20.00	10.00
439	Jim Clancy	.10	.08	.04
440	Mike Moore	.08	.06	.03
441	Doug Sisk	.08	.06	.03
442	Dennis Eckersley	.15	.11	.06
443	Gerald Perry	.25	.20	.10
444	Dale Berra	.08	.06	.03
445	Dusty Baker	.10	.08	.04
446	Ed Whitson	.08	.06	.03
447	Cesar Cedeno	.12	.09	.05
448	*Rick Schu*(FC)	.20	.15	.08
449	Joaquin Andujar	.10	.08	.04
450	*Mark Bailey*(FC)	.12	.09	.05
451	*Ron Romanick*(FC)	.12	.09	.05
452	Julio Cruz	.08	.06	.03
453	Miguel Dilone	.08	.06	.03
454	Storm Davis	.12	.09	.05
455	Jaime Cocanower	.08	.06	.03
456	Barbaro Garbey	.12	.09	.05
457	Rich Gedman	.12	.09	.05
458	Phil Niekro	.30	.25	.12
459	Mike Scioscia	.10	.08	.04
460	Pat Tabler	.10	.08	.04
461	Darryl Motley	.08	.06	.03
462	Chris Codoroli (Codiroli)	.08	.06	.03
463	Doug Flynn	.08	.06	.03
464	Billy Sample	.08	.06	.03
465	Mickey Rivers	.10	.08	.04
466	John Wathan	.10	.08	.04
467	Bill Krueger	.08	.06	.03
468	Andre Thornton	.12	.09	.05
469	Rex Hudler	.12	.09	.05
470	*Sid Bream*(FC)	.80	.60	.30
471	Kirk Gibson	.40	.30	.15
472	John Shelby	.10	.08	.04
473	Moose Haas	.08	.06	.03
474	Doug Corbett	.08	.06	.03
475	Willie McGee	.35	.25	.14
476	Bob Knepper	.10	.08	.04
477	Kevin Gross	.12	.09	.05
478	Carmelo Martinez	.10	.08	.04
479	Kent Tekulve	.10	.08	.04
480	Chili Davis	.12	.09	.05
481	Bobby Clark	.08	.06	.03
482	Mookie Wilson	.12	.09	.05
483	Dave Owen	.08	.06	.03
484	Ed Nunez	.08	.06	.03
485	Rance Mulliniks	.08	.06	.03
486	Ken Schrom	.08	.06	.03
487	Jeff Russell	.08	.06	.03
488	Tom Paciorek	.08	.06	.03
489	Dan Ford	.08	.06	.03
490	Mike Caldwell	.08	.06	.03
491	Scottie Earl	.08	.06	.03
492	*Jose Rijo*(FC)	2.00	1.50	.80
493	Bruce Hurst	.15	.11	.06
494	Ken Landreaux	.08	.06	.03
495	Mike Fischlin	.08	.06	.03
496	Don Slaught	.08	.06	.03
497	Steve McCatty	.08	.06	.03
498	Gary Lucas	.08	.06	.03
499	Gary Pettis	.10	.08	.04
500	Marvis Foley	.08	.06	.03
501	Mike Squires	.08	.06	.03
502	*Jim Pankovitz*(FC)	.15	.11	.06
503	Luis Aguayo	.08	.06	.03
504	Ralph Citarella	.08	.06	.03
505	Bruce Bochy	.08	.06	.03
506	Bob Owchinko	.08	.06	.03
507	Pascual Perez	.10	.08	.04
508	Lee Lacy	.08	.06	.03
509	Atlee Hammaker	.08	.06	.03
510	Bob Dernier	.08	.06	.03
511	Ed Vande Berg	.08	.06	.03
512	Cliff Johnson	.08	.06	.03
513	Len Whitehouse	.08	.06	.03
514	Dennis Martinez	.10	.08	.04
515	Ed Romero	.08	.06	.03
516	Rusty Kuntz	.08	.06	.03
517	Rick Miller	.08	.06	.03
518	Dennis Rasmussen	.15	.11	.06
519	Steve Yeager	.08	.06	.03
520	Chris Bando	.08	.06	.03
521	U.L. Washington	.08	.06	.03
522	*Curt Young*(FC)	.40	.30	.15
523	Angel Salazar	.08	.06	.03
524	Curt Kaufman	.08	.06	.03
525	Odell Jones	.08	.06	.03
526	Juan Agosto	.08	.06	.03

		MT	NR MT	EX
527	Denny Walling	.08	.06	.03
528	Andy Hawkins(FC)	.20	.15	.08
529	Sixto Lezcano	.08	.06	.03
530	Skeeter Barnes	.08	.06	.03
531	Randy Johnson	.08	.06	.03
532	Jim Morrison	.08	.06	.03
533	Warren Brusstar	.08	.06	.03
534a	*Jeff Pendleton* (first name incorrect)(FC)	1.50	1.25	.60
534b	*Terry Pendleton* (first name correct)(FC)	5.00	3.75	2.00
535	Vic Rodriguez	.08	.06	.03
536	Bob McClure	.08	.06	.03
537	Dave Bergman	.08	.06	.03
538	Mark Clear	.08	.06	.03
539	*Mike Pagliarulo*(FC)	1.00	.70	.40
540	Terry Whitfield	.08	.06	.03
541	Joe Beckwith	.08	.06	.03
542	Jeff Burroughs	.10	.08	.04
543	Dan Schatzeder	.08	.06	.03
544	Donnie Scott	.08	.06	.03
545	Jim Slaton	.08	.06	.03
546	Greg Luzinski	.12	.09	.05
547	*Mark Salas*(FC)	.15	.11	.06
548	Dave Smith	.10	.08	.04
549	John Wockenfuss	.08	.06	.03
550	Frank Pastore	.08	.06	.03
551	Tim Flannery	.08	.06	.03
552	Rick Rhoden	.12	.09	.05
553	Mark Davis	.08	.06	.03
554	*Jeff Dedmon*(FC)	.15	.11	.06
555	Gary Woods	.08	.06	.03
556	Danny Heep	.08	.06	.03
557	*Mark Langston*(FC)	5.00	3.75	2.00
558	Darrell Brown	.08	.06	.03
559	*Jimmy Key*(FC)	2.00	1.50	.80
560	Rick Lysander	.08	.06	.03
561	Doyle Alexander	.12	.09	.05
562	Mike Stanton	.08	.06	.03
563	Sid Fernandez	.50	.40	.20
564	Richie Hebner	.08	.06	.03
565	Alex Trevino	.08	.06	.03
566	Brian Harper	.08	.06	.03
567	*Dan Gladden*(FC)	.60	.45	.25
568	Luis Salazar	.08	.06	.03
569	Tom Foley	.08	.06	.03
570	Larry Andersen	.08	.06	.03
571	Danny Cox	.12	.09	.05
572	Joe Sambito	.08	.06	.03
573	Juan Beniquez	.08	.06	.03
574	Joel Skinner	.08	.06	.03
575	*Randy St. Claire*(FC)	.15	.11	.06
576	Floyd Rayford	.08	.06	.03
577	Roy Howell	.08	.06	.03
578	John Grubb	.08	.06	.03
579	Ed Jurak	.08	.06	.03
580	John Montefusco	.08	.06	.03
581	*Orel Hershiser*(FC)	6.00	4.50	2.50
582	*Tom Waddell*(FC)	.08	.06	.03
583	Mark Huismann	.08	.06	.03
584	Joe Morgan	.30	.25	.12
585	Jim Wohlford	.08	.06	.03
586	Dave Schmidt	.08	.06	.03
587	*Jeff Kunkel*(FC)	.12	.09	.05
588	Hal McRae	.12	.09	.05
589	Bill Almon	.08	.06	.03
590	Carmen Castillo(FC)	.10	.08	.04
591	Omar Moreno	.08	.06	.03
592	*Ken Howell*(FC)	.20	.15	.08
593	Tom Brookens	.08	.06	.03
594	Joe Nolan	.08	.06	.03
595	Willie Lozado	.08	.06	.03
596	*Tom Nieto*(FC)	.12	.09	.05
597	Walt Terrell	.10	.08	.04
598	Al Oliver	.15	.11	.06
599	Shane Rawley	.12	.09	.05
600	*Denny Gonzalez*(FC)	.10	.08	.04
601	*Mark Grant*(FC)	.15	.11	.06
602	Mike Armstrong	.08	.06	.03
603	George Foster	.15	.11	.06
604	Davey Lopes	.10	.08	.04
605	Salome Barojas	.08	.06	.03
606	Roy Lee Jackson	.08	.06	.03
607	Pete Filson	.08	.06	.03
608	Duane Walker	.08	.06	.03
609	Glenn Wilson	.10	.08	.04
610	*Rafael Santana*(FC)	.20	.15	.08
611	Roy Smith	.08	.06	.03
612	Ruppert Jones	.08	.06	.03
613	Joe Cowley(FC)	.08	.06	.03
614	*Al Nipper* (photo actually Mike Brown)(FC)	.20	.15	.08

		MT	NR MT	EX
615	Gene Nelson	.08	.06	.03
616	Joe Carter	5.00	3.75	2.00
617	Ray Knight	.12	.09	.05
618	Chuck Rainey	.08	.06	.03
619	Dan Driessen	.10	.08	.04
620	Daryl Sconiers	.08	.06	.03
621	Bill Stein	.08	.06	.03
622	Roy Smalley	.08	.06	.03
623	Ed Lynch	.08	.06	.03
624	*Jeff Stone*(FC)	.15	.11	.06
625	Bruce Berenyi	.08	.06	.03
626	Kelvin Chapman	.08	.06	.03
627	Joe Price	.08	.06	.03
628	Steve Bedrosian	.12	.09	.05
629	Vic Mata	.08	.06	.03
630	Mike Krukow	.10	.08	.04
631	*Phil Bradley*(FC)	.90	.70	.35
632	Jim Gott	.08	.06	.03
633	Randy Bush	.08	.06	.03
634	*Tom Browning*(FC)	2.00	1.50	.80
635	Lou Gehrig Puzzle Card	.08	.06	.03
636	Reid Nichols	.08	.06	.03
637	*Dan Pasqua*(FC)	.60	.45	.25
638	German Rivera	.08	.06	.03
639	*Don Schulze*(FC)	.10	.08	.04
640a	Mike Jones (last line of highlights begins "Was 11-7...")	.10	.08	.04
640b	Mike Jones (last line of highlights begins "Spent some ...")	1.25	.90	.50
641	Pete Rose	1.25	.90	.50
642	*Wade Rowdon*(FC)	.10	.08	.04
643	Jerry Narron	.08	.06	.03
644	*Darrell Miller*(FC)	.15	.11	.06
645	*Tim Hulett*(FC)	.15	.11	.06
646	Andy McGaffigan	.08	.06	.03
647	Kurt Bevacqua	.08	.06	.03
648	*John Russell*(FC)	.20	.15	.08
649	*Ron Robinson*(FC)	.25	.20	.10
650	Donnie Moore(FC)	.08	.06	.03
651a	Two for the Title (Don Mattingly, Dave Winfield) (player names in yellow)	8.00	6.00	3.25
651b	Two for the Title (Don Mattingly, Dave Winfield) (player names in white)	6.00	4.50	2.50
652	Tim Laudner	.08	.06	.03
653	*Steve Farr*(FC)	.40	.30	.15
----	Checklist 1-26 DK	.08	.06	.03
----	Checklist 27-130	.08	.06	.03
----	Checklist 131-234	.08	.06	.03
----	Checklist 235-338	.08	.06	.03
----	Checklist 339-442	.08	.06	.03
----	Checklist 443-546	.08	.06	.03
----	Checklist 547-653	.08	.06	.03

1985 Donruss Action All-Stars

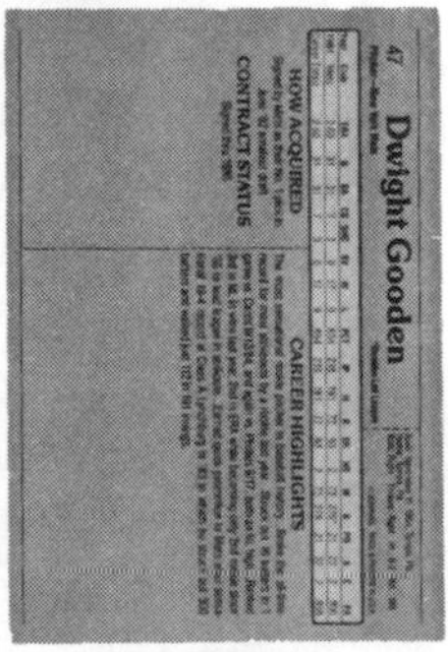

In 1985, Donruss issued an Action All-Stars set for the third consecutive year. The card fronts feature an action photo with an inset head-shot of the player inside a black border with grey boxes through it. The card backs have black print on blue and white and include statistical and biographical information. The cards were issued with a Lou Gehrig puzzle.

	MT	NR MT	EX
Complete Set:	8.00	6.00	3.25
Common Player:	.09	.07	.04

1	Tim Raines	.25	.20	.10
2	Jim Gantner	.09	.07	.04
3	Mario Soto	.09	.07	.04
4	Spike Owen	.09	.07	.04
5	Lloyd Moseby	.09	.07	.04
6	Damaso Garcia	.09	.07	.04
7	Cal Ripken	.60	.45	.25
8	Dan Quisenberry	.09	.07	.04
9	Eddie Murray	.12	.09	.05
10	Tony Pena	.09	.07	.04
11	Buddy Bell	.09	.07	.04
12	Dave Winfield	.30	.25	.12
13	Ron Kittle	.12	.09	.05
14	Rich Gossage	.12	.09	.05
15	Dwight Evans	.15	.11	.06
16	Al Davis	.15	.11	.06
17	Mike Schmidt	.40	.30	.15
18	Pascual Perez	.09	.07	.04
19	Tony Gwynn	.30	.25	.12
20	Nolan Ryan	1.25	.90	.50
21	Robin Yount	.50	.40	.20
22	Mike Marshall	.12	.09	.05
23	Brett Butler	.09	.07	.04
24	Ryne Sandberg	.50	.40	.20
25	Dale Murphy	.40	.30	.15
26	George Brett	.40	.30	.15
27	Jim Rice	.15	.11	.06
28	Ozzie Smith	.15	.11	.06
29	Larry Parrish	.09	.07	.04
30	Jack Clark	.15	.11	.06
31	Manny Trillo	.09	.07	.04
32	Dave Kingman	.12	.09	.05
33	Geoff Zahn	.09	.07	.04
34	Pedro Guerrero	.15	.11	.06
35	Dave Parker	.20	.15	.08
36	Rollie Fingers	.15	.11	.06
37	Fernando Valenzuela	.12	.09	.05
38	Wade Boggs	.60	.45	.25
39	Reggie Jackson	.30	.25	.12
40	Kent Hrbek	.20	.15	.08
41	Keith Hernandez	.25	.20	.10
42	Lou Whitaker	.15	.11	.06
43	Tom Herr	.09	.07	.04
44	Alan Trammell	.20	.15	.08
45	Butch Wynegar	.09	.07	.04
46	Leon Durham	.09	.07	.04
47	Dwight Gooden	.80	.60	.30
48	Don Mattingly	1.00	.70	.40
49	Phil Niekro	.20	.15	.08
50	Johnny Ray	.09	.07	.04
51	Doug DeCinces	.09	.07	.04
52	Willie Upshaw	.09	.07	.04
53	Lance Parrish	.15	.11	.06
54	Jody Davis	.09	.07	.04
55	Steve Carlton	.30	.25	.12
56	Juan Samuel	.09	.07	.04
57	Gary Carter	.12	.09	.05
58	Harold Baines	.15	.11	.06
59	Eric Show	.09	.07	.04
60	Checklist	.09	.07	.04

1985 Donruss Box Panels

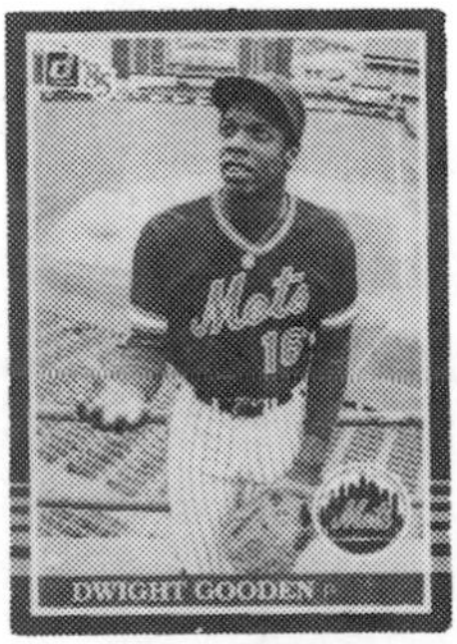

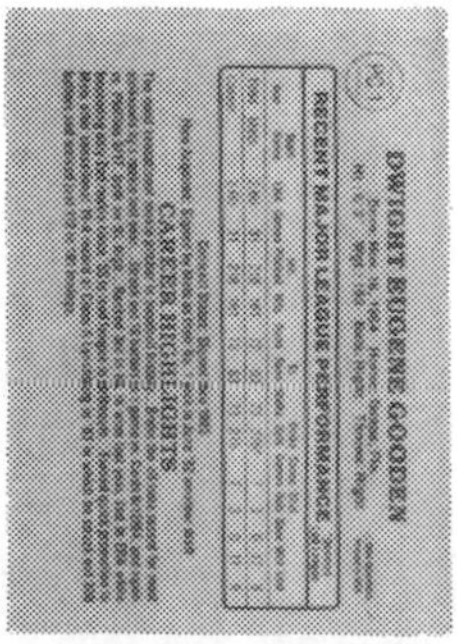

In 1985, Donruss placed on the bottoms of their wax pack boxes a four-card panel which included three player cards and a Lou Gehrig puzzle card. The player cards, numbered PC 1 through PC 3, have backs identical to the regular 1985 Donruss issue. The card fronts are identical in design to the regular

issue, but carry different picture poses.

		MT	NR MT	EX
Complete Panel Set:		7.00	5.25	2.75
Complete Singles Set:		5.00	3.75	2.00
Common Single Player:		.10	.08	.04
	Panel	7.00	5.25	2.75
1	Dwight Gooden	3.00	2.25	1.25
2	Ryne Sanberg	2.00	1.50	.80
3	Ron Kittle	.10	.08	.04
---	Lou Gehrig Puzzle Card	.05	.04	.02

1985 Donruss Diamond Kings Supers

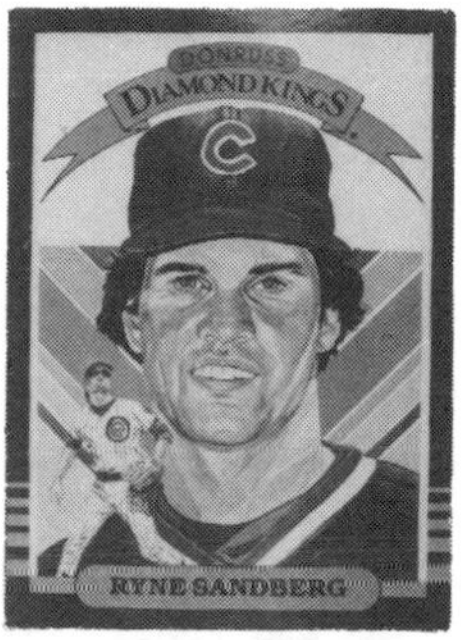

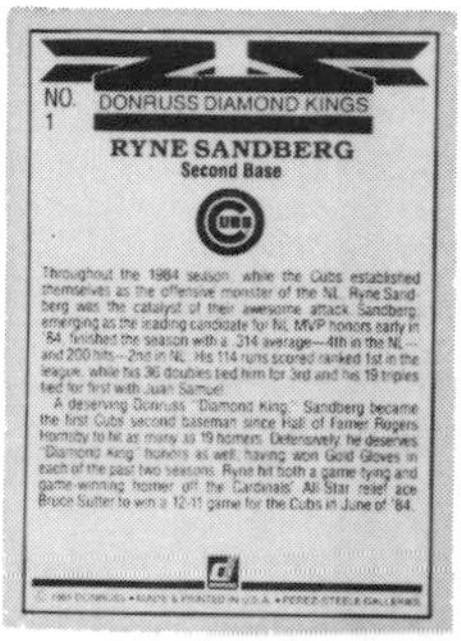

The 1985 Donruss Diamond Kings Supers are enlarged versions of the Diamond Kings card (#'s 1-26) in the regular 1985 Donruss set. The cards measure 4-15/16" by 6-3/4". The Diamond Kings series features the artwork of Dick Perez. Twenty-eight cards make up the set - 26 DK cards, an unnumbered checklist, and an unnumbered Dick Perez card. The back of the Perez card contains a brief history of Dick Perez and the Perez-Steele Galleries. The set could be obtained through a write-in offer found on the wrappers of the regular issue wax packs.

		MT	NR MT	EX
Complete Set:		15.00	11.00	6.00
Common Player:		.20	.15	.08
1	Ryne Sandberg	2.00	1.50	.80
2	Doug DeCinces	.20	.15	.08
3	Richard Dotson	.20	.15	.08
4	Bert Blyleven	.25	.20	.10
5	Lou Whitaker	.30	.25	.12
6	Dan Quisenberry	.20	.15	.08
7	Don Mattingly	3.00	2.25	1.25
8	Carney Lansford	.20	.15	.08
9	Frank Tanana	.20	.15	.08
10	Willie Upshaw	.20	.15	.08
11	Claudell Washington	.20	.15	.08
12	Mike Marshall	.25	.20	.10
13	Joaquin Andujar	.20	.15	.08
14	Cal Ripken, Jr.	2.00	1.50	.80
15	Jim Rice	.35	.25	.14
16	Don Sutton	.30	.25	.12
17	Frank Viola	.35	.25	.14
18	Alvin Davis	.30	.25	.12
19	Mario Soto	.20	.15	.08
20	Jose Cruz	.20	.15	.08
21	Charlie Lea	.20	.15	.08
22	Jesse Orosco	.20	.15	.08
23	Juan Samuel	.20	.15	.08
24	Tony Pena	.20	.15	.08
25	Tony Gwynn	.40	.30	.15
26	Bob Brenly	.20	.15	.08
---	Checklist	.12	.09	.05
---	Dick Perez (DK artist)	.12	.09	.05

NOTE: A card number in parentheses ( ) indicates the set is unnumbered.

1985 Donruss Highlights

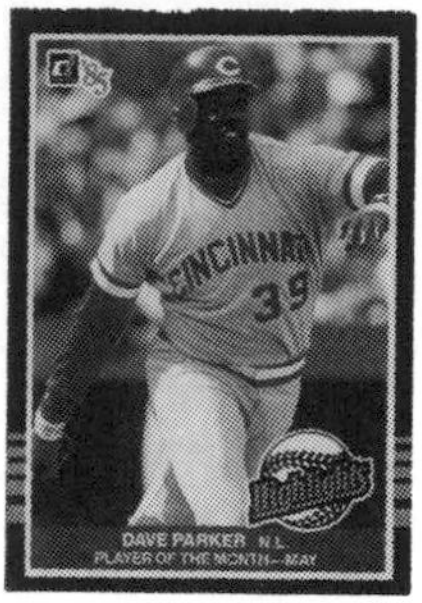

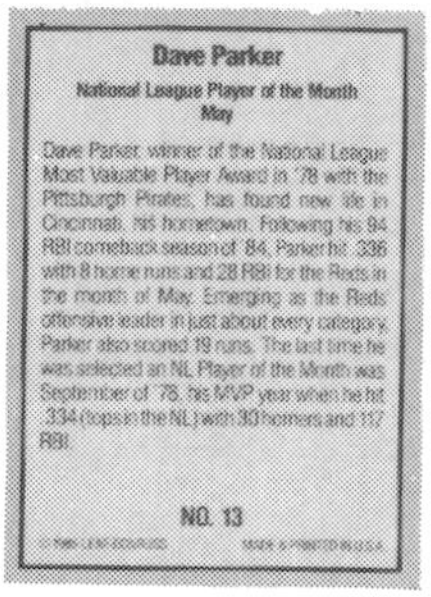

Designed in the style of the regular 1985 Donruss set, this issue features the Player of the Month in the major leagues plus highlight cards of special baseball events and milestones that occurred during the 1985 season. Fifty-six cards, including an unnumbered checklist, comprise the set which was available only through hobby dealers. The cards measure 2-1/2" by 3-1/2" and have glossy fronts. The last two cards in the set feature Donruss' picks for the A.L. and N.L. Rookies of the Year. The set was issued in a specially designed box.

		MT	NR MT	EX
Complete Set:		30.00	22.00	12.00
Common Player:		.12	.09	.05
1	Sets Opening Day Record (Tom Seaver)	.40	.30	.15
2	Establishes A.L. Save Mark (Rollie Fingers)	.15	.11	.06
3	A.L. Player of the Month - April (Mike Davis)	.12	.09	.05
4	A.L. Pitcher of the Month - April (Charlie Leibrandt)	.12	.09	.05
5	N.L. Player of the Month - April (Dale Murphy)	.40	.30	.15
6	N.L. Pitcher of the Month - April (Fernando Valenzuela)	.12	.09	.05
7	N.L. Shortstop Record (Larry Bowa)	.12	.09	.05
8	Joins Reds 2000 Hit Club (Dave Concepcion)	.12	.09	.05
9	Eldest Grand Slammer (Tony Perez)	.15	.11	.06
10	N.L. Career Run Leader (Pete Rose)	1.25	.90	.50
11	A.L. Player of the Month - May (George Brett)	.90	.70	.35
12	A.L. Pitcher of the Month - May (Dave Stieb)	.12	.09	.05
13	N.L. Player of the Month - May (Dave Parker)	.20	.15	.08
14	N.L. Pitcher of the Month - May (Andy Hawkins)	.12	.09	.05
15	Records 11th Straight Win (Andy Hawkins)	.12	.09	.05
16	Two Homers In First Inning (Von Hayes)	.15	.11	.06
17	A.L. Player of the Month - June (Rickey Henderson)	1.00	.70	.40
18	A.L. Pitcher of the Month - June (Jay Howell)	.12	.09	.05
19	N.L. Player of the Month - June (Pedro Guerrero)	.20	.15	.08
20	N.L. Pitcher of the Month - June (John Tudor)	.12	.09	.05
21	Marathon Game Iron Men (Gary Carter, Keith Hernandez)	.35	.25	.14
22	Records 4000th K (Nolan Ryan)	1.25	.90	.50
23	All-Star Game MVP (LaMarr Hoyt)	.12	.09	.05
24	1st Ranger To Hit For Cycle (Oddibe McDowell)	.40	.30	.15
25	A.L. Player of the Month - July (George Brett)	.90	.70	.35
26	A.L. Pitcher of the Month - July (Bret Saberhagen)	1.50	1.25	.60
27	N.L. Player of the Month - July (Keith Hernandez)	.35	.25	.14

		MT	NR MT	EX
28	N.L. Pitcher of the Month - July (Fernando Valenzuela)	.12	.09	.05
29	Record Setting Base Stealers (Vince Coleman, Willie McGee)	.80	.60	.30
30	Notches 300th Career Win (Tom Seaver)	.35	.25	.14
31	Strokes 3000th Hit (Rod Carew)	.40	.30	.15
32	Establishes Met Record (Dwight Gooden)	2.25	1.75	.90
33	Achieves Strikeout Milestone (Dwight Gooden)	2.25	1.75	.90
34	Explodes For 9 RBI (Eddie Murray)	.70	.50	.30
35	A.L. Career Hbp Leader (Don Baylor)	.15	.11	.06
36	A.L. Player of the Month - August (Don Mattingly)	3.25	2.50	1.25
37	A.L. Pitcher of the Month - August (Dave Righetti)	.20	.15	.08
38	N.L. Player of the Month (Willie McGee)	.20	.15	.08
39	N.L. Pitcher of the Month - August (Shane Rawley)	.12	.09	.05
40	Ty-Breaking Hit (Pete Rose)	.90	.70	.35
41	Hits 3 Hrs Drives In 8 Runs (Andre Dawson)	.20	.15	.08
42	Sets Yankee Theft Mark (Rickey Henderson)	1.00	.70	.40
43	20 Wins In Rookie Season (Tom Browning)	.35	.25	.14
44	Yankee Milestone For Hits (Don Mattingly)	3.25	2.50	1.25
45	A.L. Player of the Month - September (Don Mattingly)	3.25	2.50	1.25
46	A.L. Pitcher of the Month - September (Charlie Leibrandt)	.12	.09	.05
47	N.L. Player of the Month - September (Gary Carter)	.12	.09	.05
48	N.L. Pitcher of the Month - September (Dwight Gooden)	2.25	1.75	.90
49	Major League Record Setter (Wade Boggs)	2.00	1.50	.80
50	Hurls Shutout For 300th Win (Phil Niekro)	.30	.25	.12
51	Venerable HR King (Darrell Evans)	.15	.11	.06
52	N.L. Switch-hitting Record (Willie McGee)	.20	.15	.08
53	Equals DiMaggio Feat (Dave Winfield)	.30	.25	.12
54	Donruss N.L. Rookie of the Year (Vince Coleman)	2.25	1.75	.90
55	Donruss A.L. Rookie of the Year (Ozzie Guillen)	.50	.40	.20
----	Checklist	.20	.15	.08

1985 Donruss Sluggers of the Hall of Fame

In much the same manner as the first Bazooka cards were issued in 1959, this eight-player set from Donruss consists of cards which formed the bottom panel of a box of bubble gum. When cut off the box, cards measure 3-1/2" by 6-1/2", with blank backs. Players are pictured on the cards in paintings done by Dick Perez.

		MT	NR MT	EX
Complete Set:		12.00	9.00	4.75
Common Player:		.60	.45	.25
1	Babe Ruth	2.00	1.50	.80
2	Ted Williams	1.00	.70	.40
3	Lou Gehrig	1.75	1.25	.70
4	Johnny Mize	.60	.45	.25
5	Stan Musial	1.00	.70	.40
6	Mickey Mantle	3.00	2.25	1.25
7	Hank Aaron	2.00	1.50	.80
8	Frank Robinson	.90	.70	.35

1986 Donruss

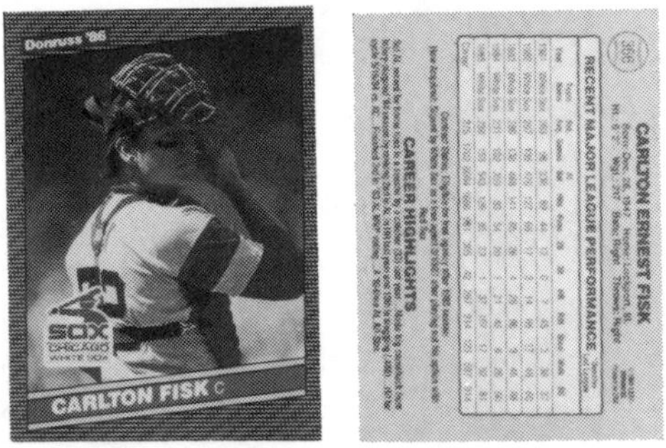

In 1986, Donruss issued a 660-card set which included 653 numbered cards and seven unnumbered checklists. The cards, which measure 2-1/2" by 3-1/2", have fronts that feature blue borders and backs that have black print on blue and white. For the fifth year in a row, the first 26 cards in the set are Diamond Kings. The Rated Rookies subset (card #'s 27-46) appears once again. The cards were distributed with a Hank Aaron puzzle. The complete set price does not include the higher priced variations. In the checklist that follows, (DK) and (RR) refer to the Diamond Kings and Rated Rookies series.

		MT	NR MT	EX
Complete Set:		200.00	150.00	80.00
Common Player:		.06	.05	.02
1	Kirk Gibson (DK)	.30	.25	.12
2	Goose Gossage (DK)	.20	.15	.08
3	Willie McGee (DK)	.15	.11	.06
4	George Bell (DK)	.30	.25	.12
5	Tony Armas (DK)	.10	.08	.04
6	Chili Davis (DK)	.10	.08	.04
7	Cecil Cooper (DK)	.12	.09	.05
8	Mike Boddicker (DK)	.10	.08	.04
9	Davey Lopes (DK)	.10	.08	.04
10	Bill Doran (DK)	.12	.09	.05
11	Bret Saberhagen (DK)	.25	.20	.10
12	Brett Butler (DK)	.10	.08	.04
13	Harold Baines (DK)	.15	.11	.06
14	Mike Davis (DK)	.10	.08	.04
15	Tony Perez (DK)	.15	.11	.06
16	Willie Randolph (DK)	.12	.09	.05
17	Bob Boone (DK)	.10	.08	.04
18	Orel Hershiser (DK)	.40	.30	.15
19	Johnny Ray (DK)	.12	.09	.05
20	Gary Ward (DK)	.10	.08	.04
21	Rick Mahler (DK)	.08	.06	.03
22	Phil Bradley (DK)	.20	.15	.08
23	Jerry Koosman (DK)	.12	.09	.05
24	Tom Brunansky (DK)	.15	.11	.06
25	Andre Dawson (DK)	.30	.25	.12
26	Dwight Gooden (DK)	1.00	.70	.40
27	*Kal Daniels (RR)*(FC)	4.00	3.00	1.50
28	*Fred McGriff (RR)*(FC)	25.00	18.00	10.00
29	*Cory Snyder (RR)*(FC)	1.00	.70	.40
30	*Jose Guzman (RR)*(FC)	.40	.30	.15
31	*Ty Gainey (RR)*(FC)	.10	.08	.04
32	*Johnny Abrego (RR)*(FC)	.08	.06	.03
33a	*Andres Galarraga (RR)* (no accent mark above "e" in Andres on back)(FC)	1.50	1.25	.60
33b	*Andres Galarraga (RR)* (accent mark above "e" in Andres on back)(FC)	2.00	2.50	.80
34	*Dave Shipanoff (RR)*(FC)	.08	.06	.03

		MT	NR MT	EX
35	*Mark McLemore (RR)*(FC)	.20	.15	.08
36	*Marty Clary (RR)*(FC)	.08	.06	.03
37	*Paul O'Neill (RR)*(FC)	3.50	2.75	1.50
38	Danny Tartabull (RR)	1.50	1.25	.60
39	*Jose Canseco (RR)*(FC)	90.00	67.00	35.00
40	*Juan Nieves (RR)*(FC)	.20	.15	.08
41	*Lance McCullers (RR)*(FC)	.35	.25	.14
42	*Rick Surhoff (RR)*(FC)	.08	.06	.03
43	*Todd Worrell (RR)*(FC)	.40	.30	.15
44	*Bob Kipper (RR)*(FC)	.20	.15	.08
45	*John Habyan (RR)*(FC)	.15	.11	.06
46	*Mike Woodard (RR)*(FC)	.10	.08	.04
47	Mike Boddicker	.10	.08	.04
48	Robin Yount	1.00	.70	.40
49	Lou Whitaker	.30	.25	.12
50	"Oil Can" Boyd	.08	.06	.03
51	Rickey Henderson	2.50	2.00	1.00
52	Mike Marshall	.15	.11	.06
53	George Brett	.80	.60	.30
54	Dave Kingman	.15	.11	.06
55	Hubie Brooks	.10	.08	.04
56	*Oddibe McDowell*(FC)	.20	.15	.08
57	Doug DeCinces	.10	.08	.04
58	Britt Burns	.06	.05	.02
59	Ozzie Smith	.60	.45	.25
60	Jose Cruz	.10	.08	.04
61	Mike Schmidt	2.00	1.50	.80
62	Pete Rose	.80	.60	.30
63	Steve Garvey	.40	.30	.15
64	Tony Pena	.10	.08	.04
65	Chili Davis	.10	.08	.04
66	Dale Murphy	.60	.45	.25
67	Ryne Sandberg	3.00	2.25	1.25
68	Gary Carter	.35	.25	.14
69	Alvin Davis	.30	.25	.12
70	Kent Hrbek	.25	.20	.10
71	George Bell	.30	.25	.12
72	Kirby Puckett	6.00	4.50	2.50
73	Lloyd Moseby	.10	.08	.04
74	Bob Kearney	.06	.05	.02
75	Dwight Gooden	3.00	2.25	1.25
76	Gary Matthews	.10	.08	.04
77	Rick Mahler	.06	.05	.02
78	Benny Distefano	.06	.05	.02
79	Jeff Leonard	.08	.06	.03
80	Kevin McReynolds	.30	.25	.12
81	Ron Oester	.06	.05	.02
82	John Russell	.06	.05	.02
83	Tommy Herr	.10	.08	.04
84	Jerry Mumphrey	.06	.05	.02
85	Ron Romanick	.06	.05	.02
86	Daryl Boston	.08	.06	.03
87	Andre Dawson	.50	.40	.20
88	Eddie Murray	.50	.40	.20
89	Dion James	.08	.06	.03
90	Chet Lemon	.08	.06	.03
91	Bob Stanley	.06	.05	.02
92	Willie Randolph	.10	.08	.04
93	Mike Scioscia	.08	.06	.03
94	Tom Waddell	.06	.05	.02
95	Danny Jackson	.30	.25	.12
96	Mike Davis	.08	.06	.03
97	Mike Fitzgerald	.06	.05	.02
98	Gary Ward	.08	.06	.03
99	Pete O'Brien	.10	.08	.04
100	Bret Saberhagen	.60	.45	.25
101	Alfredo Griffin	.08	.06	.03
102	Brett Butler	.08	.06	.03
103	Ron Guidry	.20	.15	.08
104	Jerry Reuss	.08	.06	.03
105	Jack Morris	.30	.25	.12
106	Rick Dempsey	.08	.06	.03
107	Ray Burris	.06	.05	.02
108	Brian Downing	.10	.08	.04
109	Willie McGee	.15	.11	.06
110	Bill Doran	.10	.08	.04
111	Kent Tekulve	.08	.06	.03
112	Tony Gwynn	1.50	1.25	.60
113	Marvell Wynne	.06	.05	.02
114	David Green	.06	.05	.02
115	Jim Gantner	.08	.06	.03
116	George Foster	.15	.11	.06
117	Steve Trout	.06	.05	.02
118	Mark Langston	.30	.25	.12
119	Tony Fernandez	.20	.15	.08
120	John Butcher	.06	.05	.02
121	Ron Robinson	.08	.06	.03
122	Dan Spillner	.06	.05	.02
123	Mike Young	.06	.05	.02
124	Paul Molitor	.15	.11	.06
125	Kirk Gibson	.35	.25	.14
126	Ken Griffey	.12	.09	.05
127	Tony Armas	.08	.06	.03
128	*Mariano Duncan*(FC)	.15	.11	.06
129	Mr. Clutch (Pat Tabler)	.08	.06	.03
130	Frank White	.10	.08	.04
131	Carney Lansford	.10	.08	.04
132	Vance Law	.08	.06	.03
133	Dick Schofield	.06	.05	.02
134	Wayne Tolleson	.06	.05	.02
135	Greg Walker	.10	.08	.04
136	Denny Walling	.06	.05	.02
137	Ozzie Virgil	.06	.05	.02
138	Ricky Horton	.08	.06	.03
139	LaMarr Hoyt	.06	.05	.02
140	Wayne Krenchicki	.06	.05	.02
141	Glenn Hubbard	.06	.05	.02
142	Cecilio Guante	.06	.05	.02
143	Mike Krukow	.08	.06	.03
144	Lee Smith	.10	.08	.04
145	Edwin Nunez	.06	.05	.02
146	Dave Stieb	.12	.09	.05
147	Mike Smithson	.06	.05	.02
148	Ken Dixon	.06	.05	.02
149	Danny Darwin	.06	.05	.02
150	Chris Pittaro	.06	.05	.02
151	Bill Buckner	.12	.09	.05
152	Mike Pagliarulo	.20	.15	.08
153	Bill Russell	.08	.06	.03
154	Brook Jacoby	.10	.08	.04
155	Pat Sheridan	.06	.05	.02
156	*Mike Gallego*(FC)	.15	.11	.06
157	Jim Wohlford	.06	.05	.02
158	Gary Pettis	.06	.05	.02
159	Toby Harrah	.08	.06	.03
160	Richard Dotson	.10	.08	.04
161	Bob Knepper	.08	.06	.03
162	Dave Dravecky	.08	.06	.03
163	Greg Gross	.06	.05	.02
164	Eric Davis	3.00	2.25	1.25
165	Gerald Perry	.15	.11	.06
166	Rick Rhoden	.10	.08	.04
167	Keith Moreland	.08	.06	.03
168	Jack Clark	.20	.15	.08
169	Storm Davis	.10	.08	.04
170	Cecil Cooper	.12	.09	.05
171	Alan Trammell	.35	.25	.14
172	Roger Clemens	6.00	4.50	2.50
173	Don Mattingly	5.00	3.75	2.00
174	Pedro Guerrero	.20	.15	.08
175	Willie Wilson	.12	.09	.05
176	Dwayne Murphy	.08	.06	.03
177	Tim Raines	.40	.30	.15
178	Larry Parrish	.10	.08	.04
179	Mike Witt	.10	.08	.04
180	Harold Baines	.15	.11	.06
181	*Vince Coleman*(FC)	5.00	3.75	2.00
182	*Jeff Heathcock*(FC)	.10	.08	.04
183	Steve Carlton	.50	.40	.20
184	Mario Soto	.08	.06	.03
185	Goose Gossage	.20	.15	.08
186	Johnny Ray	.12	.09	.05
187	Dan Gladden	.08	.06	.03
188	Bob Horner	.12	.09	.05
189	Rick Sutcliffe	.12	.09	.05
190	Keith Hernandez	.25	.20	.10
191	Phil Bradley	.20	.15	.08
192	Tom Brunansky	.12	.09	.05
193	Jesse Barfield	.20	.15	.08
194	Frank Viola	.20	.15	.08
195	Willie Upshaw	.08	.06	.03
196	Jim Beattie	.06	.05	.02
197	Darryl Strawberry	4.00	3.00	1.50
198	Ron Cey	.10	.08	.04
199	Steve Bedrosian	.12	.09	.05
200	Steve Kemp	.08	.06	.03
201	Manny Trillo	.08	.06	.03
202	Garry Templeton	.08	.06	.03
203	Dave Parker	.25	.20	.10
204	John Denny	.06	.05	.02
205	Terry Pendleton	.15	.11	.06
206	Terry Puhl	.06	.05	.02
207	Bobby Grich	.10	.08	.04
208	*Ozzie Guillen*(FC)	1.25	.90	.50
209	Jeff Reardon	.12	.09	.05
210	Cal Ripken Jr.	3.00	2.25	1.25
211	Bill Schroeder	.06	.05	.02
212	Dan Petry	.08	.06	.03
213	Jim Rice	.40	.30	.15
214	Dave Righetti	.20	.15	.08
215	Fernando Valenzuela	.35	.25	.14
216	Julio Franco	.50	.40	.20

		MT	NR MT	EX
217	Darryl Motley	.06	.05	.02
218	Dave Collins	.08	.06	.03
219	Tim Wallach	.12	.09	.05
220	George Wright	.06	.05	.02
221	Tommy Dunbar	.06	.05	.02
222	Steve Balboni	.08	.06	.03
223	Jay Howell	.08	.06	.03
224	Joe Carter	1.25	.90	.50
225	Ed Whitson	.06	.05	.02
226	Orel Hershiser	1.25	.90	.50
227	Willie Hernandez	.08	.06	.03
228	Lee Lacy	.06	.05	.02
229	Rollie Fingers	.20	.15	.08
230	Bob Boone	.08	.06	.03
231	Joaquin Andujar	.08	.06	.03
232	Craig Reynolds	.06	.05	.02
233	Shane Rawley	.10	.08	.04
234	Eric Show	.08	.06	.03
235	Jose DeLeon	.08	.06	.03
236	*Jose Uribe*(FC)	.25	.20	.10
237	Moose Haas	.06	.05	.02
238	Wally Backman	.08	.06	.03
239	Dennis Eckersley	.12	.09	.05
240	Mike Moore	.06	.05	.02
241	Damaso Garcia	.06	.05	.02
242	Tim Teufel	.06	.05	.02
243	Dave Concepcion	.12	.09	.05
244	Floyd Bannister	.10	.08	.04
245	Fred Lynn	.20	.15	.08
246	Charlie Moore	.06	.05	.02
247	Walt Terrell	.08	.06	.03
248	Dave Winfield	.40	.30	.15
249	Dwight Evans	.12	.09	.05
250	*Dennis Powell*(FC)	.10	.08	.04
251	Andre Thornton	.10	.08	.04
252	Onix Concepcion	.06	.05	.02
253	Mike Heath	.06	.05	.02
254a	David Palmer (2B on front)	.06	.05	.02
254b	David Palmer (P on front)	1.00	.70	.40
255	Donnie Moore	.06	.05	.02
256	Curtis Wilkerson	.06	.05	.02
257	Julio Cruz	.06	.05	.02
258	Nolan Ryan	3.00	2.25	1.25
259	Jeff Stone	.06	.05	.02
260a	John Tudor (1981 Games is .18)	.10	.08	.04
260b	John Tudor (1981 Games is 18)	1.00	.70	.40
261	Mark Thurmond	.06	.05	.02
262	Jay Tibbs	.06	.05	.02
263	Rafael Ramirez	.06	.05	.02
264	Larry McWilliams	.06	.05	.02
265	Mark Davis	.06	.05	.02
266	Bob Dernier	.06	.05	.02
267	Matt Young	.06	.05	.02
268	Jim Clancy	.08	.06	.03
269	Mickey Hatcher	.06	.05	.02
270	Sammy Stewart	.06	.05	.02
271	Bob Gibson	.06	.05	.02
272	Nelson Simmons	.06	.05	.02
273	Rich Gedman	.10	.08	.04
274	Butch Wynegar	.06	.05	.02
275	Ken Howell	.06	.05	.02
276	Mel Hall	.08	.06	.03
277	Jim Sundberg	.08	.06	.03
278	Chris Codiroli	.06	.05	.02
279	*Herman Winningham*(FC)	.15	.11	.06
280	Rod Carew	.70	.50	.30
281	Don Slaught	.06	.05	.02
282	Scott Fletcher	.08	.06	.03
283	Bill Dawley	.06	.05	.02
284	Andy Hawkins	.06	.05	.02
285	Glenn Wilson	.08	.06	.03
286	Nick Esasky	.08	.06	.03
287	Claudell Washington	.08	.06	.03
288	Lee Mazzilli	.08	.06	.03
289	Jody Davis	.10	.08	.04
290	Darrell Porter	.08	.06	.03
291	Scott McGregor	.08	.06	.03
292	Ted Simmons	.12	.09	.05
293	Aurelio Lopez	.06	.05	.02
294	Marty Barrett	.10	.08	.04
295	Dale Berra	.06	.05	.02
296	Greg Brock	.08	.06	.03
297	Charlie Leibrandt	.08	.06	.03
298	Bill Krueger	.06	.05	.02
299	Bryn Smith	.06	.05	.02
300	Burt Hooton	.08	.06	.03
301	*Stu Cliburn*(FC)	.12	.09	.05
302	Luis Salazar	.06	.05	.02
303	Ken Dayley	.06	.05	.02
304	Frank DiPino	.06	.05	.02
305	Von Hayes	.10	.08	.04

		MT	NR MT	EX
306a	Gary Redus (1983 2B is .20)	.08	.06	.03
306b	Gary Redus (1983 2B is 20)	1.00	.70	.40
307	Craig Lefferts	.06	.05	.02
308	Sam Khalifa	.06	.05	.02
309	Scott Garrelts	.06	.05	.02
310	Rick Cerone	.06	.05	.02
311	Shawon Dunston	.20	.15	.08
312	Howard Johnson	.12	.09	.05
313	Jim Presley	.15	.11	.06
314	Gary Gaetti	.25	.20	.10
315	Luis Leal	.06	.05	.02
316	Mark Salas	.06	.05	.02
317	Bill Caudill	.06	.05	.02
318	Dave Henderson	.10	.08	.04
319	Rafael Santana	.06	.05	.02
320	Leon Durham	.08	.06	.03
321	Bruce Sutter	.15	.11	.06
322	Jason Thompson	.06	.05	.02
323	Bob Brenly	.06	.05	.02
324	Carmelo Martinez	.08	.06	.03
325	Eddie Milner	.06	.05	.02
326	Juan Samuel	.15	.11	.06
327	Tom Nieto	.06	.05	.02
328	Dave Smith	.08	.06	.03
329	*Urbano Lugo*(FC)	.08	.06	.03
330	Joel Skinner	.06	.05	.02
331	Bill Gullickson	.06	.05	.02
332	Floyd Rayford	.06	.05	.02
333	Ben Oglivie	.08	.06	.03
334	Lance Parrish	.30	.25	.12
335	Jackie Gutierrez	.06	.05	.02
336	Dennis Rasmussen	.12	.09	.05
337	Terry Whitfield	.06	.05	.02
338	Neal Heaton	.06	.05	.02
339	Jorge Orta	.06	.05	.02
340	Donnie Hill	.06	.05	.02
341	Joe Hesketh	.06	.05	.02
342	Charlie Hough	.10	.08	.04
343	Dave Rozema	.06	.05	.02
344	Greg Pryor	.06	.05	.02
345	*Mickey Tettleton*(FC)	1.25	.90	.50
346	George Vukovich	.06	.05	.02
347	Don Baylor	.12	.09	.05
348	Carlos Diaz	.06	.05	.02
349	Barbaro Garbey	.06	.05	.02
350	Larry Sheets	.12	.09	.05
351	*Ted Higuera*(FC)	1.00	.70	.40
352	Juan Beniquez	.06	.05	.02
353	Bob Forsch	.08	.06	.03
354	Mark Bailey	.06	.05	.02
355	Larry Andersen	.06	.05	.02
356	Terry Kennedy	.08	.06	.03
357	Don Robinson	.08	.06	.03
358	Jim Gott	.06	.05	.02
359	*Earnest Riles*(FC)	.30	.25	.12
360	*John Christensen*(FC)	.10	.08	.04
361	Ray Fontenot	.06	.05	.02
362	Spike Owen	.06	.05	.02
363	Jim Acker	.06	.05	.02
364a	Ron Davis (last line in highlights ends with "...in May.")	.08	.06	.03
364b	Ron Davis (last line in highlights ends with "...relievers (9).")	1.00	.70	.40
365	Tom Hume	.06	.05	.02
366	Carlton Fisk	.60	.45	.25
367	Nate Snell	.06	.05	.02
368	Rick Manning	.06	.05	.02
369	Darrell Evans	.15	.11	.06
370	Ron Hassey	.06	.05	.02
371	Wade Boggs	2.50	2.00	1.00
372	Rick Honeycutt	.06	.05	.02
373	Chris Bando	.06	.05	.02
374	Bud Black	.06	.05	.02
375	Steve Henderson	.06	.05	.02
376	Charlie Lea	.06	.05	.02
377	Reggie Jackson	.40	.30	.15
378	Dave Schmidt	.06	.05	.02
379	Bob James	.06	.05	.02
380	Glenn Davis(FC)	4.00	3.00	1.50
381	Tim Corcoran	.06	.05	.02
382	Danny Cox	.10	.08	.04
383	Tim Flannery	.06	.05	.02
384	Tom Browning	.20	.15	.08
385	Rick Camp	.06	.05	.02
386	Jim Morrison	.06	.05	.02
387	Dave LaPoint	.08	.06	.03
388	Davey Lopes	.08	.06	.03
389	Al Cowens	.06	.05	.02
390	Doyle Alexander	.10	.08	.04
391	Tim Laudner	.06	.05	.02
392	Don Aase	.06	.05	.02

		MT	NR MT	EX
393	Jaime Cocanower	.06	.05	.02
394	Randy O'Neal(FC)	.08	.06	.03
395	Mike Easler	.08	.06	.03
396	Scott Bradley	.06	.05	.02
397	Tom Niedenfuer	.08	.06	.03
398	Jerry Willard	.06	.05	.02
399	Lonnie Smith	.08	.06	.03
400	Bruce Bochte	.06	.05	.02
401	Terry Francona	.06	.05	.02
402	Jim Slaton	.06	.05	.02
403	Bill Stein	.06	.05	.02
404	Tim Hulett	.06	.05	.02
405	Alan Ashby	.06	.05	.02
406	Tim Stoddard	.06	.05	.02
407	Garry Maddox	.08	.06	.03
408	Ted Power	.06	.05	.02
409	Len Barker	.08	.06	.03
410	Denny Gonzalez	.06	.05	.02
411	George Frazier	.06	.05	.02
412	Andy Van Slyke	.15	.11	.06
413	Jim Dwyer	.06	.05	.02
414	Paul Householder	.06	.05	.02
415	Alejandro Sanchez	.06	.05	.02
416	Steve Crawford	.06	.05	.02
417	Dan Pasqua	.15	.11	.06
418	Enos Cabell	.06	.05	.02
419	Mike Jones	.06	.05	.02
420	Steve Kiefer	.06	.05	.02
421	*Tim Burke*(FC)	.30	.25	.12
422	Mike Mason	.06	.05	.02
423	Ruppert Jones	.06	.05	.02
424	Jerry Hairston	.06	.05	.02
425	Tito Landrum	.06	.05	.02
426	Jeff Calhoun	.06	.05	.02
427	*Don Carman*(FC)	.20	.15	.08
428	Tony Perez	.15	.11	.06
429	Jerry Davis	.06	.05	.02
430	Bob Walk	.06	.05	.02
431	Brad Wellman	.06	.05	.02
432	Terry Forster	.08	.06	.03
433	Billy Hatcher	.10	.08	.04
434	Clint Hurdle	.06	.05	.02
435	*Ivan Calderon*(FC)	2.00	1.50	.80
436	Pete Filson	.06	.05	.02
437	Tom Henke	.08	.06	.03
438	Dave Engle	.06	.05	.02
439	Tom Filer	.06	.05	.02
440	Gorman Thomas	.10	.08	.04
441	*Rick Aguilera*(FC)	.50	.40	.20
442	Scott Sanderson	.06	.05	.02
443	Jeff Dedmon	.06	.05	.02
444	*Joe Orsulak*(FC)	.15	.11	.06
445	Atlee Hammaker	.06	.05	.02
446	Jerry Royster	.06	.05	.02
447	Buddy Bell	.10	.08	.04
448	Dave Rucker	.06	.05	.02
449	Ivan DeJesus	.06	.05	.02
450	Jim Pankovits	.06	.05	.02
451	Jerry Narron	.06	.05	.02
452	Bryan Little	.06	.05	.02
453	Gary Lucas	.06	.05	.02
454	Dennis Martinez	.08	.06	.03
455	Ed Romero	.06	.05	.02
456	*Bob Melvin*(FC)	.12	.09	.05
457	Glenn Hoffman	.06	.05	.02
458	Bob Shirley	.06	.05	.02
459	Bob Welch	.12	.09	.05
460	Carmen Castillo	.06	.05	.02
461	Dave Leeper	.06	.05	.02
462	*Tim Birtsas*(FC)	.12	.09	.05
463	Randy St. Claire	.06	.05	.02
464	Chris Welsh	.06	.05	.02
465	Greg Harris	.06	.05	.02
466	Lynn Jones	.06	.05	.02
467	Dusty Baker	.08	.06	.03
468	Roy Smith	.06	.05	.02
469	Andre Robertson	.06	.05	.02
470	Ken Landreaux	.06	.05	.02
471	Dave Bergman	.06	.05	.02
472	Gary Roenicke	.06	.05	.02
473	Pete Vuckovich	.08	.06	.03
474	*Kirk McCaskill*(FC)	.40	.30	.15
475	Jeff Lahti	.06	.05	.02
476	Mike Scott	.20	.15	.08
477	*Darren Daulton*(FC)	.12	.09	.05
478	Graig Nettles	.15	.11	.06
479	Bill Almon	.06	.05	.02
480	Greg Minton	.06	.05	.02
481	Randy Ready(FC)	.10	.08	.04
482	*Lenny Dykstra*(FC)	3.50	2.75	1.50
483	Thad Bosley	.06	.05	.02

		MT	NR MT	EX
484	*Harold Reynolds*(FC)	1.00	.70	.40
485	Al Oliver	.12	.09	.05
486	Roy Smalley	.06	.05	.02
487	John Franco	.15	.11	.06
488	Juan Agosto	.06	.05	.02
489	Al Pardo	.06	.05	.02
490	*Bill Wegman*(FC)	.25	.20	.10
491	Frank Tanana	.10	.08	.04
492	*Brian Fisher*(FC)	.20	.15	.08
493	Mark Clear	.06	.05	.02
494	Len Matuszek	.06	.05	.02
495	Ramon Romero	.06	.05	.02
496	John Wathan	.08	.06	.03
497	Rob Picciolo	.06	.05	.02
498	U.L. Washington	.06	.05	.02
499	John Candelaria	.10	.08	.04
500	Duane Walker	.06	.05	.02
501	Gene Nelson	.06	.05	.02
502	John Mizerock	.06	.05	.02
503	Luis Aguayo	.06	.05	.02
504	Kurt Kepshire	.06	.05	.02
505	Ed Wojna	.06	.05	.02
506	Joe Price	.06	.05	.02
507	*Milt Thompson*(FC)	.30	.25	.12
508	Junior Ortiz	.06	.05	.02
509	Vida Blue	.10	.08	.04
510	Steve Engel	.06	.05	.02
511	Karl Best	.06	.05	.02
512	*Cecil Fielder*(FC)	20.00	15.00	8.00
513	Frank Eufemia	.06	.05	.02
514	Tippy Martinez	.06	.05	.02
515	*Billy Robidoux*(FC)	.10	.08	.04
516	Bill Scherrer	.06	.05	.02
517	Bruce Hurst	.12	.09	.05
518	Rich Bordi	.06	.05	.02
519	Steve Yeager	.06	.05	.02
520	Tony Bernazard	.06	.05	.02
521	Hal McRae	.10	.08	.04
522	Jose Rijo	.10	.08	.04
523	*Mitch Webster*(FC)	.25	.20	.10
524	*Jack Howell*(FC)	.35	.25	.14
525	Alan Bannister	.06	.05	.02
526	Ron Kittle	.10	.08	.04
527	Phil Garner	.08	.06	.03
528	Kurt Bevacqua	.06	.05	.02
529	Kevin Gross	.08	.06	.03
530	Bo Diaz	.08	.06	.03
531	Ken Oberkfell	.06	.05	.02
532	Rick Reuschel	.10	.08	.04
533	Ron Meridith	.06	.05	.02
534	Steve Braun	.06	.05	.02
535	Wayne Gross	.06	.05	.02
536	Ray Searage	.06	.05	.02
537	Tom Brookens	.06	.05	.02
538	Al Nipper	.06	.05	.02
539	Billy Sample	.06	.05	.02
540	Steve Sax	.20	.15	.08
541	Dan Quisenberry	.10	.08	.04
542	Tony Phillips	.06	.05	.02
543	*Floyd Youmans*(FC)	.20	.15	.08
544	*Steve Buechele*(FC)	.60	.45	.25
545	Craig Gerber	.06	.05	.02
546	Joe DeSa	.06	.05	.02
547	Brian Harper	.06	.05	.02
548	Kevin Bass	.10	.08	.04
549	Tom Foley	.06	.05	.02
550	Dave Van Gorder	.06	.05	.02
551	Bruce Bochy	.06	.05	.02
552	R.J. Reynolds	.08	.06	.03
553	*Chris Brown*(FC)	.20	.15	.08
554	Bruce Benedict	.06	.05	.02
555	Warren Brusstar	.06	.05	.02
556	Danny Heep	.06	.05	.02
557	Darnell Coles	.08	.06	.03
558	Greg Gagne	.08	.06	.03
559	Ernie Whitt	.08	.06	.03
560	Ron Washington	.06	.05	.02
561	Jimmy Key	.15	.11	.06
562	Billy Swift(FC)	.15	.11	.06
563	Ron Darling	.15	.11	.06
564	Dick Ruthven	.06	.05	.02
565	Zane Smith(FC)	.15	.11	.06
566	Sid Bream	.10	.08	.04
567a	Joel Youngblood (P on front)	.08	.06	.03
567b	Joel Youngblood (IF on front)	1.00	.70	.40
568	Mario Ramirez	.06	.05	.02
569	Tom Runnells	.06	.05	.02
570	Rick Schu	.06	.05	.02
571	Bill Campbell	.06	.05	.02
572	Dickie Thon	.08	.06	.03
573	Al Holland	.06	.05	.02

		MT	NR MT	EX
574	Reid Nichols	.06	.05	.02
575	Bert Roberge	.06	.05	.02
576	Mike Flanagan	.10	.08	.04
577	Tim Leary(FC)	.35	.25	.14
578	Mike Laga	.06	.05	.02
579	Steve Lyons	.06	.05	.02
580	Phil Niekro	.30	.25	.12
581	Gilberto Reyes	.06	.05	.02
582	Jamie Easterly	.06	.05	.02
583	Mark Gubicza	.12	.09	.05
584	*Stan Javier*(FC)	.15	.11	.06
585	Bill Laskey	.06	.05	.02
586	Jeff Russell	.06	.05	.02
587	Dickie Noles	.06	.05	.02
588	Steve Farr	.08	.06	.03
589	*Steve Ontiveros*(FC)	.15	.11	.06
590	Mike Hargrove	.06	.05	.02
591	Marty Bystrom	.06	.05	.02
592	Franklin Stubbs	.08	.06	.03
593	Larry Herndon	.08	.06	.03
594	Bill Swaggerty	.06	.05	.02
595	Carlos Ponce	.06	.05	.02
596	*Pat Perry*(FC)	.12	.09	.05
597	Ray Knight	.08	.06	.03
598	*Steve Lombardozzi*(FC)	.15	.11	.06
599	Brad Havens	.06	.05	.02
600	*Pat Clements*(FC)	.12	.09	.05
601	Joe Niekro	.12	.09	.05
602	Hank Aaron Puzzle Card	.06	.05	.02
603	*Dwayne Henry*(FC)	.10	.08	.04
604	Mookie Wilson	.10	.08	.04
605	Buddy Biancalana	.06	.05	.02
606	Rance Mulliniks	.06	.05	.02
607	Alan Wiggins	.06	.05	.02
608	Joe Cowley	.06	.05	.02
609a	Tom Seaver (green stripes around name)	.60	.45	.25
609b	Tom Seaver (yellow stripes around name)	2.00	1.50	.80
610	Neil Allen	.06	.05	.02
611	Don Sutton	.30	.25	.12
612	*Fred Toliver*(FC)	.15	.11	.06
613	Jay Baller	.06	.05	.02
614	Marc Sullivan	.06	.05	.02
615	John Grubb	.06	.05	.02
616	Bruce Kison	.06	.05	.02
617	Bill Madlock	.12	.09	.05
618	Chris Chambliss	.08	.06	.03
619	Dave Stewart	.12	.09	.05
620	Tim Lollar	.06	.05	.02
621	Gary Lavelle	.06	.05	.02
622	Charles Hudson	.06	.05	.02
623	*Joel Davis*(FC)	.08	.06	.03
624	*Joe Johnson*(FC)	.08	.06	.03
625	Sid Fernandez	.12	.09	.05
626	Dennis Lamp	.06	.05	.02
627	Terry Harper	.06	.05	.02
628	Jack Lazorko	.06	.05	.02
629	*Roger McDowell*(FC)	.60	.45	.25
630	Mark Funderburk	.06	.05	.02
631	Ed Lynch	.06	.05	.02
632	Rudy Law	.06	.05	.02
633	*Roger Mason*(FC)	.08	.06	.03
634	*Mike Felder*(FC)	.15	.11	.06
635	Ken Schrom	.06	.05	.02
636	Bob Ojeda	.08	.06	.03
637	Ed Vande Berg	.06	.05	.02
638	Bobby Meacham	.06	.05	.02
639	Cliff Johnson	.06	.05	.02
640	Garth Iorg	.06	.05	.02
641	Dan Driessen	.08	.06	.03
642	Mike Brown	.06	.05	.02
643	John Shelby	.06	.05	.02
644	Ty-Breaking Hit (Pete Rose)	.50	.40	.20
645	Knuckle Brothers (Joe Niekro, Phil Niekro)	.15	.11	.06
646	Jesse Orosco	.08	.06	.03
647	*Billy Beane*(FC)	.06	.05	.02
648	Cesar Cedeno	.10	.08	.04
649	Bert Blyleven	.15	.11	.06
650	Max Venable	.06	.05	.02
651	Fleet Feet (Vince Coleman, Willie McGee)	.35	.25	.14
652	Calvin Schiraldi	.08	.06	.03
653	King of Kings (Pete Rose)	.70	.50	.30
----	Checklist 1-26 DK	.06	.05	.02
---a	Checklist 27-130 (45 is Beane)	.08	.06	.03
---b	Checklist 27-130 (45 is Habyan)	.60	.45	.25
----	Checklist 131-234	.06	.05	.02
----	Checklist 235-338	.06	.05	.02
----	Checklist 339-442	.06	.05	.02
----	Checklist 443-546	.06	.05	.02
----	Checklist 547-653	.06	.05	.02

1986 Donruss All-Stars

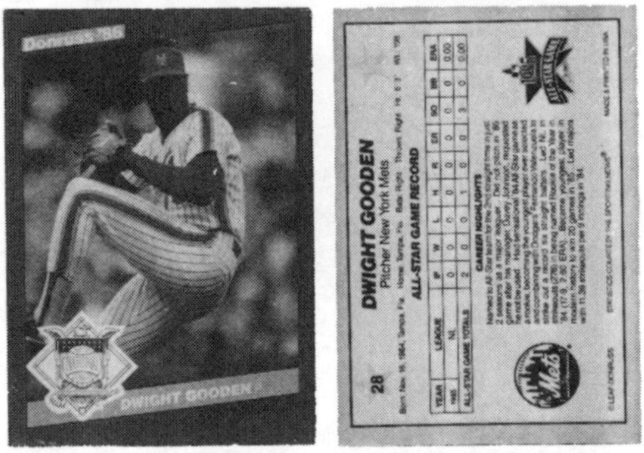

Issued in conjunction with the 1986 Donruss Pop-Ups set, the Donruss All-Stars set consists of 60 cards that measure 3-1/2" by 5". Fifty-nine players involved in the 1985 All-Star game plus an unnumbered checklist comprise the set. The card fronts have the same blue border found on the regular 1986 Donruss issue. Retail packs included one Pop-up card, three All-Star cards and one Hank Aaron puzzle card.

		MT	NR MT	EX
Complete Set:		8.00	6.00	3.25
Common Player:		.09	.07	.04
1	Tony Gwynn	.30	.25	.12
2	Tommy Herr	.09	.07	.04
3	Steve Garvey	.30	.25	.12
4	Dale Murphy	.40	.30	.15
5	Darryl Strawberry	.60	.45	.25
6	Graig Nettles	.12	.09	.05
7	Terry Kennedy	.09	.07	.04
8	Ozzie Smith	.15	.11	.06
9	LaMarr Hoyt	.09	.07	.04
10	Rickey Henderson	1.25	.90	.50
11	Lou Whitaker	.15	.11	.06
12	George Brett	.40	.30	.15
13	Eddie Murray	.12	.09	.05
14	Cal Ripken, Jr.	.35	.25	.14
15	Dave Winfield	.25	.20	.10
16	Jim Rice	.12	.09	.05
17	Carlton Fisk	.15	.11	.06
18	Jack Morris	.15	.11	.06
19	Jose Cruz	.09	.07	.04
20	Tim Raines	.25	.20	.10
21	Nolan Ryan	1.25	.90	.50
22	Tony Pena	.09	.07	.04
23	Jack Clark	.15	.11	.06
24	Dave Parker	.15	.11	.06
25	Tim Wallach	.12	.09	.05
26	Ozzie Virgil	.09	.07	.04
27	Fernando Valenzuela	.12	.09	.05
28	Dwight Gooden	.40	.30	.15
29	Glenn Wilson	.09	.07	.04
30	Garry Templeton	.09	.07	.04
31	Goose Gossage	.12	.09	.05
32	Ryne Sandberg	.25	.20	.10
33	Jeff Reardon	.12	.09	.05
34	Pete Rose	.35	.25	.14
35	Scott Garrelts	.09	.07	.04
36	Willie McGee	.12	.09	.05
37	Ron Darling	.12	.09	.05
38	Dick Williams	.09	.07	.04
39	Paul Molitor	.15	.11	.06
40	Damaso Garcia	.09	.07	.04
41	Phil Bradley	.12	.09	.05
42	Dan Petry	.09	.07	.04
43	Willie Hernandez	.09	.07	.04
44	Tom Brunansky	.12	.09	.05
45	Alan Trammell	.20	.15	.08
46	Donnie Moore	.09	.07	.04
47	Wade Boggs	.60	.45	.25
48	Ernie Whitt	.09	.07	.04
49	Harold Baines	.15	.11	.06

		MT	NR MT	EX
50	Don Mattingly	1.50	1.25	.60
51	Gary Ward	.09	.07	.04
52	Bert Blyleven	.12	.09	.05
53	Jimmy Key	.12	.09	.05
54	Cecil Cooper	.12	.09	.05
55	Dave Stieb	.12	.09	.05
56	Rich Gedman	.09	.07	.04
57	Jay Howell	.09	.07	.04
58	Sparky Anderson	.09	.07	.04
59	Minneapolis Metrodome	.09	.07	.04
----	Checklist	.09	.07	.04

1986 Donruss Box Panels

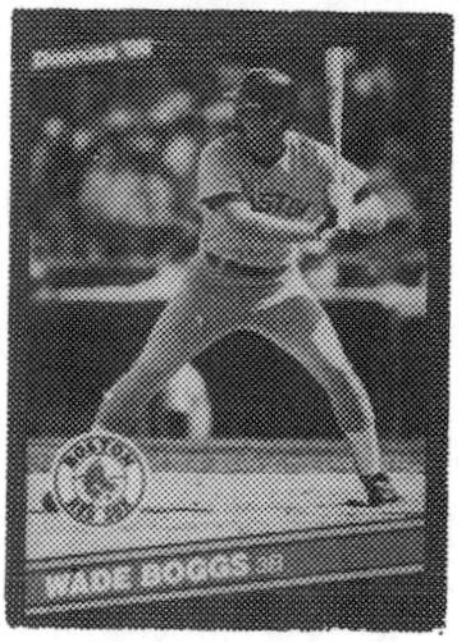

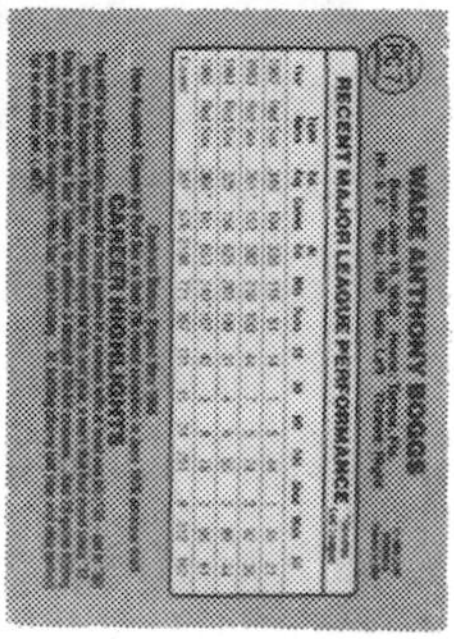

For the second year in a row, Donruss placed baseball cards on the bottom of their wax and cello pack boxes. The cards, which come four to a panel, are the standard 2-1/2" by 3-1/2" in size. With numbering that begins where Donruss left off in 1985, cards PC 4 through PC 6 were found on boxes of regular Donruss issue wax packs. Cards PC 7 through PC 9 were found on boxes of the 1986 All-Star/Pop-up packs. An unnumbered Hank Aaron puzzle card was included on each box.

	MT	NR MT	EX
Complete Panel Set:	5.00	3.75	2.00
Complete Singles Set:	3.00	2.25	1.25
Common Single Player:	.15	.11	.06

		MT	NR MT	EX
	Panel	1.00	.70	.40
4	Kirk Gibson	.35	.25	.14
5	Willie Hernandez	.15	.11	.06
6	Doug DeCinces	.15	.11	.06
----	Aaron Puzzle Card	.04	.03	.02
	Panel	3.00	2.25	1.25
7	Wade Boggs	1.00	.70	.40
8	Lee Smith	.15	.11	.06
9	Cecil Cooper	.20	.15	.08
----	Aaron Puzzle Card	.04	.03	.02

1986 Donruss Diamond Kings Supers

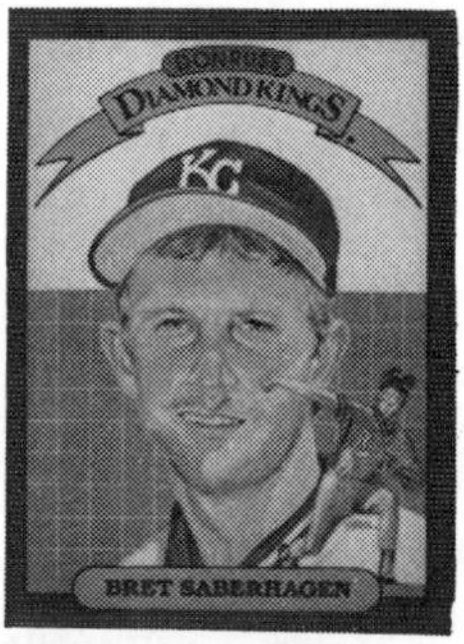

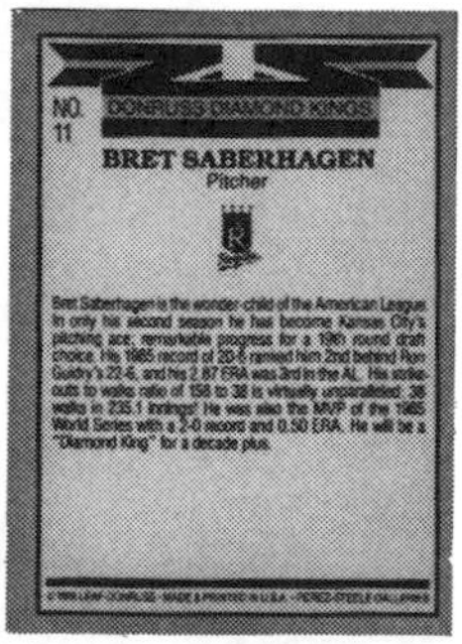

Donruss produced a set of giant-size Diamond Kings in 1986 for the second year in a row. The cards, which measure 4-11/6" by 6-3/4", are enlarged versions of the 26 Diamond Kings cards found in the regular 1986 Donruss set. Featuring the artwork of Dick Perez, the set consists of 28 cards - 26 DKs, an unnumbered checklist and an unnumbered Pete Rose "King of Kings" card.

	MT	NR MT	EX
Complete Set:	10.00	7.50	4.00
Common Player:	.20	.15	.08

		MT	NR MT	EX
1	Kirk Gibson	.50	.40	.20
2	Goose Gossage	.30	.25	.12
3	Willie McGee	.30	.25	.12
4	George Bell	.30	.25	.12
5	Tony Armas	.20	.15	.08
6	Chili Davis	.20	.15	.08
7	Cecil Cooper	.25	.20	.10
8	Mike Boddicker	.20	.15	.08
9	Davey Lopes	.20	.15	.08
10	Bill Doran	.25	.20	.10
11	Bret Saberhagen	.70	.50	.30
12	Brett Butler	.20	.15	.08
13	Harold Baines	.30	.25	.12
14	Mike Davis	.20	.15	.08
15	Tony Perez	.25	.20	.10
16	Willie Randolph	.25	.20	.10
18	Orel Hershiser	.70	.50	.30
19	Johnny Ray	.25	.20	.10
20	Gary Ward	.20	.15	.08
21	Rick Mahler	.20	.15	.08
22	Phil Bradley	.30	.25	.12
23	Jerry Koosman	.20	.15	.08
24	Tom Brunansky	.25	.20	.10
25	Andre Dawson	.35	.25	.14
26	Dwight Gooden	1.00	.70	.40
----	Checklist	.15	.11	.06
----	King of Kings (Pete Rose)	1.50	1.25	.60

1986 Donruss Highlights

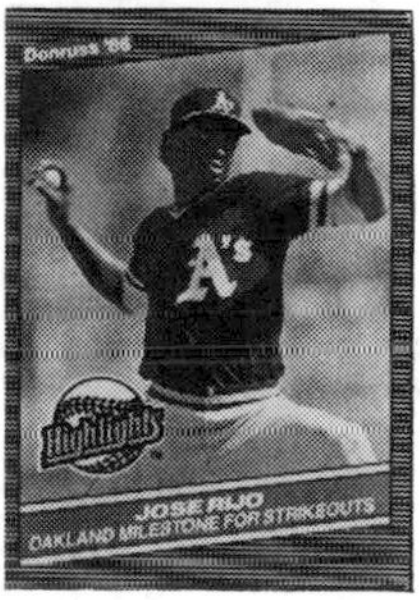

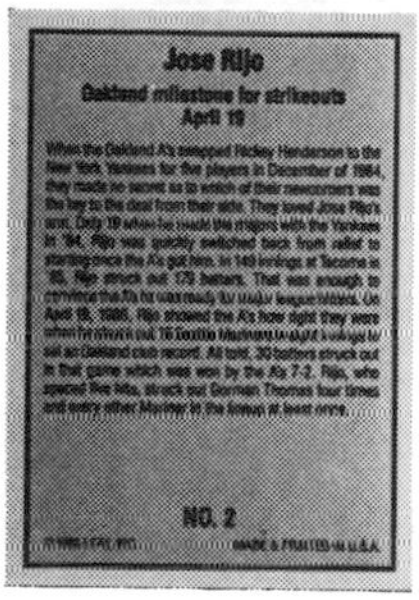

Donruss, for the second year in a row, issued a 56-card highlights set which featured cards of the A.L. and N.L. Player of the Month plus significant events that took place during the 1986 season. The cards, which measure 2-1/2" by 3-1/2" in size, are similar in design to the regular 1986 Donruss set but have a gold border instead of blue. A "Highlights" logo appears in the lower left corner of each card front. The card backs are designed on a vertical format and feature black print on a yellow background. As in 1985, the set includes Donruss' picks for the Rookies of the Year awards. A new feature was three cards honoring the 1986 Hall of Fame inductees. The set, available only through hobby dealers, was issued in a specially designed box.

	MT	NR MT	EX
Complete Set:	12.00	9.00	4.75
Common Player:	.10	.08	.04

		MT	NR MT	EX
1	Homers In First At-Bat (Will Clark)	2.00	1.50	.80
2	Oakland Milestone For Strikeouts (Jose Rijo)	.10	.08	.04
3	Royals' All-Time Hit Man (George Brett)	.20	.15	.08

		MT	NR MT	EX
4	Phillies RBI Leader (Mike Schmidt)	.30	.25	.12
5	KKKKKKKKKKKKKKKKKKKK (Roger Clemens)	.75	.55	.20
6	A.L. Pitcher of the Month-April (Roger Clemens)	.50	.40	.20
7	A.L. Player of the Month-April (Kirby Puckett)	.50	.40	.20
8	N.L. Pitcher of the Month-April (Dwight Gooden)	.50	.40	.20
9	N.L. Player of the Month-April (Johnny Ray)	.10	.08	.04
10	Eclipses Mantle HR Record (Reggie Jackson)	.25	.20	.10
11	First Five Hit Game of Career (Wade Boggs)	.50	.40	.20
12	A.L. Pitcher of the Month-May (Don Aase)	.10	.08	.04
13	A.L. Player of the Month-May (Wade Boggs)	.50	.40	.20
14	N.L. Pitcher of the Month-May (Jeff Reardon)	.15	.11	.06
15	N.L. Player of the Month-May (Hubie Brooks)	.10	.08	.04
16	Notches 300th Career Win (Don Sutton)	.10	.08	.04
17	Starts Season 14-0 (Roger Clemens)	.50	.40	.20
18	A.L. Pitcher of the Month-June (Roger Clemens)	.50	.40	.20
19	A.L. Player of the Month-June (Kent Hrbek)	.10	.08	.04
20	N.L. Pitcher of the Month-June (Rick Rhoden)	.10	.08	.04
21	N.L. Player of the Month-June (Kevin Bass)	.10	.08	.04
22	Blasts 4 HRS in 1 Game (Bob Horner)	.10	.08	.04
23	Starting All Star Rookie (Wally Joyner)	.50	.40	.20
24	Starts 3rd Straight All Star Game (Darryl Strawberry)	.25	.20	.10
25	Ties All Star Game Record (Fernando Valenzuela)	.10	.08	.04
26	All Star Game MVP (Roger Clemens)	.50	.40	.20
27	A.L. Pitcher of the Month-July (Jack Morris)	.10	.08	.04
28	A.L. Player of the Month-July (Scott Fletcher)	.10	.08	.04
29	N.L. Pitcher of the Month-July (Todd Worrell)	.25	.20	.10
30	N.L. PLayer of the Month-July (Eric Davis)	.40	.30	.15
31	Records 3000th Strikeout (Bert Blyleven)	.15	.11	.06
32	1986 Hall of Fame Inductee (Bobby Doerr)	.15	.11	.06
33	1986 Hall of Fame Inductee (Ernie Lombardi)	.15	.11	.06
34	1986 Hall of Fame Inductee (Willie McCovey)	.20	.15	.08
35	Notches 4000th K (Steve Carlton)	.25	.20	.10
36	Surpasses DiMaggio Record (Mike Schmidt)	.40	.30	.15
37	Records 3rd "Quadruple Double" (Juan Samuel)	.10	.08	.04
38	A.L. Pitcher of the Month-August (Mike Witt)	.10	.08	.04
39	A.L. Player of the Month-August (Doug DeCinces)	.10	.08	.04
40	N.L. Pitcher of the Month-August (Bill Gullickson)	.10	.08	.04
41	N.L. Player of the Month-August (Dale Murphy)	.20	.15	.08
42	Sets Tribe Offensive Record (Joe Carter)	.25	.20	.10
43	Longest HR In Royals Stadium (Bo Jackson)	2.00	1.50	.80
44	Majors 1st No-Hitter In 2 Years (Joe Cowley)	.10	.08	.04
45	Sets M.L. Strikeout Record (Jim Deshaies)	.15	.11	.06
46	No Hitter Clinches Division (Mike Scott)	.10	.08	.04
47	A.L. Pitcher of the Month-September (Bruce Hurst)	.10	.08	.04
48	A.L. Player of the Month-September (Don Mattingly)	1.00	.70	.40
49	N.L. Pitcher of the Month-September (Mike Krukow)	.10	.08	.04
50	N.L. Player of the Month-September (Steve Sax)	.10	.08	.04
51	A.L. Record For Steals By A Rookie (John Cangelosi)	.10	.08	.04
52	Shatters M.L. Save Mark (Dave Righetti)	.10	.08	.04
53	Yankee Record For Hits & Doubles (Don Mattingly)	1.00	.70	.40
54	Donruss N.L. Rookie of the Year (Todd Worrell)	.25	.20	.10
55	Donruss A.L. Rookie of the Year (Jose Canseco)	3.00	2.25	1.25
56	Highlight Checklist	.10	.08	.04

1986 Donruss Pop-Ups

Issued in conjunction with the 1986 Donruss All-Stars set, the Donruss Pop-Ups (18 unnumbered cards) feature the 1985 All-Star Game starting lineups. The cards, which measure 2-1/2" by 5", are die-cut and fold out to form a three-dimensional stand-up card. The background for the cards is the Minneapolis Metrodome, site of the 1985 All-Star Game. Retail packs included one Pop-Up card, three All-Star cards and one Hank Aaron puzzle card.

		MT	NR MT	EX
Complete Set:		5.00	3.75	2.00
Common Player:		.20	.15	.08
(1)	George Brett	.60	.45	.25
(2)	Carlton Fisk	.30	.25	.12
(3)	Steve Garvey	.20	.15	.08
(4)	Tony Gwynn	.50	.40	.20
(5)	Rickey Henderson	.70	.50	.30
(6)	Tommy Herr	.20	.15	.08
(7)	LaMarr Hoyt	.20	.15	.08
(8)	Terry Kennedy	.20	.15	.08
(9)	Jack Morris	.20	.15	.08
(10)	Dale Murphy	.30	.25	.12
(11)	Eddie Murray	.30	.25	.12
(12)	Graig Nettles	.20	.15	.08
(13)	Jim Rice	.20	.15	.08
(14)	Cal Ripken Jr.	.50	.40	.20
(15)	Ozzie Smith	.30	.25	.12
(16)	Darryl Strawberry	.70	.50	.30
(17)	Lou Whitaker	.30	.25	.12
(18)	Dave Winfield	.30	.25	.12

1986 Donruss Rookies

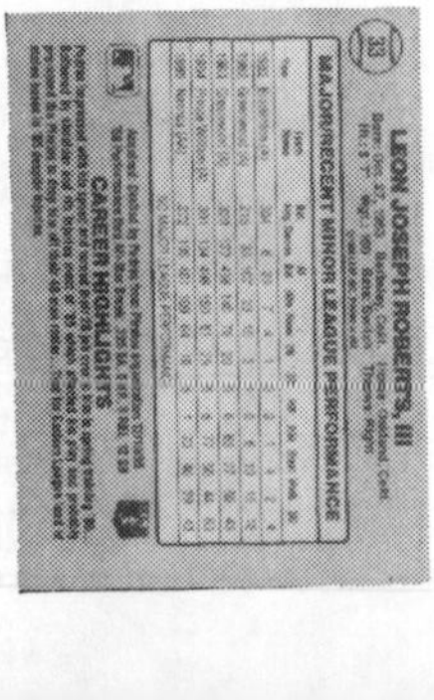

Entitled "The Rookies," this 56-card set includes the top 55 rookies of 1986 plus an unnumbered checklist. The cards, which measure 2-1/2" by 3-1/2", are similar to the format used for the 1986 Donruss regular issue, except that the borders are green rather than blue. Several of the rookies who had cards in the regular 1986 Donruss set appear again in "The Rookies" set. The sets, which were only available through hobby dealers, came in a specially designed box.

		MT	NR MT	EX
Complete Set:		60.00	45.00	25.00
Common Player:		.15	.11	.06
1	Wally Joyner(FC)	3.00	2.25	1.25
2	Tracy Jones(FC)	.20	.15	.08
3	Allan Anderson(FC)	.20	.15	.08
4	Ed Correa(FC)	.25	.20	.10
5	Reggie Williams	.20	.15	.08
6	Charlie Kerfeld(FC)	.15	.11	.06
7	Andres Galarraga	.50	.40	.20
8	Bob Tewksbury(FC)	.15	.11	.06
9	Al Newman	.15	.11	.06
10	Andres Thomas(FC)	.20	.15	.08
11	Barry Bonds(FC)	8.00	6.00	3.25
12	Juan Nieves	.15	.11	.06
13	Mark Eichhorn(FC)	.25	.20	.10
14	Dan Plesac(FC)	.25	.20	.10
15	Cory Snyder	.80	.60	.30
16	Kelly Gruber	3.50	2.75	1.50
17	Kevin Mitchell(FC)	7.00	5.25	2.75
18	Steve Lombardozzi	.15	.11	.06
19	Mitch Williams	.50	.40	.20
20	John Cerutti(FC)	.25	.20	.10
21	Todd Worrell	.35	.25	.14
22	Jose Canseco	12.00	9.00	5.00
23	Pete Incaviglia(FC)	.70	.50	.30
24	Jose Guzman	.25	.20	.10
25	Scott Bailes(FC)	.25	.20	.10
26	Greg Mathews(FC)	.25	.20	.10
27	Eric King(FC)	.20	.15	.08
28	Paul Assenmacher	.20	.15	.08
29	Jeff Sellers	.25	.20	.10
30	Bobby Bonilla(FC)	7.00	5.25	2.75
31	Doug Drabek(FC)	1.50	1.25	.60
32	Will Clark(FC)	15.00	11.00	6.00
33	Bip Roberts	.80	.60	.30
34	Jim Deshaies(FC)	.25	.20	.10
35	Mike Lavalliere (LaValliere)(FC)	.40	.30	.15
36	Scott Bankhead(FC)	.20	.15	.08
37	Dale Sveum(FC)	.25	.20	.10
38	Bo Jackson(FC)	10.00	7.50	4.00
39	Rob Thompson(FC)	.50	.40	.20
40	Eric Plunk(FC)	.20	.15	.08
41	Bill Bathe	.15	.11	.06
42	John Kruk(FC)	.70	.50	.30
43	Andy Allanson(FC)	.20	.15	.08
44	Mark Portugal	.15	.11	.06
45	Danny Tartabull	1.25	.90	.50
46	Bob Kipper	.15	.11	.06
47	Gene Walter	.15	.11	.06
48	Rey Quinonez	.15	.11	.06
49	Bobby Witt(FC)	.80	.60	.30
50	Bill Mooneyham	.15	.11	.06
51	John Cangelosi(FC)	.20	.15	.08
52	Ruben Sierra(FC)	10.00	7.50	4.00
53	Rob Woodward	.15	.11	.06
54	Ed Hearn	.15	.11	.06
55	Joel McKeon	.15	.11	.06
56	Checklist 1-56	.05	.04	.02

1987 Donruss

The 1987 Donruss set consists of 660 numbered cards, each measuring 2-1/2" by 3-1/2" in size. Full color photos are surrounded by a bold black border separated by two narrow bands of yellow which enclose a brown area filled with baseballs. The player's name, team and team logo appear on the card fronts along with the words "Donruss '87." The card backs are designed on a horizontal format and contain black print on a yellow and white background. The backs are very similar to those in previous years' sets. Backs of cards issued in wax and rack packs

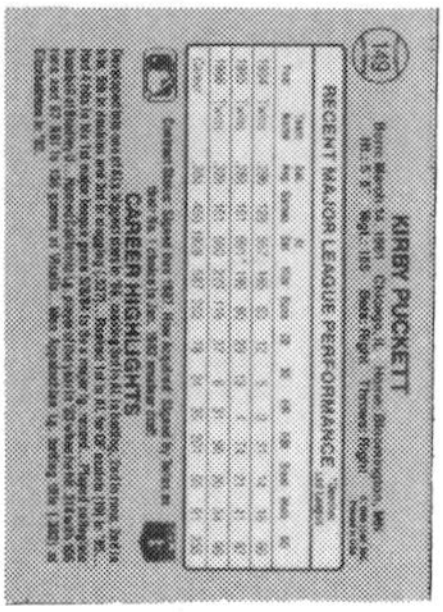

face to the left when turned over, while those issued in vending sets face to the right.

		MT	NR MT	EX
Complete Set:		80.00	60.00	32.00
Common Player:		.05	.04	.02
1	Wally Joyner (DK)	.50	.40	.20
2	Roger Clemens (DK)	.70	.50	.30
3	Dale Murphy (DK)	.30	.25	.12
4	Darryl Strawberry (DK)	.40	.30	.15
5	Ozzie Smith (DK)	.12	.09	.05
6	Jose Canseco (DK)	1.25	.90	.50
7	Charlie Hough (DK)	.07	.05	.03
8	Brook Jacoby (DK)	.10	.08	.04
9	Fred Lynn (DK)	.12	.09	.05
10	Rick Rhoden (DK)	.10	.08	.04
11	Chris Brown (DK)	.10	.08	.04
12	Von Hayes (DK)	.10	.08	.04
13	Jack Morris (DK)	.20	.15	.08
14a	Kevin McReynolds (DK) ("Donruss Diamond Kings" in white band on back)	1.25	.90	.50
14b	Kevin McReynolds (DK) ("Donruss Diamond Kings" in yellow band on back)	.20	.15	.08
15	George Brett (DK)	.40	.30	.15
16	Ted Higuera (DK)	.20	.15	.08
17	Hubie Brooks (DK)	.10	.08	.04
18	Mike Scott (DK)	.12	.09	.05
19	Kirby Puckett (DK)	.40	.30	.15
20	Dave Winfield (DK)	.25	.20	.10
21	Lloyd Moseby (DK)	.10	.08	.04
22a	Eric Davis (DK) ("Donruss Diamond Kings" in white band on back)	1.00	.70	.40
22b	Eric Davis (DK) ("Donruss Diamond Kings" in yellow band on back)	.80	.60	.30
23	Jim Presley (DK)	.12	.09	.05
24	Keith Moreland (DK)	.07	.05	.03
25a	Greg Walker (DK) ("Donruss Diamond Kings" in white band on back)	.50	.40	.20
25b	Greg Walker (DK) ("Donruss Diamond Kings" in yellow band on back)	.10	.08	.04
26	Steve Sax (DK)	.12	.09	.05
27	Checklist 1-27	.05	.04	.02
28	*B.J. Surhoff (RR)*(FC)	.50	.40	.20
29	*Randy Myers (RR)*(FC)	.60	.45	.25
30	*Ken Gerhart (RR)*(FC)	.15	.11	.06
31	Benito Santiago (RR)(FC)	1.50	1.25	.60
32	*Greg Swindell (RR)*(FC)	1.00	.70	.40
33	*Mike Birkbeck (RR)*(FC)	.20	.15	.08
34	*Terry Steinbach (RR)*(FC)	1.00	.70	.40
35	*Bo Jackson (RR)*	10.00	7.50	4.00
36	*Greg Maddux (RR)*(FC)	1.75	1.25	.70
37	*Jim Lindeman (RR)*(FC)	.15	.11	.06
38	*Devon White (RR)*(FC)	.80	.60	.30
39	*Eric Bell (RR)*(FC)	.12	.09	.05
40	*Will Fraser (RR)*(FC)	.20	.15	.08
41	*Jerry Browne (RR)*(FC)	.40	.30	.15
42	*Chris James (RR)*(FC)	.70	.50	.30
43	*Rafael Palmeiro (RR)*(FC)	5.00	3.75	2.00
44	*Pat Dodson (RR)*(FC)	.12	.09	.05
45	*Duane Ward (RR)*(FC)	.30	.25	.12
46	*Mark McGwire (RR)*(FC)	7.00	5.25	2.75
47	*Bruce Fields (RR)* (photo actually Darnell Coles)(FC)	.10	.08	.04
48	Eddie Murray	.35	.25	.14
49	Ted Higuera	.20	.15	.08
50	Kirk Gibson	.25	.20	.10
51	Oil Can Boyd	.07	.05	.03
52	Don Mattingly	1.25	.90	.50

		MT	NR MT	EX
53	Pedro Guerrero	.15	.11	.06
54	George Brett	.40	.30	.15
55	Jose Rijo	.07	.05	.03
56	Tim Raines	.30	.25	.12
57	*Ed Correa*	.15	.11	.06
58	Mike Witt	.10	.08	.04
59	Greg Walker	.10	.08	.04
60	Ozzie Smith	.15	.11	.06
61	Glenn Davis	.35	.25	.14
62	Glenn Wilson	.07	.05	.03
63	Tom Browning	.10	.08	.04
64	Tony Gwynn	.35	.25	.14
65	R.J. Reynolds	.07	.05	.03
66	*Will Clark*	12.00	9.00	4.75
67	Ozzie Virgil	.05	.04	.02
68	Rick Sutcliffe	.12	.09	.05
69	Gary Carter	.30	.25	.12
70	Mike Moore	.05	.04	.02
71	Bert Blyleven	.12	.09	.05
72	Tony Fernandez	.12	.09	.05
73	Kent Hrbek	.15	.11	.06
74	Lloyd Moseby	.10	.08	.04
75	Alvin Davis	.12	.09	.05
76	Keith Hernandez	.25	.20	.10
77	Ryne Sandberg	1.00	.70	.40
78	Dale Murphy	.40	.30	.15
79	Sid Bream	.07	.05	.03
80	Chris Brown	.07	.05	.03
81	Steve Garvey	.25	.20	.10
82	Mario Soto	.07	.05	.03
83	Shane Rawley	.07	.05	.03
84	Willie McGee	.12	.09	.05
85	Jose Cruz	.10	.08	.04
86	Brian Downing	.07	.05	.03
87	Ozzie Guillen	.10	.08	.04
88	Hubie Brooks	.10	.08	.04
89	Cal Ripken	.70	.50	.30
90	Juan Nieves	.07	.05	.03
91	Lance Parrish	.20	.15	.08
92	Jim Rice	.30	.25	.12
93	Ron Guidry	.15	.11	.06
94	Fernando Valenzuela	.25	.20	.10
95	*Andy Allanson*	.15	.11	.06
96	Willie Wilson	.12	.09	.05
97	Jose Canseco	10.00	7.50	4.00
98	Jeff Reardon	.10	.08	.04
99	*Bobby Witt*	.70	.50	.30
100	Checklist 28-133	.05	.04	.02
101	Jose Guzman	.10	.08	.04
102	Steve Balboni	.07	.05	.03
103	Tony Phillips	.05	.04	.02
104	Brook Jacoby	.10	.08	.04
105	Dave Winfield	.30	.25	.12
106	Orel Hershiser	.40	.30	.15
107	Lou Whitaker	.25	.20	.10
108	Fred Lynn	.15	.11	.06
109	Bill Wegman	.07	.05	.03
110	Donnie Moore	.05	.04	.02
111	Jack Clark	.15	.11	.06
112	Bob Knepper	.07	.05	.03
113	Von Hayes	.10	.08	.04
114	*Leon "Bip" Roberts*	.50	.40	.20
115	Tony Pena	.08	.06	.03
116	Scott Garrelts	.05	.04	.02
117	Paul Molitor	.15	.11	.06
118	Darryl Strawberry	1.00	.70	.40
119	Shawon Dunston	.10	.08	.04
120	Jim Presley	.10	.08	.04
121	Jesse Barfield	.20	.15	.08
122	Gary Gaetti	.15	.11	.06
123	*Kurt Stillwell*	.40	.30	.15
124	Joel Davis	.05	.04	.02
125	Mike Boddicker	.07	.05	.03
126	Robin Yount	.50	.40	.20
127	Alan Trammell	.25	.20	.10
128	Dave Righetti	.15	.11	.06
129	Dwight Evans	.12	.09	.05
130	Mike Scioscia	.07	.05	.03
131	Julio Franco	.10	.08	.04
132	Bret Saberhagen	.25	.20	.10
133	Mike Davis	.07	.05	.03
134	Joe Hesketh	.05	.04	.02
135	*Wally Joyner*	1.75	1.25	.70
136	Don Slaught	.05	.04	.02
137	Daryl Boston	.05	.04	.02
138	Nolan Ryan	1.25	.90	.50
139	Mike Schmidt	1.00	.70	.40
140	Tommy Herr	.10	.08	.04
141	Garry Templeton	.07	.05	.03
142	Kal Daniels	.80	.60	.30
143	Billy Sample	.05	.04	.02
144	Johnny Ray	.10	.08	.04
145	*Rob Thompson*	.30	.25	.12
146	Bob Dernier	.05	.04	.02
147	Danny Tartabull	.25	.20	.10
148	Ernie Whitt	.07	.05	.03
149	Kirby Puckett	1.50	1.25	.60
150	Mike Young	.05	.04	.02
151	Ernest Riles	.05	.04	.02
152	Frank Tanana	.07	.05	.03
153	Rich Gedman	.10	.08	.04
154	Willie Randolph	.10	.08	.04
155a	Bill Madlock (name in brown band)	.12	.09	.05
155b	Bill Madlock (name in red band)	.70	.50	.30
156a	Joe Carter (name in brown band)	.15	.11	.06
156b	Joe Carter (name in red band)	.70	.50	.30
157	Danny Jackson	.15	.11	.06
158	Carney Lansford	.10	.08	.04
159	Bryn Smith	.05	.04	.02
160	Gary Pettis	.05	.04	.02
161	Oddibe McDowell	.10	.08	.04
162	*John Cangelosi*	.12	.09	.05
163	Mike Scott	.15	.11	.06
164	Eric Show	.07	.05	.03
165	Juan Samuel	.12	.09	.05
166	Nick Esasky	.07	.05	.03
167	Zane Smith	.07	.05	.03
168	Mike Brown	.05	.04	.02
169	Keith Moreland	.07	.05	.03
170	John Tudor	.10	.08	.04
171	Ken Dixon	.05	.04	.02
172	Jim Gantner	.07	.05	.03
173	Jack Morris	.20	.15	.08
174	Bruce Hurst	.10	.08	.04
175	Dennis Rasmussen	.10	.08	.04
176	Mike Marshall	.12	.09	.05
177	Dan Quisenberry	.07	.05	.03
178	Eric Plunk(FC)	.10	.08	.04
179	Tim Wallach	.12	.09	.05
180	Steve Buechele	.07	.05	.03
181	Don Sutton	.20	.15	.08
182	Dave Schmidt	.05	.04	.02
183	Terry Pendleton	.10	.08	.04
184	*Jim Deshaies*	.35	.25	.14
185	Steve Bedrosian	.12	.09	.05
186	Pete Rose	.60	.45	.25
187	Dave Dravecky	.07	.05	.03
188	Rick Reuschel	.10	.08	.04
189	Dan Gladden	.05	.04	.02
190	Rick Mahler	.05	.04	.02
191	Thad Bosley	.05	.04	.02
192	Ron Darling	.15	.11	.06
193	Matt Young	.05	.04	.02
194	Tom Brunansky	.10	.08	.04
195	Dave Stieb	.12	.09	.05
196	Frank Viola	.15	.11	.06
197	Tom Henke	.07	.05	.03
198	Karl Best	.05	.04	.02
199	Dwight Gooden	.90	.70	.35
200	Checklist 134-239	.05	.04	.02
201	Steve Trout	.05	.04	.02
202	Rafael Ramirez	.05	.04	.02
203	Bob Walk	.05	.04	.02
204	Roger Mason	.05	.04	.02
205	Terry Kennedy	.07	.05	.03
206	Ron Oester	.05	.04	.02
207	John Russell	.05	.04	.02
208	*Greg Mathews*	.20	.15	.08
209	Charlie Kerfeld	.10	.08	.04
210	Reggie Jackson	.35	.25	.14
211	Floyd Bannister	.10	.08	.04
212	Vance Law	.07	.05	.03
213	Rich Bordi	.05	.04	.02
214	*Dan Plesac*	.35	.25	.14
215	Dave Collins	.07	.05	.03
216	Bob Stanley	.05	.04	.02
217	Joe Niekro	.10	.08	.04
218	Tom Niedenfuer	.07	.05	.03
219	Brett Butler	.07	.05	.03
220	Charlie Leibrandt	.07	.05	.03
221	Steve Ontiveros	.05	.04	.02
222	Tim Burke	.05	.04	.02
223	Curtis Wilkerson	.05	.04	.02
224	*Pete Incaviglia*	.60	.45	.25
225	Lonnie Smith	.07	.05	.03
226	Chris Codiroli	.05	.04	.02
227	*Scott Bailes*	.20	.15	.08
228	Rickey Henderson	1.00	.70	.40
229	Ken Howell	.05	.04	.02
230	Darnell Coles	.07	.05	.03
231	Don Aase	.05	.04	.02
232	Tim Leary	.07	.05	.03

		MT	NR MT	EX
233	Bob Boone	.07	.05	.03
234	Ricky Horton	.07	.05	.03
235	Mark Bailey	.05	.04	.02
236	Kevin Gross	.07	.05	.03
237	Lance McCullers	.07	.05	.03
238	Cecilio Guante	.05	.04	.02
239	Bob Melvin	.05	.04	.02
240	Billy Jo Robidoux	.05	.04	.02
241	Roger McDowell	.12	.09	.05
242	Leon Durham	.07	.05	.03
243	Ed Nunez	.05	.04	.02
244	Jimmy Key	.12	.09	.05
245	Mike Smithson	.05	.04	.02
246	Bo Diaz	.07	.05	.03
247	Carlton Fisk	.20	.15	.08
248	Larry Sheets	.08	.06	.03
249	*Juan Castillo*(FC)	.10	.08	.04
250	*Eric King*	.25	.20	.10
251	*Doug Drabek*	1.50	1.25	.60
252	Wade Boggs	1.00	.70	.40
253	Mariano Duncan	.05	.04	.02
254	Pat Tabler	.07	.05	.03
255	Frank White	.10	.08	.04
256	Alfredo Griffin	.07	.05	.03
257	Floyd Youmans	.07	.05	.03
258	Rob Wilfong	.05	.04	.02
259	Pete O'Brien	.10	.08	.04
260	Tim Hulett	.05	.04	.02
261	Dickie Thon	.07	.05	.03
262	Darren Daulton	.05	.04	.02
263	Vince Coleman	.50	.40	.20
264	Andy Hawkins	.05	.04	.02
265	Eric Davis	1.25	.90	.50
266	*Andres Thomas*	.15	.11	.06
267	*Mike Diaz*(FC)	.15	.11	.06
268	Chili Davis	.07	.05	.03
269	Jody Davis	.07	.05	.03
270	Phil Bradley	.12	.09	.05
271	George Bell	.25	.20	.10
272	Keith Atherton	.05	.04	.02
273	Storm Davis	.10	.08	.04
274	Rob Deer(FC)	.20	.15	.08
275	Walt Terrell	.07	.05	.03
276	Roger Clemens	2.00	1.50	.80
277	Mike Easler	.07	.05	.03
278	Steve Sax	.15	.11	.06
279	Andre Thornton	.07	.05	.03
280	Jim Sundberg	.07	.05	.03
281	Bill Bathe	.05	.04	.02
282	Jay Tibbs	.05	.04	.02
283	Dick Schofield	.05	.04	.02
284	Mike Mason	.05	.04	.02
285	Jerry Hairston	.05	.04	.02
286	Bill Doran	.10	.08	.04
287	Tim Flannery	.05	.04	.02
288	Gary Redus	.05	.04	.02
289	John Franco	.10	.08	.04
290	*Paul Assenmacher*	.15	.11	.06
291	Joe Orsulak	.05	.04	.02
292	Lee Smith	.10	.08	.04
293	Mike Laga	.05	.04	.02
294	Rick Dempsey	.07	.05	.03
295	Mike Felder	.05	.04	.02
296	Tom Brookens	.05	.04	.02
297	Al Nipper	.05	.04	.02
298	Mike Pagliarulo	.10	.08	.04
299	Franklin Stubbs	.07	.05	.03
300	Checklist 240-345	.05	.04	.02
301	Steve Farr	.05	.04	.02
302	*Bill Mooneyham*	.10	.08	.04
303	Andres Galarraga	.25	.20	.10
304	Scott Fletcher	.07	.05	.03
305	Jack Howell	.07	.05	.03
306	*Russ Morman*(FC)	.10	.08	.04
307	Todd Worrell	.20	.15	.08
308	Dave Smith	.07	.05	.03
309	Jeff Stone	.05	.04	.02
310	Ron Robinson	.05	.04	.02
311	Bruce Bochy	.05	.04	.02
312	Jim Winn	.05	.04	.02
313	Mark Davis	.05	.04	.02
314	Jeff Dedmon	.05	.04	.02
315	*Jamie Moyer*(FC)	.20	.15	.08
316	Wally Backman	.07	.05	.03
317	Ken Phelps	.07	.05	.03
318	Steve Lombardozzi	.05	.04	.02
319	Rance Mulliniks	.05	.04	.02
320	Tim Laudner	.05	.04	.02
321	*Mark Eichhorn*	.15	.11	.06
322	*Lee Guetterman*	.15	.11	.06
323	Sid Fernandez	.12	.09	.05
324	Jerry Mumphrey	.05	.04	.02
325	David Palmer	.05	.04	.02
326	Bill Almon	.05	.04	.02
327	Candy Maldonado	.07	.05	.03
328	*John Kruk*	.60	.45	.25
329	John Denny	.05	.04	.02
330	Milt Thompson	.07	.05	.03
331	*Mike LaValliere*	.25	.20	.10
332	Alan Ashby	.05	.04	.02
333	Doug Corbett	.05	.04	.02
334	*Ron Karkovice*(FC)	.10	.08	.04
335	Mitch Webster	.07	.05	.03
336	Lee Lacy	.05	.04	.02
337	*Glenn Braggs*(FC)	.30	.25	.12
338	Dwight Lowry	.05	.04	.02
339	Don Baylor	.12	.09	.05
340	Brian Fisher	.07	.05	.03
341	*Reggie Williams*	.10	.08	.04
342	Tom Candiotti	.05	.04	.02
343	Rudy Law	.05	.04	.02
344	Curt Young	.07	.05	.03
345	Mike Fitzgerald	.05	.04	.02
346	*Ruben Sierra*	10.00	7.50	4.00
347	*Mitch Williams*	.40	.30	.15
348	Jorge Orta	.05	.04	.02
349	Mickey Tettleton	.10	.08	.04
350	Ernie Camacho	.05	.04	.02
351	Ron Kittle	.10	.08	.04
352	Ken Landreaux	.05	.04	.02
353	Chet Lemon	.07	.05	.03
354	John Shelby	.05	.04	.02
355	Mark Clear	.05	.04	.02
356	Doug DeCinces	.07	.05	.03
357	Ken Dayley	.05	.04	.02
358	Phil Garner	.05	.04	.02
359	Steve Jeltz	.05	.04	.02
360	Ed Whitson	.05	.04	.02
361	*Barry Bonds*	8.00	6.00	3.25
362	Vida Blue	.10	.08	.04
363	Cecil Cooper	.12	.09	.05
364	Bob Ojeda	.07	.05	.03
365	Dennis Eckersley	.12	.09	.05
366	Mike Morgan	.05	.04	.02
367	Willie Upshaw	.07	.05	.03
368	*Allan Anderson*(FC)	.25	.20	.10
369	Bill Gullickson	.07	.05	.03
370	*Bobby Thigpen*(FC)	1.25	.90	.50
371	Juan Beniquez	.05	.04	.02
372	Charlie Moore	.05	.04	.02
373	Dan Petry	.07	.05	.03
374	Rod Scurry	.05	.04	.02
375	Tom Seaver	.40	.30	.15
376	Ed Vande Berg	.05	.04	.02
377	Tony Bernazard	.05	.04	.02
378	Greg Pryor	.05	.04	.02
379	Dwayne Murphy	.07	.05	.03
380	Andy McGaffigan	.05	.04	.02
381	Kirk McCaskill	.07	.05	.03
382	Greg Harris	.05	.04	.02
383	Rich Dotson	.07	.05	.03
384	Craig Reynolds	.05	.04	.02
385	Greg Gross	.05	.04	.02
386	Tito Landrum	.05	.04	.02
387	Craig Lefferts	.05	.04	.02
388	Dave Parker	.20	.15	.08
389	Bob Horner	.10	.08	.04
390	Pat Clements	.05	.04	.02
391	Jeff Leonard	.07	.05	.03
392	Chris Speier	.05	.04	.02
393	John Moses	.05	.04	.02
394	Garth Iorg	.05	.04	.02
395	Greg Gagne	.05	.04	.02
396	Nate Snell	.05	.04	.02
397	*Bryan Clutterbuck*(FC)	.10	.08	.04
398	Darrell Evans	.12	.09	.05
399	Steve Crawford	.05	.04	.02
400	Checklist 346-451	.05	.04	.02
401	*Phil Lombardi*(FC)	.10	.08	.04
402	Rick Honeycutt	.05	.04	.02
403	Ken Schrom	.05	.04	.02
404	Bud Black	.05	.04	.02
405	Donnie Hill	.05	.04	.02
406	Wayne Krenchicki	.05	.04	.02
407	*Chuck Finley*(FC)	2.00	1.50	.80
408	Toby Harrah	.07	.05	.03
409	Steve Lyons	.05	.04	.02
410	Kevin Bass	.10	.08	.04
411	Marvell Wynne	.05	.04	.02
412	Ron Roenicke	.05	.04	.02
413	*Tracy Jones*	.25	.20	.10
414	Gene Garber	.05	.04	.02

		MT	NR MT	EX
415	Mike Dielecki	.05	.04	.02
416	Frank DiPino	.05	.04	.02
417	Andy Van Slyke	.12	.09	.05
418	Jim Dwyer	.05	.04	.02
419	Ben Oglivie	.07	.05	.03
420	Dave Bergman	.05	.04	.02
421	Joe Sambito	.05	.04	.02
422	*Bob Tewksbury*	.12	.09	.05
423	Len Matuszek	.05	.04	.02
424	*Mike Kingery*(FC)	.15	.11	.06
425	Dave Kingman	.12	.09	.05
426	*Al Newman*	.07	.05	.03
427	Gary Ward	.07	.05	.03
428	Ruppert Jones	.05	.04	.02
429	Harold Baines	.15	.11	.06
430	Pat Perry	.05	.04	.02
431	Terry Puhl	.05	.04	.02
432	Don Carman	.07	.05	.03
433	Eddie Milner	.05	.04	.02
434	LaMarr Hoyt	.05	.04	.02
435	Rick Rhoden	.10	.08	.04
436	Jose Uribe	.07	.05	.03
437	Ken Oberkfell	.05	.04	.02
438	Ron Davis	.05	.04	.02
439	Jesse Orosco	.07	.05	.03
440	Scott Bradley	.05	.04	.02
441	Randy Bush	.05	.04	.02
442	*John Cerutti*	.20	.15	.08
443	Roy Smalley	.05	.04	.02
444	Kelly Gruber	2.50	2.00	1.00
445	Bob Kearney	.05	.04	.02
446	*Ed Hearn*	.10	.08	.04
447	Scott Sanderson	.05	.04	.02
448	Bruce Benedict	.05	.04	.02
449	Junior Ortiz	.05	.04	.02
450	*Mike Aldrete*	.15	.11	.06
451	Kevin McReynolds	.15	.11	.06
452	*Rob Murphy*(FC)	.20	.15	.08
453	Kent Tekulve	.07	.05	.03
454	Curt Ford(FC)	.07	.05	.03
455	Davey Lopes	.07	.05	.03
456	Bobby Grich	.10	.08	.04
457	Jose DeLeon	.07	.05	.03
458	Andre Dawson	.20	.15	.08
459	Mike Flanagan	.07	.05	.03
460	*Joey Meyer*(FC)	.20	.15	.08
461	*Chuck Cary*(FC)	.10	.08	.04
462	Bill Buckner	.10	.08	.04
463	Bob Shirley	.05	.04	.02
464	*Jeff Hamilton*(FC)	.20	.15	.08
465	Phil Niekro	.20	.15	.08
466	Mark Gubicza	.12	.09	.05
467	Jerry Willard	.05	.04	.02
468	*Bob Sebra*(FC)	.10	.08	.04
469	Larry Parrish	.10	.08	.04
470	Charlie Hough	.07	.05	.03
471	Hal McRae	.10	.08	.04
472	*Dave Leiper*(FC)	.10	.08	.04
473	Mel Hall	.07	.05	.03
474	Dan Pasqua	.10	.08	.04
475	Bob Welch	.10	.08	.04
476	Johnny Grubb	.05	.04	.02
477	Jim Traber	.07	.05	.03
478	*Chris Bosio*(FC)	.40	.30	.15
479	Mark McLemore	.07	.05	.03
480	John Morris	.05	.04	.02
481	Billy Hatcher	.07	.05	.03
482	Dan Schatzeder	.05	.04	.02
483	Rich Gossage	.15	.11	.06
484	Jim Morrison	.05	.04	.02
485	Bob Brenly	.05	.04	.02
486	Bill Schroeder	.05	.04	.02
487	Mookie Wilson	.10	.08	.04
488	*Dave Martinez*(FC)	.25	.20	.10
489	Harold Reynolds	.10	.08	.04
490	Jeff Hearron	.05	.04	.02
491	Mickey Hatcher	.05	.04	.02
492	*Barry Larkin*(FC)	5.00	3.75	2.00
493	Bob James	.05	.04	.02
494	John Habyan	.05	.04	.02
495	*Jim Adduci*(FC)	.07	.05	.03
496	Mike Heath	.05	.04	.02
497	Tim Stoddard	.05	.04	.02
498	Tony Armas	.07	.05	.03
499	Dennis Powell	.05	.04	.02
500	Checklist 452-557	.05	.04	.02
501	Chris Bando	.05	.04	.02
502	*David Cone*(FC)	3.00	2.25	1.25
503	Jay Howell	.07	.05	.03
504	Tom Foley	.05	.04	.02
505	*Ray Chadwick*(FC)	.10	.08	.04
506	*Mike Loynd*(FC)	.15	.11	.06
507	Neil Allen	.05	.04	.02
508	Danny Darwin	.05	.04	.02
509	Rick Schu	.05	.04	.02
510	Jose Oquendo	.05	.04	.02
511	Gene Walter	.07	.05	.03
512	*Terry McGriff*(FC)	.12	.09	.05
513	Ken Griffey	.10	.08	.04
514	Benny Distefano	.05	.04	.02
515	*Terry Mulholland*(FC)	.12	.09	.05
516	Ed Lynch	.05	.04	.02
517	Bill Swift	.05	.04	.02
518	Manny Lee(FC)	.07	.05	.03
519	Andre David	.05	.04	.02
520	Scott McGregor	.07	.05	.03
521	Rick Manning	.05	.04	.02
522	Willie Hernandez	.07	.05	.03
523	Marty Barrett	.10	.08	.04
524	Wayne Tolleson	.05	.04	.02
525	*Jose Gonzalez*(FC)	.15	.11	.06
526	Cory Snyder	.35	.25	.14
527	Buddy Biancalana	.05	.04	.02
528	Moose Haas	.05	.04	.02
529	*Wilfredo Tejada*(FC)	.10	.08	.04
530	Stu Cliburn	.05	.04	.02
531	*Dale Mohorcic*(FC)	.20	.15	.08
532	Ron Hassey	.05	.04	.02
533	Ty Gainey	.05	.04	.02
534	Jerry Royster	.05	.04	.02
535	*Mike Maddux*(FC)	.20	.15	.08
536	Ted Power	.05	.04	.02
537	Ted Simmons	.12	.09	.05
538	*Rafael Belliard*(FC)	.12	.09	.05
539	Chico Walker	.05	.04	.02
540	Bob Forsch	.07	.05	.03
541	John Stefero	.05	.04	.02
542	*Dale Sveum*	.20	.15	.08
543	Mark Thurmond	.05	.04	.02
544	*Jeff Sellers*	.20	.15	.08
545	Joel Skinner	.05	.04	.02
546	Alex Trevino	.05	.04	.02
547	*Randy Kutcher*(FC)	.10	.08	.04
548	Joaquin Andujar	.07	.05	.03
549	*Casey Candaele*(FC)	.15	.11	.06
550	Jeff Russell	.05	.04	.02
551	John Candelaria	.10	.08	.04
552	Joe Cowley	.05	.04	.02
553	Danny Cox	.07	.05	.03
554	Denny Walling	.05	.04	.02
555	*Bruce Ruffin*(FC)	.20	.15	.08
556	Buddy Bell	.10	.08	.04
557	*Jimmy Jones*(FC)	.20	.15	.08
558	*Bobby Bonilla*	7.00	5.25	2.75
559	Jeff Robinson	.07	.05	.03
560	Ed Olwine	.05	.04	.02
561	*Glenallen Hill*(FC)	1.00	.70	.40
562	Lee Mazzilli	.07	.05	.03
563	Mike Brown	.05	.04	.02
564	George Frazier	.05	.04	.02
565	*Mike Sharperson*(FC)	.10	.08	.04
566	*Mark Portugal*	.10	.08	.04
567	Rick Leach	.05	.04	.02
568	Mark Langston	.12	.09	.05
569	Rafael Santana	.05	.04	.02
570	Manny Trillo	.07	.05	.03
571	Cliff Speck	.05	.04	.02
572	Bob Kipper	.05	.04	.02
573	*Kelly Downs*(FC)	.30	.25	.12
574	*Randy Asadoor*(FC)	.10	.08	.04
575	*Dave Magadan*(FC)	2.00	1.50	.80
576	*Marvin Freeman*(FC)	.12	.09	.05
577	Jeff Lahti	.05	.04	.02
578	Jeff Calhoun	.05	.04	.02
579	Gus Polidor(FC)	.07	.05	.03
580	Gene Nelson	.05	.04	.02
581	Tim Teufel	.05	.04	.02
582	Odell Jones	.05	.04	.02
583	Mark Ryal	.05	.04	.02
584	Randy O'Neal	.05	.04	.02
585	*Mike Greenwell*(FC)	7.00	5.25	2.75
586	Ray Knight	.07	.05	.03
587	*Ralph Bryant*(FC)	.12	.09	.05
588	Carmen Castillo	.05	.04	.02
589	Ed Wojna	.05	.04	.02
590	Stan Javier	.05	.04	.02
591	*Jeff Musselman*(FC)	.20	.15	.08
592	*Mike Stanley*(FC)	.20	.15	.08
593	Darrell Porter	.07	.05	.03
594	*Drew Hall*(FC)	.20	.15	.08
595	*Rob Nelson*(FC)	.10	.08	.04
596	Bryan Oelkers	.05	.04	.02

		MT	NR MT	EX
597	*Scott Nielsen*(FC)	.10	.08	.04
598	*Brian Holton*(FC)	.20	.15	.08
599	*Kevin Mitchell*	5.00	3.75	2.00
600	Checklist 558-660	.05	.04	.02
601	Jackie Gutierrez	.05	.04	.02
602	*Barry Jones*(FC)	.12	.09	.05
603	Jerry Narron	.05	.04	.02
604	Steve Lake	.05	.04	.02
605	Jim Pankovits	.05	.04	.02
606	Ed Romero	.05	.04	.02
607	Dave LaPoint	.07	.05	.03
608	Don Robinson	.07	.05	.03
609	Mike Krukow	.07	.05	.03
610	*Dave Valle*(FC)	.12	.09	.05
611	Len Dykstra	.80	.60	.30
612	Roberto Clemente Puzzle Card	.05	.04	.02
613	Mike Trujillo(FC)	.05	.04	.02
614	Damaso Garcia	.05	.04	.02
615	Neal Heaton	.05	.04	.02
616	Juan Berenguer	.05	.04	.02
617	Steve Carlton	.25	.20	.10
618	Gary Lucas	.05	.04	.02
619	Geno Petralli	.05	.04	.02
620	Rick Aguilera	.07	.05	.03
621	Fred McGriff	4.00	3.00	1.50
622	Dave Henderson	.10	.08	.04
623	*Dave Clark*(FC)	.20	.15	.08
624	Angel Salazar	.05	.04	.02
625	Randy Hunt	.05	.04	.02
626	John Gibbons	.05	.04	.02
627	*Kevin Brown*(FC)	1.00	.70	.40
628	Bill Dawley	.05	.04	.02
629	Aurelio Lopez	.05	.04	.02
630	Charlie Hudson	.05	.04	.02
631	Ray Soff	.05	.04	.02
632	*Ray Hayward*(FC)	.12	.09	.05
633	Spike Owen	.05	.04	.02
634	Glenn Hubbard	.05	.04	.02
635	*Kevin Elster*(FC)	.40	.30	.15
636	Mike LaCoss	.05	.04	.02
637	Dwayne Henry	.05	.04	.02
638	*Rey Quinones*	.15	.11	.06
639	Jim Clancy	.07	.05	.03
640	Larry Andersen	.05	.04	.02
641	Calvin Schiraldi	.05	.04	.02
642	*Stan Jefferson*(FC)	.15	.11	.06
643	Marc Sullivan	.05	.04	.02
644	Mark Grant	.05	.04	.02
645	Cliff Johnson	.05	.04	.02
646	Howard Johnson	.25	.20	.10
647	Dave Sax	.05	.04	.02
648	Dave Stewart	.25	.20	.10
649	Danny Heep	.05	.04	.02
650	Joe Johnson	.05	.04	.02
651	*Bob Brower*(FC)	.15	.11	.06
652	Rob Woodward	.07	.05	.03
653	John Mizerock	.05	.04	.02
654	*Tim Pyznarski*(FC)	.10	.08	.04
655	*Luis Aquino*(FC)	.10	.08	.04
656	Mickey Brantley(FC)	.10	.08	.04
657	Doyle Alexander	.07	.05	.03
658	Sammy Stewart	.05	.04	.02
659	Jim Acker	.05	.04	.02
660	Pete Ladd	.05	.04	.02

1987 Donruss All-Stars

Issued in conjunction with the Donruss Pop-Ups set for the second consecutive year, the 1987 Donruss All-Stars set consists of 59 players (plus a checklist) who were selected to the 1986 All-Star Game. Measuring 3-1/2" by 5" in size, the card fronts feature black borders and American or National League logos. Included on the backs are the player's career highlights and All-Star Game statistics. Retail packs included one pop-Up card, three All-Star cards and one Roberto Clemente puzzle.

		MT	NR MT	EX
Complete Set:		7.00	5.25	2.75
Common Player:		.09	.07	.04
1	Wally Joyner	.80	.60	.30
2	Dave Winfield	.25	.20	.10
3	Lou Whitaker	.15	.11	.06
4	Kirby Puckett	.50	.40	.20
5	Cal Ripken, Jr.	.60	.45	.25
6	Rickey Henderson	.50	.40	.20
7	Wade Boggs	.60	.45	.25
8	Roger Clemens	.50	.40	.20
9	Lance Parrish	.09	.07	.04
10	Dick Howser	.09	.07	.04
11	Keith Hernandez	.10	.08	.04
12	Darryl Strawberry	.50	.40	.20
13	Ryne Sandberg	.60	.45	.25
14	Dale Murphy	.40	.30	.15
15	Ozzie Smith	.15	.11	.06
16	Tony Gwynn	.30	.25	.12
17	Mike Schmidt	.40	.30	.15
18	Dwight Gooden	.60	.45	.25
19	Gary Carter	.15	.11	.06
20	Whitey Herzog	.09	.07	.04
21	Jose Canseco	1.50	1.25	.60
22	John Franco	.09	.07	.04
23	Jesse Barfield	.12	.09	.05
24	Rick Rhoden	.09	.07	.04
25	Harold Baines	.15	.11	.06
26	Sid Fernandez	.12	.09	.05
27	George Brett	.40	.30	.15
28	Steve Sax	.15	.11	.06
29	Jim Presley	.12	.09	.05
30	Dave Smith	.09	.07	.04
31	Eddie Murray	.10	.08	.04
32	Mike Scott	.12	.09	.05
33	Don Mattingly	1.00	.70	.40
34	Dave Parker	.15	.11	.06
35	Tony Fernandez	.15	.11	.06
36	Tim Raines	.25	.20	.10
37	Brook Jacoby	.12	.09	.05
38	Chili Davis	.09	.07	.04
39	Rich Gedman	.09	.07	.04
40	Kevin Bass	.09	.07	.04
41	Frank White	.09	.07	.04
42	Glenn Davis	.15	.11	.06
43	Willie Hernandez	.09	.07	.04
44	Chris Brown	.09	.07	.04
45	Jim Rice	.10	.08	.04
46	Tony Pena	.09	.07	.04
47	Don Aase	.09	.07	.04
48	Hubie Brooks	.09	.07	.04
49	Charlie Hough	.09	.07	.04
50	Jody Davis	.09	.07	.04
51	Mike Witt	.09	.07	.04
52	Jeff Reardon	.12	.09	.05
53	Ken Schrom	.09	.07	.04
54	Fernando Valenzuela	.10	.08	.04
55	Dave Righetti	.15	.11	.06
56	Shane Rawley	.09	.07	.04
57	Ted Higuera	.12	.09	.05
58	Mike Krukow	.09	.07	.04
59	Lloyd Moseby	.09	.07	.04
60	Checklist	.09	.07	.04

1987 Donruss Box Panels

Continuing with an idea they initiated in 1985, Donruss once again placed baseball cards on the bottoms of their retail boxes. The cards, which are 2-1/2" by 3-1/2" in size, come four to a panel with each panel containing an unnumbered Roberto Clemente puzzle card. With numbering that begins where Donruss left off in 1986, cards PC 10 through PC 12 were found on boxes of Donruss regular issue wax packs. Cards PC 13 through PC 15 were located on boxes of the 1987 All-Star/Pop-Up packs.

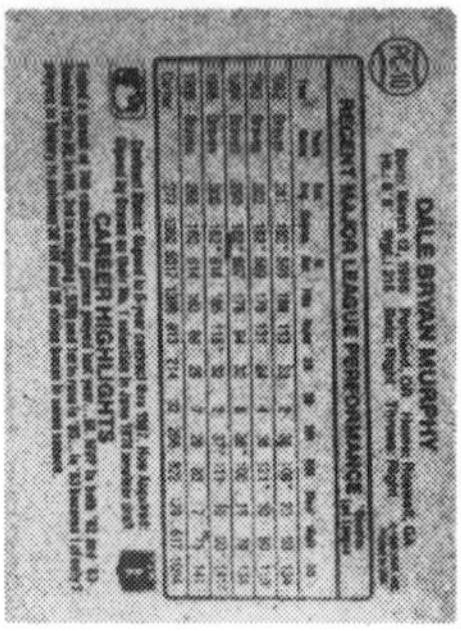

	MT	NR MT	EX
Complete Panel Set:	5.00	3.75	2.00
Complete Singles Set:	3.00	2.25	1.25
Common Single Player:	.15	.11	.06

		MT	NR MT	EX
	Panel	4.00	3.00	1.50
10	Dale Murphy	.35	.25	.14
11	Jeff Reardon	.20	.15	.08
12	Jose Canseco	2.00	1.50	.80
---	Roberto Clemente Puzzle Card	.04	.03	.02
	Panel	2.25	1.75	.90
13	Mike Scott	.20	.15	.08
14	Roger Clemens	1.00	.70	.40
15	Mike Krukow	.15	.11	.06
---	Roberto Clemente Puzzle Card	.04	.03	.02

1987 Donruss Diamond Kings Supers

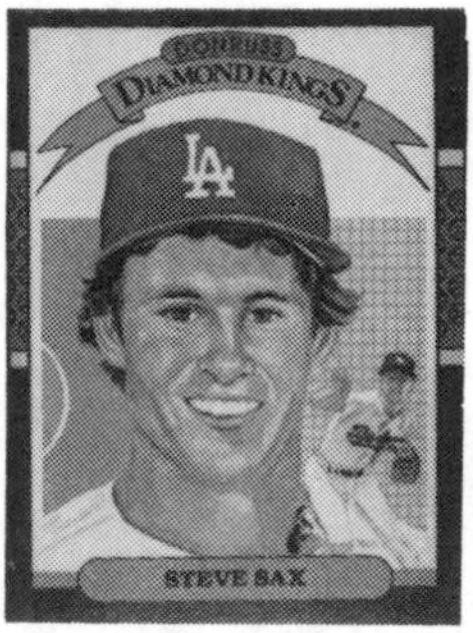

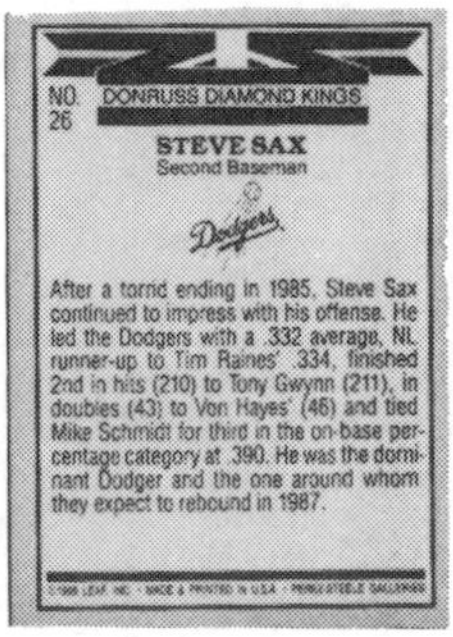

For a third straight baseball card season, Donruss produced a set of enlarged size Diamond Kings. The cards, which measure 4-11/16" by 6-3/4", are giant versions of the Diamond Kings subset found in the regular 1987 Donruss set. The 28-card set, which features the artwork of Dick Perez, contains 26 player cards, a checklist and a Roberto Clemente puzzle card. The set was available through a mail-in offer for $9.50 plus three wrappers.

	MT	NR MT	EX
Complete Set:	12.00	9.00	4.75
Common Player:	.20	.15	.08

		MT	NR MT	EX
1	Wally Joyner	.90	.70	.35
2	Roger Clemens	1.00	.70	.40
3	Dale Murphy	.40	.30	.15
4	Darryl Strawberry	.90	.70	.35
5	Ozzie Smith	.30	.25	.12
6	Jose Canseco	2.00	1.50	.80
7	Charlie Hough	.20	.15	.08
8	Brook Jacoby	.20	.15	.08
9	Fred Lynn	.20	.15	.08
10	Rick Rhoden	.20	.15	.08
11	Chris Brown	.25	.20	.10
12	Von Hayes	.25	.20	.10
13	Jack Morris	.20	.15	.08
14	Kevin McReynolds	.35	.25	.14
15	George Brett	.70	.50	.30
16	Ted Higuera	.20	.15	.08
17	Hubie Brooks	.20	.15	.08
18	Mike Scott	.20	.15	.08
19	Kirby Puckett	.90	.70	.35
20	Dave Winfield	.30	.25	.12
21	Lloyd Moseby	.20	.15	.08
22	Eric Davis	.90	.70	.35
23	Jim Presley	.25	.20	.10
24	Keith Moreland	.20	.15	.08
25	Greg Walker	.20	.15	.08
26	Steve Sax	.30	.25	.12
27	Checklist	.15	.11	.06
---	Roberto Clemente Puzzle Card	.15	.11	.06

1987 Donruss Highlights

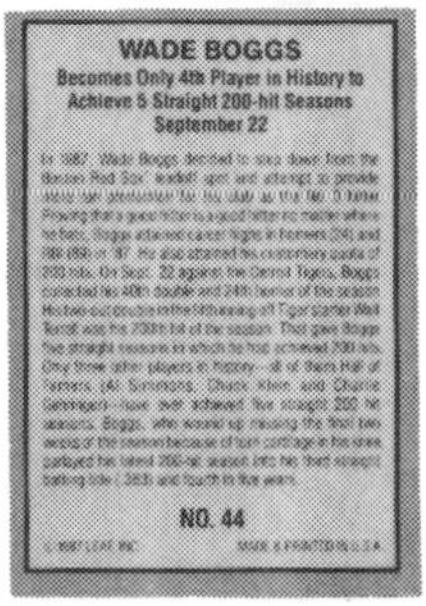

For a third consecutive year, Donruss produced a 56-card set which highlighted the special events of the 1987 baseball season. The cards, which measure 2-1/2" by 3-1/2", have a front design similar to the regular 1987 Donruss set. A blue border and the "Highlights" logo are the significant differences. The card backs feature black print on a white background and include the date the event took place plus the particulars about it. As in the past, the set includes Donruss' picks for the A.L. and N.L. Rookies of the Year. The set was issued in a specially designed box and was available only through hobby dealers.

	MT	NR MT	EX
Complete Set:	8.00	6.00	3.25
Common Player:	.10	.08	.04

		MT	NR MT	EX
1	First No-Hitter For Brewers (Juan Nieves)	.15	.11	.06
2	Hits 500th Homer (Mike Schmidt)	.40	.30	.15
3	N.L. Player of the Month - April (Eric Davis)	.50	.40	.20
4	N.L. Pitcher of the Month - April (Sid Fernandez)	.10	.08	.04
5	A.L. Player of the Month - April (Brian Downing)	.10	.08	.04
6	A.L. Pitcher of the Month - April (Bret Saberhagen)	.30	.25	.12
7	Free Agent Holdout Returns (Tim Raines)	.25	.20	.10
8	N.L. Player of the Month - May (Eric Davis)	.50	.40	.20
9	N.L. Pitcher of the Month - May (Steve Bedrosian)	.15	.11	.06
10	A.L. Player of the Month - May (Larry Parrish)	.10	.08	.04
11	A.L. Pitcher of the Month - May (Jim Clancy)	.10	.08	.04
12	N.L. Player of the Month - June (Tony Gwynn)	.30	.25	.12
13	N.L. Pitcher of the Month - June (Orel Hershiser)	.25	.20	.10
14	A.L. Player of the Month - June (Wade Boggs)	.80	.60	.30
15	A.L. Pitcher of the Month - June (Steve Ontiveros)	.10	.08	.04
16	All Star Game Hero (Tim Raines)	.25	.20	.10
17	Consecutive Game Homer Streak (Don Mattingly)	1.00	.70	.40
18	1987 Hall of Fame Inductee (Jim "Catfish" Hunter)	.20	.15	.08

		MT	NR MT	EX
19	1987 Hall of Fame Inductee (Ray Dandridge)	.10	.08	.04
20	1987 Hall of Fame Inductee (Billy Williams)	.20	.15	.08
21	N.L. Player of the Month - July (Bo Diaz)	.10	.08	.04
22	N.L. Pitcher of the Month - July (Floyd Youmans)	.10	.08	.04
23	A.L. Player of the Month - July (Don Mattingly)	1.00	.70	.40
24	A.L. Pitcher of the Month - July (Frank Viola)	.20	.15	.08
25	Strikes Out 4 Batters In 1 Inning (Bobby Witt)	.15	.11	.06
26	Ties A.L. 9-Inning Game Hit Mark (Kevin Seitzer)	.50	.40	.20
27	Sets Rookie Home Run Record (Mark McGwire)	1.25	.90	.50
28	Sets Cubs' 1st Year Homer Mark (Andre Dawson)	.20	.15	.08
29	Hits In 39 Straight Games (Paul Molitor)	.15	.11	.06
30	Record Weekend (Kirby Puckett)	.50	.40	.20
31	N.L. Player of the Month - August (Andre Dawson)	.20	.15	.08
32	N.L. Pitcher of the Month - August (Doug Drabek)	.10	.08	.04
33	A.L. Player of the Month - August (Dwight Evans)	.15	.11	.06
34	A.L. Pitcher of the Month - August (Mark Langston)	.25	.20	.10
35	100 RBI In 1st 2 Major League Seasons (Wally Joyner)	.40	.30	.15
36	100 SB In 1st 3 Major League Seasons (Vince Coleman)	.20	.15	.08
37	Orioles' All Time Homer King (Eddie Murray)	.10	.08	.04
38	Ends Consecutive Innings Streak (Cal Ripken)	.30	.25	.12
39	Blue Jays Hit Record 10 Homers In 1 Gamelers. (Rob Ducey, Fred McGriff, Ernie Whitt)	.50	.40	.20
40	Equal A's RBI Marks (Jose Canseco, Mark McGwire)	2.50	2.00	1.00
41	Sets All-Time Catching Record (Bob Boone)	.10	.08	.04
42	Sets Mets' One-Season HR Mark (Darryl Strawberry)	.50	.40	.20
43	N.L.'s All-Time Switch Hit HR King (Howard Johnson)	.15	.11	.06
44	Five Straight 200-Hit Seasons (Wade Boggs)	.80	.60	.30
45	Eclipses Rookie Game Hitting Streak (Benito Santiago)	.40	.30	.15
46	Eclipses Jackson's A's HR Record (Mark McGwire)	1.25	.90	.50
47	13th Rookie To Collect 200 Hits (Kevin Seitzer)	.50	.40	.20
48	Sets Slam Record (Don Mattingly)	1.00	.70	.40
49	N.L. Player of the Month - September (Darryl Strawberry)	.50	.40	.20
50	N.L. Pitcher of the Month - September (Pascual Perez)	.10	.08	.04
51	A.L. Player of the Month - September (Alan Trammell)	.20	.15	.08
52	A.L. Pitcher of the Month - September (Doyle Alexander)	.10	.08	.04
53	Strikeout King - Again (Nolan Ryan)	1.00	.70	.40
54	Donruss A.L. Rookie of the Year (Mark McGwire)	1.25	.90	.50
55	Donruss N.L. Rookie of the Year (Benito Santiago)	.40	.30	.15
56	Highlight Checklist	.10	.08	.04

1987 Donruss Opening Day

The Donruss Opening Day set includes all players in major league baseball's starting lineups on the opening day of the 1987 baseball season. Cards in the 272-piece set measure 2-1/2" by 3-1/2" and have a glossy coating. The card fronts are identical in design to the regular Donruss set, but new photos were utilized and the fronts contain maroon borders as

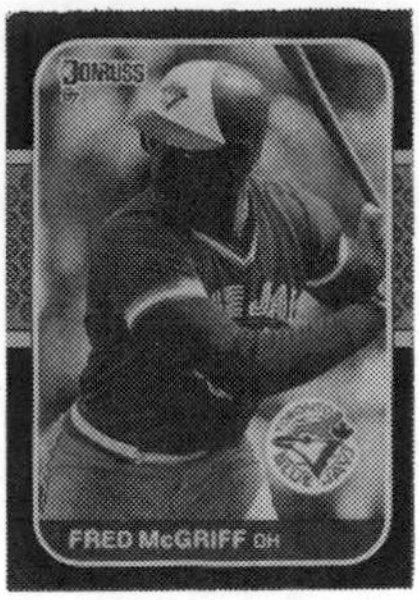

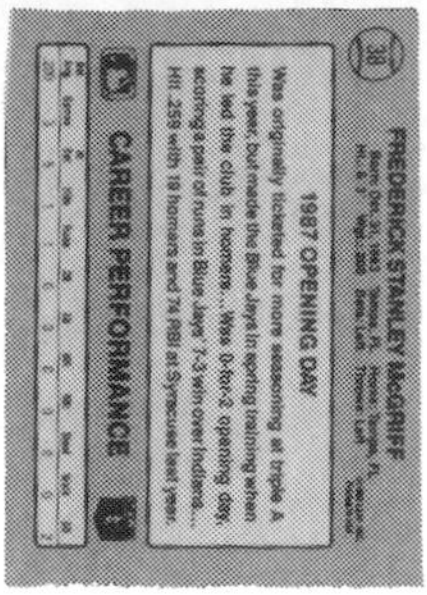

opposed to black. The backs carry black printing on white and yellow and carry a brief player biography plus the player's career statistics. The set was packaged in a sturdy 15" by 5" by 2" box with a clear acetate lid.

		MT	NR MT	EX
Complete Set:		25.00	18.50	10.00
Common Player:		.05	.04	.02
1	Doug DeCinces	.07	.05	.03
2	Mike Witt	.12	.09	.05
3	George Hendrick	.07	.05	.03
4	Dick Schofield	.05	.04	.02
5	Devon White	.50	.40	.20
6	Butch Wynegar	.05	.04	.02
7	Wally Joyner	.75	.55	.30
8	Mark McLemore	.05	.04	.02
9	Brian Downing	.07	.05	.03
10	Gary Pettis	.05	.04	.02
11	Bill Doran	.07	.05	.03
12	Phil Garner	.05	.04	.02
13	Jose Cruz	.07	.05	.03
14	Kevin Bass	.07	.05	.03
15	Mike Scott	.12	.09	.05
16	Glenn Davis	.15	.11	.06
17	Alan Ashby	.05	.04	.02
18	Billy Hatcher	.07	.05	.03
19	Craig Reynolds	.05	.04	.02
20	Carney Lansford	.07	.05	.03
21	Mike Davis	.05	.04	.02
22	Reggie Jackson	.30	.25	.12
23	Mickey Tettleton	.07	.05	.03
24	Jose Canseco	2.50	2.00	1.00
25	Rob Nelson	.05	.04	.02
26	Tony Phillips	.05	.04	.02
27	Dwayne Murphy	.05	.04	.02
28	Alfredo Griffin	.07	.05	.03
29	Curt Young	.05	.04	.02
30	Willie Upshaw	.05	.04	.02
31	Mike Sharperson	.05	.04	.02
32	Rance Mulliniks	.05	.04	.02
33	Ernie Whitt	.05	.04	.02
34	Jesse Barfield	.12	.09	.05
35	Tony Fernandez	.12	.09	.05
36	Lloyd Moseby	.07	.05	.03
37	Jimmy Key	.10	.08	.04
38	Fred McGriff	1.50	1.25	.60
39	George Bell	.25	.20	.10
40	Dale Murphy	.40	.30	.15
41	Rick Mahler	.05	.04	.02
42	Ken Griffey	.07	.05	.03
43	Andres Thomas	.10	.08	.04
44	Dion James	.05	.04	.02
45	Ozzie Virgil	.05	.04	.02
46	Ken Oberkfell	.05	.04	.02
47	Gary Roenicke	.05	.04	.02
48	Glenn Hubbard	.05	.04	.02
49	Bill Schroeder	.05	.04	.02
50	Greg Brock	.07	.05	.03
51	Billy Jo Robidoux	.05	.04	.02
52	Glenn Braggs	.12	.09	.05
53	Jim Gantner	.05	.04	.02
54	Paul Molitor	.15	.11	.06
55	Dale Sveum	.15	.11	.06
56	Ted Higuera	.12	.09	.05
57	Rob Deer	.07	.05	.03
58	Robin Yount	.35	.25	.14
59	Jim Lindeman	.10	.08	.04
60	Vince Coleman	.15	.11	.06

		MT	NR MT	EX
61	Tommy Herr	.07	.05	.03
62	Terry Pendleton	.07	.05	.03
63	John Tudor	.10	.08	.04
64	Tony Pena	.07	.05	.03
65	Ozzie Smith	.15	.11	.06
66	Tito Landrum	.05	.04	.02
67	Jack Clark	.15	.11	.06
68	Bob Dernier	.05	.04	.02
69	Rick Sutcliffe	.10	.08	.04
70	Andre Dawson	.20	.15	.08
71	Keith Moreland	.07	.05	.03
72	Jody Davis	.07	.05	.03
73	Brian Dayett	.05	.04	.02
74	Leon Durham	.07	.05	.03
75	Ryne Sandberg	.25	.20	.10
76	Shawon Dunston	.20	.15	.08
77	Mike Marshall	.10	.08	.04
78	Bill Madlock	.07	.05	.03
79	Orel Hershiser	.30	.25	.12
80	Mike Ramsey	.05	.04	.02
81	Ken Landreaux	.05	.04	.02
82	Mike Scioscia	.05	.04	.02
83	Franklin Stubbs	.07	.05	.03
84	Mariano Duncan	.05	.04	.02
85	Steve Sax	.15	.11	.06
86	Mitch Webster	.07	.05	.03
87	Reid Nichols	.05	.04	.02
88	Tim Wallach	.10	.08	.04
89	Floyd Youmans	.07	.05	.03
90	Andres Galarraga	.25	.20	.10
91	Hubie Brooks	.07	.05	.03
92	Jeff Reed	.05	.04	.02
93	Alonzo Powell	.05	.04	.02
94	Vance Law	.05	.04	.02
95	Bob Brenly	.05	.04	.02
96	Will Clark	2.50	2.00	1.00
97	Chili Davis	.07	.05	.03
98	Mike Krukow	.05	.04	.02
99	Jose Uribe	.05	.04	.02
100	Chris Brown	.07	.05	.03
101	Rob Thompson	.10	.08	.04
102	Candy Maldonado	.07	.05	.03
103	Jeff Leonard	.07	.05	.03
104	Tom Candiotti	.05	.04	.02
105	Chris Bando	.05	.04	.02
106	Cory Snyder	.30	.25	.12
107	Pat Tabler	.07	.05	.03
108	Andre Thornton	.07	.05	.03
109	Joe Carter	.25	.20	.10
110	Tony Bernazard	.05	.04	.02
111	Julio Franco	.10	.08	.04
112	Brook Jacoby	.10	.08	.04
113	Brett Butler	.07	.05	.03
114	Donnell Nixon	.05	.04	.02
115	Alvin Davis	.12	.09	.05
116	Mark Langston	.25	.20	.10
117	Harold Reynolds	.07	.05	.03
118	Ken Phelps	.05	.04	.02
119	Mike Kingery	.10	.08	.04
120	Dave Valle	.07	.05	.03
121	Rey Quinones	.07	.05	.03
122	Phil Bradley	.12	.09	.05
123	Jim Presley	.12	.09	.05
124	Keith Hernandez	.12	.09	.05
125	Kevin McReynolds	.12	.09	.05
126	Rafael Santana	.05	.04	.02
127	Bob Ojeda	.07	.05	.03
128	Darryl Strawberry	.60	.45	.25
129	Mookie Wilson	.07	.05	.03
130	Gary Carter	.15	.11	.06
131	Tim Teufel	.05	.04	.02
132	Howard Johnson	.20	.15	.08
133	Cal Ripken	.30	.25	.12
134	Rick Burleson	.05	.04	.02
135	Fred Lynn	.12	.09	.05
136	Eddie Murray	.15	.11	.06
137	Ray Knight	.07	.05	.03
138	Alan Wiggins	.05	.04	.02
139	John Shelby	.05	.04	.02
140	Mike Boddicker	.07	.05	.03
141	Ken Gerhart	.07	.05	.03
142	Terry Kennedy	.07	.05	.03
143	Steve Garvey	.30	.25	.12
144	Marvell Wynne	.05	.04	.02
145	Kevin Mitchell	1.50	1.25	.60
146	Tony Gwynn	.35	.25	.14
147	Joey Cora	.10	.08	.04
148	Benito Santiago	.60	.45	.25
149	Eric Show	.07	.05	.03
150	Garry Templeton	.07	.05	.03
151	Carmelo Martinez	.05	.04	.02

		MT	NR MT	EX
152	Von Hayes	.10	.08	.04
153	Lance Parrish	.10	.08	.04
154	Milt Thompson	.07	.05	.03
155	Mike Easler	.05	.04	.02
156	Juan Samuel	.10	.08	.04
157	Steve Jeltz	.05	.04	.02
158	Glenn Wilson	.05	.04	.02
159	Shane Rawley	.07	.05	.03
160	Mike Schmidt	.40	.30	.15
161	Andy Van Slyke	.10	.08	.04
162	Johnny Ray	.07	.05	.03
163a	Barry Bonds (dark jersey, photo actually Johnny Ray)	125.00	94.00	50.00
163b	Barry Bonds (white jersey, correct photo)	.50	.40	.20
164	Junior Ortiz	.05	.04	.02
165	Rafael Belliard	.05	.04	.02
166	Bob Patterson	.05	.04	.02
167	Bobby Bonilla	.50	.40	.20
168	Sid Bream	.07	.05	.03
169	Jim Morrison	.05	.04	.02
170	Jerry Browne	.10	.08	.04
171	Scott Fletcher	.05	.04	.02
172	Ruben Sierra	1.50	1.25	.60
173	Larry Parrish	.07	.05	.03
174	Pete O'Brien	.07	.05	.03
175	Pete Incaviglia	.35	.25	.14
176	Don Slaught	.05	.04	.02
177	Oddibe McDowell	.10	.08	.04
178	Charlie Hough	.07	.05	.03
179	Steve Buechele	.05	.04	.02
180	Bob Stanley	.05	.04	.02
181	Wade Boggs	1.00	.70	.40
182	Jim Rice	.10	.08	.04
183	Bill Buckner	.07	.05	.03
184	Dwight Evans	.10	.08	.04
185	Spike Owen	.05	.04	.02
186	Don Baylor	.10	.08	.04
187	Marc Sullivan	.05	.04	.02
188	Marty Barrett	.07	.05	.03
189	Dave Henderson	.07	.05	.03
190	Bo Diaz	.05	.04	.02
191	Barry Larkin	.90	.70	.35
192	Kal Daniels	.25	.20	.10
193	Terry Francona	.05	.04	.02
194	Tom Browning	.07	.05	.03
195	Ron Oester	.05	.04	.02
196	Buddy Bell	.07	.05	.03
197	Eric Davis	.60	.45	.25
198	Dave Parker	.15	.11	.06
199	Steve Balboni	.05	.04	.02
200	Danny Tartabull	.30	.25	.12
201	Ed Hearn	.05	.04	.02
202	Buddy Biancalana	.05	.04	.02
203	Danny Jackson	.05	.04	.02
204	Frank White	.08	.06	.03
205	Bo Jackson	2.50	2.00	1.00
206	George Brett	.40	.30	.15
207	Kevin Seitzer	.90	.70	.35
208	Willie Wilson	.10	.08	.04
209	Orlando Mercado	.05	.04	.02
210	Darrell Evans	.07	.05	.03
211	Larry Herndon	.05	.04	.02
212	Jack Morris	.15	.11	.06
213	Chet Lemon	.07	.05	.03
214	Mike Heath	.05	.04	.02
215	Darnell Coles	.07	.05	.03
216	Alan Trammell	.20	.15	.08
217	Terry Harper	.05	.04	.02
218	Lou Whitaker	.15	.11	.06
219	Gary Gaetti	.15	.11	.06
220	Tom Nieto	.05	.04	.02
221	Kirby Puckett	.80	.60	.30
222	Tom Brunansky	.10	.08	.04
223	Greg Gagne	.05	.04	.02
224	Dan Gladden	.07	.05	.03
225	Mark Davidson	.07	.05	.03
226	Bert Blyleven	.10	.08	.04
227	Steve Lombardozzi	.05	.04	.02
228	Kent Hrbek	.15	.11	.06
229	Gary Redus	.05	.04	.02
230	Ivan Calderon	.10	.08	.04
231	Tim Hulett	.05	.04	.02
232	Carlton Fisk	.15	.11	.06
233	Greg Walker	.07	.05	.03
234	Ron Karkovice	.05	.04	.02
235	Ozzie Guillen	.07	.05	.03
236	Harold Baines	.12	.09	.05
237	Donnie Hill	.05	.04	.02
238	Rich Dotson	.07	.05	.03
239	Mike Pagliarulo	.10	.08	.04

		MT	NR MT	EX
240	Joel Skinner	.05	.04	.02
241	Don Mattingly	1.50	1.25	.60
242	Gary Ward	.05	.04	.02
243	Dave Winfield	.20	.15	.08
244	Dan Pasqua	.10	.08	.04
245	Wayne Tolleson	.05	.04	.02
246	Willie Randolph	.07	.05	.03
247	Dennis Rasmussen	.07	.05	.03
248	Rickey Henderson	.50	.40	.20
249	Angels Logo/Checklist	.05	.04	.02
250	Astros Logo/Checklist	.05	.04	.02
251	Athletics Logo/Checklist	.05	.04	.02
252	Blue Jays Logo/Checklist	.05	.04	.02
253	Braves Logo/Checklist	.05	.04	.02
254	Brewers Logo/Checklist	.05	.04	.02
255	Cardinals Logo/Checklist	.05	.04	.02
256	Dodgers Logo/Checklist	.05	.04	.02
257	Expos Logo/Checklist	.05	.04	.02
258	Giants Logo/Checklist	.05	.04	.02
259	Indians Logo/Checklist	.05	.04	.02
260	Mariners Logo/Checklist	.05	.04	.02
261	Orioles Logo/Checklist	.05	.04	.02
262	Padres Logo/Checklist	.05	.04	.02
263	Phillies Logo/Checklist	.05	.04	.02
264	Pirates Logo/Checklist	.05	.04	.02
265	Rangers Logo/Checklist	.05	.04	.02
266	Red Sox Logo/Checklist	.05	.04	.02
267	Reds Logo/Checklist	.05	.04	.02
268	Royals Logo/Checklist	.05	.04	.02
269	Tigers Logo/Checklist	.05	.04	.02
270	Twins Logo/Checklist	.05	.04	.02
271	White Sox-Cubs Logos/Checklist	.05	.04	.02
272	Yankees-Mets Logos/Checklist	.05	.04	.02

1987 Donruss Pop-Ups

For the second straight year, Donruss released in conjunction with its All-Stars issue a set of cards designed to fold out to form a three-dimensional stand-up card. Consisting of 20 cards, as opposed to the previous year's 18, the 1987 Donruss Pop-Ups set contains players selected to the 1986 All Star Game. Background for the 2-1/2" by 5" cards is the Houston Astrodome, site of the 1986 mid-summer classic. Retail packs included one Pop-Up card, three All-Star cards and one Roberto Clemente puzzle card.

		MT	NR MT	EX
Complete Set:		4.00	3.00	1.50
Common Player:		.20	.15	.08
(1)	Wade Boggs	.70	.50	.30
(2)	Gary Carter	.25	.20	.10
(3)	Roger Clemens	.80	.60	.30
(4)	Dwight Gooden	.80	.60	.30
(5)	Tony Gwynn	.50	.40	.20
(6)	Rickey Henderson	.75	.55	.30
(7)	Keith Hernandez	.25	.20	.10
(8)	Whitey Herzog	.20	.15	.08
(9)	Dick Howser	.20	.15	.08
(10)	Wally Joyner	.40	.30	.15
(11)	Dale Murphy	.40	.30	.15
(12)	Lance Parrish	.20	.15	.08
(13)	Kirby Puckett	.75	.55	.30
(14)	Cal Ripken	.50	.40	.20
(15)	Ryne Sandberg	.80	.60	.30
(16)	Mike Schmidt	.60	.45	.25
(17)	Ozzie Smith	.30	.25	.12
(18)	Darryl Strawberry	.50	.40	.20
(19)	Lou Whitaker	.20	.15	.08
(20)	Dave Winfield	.30	.25	.12

1987 Donruss Rookies

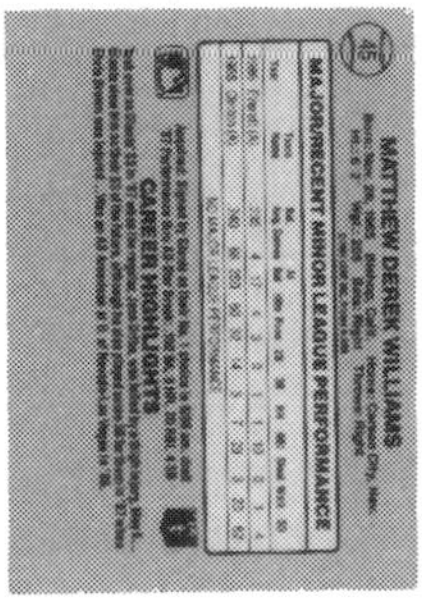

As they did in 1986, Donruss issued a 56-card set highlighting the major league's most promising rookies. The cards are the standard 2-1/2" by 3-1/2" size and are identical in design to the regular Donruss issue. The card fronts have green borders as opposed to the black found in the regular issue and carry the words "The Rookies" in the lower left portion of the card. The set came housed in a specially designed box and was available only through hobby dealers.

		MT	NR MT	EX
Complete Set:		20.00	15.00	8.00
Common Player:		.10	.08	.04
1	Mark McGwire	3.00	2.25	1.25
2	Eric Bell	.10	.08	.04
3	Mark Williamson(FC)	.15	.11	.06
4	Mike Greenwell	2.50	2.00	1.00
5	Ellis Burks(FC)	3.50	2.75	1.50
6	DeWayne Buice(FC)	.20	.15	.08
7	Mark Mclemore (McLemore)	.10	.08	.04
8	Devon White	.40	.30	.15
9	Willie Fraser	.15	.11	.06
10	Lester Lancaster(FC)	.15	.11	.06
11	Ken Williams(FC)	.20	.15	.08
12	Matt Nokes(FC)	.50	.40	.20
13	Jeff Robinson(FC)	.30	.25	.12
14	Bo Jackson	4.00	3.00	1.50
15	Kevin Seitzer(FC)	.50	.40	.20
16	Billy Ripken(FC)	.25	.20	.10
17	B.J. Surhoff	.20	.15	.08
18	Chuck Crim(FC)	.15	.11	.06
19	Mike Birbeck	.10	.08	.04
20	Chris Bosio	.10	.08	.04
21	Les Straker(FC)	.20	.15	.08
22	Mark Davidson(FC)	.15	.11	.06
23	Gene Larkin(FC)	.35	.25	.14
24	Ken Gerhart	.15	.11	.06
25	Luis Polonia(FC)	.50	.40	.20
26	Terry Steinbach	.25	.20	.10
27	Mickey Brantley	.10	.08	.04
28	Mike Stanley	.20	.15	.08
29	Jerry Browne	.10	.08	.04
30	Todd Benzinger(FC)	.30	.25	.12
31	Fred McGriff	2.50	2.00	1.00
32	Mike Henneman(FC)	.35	.25	.14
33	Casey Candaele	.10	.08	.04
34	Dave Magadan	.80	.60	.30
35	David Cone	1.00	.70	.40
36	Mike Jackson(FC)	.20	.15	.08
37	John Mitchell(FC)	.20	.15	.08
38	Mike Dunne(FC)	.15	.11	.06
39	John Smiley(FC)	1.00	.70	.40
40	Joe Magrane(FC)	.60	.45	.25
41	Jim Lindeman	.10	.08	.04
42	Shane Mack(FC)	1.00	.70	.40
43	Stan Jefferson	.10	.08	.04
44	Benito Santiago	.80	.60	.30
45	Matt Williams(FC)	6.00	4.50	2.50

		MT	NR MT	EX
46	Dave Meads(FC)	.20	.15	.08
47	Rafael Palmeiro	2.00	1.50	.80
48	Bill Long(FC)	.20	.15	.08
49	Bob Brower	.10	.08	.04
50	James Steels(FC)	.15	.11	.06
51	Paul Noce(FC)	.15	.11	.06
52	Greg Maddux	.60	.45	.25
53	Jeff Musselman	.15	.11	.06
54	Brian Holton	.15	.11	.06
55	Chuck Jackson(FC)	.20	.15	.08
56	Checklist 1-56	.10	.08	.04

1988 Donruss

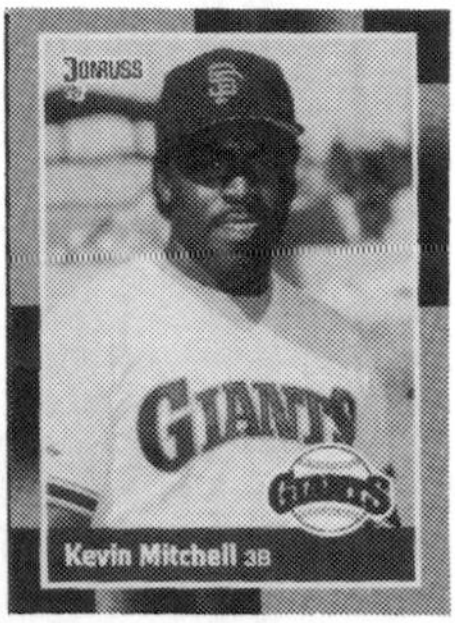

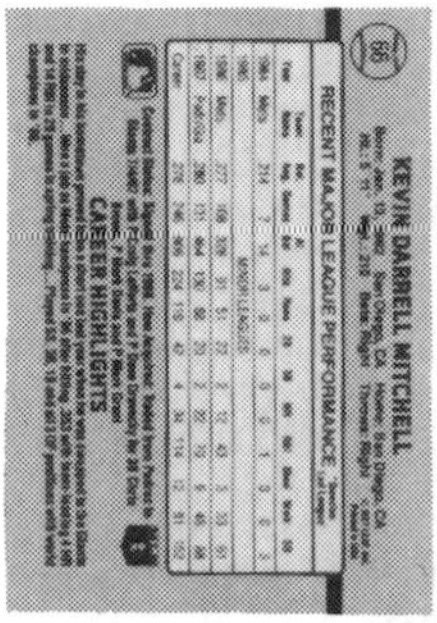

The 1988 Donruss set consists of 660 cards, each measuring 2-1/2" by 3-1/2" in size. The card fronts feature a full-color photo surrounded by a colorful border - alternating stripes of black, red, black, blue, black, blue, black, red and black (in that order), separated by soft-focus edges and airbrushed fades. The player's name and position appear in a red band at the bottom of the card. The Donruss logo is situated in the upper left corner of the card, while the team logo is located in the lower right corner. For the seventh consecutive season, Donruss included a subset of "Diamond Kings" cards (#'s 1-27) in the issue. And for the fifth straight year, Donruss incorporated their highly popular "Rated Rookies" (card #'s 28-47) with the set.

		MT	NR MT	EX
Complete Set:		20.00	15.00	8.00
Common Player		.05	.04	.02
1	Mark McGwire (DK)	.25	.20	.10
2	Tim Raines (DK)	.25	.20	.10
3	Benito Santiago (DK)	.30	.25	.12
4	Alan Trammell (DK)	.25	.20	.10
5	Danny Tartabull (DK)	.20	.15	.08
6	Ron Darling (DK)	.12	.09	.05
7	Paul Molitor (DK)	.12	.09	.05
8	Devon White (DK)	.10	.08	.04
9	Andre Dawson (DK)	.20	.15	.08
10	Julio Franco (DK)	.10	.08	.04
11	Scott Fletcher (DK)	.07	.05	.03
12	Tony Fernandez (DK)	.12	.09	.05
13	Shane Rawley (DK)	.07	.05	.03
14	Kal Daniels (DK)	.20	.15	.08
15	Jack Clark (DK)	.15	.11	.06
16	Dwight Evans (DK)	.12	.09	.05
17	Tommy John (DK)	.15	.11	.06
18	Andy Van Slyke (DK)	.15	.11	.06
19	Gary Gaetti (DK)	.12	.09	.05
20	Mark Langston (DK)	.10	.08	.04
21	Will Clark (DK)	.60	.45	.25
22	Glenn Hubbard (DK)	.07	.05	.03
23	Billy Hatcher (DK)	.07	.05	.03
24	Bob Welch (DK)	.10	.08	.04
25	Ivan Calderon (DK)	.10	.08	.04
26	Cal Ripken, Jr. (DK)	.35	.25	.14
27	Checklist 1-27	.05	.04	.02
28	*Mackey Sasser* (RR)(FC)	.20	.15	.08
29	*Jeff Treadway* (RR)(FC)	.30	.25	.12
30	*Mike Campbell* (RR)(FC)	.12	.09	.05
31	*Lance Johnson* (RR)(FC)	.30	.25	.12
32	*Nelson Liriano* (RR)(FC)	.15	.11	.06
33	Shawn Abner (RR)(FC)	.20	.15	.08

		MT	NR MT	EX
34	*Roberto Alomar* (RR)(FC)	3.00	2.25	1.25
35	*Shawn Hillegas* (RR)(FC)	.25	.20	.10
36	Joey Meyer (RR)	.20	.15	.08
37	Kevin Elster (RR)	.30	.25	.12
38	*Jose Lind* (RR)(FC)	.30	.25	.12
39	*Kirt Manwaring* (RR)(FC)	.20	.15	.08
40	*Mark Grace* (RR)(FC)	3.00	2.25	1.25
41	*Jody Reed* (RR)(FC)	.40	.30	.15
42	*John Farrell* (RR)(FC)	.15	.11	.06
43	*Al Leiter* (RR)(FC)	.12	.09	.05
44	*Gary Thurman* (RR)(FC)	.20	.15	.18
45	*Vicente Palacios* (RR)(FC)	.30	.25	.12
46	*Eddie Williams* (RR)(FC)	.15	.11	.06
47	*Jack McDowell* (RR)(FC)	1.00	.70	.40
48	Ken Dixon	.05	.04	.02
49	Mike Birkbeck	.07	.05	.03
50	Eric King	.07	.05	.03
51	Roger Clemens	.60	.45	.25
52	Pat Clements	.05	.04	.02
53	Fernando Valenzuela	.25	.20	.10
54	Mark Gubicza	.12	.09	.05
55	Jay Howell	.07	.05	.03
56	Floyd Youmans	.05	.04	.02
57	Ed Correa	.05	.04	.02
58	*DeWayne Buice*	.15	.11	.06
59	Jose DeLeon	.07	.05	.03
60	Danny Cox	.07	.05	.03
61	Nolan Ryan	.50	.40	.20
62	Steve Bedrosian	.12	.09	.05
63	Tom Browning	.10	.08	.04
64	Mark Davis	.05	.04	.02
65	R.J. Reynolds	.05	.04	.02
66	Kevin Mitchell	.60	.45	.25
67	Ken Oberkfell	.05	.04	.02
68	Rick Sutcliffe	.10	.08	.04
69	Dwight Gooden	.60	.45	.25
70	Scott Bankhead	.07	.05	.03
71	Bert Blyleven	.12	.09	.05
72	Jimmy Key	.10	.08	.04
73	*Les Straker*	.15	.11	.06
74	Jim Clancy	.07	.05	.03
75	Mike Moore	.05	.04	.02
76	Ron Darling	.12	.09	.05
77	Ed Lynch	.05	.04	.02
78	Dale Murphy	.40	.30	.15
79	Doug Drabek	.07	.05	.03
80	Scott Garrelts	.05	.04	.02
81	Ed Whitson	.05	.04	.02
82	Rob Murphy	.07	.05	.03
83	Shane Rawley	.07	.05	.03
84	Greg Mathews	.07	.05	.03
85	Jim Deshaies	.07	.05	.03
86	Mike Witt	.07	.05	.03
87	Donnie Hill	.05	.04	.02
88	Jeff Reed	.05	.04	.02
89	Mike Boddicker	.07	.05	.03
90	Ted Higuera	.10	.08	.04
91	Walt Terrell	.07	.05	.03
92	Bob Stanley	.05	.04	.02
93	Dave Righetti	.15	.11	.06
94	Orel Hershiser	.25	.20	.10
95	Chris Bando	.05	.04	.02
96	Bret Saberhagen	.15	.11	.06
97	Curt Young	.07	.05	.03
98	Tim Burke	.05	.04	.02
99	Charlie Hough	.07	.05	.03
100a	Checklist 28-137	.05	.04	.02
100b	Checklist 28-133	.10	.08	.04
101	Bobby Witt	.10	.08	.04
102	George Brett	.40	.30	.15
103	Mickey Tettleton	.25	.20	.10
104	Scott Bailes	.07	.05	.03
105	Mike Pagliarulo	.10	.08	.04
106	Mike Scioscia	.07	.05	.03
107	Tom Brookens	.05	.04	.02
108	Ray Knight	.07	.05	.03
109	Dan Plesac	.10	.08	.04
110	Wally Joyner	.30	.25	.12
111	Bob Forsch	.07	.05	.03
112	Mike Scott	.12	.09	.05
113	Kevin Gross	.07	.05	.03
114	Benito Santiago	.35	.25	.14
115	Bob Kipper	.05	.04	.02
116	Mike Krukow	.07	.05	.03
117	Chris Bosio	.07	.05	.03
118	Sid Fernandez	.10	.08	.04
119	Jody Davis	.07	.05	.03
120	Mike Morgan	.05	.04	.02
121	Mark Eichhorn	.07	.05	.03
122	Jeff Reardon	.10	.08	.04
123	John Franco	.10	.08	.04
124	Richard Dotson	.07	.05	.03

		MT	NR MT	EX
125	Eric Bell	.05	.04	.02
126	Juan Nieves	.07	.05	.03
127	Jack Morris	.20	.15	.08
128	Rick Rhoden	.07	.05	.03
129	Rich Gedman	.07	.05	.03
130	Ken Howell	.05	.04	.02
131	Brook Jacoby	.10	.08	.04
132	Danny Jackson	.12	.09	.05
133	Gene Nelson	.05	.04	.02
134	Neal Heaton	.05	.04	.02
135	Willie Fraser	.05	.04	.02
136	Jose Guzman	.07	.05	.03
137	Ozzie Guillen	.07	.05	.03
138	Bob Knepper	.07	.05	.03
139	*Mike Jackson*	.20	.15	.08
140	*Joe Magrane*	.30	.25	.12
141	Jimmy Jones	.07	.05	.03
142	Ted Power	.05	.04	.02
143	Ozzie Virgil	.05	.04	.02
144	*Felix Fermin*(FC)	.15	.11	.06
145	Kelly Downs	.10	.08	.04
146	Shawon Dunston	.10	.08	.04
147	Scott Bradley	.05	.04	.02
148	Dave Stieb	.10	.08	.04
149	Frank Viola	.15	.11	.06
150	Terry Kennedy	.07	.05	.03
151	Bill Wegman	.05	.04	.02
152	*Matt Nokes*	.50	.40	.20
153	Wade Boggs	.60	.45	.25
154	Wayne Tolleson	.05	.04	.02
155	Mariano Duncan	.05	.04	.02
156	Julio Franco	.10	.08	.04
157	Charlie Leibrandt	.07	.05	.03
158	Terry Steinbach	.10	.08	.04
159	Mike Fitzgerald	.05	.04	.02
160	Jack Lazorko	.05	.04	.02
161	Mitch Williams	.07	.05	.03
162	Greg Walker	.07	.05	.03
163	Alan Ashby	.05	.04	.02
164	Tony Gwynn	.35	.25	.14
165	Bruce Ruffin	.07	.05	.03
166	Ron Robinson	.05	.04	.02
167	Zane Smith	.07	.05	.03
168	Junior Ortiz	.05	.04	.02
169	Jamie Moyer	.07	.05	.03
170	Tony Pena	.07	.05	.03
171	Cal Ripken	.35	.25	.14
172	B.J. Surhoff	.12	.09	.05
173	Lou Whitaker	.25	.20	.10
174	*Ellis Burks*	1.00	.70	.40
175	Ron Guidry	.15	.11	.06
176	Steve Sax	.15	.11	.06
177	Danny Tartabull	.20	.15	.08
178	Carney Lansford	.10	.08	.04
179	Casey Candaele	.05	.04	.02
180	Scott Fletcher	.07	.05	.03
181	Mark McLemore	.05	.04	.02
182	Ivan Calderon	.10	.08	.04
183	Jack Clark	.15	.11	.06
184	Glenn Davis	.15	.11	.06
185	Luis Aguayo	.05	.04	.02
186	Bo Diaz	.07	.05	.03
187	Stan Jefferson	.07	.05	.03
188	Sid Bream	.07	.05	.03
189	Bob Brenly	.05	.04	.02
190	Dion James	.07	.05	.03
191	Leon Durham	.07	.05	.03
192	Jesse Orosco	.07	.05	.03
193	Alvin Davis	.12	.09	.05
194	Gary Gaetti	.12	.09	.05
195	Fred McGriff	.40	.30	.15
196	Steve Lombardozzi	.05	.04	.02
197	Rance Mulliniks	.05	.04	.02
198	Rey Quinones	.05	.04	.02
199	Gary Carter	.25	.20	.10
200a	Checklist 138-247	.05	.04	.02
200b	Checklist 134-239	.10	.08	.04
201	Keith Moreland	.07	.05	.03
202	Ken Griffey	.07	.05	.03
203	*Tommy Gregg*(FC)	.20	.15	.08
204	Will Clark	1.00	.70	.40
205	John Kruk	.10	.08	.04
206	Buddy Bell	.07	.05	.03
207	Von Hayes	.07	.05	.03
208	Tommy Herr	.07	.05	.03
209	Craig Reynolds	.05	.04	.02
210	Gary Pettis	.05	.04	.02
211	Harold Baines	.12	.09	.05
212	Vance Law	.07	.05	.03
213	Ken Gerhart	.07	.05	.03
214	Jim Gantner	.05	.04	.02

		MT	NR MT	EX
215	Chet Lemon	.07	.05	.03
216	Dwight Evans	.12	.09	.05
217	Don Mattingly	.80	.60	.30
218	Franklin Stubbs	.07	.05	.03
219	Pat Tabler	.07	.05	.03
220	Bo Jackson	1.00	.70	.40
221	Tony Phillips	.05	.04	.02
222	Tim Wallach	.10	.08	.04
223	Ruben Sierra	.60	.45	.25
224	Steve Buechele	.05	.04	.02
225	Frank White	.07	.05	.03
226	Alfredo Griffin	.07	.05	.03
227	Greg Swindell	.20	.15	.08
228	Willie Randolph	.07	.05	.03
229	Mike Marshall	.12	.09	.05
230	Alan Trammell	.25	.20	.10
231	Eddie Murray	.35	.25	.14
232	Dale Sveum	.07	.05	.03
233	Dick Schofield	.05	.04	.02
234	Jose Oquendo	.05	.04	.02
235	Bill Doran	.07	.05	.03
236	Milt Thompson	.05	.04	.02
237	Marvell Wynne	.05	.04	.02
238	Bobby Bonilla	.40	.30	.15
239	Chris Speier	.05	.04	.02
240	Glenn Braggs	.10	.08	.04
241	Wally Backman	.07	.05	.03
242	Ryne Sandberg	.50	.40	.20
243	Phil Bradley	.10	.08	.04
244	Kelly Gruber	.05	.04	.02
245	Tom Brunansky	.10	.08	.04
246	Ron Oester	.05	.04	.02
247	Bobby Thigpen	.10	.08	.04
248	Fred Lynn	.15	.11	.06
249	Paul Molitor	.12	.09	.05
250	Darrell Evans	.10	.08	.04
251	Gary Ward	.07	.05	.03
252	Bruce Hurst	.10	.08	.04
253	Bob Welch	.10	.08	.04
254	Joe Carter	.12	.09	.05
255	Willie Wilson	.10	.08	.04
256	Mark McGwire	.50	.40	.20
257	Mitch Webster	.07	.05	.03
258	Brian Downing	.07	.05	.03
259	Mike Stanley	.10	.08	.04
260	Carlton Fisk	.20	.15	.08
261	Billy Hatcher	.07	.05	.03
262	Glenn Wilson	.07	.05	.03
263	Ozzie Smith	.15	.11	.06
264	Randy Ready	.05	.04	.02
265	Kurt Stillwell	.10	.08	.04
266	David Palmer	.05	.04	.02
267	Mike Diaz	.07	.05	.03
268	Rob Thompson	.07	.05	.03
269	Andre Dawson	.20	.15	.08
270	Lee Guetterman	.05	.04	.02
271	Willie Upshaw	.07	.05	.03
272	Randy Bush	.05	.04	.02
273	Larry Sheets	.07	.05	.03
274	Rob Deer	.07	.05	.03
275	Kirk Gibson	.20	.15	.08
276	Marty Barrett	.07	.05	.03
277	Rickey Henderson	.40	.30	.15
278	Pedro Guerrero	.15	.11	.06
279	Brett Butler	.07	.05	.03
280	Kevin Seitzer	.40	.30	.15
281	Mike Davis	.07	.05	.03
282	Andres Galarraga	.15	.11	.06
283	Devon White	.30	.25	.12
284	Pete O'Brien	.07	.05	.03
285	Jerry Hairston	.05	.04	.02
286	Kevin Bass	.07	.05	.03
287	Carmelo Martinez	.07	.05	.03
288	Juan Samuel	.12	.09	.05
289	Kal Daniels	.20	.15	.08
290	Albert Hall	.05	.04	.02
291	Andy Van Slyke	.12	.09	.05
292	Lee Smith	.10	.08	.04
293	Vince Coleman	.20	.15	.08
294	Tom Niedenfuer	.07	.05	.03
295	Robin Yount	.30	.25	.12
296	*Jeff Robinson*	.15	.11	.06
297	*Todd Benzinger*	.30	.25	.12
298	Dave Winfield	.30	.25	.12
299	Mickey Hatcher	.05	.04	.02
300a	Checklist 248-357	.05	.04	.02
300b	Checklist 240-345	.10	.08	.04
301	Bud Black	.05	.04	.02
302	Jose Canseco	1.50	1.25	.60
303	Tom Foley	.05	.04	.02
304	Pete Incaviglia	.15	.11	.06

		MT	NR MT	EX
305	Bob Boone	.07	.05	.03
306	*Bill Long*	.20	.15	.08
307	Willie McGee	.12	.09	.05
308	*Ken Caminiti*(FC)	.30	.25	.12
309	Darren Daulton	.05	.04	.02
310	Tracy Jones	.12	.09	.05
311	Greg Booker	.07	.05	.03
312	Mike LaValliere	.07	.05	.03
313	Chili Davis	.07	.05	.03
314	Glenn Hubbard	.05	.04	.02
315	*Paul Noce*	.10	.08	.04
316	Keith Hernandez	.20	.15	.08
317	Mark Langston	.12	.09	.05
318	Keith Atherton	.05	.04	.02
319	Tony Fernandez	.12	.09	.05
320	Kent Hrbek	.15	.11	.06
321	John Cerutti	.07	.05	.03
322	Mike Kingery	.05	.04	.02
323	Dave Magadan	.12	.09	.05
324	Rafael Palmeiro	.40	.30	.15
325	Jeff Dedmon	.05	.04	.02
326	Barry Bonds	.40	.30	.15
327	Jeffrey Leonard	.07	.05	.03
328	Tim Flannery	.05	.04	.02
329	Dave Concepcion	.07	.05	.03
330	Mike Schmidt	.50	.40	.20
331	Bill Dawley	.05	.04	.02
332	Larry Andersen	.05	.04	.02
333	Jack Howell	.07	.05	.03
334	*Ken Williams*	.20	.15	.08
335	Bryn Smith	.05	.04	.02
336	*Billy Ripken*	.25	.20	.10
337	Greg Brock	.07	.05	.03
338	Mike Heath	.05	.04	.02
339	Mike Greenwell	.50	.40	.20
340	Claudell Washington	.07	.05	.03
341	Jose Gonzalez	.05	.04	.02
342	Mel Hall	.07	.05	.03
343	Jim Eisenreich	.07	.05	.03
344	Tony Bernazard	.05	.04	.02
345	Tim Raines	.25	.20	.10
346	Bob Brower	.07	.05	.03
347	Larry Parrish	.07	.05	.03
348	Thad Bosley	.05	.04	.02
349	Dennis Eckersley	.12	.09	.05
350	Cory Snyder	.20	.15	.08
351	Rick Cerone	.05	.04	.02
352	John Shelby	.05	.04	.02
353	Larry Herndon	.05	.04	.02
354	John Habyan	.05	.04	.02
355	*Chuck Crim*	.12	.09	.05
356	Gus Polidor	.05	.04	.02
357	Ken Dayley	.05	.04	.02
358	Danny Darwin	.05	.04	.02
359	Lance Parrish	.15	.11	.06
360	*James Steels*	.12	.09	.05
361	*Al Pedrique*(FC)	.15	.11	.06
362	Mike Aldrete	.07	.05	.03
363	Juan Castillo	.05	.04	.02
364	Len Dykstra	.10	.08	.04
365	Luis Quinones	.05	.04	.02
366	Jim Presley	.10	.08	.04
367	Lloyd Moseby	.07	.05	.03
368	Kirby Puckett	.50	.40	.25
369	Eric Davis	.60	.45	.25
370	Gary Redus	.05	.04	.02
371	Dave Schmidt	.05	.04	.02
372	Mark Clear	.05	.04	.02
373	Dave Bergman	.05	.04	.02
374	Charles Hudson	.05	.04	.02
375	Calvin Schiraldi	.05	.04	.02
376	Alex Trevino	.05	.04	.02
377	Tom Candiotti	.05	.04	.02
378	Steve Farr	.05	.04	.02
379	Mike Gallego	.05	.04	.02
380	Andy McGaffigan	.05	.04	.02
381	Kirk McCaskill	.07	.05	.03
382	Oddibe McDowell	.07	.05	.03
383	Floyd Bannister	.07	.05	.03
384	Denny Walling	.05	.04	.02
385	Don Carman	.07	.05	.03
386	Todd Worrell	.10	.08	.04
387	Eric Show	.07	.05	.03
388	Dave Parker	.20	.15	.08
389	Rick Mahler	.05	.04	.02
390	*Mike Dunne*	.15	.11	.06
391	Candy Maldonado	.07	.05	.03
392	Bob Dernier	.05	.04	.02
393	Dave Valle	.05	.04	.02
394	Ernie Whitt	.07	.05	.03
395	Juan Berenguer	.05	.04	.02

		MT	NR MT	EX
396	Mike Young	.05	.04	.02
397	Mike Felder	.05	.04	.02
398	Willie Hernandez	.07	.05	.03
399	Jim Rice	.30	.25	.12
400a	Checklist 358-467	.05	.04	.02
400b	Checklist 346-451	.10	.08	.04
401	Tommy John	.15	.11	.06
402	Brian Holton	.07	.05	.03
403	Carmen Castillo	.05	.04	.02
404	Jamie Quirk	.05	.04	.02
405	Dwayne Murphy	.07	.05	.03
406	*Jeff Parrett*(FC)	.25	.20	.10
407	Don Sutton	.20	.15	.08
408	Jerry Browne	.07	.05	.03
409	Jim Winn	.05	.04	.02
410	Dave Smith	.07	.05	.03
411	*Shane Mack*	.15	.11	.06
412	Greg Gross	.05	.04	.02
413	Nick Esasky	.07	.05	.03
414	Damaso Garcia	.05	.04	.02
415	Brian Fisher	.07	.05	.03
416	Brian Dayett	.05	.04	.02
417	Curt Ford	.05	.04	.02
418	*Mark Williamson*	.12	.09	.05
419	Bill Schroeder	.05	.04	.02
420	*Mike Henneman*	.25	.20	.10
421	*John Marzano*(FC)	.20	.15	.08
422	Ron Kittle	.07	.05	.03
423	Matt Young	.05	.04	.02
424	Steve Balboni	.07	.05	.03
425	*Luis Polonia*	.30	.25	.12
426	Randy St. Claire	.05	.04	.02
427	Greg Harris	.05	.04	.02
428	Johnny Ray	.07	.05	.03
429	Ray Searage	.05	.04	.02
430	Ricky Horton	.07	.05	.03
431	*Gerald Young*(FC)	.20	.15	.08
432	Rick Schu	.05	.04	.02
433	Paul O'Neill	.07	.05	.03
434	Rich Gossage	.15	.11	.06
435	John Cangelosi	.05	.04	.02
436	Mike LaCoss	.05	.04	.02
437	Gerald Perry	.10	.08	.04
438	Dave Martinez	.07	.05	.03
439	Darryl Strawberry	.35	.25	.14
440	John Moses	.05	.04	.02
441	Greg Gagne	.05	.04	.02
442	Jesse Barfield	.12	.09	.05
443	George Frazier	.05	.04	.02
444	Garth Iorg	.05	.04	.02
445	Ed Nunez	.05	.04	.02
446	Rick Aguilera	.05	.04	.02
447	Jerry Mumphrey	.05	.04	.02
448	Rafael Ramirez	.05	.04	.02
449	*John Smiley*	.40	.30	.15
450	Atlee Hammaker	.05	.04	.02
451	Lance McCullers	.07	.05	.03
452	Guy Hoffman(FC)	.07	.05	.03
453	Chris James	.12	.09	.05
454	Terry Pendleton	.07	.05	.03
455	*Dave Meads*	.15	.11	.06
456	Bill Buckner	.10	.08	.04
457	*John Pawlowski*(FC)	.10	.08	.04
458	Bob Sebra	.05	.04	.02
459	Jim Dwyer	.05	.04	.02
460	*Jay Aldrich*(FC)	.12	.09	.05
461	Frank Tanana	.07	.05	.03
462	Oil Can Boyd	.07	.05	.03
463	Dan Pasqua	.10	.08	.04
464	*Tim Crews*(FC)	.15	.11	.06
465	Andy Allanson	.07	.05	.03
466	*Bill Pecota*(FC)	.15	.11	.06
467	Steve Ontiveros	.05	.04	.02
468	Hubie Brooks	.10	.08	.04
469	*Paul Kilgus*(FC)	.15	.11	.06
470	Dale Mohorcic	.05	.04	.02
471	Dan Quisenberry	.07	.05	.03
472	Dave Stewart	.10	.08	.04
473	Dave Clark	.07	.05	.03
474	Joel Skinner	.05	.04	.02
475	Dave Anderson	.05	.04	.02
476	Dan Petry	.07	.05	.03
477	*Carl Nichols*(FC)	.12	.09	.05
478	Ernest Riles	.05	.04	.02
479	George Hendrick	.07	.05	.03
480	John Morris	.05	.04	.02
481	*Manny Hernandez*(FC)	.10	.08	.04
482	Jeff Stone	.05	.04	.02
483	Chris Brown	.07	.05	.03
484	Mike Bielecki	.05	.04	.02
485	Dave Dravecky	.07	.05	.03

No.	Player	MT	NR MT	EX
486	Rick Manning	.05	.04	.02
487	Bill Almon	.05	.04	.02
488	Jim Sundberg	.07	.05	.03
489	Ken Phelps	.07	.05	.03
490	Tom Henke	.07	.05	.03
491	Dan Gladden	.05	.04	.02
492	Barry Larkin	.40	.30	.15
493	*Fred Manrique*(FC)	.15	.11	.06
494	Mike Griffin	.05	.04	.02
495	*Mark Knudson*(FC)	.10	.08	.04
496	Bill Madlock	.10	.08	.04
497	Tim Stoddard	.05	.04	.02
498	*Sam Horn*(FC)	.30	.25	.12
499	*Tracy Woodson*(FC)	.15	.11	.06
500a	Checklist 468-577	.05	.04	.02
500b	Checklist 452-557	.10	.08	.04
501	Ken Schrom	.05	.04	.02
502	Angel Salazar	.05	.04	.02
503	Eric Plunk	.05	.04	.02
504	Joe Hesketh	.05	.04	.02
505	Greg Minton	.05	.04	.02
506	Geno Petralli	.05	.04	.02
507	Bob James	.05	.04	.02
508	*Robbie Wine*(FC)	.12	.09	.05
509	Jeff Calhoun	.05	.04	.02
510	Steve Lake	.05	.04	.02
511	Mark Grant	.05	.04	.02
512	Frank Williams	.05	.04	.02
513	*Jeff Blauser*(FC)	.30	.25	.12
514	Bob Walk	.05	.04	.02
515	Craig Lefferts	.05	.04	.02
516	Manny Trillo	.07	.05	.03
517	Jerry Reed	.05	.04	.02
518	Rick Leach	.05	.04	.02
519	*Mark Davidson*	.12	.09	.05
520	*Jeff Ballard*(FC)	.15	.11	.06
521	*Dave Stapleton*(FC)	.10	.08	.04
522	Pat Sheridan	.05	.04	.02
523	Al Nipper	.05	.04	.02
524	Steve Trout	.05	.04	.02
525	Jeff Hamilton	.07	.05	.03
526	*Tommy Hinzo*(FC)	.15	.11	.06
527	Lonnie Smith	.07	.05	.03
528	*Greg Cadaret*(FC)	.20	.15	.08
529	Rob McClure (Bob)	.05	.04	.02
530	Chuck Finley	.10	.08	.04
531	Jeff Russell	.05	.04	.02
532	Steve Lyons	.05	.04	.02
533	Terry Puhl	.05	.04	.02
534	*Eric Nolte*(FC)	.15	.11	.06
535	Kent Tekulve	.07	.05	.03
536	*Pat Pacillo*(FC)	.15	.11	.06
537	Charlie Puleo	.05	.04	.02
538	*Tom Prince*(FC)	.15	.11	.06
539	Greg Maddux	.15	.11	.06
540	Jim Lindeman	.07	.05	.03
541	*Pete Stanicek*(FC)	.15	.11	.06
542	Steve Kiefer	.05	.04	.02
543	Jim Morrison	.05	.04	.02
544	Spike Owen	.05	.04	.02
545	*Jay Buhner*(FC)	.50	.40	.20
546	*Mike Devereaux*(FC)	.30	.25	.12
547	Jerry Don Gleaton	.05	.04	.02
548	Jose Rijo	.07	.05	.03
549	Dennis Martinez	.05	.04	.02
550	Mike Loynd	.05	.04	.02
551	Darrell Miller	.05	.04	.02
552	Dave LaPoint	.07	.05	.03
553	John Tudor	.10	.08	.04
554	*Rocky Childress*(FC)	.12	.09	.05
555	*Wally Ritchie*(FC)	.15	.11	.06
556	Terry McGriff	.05	.04	.02
557	Dave Leiper	.05	.04	.02
558	Jeff Robinson	.07	.05	.03
559	Jose Uribe	.05	.04	.02
560	Ted Simmons	.10	.08	.04
561	*Lester Lancaster*	.15	.11	.06
562	*Keith Miller*(FC)	.25	.20	.10
563	Harold Reynolds	.07	.05	.03
564	*Gene Larkin*	.20	.15	.08
565	Cecil Fielder	.70	.50	.30
566	Roy Smalley	.05	.04	.02
567	Duane Ward	.07	.05	.03
568	*Bill Wilkinson*(FC)	.15	.11	.06
569	Howard Johnson	.10	.08	.04
570	Frank DiPino	.05	.04	.02
571	*Pete Smith*(FC)	.15	.11	.06
572	Darnell Coles	.07	.05	.03
573	Don Robinson	.07	.05	.03
574	Rob Nelson	.05	.04	.02
575	Dennis Rasmussen	.10	.08	.04
576	Steve Jeltz (photo actually Juan Samuel)	.05	.04	.02
577	*Tom Pagnozzi*(FC)	.30	.25	.12
578	Ty Gainey	.05	.04	.02
579	Gary Lucas	.05	.04	.02
580	Ron Hassey	.05	.04	.02
581	Herm Winningham	.05	.04	.02
582	*Rene Gonzales*(FC)	.15	.11	.06
583	Brad Komminsk	.05	.04	.02
584	Doyle Alexander	.07	.05	.03
585	Jeff Sellers	.07	.05	.03
586	Bill Gullickson	.05	.04	.02
587	Tim Belcher(FC)	.35	.25	.14
588	*Doug Jones*(FC)	.25	.20	.10
589	*Melido Perez*(FC)	.30	.25	.12
590	Rick Honeycutt	.05	.04	.02
591	Pascual Perez	.07	.05	.03
592	Curt Wilkerson	.05	.04	.02
593	Steve Howe	.07	.05	.03
594	*John Davis*(FC)	.15	.11	.06
595	Storm Davis	.10	.08	.04
596	Sammy Stewart	.05	.04	.02
597	Neil Allen	.05	.04	.02
598	Alejandro Pena	.07	.05	.03
599	Mark Thurmond	.05	.04	.02
600a	Checklist 578-BC26	.05	.04	.02
600b	Checklist 558-660	.10	.08	.04
601	*Jose Mesa*(FC)	.20	.15	.08
602	*Don August*(FC)	.15	.11	.06
603	Terry Leach	.10	.08	.04
604	*Tom Newell*(FC)	.15	.11	.06
605	*Randall Byers*(FC)	.15	.11	.06
606	Jim Gott	.05	.04	.02
607	Harry Spilman	.05	.04	.02
608	John Candelaria	.07	.05	.03
609	*Mike Brumley*(FC)	.15	.11	.06
610	Mickey Brantley	.07	.05	.03
611	*Jose Nunez*(FC)	.15	.11	.06
612	Tom Nieto	.05	.04	.02
613	Rick Reuschel	.10	.08	.04
614	Lee Mazzilli	.12	.09	.05
615	*Scott Lusader*(FC)	.15	.11	.06
616	Bobby Meacham	.05	.04	.02
617	Kevin McReynolds	.15	.11	.06
618	Gene Garber	.05	.04	.02
619	*Barry Lyons*(FC)	.15	.11	.06
620	Randy Myers	.10	.08	.04
621	Donnie Moore	.05	.04	.02
622	Domingo Ramos	.05	.04	.02
623	Ed Romero	.05	.04	.02
624	*Greg Myers*(FC)	.25	.20	.10
625	Ripken Baseball Family (Billy Ripken, Cal Ripken, Jr., Cal Ripken, Sr.)	.15	.11	.06
626	Pat Perry	.05	.04	.02
627	Andres Thomas	.10	.08	.04
628	*Matt Williams*	3.00	2.25	1.25
629	*Dave Hengel*(FC)	.15	.11	.06
630	Jeff Musselman	.07	.05	.03
631	Tim Laudner	.05	.04	.02
632	Bob Ojeda	.07	.05	.03
633	Rafael Santana	.05	.04	.02
634	*Wes Gardner*(FC)	.15	.11	.06
635	*Roberto Kelly*(FC)	1.50	1.25	.60
636	Mike Flanagan	.12	.09	.05
637	*Jay Bell*(FC)	.50	.40	.20
638	Bob Melvin	.05	.04	.02
639	*Damon Berryhill*(FC)	.20	.15	.08
640	*David Wells*(FC)	.25	.20	.10
641	Stan Musial Puzzle Card	.05	.04	.02
642	Doug Sisk	.05	.04	.02
643	*Keith Hughes*(FC)	.20	.15	.08
644	*Tom Glavine*(FC)	.60	.45	.25
645	Al Newman	.05	.04	.02
646	Scott Sanderson	.05	.04	.02
647	Scott Terry	.10	.08	.04
648	Tim Teufel	.12	.09	.05
649	Garry Templeton	.12	.09	.05
650	Manny Lee	.05	.04	.02
651	Roger McDowell	.10	.08	.04
652	Mookie Wilson	.15	.11	.06
653	David Cone	.60	.45	.25
654	*Ron Gant*(FC)	3.00	2.25	1.25
655	Joe Price	.12	.09	.05
656	George Bell	.25	.20	.10
657	*Gregg Jefferies*(FC)	3.00	2.25	1.25
658	*Todd Stottlemyre*(FC)	.50	.40	.20
659	*Geronimo Berroa*(FC)	.25	.20	.10
660	Jerry Royster	.12	.09	.05

1988 Donruss All-Stars

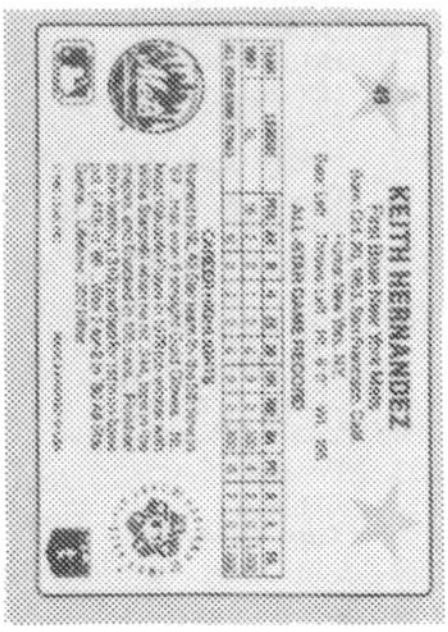

For the third consecutive year, this set of 64 cards featuring major league All-Stars was marketed in conjunction with Donruss Pop-Ups. The 1988 issue included a major change - the cards were reduced in size from 3-1/2" x 5" to a standard 2-1/2" x 3-1/2". The set features players from the 1987 All-Star Game starting lineup. Card fronts feature full-color photos, framed in blue, black and white, with a Donruss logo upper left. Player name and position appear in a red banner below the photo, along with the appropriate National or American League logo. All-Stars card backs include player stats and All-Star Game record. In 1988, All-Stars cards were distributed in individual packages containing three All-Stars, one Pop-Up and three Donruss puzzle pieces.

		MT	NR MT	EX
Complete Set:		7.00	5.25	2.75
Common Player:		.09	.07	.04
1	Don Mattingly	1.25	.90	.50
2	Dave Winfield	.25	.20	.10
3	Willie Randolph	.09	.07	.04
4	Rickey Henderson	.50	.40	.20
5	Cal Ripken, Jr.	.30	.25	.12
6	George Bell	.20	.15	.08
7	Wade Boggs	.80	.60	.30
8	Bret Saberhagen	.15	.11	.06
9	Terry Kennedy	.09	.07	.04
10	John McNamara	.09	.07	.04
11	Jay Howell	.09	.07	.04
12	Harold Baines	.12	.09	.05
13	Harold Reynolds	.09	.07	.04
14	Bruce Hurst	.09	.07	.04
15	Kirby Puckett	.50	.40	.20
16	Matt Nokes	.20	.15	.08
17	Pat Tabler	.09	.07	.04
18	Dan Plesac	.12	.09	.05
19	Mark McGwire	.60	.45	.25
20	Mike Witt	.09	.07	.04
21	Larry Parrish	.09	.07	.04
22	Alan Trammell	.20	.15	.08
23	Dwight Evans	.12	.09	.05
24	Jack Morris	.12	.09	.05
25	Tony Fernandez	.12	.09	.05
26	Mark Langston	.20	.15	.08
27	Kevin Seitzer	.40	.30	.15
28	Tom Henke	.09	.07	.04
29	Dave Righetti	.12	.09	.05
30	Oakland Coliseum	.09	.07	.04
31	Top Vote Getter (Wade Boggs)	.60	.45	.25
32	Checklist 1-32	.09	.07	.04
33	Jack Clark	.15	.11	.06
34	Darryl Strawberry	.40	.30	.15
35	Ryne Sandberg	.20	.15	.08
36	Andre Dawson	.20	.15	.08
37	Ozzie Smith	.15	.11	.06
38	Eric Davis	.50	.40	.20
39	Mike Schmidt	.80	.60	.30
40	Mike Scott	.12	.09	.05
41	Gary Carter	.12	.09	.05
42	Davey Johnson	.09	.07	.04
43	Rick Sutcliffe	.12	.09	.05
44	Willie McGee	.12	.09	.05
45	Hubie Brooks	.09	.07	.04
46	Dale Murphy	.40	.30	.15
47	Bo Diaz	.09	.07	.04
48	Pedro Guerrero	.15	.11	.06
49	Keith Hernandez	.15	.11	.06
50	Ozzie Virgil	.09	.07	.04
51	Tony Gwynn	.25	.20	.10
52	Rick Reuschel	.12	.09	.05
53	John Franco	.12	.09	.05
54	Jeffrey Leonard	.09	.07	.04
55	Juan Samuel	.15	.11	.06
56	Orel Hershiser	.20	.15	.08
57	Tim Raines	.20	.15	.08
58	Sid Fernandez	.12	.09	.05
59	Tim Wallach	.12	.09	.05
60	Lee Smith	.09	.07	.04
61	Steve Bedrosian	.12	.09	.05
62	MVP (Tim Raines)	.20	.15	.08
63	Top Vote Getter (Ozzie Smith)	.15	.11	.06
64	Checklist 33-64	.09	.07	.04

1988 Donruss Baseball's Best

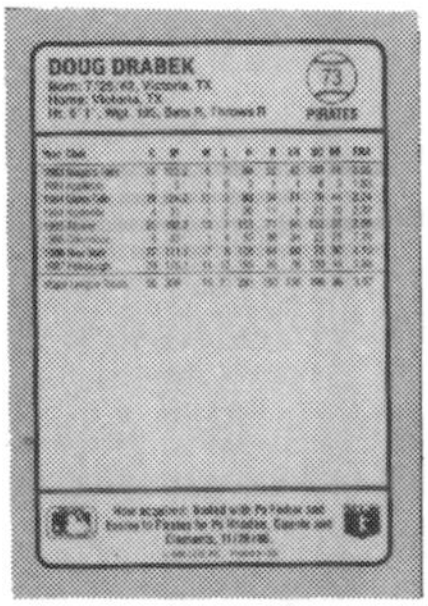

The design of this 336-card set (2-1/2" by 3-1/2") is similar to the regular 1988 Donruss issue with the exception of the borders which are orange, instead of blue. Full-color player photos are framed by the Donruss logo upper left, team logo lower right and a bright red and white player name that spans the bottom margin. The backs are black and white, framed by a yellow border, and include personal information, year-by-year stats and major league totals. This set was packaged in a bright red cardboard box (10" x 11" x 12") that contained six individually shrink-wrapped packs of 56 cards. Donruss marketed the set via retail chain outlets including Walgreens, Venture, Wall-Mart, Ben Franklin, Shopko, Super X, Target, McCrory's, Osco, Woolworth and J.C. Murphy.

		MT	NR MT	EX
Complete Set:		18.00	13.50	7.25
Common Player:		.05	.04	.02
1	Don Mattingly	1.00	.70	.40
2	Ron Gant	.50	.40	.20
3	Bob Boone	.05	.04	.02
4	Mark Grace	1.00	.70	.40
5	Andy Allanson	.05	.04	.02
6	Kal Daniels	.12	.09	.05
7	Floyd Bannister	.07	.05	.03
8	Alan Ashby	.05	.04	.02
9	Marty Barrett	.07	.05	.03
10	Tim Belcher	.10	.08	.04
11	Harold Baines	.12	.09	.05
12	Hubie Brooks	.07	.05	.03
13	Doyle Alexander	.07	.05	.03
14	Gary Carter	.15	.11	.06
15	Glenn Braggs	.07	.05	.03
16	Steve Bedrosian	.07	.05	.03
17	Barry Bonds	.50	.40	.20
18	Bert Blyleven	.10	.08	.04
19	Tom Brunansky	.10	.08	.04
20	John Candelaria	.07	.05	.03
21	Shawn Abner	.15	.11	.06
22	Jose Canseco	1.25	.90	.50
23	Brett Butler	.07	.05	.03

		MT	NR MT	EX
24	Scott Bradley	.05	.04	.02
25	Ivan Calderon	.10	.08	.04
26	Rich Gossage	.10	.08	.04
27	Brian Downing	.07	.05	.03
28	Jim Rice	.10	.08	.04
29	Dion James	.05	.04	.02
30	Terry Kennedy	.07	.05	.03
31	George Bell	.10	.08	.04
32	Scott Fletcher	.05	.04	.02
33	Bobby Bonilla	.50	.40	.20
34	Tim Burke	.05	.04	.02
35	Darrell Evans	.07	.05	.03
36	Mike Davis	.05	.04	.02
37	Shawon Dunston	.15	.11	.06
38	Kevin Bass	.07	.05	.03
39	George Brett	.40	.30	.15
40	David Cone	.25	.20	.10
41	Ron Darling	.10	.08	.04
42	Roberto Alomar	.20	.15	.08
43	Dennis Eckersley	.10	.08	.04
44	Vince Coleman	.15	.11	.06
45	Sid Bream	.07	.05	.03
46	Gary Gaetti	.12	.09	.05
47	Phil Bradley	.12	.09	.05
48	Jim Clancy	.05	.04	.02
49	Jack Clark	.15	.11	.06
50	Mike Krukow	.05	.04	.02
51	Henry Cotto	.05	.04	.02
52	Rich Dotson	.07	.05	.03
53	Jim Gantner	.05	.04	.02
54	John Franco	.07	.05	.03
55	Pete Incaviglia	.12	.09	.05
56	Joe Carter	.20	.15	.08
57	Roger Clemens	.70	.50	.30
58	Gerald Perry	.10	.08	.04
59	Jack Howell	.05	.04	.02
60	Vance Law	.05	.04	.02
61	Jay Bell	.07	.05	.03
62	Eric Davis	.70	.50	.30
63	Gene Garber	.05	.04	.02
64	Glenn Davis	.12	.09	.05
65	Wade Boggs	.80	.60	.30
66	Kirk Gibson	.20	.15	.08
67	Carlton Fisk	.15	.11	.06
68	Casey Candaele	.05	.04	.02
69	Mike Heath	.05	.04	.02
70	Kevin Elster	.15	.11	.06
71	Greg Brock	.07	.05	.03
72	Don Carman	.05	.04	.02
73	Doug Drabek	.12	.09	.05
74	Greg Gagne	.05	.04	.02
75	Danny Cox	.07	.05	.03
76	Rickey Henderson	.60	.45	.25
77	Chris Brown	.07	.05	.03
78	Terry Steinbach	.15	.11	.06
79	Will Clark	.80	.60	.30
80	Mickey Brantley	.05	.04	.02
81	Ozzie Guillen	.12	.09	.05
82	Greg Maddux	.12	.09	.05
83	Kirk McCaskill	.05	.04	.02
84	Dwight Evans	.10	.08	.04
85	Ozzie Virgil	.05	.04	.02
86	Mike Morgan	.05	.04	.02
87	Tony Fernandez	.10	.08	.04
88	Jose Guzman	.05	.04	.02
89	Mike Dunne	.12	.09	.05
90	Andres Galarraga	.15	.11	.06
91	Mike Henneman	.10	.08	.04
92	Alfredo Griffin	.07	.05	.03
93	Rafael Palmeiro	.12	.09	.05
94	Jim Deshaies	.07	.05	.03
95	Mark Gubicza	.07	.05	.03
96	Dwight Gooden	.70	.50	.30
97	Howard Johnson	.25	.20	.10
98	Mark Davis	.05	.04	.02
99	Dave Stewart	.10	.08	.04
100	Joe Magrane	.12	.09	.05
101	Brian Fisher	.07	.05	.03
102	Kent Hrbek	.15	.11	.06
103	Kevin Gross	.05	.04	.02
104	Tom Henke	.07	.05	.03
105	Mike Pagliarulo	.10	.08	.04
106	Kelly Downs	.10	.08	.04
107	Alvin Davis	.12	.09	.05
108	Willie Randolph	.07	.05	.03
109	Rob Deer	.07	.05	.03
110	Bo Diaz	.05	.04	.02
111	Paul Kilgus	.10	.08	.04
112	Tom Candiotti	.05	.04	.02
113	Dale Murphy	.40	.30	.15
114	Rick Mahler	.05	.04	.02
115	Wally Joyner	.40	.30	.15
116	Ryne Sandberg	.25	.20	.10
117	John Farrell	.12	.09	.05
118	Nick Esasky	.05	.04	.02
119	Bo Jackson	.90	.70	.35
120	Bill Doran	.07	.05	.03
121	Ellis Burks	.70	.50	.30
122	Pedro Guerrero	.12	.09	.05
123	Dave LaPoint	.05	.04	.02
124	Neal Heaton	.05	.04	.02
125	Willie Hernandez	.05	.04	.02
126	Roger McDowell	.07	.05	.03
127	Ted Higuera	.10	.08	.04
128	Von Hayes	.10	.08	.04
129	Mike LaValliere	.07	.05	.03
130	Dan Gladden	.07	.05	.03
131	Willie McGee	.12	.09	.05
132	Al Lieter	.20	.15	.08
133	Mark Grant	.05	.04	.02
134	Bob Welch	.07	.05	.03
135	Dave Dravecky	.05	.04	.02
136	Mark Langston	.10	.08	.04
137	Dan Pasqua	.10	.08	.04
138	Rick Sutcliffe	.12	.09	.05
139	Dan Petry	.05	.04	.02
140	Rich Gedman	.07	.05	.03
141	Ken Griffey	.07	.05	.03
142	Eddie Murray	.10	.08	.04
143	Jimmy Key	.10	.08	.04
144	Dale Mohoric	.05	.04	.02
145	Jose Lind	.15	.11	.06
146	Dennis Martinez	.05	.04	.02
147	Chet Lemon	.07	.05	.03
148	Orel Hershiser	.20	.15	.08
149	Dave Martinez	.07	.05	.03
150	Billy Hatcher	.07	.05	.03
151	Charlie Leibrandt	.07	.05	.03
152	Keith Hernandez	.10	.08	.04
153	Kevin McReynolds	.12	.09	.05
154	Tony Gwynn	.50	.40	.20
155	Stan Javier	.05	.04	.02
156	Tony Pena	.07	.05	.03
157	Andy Van Slyke	.10	.08	.04
158	Gene Larkin	.07	.05	.03
159	Chris James	.10	.08	.04
160	Fred McGriff	.50	.40	.20
161	Rick Rhoden	.07	.05	.03
162	Scott Garrelts	.05	.04	.02
163	Mike Campbell	.12	.09	.05
164	Dave Righetti	.12	.09	.05
165	Paul Molitor	.15	.11	.06
166	Danny Jackson	.10	.08	.04
167	Pete O'Brien	.07	.05	.03
168	Julio Franco	.10	.08	.04
169	Mark McGwire	.80	.60	.30
170	Zane Smith	.07	.05	.03
171	Johnny Ray	.07	.05	.03
172	Lester Lancaster	.07	.05	.03
173	Mel Hall	.05	.04	.02
174	Tracy Jones	.12	.09	.05
175	Kevin Seitzer	.35	.25	.14
176	Bob Knepper	.07	.05	.03
177	Mike Greenwell	.60	.45	.25
178	Mike Marshall	.10	.08	.04
179	Melido Perez	.15	.11	.06
180	Tim Raines	.50	.40	.20
181	Jack Morris	.12	.09	.05
182	Darryl Strawberry	.60	.45	.25
183	Robin Yount	.35	.25	.14
184	Lance Parrish	.15	.11	.06
185	Darnell Coles	.07	.05	.03
186	Kirby Puckett	.40	.30	.15
187	Terry Pendleton	.07	.05	.03
188	Don Slaught	.05	.04	.02
189	Jimmy Jones	.07	.05	.03
190	Dave Parker	.12	.09	.05
191	Mike Aldrete	.07	.05	.03
192	Mike Moore	.05	.04	.02
193	Greg Walker	.07	.05	.03
194	Calvin Schiraldi	.07	.05	.03
195	Dick Schofield	.05	.04	.02
196	Jody Reed	.25	.20	.10
197	Pete Smith	.10	.08	.04
198	Cal Ripken	.50	.40	.20
199	Lloyd Moseby	.07	.05	.03
200	Ruben Sierra	.25	.20	.10
201	R.J. Reynolds	.07	.05	.03
202	Bryn Smith	.05	.04	.02
203	Gary Pettis	.05	.04	.02
204	Steve Sax	.12	.09	.05
205	Frank DiPino	.05	.04	.02

		MT	NR MT	EX
206	Mike Scott	.12	.09	.05
207	Kurt Stillwell	.12	.09	.05
208	Mookie Wilson	.07	.05	.03
209	Lee Mazzilli	.05	.04	.02
210	Lance McCullers	.07	.05	.03
211	Rick Honeycutt	.05	.04	.02
212	John Tudor	.10	.08	.04
213	Jim Gott	.05	.04	.02
214	Frank Viola	.12	.09	.05
215	Juan Samuel	.10	.08	.04
216	Jesse Barfield	.12	.09	.05
217	Claudell Washington	.05	.04	.02
218	Rick Reuschel	.07	.05	.03
219	Jim Presley	.10	.08	.04
220	Tommy John	.12	.09	.05
221	Dan Plesac	.10	.08	.04
222	Barry Larkin	.20	.15	.08
223	Mike Stanley	.07	.05	.03
224	Cory Snyder	.25	.20	.10
225	Andre Dawson	.20	.15	.08
226	Ken Oberkfell	.05	.04	.02
227	Devon White	.20	.15	.08
228	Jamie Moyer	.05	.04	.02
229	Brook Jacoby	.10	.08	.04
230	Rob Murphy	.10	.08	.04
231	Bret Saberhagen	.20	.15	.08
232	Nolan Ryan	.50	.40	.20
233	Bruce Hurst	.10	.08	.04
234	Jesse Orosco	.07	.05	.03
235	Bobby Thigpen	.07	.05	.03
236	Pascual Perez	.05	.04	.02
237	Matt Nokes	.20	.15	.08
238	Bob Ojeda	.07	.05	.03
239	Joey Meyer	.07	.05	.03
240	Shane Rawley	.07	.05	.03
241	Jeff Robinson	.07	.05	.03
242	Jeff Reardon	.10	.08	.04
243	Ozzie Smith	.15	.11	.06
244	Dave Winfield	.50	.40	.20
245	John Kruk	.12	.09	.05
246	Carney Lansford	.07	.05	.03
247	Candy Maldonado	.07	.05	.03
248	Ken Phelps	.05	.04	.02
249	Ken Williams	.10	.08	.04
250	Al Nipper	.05	.04	.02
251	Mark McLemore	.05	.04	.02
252	Lee Smith	.07	.05	.03
253	Albert Hall	.05	.04	.02
254	Billy Ripken	.15	.11	.06
255	Kelly Gruber	.20	.15	.08
256	Charlie Hough	.07	.05	.03
257	John Smiley	.07	.05	.03
258	Tim Wallach	.10	.08	.04
259	Frank Tanana	.07	.05	.03
260	Mike Scioscia	.05	.04	.02
261	Damon Berryhill	.10	.08	.04
262	Dave Smith	.07	.05	.03
263	Willie Wilson	.10	.08	.04
264	Len Dykstra	.07	.05	.03
265	Randy Myers	.10	.08	.04
266	Keith Moreland	.07	.05	.03
267	Eric Plunk	.05	.04	.02
268	Todd Worrell	.10	.08	.04
269	Bob Walk	.05	.04	.02
270	Keith Atherton	.05	.04	.02
271	Mike Schmidt	.40	.30	.15
272	Mike Flanagan	.07	.05	.03
273	Rafael Santana	.05	.04	.02
274	Rob Thompson	.10	.08	.04
275	Rey Quinones	.05	.04	.02
276	Cecilio Guante	.05	.04	.02
277	B.J. Surhoff	.15	.11	.06
278	Chris Sabo	.80	.60	.30
279	Mitch Williams	.07	.05	.03
280	Greg Swindell	.10	.08	.04
281	Alan Trammell	.20	.15	.08
282	Storm Davis	.07	.05	.03
283	Chuck Finley	.05	.04	.02
284	Dave Stieb	.10	.08	.04
285	Scott Bailes	.05	.04	.02
286	Larry Sheets	.07	.05	.03
287	Danny Tartabull	.20	.15	.08
288	Checklist	.05	.04	.02
289	Todd Benzinger	.15	.11	.06
290	John Shelby	.05	.04	.02
291	Steve Lyons	.05	.04	.02
292	Mitch Webster	.05	.04	.02
293	Walt Terrell	.05	.04	.02
294	Pete Stanicek	.12	.09	.05
295	Chris Bosio	.05	.04	.02
296	Milt Thompson	.07	.05	.03
297	Fred Lynn	.12	.09	.05
298	Juan Berenguer	.05	.04	.02
299	Ken Dayley	.05	.04	.02
300	Joel Skinner	.05	.04	.02
301	Benito Santiago	.50	.40	.20
302	Ron Hassey	.05	.04	.02
303	Jose Uribe	.05	.04	.02
304	Harold Reynolds	.07	.05	.03
305	Dale Sveum	.07	.05	.03
306	Glenn Wilson	.05	.04	.02
307	Mike Witt	.07	.05	.03
308	Ron Robinson	.05	.04	.02
309	Denny Walling	.05	.04	.02
310	Joe Orsulak	.05	.04	.02
311	David Wells	.10	.08	.04
312	Steve Buechele	.05	.04	.02
313	Jose Oquendo	.05	.04	.02
314	Floyd Youmans	.07	.05	.03
315	Lou Whitaker	.12	.09	.05
316	Fernando Valenzuela	.12	.09	.05
317	Mike Boddicker	.07	.05	.03
318	Gerald Young	.15	.11	.06
319	Frank White	.07	.05	.03
320	Bill Wegman	.05	.04	.02
321	Tom Niedenfuer	.05	.04	.02
322	Ed Whitson	.05	.04	.02
323	Curt Young	.05	.04	.02
324	Greg Mathews	.10	.08	.04
325	Doug Jones	.07	.05	.03
326	Tommy Herr	.07	.05	.03
327	Kent Tekulve	.07	.05	.03
328	Rance Mulliniks	.05	.04	.02
329	Checklist	.05	.04	.02
330	Craig Lefferts	.05	.04	.02
331	Franklin Stubbs	.07	.05	.03
332	Rick Cerone	.05	.04	.02
333	Dave Schmidt	.05	.04	.02
334	Larry Parrish	.07	.05	.03
335	Tom Browning	.07	.05	.03
336	Checklist	.05	.04	.02

1988 Donruss Boston Team Book

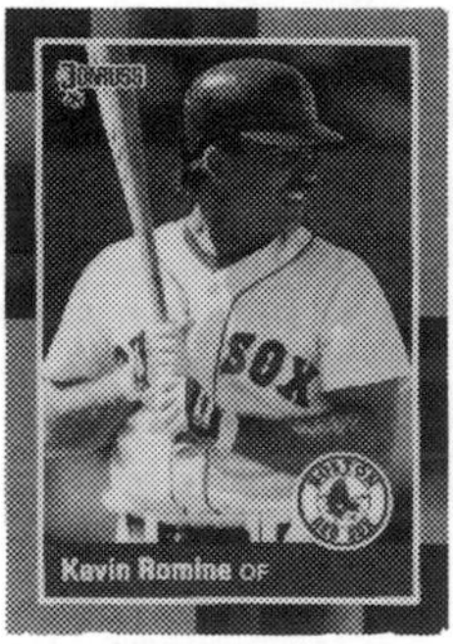

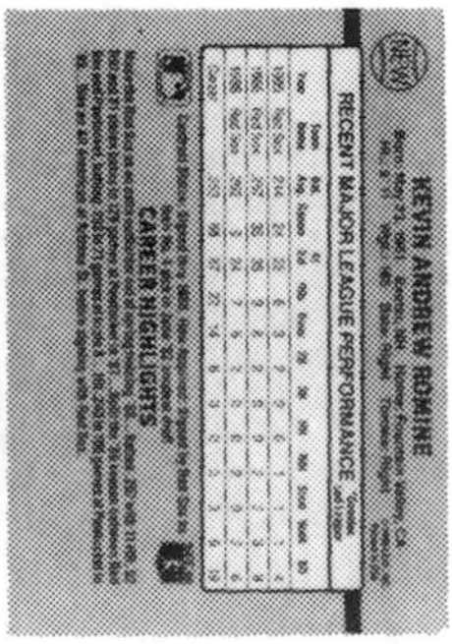

Three pages of cards and a Stan Musial puzzle highlight this special team collection book. The cards feature the same design as the regular 1988 Donruss cards, but contain a 1988 copyright date instead of 1987 like the regular set. The cards are numbered like the regular issue with the exception of eight new cards which were produced especially for the Red Sox collection book. The book is commonly found complete with the cards and puzzle. The puzzle pieces are perforated for removal, but the card sheet is not.

		MT	NR MT	EX
Complete Set:		4.00	3.00	1.50
Common Player:		.08	.06	.03
41	Jody Reed	.35	.25	.14
51	Roger Clemens	.80	.60	.30
92	Bob Stanley	.08	.06	.03
129	Rich Gedman	.08	.06	.03
153	Wade Boggs	.80	.60	.30
174	Ellis Burks	1.00	.70	.40
216	Dwight Evans	.25	.20	.10

		MT	NR MT	EX
252	Bruce Hurst	.25	.20	.10
276	Marty Barrett	.12	.09	.05
297	Todd Benzinger	.15	.11	.06
339	Mike Greenwell	.90	.70	.35
399	Jim Rice	.20	.15	.08
421	John Marzano	.12	.09	.05
462	Oil Can Boyd	.12	.09	.05
498	Sam Horn	.20	.15	.08
544	Spike Owen	.12	.09	.05
585	Jeff Sellers	.08	.06	.03
623	Ed Romero	.08	.06	.03
634	Wes Gardner	.12	.09	.05
----	Brady Anderson	.20	.15	.08
----	Rick Cerone	.08	.06	.03
----	Steve Ellsworth	.08	.06	.03
----	Dennis Lamp	.08	.06	.03
----	Kevin Romine	.15	.11	.06
----	Lee Smith	.20	.15	.08
----	Mike Smithson	.08	.06	.03
----	John Trautwein	.08	.06	.03

1988 Donruss Chicago Cubs Team Book

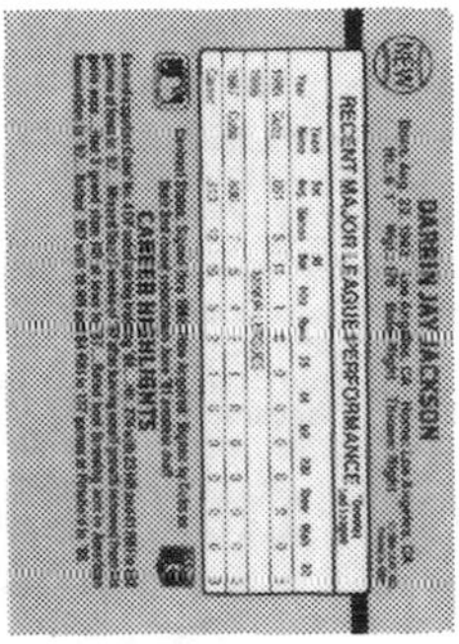

Primarily sold intact, the 1988 Donruss Chicago Cubs team book features three pages of cards and a fourth page featuring a Stan Musial puzzle. The inside cover provides space for autographs and the back inside cover provides team and ballpark history. The card fronts feature the design of the regular Donruss set. Eight "New" players are included in the team book. The cards have a 1988 copyright on the back in contrast with the 1987 copyright on the regular Donruss cards.

		MT	NR MT	EX
Complete Set:		5.00	3.75	2.00
Common Player:		.08	.06	.03
40	Mark Grace	1.75	1.25	.70
68	Rick Sutcliffe	.15	.11	.06
119	Jody Davis	.08	.06	.03
146	Shawon Dunston	.35	.25	.14
169	Jamie Moyer	.08	.06	.03
191	Leon Durham	.08	.06	.03
242	Ryne Sandberg	.70	.50	.30
269	Andre Dawson	.40	.30	.15
315	Paul Noce	.08	.06	.03
324	Rafael Palmeiro	.70	.50	.30
438	Dave Martinez	.15	.11	.06
447	Jerry Mumphrey	.08	.06	.03
488	Jim Sundberg	.08	.06	.03
516	Manny Trillo	.10	.08	.04
539	Greg Maddux	.50	.40	.20
561	Les Lancaster	.08	.06	.03
570	Frank DiPino	.08	.06	.03
639	Damon Berryhill	.30	.25	.12
646	Scott Sanderson	.08	.06	.03
----	Mike Bielecki	.20	.15	.08
----	Rich Gossage	.10	.08	.04
----	Drew Hall	.10	.08	.04
----	Darrin Jackson	.10	.08	.04
----	Vance Law	.08	.06	.03
----	Al Nipper	.08	.06	.03
----	Angel Salazar	.08	.06	.03
----	Calvin Schiraldi	.08	.06	.03

1988 Donruss Diamond Kings Supers

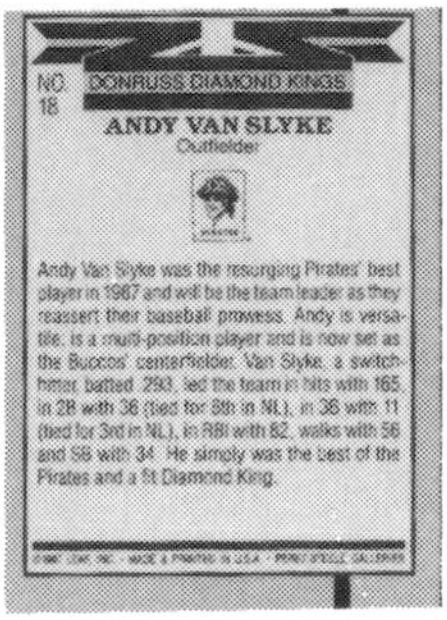

This 28-card set (including the checklist) marks the fourth edition of Donruss' super-size (5"x7") set. These cards, exact duplicates of the 1988 Diamond Kings that feature player portraits by Dick Perez, have a red, blue and black striped border. A gold Diamond Kings banner curves above the player portrait and a matching oval name banner is printed below. Each card features a large player closeup and a smaller full-figure inset on a split background that is white at the top and striped with multi-colors on the lower portion. Card backs are black and white with a blue border and contain the card number, DK logo, player name, team logo and a paragraph style career summary. A 12-piece Stan Musial puzzle was also included with the purchase of the super-size set which was marketed via a mail-in offer printed on Donruss wrappers.

		MT	NR MT	EX
Complete Set:		10.00	7.50	4.00
Common Player:		.20	.15	.08
1	Mark McGwire	.70	.50	.30
2	Tim Raines	.30	.25	.12
3	Benito Santiago	.30	.25	.12
4	Alan Trammell	.30	.25	.12
5	Danny Tartabull	.35	.25	.14
6	Ron Darling	.30	.25	.12
7	Paul Molitor	.30	.25	.12
8	Devon White	.35	.25	.14
9	Andre Dawson	.30	.25	.12
10	Julio Franco	.25	.20	.10
11	Scott Fletcher	.20	.15	.08
12	Tony Fernandez	.30	.25	.12
13	Shane Rawley	.20	.15	.08
14	Kal Daniels	.30	.25	.12
15	Jack Clark	.30	.25	.12
16	Dwight Evans	.25	.20	.10
17	Tommy John	.25	.20	.10
18	Andy Van Slyke	.25	.20	.10
19	Gary Gaetti	.30	.25	.12
20	Mark Langston	.35	.25	.14
21	Will Clark	1.75	1.25	.70
22	Glenn Hubbard	.20	.15	.08
23	Billy Hatcher	.20	.15	.08
24	Bob Welch	.20	.15	.08
25	Ivan Calderon	.20	.15	.08
26	Cal Ripken, Jr.	.60	.45	.25
27	Checklist	.20	.15	.08
641	Stan Musial Puzzle Card	.20	.15	.08

1988 Donruss MVP

This 26-card set of standard-size player cards replaced the Donruss box-bottom cards in 1988. Instead of box-bottoms, the bonus cards (numbered BC-1 through BC-26) were randomly inserted in Donruss wax or rack packs. Cards feature the

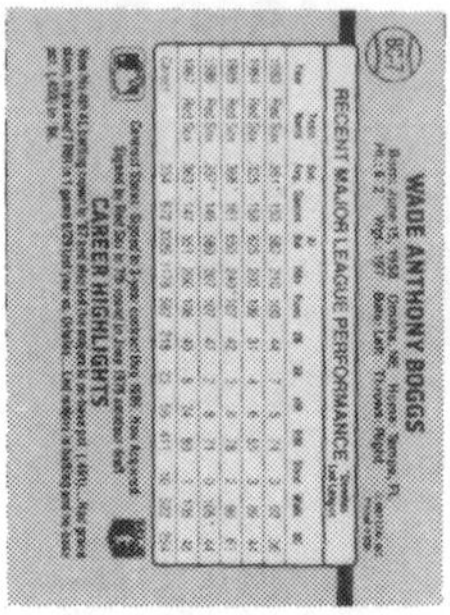

company's choice of Most Valuable Player for each major league team and are titled "Donruss MVP." The MVP cards were not included in the factory-collated sets. Card fronts carry the same basic red-blue-black flowing border design as the 1988 Donruss basic 660-card issue (with the exception of the Donruss MVP logo). Card backs are the same as the regular issue, except for the numbering system.

		MT	NR MT	EX
Complete Set:		7.00	5.25	2.75
Common Player:		.15	.11	.06
1	Cal Ripken	.30	.25	.12
2	Eric Davis	.50	.40	.20
3	Paul Molitor	.20	.15	.08
4	Mike Schmidt	.35	.25	.14
5	Ivan Calderon	.15	.11	.06
6	Tony Gwynn	.30	.25	.12
7	Wade Boggs	.75	.55	.30
8	Andy Van Slyke	.15	.11	.06
9	Joe Carter	.25	.20	.10
10	Andre Dawson	.25	.20	.10
11	Alan Trammell	.25	.20	.10
12	Mike Scott	.15	.11	.06
13	Wally Joyner	.25	.20	.10
14	Dale Murphy	.35	.25	.14
15	Kirby Puckett	.50	.40	.30
16	Pedro Guerrero	.20	.15	.08
17	Kevin Seitzer	.50	.40	.30
18	Tim Raines	.25	.20	.10
19	George Bell	.25	.20	.10
20	Darryl Strawberry	.50	.40	.30
21	Don Mattingly	1.00	.70	.40
22	Ozzie Smith	.20	.15	.08
23	Mark McGwire	.70	.50	.30
24	Will Clark	.90	.70	.35
25	Alvin Davis	.15	.11	.06
26	Ruben Sierra	.35	.25	.14

1988 Donruss New York Mets Team Book

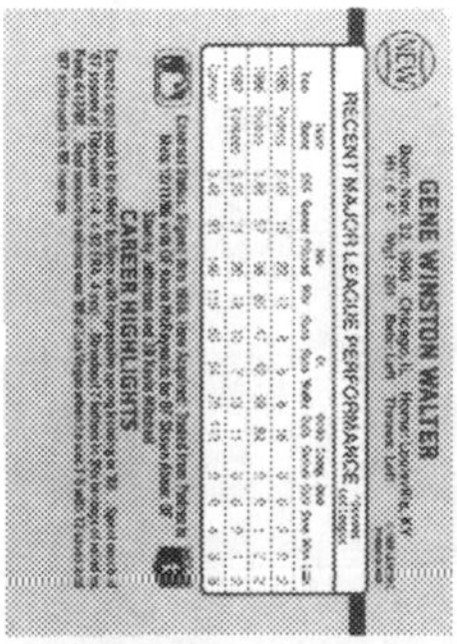

Distributed in book form, the 1988 Donruss New York Mets team book is still usually found intact. The team book features three pages of player cards, a full page featuring a perforated Stan Musial puzzle, space for autographs on the inside cover and team history information on the back inside cover. The outside covers of the Donruss team books are bright red. The player cards are the same as the regular Donruss issue with the exception of the copyright date. Three "New" Mets are featured in the team book.

		MT	NR MT	EX
Complete Set:		4.00	3.00	1.50
Common Player:		.08	.06	.03
37	Kevin Elster	.10	.08	.04
69	Dwight Gooden	.60	.45	.25
76	Ron Darling	.10	.08	.04
118	Sid Fernandez	.15	.11	.06
199	Gary Carter	.20	.15	.08
241	Wally Backman	.08	.06	.03
316	Keith Hernandez	.20	.15	.08
323	Dave Magadan	.30	.25	.12
364	Len Dykstra	.15	.11	.06
439	Darryl Strawberry	.70	.50	.30
446	Rick Aguilera	.10	.08	.04
562	Keith Miller	.10	.08	.04
569	Howard Johnson	.25	.20	.10
603	Terry Leach	.08	.06	.03
614	Lee Mazzilli	.08	.06	.03
617	Kevin McReynolds	.20	.15	.08
619	Barry Lyons	.08	.06	.03
620	Randy Myers	.20	.15	.08
632	Bob Ojeda	.08	.06	.03
648	Tim Teufel	.08	.06	.03
651	Roger McDowell	.15	.11	.06
652	Mookie Wilson	.10	.08	.04
653	David Cone	.30	.25	.12
657	Gregg Jefferies	2.00	1.50	.80
----	Jeff Innis	.15	.11	.06
----	Mackey Sasser	.30	.25	.12
----	Gene Walter	.08	.06	.03

1988 Donruss New York Yankees Team Book

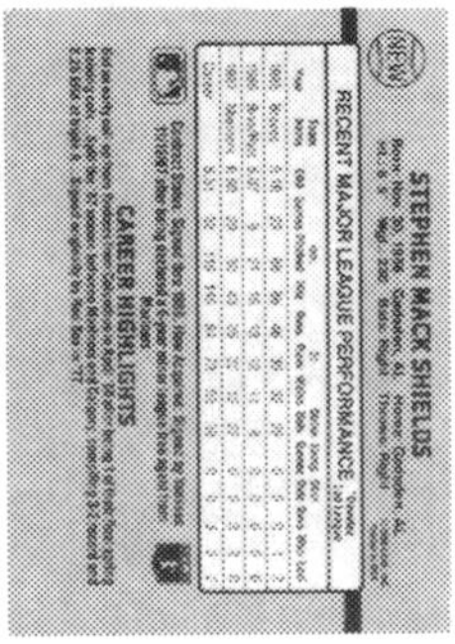

The 1988 Donruss New York Yankees team book includes the same features as the other team collection books. Three pages of cards, a Stan Musial puzzle, autograph space and team history information are provided. The team book is updated for 1988 trades. Nine "New" Yankees are included. The player cards are the same as the regular Donruss cards with the exception of the copyright dates. The team collection books are most often sold intact.

		MT	NR MT	EX
Complete Set:		5.00	3.75	2.00
Common Player:		.08	.06	.03
43	Al Leiter	.08	.06	.03
93	Dave Righetti	.15	.11	.06
105	Mike Pagliarulo	.10	.08	.04
128	Rick Rhoden	.08	.06	.03
175	Ron Guidry	.15	.11	.06
217	Don Mattingly	1.25	.90	.50
228	Willie Randolph	.15	.11	.06
251	Gary Ward	.08	.06	.03
277	Rickey Henderson	.70	.50	.30
278	Dave Winfield	.25	.20	.10

		MT	NR MT	EX
340	Claudell Washington	.08	.06	.03
374	Charles Hudson	.08	.06	.03
401	Tommy John	.15	.11	.06
474	Joel Skinner	.08	.06	.03
497	Tim Stoddard	.08	.06	.03
545	Jay Buhner	.30	.25	.12
616	Bobby Meacham	.08	.06	.03
635	Roberto Kelly	.90	.70	.35
---	John Candelaria	.10	.08	.04
---	Jack Clark	.25	.20	.10
---	Jose Cruz	.08	.06	.03
---	Richard Dotson	.08	.06	.03
---	Cecilio Guante	.08	.06	.03
---	Lee Guetterman	.08	.06	.03
---	Rafael Santana	.08	.06	.03
---	Steve Shields	.08	.06	.03
---	Don Slaught	.10	.08	.04

1988 Donruss Oakland Team Book

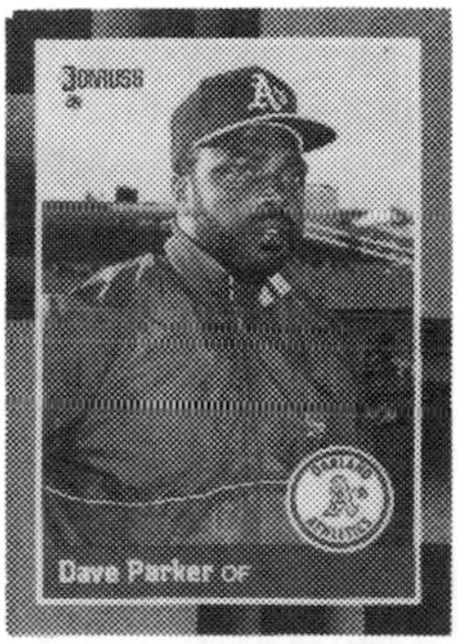

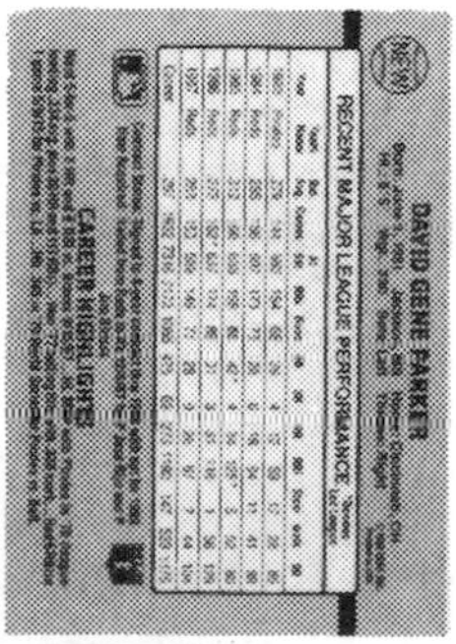

Eleven "New" players are among the featured cards in this unique collectible. The team book includes three pages of player cards, a Stan Musial puzzle, autograph space and team history information. The team books are most often sold intact. The player cards feature the same design as the regular Donruss cards.

		MT	NR MT	EX
Complete Set:		6.00	4.50	2.50
Common Player:		.08	.06	.03
97	Curt Young	.08	.06	.03
133	Gene Nelson	.08	.06	.03
158	Terry Steinbach	.20	.15	.08
178	Carney Lansford	.20	.15	.08
221	Tony Phillips	.08	.06	.03
256	Mark McGwire	.80	.60	.30
302	Jose Canseco	1.75	1.25	.70
349	Dennis Eckersley	.40	.30	.15
379	Mike Gallego	.08	.06	.03
425	Luis Polonia	.08	.06	.03
467	Steve Ontiveros	.08	.06	.03
472	Dave Stewart	.40	.30	.15
503	Eric Plunk	.08	.06	.03
528	Greg Cadaret	.08	.06	.03
590	Rick Honeycutt	.08	.06	.03
595	Storm Davis	.08	.06	.03
	Don Baylor	.20	.15	.08
---	Ron Hassey	.12	.09	.05
---	Dave Henderson	.20	.15	.08
---	Glenn Hubbard	.08	.06	.03
---	Stan Javier	.10	.08	.04
---	Doug Jennings	.20	.15	.08
---	Edward Jurak	.08	.06	.03
---	Dave Parker	.35	.25	.14
---	Walt Weiss	.80	.60	.30
---	Bob Welch	.30	.25	.12
---	Matt Young	.08	.06	.03

Definitions for grading conditions are located in the introduction section at the front of this book.

1988 Donruss Pop-Ups

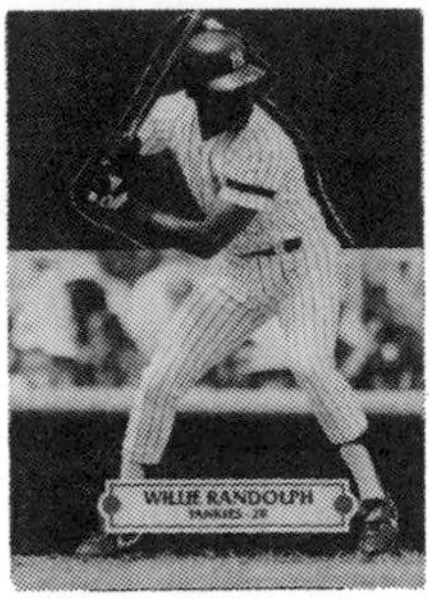

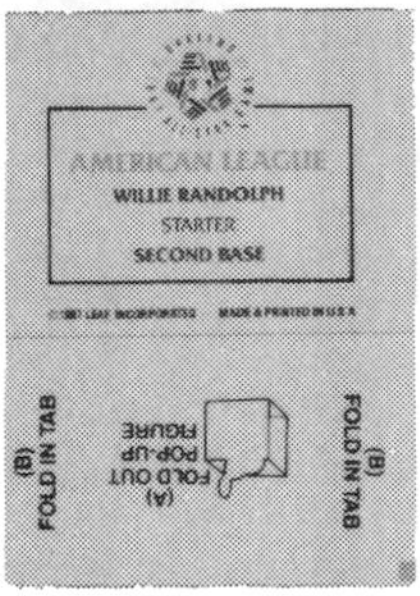

Donruss introduced its Pop-Up cards in 1986. The first two annual issues featured 2-1/2" x 5" cards. In 1988, Donruss reduced the size of the Pop-Ups cards to a standard 2-1/2"x 3-1/2". The 1988 set includes 20 cards that fold out so that the upper portion of the player stands upright, giving a three-dimensional effect. Pop-ups feature players from the All-Star Game starting lineup. Card fronts feature full-color photos, with the player's name, team and position printed in black on a yellow banner near the bottom of the card front. As in previous issues, the card backs contain only the player's name, league and position. Pop-Ups were distributed in individual packages containing one Pop-Up, three puzzle pieces and three All-Star cards.

		MT	NR MT	EX
Complete Set:		4.00	3.00	1.50
Common Player:		.15	.11	.06
(1)	George Bell	.20	.15	.08
(2)	Wade Boggs	.50	.40	.20
(3)	Gary Carter	.20	.15	.08
(4)	Jack Clark	.20	.15	.08
(5)	Eric Davis	.30	.25	.12
(6)	Andre Dawson	.20	.15	.08
(7)	Rickey Henderson	.50	.40	.20
(8)	Davey Johnson	.15	.11	.06
(9)	Don Mattingly	.50	.40	.20
(10)	Terry Kennedy	.15	.11	.06
(11)	John McNamara	.15	.11	.06
(12)	Willie Randolph	.15	.11	.06
(13)	Cal Ripken, Jr.	.60	.45	.25
(14)	Bret Saberhagen	.35	.25	.14
(15)	Ryne Sandberg	.60	.45	.25
(16)	Mike Schmidt	.60	.45	.25
(17)	Mike Scott	.15	.11	.06
(18)	Ozzie Smith	.30	.25	.12
(19)	Darryl Strawberry	.50	.40	.20
(20)	Dave Winfield	.25	.20	.10

1988 Donruss Rookies

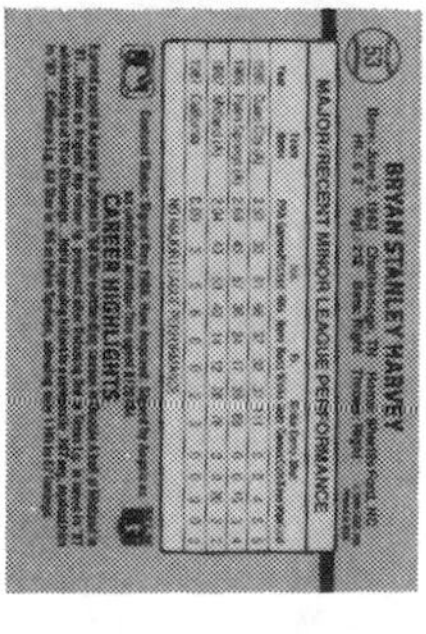

For the third consecutive year, Donruss issued this 56-card boxed set highlighting current rookies. The

complete set includes a checklist and a 15-piece Stan Musial Diamond Kings puzzle. As in previous years, the set is similar to the company's basic issue, with the exception of the logo and border color. Card fronts feature red, green and black-striped borders, with a red-and-white player name printed in the lower left corner beneath the full-color photo. "The Rookies" logo is printed in red, white and black in the lower right corner. The card backs are printed in black on bright aqua and include personal data, recent performance stats and major league totals, as well as 1984-88 year-by-year minor league stats. The cards are the standard 2-1/2" by 3-1/2" size.

		MT	NR MT	EX
Complete Set:		12.00	9.00	4.75
Common Player:		.10	.08	.04
1	Mark Grace	3.00	2.25	1.25
2	Mike Campbell	.10	.08	.04
3	Todd Frowirth(FC)	.20	.15	.08
4	Dave Stapleton	.10	.08	.04
5	Shawn Abner	.15	.11	.06
6	Jose Cecena(FC)	.25	.20	.10
7	Dave Gallagher(FC)	.20	.15	.08
8	Mark Parent(FC)	.20	.15	.08
9	Cecil Espy(FC)	.15	.11	.06
10	Pete Smith	.10	.08	.04
11	Jay Buhner	.20	.15	.08
12	Pat Borders(FC)	.25	.20	.10
13	Doug Jennings(FC)	.15	.11	.06
14	Brady Anderson(FC)	.20	.15	.08
15	Pete Stanicek	.15	.11	.06
16	Roberto Kelly	.70	.50	.30
17	Jeff Treadway	.15	.11	.06
18	Walt Weiss(FC)	.60	.45	.25
19	Paul Gibson(FC)	.20	.15	.08
20	Tim Crews	.10	.08	.04
21	Melido Perez	.25	.20	.10
22	Steve Peters(FC)	.20	.15	.08
23	Craig Worthington(FC)	.20	.15	.08
24	John Trautwein(FC)	.15	.11	.06
25	DeWayne Vaughn(FC)	.15	.11	.06
26	David Wells	.10	.08	.04
27	Al Leiter	.10	.08	.04
28	Tim Belcher	.20	.15	.08
29	Johnny Paredes(FC)	.20	.15	.08
30	Chris Sabo(FC)	2.00	1.50	.80
31	Damon Berryhill	.25	.20	.10
32	Randy Milligan(FC)	.50	.40	.20
33	Gary Thurman	.20	.15	.08
34	Kevin Elster	.20	.15	.08
35	Roberto Alomar	2.50	2.00	1.00
36	Edgar Martinez(FC)	.80	.60	.30
37	Todd Stottlemyre	.25	.20	.10
38	Joey Meyer	.15	.11	.06
39	Carl Nichols	.10	.08	.04
40	Jack McDowell	.60	.45	.25
41	Jose Bautista(FC)	.20	.15	.08
42	Sil Campusano(FC)	.15	.11	.06
43	John Dopson(FC)	.20	.15	.08
44	Jody Reed	.35	.25	.14
45	Darrin Jackson(FC)	.20	.15	.08
46	Mike Capel(FC)	.20	.15	.08
47	Ron Gant	1.50	1.25	.60
48	John Davis	.10	.08	.04
49	Kevin Coffman(FC)	.15	.11	.06
50	Cris Carpenter(FC)	.20	.15	.08
51	Mackey Sasser	.10	.08	.04
52	Luis Alicea(FC)	.25	.20	.10
53	Bryan Harvey(FC)	.40	.30	.15
54	Steve Ellsworth(FC)	.15	.11	.06
55	Mike Macfarlane(FC)	.25	.20	.10
56	Checklist 1-56	.10	.08	.04

1989 Donruss

This basic annual issue consists of 660 standard-size (2-1/2" by 3-1/2") cards, including 26 Diamond Kings portrait cards and 20 Rated Rookies cards. Top and bottom borders of the cards are printed in a variety of colors that fade from dark to light (i.e. dark blue to light purple, bright red to pale yellow). A white-lettered player name is printed across the top margin. The team logo appears upper right and the Donruss logo lower left. A black stripe and thin white

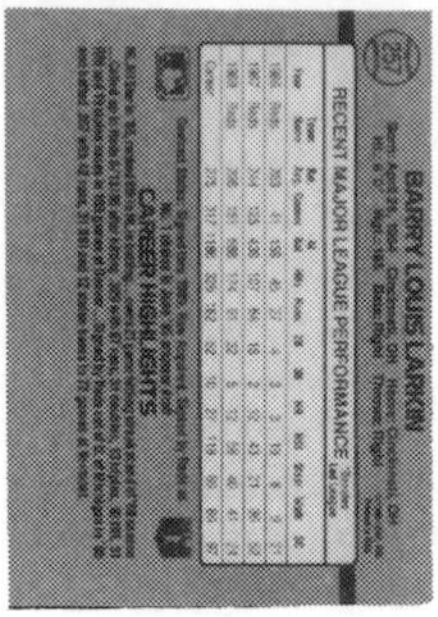

line make up the vertical side borders. The black outer stripe has a special varnish that gives a faintly visible filmstrip texture to the border. The backs (horizontal format) are printed in orange and black, similar to the 1988 design, with personal info, recent stats and major league totals. Team logo sticker cards (22 total) and Warren Spahn puzzle cards (63 total) are included in individual wax packs of cards.

		MT	NR MT	EX
Complete Set:		20.00	15.00	8.00
Common Player:		.04	.03	.02
1	Mike Greenwell (DK)	.20	.15	.08
2	Bobby Bonilla (DK)	.12	.09	.05
3	Pete Incaviglia (DK)	.12	.09	.05
4	Chris Sabo (DK)	.25	.20	.10
5	Robin Yount (DK)	.25	.20	.10
6	Tony Gwynn (DK)	.35	.25	.14
7	Carlton Fisk (DK)	.12	.09	.05
8	Cory Snyder (DK)	.15	.11	.06
9	David Cone (DK)	.20	.15	.08
10	Kevin Seitzer (DK)	.25	.20	.10
11	Rick Reuschel (DK)	.10	.08	.04
12	Johnny Ray (DK)	.10	.08	.04
13	Dave Schmidt (DK)	.08	.06	.03
14	Andres Galarraga (DK)	.15	.11	.06
15	Kirk Gibson (DK)	.20	.15	.08
16	Fred McGriff (DK)	.25	.20	.10
17	Mark Grace (DK)	.20	.15	.08
18	Jeff Robinson (DK)	.12	.09	.05
19	Vince Coleman (DK)	.20	.15	.08
20	Dave Henderson (DK)	.10	.08	.04
21	Harold Reynolds (DK)	.08	.06	.03
22	Gerald Perry (DK)	.10	.08	.04
23	Frank Viola (DK)	.15	.11	.06
24	Steve Bedrosian (DK)	.10	.08	.04
25	Glenn Davis (DK)	.15	.11	.06
26	Don Mattingly (DK)	1.25	.90	.50
27	Checklist 1-27	.04	.03	.02
28	*Sandy Alomar, Jr.* (RR)(FC)	.70	.50	.30
29	*Steve Searcy* (RR)(FC)	.15	.11	.06
30	*Cameron Drew* (RR)(FC)	.15	.11	.06
31	*Gary Sheffield* (RR)(FC)	.70	.50	.30
32	*Erik Hanson* (RR)(FC)	.70	.50	.30
33	*Ken Griffey, Jr.* (RR)(FC)	10.00	7.50	4.00
34	*Greg Harris* (RR)(FC)	.25	.20	.10
35	Gregg Jefferies (RR)	.80	.60	.30
36	*Luis Medina* (RR)(FC)	.20	.15	.08
37	*Carlos Quintana* (RR)	.50	.40	.20
38	*Felix Jose* (RR)(FC)	1.25	.90	.50
39	*Cris Carpenter* (RR)(FC)	.20	.15	.08
40	*Ron Jones* (RR)(FC)	.20	.15	.08
41	*Dave West* (RR)(FC)	.20	.15	.08
42	*Randy Johnson* (RR)(FC)	.40	.30	.15
43	*Mike Harkey* (RR)(FC)	.30	.25	.12
44	*Pete Harnisch* (RR)(FC)	.35	.25	.14
45	*Tom Gordon* (RR)(FC)	.40	.30	.15
46	*Gregg Olson* (RR)(FC)	.60	.45	.25
47	*Alex Sanchez* (RR)(FC)	.15	.11	.06
48	Ruben Sierra	.35	.25	.14
49	Rafael Palmeiro	.25	.20	.10
50	Ron Gant	.20	.15	.08
51	Cal Ripken, Jr.	.30	.25	.12
52	Wally Joyner	.20	.15	.08
53	Gary Carter	.20	.15	.08
54	Andy Van Slyke	.12	.09	.05
55	Robin Yount	.25	.20	.10
56	Pete Incaviglia	.10	.08	.04
57	Greg Brock	.06	.05	.02

		MT	NR MT	EX
58	Melido Perez	.08	.06	.03
59	Craig Lefferts	.04	.03	.02
60	Gary Pettis	.04	.03	.02
61	Danny Tartabull	.15	.11	.06
62	Guillermo Hernandez	.06	.05	.02
63	Ozzie Smith	.12	.09	.05
64	Gary Gaetti	.12	.09	.05
65	Mark Davis	.04	.03	.02
66	Lee Smith	.08	.06	.03
67	Dennis Eckersley	.10	.08	.04
68	Wade Boggs	.90	.70	.35
69	Mike Scott	.10	.08	.04
70	Fred McGriff	.50	.40	.20
71	Tom Browning	.08	.06	.03
72	Claudell Washington	.06	.05	.02
73	Mel Hall	.06	.05	.02
74	Don Mattingly	.50	.40	.20
75	Steve Bedrosian	.08	.06	.03
76	Juan Samuel	.10	.08	.04
77	Mike Scioscia	.06	.05	.02
78	Dave Righetti	.12	.09	.05
79	Alfredo Griffin	.06	.05	.02
80	Eric Davis	.40	.30	.15
81	Juan Berenguer	.04	.03	.02
82	Todd Worrell	.08	.06	.03
83	Joe Carter	.12	.09	.05
84	Steve Sax	.12	.09	.05
85	Frank White	.06	.05	.02
86	John Kruk	.06	.05	.02
87	Rance Mulliniks	.04	.03	.02
88	Alan Ashby	.04	.03	.02
89	Charlie Leibrandt	.06	.05	.02
90	Frank Tanana	.06	.05	.02
91	Jose Canseco	.70	.50	.30
92	Barry Bonds	.30	.25	.12
93	Harold Reynolds	.06	.05	.02
94	Mark McLemore	.04	.03	.02
95	Mark McGwire	.30	.25	.12
96	Eddie Murray	.25	.20	.10
97	Tim Raines	.25	.20	.10
98	Rob Thompson	.06	.05	.02
99	Kevin McReynolds	.12	.09	.05
100	Checklist 28-137	.04	.03	.02
101	Carlton Fisk	.20	.15	.08
102	Dave Martinez	.06	.05	.02
103	Glenn Braggs	.06	.05	.02
104	Dale Murphy	.30	.25	.12
105	Ryne Sandberg	.40	.30	.15
106	Dennis Martinez	.06	.05	.02
107	Pete O'Brien	.06	.05	.02
108	Dick Schofield	.04	.03	.02
109	Henry Cotto	.04	.03	.02
110	Mike Marshall	.12	.09	.05
111	Keith Moreland	.06	.05	.02
112	Tom Brunansky	.10	.08	.04
113	Kelly Gruber	.04	.03	.02
114	Brook Jacoby	.08	.06	.03
115	*Keith Brown*(FC)	.15	.11	.06
116	Matt Nokes	.15	.11	.06
117	Keith Hernandez	.20	.15	.08
118	Bob Forsch	.06	.05	.02
119	Bert Blyleven	.10	.08	.04
120	Willie Wilson	.08	.06	.03
121	Tommy Gregg	.08	.06	.03
122	Jim Rice	.25	.20	.10
123	Bob Knepper	.06	.05	.02
124	Danny Jackson	.12	.09	.05
125	Eric Plunk	.04	.03	.02
126	Brian Fisher	.06	.05	.02
127	Mike Pagliarulo	.08	.06	.03
128	Tony Gwynn	.30	.25	.12
129	Lance McCullers	.06	.05	.02
130	Andres Galarraga	.15	.11	.06
131	Jose Uribe	.04	.03	.02
132	Kirk Gibson	.20	.15	.08
133	David Palmer	.04	.03	.02
134	R.J. Reynolds	.04	.03	.02
135	Greg Walker	.06	.05	.02
136	Kirk McCaskill	.06	.05	.02
137	Shawon Dunston	.08	.06	.03
138	Andy Allanson	.04	.03	.02
139	Rob Murphy	.04	.03	.02
140	Mike Aldrete	.06	.05	.02
141	Terry Kennedy	.06	.05	.02
142	Scott Fletcher	.06	.05	.02
143	Steve Balboni	.06	.05	.02
144	Bret Saberhagen	.12	.09	.05
145	Ozzie Virgil	.04	.03	.02
146	Dale Sveum	.06	.05	.02
147	Darryl Strawberry	.40	.30	.15
148	Harold Baines	.10	.08	.04

		MT	NR MT	EX
149	George Bell	.25	.20	.10
150	Dave Parker	.12	.09	.05
151	Bobby Bonilla	.25	.20	.10
152	Mookie Wilson	.06	.05	.02
153	Ted Power	.04	.03	.02
154	Nolan Ryan	.60	.45	.25
155	Jeff Reardon	.08	.06	.03
156	Tim Wallach	.08	.06	.03
157	Jamie Moyer	.04	.03	.02
158	Rich Gossage	.10	.08	.04
159	Dave Winfield	.25	.20	.10
160	Von Hayes	.08	.06	.03
161	Willie McGee	.10	.08	.04
162	Rich Gedman	.06	.05	.02
163	Tony Pena	.06	.05	.02
164	Mike Morgan	.04	.03	.02
165	Charlie Hough	.06	.05	.02
166	Mike Stanley	.04	.03	.02
167	Andre Dawson	.20	.15	.08
168	Joe Boever(FC)	.04	.03	.02
169	Pete Stanicek	.08	.06	.03
170	Bob Boone	.06	.05	.02
171	Ron Darling	.10	.08	.04
172	Bob Walk	.04	.03	.02
173	Rob Deer	.06	.05	.02
174	Steve Buechele	.04	.03	.02
175	Ted Higuera	.08	.06	.03
176	Ozzie Guillen	.06	.05	.02
177	Candy Maldonado	.06	.05	.02
178	Doyle Alexander	.06	.05	.02
179	Mark Gubicza	.10	.08	.04
180	Alan Trammell	.15	.11	.06
181	Vince Coleman	.15	.11	.06
182	Kirby Puckett	.30	.25	.12
183	Chris Brown	.06	.05	.02
184	Marty Barrett	.06	.05	.02
185	Stan Javier	.04	.03	.02
186	Mike Greenwell	.30	.25	.12
187	Billy Hatcher	.06	.05	.02
188	Jimmy Key	.08	.06	.03
189	Nick Esasky	.06	.05	.02
190	Don Slaught	.04	.03	.02
191	Cory Snyder	.15	.11	.06
192	John Candelaria	.06	.05	.02
193	Mike Schmidt	.40	.30	.15
194	Kevin Gross	.06	.05	.02
195	John Tudor	.08	.06	.03
196	Neil Allen	.04	.03	.02
197	Orel Hershiser	.25	.20	.10
198	Kal Daniels	.15	.11	.06
199	Kent Hrbek	.15	.11	.06
200	Checklist 138-247	.04	.03	.02
201	Joe Magrane	.08	.06	.03
202	Scott Bailes	.04	.03	.02
203	Tim Belcher	.10	.08	.04
204	George Brett	.30	.25	.12
205	Benito Santiago	.12	.09	.05
206	Tony Fernandez	.10	.08	.04
207	Gerald Young	.10	.08	.04
208	Bo Jackson	.60	.45	.25
209	Chet Lemon	.06	.05	.02
210	Storm Davis	.08	.06	.03
211	Doug Drabek	.06	.05	.02
212	Mickey Brantley (photo actually Nelson Simmons)	.04	.03	.02
213	Devon White	.10	.08	.04
214	Dave Stewart	.08	.06	.03
215	Dave Schmidt	.04	.03	.02
216	Bryn Smith	.04	.03	.02
217	Brett Butler	.06	.05	.02
218	Bob Ojeda	.06	.05	.02
219	*Steve Rosenberg*(FC)	.15	.11	.06
220	Hubie Brooks	.08	.06	.03
221	B.J. Surhoff	.08	.06	.03
222	Rick Mahler	.04	.03	.02
223	Rick Sutcliffe	.08	.06	.03
224	Neal Heaton	.04	.03	.02
225	Mitch Williams	.06	.05	.02
226	Chuck Finley	.08	.06	.03
227	Mark Langston	.10	.08	.04
228	Jesse Orosco	.06	.05	.02
229	Ed Whitson	.04	.03	.02
230	Terry Pendleton	.08	.06	.03
231	Lloyd Moseby	.06	.05	.02
232	Greg Swindell	.10	.08	.04
233	John Franco	.08	.06	.03
234	Jack Morris	.15	.11	.06
235	Howard Johnson	.08	.06	.03
236	Glenn Davis	.12	.09	.05
237	Frank Viola	.12	.09	.05
238	Kevin Seitzer	.25	.20	.10

		MT	NR MT	EX
239	Gerald Perry	.08	.06	.03
240	Dwight Evans	.10	.08	.04
241	Jim Deshaies	.04	.03	.02
242	Bo Diaz	.06	.05	.02
243	Carney Lansford	.06	.05	.02
244	Mike LaValliere	.06	.05	.02
245	Rickey Henderson	.40	.30	.15
246	Roberto Alomar	.25	.20	.10
247	Jimmy Jones	.04	.03	.02
248	Pascual Perez	.06	.05	.02
249	Will Clark	.60	.45	.25
250	Fernando Valenzuela	.15	.11	.06
251	Shane Rawley	.06	.05	.02
252	Sid Bream	.06	.05	.02
253	Steve Lyons	.04	.03	.02
254	Brian Downing	.06	.05	.02
255	Mark Grace	.60	.45	.25
256	Tom Candiotti	.04	.03	.02
257	Barry Larkin	.30	.25	.12
258	Mike Krukow	.06	.05	.02
259	Billy Ripken	.06	.05	.02
260	Cecilio Guante	.04	.03	.02
261	Scott Bradley	.04	.03	.02
262	Floyd Bannister	.06	.05	.02
263	Pete Smith	.08	.06	.03
264	Jim Gantner	.04	.03	.02
265	Roger McDowell	.08	.06	.03
266	Bobby Thigpen	.08	.06	.03
267	Jim Clancy	.06	.05	.02
268	Terry Steinbach	.08	.06	.03
269	Mike Dunne	.08	.06	.03
270	Dwight Gooden	.50	.40	.20
271	Mike Heath	.04	.03	.02
272	Dave Smith	.06	.05	.02
273	Keith Atherton	.04	.03	.02
274	Tim Burke	.04	.03	.02
275	Damon Berryhill	.12	.09	.05
276	Vance Law	.06	.05	.02
277	Rich Dotson	.06	.05	.02
278	Lance Parrish	.15	.11	.06
279	Denny Walling	.04	.03	.02
280	Roger Clemens	.40	.30	.15
281	Greg Mathews	.06	.05	.02
282	Tom Niedenfuer	.06	.05	.02
283	Paul Kilgus	.10	.08	.04
284	Jose Guzman	.08	.06	.03
285	Calvin Schiraldi	.04	.03	.02
286	Charlie Puleo	.04	.03	.02
287	Joe Orsulak	.04	.03	.02
288	Jack Howell	.06	.05	.02
289	Kevin Elster	.08	.06	.03
290	Jose Lind	.10	.08	.04
291	Paul Molitor	.12	.09	.05
292	Cecil Espy	.08	.06	.03
293	Bill Wegman	.04	.03	.02
294	Dan Pasqua	.08	.06	.03
295	Scott Garrelts	.04	.03	.02
296	Walt Terrell	.06	.05	.02
297	Ed Hearn	.04	.03	.02
298	Lou Whitaker	.20	.15	.08
299	Ken Dayley	.04	.03	.02
300	Checklist 248-357	.04	.03	.02
301	Tommy Herr	.06	.05	.02
302	Mike Brumley	.06	.05	.02
303	Ellis Burks	.60	.45	.25
304	Curt Young	.06	.05	.02
305	Jody Reed	.10	.08	.04
306	Bill Doran	.06	.05	.02
307	David Wells	.06	.05	.02
308	Ron Robinson	.04	.03	.02
309	Rafael Santana	.04	.03	.02
310	Julio Franco	.10	.08	.04
311	Jack Clark	.15	.11	.06
312	Chris James	.08	.06	.03
313	Milt Thompson	.04	.03	.02
314	John Shelby	.04	.03	.02
315	Al Leiter	.15	.11	.06
316	Mike Davis	.06	.05	.02
317	*Chris Sabo*	.60	.45	.25
318	Greg Gagne	.04	.03	.02
319	Jose Oquendo	.04	.03	.02
320	John Farrell	.10	.08	.04
321	Franklin Stubbs	.04	.03	.02
322	Kurt Stillwell	.06	.05	.02
323	Shawn Abner	.10	.08	.04
324	Mike Flanagan	.06	.05	.02
325	Kevin Bass	.06	.05	.02
326	Pat Tabler	.06	.05	.02
327	Mike Henneman	.08	.06	.03
328	Rick Honeycutt	.04	.03	.02
329	John Smiley	.10	.08	.04

		MT	NR MT	EX
330	Rey Quinones	.04	.03	.02
331	Johnny Ray	.06	.05	.02
332	Bob Welch	.08	.06	.03
333	Larry Sheets	.06	.05	.02
334	Jeff Parrett	.08	.06	.03
335	Rick Reuschel	.08	.06	.03
336	Randy Myers	.10	.08	.04
337	Ken Williams	.06	.05	.02
338	Andy McGaffigan	.04	.03	.02
339	Joey Meyer	.08	.06	.03
340	Dion James	.04	.03	.02
341	Les Lancaster	.06	.05	.02
342	Tom Foley	.04	.03	.02
343	Geno Petralli	.04	.03	.02
344	Dan Petry	.06	.05	.02
345	Alvin Davis	.12	.09	.05
346	Mickey Hatcher	.04	.03	.02
347	Marvell Wynne	.04	.03	.02
348	Danny Cox	.06	.05	.02
349	Dave Stieb	.08	.06	.03
350	Jay Bell	.06	.05	.02
351	Jeff Treadway	.10	.08	.04
352	Luis Salazar	.04	.03	.02
353	Lenny Dykstra	.08	.06	.03
354	Juan Agosto	.04	.03	.02
355	Gene Larkin	.10	.08	.04
356	Steve Farr	.04	.03	.02
357	Paul Assenmacher	.04	.03	.02
358	Todd Benzinger	.12	.09	.05
359	Larry Andersen	.04	.03	.02
360	Paul O'Neill	.04	.03	.02
361	Ron Hassey	.04	.03	.02
362	Jim Gott	.04	.03	.02
363	Ken Phelps	.06	.05	.02
364	Tim Flannery	.04	.03	.02
365	Randy Ready	.04	.03	.02
366	*Nelson Santovenia*(FC)	.15	.11	.06
367	Kelly Downs	.08	.06	.03
368	Danny Heep	.04	.03	.02
369	Phil Bradley	.08	.06	.03
370	Jeff Robinson	.06	.05	.02
371	Ivan Calderon	.06	.05	.02
372	Mike Witt	.06	.05	.02
373	Greg Maddux	.10	.08	.04
374	Carmen Castillo	.04	.03	.02
375	Jose Rijo	.06	.05	.02
376	Joe Price	.04	.03	.02
377	R.C. Gonzalez	.04	.03	.02
378	Oddibe McDowell	.06	.05	.02
379	Jim Presley	.06	.05	.02
380	Brad Wellman	.04	.03	.02
381	Tom Glavine	.10	.08	.04
382	Dan Plesac	.08	.06	.03
383	Wally Backman	.06	.05	.02
384	*Dave Gallagher*	.25	.20	.10
385	Tom Henke	.06	.05	.02
386	Luis Polonia	.06	.05	.02
387	Junior Ortiz	.04	.03	.02
388	David Cone	.35	.25	.14
389	Dave Bergman	.04	.03	.02
390	Danny Darwin	.04	.03	.02
391	Dan Gladden	.04	.03	.02
392	*John Dopson*	.25	.20	.10
393	Frank DiPino	.04	.03	.02
394	Al Nipper	.04	.03	.02
395	Willie Randolph	.06	.05	.02
396	Don Carman	.06	.05	.02
397	Scott Terry	.06	.05	.02
398	Rick Cerone	.04	.03	.02
399	Tom Pagnozzi	.06	.05	.02
400	Checklist 358-467	.04	.03	.02
401	Mickey Tettleton	.08	.06	.03
402	Curtis Wilkerson	.04	.03	.02
403	Jeff Russell	.04	.03	.02
404	Pat Perry	.04	.03	.02
405	*Jose Alvarez*(FC)	.15	.11	.06
406	Rick Schu	.04	.03	.02
407	*Sherman Corbett*(FC)	.15	.11	.06
408	Dave Magadan	.10	.08	.04
409	Bob Kipper	.04	.03	.02
410	Don August	.08	.06	.03
411	Bob Brower	.04	.03	.02
412	Chris Bosio	.04	.03	.02
413	Jerry Reuss	.06	.05	.02
414	Atlee Hammaker	.04	.03	.02
415	Jim Walewander(FC)	.06	.05	.02
416	*Mike Macfarlane*	.25	.20	.10
417	Pat Sheridan	.04	.03	.02
418	Pedro Guerrero	.15	.11	.06
419	Allan Anderson	.06	.05	.02
420	*Mark Parent*	.20	.15	.08

		MT	NR MT	EX
421	Bob Stanley	.04	.03	.02
422	Mike Gallego	.04	.03	.02
423	Bruce Hurst	.08	.06	.03
424	Dave Meads	.04	.03	.02
425	Jesse Barfield	.10	.08	.04
426	*Rob Dibble*(FC)	.50	.40	.20
427	Joel Skinner	.04	.03	.02
428	Ron Kittle	.06	.05	.02
429	Rick Rhoden	.08	.06	.03
430	Bob Dernier	.04	.03	.02
431	Steve Jeltz	.04	.03	.02
432	Rick Dempsey	.06	.05	.02
433	Roberto Kelly	.10	.08	.04
434	Dave Anderson	.04	.03	.02
435	Herm Winningham	.04	.03	.02
436	Al Newman	.04	.03	.02
437	Jose DeLeon	.06	.05	.02
438	Doug Jones	.10	.08	.04
439	Brian Holton	.06	.05	.02
440	Jeff Montgomery(FC)	.06	.05	.02
441	Dickie Thon	.04	.03	.02
442	Cecil Fielder	.35	.25	.14
443	*John Fishel*(FC)	.15	.11	.06
444	Jerry Don Gleaton	.04	.03	.02
445	*Paul Gibson*	.15	.11	.06
446	Walt Weiss	.40	.30	.15
447	Glenn Wilson	.06	.05	.02
448	Mike Moore	.04	.03	.02
449	Chili Davis	.06	.05	.02
450	Dave Henderson	.08	.06	.03
451	*Jose Bautista*	.20	.15	.08
452	Rex Hudler	.04	.03	.02
453	Bob Brenly	.04	.03	.02
454	Mackey Sasser	.06	.05	.02
455	Daryl Boston	.04	.03	.02
456	Mike Fitzgerald	.04	.03	.02
457	Jeffery Leonard	.06	.05	.02
458	Bruce Sutter	.08	.06	.03
459	Mitch Webster	.06	.05	.02
460	Joe Hesketh	.04	.03	.02
461	Bobby Witt	.08	.06	.03
462	Stew Cliburn	.04	.03	.02
463	Scott Bankhead	.04	.03	.02
464	*Ramon Martinez*(FC)	2.00	1.50	.80
465	Dave Leiper	.04	.03	.02
466	*Luis Alicea*	.20	.15	.08
467	John Cerutti	.06	.05	.02
468	Ron Washington	.04	.03	.02
469	Jeff Reed	.04	.03	.02
470	Jeff Robinson	.12	.09	.05
471	Sid Fernandez	.08	.06	.03
472	Terry Puhl	.04	.03	.02
473	Charlie Lea	.04	.03	.02
474	*Israel Sanchez*(FC)	.15	.11	.06
475	Bruce Benedict	.04	.03	.02
476	Oil Can Boyd	.06	.05	.02
477	Craig Reynolds	.04	.03	.02
478	Frank Williams	.04	.03	.02
479	Greg Cadaret	.10	.08	.04
480	*Randy Kramer*(FC)	.15	.11	.06
481	*Dave Eiland*(FC)	.20	.15	.08
482	Eric Show	.06	.05	.02
483	Garry Templeton	.06	.05	.02
484	Wallace Johnson(FC)	.04	.03	.02
485	Kevin Mitchell	.60	.45	.25
486	Tim Crews	.06	.05	.02
487	Mike Maddux	.04	.03	.02
488	Dave LaPoint	.06	.05	.02
489	Fred Manrique	.06	.05	.02
490	Greg Minton	.04	.03	.02
491	*Doug Dascenzo*(FC)	.25	.20	.10
492	Willie Upshaw	.06	.05	.02
493	*Jack Armstrong*(FC)	.30	.25	.12
494	Kirt Manwaring	.10	.08	.04
495	Jeff Ballard	.06	.05	.02
496	Jeff Kunkel	.04	.03	.02
497	Mike Campbell	.08	.06	.03
498	Gary Thurman	.10	.08	.04
499	Zane Smith	.06	.05	.02
500	Checklist 468-577	.04	.03	.02
501	Mike Birkbeck	.04	.03	.02
502	Terry Leach	.04	.03	.02
503	Shawn Hillegas	.06	.05	.02
504	Manny Lee	.04	.03	.02
505	*Doug Jennings*	.15	.11	.06
506	Ken Oberkfell	.04	.03	.02
507	Tim Teufel	.04	.03	.02
508	Tom Brookens	.04	.03	.02
509	Rafael Ramirez	.04	.03	.02
510	Fred Toliver	.04	.03	.02
511	*Brian Holman*(FC)	.30	.25	.12

		MT	NR MT	EX
512	Mike Bielecki	.04	.03	.02
513	*Jeff Pico*(FC)	.15	.11	.06
514	Charles Hudson	.04	.03	.02
515	Bruce Ruffin	.04	.03	.02
516	Larry McWilliams	.04	.03	.02
517	Jeff Sellers	.04	.03	.02
518	*John Costello*(FC)	.15	.11	.06
519	*Brady Anderson*	.20	.15	.08
520	Craig McMurtry	.04	.03	.02
521	Ray Hayward	.08	.06	.03
522	Drew Hall	.08	.06	.03
523	*Mark Lemke*(FC)	.20	.15	.08
524	*Oswald Peraza*(FC)	.15	.11	.06
525	*Bryan Harvey*	.30	.25	.12
526	Rick Aguilera	.04	.03	.02
527	Tom Prince	.06	.05	.02
528	Mark Clear	.04	.03	.02
529	Jerry Browne	.04	.03	.02
530	Juan Castillo	.04	.03	.02
531	Jack McDowell	.08	.06	.03
532	Chris Speier	.04	.03	.02
533	Darrell Evans	.08	.06	.03
534	Luis Aquino	.04	.03	.02
535	Eric King	.04	.03	.02
536	*Ken Hill*(FC)	.25	.20	.10
537	Randy Bush	.04	.03	.02
538	Shane Mack	.06	.05	.02
539	Tom Bolton(FC)	.06	.05	.02
540	Gene Nelson	.04	.03	.02
541	Wes Gardner	.06	.05	.02
542	Ken Caminiti	.06	.05	.02
543	Duane Ward	.04	.03	.02
544	*Norm Charlton*(FC)	.30	.25	.12
545	*Hal Morris*(FC)	1.25	.90	.50
546	Rich Yett(FC)	.04	.03	.02
547	*Hensley Meulens*(FC)	.60	.45	.25
548	Greg Harris	.04	.03	.02
549	Darren Daulton	.04	.03	.02
550	Jeff Hamilton	.06	.05	.02
551	Luis Aguayo	.04	.03	.02
552	Tim Leary	.06	.05	.02
553	Ron Oester	.04	.03	.02
554	Steve Lombardozzi	.04	.03	.02
555	*Tim Jones*(FC)	.15	.11	.06
556	Bud Black	.04	.03	.02
557	Alejandro Pena	.04	.03	.02
558	*Jose DeJesus*(FC)	.15	.11	.06
559	Dennis Rasmussen	.08	.06	.03
560	*Pat Borders*	.20	.15	.08
561	*Craig Biggio*(FC)	.60	.45	.25
562	*Luis de los Santos*(FC)	.15	.11	.06
563	Fred Lynn	.10	.08	.04
564	*Todd Burns*(FC)	.20	.15	.08
565	Felix Fermin	.06	.05	.02
566	Darnell Coles	.06	.05	.02
567	Willie Fraser	.04	.03	.02
568	Glenn Hubbard	.04	.03	.02
569	*Craig Worthington*	.30	.25	.12
570	*Johnny Paredes*	.15	.11	.06
571	Don Robinson	.04	.03	.02
572	Barry Lyons	.04	.03	.02
573	Bill Long	.06	.05	.02
574	Tracy Jones	.10	.08	.04
575	Juan Nieves	.06	.05	.02
576	Andres Thomas	.06	.05	.02
577	*Rolando Roomes*(FC)	.15	.11	.06
578	Luis Rivera(FC)	.04	.03	.02
579	*Chad Kreuter*(FC)	.15	.11	.06
580	Tony Armas	.06	.05	.02
581	Jay Buhner	.10	.08	.04
582	Ricky Horton	.06	.05	.02
583	Andy Hawkins	.04	.03	.02
584	*Sil Campusano*	.15	.11	.06
585	Dave Clark	.06	.05	.02
586	*Van Snider*(FC)	.15	.11	.06
587	Todd Frohwirth(FC)	.06	.05	.02
588	Warren Spahn Puzzle Card	.04	.03	.02
589	*William Brennan*(FC)	.15	.11	.06
590	*German Gonzalez*(FC)	.15	.11	.06
591	Ernie Whitt	.06	.05	.02
592	Jeff Blauser	.08	.06	.03
593	Spike Owen	.04	.03	.02
594	Matt Williams	.40	.30	.15
595	Lloyd McClendon(FC)	.04	.03	.02
596	Steve Ontiveros	.04	.03	.02
597	*Scott Medvin*(FC)	.15	.11	.06
598	*Hipolito Pena*(FC)	.15	.11	.06
599	*Jerald Clark*(FC)	.30	.25	.12
600a	Checklist 578-BC26 (#635 is Kurt Schilling)	.15	.11	.06
600b	Checklist 578-BC26 (#635 is Curt Schilling)	.06	.05	.02

		MT	NR MT	EX
601	Carmelo Martinez	.04	.03	.02
602	Mike LaCoss	.04	.03	.02
603	Mike Devereaux	.15	.11	.06
604	*Alex Madrid*(FC)	.15	.11	.06
605	Gary Redus	.04	.03	.02
606	Lance Johnson	.06	.05	.02
607	*Terry Clark*(FC)	.15	.11	.06
608	Manny Trillo	.04	.03	.02
609	*Scott Jordan*(FC)	.15	.11	.06
610	Jay Howell	.06	.05	.02
611	*Francisco Melendez*(FC)	.15	.11	.06
612	Mike Boddicker	.06	.05	.02
613	Kevin Brown	.20	.15	.08
614	Dave Valle	.04	.03	.02
615	Tim Laudner	.04	.03	.02
616	*Andy Nezelek*(FC)	.15	.11	.06
617	Chuck Crim	.04	.03	.02
618	Jack Savage(FC)	.10	.08	.04
619	Adam Peterson(FC)	.10	.08	.04
620	Todd Stottlemyre	.10	.08	.04
621	*Lance Blankenship*(FC)	.25	.20	.10
622	*Miguel Garcia*(FC)	.15	.11	.06
623	Keith Miller	.06	.05	.02
624	*Ricky Jordan*(FC)	.40	.30	.15
625	Ernest Riles	.04	.03	.02
626	John Moses	.04	.03	.02
627	Nelson Liriano	.06	.05	.02
628	Mike Smithson	.04	.03	.02
629	Scott Sanderson	.04	.03	.02
630	Dale Mohorcic	.04	.03	.02
631	Marvin Freeman	.04	.03	.02
632	Mike Young	.04	.03	.02
633	Dennis Lamp	.04	.03	.02
634	*Dante Bichette*(FC)	.25	.20	.10
635	*Curt Schilling*(FC)	.25	.20	.10
636	*Scott May*(FC)	.15	.11	.06
637	*Mike Schooler*(FC)	.25	.20	.10
638	Rick Leach	.04	.03	.02
639	*Tom Lampkin*(FC)	.15	.11	.06
640	*Brian Meyer*(FC)	.15	.11	.06
641	Brian Harper	.04	.03	.02
642	*John Smoltz*(FC)	.50	.40	.20
643	40/40 Club (Jose Canseco)	.35	.25	.14
644	Bill Schroeder	.04	.03	.02
645	*Edgar Martinez*	.40	.30	.15
646	*Dennis Cook*(FC)	.20	.15	.08
647	Barry Jones	.04	.03	.02
648	59 and Counting (Orel Hershiser)	.15	.11	.06
649	*Rod Nichols*(FC)	.15	.11	.06
650	Jody Davis	.06	.05	.02
651	*Bob Milacki*(FC)	.25	.20	.10
652	Mike Jackson	.06	.05	.02
653	*Derek Lilliquist*(FC)	.15	.11	.06
654	Paul Mirabella	.04	.03	.02
655	Mike Diaz	.06	.05	.02
656	Jeff Musselman	.06	.05	.02
657	Jerry Reed	.04	.03	.02
658	*Kevin Blankenship*(FC)	.15	.11	.06
659	Wayne Tolleson	.04	.03	.02
660	*Eric Hetzel*(FC)	.15	.11	.06

1989 Donruss Grand Slammers

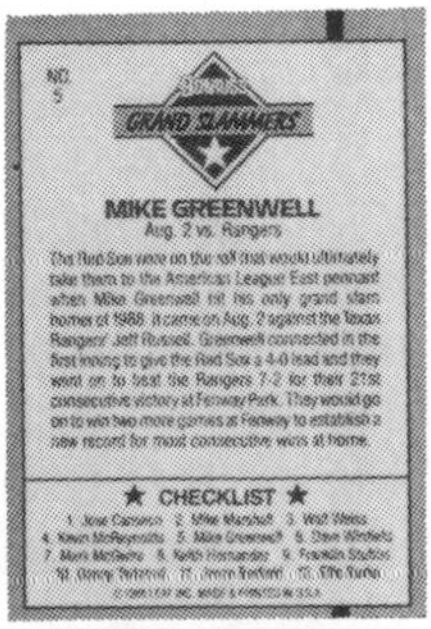

One card from this 12-card set was included in each Donruss cello pack. The featured players all hit grand slams in 1988. The 2-1/2" by 3-1/2" cards feature full color action photos. The card backs feature the story of the player's grand slam. Border variations on the front of the card have been discovered, but the prices are consistent with all forms of the cards.

		MT	NR MT	EX
Complete Set:		4.00	3.00	1.50
Common Player:		.12	.09	.05
1	Jose Canseco	1.00	.70	.40
2	Mike Marshall	.12	.09	.05
3	Walt Weiss	.12	.09	.05
4	Kevin McReynolds	.15	.11	.06
5	Mike Greenwell	.25	.20	.10
6	Dave Winfield	.40	.30	.15
7	Mark McGwire	.40	.30	.15
8	Keith Hernandez	.15	.11	.06
9	Franklin Stubbs	.12	.09	.05
10	Danny Tartabull	.30	.25	.12
11	Jesse Barfield	.15	.11	.06
12	Ellis Burks	.30	.25	.12

1989 Donruss Traded

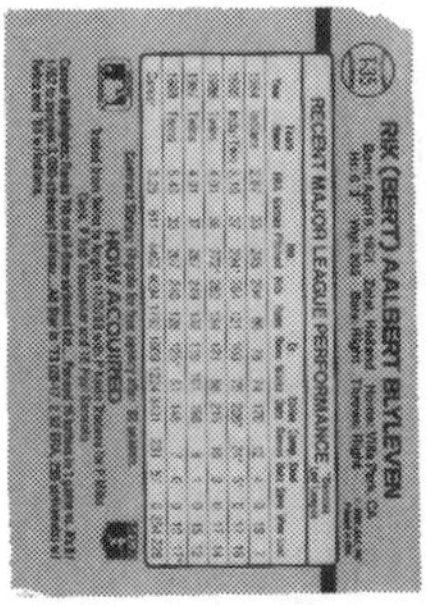

Donruss issued its first "Traded" set in 1989, releasing a 56-card boxed set designed in the same style as the regular 1989 Donruss set. The set included a Stan Musial puzzle card and a checklist.

		MT	NR MT	EX
Complete Set:		4.00	3.00	1.50
Common Player:		.06	.05	.02
1	Jeffrey Leonard	.08	.06	.03
2	Jack Clark	.15	.11	.06
3	Kevin Gross	.06	.05	.02
4	Tommy Herr	.08	.06	.03
5	Bob Boone	.10	.08	.04
6	Rafael Palmeiro	.30	.25	.12
7	John Dopson	.15	.11	.06
8	Willie Randolph	.08	.06	.03
9	Chris Brown	.06	.05	.02
10	Wally Backman	.06	.05	.02
11	Steve Ontiveros	.06	.05	.02
12	Eddie Murray	.30	.25	.12
13	Lance McCullers	.08	.06	.03
14	Spike Owen	.06	.05	.02
15	Rob Murphy	.06	.05	.02
16	Pete O'Brien	.08	.06	.03
17	Ken Williams	.06	.05	.02
18	Nick Esasky	.06	.05	.02
19	Nolan Ryan	1.50	1.25	.60
20	Brian Holton	.06	.05	.02
21	Mike Moore	.08	.06	.03
22	Joel Skinner	.06	.05	.02
23	Steve Sax	.15	.11	.06
24	Rick Mahler	.06	.05	.02
25	Mike Aldrete	.06	.05	.02
26	Jesse Orosco	.08	.06	.03
27	Dave LaPoint	.06	.05	.02
28	Walt Terrell	.08	.06	.03
29	Eddie Williams	.08	.06	.03
30	Mike Devereaux	.10	.08	.04
31	Julio Franco	.15	.11	.06
32	Jim Clancy	.06	.05	.02
33	Felix Fermin	.06	.05	.02
34	Curtis Wilkerson	.06	.05	.02
35	Bert Blyleven	.12	.09	.05

		MT	NR MT	EX
36	Mel Hall	.08	.06	.03
37	Eric King	.06	.05	.02
38	Mitch Williams	.12	.09	.05
39	Jamie Moyer	.06	.05	.02
40	Rick Rhoden	.08	.06	.03
41	Phil Bradley	.08	.06	.03
42	Paul Kilgus	.08	.06	.03
43	Milt Thompson	.06	.05	.02
44	Jerry Browne	.08	.06	.03
45	Bruce Hurst	.08	.06	.03
46	Claudell Washington	.08	.06	.03
47	Todd Benzinger	.12	.09	.05
48	Steve Balboni	.06	.05	.02
49	Oddibe McDowell	.08	.06	.03
50	Charles Hudson	.06	.05	.02
51	Ron Kittle	.08	.06	.03
52	Andy Hawkins	.06	.05	.02
53	Tom Brookens	.06	.05	.02
54	Tom Niedenfuer	.06	.05	.02
55	Jeff Parrett	.08	.06	.03
56	Checklist	.06	.05	.02

1989 Donruss Rookies

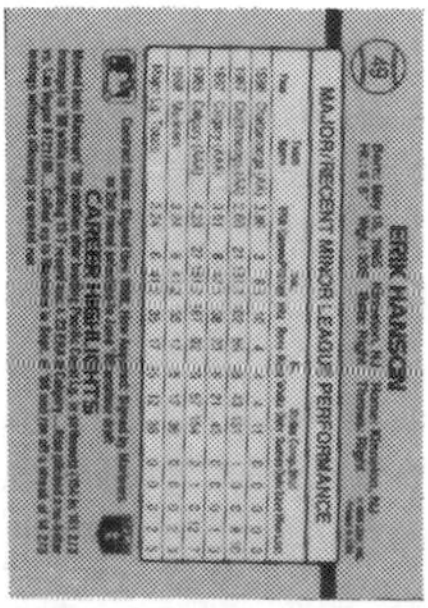

For the fourth straight year, Donruss issued a 56-card "Rookies" set in 1989. As in previous years, the set is similar in design to the regular Donruss set, except for a new "The Rookies" logo and a green and black border.

		MT	NR MT	EX
	Complete Set:	18.00	13.50	7.25
	Common Player:	.10	.08	.04
1	Gary Sheffield	.80	.60	.30
2	Gregg Jefferies	.60	.45	.25
3	Ken Griffey, Jr.	8.00	6.00	3.25
4	Tom Gordon	.40	.30	.15
5	Billy Spiers(FC)	.25	.20	.10
6	Deion Sanders(FC)	.60	.45	.25
7	Donn Pall(FC)	.20	.15	.08
8	Steve Carter(FC)	.20	.15	.08
9	Francisco Oliveras(FC)	.15	.11	.06
10	Steve Wilson(FC)	.20	.15	.08
11	Bob Geren(FC)	.20	.15	.08
12	Tony Castillo(FC)	.15	.11	.06
13	Kenny Rogers(FC)	.20	.15	.08
14	Carlos Martinez(FC)	.30	.25	.12
15	Edgar Martinez	.35	.25	.14
16	Jim Abbott(FC)	.80	.60	.30
17	Torey Lovullo(FC)	.20	.15	.08
18	Mark Carreon(FC)	.15	.11	.06
19	Geronimo Berroa	.10	.08	.04
20	Luis Medina	.10	.08	.04
21	Sandy Alomar, Jr.	.80	.60	.30
22	Bob Milacki	.10	.08	.04
23	Joe Girardi(FC)	.30	.25	.12
24	German Gonzalez	.10	.08	.04
25	Craig Worthington	.15	.11	.06
26	Jerome Walton(FC)	.60	.45	.25
27	Gary Wayne(FC)	.20	.15	.08
28	Tim Jones	.10	.08	.04
29	Dante Bichette	.10	.08	.04
30	Alexis Infante(FC)	.15	.11	.06
31	Ken Hill	.10	.08	.04
32	Dwight Smith(FC)	.30	.25	.12
33	Luis de los Santos	.10	.08	.04
34	Eric Yelding(FC)	.40	.30	.15

		MT	NR MT	EX
35	Gregg Olson	.80	.60	.30
36	Phil Stephenson(FC)	.15	.11	.06
37	Ken Patterson(FC)	.15	.11	.06
38	Rick Wrona(FC)	.15	.11	.06
39	Mike Brumley	.10	.08	.04
40	Cris Carpenter	.10	.08	.04
41	Jeff Brantley(FC)	.20	.15	.08
42	Ron Jones	.10	.08	.04
43	Randy Johnson	.10	.08	.04
44	Kevin Brown	.10	.08	.04
45	Ramon Martinez	2.00	1.50	.80
46	Greg Harris	.10	.08	.04
47	Steve Finley(FC)	.40	.30	.15
48	Randy Kramer	.10	.08	.04
49	Erik Hanson	.70	.50	.30
50	Matt Merullo(FC)	.15	.11	.06
51	Mike Devereaux	.10	.08	.04
52	Clay Parker(FC)	.15	.11	.06
53	Omar Vizquel(FC)	.20	.15	.08
54	Derek Lilliquist	.10	.08	.04
55	Junior Felix(FC)	.30	.25	.12
56	Checklist	.10	.08	.04

1989 Donruss Pop-Ups

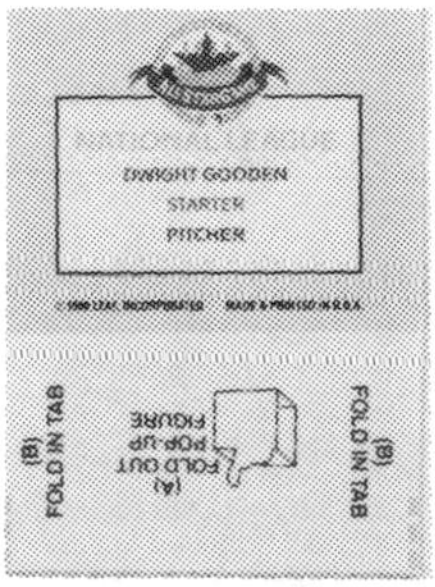

This set features the eighteen starters from the 1988 Major League All-Star game. The cards are designed with a perforated outline so each player can be popped out and made to stand upright. On the front side, each player's name, team, and position is featured in an orange-and-yellow rectangle below the borderless full-color photo. Each Pop-Up includes a unique double card, folded over and glued together on the back. The flip side features a red, white, and blue "Cincinnati Reds All-Star Game" logo at the top, a blue-lettered league designation, and the player's name and position in red. The lower portion of the flip side displays illustrated instructions for creating the base of the Pop-Up. The Pop-Ups were marketed in conjunction with All-Star and Warren Spahn Puzzle Cards.

		MT	NR MT	EX
	Complete Set:	5.00	3.75	2.00
	Common Player:	.20	.15	.08
(1)	Mark McGwire	.40	.30	.15
(2)	Jose Canseco	.80	.60	.30
(3)	Paul Molitor	.30	.25	.12
(4)	Rickey Henderson	.50	.40	.20
(5)	Cal Ripken, Jr.	.50	.40	.20
(6)	Dave Winfield	.40	.30	.15
(7)	Wade Boggs	.50	.40	.20
(8)	Frank Viola	.25	.20	.10
(9)	Terry Steinbach	.20	.15	.08
(10)	Tom Kelly	.20	.15	.08
(11)	Will Clark	1.00	.70	.40
(12)	Darryl Strawberry	.50	.40	.20
(13)	Ryne Sandberg	.50	.40	.20
(14)	Andre Dawson	.35	.25	.14
(15)	Ozzie Smith	.30	.25	.12
(16)	Vince Coleman	.20	.15	.08
(17)	Bobby Bonilla	.30	.25	.12
(18)	Dwight Gooden	.50	.40	.20
(19)	Gary Carter	.20	.15	.08
(20)	Whitey Herzog	.20	.15	.08

1989 Donruss All-Stars

For the fourth consecutive year in conjunction with the Pop-Ups, Donruss featured a 64-card set with players from the 1988 All-Star Game. The card fronts include a red- to-gold fade or gold-to-red fade border and blue vertical side borders. The top border features the player's name and position along with the "Donruss 89" logo. Each full-color player photo is highlighted by a thin white line and includes a league logo in the lower right corner. Card backs reveal an orange-gold border and black and white printing. The player's ID and personal information is displayed with a gold star on both sides. The star in the left corner includes the card number. 1988 All-Star game statistics and run totals follow along with a career highlights feature surrounded by the team, All-Star Game MLB, MLBPA, and Leaf Inc. logos. The All-Stars were distributed in wax packages containing five All-Stars, one Pop-Up, and one three-piece Warren Spahn puzzle card.

		MT	NR MT	EX
Complete Set:		9.00	6.75	3.50
Common Player:		.09	.07	.04
1	Mark McGwire	.50	.40	.20
2	Jose Canseco	1.00	.70	.40
3	Paul Molitor	.12	.09	.05
4	Rickey Henderson	.30	.25	.12
5	Cal Ripken, Jr.	.30	.25	.12
6	Dave Winfield	.20	.15	.08
7	Wade Boggs	.50	.40	.20
8	Frank Viola	.15	.11	.06
9	Terry Steinbach	.09	.07	.04
10	Tom Kelly	.09	.07	.04
11	George Brett	.12	.09	.05
12	Doyle Alexander	.09	.07	.04
13	Gary Gaetti	.12	.09	.05
14	Roger Clemens	.40	.30	.15
15	Mike Greenwell	.25	.20	.10
16	Dennis Eckersley	.12	.09	.05
17	Carney Lansford	.09	.07	.04
18	Mark Gubicza	.09	.07	.04
19	Tim Laudner	.09	.07	.04
20	Doug Jones	.09	.07	.04
21	Don Mattingly	1.00	.70	.40
22	Dan Plesac	.12	.09	.05
23	Kirby Puckett	.30	.25	.12
24	Jeff Reardon	.09	.07	.04
25	Johnny Ray	.09	.07	.04
26	Jeff Russell	.09	.07	.04
27	Harold Reynolds	.09	.07	.04
28	Dave Stieb	.09	.07	.04
29	Kurt Stillwell	.09	.07	.04
30	Jose Canseco	1.00	.70	.40
31	Terry Steinbach	.09	.07	.04
32	AL Checklist	.09	.07	.05
33	Will Clark	1.00	.70	.40
34	Darryl Strawberry	.60	.45	.25
35	Ryne Sandberg	.40	.30	.15
36	Andre Dawson	.20	.15	.08
37	Ozzie Smith	.20	.15	.08
38	Vince Coleman	.15	.11	.06
39	Bobby Bonilla	.15	.11	.06
40	Dwight Gooden	.40	.30	.15
41	Gary Carter	.10	.08	.04
42	Whitey Herzog	.09	.07	.05
43	Shawon Dunston	.09	.07	.05
44	David Cone	.12	.09	.05
45	Andres Galarraga	.09	.07	.04
46	Mark Davis	.09	.07	.04
47	Barry Larkin	.12	.09	.05
48	Kevin Gross	.09	.07	.04
49	Vance Law	.09	.07	.04
50	Orel Hershiser	.20	.15	.08
51	Willie McGee	.09	.07	.04
52	Danny Jackson	.09	.07	.04
53	Rafael Palmeiro	.20	.15	.08
54	Bob Knepper	.09	.07	.04
55	Lance Parrish	.09	.07	.04
56	Greg Maddux	.15	.11	.06
57	Gerald Perry	.09	.07	.04
58	Bob Walk	.09	.07	.04
59	Chris Sabo	.12	.09	.04
60	Todd Worrell	.09	.07	.04
61	Andy Van Slyke	.12	.09	.04
62	Ozzie Smith	.20	.15	.08
63	Riverfront Stadium	.09	.07	.04
64	NL Checklist	.09	.07	.04

1989 Donruss MVP

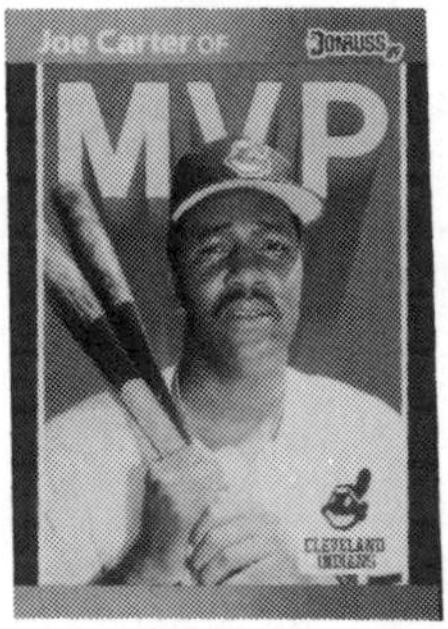

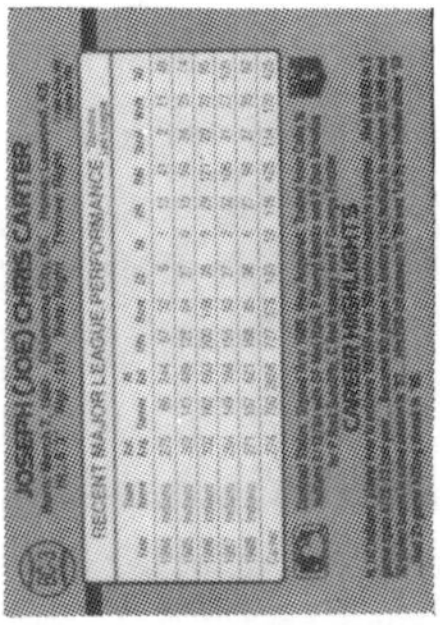

This 26-card set, numbered BC-1 through BC-26, was randomly packed in Donruss wax packs, but were not included in factory sets or other card packs. Players highlighted in this set are selected by Donruss, one player per team. MVP cards feature a variation of the design in the basic Donruss issue, with multi-color upper and lower borders and black side borders. The player name and Donruss '89 logos appear in the upper margin with the team logo appearing lower right. The "MVP" designation in large, bright letters serves as a backdrop for the full-color player photo. The cards measure 2-1/2" by 3-1/2" in size.

		MT	NR MT	EX
Complete Set:		4.00	3.00	1.50
Common Player:		.15	.11	.06
1	Kirby Puckett	.50	.40	.20
2	Mike Scott	.15	.11	.06
3	Joe Carter	.30	.25	.12
4	Orel Hershiser	.25	.20	.10
5	Jose Canseco	.75	.55	.30
6	Darryl Strawberry	.60	.45	.25
7	George Brett	.35	.25	.14
8	Andre Dawson	.25	.20	.10
9	Paul Molitor	.20	.15	.08
10	Andy Van Slyke	.15	.11	.06
11	Dave Winfield	.20	.15	.08
12	Kevin Gross	.15	.11	.06
13	Mike Greenwell	.30	.25	.12
14	Ozzie Smith	.20	.15	.08
15	Cal Ripken	.50	.40	.20
16	Andres Galarraga	.15	.11	.06
17	Alan Trammell	.25	.20	.10
18	Kal Daniels	.20	.15	.08
19	Fred McGriff	.35	.25	.14
20	Tony Gwynn	.30	.25	.12
21	Wally Joyner	.30	.25	.12
22	Will Clark	.75	.55	.30
23	Ozzie Guillen	.15	.11	.06
24	Gerald Perry	.15	.11	.06
25	Alvin Davis	.15	.11	.06
26	Ruben Sierra	.25	.20	.10

1989 Donruss Baseball's Best

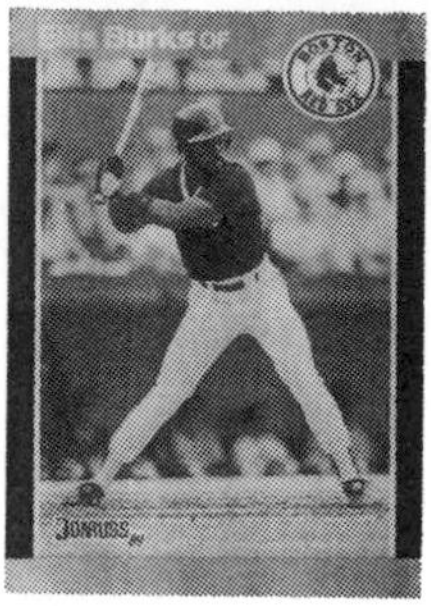

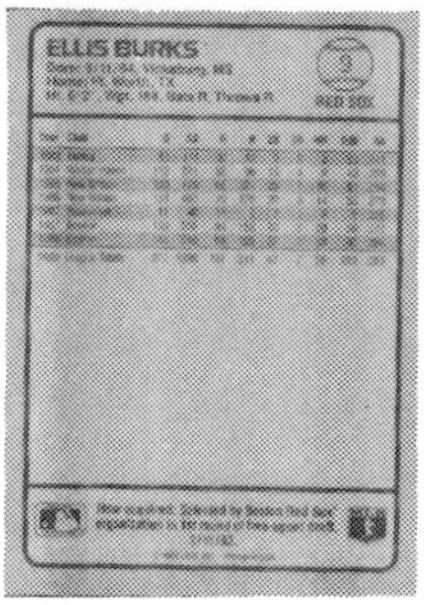

For the second consecutive year, Donruss issued a "Baseball's Best" set in 1989 to highlight the game's top players. The special 336-card set was packaged in a special box and was sold at various retail chains nationwide following the conclusion of the 1989 baseball season. The cards are styled after the regular 1989 Donruss set with green borders and a glossy finish. The set included a Warren Spahn puzzle.

		MT	NR MT	EX
Complete Set:		20.00	15.00	8.00
Common Player:		.05	.04	.02
1	Don Mattingly	1.00	.70	.40
2	Tom Glavine	.15	.11	.06
3	Bert Blyleven	.08	.06	.03
4	Andre Dawson	.10	.08	.04
5	Pete O'Brien	.05	.04	.02
6	Eric Davis	.40	.30	.15
7	George Brett	.10	.08	.04
8	Glenn Davis	.10	.08	.04
9	Ellis Burks	.30	.25	.12
10	Kirk Gibson	.08	.06	.03
11	Carlton Fisk	.08	.06	.03
12	Andres Galarraga	.08	.06	.03
13	Alan Trammell	.06	.05	.02
14	Dwight Gooden	.30	.25	.12
15	Paul Molitor	.10	.08	.04
16	Roger McDowell	.05	.04	.02
17	Doug Drabek	.05	.04	.02
18	Kent Hrbek	.08	.06	.03
19	Vince Coleman	.08	.06	.03
20	Steve Sax	.08	.06	.03
21	Roberto Alomar	.30	.25	.12
22	Carney Lansford	.06	.05	.02
23	Will Clark	1.50	1.25	.60
24	Alvin Davis	.08	.06	.03
25	Bobby Thigpen	.08	.06	.03
26	Ryne Sandberg	.60	.45	.25
27	Devon White	.08	.06	.03
28	Mike Greenwell	.40	.30	.15
29	Dale Murphy	.10	.08	.04
30	Jeff Ballard	.10	.08	.04
31	Kelly Gruber	.08	.06	.03
32	Julio Franco	.15	.11	.06
33	Bobby Bonilla	.15	.11	.06
34	Tim Wallach	.05	.04	.02
35	Lou Whitaker	.07	.05	.03
36	Jay Howell	.07	.05	.03
37	Greg Maddux	.30	.25	.12
38	Bill Doran	.07	.05	.03
39	Danny Tartabull	.12	.09	.05
40	Darryl Strawberry	.50	.40	.20
41	Ron Darling	.10	.08	.06
42	Tony Gwynn	.30	.25	.12
43	Mark McGwire	.40	.30	.15
44	Ozzie Smith	.15	.11	.06
45	Andy Van Slyke	.12	.09	.05
46	Juan Berenguer	.05	.04	.02
47	Von Hayes	.08	.06	.03
48	Tony Fernandez	.12	.09	.05
49	Eric Plunk	.05	.04	.02
50	Ernest Riles	.05	.04	.02

		MT	NR MT	EX
51	Harold Reynolds	.07	.05	.03
52	Andy Hawkins	.06	.05	.02
53	Robin Yount	.35	.25	.14
54	Danny Jackson	.06	.05	.02
55	Nolan Ryan	1.25	.90	.50
56	Joe Carter	.12	.09	.05
57	Jose Canseco	1.00	.70	.40
58	Jody Davis	.05	.04	.02
59	Lance Parrish	.06	.05	.02
60	Mitch Williams	.15	.11	.06
61	Brook Jacoby	.06	.05	.02
62	Tom Browning	.10	.08	.06
63	Kurt Stillwell	.06	.05	.02
64	Rafael Ramirez	.05	.04	.02
65	Roger Clemens	.50	.40	.20
66	Mike Scioscia	.07	.05	.02
67	Dave Gallagher	.07	.05	.02
68	Mark Langston	.15	.11	.06
69	Chet Lemon	.06	.05	.02
70	Kevin McReynolds	.25	.20	.10
71	Rob Deer	.06	.05	.02
72	Tommy Herr	.07	.05	.03
73	Barry Bonds	.12	.09	.05
74	Frank Viola	.15	.11	.06
75	Pedro Guerrero	.15	.11	.06
76	Dave Righetti	.07	.05	.03
77	Bruce Hurst	.08	.06	.03
78	Rickey Henderson	.40	.30	.15
79	Robby Thompson	.08	.06	.03
80	Randy Johnson	.25	.20	.10
81	Harold Baines	.12	.09	.05
82	Calvin Schiraldi	.05	.04	.02
83	Kirk McCaskill	.05	.04	.02
84	Lee Smith	.07	.05	.03
85	John Smoltz	.25	.20	.10
86	Mickey Tettleton	.20	.15	.08
87	Jimmy Key	.08	.06	.03
88	Rafael Palmeiro	.10	.08	.04
89	Sid Bream	.05	.04	.02
90	Dennis Martinez	.05	.04	.02
91	Frank Tanana	.05	.04	.02
92	Eddie Murray	.15	.11	.06
93	Shawon Dunston	.15	.11	.06
94	Mike Scott	.10	.08	.04
95	Bret Saberhagen	.25	.20	.10
96	David Cone	.20	.15	.08
97	Kevin Elster	.05	.04	.02
98	Jack Clark	.20	.15	.08
99	Dave Stewart	.20	.15	.08
100	Jose Oquendo	.06	.05	.02
101	Jose Lind	.05	.04	.02
102	Gary Gaetti	.12	.09	.05
103	Ricky Jordan	.25	.20	.10
104	Fred McGriff	.50	.40	.20
105	Don Slaught	.05	.04	.02
106	Jose Uribe	.05	.04	.02
107	Jeffrey Leonard	.07	.05	.02
108	Lee Guetterman	.05	.04	.02
109	Chris Bosio	.08	.06	.03
110	Barry Larkin	.15	.11	.06
111	Ruben Sierra	.30	.25	.12
112	Greg Swindell	.12	.09	.05
113	Gary Sheffield	.40	.30	.15
114	Lonnie Smith	.10	.08	.04
115	Chili Davis	.08	.06	.03
116	Damon Berryhill	.08	.06	.03
117	Tom Candiotti	.05	.04	.02
118	Kal Daniels	.10	.08	.04
119	Mark Gubicza	.10	.08	.04
120	Jim Deshaies	.08	.06	.03
121	Dwight Evans	.10	.08	.04
122	Mike Morgan	.05	.04	.02
123	Dan Pasqua	.05	.04	.02
124	Bryn Smith	.07	.05	.03
125	Doyle Alexander	.07	.05	.03
126	Howard Johnson	.25	.20	.10
127	Chuck Crim	.07	.05	.03
128	Darren Daulton	.05	.04	.02
129	Jeff Robinson	.08	.06	.03
130	Kirby Puckett	.50	.40	.20
131	Joe Magrane	.10	.08	.04
132	Jesse Barfield	.07	.05	.03
133	Mark Davis (Photo actually Dave Leiper)	.25	.20	.10
134	Dennis Eckersley	.10	.08	.04
135	Mike Krukow	.05	.04	.02
136	Jay Buhner	.10	.08	.04
137	Ozzie Guillen	.08	.06	.03
138	Rick Sutcliffe	.12	.09	.05
139	Wally Joyner	.25	.20	.10
140	Wade Boggs	.60	.45	.25

		MT	NR MT	EX
141	Jeff Treadway	.08	.06	.05
142	Cal Ripken	.30	.25	.12
143	Dave Steib	.10	.08	.04
144	Pete Incaviglia	.07	.05	.03
145	Bob Walk	.05	.04	.02
146	Nelson Santovenia	.10	.08	.04
147	Mike Heath	.05	.04	.02
148	Willie Randolph	.08	.06	.03
149	Paul Kilgus	.05	.04	.02
150	Billy Hatcher	.07	.05	.03
151	Steve Farr	.05	.04	.02
152	Gregg Jefferies	.40	.30	.15
153	Randy Myers	.06	.05	.02
154	Garry Templeton	.06	.05	.02
155	Walt Weiss	.10	.08	.04
156	Terry Pendleton	.10	.08	.04
157	John Smiley	.08	.06	.03
158	Greg Gagne	.05	.04	.02
159	Lenny Dykstra	.08	.06	.03
160	Nelson Liriano	.05	.04	.02
161	Alvaro Espinoza	.10	.08	.04
162	Rick Reuschel	.08	.06	.03
163	Omar Vizquel	.15	.11	.06
164	Clay Parker	.15	.11	.06
165	Dan Plesac	.06	.05	.02
166	John Franco	.06	.05	.02
167	Scott Fletcher	.06	.05	.02
168	Cory Snyder	.12	.09	.05
169	Bo Jackson	1.00	.70	.40
170	Tommy Gregg	.08	.06	.03
171	Jim Abbott	.50	.40	.20
172	Jerome Walton	.50	.40	.20
173	Doug Jones	.06	.05	.02
174	Todd Benzinger	.08	.06	.03
175	Frank White	.08	.06	.03
176	Craig Biggio	.20	.15	.08
177	John Dopson	.10	.08	.06
178	Alfredo Griffin	.06	.05	.02
179	Melido Perez	.06	.05	.02
180	Tim Burke	.06	.05	.02
181	Matt Nokes	.10	.08	.04
182	Gary Carter	.10	.08	.04
183	Ted Higuera	.08	.06	.03
184	Ken Howell	.05	.04	.02
185	Rey Quinones	.05	.04	.02
186	Wally Backman	.07	.05	.03
187	Tom Brunansky	.07	.05	.03
188	Steve Balboni	.05	.04	.02
189	Marvell Wynne	.05	.04	.02
190	Dave Henderson	.08	.06	.03
191	Don Robinson	.05	.04	.02
192	Ken Griffey, Jr.	4.00	3.00	1.50
193	Ivan Calderon	.05	.04	.02
194	Mike Bielecki	.07	.05	.03
195	Johnny Ray	.07	.05	.03
196	Rob Murphy	.05	.04	.02
197	Andres Thomas	.05	.04	.02
198	Phil Bradley	.06	.05	.02
199	Junior Felix	.30	.25	.12
200	Jeff Russell	.08	.06	.03
201	Mike LaValliere	.05	.04	.02
202	Kevin Gross	.06	.05	.02
203	Keith Moreland	.06	.05	.02
204	Mike Marshall	.06	.05	.02
205	Dwight Smith	.30	.25	.12
206	Jim Clancy	.05	.04	.02
207	Kevin Seitzer	.10	.08	.04
208	Keith Hernandez	.10	.08	.04
209	Bob Ojeda	.06	.05	.02
210	Ed Whitson	.06	.05	.02
211	Tony Phillips	.06	.05	.02
212	Milt Thompson	.05	.04	.02
213	Randy Kramer	.05	.04	.02
214	Randy Bush	.05	.04	.02
215	Randy Ready	.05	.04	.02
216	Duane Ward	.05	.04	.02
217	Jimmy Jones	.05	.04	.02
218	Scott Garrelts	.08	.06	.03
219	Scott Bankhead	.10	.08	.04
220	Lance McCullers	.06	.05	.02
221	B.J. Surhoff	.06	.05	.02
222	Chris Sabo	.06	.05	.02
223	Steve Buechele	.06	.05	.02
224	Joel Skinner	.05	.04	.02
225	Orel Hershiser	.15	.11	.06
226	Derek Lilliquist	.10	.08	.06
227	Claudell Washington	.08	.06	.05
228	Lloyd McClendon	.10	.08	.04
229	Felix Fermin	.05	.04	.02
230	Paul O'Neill	.08	.06	.03
231	Charlie Leibrandt	.05	.04	.02

		MT	NR MT	EX
232	Dave Smith	.06	.05	.02
233	Bob Stanley	.05	.04	.02
234	Tim Belcher	.15	.11	.06
235	Eric King	.05	.04	.02
236	Spike Owen	.05	.04	.02
237	Mike Henneman	.05	.04	.02
238	Juan Samuel	.06	.05	.02
239	Greg Brock	.06	.05	.02
240	John Kruk	.06	.05	.02
241	Glenn Wilson	.06	.05	.02
242	Jeff Reardon	.06	.05	.02
243	Todd Worrell	.08	.06	.03
244	Dave LaPoint	.05	.04	.02
245	Walt Terrell	.05	.04	.02
246	Mike Moore	.08	.06	.03
247	Kelly Downs	.05	.04	.02
248	Dave Valle	.05	.04	.02
249	Ron Kittle	.06	.05	.04
250	Steve Wilson	.10	.08	.04
251	Dick Schofield	.05	.04	.02
252	Marty Barrett	.06	.05	.02
253	Dion James	.06	.05	.02
254	Bob Milacki	.10	.08	.04
255	Ernie Whitt	.06	.05	.02
256	Kevin Brown	.08	.06	.03
257	R.J. Reynolds	.05	.04	.02
258	Tim Raines	.10	.08	.04
259	Frank Williams	.05	.04	.02
260	Jose Gonzalez	.05	.04	.02
261	Mitch Webster	.05	.04	.02
262	Ken Caminiti	.07	.05	.03
263	Bob Boone	.07	.05	.03
264	Dave Magadan	.07	.05	.03
265	Rick Aguilera	.05	.04	.02
266	Chris James	.05	.04	.02
267	Bob Welch	.07	.05	.03
268	Ken Dayley	.05	.04	.02
269	Junior Ortiz	.05	.04	.02
270	Allan Anderson	.08	.06	.03
271	Steve Jeltz	.05	.04	.02
272	George Bell	.10	.08	.04
273	Roberto Kelly	.10	.08	.04
274	Brett Butler	.07	.05	.03
275	Mike Schooler	.07	.05	.02
276	Ken Phelps	.05	.04	.02
277	Glenn Braggs	.06	.05	.02
278	Jose Rijo	.06	.05	.02
279	Bobby Witt	.06	.05	.02
280	Jerry Browne	.06	.05	.02
281	Kevin Mitchell	.40	.30	.15
282	Craig Worthington	.15	.11	.06
283	Greg Minton	.05	.04	.02
284	Nick Esasky	.07	.05	.03
285	John Farrell	.05	.04	.02
286	Rick Mahler	.05	.04	.02
287	Tom Gordon	.40	.30	.15
288	Gerald Young	.05	.04	.02
289	Jody Reed	.08	.06	.03
290	Jeff Hamilton	.05	.04	.02
291	Gerald Perry	.05	.04	.02
292	Hubie Brooks	.05	.04	.02
293	Bo Diaz	.05	.04	.02
294	Terry Puhl	.05	.04	.02
295	Jim Gantner	.05	.04	.02
296	Jeff Parrett	.05	.04	.02
297	Mike Boddicker	.05	.04	.02
298	Dan Gladden	.05	.04	.02
299	Tony Pena	.07	.05	.03
300	Checklist	.05	.04	.02
301	Tom Henke	.05	.04	.02
302	Pascual Perez	.05	.04	.02
303	Steve Bedrosian	.05	.04	.02
304	Ken Hill	.10	.08	.04
305	Jerry Reuss	.07	.05	.03
306	Jim Eisenreich	.05	.04	.02
307	Jack Howell	.05	.04	.02
308	Rick Cerone	.05	.04	.02
309	Tim Leary	.05	.04	.02
310	Joe Orsulak	.05	.04	.02
311	Jim Dwyer	.05	.04	.02
312	Geno Petralli	.05	.04	.02
313	Rick Honeycutt	.05	.04	.02
314	Tom Foley	.05	.04	.02
315	Kenny Rogers	.10	.08	.04
316	Mike Flanagan	.06	.05	.02
317	Bryan Harvey	.06	.05	.02
318	Billy Ripken	.05	.04	.02
319	Jeff Montgomery	.05	.04	.02
320	Erik Hanson	.12	.09	.05
321	Brian Downing	.06	.05	.02
322	Gregg Olson	.40	.30	.15

		MT	NR MT	EX
323	Terry Steinbach	.12	.09	.05
324	Sammy Sosa	.40	.30	.15
325	Gene Harris	.05	.04	.02
326	Mike Devereaux	.10	.08	.04
327	Dennis Cook	.12	.09	.05
328	David Wells	.08	.06	.03
329	Checklist	.05	.04	.02
330	Kirt Manwaring	.10	.08	.04
331	Jim Presley	.05	.04	.02
332	Checklist	.05	.04	.02
333	Chuck Finley	.05	.04	.02
334	Rob Dibble	.08	.06	.03
335	Cecil Espy	.06	.05	.02
336	Dave Parker	.08	.06	.02

1990 Donruss MVP

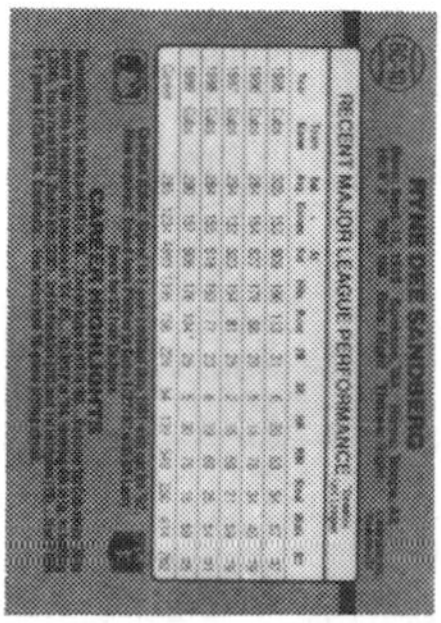

This special 26-card set includes one player from each Major League team. Numbered BC-1 (the "BC" stands for "Bonus Card") through BC-26, the cards from this set were randomly packed in 1990 Donruss wax packs and were not available in factory sets or other types of packaging. The red-bordered cards are similar in design to the regular 1990 Donruss set, except the player photos are set against a special background made up of the "MVP" logo.

		MT	NR MT	EX
Complete Set:		4.00	3.00	1.50
Common Player:		.08	.06	.03
1	Bo Jackson	.30	.25	.12
2	Howard Johnson	.10	.08	.04
3	Dave Stewart	.08	.06	.03
4	Tony Gwynn	.15	.11	.06
5	Orel Hershiser	.10	.08	.04
6	Pedro Guerrero	.10	.08	.04
7	Tim Raines	.10	.08	.04
8	Kirby Puckett	.30	.25	.12
9	Alvin Davis	.08	.06	.03
10	Ryne Sandberg	.30	.25	.12
11	Kevin Mitchell	.20	.15	.08
12a	John Smoltz (photo of Tom Glavine)	2.00	1.50	.80
12b	John Smoltz (corrected)	.40	.30	.15
13	George Bell	.10	.08	.04
14	Julio Franco	.15	.11	.06
15	Paul Molitor	.10	.08	.04
16	Bobby Bonilla	.15	.11	.06
17	Mike Greenwell	.15	.11	.06
18	Cal Ripken	.30	.25	.12
19	Carlton Fisk	.12	.09	.05
20	Chili Davis	.08	.06	.03
21	Glenn Davis	.10	.08	.04
22	Steve Sax	.10	.08	.04
23	Eric Davis	.20	.15	.08
24	Greg Swindell	.08	.06	.03
25	Von Hayes	.08	.06	.03
26	Alan Trammell	.10	.08	.04

A player's name in *italic* type indicates a rookie card. An (FC) indicates a player's first card for that particular card company.

1990 Donruss

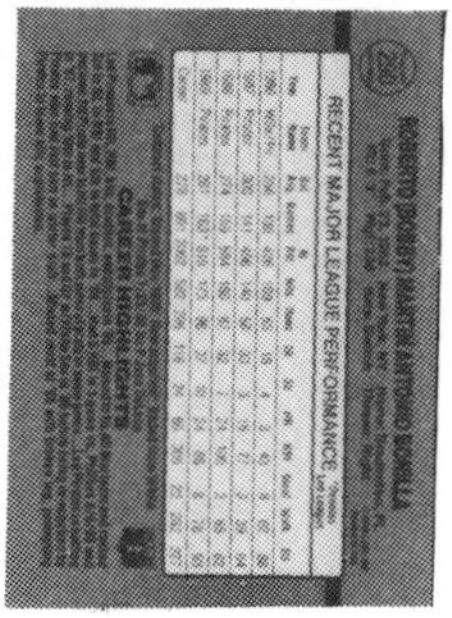

Donruss celebrated its 10th anniversary in the baseball card hobby with a 715-card set in 1990, up from the 660-card sets of previous years. The standard-size cards feature bright red borders with the player's name in script along the top. The 1990 set included 26 "Diamond Kings" and 20 "Rated Rookies," along with a Carl Yastrzemski puzzle.

		MT	NR MT	EX
Complete Set:		20.00	15.00	8.00
Common Player:		.04	.03	.02
1	Bo Jackson (DK)	.40	.30	.15
2	Steve Sax (DK)	.12	.09	.05
3a	Ruben Sierra (DK - missing line on top border)	1.25	.90	.50
3b	Ruben Sierra (DK)	.30	.25	.12
4	Ken Griffey, Jr. (DK)	.80	.60	.30
5	Mickey Tettleton (DK)	.12	.09	.05
6	Dave Stewart (DK)	.12	.09	.05
7	Jim Deshaies (DK)	.07	.05	.03
8	John Smoltz (DK)	.25	.20	.10
9	Mike Bielecki (DK)	.07	.05	.03
10a	Brian Downing DK (Reverse Negative)	1.00	.70	.40
10b	Brian Downing DK (Corrected)	.25	.20	.10
11	Kevin Mitchell (DK)	.35	.25	.14
12	Kelly Gruber (DK)	.08	.06	.03
13	Joe Magrane (DK)	.08	.06	.03
14	John Franco (DK)	.08	.06	.03
15	Ozzie Guillen (DK)	.08	.06	.03
16	Lou Whitaker (DK)	.08	.06	.03
17	John Smiley (DK)	.08	.06	.03
18	Howard Johnson (DK)	.30	.25	.12
19	Willie Randolph (DK)	.08	.06	.03
20	Chris Bosio (DK)	.07	.05	.03
21	Tommy Herr (DK)	.07	.05	.03
22	Dan Gladden (DK)	.07	.05	.03
23	Ellis Burks (DK)	.20	.15	.08
24	Pete O'Brien (DK)	.08	.06	.03
25	Bryn Smith (DK)	.07	.05	.03
26	Ed Whitson (DK)	.07	.05	.03
27	Checklist 1-27	.04	.03	.02
28	Robin Ventura (RR)(FC)	.80	.60	.30
29	*Todd Zeile* (RR)(FC)	.70	.50	.30
30	Sandy Alomar, Jr. (RR)	.35	.25	.14
31	*Kent Mercker* (RR)(FC)	.30	.25	.12
32	*Ben McDonald* (RR)(FC)	2.00	1.50	.80
33a	*Juan Gonzalez RR* (Reverse Negative)(FC)	5.00	3.75	2.00
33b	*Juan Gonzalez RR* (Corrected)(FC)	3.00	2.25	1.25
34	*Eric Anthony* (RR)(FC)	.50	.40	.20
35	*Mike Fetters* (RR)(FC)	.20	.15	.08
36	*Marquis Grissom* (RR)(FC)	.60	.45	.25
37	*Greg Vaughn* (RR)(FC)	.60	.45	.25
38	*Brian Dubois* (RR)(FC)	.15	.11	.06
39	Steve Avery (RR)(FC)	.50	.40	.20
40	*Mark Gardner* (RR)(FC)	.20	.15	.08
41	Andy Benes (RR)(FC)	.40	.30	.15
42	*Delino Deshields* (RR)(FC)	.50	.40	.20
43	*Scott Coolbaugh* (RR)(FC)	.25	.20	.10
44	*Pat Combs* (RR)(FC)	.25	.20	.10
45	Alex Sanchez (RR)	.15	.11	.06
46	*Kelly Mann* (RR)(FC)	.20	.15	.08
47	*Julio Machado* (RR)(FC)	.20	.15	.08
48	Pete Incaviglia	.05	.04	.02
49	Shawon Dunston	.07	.05	.03

		MT	NR MT	EX
50	Jeff Treadway	.05	.04	.02
51	Jeff Ballard	.10	.08	.04
52	Claudell Washington	.08	.06	.03
53	Juan Samuel	.10	.08	.04
54	John Smiley	.08	.06	.03
55	Rob Deer	.06	.05	.02
56	Geno Petralli	.04	.03	.02
57	Chris Bosio	.10	.08	.04
58	Carlton Fisk	.12	.09	.05
59	Kirt Manwaring	.10	.08	.04
60	Chet Lemon	.06	.05	.02
61	Bo Jackson	.40	.30	.15
62	Doyle Alexander	.05	.04	.02
63	Pedro Guerrero	.12	.09	.05
64	Allan Anderson	.07	.05	.03
65	Greg Harris	.07	.05	.03
66	Mike Greenwell	.25	.20	.10
67	Walt Weiss	.08	.06	.03
68	Wade Boggs	.30	.25	.12
69	Jim Clancy	.04	.03	.02
70	*Junior Felix*	.20	.15	.08
71	Barry Larkin	.12	.09	.05
72	Dave LaPoint	.05	.04	.02
73	Joel Skinner	.04	.03	.02
74	Jesse Barfield	.08	.06	.03
75	Tommy Herr	.08	.06	.03
76	Ricky Jordan	.20	.15	.08
77	Eddie Murray	.15	.11	.06
78	Steve Sax	.10	.08	.04
79	Tim Belcher	.10	.08	.04
80	Danny Jackson	.06	.05	.02
81	Kent Hrbek	.10	.08	.04
82	Milt Thompson	.05	.04	.02
83	Brook Jacoby	.07	.05	.03
84	Mike Marshall	.08	.06	.03
85	Kevin Seitzer	.12	.09	.05
86	Tony Gwynn	.15	.11	.06
87	Dave Steib	.08	.06	.03
88	Dave Smith	.06	.05	.02
89	Bret Saberhagen	.15	.11	.06
90	Alan Trammell	.10	.08	.04
91	Tony Phillips	.05	.04	.03
92	Doug Drabek	.05	.04	.03
93	Jeffrey Leonard	.09	.07	.04
94	Wally Joyner	.15	.11	.06
95	Carney Lansford	.09	.07	.04
96	Cal Ripken	.15	.11	.06
97	Andres Galarraga	.15	.11	.06
98	Kevin Mitchell	.30	.25	.12
99	Howard Johnson	.15	.11	.06
100	Checklist	.04	.03	.02
101	Melido Perez	.07	.05	.03
102	Spike Owen	.05	.04	.02
103	Paul Molitor	.10	.08	.04
104	Geronimo Berroa	.06	.05	.02
105	Ryne Sandberg	.25	.20	.10
106	Bryn Smith	.06	.05	.02
107	Steve Buechele	.04	.03	.02
108	Jim Abbott	.30	.25	.12
109	Alvin Davis	.10	.08	.04
110	Lee Smith	.05	.04	.02
111	Roberto Alomar	.15	.11	.06
112	Rick Reuschel	.09	.07	.04
113	Kelly Gruber	.09	.07	.04
114	Joe Carter	.09	.07	.04
115	Jose Rijo	.06	.05	.02
116	Greg Minton	.04	.03	.02
117	Bob Ojeda	.04	.03	.02
118	Glenn Davis	.08	.06	.03
119	Jeff Reardon	.05	.04	.02
120	Kurt Stillwell	.05	.04	.02
121	John Smoltz	.15	.11	.06
122	Dwight Evans	.08	.06	.03
123	Eric Yelding	.08	.06	.03
124	John Franco	.05	.04	.02
125	Jose Canseco	.50	.40	.20
126	Barry Bonds	.25	.20	.10
127	Lee Guetterman	.04	.03	.02
128	Jack Clark	.10	.08	.04
129	Dave Valle	.04	.03	.02
130	Hubie Brooks	.05	.04	.02
131	Ernest Riles	.04	.03	.02
132	Mike Morgan	.04	.03	.02
133	Steve Jeltz	.04	.03	.02
134	Jeff Robinson	.05	.04	.02
135	Ozzie Guillen	.05	.04	.02
136	Chili Davis	.06	.05	.02
137	Mitch Webster	.04	.03	.02
138	Jerry Browne	.06	.05	.02
139	Bo Diaz	.04	.03	.02
140	Robby Thompson	.07	.05	.03

		MT	NR MT	EX
141	Craig Worthington	.09	.07	.04
142	Julio Franco	.09	.07	.04
143	Brian Holman	.05	.04	.02
144	George Brett	.10	.08	.04
145	Tom Glavine	.10	.08	.04
146	Robin Yount	.20	.15	.08
147	Gary Carter	.06	.05	.02
148	Ron Kittle	.06	.05	.02
149	Tony Fernandez	.07	.05	.03
150	Dave Stewart	.07	.05	.03
151	Gary Gaetti	.07	.05	.03
152	Kevin Elster	.04	.03	.02
153	Gerald Perry	.05	.04	.02
154	Jesse Orosco	.05	.04	.02
155	Wally Backman	.05	.04	.02
156	Dennis Martinez	.05	.04	.02
157	Rick Sutcliffe	.08	.06	.03
158	Greg Maddux	.12	.09	.05
159	Andy Hawkins	.05	.04	.02
160	John Kruk	.05	.04	.02
161	Jose Oquendo	.05	.04	.02
162	John Dopson	.08	.06	.03
163	Joe Magrane	.08	.06	.03
164	Billy Ripken	.04	.03	.02
165	Fred Manrique	.04	.03	.02
166	Nolan Ryan	.40	.30	.15
167	Damon Berryhill	.06	.05	.02
168	Dale Murphy	.09	.07	.04
169	Mickey Tettleton	.08	.06	.03
170	Kirk McCaskill	.05	.04	.02
171	Dwight Gooden	.15	.11	.06
172	Jose Lind	.04	.03	.02
173	B.J. Surhoff	.07	.05	.03
174	Ruben Sierra	.15	.11	.06
175	Dan Plesac	.08	.06	.03
176	Dan Pasqua	.05	.04	.02
177	Kelly Downs	.05	.04	.02
178	Matt Nokes	.08	.06	.03
179	Luis Aquino	.04	.03	.02
180	Frank Tanana	.04	.03	.02
181	Tony Pena	.07	.05	.03
182	Dan Gladden	.05	.04	.02
183	Bruce Hurst	.05	.04	.02
184	Roger Clemens	.20	.15	.08
185	Mark McGwire	.30	.25	.12
186	Rob Murphy	.04	.03	.02
187	Jim Deshaies	.06	.05	.02
188	Fred McGriff	.20	.15	.08
189	Rob Dibble	.06	.05	.02
190	Don Mattingly	.40	.30	.15
191	Felix Fermin	.04	.03	.02
192	Roberto Kelly	.08	.06	.03
193	Dennis Cook	.08	.06	.03
194	Darren Daulton	.04	.03	.02
195	Alfredo Griffin	.05	.04	.02
196	Eric Plunk	.05	.04	.02
197	Orel Hershiser	.20	.15	.08
198	Paul O'Neil	.07	.05	.03
199	Randy Bush	.04	.03	.02
200	Checklist	.04	.03	.02
201	Ozzie Smith	.10	.08	.04
202	Pete O'Brien	.06	.05	.02
203	Jay Howell	.06	.05	.02
204	Mark Gibicza	.08	.06	.03
205	Ed Whitson	.04	.03	.02
206	George Bell	.09	.07	.04
207	Mike Scott	.09	.07	.04
208	Charlie Leibrandt	.04	.03	.02
209	Mike Heath	.04	.03	.02
210	Dennis Eckersley	.09	.07	.04
211	Mike LaValliere	.04	.03	.02
212	Darnell Coles	.04	.03	.02
213	Lance Parrish	.07	.05	.03
214	Mike Moore	.07	.05	.03
215	*Steve Finley*	.20	.15	.08
216	Tim Raines	.09	.07	.04
217	Scott Garrelts	.06	.05	.02
218	Kevin McReynolds	.09	.07	.04
219	Dave Gallagher	.08	.06	.03
220	Tim Wallach	.08	.06	.03
221	Chuck Crim	.04	.03	.02
222	Lonnie Smith	.08	.06	.03
223	Andre Dawson	.10	.08	.04
224	Nelson Santovenia	.07	.05	.03
225	Rafael Palmeiro	.07	.05	.03
226	Devon White	.07	.05	.03
227	Harold Reynolds	.07	.05	.03
228	Ellis Burks	.15	.11	.06
229	Mark Parent	.04	.03	.02
230	Will Clark	.40	.30	.15
231	Jimmy Key	.08	.06	.03

		MT	NR MT	EX
232	John Farrell	.04	.03	.02
233	Eric Davis	.30	.25	.12
234	Johnny Ray	.05	.04	.02
235	Darryl Strawberry	.30	.25	.12
236	Bill Doran	.05	.04	.02
237	Greg Gagne	.05	.04	.02
238	Jim Eisenreich	.04	.03	.02
239	Tommy Gregg	.06	.05	.02
240	Marty Barrett	.05	.04	.02
241	Rafael Ramirez	.05	.04	.02
242	Chris Sabo	.10	.08	.04
243	Dave Henderson	.07	.05	.03
244	Andy Van Slyke	.07	.05	.03
245	Alvaro Espinoza	.10	.07	.04
246	Garry Templeton	.06	.05	.02
247	Gene Harris	.04	.03	.02
248	Kevin Gross	.05	.04	.02
249	Brett Butler	.09	.07	.04
250	Willie Randolph	.07	.05	.03
251	Roger McDowell	.05	.04	.02
252	Rafael Belliard	.04	.03	.02
253	Steve Rosenberg	.04	.03	.02
254	Jack Howell	.04	.03	.02
255	Marvell Wynne	.04	.03	.02
256	Tom Candiotti	.05	.04	.02
257	Todd Benzinger	.05	.04	.02
258	Don Robinson	.04	.03	.02
259	Phil Bradley	.08	.06	.03
260	Cecil Espy	.05	.04	.02
261	Scott Bankhead	.05	.04	.02
262	Frank White	.07	.05	.03
263	Andres Thomas	.05	.04	.02
264	Glenn Braggs	.05	.04	.02
265	David Cone	.10	.08	.04
266	Bobby Thigpen	.07	.05	.03
267	Nelson Liriano	.04	.03	.02
268	Terry Steinbach	.09	.07	.04
269	Kirby Puckett	.30	.25	.12
270	Gregg Jefferies	.25	.20	.10
271	Jeff Blauser	.05	.04	.02
272	Cory Snyder	.07	.05	.03
273	Roy Smith	.05	.04	.02
274	Tom Foley	.04	.03	.02
275	Mitch Williams	.09	.07	.04
276	Paul Kilgus	.04	.03	.02
277	Don Slaught	.04	.03	.02
278	Von Hayes	.08	.06	.03
279	Vince Coleman	.10	.08	.04
280	Mike Boddicker	.05	.04	.02
281	Ken Dayley	.04	.03	.02
282	Mike Devereaux	.07	.05	.03
283	*Kenny Rogers*	.09	.07	.04
284	Jeff Russell	.07	.05	.04
285	*Jerome Walton*	.35	.25	.14
286	Derek Lilliquist	.08	.06	.03
287	Joe Orsulak	.04	.03	.02
288	Dick Schofield	.04	.03	.02
289	Ron Darling	.09	.07	.04
290	Bobby Bonilla	.10	.07	.04
291	Jim Gantner	.05	.04	.02
292	Bobby Witt	.05	.04	.02
293	Greg Brock	.05	.04	.02
294	Ivan Calderon	.05	.04	.02
295	Steve Bedrosian	.06	.05	.02
296	Mike Henneman	.06	.05	.02
297	Tom Gordon	.25	.20	.10
298	Lou Whitaker	.08	.06	.03
299	Terry Pendleton	.07	.05	.03
300	Checklist	.04	.03	.02
301	Juan Berenguer	.04	.03	.02
302	Mark Davis	.09	.07	.05
303	Nick Esasky	.09	.07	.05
304	Rickey Henderson	.15	.11	.06
305	Rick Cerone	.04	.03	.02
306	Craig Biggio	.15	.11	.06
307	Duane Ward	.04	.03	.02
308	Tom Browning	.07	.05	.03
309	Walt Terrell	.05	.04	.02
310	Greg Swindell	.10	.08	.04
311	Dave Righetti	.07	.05	.03
312	Mike Maddux	.04	.03	.02
313	Lenny Dykstra	.07	.05	.03
314	Jose Gonzalez	.08	.06	.03
315	Steve Balboni	.04	.03	.02
316	Mike Scioscia	.07	.05	.02
317	Ron Oester	.04	.03	.02
318	*Gary Wayne*	.09	.07	.04
319	Todd Worrell	.06	.05	.02
320	Doug Jones	.05	.04	.02
321	Jeff Hamilton	.05	.04	.02
322	Danny Tartabull	.09	.07	.04
323	Chris James	.05	.04	.02
324	Mike Flanagan	.05	.04	.02
325	Gerald Young	.05	.04	.02
326	Bob Boone	.09	.07	.04
327	Frank Williams	.04	.03	.02
328	Dave Parker	.09	.07	.04
329	Sid Bream	.04	.03	.02
330	Mike Schooler	.06	.05	.02
331	Bert Blyleven	.08	.06	.03
332	Bob Welch	.07	.05	.03
333	Bob Milacki	.06	.05	.02
334	Tim Burke	.05	.04	.02
335	Jose Uribe	.05	.04	.02
336	Randy Myers	.05	.04	.02
337	Eric King	.04	.03	.02
338	Mark Langston	.12	.09	.05
339	Ted Higuera	.08	.06	.03
340	Oddibe McDowell	.06	.05	.02
341	Lloyd McClendon	.07	.05	.03
342	Pascual Perez	.05	.04	.02
343	Kevin Brown	.08	.06	.03
344	Chuck Finley	.05	.04	.02
345	Erik Hanson	.09	.07	.05
346	Rich Gedman	.05	.04	.02
347	Bip Roberts	.10	.08	.04
348	Matt Williams	.20	.15	.08
349	Tom Henke	.05	.04	.02
350	Brad Komminsk	.05	.04	.02
351	Jeff Reed	.04	.03	.02
352	Brian Downing	.05	.04	.02
353	Frank Viola	.09	.07	.04
354	Terry Puhl	.05	.04	.02
355	Brian Harper	.05	.04	.02
356	Steve Farr	.05	.04	.02
357	Joe Boever	.05	.04	.02
358	Danny Heep	.04	.03	.02
359	Larry Andersen	.04	.03	.02
360	Rolando Roomes	.10	.08	.04
361	Mike Gallego	.05	.04	.02
362	Bob Kipper	.04	.03	.02
363	Clay Parker	.07	.05	.03
364	Mike Pagliarulo	.05	.04	.02
365	Ken Griffey, Jr.	3.00	2.25	1.25
366	Rex Hudler	.04	.03	.02
367	Pat Sheridan	.04	.03	.02
368	Kirk Gibson	.09	.07	.04
369	Jeff Parrett	.05	.04	.02
370	Bob Walk	.05	.04	.02
371	Ken Patterson	.04	.03	.02
372	Bryan Harvey	.05	.04	.02
373	Mike Bielecki	.07	.05	.03
374	*Tom Magrann*(FC)	.12	.09	.05
375	Rick Mahler	.05	.04	.02
376	Craig Lefferts	.05	.04	.02
377	Gregg Olson	.20	.15	.08
378	Jamie Moyer	.04	.03	.02
379	Randy Johnson	.09	.07	.04
380	Jeff Montgomery	.06	.05	.02
381	Marty Clary	.06	.05	.02
382	*Bill Spiers*	.15	.11	.06
383	Dave Magadan	.06	.05	.02
384	*Greg Hibbard*(FC)	.20	.15	.08
385	Ernie Whitt	.05	.04	.02
386	Rick Honeycutt	.04	.03	.02
387	Dave West	.08	.06	.03
388	Keith Hernandez	.07	.05	.03
389	Jose Alvarez	.04	.03	.02
390	*Joey Belle*(FC)	.70	.50	.30
391	Rick Aguilera	.05	.04	.02
392	Mike Fitzgerald	.04	.03	.02
393	*Dwight Smith*	.25	.20	.10
394	*Steve Wilson*	.09	.07	.04
395	*Bob Geren*	.20	.15	.08
396	Randy Ready	.04	.03	.02
397	Ken Hill	.07	.05	.03
398	Jody Reed	.05	.04	.02
399	Tom Brunansky	.07	.05	.03
400	Checklist	.04	.03	.02
401	Rene Gonzales	.04	.03	.02
402	Harold Baines	.09	.07	.04
403	Cecilio Guante	.04	.03	.02
404	Joe Girardi	.15	.11	.06
405	*Sergio Valdez*(FC)	.30	.25	.12
406	Mark Williamson	.04	.03	.02
407	Glenn Hoffman	.04	.03	.02
408	*Jeff Innis*(FC)	.10	.08	.04
409	Randy Kramer	.04	.03	.02
410	Charlie O'Brien(FC)	.04	.03	.02
411	Charlie Hough	.06	.05	.02
412	Gus Polidor	.04	.03	.02
413	Ron Karkovice	.04	.03	.02

		MT	NR MT	EX
414	Trevor Wilson(FC)	.07	.05	.03
415	*Kevin Ritz*(FC)	.20	.15	.08
416	Gary Thurman	.04	.03	.02
417	Jeff Robinson	.04	.03	.02
418	Scott Terry	.05	.04	.02
419	Tim Laudner	.04	.03	.02
420	Dennis Rasmussen	.04	.03	.02
421	Luis Rivera	.04	.03	.02
422	Jim Corsi(FC)	.07	.05	.03
423	Dennis Lamp	.04	.03	.02
424	Ken Caminiti	.06	.05	.02
425	David Wells	.06	.05	.02
426	Norm Charlton	.09	.07	.04
427	*Deion Sanders*	.35	.25	.14
428	Dion James	.05	.04	.02
429	Chuck Cary	.05	.04	.02
430	Ken Howell	.04	.03	.02
431	Steve Lake	.04	.03	.02
432	Kal Daniels	.09	.07	.04
433	Lance McCullers	.05	.04	.02
434	Lenny Harris(FC)	.10	.08	.04
435	*Scott Scudder*(FC)	.20	.15	.08
436	Gene Larkin	.04	.03	.02
437	Dan Quisenberry	.05	.04	.02
438	*Steve Olin*(FC)	.15	.11	.06
439	Mickey Hatcher	.05	.04	.02
440	Willie Wilson	.05	.04	.02
441	Mark Grant	.05	.04	.02
442	Mookie Wilson	.07	.05	.03
443	Alex Trevino	.04	.03	.02
444	Pat Tabler	.05	.04	.02
445	Dave Bergman	.04	.03	.02
446	Todd Burns	.05	.04	.02
447	R.J. Reynolds	.04	.03	.02
448	Jay Buhner	.08	.06	.03
449	*Lee Stevens*(FC)	.20	.15	.08
450	Ron Hassey	.04	.03	.02
451	Bob Melvin	.04	.03	.02
452	Dave Martinez	.05	.04	.02
453	*Greg Litton*(FC)	.15	.11	.06
454	Mark Carreon	.10	.07	.04
455	Scott Fletcher	.05	.04	.02
456	Otis Nixon	.04	.03	.02
457	*Tony Fossas*(FC)	.10	.08	.04
458	John Russell	.04	.03	.02
459	Paul Assenmacher	.04	.03	.02
460	Zane Smith	.04	.03	.02
461	*Jack Daugherty*	.25	.20	.10
462	*Rich Monteleone*(FC)	.15	.11	.06
463	Greg Briley(FC)	.25	.20	.10
464	Mike Smithson	.04	.03	.02
465	Benito Santiago	.09	.07	.04
466	*Jeff Brantley*	.10	.08	.04
467	Jose Nunez	.07	.05	.03
468	Scott Bailes	.04	.03	.02
469	Ken Griffey	.06	.05	.02
470	Bob McClure	.04	.03	.02
471	Mackey Sasser	.04	.03	.02
472	Glenn Wilson	.04	.03	.02
473	*Kevin Tapani*(FC)	.30	.25	.15
474	Bill Buckner	.05	.04	.02
475	Ron Gant	.05	.04	.02
476	Kevin Romine(FC)	.05	.04	.02
477	Juan Agosto	.04	.03	.02
478	Herm Winningham	.04	.03	.02
479	Storm Davis	.05	.04	.02
480	Jeff King(FC)	.09	.07	.04
481	*Kevin Mmahat*(FC)	.25	.20	.10
482	Carmelo Martinez	.05	.04	.02
483	*Omar Vizquel*	.10	.08	.04
484	Jim Dwyer	.04	.03	.02
485	Bob Knepper	.04	.03	.02
486	Dave Anderson	.04	.03	.02
487	Ron Jones	.09	.07	.04
488	Jay Bell	.05	.04	.02
489	*Sammy Sosa*(FC)	.35	.25	.14
490	*Kent Anderson*(FC)	.15	.11	.06
491	Domingo Ramos	.04	.03	.02
492	Dave Clark	.05	.04	.02
493	Tim Birtsas	.04	.03	.02
494	Ken Oberkfell	.04	.03	.02
495	Larry Sheets	.04	.03	.02
496	Jeff Kunkel	.04	.03	.02
497	Jim Presley	.04	.03	.02
498	Mike Macfarlane	.04	.03	.02
499	Pete Smith	.05	.04	.02
500	Checklist	.04	.03	.02
501	Gary Sheffield	.25	.20	.10
502	*Terry Bross*(FC)	.15	.11	.06
503	*Jerry Kutzler*(FC)	.20	.15	.08
504	Lloyd Moseby	.05	.04	.02
505	Curt Young	.04	.03	.02
506	Al Newman	.04	.03	.02
507	Keith Miller	.04	.03	.02
508	*Mike Stanton*(FC)	.20	.15	.08
509	Rich Yett	.04	.03	.02
510	*Tim Drummond*(FC)	.20	.15	.08
511	Joe Hesketh	.04	.03	.02
512	*Rick Wrona*	.10	.08	.04
513	Luis Salazar	.04	.03	.02
514	Hal Morris	.06	.05	.02
515	Terry Mullholland	.07	.05	.03
516	John Morris	.05	.04	.02
517	Carlos Quintana	.08	.06	.03
518	Frank DiPino	.04	.03	.02
519	Randy Milligan	.06	.05	.02
520	Chad Kreuter	.07	.05	.03
521	Mike Jeffcoat	.04	.03	.02
522	Mike Harkey	.10	.08	.04
523	Andy Nezelek	.07	.05	.03
524	Dave Schmidt	.04	.03	.02
525	Tony Armas	.04	.03	.02
526	Barry Lyons	.04	.03	.02
527	*Rick Reed*(FC)	.20	.15	.08
528	Jerry Reuss	.06	.05	.02
529	*Dean Palmer*(FC)	.80	.60	.30
530	*Jeff Peterek*(FC)	.20	.15	.08
531	*Carlos Martinez*	.20	.15	.08
532	Atlee Hammaker	.05	.04	.02
533	Mike Brumley	.04	.03	.02
534	Terry Leach	.04	.03	.02
535	*Doug Strange*(FC)	.20	.15	.08
536	Jose DeLeon	.05	.04	.02
537	Shane Rawley	.05	.04	.02
538	Joey Cora(FC)	.10	.08	.04
539	Eric Hetzel	.08	.06	.03
540	Gene Nelson	.04	.03	.02
541	Wes Gardner	.04	.03	.02
542	Mark Portugal	.04	.03	.02
543	Al Leiter	.05	.04	.02
544	Jack Armstrong	.04	.03	.02
545	Greg Cadaret	.04	.03	.02
546	Rod Nichols	.04	.03	.02
547	Luis Polonia	.05	.04	.02
548	Charlie Hayes(FC)	.20	.15	.08
549	Dickie Thon	.04	.03	.02
550	Tim Crews	.04	.03	.02
551	Dave Winfield	.20	.15	.08
552	Mike Davis	.04	.03	.02
553	Ron Robinson	.04	.03	.02
554	Carmen Castillo	.04	.03	.02
555	John Costello	.04	.03	.02
556	Bud Black	.04	.03	.02
557	Rick Dempsey	.04	.03	.02
558	Jim Acker	.04	.03	.02
559	Eric Show	.06	.05	.02
560	Pat Borders	.06	.05	.02
561	Danny Darwin	.04	.03	.02
562	*Rick Luecken*(FC)	.20	.15	.08
563	Edwin Nunez	.05	.04	.02
564	Felix Jose	.09	.07	.04
565	John Cangelosi	.04	.03	.02
566	Billy Swift	.04	.03	.02
567	Bill Schroeder	.04	.03	.02
568	Stan Javier	.04	.03	.02
569	Jim Traber	.04	.03	.02
570	Wallace Johnson	.04	.03	.02
571	Donell Nixon	.04	.03	.02
572	Sid Fernandez	.08	.06	.03
573	Lance Johnson	.09	.07	.04
574	Andy McGaffigan	.04	.03	.02
575	Mark Knudson	.04	.03	.02
576	*Tommy Greene*(FC)	.30	.25	.12
577	Mark Grace	.25	.20	.10
578	*Larry Walker*(FC)	.35	.25	.14
579	Mike Stanley	.04	.03	.02
580	Mike Witt	.05	.04	.02
581	Scott Bradley	.04	.03	.02
582	Greg Harris	.07	.05	.03
583	Kevin Hickey	.04	.03	.02
584	Lee Mazzilli	.04	.03	.02
585	Jeff Pico	.04	.03	.02
586	*Joe Oliver*(FC)	.20	.15	.08
587	Willie Fraser	.04	.03	.02
588	Puzzle Card	.04	.03	.02
589	Kevin Bass	.06	.05	.03
590	John Moses	.04	.03	.02
591	Tom Pagnozzi	.04	.03	.02
592	*Tony Castillo*	.10	.08	.04
593	Jerald Clark	.06	.05	.03
594	Dan Schatzeder	.04	.03	.02
595	Luis Quinones	.04	.03	.02

		MT	NR MT	EX
596	Pete Harnisch	.08	.06	.03
597	Gary Redus	.04	.03	.02
598	Mel Hall	.05	.04	.02
599	Rick Schu	.04	.03	.02
600	Checklist	.04	.03	.02
601	Mike Kingery	.04	.03	.02
602	Terry Kennedy	.04	.03	.02
603	Mike Sharperson	.06	.05	.02
604	Don Carman	.04	.03	.02
605	Jim Gott	.05	.04	.03
606	Donn Pall	.05	.04	.03
607	Rance Mulliniks	.04	.03	.02
608	Curt Wilkerson	.04	.03	.02
609	Mike Felder	.04	.03	.02
610	Guillermo Hernandez	.04	.03	.02
611	Candy Maldonado	.05	.04	.02
612	Mark Thurmond	.04	.03	.02
613	Rick Leach	.04	.03	.02
614	Jerry Reed	.04	.03	.02
615	Franklin Stubbs	.05	.04	.02
616	Billy Hatcher	.05	.04	.02
617	Don August	.05	.04	.02
618	Tim Teufel	.04	.03	.02
619	Shawn Hillegas	.04	.03	.02
620	Manny Lee	.04	.03	.02
621	Gary Ward	.05	.04	.02
622	*Mark Guthrie*(FC)	.20	.15	.08
623	Jeff Musselman	.05	.04	.02
624	Mark Lemke	.07	.05	.03
625	Fernando Valenzuela	.07	.05	.03
626	*Paul Sorrento*(FC)	.25	.20	.10
627	Glenallen Hill	.20	.15	.08
628	Les Lancaster	.05	.04	.03
629	Vance Law	.04	.03	.02
630	Randy Velarde(FC)	.10	.08	.04
631	Todd Frohwirth	.04	.03	.02
632	Willie McGee	.06	.05	.02
633	Oil Can Boyd	.06	.05	.02
634	Cris Carpenter	.09	.07	.04
635	Brian Holton	.04	.03	.02
636	Tracy Jones	.05	.04	.02
637	Terry Steinbach (AS)	.09	.07	.04
638	Brady Anderson	.09	.07	.04
639	Jack Morris	.06	.05	.02
640	*Jaime Navarro*(FC)	.25	.20	.10
641	Darrin Jackson	.05	.04	.02
642	*Mike Dyer*(FC)	.20	.15	.08
643	Mike Schmidt	.40	.30	.15
644	Henry Cotto	.04	.03	.02
645	John Cerutti	.05	.04	.02
646	*Francisco Cabrera*(FC)	.40	.30	.15
647	Scott Sanderson	.05	.04	.02
648	Brian Meyer	.05	.04	.02
649	Ray Searage	.05	.04	.02
650a	Bo Jackson AS (Recent Major League Performance on back)	1.50	1.25	.60
650b	Bo Jackson AS (Corrected)	.50	.40	.20
651	Steve Lyons	.04	.03	.02
652	Mike LaCoss	.04	.03	.02
653	Ted Power	.04	.03	.02
654	Howard Johnson (AS)	.20	.15	.08
655	*Mauro Gozzo*(FC)	.15	.11	.06
656	*Mike Blowers*(FC)	.25	.20	.10
657	Paul Gibson	.05	.04	.02
658	Neal Heaton	.05	.04	.02
659a	5000 K (Nolan Ryan) (King card number 665 back)	9.00	6.75	3.50
659b	5000 K (Nolan Ryan) (Corrected)	1.00	.70	.40
660a	Harold Baines (AS - recent major league performance on back)	5.00	3.75	2.00
660b	Harold Baines (AS - line through star on front-incorrect back)	7.00	5.25	2.75
660c	Harold Baines (AS - Incorrect front and back)	7.00	5.25	2.75
660d	Harold Baines (AS - Corrected)	.10	.08	.04
661	Gary Pettis	.05	.04	.02
662	*Clint Zavaras*(FC)	.20	.15	.08
663	Rick Reuschel	.08	.06	.03
664	Alejandro Pena	.05	.04	.02
665a	King of Kings (Nolan Ryan) (5000 K card number 659 back)	10.00	7.50	4.00
665b	King of Kings (Nolan Ryan) (Corrected)	1.00	.70	.40
665c	King of Kings (Nolan Ryan) (No card #)	5.00	3.75	2.00
666	Ricky Horton	.04	.03	.02
667	Curt Schilling	.06	.05	.02
668	Bill Landrum(FC)	.05	.04	.02
669	Todd Stottlemyre	.05	.04	.02
670	Tim Leary	.05	.04	.02
671	*John Wetteland*(FC)	.25	.20	.10

		MT	NR MT	EX
672	Calvin Schiraldi	.04	.03	.02
673	Ruben Sierra (AS)	.09	.07	.04
674	Pedro Guerrero (AS)	.09	.07	.04
675	Ken Phelps	.04	.03	.02
676	Cal Ripken (AS)	.09	.07	.04
677	Denny Walling	.04	.03	.02
678	Goose Gossage	.04	.03	.02
679	*Gary Mielke*(FC)	.20	.15	.08
680	Bill Bathe	.04	.03	.02
681	Tom Lawless	.04	.03	.02
682	*Xavier Hernandez*(FC)	.20	.15	.08
683	Kirby Puckett (AS)	.09	.07	.04
684	Mariano Duncan	.05	.04	.02
685	Ramon Martinez	.10	.08	.04
686	Tim Jones	.05	.04	.02
687	Tom Filer	.04	.03	.02
688	Steve Lombardozzi	.04	.03	.02
689	*Bernie Williams*(FC)	.50	.40	.20
690	*Chip Hale*(FC)	.15	.11	.06
691	*Beau Allred*(FC)	.15	.11	.06
692	Ryne Sandberg (AS)	.09	.07	.04
693	*Jeff Huson*(FC)	.25	.20	.10
694	Curt Ford	.04	.03	.02
695	Eric Davis (AS)	.09	.07	.04
696	Scott Lusader	.05	.04	.02
697	Mark McGwire (AS)	.09	.07	.04
698	*Steve Cummings*(FC)	.15	.11	.06
699	*George Canale*(FC)	.15	.11	.06
700	Checklist	.04	.03	.02
701	Julio Franco (AS)	.09	.07	.04
702	*Dave Johnson*(FC)	.10	.08	.04
703	Dave Stewart (AS)	.08	.06	.03
704	*Dave Justice*(FC)	3.00	2.25	1.25
705	Tony Gwynn (AS)	.09	.07	.04
706	Greg Myers	.06	.05	.02
707	Will Clark (AS)	.15	.11	.06
708	Benito Santiago (AS)	.08	.06	.03
709	Larry McWilliams	.04	.03	.02
710	Ozzie Smith (AS)	.08	.06	.03
711	*John Olerud*(FC)	1.25	.90	.50
712	Wade Boggs (AS)	.09	.07	.04
713	*Gary Eave*(FC)	.15	.11	.06
714	Bob Tewksbury	.05	.04	.02
715	Kevin Mitchell (AS)	.09	.07	.04
716	A. Bartlett Giamatti	1.25	.90	.50

1990 Donruss A.L. Best

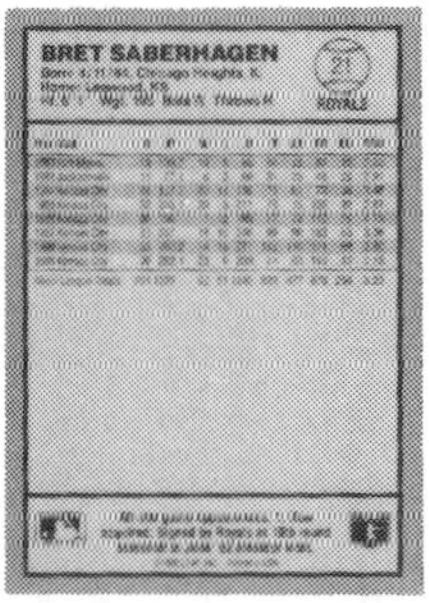

This 144-card set features the top players of the American League. The cards measure 2-1/2" by 3-1/2" and feature the same card front design as the regular Donruss set with the exception of having blue borders instead of red. The card backs feature a yellow frame with complete statistics and biographical information provided. 1990 marks the first year that Donruss divided its baseball best issue into two sets designated by league.

		MT	NR MT	EX
Complete Set:		12.00	9.00	4.75
Common Player:		.04	.03	.02
1	Ken Griffey,Jr.	1.50	1.25	.90
2	Bob Milacki	.04	.03	.02
3	Mike Boddicker	.06	.05	.02
4	Bert Blyleven	.08	.06	.03
5	Carlton Fisk	.10	.08	.04
6	Greg Swindell	.06	.05	.02

		MT	NR MT	EX
7	Alan Trammell	.10	.08	.04
8	Mark Davis	.05	.04	.02
9	Chris Bosio	.04	.03	.02
10	Gary Gaetti	.10	.08	.04
11	Matt Nokes	.06	.05	.02
12	Dennis Eckersley	.10	.08	.04
13	Kevin Brown	.08	.06	.03
14	Tom Henke	.06	.05	.02
15	Mickey Tettleton	.08	.06	.03
16	Jody Reed	.08	.06	.03
17	Mark Langston	.08	.06	.03
18	Melido Perez	.06	.05	.02
19	John Farrell	.04	.03	.02
20	Tony Phillips	.04	.03	.02
21	Bret Saberhagen	.10	.08	.04
22	Robin Yount	.10	.08	.04
23	Kirby Puckett	.15	.11	.06
24	Steve Sax	.10	.08	.04
25	Dave Stewart	.10	.08	.04
26	Alvin Davis	.08	.06	.03
27	Geno Petralli	.04	.03	.02
28	Mookie Wilson	.05	.04	.02
29	Jeff Ballard	.04	.03	.02
30	Ellis Burks	.10	.08	.04
31	Wally Joyner	.08	.06	.03
32	Bobby Thigpen	.10	.08	.04
33	Keith Hernandez	.06	.05	.02
34	Jack Morris	.06	.05	.02
35	George Brett	.10	.08	.04
36	Dan Plesac	.08	.06	.03
37	Brian Harper	.05	.04	.02
38	Don Mattingly	.25	.20	.10
39	Dave Henderson	.08	.06	.03
40	Scott Bankhead	.06	.05	.02
41	Rafael Palmeiro	.10	.08	.04
42	Jimmy Key	.06	.05	.02
43	Gregg Olson	.10	.08	.04
44	Tony Pena	.06	.05	.02
45	Jack Howell	.04	.03	.02
46	Eric King	.04	.03	.02
47	Cory Snyder	.06	.05	.02
48	Frank Tanana	.04	.03	.02
49	Nolan Ryan	.60	.45	.25
50	Bob Boone	.06	.05	.02
51	Dave Parker	.10	.08	.04
52	Allan Anderson	.04	.03	.02
53	Tim Leary	.05	.04	.02
54	Mark McGwire	.25	.20	.10
55	Dave Valle	.04	.03	.02
56	Fred McGriff	.25	.20	.10
57	Cal Ripken	.15	.11	.06
58	Roger Clemens	.30	.25	.12
59	Lance Parrish	.08	.06	.03
60	Robin Ventura	.30	.25	.12
61	Doug Jones	.08	.06	.03
62	Lloyd Moseby	.06	.05	.02
63	Bo Jackson	.80	.60	.30
64	Paul Molitor	.08	.06	.03
65	Kent Hrbek	.08	.06	.03
66	Mel Hall	.04	.03	.02
67	Bob Welch	.10	.08	.04
68	Erik Hanson	.10	.08	.04
69	Harold Baines	.08	.06	.03
70	Junior Felix	.10	.08	.04
71	Craig Worthington	.06	.05	.02
72	Jeff Reardon	.08	.06	.03
73	Johnny Ray	.05	.04	.02
74	Ozzie Guillen	.10	.08	.04
75	Brook Jacoby	.08	.06	.03
76	Chet Lemon	.05	.04	.02
77	Mark Gubicza	.08	.06	.03
78	B.J. Surhoff	.08	.06	.03
79	Rick Aguilera	.05	.04	.02
80	Pascual Perez	.04	.03	.02
81	Jose Canseco	.70	.50	.30
82	Mike Schooler	.08	.06	.03
83	Jeff Huson	.12	.09	.05
84	Kelly Gruber	.15	.11	.06
85	Randy Milligan	.08	.06	.03
86	Wade Boggs	.35	.25	.14
87	Dave Winfield	.20	.15	.08
88	Scott Fletcher	.04	.03	.02
89	Tom Candiotti	.04	.03	.02
90	Mike Heath	.04	.03	.02
91	Kevin Seitzer	.08	.06	.03
92	Ted Higuera	.08	.06	.03
93	Kevin Tapani	.15	.11	.06
94	Roberto Kelly	.08	.06	.03
95	Walt Weiss	.06	.05	.02
96	Checklist	.04	.03	.02
97	Sandy Alomar	.30	.25	.12
98	Pete O'Brien	.05	.04	.02
99	Jeff Russell	.06	.05	.02
100	John Olerud	.50	.40	.20
101	Pete Harnisch	.05	.04	.02
102	Dwight Evans	.08	.06	.03
103	Chuck Finley	.08	.06	.03
104	Sammy Sosa	.25	.20	.10
105	Mike Henneman	.06	.05	.02
106	Kurt Stillwell	.06	.05	.02
107	Greg Vaughn	.30	.25	.12
108	Dan Gladden	.05	.04	.02
109	Jesse Barfield	.06	.05	.02
110	Willie Randolph	.06	.05	.02
111	Randy Johnson	.08	.06	.03
112	Julio Franco	.08	.06	.03
113	Tony Fernandez	.08	.06	.03
114	Ben McDonald	.50	.40	.20
115	Mike Greenwell	.20	.15	.08
116	Luis Polonia	.04	.03	.02
117	Carney Lansford	.06	.05	.02
118	Bud Black	.05	.04	.02
119	Lou Whitaker	.08	.06	.03
120	Jim Eisenreich	.04	.03	.02
121	Gary Sheffield	.25	.20	.10
122	Shane Mack	.08	.06	.03
123	Alvaro Espinoza	.04	.03	.02
124	Rickey Henderson	.40	.30	.15
125	Jeffrey Leonard	.05	.04	.02
126	Gary Pettis	.04	.03	.02
127	Dave Steib	.08	.06	.03
128	Danny Tartabull	.08	.06	.03
129	Joe Orsulak	.04	.03	.02
130	Tom Brunansky	.06	.05	.02
131	Dick Schofield	.04	.03	.02
132	Candy Maldonado	.06	.05	.02
133	Cecil Fielder	.30	.25	.12
134	Terry Shumpert	.20	.15	.08
135	Greg Gagne	.05	.04	.02
136	Dave Righetti	.08	.06	.03
137	Terry Steinbach	.06	.05	.02
138	Harold Reynolds	.08	.06	.03
139	George Bell	.08	.06	.03
140	Carlos Quintana	.06	.05	.02
141	Ivan Calderon	.08	.06	.03
142	Greg Brock	.04	.03	.02
143	Ruben Sierra	.15	.11	.06
144	Checklist	.04	.03	.02

1990 Donruss Diamond Kings Supers

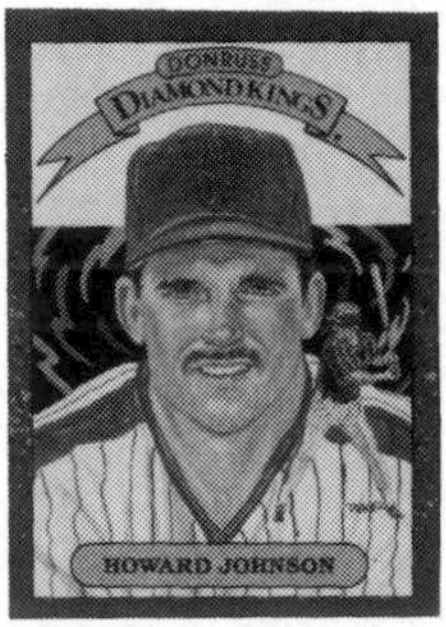

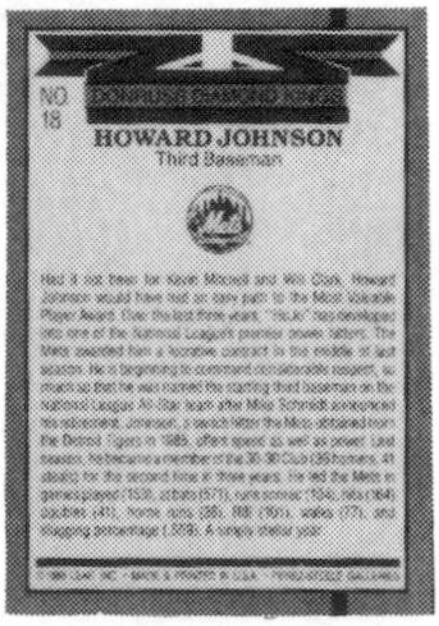

Donruss made this set available through a mail-in offer. Three wrappers, $10 and $2 for postage were necessary to obtain this set. The cards are exactly the same design as the regular Donruss Diamond Kings except they measure approximately 5" by 6-3/4" in size. The artwork of Dick Perez is featured.

		MT	NR MT	EX
Complete Set:		10.00	7.50	4.00
Common Player:		.10	.08	.04
1	Bo Jackson	1.25	.90	.50
2	Steve Sax	.15	.11	.06
3	Ruben Sierra	.35	.25	.12
4	Ken Griffey,Jr.	2.00	1.50	.80
5	Mickey Tettleton	.10	.08	.04
6	Dave Stewart	.20	.15	.08

		MT	NR MT	EX
7	Jim Deshaies	.10	.08	.04
8	John Smoltz	.20	.15	.08
9	Mike Bielecki	.10	.08	.04
10	Brian Downing	.10	.08	.04
11	Kevin Mitchell	.20	.15	.08
12	Kelly Gruber	.25	.20	.10
13	Joe Magrane	.15	.11	.06
14	John Franco	.15	.11	.06
15	Ozzie Guillen	.20	.15	.08
16	Lou Whitaker	.15	.11	.06
17	John Smiley	.10	.08	.04
18	Howard Johnson	.25	.20	.10
19	Willie Randolph	.10	.08	.04
20	Chris Bosio	.10	.08	.04
21	Tommy Herr	.10	.08	.04
22	Dan Gladden	.10	.08	.04
23	Ellis Burks	.20	.15	.08
24	Pete O'Brien	.10	.08	.04
25	Bryn Smith	.10	.08	.04
26	Ed Whitson	.10	.08	.04

1990 Donruss N.L. Best

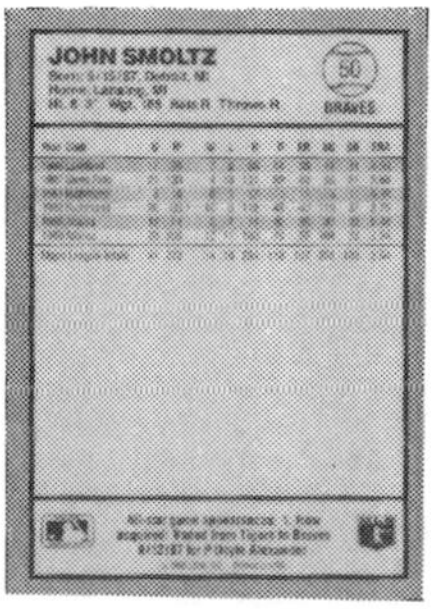

This 144-card set features the top players in the National League for 1990. The cards measure 2-1/2" by 3-1/2" and feature the same design as the regular Donruss cards. The only difference on the card fronts is the border color. The N.L. Best cards contain blue borders, while the regular cards featured red borders. Traded players are featured with their new teams. This set along with the A.L. Best set was available at select retail stores and within the hobby.

		MT	NR MT	EX
Complete Set:		12.00	9.00	4.75
Common Player:		.04	.03	.02
1	Eric Davis	.20	.15	.08
2	Tom Glavine	.10	.08	.04
3	Mike Bielecki	.05	.04	.02
4	Jim Deshaies	.05	.04	.02
5	Mike Scioscia	.05	.04	.02
6	Spike Owen	.05	.04	.02
7	Dwight Gooden	.20	.15	.08
8	Ricky Jordan	.08	.06	.03
9	Doug Drabek	.10	.08	.04
10	Bryn Smith	.04	.03	.02
11	Tony Gwynn	.10	.08	.04
12	John Burkett	.10	.08	.04
13	Nick Esasky	.06	.05	.02
14	Greg Maddux	.08	.06	.03
15	Joe Oliver	.08	.06	.03
16	Mike Scott	.08	.06	.03
17	Tim Belcher	.08	.06	.03
18	Kevin Gross	.06	.05	.02
19	Howard Johnson	.10	.08	.04
20	Darren Daulton	.06	.05	.02
21	John Smiley	.06	.05	.02
22	Ken Dayley	.05	.04	.02
23	Craig Lefferts	.05	.04	.02
24	Will Clark	.60	.45	.25
25	Greg Olson	.12	.09	.05
26	Ryne Sandberg	.50	.40	.20
27	Tom Browning	.06	.05	.02
28	Eric Anthony	.20	.15	.08
29	Juan Samuel	.06	.05	.02
30	Dennis Martinez	.06	.05	.02
31	Kevin Elster	.05	.04	.02
32	Tom Herr	.06	.05	.02
33	Sid Bream	.06	.05	.02
34	Terry Pendleton	.06	.05	.02
35	Roberto Alomar	.20	.15	.08
36	Kevin Bass	.06	.05	.02
37	Jim Presley	.06	.05	.02
38	Les Lancaster	.04	.03	.02
39	Paul O'Neill	.08	.06	.03
40	Dave Smith	.06	.05	.02
41	Kirk Gibson	.10	.08	.04
42	Tim Burke	.06	.05	.02
43	David Cone	.10	.08	.04
44	Ken Howell	.06	.05	.02
45	Barry Bonds	.20	.15	.08
46	Joe Magrane	.08	.06	.03
47	Andy Benes	.08	.06	.03
48	Gary Carter	.10	.08	.04
49	Pat Combs	.08	.06	.03
50	John Smoltz	.10	.08	.04
51	Mark Grace	.10	.08	.04
52	Barry Larkin	.10	.08	.04
53	Danny Darwin	.08	.06	.03
54	Orel Hershiser	.10	.08	.04
55	Tim Wallach	.08	.06	.03
56	Dave Magadan	.10	.08	.04
57	Roger McDowell	.08	.06	.03
58	Bill Landrum	.06	.05	.02
59	Jose DeLeon	.06	.05	.02
60	Bip Roberts	.06	.05	.02
61	Matt Williams	.10	.08	.04
62	Dale Murphy	.08	.06	.03
63	Dwight Smith	.08	.06	.03
64	Chris Sabo	.10	.08	.04
65	Glenn Davis	.10	.08	.04
66	Jay Howell	.06	.05	.02
67	Andres Galarraga	.08	.06	.03
68	Frank Viola	.10	.08	.04
69	John Kruk	.06	.05	.02
70	Bobby Bonilla	.15	.11	.06
71	Todd Zeile	.60	.45	.25
72	Joe Carter	.10	.08	.04
73	Robby Thompson	.06	.05	.02
74	Jeff Blauser	.04	.03	.02
75	Mitch Williams	.08	.06	.03
76	Rob Dibble	.10	.08	.04
77	Rafael Ramirez	.04	.03	.02
78	Eddie Murray	.10	.08	.04
79	Dave Martinez	.05	.04	.02
80	Darryl Strawberry	.50	.40	.20
81	Dickie Thon	.04	.03	.02
82	Jose Lind	.05	.04	.02
83	Ozzie Smith	.10	.08	.04
84	Bruce Hurst	.06	.05	.02
85	Kevin Mitchell	.20	.15	.08
86	Lonnie Smith	.05	.04	.02
87	Joe Girardi	.08	.06	.03
88	Randy Myers	.10	.08	.04
89	Craig Biggio	.08	.06	.03
90	Fernando Valenzuela	.06	.05	.02
91	Larry Walker	.20	.15	.08
92	John Franco	.10	.08	.04
93	Dennis Cook	.06	.05	.02
94	Bob Walk	.05	.04	.02
95	Pedro Guerrero	.08	.06	.03
96	Checklist	.04	.03	.02
97	Andre Dawson	.10	.08	.04
98	Ed Whitson	.06	.05	.02
99	Steve Bedrosian	.06	.05	.02
100	Oddibe McDowell	.06	.05	.02
101	Todd Benzinger	.06	.05	.02
102	Bill Doran	.08	.06	.03
103	Alfredo Griffin	.04	.03	.02
104	Tim Raines	.10	.08	.04
105	Sid Fernandez	.08	.06	.03
106	Charlie Hayes	.08	.06	.03
107	Mike LaValliere	.05	.04	.02
108	Jose Oquendo	.04	.03	.02
109	Jack Clark	.08	.06	.03
110	Scott Garrelts	.06	.05	.02
111	Ron Gant	.10	.08	.04
112	Shawon Dunston	.10	.08	.04
113	Mariano Duncan	.06	.05	.02
114	Eric Yelding	.10	.08	.04
115	Hubie Brooks	.08	.06	.03
116	Delino DeShields	.25	.20	.10
117	Gregg Jefferies	.20	.15	.08
118	Len Dykstra	.10	.08	.04
119	Andy Van Slyke	.10	.08	.04
120	Lee Smith	.08	.06	.03

		MT	NR MT	EX
121	Benito Santiago	.10	.08	.04
122	Jose Uribe	.04	.03	.02
123	Jeff Treadway	.05	.04	.02
124	Jerome Walton	.10	.08	.04
125	Billy Hatcher	.06	.05	.02
126	Ken Caminiti	.04	.03	.02
127	Kal Daniels	.08	.06	.03
128	Marquis Grissom	.30	.25	.12
129	Kevin McReynolds	.08	.06	.03
130	Wally Backman	.04	.03	.02
131	Willie McGee	.10	.08	.04
132	Terry Kennedy	.04	.03	.02
133	Garry Templeton	.04	.03	.02
134	Lloyd McClendon	.04	.03	.02
135	Daryl Boston	.04	.03	.02
136	Jay Bell	.08	.06	.03
137	Mike Pagliarulo	.06	.05	.02
138	Vince Coleman	.08	.06	.03
139	Brett Butler	.06	.05	.02
140	Von Hayes	.08	.06	.03
141	Ramon Martinez	.20	.15	.08
142	Jack Armstrong	.10	.08	.04
143	Franklin Stubbs	.05	.04	.02
144	Checklist	.04	.03	.02

1990 Donruss Rookies

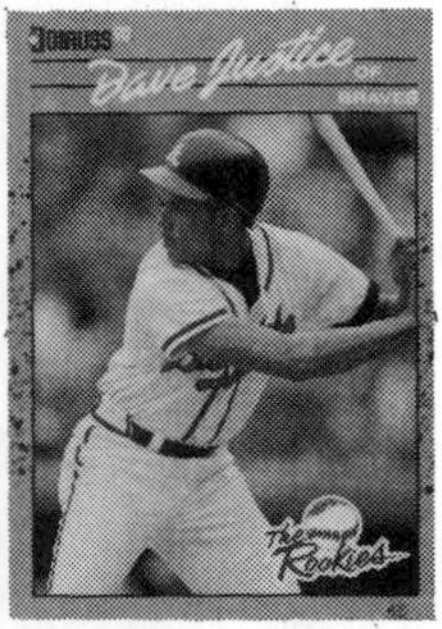

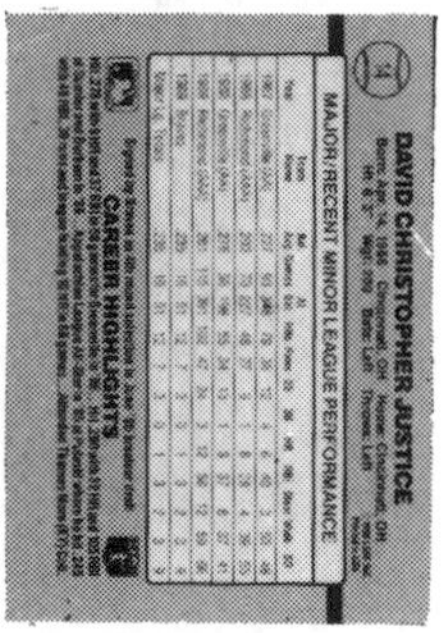

For the fifth straight year, Donruss issued a 56-card "Rookies" set in 1990. As in previous years, the set is similar in design to the regular Donruss set, except for a new "The Rookies" logo and green borders instead of red. The set is packaged in a special box and includes a special Carl Yastrzemski puzzle card.

		MT	NR MT	EX
Complete Set:		12.00	9.00	4.75
Common Player:		.10	.08	.04
1	Sandy Alomar	.25	.20	.10
2	John Olerud	1.25	.90	.50
3	Pat Combs	.20	.15	.08
4	Brian Dubois	.10	.08	.04
5	Felix Jose	.12	.09	.05
6	Delino DeShields	.50	.40	.20
7	Mike Stanton	.10	.08	.04
8	Mike Munoz(FC)	.10	.08	.04
9	Craig Grebeck(FC)	.15	.11	.06
10	Joe Kraemer(FC)	.10	.08	.04
11	Jeff Huson	.10	.08	.04
12	Bill Sampen(FC)	.30	.25	.12
13	Brian Bohanon(FC)	.12	.09	.05
14	Dave Justice	2.50	2.00	1.00
15	Robin Ventura	.80	.60	.30
16	Greg Vaughn	.60	.45	.25
17	Wayne Edwards(FC)	.15	.11	.06
18	Shawn Boskie	.25	.20	.10
19	Carlos Baerga(FC)	.50	.40	.20
20	Mark Gardner	.20	.15	.08
21	Kevin Appier(FC)	.30	.25	.12
22	Mike Harkey	.20	.15	.08
23	Tim Layana(FC)	.20	.15	.08
24	Glenallen Hill	.20	.15	.08
25	Jerry Kutzler	.10	.08	.04
26	Mike Blowers	.15	.11	.06
27	Scott Ruskin(FC)	.25	.20	.10
28	Dana Kiecker(FC)	.15	.11	.06
29	Willie Blair(FC)	.10	.08	.04
30	Ben McDonald	1.00	.70	.40

		MT	NR MT	EX
31	Todd Zeile	.60	.45	.25
32	Scott Coolbaugh	.12	.09	.05
33	Xavier Hernandez	.10	.08	.04
34	Mike Hartley(FC)	.15	.11	.06
35	Kevin Tapani	.30	.25	.12
36	Kevin Wickander(FC)	.10	.08	.04
37	Carlos Hernandez(FC)	.15	.11	.06
38	Brian Traxler(FC)	.20	.15	.08
39	Marty Brown(FC)	.10	.08	.04
40	Scott Radinsky(FC)	.25	.20	.10
41	Julio Machado	.15	.11	.06
42	Steve Avery	.90	.70	.35
43	Mark Lemke	.12	.09	.05
44	Alan Mills(FC)	.25	.20	.10
45	Marquis Grissom	.50	.40	.20
46	Greg Olson(FC)	.15	.11	.06
47	Dave Hollins(FC)	.25	.20	.10
48	Jerald Clark	.10	.08	.04
49	Eric Anthony	.35	.25	.14
50	Tim Drummond	.10	.08	.04
51	John Burkett(FC)	.20	.15	.08
52	Brent Knackert(FC)	.12	.09	.05
53	Jeff Shaw(FC)	.12	.09	.05
54	John Orton(FC)	.10	.08	.04
55	Terry Shumpert(FC)	.15	.11	.06
56	Checklist	.10	.08	.04

A player's name in *italic* indicates a rookie card. An (FC) indicates a player's first card for that particular card company.

1990 Donruss Grand Slammers

For the second consecutive year Donruss produced a set in honor of players who hit grand slams in the previous season. The cards are styled after the 1990 Donruss regular issue. The cards were inserted into 1990 Donruss factory sets.

		MT	NR MT	EX
Complete Set:		2.00	1.50	.80
Common Player:		.12	.09	.05
1	Matt Williams	.25	.20	.10
2	Jeffrey Leonard	.12	.09	.05
3	Chris James	.12	.09	.05
4	Mark McGwire	.30	.25	.12
5	Dwight Evans	.15	.11	.06
6	Will Clark	.60	.45	.25
7	Mike Scioscia	.12	.09	.05
8	Todd Benzinger	.12	.09	.05
9	Fred McGriff	.25	.20	.10
10	Kevin Bass	.12	.09	.05
11	Jack Clark	.12	.09	.05
12	Bo Jackson	.60	.45	.25

1991 Donruss

Donruss decided to use a two series format in 1991. The first series was released in December and the second in February. The 1991 design is somewhat reminiscent of the 1986 set. Blue borders are used. Limited edition cards including an autographed Ryne Sandberg card (5,000) were randomly inserted in wax packs. Other features of the set include 40 Rated Rookies, a "Legends Series," Elite Series,

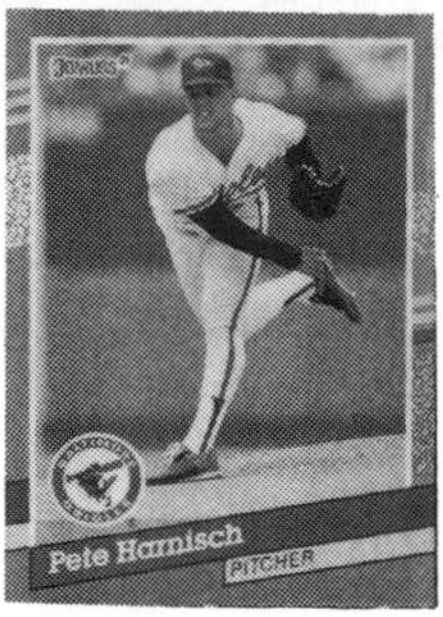

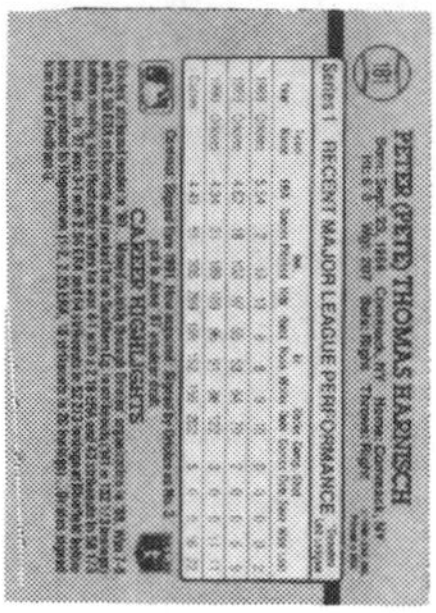

and another Diamond King subset. Collectors could also take part in Donruss' Instant Win promotion.

		MT	NR MT	EX
Complete Set:		25.00	20.00	10.00
Common Player:		.04	.03	.02
1	Dave Steib (DK)	.04	.03	.02
2	Craig Biggio (DK)	.05	.04	.02
3	Cecil Fielder (DK)	.15	.11	.06
4	Barry Bonds (DK)	.10	.08	.04
5	Barry Larkin (DK)	.06	.05	.02
6	Dave Parker (DK)	.05	.04	.03
7	Len Dykstra (DK)	.06	.05	.02
8	Bobby Thigpen (DK)	.05	.04	.02
9	Roger Clemens (DK)	.10	.08	.04
10	Ron Gant (DK)	.08	.06	.03
11	Delino DeShields (DK)	.08	.06	.03
12	Roberto Alomar (DK)	.08	.06	.03
13	Sandy Alomar (DK)	.12	.09	.05
14	Ryne Sandberg (DK)	.15	.11	.06
15	Ramon Martinez (DK)	.06	.05	.02
16	Edgar Martinez (DK)	.08	.06	.03
17	Dave Magadan (DK)	.04	.03	.02
18	Matt Williams (DK)	.12	.09	.05
19	Rafael Palmeiro (DK)	.05	.04	.02
20	Bob Welch (DK)	.06	.05	.02
21	Dave Righetti (DK)	.04	.03	.02
22	Brian Harper (DK)	.04	.03	.02
23	Gregg Olson (DK)	.05	.04	.02
24	Kurt Stillwell (DK)	.04	.03	.02
25	Pedro Guerrero (DK)	.05	.04	.02
26	Chuck Finley (DK)	.05	.04	.02
27	DK Checklist	.04	.03	.02
28	Tino Martinez (RR)(FC)	.30	.25	.12
29	Mark Lewis (RR)(FC)	.35	.25	.14
30	*Bernard Gilkey* (RR)(FC)	.30	.25	.12
31	Hensley Meulens (RR)	.08	.06	.03
32	*Derek Bell* (RR)(FC)	.35	.25	.14
33	Jose Offerman (RR)(FC)	.25	.20	.10
34	Terry Bross (RR)	.10	.08	.04
35	*Leo Gomez* (RR)(FC)	.50	.40	.20
36	Derrick May (RR)(FC)	.25	.20	.10
37	*Kevin Morton* (RR)(FC)	.25	.20	.10
38	Moises Alou (RR)(FC)	.10	.08	.04
39	*Julio Valera* (RR)(FC)	.15	.11	.06
40	Milt Cuyler (RR)(FC)	.10	.08	.04
41	*Phil Plantier* (RR)(FC)	1.25	.90	.50
42	*Scott Chiamparino* (RR)(FC)	.30	.25	.12
43	*Ray Lankford* (RR)(FC)	.40	.30	.15
44	*Mickey Morandini* (RR)(FC)	.20	.15	.08
45	Dave Hansen (RR)(FC)	.10	.08	.04
46	*Kevin Belcher* (RR)(FC)	.15	.11	.06
47	Darrin Fletcher (RR)(FC)	.10	.08	.04
48	Steve Sax (AS)	.05	.04	.02
49	Ken Griffey,Jr. (AS)	.40	.30	.15
50	Jose Canseco (AS)	.25	.20	.10
51	Sandy Alomar (AS)	.10	.08	.04
52	Cal Ripken (AS)	.05	.04	.02
53	Rickey Henderson (AS)	.15	.11	.06
54	Bob Welch (AS)	.05	.04	.02
55	Wade Boggs (AS)	.10	.08	.04
56	Mark McGwire (AS)	.10	.08	.04
57	Jack McDowell	.06	.05	.02
58	Jose Lind	.05	.04	.02
59	*Alex Fernandez*(FC)	.50	.40	.20
60	Pat Combs	.08	.06	.03
61	*Mike Walker*(FC)	.15	.11	.06
62	Juan Samuel	.05	.04	.02
63	Mike Blowers	.05	.04	.02
64	Mark Guthrie	.05	.04	.02

		MT	NR MT	EX
65	Mark Salas	.04	.03	.02
66	Tim Jones	.04	.03	.02
67	Tim Leary	.05	.04	.02
68	Andres Galarraga	.08	.06	.03
69	Bob Milacki	.05	.04	.02
70	Tim Belcher	.08	.06	.03
71	Todd Zeile	.20	.15	.08
72	Jerome Walton	.08	.06	.03
73	Kevin Seitzer	.06	.05	.02
74	Jerald Clark	.06	.05	.02
75	John Smoltz	.08	.06	.03
76	Mike Henneman	.05	.04	.02
77	Ken Griffey,Jr.	1.00	.70	.40
78	Jim Abbott	.06	.05	.02
79	Gregg Jefferies	.15	.11	.06
80	Kevin Reimer(FC)	.20	.15	.08
81	Roger Clemens	.15	.11	.06
82	Mike Fitzgerald	.04	.03	.02
83	Bruce Hurst	.06	.05	.02
84	Eric Davis	.15	.11	.06
85	Paul Molitor	.08	.06	.03
86	Will Clark	.25	.20	.10
87	Mike Bielecki	.04	.03	.02
88	Bret Saberhagen	.10	.08	.04
89	Nolan Ryan	.25	.20	.10
90	Bobby Thigpen	.08	.06	.03
91	Dickie Thon	.04	.03	.02
92	Duane Ward	.04	.03	.02
93	Luis Polonia	.04	.03	.02
94	Terry Kennedy	.04	.03	.02
95	Kent Hrbek	.08	.06	.03
96	Danny Jackson	.06	.05	.02
97	Sid Fernandez	.08	.06	.03
98	Jimmy Key	.06	.05	.02
99	Franklin Stubbs	.05	.04	.02
100	Checklist	.04	.03	.02
101	R.J. Reynolds	.04	.03	.02
102	Dave Stewart	.08	.06	.03
103	Dan Pasqua	.05	.04	.02
104	Dan Plesac	.06	.05	.02
105	Mark McGwire	.20	.15	.08
106	John Farrell	.04	.03	.02
107	Don Mattingly	.20	.15	.08
108	Carlton Fisk	.10	.08	.04
109	Ken Oberkfell	.04	.03	.02
110	Darrel Akerfelds	.04	.03	.02
111	Gregg Olson	.08	.06	.03
112	Mike Scioscia	.06	.05	.02
113	Bryn Smith	.04	.03	.02
114	Bob Geren	.05	.04	.02
115	Tom Candiotti	.04	.03	.02
116	Kevin Tapani	.15	.11	.06
117	Jeff Treadway	.05	.04	.02
118	Alan Trammell	.08	.06	.03
119	Pete O'Brien	.04	.03	.02
120	Joel Skinner	.04	.03	.02
121	Mike LaValliere	.05	.04	.02
122	Dwight Evans	.08	.06	.03
123	Jody Reed	.08	.06	.03
124	Lee Guetterman	.04	.03	.02
125	Tim Burke	.05	.04	.02
126	Dave Johnson	.04	.03	.02
127	Fernando Valenzuela	.08	.06	.03
128	Jose DeLeon	.06	.05	.02
129	Andre Dawson	.10	.08	.04
130	Gerald Perry	.05	.04	.02
131	Greg Harris	.04	.03	.02
132	Tom Glavine	.08	.06	.03
133	Lance McCullers	.04	.03	.02
134	Randy Johnson	.08	.06	.03
135	Lance Parrish	.08	.06	.03
136	Mackey Sasser	.08	.06	.03
137	Geno Petralli	.04	.03	.02
138	Dennis Lamp	.04	.03	.02
139	Dennis Martinez	.06	.05	.02
140	Mike Pagliarulo	.05	.04	.02
141	Hal Morris	.10	.08	.04
142	Dave Parker	.10	.08	.04
143	Brett Butler	.06	.05	.02
144	Paul Assenmacher	.04	.03	.02
145	Mark Gubicza	.06	.05	.02
146	Charlie Hough	.05	.04	.02
147	Sammy Sosa	.15	.11	.06
148	Randy Ready	.04	.03	.02
149	Kelly Gruber	.08	.06	.03
150	Devon White	.06	.05	.02
151	Gary Carter	.08	.06	.03
152	Gene Larkin	.05	.04	.02
153	Chris Sabo	.08	.06	.03
154	David Cone	.08	.06	.03
155	Todd Stottlemyre	.06	.05	.02

		MT	NR MT	EX
156	Glenn Wilson	.05	.04	.02
157	Bob Walk	.05	.04	.02
158	Mike Gallego	.04	.03	.02
159	Greg Hibbard	.06	.05	.02
160	Chris Bosio	.05	.04	.02
161	Mike Moore	.06	.05	.02
162	Jerry Browne	.06	.05	.02
163	Steve Sax	.08	.06	.03
164	Melido Perez	.06	.05	.02
165	Danny Darwin	.05	.04	.02
166	Roger McDowell	.06	.05	.02
167	Bill Ripken	.04	.03	.02
168	Mike Sharperson	.05	.04	.02
169	Lee Smith	.08	.06	.03
170	Matt Nokes	.06	.05	.02
171	Jesse Orosco	.05	.04	.02
172	Rick Aguilera	.06	.05	.02
173	Jim Presley	.06	.05	.02
174	Lou Whitaker	.08	.06	.03
175	Harold Reynolds	.08	.06	.03
176	Brook Jacoby	.06	.05	.02
177	Wally Backman	.05	.04	.02
178	Wade Boggs	.20	.15	.08
179	Chuck Cary	.04	.03	.02
180	Tom Foley	.04	.03	.02
181	Pete Harnisch	.05	.04	.02
182	Mike Morgan	.05	.04	.02
183	Bob Tewksbury	.05	.04	.02
184	Joe Girardi	.06	.05	.02
185	Storm Davis	.05	.04	.02
186	Ed Whitson	.06	.05	.02
187	Steve Avery	.25	.20	.10
188	Lloyd Moseby	.06	.05	.02
189	Scott Bankhead	.06	.05	.02
190	Mark Langston	.08	.06	.03
191	Kevin McReynolds	.06	.05	.02
192	Julio Franco	.08	.06	.03
193	John Dopson	.05	.04	.02
194	Oil Can Boyd	.05	.04	.02
195	Bip Roberts	.06	.05	.02
196	Billy Hatcher	.06	.05	.02
197	Edgar Diaz(FC)	.08	.06	.03
198	Greg Litton	.05	.04	.02
199	Mark Grace	.10	.08	.04
200	Checklist	.04	.03	.02
201	George Brett	.10	.08	.04
202	Jeff Russell	.06	.05	.02
203	Ivan Calderon	.08	.06	.03
204	Ken Howell	.04	.03	.02
205	Tom Henke	.08	.06	.03
206	Bryan Harvey	.06	.05	.02
207	Steve Bedrosian	.08	.06	.03
208	Al Newman	.04	.03	.02
209	Randy Myers	.08	.06	.03
210	Daryl Boston	.04	.03	.02
211	Manny Lee	.06	.05	.02
212	Dave Smith	.06	.05	.02
213	Don Slaught	.04	.03	.02
214	Walt Weiss	.06	.05	.02
215	Donn Pall	.04	.03	.02
216	Jamie Navarro	.06	.05	.02
217	Willie Randolph	.06	.05	.02
218	Rudy Seanez(FC)	.08	.06	.03
219	*Jim Leyritz*(FC)	.15	.11	.06
220	Ron Karkovice	.05	.04	.02
221	Ken Caminiti	.05	.04	.02
222	Von Hayes	.08	.06	.03
223	Cal Ripken	.10	.08	.04
224	Lenny Harris	.06	.05	.02
225	Milt Thompson	.05	.04	.02
226	Alvaro Espinoza	.05	.04	.02
227	Chris James	.06	.05	.02
228	Dan Gladden	.06	.05	.02
229	Jeff Blauser	.05	.04	.02
230	Mike Heath	.04	.03	.02
231	Omar Vizquel	.05	.04	.02
232	Doug Jones	.08	.06	.03
233	Jeff King	.06	.05	.02
234	Luis Rivera	.04	.03	.02
235	Ellis Burks	.10	.08	.04
236	Greg Cadaret	.04	.03	.02
237	Dave Martinez	.05	.04	.02
238	Mark Williamson	.04	.03	.02
239	Stan Javier	.05	.04	.02
240	Ozzie Smith	.10	.08	.04
241	*Shawn Boskie*	.15	.11	.06
242	Tom Gordon	.10	.08	.04
243	Tony Gwynn	.10	.08	.04
244	Tommy Gregg	.04	.03	.02
245	Jeff Robinson	.05	.04	.02
246	Keith Comstock	.04	.03	.02
247	Jack Howell	.05	.04	.02
248	Keith Miller	.05	.04	.02
249	Bobby Witt	.08	.06	.03
250	Rob Murphy	.04	.03	.02
251	Spike Owen	.06	.05	.02
252	Garry Templeton	.06	.05	.02
253	Glenn Braggs	.06	.05	.02
254	Ron Robinson	.06	.05	.02
255	Kevin Mitchell	.20	.15	.08
256	Les Lancaster	.04	.03	.02
257	*Mel Stottlemyre*(FC)	.10	.08	.04
258	Kenny Rogers	.06	.05	.02
259	Lance Johnson	.06	.05	.02
260	John Kruk	.06	.05	.02
261	Fred McGriff	.15	.11	.06
262	Dick Schofield	.04	.03	.02
263	Trevor Wilson	.05	.04	.02
264	Scott Scudder, David West	.05	.04	.02
266	Dwight Gooden	.20	.15	.08
267	*Willie Blair*(FC)	.15	.11	.06
268	Mark Portugal	.04	.03	.02
269	Doug Drabek	.10	.08	.04
270	Dennis Eckersley	.10	.08	.04
271	Eric King	.05	.04	.02
272	Robin Yount	.10	.08	.04
273	Carney Lansford	.08	.06	.02
274	*Carlos Baerga*	.25	.20	.10
275	Dave Righetti	.08	.06	.03
276	Scott Fletcher	.04	.03	.02
277	Eric Yelding	.08	.06	.03
278	Charlie Hayes	.08	.06	.03
279	Jeff Ballard	.05	.04	.02
280	Orel Hershiser	.10	.08	.04
281	Jose Oquendo	.04	.03	.02
282	Mike Witt	.05	.04	.02
283	Mitch Webster	.04	.03	.02
284	Greg Gagne	.05	.04	.02
285	*Greg Olson*	.10	.08	.04
286	Tony Phillips	.05	.04	.02
287	Scott Bradley	.04	.03	.02
288	Cory Snyder	.08	.06	.03
289	Jay Bell	.06	.05	.02
290	Kevin Romine	.04	.03	.02
291	Jeff Robinson	.05	.04	.02
292	Steve Frey(FC)	.06	.05	.02
293	Craig Worthington	.05	.04	.02
294	Tim Crews	.04	.03	.02
295	Joe Magrane	.08	.06	.03
296	*Hector Villanueva*(FC)	.20	.15	.08
297	*Terry Shumpert*	.10	.08	.04
298	Joe Carter	.10	.08	.04
299	Kent Mercker	.10	.08	.04
300	Checklist	.04	.03	.02
301	Chet Lemon	.05	.04	.02
302	Mike Schooler	.08	.06	.03
303	Dante Bichette	.06	.05	.02
304	Kevin Elster	.05	.04	.02
305	Jeff Huson	.06	.05	.02
306	Greg Harris	.05	.04	.02
307	Marquis Grissom	.10	.08	.04
308	Calvin Schiraldi	.04	.03	.02
309	Mariano Duncan	.06	.05	.02
310	Bill Spiers	.06	.05	.02
311	Scott Garrelts	.06	.05	.02
312	Mitch Williams	.08	.06	.03
313	Mike Macfarlane	.05	.04	.02
314	Kevin Brown	.06	.05	.02
315	Robin Ventura	.10	.08	.04
316	Darren Daulton	.06	.05	.02
317	PUuat Borders	.06	.05	.02
318	Mark Eichhorn	.04	.03	.02
319	Jeff Brantley	.08	.06	.03
320	Shane Mack	.05	.04	.02
321	Rob Dibble	.10	.08	.04
322	John Franco	.10	.08	.04
323	Junior Felix	.08	.06	.03
324	Casey Candaele	.04	.03	.02
325	Bobby Bonilla	.10	.08	.04
326	Dave Henderson	.06	.05	.02
327	Wayne Edwards	.06	.05	.02
328	Mark Knudson	.04	.03	.02
329	Terry Steinbach	.06	.05	.02
330	*Colby Ward*(FC)	.20	.15	.08
331	*Oscar Azocar*(FC)	.15	.11	.06
332	*Scott Radinsky*	.15	.11	.06
333	Eric Anthony	.10	.08	.04
334	Steve Lake	.04	.03	.02
335	Bob Melvin	.04	.03	.02
336	Kal Daniels	.08	.06	.03
337	Tom Pagnozzi	.05	.04	.02
338	*Alan Mills*	.15	.11	.06

		MT	NR MT	EX
339	Steve Olin	.06	.05	.02
340	Juan Berenguer	.04	.03	.02
341	Francisco Cabrera	.06	.05	.02
342	Dave Bergman	.04	.03	.02
343	Henry Cotto	.04	.03	.02
344	Sergio Valdez	.08	.06	.03
345	Bob Patterson	.04	.03	.02
346	John Marzano	.05	.04	.02
347	*Dana Kiecker*	.08	.06	.03
348	Dion James	.04	.03	.02
349	Hubie Brooks	.08	.06	.03
350	Bill Landrum	.05	.04	.02
351	*Bill Sampen*	.20	.15	.08
352	Greg Briley	.05	.04	.02
353	Paul Gibson	.04	.03	.02
354	Dave Eiland	.04	.03	.02
355	Steve Finley	.06	.05	.02
356	Bob Boone	.06	.05	.02
357	Steve Buechele	.06	.05	.02
358	*Chris Hoiles*(FC)	.20	.15	.08
359	Larry Walker	.10	.08	.04
360	Frank DiPino	.04	.03	.02
361	Mark Grant	.04	.03	.02
362	Dave Magadan	.08	.06	.03
363	Robby Thompson	.06	.05	.02
364	Lonnie Smith	.05	.04	.02
365	Steve Farr	.05	.04	.02
366	Dave Valle	.05	.04	.02
367	*Tim Naehring*(FC)	.25	.20	.10
368	Jim Acker	.04	.03	.02
369	Jeff Reardon	.08	.06	.04
370	Tim Teufel	.04	.03	.02
371	Juan Gonzalez	.35	.25	.14
372	Luis Salazar	.04	.03	.02
373	Rick Honeycutt	.04	.03	.02
374	Greg Maddux	.08	.06	.03
375	Jose Uribe	.05	.04	.02
376	Donnie Hill	.04	.03	.02
377	Don Carman	.04	.03	.02
378	*Craig Grebeck*	.06	.05	.02
379	Willie Fraser	.05	.04	.02
380	Glenallen Hill	.08	.06	.03
381	Joe Oliver	.06	.05	.02
382	Randy Bush	.04	.03	.02
383	Alex Cole(FC)	.30	.25	.12
384	Norm Charlton	.08	.06	.03
385	Gene Nelson	.04	.03	.02
386	Checklist	.04	.03	.02
387	Rickey Henderson (MVP)	.15	.11	.06
388	Lance Parrish (MVP)	.05	.04	.02
389	Fred McGriff (MVP)	.10	.08	.04
390	Dave Parker (MVP)	.10	.08	.04
391	Candy Maldonado	.05	.04	.02
392	Ken Griffey,Jr. (MVP)	.40	.30	.15
393	Gregg Olson (MVP)	.10	.08	.04
394	Rafael Palmeiro (MVP)	.10	.08	.04
395	Roger Clemens (MVP)	.15	.11	.06
396	George Brett (MVP)	.10	.08	.04
397	Cecil Fielder (MVP)	.15	.11	.06
398	Brian Harper (MVP)	.05	.04	.02
399	Bobby Thigpen (MVP)	.06	.05	.02
400	Roberto Kelly (MVP)	.08	.06	.03
401	Danny Darwin (MVP)	.05	.04	.02
402	Dave Justice (MVP)	.25	.20	.10
403	Lee Smith (MVP)	.05	.04	.02
404	Ryne Sanberg (MVP)	.15	.11	.06
405	Eddie Murray (MVP)	.10	.08	.04
406	Tim Wallach (MVP)	.06	.05	.02
407	Kevin Mitchell (MVP)	.10	.08	.04
408	Darryl Strawberry (MVP)	.15	.11	.06
409	Joe Carter (MVP)	.06	.05	.02
410	Len Dykstra (MVP)	.06	.05	.02
411	Doug Drabek (MVP)	.06	.05	.02
412	Chris Sabo (MVP)	.08	.06	.03
413	*Paul Marak* (RR)(FC)	.15	.11	.06
414	Tim MCIntosh (RR)(FC)	.10	.08	.04
415	*Brian Barnes* (RR)(FC)	.20	.15	.08
416	*Eric Gunderson* (RR)(FC)	.15	.11	.06
417	*Mike Gardiner* (RR)(FC)	.20	.15	.08
418	Steve Carter (RR)	.08	.06	.03
419	*Gerald Alexander* (RR)(FC)	.15	.11	.06
420	*Rich Garces* (RR)(FC)	.20	.15	.08
421	Chuck Knoblauch (RR)(FC)	.50	.40	.20
422	*Scott Aldred* (RR)(FC)	.15	.11	.06
423	*Wes Chamberlain* (RR)(FC)	.40	.30	.15
424	*Lance Dickson* (RR)(FC)	.25	.20	.10
425	*Greg Colbrunn* (RR)(FC)	.30	.25	.12
426	*Rich Delucia* (RR)(FC)	.20	.15	.08
427	*Jeff Conine* (RR)(FC)	.30	.25	.12
428	*Steve Decker* (RR)(FC)	.40	.30	.15
429	*Turner Ward* (RR)(FC)	.20	.15	.08

		MT	NR MT	EX
430	Mo Vaughn (RR)(FC)	.60	.45	.25
431	*Steve Chitren* (RR)(FC)	.20	.15	.08
432	Mike Benjamin (RR)(FC)	.10	.08	.04
433	Ryne Sandberg (All-Star)	.10	.08	.04
434	Len Dykstra (All-Star)	.06	.05	.02
435	Andre Dawson (All-Star)	.10	.08	.04
436	Mike Scioscia (All-Star)	.06	.05	.02
437	Ozzie Smith (All-Star)	.10	.08	.04
438	Kevin Mitchell (All-Star)	.10	.08	.04
439	Jack Armstrong (All-Star)	.06	.05	.02
440	Chris Sabo (All-Star)	.08	.06	.03
441	Will Clark (All-Star)	.15	.11	.06
442	Mel Hall	.05	.04	.02
443	Mark Gardner	.06	.05	.02
444	Mike Devereaux	.06	.05	.02
445	Kirk Gibson	.06	.05	.02
446	Terry Pendleton	.08	.06	.03
447	Mike Harkey	.08	.06	.03
448	Jim Eisenreich	.04	.03	.02
449	Benito Santiago	.08	.06	.03
450	Oddibe McDowell	.04	.03	.02
451	Cecil Fielder	.20	.15	.08
452	Ken Griffey,Sr.	.08	.06	.03
453	Bert Blyleven	.06	.05	.02
454	Howard Johnson	.10	.08	.04
455	Monty Farris(FC)	.15	.11	.06
456	Tony Pena	.05	.04	.02
457	Tim Raines	.08	.06	.03
458	Dennis Rasmussen	.04	.03	.02
459	Luis Quinones	.04	.03	.02
460	B.J. Surhoff	.06	.05	.02
461	Ernest Riles	.04	.03	.02
462	Rick Sutcliffe	.06	.05	.02
463	Danny Tartabull	.10	.08	.04
464	Pete Incaviglia	.06	.05	.02
465	Carlos Martinez	.05	.04	.02
466	Ricky Jordan	.06	.05	.02
467	John Cerutti	.04	.03	.02
468	Dave Winfield	.12	.09	.05
469	Francisco Oliveras	.04	.03	.02
470	Roy Smith	.04	.03	.02
471	Barry Larkin	.12	.09	.05
472	Ron Darling	.06	.05	.02
473	David Wells	.06	.05	.02
474	Glenn Davis	.10	.08	.04
475	Neal Heaton	.04	.03	.02
476	Ron Hassey	.04	.03	.02
477	Frank Thomas(FC)	1.25	.90	.50
478	Greg Vaughn	.15	.11	.06
479	Todd Burns	.04	.03	.02
480	Candy Maldonado	.05	.04	.02
481	Dave LaPoint	.04	.03	.02
482	Alvin Davis	.08	.06	.03
483	Mike Scott	.06	.05	.02
484	Dale Murphy	.12	.09	.05
485	Ben McDonald	.35	.25	.14
486	Jay Howell	.06	.05	.02
487	Vince Coleman	.08	.06	.03
488	Alfredo Griffin	.05	.04	.02
489	Sandy Alomar	.15	.11	.06
490	Kirby Puckett	.15	.11	.06
491	Andres Thomas	.04	.03	.02
492	Jack Morris	.08	.06	.03
493	Matt Young	.04	.03	.02
494	Greg Myers	.04	.03	.02
495	Barry Bonds	.15	.11	.06
496	Scott Cooper(FC)	.20	.15	.08
497	Dan Schatzeder	.04	.03	.02
498	Jesse Barfield	.06	.05	.02
499	Jerry Goff(FC)	.05	.04	.02
500	Checklist	.04	.03	.02
501	*Anthony Telford*(FC)	.15	.11	.06
502	Eddie Murray	.12	.09	.05
503	*Omar Olivares*(FC)	.12	.09	.05
504	Ryne Sandberg	.15	.11	.06
505	Jeff Montgomery	.06	.05	.02
506	Mark Parent	.04	.03	.02
507	Ron Gant	.15	.11	.06
508	Frank Tanana	.05	.04	.02
509	Jay Buhner	.06	.05	.02
510	Max Venable	.04	.03	.02
511	Wally Whitehurst	.06	.05	.02
512	Gary Pettis	.04	.03	.02
513	Tom Brunansky	.06	.05	.02
514	Tim Wallach	.08	.06	.03
515	Craig Lefferts	.05	.04	.02
516	*Tim Layana*	.10	.08	.04
517	Darryl Hamilton	.08	.06	.03
518	Rick Reuschel	.05	.04	.02
519	Steve Wilson	.06	.05	.02
520	Kurt Stillwell	.05	.04	.02

		MT	NR MT	EX
521	Rafael Palmeiro	.12	.09	.05
522	Ken Patterson	.04	.03	.02
523	Len Dykstra	.12	.09	.05
524	Tony Fernandez	.06	.05	.02
525	Kent Anderson	.04	.03	.02
526	*Mark Leonard*(FC)	.20	.15	.08
527	Allan Anderson	.04	.03	.02
528	Tom Browning	.06	.05	.02
529	Frank Viola	.12	.09	.05
530	John Olerud	.30	.25	.12
531	Juan Agosto	.04	.03	.02
532	Zane Smith	.06	.05	.02
533	Scott Sanderson	.06	.05	.02
534	Barry Jones	.05	.04	.02
535	Mike Felder	.04	.03	.02
536	Jose Canseco	.30	.25	.12
537	Felix Fermin	.04	.03	.02
538	Roberto Kelly	.08	.06	.03
539	Brian Holman	.05	.04	.02
540	Mark Davidson	.04	.03	.02
541	Terry Mulholland	.06	.05	.02
542	Randy Milligan	.06	.05	.02
543	Jose Gonzalez	.04	.03	.02
544	*Craig Wilson*(FC)	.10	.08	.04
545	Mike Hartley	.04	.03	.02
546	Greg Swindell	.06	.05	.02
547	Gary Gaetti	.08	.06	.03
548	Dave Justice	.50	.40	.20
549	Steve Searcy	.04	.03	.02
550	Erik Hanson	.12	.09	.05
551	Dave Stieb	.08	.06	.03
552	Andy Van Slyke	.08	.06	.03
553	Mike Greenwell	.12	.09	.05
554	Kevin Maas	.30	.25	.12
555	Delino Deshields	.20	.15	.08
556	Curt Schilling	.05	.04	.02
557	Ramon Martinez	.20	.15	.08
558	Pedro Guerrero	.08	.06	.03
559	Dwight Smith	.05	.04	.02
560	Mark Davis	.04	.03	.02
561	Shawn Abner	.05	.04	.02
562	Charlie Leibrandt	.05	.04	.02
563	John Shelby	.04	.03	.02
564	Bill Swift	.05	.04	.02
565	Mike Fetters	.06	.05	.02
566	Alejandro Pena	.05	.04	.02
567	Ruben Sierra	.15	.11	.06
568	Calos Quintana	.08	.06	.03
569	Kevin Gross	.05	.04	.02
570	Derek Lilliquist	.04	.03	.02
571	Jack Armstrong	.06	.05	.02
572	Greg Brock	.04	.03	.02
573	Mike Kingery	.04	.03	.02
574	Greg Smith(FC)	.06	.05	.02
575	*Brian McRae*(FC)	.70	.50	.30
576	Jack Daugherty	.05	.04	.02
577	Ozzie Guillen	.06	.05	.02
578	Joe Boever	.04	.03	.02
579	Luis Sojo	.06	.05	.02
580	Chili Davis	.06	.05	.02
581	Don Robinson	.04	.03	.02
582	Brian Harper	.06	.05	.02
583	Paul O'Neill	.06	.05	.02
584	Bob Ojeda	.05	.04	.02
585	Mookie Wilson	.05	.04	.02
586	Rafael Ramirez	.04	.03	.02
587	Gary Redus	.04	.03	.02
588	Jamie Quirk	.04	.03	.02
589	Shawn Hilligas	.04	.03	.02
590	*Tom Edens*(FC)	.08	.06	.03
591	Joe Klink(FC)	.05	.04	.02
592	Charles Nagy(FC)	.15	.11	.06
593	Eric Plunk	.04	.03	.02
594	Tracy Jones	.04	.03	.02
595	Craig Biggio	.08	.06	.03
596	Jose DeJesus	.06	.05	.02
597	Mickey Tettleton	.08	.06	.03
598	Chris Gwynn	.05	.04	.02
599	Rex Hudler	.06	.05	.02
600	Checklist	.04	.03	.02
601	Jim Gott	.04	.03	.02
602	Jeff Manto(FC)	.12	.09	.05
603	Nelson Liriano	.04	.03	.02
604	Mark Lemke	.06	.05	.02
605	Clay Parker	.04	.03	.02
606	Edgar Martinez	.08	.06	.03
607	*Mark Whiten*(FC)	.35	.25	.14
608	Ted Power	.04	.03	.02
609	Tom Bolton	.05	.04	.02
610	Tom Herr	.05	.04	.02
611	Andy Hawkins	.04	.03	.02

		MT	NR MT	EX
612	Scott Ruskin	.04	.03	.02
613	Ron Kittle	.05	.04	.02
614	John Wetteland	.06	.05	.02
615	*Mike Perez*(FC)	.12	.09	.05
616	Dave Clark	.04	.03	.02
617	Brent Mayne(FC)	.12	.09	.05
618	Jack Clark	.08	.06	.03
619	Marvin Freeman	.04	.03	.02
620	Edwin Nunez	.04	.03	.02
621	Russ Swan(FC)	.08	.06	.03
622	Johnny Ray	.04	.03	.02
623	Charlie O'Brien	.04	.03	.02
624	*Joe Bitker*(FC)	.12	.09	.05
625	Mike Marshall	.04	.03	.02
626	Otis Nixon	.05	.04	.02
627	Andy Benes	.15	.11	.06
628	Ron Oester	.04	.03	.02
629	Ted Higuera	.06	.05	.02
630	Kevin Bass	.05	.04	.02
631	Damon Berryhill	.05	.04	.02
632	Bo Jackson	.30	.25	.12
633	Brad Arnsberg	.05	.04	.02
634	Jerry Willard	.04	.03	.02
635	Tommy Greene	.06	.05	.02
636	*Bob MacDonald*(FC)	.15	.11	.06
637	Kirk McCaskill	.05	.04	.02
638	John Burkett	.05	.04	.02
639	*Paul Abbott*(FC)	.15	.11	.06
640	Todd Benzinger	.05	.04	.02
641	Todd Hundley(FC)	.10	.08	.04
642	George Bell	.10	.08	.04
643	*Javier Ortiz*(FC)	.12	.09	.05
644	Sid Bream	.05	.04	.02
645	Bob Welch	.06	.05	.02
646	Phil Bradley	.05	.04	.02
647	Bill Krueger	.04	.03	.02
648	Rickey Henderson	.20	.15	.08
649	Kevin Wickander	.05	.04	.02
650	Steve Balboni	.04	.03	.02
651	Gene Harris	.05	.04	.02
652	Jim Deshaies	.04	.03	.02
653	Jason Grimsley(FC)	.12	.09	.05
654	Joe Orsulak	.05	.04	.02
655	*Jimmy Poole*(FC)	.12	.09	.05
656	Felix Jose	.10	.08	.04
657	Dennis Cook	.05	.04	.02
658	Tom Brookens	.04	.03	.02
659	Junior Ortiz	.04	.03	.02
660	Jeff Parrett	.04	.03	.02
661	Jerry Don Gleaton	.04	.03	.02
662	Brent Knackert	.04	.03	.02
663	Rance Mulliniks	.04	.03	.02
664	John Smiley	.06	.05	.02
665	Larry Andersen	.04	.03	.02
666	Willie McGee	.08	.06	.03
667	*Chris Nabholz*(FC)	.20	.15	.08
668	Brady Anderson	.04	.03	.02
669	*Darren Holmes*(FC)	.12	.09	.05
670	Ken Hill	.06	.05	.02
671	Gary Varsho	.04	.03	.02
672	Bill Pecota	.05	.04	.02
673	Fred Lynn	.05	.04	.02
674	Kevin D. Brown(FC)	.10	.08	.04
675	Dan Petry	.04	.03	.02
676	Mike Jackson	.05	.04	.02
677	Wally Joyner	.12	.09	.05
678	Danny Jackson	.05	.04	.02
679	*Bill Haselman*(FC)	.12	.09	.05
680	Mike Boddicker	.06	.05	.02
681	*Mel Rojas*(FC)	.12	.09	.05
682	Roberto Alomar	.12	.09	.05
683	Dave Justice (R.O.Y.)	.25	.20	.10
684	Chuck Crim	.04	.03	.02
685	Matt Williams	.12	.09	.05
686	Shawon Dunston	.06	.05	.02
687	*Jeff Schulz*(FC)	.08	.06	.03
688	*John Barfield*(FC)	.08	.06	.03
689	Gerald Young	.04	.03	.02
690	*Luis Gonzalez*(FC)	.50	.40	.20
691	Frank Wills	.05	.04	.02
692	Chuck Finley	.08	.06	.03
693	Sandy Alomar (R.O.Y.)	.15	.11	.06
694	Tim Drummond	.05	.04	.02
695	Herm Winningham	.04	.03	.02
696	Darryl Strawberry	.25	.20	.10
697	Al Leiter	.04	.03	.02
698	*Karl Rhodes*(FC)	.25	.20	.10
699	Stan Belinda(FC)	.08	.06	.03
700	Checklist	.04	.03	.02
701	Lance Blankenship	.04	.03	.02
702	Willie Stargell (Puzzle Card)	.10	.08	.04

		MT	NR MT	EX
703	Jim Gantner	.05	.04	.02
704	*Reggie Harris*(FC)	.15	.11	.06
705	Rob Ducey	.04	.03	.02
706	Tim Hulett	.04	.03	.02
707	Atlee Hammaker	.04	.03	.02
708	Xavier Hernandez	.04	.03	.02
709	Chuck McElroy(FC)	.08	.06	.03
710	John Mitchell	.04	.03	.02
711	Carlos Hernandez	.05	.04	.02
712	Geronimo Pena(FC)	.10	.08	.04
713	*Jim Neidlinger*(FC)	.15	.11	.06
714	John Orton	.04	.03	.02
715	Terry Leach	.04	.03	.02
716	Mike Stanton	.06	.05	.02
717	Walt Terrell	.04	.03	.02
718	Luis Aquino	.05	.04	.02
719	Bud Black	.05	.04	.02
720	Bob Kipper	.04	.03	.02
721	*Jeff Gray*(FC)	.15	.11	.06
722	Jose Rijo	.08	.06	.03
723	Curt Young	.04	.03	.02
724	Jose Vizcaino(FC)	.08	.06	.03
725	*Randy Tomlin*(FC)	.15	.11	.06
726	Junior Noboa	.05	.04	.02
727	Bob Welch (Award Winner)	.08	.06	.03
728	Gary Ward	.04	.03	.02
729	Rob Deer	.05	.04	.02
730	*David Segui*(FC)	.25	.20	.10
731	Mark Carreon	.04	.03	.02
732	Vicente Palacios	.04	.03	.02
733	Sam Horn	.05	.04	.02
734	*Howard Farmer*(FC)	.15	.11	.06
735	Ken Dayley	.04	.03	.02
736	Kelly Mann	.08	.06	.03
737	*Joe Grahe*(FC)	.12	.09	.05
738	Kelly Downs	.04	.03	.02
739	*Jimmy Kremers*(FC)	.15	.11	.06
740	Kevin Appier	.12	.09	.05
741	Jeff Reed	.04	.03	.02
742	Jose Rijo (World Series)	.08	.06	.03
743	*Dave Rohde*(FC)	.12	.09	.05
744	Dr. Dirt/ Mr. Clean (Len Dykstra, Dale Murphy)	.25	.20	.10
745	Paul Sorrento	.06	.05	.02
746	Thomas Howard(FC)	.10	.08	.04
747	*Matt Stark*(FC)	.20	.15	.08
748	Harold Baines	.08	.06	.03
749	Doug Dascenzo	.05	.04	.02
750	Doug Drabek (Award Winner)	.08	.06	.03
751	Gary Sheffield	.15	.11	.06
752	*Terry Lee*(FC)	.20	.15	.08
753	*Jim Vatcher*(FC)	.08	.06	.03
754	Lee Stevens	.12	.09	.05
755	Randy Veres(FC)	.08	.06	.03
756	Bill Doran	.06	.05	.02
757	Gary Wayne	.04	.03	.02
758	*Pedro Munoz*(FC)	.30	.25	.12
759	Chris Hammond(FC)	.08	.06	.03
760	Checklist	.04	.03	.02
761	Rickey Henderson (MVP)	.12	.09	.05
762	Barry Bonds (MVP)	.12	.09	.05
763	Billy Hatcher (World Series)	.05	.04	.02
764	Julio Machado	.05	.04	.02
765	Jose Mesa	.05	.04	.02
766	Willie Randolph (World Series)	.05	.04	.02
767	*Scott Erickson*(FC)	1.25	.90	.50
768	*Travis Fryman*(FC)	.50	.40	.20
769	*Rich Rodriguez*(FC)	.12	.09	.05
770	Checklist, Checklist	.04	.03	.02

1991 Donruss Highlights

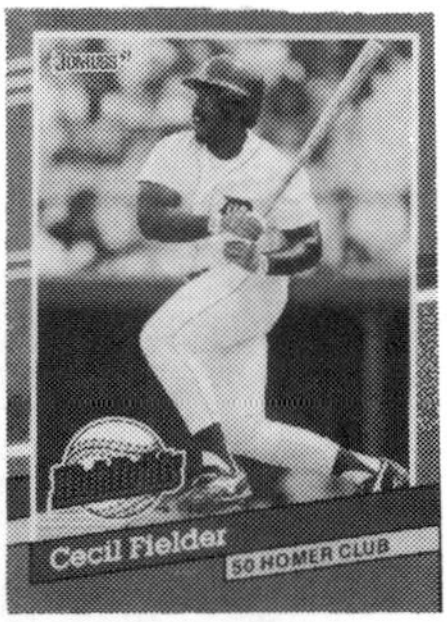

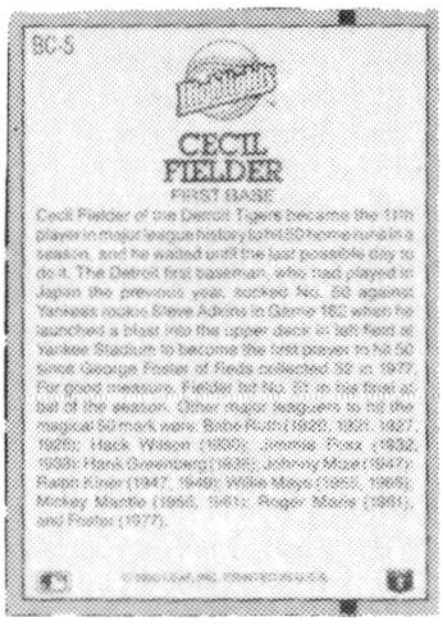

This 22-card subset features highlights from the 1990 season. The cards feature a "BC" designation along with the number and are styled after the 1991 regular issue Donruss Cards. Cards 1-10 feature blue borders due to their release with Series I cards. Cards 11-22 feature green borders and were released with Series II cards. A highlight logo appears on the front of the card. Each highlight is explained in depth on the card back.

		MT	NR MT	EX
	Complete Set:	3.00	2.25	1.25
	Common Player:	.10	.08	.04
1	Langston/Witt (No-Hit Mariners)	.15	.11	.06
2	Randy Johnson (No-Hits Tigers)	.15	.11	.06
3	Nolan Ryan (No-Hits A's)	.40	.30	.15
4	Dave Stewart (No-Hits Blue Jays)	.15	.11	.06
5	Cecil Fielder (50 Homer Club)	.25	.20	.10
6	Carlton Fisk (Record Home Run)	.20	.15	.08
7	Ryne Sandberg (Sets Fielding Records)	.20	.15	.08
8	Gary Carter (Breaks Catching Mark)	.15	.11	.06
9	Mark McGwire (Home Run Milestone)	.15	.11	.06
10	Bo Jackson (4 Consecutive HRs)	.25	.20	.10
11	Fernando Valenzuela (No-Hits Cardinals)	.15	.11	.06
12	Andy Hawkins (No-Hits White Sox)	.10	.08	.04
13	Melido Perez (No-Hits Yankees)	.10	.08	.04
14	Terry Mulholland (No-Hits Giants)	.10	.08	.04
15	Nolan Ryan (300th Win)	.40	.30	.15
16	Delino DeShields (4 Hits In Debut)	.15	.11	.06
17	Cal Ripken (Errorless Games)	.20	.15	.08
18	Eddie Murray (Switch Hit Homers)	.15	.11	.06
19	George Brett (3 Decade Champ)	.20	.15	.08
20	Bobby Thigpen (Shatters Save Mark)	.15	.11	.06
21	Dave Stieb (No-Hits Indians)	.10	.08	.06
22	Willie McGee (NL Batting Champ)	.10	.08	.04

1991 Donruss Rookies

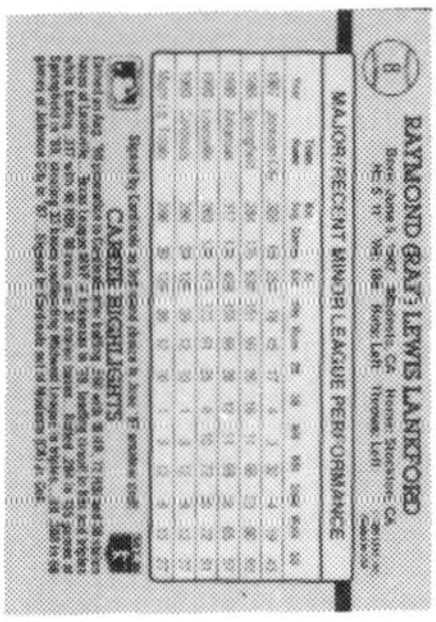

Red borders highlight the 1991 Donruss Rookies cards. This set marks the sixth year that Donruss has produced such an issue. Like in past years, "The Rookies" logo appears on the card fronts. The set is packaged in a special box and includes a Willie Stargell puzzle card.

		MT	NR MT	EX
	Complete Set:	12.00	9.00	4.75
	Common Player:	.10	.08	.04
1	Pat Kelly(FC)	.25	.20	.10
2	Rich DeLucia	.10	.08	.04
3	Wes Chamberlain	.40	.30	.15
4	Scott Leius(FC)	.10	.08	.04
5	Darryl Kile(FC)	.15	.11	.06
6	Milt Cuyler	.15	.11	.06
7	Todd Van Poppel(FC)	1.00	.70	.40
8	Ray Lankford	.20	.15	.08
9	Brian Hunter(FC)	.70	.50	.30
10	Tony Perezchica	.10	.08	.04
11	Ced Landrum(FC)	.10	.08	.04
12	Dave Burba(FC)	.10	.08	.04
13	Ramon Garcia(FC)	.20	.15	.08

		MT	NR MT	EX
14	Ed Sprague(FC)	.15	.11	.06
15	Warren Newson(FC)	.15	.11	.06
16	Paul Faries(FC)	.10	.08	.04
17	Luis Gonzalez	.35	.25	.14
18	Charles Nagy	.15	.11	.06
19	Chris Hammond	.10	.08	.04
20	Frank Castillo(FC)	.25	.20	.10
21	Pedro Munoz	.20	.15	.08
22	Orlando Merced(FC)	.40	.30	.15
23	Jose Melendez(FC)	.10	.08	.04
24	Kirk Dressendorfer(FC)	.30	.25	.12
25	Heathcliff Slocumb(FC)	.10	.08	.04
26	Doug Simons(FC)	.10	.08	.04
27	Mike Timlin(FC)	.20	.15	.08
28	Jeff Fassero(FC)	.10	.08	.04
29	Mark Leiter(FC)	.10	.08	.04
30	Jeff Bagwell(FC)	2.50	2.00	1.00
31	Brian McRae	.35	.25	.14
32	Mark Whiten	.20	.15	.08
33	Ivan Rodriguez(FC)	2.00	1.50	.80
34	Wade Taylor(FC)	.10	.08	.04
35	Darren Lewis(FC)	.35	.25	.12
36	Mo Vaughn	.40	.30	.15
37	Mike Remlinger(FC)	.10	.08	.04
38	Rick Wilkins(FC)	.20	.15	.08
39	Chuck Knoblauch	.35	.25	.14
40	Kevin Morton	.15	.11	.06
41	Carlos Rodriguez(FC)	.10	.08	.04
42	Mark Lewis	.20	.15	.08
43	Brent Mayne	.10	.08	.04
44	Chris Haney(FC)	.15	.11	.06
45	Denis Boucher(FC)	.15	.11	.06
46	Mike Gardiner	.10	.08	.04
47	Jeff Johnson(FC)	.15	.11	.06
48	Dean Palmer	.25	.20	.10
49	Chuck McElroy	.10	.08	.04
50	Chris Jones(FC)	.10	.08	.04
51	Scott Kamieniecki(FC)	.10	.08	.04
52	Al Osuna(FC)	.10	.08	.04
53	Rusty Meacham(FC)	.15	.11	.06
54	Chito Martinez(FC)	.60	.45	.25
55	Reggie Jefferson(FC)	.40	.30	.15
56	Checklist	.05	.04	.02

1991 Donruss Grand Slammers

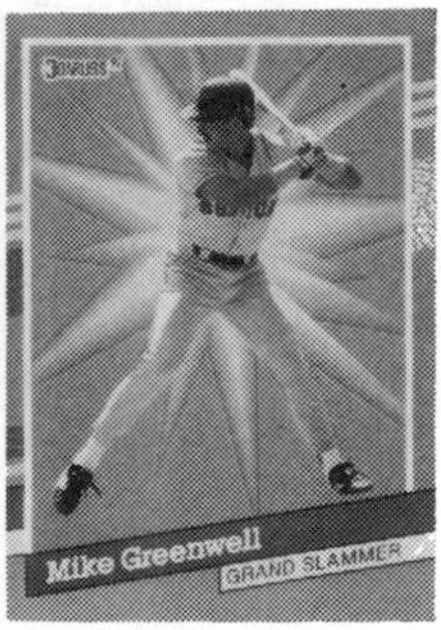

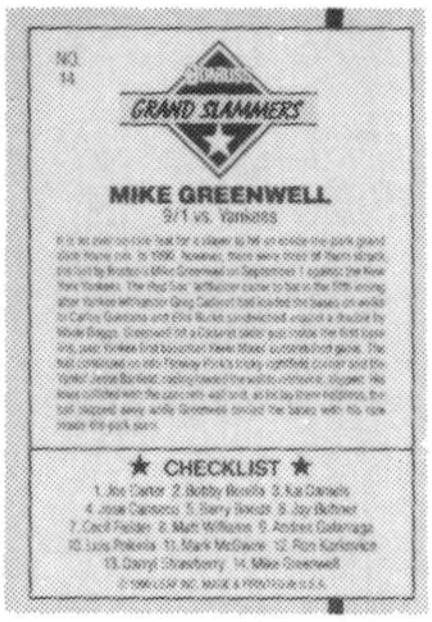

This 14-card set features players who hit grand slams in 1990. The cards are styled after the 1991 Donruss regular issue cards. The featured player is showcased with a star in the background. This set is the third Donruss Grand Slammers issue.

		MT	NR MT	EX
Complete Set:		2.50	2.00	1.00
Common Player:		.10	.08	.04
1	Joe Carter	.20	.15	.08
2	Bobby Bonilla	.20	.15	.08
3	Kal Daniels	.15	.11	.06
4	Jose Canseco	.30	.25	.12
5	Barry Bonds	.25	.20	.10
6	Jay Buhner	.15	.11	.06
7	Cecil Fielder	.30	.25	.12
8	Matt Williams	.20	.15	.08
9	Andres Galarraga	.10	.08	.04
10	Luis Polonia	.10	.08	.04
11	Mark McGwire	.20	.15	.08
12	Ron Karkovice	.10	.08	.04
13	Darryl Strawberry	.25	.20	.10
14	Mike Greenwell	.20	.15	.06

1991 Donruss Studio

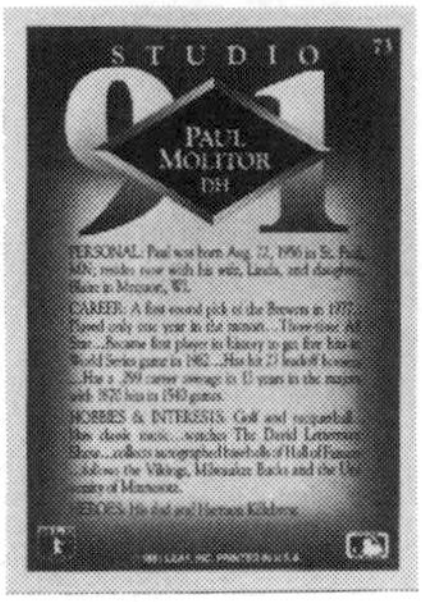

Donruss introduced this 264-card set in 1991. The cards feature marron borders surrounding black and white posed player photos. The card backs are printed in black and white and feature personal data, career highlights, hobbies and interests and the player's hero. The cards were released in foil packs only and feature a special Rod Carew puzzle.

		MT	NR MT	EX
Complete Set:		60.00	45.00	25.00
Common Player:		.12	.09	.05
1	Glenn Davis	.15	.11	.06
2	Dwight Evans	.15	.11	.06
3	Leo Gomez	.50	.40	.20
4	Chris Hoiles	.25	.20	.10
5	Sam Horn	.12	.09	.05
6	Ben McDonald	.50	.40	.20
7	Randy Milligan	.12	.09	.05
8	Gregg Olson	.15	.11	.06
9	Cal Ripken,Jr.	1.25	.90	.50
10	David Segui	.20	.15	.08
11	Wade Boggs	.60	.45	.25
12	Ellis Burks	.25	.20	.10
13	Jack Clark	.12	.09	.05
14	Roger Clemens	1.00	.70	.40
15	Mike Greenwell	.20	.15	.08
16	Tim Naehring	.15	.11	.06
17	Tony Pena	.12	.09	.05
18	Phil Plantier	5.00	3.75	2.00
19	Jeff Reardon	.15	.11	.06
20	Mo Vaughn	1.50	1.25	.60
21	Jimmy Reese	.15	.11	.06
22	Jim Abbott	.30	.25	.12
23	Bert Blyleven	.15	.11	.06
24	Chuck Finley	.20	.15	.08
25	Gary Gaetti	.12	.09	.05
26	Wally Joyner	.30	.25	.12
27	Mark Langston	.25	.20	.10
28	Kirk McCaskill	.12	.09	.05
29	Lance Parrish	.15	.11	.06
30	Dave Winfield	.25	.20	.10
31	Alex Fernandez	.50	.40	.20
32	Carlton Fisk	.35	.25	.14
33	Scott Fletcher	.12	.09	.05
34	Greg Hibbard	.12	.09	.05
35	Charlie Hough	.12	.09	.05
36	Jack McDowell	.25	.20	.10
37	Tim Rock Raines	.25	.20	.10
38	Sammy Sosa	.20	.15	.08
39	Bobby Thigpen	.25	.20	.10
40	Frank Thomas	7.00	5.25	2.75
41	Sandy Alomar	.30	.25	.12
42	John Farrell	.12	.09	.05
43	Glenallen Hill	.15	.11	.06
44	Brook Jacoby	.12	.09	.05
45	Chris James	.12	.09	.05
46	Doug Jones	.12	.09	.05
47	Eric King	.12	.09	.05
48	Mark Lewis	.60	.45	.25
49	Greg Swindell	.15	.11	.06

		MT	NR MT	EX
50	Mark Whiten	.50	.40	.20
51	Milt Cuyler	.30	.25	.12
52	Rob Deer	.12	.09	.05
53	Cecil Fielder	1.00	.70	.40
54	Travis Fryman	2.00	1.50	.80
55	Bill Gullickson	.12	.09	.05
56	Lloyd Moseby	.12	.09	.05
57	Frank Tanana	.12	.09	.05
58	Mickey Tettleton	.20	.15	.08
59	Alan Trammell	.25	.20	.10
60	Lou Whitaker	.20	.15	.08
61	Mike Boddicker	.12	.09	.05
62	George Brett	.30	.25	.12
63	Jeff Conine	.40	.30	.15
64	Warren Cromartie	.12	.09	.05
65	Storm Davis	.12	.09	.05
66	Kirk Gibson	.20	.15	.08
67	Mark Gubicza	.15	.11	.06
68	Brian McRae	2.00	1.50	.80
69	Bret Saberhagen	.15	.11	.06
70	Kurt Stillwell	.12	.09	.05
71	Tim McIntosh	.15	.11	.06
72	Candy Maldonado	.12	.09	.05
73	Paul Molitor	.20	.15	.08
74	Willie Randolph	.12	.09	.05
75	Ron Robinson	.12	.09	.05
76	Gary Sheffield	.25	.20	.10
77	Franklin Stubbs	.12	.09	.05
78	B.J. Surhoff	.12	.09	.05
79	Greg Vaughn	.25	.20	.10
80	Robin Yount	.35	.25	.14
81	Rick Aguilera	.20	.15	.08
82	Steve Bedrosian	.12	.09	.05
83	Scott Erickson	3.00	2.25	1.25
84	Greg Gagne	.12	.09	.05
85	Dan Gladden	.12	.09	.05
86	Brian Harper	.15	.11	.06
87	Kent Hrbek	.15	.11	.06
88	Shane Mack	.25	.20	.10
89	Jack Morris	.20	.15	.08
90	Kirby Puckett	.70	.50	.30
91	Jesse Barfield	.12	.09	.05
92	Steve Farr	.12	.09	.05
93	Steve Howe	.12	.09	.05
94	Roberto Kelly	.20	.15	.08
95	Tim Leary	.12	.09	.05
96	Kevin Maas	.50	.40	.20
97	Don Mattingly	.50	.40	.20
98	Hensley Meulens	.20	.15	.08
99	Scott Sanderson	.12	.09	.05
100	Steve Sax	.15	.11	.06
101	Jose Canseco	1.50	1.25	.60
102	Dennis Eckersley	.25	.20	.10
103	Dave Henderson	.15	.11	.06
104	Rickey Henderson	1.00	.70	.40
105	Rick Honeycutt	.12	.09	.05
106	Mark McGwire	.30	.25	.12
107	Dave Stewart	.20	.15	.08
108	Eric Show	.12	.09	.05
109	Todd Van Poppel	3.00	2.25	1.25
110	Bob Welch	.15	.11	.06
111	Alvin Davis	.12	.09	.05
112	Ken Griffey,Jr.	5.00	3.75	2.00
113	Ken Griffey,Sr.	.20	.15	.08
114	Erik Hanson	.15	.11	.06
115	Brian Holman	.12	.09	.05
116	Randy Johnson	.15	.11	.06
117	Edgar Martinez	.15	.11	.06
118	Tino Martinez	.35	.25	.14
119	Harold Reynolds	.15	.11	.06
120	David Valle	.12	.09	.05
121	Kevin Belcher	.12	.09	.05
122	Scott Chiamparino	.12	.09	.05
123	Julio Franco	.20	.15	.08
124	Juan Gonzalez	4.00	3.00	1.50
125	Rich Gossage	.15	.11	.06
126	Jeff Kunkel	.12	.09	.05
127	Rafael Palmeiro	.30	.25	.12
128	Nolan Ryan	2.00	1.50	.80
129	Ruben Sierra	.60	.45	.25
130	Bobby Witt	.15	.11	.06
131	Roberto Alomar	.40	.30	.15
132	Tom Candiotti	.12	.09	.05
133	Joe Carter	.30	.25	.12
134	Ken Dayley	.12	.09	.05
135	Kelly Gruber	.15	.11	.06
136	John Olerud	.40	.30	.15
137	Dave Stieb	.15	.11	.06
138	Turner Ward	.25	.20	.10
139	Devon White	.15	.11	.06
140	Mookie Wilson	.12	.09	.05

		MT	NR MT	EX
141	Steve Avery	2.00	1.50	.80
142	Sid Bream	.12	.09	.05
143	Nick Esasky	.12	.09	.05
144	Ron Gant	.50	.40	.20
145	Tom Glavine	.20	.15	.08
146	David Justice	3.00	2.25	1.25
147	Kelly Mann	.12	.09	.05
148	Terry Pendleton	.15	.11	.06
149	John Smoltz	.20	.15	.08
150	Jeff Treadway	.12	.09	.05
151	George Bell	.20	.15	.08
152	Shawn Boskie	.12	.09	.05
153	Andre Dawson	.30	.25	.12
154	Lance Dickson	.25	.20	.10
155	Shawon Dunston	.20	.15	.08
156	Joe Girardi	.12	.09	.05
157	Mark Grace	.40	.30	.15
158	Ryne Sandberg	1.00	.70	.40
159	Gary Scott	.25	.20	.10
160	Dave Smith	.12	.09	.05
161	Tom Browning	.15	.11	.06
162	Eric Davis	.30	.25	.12
163	Rob Dibble	.20	.15	.08
164	Mariano Duncan	.12	.09	.05
165	Chris Hammond	.12	.09	.05
166	Billy Hatcher	.12	.09	.05
167	Barry Larkin	.30	.25	.12
168	Hal Morris	.30	.25	.12
169	Paul O'Neill	.15	.11	.06
170	Chris Sabo	.15	.11	.06
171	Eric Anthony	.15	.11	.06
172	Jeff Bagwell	6.00	4.50	2.50
173	Craig Biggio	.20	.15	.08
174	Ken Caminitti	.15	.11	.06
175	Jim Deshaies	.12	.09	.05
176	Steve Finley	.15	.11	.06
177	Pete Harnisch	.15	.11	.06
178	Darryl Kile	.20	.15	.08
179	Curt Schilling	.12	.09	.05
180	Mike Scott	.12	.09	.05
181	Brett Butler	.15	.11	.06
182	Gary Carter	.15	.11	.06
183	Orel Hershiser	.20	.15	.08
184	Ramon Martinez	.60	.45	.25
185	Eddie Murray	.30	.25	.12
186	Jose Offerman	.25	.20	.10
187	Bob Ojeda	.12	.09	.05
188	Juan Samuel	.15	.11	.06
189	Mike Scioscia	.15	.11	.06
190	Darryl Strawberry	1.00	.70	.40
191	Moises Alou	.15	.11	.06
192	Brian Barnes	.15	.11	.06
193	Oil Can Boyd	.15	.11	.06
194	Ivan Calderon	.15	.11	.06
195	Delino DeShields	.20	.15	.08
196	Mike Fitzgerald	.12	.09	.05
197	Andres Galarraga	.15	.11	.06
198	Marquis Grissom	.30	.25	.12
199	Bill Sampen	.12	.09	.05
200	Tim Wallach	.12	.09	.05
201	Daryl Boston	.12	.09	.05
202	Vince Coleman	.20	.15	.08
203	John Franco	.15	.11	.06
204	Dwight Gooden	.35	.25	.14
205	Tom Herr	.12	.09	.05
206	Gregg Jefferies	.20	.15	.08
207	Howard Johnson	.20	.15	.08
208	Dave Magadan	.20	.15	.08
209	Kevin McReynolds	.15	.11	.06
210	Frank Viola	.20	.15	.08
211	Wes Chamberlain	1.50	1.25	.60
212	Darren Daulton	.12	.09	.05
213	Lenny Dykstra	.20	.15	.08
214	Charlie Hayes	.15	.11	.06
215	Ricky Jordan	.15	.11	.06
216	Steve Lake	.12	.09	.05
217	Roger McDowell	.12	.09	.05
218	Mickey Morandini	.15	.11	.06
219	Terry Mulholland	.15	.11	.06
220	Dale Murphy	.20	.15	.08
221	Jay Bell	.15	.11	.06
222	Barry Bonds	.60	.45	.25
223	Bobby Bonilla	.60	.45	.25
224	Doug Drabek	.15	.11	.06
225	Bill Landrum	.12	.09	.05
226	Mike LaValliere	.12	.09	.05
227	Jose Lind	.12	.09	.05
228	Don Slaught	.12	.09	.05
229	John Smiley	.15	.11	.06
230	Andy Van Slyke	.20	.15	.08
231	Bernard Gilkey	.20	.15	.08

		MT	NR MT	EX
232	Pedro Guerrero	.20	.15	.08
233	Rex Hudler	.12	.09	.05
234	Ray Lankford	.80	.60	.30
235	Joe Magrane	.12	.09	.05
236	Jose Oquendo	.12	.09	.05
237	Lee Smith	.15	.11	.06
238	Ozzie Smith	.40	.30	.15
239	Milt Thompson	.12	.09	.05
240	Todd Zeile	.30	.25	.12
241	Larry Andersen	.12	.09	.05
242	Andy Benes	.30	.25	.12
243	Paul Faries	.12	.09	.05
244	Tony Fernandez	.12	.09	.05
245	Tony Gwynn	.50	.40	.20
246	Atlee Hammaker	.12	.09	.05
247	Fred McGriff	.35	.25	.14
248	Bip Roberts	.12	.09	.05
249	Benito Santiago	.15	.11	.06
250	Ed Whitson	.12	.09	.05
251	Dave Anderson	.12	.09	.05
252	Mike Benjamin	.15	.11	.06
253	John Burkett	.15	.11	.06
254	Will Clark	1.00	.70	.40
255	Scott Garrelts	.12	.09	.05
256	Willie McGee	.15	.11	.06
257	Kevin Mitchell	.30	.25	.12
258	Dave Righetti	.15	.11	.06
259	Matt Williams	.30	.25	.12
260	Black & Decker	.20	.15	.08
261	Checklist	.10	.08	.04
262	Checklist	.10	.08	.04
263	Checklist	.10	.08	.04
264	Checklist	.10	.08	.04

1992 Donruss Series I

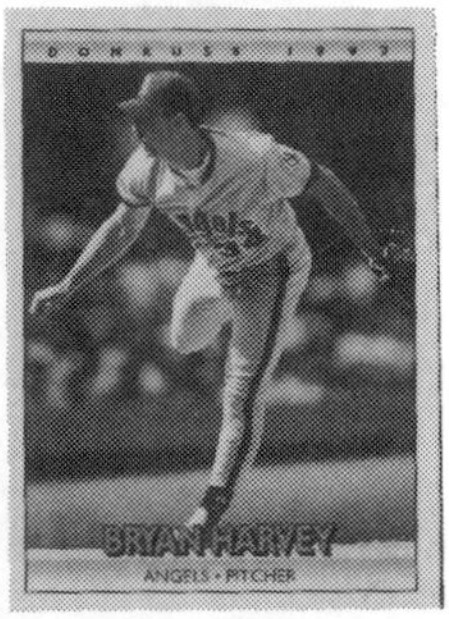

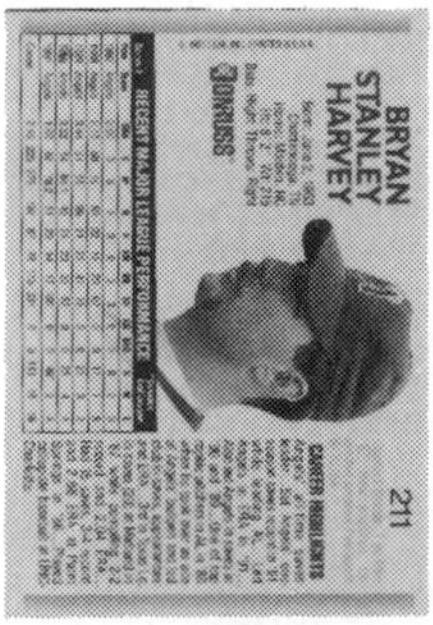

For the second consecutive year, Donruss chose to release its card set in two series. The 1992 cards feature improved stock, an anti-couterfeit feature and include both front and back photos. Once again Rated Rookies and All-Stars are included in the set. Special highlight cards also can be found in the 1992 Donruss set. Production was reduced in 1992 compared to other years.

		MT	NR MT	EX
Complete Set:		15.00	11.00	6.00
Common Player:		.05	.04	.02

		MT	NR MT	EX
1	*Mark Wohlers* (RR)(FC)	.35	.25	.14
2	Will Cordero (RR)(FC)	.30	.25	.12
3	Kyle Abbott (RR)(FC)	.30	.25	.12
4	*Dave Nilsson* (RR)(FC)	.70	.50	.30
5	*Kenny Lofton* (RR)(FC)	.70	.50	.30
6	*Luis Mercedes* (RR)(FC)	.35	.25	.14
7	Roger Salkeld (RR)(FC)	.30	.25	.12
8	Eddie Zosky (RR)(FC)	.25	.20	.10
9	Todd Van Poppel (RR)	1.00	.70	.40
10	*Frank Seminara* (RR)(FC)	.40	.30	.15
11	*Andy Ashby* (RR)(FC)	.40	.30	.15
12	Reggie Jefferson (RR)(FC)	.35	.25	.14
13	*Ryan Klesko* (RR)(FC)	1.50	1.25	.60
14	*Carlos Garcia* (RR)(FC)	.35	.25	.14
15	*John Ramos* (RR)(FC)	.30	.25	.12
16	Eric Karros (RR)(FC)	.60	.45	.25
17	*Pat Lennon* (RR)(FC)	.35	.25	.14
18	*Eddie Taubensee* (RR)(FC)	.35	.25	.14
19	*Roberto Hernandez* (RR)(FC)	.35	.25	.14
20	D.J. Dozier (RR)(FC)	.20	.15	.08
21	Dave Henderson (AS)	.10	.08	.04
22	Cal Ripken (AS)	.20	.15	.08
23	Wade Boggs (AS)	.20	.15	.08
24	Ken Griffey,Jr. (AS)	.60	.45	.25
25	Jack Morris (AS)	.10	.08	.04
26	Danny Tartabull (AS)	.10	.08	.04
27	Cecil Fielder (AS)	.20	.15	.08
28	Roberto Alomar (AS)	.20	.15	.08
29	Sandy Alomar (AS)	.10	.08	.04
30	Rickey Henderson (AS)	.20	.15	.08
31	Ken Hill	.06	.05	.02
32	John Habyan	.05	.04	.02
33	Otis Nixon (Highlight)	.10	.08	.04
34	Tim Wallach	.08	.06	.03
35	Cal Ripken	.25	.20	.10
36	Gary Carter	.08	.06	.03
37	Juan Agosto	.05	.04	.02
38	Doug Dascenzo	.05	.04	.02
39	Kirk Gibson	.08	.06	.03
40	Benito Santiago	.08	.06	.03
41	Otis Nixon	.06	.05	.02
42	Andy Allanson	.05	.04	.02
43	Brian Holman	.06	.05	.02
44	Dick Schofield	.05	.04	.02
45	Dave Magadan	.08	.06	.03
46	Rafael Palmeiro	.10	.08	.04
47	Jody Reed	.06	.03	.02
48	Ivan Calderon	.08	.06	.03
49	Greg Harris	.05	.04	.02
50	Chris Sabo	.08	.06	.03
51	Paul Molitor	.10	.08	.04
52	Robby Thompson	.06	.05	.02
53	Dave Smith	.05	.04	.02
54	Mark Davis	.05	.04	.02
55	Kevin Brown	.06	.05	.02
56	Donn Pall	.05	.04	.02
57	Lenny Dykstra	.08	.06	.03
58	Roberto Alomar	.15	.11	.06
59	Jeff Robinson	.05	.04	.02
60	Willie McGee	.08	.06	.03
61	Jay Buhner	.08	.06	.03
62	Mike Pagliarulo	.05	.04	.02
63	Paul O'Neill	.08	.06	.03
64	Hubie Brooks	.06	.05	.02
65	Kelly Gruber	.08	.06	.03
66	Ken Caminiti	.06	.05	.02
67	Gary Redus	.05	.04	.02
68	Harold Baines	.08	.06	.03
69	Charlie Hough	.06	.05	.02
70	B.J. Surhoff	.06	.05	.02
71	Walt Weiss	.06	.05	.02
72	Shawn Hillegas	.05	.04	.02
73	Roberto Kelly	.08	.06	.03
74	Jeff Ballard	.05	.04	.02
75	Craig Biggio	.08	.06	.03
76	Pat Combs	.06	.05	.02
77	Jeff Robinson	.05	.04	.02
78	Tim Belcher	.06	.05	.02
79	Cris Carpenter	.06	.05	.02
80	Checklist	.05	.04	.02
81	Steve Avery	.25	.20	.10
82	Chris James	.05	.04	.02
83	Brian Harper	.06	.05	.02
84	Charlie Leibrandt	.06	.05	.02
85	Mickey Tettleton	.08	.06	.03
86	Pete O'Brien	.06	.05	.02
87	Danny Darwin	.05	.04	.02
88	Bob Walk	.05	.04	.02
89	Jeff Reardon	.08	.06	.03
90	Bobby Rose	.08	.06	.03
91	Danny Jackson	.06	.05	.02
92	John Morris	.05	.04	.02
93	Bud Black	.06	.05	.02
94	Tommy Greene (Highlight)	.10	.08	.04
95	Rick Aguilera	.08	.06	.03
96	Gary Gaetti	.08	.06	.03
97	David Cone	.08	.06	.03
98	John Olerud	.20	.15	.08
99	Joel Skinner	.05	.04	.02
100	Jay Bell	.08	.06	.03
101	Bob Milacki	.05	.04	.02
102	Norm Charlton	.06	.05	.02
103	Chuck Crim	.05	.04	.02
104	Terry Steinbach	.06	.05	.02
105	Juan Samuel	.08	.06	.03
106	Steve Howe	.06	.05	.02
107	Rafael Belliard	.05	.04	.02
108	Joey Cora	.05	.04	.02
109	Tommy Greene	.08	.06	.03
110	Gregg Olson	.08	.06	.03
111	Frank Tanana	.06	.05	.02

		MT	NR MT	EX
112	Lee Smith	.08	.06	.03
113	Greg Harris	.05	.04	.02
114	Dwayne Henry	.05	.04	.02
115	Chili Davis	.08	.06	.03
116	Kent Mercker	.08	.06	.03
117	Brian Barnes	.08	.06	.03
118	Rich DeLucia	.06	.05	.02
119	Andre Dawson	.15	.11	.06
120	Carlos Baerga	.08	.06	.03
121	Mike LaValliere	.06	.05	.02
122	Jeff Gray	.06	.05	.02
123	Bruce Hurst	.08	.06	.03
124	Alvin Davis	.08	.06	.03
125	John Candelaria	.06	.05	.02
126	Matt Nokes	.08	.06	.03
127	George Bell	.10	.08	.04
128	Bret Saberhagen	.10	.08	.04
129	Jeff Russell	.08	.06	.03
130	Jim Abbott	.15	.11	.06
131	Bill Gullickson	.06	.05	.02
132	Todd Zeile	.15	.11	.06
133	Dave Winfield	.10	.08	.04
134	Wally Whitehurst	.06	.05	.02
135	Matt Williams	.15	.11	.06
136	Tom Browning	.08	.06	.03
137	Marquis Grissom	.15	.11	.06
138	Erik Hanson	.10	.08	.04
139	Rob Dibble	.08	.06	.03
140	Don August	.05	.04	.02
141	Tom Henke	.08	.06	.03
142	Dan Pasqua	.06	.05	.02
143	George Brett	.15	.11	.06
144	Jerald Clark	.06	.05	.02
145	Robin Ventura	.25	.20	.10
146	Dale Murphy	.10	.08	.04
147	Dennis Eckersley	.10	.08	.04
148	Eric Yelding	.05	.04	.02
149	Mario Diaz	.05	.04	.02
150	Casey Candaele	.05	.04	.02
151	Steve Olin	.06	.05	.02
152	Luis Salazar	.05	.04	.02
153	Kevin Maas	.20	.15	.08
154	Nolan Ryan (Highlight)	.60	.45	.25
155	Barry Jones	.05	.04	.02
156	Chris Hoiles	.15	.11	.06
157	Bobby Ojeda	.06	.05	.02
158	Pedro Guerrero	.08	.06	.03
159	Paul Assenmacher	.05	.04	.02
160	Checklist	.05	.04	.02
161	Mike Macfarlane	.06	.05	.02
162	Craig Lefferts	.06	.05	.02
163	*Brian Hunter*	.70	.50	.30
164	Alan Trammell	.10	.08	.04
165	Ken Griffey,Jr.	.80	.60	.30
166	Lance Parrish	.08	.06	.03
167	Brian Downing	.05	.04	.02
168	John Barfield	.06	.05	.02
169	Jack Clark	.08	.06	.03
170	Chris Nabholz	.06	.05	.02
171	Tim Teufel	.05	.04	.02
172	Chris Hammond	.08	.06	.03
173	Robin Yount	.20	.15	.08
174	Dave Righetti	.08	.04	.02
175	Joe Girardi	.06	.05	.02
176	Mike Boddicker	.06	.05	.02
177	Dean Palmer	.25	.20	.10
178	Greg Hibbard	.06	.05	.02
179	Randy Ready	.05	.04	.02
180	Devon White	.08	.06	.03
181	Mark Eichhorn	.05	.04	.02
182	Mike Felder	.05	.04	.02
183	Joe Klink	.05	.04	.02
184	Steve Bedrosian	.06	.05	.02
185	Barry Larkin	.15	.11	.06
186	John Franco	.08	.06	.03
187	*Ed Sprague*	.25	.20	.10
188	Mark Portugal	.05	.04	.02
189	Jose Lind	.05	.04	.02
190	Bob Welch	.08	.06	.03
191	Alex Fernandez	.25	.20	.10
192	Gary Sheffield	.15	.11	.06
193	Rickey Henderson	.20	.15	.08
194	Rod Nichols	.05	.04	.02
195	*Scott Kamieniecki*	.15	.11	.06
196	Mike Flanagan	.05	.04	.02
197	Steve Finley	.08	.06	.03
198	Darren Daulton	.06	.05	.02
199	Leo Gomez	.15	.11	.06
200	Mike Morgan	.06	.05	.02
201	Bob Tewksbury	.05	.04	.02
202	Sid Bream	.08	.06	.03

		MT	NR MT	EX
203	Sandy Alomar	.15	.11	.06
204	Greg Gagne	.05	.04	.02
205	Juan Berenguer	.05	.04	.02
206	Cecil Fielder	.25	.20	.10
207	Randy Johnson	.08	.06	.03
208	Tony Pena	.06	.05	.02
209	Doug Drabek	.10	.08	.04
210	Wade Boggs	.20	.15	.08
211	Bryan Harvey	.08	.06	.03
212	Jose Vizcaino	.06	.05	.02
213	*Alonzo Powell*(FC)	.15	.11	.06
214	Will Clark	.30	.25	.12
215	Rickey Henderson (Highlight)	.30	.25	.12
216	Jack Morris	.08	.06	.03
217	Junior Felix	.06	.05	.02
218	Vince Coleman	.08	.06	.03
219	Jimmy Key	.08	.06	.03
220	Alex Cole	.08	.06	.03
221	Bill Landrum	.06	.05	.02
222	Randy Milligan	.08	.06	.03
223	Jose Rijo	.08	.06	.03
224	Greg Vaughn	.10	.08	.04
225	Dave Stewart	.08	.06	.03
226	Lenny Harris	.06	.05	.02
227	Scott Sanderson	.06	.05	.02
228	Jeff Blauser	.06	.05	.02
229	Ozzie Guillen	.08	.06	.03
230	John Kruk	.08	.06	.03
231	Bob Melvin	.05	.04	.02
232	Milt Cuyler	.15	.11	.06
233	Felix Jose	.15	.11	.06
234	Ellis Burks	.10	.08	.04
235	Pete Harnisch	.06	.05	.02
236	Kevin Tapani	.08	.06	.03
237	Terry Pendleton	.08	.06	.03
238	Mark Gardner	.08	.06	.03
239	Harold Reynolds	.06	.05	.02
240	Checklist	.05	.04	.02
241	Mike Harkey	.06	.05	.02
242	Felix Fermin	.05	.04	.02
243	Barry Bonds	.20	.15	.08
244	Roger Clemens	.25	.20	.10
245	Dennis Rasmussen	.05	.04	.02
246	Jose DeLeon	.06	.05	.02
247	Orel Hershiser	.10	.08	.04
248	Mel Hall	.06	.05	.02
249	*Rick Wilkins*	.25	.20	.10
250	Tom Gordon	.08	.06	.03
251	Kevin Reimer	.06	.05	.02
252	Luis Polonia	.06	.05	.02
253	Mike Henneman	.06	.05	.02
254	Tom Pagnozzi	.06	.05	.02
255	Chuck Finley	.10	.08	.04
256	Mackey Sasser	.05	.04	.02
257	John Burkett	.06	.05	.02
258	Hal Morris	.15	.11	.06
259	Larry Walker	.10	.08	.04
260	Billy Swift	.06	.05	.02
261	Joe Oliver	.06	.05	.02
262	Julio Machado	.05	.04	.02
263	Todd Stottlemyre	.08	.06	.03
264	Matt Merullo	.05	.04	.02
265	Brent Mayne	.08	.06	.03
266	Thomas Howard	.06	.05	.02
267	Lance Johnson	.06	.05	.02
268	Terry Mulholland	.08	.06	.03
269	Rick Honeycutt	.05	.04	.02
270	Luis Gonzalez	.25	.20	.10
271	Jose Guzman	.06	.05	.02
272	Jimmy Jones	.05	.04	.02
273	Mark Lewis	.20	.15	.08
274	Rene Gonzales	.05	.04	.02
275	*Jeff Johnson*	.25	.20	.10
276	Dennis Martinez (Highlight)	.10	.08	.04
277	Delino DeShields	.08	.06	.03
278	Sam Horn	.05	.04	.02
279	Kevin Gross	.06	.05	.02
280	Jose Oquendo	.05	.04	.02
281	Mark Grace	.15	.11	.06
282	Mark Gubicza	.08	.06	.03
283	Fred McGriff	.10	.08	.04
284	Ron Gant	.15	.11	.06
285	Lou Whitaker	.08	.06	.03
286	Edgar Martinez	.08	.06	.03
287	Ron Tingley	.05	.04	.02
288	Kevin McReynolds	.08	.06	.03
289	*Ivan Rodriguez*	1.75	1.25	.70
290	Mike Gardiner	.08	.06	.03
291	*Chris Haney*	.20	.15	.08
292	Darrin Jackson	.06	.05	.02
293	Bill Doran	.08	.06	.03

		MT	NR MT	EX
294	Ted Higuera	.08	.06	.03
295	Jeff Brantley	.08	.06	.03
296	Les Lancaster	.05	.04	.02
297	Jim Eisenreich	.05	.04	.02
298	Ruben Sierra	.20	.15	.08
299	Scott Radinsky	.08	.06	.03
300	Jose DeJesus	.08	.06	.03
301	*Mike Timlin*	.20	.15	.08
302	Luis Sojo	.08	.06	.03
303	Kelly Downs	.05	.04	.02
304	Scott Bankhead	.06	.05	.02
305	Pedro Munoz	.20	.15	.08
306	Scott Scudder	.06	.05	.02
307	Kevin Elster	.06	.05	.02
308	Duane Ward	.06	.05	.02
309	*Darryl Kile*	.15	.11	.06
310	Orlando Merced	.35	.25	.14
311	Dave Henderson	.10	.08	.04
312	Tim Raines	.10	.08	.04
313	Mark Lee(FC)	.06	.05	.02
314	Mike Gallego	.06	.05	.02
315	Charles Nagy	.10	.08	.04
316	Jesse Barfield	.08	.06	.03
317	Todd Frohwirth	.05	.04	.02
318	Al Osuna	.06	.05	.02
319	Darrin Fletcher	.06	.05	.02
320	Checklist	.05	.04	.02
321	David Segui	.10	.08	.04
322	Stan Javier	.05	.04	.02
323	Bryn Smith	.05	.04	.02
324	Jeff Treadway	.06	.05	.02
325	Mark Whiten	.15	.11	.06
326	Kent Hrbek	.08	.06	.03
327	David Justice	.35	.25	.14
328	Tony Phillips	.06	.05	.02
329	Rob Murphy	.05	.04	.02
330	Kevin Morton	.10	.08	.04
331	John Smiley	.08	.06	.03
332	Luis Rivera	.05	.04	.02
333	Wally Joyner	.15	.11	.06
334	*Heathcliff Slocumb*	.15	.11	.06
335	Rick Cerone	.05	.04	.02
336	*Mike Remlinger*(FC)	.15	.11	.06
337	Mike Moore	.06	.05	.02
338	Lloyd McClendon	.05	.04	.02
339	Al Newman	.05	.04	.02
340	Kirk McCaskill	.08	.06	.03
341	Howard Johnson	.15	.11	.06
342	Greg Myers	.05	.04	.02
343	Kal Daniels	.08	.06	.03
344	Bernie Williams	.30	.25	.12
345	Shane Mack	.10	.08	.04
346	Gary Thurman	.05	.04	.02
347	Dante Bichette	.06	.05	.02
348	Mark McGwire	.15	.11	.06
349	Travis Fryman	.25	.20	.10
350	Ray Lankford	.20	.15	.08
351	Mike Jeffcoat	.05	.04	.02
352	Jack McDowell	.10	.08	.04
353	Mitch Williams	.08	.06	.03
354	Mike Devereaux	.06	.05	.02
355	Andre Galarraga	.06	.05	.02
356	Henry Cotto	.05	.04	.02
357	Scott Bailes	.05	.04	.02
358	*Jeff Bagwell*	1.75	1.25	.70
359	Scott Leius	.08	.06	.03
360	Zane Smith	.06	.05	.02
361	Bill Pecota	.06	.05	.02
362	Tony Fernandez	.08	.06	.03
363	Glenn Braggs	.06	.05	.02
364	Bill Spiers	.06	.05	.02
365	Vicente Palacios	.05	.04	.02
366	Tim Burke	.06	.05	.02
367	Randy Tomlin	.06	.05	.02
368	Kenny Rogers	.06	.05	.02
369	Brett Butler	.08	.06	.03
370	Pat Kelly	.20	.15	.08
371	Bip Roberts	.06	.05	.02
372	Gregg Jefferies	.15	.11	.06
373	Kevin Bass	.06	.05	.02
374	Ron Karkovice	.05	.04	.02
375	Paul Gibson	.05	.04	.02
376	Bernard Gilkey	.10	.08	.04
377	Dave Gallagher	.06	.05	.02
378	Bill Wegman	.06	.05	.02
379	Pat Borders	.06	.05	.02
380	Ed Whitson	.06	.05	.02
381	Gilberto Reyes	.08	.06	.03
382	Russ Swan	.08	.06	.03
383	Andy Van Slyke	.10	.08	.04
384	Wes Chamberlain	.20	.15	.08
385	Steve Chitren	.08	.06	.03
386	Greg Olson	.06	.05	.02
387	Brian McRae	.20	.15	.08
388	Rich Rodriguez	.06	.05	.02
389	Steve Decker	.15	.11	.06
390	Chuck Knoblauch	.15	.11	.06
391	Bobby Witt	.06	.05	.02
392	Eddie Murray	.10	.08	.04
393	Juan Gonzalez	.25	.20	.10
394	Scott Ruskin	.05	.04	.02
395	Jay Howell	.06	.05	.02
396	Checklist	.05	.04	.02

1986 Dorman's Cheese

Found in specially-marked packages of Dorman's American Cheese Singles, the Dorman's set consists of ten two-card panels of baseball superstars. Labeled as a "Super Star Limited Edition" set, the panels measure 1-1/2" by 2" each and have a perforation line in the center. The fronts contain a color photo along with the Dorman's logo and the player's name, team and position. Due to a lack of proper licensing, all team insignias have been airbrushed from the players' caps. The backs of the cards contain brief player statistics.

		MT	NR MT	EX
Complete Panel Set:		35.00	26.00	14.00
Complete Singles Set:		20.00	15.00	8.00
Common Panel:		1.25	.90	.50
Common Single Player:		.20	.15	.08
()	Panel	2.00	1.50	.80
(1)	George Brett	.50	.40	.20
(2)	Jack Morris	.20	.15	.08
()	Panel	2.00	1.50	.80
(3)	Gary Carter	.30	.25	.12
(4)	Cal Ripken	.40	.30	.15
()	Panel	2.00	1.50	.80
(5)	Dwight Gooden	.60	.45	.25
(6)	Kent Hrbek	.20	.15	.08
()	Panel	3.00	1.50	.90
(7)	Rickey Henderson	.60	.45	.25
(8)	Mike Schmidt	.80	.60	.30
()	Panel	2.00	1.50	.80
(9)	Keith Hernandez	.30	.25	.12
(10)	Dale Murphy	.30	.25	.12
()	Panel	2.00	1.50	.80
(11)	Reggie Jackson	.40	.30	.15
(12)	Eddie Murray	.40	.30	.15
()	Panel	4.00	3.00	1.50
(13)	Don Mattingly	1.00	.70	.40
(14)	Ryne Sandberg	.60	.45	.25
()	Panel	1.25	.90	.50
(15)	Willie McGee	.20	.15	.08
(16)	Robin Yount	.30	.25	.12
()	Panel	2.25	1.75	.90
(17)	Rick Sutcliff (Sutcliffe)	.20	.15	.08
(18)	Wade Boggs	.80	.60	.30
()	Panel	1.50	1.25	.60
(19)	Dave Winfield	.40	.30	.15
(20)	Jim Rice	.20	.15	.10

NOTE: A card number in parentheses ( ) indicates the set is unnumbered.

1950 Drake's

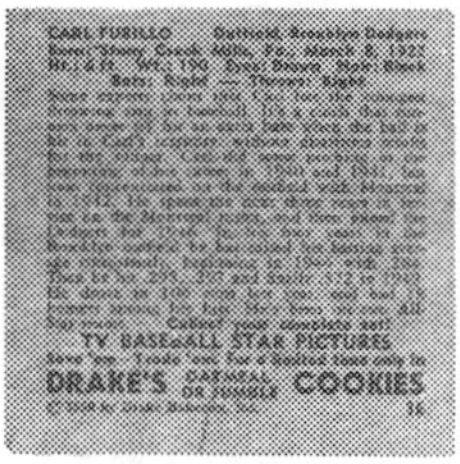

Entitled "TV Baseball Series", the 1950 Drake's Bakeries set pictures 36 different players on a television screen format. The cards, which measure 2-1/2" by 2-1/2", contain black and white photos surrounded by a black border. The card backs carry a player biography plus an advertisement advising collectors to look for the cards in packages of Oatmeal or Jumble cookies. The ACC designation for the set is D358.

		NR MT	EX	VG
Complete Set:		5000.00	3000.00	1500.
Common Player:		50.00	25.00	15.00
1	Elwin "Preacher" Roe	100.00	50.00	30.00
2	Clint Hartung	50.00	25.00	15.00
3	Earl Torgeson	50.00	25.00	15.00
4	Leland "Lou" Brissie	50.00	25.00	15.00
5	Edwin "Duke" Snider	350.00	175.00	100.00
6	Roy Campanella	400.00	200.00	125.00
7	Sheldon "Available" Jones	50.00	25.00	15.00
8	Carroll "Whitey" Lockman	50.00	25.00	15.00
9	Bobby Thomson	80.00	40.00	25.00
10	Dick Sisler	50.00	25.00	15.00
11	Gil Hodges	200.00	100.00	60.00
12	Eddie Waitkus	50.00	25.00	15.00
13	Bobby Doerr	150.00	75.00	45.00
14	Warren Spahn	250.00	125.00	75.00
15	John "Buddy" Kerr	50.00	25.00	15.00
16	Sid Gordon	50.00	25.00	15.00
17	Willard Marshall	50.00	25.00	15.00
18	Carl Furillo	90.00	45.00	25.00
19	Harold "Pee Wee" Reese	300.00	150.00	90.00
20	Alvin Dark	70.00	35.00	20.00
21	Del Ennis	50.00	25.00	15.00
22	Ed Stanky	70.00	35.00	20.00
23	Tommy "Old Reliable" Henrich	90.00	45.00	25.00
24	Larry "Yogi" Berra	400.00	200.00	125.00
25	Phil "Scooter" Rizzuto	275.00	150.00	100.00
26	Jerry Coleman	70.00	35.00	20.00
27	Joe Page	70.00	35.00	20.00
28	Allie Reynolds	90.00	45.00	25.00
29	Ray Scarborough	50.00	25.00	15.00
30	George "Birdie" Tebbetts	50.00	25.00	15.00
31	Maurice "Lefty" McDermott	50.00	25.00	15.00
32	Johnny Pesky	70.00	35.00	20.00
33	Dom "Little Professor" DiMaggio	80.00	40.00	25.00
34	Vern "Junior" Stephens	50.00	25.00	15.00
35	Bob Elliott	50.00	25.00	15.00
36	Enos "Country" Slaughter	250.00	125.00	75.00

1981 Drake's

Producing their first baseball card set since 1950, Drake Bakeries, in conjunction with Topps, issued a 33-card set entitled "Big Hitters." The cards, which are the standard 2-1/2" by 3-1/2" in size, feature 19 American League and 14 National League sluggers. Full-color photos, containing a facsimile autograph, are positioned in red frames for A.L. players and blue frames for N.L. hitters. The player's name, team, position, and the Drake's logo are also included on the card fronts. The card backs, which are similar to

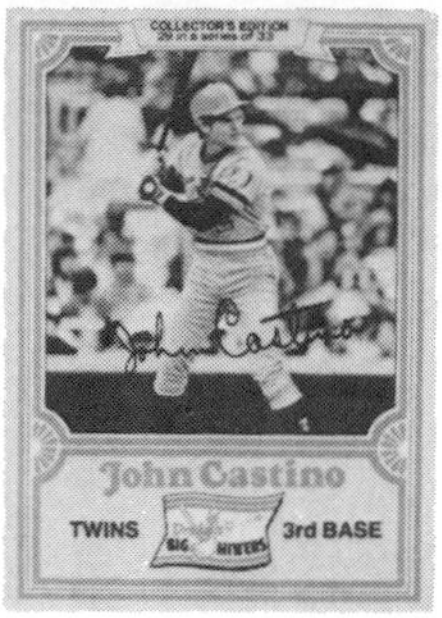

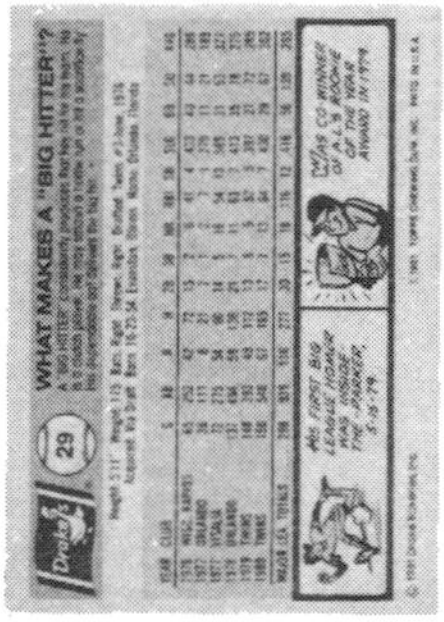

the regular 1981 Topps issue, contain the card number (1-33), statistical and biographical information, and the Drake's logo.

		MT	NR MT	EX
Complete Set:		8.00	6.00	3.25
Common Player:		.12	.09	.05
1	Carl Yastrzemski	.70	.50	.30
2	Rod Carew	.60	.45	.25
3	Pete Rose	1.00	.70	.40
4	Dave Parker	.25	.20	.10
5	George Brett	.70	.50	.30
6	Eddie Murray	.60	.45	.25
7	Mike Schmidt	1.00	.70	.40
8	Jim Rice	.45	.35	.20
9	Fred Lynn	.25	.20	.10
10	Reggie Jackson	.60	.45	.25
11	Steve Garvey	.45	.35	.20
12	Ken Singleton	.12	.09	.05
13	Bill Buckner	.12	.09	.05
14	Dave Winfield	.60	.45	.25
15	Jack Clark	.30	.25	.12
16	Cecil Cooper	.20	.15	.08
17	Bob Horner	.20	.15	.08
18	George Foster	.20	.15	.08
19	Dave Kingman	.20	.15	.08
20	Cesar Cedeno	.12	.09	.05
21	Joe Charboneau	.12	.09	.05
22	George Hendrick	.12	.09	.05
23	Gary Carter	.45	.35	.20
24	Al Oliver	.20	.15	.08
25	Bruce Bochte	.12	.09	.05
26	Jerry Mumphrey	.12	.09	.05
27	Steve Kemp	.12	.09	.05
28	Bob Watson	.12	.09	.05
29	John Castino	.12	.09	.05
30	Tony Armas	.12	.09	.05
31	John Mayberry	.12	.09	.05
32	Carlton Fisk	.30	.25	.12
33	Lee Mazzilli	.12	.09	.05

1982 Drake's

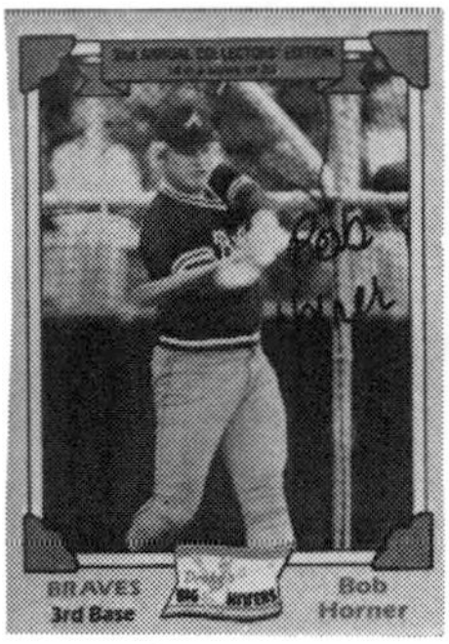

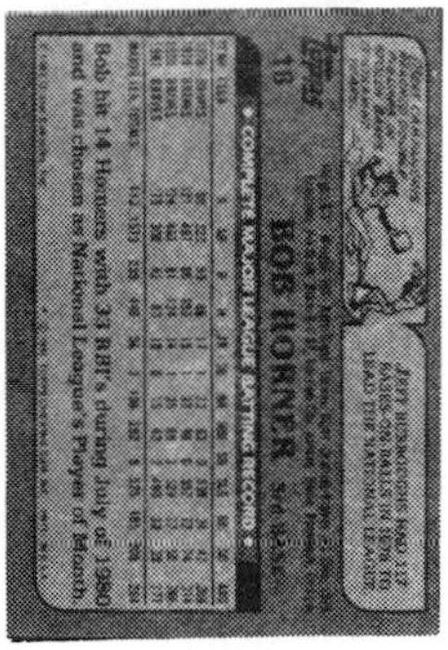

Drake Bakeries produced, in conjunction with Topps, a "2nd Annual Collectors' Edition" in 1982. Thirty-three standard-size cards (2-1/2" by 3-1/2") make up the set. Like the previous year, the set is entitled "Big Hitters" and is comprised of 19

American League players and 14 from the National League. The card fronts have a mounted photo appearance and contain a facsimile autograph. The player's name, team, position, and the Drake's logo also are located on the fronts. The card backs, other than being numbered 1-33 and containing a Drake's copyright line, are identical to the regular 1982 Topps issue.

		MT	NR MT	EX
Complete Set:		9.00	6.75	3.50
Common Player:		.12	.09	.05
1	Tony Armas	.12	.09	.05
2	Buddy Bell	.20	.15	.08
3	Johnny Bench	.50	.40	.20
4	George Brett	.70	.50	.30
5	Bill Buckner	.12	.09	.05
6	Rod Carew	.50	.40	.20
7	Gary Carter	.45	.35	.20
8	Jack Clark	.30	.25	.12
9	Cecil Cooper	.20	.15	.08
10	Jose Cruz	.12	.09	.05
11	Dwight Evans	.20	.15	.08
12	Carlton Fisk	.30	.25	.12
13	George Foster	.20	.15	.08
14	Steve Garvey	.45	.35	.20
15	Kirk Gibson	.40	.30	.15
16	Mike Hargrove	.12	.09	.05
17	George Hendrick	.12	.09	.05
18	Bob Horner	.20	.15	.08
19	Reggie Jackson	.80	.60	.30
20	Terry Kennedy	.12	.09	.05
21	Dave Kingman	.20	.15	.08
22	Greg Luzinski	.20	.15	.08
23	Bill Madlock	.20	.15	.08
24	John Mayberry	.12	.09	.05
25	Eddie Murray	.50	.40	.20
26	Graig Nettles	.20	.15	.08
27	Jim Rice	.45	.35	.20
28	Pete Rose	1.00	.70	.40
29	Mike Schmidt	1.00	.70	.40
30	Ken Singleton	.12	.09	.05
31	Dave Winfield	.50	.40	.20
32	Butch Wynegar	.12	.09	.05
33	Richie Zisk	.12	.09	.05

1983 Drake's

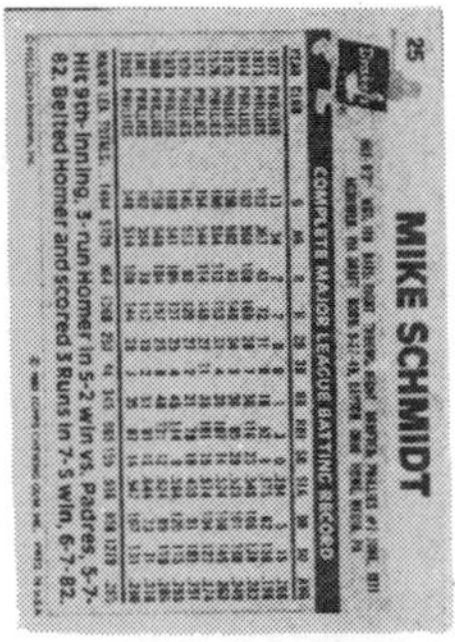

Seventeen American League and 16 National League "Big Hitters" make up the 33-card "3rd Annual Collectors' Edition" set issued by Drake Bakeries in 1983. The Topps-produced set contains 33 cards which measure 2-1/2" by 3-1/2" in size. The card fronts are somewhat similar in design to the previous year's set. The backs are identical to the 1983 Topps regular issue except for being numbered 1-33 and containing a Drake's logo and copyright line.

		MT	NR MT	EX
Complete Set:		7.00	5.25	2.75
Common Player:		.12	.09	.05
1	Don Baylor	.20	.15	.08
2	Bill Buckner	.12	.09	.05
3	Rod Carew	.50	.40	.20
4	Gary Carter	.45	.35	.20
5	Jack Clark	.25	.20	.10
6	Cecil Cooper	.20	.15	.08
7	Dwight Evans	.20	.15	.08
8	George Foster	.20	.15	.08
9	Pedro Guerrero	.25	.20	.10
10	George Hendrick	.12	.09	.05
11	Bob Horner	.20	.15	.08
12	Reggie Jackson	.60	.45	.25
13	Steve Kemp	.12	.09	.05
14	Dave Kingman	.20	.15	.08
15	Bill Madlock	.20	.15	.08
16	Gary Matthews	.12	.09	.05
17	Hal McRae	.12	.09	.05
18	Dale Murphy	.40	.30	.15
19	Eddie Murray	.50	.40	.20
20	Ben Oglivie	.12	.09	.05
21	Al Oliver	.20	.15	.08
22	Jim Rice	.45	.35	.20
23	Cal Ripken	.60	.45	.25
24	Pete Rose	1.00	.70	.40
25	Mike Schmidt	1.00	.70	.40
26	Ken Singleton	.12	.09	.05
27	Gorman Thomas	.12	.09	.05
28	Jason Thompson	.12	.09	.05
29	Mookie Wilson	.10	.08	.04
30	Willie Wilson	.20	.15	.08
31	Dave Winfield	.50	.40	.20
32	Carl Yastrzemski	.40	.30	.15
33	Robin Yount	.40	.30	.15

1984 Drake's

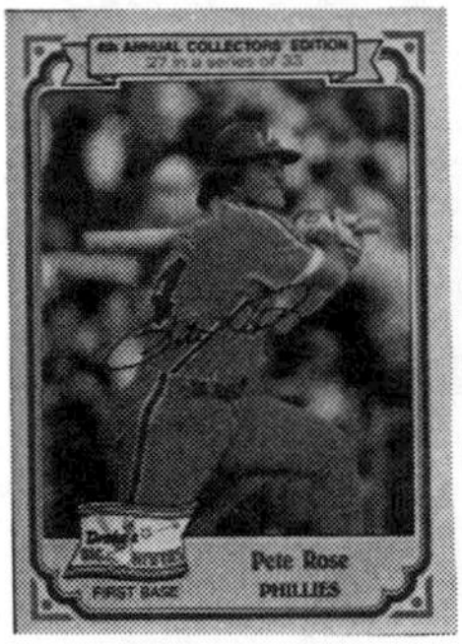

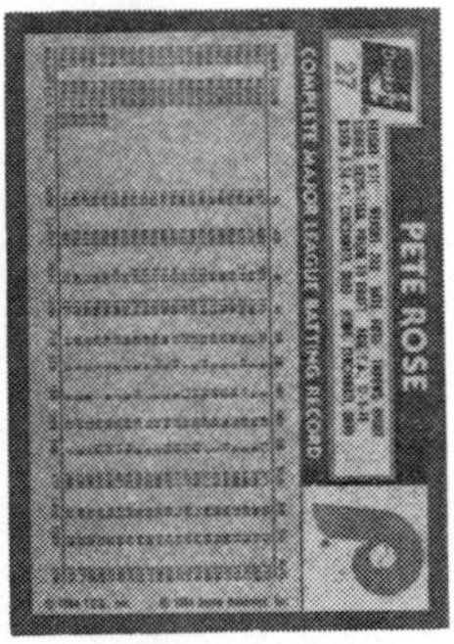

For the fourth year in a row, Drake Bakeries issued a 33-card "Big Hitters" set. The 1984 edition, produced again by Topps, includes 17 National League players and 16 from the American League. As in all previous years, the card fronts feature the player in a batting pose. The backs are identical to the 1984 Topps regular issue except for being numbered 1-33 and carrying the Drake's logo and copyright line. The cards are the standard size 2-1/2" by 3-1/2".

		MT	NR MT	EX
Complete Set:		9.00	6.75	3.50
Complete Set:		.12	.09	.05
1	Don Baylor	.20	.15	.08
2	Wade Boggs	1.25	.90	.50
3	George Brett	.70	.50	.30
4	Bill Buckner	.12	.09	.05
5	Rod Carew	.60	.45	.25
6	Gary Carter	.45	.35	.20
7	Ron Cey	.12	.09	.05
8	Cecil Cooper	.20	.15	.08
9	Andre Dawson	.35	.25	.14
10	Steve Garvey	.45	.35	.20
11	Pedro Guerrero	.25	.20	.10
12	George Hendrick	.12	.09	.05
13	Keith Hernandez	.40	.30	.15
14	Bob Horner	.20	.15	.08
15	Reggie Jackson	.60	.45	.25
16	Steve Kemp	.12	.09	.05
17	Ron Kittle	.20	.15	.08
18	Greg Luzinski	.20	.15	.08
19	Fred Lynn	.20	.15	.08
20	Bill Madlock	.20	.15	.08
21	Gary Matthews	.12	.09	.05

		MT	NR MT	EX
22	Dale Murphy	.70	.50	.30
23	Eddie Murray	.60	.45	.25
24	Al Oliver	.20	.15	.08
25	Jim Rice	.45	.35	.20
26	Cal Ripken	.60	.45	.25
27	Pete Rose	1.00	.70	.40
28	Mike Schmidt	1.00	.70	.40
29	Darryl Strawberry	1.25	.90	.50
30	Alan Trammell	.30	.25	.12
31	Mookie Wilson	.12	.09	.05
32	Dave Winfield	.60	.45	.25
33	Robin Yount	.40	.30	.15

1985 Drake's

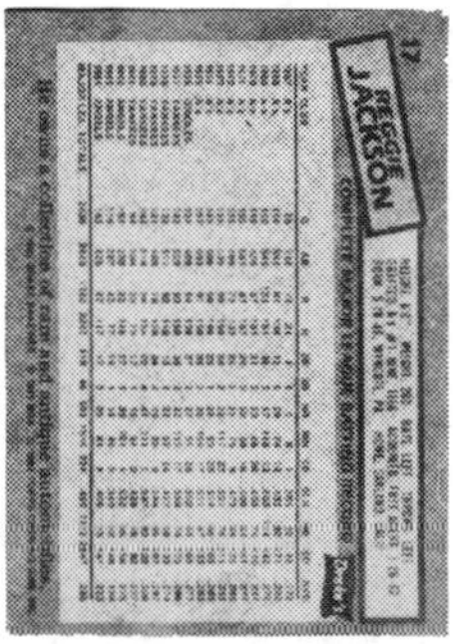

The "5th Annual Collectors' Edition" set produced by Topps for Drake Bakeries consists of 33 "Big Hitters" and 11 "Super Pitchers." The new "Super Pitchers" feature increased the set's size from the usual 33 cards to 44. The cards, which measure 2-1/2" by 3-1/2", show the player in either a batting or pitching pose. The backs differ only from the regular 1985 Topps issue in that they are numbered 1-44 and carry the Drake's logo.

		MT	NR MT	EX
Complete Set:		12.00	9.00	4.75
Commmon Player:		.12	.09	.05
1	Tony Armas	.12	.09	.05
2	Harold Baines	.20	.15	.08
3	Don Baylor	.20	.15	.08
4	George Brett	.70	.50	.30
5	Gary Carter	.45	.35	.20
6	Ron Cey	.12	.09	.05
7	Jose Cruz	.12	.09	.05
8	Alvin Davis	.25	.20	.10
9	Chili Davis	.12	.09	.05
10	Dwight Evans	.20	.15	.08
11	Steve Garvey	.45	.35	.20
12	Kirk Gibson	.35	.25	.14
13	Pedro Guerrero	.25	.20	.10
14	Tony Gwynn	.60	.45	.25
15	Keith Hernandez	.40	.30	.15
16	Kent Hrbek	.35	.25	.14
17	Reggie Jackson	.60	.45	.25
18	Gary Matthews	.12	.09	.05
19	Don Mattingly	1.50	1.25	.60
20	Dale Murphy	.70	.50	.30
21	Eddie Murray	.45	.35	.20
22	Dave Parker	.20	.15	.08
23	Lance Parrish	.25	.20	.10
24	Tim Raines	.45	.35	.20
25	Jim Rice	.45	.35	.20
26	Cal Ripken	.60	.45	.25
27	Juan Samuel	.25	.20	.10
28	Ryne Sandberg	.40	.30	.15
29	Mike Schmidt	1.00	.70	.40
30	Darryl Strawberry	.90	.70	.35
31	Alan Trammell	.30	.25	.12
32	Dave Winfield	.50	.40	.20
33	Robin Yount	.40	.30	.15
34	Mike Boddicker	.12	.09	.05
35	Steve Carlton	.40	.30	.15
36	Dwight Gooden	1.00	.70	.40
37	Willie Hernandez	.12	.09	.05
38	Mark Langston	.20	.15	.08
39	Dan Quisenberry	.12	.09	.05
40	Dave Righetti	.20	.15	.08
41	Tom Seaver	.40	.30	.15
42	Bob Stanley	.12	.09	.05
43	Rick Sutcliffe	.20	.15	.08
44	Bruce Sutter	.20	.15	.08

1986 Drake's

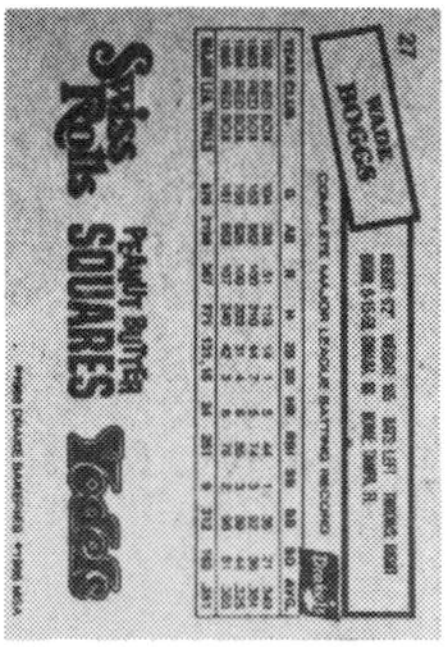

For the sixth year in a row, Drake Bakeries issued a baseball card set. Produced for Drake's by Topps in the past, the 1986 set was not and was available only by buying the actual products the cards were printed on. The cards, which measure 2-1/2" by 3-1/2", were issued in either two-, three-, or four-card panels. Fourteen panels, consisting of 37 different players, comprise the set. The players who make up the set are tabbed as either "Big Hitters" or "Super Pitchers." Logos of various Drake's products can be found on the panel backs. The value of the set is higher when collected in either panel or complete box form.

		MT	NR MT	EX
Complete Panel Set:		45.00	34.00	18.00
Complete Singles Set:		35.00	26.00	14.00
Common Panel:		1.75	1.25	.70
Common Single Player:		.20	.15	.08
	Panel	1.75	1.25	.70
1	Gary Carter	.50	.40	.20
2	Dwight Evans	.25	.20	.10
	Panel	2.00	1.50	.80
3	Reggie Jackson	.60	.45	.25
4	Dave Parker	.25	.20	.10
	Panel	2.00	1.50	.80
5	Rickey Henderson	1.00	.70	.40
6	Pedro Guerrero	.30	.25	.12
	Panel	5.00	3.75	2.00
7	Don Mattingly	2.00	1.50	.80
8	Mike Marshall	.25	.20	.10
9	Keith Moreland	.20	.15	.08
	Panel	2.00	1.50	.80
10	Keith Hernandez	.40	.30	.15
11	Cal Ripken	.60	.45	.25
	Panel	2.25	1.75	.90
12	Dale Murphy	.60	.45	.25
13	Jim Rice	.40	.30	.15
	Panel	2.25	1.75	.90
14	George Brett	.60	.45	.25
15	Tim Raines	.50	.40	.20
	Panel	2.00	1.50	.80
16	Darryl Strawberry	.80	.60	.30
17	Bill Buckner	.20	.15	.08
	Panel	2.75	2.00	1.00
18	Dave Winfield	.50	.40	.20
19	Ryne Sandberg	.40	.30	.15
20	Steve Balboni	.20	.15	.08
21	Tom Herr	.25	.20	.10
	Panel	3.75	2.75	1.50
22	Pete Rose	.90	.70	.35
23	Willie McGee	.25	.20	.10
24	Harold Baines	.25	.20	.10
25	Eddie Murray	.50	.40	.20
	Panel	4.00	3.00	1.50
26	Mike Schmidt	1.00	.70	.40
27	Wade Boggs	1.25	.90	.50
28	Kirk Gibson	.35	.25	.14

		MT	NR MT	EX
	Panel	2.00	1.50	.80
29	Bret Saberhagen	.35	.25	.14
30	John Tudor	.20	.15	.08
31	Orel Hershiser	.40	.30	.15
	Panel	2.00	1.50	.80
32	Ron Guidry	.25	.20	.10
33	Nolan Ryan	1.00	.70	.40
34	Dave Stieb	.25	.20	.10
	Panel	2.75	2.00	1.00
35	Dwight Gooden	.80	.60	.30
36	Fernando Valenzuela	.35	.25	.14
37	Tom Browning	.25	.20	.10

1987 Drake's

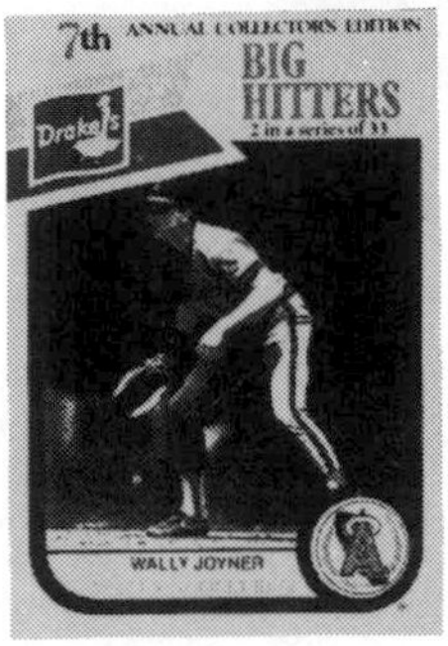

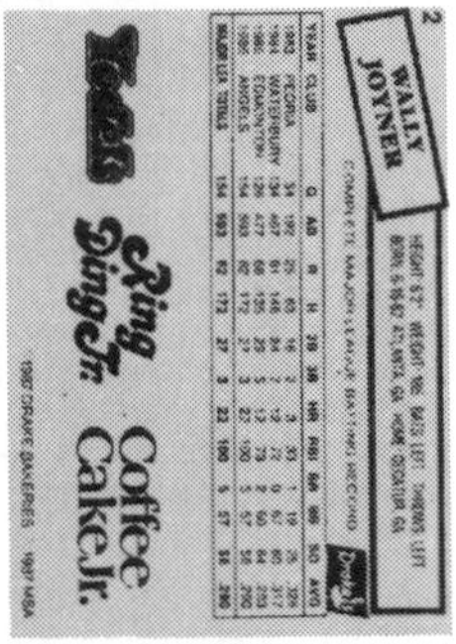

For the seventh consecutive season, Drake Bakeries produced a baseball card set. The cards, which measure 2-1/2" by 3-1/2", were included in either two-, three-, or four-card panels on boxes of various Drake's products distributed in the eastern United States. The set is comprised of 33 cards, with 25 players branded as "Big Hitters" and 8 as "Super Pitchers". The card fronts carry a full-color photo and the Drake's logo surrounded by a brown and yellow border. The backs contain the player's complete major league record.

	MT	NR MT	EX
Complete Panel Set:	45.00	34.00	18.00
Complete Singles Set:	30.00	22.00	12.00
Common Panel:	1.75	1.25	.70
Common Single Player:	.20	.15	.08

		MT	NR MT	EX
	Panel	4.00	3.00	1.50
1	Darryl Strawberry	.80	.60	.30
2	Wally Joyner	1.25	.90	.50
	Panel	3.75	2.75	1.50
3	Von Hayes	.25	.20	.10
4	Jose Canseco	1.75	1.25	.70
	Panel	2.00	1.50	.80
5	Dave Winfield	.50	.40	.20
6	Cal Ripken	.60	.45	.25
	Panel	4.50	3.50	1.75
7	Keith Moreland	.20	.15	.08
8	Don Mattingly	2.00	1.50	.80
9	Willie McGee	.25	.20	.10
	Panel	2.00	1.50	.80
10	Keith Hernandez	.40	.30	.15
11	Tony Gwynn	.60	.45	.25
	Panel	4.25	3.25	1.75
12	Rickey Henderson	1.00	.70	.40
13	Dale Murphy	.60	.45	.25
14	George Brett	.60	.45	.25
15	Jim Rice	.40	.30	.15
	Panel	4.00	3.00	1.50
16	Wade Boggs	1.25	.90	.50
17	Kevin Bass	.20	.15	.08
18	Dave Parker	.25	.20	.10
19	Kirby Puckett	.50	.40	.20
	Panel	2.00	1.50	.80
20	Gary Carter	.50	.40	.20
21	Ryne Sandberg	.40	.30	.15
22	Harold Baines	.25	.20	.10
	Panel	2.75	2.00	1.00
23	Mike Schmidt	1.00	.70	.40
24	Eddie Murray	.50	.40	.20
25	Steve Sax	.25	.20	.10

		MT	NR MT	EX
	Panel	1.75	1.25	.70
26	Dwight Gooden	.80	.60	.30
27	Jack Morris	.25	.20	.10
	Panel	1.75	1.25	.70
28	Ron Darling	.25	.20	.10
29	Fernando Valenzuela	.35	.25	.14
30	John Tudor	.20	.15	.08
	Panel	2.50	2.00	1.00
31	Roger Clemens	.80	.60	.30
32	Nolan Ryan	1.00	.70	.40
33	Mike Scott	.25	.20	.10

1988 Drake's

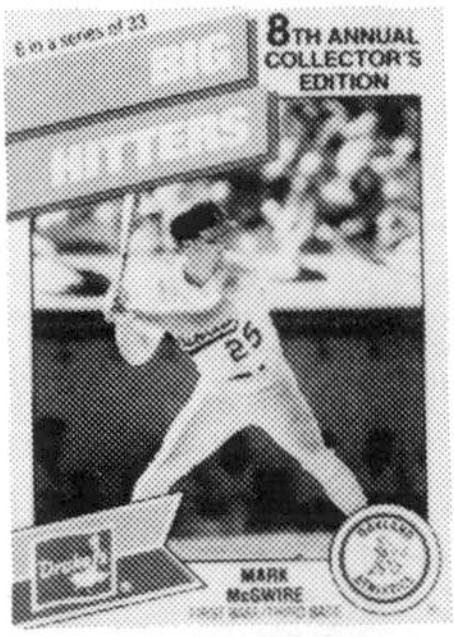

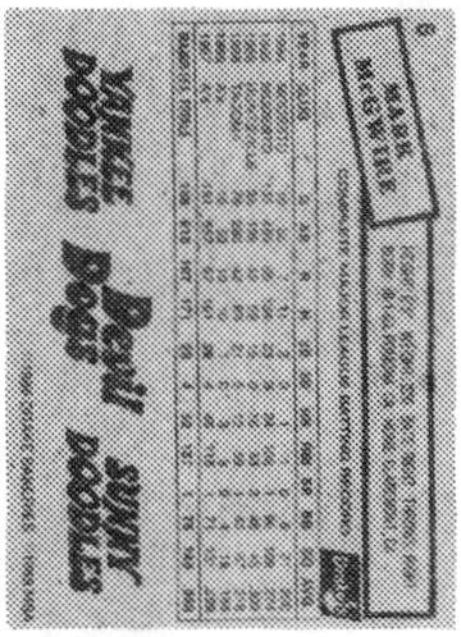

The 8th annual edition of this set includes 33 glossy full-color cards printed on cut-out panels of 2, 3 or 4 cards on Drake's dessert snack boxes. Card fronts have white borders with a large red and blue "Super Pitchers" (6 cards) or "Big Hitters" (27 cards) caption upper left, beside the "8th Annual Collector's Edition label. The Drake logo, player name and team logo are printed in black and include the card number, personal data, batting/pitching record and sponsor logos. Sets were available exclusively on 12 different Drake's packages. To complete the set, collectors had to purchase all 12 products.

	MT	NR MT	EX
Complete Panel Set:	45.00	34.00	18.00
Complete Singles Set:	30.00	22.00	12.00
Common Panel:	1.75	1.25	.70
Common Single Player:	.20	.15	.08

		MT	NR MT	EX
	Panel	4.25	3.25	1.75
1	Don Mattingly	2.00	1.50	.80
2	Tim Raines	.50	.40	.20
	Panel	3.75	2.75	1.50
3	Darryl Strawberry	.80	.60	.30
4	Wade Boggs	1.25	.90	.50
	Panel	3.25	2.50	1.25
5	Keith Hernandez	.40	.30	.15
6	Mark McGwire	1.25	.90	.50
	Panel	2.75	2.00	1.00
7	Rickey Henderson	1.00	.70	.40
8	Mike Schmidt	.60	.45	.25
9	Dwight Evans	.25	.20	.10
	Panel	1.75	1.25	.70
10	Gary Carter	.50	.40	.20
11	Paul Molitor	.30	.25	.12
	Panel	2.75	2.00	1.00
12	Dave Winfield	.50	.40	.20
13	Alan Trammell	.35	.25	.14
14	Tony Gwynn	.50	.40	.20
	Panel	2.50	2.00	1.00
15	Dale Murphy	.60	.45	.25
16	Andre Dawson	.30	.25	.12
17	Von Hayes	.20	.15	.08
18	Willie Randolph	.20	.15	.08
	Panel	2.00	1.50	.80
19	Kirby Puckett	.50	.40	.20
20	Juan Samuel	.25	.20	.10
21	Eddie Murray	.40	.30	.15
	Panel	3.00	2.25	1.25
22	George Bell	.35	.25	.14
23	Larry Sheets	.20	.15	.08
24	Eric Davis	.70	.50	.30
	Panel	2.25	1.75	.90

		MT	NR MT	EX
25	Cal Ripken	.60	.45	.25
26	Pedro Guerrero	.25	.20	.10
27	Will Clark	1.75	1.25	.70
	Panel	2.00	1.50	.80
28	Dwight Gooden	.80	.60	.30
29	Frank Viola	.25	.20	.10
	Panel	3.00	2.25	1.25
30	Roger Clemens	.80	.60	.30
31	Rick Sutcliffe	.20	.15	.08
32	Jack Morris	.25	.20	.10
33	John Tudor	.20	.15	.08

E

1966 East Hills Pirates

Stores in the East Hills Shopping Center, a large mall located in suburban Pittsburgh, distributed cards from this 25-card full-color set in 1966. The cards, which measure 3-1/4" by 4-1/4", are blank-backed and are numbered by the players' uniform numbers. The numbers appear in the lower right corners of the cards.

		NR MT	EX	VG
Complete Set:		40.00	20.00	12.00
Common Player:		.50	.25	.15
3	Harry Walker	.70	.35	.20
7	Bob Bailey	.50	.25	.15
8	Willie Stargell	8.00	4.00	2.50
9	Bill Mazeroski	3.00	1.50	.90
10	Jim Pagliaroni	.50	.25	.15
11	Jose Pagan	.50	.25	.15
12	Jerry May	.50	.25	.15
14	Gene Alley	.60	.30	.20
15	Manny Mota	.80	.40	.25
16	Andy Rodgers	.50	.25	.15
17	Donn Clendenon	.60	.30	.20
18	Matty Alou	.80	.40	.25
19	Pete Mikkelsen	.50	.25	.15
20	Jesse Gonder	.50	.25	.15
21	Bob Clemente	20.00	10.00	6.00
22	Woody Fryman	.60	.30	.20
24	Jerry Lynch	.50	.25	.15
25	Tommie Sisk	.50	.25	.15
26	Roy Face	1.25	.60	.40
28	Steve Blass	.60	.30	.20
32	Vernon Law	1.25	.60	.40
34	Al McBean	.50	.25	.15
39	Bob Veale	.60	.30	.20
43	Don Cardwell	.50	.25	.15
45	Gene Michael	.60	.30	.20

1900 Exhibits - 1947-1966

Called "Exhibits" as they were produced by the Exhibit Supply Co. of Chicago, Ill., this group covers a span of twenty years. Each unnumbered, black and

white card, printed on heavy stock, measures 3-3/8" by 5-3/8" and is blank-backed. The Exhibit Supply Co. issued new sets each year, with many players being repeated year after year. Other players appeared in only one or two years, thereby creating levels of scarcity. Many variations of the same basic pose are found in the group. Those cards are listed in the checklist that follows with an "a", "b", etc. following the assigned card number. The complete set includes all variations

		NR MT	EX	VG
Complete Set:		5000.00	2500.00	1500.
Common Player:		4.00	2.00	1.25
(1)	Hank Aaron	30.00	15.00	9.00
(2a)	Joe Adcock (script signature)	4.00	2.00	1.25
(2b)	Joe Adcock (plain signature)	5.00	2.50	1.50
(3)	Max Alvis	25.00	12.50	7.50
(4)	Johnny Antonelli (Braves)	4.00	2.00	1.25
(5)	Johnny Antonelli (Giants)	5.00	2.50	1.50
(6)	Luis Aparicio (portrait)	7.00	3.50	2.00
(7)	Luis Aparicio (batting)	25.00	12.50	7.50
(8)	Luke Appling	7.00	3.50	2.00
(9a)	Ritchie Ashburn (Phillies, first name incorrect)	5.00	2.50	1.50
(9b)	Richie Ashburn (Phillies, first name correct)	7.00	3.50	2.00
(10)	Richie Ashburn (Cubs)	13.00	6.50	4.00
(11)	Bob Aspromonte	4.00	2.00	1.25
(12)	Toby Atwell	4.00	2.00	1.25
(13)	Ed Bailey (with cap)	5.00	2.50	1.50
(14)	Ed Bailey (no cap)	4.00	2.00	1.25
(15)	Gene Baker	4.00	2.00	1.25
(16a)	Ernie Banks (bat on shoulder, script signature)	25.00	12.50	7.50
(16b)	Ernie Banks (bat on shoulder, plain signature)	10.00	5.00	3.00
(17)	Ernie Banks (portrait)	25.00	12.50	7.50
(18)	Steve Barber	4.00	2.00	1.25
(19)	Earl Battey	5.00	2.50	1.50
(20)	Matt Batts	4.00	2.00	1.25
(21a)	Hank Bauer (N.Y. cap)	5.00	2.50	1.50
(21b)	Hank Bauer (plain cap)	7.00	3.50	2.00
(22)	Frank Baumholtz	4.00	2.00	1.25
(23)	Gene Bearden	4.00	2.00	1.25
(24)	Joe Beggs	12.00	6.00	3.50
(25)	Larry "Yogi" Berra	30.00	15.00	9.00
(26)	Yogi Berra	10.00	5.00	3.00
(27)	Steve Bilko	5.00	2.50	1.50
(28)	Ewell Blackwell (pitching)	7.00	3.50	2.00
(29)	Ewell Blackwell (portrait)	4.00	2.00	1.25
(30a)	Don Blasingame (St. Louis cap)	4.00	2.00	1.25
(30b)	Don Blasingame (plain cap)	6.00	3.00	1.75
(31)	Ken Boyer	7.00	3.50	2.00
(32)	Ralph Branca	7.00	3.50	2.00
(33)	Jackie Brandt	50.00	25.00	15.00
(34)	Harry Brecheen	4.00	2.00	1.25
(35)	Tom Brewer	12.00	6.00	3.50
(36)	Lou Brissie	5.00	2.50	1.50
(37)	Bill Bruton	4.00	2.00	1.25
(38)	Lew Burdette (pitching, side view)	4.00	2.00	1.25
(39)	Lew Burdette (pitching, front view)	6.00	3.00	1.75
(40)	Johnny Callison	7.00	3.50	2.00
(41)	Roy Campanella	13.00	6.50	4.00
(42)	Chico Carrasquel (portrait)	13.00	6.50	4.00
(43)	Chico Carrasquel (leaping)	4.00	2.00	1.25
(44)	George Case	12.00	6.00	3.50

		NR MT	EX	VG
(45)	Hugh Casey	5.00	2.50	1.50
(46)	Norm Cash	7.00	3.50	2.00
(47)	Orlando Cepeda (portrait)	7.00	3.50	2.00
(48)	Orlando Cepeda (batting)	7.00	3.50	2.00
(49a)	Bob Cerv (A's cap)	7.00	3.50	2.00
(49b)	Bob Cerv (plain cap)	16.00	8.00	4.75
(50)	Dean Chance	4.00	2.00	1.25
(51)	Spud Chandler	12.00	6.00	3.50
(52)	Tom Cheney	4.00	2.00	1.25
(53)	Bubba Church	5.00	2.50	1.50
(54)	Roberto Clemente	30.00	15.00	9.00
(55)	Rocky Colavito (portrait)	30.00	15.00	9.00
(56)	Rocky Colavito (batting)	7.00	3.50	2.00
(57)	Choo Choo Coleman	13.00	6.50	4.00
(58)	Gordy Coleman	25.00	12.50	7.50
(59)	Jerry Coleman	5.00	2.50	1.50
(60)	Mort Cooper	12.00	6.00	3.50
(61)	Walker Cooper	4.00	2.00	1.25
(62)	Roger Craig	12.00	6.00	3.50
(63)	Delmar Crandall	4.00	2.00	1.25
(64)	Joe Cunningham (batting)	30.00	15.00	9.00
(65)	Joe Cunningham (portrait)	7.00	3.50	2.00
(66)	Guy Curtwright (Curtright)	5.00	2.50	1.50
(67)	Bud Daley	35.00	17.50	10.50
(68a)	Alvin Dark (Braves)	7.00	3.50	2.00
(68b)	Alvin Dark (Giants)	5.00	2.50	1.50
(69)	Alvin Dark (Cubs)	7.00	3.50	2.00
(70)	Murray Dickson (Murry)	5.00	2.50	1.50
(71)	Bob Dillinger	7.00	3.50	2.00
(72)	Dom DiMaggio	18.00	9.00	5.50
(73)	Joe Dobson	7.00	3.50	2.00
(74)	Larry Doby	4.00	2.00	1.25
(75)	Bobby Doerr	12.00	6.00	3.50
(76)	Dick Donovan (plain cap)	7.00	3.50	2.00
(77)	Dick Donovan (Sox cap)	4.00	2.00	1.25
(78)	Walter Dropo	4.00	2.00	1.25
(79)	Don Drysdale (glove at waist)	30.00	15.00	9.00
(80)	Don Drysdale (portrait)	30.00	15.00	9.00
(81)	Luke Easter	5.00	2.50	1.50
(82)	Bruce Edwards	5.00	2.50	1.50
(83)	Del Ennis	4.00	2.00	1.25
(84)	Al Evans	4.50	2.25	1.25
(85)	Walter Evers	4.00	2.00	1.25
(86)	Ferris Fain (fielding)	7.00	3.50	2.00
(87)	Ferris Fain (portrait)	4.00	2.00	1.25
(88)	Dick Farrell	4.00	2.00	1.25
(89)	Ed "Whitey" Ford	15.00	7.50	4.50
(90)	Whitey Ford (pitching)	10.00	5.00	3.00
(91)	Whitey Ford (portrait)	60.00	30.00	17.50
(92)	Dick Fowler	7.00	3.50	2.00
(93)	Nelson Fox	5.00	2.50	1.50
(94)	Tito Francona	4.00	2.00	1.25
(95)	Bob Friend	4.00	2.00	1.25
(96)	Carl Furillo	7.00	3.50	2.00
(97)	Augie Galan	7.00	3.50	2.00
(98)	Jim Gentile	4.00	2.00	1.25
(99)	Tony Gonzalez	4.00	2.00	1.25
(100)	Billy Goodman (leaping)	4.00	2.00	1.25
(101)	Billy Goodman (batting)	7.00	3.50	2.00
(102)	Ted Greengrass (Jim)	4.00	2.00	1.25
(103)	Dick Groat	7.00	3.50	2.00
(104)	Steve Gromek	4.00	2.00	1.25
(105)	Johnny Groth	4.00	2.00	1.25
(106)	Orval Grove	13.00	6.50	4.00
(107a)	Frank Gustine (Pirates uniform)	5.00	2.50	1.50
(107b)	Frank Gustine (plain uniform)	5.00	2.50	1.50
(108)	Berthold Haas	13.00	6.50	4.00
(109)	Grady Hatton	5.00	2.50	1.50
(110)	Jim Hegan	4.00	2.00	1.25
(111)	Tom Henrich	7.00	3.50	2.00
(112)	Ray Herbert	25.00	12.50	7.50
(113)	Gene Hermanski	4.50	2.25	1.25
(114)	Whitey Herzog	7.00	3.50	2.00
(115)	Kirby Higbe	13.00	6.50	4.00
(116)	Chuck Hinton	4.00	2.00	1.25
(117)	Don Hoak	13.00	6.50	4.00
(118a)	Gil Hodges ("B" on cap)	9.00	4.50	2.75
(118b)	Gil Hodges ("LA" on cap)	9.00	4.50	2.75
(119)	Johnny Hopp	12.00	6.00	3.50
(120)	Elston Howard	4.00	2.00	1.25
(121)	Frank Howard	7.00	3.50	2.00
(122)	Ken Hubbs	35.00	17.50	10.50
(123)	Tex Hughson	12.00	6.00	3.50
(124)	Fred Hutchinson	4.50	2.25	1.25
(125)	Monty Irvin	7.00	3.50	2.00
(126)	Joey Jay	4.00	2.00	1.25
(127)	Jackie Jensen	30.00	15.00	9.00
(128)	Sam Jethroe	5.00	2.50	1.50
(129)	Bill Johnson	5.00	2.50	1.50
(130)	Walter Judnich	12.00	6.00	3.50
(131)	Al Kaline (kneeling)	30.00	15.00	9.00
(132)	Al Kaline (portrait)	30.00	15.00	9.00

		NR MT	EX	VG
(133)	George Kell	7.00	3.50	2.00
(134)	Charley Keller	4.50	2.25	1.25
(135)	Alex Kellner	4.00	2.00	1.25
(136)	Kenn Keltner (Ken)	5.00	2.50	1.50
(137)	Harmon Killebrew (batting)	30.00	15.00	9.00
(138)	Harmon Killebrew (throwing)	30.00	15.00	9.00
(139)	Harmon Killibrew (Killebrew) (portrait)	30.00	15.00	9.00
(140)	Ellis Kinder	4.00	2.00	1.25
(141)	Ralph Kiner	6.00	3.00	1.75
(142)	Billy Klaus	25.00	12.50	7.50
(143)	Ted Kluzewski (Kluszewski) (batting)	5.00	2.50	1.50
(144a)	Ted Kluzewski (Kluszewski) (Pirates uniform)	5.00	2.50	1.50
(144b)	Ted Kluzewski (Kluszewski) (plain uniform)	13.00	6.50	4.00
(145)	Don Kolloway	7.00	3.50	2.00
(146)	Jim Konstanty	5.00	2.50	1.50
(147)	Sandy Koufax	25.00	12.50	7.50
(148)	Ed Kranepool	50.00	25.00	15.00
(149a)	Tony Kubek (light background)	7.00	3.50	2.00
(149b)	Tony Kubek (dark background)	5.00	2.50	1.50
(150a)	Harvey Kuenn ("D" on cap)	12.00	6.00	3.50
(150b)	Harvey Kuenn (plain cap)	13.00	6.50	4.00
(151)	Harvey Kuenn ("SF" on cap)	7.00	3.50	2.00
(152)	Kurowski (Whitey)	4.50	2.25	1.25
(153)	Eddie Lake	5.00	2.50	1.50
(154)	Jim Landis	4.00	2.00	1.25
(155)	Don Larsen	4.00	2.00	1.25
(156)	Bob Lemon (glove not visible)	7.00	3.50	2.00
(157)	Bob Lemon (glove partially visible)	30.00	15.00	9.00
(158)	Buddy Lewis	12.00	6.00	3.50
(159)	Johnny Lindell	25.00	12.50	7.50
(160)	Phil Linz	25.00	12.50	7.50
(161)	Don Lock	25.00	12.50	7.50
(162)	Whitey Lockman	4.00	2.00	1.25
(163)	Johnny Logan	4.00	2.00	1.25
(164)	Dale Long ("P" on cap)	4.00	2.00	1.25
(165)	Dale Long ("C" on cap)	7.00	3.50	2.00
(166)	Ed Lopat	5.00	2.50	1.50
(167a)	Harry Lowery (name misspelled)	5.00	2.50	1.50
(167b)	Harry Lowrey (name correct)	5.00	2.50	1.50
(168)	Sal Maglie	4.00	2.00	1.25
(169)	Art Mahaffey	5.00	2.50	1.50
(170)	Hank Majeski	4.00	2.00	1.25
(171)	Frank Malzone	4.00	2.00	1.25
(172)	Mickey Mantle (batting, pinstriped uniform)	100.00	50.00	30.00
(173a)	Mickey Mantle (batting, no pinstripes, first name outlined in white)	75.00	38.00	23.00
173b	Mickey Mantle (batting, no pinstripes, first name not outlined in white)	75.00	38.00	23.00
(174)	Mickey Mantle (portrait)	400.00	200.00	120.00
(175)	Martin Marion	7.00	3.50	2.00
(176)	Roger Maris	25.00	12.50	7.50
(177)	Willard Marshall	5.00	2.50	1.50
(178a)	Eddie Matthews (name incorrect)	12.00	6.00	3.50
(178b)	Eddie Mathews (name correct)	13.00	6.50	4.00
(179)	Ed Mayo	5.00	2.50	1.50
(180)	Willie Mays (batting)	18.00	9.00	5.50
(181)	Willie Mays (portrait)	25.00	12.50	7.50
(182)	Bill Mazeroski (portrait)	7.00	3.50	2.00
(183)	Bill Mazeroski (batting)	7.00	3.50	2.00
(184)	Ken McBride	4.00	2.00	1.25
(185a)	Barney McCaskey (McCosky)	13.00	6.50	4.00
(185b)	Barney McCoskey (McCosky)	90.00	45.00	27.00
(186)	Lindy McDaniel	4.00	2.00	1.25
(187)	Gil McDougald	4.00	2.00	1.25
(188)	Albert Mele	13.00	6.50	4.00
(189)	Sam Mele	5.00	2.50	1.50
(190)	Orestes Minoso ("C" on cap)	7.00	3.50	2.00
(191)	Orestes Minoso (Sox on cap)	4.00	2.00	1.25
(192)	Dale Mitchell	4.00	2.00	1.25
(193)	Wally Moon	7.00	3.50	2.00
(194)	Don Mueller	5.00	2.50	1.50
(195)	Stan Musial (kneeling)	15.00	7.50	4.50
(196)	Stan Musial (batting)	35.00	17.50	10.50
(197)	Charley Neal	18.00	9.00	5.50
(198)	Don Newcombe (shaking hands)	7.00	3.50	2.00
(199a)	Don Newcombe (Dodgers on jacket)	5.00	2.50	1.50
(199b)	Don Newcombe (plain jacket)	5.00	2.50	1.50
(200)	Hal Newhouser	4.00	2.00	1.25
(201)	Ron Northey	12.00	6.00	3.50
(202)	Bill O'Dell	4.00	2.00	1.25
(203)	Joe Page	12.00	6.00	3.50
(204)	Satchel Paige	35.00	17.50	10.50
(205)	Milt Pappas	4.00	2.00	1.25

	NR MT	EX	VG
(206) Camilo Pascual	4.00	2.00	1.25
(207) Albie Pearson	25.00	12.50	7.50
(208) Johnny Pesky	4.00	2.00	1.25
(209) Gary Peters	25.00	12.50	7.50
(210) Dave Philley	4.00	2.00	1.25
(211) Billy Pierce	4.00	2.00	1.25
(212) Jimmy Piersall	16.00	8.00	4.75
(213) Vada Pinson	7.00	3.50	2.00
(214) Bob Porterfield	4.00	2.00	1.25
(215) John "Boog" Powell	35.00	17.50	10.50
(216) Vic Raschi	4.50	2.25	1.25
(217a) Harold "Peewee" Reese (fielding, ball partially visible)	10.00	5.00	3.00
(217b) Harold "Peewee" Reese (fielding, ball not visible)	10.00	5.00	3.00
(218) Del Rice	4.00	2.00	1.25
(219) Bobby Richardson	55.00	28.00	16.50
(220) Phil Rizzuto	6.00	3.00	1.75
(221a) Robin Roberts (script signature)	12.00	6.00	3.50
(221b) Robin Roberts (plain signature)	6.00	3.00	1.75
(222) Brooks Robinson	30.00	15.00	9.00
(223) Eddie Robinson	4.00	2.00	1.25
(224) Floyd Robinson	25.00	12.50	7.50
(225) Frankie Robinson	18.00	9.00	5.50
(226) Jackie Robinson	30.00	15.00	9.00
(227) Preacher Roe	4.50	2.25	1.25
(228) Bob Rogers (Rodgers)	25.00	12.50	7.50
(229) Richard Rollins	25.00	12.50	7.50
(230) Pete Runnels	12.00	6.00	3.50
(231) John Sain	5.00	2.50	1.50
(232) Ron Santo	6.00	3.00	1.75
(233) Henry Sauer	5.00	2.50	1.50
(234a) Carl Sawatski ("M" on cap)	4.00	2.00	1.25
(234b) Carl Sawatski ("P" on cap)	4.00	2.00	1.25
(234c) Carl Sawatski (plain cap)	13.00	6.50	4.00
(235) Johnny Schmitz	5.00	2.50	1.50
(236a) Red Schoendeinst (Schoendienst) (fielding, name in white)	5.00	2.50	1.50
(236b) Red Schoendeinst (Schoendienst) (fielding, name in red-brown)	7.00	3.50	2.00
(237) Red Schoendinst (Schoendienst) (batting)	4.00	2.00	1.25
(238a) Herb Score ("C" on cap)	5.00	2.50	1.50
(238b) Herb Score (plain cap)	12.00	6.00	3.50
(239) Andy Seminick	4.00	2.00	1.25
(240) Rip Sewell	7.00	3.50	2.00
(241) Norm Siebern	4.00	2.00	1.25
(242) Roy Sievers (batting)	5.00	2.50	1.50
(243a) Roy Sievers (portrait, "W" on cap, light background)	7.00	3.50	2.00
(243b) Roy Sievers (portrait, "W" on cap, dark background)	5.00	2.50	1.50
(243c) Roy Sievers (portrait, plain cap)	4.50	2.25	1.25
(244) Curt Simmons	5.00	2.50	1.50
(245) Dick Sisler	5.00	2.50	1.50
(246) Bill Skowron	5.00	2.50	1.50
(247) Bill "Moose" Skowron	55.00	28.00	16.50
(248) Enos Slaughter	7.00	3.50	2.00
(249a) Duke Snider ("B" on cap)	8.50	4.25	2.50
(249b) Duke Snider ("LA" on cap)	18.00	9.00	5.50
(250a) Warren Spahn ("B" on cap)	10.00	5.00	3.00
(250b) Warren Spahn ("M" on cap)	12.00	6.00	3.50
(251) Stanley Spence	13.00	6.50	4.00
(252) Ed Stanky (plain uniform)	5.00	2.50	1.50
(253) Ed Stanky (Giants uniform)	5.00	2.50	1.50
(254) Vern Stephens (batting)	5.00	2.50	1.50
(255) Vern Stephens (portrait)	5.00	2.50	1.50
(256) Ed Stewart	5.00	2.50	1.50
(257) Snuffy Stirnweiss	13.00	6.50	4.00
(258) George "Birdie" Tebbetts	12.00	6.00	3.50
(259) Frankie Thomas (photo actually Bob Skinner)	30.00	15.00	9.00
(260) Frank Thomas (portrait)	13.00	6.50	4.00
(261) Lee Thomas	4.00	2.00	1.25
(262) Bobby Thomson	7.00	3.50	2.00
(263a) Earl Torgeson (Braves uniform)	4.00	2.00	1.25
(263b) Earl Torgeson (plain uniform)	5.00	2.50	1.50
(264) Gus Triandos	7.00	3.50	2.00
(265) Virgil Trucks	4.00	2.00	1.25
(266) Johnny Vandermeer (VanderMeer)	13.00	6.50	4.00
(267) Emil Verban	7.00	3.50	2.00
(268) Mickey Vernon (throwing)	4.00	2.00	1.25
(269) Mickey Vernon (batting)	4.00	2.00	1.25
(270) Bill Voiselle	7.00	3.50	2.00
(271) Leon Wagner	4.00	2.00	1.25
(272a) Eddie Waitkus (throwing, Chicago uniform)	7.00	3.50	2.00
(272b) Eddie Waitkus (throwing, plain uniform)	5.00	2.50	1.50
(273) Eddie Waitkus (portrait)	13.00	6.50	4.00
(274) Dick Wakefield	5.00	2.50	1.50
(275) Harry Walker	7.00	3.50	2.00
(276) Bucky Walters	4.50	2.25	1.25
(277) Pete Ward	30.00	15.00	9.00
(278) Herman Wehmeier	5.00	2.50	1.50
(279) Vic Wertz (batting)	4.00	2.00	1.25
(280) Vic Wertz (portrait)	4.00	2.00	1.25
(281) Wally Westlake	5.00	2.50	1.50
(282) Wes Westrum	13.00	6.50	4.00
(283) Billy Williams	13.00	6.50	4.00
(284) Maurice Wills	12.00	6.00	3.50
(285a) Gene Woodling (script signature)	4.00	2.00	1.25
(285b) Gene Woodling (plain signature)	7.00	3.50	2.00
(286) Taffy Wright	5.00	2.50	1.50
(287) Carl Yastrazemski (Yastrzemski)	175.00	90.00	50.00
(288) Al Zarilla	5.00	2.50	1.50
(289a) Gus Zernial (script signature)	4.00	2.00	1.25
(289b) Gus Zernial (plain signature)	7.00	3.50	2.00
(290) Braves Team - 1948	18.00	9.00	5.50
(291) Dodgers Team - 1949	25.00	12.50	7.50
(292) Dodgers Team - 1952	25.00	12.50	7.50
(293) Dodgers Team - 1955	25.00	12.50	7.50
(294) Dodgers Team - 1956	25.00	12.50	7.50
(295) Giants Team - 1951	18.00	9.00	5.50
(296) Giants Team - 1954	18.00	9.00	5.50
(297) Indians Team - 1948	18.00	9.00	5.50
(298) Indians Team - 1954	18.00	9.00	5.50
(299) Phillies Team - 1950	18.00	9.00	5.50
(300) Yankees Team - 1949	30.00	15.00	9.00
(301) Yankees Team - 1950	30.00	15.00	9.00
(302) Yankees Team - 1951	30.00	15.00	9.00
(303) Yankees Team - 1952	30.00	15.00	9.00
(304) Yankees Team - 1955	30.00	15.00	9.00
(305) Yankees Team - 1956	30.00	15.00	9.00

1962 Exhibit Supply Co. Statistic Backs

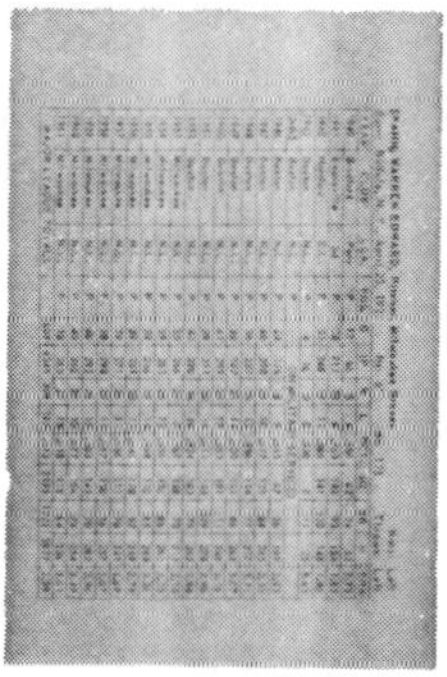

In 1962, the Exhibit Supply Co. added career statistics to the yearly set they produced. The black and white, unnumbered cards measure 3-3/8" by 5-3/8". The statistics found on the back are printed in black or red. The red backs are three times greater in value. The set is comprised of 32 cards.

	NR MT	EX	VG
Complete Set:	425.00	212.00	127.00
Common Player:	3.00	1.50	.90
(1) Hank Aaron	35.00	17.50	10.50
(2) Luis Aparicio	4.00	2.00	1.25
(3) Ernie Banks	7.00	3.50	2.00
(4) Larry "Yogi" Berra	10.00	5.00	3.00
(5) Ken Boyer	4.00	2.00	1.25
(6) Lew Burdette	3.50	1.75	1.00
(7) Norm Cash	3.50	1.75	1.00
(8) Orlando Cepeda	3.00	1.50	.90
(9) Roberto Clemente	35.00	17.50	10.50
(10) Rocky Colavito	4.00	2.00	1.25
(11) Ed "Whitey" Ford	7.00	3.50	2.00
(12) Nelson Fox	3.00	1.50	.90
(13) Tito Francona	3.00	1.50	.90
(14) Jim Gentile	3.00	1.50	.90
(15) Dick Groat	3.50	1.75	1.00
(16) Don Hoak	3.50	1.75	1.00
(17) Al Kaline	10.00	5.00	3.00

		NR MT	EX	VG
(18)	Harmon Killebrew	10.00	5.00	3.00
(19)	Sandy Koufax	25.00	12.50	7.50
(20)	Jim Landis	3.00	1.50	.90
(21)	Art Mahaffey	3.00	1.50	.90
(22)	Frank Malzone	3.00	1.50	.90
(23)	Mickey Mantle	90.00	45.00	27.00
(24)	Roger Maris	10.00	5.00	3.00
(25)	Eddie Mathews	5.00	2.50	1.50
(26)	Willie Mays	35.00	17.50	10.50
(27)	Wally Moon	3.50	1.75	1.00
(28)	Stan Musial	35.00	17.50	10.50
(29)	Milt Pappas	3.50	1.75	1.00
(30)	Vada Pinson	4.00	2.00	1.25
(31)	Norm Siebern	3.00	1.50	.90
(32)	Warren Spahn	10.00	5.00	3.00

1963 Exhibit Supply Co. Statistic Backs

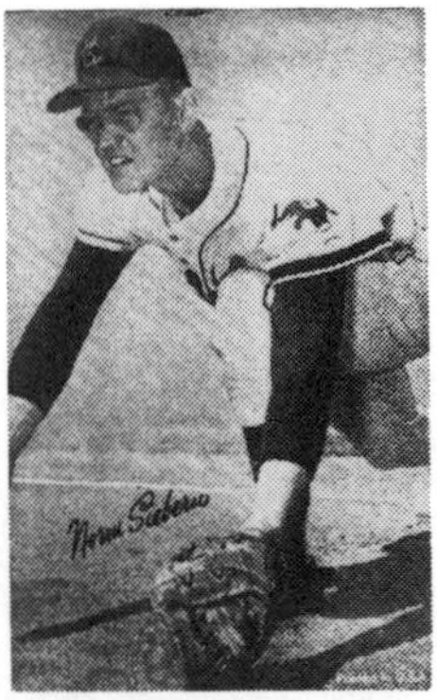

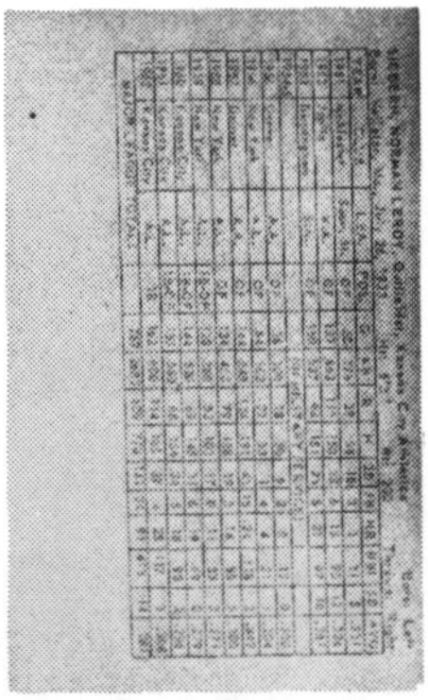

The Exhibit Supply Co. issued a 64-card set with career statistics on the backs of the cards in 1963. The unnumbered, black and white cards are printed on thick cardboard and measure 3-3/8" by 5-3/8" in size. The statistics on the back are printed in black.

		NR MT	EX	VG
Complete Set:		525.00	262.00	157.00
Common Player:		3.00	1.50	.90
(1)	Hank Aaron	35.00	17.50	10.50
(2)	Luis Aparicio	4.00	2.00	1.25
(3)	Bob Aspromonte	3.00	1.50	.90
(4)	Ernie Banks	20.00	10.00	6.00
(5)	Steve Barber	3.00	1.50	.90
(6)	Earl Battey	3.00	1.50	.90
(7)	Larry "Yogi" Berra	12.00	6.00	3.50
(8)	Ken Boyer	4.00	2.00	1.25
(9)	Lew Burdette	3.50	1.75	1.00
(10)	Johnny Callison	3.50	1.75	1.00
(11)	Norm Cash	3.50	1.75	1.00
(12)	Orlando Cepeda	3.00	1.50	.90
(13)	Dean Chance	3.00	1.50	.90
(14)	Tom Cheney	3.00	1.50	.90
(15)	Roberto Clemente	35.00	17.50	10.50
(16)	Rocky Colavito	4.00	2.00	1.25
(17)	Choo Choo Coleman	3.00	1.50	.90
(18)	Roger Craig	3.50	1.75	1.00
(19)	Joe Cunningham	3.00	1.50	.90
(20)	Don Drysdale	7.00	3.50	2.00
(21)	Dick Farrell	3.00	1.50	.90
(22)	Ed "Whitey" Ford	15.00	7.50	4.50
(23)	Nelson Fox	3.00	1.50	.90
(24)	Tito Francona	3.00	1.50	.90
(25)	Jim Gentile	3.00	1.50	.90
(26)	Tony Gonzalez	3.00	1.50	.90
(27)	Dick Groat	3.50	1.75	1.00
(28)	Ray Herbert	3.00	1.50	.90
(29)	Chuck Hinton	3.00	1.50	.90
(30)	Don Hoak	3.50	1.75	1.00
(31)	Frank Howard	4.00	2.00	1.25
(32)	Ken Hubbs	3.50	1.75	1.00
(33)	Joey Jay	3.00	1.50	.90
(34)	Al Kaline	15.00	7.50	4.50
(35)	Harmon Killebrew	15.00	7.50	4.50
(36)	Sandy Koufax	20.00	10.00	6.00
(37)	Harvey Kuenn	4.00	2.00	1.25
(38)	Jim Landis	3.00	1.50	.90
(39)	Art Mahaffey	3.00	1.50	.90
(40)	Frank Malzone	3.00	1.50	.90
(41)	Mickey Mantle	150.00	75.00	45.00
(42)	Roger Maris	15.00	7.50	4.50
(43)	Eddie Mathews	5.00	2.50	1.50
(44)	Willie Mays	35.00	17.50	10.50
(45)	Bill Mazeroski	4.00	2.00	1.25
(46)	Ken McBride	3.00	1.50	.90
(47)	Wally Moon	3.50	1.75	1.00
(48)	Stan Musial	35.00	17.50	10.50
(49)	Charlie Neal	3.00	1.50	.90
(50)	Bill O'Dell	3.00	1.50	.90
(51)	Milt Pappas	3.50	1.75	1.00
(52)	Camilo Pascual	3.50	1.75	1.00
(53)	Jimmy Piersall	4.00	2.00	1.25
(54)	Vada Pinson	4.00	2.00	1.25
(55)	Brooks Robinson	15.00	7.50	4.50
(56)	Frankie Robinson	15.00	7.50	4.50
(57)	Pete Runnels	3.50	1.75	1.00
(58)	Ron Santo	4.00	2.00	1.25
(59)	Norm Siebern	3.00	1.50	.90
(60)	Warren Spahn	12.00	6.00	3.50
(61)	Lee Thomas	3.00	1.50	.90
(62)	Leon Wagner	3.00	1.50	.90
(63)	Billy Williams	4.00	2.00	1.25
(64)	Maurice Wills	3.00	1.50	.90

F

1988 Fantastic Sam's

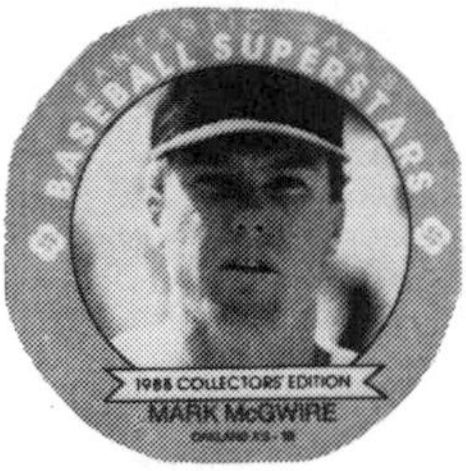

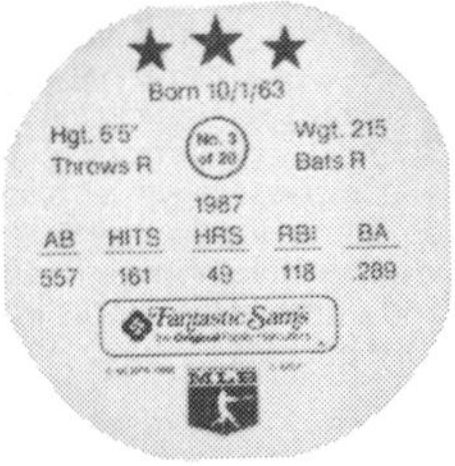

This set of 20 full-color player discs (2-1/2" diameter) was distributed during a Superstar Sweepstakes sponsored by Fantastic Sam's Family Haircutters' 1,800 stores nationwide. Each sweepstakes card consists of two connected discs (bright orange fronts, white backs) perforated for easy separation. One disc features the baseball player photo, the other carries the sweepstakes logo and a list of prizes. Player discs carry a Fantastic Sam's Baseball Superstars header curved above the photo, with his name, team and position printed in black. The disc backs are black and white and include personal info, card number and 1987 player stats. Sweepstakes discs list contest prizes (Grand Prize was 4 tickets to a 1988 Championship game) on the front and an entry form on the flipside. Below the prize list is a silver scratch-off rectangle which may reveal an instant prize.

		MT	NR MT	EX
Complete Set:		7.00	5.25	2.75
Common Player:		.20	.15	.08
1	Kirby Puckett	.75	.60	.30
2	George Brett	1.00	.70	.40
3	Mark McGwire	1.25	.90	.50
4	Wally Joyner	1.25	.90	.50
5	Paul Molitor	.20	.15	.08
6	Alan Trammell	.40	.30	.15
7	George Bell	.50	.40	.20

		MT	NR MT	EX
8	Wade Boggs	1.25	.90	.50
9	Don Mattingly	2.00	1.50	.80
10	Julio Franco	.20	.15	.08
11	Ozzie Smith	.20	.15	.08
12	Will Clark	.75	.60	.30
13	Dale Murphy	1.00	.70	.40
14	Eric Davis	1.50	1.25	.60
15	Andre Dawson	.50	.40	.20
16	Tim Raines	.60	.45	.25
17	Darryl Strawberry	1.25	.90	.50
18	Tony Gwynn	.75	.60	.30
19	Mike Schmidt	1.50	1.25	.60
20	Pedro Guerrero	.20	.15	.08

1987 Farmland Dairies Mets

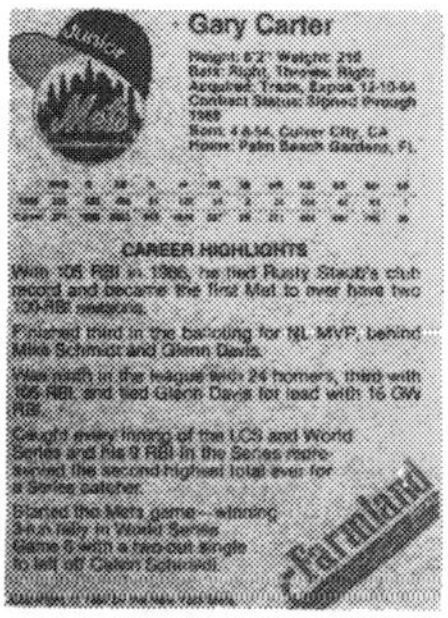

The New York Mets and Farmland Dairies produced a nine-card panel of baseball cards for members of the Junior Mets Club. Members of the club, kids 14 years of age and younger, received the perforated panel as part of a package featuring gifts and special privileges. The cards are the standard 2-1/2" by 3-1/2" with fronts containing a full-color photo encompassed by a blue border. The backs are designed on a vertical format and have player statistics and career highlights. The Farmland Dairies and Junior Mets Club logos are also carried on the card backs.

		MT	NR MT	EX
Complete Panel Set:		15.00	11.00	6.00
Complete Singles Set:		6.00	4.50	2.50
Common Single Player:		.25	.20	.10
	Panel	12.00	9.00	4.75
1	Mookie Wilson	.25	.20	.10
4	Len Dykstra	.60	.45	.25
8	Gary Carter	.70	.50	.30
12	Ron Darling	.40	.30	.15
18	Darryl Strawberry	1.50	1.25	.60
19	Bob Ojeda	.25	.20	.10
22	Kevin McReynolds	.40	.30	.15
42	Roger McDowell	.35	.25	.14
----	Team Card	.25	.20	.10

1988 Farmland Dairies Mets

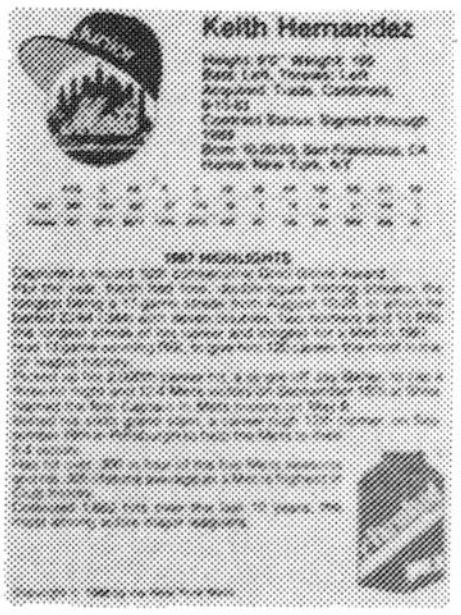

Part of the Junior Mets Fan Club membership package, this set of 9 standard size cards was printed on a single panel. Card fronts feature full-color action shots framed in orange and blue. A white player name runs across the top border, with a large team logo, uniform number and position printed below the photo. Card backs are blue on brown and include personal data, stats and 1987 season highlights. The set was offered to fans 14 years and younger for a $6 fan club membership fee, with a $1 discount for those who sent in two proofs of purchase from Farmland Dairies milk cartons.

		MT	NR MT	EX
Complete Panel Set:		15.00	11.00	6.00
Complete Singles Set:		6.00	4.50	2.50
Common Single Player:		.25	.20	.10
	Panel	12.00	9.00	4.75
8	Gary Carter	.70	.50	.30
16	Dwight Gooden	1.25	.90	.50
17	Keith Hernandez	.40	.30	.15
18	Darryl Strawberry	1.25	.90	.50
20	Howard Johnson	.70	.50	.30
21	Kevin Elster	.35	.25	.14
42	Roger McDowell	.25	.20	.10
48	Randy Myers	.35	.25	.14

1959 Fleer Ted Williams

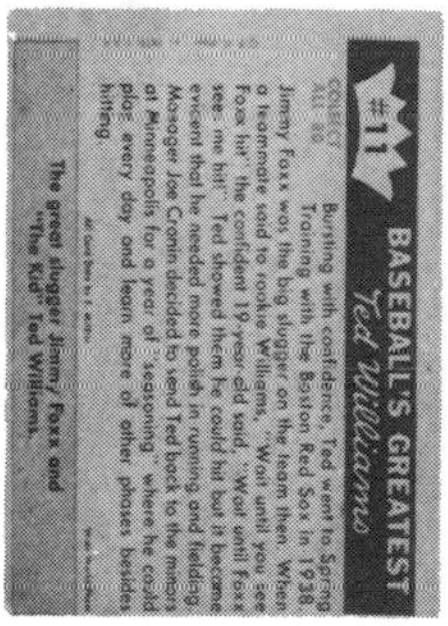

This 80-card 1959 Fleer set tells of the life of baseball great Ted Williams, from his childhood years up to 1958. The full-color cards measure 2-1/2" by 3-1/2" in size and make use of both horizontal and vertical formats. The card backs, all designed horizontally, contain a continuing biography of Williams. Card #68 was withdrawn from the set early in production and is scarce. Counterfeit cards of #68 have been produced and can be distinguished by a cross-hatch pattern which appears over the photo on the card fronts.

		NR MT	EX	VG
Complete Set:		1000.00	500.00	300.00
Common Player:		5.00	2.50	1.50
1	The Early Years	25.00	12.50	7.50
2	Ted's Idol - Babe Ruth	25.00	12.50	7.50
3	Practice Makes Perfect	5.00	2.50	1.50
4	1934 - Ted Learns The Fine Points	5.00	2.50	1.50
5	Ted's Fame Spreads - 1935-36	5.00	2.50	1.50
6	Ted Turns Professional	5.00	2.50	1.50
7	1936 - From Mound To Plate	5.00	2.50	1.50
8	1937 - First Full Season	5.00	2.50	1.50
9	1937 - First Step To The Majors	5.00	2.50	1.50
10	1938 - Gunning As A Pastime	5.00	2.50	1.50
11	1938 - First Spring Training	4.00	2.00	1.25
12	1939 - Burning Up The Minors	5.00	2.50	1.50
13	1939 - Ted Shows He Will Stay	5.00	2.50	1.50
14	Outstanding Rookie of 1939	5.00	2.50	1.50
15	1940 - Williams Licks Sophomore Jinx	5.00	2.50	1.50
16	1941 - Williams' Greatest Year	5.00	2.50	1.50
17	1941 - How Ted Hit .400	5.00	2.50	1.50
18	1941 - All-Star Hero	5.00	2.50	1.50

		NR MT	EX	VG
19	1942 - Ted Wins Triple Crown	5.00	2.50	1.50
20	1942 - On To Naval Training	5.00	2.50	1.50
21	1943 - Honors For Williams	5.00	2.50	1.50
22	1944 - Ted Solos	5.00	2.50	1.50
23	1944 - Williams Wins His Wings	5.00	2.50	1.50
24	1945 - Sharpshooter	5.00	2.50	1.50
25	1945 - Ted Is Discharged	5.00	2.50	1.50
26	1946 - Off To A Flying Start	5.00	2.50	1.50
27	July 9, 1946 - One Man Show	5.00	2.50	1.50
28	July 14, 1946 - The Williams Shift	5.00	2.50	1.50
29	July 21, 1946, Ted Hits For The Cycle	5.00	2.50	1.50
30	1946 - Beating The Williams Shift	5.00	2.50	1.50
31	Oct. 1946 - Sox Lose The Series	5.00	2.50	1.50
32	1946 - Most Valuable Player	5.00	2.50	1.50
33	1947 - Another Triple Crown For Ted	5.00	2.50	1.50
34	1947 - Ted Sets Runs-Scored Record	5.00	2.50	1.50
35	1948 - The Sox Miss The Pennant	5.00	2.50	1.50
36	1948 - Banner Year For Ted	5.00	2.50	1.50
37	1949 - Sox Miss Out Again	5.00	2.50	1.50
38	1949 - Power Rampage	5.00	2.50	1.50
39	1950 - Great Start	4.50	2.25	1.25
40	July 11, 1950 - Ted Crashes Into Wall	5.00	2.50	1.50
41	1950 - Ted Recovers	5.00	2.50	1.50
42	1951 - Williams Slowed By Injury	5.00	2.50	1.50
43	1951 - Leads Outfielders In Double Plays	5.00	2.50	1.50
44	1952 - Back To The Marines	5.00	2.50	1.50
45	1952 - Farewell To Baseball?	5.00	2.50	1.50
46	1952 - Ready For Combat	5.00	2.50	1.50
47	1953 - Ted Crash Lands Jet	5.00	2.50	1.50
48	July 14, 1953 - Ted Returns	5.00	2.50	1.50
49	1953 - Smash Return	5.00	2.50	1.50
50	March 1954 - Spring Injury	5.00	2.50	1.50
51	May 16, 1954 - Ted Is Patched Up	5.00	2.50	1.50
52	1954 - Ted's Comeback	5.00	2.50	1.50
53	1954 - Ted's Comeback Is A Sucess	5.00	2.50	1.50
54	Dec. 1954, Fisherman Ted Hooks a Big One	5.00	2.50	1.50
55	1955 - Ted Decides Retirement Is "No Go"	5.00	2.50	1.50
56	1956 - Ted Reaches 400th Homer,	5.00	2.50	1.50
58	1957 - Williams Hits .388	5.00	2.50	1.50
59	1957 - Hot September For Ted	5.00	2.50	1.50
60	1957 - More Records For Ted	5.00	2.50	1.50
61	1957 - Outfielder Ted	5.00	2.50	1.50
62	1958 - 6th Batting Title For Ted	5.00	2.50	1.50
63	Ted's All-Star Record	5.00	2.50	1.50
64	1958 - Daughter And Famous Daddy	5.00	2.50	1.50
65	August 30, 1958	5.00	2.50	1.50
66	1958 - Powerhouse	5.00	2.50	1.50
67	Two Famous Fisherman	4.50	2.25	1.25
68	Jan. 23, 1959 - Ted Signs For 1959	525.00	262.00	157.00
69	A Future Ted Williams?	5.00	2.50	1.50
70	Ted Williams & Jim Thorpe	4.50	2.25	1.25
71	Ted's Hitting Fundamentals #1	5.00	2.50	1.50
72	Ted's Hitting Fundamentals #2	5.00	2.50	1.50
73	Ted's Hitting Fundamentals #3	5.00	2.50	1.50
74	Here's How!	5.00	2.50	1.50
75	Williams' Value To Red Sox	12.00	6.00	3.50
76	Ted's Remarkable "On Base" Record	5.00	2.50	1.50
77	Ted Relaxes	5.00	2.50	1.50
78	Honors For Williams	5.00	2.50	1.50
79	Where Ted Stands	5.00	2.50	1.50
80	Ted's Goals For 1959	12.00	6.00	3.50

1960 Fleer

The 1960 Fleer Baseball Greats set consists of 79 cards of the game's top players from the past. (The set does include a card of Ted Williams, who was in his final major league season). The cards are standard size (2-1/2" by 3-1/2") and feature color photos inside blue, green, red or yellow borders. The card backs carry a short player biography plus career hitting or pitching statistics. Cards with a Pepper Martin back (#80), but with another player pictured on the front are in existence.

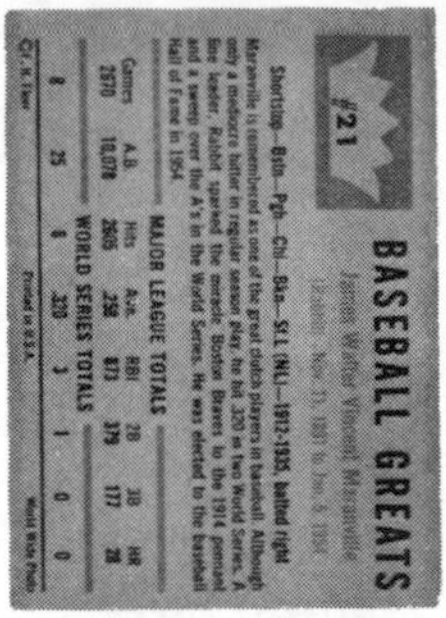

		NR MT	EX	VG
Complete Set:		400.00	200.00	120.00
Common Player:		2.00	1.00	.60
1	Nap Lajoie	8.00	4.00	2.50
2	Christy Mathewson	8.00	4.00	2.50
3	Babe Ruth	70.00	35.00	21.00
4	Carl Hubbell	2.50	1.25	.70
5	Grover Cleveland Alexander	4.00	2.00	1.25
6	Walter Johnson	8.00	4.00	2.50
7	Chief Bender	2.00	1.00	.60
8	Roger Bresnahan	2.00	1.00	.60
9	Mordecai Brown	2.00	1.00	.60
10	Tris Speaker	2.50	1.25	.70
11	Arky Vaughan	2.00	1.00	.60
12	Zack Wheat	2.00	1.00	.60
13	George Sisler	2.50	1.25	.70
14	Connie Mack	4.00	2.00	1.25
15	Clark Griffith	2.00	1.00	.60
16	Lou Boudreau	2.00	1.00	.60
17	Ernie Lombardi	2.00	1.00	.60
18	Heinie Manush	2.00	1.00	.60
19	Marty Marion	2.00	1.00	.60
20	Eddie Collins	2.50	1.25	.70
21	Rabbit Maranville	2.00	1.00	.60
22	Joe Medwick	2.00	1.00	.60
23	Ed Barrow	2.00	1.00	.60
24	Mickey Cochrane	2.50	1.25	.70
25	Jimmy Collins	2.00	1.00	.60
26	Bob Feller	7.00	3.50	2.00
27	Luke Appling	2.00	1.00	.60
28	Lou Gehrig	35.00	17.50	10.50
29	Gabby Hartnett	2.00	1.00	.60
30	Chuck Klein	2.00	1.00	.60
31	Tony Lazzeri	2.00	1.00	.60
32	Al Simmons	2.00	1.00	.60
33	Wilbert Robinson	2.00	1.00	.60
34	Sam Rice	2.00	1.00	.60
35	Herb Pennock	2.00	1.00	.60
36	Mel Ott	2.50	1.25	.70
37	Lefty O'Doul	2.00	1.00	.60
38	Johnny Mize	2.50	1.25	.70
39	Bing Miller	2.00	1.00	.60
40	Joe Tinker	2.00	1.00	.60
41	Frank Baker	2.00	1.00	.60
42	Ty Cobb	35.00	17.50	10.50
43	Paul Derringer	2.00	1.00	.60
44	Cap Anson	2.50	1.25	.70
45	Jim Bottomley	2.00	1.00	.60
46	Eddie Plank	2.00	1.00	.60
47	Cy Young	5.00	2.50	1.50
48	Hack Wilson	2.00	1.00	.60
49	Ed Walsh	2.00	1.00	.60
50	Frank Chance	2.00	1.00	.60
51	Dazzy Vance	2.00	1.00	.60
52	Bill Terry	2.50	1.25	.70
53	Jimmy Foxx	4.00	2.00	1.25
54	Lefty Gomez	2.50	1.25	.70
55	Branch Rickey	2.00	1.00	.60
56	Ray Schalk	2.00	1.00	.60
57	Johnny Evers	2.00	1.00	.60
58	Charlie Gehringer	2.50	1.25	.70
59	Burleigh Grimes	2.00	1.00	.60
60	Lefty Grove	2.50	1.25	.70
61	Rube Waddell	2.00	1.00	.60
62	Honus Wagner	8.00	4.00	2.50
63	Red Ruffing	2.00	1.00	.60
64	Judge Landis	2.00	1.00	.60
65	Harry Heilmann	2.00	1.00	.60
66	John McGraw	2.50	1.25	.70
67	Hughie Jennings	2.00	1.00	.60
68	Hal Newhouser	2.00	1.00	.60

		NR MT	EX	VG
69	Waite Hoyt	2.00	1.00	.60
70	Bobo Newsom	2.00	1.00	.60
71	Earl Averill	2.00	1.00	.60
72	Ted Williams	55.00	27.00	16.50
73	Warren Giles	2.00	1.00	.60
74	Ford Frick	2.00	1.00	.60
75	Ki Ki Cuyler	2.00	1.00	.60
76	Paul Waner	2.00	1.00	.60
77	Pie Traynor	2.00	1.00	.60
78	Lloyd Waner	2.00	1.00	.60
79	Ralph Kiner	8.00	4.00	2.50

1961 Fleer

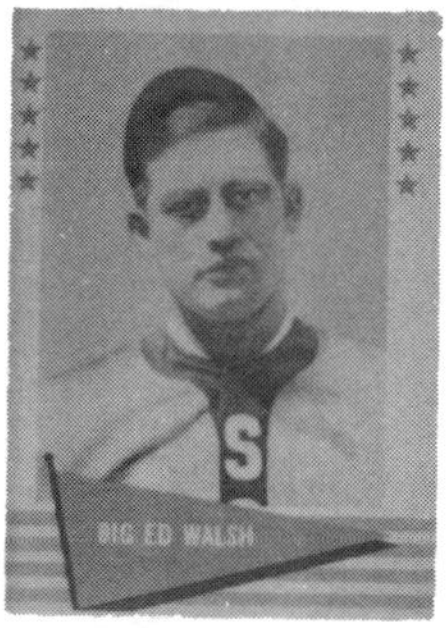

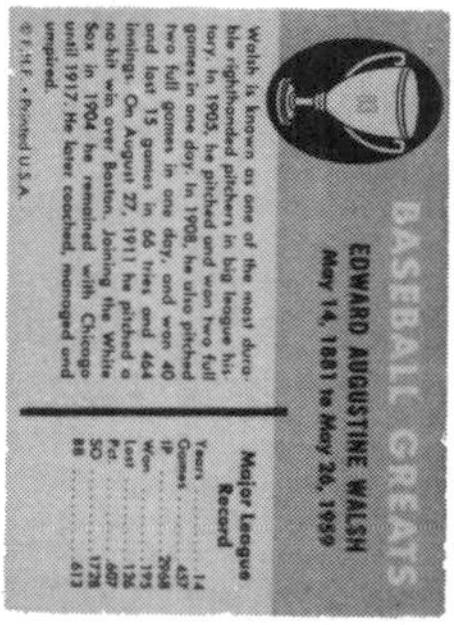

Over a two-year period, Fleer issued another set utilizing the Baseball Greats theme. The 154-card set was issued in two series and features a color player portrait against a color background. The player's name is located in a pennant set at the bottom of the card. The card backs feature orange and black on white stock and contain player biographical and statistical information. The cards measure 2-1/2" by 3-1/2" in size. The second series cards (#'s 89-154) were issued in 1962.

	NR MT	EX	VG
Complete Set:	800.00	400.00	240.00
Common Player: 1-88	2.00	1.00	.60
Common Player: 89-154	4.00	2.00	1.25

		NR MT	EX	VG
1	Baker, Cobb, Wheat/Checklist	35.00	17.50	10.50
2	G.C. Alexander	4.00	2.00	1.25
3	Nick Altrock	2.00	1.00	.60
4	Cap Anson	2.50	1.25	.70
5	Earl Averill	2.00	1.00	.60
6	Home Run Baker	2.00	1.00	.60
7	Dave Bancroft	2.00	1.00	.60
8	Chief Bender	2.00	1.00	.60
9	Jim Bottomley	2.00	1.00	.60
10	Roger Bresnahan	2.00	1.00	.60
11	Mordecai Brown	2.00	1.00	.60
12	Max Carey	2.00	1.00	.60
13	Jack Chesbro	2.00	1.00	.60
14	Ty Cobb	35.00	17.50	10.50
15	Mickey Cochrane	2.50	1.25	.70
16	Eddie Collins	2.50	1.25	.70
17	Earle Combs	2.00	1.00	.60
18	Charles Comiskey	2.00	1.00	.60
19	Ki Ki Cuyler	2.00	1.00	.60
20	Paul Derringer	2.00	1.00	.60
21	Howard Ehmke	2.00	1.00	.60
22	Billy Evans	2.00	1.00	.60
23	Johnny Evers	2.00	1.00	.60
24	Red Faber	2.00	1.00	.60
25	Bob Feller	6.00	3.00	1.75
26	Wes Ferrell	2.00	1.00	.60
27	Lew Fonseca	2.00	1.00	.60
28	Jimmy Foxx	4.00	2.00	1.25
29	Ford Frick	2.00	1.00	.60
30	Frankie Frisch	2.50	1.25	.70
31	Lou Gehrig	35.00	17.50	10.50
32	Charlie Gehringer	2.50	1.25	.70
33	Warren Giles	2.00	1.00	.60
34	Lefty Gomez	2.50	1.25	.70
35	Goose Goslin	2.00	1.00	.60
36	Clark Griffith	2.00	1.00	.60
37	Burleigh Grimes	2.00	1.00	.60
38	Lefty Grove	1.50	.70	.45
39	Chick Hafey	2.00	1.00	.60
40	Jesse Haines	2.00	1.00	.60
41	Gabby Hartnett	2.00	1.00	.60
42	Harry Heilmann	2.00	1.00	.60
43	Rogers Hornsby	4.00	2.00	1.25
44	Waite Hoyt	2.00	1.00	.60
45	Carl Hubbell	1.50	.70	.45
46	Miller Huggins	2.00	1.00	.60
47	Hughie Jennings	2.00	1.00	.60
48	Ban Johnson	2.00	1.00	.60
49	Walter Johnson	4.00	2.00	1.25
50	Ralph Kiner	2.50	1.25	.70
51	Chuck Klein	2.00	1.00	.60
52	Johnny Kling	2.00	1.00	.60
53	Judge Landis	2.00	1.00	.60
54	Tony Lazzeri	2.00	1.00	.60
55	Ernie Lombardi	2.00	1.00	.60
56	Dolf Luque	2.00	1.00	.60
57	Heinie Manush	2.00	1.00	.60
58	Marty Marion	2.00	1.00	.60
59	Christy Mathewson	2.50	1.25	.70
60	John McGraw	2.50	1.25	.70
61	Joe Medwick	2.00	1.00	.60
62	Bing Miller	2.00	1.00	.60
63	Johnny Mize	2.50	1.25	.70
64	Johnny Mostil	2.00	1.00	.60
65	Art Nehf	2.00	1.00	.60
66	Hal Newhouser	2.00	1.00	.60
67	Bobo Newsom	2.00	1.00	.60
68	Mel Ott	1.50	.70	.45
69	Allie Reynolds	2.00	1.00	.60
70	Sam Rice	2.00	1.00	.60
71	Eppa Rixey	2.00	1.00	.60
72	Edd Roush	2.00	1.00	.60
73	Schoolboy Rowe	2.00	1.00	.60
74	Red Ruffing	2.00	1.00	.60
75	Babe Ruth	65.00	32.00	19.50
76	Joe Sewell	2.00	1.00	.60
77	Al Simmons	2.00	1.00	.60
78	George Sisler	2.50	1.25	.70
79	Tris Speaker	1.50	.70	.45
80	Fred Toney	2.00	1.00	.60
81	Dazzy Vance	2.00	1.00	.60
82	Jim Vaughn	2.00	1.00	.60
83	Big Ed Walsh	2.00	1.00	.60
84	Lloyd Waner	2.00	1.00	.60
85	Paul Waner	2.00	1.00	.60
86	Zach Wheat	2.00	1.00	.60
87	Hack Wilson	2.00	1.00	.60
88	Jimmy Wilson	2.00	1.00	.60
89	Sisler & Traynor/Checklist	35.00	17.50	10.50
90	Babe Adams	4.00	2.00	1.25
91	Dale Alexander	4.00	2.00	1.25
92	Jim Bagby	4.00	2.00	1.25
93	Ossie Bluege	4.00	2.00	1.25
94	Lou Boudreau	6.00	3.00	1.75
95	Tommy Bridges	4.00	2.00	1.25
96	Donnie Bush (Donie)	4.00	2.00	1.25
97	Dolph Camilli	4.00	2.00	1.25
98	Frank Chance	6.00	3.00	1.75
99	Jimmy Collins	4.00	2.00	1.25
100	Stanley Coveleskie (Coveleski)	4.00	2.00	1.25
101	Hughie Critz	4.00	2.00	1.25
102	General Crowder	4.00	2.00	1.25
103	Joe Dugan	4.00	2.00	1.25
104	Bibb Falk	4.00	2.00	1.25
105	Rick Ferrell	4.00	2.00	1.25
106	Art Fletcher	4.00	2.00	1.25
107	Dennis Galehouse	4.00	2.00	1.25
108	Chick Galloway	4.00	2.00	1.25
109	Mule Haas	4.00	2.00	1.25
110	Stan Hack	4.00	2.00	1.25
111	Bump Hadley	4.00	2.00	1.25
112	Billy Hamilton	4.00	2.00	1.25
113	Joe Hauser	4.00	2.00	1.25
114	Babe Herman	4.00	2.00	1.25
115	Travis Jackson	4.00	2.00	1.25
116	Eddie Joost	4.00	2.00	1.25
117	Addie Joss	4.00	2.00	1.25
118	Joe Judge	4.00	2.00	1.25
119	Joe Kuhel	4.00	2.00	1.25
120	Nap Lajoie	8.00	4.00	2.50
121	Dutch Leonard	4.00	2.00	1.25
122	Ted Lyons	4.00	2.00	1.25
123	Connie Mack	8.00	4.00	2.50
124	Rabbit Maranville	4.00	2.00	1.25
125	Fred Marberry	4.00	2.00	1.25
126	Iron Man McGinnity	4.00	2.00	1.25
127	Oscar Melillo	4.00	2.00	1.25
128	Ray Mueller	4.00	2.00	1.25

		NR MT	EX	VG
129	Kid Nichols	4.00	2.00	1.25
130	Lefty O'Doul	4.00	2.00	1.25
131	Bob O'Farrell	4.00	2.00	1.25
132	Roger Peckinpaugh	4.00	2.00	1.25
133	Herb Pennock	4.00	2.00	1.25
134	George Pipgras	4.00	2.00	1.25
135	Eddie Plank	4.00	2.00	1.25
136	Ray Schalk	4.00	2.00	1.25
137	Hal Schumacher	4.00	2.00	1.25
138	Luke Sewell	4.00	2.00	1.25
139	Bob Shawkey	4.00	2.00	1.25
140	Riggs Stephenson	4.00	2.00	1.25
141	Billy Sullivan	4.00	2.00	1.25
142	Bill Terry	7.00	3.50	2.00
143	Joe Tinker	2.75	1.50	.80
144	Pie Traynor	6.00	3.00	1.75
145	George Uhle	4.00	2.00	1.25
146	Hal Troskey (Trosky)	4.00	2.00	1.25
147	Arky Vaughan	4.00	2.00	1.25
148	Johnny Vander Meer	4.00	2.00	1.25
149	Rube Waddell	4.00	2.00	1.25
150	Honus Wagner	35.00	17.50	10.50
151	Dixie Walker	4.00	2.00	1.25
152	Ted Williams	65.00	32.00	19.50
153	Cy Young	10.00	5.00	3.00
154	Ross Young (Youngs)	8.00	4.00	2.50

1963 Fleer

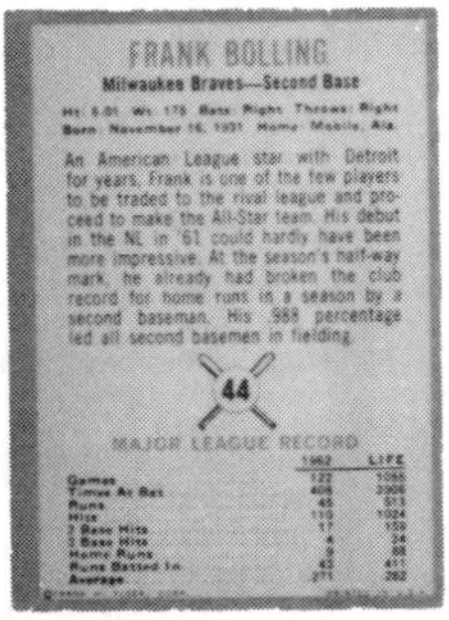

A lawsuit by Topps stopped Fleer's 1963 set at one series of 66 cards. Issued with a cookie rather than gum, the set features color photos of current players. The card backs include statistical information for 1962 and career plus a brief player biography. The cards, which measure 2-1/2" by 3-1/2", are numbered 1-66. An unnumbered checklist was issued with the set and is included in the complete set price in the checklist that follows. The checklist and #46 Adcock are scarce.

	NR MT	EX	VG
Complete Set:	1000.00	500.00	300.00
Common Player:	6.00	3.00	1.75

1	Steve Barber	10.00	2.00	1.25
2	Ron Hansen	6.00	3.00	1.75
3	Milt Pappas	2.25	1.25	.70
4	Brooks Robinson	30.00	15.00	9.00
5	Willie Mays	80.00	40.00	25.00
6	Lou Clinton	6.00	3.00	1.75
7	Bill Monbouquette	6.00	3.00	1.75
8	Carl Yastrzemski	75.00	38.00	23.00
9	Ray Herbert	6.00	3.00	1.75
10	Jim Landis	6.00	3.00	1.75
11	Dick Donovan	6.00	3.00	1.75
12	Tito Francona	6.00	3.00	1.75
13	Jerry Kindall	6.00	3.00	1.75
14	Frank Lary	2.25	1.25	.70
15	Dick Howser	4.00	2.00	1.25
16	Jerry Lumpe	6.00	3.00	1.75
17	Norm Siebern	6.00	3.00	1.75
18	Don Lee	6.00	3.00	1.75
19	Albie Pearson	6.00	3.00	1.75
20	Bob Rodgers	2.25	1.25	.70
21	Leon Wagner	6.00	3.00	1.75
22	Jim Kaat	7.00	3.50	2.00
23	Vic Power	6.00	3.00	1.75

		NR MT	EX	VG
24	Rich Rollins	6.00	3.00	1.75
25	Bobby Richardson	7.00	3.50	2.00
26	Ralph Terry	2.50	1.25	.70
27	Tom Cheney	2.25	1.25	.70
28	Chuck Cottier	6.00	3.00	1.75
29	Jimmy Piersall	2.50	1.25	.70
30	Dave Stenhouse	6.00	3.00	1.75
31	Glen Hobbie	6.00	3.00	1.75
32	Ron Santo	10.00	5.00	3.00
33	Gene Freese	6.00	3.00	1.75
34	Vada Pinson	10.00	5.00	3.00
35	Bob Purkey	6.00	3.00	1.75
36	Joe Amalfitano	6.00	3.00	1.75
37	Bob Aspromonte	6.00	3.00	1.75
38	Dick Farrell	6.00	3.00	1.75
39	Al Spangler	6.00	3.00	1.75
40	Tommy Davis	2.50	1.25	.70
41	Don Drysdale	30.00	15.00	9.00
42	Sandy Koufax	100.00	50.00	30.00
43	Maury Wills	50.00	25.00	15.00
44	Frank Bolling	6.00	3.00	1.75
45	Warren Spahn	40.00	20.00	12.00
46	Joe Adcock	125.00	62.00	37.00
47	Roger Craig	10.00	5.00	3.00
48	Al Jackson	2.25	1.25	.70
49	Rod Kanehl	2.25	1.25	.70
50	Ruben Amaro	6.00	3.00	1.75
51	John Callison	2.25	1.25	.70
52	Clay Dalrymple	6.00	3.00	1.75
53	Don Demeter	6.00	3.00	1.75
54	Art Mahaffey	6.00	3.00	1.75
55	"Smoky" Burgess	2.25	1.25	.70
56	Roberto Clemente	80.00	40.00	25.00
57	Elroy Face	2.25	1.25	.70
58	Vernon Law	2.25	1.25	.70
59	Bill Mazeroski	10.00	5.00	3.00
60	Ken Boyer	10.00	5.00	3.00
61	Bob Gibson	30.00	15.00	9.00
62	Gene Oliver	6.00	3.00	1.75
63	Bill White	9.00	4.50	2.75
64	Orlando Cepeda	10.00	5.00	3.00
65	Jimmy Davenport	6.00	3.00	1.75
66	Billy O'Dell	6.00	3.00	1.75
----	Checklist 1-66	325.00	130.00	81.00

1981 Fleer

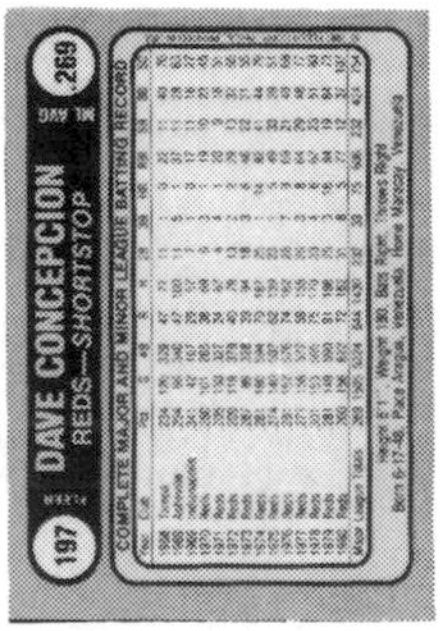

For the first time in 18 years, Fleer issued a baseball card set featuring current players. Fleer's 660-card effort included numerous errors in the first printing run which were subsequently corrected in additional runs. The cards, which measure 2-1/2" by 3-1/2", are numbered alphabetically by team. The card fronts feature a full-color photo inside a border which is color-coded by team. The card backs have black, grey and yellow ink on white stock and carry player statistical information. The player's batting average or earned run average is located in a circle in the upper right corner of the card. The complete set price in the checklist that follows does not include the higher priced variations.

	MT	NR MT	EX
Complete Set:	55.00	40.00	22.00
Common Player:	.06	.05	.02

1	Pete Rose	1.75	1.25	.70

		MT	NR MT	EX
2	Larry Bowa	.15	.11	.06
3	Manny Trillo	.08	.06	.03
4	Bob Boone	.10	.08	.04
5a	Mike Schmidt (portrait)	2.00	1.50	.80
5b	Mike Schmidt (batting)	2.00	1.50	.80
6a	Steve Carlton ("Lefty" on front)	1.00	.70	.40
6b	Steve Carlton (Pitcher of the Year on front, date 1066 on back)	2.00	1.50	.80
6c	Steve Carlton (Pitcher of the Year on front, date 1966 on back)	3.00	2.25	1.25
7a	Tug McGraw (Game Saver on front)	.50	.40	.20
7b	Tug McGraw (Pitcher on front)	.12	.09	.05
8	Larry Christenson	.06	.05	.02
9	Bake McBride	.06	.05	.02
10	Greg Luzinski	.15	.11	.06
11	Ron Reed	.06	.05	.02
12	Dickie Noles	.06	.05	.02
13	*Keith Moreland*	.20	.15	.08
14	*Bob Walk*	.25	.20	.10
15	Lonnie Smith	.08	.06	.03
16	Dick Ruthven	.06	.05	.02
17	Sparky Lyle	.10	.08	.04
18	Greg Gross	.06	.05	.02
19	Garry Maddox	.10	.08	.04
20	Nino Espinosa	.06	.05	.02
21	George Vukovich	.06	.05	.02
22	John Vukovich	.06	.05	.02
23	Ramon Aviles	.06	.05	.02
24a	Kevin Saucier (Ken Saucier on back)	.15	.11	.06
24b	Kevin Saucier (Kevin Saucier on back)	.70	.50	.30
25	Randy Lerch	.06	.05	.02
26	Del Unser	.06	.05	.02
27	Tim McCarver	.15	.11	.06
28a	George Brett (batting)	2.00	1.50	.80
28b	George Brett (portrait)	1.00	.70	.40
29a	Willie Wilson (portrait)	.60	.45	.25
29b	Willie Wilson (batting)	.15	.11	.06
30	Paul Splittorff	.06	.05	.02
31	Dan Quisenberry	.15	.11	.06
32a	Amos Otis (batting)	.50	.40	.20
32b	Amos Otis (portrait)	.10	.08	.04
33	Steve Busby	.08	.06	.03
34	U.L. Washington	.06	.05	.02
35	Dave Chalk	.06	.05	.02
36	Darrell Porter	.08	.06	.03
37	Marty Pattin	.06	.05	.02
38	Larry Gura	.06	.05	.02
39	Renie Martin	.06	.05	.02
40	Rich Gale	.06	.05	.02
41a	Hal McRae (dark blue "Royals" on front)	.40	.30	.15
41b	Hal McRae (light blue "Royals" on front)	.10	.08	.04
42	Dennis Leonard	.08	.06	.03
43	Willie Aikens	.06	.05	.02
44	Frank White	.10	.08	.04
45	Clint Hurdle	.06	.05	.02
46	John Wathan	.08	.06	.03
47	Pete LaCock	.06	.05	.02
48	Rance Mulliniks	.06	.05	.02
49	Jeff Twitty	.06	.05	.02
50	Jamie Quirk	.06	.05	.02
51	Art Howe	.06	.05	.02
52	Ken Forsch	.06	.05	.02
53	Vern Ruhle	.06	.05	.02
54	Joe Niekro	.12	.09	.05
55	Frank LaCorte	.06	.05	.02
56	J.R. Richard	.10	.08	.04
57	Nolan Ryan	6.00	4.50	2.50
58	Enos Cabell	.06	.05	.02
59	Cesar Cedeno	.12	.09	.05
60	Jose Cruz	.12	.09	.05
61	Bill Virdon	.06	.05	.02
62	Terry Puhl	.06	.05	.02
63	Joaquin Andujar	.10	.08	.04
64	Alan Ashby	.06	.05	.02
65	Joe Sambito	.06	.05	.02
66	Denny Walling	.06	.05	.02
67	Jeff Leonard	.12	.09	.05
68	Luis Pujols	.06	.05	.02
69	Bruce Bochy	.06	.05	.02
70	Rafael Landestoy	.06	.05	.02
71	*Dave Smith*	.30	.25	.12
72	*Danny Heep*	.10	.08	.04
73	Julio Gonzalez	.06	.05	.02
74	Craig Reynolds	.06	.05	.02
75	Gary Woods	.06	.05	.02
76	Dave Bergman	.06	.05	.02

		MT	NR MT	EX
77	Randy Niemann	.06	.05	.02
78	Joe Morgan	.60	.45	.25
79a	Reggie Jackson (portrait)	2.00	1.50	.80
79b	Reggie Jackson (batting)	.75	.60	.30
80	Bucky Dent	.10	.08	.04
81	Tommy John	.20	.15	.08
82	Luis Tiant	.12	.09	.05
83	Rick Cerone	.06	.05	.02
84	Dick Howser	.06	.05	.02
85	Lou Piniella	.12	.09	.05
86	Ron Davis	.08	.06	.03
87a	Graig Nettles (Craig on back)	12.00	9.00	4.75
87b	Graig Nettles (Graig on back)	.30	.25	.12
88	Ron Guidry	.25	.20	.10
89	Rich Gossage	.20	.15	.08
90	Rudy May	.06	.05	.02
91	Gaylord Perry	.60	.45	.25
92	Eric Soderholm	.06	.05	.02
93	Bob Watson	.08	.06	.03
94	Bobby Murcer	.10	.08	.04
95	Bobby Brown	.06	.05	.02
96	Jim Spencer	.06	.05	.02
97	Tom Underwood	.06	.05	.02
98	Oscar Gamble	.08	.06	.03
99	Johnny Oates	.06	.05	.02
100	Fred Stanley	.06	.05	.02
101	Ruppert Jones	.06	.05	.02
102	Dennis Werth	.06	.05	.02
103	Joe Lefebvre	.06	.05	.02
104	Brian Doyle	.06	.05	.02
105	Aurelio Rodriguez	.08	.06	.03
106	Doug Bird	.06	.05	.02
107	Mike Griffin	.06	.05	.02
108	Tim Lollar	.06	.05	.02
109	Willie Randolph	.10	.08	.04
110	Steve Garvey	.70	.50	.30
111	Reggie Smith	.10	.08	.04
112	Don Sutton	.30	.25	.12
113	Burt Hooton	.08	.06	.03
114a	Davy Lopes (Davey) (no finger on back)	.10	.08	.04
114b	Davy Lopes (Davey) (small finger on back)	1.00	.70	.40
115	Dusty Baker	.10	.08	.04
116	Tom Lasorda	.10	.08	.04
117	Bill Russell	.08	.06	.03
118	Jerry Reuss	.10	.08	.04
119	Terry Forster	.08	.06	.03
120a	Robert Welch (Bob Welch on back)	.60	.45	.25
120b	Robert Welch (Robert Welch on back)	1.00	.70	.40
121	Don Stanhouse	.06	.05	.02
122	Rick Monday	.10	.08	.04
123	Derrel Thomas	.06	.05	.02
124	Joe Ferguson	.06	.05	.02
125	Rick Sutcliffe	.20	.15	.08
126a	Ron Cey (no finger on back)	.12	.09	.05
126b	Ron Cey (small finger on back)	1.00	.70	.40
127	Dave Goltz	.08	.06	.03
128	Jay Johnstone	.08	.06	.03
129	Steve Yeager	.06	.05	.02
130	Gary Weiss	.06	.05	.02
131	*Mike Scioscia*	1.00	.70	.40
132	Vic Davalillo	.08	.06	.03
133	Doug Rau	.06	.05	.02
134	Pepe Frias	.06	.05	.02
135	Mickey Hatcher	.08	.06	.03
136	*Steve Howe*	.10	.08	.04
137	Robert Castillo	.06	.05	.02
138	Gary Thomasson	.06	.05	.02
139	Rudy Law	.06	.05	.02
140	*Fernand Valenzuela (Fernando)*	3.00	2.25	1.25
141	Manny Mota	.08	.06	.03
142	Gary Carter	.40	.30	.15
143	Steve Rogers	.08	.06	.03
144	Warren Cromartie	.06	.05	.02
145	Andre Dawson	1.50	1.25	.60
146	Larry Parrish	.10	.08	.04
147	Rowland Office	.06	.05	.02
148	Ellis Valentine	.06	.05	.02
149	Dick Williams	.06	.05	.02
150	*Bill Gullickson*	.15	.11	.06
151	Elias Sosa	.06	.05	.02
152	John Tamargo	.06	.05	.02
153	Chris Speier	.06	.05	.02
154	Ron LeFlore	.08	.06	.03
155	Rodney Scott	.06	.05	.02
156	Stan Bahnsen	.06	.05	.02
157	Bill Lee	.08	.06	.03
158	Fred Norman	.06	.05	.02
159	Woodie Fryman	.08	.06	.03

		MT	NR MT	EX
160	Dave Palmer	.06	.05	.02
161	Jerry White	.06	.05	.02
162	Roberto Ramos	.06	.05	.02
163	John D'Acquisto	.06	.05	.02
164	Tommy Hutton	.06	.05	.02
165	*Charlie Lea*	.12	.09	.05
166	Scott Sanderson	.06	.05	.02
167	Ken Macha	.06	.05	.02
168	Tony Bernazard	.06	.05	.02
169	Jim Palmer	1.00	.70	.40
170	Steve Stone	.08	.06	.03
171	Mike Flanagan	.10	.08	.04
172	Al Bumbry	.08	.06	.03
173	Doug DeCinces	.10	.08	.04
174	Scott McGregor	.08	.06	.03
175	Mark Belanger	.08	.06	.03
176	Tim Stoddard	.06	.05	.02
177a	Rick Dempsey (no finger on front)	.10	.08	.04
177b	Rick Dempsey (small finger on front)	1.00	.70	.40
178	Earl Weaver	.10	.08	.04
179	Tippy Martinez	.06	.05	.02
180	Dennis Martinez	.08	.06	.03
181	Sammy Stewart	.06	.05	.02
182	Rich Dauer	.06	.05	.02
183	Lee May	.08	.06	.03
184	Eddie Murray	1.25	.90	.50
185	Benny Ayala	.06	.05	.02
186	John Lowenstein	.06	.05	.02
187	Gary Roenicke	.06	.05	.02
188	Ken Singleton	.10	.08	.04
189	Dan Graham	.06	.05	.02
190	Terry Crowley	.06	.05	.02
191	Kiko Garcia	.06	.05	.02
192	Dave Ford	.06	.05	.02
193	Mark Corey	.06	.05	.02
194	Lenn Sakata	.06	.05	.02
195	Doug DeCinces	.10	.08	.04
196	Johnny Bench	1.00	.70	.40
197	Dave Concepcion	.15	.11	.06
198	Ray Knight	.10	.08	.04
199	Ken Griffey	.12	.09	.05
200	Tom Seaver	1.50	1.25	.60
201	Dave Collins	.08	.06	.03
202	George Foster	.20	.15	.08
203	Junior Kennedy	.06	.05	.02
204	Frank Pastore	.06	.05	.02
205	Dan Driessen	.08	.06	.03
206	Hector Cruz	.06	.05	.02
207	Paul Moskau	.06	.05	.02
208	*Charlie Leibrandt*	.40	.30	.15
209	Harry Spilman	.06	.05	.02
210	*Joe Price*	.12	.09	.05
211	Tom Hume	.06	.05	.02
212	Joe Nolan	.06	.05	.02
213	Doug Bair	.06	.05	.02
214	Mario Soto	.08	.06	.03
215a	Bill Bonham (no finger on back)	.08	.06	.03
215b	Bill Bonham (small finger on back)	1.00	.70	.40
216a	George Foster (Slugger on front)	.25	.20	.10
216b	George Foster (Outfield on front)	.20	.15	.08
217	Paul Householder	.06	.05	.02
218	Ron Oester	.06	.05	.02
219	Sam Mejias	.06	.05	.02
220	Sheldon Burnside	.06	.05	.02
221	Carl Yastrzemski	1.25	.90	.50
222	Jim Rice	.50	.40	.20
223	Fred Lynn	.20	.15	.08
224	Carlton Fisk	.60	.45	.25
225	Rick Burleson	.08	.06	.03
226	Dennis Eckersley	.50	.40	.20
227	Butch Hobson	.06	.05	.02
228	Tom Burgmeier	.06	.05	.02
229	Garry Hancock	.06	.05	.02
230	Don Zimmer	.06	.05	.02
231	Steve Renko	.06	.05	.02
232	Dwight Evans	.15	.11	.06
233	Mike Torrez	.08	.06	.03
234	Bob Stanley	.06	.05	.02
235	Jim Dwyer	.06	.05	.02
236	Dave Stapleton	.06	.05	.02
237	Glenn Hoffman	.06	.05	.02
238	Jerry Remy	.06	.05	.02
239	Dick Drago	.06	.05	.02
240	Bill Campbell	.06	.05	.02
241	Tony Perez	.20	.15	.08
242	Phil Niekro	.30	.25	.12
243	Dale Murphy	.90	.70	.35
244	Bob Horner	.12	.09	.05
245	Jeff Burroughs	.08	.06	.03
246	Rick Camp	.06	.05	.02
247	Bob Cox	.06	.05	.02
248	Bruce Benedict	.06	.05	.02
249	Gene Garber	.06	.05	.02
250	Jerry Royster	.06	.05	.02
251a	Gary Matthews (no finger on back)	.12	.09	.05
251b	Gary Matthews (small finger on back)	1.00	.70	.40
252	Chris Chambliss	.08	.06	.03
253	Luis Gomez	.06	.05	.02
254	Bill Nahorodny	.06	.05	.02
255	Doyle Alexander	.10	.08	.04
256	Brian Asselstine	.06	.05	.02
257	Biff Pocoroba	.06	.05	.02
258	Mike Lum	.06	.05	.02
259	Charlie Spikes	.06	.05	.02
260	Glenn Hubbard	.08	.06	.03
261	Tommy Boggs	.06	.05	.02
262	Al Hrabosky	.08	.06	.03
263	Rick Matula	.06	.05	.02
264	Preston Hanna	.06	.05	.02
265	Larry Bradford	.06	.05	.02
266	*Rafael Ramirez*	.20	.15	.08
267	Larry McWilliams	.06	.05	.02
268	Rod Carew	1.50	1.25	.60
269	Bobby Grich	.10	.08	.04
270	Carney Lansford	.10	.08	.04
271	Don Baylor	.12	.09	.05
272	Joe Rudi	.10	.08	.04
273	Dan Ford	.06	.05	.02
274	Jim Fregosi	.08	.06	.03
275	Dave Frost	.06	.05	.02
276	Frank Tanana	.10	.08	.04
277	Dickie Thon	.08	.06	.03
278	Jason Thompson	.06	.05	.02
279	Rick Miller	.06	.05	.02
280	Bert Campaneris	.10	.08	.04
281	Tom Donohue	.06	.05	.02
282	Brian Downing	.10	.08	.04
283	Fred Patek	.06	.05	.02
284	Bruce Kison	.06	.05	.02
285	Dave LaRoche	.06	.05	.02
286	Don Aase	.06	.05	.02
287	Jim Barr	.06	.05	.02
288	Alfredo Martinez	.06	.05	.02
289	Larry Harlow	.06	.05	.02
290	Andy Hassler	.06	.05	.02
291	Dave Kingman	.15	.11	.06
292	Bill Buckner	.12	.09	.05
293	Rick Reuschel	.10	.08	.04
294	Bruce Sutter	.15	.11	.06
295	Jerry Martin	.06	.05	.02
296	Scot Thompson	.06	.05	.02
297	Ivan DeJesus	.06	.05	.02
298	Steve Dillard	.06	.05	.02
299	Dick Tidrow	.06	.05	.02
300	Randy Martz	.06	.05	.02
301	Lenny Randle	.06	.05	.02
302	Lynn McGlothen	.06	.05	.02
303	Cliff Johnson	.06	.05	.02
304	Tim Blackwell	.06	.05	.02
305	Dennis Lamp	.06	.05	.02
306	Bill Caudill	.06	.05	.02
307	Carlos Lezcano	.06	.05	.02
308	Jim Tracy	.06	.05	.02
309	Doug Capilla	.06	.05	.02
310	Willie Hernandez	.10	.08	.04
311	Mike Vail	.06	.05	.02
312	Mike Krukow	.08	.06	.03
313	Barry Foote	.06	.05	.02
314	Larry Biittner	.06	.05	.02
315	Mike Tyson	.06	.05	.02
316	Lee Mazzilli	.08	.06	.03
317	John Stearns	.06	.05	.02
318	Alex Trevino	.06	.05	.02
319	Craig Swan	.06	.05	.02
320	Frank Taveras	.06	.05	.02
321	Steve Henderson	.06	.05	.02
322	Neil Allen	.08	.06	.03
323	Mark Bomback	.06	.05	.02
324	Mike Jorgensen	.06	.05	.02
325	Joe Torre	.08	.06	.03
326	Elliott Maddox	.06	.05	.02
327	Pete Falcone	.06	.05	.02
328	Ray Burris	.06	.05	.02
329	Claudell Washington	.08	.06	.03
330	Doug Flynn	.06	.05	.02
331	Joel Youngblood	.06	.05	.02
332	Bill Almon	.06	.05	.02
333	Tom Hausman	.06	.05	.02
334	Pat Zachry	.06	.05	.02

		MT	NR MT	EX
335	*Jeff Reardon*	3.00	2.25	1.25
336	*Wally Backman*	.35	.25	.14
337	Dan Norman	.06	.05	.02
338	Jerry Morales	.06	.05	.02
339	Ed Farmer	.06	.05	.02
340	Bob Molinaro	.06	.05	.02
341	Todd Cruz	.06	.05	.02
342a	*Britt Burns* (no finger on front)	.20	.15	.08
342b	*Britt Burns* (small finger on front)	1.00	.70	.40
343	Kevin Bell	.06	.05	.02
344	Tony LaRussa	.08	.06	.03
345	Steve Trout	.06	.05	.02
346	*Harold Baines*	5.00	3.75	2.00
347	Richard Wortham	.06	.05	.02
348	Wayne Nordhagen	.06	.05	.02
349	Mike Squires	.06	.05	.02
350	Lamar Johnson	.06	.05	.02
351	Rickey Henderson	15.00	11.00	6.00
352	Francisco Barrios	.06	.05	.02
353	Thad Bosley	.06	.05	.02
354	Chet Lemon	.08	.06	.03
355	Bruce Kimm	.06	.05	.02
356	*Richard Dotson*	.25	.20	.10
357	Jim Morrison	.06	.05	.02
358	Mike Proly	.06	.05	.02
359	Greg Pryor	.06	.05	.02
360	Dave Parker	.30	.25	.12
361	Omar Moreno	.06	.05	.02
362a	Kent Tekulve (1071 Waterbury on back)	.15	.11	.06
362b	Kent Tekulve (1971 Waterbury on back)	.70	.50	.30
363	Willie Stargell	.40	.30	.15
364	Phil Garner	.08	.06	.03
365	Ed Ott	.06	.05	.02
366	Don Robinson	.08	.06	.03
367	Chuck Tanner	.06	.05	.02
368	Jim Rooker	.06	.05	.02
369	Dale Berra	.06	.05	.02
370	Jim Bibby	.06	.05	.02
371	Steve Nicosia	.06	.05	.02
372	Mike Easler	.08	.06	.03
373	Bill Robinson	.06	.05	.02
374	Lee Lacy	.06	.05	.02
375	John Candelaria	.10	.08	.04
376	Manny Sanguillen	.06	.05	.02
377	Rick Rhoden	.10	.08	.04
378	Grant Jackson	.06	.05	.02
379	Tim Foli	.06	.05	.02
380	*Rod Scurry*	.08	.06	.03
381	Bill Madlock	.12	.09	.05
382a	Kurt Bevacqua (photo reversed, backwards "P" on cap)	.15	.11	.06
382b	Kurt Bevacqua (correct photo)	.70	.50	.30
383	Bert Blyleven	.12	.09	.05
384	Eddie Solomon	.06	.05	.02
385	Enrique Romo	.06	.05	.02
386	John Milner	.06	.05	.02
387	Mike Hargrove	.06	.05	.02
388	Jorge Orta	.06	.05	.02
389	Toby Harrah	.08	.06	.03
390	Tom Veryzer	.06	.05	.02
391	Miguel Dilone	.06	.05	.02
392	Dan Spillner	.06	.05	.02
393	Jack Brohamer	.06	.05	.02
394	Wayne Garland	.06	.05	.02
395	Sid Monge	.06	.05	.02
396	Rick Waits	.06	.05	.02
397	*Joe Charboneau*	.10	.08	.04
398	Gary Alexander	.06	.05	.02
399	Jerry Dybzinski	.06	.05	.02
400	Mike Stanton	.06	.05	.02
401	Mike Paxton	.06	.05	.02
402	Gary Gray	.06	.05	.02
403	Rick Manning	.06	.05	.02
404	Bo Diaz	.08	.06	.03
405	Ron Hassey	.06	.05	.02
406	Ross Grimsley	.06	.05	.02
407	Victor Cruz	.06	.05	.02
408	Len Barker	.08	.06	.03
409	Bob Bailor	.06	.05	.02
410	Otto Velez	.06	.05	.02
411	Ernie Whitt	.08	.06	.03
412	Jim Clancy	.08	.06	.03
413	Barry Bonnell	.06	.05	.02
414	Dave Stieb	.60	.45	.25
415	*Damaso Garcia*	.10	.08	.04
416	John Mayberry	.08	.06	.03
417	Roy Howell	.06	.05	.02
418	*Dan Ainge*	.25	.20	.10
419a	Jesse Jefferson (Pirates on back)	.10	.08	.04

		MT	NR MT	EX
419b	Jesse Jefferson (Blue Jays on back)	.50	.40	.20
420	Joey McLaughlin	.06	.05	.02
421	*Lloyd Moseby*	.80	.60	.30
422	Al Woods	.06	.05	.02
423	Garth Iorg	.06	.05	.02
424	Doug Ault	.06	.05	.02
425	*Ken Schrom*	.06	.05	.02
426	Mike Willis	.06	.05	.02
427	Steve Braun	.06	.05	.02
428	Bob Davis	.06	.05	.02
429	Jerry Garvin	.06	.05	.02
430	Alfredo Griffin	.08	.06	.03
431	Bob Mattick	.06	.05	.02
432	Vida Blue	.12	.09	.05
433	Jack Clark	.25	.20	.10
434	Willie McCovey	.40	.30	.15
435	Mike Ivie	.06	.05	.02
436a	Darrel Evans (Darrel on front)	.15	.11	.06
436b	Darrell Evans (Darrell on front)	.70	.50	.30
437	Terry Whitfield	.06	.05	.02
438	Rennie Stennett	.06	.05	.02
439	John Montefusco	.08	.06	.03
440	Jim Wohlford	.06	.05	.02
441	Bill North	.06	.05	.02
442	Milt May	.06	.05	.02
443	Max Venable	.06	.05	.02
444	Ed Whitson	.06	.05	.02
445	*Al Holland*	.08	.06	.03
446	Randy Moffitt	.06	.05	.02
447	Bob Knepper	.08	.06	.03
448	Gary Lavelle	.06	.05	.02
449	Greg Minton	.06	.05	.02
450	Johnnie LeMaster	.06	.05	.02
451	Larry Herndon	.08	.06	.03
452	Rich Murray	.06	.05	.02
453	Joe Pettini	.06	.05	.02
454	Allen Ripley	.06	.05	.02
455	Dennis Littlejohn	.06	.05	.02
456	Tom Griffin	.06	.05	.02
457	Alan Hargesheimer	.06	.05	.02
458	Joe Strain	.06	.05	.02
459	Steve Kemp	.08	.06	.03
460	Sparky Anderson	.10	.08	.04
461	Alan Trammell	.40	.30	.15
462	Mark Fidrych	.08	.06	.03
463	Lou Whitaker	.40	.30	.15
464	Dave Rozema	.06	.05	.02
465	Milt Wilcox	.06	.05	.02
466	Champ Summers	.06	.05	.02
467	Lance Parrish	.35	.25	.14
468	Dan Petry	.08	.06	.03
469	Pat Underwood	.06	.05	.02
470	Rick Peters	.06	.05	.02
471	Al Cowens	.06	.05	.02
472	John Wockenfuss	.06	.05	.02
473	Tom Brookens	.08	.06	.03
474	Richie Hebner	.06	.05	.02
475	Jack Morris	.30	.25	.12
476	Jim Lentine	.06	.05	.02
477	Bruce Robbins	.06	.05	.02
478	Mark Wagner	.06	.05	.02
479	Tim Corcoran	.06	.05	.02
480a	Stan Papi (Pitcher on front)	.15	.11	.06
480b	Stan Papi (Shortstop on front)	.70	.50	.30
481	*Kirk Gibson*	4.00	3.00	1.50
482	Dan Schatzeder	.06	.05	.02
483	Amos Otis	.70	.50	.30
484	Dave Winfield	1.25	.90	.50
485	Rollie Fingers	1.00	.70	.40
486	Gene Richards	.06	.05	.02
487	Randy Jones	.08	.06	.03
488	Ozzie Smith	1.50	1.25	.60
489	Gene Tenace	.08	.06	.03
490	Bill Fahey	.06	.05	.02
491	John Curtis	.06	.05	.02
492	Dave Cash	.06	.05	.02
493a	Tim Flannery (photo reversed, batting righty)	.15	.11	.06
493b	Tim Flannery (photo correct, batting lefty)	.70	.50	.30
494	Jerry Mumphrey	.06	.05	.02
495	Bob Shirley	.06	.05	.02
496	Steve Mura	.06	.05	.02
497	Eric Rasmussen	.06	.05	.02
498	Broderick Perkins	.06	.05	.02
499	Barry Evans	.06	.05	.02
500	Chuck Baker	.06	.05	.02
501	*Luis Salazar*	.15	.11	.06
502	Gary Lucas	.08	.06	.03
503	Mike Armstrong	.06	.05	.02

		MT	NR MT	EX
504	Jerry Turner	.06	.05	.02
505	Dennis Kinney	.06	.05	.02
506	Willy Montanez (Willie)	.06	.05	.02
507	Gorman Thomas	.10	.08	.04
508	Ben Oglivie	.08	.06	.03
509	Larry Hisle	.08	.06	.03
510	Sal Bando	.10	.08	.04
511	Robin Yount	2.00	1.50	.80
512	Mike Caldwell	.06	.05	.02
513	Sixto Lezcano	.06	.05	.02
514a	Jerry Augustine (Billy Travers photo)	.15	.11	.06
514b	Billy Travers (correct name with photo)	.70	.50	.30
515	Paul Molitor	.20	.15	.08
516	Moose Haas	.06	.05	.02
517	Bill Castro	.06	.05	.02
518	Jim Slaton	.06	.05	.02
519	Lary Sorensen	.06	.05	.02
520	Bob McClure	.06	.05	.02
521	Charlie Moore	.06	.05	.02
522	Jim Gantner	.08	.06	.03
523	Reggie Cleveland	.06	.05	.02
524	Don Money	.06	.05	.02
525	Billy Travers	.06	.05	.02
526	Buck Martinez	.06	.05	.02
527	Dick Davis	.06	.05	.02
528	Ted Simmons	.12	.09	.05
529	Garry Templeton	.10	.08	.04
530	Ken Reitz	.06	.05	.02
531	Tony Scott	.06	.05	.02
532	Ken Oberkfell	.06	.05	.02
533	Bob Sykes	.06	.05	.02
534	Keith Smith	.06	.05	.02
535	John Littlefield	.06	.05	.02
536	Jim Kaat	.15	.11	.06
537	Bob Forsch	.08	.06	.03
538	Mike Phillips	.06	.05	.02
539	*Terry Landrum*	.10	.08	.04
540	*Leon Durham*	.20	.15	.08
541	Terry Kennedy	.08	.06	.03
542	George Hendrick	.08	.06	.03
543	Dane Iorg	.06	.05	.02
544	Mark Littell (photo actually Jeff Little)	.06	.05	.02
545	Keith Hernandez	.40	.30	.15
546	Silvio Martinez	.06	.05	.02
547a	Pete Vuckovich (photo actually Don Hood)	.15	.11	.06
547b	Don Hood (correct name with photo)	.70	.50	.30
548	Bobby Bonds	.10	.08	.04
549	Mike Ramsey	.06	.05	.02
550	Tom Herr	.10	.08	.04
551	Roy Smalley	.06	.05	.02
552	Jerry Koosman	.10	.08	.04
553	Ken Landreaux	.06	.05	.02
554	John Castino	.06	.05	.02
555	Doug Corbett	.06	.05	.02
556	Bombo Rivera	.06	.05	.02
557	Ron Jackson	.06	.05	.02
558	Butch Wynegar	.06	.05	.02
559	Hosken Powell	.06	.05	.02
560	Pete Redfern	.06	.05	.02
561	Roger Erickson	.06	.05	.02
562	Glenn Adams	.06	.05	.02
563	Rick Sofield	.06	.05	.02
564	Geoff Zahn	.06	.05	.02
565	Pete Mackanin	.06	.05	.02
566	Mike Cubbage	.06	.05	.02
567	Darrell Jackson	.06	.05	.02
568	Dave Edwards	.06	.05	.02
569	Rob Wilfong	.06	.05	.02
570	Sal Butera	.06	.05	.02
571	Jose Morales	.06	.05	.02
572	Rick Langford	.06	.05	.02
573	Mike Norris	.06	.05	.02
574	Rickey Henderson	20.00	15.00	8.00
575	Tony Armas	.10	.08	.04
576	Dave Revering	.06	.05	.02
577	Jeff Newman	.06	.05	.02
578	Bob Lacey	.06	.05	.02
579	Brian Kingman (photo actually Alan Wirth)	.06	.05	.02
580	Mitchell Page	.06	.05	.02
581	Billy Martin	.12	.09	.05
582	Rob Picciolo	.06	.05	.02
583	Mike Heath	.06	.05	.02
584	Mickey Klutts	.06	.05	.02
585	Orlando Gonzalez	.06	.05	.02
586	*Mike Davis*	.25	.20	.10
587	Wayne Gross	.06	.05	.02
588	Matt Keough	.06	.05	.02
589	Steve McCatty	.06	.05	.02
590	Dwayne Murphy	.08	.06	.03
591	Mario Guerrero	.06	.05	.02
592	Dave McKay	.06	.05	.02
593	Jim Essian	.06	.05	.02
594	Dave Heaverlo	.06	.05	.02
595	Maury Wills	.10	.08	.04
596	Juan Beniquez	.06	.05	.02
597	Rodney Craig	.06	.05	.02
598	Jim Anderson	.06	.05	.02
599	Floyd Bannister	.10	.08	.04
600	Bruce Bochte	.06	.05	.02
601	Julio Cruz	.06	.05	.02
602	Ted Cox	.06	.05	.02
603	Dan Meyer	.06	.05	.02
604	Larry Cox	.06	.05	.02
605	Bill Stein	.06	.05	.02
606	Steve Garvey	.50	.40	.20
607	Dave Roberts	.06	.05	.02
608	Leon Roberts	.06	.05	.02
609	Reggie Walton	.06	.05	.02
610	Dave Edler	.06	.05	.02
611	Larry Milbourne	.06	.05	.02
612	Kim Allen	.06	.05	.02
613	Mario Mendoza	.06	.05	.02
614	Tom Paciorek	.06	.05	.02
615	Glenn Abbott	.06	.05	.02
616	Joe Simpson	.06	.05	.02
617	Mickey Rivers	.08	.06	.03
618	Jim Kern	.06	.05	.02
619	Jim Sundberg	.08	.06	.03
620	Richie Zisk	.08	.06	.03
621	Jon Matlack	.08	.06	.03
622	Ferguson Jenkins	.50	.40	.20
623	Pat Corrales	.06	.05	.02
624	Ed Figueroa	.06	.05	.02
625	Buddy Bell	.12	.09	.05
626	Al Oliver	.15	.11	.06
627	Doc Medich	.06	.05	.02
628	Bump Wills	.06	.05	.02
629	Rusty Staub	.10	.08	.04
630	Pat Putnam	.06	.05	.02
631	John Grubb	.06	.05	.02
632	Danny Darwin	.06	.05	.02
633	Ken Clay	.06	.05	.02
634	Jim Norris	.06	.05	.02
635	John Butcher	.06	.05	.02
636	Dave Roberts	.06	.05	.02
637	Billy Sample	.06	.05	.02
638	Carl Yastrzemski	1.00	.70	.40
639	Cecil Cooper	.15	.11	.06
640	Mike Schmidt	2.00	1.50	.80
641a	Checklist 1-50 (41 Hal McRae)	.10	.08	.04
641b	Checklist 1-50 (41 Hal McRae Double Threat)	.40	.30	.15
642	Checklist 51-109	.06	.05	.02
643	Checklist 110-168	.06	.05	.02
644a	Checklist 169-220 (202 George Foster)	.10	.08	.04
644b	Checklist 169-220 (202 George Foster "Slugger")	.40	.30	.15
645a	Triple Threat (Larry Bowa, Pete Rose, Mike Schmidt) (no number on back)	1.00	.70	.40
645b	Triple Threat (Larry Bowa, Pete Rose, Mike Schmidt) (645 on back)	2.00	1.50	.80
646	Checklist 221-267	.06	.05	.02
647	Checklist 268-315	.06	.05	.02
648	Checklist 316-359	.06	.05	.02
649	Checklist 360-408	.06	.05	.02
650	Reggie Jackson	3.00	2.25	1.25
651	Checklist 409-458	.06	.05	.02
652a	Checklist 459-509 (483 Aurelio Lopez)	.10	.08	.04
652b	Checklist 459-506 (no 483)	.40	.30	.15
653	Willie Wilson	1.00	.70	.40
654a	Checklist 507-550 (514 Jerry Augustine)	.10	.08	.04
654b	Checklist 507-550 (514 Billy Travers)	.40	.30	.15
655	George Brett	2.00	1.50	.80
656	Checklist 551-593	.06	.05	.02
657	Tug McGraw	1.00	.70	.40
658	Checklist 594-637	.06	.05	.02
659a	Checklist 640-660 (last number on front is 551)	.10	.08	.04
659b	Checklist 640-660 (last number on front is 483)	.40	.30	.15
660a	Steve Carlton (date 1066 on back)	1.00	.70	.40

		MT	NR MT	EX
660b	Steve Carlton (date 1966 on back)	2.00	1.50	.80

1981 Fleer Star Stickers

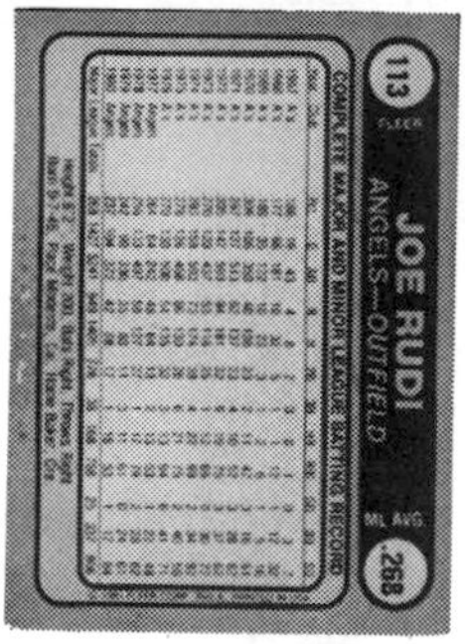

The 128-card 1981 Fleer Star Sticker set was designed for the card fronts to be peeled away from the cardboard backs. The card obverses feature color photos with blue and yellow trim. The card backs are identical in design to the regular 1981 Fleer set except for color and numbering. The set contains three unnumbered checklist cards whose fronts depict Reggie Jackson (#'s 1-42), George Brett (#'s 43-83) and Mike Schmidt (#'s 84-125). The cards, which are the standard 2-1/2" by 3-1/2", were issued in gum wax packs.

		MT	NR MT	EX
	Complete Set	65.00	49.00	26.00
	Common Player	.10	.08	.04
1	Steve Garvey	1.00	.70	.40
2	Ron LeFlore	.10	.08	.04
3	Ron Cey	.25	.20	.10
4	Dave Revering	.10	.08	.04
5	Tony Armas	.15	.11	.06
6	Mike Norris	.10	.08	.04
7	Steve Kemp	.15	.11	.06
8	Bruce Bochte	.10	.08	.04
9	Mike Schmidt	4.00	3.00	1.50
10	Scott McGregor	.10	.08	.04
11	Buddy Bell	.20	.15	.08
12	Carney Lansford	.20	.15	.08
13	Carl Yastrzemski	4.00	3.00	1.50
14	Ben Oglivie	.10	.08	.04
15	Willie Stargell	4.00	3.00	1.50
16	Cecil Cooper	.15	.11	.06
17	Gene Richards	.10	.08	.04
18	Jim Kern	.10	.08	.04
19	Jerry Koosman	.15	.11	.06
20	Larry Bowa	.20	.15	.08
21	Kent Tekulve	.15	.11	.06
22	Dan Driessen	.10	.08	.04
23	Phil Niekro	1.00	.70	.40
24	Dan Quisenberry	.30	.25	.12
25	Dave Winfield	1.00	.70	.40
26	Dave Parker	1.00	.70	.40
27	Rick Langford	.10	.08	.04
28	Amos Otis	.15	.11	.06
29	Bill Buckner	.15	.11	.06
30	Al Bumbry	.10	.08	.04
31	Bake McBride	.10	.08	.04
32	Mickey Rivers	.10	.08	.04
33	Rick Burleson	.10	.08	.04
34	Dennis Eckersley	.60	.45	.25
35	Cesar Cedeno	.20	.15	.08
36	Enos Cabell	.10	.08	.04
37	Johnny Bench	4.00	3.00	1.50
38	Robin Yount	4.00	3.00	1.50
39	Mark Belanger	.10	.08	.04
40	Rod Carew	1.00	.70	.40
41	George Foster	.40	.30	.15
42	Lee Mazzilli	.15	.11	.06
43	Triple Threat (Larry Bowa, Pete Rose, Mike Schmidt)	2.00	1.50	.80
44	J.R. Richard	.15	.11	.06
45	Lou Piniella	.30	.25	.12
46	Ken Landreaux	.10	.08	.04
47	Rollie Fingers	1.00	.70	.40
48	Joaquin Andujar	.10	.08	.04
49	Tom Seaver	4.00	3.00	1.50
50	Bobby Grich	.20	.15	.08
51	Jon Matlack	.10	.08	.04
52	Jack Clark	.25	.20	.10
53	Jim Rice	.25	.20	.10
54	Rickey Henderson	4.00	3.00	1.50
55	Roy Smalley	.10	.08	.04
56	Mike Flanagan	.15	.11	.06
57	Steve Rogers	.10	.08	.04
58	Carlton Fisk	.60	.45	.25
59	Don Sutton	1.00	.70	.40
60	Ken Griffey	.20	.15	.08
61	Burt Hooton	.10	.08	.04
62	Dusty Baker	.20	.15	.08
63	Vida Blue	.25	.20	.10
64	Al Oliver	.30	.25	.12
65	Jim Bibby	.10	.08	.04
66	Tony Perez	1.00	.70	.40
67	Davy Lopes (Davey)	.15	.11	.06
68	Bill Russell	.15	.11	.06
69	Larry Parrish	.20	.15	.08
70	Garry Maddox	.15	.11	.06
71	Phil Garner	.15	.11	.06
72	Graig Nettles	.35	.25	.14
73	Gary Carter	1.00	.70	.40
74	Pete Rose	4.00	3.00	1.50
75	Greg Luzinski	.30	.25	.12
76	Ron Guidry	.25	.20	.10
77	Gorman Thomas	.15	.11	.06
78	Jose Cruz	.20	.15	.08
79	Bob Boone	.15	.11	.06
80	Bruce Sutter	.35	.25	.14
81	Chris Chambliss	.15	.11	.06
82	Paul Molitor	.60	.45	.25
83	Tug McGraw	.25	.20	.10
84	Ferguson Jenkins	.40	.30	.15
85	Steve Carlton	5.00	3.75	2.00
86	Miguel Dilone	.10	.08	.04
87	Reggie Smith	.20	.15	.08
88	Rick Cerone	.10	.08	.04
89	Alan Trammell	1.00	.70	.40
90	Doug DeCinces	.20	.15	.08
91	Sparky Lyle	.15	.11	.06
92	Warren Cromartie	.10	.08	.04
93	Rick Reuschel	.25	.20	.10
94	Larry Hisle	.10	.08	.04
95	Paul Splittorff	.10	.08	.04
96	Manny Trillo	.10	.08	.04
97	Frank White	.20	.15	.08
98	Fred Lynn	.25	.20	.10
99	Bob Horner	.15	.11	.06
100	Omar Moreno	.10	.08	.04
101	Dave Concepcion	.20	.15	.08
102	Larry Gura	.10	.08	.04
103	Ken Singleton	.20	.15	.08
104	Steve Stone	.15	.11	.06
105	Richie Zisk	.10	.08	.04
106	Willie Wilson	.40	.30	.15
107	Willie Randolph	.20	.15	.08
108	Nolan Ryan	6.00	4.50	2.50
109	Joe Morgan	1.00	.70	.40
110	Bucky Dent	.20	.15	.08
111	Dave Kingman	.40	.30	.15
112	John Castino	.10	.08	.04
113	Joe Rudi	.20	.15	.08
114	Ed Farmer	.10	.08	.04
115	Reggie Jackson	4.00	3.00	1.50
116	George Brett	1.00	.70	.40
117	Eddie Murray	.25	.20	.10
118	Rich Gossage	.25	.20	.10
119	Dale Murphy	1.00	.70	.40
120	Ted Simmons	.15	.11	.06
121	Tommy John	.25	.20	.10
122	Don Baylor	.30	.25	.12
123	Andre Dawson	1.00	.70	.40
124	Jim Palmer	4.00	3.00	1.50
125	Garry Templeton	.20	.15	.08
----	Reggie Jackson/Checklist 1-42	4.00	3.00	1.50
----	George Brett/Checklist 43-83	4.00	3.00	1.50
----	Mike Schmidt/Checklist 84-125	4.00	3.00	1.50

Definitions for grading conditions are located in the introduction section at the front of this book.

1982 Fleer

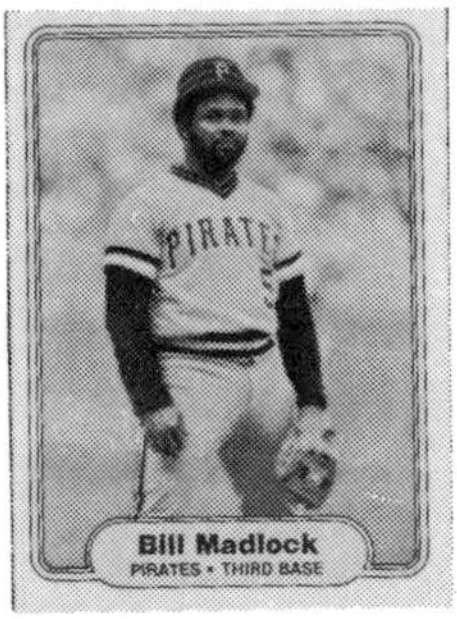

Fleer's 1982 set did not match the quality of the previous year's effort. Many of the photos in the set are blurred and have muddied backgrounds. The cards, which measure 2-1/2" by 3-1/2", feature color photos surrounded by a border frame which is color-coded by team. The card backs are blue, white, and yellow and contain the player's team logo plus the logos of Major League Baseball and the Major League Baseball Players Association. Due to a lawsuit by Topps, Fleer was forced to issue the set with team logo stickers rather than gum. The complete set price does not include the higher priced variations.

		MT	NR MT	EX
Complete Set:		70.00	52.00	27.00
Common Player:		.06	.05	.02
1	Dusty Baker	.10	.08	.04
2	Robert Castillo	.06	.05	.02
3	Ron Cey	.12	.09	.05
4	Terry Forster	.08	.06	.03
5	Steve Garvey	.50	.40	.20
6	Dave Goltz	.08	.06	.03
7	Pedro Guerrero(FC)	.60	.45	.25
8	Burt Hooton	.08	.06	.03
9	Steve Howe	.08	.06	.03
10	Jay Johnstone	.08	.06	.03
11	Ken Landreaux	.06	.05	.02
12	Davey Lopes	.10	.08	.04
13	*Mike Marshall*(FC)	.50	.40	.20
14	Bobby Mitchell	.06	.05	.02
15	Rick Monday	.10	.08	.04
16	*Tom Niedenfuer*(FC)	.20	.15	.08
17	*Ted Power*(FC)	.20	.15	.08
18	Jerry Reuss	.10	.08	.04
19	Ron Roenicke	.06	.05	.02
20	Bill Russell	.08	.06	.03
21	*Steve Sax*(FC)	4.00	3.00	1.50
22	Mike Scioscia	.08	.06	.03
23	Reggie Smith	.10	.08	.04
24	*Dave Stewart*(FC)	6.00	4.50	2.50
25	Rick Sutcliffe	.15	.11	.06
26	Derrel Thomas	.06	.05	.02
27	Fernando Valenzuela	.60	.45	.25
28	Bob Welch	.12	.09	.05
29	Steve Yeager	.06	.05	.02
30	Bobby Brown	.06	.05	.02
31	Rick Cerone	.06	.05	.02
32	Ron Davis	.06	.05	.02
33	Bucky Dent	.10	.08	.04
34	Barry Foote	.06	.05	.02
35	George Frazier	.06	.05	.02
36	Oscar Gamble	.08	.06	.03
37	Rich Gossage	.20	.15	.08
38	Ron Guidry	.25	.20	.10
39	Reggie Jackson	1.00	.70	.40
40	Tommy John	.20	.15	.08
41	Rudy May	.06	.05	.02
42	Larry Milbourne	.06	.05	.02
43	Jerry Mumphrey	.06	.05	.02
44	Bobby Murcer	.10	.08	.04
45	*Gene Nelson*	.12	.09	.05
46	Graig Nettles	.15	.11	.06
47	Johnny Oates	.06	.05	.02
48	Lou Piniella	.12	.09	.05
49	Willie Randolph	.10	.08	.04
50	Rick Reuschel	.10	.08	.04
51	Dave Revering	.06	.05	.02
52	*Dave Righetti*(FC)	2.00	1.50	.80
53	Aurelio Rodriguez	.08	.06	.03
54	Bob Watson	.08	.06	.03
55	Dennis Werth	.06	.05	.02
56	Dave Winfield	.60	.45	.25
57	Johnny Bench	.80	.60	.30
58	Bruce Berenyi	.06	.05	.02
59	Larry Biittner	.06	.05	.02
60	Scott Brown	.06	.05	.02
61	Dave Collins	.08	.06	.03
62	Geoff Combe	.06	.05	.02
63	Dave Concepcion	.12	.09	.05
64	Dan Driessen	.08	.06	.03
65	Joe Edelen	.06	.05	.02
66	George Foster	.20	.15	.08
67	Ken Griffey	.12	.09	.05
68	Paul Householder	.06	.05	.02
69	Tom Hume	.06	.05	.02
70	Junior Kennedy	.06	.05	.02
71	Ray Knight	.10	.08	.04
72	Mike LaCoss	.06	.05	.02
73	Rafael Landestoy	.06	.05	.02
74	Charlie Leibrandt	.10	.08	.04
75	Sam Mejias	.06	.05	.02
76	Paul Moskau	.06	.05	.02
77	Joe Nolan	.06	.05	.02
78	Mike O'Berry	.06	.05	.02
79	Ron Oester	.06	.05	.02
80	Frank Pastore	.06	.05	.02
81	Joe Price	.06	.05	.02
82	Tom Seaver	.60	.45	.25
83	Mario Soto	.08	.06	.03
84	Mike Vail	.06	.05	.02
85	Tony Armas	.10	.08	.04
86	Shooty Babitt	.06	.05	.02
87	Dave Beard	.06	.05	.02
88	Rick Bosetti	.06	.05	.02
89	Keith Drumright	.06	.05	.02
90	Wayne Gross	.06	.05	.02
91	Mike Heath	.06	.05	.02
92	Rickey Henderson	5.00	3.75	2.00
93	Cliff Johnson	.06	.05	.02
94	Jeff Jones	.06	.05	.02
95	Matt Keough	.06	.05	.02
96	Brian Kingman	.06	.05	.02
97	Mickey Klutts	.06	.05	.02
98	Rick Langford	.06	.05	.02
99	Steve McCatty	.06	.05	.02
100	Dave McKay	.06	.05	.02
101	Dwayne Murphy	.08	.06	.03
102	Jeff Newman	.06	.05	.02
103	Mike Norris	.06	.05	.02
104	Bob Owchinko	.06	.05	.02
105	Mitchell Page	.06	.05	.02
106	Rob Picciolo	.06	.05	.02
107	Jim Spencer	.06	.05	.02
108	Fred Stanley	.06	.05	.02
109	Tom Underwood	.06	.05	.02
110	Joaquin Andujar	.08	.06	.03
111	Steve Braun	.06	.05	.02
112	Bob Forsch	.08	.06	.03
113	George Hendrick	.08	.06	.03
114	Keith Hernandez	.40	.30	.15
115	Tom Herr	.10	.08	.04
116	Dane Iorg	.06	.05	.02
117	Jim Kaat	.15	.11	.06
118	Tito Landrum	.06	.05	.02
119	Sixto Lezcano	.06	.05	.02
120	Mark Littell	.06	.05	.02
121	John Martin	.06	.05	.02
122	Silvio Martinez	.06	.05	.02
123	Ken Oberkfell	.06	.05	.02
124	Darrell Porter	.08	.06	.03
125	Mike Ramsey	.06	.05	.02
126	Orlando Sanchez	.06	.05	.02
127	Bob Shirley	.06	.05	.02
128	Lary Sorensen	.06	.05	.02
129	Bruce Sutter	.15	.11	.06
130	Bob Sykes	.06	.05	.02
131	Garry Templeton	.10	.08	.04
132	Gene Tenace	.08	.06	.03
133	Jerry Augustine	.06	.05	.02
134	Sal Bando	.08	.06	.03
135	Mark Brouhard	.06	.05	.02
136	Mike Caldwell	.06	.05	.02
137	Reggie Cleveland	.06	.05	.02
138	Cecil Cooper	.15	.11	.06
139	Jamie Easterly	.06	.05	.02
140	Marshall Edwards	.06	.05	.02
141	Rollie Fingers	.20	.15	.08

		MT	NR MT	EX
142	Jim Gantner	.08	.06	.03
143	Moose Haas	.06	.05	.02
144	Larry Hisle	.08	.06	.03
145	Roy Howell	.06	.05	.02
146	Rickey Keeton	.06	.05	.02
147	Randy Lerch	.06	.05	.02
148	Paul Molitor	.20	.15	.08
149	Don Money	.06	.05	.02
150	Charlie Moore	.06	.05	.02
151	Ben Oglivie	.08	.06	.03
152	Ted Simmons	.12	.09	.05
153	Jim Slaton	.06	.05	.02
154	Gorman Thomas	.10	.08	.04
155	Robin Yount	1.50	1.25	.60
156	Pete Vukovich	.08	.06	.03
157	Benny Ayala	.06	.05	.02
158	Mark Belanger	.08	.06	.03
159	Al Bumbry	.08	.06	.03
160	Terry Crowley	.06	.05	.02
161	Rich Dauer	.06	.05	.02
162	Doug DeCinces	.10	.08	.04
163	Rick Dempsey	.08	.06	.03
164	Jim Dwyer	.06	.05	.02
165	Mike Flanagan	.10	.08	.04
166	Dave Ford	.06	.05	.02
167	Dan Graham	.06	.05	.02
168	Wayne Krenchicki	.06	.05	.02
169	John Lowenstein	.06	.05	.02
170	Dennis Martinez	.08	.06	.03
171	Tippy Martinez	.06	.05	.02
172	Scott McGregor	.08	.06	.03
173	Jose Morales	.06	.05	.02
174	Eddie Murray	.80	.60	.30
175	Jim Palmer	.60	.45	.25
176	*Cal Ripken, Jr.*(FC)	50.00	37.00	20.00
177	Gary Roenicke	.06	.05	.02
178	Lenn Sakata	.06	.05	.02
179	Ken Singleton	.10	.08	.04
180	Sammy Stewart	.06	.05	.02
181	Tim Stoddard	.06	.05	.02
182	Steve Stone	.08	.06	.03
183	Stan Bahnsen	.06	.05	.02
184	Ray Burris	.06	.05	.02
185	Gary Carter	.35	.25	.14
186	Warren Cromartie	.06	.05	.02
187	Andre Dawson	1.00	.70	.40
188	*Terry Francona*(FC)	.10	.08	.04
189	Woodie Fryman	.08	.06	.03
190	Bill Gullickson	.08	.06	.03
191	Grant Jackson	.06	.05	.02
192	Wallace Johnson	.06	.05	.02
193	Charlie Lea	.06	.05	.02
194	Bill Lee	.08	.06	.03
195	Jerry Manuel	.06	.05	.02
196	Brad Mills	.06	.05	.02
197	John Milner	.06	.05	.02
198	Rowland Office	.06	.05	.02
199	David Palmer	.06	.05	.02
200	Larry Parrish	.10	.08	.04
201	Mike Phillips	.06	.05	.02
202	Tim Raines	1.50	1.25	.60
203	Bobby Ramos	.06	.05	.02
204	Jeff Reardon	.20	.15	.08
205	Steve Rogers	.08	.06	.03
206	Scott Sanderson	.06	.05	.02
207	Rodney Scott (photo actually Tim Raines)	.10	.08	.04
208	Elias Sosa	.06	.05	.02
209	Chris Speier	.06	.05	.02
210	*Tim Wallach*(FC)	2.00	1.50	.80
211	Jerry White	.06	.05	.02
212	Alan Ashby	.06	.05	.02
213	Cesar Cedeno	.12	.09	.05
214	Jose Cruz	.12	.09	.05
215	Kiko Garcia	.06	.05	.02
216	Phil Garner	.08	.06	.03
217	Danny Heep	.06	.05	.02
218	Art Howe	.06	.05	.02
219	Bob Knepper	.08	.06	.03
220	Frank LaCorte	.06	.05	.02
221	Joe Niekro	.12	.09	.05
222	Joe Pittman	.06	.05	.02
223	Terry Puhl	.06	.05	.02
224	Luis Pujols	.06	.05	.02
225	Craig Reynolds	.06	.05	.02
226	J.R. Richard	.10	.08	.04
227	Dave Roberts	.06	.05	.02
228	Vern Ruhle	.06	.05	.02
229	Nolan Ryan	5.00	3.75	2.00
230	Joe Sambito	.06	.05	.02
231	Tony Scott	.06	.05	.02

		MT	NR MT	EX
232	Dave Smith	.10	.08	.04
233	Harry Spilman	.06	.05	.02
234	Don Sutton	.30	.25	.12
235	Dickie Thon	.08	.06	.03
236	Denny Walling	.06	.05	.02
237	Gary Woods	.06	.05	.02
238	*Luis Aguayo*(FC)	.10	.08	.04
239	Ramon Aviles	.06	.05	.02
240	Bob Boone	.10	.08	.04
241	Larry Bowa	.15	.11	.06
242	Warren Brusstar	.06	.05	.02
243	Steve Carlton	1.00	.70	.40
244	Larry Christenson	.06	.05	.02
245	Dick Davis	.06	.05	.02
246	Greg Gross	.06	.05	.02
247	Sparky Lyle	.10	.08	.04
248	Garry Maddox	.10	.08	.04
249	Gary Matthews	.10	.08	.04
250	Bake McBride	.06	.05	.02
251	Tug McGraw	.12	.09	.05
252	Keith Moreland	.10	.08	.04
253	Dickie Noles	.06	.05	.02
254	Mike Proly	.06	.05	.02
255	Ron Reed	.06	.05	.02
256	Pete Rose	1.00	.70	.40
257	Dick Ruthven	.06	.05	.02
258	Mike Schmidt	2.00	1.50	.80
259	Lonnie Smith	.08	.06	.03
260	Manny Trillo	.08	.06	.03
261	Del Unser	.06	.05	.02
262	George Vukovich	.06	.05	.02
263	Tom Brookens	.06	.05	.02
264	George Cappuzzello	.06	.05	.02
265	Marty Castillo	.06	.05	.02
266	Al Cowens	.06	.05	.02
267	Kirk Gibson	.70	.50	.30
268	Richie Hebner	.06	.05	.02
269	Ron Jackson	.06	.05	.02
270	Lynn Jones	.06	.05	.02
271	Steve Kemp	.08	.06	.03
272	*Rick Leach*(FC)	.12	.09	.05
273	Aurelio Lopez	.06	.05	.02
274	Jack Morris	.30	.25	.12
275	Kevin Saucier	.06	.05	.02
276	Lance Parrish	.35	.25	.14
277	Rick Peters	.06	.05	.02
278	Dan Petry	.08	.06	.03
279	David Rozema	.06	.05	.02
280	Stan Papi	.06	.05	.02
281	Dan Schatzeder	.06	.05	.02
282	Champ Summers	.06	.05	.02
283	Alan Trammell	.40	.30	.15
284	Lou Whitaker	.40	.30	.15
285	Milt Wilcox	.06	.05	.02
286	John Wockenfuss	.06	.05	.02
287	Gary Allenson	.06	.05	.02
288	Tom Burgmeier	.06	.05	.02
289	Bill Campbell	.06	.05	.02
290	Mark Clear	.06	.05	.02
291	Steve Crawford	.06	.05	.02
292	Dennis Eckersley	.12	.09	.05
293	Dwight Evans	.15	.11	.06
294	*Rich Gedman*(FC)	.25	.20	.10
295	Garry Hancock	.06	.05	.02
296	Glenn Hoffman	.06	.05	.02
297	Bruce Hurst(FC)	.30	.25	.12
298	Carney Lansford	.08	.06	.03
299	Rick Miller	.06	.05	.02
300	Reid Nichols	.06	.05	.02
301	*Bob Ojeda*(FC)	.50	.40	.20
302	Tony Perez	.20	.15	.08
303	Chuck Rainey	.06	.05	.02
304	Jerry Remy	.06	.05	.02
305	Jim Rice	.40	.30	.15
306	Joe Rudi	.10	.08	.04
307	Bob Stanley	.06	.05	.02
308	Dave Stapleton	.06	.05	.02
309	Frank Tanana	.10	.08	.04
310	Mike Torrez	.08	.06	.03
311	John Tudor(FC)	.25	.20	.10
312	Carl Yastrzemski	1.00	.70	.40
313	Buddy Bell	.12	.09	.05
314	Steve Comer	.06	.05	.02
315	Danny Darwin	.06	.05	.02
316	John Ellis	.06	.05	.02
317	John Grubb	.06	.05	.02
318	Rick Honeycutt	.06	.05	.02
319	Charlie Hough	.10	.08	.04
320	Ferguson Jenkins	.15	.11	.06
321	John Henry Johnson	.06	.05	.02
322	Jim Kern	.06	.05	.02

		MT	NR MT	EX
323	Jon Matlack	.08	.06	.03
324	Doc Medich	.06	.05	.02
325	Mario Mendoza	.06	.05	.02
326	Al Oliver	.15	.11	.06
327	Pat Putnam	.06	.05	.02
328	Mickey Rivers	.08	.06	.03
329	Leon Roberts	.06	.05	.02
330	Billy Sample	.06	.05	.02
331	Bill Stein	.06	.05	.02
332	Jim Sundberg	.08	.06	.03
333	Mark Wagner	.06	.05	.02
334	Bump Wills	.06	.05	.02
335	Bill Almon	.06	.05	.02
336	Harold Baines	.30	.25	.12
337	Ross Baumgarten	.06	.05	.02
338	Tony Bernazard	.06	.05	.02
339	Britt Burns	.06	.05	.02
340	Richard Dotson	.10	.08	.04
341	Jim Essian	.06	.05	.02
342	Ed Farmer	.06	.05	.02
343	Carlton Fisk	.80	.60	.30
344	Kevin Hickey	.06	.05	.02
345	Lamarr Hoyt (LaMarr)	.06	.05	.02
346	Lamar Johnson	.06	.05	.02
347	Jerry Koosman	.10	.08	.04
348	Rusty Kuntz	.06	.05	.02
349	Dennis Lamp	.06	.05	.02
350	Ron LeFlore	.08	.06	.03
351	Chet Lemon	.08	.06	.03
352	Greg Luzinski	.15	.11	.06
353	Bob Molinaro	.06	.05	.02
354	Jim Morrison	.06	.05	.02
355	Wayne Nordhagen	.06	.05	.02
356	Greg Pryor	.06	.05	.02
357	Mike Squires	.06	.05	.02
358	Steve Trout	.06	.05	.02
359	Alan Bannister	.06	.05	.02
360	Len Barker	.08	.06	.03
361	Bert Blyleven	.12	.09	.05
362	Joe Charboneau	.08	.06	.03
363	John Denny	.06	.05	.02
364	Bo Diaz	.08	.06	.03
365	Miguel Dilone	.06	.05	.02
366	Jerry Dybzinski	.06	.05	.02
367	Wayne Garland	.06	.05	.02
368	Mike Hargrove	.06	.05	.02
369	Toby Harrah	.08	.06	.03
370	Ron Hassey	.06	.05	.02
371	*Von Hayes*(FC)	1.00	.70	.40
372	Pat Kelly	.06	.05	.02
373	Duane Kuiper	.06	.05	.02
374	Rick Manning	.06	.05	.02
375	Sid Monge	.06	.05	.02
376	Jorge Orta	.06	.05	.02
377	Dave Rosello	.06	.05	.02
378	Dan Spillner	.06	.05	.02
379	Mike Stanton	.06	.05	.02
380	Andre Thornton	.10	.08	.04
381	Tom Veryzer	.06	.05	.02
382	Rick Waits	.06	.05	.02
383	Doyle Alexander	.10	.08	.04
384	Vida Blue	.12	.09	.05
385	Fred Breining	.06	.05	.02
386	Enos Cabell	.06	.05	.02
387	Jack Clark	.25	.20	.10
388	Darrell Evans	.15	.11	.06
389	Tom Griffin	.06	.05	.02
390	Larry Herndon	.08	.06	.03
391	Al Holland	.06	.05	.02
392	Gary Lavelle	.06	.05	.02
393	Johnnie LeMaster	.06	.05	.02
394	Jerry Martin	.06	.05	.02
395	Milt May	.06	.05	.02
396	Greg Minton	.06	.05	.02
397	Joe Morgan	.50	.40	.20
398	Joe Pettini	.06	.05	.02
399	Alan Ripley	.06	.05	.02
400	Billy Smith	.06	.05	.02
401	Rennie Stennett	.06	.05	.02
402	Ed Whitson	.06	.05	.02
403	Jim Wohlford	.06	.05	.02
404	Willie Aikens	.06	.05	.02
405	George Brett	1.25	.90	.50
406	Ken Brett	.08	.06	.03
407	Dave Chalk	.06	.05	.02
408	Rich Gale	.06	.05	.02
409	Cesar Geronimo	.06	.05	.02
410	Larry Gura	.06	.05	.02
411	Clint Hurdle	.06	.05	.02
412	Mike Jones	.06	.05	.02
413	Dennis Leonard	.08	.06	.03

		MT	NR MT	EX
414	Renie Martin	.06	.05	.02
415	Lee May	.08	.06	.03
416	Hal McRae	.12	.09	.05
417	Darryl Motley	.06	.05	.02
418	Rance Mulliniks	.06	.05	.02
419	Amos Otis	.08	.06	.03
420	*Ken Phelps*(FC)	.30	.25	.12
421	Jamie Quirk	.06	.05	.02
422	Dan Quisenberry	.15	.11	.06
423	Paul Splittorff	.06	.05	.02
424	U.L. Washington	.06	.05	.02
425	John Wathan	.08	.06	.03
426	Frank White	.10	.08	.04
427	Willie Wilson	.15	.11	.06
428	Brian Asselstine	.06	.05	.02
429	Bruce Benedict	.06	.05	.02
430	Tom Boggs	.06	.05	.02
431	Larry Bradford	.06	.05	.02
432	Rick Camp	.06	.05	.02
433	Chris Chambliss	.08	.06	.03
434	Gene Garber	.06	.05	.02
435	Preston Hanna	.06	.05	.02
436	Bob Horner	.12	.09	.05
437	Glenn Hubbard	.08	.06	.03
438a	Al Hrabosky (All Hrabosky, 5'1" on back)	20.00	15.00	8.00
438b	Al Hrabosky (Al Hrabosky, 5'1" on back)	1.25	.90	.50
438c	Al Hrabosky (Al Hrabosky, 5'10" on back)	.35	.25	.14
439	Rufino Linares	.06	.05	.02
440	*Rick Mahler*(FC)	.25	.20	.10
441	Ed Miller	.06	.05	.02
442	John Montefusco	.08	.06	.03
443	Dale Murphy	.90	.70	.35
444	Phil Niekro	.30	.25	.12
445	Gaylord Perry	.40	.30	.15
446	Biff Pocoroba	.06	.05	.02
447	Rafael Ramirez	.08	.06	.03
448	Jerry Royster	.06	.05	.02
449	Claudell Washington	.08	.06	.03
450	Don Aase	.06	.05	.02
451	Don Baylor	.12	.09	.05
452	Juan Beniquez	.06	.05	.02
453	Rick Burleson	.08	.06	.03
454	Bert Campaneris	.10	.08	.04
455	Rod Carew	.90	.70	.35
456	Bob Clark	.06	.05	.02
457	Brian Downing	.10	.08	.04
458	Dan Ford	.06	.05	.02
459	Ken Forsch	.06	.05	.02
460	Dave Frost	.06	.05	.02
461	Bobby Grich	.10	.08	.04
462	Larry Harlow	.06	.05	.02
463	John Harris	.06	.05	.02
464	Andy Hassler	.06	.05	.02
465	Butch Hobson	.06	.05	.02
466	Jesse Jefferson	.06	.05	.02
467	Bruce Kison	.06	.05	.02
468	Fred Lynn	.20	.15	.08
469	Angel Moreno	.06	.05	.02
470	Ed Ott	.06	.05	.02
471	Fred Patek	.06	.05	.02
472	Steve Renko	.06	.05	.02
473	*Mike Witt*(FC)	.35	.25	.12
474	Geoff Zahn	.06	.05	.02
475	Gary Alexander	.06	.05	.02
476	Dale Berra	.06	.05	.02
477	Kurt Bevacqua	.06	.05	.02
478	Jim Bibby	.06	.05	.02
479	John Candelaria	.10	.08	.04
480	Victor Cruz	.06	.05	.02
481	Mike Easler	.08	.06	.03
482	Tim Foli	.06	.05	.02
483	Lee Lacy	.06	.05	.02
484	Vance Law(FC)	.12	.09	.05
485	Bill Madlock	.12	.09	.05
486	Willie Montanez	.06	.05	.02
487	Omar Moreno	.06	.05	.02
488	Steve Nicosia	.06	.05	.02
489	Dave Parker	.30	.25	.12
490	Tony Pena(FC)	.25	.20	.10
491	Pascual Perez(FC)	.15	.11	.06
492	*Johnny Ray*(FC)	.30	.25	.12
493	Rick Rhoden	.10	.08	.04
494	Bill Robinson	.06	.05	.02
495	Don Robinson	.08	.06	.03
496	Enrique Romo	.06	.05	.02
497	Rod Scurry	.06	.05	.02
498	Eddie Solomon	.06	.05	.02
499	Willie Stargell	.40	.30	.15

		MT	NR MT	EX
500	Kent Tekulve	.08	.06	.03
501	Jason Thompson	.06	.05	.02
502	Glenn Abbott	.06	.05	.02
503	Jim Anderson	.06	.05	.02
504	Floyd Bannister	.10	.08	.04
505	Bruce Bochte	.06	.05	.02
506	Jeff Burroughs	.08	.06	.03
507	Bryan Clark	.06	.05	.02
508	Ken Clay	.06	.05	.02
509	Julio Cruz	.06	.05	.02
510	Dick Drago	.06	.05	.02
511	Gary Gray	.06	.05	.02
512	Dan Meyer	.06	.05	.02
513	Jerry Narron	.06	.05	.02
514	Tom Paciorek	.06	.05	.02
515	Casey Parsons	.06	.05	.02
516	Lenny Randle	.06	.05	.02
517	Shane Rawley	.10	.08	.04
518	Joe Simpson	.06	.05	.02
519	Richie Zisk	.08	.06	.03
520	Neil Allen	.06	.05	.02
521	Bob Bailor	.06	.05	.02
522	Hubie Brooks(FC)	.50	.40	.20
523	Mike Cubbage	.06	.05	.02
524	Pete Falcone	.06	.05	.02
525	Doug Flynn	.06	.05	.02
526	Tom Hausman	.06	.05	.02
527	Ron Hodges	.06	.05	.02
528	Randy Jones	.08	.06	.03
529	Mike Jorgensen	.06	.05	.02
530	Dave Kingman	.15	.11	.06
531	Ed Lynch	.06	.05	.02
532	Mike Marshall	.10	.08	.04
533	Lee Mazzilli	.08	.06	.03
534	Dyar Miller	.06	.05	.02
535	Mike Scott(FC)	.50	.40	.20
536	Rusty Staub	.10	.08	.04
537	John Stearns	.06	.05	.02
538	Craig Swan	.06	.05	.02
539	Frank Taveras	.06	.05	.02
540	Alex Trevino	.06	.05	.02
541	Ellis Valentine	.06	.05	.02
542	Mookie Wilson(FC)	.15	.11	.06
543	Joel Youngblood	.06	.05	.02
544	Pat Zachry	.06	.05	.02
545	Glenn Adams	.06	.05	.02
546	Fernando Arroyo	.06	.05	.02
547	John Verhoeven	.06	.05	.02
548	Sal Butera	.06	.05	.02
549	John Castino	.06	.05	.02
550	Don Cooper	.06	.05	.02
551	Doug Corbett	.06	.05	.02
552	Dave Engle	.06	.05	.02
553	Roger Erickson	.06	.05	.02
554	Danny Goodwin	.06	.05	.02
555a	Darrell Jackson (black cap)	1.00	.70	.40
555b	Darrell Jackson (red cap with emblem)	.10	.08	.04
555c	Darrell Jackson (red cap, no emblem)	.25	.20	.10
556	Pete Mackanin	.06	.05	.02
557	Jack O'Connor	.06	.05	.02
558	Hosken Powell	.06	.05	.02
559	Pete Redfern	.06	.05	.02
560	Roy Smalley	.06	.05	.02
561	Chuck Baker	.06	.05	.02
562	Gary Ward	.08	.06	.03
563	Rob Wilfong	.06	.05	.02
564	Al Williams	.06	.05	.02
565	Butch Wynegar	.06	.05	.02
566	Randy Bass	.06	.05	.02
567	Juan Bonilla	.06	.05	.02
568	Danny Boone	.06	.05	.02
569	John Curtis	.06	.05	.02
570	Juan Eichelberger	.06	.05	.02
571	Barry Evans	.06	.05	.02
572	Tim Flannery	.06	.05	.02
573	Ruppert Jones	.06	.05	.02
574	Terry Kennedy	.08	.06	.03
575	Joe Lefebvre	.06	.05	.02
576a	John Littlefield (pitching lefty)	175.00	125.00	70.00
576b	John Littlefield (pitching righty)	.08	.06	.03
577	Gary Lucas	.06	.05	.02
578	Steve Mura	.06	.05	.02
579	Broderick Perkins	.06	.05	.02
580	Gene Richards	.06	.05	.02
581	Luis Salazar	.06	.05	.02
582	Ozzie Smith	1.00	.70	.40
583	John Urrea	.06	.05	.02
584	Chris Welsh	.06	.05	.02
585	Rick Wise	.08	.06	.03

		MT	NR MT	EX
586	Doug Bird	.06	.05	.02
587	Tim Blackwell	.06	.05	.02
588	Bobby Bonds	.10	.08	.04
589	Bill Buckner	.12	.09	.05
590	Bill Caudill	.06	.05	.02
591	Hector Cruz	.06	.05	.02
592	*Jody Davis*(FC)	.30	.25	.12
593	Ivan DeJesus	.06	.05	.02
594	Steve Dillard	.06	.05	.02
595	Leon Durham	.08	.06	.03
596	Rawly Eastwick	.06	.05	.02
597	Steve Henderson	.06	.05	.02
598	Mike Krukow	.08	.06	.03
599	Mike Lum	.06	.05	.02
600	Randy Martz	.06	.05	.02
601	Jerry Morales	.06	.05	.02
602	Ken Reitz	.06	.05	.02
603a	*Lee Smith* (Cubs logo reversed on back)(FC)	2.00	1.50	.80
603b	*Lee Smith* (Cubs logo correct)(FC)	1.00	.70	.40
604	Dick Tidrow	.06	.05	.02
605	Jim Tracy	.06	.05	.02
606	Mike Tyson	.06	.05	.02
607	Ty Waller	.06	.05	.02
608	Danny Ainge	.12	.09	.05
609	*Jorge Bell*(FC)	8.00	6.00	3.25
610	Mark Bomback	.06	.05	.02
611	Barry Bonnell	.06	.05	.02
612	Jim Clancy	.08	.06	.03
613	Damaso Garcia	.06	.05	.02
614	Jerry Garvin	.06	.05	.02
615	Alfredo Griffin	.08	.06	.03
616	Garth Iorg	.06	.05	.02
617	Luis Leal	.06	.05	.02
618	Ken Macha	.06	.05	.02
619	John Mayberry	.08	.06	.03
620	Joey McLaughlin	.06	.05	.02
621	Lloyd Moseby	.12	.09	.05
622	Dave Stieb	.12	.09	.05
623	Jackson Todd	.06	.05	.02
624	Willie Upshaw(FC)	.15	.11	.06
625	Otto Velez	.06	.05	.02
626	Ernie Whitt	.08	.06	.03
627	Al Woods	.06	.05	.02
628	1981 All-Star Game	.08	.06	.03
629	All-Star Infielders (Bucky Dent, Frank White)	.10	.08	.04
630	Big Red Machine (Dave Concepcion, Dan Driessen, George Foster)	.15	.11	.06
631	Top N.L. Relief Pitcher (Bruce Sutter)	.15	.11	.06
632	Steve & Carlton (Steve Carlton, Carlton Fisk)	.25	.20	.10
633	3000th Game, May 25, 1981 (Carl Yastrzemski)	.35	.25	.14
634	Dynamic Duo (Johnny Bench, Tom Seaver)	.30	.25	.12
635	West Meets East (Gary Carter, Fernando Valenzuela)	.30	.25	.12
636a	N.L. Strikeout King (Fernando Valenzuela) ("...led he National League...")	1.00	.70	.40
636b	N.L. Strikeout King (Fernando Valenzuela) ("...led the National League...")	.50	.40	.20
637	1981 Home Run King (Mike Schmidt)	.40	.30	.15
638	N.L. All-Stars (Gary Carter, Dave Parker)	.25	.20	.10
639	Perfect Game! (Len Barker, Bo Diaz)	.08	.06	.03
640	Pete & Re-Pete (Pete Rose, Pete Rose, Jr.)	2.50	2.00	1.00
641	Phillies' Finest (Steve Carlton, Mike Schmidt, Lonnie Smith)	.50	.40	.20
642	Red Sox Reunion (Dwight Evans, Fred Lynn)	.15	.11	.06
643	1981 Most Hits, Most Runs (Rickey Henderson)	3.00	2.25	1.25
644	Most Saves 1981 A.L. (Rollie Fingers)	.15	.11	.06
645	Most 1981 Wins (Tom Seaver)	.25	.20	.10
646a	Yankee Powerhouse (Reggie Jackson, Dave Winfield) (comma after "outfielder" on back)	1.25	.90	.50
646b	Yankee Powerhouse (Reggie Jackson, Dave Winfield) (no comma after "oufielder")	.60	.45	.25
647	Checklist 1-56	.06	.05	.02
648	Checklist 57-109	.06	.05	.02
649	Checklist 110-156	.06	.05	.02
650	Checklist 157-211	.06	.05	.02

		MT	NR MT	EX
651	Checklist 212-262	.06	.05	.02
652	Checklist 263-312	.06	.05	.02
653	Checklist 313-358	.06	.05	.02
654	Checklist 359-403	.06	.05	.02
655	Checklist 404-449	.06	.05	.02
656	Checklist 450-501	.06	.05	.02
657	Checklist 502-544	.06	.05	.02
658	Checklist 545-585	.06	.05	.02
659	Checklist 586-627	.06	.05	.02
660	Checklist 628-646	.06	.05	.02

1983 Fleer

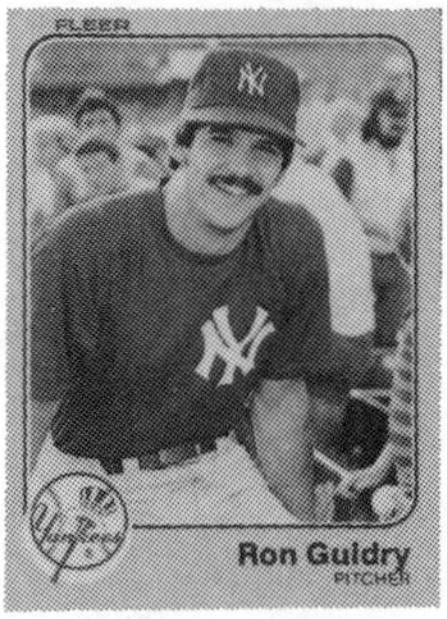

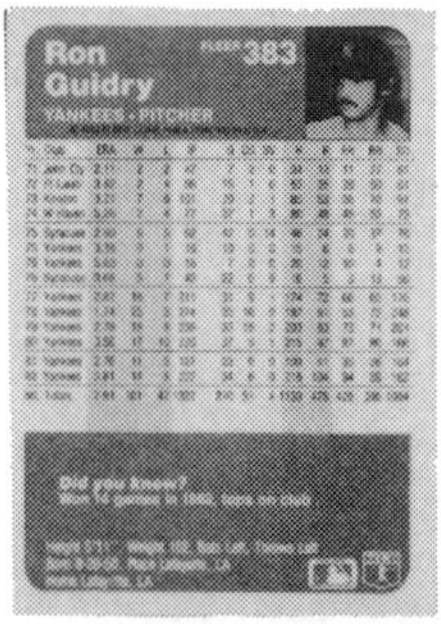

The 1983 Fleer set features color photos set inside a light brown border. The cards are the standard size of 2-1/2" by 3-1/2". A team logo is located at the card bottom and the word "Fleer" is found at the top. The card backs are designed on a vertical format and include a small black and white photo of the player along with biographical and statistical information. The reverses are done in two shades of brown on white stock. The set was issued with team logo stickers.

		MT	NR MT	EX
Complete Set:		110.00	82.00	45.00
Common Player:		.06	.05	.02
1	Joaquin Andujar	.08	.06	.03
2	Doug Bair	.06	.05	.02
3	Steve Braun	.06	.05	.02
4	Glenn Brummer	.06	.05	.02
5	Bob Forsch	.08	.06	.03
6	David Green	.06	.05	.02
7	George Hendrick	.08	.06	.03
8	Keith Hernandez	.40	.30	.15
9	Tom Herr	.10	.08	.04
10	Dane Iorg	.06	.05	.02
11	Jim Kaat	.15	.11	.06
12	Jeff Lahti	.06	.05	.02
13	Tito Landrum	.06	.05	.02
14	*Dave LaPoint*(FC)	.30	.25	.12
15	*Willie McGee*(FC)	4.00	3.00	1.50
16	Steve Mura	.06	.05	.02
17	Ken Oberkfell	.06	.05	.02
18	Darrell Porter	.08	.06	.03
19	Mike Ramsey	.06	.05	.02
20	Gene Roof	.06	.05	.02
21	Lonnie Smith	.08	.06	.03
22	Ozzie Smith	1.00	.70	.40
23	John Stuper	.06	.05	.02
24	Bruce Sutter	.15	.11	.06
25	Gene Tenace	.08	.06	.03
26	Jerry Augustine	.06	.05	.02
27	Dwight Bernard	.06	.05	.02
28	Mark Brouhard	.06	.05	.02
29	Mike Caldwell	.06	.05	.02
30	Cecil Cooper	.15	.11	.06
31	Jamie Easterly	.06	.05	.02
32	Marshall Edwards	.06	.05	.02
33	Rollie Fingers	.20	.15	.08
34	Jim Gantner	.08	.06	.03
35	Moose Haas	.06	.05	.02
36	Roy Howell	.06	.05	.02
37	Peter Ladd	.06	.05	.02
38	Bob McClure	.06	.05	.02
39	Doc Medich	.06	.05	.02
40	Paul Molitor	.20	.15	.08
41	Don Money	.06	.05	.02
42	Charlie Moore	.06	.05	.02
43	Ben Oglivie	.08	.06	.03
44	Ed Romero	.06	.05	.02
45	Ted Simmons	.12	.09	.05
46	Jim Slaton	.06	.05	.02
47	Don Sutton	.30	.25	.12
48	Gorman Thomas	.10	.08	.04
49	Pete Vuckovich	.08	.06	.03
50	Ned Yost	.06	.05	.02
51	Robin Yount	1.00	.70	.40
52	Benny Ayala	.06	.05	.02
53	Bob Bonner	.06	.05	.02
54	Al Bumbry	.08	.06	.03
55	Terry Crowley	.06	.05	.02
56	*Storm Davis*(FC)	.40	.30	.15
57	Rich Dauer	.06	.05	.02
58	Rick Dempsey	.08	.06	.03
59	Jim Dwyer	.06	.05	.02
60	Mike Flanagan	.10	.08	.04
61	Dan Ford	.06	.05	.02
62	Glenn Gulliver	.06	.05	.02
63	John Lowenstein	.06	.05	.02
64	Dennis Martinez	.08	.06	.03
65	Tippy Martinez	.06	.05	.02
66	Scott McGregor	.08	.06	.03
67	Eddie Murray	1.00	.70	.40
68	Joe Nolan	.06	.05	.02
69	Jim Palmer	.50	.40	.20
70	Cal Ripken, Jr.	12.00	9.00	4.75
71	Gary Roenicke	.06	.05	.02
72	Lenn Sakata	.06	.05	.02
73	Ken Singleton	.10	.08	.04
74	Sammy Stewart	.06	.05	.02
75	Tim Stoddard	.06	.05	.02
76	Don Aase	.06	.05	.02
77	Don Baylor	.12	.09	.05
78	Juan Beniquez	.06	.05	.02
79	Bob Boone	.10	.08	.04
80	Rick Burleson	.08	.06	.03
81	Rod Carew	.50	.40	.20
82	Bobby Clark	.06	.05	.02
83	Doug Corbett	.06	.05	.02
84	John Curtis	.06	.05	.02
85	Doug DeCinces	.10	.08	.04
86	Brian Downing	.10	.08	.04
87	Joe Ferguson	.06	.05	.02
88	Tim Foli	.06	.05	.02
89	Ken Forsch	.06	.05	.02
90	Dave Goltz	.08	.06	.03
91	Bobby Grich	.10	.08	.04
92	Andy Hassler	.06	.05	.02
93	Reggie Jackson	.50	.40	.20
94	Ron Jackson	.06	.05	.02
95	Tommy John	.20	.15	.08
96	Bruce Kison	.06	.05	.02
97	Fred Lynn	.20	.15	.08
98	Ed Ott	.06	.05	.02
99	Steve Renko	.06	.05	.02
100	Luis Sanchez	.06	.05	.02
101	Rob Wilfong	.06	.05	.02
102	Mike Witt	.15	.11	.06
103	Geoff Zahn	.06	.05	.02
104	Willie Aikens	.06	.05	.02
105	Mike Armstrong	.06	.05	.02
106	Vida Blue	.12	.09	.05
107	*Bud Black*(FC)	.50	.40	.20
108	George Brett	1.00	.70	.40
109	Bill Castro	.06	.05	.02
110	Onix Concepcion	.06	.05	.02
111	Dave Frost	.06	.05	.02
112	Cesar Geronimo	.06	.05	.02
113	Larry Gura	.06	.05	.02
114	Steve Hammond	.06	.05	.02
115	Don Hood	.06	.05	.02
116	Dennis Leonard	.08	.06	.03
117	Jerry Martin	.06	.05	.02
118	Lee May	.08	.06	.03
119	Hal McRae	.12	.09	.05
120	Amos Otis	.08	.06	.03
121	Greg Pryor	.06	.05	.02
122	Dan Quisenberry	.15	.11	.06
123	*Don Slaught*(FC)	.20	.15	.08
124	Paul Splittorff	.06	.05	.02
125	U.L. Washington	.06	.05	.02
126	John Wathan	.08	.06	.03
127	Frank White	.10	.08	.04
128	Willie Wilson	.15	.11	.06
129	Steve Bedrosian(FC)	.35	.25	.14
130	Bruce Benedict	.06	.05	.02
131	Tommy Boggs	.06	.05	.02

		MT	NR MT	EX
132	Brett Butler(FC)	.15	.11	.06
133	Rick Camp	.06	.05	.02
134	Chris Chambliss	.08	.06	.03
135	Ken Dayley(FC)	.10	.08	.04
136	Gene Garber	.06	.05	.02
137	Terry Harper	.06	.05	.02
138	Bob Horner	.12	.09	.05
139	Glenn Hubbard	.08	.06	.03
140	Rufino Linares	.06	.05	.02
141	Rick Mahler	.08	.06	.03
142	Dale Murphy	.90	.70	.35
143	Phil Niekro	.30	.25	.12
144	Pascual Perez	.08	.06	.03
145	Biff Pocoroba	.06	.05	.02
146	Rafael Ramirez	.06	.05	.02
147	Jerry Royster	.06	.05	.02
148	Ken Smith	.06	.05	.02
149	Bob Walk	.08	.06	.03
150	Claudell Washington	.08	.06	.03
151	Bob Watson	.08	.06	.03
152	Larry Whisenton	.06	.05	.02
153	Porfirio Altamirano	.06	.05	.02
154	Marty Bystrom	.06	.05	.02
155	Steve Carlton	.50	.40	.20
156	Larry Christenson	.06	.05	.02
157	Ivan DeJesus	.06	.05	.02
158	John Denny	.06	.05	.02
159	Bob Dernier(FC)	.10	.08	.04
160	Bo Diaz	.08	.06	.03
161	Ed Farmer	.06	.05	.02
162	Greg Gross	.06	.05	.02
163	Mike Krukow	.08	.06	.03
164	Garry Maddox	.10	.08	.04
165	Gary Matthews	.10	.08	.04
166	Tug McGraw	.12	.09	.05
167	Bob Molinaro	.06	.05	.02
168	Sid Monge	.06	.05	.02
169	Ron Reed	.06	.05	.02
170	Bill Robinson	.06	.05	.02
171	Pete Rose	1.00	.70	.40
172	Dick Ruthven	.06	.05	.02
173	Mike Schmidt	1.50	1.25	.60
174	Manny Trillo	.08	.06	.03
175	Ozzie Virgil(FC)	.10	.08	.04
176	George Vukovich	.06	.05	.02
177	Gary Allenson	.06	.05	.02
178	Luis Aponte	.06	.05	.02
179	*Wade Boggs*(FC)	20.00	15.00	8.00
180	Tom Burgmeier	.06	.05	.02
181	Mark Clear	.06	.05	.02
182	Dennis Eckersley	.12	.09	.05
183	Dwight Evans	.15	.11	.06
184	Rich Gedman	.08	.06	.03
185	Glenn Hoffman	.06	.05	.02
186	Bruce Hurst	.10	.08	.04
187	Carney Lansford	.08	.06	.03
188	Rick Miller	.06	.05	.02
189	Reid Nichols	.06	.05	.02
190	Bob Ojeda	.12	.09	.05
191	Tony Perez	.20	.15	.08
192	Chuck Rainey	.06	.05	.02
193	Jerry Remy	.06	.05	.02
194	Jim Rice	.40	.30	.15
195	Bob Stanley	.06	.05	.02
196	Dave Stapleton	.06	.05	.02
197	Mike Torrez	.08	.06	.03
198	John Tudor	.10	.08	.04
199	Julio Valdez	.06	.05	.02
200	Carl Yastrzemski	1.00	.70	.40
201	Dusty Baker	.10	.08	.04
202	Joe Beckwith	.06	.05	.02
203	*Greg Brock*(FC)	.35	.25	.14
204	Ron Cey	.12	.09	.05
205	Terry Forster	.08	.06	.03
206	Steve Garvey	.40	.30	.15
207	Pedro Guerrero	.25	.20	.10
208	Burt Hooton	.08	.06	.03
209	Steve Howe	.08	.06	.03
210	Ken Landreaux	.06	.05	.02
211	Mike Marshall	.20	.15	.08
212	*Candy Maldonado*(FC)	.80	.60	.30
213	Rick Monday	.10	.08	.04
214	Tom Niedenfuer	.10	.08	.04
215	Jorge Orta	.06	.05	.02
216	Jerry Reuss	.10	.08	.04
217	Ron Roenicke	.06	.05	.02
218	Vicente Romo	.06	.05	.02
219	Bill Russell	.08	.06	.03
220	Steve Sax	.30	.25	.12
221	Mike Scioscia	.08	.06	.03
222	Dave Stewart	1.00	.70	.40

		MT	NR MT	EX
223	Derrel Thomas	.06	.05	.02
224	Fernando Valenzuela	.30	.25	.12
225	Bob Welch	.12	.09	.05
226	Ricky Wright	.06	.05	.02
227	Steve Yeager	.06	.05	.02
228	Bill Almon	.06	.05	.02
229	Harold Baines	.15	.11	.06
230	Salome Barojas	.06	.05	.02
231	Tony Bernazard	.06	.05	.02
232	Britt Burns	.06	.05	.02
233	Richard Dotson	.10	.08	.04
234	Ernesto Escarrega	.06	.05	.02
235	Carlton Fisk	.50	.40	.20
236	Jerry Hairston	.06	.05	.02
237	Kevin Hickey	.06	.05	.02
238	LaMarr Hoyt	.06	.05	.02
239	Steve Kemp	.10	.08	.04
240	Jim Kern	.06	.05	.02
241	*Ron Kittle*(FC)	.50	.40	.20
242	Jerry Koosman	.10	.08	.04
243	Dennis Lamp	.06	.05	.02
244	Rudy Law	.06	.05	.02
245	Vance Law	.08	.06	.03
246	Ron LeFlore	.08	.06	.03
247	Greg Luzinski	.12	.09	.05
248	Tom Paciorek	.06	.05	.02
249	Aurelio Rodriguez	.08	.06	.03
250	Mike Squires	.06	.05	.02
251	Steve Trout	.06	.05	.02
252	Jim Barr	.06	.05	.02
253	Dave Bergman	.06	.05	.02
254	Fred Breining	.06	.05	.02
255	Bob Brenly(FC)	.08	.06	.03
256	Jack Clark	.25	.20	.10
257	Chili Davis(FC)	.20	.15	.08
258	Darrell Evans	.15	.11	.06
259	Alan Fowlkes	.06	.05	.02
260	Rich Gale	.06	.05	.02
261	Atlee Hammaker(FC)	.12	.09	.05
262	Al Holland	.06	.05	.02
263	Duane Kuiper	.06	.05	.02
264	Bill Laskey	.06	.05	.02
265	Gary Lavelle	.06	.05	.02
266	Johnnie LeMaster	.06	.05	.02
267	Renie Martin	.06	.05	.02
268	Milt May	.06	.05	.02
269	Greg Minton	.06	.05	.02
270	Joe Morgan	.50	.40	.20
271	Tom O'Malley	.06	.05	.02
272	Reggie Smith	.10	.08	.04
273	Guy Sularz	.06	.05	.02
274	Champ Summers	.06	.05	.02
275	Max Venable	.06	.05	.02
276	Jim Wohlford	.06	.05	.02
277	Ray Burris	.06	.05	.02
278	Gary Carter	.35	.25	.14
279	Warren Cromartie	.06	.05	.02
280	Andre Dawson	.50	.40	.20
281	Terry Francona	.06	.05	.02
282	Doug Flynn	.06	.05	.02
283	Woody Fryman	.08	.06	.03
284	Bill Gullickson	.06	.05	.02
285	Wallace Johnson	.06	.05	.02
286	Charlie Lea	.06	.05	.02
287	Randy Lerch	.06	.05	.02
288	Brad Mills	.06	.05	.02
289	Dan Norman	.06	.05	.02
290	Al Oliver	.15	.11	.06
291	David Palmer	.06	.05	.02
292	Tim Raines	.35	.25	.14
293	Jeff Reardon	.12	.09	.05
294	Steve Rogers	.08	.06	.03
295	Scott Sanderson	.06	.05	.02
296	Dan Schatzeder	.06	.05	.02
297	Bryn Smith	.08	.06	.03
298	Chris Speier	.06	.05	.02
299	Tim Wallach	.20	.15	.08
300	Jerry White	.06	.05	.02
301	Joel Youngblood	.06	.05	.02
302	Ross Baumgarten	.06	.05	.02
303	Dale Berra	.06	.05	.02
304	John Candelaria	.10	.08	.04
305	Dick Davis	.06	.05	.02
306	Mike Easler	.08	.06	.03
307	Richie Hebner	.06	.05	.02
308	Lee Lacy	.06	.05	.02
309	Bill Madlock	.12	.09	.05
310	Larry McWilliams	.06	.05	.02
311	John Milner	.06	.05	.02
312	Omar Moreno	.06	.05	.02
313	Jim Morrison	.06	.05	.02

		MT	NR MT	EX
314	Steve Nicosia	.06	.05	.02
315	Dave Parker	.30	.25	.12
316	Tony Pena	.10	.08	.04
317	Johnny Ray	.12	.09	.05
318	Rick Rhoden	.10	.08	.04
319	Don Robinson	.08	.06	.03
320	Enrique Romo	.06	.05	.02
321	Manny Sarmiento	.06	.05	.02
322	Rod Scurry	.06	.05	.02
323	Jim Smith	.06	.05	.02
324	Willie Stargell	.40	.30	.15
325	Jason Thompson	.06	.05	.02
326	Kent Tekulve	.08	.06	.03
327a	Tom Brookens (narrow (1/4") brown box at bottom on back)	.30	.25	.12
327b	Tom Brookens (wide (1 1/4") brown box at bottom on back)	.08	.06	.03
328	Enos Cabell	.06	.05	.02
329	Kirk Gibson	.40	.30	.15
330	Larry Herndon	.08	.06	.03
331	Mike Ivie	.06	.05	.02
332	*Howard Johnson*(FC)	12.00	9.00	4.75
333	Lynn Jones	.06	.05	.02
334	Rick Leach	.06	.05	.02
335	Chet Lemon	.08	.06	.03
336	Jack Morris	.30	.25	.12
337	Lance Parrish	.35	.25	.14
338	Larry Pashnick	.06	.05	.02
339	Dan Petry	.08	.06	.03
340	Dave Rozema	.06	.05	.02
341	Dave Rucker	.06	.05	.02
342	Elias Sosa	.06	.05	.02
343	Dave Tobik	.06	.05	.02
344	Alan Trammell	.40	.30	.15
345	Jerry Turner	.06	.05	.02
346	Jerry Ujdur	.06	.05	.02
347	Pat Underwood	.06	.05	.02
348	Lou Whitaker	.40	.30	.15
349	Milt Wilcox	.06	.05	.02
350	*Glenn Wilson*(FC)	.35	.25	.14
351	John Wockenfuss	.06	.05	.02
352	Kurt Bevacqua	.06	.05	.02
353	Juan Bonilla	.06	.05	.02
354	Floyd Chiffer	.06	.05	.02
355	Luis DeLeon	.06	.05	.02
356	*Dave Dravecky*(FC)	.60	.45	.25
357	Dave Edwards	.06	.05	.02
358	Juan Eichelberger	.06	.05	.02
359	Tim Flannery	.06	.05	.02
360	*Tony Gwynn*(FC)	20.00	15.00	8.00
361	Ruppert Jones	.06	.05	.02
362	Terry Kennedy	.08	.06	.03
363	Joe Lefebvre	.06	.05	.02
364	Sixto Lezcano	.06	.05	.02
365	Tim Lollar	.06	.05	.02
366	Gary Lucas	.06	.05	.02
367	John Montefusco	.06	.05	.02
368	Broderick Perkins	.06	.05	.02
369	Joe Pittman	.06	.05	.02
370	Gene Richards	.06	.05	.02
371	Luis Salazar	.06	.05	.02
372	*Eric Show*(FC)	.30	.25	.12
373	Garry Templeton	.10	.08	.04
374	Chris Welsh	.06	.05	.02
375	Alan Wiggins	.06	.05	.02
376	Rick Cerone	.06	.05	.02
377	Dave Collins	.08	.06	.03
378	Roger Erickson	.06	.05	.02
379	George Frazier	.06	.05	.02
380	Oscar Gamble	.08	.06	.03
381	Goose Gossage	.20	.15	.08
382	Ken Griffey	.12	.09	.05
383	Ron Guidry	.25	.20	.10
384	Dave LaRoche	.06	.05	.02
385	Rudy May	.06	.05	.02
386	John Mayberry	.08	.06	.03
387	Lee Mazzilli	.08	.06	.03
388	Mike Morgan(FC)	.12	.09	.05
389	Jerry Mumphrey	.06	.05	.02
390	Bobby Murcer	.10	.08	.04
391	Graig Nettles	.15	.11	.06
392	Lou Piniella	.12	.09	.05
393	Willie Randolph	.10	.08	.04
394	Shane Rawley	.10	.08	.04
395	Dave Righetti	.25	.20	.10
396	Andre Robertson	.06	.05	.02
397	Roy Smalley	.06	.05	.02
398	Dave Winfield	.40	.30	.15
399	Butch Wynegar	.06	.05	.02
400	Chris Bando	.06	.05	.02
401	Alan Bannister	.06	.05	.02

		MT	NR MT	EX
402	Len Barker	.08	.06	.03
403	Tom Brennan	.06	.05	.02
404	*Carmelo Castillo*(FC)	.12	.09	.05
405	Miguel Dilone	.06	.05	.02
406	Jerry Dybzinski	.06	.05	.02
407	Mike Fischlin	.06	.05	.02
408	Ed Glynn (photo actually Bud Anderson)	.06	.05	.02
409	Mike Hargrove	.06	.05	.02
410	Toby Harrah	.08	.06	.03
411	Ron Hassey	.06	.05	.02
412	Von Hayes	.15	.11	.06
413	Rick Manning	.06	.05	.02
414	Bake McBride	.06	.05	.02
415	Larry Milbourne	.06	.05	.02
416	Bill Nahorodny	.06	.05	.02
417	Jack Perconte	.06	.05	.02
418	Lary Sorensen	.06	.05	.02
419	Dan Spillner	.06	.05	.02
420	Rick Sutcliffe	.12	.09	.05
421	Andre Thornton	.10	.08	.04
422	Rick Waits	.06	.05	.02
423	Eddie Whitson	.06	.05	.02
424	Jesse Barfield(FC)	.60	.45	.25
425	Barry Bonnell	.06	.05	.02
426	Jim Clancy	.08	.06	.03
427	Damaso Garcia	.06	.05	.02
428	Jerry Garvin	.06	.05	.02
429	Alfredo Griffin	.08	.06	.03
430	Garth Iorg	.06	.05	.02
431	Roy Lee Jackson	.06	.05	.02
432	Luis Leal	.06	.05	.02
433	Buck Martinez	.06	.05	.02
434	Joey McLaughlin	.06	.05	.02
435	Lloyd Moseby	.12	.09	.05
436	Rance Mulliniks	.06	.05	.02
437	Dale Murray	.06	.05	.02
438	Wayne Nordhagen	.06	.05	.02
439	*Gene Petralli*(FC)	.15	.11	.06
440	Hosken Powell	.06	.05	.02
441	Dave Stieb	.12	.09	.05
442	Willie Upshaw	.08	.06	.03
443	Ernie Whitt	.08	.06	.03
444	Al Woods	.06	.05	.02
445	Alan Ashby	.06	.05	.02
446	Jose Cruz	.12	.09	.05
447	Kiko Garcia	.06	.05	.02
448	Phil Garner	.08	.06	.03
449	Danny Heep	.06	.05	.02
450	Art Howe	.06	.05	.02
451	Bob Knepper	.08	.06	.03
452	Alan Knicely	.06	.05	.02
453	Ray Knight	.10	.08	.04
454	Frank LaCorte	.06	.05	.02
455	Mike LaCoss	.06	.05	.02
456	Randy Moffitt	.06	.05	.02
457	Joe Niekro	.12	.09	.05
458	Terry Puhl	.06	.05	.02
459	Luis Pujols	.06	.05	.02
460	Craig Reynolds	.06	.05	.02
461	Bert Roberge	.06	.05	.02
462	Vern Ruhle	.06	.05	.02
463	Nolan Ryan	5.00	3.75	2.00
464	Joe Sambito	.06	.05	.02
465	Tony Scott	.06	.05	.02
466	Dave Smith	.08	.06	.03
467	Harry Spilman	.06	.05	.02
468	Dickie Thon	.08	.06	.03
469	Denny Walling	.06	.05	.02
470	Larry Andersen	.06	.05	.02
471	Floyd Bannister	.10	.08	.04
472	Jim Beattie	.06	.05	.02
473	Bruce Bochte	.06	.05	.02
474	Manny Castillo	.06	.05	.02
475	Bill Caudill	.06	.05	.02
476	Bryan Clark	.06	.05	.02
477	Al Cowens	.06	.05	.02
478	Julio Cruz	.06	.05	.02
479	Todd Cruz	.06	.05	.02
480	Gary Gray	.06	.05	.02
481	Dave Henderson(FC)	.20	.15	.08
482	*Mike Moore*(FC)	1.00	.70	.40
483	Gaylord Perry	.40	.30	.15
484	Dave Revering	.06	.05	.02
485	Joe Simpson	.06	.05	.02
486	Mike Stanton	.06	.05	.02
487	Rick Sweet	.06	.05	.02
488	*Ed Vande Berg*(FC)	.10	.08	.04
489	Richie Zisk	.08	.06	.03
490	Doug Bird	.06	.05	.02
491	Larry Bowa	.12	.09	.05

		MT	NR MT	EX
492	Bill Buckner	.12	.09	.05
493	Bill Campbell	.06	.05	.02
494	Jody Davis	.10	.08	.04
495	Leon Durham	.08	.06	.03
496	Steve Henderson	.06	.05	.02
497	Willie Hernandez	.08	.06	.03
498	Ferguson Jenkins	.15	.11	.06
499	Jay Johnstone	.08	.06	.03
500	Junior Kennedy	.06	.05	.02
501	Randy Martz	.06	.05	.02
502	Jerry Morales	.06	.05	.02
503	Keith Moreland	.08	.06	.03
504	Dickie Noles	.06	.05	.02
505	Mike Proly	.06	.05	.02
506	Allen Ripley	.06	.05	.02
507	*Ryne Sandberg*(FC)	35.00	27.00	15.00
508	Lee Smith	.15	.11	.06
509	Pat Tabler(FC)	.15	.11	.06
510	Dick Tidrow	.06	.05	.02
511	Bump Wills	.06	.05	.02
512	Gary Woods	.06	.05	.02
513	Tony Armas	.10	.08	.04
514	Dave Beard	.06	.05	.02
515	Jeff Burroughs	.08	.06	.03
516	John D'Acquisto	.06	.05	.02
517	Wayne Gross	.06	.05	.02
518	Mike Heath	.06	.05	.02
519	Rickey Henderson	5.00	3.75	2.00
520	Cliff Johnson	.06	.05	.02
521	Matt Keough	.06	.05	.02
522	Brian Kingman	.06	.05	.02
523	Rick Langford	.06	.05	.02
524	Davey Lopes	.10	.08	.04
525	Steve McCatty	.06	.05	.02
526	Dave McKay	.06	.05	.02
527	Dan Meyer	.06	.05	.02
528	Dwayne Murphy	.08	.06	.03
529	Jeff Newman	.06	.05	.02
530	Mike Norris	.06	.05	.02
531	Bob Owchinko	.06	.05	.02
532	Joe Rudi	.10	.08	.04
533	Jimmy Sexton	.06	.05	.02
534	Fred Stanley	.06	.05	.02
535	Tom Underwood	.06	.05	.02
536	Neil Allen	.06	.05	.02
537	Wally Backman	.08	.06	.03
538	Bob Bailor	.06	.05	.02
539	Hubie Brooks	.12	.09	.05
540	Carlos Diaz	.06	.05	.02
541	Pete Falcone	.06	.05	.02
542	George Foster	.15	.11	.06
543	Ron Gardenhire	.06	.05	.02
544	Brian Giles	.06	.05	.02
545	Ron Hodges	.06	.05	.02
546	Randy Jones	.08	.06	.03
547	Mike Jorgensen	.06	.05	.02
548	Dave Kingman	.15	.11	.06
549	Ed Lynch	.06	.05	.02
550	Jesse Orosco(FC)	.15	.11	.06
551	Rick Ownbey	.06	.05	.02
552	*Charlie Puleo*(FC)	.12	.09	.05
553	Gary Rajsich	.06	.05	.02
554	Mike Scott	.15	.11	.06
555	Rusty Staub	.10	.08	.04
556	John Stearns	.06	.05	.02
557	Craig Swan	.06	.05	.02
558	Ellis Valentine	.06	.05	.02
559	Tom Veryzer	.06	.05	.02
560	Mookie Wilson	.10	.08	.04
561	Pat Zachry	.06	.05	.02
562	Buddy Bell	.12	.09	.05
563	John Butcher	.06	.05	.02
564	Steve Comer	.06	.05	.02
565	Danny Darwin	.06	.05	.02
566	Bucky Dent	.10	.08	.04
567	John Grubb	.06	.05	.02
568	Rick Honeycutt	.06	.05	.02
569	Dave Hostetler	.06	.05	.02
570	Charlie Hough	.10	.08	.04
571	Lamar Johnson	.06	.05	.02
572	Jon Matlack	.08	.06	.03
573	Paul Mirabella	.06	.05	.02
574	Larry Parrish	.10	.08	.04
575	Mike Richardt	.06	.05	.02
576	Mickey Rivers	.08	.06	.03
577	Billy Sample	.06	.05	.02
578	*Dave Schmidt*(FC)	.10	.08	.04
579	Bill Stein	.06	.05	.02
580	Jim Sundberg	.08	.06	.03
581	Frank Tanana	.10	.08	.04
582	Mark Wagner	.06	.05	.02

		MT	NR MT	EX
583	George Wright	.06	.05	.02
584	Johnny Bench	.40	.30	.15
585	Bruce Berenyi	.06	.05	.02
586	Larry Biittner	.06	.05	.02
587	Cesar Cedeno	.12	.09	.05
588	Dave Concepcion	.12	.09	.05
589	Dan Driessen	.08	.06	.03
590	Greg Harris(FC)	.08	.06	.03
591	Ben Hayes	.06	.05	.02
592	Paul Householder	.06	.05	.02
593	Tom Hume	.06	.05	.02
594	Wayne Krenchicki	.06	.05	.02
595	Rafael Landestoy	.06	.05	.02
596	Charlie Leibrandt	.08	.06	.03
597	*Eddie Milner*(FC)	.10	.08	.04
598	Ron Oester	.06	.05	.02
599	Frank Pastore	.06	.05	.02
600	Joe Price	.06	.05	.02
601	Tom Seaver	.50	.40	.20
602	Bob Shirley	.06	.05	.02
603	Mario Soto	.08	.06	.03
604	Alex Trevino	.06	.05	.02
605	Mike Vail	.06	.05	.02
606	Duane Walker	.06	.05	.02
607	Tom Brunansky(FC)	.25	.20	.10
608	Bobby Castillo	.06	.05	.02
609	John Castino	.06	.05	.02
610	Ron Davis	.06	.05	.02
611	Lenny Faedo	.06	.05	.02
612	Terry Felton	.06	.05	.02
613	*Gary Gaetti*(FC)	1.50	1.25	.60
614	Mickey Hatcher	.08	.06	.03
615	Brad Havens	.06	.05	.02
616	Kent Hrbek(FC)	1.75	1.25	.70
617	Randy Johnson	.06	.05	.02
618	Tim Laudner(FC)	.12	.09	.05
619	Jeff Little	.06	.05	.02
620	Bob Mitchell	.06	.05	.02
621	Jack O'Connor	.06	.05	.02
622	John Pacella	.06	.05	.02
623	Pete Redfern	.06	.05	.02
624	Jesus Vega	.06	.05	.02
625	*Frank Viola*(FC)	5.00	3.75	2.00
626	Ron Washington	.06	.05	.02
627	Gary Ward	.08	.06	.03
628	Al Williams	.06	.05	.02
629	Red Sox All-Stars (Mark Clear, Dennis Eckersley, Carl Yastrzemski)	.25	.20	.10
630	300 Career Wins (Terry Bulling, Gaylord Perry)	.15	.11	.06
631	Pride of Venezuela (Dave Concepcion, Manny Trillo)	.10	.08	.04
632	All-Star Infielders (Buddy Bell, Robin Yount)	.15	.11	.06
633	Mr. Vet & Mr. Rookie (Kent Hrbek, Dave Winfield)	.25	.20	.10
634	Fountain of Youth (Pete Rose, Willie Stargell)	.40	.30	.15
635	Big Chiefs (Toby Harrah, Andre Thornton)	.08	.06	.03
636	"Smith Bros." (Lonnie Smith, Ozzie Smith)	.10	.08	.04
637	Base Stealers' Threat (Gary Carter, Bo Diaz)	.15	.11	.06
638	All-Star Catchers (Gary Carter, Carlton Fisk)	.20	.15	.08
639	The Silver Shoe (Rickey Henderson)	2.00	1.50	.80
640	Home Run Threats (Reggie Jackson, Ben Oglivie)	.25	.20	.10
641	Two Teams - Same Day (Joel Youngblood)	.08	.06	.03
642	Last Perfect Game (Len Barker, Ron Hassey)	.08	.06	.03
643	Blue (Vida Blue)	.10	.08	.04
644	Black & (Bud Black)	.10	.08	.04
645	Power (Reggie Jackson)	.30	.25	.12
646	Speed & (Rickey Henderson)	.30	.25	.12
647	Checklist 1-51	.06	.05	.02
648	Checklist 52-103	.06	.05	.02
649	Checklist 104-152	.06	.05	.02
650	Checklist 153-200	.06	.05	.02
651	Checklist 201-251	.06	.05	.02
652	Checklist 252-301	.06	.05	.02
653	Checklist 302-351	.06	.05	.02
654	Checklist 352-399	.06	.05	.02
655	Checklist 400-444	.06	.05	.02
656	Checklist 445-489	.06	.05	.02
657	Checklist 490-535	.06	.05	.02
658	Checklist 536-583	.06	.05	.02
659	Checklist 584-628	.06	.05	.02

		MT	NR MT	EX
660	Checklist 629-646	.06	.05	.02

1984 Fleer

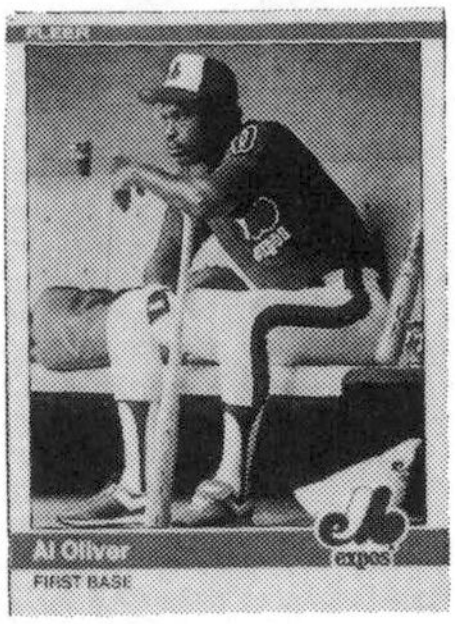

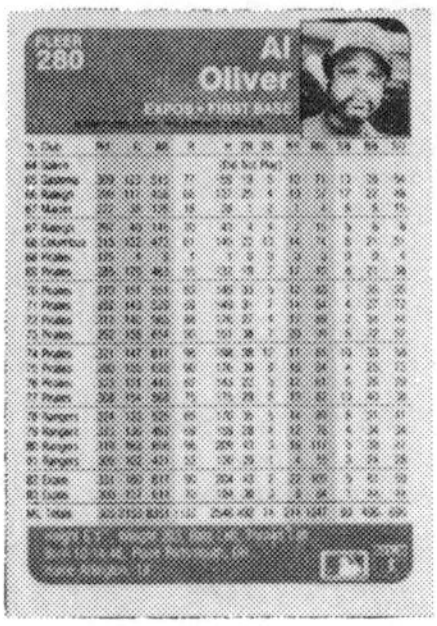

The 1984 Fleer set contained 660 cards for the fourth consecutive year. The cards, which measure 2-1/2" by 3-1/2", feature a color photo surrounded by four white borders and two blue stripes. The top stripe contains the word "Fleer" with the lower carrying the player's name. The card backs contain a small black and white photo of the player and are done in blue ink on white stock. The set was issued with team logo stickers.

		MT	NR MT	EX
Complete Set:		200.00	150.00	80.00
Common Player:		.08	.06	.03
1	Mike Boddicker(FC)	.20	.15	.08
2	Al Bumbry	.10	.08	.04
3	Todd Cruz	.08	.06	.03
4	Rich Dauer	.08	.06	.03
5	Storm Davis	.12	.09	.05
6	Rick Dempsey	.10	.08	.04
7	Jim Dwyer	.08	.06	.03
8	Mike Flanagan	.12	.09	.05
9	Dan Ford	.08	.06	.03
10	John Lowenstein	.08	.06	.03
11	Dennis Martinez	.10	.08	.04
12	Tippy Martinez	.08	.06	.03
13	Scott McGregor	.10	.08	.04
14	Eddie Murray	2.00	1.50	.80
15	Joe Nolan	.08	.06	.03
16	Jim Palmer	1.25	.90	.50
17	Cal Ripken, Jr.	15.00	11.00	6.00
18	Gary Roenicke	.08	.06	.03
19	Lenn Sakata	.08	.06	.03
20	*John Shelby*(FC)	.25	.20	.10
21	Ken Singleton	.12	.09	.05
22	Sammy Stewart	.08	.06	.03
23	Tim Stoddard	.08	.06	.03
24	Marty Bystrom	.08	.06	.03
25	Steve Carlton	1.25	.90	.50
26	Ivan DeJesus	.08	.06	.03
27	John Denny	.08	.06	.03
28	Bob Dernier	.08	.06	.03
29	Bo Diaz	.10	.08	.04
30	Kiko Garcia	.08	.06	.03
31	Greg Gross	.08	.06	.03
32	*Kevin Gross*(FC)	.35	.25	.14
33	Von Hayes	.15	.11	.06
34	Willie Hernandez	.12	.09	.05
35	Al Holland	.08	.06	.03
36	*Charles Hudson*(FC)	.20	.15	.08
37	Joe Lefebvre	.08	.06	.03
38	Sixto Lezcano	.08	.06	.03
39	Garry Maddox	.10	.08	.04
40	Gary Matthews	.12	.09	.05
41	Len Matuszek	.08	.06	.03
42	Tug McGraw	.12	.09	.05
43	Joe Morgan	.40	.30	.15
44	Tony Perez	.20	.15	.08
45	Ron Reed	.08	.06	.03
46	Pete Rose	1.00	.70	.40
47	*Juan Samuel*(FC)	5.00	3.75	2.00
48	Mike Schmidt	7.00	5.25	2.75
49	Ozzie Virgil	.08	.06	.03
50	*Juan Agosto*(FC)	.15	.11	.06

		MT	NR MT	EX
51	Harold Baines	.25	.20	.10
52	Floyd Bannister	.12	.09	.05
53	Salome Barojas	.08	.06	.03
54	Britt Burns	.08	.06	.03
55	Julio Cruz	.08	.06	.03
56	Richard Dotson	.12	.09	.05
57	Jerry Dybzinski	.08	.06	.03
58	Carlton Fisk	1.25	.90	.50
59	Scott Fletcher(FC)	.15	.11	.06
60	Jerry Hairston	.08	.06	.03
61	Kevin Hickey	.08	.06	.03
62	Marc Hill	.08	.06	.03
63	LaMarr Hoyt	.08	.06	.03
64	Ron Kittle	.15	.11	.06
65	Jerry Koosman	.12	.09	.05
66	Dennis Lamp	.08	.06	.03
67	Rudy Law	.08	.06	.03
68	Vance Law	.10	.08	.04
69	Greg Luzinski	.12	.09	.05
70	Tom Paciorek	.08	.06	.03
71	Mike Squires	.08	.06	.03
72	Dick Tidrow	.08	.06	.03
73	*Greg Walker*(FC)	.45	.35	.20
74	Glenn Abbott	.08	.06	.03
75	Howard Bailey	.08	.06	.03
76	Doug Bair	.08	.06	.03
77	Juan Berenguer	.08	.06	.03
78	Tom Brookens	.08	.06	.03
79	Enos Cabell	.08	.06	.03
80	Kirk Gibson	.40	.30	.15
81	John Grubb	.08	.06	.03
82	Larry Herndon	.10	.08	.04
83	Wayne Krenchicki	.08	.06	.03
84	Rick Leach	.08	.06	.03
85	Chet Lemon	.10	.08	.04
86	Aurelio Lopez	.08	.06	.03
87	Jack Morris	.30	.25	.12
88	Lance Parrish	.35	.25	.14
89	Dan Petry	.10	.08	.04
90	Dave Rozema	.08	.06	.03
91	Alan Trammell	.40	.30	.15
92	Lou Whitaker	.40	.30	.15
93	Milt Wilcox	.08	.06	.03
94	Glenn Wilson	.10	.08	.04
95	John Wockenfuss	.08	.06	.03
96	Dusty Baker	.12	.09	.05
97	Joe Beckwith	.08	.06	.03
98	Greg Brock	.12	.09	.05
99	Jack Fimple	.08	.06	.03
100	Pedro Guerrero	.35	.25	.14
101	Rick Honeycutt	.08	.06	.03
102	Burt Hooton	.10	.08	.04
103	Steve Howe	.12	.09	.05
104	Ken Landreaux	.08	.06	.03
105	Mike Marshall	.15	.11	.06
106	Rick Monday	.10	.08	.04
107	Jose Morales	.08	.06	.03
108	Tom Niedenfuer	.10	.08	.04
109	*Alejandro Pena*(FC)	.30	.25	.12
110	Jerry Reuss	.12	.09	.05
111	Bill Russell	.10	.08	.04
112	Steve Sax	.20	.15	.08
113	Mike Scioscia	.10	.08	.04
114	Derrel Thomas	.08	.06	.03
115	Fernando Valenzuela	.40	.30	.15
116	Bob Welch	.15	.11	.06
117	Steve Yeager	.08	.06	.03
118	Pat Zachry	.08	.06	.03
119	Don Baylor	.15	.11	.06
120	Bert Campaneris	.12	.09	.05
121	Rick Cerone	.08	.06	.03
122	*Ray Fontenot*(FC)	.10	.08	.04
123	George Frazier	.08	.06	.03
124	Oscar Gamble	.10	.08	.04
125	Goose Gossage	.25	.20	.10
126	Ken Griffey	.12	.09	.05
127	Ron Guidry	.30	.25	.12
128	Jay Howell(FC)	.15	.11	.06
129	Steve Kemp	.10	.08	.04
130	Matt Keough	.08	.06	.03
131	*Don Mattingly*(FC)	40.00	30.00	15.00
132	John Montefusco	.08	.06	.03
133	Omar Moreno	.08	.06	.03
134	Dale Murray	.08	.06	.03
135	Graig Nettles	.20	.15	.08
136	Lou Piniella	.15	.11	.06
137	Willie Randolph	.12	.09	.05
138	Shane Rawley	.12	.09	.05
139	Dave Righetti	.25	.20	.10
140	Andre Robertson	.08	.06	.03
141	Bob Shirley	.08	.06	.03
142	Roy Smalley	.08	.06	.03

		MT	NR MT	EX
143	Dave Winfield	1.25	.90	.50
144	Butch Wynegar	.08	.06	.03
145	*Jim Acker*(FC)	.12	.09	.05
146	Doyle Alexander	.12	.09	.05
147	Jesse Barfield	.25	.20	.10
148	Jorge Bell	2.00	1.50	.80
149	Barry Bonnell	.08	.06	.03
150	Jim Clancy	.10	.08	.04
151	Dave Collins	.10	.08	.04
152	*Tony Fernandez*(FC)	6.00	4.50	2.50
153	Damaso Garcia	.08	.06	.03
154	Dave Geisel	.08	.06	.03
155	Jim Gott(FC)	.10	.08	.04
156	Alfredo Griffin	.10	.08	.04
157	Garth Iorg	.08	.06	.03
158	Roy Lee Jackson	.08	.06	.03
159	Cliff Johnson	.08	.06	.03
160	Luis Leal	.08	.06	.03
161	Buck Martinez	.08	.06	.03
162	Joey McLaughlin	.08	.06	.03
163	Randy Moffitt	.08	.06	.03
164	Lloyd Moseby	.12	.09	.05
165	Rance Mulliniks	.08	.06	.03
166	Jorge Orta	.08	.06	.03
167	Dave Stieb	.15	.11	.06
168	Willie Upshaw	.10	.08	.04
169	Ernie Whitt	.10	.08	.04
170	Len Barker	.10	.08	.04
171	Steve Bedrosian	.12	.09	.05
172	Bruce Benedict	.08	.06	.03
173	Brett Butler	.10	.08	.04
174	Rick Camp	.08	.06	.03
175	Chris Chambliss	.10	.08	.04
176	Ken Dayley	.08	.06	.03
177	Pete Falcone	.08	.06	.03
178	Terry Forster	.10	.08	.04
179	Gene Garber	.08	.06	.03
180	Terry Harper	.08	.06	.03
181	Bob Horner	.12	.09	.05
182	Glenn Hubbard	.10	.08	.04
183	Randy Johnson	.08	.06	.03
184	*Craig McMurtry*(FC)	.12	.09	.05
185	Donnie Moore(FC)	.10	.08	.04
186	Dale Murphy	1.00	.70	.40
187	Phil Niekro	.30	.25	.12
188	Pascual Perez	.10	.08	.04
189	Biff Pocoroba	.08	.06	.03
190	Rafael Ramirez	.08	.06	.03
191	Jerry Royster	.08	.06	.03
192	Claudell Washington	.10	.08	.04
193	Bob Watson	.10	.08	.04
194	Jerry Augustine	.08	.06	.03
195	Mark Brouhard	.08	.06	.03
196	Mike Caldwell	.08	.06	.03
197	*Tom Candiotti*(FC)	.25	.20	.10
198	Cecil Cooper	.15	.11	.06
199	Rollie Fingers	.25	.20	.10
200	Jim Gantner	.10	.08	.04
201	Bob Gibson	.08	.06	.03
202	Moose Haas	.08	.06	.03
203	Roy Howell	.08	.06	.03
204	Pete Ladd	.08	.06	.03
205	Rick Manning	.08	.06	.03
206	Bob McClure	.08	.06	.03
207	Paul Molitor	.20	.15	.08
208	Don Money	.08	.06	.03
209	Charlie Moore	.08	.06	.03
210	Ben Oglivie	.10	.08	.04
211	Chuck Porter	.08	.06	.03
212	Ed Romero	.08	.06	.03
213	Ted Simmons	.15	.11	.06
214	Jim Slaton	.08	.06	.03
215	Don Sutton	.30	.25	.12
216	Tom Tellmann	.08	.06	.03
217	Pete Vuckovich	.10	.08	.04
218	Ned Yost	.08	.06	.03
219	Robin Yount	3.00	2.25	1.25
220	Alan Ashby	.08	.06	.03
221	Kevin Bass(FC)	.20	.15	.08
222	Jose Cruz	.12	.09	.05
223	*Bill Dawley*(FC)	.10	.08	.04
224	Frank DiPino	.08	.06	.03
225	*Bill Doran*(FC)	1.00	.70	.50
226	Phil Garner	.10	.08	.04
227	Art Howe	.08	.06	.03
228	Bob Knepper	.10	.08	.04
229	Ray Knight	.12	.09	.05
230	Frank LaCorte	.08	.06	.03
231	Mike LaCoss	.08	.06	.03
232	Mike Madden	.08	.06	.03
233	Jerry Mumphrey	.08	.06	.03
235	Terry Puhl	.08	.06	.03
236	Luis Pujols	.08	.06	.03
237	Craig Reynolds	.08	.06	.03
238	Vern Ruhle	.08	.06	.03
239	Nolan Ryan	10.00	7.50	4.00
240	Mike Scott	.20	.15	.08
241	Tony Scott	.08	.06	.03
242	Dave Smith	.10	.08	.04
243	Dickie Thon	.10	.08	.04
244	Denny Walling	.08	.06	.03
245	Dale Berra	.08	.06	.03
246	Jim Bibby	.08	.06	.03
247	John Candelaria	.12	.09	.05
248	*Jose DeLeon*(FC)	.50	.40	.20
249	Mike Easler	.10	.08	.04
250	Cecilio Guante(FC)	.10	.08	.04
251	Richie Hebner	.08	.06	.03
252	Lee Lacy	.08	.06	.03
253	Bill Madlock	.12	.09	.05
254	Milt May	.08	.06	.03
255	Lee Mazzilli	.10	.08	.04
256	Larry McWilliams	.08	.06	.03
257	Jim Morrison	.08	.06	.03
258	Dave Parker	.30	.25	.12
259	Tony Pena	.12	.09	.05
260	Johnny Ray	.12	.09	.05
261	Rick Rhoden	.12	.09	.05
262	Don Robinson	.10	.08	.04
263	Manny Sarmiento	.08	.06	.03
264	Rod Scurry	.08	.06	.03
265	Kent Tekulve	.10	.08	.04
266	Gene Tenace	.10	.08	.04
267	Jason Thompson	.08	.06	.03
268	*Lee Tunnell*(FC)	.10	.08	.04
269	*Marvell Wynne*(FC)	.20	.15	.08
270	Ray Burris	.08	.06	.03
271	Gary Carter	.40	.30	.15
272	Warren Cromartie	.08	.06	.03
273	Andre Dawson	3.00	2.25	1.25
274	Doug Flynn	.08	.06	.03
275	Terry Francona	.08	.06	.03
276	Bill Gullickson	.08	.06	.03
277	Bob James	.08	.06	.03
278	Charlie Lea	.08	.06	.03
279	Bryan Little	.08	.06	.03
280	Al Oliver	.20	.15	.08
281	Tim Raines	.70	.50	.30
282	Bobby Ramos	.08	.06	.03
283	Jeff Reardon	.15	.11	.06
284	Steve Rogers	.10	.08	.04
285	Scott Sanderson	.08	.06	.03
286	Dan Schatzeder	.08	.06	.03
287	Bryn Smith	.08	.06	.03
288	Chris Speier	.08	.06	.03
289	Manny Trillo	.10	.08	.04
290	Mike Vail	.08	.06	.03
291	Tim Wallach	.15	.11	.06
292	Chris Welsh	.08	.06	.03
293	Jim Wohlford	.08	.06	.03
294	Kurt Bevacqua	.08	.06	.03
295	Juan Bonilla	.08	.06	.03
296	Bobby Brown	.08	.06	.03
297	Luis DeLeon	.08	.06	.03
298	Dave Dravecky	.10	.08	.04
299	Tim Flannery	.08	.06	.03
300	Steve Garvey	.50	.40	.20
301	Tony Gwynn	8.00	6.00	3.25
302	*Andy Hawkins*(FC)	.40	.30	.15
303	Ruppert Jones	.08	.06	.03
304	Terry Kennedy	.10	.08	.04
305	Tim Lollar	.08	.06	.03
306	Gary Lucas	.08	.06	.03
307	*Kevin McReynolds*(FC)	7.00	5.25	2.75
308	Sid Monge	.08	.06	.03
309	Mario Ramirez	.08	.06	.03
310	Gene Richards	.08	.06	.03
311	Luis Salazar	.08	.06	.03
312	Eric Show	.12	.09	.05
313	Elias Sosa	.08	.06	.03
314	Garry Templeton	.12	.09	.05
315	*Mark Thurmond*(FC)	.10	.08	.04
316	Ed Whitson	.08	.06	.03
317	Alan Wiggins	.08	.06	.03
318	Neil Allen	.08	.06	.03
319	Joaquin Andujar	.10	.08	.04
320	Steve Braun	.08	.06	.03
321	Glenn Brummer	.08	.06	.03
322	Bob Forsch	.10	.08	.04
323	David Green	.08	.06	.03
324	George Hendrick	.10	.08	.04
325	Tom Herr	.12	.09	.05

		MT	NR MT	EX
326	Dane Iorg	.08	.06	.03
327	Jeff Lahti	.08	.06	.03
328	Dave LaPoint	.10	.08	.04
329	Willie McGee	.35	.25	.14
330	Ken Oberkfell	.08	.06	.03
331	Darrell Porter	.10	.08	.04
332	Jamie Quirk	.08	.06	.03
333	Mike Ramsey	.08	.06	.03
334	Floyd Rayford	.08	.06	.03
335	Lonnie Smith	.10	.08	.04
336	Ozzie Smith	1.50	1.25	.60
337	John Stuper	.08	.06	.03
338	Bruce Sutter	.20	.15	.08
339	*Andy Van Slyke*(FC)	4.00	3.00	1.50
340	Dave Von Ohlen	.08	.06	.03
341	Willie Aikens	.08	.06	.03
342	Mike Armstrong	.08	.06	.03
343	Bud Black	.10	.08	.04
344	George Brett	2.00	1.50	.80
345	Onix Concepcion	.08	.06	.03
346	Keith Creel	.08	.06	.03
347	Larry Gura	.08	.06	.03
348	Don Hood	.08	.06	.03
349	Dennis Leonard	.10	.08	.04
350	Hal McRae	.12	.09	.05
351	Amos Otis	.12	.09	.05
352	Gaylord Perry	.40	.30	.15
353	Greg Pryor	.08	.06	.03
354	Dan Quisenberry	.12	.09	.05
355	Steve Renko	.08	.06	.03
356	Leon Roberts	.08	.06	.03
357	*Pat Sheridan*(FC)	.15	.11	.06
358	Joe Simpson	.08	.06	.03
359	Don Slaught	.08	.06	.03
360	Paul Splittorff	.08	.06	.03
361	U.L. Washington	.08	.06	.03
362	John Wathan	.10	.08	.04
363	Frank White	.12	.09	.05
364	Willie Wilson	.15	.11	.06
365	Jim Barr	.08	.06	.03
366	Dave Bergman	.08	.06	.03
367	Fred Breining	.08	.06	.03
368	Bob Brenly	.08	.06	.03
369	Jack Clark	.25	.20	.10
370	Chili Davis	.12	.09	.05
371	Mark Davis(FC)	.20	.15	.08
372	Darrell Evans	.15	.11	.06
373	Atlee Hammaker	.08	.06	.03
374	Mike Krukow	.10	.08	.04
375	Duane Kuiper	.08	.06	.03
376	Bill Laskey	.08	.06	.03
377	Gary Lavelle	.08	.06	.03
378	Johnnie LeMaster	.08	.06	.03
379	Jeff Leonard	.12	.09	.05
380	Randy Lerch	.08	.06	.03
381	Renie Martin	.08	.06	.03
382	Andy McGaffigan	.08	.06	.03
383	Greg Minton	.08	.06	.03
384	Tom O'Malley	.08	.06	.03
385	Max Venable	.08	.06	.03
386	Brad Wellman	.08	.06	.03
387	Joel Youngblood	.08	.06	.03
388	Gary Allenson	.08	.06	.03
389	Luis Aponte	.08	.06	.03
390	Tony Armas	.12	.09	.05
391	Doug Bird	.08	.06	.03
392	Wade Boggs	8.00	6.00	3.25
393	*Dennis Boyd*(FC)	.70	.50	.30
394	Mike Brown	.08	.06	.03
395	Mark Clear	.08	.06	.03
396	Dennis Eckersley	.15	.11	.06
397	Dwight Evans	.20	.15	.08
398	Rich Gedman	.10	.08	.04
399	Glenn Hoffman	.08	.06	.03
400	Bruce Hurst	.15	.11	.06
401	John Henry Johnson	.08	.06	.03
402	Ed Jurak	.08	.06	.03
403	Rick Miller	.08	.06	.03
404	Jeff Newman	.08	.06	.03
405	Reid Nichols	.08	.06	.03
406	Bob Ojeda	.12	.09	.05
407	Jerry Remy	.08	.06	.03
408	Jim Rice	.40	.30	.15
409	Bob Stanley	.08	.06	.03
410	Dave Stapleton	.08	.06	.03
411	John Tudor	.12	.09	.05
412	Carl Yastrzemski	.80	.60	.30
413	Buddy Bell	.12	.09	.05
414	Larry Biittner	.08	.06	.03
415	John Butcher	.08	.06	.03
416	Danny Darwin	.08	.06	.03

		MT	NR MT	EX
417	Bucky Dent	.12	.09	.05
418	Dave Hostetler	.08	.06	.03
419	Charlie Hough	.12	.09	.05
420	Bobby Johnson	.08	.06	.03
421	Odell Jones	.08	.06	.03
422	Jon Matlack	.10	.08	.04
423	*Pete O'Brien*(FC)	.80	.60	.30
424	Larry Parrish	.12	.09	.05
425	Mickey Rivers	.10	.08	.04
426	Billy Sample	.08	.06	.03
427	Dave Schmidt	.08	.06	.03
428	*Mike Smithson*(FC)	.15	.11	.06
429	Bill Stein	.08	.06	.03
430	Dave Stewart	.15	.11	.06
431	Jim Sundberg	.10	.08	.04
432	Frank Tanana	.12	.09	.05
433	Dave Tobik	.08	.06	.03
434	Wayne Tolleson(FC)	.10	.08	.04
435	George Wright	.08	.06	.03
436	Bill Almon	.08	.06	.03
437	*Keith Atherton*(FC)	.20	.15	.08
438	Dave Beard	.08	.06	.03
439	Tom Burgmeier	.08	.06	.03
440	Jeff Burroughs	.10	.08	.04
441	*Chris Codiroli*(FC)	.10	.08	.04
442	*Tim Conroy*(FC)	.12	.09	.05
443	Mike Davis	.10	.08	.04
444	Wayne Gross	.08	.06	.03
445	Garry Hancock	.08	.06	.03
446	Mike Heath	.08	.06	.03
447	Rickey Henderson	10.00	7.50	4.00
448	*Don Hill*(FC)	.15	.11	.06
449	Bob Kearney	.08	.06	.03
450	Bill Krueger	.08	.06	.03
451	Rick Langford	.08	.06	.03
452	Carney Lansford	.12	.09	.05
453	Davey Lopes	.10	.08	.04
454	Steve McCatty	.08	.06	.03
455	Dan Meyer	.08	.06	.03
456	Dwayne Murphy	.10	.08	.04
457	Mike Norris	.08	.06	.03
458	Ricky Peters	.08	.06	.03
459	*Tony Phillips*(FC)	.15	.11	.06
460	Tom Underwood	.08	.06	.03
461	Mike Warren	.08	.06	.03
462	Johnny Bench	.80	.60	.30
463	Bruce Berenyi	.08	.06	.03
464	Dann Bilardello	.08	.06	.03
465	Cesar Cedeno	.12	.09	.05
466	Dave Concepcion	.15	.11	.06
467	Dan Driessen	.10	.08	.04
468	*Nick Esasky*(FC)	.70	.50	.30
469	Rich Gale	.08	.06	.03
470	Ben Hayes	.08	.06	.03
471	Paul Householder	.08	.06	.03
472	Tom Hume	.08	.06	.03
473	Alan Knicely	.08	.06	.03
474	Eddie Milner	.08	.06	.03
475	Ron Oester	.08	.06	.03
476	Kelly Paris	.08	.06	.03
477	Frank Pastore	.08	.06	.03
478	Ted Power	.10	.08	.04
479	Joe Price	.08	.06	.03
480	Charlie Puleo	.08	.06	.03
481	*Gary Redus*(FC)	.25	.20	.10
482	Bill Scherrer	.08	.06	.03
483	Mario Soto	.10	.08	.04
484	Alex Trevino	.08	.06	.03
485	Duane Walker	.08	.06	.03
486	Larry Bowa	.15	.11	.06
487	Warren Brusstar	.08	.06	.03
488	Bill Buckner	.15	.11	.06
489	Bill Campbell	.08	.06	.03
490	Ron Cey	.12	.09	.05
491	Jody Davis	.10	.08	.04
492	Leon Durham	.10	.08	.04
493	Mel Hall(FC)	.20	.15	.08
494	Ferguson Jenkins	.20	.15	.08
495	Jay Johnstone	.10	.08	.04
496	*Craig Lefferts*(FC)	.20	.15	.08
497	*Carmelo Martinez*(FC)	.25	.20	.10
498	Jerry Morales	.08	.06	.03
499	Keith Moreland	.10	.08	.04
500	Dickie Noles	.08	.06	.03
501	Mike Proly	.08	.06	.03
502	Chuck Rainey	.08	.06	.03
503	Dick Ruthven	.08	.06	.03
504	Ryne Sandberg	15.00	11.00	6.00
505	Lee Smith	.15	.11	.06
506	Steve Trout	.08	.06	.03
507	Gary Woods	.08	.06	.03

		MT	NR MT	EX
508	Juan Beniquez	.08	.06	.03
509	Bob Boone	.10	.08	.04
510	Rick Burleson	.10	.08	.04
511	Rod Carew	1.25	.90	.50
512	Bobby Clark	.08	.06	.03
513	John Curtis	.08	.06	.03
514	Doug DeCinces	.12	.09	.05
515	Brian Downing	.12	.09	.05
516	Tim Foli	.08	.06	.03
517	Ken Forsch	.08	.06	.03
518	Bobby Grich	.12	.09	.05
519	Andy Hassler	.08	.06	.03
520	Reggie Jackson	1.25	.90	.50
521	Ron Jackson	.08	.06	.03
522	Tommy John	.25	.20	.10
523	Bruce Kison	.08	.06	.03
524	Steve Lubratich	.08	.06	.03
525	Fred Lynn	.25	.20	.10
526	*Gary Pettis*(FC)	.25	.20	.10
527	Luis Sanchez	.08	.06	.03
528	Daryl Sconiers	.08	.06	.03
529	Ellis Valentine	.08	.06	.03
530	Rob Wilfong	.08	.06	.03
531	Mike Witt	.15	.11	.06
532	Geoff Zahn	.08	.06	.03
533	Bud Anderson	.08	.06	.03
534	Chris Bando	.08	.06	.03
535	Alan Bannister	.08	.06	.03
536	Bert Blyleven	.20	.15	.08
537	Tom Brennan	.08	.06	.03
538	Jamie Easterly	.08	.06	.03
539	Juan Eichelberger	.08	.06	.03
540	Jim Essian	.08	.06	.03
541	Mike Fischlin	.08	.06	.03
542	Julio Franco(FC)	3.00	2.25	1.25
543	Mike Hargrove	.08	.06	.03
544	Toby Harrah	.10	.08	.04
545	Ron Hassey	.08	.06	.03
546	*Neal Heaton*(FC)	.15	.11	.06
547	Bake McBride	.08	.06	.03
548	Broderick Perkins	.08	.06	.03
549	Lary Sorensen	.08	.06	.03
550	Dan Spillner	.08	.06	.03
551	Rick Sutcliffe	.15	.11	.06
552	Pat Tabler	.10	.08	.04
553	Gorman Thomas	.10	.08	.04
554	Andre Thornton	.12	.09	.05
555	George Vukovich	.08	.06	.03
556	Darrell Brown	.08	.06	.03
557	Tom Brunansky	.20	.15	.08
558	*Randy Bush*(FC)	.15	.11	.06
559	Bobby Castillo	.08	.06	.03
560	John Castino	.08	.06	.03
561	Ron Davis	.08	.06	.03
562	Dave Engle	.08	.06	.03
563	Lenny Faedo	.08	.06	.03
564	Pete Filson	.08	.06	.03
565	Gary Gaetti	.60	.45	.25
566	Mickey Hatcher	.10	.08	.04
567	Kent Hrbek	.40	.30	.15
568	Rusty Kuntz	.08	.06	.03
569	Tim Laudner	.08	.06	.03
570	Rick Lysander	.08	.06	.03
571	Bobby Mitchell	.08	.06	.03
572	Ken Schrom	.08	.06	.03
573	Ray Smith	.08	.06	.03
574	*Tim Teufel*(FC)	.30	.25	.12
575	Frank Viola	2.00	1.50	.80
576	Gary Ward	.10	.08	.04
577	Ron Washington	.08	.06	.03
578	Len Whitehouse	.08	.06	.03
579	Al Williams	.08	.06	.03
580	Bob Bailor	.08	.06	.03
581	Mark Bradley	.08	.06	.03
582	Hubie Brooks	.15	.11	.06
583	Carlos Diaz	.08	.06	.03
584	George Foster	.20	.15	.08
585	Brian Giles	.08	.06	.03
586	Danny Heep	.08	.06	.03
587	Keith Hernandez	.40	.30	.15
588	Ron Hodges	.08	.06	.03
589	Scott Holman	.08	.06	.03
590	Dave Kingman	.15	.11	.06
591	Ed Lynch	.08	.06	.03
592	*Jose Oquendo*(FC)	.15	.11	.06
593	Jesse Orosco	.10	.08	.04
594	*Junior Ortiz*(FC)	.10	.08	.04
595	Tom Seaver	3.00	2.25	1.25
596	*Doug Sisk*(FC)	.10	.08	.04
597	Rusty Staub	.12	.09	.05
598	John Stearns	.08	.06	.03

		MT	NR MT	EX
599	*Darryl Strawberry*(FC)	40.00	30.00	15.00
600	Craig Swan	.08	.06	.03
601	*Walt Terrell*(FC)	.25	.20	.10
602	Mike Torrez	.10	.08	.04
603	Mookie Wilson	.12	.09	.05
604	Jamie Allen	.08	.06	.03
605	Jim Beattie	.08	.06	.03
606	Tony Bernazard	.08	.06	.03
607	Manny Castillo	.08	.06	.03
608	Bill Caudill	.08	.06	.03
609	Bryan Clark	.08	.06	.03
610	Al Cowens	.08	.06	.03
611	Dave Henderson	.12	.09	.05
612	Steve Henderson	.08	.06	.03
613	Orlando Mercado	.08	.06	.03
614	Mike Moore	.10	.08	.04
615	Ricky Nelson	.08	.06	.03
616	*Spike Owen*(FC)	.20	.15	.08
617	Pat Putnam	.08	.06	.03
618	Ron Roenicke	.08	.06	.03
619	Mike Stanton	.08	.06	.03
620	Bob Stoddard	.08	.06	.03
621	Rick Sweet	.08	.06	.03
622	Roy Thomas	.08	.06	.03
623	Ed Vande Berg	.08	.06	.03
624	*Matt Young*(FC)	.15	.11	.06
625	Richie Zisk	.10	.08	.04
626	'83 All-Star Game Record Breaker (Fred Lynn)	.12	.09	.05
627	'83 All-Star Game Record Breaker (Manny Trillo)	.10	.08	.04
628	N.L. Iron Man (Steve Garvey)	.20	.15	.08
629	A.L. Batting Runner-Up (Rod Carew)	.25	.20	.10
630	A.L. Batting Champion (Wade Boggs)	.60	.45	.25
631	Letting Go Of The Raines (Tim Raines)	.20	.15	.08
632	Double Trouble (Al Oliver)	.10	.08	.04
633	All-Star Second Base (Steve Sax)	.15	.11	.06
634	All-Star Shortstop (Dickie Thon)	.10	.08	.04
635	Ace Firemen (Tippy Martinez, Dan Quisenberry)	.10	.08	.04
636	Reds Reunited (Joe Morgan, Tony Perez, Pete Rose)	.50	.40	.20
637	Backstop Stars (Bob Boone, Lance Parrish)	.15	.11	.06
638	The Pine Tar Incident, 7/24/83 (George Brett, Gaylord Perry)	.30	.25	.12
639	1983 No-Hitters (Bob Forsch, Dave Righetti, Mike Warren)	.10	.08	.04
640	Retiring Superstars (Johnny Bench, Carl Yastrzemski)	1.50	1.25	.60
641	Going Out In Style (Gaylord Perry)	.15	.11	.06
642	300 Club & Strikeout Record (Steve Carlton)	.20	.15	.08
643	The Managers (Joe Altobelli, Paul Owens)	.10	.08	.04
644	The MVP (Rick Dempsey)	.10	.08	.04
645	The Rookie Winner (Mike Boddicker)(FC)	.12	.09	.05
646	The Clincher (Scott McGregor)	.10	.08	.04
647	Checklist: Orioles/Royals (Joe Altobelli)	.08	.06	.03
648	Checklist: Phillies/Giants (Paul Owens)	.08	.06	.03
649	Checklist: White Sox/Red Sox (Tony LaRussa)	.08	.06	.03
650	Checklist: Tigers/Rangers (Sparky Anderson)	.08	.06	.03
651	Checklist: Dodgers/A's (Tom Lasorda)	.08	.06	.03
652	Checklist: Yankees/Reds (Billy Martin)	.08	.06	.03
653	Checklist: Blue Jays/Cubs (Bobby Cox)	.08	.06	.03
654	Checklist: Braves/Angels (Joe Torre)	.08	.06	.03
655	Checklist: Brewers/Indians (Rene Lachemann)	.08	.06	.03
656	Checklist: Astros/Twins (Bob Lillis)	.08	.06	.03
657	Checklist: Pirates/Mets (Chuck Tanner)	.08	.06	.03
658	Checklist: Expos/Mariners (Bill Virdon)	.08	.06	.03
659	Checklist: Padres/Specials (Dick Williams)	.08	.06	.03
660	Checklist: Cardinals/Specials (Whitey Herzog)	.08	.06	.03

1984 Fleer Update

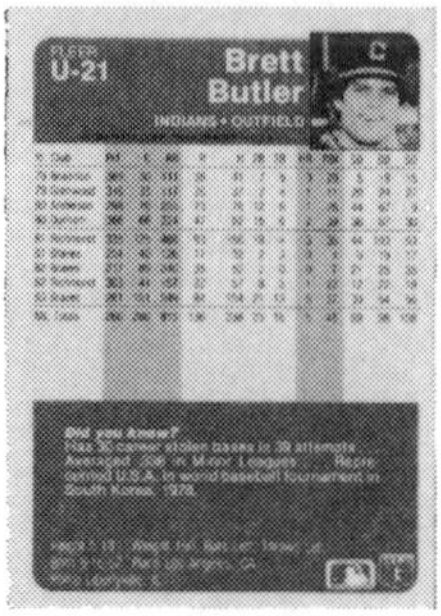

Following the lead of Topps, Fleer issued near the end of the baseball season a 132-card set to update player trades and include rookies not depicted in the regular issue. The cards, which measure 2-1/2" by 3-1/2", are identical in design to the regular issue but are numbered U-1 through U-132. Available to the collecting public only through hobby dealers, the set was printed in limited quantities and has escalated in price quite rapidly the past several years. The set was issued with team logo stickers in a specially designed box.

		MT	NR MT	EX
Complete Set:		650.00	475.00	275.00
Common Player:		.15	.11	.06
1	Willie Aikens	.15	.11	.06
2	Luis Aponte	.15	.11	.06
3	Mark Bailey(FC)	.20	.15	.08
4	Bob Bailor	.15	.11	.06
5	Dusty Baker	.30	.25	.12
6	Steve Balboni(FC)	.40	.30	.15
7	Alan Bannister	.15	.11	.06
8	Marty Barrett(FC)	2.00	1.50	.80
9	Dave Beard	.15	.11	.06
10	Joe Beckwith	.15	.11	.06
11	Dave Bergman	.15	.11	.06
12	Tony Bernazard	.15	.11	.06
13	Bruce Bochte	.15	.11	.06
14	Barry Bonnell	.15	.11	.06
15	Phil Bradley(FC)	4.00	3.00	1.50
16	Fred Breining	.15	.11	.06
17	Mike Brown	.15	.11	.06
18	Bill Buckner	.50	.40	.20
19	Ray Burris	.15	.11	.06
20	John Butcher	.15	.11	.06
21	Brett Butler	.30	.25	.12
22	Enos Cabell	.15	.11	.06
23	Bill Campbell	.15	.11	.06
24	Bill Caudill	.15	.11	.06
25	Bobby Clark	.15	.11	.06
26	Bryan Clark	.15	.11	.06
27	Roger Clemens(FC)	250.00	200.00	100.00
28	Jaime Cocanower	.15	.11	.06
29	Ron Darling(FC)	7.00	5.25	2.75
30	Alvin Davis(FC)	10.00	7.50	4.00
31	Bob Dernier	.15	.11	.06
32	Carlos Diaz	.15	.11	.06
33	Mike Easler	.20	.15	.08
34	Dennis Eckersley	5.00	3.75	2.00
35	Jim Essian	.15	.11	.06
36	Darrell Evans	.60	.45	.25
37	Mike Fitzgerald(FC)	.20	.15	.08
38	Tim Foli	.15	.11	.06
39	John Franco(FC)	10.00	7.50	4.00
40	George Frazier	.15	.11	.06
41	Rich Gale	.15	.11	.06
42	Barbaro Garbey	.20	.15	.08
43	Dwight Gooden(FC)	125.00	90.00	50.00
44	Goose Gossage	1.00	.70	.40
45	Wayne Gross	.15	.11	.06
46	Mark Gubicza(FC)	6.00	4.50	2.50
47	Jackie Gutierrez	.15	.11	.06
48	Toby Harrah	.20	.15	.08
49	Ron Hassey	.15	.11	.06
50	Richie Hebner	.15	.11	.06
51	Willie Hernandez	.40	.30	.15
52	Ed Hodge	.15	.11	.06
53	Ricky Horton(FC)	.50	.40	.20
54	Art Howe	.15	.11	.06
55	Dane Iorg	.15	.11	.06
56	Brook Jacoby(FC)	4.00	3.00	1.50
57	Dion James(FC)	.30	.25	.12
58	Mike Jeffcoat(FC)	.20	.15	.08
59	Ruppert Jones	.15	.11	.06
60	Bob Kearney	.15	.11	.06
61	Jimmy Key(FC)	8.00	6.00	3.25
62	Dave Kingman	.70	.50	.30
63	Brad Komminsk(FC)	.20	.15	.08
64	Jerry Koosman	.50	.40	.20
65	Wayne Krenchicki	.15	.11	.06
66	Rusty Kuntz	.15	.11	.06
67	Frank LaCorte	.15	.11	.06
68	Dennis Lamp	.15	.11	.06
69	Tito Landrum	.15	.11	.06
70	Mark Langston(FC)	20.00	15.00	8.00
71	Rick Leach	.15	.11	.06
72	Craig Lefferts(FC)	.30	.25	.12
73	Gary Lucas	.15	.11	.06
74	Jerry Martin	.15	.11	.06
75	Carmelo Martinez	.30	.25	.12
76	Mike Mason(FC)	.20	.15	.08
77	Gary Matthews	.30	.25	.12
78	Andy McGaffigan	.15	.11	.06
79	Joey McLaughlin	.15	.11	.06
80	Joe Morgan	5.00	3.75	2.00
81	Darryl Motley	.15	.11	.06
82	Graig Nettles	1.00	.70	.40
83	Phil Niekro	4.00	3.00	1.50
84	Ken Oberkfell	.15	.11	.06
85	Al Oliver	.80	.60	.30
86	Jorge Orta	.15	.11	.06
87	Amos Otis	.30	.25	.12
88	Bob Owchinko	.15	.11	.06
89	Dave Parker	4.00	3.00	1.50
90	Jack Perconte	.15	.11	.06
91	Tony Perez	4.00	3.00	1.50
92	Gerald Perry(FC)	1.25	.90	.50
93	Kirby Puckett(FC)	200.00	150.00	80.00
94	Shane Rawley	.35	.30	.14
95	Floyd Rayford	.15	.11	.06
96	Ron Reed	.20	.15	.08
97	R.J. Reynolds(FC)	.90	.70	.35
98	Gene Richards	.15	.11	.06
99	Jose Rijo(FC)	10.00	7.50	4.00
100	Jeff Robinson(FC)	.50	.40	.20
101	Ron Romanick(FC)	.20	.15	.08
102	Pete Rose	15.00	11.00	6.00
103	Bret Saberhagen(FC)	30.00	22.00	12.00
104	Scott Sanderson	.15	.11	.06
105	Dick Schofield(FC)	.40	.30	.15
106	Tom Seaver	20.00	15.00	8.00
107	Jim Slaton	.15	.11	.06
108	Mike Smithson	.20	.15	.08
109	Lary Sorensen	.15	.11	.06
110	Tim Stoddard	.15	.11	.06
111	Jeff Stone(FC)	.30	.25	.12
112	Champ Summers	.15	.11	.06
113	Jim Sundberg	.20	.15	.08
114	Rick Sutcliffe	.80	.60	.30
115	Craig Swan	.15	.11	.06
116	Derrel Thomas	.15	.11	.06
117	Gorman Thomas	.35	.30	.14
118	Alex Trevino	.15	.11	.06
119	Manny Trillo	.20	.15	.08
120	John Tudor	.60	.45	.25
121	Tom Underwood	.15	.11	.06
122	Mike Vail	.15	.11	.06
123	Tom Waddell(FC)	.15	.11	.06
124	Gary Ward	.20	.15	.08
125	Terry Whitfield	.15	.11	.06
126	Curtis Wilkerson	.15	.11	.06
127	Frank Williams(FC)	.35	.25	.14
128	Glenn Wilson	.25	.20	.10
129	John Wockenfuss	.15	.11	.06
130	Ned Yost	.15	.11	.06
131	Mike Young(FC)	.35	.25	.14
132	Checklist 1-132	.15	.11	.06

1985 Fleer

The 1985 Fleer set consists of 660 cards, each measuring 2-1/2" by 3-1/2" in size. The card fronts feature a color photo plus the player's team logo and the word "Fleer." The photos have a color-coded

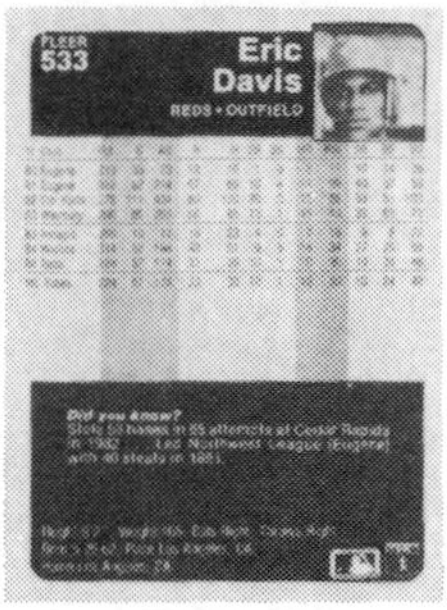

frame which corresponds to the player's team. A grey border surrounds the color-coded frame. The card backs are similar in design to the previous two years, but have two shades of red and black ink on white stock. For the fourth consecutive year, Fleer included special cards and team checklists in the set. Also incorporated in a set for the first time were ten "Major League Prospect" cards, each featuring two rookie hopefuls. The set was issued with team logo stickers.

		MT	NR MT	EX
Complete Set:		175.00	130.00	70.00
Common Player:		.06	.05	.02
1	Doug Bair	.06	.05	.02
2	Juan Berenguer	.06	.05	.02
3	Dave Bergman	.06	.05	.02
4	Tom Brookens	.06	.05	.02
5	Marty Castillo	.06	.05	.02
6	Darrell Evans	.12	.09	.05
7	Barbaro Garbey	.12	.09	.05
8	Kirk Gibson	.35	.25	.14
9	John Grubb	.06	.05	.02
10	Willie Hernandez	.08	.06	.03
11	Larry Herndon	.08	.06	.03
12	Howard Johnson	2.00	1.50	.80
13	Ruppert Jones	.06	.05	.02
14	Rusty Kuntz	.06	.05	.02
15	Chet Lemon	.08	.06	.03
16	Aurelio Lopez	.06	.05	.02
17	Sid Monge	.06	.05	.02
18	Jack Morris	.25	.20	.10
19	Lance Parrish	.30	.25	.12
20	Dan Petry	.08	.06	.03
21	Dave Rozema	.06	.05	.02
22	Bill Scherrer	.06	.05	.02
23	Alan Trammell	.35	.25	.14
24	Lou Whitaker	.35	.25	.14
25	Milt Wilcox	.06	.05	.02
26	Kurt Bevacqua	.06	.05	.02
27	*Greg Booker*(FC)	.15	.11	.06
28	Bobby Brown	.06	.05	.02
29	Luis DeLeon	.06	.05	.02
30	Dave Dravecky	.08	.06	.03
31	Tim Flannery	.06	.05	.02
32	Steve Garvey	.40	.30	.15
33	Goose Gossage	.20	.15	.08
34	Tony Gwynn	3.00	2.25	1.25
35	Greg Harris	.06	.05	.02
36	Andy Hawkins	.08	.06	.03
37	Terry Kennedy	.08	.06	.03
38	Craig Lefferts	.08	.06	.03
39	Tim Lollar	.06	.05	.02
40	Carmelo Martinez	.08	.06	.03
41	Kevin McReynolds	1.00	.70	.40
42	Graig Nettles	.15	.11	.06
43	Luis Salazar	.06	.05	.02
44	Eric Show	.08	.06	.03
45	Garry Templeton	.08	.06	.03
46	Mark Thurmond	.06	.05	.02
47	Ed Whitson	.06	.05	.02
48	Alan Wiggins	.06	.05	.02
49	Rich Bordi	.06	.05	.02
50	Larry Bowa	.12	.09	.05
51	Warren Brusstar	.06	.05	.02
52	Ron Cey	.10	.08	.04
53	*Henry Cotto*(FC)	.15	.11	.06
54	Jody Davis	.10	.08	.04
55	Bob Dernier	.06	.05	.02
56	Leon Durham	.08	.06	.03
57	Dennis Eckersley	.12	.09	.05
58	George Frazier	.06	.05	.02
59	Richie Hebner	.06	.05	.02
60	Dave Lopes	.08	.06	.03
61	Gary Matthews	.10	.08	.04
62	Keith Moreland	.08	.06	.03
63	Rick Reuschel	.10	.08	.04
64	Dick Ruthven	.06	.05	.02
65	Ryne Sandberg	6.00	4.50	2.50
66	Scott Sanderson	.06	.05	.02
67	Lee Smith	.10	.08	.04
68	Tim Stoddard	.06	.05	.02
69	Rick Sutcliffe	.12	.09	.05
70	Steve Trout	.06	.05	.02
71	Gary Woods	.06	.05	.02
72	Wally Backman	.08	.06	.03
73	Bruce Berenyi	.06	.05	.02
74	Hubie Brooks	.10	.08	.04
75	Kelvin Chapman	.06	.05	.02
76	Ron Darling	.80	.60	.30
77	Sid Fernandez(FC)	1.00	.70	.40
78	Mike Fitzgerald	.08	.06	.03
79	George Foster	.15	.11	.06
80	Brent Gaff	.06	.05	.02
81	Ron Gardenhire	.06	.05	.02
82	*Dwight Gooden*	15.00	11.00	6.00
83	Tom Gorman	.06	.05	.02
84	Danny Heep	.06	.05	.02
85	Keith Hernandez	.30	.25	.12
86	Ray Knight	.10	.08	.04
87	Ed Lynch	.06	.05	.02
88	Jose Oquendo	.08	.06	.03
89	Jesse Orosco	.08	.06	.03
90	*Rafael Santana*(FC)	.20	.15	.08
91	Doug Sisk	.06	.05	.02
92	Rusty Staub	.12	.09	.05
93	Darryl Strawberry	10.00	7.50	4.00
94	Walt Terrell	.08	.06	.03
95	Mookie Wilson	.10	.08	.04
96	Jim Acker	.06	.05	.02
97	Willie Aikens	.06	.05	.02
98	Doyle Alexander	.10	.08	.04
99	Jesse Barfield	.25	.20	.10
100	George Bell	.50	.40	.20
101	Jim Clancy	.08	.06	.03
102	Dave Collins	.08	.06	.03
103	Tony Fernandez	.35	.25	.14
104	Damaso Garcia	.06	.05	.02
105	Jim Gott	.06	.05	.02
106	Alfredo Griffin	.08	.06	.03
107	Garth Iorg	.06	.05	.02
108	Roy Lee Jackson	.06	.05	.02
109	Cliff Johnson	.06	.05	.02
110	*Jimmy Key*	2.00	1.50	.80
111	Dennis Lamp	.06	.05	.02
112	Rick Leach	.06	.05	.02
113	Luis Leal	.06	.05	.02
114	Buck Martinez	.06	.05	.02
115	Lloyd Moseby	.10	.08	.04
116	Rance Mulliniks	.06	.05	.02
117	Dave Stieb	.12	.09	.05
118	Willie Upshaw	.08	.06	.03
119	Ernie Whitt	.08	.06	.03
120	Mike Armstrong	.06	.05	.02
121	Don Baylor	.12	.09	.05
122	Marty Bystrom	.06	.05	.02
123	Rick Cerone	.06	.05	.02
124	Joe Cowley(FC)	.06	.05	.02
125	Brian Dayett(FC)	.06	.05	.02
126	Tim Foli	.06	.05	.02
127	Ray Fontenot	.06	.05	.02
128	Ken Griffey	.10	.08	.04
129	Ron Guidry	.25	.20	.10
130	Toby Harrah	.08	.06	.03
131	Jay Howell	.08	.06	.03
132	Steve Kemp	.08	.06	.03
133	Don Mattingly	10.00	7.50	4.50
134	Bobby Meacham	.06	.05	.02
135	John Montefusco	.06	.05	.02
136	Omar Moreno	.06	.05	.02
137	Dale Murray	.06	.05	.02
138	Phil Niekro	.25	.20	.10
139	*Mike Pagliarulo*(FC)	.70	.50	.30
140	Willie Randolph	.10	.08	.04
141	Dennis Rasmussen(FC)	.30	.25	.12
142	Dave Righetti	.20	.15	.08
143	*Jose Rijo*	2.00	1.50	.80
144	Andre Robertson	.06	.05	.02
145	Bob Shirley	.06	.05	.02
146	Dave Winfield	.35	.25	.14
147	Butch Wynegar	.06	.05	.02

		MT	NR MT	EX
148	Gary Allenson	.06	.05	.02
149	Tony Armas	.10	.08	.04
150	Marty Barrett	.20	.15	.08
151	Wade Boggs	4.00	3.00	1.50
152	Dennis Boyd	.10	.08	.04
153	Bill Buckner	.12	.09	.05
154	Mark Clear	.06	.05	.02
155	*Roger Clemens*	35.00	27.00	15.00
156	Steve Crawford	.06	.05	.02
157	Mike Easler	.08	.06	.03
158	Dwight Evans	.12	.09	.05
159	Rich Gedman	.10	.08	.04
160	Jackie Gutierrez	.06	.05	.02
161	Bruce Hurst	.12	.09	.05
162	John Henry Johnson	.06	.05	.02
163	Rick Miller	.06	.05	.02
164	Reid Nichols	.06	.05	.02
165	*Al Nipper*(FC)	.15	.11	.06
166	Bob Ojeda	.10	.08	.04
167	Jerry Remy	.06	.05	.02
168	Jim Rice	.35	.25	.14
169	Bob Stanley	.06	.05	.02
170	Mike Boddicker	.10	.08	.04
171	Al Bumbry	.08	.06	.03
172	Todd Cruz	.06	.05	.02
173	Rich Dauer	.06	.05	.02
174	Storm Davis	.10	.08	.04
175	Rick Dempsey	.08	.06	.03
176	Jim Dwyer	.06	.05	.02
177	Mike Flanagan	.10	.08	.04
178	Dan Ford	.06	.05	.02
179	Wayne Gross	.06	.05	.02
180	John Lowenstein	.06	.05	.02
181	Dennis Martinez	.08	.06	.03
182	Tippy Martinez	.06	.05	.02
183	Scott McGregor	.08	.06	.03
184	Eddie Murray	.50	.40	.20
185	Joe Nolan	.06	.05	.02
186	Floyd Rayford	.06	.05	.02
187	Cal Ripken, Jr.	5.00	3.75	2.00
188	Gary Roenicke	.06	.05	.02
189	Lenn Sakata	.06	.05	.02
190	John Shelby	.08	.06	.03
191	Ken Singleton	.08	.06	.03
192	Sammy Stewart	.06	.05	.02
193	Bill Swaggerty	.06	.05	.02
194	Tom Underwood	.06	.05	.02
195	Mike Young	.12	.09	.05
196	Steve Balboni	.08	.06	.03
197	Joe Beckwith	.06	.05	.02
198	Bud Black	.06	.05	.02
199	George Brett	.50	.40	.20
200	Onix Concepcion	.06	.05	.02
201	*Mark Gubicza*	1.75	1.25	.70
202	Larry Gura	.06	.05	.02
203	Mark Huismann(FC)	.06	.05	.02
204	Dane Iorg	.06	.05	.02
205	Danny Jackson(FC)	1.00	.70	.40
206	Charlie Leibrandt	.08	.06	.03
207	Hal McRae	.10	.08	.04
208	Darryl Motley	.06	.05	.02
209	Jorge Orta	.06	.05	.02
210	Greg Pryor	.06	.05	.02
211	Dan Quisenberry	.10	.08	.04
212	*Bret Saberhagen*	7.00	5.25	2.75
213	Pat Sheridan	.06	.05	.02
214	Don Slaught	.06	.05	.02
215	U.L. Washington	.06	.05	.02
216	John Wathan	.08	.06	.03
217	Frank White	.10	.08	.04
218	Willie Wilson	.12	.09	.05
219	Neil Allen	.06	.05	.02
220	Joaquin Andujar	.08	.06	.03
221	Steve Braun	.06	.05	.02
222	Danny Cox(FC)	.20	.20	.10
223	Bob Forsch	.08	.06	.03
224	David Green	.06	.05	.02
225	George Hendrick	.08	.06	.03
226	Tom Herr	.10	.08	.04
227	*Ricky Horton*	.30	.25	.12
228	Art Howe	.06	.05	.02
229	Mike Jorgensen	.06	.05	.02
230	Kurt Kepshire	.06	.05	.02
231	Jeff Lahti	.06	.05	.02
232	Tito Landrum	.06	.05	.02
233	Dave LaPoint	.08	.06	.03
234	Willie McGee	.30	.25	.12
235	*Tom Nieto*(FC)	.10	.08	.04
236	*Terry Pendleton*(FC)	2.00	1.50	.80
237	Darrell Porter	.08	.06	.03
238	Dave Rucker	.06	.05	.02

		MT	NR MT	EX
239	Lonnie Smith	.08	.06	.03
240	Ozzie Smith	.15	.11	.06
241	Bruce Sutter	.12	.09	.05
242	Andy Van Slyke	.35	.25	.14
243	Dave Von Ohlen	.06	.05	.02
244	Larry Andersen	.06	.05	.02
245	Bill Campbell	.06	.05	.02
246	Steve Carlton	.40	.30	.15
247	Tim Corcoran	.06	.05	.02
248	Ivan DeJesus	.06	.05	.02
249	John Denny	.06	.05	.02
250	Bo Diaz	.08	.06	.03
251	Greg Gross	.06	.05	.02
252	Kevin Gross	.10	.08	.04
253	Von Hayes	.12	.09	.05
254	Al Holland	.06	.05	.02
255	Charles Hudson	.08	.06	.03
256	Jerry Koosman	.10	.08	.04
257	Joe Lefebvre	.06	.05	.02
258	Sixto Lezcano	.06	.05	.02
259	Garry Maddox	.10	.08	.04
260	Len Matuszek	.06	.05	.02
261	Tug McGraw	.10	.08	.04
262	Al Oliver	.12	.09	.05
263	Shane Rawley	.10	.08	.04
264	Juan Samuel	.40	.30	.15
265	Mike Schmidt	2.00	1.50	.80
266	*Jeff Stone*	.12	.09	.05
267	Ozzie Virgil	.06	.05	.02
268	Glenn Wilson	.08	.06	.03
269	John Wockenfuss	.06	.05	.02
270	Darrell Brown	.06	.05	.02
271	Tom Brunansky	.12	.09	.05
272	Randy Bush	.06	.05	.02
273	John Butcher	.06	.05	.02
274	Bobby Castillo	.06	.05	.02
275	Ron Davis	.06	.05	.02
276	Dave Engle	.06	.05	.02
277	Pete Filson	.06	.05	.02
278	Gary Gaetti	.25	.20	.10
279	Mickey Hatcher	.06	.05	.02
280	Ed Hodge	.06	.05	.02
281	Kent Hrbek	.25	.20	.10
282	Houston Jimenez	.06	.05	.02
283	Tim Laudner	.06	.05	.02
284	Rick Lysander	.06	.05	.02
285	Dave Meier	.06	.05	.02
286	*Kirby Puckett*	25.00	18.00	10.00
287	Pat Putnam	.06	.05	.02
288	Ken Schrom	.06	.05	.02
289	Mike Smithson	.06	.05	.02
290	Tim Teufel	.08	.06	.03
291	Frank Viola	.20	.15	.08
292	Ron Washington	.06	.05	.02
293	Don Aase	.06	.05	.02
294	Juan Beniquez	.06	.05	.02
295	Bob Boone	.08	.06	.03
296	Mike Brown	.06	.05	.02
297	Rod Carew	.40	.30	.15
298	Doug Corbett	.06	.05	.02
299	Doug DeCinces	.10	.08	.04
300	Brian Downing	.10	.08	.04
301	Ken Forsch	.06	.05	.02
302	Bobby Grich	.10	.08	.04
303	Reggie Jackson	.40	.30	.15
304	Tommy John	.20	.15	.08
305	Curt Kaufman	.06	.05	.02
306	Bruce Kison	.06	.05	.02
307	Fred Lynn	.20	.15	.08
308	Gary Pettis	.08	.06	.03
309	*Ron Romanick*	.10	.08	.04
310	Luis Sanchez	.06	.05	.02
311	Dick Schofield	.12	.09	.05
312	Daryl Sconiers	.06	.05	.02
313	Jim Slaton	.06	.05	.02
314	Derrel Thomas	.06	.05	.02
315	Rob Wilfong	.06	.05	.02
316	Mike Witt	.12	.09	.05
317	Geoff Zahn	.06	.05	.02
318	Len Barker	.08	.06	.03
319	Steve Bedrosian	.12	.09	.05
320	Bruce Benedict	.06	.05	.02
321	Rick Camp	.06	.05	.02
322	Chris Chambliss	.08	.06	.03
323	*Jeff Dedmon*(FC)	.12	.09	.05
324	Terry Forster	.08	.06	.03
325	Gene Garber	.06	.05	.02
326	*Albert Hall*(FC)	.15	.11	.06
327	Terry Harper	.06	.05	.02
328	Bob Horner	.12	.09	.05
329	Glenn Hubbard	.06	.05	.02

		MT	NR MT	EX
330	Randy Johnson	.06	.05	.02
331	Brad Komminsk	.06	.05	.02
332	Rick Mahler	.06	.05	.02
333	Craig McMurtry	.06	.05	.02
334	Donnie Moore	.06	.05	.02
335	Dale Murphy	.60	.45	.25
336	Ken Oberkfell	.06	.05	.02
337	Pascual Perez	.08	.06	.03
338	Gerald Perry	.35	.25	.14
339	Rafael Ramirez	.06	.05	.02
340	Jerry Royster	.06	.05	.02
341	Alex Trevino	.06	.05	.02
342	Claudell Washington	.08	.06	.03
343	Alan Ashby	.06	.05	.02
344	*Mark Bailey*	.10	.08	.04
345	Kevin Bass	.10	.08	.04
346	Enos Cabell	.06	.05	.02
347	Jose Cruz	.10	.08	.04
348	Bill Dawley	.06	.05	.02
349	Frank DiPino	.06	.05	.02
350	Bill Doran	.12	.09	.05
351	Phil Garner	.08	.06	.03
352	Bob Knepper	.08	.06	.03
353	Mike LaCoss	.06	.05	.02
354	Jerry Mumphrey	.06	.05	.02
355	Joe Niekro	.10	.08	.04
356	Terry Puhl	.06	.05	.02
357	Craig Reynolds	.06	.05	.02
358	Vern Ruhle	.06	.05	.02
359	Nolan Ryan	6.00	4.50	2.50
360	Joe Sambito	.06	.05	.02
361	Mike Scott	.15	.11	.06
362	Dave Smith	.08	.06	.03
363	*Julio Solano*(FC)	.08	.06	.03
364	Dickie Thon	.08	.06	.03
365	Denny Walling	.06	.05	.02
366	Dave Anderson	.06	.05	.02
367	Bob Bailor	.06	.05	.02
368	Greg Brock	.08	.06	.03
369	Carlos Diaz	.06	.05	.02
370	Pedro Guerrero	.25	.20	.10
371	*Orel Hershiser*(FC)	6.00	4.50	2.50
372	Rick Honeycutt	.06	.05	.02
373	Burt Hooton	.08	.06	.03
374	*Ken Howell*(FC)	.15	.11	.06
375	Ken Landreaux	.08	.06	.03
376	Candy Maldonado	.10	.08	.04
377	Mike Marshall	.15	.11	.06
378	Tom Niedenfuer	.08	.06	.03
379	Alejandro Pena	.08	.06	.03
380	Jerry Reuss	.08	.06	.03
381	*R.J. Reynolds*	.25	.20	.10
382	German Rivera	.06	.05	.02
383	Bill Russell	.08	.06	.03
384	Steve Sax	.20	.15	.08
385	Mike Scioscia	.08	.06	.03
386	*Franklin Stubbs*(FC)	.60	.45	.25
387	Fernando Valenzuela	.35	.25	.14
388	Bob Welch	.12	.09	.05
389	Terry Whitfield	.06	.05	.02
390	Steve Yeager	.06	.05	.02
391	Pat Zachry	.06	.05	.02
392	Fred Breining	.06	.05	.02
393	Gary Carter	.35	.25	.14
394	Andre Dawson	.60	.45	.25
395	Miguel Dilone	.06	.05	.02
396	Dan Driessen	.08	.06	.03
397	Doug Flynn	.06	.05	.02
398	Terry Francona	.06	.05	.02
399	Bill Gullickson	.06	.05	.02
400	Bob James	.06	.05	.02
401	Charlie Lea	.06	.05	.02
402	Bryan Little	.06	.05	.02
403	Gary Lucas	.06	.05	.02
404	David Palmer	.06	.05	.02
405	Tim Raines	.35	.25	.14
406	Mike Ramsey	.06	.05	.02
407	Jeff Reardon	.12	.09	.05
408	Steve Rogers	.08	.06	.03
409	Dan Schatzeder	.06	.05	.02
410	Bryn Smith	.06	.05	.02
411	Mike Stenhouse	.06	.05	.02
412	Tim Wallach	.12	.09	.05
413	Jim Wohlford	.06	.05	.02
414	Bill Almon	.06	.05	.02
415	Keith Atherton	.06	.05	.02
416	Bruce Bochte	.06	.05	.02
417	Tom Burgmeier	.06	.05	.02
418	Ray Burris	.06	.05	.02
419	Bill Caudill	.06	.05	.02
420	Chris Codiroli	.06	.05	.02

		MT	NR MT	EX
421	Tim Conroy	.06	.05	.02
422	Mike Davis	.08	.06	.03
423	Jim Essian	.06	.05	.02
424	Mike Heath	.06	.05	.02
425	Rickey Henderson	4.00	3.00	1.50
426	Donnie Hill	.06	.05	.02
427	Dave Kingman	.15	.11	.06
428	Bill Krueger	.06	.05	.02
429	Carney Lansford	.10	.08	.04
430	Steve McCatty	.06	.05	.02
431	Joe Morgan	.30	.25	.12
432	Dwayne Murphy	.08	.06	.03
433	Tony Phillips	.06	.05	.02
434	Lary Sorensen	.06	.05	.02
435	Mike Warren	.06	.05	.02
436	*Curt Young*(FC)	.35	.25	.14
437	Luis Aponte	.06	.05	.02
438	Chris Bando	.06	.05	.02
439	Tony Bernazard	.06	.05	.02
440	Bert Blyleven	.15	.11	.06
441	Brett Butler	.10	.08	.04
442	Ernie Camacho	.06	.05	.02
443	Joe Carter(FC)	6.00	4.50	2.50
444	Carmelo Castillo	.06	.05	.02
445	Jamie Easterly	.06	.05	.02
446	*Steve Farr*(FC)	.40	.30	.15
447	Mike Fischlin	.06	.05	.02
448	Julio Franco	.12	.09	.05
449	Mel Hall	.08	.06	.03
450	Mike Hargrove	.06	.05	.02
451	Neal Heaton	.06	.05	.02
452	Brook Jacoby	.30	.25	.12
453	*Mike Jeffcoat*	.08	.06	.03
454	*Don Schulze*(FC)	.08	.06	.03
455	Roy Smith	.06	.05	.02
456	Pat Tabler	.08	.06	.03
457	Andre Thornton	.10	.08	.04
458	George Vukovich	.06	.05	.02
459	Tom Waddell	.06	.05	.02
460	Jerry Willard	.06	.05	.02
461	Dale Berra	.06	.05	.02
462	John Candelaria	.10	.08	.04
463	Jose DeLeon	.08	.06	.03
464	Doug Frobel	.06	.05	.02
465	Cecilio Guante	.06	.05	.02
466	Brian Harper	.06	.05	.02
467	Lee Lacy	.06	.05	.02
468	Bill Madlock	.12	.09	.05
469	Lee Mazzilli	.08	.06	.03
470	Larry McWilliams	.06	.05	.02
471	Jim Morrison	.06	.05	.02
472	Tony Pena	.10	.08	.04
473	Johnny Ray	.12	.09	.05
474	Rick Rhoden	.10	.08	.04
475	Don Robinson	.08	.06	.03
476	Rod Scurry	.06	.05	.02
477	Kent Tekulve	.08	.06	.03
478	Jason Thompson	.06	.05	.02
479	John Tudor	.10	.08	.04
480	Lee Tunnell	.06	.05	.02
481	Marvell Wynne	.06	.05	.02
482	Salome Barojas	.06	.05	.02
483	Dave Beard	.06	.05	.02
484	Jim Beattie	.06	.05	.02
485	Barry Bonnell	.06	.05	.02
486	*Phil Bradley*	.90	.70	.35
487	Al Cowens	.06	.05	.02
488	*Alvin Davis*	2.50	2.00	1.00
489	Dave Henderson	.10	.08	.04
490	Steve Henderson	.06	.05	.02
491	Bob Kearney	.06	.05	.02
492	*Mark Langston*	5.00	3.75	2.00
493	Larry Milbourne	.06	.05	.02
494	Paul Mirabella	.06	.05	.02
495	Mike Moore	.06	.05	.02
496	Edwin Nunez(FC)	.08	.06	.03
497	Spike Owen	.08	.06	.03
498	Jack Perconte	.06	.05	.02
499	Ken Phelps	.10	.08	.04
500	*Jim Presley*(FC)	.50	.40	.20
501	Mike Stanton	.06	.05	.02
502	Bob Stoddard	.06	.05	.02
503	Gorman Thomas	.10	.08	.04
504	Ed Vande Berg	.06	.05	.02
505	Matt Young	.06	.05	.02
506	Juan Agosto	.06	.05	.02
507	Harold Baines	.15	.11	.06
508	Floyd Bannister	.10	.08	.04
509	Britt Burns	.06	.05	.02
510	Julio Cruz	.06	.05	.02
511	Richard Dotson	.10	.08	.04

		MT	NR MT	EX
512	Jerry Dybzinski	.06	.05	.02
513	Carlton Fisk	.40	.30	.15
514	Scott Fletcher	.08	.06	.03
515	Jerry Hairston	.06	.05	.02
516	Marc Hill	.06	.05	.02
517	LaMarr Hoyt	.06	.05	.02
518	Ron Kittle	.10	.08	.04
519	Rudy Law	.06	.05	.02
520	Vance Law	.08	.06	.03
521	Greg Luzinski	.10	.08	.04
522	Gene Nelson	.06	.05	.02
523	Tom Paciorek	.06	.05	.02
524	Ron Reed	.06	.05	.02
525	Bert Roberge	.06	.05	.02
526	Tom Seaver	.40	.30	.15
527	Roy Smalley	.06	.05	.02
528	Dan Spillner	.06	.05	.02
529	Mike Squires	.06	.05	.02
530	Greg Walker	.12	.09	.05
531	Cesar Cedeno	.10	.08	.04
532	Dave Concepcion	.12	.09	.05
533	*Eric Davis*(FC)	18.00	13.50	7.25
534	Nick Esasky	.08	.06	.03
535	Tom Foley	.06	.05	.02
536	*John Franco*	2.00	1.50	.80
537	Brad Gulden	.06	.05	.02
538	Tom Hume	.06	.05	.02
539	Wayne Krenchicki	.06	.05	.02
540	Andy McGaffigan	.06	.05	.02
541	Eddie Milner	.06	.05	.02
542	Ron Oester	.06	.05	.02
543	Bob Owchinko	.06	.05	.02
544	Dave Parker	.25	.20	.10
545	Frank Pastore	.06	.05	.02
546	Tony Perez	.15	.11	.06
547	Ted Power	.06	.05	.02
548	Joe Price	.06	.05	.02
549	Gary Redus	.08	.06	.03
550	Pete Rose	1.00	.70	.40
551	Jeff Russell(FC)	.10	.08	.04
552	Mario Soto	.08	.06	.03
553	*Jay Tibbs*(FC)	.15	.11	.06
554	Duane Walker	.06	.05	.02
555	Alan Bannister	.06	.05	.02
556	Buddy Bell	.12	.09	.05
557	Danny Darwin	.06	.05	.02
558	Charlie Hough	.08	.06	.03
559	Bobby Jones	.06	.05	.02
560	Odell Jones	.06	.05	.02
561	*Jeff Kunkel*(FC)	.10	.08	.04
562	*Mike Mason*	.10	.08	.04
563	Pete O'Brien	.12	.09	.05
564	Larry Parrish	.10	.08	.04
565	Mickey Rivers	.08	.06	.03
566	Billy Sample	.06	.05	.02
567	Dave Schmidt	.06	.05	.02
568	Donnie Scott	.06	.05	.02
569	Dave Stewart	.12	.09	.05
570	Frank Tanana	.10	.08	.04
571	Wayne Tolleson	.06	.05	.02
572	Gary Ward	.08	.06	.03
573	Curtis Wilkerson	.08	.06	.03
574	George Wright	.06	.05	.02
575	Ned Yost	.06	.05	.02
576	Mark Brouhard	.06	.05	.02
577	Mike Caldwell	.06	.05	.02
578	Bobby Clark	.06	.05	.02
579	Jaime Cocanower	.06	.05	.02
580	Cecil Cooper	.15	.11	.06
581	Rollie Fingers	.20	.15	.08
582	Jim Gantner	.08	.06	.03
583	Moose Haas	.06	.05	.02
584	Dion James	.12	.09	.05
585	Pete Ladd	.06	.05	.02
586	Rick Manning	.06	.05	.02
587	Bob McClure	.06	.05	.02
588	Paul Molitor	.15	.11	.06
589	Charlie Moore	.06	.05	.02
590	Ben Oglivie	.08	.06	.03
591	Chuck Porter	.06	.05	.02
592	*Randy Ready*(FC)	.20	.15	.08
593	Ed Romero	.06	.05	.02
594	Bill Schroeder(FC)	.10	.08	.04
595	Ray Searage	.06	.05	.02
596	Ted Simmons	.12	.09	.05
597	Jim Sundberg	.08	.06	.03
598	Don Sutton	.30	.25	.12
599	Tom Tellmann	.06	.05	.02
600	Rick Waits	.06	.05	.02
601	Robin Yount	.70	.50	.30
602	Dusty Baker	.08	.06	.03

		MT	NR MT	EX
603	Bob Brenly	.06	.05	.02
604	Jack Clark	.20	.15	.08
605	Chili Davis	.10	.08	.04
606	Mark Davis	.06	.05	.02
607	*Dan Gladden*(FC)	.50	.40	.20
608	Atlee Hammaker	.06	.05	.02
609	Mike Krukow	.08	.06	.03
610	Duane Kuiper	.06	.05	.02
611	Bob Lacey	.06	.05	.02
612	Bill Laskey	.06	.05	.02
613	Gary Lavelle	.06	.05	.02
614	Johnnie LeMaster	.06	.05	.02
615	Jeff Leonard	.10	.08	.04
616	Randy Lerch	.06	.05	.02
617	Greg Minton	.06	.05	.02
618	Steve Nicosia	.06	.05	.02
619	Gene Richards	.06	.05	.02
620	*Jeff Robinson*	.30	.25	.12
621	Scot Thompson	.06	.05	.02
622	Manny Trillo	.08	.06	.03
623	Brad Wellman	.06	.05	.02
624	*Frank Williams*	.15	.11	.06
625	Joel Youngblood	.06	.05	.02
626	Ripken-In-Action (Cal Ripken)	.30	.25	.12
627	Schmidt-In-Action (Mike Schmidt)	.30	.25	.12
628	Giving the Signs (Sparky Anderson)	.08	.06	.03
629	A.L. Pitcher's Nightmare (Rickey Henderson, Dave Winfield)	.30	.25	.12
630	N.L. Pitcher's Nightmare (Ryne Sandberg, Mike Schmidt)	.30	.25	.12
631	N.L. All-Stars (Gary Carter, Steve Garvey, Ozzie Smith, Darryl Strawberry)	.30	.25	.12
632	All-Star Game Winning Battery (Gary Carter, Charlie Lea)	.15	.11	.06
633	N.L. Pennant Clinchers (Steve Garvey, Goose Gossage)	.20	.15	.08
634	N.L. Rookie Phenoms (Dwight Gooden, Juan Samuel)	1.00	.70	.40
635	Toronto's Big Guns (Willie Upshaw)	.08	.06	.03
636	Toronto's Big Guns (Lloyd Moseby)	.08	.06	.03
637	Holland (Al Holland)	.08	.06	.03
638	Tunnell (Lee Tunnell)	.08	.06	.03
639	500th Homer (Reggie Jackson)	.30	.25	.12
640	4,000th Hit (Pete Rose)	.50	.40	.20
641	Father & Son (Cal Ripken, Jr., Cal Ripken, Sr.)	.30	.25	.12
642	Cubs Team	.08	.06	.03
643	1984's Two Perfect Games & One No Hitter (Jack Morris, David Palmer, Mike Witt)	.15	.11	.06
644	Major League Prospect (Willie Lozado, Vic Mata)	.06	.05	.02
645	Major League Prospect *(Kelly Gruber, Randy O'Neal)*(FC)	10.00	7.50	4.00
646	Major League Prospect *(Jose Roman, Joel Skinner)*(FC)	.12	.09	.05
647	Major League Prospect *(Steve Kiefer, Danny Tartabull)*(FC)	6.00	4.50	2.50
648	Major League Prospect *(Rob Deer, Alejandro Sanchez)*(FC)	1.75	1.25	.70
649	Major League Prospect *(Shawon Dunston, Bill Hatcher)*(FC)	6.00	4.50	2.50
650	Major League Prospect *(Mike Bielecki, Ron Robinson)*(FC)	.30	.25	.12
651	Major League Prospect *(Zane Smith, Paul Zuvella)*(FC)	1.25	.90	.50
652	Major League Prospect *(Glenn Davis, Joe Hesketh)*(FC)	10.00	7.50	4.00
653	Major League Prospect *(Steve Jeltz, John Russell)*(FC)	.20	.15	.08
654	Checklist 1-95	.06	.05	.02
655	Checklist 96-195	.06	.05	.02
656	Checklist 196-292	.06	.05	.02
657	Checklist 293-391	.06	.05	.02
658	Checklist 392-481	.06	.05	.02
659	Checklist 482-575	.06	.05	.02
660	Checklist 576-660	.06	.05	.02

1985 Fleer Limited Edition

The 1985 Fleer Limited Edition 44-card set was distributed through McCrory's, J.J. Newbury, McClellan, Kress, YDC, and Green stores. The cards, which are the standard 2-1/2" by 3-1/2" size, have full-color photos inside a red and yellow frame. The card backs are set in black type against two different shades of yellow and contain the player's personal

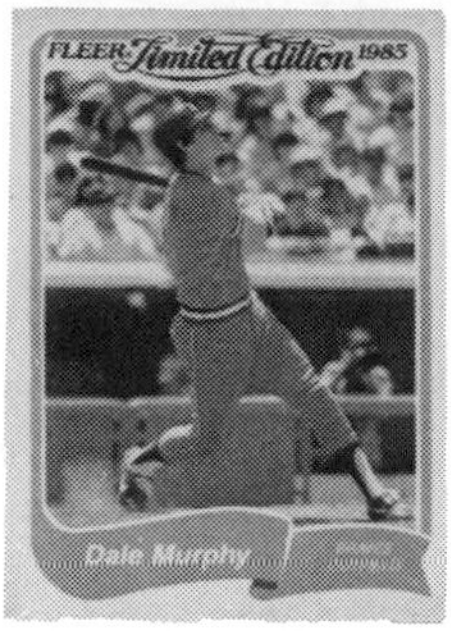

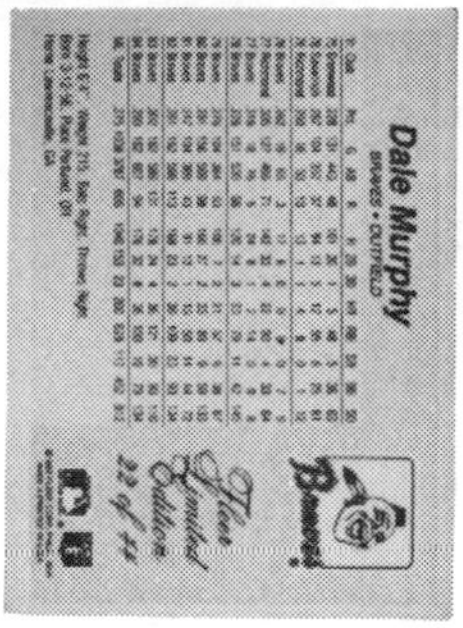

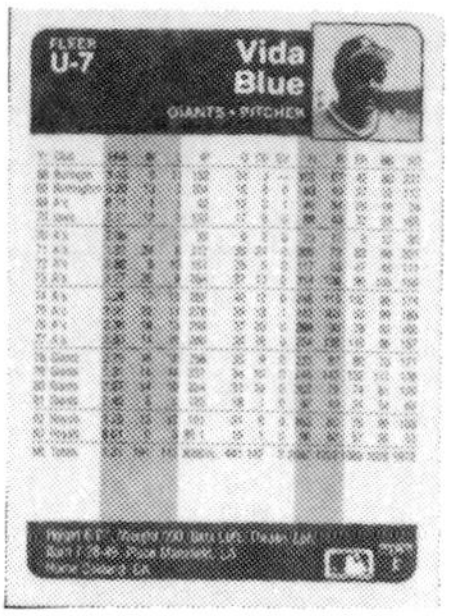

and statistical information. The set was issued in a specially designed box which carried the complete checklist for the set on the back. Six team logo stickers were also included with the set.

		MT	NR MT	EX
Complete Set:		6.00	4.50	2.50
Common Player:		.05	.04	.02
1	Buddy Bell	.07	.05	.03
2	Bert Blyleven	.10	.08	.04
3	Wade Boggs	.70	.50	.30
4	George Brett	.30	.25	.12
5	Rod Carew	.30	.25	.12
6	Steve Carlton	.25	.20	.10
7	Alvin Davis	.20	.15	.08
8	Andre Dawson	.15	.11	.06
9	Steve Garvey	.25	.20	.10
10	Goose Gossage	.12	.09	.05
11	Tony Gwynn	.40	.30	.15
12	Keith Hernandez	.20	.15	.08
13	Kent Hrbek	.15	.11	.06
14	Reggie Jackson	.30	.25	.12
15	Dave Kingman	.10	.08	.04
16	Ron Kittle	.07	.05	.03
17	Mark Langston	.25	.20	.10
18	Jeff Leonard	.05	.04	.02
19	Bill Madlock	.07	.05	.03
20	Don Mattingly	.70	.50	.30
21	Jack Morris	.15	.11	.06
22	Dale Murphy	.30	.25	.12
23	Eddie Murray	.25	.20	.10
24	Tony Pena	.07	.05	.03
25	Dan Quisenberry	.07	.05	.03
26	Tim Raines	.25	.20	.10
27	Jim Rice	.25	.20	.10
28	Cal Ripken, Jr.	.60	.45	.25
29	Pete Rose	.60	.45	.25
30	Nolan Ryan	1.25	.90	.50
31	Ryne Sandberg	.70	.50	.30
32	Steve Sax	.15	.11	.06
33	Mike Schmidt	.50	.40	.20
34	Tom Seaver	.50	.40	.20
35	Ozzie Smith	.12	.09	.05
36	Mario Soto	.05	.04	.02
37	Dave Stieb	.10	.08	.04
38	Darryl Strawberry	.60	.45	.25
39	Rick Sutcliffe	.10	.08	.04
40	Alan Trammell	.20	.15	.08
41	Willie Upshaw	.05	.04	.02
42	Fernando Valenzuela	.20	.15	.08
43	Dave Winfield	.25	.20	.10
44	Robin Yount	.50	.40	.20

1985 Fleer Update

For the second straight year, Fleer issued a 132-card update set. The cards, which measure 2-1/2" by 3-1/2", portray players on their new teams and also includes rookies not depicted in the regular issue. The cards are identical in design to the 1985 Fleer set but are numbered U-1 through U-132. The set was issued with team logo stickers in a specially designed box and was available only through hobby dealers.

		MT	NR MT	EX
Complete Set:		25.00	20.00	10.00
Common Player:		.10	.08	.04
1	Don Aase	.15	.11	.06
2	Bill Almon	.10	.08	.04
3	Dusty Baker	.15	.11	.06
4	Dale Berra	.10	.08	.04
5	Karl Best(FC)	.10	.08	.04
6	Tim Birtsas(FC)	.20	.15	.08
7	Vida Blue	.20	.15	.08
8	Rich Bordi	.10	.08	.04
9	Daryl Boston(FC)	.20	.15	.08
10	Hubie Brooks	.20	.15	.08
11	Chris Brown(FC)	.25	.20	.10
12	Tom Browning(FC)	1.50	1.25	.60
13	Al Bumbry	.10	.08	.04
14	Tim Burke(FC)	.50	.40	.20
15	Ray Burris	.10	.08	.04
16	Jeff Burroughs	.15	.11	.06
17	Ivan Calderon(FC)	3.00	2.25	1.25
18	Jeff Calhoun	.10	.08	.04
19	Bill Campbell	.10	.08	.04
20	Don Carman(FC)	.15	.11	.06
21	Gary Carter	.80	.60	.30
22	Bobby Castillo	.10	.08	.04
23	Bill Caudill	.10	.08	.04
24	Rick Cerone	.10	.08	.04
25	Jack Clark	.35	.25	.14
26	Pat Clements(FC)	.20	.15	.08
27	Stewart Cliburn(FC)	.15	.11	.06
28	Vince Coleman(FC)	12.00	9.00	4.75
29	Dave Collins	.15	.11	.06
30	Fritz Connally	.10	.08	.04
31	Henry Cotto(FC)	.20	.15	.08
32	Danny Darwin	.15	.11	.06
33	Darren Daulton(FC)	.60	.45	.25
34	Jerry Davis	.10	.08	.04
35	Brian Dayett	.10	.08	.04
36	Ken Dixon(FC)	.10	.08	.04
37	Tommy Dunbar	.10	.08	.04
38	Mariano Duncan(FC)	.80	.60	.30
39	Bob Fallon	.10	.08	.04
40	Brian Fisher(FC)	.15	.11	.06
41	Mike Fitzgerald	.10	.08	.04
42	Ray Fontenot	.10	.08	.04
43	Greg Gagne(FC)	.35	.25	.14
44	Oscar Gamble	.15	.11	.06
45	Jim Gott	.10	.08	.04
46	David Green	.10	.08	.04
47	Alfredo Griffin	.15	.11	.06
48	Ozzie Guillen(FC)	2.50	2.00	1.00
49	Toby Harrah	.15	.11	.06
50	Ron Hassey	.10	.08	.04
51	Rickey Henderson	5.00	3.75	2.00
52	Steve Henderson	.10	.08	.04
53	George Hendrick	.15	.11	.06
54	Teddy Higuera(FC)	1.00	.70	.40
55	Al Holland	.10	.08	.04
56	Burt Hooton	.15	.11	.06
57	Jay Howell	.15	.11	.06
58	LaMarr Hoyt	.10	.08	.04
59	Tim Hulett(FC)	.20	.15	.08
60	Bob James	.10	.08	.04
61	Cliff Johnson	.10	.08	.04
62	Howard Johnson	2.50	2.00	1.00
63	Ruppert Jones	.10	.08	.04
64	Steve Kemp	.15	.11	.06
65	Bruce Kison	.10	.08	.04
66	Mike LaCoss	.15	.11	.06
67	Lee Lacy	.15	.11	.06
68	Dave LaPoint	.20	.15	.08

		MT	NR MT	EX
69	Gary Lavelle	.10	.08	.04
70	Vance Law	.15	.11	.06
71	Manny Lee(FC)	.20	.15	.08
72	Sixto Lezcano	.10	.08	.04
73	Tim Lollar	.10	.08	.04
74	Urbano Lugo(FC)	.15	.11	.06
75	Fred Lynn	.30	.25	.12
76	Steve Lyons(FC)	.15	.11	.06
77	Mickey Mahler	.10	.08	.04
78	Ron Mathis(FC)	.10	.08	.04
79	Len Matuszek	.10	.08	.04
80	Oddibe McDowell(FC)	.25	.20	.10
81	Roger McDowell(FC)	.50	.40	.20
82	Donnie Moore	.10	.08	.04
83	Ron Musselman	.10	.08	.04
84	Al Oliver	.25	.20	.10
85	Joe Orsulak(FC)	.20	.15	.08
86	Dan Pasqua(FC)	.60	.45	.25
87	Chris Pittaro(FC)	.10	.08	.04
88	Rick Reuschel	.20	.15	.08
89	Earnie Riles(FC)	.20	.15	.08
90	Jerry Royster	.10	.08	.04
91	Dave Rozema	.10	.08	.04
92	Dave Rucker	.10	.08	.04
93	Vern Ruhle	.10	.08	.04
94	Mark Salas(FC)	.20	.15	.08
95	Luis Salazar	.10	.08	.04
96	Joe Sambito	.10	.08	.04
97	Billy Sample	.10	.08	.04
98	Alex Sanchez	.10	.08	.04
99	Calvin Schiraldi(FC)	.25	.20	.10
100	Rick Schu(FC)	.20	.15	.08
101	Larry Sheets(FC)	.50	.40	.20
102	Ron Shepherd	.10	.08	.04
103	Nelson Simmons(FC)	.10	.08	.04
104	Don Slaught	.10	.08	.04
105	Roy Smalley	.15	.11	.06
106	Lonnie Smith	.15	.11	.06
107	Nate Snell(FC)	.10	.08	.04
108	Lary Sorensen	.10	.08	.04
109	Chris Speier	.10	.08	.04
110	Mike Stenhouse	.10	.08	.04
111	Tim Stoddard	.10	.08	.04
112	John Stuper	.10	.08	.04
113	Jim Sundberg	.15	.11	.06
114	Bruce Sutter	.25	.20	.10
115	Don Sutton	.60	.45	.25
116	Bruce Tanner(FC)	.10	.08	.04
117	Kent Tekulve	.15	.11	.06
118	Walt Terrell	.15	.11	.06
119	Mickey Tettleton(FC)	1.50	1.25	.60
120	Rich Thompson	.10	.08	.04
121	Louis Thornton(FC)	.10	.08	.04
122	Alex Trevino	.10	.08	.04
123	John Tudor	.30	.25	.12
124	Jose Uribe(FC)	.25	.20	.10
125	Dave Valle(FC)	.20	.15	.08
126	Dave Von Ohlen	.10	.08	.04
127	Curt Wardle	.10	.08	.04
128	U.L. Washington	.10	.08	.04
129	Ed Whitson	.10	.08	.04
130	Herm Winningham(FC)	.20	.15	.08
131	Rich Yett(FC)	.15	.11	.06
132	Checklist	.10	.08	.04

1986 Fleer

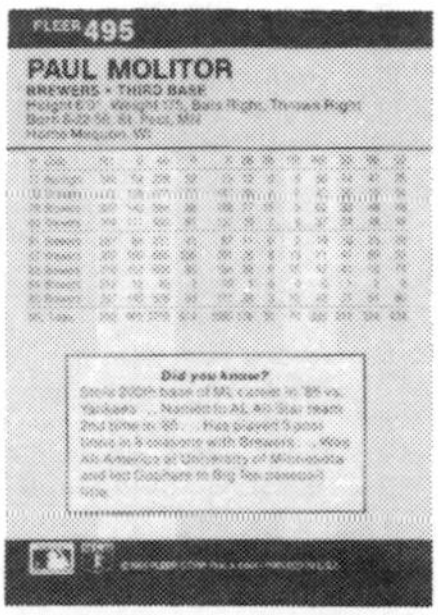

The 1986 Fleer set contains 660 color photos, with each card measuring 2-1/2" by 3-1/2" in size. The card fronts include the word "Fleer," the player's team logo, and a player picture enclosed by a dark blue border. The card reverses are minus the black and white photo that was included in past Fleer efforts. Player biographical and statistical information appear in black and yellow ink on white stock. As in 1985, Fleer devoted ten cards, entitled "Major League Prospects," to twenty promising rookie players. The 1986 set, as in the previous four years, was issued with team logo stickers.

		MT	NR MT	EX
Complete Set:		125.00	90.00	50.00
Common Player:		.06	.05	.02
1	Steve Balboni	.08	.06	.03
2	Joe Beckwith	.06	.05	.02
3	Buddy Biancalana	.06	.05	.02
4	Bud Black	.06	.05	.02
5	George Brett	.60	.45	.25
6	Onix Concepcion	.06	.05	.02
7	Steve Farr	.08	.06	.03
8	Mark Gubicza	.12	.09	.05
9	Dane Iorg	.06	.05	.02
10	Danny Jackson	.20	.15	.08
11	Lynn Jones	.06	.05	.02
12	Mike Jones	.06	.05	.02
13	Charlie Leibrandt	.08	.06	.03
14	Hal McRae	.10	.08	.04
15	Omar Moreno	.06	.05	.02
16	Darryl Motley	.06	.05	.02
17	Jorge Orta	.06	.05	.02
18	Dan Quisenberry	.08	.06	.03
19	Bret Saberhagen	1.00	.70	.40
20	Pat Sheridan	.06	.05	.02
21	Lonnie Smith	.08	.06	.03
22	Jim Sundberg	.08	.06	.03
23	John Wathan	.08	.06	.03
24	Frank White	.10	.08	.04
25	Willie Wilson	.12	.09	.05
26	Joaquin Andujar	.08	.06	.03
27	Steve Braun	.06	.05	.02
28	Bill Campbell	.06	.05	.02
29	Cesar Cedeno	.10	.08	.04
30	Jack Clark	.20	.15	.08
31	*Vince Coleman*	6.00	4.50	2.50
32	Danny Cox	.10	.08	.04
33	Ken Dayley	.06	.05	.02
34	Ivan DeJesus	.06	.05	.02
35	Bob Forsch	.08	.06	.03
36	Brian Harper	.06	.05	.02
37	Tom Herr	.10	.08	.04
38	Ricky Horton	.08	.06	.03
39	Kurt Kepshire	.06	.05	.02
40	Jeff Lahti	.06	.05	.02
41	Tito Landrum	.06	.05	.02
42	Willie McGee	.15	.11	.06
43	Tom Nieto	.06	.05	.02
44	Terry Pendleton	.15	.11	.06
45	Darrell Porter	.08	.06	.03
46	Ozzie Smith	.50	.40	.20
47	John Tudor	.10	.08	.04
48	Andy Van Slyke	.15	.11	.06
49	*Todd Worrell*(FC)	.40	.30	.15
50	Jim Acker	.06	.05	.02
51	Doyle Alexander	.10	.08	.04
52	Jesse Barfield	.20	.15	.08
53	George Bell	.30	.25	.12
54	Jeff Burroughs	.08	.06	.03
55	Bill Caudill	.06	.05	.02
56	Jim Clancy	.08	.06	.03
57	Tony Fernandez	.20	.15	.08
58	Tom Filer	.06	.05	.02
59	Damaso Garcia	.06	.05	.02
60	Tom Henke(FC)	.15	.11	.06
61	Garth Iorg	.06	.05	.02
62	Cliff Johnson	.06	.05	.02
63	Jimmy Key	.15	.11	.06
64	Dennis Lamp	.06	.05	.02
65	Gary Lavelle	.06	.05	.02
66	Buck Martinez	.06	.05	.02
67	Lloyd Moseby	.10	.08	.04
68	Rance Mulliniks	.06	.05	.02
69	Al Oliver	.10	.08	.04
70	Dave Stieb	.12	.09	.05
71	Louis Thornton	.06	.05	.02
72	Willie Upshaw	.08	.06	.03
73	Ernie Whitt	.08	.06	.03
74	*Rick Aguilera*(FC)	.60	.45	.25
75	Wally Backman	.08	.06	.03
76	Gary Carter	.25	.20	.10

		MT	NR MT	EX
77	Ron Darling	.15	.11	.06
78	*Len Dykstra*(FC)	3.00	2.25	1.25
79	Sid Fernandez	.12	.09	.05
80	George Foster	.15	.11	.06
81	Dwight Gooden	3.00	2.25	1.25
82	Tom Gorman	.06	.05	.02
83	Danny Heep	.06	.05	.02
84	Keith Hernandez	.30	.25	.12
85	Howard Johnson	.50	.40	.20
86	Ray Knight	.08	.06	.03
87	Terry Leach	.08	.06	.03
88	Ed Lynch	.06	.05	.02
89	*Roger McDowell*(FC)	.60	.45	.25
90	Jesse Orosco	.08	.06	.03
91	Tom Paciorek	.06	.05	.02
92	Ronn Reynolds	.06	.05	.02
93	Rafael Santana	.06	.05	.02
94	Doug Sisk	.06	.05	.02
95	Rusty Staub	.10	.08	.04
96	Darryl Strawberry	4.00	3.00	1.50
97	Mookie Wilson	.10	.08	.04
98	Neil Allen	.06	.05	.02
99	Don Baylor	.12	.09	.05
100	Dale Berra	.06	.05	.02
101	Rich Bordi	.06	.05	.02
102	Marty Bystrom	.06	.05	.02
103	Joe Cowley	.06	.05	.02
104	*Brian Fisher*	.15	.11	.06
105	Ken Griffey	.10	.08	.04
106	Ron Guidry	.20	.15	.08
107	Ron Hassey	.06	.05	.02
108	Rickey Henderson	2.00	1.50	.80
109	Don Mattingly	4.00	3.00	1.50
110	Bobby Meacham	.06	.05	.02
111	John Montefusco	.06	.05	.02
112	Phil Niekro	.25	.20	.10
113	Mike Pagliarulo	.20	.15	.08
114	Dan Pasqua	.20	.15	.08
115	Willie Randolph	.10	.08	.04
116	Dave Righetti	.20	.15	.08
117	Andre Robertson	.06	.05	.02
118	Billy Sample	.06	.05	.02
119	Bob Shirley	.06	.05	.02
120	Ed Whitson	.06	.05	.02
121	Dave Winfield	.50	.40	.20
122	Butch Wynegar	.06	.05	.02
123	Dave Anderson	.06	.05	.02
124	Bob Bailor	.06	.05	.02
125	Greg Brock	.08	.06	.03
126	Enos Cabell	.06	.05	.02
127	Bobby Castillo	.06	.05	.02
128	Carlos Diaz	.06	.05	.02
129	*Mariano Duncan*	.15	.11	.06
130	Pedro Guerrero	.20	.15	.08
131	Orel Hershiser	.70	.50	.30
132	Rick Honeycutt	.06	.05	.02
133	Ken Howell	.06	.05	.02
134	Ken Landreaux	.06	.05	.02
135	Bill Madlock	.12	.09	.05
136	Candy Maldonado	.10	.08	.04
137	Mike Marshall	.15	.11	.06
138	Len Matuszek	.06	.05	.02
139	Tom Niedenfuer	.08	.06	.03
140	Alejandro Pena	.08	.06	.03
141	Jerry Reuss	.08	.06	.03
142	Bill Russell	.08	.06	.03
143	Steve Sax	.20	.15	.08
144	Mike Scioscia	.08	.06	.03
145	Fernando Valenzuela	.30	.25	.12
146	Bob Welch	.12	.09	.05
147	Terry Whitfield	.06	.05	.02
148	Juan Beniquez	.06	.05	.02
149	Bob Boone	.08	.06	.03
150	John Candelaria	.10	.08	.04
151	Rod Carew	.70	.50	.30
152	*Stewart Cliburn*(FC)	.12	.09	.05
153	Doug DeCinces	.10	.08	.04
154	Brian Downing	.08	.06	.03
155	Ken Forsch	.06	.05	.02
156	Craig Gerber	.06	.05	.02
157	Bobby Grich	.10	.08	.04
158	George Hendrick	.08	.06	.03
159	Al Holland	.06	.05	.02
160	Reggie Jackson	.35	.25	.14
161	Ruppert Jones	.06	.05	.02
162	*Urbano Lugo*	.08	.06	.03
163	*Kirk McCaskill*(FC)	.35	.25	.14
164	Donnie Moore	.06	.05	.02
165	Gary Pettis	.06	.05	.02
166	Ron Romanick	.06	.05	.02
167	Dick Schofield	.06	.05	.02

		MT	NR MT	EX
168	Daryl Sconiers	.06	.05	.02
169	Jim Slaton	.06	.05	.02
170	Don Sutton	.25	.20	.10
171	Mike Witt	.10	.08	.04
172	Buddy Bell	.10	.08	.04
173	Tom Browning	.30	.25	.12
174	Dave Concepcion	.12	.09	.05
175	Eric Davis	2.25	1.75	.90
176	Bo Diaz	.08	.06	.03
177	Nick Esasky	.08	.06	.03
178	John Franco	.12	.09	.05
179	Tom Hume	.06	.05	.02
180	Wayne Krenchicki	.06	.05	.02
181	Andy McGaffigan	.06	.05	.02
182	Eddie Milner	.06	.05	.02
183	Ron Oester	.06	.05	.02
184	Dave Parker	.20	.15	.08
185	Frank Pastore	.06	.05	.02
186	Tony Perez	.15	.11	.06
187	Ted Power	.08	.06	.03
188	Joe Price	.06	.05	.02
189	Gary Redus	.06	.05	.02
190	Ron Robinson	.08	.06	.03
191	Pete Rose	.70	.50	.30
192	Mario Soto	.08	.06	.03
193	John Stuper	.06	.05	.02
194	Jay Tibbs	.06	.05	.02
195	Dave Van Gorder	.06	.05	.02
196	Max Venable	.06	.05	.02
197	Juan Agosto	.06	.05	.02
198	Harold Baines	.15	.11	.06
199	Floyd Bannister	.10	.08	.04
200	Britt Burns	.06	.05	.02
201	Julio Cruz	.06	.05	.02
202	*Joel Davis*(FC)	.08	.06	.03
203	Richard Dotson	.10	.08	.04
204	Carlton Fisk	.50	.40	.20
205	Scott Fletcher	.08	.06	.03
206	*Ozzie Guillen*	1.25	.90	.50
207	Jerry Hairston	.06	.05	.02
208	Tim Hulett	.08	.06	.03
209	Bob James	.06	.05	.02
210	Ron Kittle	.10	.08	.04
211	Rudy Law	.06	.05	.02
212	Bryan Little	.06	.05	.02
213	Gene Nelson	.06	.05	.02
214	Reid Nichols	.06	.05	.02
215	Luis Salazar	.06	.05	.02
216	Tom Seaver	.50	.40	.20
217	Dan Spillner	.06	.05	.02
218	Bruce Tanner	.06	.05	.02
219	Greg Walker	.10	.08	.04
220	Dave Wehrmeister	.06	.05	.02
221	Juan Berenguer	.06	.05	.02
222	Dave Bergman	.06	.05	.02
223	Tom Brookens	.06	.05	.02
224	Darrell Evans	.12	.09	.05
225	Barbaro Garbey	.06	.05	.02
226	Kirk Gibson	.30	.25	.12
227	John Grubb	.06	.05	.02
228	Willie Hernandez	.08	.06	.03
229	Larry Herndon	.08	.06	.03
230	Chet Lemon	.08	.06	.03
231	Aurelio Lopez	.06	.05	.02
232	Jack Morris	.20	.15	.08
233	Randy O'Neal	.06	.05	.02
234	Lance Parrish	.20	.15	.08
235	Dan Petry	.08	.06	.03
236	Alex Sanchez	.06	.05	.02
237	Bill Scherrer	.06	.05	.02
238	Nelson Simmons	.06	.05	.02
239	Frank Tanana	.10	.08	.04
240	Walt Terrell	.08	.06	.03
241	Alan Trammell	.30	.25	.12
242	Lou Whitaker	.30	.25	.12
243	Milt Wilcox	.06	.05	.02
244	Hubie Brooks	.10	.08	.04
245	*Tim Burke*(FC)	.30	.25	.12
246	Andre Dawson	.30	.25	.12
247	Mike Fitzgerald	.06	.05	.02
248	Terry Francona	.06	.05	.02
249	Bill Gullickson	.06	.05	.02
250	Joe Hesketh	.06	.05	.02
251	Bill Laskey	.06	.05	.02
252	Vance Law	.08	.06	.03
253	Charlie Lea	.06	.05	.02
254	Gary Lucas	.06	.05	.02
255	David Palmer	.06	.05	.02
256	Tim Raines	.30	.25	.12
257	Jeff Reardon	.12	.09	.05
258	Bert Roberge	.06	.05	.02

		MT	NR MT	EX
259	Dan Schatzeder	.06	.05	.02
260	Bryn Smith	.06	.05	.02
261	Randy St. Claire(FC)	.08	.06	.03
262	Scot Thompson	.06	.05	.02
263	Tim Wallach	.12	.09	.05
264	U.L. Washington	.06	.05	.02
265	*Mitch Webster*(FC)	.25	.20	.10
266	*Herm Winningham*	.15	.11	.06
267	*Floyd Youmans*(FC)	.15	.11	.06
268	Don Aase	.06	.05	.02
269	Mike Boddicker	.08	.06	.03
270	Rich Dauer	.06	.05	.02
271	Storm Davis	.10	.08	.04
272	Rick Dempsey	.08	.06	.03
273	Ken Dixon	.06	.05	.02
274	Jim Dwyer	.06	.05	.02
275	Mike Flanagan	.10	.08	.04
276	Wayne Gross	.06	.05	.02
277	Lee Lacy	.06	.05	.02
278	Fred Lynn	.20	.15	.08
279	Tippy Martinez	.06	.05	.02
280	Dennis Martinez	.08	.06	.03
281	Scott McGregor	.08	.06	.03
282	Eddie Murray	.40	.30	.15
283	Floyd Rayford	.06	.05	.02
284	Cal Ripken, Jr.	2.50	2.00	1.00
285	Gary Roenicke	.06	.05	.02
286	Larry Sheets	.20	.15	.08
287	John Shelby	.06	.05	.02
288	Nate Snell	.06	.05	.02
289	Sammy Stewart	.06	.05	.02
290	Alan Wiggins	.06	.05	.02
291	Mike Young	.06	.05	.02
292	Alan Ashby	.06	.05	.02
293	Mark Bailey	.06	.05	.02
294	Kevin Bass	.10	.08	.04
295	Jeff Calhoun	.06	.05	.02
296	Jose Cruz	.10	.08	.04
297	Glenn Davis	2.00	1.50	.80
298	Bill Dawley	.06	.05	.02
299	Frank DiPino	.06	.05	.02
300	Bill Doran	.10	.08	.04
301	Phil Garner	.08	.06	.03
302	*Jeff Heathcock*(FC)	.10	.08	.04
303	*Charlie Kerfeld*(FC)	.15	.11	.06
304	Bob Knepper	.08	.06	.03
305	Ron Mathis	.06	.05	.02
306	Jerry Mumphrey	.06	.05	.02
307	Jim Pankovits	.06	.05	.02
308	Terry Puhl	.06	.05	.02
309	Craig Reynolds	.06	.05	.02
310	Nolan Ryan	3.50	2.75	1.50
311	Mike Scott	.15	.11	.06
312	Dave Smith	.08	.06	.03
313	Dickie Thon	.08	.06	.03
314	Denny Walling	.06	.05	.02
315	Kurt Bevacqua	.06	.05	.02
316	Al Bumbry	.06	.05	.02
317	Jerry Davis	.06	.05	.02
318	Luis DeLeon	.06	.05	.02
319	Dave Dravecky	.08	.06	.03
320	Tim Flannery	.06	.05	.02
321	Steve Garvey	.30	.25	.12
322	Goose Gossage	.20	.15	.08
323	Tony Gwynn	.70	.50	.30
324	Andy Hawkins	.06	.05	.02
325	LaMarr Hoyt	.06	.05	.02
326	Roy Lee Jackson	.06	.05	.02
327	Terry Kennedy	.08	.06	.03
328	Craig Lefferts	.06	.05	.02
329	Carmelo Martinez	.08	.06	.03
330	*Lance McCullers*(FC)	.25	.20	.10
331	Kevin McReynolds	.30	.25	.12
332	Graig Nettles	.15	.11	.06
333	Jerry Royster	.06	.05	.02
334	Eric Show	.08	.06	.03
335	Tim Stoddard	.06	.05	.02
336	Garry Templeton	.08	.06	.03
337	Mark Thurmond	.06	.05	.02
338	Ed Wojna	.06	.05	.02
339	Tony Armas	.08	.06	.03
340	Marty Barrett	.10	.08	.04
341	Wade Boggs	2.25	1.75	.90
342	Dennis Boyd	.08	.06	.03
343	Bill Buckner	.12	.09	.05
344	Mark Clear	.06	.05	.02
345	Roger Clemens	7.00	5.25	2.75
346	Steve Crawford	.06	.05	.02
347	Mike Easler	.08	.06	.03
348	Dwight Evans	.12	.09	.05
349	Rich Gedman	.10	.08	.04

		MT	NR MT	EX
350	Jackie Gutierrez	.06	.05	.02
351	Glenn Hoffman	.06	.05	.02
352	Bruce Hurst	.12	.09	.05
353	Bruce Kison	.06	.05	.02
354	Tim Lollar	.06	.05	.02
355	Steve Lyons	.08	.06	.03
356	Al Nipper	.08	.06	.03
357	Bob Ojeda	.08	.06	.03
358	Jim Rice	.30	.25	.12
359	Bob Stanley	.06	.05	.02
360	Mike Trujillo	.06	.05	.02
361	Thad Bosley	.06	.05	.02
362	Warren Brusstar	.06	.05	.02
363	Ron Cey	.10	.08	.04
364	Jody Davis	.10	.08	.04
365	Bob Dernier	.06	.05	.02
366	Shawon Dunston	.70	.50	.30
367	Leon Durham	.08	.06	.03
368	Dennis Eckersley	.12	.09	.05
369	Ray Fontenot	.06	.05	.02
370	George Frazier	.06	.05	.02
371	Bill Hatcher	.10	.08	.04
372	Dave Lopes	.08	.06	.03
373	Gary Matthews	.10	.08	.04
374	Ron Meredith	.06	.05	.02
375	Keith Moreland	.08	.06	.03
376	Reggie Patterson	.06	.05	.02
377	Dick Ruthven	.06	.05	.02
378	Ryne Sandberg	3.00	2.25	1.25
379	Scott Sanderson	.06	.05	.02
380	Lee Smith	.10	.08	.04
381	Lary Sorensen	.06	.05	.02
382	Chris Speier	.06	.05	.02
383	Rick Sutcliffe	.12	.09	.05
384	Steve Trout	.06	.05	.02
385	Gary Woods	.06	.05	.02
386	Bert Blyleven	.15	.11	.06
387	Tom Brunansky	.12	.09	.05
388	Randy Bush	.06	.05	.02
389	John Butcher	.06	.05	.02
390	Ron Davis	.06	.05	.02
391	Dave Engle	.06	.05	.02
392	Frank Eufemia	.06	.05	.02
393	Pete Filson	.06	.05	.02
394	Gary Gaetti	.20	.15	.08
395	Greg Gagne	.10	.08	.04
396	Mickey Hatcher	.06	.05	.02
397	Kent Hrbek	.20	.15	.08
398	Tim Laudner	.06	.05	.02
399	Rick Lysander	.06	.05	.02
400	Dave Meier	.06	.05	.02
401	Kirby Puckett	6.00	4.50	2.50
402	Mark Salas	.08	.06	.03
403	Ken Schrom	.06	.05	.02
404	Roy Smalley	.06	.05	.02
405	Mike Smithson	.06	.05	.02
406	Mike Stenhouse	.06	.05	.02
407	Tim Teufel	.06	.05	.02
408	Frank Viola	.15	.11	.06
409	Ron Washington	.06	.05	.02
410	Keith Atherton	.06	.05	.02
411	Dusty Baker	.08	.06	.03
412	*Tim Birtsas*	.12	.09	.05
413	Bruce Bochte	.06	.05	.02
414	Chris Codiroli	.06	.05	.02
415	Dave Collins	.08	.06	.03
416	Mike Davis	.08	.06	.03
417	Alfredo Griffin	.08	.06	.03
418	Mike Heath	.06	.05	.02
419	Steve Henderson	.06	.05	.02
420	Donnie Hill	.06	.05	.02
421	Jay Howell	.08	.06	.03
422	Tommy John	.20	.15	.08
423	Dave Kingman	.15	.11	.06
424	Bill Krueger	.06	.05	.02
425	Rick Langford	.06	.05	.02
426	Carney Lansford	.10	.08	.04
427	Steve McCatty	.06	.05	.02
428	Dwayne Murphy	.08	.06	.03
429	*Steve Ontiveros*(FC)	.12	.09	.05
430	Tony Phillips	.06	.05	.02
431	Jose Rijo	.10	.08	.04
432	*Mickey Tettleton*	1.00	.70	.40
433	Luis Aguayo	.06	.05	.02
434	Larry Andersen	.06	.05	.02
435	Steve Carlton	.30	.25	.12
436	*Don Carman*	.30	.25	.12
437	Tim Corcoran	.06	.05	.02
438	*Darren Daulton*	.12	.09	.05
439	John Denny	.06	.05	.02
440	Tom Foley	.06	.05	.02

		MT	NR MT	EX
441	Greg Gross	.06	.05	.02
442	Kevin Gross	.08	.06	.03
443	Von Hayes	.10	.08	.04
444	Charles Hudson	.06	.05	.02
445	Garry Maddox	.08	.06	.03
446	Shane Rawley	.10	.08	.04
447	Dave Rucker	.06	.05	.02
448	John Russell	.06	.05	.02
449	Juan Samuel	.12	.09	.05
450	Mike Schmidt	2.00	1.50	.80
451	Rick Schu	.08	.06	.03
452	Dave Shipanoff	.06	.05	.02
453	Dave Stewart	.12	.09	.05
454	Jeff Stone	.06	.05	.02
455	Kent Tekulve	.08	.06	.03
456	Ozzie Virgil	.06	.05	.02
457	Glenn Wilson	.08	.06	.03
458	Jim Beattie	.06	.05	.02
459	Karl Best	.06	.05	.02
460	Barry Bonnell	.06	.05	.02
461	Phil Bradley	.20	.15	.08
462	*Ivan Calderon*	2.00	1.50	.80
463	Al Cowens	.06	.05	.02
464	Alvin Davis	.30	.25	.12
465	Dave Henderson	.10	.08	.04
466	Bob Kearney	.06	.05	.02
467	Mark Langston	.30	.25	.12
468	Bob Long	.06	.05	.02
469	Mike Moore	.06	.05	.02
470	Edwin Nunez	.06	.05	.02
471	Spike Owen	.06	.05	.02
472	Jack Perconte	.06	.05	.02
473	Jim Presley	.15	.11	.06
474	Donnie Scott	.06	.05	.02
475	Bill Swift(FC)	.12	.09	.05
476	Danny Tartabull	.70	.50	.30
477	Gorman Thomas	.10	.08	.04
478	Roy Thomas	.06	.05	.02
479	Ed Vande Berg	.06	.05	.02
480	Frank Wills	.06	.05	.02
481	Matt Young	.06	.05	.02
482	Ray Burris	.06	.05	.02
483	Jaime Cocanower	.06	.05	.02
484	Cecil Cooper	.12	.09	.05
485	Danny Darwin	.06	.05	.02
486	Rollie Fingers	.20	.15	.08
487	Jim Gantner	.08	.06	.03
488	Bob Gibson	.06	.05	.02
489	Moose Haas	.06	.05	.02
490	*Teddy Higuera*	.60	.45	.25
491	Paul Householder	.06	.05	.02
492	Pete Ladd	.06	.05	.02
493	Rick Manning	.06	.05	.02
494	Bob McClure	.06	.05	.02
495	Paul Molitor	.15	.11	.06
496	Charlie Moore	.06	.05	.02
497	Ben Oglivie	.08	.06	.03
498	Randy Ready	.06	.05	.02
499	*Earnie Riles*	.20	.15	.08
500	Ed Romero	.06	.05	.02
501	Bill Schroeder	.06	.05	.02
502	Ray Searage	.06	.05	.02
503	Ted Simmons	.12	.09	.05
504	Pete Vuckovich	.08	.06	.03
505	Rick Waits	.06	.05	.02
506	Robin Yount	.60	.45	.25
507	Len Barker	.08	.06	.03
508	Steve Bedrosian	.12	.09	.05
509	Bruce Benedict	.06	.05	.02
510	Rick Camp	.06	.05	.02
511	Rick Cerone	.06	.05	.02
512	Chris Chambliss	.08	.06	.03
513	Jeff Dedmon	.06	.05	.02
514	Terry Forster	.08	.06	.03
515	Gene Garber	.06	.05	.02
516	Terry Harper	.06	.05	.02
517	Bob Horner	.12	.09	.05
518	Glenn Hubbard	.06	.05	.02
519	*Joe Johnson*(FC)	.08	.06	.03
520	Brad Komminsk	.06	.05	.02
521	Rick Mahler	.06	.05	.02
522	Dale Murphy	.50	.40	.20
523	Ken Oberkfell	.06	.05	.02
524	Pascual Perez	.08	.06	.03
525	Gerald Perry	.12	.09	.05
526	Rafael Ramirez	.06	.05	.02
527	*Steve Shields*(FC)	.12	.09	.05
528	Zane Smith	.10	.08	.04
529	Bruce Sutter	.12	.09	.05
530	*Milt Thompson*(FC)	.30	.25	.12
531	Claudell Washington	.08	.06	.03

		MT	NR MT	EX
532	Paul Zuvella	.06	.05	.02
533	Vida Blue	.10	.08	.04
534	Bob Brenly	.06	.05	.02
535	*Chris Brown*	.20	.15	.08
536	Chili Davis	.10	.08	.04
537	Mark Davis	.06	.05	.02
538	Rob Deer	.12	.09	.05
539	Dan Driessen	.08	.06	.03
540	Scott Garrelts	.08	.06	.03
541	Dan Gladden	.08	.06	.03
542	Jim Gott	.06	.05	.02
543	David Green	.06	.05	.02
544	Atlee Hammaker	.06	.05	.02
545	Mike Jeffcoat	.06	.05	.02
546	Mike Krukow	.08	.06	.03
547	Dave LaPoint	.08	.06	.03
548	Jeff Leonard	.08	.06	.03
549	Greg Minton	.06	.05	.02
550	Alex Trevino	.06	.05	.02
551	Manny Trillo	.08	.06	.03
552	*Jose Uribe*	.20	.15	.08
553	Brad Wellman	.06	.05	.02
554	Frank Williams	.06	.05	.02
555	Joel Youngblood	.06	.05	.02
556	Alan Bannister	.06	.05	.02
557	Glenn Brummer	.06	.05	.02
558	*Steve Buechele*(FC)	.20	.15	.08
559	*Jose Guzman*(FC)	.20	.15	.08
560	Toby Harrah	.08	.06	.03
561	Greg Harris	.06	.05	.02
562	*Dwayne Henry*(FC)	.10	.08	.04
563	Burt Hooton	.08	.06	.03
564	Charlie Hough	.08	.06	.03
565	Mike Mason	.06	.05	.02
566	*Oddibe McDowell*	.20	.15	.08
567	Dickie Noles	.06	.05	.02
568	Pete O'Brien	.10	.08	.04
569	Larry Parrish	.10	.08	.04
570	Dave Rozema	.06	.05	.02
571	Dave Schmidt	.06	.05	.02
572	Don Slaught	.06	.05	.02
573	Wayne Tolleson	.06	.05	.02
574	Duane Walker	.06	.05	.02
575	Gary Ward	.08	.06	.03
576	Chris Welsh	.06	.05	.02
577	Curtis Wilkerson	.06	.05	.02
578	George Wright	.06	.05	.02
579	Chris Bando	.06	.05	.02
580	Tony Bernazard	.06	.05	.02
581	Brett Butler	.08	.06	.03
582	Ernie Camacho	.06	.05	.02
583	Joe Carter	.20	.15	.08
584	Carmello Castillo (Carmelo)	.06	.05	.02
585	Jamie Easterly	.06	.05	.02
586	Julio Franco	.10	.08	.04
587	Mel Hall	.08	.06	.03
588	Mike Hargrove	.06	.05	.02
589	Neal Heaton	.06	.05	.02
590	Brook Jacoby	.10	.08	.04
591	*Otis Nixon*(FC)	.12	.09	.05
592	Jerry Reed	.06	.05	.02
593	Vern Ruhle	.06	.05	.02
594	Pat Tabler	.08	.06	.03
595	Rich Thompson	.06	.05	.02
596	Andre Thornton	.08	.06	.03
597	Dave Von Ohlen	.06	.05	.02
598	George Vukovich	.06	.05	.02
599	Tom Waddell	.06	.05	.02
600	Curt Wardle	.06	.05	.02
601	Jerry Willard	.06	.05	.02
602	Bill Almon	.06	.05	.02
603	Mike Bielecki	.08	.06	.03
604	Sid Bream	.10	.08	.04
605	Mike Brown	.06	.05	.02
606	*Pat Clements*	.12	.09	.05
607	Jose DeLeon	.08	.06	.03
608	Denny Gonzalez	.06	.05	.02
609	Cecilio Guante	.06	.05	.02
610	Steve Kemp	.08	.06	.03
611	Sam Khalifa	.06	.05	.02
612	Lee Mazzilli	.08	.06	.03
613	Larry McWilliams	.06	.05	.02
614	Jim Morrison	.06	.05	.02
615	*Joe Orsulak*	.15	.11	.06
616	Tony Pena	.10	.08	.04
617	Johnny Ray	.10	.08	.04
618	Rick Reuschel	.10	.08	.04
619	R.J. Reynolds	.08	.06	.03
620	Rick Rhoden	.10	.08	.04
621	Don Robinson	.08	.06	.03
622	Jason Thompson	.06	.05	.02

		MT	NR MT	EX
623	Lee Tunnell	.06	.05	.02
624	Jim Winn	.06	.05	.02
625	Marvell Wynne	.06	.05	.02
626	Gooden In Action (Dwight Gooden)	.50	.40	.20
627	Mattingly In Action (Don Mattingly)	1.25	.90	.50
628	4,192! (Pete Rose)	.50	.40	.20
629	3,000 Career Hits (Rod Carew)	.20	.15	.08
630	300 Career Wins (Phil Niekro, Tom Seaver)	.20	.15	.08
631	Ouch! (Don Baylor)	.08	.06	.03
632	Instant Offense (Tim Raines, Darryl Strawberry)	.30	.25	.12
633	Shortstops Supreme (Cal Ripken, Jr., Alan Trammell)	.30	.25	.12
634	Boggs & "Hero" (Wade Boggs, George Brett)	.60	.45	.25
635	Braves Dynamic Duo (Bob Horner, Dale Murphy)	.30	.25	.12
636	Cardinal Ignitors (Vince Coleman, Willie McGee)	.35	.25	.14
637	Terror on the Basepaths (Vince Coleman)	.50	.40	.20
638	Charlie Hustle & Dr. K (Dwight Gooden, Pete Rose)	.70	.50	.30
639	1984 and 1985 A.L. Batting Champs (Wade Boggs, Don Mattingly)	1.75	1.25	.70
640	N.L. West Sluggers (Steve Garvey, Dale Murphy, Dave Parker)	.30	.25	.12
641	Staff Aces (Dwight Gooden, Fernando Valenzuela)	.40	.30	.15
642	Blue Jay Stoppers (Jimmy Key, Dave Stieb)	.10	.08	.04
643	A.L. All-Star Backstops (Carlton Fisk, Rich Gedman)	.10	.08	.04
644	Major League Prospect *(Benito Santiago, Gene Walter)*(FC)	5.00	3.75	2.00
645	Major League Prospect *(Colin Ward, Mike Woodard)*(FC)	.10	.08	.04
646	Major League Prospect *(Kal Daniels, Paul O'Neill)*(FC)	7.00	5.25	2.75
647	Major League Prospect *(Andres Galarraga, Fred Toliver)*(FC)	1.25	.90	.50
648	Major League Prospect *(Curt Ford, Bob Kipper)*(FC)	.25	.20	.10
649	Major League Prospect *(Jose Canseco, Eric Plunk)*(FC)	50.00	37.00	20.00
650	Major League Prospect *(Mark McLemore, Gus Polidor)*(FC)	.15	.11	.06
651	Major League Prospect *(Mickey Brantley, Rob Woodward)*(FC)	.15	.11	.06
652	Major League Prospect *(Mark Funderburk, Billy Joe Robidoux)*(FC)	.10	.08	.04
653	Major League Prospect *(Cecil Fielder, Cory Snyder)*(FC)	20.00	15.00	8.00
654	Checklist 1-97	.06	.05	.02
655	Checklist 98-196	.06	.05	.02
656	Checklist 197-291	.06	.05	.02
657	Checklist 292-385	.06	.05	.02
658	Checklist 386-482	.06	.05	.02
659	Checklist 483-578	.06	.05	.02
660	Checklist 579-660	.06	.05	.02

1986 Fleer All Star Team

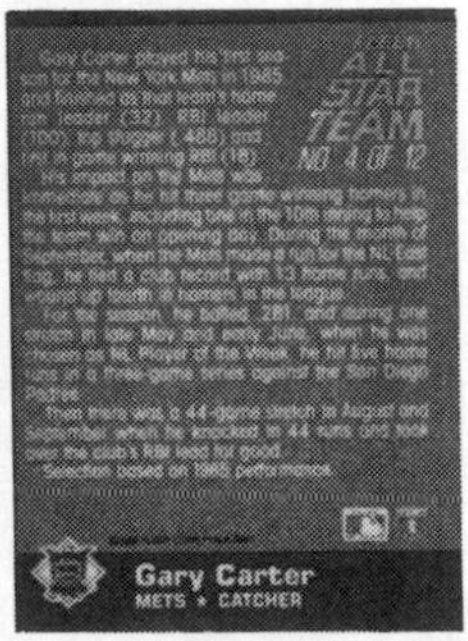

Fleer's choices for a major league All-Star team make up this 12-card set. The cards, which measure 2-1/2" by 3-1/2", were randomly inserted in 35¢ wax packs and 59¢ cello packs. The card fronts have a color photo set against a bright red background for A.L. players or a bright blue background for N.L. players. The card backs feature the player's career highlights set in white type against a red and blue background.

		MT	NR MT	EX
	Complete Set:	16.00	12.00	6.50
	Common Player:	.60	.45	.25
1	Don Mattingly	4.00	3.00	1.50
2	Tom Herr	.60	.45	.25
3	George Brett	2.00	1.50	.80
4	Gary Carter	1.00	.70	.40
5	Cal Ripken, Jr.	2.50	2.00	1.00
6	Dave Parker	.75	.60	.30
7	Rickey Henderson	3.00	2.25	1.25
8	Pedro Guerrero	.75	.60	.30
9	Dan Quisenberry	.60	.45	.25
10	Dwight Gooden	3.00	2.25	1.25
11	Gorman Thomas	.60	.45	.25
12	John Tudor	.60	.45	.25

1986 Fleer Baseball's Best

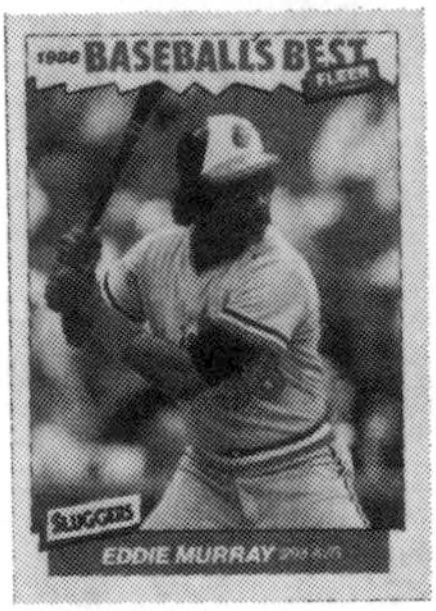

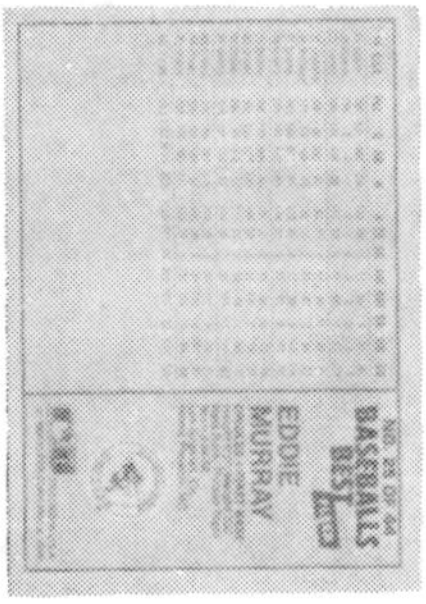

The 1986 Fleer Baseball's Best set consists of 44 cards and was produced for the McCrory's store chain and their affiliated stores. Subtitled "Sluggers vs. Pitchers," the set contains 22 each of the game's best hitters and pitchers. The cards, which measure 2-1/2" by 3-1/2", have color photos depicting an action pose. The backs are done in blue and red ink on white stock and carry the player's personal and statistical information. The sets were issued in a specially designed box with six team logo stickers.

		MT	NR MT	EX
	Complete Set:	7.00	5.25	2.75
	Common Player:	.05	.04	.02
1	Bert Blyleven	.10	.08	.04
2	Wade Boggs	.70	.50	.30
3	George Brett	.30	.25	.12
4	Tom Browning	.15	.11	.06
5	Jose Canseco	2.50	2.00	1.00
6	Will Clark	1.50	1.25	.60
7	Roger Clemens	.70	.50	.30
8	Alvin Davis	.10	.08	.04
9	Julio Franco	.10	.08	.04
10	Kirk Gibson	.20	.15	.08
11	Dwight Gooden	.70	.50	.30
12	Goose Gossage	.12	.09	.05
13	Pedro Guerrero	.15	.11	.06
14	Ron Guidry	.12	.09	.05
15	Tony Gwynn	.25	.20	.10
16	Orel Hershiser	.20	.15	.08
17	Kent Hrbek	.15	.11	.06
18	Reggie Jackson	.25	.20	.10
19	Wally Joyner	.50	.40	.20
20	Charlie Leibrandt	.05	.04	.02
21	Don Mattingly	1.00	.70	.40
22	Willie McGee	.12	.09	.05

		MT	NR MT	EX
23	Jack Morris	.15	.11	.06
24	Dale Murphy	.30	.25	.12
25	Eddie Murray	.25	.20	.10
26	Jeff Reardon	.07	.05	.03
27	Rick Reuschel	.07	.05	.03
28	Cal Ripken, Jr	.80	.60	.30
29	Pete Rose	.60	.45	.25
30	Nolan Ryan	1.75	1.25	.70
31	Bret Saberhagen	.15	.11	.06
32	Ryne Sandberg	.60	.45	.25
33	Mike Schmidt	.30	.25	.12
34	Tom Seaver	.25	.20	.10
35	Bryn Smith	.05	.04	.02
36	Mario Soto	.05	.04	.02
37	Dave Stieb	.10	.08	.04
38	Darryl Strawberry	.40	.30	.15
39	Rick Sutcliffe	.10	.08	.04
40	John Tudor	.10	.08	.04
41	Fernando Valenzuela	.20	.15	.08
42	Bobby Witt	.15	.11	.06
43	Mike Witt	.07	.05	.03
44	Robin Yount	.35	.25	.14

1986 Fleer Box Panels

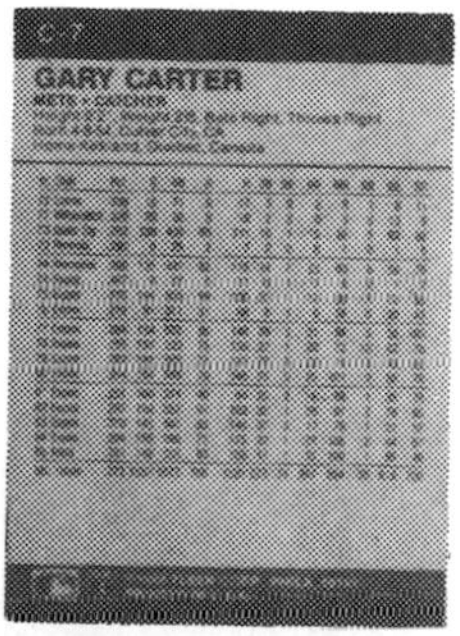

Picking up on a Donruss idea, Fleer issued eight cards in panels of four on the bottoms of the wax and cello pack boxes. The cards are numbered C-1 through C-8 and are 2-1/2" by 3-1/2", with a complete panel measuring 5" by 7-1/8" in size. Included in the eight cards are six player cards and two team logo/checklist cards.

		MT	NR MT	EX
Complete Panel Set:		3.50	2.75	1.50
Complete Singles Set:		1.75	1.25	.70
Common Single Player:		.20	.15	.08
	Panel	2.00	1.50	.80
1	Royals Logo/Checklist	.05	.04	.02
2	George Brett	.60	.45	.25
3	Ozzie Guillen	.40	.30	.15
4	Dale Murphy	.40	.30	.15
	Panel	1.50	1.25	.60
5	Cardinals Logo/Checklist	.05	.04	.02
6	Tom Browning	.20	.15	.08
7	Gary Carter	.35	.25	.14
8	Carlton Fisk	.20	.15	.08

1986 Fleer Future Hall Of Famers

The 1986 Fleer Future Hall of Famers set is comprised of six players Fleer felt would gain eventual entrance into the Baseball Hall of Fame. The cards are the standard 2-1/2" by 3-1/2" in size and were randomly inserted in three-pack cello packs. The card fronts feature a player photo set against a blue background with horizontal light blue stripes. The card backs are printed in black on a blue background and feature player highlights in paragraph form.

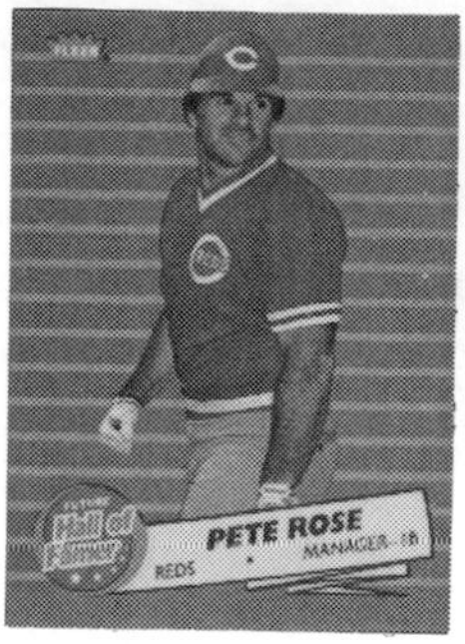

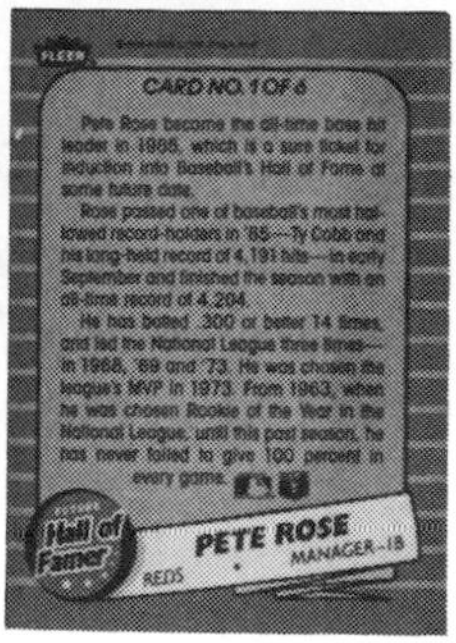

		MT	NR MT	EX
Complete Set:		12.00	9.00	4.75
Common Player:		1.75	1.25	.70
1	Pete Rose	1.75	1.25	.70
2	Steve Carlton	1.75	1.25	.70
3	Tom Seaver	1.75	1.25	.70
4	Rod Carew	1.75	1.25	.70
5	Nolan Ryan	3.00	2.25	1.25
6	Reggie Jackson	1.75	1.25	.70

1986 Fleer League Leaders

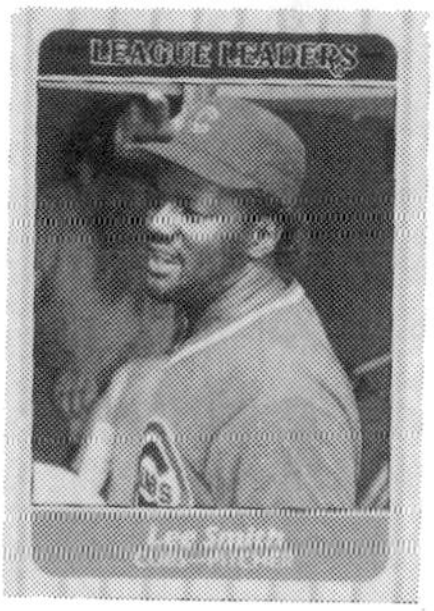

Fleer's 1986 "League Leaders" set features 44 of the game's top players and was issued through the Walgreens drug store chain. The card fronts contain a color photo and feature the player's name, team and postition in a blue band near the bottom of the card. The words "League Leaders" appear in a red band at the top of the card. The background for the card fronts is alternating blue and white stripes. The card backs are printed in blue, red and white and carry the player's statistical information and team logo. The cards are the standard 2-1/2" by 3-1/2" size. The set was issued in a special cardboard box, along with six team logo stickers.

		MT	NR MT	EX
Complete Set:		7.00	5.25	2.75
Common Player:		.05	.04	.02
1	Wade Boggs	.60	.45	.25
2	George Brett	.30	.25	.12
3	Jose Canseco	2.50	2.00	1.00
4	Rod Carew	.30	.25	.12
5	Gary Carter	.25	.20	.10
6	Jack Clark	.12	.09	.05
7	Vince Coleman	.30	.25	.12
8	Jose Cruz	.05	.04	.02
9	Alvin Davis	.10	.08	.04
10	Mariano Duncan	.05	.04	.02
11	Leon Durham	.05	.04	.02
12	Carlton Fisk	.15	.11	.06
13	Julio Franco	.10	.08	.04
14	Scott Garrelts	.05	.04	.02
15	Steve Garvey	.25	.20	.10

		MT	NR MT	EX
16	Dwight Gooden	.60	.45	.25
17	Ozzie Guillen	.10	.08	.04
18	Willie Hernandez	.05	.04	.02
19	Bob Horner	.07	.05	.03
20	Kent Hrbek	.15	.11	.06
21	Charlie Leibrandt	.05	.04	.02
22	Don Mattingly	.80	.60	.30
23	Oddibe McDowell	.12	.09	.05
24	Willie McGee	.10	.08	.04
25	Keith Moreland	.05	.04	.02
26	Lloyd Moseby	.07	.05	.03
27	Dale Murphy	.30	.25	.12
28	Phil Niekro	.15	.11	.06
29	Joe Orsulak	.05	.04	.02
30	Dave Parker	.12	.09	.05
31	Lance Parrish	.15	.11	.06
32	Kirby Puckett	.70	.50	.30
33	Tim Raines	.25	.20	.10
34	Earnie Riles	.07	.05	.03
35	Cal Ripken, Jr.	.80	.60	.30
36	Pete Rose	.60	.45	.25
37	Bret Saberhagen	.15	.11	.06
38	Juan Samuel	.10	.08	.04
39	Ryne Sandberg	.60	.45	.25
40	Tom Seaver	.25	.20	.10
41	Lee Smith	.07	.05	.03
42	Ozzie Smith	.12	.09	.05
43	Dave Stieb	.10	.08	.04
44	Robin Yount	.35	.25	.12

1986 Fleer Limited Edition

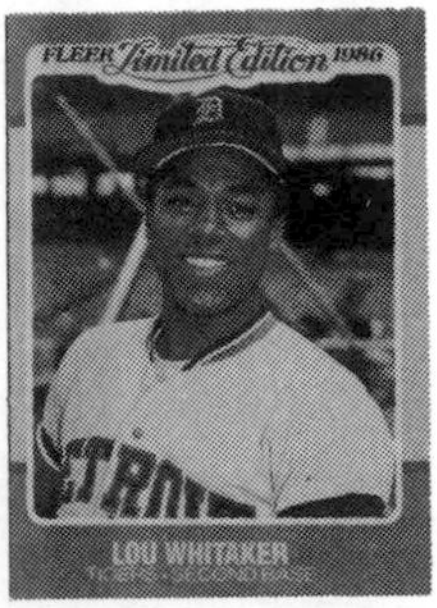

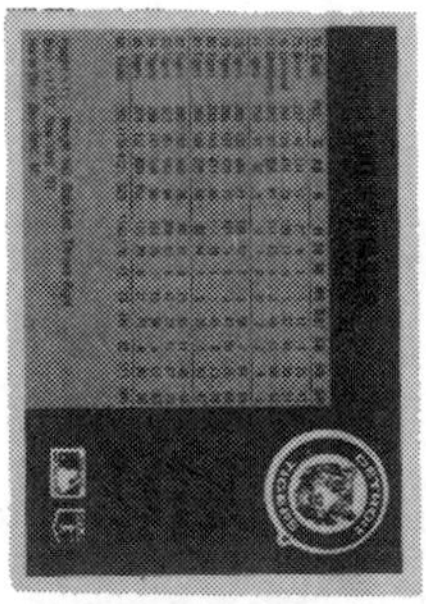

Produced for the McCrory's store chain and their affiliates for the second year in a row, the 1986 Fleer Limited Edition set contains 44 cards. The cards, which are the standard 2-1/2" by 3-1/2" size, have color photos enclosed by green, red and yellow trim. The card backs carry black print on two shades of red. The set was issued in a special cardboard box, along with six team logo stickers.

		MT	NR MT	EX
	Complete Set:	6.00	4.50	2.50
	Common Player:	.05	.04	.02
1	Doyle Alexander	.05	.04	.02
2	Joaquin Andujar	.05	.04	.02
3	Harold Baines	.12	.09	.05
4	Wade Boggs	.70	.50	.30
5	Phil Bradley	.12	.09	.05
6	George Brett	.30	.25	.12
7	Hubie Brooks	.07	.05	.03
8	Chris Brown	.12	.09	.05
9	Tom Brunansky	.10	.08	.04
10	Gary Carter	.25	.20	.10
11	Vince Coleman	.60	.45	.25
12	Cecil Cooper	.07	.05	.03
13	Jose Cruz	.05	.04	.02
14	Mike Davis	.05	.04	.02
15	Carlton Fisk	.15	.11	.06
16	Julio Franco	.10	.08	.04
17	Damaso Garcia	.05	.04	.02
18	Rich Gedman	.05	.04	.02
19	Kirk Gibson	.20	.15	.08
20	Dwight Gooden	.70	.50	.30
21	Pedro Guerrero	.15	.11	.06
22	Tony Gwynn	.25	.20	.10
23	Rickey Henderson	.50	.40	.20
24	Orel Hershiser	.20	.15	.08
25	LaMarr Hoyt	.05	.04	.02
26	Reggie Jackson	.30	.25	.12
27	Don Mattingly	.90	.70	.35
28	Oddibe McDowell	.12	.09	.05
29	Willie McGee	.10	.08	.04
30	Paul Molitor	.12	.09	.05
31	Dale Murphy	.30	.25	.12
32	Eddie Murray	.25	.20	.10
33	Dave Parker	.12	.09	.05
34	Tony Pena	.07	.05	.03
35	Jeff Reardon	.07	.05	.03
36	Cal Ripken, Jr.	.60	.45	.25
37	Pete Rose	.60	.45	.25
38	Bret Saberhagen	.15	.11	.06
39	Juan Samuel	.10	.08	.04
40	Ryne Sandberg	.60	.45	.25
41	Mike Schmidt	.30	.25	.12
42	Lee Smith	.07	.05	.03
43	Don Sutton	.12	.09	.05
44	Lou Whitaker	.15	.11	.06

1986 Fleer Mini

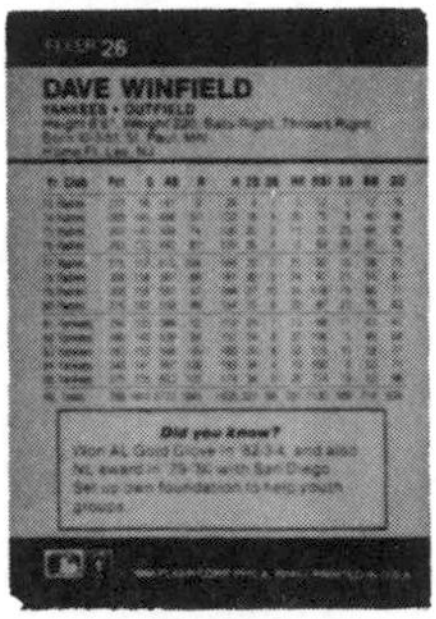

Fleer's 1986 "Classic Miniatures" set contains 120 cards that measure 1-13/16" by 2-9/16" in size. The design of the high-gloss cards is identical to the regular 1986 Fleer set but the player photos are entirely different. The set, which was issued in a specially designed box along with 18 team logo stickers, was available to the collecting public only through hobby dealers.

		MT	NR MT	EX
	Complete Set:	15.00	11.00	6.00
	Common Player:	.05	.04	.02
1	George Brett	.30	.25	.12
2	Dan Quisenberry	.07	.05	.03
3	Bret Saberhagen	.15	.11	.06
4	Lonnie Smith	.05	.04	.02
5	Willie Wilson	.10	.08	.04
6	Jack Clark	.12	.09	.05
7	Vince Coleman	.50	.40	.20
8	Tom Herr	.07	.05	.03
9	Willie McGee	.10	.08	.04
10	Ozzie Smith	.12	.09	.05
11	John Tudor	.07	.05	.03
12	Jesse Barfield	.12	.09	.05
13	George Bell	.20	.15	.08
14	Tony Fernandez	.10	.08	.04
15	Damaso Garcia	.05	.04	.02
16	Dave Stieb	.07	.05	.03
17	Gary Carter	.20	.15	.08
18	Ron Darling	.10	.08	.04
19	Dwight Gooden	.60	.45	.25
20	Keith Hernandez	.20	.15	.08
21	Darryl Strawberry	.50	.40	.20
22	Ron Guidry	.15	.11	.06
23	Rickey Henderson	1.00	.70	.40
24	Don Mattingly	1.25	.90	.50
25	Dave Righetti	.12	.09	.05
26	Dave Winfield	.20	.15	.08
27	Mariano Duncan	.07	.05	.03
28	Pedro Guerrero	.12	.09	.05
29	Bill Madlock	.10	.08	.04

		MT	NR MT	EX
30	Mike Marshall	.10	.08	.04
31	Fernando Valenzuela	.10	.08	.04
32	Reggie Jackson	.30	.25	.12
33	Gary Pettis	.05	.04	.02
34	Ron Romanick	.05	.04	.02
35	Don Sutton	.12	.09	.05
36	Mike Witt	.07	.05	.03
37	Buddy Bell	.07	.05	.03
38	Tom Browning	.10	.08	.04
39	Dave Parker	.12	.09	.05
40	Pete Rose	.60	.45	.25
41	Mario Soto	.05	.04	.02
42	Harold Baines	.12	.09	.05
43	Carlton Fisk	.15	.11	.06
44	Ozzie Guillen	.12	.09	.05
45	Ron Kittle	.07	.05	.03
46	Tom Seaver	.20	.15	.08
47	Kirk Gibson	.20	.15	.08
48	Jack Morris	.15	.11	.06
49	Lance Parrish	.15	.11	.06
50	Alan Trammell	.20	.15	.08
51	Lou Whitaker	.15	.11	.06
52	Hubie Brooks	.07	.05	.03
53	Andre Dawson	.15	.11	.06
54	Tim Raines	.20	.15	.08
55	Bryn Smith	.05	.04	.02
56	Tim Wallach	.10	.08	.04
57	Mike Boddicker	.05	.04	.02
58	Eddie Murray	.25	.20	.10
59	Cal Ripken	1.00	.70	.40
60	John Shelby	.05	.04	.02
61	Mike Young	.05	.04	.02
62	Jose Cruz	.07	.05	.03
63	Glenn Davis	.15	.11	.06
64	Phil Garner	.05	.04	.02
65	Nolan Ryan	2.00	1.50	.80
66	Mike Scott	.12	.09	.05
67	Steve Garvey	.20	.15	.08
68	Goose Gossage	.12	.09	.05
69	Tony Gwynn	.25	.20	.10
70	Andy Hawkins	.05	.04	.02
71	Garry Templeton	.05	.04	.02
72	Wade Boggs	.80	.60	.30
73	Roger Clemens	.80	.60	.30
74	Dwight Evans	.12	.09	.05
75	Rich Gedman	.05	.04	.02
76	Jim Rice	.20	.15	.08
77	Shawon Dunston	.10	.08	.04
78	Leon Durham	.05	.04	.02
79	Keith Moreland	.05	.04	.02
80	Ryne Sandberg	.20	.15	.08
81	Rick Sutcliffe	.10	.08	.04
82	Bert Blyleven	.12	.09	.05
83	Tom Brunansky	.10	.08	.04
84	Kent Hrbek	.15	.11	.06
85	Kirby Puckett	.70	.50	.30
86	Bruce Bochte	.05	.04	.02
87	Jose Canseco	3.00	2.25	1.25
88	Mike Davis	.05	.04	.02
89	Jay Howell	.07	.05	.03
90	Dwayne Murphy	.05	.04	.02
91	Steve Carlton	.20	.15	.08
92	Von Hayes	.10	.08	.04
93	Juan Samuel	.12	.09	.05
94	Mike Schmidt	.30	.25	.12
95	Glenn Wilson	.05	.04	.02
96	Phil Bradley	.10	.08	.04
97	Alvin Davis	.10	.08	.04
98	Jim Presley	.10	.08	.04
99	Danny Tartabull	.15	.11	.06
100	Cecil Cooper	.10	.08	.04
101	Paul Molitor	.12	.09	.05
102	Earnie Riles	.07	.05	.03
103	Robin Yount	.30	.25	.12
104	Bob Horner	.10	.08	.04
105	Dale Murphy	.30	.25	.12
106	Bruce Sutter	.10	.08	.04
107	Claudell Washington	.05	.04	.02
108	Chris Brown	.12	.09	.05
109	Chili Davis	.05	.04	.02
110	Scott Garrelts	.05	.04	.02
111	Oddibe McDowell	.12	.09	.05
112	Pete O'Brien	.07	.05	.03
113	Gary Ward	.05	.04	.02
114	Brett Butler	.05	.04	.02
115	Julio Franco	.10	.08	.04
116	Brook Jacoby	.10	.08	.04
117	Mike Brown	.05	.04	.02
118	Joe Orsulak	.05	.04	.02
119	Tony Pena	.07	.05	.03
120	R.J. Reynolds	.05	.04	.02

1986 Fleer Star Stickers

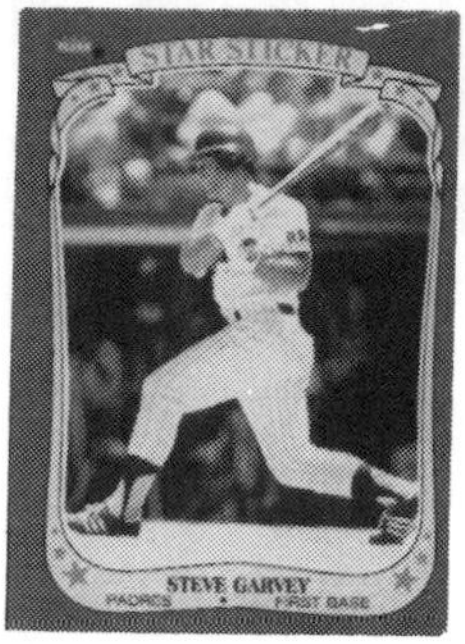

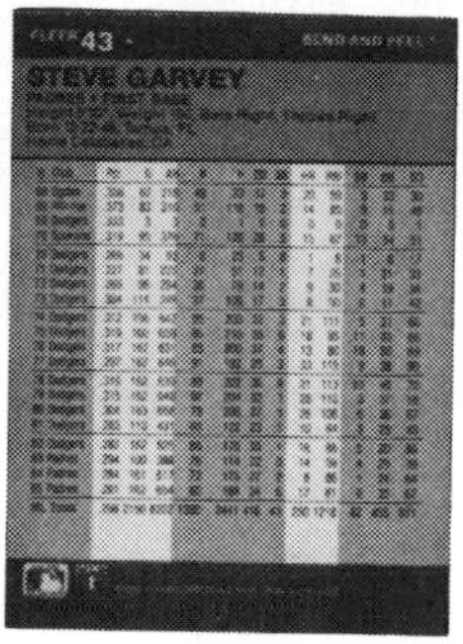

After a five-year layoff, Fleer once again produced a Star Sticker set. The cards, which measure 2-1/2" by 3-1/2", have color photos inside dark maroon borders. The card backs are identical to the 1986 regular issue except for the 1-132 numbering system and blue ink instead of yellow. The words "Bend and Peel" are found in the upper right corner of the card backs. Card #132 is a multi-player card featuring Dwight Gooden and Dale Murphy on the front and a complete checklist for the set on the reverse. The cards were sold in wax packs with team logo stickers.

		MT	NR MT	EX
Complete Set		30.00	22.00	12.00
Common Player		.05	.04	.02
1	Harold Baines	.20	.15	.08
2	Jesse Barfield	.20	.15	.08
3	Don Baylor	.12	.09	.05
4	Juan Beniquez	.05	.04	.02
5	Tim Birtsas	.08	.06	.03
6	Bert Blyleven	.15	.11	.06
7	Bruce Bochte	.05	.04	.02
8	Wade Boggs	1.00	.70	.40
9	Dennis Boyd	.12	.09	.05
10	Phil Bradley	.20	.15	.08
11	George Brett	.50	.40	.20
12	Hubie Brooks	.12	.09	.05
13	Chris Brown	.45	.35	.20
14	Tom Browning	.15	.11	.06
15	Tom Brunansky	.15	.11	.06
16	Bill Buckner	.10	.08	.04
17	Britt Burns	.05	.04	.02
18	Brett Butler	.08	.06	.03
19	Jose Canseco	3.00	2.25	1.25
20	Rod Carew	.40	.30	.15
21	Steve Carlton	.40	.30	.15
22	Don Carman	.20	.15	.08
23	Gary Carter	.40	.30	.15
24	Jack Clark	.20	.15	.08
25	Vince Coleman	.70	.50	.30
26	Cecil Cooper	.15	.11	.06
27	Jose Cruz	.10	.08	.04
28	Ron Darling	.20	.15	.08
29	Alvin Davis	.20	.15	.08
30	Jody Davis	.08	.06	.03
31	Mike Davis	.05	.04	.02
32	Andre Dawson	.25	.20	.10
33	Mariano Duncan	.10	.08	.04
34	Shawon Dunston	.15	.11	.06
35	Leon Durham	.08	.06	.03
36	Darrell Evans	.12	.09	.05
37	Tony Fernandez	.15	.11	.06
38	Carlton Fisk	.20	.15	.08
39	John Franco	.10	.08	.04
40	Julio Franco	.12	.09	.05
41	Damaso Garcia	.05	.04	.02
42	Scott Garrelts	.05	.04	.02
43	Steve Garvey	.25	.20	.10
44	Rich Gedman	.10	.08	.04
45	Kirk Gibson	.30	.25	.12
46	Dwight Gooden	.90	.70	.35
47	Pedro Guerrero	.20	.15	.08
48	Ron Guidry	.20	.15	.08
49	Ozzie Guillen	.30	.25	.12

		MT	NR MT	EX
50	Tony Gwynn	.40	.30	.15
51	Andy Hawkins	.08	.06	.03
52	Von Hayes	.12	.09	.05
53	Rickey Henderson	1.00	.70	.40
54	Tom Henke	.12	.09	.05
55	Keith Hernandez	.35	.25	.14
56	Willie Hernandez	.05	.04	.02
57	Tom Herr	.10	.08	.04
58	Orel Hershiser	.30	.25	.12
59	Teddy Higuera	.60	.45	.25
60	Bob Horner	.12	.09	.05
61	Charlie Hough	.08	.06	.03
62	Jay Howell	.08	.06	.03
63	LaMarr Hoyt	.05	.04	.02
64	Kent Hrbek	.30	.25	.12
65	Reggie Jackson	.50	.40	.20
66	Bob James	.05	.04	.02
67	Dave Kingman	.12	.09	.05
68	Ron Kittle	.12	.09	.05
69	Charlie Leibrandt	.08	.06	.03
70	Fred Lynn	.25	.20	.10
71	Mike Marshall	.20	.15	.08
72	Don Mattingly	1.75	1.25	.70
73	Oddibe McDowell	.25	.20	.10
74	Willie McGee	.20	.15	.08
75	Scott McGregor	.05	.04	.02
76	Paul Molitor	.20	.15	.08
77	Donnie Moore	.05	.04	.02
78	Keith Moreland	.08	.06	.03
79	Jack Morris	.25	.20	.10
80	Dale Murphy	.40	.30	.15
81	Eddie Murray	.50	.40	.20
82	Phil Niekro	.25	.20	.10
83	Joe Orsulak	.10	.08	.04
84	Dave Parker	.25	.20	.10
85	Lance Parrish	.25	.20	.10
86	Larry Parrish	.08	.06	.03
87	Tony Pena	.10	.08	.04
88	Gary Pettis	.05	.04	.02
89	Jim Presley	.15	.11	.06
90	Kirby Puckett	1.00	.70	.40
91	Dan Quisenberry	.12	.09	.05
92	Tim Raines	.35	.25	.14
93	Johnny Ray	.10	.08	.04
94	Jeff Reardon	.10	.08	.04
95	Rick Reuschel	.10	.08	.04
96	Jim Rice	.15	.11	.06
97	Dave Righetti	.20	.15	.08
98	Earnie Riles	.12	.09	.05
99	Cal Ripken, Jr.	1.00	.70	.40
100	Ron Romanick	.05	.04	.02
101	Pete Rose	1.00	.70	.40
102	Nolan Ryan	2.00	1.50	.80
103	Bret Saberhagen	.25	.20	.10
104	Mark Salas	.05	.04	.02
105	Juan Samuel	.15	.11	.06
106	Ryne Sandberg	.70	.50	.30
107	Mike Schmidt	1.00	.70	.40
108	Mike Scott	.15	.11	.06
109	Tom Seaver	.30	.25	.12
110	Bryn Smith	.05	.04	.02
111	Dave Smith	.05	.04	.02
112	Lee Smith	.10	.08	.04
113	Ozzie Smith	.20	.15	.08
114	Mario Soto	.05	.04	.02
115	Dave Stieb	.12	.09	.05
116	Darryl Strawberry	1.00	.70	.40
117	Bruce Sutter	.10	.08	.04
118	Garry Templeton	.08	.06	.03
119	Gorman Thomas	.08	.06	.03
120	Andre Thornton	.10	.08	.04
121	Allan Trammell	.20	.15	.08
122	John Tudor	.12	.09	.05
123	Fernando Valenzuela	.30	.25	.12
124	Frank Viola	.20	.15	.08
125	Gary Ward	.05	.04	.02
126	Lou Whitaker	.25	.20	.10
127	Frank White	.10	.08	.04
128	Glenn Wilson	.08	.06	.03
129	Willie Wilson	.15	.11	.06
130	Dave Winfield	.40	.30	.15
131	Robin Yount	.35	.25	.14
132	Dwight Gooden, Dale Murphy/Checklist	1.25	.90	.50

A player's name in *italic* type indicates a rookie card. An (FC) indicates a player's first card for that particular card company.

1986 Fleer Star Stickers Box Panels

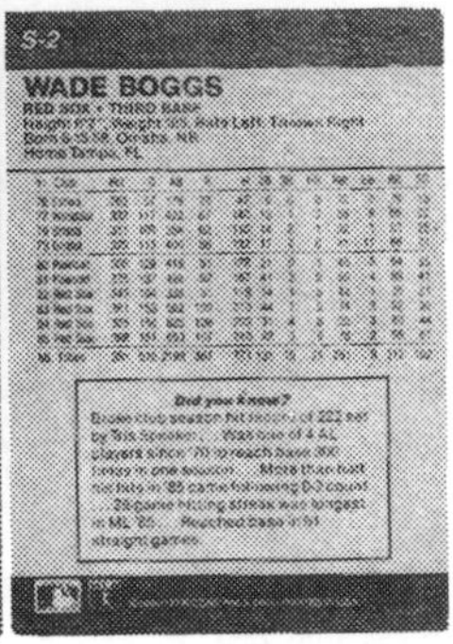

Four cards, numbered S-1 through S-4, were placed on the bottoms of 1986 Fleer Star Stickers wax pack boxes. The cards are nearly identical in format to the regular issue sticker cards. Individual cards measure 2-1/2" by 3-1/2" in size, while a complete panel of four measures 5" by 7-1/8".

		MT	NR MT	EX
Complete Panel Set:		2.00	1.50	.80
Complete Singles Set:		1.00	.70	.40
Common Single Player:		.30	.25	.12
	Panel	2.00	1.50	.80
1	Dodgers Logo	.05	.04	.02
2	Wade Boggs	1.00	.70	.40
3	Steve Garvey	.30	.25	.12
4	Dave Winfield	.30	.25	.12

1986 Fleer Update

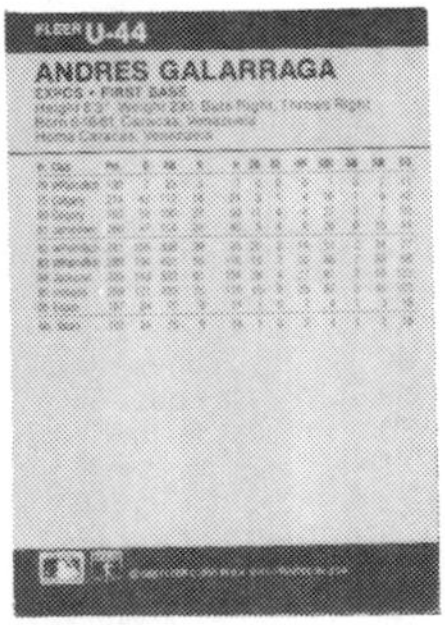

Issued near the end of the baseball season, the 1986 Fleer Update set consists of 132 cards numbered U-1 through U-132. The cards, which measure 2-1/2" by 3-1/2" in size, are identical in design to the regular 1986 Fleer set. The purpose of the set is to update player trades and include new players not depicted in the regular issue. The set was issued with team logo stickers in a specially designed box and was available only through hobby dealers.

		MT	NR MT	EX
Complete Set:		40.00	30.00	15.00
Common Player:		.08	.06	.03
1	Mike Aldrete(FC)	.15	.11	.06
2	Andy Allanson(FC)	.20	.15	.08
3	Neil Allen	.08	.06	.03
4	Joaquin Andujar	.10	.08	.04
5	Paul Assenmacher(FC)	.20	.15	.08
6	Scott Bailes(FC)	.15	.11	.06
7	Jay Baller(FC)	.15	.11	.06
8	Scott Bankhead(FC)	.20	.15	.08

		MT	NR MT	EX
9	Bill Bathe(FC)	.08	.06	.03
10	Don Baylor	.15	.11	.06
11	Billy Beane(FC)	.08	.06	.03
12	Steve Bedrosian	.15	.11	.06
13	Juan Beniquez	.08	.06	.03
14	Barry Bonds(FC)	7.00	5.25	2.75
15	Bobby Bonilla(FC)	5.00	3.75	2.00
16	Rich Bordi	.08	.06	.03
17	Bill Campbell	.08	.06	.03
18	Tom Candiotti	.08	.06	.03
19	John Cangelosi(FC)	.20	.15	.08
20	Jose Canseco	12.00	9.00	4.75
21	Chuck Cary(FC)	.15	.11	.06
22	Juan Castillo(FC)	.10	.08	.04
23	Rick Cerone	.08	.06	.03
24	John Cerutti(FC)	.25	.20	.10
25	Will Clark(FC)	12.00	9.00	4.75
26	Mark Clear	.08	.06	.03
27	Darnell Coles(FC)	.15	.11	.06
28	Dave Collins	.10	.08	.04
29	Tim Conroy	.08	.06	.03
30	Ed Correa(FC)	.20	.15	.08
31	Joe Cowley	.08	.06	.03
32	Bill Dawley	.08	.06	.03
33	Rob Deer	.15	.11	.06
34	John Denny	.08	.06	.03
35	Jim DeShaies (Deshaies)(FC)	.25	.20	.10
36	Doug Drabek(FC)	1.25	.90	.50
37	Mike Easler	.12	.09	.05
38	Mark Eichhorn(FC)	.20	.15	.08
39	Dave Engle	.08	.06	.03
40	Mike Fischlin	.08	.06	.03
41	Scott Fletcher	.15	.11	.06
42	Terry Forster	.12	.09	.05
43	Terry Francona	.08	.06	.03
44	Andres Galarraga	.70	.50	.30
45	Lee Guetterman(FC)	.20	.15	.08
46	Bill Gullickson	.08	.06	.03
47	Jackie Gutierrez	.08	.06	.03
48	Moose Haas	.08	.06	.03
49	Billy Hatcher	.15	.11	.06
50	Mike Heath	.08	.06	.03
51	Guy Hoffman(FC)	.10	.08	.04
52	Tom Hume	.08	.06	.03
53	Pete Incaviglia(FC)	.70	.50	.30
54	Dane Iorg	.08	.06	.03
55	Chris James(FC)	.50	.40	.20
56	Stan Javier(FC)	.25	.20	.10
57	Tommy John	.20	.15	.08
58	Tracy Jones(FC)	.20	.15	.08
59	Wally Joyner(FC)	2.50	2.00	1.00
60	Wayne Krenchicki	.08	.06	.03
61	John Kruk(FC)	.60	.45	.25
62	Mike LaCoss	.08	.06	.03
63	Pete Ladd	.08	.06	.03
64	Dave LaPoint	.15	.11	.06
65	Mike LaValliere(FC)	.40	.30	.15
66	Rudy Law	.08	.06	.03
67	Dennis Leonard	.10	.08	.04
68	Steve Lombardozzi(FC)	.20	.15	.08
69	Aurelio Lopez	.08	.06	.03
70	Mickey Mahler	.08	.06	.03
71	Candy Maldonado	.15	.11	.06
72	Roger Mason(FC)	.10	.08	.04
73	Greg Mathews(FC)	.25	.20	.10
74	Andy McGaffigan	.08	.06	.03
75	Joel McKeon(FC)	.12	.09	.05
76	Kevin Mitchell(FC)	6.00	4.50	2.50
77	Bill Mooneyham(FC)	.12	.09	.05
78	Omar Moreno	.08	.06	.03
79	Jerry Mumphrey	.08	.06	.03
80	Al Newman(FC)	.12	.09	.05
81	Phil Niekro	.40	.30	.15
82	Randy Niemann	.08	.06	.03
83	Juan Nieves(FC)	.20	.15	.08
84	Bob Ojeda	.12	.09	.05
85	Rick Ownbey	.08	.06	.03
86	Tom Paciorek	.08	.06	.03
87	David Palmer	.08	.06	.03
88	Jeff Parrett(FC)	.25	.20	.10
89	Pat Perry(FC)	.15	.11	.06
90	Dan Plesac(FC)	.25	.20	.10
91	Darrell Porter	.12	.09	.05
92	Luis Quinones(FC)	.12	.09	.05
93	Rey Quinonez(FC)	.20	.15	.08
94	Gary Redus	.10	.08	.04
95	Jeff Reed(FC)	.12	.09	.05
96	Bip Roberts(FC)	.08	.06	.03
97	Billy Joe Robidoux	.12	.09	.05
98	Gary Roenicke	.08	.06	.03
99	Ron Roenicke	.08	.06	.03
100	Angel Salazar	.08	.06	.03
101	Joe Sambito	.08	.06	.03
102	Billy Sample	.08	.06	.03
103	Dave Schmidt	.08	.06	.03
104	Ken Schrom	.08	.06	.03
105	Ruben Sierra(FC)	9.00	6.75	3.50
106	Ted Simmons	.20	.15	.08
107	Sammy Stewart	.08	.06	.03
108	Kurt Stillwell(FC)	.30	.25	.12
109	Dale Sveum(FC)	.25	.20	.10
110	Tim Teufel	.08	.06	.03
111	Bob Tewksbury(FC)	.12	.09	.05
112	Andres Thomas(FC)	.15	.11	.06
113	Jason Thompson	.08	.06	.03
114	Milt Thompson	.12	.09	.05
115	Rob Thompson(FC)	.40	.30	.15
116	Jay Tibbs	.08	.06	.03
117	Fred Toliver	.12	.09	.05
118	Wayne Tolleson	.08	.06	.03
119	Alex Trevino	.08	.06	.03
120	Manny Trillo	.10	.08	.04
121	Ed Vande Berg	.08	.06	.03
122	Ozzie Virgil	.08	.06	.03
123	Tony Walker(FC)	.08	.06	.03
124	Gene Walter	.12	.09	.05
125	Duane Ward(FC)	.30	.25	.12
126	Jerry Willard	.08	.06	.03
127	Mitch Williams(FC)	.40	.30	.15
128	Reggie Williams(FC)	.20	.15	.08
129	Bobby Witt(FC)	.70	.50	.30
130	Marvell Wynne	.08	.06	.03
131	Steve Yeager	.08	.06	.03
132	Checklist	.08	.06	.03

1987 Fleer

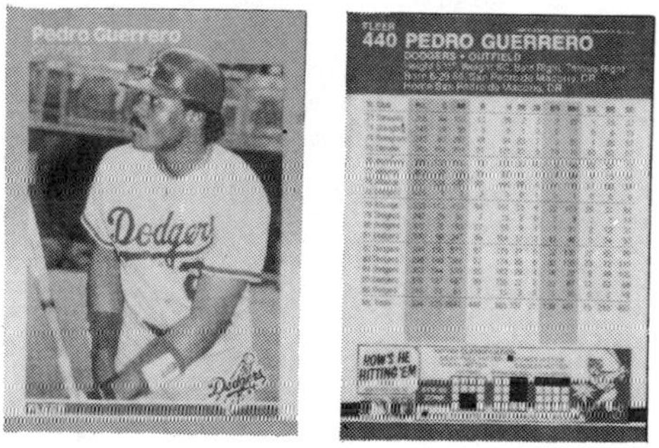

The 1987 Fleer set consists of 660 cards, each measuring 2-1/2" by 3-1/2". The card fronts feature an attractive blue and white border. The player's name and position appears in the upper left corner of the card. The player's team logo is located in the lower right corner. The card backs are done in blue, red and white and contain an innovative "Pro Scouts Report" feature which lists the hitter's or pitcher's batting and pitching strengths. For the third year in a row, Fleer included its "Major League Prospects" subset. Fleer produced a glossy-finish Collectors Edition set which came housed in a specially-designed tin box. It was speculated that 100,000 of the glossy sets were produced. After experiencing a dramatic drop in price during 1987, the glossy set now sells for only a few dollars more than the regular issue.

		MT	NR MT	EX
Complete Set:		125.00	90.00	50.00
Common Player:		.06	.05	.02
1	Rick Aguilera	.08	.06	.03
2	Richard Anderson	.06	.05	.02
3	Wally Backman	.08	.06	.03
4	Gary Carter	.25	.20	.10
5	Ron Darling	.15	.11	.06
6	Len Dykstra	.70	.50	.30
7	*Kevin Elster*(FC)	.50	.40	.20
8	Sid Fernandez	.12	.09	.05
9	Dwight Gooden	1.00	.70	.40
10	*Ed Hearn*(FC)	.10	.08	.04
11	Danny Heep	.06	.05	.02

		MT	NR MT	EX
12	Keith Hernandez	.25	.20	.10
13	Howard Johnson	.10	.08	.04
14	Ray Knight	.08	.06	.03
15	Lee Mazzilli	.08	.06	.03
16	Roger McDowell	.12	.09	.05
17	*Kevin Mitchell*	12.00	9.00	4.75
18	Randy Niemann	.06	.05	.02
19	Bob Ojeda	.08	.06	.03
20	Jesse Orosco	.08	.06	.03
21	Rafael Santana	.06	.05	.02
22	Doug Sisk	.06	.05	.02
23	Darryl Strawberry	2.00	1.50	.80
24	Tim Teufel	.06	.05	.02
25	Mookie Wilson	.10	.08	.04
26	Tony Armas	.08	.06	.03
27	Marty Barrett	.10	.08	.04
28	Don Baylor	.12	.09	.05
29	Wade Boggs	1.50	1.25	.60
30	Oil Can Boyd	.08	.06	.03
31	Bill Buckner	.10	.08	.04
32	Roger Clemens	3.00	2.25	1.25
33	Steve Crawford	.06	.05	.02
34	Dwight Evans	.12	.09	.05
35	Rich Gedman	.10	.08	.04
36	Dave Henderson	.10	.08	.04
37	Bruce Hurst	.10	.08	.04
38	Tim Lollar	.06	.05	.02
39	Al Nipper	.06	.05	.02
40	Spike Owen	.06	.05	.02
41	Jim Rice	.20	.15	.08
42	Ed Romero	.06	.05	.02
43	Joe Sambito	.06	.05	.02
44	Calvin Schiraldi	.10	.08	.04
45	Tom Seaver	.40	.30	.15
46	*Jeff Sellers*(FC)	.20	.15	.08
47	Bob Stanley	.06	.05	.02
48	Sammy Stewart	.06	.05	.02
49	Larry Andersen	.06	.05	.02
50	Alan Ashby	.06	.05	.02
51	Kevin Bass	.10	.08	.04
52	Jeff Calhoun	.06	.05	.02
53	Jose Cruz	.10	.08	.04
54	Danny Darwin	.06	.05	.02
55	Glenn Davis	.40	.30	.15
56	*Jim Deshaies*	.25	.20	.10
57	Bill Doran	.10	.08	.04
58	Phil Garner	.06	.05	.02
59	Billy Hatcher	.08	.06	.03
60	Charlie Kerfeld	.06	.05	.02
61	Bob Knepper	.08	.06	.03
62	Dave Lopes	.08	.06	.03
63	Aurelio Lopez	.06	.05	.02
64	Jim Pankovits	.06	.05	.02
65	Terry Puhl	.06	.05	.02
66	Craig Reynolds	.06	.05	.02
67	Nolan Ryan	3.00	2.25	1.25
68	Mike Scott	.15	.11	.06
69	Dave Smith	.08	.06	.03
70	Dickie Thon	.08	.06	.03
71	Tony Walker	.06	.05	.02
72	Denny Walling	.06	.05	.02
73	Bob Boone	.08	.06	.03
74	Rick Burleson	.08	.06	.03
75	John Candelaria	.10	.08	.04
76	Doug Corbett	.06	.05	.02
77	Doug DeCinces	.08	.06	.03
78	Brian Downing	.08	.06	.03
79	*Chuck Finley*(FC)	3.50	2.75	1.50
80	Terry Forster	.08	.06	.03
81	Bobby Grich	.10	.08	.04
82	George Hendrick	.08	.06	.03
83	Jack Howell(FC)	.10	.08	.04
84	Reggie Jackson	.35	.25	.14
85	Ruppert Jones	.06	.05	.02
86	*Wally Joyner*	4.00	3.00	1.50
87	Gary Lucas	.06	.05	.02
88	Kirk McCaskill	.08	.06	.03
89	Donnie Moore	.06	.05	.02
90	Gary Pettis	.06	.05	.02
91	Vern Ruhle	.06	.05	.02
92	Dick Schofield	.06	.05	.02
93	Don Sutton	.20	.15	.08
94	Rob Wilfong	.06	.05	.02
95	Mike Witt	.10	.08	.04
96	*Doug Drabek*	3.00	2.25	1.25
97	Mike Easler	.08	.06	.03
98	Mike Fischlin	.06	.05	.02
99	Brian Fisher	.08	.06	.03
100	Ron Guidry	.15	.11	.06
101	Rickey Henderson	2.00	1.50	.80
102	Tommy John	.20	.15	.08
103	Ron Kittle	.10	.08	.04

		MT	NR MT	EX
104	Don Mattingly	3.00	2.25	1.25
105	Bobby Meacham	.06	.05	.02
106	Joe Niekro	.10	.08	.04
107	Mike Pagliarulo	.10	.08	.04
108	Dan Pasqua	.10	.08	.04
109	Willie Randolph	.10	.08	.04
110	Dennis Rasmussen	.10	.08	.04
111	Dave Righetti	.15	.11	.06
112	Gary Roenicke	.06	.05	.02
113	Rod Scurry	.06	.05	.02
114	Bob Shirley	.06	.05	.02
115	Joel Skinner	.06	.05	.02
116	Tim Stoddard	.06	.05	.02
117	*Bob Tewksbury*	.12	.09	.05
118	Wayne Tolleson	.06	.05	.02
119	Claudell Washington	.08	.06	.03
120	Dave Winfield	.30	.25	.12
121	Steve Buechele	.08	.06	.03
122	*Ed Correa*	.15	.11	.06
123	Scott Fletcher	.08	.06	.03
124	Jose Guzman	.10	.08	.04
125	Toby Harrah	.08	.06	.03
126	Greg Harris	.06	.05	.02
127	Charlie Hough	.08	.06	.03
128	*Pete Incaviglia*	.60	.45	.25
129	Mike Mason	.06	.05	.02
130	Oddibe McDowell	.10	.08	.04
131	*Dale Mohorcic*(FC)	.20	.15	.08
132	Pete O'Brien	.10	.08	.04
133	Tom Paciorek	.06	.05	.02
134	Larry Parrish	.08	.06	.03
135	Geno Petralli	.06	.05	.02
136	Darrell Porter	.08	.06	.03
137	Jeff Russell	.06	.05	.02
138	*Ruben Sierra*	13.00	9.75	5.25
139	Don Slaught	.06	.05	.02
140	Gary Ward	.08	.06	.03
141	Curtis Wilkerson	.06	.05	.02
142	*Mitch Williams*	.60	.45	.25
143	*Bobby Witt*	1.50	1.25	.60
144	Dave Bergman	.06	.05	.02
145	Tom Brookens	.06	.05	.02
146	Bill Campbell	.06	.05	.02
147	*Chuck Cary*	.10	.08	.04
148	Darnell Coles	.08	.06	.03
149	Dave Collins	.08	.06	.03
150	Darrell Evans	.12	.09	.05
151	Kirk Gibson	.25	.20	.10
152	John Grubb	.06	.05	.02
153	Willie Hernandez	.08	.06	.03
154	Larry Herndon	.08	.06	.03
155	*Eric King*	.25	.20	.10
156	Chet Lemon	.08	.06	.03
157	Dwight Lowry	.06	.05	.02
158	Jack Morris	.20	.15	.08
159	Randy O'Neal	.06	.05	.02
160	Lance Parrish	.20	.15	.08
161	Dan Petry	.08	.06	.03
162	Pat Sheridan	.06	.05	.02
163	Jim Slaton	.06	.05	.02
164	Frank Tanana	.08	.06	.03
165	Walt Terrell	.08	.06	.03
166	Mark Thurmond	.06	.05	.02
167	Alan Trammell	.25	.20	.10
168	Lou Whitaker	.25	.20	.10
169	Luis Aguayo	.06	.05	.02
170	Steve Bedrosian	.12	.09	.05
171	Don Carman	.10	.08	.04
172	Darren Daulton	.06	.05	.02
173	Greg Gross	.06	.05	.02
174	Kevin Gross	.08	.06	.03
175	Von Hayes	.10	.08	.04
176	Charles Hudson	.06	.05	.02
177	Tom Hume	.06	.05	.02
178	Steve Jeltz	.06	.05	.02
179	*Mike Maddux*(FC)	.20	.15	.08
180	Shane Rawley	.08	.06	.03
181	Gary Redus	.06	.05	.02
182	Ron Roenicke	.06	.05	.02
183	*Bruce Ruffin*(FC)	.20	.15	.08
184	John Russell	.06	.05	.02
185	Juan Samuel	.12	.09	.05
186	Dan Schatzeder	.06	.05	.02
187	Mike Schmidt	1.50	1.25	.60
188	Rick Schu	.06	.05	.02
189	Jeff Stone	.06	.05	.02
190	Kent Tekulve	.08	.06	.03
191	Milt Thompson	.08	.06	.03
192	Glenn Wilson	.08	.06	.03
193	Buddy Bell	.10	.08	.04
194	Tom Browning	.10	.08	.04

		MT	NR MT	EX
195	Sal Butera	.06	.05	.02
196	Dave Concepcion	.12	.09	.05
197	Kal Daniels	.80	.60	.30
198	Eric Davis	1.50	1.25	.60
199	John Denny	.06	.05	.02
200	Bo Diaz	.08	.06	.03
201	Nick Esasky	.08	.06	.03
202	John Franco	.10	.08	.04
203	Bill Gullickson	.06	.05	.02
204	*Barry Larkin*(FC)	7.00	5.25	2.75
205	Eddie Milner	.06	.05	.02
206	*Rob Murphy*(FC)	.20	.15	.08
207	Ron Oester	.06	.05	.02
208	Dave Parker	.20	.15	.08
209	Tony Perez	.15	.11	.06
210	Ted Power	.06	.05	.02
211	Joe Price	.06	.05	.02
212	Ron Robinson	.06	.05	.02
213	Pete Rose	.60	.45	.25
214	Mario Soto	.08	.06	.03
215	*Kurt Stillwell*	.60	.45	.25
216	Max Venable	.06	.05	.02
217	Chris Welsh	.06	.05	.02
218	*Carl Willis*(FC)	.10	.08	.04
219	Jesse Barfield	.15	.11	.06
220	George Bell	.25	.20	.10
221	Bill Caudill	.06	.05	.02
222	*John Cerutti*	.20	.15	.08
223	Jim Clancy	.08	.06	.03
224	*Mark Eichhorn*	.15	.11	.06
225	Tony Fernandez	.12	.09	.05
226	Damaso Garcia	.06	.05	.02
227	Kelly Gruber	1.00	.70	.40
228	Tom Henke	.08	.06	.03
229	Garth Iorg	.06	.05	.02
230	Cliff Johnson	.06	.05	.02
231	Joe Johnson	.06	.05	.02
232	Jimmy Key	.12	.09	.05
233	Dennis Lamp	.06	.05	.02
234	Rick Leach	.06	.05	.02
235	Buck Martinez	.06	.05	.02
236	Lloyd Moseby	.10	.08	.04
237	Rance Mulliniks	.06	.05	.02
238	Dave Stieb	.12	.09	.05
239	Willie Upshaw	.08	.06	.03
240	Ernie Whitt	.08	.06	.03
241	*Andy Allanson*	.15	.11	.06
242	*Scott Bailes*	.20	.15	.08
243	Chris Bando	.06	.05	.02
244	Tony Bernazard	.06	.05	.02
245	John Butcher	.06	.05	.02
246	Brett Butler	.08	.06	.03
247	Ernie Camacho	.06	.05	.02
248	Tom Candiotti	.06	.05	.02
249	Joe Carter	.50	.40	.20
250	Carmen Castillo	.06	.05	.02
251	Julio Franco	.10	.08	.04
252	Mel Hall	.08	.06	.03
253	Brook Jacoby	.10	.08	.04
254	Phil Niekro	.20	.15	.08
255	Otis Nixon	.06	.05	.02
256	Dickie Noles	.06	.05	.02
257	Bryan Oelkers	.06	.05	.02
258	Ken Schrom	.06	.05	.02
259	Don Schulze	.06	.05	.02
260	Cory Snyder	.50	.40	.20
261	Pat Tabler	.08	.06	.03
262	Andre Thornton	.08	.06	.03
263	*Rich Yett*(FC)	.12	.09	.05
264	*Mike Aldrete*	.25	.20	.10
265	Juan Berenguer	.06	.05	.02
266	Vida Blue	.10	.08	.04
267	Bob Brenly	.06	.05	.02
268	Chris Brown	.08	.06	.03
269	*Will Clark*	30.00	22.00	12.00
270	Chili Davis	.08	.06	.03
271	Mark Davis	.06	.05	.02
272	*Kelly Downs*(FC)	.30	.25	.12
273	Scott Garrelts	.06	.05	.02
274	Dan Gladden	.06	.05	.02
275	Mike Krukow	.08	.06	.03
276	*Randy Kutcher*(FC)	.10	.08	.04
277	Mike LaCoss	.06	.05	.02
278	Jeff Leonard	.08	.06	.03
279	Candy Maldonado	.08	.06	.03
280	Roger Mason	.06	.05	.02
281	Bob Melvin(FC)	.08	.06	.03
282	Greg Minton	.06	.05	.02
283	Jeff Robinson	.08	.06	.03
284	Harry Spilman	.06	.05	.02
285	*Rob Thompson*	.35	.25	.14

		MT	NR MT	EX
286	Jose Uribe	.08	.06	.03
287	Frank Williams	.06	.05	.02
288	Joel Youngblood	.06	.05	.02
289	Jack Clark	.15	.11	.06
290	Vince Coleman	.70	.50	.30
291	Tim Conroy	.06	.05	.02
292	Danny Cox	.08	.06	.03
293	Ken Dayley	.06	.05	.02
294	Curt Ford	.06	.05	.02
295	Bob Forsch	.08	.06	.03
296	Tom Herr	.10	.08	.04
297	Ricky Horton	.08	.06	.03
298	Clint Hurdle	.06	.05	.02
299	Jeff Lahti	.06	.05	.02
300	Steve Lake	.06	.05	.02
301	Tito Landrum	.06	.05	.02
302	*Mike LaValliere*	.25	.20	.10
303	*Greg Mathews*(FC)	.20	.15	.08
304	Willie McGee	.12	.09	.05
305	Jose Oquendo	.06	.05	.02
306	Terry Pendleton	.10	.08	.04
307	Pat Perry	.08	.06	.03
308	Ozzie Smith	.15	.11	.06
309	Ray Soff	.06	.05	.02
310	John Tudor	.10	.08	.04
311	Andy Van Slyke	.12	.09	.05
312	Todd Worrell	.20	.15	.08
313	Dann Bilardello	.06	.05	.02
314	Hubie Brooks	.10	.08	.04
315	Tim Burke	.06	.05	.02
316	Andre Dawson	.20	.15	.08
317	Mike Fitzgerald	.06	.05	.02
318	Tom Foley	.06	.05	.02
319	Andres Galarraga	.40	.30	.15
320	Joe Hesketh	.06	.05	.02
321	Wallace Johnson	.06	.05	.02
322	Wayne Krenchicki	.06	.05	.02
323	Vance Law	.08	.06	.03
324	Dennis Martinez	.08	.06	.03
325	Bob McClure	.06	.05	.02
326	Andy McGaffigan	.06	.05	.02
327	*Al Newman*	.08	.06	.03
328	Tim Raines	.30	.25	.12
329	Jeff Reardon	.10	.08	.04
330	*Luis Rivera*(FC)	.10	.08	.04
331	*Bob Sebra*(FC)	.10	.08	.04
332	Bryn Smith	.06	.05	.02
333	Jay Tibbs	.06	.05	.02
334	Tim Wallach	.12	.09	.05
335	Mitch Webster	.08	.06	.03
336	Jim Wohlford	.06	.05	.02
337	Floyd Youmans	.08	.06	.03
338	*Chris Bosio*(FC)	.40	.30	.15
339	*Glenn Braggs*(FC)	.40	.30	.15
340	Rick Cerone	.06	.05	.02
341	Mark Clear	.06	.05	.02
342	*Bryan Clutterbuck*(FC)	.10	.08	.04
343	Cecil Cooper	.12	.09	.05
344	Rob Deer	.10	.08	.04
345	Jim Gantner	.08	.06	.03
346	Ted Higuera	.20	.15	.08
347	John Henry Johnson	.06	.05	.02
348	Tim Leary(FC)	.30	.25	.12
349	Rick Manning	.06	.05	.02
350	Paul Molitor	.15	.11	.06
351	Charlie Moore	.06	.05	.02
352	Juan Nieves	.10	.08	.04
353	Ben Oglivie	.08	.06	.03
354	*Dan Plesac*	.35	.25	.14
355	Ernest Riles	.06	.05	.02
356	Billy Joe Robidoux	.06	.05	.02
357	Bill Schroeder	.06	.05	.02
358	*Dale Sveum*	.20	.15	.08
359	Gorman Thomas	.10	.08	.04
360	Bill Wegman(FC)	.10	.08	.04
361	Robin Yount	.50	.40	.20
362	Steve Balboni	.08	.06	.03
363	*Scott Bankhead*	.30	.25	.12
364	Buddy Biancalana	.06	.05	.02
365	Bud Black	.06	.05	.02
366	George Brett	.50	.40	.20
367	Steve Farr	.06	.05	.02
368	Mark Gubicza	.12	.09	.05
369	*Bo Jackson*	20.00	15.00	8.00
370	Danny Jackson	.15	.11	.06
371	*Mike Kingery*	.15	.11	.06
372	Rudy Law	.06	.05	.02
373	Charlie Leibrandt	.08	.06	.03
374	Dennis Leonard	.08	.06	.03
375	Hal McRae	.10	.08	.04
376	Jorge Orta	.06	.05	.02

		MT	NR MT	EX
377	Jamie Quirk	.06	.05	.02
378	Dan Quisenberry	.08	.06	.03
379	Bret Saberhagen	.30	.25	.12
380	Angel Salazar	.06	.05	.02
381	Lonnie Smith	.08	.06	.03
382	Jim Sundberg	.08	.06	.03
383	Frank White	.10	.08	.04
384	Willie Wilson	.12	.09	.05
385	Joaquin Andujar	.08	.06	.03
386	Doug Bair	.06	.05	.02
387	Dusty Baker	.08	.06	.03
388	Bruce Bochte	.06	.05	.02
389	Jose Canseco	12.00	9.00	4.75
390	Chris Codiroli	.06	.05	.02
391	Mike Davis	.08	.06	.03
392	Alfredo Griffin	.08	.06	.03
393	Moose Haas	.06	.05	.02
394	Donnie Hill	.06	.05	.02
395	Jay Howell	.08	.06	.03
396	Dave Kingman	.12	.09	.05
397	Carney Lansford	.10	.08	.04
398	*David Leiper*(FC)	.12	.09	.05
399	*Bill Mooneyham*	.10	.08	.04
400	Dwayne Murphy	.08	.06	.03
401	Steve Ontiveros	.06	.05	.02
402	Tony Phillips	.06	.05	.02
403	Eric Plunk	.08	.06	.03
404	Jose Rijo	.08	.06	.03
405	*Terry Steinbach*(FC)	.90	.70	.35
406	Dave Stewart	.12	.09	.05
407	Mickey Tettleton	.06	.05	.02
408	Dave Von Ohlen	.06	.05	.02
409	Jerry Willard	.06	.05	.02
410	Curt Young	.08	.06	.03
411	Bruce Bochy	.06	.05	.02
412	Dave Dravecky	.08	.06	.03
413	Tim Flannery	.06	.05	.02
414	Steve Garvey	.25	.20	.10
415	Goose Gossage	.15	.11	.06
416	Tony Gwynn	1.00	.70	.40
417	Andy Hawkins	.06	.05	.02
418	LaMarr Hoyt	.06	.05	.02
419	Terry Kennedy	.08	.06	.03
420	*John Kruk*	.70	.50	.30
421	Dave LaPoint	.08	.06	.03
422	Craig Lefferts	.06	.05	.02
423	Carmelo Martinez	.08	.06	.03
424	Lance McCullers	.08	.06	.03
425	Kevin McReynolds	.15	.11	.06
426	Graig Nettles	.12	.09	.05
427	*Bip Roberts*	.80	.60	.30
428	Jerry Royster	.06	.05	.02
429	Benito Santiago	.70	.50	.30
430	Eric Show	.08	.06	.03
431	Bob Stoddard	.06	.05	.02
432	Garry Templeton	.08	.06	.03
433	Gene Walter	.06	.05	.02
434	Ed Whitson	.06	.05	.02
435	Marvell Wynne	.06	.05	.02
436	Dave Anderson	.06	.05	.02
437	Greg Brock	.08	.06	.03
438	Enos Cabell	.06	.05	.02
439	Mariano Duncan	.06	.05	.02
440	Pedro Guerrero	.15	.11	.06
441	Orel Hershiser	.40	.30	.15
442	Rick Honeycutt	.06	.05	.02
443	Ken Howell	.06	.05	.02
444	Ken Landreaux	.06	.05	.02
445	Bill Madlock	.12	.09	.05
446	Mike Marshall	.12	.09	.05
447	Len Matuszek	.06	.05	.02
448	Tom Niedenfuer	.08	.06	.03
449	Alejandro Pena	.08	.06	.03
450	Dennis Powell(FC)	.08	.06	.03
451	Jerry Reuss	.08	.06	.03
452	Bill Russell	.08	.06	.03
453	Steve Sax	.15	.11	.06
454	Mike Scioscia	.08	.06	.03
455	Franklin Stubbs	.08	.06	.03
456	Alex Trevino	.06	.05	.02
457	Fernando Valenzuela	.25	.20	.10
458	Ed Vande Berg	.06	.05	.02
459	Bob Welch	.10	.08	.04
460	*Reggie Williams*	.10	.08	.04
461	Don Aase	.06	.05	.02
462	Juan Beniquez	.06	.05	.02
463	Mike Boddicker	.08	.06	.03
464	Juan Bonilla	.06	.05	.02
465	Rich Bordi	.06	.05	.02
466	Storm Davis	.10	.08	.04
467	Rick Dempsey	.08	.06	.03

		MT	NR MT	EX
468	Ken Dixon	.06	.05	.02
469	Jim Dwyer	.06	.05	.02
470	Mike Flanagan	.08	.06	.03
471	Jackie Gutierrez	.06	.05	.02
472	Brad Havens	.06	.05	.02
473	Lee Lacy	.06	.05	.02
474	Fred Lynn	.15	.11	.06
475	Scott McGregor	.08	.06	.03
476	Eddie Murray	.35	.25	.14
477	Tom O'Malley	.06	.05	.02
478	Cal Ripken, Jr.	.70	.50	.30
479	Larry Sheets	.08	.06	.03
480	John Shelby	.06	.05	.02
481	Nate Snell	.06	.05	.02
482	Jim Traber(FC)	.10	.08	.04
483	Mike Young	.06	.05	.02
484	Neil Allen	.06	.05	.02
485	Harold Baines	.15	.11	.06
486	Floyd Bannister	.10	.08	.04
487	Daryl Boston	.08	.06	.03
488	Ivan Calderon	.50	.40	.20
489	*John Cangelosi*	.12	.09	.05
490	Steve Carlton	.25	.20	.10
491	Joe Cowley	.06	.05	.02
492	Julio Cruz	.06	.05	.02
493	Bill Dawley	.06	.05	.02
494	Jose DeLeon	.08	.06	.03
495	Richard Dotson	.08	.06	.03
496	Carlton Fisk	.30	.25	.12
497	Ozzie Guillen	.10	.08	.04
498	Jerry Hairston	.06	.05	.02
499	Ron Hassey	.06	.05	.02
500	Tim Hulett	.06	.05	.02
501	Bob James	.06	.05	.02
502	Steve Lyons	.06	.05	.02
503	*Joel McKeon*	.10	.08	.04
504	Gene Nelson	.06	.05	.02
505	Dave Schmidt	.06	.05	.02
506	Ray Searage	.06	.05	.02
507	*Bobby Thigpen*(FC)	2.75	2.00	1.00
508	Greg Walker	.10	.08	.04
509	Jim Acker	.06	.05	.02
510	Doyle Alexander	.08	.06	.03
511	*Paul Assenmacher*	.15	.11	.06
512	Bruce Benedict	.06	.05	.02
513	Chris Chambliss	.08	.06	.03
514	Jeff Dedmon	.06	.05	.02
515	Gene Garber	.06	.05	.02
516	Ken Griffey	.10	.08	.04
517	Terry Harper	.06	.05	.02
518	Bob Horner	.10	.08	.04
519	Glenn Hubbard	.06	.05	.02
520	Rick Mahler	.06	.05	.02
521	Omar Moreno	.06	.05	.02
522	Dale Murphy	.40	.30	.15
523	Ken Oberkfell	.06	.05	.02
524	Ed Olwine	.06	.05	.02
525	David Palmer	.06	.05	.02
526	Rafael Ramirez	.06	.05	.02
527	Billy Sample	.06	.05	.02
528	Ted Simmons	.12	.09	.05
529	Zane Smith	.08	.06	.03
530	Bruce Sutter	.12	.09	.05
531	*Andres Thomas*	.15	.11	.06
532	Ozzie Virgil	.06	.05	.02
533	*Allan Anderson*(FC)	.25	.20	.10
534	Keith Atherton	.06	.05	.02
535	Billy Beane	.06	.05	.02
536	Bert Blyleven	.12	.09	.05
537	Tom Brunansky	.10	.08	.04
538	Randy Bush	.06	.05	.02
539	George Frazier	.06	.05	.02
540	Gary Gaetti	.15	.11	.06
541	Greg Gagne	.06	.05	.02
542	Mickey Hatcher	.06	.05	.02
543	Neal Heaton	.06	.05	.02
544	Kent Hrbek	.15	.11	.06
545	Roy Lee Jackson	.06	.05	.02
546	Tim Laudner	.06	.05	.02
547	Steve Lombardozzi	.10	.08	.04
548	*Mark Portugal*(FC)	.10	.08	.04
549	Kirby Puckett	2.25	1.75	.90
550	Jeff Reed	.08	.06	.03
551	Mark Salas	.06	.05	.02
552	Roy Smalley	.06	.05	.02
553	Mike Smithson	.06	.05	.02
554	Frank Viola	.15	.11	.06
555	Thad Bosley	.06	.05	.02
556	Ron Cey	.10	.08	.04
557	Jody Davis	.08	.06	.03
558	Ron Davis	.06	.05	.02

		MT	NR MT	EX
559	Bob Dernier	.06	.05	.02
560	Frank DiPino	.06	.05	.02
561	Shawon Dunston	.35	.25	.14
562	Leon Durham	.08	.06	.03
563	Dennis Eckersley	.12	.09	.05
564	Terry Francona	.06	.05	.02
565	Dave Gumpert	.06	.05	.02
566	Guy Hoffman	.08	.06	.03
567	Ed Lynch	.06	.05	.02
568	Gary Matthews	.10	.08	.04
569	Keith Moreland	.08	.06	.03
570	*Jamie Moyer*(FC)	.20	.15	.08
571	Jerry Mumphrey	.06	.05	.02
572	Ryne Sandberg	1.50	1.25	.60
573	Scott Sanderson	.06	.05	.02
574	Lee Smith	.10	.08	.04
575	Chris Speier	.06	.05	.02
576	Rick Sutcliffe	.12	.09	.05
577	Manny Trillo	.08	.06	.03
578	Steve Trout	.06	.05	.02
579	Karl Best	.06	.05	.02
580	Scott Bradley(FC)	.08	.06	.03
581	Phil Bradley	.12	.09	.05
582	Mickey Brantley	.08	.06	.03
583	Mike Brown	.06	.05	.02
584	Alvin Davis	.12	.09	.05
585	*Lee Guetterman*(FC)	.15	.11	.06
586	Mark Huismann	.06	.05	.02
587	Bob Kearney	.06	.05	.02
588	Pete Ladd	.06	.05	.02
589	Mark Langston	.12	.09	.05
590	Mike Moore	.06	.05	.02
591	Mike Morgan	.06	.05	.02
592	John Moses	.06	.05	.02
593	Ken Phelps	.08	.06	.03
594	Jim Presley	.10	.08	.04
595	*Rey Quinonez (Quinones)*	.15	.11	.06
596	Harold Reynolds	.15	.11	.06
597	Billy Swift	.06	.05	.02
598	Danny Tartabull	.50	.40	.20
599	Steve Yeager	.06	.05	.02
600	Matt Young	.06	.05	.02
601	Bill Almon	.06	.05	.02
602	*Rafael Belliard*(FC)	.12	.09	.05
603	Mike Bielecki	.06	.05	.02
604	*Barry Bonds*	12.00	9.00	4.75
605	*Bobby Bonilla*	9.00	6.75	3.50
606	Sid Bream	.08	.06	.03
607	Mike Brown	.06	.05	.02
608	Pat Clements	.06	.05	.02
609	*Mike Diaz*(FC)	.15	.11	.06
610	Cecilio Guante	.06	.05	.02
611	*Barry Jones*(FC)	.12	.09	.05
612	Bob Kipper	.06	.05	.02
613	Larry McWilliams	.06	.05	.02
614	Jim Morrison	.06	.05	.02
615	Joe Orsulak	.06	.05	.02
616	Junior Ortiz	.06	.05	.02
617	Tony Pena	.08	.06	.03
618	Johnny Ray	.10	.08	.04
619	Rick Reuschel	.10	.08	.04
620	R.J. Reynolds	.06	.05	.02
621	Rick Rhoden	.10	.08	.04
622	Don Robinson	.08	.06	.03
623	Bob Walk	.06	.05	.02
624	Jim Winn	.06	.05	.02
625	Youthful Power (Jose Canseco, Pete Incaviglia)	.70	.50	.30
626	300 Game Winners (Phil Niekro, Don Sutton)	.12	.09	.05
627	A.L. Firemen (Don Aase, Dave Righetti)	.08	.06	.03
628	Rookie All-Stars (Jose Canseco, Wally Joyner)	1.50	1.25	.60
629	Magic Mets (Gary Carter, Sid Fernandez, Dwight Gooden, Keith Hernandez, Darryl Strawberry)	.60	.45	.25
630	N.L. Best Righties (Mike Krukow, Mike Scott)	.08	.06	.03
631	Sensational Southpaws (John Franco, Fernando Valenzuela)	.10	.08	.04
632	Count 'Em (Bob Horner)	.08	.06	.03
633	A.L. Pitcher's Nightmare (Jose Canseco, Kirby Puckett, Jim Rice)	.70	.50	.30
634	All Star Battery (Gary Carter, Roger Clemens)	.25	.20	.10
635	4,000 Strikeouts (Steve Carlton)	.12	.09	.05
636	Big Bats At First Sack (Glenn Davis, Eddie Murray)	.20	.15	.08
637	On Base (Wade Boggs, Keith Hernandez)	.35	.25	.14
638	Sluggers From Left Side (Don Mattingly, Darryl Strawberry)	.90	.70	.35
639	Former MVP's (Dave Parker, Ryne Sandberg)	.12	.09	.05
640	Dr. K. & Super K (Roger Clemens, Dwight Gooden)	.50	.40	.20
641	A.L. West Stoppers (Charlie Hough, Mike Witt)	.08	.06	.03
642	Doubles & Triples (Tim Raines, Juan Samuel)	.12	.09	.05
643	Outfielders With Punch (Harold Baines, Jesse Barfield)	.10	.08	.04
644	Major League Prospects *(Dave Clark, Greg Swindell)*(FC)	1.50	1.25	.60
645	Major League Prospects *(Ron Karkovice, Russ Morman)*(FC)	.12	.09	.05
646	Major League Prospects *(Willie Fraser, Devon White)*(FC)	1.50	1.25	.60
647	Major League Prospects *(Jerry Browne, Mike Stanley)*(FC)	.40	.30	.15
648	Major League Prospects *(Phil Lombardi, Dave Magadan)*(FC)	4.00	3.00	1.50
649	Major League Prospects *(Ralph Bryant, Jose Gonzalez)*(FC)	.20	.15	.08
650	Major League Prospects *(Randy Asadoor, Jimmy Jones)*(FC)	.20	.15	.08
651	Major League Prospects *(Marvin Freeman, Tracy Jones)*	.25	.20	.10
652	Major League Prospects *(Kevin Seitzer,* John Stefero)(FC)	2.00	1.50	.80
653	Major League Prospects *(Steve Fireovid, Rob Nelson)*(FC)	.10	.08	.04
654	Checklist 1-95	.06	.05	.02
655	Checklist 96-192	.06	.05	.02
656	Checklist 193-288	.06	.05	.02
657	Checklist 289-384	.06	.05	.02
658	Checklist 385-483	.06	.05	.02
659	Checklist 484-578	.06	.05	.02
660	Checklist 579-660	.06	.05	.02

1987 Fleer All Star Team

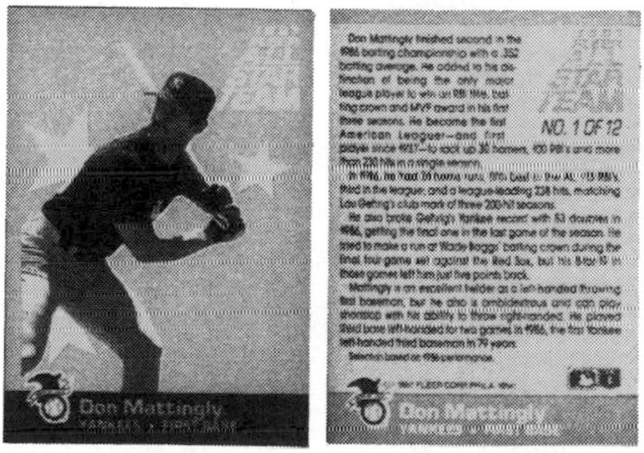

As in 1986, Fleer All Star Team cards were randomly inserted in Fleer wax and cello packs. Twelve cards, each measuring the standard 2-1/2" by 3-1/2", comprise the set. The card fronts feature a full-color player photo set against a gray background for American League players and a black background for National Leaguers. Card backs are printed in black, red and white and feature a lengthy player biography. Fleer's choices for a major league All-Star team is once again the theme for the set.

		MT	NR MT	EX
Complete Set:		18.00	13.50	7.25
Common Player:		.60	.45	.25
1	Don Mattingly	4.00	3.00	1.50
2	Gary Carter	1.00	.70	.40
3	Tony Fernandez	.75	.60	.30
4	Steve Sax	.75	.60	.30
5	Kirby Puckett	3.00	2.25	1.25
6	Mike Schmidt	2.00	1.50	.80
7	Mike Easler	.60	.45	.25
8	Todd Worrell	.75	.60	.30

		MT	NR MT	EX
9	George Bell	1.00	.70	.40
10	Fernando Valenzuela	1.00	.70	.40
11	Roger Clemens	2.25	1.75	.90
12	Tim Raines	1.25	.90	.50

1987 Fleer Baseball's Award Winners

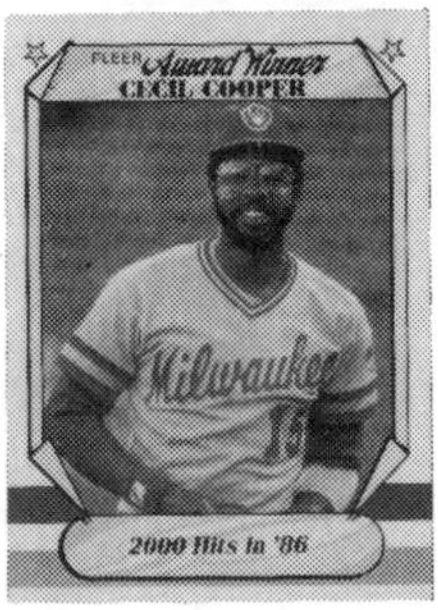

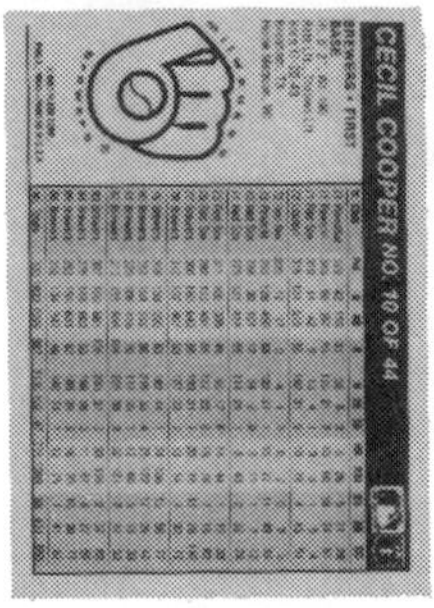

The 1987 Fleer Award Winners boxed set was prepared by Fleer for distribution by 7-Eleven stores. The cards, which measure 2-1/2" by 3-1/2", feature players who have won various major league awards during their careers. The card fronts contain full-color photos surrounded by a yellow border. The name of the award the player won is printed at the bottom of the card in an oval-shaped band designed to resemble a metal nameplate on a trophy. Card backs, printed in black, yellow and white, include lifetime major and minor league statistics along with typical personal information. Each boxed set contained six team logo stickers.

		MT	NR MT	EX
Complete Set:		6.00	4.50	2.50
Common Player:		.05	.04	.02
1	Marty Barrett	.07	.05	.03
2	George Bell	.20	.15	.08
3	Bert Blyleven	.10	.08	.04
4	Bob Boone	.05	.04	.02
5	John Candelaria	.05	.04	.02
6	Jose Canseco	1.00	.70	.40
7	Gary Carter	.25	.20	.10
8	Joe Carter	.25	.20	.10
9	Roger Clemens	.50	.40	.20
10	Cecil Cooper	.10	.08	.04
11	Eric Davis	.60	.45	.25
12	Tony Fernandez	.10	.08	.04
13	Scott Fletcher	.05	.04	.02
14	Bob Forsch	.05	.04	.02
15	Dwight Gooden	.50	.40	.20
16	Ron Guidry	.12	.09	.05
17	Ozzie Guillen	.07	.05	.03
18	Bill Gullickson	.05	.04	.02
19	Tony Gwynn	.25	.20	.10
20	Bob Knepper	.05	.04	.02
21	Ray Knight	.05	.04	.02
22	Mark Langston	.20	.15	.08
23	Candy Maldonado	.05	.04	.02
24	Don Mattingly	1.00	.70	.40
25	Roger McDowell	.07	.05	.03
26	Dale Murphy	.30	.25	.12
27	Dave Parker	.12	.09	.05
28	Lance Parrish	.15	.11	.06
29	Gary Pettis	.05	.04	.02
30	Kirby Puckett	.70	.50	.40
31	Johnny Ray	.07	.05	.03
32	Dave Righetti	.12	.09	.05
33	Cal Ripken, Jr.	.60	.45	.25
34	Bret Saberhagen	.15	.11	.06
35	Ryne Sandberg	.20	.15	.08
36	Mike Schmidt	.30	.25	.12
37	Mike Scott	.12	.09	.05
38	Ozzie Smith	.12	.09	.05
39	Robbie Thompson	.10	.08	.04
40	Fernando Valenzuela	.20	.15	.08

		MT	NR MT	EX
41	Mitch Webster	.05	.04	.02
42	Frank White	.07	.05	.03
43	Mike Witt	.07	.05	.03
44	Todd Worrell	.15	.11	.06

1987 Fleer Baseball All Stars

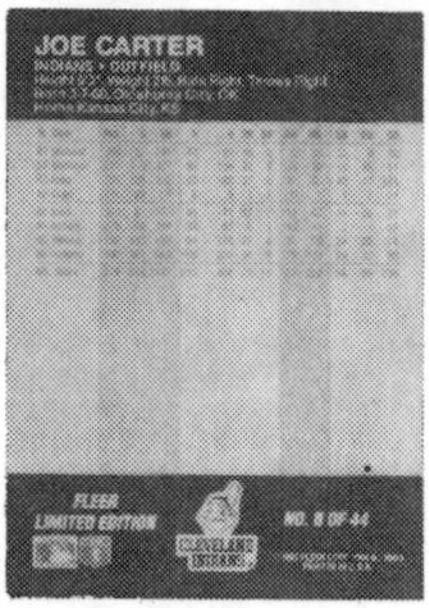

Produced by Fleer for exclusive distribution through Ben Franklin stores, the "Baseball All Stars" set is comprised of 44 cards which are the standard 2-1/2" by 3-1/2" size. The cards have full-color photos surrounded by a bright red border with white pinstripes at the top and bottom. The card backs are printed in blue, white and dark red and include complete major and minor league statistics. The set was issued in a special cardboard box.

		MT	NR MT	EX
Complete Set:		6.00	4.50	2.50
Common Player:		.05	.04	.02
1	Harold Baines	.10	.08	.04
2	Jesse Barfield	.12	.09	.05
3	Wade Boggs	.60	.45	.25
4	Dennis "Oil Can" Boyd	.05	.04	.02
5	Scott Bradley	.05	.04	.02
6	Jose Canseco	1.00	.70	.40
7	Gary Carter	.25	.20	.10
8	Joe Carter	.25	.20	.10
9	Mark Clear	.05	.04	.02
10	Roger Clemens	.50	.40	.20
11	Jose Cruz	.05	.04	.02
12	Chili Davis	.07	.05	.03
13	Jody Davis	.05	.04	.02
14	Rob Deer	.05	.04	.02
15	Brian Downing	.05	.04	.02
16	Sid Fernandez	.07	.05	.03
17	John Franco	.07	.05	.03
18	Andres Galarraga	.15	.11	.06
19	Dwight Gooden	.50	.40	.20
20	Tony Gwynn	.25	.20	.10
21	Charlie Hough	.05	.04	.02
22	Bruce Hurst	.10	.08	.04
23	Wally Joyner	.70	.50	.30
24	Carney Lansford	.05	.04	.02
25	Fred Lynn	.12	.09	.05
26	Don Mattingly	1.50	1.25	.60
27	Willie McGee	.10	.08	.04
28	Jack Morris	.15	.11	.06
29	Dale Murphy	.30	.25	.12
30	Bob Ojeda	.07	.05	.03
31	Tony Pena	.07	.05	.03
32	Kirby Puckett	.70	.50	.30
33	Dan Quisenberry	.07	.05	.03
34	Tim Raines	.25	.20	.10
35	Willie Randolph	.07	.05	.03
36	Cal Ripken, Jr.	.50	.40	.20
37	Pete Rose	.50	.40	.20
38	Nolan Ryan	1.00	.70	.40
39	Juan Samuel	.10	.08	.04
40	Mike Schmidt	.30	.25	.12
41	Ozzie Smith	.12	.09	.05
42	Andres Thomas	.10	.08	.04
43	Fernando Valenzuela	.20	.15	.08
44	Mike Witt	.07	.05	.03

1987 Fleer Baseball's Best

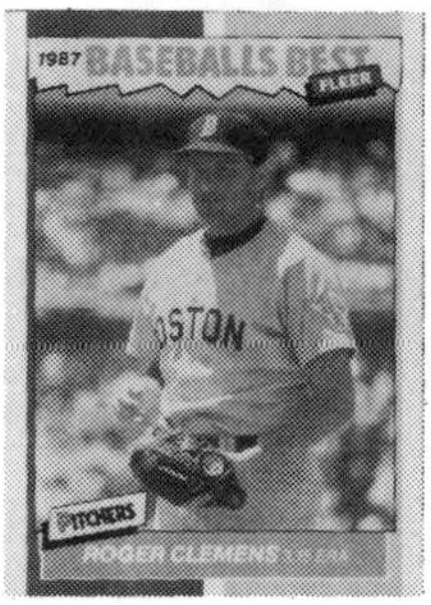

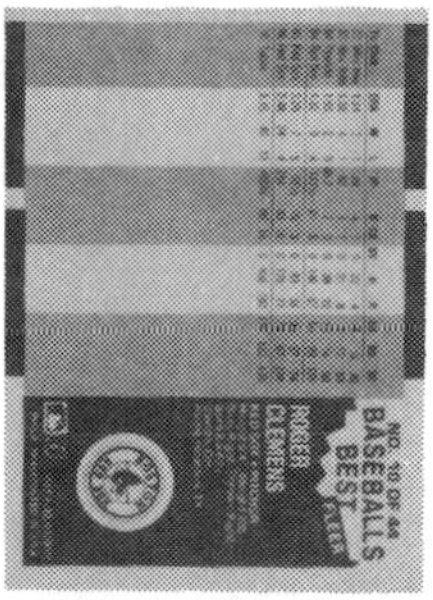

For a second straight baseball card season, Fleer produced for McCrory's stores and their affiliates a 44-card "Baseball's Best" set. Subtitled "Sluggers vs. Pitchers," 28 everyday players and 16 pitchers are featured. The card design is nearly identical to the previous year's effort. The cards, which measure 2-1/2" by 3-1/2", were housed in a specially designed box along with six team logo stickers.

		MT	NR MT	EX
Complete Set:		6.00	4.50	2.50
Common Player:		.05	.04	.02
1	Kevin Bass	.07	.05	.03
2	Jesse Barfield	.12	.09	.05
3	George Bell	.20	.15	.08
4	Wade Boggs	.60	.45	.25
5	Sid Bream	.05	.04	.02
6	George Brett	.30	.25	.12
7	Ivan Calderon	.10	.08	.04
8	Jose Canseco	1.00	.70	.40
9	Jack Clark	.12	.09	.05
10	Roger Clemens	.50	.40	.20
11	Eric Davis	.50	.40	.20
12	Andre Dawson	.15	.11	.06
13	Sid Fernandez	.07	.05	.03
14	John Franco	.07	.05	.03
15	Dwight Gooden	.50	.40	.20
16	Pedro Guerrero	.15	.11	.06
17	Tony Gwynn	.25	.20	.10
18	Rickey Henderson	.30	.25	.12
19	Tom Henke	.05	.04	.02
20	Ted Higuera	.10	.08	.04
21	Pete Incaviglia	.30	.25	.12
22	Wally Joyner	.50	.40	.20
23	Jeff Leonard	.05	.04	.02
24	Joe Magrane	.15	.11	.06
25	Don Mattingly	1.00	.70	.40
26	Mark McGwire	.60	.45	.25
27	Jack Morris	.15	.11	.06
28	Dale Murphy	.30	.25	.12
29	Dave Parker	.12	.09	.05
30	Ken Phelps	.05	.04	.02
31	Kirby Puckett	.70	.50	.30
32	Tim Raines	.25	.20	.10
33	Jeff Reardon	.10	.08	.04
34	Dave Righetti	.12	.09	.05
35	Cal Ripken, Jr.	.60	.45	.25
36	Bret Saberhagen	.15	.11	.06
37	Mike Schmidt	.30	.25	.12
38	Mike Scott	.12	.09	.05
39	Kevin Seitzer	.50	.40	.20
40	Darryl Strawberry	.40	.30	.15
41	Rick Sutcliffe	.10	.08	.04
42	Pat Tabler	.05	.04	.02
43	Fernando Valenzuela	.10	.08	.04
44	Mike Witt	.07	.05	.03

A player's name in italic type indicates a rookie card. An (FC) indicates a player's first card for that particular card company.

1987 Fleer Baseball's Exciting Stars

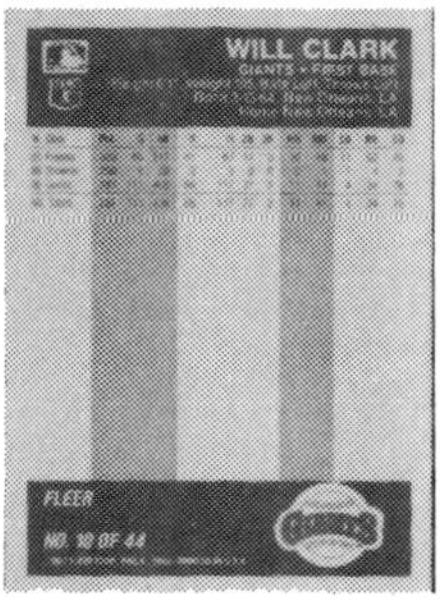

Another entry into the Fleer lineup of individual boxed sets, the "Baseball's Exciting Stars" set was produced by Fleer for Cumberland Farms stores. The card fronts feature a red, white and blue border with the words "Exciting Stars" printed in yellow at the top. The backs are printed in red and blue and carry complete major and minor league statistics. Included with the boxed set of 44 cards were six team logo stickers.

		MT	NR MT	EX
Complete Set:		6.00	4.50	2.50
Common Player:		.05	.04	.02
1	Don Aase	.05	.04	.02
2	Rick Aguilera	.07	.05	.03
3	Jesse Barfield	.12	.09	.05
4	Wade Boggs	.60	.45	.25
5	Dennis "Oil Can" Boyd	.05	.04	.02
6	Sid Bream	.07	.05	.03
7	Jose Canseco	1.00	.70	.40
8	Steve Carlton	.25	.20	.10
9	Gary Carter	.25	.20	.10
10	Will Clark	1.00	.70	.40
11	Roger Clemens	.40	.30	.15
12	Danny Cox	.07	.05	.03
13	Alvin Davis	.10	.08	.04
14	Eric Davis	.50	.40	.20
15	Rob Deer	.07	.05	.03
16	Brian Downing	.05	.04	.02
17	Gene Garber	.05	.04	.02
18	Steve Garvey	.25	.20	.10
19	Dwight Gooden	.50	.40	.20
20	Mark Gubicza	.10	.08	.04
21	Mel Hall	.05	.04	.02
22	Terry Harper	.05	.04	.02
23	Von Hayes	.10	.08	.04
24	Rickey Henderson	.60	.45	.25
25	Tom Henke	.05	.04	.02
26	Willie Hernandez	.05	.04	.02
27	Ted Higuera	.10	.08	.04
28	Rick Honeycutt	.05	.04	.02
29	Kent Hrbek	.15	.11	.06
30	Wally Joyner	.60	.45	.25
31	Charlie Kerfeld	.05	.04	.02
32	Fred Lynn	.12	.09	.05
33	Don Mattingly	1.50	1.25	.60
34	Tim Raines	.25	.20	.10
35	Dennis Rasmussen	.07	.05	.03
36	Johnny Ray	.07	.05	.03
37	Jim Rice	.20	.15	.08
38	Pete Rose	.50	.40	.20
39	Lee Smith	.07	.05	.03
40	Cory Snyder	.25	.20	.10
41	Darryl Strawberry	.40	.30	.15
42	Kent Tekulve	.05	.04	.02
43	Willie Wilson	.10	.08	.04
44	Bobby Witt	.12	.09	.05

1987 Fleer Baseball's Game Winners

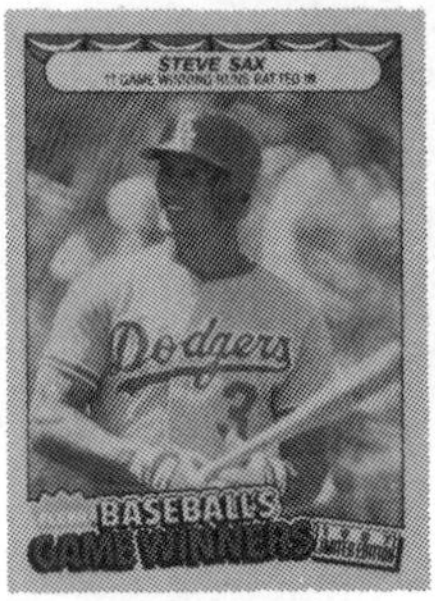

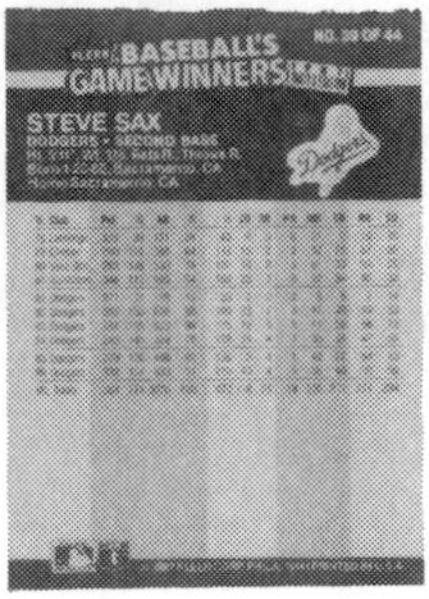

The 1987 Fleer "Baseball's Game Winners" boxed set of 44 cards was produced for distribution through Bi-Mart Discount Drug, Pay'n-Save, Mott's 5 & 10, M.E. Moses, and Winn's stores. The cards, which measure 2-1/2" by 3-1/2", have a light blue border with the player's name and game winning RBI or games won statistics in a yellow oval band at the top of the card. Below the full-color player photo is the name of the set in blue, yellow and red. Included with the boxed set were six team logo stickers.

		MT	NR MT	EX
Complete Set:		6.00	4.50	2.50
Common Player:		.05	.04	.02
1	Harold Baines	.10	.08	.04
2	Don Baylor	.10	.08	.04
3	George Bell	.20	.15	.08
4	Tony Bernazard	.05	.04	.02
5	Wade Boggs	.60	.45	.25
6	George Brett	.40	.30	.15
7	Hubie Brooks	.07	.05	.03
8	Jose Canseco	1.00	.70	.40
9	Gary Carter	.20	.15	.08
10	Roger Clemens	.40	.30	.15
11	Eric Davis	.50	.40	.20
12	Glenn Davis	.15	.11	.06
13	Shawon Dunston	.07	.05	.03
14	Mark Eichhorn	.10	.08	.04
15	Gary Gaetti	.12	.09	.05
16	Steve Garvey	.25	.20	.10
17	Kirk Gibson	.20	.15	.08
18	Dwight Gooden	.50	.40	.20
19	Von Hayes	.07	.05	.03
20	Willie Hernandez	.07	.05	.03
21	Ted Higuera	.10	.08	.04
22	Wally Joyner	.80	.60	.30
23	Bob Knepper	.05	.04	.02
24	Mike Krukow	.05	.04	.02
25	Jeff Leonard	.05	.04	.02
26	Don Mattingly	1.00	.70	.40
27	Kirk McCaskill	.07	.05	.03
28	Kevin McReynolds	.12	.09	.05
29	Jim Morrison	.05	.04	.02
30	Dale Murphy	.30	.25	.12
31	Pete O'Brien	.07	.05	.03
32	Bob Ojeda	.07	.05	.03
33	Larry Parrish	.05	.04	.02
34	Ken Phelps	.05	.04	.02
35	Dennis Rasmussen	.07	.05	.03
36	Ernest Riles	.07	.05	.03
37	Cal Ripken, Jr.	.60	.45	.25
38	Ron Robinson	.05	.04	.02
39	Steve Sax	.15	.11	.06
40	Mike Schmidt	.30	.25	.12
41	John Tudor	.07	.05	.03
42	Fernando Valenzuela	.20	.15	.08
43	Mike Witt	.07	.05	.03
44	Curt Young	.05	.04	.02

Definitions for grading conditions are located in the introduction section at the front of this book.

1987 Fleer Baseball's Hottest Stars

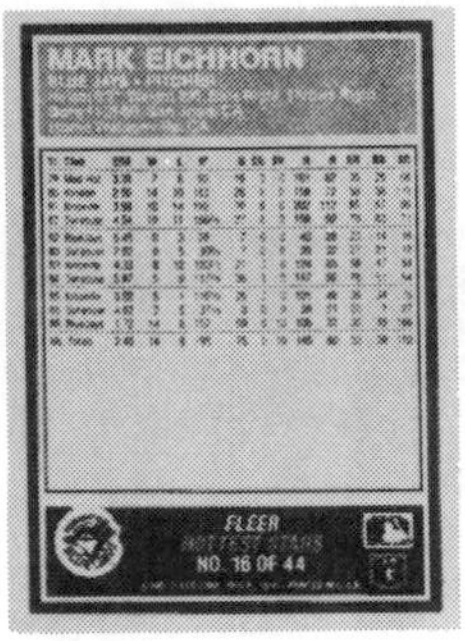

The "Baseball's Hottest Stars" 44-card set was produced by Fleer for the Revco Drug Store chain. Measuring the standard 2-1/2" by 3-1/2", the cards feature full-color photos surrounded by a red, white and blue border. The player's name, position and team appear in a blue band at the bottom of the card. Card backs are printed in red, white and black and contain the player's lifetime professional statistics. The set was housed in a special cardboard box with six team logo stickers.

		MT	NR MT	EX
Complete Set:		6.00	4.50	2.50
Common Player:		.05	.04	.02
1	Joaquin Andujar	.05	.04	.02
2	Harold Baines	.10	.08	.04
3	Kevin Bass	.07	.05	.03
4	Don Baylor	.10	.08	.04
5	Barry Bonds	.20	.15	.08
6	George Brett	.30	.25	.12
7	Tom Brunansky	.10	.08	.04
8	Brett Butler	.05	.04	.02
9	Jose Canseco	1.00	.70	.40
10	Roger Clemens	.50	.40	.20
11	Ron Darling	.10	.08	.04
12	Eric Davis	.50	.40	.20
13	Andre Dawson	.15	.11	.06
14	Doug DeCinces	.05	.04	.02
15	Leon Durham	.07	.05	.03
16	Mark Eichhorn	.10	.08	.04
17	Scott Garrelts	.05	.04	.02
18	Dwight Gooden	.50	.40	.20
19	Dave Henderson	.05	.04	.02
20	Rickey Henderson	.50	.40	.20
21	Keith Hernandez	.15	.11	.06
22	Ted Higuera	.10	.08	.04
23	Bob Horner	.07	.05	.03
24	Pete Incaviglia	.40	.30	.15
25	Wally Joyner	.50	.40	.20
26	Mark Langston	.07	.05	.03
27	Don Mattingly	1.00	.70	.40
28	Dale Murphy	.30	.25	.12
29	Kirk McCaskill	.07	.05	.03
30	Willie McGee	.10	.08	.04
31	Dave Righetti	.12	.09	.05
32	Pete Rose	.40	.30	.15
33	Bruce Ruffin	.15	.11	.06
34	Steve Sax	.15	.11	.06
35	Mike Schmidt	.30	.25	.12
36	Larry Sheets	.10	.08	.04
37	Eric Show	.07	.05	.03
38	Dave Smith	.05	.04	.02
39	Cory Snyder	.07	.05	.03
40	Frank Tanana	.05	.04	.02
41	Alan Trammell	.20	.15	.08
42	Reggie Williams	.07	.05	.03
43	Mookie Wilson	.07	.05	.03
44	Todd Worrell	.15	.11	.06

A player's name in italic indicates a rookie card. An (FC) indicates a player's first card for that particular card company.

1987 Fleer Box Panels

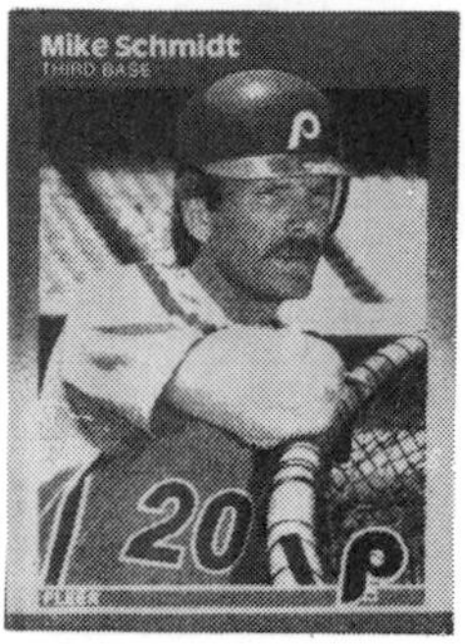

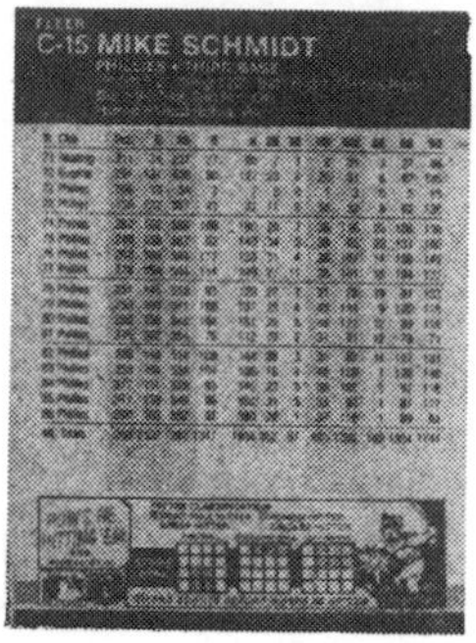

For the second straight year, Fleer produced a special set of cards designed to stimulate sales of their wax and cello pack boxes. In 1987, Fleer issued 16 cards in panels of four on the bottoms of retail boxes. The cards are numbered C-1 through C-16 and are 2-1/2" by 3-1/2" in size. The cards have the same design as the regular issue set with the player photos and card numbers being different.

	MT	NR MT	EX
Complete Panel Set:	8.00	6.00	3.25
Complete Singles Set:	3.50	2.75	1.50
Common Panel:	2.25	1.75	.90
Common Single Player:	.20	.15	.08

		MT	NR MT	EX
	Panel	2.50	2.00	1.00
1	Mets Logo	.05	.04	.02
6	Keith Hernandez	.30	.25	.12
8	Dale Murphy	.60	.45	.25
14	Ryne Sandberg	.30	.25	.12
	Panel	2.25	1.75	.90
2	Jesse Barfield	.20	.15	.08
3	George Brett	.60	.45	.25
5	Red Sox Logo	.05	.04	.02
11	Kirby Puckett	.30	.25	.12
	Panel	2.75	2.00	1.00
4	Dwight Gooden	.80	.60	.30
9	Astros Logo	.05	.04	.02
10	Dave Parker	.25	.20	.10
15	Mike Schmidt	.60	.45	.25
	Panel	2.75	2.00	1.00
7	Wally Joyner	1.00	.70	.40
12	Dave Righetti	.20	.15	.08
13	Angels Logo	.05	.04	.02
16	Robin Yount	.25	.20	.10

1987 Fleer '86 World Series

Fleer issued a set of 12 cards highlighting the 1986 World Series between the Boston Red Sox and New York Mets. The sets were available only with Fleer factory-packaged sets of 660 regular issue cards. The cards, which are the standard 2-1/2" by 3-1/2" size, have either horizontal or vertical formats. The fronts are bordered in red, white and blue stars and stripes with a thin gold frame around the photo. The backs are printed in red and blue ink on white stock and include information regarding the photo on the card fronts.

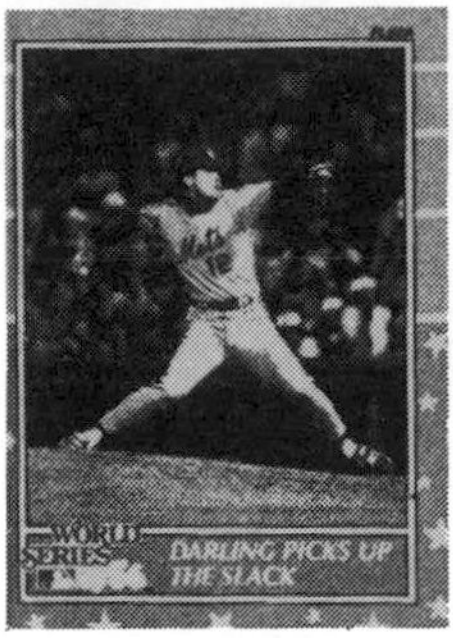

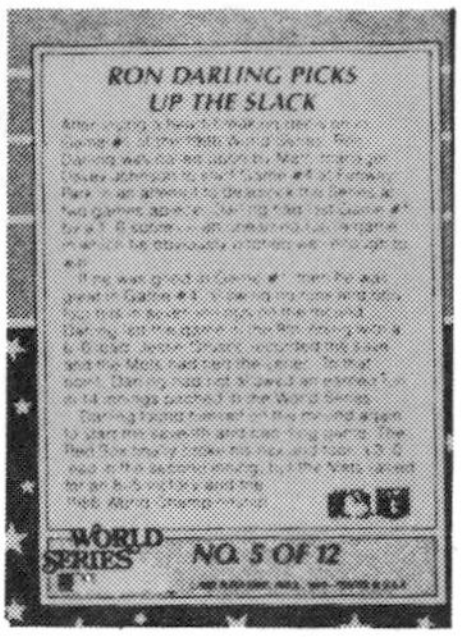

	MT	NR MT	EX
Complete Set:	5.00	3.75	2.00
Common Player:	.50	.40	.20

		MT	NR MT	EX
1	Left-Hand Finesse Beats Mets (Bruce Hurst)	.50	.40	.20
2	Hernandez And Boggs (Wade Boggs, Keith Hernandez)	1.00	.70	.40
3	Roger Clemens	.70	.50	.30
4	Clutch Hitting (Gary Carter)	.50	.40	.20
5	Darling Picks Up The Slack (Ron Darling)	.50	.40	.20
6	.433 Series Batting Average (Marty Barrett)	.50	.40	.20
7	Dwight Gooden	.70	.50	.30
8	Strategy At Work	.50	.40	.20
9	Dewey! (Dwight Evans)	.50	.40	.20
10	One Strike From Boston Victory (Dave Henderson, Spike Owen)	.50	.40	.20
11	Series Home Run Duo (Ray Knight, Darryl Strawberry)	.50	.40	.20
12	Series M.V.P. (Ray Knight)	.50	.40	.20

1987 Fleer Headliners

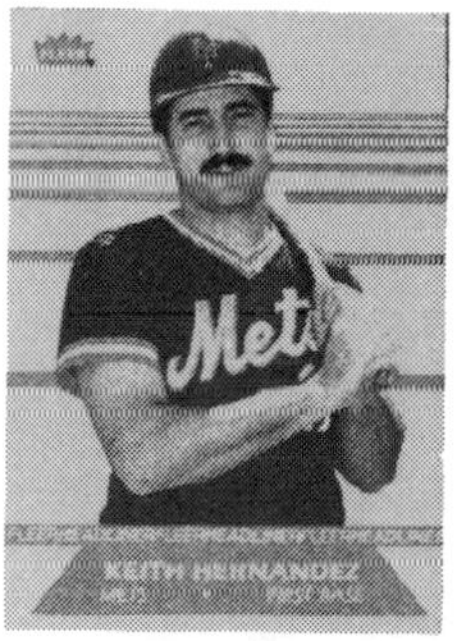

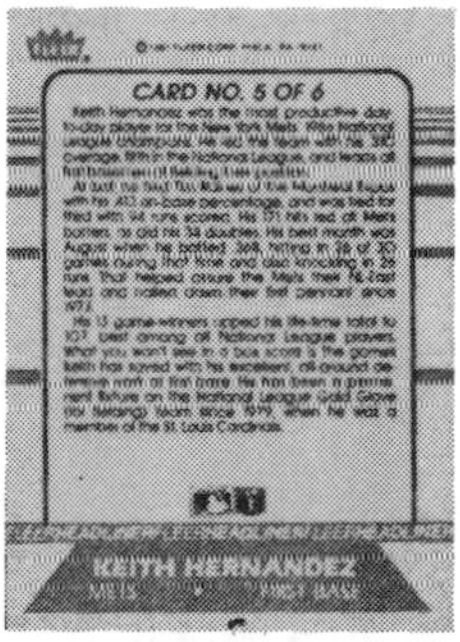

A continuation of the 1986 Future Hall of Famers idea, Fleer encountered legal problems with using the Hall of Fame name and abated them by entitling the set "Headliners." The cards, which are the standard 2-1/2" by 3-1/2" size, were randomly inserted in three-pack cello packs. Card fronts feature a player photo set against a beige background with bright red stripes. The card backs are printed in black, red and gray and offer a brief biography with an emphasis on the player's performance during the 1986 season.

	MT	NR MT	EX
Complete Set:	10.00	7.50	4.00
Common Player:	1.00	.70	.40

		MT	NR MT	EX
1	Wade Boggs	2.25	1.75	.90
2	Jose Canseco	3.00	2.25	1.25
3	Dwight Gooden	1.50	1.25	.60
4	Rickey Henderson	2.00	1.50	.80
5	Keith Hernandez	1.00	.70	.40
6	Jim Rice	1.00	.70	.40

1987 Fleer League Leaders

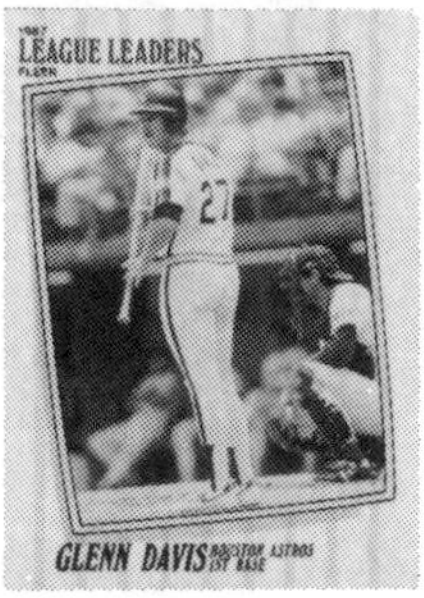

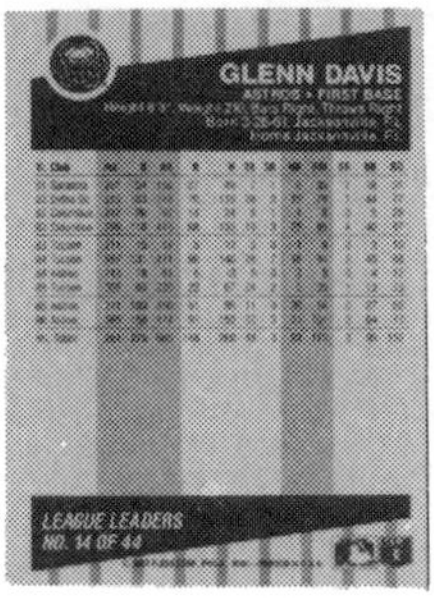

For the second year in a row, Fleer produced a 44-card "League Leaders" set for Walgreens. The card fronts feature a border style which is identical to that used in 1986. However, an elliptical shaped full-color player photo is placed diagonally on the front. "1987 Fleer League Leaders" appears in the upper left corner of the front although nowhere on the card does it state in which pitching, hitting or fielding department was the player a league leader. The card backs are printed in red and blue on white stock. The cards in the boxed set are the standard 2-1/2" by 3-1/2" size.

		MT	NR MT	EX
Complete Set:		5.00	3.75	2.00
Common Player:		.05	.04	.02
1	Jesse Barfield	.12	.09	.05
2	Mike Boddicker	.07	.05	.03
3	Wade Boggs	.60	.45	.25
4	Phil Bradley	.10	.08	.04
5	George Brett	.30	.25	.12
6	Hubie Brooks	.07	.05	.03
7	Chris Brown	.07	.05	.03
8	Jose Canseco	.70	.50	.30
9	Joe Carter	.12	.09	.05
10	Roger Clemens	.40	.30	.15
11	Vince Coleman	.15	.11	.06
12	Joe Cowley	.05	.04	.02
13	Kal Daniels	.20	.15	.08
14	Glenn Davis	.15	.11	.06
15	Jody Davis	.07	.05	.03
16	Darrell Evans	.07	.05	.03
17	Dwight Evans	.10	.08	.04
18	John Franco	.07	.05	.03
19	Julio Franco	.10	.08	.04
20	Dwight Gooden	.40	.30	.15
21	Goose Gossage	.12	.09	.05
22	Tom Herr	.07	.05	.03
23	Ted Higuera	.10	.08	.04
24	Bob Horner	.07	.05	.03
25	Pete Incaviglia	.40	.30	.15
26	Wally Joyner	.40	.30	.15
27	Dave Kingman	.10	.08	.04
28	Don Mattingly	1.00	.70	.40
29	Willie McGee	.10	.08	.04
30	Donnie Moore	.05	.04	.02
31	Keith Moreland	.05	.04	.02
32	Eddie Murray	.25	.20	.10
33	Mike Pagliarulo	.10	.08	.04
34	Larry Parrish	.05	.04	.02
35	Tony Pena	.07	.05	.03
36	Kirby Puckett	.50	.40	.20
37	Pete Rose	.50	.40	.20
38	Juan Samuel	.12	.09	.05
39	Ryne Sandberg	.20	.15	.08
40	Mike Schmidt	.30	.25	.12
41	Darryl Strawberry	.40	.30	.15
42	Greg Walker	.07	.05	.03
43	Bob Welch	.07	.05	.03
44	Todd Worrell	.12	.09	.05

1987 Fleer Limited Edition

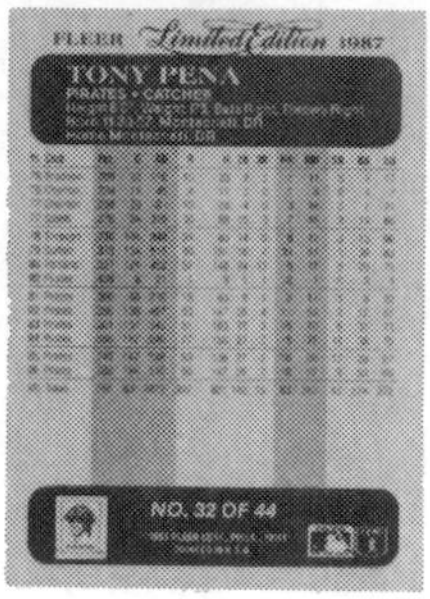

For the third straight year, Fleer produced a Limited Edition set for the McCrory's store chain and their affiliates. The cards are the standard 2-1/2" by 3-1/2" size and feature light blue borders at the top and bottom and a diagonal red and white border running along both sides. The set was issued in a specially prepared cardboard box, along with six team logo stickers.

		MT	NR MT	EX
Complete Set:		5.00	3.75	2.00
Common Player:		.05	.04	.02
1	Floyd Bannister	.05	.04	.02
2	Marty Barrett	.07	.05	.03
3	Steve Bedrosian	.10	.08	.04
4	George Bell	.20	.15	.08
5	George Brett	.30	.25	.12
6	Jose Canseco	1.00	.70	.40
7	Joe Carter	.12	.09	.05
8	Will Clark	1.00	.70	.40
9	Roger Clemens	.40	.30	.15
10	Vince Coleman	.15	.11	.06
11	Glenn Davis	.15	.11	.06
12	Mike Davis	.05	.04	.02
13	Len Dykstra	.07	.05	.03
14	John Franco	.07	.05	.03
15	Julio Franco	.10	.08	.04
16	Steve Garvey	.25	.20	.10
17	Kirk Gibson	.20	.15	.08
18	Dwight Gooden	.40	.30	.15
19	Tony Gwynn	.25	.20	.10
20	Keith Hernandez	.20	.15	.08
21	Teddy Higuera	.10	.08	.04
22	Kent Hrbek	.15	.11	.06
23	Wally Joyner	.50	.40	.20
24	Mike Krukow	.05	.04	.02
25	Mike Marshall	.10	.08	.04
26	Don Mattingly	1.00	.70	.40
27	Oddibe McDowell	.10	.08	.04
28	Jack Morris	.15	.11	.06
29	Lloyd Moseby	.07	.05	.03
30	Dale Murphy	.30	.25	.12
31	Eddie Murray	.25	.20	.10
32	Tony Pena	.07	.05	.03
33	Jim Presley	.10	.08	.04
34	Jeff Reardon	.10	.08	.04
35	Jim Rice	.20	.15	.08
36	Pete Rose	.40	.30	.15
37	Mike Schmidt	.30	.25	.12
38	Mike Scott	.12	.09	.05
39	Lee Smith	.07	.05	.03
40	Lonnie Smith	.05	.04	.02
41	Gary Ward	.05	.04	.02
42	Dave Winfield	.25	.20	.10
43	Todd Worrell	.12	.09	.05
44	Robin Yount	.20	.15	.08

A player's name in italic type indicates a rookie card. An (FC) indicates a player's first card for that particular card company.

1987 Fleer Mini

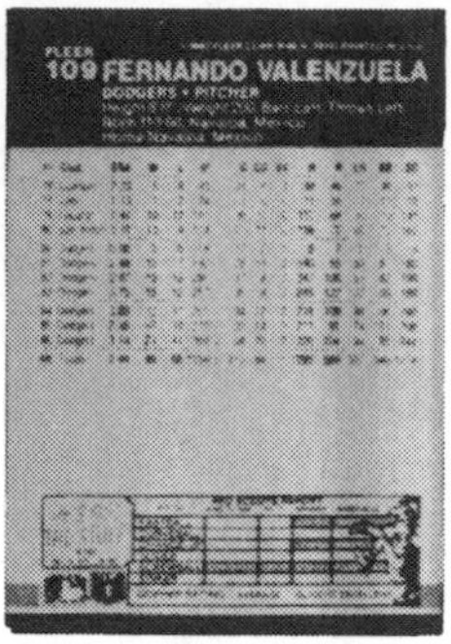

Continuing with an idea originated the previous year, the Fleer "Classic Miniatures" set consists of 120 cards that measure 1-13/16" by 2-9/16" in size. The cards are identical in design to the regular issue set produced by Fleer, but use completely different photos. The set was issued in a specially prepared collectors box along with 18 team logo stickers. The Fleer Mini set was available only through hobby dealers.

		MT	NR MT	EX
Complete Set:		9.00	6.75	3.50
Common Player:		.05	.04	.02
1	Don Aase	.05	.04	.02
2	Joaquin Andujar	.05	.04	.02
3	Harold Baines	.12	.09	.05
4	Jesse Barfield	.12	.09	.05
5	Kevin Bass	.05	.04	.02
6	Don Baylor	.10	.08	.04
7	George Bell	.20	.15	.08
8	Tony Bernazard	.05	.04	.02
9	Bert Blyleven	.12	.09	.05
10	Wade Boggs	.60	.45	.25
11	Phil Bradley	.10	.08	.04
12	Sid Bream	.05	.04	.02
13	George Brett	.30	.25	.12
14	Hubie Brooks	.07	.05	.03
15	Chris Brown	.07	.05	.03
16	Tom Candiotti	.05	.04	.02
17	Jose Canseco	1.00	.70	.40
18	Gary Carter	.20	.15	.08
19	Joe Carter	.12	.09	.05
20	Roger Clemens	.60	.45	.25
21	Vince Coleman	.15	.11	.06
22	Cecil Cooper	.10	.08	.04
23	Ron Darling	.10	.08	.04
24	Alvin Davis	.10	.08	.04
25	Chili Davis	.05	.04	.02
26	Eric Davis	.60	.45	.25
27	Glenn Davis	.15	.11	.06
28	Mike Davis	.05	.04	.02
29	Doug DeCinces	.05	.04	.02
30	Rob Deer	.07	.05	.03
31	Jim Deshaies	.10	.08	.04
32	Bo Diaz	.05	.04	.02
33	Richard Dotson	.07	.05	.03
34	Brian Downing	.05	.04	.02
35	Shawon Dunston	.07	.05	.03
36	Mark Eichhorn	.10	.08	.04
37	Dwight Evans	.12	.09	.05
38	Tony Fernandez	.10	.08	.04
39	Julio Franco	.10	.08	.04
40	Gary Gaetti	.12	.09	.05
41	Andres Galarraga	.15	.11	.06
42	Scott Garrelts	.05	.04	.02
43	Steve Garvey	.20	.15	.08
44	Kirk Gibson	.20	.15	.08
45	Dwight Gooden	.60	.45	.25
46	Ken Griffey	.07	.05	.03
47	Mark Gubicza	.10	.08	.04
48	Ozzie Guillen	.07	.05	.03
49	Bill Gullickson	.05	.04	.02
50	Tony Gwynn	.25	.20	.10
51	Von Hayes	.10	.08	.04
52	Rickey Henderson	.80	.60	.30
53	Keith Hernandez	.15	.11	.06
54	Willie Hernandez	.05	.04	.02
55	Ted Higuera	.10	.08	.04
56	Charlie Hough	.05	.04	.02
57	Kent Hrbek	.15	.11	.06
58	Pete Incaviglia	.40	.30	.15
59	Wally Joyner	.80	.60	.30
60	Bob Knepper	.07	.05	.03
61	Mike Krukow	.05	.04	.02
62	Mark Langston	.10	.08	.04
63	Carney Lansford	.07	.05	.03
64	Jim Lindeman	.12	.09	.05
65	Bill Madlock	.10	.08	.04
66	Don Mattingly	.80	.60	.30
67	Kirk McCaskill	.05	.04	.02
68	Lance McCullers	.10	.08	.04
69	Keith Moreland	.05	.04	.02
70	Jack Morris	.15	.11	.06
71	Jim Morrison	.05	.04	.02
72	Lloyd Moseby	.07	.05	.03
73	Jerry Mumphrey	.05	.04	.02
74	Dale Murphy	.30	.25	.12
75	Eddie Murray	.25	.20	.10
76	Pete O'Brien	.07	.05	.03
77	Bob Ojeda	.07	.05	.03
78	Jesse Orosco	.05	.04	.02
79	Dan Pasqua	.10	.08	.04
80	Dave Parker	.12	.09	.05
81	Larry Parrish	.05	.04	.02
82	Jim Presley	.10	.08	.04
83	Kirby Puckett	.50	.40	.20
84	Dan Quisenberry	.07	.05	.03
85	Tim Raines	.20	.15	.08
86	Dennis Rasmussen	.07	.05	.03
87	Johnny Ray	.07	.05	.03
88	Jeff Reardon	.07	.05	.03
89	Jim Rice	.20	.15	.08
90	Dave Righetti	.12	.09	.05
91	Earnest Riles	.05	.04	.02
92	Cal Ripken, Jr.	.60	.45	.25
93	Ron Robinson	.05	.04	.02
94	Juan Samuel	.12	.09	.05
95	Ryne Sandberg	.20	.15	.08
96	Steve Sax	.15	.11	.06
97	Mike Schmidt	.30	.25	.12
98	Ken Schrom	.05	.04	.02
99	Mike Scott	.12	.09	.05
100	Ruben Sierra	1.50	1.25	.60
101	Lee Smith	.07	.05	.03
102	Ozzie Smith	.12	.09	.05
103	Cory Snyder	.20	.15	.08
104	Kent Tekulve	.05	.04	.02
105	Andres Thomas	.10	.08	.04
106	Rob Thompson	.10	.08	.04
107	Alan Trammell	.20	.15	.08
108	John Tudor	.07	.05	.03
109	Fernando Valenzuela	.20	.15	.08
110	Greg Walker	.07	.05	.03
111	Mitch Webster	.05	.04	.02
112	Lou Whitaker	.15	.11	.06
113	Frank White	.07	.05	.03
114	Reggie Williams	.10	.08	.04
115	Glenn Wilson	.05	.04	.02
116	Willie Wilson	.10	.08	.04
117	Dave Winfield	.20	.15	.08
118	Mike Witt	.07	.05	.03
119	Todd Worrell	.12	.09	.05
120	Floyd Youmans	.05	.04	.02

1987 Fleer Baseball Record Setters

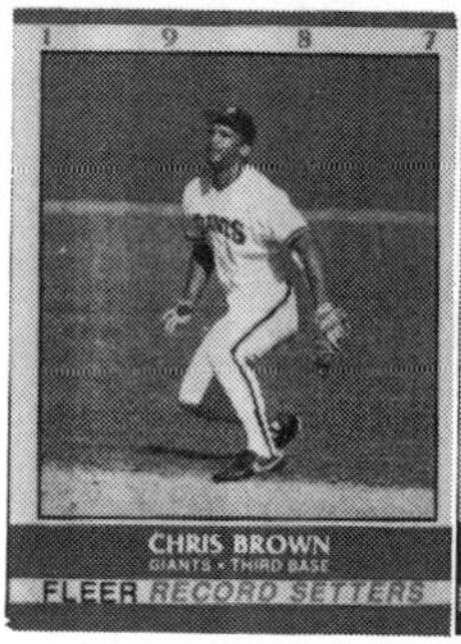

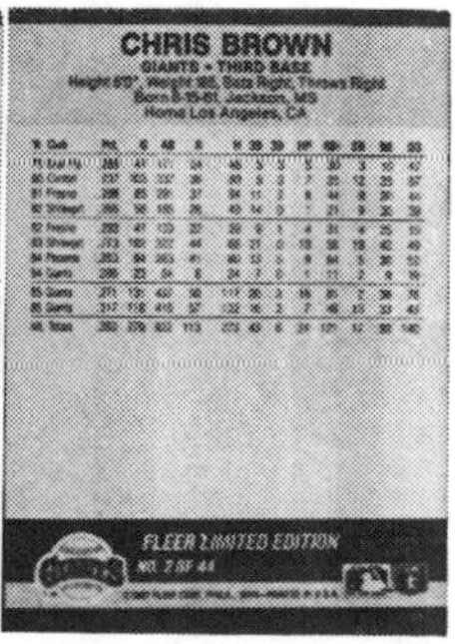

Produced by Fleer for the Eckerd Drug chain, the

1987 Fleer Record Setters set contains 44 cards that measure the standard 2-1/2" by 3-1/2" size. Although the set is titled "Record Setters," the actual records the players have set is not specified anywhere on the cards. Given that several players included in the set were young prospects, a better title for those cards might have been "Possible Record Setters." The set came housed in a special cardboard box with six team logo stickers.

		MT	NR MT	EX
Complete Set:		5.00	3.75	2.00
Common Player:		.05	.04	.02
1	George Brett	.30	.25	.12
2	Chris Brown	.07	.05	.03
3	Jose Canseco	1.00	.70	.40
4	Roger Clemens	.40	.30	.15
5	Alvin Davis	.10	.08	.04
6	Shawon Dunston	.07	.05	.03
7	Tony Fernandez	.10	.08	.04
8	Carlton Fisk	.12	.09	.05
9	Gary Gaetti	.10	.08	.04
10	Gene Garber	.05	.04	.02
11	Rich Gedman	.05	.04	.02
12	Dwight Gooden	.40	.30	.15
13	Ozzie Guillen	.07	.05	.03
14	Bill Gullickson	.05	.04	.02
15	Billy Hatcher	.07	.05	.03
16	Orel Hershiser	.20	.15	.08
17	Wally Joyner	.70	.50	.30
18	Ray Knight	.05	.04	.02
19	Craig Lefferts	.05	.04	.02
20	Don Mattingly	1.00	.70	.40
21	Kevin Mitchell	.70	.50	.30
22	Lloyd Moseby	.07	.05	.03
23	Dale Murphy	.30	.25	.12
24	Eddie Murray	.25	.20	.10
25	Phil Niekro	.15	.11	.06
26	Ben Oglivie	.05	.04	.02
27	Jesse Orosco	.05	.04	.02
28	Joe Orsulak	.05	.04	.02
29	Larry Parrish	.05	.04	.02
30	Tim Raines	.25	.20	.10
31	Shane Rawley	.07	.05	.03
32	Dave Righetti	.12	.09	.05
33	Pete Rose	.40	.30	.15
34	Steve Sax	.15	.11	.06
35	Mike Schmidt	.30	.25	.12
36	Mike Scott	.12	.09	.05
37	Don Sutton	.12	.09	.05
38	Alan Trammell	.20	.15	.08
39	John Tudor	.10	.08	.04
40	Gary Ward	.05	.04	.02
41	Lou Whitaker	.15	.11	.06
42	Willie Wilson	.10	.08	.04
43	Todd Worrell	.15	.11	.06
44	Floyd Youmans	.10	.08	.04

1987 Fleer Star Stickers

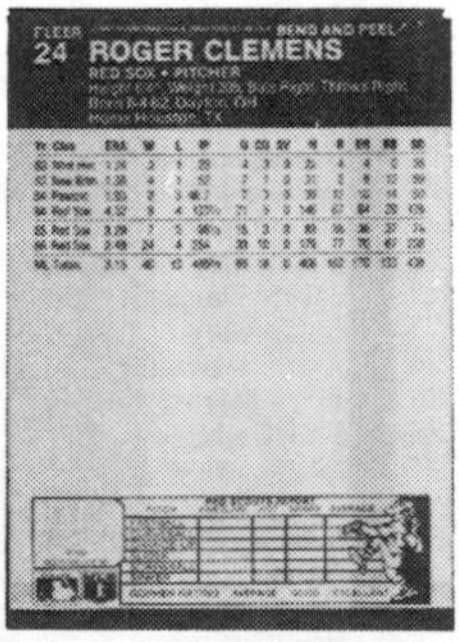

The 1987 Fleer Star Stickers set contains 132 cards which become stickers if the back is bent and peeled off. As in the previous year, the card backs are identical, save the numbering system, to the regular issue cards. The cards measure 2-1/2" by 3-1/2" and were sold in wax packs with team logo stickers. The fronts have a green border with a red and white banner wrapped across the upper left corner and the sides. The backs are printed in green and yellow.

		MT	NR MT	EX
Complete Set:		20.00	15.00	8.00
Common Player:		.05	.04	.02
1	Don Aase	.05	.04	.02
2	Harold Baines	.20	.15	.08
3	Floyd Bannister	.08	.06	.03
4	Jesse Barfield	.20	.15	.08
5	Marty Barrett	.10	.08	.04
6	Kevin Bass	.10	.08	.04
7	Don Baylor	.12	.09	.05
8	Steve Bedrosian	.15	.11	.06
9	George Bell	.35	.25	.14
10	Bert Blyleven	.15	.11	.06
11	Mike Boddicker	.08	.06	.03
12	Wade Boggs	1.00	.70	.40
13	Phil Bradley	.15	.11	.06
14	Sid Bream	.08	.06	.03
15	George Brett	.70	.50	.30
16	Hubie Brooks	.10	.08	.04
17	Tom Brunansky	.15	.11	.06
18	Tom Candiotti	.05	.04	.02
19	Jose Canseco	1.00	.70	.40
20	Gary Carter	.40	.30	.15
21	Joe Carter	.20	.15	.08
22	Will Clark	1.00	.70	.40
23	Mark Clear	.05	.04	.02
24	Roger Clemens	.90	.70	.35
25	Vince Coleman	.25	.20	.10
26	Jose Cruz	.10	.08	.04
27	Ron Darling	.20	.15	.08
28	Alvin Davis	.20	.15	.08
29	Chili Davis	.10	.08	.04
30	Eric Davis	.60	.45	.25
31	Glenn Davis	.20	.15	.08
32	Mike Davis	.05	.04	.02
33	Andre Dawson	.25	.20	.10
34	Doug DeCinces	.08	.06	.03
35	Brian Downing	.08	.06	.03
36	Shawon Dunston	.12	.09	.05
37	Mark Eichhorn	.12	.09	.05
38	Dwight Evans	.15	.11	.06
39	Tony Fernandez	.15	.11	.06
40	Bob Forsch	.05	.04	.02
41	John Franco	.10	.08	.04
42	Julio Franco	.12	.09	.05
43	Gary Gaetti	.20	.15	.08
44	Gene Garber	.05	.04	.02
45	Scott Garrelts	.05	.04	.02
46	Steve Garvey	.40	.30	.15
47	Kirk Gibson	.30	.25	.12
48	Dwight Gooden	.90	.70	.35
49	Ken Griffey	.10	.08	.04
50	Ozzie Guillen	.10	.08	.04
51	Bill Gullickson	.05	.04	.02
52	Tony Gwynn	.40	.30	.15
53	Mel Hall	.08	.06	.03
54	Greg Harris	.05	.04	.02
55	Von Hayes	.12	.09	.05
56	Rickey Henderson	1.00	.70	.40
57	Tom Henke	.10	.08	.04
58	Keith Hernandez	.35	.25	.14
59	Willie Hernandez	.05	.04	.02
60	Ted Higuera	.20	.15	.08
61	Bob Horner	.12	.09	.05
62	Charlie Hough	.08	.06	.03
63	Jay Howell	.08	.06	.03
64	Kent Hrbek	.30	.25	.12
65	Bruce Hurst	.12	.09	.05
66	Pete Incaviglia	.60	.45	.25
67	Bob James	.05	.04	.02
68	Wally Joyner	.50	.40	.20
69	Mike Krukow	.05	.04	.02
70	Mark Langston	.15	.11	.06
71	Carney Lansford	.08	.06	.03
72	Fred Lynn	.25	.20	.10
73	Bill Madlock	.12	.09	.05
74	Don Mattingly	1.00	.70	.40
75	Kirk McCaskill	.05	.04	.02
76	Lance McCullers	.12	.09	.05
77	Oddibe McDowell	.15	.11	.06
78	Paul Molitor	.20	.15	.08
79	Keith Moreland	.08	.06	.03
80	Jack Morris	.25	.20	.10
81	Jim Morrison	.05	.04	.02
82	Jerry Mumphrey	.05	.04	.02
83	Dale Murphy	.70	.50	.30
84	Eddie Murray	.50	.40	.20

		MT	NR MT	EX
85	Ben Oglivie	.05	.04	.02
86	Bob Ojeda	.10	.08	.04
87	Jesse Orosco	.08	.06	.03
88	Dave Parker	.25	.20	.10
89	Larry Parrish	.08	.06	.03
90	Tony Pena	.10	.08	.04
91	Jim Presley	.15	.11	.06
92	Kirby Puckett	.70	.50	.30
93	Dan Quisenberry	.12	.09	.05
94	Tim Raines	.35	.25	.14
95	Dennis Rasmussen	.10	.08	.04
96	Shane Rawley	.08	.06	.03
97	Johnny Ray	.10	.08	.04
98	Jeff Reardon	.10	.08	.04
99	Jim Rice	.35	.25	.14
100	Dave Righetti	.20	.15	.08
101	Cal Ripken, Jr.	1.00	.70	.40
102	Pete Rose	1.00	.70	.40
103	Nolan Ryan	2.00	1.50	.80
104	Juan Samuel	.15	.11	.06
105	Ryne Sandberg	.60	.45	.25
106	Steve Sax	.20	.15	.08
107	Mike Schmidt	1.25	.90	.50
108	Mike Scott	.15	.11	.06
109	Dave Smith	.05	.04	.02
110	Lee Smith	.10	.08	.04
111	Lonnie Smith	.05	.04	.02
112	Ozzie Smith	.20	.15	.08
113	Cory Snyder	.50	.40	.20
114	Darryl Strawberry	.70	.50	.30
115	Don Sutton	.25	.20	.10
116	Kent Tekulve	.08	.06	.03
117	Gorman Thomas	.08	.06	.03
118	Alan Trammell	.30	.25	.12
119	John Tudor	.12	.09	.05
120	Fernando Valenzuela	.12	.09	.05
121	Bob Welch	.12	.09	.05
122	Lou Whitaker	.25	.20	.10
123	Frank White	.10	.08	.04
124	Reggie Williams	.12	.09	.05
125	Willie Wilson	.15	.11	.06
126	Dave Winfield	.40	.30	.15
127	Mike Witt	.10	.08	.04
128	Todd Worrell	.25	.20	.10
129	Curt Young	.08	.06	.03
130	Robin Yount	.30	.25	.12
131	Jose Canseco, Don Mattingly/Checklist	2.50	2.00	1.00
132	Eric Davis, Bo Jackson/Checklist	1.25	.90	.50

1987 Fleer Star Sticker Box Panels

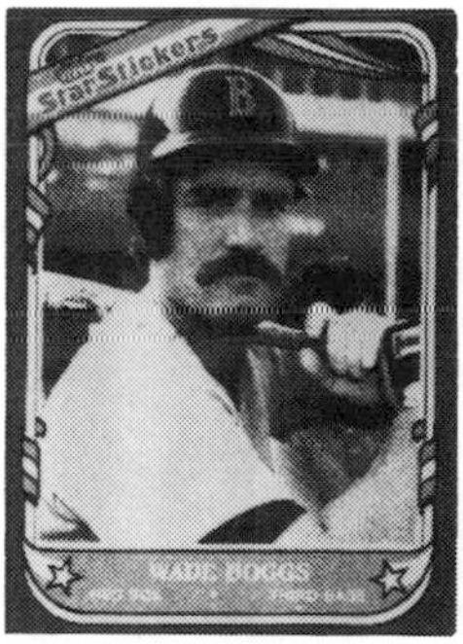

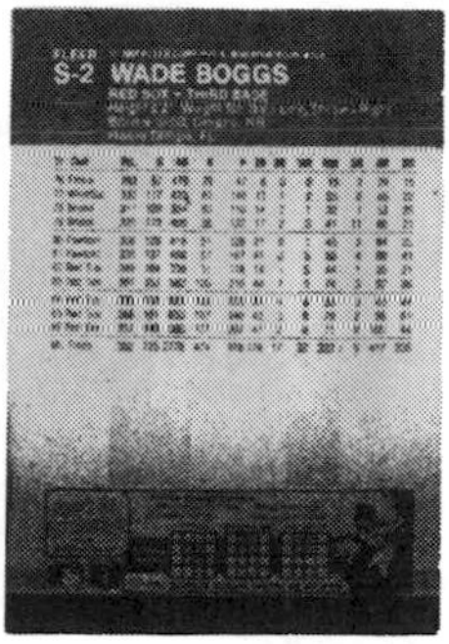

Fleer issued on the bottoms of their Fleer Star Stickers wax pack boxes six player cards plus two team logo/checklist cards. The cards, which measure 2-1/2" by 3-1/2", are numbered S-1 through S-8. The cards are identical in design to the Star Stickers.

		MT	NR MT	EX
Complete Panel Set:		6.00	4.50	2.50
Complete Singles Set:		3.25	2.50	1.25
Common Single Player:		.15	.11	.06
	Panel	5.00	3.75	2.00
2	Wade Boggs	.60	.45	.25
3	Bert Blyleven	.20	.15	.08
6	Phillies Logo	.05	.04	.02
8	Don Mattingly	1.50	1.25	.60
	Panel	1.00	.70	.40
1	Tigers Logo	.05	.04	.02
4	Jose Cruz	.15	.11	.06
5	Glenn Davis	.20	.15	.08
7	Bob Horner	.15	.11	.06

1987 Fleer Update

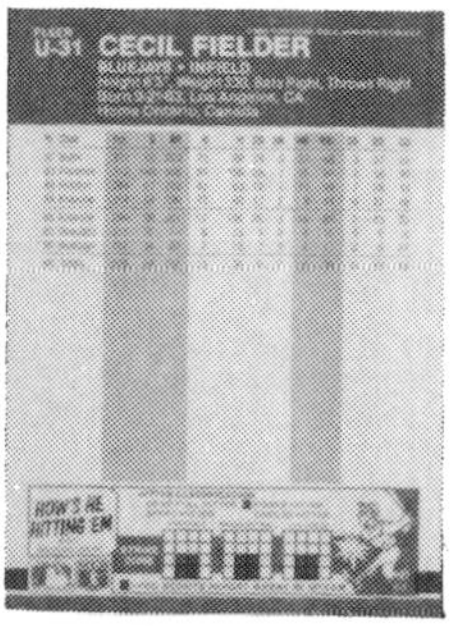

Fleer followed suit on a Topps idea in 1984 and began producing "Update" sets. The 1987 edition brings the regular Fleer set to date by including traded players and hot rookies. The cards measure 2-1/2" by 3-1/2" and are housed in a specially designed box with 25 team logo stickers. As a companion to the glossy-coated Fleer Collectors Edition set, Fleer produced a special edition Update set in its own tin box. Values of the glossy-coated cards are only a few dollars more than the regular Update cards.

		MT	NR MT	EX
Complete Set:		18.00	13.50	7.25
Common Player:		.06	.05	.02
1	Scott Bankhead	.08	.06	.03
2	Eric Bell(FC)	.15	.11	.06
3	Juan Beniquez	.06	.05	.02
4	Juan Berenguer	.06	.05	.02
5	Mike Birkbeck(FC)	.20	.15	.08
6	Randy Bockus(FC)	.15	.11	.06
7	Rod Booker(FC)	.15	.11	.06
8	Thad Bosley	.06	.05	.02
9	Greg Brock	.10	.08	.04
10	Bob Brower(FC)	.15	.11	.06
11	Chris Brown	.12	.09	.05
12	Jerry Browne	.15	.11	.06
13	Ralph Bryant	.10	.08	.04
14	DeWayne Buice(FC)	.20	.15	.08
15	Ellis Burks(FC)	3.00	2.25	1.25
16	Casey Candaele(FC)	.15	.11	.06
17	Steve Carlton	.40	.30	.15
18	Juan Castillo	.08	.06	.03
19	Chuck Crim(FC)	.15	.11	.06
20	Mark Davidson(FC)	.20	.15	.08
21	Mark Davis	.06	.05	.02
22	Storm Davis	.12	.09	.05
23	Bill Dawley	.06	.05	.02
24	Andre Dawson	.40	.30	.15
25	Brian Dayett	.06	.05	.02
26	Rick Dempsey	.08	.06	.03
27	Ken Dowell(FC)	.15	.11	.06
28	Dave Dravecky	.10	.08	.04
29	Mike Dunne(FC)	.20	.15	.08
30	Dennis Eckersley	.30	.25	.12
31	Cecil Fielder	3.00	2.25	1.25
32	Brian Fisher	.10	.08	.04
33	Willie Fraser	.10	.08	.04
34	Ken Gerhart(FC)	.15	.11	.06
35	Jim Gott	.06	.05	.02
36	Dan Gladden	.06	.05	.02
37	Mike Greenwell(FC)	2.00	1.50	.80
38	Cecilio Guante	.06	.05	.02
39	Albert Hall	.06	.05	.02
40	Atlee Hammaker	.06	.05	.02

		MT	NR MT	EX
41	Mickey Hatcher	.06	.05	.02
42	Mike Heath	.06	.05	.02
43	Neal Heaton	.06	.05	.02
44	Mike Henneman(FC)	.30	.25	.12
45	Guy Hoffman	.06	.05	.02
46	Charles Hudson	.06	.05	.02
47	Chuck Jackson(FC)	.20	.15	.08
48	Mike Jackson(FC)	.20	.15	.08
49	Reggie Jackson	.50	.40	.20
50	Chris James	.35	.25	.14
51	Dion James	.12	.09	.05
52	Stan Javier	.06	.05	.02
53	Stan Jefferson(FC)	.20	.15	.08
54	Jimmy Jones	.10	.08	.04
55	Tracy Jones	.20	.15	.08
56	Terry Kennedy	.08	.06	.03
57	Mike Kingery	.08	.06	.03
58	Ray Knight	.10	.08	.04
59	Gene Larkin(FC)	.30	.25	.12
60	Mike LaValliere	.12	.09	.05
61	Jack Lazorko(FC)	.06	.05	.02
62	Terry Leach	.06	.05	.02
63	Rick Leach	.06	.05	.02
64	Craig Lefferts	.06	.05	.02
65	Jim Lindeman(FC)	.15	.11	.06
66	Bill Long(FC)	.20	.15	.08
67	Mike Loynd(FC)	.15	.11	.06
68	Greg Maddux(FC)	1.00	.70	.40
69	Bill Madlock	.15	.11	.06
70	Dave Magadan	.80	.60	.30
71	Joe Magrane(FC)	.60	.45	.25
72	Fred Manrique(FC)	.20	.15	.08
73	Mike Mason	.06	.05	.02
74	Lloyd McClendon(FC)	.15	.11	.06
75	Fred McGriff(FC)	3.00	2.25	1.25
76	Mark McGwire(FC)	2.00	1.50	.80
77	Mark McLemore	.06	.05	.02
78	Kevin McReynolds	.30	.25	.12
79	Dave Meads(FC)	.15	.11	.06
80	Greg Minton	.06	.05	.02
81	John Mitchell(FC)	.15	.11	.06
82	Kevin Mitchell	1.50	1.25	.60
83	John Morris	.06	.05	.02
84	Jeff Musselman(FC)	.15	.11	.06
85	Randy Myers(FC)	.50	.40	.20
86	Gene Nelson	.06	.05	.02
87	Joe Niekro	.10	.08	.04
88	Tom Nieto	.06	.05	.02
89	Reid Nichols	.06	.05	.02
90	Matt Nokes(FC)	.40	.30	.15
91	Dickie Noles	.06	.05	.02
92	Edwin Nunez	.06	.05	.02
93	Jose Nunez(FC)	.12	.09	.05
94	Paul O'Neill	.50	.40	.20
95	Jim Paciorek(FC)	.06	.05	.02
96	Lance Parrish	.20	.15	.08
97	Bill Pecota(FC)	.20	.15	.08
98	Tony Pena	.12	.09	.05
99	Luis Polonia(FC)	.40	.30	.15
100	Randy Ready	.06	.05	.02
101	Jeff Reardon	.15	.11	.06
102	Gary Redus	.08	.06	.03
103	Rick Rhoden	.10	.08	.04
104	Wally Ritchie(FC)	.15	.11	.06
105	Jeff Robinson(FC)	.30	.25	.12
106	Mark Salas	.06	.05	.02
107	Dave Schmidt	.06	.05	.02
108	Kevin Seitzer	.60	.45	.25
109	John Shelby	.06	.05	.02
110	John Smiley(FC)	.90	.70	.35
111	Lary Sorenson	.06	.05	.02
112	Chris Speier	.06	.05	.02
113	Randy St. Claire	.06	.05	.02
114	Jim Sundberg	.08	.06	.03
115	B.J. Surhoff(FC)	.35	.25	.14
116	Greg Swindell	.50	.40	.20
117	Danny Tartabull	.40	.30	.15
118	Dorn Taylor(FC)	.12	.09	.05
119	Lee Tunnell	.06	.05	.02
120	Ed Vande Berg	.06	.05	.02
121	Andy Van Slyke	.20	.15	.08
122	Gary Ward	.06	.05	.02
123	Devon White	.40	.30	.15
124	Alan Wiggins	.06	.05	.02
125	Bill Wilkinson(FC)	.15	.11	.06
126	Jim Winn	.06	.05	.02
127	Frank Williams	.06	.05	.02
128	Ken Williams(FC)	.20	.15	.08
129	Matt Williams(FC)	6.00	4.50	2.50
130	Herm Winningham	.06	.05	.02
131	Matt Young	.06	.05	.02
132	Checklist 1-132	.06	.05	.02

1988 Fleer

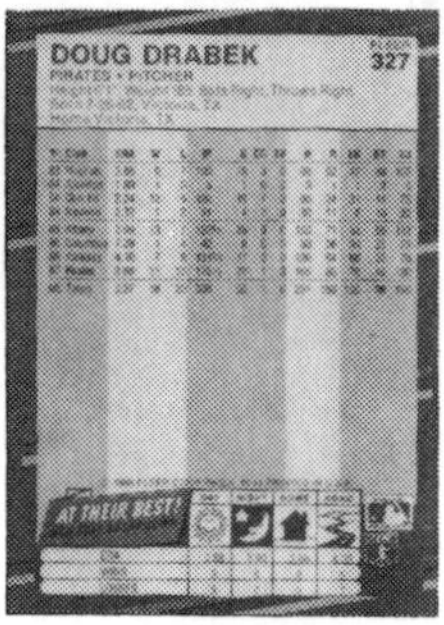

A clean, uncluttered look was the trademark of the 660-card 1988 Fleer set. The cards, which are the standard 2-1/2" by 3-1/2", feature blue and red diagonal lines set inside a white border. The player name and position are located on a slant in the upper left corner of the card. The player's team logo appears in the upper right corner. Below the player photo a blue and red band with the word "Fleer" appears. The backs of the cards include the card number, player personal information, and career statistics, plus a new feature called "At Their Best." This feature graphically shows a player's pitching or hitting statistics for home and road games and how he fared during day games as opposed to night contests. The set includes 19 special cards (#'s 622-640) and 12 "Major League Prospects" cards (#'s 641-653).

		MT	NR MT	EX
Complete Set:		45.00	33.00	17.00
Common Player:		.06	.05	.02
1	Keith Atherton	.06	.05	.02
2	Don Baylor	.10	.08	.04
3	Juan Berenguer	.06	.05	.02
4	Bert Blyleven	.12	.09	.05
5	Tom Brunansky	.10	.08	.04
6	Randy Bush	.06	.05	.02
7	Steve Carlton	.25	.20	.10
8	*Mark Davidson*(FC)	.12	.09	.05
9	George Frazier	.06	.05	.02
10	Gary Gaetti	.15	.11	.06
11	Greg Gagne	.06	.05	.02
12	Dan Gladden	.06	.05	.02
13	Kent Hrbek	.15	.11	.06
14	*Gene Larkin*	.20	.15	.08
15	Tim Laudner	.06	.05	.02
16	Steve Lombardozzi	.06	.05	.02
17	Al Newman	.06	.05	.02
18	Joe Niekro	.08	.06	.03
19	Kirby Puckett	.60	.45	.25
20	Jeff Reardon	.10	.08	.04
21a	Dan Schatzader (incorrect spelling)	.20	.15	.08
21b	Dan Schatzeder (correct spelling)	.06	.05	.02
22	Roy Smalley	.06	.05	.02
23	Mike Smithson	.06	.05	.02
24	*Les Straker*(FC)	.15	.11	.06
25	Frank Viola	.15	.11	.06
26	Jack Clark	.15	.11	.06
27	Vince Coleman	.20	.15	.08
28	Danny Cox	.08	.06	.03
29	Bill Dawley	.06	.05	.02
30	Ken Dayley	.06	.05	.02
31	Doug DeCinces	.08	.06	.03
32	Curt Ford	.06	.05	.02
33	Bob Forsch	.08	.06	.03
34	David Green	.06	.05	.02
35	Tom Herr	.08	.06	.03
36	Ricky Horton	.08	.06	.03
37	*Lance Johnson*(FC)	.40	.30	.15
38	Steve Lake	.06	.05	.02

		MT	NR MT	EX
39	Jim Lindeman	.10	.08	.04
40	*Joe Magrane*	.30	.25	.12
41	Greg Mathews	.08	.06	.03
42	Willie McGee	.12	.09	.05
43	John Morris	.06	.05	.02
44	Jose Oquendo	.06	.05	.02
45	Tony Pena	.08	.06	.03
46	Terry Pendleton	.08	.06	.03
47	Ozzie Smith	.15	.11	.06
48	John Tudor	.10	.08	.04
49	Lee Tunnell	.06	.05	.02
50	Todd Worrell	.10	.08	.04
51	Doyle Alexander	.08	.06	.03
52	Dave Bergman	.06	.05	.02
53	Tom Brookens	.06	.05	.02
54	Darrell Evans	.10	.08	.04
55	Kirk Gibson	.20	.15	.08
56	Mike Heath	.06	.05	.02
57	*Mike Henneman*	.25	.20	.10
58	Willie Hernandez	.08	.06	.03
59	Larry Herndon	.06	.05	.02
60	Eric King	.08	.06	.03
61	Chet Lemon	.08	.06	.03
62	*Scott Lusader*(FC)	.15	.11	.06
63	Bill Madlock	.10	.08	.04
64	Jack Morris	.20	.15	.08
65	Jim Morrison	.06	.05	.02
66	*Matt Nokes*	.50	.40	.20
67	Dan Petry	.08	.06	.03
68a	*Jeff Robinson* (Born 12-13-60 on back)	.80	.60	.30
68b	*Jeff Robinson* (Born 12/14/61 on back)	.30	.25	.12
69	Pat Sheridan	.06	.05	.02
70	Nate Snell	.06	.05	.02
71	Frank Tanana	.08	.06	.03
72	Walt Terrell	.08	.06	.03
73	Mark Thurmond	.06	.05	.02
74	Alan Trammell	.25	.20	.10
75	Lou Whitaker	.25	.20	.10
76	Mike Aldrete	.08	.06	.03
77	Bob Brenly	.06	.05	.02
78	Will Clark	4.00	3.00	1.50
79	Chili Davis	.08	.06	.03
80	Kelly Downs	.10	.08	.04
81	Dave Dravecky	.08	.06	.03
82	Scott Garrelts	.06	.05	.02
83	Atlee Hammaker	.06	.05	.02
84	Dave Henderson	.10	.08	.04
85	Mike Krukow	.08	.06	.03
86	Mike LaCoss	.06	.05	.02
87	Craig Lefferts	.06	.05	.02
88	Jeff Leonard	.08	.06	.03
89	Candy Maldonado	.08	.06	.03
90	Ed Milner	.06	.05	.02
91	Bob Melvin	.06	.05	.02
92	Kevin Mitchell	1.00	.70	.40
93	*Jon Perlman*(FC)	.12	.09	.05
94	Rick Reuschel	.10	.08	.04
95	Don Robinson	.08	.06	.03
96	Chris Speier	.06	.05	.02
97	Harry Spilman	.06	.05	.02
98	Robbie Thompson	.08	.06	.03
99	Jose Uribe	.06	.05	.02
100	*Mark Wasinger*(FC)	.15	.11	.06
101	*Matt Williams*	5.00	3.75	2.00
102	Jesse Barfield	.15	.11	.06
103	George Bell	.25	.20	.10
104	Juan Beniquez	.06	.05	.02
105	John Cerutti	.08	.06	.03
106	Jim Clancy	.08	.06	.03
107	*Rob Ducey*(FC)	.15	.11	.06
108	Mark Eichhorn	.08	.06	.03
109	Tony Fernandez	.12	.09	.05
110	Cecil Fielder	1.50	1.25	.60
111	Kelly Gruber	.50	.40	.20
112	Tom Henke	.08	.06	.03
113	Garth Iorq (Iorg)	.06	.05	.02
114	Jimmy Key	.10	.08	.04
115	Rick Leach	.06	.05	.02
116	Manny Lee	.08	.06	.03
117	*Nelson Liriano*(FC)	.15	.11	.06
118	*Fred McGriff*	2.50	2.00	1.00
119	Lloyd Moseby	.08	.06	.03
120	Rance Mulliniks	.06	.05	.02
121	Jeff Musselman	.10	.08	.04
122	*Jose Nunez*	.15	.11	.06
123	Dave Stieb	.10	.08	.04
124	Willie Upshaw	.08	.06	.03
125	Duane Ward(FC)	.08	.06	.03
126	Ernie Whitt	.08	.06	.03

		MT	NR MT	EX
127	Rick Aguilera	.06	.05	.02
128	Wally Backman	.08	.06	.03
129	*Mark Carreon*(FC)	.12	.09	.05
130	Gary Carter	.25	.20	.10
131	David Cone(FC)	.70	.50	.30
132	Ron Darling	.12	.09	.05
133	Len Dykstra	.10	.08	.04
134	Sid Fernandez	.10	.08	.04
135	Dwight Gooden	.60	.45	.25
136	Keith Hernandez	.20	.15	.08
137	*Gregg Jefferies*(FC)	4.00	3.00	1.50
138	Howard Johnson	.10	.08	.04
139	Terry Leach	.06	.05	.02
140	*Barry Lyons*(FC)	.15	.11	.06
141	Dave Magadan	.30	.25	.12
142	Roger McDowell	.10	.08	.04
143	Kevin McReynolds	.15	.11	.06
144	*Keith Miller*(FC)	.15	.11	.06
145	*John Mitchell*(FC)	.20	.15	.08
146	Randy Myers	.15	.11	.06
147	Bob Ojeda	.08	.06	.03
148	Jesse Orosco	.08	.06	.03
149	Rafael Santana	.06	.05	.02
150	Doug Sisk	.06	.05	.02
151	Darryl Strawberry	.60	.45	.25
152	Tim Teufel	.06	.05	.02
153	Gene Walter	.06	.05	.02
154	Mookie Wilson	.08	.06	.03
155	*Jay Aldrich*(FC)	.12	.09	.05
156	Chris Bosio	.08	.06	.03
157	Glenn Braggs	.10	.08	.04
158	Greg Brock	.08	.06	.03
159	Juan Castillo	.06	.05	.02
160	Mark Clear	.06	.05	.02
161	Cecil Cooper	.10	.08	.04
162	*Chuck Crim*	.12	.09	.05
163	Rob Deer	.08	.06	.03
164	Mike Felder	.06	.05	.02
165	Jim Gantner	.06	.05	.02
166	Ted Higuera	.10	.08	.04
167	Steve Kiefer	.06	.05	.02
168	Rick Manning	.06	.05	.02
169	Paul Molitor	.12	.09	.05
170	Juan Nieves	.08	.06	.03
171	Dan Plesac	.10	.08	.04
172	Earnest Riles	.06	.05	.02
173	Bill Schroeder	.06	.05	.02
174	*Steve Stanicek*(FC)	.15	.11	.06
175	B.J. Surhoff	.15	.11	.06
176	Dale Sveum	.08	.06	.03
177	Bill Wegman	.06	.05	.02
178	Robin Yount	.30	.25	.12
179	Hubie Brooks	.10	.08	.04
180	Tim Burke	.06	.05	.02
181	Casey Candaele	.06	.05	.02
182	Mike Fitzgerald	.06	.05	.02
183	Tom Foley	.06	.05	.02
184	Andres Galarraga	.15	.11	.06
185	Neal Heaton	.06	.05	.02
186	Wallace Johnson	.06	.05	.02
187	Vance Law	.08	.06	.03
188	Dennis Martinez	.08	.06	.03
189	Bob McClure	.06	.05	.02
190	Andy McGaffigan	.06	.05	.02
191	Reid Nichols	.06	.05	.02
192	Pascual Perez	.08	.06	.03
193	Tim Raines	.25	.20	.10
194	Jeff Reed	.06	.05	.02
195	Bob Sebra	.06	.05	.02
196	Bryn Smith	.06	.05	.02
197	Randy St. Claire	.06	.05	.02
198	Tim Wallach	.10	.08	.04
199	Mitch Webster	.08	.06	.03
200	Herm Winningham	.06	.05	.02
201	Floyd Youmans	.06	.05	.02
202	*Brad Arnsberg*(FC)	.20	.15	.08
203	Rick Cerone	.06	.05	.02
204	Pat Clements	.06	.05	.02
205	Henry Cotto	.06	.05	.02
206	Mike Easler	.08	.06	.03
207	Ron Guidry	.15	.11	.06
208	Bill Gullickson	.06	.05	.02
209	Rickey Henderson	.60	.45	.25
210	Charles Hudson	.06	.05	.02
211	Tommy John	.15	.11	.06
212	*Roberto Kelly*(FC)	2.00	1.50	.80
213	Ron Kittle	.08	.06	.03
214	Don Mattingly	.80	.60	.30
215	Bobby Meacham	.06	.05	.02
216	Mike Pagliarulo	.10	.08	.04
217	Dan Pasqua	.10	.08	.04

		MT	NR MT	EX
218	Willie Randolph	.08	.06	.03
219	Rick Rhoden	.08	.06	.03
220	Dave Righetti	.15	.11	.06
221	Jerry Royster	.06	.05	.02
222	Tim Stoddard	.06	.05	.02
223	Wayne Tolleson	.06	.05	.02
224	Gary Ward	.08	.06	.03
225	Claudell Washington	.08	.06	.03
226	Dave Winfield	.30	.25	.12
227	Buddy Bell	.08	.06	.03
228	Tom Browning	.10	.08	.04
229	Dave Concepcion	.08	.06	.03
230	Kal Daniels	.20	.15	.08
231	Eric Davis	.80	.60	.30
232	Bo Diaz	.08	.06	.03
233	Nick Esasky	.08	.06	.03
234	John Franco	.10	.08	.04
235	Guy Hoffman	.06	.05	.02
236	Tom Hume	.06	.05	.02
237	Tracy Jones	.12	.09	.05
238	*Bill Landrum*(FC)	.10	.08	.04
239	Barry Larkin	1.50	1.25	.60
240	Terry McGriff(FC)	.06	.05	.02
241	Rob Murphy	.08	.06	.03
242	Ron Oester	.06	.05	.02
243	Dave Parker	.20	.15	.08
244	Pat Perry	.06	.05	.02
245	Ted Power	.06	.05	.02
246	Dennis Rasmussen	.10	.08	.04
247	Ron Robinson	.06	.05	.02
248	Kurt Stillwell	.10	.08	.04
249	*Jeff Treadway*(FC)	.40	.30	.15
250	Frank Williams	.06	.05	.02
251	Steve Balboni	.08	.06	.03
252	Bud Black	.06	.05	.02
253	Thad Bosley	.06	.05	.02
254	George Brett	.40	.30	.15
255	*John Davis*(FC)	.15	.11	.06
256	Steve Farr	.06	.05	.02
257	Gene Garber	.06	.05	.02
258	Jerry Gleaton	.06	.05	.02
259	Mark Gubicza	.12	.09	.05
260	Bo Jackson	3.00	2.25	1.25
261	Danny Jackson	.12	.09	.05
262	*Ross Jones*(FC)	.12	.09	.05
263	Charlie Leibrandt	.08	.06	.03
264	*Bill Pecota*	.15	.11	.06
265	*Melido Perez*(FC)	.30	.25	.12
266	Jamie Quirk	.06	.05	.02
267	Dan Quisenberry	.08	.06	.03
268	Bret Saberhagen	.15	.11	.06
269	Angel Salazar	.06	.05	.02
270	Kevin Seitzer	.50	.40	.20
271	Danny Tartabull	.30	.25	.12
272	*Gary Thurman*(FC)	.20	.15	.08
273	Frank White	.08	.06	.03
274	Willie Wilson	.10	.08	.04
275	Tony Bernazard	.06	.05	.02
276	Jose Canseco	3.25	2.50	1.25
277	Mike Davis	.08	.06	.03
278	Storm Davis	.10	.08	.04
279	Dennis Eckersley	.12	.09	.05
280	Alfredo Griffin	.08	.06	.03
281	Rick Honeycutt	.06	.05	.02
282	Jay Howell	.08	.06	.03
283	Reggie Jackson	.50	.40	.20
284	Dennis Lamp	.06	.05	.02
285	Carney Lansford	.10	.08	.04
286	Mark McGwire	3.00	2.25	1.25
287	Dwayne Murphy	.08	.06	.03
288	Gene Nelson	.06	.05	.02
289	Steve Ontiveros	.06	.05	.02
290	Tony Phillips	.06	.05	.02
291	Eric Plunk	.06	.05	.02
292	*Luis Polonia*	.40	.30	.15
293	*Rick Rodriguez*(FC)	.12	.09	.05
294	Terry Steinbach	.10	.08	.04
295	Dave Stewart	.10	.08	.04
296	Curt Young	.08	.06	.03
297	Luis Aguayo	.06	.05	.02
298	Steve Bedrosian	.12	.09	.05
299	Jeff Calhoun	.06	.05	.02
300	Don Carman	.08	.06	.03
301	*Todd Frohwirth*(FC)	.20	.15	.08
302	Greg Gross	.06	.05	.02
303	Kevin Gross	.08	.06	.03
304	Von Hayes	.08	.06	.03
305	*Keith Hughes*(FC)	.15	.11	.06
306	*Mike Jackson*	.20	.15	.08
307	Chris James	.20	.15	.08
308	Steve Jeltz	.06	.05	.02

		MT	NR MT	EX
309	Mike Maddux	.07	.05	.03
310	Lance Parrish	.15	.11	.06
311	Shane Rawley	.08	.06	.03
312	*Wally Ritchie*	.15	.11	.06
313	Bruce Ruffin	.08	.06	.03
314	Juan Samuel	.12	.09	.05
315	Mike Schmidt	.50	.40	.20
316	Rick Schu	.06	.05	.02
317	Jeff Stone	.06	.05	.02
318	Kent Tekulve	.08	.06	.03
319	Milt Thompson	.06	.05	.02
320	Glenn Wilson	.08	.06	.03
321	Rafael Belliard	.06	.05	.02
322	Barry Bonds	1.75	1.25	.70
323	Bobby Bonilla	1.25	.90	.50
324	Sid Bream	.08	.06	.03
325	John Cangelosi	.06	.05	.02
326	Mike Diaz	.08	.06	.03
327	Doug Drabek	.08	.06	.03
328	*Mike Dunne*	.15	.11	.06
329	Brian Fisher	.08	.06	.03
330	*Brett Gideon*(FC)	.12	.09	.05
331	Terry Harper	.06	.05	.02
332	Bob Kipper	.06	.05	.02
333	Mike LaValliere	.08	.06	.03
334	*Jose Lind*(FC)	.30	.25	.12
335	Junior Ortiz	.06	.05	.02
336	*Vicente Palacios*(FC)	.30	.25	.12
337	*Bob Patterson*(FC)	.12	.09	.05
338	*Al Pedrique*(FC)	.15	.11	.06
339	R.J. Reynolds	.06	.05	.02
340	*John Smiley*	.90	.70	.35
341	Andy Van Slyke	.12	.09	.05
342	Bob Walk	.06	.05	.02
343	Marty Barrett	.08	.06	.03
344	*Todd Benzinger*(FC)	.30	.25	.12
345	Wade Boggs	.70	.50	.30
346	*Tom Bolton*(FC)	.15	.11	.06
347	Oil Can Boyd	.08	.06	.03
348	*Ellis Burks*	3.00	2.25	1.25
349	Roger Clemens	1.00	.70	.40
350	Steve Crawford	.06	.05	.02
351	Dwight Evans	.12	.09	.05
352	*Wes Gardner*(FC)	.25	.20	.10
353	Rich Gedman	.08	.06	.03
354	Mike Greenwell	2.00	1.50	.80
355	*Sam Horn*(FC)	.30	.25	.12
356	Bruce Hurst	.10	.08	.04
357	*John Marzano*(FC)	.20	.15	.08
358	Al Nipper	.06	.05	.02
359	Spike Owen	.06	.05	.02
360	*Jody Reed*(FC)	.60	.45	.25
361	Jim Rice	.30	.25	.12
362	Ed Romero	.06	.05	.02
363	Kevin Romine(FC)	.08	.06	.03
364	Joe Sambito	.06	.05	.02
365	Calvin Schiraldi	.06	.05	.02
366	Jeff Sellers	.08	.06	.03
367	Bob Stanley	.06	.05	.02
368	Scott Bankhead	.06	.05	.02
369	Phil Bradley	.10	.08	.04
370	Scott Bradley	.06	.05	.02
371	Mickey Brantley	.06	.05	.02
372	*Mike Campbell*(FC)	.15	.11	.06
373	Alvin Davis	.12	.09	.05
374	Lee Guetterman	.06	.05	.02
375	*Dave Hengel*(FC)	.20	.15	.08
376	Mike Kingery	.06	.05	.02
377	Mark Langston	.12	.09	.05
378	*Edgar Martinez*(FC)	1.00	.70	.40
379	Mike Moore	.06	.05	.02
380	Mike Morgan	.06	.05	.02
381	John Moses	.06	.05	.02
382	*Donnell Nixon*(FC)	.20	.15	.08
383	Edwin Nunez	.06	.05	.02
384	Ken Phelps	.08	.06	.03
385	Jim Presley	.10	.08	.04
386	Rey Quinones	.06	.05	.02
387	Jerry Reed	.06	.05	.02
388	Harold Reynolds	.08	.06	.03
389	Dave Valle	.08	.06	.03
390	*Bill Wilkinson*	.15	.11	.06
391	Harold Baines	.12	.09	.05
392	Floyd Bannister	.08	.06	.03
393	Daryl Boston	.06	.05	.02
394	Ivan Calderon	.30	.25	.12
395	Jose DeLeon	.08	.06	.03
396	Richard Dotson	.08	.06	.03
397	Carlton Fisk	.20	.15	.08
398	Ozzie Guillen	.08	.06	.03
399	Ron Hassey	.06	.05	.02

		MT	NR MT	EX
400	Donnie Hill	.06	.05	.02
401	Bob James	.06	.05	.02
402	Dave LaPoint	.08	.06	.03
403	*Bill Lindsey*(FC)	.12	.09	.05
404	*Bill Long*(FC)	.15	.11	.06
405	Steve Lyons	.06	.05	.02
406	*Fred Manrique*	.15	.11	.06
407	*Jack McDowell*(FC)	2.00	1.50	.80
408	Gary Redus	.06	.05	.02
409	Ray Searage	.06	.05	.02
410	Bobby Thigpen	.20	.15	.08
411	Greg Walker	.08	.06	.03
412	*Kenny Williams*	.20	.15	.08
413	Jim Winn	.06	.05	.02
414	Jody Davis	.08	.06	.03
415	Andre Dawson	.20	.15	.08
416	Brian Dayett	.06	.05	.02
417	Bob Dernier	.06	.05	.02
418	Frank DiPino	.06	.05	.02
419	Shawon Dunston	.10	.08	.04
420	Leon Durham	.08	.06	.03
421	*Les Lancaster*(FC)	.20	.15	.08
422	Ed Lynch	.06	.05	.02
423	Greg Maddux	.35	.25	.14
424	Dave Martinez(FC)	.07	.05	.03
425a	Keith Moreland (bunting, photo actually Jody Davis)	3.00	2.25	1.25
425b	Keith Moreland (standing upright, correct photo)	.08	.06	.03
426	Jamie Moyer	.08	.06	.03
427	Jerry Mumphrey	.06	.05	.02
428	*Paul Noce*(FC)	.10	.08	.04
429	Rafael Palmeiro(FC)	1.75	1.25	.70
430	Wade Rowdon(FC)	.08	.06	.03
431	Ryne Sandberg	1.00	.70	.40
432	Scott Sanderson	.06	.05	.02
433	Lee Smith	.10	.08	.04
434	Jim Sundberg	.08	.06	.03
435	Rick Sutcliffe	.10	.08	.04
436	Manny Trillo	.08	.06	.03
437	Juan Agosto	.06	.05	.02
438	Larry Andersen	.06	.05	.02
439	Alan Ashby	.06	.05	.02
440	Kevin Bass	.08	.06	.03
441	*Ken Caminiti*(FC)	.35	.25	.14
442	*Rocky Childress*(FC)	.12	.09	.05
443	Jose Cruz	.08	.06	.03
444	Danny Darwin	.06	.05	.02
445	Glenn Davis	.15	.11	.06
446	Jim Deshaies	.08	.06	.03
447	Bill Doran	.08	.06	.03
448	Ty Gainey	.06	.05	.02
449	Billy Hatcher	.08	.06	.03
450	Jeff Heathcock	.06	.05	.02
451	Bob Knepper	.08	.06	.03
452	*Rob Mallicoat*(FC)	.12	.09	.05
453	*Dave Meads*	.15	.11	.06
454	Craig Reynolds	.06	.05	.02
455	Nolan Ryan	1.00	.70	.40
456	Mike Scott	.12	.09	.05
457	Dave Smith	.08	.06	.03
458	Denny Walling	.06	.05	.02
459	*Robbie Wine*(FC)	.12	.09	.05
460	*Gerald Young*(FC)	.15	.11	.06
461	Bob Brower	.08	.06	.03
462a	Jerry Browne (white player, photo actually Bob Brower)	3.50	2.75	1.50
462b	Jerry Browne (black player, correct photo)	.08	.06	.03
463	Steve Buechele	.06	.05	.02
464	Edwin Correa	.06	.05	.02
465	*Cecil Espy*(FC)	.15	.11	.06
466	Scott Fletcher	.08	.06	.03
467	Jose Guzman	.08	.06	.03
468	Greg Harris	.06	.05	.02
469	Charlie Hough	.08	.06	.03
470	Pete Incaviglia	.15	.11	.06
471	*Paul Kilgus*(FC)	.15	.11	.06
472	Mike Loynd	.08	.06	.03
473	Oddibe McDowell	.08	.06	.03
474	Dale Mohorcic	.08	.06	.03
475	Pete O'Brien	.08	.06	.03
476	Larry Parrish	.08	.06	.03
477	Geno Petralli	.06	.05	.02
478	Jeff Russell	.06	.05	.02
479	Ruben Sierra	2.00	1.50	.80
480	Mike Stanley	.08	.06	.03
481	Curtis Wilkerson	.06	.05	.02
482	Mitch Williams	.08	.06	.03
483	Bobby Witt	.10	.08	.04
484	Tony Armas	.08	.06	.03
485	Bob Boone	.08	.06	.03
486	Bill Buckner	.10	.08	.04
487	*DeWayne Buice*	.15	.11	.06
488	Brian Downing	.08	.06	.03
489	Chuck Finley	.06	.05	.02
490	Willie Fraser	.06	.05	.02
491	Jack Howell	.08	.06	.03
492	Ruppert Jones	.06	.05	.02
493	Wally Joyner	.40	.30	.15
494	Jack Lazorko	.06	.05	.02
495	Gary Lucas	.06	.05	.02
496	Kirk McCaskill	.08	.06	.03
497	Mark McLemore	.06	.05	.02
498	Darrell Miller	.06	.05	.02
499	Greg Minton	.06	.05	.02
500	Donnie Moore	.06	.05	.02
501	Gus Polidor	.06	.05	.02
502	Johnny Ray	.08	.06	.03
503	Mark Ryal(FC)	.06	.05	.02
504	Dick Schofield	.06	.05	.02
505	Don Sutton	.20	.15	.08
506	Devon White	.25	.20	.10
507	Mike Witt	.08	.06	.03
508	Dave Anderson	.06	.05	.02
509	Tim Belcher(FC)	.60	.45	.25
510	Ralph Bryant	.06	.05	.02
511	*Tim Crews*(FC)	.15	.11	.06
512	*Mike Devereaux*(FC)	.40	.30	.15
513	Mariano Duncan	.06	.05	.02
514	Pedro Guerrero	.15	.11	.06
515	Jeff Hamilton(FC)	.12	.09	.05
516	Mickey Hatcher	.06	.05	.02
517	Brad Havens	.06	.05	.02
518	Orel Hershiser	.25	.20	.10
519	*Shawn Hillegas*(FC)	.20	.15	.08
520	Ken Howell	.06	.05	.02
521	Tim Leary	.08	.06	.03
522	Mike Marshall	.12	.09	.05
523	Steve Sax	.15	.11	.06
524	Mike Scioscia	.08	.06	.03
525	Mike Sharperson(FC)	.06	.05	.02
526	John Shelby	.06	.05	.02
527	Franklin Stubbs	.08	.06	.03
528	Fernando Valenzuela	.20	.15	.08
529	Bob Welch	.10	.08	.04
530	Matt Young	.06	.05	.02
531	Jim Acker	.06	.05	.02
532	Paul Assenmacher	.06	.05	.02
533	*Jeff Blauser*(FC)	.25	.20	.10
534	*Joe Boever*(FC)	.25	.20	.10
535	Martin Clary(FC)	.06	.05	.02
536	*Kevin Coffman*(FC)	.12	.09	.05
537	Jeff Dedmon	.06	.05	.02
538	*Ron Gant*(FC)	5.00	3.75	2.00
539	*Tom Glavine*(FC)	2.00	1.50	.80
540	Ken Griffey	.08	.06	.03
541	Al Hall	.06	.05	.02
542	Glenn Hubbard	.06	.05	.02
543	Dion James	.08	.06	.03
544	Dale Murphy	.40	.30	.15
545	Ken Oberkfell	.06	.05	.02
546	David Palmer	.06	.05	.02
547	Gerald Perry	.10	.08	.04
548	Charlie Puleo	.06	.05	.02
549	Ted Simmons	.10	.08	.04
550	Zane Smith	.08	.06	.03
551	Andres Thomas	.08	.06	.03
552	Ozzie Virgil	.06	.05	.02
553	Don Aase	.06	.05	.02
554	*Jeff Ballard*(FC)	.35	.25	.14
555	Eric Bell	.08	.06	.03
556	Mike Boddicker	.08	.06	.03
557	Ken Dixon	.06	.05	.02
558	Jim Dwyer	.06	.05	.02
559	Ken Gerhart	.08	.06	.03
560	*Rene Gonzales*(FC)	.15	.11	.06
561	Mike Griffin	.06	.05	.02
562	John Hayban (Habyan)	.06	.05	.02
563	Terry Kennedy	.08	.06	.03
564	Ray Knight	.08	.06	.03
565	Lee Lacy	.06	.05	.02
566	Fred Lynn	.15	.11	.06
567	Eddie Murray	.35	.25	.14
568	Tom Niedenfuer	.08	.06	.03
569	*Bill Ripken*(FC)	.25	.20	.10
570	Cal Ripken, Jr.	.60	.45	.25
571	Dave Schmidt	.06	.05	.02
572	Larry Sheets	.08	.06	.03
573	*Pete Stanicek*(FC)	.15	.11	.06
574	*Mark Williamson*(FC)	.12	.09	.05
575	Mike Young	.06	.05	.02

		MT	NR MT	EX
576	Shawn Abner(FC)	.20	.15	.08
577	Greg Booker	.06	.05	.02
578	Chris Brown	.08	.06	.03
579	*Keith Comstock*(FC)	.12	.09	.05
580	*Joey Cora*(FC)	.12	.09	.05
581	Mark Davis	.06	.05	.02
582	Tim Flannery	.06	.05	.02
583	Goose Gossage	.15	.11	.06
584	Mark Grant	.06	.05	.02
585	Tony Gwynn	.35	.25	.14
586	Andy Hawkins	.06	.05	.02
587	Stan Jefferson	.10	.08	.04
588	Jimmy Jones	.08	.06	.03
589	John Kruk	.10	.08	.04
590	*Shane Mack*(FC)	.20	.15	.08
591	Carmelo Martinez	.08	.06	.03
592	Lance McCullers	.08	.06	.03
593	*Eric Nolte*(FC)	.15	.11	.06
594	Randy Ready	.06	.05	.02
595	Luis Salazar	.06	.05	.02
596	Benito Santiago	.35	.25	.14
597	Eric Show	.08	.06	.03
598	Garry Templeton	.08	.06	.03
599	Ed Whitson	.06	.05	.02
600	Scott Bailes	.08	.06	.03
601	Chris Bando	.06	.05	.02
602	*Jay Bell*(FC)	.60	.45	.25
603	Brett Butler	.08	.06	.03
604	Tom Candiotti	.06	.05	.02
605	Joe Carter	.12	.09	.05
606	Carmen Castillo	.06	.05	.02
607	*Brian Dorsett*(FC)	.15	.11	.06
608	*John Farrell*(FC)	.20	.15	.08
609	Julio Franco	.10	.08	.04
610	Mel Hall	.08	.06	.03
611	*Tommy Hinzo*(FC)	.15	.11	.06
612	Brook Jacoby	.10	.08	.04
613	*Doug Jones*(FC)	.40	.30	.15
614	Ken Schrom	.06	.05	.02
615	Cory Snyder	.20	.15	.08
616	Sammy Stewart	.06	.05	.02
617	Greg Swindell	.25	.20	.10
618	Pat Tabler	.08	.06	.03
619	Ed Vande Berg	.06	.05	.02
620	*Eddie Williams*(FC)	.15	.11	.06
621	Rich Yett	.06	.05	.02
622	Slugging Sophomores (Wally Joyner, Cory Snyder)	.35	.25	.14
623	Dominican Dynamite (George Bell, Pedro Guerrero)	.12	.09	.05
624	Oakland's Power Team (Jose Canseco, Mark McGwire)	1.00	.70	.40
625	Classic Relief (Dan Plesac, Dave Righetti)	.08	.06	.03
626	All Star Righties (Jack Morris, Bret Saberhagen, Mike Witt)	.10	.08	.04
627	Game Closers (Steve Bedrosian, John Franco)	.08	.06	.03
628	Masters of the Double Play (Ryne Sandberg, Ozzie Smith)	.12	.09	.05
629	Rookie Record Setter (Mark McGwire)	1.00	.70	.40
630	Changing the Guard in Boston (Todd Benzinger, Ellis Burks, Mike Greenwell)	1.00	.70	.40
631	N.L. Batting Champs (Tony Gwynn, Tim Raines)	.15	.11	.06
632	Pitching Magic (Orel Hershiser, Mike Scott)	.12	.09	.05
633	Big Bats At First (Mark McGwire, Pat Tabler)	.60	.45	.25
634	Hitting King and the Thief (Vince Coleman, Tony Gwynn)	.12	.09	.05
635	A.L. Slugging Shortstops (Tony Fernandez, Cal Ripken, Jr., Alan Trammell)	.15	.11	.06
636	Tried and True Sluggers (Gary Carter, Mike Schmidt)	.20	.15	.08
637	Crunch Time (Eric Davis, Darryl Strawberry)	.70	.50	.30
638	A.L. All Stars (Matt Nokes, Kirby Puckett)	.20	.15	.08
639	N.L. All Stars (Keith Hernandez, Dale Murphy)	.20	.15	.08
640	The "O's" Brothers (Bill Ripken, Cal Ripken, Jr.)	.12	.09	.05
641	Major League Prospects *(Mark Grace, Darrin Jackson)*(FC)	7.00	5.25	2.75
642	Major League Prospects *(Damon Berryhill, Jeff Montgomery)*(FC)	.80	.60	.30
643	Major League Prospects *(Felix Fermin, Jessie Reid)*(FC)	.20	.15	.08
644	Major League Prospects *(Greg Myers, Greg Tabor)*(FC)	.20	.15	.08
645	Major League Prospects *(Jim Eppard,* Joey Meyer)(FC)	.20	.15	.08
646	Major League Prospects *(Adam Peterson, Randy Velarde)*(FC)	.20	.15	.08
647	Major League Prospects *(Chris Gwynn, Peter Smith)*(FC)	.25	.20	.10
648	Major League Prospects *(Greg Jelks, Tom Newell)*(FC)	.25	.20	.10
649	Major League Prospects *(Mario Diaz, Clay Parker)*(FC)	.25	.20	.10
650	Major League Prospects *(Jack Savage, Todd Simmons)*(FC)	.25	.20	.10
651	Major League Prospects *(John Burkett, Kirt Manwaring)*(FC)	.70	.50	.30
652	Major League Prospects *(Dave Otto, Walt Weiss)*(FC)	.70	.50	.30
653	Major League Prospects *(Randell Byers (Randall), Jeff King)*(FC)	.50	.40	.20
654a	Checklist 1-101 (21 is Schatzader)	.10	.08	.04
654b	Checklist 1-101 (21 is Schatzeder)	.06	.05	.02
655	Checklist 102-201	.06	.05	.02
656	Checklist 202-296	.06	.05	.02
657	Checklist 297-390	.06	.05	.02
658	Checklist 391-483	.06	.05	.02
659	Checklist 484-575	.06	.05	.02
660	Checklist 576-660	.06	.05	.02

1988 Fleer All Star Team

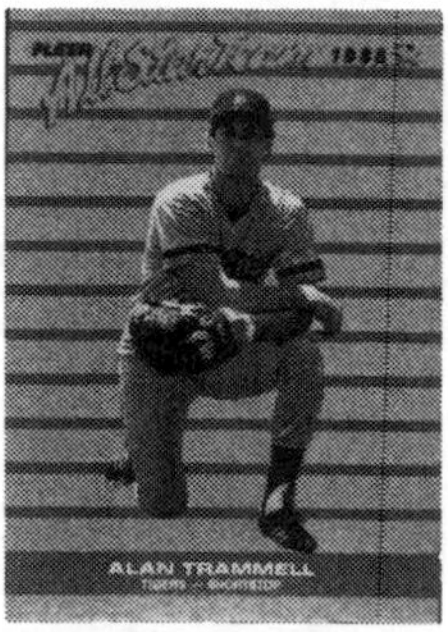

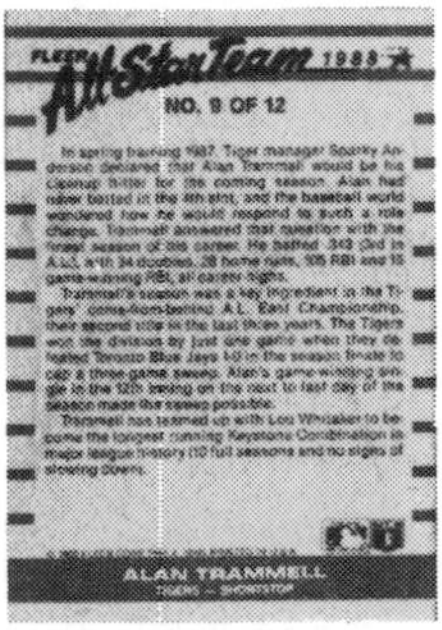

For the third consecutive year, Fleer randomly inserted All Star Team cards in their wax and cello packs. Twelve cards make up the set, each card measuring 2-1/2" by 3-1/2" in size. Players chosen for the set are Fleer's choices for a major league All-Star team.

		MT	NR MT	EX
Complete Set:		15.00	11.00	6.00
Common Player:		.60	.45	.25
1	Matt Nokes	.75	.60	.30
2	Tom Henke	.60	.45	.25
3	Ted Higuera	.60	.45	.25
4	Roger Clemens	2.25	1.75	.90
5	George Bell	1.00	.70	.40
6	Andre Dawson	1.00	.70	.40
7	Eric Davis	2.25	1.75	.90
8	Wade Boggs	2.50	2.00	1.00
9	Alan Trammell	1.00	.70	.40
10	Juan Samuel	.75	.60	.30
11	Jack Clark	.75	.60	.30
12	Paul Molitor	.75	.60	.30

A player's name in italic indicates a rookie card. An (FC) indicates a player's first card for that particular card company.

1988 Fleer Award Winners

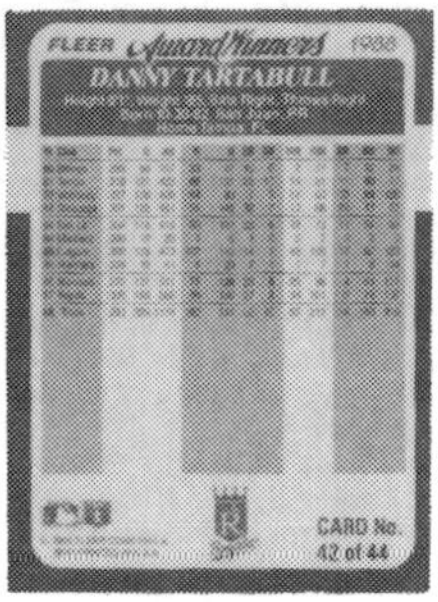

This limited edition 44-card boxed set of 1987 award-winning player cards also includes six team logo sticker cards. Red, white, blue and yellow bands border the sharp, full-color player photos printed below a "Fleer Award Winners 1988" banner. The player's name and award are printed beneath the photo. Flip sides are red, white and blue and list personal information, career data, team logo and card number. This set was sold exclusively at 7-11 stores nationwide.

		MT	NR MT	EX
Complete Set:		5.00	3.75	2.00
Common Player:		.05	.04	.02
1	Steve Bedrosian	.10	.08	.04
2	George Bell	.20	.15	.08
3	Wade Boggs	.70	.50	.30
4	Jose Canseco	.70	.50	.30
5	Will Clark	.50	.40	.20
6	Roger Clemens	.40	.30	.15
7	Kal Daniels	.20	.15	.08
8	Eric Davis	.50	.40	.20
9	Andre Dawson	.15	.11	.06
10	Mike Dunne	.10	.08	.04
11	Dwight Evans	.10	.08	.04
12	Carlton Fisk	.15	.11	.06
13	Julio Franco	.07	.05	.03
14	Dwight Gooden	.40	.30	.15
15	Pedro Guerrero	.15	.11	.06
16	Tony Gwynn	.25	.20	.10
17	Orel Hershiser	.20	.15	.08
18	Tom Henke	.05	.04	.02
19	Ted Higuera	.10	.08	.04
20	Charlie Hough	.05	.04	.02
21	Wally Joyner	.30	.25	.12
22	Jimmy Key	.07	.05	.03
23	Don Mattingly	.70	.50	.30
24	Mark McGwire	.70	.50	.30
25	Paul Molitor	.12	.09	.05
26	Jack Morris	.12	.09	.05
27	Dale Murphy	.30	.25	.12
28	Terry Pendleton	.05	.04	.02
29	Kirby Puckett	.70	.50	.30
30	Tim Raines	.25	.20	.10
31	Jeff Reardon	.07	.05	.03
32	Harold Reynolds	.05	.04	.02
33	Dave Righetti	.12	.09	.05
34	Benito Santiago	.25	.20	.10
35	Mike Schmidt	.30	.25	.12
36	Mike Scott	.10	.08	.04
37	Kevin Seitzer	.60	.45	.25
38	Larry Sheets	.07	.05	.03
39	Ozzie Smith	.15	.11	.06
40	Darryl Strawberry	.40	.30	.15
41	Rick Sutcliffe	.10	.08	.04
42	Danny Tartabull	.12	.09	.05
43	Alan Trammell	.15	.11	.06
44	Tim Wallach	.10	.08	.04

NOTE: A card number in parentheses ( ) indicates the set is unnumbered.

1988 Fleer Baseball All Stars

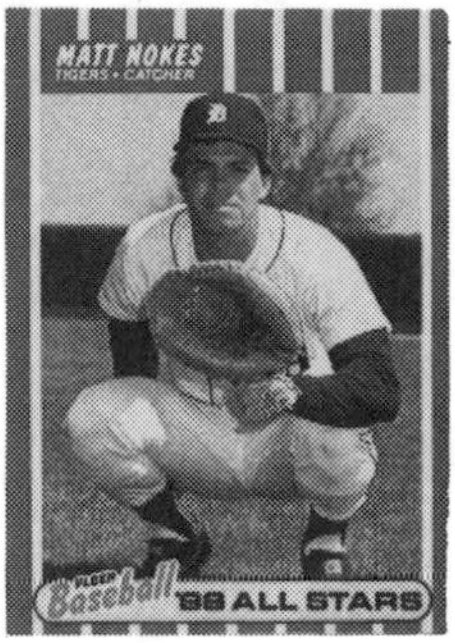

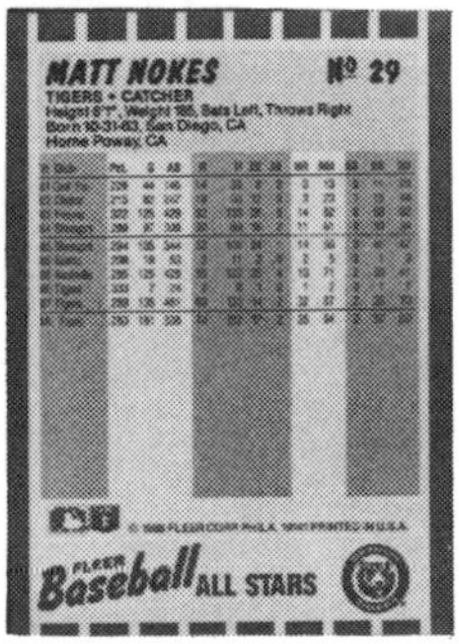

This limited edition 44-card boxed set features excellent photography of major league All-Stars. The standard-size cards feature a sporty bright blue- and yellow-striped background. The player name is printed in white across the upper left front corner. "Fleer Baseball 88 All Stars" appears on a yellow band beneath the photo. Card backs feature a blue- and white-striped design with a yellow highlighted section at the top that contains the player name, card number, team, position and personal data, followed by lifetime career stats. Fleer All Stars are cello-wrapped in blue and yellow striped boxes with checklist backs. The set includes six team logo sticker cards that feature black and white aerial shots of major league ballparks. The set was marketed exclusively by Ben Franklin stores.

		MT	NR MT	EX
Complete Set:		6.00	4.50	2.50
Common Player:		.05	.04	.02
1	George Bell	.20	.15	.08
2	Wade Boggs	.70	.50	.30
3	Bobby Bonilla	.12	.09	.05
4	George Brett	.30	.25	.12
5	Jose Canseco	.70	.50	.30
6	Jack Clark	.15	.11	.06
7	Will Clark	.70	.50	.30
8	Roger Clemens	.40	.30	.15
9	Eric Davis	.50	.40	.20
10	Andre Dawson	.15	.11	.06
11	Julio Franco	.07	.05	.03
12	Dwight Gooden	.40	.30	.15
13	Tony Gwynn	.25	.20	.10
14	Orel Hershiser	.20	.15	.08
15	Teddy Higuera	.10	.08	.04
16	Charlie Hough	.05	.04	.02
17	Kent Hrbek	.15	.11	.06
18	Bruce Hurst	.10	.08	.04
19	Wally Joyner	.30	.25	.12
20	Mark Langston	.10	.08	.04
21	Dave LaPoint	.05	.04	.02
22	Candy Maldonado	.05	.04	.02
23	Don Mattingly	.70	.50	.30
24	Roger McDowell	.07	.05	.03
25	Mark McGwire	.70	.50	.30
26	Jack Morris	.12	.09	.05
27	Dale Murphy	.30	.25	.12
28	Eddie Murray	.20	.15	.08
29	Matt Nokes	.30	.25	.12
30	Kirby Puckett	.70	.50	.30
31	Tim Raines	.25	.20	.10
32	Willie Randolph	.07	.05	.03
33	Jeff Reardon	.07	.05	.03
34	Nolan Ryan	1.50	1.25	.60
35	Juan Samuel	.10	.08	.04
36	Mike Schmidt	.30	.25	.12
37	Mike Scott	.10	.08	.04
38	Kevin Seitzer	.60	.45	.25
39	Ozzie Smith	.15	.11	.06
40	Darryl Strawberry	.40	.30	.15
41	Rick Sutcliffe	.10	.08	.04
42	Alan Trammell	.15	.11	.06
43	Tim Wallach	.10	.08	.04

		MT	NR MT	EX
44	Dave Winfield	.20	.15	.08

1988 Fleer Baseball MVP

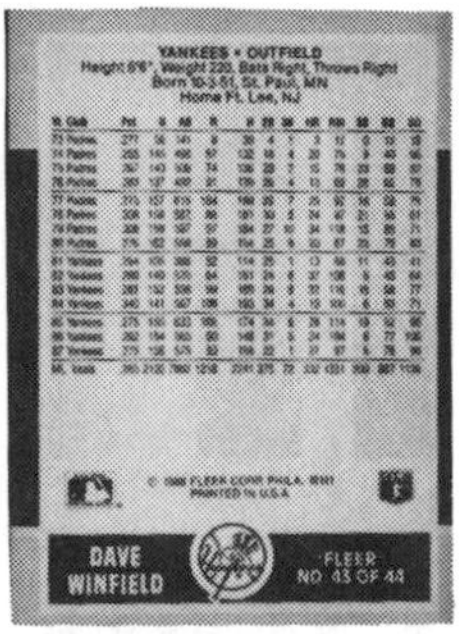

This boxed set of 44 standard-size cards and six team logo stickers was produced by Fleer for exclusive distribution at Toys "R" Us stores. This premiere edition features full-color player photos framed by a yellow and blue border. The player's name is printed in red below and to the left of the photo; team and position are printed in black in the lower right corner. The "Fleer Baseball MVP" logo appears bottom center. Card backs are yellow and blue on a white background. The player's team, position and personal data are followed by stats, logo and a blue banner bearing the player's name, team logo and card number. The six sticker cards feature black and white stadium photos on the backs.

		MT	NR MT	EX
Complete Set:		6.00	4.50	2.50
Common Player:		.05	.04	.02
1	George Bell	.20	.15	.08
2	Wade Boggs	.80	.60	.30
3	Jose Canseco	.80	.60	.30
4	Ivan Calderon	.07	.05	.03
5	Will Clark	.80	.60	.30
6	Roger Clemens	.40	.30	.15
7	Vince Coleman	.15	.11	.06
8	Eric Davis	.50	.40	.20
9	Andre Dawson	.15	.11	.06
10	Dave Dravecky	.05	.04	.02
11	Mike Dunne	.10	.08	.04
12	Dwight Evans	.10	.08	.04
13	Sid Fernandez	.07	.05	.03
14	Tony Fernandez	.10	.08	.04
15	Julio Franco	.07	.05	.03
16	Dwight Gooden	.40	.30	.15
17	Tony Gwynn	.25	.20	.10
18	Ted Higuera	.10	.08	.04
19	Charlie Hough	.05	.04	.02
20	Wally Joyner	.30	.25	.12
21	Mark Langston	.10	.08	.04
22	Don Mattingly	.80	.60	.30
23	Mark McGwire	.80	.60	.30
24	Jack Morris	.12	.09	.05
25	Dale Murphy	.30	.25	.12
26	Kirby Puckett	.50	.40	.20
27	Tim Raines	.25	.20	.10
28	Willie Randolph	.07	.05	.03
29	Ryne Sandberg	.20	.15	.08
30	Benito Santiago	.25	.20	.10
31	Mike Schmidt	.30	.25	.12
32	Mike Scott	.10	.08	.04
33	Kevin Seitzer	.60	.45	.25
34	Larry Sheets	.07	.05	.03
35	Ozzie Smith	.15	.11	.06
36	Dave Stewart	.10	.08	.04
37	Darryl Strawberry	.40	.30	.15
38	Rick Sutcliffe	.10	.08	.04
39	Alan Trammell	.15	.11	.06
40	Fernando Valenzuela	.20	.15	.08
41	Frank Viola	.12	.09	.05
42	Tim Wallach	.10	.08	.04

		MT	NR MT	EX
43	Dave Winfield	.20	.15	.08
44	Robin Yount	.25	.20	.10

1988 Fleer Baseball's Best

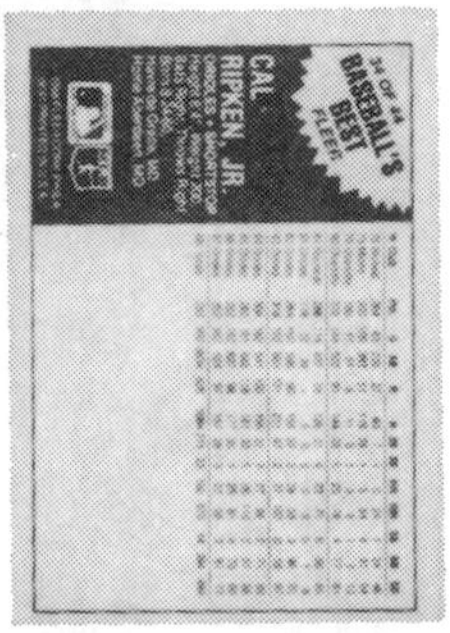

This boxed set of 44 standard-size cards (2-1/2" by 3-1/2") and six team logo stickers is the third annual issue from Fleer highlighting the best major league sluggers and pitchers. Five additional player cards were printed on retail display box bottoms, along with a checklist logo card (numbered C-1 through C-6). Full-color player photos are framed by a green border that fades to yellow. A red (slugger) or blue (pitcher) player name is printed beneath the photo. The card backs are printed in green on a white background with yellow highlights. Card number, player name and personal info appear in a green vertical box on the left-hand side of the card back with a yellow cartoon-style team logo overprinted across a stats chart on the right. This set was produced by Fleer for exclusive distribution by McCrory's stores (McCrory, McClellan, J.J. Newberry, H.L. Green, TG&Y).

		MT	NR MT	EX
Complete Set:		6.00	4.50	2.50
Common Player:		.05	.04	.02
1	George Bell	.20	.15	.08
2	Wade Boggs	.80	.60	.30
3	Bobby Bonilla	.12	.09	.05
4	Tom Brunansky	.10	.08	.04
5	Ellis Burks	.80	.60	.30
6	Jose Canseco	.80	.60	.30
7	Joe Carter	.12	.09	.05
8	Will Clark	.80	.60	.30
9	Roger Clemens	.40	.30	.15
10	Eric Davis	.50	.40	.20
11	Glenn Davis	.12	.09	.05
12	Andre Dawson	.15	.11	.06
13	Dennis Eckersley	.07	.05	.03
14	Andres Galarraga	.15	.11	.06
15	Dwight Gooden	.40	.30	.15
16	Pedro Guerrero	.15	.11	.06
17	Tony Gwynn	.25	.20	.10
18	Orel Hershiser	.20	.15	.08
19	Ted Higuera	.10	.08	.04
20	Pete Incaviglia	.12	.09	.05
21	Danny Jackson	.10	.08	.04
22	Doug Jennings	.07	.05	.03
23	Mark Langston	.10	.08	.04
24	Dave LaPoint	.05	.04	.02
25	Mike LaValliere	.07	.05	.03
26	Don Mattingly	.80	.60	.30
27	Mark McGwire	.80	.60	.30
28	Dale Murphy	.30	.25	.12
29	Ken Phelps	.05	.04	.02
30	Kirby Puckett	.50	.40	.20
31	Johnny Ray	.05	.04	.02
32	Jeff Reardon	.07	.05	.03
33	Dave Righetti	.12	.09	.05
34	Cal Ripkin, Jr. (Ripken)	.60	.45	.25
35	Chris Sabo	.90	.70	.35
36	Mike Schmidt	.30	.25	.12
37	Mike Scott	.10	.08	.04

		MT	NR MT	EX
38	Kevin Seitzer	.60	.45	.25
39	Dave Stewart	.10	.08	.04
40	Darryl Strawberry	.40	.30	.15
41	Greg Swindell	.10	.08	.04
42	Frank Tanana	.05	.04	.02
43	Dave Winfield	.20	.15	.08
44	Todd Worrell	.10	.08	.04

1988 Fleer Baseball's Best Box Panel

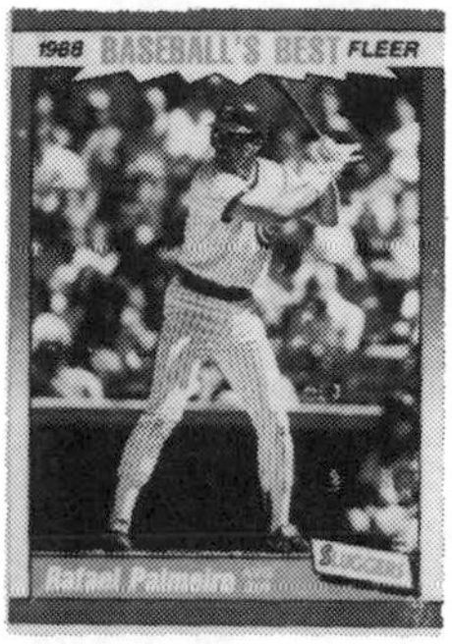

Six cards were placed on the bottoms of retail boxes of the Fleer 44-card Baseball's Best boxed sets in 1988. The cards, which measure 2-1/2" by 3-1/2", are identical in design to cards found in the 44-card set. The cards are numbered C-1 through C-6 and were produced by Fleer for distribution by McCrory stores and its affiliates.

		MT	NR MT	EX
Complete Panel Set:		1.50	1.25	.60
Complete Singles Set:		.90	.70	.35
Common Single Player:		.15	.11	.06
	Panel	1.50	1.25	.60
1	Ron Darling	.20	.15	.08
2	Rickey Henderson	.60	.45	.25
3	Carney Lansford	.15	.11	.06
4	Rafael Palmeiro	.20	.15	.08
5	Frank Viola	.20	.15	.08
6	Twins Logo	.05	.04	.02

1988 Fleer Baseball's Exciting Stars

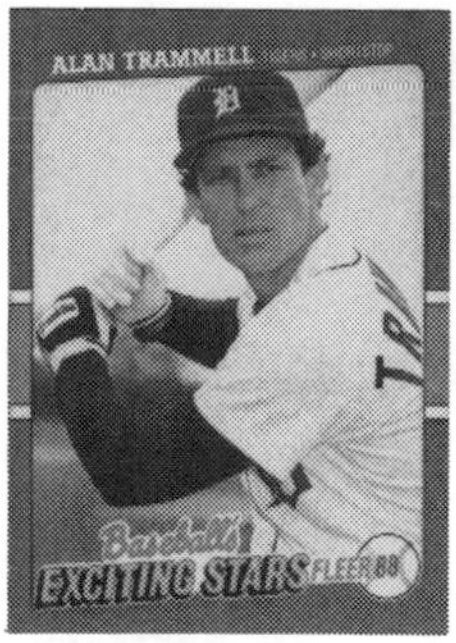

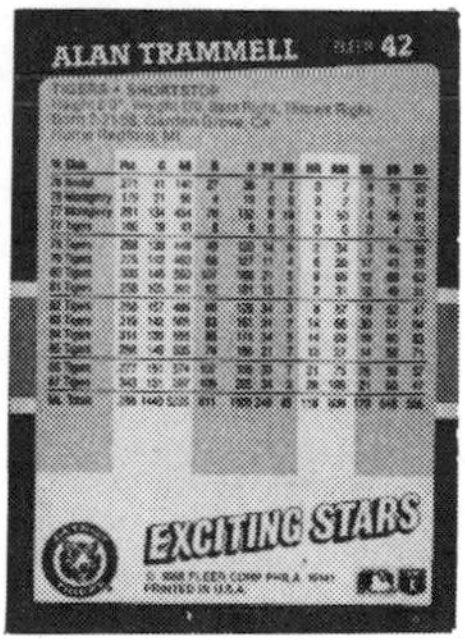

This 44-card limited-edition boxed set showcases star major leaguers. Player photos are slanted upwards to the right, framed by a blue border with a red and white bar stripe across the middle. The player's name is printed in white above the photo. "Baseball's Exciting Stars" is printed in red and yellow across the bottom margin, following the upward slant of the photo. Fleer's logo appears lower right intersecting a white baseball bearing the number "88." Card backs are numbered and printed in red, white and blue. The set was packaged in a checklist box, with six team logo sticker cards featuring black and white stadium photos on the flip sides. Exciting Stars was distributed via Cumberland Farm stores throughout the northeastern U.S. and Florida.

		MT	NR MT	EX
Complete Set:		5.00	3.75	2.00
Common Player:		.05	.04	.02
1	Harold Baines	.10	.08	.04
2	Kevin Bass	.07	.05	.03
3	George Bell	.20	.15	.08
4	Wade Boggs	.80	.60	.30
5	Mickey Brantley	.05	.04	.02
6	Sid Bream	.05	.04	.02
7	Jose Canseco	.80	.60	.30
8	Jack Clark	.15	.11	.06
9	Will Clark	.80	.60	.30
10	Roger Clemens	.40	.30	.15
11	Vince Coleman	.15	.11	.06
12	Eric Davis	.50	.40	.20
13	Andre Dawson	.15	.11	.06
14	Julio Franco	.07	.05	.03
15	Dwight Gooden	.40	.30	.15
16	Mike Greenwell	.40	.30	.15
17	Tony Gwynn	.25	.20	.10
18	Von Hayes	.07	.05	.03
19	Tom Henke	.05	.04	.02
20	Orel Hershiser	.20	.15	.08
21	Teddy Higuera	.10	.08	.04
22	Brook Jacoby	.07	.05	.03
23	Wally Joyner	.30	.25	.12
24	Jimmy Key	.07	.05	.03
25	Don Mattingly	.80	.60	.30
26	Mark McGwire	.80	.60	.30
27	Jack Morris	.12	.09	.05
28	Dale Murphy	.30	.25	.12
29	Matt Nokes	.30	.25	.12
30	Kirby Puckett	.50	.40	.20
31	Tim Raines	.25	.20	.10
32	Ryne Sandberg	.20	.15	.08
33	Benito Santiago	.25	.20	.10
34	Mike Schmidt	.30	.25	.12
35	Mike Scott	.10	.08	.04
36	Kevin Seitzer	.60	.45	.25
37	Larry Sheets	.07	.05	.03
38	Ruben Sierra	.12	.09	.05
39	Darryl Strawberry	.40	.30	.15
40	Ozzie Smith	.15	.11	.06
41	Danny Tartabull	.10	.08	.04
42	Alan Trammell	.15	.11	.06
43	Fernando Valenzuela	.20	.15	.08
44	Devon White	.20	.15	.08

1988 Fleer Baseball's Hottest Stars

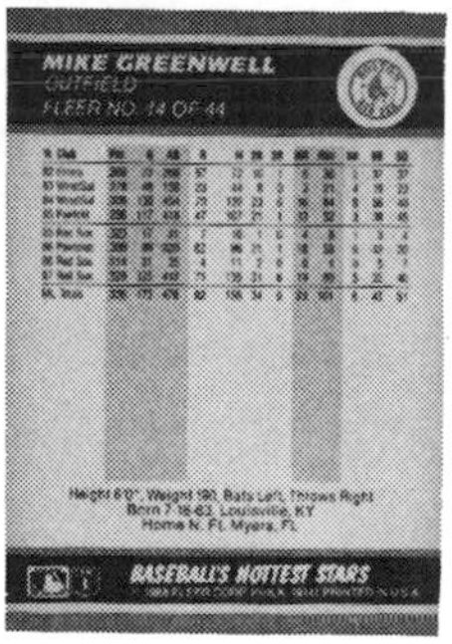

This boxed set of 44 standard-size player cards and six team logo sticker cards was produced by Fleer for exclusive distribution at Revco drug stores nationwide. Card fronts feature full-color photos of players representing every major league team. Photos are framed in red, orange and yellow, with a blue and white player name printed across the bottom of the card front. A flaming baseball logo bearing the words

"Hottest Stars" appears in the lower left corner of the player photo. Card backs are red, white and blue. The player's name, position, card number and team logo are printed across the top section, followed by a stats box, personal data, batting and throwing preferences. The set also includes six team logo sticker cards with flipside stadium photos in black and white.

		MT	NR MT	EX
Complete Set:		6.00	4.50	2.50
Common Player:		.05	.04	.02
1	George Bell	.20	.15	.08
2	Wade Boggs	.80	.60	.30
3	Bobby Bonilla	.12	.09	.05
4	George Brett	.30	.25	.12
5	Jose Canseco	.80	.60	.30
6	Will Clark	.80	.60	.30
7	Roger Clemens	.40	.30	.15
8	Eric Davis	.50	.40	.20
9	Andre Dawson	.15	.11	.06
10	Tony Fernandez	.10	.08	.04
11	Julio Franco	.07	.05	.03
12	Gary Gaetti	.10	.08	.04
13	Dwight Gooden	.40	.30	.15
14	Mike Greenwell	.40	.30	.15
15	Tony Gwynn	.25	.20	.10
16	Rickey Henderson	.50	.40	.20
17	Keith Hernandez	.15	.11	.06
18	Tom Herr	.07	.05	.03
19	Orel Hershiser	.20	.15	.08
20	Ted Higuera	.10	.08	.04
21	Wally Joyner	.30	.25	.12
22	Jimmy Key	.07	.05	.03
23	Mark Langston	.10	.08	.04
24	Don Mattingly	.80	.60	.30
25	Jack McDowell	.20	.15	.08
26	Mark McGwire	.80	.60	.30
27	Kevin Mitchell	.50	.40	.20
28	Jack Morris	.12	.09	.05
29	Dale Murphy	.30	.25	.12
30	Kirby Puckett	.50	.40	.20
31	Tim Raines	.25	.20	.10
32	Shane Rawley	.05	.04	.02
33	Benito Santiago	.25	.20	.10
34	Mike Schmidt	.30	.25	.12
35	Mike Scott	.10	.08	.04
36	Kevin Seitzer	.60	.45	.25
37	Larry Sheets	.07	.05	.03
38	Ruben Sierra	.50	.40	.20
39	Dave Smith	.05	.04	.02
41	Darryl Strawberry	.40	.30	.15
42	Rick Sutcliffe	.10	.08	.04
43	Pat Tabler	.05	.04	.02
44	Alan Trammell	.15	.11	.06

1988 Fleer Box Panels

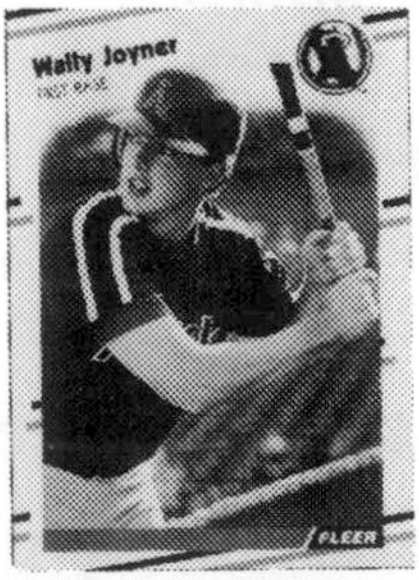

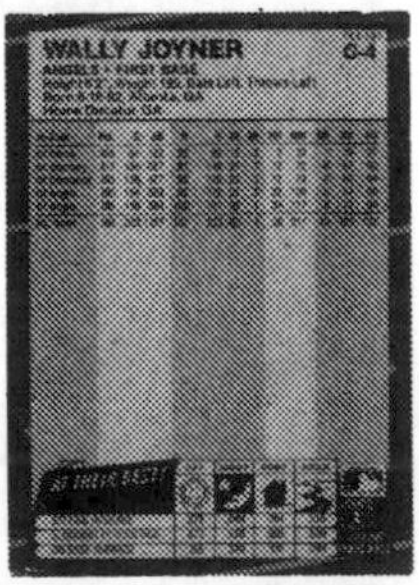

Fleer's third annual box-bottom issue once again included 16 full-color trading cards printed on the bottoms of four different wax and cello pack retail display boxes. Each box contains three player cards and one team logo card. Player cards follow the same design as the basic 1988 Fleer issue - full-color player photo, name upper left, team logo upper right, Fleer logo lower right. Card fronts feature a blue and red striped border, with a thin white line framing the photo. Card backs are printed in blue and red and include personal information and statistics. Standard- size, the cards are numbered C-1 through C-16.

		MT	NR MT	EX
Complete Panel Set:		6.25	4.75	2.50
Complete Singles Set:		2.50	2.00	1.00
Common Panel:		1.25	.90	.50
Common Single Player:		.15	.11	.06
	Panel	2.00	1.50	.80
1	Cardinals Logo	.05	.04	.02
11	Mike Schmidt	.60	.45	.25
14	Dave Stewart	.15	.11	.06
15	Tim Wallach	.20	.15	.08
	Panel	1.25	.90	.50
2	Dwight Evans	.15	.11	.06
8	Shane Rawley	.15	.11	.06
10	Ryne Sandberg	.30	.25	.12
13	Tigers Logo	.05	.04	.02
	Panel	2.75	2.00	1.00
3	Andres Galarraga	.25	.20	.10
6	Dale Murphy	.60	.45	.25
9	Giants Logo	.05	.04	.02
12	Kevin Seitzer	.80	.60	.30
	Panel	2.25	1.75	.90
4	Wally Joyner	.60	.45	.25
5	Twins Logo	.05	.04	.02
7	Kirby Puckett	.40	.30	.15
16	Todd Worrell	.20	.15	.08

1988 Fleer '87 World Series

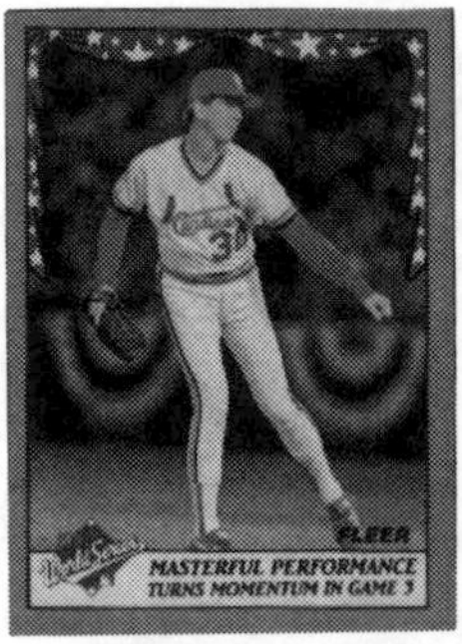

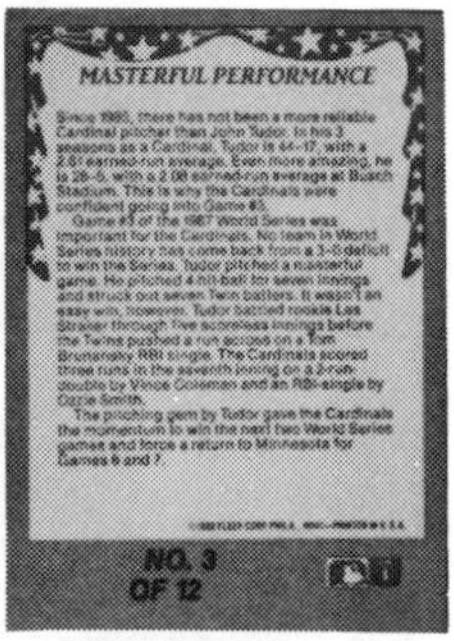

Highlights of the 1987 Series are captured in this full-color insert set found only in Fleer's regular 660-card factory sealed sets. This second World Series edition by Fleer features cards framed in red, with a blue and white starred bunting draped over the upper edges of the photo and a brief photo caption printed on a yellow band across the lower border. Numbered card backs are red, white and blue and include a description of the action pictured on the front, with stats for the Series.

		MT	NR MT	EX
Complete Set:		3.00	2.25	1.25
Common Player:		.30	.25	.12
1	"Grand" Hero In Game 1 (Dan Gladden)	.30	.25	.12
2	The Cardinals "Bush" Whacked (Randy Bush, Tony Pena)	.30	.25	.12
3	Masterful Performance Turns Momentum (John Tudor)	.30	.25	.12
4	The Wizard (Ozzie Smith)	.35	.25	.14
5	Throw Smoke! (Tony Pena, Todd Worrell)	.35	.25	.14
6	Cardinal Attack - Disruptive Speed (Vince Coleman)	.40	.30	.15
7	Herr's Wallop (Dan Driessen, Tom Herr)	.30	.25	.12
8	Kirby's Bat Comes Alive in Game 6 (Kirby Puckett)	1.00	.70	.40
9	Hrbek's Slam Forces Game 7 (Kent Hrbek)	.30	.25	.12
10	Herr, Out At First? (Rich Hacker (coach), Tom Herr, Lee Weyer (umpire))	.30	.25	.12

		MT	NR MT	EX
11	Game 7's Play At The Plate (Don Baylor, Dave Phillips (umpire))	.30	.25	.12
12	Series MVP with 16 K's (Frank Viola)	.35	.25	.14

1988 Fleer Headliners

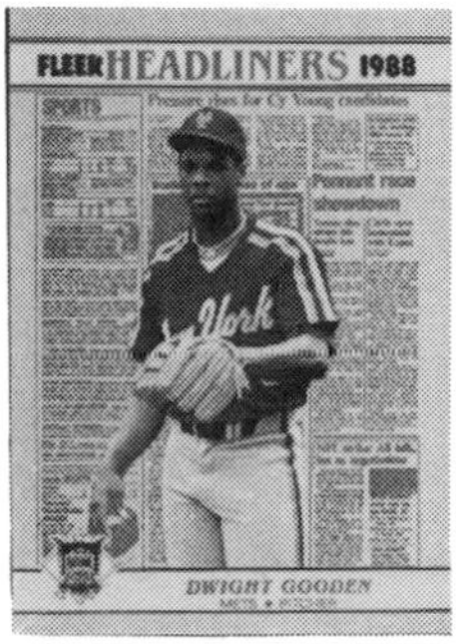

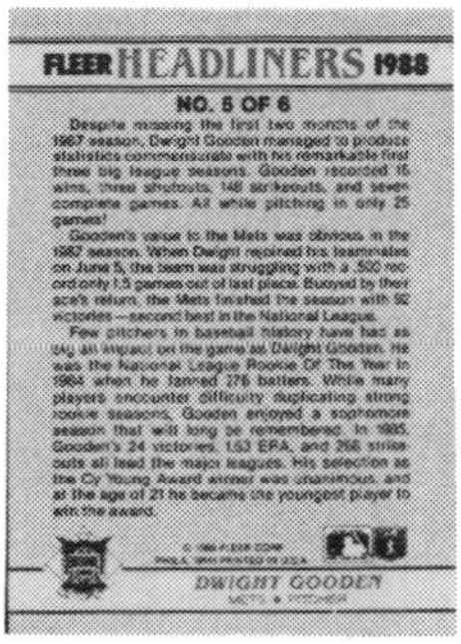

This six-card special set was inserted in Fleer three-packs, sold by retail outlets and hobby dealers nationwide. The card fronts feature crisp full-color player cut-outs printed on a grey and white USA Today-style sports page. "Fleer Headliners 1988" is printed in black and red on a white banner across the top of the card, both front and back. A similar white banner across the card bottom bears the black and white National or American League logo and a red player/team name. Card backs are black on grey with red accents and include the card number and a three-paragraph career summary.

		MT	NR MT	EX
Complete Set:		8.00	6.00	3.25
Common Player:		1.00	.70	.40
1	Don Mattingly	2.00	1.50	.80
2	Mark McGwire	1.50	1.25	.60
3	Jack Morris	1.00	.70	.40
4	Darryl Strawberry	1.50	1.25	.60
5	Dwight Gooden	1.50	1.25	.60
6	Tim Raines	1.25	.90	.50

1988 Fleer League Leaders

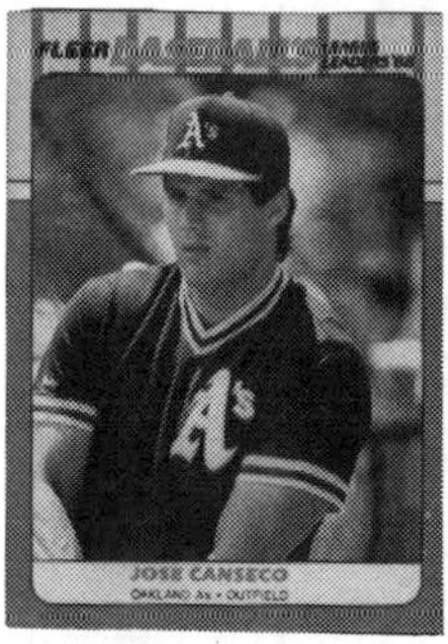

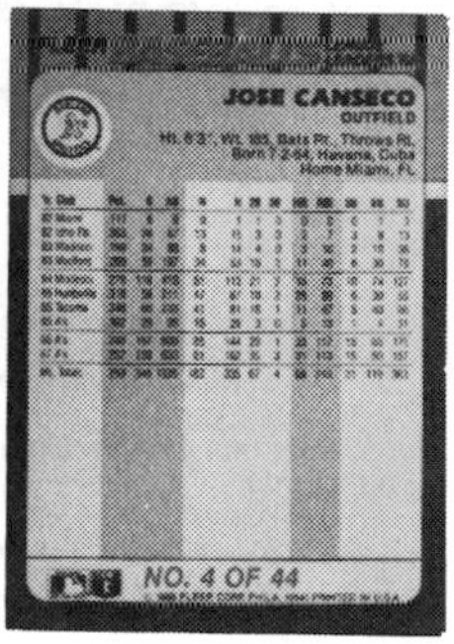

This 44-card boxed set is the third annual limited edition set from Fleer highlighting leading players. The 1988 edition contains the same type of information, front and back, as the previous sets, with a new color scheme and design. Card fronts have bright blue borders, solid on the lower portion, striped on the upper, with a gold bar separating the two sections. "Fleer's Baseball's League Leaders '88" headlines the card face. The full-color player photo is centered above a yellow player name banner. The numbered card backs are blue, pink and white, and contain player stats and personal notes. Six team logo sticker cards, with flipside black and white photos of ballparks, accompany this set which was marketed exclusively by Walgreen drug stores.

		MT	NR MT	EX
Complete Set:		6.00	4.50	2.50
Common Player:		.05	.04	.02
1	George Bell	.20	.15	.08
2	Wade Boggs	.80	.60	.30
3	Ivan Calderon	.07	.05	.03
4	Jose Canseco	.80	.60	.30
5	Will Clark	.80	.60	.30
6	Roger Clemens	.40	.30	.15
7	Vince Coleman	.15	.11	.06
8	Eric Davis	.50	.40	.20
9	Andre Dawson	.15	.11	.06
10	Bill Doran	.07	.05	.03
11	Dwight Evans	.10	.08	.04
12	Julio Franco	.07	.05	.03
13	Gary Gaetti	.10	.08	.04
14	Andres Galarraga	.15	.11	.06
15	Dwight Gooden	.40	.30	.15
16	Tony Gwynn	.25	.20	.10
17	Tom Henke	.05	.04	.02
18	Keith Hernandez	.20	.15	.08
19	Orel Hershiser	.20	.15	.08
20	Ted Higuera	.10	.08	.04
21	Kent Hrbek	.15	.11	.06
22	Wally Joyner	.30	.25	.12
23	Jimmy Key	.07	.05	.03
24	Mark Langston	.10	.08	.04
25	Don Mattingly	.80	.60	.30
26	Mark McGwire	.80	.60	.30
27	Paul Molitor	.12	.09	.05
28	Jack Morris	.12	.09	.05
29	Dale Murphy	.30	.25	.12
30	Kirby Puckett	.50	.40	.20
31	Tim Raines	.25	.20	.10
32	Rick Rueschel	.07	.05	.03
33	Bret Saberhagen	.15	.11	.06
34	Benito Santiago	.25	.20	.10
35	Mike Schmidt	.30	.25	.12
36	Mike Scott	.10	.08	.04
37	Kevin Seitzer	.60	.45	.25
38	Larry Sheets	.07	.05	.03
39	Ruben Sierra	.50	.40	.20
40	Darryl Strawberry	.40	.30	.15
41	Rick Sutcliffe	.10	.08	.04
42	Alan Trammell	.15	.11	.06
43	Andy Van Slyke	.10	.08	.04
44	Todd Worrell	.10	.08	.04

1988 Fleer Mini

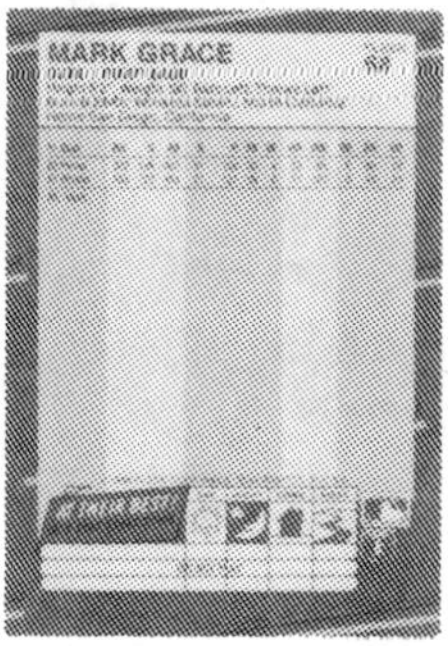

This third annual issue of miniatures (1-7/8" by 2-5/8") includes 120 high-gloss cards featuring new photos, not copies from the regular issue, although the card designs are identical. Card fronts have white borders, with red and blue striping and a bright color band beneath the photo leading to a blue Fleet logo lower right. The player name is printed upper left; the full-color team logo appears upper right. Card backs

are red, white and blue and include personal data, yearly career stats and a stats breakdown of batting average, slugging percentage and on-base average, listed for day, night, home and road games. Card backs are numbered in alphabetical order by teams which are also listed alphabetically. The set includes 18 team logo stickers with black and white aerial stadium photos on the flip sides.

		MT	NR MT	EX
Complete Set:		12.00	9.00	4.75
Common Player:		.05	.04	.02
1	Eddie Murray	.25	.20	.10
2	Dave Schmidt	.05	.04	.02
3	Larry Sheets	.07	.05	.03
4	Wade Boggs	.70	.50	.30
5	Roger Clemens	.80	.60	.30
6	Dwight Evans	.12	.09	.05
7	Mike Greenwell	.40	.30	.15
8	Sam Horn	.20	.15	.08
9	Lee Smith	.07	.05	.03
10	Brian Downing	.05	.04	.02
11	Wally Joyner	.30	.25	.12
12	Devon White	.10	.08	.04
13	Mike Witt	.07	.05	.03
14	Ivan Calderon	.15	.11	.06
15	Ozzie Guillen	.07	.05	.03
16	Jack McDowell	.50	.40	.20
17	Kenny Williams	.12	.09	.05
18	Joe Carter	.20	.15	.08
19	Julio Franco	.20	.15	.08
20	Pat Tabler	.05	.04	.02
21	Doyle Alexander	.05	.04	.02
22	Jack Morris	.15	.11	.06
23	Matt Nokes	.30	.25	.12
24	Walt Terrell	.05	.04	.02
25	Alan Trammell	.20	.15	.08
26	Bret Saberhagen	.15	.11	.06
27	Kevin Seitzer	.20	.15	.08
28	Danny Tartabull	.15	.11	.06
29	Gary Thurman	.20	.15	.08
30	Ted Higuera	.10	.08	.04
31	Paul Molitor	.12	.09	.05
32	Dan Plesac	.10	.08	.04
33	Robin Yount	.25	.20	.10
34	Gary Gaetti	.12	.09	.05
35	Kent Hrbek	.15	.11	.06
36	Kirby Puckett	.50	.40	.20
37	Jeff Reardon	.07	.05	.03
38	Frank Viola	.12	.09	.05
39	Jack Clark	.12	.09	.05
40	Rickey Henderson	.80	.60	.30
41	Don Mattingly	.80	.60	.30
42	Willie Randolph	.05	.04	.02
43	Dave Righetti	.12	.09	.05
44	Dave Winfield	.20	.15	.08
45	Jose Canseco	.80	.60	.30
46	Mark McGwire	.60	.45	.25
47	Dave Parker	.12	.09	.05
48	Dave Stewart	.07	.05	.03
49	Walt Weiss	.60	.45	.25
50	Bob Welch	.07	.05	.03
51	Mickey Brantley	.05	.04	.02
52	Mark Langston	.10	.08	.04
53	Harold Reynolds	.07	.05	.03
54	Scott Fletcher	.05	.04	.02
55	Charlie Hough	.05	.04	.02
56	Pete Incaviglia	.12	.09	.05
57	Larry Parrish	.05	.04	.02
58	Ruben Sierra	.35	.25	.14
59	George Bell	.20	.15	.08
60	Mark Eichhorn	.05	.04	.02
61	Tony Fernandez	.10	.08	.04
62	Tom Henke	.05	.04	.02
63	Jimmy Key	.07	.05	.03
64	Dion James	.05	.04	.02
65	Dale Murphy	.30	.25	.12
66	Zane Smith	.05	.04	.02
67	Andre Dawson	.15	.11	.06
68	Mark Grace	1.00	.70	.40
69	Jerry Mumphrey	.05	.04	.02
70	Ryne Sandberg	.40	.30	.15
71	Rick Sutcliffe	.10	.08	.04
72	Kal Daniels	.12	.09	.05
73	Eric Davis	.40	.30	.15
74	John Franco	.07	.05	.03
75	Ron Robinson	.05	.04	.02
76	Jeff Treadway	.20	.15	.08
77	Kevin Bass	.07	.05	.03
78	Glenn Davis	.15	.11	.06
79	Nolan Ryan	1.00	.70	.40
80	Mike Scott	.12	.09	.05
81	Dave Smith	.05	.04	.02
82	Kirk Gibson	.20	.15	.08
83	Pedro Guerrero	.12	.09	.05
84	Orel Hershiser	.20	.15	.08
85	Steve Sax	.15	.11	.06
86	Fernando Valenzuela	.15	.11	.06
87	Tim Burke	.05	.04	.02
88	Andres Galarraga	.15	.11	.06
89	Neal Heaton	.05	.04	.02
90	Tim Raines	.20	.15	.08
91	Tim Wallach	.10	.08	.04
92	Dwight Gooden	.40	.30	.15
93	Keith Hernandez	.15	.11	.06
94	Gregg Jefferies	.70	.50	.30
95	Howard Johnson	.10	.08	.04
96	Roger McDowell	.05	.04	.02
97	Darryl Strawberry	.50	.40	.20
98	Steve Bedrosian	.10	.08	.04
99	Von Hayes	.10	.08	.04
100	Shane Rawley	.05	.04	.02
101	Juan Samuel	.12	.09	.05
102	Mike Schmidt	.30	.25	.12
103	Bobby Bonilla	.30	.25	.12
104	Mike Dunne	.07	.05	.03
105	Andy Van Slyke	.10	.08	.04
106	Vince Coleman	.15	.11	.06
107	Bob Horner	.07	.05	.03
108	Willie McGee	.10	.08	.04
109	Ozzie Smith	.12	.09	.05
110	John Tudor	.07	.05	.03
111	Todd Worrell	.10	.08	.04
112	Tony Gwynn	.25	.20	.10
113	John Kruk	.12	.09	.05
114	Lance McCullers	.05	.04	.02
115	Benito Santiago	.15	.11	.06
116	Will Clark	.40	.30	.15
117	Jeff Leonard	.05	.04	.02
118	Candy Maldonado	.05	.04	.02
119	Rick Rueschel	.07	.05	.03
120	Don Robinson	.05	.04	.02

1988 Fleer Record Setters

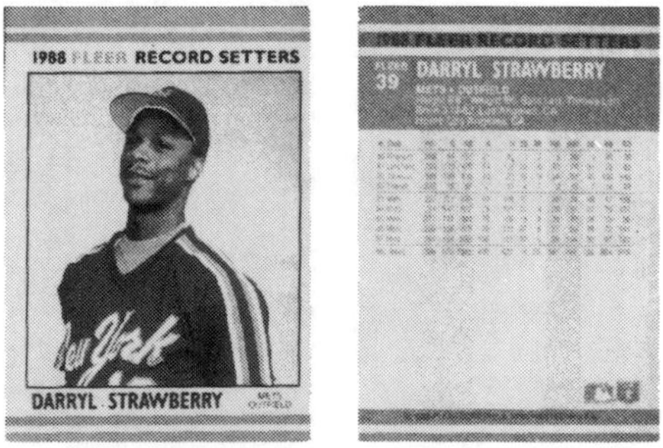

For the second consecutive year, Fleer Corp. issued this special limited-edition 44-card set for exclusive distribution by Eckerd Drug stores. Cards are standard-size with red and blue borders framing the full-color player photos. A "1988 Fleer Record Setters" headline is printed on a yellow strip above the player's photo. The player's name, team and position appear beneath the pose. Card backs list personal information and career stats in red and blue ink on a white background. Each 44-card set comes cello-wrapped in a checklist box that contains six additional cards with peel-off team logo stickers. The sticker cards feature black and white aerial photos of major league ballparks, along with stadium statistics such as field size, seating capacity and date of the first game played.

		MT	NR MT	EX
Complete Set:		5.00	3.75	2.00
Common Player:		.05	.04	.02
1	Jesse Barfield	.10	.08	.04
2	George Bell	.20	.15	.08
3	Wade Boggs	.80	.60	.30
4	Jose Canseco	.80	.60	.30
5	Jack Clark	.15	.11	.06
6	Will Clark	.80	.60	.30
7	Roger Clemens	.40	.30	.15
8	Alvin Davis	.10	.08	.04
9	Eric Davis	.50	.40	.20
10	Andre Dawson	.15	.11	.06
11	Mike Dunne	.10	.08	.04
12	John Franco	.07	.05	.03
13	Julio Franco	.07	.05	.03
14	Dwight Gooden	.40	.30	.15
15	Mark Gubicza	.07	.05	.03
16	Ozzie Guillen	.07	.05	.03
17	Tony Gwynn	.25	.20	.10
18	Orel Hershiser	.20	.15	.08
19	Teddy Higuera	.10	.08	.04
20	Howard Johnson	.07	.05	.03
21	Wally Joyner	.30	.25	.12
22	Jimmy Key	.07	.05	.03
23	Jeff Leonard	.05	.04	.02
24	Don Mattingly	.80	.60	.30
25	Mark McGwire	.80	.60	.30
26	Jack Morris	.12	.09	.05
27	Dale Murphy	.30	.25	.12
28	Larry Parrish	.05	.04	.02
29	Kirby Puckett	.50	.40	.20
30	Tim Raines	.25	.20	.10
31	Harold Reynolds	.07	.05	.03
32	Dave Righetti	.12	.09	.05
33	Cal Ripken, Jr.	.60	.45	.25
34	Benito Santiago	.25	.20	.10
35	Mike Schmidt	.30	.25	.12
36	Mike Scott	.10	.08	.04
37	Kevin Seitzer	.60	.45	.25
38	Ozzie Smith	.12	.09	.05
39	Darryl Strawberry	.40	.30	.15
40	Rick Sutcliffe	.10	.08	.04
41	Alan Trammell	.15	.11	.06
42	Frank Viola	.12	.09	.05
43	Mitch Williams	.05	.04	.02
44	Todd Worrell	.10	.08	.04

1988 Fleer Star Stickers

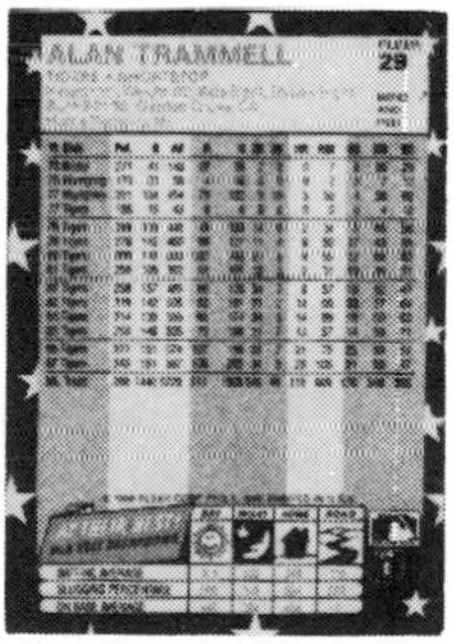

This set of 132 standard-size sticker cards (including a checklist card) features exclusive player photos, different from those in the Fleer regular issue. Card fronts have light gray borders sprinkled with multi-colored stars. The "Fleer Star Stickers" logo appears upper left, player names are printed beneath the photos. Card backs are printed in red, gray and black on white and include personal data and a breakdown of pitching and batting stats into day, night, home and road categories. Cards were marketed in two different display boxes that feature six players and two team logos from Fleer's 1988 Limited Edition box-bottom set.

		MT	NR MT	EX
Complete Set:		20.00	15.00	8.00
Common Player:		.05	.04	.02
1	Mike Boddicker	.08	.06	.03
2	Eddie Murray	.50	.40	.20
3	Cal Ripken, Jr.	.60	.45	.25
4	Larry Sheets	.15	.11	.06
5	Wade Boggs	.80	.60	.30
6	Ellis Burks	.60	.45	.25
7	Roger Clemens	.90	.70	.35
8	Dwight Evans	.15	.11	.06
9	Mike Greenwell	.40	.30	.15
10	Bruce Hurst	.12	.09	.05
11	Brian Downing	.08	.06	.03
12	Wally Joyner	.40	.30	.15
13	Mike Witt	.10	.08	.04
14	Ivan Calderon	.12	.09	.05
15	Jose DeLeon	.05	.04	.02
16	Ozzie Guillen	.15	.11	.06
17	Bobby Thigpen	.10	.08	.04
18	Joe Carter	.20	.15	.08
19	Julio Franco	.12	.09	.05
20	Brook Jacoby	.12	.09	.05
21	Cory Snyder	.05	.04	.02
22	Pat Tabler	.10	.08	.04
23	Doyle Alexander	.08	.06	.03
24	Kirk Gibson	.30	.25	.12
25	Mike Henneman	.20	.15	.08
26	Jack Morris	.25	.20	.10
27	Matt Nokes	.30	.25	.12
28	Walt Terrell	.05	.04	.02
29	Alan Trammell	.30	.25	.12
30	George Brett	.70	.50	.30
31	Charlie Leibrandt	.05	.04	.02
32	Bret Saberhagen	.25	.20	.10
33	Kevin Seitzer	.15	.11	.06
34	Danny Tartabull	.25	.20	.10
35	Frank White	.10	.08	.04
36	Rob Deer	.10	.08	.04
37	Ted Higuera	.15	.11	.06
38	Paul Molitor	.20	.15	.08
39	Dan Plesac	.12	.09	.05
40	Robin Yount	.30	.25	.12
41	Bert Blyleven	.15	.11	.06
42	Tom Brunansky	.15	.11	.06
43	Gary Gaetti	.20	.15	.08
44	Kent Hrbek	.30	.25	.12
45	Kirby Puckett	.50	.40	.20
46	Jeff Reardon	.10	.08	.04
47	Frank Viola	.15	.11	.06
48	Don Mattingly	1.00	.70	.40
49	Mike Pagliarulo	.12	.09	.05
50	Willie Randolph	.08	.06	.03
51	Rick Rhoden	.08	.06	.03
52	Dave Righetti	.20	.15	.08
53	Dave Winfield	.40	.30	.15
54	Jose Canseco	1.00	.70	.40
55	Carney Lansford	.08	.06	.03
56	Mark McGwire	.60	.45	.25
57	Dave Stewart	.12	.09	.05
58	Curt Young	.08	.06	.03
59	Alvin Davis	.15	.11	.06
60	Mark Langston	.15	.11	.06
61	Ken Phelps	.05	.04	.02
62	Harold Reynolds	.10	.08	.04
63	Scott Fletcher	.05	.04	.02
64	Charlie Hough	.08	.06	.03
65	Pete Incaviglia	.25	.20	.10
66	Oddibe McDowell	.10	.08	.04
67	Pete O'Brien	.10	.08	.04
68	Larry Parrish	.08	.06	.03
69	Ruben Sierra	.25	.20	.10
70	Jesse Barfield	.12	.09	.05
71	George Bell	.25	.20	.10
72	Tony Fernandez	.12	.09	.05
73	Tom Henke	.10	.08	.04
74	Jimmy Key	.12	.09	.05
75	Lloyd Moseby	.10	.08	.04
76	Dion James	.05	.04	.02
77	Dale Murphy	.35	.25	.12
78	Zane Smith	.08	.06	.03
79	Andre Dawson	.25	.20	.10
80	Ryne Sandberg	.35	.25	.14
81	Rick Sutcliffe	.15	.11	.06
82	Kal Daniels	.25	.20	.10
83	Eric Davis	.30	.25	.12
84	John Franco	.10	.08	.04
85	Kevin Bass	.10	.08	.04
86	Glenn Davis	.20	.15	.08
87	Bill Doran	.10	.08	.04
88	Nolan Ryan	1.00	.70	.40
89	Mike Scott	.15	.11	.06
90	Dave Smith	.05	.04	.02
91	Pedro Guerrero	.20	.15	.08

		MT	NR MT	EX
92	Orel Hershiser	.35	.25	.14
93	Steve Sax	.20	.15	.08
94	Fernando Valenzuela	.25	.20	.10
95	Tim Burke	.05	.04	.02
96	Andres Galarraga	.20	.15	.08
97	Tim Raines	.25	.20	.10
98	Tim Wallach	.12	.09	.05
99	Mitch Webster	.05	.04	.02
100	Ron Darling	.20	.15	.08
101	Sid Fernandez	.10	.08	.04
102	Dwight Gooden	.90	.70	.35
103	Keith Hernandez	.30	.25	.12
104	Howard Johnson	.12	.09	.05
105	Roger McDowell	.10	.08	.04
106	Darryl Strawberry	.70	.50	.30
107	Steve Bedrosian	.12	.09	.05
108	Von Hayes	.12	.09	.05
109	Shane Rawley	.08	.06	.03
110	Juan Samuel	.15	.11	.06
111	Mike Schmidt	.70	.50	.30
112	Milt Thompson	.05	.04	.02
113	Sid Bream	.08	.06	.03
114	Bobby Bonilla	.35	.25	.14
115	Mike Dunne	.15	.11	.06
116	Andy Van Slyke	.12	.09	.05
117	Vince Coleman	.25	.20	.10
118	Willie McGee	.15	.11	.06
119	Terry Pendleton	.10	.08	.04
120	Ozzie Smith	.20	.15	.08
121	John Tudor	.12	.09	.05
122	Todd Worrell	.20	.15	.08
123	Tony Gwynn	.40	.30	.15
124	John Kruk	.20	.15	.08
125	Benito Santiago	.30	.25	.12
126	Will Clark	1.00	.70	.40
127	Dave Dravecky	.05	.04	.02
128	Jeff Leonard	.05	.04	.02
129	Candy Maldonado	.05	.04	.02
130	Rick Rueschel	.10	.08	.04
131	Don Robinson	.05	.04	.02
132	Checklist	.05	.04	.02

1988 Fleer Star Stickers Box Panels

This set of eight box-bottom cards was printed on two different retail display boxes. Six players and two team logo sticker cards are included in the set, three player photos and one team photo per box. The full-color player photos are exclusively limited to the Fleer Star Sticker set. The cards, which measure 2-1/2" by 3-1/2", have a light gray border sprinkled with multi-color stars. The backs are printed in navy blue and red.

		MT	NR MT	EX
	Complete Panel Set:	3.50	2.75	1.50
	Complete Singles Set:	1.75	1.25	.70
	Common Singles Player:	.15	.11	.06
	Panel	2.50	2.00	1.00
1	Eric Davis, Mark McGwire	.70	.50	.30
3	Kevin Mitchell	.50	.40	.20
5	Rickey Henderson	.50	.40	.20
7	Tigers Logo	.05	.04	.02
	Panel	1.25	.90	.50
2	Gary Carter	.35	.25	.14
4	Ron Guidry	.20	.15	.08
6	Don Baylor	.15	.11	.06
8	Giants Logo	.05	.04	.02

1988 Fleer Superstars

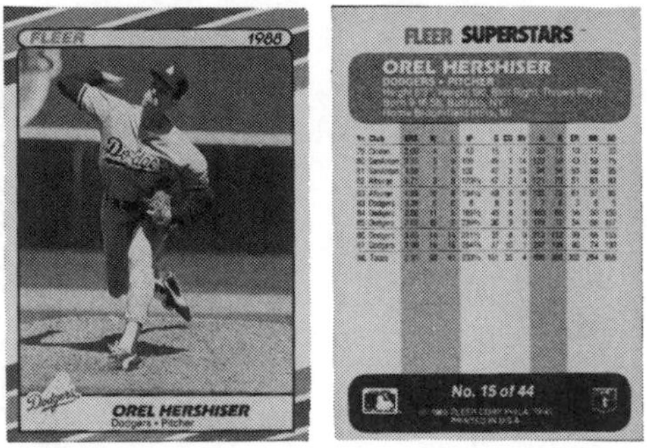

This is the fourth edition of Fleer's 44-card boxed set produced for distribution by McCrory's (1985-87 issues were simply titled "Fleer Limited Edition"). The Superstars standard-size card set features full-color player photos framed by red, white and blue striped top and bottom borders. "Fleer 1988" is printed in an elongated yellow oval banner above the photo. A pale yellow rectangle below the photo carries the player's name and team logo. Card fronts have a semi-glossy slightly textured finish. Card backs are red and blue on white and include card numbers, personal data and statistics. Six team logo sticker cards are also included in this set which was marketed in red, white and blue boxes with checklist backs. Boxed sets were sold exclusively at McCrory's stores and its affiliates.

		MT	NR MT	EX
	Complete Set:	6.00	4.50	2.50
	Common Player:	.05	.04	.02
1	Steve Bedrosian	.10	.08	.04
2	George Bell	.20	.15	.08
3	Wade Boggs	.80	.60	.30
4	Barry Bonds	.12	.09	.05
5	Jose Canseco	.80	.60	.30
6	Joe Carter	.12	.09	.05
7	Jack Clark	.15	.11	.06
8	Will Clark	.80	.60	.30
9	Roger Clemens	.40	.30	.15
10	Alvin Davis	.10	.08	.04
11	Eric Davis	.50	.40	.20
12	Glenn Davis	.12	.09	.05
13	Andre Dawson	.15	.11	.06
14	Dwight Gooden	.40	.30	.15
15	Orel Hershiser	.20	.15	.08
16	Teddy Higuera	.10	.08	.04
17	Kent Hrbek	.15	.11	.06
18	Wally Joyner	.30	.25	.12
19	Jimmy Key	.07	.05	.03
20	John Kruk	.10	.08	.04
21	Jeff Leonard	.05	.04	.02
22	Don Mattingly	.80	.60	.30
23	Mark McGwire	.80	.60	.30
24	Kevin McReynolds	.12	.09	.05
25	Dale Murphy	.30	.25	.12
26	Matt Nokes	.30	.25	.12
27	Terry Pendleton	.05	.04	.02
28	Kirby Puckett	.50	.40	.20
29	Tim Raines	.25	.20	.10
30	Rick Rhoden	.07	.05	.03
31	Cal Ripken, Jr.	.60	.45	.25
32	Benito Santiago	.25	.20	.10
33	Mike Schmidt	.30	.25	.12
34	Mike Scott	.10	.08	.04
35	Kevin Seitzer	.60	.45	.25
36	Ruben Sierra	.25	.20	.10
37	Cory Snyder	.12	.09	.05
38	Darryl Strawberry	.40	.30	.15
39	Rick Sutcliffe	.10	.08	.04
40	Danny Tartabull	.12	.09	.05

		MT	NR MT	EX
41	Alan Trammell	.15	.11	.06
42	Ken Williams	.07	.05	.03
43	Mike Witt	.07	.05	.03
44	Robin Yount	.15	.11	.06

1988 Fleer Update

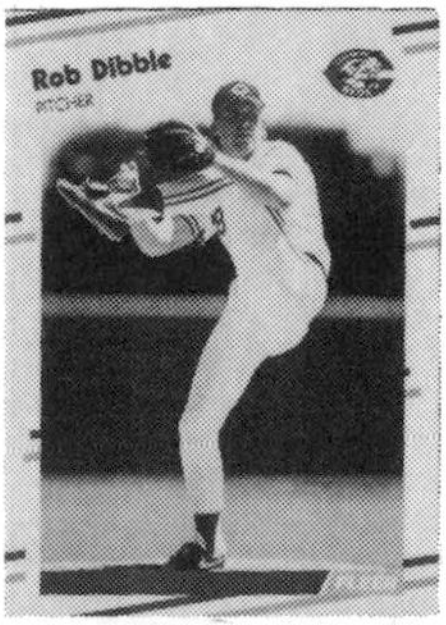

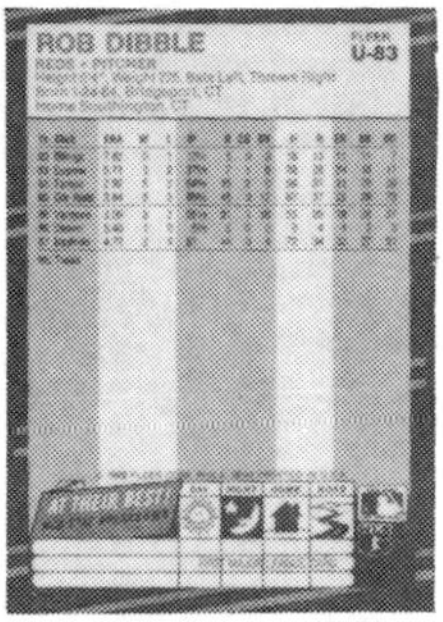

This 132-card update set (numbered U-1 through U-132 and 2-1/2" by 3-1/2") features traded veterans and rookies in a mixture of full-color action shots and close-ups, framed by white borders with red and blue stripes. Player name and position appear upper left, printed on an upward slant leading into the team logo, upper right. A bright stripe in a variety of colors (blue, red, green, yellow) edges the bottom of the photo and leads into the Fleer logo at lower right. The backs are red, white and blue-grey and include personal info, along with yearly and "At Their Best" (day, night, home, road) stats charts. The set was packaged in white cardboard boxes with red and blue stripes. A glossy-coated edition of the update set was issued in its own tin box and is valued at two times greater than the regular issue.

		MT	NR MT	EX
Complete Set:		13.00	9.75	5.25
Common Player:		.06	.05	.02
1	Jose Bautista(FC)	.20	.15	.08
2	Joe Orsulak	.06	.05	.02
3	Doug Sisk	.06	.05	.02
4	Craig Worthington(FC)	.20	.15	.08
5	Mike Boddicker	.08	.06	.03
6	Rick Cerone	.06	.05	.02
7	Larry Parrish	.08	.06	.03
8	Lee Smith	.10	.08	.04
9	Mike Smithson	.06	.05	.02
10	John Trautwein(FC)	.15	.11	.06
11	Sherman Corbett(FC)	.15	.11	.06
12	Chili Davis	.10	.08	.04
13	Jim Eppard	.08	.06	.03
14	Bryan Harvey(FC)	.50	.40	.20
15	John Davis	.08	.06	.03
16	Dave Gallagher(FC)	.20	.15	.08
17	Ricky Horton	.08	.06	.03
18	Dan Pasqua	.10	.08	.04
19	Melido Perez	.12	.09	.05
20	Jose Segura(FC)	.15	.11	.06
21	Andy Allanson	.08	.06	.03
22	Jon Perlman	.06	.05	.02
23	Domingo Ramos	.06	.05	.02
24	Rick Rodriguez	.08	.06	.03
25	Willie Upshaw	.10	.08	.04
26	Paul Gibson(FC)	.15	.11	.06
27	Don Heinkel(FC)	.15	.11	.06
28	Ray Knight	.08	.06	.03
29	Gary Pettis	.08	.06	.03
30	Luis Salazar	.06	.05	.02
31	Mike MacFarlane (Macfarlane)(FC)	.25	.20	.10
32	Jeff Montgomery	.08	.06	.03
33	Ted Power	.06	.05	.02
34	Israel Sanchez(FC)	.15	.11	.06
35	Kurt Stillwell	.10	.08	.04
36	Pat Tabler	.08	.06	.03
37	Don August(FC)	.15	.11	.06
38	Darryl Hamilton(FC)	.30	.25	.12
39	Jeff Leonard	.08	.06	.03
40	Joey Meyer	.15	.11	.06
41	Allan Anderson	.10	.08	.04
42	Brian Harper	.06	.05	.02
43	Tom Herr	.10	.08	.04
44	Charlie Lea	.06	.05	.02
45	John Moses	.06	.05	.02
46	John Candelaria	.10	.08	.04
47	Jack Clark	.15	.11	.06
48	Richard Dotson	.10	.08	.04
49	Al Leiter(FC)	.15	.11	.06
50	Rafael Santana	.06	.05	.02
51	Don Slaught	.06	.05	.02
52	Todd Burns(FC)	.25	.20	.10
53	Dave Henderson	.10	.08	.04
54	Doug Jennings(FC)	.20	.15	.08
55	Dave Parker	.12	.09	.05
56	Walt Weiss	.40	.30	.15
57	Bob Welch	.10	.08	.04
58	Henry Cotto	.06	.05	.02
59	Marion Diaz (Mario)	.08	.06	.03
60	Mike Jackson	.06	.05	.02
61	Bill Swift	.06	.05	.02
62	Jose Cecena(FC)	.15	.11	.06
63	Ray Hayward(FC)	.08	.06	.03
64	Jim Steels(FC)	.08	.06	.03
65	Pat Borders(FC)	.30	.25	.12
66	Sil Campusano(FC)	.20	.15	.08
67	Mike Flanagan	.10	.08	.04
68	Todd Stottlemyre(FC)	.70	.50	.30
69	David Wells(FC)	.08	.06	.03
70	Jose Alvarez(FC)	.15	.11	.06
71	Paul Runge	.06	.05	.02
72	Cesar Jimenez (German)(FC)	.15	.11	.06
73	Pete Smith	.08	.06	.03
74	John Smoltz(FC)	1.25	.90	.50
75	Damon Berryhill	.10	.08	.04
76	Goose Gossage	.15	.11	.06
77	Mark Grace	4.00	3.00	1.50
78	Darrin Jackson	.08	.06	.03
79	Vance Law	.08	.06	.03
80	Jeff Pico(FC)	.20	.15	.08
81	Gary Varsho(FC)	.20	.15	.08
82	Tim Birtsas	.06	.05	.02
83	Rob Dibble(FC)	1.25	.90	.50
84	Danny Jackson	.15	.11	.06
85	Paul O'Neill	.08	.06	.03
86	Jose Rijo	.08	.06	.03
87	Chris Sabo(FC)	2.00	1.50	.80
88	John Fishel(FC)	.15	.11	.06
89	Craig Biggio(FC)	1.25	.90	.50
90	Terry Puhl	.06	.05	.02
91	Rafael Ramirez	.06	.05	.02
92	Louie Meadows(FC)	.15	.11	.06
93	Kirk Gibson(FC)	.20	.15	.08
94	Alfredo Griffin	.08	.06	.03
95	Jay Howell	.08	.06	.03
96	Jesse Orosco	.08	.06	.03
97	Alejandro Pena	.08	.06	.03
98	Tracy Woodson(FC)	.10	.08	.04
99	John Dopson(FC)	.25	.20	.10
100	Brian Holman(FC)	.40	.30	.15
101	Rex Hudler(FC)	.08	.06	.03
102	Jeff Parrett(FC)	.10	.08	.04
103	Nelson Santovenia(FC)	.15	.11	.06
104	Kevin Elster	.12	.09	.05
105	Jeff Innis(FC)	.20	.15	.08
106	Mackey Sasser(FC)	.10	.08	.04
107	Phil Bradley	.10	.08	.04
108	Danny Clay(FC)	.15	.11	.06
109	Greg Harris	.06	.05	.02
110	Ricky Jordan(FC)	.70	.50	.30
111	David Palmer	.06	.05	.02
112	Jim Gott	.06	.05	.02
113	Tommy Gregg (photo actually Randy Milligan)(FC)	.10	.08	.04
114	Barry Jones	.06	.05	.02
115	Randy Milligan(FC)	.60	.45	.25
116	Luis Alicea(FC)	.15	.11	.06
117	Tom Brunansky	.12	.09	.05
118	John Costello(FC)	.15	.11	.06
119	Jose DeLeon	.08	.06	.03
120	Bob Horner	.10	.08	.04
121	Scott Terry(FC)	.10	.08	.04
122	Roberto Alomar(FC)	2.50	2.00	1.00
123	Dave Leiper	.06	.05	.02
124	Keith Moreland	.08	.06	.03
125	Mark Parent(FC)	.20	.15	.08
126	Dennis Rasmussen	.10	.08	.04
127	Randy Bockus	.06	.05	.02
128	Brett Butler	.08	.06	.03
129	Donell Nixon	.06	.05	.02

		MT	NR MT	EX
130	Earnest Riles	.06	.05	.02
131	Roger Samuels(FC)	.15	.11	.06
132	Checklist	.06	.05	.02

1989 Fleer

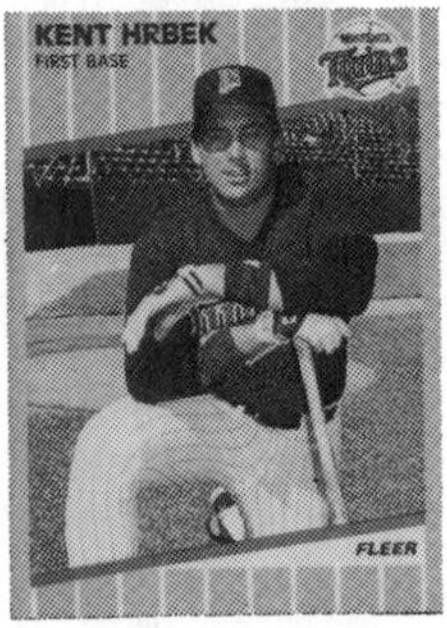

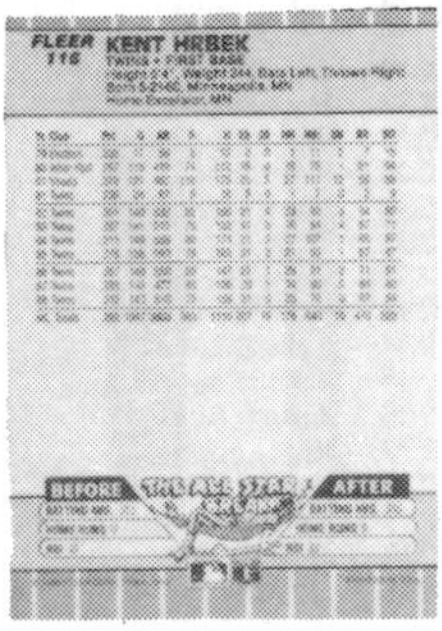

This set includes 660 standard-size cards and was issued with 45 team logo stickers. Individual card fronts feature a grey and white striped background with full-color player photos framed by a bright line of color that slants upward to the right. The set also includes two subsets: 15 Major League Prospects and 12 SuperStar Specials. A special bonus set of 12 All-Star Team cards was randomly inserted in individual wax packs of 15 cards. The last seven cards in the set are checklists, with players listed alphabetically by teams.

	MT	NR MT	EX
Complete Set:	28.00	21.00	12.00
Common Player:	.05	.04	.02

		MT	NR MT	EX
1	Don Baylor	.10	.08	.04
2	*Lance Blankenship*(FC)	.15	.11	.06
3	*Todd Burns*	.15	.11	.06
4	Greg Cadaret(FC)	.07	.05	.03
5	Jose Canseco	1.25	.90	.50
6	Storm Davis	.10	.08	.04
7	Dennis Eckersley	.12	.09	.05
8	Mike Gallego(FC)	.05	.04	.02
9	Ron Hassey	.05	.04	.02
10	Dave Henderson	.10	.08	.04
11	Rick Honeycutt	.05	.04	.02
12	Glenn Hubbard	.05	.04	.02
13	Stan Javier	.05	.04	.02
14	*Doug Jennings*	.15	.11	.06
15	*Felix Jose*(FC)	1.50	1.25	.60
16	Carney Lansford	.07	.05	.03
17	Mark McGwire	.70	.50	.30
18	Gene Nelson	.05	.04	.02
19	Dave Parker	.12	.09	.05
20	Eric Plunk	.05	.04	.02
21	Luis Polonia	.07	.05	.03
22	Terry Steinbach	.10	.08	.04
23	Dave Stewart	.10	.08	.04
24	Walt Weiss	.30	.25	.12
25	Bob Welch	.10	.08	.04
26	Curt Young	.07	.05	.03
27	Rick Aguilera	.05	.04	.02
28	Wally Backman	.07	.05	.03
29	Mark Carreon	.07	.05	.03
30	Gary Carter	.20	.15	.08
31	David Cone	.25	.20	.10
32	Ron Darling	.12	.09	.05
33	Len Dykstra	.10	.08	.04
34	Kevin Elster	.10	.08	.04
35	Sid Fernandez	.10	.08	.04
36	Dwight Gooden	.50	.40	.20
37	Keith Hernandez	.25	.20	.10
38	Gregg Jefferies	.70	.50	.30
39	Howard Johnson	.10	.08	.04
40	Terry Leach	.05	.04	.02
41	Dave Magadan	.10	.08	.04
42	Bob McClure	.05	.04	.02
43	Roger McDowell	.10	.08	.04
44	Kevin McReynolds	.15	.11	.06
45	Keith Miller	.10	.08	.04
46	Randy Myers	.10	.08	.04
47	Bob Ojeda	.07	.05	.03
48	Mackey Sasser	.07	.05	.03
49	Darryl Strawberry	.40	.30	.15
50	Tim Teufel	.05	.04	.02
51	*Dave West*(FC)	.20	.15	.08
52	Mookie Wilson	.07	.05	.03
53	Dave Anderson	.05	.04	.02
54	Tim Belcher	.10	.08	.04
55	Mike Davis	.07	.05	.03
56	Mike Devereaux	.15	.11	.06
57	Kirk Gibson	.20	.15	.08
58	Alfredo Griffin	.07	.05	.03
59	Chris Gwynn	.12	.09	.05
60	Jeff Hamilton	.07	.05	.03
61a	Danny Heep (Home: San Antonio, TX)	.70	.50	.30
61b	Danny Heep (Home: Lake Hills, TX)	.05	.04	.02
62	Orel Hershiser	.25	.20	.10
63	Brian Holton(FC)	.07	.05	.03
64	Jay Howell	.07	.05	.03
65	Tim Leary	.07	.05	.03
66	Mike Marshall	.12	.09	.05
67	*Ramon Martinez*(FC)	3.00	2.25	1.25
68	Jesse Orosco	.07	.05	.03
69	Alejandro Pena	.07	.05	.03
70	Steve Sax	.15	.11	.06
71	Mike Scioscia	.07	.05	.03
72	Mike Sharperson	.05	.04	.02
73	John Shelby	.05	.04	.02
74	Franklin Stubbs	.05	.04	.02
75	John Tudor	.10	.08	.04
76	Fernando Valenzuela	.20	.15	.08
77	Tracy Woodson	.10	.08	.04
78	Marty Barrett	.07	.05	.03
79	Todd Benzinger	.12	.09	.05
80	Mike Boddicker	.07	.05	.03
81	Wade Boggs	.50	.40	.20
82	"Oil Can" Boyd	.07	.05	.03
83	Ellis Burks	.40	.30	.15
84	Rick Cerone	.05	.04	.02
85	Roger Clemens	.50	.40	.20
86	*Steve Curry*(FC)	.20	.15	.08
87	Dwight Evans	.10	.08	.04
88	Wes Gardner	.07	.05	.03
89	Rich Gedman	.07	.05	.03
90	Mike Greenwell	.40	.30	.15
91	Bruce Hurst	.10	.08	.04
92	Dennis Lamp	.05	.04	.02
93	Spike Owen	.05	.04	.02
94	Larry Parrish	.07	.05	.03
95	*Carlos Quintana*(FC)	.50	.40	.20
96	Jody Reed	.12	.09	.05
97	Jim Rice	.25	.20	.10
98a	Kevin Romine (batting follow-thru, photo actually Randy Kutcher)	.50	.40	.20
98b	Kevin Romine (arms crossed on chest, correct photo)	.60	.45	.25
99	Lee Smith	.10	.08	.04
100	Mike Smithson	.05	.04	.02
101	Bob Stanley	.05	.04	.02
102	Allan Anderson	.07	.05	.03
103	Keith Atherton	.05	.04	.02
104	Juan Berenguer	.05	.04	.02
105	Bert Blyleven	.12	.09	.05
106	*Eric Bullock*(FC)	.15	.11	.06
107	Randy Bush	.05	.04	.02
108	John Christensen(FC)	.05	.04	.02
109	Mark Davidson	.07	.05	.03
110	Gary Gaetti	.15	.11	.06
111	Greg Gagne	.05	.04	.02
112	Dan Gladden	.05	.04	.02
113	*German Gonzalez*(FC)	.20	.15	.08
114	Brian Harper	.05	.04	.02
115	Tom Herr	.07	.05	.03
116	Kent Hrbek	.20	.15	.08
117	Gene Larkin	.10	.08	.04
118	Tim Laudner	.05	.04	.02
119	Charlie Lea	.05	.04	.02
120	Steve Lombardozzi	.05	.04	.02
121a	John Moses (Home: Phoenix, AZ)	1.00	.70	.40
121b	John Moses (Home: Tempe, AZ)	.05	.04	.02
122	Al Newman	.05	.04	.02
123	Mark Portugal	.05	.04	.02
124	Kirby Puckett	.35	.25	.14
125	Jeff Reardon	.10	.08	.04
126	Fred Toliver	.05	.04	.02
127	Frank Viola	.15	.11	.06
128	Doyle Alexander	.07	.05	.03
129	Dave Bergman	.05	.04	.02

		MT	NR MT	EX
130a	Tom Brookens (Mike Heath stats on back)	2.25	1.75	.90
130b	Tom Brookens (correct stats on back)	.30	.25	.12
131	*Paul Gibson*	.15	.11	.06
132a	Mike Heath (Tom Brookens stats on back)	2.25	1.75	.90
132b	Mike Heath (correct stats on back)	.30	.25	.12
133	*Don Heinkel*	.15	.11	.06
134	Mike Henneman	.10	.08	.04
135	Guillermo Hernandez	.07	.05	.03
136	Eric King	.05	.04	.02
137	Chet Lemon	.07	.05	.03
138	Fred Lynn	.10	.08	.04
139	Jack Morris	.15	.11	.06
140	Matt Nokes	.20	.15	.08
141	Gary Pettis	.05	.04	.02
142	Ted Power	.05	.04	.02
143	Jeff Robinson	.12	.09	.05
144	Luis Salazar	.05	.04	.02
145	*Steve Searcy*(FC)	.20	.15	.08
146	Pat Sheridan	.05	.04	.02
147	Frank Tanana	.07	.05	.03
148	Alan Trammell	.20	.15	.08
149	Walt Terrell	.07	.05	.03
150	Jim Walewander(FC)	.07	.05	.03
151	Lou Whitaker	.20	.15	.08
152	Tim Birtsas	.05	.04	.02
153	Tom Browning	.10	.08	.04
154	*Keith Brown*(FC)	.15	.11	.06
155	*Norm Charlton*(FC)	.30	.25	.12
156	Dave Concepcion	.10	.08	.04
157	Kal Daniels	.15	.11	.06
158	Eric Davis	.50	.40	.20
159	Bo Diaz	.07	.05	.03
160	*Rob Dibble*	.80	.60	.30
161	Nick Esasky	.07	.05	.03
162	John Franco	.10	.08	.04
163	Danny Jackson	.15	.11	.06
164	Barry Larkin	.25	.20	.10
165	Rob Murphy	.05	.04	.02
166	Paul O'Neill	.05	.04	.02
167	Jeff Reed	.05	.04	.02
168	Jose Rijo	.07	.05	.03
169	Ron Robinson	.05	.04	.02
170	*Chris Sabo*	.60	.45	.25
171	*Candy Sierra*(FC)	.15	.11	.06
172	*Van Snider*(FC)	.15	.11	.06
173	Jeff Treadway	.12	.09	.05
174	Frank Williams	.05	.04	.02
175	Herm Winningham	.05	.04	.02
176	Jim Adduci(FC)	.05	.04	.02
177	Don August	.10	.08	.04
178	Mike Birkbeck	.05	.04	.02
179	Chris Bosio	.05	.04	.02
180	Glenn Braggs	.07	.05	.03
181	Greg Brock	.07	.05	.03
182	Mark Clear	.05	.04	.02
183	Chuck Crim	.05	.04	.02
184	Rob Deer	.07	.05	.03
185	Tom Filer	.05	.04	.02
186	Jim Gantner	.05	.04	.02
187	*Darryl Hamilton*	.30	.25	.12
188	Ted Higuera	.10	.08	.04
189	Odell Jones	.05	.04	.02
190	Jeffrey Leonard	.07	.05	.03
191	Joey Meyer	.10	.08	.04
192	Paul Mirabella	.05	.04	.02
193	Paul Molitor	.15	.11	.06
194	Charlie O'Brien(FC)	.07	.05	.03
195	Dan Plesac	.10	.08	.04
196	*Gary Sheffield*(FC)	1.25	.90	.50
197	B.J. Surhoff	.10	.08	.04
198	Dale Sveum	.07	.05	.03
199	Bill Wegman	.05	.04	.02
200	Robin Yount	.25	.20	.10
201	Rafael Belliard	.05	.04	.02
202	Barry Bonds	.40	.30	.15
203	Bobby Bonilla	.30	.25	.12
204	Sid Bream	.07	.05	.03
205	Benny Distefano(FC)	.05	.04	.02
206	Doug Drabek	.07	.05	.03
207	Mike Dunne	.10	.08	.04
208	Felix Fermin	.07	.05	.03
209	Brian Fisher	.07	.05	.03
210	Jim Gott	.05	.04	.02
211	Bob Kipper	.05	.04	.02
212	Dave LaPoint	.07	.05	.03
213	Mike LaValliere	.07	.05	.03
214	Jose Lind	.10	.08	.04
215	Junior Ortiz	.05	.04	.02

		MT	NR MT	EX
216	Vicente Palacios	.07	.05	.03
217	Tom Prince(FC)	.10	.08	.04
218	Gary Redus	.05	.04	.02
219	R.J. Reynolds	.05	.04	.02
220	Jeff Robinson	.07	.05	.03
221	John Smiley	.12	.09	.05
222	Andy Van Slyke	.12	.09	.05
223	Bob Walk	.05	.04	.02
224	Glenn Wilson	.07	.05	.03
225	Jesse Barfield	.10	.08	.04
226	George Bell	.25	.20	.10
227	*Pat Borders*	.25	.20	.10
228	John Cerutti	.07	.05	.03
229	Jim Clancy	.07	.05	.03
230	Mark Eichhorn	.07	.05	.03
231	Tony Fernandez	.12	.09	.05
232	Cecil Fielder	.05	.04	.02
233	Mike Flanagan	.07	.05	.03
234	Kelly Gruber	.05	.04	.02
235	Tom Henke	.07	.05	.03
236	Jimmy Key	.10	.08	.04
237	Rick Leach	.05	.04	.02
238	Manny Lee	.05	.04	.02
239	Nelson Liriano	.07	.05	.03
240	Fred McGriff	.50	.40	.20
241	Lloyd Moseby	.07	.05	.03
242	Rance Mulliniks	.05	.04	.02
243	Jeff Musselman	.07	.05	.03
244	Dave Stieb	.10	.08	.04
245	Todd Stottlemyre	.10	.08	.04
246	Duane Ward	.05	.04	.02
247	David Wells	.10	.08	.04
248	Ernie Whitt	.07	.05	.03
249	Luis Aguayo	.05	.04	.02
250a	Neil Allen (Home: Sarasota, FL)	1.50	1.25	.60
250b	Neil Allen (Home: Syosset, NY)	.05	.04	.02
251	John Candelaria	.07	.05	.03
252	Jack Clark	.15	.11	.06
253	Richard Dotson	.07	.05	.03
254	Rickey Henderson	.35	.25	.14
255	Tommy John	.12	.09	.05
256	Roberto Kelly	.20	.15	.08
257	Al Leiter	.15	.11	.06
258	Don Mattingly	.80	.60	.30
259	Dale Mohorcic	.05	.04	.02
260	*Hal Morris*(FC)	2.50	2.00	1.00
261	Scott Nielsen(FC)	.10	.08	.04
262	Mike Pagliarulo	.10	.08	.04
263	*Hipolito Pena*(FC)	.15	.11	.06
264	Ken Phelps	.07	.05	.03
265	Willie Randolph	.07	.05	.03
266	Rick Rhoden	.07	.05	.03
267	Dave Righetti	.12	.09	.05
268	Rafael Santana	.05	.04	.02
269	Steve Shields(FC)	.07	.05	.03
270	Joel Skinner	.05	.04	.02
271	Don Slaught	.05	.04	.02
272	Claudell Washington	.07	.05	.03
273	Gary Ward	.07	.05	.03
274	Dave Winfield	.30	.25	.12
275	Luis Aquino(FC)	.05	.04	.02
276	Floyd Bannister	.07	.05	.03
277	George Brett	.35	.25	.14
278	Bill Buckner	.10	.08	.04
279	*Nick Capra*(FC)	.15	.11	.06
280	*Jose DeJesus*(FC)	.15	.11	.06
281	Steve Farr	.05	.04	.02
282	Jerry Gleaton	.05	.04	.02
283	Mark Gubicza	.10	.08	.04
284	*Tom Gordon*(FC)	.40	.30	.15
285	Bo Jackson	.80	.60	.30
286	Charlie Leibrandt	.07	.05	.03
287	*Mike Macfarlane*	.20	.15	.08
288	Jeff Montgomery	.07	.05	.03
289	Bill Pecota	.07	.05	.03
290	Jamie Quirk	.05	.04	.02
291	Bret Saberhagen	.15	.11	.06
292	Kevin Seitzer	.30	.25	.12
293	Kurt Stillwell	.07	.05	.03
294	Pat Tabler	.07	.05	.03
295	Danny Tartabull	.20	.15	.08
296	Gary Thurman	.12	.09	.05
297	Frank White	.07	.05	.03
298	Willie Wilson	.10	.08	.04
299	Roberto Alomar	1.00	.70	.40
300	*Sandy Alomar, Jr.*(FC)	1.25	.90	.50
301	Chris Brown	.07	.05	.03
302	Mike Brumley(FC)	.07	.05	.03
303	Mark Davis	.05	.04	.02
304	Mark Grant	.05	.04	.02
305	Tony Gwynn	.35	.25	.14

		MT	NR MT	EX
306	*Greg Harris*(FC)	.20	.15	.08
307	Andy Hawkins	.05	.04	.02
308	Jimmy Jones	.05	.04	.02
309	John Kruk	.07	.05	.03
310	Dave Leiper	.05	.04	.02
311	Carmelo Martinez	.05	.04	.02
312	Lance McCullers	.07	.05	.03
313	Keith Moreland	.07	.05	.03
314	Dennis Rasmussen	.10	.08	.04
315	Randy Ready	.05	.04	.02
316	Benito Santiago	.15	.11	.06
317	Eric Show	.07	.05	.03
318	Todd Simmons	.10	.08	.04
319	Garry Templeton	.07	.05	.03
320	Dickie Thon	.05	.04	.02
321	Ed Whitson	.05	.04	.02
322	Marvell Wynne	.05	.04	.02
323	Mike Aldrete	.07	.05	.03
324	Brett Butler	.07	.05	.03
325	Will Clark	.80	.60	.30
326	Kelly Downs	.10	.08	.04
327	Dave Dravecky	.07	.05	.03
328	Scott Garrelts	.05	.04	.02
329	Atlee Hammaker	.05	.04	.02
330	*Charlie Hayes*(FC)	.30	.25	.12
331	Mike Krukow	.07	.05	.03
332	Craig Lefferts	.05	.04	.02
333	Candy Maldonado	.07	.05	.03
334	Kirt Manwaring	.10	.08	.04
335	Bob Melvin	.05	.04	.02
336	Kevin Mitchell	.60	.45	.25
337	Donell Nixon	.05	.04	.02
338	*Tony Perezchica*(FC)	.15	.11	.06
339	Joe Price	.05	.04	.02
340	Rick Reuschel	.10	.08	.04
341	Earnest Riles	.05	.04	.02
342	Don Robinson	.05	.04	.02
343	Chris Speier	.05	.04	.02
344	Robby Thompson	.07	.05	.03
345	Jose Uribe	.05	.04	.02
346	Matt Williams	.12	.09	.05
347	*Trevor Wilson*(FC)	.15	.11	.06
348	Juan Agosto	.05	.04	.02
349	Larry Andersen	.05	.04	.02
350	Alan Ashby	.05	.04	.02
351	Kevin Bass	.07	.05	.03
352	Buddy Bell	.07	.05	.03
353	*Craig Biggio*	.60	.45	.25
354	Danny Darwin	.05	.04	.02
355	Glenn Davis	.25	.20	.10
356	Jim Deshaies	.05	.04	.02
357	Bill Doran	.07	.05	.03
358	*John Fishel*	.20	.15	.08
359	Billy Hatcher	.07	.05	.03
360	Bob Knepper	.07	.05	.03
361	*Louie Meadows*	.15	.11	.06
362	Dave Meads	.05	.04	.02
363	Jim Pankovits	.05	.04	.02
364	Terry Puhl	.05	.04	.02
365	Rafael Ramirez	.05	.04	.02
366	Craig Reynolds	.05	.04	.02
367	Mike Scott	.12	.09	.05
368	Nolan Ryan	.40	.30	.15
369	Dave Smith	.07	.05	.03
370	Gerald Young	.12	.09	.05
371	Hubie Brooks	.10	.08	.04
372	Tim Burke	.05	.04	.02
373	*John Dopson*	.25	.20	.10
374	Mike Fitzgerald	.05	.04	.02
375	Tom Foley	.05	.04	.02
376	Andres Galarraga	.15	.11	.06
377	Neal Heaton	.05	.04	.02
378	Joe Hesketh	.05	.04	.02
379	*Brian Holman*	.35	.25	.14
380	Rex Hudler	.05	.04	.02
381	*Randy Johnson*(FC)	.50	.40	.20
382	Wallace Johnson	.05	.04	.02
383	Tracy Jones	.10	.08	.04
384	Dave Martinez	.07	.05	.03
385	Dennis Martinez	.07	.05	.03
386	Andy McGaffigan	.05	.04	.02
387	Otis Nixon	.05	.04	.02
388	*Johnny Paredes*(FC)	.12	.09	.05
389	Jeff Parrett	.10	.08	.04
390	Pascual Perez	.07	.05	.03
391	Tim Raines	.25	.20	.10
392	Luis Rivera	.05	.04	.02
393	*Nelson Santovenia*	.15	.11	.06
394	Bryn Smith	.05	.04	.02
395	Tim Wallach	.10	.08	.04
396	Andy Allanson	.05	.04	.02

		MT	NR MT	EX
397	*Rod Allen*	.15	.11	.06
398	Scott Bailes	.05	.04	.02
399	Tom Candiotti	.05	.04	.02
400	Joe Carter	.12	.09	.05
401	Carmen Castillo	.05	.04	.02
402	Dave Clark	.07	.05	.03
403	John Farrell	.10	.08	.04
404	Julio Franco	.10	.08	.04
405	Don Gordon	.05	.04	.02
406	Mel Hall	.07	.05	.03
407	Brad Havens	.05	.04	.02
408	Brook Jacoby	.10	.08	.04
409	Doug Jones	.12	.09	.05
410	*Jeff Kaiser*(FC)	.15	.11	.06
411	*Luis Medina*(FC)	.20	.15	.08
412	Cory Snyder	.15	.11	.06
413	Greg Swindell	.12	.09	.05
414	*Ron Tingley*(FC)	.15	.11	.06
415	Willie Upshaw	.07	.05	.03
416	Ron Washington	.05	.04	.02
417	Rich Yett	.05	.04	.02
418	Damon Berryhill	.12	.09	.05
419	Mike Bielecki	.05	.04	.02
420	*Doug Dascenzo*(FC)	.20	.15	.08
421	Jody Davis	.07	.05	.03
422	Andre Dawson	.20	.15	.08
423	Frank DiPino	.05	.04	.02
424	Shawon Dunston	.10	.08	.04
425	"Goose" Gossage	.12	.09	.05
426	Mark Grace	1.00	.70	.40
427	*Mike Harkey*(FC)	.35	.25	.14
428	Darrin Jackson	.07	.05	.03
429	Les Lancaster	.07	.05	.03
430	Vance Law	.07	.05	.03
431	Greg Maddux	.12	.09	.05
432	Jamie Moyer	.05	.04	.02
433	Al Nipper	.05	.04	.02
434	Rafael Palmeiro	.20	.15	.08
435	Pat Perry	.05	.04	.02
436	*Jeff Pico*	.12	.09	.05
437	Ryne Sandberg	.40	.30	.15
438	Calvin Schiraldi	.05	.04	.02
439	Rick Sutcliffe	.10	.08	.04
440	Manny Trillo	.05	.04	.02
441	*Gary Varsho*	.20	.15	.08
442	Mitch Webster	.07	.05	.03
443	*Luis Alicea*	.15	.11	.06
444	Tom Brunansky	.12	.09	.05
445	Vince Coleman	.15	.11	.06
446	*John Costello*	.15	.11	.06
447	Danny Cox	.07	.05	.03
448	Ken Dayley	.05	.04	.02
449	Jose DeLeon	.07	.05	.03
450	Curt Ford	.05	.04	.02
451	Pedro Guerrero	.15	.11	.06
452	Bob Horner	.10	.08	.04
453	*Tim Jones*(FC)	.15	.11	.06
454	Steve Lake	.05	.04	.02
455	Joe Magrane	.10	.08	.04
456	Greg Mathews	.07	.05	.03
457	Willie McGee	.12	.09	.05
458	Larry McWilliams	.05	.04	.02
459	Jose Oquendo	.05	.04	.02
460	Tony Pena	.07	.05	.03
461	Terry Pendleton	.10	.08	.04
462	*Steve Peters*(FC)	.15	.11	.06
463	Ozzie Smith	.15	.11	.06
464	Scott Terry	.08	.06	.03
465	Denny Walling	.05	.04	.02
466	Todd Worrell	.10	.08	.04
467	Tony Armas	.07	.05	.03
468	*Dante Bichette*(FC)	.30	.25	.12
469	Bob Boone	.07	.05	.03
470	*Terry Clark*(FC)	.15	.11	.06
471	Stew Cliburn(FC)	.05	.04	.02
472	*Mike Cook*(FC)	.15	.11	.06
473	*Sherman Corbett*	.15	.11	.06
474	Chili Davis	.07	.05	.03
475	Brian Downing	.07	.05	.03
476	Jim Eppard	.07	.05	.03
477	Chuck Finley	.05	.04	.02
478	Willie Fraser	.05	.04	.02
479	*Bryan Harvey*	.30	.25	.12
480	Jack Howell	.07	.05	.03
481	Wally Joyner	.25	.20	.10
482	Jack Lazorko	.05	.04	.02
483	Kirk McCaskill	.07	.05	.03
484	Mark McLemore	.05	.04	.02
485	Greg Minton	.05	.04	.02
486	Dan Petry	.07	.05	.03
487	Johnny Ray	.07	.05	.03

		MT	NR MT	EX
488	Dick Schofield	.05	.04	.02
489	Devon White	.12	.09	.05
490	Mike Witt	.07	.05	.03
491	Harold Baines	.12	.09	.05
492	Daryl Boston	.05	.04	.02
493	Ivan Calderon	.07	.05	.03
494	Mike Diaz	.07	.05	.03
495	Carlton Fisk	.20	.15	.08
496	*Dave Gallagher*	.15	.11	.06
497	Ozzie Guillen	.07	.05	.03
498	Shawn Hillegas	.07	.05	.03
499	Lance Johnson	.07	.05	.03
500	Barry Jones	.05	.04	.02
501	Bill Long	.07	.05	.03
502	Steve Lyons	.05	.04	.02
503	Fred Manrique	.07	.05	.03
504	Jack McDowell	.10	.08	.04
505	*Donn Pall*	.15	.11	.06
506	Kelly Paris	.05	.04	.02
507	Dan Pasqua	.10	.08	.04
508	*Ken Patterson*	.15	.11	.06
509	Melido Perez	.10	.08	.04
510	Jerry Reuss	.07	.05	.03
511	Mark Salas	.05	.04	.02
512	Bobby Thigpen	.10	.08	.04
513	Mike Woodard	.05	.04	.02
514	Bob Brower	.05	.04	.02
515	Steve Buechele	.05	.04	.02
516	*Jose Cecena*	.15	.11	.06
517	Cecil Espy	.07	.05	.03
518	Scott Fletcher	.07	.05	.03
519	Cecilio Guante	.05	.04	.02
520	Jose Guzman	.10	.08	.04
521	Ray Hayward	.05	.04	.02
522	Charlie Hough	.07	.05	.03
523	Pete Incaviglia	.12	.09	.05
524	Mike Jeffcoat	.05	.04	.02
525	Paul Kilgus	.10	.08	.04
526	*Chad Kreuter*(FC)	.15	.11	.06
527	Jeff Kunkel	.05	.04	.02
528	Oddibe McDowell	.07	.05	.03
529	Pete O'Brien	.07	.05	.03
530	Geno Petralli	.05	.04	.02
531	Jeff Russell	.05	.04	.02
532	Ruben Sierra	.35	.25	.12
533	Mike Stanley	.05	.04	.02
534	Ed Vande Berg	.05	.04	.02
535	Curtis Wilkerson	.05	.04	.02
536	Mitch Williams	.07	.05	.03
537	Bobby Witt	.10	.08	.04
538	Steve Balboni	.07	.05	.03
539	Scott Bankhead	.05	.04	.02
540	Scott Bradley	.05	.04	.02
541	Mickey Brantley	.05	.04	.02
542	Jay Buhner(FC)	.10	.08	.04
543	Mike Campbell	.10	.08	.04
544	Darnell Coles	.07	.05	.03
545	Henry Cotto	.05	.04	.02
546	Alvin Davis	.12	.09	.05
547	Mario Diaz	.07	.05	.03
548	*Ken Griffey, Jr.*(FC)	12.00	9.00	4.75
549	*Erik Hanson*(FC)	1.00	.70	.40
550	Mike Jackson	.07	.05	.03
551	Mark Langston	.10	.08	.04
552	Edgar Martinez	.20	.15	.08
553	*Bill McGuire*(FC)	.15	.11	.06
554	Mike Moore	.05	.04	.02
555	Jim Presley	.07	.05	.03
556	Rey Quinones	.05	.04	.02
557	Jerry Reed	.05	.04	.02
558	Harold Reynolds	.07	.05	.03
559	*Mike Schooler*(FC)	.35	.25	.14
560	Bill Swift	.05	.04	.02
561	Dave Valle	.05	.04	.02
562	Steve Bedrosian	.10	.08	.04
563	Phil Bradley	.10	.08	.04
564	Don Carman	.07	.05	.03
565	Bob Dernier	.05	.04	.02
566	Marvin Freeman	.05	.04	.02
567	Todd Frohwirth	.07	.05	.03
568	Greg Gross	.05	.04	.02
569	Kevin Gross	.07	.05	.03
570	Greg Harris	.05	.04	.02
571	Von Hayes	.10	.08	.04
572	Chris James	.10	.08	.04
573	Steve Jeltz	.05	.04	.02
574	*Ron Jones*(FC)	.15	.11	.06
575	*Ricky Jordan*	.50	.40	.20
576	Mike Maddux	.05	.04	.02
577	David Palmer	.05	.04	.02
578	Lance Parrish	.15	.11	.06

		MT	NR MT	EX
579	Shane Rawley	.07	.05	.03
580	Bruce Ruffin	.05	.04	.02
581	Juan Samuel	.12	.09	.05
582	Mike Schmidt	.50	.40	.20
583	Kent Tekulve	.07	.05	.03
584	Milt Thompson	.05	.04	.02
585	*Jose Alvarez*	.15	.11	.06
586	Paul Assenmacher	.05	.04	.02
587	Bruce Benedict	.05	.04	.02
588	Jeff Blauser	.10	.08	.04
589	*Terry Blocker*(FC)	.15	.11	.06
590	Ron Gant	.12	.09	.05
591	Tom Glavine	.10	.08	.04
592	Tommy Gregg	.10	.08	.04
593	Albert Hall	.05	.04	.02
594	Dion James	.05	.04	.02
595	Rick Mahler	.05	.04	.02
596	Dale Murphy	.40	.30	.15
597	Gerald Perry	.10	.08	.04
598	Charlie Puleo	.05	.04	.02
599	Ted Simmons	.10	.08	.04
600	Pete Smith	.10	.08	.04
601	Zane Smith	.07	.05	.03
602	*John Smoltz*	.50	.40	.20
603	Bruce Sutter	.10	.08	.04
604	Andres Thomas	.07	.05	.03
605	Ozzie Virgil	.05	.04	.02
606	*Brady Anderson*(FC)	.25	.20	.10
607	Jeff Ballard	.07	.05	.03
608	*Jose Bautista*	.20	.15	.08
609	Ken Gerhart	.07	.05	.03
610	Terry Kennedy	.07	.05	.03
611	Eddie Murray	.30	.25	.12
612	Carl Nichols(FC)	.10	.08	.04
613	Tom Niedenfuer	.07	.05	.03
614	Joe Orsulak	.05	.04	.02
615	*Oswaldo Peraza (Oswald)*(FC)	.15	.11	.06
616a	Bill Ripken (obscenity on bat)	15.00	11.00	6.00
616b	Bill Ripken (obscenity on bat scrawled out in black)	15.00	11.00	6.00
616c	Bill Ripken (obscenity on bat blocked out in black)	.60	.45	.25
616d	Bill Ripken (obscenity on bat whiteout)	30.00	22.00	12.50
617	Cal Ripken, Jr.	.40	.30	.15
618	Dave Schmidt	.05	.04	.02
619	Rick Schu	.05	.04	.02
620	Larry Sheets	.07	.05	.03
621	Doug Sisk	.05	.04	.02
622	Pete Stanicek	.10	.08	.04
623	Mickey Tettleton	.05	.04	.02
624	Jay Tibbs	.05	.04	.02
625	Jim Traber	.07	.05	.03
626	Mark Williamson	.07	.05	.03
627	*Craig Worthington*	.20	.15	.08
628	Speed and Power (Jose Canseco)	.60	.45	.25
629	Pitcher Perfect (Tom Browning)	.10	.08	.04
630	Like Father - Like Sons (Roberto Alomar, Sandy Alomar, Jr.)	.50	.40	.20
631	N.L. All-Stars (Will Clark, Rafael Palmeiro)	.40	.30	.15
632	Homeruns Coast to Coast (Will Clark, Darryl Strawberry)	.30	.25	.12
633	Hot Corner's - Hot Hitters (Wade Boggs, Carney Lansford)	.40	.30	.15
634	Triple A's (Jose Canseco, Mark McGwire, Terry Steinbach)	.30	.25	.12
635	Dual Heat (Mark Davis, Dwight Gooden)	.20	.15	.08
636	N.L. Pitching Power (David Cone, Danny Jackson)	.15	.11	.06
637	Cannon Arms (Bobby Bonilla, Chris Sabo)	.20	.15	.08
638	Double Trouble (Andres Galarraga, Gerald Perry)	.10	.08	.04
639	Power Center (Eric Davis, Kirby Puckett)	.15	.11	.06
640	Major League Prospects *(Cameron Drew, Steve Wilson)*(FC)	.15	.11	.06
641	Major League Prospects (Kevin Brown, *Kevin Reimer*)(FC)	.60	.45	.25
642	Major League Prospects *(Jerald Clark, Brad Pounders)*(FC)	.40	.30	.15
643	Major League Prospects *(Mike Capel, Drew Hall)*(FC)	.15	.11	.06
644	Major League Prospects *(Joe Girardi, Rolando Roomes)*(FC)	.30	.25	.12
645	Major League Prospects *(Marty Brown, Lenny Harris)*(FC)	.40	.30	.15
646	Major League Prospects *(Luis de los Santos, Jim Campbell)*(FC)	.20	.15	.08

		MT	NR MT	EX
647	Major League Prospects *(Miguel Garcia, Randy Kramer)*(FC)	.15	.11	.06
648	Major League Prospects *(Torey Lovullo, Robert Palacios)*(FC)	.15	.11	.06
649	Major League Prospects *(Jim Corsi, Bob Milacki)*(FC)	.25	.20	.10
650	Major League Prospects *(Grady Hall, Mike Rochford)*(FC)	.15	.11	.06
651	Major League Prospects *(Vance Lovelace, Terry Taylor)*(FC)	.15	.11	.06
652	Major League Prospects *(Dennis Cook, Ken Hill)*(FC)	.35	.25	.14
653	Major League Prospects *(Scott Service, Shane Turner)*(FC)	.15	.11	.06
654	Checklist 1-101	.05	.04	.02
655	Checklist 102-200	.05	.04	.02
656	Checklist 201-298	.05	.04	.02
657	Checklist 299-395	.05	.04	.02
658	Checklist 396-490	.05	.04	.02
659	Checklist 491-584	.05	.04	.02
660	Checklist 585-660	.05	.04	.02

1989 Fleer All Star Team

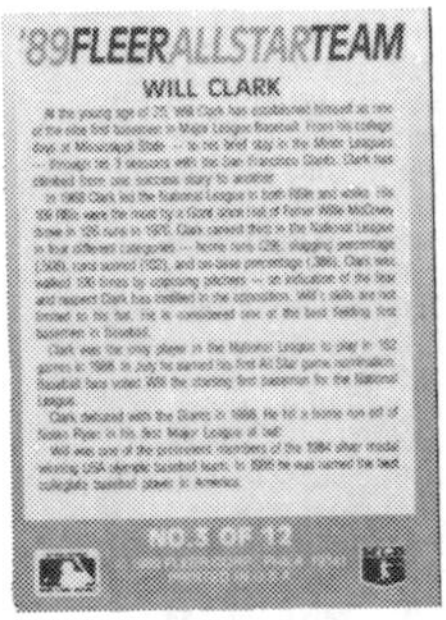

This special 12-card set represents Fleer's choices for its 1989 Major League All-Star Team. For the fourth consecutive year, Fleer inserted the special cards randomly inside their regular 1989 wax and cello packs. The cards feature two player photos set against a green background with the "1989 Fleer All Star Team" logo bannered across the top, and the player's name, position and team in the lower left corner. The backs contain a several-paragraph player profile.

		MT	NR MT	EX
	Complete Set:	15.00	11.00	6.00
	Common Player:	.50	.40	.20
1	Bobby Bonilla	1.25	.90	.50
2	Jose Canseco	2.00	1.50	.80
3	Will Clark	2.50	2.00	1.00
4	Dennis Eckersley	.80	.60	.30
5	Julio Franco	.80	.60	.30
6	Mike Greenwell	.50	.40	.20
7	Orel Hershiser	.70	.50	.30
8	Paul Molitor	.70	.50	.30
9	Mike Scioscia	.50	.40	.20
10	Darryl Strawberry	1.25	.90	.50
11	Alan Trammell	.70	.50	.30
12	Frank Viola	.80	.60	.30

1989 Fleer Baseball All Stars

This specially-boxed set was produced by Fleer for the Ben Franklin store chain. The full-color player photos are surrounded by a border of pink and yellow vertical bands. "Fleer Baseball All-Stars" appears along the top in red, white and blue. The set was sold in a box with a checklist on the back.

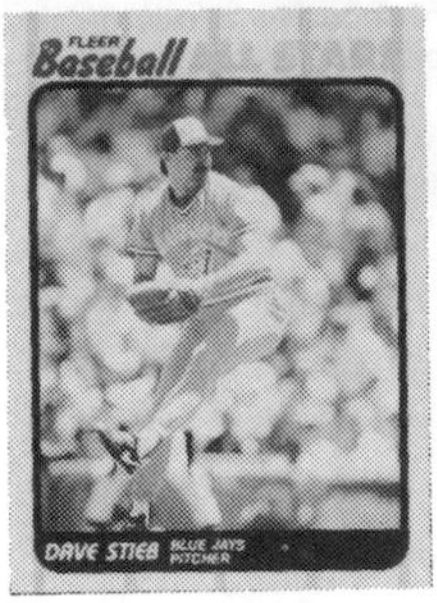

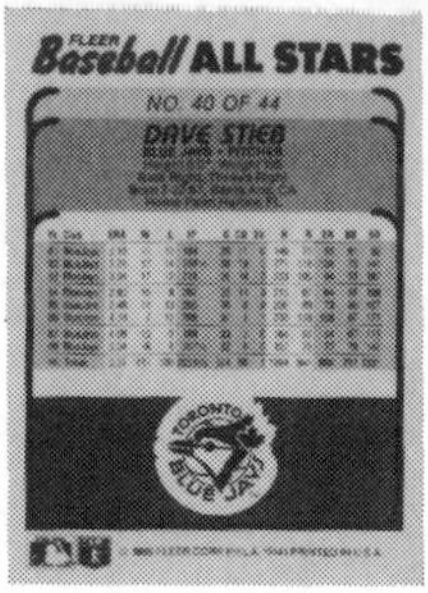

		MT	NR MT	EX
	Complete Set:	4.00	3.00	1.50
	Common Player:	.05	.04	.02
1	Doyle Alexander	.05	.04	.02
2	George Bell	.12	.09	.05
3	Wade Boggs	.40	.30	.15
4	Bobby Bonilla	.08	.06	.04
5	Jose Canseco	.50	.40	.20
6	Will Clark	.90	.70	.35
7	Roger Clemens	.30	.25	.12
8	Vince Coleman	.15	.11	.06
9	David Cone	.15	.11	.06
10	Mark Davis	.08	.06	.03
11	Andre Dawson	.10	.08	.04
12	Dennis Eckersley	.08	.06	.03
13	Andres Galarraga	.12	.09	.05
14	Kirk Gibson	.12	.09	.05
15	Dwight Gooden	.30	.25	.12
16	Mike Greenwell	.40	.30	.15
17	Mark Gubicza	.08	.06	.03
18	Ozzie Guillen	.05	.04	.02
19	Tony Gwynn	.20	.15	.08
20	Rickey Henderson	.15	.08	.04
21	Orel Hershiser	.20	.15	.08
22	Danny Jackson	.05	.04	.02
23	Doug Jones	.05	.04	.02
24	Ricky Jordan	.25	.20	.10
25	Bob Knepper	.05	.04	.02
26	Barry Larkin	.20	.15	.08
27	Vance Law	.05	.04	.02
28	Don Mattingly	.80	.60	.30
29	Mark McGwire	.50	.40	.20
30	Paul Molitor	.08	.06	.02
31	Gerald Perry	.05	.04	.02
32	Kirby Puckett	.35	.25	.12
33	Johnny Ray	.05	.04	.02
34	Harold Reynolds	.08	.06	.03
35	Cal Ripken, Jr.	.30	.25	.12
36	Don Robinson	.05	.04	.02
37	Ruben Sierra	.30	.25	.12
38	Dave Smith	.05	.04	.02
39	Darryl Strawberry	.35	.25	.14
40	Dave Steib	.08	.06	.03
41	Alan Trammell	.15	.11	.06
42	Andy Van Slyke	.10	.08	.04
43	Frank Viola	.15	.11	.06
44	Dave Winfield	.15	.11	.06

1989 Fleer Update

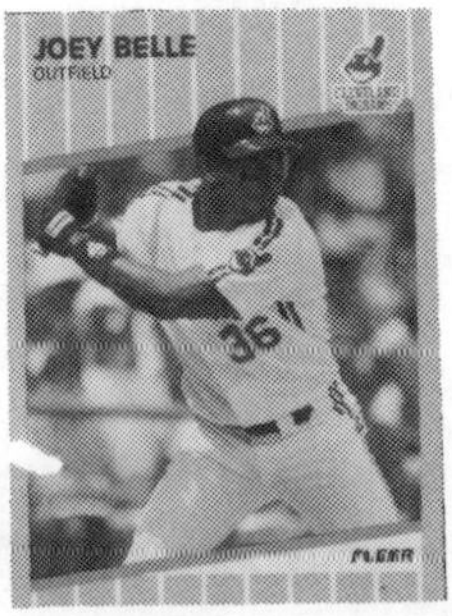

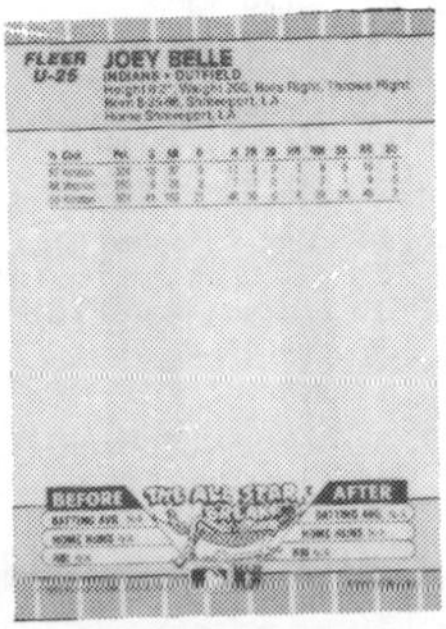

Fleer produced its sixth consecutive "Update" set in 1989 to supplement the company's regular set. As in the past, the set consisted of 132 cards (numbered U-1 through U-132) that were sold by hobby dealers in special collector's boxes.

		MT	NR MT	EX
Complete Set:		13.00	9.75	5.25
Common Player:		.06	.05	.02
1	Phil Bradley	.06	.05	.02
2	Mike Devereaux	.10	.08	.04
3	Steve Finley(FC)	.40	.30	.15
4	Kevin Hickey	.06	.05	.02
5	Brian Holton	.06	.05	.02
6	Bob Milacki	.20	.15	.08
7	Randy Milligan	.10	.08	.04
8	John Dopson	.15	.11	.06
9	Nick Esasky	.10	.08	.04
10	Rob Murphy	.06	.05	.02
11	Jim Abbott(FC)	1.00	.70	.40
12	Bert Blyleven	.06	.05	.02
13	Jeff Manto(FC)	.30	.25	.12
14	Bob McClure	.06	.05	.02
15	Lance Parrish	.06	.05	.02
16	Lee Stevens(FC)	.60	.45	.25
17	Claudell Washington	.06	.05	.02
18	Mark Davis	.06	.05	.02
19	Eric King	.06	.05	.02
20	Ron Kittle	.06	.05	.02
21	Matt Merullo(FC)	.15	.11	.06
22	Steve Rosenberg(FC)	.08	.06	.03
23	Robin Ventura(FC)	2.00	1.00	.60
24	Keith Atherton	.06	.05	.02
25	Joey Belle(FC)	1.75	1.25	.70
26	Jerry Browne	.06	.05	.02
27	Felix Fermin	.06	.05	.02
28	Brad Komminsk	.06	.05	.02
29	Pete O'Brien	.06	.05	.02
30	Mike Brumley	.06	.05	.02
31	Tracy Jones	.06	.05	.02
32	Mike Schwabe(FC)	.30	.25	.12
33	Gary Ward	.06	.05	.02
34	Frank Williams	.06	.05	.02
35	Kevin Appier(FC)	.50	.40	.20
36	Bob Boone	.06	.05	.02
37	Luis de los Santos	.10	.08	.04
38	Jim Eisenreich(FC)	.06	.05	.02
39	Jaime Navarro(FC)	.30	.25	.12
40	Bill Spiers(FC)	.40	.30	.15
41	Greg Vaughn(FC)	2.00	1.50	.80
42	Randy Veres(FC)	.15	.11	.06
43	Wally Backman	.06	.05	.02
44	Shane Rawley	.06	.05	.02
45	Steve Balboni	.06	.05	.02
46	Jesse Barfield	.06	.05	.02
47	Alvaro Espinoza(FC)	.25	.20	.10
48	Bob Geren(FC)	.40	.30	.15
49	Mel Hall	.06	.05	.02
50	Andy Hawkins	.06	.05	.02
51	Hensley Meulens(FC)	.50	.40	.20
52	Steve Sax	.15	.11	.06
53	Deion Sanders(FC)	.60	.45	.25
54	Rickey Henderson	.50	.40	.20
55	Mike Moore	.10	.08	.04
56	Tony Phillips	.06	.05	.02
57	Greg Briley(FC)	.35	.25	.14
58	Gene Harris	.10	.08	.04
59	Randy Johnson	.08	.06	.03
60	Jeffrey Leonard	.06	.05	.02
61	Dennis Powell	.06	.05	.02
62	Omar Vizquel(FC)	.20	.15	.08
63	Kevin Brown	.08	.06	.03
64	Julio Franco	.25	.20	.10
65	Jamie Moyer	.06	.05	.02
66	Rafael Palmeiro	.15	.11	.06
67	Nolan Ryan	1.75	1.25	.70
68	Francisco Cabrera(FC)	.20	.15	.08
69	Junior Felix(FC)	.40	.30	.15
70	Al Leiter	.06	.05	.02
71	Alex Sanchez(FC)	.12	.09	.05
72	Geronimo Berroa(FC)	.08	.06	.03
73	Derek Lilliquist(FC)	.15	.11	.06
74	Lonnie Smith	.10	.08	.04
75	Jeff Treadway	.06	.05	.02
76	Paul Kilgus	.06	.05	.02
77	Lloyd McClendon	.15	.11	.06
78	Scott Sanderson	.06	.05	.02
79	Dwight Smith(FC)	.40	.30	.15
80	Jerome Walton(FC)	1.00	.70	.40
81	Mitch Williams	.15	.11	.06
82	Steve Wilson	.25	.20	.10
83	Todd Benzinger	.06	.05	.02
84	Ken Griffey	.20	.15	.08
85	Rick Mahler	.06	.05	.02
86	Rolando Roomes	.15	.11	.06
87	Scott Scudder(FC)	.20	.15	.08
88	Jim Clancy	.06	.05	.02
89	Rick Rhoden	.06	.05	.02
90	Dan Schatzeder	.06	.05	.02
91	Mike Morgan	.06	.05	.02
92	Eddie Murray	.20	.15	.08
93	Willie Randolph	.06	.05	.02
94	Ray Searage	.06	.05	.02
95	Mike Aldrete	.06	.05	.02
96	Kevin Gross	.06	.05	.02
97	Mark Langston	.15	.11	.06
98	Spike Owen	.06	.05	.02
99	Zane Smith	.06	.05	.02
100	Don Aase	.06	.05	.02
101	Barry Lyons	.06	.05	.02
102	Juan Samuel	.06	.05	.02
103	Wally Whitehurst(FC)	.20	.15	.08
104	Dennis Cook	.15	.11	.06
105	Lenny Dykstra	.06	.05	.02
106	Charlie Hayes(FC)	.10	.08	.04
107	Tommy Herr	.06	.05	.02
108	Ken Howell	.06	.05	.02
109	John Kruk	.06	.05	.02
110	Roger McDowell	.06	.05	.02
111	Terry Mulholland(FC)	.06	.05	.02
112	Jeff Parrett	.06	.05	.02
113	Neal Heaton	.06	.05	.02
114	Jeff King	.10	.08	.04
115	Randy Kramer	.06	.05	.02
116	Bill Landrum	.06	.05	.02
117	Cris Carpenter(FC)	.15	.11	.06
118	Frank DiPino	.06	.05	.02
119	Ken Hill	.15	.11	.06
120	Dan Quisenberry	.06	.05	.02
121	Milt Thompson	.06	.05	.02
122	Todd Zeile(FC)	1.50	1.15	.60
123	Jack Clark	.10	.08	.04
124	Bruce Hurst	.06	.05	.02
125	Mark Parent	.06	.05	.02
126	Bip Roberts	.06	.05	.02
127	Jeff Brantley(FC)	.25	.20	.10
128	Terry Kennedy	.06	.05	.02
129	Mike LaCoss	.06	.05	.02
130	Greg Litton(FC)	.25	.20	.10
131	Mike Schmidt	1.50	1.25	.60
132	Checklist	.06	.05	.02

1989 Fleer Baseball MVP

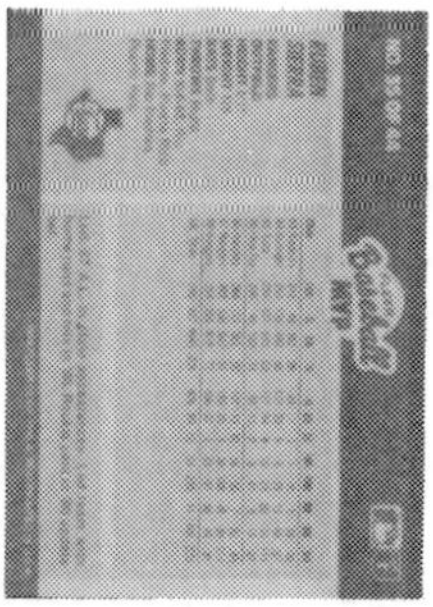

Filled with superstars, this 44-card boxed set was produced by Fleer in 1989 for the Toys 'R' Us chain. The fronts of the cards are designed in a yellow and green color scheme and include a "Fleer Baseball MVP" logo above the color player photo. The backs are printed in shades of green and yellow and include biographical notes and stats. The set was issued in a special box with a checklist on the back.

	MT	NR MT	EX
Complete Set:	3.75	2.75	1.50
Common Player:	.05	.04	.02

		MT	NR MT	EX
1	Steve Bedrosian	.05	.04	.02
2	George Bell	.12	.09	.05
3	Wade Boggs	.70	.50	.30
4	George Brett	.15	.11	.06
5	Hubie Brooks	.05	.04	.02
6	Jose Canseco	.90	.70	.35
7	Will Clark	.90	.70	.35
8	Roger Clemens	.30	.25	.12
9	Eric Davis	.20	.15	.08
10	Glenn Davis	.12	.09	.05
11	Andre Dawson	.12	.09	.05
12	Andres Galarraga	.12	.09	.05
13	Kirk Gibson	.15	.11	.06
14	Dwight Gooden	.30	.25	.12
15	Mark Grace	.25	.20	.10
16	Mike Greenwell	.50	.40	.20
17	Tony Gwynn	.20	.15	.08
18	Bryan Harvey	.05	.04	.02
19	Orel Hershiser	.25	.20	.10
20	Ted Higuera	.07	.05	.03
21	Danny Jackson	.05	.04	.02
22	Mike Jackson	.05	.04	.02
23	Doug Jones	.05	.04	.02
24	Greg Maddux	.07	.05	.03
25	Mike Marshall	.05	.04	.02
26	Don Mattingly	.80	.60	.30
27	Fred McGriff	.30	.25	.12
28	Mark McGwire	.80	.60	.30
29	Kevin McReynolds	.15	.11	.06
30	Jack Morris	.05	.04	.02
31	Gerald Perry	.05	.04	.02
32	Kirby Puckett	.35	.25	.12
33	Chris Sabo	.20	.15	.08
34	Mike Scott	.12	.09	.05
35	Ruben Sierra	.25	.20	.10
36	Darryl Strawberry	.35	.25	.12
37	Danny Tartabull	.09	.07	.04
38	Bobby Thigpen	.09	.07	.04
39	Alan Trammell	.15	.11	.06
40	Andy Van Slyke	.12	.09	.05
41	Frank Viola	.12	.09	.05
42	Walt Weiss	.20	.15	.08
43	Dave Winfield	.15	.11	.06
44	Todd Worrell	.07	.05	.03

1989 Fleer Baseball's Exciting Stars

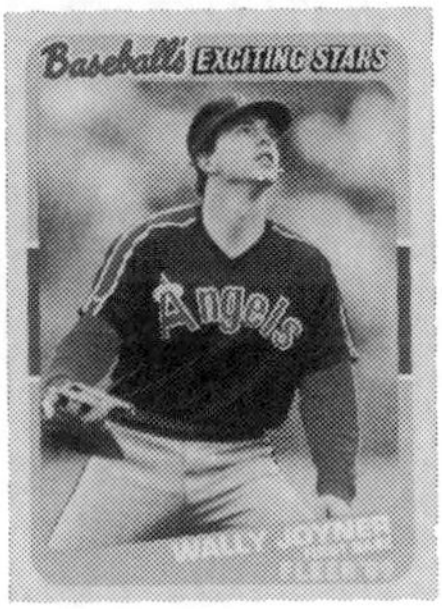

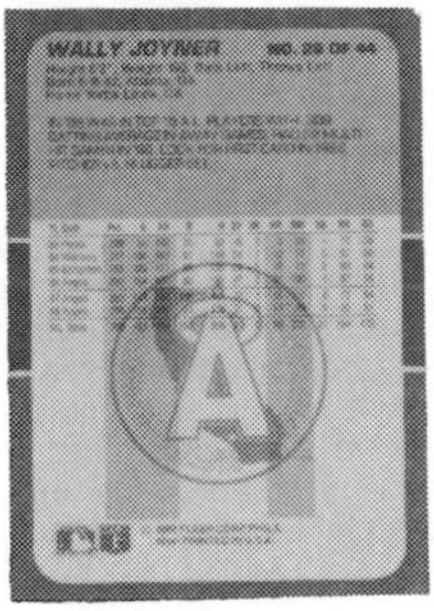

Sold exclusively in Cumberland Farm stores, this 44-card boxed set pictures the game's top stars. The card fronts feature a color player photo surrounded by a blue border with "Baseball's Exciting Stars" along the top. The cards were were numbered alphabetically and packed in a special box with a complete checklist on the back.

		MT	NR MT	EX
Complete Set:		3.50	2.75	1.50
Common Player:		.05	.04	.02
1	Harold Baines	.07	.05	.03
2	Wade Boggs	.70	.50	.30
3	Jose Canseco	.90	.70	.35
4	Joe Carter	.12	.09	.05
5	Will Clark	.90	.70	.35
6	Roger Clemens	.30	.25	.12
7	Vince Coleman	.15	.11	.06
8	David Cone	.15	.11	.06
9	Eric Davis	.20	.15	.08
10	Glenn Davis	.15	.11	.06
11	Andre Dawson	.12	.09	.05
12	Dwight Evans	.09	.07	.04
13	Andres Galarraga	.12	.09	.05
14	Kirk Gibson	.12	.09	.05
15	Dwight Gooden	.30	.25	.12
16	Jim Gott	.05	.04	.02
17	Mark Grace	.30	.25	.12
18	Mike Greenwell	.40	.30	.15
19	Mark Gibicza	.07	.05	.03
20	Tony Gwynn	.20	.15	.08
21	Rickey Henderson	.40	.30	.15
22	Tom Henke	.05	.04	.02
23	Mike Henneman	.05	.04	.02
24	Orel Hershiser	.25	.20	.10
25	Danny Jackson	.05	.04	.02
26	Gregg Jefferies	.40	.30	.15
27	Ricky Jordan	.30	.25	.12
28	Wally Joyner	.15	.11	.06
29	Mark Langston	.15	.11	.06
30	Tim Leary	.05	.04	.02
31	Don Mattingly	.70	.50	.30
32	Mark McGwire	.80	.60	.30
33	Dale Murphy	.15	.11	.06
34	Kirby Puckett	.35	.25	.14
35	Chris Sabo	.30	.25	.12
36	Kevin Seitzer	.15	.11	.06
37	Ruben Sierra	.30	.25	.12
38	Ozzie Smith	.15	.11	.06
39	Dave Stewart	.07	.05	.03
40	Darryl Strawberry	.35	.25	.14
41	Alan Trammell	.15	.11	.06
42	Frank Viola	.15	.11	.06
43	Dave Winfield	.15	.11	.06
44	Robin Yount	.15	.11	.06

1989 Fleer Heroes of Baseball

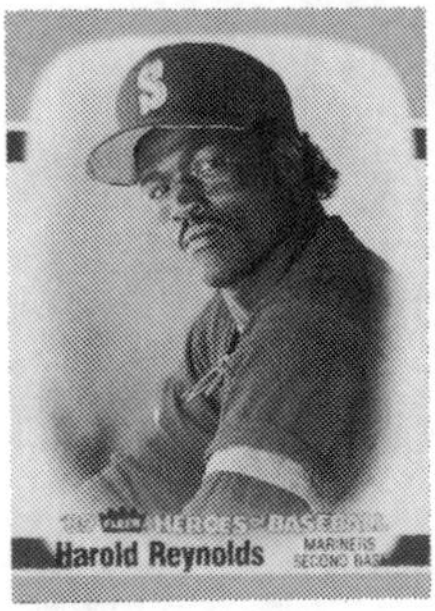

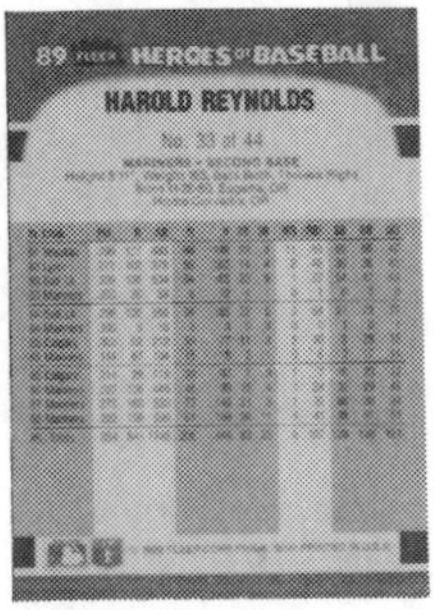

This 44-card boxed set was produced by Fleer for the Woolworth store chain. The fronts of the cards are designed in a red and blue color scheme and feature full-color photos that fade into a soft focus on all edges. "Fleer Heroes of Baseball" appears just above the player's name, team and position at the bottom of the card. The set is numbered alphabetically and was packaged in a special box with a checklist on the back.

		MT	NR MT	EX
Complete Set:		3.50	2.75	1.50
Common Player:		.05	.04	.02
1	George Bell	.12	.09	.05
2	Wade Boggs	.70	.50	.30
3	Barry Bonds	.12	.09	.05
4	Tom Brunansky	.08	.06	.03
5	Jose Canseco	.90	.70	.35
6	Joe Carter	.12	.09	.05
7	Will Clark	.90	.70	.35
8	Roger Clemens	.30	.25	.12
9	David Cone	.15	.11	.06
10	Eric Davis	.40	.30	.15
11	Glenn Davis	.12	.09	.05
12	Andre Dawson	.12	.09	.05
13	Dennis Eckersley	.07	.05	.03

		MT	NR MT	EX
14	John Franco	.05	.04	.02
15	Gary Gaetti	.12	.09	.05
16	Andres Galarraga	.15	.11	.06
17	Kirk Gibson	.12	.09	.05
18	Dwight Gooden	.30	.25	.12
19	Mike Greenwell	.50	.40	.20
20	Tony Gwynn	.25	.20	.10
21	Bryan Harvey	.05	.04	.02
22	Orel Hershiser	.20	.15	.08
23	Ted Higuera	.07	.05	.03
24	Danny Jackson	.05	.04	.02
25	Ricky Jordan	.40	.30	.15
26	Don Mattingly	.70	.50	.30
27	Fred McGriff	.30	.25	.12
28	Mark McGwire	.60	.45	.25
29	Kevin McReynolds	.15	.11	.06
30	Gerald Perry	.05	.04	.02
31	Kirby Puckett	.30	.25	.12
32	Johnny Ray	.05	.04	.02
33	Harold Reynolds	.05	.04	.02
34	Cal Ripken, Jr.	.15	.11	.06
35	Ryne Sandberg	.15	.11	.06
36	Kevin Seitzer	.15	.11	.06
37	Ruben Sierra	.30	.25	.12
38	Darryl Strawberry	.30	.25	.12
39	Bobby Thigpen	.05	.04	.02
40	Alan Trammell	.12	.09	.05
41	Andy Van Slyke	.10	.08	.04
42	Frank Viola	.15	.11	.06
43	Dave Winfield	.15	.11	.06
44	Robin Yount	.20	.15	.08

1989 Fleer League Leaders

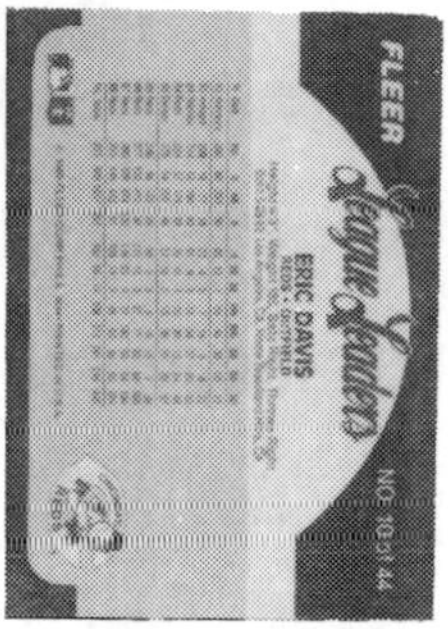

Another of the various small, boxed sets issued by Fleer, the 44-card "League Leaders" set was produced for Walgreen stores. The standard-size cards feature color photos on the front surrounded by a red border with "Fleer League Leaders" across the top. The player's name, team and position appear in a yellow band at the bottom. The backs include player stats and data and the team logo. The cards are numbered alphabetically and packaged in a special box that includes the full checklist on the back.

		MT	NR MT	EX
	Complete Set:	4.00	3.00	1.50
	Common Player:	.05	.04	.02
1	Allan Anderson	.05	.04	.02
2	Wade Boggs	.70	.50	.30
3	Jose Canseco	.90	.70	.35
4	Will Clark	.90	.70	.35
5	Roger Clemens	.40	.30	.15
6	Vince Coleman	.15	.11	.06
7	David Cone	.15	.11	.06
8	Kal Daniels	.12	.09	.05
9	Chili Davis	.05	.04	.02
10	Eric Davis	.20	.15	.08
11	Glenn Davis	.15	.11	.06
12	Andre Dawson	.12	.09	.05
13	John Franco	.05	.04	.02
14	Andres Galarraga	.12	.09	.05
15	Kirk Gibson	.12	.09	.05
16	Dwight Gooden	.30	.25	.12
17	Mark Grace	.30	.25	.12
18	Mike Greenwell	.60	.45	.25
19	Tony Gwynn	.20	.15	.08
20	Orel Hershiser	.25	.20	.10
21	Pete Incaviglia	.05	.04	.02
22	Danny Jackson	.05	.04	.02
23	Gregg Jefferies	.90	.70	.35
24	Joe Magrane	.09	.07	.05
25	Don Mattingly	.70	.50	.30
26	Fred McGriff	.30	.25	.12
27	Mark McGwire	.80	.60	.30
28	Dale Murphy	.15	.11	.06
29	Dan Plesac	.07	.05	.03
30	Kirby Puckett	.40	.30	.15
31	Harold Reynolds	.12	.09	.05
32	Cal Ripken, Jr.	.15	.11	.06
33	Jeff Robinson	.05	.04	.02
34	Mike Scott	.12	.09	.05
35	Ozzie Smith	.15	.09	.05
36	Dave Stewart	.07	.05	.03
37	Darryl Strawberry	.30	.25	.12
38	Greg Swindell	.15	.11	.06
39	Bobby Thigpen	.08	.06	.03
40	Alan Trammell	.12	.09	.05
41	Andy Van Slyke	.12	.09	.05
42	Frank Viola	.12	.09	.05
43	Dave Winfield	.12	.09	.05
44	Robin Yount	.20	.15	.08

1989 Fleer Superstars

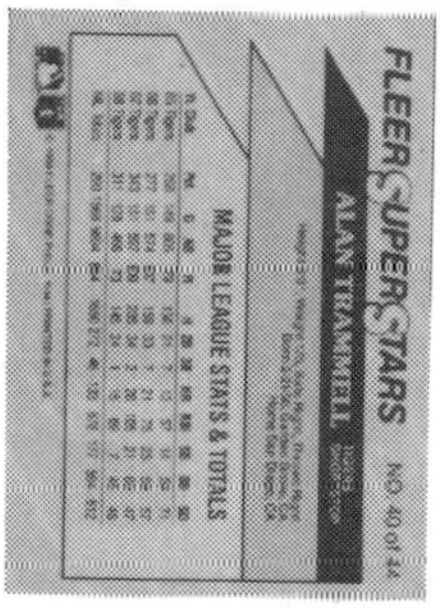

This 44-card boxed set was produced by Fleer for the McCrory store chain. The cards are the standard 2-1/2" by 3-1/2" and the full-color player photos are outlined in red with a tan-and-white striped border. The player's name, position and team logo appear at the bottom of the card. The backs carry yellow and white stripes and include the Fleer "SuperStars" logo, player stats and biographical information. The cards are numbered alphabetically and packaged in a special box that includes a checklist on the back.

		MT	NR MT	EX
	Complete Set:	4.00	3.00	1.50
	Common Player:	.05	.04	.02
1	Roberto Alomar	.20	.15	.08
2	Harold Baines	.12	.09	.05
3	Tim Belcher	.12	.09	.05
4	Wade Boggs	.70	.50	.30
5	George Brett	.15	.11	.06
6	Jose Canseco	.90	.70	.35
7	Gary Carter	.05	.04	.02
8	Will Clark	.90	.70	.35
9	Roger Clemens	.30	.25	.12
10	Kal Daniels	.15	.11	.06
11	Eric Davis	.20	.15	.08
12	Andre Dawson	.12	.09	.05
13	Tony Fernandez	.12	.09	.05
14	Scott Fletcher	.05	.04	.02
15	Andres Galarraga	.15	.11	.06
16	Kirk Gibson	.15	.11	.06
17	Dwight Gooden	.30	.25	.12

		MT	NR MT	EX
18	Jim Gott	.05	.04	.02
19	Mark Grace	.30	.25	.12
20	Mike Greenwell	.50	.40	.20
21	Tony Gwynn	.20	.15	.08
22	Rickey Henderson	.20	.15	.08
23	Orel Hershiser	.20	.15	.08
24	Ted Higuera	.07	.05	.02
25	Gregg Jefferies	.90	.70	.35
26	Wally Joyner	.15	.11	.06
27	Mark Langston	.15	.11	.06
28	Greg Maddux	.15	.11	.06
29	Don Mattingly	.70	.50	.30
30	Fred McGriff	.30	.25	.12
31	Mark McGwire	.80	.60	.30
32	Dan Plesac	.09	.07	.04
33	Kirby Puckett	.30	.25	.12
34	Jeff Reardon	.05	.04	.02
35	Chris Sabo	.12	.09	.05
36	Mike Schmidt	.25	.20	.10
37	Mike Scott	.10	.08	.04
38	Cory Snyder	.10	.08	.04
39	Darryl Strawberry	.30	.25	.12
40	Alan Trammell	.12	.09	.05
41	Frank Viola	.12	.09	.05
42	Walt Weiss	.12	.09	.05
43	Dave Winfield	.12	.09	.05
44	Todd Worrell	.05	.04	.02

1989 Fleer Box Panels

For the fourth consecutive year, Fleer issued a series of cards on the bottom panels of its regular 1989 wax pack boxes. The 28-card set includes 20 players and eight team logo cards, all designed in the identical style of the regular 1989 Fleer set. The box-bottom cards were randomly printed, four cards (three player cards and one team logo) on each bottom panel. The cards were numbered from C-1 to C-28.

	MT	NR MT	EX
Complete Panel Set:	6.00	4.50	2.50
Complete Singles Set:	3.00	2.25	1.25
Common Single Player:	.15	.11	.06

		MT	NR MT	EX
1	Mets Logo	.05	.04	.02
2	Wade Boggs	.40	.30	.15
3	George Brett	.25	.20	.10
4	Jose Canseco	.50	.40	.20
5	A's Logo	.05	.04	.02
6	Will Clark	.50	.40	.20
7	David Cone	.25	.20	.10
8	Andres Galarraga	.25	.20	.10
9	Dodgers Logo	.05	.04	.02
10	Kirk Gibson	.15	.11	.06
11	Mike Greenwell	.25	.20	.10
12	Tony Gwynn	.25	.20	.10
13	Tigers Logo	.05	.04	.02
14	Orel Hershiser	.20	.15	.08
15	Danny Jackson	.15	.11	.06
16	Wally Joyner	.50	.40	.20
17	Red Sox Logo	.05	.04	.02
18	Yankees Logo	.05	.04	.02
19	Fred McGriff	.60	.45	.25
20	Kirby Puckett	.30	.25	.12
21	Chris Sabo	.15	.11	.06
22	Kevin Seltzer	.30	.25	.12
23	Pirates Logo	.05	.04	.02
24	Astros Logo	.05	.04	.02
25	Darryl Strawberry	.40	.30	.15
26	Alan Trammell	.20	.15	.08
27	Andy Van Slyke	.25	.20	.10
28	Frank Viola	.20	.15	.08

1989 Fleer For The Record

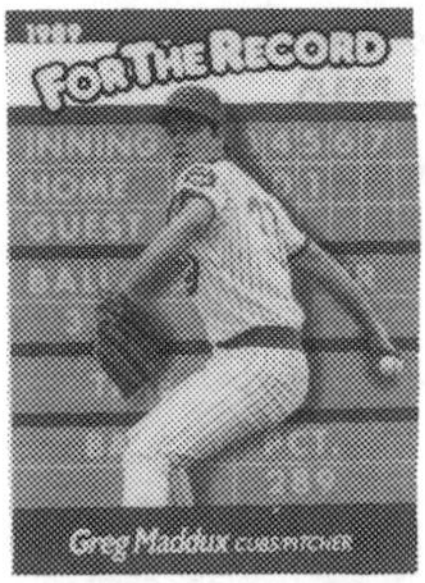

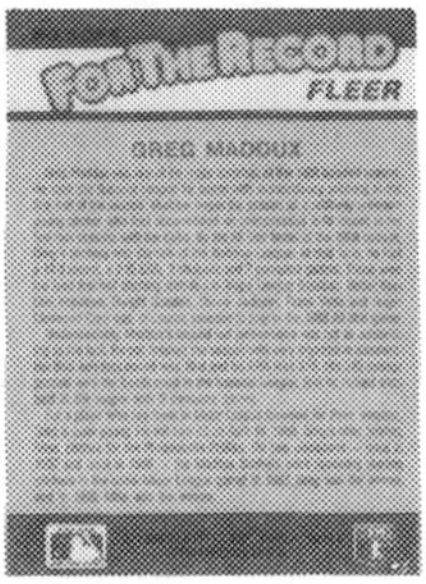

Fleer's "For the Record" set features six players and their achievements from 1988. Fronts of the standard 2-1/2" by 3-1/2" cards feature a full color photo of the player set against a red background. The words "For the Record" appear in blue script at the top of the card and the players name on the bottom, printed in white type. Card backs are grey and describe individual accomplishments. The cards were distributed randomly in rack packs.

	MT	NR MT	EX
Complete Set:	4.00	3.00	1.50
Common Player:	.80	.60	.30

		MT	NR MT	EX
1	Wade Boggs	1.00	.70	.40
2	Roger Clemens	1.25	.90	.50
3	Andres Galarraga	.80	.60	.30
4	Kirk Gibson	.80	.60	.30
5	Greg Maddux	.80	.60	.30
6	Don Mattingly	1.00	.70	.40

1989 Fleer '88 World Series

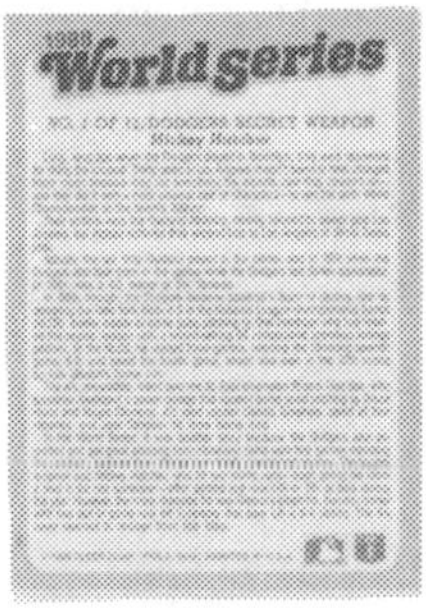

This 12-card set, which depicts highlights of the 1988 World Series, was included as a special sub-set with the regular factory-collated Fleer set. It was not available as individual cards in wax packs, cello packs or any other form.

	MT	NR MT	EX
Complete Set:	3.00	2.25	1.25
Common Player:	.25	.20	.10

		MT	NR MT	EX
1	Dodgers' Secret Weapon (Mickey Hatcher)	.25	.20	.10
2	Rookie Starts Series (Tim Belcher)	.35	.25	.14
3	Canseco Slams L.A. (Jose Canseco)	.40	.30	.20
4	Dramatic Comeback (Mike Scioscia)	.25	.20	.10
5	Gibson Steals The Show (Kirk Gibson)	.40	.30	.15
6	"Bulldog" (Orel Hershiser)	.30	.25	.12
7	One Swing, Three RBI's (Mike Marshall)	.25	.20	.10
8	Game-Winning Home Run (Mark McGwire)	.40	.30	.15
9	Sax's Speed Wins Game 4 (Steve Sax)	.25	.20	.10
10	Series Caps Award-Winning Year (Walt Weiss)	.25	.20	.10
11	The M.V.P. And His Shutout Magic (Orel Hershiser)	.35	.25	.14
12	Dodger Blue, World Champs	.25	.20	.10

1990 Fleer

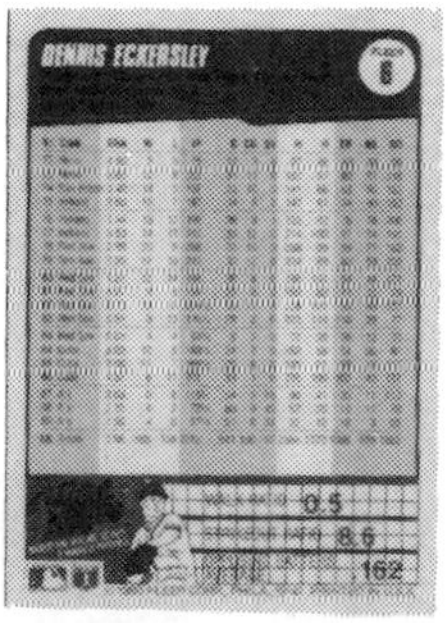

Fleer's 1990 set, its 10th consecutive baseball card offering, again consisted of 660 cards numbered by team. The front of the cards feature mostly action photos surrounded by one of several different color bands and a white border. The "Fleer '90" logo appears in the upper left corner, while the team logo is the upper right. The player's name and position are printed in a flowing banner below the photo. The set includes various special cards, including a series of "Major League Prospects," Players of the Decade, team checklist cards and a series of multi-player cards. The backs include complete career stats, player data, and a special "Vital Signs" section showing on-base percentage, slugging percentage, etc. for batters; and strikeout and walk ratios, opposing batting averages, etc. for pitchers.

	MT	NR MT	EX
Complete Set:	20.00	15.00	8.00
Common Player:	.05	.04	.02

		MT	NR MT	EX
1	Lance Blankenship	.07	.05	.03
2	Todd Burns	.06	.05	.02
3	Jose Canseco	.50	.40	.20
4	Jim Corsi	.09	.07	.04
5	Storm Davis	.06	.05	.02
6	Dennis Eckersley	.12	.09	.05
7	Mike Gallego	.06	.05	.02
8	Ron Hassey	.05	.04	.02
9	Dave Henderson	.10	.08	.06
10	Rickey Henderson	.30	.25	.12
11	Rick Honeycutt	.05	.04	.02
12	Stan Javier	.05	.04	.02
13	Felix Jose	.20	.15	.08
14	Carney Lansford	.07	.05	.03
15	Mark McGwire	.25	.20	.10
16	Mike Moore	.10	.08	.04
17	Gene Nelson	.05	.04	.02
18	Dave Parker	.12	.09	.05
19	Tony Phillips	.05	.04	.02
20	Terry Steinbach	.10	.08	.06
21	Dave Stewart	.10	.08	.06
22	Walt Weiss	.10	.08	.06
23	Bob Welch	.06	.05	.03
24	Curt Young	.05	.04	.02
25	Paul Assenmacher	.05	.04	.02
26	Damon Berryhill	.10	.08	.04
27	Mike Bielecki	.10	.08	.04
28	Kevin Blankenship	.07	.05	.03
29	Andre Dawson	.12	.09	.05
30	Shawon Dunston	.09	.07	.04
31	Joe Girardi	.12	.09	.05
32	Mark Grace	.25	.20	.10
33	Mike Harkey	.12	.09	.05
34	Paul Kilgus	.05	.04	.02
35	Les Lancaster	.06	.05	.02
36	Vance Law	.05	.04	.02
37	Greg Maddux	.10	.08	.04
38	Lloyd McClendon	.10	.08	.04
39	Jeff Pico	.05	.04	.02
40	Ryne Sandberg	.35	.25	.14
41	Scott Sanderson	.05	.04	.02
42	Dwight Smith	.25	.20	.10
43	Rick Sutcliffe	.08	.06	.03
44	*Jerome Walton*	.30	.25	.12
45	Mitch Webster	.05	.04	.02
46	Curt Wilkerson	.05	.04	.02
47	*Dean Wilkins*(FC)	.15	.11	.06
48	Mitch Williams	.08	.06	.03
49	Steve Wilson	.15	.11	.06
50	Steve Bedrosian	.06	.05	.02
51	*Mike Benjamin*(FC)	.25	.20	.10
52	*Jeff Brantley*	.25	.20	.10
53	Brett Butler	.07	.05	.03
54	Will Clark	.40	.30	.15
55	Kelly Downs	.05	.04	.02
56	Scott Garrelts	.09	.07	.04
57	Atlee Hammaker	.05	.04	.02
58	Terry Kennedy	.05	.04	.02
59	Mike LaCoss	.05	.04	.02
60	Craig Lefferts	.06	.05	.02
61	*Greg Litton*	.25	.20	.10
62	Candy Maldonado	.06	.05	.02
63	Kirt Manwaring	.09	.07	.04
64	*Randy McCament*(FC)	.20	.15	.08
65	Kevin Mitchell	.30	.25	.12
66	Donell Nixon	.05	.04	.02
67	Ken Oberkfell	.05	.04	.02
68	Rick Reuschel	.09	.07	.04
69	Ernest Riles	.05	.04	.02
70	Don Robinson	.05	.04	.02
71	Pat Sheridan	.05	.04	.02
72	Chris Speier	.05	.04	.02
73	Robby Thompson	.07	.05	.03
74	Jose Uribe	.06	.05	.02
75	Matt Williams	.20	.15	.08
76	George Bell	.10	.08	.04
77	Pat Borders	.07	.05	.03
78	John Cerutti	.05	.04	.02
79	*Junior Felix*	.20	.15	.08
80	Tony Fernandez	.09	.07	.04
81	Mike Flanagan	.05	.04	.02
82	*Mauro Gozzo*(FC)	.15	.11	.06
83	Kelly Gruber	.07	.05	.03
84	Tom Henke	.05	.04	.02
85	Jimmy Key	.07	.05	.03
86	Manny Lee	.05	.04	.02
87	Nelson Liriano	.05	.04	.02
88	Lee Mazzllli	.05	.04	.02
89	Fred McGriff	.25	.20	.10
90	Lloyd Moseby	.06	.05	.02
91	Rance Mulliniks	.05	.04	.02
92	Alex Sanchez	.15	.11	.06
93	Dave Steib	.09	.07	.05
94	Todd Stottlemyre	.09	.07	.05
95	Duane Ward	.05	.04	.02
96	David Wells	.05	.04	.02
97	Ernie Whitt	.06	.05	.02
98	Frank Wills	.05	.04	.02
99	Mookie Wilson	.09	.07	.04
100	*Kevin Appier*(FC)	.25	.20	.10
101	Luis Aquino	.05	.04	.02
102	Bob Boone	.07	.05	.03
103	George Brett	.15	.11	.06
104	Jose DeJesus	.08	.06	.03
105	Luis de los Santos	.08	.06	.03
106	Jim Eisenreich	.05	.04	.02
107	Steve Farr	.05	.04	.02
108	Tom Gordon	.25	.20	.10
109	Mark Gubicza	.09	.07	.04
110	Bo Jackson	.35	.25	.14
111	Terry Leach	.05	.04	.02
112	Charlie Leibrandt	.05	.04	.02
113	*Rick Luecken*(FC)	.20	.15	.08

		MT	NR MT	EX
114	Mike Macfarlane	.05	.04	.02
115	Jeff Montgomery	.06	.05	.03
116	Bret Saberhagen	.10	.08	.04
117	Kevin Seitzer	.10	.08	.04
118	Kurt Stillwell	.06	.05	.02
119	Pat Tabler	.05	.04	.02
121	Gary Thurman	.05	.04	.02
122	Frank White	.07	.05	.03
123	Willie Wilson	.06	.05	.03
124	*Matt Winters*(FC)	.20	.15	.08
125	Jim Abbott	.35	.25	.14
126	Tony Armas	.05	.04	.02
127	Dante Bichette	.09	.07	.04
128	Bert Blyleven	.09	.07	.04
129	Chili Davis	.06	.05	.02
130	Brian Downing	.06	.05	.02
131	*Mike Fetters*(FC)	.20	.15	.08
132	Chuck Finley	.06	.05	.02
133	Willie Fraser	.05	.04	.02
134	Bryan Harvey	.05	.04	.02
135	Jack Howell	.05	.04	.02
136	Wally Joyner	.10	.08	.04
137	*Jeff Manto*	.20	.15	.08
138	Kirk McCaskill	.06	.05	.02
139	Bob McClure	.05	.04	.02
140	Greg Minton	.05	.04	.02
141	Lance Parrish	.07	.05	.02
142	Dan Petry	.05	.04	.02
143	Johnny Ray	.05	.04	.02
144	Dick Schofield	.06	.05	.02
145	*Lee Stevens*	.20	.15	.08
146	Claudell Washington	.06	.05	.02
147	Devon White	.08	.06	.03
148	Mike Witt	.06	.05	.02
149	Roberto Alomar	.10	.08	.04
150	Sandy Alomar, Jr.	.25	.20	.10
151	Andy Benes(FC)	.30	.25	.12
152	Jack Clark	.06	.05	.02
153	Pat Clements	.05	.04	.02
154	Joey Cora	.15	.11	.06
155	Mark Davis	.09	.07	.04
156	Mark Grant	.05	.04	.02
157	Tony Gwynn	.25	.20	.10
158	Greg Harris	.10	.08	.04
159	Bruce Hurst	.06	.05	.02
160	Darrin Jackson	.05	.04	.02
161	Chris James	.06	.05	.02
162	Carmelo Martinez	.06	.05	.02
163	Mike Pagliarulo	.06	.05	.02
164	Mark Parent	.05	.04	.02
165	Dennis Rasmussen	.05	.04	.02
166	Bip Roberts	.08	.06	.03
167	Benito Santiago	.12	.09	.05
168	Calvin Schiraldi	.05	.04	.02
169	Eric Show	.06	.05	.02
170	Garry Templeton	.06	.05	.02
171	Ed Whitson	.06	.05	.02
172	Brady Anderson	.07	.05	.03
173	Jeff Ballard	.07	.05	.03
174	Phil Bradley	.07	.05	.03
175	Mike Devereaux	.07	.05	.03
176	*Steve Finley*	.20	.15	.08
177	Pete Harnisch(FC)	.10	.08	.04
178	Kevin Hickey	.10	.08	.04
179	Brian Holton	.05	.04	.02
180	*Ben McDonald*(FC)	1.00	.70	.40
181	Bob Melvin	.05	.04	.02
182	Bob Milacki	.07	.05	.03
183	Randy Milligan	.06	.05	.02
184	Gregg Olson(FC)	.30	.25	.12
185	Joe Orsulak	.05	.04	.02
186	Bill Ripken	.05	.04	.02
187	Cal Ripken, Jr.	.15	.11	.06
188	Dave Schmidt	.05	.04	.02
189	Larry Sheets	.05	.04	.02
190	Mickey Tettleton	.08	.06	.03
191	Mark Thurmond	.05	.04	.02
192	Jay Tibbs	.05	.04	.02
193	Jim Traber	.05	.04	.02
194	Mark Williamson	.05	.04	.02
195	Craig Worthington	.15	.11	.06
196	Don Aase	.05	.04	.02
197	*Blaine Beatty*(FC)	.25	.20	.10
198	Mark Carreon	.10	.08	.04
199	Gary Carter	.06	.05	.02
200	David Cone	.10	.08	.04
201	Ron Darling	.07	.05	.03
202	Kevin Elster	.05	.04	.02
203	Sid Fernandez	.09	.07	.04
204	Dwight Gooden	.20	.15	.08
205	Keith Hernandez	.06	.05	.02

		MT	NR MT	EX
206	*Jeff Innis*	.15	.11	.06
207	Gregg Jefferies	.20	.15	.08
208	Howard Johnson	.15	.11	.06
209	Barry Lyons	.05	.04	.02
210	Dave Magadan	.06	.05	.02
211	Kevin McReynolds	.07	.05	.03
212	Jeff Musselman	.05	.04	.02
213	Randy Myers	.06	.05	.02
214	Bob Ojeda	.06	.05	.02
215	Juan Samuel	.06	.05	.02
216	Mackey Sasser	.05	.04	.02
217	Darryl Strawberry	.25	.20	.10
218	Tim Teufel	.05	.04	.02
219	Frank Viola	.10	.08	.04
220	Juan Agosto	.05	.04	.02
221	Larry Anderson	.05	.04	.02
222	*Eric Anthony*(FC)	.50	.40	.20
223	Kevin Bass	.08	.06	.03
224	Craig Biggio	.10	.08	.04
225	Ken Caminiti	.06	.05	.02
226	Jim Clancy	.05	.04	.02
227	Danny Darwin	.05	.04	.02
228	Glenn Davis	.09	.07	.04
229	Jim Deshaies	.07	.05	.02
230	Bill Doran	.06	.05	.02
231	Bob Forsch	.05	.04	.02
233	Terry Puhl	.05	.04	.02
234	Rafael Ramirez	.05	.04	.02
235	Rick Rhoden	.05	.04	.02
236	Dan Schatzeder	.05	.04	.02
237	Mike Scott	.08	.06	.03
238	Dave Smith	.06	.05	.02
239	Alex Trevino	.05	.04	.02
240	Glenn Wilson	.05	.04	.02
241	Gerald Young	.05	.04	.02
242	Tom Brunansky	.07	.05	.03
243	Cris Carpenter	.10	.08	.04
244	*Alex Cole*(FC)	.40	.30	.15
245	Vince Coleman	.10	.08	.04
246	John Costello	.05	.04	.02
247	Ken Dayley	.05	.04	.02
248	Jose DeLeon	.06	.05	.02
249	Frank DiPino	.05	.04	.02
250	Pedro Guerrero	.09	.07	.04
251	Ken Hill	.09	.07	.04
252	Joe Magrane	.09	.07	.04
253	Willie McGee	.06	.05	.02
254	John Morris	.05	.04	.02
255	Jose Oquendo	.06	.05	.02
256	Tony Pena	.06	.05	.02
257	Terry Pendleton	.06	.05	.02
258	Ted Power	.05	.04	.02
259	Dan Quisenberry	.05	.04	.02
260	Ozzie Smith	.09	.07	.04
261	Scott Terry	.06	.05	.02
262	Milt Thompson	.05	.04	.02
263	Denny Walling	.05	.04	.02
264	Todd Worrell	.06	.05	.02
265	*Todd Zeile*	.70	.50	.30
266	Marty Barrett	.05	.04	.02
267	Mike Boddicker	.05	.04	.02
268	Wade Boggs	.40	.30	.15
269	Ellis Burks	.35	.25	.12
270	Rick Cerone	.05	.04	.02
271	Roger Clemens	.25	.20	.10
272	John Dopson	.06	.05	.02
273	Nick Esasky	.07	.05	.03
274	Dwight Evans	.09	.07	.05
275	Wes Gardner	.05	.04	.02
276	Rich Gedman	.05	.04	.02
277	Mike Greenwell	.50	.40	.20
278	Danny Heep	.05	.04	.02
279	Eric Hetzel	.10	.08	.04
280	Dennis Lamp	.05	.04	.02
281	Rob Murphy	.05	.04	.02
282	Joe Price	.05	.04	.02
283	Carlos Quintana	.10	.07	.04
284	Jody Reed	.06	.05	.02
285	Luis Rivera	.05	.04	.02
286	Kevin Romine	.05	.04	.02
287	Lee Smith	.05	.04	.02
288	Mike Smithson	.05	.04	.02
289	Bob Stanley	.05	.04	.02
290	Harold Baines	.09	.07	.04
291	Kevin Brown	.09	.07	.04
292	Steve Buechele	.05	.04	.02
293	*Scott Coolbaugh*(FC)	.25	.20	.10
294	*Jack Daugherty*(FC)	.25	.20	.10
295	Cecil Espy	.06	.05	.02
296	Julio Franco	.07	.05	.03
297	*Juan Gonzalez*(FC)	3.00	2.25	1.25

		MT	NR MT	EX
298	Cecilio Guante	.05	.04	.02
299	Drew Hall	.05	.04	.02
300	Charlie Hough	.06	.05	.02
301	Pete Incaviglia	.08	.06	.03
302	Mike Jeffcoat	.05	.04	.02
303	Chad Kreuter	.08	.06	.03
304	Jeff Kunkel	.05	.04	.02
305	Rick Leach	.05	.04	.02
306	Fred Manrique	.05	.04	.02
307	Jamie Moyer	.06	.05	.02
308	Rafael Palmeiro	.07	.05	.02
309	Geno Petralli	.05	.04	.02
310	Kevin Reimer	.10	.08	.06
311	*Kenny Rogers*(FC)	.20	.15	.08
312	Jeff Russell	.06	.05	.02
313	Nolan Ryan	.50	.40	.20
314	Ruben Sierra	.15	.11	.06
315	Bobby Witt	.05	.04	.02
316	Chris Bosio	.07	.05	.02
317	Glenn Braggs	.07	.05	.02
318	Greg Brock	.05	.04	.02
319	Chuck Crim	.05	.04	.02
320	Rob Deer	.06	.05	.02
321	Mike Felder	.05	.04	.02
322	Tom Filer	.05	.04	.02
323	*Tony Fossas*(FC)	.10	.08	.04
324	Jim Gantner	.06	.05	.02
325	Darryl Hamilton	.08	.06	.03
326	Ted Higuera	.08	.06	.03
327	Mark Knudson(FC)	.10	.08	.04
328	Bill Krueger	.05	.04	.02
329	*Tim McIntosh*(FC)	.20	.15	.08
330	Paul Molitor	.08	.06	.03
331	*Jaime Navarro*	.25	.20	.10
332	Charlie O'Brien	.05	.04	.02
333	*Jeff Peterek*(FC)	.15	.11	.06
334	Dan Plesac	.07	.05	.03
335	Jerry Reuss	.06	.05	.02
336	Gary Sheffield	.25	.20	.10
337	*Bill Spiers*	.35	.25	.12
338	B.J. Surhoff	.07	.05	.02
339	*Greg Vaughn*	.60	.45	.25
340	Robin Yount	.20	.15	.08
341	Hubie Brooks	.06	.05	.02
342	Tim Burke	.06	.05	.02
343	Mike Fitzgerald	.05	.04	.02
344	Tom Foley	.05	.04	.02
345	Andres Galarraga	.15	.11	.06
346	Damaso Garcia	.05	.04	.02
347	*Marquis Grissom*(FC)	.50	.40	.20
348	Kevin Gross	.06	.05	.02
349	Joe Hesketh	.05	.04	.02
350	*Jeff Huson*(FC)	.25	.20	.10
351	Wallace Johnson	.05	.04	.02
352	Mark Langston	.15	.11	.06
353	Dave Martinez	.06	.05	.02
354	Dennis Martinez	.06	.05	.02
355	Andy McGaffigan	.05	.04	.02
356	Otis Nixon	.05	.04	.02
357	Spike Owen	.05	.04	.02
358	Pascual Perez	.06	.05	.02
359	Tim Raines	.10	.08	.04
360	Nelson Santovenia	.10	.08	.04
361	Bryn Smith	.06	.05	.02
362	Zane Smith	.05	.04	.02
363	*Larry Walker*(FC)	.35	.25	.14
364	Tim Wallach	.06	.05	.02
365	Rick Aguilera	.05	.04	.02
366	Allan Anderson	.06	.05	.02
367	Wally Backman	.06	.05	.02
368	Doug Baker(FC)	.08	.06	.03
369	Juan Berenguer	.05	.04	.02
370	Randy Bush	.05	.04	.02
371	Carmen Castillo	.05	.04	.02
372	*Mike Dyer*(FC)	.15	.11	.06
373	Gary Gaetti	.07	.05	.03
374	Greg Gagne	.05	.04	.02
375	Dan Gladden	.05	.04	.02
376	German Gonzalez	.05	.04	.02
377	Brian Harper	.06	.05	.02
378	Kent Hrbek	.10	.08	.04
379	Gene Larkin	.05	.04	.02
380	Tim Laudner	.05	.04	.02
381	John Moses	.05	.04	.02
382	Al Newman	.05	.04	.02
383	Kirby Puckett	.40	.30	.15
384	Shane Rawley	.06	.05	.02
385	Jeff Reardon	.06	.05	.02
386	Roy Smith	.05	.04	.02
387	*Gary Wayne*(FC)	.15	.11	.06
388	Dave West	.25	.20	.10

		MT	NR MT	EX
389	Tim Belcher	.12	.09	.05
390	Tim Crews	.05	.04	.02
391	Mike Davis	.05	.04	.02
392	Rick Dempsey	.05	.04	.02
393	Kirk Gibson	.09	.07	.04
394	Jose Gonzalez	.05	.04	.02
395	Alfredo Griffin	.06	.05	.02
396	Jeff Hamilton	.06	.05	.02
397	Lenny Harris	.10	.08	.06
398	Mickey Hatcher	.05	.04	.02
399	Orel Hershiser	.12	.09	.05
400	Jay Howell	.06	.05	.02
401	Mike Marshall	.06	.05	.02
402	Ramon Martinez	.35	.25	.14
403	Mike Morgan	.05	.04	.02
404	Eddie Murray	.10	.08	.04
405	Alejandro Pena	.05	.04	.02
406	Willie Randolph	.08	.06	.03
407	Mike Scioscia	.06	.05	.02
408	Ray Searage	.05	.04	.02
409	Fernando Valenzuela	.07	.05	.03
410	*Jose Vizcaino*(FC)	.20	.15	.08
411	*John Wetteland*(FC)	.15	.11	.06
412	Jack Armstrong	.05	.04	.02
413	Todd Benzinger	.07	.05	.03
414	Tim Birtsas	.05	.04	.02
415	Tom Browning	.07	.05	.03
416	Norm Charlton	.08	.06	.03
417	Eric Davis	.20	.15	.08
418	Rob Dibble	.15	.11	.06
419	John Franco	.07	.05	.03
420	Ken Griffey, Sr.	.07	.05	.03
421	*Chris Hammond*(FC)	.25	.20	.10
422	Danny Jackson	.06	.05	.02
423	Barry Larkin	.15	.11	.06
424	Tim Leary	.06	.05	.02
425	Rick Mahler	.05	.04	.02
426	*Joe Oliver*(FC)	.30	.25	.12
427	Paul O'Neill	.07	.05	.03
428	Luis Quinones	.05	.04	.02
429	Jeff Reed	.05	.04	.02
430	Jose Rijo	.07	.05	.03
431	Ron Robinson	.05	.04	.02
432	Rolando Roomes	.10	.08	.04
433	Chris Sabo	.15	.11	.06
434	*Scott Scudder*	.30	.25	.12
435	Herm Winningham	.05	.04	.02
436	Steve Balboni	.05	.04	.02
437	Jesse Barfield	.08	.06	.03
438	*Mike Blowers*(FC)	.20	.15	.08
439	Tom Brookens	.05	.04	.02
440	Greg Cadaret	.05	.04	.02
441	Alvaro Espinoza	.25	.20	.10
442	*Bob Geren*	.15	.11	.06
443	Lee Guetterman	.05	.04	.02
444	Mel Hall	.06	.05	.02
445	Andy Hawkins	.06	.05	.02
446	Roberto Kelly	.15	.11	.06
447	Don Mattingly	.35	.25	.14
448	Lance McCullers	.05	.04	.02
449	Hensley Meulens	.35	.25	.14
450	Dale Mohorcic	.05	.04	.02
451	Clay Parker	.10	.07	.04
452	Eric Plunk	.05	.04	.02
453	Dave Righetti	.07	.05	.03
454	*Deion Sanders*	.30	.25	.12
455	Steve Sax	.07	.05	.03
456	Don Slaught	.05	.04	.02
457	Walt Terrell	.05	.04	.02
458	Dave Winfield	.15	.11	.06
459	Jay Bell	.05	.04	.02
460	Rafael Belliard	.05	.04	.02
461	Barry Bonds	.10	.08	.04
462	Bobby Bonilla	.10	.08	.04
463	Sid Bream	.05	.04	.02
464	Benny Distefano	.06	.05	.02
465	Doug Drabek	.06	.05	.02
466	Jim Gott	.06	.05	.02
467	Billy Hatcher	.06	.05	.02
468	Neal Heaton	.06	.05	.02
469	Jeff King	.20	.15	.08
470	Bob Kipper	.05	.04	.02
471	Randy Kramer	.05	.04	.02
472	Bill Landrum	.06	.05	.02
473	Mike LaValliere	.06	.05	.02
474	Jose Lind	.06	.05	.02
475	Junior Ortiz	.05	.04	.02
476	Gary Redus	.05	.04	.02
477	*Rick Reed*(FC)	.15	.11	.06
478	R.J. Reynolds	.05	.04	.02
479	Jeff Robinson	.05	.04	.02

		MT	NR MT	EX
480	John Smiley	.07	.05	.03
481	Andy Van Slyke	.09	.07	.04
482	Bob Walk	.06	.05	.04
483	Andy Allanson	.05	.04	.02
484	Scott Bailes	.05	.04	.02
485	*Joey Belle*	.60	.45	.25
486	Bud Black	.05	.04	.02
487	Jerry Browne	.07	.05	.03
488	Tom Candiotti	.05	.04	.02
489	Joe Carter	.08	.06	.03
490	David Clark	.06	.05	.02
491	John Farrell	.06	.05	.02
492	Felix Fermin	.05	.04	.02
493	Brook Jacoby	.06	.05	.02
494	Dion James	.06	.05	.02
495	Doug Jones	.06	.05	.02
496	Brad Komminsk	.05	.04	.02
497	Rod Nichols	.05	.04	.02
498	Pete O'Brien	.07	.05	.03
499	*Steve Olin*(FC)	.35	.25	.12
500	Jesse Orosco	.05	.04	.02
501	Joel Skinner	.05	.04	.02
502	Cory Snyder	.09	.07	.04
503	Greg Swindell	.10	.08	.04
504	Rich Yett	.05	.04	.02
505	Scott Bankhead	.07	.05	.03
506	Scott Bradley	.05	.04	.02
507	Greg Briley	.15	.11	.06
508	Jay Buhner	.07	.05	.03
509	Darnell Coles	.05	.04	.02
510	Keith Comstock	.05	.04	.02
511	Henry Cotto	.05	.04	.02
512	Alvin Davis	.12	.09	.05
513	Ken Griffey, Jr.	2.75	2.00	1.00
514	Erik Hanson	.20	.15	.08
515	Gene Harris	.15	.11	.06
516	Brian Holman	.07	.05	.03
517	Mike Jackson	.05	.04	.02
518	Randy Johnson	.15	.11	.06
519	Jeffrey Leonard	.08	.06	.03
520	Edgar Martinez	.10	.08	.04
521	Dennis Powell	.05	.04	.02
522	Jim Presley	.06	.05	.02
523	Jerry Reed	.05	.04	.02
524	Harold Reynolds	.07	.05	.03
525	Mike Schooler	.06	.05	.04
526	Bill Swift	.05	.04	.02
527	David Valle	.05	.04	.02
528	*Omar Vizquel*	.20	.15	.08
529	Ivan Calderon	.06	.05	.02
530	Carlton Fisk	.10	.08	.04
531	Scott Fletcher	.06	.05	.02
532	Dave Gallagher	.09	.07	.04
533	Ozzie Guillen	.07	.05	.03
534	*Greg Hibbard*(FC)	.20	.15	.08
535	Shawn Hillegas	.05	.04	.02
536	Lance Johnson	.07	.05	.03
537	Eric King	.05	.04	.02
538	Ron Kittle	.07	.05	.02
539	Steve Lyons	.05	.04	.02
540	Carlos Martinez	.15	.11	.06
541	*Tom McCarthy*(FC)	.10	.07	.04
542	*Matt Merullo*	.25	.20	.10
543	Donn Pall	.05	.04	.02
544	Dan Pasqua	.06	.05	.02
545	Ken Patterson	.06	.05	.02
546	Melido Perez	.07	.05	.03
547	Steve Rosenberg	.07	.05	.03
548	*Sammy Sosa*(FC)	.40	.30	.15
549	Bobby Thigpen	.07	.05	.03
550	Robin Ventura	.60	.45	.25
551	Greg Walker	.06	.05	.02
552	Don Carman	.05	.04	.02
553	*Pat Combs*(FC)	.25	.20	.10
554	Dennis Cook	.20	.15	.08
555	Darren Daulton	.05	.04	.02
556	Lenny Dykstra	.07	.05	.03
557	Curt Ford	.05	.04	.02
558	Charlie Hayes	.10	.08	.04
559	Von Hayes	.07	.05	.03
560	Tom Herr	.06	.05	.02
561	Ken Howell	.05	.04	.02
562	Steve Jeltz	.05	.04	.02
563	Ron Jones	.15	.11	.06
564	Ricky Jordan	.35	.25	.14
565	John Kruk	.07	.05	.03
566	Steve Lake	.05	.04	.02
567	Roger McDowell	.06	.05	.02
568	Terry Mulholland	.05	.04	.02
569	Dwayne Murphy	.05	.04	.02
570	Jeff Parrett	.06	.05	.02
571	Randy Ready	.05	.04	.02
572	Bruce Ruffin	.05	.04	.02
573	Dickie Thon	.05	.04	.02
574	Jose Alvarez	.05	.04	.02
575	Geronimo Berroa	.06	.05	.03
576	Jeff Blauser	.05	.04	.02
577	Joe Boever	.07	.05	.03
578	Marty Clary	.05	.04	.02
579	Jody Davis	.05	.04	.02
580	Mark Eichhorn	.05	.04	.02
581	Darrell Evans	.06	.05	.02
582	Ron Gant	.06	.05	.02
583	Tom Glavine	.09	.07	.04
584	*Tommy Greene*(FC)	.35	.25	.14
585	Tommy Gregg	.10	.07	.04
586	*David Justice*(FC)	3.00	2.25	1.25
587	Mark Lemke(FC)	.10	.08	.04
588	Derek Lilliquist	.10	.08	.04
589	Oddibe McDowell	.07	.05	.03
590	*Kent Mercker*(FC)	.30	.25	.12
591	Dale Murphy	.15	.11	.06
592	Gerald Perry	.06	.05	.02
593	Lonnie Smith	.06	.05	.02
594	Pete Smith	.07	.05	.03
595	John Smoltz	.15	.11	.06
596	*Mike Stanton*(FC)	.25	.20	.10
597	Andres Thomas	.06	.05	.02
598	Jeff Treadway	.06	.05	.02
599	Doyle Alexander	.06	.05	.02
600	Dave Bergman	.05	.04	.02
601	*Brian Dubois*(FC)	.15	.11	.06
602	Paul Gibson	.06	.05	.02
603	Mike Heath	.05	.04	.02
604	Mike Henneman	.07	.05	.03
605	Guillermo Hernandez	.05	.04	.02
606	*Shawn Holman*(FC)	.20	.15	.08
607	Tracy Jones	.09	.07	.04
608	Chet Lemon	.06	.05	.02
609	Fred Lynn	.06	.05	.02
610	Jack Morris	.07	.05	.02
611	Matt Nokes	.10	.08	.04
612	Gary Pettis	.05	.04	.02
613	*Kevin Ritz*(FC)	.15	.11	.06
614	Jeff Robinson	.07	.05	.03
615	Steve Searcy	.10	.08	.04
616	Frank Tanana	.06	.05	.02
617	Alan Trammell	.09	.07	.04
618	Gary Ward	.05	.04	.02
619	Lou Whitaker	.09	.07	.04
620	Frank Williams	.05	.04	.02
621a	Players Of The Decade - 1980 (George Brett) (10 .390 hitting seasons)	2.25	1.75	.90
621b	Players Of The Decade - 1980 (George Brett) (10 .300 hitting seasons)	.50	.40	.20
622	Players Of The Decade - 1981 (Fernando Valenzuela)	.20	.15	.08
623	Players Of The Decade - 1982 (Dale Murphy)	.25	.20	.10
624a	Players Of The Decade - 1983 (Cal Ripkin, Jr.)	2.00	1.50	.80
624b	Players Of The Decade - 1983 (Cal Ripken, Jr.)	.25	.20	.10
625	Players Of The Decade - 1984 (Ryne Sandberg)	.25	.20	.10
626	Players Of The Decade - 1985 (Don Mattingly)	.50	.40	.20
627	Players Of The Decade - 1986 (Roger Clemens)	.25	.20	.10
628	Players Of The Decade - 1987 (George Bell)	.20	.15	.08
629	Players Of The Decade - (Jose Canseco)	.60	.45	.25
630a	Players Of The Decade - 1989 (Will Clark) (total bases (32))	2.25	1.75	.90
630b	Players Of The Decade - 1989 (Will Clark) (total bases (321))	.60	.45	.25
631	Game Savers	.10	.08	.04
632	Boston Igniters	.10	.08	.04
633	The Starter & Stopper	.10	.08	.04
634	League's Best Shortstops	.10	.08	.04
635	Human Dynamos	.10	.08	.04
636	300 Strikeout Club	.10	.08	.04
637	The Dynamic Duo	.10	.08	.04
638	A.L. All Stars	.10	.08	.04
639	N.L. East Rivals	.10	.08	.04
640	*Rudy Seanez, Colin Charland*(FC)	.15	.11	.06
641	*George Canale, Kevin Maas*(FC)	2.50	2.00	1.00
642	*Kelly Mann, Dave Hansen*(FC)	.30	.25	.12
643	*Greg Smith, Stu Tate*(FC)	.15	.11	.06

		MT	NR MT	EX
644	*Tom Drees, Dan Howitt*(FC)	.15	.11	.06
645	*Mike Roesler, Derrick May*(FC)	.50	.40	.20
646	*Scott Hemond, Mark Gardner*(FC)	.35	.25	.14
647	*John Orton, Scott Leuis*(FC)	.25	.20	.10
648	*Rich Monteleone, Dana Williams*(FC)	.15	.11	.06
649	*Mike Huff, Steve Frey*(FC)	.25	.20	.10
650	*Chuck McElroy, Moises Alou*(FC)	.25	.20	.10
651	*Bobby Rose, Mike Hartley*(FC)	.15	.11	.06
652	*Matt Kinzer, Wayne Edwards*(FC)	.20	.15	.08
653	*Delino DeShields, Jason Grimsley*(FC)	.50	.40	.20
654	Athletics, Cubs, Giants & Blue Jays (Checklist)	.05	.04	.03
655	Royals, Angels, Padres & Orioles (Checklist)	.05	.04	.03
656	Mets, Astros, Cardinals & Red Sox (Checklist)	.05	.04	.03
657	Rangers, Brewers, Expos & Twins (Checklist)	.05	.04	.03
658	Dodgers, Reds, Yankees & Pirates (Checklist)	.05	.04	.03
659	Indians, Mariners, White Sox & Phillies (Checklist)	.05	.04	.03
660	Braves, Tigers & Special Cards (Checklist)	.05	.04	.03

A player's name in *italic* indicates a rookie card. An (FC) indicates a player's first card for that particular card company.

1990 Fleer All-Star Team

The top players at each position, as selected by Fleer, are featured in this 12-card set. The cards were inserted in cello packs and some wax packs. The cards measure 2-1/2" by 3-1/2" and feature a unique two-photo format on the card fronts.

		MT	NR MT	EX
Complete Set:		10.00	7.50	4.00
Common Player:		.20	.15	.08
1	Harold Baines	.25	.20	.10
2	Will Clark	2.00	1.50	.80
3	Mark Davis	.20	.15	.08
4	Howard Johnson	.40	.30	.15
5	Joe Magrane	.25	.20	.10
6	Kevin Mitchell	.40	.30	.15
7	Kirby Puckett	.60	.45	.25
8	Cal Ripken	1.00	.70	.40
9	Ryne Sandberg	2.00	1.50	.80
10	Mike Scott	.20	.15	.08
11	Ruben Sierra	1.00	.70	.40
12	Mickey Tettleton	.20	.15	.08

1990 Fleer Award Winners

Hill's Department Stores and 7-Eleven Outlets are exclusively carrying the 1990 Fleer "Award Winners." This 44-card boxed set includes baseball's statistical leaders of 1989, six special cards that feature peel-off team logo stickers and a baseball trivia quiz. The card fronts feature a full-color player photo framed by a winner's cup design and a blue border.

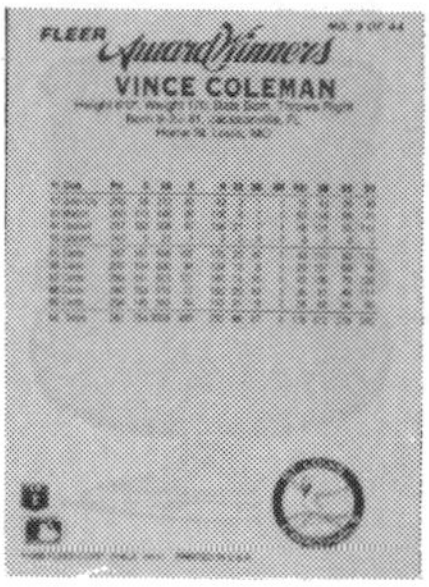

The card backs showcase player statistics in blue on a yellow and white background. The cards measure 2-1/2" by 3-1/2" in size. A complete checklist is provided on the back of each box. The checklist incorrectly lists Bob Boone's team as the Angels.

		MT	NR MT	EX
Complete Set:		3.50	2.75	1.50
Common Player:		.05	.04	.02
1	Jeff Ballard	.05	.04	.02
2	Tim Belcher	.08	.06	.03
3	Bert Blyleven	.08	.06	.03
4	Wade Boggs	.35	.25	.14
5	Bob Boone	.05	.04	.02
6	Jose Canseco	.60	.45	.25
7	Will Clark	.50	.40	.20
8	Jack Clark	.05	.04	.02
9	Vince Coleman	.05	.04	.02
10	Ron Darling	.05	.04	.02
11	Eric Davis	.40	.30	.15
12	Jose DeLeon	.05	.04	.02
13	Tony Fernandez	.05	.04	.02
14	Carlton Fisk	.10	.08	.04
15	Scott Garrelts	.05	.04	.02
16	Tom Gordon	.15	.11	.06
17	Ken Griffey,Jr.	1.75	1.25	.60
18	Von Hayes	.05	.04	.02
19	Rickey Henderson	.35	.25	.14
20	Bo Jackson	.80	.60	.30
21	Howard Johnson	.15	.11	.06
22	Don Mattingly	.40	.30	.15
23	Fred McGriff	.25	.20	.10
24	Kevin Mitchell	.30	.25	.12
25	Gregg Olson	.15	.11	.06
26	Gary Pettis	.05	.04	.02
27	Kirby Puckett	.30	.25	.12
28	Harold Reynolds	.05	.04	.02
29	Jeff Russell	.05	.04	.02
30	Nolan Ryan	.70	.50	.30
31	Bret Saberhagen	.10	.08	.04
32	Ryne Sandberg	.25	.20	.10
33	Benito Santiago	.10	.08	.04
34	Mike Scott	.05	.04	.02
35	Ruben Sierra	.25	.20	.10
36	Lonnie Smith	.05	.04	.02
37	Ozzie Smith	.10	.08	.04
38	Dave Stewart	.10	.08	.04
39	Greg Swindell	.05	.04	.02
40	Andy Van Slyke	.08	.06	.03
41	Tim Wallach	.05	.04	.02
42	Jerome Walton	.20	.15	.08
43	Mitch Williams	.08	.06	.03
44	Robin Yount	.15	.11	.06

1990 Fleer Baseball All Stars

Sold Exclusively in Ben Franklin stores, this 44-card boxed set showcases the game's top players. The card fronts feature a full color player photo surrounded by a tan border. The flip side contains individual player statistics and data printed in red and black. The cards measure 2-1/2" by 3-1/2" in size and are packed in a special box with a complete checklist on the back. Like other Fleer boxed sets, the cards are numbered alphabetically.

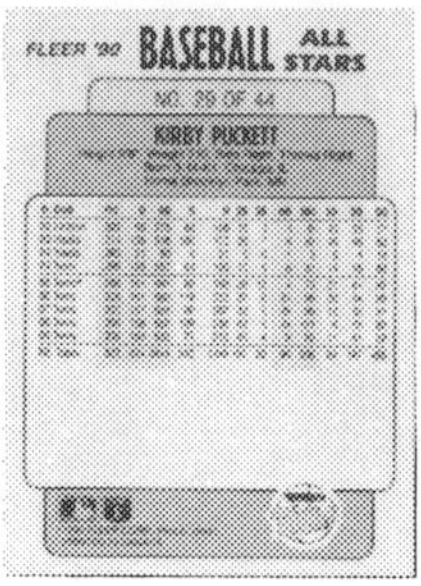

		MT	NR MT	EX
Complete Set:		4.00	3.00	1.50
Common Player:		.05	.04	.02
1	Wade Boggs	.35	.25	.14
2	Bobby Bonilla	.20	.15	.08
3	Tim Burke	.05	.04	.02
4	Jose Canseco	.60	.45	.25
5	Will Clark	.50	.40	.20
6	Eric Davis	.40	.30	.15
7	Glenn Davis	.20	.15	.08
8	Julio Franco	.10	.08	.04
9	Tony Fernandez	.10	.08	.04
10	Gary Gaetti	.10	.08	.04
11	Scott Garrelts	.05	.04	.02
12	Mark Grace	.20	.15	.08
13	Mike Greenwell	.20	.15	.08
14	Ken Griffey,Jr.	1.75	1.25	.70
15	Mark Gubicza	.05	.04	.02
16	Pedro Guerrero	.10	.08	.04
17	Von Hayes	.05	.04	.02
18	Orel Hershiser	.10	.08	.04
19	Bruce Hurst	.05	.04	.02
20	Bo Jackson	.80	.60	.30
21	Howard Johnson	.20	.15	.08
22	Doug Jones	.05	.04	.02
23	Barry Larkin	.30	.25	.12
24	Don Mattingly	.60	.45	.25
25	Mark McGwire	.50	.40	.20
26	Kevin McReynolds	.05	.04	.02
27	Kevin Mitchell	.40	.30	.15
28	Dan Plesac	.05	.04	.02
29	Kirby Puckett	.40	.30	.15
30	Cal Ripken,Jr.	.35	.25	.14
31	Bret Saberhagen	.10	.08	.04
32	Ryne Sandberg	.35	.25	.14
33	Steve Sax	.10	.08	.04
34	Ruben Sierra	.35	.25	.14
35	Ozzie Smith	.10	.08	.04
36	John Smoltz	.10	.08	.04
37	Darryl Strawberry	.30	.25	.12
38	Terry Steinbach	.05	.04	.02
39	Dave Stewart	.10	.08	.04
40	Bobby Thigpen	.10	.08	.04
41	Alan Trammell	.10	.08	.04
42	Devon White	.05	.04	.02
43	Mitch Williams	.05	.04	.02
44	Robin Yount	.15	.11	.06

1990 Fleer Baseball MVP

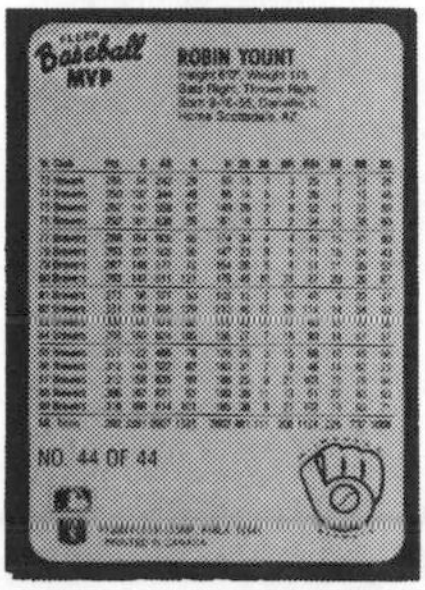

This 44-card boxed set was produced by Fleer for the Toys "R" Us chain. Card fronts are designed with graduating black-to-white borders, surrounding a color photo of each player. Card backs contain individual player data and career statistics. The back of each box carries a checklist of all the players in the set. Six peel-off team logo stickers featuring a baseball trivia quiz on the back are also included with each set. The cards are 2-1/2" by 3-1/2" in size and are numbered alphabetically.

		MT	NR MT	EX
Complete Set:		4.00	3.00	1.50
Common Player:		.05	.04	.02
1	George Bell	.10	.08	.04
2	Bert Blyleven	.10	.08	.04
3	Wade Boggs	.40	.30	.15
4	Bobby Bonilla	.15	.11	.06
5	George Brett	.15	.11	.06
6	Jose Canseco	.70	.50	.30
7	Will Clark	.60	.45	.25
8	Roger Clemens	.30	.25	.12
9	Eric Davis	.60	.45	.25
10	Glenn Davis	.15	.11	.06
11	Tony Fernandez	.08	.06	.03
12	Dwight Gooden	.25	.20	.10
13	Mike Greenwell	.20	.15	.08
14	Ken Griffey,Jr.	2.00	1.50	.80
15	Pedro Guerrero	.08	.06	.03
16	Tony Gwynn	.15	.11	.06
17	Rickey Henderson	.40	.30	.15
18	Tom Herr	.05	.04	.02
19	Orel Hershiser	.10	.08	.04
20	Kent Hrbek	.05	.04	.02
21	Bo Jackson	.80	.60	.30
22	Howard Johnson	.25	.20	.10
23	Don Mattingly	.50	.40	.20
24	Fred McGriff	.25	.20	.10
25	Mark McGwire	.50	.40	.20
26	Kevin Mitchell	.35	.25	.14
27	Paul Molitor	.10	.08	.04
28	Dale Murphy	.10	.08	.04
29	Kirby Puckett	.40	.30	.15
30	Tim Raines	.10	.08	.04
31	Cal Ripken,Jr.	.30	.25	.12
32	Bret Saberhagen	.10	.08	.04
33	Ryne Sandberg	.20	.15	.08
34	Ruben Sierra	.30	.25	.12
35	Dwight Smith	.08	.06	.03
36	Ozzie Smith	.10	.08	.04
37	Darryl Strawberry	.35	.25	.14
38	Dave Stewart	.10	.08	.04
39	Greg Swindell	.05	.04	.02
40	Bobby Thigpen	.08	.06	.03
41	Alan Trammell	.10	.08	.04
42	Jerome Walton	.25	.20	.10
43	Mitch Williams	.08	.06	.03
44	Robin Yount	.20	.15	.08

A player's name in *italic* indicates a rookie card. An (FC) indicates a player's first card for that particular card company.

1990 Fleer Box Panels

For the fifth consecutive year, Fleer issued a series of cards on the bottom panels of its regular 1990 wax pack boxes. This 28-card set features both players and team logo cards. The cards were numbered C-1 to C-28.

		MT	NR MT	EX
Complete Set:		5.00	3.75	2.00
Common Player:		.05	.04	.02
1	Giants Logo	.05	.04	.02
2	Tim Belcher	.06	.05	.02
3	Roger Clemens	.35	.25	.14
4	Eric Davis	.35	.25	.14
5	Glenn Davis	.10	.08	.04
6	Cubs Logo	.05	.04	.02
7	Jon Franco	.06	.05	.02
8	Mike Greenwell	.30	.25	.12
9	Athletics Logo	.05	.04	.02
10	Ken Griffey, Jr.	1.50	1.25	.60
11	Pedro Guerrero	.05	.04	.02
12	Tony Gwynn	.20	.15	.08
13	Blue Jays Logo	.05	.04	.02
14	Orel Hershiser	.20	.15	.08
15	Bo Jackson	.70	.50	.30
16	Howard Johnson	.15	.11	.06
17	Mets Logo	.05	.04	.02
18	Cardinals Logo	.05	.04	.02
19	Don Mattingly	.60	.45	.25
20	Mark McGwire	.40	.30	.15
21	Kevin Mitchell	.25	.20	.10
22	Kirby Puckett	.35	.25	.14
23	Royals Logo	.05	.04	.02
24	Orioles Logo	.05	.04	.02
25	Ruben Sierra	.30	.25	.12
26	Dave Stewart	.20	.15	.08
27	Jerome Walton	.50	.40	.20
28	Robin Yount	.25	.20	.10

1990 Fleer '89 World Series

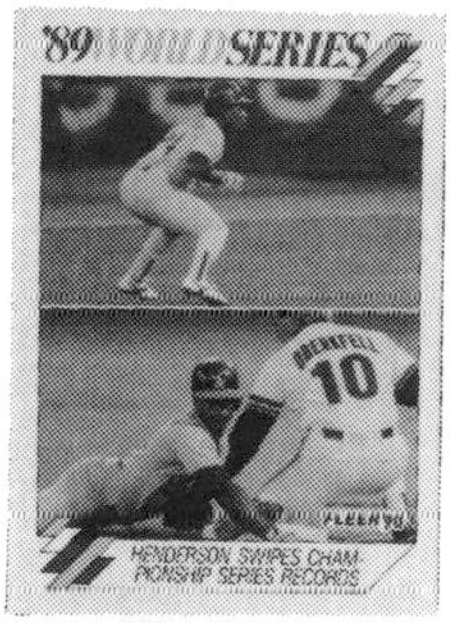

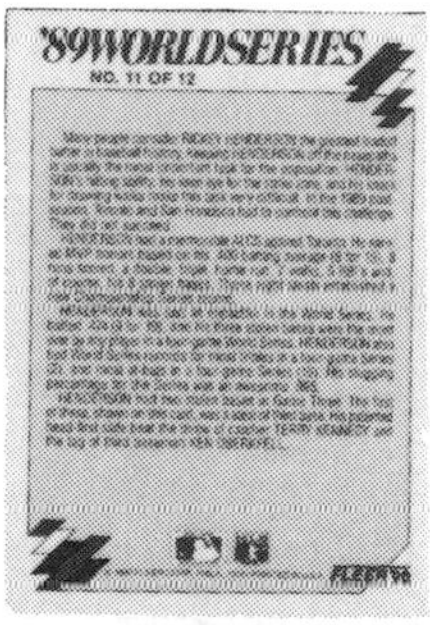

This 12-card set, which depicts highlights of the 1989 World Series, was included as a special sub-set with the regular factory-collated Fleer set. Ironically, single World Series cards were discovered in cello and three-packs. This was not intended to happen. Fronts of the 2-1/2" by 3-1/2" cards feature full color photos set against a white background with a red and blue "'89 World Series" banner. The card backs are pink and white and describe the events of the 1989 FALL Classic.

		MT	NR MT	EX
Complete Set:		3.00	2.25	1.25
Common Player:		.20	.15	.08
1	The Final Piece To The Puzzle (Mike Moore)	.20	.15	.08
2	The National League M.V.P. (Kevin Mitchell)	.30	.25	.12
3	Game Two's Crushing Blow	.20	.15	.08
4	Clark Pwers The Giants Into The Series (Will Clark)	.35	.25	.14
5	Canseco Crushed World Series Slump (Jose Canseco)	.40	.30	.15
6	Great leather In The Field	.20	.15	.08
7	Game One And A's Break Out On Top	.20	.15	.08
8	Oakland's M.V.P. (Dave Stewart)	.25	.20	.10
9	Parker's Bat Produces Power (Dave Parker)	.20	.15	.08
10	World Series Record Book Game 3	.20	.15	.08
11	Swipes Championship Series Records (Rickey Henderson)	.35	.25	.14
12	Oakland A's - Baseball's Best In '89	.25	.20	.10

1990 Fleer League Leaders

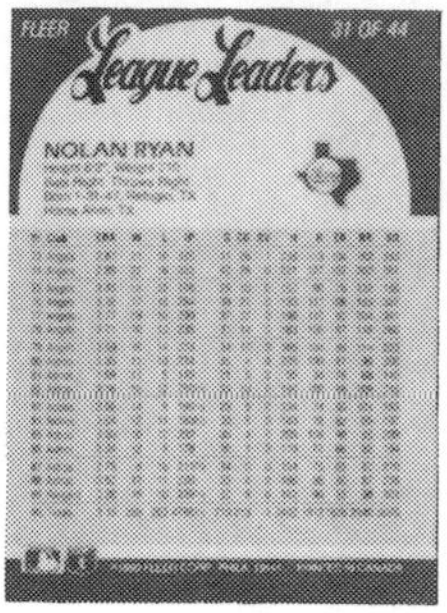

For the fifth consecutive year Fleer released a "League Leaders" trading card set. The set includes 44 top Major League players and features six special cards containing peel-off team logos and a baseball trivia quiz. Card number 42 (Jerome Walton) pictures a player other than Walton. The cards measure 2-1/2" by 3-1/2" in size. The card fronts display a full- color photo bordered by a blue frame. The card backs feature complete statistics. The cards are numbered alphabetically and a complete checklist is displayed on the back of the card box. The set is available at Walgreen Drug Stores.

		MT	NR MT	EX
Complete Set:		4.00	3.00	1.50
Common Player:		.05	.04	.02
1	Roberto Alomar	.35	.25	.14
2	Tim Belcher	.08	.06	.03
3	George Bell	.10	.08	.04
4	Wade Boggs	.35	.25	.14
5	Jose Canseco	.60	.45	.25
6	Will Clark	.50	.40	.20
7	David Cone	.08	.06	.03
8	Eric Davis	.40	.30	.15
9	Glenn Davis	.20	.15	.08
10	Nick Esasky	.10	.08	.04
11	Dennis Eckersley	.10	.08	.04
12	Mark Grace	.15	.11	.06
13	Mike Greenwell	.20	.15	.08
14	Ken Griffey,Jr.	1.75	1.25	.70
15	Mark Gubicza	.05	.04	.02
16	Pedro Guerrero	.05	.04	.02
17	Tony Gwynn	.15	.11	.06
18	Rickey Henderson	.40	.30	.15
19	Bo Jackson	.80	.60	.30
20	Doug Jones	.05	.04	.02
21	Ricky Jordan	.08	.06	.03
22	Barry Larkin	.25	.20	.10
23	Don Mattingly	.40	.30	.15
24	Fred McGriff	.25	.20	.10
25	Mark McGwire	.40	.30	.15
26	Kevin Mitchell	.40	.30	.15
27	Jack Morris	.05	.04	.02
28	Gregg Olson	.15	.11	.06
29	Dan Plesac	.05	.04	.02
30	Kirby Puckett	.30	.25	.12
31	Nolan Ryan	.50	.40	.20
32	Bret Saberhagen	.10	.08	.04
33	Ryne Sandberg	.20	.15	.08
34	Steve Sax	.10	.08	.04
35	Mike Scott	.05	.04	.02
36	Ruben Sierra	.30	.25	.12
37	Lonnie Smith	.05	.04	.02
38	Darryl Strawberry	.30	.25	.12
39	Bobby Thigpen	.08	.06	.03
40	Andy Van Slyke	.10	.08	.04
41	Tim Wallach	.05	.04	.02
42	Jerome Walton	.20	.15	.08
43	Devon White	.05	.04	.02
44	Robin Yount	.15	.11	.06

A player's name in *italic* type indicates a rookie card. An (FC) indicates a player's first card for that particular card company.

1990 Fleer League Standouts

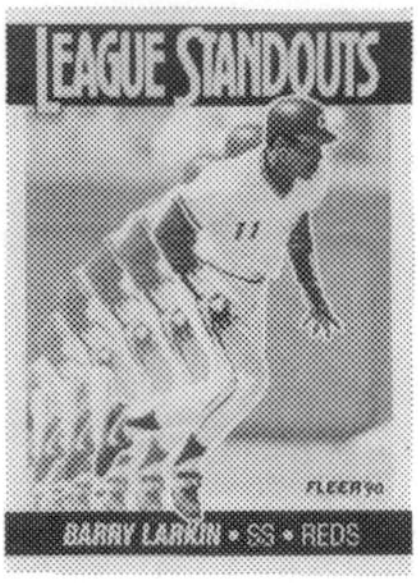

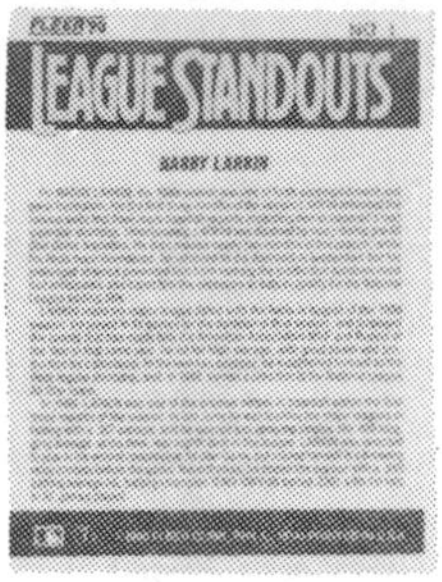

Fleer's ''League Standouts'' set features six of baseball's top players. The cards were distributed randomly in Fleer three-packs. The card fronts feature full-color photos with a six dimensional effect. An attractive black and gold frame borders the photo. The card backs are yellow and describe the player's individual accomplishments. The cards measure 2-1/2'' by 3-1/2'' in size.

		MT	NR MT	EX
Complete Set:		4.00	3.00	1.50
Common Player:		.50	.40	.20
1	Barry Larkin	.50	.40	.20
2	Mark Grace	.50	.40	.20
3	Don Mattingly	.80	.60	.30
4	Darryl Strawberry	.60	.45	.25
5	Jose Canseco	1.00	.70	.40
6	Wade Boggs	.60	.45	.25

1990 Fleer Update

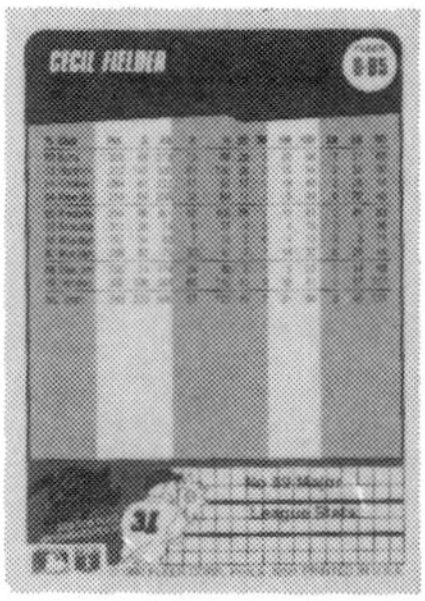

Fleer produced its seventh consecutive "Update" set in 1990 to supplement the company's regular set. As in the past, the set consists of 132 cards (numbered U-1 through U-132) that were sold by hobby dealers in special collectors boxes. The cards are designed in the exact same style as the regular issue. A special Nolan Ryan commemorative card is included in the 1990 Fleer Update set.

		MT	NR MT	EX
Complete Set:		12.00	9.00	4.75
Common Player:		.06	.05	.02
1	Steve Avery(FC)	.70	.50	.30
2	Francisco Cabrera	.20	.15	.08
3	Nick Esasky	.06	.05	.02
4	Jim Kremers(FC)	.15	.11	.06
5	Greg Olson(FC)	.12	.09	.05
6	Jim Presley	.06	.05	.02
7	Shawn Boskie(FC)	.25	.20	.10
8	Joe Kraemer(FC)	.08	.06	.03
9	Luis Salazar	.06	.05	.02
10	Hector Villanueva(FC)	.30	.25	.12
11	Glenn Braggs	.06	.05	.02
12	Mariano Duncan	.06	.05	.02
13	Billy Hatcher	.06	.05	.02
14	Tim Layana(FC)	.20	.15	.08
15	Hal Morris	.40	.30	.15
16	Javier Ortiz(FC)	.20	.15	.08
17	Dave Rohde(FC)	.15	.11	.06
18	Eric Yelding(FC)	.20	.15	.08
19	Hubie Brooks	.08	.06	.03
20	Kal Daniels	.08	.06	.03
21	Dave Hansen	.15	.11	.06
22	Mike Hartley	.15	.11	.06
23	Stan Javier	.06	.05	.02
24	Jose Offerman(FC)	.60	.45	.25
25	Juan Samuel	.06	.05	.02
26	Dennis Boyd	.06	.05	.02
27	Delino DeShields	.60	.45	.25
28	Steve Frey	.12	.09	.05
29	Mark Gardner	.15	.11	.06
30	Chris Nabholz(FC)	.40	.30	.15
31	Bill Sampen(FC)	.25	.20	.10
32	Dave Schmidt	.06	.05	.02
33	Daryl Boston	.06	.05	.02
34	Chuck Carr(FC)	.20	.15	.08
35	John Franco	.08	.06	.03
36	Todd Hundley(FC)	.25	.20	.10
37	Julio Machado(FC)	.15	.11	.06
38	Alejandro Pena	.06	.05	.02
39	Darren Reed(FC)	.25	.20	.10
40	Kelvin Torve(FC)	.12	.09	.05
41	Darrel Akerfelds(FC)	.12	.09	.05
42	Jose DeJesus	.20	.15	.08
43	Dave Hollins(FC)	.30	.25	.12
44	Carmelo Martinez	.06	.05	.02
45	Brad Moore(FC)	.15	.11	.06
46	Dale Murphy	.10	.08	.04
47	Wally Backman	.06	.05	.02
48	Stan Belinda(FC)	.20	.15	.08
49	Bob Patterson	.06	.05	.02
50	Ted Power	.06	.05	.02
51	Don Slaught	.06	.05	.02
52	Geronimo Pena(FC)	.25	.20	.10
53	Lee Smith	.08	.06	.03
54	John Tudor	.06	.05	.02
55	Joe Carter	.10	.08	.04
56	Tom Howard(FC)	.20	.15	.08
57	Craig Lefferts	.06	.05	.02
58	Rafael Valdez(FC)	.20	.15	.08
59	Dave Anderson	.06	.05	.02
60	Kevin Bass	.06	.05	.02
61	John Burkett	.25	.20	.10
62	Gary Carter	.10	.08	.04
63	Rick Parker(FC)	.10	.08	.04
64	Trevor Wilson	.10	.08	.04
65	Chris Hoiles(FC)	.25	.20	.10
66	Tim Hulett	.06	.05	.02
67	Dave Johnson(FC)	.10	.08	.04
68	Curt Schilling(FC)	.10	.08	.04
69	David Segui(FC)	.35	.25	.12
70	Tom Brunansky	.08	.06	.03
71	Greg Harris	.06	.05	.02
72	Dana Kiecker(FC)	.12	.09	.05
73	Tim Naehring(FC)	.40	.30	.15
74	Tony Pena	.06	.05	.02
75	Jeff Reardon	.08	.06	.03
76	Jerry Reed	.06	.05	.02
77	Mark Eichhorn	.06	.05	.02
78	Mark Langston	.08	.06	.03
79	John Orton	.12	.09	.05
80	Luis Polonia	.06	.05	.02
81	Dave Winfield	.12	.09	.05
82	Cliff Young(FC)	.20	.15	.08
83	Wayne Edwards	.10	.08	.04
84	Alex Fernandez(FC)	.80	.60	.30
85	Craig Grebeck(FC)	.15	.11	.06
86	Scott Radinsky(FC)	.25	.20	.10
87	Frank Thomas(FC)	6.00	4.50	2.50
88	Beau Allred(FC)	.20	.15	.08
89	Sandy Alomar,Jr.	.35	.25	.14
90	Carlos Baerga(FC)	.50	.40	.20
91	Kevin Bearse(FC)	.25	.20	.10
92	Chris James	.06	.05	.02
93	Candy Maldonado	.06	.05	.02
94	Jeff Manto	.12	.09	.05
95	Cecil Fielder	.60	.45	.25
96	Travis Fryman(FC)	1.25	.90	.50
97	Lloyd Moseby	.06	.05	.02
98	Edwin Nunez	.06	.05	.02
99	Tony Phillips	.06	.05	.02
100	Larry Sheets	.06	.05	.02
101	Mark Davis	.06	.05	.02

		MT	NR MT	EX
102	Storm Davis	.06	.05	.02
103	Gerald Perry	.06	.05	.02
104	Terry Shumpert(FC)	.15	.11	.06
105	Edgar Diaz(FC)	.15	.11	.06
106	Dave Parker	.10	.08	.04
107	Tim Drummond(FC)	.15	.11	.06
108	Junior Ortiz	.06	.05	.02
109	Park Pittman(FC)	.15	.11	.06
110	Kevin Tapani(FC)	.25	.20	.10
111	Oscar Azocar(FC)	.15	.11	.06
112	Jim Leyritz(FC)	.15	.11	.06
113	Kevin Maas	2.00	1.50	.80
114	Alan Mills(FC)	.25	.20	.10
115	Matt Nokes	.06	.05	.02
116	Pascual Perez	.06	.05	.02
117	Ozzie Canseco(FC)	.20	.15	.08
118	Scott Sanderson	.06	.05	.02
119	Tino Martinez(FC)	.60	.45	.25
120	Jeff Schaefer(FC)	.15	.11	.06
121	Matt Young	.06	.05	.02
122	Brian Bohanon(FC)	.20	.15	.08
123	Jeff Huson	.15	.11	.06
124	Ramon Manon(FC)	.20	.15	.08
125	Gary Mielke(FC)	.15	.11	.06
126	Willie Blair(FC)	.15	.11	.06
127	Glenallen Hill(FC)	.15	.11	.06
128	John Olerud(FC)	1.25	.90	.50
129	Luis Sojo(FC)	.15	.11	.06
130	Mark Whiten(FC)	.70	.50	.30
131	Three Decades Of No Hitters (Nolan Ryan)	1.00	.70	.40
132	Checklist	.06	.05	.02

1991 Fleer

Fleer expanded its 1991 set to include 720 cards. The cards feature yellow boders surrounding full-color action photos. The player's name appears above the photo, while the team and position in displayed below. The "Fleer 91" logo appears in the lower right corner of the photo. The card backs feature a player photo in a circle design, biographical information, complete statistics, and career highlights. Five special Super Star cards are among the cards in the regular set. Once again the cards are numbered according to team.

	MT	NR MT	EX
Complete Set:	22.00	16.00	9.00
Common Player:	.05	.04	.02

		MT	NR MT	EX
1	*Troy Afenir*(FC)	.10	.08	.04
2	Harold Baines	.08	.06	.03
3	Lance Blankenship	.06	.05	.02
4	Todd Burns	.05	.04	.02
5	Jose Canseco	.30	.25	.12
6	Dennis Eckersley	.10	.08	.04
7	Mike Gallego	.05	.04	.02
8	Ron Hassey	.05	.04	.02
9	Dave Henderson	.08	.06	.03
10	Rickey Henderson	.20	.15	.08
11	Rick Honeycutt	.05	.04	.02
12	Doug Jennings	.06	.05	.02
13	*Joe Klink*(FC)	.10	.08	.04
14	Carney Lansford	.08	.06	.03
15	*Darren Lewis*(FC)	.40	.30	.15
16	Willie McGee	.08	.06	.03
17	Mark McGwire	.20	.15	.08
18	Mike Moore	.06	.05	.02
19	Gene Nelson	.05	.04	.02
20	Dave Otto	.05	.04	.02
21	Jamie Quirk	.05	.04	.02
22	Willie Randolph	.06	.05	.02
23	Scott Sanderson	.06	.05	.02
24	Terry Steinbach	.06	.05	.02
25	Dave Stewart	.10	.08	.04
26	Walt Weiss	.06	.05	.02
27	Bob Welch	.08	.06	.03
28	Curt Young	.05	.04	.02
29	Wally Backman	.05	.04	.02
30	*Stan Belinda*	.10	.08	.04
31	Jay Bell	.06	.05	.02
32	Rafael Belliard	.05	.04	.02
33	Barry Bonds	.20	.15	.08
34	Bobby Bonilla	.15	.11	.06
35	Sid Bream	.06	.05	.02
36	Doug Drabek	.10	.08	.04
37	*Carlos Garcia*(FC)	.15	.11	.06
38	Neal Heaton	.06	.05	.02
39	Jeff King	.08	.06	.03
40	Bob Kipper	.05	.04	.02
41	Bill Landrum	.06	.05	.02
42	Mike LaValliere	.06	.05	.02
43	Jose Lind	.06	.05	.02
44	Carmelo Martinez	.05	.04	.02
45	Bob Patterson	.05	.04	.02
46	Ted Power	.05	.04	.02
47	Gary Redus	.05	.04	.02
48	R.J. Reynolds	.05	.04	.02
49	Don Slaught	.05	.04	.02
50	John Smiley	.05	.04	.02
51	Zane Smith	.06	.05	.02
52	*Randy Tomlin*(FC)	.20	.15	.08
53	Andy Van Slyke	.08	.06	.03
54	Bob Walk	.05	.04	.02
55	Jack Armstrong	.08	.06	.03
56	Todd Benzinger	.06	.05	.02
57	Glenn Braggs	.06	.05	.02
58	Keith Brown	.06	.05	.02
59	Tom Browning	.06	.05	.02
60	Norm Charlton	.08	.06	.03
61	Eric Davis	.20	.15	.08
62	Rob Dibble	.10	.08	.04
63	Bill Doran	.08	.06	.03
64	Mariano Duncan	.06	.05	.02
65	Chris Hammond	.06	.05	.02
66	Billy Hatcher	.06	.05	.02
67	Danny Jackson	.06	.05	.02
68	Barry Larkin	.15	.11	.06
69	*Tim Layana*	.10	.08	.04
70	*Terry Lee*(FC)	.15	.11	.06
71	Rick Mahler	.05	.04	.02
72	Hal Morris	.15	.11	.06
73	Randy Myers	.08	.06	.03
74	Ron Oester	.05	.04	.02
75	Joe Oliver	.08	.06	.03
76	Paul O'Neill	.06	.05	.02
77	Luis Quinones	.05	.04	.02
78	Jeff Reed	.05	.04	.02
79	Jose Rijo	.08	.06	.03
80	Chris Sabo	.08	.06	.03
81	Scott Scudder	.06	.05	.02
82	Herm Winningham	.05	.04	.02
83	Larry Andersen	.05	.04	.02
84	Marty Barrett	.05	.04	.02
85	Mike Boddicker	.06	.05	.02
86	Wade Boggs	.20	.15	.08
87	Tom Bolton	.05	.04	.02
88	Tom Brunansky	.06	.05	.02
89	Ellis Burks	.15	.11	.06
90	Roger Clemens	.20	.15	.08
91	Scott Cooper(FC)	.15	.11	.06
92	John Dopson	.05	.04	.02
93	Dwight Evans	.06	.05	.02
94	Wes Gardner	.05	.04	.02
95	*Jeff Gray*(FC)	.15	.11	.06
96	Mike Greenwell	.10	.08	.04
97	Greg Harris	.05	.04	.02
98	*Daryl Irvine*(FC)	.20	.15	.08
99	*Dana Kiecker*	.10	.08	.04
100	Randy Kutcher	.05	.04	.02
101	Dennis Lamp	.05	.04	.02
102	Mike Marshall	.05	.04	.02
103	John Marzano	.05	.04	.02
104	Rob Murphy	.05	.04	.02
105	*Tim Naehring*	.20	.15	.08
106	Tony Pena	.06	.05	.02
107	*Phil Plantier*(FC)	1.25	.90	.50
108	Carlos Quintana	.06	.05	.02

		MT	NR MT	EX
109	Jeff Reardon	.06	.05	.02
110	Jerry Reed	.05	.04	.02
111	Jody Reed	.06	.05	.02
112	Luis Rivera	.05	.04	.02
113	Kevin Romine	.05	.04	.02
114	Phil Bradley	.06	.05	.02
115	Ivan Calderon	.06	.05	.02
116	Wayne Edwards	.05	.04	.02
117	*Alex Fernandez*	.40	.30	.15
118	Carlton Fisk	.10	.08	.04
119	Scott Fletcher	.05	.04	.02
120	*Craig Grebeck*	.15	.11	.06
121	Ozzie Guillen	.08	.06	.03
122	Greg Hibbard	.06	.05	.02
123	Lance Johnson	.06	.05	.02
124	Barry Jones	.05	.04	.02
125	Ron Karkovice	.05	.04	.02
126	Eric King	.05	.04	.02
127	Steve Lyons	.05	.04	.02
128	Carlos Martinez	.06	.05	.02
129	Jack McDowell	.06	.05	.02
130	Donn Pall	.05	.04	.02
131	Dan Pasqua	.05	.04	.02
132	Ken Patterson	.05	.04	.02
133	Melido Perez	.06	.05	.02
134	Adam Peterson	.05	.04	.02
135	*Scott Radinsky*	.15	.11	.06
136	Sammy Sosa	.15	.11	.06
137	Bobby Thigpen	.08	.06	.03
138	Frank Thomas	1.25	.90	.50
139	Robin Ventura	.25	.20	.10
140	Daryl Boston	.05	.04	.02
141	*Chuck Carr*	.20	.15	.08
142	Mark Carreon	.05	.04	.02
143	David Cone	.06	.05	.02
144	Ron Darling	.06	.05	.02
145	Kevin Elster	.05	.04	.02
146	Sid Fernandez	.06	.05	.02
147	John Franco	.08	.06	.03
148	Dwight Gooden	.20	.15	.08
149	Tom Herr	.06	.05	.02
150	*Todd Hundley*	.20	.15	.08
151	Gregg Jefferies	.15	.11	.06
152	Howard Johnson	.08	.06	.03
153	Dave Magadan	.08	.06	.03
154	Kevin McReynolds	.08	.06	.03
155	Keith Miller	.06	.05	.02
156	Bob Ojeda	.05	.04	.02
157	Tom O'Malley	.05	.04	.02
158	Alejandro Pena	.05	.04	.02
159	*Darren Reed*	.20	.15	.08
160	Mackey Sasser	.06	.05	.02
161	Darryl Strawberry	.25	.20	.10
162	Tim Teufel	.05	.04	.02
163	Kelvin Torve	.08	.06	.03
164	Julio Valera	.25	.20	.10
165	Frank Viola	.12	.09	.05
166	Wally Whitehurst	.05	.04	.02
167	Jim Acker	.05	.04	.02
168	*Derek Bell*(FC)	.35	.25	.14
169	George Bell	.08	.06	.03
170	*Willie Blair*	.15	.11	.06
171	Pat Borders	.06	.05	.02
172	John Cerutti	.05	.04	.02
173	Juunior Felix	.12	.09	.05
174	Tony Fernandez	.08	.06	.03
175	Kelly Gruber	.12	.09	.05
176	Tom Henke	.06	.05	.02
177	Glenallen Hill	.08	.06	.03
178	Jimmy Key	.06	.05	.02
179	Manny Lee	.05	.04	.02
180	Fred McGriff	.15	.11	.06
181	Rance Mulliniks	.05	.04	.02
182	Greg Myers	.05	.04	.02
183	John Olerud	.50	.40	.20
184	Luis Sojo	.15	.11	.06
185	Dave Steib	.08	.06	.03
186	Todd Stottlemyre	.06	.05	.02
187	Duane Ward	.05	.04	.02
188	David Wells	.05	.04	.02
189	*Mark Whiten*	.40	.30	.15
190	Ken Williams	.05	.04	.02
191	Frank Wills	.05	.04	.02
192	Mookie Wilson	.05	.04	.02
193	Don Aase	.05	.04	.02
194	Tim Belcher	.08	.06	.03
195	Hubie Brooks	.08	.06	.03
196	Dennis Cook	.06	.05	.02
197	Tim Crews	.05	.04	.02
198	Kal Daniels	.06	.05	.02
199	Kirk Gibson	.08	.06	.03
200	Jim Gott	.05	.04	.02
201	Alfredo Griffin	.05	.04	.02
202	Chris Gwynn	.06	.05	.02
203	Dave Hansen	.20	.15	.08
204	Lenny Harris	.06	.05	.02
205	Mike Hartley	.10	.08	.04
206	Mickey Hatcher	.05	.04	.02
207	*Carlos Hernandez*(FC)	.20	.15	.08
208	Orel Hershiser	.10	.08	.04
209	Jay Howell	.06	.05	.02
210	Mike Huff	.10	.08	.04
211	Stan Javier	.05	.04	.02
212	Ramon Martinez	.20	.15	.08
213	Mike Morgan	.05	.04	.02
214	Eddie Murray	.08	.06	.03
215	*Jim Neidlinger*(FC)	.20	.15	.08
216	Jose Offerman	.30	.25	.12
217	*Jim Poole*(FC)	.20	.15	.08
218	Juan Samuel	.06	.05	.02
219	Mike Scioscia	.06	.05	.02
220	Ray Searage	.05	.04	.02
221	Mike Sharperson	.06	.05	.02
222	Fernando Valenzuela	.06	.05	.02
223	Jose Vizcaino	.10	.08	.04
224	Mike Aldrete	.05	.04	.02
225	*Scott Anderson*(FC)	.20	.15	.08
226	Dennis Boyd	.06	.05	.02
227	Tim Burke	.06	.05	.02
228	Delino DeShields	.30	.25	.12
229	Mike Fitzgerald	.05	.04	.02
230	Tom Foley	.05	.04	.02
231	Steve Frey	.05	.04	.02
232	Andres Galarraga	.08	.06	.03
233	Mark Gardner	.10	.08	.04
234	Marquis Grissom(FC)	.20	.15	.08
235	Kevin Gross	.06	.05	.02
236	Drew Hall	.05	.04	.02
237	Dave Martinez	.06	.05	.02
238	Dennis Martinez	.06	.05	.02
239	Dale Mohorcic	.05	.04	.02
240	*Chris Nabholz*	.25	.20	.10
241	Otis Nixon	.05	.04	.02
242	Junior Noboa(FC)	.08	.06	.03
243	Spike Owen	.06	.05	.02
244	Tim Raines	.08	.06	.03
245	*Mel Rojas*(FC)	.12	.09	.05
246	*Scott Ruskin*(FC)	.15	.11	.06
247	*Bill Sampen*	.25	.20	.10
248	Nelson Santovenia	.05	.04	.02
249	Dave Schmidt	.05	.04	.02
250	Larry Walker	.15	.11	.06
251	Tim Wallach	.08	.06	.03
252	Dave Anderson	.05	.04	.02
253	Kevin Bass	.06	.05	.02
254	Steve Bedrosian	.06	.05	.02
255	Jeff Brantley	.08	.06	.03
256	John Burkett	.12	.09	.05
257	Brett Butler	.06	.05	.02
258	Gary Carter	.08	.06	.03
259	Will Clark	.25	.20	.10
260	*Steve Decker*(FC)	.40	.30	.15
261	Kelly Downs	.05	.04	.02
262	Scott Garrelts	.06	.05	.02
263	Terry Kennedy	.05	.04	.02
264	Mike LaCoss	.05	.04	.02
265	*Mark Leonard*(FC)	.20	.15	.08
266	Greg Litton	.06	.05	.02
267	Kevin Mitchell	.20	.15	.08
268	Randy O'Neal(FC)	.05	.04	.02
269	*Rick Parker*	.15	.11	.06
270	Rick Reuschel	.06	.05	.02
271	Ernest Riles	.05	.04	.02
272	Don Robinson	.05	.04	.02
273	Robby Thompson	.06	.05	.02
274	Mark Thurmond	.05	.04	.02
275	Jose Uribe	.05	.04	.02
276	Matt Williams	.15	.11	.06
277	Trevor Wilson	.06	.05	.02
278	*Gerald Alexander*(FC)	.20	.15	.08
279	Brad Arnsberg	.06	.05	.02
280	*Kevin Belcher*(FC)	.20	.15	.08
281	*Joe Bitker*(FC)	.15	.11	.06
282	Kevin Brown	.06	.05	.02
283	Steve Buechele	.05	.04	.02
284	Jack Daugherty	.06	.05	.02
285	Julio Franco	.10	.08	.04
286	Juan Gonzalez	.30	.25	.12
287	*Bill Haselman*(FC)	.20	.15	.08
288	Charlie Hough	.05	.04	.02
289	Jeff Huson	.06	.05	.02
290	Pete Incaviglia	.06	.05	.02

		MT	NR MT	EX
291	Mike Jeffcoat	.05	.04	.02
292	Jeff Kunkel	.05	.04	.02
293	Gary Mielke	.08	.06	.03
294	Jamie Moyer	.05	.04	.02
295	Rafael Palmeiro	.08	.06	.03
296	Geno Petralli	.05	.04	.02
297	Gary Pettis	.06	.05	.02
298	Kevin Reimer	.10	.08	.04
299	Kenny Rogers	.06	.05	.02
300	Jeff Russell	.06	.05	.02
301	John Russell	.05	.04	.02
302	Nolan Ryan	.25	.20	.10
303	Ruben Sierra	.12	.09	.05
304	Bobby Witt	.08	.06	.03
305	Jim Abbott	.08	.06	.03
306	Kent Anderson(FC)	.06	.05	.02
307	Dante Bichette	.06	.05	.02
308	Bert Blyleven	.08	.06	.03
309	Chili Davis	.06	.05	.02
310	Brian Downing	.05	.04	.02
311	Mark Eichhorn	.05	.04	.02
312	Mike Fetters	.08	.06	.03
313	Chuck Finley	.08	.06	.03
314	Willie Fraser	.05	.04	.02
315	Bryan Harvey	.06	.05	.02
316	Donnie Hill	.05	.04	.02
317	Wally Joyner	.10	.08	.04
318	Mark Langston	.10	.08	.04
319	Kirk McCaskill	.06	.05	.02
320	John Orton	.06	.05	.02
321	Lance Parrish	.08	.06	.03
322	Luis Polonia	.05	.04	.02
323	Johnny Ray	.05	.04	.02
324	Bobby Rose	.06	.05	.02
325	Dick Schofield	.05	.04	.02
326	Rick Schu	.05	.04	.02
327	Lee Stevens	.10	.08	.04
328	Devon White	.06	.05	.02
329	Dave Winfield	.12	.09	.05
330	*Cliff Young*	.15	.11	.06
331	Dave Bergman	.05	.04	.02
332	*Phil Clark*(FC)	.25	.20	.10
333	Darnell Coles	.05	.04	.02
334	Milt Cuyler(FC)	.20	.15	.08
335	Cecil Fielder	.30	.25	.12
336	*Travis Fryman*	.50	.40	.20
337	Paul Gibson	.05	.04	.02
338	Jerry Don Gleaton	.05	.04	.02
339	Mike Heath	.05	.04	.02
340	Mike Henneman	.06	.05	.02
341	Chet Lemon	.06	.05	.02
342	Lance McCullers	.05	.04	.02
343	Jack Morris	.08	.06	.03
344	lloyd Moseby	.06	.05	.02
345	Edwin Nunez	.05	.04	.02
346	Clay Parker	.05	.04	.02
347	Dan Petry	.05	.04	.02
348	Tony Phillips	.06	.05	.02
349	Jeff Robinson	.06	.05	.02
350	Mark Salas	.05	.04	.02
351	*Mike Schwabe*	.15	.11	.06
352	Larry Sheets	.05	.04	.02
353	John Shelby	.05	.04	.02
354	Frank Tanana	.06	.05	.02
355	Alan Trammell	.08	.06	.03
356	Gary Ward	.05	.04	.02
357	Lou Whitaker	.08	.06	.03
358	Beau Allred	.15	.11	.06
359	Sandy Alomar,Jr.	.20	.15	.08
360	*Carlos Baerga*	.20	.15	.08
361	*Kevin Bearse*	.12	.09	.05
362	Tom Brookens	.05	.04	.02
363	Jerry Browne	.06	.05	.02
364	Tom Candiotti	.05	.04	.02
365	Alex Cole	.25	.20	.10
366	John Farrell	.05	.04	.02
367	Felix Fermin	.05	.04	.02
368	Keith Hernandez	.08	.06	.03
369	Brook Jacoby	.08	.06	.03
370	Chris James	.06	.05	.02
371	Dion James	.05	.04	.02
372	Doug Jones	.08	.06	.03
373	Candy Maldonado	.08	.06	.03
374	Steve Olin	.06	.05	.02
375	Jesse Orosco	.05	.04	.02
376	Rudy Seanez	.06	.05	.02
377	Joel Skinner	.05	.04	.02
378	Cory Snyder	.08	.06	.03
379	Greg Swindell	.06	.05	.02
380	Sergio Valdez(FC)	.08	.06	.03
381	*Mike Walker*(FC)	.15	.11	.06
382	*Colby Ward*(FC)	.20	.15	.08
383	*Turner Ward*(FC)	.20	.15	.08
384	Mitch Webster	.05	.04	.02
385	Kevin Wickander(FC)	.15	.11	.06
386	Darrel Akerfelds	.06	.05	.02
387	Joe Boever	.05	.04	.02
388	Rod Booker	.05	.04	.02
389	Sil Campusano	.05	.04	.02
390	Don Carman	.05	.04	.02
391	*Wes Chamberlain*(FC)	.50	.40	.20
392	Pat Combs	.06	.05	.02
393	Darren Daulton	.06	.05	.02
394	Jose DeJesus	.06	.05	.02
395	Len Dykstra	.08	.06	.03
396	Jason Grimsley	.06	.05	.02
397	Charlie Hayes	.08	.06	.03
398	Von Hayes	.08	.06	.03
399	*David Hollins*	.15	.11	.06
400	Ken Howell	.06	.05	.02
401	Ricky Jordan	.10	.08	.04
402	John Kruk	.06	.05	.02
403	Steve Lake	.05	.04	.02
404	*Chuck Malone*(FC)	.15	.11	.06
405	Roger McDowell	.08	.06	.03
406	Chuck McElroy	.15	.11	.06
407	*Mickey Morandini*(FC)	.15	.11	.06
408	Terry Mulholland	.06	.05	.02
409	Dale Murphy	.10	.08	.04
410	Randy Ready	.05	.04	.02
411	Bruce Ruffin	.05	.04	.02
412	Dickie Thon	.05	.04	.02
413	Paul Assenmacher	.05	.04	.02
414	Damon Berryhill	.06	.05	.02
415	Mike Bielecki	.06	.05	.02
416	*Shawn Boskie*	.15	.11	.06
417	Dave Clark	.05	.04	.02
418	Doug Dascenzo	.05	.04	.02
419	Andre Dawson	.10	.08	.04
420	Shawon Dunston	.10	.08	.04
421	Joe Girardi	.06	.05	.02
422	Mark Grace	.15	.11	.06
423	Mike Harkey	.08	.06	.03
424	Les Lancaster	.05	.04	.02
425	Bill Long	.05	.04	.02
426	Greg Maddux	.08	.06	.03
427	Derrick May	.25	.20	.10
428	Jeff Pico	.05	.04	.02
429	Domingo Ramos	.05	.04	.02
430	Luis Salazar	.05	.04	.02
431	Ryne Sandberg	.20	.15	.08
432	Dwight Smith	.06	.05	.02
433	Greg Smith	.08	.06	.03
434	Rick Sutcliffe	.08	.06	.03
435	Gary Varsho	.05	.04	.02
436	*Hector Villanueva*	.15	.11	.06
437	Jerome Walton	.08	.06	.03
438	Curtis Wilkerson	.05	.04	.02
439	Mitch Williams	.08	.06	.03
440	Steve Wilson	.06	.05	.02
441	Marvell Wynne	.05	.04	.02
442	Scott Bankhead	.06	.05	.02
443	Scott Bradley	.05	.04	.02
444	Greg Briley	.06	.05	.02
445	Mike Brumley	.05	.04	.02
446	Jay Buhner	.06	.05	.02
447	*Dave Burba*(FC)	.15	.11	.06
448	Henry Cotto	.05	.04	.02
449	Alvin Davis	.08	.06	.03
450	Ken Griffey,Jr.	1.00	.70	.40
451	Erik Hanson	.12	.09	.05
452	Gene Harris	.05	.04	.02
453	Brian Holman	.06	.05	.02
454	Mike Jackson	.06	.05	.02
455	Randy Johnson	.10	.08	.04
456	Jeffrey Leonard	.06	.05	.02
457	Edgar Martinez	.06	.05	.02
458	Tino Martinez	.35	.25	.14
459	Pete O'Brien	.05	.04	.02
460	Harold Reynolds	.08	.06	.03
461	Mike Schooler	.08	.06	.03
462	Bill Swift	.06	.05	.02
463	David Valle	.05	.04	.02
464	Omar Vizquel	.06	.05	.02
465	Matt Young	.06	.05	.02
466	Brady Anderson	.05	.04	.02
467	Jeff Ballard	.06	.05	.02
468	Juan Bell(FC)	.20	.15	.08
469	Mike Devereaux	.06	.05	.02
470	Steve Finley	.06	.05	.02
471	Dave Gallagher	.05	.04	.02
472	*Leo Gomez*(FC)	.40	.30	.15

		MT	NR MT	EX
473	Rene Gonzales	.05	.04	.02
474	Pete Harnisch	.06	.05	.02
475	Kevin Hickey	.05	.04	.02
476	*Chris Hoiles*	.20	.15	.08
477	Sam Horn	.06	.05	.02
478	Tim Hulett	.05	.04	.02
479	Dave Johnson	.05	.04	.02
480	Ron Kittle	.08	.06	.03
481	Ben McDonald	.40	.30	.15
482	Bob Melvin	.05	.04	.02
483	Bob Milacki	.06	.05	.02
484	Randy Milligan	.06	.05	.02
485	*John Mitchell*(FC)	.15	.11	.06
486	Gregg Olson	.08	.06	.03
487	Joe Orsulak	.05	.04	.02
488	Joe Price	.05	.04	.02
489	Bill Ripken	.05	.04	.02
490	Cal Ripken,Jr.	.15	.11	.06
491	Curt Schilling	.06	.05	.02
492	*David Segui*	.30	.25	.12
493	*Anthony Telford*(FC)	.20	.15	.08
494	Mickey Tettleton	.06	.05	.02
495	Mark Williamson	.05	.04	.02
496	Craig Worthington	.06	.05	.02
497	Juan Agosto	.05	.04	.02
498	Eric Anthony	.15	.11	.06
499	Craig Biggio	.08	.06	.03
500	Ken Caminiti	.06	.05	.02
501	Casey Candaele	.05	.04	.02
502	*Andujar Cedeno*(FC)	.60	.45	.25
503	Danny Darwin	.06	.05	.02
504	Mark Davidson	.05	.04	.02
505	Glenn Davis	.15	.11	.06
506	Jim Deshaies	.06	.05	.02
507	*Luis Gonzalez*(FC)	.50	.40	.20
508	Bill Gullickson	.05	.04	.02
509	Xavier Hernandez(FC)	.08	.06	.03
510	Brian Meyer	.06	.05	.02
511	Ken Oberkfell	.05	.04	.02
512	Mark Portugal	.05	.04	.02
513	Rafael Ramirez	.05	.04	.02
514	*Karl Rhodes*(FC)	.25	.20	.10
515	Mike Scott	.08	.06	.03
516	*Mike Simms*(FC)	.25	.20	.10
517	Dave Smith	.06	.05	.02
518	Franklin Stubbs	.06	.05	.02
519	Glenn Wilson	.06	.05	.02
520	Eric Yelding	.10	.08	.04
521	Gerald Young	.05	.04	.02
522	Shawn Abner	.05	.04	.02
523	Roberto Alomar	.10	.08	.04
524	Andy Benes	.15	.11	.06
525	Joe Carter	.10	.08	.04
526	Jack Clark	.08	.06	.03
527	Joey Cora	.06	.05	.02
528	*Paul Faries*(FC)	.20	.15	.08
529	Tony Gwynn	.15	.11	.06
530	Atlee Hammaker	.05	.04	.02
531	Greg Harris	.06	.05	.02
532	*Thomas Howard*	.20	.15	.08
533	Bruce Hurst	.06	.05	.02
534	Craig Lefferts	.06	.05	.02
535	Derek Lilliquist	.06	.05	.02
536	Fred Lynn	.06	.05	.02
537	Mike Pagliarulo	.06	.05	.02
538	Mark Parent	.05	.04	.02
539	Dennis Rasmussen	.05	.04	.02
540	Bip Roberts	.08	.06	.03
541	*Richard Rodriguez*(FC)	.20	.15	.08
542	Benito Santiago	.10	.08	.04
543	Calvin Schiraldi	.05	.04	.02
544	Eric Show	.06	.05	.02
545	Phil Stephenson	.05	.04	.02
546	Garry Templeton	.06	.05	.02
547	Ed Whitson	.06	.05	.02
548	Eddie Williams	.05	.04	.02
549	Kevin Appier	.10	.08	.04
550	Luis Aquino	.05	.04	.02
551	Bob Boone	.08	.06	.03
552	George Brett	.12	.09	.05
553	*Jeff Conine*(FC)	.30	.25	.12
554	Steve Crawford	.05	.04	.02
555	Mark Davis	.06	.05	.02
556	Storm Davis	.06	.05	.02
557	Jim Eisenreich	.06	.05	.02
558	Steve Farr	.05	.04	.02
559	Tom Gordon	.10	.08	.04
560	Mark Gubicza	.08	.06	.03
561	Bo Jackson	.30	.25	.12
562	Mike Macfarlane	.05	.04	.02
563	*Brian McRae*(FC)	.60	.45	.25
564	Jeff Montgomery	.06	.05	.02
565	Bill Pecota	.05	.04	.02
566	Gerald Perry	.06	.05	.02
567	Bret Saberhagen	.10	.08	.04
568	*Jeff Schulz*(FC)	.15	.11	.06
569	Kevin Seitzer	.08	.06	.03
570	*Terry Shumpert*	.15	.11	.06
571	Kurt Stillwell	.06	.05	.02
572	Danny Tartabull	.08	.06	.03
573	Gary Thurman	.05	.04	.02
574	Frank White	.06	.05	.02
575	Willie Wilson	.06	.05	.02
576	Chris Bosio	.06	.05	.02
577	Greg Brock	.06	.05	.02
578	George Canale	.06	.05	.02
579	Chuck Crim	.05	.04	.02
580	Rob Deer	.06	.05	.02
581	*Edgar Diaz*	.06	.05	.02
582	*Tom Edens*(FC)	.08	.06	.03
583	Mike Felder	.05	.04	.02
584	Jim Gantner	.06	.05	.02
585	Darryl Hamilton	.06	.05	.02
586	Ted Higuera	.08	.06	.03
587	Mark Knudson	.05	.04	.02
588	Bill Krueger	.05	.04	.02
589	Tim McIntosh	.08	.06	.03
590	Paul Mirabella	.05	.04	.02
591	Paul Molitor	.10	.08	.04
592	Jaime Navarro	.08	.06	.03
593	Dave Parker	.12	.09	.05
594	Dan Plesac	.06	.05	.02
595	Ron Robinson	.06	.05	.02
596	Gary Sheffield	.15	.11	.06
597	Bill Spiers	.06	.05	.02
598	B.J. Surhoff	.06	.05	.02
599	Greg Vaughn	.15	.11	.06
600	Randy Veres	.05	.04	.02
601	Robin Yount	.15	.11	.06
602	Rick Aguilera	.06	.05	.02
603	Allan Anderson	.05	.04	.02
604	Juan Berenguer	.05	.04	.02
605	Randy Bush	.05	.04	.02
606	Carmen Castillo	.05	.04	.02
607	Tim Drummond	.06	.05	.02
608	*Scott Erickson*(FC)	1.00	.70	.40
609	Gary Gaetti	.08	.06	.03
610	Greg Gagne	.06	.05	.02
611	Dan Gladden	.06	.05	.02
612	Mark Guthrie(FC)	.06	.05	.02
613	Brian Harper	.06	.05	.02
614	Kent Hrbek	.08	.06	.03
615	Gene Larkin	.06	.05	.02
616	Terry Leach	.05	.04	.02
617	Nelson Liriano	.05	.04	.02
618	Shane Mack	.06	.05	.02
619	John Moses	.05	.04	.02
620	*Pedro Munoz*(FC)	.30	.25	.12
621	Al Newman	.05	.04	.02
622	Junior Ortiz	.05	.04	.02
623	Kirby Puckett	.15	.11	.06
624	Roy Smith	.05	.04	.02
625	Kevin Tapani	.10	.08	.04
626	Gary Wayne	.05	.04	.02
627	David West	.06	.05	.02
628	Cris Carpenter	.06	.05	.02
629	Vince Coleman	.08	.06	.03
630	Ken Dayley	.06	.05	.02
631	Jose DeLeon	.06	.05	.02
632	Frank DiPino	.05	.04	.02
633	*Bernard Gilkey*(FC)	.25	.20	.10
634	Pedro Guerrero	.08	.06	.03
635	Ken Hill	.06	.05	.02
636	Felix Jose	.08	.06	.03
637	*Ray Lankford*(FC)	.50	.40	.20
638	Joe Magrane	.08	.06	.03
639	Tom Niedenfuer	.05	.04	.02
640	Jose Oquendo	.05	.04	.02
641	Tom Pagnozzi	.05	.04	.02
642	Terry Pendleton	.06	.05	.02
643	*Mike Perez*(FC)	.20	.15	.08
644	Bryn Smith	.05	.04	.02
645	Lee Smith	.08	.06	.03
646	Ozzie Smith	.10	.08	.04
647	Scott Terry	.05	.04	.02
648	Bob Tewksbury	.05	.04	.02
649	Milt Thompson	.05	.04	.02
650	John Tudor	.06	.05	.02
651	Denny Walling	.05	.04	.02
652	*Craig Wilson*(FC)	.15	.11	.06
653	Todd Worrell	.06	.05	.02
654	Todd Zeile	.20	.15	.08

		MT	NR MT	EX
655	*Oscar Azocar*	.20	.15	.08
656	Steve Balboni	.05	.04	.02
657	Jesse Barfield	.08	.06	.03
658	Greg Cadaret	.05	.04	.02
659	Chuck Cary	.05	.04	.02
660	Rick Cerone	.05	.04	.02
661	Dave Eiland(FC)	.06	.05	.02
662	Alvaro Espinoza	.06	.05	.02
663	Bob Geren	.06	.05	.02
664	Lee Guettuerman	.05	.04	.02
665	Mel Hall	.06	.05	.02
666	Andy Hawkins	.06	.05	.02
667	Jimmy Jones	.05	.04	.02
668	Roberto Kelly	.10	.08	.04
669	Dave LaPoint	.05	.04	.02
670	Tim Leary	.06	.05	.02
671	*Jim Leyritz*	.15	.11	.06
672	Kevin Maas	.40	.30	.15
673	Don Mattingly	.40	.30	.15
674	Matt Nokes	.06	.05	.02
675	Pascual Perez	.06	.05	.02
676	Eric Plunk	.05	.04	.02
677	Dave Righetti	.08	.06	.03
678	Jeff Robinson	.05	.04	.02
679	Steve Sax	.10	.08	.04
680	Mike Witt	.06	.05	.02
681	Steve Avery	.15	.11	.06
682	Mike Bell	.15	.11	.06
683	Jeff Blauser	.06	.05	.02
684	Francisco Cabrera	.10	.08	.04
685	Tony Castillo(FC)	.08	.06	.03
686	Marty Clary	.05	.04	.02
687	Nick Esasky	.08	.06	.03
688	Ron Gant	.10	.08	.04
689	Tom Glavine	.06	.05	.02
690	Mark Grant	.05	.04	.02
691	Tommy Gregg	.06	.05	.02
692	Dwayne Henry	.05	.04	.02
693	Dave Justice	.70	.50	.30
694	*Jimmy Kremers*	.15	.11	.06
695	Charlie Leibrandt	.06	.05	.02
696	Mark Lemke	.06	.05	.02
697	Oddibe McDowell	.06	.05	.02
698	*Greg Olson*	.08	.06	.03
699	Jeff Parrett	.06	.05	.02
700	Jim Presley	.06	.05	.02
701	*Victor Rosario*(FC)	.20	.15	.08
702	Lonnie Smith	.06	.05	.02
703	Pete Smith	.06	.05	.02
704	John Smoltz	.08	.06	.03
705	Mike Stanton	.08	.06	.03
706	Andres Thomas	.05	.04	.02
707	Jeff Treadway	.06	.05	.02
708	*Jim Vatcher*(FC)	.15	.11	.06
709	Home Run Kings (Ryne Sandberg, Cecil Fielder)	.25	.20	.10
710	Second Generation Stars (Barry Bonds, Ken Griffey,Jr.)	.40	.30	.15
711	NLCS Team Leaders (Bobby Bonilla, Barry Larkin)	.15	.11	.06
712	Top Game Savers (Bobby Thigpen, John Franco)	.10	.08	.04
713	Chicago's 100 Club (Andre Dawson, Ryne Sandberg)	.15	.11	.06
714	Checklists (Athletics, Pirates, Reds, Red Sox)	.05	.04	.02
715	Checklists (White Sox, Mets Blue Jays, Dodgers)	.05	.04	.02
716	Checklists (Expos, Giants, Rangers, Angels)	.05	.04	.02
717	Checklists (Tigers, Indians, Phillies, Cubs)	.05	.04	.02
718	Checklists (Mariners, Orioles, Astros, Padres)	.05	.04	.02
719	Checklists (Royals, Brewers, Twins, Cardinals)	.05	.04	.02
720	Checklists (Yankees, Braves, Super Stars)	.05	.04	.02

1991 Fleer All Stars

Three player photos are featured on each card in this special insert set. An action shot and facial close-up are featured on the front, while a full-figure pose is showcased on the back. The cards are horizontal and were inseted into 1991 Fleer cello packs.

		MT	NR MT	EX
Complete Set:		18.00	13.50	7.25
Common Player:		.60	.45	.25
1	Ryne Sandberg	2.50	2.00	1.00
2	Barry Larkin	1.00	.70	.40
3	Matt Williams	1.50	1.25	.60
4	Cecil Fielder	2.00	1.50	.80
5	Barry Bonds	2.00	1.50	.80
6	Rickey Henderson	2.00	1.50	.80
7	Ken Griffey,Jr.	5.00	3.75	2.00
8	Jose Canseco	2.50	2.00	1.00
9	Benito Santiago	.60	.45	.25
10	Roger Clemens	2.00	1.50	.80

A player's name in italic indicates a rookie card. An (FC) indicates a player's first card for that particular card company.

1991 Fleer Box Panels

Unlike past box panel sets, the 1991 Fleer box panels feature a theme. 1990 no-hitters are celebrated on the three different boxes. The cards feature blank backs and are numbered in order of no-hitter on the front. A team logo was included on each box. The card fronts are styled after the 1991 Fleer cards. A special no-hitter logo appears in the lower left corner.

		MT	NR MT	EX
Complete Set:		2.00	1.50	.80
Common Player:		.10	.08	.04
1	Langston/Witt	.10	.08	.04
2	Randy Johnson	.10	.08	.04
3	Nolan Ryan	.80	.60	.30
4	Dave Stewart	.15	.11	.06
5	Fernando Valenzuela	.15	.11	.06
6	Andy Hawkins	.10	.08	.04
7	Melido Perez	.10	.08	.04
8	Terry Mulholland (u)	.10	.08	.04
9	Dave Steib	.15	.11	.06
---	Team Logos	.05	.04	.02

1991 Fleer '90 World Series

Once again Fleer released a set in honor of the World Series from the previous season. The 1991 issue features only eight cards compared to twelve in

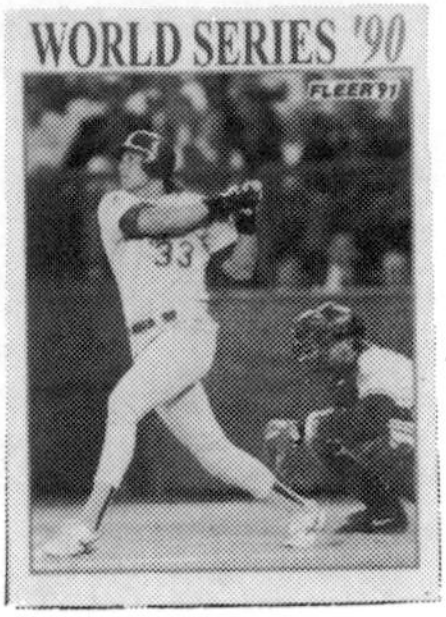

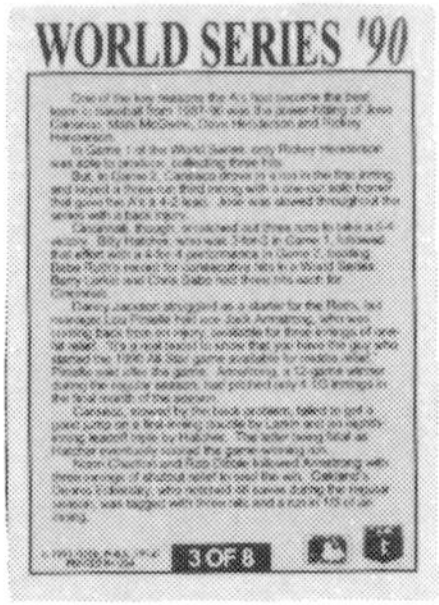

1990. The cards feature white borders surrounding full-color action shots from the 1990 Fall Classic. The card backs feature an overview of the World Series action.

		MT	NR MT	EX
Complete Set:		2.50	2.00	1.00
Common Player:		.20	.15	.08
1	Eric Davis	.25	.20	.10
2	Billy Hatcher	.20	.15	.08
3	Jose Canseco	.35	.25	.14
4	Rickey Henderson	.35	.25	.14
5	Sabo/Lansford	.20	.15	.08
6	Dave Stewart	.25	.20	.10
7	Jose Rijo	.25	.20	.10
8	Reds Celebrate	.20	.15	.08

1991 Fleer Pro Visions

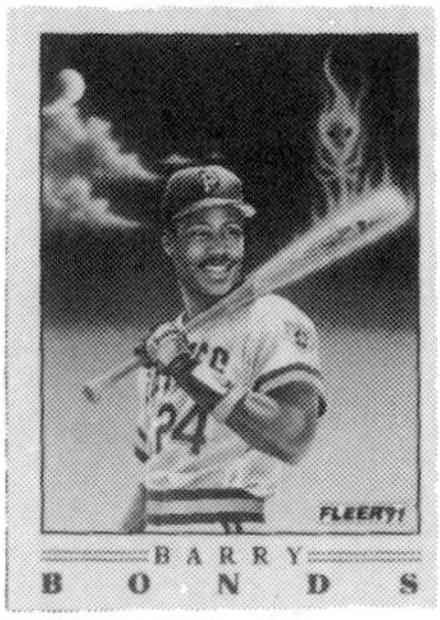

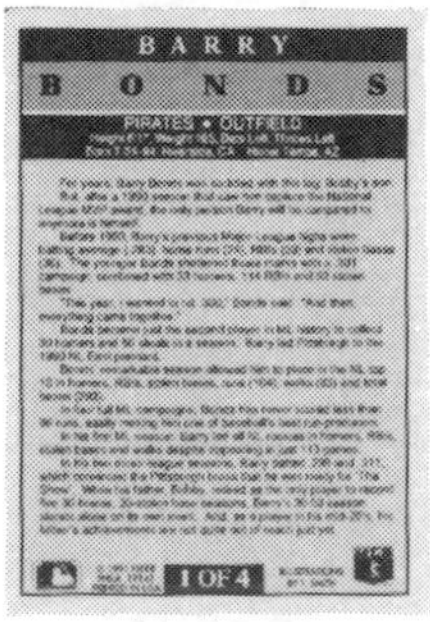

The illustrations of artist Terry Smith are showcased in this special set. Twelve fantasy portraits were produced for cards inserted into rack packs. Four other pro vision cards were inserted into factory sets. The rack pack cards feature black borders, while the factory set cards have white borders. Information on the card backs supports the manner in which Smith painted each player.

		MT	NR MT	EX
Complete Set:		4.00	3.00	1.50
Common Player:		.25	.20	.10
Complete Factory Set:		3.00	2.25	1.25
Common Player:		.40	.30	.15
1	Kirby Puckett	.40	.30	.15
2	Will Clark	.60	.45	.25
3	Ruben Sierra	.40	.30	.15
4	Mark McGwire	.25	.20	.10
5	Bo Jackson	.60	.45	.25
6	Jose Canseco	.60	.45	.25
7	Dwight Gooden	.25	.20	.10
8	Mike Greenwell	.25	.20	.10
9	Roger Clemens	.40	.30	.15
10	Eric Davis	.25	.20	.10
11	Don Mattingly	.40	.30	.15
12	Darryl Strawberry	.40	.30	.15
----	Barry Bonds (1 of 4)	.70	.50	.30
----	Rickey Henderson (2 of 4)	1.00	.70	.40
----	Ryne Sandberg (3 of 4)	1.00	.70	.40
----	Dave Stewart (4 of 4)	.40	.30	.15

1991 Fleer Update

Fleer produced its eight consecutive "Update" set in 1991 to supplement the company's regular set. As in the past, the set consists of 132 cards that were sold by hobby dealers in special collectors boxes. The cards are designed in the same style as the regular Fleer issue.

		MT	NR MT	EX
Complete Set:		12.00	9.00	4.75
Common Player:		.06	.05	.02
1	Glenn Davis	.12	.09	.05
2	Dwight Evans	.08	.06	.03
3	Jose Mesa(FC)	.08	.06	.03
4	Jack Clark	.12	.09	.05
5	Danny Darwin	.06	.05	.02
6	Steve Lyons	.06	.05	.02
7	Mo Vaughn(FC)	.70	.50	.30
8	Floyd Bannister	.06	.05	.02
9	Gary Gaetti	.08	.06	.03
10	Dave Parker	.10	.08	.04
11	Joey Cora	.06	.05	.02
12	Charlie Hough	.06	.05	.02
13	Matt Merullo	.08	.06	.03
14	Warren Newson(FC)	.30	.25	.12
15	Tim Raines	.15	.11	.06
16	Albert Belle	.30	.25	.12
17	Glenallen Hill	.15	.11	.06
18	Shawn Hillegas	.06	.05	.02
19	Mark Lewis(FC)	.30	.25	.12
20	Charles Nagy(FC)	.20	.15	.08
21	Mark Whiten	.20	.15	.08
22	John Cerutti	.06	.05	.02
23	Rob Deer	.06	.05	.02
24	Mickey Tettleton	.08	.06	.03
25	Warren Cromartie	.06	.05	.02
26	Kirk Gibson	.08	.06	.03
27	David Howard(FC)	.25	.20	.10
28	Brent Mayne(FC)	.15	.11	.06
29	Dante Bichette	.06	.05	.02
30	Mark Lee(FC)	.08	.06	.03
31	Julio Machado	.06	.05	.02
32	Edwin Nunez	.06	.05	.02
33	Willie Randolph	.08	.06	.03
34	Franklin Stubbs	.06	.05	.02
35	Bill Wegman	.06	.05	.02
36	Chili Davis	.08	.06	.03
37	Chuck Knoblauch(FC)	.40	.30	.15
38	Scott Leius	.15	.11	.06
39	Jack Morris	.10	.08	.04
40	Mike Pagliarulo	.06	.05	.02
41	Lenny Webster(FC)	.12	.09	.05
42	John Habyan(FC)	.12	.09	.05
43	Steve Howe	.08	.06	.03
44	Jeff Johnson(FC)	.20	.15	.08
45	Scott Kamieniecki(FC)	.25	.20	.10
46	Pat Kelly(FC)	.40	.30	.15
47	Hensley Meulens	.12	.09	.05
48	Wade Taylor(FC)	.20	.15	.08
49	Bernie Williams(FC)	.35	.25	.14
50	Kirk Dressendorfer(FC)	.35	.25	.14
51	Ernest Riles	.06	.05	.02

		MT	NR MT	EX
52	Rich DeLucia(FC)	.15	.11	.06
53	Tracy Jones	.06	.05	.02
54	Bill Krueger	.06	.05	.02
55	Alonzo Powell(FC)	.15	.11	.06
56	Jeff Schaefer	.06	.05	.02
57	Russ Swan(FC)	.08	.06	.03
58	John Barfield(FC)	.15	.11	.06
59	Rich Gossage	.08	.06	.03
60	Jose Guzman	.06	.05	.02
61	Dean Palmer(FC)	.40	.30	.15
62	Ivan Rodriguez(FC)	2.50	2.00	1.00
63	Roberto Alomar	.20	.15	.08
64	Tom Candiotti	.06	.05	.02
65	Joe Carter	.15	.11	.06
66	Ed Sprague(FC)	.20	.15	.08
67	Pat Tabler	.06	.05	.02
68	Mike Timlin(FC)	.20	.15	.08
69	Devon White	.08	.06	.03
70	Rafael Belliard	.06	.05	.02
71	Juan Berenguer	.06	.05	.02
72	Sid Bream	.08	.06	.03
73	Marvin Freeman	.06	.05	.02
74	Kent Mercker	.08	.06	.03
75	Otis Nixon	.06	.05	.02
76	Terry Pendleton	.08	.06	.03
77	George Bell	.10	.08	.04
78	Danny Jackson	.06	.05	.02
79	Chuck McElroy	.06	.05	.02
80	Gary Scott(FC)	.30	.25	.12
81	Heathcliff Slocumb(FC)	.15	.11	.06
82	Dave Smith	.06	.05	.02
83	Rick Wilkins(FC)	.30	.25	.12
84	Freddie Benavides(FC)	.20	.15	.08
85	Ted Power	.06	.05	.02
86	Mo Sanford(FC)	.30	.25	.12
87	Jeff Bagwell(FC)	2.50	2.00	1.00
88	Steve Finley	.08	.06	.03
89	Pete Harnisch	.08	.06	.03
90	Darryl Kile(FC)	.20	.15	.08
91	Brett Butler	.08	.06	.03
92	John Candelaria	.06	.05	.02
93	Gary Carter	.08	.06	.03
94	Kevin Gross	.06	.05	.02
95	Bob Ojeda	.06	.05	.02
96	Darryl Strawberry	.30	.25	.12
97	Ivan Calderon	.08	.06	.03
98	Ron Hassey	.06	.05	.02
99	Gilberto Reyes	.08	.06	.03
100	Hubie Brooks	.08	.06	.03
101	Rick Cerone	.06	.05	.02
102	Vince Coleman	.08	.06	.03
103	Jeff Innis	.08	.06	.03
104	Pete Schourek(FC)	.20	.15	.08
105	Andy Ashby(FC)	.12	.09	.05
106	Wally Backman	.06	.05	.02
107	Darrin Fletcher(FC)	.12	.09	.05
108	Tommy Greene	.08	.06	.03
109	John Morris	.06	.05	.02
110	Mitch Williams	.08	.06	.03
111	Lloyd McClendon	.06	.05	.02
112	Orlando Merced(FC)	.40	.30	.15
113	Vicente Palacios	.06	.05	.02
114	Gary Varsho	.06	.05	.02
115	John Wehner(FC)	.25	.20	.10
116	Rex Hudler	.06	.05	.02
117	Tim Jones	.06	.05	.02
118	Geronimo Pena(FC)	.15	.11	.06
119	Gerald Perry	.06	.05	.02
120	Larry Andersen	.06	.05	.02
121	Jerald Clark	.06	.05	.02
122	Scott Coolbaugh	.08	.06	.03
123	Tony Fernandez	.08	.06	.03
124	Darrin Jackson	.06	.05	.02
125	Fred McGriff	.15	.11	.06
126	Jose Mota(FC)	.25	.20	.10
127	Tim Teufel	.06	.05	.02
128	Bud Black	.06	.05	.02
129	Mike Felder	.06	.05	.02
130	Willie McGee	.08	.06	.03
131	Dave Righetti	.08	.06	.03
132	Checklist	.06	.05	.02

1991 Fleer Ultra

This 400-card set was originally going to be called the Elite set, but Fleer chose to use the Ultra label. The card fronts feature gray borders surrounding full-color action photos. The backs feature three

player photos and statistics. Hot Prospects and Great Performers are among the special cards featured within the set. This set is the premier release for Fleer Ultra.

		MT	NR MT	EX
Complete Set:		40.00	30.00	15.00
Common Player:		.06	.05	.02
1	Steve Avery	2.00	1.50	.80
2	Jeff Blauser	.06	.05	.02
3	Francisco Cabrera	.08	.06	.03
4	Ron Gant	.35	.25	.14
5	Tom Glavine	.15	.11	.06
6	Tommy Gregg	.06	.05	.02
7	Dave Justice	2.00	1.50	.80
8	Oddibe McDowell	.06	.05	.02
9	Greg Olson	.08	.06	.03
10	Terry Pendleton	.15	.11	.06
11	Lonnie Smith	.06	.05	.02
12	John Smoltz	.15	.11	.06
13	Jeff Treadway	.06	.05	.02
14	Glenn Davis	.10	.08	.04
15	Mike Devereaux	.08	.06	.03
16	Leo Gomez	.40	.30	.15
17	Chris Hoiles	.15	.11	.06
18	Dave Johnson	.06	.05	.02
19	Ben McDonald	.20	.15	.08
20	Randy Milligan	.08	.06	.03
21	Gregg Olson	.10	.08	.04
22	Joe Orsulak	.06	.05	.02
23	Bill Ripken	.06	.05	.02
24	Cal Ripken,Jr.	.50	.40	.20
25	David Segui	.15	.11	.06
26	Craig Worthington	.08	.06	.03
27	Wade Boggs	.25	.20	.10
28	Tom Bolton	.06	.05	.02
29	Tom Brunansky	.08	.06	.03
30	Ellis Burks	.12	.09	.05
31	Roger Clemens	.50	.40	.20
32	Mike Greenwell	.15	.11	.06
33	Greg Harris	.06	.05	.02
34	Daryl Irvine	.15	.11	.06
35	Mike Marshall	.06	.05	.02
36	Tim Naehring	.15	.11	.06
37	Tony Pena	.06	.05	.02
38	Phil Plantier	3.00	2.25	1.25
39	Carlos Quintana	.08	.06	.03
40	Jeff Reardon	.08	.06	.03
41	Jody Reed	.06	.05	.02
42	Luis Rivera	.06	.05	.02
43	Jim Abbott	.20	.15	.08
44	Chuck Finley	.15	.11	.06
45	Bryan Harvey	.08	.06	.03
46	Donnie Hill	.06	.05	.02
47	Jack Howell	.06	.05	.02
48	Wally Joyner	.15	.11	.06
49	Mark Langston	.12	.09	.05
50	Kirk McCaskill	.06	.05	.02
51	Lance Parrish	.08	.06	.03
52	Dick Schofield	.06	.05	.02
53	Lee Stevens	.15	.11	.06
54	Dave Winfield	.15	.11	.06
55	George Bell	.12	.09	.05
56	Damon Berryhill	.06	.05	.02
57	Mike Bielecki	.06	.05	.02
58	Andre Dawson	.20	.15	.08
59	Shawon Dunston	.10	.08	.04
60	Joe Girardi	.06	.05	.02
61	Mark Grace	.15	.11	.06
62	Mike Harkey	.08	.06	.03
63	Les Lancaster	.06	.05	.02

		MT	NR MT	EX
64	Greg Maddux	.08	.06	.03
65	Derrick May	.20	.15	.08
66	Ryne Sandberg	.50	.40	.20
67	Luis Salazar	.06	.05	.02
68	Dwight Smith	.06	.05	.02
69	Hector Villanueva	.08	.06	.03
70	Jerome Walton	.12	.09	.05
71	Mitch Williams	.08	.06	.03
72	Carlton Fisk	.20	.15	.08
73	Scott Fletcher	.06	.05	.02
74	Ozzie Guillen	.10	.08	.04
75	Greg Hibbard	.08	.06	.03
76	Lance Johnson	.06	.05	.02
77	Steve Lyons	.06	.05	.02
78	Jack McDowell	.12	.09	.05
79	Dan Pasqua	.06	.05	.02
80	Melido Perez	.06	.05	.02
81	Tim Raines	.10	.08	.04
82	Sammy Sosa	.10	.08	.04
83	Cory Snyder	.06	.05	.02
84	Bobby Thigpen	.08	.06	.03
85	Frank Thomas	6.00	4.50	2.50
86	Robin Ventura	.50	.40	.20
87	Todd Benzinger	.06	.05	.02
88	Glenn Braggs	.06	.05	.02
89	Tom Browning	.08	.06	.03
90	Norm Charlton	.08	.06	.03
91	Eric Davis	.15	.11	.06
92	Rob Dibble	.10	.08	.04
93	Bill Doran	.08	.06	.03
94	Mariano Duncan	.06	.05	.02
95	Billy Hatcher	.06	.05	.02
96	Barry Larkin	.15	.11	.06
97	Randy Myers	.08	.06	.03
98	Hal Morris	.20	.15	.08
99	Joe Oliver	.06	.05	.02
100	Paul O'Neill	.08	.06	.03
101	Jeff Reed	.06	.05	.02
102	Jose Rijo	.08	.06	.03
103	Chris Sabo	.10	.08	.04
104	Beau Allred	.06	.05	.02
105	Sandy Alomar,Jr.	.10	.08	.04
106	Carlos Baerga	.15	.11	.06
107	Albert Belle	.50	.40	.20
108	Jerry Browne	.06	.05	.02
109	Tom Candiotti	.06	.05	.02
110	Alex Cole	.06	.05	.02
111	John Farrell	.06	.05	.02
112	Felix Fermin	.06	.05	.02
113	Brook Jacoby	.06	.05	.02
114	Chris James	.06	.05	.02
115	Doug Jones	.06	.05	.02
116	Steve Olin	.06	.05	.03
117	Greg Swindell	.08	.06	.03
118	Turner Ward	.20	.15	.08
119	Mitch Webster	.06	.05	.02
120	Dave Bergman	.06	.05	.02
121	Cecil Fielder	.40	.30	.15
122	Travis Fryman	1.50	1.25	.60
123	Mike Henneman	.08	.06	.03
124	Lloyd Moseby	.06	.05	.02
125	Dan Petry	.06	.05	.02
126	Tony Phillips	.06	.05	.02
127	Mark Salas	.06	.05	.02
128	Frank Tanana	.06	.05	.02
129	Alan Trammell	.15	.11	.06
130	Lou Whitaker	.08	.06	.03
131	Eric Anthony	.10	.08	.04
132	Craig Biggio	.15	.11	.06
133	Ken Caminiti	.08	.06	.03
134	Casey Candaele	.06	.05	.02
135	Andujar Cedeno	.80	.60	.30
136	Mark Davidson	.06	.05	.02
137	Jim Deshaies	.06	.05	.02
138	Mark Portugal	.06	.05	.02
139	Rafael Ramirez	.06	.05	.02
140	Mike Scott	.08	.06	.03
141	Eric Yelding	.06	.05	.02
142	Gerald Young	.06	.05	.02
143	Kevin Appier	.10	.08	.04
144	George Brett	.25	.20	.10
145	Jeff Conine	.20	.15	.08
146	Jim Eisenreich	.06	.05	.02
147	Tom Gordon	.10	.08	.04
148	Mark Gubicza	.08	.06	.03
149	Bo Jackson	.60	.45	.25
150	Brent Mayne	.20	.15	.08
151	Mike Macfarlane	.06	.05	.02
152	Brian McRae	1.00	.70	.40
153	Jeff Montgomery	.08	.06	.03
154	Bret Saberhagen	.10	.08	.04

		MT	NR MT	EX
155	Kevin Seitzer	.06	.05	.02
156	Terry Shumpert	.06	.05	.02
157	Kurt Stillwell	.06	.05	.02
158	Danny Tartabull	.15	.11	.06
159	Tim Belcher	.08	.06	.03
160	Kal Daniels	.10	.08	.04
161	Alfredo Griffin	.06	.05	.02
162	Lenny Harris	.06	.05	.02
163	Jay Howell	.06	.05	.02
164	Ramon Martinez	.40	.30	.15
165	Mike Morgan	.06	.05	.02
166	Eddie Murray	.20	.15	.08
167	Jose Offerman	.15	.11	.06
168	Juan Samuel	.08	.06	.03
169	Mike Scioscia	.08	.06	.03
170	Mike Sharperson	.06	.05	.02
171	Darryl Strawberry	.40	.30	.15
172	Greg Brock	.06	.05	.02
173	Chuck Crim	.06	.05	.02
174	Jim Gantner			
175	Ted Higuera	.08	.06	.03
176	Mark Knudson	.06	.05	.02
177	Tim McIntosh	.08	.06	.03
178	Paul Molitor	.15	.11	.06
179	Dan Plesac	.06	.05	.02
180	Gary Sheffield	.12	.09	.05
181	Bill Spiers	.06	.05	.02
182	B.J. Surhoff	.06	.05	.02
183	Greg Vaughn	.20	.15	.08
184	Robin Yount	.20	.15	.08
185	Rick Aguilera	.08	.06	.03
186	Greg Gagne	.06	.05	.02
187	Dan Gladden	.06	.05	.02
188	Brian Harper	.06	.05	.02
189	Kent Hrbek	.08	.06	.03
190	Gene Larkin	.06	.05	.04
191	Shane Mack	.08	.06	.03
192	Pedro Munoz	.50	.40	.20
193	Al Newman	.06	.05	.02
194	Junior Ortiz	.06	.05	.02
195	Kirby Puckett	.25	.20	.10
196	Kevin Tapani	.08	.06	.03
197	Dennis Boyd	.06	.05	.02
198	Tim Burke	.06	.05	.02
199	Ivan Calderon	.08	.06	.03
200	Delino DeShields	.10	.08	.04
201	Mike Fitzgerald	.06	.05	.02
202	Steve Frey	.06	.05	.02
203	Andres Galarraga	.08	.06	.03
204	Marquis Grissom	.15	.11	.06
205	Dave Martinez	.06	.05	.02
206	Dennis Martinez	.08	.06	.03
207	Junior Noboa	.06	.05	.02
208	Spike Owen	.06	.05	.02
209	Scott Ruskin	.06	.05	.02
210	Tim Wallach	.08	.06	.03
211	Daryl Boston	.06	.05	.02
212	Vince Coleman	.10	.08	.04
213	David Cone	.10	.08	.04
214	Ron Darling	.08	.06	.03
215	Kevin Elster	.06	.05	.02
216	Sid Fernandez	.08	.06	.03
217	John Franco	.08	.06	.03
218	Dwight Gooden	.20	.15	.08
219	Tom Herr	.06	.05	.02
220	Todd Hundley	.15	.11	.06
221	Gregg Jefferies	.15	.11	.06
222	Howard Johnson	.15	.11	.06
223	Dave Magadan	.10	.08	.04
224	Kevin McReynolds	.10	.08	.04
225	Keith Miller	.06	.05	.02
226	Mackey Sasser	.06	.05	.02
227	Frank Viola	.10	.08	.04
228	Jesse Barfield	.08	.06	.03
229	Greg Cadaret	.06	.05	.02
230	Alvaro Espinoza	.06	.05	.02
231	Bob Geren	.06	.05	.02
232	Lee Guetterman	.06	.05	.02
233	Mel Hall	.08	.06	.03
234	Andy Hawkins	.06	.05	.02
235	Roberto Kelly	.10	.08	.04
236	Tim Leary	.06	.05	.02
237	Jim Leyritz	.06	.05	.02
238	Kevin Maas	.25	.20	.10
239	Don Mattingly	.30	.25	.12
240	Hensley Meulens	.10	.08	.04
241	Eric Plunk	.06	.05	.02
242	Steve Sax	.08	.06	.03
243	Todd Burns	.06	.05	.02
244	Jose Canseco	.60	.45	.25
245	Dennis Eckersley	.10	.08	.04

		MT	NR MT	EX
246	Mike Gallego	.06	.05	.02
247	Dave Henderson	.10	.08	.04
248	Rickey Henderson	.50	.40	.20
249	Rick Honeycutt	.06	.05	.02
250	Carney Lansford	.08	.06	.03
251	Mark McGwire	.15	.11	.06
252	Mike Moore	.06	.05	.02
253	Terry Steinbach	.06	.05	.02
254	Dave Stewart	.10	.08	.04
255	Walt Weiss	.06	.05	.02
256	Bob Welch	.08	.06	.03
257	Curt Young	.06	.05	.02
258	Wes Chamberlain	1.25	.90	.50
259	Pat Combs	.08	.06	.03
260	Darren Daulton	.06	.05	.02
261	Jose DeJesus	.06	.05	.02
262	Len Dykstra	.10	.08	.04
263	Charlie Hayes	.08	.06	.03
264	Von Hayes	.08	.06	.03
265	Ken Howell	.06	.05	.02
266	John Kruk	.08	.06	.03
267	Roger McDowell	.08	.06	.03
268	Mickey Morandini	.15	.11	.06
269	Terry Mulholland	.08	.06	.03
270	Dale Murphy	.10	.08	.04
271	Randy Ready	.06	.05	.02
272	Dickie Thon	.06	.05	.02
273	Stan Belinda	.06	.05	.02
274	Jay Bell	.08	.06	.03
275	Barry Bonds	.25	.20	.10
276	Bobby Bonilla	.25	.20	.10
277	Doug Drabek	.10	.08	.04
278	Carlos Garcia	.20	.15	.08
279	Neal Heaton	.06	.05	.02
280	Jeff King	.08	.06	.03
281	Bill Landrum	.06	.05	.02
282	Mike LaValliere	.06	.05	.02
283	Jose Lind	.06	.05	.02
284	Orlando Merced	.70	.50	.30
285	Gary Redus	.06	.05	.02
286	Don Slaught	.06	.05	.02
287	Andy Van Slyke	.10	.08	.04
288	Jose DeLeon	.06	.05	.02
289	Pedro Guerrero	.10	.08	.04
290	Ray Lankford	.50	.40	.20
291	Joe Magrane	.08	.06	.03
292	Jose Oquendo	.06	.05	.02
293	Tom Pagnozzi	.06	.05	.02
294	Bryn Smith	.06	.05	.02
295	Lee Smith	.08	.06	.03
296	Ozzie Smith	.20	.15	.08
297	Milt Thompson	.06	.05	.02
298	Craig Wilson	.12	.09	.05
299	Todd Zeile	.20	.15	.08
300	Shawn Abner	.06	.05	.02
301	Andy Benes	.15	.11	.06
302	Paul Faries	.15	.11	.06
303	Tony Gwynn	.20	.15	.08
304	Greg Harris	.06	.05	.02
305	Thomas Howard	.10	.08	.04
306	Bruce Hurst	.08	.06	.03
307	Craig Lefferts	.06	.05	.02
308	Fred McGriff	.15	.11	.06
309	Dennis Rasmussen	.06	.05	.02
310	Bip Roberts	.08	.06	.03
311	Benito Santiago	.10	.08	.04
312	Garry Templeton	.06	.05	.02
313	Ed Whitson	.06	.05	.02
314	Dave Anderson	.06	.05	.02
315	Kevin Bass	.06	.05	.02
316	Jeff Brantley	.06	.05	.02
317	John Burkett	.08	.06	.03
318	Will Clark	.50	.40	.20
319	Steve Decker	.30	.25	.12
320	Scott Garrelts	.06	.05	.02
321	Terry Kennedy	.06	.05	.02
322	Mark Leonard	.20	.15	.08
323	Darren Lewis	.50	.40	.20
324	Greg Litton	.06	.05	.02
325	Willie McGee	.10	.08	.04
326	Kevin Mitchell	.15	.11	.06
327	Don Robinson	.06	.05	.02
328	Andres Santana	.25	.20	.10
329	Robby Thompson	.06	.05	.02
330	Jose Uribe	.06	.05	.02
331	Matt Williams	.15	.11	.06
332	Scott Bradley	.06	.05	.02
334	Alvin Davis	.08	.06	.03
335	Ken Griffey,Sr.	.08	.06	.03
336	Ken Griffey,Jr.	3.00	2.25	1.25
337	Erik Hanson	.10	.08	.04

NOTE: A card number in parentheses ( ) indicates the set is unnumbered.

		MT	NR MT	EX
338	Brian Holman	.06	.05	.02
339	Randy Johnson	.08	.06	.03
340	Edgar Martinez	.08	.06	.03
341	Tino Martinez	.20	.15	.08
342	Pete O'Brien	.06	.05	.02
343	Harold Reynolds	.08	.06	.03
344	David Valle	.06	.05	.02
345	Omar Vizquel	.06	.05	.02
346	Brad Arnsberg	.06	.05	.02
347	Kevin Brown	.06	.05	.02
348	Julio Franco	.10	.08	.04
349	Jeff Huson	.06	.05	.02
350	Rafael Palmeiro	.20	.15	.08
351	Geno Petralli	.06	.05	.02
352	Gary Pettis	.06	.05	.02
353	Kenny Rogers	.06	.05	.02
354	Jeff Russell	.06	.05	.02
355	Nolan Ryan	1.00	.70	.40
356	Ruben Sierra	.25	.20	.10
357	Bobby Witt	.08	.06	.03
358	Roberto Alomar	.25	.20	.10
359	Pat Borders	.06	.05	.02
360	Joe Carter	.15	.11	.06
361	Kelly Gruber	.08	.06	.03
362	Tom Henke	.08	.06	.03
363	Glenallen Hill	.08	.06	.03
364	Jimmy Key	.08	.06	.03
365	Manny Lee	.06	.05	.02
366	Rance Mulliniks	.06	.05	.02
367	John Olerud	.20	.15	.08
368	Dave Stieb	.08	.06	.03
369	Duane Ward	.06	.05	.02
370	David Wells	.06	.05	.02
371	Mark Whiten	.30	.25	.12
372	Mookie Wilson	.06	.05	.02
373	Willie Banks	.30	.25	.12
374	Steve Carter	.06	.05	.02
375	Scott Chiamparino	.10	.08	.04
376	Steve Chitren	.10	.08	.04
377	Darrin Fletcher	.10	.08	.04
378	Rich Garces	.10	.08	.04
379	Reggie Jefferson	.60	.45	.25
380	Eric Karros	.70	.50	.30
381	Pat Kelly	.70	.50	.30
382	Chuck Knoblauch	1.25	.90	.50
383	Denny Neagle	.50	.40	.20
384	Dan Opperman	.20	.15	.08
385	John Ramos	.20	.15	.08
386	Henry Rodriguez	.30	.25	.12
387	Maurice Vaughn	1.00	.70	.40
388	Gerald Williams	.40	.30	.15
389	Mike York	.20	.15	.08
390	Eddie Zosky	.20	.15	.08
391	Barry Bonds (Great Performer)	.20	.15	.08
392	Cecil Fielder (Great Performer)	.20	.15	.08
393	Rickey Henderson (Great Performer)	.20	.15	.08
394	Dave Justice (Great Performer)	.60	.45	.25
395	Nolan Ryan (Great Performer)	.40	.30	.15
396	Bobby Thigpen (Great Performer)	.10	.08	.04
397	Checklist	.06	.05	.02
398	Checklist	.06	.05	.02
399	Checklist	.06	.05	.02
400	Checklist	.06	.05	.02

A player's name in italic indicates a rookie card. An (FC) indicates a player's first card for that particular card company.

4-photo Ultra look is featured on each card. The cards were sold in full color, overwrapped boxes.

		MT	NR MT	EX
Complete Set:		20.00	15.00	8.00
Common Player:		.06	.05	.02
1	Dwight Evans	.08	.06	.03
2	Chito Martinez	1.25	.90	.50
3	Bob Melvin	.06	.05	.02
4	Mike Mussina	.60	.45	.25
5	Jack Clark	.08	.06	.03
6	Dana Kiecker	.06	.05	.02
7	Steve Lyons	.06	.05	.02
8	Gary Gaetti	.08	.06	.03
9	Dave Gallagher	.06	.05	.02
10	Dave Parker	.08	.06	.03
11	Luis Polonia	.06	.05	.02
12	Luis Sojo	.08	.06	.03
13	Wilson Alvarez	.20	.15	.08
14	Alex Fernandez	.40	.30	.15
15	Craig Grebeck	.06	.05	.02
16	Ron Karkovice	.06	.05	.02
17	Warren Newson	.40	.30	.15
18	Scott Radinsky	.08	.06	.03
19	Glenallen Hill	.12	.09	.05
20	Charles Nagy	.15	.11	.06
21	Mark Whiten	.30	.25	.12
22	Milt Cuyler	.35	.25	.14
23	Paul Gibson	.06	.05	.02
24	Mickey Tettleton	.08	.06	.03
25	Todd Benzinger	.08	.06	.03
26	Storm Davis	.06	.05	.02
27	Kirk Gibson	.08	.06	.03
28	Bill Pecota	.06	.05	.02
29	Gary Thurman	.06	.05	.02
30	Darryl Hamilton	.08	.06	.03
31	Jaime Navarro	.08	.06	.03
32	Willie Randolph	.08	.06	.03
33	Bill Wegman	.06	.05	.02
34	Randy Bush	.06	.05	.02
35	Chili Davis	.08	.06	.03
36	Scott Erickson	1.75	1.25	.60
37	Chuck Knoblauch	.70	.50	.30
38	Scott Leius	.15	.11	.06
39	Jack Morris	.12	.09	.05
40	John Habyan	.08	.06	.03
41	Pat Kelly	.60	.45	.25
42	Matt Nokes	.08	.06	.03
43	Scott Sanderson	.08	.06	.03
44	Bernie Williams	1.00	.70	.40
45	Harold Baines	.10	.08	.04
46	Brook Jacoby	.08	.06	.03
47	Ernest Riles	.06	.05	.02
48	Willie Wilson	.06	.05	.02
49	Jay Buhner	.08	.06	.03
50	Rich DeLucia	.20	.15	.08
51	Mike Jackson	.06	.05	.02
52	Bill Krueger	.06	.05	.02
53	Bill Swift	.06	.05	.02
54	Brian Downing	.06	.05	.02
55	Juan Gonzalez	2.00	1.50	.80
56	Dean Palmer	.80	.60	.30
57	Kevin Reimer	.20	.15	.08
58	Ivan Rodriguez	4.00	3.00	1.50
59	Tom Candiotti	.06	.05	.02
60	Juan Guzman	1.50	1.25	.60
61	Bob MacDonald	.20	.15	.08
62	Greg Myers	.06	.05	.02
63	Ed Sprague	.20	.15	.08
64	Devon White	.08	.06	.03
65	Rafael Belliard	.06	.05	.02
66	Juan Berenguer	.06	.05	.02
67	Brian Hunter	1.50	1.25	.60
68	Kent Mercker	.08	.06	.03
69	Otis Nixon	.06	.05	.02
70	Danny Jackson	.06	.05	.04
71	Chuck McElroy	.06	.05	.04
72	Gary Scott	.35	.25	.14
73	Heathcliff Slocumb	.15	.11	.06
74	Chico Walker	.10	.08	.04
75	Rick Wilkins	.35	.25	.14
76	Chris Hammond	.15	.11	.06
77	Luis Quinones	.06	.05	.02
78	Herm Winningham	.06	.05	.02
79	Jeff Bagwell	5.00	3.75	2.00
80	Jim Corsi	.06	.05	.02
81	Steve Finley	.08	.06	.03
82	Luis Gonzalez	1.75	1.25	.60
83	Pete Harnisch	.08	.06	.03
84	Darryl Kile	.25	.20	.10
85	Brett Butler	.08	.06	.03
86	Gary Carter	.15	.11	.06
87	Tim Crews	.06	.05	.02
88	Orel Hershiser	.15	.11	.06
89	Bob Ojeda	.06	.05	.02
90	Bret Barberie	.40	.30	.15
91	Barry Jones	.06	.05	.02
92	Gilberto Reyes	.08	.06	.03
93	Larry Walker	.15	.11	.06
94	Hubie Brooks	.08	.06	.03
95	Tim Burke	.06	.05	.02
96	Rick Cerone	.06	.05	.02
97	Jeff Innis	.08	.06	.03
98	Wally Backman	.06	.05	.02
99	Tommy Greene	.15	.11	.06
100	Ricky Jordan	.10	.08	.04
101	Mitch Williams	.08	.06	.03
102	John Smiley	.08	.06	.03
103	Randy Tomlin	.40	.30	.15
104	Gary Varsho	.06	.05	.02
105	Cris Carpenter	.06	.05	.02
106	Ken Hill	.08	.06	.03
107	Felix Jose	.25	.20	.10
108	Omar Oliveras	.25	.20	.10
109	Gerald Perry	.06	.05	.02
110	Jerald Clark	.08	.06	.03
111	Tony Fernandez	.08	.06	.03
112	Darrin Jackson	.08	.06	.03
113	Mike Maddux	.06	.05	.02
114	Tim Teufel	.06	.05	.02
115	Bud Black	.06	.05	.02
116	Kelly Downs	.06	.05	.02
117	Mike Felder	.06	.05	.02
118	Willie McGee	.12	.09	.05
119	Trevor Wilson	.12	.09	.05
120	Checklist	.06	.05	.02

1992 Fleer

For the second consecutive year, Fleer produced a 720-card set. The standard card fronts feature full-color action photos bordered in blue with the player's name, position and team logo on the right border. The backs feature another full-color action photo, biographical information and statistics. A special twelve card Roger Clemens subset is also included in the 1992 Fleer set. Three more Clemens cards are available through a mail-in offer, and 2,000 Roger Clemens autographed cards were inserted in 1992 packs. Once again the cards are numbered according to team.

		MT	NR MT	EX
Complete Set:		20.00	15.00	8.00
Common Player:		.04	.03	.02
1	Brady Anderson	.04	.03	.02
2	Jose Bautista	.04	.03	.02
3	Juan Bell	.06	.05	.02
4	Glenn Davis	.08	.06	.03
5	Mike Devereaux	.05	.04	.02
6	Dwight Evans	.08	.06	.03
7	Mike Flanagan	.04	.03	.02
8	Leo Gomez	.15	.11	.06
9	Chris Hoiles	.10	.08	.04
10	Sam Horn	.05	.04	.02
11	Tim Hulett	.04	.03	.02
12	Dave Johnson	.04	.03	.02
13	*Chito Martinez*(FC)	.40	.30	.15
14	Ben McDonald	.10	.08	.04
15	Bob Melvin	.04	.03	.02

		MT	NR MT	EX
16	*Luis Mercedes*(FC)	.25	.20	.10
17	Jose Mesa	.05	.04	.02
18	Bob Milacki	.05	.04	.02
19	Randy Milligan	.06	.05	.02
20	Mike Mussina	.10	.08	.04
21	Gregg Olson	.08	.06	.03
22	Joe Orsulak	.04	.03	.02
23	Jim Poole	.05	.04	.02
24	*Arthur Rhodes*(FC)	.25	.20	.10
25	Billy Ripken	.04	.03	.02
26	Cal Ripken, Jr.	.20	.15	.08
27	David Segui	.08	.06	.03
28	Roy Smith	.04	.03	.02
29	Anthony Telford	.04	.03	.02
30	Mark Williamson	.04	.03	.02
31	Craig Worthington	.06	.05	.02
32	Wade Boggs	.15	.11	.06
33	Tom Bolton	.04	.03	.02
34	Tom Brunansky	.05	.04	.02
35	Ellis Burks	.08	.06	.03
36	Jack Clark	.08	.06	.03
37	Roger Clemens	.15	.11	.06
38	Danny Darwin	.04	.03	.02
39	Mike Greenwell	.08	.06	.03
40	Joe Hesketh	.04	.03	.02
41	Daryl Irvine	.05	.04	.02
42	Dennis Lamp	.04	.03	.02
43	Tony Pena	.05	.04	.02
44	Phil Plantier	.25	.20	.10
45	Carlos Quintana	.06	.05	.02
46	Jeff Reardon	.08	.06	.03
47	Jody Reed	.05	.04	.02
48	Luis Rivera	.04	.03	.02
49	Mo Vaughn	.30	.25	.12
50	Jim Abbott	.10	.08	.04
51	Kyle Abbott	.08	.06	.03
52	*Ruben Amaro, Jr.*(FC)	.15	.11	.06
53	Scott Bailes	.04	.03	.02
54	*Chris Beasley*(FC)	.12	.09	.05
55	Mark Eichhorn	.04	.03	.02
56	Mike Fetters	.04	.03	.02
57	Chuck Finley	.08	.06	.03
58	Gary Gaetti	.08	.06	.03
59	Dave Gallagher	.05	.04	.02
60	Donnie Hill	.04	.03	.02
61	Bryan Harvey	.06	.05	.02
62	Wally Joyner	.10	.08	.04
63	Mark Langston	.10	.08	.04
64	Kirk McCaskill	.05	.04	.02
65	John Orton	.04	.03	.02
66	Lance Parrish	.06	.05	.02
67	Luis Polonia	.05	.04	.02
68	Bobby Rose	.05	.04	.02
69	Dick Schofield	.04	.03	.02
70	Luis Sojo	.05	.04	.02
71	Lee Stevens	.08	.06	.03
72	Dave Winfield	.12	.09	.05
73	Cliff Young	.06	.05	.02
74	Wilson Alvarez	.08	.06	.03
75	*Esteban Beltre*(FC)	.20	.15	.08
76	Joey Cora	.04	.03	.02
77	*Brian Drahman*(FC)	.20	.15	.08
78	Alex Fernandez	.15	.11	.06
79	Carlton Fisk	.10	.08	.04
80	Scott Fletcher	.04	.03	.02
81	Craig Grebeck	.04	.03	.02
82	Ozzie Guillen	.06	.05	.02
83	Greg Hibbard	.06	.05	.02
84	Charlie Hough	.05	.04	.02
85	Mike Huff	.05	.04	.02
86	Bo Jackson	.40	.30	.15
87	Lance Johnson	.04	.03	.02
88	Ron Karkovice	.04	.03	.02
89	Jack McDowell	.08	.06	.03
90	Matt Merullo	.04	.03	.02
91	*Warren Newson*	.15	.11	.06
92	Donn Pall	.04	.03	.02
93	Dan Pasqua	.05	.04	.02
94	Ken Patterson	.04	.03	.02
95	Melido Perez	.05	.04	.02
96	Scott Radinsky	.04	.03	.02
97	Tim Raines	.10	.08	.04
98	Sammy Sosa	.08	.06	.03
99	Bobby Thigpen	.08	.06	.03
100	Frank Thomas	.60	.45	.25
101	Robin Ventura	.15	.11	.06
102	Mike Aldrete	.04	.03	.02
103	Sandy Alomar, Jr.	.10	.08	.04
104	Carlos Baerga	.10	.08	.04
105	Albert Belle	.15	.11	.06
106	Willie Blair	.05	.04	.02
107	Jerry Browne	.04	.03	.02
108	Alex Cole	.06	.05	.02
109	Felix Fermin	.04	.03	.02
110	Glenallen Hill	.06	.05	.02
111	Shawn Hillegas	.04	.03	.02
112	Chris James	.05	.04	.02
113	Reggie Jefferson(FC)	.20	.15	.08
114	Doug Jones	.05	.04	.02
115	Eric King	.04	.03	.02
116	Mark Lewis	.15	.11	.06
117	Carlos Martinez	.05	.04	.02
118	Charles Nagy	.08	.06	.03
119	Rod Nichols	.04	.03	.02
120	Steve Olin	.04	.03	.02
121	Jesse Orosco	.04	.03	.02
122	Rudy Seanez	.04	.03	.02
123	Joel Skinner	.04	.03	.02
124	Greg Swindell	.08	.06	.03
125	*Jim Thome*(FC)	.50	.40	.20
126	Mark Whiten	.10	.08	.04
127	Scott Aldred	.10	.08	.04
128	Andy Allanson	.04	.03	.02
129	John Cerutti	.04	.03	.02
130	Milt Cuyler	.10	.08	.04
131	*Mike Dalton*(FC)	.15	.11	.06
132	Rob Deer	.05	.04	.02
133	Cecil Fielder	.15	.11	.06
134	Travis Fryman	.20	.15	.08
135	*Dan Gakeler*(FC)	.20	.15	.08
136	Paul Gibson	.04	.03	.02
137	Bill Gullickson	.05	.04	.02
138	Mike Henneman	.05	.04	.02
139	Pete Incaviglia	.05	.04	.02
140	*Mark Leiter*(FC)	.12	.09	.05
141	*Scott Livingstone*(FC)	.20	.15	.08
142	Lloyd Moseby	.04	.03	.02
143	Tony Phillips	.05	.04	.02
144	Mark Salas	.04	.03	.02
145	Frank Tanana	.05	.04	.02
146	Walt Terrell	.04	.03	.02
147	Mickey Tettleton	.06	.05	.02
148	Alan Trammell	.10	.08	.04
149	Lou Whitaker	.08	.06	.03
150	Kevin Appier	.06	.05	.02
151	Luis Aquino	.04	.03	.02
152	Todd Benzinger	.05	.04	.02
153	Mike Boddicker	.05	.04	.02
154	George Brett	.15	.11	.06
155	Storm Davis	.05	.04	.02
156	Jim Eisenreich	.04	.03	.02
157	Kirk Gibson	.08	.06	.03
158	Tom Gordon	.06	.05	.02
159	Mark Gubicza	.06	.05	.02
160	*David Howard*(FC)	.20	.15	.08
161	Mike Macfarlane	.05	.04	.02
162	Brent Mayne	.05	.04	.02
163	Brian McRae	.25	.20	.10
164	Jeff Montgomery	.05	.04	.02
165	Bill Pecota	.04	.03	.02
166	*Harvey Pulliam*(FC)	.20	.15	.08
167	Bret Saberhagen	.08	.06	.03
168	Kevin Seitzer	.05	.04	.02
169	Terry Shumpert	.05	.04	.02
170	Kurt Stillwell	.05	.04	.02
171	Danny Tartabull	.08	.06	.03
172	Gary Thurman	.04	.03	.02
173	Dante Bichette	.05	.04	.02
174	Kevin Brown	.04	.03	.02
175	Chuck Crim	.04	.03	.02
176	Jim Gantner	.05	.04	.02
177	Darryl Hamilton	.05	.04	.02
178	Ted Higuera	.06	.05	.02
179	Darren Holmes	.04	.03	.02
180	Mark Lee	.04	.03	.02
181	Julio Machado	.04	.03	.02
182	Paul Molitor	.10	.08	.04
183	Jaime Navarro	.06	.05	.02
184	Edwin Nunez	.04	.03	.02
185	Dan Plesac	.05	.04	.02
186	Willie Randolph	.05	.04	.02
187	Ron Robinson	.04	.03	.02
188	Gary Sheffield	.10	.08	.04
189	Bill Spiers	.05	.04	.02
190	B.J. Surhoff	.05	.04	.02
191	Dale Sveum	.04	.03	.02
192	Greg Vaughn	.10	.08	.04
193	Bill Wegman	.05	.04	.02
194	Robin Yount	.15	.11	.06
195	Rick Aguilera	.05	.04	.02
196	Allan Anderson	.04	.03	.02
197	Steve Bedrosian	.04	.03	.02

		MT	NR MT	EX
198	Randy Bush	.04	.03	.02
199	Larry Casian(FC)	.05	.04	.02
200	Chili Davis	.06	.05	.02
201	Scott Erickson	.20	.15	.08
202	Greg Gagne	.04	.03	.02
203	Dan Gladden	.04	.03	.02
204	Brian Harper	.05	.04	.02
205	Kent Hrbek	.06	.05	.02
206	Chuck Knoblauch	.20	.15	.08
207	Gene Larkin	.04	.03	.02
208	Terry Leach	.04	.03	.02
209	Scott Leius	.10	.08	.04
210	Shane Mack	.08	.06	.03
211	Jack Morris	.08	.06	.03
212	Pedro Munoz(FC)	.20	.15	.08
213	*Denny Neagle*(FC)	.20	.15	.08
214	Al Newman	.04	.03	.02
215	Junior Ortiz	.04	.03	.02
216	Mike Pagliarulo	.04	.03	.02
217	Kirby Puckett	.15	.11	.06
218	Paul Sorrento	.06	.05	.02
219	Kevin Tapani	.08	.06	.03
220	Lenny Webster	.06	.05	.02
221	Jesse Barfield	.06	.05	.02
222	Greg Cadaret	.04	.03	.02
223	Dave Eiland	.04	.03	.02
224	Alvaro Espinoza	.04	.03	.02
225	Steve Farr	.05	.04	.02
226	Bob Geren	.04	.03	.02
227	Lee Guetterman	.04	.03	.02
228	John Habyan	.04	.03	.02
229	Mel Hall	.06	.05	.02
230	Steve Howe	.06	.05	.02
231	*Mike Humphreys*(FC)	.20	.15	.08
232	*Scott Kamieniecki*	.15	.11	.06
233	Pat Kelly	.15	.11	.06
234	Roberto Kelly	.08	.06	.03
235	Tim Leary	.04	.03	.02
236	Kevin Maas	.15	.11	.06
237	Don Mattingly	.25	.20	.10
238	Hensley Meulens	.08	.06	.03
239	Matt Nokes	.06	.05	.02
240	Pascual Perez	.05	.04	.02
241	Eric Plunk	.04	.03	.02
242	*John Ramos*(FC)	.20	.15	.08
243	Scott Sanderson	.05	.04	.02
244	Steve Sax	.06	.05	.02
245	*Wade Taylor*	.15	.11	.06
246	Randy Velarde	.04	.03	.02
247	Bernie Williams	.20	.15	.08
248	Troy Afenir	.05	.04	.02
249	Harold Baines	.08	.06	.03
250	Lance Blankenship	.04	.03	.02
251	*Mike Bordick*(FC)	.10	.08	.04
252	Jose Canseco	.25	.20	.10
253	Steve Chitren	.06	.05	.02
254	Ron Darling	.06	.05	.02
255	Dennis Eckersley	.08	.06	.03
256	Mike Gallego	.04	.03	.02
257	Dave Henderson	.08	.06	.03
258	Rickey Henderson	.20	.15	.08
259	Rick Honeycutt	.04	.03	.02
260	Brook Jacoby	.06	.05	.02
261	Carney Lansford	.06	.05	.02
262	Mark McGwire	.12	.09	.05
263	Mike Moore	.05	.04	.02
264	Gene Nelson	.04	.03	.02
265	Jamie Quirk	.04	.03	.02
266	*Joe Slusarski*(FC)	.15	.11	.06
267	Terry Steinbach	.06	.05	.02
268	Dave Stewart	.08	.06	.03
269	Todd Van Poppel(FC)	.70	.50	.30
270	Walt Weiss	.06	.05	.02
271	Bob Welch	.06	.05	.02
272	Curt Young	.04	.03	.02
273	Scott Bradley	.04	.03	.02
274	Greg Briley	.04	.03	.02
275	Jay Buhner	.06	.05	.02
276	Henry Cotto	.04	.03	.02
277	Alvin Davis	.06	.05	.02
278	Rich DeLucia	.06	.05	.02
279	Ken Griffey, Jr.	.50	.40	.20
280	Erik Hanson	.08	.06	.03
281	Brian Holman	.05	.04	.02
282	Mike Jackson	.04	.03	.02
283	Randy Johnson	.08	.06	.03
284	Tracy Jones	.04	.03	.02
285	Bill Krueger	.04	.03	.02
286	Edgar Martinez	.06	.05	.02
287	Tino Martinez	.10	.08	.04
288	Rob Murphy	.04	.03	.02

		MT	NR MT	EX
289	Pete O'Brien	.04	.03	.02
290	Alonzo Powell	.06	.05	.02
291	Harold Reynolds	.06	.05	.02
292	Mike Schooler	.05	.04	.02
293	Russ Swan	.04	.03	.02
294	Bill Swift	.04	.03	.02
295	Dave Valle	.04	.03	.02
296	Omar Vizquel	.04	.03	.02
297	Gerald Alexander	.05	.04	.02
298	Brad Arnsberg	.05	.04	.02
299	Kevin Brown	.05	.04	.02
300	Jack Daugherty	.04	.03	.02
301	Mario Diaz	.04	.03	.02
302	Brian Downing	.05	.04	.02
303	Julio Franco	.08	.06	.03
304	Juan Gonzalez	.25	.20	.10
305	Rich Gossage	.05	.04	.02
306	Jose Guzman	.05	.04	.02
307	*Jose Hernandez*(FC)	.20	.15	.08
308	Jeff Huson	.05	.04	.02
309	Mike Jeffcoat	.04	.03	.02
310	*Terry Mathews*(FC)	.20	.15	.08
311	Rafael Palmeiro	.10	.08	.04
312	Dean Palmer	.20	.15	.08
313	Geno Petralli	.04	.03	.02
314	Gary Pettis	.04	.03	.02
315	Kevin Reimer	.05	.04	.02
316	*Ivan Rodriguez*	1.25	.90	.50
317	Kenny Rogers	.05	.04	.02
318	*Wayne Rosenthal*(FC)	.10	.08	.04
319	Jeff Russell	.05	.04	.02
320	Nolan Ryan	.25	.20	.10
321	Ruben Sierra	.15	.11	.06
322	Jim Acker	.04	.03	.02
323	Roberto Alomar	.10	.08	.04
324	Derek Bell	.35	.25	.14
325	Pat Borders	.05	.04	.02
326	Tom Candiotti	.05	.04	.02
327	Joe Carter	.08	.06	.03
328	Rob Ducey	.05	.04	.02
329	Kelly Gruber	.08	.06	.03
330	*Juan Guzman*(FC)	.50	.40	.20
331	Tom Henke	.06	.05	.02
332	Jimmy Key	.06	.05	.02
333	Manny Lee	.05	.04	.02
334	Al Leiter	.04	.03	.02
335	*Bob MacDonald*(FC)	.10	.08	.04
336	Candy Maldonado	.05	.04	.02
337	Rance Mulliniks	.04	.03	.02
338	Greg Myers	.05	.04	.02
339	John Olerud	.15	.11	.06
340	*Ed Sprague*	.10	.08	.04
341	Dave Stieb	.08	.06	.03
342	Todd Stottlemyre	.05	.04	.02
343	*Mike Timlin*	.15	.11	.06
344	Duane Ward	.05	.04	.02
345	David Wells	.05	.04	.02
346	Devon White	.08	.06	.03
347	Mookie Wilson	.04	.03	.02
348	Eddie Zosky	.08	.06	.03
349	Steve Avery	.15	.11	.06
350	Mike Bell(FC)	.08	.06	.03
351	Rafael Belliard	.04	.03	.02
352	Juan Berenguer	.04	.03	.02
353	Jeff Blauser	.05	.04	.02
354	Sid Bream	.05	.04	.02
355	Francisco Cabrera	.05	.04	.02
356	Marvin Freeman	.04	.03	.02
357	Ron Gant	.15	.11	.06
358	Tom Glavine	.10	.08	.04
359	*Brian Hunter*(FC)	.50	.40	.20
360	Dave Justice	.20	.15	.08
361	Charlie Leibrandt	.04	.03	.02
362	Mark Lemke	.05	.04	.02
363	Kent Mercker	.05	.04	.02
364	*Keith Mitchell*(FC)	.20	.15	.08
365	Greg Olson	.05	.04	.02
366	Terry Pendleton	.08	.06	.03
367	*Armando Reynoso*(FC)	.15	.11	.06
368	Deion Sanders	.15	.11	.06
369	Lonnie Smith	.04	.03	.02
370	Pete Smith	.04	.03	.02
371	John Smoltz	.10	.08	.04
372	Mike Stanton	.05	.04	.02
373	Jeff Treadway	.05	.04	.02
374	*Mark Wohlers*(FC)	.25	.20	.10
375	Paul Assenmacher	.04	.03	.02
376	George Bell	.08	.06	.03
377	Shawn Boskie	.06	.05	.02
378	*Frank Castillo*(FC)	.25	.20	.10
379	Andre Dawson	.12	.09	.05

		MT	NR MT	EX
380	Shawon Dunston	.08	.06	.03
381	Mark Grace	.08	.06	.03
382	Mike Harkey	.05	.04	.02
383	Danny Jackson	.05	.04	.02
384	Les Lancaster	.04	.03	.02
385	*Cedric Landrum*(FC)	.15	.11	.06
386	Greg Maddux	.06	.05	.02
387	Derrick May	.15	.11	.06
388	Chuck McElroy	.04	.03	.02
389	Ryne Sandberg	.20	.15	.08
390	*Heathcliff Slocumb*	.10	.08	.04
391	Dave Smith	.05	.04	.02
392	Dwight Smith	.05	.04	.02
393	Rick Sutcliffe	.05	.04	.02
394	Hector Villanueva	.06	.05	.02
395	*Chico Walker*(FC)	.10	.08	.04
396	Jerome Walton	.06	.05	.02
397	*Rick Wilkins*	.15	.11	.06
398	Jack Armstrong	.06	.05	.02
399	*Freddie Benavides*	.10	.08	.04
400	Glenn Braggs	.05	.04	.02
401	Tom Browning	.06	.05	.02
402	Norm Charlton	.06	.05	.02
403	Eric Davis	.12	.09	.05
404	Rob Dibble	.08	.06	.03
405	Bill Doran	.05	.04	.02
406	Mariano Duncan	.05	.04	.02
407	*Kip Gross*(FC)	.10	.08	.04
408	Chris Hammond	.06	.05	.02
409	Billy Hatcher	.04	.03	.02
410	*Chris Jones*(FC)	.15	.11	.06
411	Barry Larkin	.10	.08	.04
412	Hal Morris	.10	.08	.04
413	Randy Myers	.05	.04	.02
414	Joe Oliver	.05	.04	.02
415	Paul O'Neill	.06	.05	.02
416	Ted Power	.04	.03	.02
417	Luis Quinones	.04	.03	.02
418	Jeff Reed	.04	.03	.02
419	Jose Rijo	.08	.06	.03
420	Chris Sabo	.08	.06	.03
421	Reggie Sanders(FC)	.25	.20	.10
422	Scott Scudder	.05	.04	.02
423	Glenn Sutko	.05	.04	.02
424	Eric Anthony	.08	.06	.03
425	*Jeff Bagwell*	1.00	.70	.40
426	Craig Biggio	.08	.06	.03
427	Ken Caminiti	.05	.04	.02
428	Casey Candaele	.04	.03	.02
429	Mike Capel	.04	.03	.02
430	Andujar Cedeno	.15	.11	.06
431	Jim Corsi	.04	.03	.02
432	Mark Davidson	.04	.03	.02
433	Steve Finley	.06	.05	.02
434	Luis Gonzalez	.20	.15	.08
435	Pete Harnisch	.06	.05	.02
436	Dwayne Henry	.04	.03	.02
437	Xavier Hernandez	.04	.03	.02
438	Jimmy Jones	.04	.03	.02
439	*Darryl Kile*	.10	.08	.04
440	*Rob Mallicoat*(FC)	.15	.11	.06
441	*Andy Mota*(FC)	.15	.11	.06
442	Al Osuna	.05	.04	.02
443	Mark Portugal	.04	.03	.02
444	*Scott Servais*(FC)	.10	.08	.04
445	Mike Simms	.15	.11	.06
446	Gerald Young	.04	.03	.02
447	Tim Belcher	.06	.05	.02
448	Brett Butler	.08	.06	.03
449	John Candelaria	.04	.03	.02
450	Gary Carter	.08	.06	.03
451	Dennis Cook	.04	.03	.02
452	Tim Crews	.04	.03	.02
453	Kal Daniels	.08	.06	.03
454	Jim Gott	.04	.03	.02
455	Alfredo Griffin	.04	.03	.02
456	Kevin Gross	.04	.03	.02
457	Chris Gwynn	.04	.03	.02
458	Lenny Harris	.05	.04	.02
459	Orel Hershiser	.08	.06	.03
460	Jay Howell	.05	.04	.02
461	Stan Javier	.04	.03	.02
462	Eric Karros(FC)	.40	.30	.15
463	Ramon Martinez	.12	.09	.05
464	Roger McDowell	.05	.04	.02
465	Mike Morgan	.05	.04	.02
466	Eddie Murray	.12	.09	.05
467	Jose Offerman	.12	.09	.05
468	Bob Ojeda	.05	.04	.02
469	Juan Samuel	.06	.05	.02
470	Mike Scioscia	.06	.05	.02

		MT	NR MT	EX
471	Darryl Strawberry	.15	.11	.06
472	*Bret Barberie*(FC)	.15	.11	.06
473	Brian Barnes	.06	.05	.02
474	Eric Bullock	.04	.03	.02
475	Ivan Calderon	.08	.06	.03
476	Delino DeShields	.08	.06	.03
477	*Jeff Fassero*(FC)	.10	.08	.04
478	Mike Fitzgerald	.04	.03	.02
479	Steve Frey	.04	.03	.02
480	Andres Galarraga	.06	.05	.02
481	Mark Gardner	.06	.05	.02
482	Marquis Grissom	.12	.09	.05
483	*Chris Haney*(FC)	.20	.15	.08
484	Barry Jones	.04	.03	.02
485	Dave Martinez	.05	.04	.02
486	Dennis Martinez	.08	.06	.03
487	Chris Nabholz	.06	.05	.02
488	Spike Owen	.04	.03	.02
489	Gilberto Reyes	.05	.04	.02
490	Mel Rojas	.05	.04	.02
491	Scott Ruskin	.05	.04	.02
492	Bill Sampen	.05	.04	.02
493	Larry Walker	.10	.08	.04
494	Tim Wallach	.08	.06	.03
495	Daryl Boston	.04	.03	.02
496	Hubie Brooks	.06	.05	.02
497	Tim Burke	.05	.04	.02
498	Mark Carreon	.04	.03	.02
499	Tony Castillo	.04	.03	.02
500	Vince Coleman	.08	.06	.03
501	David Cone	.08	.06	.03
502	Kevin Elster	.04	.03	.02
503	Sid Fernandez	.06	.05	.02
504	John Franco	.06	.05	.02
505	Dwight Gooden	.12	.09	.05
506	Todd Hundley	.12	.09	.05
507	Jeff Innis	.04	.03	.02
508	Gregg Jefferies	.12	.09	.05
509	Howard Johnson	.12	.09	.05
510	Dave Magadan	.06	.05	.02
511	*Terry McDaniel*(FC)	.25	.20	.10
512	Kevin McReynolds	.08	.06	.03
513	Keith Miller	.04	.03	.02
514	Charlie O'Brien	.04	.03	.02
515	Mackey Sasser	.04	.03	.02
516	*Pete Schourek*	.10	.08	.04
517	Julio Valera	.06	.05	.02
518	Frank Viola	.10	.08	.04
519	Wally Whitehurst	.05	.04	.02
520	*Anthony Young*(FC)	.40	.30	.15
521	*Andy Ashby*	.10	.08	.04
522	*Kim Batiste*(FC)	.10	.08	.04
523	Joe Boever	.04	.03	.02
524	Wes Chamberlain	.20	.15	.08
525	Pat Combs	.05	.04	.02
526	Danny Cox	.04	.03	.02
527	Darren Daulton	.05	.04	.02
528	Jose DeJesus	.05	.04	.02
529	Lenny Dykstra	.08	.06	.03
530	Darrin Fletcher	.05	.04	.02
531	Tommy Greene	.06	.05	.02
532	Jason Grimsley	.05	.04	.02
533	Charlie Hayes	.05	.04	.02
534	Von Hayes	.06	.05	.02
535	Dave Hollins	.08	.06	.03
536	Ricky Jordan	.08	.06	.03
537	John Kruk	.06	.05	.02
538	Jim Lindeman	.04	.03	.02
539	Mickey Morandini	.08	.06	.03
540	Terry Mulholland	.06	.05	.02
541	Dale Murphy	.12	.09	.05
542	Randy Ready	.04	.03	.02
543	Wally Ritchie	.04	.03	.02
544	Bruce Ruffin	.04	.03	.02
545	Steve Searcy	.04	.03	.02
546	Dickie Thon	.04	.03	.02
547	Mitch Williams	.08	.06	.03
548	Stan Belinda	.04	.03	.02
549	Jay Bell	.06	.05	.02
550	Barry Bonds	.15	.11	.06
551	Bobby Bonilla	.12	.09	.05
552	Steve Buechele	.05	.04	.02
553	Doug Drabek	.08	.06	.03
554	Neal Heaton	.04	.03	.02
555	Jeff King	.05	.04	.02
556	Bob Kipper	.04	.03	.02
557	Bill Landrum	.04	.03	.02
558	Mike LaValliere	.05	.04	.02
559	Jose Lind	.04	.03	.02
560	Lloyd McClendon	.04	.03	.02
561	Orlando Merced	.25	.20	.10

		MT	NR MT	EX
562	Bob Patterson	.04	.03	.02
563	*Joe Redfield*(FC)	.10	.08	.04
564	Gary Redus	.04	.03	.02
565	Rosario Rodriguez	.04	.03	.02
566	Don Slaught	.04	.03	.02
567	John Smiley	.06	.05	.02
568	Zane Smith	.05	.04	.02
569	Randy Tomlin	.08	.06	.03
570	Andy Van Slyke	.08	.06	.03
571	Gary Varsho	.04	.03	.02
572	Bob Walk	.04	.03	.02
573	*John Wehner*(FC)	.25	.20	.10
574	Juan Agosto	.04	.03	.02
575	Cris Carpenter	.05	.04	.02
576	Jose DeLeon	.05	.04	.02
577	Rich Gedman	.04	.03	.02
578	Bernard Gilkey	.10	.08	.04
579	Pedro Guerrero	.08	.06	.03
580	Ken Hill	.05	.04	.02
581	Rex Hudler	.04	.03	.02
582	Felix Jose	.10	.08	.04
583	Ray Lankford	.15	.11	.06
584	Omar Olivares	.06	.05	.02
585	Jose Oquendo	.04	.03	.02
586	Tom Pagnozzi	.05	.04	.02
587	Geronimo Pena	.05	.04	.02
588	Mike Perez	.05	.04	.02
589	Gerald Perry	.04	.03	.02
590	Bryn Smith	.04	.03	.02
591	Lee Smith	.06	.05	.02
592	Ozzie Smith	.12	.09	.05
593	Scott Terry	.04	.03	.02
594	Bob Teksbury	.04	.03	.02
595	Milt Thompson	.04	.03	.02
596	Todd Zeile	.12	.09	.05
597	Larry Andersen	.04	.03	.02
598	Oscar Azocar	.04	.03	.02
599	Andy Benes	.10	.08	.04
600	*Ricky Bones*(FC)	.10	.08	.04
601	Jerald Clark	.05	.04	.02
602	Pat Clements	.04	.03	.02
603	Paul Faries	.06	.05	.02
604	Tony Fernandez	.06	.05	.02
605	Tony Gwynn	.12	.09	.05
606	Greg Harris	.05	.04	.02
607	Thomas Howard	.05	.04	.02
608	Bruce Hurst	.06	.05	.02
609	Darrin Jackson	.04	.03	.02
610	Tom Lampkin	.04	.03	.02
611	Craig Lefferts	.04	.03	.02
612	*Jim Lewis*(FC)	.20	.15	.08
613	Mike Maddux	.04	.03	.02
614	Fred McGriff	.10	.08	.04
615	*Jose Melendez*(FC)	.20	.15	.08
616	*Jose Mota*	.15	.11	.06
617	Dennis Rasmussen	.04	.03	.02
618	Bip Roberts	.06	.05	.02
619	Rich Rodriguez	.04	.03	.02
620	Benito Santiago	.08	.06	.03
621	*Craig Shipley*(FC)	.10	.08	.04
622	Tim Teufel	.04	.03	.02
623	*Kevin Ward*(FC)	.15	.11	.06
624	Ed Whitson	.05	.04	.02
625	Dave Anderson	.04	.03	.02
626	Kevin Bass	.05	.04	.02
627	*Rod Beck*(FC)	.10	.08	.04
628	Bud Black	.05	.04	.02
629	Jeff Brantley	.05	.04	.02
630	John Burkett	.05	.04	.02
631	Will Clark	.25	.20	.10
632	Royce Clayton(FC)	.15	.11	.06
633	Steve Decker	.10	.08	.04
634	Kelly Downs	.04	.03	.02
635	Mike Felder	.04	.03	.02
636	Scott Garrelts	.04	.03	.02
637	Eric Gunderson	.08	.06	.03
638	*Bryan Hickerson*(FC)	.20	.15	.08
639	Darren Lewis	.15	.11	.06
640	Greg Litton	.04	.03	.02
641	Kirt Manwaring	.06	.05	.02
642	*Paul McClellan*(FC)	.10	.08	.04
643	Willie McGee	.08	.06	.03
644	Kevin Mitchell	.12	.09	.05
645	Francisco Olivares	.04	.03	.02
646	*Mike Remlinger*(FC)	.10	.08	.04
647	Dave Righetti	.06	.05	.02
648	Robby Thompson	.05	.04	.02
649	Jose Uribe	.04	.03	.02
650	Matt Williams	.12	.09	.05
651	Trevor Wilson	.06	.05	.02
652	Tom Goodwin(FC)	.25	.20	.10

		MT	NR MT	EX
653	Terry Bross(FC)	.08	.06	.03
654	*Mike Christopher*(FC)	.20	.15	.08
655	*Kenny Lofton*(FC)	.35	.25	.14
656	*Chris Cron*(FC)	.20	.15	.08
657	Willie Banks(FC)	.25	.20	.10
658	*Pat Rice*(FC)	.25	.20	.10
659	*Rob Maurer*(FC)	.25	.20	.10
660	Don Harris(FC)	.20	.15	.08
661	Henry Rodriguez(FC)	.10	.08	.04
662	*Cliff Brantley*(FC)	.20	.15	.08
663	*Mike Linskey*(FC)	.20	.15	.08
664	Gary Disarcina(FC)	.08	.06	.03
665	*Gil Heredia*(FC)	.20	.15	.08
666	*Vinny Castilla*(FC)	.25	.20	.10
667	Paul Abbott(FC)	.08	.06	.03
668	Monty Fariss(FC)	.08	.06	.03
669	*Jarvis Brown*(FC)	.10	.08	.04
670	*Wayne Kirby*(FC)	.20	.15	.08
671	*Scott Brosius*(FC)	.15	.11	.06
672	Bob Hamelin(FC)	.10	.08	.04
673	*Joel Johnston*(FC)	.20	.15	.08
674	*Tim Spehr*(FC)	.15	.11	.06
675	*Jeff Gardner*(FC)	.15	.11	.06
676	*Rico Rossy*(FC)	.20	.15	.08
677	*Roberto Hernandez*(FC)	.20	.15	.08
678	*Ted Wood*(FC)	.25	.20	.10
679	Cal Eldred(FC)	.20	.15	.08
680	Sean Berry(FC)	.08	.06	.03
681	Rickey Henderson (RS)	.15	.11	.06
682	Nolan Ryan (RS)	.20	.15	.08
683	Dennis Martinez (RS)	.05	.04	.02
684	Wilson Alvarez (RS)	.05	.04	.02
685	Joe Carter (RS)	.06	.05	.02
686	Dave Winfield (RS)	.10	.08	.04
687	David Cone (RS)	.06	.05	.02
688	Jose Canseco (LL)	.15	.11	.06
689	Howard Johnson (LL)	.08	.06	.03
690	Julio Franco (LL)	.08	.06	.03
691	Terry Pendleton (LL)	.08	.06	.03
692	Cecil Fielder (LL)	.10	.08	.04
693	Scott Erickson (LL)	.10	.08	.04
694	Tom Glavine (LL)	.08	.06	.03
695	Dennis Martinez (LL)	.05	.04	.02
696	Bryan Harvey (LL)	.05	.04	.02
697	Lee Smith (LL)	.05	.04	.02
698	Super Siblings (Roberto & Sandy Alomar)	.08	.06	.03
699	The Indispensables (Bonilla & Clark)	.10	.08	.04
700	Teamwork (Wohlers, Mercker & Pena)	.06	.05	.02
701	Tiger Tandems (Jones. Jackson, Olson & Thomas)	.40	.30	.15
702	The Ignitors (Molitor & Butler)	.06	.05	.02
703	The Indespensables II (Ripken, Jr. & Carter)	.15	.11	.06
704	Power Packs (Larkin & Puckett)	.10	.08	.04
705	Today & Tomorrow (Vaughn & Fielder)	.15	.11	.06
706	Teenage Sensations (Martinez & Guillen)	.08	.06	.03
707	Designated Hitters (Baines & Boggs)	.08	.06	.03
708	Robin Yount (PV)	.40	.30	.15
709	Ken Griffey, Jr. (PV)	1.00	.70	.40
710	Nolan Ryan (PV)	1.00	.70	.40
711	Cal Ripken, Jr. (PV)	.70	.50	.30
712	Frank Thomas (PV)	1.00	.70	.40
713	Dave Justice (PV)	.70	.50	.30
714	Checklist	.04	.03	.02
715	Checklist	.04	.03	.02
716	Checklist	.04	.03	.02
717	Checklist	.04	.03	.02
718	Checklist	.04	.03	.02
719	Checklist	.04	.03	.02
720	Checklist	.04	.03	.02

A player's name in italic indicates a rookie card. An (FC) indicates a player's first card for that particular card company.

1991 Front Row Draft Picks

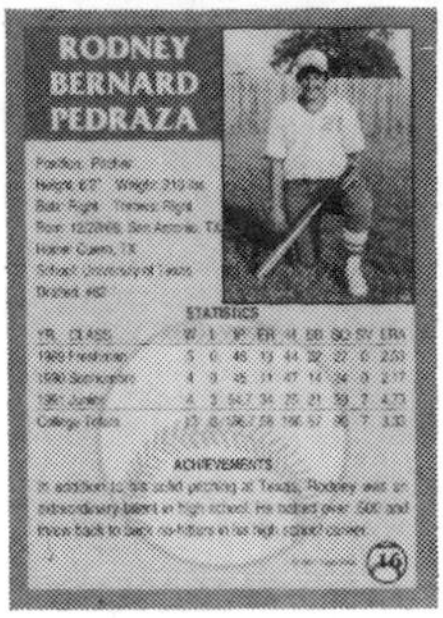

Only 240,000 of these sets were produced. The bonus card in the set must be sent in to Front Row in exchange for a special Frankie Rodriguez card. The first 120,000 collectors returning bonus cards also received Front Row's mini-update set. The cards feature full-color photos on both sides. Each set includes an official certificate of authenticity. 1991 marks the premier issue of Front Row baseball draft picks.

		MT	NR MT	EX
Complete Set:		12.00	9.00	4.75
Common Player:		.20	.15	.08
1	Frankie Rodriguez	1.50	1.25	.60
2	Aaron Sele	.25	.20	.10
3	Chad Schoenvogel	.20	.15	.08
4	Scott Ruffcorn	.20	.15	.08
5	Dan Chowlowski	.20	.15	.08
6	Gene Schall	.20	.15	.08
7	Trever Miller	.25	.20	.10
8	Chris Durkin	.20	.15	.08
9	Mike Neill	.20	.15	.08
10	Kevin Stocker	.20	.15	.08
11	Bobby Jones	.50	.40	.20
12	John Farrell	.20	.15	.08
13	Ronnie Allen	.20	.15	.08
14	Mike Rossiter	.20	.15	.08
15	Scott Hatteberg	.25	.20	.10
16	Rodney Pedraza	.20	.15	.08
17	Mike Durant	.20	.15	.08
18	Ryan Long	.20	.15	.08
19	Greg Anthony	.20	.15	.08
20	Jon Barnes	.20	.15	.08
21	Brian Barber	.20	.15	.08
22	Brent Gates	.35	.25	.14
23	Calvin Reese	.30	.25	.14
24	Terry Horn	.20	.15	.08
25	Scott Stahoviak	.35	.25	.14
26	Jason Pruitt	.30	.25	.12
27	Shawn Curran	.20	.15	.08
28	Jimmy Lewis	.25	.20	.10
29	Alex Ochoa	.20	.15	.08
30	Joe Deberry	.20	.15	.08
31	Justin Thompson	.30	.25	.12
32	Jimmy Gonzalez	.30	.25	.12
33	Eddie Ramos	.20	.15	.08
34	Tyler Green	.50	.40	.20
35	Toby Rumfield	.20	.15	.08
36	Dave Doorneweerd	.20	.15	.08
37	Jeff Hostetler	.20	.15	.08
38	Shawn Livsey	.25	.20	.10
39	Mike Groppuso	.40	.30	.15
40	Steve Whitaker	.30	.25	.12
41	Tom McKinnon	.30	.25	.12
42	Buck McNabb	.25	.20	.10
43	Al Shirley	.50	.40	.20
44	Allan Watson	.25	.20	.10
45	Bill Bliss	.20	.15	.08
46	Todd Hollandsworth	.20	.15	.08
47	Manny Ramirez	.40	.30	.15
48	J.J. Johnson	.25	.20	.10
49	Cliff Floyd	.50	.40	.20
50	Bonus Card	.25	.20	.10

G

1953 Glendale Hot Dogs Tigers

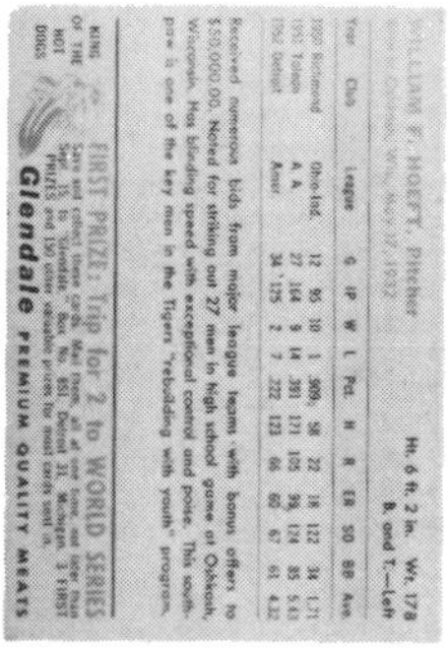

Glendale Meats issued these unnumbered, full-color cards (2-5/8" by 3-3/4") in packages of hot dogs. Featuring Detroit Tigers players, the card fronts contain a player picture plus the player's name, a facsimile autograph, and the Tigers logo. The card reverses carry player statistical and biographical information plus an offer for a trip for two to the World Series. Collectors were advised to mail all the cards they had saved to Glendale Meats. The World Series trip plus 150 other prizes were to be given to the individuals sending in the most cards. As with most cards issued with food products, quality-condition cards are tough to find because of the cards' susceptibilty to stains. The Houtteman card is extremely scarce.

		NR MT	EX	VG
Complete Set:		6000.00	3000.00	1800.
Common Player:		125.00	62.00	37.00
(1)	Matt Batts	125.00	62.00	37.00
(2)	Johnny Bucha	125.00	62.00	37.00
(3)	Frank Carswell	125.00	62.00	37.00
(4)	Jim Delsing	125.00	62.00	37.00
(5)	Walt Dropo	125.00	62.00	37.00
(6)	Hal Erickson	125.00	62.00	37.00
(7)	Paul Foytack	125.00	62.00	37.00
(8)	Owen Friend	150.00	75.00	45.00
(9)	Ned Garver	125.00	62.00	37.00
(10)	Joe Ginsberg	350.00	175.00	105.00
(11)	Ted Gray	125.00	62.00	37.00
(12)	Fred Hatfield	125.00	62.00	37.00
(13)	Ray Herbert	150.00	75.00	45.00
(14)	Bill Hitchcock	125.00	62.00	37.00
(15)	Bill Hoeft	275.00	137.00	82.00
(16)	Art Houtteman	2200.00	1100.00	660.00
(17)	Milt Jordan	200.00	100.00	60.00
(18)	Harvey Kuenn	325.00	162.00	97.00
(19)	Don Lund	125.00	62.00	37.00
(20)	Dave Madison	125.00	62.00	37.00
(21)	Dick Marlowe	125.00	62.00	37.00
(22)	Pat Mullin	125.00	62.00	37.00
(23)	Bob Neiman	125.00	62.00	37.00
(24)	Johnny Pesky	150.00	75.00	45.00
(25)	Jerry Priddy	125.00	62.00	37.00
(26)	Steve Souchock	125.00	62.00	37.00
(27)	Russ Sullivan	125.00	62.00	37.00
(28)	Bill Wight	200.00	100.00	60.00

1961 Golden Press

The 1961 Golden Press set features 33 players, all enshrined in the Baseball Hall of Fame. The full color cards measure 2-1/2" by 3-1/2" and came in a booklet with perforations so that they could be easily

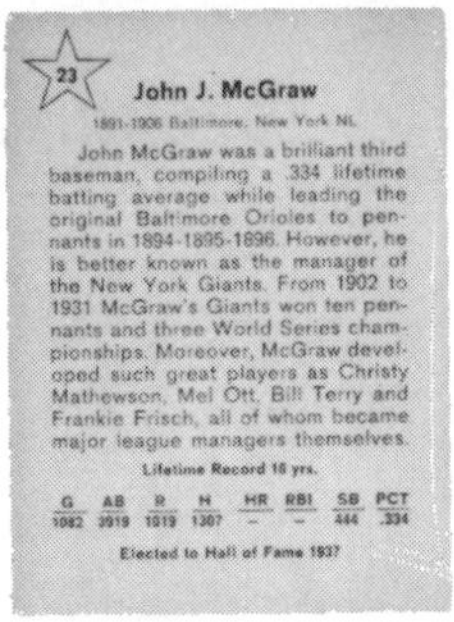

removed. Full books with the cards intact would command 50 percent over the set price in the checklist that follows. Card numbers 1-3 and 28-33 are slightly higher in price as they were located on the book's front and back covers, making them more susceptible to scuffing and wear.

		NR MT	EX	VG
Complete Set:		80.00	40.00	24.00
Common Player:		.75	.40	.25
1	Mel Ott	1.75	.90	.50
2	Grover Cleveland Alexander	1.75	.90	.50
3	Babe Ruth	25.00	12.50	7.50
4	Hank Greenberg	1.50	.70	.45
5	Bill Terry	.90	.45	.25
6	Carl Hubbell	.90	.45	.25
7	Rogers Hornsby	2.00	1.00	.60
8	Dizzy Dean	5.00	2.50	1.50
9	Joe DiMaggio	16.00	8.00	4.75
10	Charlie Gehringer	.90	.45	.25
11	Gabby Hartnett	.75	.40	.25
12	Mickey Cochrane	.90	.45	.25
13	George Sisler	.90	.45	.25
14	Joe Cronin	.90	.45	.25
15	Pie Traynor	.75	.40	.25
16	Lou Gehrig	16.00	8.00	4.75
17	Lefty Grove	1.25	.60	.40
18	Chief Bender	.75	.40	.25
19	Frankie Frisch	.90	.45	.25
20	Al Simmons	.75	.40	.25
21	Home Run Baker	.75	.40	.25
22	Jimmy Foxx	2.00	1.00	.60
23	John McGraw	1.25	.60	.40
24	Christy Mathewson	4.00	2.00	1.25
25	Ty Cobb	16.00	8.00	4.75
26	Dazzy Vance	.75	.40	.25
27	Bill Dickey	1.25	.60	.40
28	Eddie Collins	.90	.45	.25
29	Walter Johnson	4.00	2.00	1.25
30	Tris Speaker	1.75	.90	.50
31	Nap Lajoie	1.75	.90	.50
32	Honus Wagner	4.00	2.00	1.25
33	Cy Young	4.00	2.00	1.25

H

1989 Hills Team MVP's

This high-gloss, 33-card boxed set of superstars was produced by Topps for the Hills department store chain. The words "Hills Team MVP's" appear above the player photos, while the player's name and team are printed below. The front of the card carries a red, white and blue color scheme with yellow and gold accents. The horizontal backs include player data set against a green playing field background.

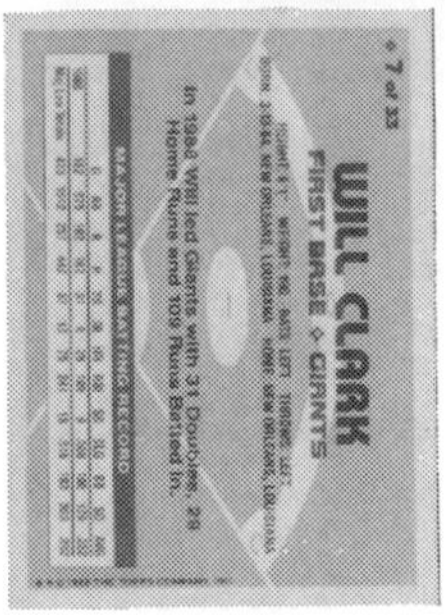

		MT	NR MT	EX
Complete Set:		3.00	2.25	1.25
Common Player:		.05	.04	.02
1	Harold Baines	.05	.04	.02
2	Wade Boggs	.30	.25	.12
3	George Brett	.09	.07	.04
4	Tom Brunansky	.05	.04	.02
5	Jose Canseco	.35	.25	.14
6	Joe Carter	.09	.07	.04
7	Will Clark	.35	.25	.12
8	Roger Clemens	.15	.11	.06
9	Dave Cone	.05	.04	.02
10	Glenn Davis	.05	.04	.02
11	Andre Dawson	.09	.07	.04
12	Dennis Eckersley	.09	.07	.04
13	Andres Galarraga	.05	.04	.02
14	Kirk Gibson	.06	.05	.02
15	Mike Greenwell	.10	.08	.04
16	Tony Gwynn	.15	.11	.06
17	Orel Hershiser	.09	.07	.03
18	Danny Jackson	.05	.04	.02
19	Mark Langston	.09	.07	.04
20	Fred McGriff	.10	.08	.04
21	Dale Murphy	.06	.05	.04
22	Eddie Murray	.06	.05	.04
23	Kirby Puckett	.20	.15	.08
24	Johnny Ray	.05	.04	.02
25	Juan Samuel	.05	.04	.02
26	Ruben Sierra	.15	.11	.06
27	Dave Stewart	.05	.04	.02
28	Darryl Strawberry	.20	.15	.08
29	Allan Trammell	.06	.05	.02
30	Andy Van Slyke	.05	.04	.02
31	Frank Viola	.06	.05	.02
32	Dave Winfield	.06	.05	.02
33	Robin Yount	.09	.07	.03

1990 Hills Hit Men

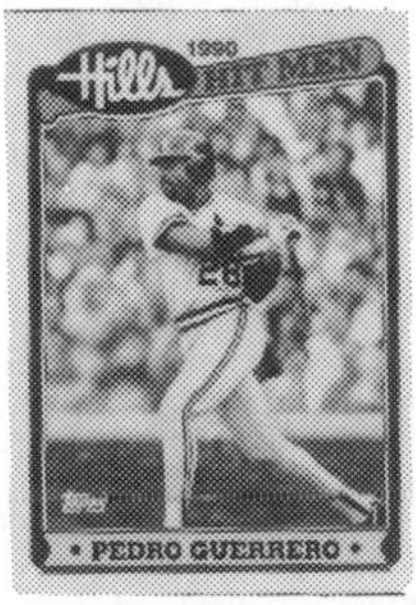

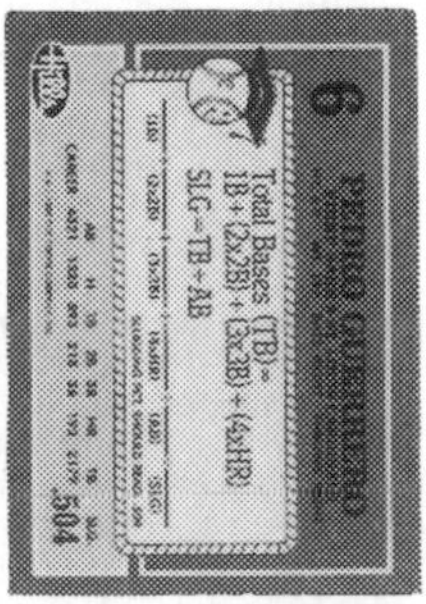

The 33 slugging percentage leaders are featured in this high-gloss set. The cards were produced by Topps for the Hills department store chain. The card fronts feature "Hit Men" ina bat design above the photo. The player's name appears on a band below the photo. The horizontal backs feature a breakdown of the player's slugging percentage and also display career statistics.

	MT	NR MT	EX
Complete Set:	3.00	2.25	1.25

		MT	NR MT	EX
Common Player:		.05	.04	.02
1	Eric Davis	.10	.08	.04
2	Will Clark	.25	.20	.10
3	Don Mattingly	.20	.15	.08
4	Darryl Strawberry	.20	.15	.08
5	Kevin Mitchell	.10	.08	.04
6	Pedro Guerrero	.05	.04	.02
7	Jose Canseco	.30	.25	.12
8	Jim Rice	.05	.04	.02
9	Danny Tartabull	.09	.07	.03
10	George Brett	.09	.07	.04
11	Kent Hrbek	.05	.04	.02
12	George Bell	.09	.07	.03
13	Eddie Murray	.08	.06	.03
14	Fred Lynn	.05	.04	.02
15	Andre Dawson	.09	.07	.04
16	Dale Murphy	.09	.07	.04
17	Dave Winfield	.09	.07	.04
18	Jack Clark	.05	.04	.02
19	Wade Boggs	.25	.20	.10
20	Ruben Sierra	.15	.11	.06
21	Dave Parker	.10	.08	.04
22	Glenn Davis	.05	.04	.02
23	Dwight Evans	.05	.04	.02
24	Jesse Barfield	.05	.04	.02
25	Kirk Gibson	.06	.05	.02
26	Alvin Davis	.05	.04	.02
27	Kirby Puckett	.20	.15	.08
28	Joe Carter	.09	.07	.03
29	Carlton Fisk	.10	.08	.04
30	Harold Baines	.05	.04	.02
31	Andres Galarraga	.05	.04	.02
32	Cal Ripken	.15	.11	.06
33	Howard Johnson	.08	.06	.03

1958 Hires Root Beer Test Set

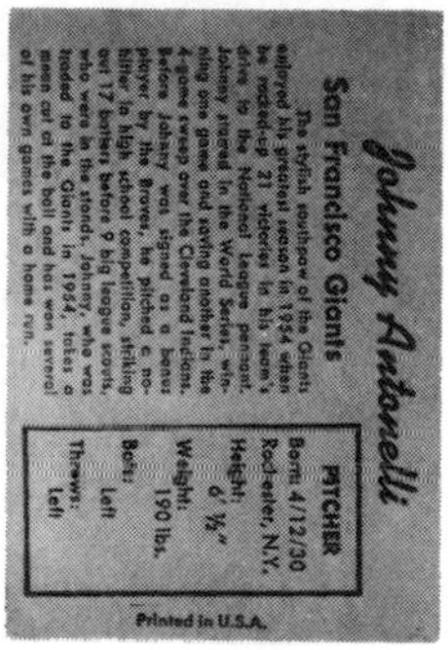

Among the scarcest of the regional issues of the late 1950s is the eight-card test issue which preceded the Hires Root Beer set of 66 cards. Probably issued in a very limited area in the Northeast, the test cards differ from the regular issue in that they have sepia-toned, rather than color pictures, which are set against plain yellow or orange backgrounds (much like the 1958 Topps), instead of viewed through a knothole. Like the regular Hires cards, the 2-5/16" by 3-1/2" cards were issued with an attached wedge-shaped tab of like size. The tab offered membership in Hires baseball fan club, and served to hold the card into the carton of bottled root beer with which it was given away. Values quoted here are for cards with tabs. Cards without tabs would be valued approximately 50 per cent lower.

		NR MT	EX	VG
Complete Set:		1550.00	775.00	465.00
Common Player:		130.00	65.00	39.00
(1)	Johnny Antonelli	150.00	75.00	45.00
(2)	Jim Busby	130.00	65.00	39.00
(3)	Chico Fernandez	130.00	65.00	39.00
(4)	Bob Friend	150.00	75.00	45.00
(5)	Vern Law	150.00	75.00	45.00
(6)	Stan Lopata	130.00	65.00	39.00
(7)	Willie Mays	550.00	280.00	165.00
(8)	Al Pilarcik	130.00	65.00	39.00

1958 Hires Root Beer

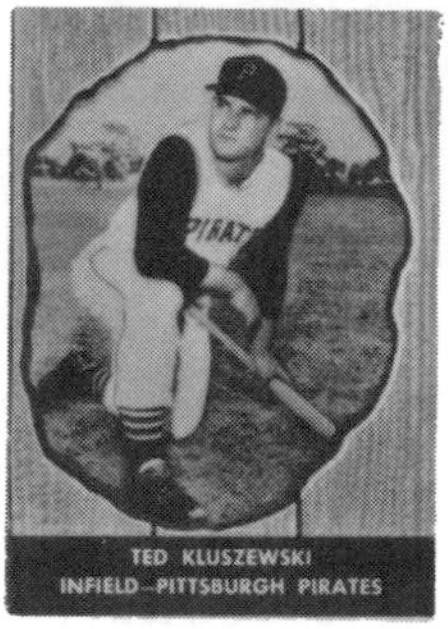

Like most baseball cards issued with a tab in the 1950s, the Hires cards are extremely scarce today in their original form. The basic card was attached to a wedge-shaped tab that served the dual purpose of offering a fan club membership and of holding the card into the cardboard carton of soda bottles with which it was distributed. The card itself measures 2-5/16" by 3-1/2". The tab extends for another 3-1/2". Numbering of the Hires set begins at 10 and goes through 76, with card #69 never issued, making a set complete at 66 cards. Values given below are for cards with tabs. Cards without tabs would be valued approximately 50 per cent lower.

		NR MT	EX	VG
Complete Set:		2400.00	1200.00	720.00
Common Player:		25.00	12.50	7.50
10	Richie Ashburn	100.00	50.00	30.00
11	Chico Carrasquel	25.00	12.50	7.50
12	Dave Philley	25.00	12.50	7.50
13	Don Newcombe	28.00	14.00	8.50
14	Wally Post	25.00	12.50	7.50
15	Rip Repulski	25.00	12.50	7.50
16	Chico Fernandez	25.00	12.50	7.50
17	Larry Doby	28.00	14.00	8.50
18	Hector Brown	25.00	12.50	7.50
19	Danny O'Connell	25.00	12.50	7.50
20	Granny Hamner	25.00	12.50	7.50
21	Dick Groat	30.00	15.00	9.00
22	Ray Narleski	25.00	12.50	7.50
23	Pee Wee Reese	100.00	50.00	30.00
24	Bob Friend	30.00	15.00	9.00
25	Willie Mays	275.00	150.00	80.00
26	Bob Nieman	25.00	12.50	7.50
27	Frank Thomas	25.00	12.50	7.50
28	Curt Simmons	30.00	15.00	9.00
29	Stan Lopata	25.00	12.50	7.50
30	Bob Skinner	25.00	12.50	7.50
31	Ron Kline	25.00	12.50	7.50
32	Willie Miranda	25.00	12.50	7.50
33	Bob Avila	25.00	12.50	7.50
34	Clem Labine	30.00	15.00	9.00
35	Ray Jablonski	25.00	12.50	7.50
36	Bill Mazeroski	28.00	14.00	8.50
37	Billy Gardner	25.00	12.50	7.50
38	Pete Runnels	30.00	15.00	9.00
39	Jack Sanford	25.00	12.50	7.50
40	Dave Sisler	25.00	12.50	7.50
41	Don Zimmer	30.00	15.00	9.00
42	Johnny Podres	28.00	14.00	8.50
43	Dick Farrell	25.00	12.50	7.50
44	Hank Aaron	275.00	150.00	80.00
45	Bill Virdon	30.00	15.00	9.00
46	Bobby Thomson	30.00	15.00	9.00
47	Willard Nixon	25.00	12.50	7.50
48	Billy Loes	25.00	12.50	7.50
49	Hank Sauer	25.00	12.50	7.50
50	Johnny Antonelli	30.00	15.00	9.00
51	Daryl Spencer	25.00	12.50	7.50
52	Ken Lehman	25.00	12.50	7.50
53	Sammy White	25.00	12.50	7.50
54	Charley Neal	25.00	12.50	7.50
55	Don Drysdale	80.00	40.00	24.00
56	Jack Jensen	28.00	14.00	8.50

		NR MT	EX	VG
57	Ray Katt	25.00	12.50	7.50
58	Franklin Sullivan	25.00	12.50	7.50
59	Roy Face	30.00	15.00	9.00
60	Willie Jones	25.00	12.50	7.50
61	Duke Snider	125.00	62.00	37.00
62	Whitey Lockman	25.00	12.50	7.50
63	Gino Cimoli	30.00	15.00	9.00
64	Marv Grissom	25.00	12.50	7.50
65	Gene Baker	25.00	12.50	7.50
66	George Zuverink	25.00	12.50	7.50
67	Ted Kluszewski	28.00	14.00	8.50
68	Jim Busby	25.00	12.50	7.50
69	Not Issued			
70	Curt Barclay	25.00	12.50	7.50
71	Hank Foiles	25.00	12.50	7.50
72	Gene Stephens	25.00	12.50	7.50
73	Al Worthington	25.00	12.50	7.50
74	Al Walker	25.00	12.50	7.50
75	Bob Boyd	25.00	12.50	7.50
76	Al Pilarcik	30.00	9.00	5.50

1959 Home Run Derby

This 20-card unnumbered set was produced by American Motors to publicize the Home Run Derby television program. The cards measure approximately 3-1/4" by 5-1/4" and feature black and white player photos on black-backed white stock. The player name and team are printed beneath the photo. This set was reprinted (and marked as such) in 1988 by Card Collectors' Company of New York.

		NR MT	EX	VG
Complete Set:		4000.00	2000.00	1200.
Common Player:		100.00	50.00	30.00
(1)	Hank Aaron	450.00	225.00	135.00
(2)	Bob Allison	100.00	50.00	30.00
(3)	Ernie Banks	300.00	150.00	90.00
(4)	Ken Boyer	175.00	87.00	52.00
(5)	Bob Cerv	100.00	50.00	30.00
(6)	Rocky Colavito	175.00	87.00	52.00
(7)	Gil Hodges	225.00	112.00	67.00
(8)	Jackie Jensen	175.00	87.00	52.00
(9)	Al Kaline	300.00	150.00	90.00
(10)	Harmon Killebrew	225.00	112.00	67.00
(11)	Jim Lemon	100.00	50.00	30.00
(12)	Mickey Mantle	1200.00	600.00	400.00
(13)	Ed Mathews	275.00	137.00	82.00
(14)	Willie Mays	450.00	225.00	135.00
(15)	Wally Post	100.00	50.00	30.00
(16)	Frank Robinson	275.00	137.00	82.00
(17)	Mark Scott (host)	175.00	87.00	52.00
(18)	Duke Snider	450.00	225.00	135.00
(19)	Dick Stuart	100.00	50.00	30.00
(20)	Gus Triandos	100.00	50.00	30.00

1975 Hostess

The first of what would become five annual issues, the 1975 Hostess set consists of 50 three-card panels which formed the bottom of boxes of family-size snack cake products. Unlike many similar issues, the Hostess cards do not share common borders, so it

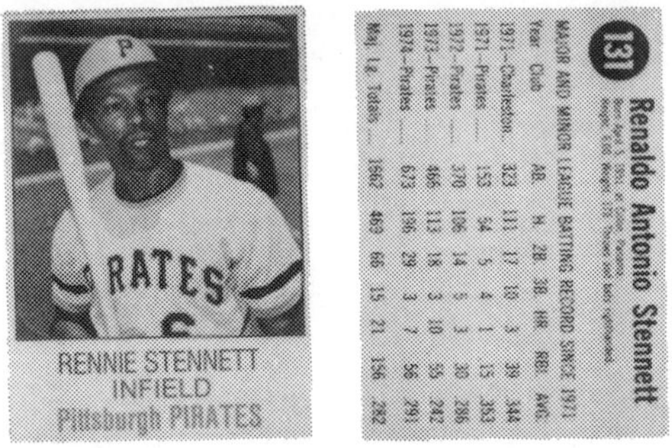

was possible to cut them neatly and evenly from the box. Well-cut single cards measure 2-1/4" by 3-1/4", while a three-card panel measures 7-1/4" by 3-1/4". Because some of the panels were issued on packages of less popular snack cakes, they are somewhat scarcer today. Since the hobby was quite well- developed when the Hostess cards were first issued, there is no lack of complete panels. Even unused complete boxes are available today. Some of the photos in this issue also appear on Topps cards of the era.

		NR MT	EX	VG
Complete Panel Set:		400.00	200.00	120.00
Complete Singles Set:		200.00	100.00	60.00
Common Panel:		2.50	1.25	.70
Common Single Player:		.40	.20	.12
	Panel 1	2.50	1.25	.70
1	Bobby Tolan	.40	.20	.12
2	Cookie Rojas	.40	.20	.12
3	Darrell Evans	.70	.35	.20
	Panel 2	5.50	2.75	1.75
4	Sal Bando	.50	.25	.15
5	Joe Morgan	2.00	1.00	.60
6	Mickey Lolich	.60	.30	.20
	Panel 3	4.00	2.00	1.25
7	Don Sutton	1.50	.70	.45
8	Bill Melton	.40	.20	.12
9	Tim Foli	.40	.20	.12
	Panel 4	5.00	2.50	1.50
10	Joe Lahoud	.40	.20	.12
11a	Bert Hooten (incorrect spelling)	1.50	.70	.45
11b	Burt Hooton (correct spelling)	1.50	.70	.45
12	Paul Blair	.40	.20	.12
	Panel 5	2.50	1.25	.70
13	Jim Barr	.40	.20	.12
14	Toby Harrah	.50	.25	.15
15	John Milner	.40	.20	.12
	Panel 6	3.50	1.75	1.00
16	Ken Holtzman	.50	.25	.15
17	Cesar Cedeno	.50	.25	.15
18	Dwight Evans	.90	.45	.25
	Panel 7	7.50	3.75	2.25
19	Willie McCovey	3.00	1.50	.90
20	Tony Oliva	.70	.35	.20
21	Manny Sanguillen	.40	.20	.12
	Panel 8	8.00	4.00	2.50
22	Mickey Rivers	.50	.25	.15
23	Lou Brock	3.00	1.50	.90
24	Craig Nettles	.90	.45	.25
	Panel 9	3.00	1.50	.90
25	Jimmy Wynn	.50	.25	.15
26	George Scott	.50	.25	.15
27	Greg Luzinski	.50	.25	.15
	Panel 10	20.00	10.00	6.00
28	Bert Campaneris	.50	.25	.15
29	Pete Rose	8.00	4.00	2.50
30	Buddy Bell	.50	.25	.15
	Panel 11	2.50	1.25	.70
31	Gary Matthews	.50	.25	.15
32	Fred Patek	.40	.20	.12
33	Mike Lum	.40	.20	.12
	Panel 12	2.50	1.25	.70
34	Ellie Rodriguez	.40	.20	.12
35	Milt May	.40	.20	.12
36	Willie Horton	.50	.25	.15
	Panel 13	10.00	5.00	3.00
37	Dave Winfield	4.50	2.25	1.25
38	Tom Grieve	.40	.20	.12
39	Barry Foote	.40	.20	.12

		NR MT	EX	VG
	Panel 14	2.50	1.25	.70
40	Joe Rudi	.50	.25	.15
41	Bake McBride	.40	.20	.12
42	Mike Cuellar	.50	.25	.15
	Panel 15	2.50	1.25	.70
43	Garry Maddox	.50	.25	.15
44	Carlos May	.40	.20	.12
45	Bud Harrelson	.40	.20	.12
	Panel 16	15.00	7.50	4.50
46	Dave Chalk	.40	.20	.12
47	Dave Concepcion	.50	.25	.15
48	Carl Yastrzemski	6.50	3.25	2.00
	Panel 17	9.00	4.50	2.75
49	Steve Garvey	4.00	2.00	1.25
50	Amos Otis	.50	.25	.15
51	Rickey Reuschel	.50	.25	.15
	Panel 18	3.75	2.00	1.25
52	Rollie Fingers	1.25	.60	.40
53	Bob Watson	.40	.20	.12
54	John Ellis	.40	.20	.12
	Panel 19	9.50	4.75	2.75
55	Bob Bailey	.40	.20	.12
56	Rod Carew	4.00	2.00	1.25
57	Richie Hebner	.40	.20	.12
	Panel 20	15.00	7.50	4.50
58	Nolan Ryan	10.00	5.00	3.00
59	Reggie Smith	.50	.25	.15
60	Joe Coleman	.40	.20	.12
	Panel 21	10.00	5.00	3.00
61	Ron Cey	.50	.25	.15
62	Darrell Porter	.50	.25	.15
63	Steve Carlton	4.00	2.00	1.25
	Panel 22	2.50	1.25	.70
64	Gene Tenace	.40	.20	.12
65	Jose Cardenal	.40	.20	.12
66	Bill Lee	.40	.20	.12
	Panel 23	2.50	1.25	.70
67	Dave Lopes	.50	.25	.15
68	Wilbur Wood	.50	.25	.15
69	Steve Renko	.40	.20	.12
	Panel 24	3.00	1.50	.90
70	Joe Torre	.50	.25	.15
71	Ted Sizemore	.40	.20	.12
72	Bobby Grich	.50	.25	.15
	Panel 25	11.00	5.50	3.25
73	Chris Speier	.40	.20	.12
74	Bert Blyleven	.70	.35	.20
75	Tom Seaver	4.50	2.25	1.25
	Panel 26	2.50	1.25	.70
76	Nate Colbert	.40	.20	.12
77	Don Kessinger	.40	.20	.12
78	George Medich	.40	.20	.12
	Panel 27	30.00	15.00	9.00
79	Andy Messersmith	.70	.35	.20
80	Robin Yount	20.00	10.00	6.00
81	Al Oliver	1.50	.70	.45
	Panel 28	18.00	9.00	5.50
82	Bill Singer	.50	.25	.15
83	Johnny Bench	6.00	3.00	1.75
84	Gaylord Perry	3.00	1.50	.90
	Panel 29	5.00	2.50	1.50
85	Dave Kingman	1.25	.60	.40
86	Ed Herrmann	.50	.25	.15
87	Ralph Garr	.60	.30	.20
	Panel 30	23.00	11.50	7.00
88	Reggie Jackson	9.00	4.50	2.75
89a	Doug Radar (incorrect spelling)	2.00	1.00	.60
89b	Doug Rader (correct spelling)	2.00	1.00	.60
90	Elliott Maddox	.50	.25	.15
	Panel 31	3.50	1.75	1.00
91	Bill Russell	.60	.30	.20
92	John Mayberry	.50	.25	.15
93	Dave Cash	.50	.25	.15
	Panel 32	5.00	2.50	1.50
94	Jeff Burroughs	.60	.30	.20
95	Ted Simmons	1.25	.60	.40
96	Joe Decker	.50	.25	.15
	Panel 33	10.00	5.00	3.00
97	Bill Buckner	1.00	.50	.30
98	Bobby Darwin	.50	.25	.15
99	Phil Niekro	3.50	1.75	1.00
	Panel 34	3.00	1.50	.90
100	Mike Sundberg (Jim)	.50	.25	.15
101	Greg Gross	.40	.20	.12
102	Luis Tiant	.70	.35	.20
	Panel 35	2.50	1.25	.70
103	Glenn Beckert	.40	.20	.12
104	Hal McRae	.50	.25	.15
105	Mike Jorgensen	.40	.20	.12
	Panel 36	2.50	1.25	.70
106	Mike Hargrove	.40	.20	.12
107	Don Gullett	.40	.20	.12

		NR MT	EX	VG
108	Tito Fuentes	.40	.20	.12
	Panel 37	3.50	1.75	1.00
109	John Grubb	.40	.20	.12
110	Jim Kaat	.90	.45	.25
111	Felix Millan	.40	.20	.12
	Panel 38	2.50	1.25	.70
112	Don Money	.40	.20	.12
113	Rick Monday	.50	.25	.15
114	Dick Bosman	.40	.20	.12
	Panel 39	3.50	1.75	1.00
115	Roger Metzger	.40	.20	.12
116	Fergie Jenkins	.90	.45	.25
117	Dusky Baker	.50	.25	.15
	Panel 40	10.00	5.00	3.00
118	Billy Champion	.50	.25	.15
119	Bob Gibson	3.50	1.75	1.00
120	Bill Freehan	.80	.40	.25
	Panel 41	2.50	1.25	.70
121	Cesar Geronimo	.40	.20	.12
122	Jorge Orta	.40	.20	.12
123	Cleon Jones	.40	.20	.12
	Panel 42	10.50	5.25	3.25
124	Steve Busby	.40	.20	.12
125a	Bill Madlock (Pitcher)	2.00	1.00	.60
125b	Bill Madlock (Third Base)	2.00	1.00	.60
126	Jim Palmer	2.75	1.50	.80
	Panel 43	4.25	2.25	1.25
127	Tony Perez	1.00	.50	.30
128	Larry Hisle	.40	.20	.12
129	Rusty Staub	.70	.35	.20
	Panel 44	20.00	10.00	6.00
130	Hank Aaron	9.00	4.50	2.75
131	Rennie Stennett	.50	.25	.15
132	Rico Petrocelli	.70	.35	.20
	Panel 45	16.00	8.00	4.75
133	Mike Schmidt	6.00	3.00	1.75
134	Sparky Lyle	.50	.25	.15
135	Willie Stargell	3.00	1.50	.90
	Panel 46	7.00	3.50	2.00
136	Ken Henderson	.40	.20	.12
137	Willie Montanez	.40	.20	.12
138	Thurman Munson	2.50	1.25	.70
	Panel 47	2.50	1.25	.70
139	Richie Zisk	.40	.20	.12
140	Geo. Hendricks (Hendrick)	.50	.25	.15
141	Bobby Murcer	.50	.25	.15
	Panel 48	10.00	5.00	3.00
142	Lee May	.50	.25	.15
143	Carlton Fisk	1.00	.50	.30
144	Brooks Robinson	3.50	1.75	1.00
	Panel 49	2.50	1.25	.70
145	Bobby Bonds	.50	.25	.15
146	Gary Sutherland	.40	.20	.12
147	Oscar Gamble	.40	.20	.12
	Panel 50	6.00	3.00	1.75
148	Jim Hunter	2.50	1.25	.70
149	Tug McGraw	.50	.25	.15
150	Dave McNally	.50	.25	.15

1975 Hostess Twinkies

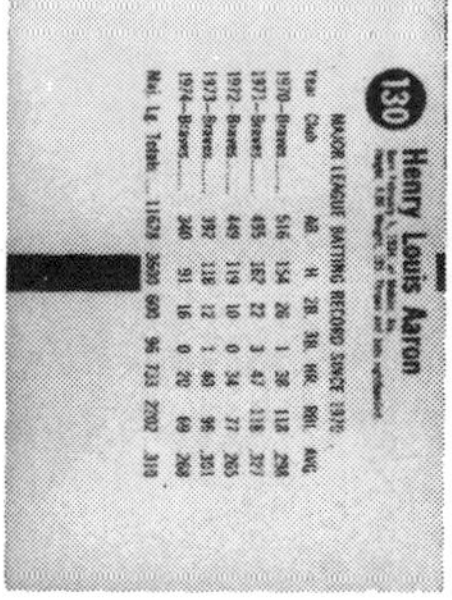

Believed to have been issued only in the Western states, and on a limited basis at that, the 1975 Hostess Twinkie set features 60 of the cards from the "regular" Hostess set of that year. The cards were issued one per pack with the popular snack cake. Card #'s 1-36 are a direct pick-up from the Hostess set, while the remaining 24 cards in the set were selected from the more popular names in the

remainder of the Hostess issue - with an emphasis on West Coast players. Thus, after card #36, the '75 Twinkie cards are skip-numbered from 40-136. In identical 2-1/4" by 3-1/4" size, the Twinkie cards differ from the Hostess issue only in the presence of small black bars at top and bottom center of the back of the card. Values quoted are for full bottom panels.

		NR MT	EX	VG
Complete Set:		200.00	100.00	60.00
Common Player:		.90	.45	.25
1	Bobby Tolan	.90	.45	.25
2	Cookie Rojas	.90	.45	.25
3	Darrell Evans	2.00	1.00	.60
4	Sal Bando	1.25	.60	.40
5	Joe Morgan	5.00	2.50	1.50
6	Mickey Lolich	2.00	1.00	.60
7	Don Sutton	4.50	2.25	1.25
8	Bill Melton	.90	.45	.25
9	Tim Foli	.90	.45	.25
10	Joe Lahoud	.90	.45	.25
11	Bert Hooten (Burt Hooton)	1.25	.60	.40
12	Paul Blair	.90	.45	.25
13	Jim Barr	.90	.45	.25
14	Toby Harrah	.90	.45	.25
15	John Milner	.90	.45	.25
16	Ken Holtzman	1.00	.50	.30
17	Cesar Cedeno	1.25	.60	.40
18	Dwight Evans	3.00	1.50	.90
19	Willie McCovey	7.00	3.50	2.00
20	Tony Oliva	2.00	1.00	.60
21	Manny Sanguillen	.90	.45	.25
22	Mickey Rivers	.90	.45	.25
23	Lou Brock	6.50	3.25	2.00
24	Graig Nettles	3.00	1.50	.90
25	Jim Wynn	.90	.45	.25
26	George Scott	.90	.45	.25
27	Greg Luzinski	1.25	.60	.40
28	Bert Campaneris	1.25	.60	.40
29	Pete Rose	20.00	10.00	6.00
30	Buddy Bell	1.75	.90	.50
31	Gary Matthews	1.25	.60	.40
32	Fred Patek	.90	.45	.25
33	Mike Lum	.90	.45	.25
34	Ellie Rodriguez	.90	.45	.25
35	Milt May (photo actually Lee May)	1.25	.60	.40
36	Willie Horton	.90	.45	.25
40	Joe Rudi	1.25	.60	.40
43	Garry Maddox	.90	.45	.25
46	Dave Chalk	.90	.45	.25
49	Steve Garvey	10.00	5.00	3.00
52	Rollie Fingers	4.00	2.00	1.25
58	Nolan Ryan	12.00	6.00	3.50
61	Ron Cey	1.50	.70	.45
64	Gene Tenace	.90	.45	.25
65	Jose Cardenal	.90	.45	.25
67	Dave Lopes	1.25	.60	.40
68	Wilbur Wood	.90	.45	.25
73	Chris Speier	.90	.45	.25
77	Don Kessinger	.90	.45	.25
79	Andy Messersmith	.90	.45	.25
80	Robin Yount	20.00	10.00	6.00
82	Bill Singer	.90	.45	.25
103	Glenn Beckert	.90	.45	.25
110	Jim Kaat	2.50	1.25	.70
112	Don Money	.90	.45	.25
113	Rick Monday	1.25	.60	.40
122	Jorge Orta	.90	.45	.25
125	Bill Madlock	2.25	1.25	.70
130	Hank Aaron	15.00	7.50	4.50
136	Ken Henderson	.90	.45	.25

1976 Hostess

The second of five annual Hostess issues, the 1976 cards carried a "Bicentennial" color theme, with red, white and blue stripes at the bottom of the 2-1/4" by 3-1/4" cards. Like other Hostess issues, the cards were printed in panels of three as the bottom of family-size boxes of snack cake products. This leads to a degree of scarcity for some of the 150 cards in the set; those which were found on less-popular brands. A well-trimmed three-card panel measures 7-1/4" by 3-1/4" size. Some of the photos used in the 1976 Hostess set can also be found on Topps

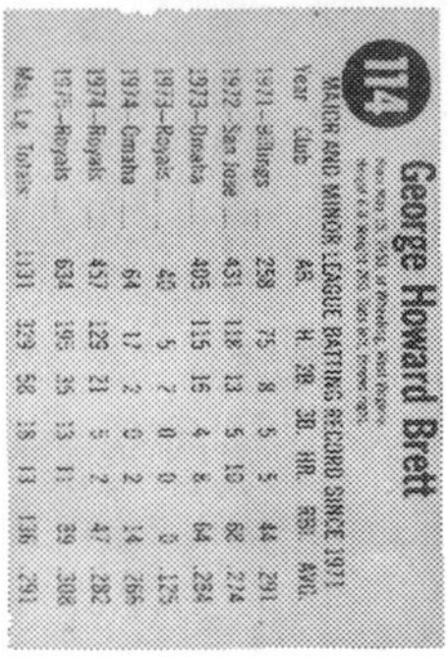

issues of the era.

		NR MT	EX	VG
Complete Panel Set:		400.00	200.00	120.00
Complete Singles Set:		225.00	112.00	67.00
Common Panel:		2.50	1.25	.70
Common Single Player:		.40	.20	.12
	Panel 1	11.75	6.00	3.50
1	Fred Lynn	1.25	.60	.40
2	Joe Morgan	2.00	1.00	.60
3	Phil Niekro	2.25	1.25	.70
	Panel 2	4.50	2.25	1.25
4	Gaylord Perry	1.75	.90	.50
5	Bob Watson	.40	.20	.12
6	Bill Freehan	.50	.25	.15
	Panel 3	6.50	3.25	2.00
7	Lou Brock	3.00	1.50	.90
8	Al Fitzmorris	.40	.20	.12
9	Rennie Stennett	.40	.20	.12
	Panel 4	9.00	4.50	2.75
10	Tony Oliva	.70	.35	.20
11	Robin Yount	10.00	5.00	3.00
12	Rick Manning	.40	.20	.12
	Panel 5	3.50	1.75	1.00
13	Bobby Grich	.50	.25	.15
14	Terry Forster	.40	.20	.12
15	Dave Kingman	.70	.35	.20
	Panel 6	7.00	3.50	2.00
16	Thurman Munson	2.50	1.25	.70
17	Rick Reuschel	.50	.25	.15
18	Bobby Bonds	.50	.25	.15
	Panel 7	9.50	4.75	2.75
19	Steve Garvey	4.00	2.00	1.25
20	Vida Blue	.50	.25	.15
21	Dave Rader	.40	.20	.12
	Panel 8	9.00	4.50	2.75
22	Johnny Bench	4.00	2.00	1.25
23	Luis Tiant	.50	.25	.15
24	Darrell Evans	.70	.35	.20
	Panel 9	2.50	1.25	.70
25	Larry Dierker	.40	.20	.12
26	Willie Horton	.50	.25	.15
27	John Ellis	.40	.20	.12
	Panel 10	3.00	1.50	.90
28	Al Cowens	.40	.20	.12
29	Jerry Reuss	.50	.25	.15
30	Reggie Smith	.50	.25	.15
	Panel 11	13.00	6.50	4.00
31	Bobby Darwin	.50	.25	.15
32	Fritz Peterson	.50	.25	.15
33	Rod Carew	6.00	3.00	1.75
	Panel 12	21.00	10.50	6.25
34	Carlos May	.50	.25	.15
35	Tom Seaver	6.00	3.00	1.75
36	Brooks Robinson	5.00	2.50	1.50
	Panel 13	2.50	1.25	.70
37	Jose Cardenal	.40	.20	.12
38	Ron Blomberg	.40	.20	.12
39	Lee Stanton	.40	.20	.12
	Panel 14	2.50	1.25	.70
40	Dave Cash	.40	.20	.12
41	John Montefusco	.40	.20	.12
42	Bob Tolan	.40	.20	.12
	Panel 15	2.50	1.25	.70
43	Carl Morton	.40	.20	.12
44	Rick Burleson	.50	.25	.15
45	Don Gullett	.40	.20	.12
	Panel 16	2.50	1.25	.70
46	Vern Ruhle	.40	.20	.12

		NR MT	EX	VG
47	Cesar Cedeno	.50	.25	.15
48	Toby Harrah	.50	.25	.15
	Panel 17	6.00	3.00	1.75
49	Willie Stargell	3.00	1.50	.90
50	Al Hrabosky	.40	.20	.12
51	Amos Otis	.50	.25	.15
	Panel 18	2.50	1.25	.70
52	Bud Harrelson	.50	.25	.15
53	Jim Hughes	.40	.20	.12
54	George Scott	.50	.25	.15
	Panel 19	9.50	4.75	2.75
55	Mike Vail	.50	.25	.15
56	Jim Palmer	4.00	2.00	1.25
57	Jorge Orta	.80	.40	.25
	Panel 20	3.50	1.75	1.00
58	Chris Chambliss	.80	.40	.25
59	Dave Chalk	.50	.25	.15
60	Ray Burris	.50	.25	.15
	Panel 21	14.00	7.00	4.25
61	Bert Campaneris	.80	.40	.25
62	Gary Carter	6.00	3.00	1.75
63	Ron Cey	.90	.45	.25
	Panel 22	28.00	14.00	8.50
64	Carlton Fisk	2.00	1.00	.60
65	Marty Perez	.50	.25	.15
66	Pete Rose	10.00	5.00	3.00
	Panel 23	3.50	1.75	1.00
67	Roger Metzger	.50	.25	.15
68	Jim Sundberg	.60	.30	.20
69	Ron LeFlore	.60	.30	.20
	Panel 24	3.50	1.75	1.00
70	Ted Sizemore	.50	.25	.15
71	Steve Busby	.50	.25	.15
72	Manny Sanguillen	.50	.25	.15
	Panel 25	5.00	2.50	1.50
73	Larry Hisle	.60	.30	.20
74	Pete Broberg	.50	.25	.15
75	Boog Powell	1.25	.60	.40
	Panel 26	6.50	3.25	2.00
76	Ken Singleton	.80	.40	.25
77	Rich Gossage	2.00	1.00	.60
78	Jerry Grote	.50	.25	.15
	Panel 27	16.00	8.00	4.75
79	Nolan Ryan	12.00	6.00	3.50
80	Rick Monday	.70	.35	.20
81	Graig Nettles	1.25	.60	.40
	Panel 28	18.00	9.00	5.50
82	Chris Speier	.40	.20	.12
83	Dave Winfield	4.00	2.00	1.25
84	Mike Schmidt	6.00	3.00	1.75
	Panel 29	4.00	2.00	1.25
85	Buzz Capra	.40	.20	.12
86	Tony Perez	1.00	.50	.30
87	Dwight Evans	.90	.45	.25
	Panel 30	2.50	1.25	.70
88	Mike Hargrove	.40	.20	.12
89	Joe Coleman	.40	.20	.12
90	Greg Gross	.40	.20	.12
	Panel 31	2.50	1.25	.70
91	John Mayberry	.40	.20	.12
92	John Candelaria	.50	.25	.15
93	Bake McBride	.40	.20	.12
	Panel 32	15.00	7.50	4.50
94	Hank Aaron	7.00	3.50	2.00
95	Buddy Bell	.50	.25	.15
96	Steve Braun	.40	.20	.12
	Panel 33	2.50	1.25	.70
97	Jon Matlack	.40	.20	.12
98	Lee May	.50	.25	.15
99	Wilbur Wood	.50	.25	.15
	Panel 34	4.00	2.00	1.25
100	Bill Madlock	.90	.45	.25
101	Frank Tanana	.50	.25	.15
102	Mickey Rivers	.50	.25	.15
	Panel 35	3.75	2.00	1.25
103	Mike Ivie	.40	.20	.12
104	Rollie Fingers	1.25	.60	.40
105	Dave Lopes	.50	.25	.15
	Panel 36	3.50	1.75	1.00
106	George Foster	.90	.45	.25
107	Denny Doyle	.40	.20	.12
108	Earl Williams	.40	.20	.12
	Panel 37	2.50	1.25	.70
109	Tom Veryzer	.40	.20	.12
110	J.R. Richard	.50	.25	.15
111	Jeff Burroughs	.40	.20	.12
	Panel 38	14.00	7.00	4.25
112	Al Oliver	.90	.45	.25
113	Ted Simmons	.80	.40	.25
114	George Brett	5.00	2.50	1.50
	Panel 39	3.00	1.50	.90

		NR MT	EX	VG
115	Frank Duffy	.40	.20	.12
116	Bert Blyleven	.80	.40	.25
117	Darrell Porter	.50	.25	.15
	Panel 40	2.50	1.25	.70
118	Don Baylor	.70	.35	.20
119	Bucky Dent	.50	.25	.15
120	Felix Millan	.40	.20	.12
	Panel 41	2.50	1.25	.70
121	Mike Cuellar	.50	.25	.15
122	Gene Tenace	.40	.20	.12
123	Bobby Murcer	.50	.25	.15
	Panel 42	7.00	3.50	2.00
124	Willie McCovey	3.00	1.50	.90
125	Greg Luzinski	.50	.25	.15
126	Larry Parrish	.50	.25	.15
	Panel 43	10.00	5.00	3.00
127	Jim Rice	4.00	2.00	1.25
128	Dave Concepcion	.50	.25	.15
129	Jim Wynn	.50	.25	.15
	Panel 44	2.50	1.25	.70
130	Tom Grieve	.40	.20	.12
131	Mike Cosgrove	.40	.20	.12
132	Dan Meyer	.40	.20	.12
	Panel 45	5.00	2.50	1.50
133	Dave Parker	1.50	.70	.45
134	Don Kessinger	.40	.20	.12
135	Hal McRae	.50	.25	.15
	Panel 46	4.00	2.00	1.25
136	Don Money	.70	.35	.20
137	Dennis Eckersley	.90	.45	.25
138	Fergie Jenkins	.80	.40	.25
	Panel 47	4.00	2.00	1.25
139	Mike Torrez	.40	.20	.12
140	Jerry Morales	.40	.20	.12
141	Jim Hunter	1.25	.60	.40
	Panel 48	2.50	1.25	.70
142	Gary Matthews	.50	.25	.15
143	Randy Jones	.40	.20	.12
144	Mike Jorgensen	.40	.20	.12
	Panel 49	13.00	6.50	4.00
145	Larry Bowa	.60	.30	.20
146	Reggie Jackson	5.00	2.50	1.50
147	Steve Yeager	.40	.20	.12
	Panel 50	15.00	7.50	4.50
148	Dave May	.40	.20	.12
149	Carl Yastrzemski	6.50	3.25	2.00
150	Cesar Geronimo	.40	.20	.12

1976 Hostess Twinkies

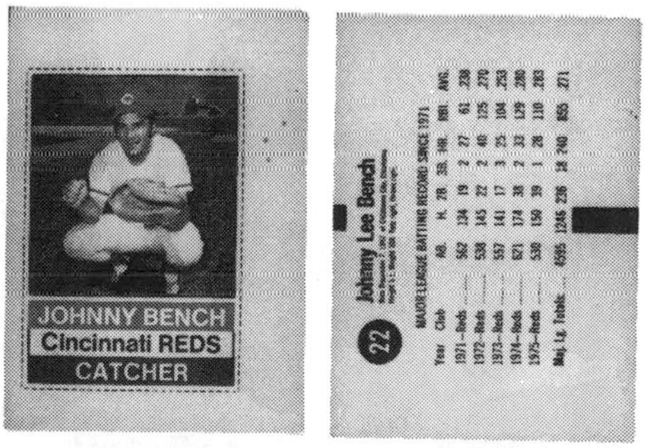

The 60 cards in this regionally-issued (West Coast only) set closely parallel the first 60 cards in the numerical sequence of the "regular" 1976 Hostess issue. The singular difference is the appearance on the back of a black band toward the center of the card at top and bottom. Also unlike the three-card panels of the regular Hostess issue, the 2-1/4" by 3-1/4" Twinkie cards were issued singly, as the cardboard stiffener for the cellophane-wrapped snack cakes. Values quoted are for complete bottom panels.

		NR MT	EX	VG
Complete Set:		200.00	100.00	60.00
Common Player:		.90	.45	.25
1	Fred Lynn	3.00	1.50	.90

		NR MT	EX	VG
2	Joe Morgan	5.00	2.50	1.50
3	Phil Niekro	4.50	2.25	1.25
4	Gaylord Perry	5.00	2.50	1.50
5	Bob Watson	.90	.45	.25
6	Bill Freehan	1.25	.60	.40
7	Lou Brock	7.00	3.50	2.00
8	Al Fitzmorris	.90	.45	.25
9	Rennie Stennett	.90	.45	.25
10	Tony Oliva	2.00	1.00	.60
11	Robin Yount	12.00	6.00	3.50
12	Rick Manning	.90	.45	.25
13	Bobby Grich	1.25	.60	.40
14	Terry Forster	.90	.45	.25
15	Dave Kingman	2.00	1.00	.60
16	Thurman Munson	6.50	3.25	2.00
17	Rick Reuschel	1.25	.60	.40
18	Bobby Bonds	1.25	.60	.40
19	Steve Garvey	10.00	5.00	3.00
20	Vida Blue	1.75	.90	.50
21	Dave Rader	.90	.45	.25
22	Johnny Bench	10.00	5.00	3.00
23	Luis Tiant	1.50	.70	.45
24	Darrell Evans	2.00	1.00	.60
25	Larry Dierker	.90	.45	.25
26	Willie Horton	.90	.45	.25
27	John Ellis	.90	.45	.25
28	Al Cowens	.90	.45	.25
29	Jerry Reuss	1.25	.60	.40
30	Reggie Smith	1.25	.60	.40
31	Bobby Darwin	.90	.45	.25
32	Fritz Peterson	.90	.45	.25
33	Rod Carew	10.00	5.00	3.00
34	Carlos May	.90	.45	.25
35	Tom Seaver	10.00	5.00	3.00
36	Brooks Robinson	9.00	4.50	2.75
37	Jose Cardenal	.90	.45	.25
38	Ron Blomberg	.90	.45	.25
39	Lee Stanton	.90	.45	.25
40	Dave Cash	.90	.45	.25
41	John Montefusco	.90	.45	.25
42	Bob Tolan	.90	.45	.25
43	Carl Morton	.90	.45	.25
44	Rick Burleson	.90	.45	.25
45	Don Gullett	.90	.45	.25
46	Vern Ruhle	.90	.45	.25
47	Cesar Cedeno	1.25	.60	.40
48	Toby Harrah	.90	.45	.25
49	Willie Stargell	7.00	3.50	2.00
50	Al Hrabosky	.90	.45	.25
51	Amos Otis	.90	.45	.25
52	Bud Harrelson	.90	.45	.25
53	Jim Hughes	.90	.45	.25
54	George Scott	.90	.45	.25
55	Mike Vail	.90	.45	.25
56	Jim Palmer	7.00	3.50	2.00
57	Jorge Orta	.90	.45	.25
58	Chris Chambliss	1.25	.60	.40
59	Dave Chalk	.90	.45	.25
60	Ray Burris	.90	.45	.25

1977 Hostess

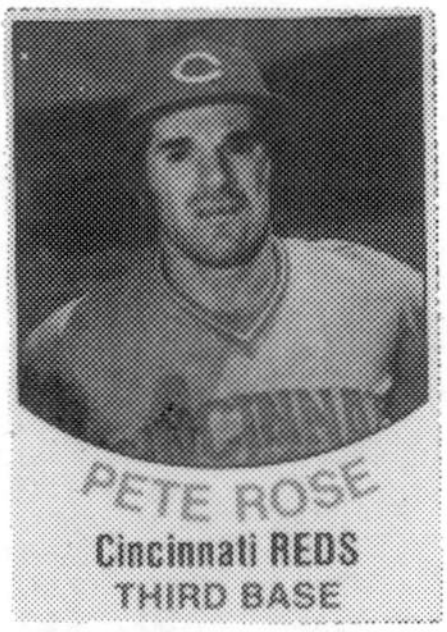

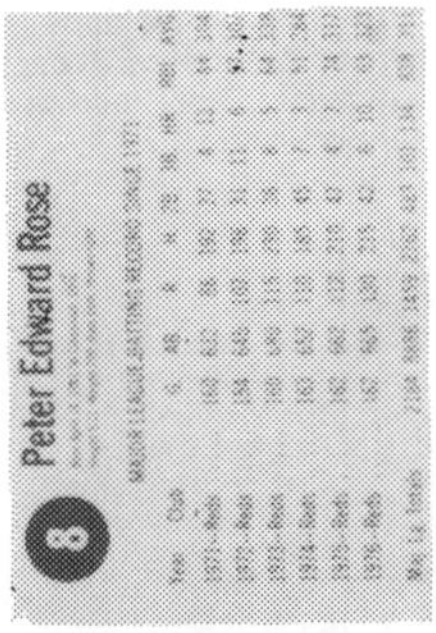

The third of five consecutive annual issues, the 1977 Hostess cards retained the same card size 2-1/4" by 3-1/4", set size - 150 cards, and mode of issue - three cards on a 7-1/4" by 3-1/4" panel, as the previous two efforts. Because they were issued as the bottom panel of snack cake boxes, and because some brands of Hostess products were more popular than others, certain cards in the set are scarcer than others.

		NR MT	EX	VG
Complete Panel Set:		350.00	175.00	105.00
Complete Singles Set:		225.00	112.00	70.00
Common Panel:		2.50	1.25	.70
Common Single Player:		.40	.20	.12
	Panel 1	20.00	10.00	6.00
1	Jim Palmer	3.00	1.50	.80
2	Joe Morgan	3.00	1.50	.80
3	Reggie Jackson	5.00	2.50	1.50
	Panel 2	23.00	11.50	7.00
4	Carl Yastrzemski	6.00	3.00	1.75
5	Thurman Munson	2.50	1.25	.70
6	Johnny Bench	4.00	2.00	1.25
	Panel 3	32.00	16.00	9.50
7	Tom Seaver	3.00	1.50	.90
8	Pete Rose	8.00	4.00	2.50
9	Rod Carew	4.00	2.00	1.25
	Panel 4	2.50	1.25	.70
10	Luis Tiant	.60	.30	.20
11	Phil Garner	.50	.25	.15
12	Sixto Lezcano	.40	.20	.12
	Panel 5	2.50	1.25	.70
13	Mike Torrez	.40	.20	.12
14	Dave Lopes	.50	.25	.15
15	Doug DeCinces	.50	.25	.15
	Panel 6	2.50	1.25	.70
16	Jim Spencer	.40	.20	.12
17	Hal McRae	.50	.25	.15
18	Mike Hargrove	.40	.20	.12
	Panel 7	4.50	2.25	1.25
19	Willie Montanez	.50	.25	.15
20	Roger Metzger	.50	.25	.15
21	Dwight Evans	1.50	.70	.45
	Panel 8	10.00	5.00	3.00
22	Steve Rogers	.50	.25	.15
23	Jim Rice	4.00	2.00	1.25
24	Pete Falcone	.50	.25	.15
	Panel 9	9.00	4.50	2.75
25	Greg Luzinski	.90	.45	.25
26	Randy Jones	.50	.25	.15
27	Willie Stargell	3.00	1.50	.90
	Panel 10	3.50	1.75	1.00
28	John Hiller	.50	.25	.15
29	Bobby Murcer	.70	.35	.20
30	Rick Monday	.70	.35	.20
	Panel 11	9.00	4.50	2.75
31	John Montefusco	.50	.25	.15
32	Lou Brock	4.00	2.00	1.25
33	Bill North	.50	.25	.15
	Panel 12	32.00	16.00	9.50
34	Robin Yount	8.00	4.00	2.50
35	Steve Garvey	5.00	2.50	1.50
36	George Brett	8.00	4.00	2.50
	Panel 13	3.50	1.75	1.00
37	Toby Harrah	.70	.35	.20
38	Jerry Royster	.50	.25	.15
39	Bob Watson	.60	.30	.20
	Panel 14	9.50	4.75	2.75
40	George Foster	.90	.45	.25
41	Gary Carter	3.50	1.75	1.00
42	John Denny	.40	.20	.12
	Panel 15	18.00	9.00	5.50
43	Mike Schmidt	5.00	2.50	1.50
44	Dave Winfield	3.75	2.00	1.25
45	Al Oliver	.90	.45	.25
	Panel 16	3.00	1.50	.90
46	Mark Fidrych	.60	.30	.20
47	Larry Herndon	.50	.25	.15
48	Dave Goltz	.40	.20	.12
	Panel 17	3.50	1.75	1.00
49	Jerry Morales	.40	.20	.12
50	Ron LeFlore	.50	.25	.15
51	Fred Lynn	.90	.45	.25
	Panel 18	3.50	1.75	1.00
52	Vida Blue	.50	.25	.15
53	Rick Manning	.40	.20	.12
54	Bill Buckner	.70	.35	.20
	Panel 19	2.50	1.25	.70
55	Lee May	.50	.25	.15
56	John Mayberry	.40	.20	.12
57	Darrel Chaney	.40	.20	.12
	Panel 20	3.50	1.75	1.00
58	Cesar Cedeno	.50	.25	.15
59	Ken Griffey	.50	.25	.15
60	Dave Kingman	.80	.40	.25
	Panel 21	3.50	1.75	1.00
61	Ted Simmons	.80	.40	.25

		NR MT	EX	VG
62	Larry Bowa	.50	.25	.15
63	Frank Tanana	.50	.25	.15
	Panel 22	2.50	1.25	.70
64	Jason Thompson	.40	.20	.12
65	Ken Brett	.40	.20	.12
66	Roy Smalley	.40	.20	.12
	Panel 23	2.50	1.25	.70
67	Ray Burris	.40	.20	.12
68	Rick Burleson	.40	.20	.12
69	Buddy Bell	.50	.25	.15
	Panel 24	5.00	2.50	1.50
70	Don Sutton	2.00	1.00	.60
71	Mark Belanger	.40	.20	.12
72	Dennis Leonard	.40	.20	.12
	Panel 25	5.00	2.50	1.50
73	Gaylord Perry	1.50	.70	.45
74	Dick Ruthven	.40	.20	.12
75	Jose Cruz	.50	.25	.15
	Panel 26	4.25	2.25	1.25
76	Cesar Geronimo	.40	.20	.12
77	Jerry Koosman	.50	.25	.15
78	Garry Templeton	.80	.40	.25
	Panel 27	15.00	7.50	4.50
79	Jim Hunter	1.25	.60	.40
80	John Candelaria	.50	.25	.15
81	Nolan Ryan	10.00	5.00	3.00
	Panel 28	2.50	1.25	.70
82	Rusty Staub	.50	.25	.15
83	Jim Barr	.40	.20	.12
84	Butch Wynegar	.50	.25	.15
	Panel 29	2.50	1.25	.70
85	Jose Cardenal	.40	.20	.12
86	Claudell Washington	.50	.25	.15
87	Bill Travers	.40	.20	.12
	Panel 30	2.50	1.25	.70
88	Rick Waits	.40	.20	.12
89	Ron Cey	.50	.25	.15
90	Al Bumbry	.40	.20	.12
	Panel 31	2.50	1.25	.70
91	Bucky Dent	.50	.25	.15
92	Amos Otis	.50	.25	.15
93	Tom Grieve	.40	.20	.12
	Panel 32	2.50	1.25	.70
94	Enos Cabell	.40	.20	.12
95	Dave Concepcion	.50	.25	.15
96	Felix Millan	.40	.20	.12
	Panel 33	2.50	1.25	.70
97	Bake McBride	.40	.20	.12
98	Chris Chambliss	.50	.25	.15
99	Butch Metzger	.40	.20	.12
	Panel 34	2.50	1.25	.70
100	Rennie Stennett	.40	.20	.12
101	Dave Roberts	.40	.20	.12
102	Lyman Bostock	.50	.25	.15
	Panel 35	3.50	1.75	1.00
103	Rick Reuschel	.50	.25	.15
104	Carlton Fisk	1.00	.50	.30
105	Jim Slaton	.40	.20	.12
	Panel 36	2.50	1.25	.70
106	Dennis Eckersley	.60	.30	.20
107	Ken Singleton	.50	.25	.15
108	Ralph Garr	.40	.20	.12
	Panel 37	8.00	4.00	2.50
109	Freddie Patek	.50	.25	.15
110	Jim Sundberg	.60	.30	.20
111	Phil Niekro	3.25	1.75	1.00
	Panel 38	3.50	1.75	1.00
112	J.R. Richard	.70	.35	.20
113	Gary Nolan	.50	.25	.15
114	Jon Matlack	.60	.30	.20
	Panel 39	20.00	10.00	6.00
115	Keith Hernandez	4.00	2.00	1.25
116	Graig Nettles	.70	.35	.20
117	Steve Carlton	4.50	2.25	1.25
	Panel 40	6.50	3.25	2.00
118	Bill Madlock	1.50	.70	.45
119	Jerry Reuss	.80	.40	.25
120	Aurelio Rodriguez	.50	.25	.15
	Panel 41	3.50	1.75	1.00
121	Dan Ford	.50	.25	.15
122	Ray Fosse	.50	.25	.15
123	George Hendrick	.70	.35	.20
	Panel 42	2.50	1.25	.70
124	Alan Ashby	.40	.20	.12
125	Joe Lis	.40	.20	.12
126	Sal Bando	.50	.25	.15
	Panel 43	4.00	2.00	1.25
127	Richie Zisk	.50	.25	.15
128	Rich Gossage	.90	.45	.25
129	Don Baylor	.60	.30	.20
	Panel 44	2.50	1.25	.70
130	Dave McKay	.40	.20	.12
131	Bob Grich	.50	.25	.15
132	Dave Pagan	.40	.20	.12
	Panel 45	2.50	1.25	.70
133	Dave Cash	.40	.20	.12
134	Steve Braun	.40	.20	.12
135	Dan Meyer	.40	.20	.12
	Panel 46	4.25	2.25	1.25
136	Bill Stein	.40	.20	.12
137	Rollie Fingers	1.50	.70	.45
138	Brian Downing	.50	.25	.15
	Panel 47	2.50	1.25	.70
139	Bill Singer	.40	.20	.12
140	Doyle Alexander	.50	.25	.15
141	Gene Tenace	.40	.20	.12
	Panel 48	2.50	1.25	.70
142	Gary Matthews	.50	.25	.15
143	Don Gullett	.40	.20	.12
144	Wayne Garland	.40	.20	.12
	Panel 49	2.50	1.25	.70
145	Pete Broberg	.40	.20	.12
146	Joe Rudi	.50	.25	.15
147	Glenn Abbott	.40	.20	.12
	Panel 50	2.50	1.25	.70
148	George Scott	.50	.25	.15
149	Bert Campaneris	.50	.25	.15
150	Andy Messersmith	.50	.25	.15

1977 Hostess Twinkies

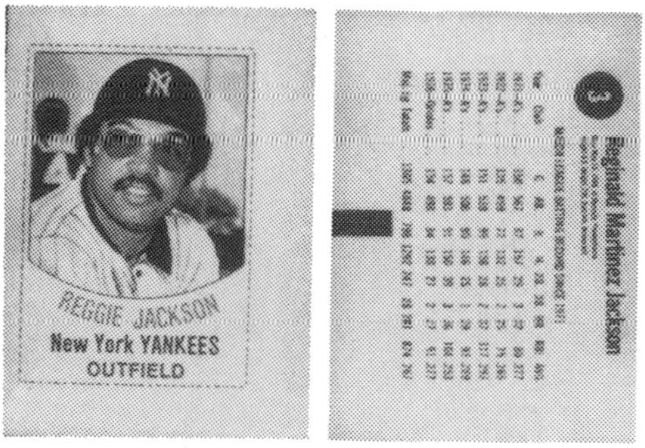

The 1977 Hostess Twinkie issue, at 150 different cards, is the largest of the single-panel Twinkie sets. It is also the most obscure. The cards, which measure 2-1/4" by 3-1/4", but are part of a larger panel, were found not only with Twinkies, but with Hostess Cupcakes as well. Card #'s 1-30 and 111-150 are Twinkies panels and #'s 31-135 are Cupcakes panels. Complete Cupcakes panels are approximately 2-1/4" by 4-1/2" in size, while complete Twinkies panels measure 3-1/8" by 4-1/4". The photos used in the set are identical to those in the 1977 Hostess three-card panel set. The main difference is the appearance of a black band at the center of the card back. The values quoted in the checklist that follows are for complete bottom panels.

		NR MT	EX	VG
Complete Set:		300.00	150.00	90.00
Common Player:		.80	.40	.25
1	Jim Palmer	6.00	3.00	1.75
2	Joe Morgan	4.00	2.00	1.25
3	Reggie Jackson	10.00	5.00	3.00
4	Carl Yastrzemski	12.00	6.00	3.50
5	Thurman Munson	5.00	2.50	1.50
6	Johnny Bench	8.00	4.00	2.50
7	Tom Seaver	7.00	3.50	2.00
8	Pete Rose	15.00	7.50	4.50
9	Rod Carew	8.00	4.00	2.50
10	Luis Tiant	1.00	.50	.30
11	Phil Garner	.80	.40	.25
12	Sixto Lezcano	.80	.40	.25
13	Mike Torrez	.80	.40	.25
14	Dave Lopes	1.00	.50	.30
15	Doug DeCinces	1.00	.50	.30
16	Jim Spencer	.80	.40	.25
17	Hal McRae	1.00	.50	.30

		NR MT	EX	VG
18	Mike Hargrove	.80	.40	.25
19	Willie Montanez	.80	.40	.25
20	Roger Metzger	.80	.40	.25
21	Dwight Evans	2.00	1.00	.60
22	Steve Rogers	.80	.40	.25
23	Jim Rice	6.00	3.00	1.75
24	Pete Falcone	.80	.40	.25
25	Greg Luzinski	1.50	.70	.45
26	Randy Jones	.80	.40	.25
27	Willie Stargell	6.00	3.00	1.75
28	John Hiller	.80	.40	.25
29	Bobby Murcer	1.25	.60	.40
30	Rick Monday	1.00	.50	.30
31	John Montefusco	.80	.40	.25
32	Lou Brock	6.00	3.00	1.75
33	Bill North	.80	.40	.25
34	Robin Yount	8.00	4.00	2.50
35	Steve Garvey	7.00	3.50	2.00
36	George Brett	10.00	5.00	3.00
37	Toby Harrah	.80	.40	.25
38	Jerry Royster	.80	.40	.25
39	Bob Watson	1.00	.50	.30
40	George Foster	1.75	.90	.50
41	Gary Carter	7.00	3.50	2.00
42	John Denny	.80	.40	.25
43	Mike Schmidt	9.00	4.50	2.75
44	Dave Winfield	7.00	3.50	2.00
45	Al Oliver	1.75	.90	.50
46	Mark Fidrych	1.50	.70	.45
47	Larry Herndon	1.00	.50	.30
48	Dave Goltz	.80	.40	.25
49	Jerry Morales	.80	.40	.25
50	Ron LeFlore	1.00	.50	.30
51	Fred Lynn	1.75	.90	.50
52	Vida Blue	1.00	.50	.30
53	Rick Manning	.80	.40	.25
54	Bill Buckner	1.50	.70	.45
55	Lee May	1.00	.50	.30
56	John Mayberry	.80	.40	.25
57	Darrel Chaney	.80	.40	.25
58	Cesar Cedeno	1.25	.60	.40
59	Ken Griffey	1.25	.60	.40
60	Dave Kingman	1.75	.90	.50
61	Ted Simmons	1.50	.70	.45
62	Larry Bowa	1.25	.60	.40
63	Frank Tanana	1.00	.50	.30
64	Jason Thompson	.80	.40	.25
65	Ken Brett	.80	.40	.25
66	Roy Smalley	.80	.40	.25
67	Ray Burris	.80	.40	.25
68	Rick Burleson	.80	.40	.25
69	Buddy Bell	1.25	.60	.40
70	Don Sutton	3.50	1.75	1.00
71	Mark Belanger	.80	.40	.25
72	Dennis Leonard	.80	.40	.25
73	Gaylord Perry	4.00	2.00	1.25
74	Dick Ruthven	.80	.40	.25
75	Jose Cruz	1.25	.60	.40
76	Cesar Geronimo	.80	.40	.25
77	Jerry Koosman	1.25	.60	.40
78	Garry Templeton	2.50	1.25	.70
79	Jim Hunter	4.00	2.00	1.25
80	John Candelaria	1.00	.50	.30
81	Nolan Ryan	10.00	5.00	3.00
82	Rusty Staub	1.50	.70	.45
83	Jim Barr	.80	.40	.25
84	Butch Wynegar	1.00	.50	.30
85	Jose Cardenal	.80	.40	.25
86	Claudell Washington	1.00	.50	.30
87	Bill Travers	.80	.40	.25
88	Rick Waits	.80	.40	.25
89	Ron Cey	1.25	.60	.40
90	Al Bumbry	.80	.40	.25
91	Bucky Dent	1.00	.50	.30
92	Amos Otis	1.00	.50	.30
93	Tom Grieve	.80	.40	.25
94	Enos Cabell	.80	.40	.25
95	Dave Concepcion	1.25	.60	.40
96	Felix Millan	.80	.40	.25
97	Bake McBride	.80	.40	.25
98	Chris Chambliss	1.00	.50	.30
99	Butch Metzger	.80	.40	.25
100	Rennie Stennett	.80	.40	.25
101	Dave Roberts	.80	.40	.25
102	Lyman Bostock	1.00	.50	.30
103	Rick Reuschel	1.00	.50	.30
104	Carlton Fisk	2.25	1.25	.70
105	Jim Slaton	.80	.40	.25
106	Dennis Eckersley	1.25	.60	.40
107	Ken Singleton	1.00	.50	.30
108	Ralph Garr	.80	.40	.25
109	Freddie Patek	.80	.40	.25
110	Jim Sundberg	.80	.40	.25
111	Phil Niekro	3.50	1.75	1.00
112	J. R. Richard	1.00	.50	.30
113	Gary Nolan	.80	.40	.25
114	Jon Matlack	.80	.40	.25
115	Keith Hernandez	5.00	2.50	1.50
116	Graig Nettles	2.00	1.00	.60
117	Steve Carlton	7.00	3.50	2.00
118	Bill Madlock	1.50	.70	.45
119	Jerry Reuss	1.00	.50	.30
120	Aurelio Rodriguez	.80	.40	.25
121	Dan Ford	.80	.40	.25
122	Ray Fosse	.80	.40	.25
123	George Hendrick	1.00	.50	.30
124	Alan Ashby	.80	.40	.25
125	Joe Lis	.80	.40	.25
126	Sal Bando	1.00	.50	.30
127	Richie Zisk	1.00	.50	.30
128	Rich Gossage	1.75	.90	.50
129	Don Baylor	1.50	.70	.45
130	Dave McKay	.80	.40	.25
131	Bob Grich	1.00	.50	.30
132	Dave Pagan	.80	.40	.25
133	Dave Cash	.80	.40	.25
134	Steve Braun	.80	.40	.25
135	Dan Meyer	.80	.40	.25
136	Bill Stein	.80	.40	.25
137	Rollie Fingers	3.00	1.50	.90
138	Brian Downing	1.00	.50	.30
139	Bill Singer	.80	.40	.25
140	Doyle Alexander	1.00	.50	.30
141	Gene Tenace	1.00	.50	.30
142	Gary Matthews	1.00	.50	.30
143	Don Gullett	.80	.40	.25
144	Wayne Garland	.80	.40	.25
145	Pete Broberg	.80	.40	.25
146	Joe Rudi	1.00	.50	.30
147	Glenn Abbott	.80	.40	.25
148	George Scott	1.00	.50	.30
149	Bert Campaneris	1.25	.60	.40
150	Andy Messersmith	1.00	.50	.30

1978 Hostess

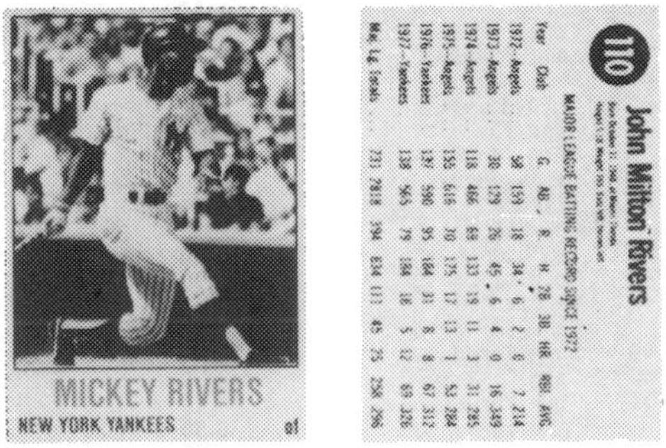

Other than the design on the front of the card, there was little different about the 1978 Hostess cards from the three years' issues which had preceded it, or the one which followed. The 2-1/4" by 3-1/4" cards were printed in panels of three (7-1/4" by 3-1/4") as the bottom of family-sized boxes of snake cakes. The 1978 set was again complete at 150 cards. Like other years of Hostess issues, there are scarcities within the 1978 set that are the result of those panels having been issued with less-popular brands of snack cakes.

		NR MT	EX	VG
Complete Panel:		325.00	162.00	97.00
Complete Singles Set:		225.00	112.00	70.00
Common Panel:		2.50	1.25	.70
Common Single Player:		.40	.20	.12
	Panel 1	4.00	2.00	1.25
1	Butch Hobson	.40	.20	.12
2	George Foster	.90	.45	.25
3	Bob Forsch	.50	.25	.15
	Panel 2	5.00	2.50	1.50

		NR MT	EX	VG
4	Tony Perez	1.00	.50	.30
5	Bruce Sutter	.90	.45	.25
6	Hal McRae	.50	.25	.15
	Panel 3	6.00	3.00	1.75
7	Tommy John	1.50	.70	.45
8	Greg Luzinski	.50	.25	.15
9	Enos Cabell	.40	.20	.12
	Panel 4	7.00	3.50	2.00
10	Doug DeCinces	.50	.25	.15
11	Willie Stargell	3.00	1.50	.90
12	Ed Halicki	.40	.20	.12
	Panel 5	2.50	1.25	.70
13	Larry Hisle	.40	.20	.12
14	Jim Slaton	.40	.20	.12
15	Buddy Bell	.50	.25	.15
	Panel 6	2.50	1.25	.70
16	Earl Williams	.40	.20	.12
17	Glenn Abbott	.40	.20	.12
18	Dan Ford	.40	.20	.12
	Panel 7	2.50	1.25	.70
19	Gary Mathews	.50	.25	.15
20	Eric Soderholm	.40	.20	.12
21	Bump Wills	.40	.20	.12
	Panel 8	7.00	3.50	2.00
22	Keith Hernandez	2.50	1.25	.70
23	Dave Cash	.40	.20	.12
24	George Scott	.50	.25	.15
	Panel 9	15.00	7.50	4.50
25	Ron Guidry	1.50	.70	.45
26	Dave Kingman	.80	.40	.25
27	George Brett	7.00	3.50	2.00
	Panel 10	3.50	1.75	1.00
28	Bob Watson	.50	.25	.15
29	Bob Boone	.70	.35	.20
30	Reggie Smith	.70	.35	.20
	Panel 11	20.00	10.00	6.00
31	Eddie Murray	10.00	5.00	3.00
32	Gary Lavelle	.50	.25	.15
33	Rennie Stennett	.50	.25	.15
	Panel 12	3.50	1.75	1.00
34	Duane Kuiper	.50	.25	.15
35	Sixto Lezcano	.50	.25	.15
36	Dave Rozema	.50	.25	.15
	Panel 13	3.50	1.75	1.00
37	Butch Wynegar	.50	.25	.15
38	Mitchell Page	.50	.25	.15
39	Bill Stein	.50	.25	.15
	Panel 14	2.50	1.25	.70
40	Elliott Maddox	.40	.20	.12
41	Mike Hargrove	.40	.20	.12
42	Bobby Bonds	.50	.25	.15
	Panel 15	15.00	7.50	4.50
43	Garry Templeton	.80	.40	.25
44	Johnny Bench	4.00	2.00	1.25
45	Jim Rice	4.00	2.00	1.25
	Panel 16	13.00	6.50	4.00
46	Bill Buckner	.80	.40	.25
47	Reggie Jackson	5.00	2.50	1.50
48	Freddie Patek	.40	.20	.12
	Panel 17	8.50	4.25	2.50
49	Steve Carlton	3.50	1.75	1.00
50	Cesar Cedeno	.50	.25	.15
51	Steve Yeager	.40	.20	.12
	Panel 18	3.50	1.75	1.00
52	Phil Garner	.50	.25	.15
53	Lee May	.50	.25	.15
54	Darrell Evans	.70	.35	.20
	Panel 19	2.50	1.25	.70
55	Steve Kemp	.50	.25	.15
56	Dusty Baker	.50	.25	.15
57	Ray Fosse	.40	.20	.12
	Panel 20	2.50	1.25	.70
58	Manny Sanguillen	.40	.20	.12
59	Tom Johnson	.40	.20	.12
60	Lee Stanton	.40	.20	.12
	Panel 21	10.00	5.00	3.00
61	Jeff Burroughs	.40	.20	.12
62	Bobby Grich	.50	.25	.15
63	Dave Winfield	4.00	2.00	1.25
	Panel 22	3.50	1.75	1.00
64	Dan Driessen	.50	.25	.15
65	Ted Simmons	.80	.40	.25
66	Jerry Remy	.40	.20	.12
	Panel 23	2.50	1.25	.70
67	Al Cowens	.40	.20	.12
68	Sparky Lyle	.50	.25	.15
69	Manny Trillo	.50	.25	.15
	Panel 24	5.00	2.50	1.50
70	Don Sutton	1.50	.70	.45
71	Larry Bowa	.50	.25	.15
72	Jose Cruz	.50	.25	.15
	Panel 25	8.00	4.00	2.50
73	Willie McCovey	3.00	1.50	.90
74	Bert Blyleven	.70	.35	.20
75	Ken Singleton	.50	.25	.15
	Panel 26	2.50	1.25	.70
76	Bill North	.40	.20	.12
77	Jason Thompson	.40	.20	.12
78	Dennis Eckersley	.50	.25	.15
	Panel 27	2.50	1.25	.70
79	Jim Sundberg	.50	.25	.15
80	Jerry Koosman	.50	.25	.15
81	Bruce Bochte	.40	.20	.12
	Panel 28	15.00	7.50	4.50
82	George Hendrick	.50	.25	.15
83	Nolan Ryan	10.00	5.00	3.00
84	Roy Howell	.40	.20	.12
	Panel 29	5.50	2.75	1.75
85	Butch Metzger	.40	.20	.12
86	George Medich	.40	.20	.12
87	Joe Morgan	2.00	1.00	.60
	Panel 30	3.00	1.50	.90
88	Dennis Leonard	.50	.25	.15
89	Willie Randolph	.50	.25	.15
90	Bobby Murcer	.50	.25	.15
	Panel 31	3.00	1.50	.90
91	Rick Manning	.40	.20	.12
92	J.R. Richard	.50	.25	.15
93	Ron Cey	.60	.30	.20
	Panel 32	2.50	1.25	.70
94	Sal Bando	.50	.25	.15
95	Ron LeFlore	.50	.25	.15
96	Dave Goltz	.40	.20	.12
	Panel 33	2.50	1.25	.70
97	Dan Meyer	.40	.20	.12
98	Chris Chambliss	.50	.25	.15
99	Biff Pocoroba	.40	.20	.12
	Panel 34	2.50	1.25	.70
100	Oscar Gamble	.40	.20	.12
101	Frank Tanana	.50	.25	.15
102	Lenny Randle	.40	.20	.12
	Panel 35	2.50	1.25	.70
103	Tommy Hutton	.40	.20	.12
104	John Candelaria	.50	.25	.15
105	Jorge Orta	.40	.20	.12
	Panel 36	3.00	1.50	.90
106	Ken Reitz	.40	.20	.12
107	Bill Campbell	.40	.20	.12
108	Dave Concepcion	.70	.35	.20
	Panel 37	2.50	1.25	.70
109	Joe Ferguson	.40	.20	.12
110	Mickey Rivers	.50	.25	.15
111	Paul Splittorff	.40	.20	.12
	Panel 38	12.00	6.00	3.50
112	Davey Lopes	.50	.25	.15
113	Mike Schmidt	7.00	3.50	2.00
114	Joe Rudi	.50	.25	.15
	Panel 39	7.00	3.50	2.00
115	Milt May	.40	.20	.12
116	Jim Palmer	3.00	1.50	.90
117	Bill Madlock	.70	.35	.20
	Panel 40	2.50	1.25	.70
118	Roy Smalley	.40	.20	.12
119	Cecil Cooper	.50	.25	.15
120	Rick Langford	.40	.20	.12
	Panel 41	5.75	3.00	1.75
121	Ruppert Jones	.40	.20	.12
122	Phil Niekro	2.25	1.25	.70
123	Toby Harrah	.50	.25	.15
	Panel 42	2.50	1.25	.70
124	Chet Lemon	.50	.25	.15
125	Gene Tenace	.40	.20	.12
126	Steve Henderson	.40	.20	.12
	Panel 43	20.00	10.00	6.00
127	Mike Torrez	.40	.20	.12
128	Pete Rose	8.00	4.00	2.50
129	John Denny	.50	.25	.15
	Panel 44	4.00	2.00	1.25
130	Darrell Porter	.50	.25	.15
131	Rick Reuschel	.50	.25	.15
132	Graig Nettles	.90	.45	.25
	Panel 45	4.50	2.25	1.25
133	Garry Maddox	.50	.25	.15
134	Mike Flanagan	.50	.25	.15
135	Dave Parker	1.25	.60	.40
	Panel 46	12.00	6.00	3.50
136	Terry Whitfield	.40	.20	.12
137	Wayne Garland	.40	.20	.12
138	Robin Yount	8.00	4.00	2.50
	Panel 47	12.00	6.00	3.50
139	Gaylord Perry	2.50	1.25	.70
140	Rod Carew	4.00	2.00	1.25

		NR MT	EX	VG
141	Wayne Gross	.40	.20	.12
	Panel 48	5.00	2.50	1.50
142	Barry Bonnell	.40	.20	.12
143	Willie Montanez	.40	.20	.12
144	Rollie Fingers	1.75	.90	.50
	Panel 49	12.00	6.00	3.50
145	Bob Bailor	.40	.20	.12
146	Tom Seaver	3.50	1.75	1.00
147	Thurman Munson	2.50	1.25	.70
	Panel 50	8.00	4.00	2.50
148	Lyman Bostock	.50	.25	.15
149	Gary Carter	3.50	1.75	1.00
150	Ron Blomberg	.40	.20	.12

1979 Hostess

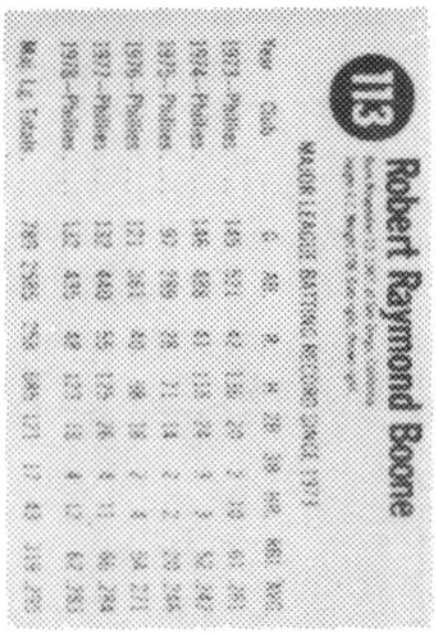

The last of five consecutive annual issues, the 1979 Hostess set retained the 150-card set size, 2-1/4" by 3-1/4" single-card size and 7-1/4" by 3-1/4" three-card panel format from the previous years. The cards were printed as the bottom panel on family-size boxes of Hostess snack cakes. Some panels, which were printed on less-popular brands, are somewhat scarcer today than the rest of the set. Like all Hostess issues, because the hobby was in a well-developed state at the time of issue, the 1979s survive today in complete panels and complete unused boxes, for collectors who like original packaging.

	NR MT	EX	VG
Complete Panel Set:	350.00	175.00	105.00
Complete Singles Set:	200.00	100.00	60.00
Common Panel:	2.50	1.25	.70
Common Single Player:	.40	.20	.12

		NR MT	EX	VG
	Panel 1	9.50	4.75	2.75
1	John Denny	.40	.20	.12
2	Jim Rice	4.00	2.00	1.25
3	Doug Bair	.40	.20	.12
	Panel 2	2.50	1.25	.70
4	Darrell Porter	.50	.25	.15
5	Ross Grimsley	.40	.20	.12
6	Bobby Murcer	.50	.25	.15
	Panel 3	18.00	9.00	5.50
7	Lee Mazzilli	.50	.25	.15
8	Steve Garvey	4.00	2.00	1.25
9	Mike Schmidt	5.00	2.50	1.50
	Panel 4	6.50	3.25	2.00
10	Terry Whitfield	.40	.20	.12
11	Jim Palmer	3.00	1.50	.90
12	Omar Moreno	.40	.20	.12
	Panel 5	2.50	1.25	.70
13	Duane Kuiper	.40	.20	.12
14	Mike Caldwell	.40	.20	.12
15	Steve Kemp	.50	.25	.15
	Panel 6	2.50	1.25	.70
16	Dave Goltz	.40	.20	.12
17	Mitchell Page	.40	.20	.12
18	Bill Stein	.40	.20	.12
	Panel 7	2.50	1.25	.70
19	Gene Tenace	.40	.20	.12
20	Jeff Burroughs	.40	.20	.12
21	Francisco Barrios	.40	.20	.12
	Panel 8	8.00	4.00	2.50
22	Mike Torrez	.40	.20	.12
23	Ken Reitz	.40	.20	.12
24	Gary Carter	3.50	1.75	1.00
	Panel 9	8.00	4.00	2.50
25	Al Hrabosky	.50	.25	.15
26	Thurman Munson	2.50	1.25	.70
27	Bill Buckner	.80	.40	.25
	Panel 10	5.00	2.50	1.50
28	Ron Cey	.90	.45	.25
29	J.R. Richard	.70	.35	.20
30	Greg Luzinski	.90	.45	.25
	Panel 11	5.00	2.50	1.50
31	Ed Ott	.50	.25	.15
32	Denny Martinez	.50	.25	.15
33	Darrell Evans	1.25	.60	.40
	Panel 12	2.50	1.25	.70
34	Ron LeFlore	.50	.25	.15
35	Rick Waits	.40	.20	.12
36	Cecil Cooper	.50	.25	.15
	Panel 13	9.50	4.75	2.75
37	Leon Roberts	.40	.20	.12
38	Rod Carew	4.00	2.00	1.25
39	John Henry Johnson	.40	.20	.12
	Panel 14	2.50	1.25	.70
40	Chet Lemon	.50	.25	.15
41	Craig Swan	.40	.20	.12
42	Gary Matthews	.50	.25	.15
	Panel 15	3.50	1.75	1.00
43	Lamar Johnson	.40	.20	.12
44	Ted Simmons	.80	.40	.25
45	Ken Griffey	.50	.25	.15
	Panel 16	4.00	2.00	1.25
46	Freddie Patek	.40	.20	.12
47	Frank Tanana	.50	.25	.15
48	Rich Gossage	1.25	.60	.40
	Panel 17	2.50	1.25	.70
49	Burt Hooton	.40	.20	.12
50	Ellis Valentine	.40	.20	.12
51	Ken Forsch	.40	.20	.12
	Panel 18	5.00	2.50	1.50
52	Bob Knepper	.50	.25	.15
53	Dave Parker	1.50	.70	.45
54	Doug DeCinces	.50	.25	.15
	Panel 19	12.00	6.00	3.50
55	Robin Yount	6.00	3.00	1.75
56	Rusty Staub	.80	.40	.25
57	Gary Alexander	.40	.20	.12
	Panel 20	2.50	1.25	.70
58	Julio Cruz	.40	.20	.12
59	Matt Keough	.40	.20	.12
60	Roy Smalley	.40	.20	.12
	Panel 21	10.00	5.00	3.00
61	Joe Morgan	2.50	1.25	.70
62	Phil Niekro	2.50	1.25	.70
63	Don Baylor	.80	.40	.25
	Panel 22	10.00	5.00	3.00
64	Dwight Evans	.90	.45	.25
65	Tom Seaver	4.00	2.00	1.25
66	George Hendrick	.50	.25	.15
	Panel 23	14.00	7.00	4.25
67	Rick Reuschel	.50	.25	.15
68	Geroge Brett	6.00	3.00	1.75
69	Lou Piniella	.80	.40	.25
	Panel 24	8.50	4.25	2.50
70	Enos Cabell	.40	.20	.12
71	Steve Carlton	3.50	1.75	1.00
72	Reggie Smith	.50	.25	.15
	Panel 25	4.00	2.00	1.25
73	Rick Dempsey	.50	.25	.15
74	Vida Blue	.80	.40	.25
75	Phil Garner	.70	.35	.20
	Panel 26	3.50	1.75	1.00
76	Rick Manning	.50	.25	.15
77	Mark Fidrych	.80	.40	.25
78	Mario Guerrero	.50	.25	.15
	Panel 27	5.00	2.50	1.50
79	Bob Stinson	.50	.25	.15
80	Al Oliver	1.25	.60	.40
81	Doug Flynn	.50	.25	.15
	Panel 28	6.00	3.00	1.75
82	John Mayberry	.40	.20	.12
83	Gaylord Perry	2.50	1.25	.70
84	Joe Rudi	.50	.25	.15
	Panel 29	3.50	1.75	1.00
85	Dave Concepcion	.70	.35	.20
86	John Candelaria	.50	.25	.15
87	Pete Vuckovich	.50	.25	.15
	Panel 30	5.00	2.50	1.50
88	Ivan DeJesus	.40	.20	.12
89	Ron Guidry	1.50	.70	.45
90	Hal McRae	.50	.25	.15
	Panel 31	5.50	2.75	1.75
91	Cesar Cedeno	.50	.25	.15

		NR MT	EX	VG
92	Don Sutton	2.00	1.00	.60
93	Andre Thornton	.50	.25	.15
	Panel 32	2.50	1.25	.70
94	Roger Erickson	.40	.20	.12
95	Larry Hisle	.40	.20	.12
96	Jason Thompson	.40	.20	.12
	Panel 33	7.50	3.75	2.25
97	Jim Sundberg	.50	.25	.15
98	Bob Horner	3.00	1.50	.90
99	Ruppert Jones	.40	.20	.12
	Panel 34	20.00	10.00	6.00
100	Willie Montanez	.40	.20	.12
101	Nolan Ryan	8.00	4.00	2.50
102	Ozzie Smith	12.00	6.00	3.50
	Panel 35	7.50	3.75	2.25
103	Eric Soderholm	.40	.20	.12
104	Willie Stargell	3.00	1.50	.90
105	Bob Bailor	.40	.20	.12
	Panel 36	9.00	4.50	2.75
106	Carlton Fisk	1.25	.60	.40
107	George Foster	.90	.45	.25
108	Keith Hernandez	2.50	1.25	.70
	Panel 37	4.00	2.00	1.25
109	Dennis Leonard	.50	.25	.15
110	Graig Nettles	.90	.45	.25
111	Jose Cruz	.50	.25	.15
	Panel 38	3.50	1.75	1.00
112	Bobby Grich	.50	.25	.15
113	Bob Boone	.50	.25	.15
114	Dave Lopes	.50	.25	.15
	Panel 39	15.00	7.50	4.50
115	Eddie Murray	4.50	2.25	1.25
116	Jack Clark	.90	.45	.25
117	Lou Whitaker	.50	.25	.15
	Panel 40	10.00	5.00	3.00
118	Miguel Dilone	.40	.20	.12
119	Sal Bando	.50	.25	.15
120	Reggie Jackson	4.50	2.25	1.25
	Panel 41	14.00	7.00	4.25
121	Dale Murphy	7.00	3.50	2.00
122	Jon Matlack	.40	.20	.12
123	Bruce Bochte	.40	.20	.12
	Panel 42	9.00	4.50	2.75
124	John Stearns	.40	.20	.12
125	Dave Winfield	3.50	1.75	1.00
126	Jorge Orta	.40	.20	.12
	Panel 43	9.00	4.50	2.75
127	Garry Templeton	.70	.35	.20
128	Johnny Bench	4.00	2.00	1.25
129	Butch Hobson	.40	.20	.12
	Panel 44	4.50	2.25	1.25
130	Bruce Sutter	1.25	.60	.40
131	Bucky Dent	.50	.25	.15
132	Amos Otis	.50	.25	.15
	Panel 45	3.50	1.75	1.00
133	Bert Blyleven	.70	.35	.20
134	Larry Bowa	.50	.25	.15
135	Ken Singleton	.50	.25	.15
	Panel 46	3.50	1.75	1.00
136	Sixto Lezcano	.40	.20	.12
137	Roy Howell	.40	.20	.12
138	Bill Madlock	.80	.40	.25
	Panel 47	2.50	1.25	.70
139	Dave Revering	.40	.20	.12
140	Richie Zisk	.50	.25	.15
141	Butch Wynegar	.50	.25	.15
	Panel 48	18.00	9.00	5.50
142	Alan Ashby	.40	.20	.12
143	Sparky Lyle	.50	.25	.15
144	Pete Rose	8.00	4.00	2.50
	Panel 49	4.00	2.00	1.25
145	Dennis Eckersley	.60	.30	.20
146	Dave Kingman	.80	.40	.25
147	Buddy Bell	.60	.30	.20
	Panel 50	2.50	1.25	.70
148	Mike Hargrove	.40	.20	.12
149	Jerry Koosman	.50	.25	.15
150	Toby Harrah	.50	.25	.15

1985 Hostess Braves

After a five-year hiatus, Hostess returned to the production of baseball cards in 1985 with an Atlanta Braves team set. The 22 cards in the set were printed by Topps and inserted into packages of snack cake products, three cello-wrapped player cards and a header card per box. The 2-1/2" by 3-1/2" cards

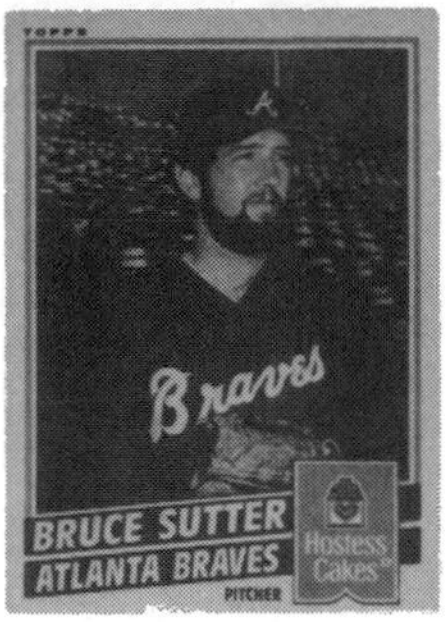

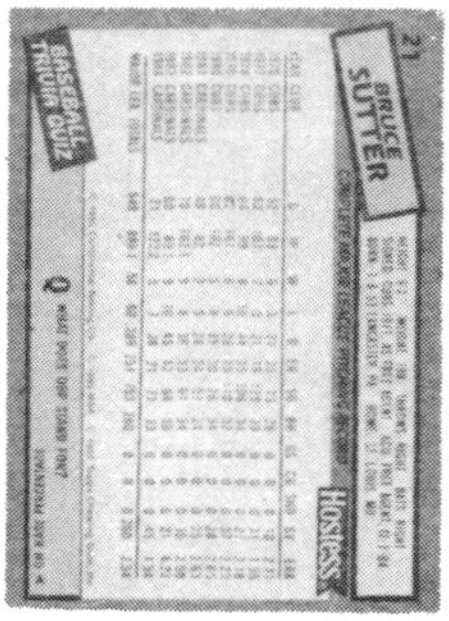

share a common back design with the regular-issue Topps cards of 1985.

		MT	NR MT	EX
Complete Set:		7.00	5.25	2.75
Common Player:		.35	.25	.14
1	Eddie Haas	.35	.25	.14
2	Len Barker	.35	.25	.14
3	Steve Bedrosian	.50	.40	.20
4	Bruce Benedict	.35	.25	.14
5	Rick Camp	.35	.25	.14
6	Rick Cerone	.35	.25	.14
7	Chris Chambliss	.40	.30	.15
8	Terry Forster	.35	.25	.14
9	Gene Garber	.35	.25	.14
10	Albert Hall	.35	.25	.14
11	Bob Horner	.50	.40	.20
12	Glenn Hubbard	.35	.25	.14
13	Brad Komminsk	.35	.25	.14
14	Rick Mahler	.40	.30	.15
15	Craig McMurtry	.35	.25	.14
16	Dale Murphy	2.00	1.50	.80
17	Ken Oberkfell	.40	.30	.15
18	Pascual Perez	.40	.30	.15
19	Gerald Perry	.50	.40	.20
20	Rafael Ramirez	.35	.25	.14
21	Bruce Sutter	.70	.50	.30
22	Claudell Washington	.40	.30	.15
----	Header Card	.10	.08	.04

1987 Hostess Stickers

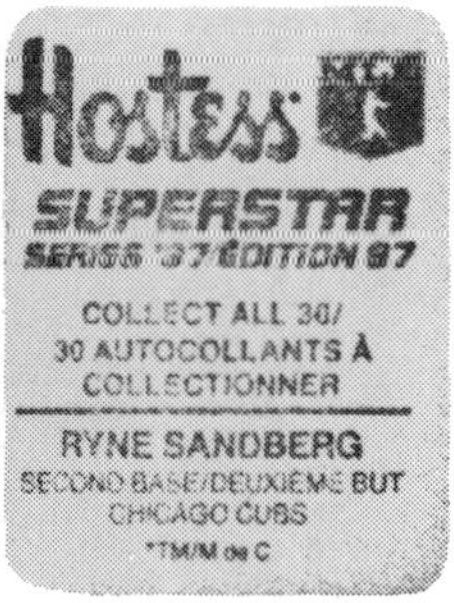

Hostess of Canada issued a 30-card set of stickers in specially marked bags of potato chips. One sticker, measuring 1-3/4" by 1-3/8" in size, was found in each bag. The stickers have full-color fronts with the player's name appearing in black type in a white band. The Hostess logo and the sticker number are also included on the fronts. The backs are written in both English and French and contain the player's name, position and team.

	MT	NR MT	EX
Complete Set:	25.00	18.50	10.00
Common Player:	.15	.11	.06

		MT	NR MT	EX
1	Jesse Barfield	.25	.20	.10
2	Ernie Whitt	.15	.11	.06
3	George Bell	1.00	.70	.40
4	Hubie Brooks	.15	.11	.06
5	Tim Wallach	.25	.20	.10
6	Floyd Youmans	.15	.11	.06
7	Dale Murphy	1.50	1.25	.60
8	Ryne Sandberg	1.00	.70	.40
9	Eric Davis	2.00	1.50	.80
10	Mike Scott	.25	.20	.10
11	Fernando Valenzuela	.75	.60	.30
12	Gary Carter	1.00	.70	.40
13	Mike Schmidt	1.50	1.25	.60
14	Tony Pena	.15	.11	.06
15	Ozzie Smith	.60	.45	.25
16	Tony Gwynn	1.25	.90	.50
17	Mike Krukow	.15	.11	.06
18	Eddie Murray	1.25	.90	.50
19	Wade Boggs	1.75	1.25	.70
20	Wally Joyner	2.00	1.50	.80
21	Harold Baines	.25	.20	.10
22	Brook Jacoby	.25	.20	.10
23	Lou Whitaker	.50	.40	.20
24	George Brett	1.50	1.25	.60
25	Robin Yount	.75	.60	.30
26	Kirby Puckett	1.25	.90	.50
27	Don Mattingly	2.50	2.00	1.00
28	Jose Canseco	3.00	2.25	1.25
29	Phil Bradley	.25	.20	.10
30	Pete O'Brien	.15	.11	.06

1988 Hostess Potato Chips Expos

The Expos and Blue Jays are showcased in this set of 24 discs (1-1/2" diameter). Full-color head shots are framed in white, surrounded by red stars. A yellow-banner "1988 Collectors Edition" label is printed (English and French) beneath the photo, followed by the player's name in black. Numbered disc backs are bilingual, blue and white, and include player name and stats. This set was distributed inside Hostess potato chip packages sold in Canada.

		MT	NR MT	EX
Complete Panel Set:		15.00	11.00	6.00
Complete Singles Set:		9.00	6.75	3.50
Common Panel:		.75	.60	.30
Common Single Player:		.25	.20	.10
	Panel	.90	.70	.35
1	Mitch Webster	.25	.20	.10
20	Lloyd Moseby	.40	.30	.15
	Panel	.90	.70	.35
2	Tim Burke	.25	.20	.10
23	Tom Henke	.40	.30	.15
	Panel	.80	.60	.30
3	Tom Foley	.25	.20	.10
13	Jim Clancy	.30	.25	.12
	Panel	.75	.60	.30
4	Herm Winningham	.25	.20	.10
14	Rance Mulliniks	.25	.20	.10
	Panel	1.25	.90	.50
5	Hubie Brooks	.40	.30	.15
24	Jimmy Key	.60	.45	.25
	Panel	1.50	1.25	.60
6	Mike Fitzgerald	.25	.20	.10
17	Dave Stieb	.60	.45	.25
	Panel	2.25	1.75	.90
7	Tim Wallach	.70	.50	.30
15	Fred McGriff	1.50	1.25	.60
	Panel	2.25	1.75	.90
8	Andres Galarraga	1.50	1.25	.60
21	Tony Fernandez	.70	.50	.30
	Panel	.80	.60	.30
9	Floyd Youmans	.30	.25	.12
18	Mark Eichhorn	.30	.25	.12
	Panel	1.50	1.25	.60
10	Neal Heaton	.25	.20	.10
19	Jesse Barfield	.70	.50	.30
	Panel	2.00	1.50	.80
11	Tim Raines	1.25	.90	.50
16	Ernie Whitt	.25	.20	.10
	Panel	1.75	1.25	.70
12	Casey Candaele	.25	.20	.10
22	George Bell	1.50	1.25	.60

1982 Hygrade Expos

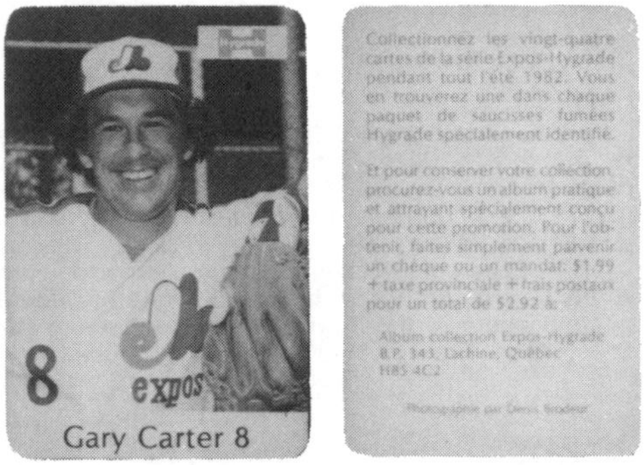

This 24-card Montreal Expos team set was the object of intense collector speculation when it was first issued. Single cello-wrapped cards were included in packages of Hygrade luncheon meat in the province of Quebec only. Until a mail-in offer for the complete set appeared later in the season, the set was selling for as high as $50. It remains a relatively scarce issue today. The 2" by 3" cards are printed on heavy paper, with round corners. Backs are printed only in French, and contain an offer for an album to house the set.

		MT	NR MT	EX
Complete Set:		45.00	34.00	18.00
Common Player:		1.00	.70	.40
Album:		8.00	6.00	3.25
0	Al Oliver	2.25	1.75	.90
4	Chris Speier	1.00	.70	.40
5	John Milner	1.00	.70	.40
6	Jim Fanning	1.00	.70	.40
8	Gary Carter	7.00	5.25	2.75
10	Andre Dawson	5.00	3.75	2.00
11	Frank Tavaras (Taveras)	1.00	.70	.40
16	Terry Francona	1.25	.90	.50
17	Tim Blackwell	1.00	.70	.40
18	Jerry White	1.00	.70	.40
20	Bob James	1.25	.90	.50
21	Scott Sanderson	1.00	.70	.40
24	Brad Mills	1.00	.70	.40
29	Tim Wallach	3.00	2.25	1.25
30	Tim Raines	7.00	5.25	2.75
34	Bill Gullickson	1.25	.90	.50
35	Woodie Fryman	1.00	.70	.40
38	Bryn Smith	1.50	1.25	.60
41	Jeff Reardon	3.00	2.25	1.25
44	Dan Norman	1.00	.70	.40
45	Steve Rogers	1.25	.90	.50
48	Ray Burris	1.00	.70	.40
49	Warren Cromartie	1.00	.70	.40
53	Charlie Lea	1.00	.70	.40

J

1984 Jarvis Press Rangers

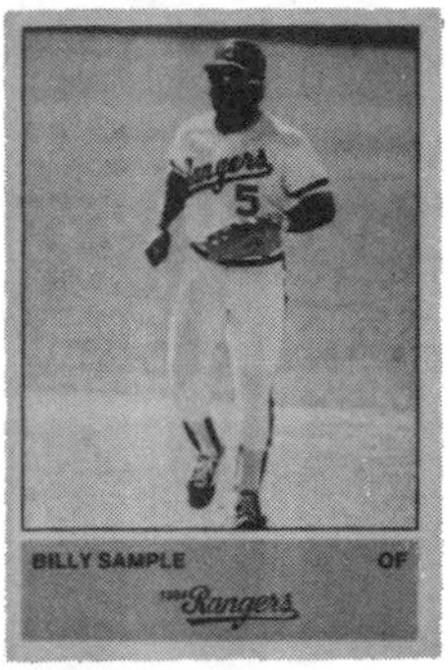

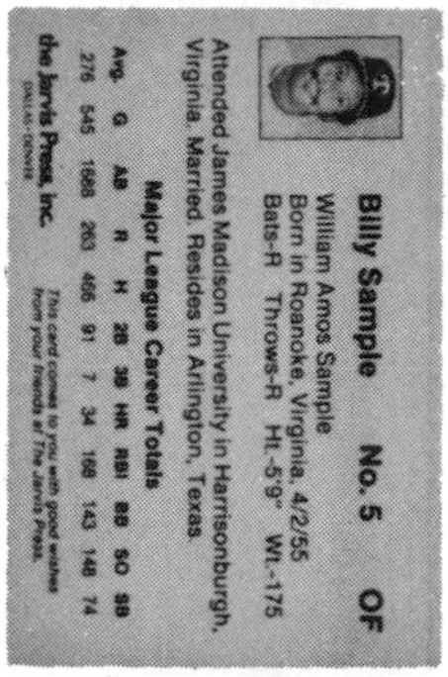

For its second annual "Baseball Card Day" game promotional set, the Rangers picked up a new sponsor, Jarvis Press of Dallas. The 30 cards in the set include 27 players, the manager, trainer and a group card of the coaches. Cards measure 2-3/8" by 3-1/2". Color game-action photos make up the card fronts. Backs, printed in black and white, include a portrait photo of the player. A source close to the promotion indicated 10,000 sets were produced.

		MT	NR MT	EX
Complete Set:		5.00	3.75	2.00
Common Player:		.12	.09	.05
1	Bill Stein	.12	.09	.05
2	Alan Bannister	.12	.09	.05
3	Wayne Tolleson	.12	.09	.05
5	Billy Sample	.12	.09	.05
6	Bobby Jones	.12	.09	.05
7	Ned Yost	.12	.09	.05
9	Pete O'Brien	.30	.25	.12
11	Doug Rader	.12	.09	.05
13	Tommy Dunbar	.12	.09	.05
14	Jim Anderson	.12	.09	.05
15	Larry Parrish	.20	.15	.08
16	Mike Mason	.12	.09	.05
17	Mickey Rivers	.20	.15	.08
19	Curtis Wilkerson	.12	.09	.05
20	Jeff Kunkel	.12	.09	.05
21	Odell Jones	.12	.09	.05
24	Dave Schmidt	.15	.11	.06
25	Buddy Bell	.35	.25	.14
26	George Wright	.12	.09	.05
28	Frank Tanana	.20	.15	.08
30	Marv Foley	.12	.09	.05
31	Dave Stewart	1.00	.70	.40
32	Gary Ward	.20	.15	.08
36	Dickie Noles	.12	.09	.05
43	Donnie Scott	.12	.09	.05
44	Danny Darwin	.25	.20	.10
49	Charlie Hough	.30	.25	.12
53	Joey McLaughlin	.12	.09	.05
----	Coaching Staff (Rich Donnelly, Glenn Ezell, Merv Rettenmund, Dick Such, Wayne Terwilliger)	.12	.09	.05
----	Trainer (Bill Zeigler)	.12	.09	.05

1986 Jays Potato Chips

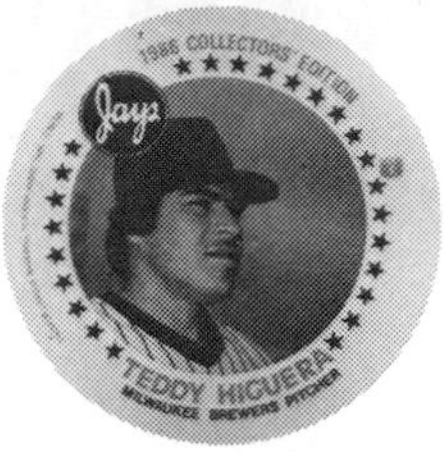

One of a handful of round baseball cards produced for inclusion in boxes of potato chips on a regional basis in 1986, the Jays set of 2-7/8" discs is believed to be the scarcest of the type. The 20 cards in the issue include the most popular Milwaukee Brewers and Chicago Cubs and White Sox players; the set having been distributed in the southern Wisconsin-northern Illinois area. Like many of the recent sets produced by Mike Schecter Associates, the '86 Jays cards feature player photos on which the team logos have been airbrushed off the caps.

		MT	NR MT	EX
Complete Set:		20.00	15.00	8.00
Common Player:		.60	.45	.25
(1)	Harold Baines	1.00	.70	.40
(2)	Cecil Cooper	.80	.60	.30
(3)	Jody Davis	.60	.45	.25
(4)	Bob Dernier	.60	.45	.25
(5)	Richard Dotson	.60	.45	.25
(6)	Shawon Dunston	1.00	.70	.40
(7)	Carlton Fisk	1.50	1.25	.60
(8)	Jim Gantner	.60	.45	.25
(9)	Ozzie Guillen	1.00	.70	.40
(10)	Teddy Higuera	1.00	.70	.40
(11)	Ron Kittle	.75	.60	.30
(12)	Paul Molitor	1.50	1.25	.60
(13)	Keith Moreland	.60	.45	.25
(14)	Ernie Riles	.60	.45	.25
(15)	Ryne Sandberg	3.00	2.25	1.25
(16)	Tom Seaver	2.00	1.50	.80
(17)	Lee Smith	.90	.70	.35
(18)	Rick Sutcliffe	.90	.70	.35
(19)	Greg Walker	.60	.45	.25
(20)	Robin Yount	2.00	1.50	.80

1962 Jell-O

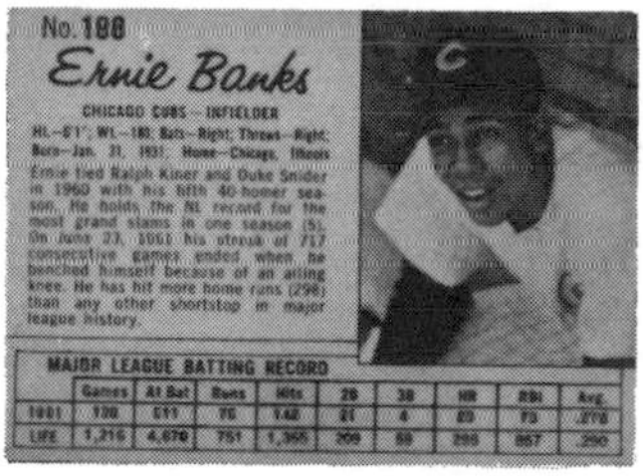

Virtually identical in content to the 1962 Post cereal cards, the '62 Jell-O set of 197 was only issued in the Midwest. Players and card numbers are identical in the two sets, except Brooks Robinson (#29), Ted Kluszewski (#82) and Smoky Burgess (#176) were not issued in the Jell-O version. The Jell-O cards are easy to distinguish from the Post of that year by the absence of the red oval Post logo and red or blue border around the stat box. Cards which have been neatly trimmed from the box which they were printed will measure 3-1/2" by 2-1/2".

A player's name in *italic* type indicates a rookie card. An (FC) indicates a player's first card for that particular card company.

		NR MT	EX	VG
Complete Set:		4500.00	2250.00	1350.
Common Player:		5.00	2.50	1.50
1	Bill Skowron	20.00	10.00	6.00
2	Bobby Richardson	20.00	10.00	6.00
3	Cletis Boyer	10.00	5.00	3.00
4	Tony Kubek	15.00	7.50	4.50
5	Mickey Mantle	700.00	350.00	210.00
6	Roger Maris	125.00	62.00	37.00
7	Yogi Berra	60.00	30.00	18.00
8	Elston Howard	15.00	7.50	4.50
9	Whitey Ford	40.00	20.00	12.00
10	Ralph Terry	10.00	5.00	3.00
11	John Blanchard	6.00	3.00	1.75
12	Luis Arroyo	6.00	3.00	1.75
13	Bill Stafford	20.00	10.00	6.00
14	Norm Cash	10.00	5.00	3.00
15	Jake Wood	5.00	2.50	1.50
16	Steve Boros	5.00	2.50	1.50
17	Chico Fernandez	5.00	2.50	1.50
18	Billy Bruton	5.00	2.50	1.50
19	Ken Aspromonte	5.00	2.50	1.50
20	Al Kaline	40.00	20.00	12.00
21	Dick Brown	5.00	2.50	1.50
22	Frank Lary	6.00	3.00	1.75
23	Don Mossi	6.00	3.00	1.75
24	Phil Regan	5.00	2.50	1.50
25	Charley Maxwell	5.00	2.50	1.50
26	Jim Bunning	15.00	7.50	4.50
27	Jim Gentile	6.00	3.00	1.75
28	Marv Breeding	5.00	2.50	1.50
29	Not Issued			
30	Ron Hansen	5.00	2.50	1.50
31	Jackie Brandt	20.00	10.00	6.00
32	Dick Williams	6.00	3.00	1.75
33	Gus Triandos	6.00	3.00	1.75
34	Milt Pappas	6.00	3.00	1.75
35	Hoyt Wilhelm	25.00	12.50	7.50
36	Chuck Estrada	5.00	2.50	1.50
37	Vic Power	5.00	2.50	1.50
38	Johnny Temple	5.00	2.50	1.50
39	Bubba Phillips	20.00	10.00	6.00
40	Tito Francona	6.00	3.00	1.75
41	Willie Kirkland	5.00	2.50	1.50
42	John Romano	5.00	2.50	1.50
43	Jim Perry	10.00	5.00	3.00
44	Woodie Held	5.00	2.50	1.50
45	Chuck Essegian	5.00	2.50	1.50
46	Roy Sievers	6.00	3.00	1.75
47	Nellie Fox	15.00	7.50	4.50
48	Al Smith	5.00	2.50	1.50
49	Luis Aparicio	25.00	12.50	7.50
50	Jim Landis	5.00	2.50	1.50
51	Minnie Minoso	10.00	5.00	3.00
52	Andy Carey	20.00	10.00	6.00
53	Sherman Lollar	6.00	3.00	1.75
54	Bill Pierce	6.00	3.00	1.75
55	Early Wynn	25.00	12.50	7.50
56	Chuck Schilling	20.00	10.00	6.00
57	Pete Runnels	6.00	3.00	1.75
58	Frank Malzone	6.00	3.00	1.75
59	Don Buddin	10.00	5.00	3.00
60	Gary Geiger	5.00	2.50	1.50
61	Carl Yastrzemski	200.00	100.00	60.00
62	Jackie Jensen	20.00	10.00	6.00
63	Jim Pagliaroni	20.00	10.00	6.00
64	Don Schwall	5.00	2.50	1.50
65	Dale Long	6.00	3.00	1.75
66	Chuck Cottier	10.00	5.00	3.00
67	Billy Klaus	20.00	10.00	6.00
68	Coot Veal	5.00	2.50	1.50
69	Marty Keough	40.00	20.00	12.00
70	Willie Tasby	40.00	20.00	12.00
71	Gene Woodling	6.00	3.00	1.75
72	Gene Green	40.00	20.00	12.00
73	Dick Donovan	10.00	5.00	3.00
74	Steve Bilko	10.00	5.00	3.00
75	Rocky Bridges	20.00	10.00	6.00
76	Eddie Yost	10.00	5.00	3.00
77	Leon Wagner	10.00	5.00	3.00
78	Albie Pearson	10.00	5.00	3.00
79	Ken Hunt	10.00	5.00	3.00
80	Earl Averill	40.00	20.00	12.00
81	Ryne Duren	10.00	5.00	3.00
82	Not Issued			
83	Bob Allison	6.00	3.00	1.75
84	Billy Martin	15.00	7.50	4.50
85	Harmon Killebrew	40.00	20.00	12.00
86	Zorro Versalles	6.00	3.00	1.75
87	Lennie Green	20.00	10.00	6.00
88	Bill Tuttle	5.00	2.50	1.50

		NR MT	EX	VG
89	Jim Lemon	6.00	3.00	1.75
90	Earl Battey	20.00	10.00	6.00
91	Camilo Pascual	6.00	3.00	1.75
92	Norm Siebern	10.00	5.00	3.00
93	Jerry Lumpe	10.00	5.00	3.00
94	Dick Howser	10.00	5.00	3.00
95	Gene Stephens	40.00	20.00	12.00
96	Leo Posada	10.00	5.00	3.00
97	Joe Pignatano	10.00	5.00	3.00
98	Jim Archer	10.00	5.00	3.00
99	Haywood Sullivan	20.00	10.00	6.00
100	Art Ditmar	10.00	5.00	3.00
101	Gil Hodges	40.00	20.00	12.00
102	Charlie Neal	10.00	5.00	3.00
103	Daryl Spencer	10.00	5.00	3.00
104	Maury Wills	20.00	10.00	6.00
105	Tommy Davis	10.00	5.00	3.00
106	Willie Davis	10.00	5.00	3.00
107	John Roseboro	40.00	20.00	12.00
108	John Podres	10.00	5.00	3.00
109	Sandy Koufax	80.00	40.00	24.00
110	Don Drysdale	50.00	25.00	15.00
111	Larry Sherry	20.00	10.00	6.00
112	Jim Gilliam	20.00	10.00	6.00
113	Norm Larker	40.00	20.00	12.00
114	Duke Snider	70.00	35.00	21.00
115	Stan Williams	20.00	10.00	6.00
116	Gordon Coleman	70.00	35.00	21.00
117	Don Blasingame	20.00	10.00	6.00
118	Gene Freese	40.00	20.00	12.00
119	Ed Kasko	40.00	20.00	12.00
120	Gus Bell	20.00	10.00	6.00
121	Vada Pinson	10.00	5.00	3.00
122	Frank Robinson	40.00	20.00	12.00
123	Bob Purkey	10.00	5.00	3.00
124	Joey Jay	10.00	5.00	3.00
125	Jim Brosnan	10.00	5.00	3.00
126	Jim O'Toole	10.00	5.00	3.00
127	Jerry Lynch	10.00	5.00	3.00
128	Wally Post	10.00	5.00	3.00
129	Ken Hunt	10.00	5.00	3.00
130	Jerry Zimmerman	10.00	5.00	3.00
131	Willie McCovey	40.00	20.00	12.00
132	Jose Pagan	20.00	10.00	6.00
133	Felipe Alou	10.00	5.00	3.00
134	Jim Davenport	10.00	5.00	3.00
135	Harvey Kuenn	10.00	5.00	3.00
136	Orlando Cepeda	15.00	7.50	4.50
137	Ed Bailey	10.00	5.00	3.00
138	Sam Jones	10.00	5.00	3.00
139	Mike McCormick	10.00	5.00	3.00
140	Juan Marichal	40.00	20.00	12.00
141	Jack Sanford	10.00	5.00	3.00
142	Willie Mays	150.00	75.00	45.00
143	Stu Miller	70.00	35.00	21.00
144	Joe Amalfitano	10.00	5.00	3.00
145	Joe Adcock	10.00	5.00	3.00
146	Frank Bolling	5.00	2.50	1.50
147	Ed Mathews	40.00	20.00	12.00
148	Roy McMillan	6.00	3.00	1.75
149	Hank Aaron	150.00	75.00	45.00
150	Gino Cimoli	20.00	10.00	6.00
151	Frank Thomas	6.00	3.00	1.75
152	Joe Torre	10.00	5.00	3.00
153	Lou Burdette	10.00	5.00	3.00
154	Bob Buhl	6.00	3.00	1.75
155	Carlton Willey	5.00	2.50	1.50
156	Lee Maye	18.00	9.00	5.50
157	Al Spangler	40.00	20.00	12.00
158	Bill White	40.00	20.00	12.00
159	Ken Boyer	15.00	7.50	4.50
160	Joe Cunningham	10.00	5.00	3.00
161	Carl Warwick	10.00	5.00	3.00
162	Carl Sawatski	5.00	2.50	1.50
163	Lindy McDaniel	5.00	2.50	1.50
164	Ernie Broglio	10.00	5.00	3.00
165	Larry Jackson	5.00	2.50	1.50
166	Curt Flood	15.00	7.50	4.50
167	Curt Simmons	40.00	20.00	12.00
168	Alex Grammas	20.00	10.00	6.00
169	Dick Stuart	6.00	3.00	1.75
170	Bill Mazeroski	20.00	10.00	6.00
171	Don Hoak	10.00	5.00	3.00
172	Dick Groat	10.00	5.00	3.00
173	Roberto Clemente	150.00	75.00	45.00
174	Bob Skinner	20.00	10.00	6.00
175	Bill Virdon	40.00	20.00	12.00
176	Not Issued			
177	Elroy Face	10.00	5.00	3.00
178	Bob Friend	6.00	3.00	1.75
179	Vernon Law	20.00	10.00	6.00

		NR MT	EX	VG
180	Harvey Haddix	40.00	20.00	12.00
181	Hal Smith	20.00	10.00	6.00
182	Ed Bouchee	20.00	10.00	6.00
183	Don Zimmer	6.00	3.00	1.75
184	Ron Santo	10.00	5.00	3.00
185	Andre Rodgers	5.00	2.50	1.50
186	Richie Ashburn	15.00	7.50	4.50
187	George Altman	5.00	2.50	1.50
188	Ernie Banks	40.00	20.00	12.00
189	Sam Taylor	5.00	2.50	1.50
190	Don Elston	5.00	2.50	1.50
191	Jerry Kindall	20.00	10.00	6.00
192	Pancho Herrera	5.00	2.50	1.50
193	Tony Taylor	5.00	2.50	1.50
194	Ruben Amaro	20.00	10.00	6.00
195	Don Demeter	5.00	2.50	1.50
196	Bobby Gene Smith	5.00	2.50	1.50
197	Clay Dalrymple	5.00	2.50	1.50
198	Robin Roberts	25.00	12.50	7.50
199	Art Mahaffey	5.00	2.50	1.50
200	John Buzhardt	5.00	2.50	1.50

1963 Jell-O

Like the other Post and Jell-O issues of the era, the '63 Jell-O set includes many scarce cards; primarily those which were printed as the backs of less popular brands and sizes of the gelatin dessert. Slightly smaller than the virtually identical Post cereal cards of the same year, the 200 cards in the Jell-O issue measure 3-3/8" by 2-1/2". The easiest way to distinguish 1963 Jell-O cards from Post cards is by the red line that separates the 1962 stats from the lifetime stats. On Post cards, the line extends almost all the way to the side borders, on the Jell-O cards, the line begins and ends much closer to the stats.

		NR MT	EX	VG
Complete Set:		3000.00	1500.00	900.00
Common Player:		2.00	1.00	.60
1	Vic Power	2.50	1.25	.70
2	Bernie Allen	20.00	10.00	6.00
3	Zoilo Versalles	20.00	10.00	6.00
4	Rich Rollins	2.00	1.00	.60
5	Harmon Killebrew	8.00	4.00	2.50
6	Lenny Green	20.00	10.00	6.00
7	Bob Allison	3.00	1.50	.90
8	Earl Battey	15.00	7.50	4.50
9	Camilo Pascual	2.50	1.25	.70
10	Jim Kaat	35.00	17.50	10.50
11	Jack Kralick	2.00	1.00	.60
12	Bill Skowron	20.00	10.00	6.00
13	Bobby Richardson	5.00	2.50	1.50
14	Cletis Boyer	2.50	1.25	.70
15	Mickey Mantle	250.00	125.00	75.00
16	Roger Maris	20.00	10.00	6.00
17	Yogi Berra	20.00	10.00	6.00
18	Elston Howard	20.00	10.00	6.00
19	Whitey Ford	10.00	5.00	3.00
20	Ralph Terry	2.00	1.00	.60
21	John Blanchard	15.00	7.50	4.50
22	Bill Stafford	20.00	10.00	6.00
23	Tom Tresh	2.50	1.25	.70
24	Steve Bilko	2.00	1.00	.60
25	Bill Moran	2.00	1.00	.60
26	Joe Koppe	2.00	1.00	.60
27	Felix Torres	2.00	1.00	.60
28	Leon Wagner	2.50	1.25	.70
29	Albie Pearson	2.00	1.00	.60
30	Lee Thomas	2.00	1.00	.60
31	Bob Rodgers	20.00	10.00	6.00
32	Dean Chance	1.50	.70	.45
33	Ken McBride	20.00	10.00	6.00
34	George Thomas	20.00	10.00	6.00
35	Joe Cunningham	20.00	10.00	6.00
36	Nelson Fox	5.00	2.50	1.50
37	Luis Aparicio	6.00	3.00	1.75
38	Al Smith	2.00	1.00	.60
39	Floyd Robinson	2.00	1.00	.60
40	Jim Landis	2.00	1.00	.60
41	Charlie Maxwell	2.00	1.00	.60
42	Sherman Lollar	2.00	1.00	.60
43	Early Wynn	6.00	3.00	1.75
44	Juan Pizarro	20.00	10.00	6.00
45	Ray Herbert	20.00	10.00	6.00
46	Norm Cash	3.50	1.75	1.00
47	Steve Boros	20.00	10.00	6.00
48	Dick McAuliffe	2.00	1.00	.60
49	Bill Bruton	2.00	1.00	.60
50	Rocky Colavito	5.00	2.50	1.50
51	Al Kaline	12.00	6.00	3.50
52	Dick Brown	20.00	10.00	6.00
53	Jim Bunning	5.00	2.50	1.50
54	Hank Aguirre	2.00	1.00	.60
55	Frank Lary	20.00	10.00	6.00
56	Don Mossi	20.00	10.00	6.00
57	Jim Gentile	2.00	1.00	.60
58	Jackie Brandt	2.00	1.00	.60
59	Brooks Robinson	15.00	7.50	4.50
60	Ron Hansen	2.00	1.00	.60
61	Jerry Adair	55.00	27.00	16.50
62	John Powell	3.50	1.75	1.00
63	Russ Snyder	20.00	10.00	6.00
64	Steve Barber	2.00	1.00	.60
65	Milt Pappas	20.00	10.00	6.00
66	Robin Roberts	6.00	3.00	1.75
67	Tito Francona	2.00	1.00	.60
68	Jerry Kindall	20.00	10.00	6.00
69	Woodie Held	2.00	1.00	.60
70	Bubba Phillips	2.00	1.00	.60
71	Chuck Essegian	2.00	1.00	.60
72	Willie Kirkland	20.00	10.00	6.00
73	Al Luplow	2.00	1.00	.60
74	Ty Cline	20.00	10.00	6.00
75	Dick Donovan	2.00	1.00	.60
76	John Romano	2.00	1.00	.60
77	Pete Runnels	2.00	1.00	.60
78	Ed Bressoud	20.00	10.00	6.00
79	Frank Malzone	2.00	1.00	.60
80	Carl Yastrzemski	70.00	35.00	21.00
81	Gary Geiger	2.00	1.00	.60
82	Lou Clinton	20.00	10.00	6.00
83	Earl Wilson	2.50	1.25	.70
84	Bill Monbouquette	2.50	1.25	.70
85	Norm Siebern	2.50	1.25	.70
86	Jerry Lumpe	2.50	1.25	.70
87	Manny Jimenez	2.00	1.00	.60
88	Gino Cimoli	2.00	1.00	.60
89	Ed Charles	55.00	27.00	16.50
90	Ed Rakow	2.00	1.00	.60
91	Bob Del Greco	20.00	10.00	6.00
92	Haywood Sullivan	20.00	10.00	6.00
93	Chuck Hinton	2.00	1.00	.60
94	Ken Retzer	20.00	10.00	6.00
95	Harry Bright	20.00	10.00	6.00
96	Bob Johnson	2.00	1.00	.60
97	Dave Stenhouse	20.00	10.00	6.00
98	Chuck Cottier	2.00	1.00	.60
99	Tom Cheney	2.00	1.00	.60
100	Claude Osteen	20.00	10.00	6.00
101	Orlando Cepeda	5.00	2.50	1.50
102	Charley Hiller	20.00	10.00	6.00
103	Jose Pagan	20.00	10.00	6.00
104	Jim Davenport	2.00	1.00	.60
105	Harvey Kuenn	3.50	1.75	1.00
106	Willie Mays	75.00	37.00	22.00
107	Felipe Alou	3.00	1.50	.90
108	Tom Haller	2.00	1.00	.60
109	Juan Marichal	6.00	3.00	1.75
110	Jack Sanford	2.00	1.00	.60
111	Bill O'Dell	2.00	1.00	.60
112	Willie McCovey	90.00	45.00	27.00
113	Lee Walls	20.00	10.00	6.00
114	Jim Gilliam	20.00	10.00	6.00
115	Maury Wills	5.00	2.50	1.50
116	Ron Fairly	2.00	1.00	.60
117	Tommy Davis	3.00	1.50	.90

		NR MT	EX	VG
118	Duke Snider	9.00	4.50	2.75
119	Willie Davis	3.00	1.50	.90
120	John Roseboro	2.00	1.00	.60
121	Sandy Koufax	20.00	10.00	6.00
122	Stan Williams	20.00	10.00	6.00
123	Don Drysdale	9.00	4.50	2.75
124	Daryl Spencer	2.00	1.00	.60
125	Gordy Coleman	2.00	1.00	.60
126	Don Blasingame	20.00	10.00	6.00
127	Leo Cardenas	2.00	1.00	.60
128	Eddie Kasko	20.00	10.00	6.00
129	Jerry Lynch	2.00	1.00	.60
130	Vada Pinson	4.00	2.00	1.25
131	Frank Robinson	9.00	4.50	2.75
132	John Edwards	20.00	10.00	6.00
133	Joey Jay	2.00	1.00	.60
134	Bob Purkey	2.00	1.00	.60
135	Marty Keough	55.00	27.00	16.50
136	Jim O'Toole	20.00	10.00	6.00
137	Dick Stuart	2.00	1.00	.60
138	Bill Mazeroski	3.50	1.75	1.00
139	Dick Groat	3.00	1.50	.90
140	Don Hoak	2.00	1.00	.60
141	Bob Skinner	2.00	1.00	.60
142	Bill Virdon	3.00	1.50	.90
143	Roberto Clemente	75.00	37.00	22.00
144	Smoky Burgess	3.00	1.50	.90
145	Bob Friend	2.00	1.00	.60
146	Al McBean	20.00	10.00	6.00
147	ElRoy Face	3.00	1.50	.90
148	Joe Adcock	3.50	1.75	1.00
149	Frank Bolling	2.00	1.00	.60
150	Roy McMillan	2.00	1.00	.60
151	Eddie Mathews	8.00	4.00	2.50
152	Hank Aaron	75.00	37.00	22.00
153	Del Crandall	20.00	10.00	6.00
154	Bob Shaw	2.00	1.00	.60
155	Lew Burdette	3.50	1.75	1.00
156	Joe Torre	20.00	10.00	6.00
157	Tony Cloninger	35.00	17.50	10.50
158	Bill White	2.50	1.25	.70
159	Julian Javier	20.00	10.00	6.00
160	Ken Boyer	4.00	2.00	1.25
161	Julio Gotay	20.00	10.00	6.00
162	Curt Flood	3.00	1.50	.90
163	Charlie James	35.00	17.50	10.50
164	Gene Oliver	20.00	10.00	6.00
165	Ernie Broglio	2.00	1.00	.60
166	Bob Gibson	75.00	37.00	22.00
167	Lindy McDaniel	20.00	10.00	6.00
168	Ray Washburn	2.00	1.00	.60
169	Ernie Banks	12.00	6.00	3.50
170	Ron Santo	3.50	1.75	1.00
171	George Altman	2.00	1.00	.60
172	Billy Williams	75.00	37.00	22.00
173	Andre Rodgers	20.00	10.00	6.00
174	Ken Hubbs	3.00	1.50	.90
175	Don Landrum	20.00	10.00	6.00
176	Dick Bertell	20.00	10.00	6.00
177	Roy Sievers	2.50	1.25	.70
178	Tony Taylor	20.00	10.00	6.00
179	John Callison	2.50	1.25	.70
180	Don Demeter	2.00	1.00	.60
181	Tony Gonzalez	20.00	10.00	6.00
182	Wes Covington	20.00	10.00	6.00
183	Art Mahaffey	2.00	1.00	.60
184	Clay Dalrymple	2.00	1.00	.60
185	Al Spangler	2.00	1.00	.60
186	Roman Mejias	2.00	1.00	.60
187	Bob Aspromonte	50.00	25.00	15.00
188	Norm Larker	2.00	1.00	.60
189	Johnny Temple	2.00	1.00	.60
190	Carl Warwick	20.00	10.00	6.00
191	Bob Lillis	20.00	10.00	6.00
192	Dick Farrell	50.00	25.00	15.00
193	Gil Hodges	8.00	4.00	2.50
194	Marv Throneberry	3.00	1.50	.90
195	Charlie Neal	20.00	10.00	6.00
196	Frank Thomas	2.00	1.00	.60
197	Richie Ashburn	5.00	2.50	1.50
198	Felix Mantilla	20.00	10.00	6.00
199	Rod Kanehl	20.00	10.00	6.00
200	Roger Craig	20.00	10.00	6.00

A player's name in *italic* type indicates a rookie card. An (FC) indicates a player's first card for that particular card company.

1986 Jiffy Pop

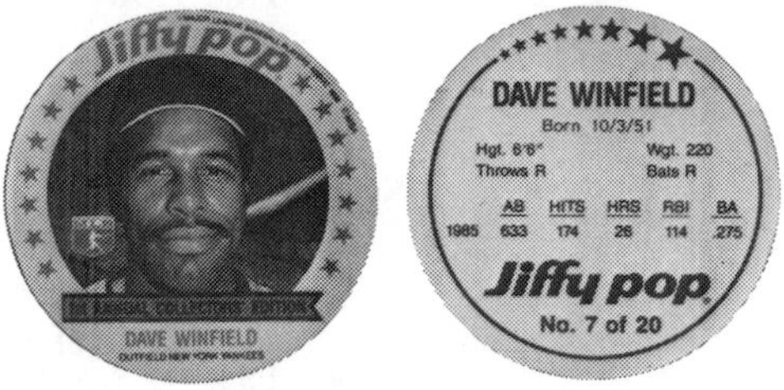

One of the scarcer of the 1986 "regionals," the 20-card Jiffy Pop issue was inserted in packages of heat-and-eat popcorn. A production of Mike Schecter Associates, the 2-7/8" round discs feature 20 popular stars, many in the same pictures found in other '86 regionals. Like other MSA issues, caps have had the team logos erased, allowing Jiffy Pop to avoid having to pay a licensing fee to the teams.

		MT	NR MT	EX
Complete Set:		30.00	22.00	12.00
Common Player:		1.00	.70	.40
1	Jim Rice	2.50	2.00	1.00
2	Wade Boggs	2.00	1.50	.80
3	Lance Parrish	1.00	.70	.40
4	George Brett	2.50	2.00	1.00
5	Robin Yount	2.50	2.00	1.00
6	Don Mattingly	3.50	2.75	1.50
7	Dave Winfield	2.00	1.50	.80
8	Reggie Jackson	2.50	2.00	1.00
9	Cal Ripken	2.50	2.00	1.00
10	Eddie Murray	2.00	1.50	.80
11	Pete Rose	2.00	1.50	.80
12	Ryne Sandberg	2.50	2.00	1.00
13	Nolan Ryan	4.00	3.00	1.50
14	Fernando Valenzuela	1.25	.90	.50
15	Willie McGee	1.00	.70	.40
16	Dale Murphy	2.50	2.00	1.00
17	Mike Schmidt	2.50	2.00	1.00
18	Steve Garvey	2.00	1.50	.80
19	Gary Carter	2.00	1.50	.80
20	Dwight Gooden	2.00	1.50	.80

1987 Jiffy Pop

For the second year in a row, Jiffy Pop inserted baseball discs in their packages of popcorn. The full-color discs measure 2-7/8" in diameter and were produced by Mike Schecter Associates of Cos Cob, Conn. Titled "2nd Annual Collectors' Edition," the card fronts feature player photos with all team insignias airbrushed away. Information on the backs of the discs are printed in bright red on white stock. Die-cut press sheets containing all 20 discs were

available via a mail-in offer.

		MT	NR MT	EX
Complete Set:		25.00	18.50	10.00
Common Player:		1.00	.70	.40
1	Ryne Sandberg	2.50	2.00	1.00
2	Dale Murphy	2.50	2.00	1.00
3	Jack Morris	1.00	.70	.40
4	Keith Hernandez	1.50	1.25	.60
5	George Brett	2.50	2.00	1.00
6	Don Mattingly	3.50	2.75	1.50
7	Ozzie Smith	1.00	.70	.40
8	Cal Ripken	2.50	2.00	1.00
9	Dwight Gooden	3.00	2.25	1.25
10	Pedro Guerrero	1.00	.70	.40
11	Lou Whitaker	1.00	.70	.40
12	Roger Clemens	3.00	2.25	1.25
13	Lance Parrish	1.00	.70	.40
14	Rickey Henderson	2.50	2.00	1.00
15	Fernando Valenzuela	1.25	.90	.50
16	Mike Schmidt	2.50	2.00	1.00
17	Darryl Strawberry	2.75	2.00	1.00
18	Mike Scott	1.00	.70	.40
19	Jim Rice	2.75	2.00	1.00
20	Wade Boggs	2.50	2.00	1.00

1988 Jiffy Pop

This 20-disc set is the third Jiffy Pop issue spotlighting leading players. Discs are 2-/12" in diameter, with a semi-gloss finish, and feature full-color closeups on white stock. Team logos have been airbrushed off the player's caps. The Jiffy Pop logo appears in red at the top of the disc; a banner running across the bottom encloses a "1988" and player name, also in red. The circular border is blue, with two large baseballs streaking toward the top logo. A third baseball appears lower right under the curved label "3rd Annual Collector's Edition." Dsic backs are white, with dark blue lettering, and contain player information and disc number.

		MT	NR MT	EX
Complete Set:		18.00	13.50	7.25
Common Player:		.60	.45	.25
1	Buddy Bell	.60	.45	.25
2	Wade Boggs	2.25	1.75	.90
3	Gary Carter	1.50	1.25	.60
4	Jack Clark	.80	.60	.30
5	Will Clark	1.50	1.25	.60
6	Roger Clemens	2.25	1.75	.90
7	Vince Coleman	.80	.60	.30
8	Andre Dawson	1.25	.90	.50
9	Keith Hernandez	1.25	.90	.50
10	Kent Hrbek	1.25	.90	.50
11	Wally Joyner	1.50	1.25	.60
12	Paul Molitor	.80	.60	.30
13	Eddie Murray	1.50	1.25	.60
14	Tim Raines	1.50	1.25	.60
15	Bret Saberhagen	1.25	.90	.50
16	Alan Trammell	1.25	.90	.50
17	Ozzie Virgil	.60	.45	.25
18	Tim Wallach	.60	.45	.25
19	Dave Winfield	1.50	1.25	.60
20	Robin Yount	1.25	.90	.50

1991 Jimmy Dean

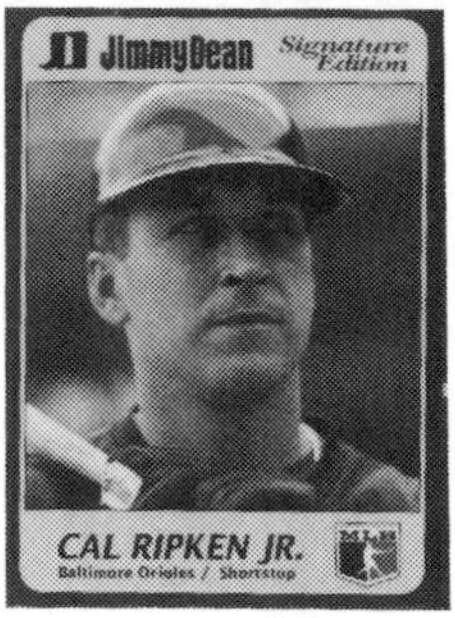

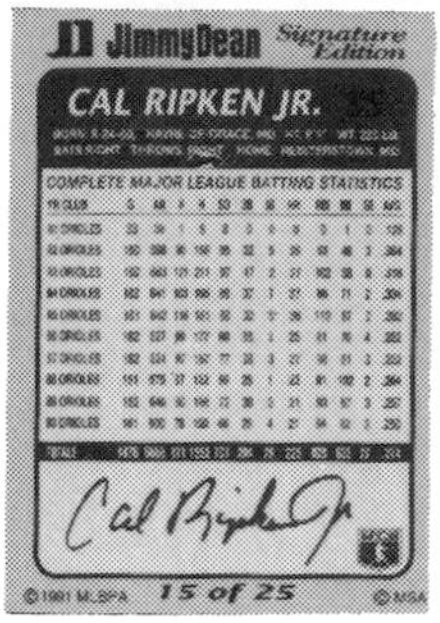

Baseball cards were inserted into packages of Jimmy Dean sausages in 1991. The complete set consists of 25 cards. Star players are featured in the set. Red and yellow borders surround fll-color player photos on the card fronts. No team logos appear on the cards. The card backs feature statistics, biographical information and a facsimile autograph. The set is entitled the "Signature Edition."

		MT	NR MT	EX
Complete Set:		12.00	9.00	4.75
Common Player:		.30	.25	.12
1	Will Clark	.70	.50	.30
2	Ken Griffey, Jr.	1.50	1.25	.60
3	Dale Murphy	.30	.25	.12
4	Barry Bonds	.40	.30	.15
5	Darryl Strawberry	.40	.30	.15
6	Ryne Sandberg	.50	.40	.20
7	Gary Sheffield	.40	.30	.15
8	Sandy Alomar, Jr.	.35	.25	.14
9	Frank Thomas	1.50	1.25	.60
10	Barry Larkin	.35	.25	.14
11	Kirby Puckett	.35	.25	.14
12	George Brett	.40	.30	.15
13	Kevin Mitchell	.35	.25	.14
14	Dave Justice	1.00	.70	.40
15	Cal Ripken, Jr.	.50	.40	.20
16	Craig Biggio	.30	.25	.12
17	Rickey Henderson	.50	.40	.20
18	Roger Clemens	.50	.40	.20
19	Jose Canseco	.70	.50	.30
20	Ozzie Smith	.40	.30	.15
21	Cecil Fielder	.50	.40	.20
22	Dave Winfield	.35	.25	.14
23	Kevin Maas	.50	.40	.20
24	Nolan Ryan	.80	.60	.30
25	Dwight Gooden	.40	.30	.15

1953 Johnston Cookies Braves

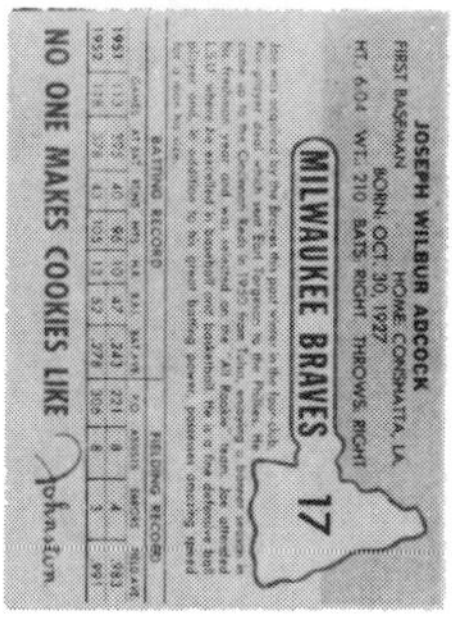

The first and most common of three annual issues, the '53 Johnston's were inserted into boxes of cookies on a regional basis. Complete sets were also available from the company, whose factory sits in the shadow of Milwaukee County Stadium. While at first glance appearing to be color photos, the pictures on

the 25 cards in the set are actually well-done colorizations of black and white photos. Cards measure 2-9/16" by 3-5/8". Write-ups on the backs were "borrowed" from the Braves' 1953 yearbook.

		NR MT	EX	VG
Complete Set:		325.00	175.00	100.00
Common Player:		8.00	4.00	2.50
1	Charlie Grimm	10.00	5.00	3.00
2	John Antonelli	10.00	5.00	3.00
3	Vern Bickford	8.00	4.00	2.50
4	Bob Buhl	10.00	5.00	3.00
5	Lew Burdette	15.00	7.50	4.50
6	Dave Cole	8.00	4.00	2.50
7	Ernie Johnson	8.00	4.00	2.50
8	Dave Jolly	8.00	4.00	2.50
9	Don Liddle	8.00	4.00	2.50
10	Warren Spahn	55.00	27.00	16.50
11	Max Surkont	8.00	4.00	2.50
12	Jim Wilson	8.00	4.00	2.50
13	Sibby Sisti	8.00	4.00	2.50
14	Walker Cooper	8.00	4.00	2.50
15	Del Crandall	15.00	7.50	4.50
16	Ebba St. Claire	8.00	4.00	2.50
17	Joe Adcock	15.00	7.50	4.50
18	George Crowe	8.00	4.00	2.50
19	Jack Dittmer	8.00	4.00	2.50
20	Johnny Logan	10.00	5.00	3.00
21	Ed Mathews	55.00	27.00	16.50
22	Bill Bruton	10.00	5.00	3.00
23	Sid Gordon	8.00	4.00	2.50
24	Andy Pafko	10.00	5.00	3.00
25	Jim Pendleton	8.00	4.00	2.50

1954 Johnston Cookies Braves

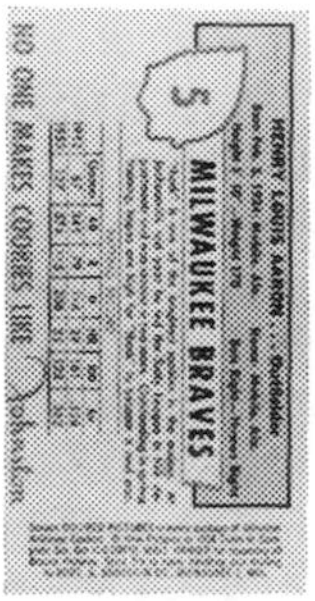

In its second of three annual issues, Johnston's increased the number of cards in its 1954 Braves issue to 35, and switched to an unusual size, a narrow format, 2" by 3-7/8". Besides the players and managers, the '54 set also includes unnumbered cards of the team trainer and equipment manager. Other cards are numbered by uniform number. After his early-season injury (which gave Hank Aaron a chance to play regularly), Bobby Thomson's card was withdrawn, accounting for its scarcity and high value. A cardboard wall-hanging display into which cards could be inserted was available as a premium offer.

		NR MT	EX	VG
Complete Set:		1250.00	625.00	375.00
Common Player:		10.00	5.00	3.00
1	Del Crandall	15.00	7.50	4.50
3	Jim Pendleton	10.00	5.00	3.00
4	Danny O'Connell	10.00	5.00	3.00
5	Henry Aaron	500.00	250.00	150.00
6	Jack Dittmer	10.00	5.00	3.00
9	Joe Adcock	15.00	7.50	4.50
10	Robert Buhl	15.00	7.50	4.50
11	Phillip Paine (Phillips)	10.00	5.00	3.00
12	Ben Johnson	10.00	5.00	3.00
13	Sibby Sisti	10.00	5.00	3.00
15	Charles Gorin	10.00	5.00	3.00
16	Chet Nichols	10.00	5.00	3.00
17	Dave Jolly	10.00	5.00	3.00

		NR MT	EX	VG
19	Jim Wilson	10.00	5.00	3.00
20	Ray Crone	10.00	5.00	3.00
21	Warren Spahn	65.00	32.00	19.50
22	Gene Conley	10.00	5.00	3.00
23	Johnny Logan	12.00	6.00	3.50
24	Charlie White	10.00	5.00	3.00
27	George Metkovich	10.00	5.00	3.00
28	John Cooney	10.00	5.00	3.00
29	Paul Burris	10.00	5.00	3.00
31	Wm. Walters	10.00	5.00	3.00
32	Ernest T. Johnson	10.00	5.00	3.00
33	Lew Burdette	20.00	10.00	6.00
34	Bob Thomson	200.00	100.00	60.00
35	Robert Keely	10.00	5.00	3.00
38	Billy Bruton	10.00	5.00	3.00
40	Charles Grimm	10.00	5.00	3.00
41	Ed Mathews	65.00	32.00	19.50
42	Sam Calderone	10.00	5.00	3.00
47	Joey Jay	10.00	5.00	3.00
48	Andy Pafko	12.00	6.00	3.50
----	Dr. Charles Lacks (trainer)	10.00	5.00	3.00
----	Joseph F. Taylor (asst. trainer)	10.00	5.00	3.00

1955 Johnston Cookies Braves

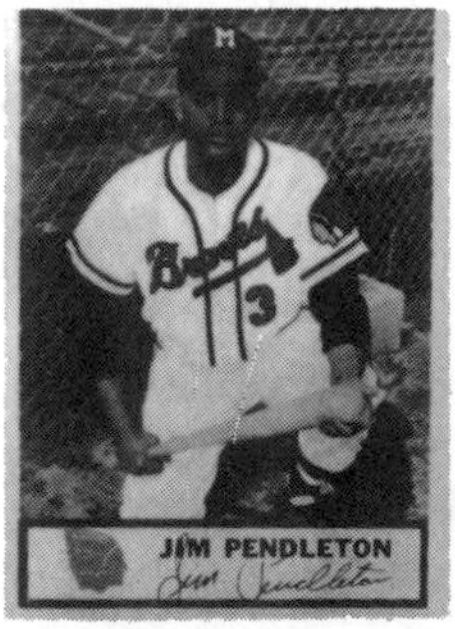

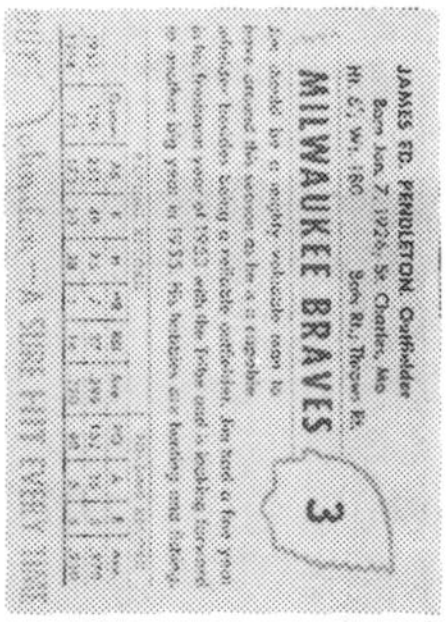

A third change in size and format was undertaken in the third and final year of Braves sets produced by Johnston's. The 35 cards in the 1955 set were issued in six fold-out panels of six cards each (Andy Pafko was double-printed). As in 1954, cards are numbered by uniform number, except those of the team equipment manager, trainer and road secretary (former Boston star Duffy Lewis). Single cards measure 2-7/8" by 4". Besides including panels in boxes of cookies, the '55 Johnston's could be ordered for 5¢ per panel by mail. The scarcest of the Johnston's issues, the 1955 set can be found today still in complete panels, or as single cards.

		NR MT	EX	VG
Complete Folder Set:		1500.00	750.00	450.00
Complete Singles Set:		1000.00	500.00	300.00
Common Player:		15.00	7.50	4.50
Common Folder:		125.00	62.00	37.00
1	Del Crandall	25.00	12.50	7.50
3	Jim Pendleton	15.00	7.50	4.50
4	Danny O'Connell	15.00	7.50	4.50
6	Jack Dittmer	15.00	7.50	4.50
9	Joe Adcock	25.00	12.50	7.50
10	Bob Buhl	20.00	10.00	6.00
11	Phil Paine	15.00	7.50	4.50
12	Ray Crone	15.00	7.50	4.50
15	Charlie Gorin	15.00	7.50	4.50
16	Dave Jolly	15.00	7.50	4.50
17	Chet Nichols	15.00	7.50	4.50
18	Chuck Tanner	25.00	12.50	7.50
19	Jim Wilson	15.00	7.50	4.50
20	Dave Koslo	15.00	7.50	4.50
21	Warren Spahn	80.00	40.00	24.00
22	Gene Conley	20.00	10.00	6.00
23	John Logan	20.00	10.00	6.00
24	Charlie White	15.00	7.50	4.50
28	Johnny Cooney	15.00	7.50	4.50
30	Roy Smalley	15.00	7.50	4.50
31	Bucky Walters	15.00	7.50	4.50
32	Ernie Johnson	15.00	7.50	4.50

		NR MT	EX	VG
33	Lew Burdette	25.00	12.50	7.50
34	Bobby Thomson	25.00	12.50	7.50
35	Bob Keely	15.00	7.50	4.50
38	Billy Bruton	20.00	10.00	6.00
39	George Crowe	15.00	7.50	4.50
40	Charlie Grimm	20.00	10.00	6.00
41	Eddie Mathews	80.00	40.00	24.00
44	Hank Aaron	400.00	200.00	120.00
47	Joe Jay	15.00	7.50	4.50
48	Andy Pakfo	20.00	10.00	6.00
---	Dr. Charles K. Lacks	15.00	7.50	4.50
---	Duffy Lewis	15.00	7.50	4.50
---	Joe Taylor	15.00	7.50	4.50
---	Series 1 Folder (Hank Aaron, Lew Burdette, Del Crandall, Charlie Gorin, Bob Keely, Danny O'Connell)	400.00	200.00	120.00
---	Series 2 Folder (Joe Adcock, Joe Jay, Dr. Charles K. Lacks, Chet Nichols, Andy Pafko, Charlie White)	125.00	62.00	37.00
---	Series 3 Folder (Gene Conley, George Crowe, Jim Pendleton, Roy Smalley, Warren Spahn, Joe Taylor)	175.00	87.00	52.00
---	Series 4 Folder (Billy Bruton, John Cooney, Dave Jolly, Dave Koslo, Johnny Logan, Andy Pafko)	125.00	62.00	37.00
---	Series 5 Folder (Ray Crone, Ernie Johnson, Duffy Lewis, Eddie Mathews, Phil Paine, Chuck Tanner)	200.00	100.00	60.00
---	Series 6 Folder (Bob Buhl, Jack Dittmer, Charlie Grimm, Bobby Thomson, Bucky Walters, Jim Wilson)	125.00	62.00	37.00

K

1982 K-Mart

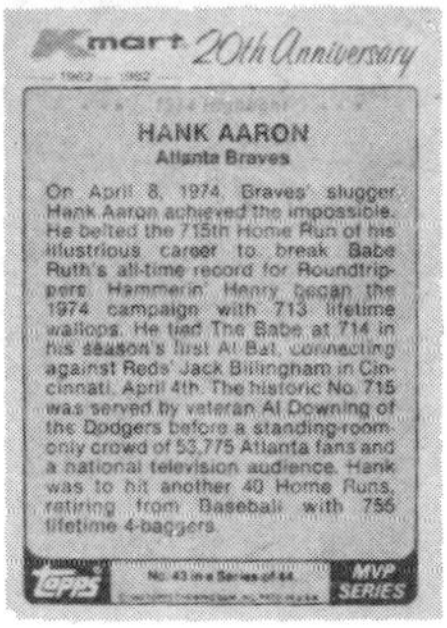

The first of what became dozens of boxed sets specially produced for retail chain stores by the major card producers, the 1982 K-Mart set has not enjoyed any collector popularity. The theme of the set is Most Valuable Players and selected record-breaking performances of the 1962-1981 seasons. The design used miniature reproductions of Topps cards of the era, except in a few cases where designs had to be created because original cards were never issued (1962 Maury Wills, 1975 Fred Lynn.) Originally sold for about $2 per boxed set of 44, large quantities were bought up by speculators who got burned when over-production and lack of demand caused the set to drop as low as 10¢. The 2-1/2" by 3-1/2" cards were printed by Topps.

		MT	NR MT	EX
Complete Set:		1.00	.70	.40
Common Player:		.03	.02	.01
1	Mickey Mantle	.25	.20	.10
2	Maury Wills	.05	.04	.02
3	Elston Howard	.03	.02	.01
4	Sandy Koufax	.10	.08	.04
5	Brooks Robinson	.05	.04	.02
6	Ken Boyer	.03	.02	.01
7	Zoilo Versalles	.03	.02	.01
8	Willie Mays	.10	.08	.04
9	Frank Robinson	.05	.04	.02
10	Bob Clemente	.10	.08	.04
11	Carl Yastrzemski	.10	.08	.04
12	Orlando Cepeda	.03	.02	.01
13	Denny McLain	.03	.02	.01
14	Bob Gibson	.05	.04	.02
15	Harmon Killebrew	.05	.04	.02
16	Willie McCovey	.05	.04	.02
17	Boog Powell	.03	.02	.01
18	Johnny Bench	.07	.05	.03
19	Vida Blue	.03	.02	.01
20	Joe Torre	.03	.02	.01
21	Rich Allen	.03	.02	.01
22	Johnny Bench	.07	.05	.03
23	Reggie Jackson	.07	.05	.03
24	Pete Rose	.12	.09	.05
25	Jeff Burroughs	.03	.02	.01
26	Steve Garvey	.07	.05	.03
27	Fred Lynn	.03	.02	.01
28	Joe Morgan	.05	.04	.02
29	Thurman Munson	.05	.04	.02
30	Joe Morgan	.05	.04	.02
31	Rod Carew	.07	.05	.03
32	George Foster	.03	.02	.01
33	Jim Rice	.05	.04	.02
34	Dave Parker	.05	.04	.02
35	Don Baylor	.03	.02	.01
36	Keith Hernandez	.03	.02	.01
37	Willie Stargell	.05	.04	.02
38	George Brett	.07	.05	.03
39	Mike Schmidt	.07	.05	.03
40	Rollie Fingers	.05	.04	.02
41	Mike Schmidt	.07	.05	.03
42	Don Drysdale	.05	.04	.02
43	Hank Aaron	.10	.08	.04
44	Pete Rose	.12	.09	.05

1987 K-Mart

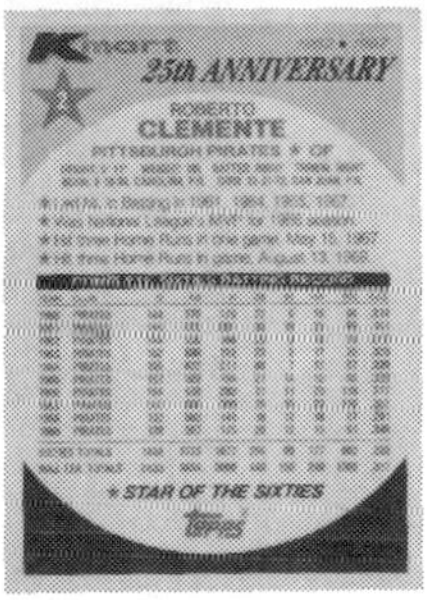

Produced by Topps for K-Mart, the 1987 K-Mart set was distributed by the department stores to celebrate their 25th anniversary. Entitled "Baseball's Stars of the Decades," the 33-card set was issued in a special cardboard box with one stick of bubblegum. The card fronts feature a full-color photo set diagonally against a red background. The backs contain career highlights plus pitching or batting statistics for the decade in which the player enjoyed his greatest success. Cards are the standard 2-1/2" by 3-1/2" size.

		MT	NR MT	EX
Complete Set:		4.00	3.00	1.50
Common Player:		.10	.08	.04
1	Hank Aaron	.50	.40	.20
2	Roberto Clemente	.40	.30	.15
3	Bob Gibson	.10	.08	.04
4	Harmon Killebrew	.10	.08	.04
5	Mickey Mantle	1.00	.70	.40
6	Juan Marichal	.10	.08	.04
7	Roger Maris	.30	.25	.12
8	Willie Mays	.50	.40	.20
9	Brooks Robinson	.30	.25	.12

		MT	NR MT	EX
10	Frank Robinson	.20	.15	.08
11	Carl Yastrzemski	.50	.40	.20
12	Johnny Bench	.30	.25	.12
13	Lou Brock	.20	.15	.08
14	Rod Carew	.30	.25	.12
15	Steve Carlton	.20	.15	.08
16	Reggie Jackson	.30	.25	.12
17	Jim Palmer	.10	.08	.04
18	Jim Rice	.10	.08	.04
19	Pete Rose	.50	.40	.20
20	Nolan Ryan	.20	.15	.08
21	Tom Seaver	.20	.15	.08
22	Willie Stargell	.10	.08	.04
23	Wade Boggs	.50	.40	.20
24	George Brett	.40	.30	.15
25	Gary Carter	.20	.15	.08
26	Dwight Gooden	.50	.40	.20
27	Rickey Henderson	.35	.25	.12
28	Don Mattingly	.50	.40	.20
29	Dale Murphy	.40	.30	.15
30	Eddie Murray	.20	.15	.08
31	Mike Schmidt	.30	.25	.12
32	Darryl Strawberry	.40	.30	.15
33	Fernando Valenzuela	.10	.08	.04

1988 K-Mart

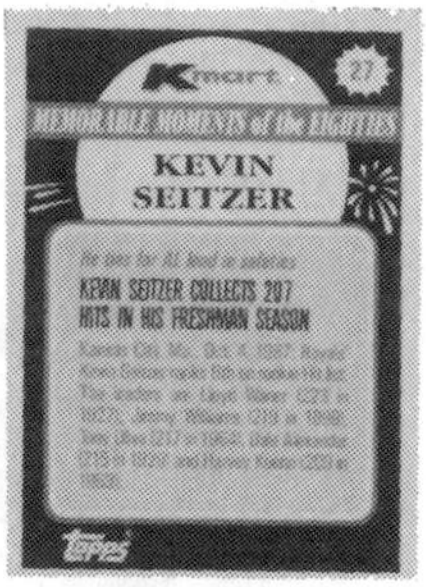

This 33-card boxed set, titled "Memorable Moments," was produced by Topps for distribution via K-Mart. Two previous Topps K-Mart sets were issued: a 44-card set in 1982 in honor of K-Mart's 20th anniversary and a 33-card set in 1987 for the company's 25th anniversary. The 1988 cards are standard-size with red, white and blue borders and a super glossy coating. Numbered card backs are printed in red and blue on white and highlight special events in the featured players' careers. The set was marketed in a bright yellow and green checklist box (gum included).

		MT	NR MT	EX
Complete Set:		3.00	2.25	1.25
Common Player:		.10	.08	.04
1	George Bell	.20	.15	.08
2	Wade Boggs	.50	.40	.20
3	George Brett	.30	.25	.12
4	Jose Canseco	.50	.40	.20
5	Jack Clark	.15	.11	.06
6	Will Clark	.25	.20	.10
7	Roger Clemens	.40	.30	.15
8	Vince Coleman	.15	.11	.06
9	Andre Dawson	.15	.11	.06
10	Dwight Gooden	.40	.30	.15
11	Pedro Guerrero	.15	.11	.06
12	Tony Gwynn	.25	.20	.10
13	Rickey Henderson	.25	.20	.10
14	Keith Hernandez	.15	.11	.06
15	Don Mattingly	.40	.30	.15
16	Mark McGwire	.40	.30	.15
17	Paul Molitor	.12	.09	.05
18	Dale Murphy	.20	.15	.08
19	Tim Raines	.20	.15	.08
20	Dave Righetti	.12	.09	.05
21	Cal Ripken	.25	.20	.10
22	Pete Rose	.50	.40	.20
23	Nolan Ryan	.25	.20	.10
24	Benny Santiago	.25	.20	.10
25	Mike Schmidt	.30	.25	.12
26	Mike Scott	.10	.08	.04
27	Kevin Seitzer	.25	.20	.10
28	Ozzie Smith	.15	.11	.06
29	Darryl Strawberry	.30	.25	.12
30	Rick Sutcliffe	.10	.08	.04
31	Fernando Valenzuela	.15	.11	.06
32	Todd Worrell	.10	.08	.04
33	Robin Yount	.15	.11	.06

1989 K-Mart

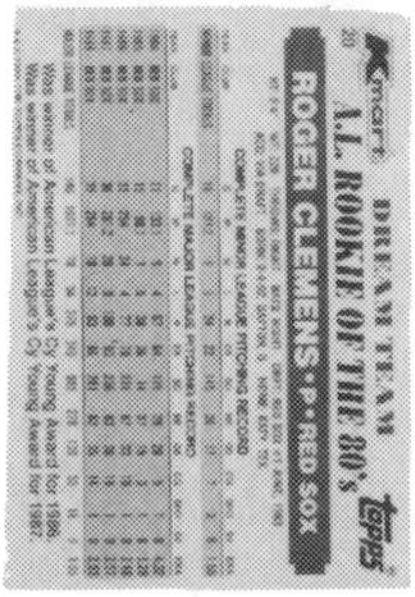

This 33-card, glossy set was produced by Topps for K-Mart, where it was sold in stores nationwide. The standard-size cards feature mostly action shots on the front, and include the Topps "Dream Team" logo at the top, with the K-Mart logo in the lower right corner. The first 11 cards in the set picture the top rookies of 1988, while next 11 picture the top A.L. rookies of the '80s, and the final 11 cards highlight the top N.L. rookies of the decade.

		MT	NR MT	EX
Complete Set:		4.00	3.00	1.50
Common Player:		.10	.08	.04
1	Mark Grace	.50	.40	.20
2	Ron Gant	.15	.11	.06
3	Chris Sabo	.15	.11	.06
4	Walt Weiss	.15	.11	.06
5	Jay Buhner	.15	.11	.06
6	Cecil Espy	.10	.08	.04
7	Dave Gallagher	.15	.11	.06
8	Damon Berryhill	.10	.08	.04
9	Tim Belcher	.20	.15	.08
10	Paul Gibson	.10	.08	.04
11	Gregg Jefferies	.50	.40	.20
12	Don Mattingly	1.00	.70	.40
13	Harold Reynolds	.15	.11	.06
14	Wade Boggs	.50	.40	.20
15	Cal Ripken	.25	.20	.10
16	Kirby Puckett	.40	.30	.15
17	George Bell	.15	.11	.06
18	Jose Canseco	.50	.40	.20
19	Terry Steinbach	.20	.15	.08
20	Roger Clemens	.40	.30	.15
21	Mark Langston	.20	.15	.08
22	Harold Baines	.15	.11	.06
23	Will Clark	.50	.40	.20
24	Ryne Sanberg	.25	.20	.10
25	Tim Wallach	.10	.08	.04
26	Shawon Dunston	.10	.08	.04
27	Rock Raines	.15	.11	.06
28	Darryl Strawberry	.35	.25	.14
29	Tony Gwynn	.35	.25	.14
30	Tony Pena	.10	.08	.04
31	Doc Gooden	.35	.25	.12
32	Fernando Valenzuela	.15	.11	.06
33	Pedro Guerrero	.15	.11	.06

A player's name in italic type indicates a rookie card. An (FC) indicates a player's first card for that particular card company.

1990 K-Mart

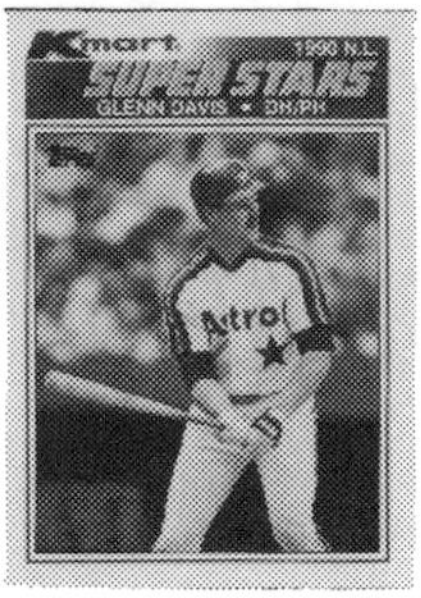

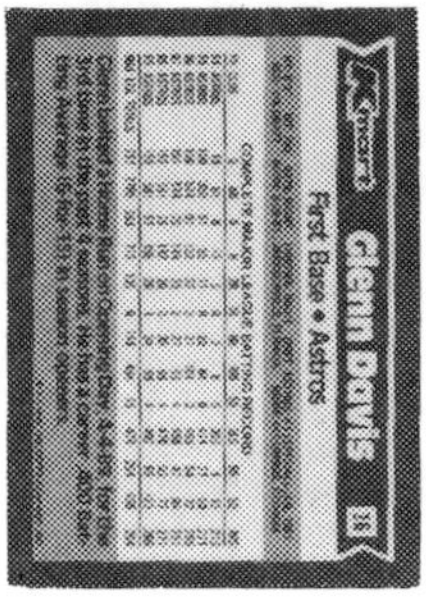

This 33-card, glossy set was produced by Topps for K-Mart, where it was available nationwide. The set is subtitled "Superstars" and features sixteen A.L. players, sixteen N.L. stars and a managers' card featuring both Tony LaRussa and Roger Craig. A special Superstars logo is featured on the card fronts. 1990 marks the fourth consecutive year that Topps has produced a set in cooperation with K-Mart.

		MT	NR MT	EX
Complete Set:		3.00	2.25	1.25
Common Player:		.08	.06	.03
1	Will Clark	.25	.20	.10
2	Ryne Sandberg	.25	.20	.10
3	Howard Johnson	.15	.11	.06
4	Ozzie Smith	.15	.11	.06
5	Tony Gwynn	.15	.11	.06
6	Kevin Mitchell	.20	.15	.08
7	Jerome Walton	.15	.11	.06
8	Craig Biggio	.08	.06	.03
9	Mike Scott	.08	.06	.03
10	Doc Gooden	.20	.15	.08
11	Sid Fernandez	.08	.06	.03
12	Joe Magrane	.08	.06	.03
13	Jay Howell	.08	.06	.03
14	Mark Davis	.08	.06	.03
15	Pedro Guerrero	.10	.08	.04
16	Glenn Davis	.15	.11	.06
17	Don Mattingly	.25	.20	.10
18	Julio Franco	.10	.08	.04
19	Wade Boggs	.20	.15	.08
20	Cal Ripken	.15	.11	.06
21	Jose Canseco	.40	.30	.15
22	Kirby Puckett	.20	.15	.08
23	Rickey Henderson	.25	.20	.10
24	Mickey Tettleton	.08	.06	.03
25	Nolan Ryan	.25	.20	.10
26	Bret Saberhagen	.10	.08	.04
27	Jeff Ballard	.08	.06	.03
28	Chuck Finley	.08	.06	.03
29	Dennis Eckersley	.15	.11	.06
30	Dan Plesac	.08	.06	.03
31	Fred McGriff	.15	.11	.06
32	Mark McGwire	.20	.15	.08
33	Managers (Tony LaRussa, Roger Craig)	.08	.06	.03

1955 Kahn's Wieners Reds

The first of what would become 15 successive years of baseball card issues by the Kahn's meat company of Cincinnati is also the rarest. The set consists of six Cincinnati Redlegs player cards, 3-1/4" by 4". Printed in black and white, with blank backs, the '55 Kahn's cards were distributed at a one-day promotional event at a Cincinnati amusement park, where the featured players were on hand to sign autographs. Like the other Kahn's issues through 1963, the '55 cards have a 1/2" white panel containing an advertising message below the player photo. These cards are sometimes found with this portion cut off, greatly reducing the value of the card.

		NR MT	EX	VG
Complete Set:		3100.00	1550.00	930.00
Common Player:		450.00	225.00	135.00
(1)	Gus Bell	800.00	400.00	240.00
(2)	Ted Kluszewski	750.00	375.00	225.00
(3)	Roy McMillan	450.00	225.00	135.00
(4)	Joe Nuxhall	450.00	225.00	135.00
(5)	Wally Post	450.00	225.00	135.00
(6)	Johnny Temple	450.00	225.00	135.00

1956 Kahn's Wieners Reds

In 1956, Kahn's expanded its baseball card program to include 15 Redlegs players, and began issuing the cards one per pack in packages of hot dogs. Because the cards were packaged in direct contact with the meat, they are often found today in stained condition. In 3-1/4" by 4" format, black and white with blank backs, the '56 Kahn's cards can be distinguished from later issues by the presence of full stadium photographic backgrounds behind the player photos. Like all Kahn's issues, the 1956 set is unnumbered; the checklists are arranged alphabetically for convenience. The set features the first-ever baseball card of Hall of Famer Frank Robinson.

		NR MT	EX	VG
Complete Set:		1600.00	800.00	480.00
Common Player:		75.00	37.00	22.00
(1)	Ed Bailey	75.00	37.00	22.00
(2)	Gus Bell	100.00	50.00	30.00
(3)	Joe Black	100.00	50.00	30.00
(4)	"Smokey" Burgess	100.00	50.00	30.00
(5)	Art Fowler	75.00	37.00	22.00
(6)	Hershell Freeman	75.00	37.00	22.00
(7)	Ray Jablonski	75.00	37.00	22.00
(8)	John Klippstein	75.00	37.00	22.00
(9)	Ted Kluszewski	150.00	75.00	45.00

(10)	Brooks Lawrence	75.00	37.00	22.00
(11)	Roy McMillan	75.00	37.00	22.00
(12)	Joe Nuxhall	100.00	50.00	30.00
(13)	Wally Post	75.00	37.00	22.00
(14)	Frank Robinson	350.00	175.00	105.00
(15)	Johnny Temple	100.00	50.00	30.00

1957 Kahn's Wieners

In its third season of baseball card issue, Kahn's kept the basic 3-1/4" by 4" format, with black and white photos and blank backs. The issue was expanded to 28 players, all Pirates or Reds. The last of the blank-backed Kahn's sets, the 1957 Reds players can be distinguished from the 1956 issue by the general lack of background photo detail, in favor of a neutral light gray background. The Dick Groat card appears with two name variations, a facsimile autograph, "Richard Groat," and a printed "Dick Groat." Both Groat varieties are included in the complete set price.

		NR MT	EX	VG
Complete Set		2600.00	1300.00	780.00
Common Player		50.00	25.00	15.00
(1)	Tom Acker	50.00	25.00	15.00
(2)	Ed Bailey	50.00	25.00	15.00
(3)	Gus Bell	70.00	35.00	21.00
(4)	Smokey Burgess	70.00	35.00	21.00
(5)	Roberto Clemente	650.00	325.00	195.00
(6)	George Crowe	50.00	25.00	15.00
(7)	Elroy Face	70.00	35.00	21.00
(8)	Hershell Freeman	50.00	25.00	15.00
(9)	Robert Friend	50.00	25.00	15.00
(10)	Don Gross	50.00	25.00	15.00
(11a)	Dick Groat	70.00	35.00	21.00
(11b)	Richard Groat	175.00	87.00	52.00
(12)	Warren Hacker	50.00	25.00	15.00
(13)	Don Hoak	70.00	35.00	21.00
(14)	Hal Jeffcoat	50.00	25.00	15.00
(15)	Ron Kline	50.00	25.00	15.00
(16)	John Klippstein	50.00	25.00	15.00
(17)	Ted Kluszewski	100.00	50.00	30.00
(18)	Brooks Lawrence	50.00	25.00	15.00
(19)	Dale Long	50.00	25.00	15.00
(20)	Wm. Mazeroski	100.00	50.00	30.00
(21)	Roy McMillan	50.00	25.00	15.00
(22)	Joe Nuxhall	50.00	25.00	15.00
(23)	Wally Post	50.00	25.00	15.00
(24)	Frank Robinson	250.00	125.00	75.00
(25)	Johnny Temple	50.00	25.00	15.00
(26)	Frank Thomas	50.00	25.00	15.00
(27)	Bob Thurman	50.00	25.00	15.00
(28)	Lee Walls	50.00	25.00	15.00

1958 Kahn's Wieners

Long-time Cincinnati favorite Wally Post became the only Philadelphia Phillies ballplayer to appear in the 15-year run of Kahn's issues when he was traded in 1958, but included as part of the otherwise exclusively Pirates-Reds set. Like previous years, the '58 Kahn's were 3-1/4" by 4", with black and white player photos. Unlike previous years, however, the cards had printing on the back, a story by the pictured player, titled "My Greatest Thrill in Baseball." Quite similar to the 1959 issue, the '58 Kahn's can be

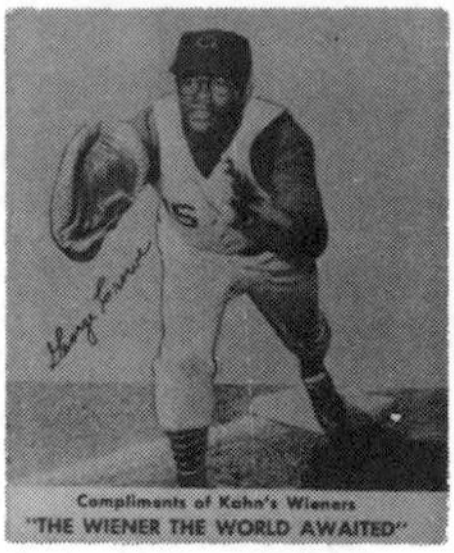

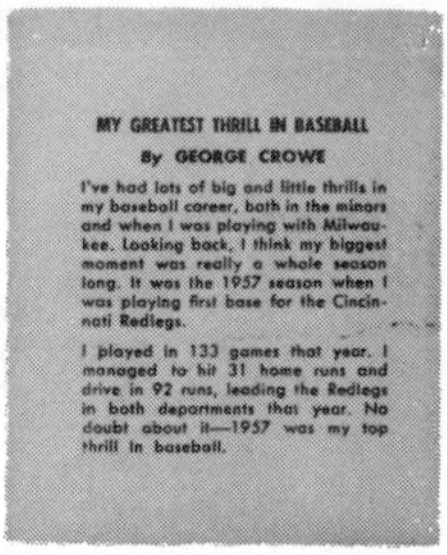

MY GREATEST THRILL IN BASEBALL

By GEORGE CROWE

I've had lots of big and little thrills in my baseball career, both in the minors and when I was playing with Milwaukee. Looking back, I think my biggest moment was really a whole season long. It was the 1957 season when I was playing first base for the Cincinnati Redlegs.

I played in 133 games that year. I managed to hit 31 home runs and drive in 92 runs, leading the Redlegs in both departments that year. No doubt about it—1957 was my top thrill in baseball.

distinguished by the fact that the top line of the advertising panel at bottom has the word "Wieners" in 1958, but not in 1959.

		NR MT	EX	VG
Complete Set:		2600.00	1300.00	780.00
Common Player:		50.00	25.00	15.00
(1)	Ed Bailey	50.00	25.00	15.00
(2)	Gene Baker	50.00	25.00	15.00
(3)	Gus Bell	60.00	30.00	18.00
(4)	Smokey Burgess	60.00	30.00	18.00
(5)	Roberto Clemente	500.00	250.00	150.00
(6)	George Crowe	50.00	25.00	15.00
(7)	Elroy Face	60.00	30.00	18.00
(8)	Henry Foiles	50.00	25.00	15.00
(9)	Dee Fondy	50.00	25.00	15.00
(10)	Robert Friend	60.00	30.00	18.00
(11)	Richard Groat	100.00	50.00	30.00
(12)	Harvey Haddix	60.00	30.00	18.00
(13)	Don Hoak	60.00	30.00	18.00
(14)	Hal Jeffcoat	60.00	30.00	18.00
(15)	Ronald L. Kline	60.00	30.00	18.00
(16)	Ted Kluszewski	100.00	50.00	30.00
(17)	Vernon Law	60.00	30.00	18.00
(18)	Brooks Lawrence	50.00	25.00	15.00
(19)	William Mazeroski	100.00	50.00	30.00
(20)	Roy McMillan	50.00	25.00	15.00
(21)	Joe Nuxhall	60.00	30.00	18.00
(22)	Wally Post	275.00	137.00	80.00
(23)	John Powers	50.00	25.00	15.00
(24)	Robert T. Purkey	50.00	25.00	15.00
(25)	Charles Rabe	275.00	137.00	80.00
(26)	Frank Robinson	275.00	137.00	80.00
(27)	Robert Skinner	50.00	25.00	15.00
(28)	Johnny Temple	50.00	25.00	15.00
(29)	Frank Thomas	275.00	137.00	80.00

1959 Kahn's Wieners

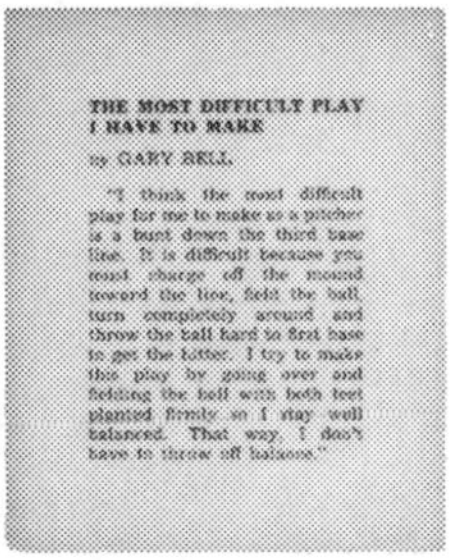

A third team was added to the Kahn's lineup in 1959, the Cleveland Indians joining the Pirates and Reds, bringing the number of cards in the set to 38. Again printed in black and white in the 3-1/4" by 4" size, the 1959 Kahn's cards can be differentiated from the previous issue by the lack of the word "Wieners" on the top line of the advertising panel at bottom. Backs again featured a story written by the pictured player, titled "The Toughest Play I Had to Make," "My Most Difficult Moment in Baseball," or

"The Toughest Batters I Have to Face."

		NR MT	EX	VG
Complete Set:		4250.00	2125.00	1275.
Common Player:		45.00	22.00	13.50
(1)	Ed Bailey	45.00	22.00	13.50
(2)	Gary Bell	45.00	22.00	13.50
(3)	Gus Bell	50.00	25.00	15.00
(4)	Richard Brodowski	500.00	250.00	150.00
(5)	Forrest Burgess	50.00	25.00	15.00
(6)	Roberto Clemente	450.00	225.00	135.00
(7)	Rocky Colavito	75.00	37.00	22.00
(8)	ElRoy Face	50.00	25.00	15.00
(9)	Robert Friend	50.00	25.00	15.00
(10)	Joe Gordon	50.00	25.00	15.00
(11)	Jim Grant	45.00	22.00	13.50
(12)	Richard M. Groat	60.00	30.00	18.00
(13)	Harvey Haddix	350.00	175.00	105.00
(14)	Woodie Held	350.00	175.00	105.00
(15)	Don Hoak	50.00	25.00	15.00
(16)	Ronald Kline	45.00	22.00	13.50
(17)	Ted Kluszewski	75.00	37.00	22.00
(18)	Vernon Law	50.00	25.00	15.00
(19)	Jerry Lynch	45.00	22.00	13.50
(20)	Billy Martin	75.00	37.00	22.00
(21)	William Mazeroski	50.00	25.00	15.00
(22)	Cal McLish	350.00	175.00	105.00
(23)	Roy McMillan	45.00	22.00	13.50
(24)	Minnie Minoso	60.00	30.00	18.00
(25)	Russell Nixon	45.00	22.00	13.50
(26)	Joe Nuxhall	50.00	25.00	15.00
(27)	Jim Perry	50.00	25.00	15.00
(28)	Vada Pinson	60.00	30.00	18.00
(29)	Vic Power	45.00	22.00	13.50
(30)	Robert Purkey	45.00	22.00	13.50
(31)	Frank Robinson	175.00	87.00	52.00
(32)	Herb Score	50.00	25.00	15.00
(33)	Robert Skinner	45.00	22.00	13.50
(34)	George Strickland	45.00	22.00	13.50
(35)	Richard L. Stuart	50.00	25.00	15.00
(36)	John Temple	45.00	22.00	13.50
(37)	Frank Thomas	50.00	25.00	15.00
(38)	George A. Witt	45.00	22.00	13.50

1960 Kahn's Wieners

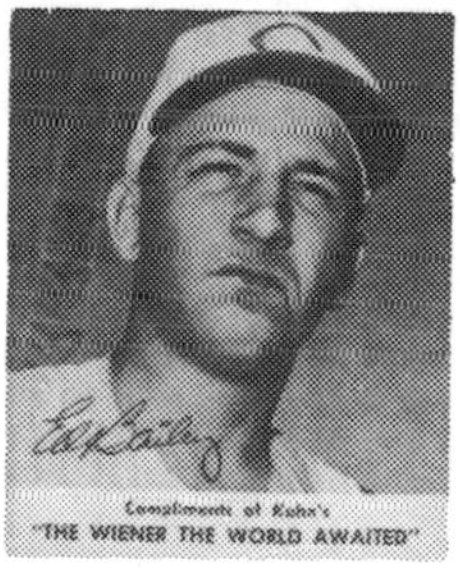

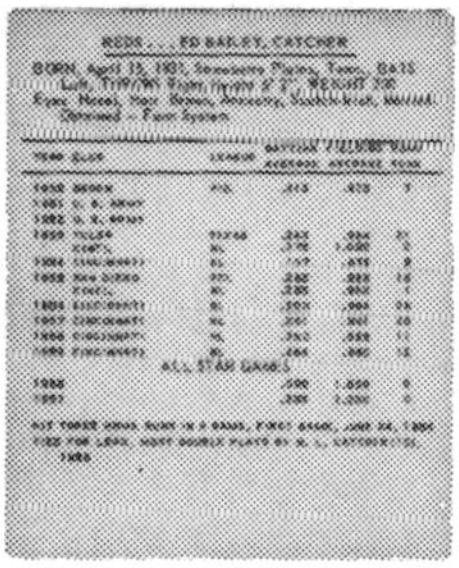

Three more teams joined the Kahn's roster in 1960, the Chicago Cubs, Chicago White Sox and St. Louis Cardinals. A total of 42 different players are represented in the set. Again 3-1/4" by 4" with black and white photos, the 1960 Kahn's cards featured for the first time player stats and personal data on the back, except Harvey Kuenn, which was issued with blank back, probably because of the lateness of his trade to the Indians.

		NR MT	EX	VG
Complete Set:		2000.00	1000.00	600.00
Common Player:		30.00	15.00	9.00
(1)	Ed Bailey	30.00	15.00	9.00
(2)	Gary Bell	30.00	15.00	9.00
(3)	Gus Bell	35.00	17.50	10.50
(4)	Forrest Burgess	35.00	17.50	10.50
(5)	Gino N. Cimoli	30.00	15.00	9.00
(6)	Roberto Clemente	300.00	150.00	90.00
(7)	ElRoy Face	35.00	17.50	10.50
(8)	Tito Francona	35.00	17.50	10.50
(9)	Robert Friend	35.00	17.50	10.50
(10)	Jim Grant	30.00	15.00	9.00
(11)	Richard Groat	40.00	20.00	12.00
(12)	Harvey Haddix	35.00	17.50	10.50
(13)	Woodie Held	30.00	15.00	9.00
(14)	Bill Henry	30.00	15.00	9.00
(15)	Don Hoak	35.00	17.50	10.50
(16)	Jay Hook	30.00	15.00	9.00
(17)	Eddie Kasko	30.00	15.00	9.00
(18)	Ronnie Kline	40.00	20.00	12.00
(19)	Ted Kluszewski	50.00	25.00	15.00
(20)	Harvey Kuenn	300.00	150.00	90.00
(21)	Vernon S. Law	35.00	17.50	10.50
(22)	Brooks Lawrence	30.00	15.00	9.00
(23)	Jerry Lynch	30.00	15.00	9.00
(24)	Billy Martin	60.00	30.00	18.00
(25)	William Mazeroski	40.00	20.00	12.00
(26)	Cal McLish	30.00	15.00	9.00
(27)	Roy McMillan	30.00	15.00	9.00
(28)	Don Newcombe	35.00	17.50	10.50
(29)	Russ Nixon	30.00	15.00	9.00
(30)	Joe Nuxhall	35.00	17.50	10.50
(31)	James J. O'Toole	30.00	15.00	9.00
(32)	Jim Perry	35.00	17.50	10.50
(33)	Vada Pinson	40.00	20.00	12.00
(34)	Vic Power	30.00	15.00	9.00
(35)	Robert T. Purkey	30.00	15.00	9.00
(36)	Frank Robinson	150.00	75.00	45.00
(37)	Herb Score	35.00	17.50	10.50
(38)	Robert R. Skinner	30.00	15.00	9.00
(39)	Richard L. Stuart	35.00	17.50	10.50
(40)	John Temple	30.00	15.00	9.00
(41)	Frank Thomas	40.00	20.00	12.00
(42)	Lee Walls	35.00	17.50	10.50

1961 Kahn's Wieners

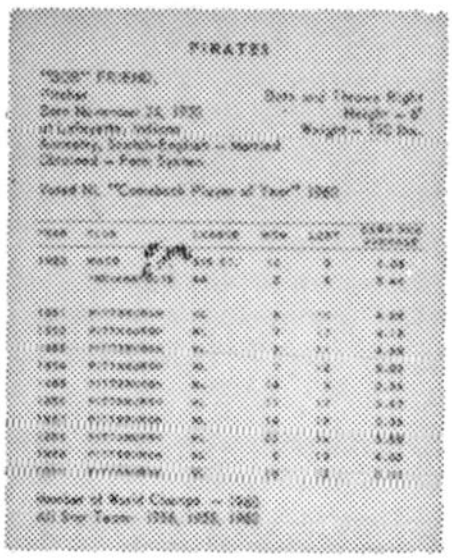

After a single season, the Chicago and St. Louis teams dropped out of the Kahn's program, but the 1961 set was larger than ever, at 43 cards. The same basic format - 3-1/4" by 4" size, black and white photos and statistical information on the back - was retained. For the first time in '61, the meat company made complete sets of the Kahn's cards available to collectors via a mail-in offer. This makes the 1961 and later Kahn's cards considerably easier to obtain than the earlier issues.

		NR MT	EX	VG
Complete Set:		1000.00	500.00	300.00
Common Player:		18.00	9.00	5.50
(1)	John A. Antonelli	20.00	10.00	6.00
(2)	Ed Bailey	18.00	9.00	5.50
(3)	Gary Bell	18.00	9.00	5.50
(4)	Gus Bell	20.00	10.00	6.00
(5)	James P. Brosnan	18.00	9.00	5.50
(6)	Forrest Burgess	20.00	10.00	6.00
(7)	Gino Cimoli	18.00	9.00	5.50
(8)	Roberto Clemente	200.00	100.00	60.00
(9)	Gordon Coleman	18.00	9.00	5.50
(10)	Jimmie Dykes	20.00	10.00	6.00
(11)	ElRoy Face	25.00	12.50	7.50
(12)	Tito Francona	20.00	10.00	6.00
(13)	Robert Friend	20.00	10.00	6.00
(14)	Gene L. Freese	18.00	9.00	5.50
(15)	Jim Grant	18.00	9.00	5.50

		NR MT	EX	VG
(16)	Richard M. Groat	30.00	15.00	9.00
(17)	Harvey Haddix	20.00	10.00	6.00
(18)	Woodie Held	18.00	9.00	5.50
(19)	Don Hoak	20.00	10.00	6.00
(20)	Jay Hook	18.00	9.00	5.50
(21)	Joe Jay	18.00	9.00	5.50
(22)	Eddie Kasko	18.00	9.00	5.50
(23)	Willie Kirkland	18.00	9.00	5.50
(24)	Vernon S. Law	25.00	12.50	7.50
(25)	Jerry Lynch	18.00	9.00	5.50
(26)	Jim Maloney	25.00	12.50	7.50
(27)	William Mazeroski	30.00	15.00	9.00
(28)	Wilmer D. Mizell	20.00	10.00	6.00
(29)	Glenn R. Nelson	18.00	9.00	5.50
(30)	James J. O'Toole	18.00	9.00	5.50
(31)	Jim Perry	20.00	10.00	6.00
(32)	John M. Phillips	18.00	9.00	5.50
(33)	Vada E. Pinson Jr.	30.00	15.00	9.00
(34)	Wally Post	18.00	9.00	5.50
(35)	Vic Power	18.00	9.00	5.50
(36)	Robert T. Purkey	18.00	9.00	5.50
(37)	Frank Robinson	125.00	62.00	37.00
(38)	John A. Romano Jr.	18.00	9.00	5.50
(39)	Dick Schofield	18.00	9.00	5.50
(40)	Robert Skinner	18.00	9.00	5.50
(41)	Hal Smith	18.00	9.00	5.50
(42)	Richard Stuart	20.00	10.00	6.00
(43)	John E. Temple	18.00	9.00	5.50

1962 Kahn's Wieners

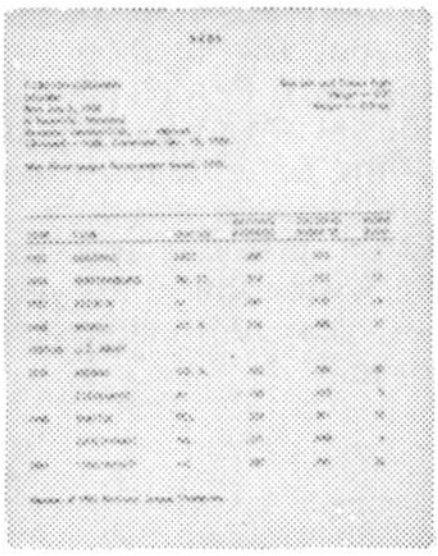

Besides the familiar Reds, Pirates and Indians players in the 1962 Kahn's set, a fourth team was added, the Minnesota Twins, though the overall size of the set was decreased from the previous year, to 38 players in 1962. The cards retained the 3-1/4" by 4" black and white format of previous years. The '62 Kahn's set is awash in variations. Besides the photo and front design variations on the Bell, Purkey and Power cards, each Cleveland player can be found with two back variations, listing the team either as "Cleveland" or "Cleveland Indians." The complete set values listed below include all variations.

		NR MT	EX	VG
Complete Set:		2000.00	1000.00	600.00
Common Player:		15.00	7.50	4.50
(1a)	Gary Bell (fat man in background)	150.00	75.00	45.00
(1b)	Gary Bell (no fat man)	40.00	20.00	12.00
(2)	James P. Brosnan	15.00	7.50	4.50
(3)	Forrest Burgess	20.00	10.00	6.00
(4)	Leonardo Cardenas	15.00	7.50	4.50
(5)	Roberto Clemente	150.00	75.00	45.00
(6a)	Ty Cline (Cleveland Indians back)	75.00	37.00	22.00
(6b)	Ty Cline (Cleveland back)	30.00	15.00	9.00
(7)	Gordon Coleman	15.00	7.50	4.50
(8)	Dick Donovan	30.00	15.00	9.00
(9)	John Edwards	15.00	7.50	4.50
(10a)	Tito Francona (Cleveland Indians back)	75.00	37.00	22.00
(10b)	Tito Francona (Cleveland back)	30.00	15.00	9.00
(11)	Gene Freese	15.00	7.50	4.50
(12)	Robert B. Friend	20.00	10.00	6.00
(13)	Joe Gibbon	90.00	45.00	27.00
(14a)	Jim Grant (Cleveland Indians back)	75.00	37.00	22.00
(14b)	Jim Grant (Cleveland back)	30.00	15.00	9.00
(15)	Richard M. Groat	25.00	12.50	7.50
(16)	Harvey Haddix	20.00	10.00	6.00
(17a)	Woodie Held (Cleveland Indians back)	90.00	45.00	27.00
(17b)	Woodie Held (Cleveland back)	30.00	15.00	9.00
(18)	Bill Henry	15.00	7.50	4.50
(19)	Don Hoak	20.00	10.00	6.00
(20)	Ken Hunt	15.00	7.50	4.50
(21)	Joseph R. Jay	15.00	7.50	4.50
(22)	Eddie Kasko	15.00	7.50	4.50
(23a)	Willie Kirkland (Cleveland Indians back)	75.00	37.00	22.00
(23b)	Willie Kirkland (Cleveland back)	30.00	15.00	9.00
(24a)	Barry Latman (Cleveland Indians back)	75.00	37.00	22.00
(24b)	Barry Latman (Cleveland back)	30.00	15.00	9.00
(25)	Jerry Lynch	15.00	7.50	4.50
(26)	Jim Maloney	20.00	10.00	6.00
(27)	William Mazeroski	25.00	12.50	7.50
(28)	Jim O'Toole	15.00	7.50	4.50
(29a)	Jim Perry (Cleveland Indians back)	90.00	45.00	27.00
(29b)	Jim Perry (Cleveland back)	30.00	15.00	9.00
(30a)	John M. Phillips (Cleveland Indians back)	75.00	37.00	22.00
(30b)	John M. Phillips (Cleveland back)	30.00	15.00	9.00
(31)	Vada E. Pinson	25.00	12.50	7.50
(32)	Wally Post	15.00	7.50	4.50
(33a)	Vic Power (Cleveland Indians back)	75.00	37.00	22.00
(33b)	Vic Power (Cleveland back)	30.00	15.00	9.00
(33c)	Vic Power (Minnesota Twins back)	150.00	75.00	45.00
(34a)	Robert T. Purkey (no autograph)	150.00	75.00	45.00
(34b)	Robert T. Purkey (with autograph)	40.00	20.00	12.00
(35)	Frank Robinson	80.00	40.00	24.00
(36a)	John Romano (Cleveland Indians back)	75.00	37.00	22.00
(36b)	John Romano (Cleveland back)	30.00	15.00	9.00
(37)	Dick Stuart	20.00	10.00	6.00
(38)	Bill Virdon	20.00	10.00	6.00

1963 Kahn's Wieners

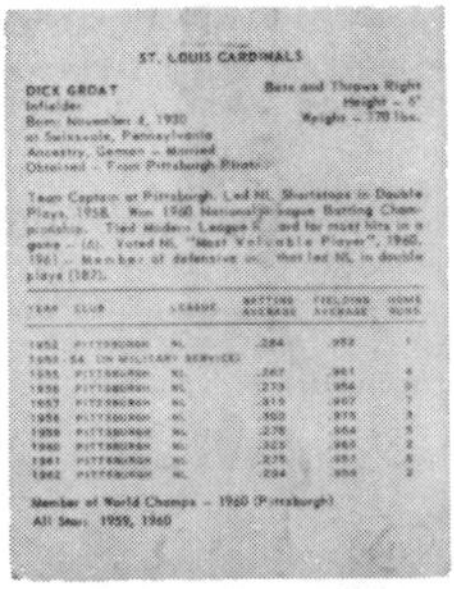
ST. LOUIS CARDINALS

DICK GROAT

In 1963, for the first time since Kahn's began issuing baseball cards in 1955, the design underwent a significant change, white borders were added to the top and sides of player photo. Also, the card size was changed to 3-3/16" by 4-1/4". Statistical and personal data continued to be printed on the card backs. Joining traditional Reds, Pirates and Indians personnel in the 30-card 1963 set were a handful of New York Yankees and Dick Groat, in his new identity as a St. Louis Cardinal.

		NR MT	EX	VG
Complete Set:		800.00	400.00	240.00
Common Player:		15.00	7.50	4.50
(1)	Robert Bailey	15.00	7.50	4.50
(2)	Don Blasingame	15.00	7.50	4.50
(3)	Clete Boyer	25.00	12.50	7.50
(4)	Forrest Burgess	20.00	10.00	6.00

		NR MT	EX	VG
(5)	Leonardo Cardenas	15.00	7.50	4.50
(6)	Roberto Clemente	150.00	75.00	45.00
(7)	Don Clendennon (Donn Clendenon)	15.00	7.50	4.50
(8)	Gordon Coleman	15.00	7.50	4.50
(9)	John A. Edwards	15.00	7.50	4.50
(10)	Gene Freese	15.00	7.50	4.50
(11)	Robert B. Friend	20.00	10.00	6.00
(12)	Joe Gibbon	15.00	7.50	4.50
(13)	Dick Groat	25.00	12.50	7.50
(14)	Harvey Haddix	20.00	10.00	6.00
(15)	Elston Howard	30.00	15.00	9.00
(16)	Joey Jay	15.00	7.50	4.50
(17)	Eddie Kasko	15.00	7.50	4.50
(18)	Tony Kubek	30.00	15.00	9.00
(19)	Jerry Lynch	15.00	7.50	4.50
(20)	Jim Maloney	20.00	10.00	6.00
(21)	William Mazeroski	25.00	12.50	7.50
(22)	Joe Nuxhall	20.00	10.00	6.00
(23)	Jim O'Toole	15.00	7.50	4.50
(24)	Vada E. Pinson	25.00	12.50	7.50
(25)	Robert T. Purkey	15.00	7.50	4.50
(26)	Bob Richardson	30.00	15.00	9.00
(27)	Frank Robinson	70.00	35.00	21.00
(28)	Bill Stafford	20.00	10.00	6.00
(29)	Ralph W. Terry	25.00	12.50	7.50
(30)	Bill Virdon	20.00	10.00	6.00

1964 Kahn's Wieners

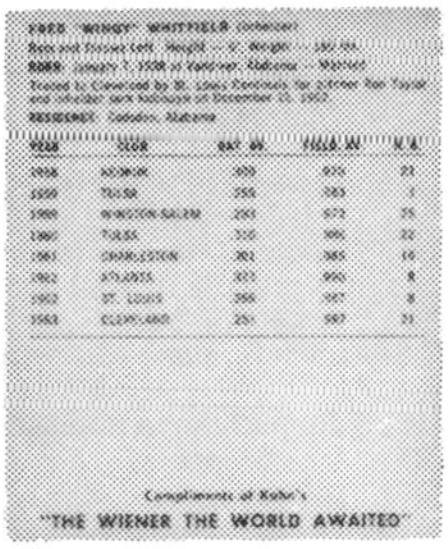
Compliments of Kahn's
"THE WIENER THE WORLD AWAITED"

After nearly a decade of virtually identical card issues, the 1964 Kahn's issue was an abrupt change. In a new size, 3" by 3-1/2", the nearly square cards featured a borderless color photo. The only other design element on the front of the card was a facsimile autograph. The advertising slogan which had traditionally appeared on the front of the card was moved to the back, where it joined the player's stats and personal data. The teams in the 1964 issue once again reverted to the Reds, Pirates and Indians, for a total of 31 cards.

		NR MT	EX	VG
Complete Set:		900.00	450.00	270.00
Common Player:		9.00	4.50	2.75
(1)	Max Alvis	9.00	4.50	2.75
(2)	Bob Bailey	9.00	4.50	2.75
(3)	Leonardo Cardenas	9.00	4.50	2.75
(4)	Roberto Clemente	150.00	75.00	45.00
(5)	Donn A. Clendenon	9.00	4.50	2.75
(6)	Victor Davalillo	9.00	4.50	2.75
(7)	Dick Donovan	9.00	4.50	2.75
(8)	John A. Edwards	9.00	4.50	2.75
(9)	Robert Friend	15.00	7.50	4.50
(10)	Jim Grant	9.00	4.50	2.75
(11)	Tommy Harper	9.00	4.50	2.75
(12)	Woodie Held	9.00	4.50	2.75
(13)	Joey Jay	9.00	4.50	2.75
(14)	Jack Kralick	9.00	4.50	2.75
(15)	Jerry Lynch	9.00	4.50	2.75
(16)	Jim Maloney	15.00	7.50	4.50
(17)	William S. Mazeroski	20.00	10.00	6.00
(18)	Alvin McBean	9.00	4.50	2.75
(19)	Joe Nuxhall	15.00	7.50	4.50
(20)	Jim Pagliaroni	9.00	4.50	2.75
(21)	Vada E. Pinson Jr.	20.00	10.00	6.00
(22)	Robert T. Purkey	9.00	4.50	2.75
(23)	Pedro Ramos	9.00	4.50	2.75
(24)	Frank Robinson	70.00	35.00	21.00
(25)	John Romano	9.00	4.50	2.75
(26)	Pete Rose	400.00	200.00	120.00
(27)	John Tsitouris	9.00	4.50	2.75
(28)	Robert A. Veale Jr.	9.00	4.50	2.75
(29)	Bill Virdon	15.00	7.50	4.50
(30)	Leon Wagner	9.00	4.50	2.75
(31)	Fred Whitfield	9.00	4.50	2.75

1965 Kahn's Wieners

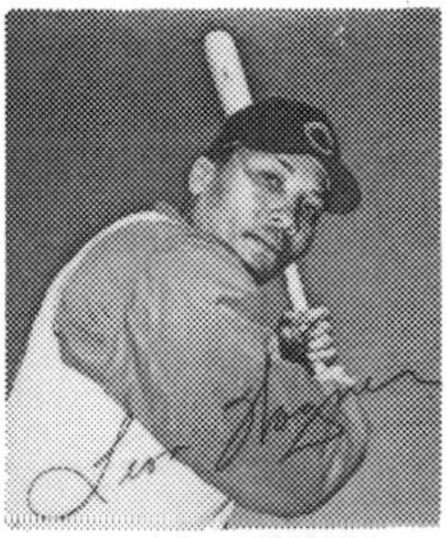

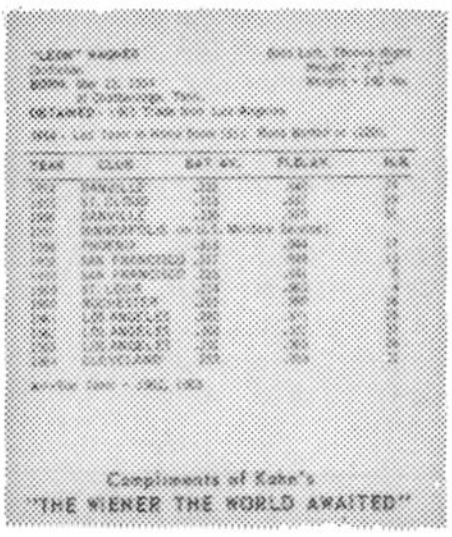
Compliments of Kahn's
"THE WIENER THE WORLD AWAITED"

There was little change for the Kahn's issue in 1965 beyond the addition of Milwaukee Braves players to the Reds, Pirates and Indians traditionally included in the set. At 45 players, the 1965 issue was the largest of the Kahn's sets. Once again in 3" by 3-1/2" size, the 1965s retained the borderless color photo design of the previous season. A look at the stats on the back will confirm the year of issue, however, since the last year of statistics is the year prior to the card's issue.

		NR MT	EX	VG
Complete Set:		1100.00	550.00	330.00
Common Player:		12.00	6.00	3.50
(1)	Hank Aaron	125.00	62.00	37.00
(2)	Max Alvis	12.00	6.00	3.50
(3)	Jose Azcue	12.00	6.00	3.50
(4)	Bob Bailey	12.00	6.00	3.50
(5)	Frank Bolling	12.00	6.00	3.50
(6)	Leonardo Cardenas	12.00	6.00	3.50
(7)	Rico Ricardo Carty	15.00	7.50	4.50
(8)	Donn A. Clendenon	12.00	6.00	3.50
(9)	Tony Cloninger	12.00	6.00	3.50
(10)	Gordon Coleman	12.00	6.00	3.50
(11)	Victor Davalillo	12.00	6.00	3.50
(12)	John A. Edwards	12.00	6.00	3.50
(13)	Sam Ellis	12.00	6.00	3.50
(14)	Robert Friend	15.00	7.50	4.50
(15)	Tommy Harper	12.00	6.00	3.50
(16)	Chuck Hinton	12.00	6.00	3.50
(17)	Dick Howser	15.00	7.50	4.50
(18)	Joey Jay	12.00	6.00	3.50
(19)	Deron Johnson	12.00	6.00	3.50
(20)	Jack Kralick	12.00	6.00	3.50
(21)	Denny Lemaster	12.00	6.00	3.50
(22)	Jerry Lynch	12.00	6.00	3.50
(23)	Jim Maloney	15.00	7.50	4.50
(24)	Lee Maye	12.00	6.00	3.50
(25)	William S. Mazeroski	20.00	10.00	6.00
(26)	Alvin McBean	12.00	6.00	3.50
(27)	Bill McCool	12.00	6.00	3.50
(28)	Sam McDowell	15.00	7.50	4.50
(29)	Donald McMahon	12.00	6.00	3.50
(30)	Denis Menke	12.00	6.00	3.50
(31)	Joe Nuxhall	15.00	7.50	4.50
(32)	Gene Oliver	12.00	6.00	3.50
(33)	Jim O'Toole	12.00	6.00	3.50
(34)	Jim Pagliaroni	12.00	6.00	3.50
(35)	Vada E. Pinson Jr.	20.00	10.00	6.00
(36)	Frank Robinson	100.00	50.00	30.00
(37)	Pete Rose	250.00	125.00	75.00
(38)	Willie Stargell	100.00	50.00	30.00
(39)	Ralph W. Terry	12.00	6.00	3.50
(40)	Luis Tiant	20.00	10.00	6.00

		NR MT	EX	VG
(41)	Joe Torre	25.00	12.50	7.50
(42)	John Tsitouris	12.00	6.00	3.50
(43)	Robert A. Veale Jr.	12.00	6.00	3.50
(44)	Bill Virdon	15.00	7.50	4.50
(45)	Leon Wagner	12.00	6.00	3.50

1966 Kahn's Wieners

The fourth new format in five years greeted collector's with the introduction of Kahn's 1966 issue of 32 cards. The design consisted of a color photo bordered by white and yellow vertical stripes. The player's name was printed above the photo, and a facsimile autograph appeared across the photo. As printed, the cards were 2-13/16" by 4" in size. However, the top portion consisted of a 2-13/16" by 1-3/8" advertising panel with a red rose logo and the word "Kahn's," separated from the player portion of the card by a black dotted line. Naturally, many of the cards are found today with the top portion cut off. Values listed here are for cards with the top portion intact. Players from the Cincinnati Reds, Pittsburgh Pirates, Cleveland Indians and Atlanta Braves were included in the set. Since the cards are blank-backed, collectors must learn to differentiate player poses to determine year of issue for some cards.

		NR MT	EX	VG
Complete Set:		1000.00	500.00	300.00
Common Player:		15.00	7.50	4.50
(1)	Henry Aaron	125.00	62.00	37.00
(2)	Felipe Alou	24.00	12.00	7.25
(3)	Max Alvis	15.00	7.50	4.50
(4)	Robert Bailey	15.00	7.50	4.50
(5)	Wade Blasingame	15.00	7.50	4.50
(6)	Frank Bolling	15.00	7.50	4.50
(7)	Leo Cardenas	15.00	7.50	4.50
(8)	Roberto Clemente	125.00	62.00	37.00
(9)	Tony Cloninger	15.00	7.50	4.50
(10)	Vic Davalillo	15.00	7.50	4.50
(11)	John Edwards	15.00	7.50	4.50
(12)	Sam Ellis	15.00	7.50	4.50
(13)	Pedro Gonzalez	15.00	7.50	4.50
(14)	Tommy Harper	15.00	7.50	4.50
(15)	Deron Johnson	15.00	7.50	4.50
(16)	Mack Jones	15.00	7.50	4.50
(17)	Denny Lemaster	15.00	7.50	4.50
(18)	Jim Maloney	24.00	12.00	7.25
(19)	William Mazeroski	28.00	14.00	8.50
(20)	Bill McCool	15.00	7.50	4.50
(21)	Sam McDowell	24.00	12.00	7.25
(22)	Denis Menke	15.00	7.50	4.50
(23)	Joe Nuxhall	24.00	12.00	7.25
(24)	Jim Pagliaroni	15.00	7.50	4.50
(25)	Milt Pappas	24.00	12.00	7.25
(26)	Vada Pinson	28.00	14.00	8.50
(27)	Pete Rose	200.00	100.00	60.00
(28)	Sonny Siebert	15.00	7.50	4.50
(29)	Willie Stargell	80.00	40.00	24.00
(30)	Joe Torre	28.00	14.00	8.50
(31)	Bob Veale	15.00	7.50	4.50
(32)	Fred Whitfield	15.00	7.50	4.50

1967 Kahn's Wieners

Retaining the basic format of the 1966 set (see listing for description), the '67 Kahn's set was expanded to 41 players through the addition of several New York Mets players to the previous season's lineup of Reds, Pirates, Indians and Braves. Making the 1967 set especially challenging for collectors is the fact that some cards are found in a smaller size and/or with different colored stripes bordering the color player photo. On the majority of cards, the size remained 2-13/16" by 4" (with ad at top; 2-13/16" by 2-5/8"without ad at top). However, because of packing in different products, the Ellis, Helms and Torre cards can be found in 2-13/16" by 3-1/4" size (with ad; 2-13/16" by 2-1/8" without ad). The handful of known border stripe variations are listed below. Values quoted are for cards with the top ad panel intact. All variation cards are included in the valuations given below for complete sets.

		NR MT	EX	VG
Complete Set:		1100.00	550.00	330.00
Common Player:		15.00	7.50	4.50
(1)	Henry Aaron	125.00	62.00	37.00
(2)	Gene Alley	15.00	7.50	4.50
(3)	Felipe Alou	24.00	12.00	7.25
(4a)	Matty Alou (yellow & white striped border)	24.00	12.00	7.25
(4b)	Matty Alou (red & white striped border)	28.00	14.00	8.50
(5)	Max Alvis	15.00	7.50	4.50
(6a)	Ken Boyer (yellow & white striped border)	30.00	15.00	9.00
(6b)	Ken Boyer (red & white striped border)	35.00	17.50	10.50
(7)	Leo Cardenas	15.00	7.50	4.50
(8)	Rico Carty	24.00	12.00	7.25
(9)	Tony Cloninger	15.00	7.50	4.50
(10)	Tommy Davis	24.00	12.00	7.25
(11)	John Edwards	15.00	7.50	4.50
(12a)	Sam Ellis (large size)	15.00	7.50	4.50
(12b)	Sam Ellis (small size)	28.00	14.00	8.50
(13)	Jack Fisher	15.00	7.50	4.50
(14)	Steve Hargan	15.00	7.50	4.50
(15)	Tom Harper	15.00	7.50	4.50
(16a)	Tom Helms (large size)	15.00	7.50	4.50
(16b)	Tom Helms (small size)	28.00	14.00	8.50
(17)	Deron Johnson	15.00	7.50	4.50
(18)	Ken Johnson	15.00	7.50	4.50
(19)	Cleon Jones	15.00	7.50	4.50
(20a)	Ed Kranepool (yellow & white striped border)	15.00	7.50	4.50
(20b)	Ed Kranepool (red & white striped border)	25.00	12.50	7.50
(21a)	James Maloney (yellow & white striped border)	24.00	12.00	7.25
(21b)	James Maloney (red & white striped border)	28.00	14.00	8.50
(22)	Lee May	24.00	12.00	7.25
(23)	Wm. Mazeroski	28.00	14.00	8.50
(24)	Wm. McCool	15.00	7.50	4.50
(25)	Sam McDowell	24.00	12.00	7.25
(26)	Dennis Menke (Denis)	15.00	7.50	4.50
(27)	Jim Pagliaroni	15.00	7.50	4.50
(28)	Don Pavletich	15.00	7.50	4.50

		NR MT	EX	VG
(29)	Tony Perez	35.00	17.50	10.50
(30)	Vada Pinson	28.00	14.00	8.50
(31)	Dennis Ribant	15.00	7.50	4.50
(32)	Pete Rose	175.00	87.00	52.00
(33)	Art Shamsky	15.00	7.50	4.50
(34)	Bob Shaw	15.00	7.50	4.50
(35)	Sonny Siebert	15.00	7.50	4.50
(36)	Wm. Stargell (first name actually Wilver)	80.00	40.00	24.00
(37a)	Joe Torre (large size)	28.00	14.00	8.50
(37b)	Joe Torre (small size)	32.00	16.00	9.50
(38)	Bob Veale	15.00	7.50	4.50
(39)	Leon Wagner	15.00	7.50	4.50
(40)	Fred Whitfield	15.00	7.50	4.50
(41)	Woody Woodward	15.00	7.50	4.50

1968 Kahn's Wieners

The number of card size and stripe color variations increased with the 1968 Kahn's issue (see 1967 listing), though the basic card design was retained from the previous two seasons: 2-13/16" by 4" size (with ad panel at top; 2-13/16" by 2-5/8" with ad panel cut off), color photo bordered by yellow and white vertical stripes. In addition to the basic issue, a number of the cards appear in a smaller, 2-13/16" by 3-1/4", size, while some of them, and others, appear with variations in the color of border stripes. One card, Maloney, can be found with a top portion advertising Blue Mountain brand meats, as well as Kahn's. All in all, quite a challenge for the specialist. The 1968 set featured the largest number of teams represented in any Kahn's issue: Atlanta Braves, Chicago Cubs and White Sox, Cincinnati Reds, Cleveland Indians, Detroit Tigers, New York Mets and Pittsburgh Pirates. Values quoted below are for cards with the ad panel at top; complete set prices include all variations.

		NR MT	EX	VG
Complete Set:		1600.00	800.00	480.00
Common Player:		15.00	7.50	4.50
(1a)	Hank Aaron (large size)	125.00	62.00	37.00
(1b)	Hank Aaron (small size)	150.00	75.00	45.00
(2)	Tommy Agee	15.00	7.50	4.50
(3a)	Gene Alley (large size)	15.00	7.50	4.50
(3b)	Gene Alley (small size)	24.00	12.00	7.25
(4)	Felipe Alou	24.00	12.00	7.25
(5a)	Matty Alou (yellow striped border)	24.00	12.00	7.25
(5b)	Matty Alou (red striped border)	28.00	14.00	8.50
(6a)	Max Alvis (large size)	15.00	7.50	4.50
(6b)	Max Alvis (small size)	24.00	12.00	7.25
(7)	Gerry Arrigo	15.00	7.50	4.50
(8)	John Bench	400.00	200.00	120.00
(9a)	Clete Boyer (large size)	15.00	7.50	4.50
(9b)	Clete Boyer (small size)	24.00	12.00	7.25
(10)	Larry Brown	15.00	7.50	4.50
(11a)	Leo Cardenas (large size)	15.00	7.50	4.50
(11b)	Leo Cardenas (small size)	24.00	12.00	7.25
(12a)	Bill Freehan (large size)	24.00	12.00	7.25
(12b)	Bill Freehan (small size)	28.00	14.00	8.50
(13)	Steve Hargan	15.00	7.50	4.50
(14)	Joel Horlen	15.00	7.50	4.50
(15)	Tony Horton	24.00	12.00	7.25
(16)	Willie Horton	24.00	12.00	7.25
(17)	Ferguson Jenkins	32.00	16.00	9.50
(18)	Deron Johnson	15.00	7.50	4.50
(19)	Mack Jones	15.00	7.50	4.50
(20)	Bob Lee	15.00	7.50	4.50
(21a)	Jim Maloney (large size, rose logo)	24.00	12.00	7.25
(21b)	Jim Maloney (large size, blue mountain logo)	28.00	14.00	8.50
(21c)	Jim Maloney (small size, yellow & white striped border)	28.00	14.00	8.50
(21d)	Jim Maloney (small size, yellow, white & green striped border)	28.00	14.00	8.50
(22a)	Lee May (large size)	24.00	12.00	7.25
(22b)	Lee May (small size)	28.00	14.00	8.50
(23a)	Wm. Mazeroski (large size)	24.00	12.00	7.25
(23b)	Wm. Mazeroski (small size)	28.00	14.00	8.50
(24)	Dick McAuliffe	15.00	7.50	4.50
(25)	Bill McCool	15.00	7.50	4.50
(26a)	Sam McDowell (yellow striped border)	24.00	12.00	7.25
(26b)	Sam McDowell (red striped border)	28.00	14.00	8.50
(27a)	Tony Perez (yellow striped border)	35.00	17.50	10.50
(27b)	Tony Perez (red striped border)	40.00	20.00	12.00
(28)	Gary Peters	15.00	7.50	4.50
(29a)	Vada Pinson (large size)	24.00	12.00	7.25
(29b)	Vada Pinson (small size)	28.00	14.00	8.50
(30)	Chico Ruiz	15.00	7.50	4.50
(31a)	Ron Santo (yellow striped border)	24.00	12.00	7.25
(31b)	Ron Santo (red striped border)	28.00	14.00	8.50
(32)	Art Shamsky	15.00	7.50	4.50
(33)	Luis Tiant	24.00	12.00	7.25
(34a)	Joe Torre (large size)	28.00	14.00	8.50
(34b)	Joe Torre (small size)	32.00	16.00	9.50
(35a)	Bob Veale (large size)	15.00	7.50	4.50
(35b)	Bob Veale (small size)	24.00	12.00	7.25
(36)	Leon Wagner	15.00	7.50	4.50
(37)	Billy Williams	50.00	25.00	15.00
(38)	Earl Wilson	15.00	7.50	4.50

1969 Kahn's Wieners

In its 15th consecutive year of baseball card issuing, Kahn's continued the basic format adopted in 1966. The basic card issue of 22 players was printed in 2-13/16" by 4" size (with ad panel at top; 2-13/16" by 2-5/8" without panel) and are blanked-backed. Teams represented in the set included the Braves, Cubs, White Sox, Reds, Cardinals, Indians and Pirates. The cards featured a color photo and facsimile autograph bordered by yellow and white vertical stripes. At top was an ad panel consisting of the Kahn's red rose logo. However, because some cards were produced for inclusion in packages other than the standard hot dogs, a number of variations in card size and stripe color were created, as noted in the listings below. The smaller size cards, 2-13/16" by 3-1/4" with ad, 2-13/16" by 2-1/8" without ad, were created by more closely cropping the player photo at top and bottom. Values quoted below are for cards with the top logo panel intact. Complete set values include all the variations.

		NR MT	EX	VG
Complete Set:		800.00	400.00	240.00
Common Player:		15.00	7.50	4.50
(1a)	Hank Aaron (large size)	125.00	62.00	37.00
(1b)	Hank Aaron (small size)	150.00	75.00	45.00
(2)	Matty Alou	24.00	12.00	7.25
(3)	Max Alvis	15.00	7.50	4.50
(4)	Gerry Arrigo	15.00	7.50	4.50
(5)	Steve Blass	15.00	7.50	4.50
(6)	Clay Carroll	15.00	7.50	4.50
(7)	Tony Cloninger	15.00	7.50	4.50
(8)	George Culver	15.00	7.50	4.50
(9)	Joel Horlen	15.00	7.50	4.50
(10)	Tony Horton	24.00	12.00	7.25
(11)	Alex Johnson	15.00	7.50	4.50
(12a)	Jim Maloney (large size)	24.00	12.00	7.25
(12b)	Jim Maloney (small size)	28.00	14.00	8.50
(13a)	Lee May (yellow striped border)	24.00	12.00	7.25
(13b)	Lee May (red striped border)	28.00	14.00	8.50
(14a)	Wm. Mazeroski (yellow striped border)	24.00	12.00	7.25
(14b)	Wm. Mazeroski (red striped border)	28.00	14.00	8.50
(15a)	Sam McDowell (yellow striped border)	24.00	12.00	7.25
(15b)	Sam McDowell (red striped border)	28.00	14.00	8.50
(16a)	Tony Perez (large size)	35.00	17.50	10.50
(16b)	Tony Perez (small size)	40.00	20.00	12.00
(17)	Gary Peters	15.00	7.50	4.50
(18a)	Ron Santo (yellow striped border)	24.00	12.00	7.25
(18b)	Ron Santo (red striped border)	28.00	14.00	8.50
(19)	Luis Tiant	24.00	12.00	7.25
(20)	Joe Torre	28.00	14.00	8.50
(21)	Bob Veale	15.00	7.50	4.50
(22)	Billy Williams	50.00	25.00	15.00

1987 Kahn's Wieners Reds

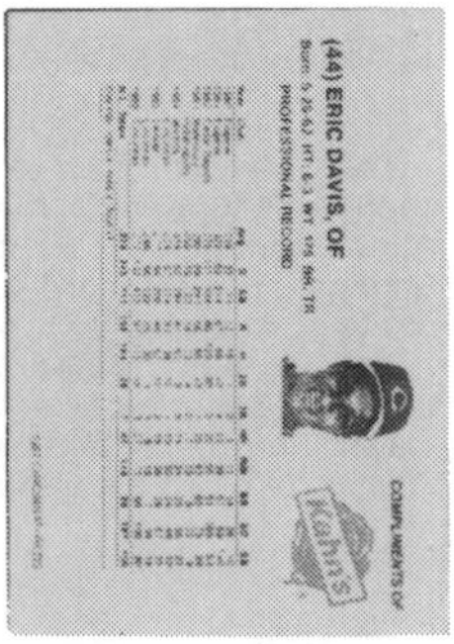

After a nearly 20-year layoff, Kahn's Wieners produced a baseball card set. Kahn's, who produced card sets between 1955 and 1968, sponsored a 28-card 9set that was distributed to fans attending the August 2nd game at Riverfront Stadium. The cards are the standard 2-1/2" by 3-1/2" size. The fronts offer a full-color player photo bordered in red and white. The backs carry the Kahn's logo and a head shot of the player.

		MT	NR MT	EX
Complete Set:		15.00	11.00	6.00
Common Player:		.25	.20	.10
6	Bo Diaz	.25	.20	.10
10	Terry Francona	.25	.20	.10
11	Kurt Stillwell	.50	.40	.20
12	Nick Esasky	.50	.40	.20
13	Dave Concepcion	.50	.40	.20
15	Barry Larkin	2.00	1.50	.80
16	Ron Oester	.25	.20	.10
21	Paul O'Neill	1.00	.70	.40
23	Lloyd McClendon	.40	.30	.15
25	Buddy Bell	.35	.25	.14
28	Kal Daniels	1.00	.70	.40
29	Tracy Jones	.50	.40	.20
30	Guy Hoffman	.25	.20	.10
31	John Franco	.80	.60	.30
32	Tom Browning	.80	.60	.30
33	Ron Robinson	.25	.20	.10
34	Bill Gullickson	.25	.20	.10
35	Pat Pacillo	.30	.25	.12
39	Dave Parker	.80	.60	.30
43	Bill Landrum	.50	.40	.20
44	Eric Davis	2.50	2.00	1.00
46	Rob Murphy	.40	.30	.15
47	Frank Williams	.25	.20	.10
48	Ted Power	.25	.20	.10

1988 Kahn's Wieners Mets

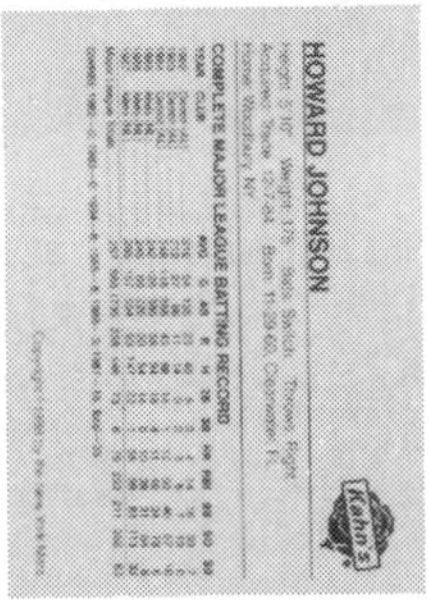

Approximately 50,000 Mets fans received this complimentary card set during a ballpark promotion sponsored by Kahn's Wieners. Twenty-five players are featured in the set, along with manager Davey Johnson, four coaches and a team photo. Card fronts have a dark blue border with an orange rectangle framing the full-color player photo. Card numbers reflecting the players' uniform numbers, are printed in white in the upper right corner of the card face, beside the team logo. The player name appears upper left and the player position is centered in the bottom margin. The card backs are black and white with red line accents. In addition to player acquisition date, birthday and residence, a paragraph-style career summary is included. The cards measure 2-1/2" by 3-1/2".

		MT	NR MT	EX
Complete Set:		14.00	10.50	5.50
Common Player:		.20	.15	.08
1	Mookie Wilson	.35	.25	.14
2	Mackey Sasser	.30	.25	.12
3	Bud Harrelson	.20	.15	.08
4	Lenny Dykstra	.40	.30	.15
5	Davey Johnson	.30	.25	.12
6	Wally Backman	.20	.15	.08
8	Gary Carter	1.00	.70	.40
11	Tim Teufel	.20	.15	.08
12	Ron Darling	.60	.45	.25
13	Lee Mazzilli	.20	.15	.08
15	Rick Aguilera	.20	.15	.08
16	Dwight Gooden	1.00	.70	.40
17	Keith Hernandez	1.00	.70	.40
18	Darryl Strawberry	2.00	1.50	.80
19	Bob Ojeda	.35	.25	.14
20	Howard Johnson	1.00	.70	.40
21	Kevin Elster	.50	.40	.20
22	Kevin McReynolds	.60	.45	.25
26	Terry Leach	.20	.15	.08
28	Bill Robinson	.20	.15	.08
29	Dave Magadan	.40	.30	.15
30	Mel Stottlemyre	.20	.15	.08
31	Gene Walter	.20	.15	.08
33	Barry Lyons	.20	.15	.08
34	Sam Perlozzo	.20	.15	.08
42	Roger McDowell	.30	.25	.12
44	David Cone	.70	.50	.30
48	Randy Myers	.50	.40	.20
50	Sid Fernandez	.35	.25	.14
52	Greg Pavlick	.20	.15	.08
---	Team Photo	.20	.15	.08

1988 Kahn's Wieners Reds

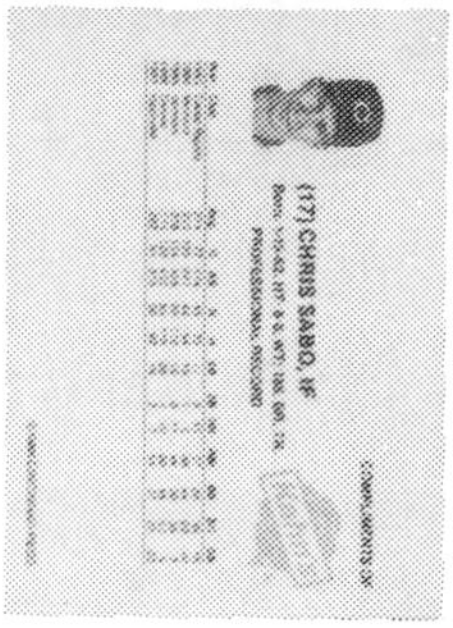

This 26-card set was a one-time giveaway during the August 14th, 1988 Cincinnati Reds game. The glossy cards (2-1/2" by 3-1/2") feature full-color action photos inside red and white borders. The Reds logo, player uniform number, name and position are printed below the photo. The backs are black and white, with small player close-ups and career stats. A promotional 25-cent coupon for Kahn's Wieners was included with each set.

		MT	NR MT	EX
Complete Set:		14.00	10.50	5.50
Common Player:		.25	.20	.10
6	Bo Diaz	.25	.20	.10
8	Terry McGriff	.25	.20	.10
9	Eddie Milner	.25	.20	.10
10	Leon Durham	.30	.25	.12
11	Barry Larkin	.70	.50	.30
12	Nick Esasky	.30	.25	.12
13	Dave Concepcion	.40	.30	.15
14	Pete Rose	1.25	.90	.50
15	Jeff Treadway	.50	.40	.20
17	Chris Sabo	1.50	1.25	.60
20	Danny Jackson	.60	.45	.25
21	Paul O'Neill	.30	.25	.12
22	Dave Collins	.25	.20	.10
27	Jose Rijo	.35	.25	.14
28	Kal Daniels	.70	.50	.30
29	Tracy Jones	.50	.40	.20
30	Lloyd McClendon	.25	.20	.10
31	John Franco	.50	.40	.20
32	Tom Browning	.50	.40	.20
33	Ron Robinson	.25	.20	.10
40	Jack Armstrong	.25	.20	.10
44	Eric Davis	1.50	1.25	.60
46	Rob Murphy	.25	.20	.10
47	Frank Williams	.25	.20	.10
48	Tim Birtsas	.25	.20	.10
---	Coaches (Scott Breeden, Tommy Helms, Bruce Kimm, Jim Lett, Lee May, Tony Perez)	.25	.20	.10

1989 Kahn's-Hillshire Farms

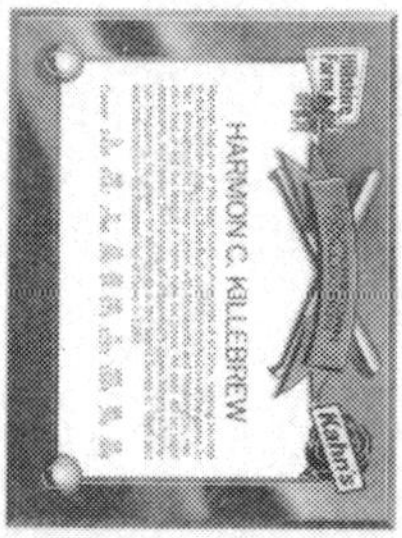

This 11-player card set was available through a mail-in offer. One dollar and three proofs of purchase from Hillshire Farms were needed to obtain the set. The card fronts feature paintings of recent Hall of Fame inductees. A coupon card was also included with each set.

		MT	NR MT	EX
Complete Set:		6.00	4.50	2.50
Common Player:		.40	.30	.10
(1)	Cool Papa Bell	.40	.30	.15
(2)	Johnny Bench	.80	.60	.30
(3)	Lou Brock	.80	.60	.30
(4)	Whitey Ford	.80	.60	.30
(5)	Bob Gibson	.80	.60	.30
(6)	Billy Herman	.40	.30	.15
(7)	Harmon Killebrew	.80	.60	.30
(8)	Eddie Mathews	1.00	.70	.40
(9)	Brooks Robinson	1.00	.70	.40
(10)	Willie Stargell	.80	.60	.30
(11)	Carl Yastrzemski	.80	.60	.30

1989 Kahn's Wieners Mets

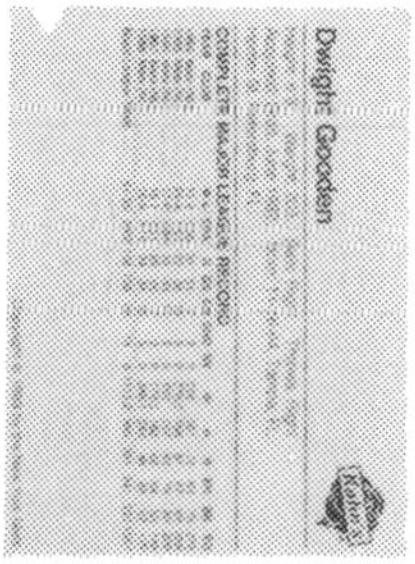

This 30-card New York Mets team set was sponsored by Kahn's Wieners and was given to fans attending the July 6, 1989 Mets game at Shea Stadium. The standard-size cards feature a full-color photo surrounded by a blue and orange border with the player's name and uniform number across the top. The backs include the Kahn's logo, along with player information and complete Major League stats. Four update cards were later added to the set.

		MT	NR MT	EX
Complete Set:		15.00	11.00	6.00
Common Player:		.20	.15	.08
1	Mookie Wilson	.35	.25	.14
2	Mackey Sasser	.25	.20	.10
3	Bud Harrelson	.20	.15	.08
5	Davey Johnson	.25	.20	.10
7	Juan Samuel	.40	.30	.15
8	Gary Carter	.50	.40	.20
9	Gregg Jefferies	1.00	.70	.40
12	Ron Darling	.50	.40	.20
13	Lee Mazzilli	.20	.15	.08
16	Dwight Gooden	1.75	1.50	.70
17	Keith Hernandez	.60	.45	.25
18	Darryl Strawberry	1.25	.90	.50
19	Bob Ojeda	.25	.20	.10
20	Howard Johnson	.70	.50	.30
21	Kevin Elster	.35	.25	.14
22	Kevin McReynolds	.50	.40	.20
28	Bill Robinson	.20	.15	.08
29	Dave Magadan	.40	.30	.15
30	Mel Stottlemyre	.20	.15	.08
32	Mark Carreon	.40	.30	.15
33	Barry Lyons	.20	.15	.08
34	Sam Perlozzo	.20	.15	.08
38	Rick Aguilera	.20	.15	.08
44	David Cone	.50	.40	.20
46	Dave West	.60	.45	.25
48	Randy Myers	.35	.25	.14
50	Sid Fernandez	.35	.25	.14
51	Don Aase	.20	.15	.08
52	Greg Pavlick	.20	.15	.08

		MT	NR MT	EX
----	Team Card	.20	.15	.08
----	Jeff Innis	.90	.70	.50
----	Keith Miller	.70	.50	.30
----	Jeff Musselman	.70	.50	.30
----	Frank Viola	1.50	1.25	.60

1989 Kahn's Wieners Reds

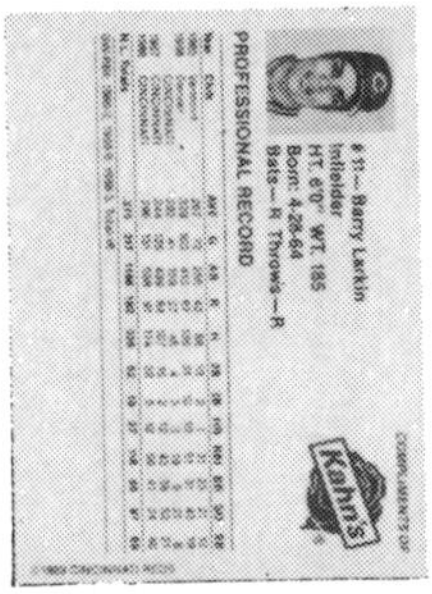

This 26-card Cincinnati Reds team set, sponsored by Kahn's Wieners, was distributed to fans attending the Aug. 6 Reds game at Riverfront Stadium. The standard-size, red-bordered cards feature action photos with the player's name in the upper left corner, his uniform number in the upper right and the Reds logo in the middle. The backs include a black-and-white head shot, player data and complete major and minor league stats. The Kahn's logo appears in the upper right corner of the back.

		MT	NR MT	EX
Complete Set:		12.00	9.00	4.75
Common Player:		.20	.15	.08
6	Bo Diaz	.20	.15	.08
7	Lenny Harris	.40	.30	.15
11	Barry Larkin	1.00	.70	.40
12	Joel Youngblood	.20	.15	.08
14	Pete Rose	1.00	.70	.40
16	Ron Oester	.25	.20	.10
17	Chris Sabo	.40	.30	.15
20	Danny Jackson	.25	.20	.15
21	Paul O'Neill	.25	.20	.15
25	Todd Benzinger	.40	.30	.15
27	Jose Rijo	.25	.20	.10
28	Kal Daniels	.40	.30	.15
29	Herm Winningham	.20	.15	.08
30	Ken Griffey	.30	.25	.12
31	John Franco	.30	.25	.12
32	Tom Browning	.35	.25	.14
33	Ron Robinson	.20	.15	.08
34	Jeff Reed	.20	.15	.08
36	Rolando Roomes	.70	.50	.30
37	Norm Charlton	.50	.40	.20
42	Rick Mahler	.25	.20	.10
43	Kent Tekulve	.20	.15	.08
44	Eric Davis	1.50	1.25	.60
48	Tim Birtsas	.20	.15	.08
49	Rob Dibble	.60	.45	.25
----	Coaches Card	.20	.15	.08

1990 Kahn's Wieners Mets

For the third consecutive year, Kahn's issued a set of baseball cards of members of the New York Mets. The sets were given out at Shea Stadium on May 3- prior to the Mets/Reds game. The cards feature blue and orange highlights like the team colors and are numbered according to uniform number. Two coupon cards were also included with each set.

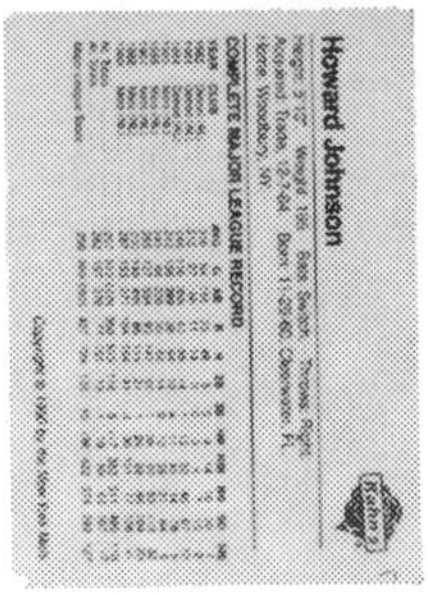

Complete Set:		9.00	6.75	3.50
Common Player:		.20	.15	.08
1	Lou Thornton	.20	.15	.08
2	Mackey Sasser	.25	.20	.10
3	Bud Harrelson	.20	.15	.08
4	Mike Cubbage	.20	.15	.08
5	Davey Johnson	.20	.15	.08
6	Mike Marshall	.25	.20	.10
9	Gregg Jefferies	.80	.60	.30
10	Dave Magadan	.40	.30	.15
11	Tim Teufel	.20	.15	.08
13	Jeff Musselman	.20	.15	.08
15	Ron Darling	.30	.25	.12
16	Dwight Gooden	.80	.60	.30
18	Darryl Strawberry	1.00	.70	.40
19	Bob Ojeda	.20	.15	.08
20	Howard Johnson	.50	.40	.20
21	Kevin Elster	.25	.20	.10
22	Kevin McReynolds	.40	.30	.15
25	Keith Miller	.25	.20	.10
26	Alejandro Pena	.20	.15	.08
27	Tom O'Malley	.20	.15	.08
29	Frank Viola	.80	.60	.30
30	Mel Stottlemyre	.20	.15	.08
31	John Franco	.40	.30	.15
32	Doc Edwards	.20	.15	.08
33	Barry Lyons	.20	.15	.08
35	Orlando Mercado	.20	.15	.08
40	Jeff Innis	.25	.20	.15
44	David Cone	.40	.30	.15
45	Mark Carreon	.30	.25	.12
47	Wally Whitehurst	.30	.25	.12
48	Julio Machado	.30	.25	.12
50	Sid Fernandez	.35	.25	.14
52	Greg Pavlick	.20	.15	.08
----	Team Card	.20	.15	.08

Note: All values listed in this guide are intended to serve only as an aid in evaluating your cards. Actual market conditions are constantly changing, especially for current players, whose on-field performance during the course of a season can affect affect the value of their cards — either up or down.

1990 Kahn's Wieners Reds

This 27-card set marks the fourth consecutive year in which Kahn's released a modern Reds issue. The cards feature full-color photos, red and white borders and the player's name, number, and postion on the card front. The flip sides feature biographical information, statistics, a posed photo and the Kahn's logo. The set is numbered by uniform.

		MT	NR MT	EX
Complete Set:		10.00	7.50	4.00
Common Player:		.25	.20	.10
7	Mariano Duncan	.40	.30	.15
9	Joe Oliver	.40	.30	.15
10	Luis Quinones	.25	.20	.10
11	Barry Larkin	.80	.60	.30
15	Glenn Braggs	.30	.25	.12
16	Ron Oester	.25	.20	.10
17	Chris Sabo	.70	.50	.30
20	Danny Jackson	.30	.25	.12
21	Paul O'Neill	.40	.30	.15
22	Billy Hatcher	.25	.20	.10
23	Hal Morris	.80	.60	.30
25	Todd Benzinger	.30	.25	.12
27	Jose Rijo	.50	.40	.20
28	Randy Myers	.35	.25	.14
29	Herm Winningham	.25	.20	.10
30	Ken Griffey	.40	.30	.15
32	Tom Browning	.40	.30	.15
34	Jeff Reed	.25	.20	.10
37	Norm Charlton	.40	.30	.15
40	Jack Armstrong	.40	.30	.15
41	Lou Pinella	.40	.30	.15
42	Rick Mahler	.25	.20	.10
43	Tim Layana	.30	.25	.12
44	Eric Davis	1.00	.70	.40
48	Tim Birtsas	.25	.20	.10
49	Rob Dibble	.50	.40	.20
----	Reds Coaches	.25	.20	.10

1991 Kahn's Wieners Reds

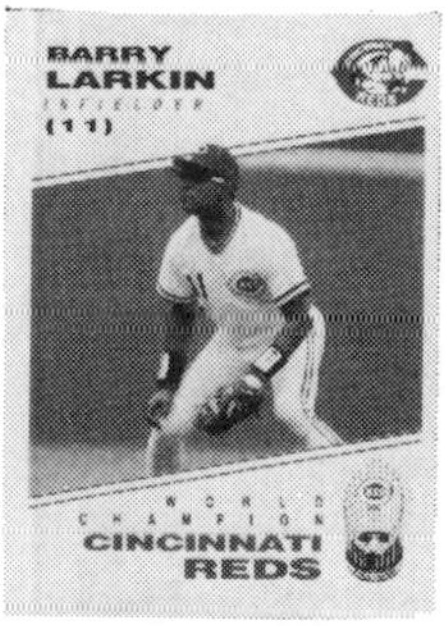

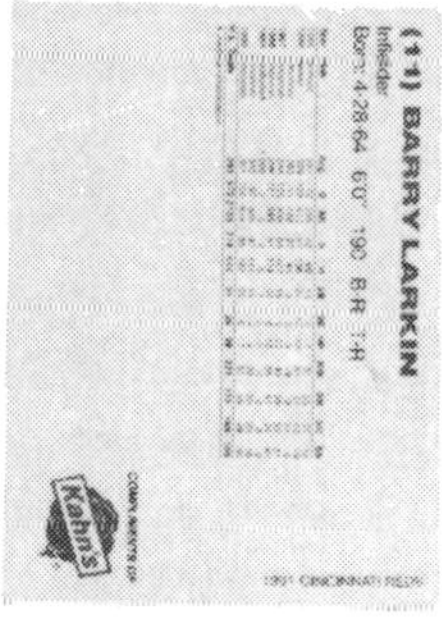

The World Champion Cincinnati Reds are showcased in this 28-card set. The card fronts feature small full-color action photos on white stock. The backs feature statistics, biographical information and the Kahn's logo. A special card of Schottzie is included in this set.

		MT	NR MT	EX
Complete Set:		8.00	6.00	3.25
Common Player:		.25	.20	.10
	Schottzie	.25	.20	.10
7	Mariano Duncan	.30	.25	.12
9	Joe Oliver	.30	.25	.12
10	Luis Quinones	.25	.20	.10
11	Barry Larkin	.80	.60	.30
15	Glenn Braggs	.30	.25	.12
17	Chris Sabo	.60	.45	.25
19	Bill Doran	.35	.25	.14
21	Paul O'Neill	.40	.30	.15
22	Billy Hatcher	.25	.20	.10
23	Hal Morris	.80	.60	.30
25	Todd Benzinger	.30	.25	.12
27	Jose Rijo	.40	.30	.15
28	Randy Myers	.35	.25	.14
29	Herm Winningham	.25	.20	.10
32	Tom Browning	.35	.25	.14
34	Jeff Reed	.25	.20	.10
36	Don Carman	.25	.20	.10
37	Norm Charlton	.30	.25	.12
40	Jack Armstrong	.35	.25	.14
41	Lou Pinella	.35	.25	.14
44	Eric Davis	.80	.60	.30
45	Chris Hammond	.40	.30	.15
47	Scott Scudder	.30	.25	.12
48	Ted Power	.25	.20	.10

		MT	NR MT	EX
49	Rob Dibble	.50	.40	.20
57	Freddie Benavides	.40	.30	.15
----	Reds Coaches	.25	.20	.10

1986 Kas Potato Chips Cardinals

One of a handful of 2-7/8" round baseball card "discs" created by Mike Schecter Associates for inclusion in boxes of potato chips, the 20-card Kas set features players of the defending National League Champion St. Louis Cardinals. Fronts feature color photo on which the team logos have been removed from the caps by airbrushing the photos, indicating Kas did not license with the Cardinals for use of its uniform logos. Card backs have minimal personal data and 1985 stats.

		MT	NR MT	EX
Complete Set:		15.00	11.00	6.00
Common Player:		.70	.50	.30
1	Vince Coleman	2.00	1.50	.80
2	Ken Dayley	.70	.50	.30
3	Tito Landrum	.70	.50	.30
4	Steve Braun	.70	.50	.30
5	Danny Cox	.80	.60	.30
6	Bob Forsch	.80	.60	.30
7	Ozzie Smith	2.00	1.50	.80
8	Brian Harper	1.00	.70	.40
9	Jack Clark	1.50	1.25	.60
10	Todd Worrell	1.00	.70	.40
11	Joaquin Andujar	.70	.50	.30
12	Tom Nieto	.70	.50	.30
13	Kurt Kepshire	.70	.50	.30
14	Terry Pendleton	1.50	1.25	.60
15	Tom Herr	1.00	.70	.40
16	Darrell Porter	.70	.50	.30
17	John Tudor	1.00	.70	.40
18	Jeff Lahti	.70	.50	.30
19	Andy Van Slyke	2.00	1.50	.80
20	Willie McGee	1.50	1.25	.60

1986 Kay Bee

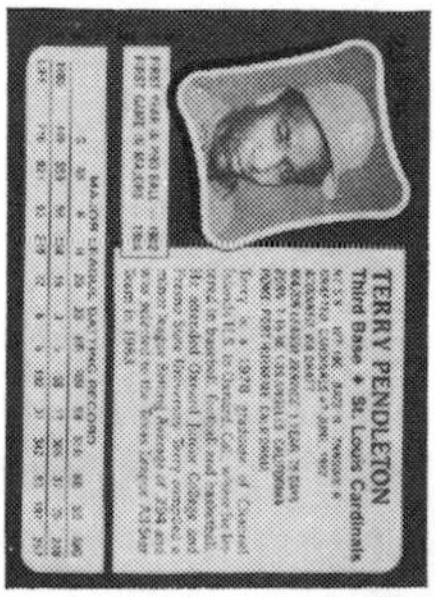

One of the most-widely distributed of the specialty boxed sets of 1986, the Kay Bee toy store chain sets of "Young Superstars of Baseball" was produced by Topps. The 2-1/2" by 3-1/2" cards are printed on white stock with a glossy surface finish. Backs, printed in red and black, are strongly reminiscent of the 1971 Topps cards. While the set concentrated on "young" stars of the game, few of the year's top rookies were included.

		MT	NR MT	EX
Complete Set:		4.00	3.00	1.50
Common Player:		.05	.04	.02
1	Rick Aguilera	.12	.09	.05
2	Chris Brown	.15	.11	.06
3	Tom Browning	.07	.05	.03
4	Tom Brunansky	.07	.05	.03
5	Vince Coleman	.25	.20	.10
6	Ron Darling	.10	.08	.04
7	Alvin Davis	.10	.08	.04
8	Mariano Duncan	.07	.05	.03
9	Shawon Dunston	.07	.05	.03
10	Sid Fernandez	.10	.08	.04
11	Tony Fernandez	.10	.08	.04
12	Brian Fisher	.10	.08	.04
13	John Franco	.07	.05	.03
14	Julio Franco	.10	.08	.04
15	Dwight Gooden	.50	.40	.20
16	Ozzie Guillen	.15	.11	.06
17	Tony Gwynn	.30	.25	.12
18	Jimmy Key	.10	.08	.04
19	Don Mattingly	.80	.60	.30
20	Oddibe McDowell	.15	.11	.06
21	Roger McDowell	.15	.11	.06
22	Dan Pasqua	.10	.08	.04
23	Terry Pendleton	.07	.05	.03
24	Jim Presley	.10	.08	.04
25	Kirby Puckett	.25	.20	.10
26	Earnie Riles	.07	.05	.03
27	Bret Saberhagen	.15	.11	.06
28	Mark Salas	.05	.04	.02
29	Juan Samuel	.12	.09	.05
30	Jeff Stone	.05	.04	.02
31	Darryl Strawberry	.40	.30	.15
32	Andy Van Slyke	.10	.08	.04
33	Frank Viola	.12	.09	.05

1987 Kay Bee

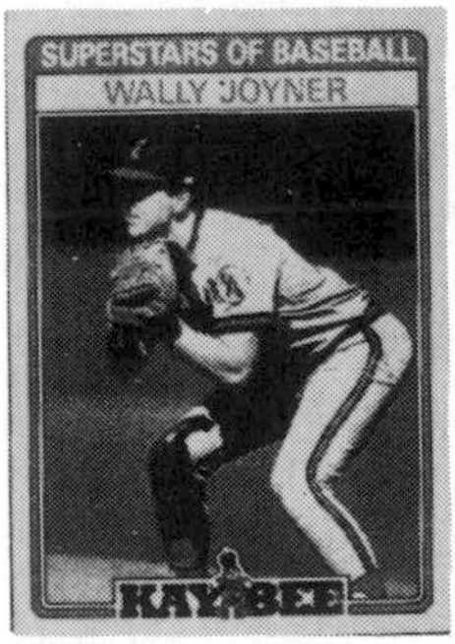

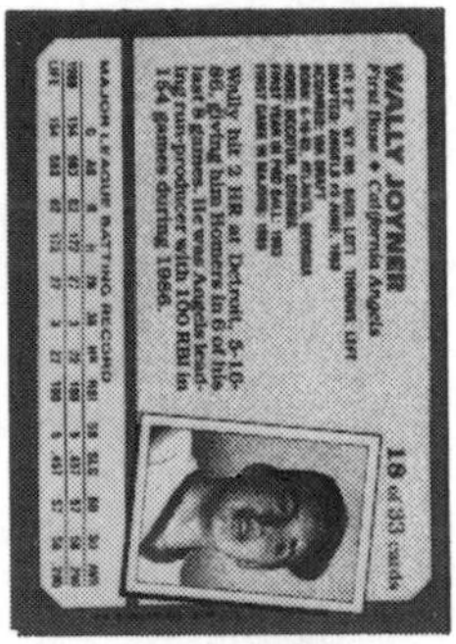

For a second straight year, Topps produced a 33-card set for the Kay Bee toy store chain. Called "Superstars of Baseball," the cards in the set measure the standard 2-1/2" by 3-1/2" size. The glossy-coated card fronts carry a full-color player photo plus the Kay Bee logo. The card backs, reminiscent of those found in the 1971 Topps set, offer a black and white head shot of the player along with his name, postion, personal information, playing record and a brief biography. The set was packaged in a specially designed box.

		MT	NR MT	EX
Complete Set:		4.00	3.00	1.50
Common Player:		.05	.04	.02
1	Harold Baines	.10	.08	.04
2	Jesse Barfield	.12	.09	.05
3	Don Baylor	.10	.08	.04
4	Wade Boggs	1.00	.70	.40
5	George Brett	.40	.30	.15
6	Hubie Brooks	.07	.05	.03
7	Jose Canseco	1.00	.70	.40
8	Gary Carter	.20	.15	.08
9	Joe Carter	.12	.09	.05
10	Roger Clemens	.40	.30	.15
11	Vince Coleman	.15	.11	.06
12	Glenn Davis	.15	.11	.06
13	Dwight Gooden	.40	.30	.15
14	Pedro Guerrero	.15	.11	.06
15	Tony Gwynn	.25	.20	.10
16	Rickey Henderson	.25	.20	.10
17	Keith Hernandez	.20	.15	.08
18	Wally Joyner	.50	.40	.20
19	Don Mattingly	.80	.60	.30
20	Jack Morris	.15	.11	.06
21	Dale Murphy	.30	.25	.12
22	Eddie Murray	.25	.20	.10
23	Dave Parker	.15	.11	.06
24	Kirby Puckett	.25	.20	.10
25	Tim Raines	.25	.20	.10
26	Jim Rice	.25	.20	.10
27	Dave Righetti	.12	.09	.05
28	Ryne Sandberg	.40	.30	.15
29	Mike Schmidt	.30	.25	.12
30	Mike Scott	.12	.09	.05
31	Darryl Strawberry	.40	.30	.15
32	Fernando Valenzuela	.20	.15	.08
33	Dave Winfield	.20	.15	.08

1988 Kay Bee
Superstars Of Baseball

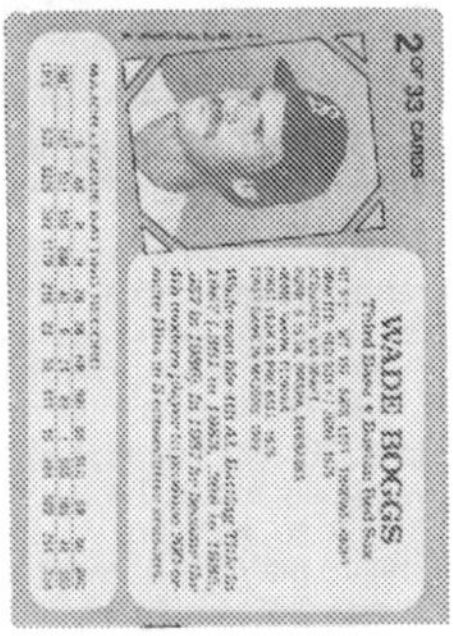

This 33-card boxed set was produced by Topps for exclusive distribution via Kay Bee toy stores nationwide. Card fronts are super glossy and feature full-color player action photos below a bright red and yellow player name banner. Photos are framed in green above a large, cartoon-style Kay Bee logo. Card backs feature player closeups in a horizontal layout in blue ink on a green and white background. Card backs are numbered and carry a player name section that includes biographical information, career data and major league batting stats.

		MT	NR MT	EX
Complete Set:		4.00	3.00	1.50
Common Player:		.10	.08	.04
1	George Bell	.20	.15	.08
2	Wade Boggs	.60	.45	.25
3	Jose Canseco	1.00	.70	.40
4	Joe Carter	.12	.09	.05
5	Jack Clark	.15	.11	.06
6	Alvin Davis	.10	.08	.04
7	Eric Davis	.80	.60	.30
8	Andre Dawson	.15	.11	.06
9	Darrell Evans	.10	.08	.04
10	Dwight Evans	.10	.08	.04
11	Gary Gaetti	.12	.09	.05
12	Pedro Guerrero	.15	.11	.06
13	Tony Gwynn	.25	.20	.10

		MT	NR MT	EX
14	Howard Johnson	.12	.09	.05
15	Wally Joyner	.30	.25	.12
16	Don Mattingly	1.00	.70	.40
17	Willie McGee	.10	.08	.04
18	Mark McGwire	.60	.45	.25
19	Paul Molitor	.12	.09	.05
20	Dale Murphy	.30	.25	.12
21	Dave Parker	.15	.11	.06
22	Lance Parrish	.15	.11	.06
23	Kirby Puckett	.25	.20	.10
24	Tim Raines	.25	.20	.10
25	Cal Ripken	.50	.40	.20
26	Juan Samuel	.12	.09	.05
27	Mike Schmidt	.30	.25	.12
28	Ruben Sierra	.12	.09	.05
29	Darryl Strawberry	.40	.30	.15
30	Danny Tartabull	.12	.09	.05
31	Alan Trammell	.15	.11	.06
32	Tim Wallach	.10	.08	.04
33	Dave Winfield	.20	.15	.08

1988 Kay Bee Team Leaders

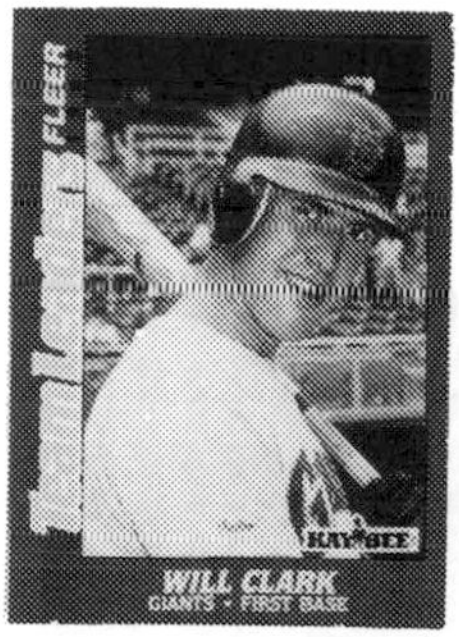

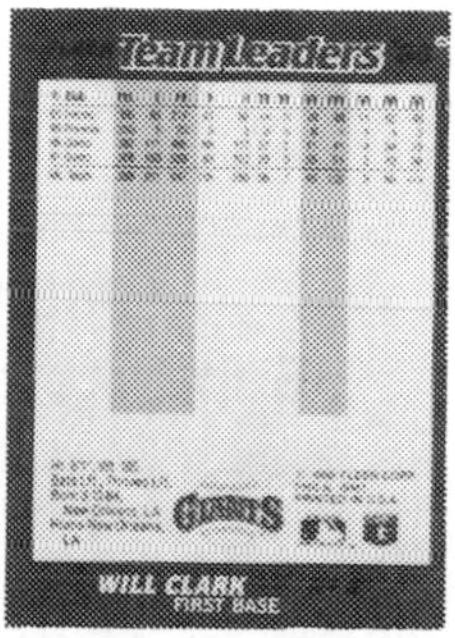

This first-year boxed edition of 44 player and 6 team logo cards was produced by Fleer for distribution by Kay Bee toy stores nationwide. Full-color player photos are framed in black against a bright red border. Lettering is blue, yellow and black. The "Fleer Team Leaders 1988" logo is printed vertically along the left side of the card front; the Kay Bee logo appears in the lower right corner of the photo; player's name, team and position are centered in the bottom margin. Card backs (red, white and pink) repeat the Team Leaders logo, followed by stats, personal data, team and major league baseball logos. The player's name, card number and position are listed on the lower border. The set includes six team logo sticker cards that feature black and white stadium photos on the backs.

		MT	NR MT	EX
Complete Set:		4.00	3.00	1.50
Common Player:		.05	.04	.02
1	George Bell	.20	.15	.08
2	Wade Boggs	.60	.45	.25
3	Jose Canseco	1.00	.70	.40
4	Will Clark	.25	.20	.10
5	Roger Clemens	.40	.30	.15
6	Eric Davis	.80	.60	.30
7	Andre Dawson	.15	.11	.06
8	Julio Franco	.07	.05	.03
9	Andres Galarraga	.15	.11	.06
10	Dwight Gooden	.40	.30	.15
11	Tony Gwynn	.25	.20	.10
12	Tom Henke	.05	.04	.02
13	Orel Hershiser	.10	.08	.04
14	Kent Hrbek	.15	.11	.06
15	Ted Higuera	.10	.08	.04
16	Wally Joyner	.30	.25	.12
17	Jimmy Key	.07	.05	.03
18	Mark Langston	.10	.08	.04
19	Don Mattingly	1.00	.70	.40
20	Willie McGee	.10	.08	.04

		MT	NR MT	EX
21	Mark McGwire	.60	.45	.25
22	Paul Molitor	.12	.09	.05
23	Jack Morris	.12	.09	.05
24	Dale Murphy	.30	.25	.12
25	Larry Parrish	.05	.04	.02
26	Kirby Puckett	.20	.15	.08
27	Tim Raines	.20	.15	.08
28	Jeff Reardon	.07	.05	.03
29	Dave Righetti	.12	.09	.05
30	Cal Ripken, Jr.	.50	.40	.20
31	Don Robinson	.05	.04	.02
32	Bret Saberhagen	.15	.11	.06
33	Juan Samuel	.12	.09	.05
34	Mike Schmidt	.30	.25	.12
35	Mike Scott	.12	.09	.05
36	Kevin Seitzer	.10	.08	.04
37	Dave Smith	.05	.04	.02
38	Ozzie Smith	.15	.11	.06
39	Zane Smith	.05	.04	.02
40	Darryl Strawberry	.40	.30	.15
41	Rick Sutcliffe	.10	.08	.04
42	Bobby Thigpen	.07	.05	.03
43	Alan Trammell	.15	.11	.06
44	Andy Van Slyke	.10	.08	.04

1989 Kay-Bee Superstars

The top stars of baseball were featured in this 33-card boxed set produced by Topps for the Kay-Bee Toy store chain. The glossy, standard- size cards display the Kee-Bee logo below the player photo on the front. The top of the card is headlined "Superstars of Baseball," with the player's name underneath. The backs of the cards include a small black-and-white player photo and personal data.

		MT	NR MT	EX
Complete Set:		5.00	3.75	2.00
Common Player:		.10	.08	.04
1	Wade Boggs	.50	.40	.20
2	George Brett	.15	.11	.08
3	Jose Canseco	1.00	.70	.40
4	Gary Carter	.10	.08	.04
5	Jack Clark	.10	.08	.04
6	Will Clark	1.00	.70	.40
7	Roger Clemens	.50	.40	.20
8	Eric Davis	.40	.30	.15
9	Andre Dawson	.15	.11	.06
10	Dwight Evans	.10	.08	.04
11	Carlton Fisk	.15	.11	.06
12	Andres Galarraga	.10	.08	.04
13	Kirk Gibson	.10	.08	.04
14	Doc Gooden	.30	.25	.12
15	Mike Greenwell	.30	.25	.12
16	Pedro Guerrero	.15	.11	.08
17	Tony Gwynn	.25	.20	.10
18	Rickey Henderson	.50	.40	.20
19	Orel Hershiser	.15	.11	.06
20	Don Mattingly	.80	.60	.30
21	Mark McGwire	.40	.30	.15
22	Dale Murphy	.20	.15	.08
23	Eddie Murray	.15	.11	.06
24	Kirby Puckett	.25	.20	.10
25	Rock Raines	.15	.11	.06
26	Ryne Sanberg	.40	.30	.15
27	Mike Schmidt	.30	.25	.12

		MT	NR MT	EX
28	Ozzie Smith	.20	.15	.08
29	Darryl Strawberry	.30	.25	.12
30	Alan Trammell	.12	.09	.05
31	Frank Viola	.12	.09	.05
32	Dave Winfield	.12	.09	.05
33	Robin Yount	.20	.15	.08

1970 Kellogg's

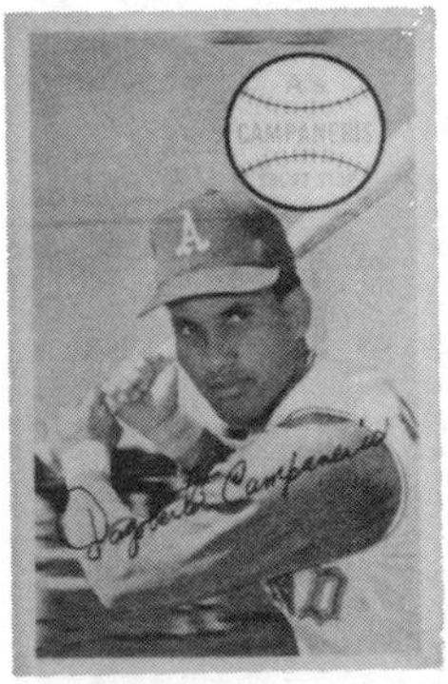

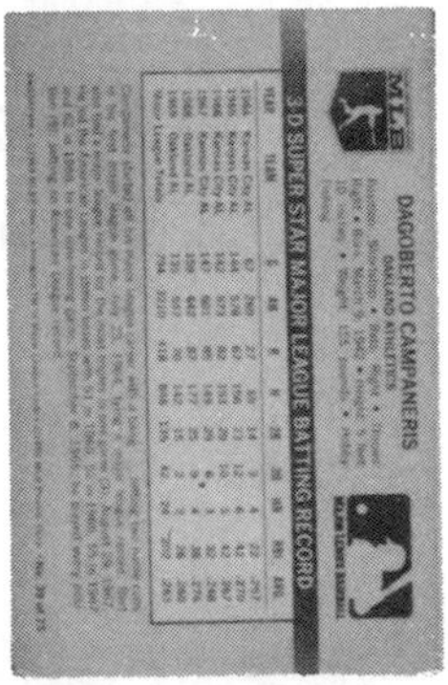

For 14 years in the 1970s and early 1980s, the Kellogg's cereal company provided Topps with virtually the only meaningful national competition in the baseball card market. Kellogg's kicked off its baseball card program in 1970 with a 75-player set of simulated 3-D cards. Single cards were available in selected brands of the company's cereal, while a mail-in program offered complete sets. The 3-D effect was achieved by the sandwiching of a clear color player photo between a purposely blurred stadium background scene and a layer of ribbed plastic. The relatively narrow dimension of the card, 2-1/4" by 3-1/2" and the nature of the plastic overlay seem to conspire to cause the cards to curl, often cracking the plastic layer, if not stored properly. Cards with major cracks in the plastic can be considered in Fair condition, at best.

		NR MT	EX	VG
Complete Set:		175.00	87.00	52.00
Common Player: 1-15		.90	.45	.25
Common Player: 16-30		1.00	.50	.30
Common Player: 31-75		.90	.45	.25
1	Ed Kranepool	1.50	.70	.45
2	Pete Rose	20.00	10.00	6.00
3	Cleon Jones	.90	.45	.25
4	Willie McCovey	3.50	1.75	1.00
5	Mel Stottlemyre	1.00	.50	.30
6	Frank Howard	1.25	.60	.40
7	Tom Seaver	10.00	5.00	3.00
8	Don Sutton	2.50	1.25	.70
9	Jim Wynn	.90	.45	.25
10	Jim Maloney	.90	.45	.25
11	Tommie Agee	.90	.45	.25
12	Willie Mays	10.00	5.00	3.00
13	Juan Marichal	3.00	1.50	.90
14	Dave McNally	1.00	.50	.30
15	Frank Robinson	3.50	1.75	1.00
16	Carlos May	1.00	.50	.30
17	Bill Singer	1.00	.50	.30
18	Rick Reichardt	1.00	.50	.30
19	Boog Powell	1.50	.70	.45
20	Gaylord Perry	3.50	1.75	1.00
21	Brooks Robinson	6.00	3.00	1.75
22	Luis Aparicio	3.50	1.75	1.00
23	Joel Horlen	1.00	.50	.30
24	Mike Epstein	1.00	.50	.30
25	Tom Haller	1.00	.50	.30
26	Willie Crawford	1.00	.50	.30
27	Roberto Clemente	10.00	5.00	3.00
28	Matty Alou	1.25	.60	.40
29	Willie Stargell	4.00	2.00	1.25
30	Tim Cullen	1.00	.50	.30
31	Randy Hundley	.90	.45	.25
32	Reggie Jackson	10.00	5.00	3.00
33	Rich Allen	1.25	.60	.40
34	Tim McCarver	1.00	.50	.30
35	Ray Culp	.90	.45	.25
36	Jim Fregosi	1.00	.50	.30
37	Billy Williams	3.00	1.50	.90
38	Johnny Odom	.90	.45	.25
39	Bert Campaneris	1.00	.50	.30
40	Ernie Banks	3.50	1.75	1.00
41	Chris Short	.90	.45	.25
42	Ron Santo	1.00	.50	.30
43	Glenn Beckert	.90	.45	.25
44	Lou Brock	3.50	1.75	1.00
45	Larry Hisle	.90	.45	.25
46	Reggie Smith	1.00	.50	.30
47	Rod Carew	4.00	2.00	1.25
48	Curt Flood	1.00	.50	.30
49	Jim Lonborg	.90	.45	.25
50	Sam McDowell	1.00	.50	.30
51	Sal Bando	1.00	.50	.30
52	Al Kaline	4.00	2.00	1.25
53	Gary Nolan	.90	.45	.25
54	Rico Petrocelli	.90	.45	.25
55	Ollie Brown	.90	.45	.25
56	Luis Tiant	1.25	.60	.40
57	Bill Freehan	1.00	.50	.30
58	Johnny Bench	10.00	5.00	3.00
59	Joe Pepitone	1.00	.50	.30
60	Bobby Murcer	1.00	.50	.30
61	Harmon Killebrew	3.50	1.75	1.00
62	Don Wilson	.90	.45	.25
63	Tony Oliva	1.25	.60	.40
64	Jim Perry	1.00	.50	.30
65	Mickey Lolich	1.25	.60	.40
66	Coco Laboy	.90	.45	.25
67	Dean Chance	.90	.45	.25
68	Ken Harrelson	1.00	.50	.30
69	Willie Horton	1.00	.50	.30
70	Wally Bunker	.90	.45	.25
71a	Bob Gibson (1959 IP blank)	5.00	2.50	1.50
71b	Bob Gibson (1959 IP 76)	3.00	1.50	.90
72	Joe Morgan	3.00	1.50	.90
73	Denny McLain	1.25	.60	.40
74	Tommy Harper	.90	.45	.25
75	Don Mincher	1.25	.60	.40

1971 Kellogg's

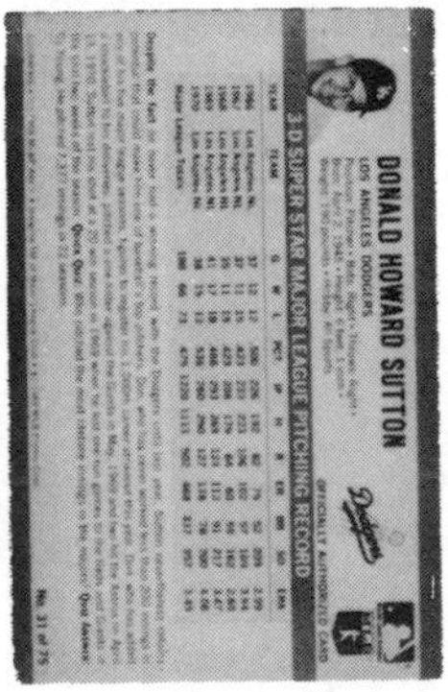

The scarcest and most valuable of the Kellogg's editions, the 75-card 1971 set was the only one not offered by the company on a mail-in basis; the only way to complete it was to buy ... and buy and buy ... boxes of cereal. Kellogg's again used the simulated 3-D effect in the cards' design, with the same result being many of the 2-1/4" by 3-1/2" cards are found today with cracks resulting from the cards' curling. A number of scarcer back variations are checklisted below. In addition, all 75 cards can be found with and without the 1970 date before the "Xograph" copyright line on the back; though there is no difference in value.

		NR MT	EX	VG
Complete Set:		850.00	425.00	255.00
Common Player:		8.00	4.00	2.50
1a	Wayne Simpson (SO 120)	12.00	6.00	3.50
1b	Wayne Simpson (SO 119)	15.00	7.50	4.50
2	Tom Seaver	30.00	15.00	9.00
3a	Jim Perry (IP 2238)	10.00	5.00	3.00

		NR MT	EX	VG
3b	Jim Perry (IP 2239)	15.00	7.50	4.50
4a	Bob Robertson (RBI 94)	8.00	4.00	2.50
4b	Bob Robertson (RBI 95)	12.00	6.00	3.50
5	Roberto Clemente	35.00	17.50	10.50
6a	Gaylord Perry (IP 2014)	15.00	7.50	4.50
6b	Gaylord Perry (IP 2015)	20.00	10.00	6.00
7a	Felipe Alou (1970 Oakland NL)	15.00	7.50	4.50
7b	Felipe Alou (1970 Oakland AL)	10.00	5.00	3.00
8	Denis Menke	8.00	4.00	2.50
9a	Don Kessinger (Hits 849)	10.00	5.00	3.00
9b	Don Kessinger (Hits 850)	15.00	7.50	4.50
10	Willie Mays	35.00	17.50	10.50
11	Jim Hickman	8.00	4.00	2.50
12	Tony Oliva	12.00	6.00	3.50
13	Manny Sanguillen	8.00	4.00	2.50
14a	Frank Howard (1968 Washington NL)	18.00	9.00	5.50
14b	Frank Howard (1968 Washington AL)	12.00	6.00	3.50
15	Frank Robinson	25.00	12.50	7.50
16	Willie Davis	10.00	5.00	3.00
17	Lou Brock	20.00	10.00	6.00
18	Cesar Tovar	8.00	4.00	2.50
19	Luis Aparicio	15.00	7.50	4.50
20	Boog Powell	12.00	6.00	3.50
21a	Dick Selma (SO 584)	8.00	4.00	2.50
21b	Dick Selma (SO 587)	12.00	6.00	3.50
22	Danny Walton	8.00	4.00	2.50
23	Carl Morton	8.00	4.00	2.50
24a	Sonny Siebert (SO 1054)	8.00	4.00	2.50
24b	Sonny Siebert (SO 1055)	12.00	6.00	3.50
25	Jim Merritt	8.00	4.00	2.50
26a	Jose Cardenal (Hits 828)	8.00	4.00	2.50
26b	Jose Cardenal (Hits 829)	12.00	6.00	3.50
27	Don Mincher	8.00	4.00	2.50
28a	Clyde Wright (California state logo)	8.00	4.00	2.50
28b	Clyde Wright (Angels crest logo)	12.00	6.00	3.50
29	Les Cain	8.00	4.00	2.50
30	Danny Cater	8.00	4.00	2.50
31	Don Sutton	15.00	7.50	4.50
32	Chuck Dobson	8.00	4.00	2.50
33	Willie McCovey	20.00	10.00	6.00
34	Mike Epstein	8.00	4.00	2.50
35a	Paul Blair (Runs 386)	8.00	4.00	2.50
35b	Paul Blair (Runs 385)	12.00	6.00	3.50
36a	Gary Nolan (SO 577)	8.00	4.00	2.50
36b	Gary Nolan (SO 581)	12.00	6.00	3.50
37	Sam McDowell	10.00	5.00	3.00
38	Amos Otis	10.00	5.00	3.00
39a	Ray Fosse (RBI 69)	8.00	4.00	2.50
39b	Ray Fosse (RBI 70)	12.00	6.00	3.50
40	Mel Stottlemyre	10.00	5.00	3.00
41	Cito Gaston	8.00	4.00	2.50
42	Dick Dietz	8.00	4.00	2.50
43	Roy White	10.00	5.00	3.00
44	Al Kaline	25.00	12.50	7.50
45	Carlos May	8.00	4.00	2.50
46a	Tommie Agee (RBI 313)	8.00	4.00	2.50
46b	Tommie Agee (RBI 314)	12.00	6.00	3.50
47	Tommy Harper	8.00	4.00	2.50
48	Larry Dierker	8.00	4.00	2.50
49	Mike Cuellar	10.00	5.00	3.00
50	Ernie Banks	25.00	12.50	7.50
51	Bob Gibson	20.00	10.00	6.00
52	Reggie Smith	10.00	5.00	3.00
53a	Matty Alou (RBI 273)	10.00	5.00	3.00
53b	Matty Alou (RBI 274)	15.00	7.50	4.50
54a	Alex Johnson (California state logo)	8.00	4.00	2.50
54b	Alex Johnson (Angels crest logo)	12.00	6.00	3.50
55	Harmon Killebrew	20.00	10.00	6.00
56	Billy Grabarkewitz	8.00	4.00	2.50
57	Rich Allen	12.00	6.00	3.50
58	Tony Perez	15.00	7.50	4.50
59a	Dave McNally (SO 1065)	10.00	5.00	3.00
59b	Dave McNally (SO 1067)	15.00	7.50	4.50
60a	Jim Palmer (SO 564)	15.00	7.50	4.50
60b	Jim Palmer (SO 567)	20.00	10.00	6.00
61	Billy Williams	15.00	7.50	4.50
62	Joe Torre	12.00	6.00	3.50
63a	Jim Northrup (AB 2773)	8.00	4.00	2.50
63b	Jim Northrup (AB 2772)	12.00	6.00	3.50
64a	Jim Fregosi (Calif. state logo - Hits 1326)	8.00	4.00	2.50
64b	Jim Fregosi (Calif. state logo - Hits 1327)	12.00	6.00	3.50
64c	Jim Fregosi (Angels crest logo)	12.00	6.00	3.50
65	Pete Rose	75.00	37.00	22.00
66a	Bud Harrelson (RBI 112)	8.00	4.00	2.50
66b	Bud Harrelson (RBI 113)	12.00	6.00	3.50
67	Tony Taylor	8.00	4.00	2.50
68	Willie Stargell	20.00	10.00	6.00
69	Tony Horton	8.50	4.25	2.50
70a	Claude Osteen (no number)	20.00	10.00	6.00
70b	Claude Osteen (#70 on back)	8.00	4.00	2.50
71	Glenn Beckert	10.00	5.00	3.00
72	Nate Colbert	8.00	4.00	2.50
73a	Rick Monday (AB 1705)	10.00	5.00	3.00
73b	Rick Monday (AB 1704)	15.00	7.50	4.50
74a	Tommy John (BB 444)	15.00	7.50	4.50
74b	Tommy John (BB 443)	20.00	10.00	6.00
75	Chris Short	12.00	6.00	3.50

1972 Kellogg's

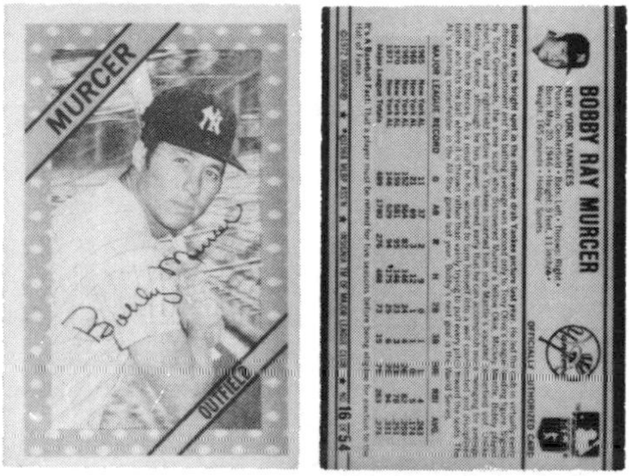

For 1972, Kellogg's reduced both the number of cards in its set and the dimensions of each card, moving to a 2-1/8" by 3-1/4" size and fixing the set at 54 cards. Once again, the cards were produced to simulate a 3-D effect (see description for 1970 Kellogg's). The set was available via a mail-in offer. The checklist includes variations which resulted from the correction of erroneous statistics on the backs of some cards. The complete set values quoted do not include the scarcer variations.

		NR MT	EX	VG
Complete Set:		75.00	37.00	22.00
Common Player:		.70	.35	.20
1a	Tom Seaver (1970 ERA 2.85)	9.00	4.50	2.75
1b	Tom Seaver (1970 ERA 2.81)	6.50	3.25	2.00
2	Amos Otis	.80	.40	.25
3a	Willie Davis (Runs 842)	1.25	.60	.40
3b	Willie Davis (Runs 841)	.80	.40	.25
4	Wilbur Wood	.80	.40	.25
5	Bill Parsons	.70	.35	.20
6	Pete Rose	20.00	10.00	6.00
7a	Willie McCovey (HR 360)	5.00	2.50	1.50
7b	Willie McCovey (HR 370)	3.50	1.75	1.00
8	Fergie Jenkins	1.25	.60	.40
9a	Vida Blue (ERA 2.35)	1.50	.70	.45
9b	Vida Blue (ERA 2.31)	.90	.45	.25
10	Joe Torre	.90	.45	.25
11	Merv Rettenmund	.70	.35	.20
12	Bill Melton	.70	.35	.20
13a	Jim Palmer (Games 170)	4.75	2.50	1.50
13b	Jim Palmer (Games 168)	3.00	1.50	.90
14	Doug Rader	.70	.35	.20
15a	Dave Roberts (...Seaver, the NL leader...)	1.25	.60	.40
15b	Dave Roberts (...Seaver, the league leader...)	.70	.35	.20
16	Bobby Murcer	.80	.40	.25
17	Wes Parker	.70	.35	.20
18a	Joe Coleman (BB 394)	1.25	.60	.40
18b	Joe Coleman (BB 393)	.70	.35	.20
19	Manny Sanguillen	.70	.35	.20
20	Reggie Jackson	8.00	4.00	2.50
21	Ralph Garr	.70	.35	.20
22	Jim "Catfish" Hunter	2.50	1.25	.70
23	Rick Wise	.70	.35	.20
24	Glenn Beckert	.70	.35	.20
25	Tony Oliva	.90	.45	.25
26a	Bob Gibson (SO 2577)	4.75	2.50	1.50
26b	Bob Gibson (SO 2578)	3.00	1.50	.90
27a	Mike Cuellar (1971 ERA 3.80)	1.25	.60	.40

		NR MT	EX	VG
27b	Mike Cuellar (1971 ERA 3.08)	.80	.40	.25
28	Chris Speier	.70	.35	.20
29a	Dave McNally (ERA 3.18)	1.25	.60	.40
29b	Dave McNally (ERA 3.15)	.80	.40	.25
30	Chico Cardenas	.70	.35	.20
31a	Bill Freehan (AVG. .263)	1.25	.60	.40
31b	Bill Freehan (AVG. .262)	.80	.40	.25
32a	Bud Harrelson (Hits 634)	1.25	.60	.40
32b	Bud Harrelson (Hits 624)	.70	.35	.20
33a	Sam McDowell (...less than 200 innings...)	1.25	.60	.40
33b	Sam McDowell (...less than 225 innings...)	.80	.40	.25
34a	Claude Osteen (1971 ERA 3.25)	1.25	.60	.40
34b	Claude Osteen (1971 ERA 3.51)	.70	.35	.20
35	Reggie Smith	.80	.40	.25
36	Sonny Siebert	.70	.35	.20
37	Lee May	.80	.40	.25
38	Mickey Lolich	.90	.45	.25
39a	Cookie Rojas (2B 149)	1.25	.60	.40
39b	Cookie Rojas (2B 150)	.70	.35	.20
40	Dick Drago	.70	.35	.20
41	Nate Colbert	.70	.35	.20
42	Andy Messersmith	.70	.35	.20
43a	Dave Johnson (AVG. .262)	1.50	.70	.45
43b	Dave Johnson (AVG. .264)	.90	.45	.25
44	Steve Blass	.70	.35	.20
45	Bob Robertson	.70	.35	.20
46a	Billy Williams (...missed only one last season...)	5.00	2.50	1.50
46b	Billy Williams (phrase omitted)	3.00	1.50	.90
47	Juan Marichal	3.00	1.50	.90
48	Lou Brock	3.50	1.75	1.00
49	Roberto Clemente	7.00	3.50	2.00
50	Mel Stottlemyre	.80	.40	.25
51	Don Wilson	.70	.35	.20
52a	Sal Bando (RBI 355)	1.25	.60	.40
52b	Sal Bando (RBI 356)	.80	.40	.25
53a	Willie Stargell (2B 197)	5.00	2.50	1.50
53b	Willie Stargell (2B 196)	3.00	1.50	.90
54a	Willie Mays (RBI 1855)	18.00	9.00	5.50
54b	Willie Mays (RBI 1856)	10.00	5.00	3.00

1972 Kellogg's All-Time Baseball Greats

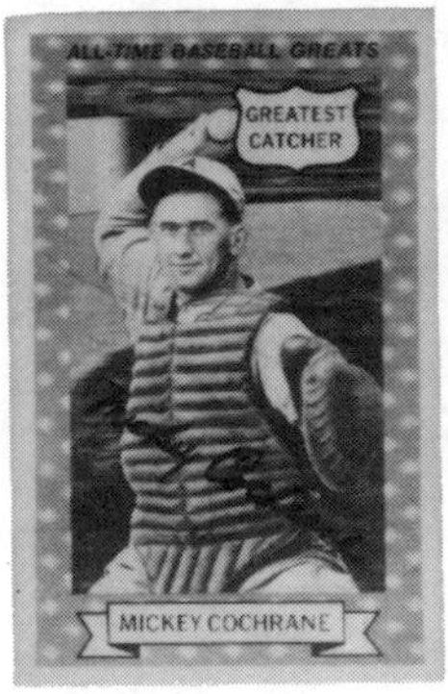

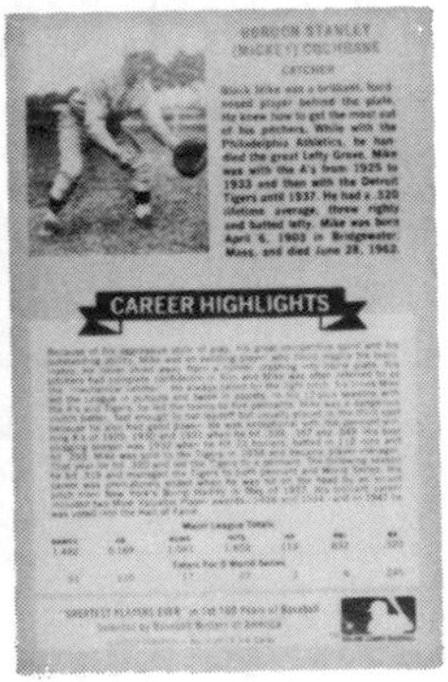

Kellogg's issued a second baseball card set in 1972, inserted into packages of breakfast rolls. The 2-1/4" by 3-1/2" cards also featured a simulated 3-D effect, but the 15 players in the set were "All-Time Baseball Greats", rather than current players. The set is virtually identical to a Rold Gold pretzel issue of 1970; the only difference being the 1972 copyright date on the back of the Kellog's cards, while the pretzel issue bears a 1970 date. The pretzel cards are considerably scarcer than the Kellogg's.

		NR MT	EX	VG
Complete Set:		15.00	7.50	4.50
Common Player:		.50	.25	.15
1	Walter Johnson	1.25	.60	.40
2	Rogers Hornsby	.80	.40	.25
3	John McGraw	.50	.25	.15
4	Mickey Cochrane	.50	.25	.15
5	George Sisler	.50	.25	.15
6	Babe Ruth	4.00	2.00	1.25
7	Robert "Lefty" Grove	.70	.35	.20
8	Harold "Pie" Traynor	.50	.25	.15
9	Honus Wagner	1.00	.50	.30
10	Eddie Collins	.50	.25	.15
11	Tris Speaker	.70	.35	.20
12	Cy Young	.80	.40	.25
13	Lou Gehrig	2.00	1.00	.60
14	Babe Ruth	4.00	2.00	1.25
15	Ty Cobb	2.00	1.00	.60

1973 Kellogg's

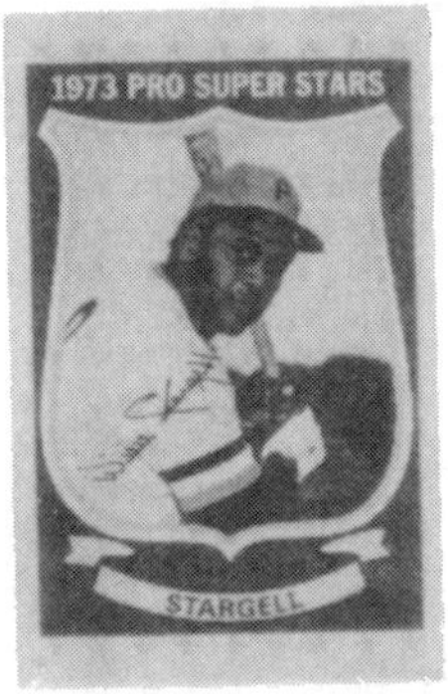

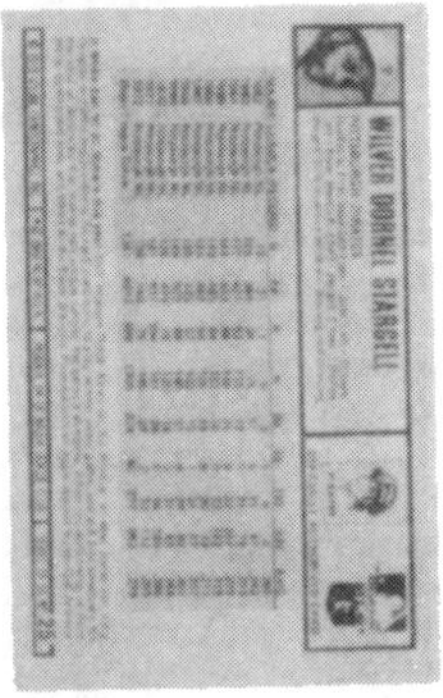

The lone exception to Kellogg's long run of simulated 3-D effect cards came in 1973, when the cereal company's 54-card set was produced by "normal" printing methods. In 2'1/4" by 3-1/2" size, the design was otherwise quite compatible with the issues which preceded and succeeded it. Because it was available via a mail-in offer, it is not as scarce as some other Kellogg's issues.

		NR MT	EX	VG
Complete Set:		75.00	37.00	22.00
Common Player:		.50	.25	.15
1	Amos Otis	.60	.30	.20
2	Ellie Rodriguez	.50	.25	.15
3	Mickey Lolich	.80	.40	.25
4	Tony Oliva	.80	.40	.25
5	Don Sutton	1.25	.60	.40
6	Pete Rose	11.00	5.50	3.25
7	Steve Carlton	4.00	2.00	1.25
8	Bobby Bonds	.70	.35	.20
9	Wilbur Wood	.60	.30	.20
10	Billy Williams	2.50	1.25	.70
11	Steve Blass	.50	.25	.15
12	Jon Matlack	.50	.25	.15
13	Cesar Cedeno	.70	.35	.20
14	Bob Gibson	2.50	1.25	.70
15	Sparky Lyle	.60	.30	.20
16	Nolan Ryan	15.00	7.50	4.50
17	Jim Palmer	2.50	1.25	.70
18	Ray Fosse	.50	.25	.15
19	Bobby Murcer	.60	.30	.20
20	Jim "Catfish" Hunter	2.50	1.25	.70
21	Tug McGraw	.80	.40	.25
22	Reggie Jackson	7.00	3.50	2.00
23	Bill Stoneman	.50	.25	.15
24	Lou Piniella	.80	.40	.25
25	Willie Stargell	2.50	1.25	.70
26	Dick Allen	.90	.45	.25
27	Carlton Fisk	1.25	.60	.40
28	Fergie Jenkins	.90	.45	.25
29	Phil Niekro	1.50	.70	.45
30	Gary Nolan	.50	.25	.15
31	Joe Torre	.80	.40	.25
32	Bobby Tolan	.50	.25	.15
33	Nate Colbert	.50	.25	.15
34	Joe Morgan	2.50	1.25	.70
35	Bert Blyleven	.90	.45	.25
36	Joe Rudi	.60	.30	.20
37	Ralph Garr	.50	.25	.15
38	Gaylord Perry	2.00	1.00	.60
39	Bobby Grich	.60	.30	.20
40	Lou Brock	2.50	1.25	.70
41	Pete Broberg	.50	.25	.15
42	Manny Sanguillen	.50	.25	.15

		NR MT	EX	VG
43	Willie Davis	.60	.30	.20
44	Dave Kingman	.90	.45	.25
45	Carlos May	.50	.25	.15
46	Tom Seaver	4.00	2.00	1.25
47	Mike Cuellar	.60	.30	.20
48	Joe Coleman	.50	.25	.15
49	Claude Osteen	.50	.25	.15
50	Steve Kline	.50	.25	.15
51	Rod Carew	4.00	2.00	1.25
52	Al Kaline	5.00	2.50	1.50
53	Larry Dierker	.50	.25	.15
54	Ron Santo	.70	.35	.20

1974 Kellogg's

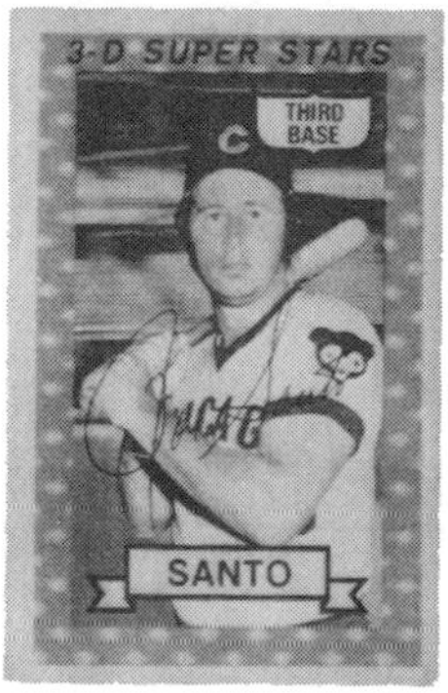

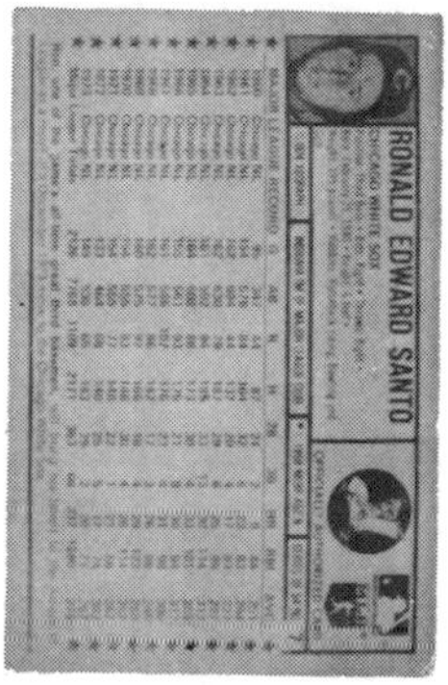

For 1974, Kellogg's returned to the use of simulated 3-D for its 54-player baseball card issue (see 1970 Kellogg's listing for description). In 2-1/8" by 3-1/4" size, the cards were available as a complete set via a mail-in offer.

		NR MT	EX	VG
Complete Set:		65.00	32.00	19.50
Common Player:		.50	.25	.15
1	Bob Gibson	5.00	2.50	1.50
2	Rick Monday	.70	.35	.20
3	Joe Coleman	.50	.25	.15
4	Bert Campaneris	.70	.35	.20
5	Carlton Fisk	1.25	.60	.40
6	Jim Palmer	2.50	1.25	.70
7a	Ron Santo (Chicago Cubs)	1.50	.70	.45
7b	Ron Santo (Chicago White Sox)	.80	.40	.25
8	Nolan Ryan	10.00	5.00	3.00
9	Greg Luzinski	.80	.40	.25
10a	Buddy Bell (Runs 134)	1.50	.70	.45
10b	Buddy Bell (Runs 135)	.80	.40	.25
11	Bob Watson	.50	.25	.15
12	Bill Singer	.50	.25	.15
13	Dave May	.50	.25	.15
14	Jim Brewer	.50	.25	.15
15	Manny Sanguillen	.50	.25	.15
16	Jeff Burroughs	.50	.25	.15
17	Amos Otis	.50	.25	.15
18	Ed Goodson	.50	.25	.15
19	Nate Colbert	.50	.25	.15
20	Reggie Jackson	4.00	2.00	1.25
21	Ted Simmons	.90	.45	.25
22	Bobby Murcer	.60	.30	.20
23	Willie Horton	.60	.30	.20
24	Orlando Cepeda	1.25	.60	.40
25	Ron Hunt	.50	.25	.15
26	Wayne Twitchell	.50	.25	.15
27	Ron Fairly	.50	.25	.15
28	Johnny Bench	5.00	2.50	1.50
29	John Mayberry	.50	.25	.15
30	Rod Carew	5.00	2.50	1.50
31	Ken Holtzman	.50	.25	.15
32	Billy Williams	2.50	1.25	.70
33	Dick Allen	.80	.40	.25
34a	Wilbur Wood (SO 959)	1.25	.60	.40
34b	Wilbur Wood (SO 960)	.70	.35	.20
35	Danny Thompson	.50	.25	.15
36	Joe Morgan	2.50	1.25	.70
37	Willie Stargell	3.00	1.50	.90
38	Pete Rose	13.00	6.50	4.00
39	Bobby Bonds	.70	.35	.20
40	Chris Speier	.50	.25	.15

		NR MT	EX	VG
41	Sparky Lyle	.60	.30	.20
42	Cookie Rojas	.50	.25	.15
43	Tommy Davis	.60	.30	.20
44	Jim "Catfish" Hunter	2.50	1.25	.70
45	Willie Davis	.60	.30	.20
46	Bert Blyleven	.90	.45	.25
47	Pat Kelly	.50	.25	.15
48	Ken Singleton	.60	.30	.20
49	Manny Mota	.60	.30	.20
50	Dave Johnson	.90	.45	.25
51	Sal Bando	.60	.30	.20
52	Tom Seaver	5.00	2.50	1.50
53	Felix Millan	.50	.25	.15
54	Ron Blomberg	.80	.40	.25

1975 Kellogg's

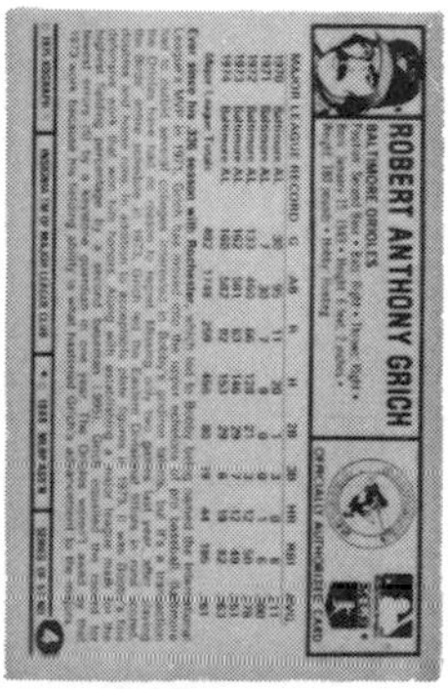

While the card size remained the same at 2-1/8" by 3-1/4", the size of the 1975 Kellogg's "3-D" set was increased by three, to 57 cards. Despite the fact cards could be obtained by a mail-in offer, as well as in cereal boxes, the '75 Kellogg's are noticeably scarcer than the company's other issues, with the exception of the 1971 set. Also helping to raise the value of the cards is the presence of an unusually large number of current and future Hall of Famers.

		NR MT	EX	VG
Complete Set:		150.00	75.00	45.00
Common Player:		2.00	1.00	.60
1	Roy White	3.50	1.75	1.00
2	Ross Grimsley	2.00	1.00	.60
3	Reggie Smith	2.50	1.25	.70
4a	Bob Grich ("...1973 work..." in last line)	4.00	2.00	1.25
4b	Bob Grich (no "...1973 work...")	2.50	1.25	.70
5	Greg Gross	2.00	1.00	.60
6	Bob Watson	2.00	1.00	.60
7	Johnny Bench	11.00	5.50	3.25
8	Jeff Burroughs	2.00	1.00	.60
9	Elliott Maddox	2.00	1.00	.60
10	Jon Matlack	2.00	1.00	.60
11	Pete Rose	24.00	12.00	7.25
12	Leroy Stanton	2.00	1.00	.60
13	Bake McBride	2.00	1.00	.60
14	Jorge Orta	2.00	1.00	.60
15	Al Oliver	2.50	1.25	.70
16	John Briggs	2.00	1.00	.60
17	Steve Garvey	9.00	4.50	2.75
18	Brooks Robinson	10.00	5.00	3.00
19	John Hiller	2.00	1.00	.60
20	Lynn McGlothen	2.00	1.00	.60
21	Cleon Jones	2.00	1.00	.60
22	Fergie Jenkins	2.50	1.25	.70
23	Bill North	2.00	1.00	.60
24	Steve Busby	2.00	1.00	.60
25	Richie Zisk	2.00	1.00	.60
26	Nolan Ryan	20.00	10.00	6.00
27	Joe Morgan	6.50	3.25	2.00
28	Joe Rudi	2.50	1.25	.70
29	Jose Cardenal	2.00	1.00	.60
30	Andy Messersmith	2.00	1.00	.60
31	Willie Montanez	2.00	1.00	.60
32	Bill Buckner	2.50	1.25	.70
33	Rod Carew	10.00	5.00	3.00
34	Lou Piniella	2.50	1.25	.70
35	Ralph Garr	2.00	1.00	.60

		NR MT	EX	VG
36	Mike Marshall	2.00	1.00	.60
37	Garry Maddox	2.00	1.00	.60
38	Dwight Evans	3.00	1.50	.90
39	Lou Brock	9.00	4.50	2.75
40	Ken Singleton	2.50	1.25	.70
41	Steve Braun	2.00	1.00	.60
42	Dick Allen	2.50	1.25	.70
43	Johnny Grubb	2.00	1.00	.60
44a	Jim Hunter (Oakland)	12.00	6.00	3.50
44b	Jim Hunter (New York)	8.00	4.00	2.50
45	Gaylord Perry	6.50	3.25	2.00
46	George Hendrick	2.00	1.00	.60
47	Sparky Lyle	2.50	1.25	.70
48	Dave Cash	2.00	1.00	.60
49	Luis Tiant	2.50	1.25	.70
50	Cesar Geronimo	2.00	1.00	.60
51	Carl Yastrzemski	16.00	8.00	4.75
52	Ken Brett	2.00	1.00	.60
53	Hal McRae	2.50	1.25	.70
54	Reggie Jackson	12.00	6.00	3.50
55	Rollie Fingers	3.50	1.75	1.00
56	Mike Schmidt	14.00	7.00	4.25
57	Richie Hebner	2.50	1.25	.70

1976 Kellogg's

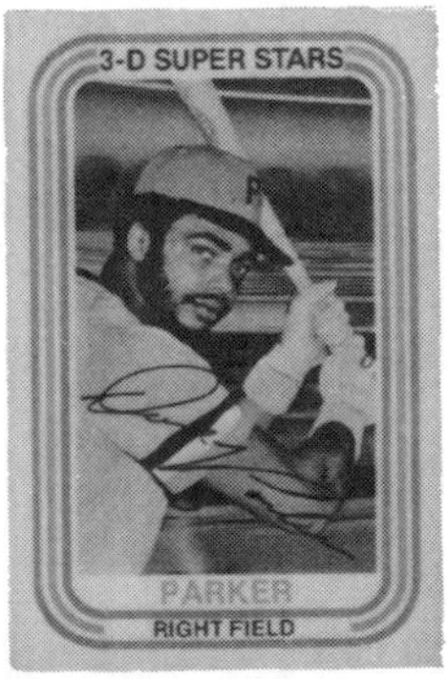

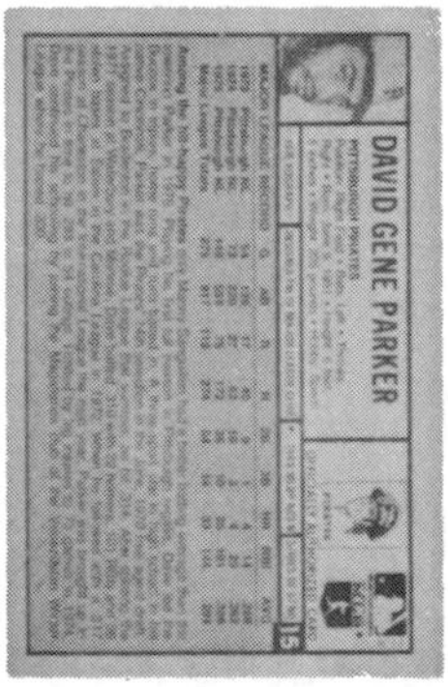

A sizeable list of corrected errors and other variation cards dots the checklist for the 57-card 1976 Kellogg's 3-D set. Again containing 57 cards, the first three cards in the set are found far less often than cards #4-57, indicating they were short-printed in relation to the rest of the set. The complete set values quoted below do not include the scarcer variation cards. Card size remained at 2-1/8" by 3-1/4".

		NR MT	EX	VG
Complete Set:		80.00	40.00	24.00
Common Player:		1.25	.60	.40
1	Steve Hargan	10.00	5.00	3.00
2	Claudell Washington	10.00	5.00	3.00
3	Don Gullett	10.00	5.00	3.00
4	Randy Jones	1.25	.60	.40
5	Jim "Catfish" Hunter	6.50	3.25	2.00
6a	Clay Carroll (Cincinnati)	3.00	1.50	.90
6b	Clay Carroll (Chicago)	1.50	.70	.45
7	Joe Rudi	1.50	.70	.45
8	Reggie Jackson	10.00	5.00	3.00
9	Felix Millan	1.25	.60	.40
10	Jim Rice	8.00	4.00	2.50
11	Bert Blyleven	2.50	1.25	.70
12	Ken Singleton	1.50	.70	.45
13	Don Sutton	2.50	1.25	.70
14	Joe Morgan	5.00	2.50	1.50
15	Dave Parker	4.00	2.00	1.25
16	Dave Cash	1.25	.60	.40
17	Ron LeFlore	1.25	.60	.40
18	Greg Luzinski	2.00	1.00	.60
19	Dennis Eckersley	2.25	1.25	.70
20	Bill Madlock	2.25	1.25	.70
21	George Scott	1.25	.60	.40
22	Willie Stargell	6.50	3.25	2.00
23	Al Hrabosky	1.25	.60	.40
24	Carl Yastrzemski	13.00	6.50	4.00
25	Jim Kaat	2.50	1.25	.70
26	Marty Perez	1.25	.60	.40
27	Bob Watson	1.25	.60	.40

		NR MT	EX	VG
28	Eric Soderholm	1.25	.60	.40
29	Bill Lee	1.25	.60	.40
30a	Frank Tanana (1975 ERA 2.63)	2.50	1.25	.70
30b	Frank Tanana (1975 ERA 2.62)	1.50	.70	.45
31	Fred Lynn	3.50	1.75	1.00
32a	Tom Seaver (1967 PCT. 552)	10.00	5.00	3.00
32b	Tom Seaver (1967 Pct. .552)	8.00	4.00	2.50
33	Steve Busby	1.25	.60	.40
34	Gary Carter	10.00	5.00	3.00
35	Rick Wise	1.25	.60	.40
36	Johnny Bench	10.00	5.00	3.00
37	Jim Palmer	8.00	4.00	2.50
38	Bobby Murcer	2.00	1.00	.60
39	Von Joshua	1.25	.60	.40
40	Lou Brock	8.00	4.00	2.50
41a	Mickey Rivers (last line begins "In three...")	2.75	1.50	.80
41b	Mickey Rivers (last line begins "The Yankees...")	1.25	.60	.40
42	Manny Sanguillen	1.25	.60	.40
43	Jerry Reuss	1.50	.70	.45
44	Ken Griffey	1.50	.70	.45
45a	Jorge Orta (AB 1616)	2.25	1.25	.70
45b	Jorge Orta (AB 1615)	1.25	.60	.40
46	John Mayberry	1.25	.60	.40
47a	Vida Blue (2nd line reads "...pitched more innings...")	3.00	1.50	.90
47b	Vida Blue (2nd line reads "...struck out more...")	2.00	1.00	.60
48	Rod Carew	10.00	5.00	3.00
49a	Jon Matlack (1975 ER 87)	2.25	1.25	.70
49b	Jon Matlack (1975 ER 86)	1.25	.60	.40
50	Boog Powell	2.50	1.25	.70
51a	Mike Hargrove (AB 935)	2.25	1.25	.70
51b	Mike Hargrove (AB 934)	1.25	.60	.40
52a	Paul Lindblad (1975 ERA 2.72)	2.25	1.25	.70
52b	Paul Lindblad (1975 ERA 2.73)	1.25	.60	.40
53	Thurman Munson	6.50	3.25	2.00
54	Steve Garvey	8.00	4.00	2.50
55	Pete Rose	18.00	9.00	5.50
56a	Greg Gross (Games 302)	2.25	1.25	.70
56b	Greg Gross (Games 334)	1.25	.60	.40
57	Ted Simmons	2.50	1.25	.70

1977 Kellogg's

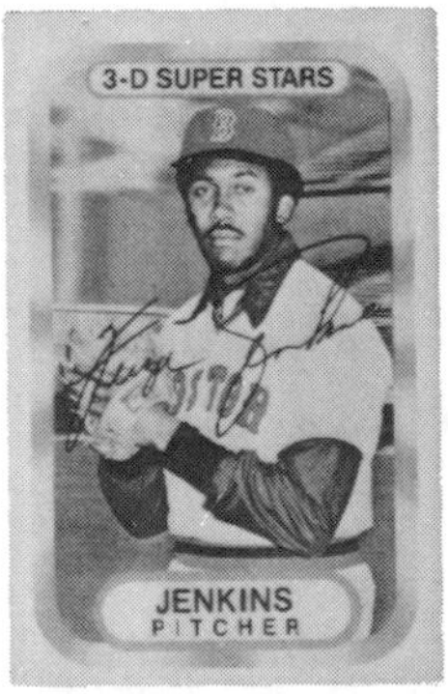

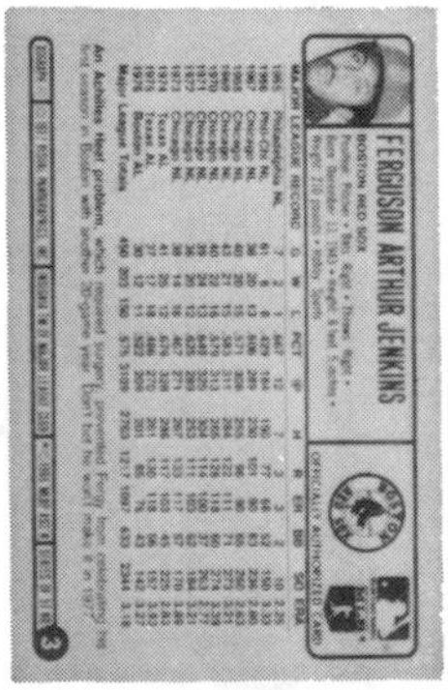

Other than another innovative card design to complement the simulated 3-D effect, there was little change in the 1977 Kellogg's issue. Set size remained at 57 cards, the set remained in the 2-1/8" by 3-1/4" format, and the cards were available either individually in boxes of cereal, or as a complete set via a mail-in box top offer. The 1977 set is the last in which Kellogg's used a player portrait photo on the back of the card.

		NR MT	EX	VG
Complete Set:		55.00	28.00	16.50
Common Player:		.40	.20	.12
1	George Foster	.90	.45	.25
2	Bert Campaneris	.60	.30	.20
3	Fergie Jenkins	.90	.45	.25
4	Dock Ellis	.40	.20	.12
5	John Montefusco	.40	.20	.12
6	George Brett	8.50	4.25	2.50
7	John Candelaria	.50	.25	.15
8	Fred Norman	.40	.20	.12

		NR MT	EX	VG
9	Bill Travers	.40	.20	.12
10	Hal McRae	.60	.30	.20
11	Doug Rau	.40	.20	.12
12	Greg Luzinski	.70	.35	.20
13	Ralph Garr	.40	.20	.12
14	Steve Garvey	4.50	2.25	1.25
15	Rick Manning	.40	.20	.12
16	Lyman Bostock	.50	.25	.15
17	Randy Jones	.40	.20	.12
18a	Ron Cey (58 homers in first sentence)	1.00	.50	.30
18b	Ron Cey (48 homers in first sentence)	.60	.30	.20
19	Dave Parker	1.25	.60	.40
20	Pete Rose	11.00	5.50	3.25
21a	Wayne Garland (last line begins "Prior to...")	.90	.45	.25
21b	Wayne Garland (last line begins "There he...")	.40	.20	.12
22	Bill North	.40	.20	.12
23	Thurman Munson	2.50	1.25	.70
24	Tom Poquette	.40	.20	.12
25	Ron LeFlore	.50	.25	.15
26	Mark Fidrych	.50	.25	.15
27	Sixto Lezcano	.40	.20	.12
28	Dave Winfield	4.00	2.00	1.25
29	Jerry Koosman	.50	.25	.15
30	Mike Hargrove	.40	.20	.12
31	Willie Montanez	.40	.20	.12
32	Don Stanhouse	.40	.20	.12
33	Jay Johnstone	.50	.25	.15
34	Bake McBride	.40	.20	.12
35	Dave Kingman	.70	.35	.20
36	Freddie Patek	.40	.20	.12
37	Garry Maddox	.50	.25	.15
38a	Ken Reitz (last line begins "The previous...")	.90	.45	.25
38b	Ken Reitz (last line begins "In late...")	.40	.20	.12
39	Bobby Grich	.60	.30	.20
40	Cesar Geronimo	.40	.20	.12
41	Jim Lonborg	.40	.20	.12
42	Ed Figueroa	.40	.20	.12
43	Bill Madlock	.80	.40	.25
44	Jerry Remy	.40	.20	.12
45	Frank Tanana	.50	.25	.15
46	Al Oliver	.90	.45	.25
47	Charlie Hough	.50	.25	.15
48	Lou Piniella	.70	.35	.20
49	Ken Griffey	.60	.30	.20
50	Jose Cruz	.60	.30	.20
51	Rollie Fingers	1.25	.60	.40
52	Chris Chambliss	.50	.25	.15
53	Rod Carew	4.00	2.00	1.25
54	Andy Messersmith	.40	.20	.12
55	Mickey Rivers	.40	.20	.12
56	Butch Wynegar	.40	.20	.12
57	Steve Carlton	5.00	2.50	1.50

1978 Kellogg's

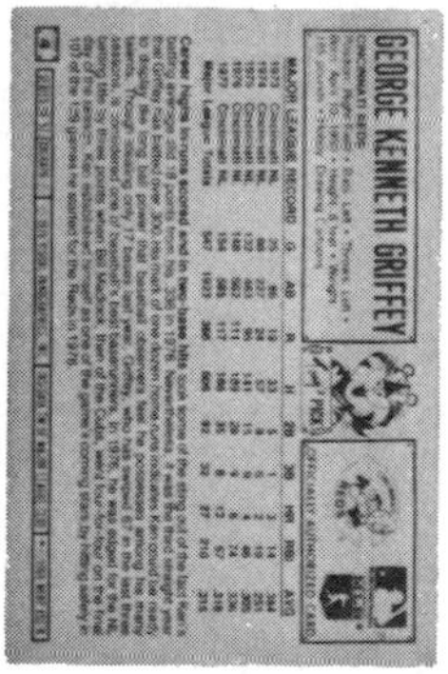

Besides the substitution of a Tony the Tiger drawing for a player portrait photo on the back of the card, the 1978 Kellogg's set offered no major changes from the previous few years issues. Cards were once again in the 2-1/8" by 3-1/4" format, with 57 cards comprising a complete set. Single cards were available in selected brands of the company's cereal, while complete sets could be obtained by a mail-in offer.

		NR MT	EX	VG
Complete Set:		55.00	27.00	16.50
Common Player:		.40	.20	.12
1	Steve Carlton	4.00	2.00	1.25
2	Bucky Dent	.50	.25	.15
3	Mike Schmidt	4.00	2.00	1.25
4	Ken Griffey	.50	.25	.15
5	Al Cowens	.40	.20	.12
6	George Brett	5.00	2.50	1.50
7	Lou Brock	3.00	1.50	.90
8	Rich Gossage	1.25	.60	.40
9	Tom Johnson	.40	.20	.12
10	George Foster	.70	.35	.20
11	Dave Winfield	3.50	1.75	1.00
12	Dan Meyer	.40	.20	.12
13	Chris Chambliss	.50	.25	.15
14	Paul Dade	.40	.20	.12
15	Jeff Burroughs	.40	.20	.12
16	Jose Cruz	.60	.30	.20
17	Mickey Rivers	.40	.20	.12
18	John Candelaria	.50	.25	.15
19	Ellis Valentine	.40	.20	.12
20	Hal McRae	.50	.25	.15
21	Dave Rozema	.40	.20	.12
22	Lenny Randle	.40	.20	.12
23	Willie McCovey	3.00	1.50	.90
24	Ron Cey	.70	.35	.20
25	Eddie Murray	12.00	6.00	3.50
26	Larry Bowa	.60	.30	.20
27	Tom Seaver	3.50	1.75	1.00
28	Garry Maddox	.50	.25	.15
29	Rod Carew	4.00	2.00	1.25
30	Thurman Munson	2.50	1.25	.70
31	Garry Templeton	.60	.30	.20
32	Eric Soderholm	.40	.20	.12
33	Greg Luzinski	.70	.35	.20
34	Reggie Smith	.50	.25	.15
35	Dave Goltz	.40	.20	.12
36	Tommy John	1.25	.60	.40
37	Ralph Garr	.40	.20	.12
38	Alan Bannister	.40	.20	.12
39	Bob Bailor	.40	.20	.12
40	Reggie Jackson	5.00	2.50	1.50
41	Cecil Cooper	.80	.40	.25
42	Burt Hooton	.40	.20	.12
43	Sparky Lyle	.50	.25	.15
44	Steve Ontiveros	.40	.20	.12
45	Rick Reuschel	.60	.30	.20
46	Lyman Bostock	.50	.25	.15
47	Mitchell Page	.40	.20	.12
48	Bruce Sutter	.70	.35	.20
49	Jim Rice	3.50	1.75	1.00
50	Bob Forsch	.40	.20	.12
51	Nolan Ryan	8.00	4.00	2.50
52	Dave Parker	1.25	.60	.40
53	Bert Blyleven	.90	.45	.25
54	Frank Tanana	.50	.25	.15
55	Ken Singleton	.50	.25	.15
56	Mike Hargrove	.40	.20	.12
57	Don Sutton	2.50	1.25	.70

1979 Kellogg's

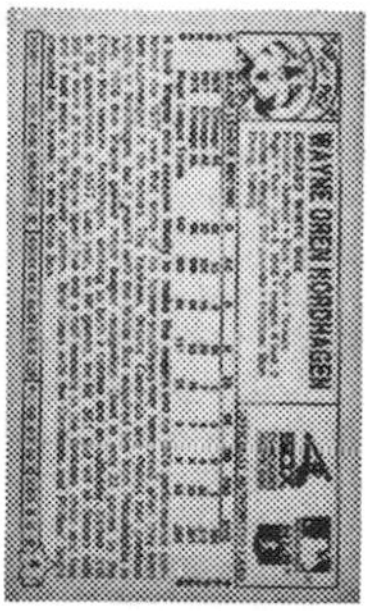

For its 1979 3-D issue, Kellogg's increased the size of the set to 60 cards, but reduced the width of the cards to 1-15/16". Depth stayed the same as in

previous years, 3-1/4". The narrower card format seems to have compounded the problem of curling and subsequent cracking of the ribbed plastic surface which helps give the card a 3-D effect. Cards with major cracks can be graded no higher than VG. The complete set price in the checklist that follows does not include the scarcer variations. Numerous minor variations featuring copyright and trademark logos can be found in the set.

		NR MT	EX	VG
Complete Set:		35.00	17.50	10.50
Common Player:		.30	.15	.09
1	Bruce Sutter	.80	.40	.25
2	Ted Simmons	.70	.35	.20
3	Ross Grimsley	.30	.15	.09
4	Wayne Nordhagen	.30	.15	.09
5a	Jim Palmer (PCT. .649)	2.25	1.25	.70
5b	Jim Palmer (PCT. .650)	1.50	.70	.45
6	John Henry Johnson	.30	.15	.09
7	Jason Thompson	.30	.15	.09
8	Pat Zachry	.30	.15	.09
9	Dennis Eckersley	1.50	1.25	.60
10a	Paul Splittorff (IP 1665)	.60	.30	.20
10b	Paul Splittorff (IP 1666)	.30	.15	.09
11a	Ron Guidry (Hits 397)	2.00	1.00	.60
11b	Ron Guidry (Hits 396)	1.25	.60	.40
12	Jeff Burroughs	.30	.15	.09
13	Rod Carew	2.50	1.25	.70
14a	Buddy Bell (no trade line in bio)	1.25	.60	.40
14b	Buddy Bell (trade line in bio)	.60	.30	.20
15	Jim Rice	2.50	1.25	.70
16	Garry Maddox	.50	.25	.15
17	Willie McCovey	2.50	1.25	.70
18	Steve Carlton	2.50	1.25	.70
19a	J. R. Richard (stats begin with 1972)	.60	.30	.20
19b	J. R. Richard (stats begin with 1971)	.30	.15	.09
20	Paul Molitor	.90	.45	.25
21a	Dave Parker (AVG. .281)	2.00	1.00	.60
21b	Dave Parker (AVG. .318)	1.00	.50	.30
22a	Pete Rose (1978 3B 3)	12.00	6.00	3.50
22b	Pete Rose (1978 3B 33)	8.00	4.00	2.50
23a	Vida Blue (Runs 819)	1.25	.60	.40
23b	Vida Blue (Runs 818)	.60	.30	.20
24	Richie Zisk	.30	.15	.09
25a	Darrell Porter (2B 101)	.80	.40	.25
25b	Darrell Porter (2B 111)	.40	.20	.12
26a	Dan Driessen (Games 642)	.80	.40	.25
26b	Dan Driessen (Games 742)	.40	.20	.12
27a	Geoff Zahn (1978 Minnessota)	.60	.30	.20
27b	Geoff Zahn (1978 Minnesota)	.30	.15	.09
28	Phil Niekro	1.25	.60	.40
29	Tom Seaver	2.50	1.25	.70
30	Fred Lynn	1.00	.50	.30
31	Bill Bonham	.30	.15	.09
32	George Foster	.70	.35	.20
33a	Terry Puhl (last line of bio begins "Terry...")	.60	.30	.20
33b	Terry Puhl (last line of bio begins "His...")	.30	.15	.09
34a	John Candelaria (age is 24)	.90	.45	.25
34b	John Candelaria (age is 25)	.50	.25	.15
35	Bob Knepper	.40	.20	.12
36	Freddie Patek	.30	.15	.09
37	Chris Chambliss	.40	.20	.12
38a	Bob Forsch (1977 Games 86)	.80	.40	.25
38b	Bob Forsch (1977 Games 35)	.40	.20	.12
39a	Ken Griffey (1978 AB 674)	.90	.45	.25
39b	Ken Griffey (1978 AB 614)	.50	.25	.15
40	Jack Clark	.90	.45	.25
41a	Dwight Evans (1978 Hits 13)	1.50	.70	.45
41b	Dwight Evans (1978 Hits 123)	.90	.45	.25
42	Lee Mazzilli	.40	.20	.12
43	Mario Guerrero	.30	.15	.09
44	Larry Bowa	.50	.25	.15
45a	Carl Yastrzemski (Games 9930)	6.00	3.00	1.75
45b	Carl Yastrzemski (Games 9929)	4.00	2.00	1.25
46a	Reggie Jackson (1978 Games 162)	5.00	2.50	1.50
46b	Reggie Jackson (1978 Games 139)	3.00	1.50	.90
47	Rick Reuschel	.60	.30	.20
48a	Mike Flanagan (1976 SO 57)	.90	.45	.25
48b	Mike Flanagan (1976 SO 56)	.50	.25	.15
49a	Gaylord Perry (1973 Hits 325)	2.00	1.00	.60
49b	Gaylord Perry (1973 Hits 315)	1.25	.60	.40
50	George Brett	3.50	1.75	1.00
51a	Craig Reynolds (last line of bio begins "He spent...")	.60	.30	.20
51b	Craig Reynolds (last line of bio begins "In those...")	.30	.15	.09
52	Davey Lopes	.40	.20	.12
53a	Bill Almon (2B 31)	.60	.30	.20
53b	Bill Almon (2B 41)	.30	.15	.09
54	Roy Howell	.30	.15	.09
55	Frank Tanana	.50	.25	.15
56a	Doug Rau (1978 PCT. .577)	.60	.30	.20
56b	Doug Rau (1978 PCT. .625)	.30	.15	.09
57a	Rick Monday (1976 Runs 197)	.90	.45	.25
57b	Rick Monday (1976 Runs 107)	.50	.25	.15
58	Jon Matlack	.30	.15	.09
59a	Ron Jackson (last line of bio begins "His best...")	.60	.30	.20
59b	Ron Jackson (last line of bio begins "The Twins...")	.30	.15	.09
60	Jim Sundberg	.50	.25	.15

1980 Kellogg's

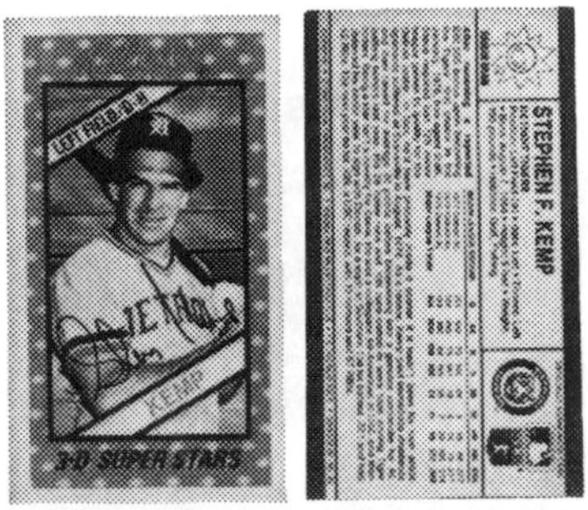

The 1980 cereal company issue featured the narrowest format of any Kellogg's card, 1-7/8" by 3-1/4". For the second straight year, set size remained at 60 cards, available either singly in boxes of cereal, or as complete sets by a mail-in offer.

		NR MT	EX	VG
Complete Set:		25.00	12.50	7.50
Common Player:		.30	.15	.09
1	Ross Grimsley	.30	.15	.09
2	Mike Schmidt	4.00	2.00	1.25
3	Mike Flanagan	.40	.20	.12
4	Ron Guidry	.90	.45	.25
5	Bert Blyleven	.80	.40	.25
6	Dave Kingman	.70	.35	.20
7	Jeff Newman	.30	.15	.09
8	Steve Rogers	.30	.15	.09
9	George Brett	4.00	2.00	1.25
10	Bruce Sutter	.70	.35	.20
11	Gorman Thomas	.40	.20	.12
12	Darrell Porter	.30	.15	.09
13	Roy Smalley	.30	.15	.09
14	Steve Carlton	1.75	.90	.50
15	Jim Palmer	1.50	.70	.45
16	Bob Bailor	.30	.15	.09
17	Jason Thompson	.30	.15	.09
18	Graig Nettles	.80	.40	.25
19	Ron Cey	.50	.25	.15
20	Nolan Ryan	5.00	2.50	1.50
21	Ellis Valentine	.30	.15	.09
22	Larry Hisle	.30	.15	.09
23	Dave Parker	.90	.45	.25
24	Eddie Murray	2.50	1.25	.70
25	Willie Stargell	1.75	.90	.50
26	Reggie Jackson	2.50	1.25	.70
27	Carl Yastrzemski	3.50	1.75	1.00
28	Andre Thornton	.40	.20	.12
29	Davey Lopes	.40	.20	.12
30	Ken Singleton	.40	.20	.12
31	Steve Garvey	2.50	1.25	.70
32	Dave Winfield	2.50	1.25	.70
33	Steve Kemp	.40	.20	.12
34	Claudell Washington	.40	.20	.12
35	Pete Rose	6.50	3.25	2.00
36	Cesar Cedeno	.40	.20	.12

		NR MT	EX	VG
37	John Stearns	.30	.15	.09
38	Lee Mazzilli	.30	.15	.09
39	Larry Bowa	.40	.20	.12
40	Fred Lynn	.80	.40	.25
41	Carlton Fisk	.90	.45	.25
42	Vida Blue	.50	.25	.15
43	Keith Hernandez	1.25	.60	.40
44	Jim Rice	1.75	.90	.50
45	Ted Simmons	.80	.40	.25
46	Chet Lemon	.30	.15	.09
47	Fergie Jenkins	.50	.25	.15
48	Gary Matthews	.40	.20	.12
49	Tom Seaver	2.50	1.25	.70
50	George Foster	.70	.35	.20
51	Phil Niekro	1.25	.60	.40
52	Johnny Bench	2.50	1.25	.70
53	Buddy Bell	.50	.25	.15
54	Lance Parrish	.90	.45	.25
55	Joaquin Andujar	.30	.15	.09
56	Don Baylor	.50	.25	.15
57	Jack Clark	.80	.40	.25
58	J.R. Richard	.30	.15	.09
59	Bruce Bochte	.30	.15	.09
60	Rod Carew	2.50	1.25	.70

1981 Kellogg's

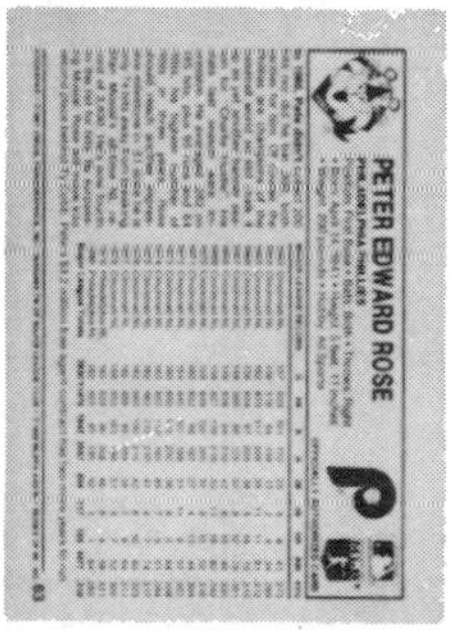

"Bigger" is the word to best describe Kellogg's 1981 card set. Not only were the cards themselves larger than ever before (or since) at 2-1/2" by 3-1/2", but the size of the set was increased to 66, the largest since the 75-card issues of 1970-1971. The '81 Kellogg's set was available only as complete sets by mail. It is thought that the wider format of the 1981s may help prevent the problems of curling and cracking from which other years of Kellogg's issues suffer.

		MT	NR MT	EX
Complete Set:		12.00	9.00	4.75
Common Player:		.08	.04	.02
1	George Foster	.15	.08	.04
2	Jim Palmer	.30	.15	.08
3	Reggie Jackson	1.25	.90	.50
4	Al Oliver	.15	.08	.04
5	Mike Schmidt	1.25	.90	.50
6	Nolan Ryan	2.00	1.50	.80
7	Bucky Dent	.10	.05	.03
8	George Brett	1.25	.90	.50
9	Jim Rice	.35	.20	.09
10	Steve Garvey	.40	.20	.10
11	Willie Stargell	.30	.15	.08
12	Phil Niekro	.25	.13	.06
13	Dave Parker	.20	.10	.05
14	Cesar Cedeno	.10	.05	.03
15	Don Baylor	.10	.05	.03
16	J.R. Richard	.08	.04	.02
17	Tony Perez	.15	.08	.04
18	Eddie Murray	.80	.60	.30
19	Chet Lemon	.08	.04	.02
20	Ben Oglivie	.08	.04	.02
21	Dave Winfield	.50	.25	.13
22	Joe Morgan	.40	.30	.15
23	Vida Blue	.10	.05	.03
24	Willie Wilson	.15	.08	.04
25	Steve Henderson	.08	.04	.02

		MT	NR MT	EX
26	Rod Carew	1.00	.70	.40
27	Garry Templeton	.08	.04	.02
28	Dave Concepcion	.10	.05	.03
29	Davey Lopes	.08	.04	.02
30	Ken Landreaux	.08	.04	.02
31	Keith Hernandez	.40	.20	.10
32	Cecil Cooper	.10	.05	.03
33	Rickey Henderson	1.00	.70	.40
34	Frank White	.10	.05	.03
35	George Hendrick	.08	.04	.02
36	Reggie Smith	.10	.05	.03
37	Tug McGraw	.10	.05	.03
38	Tom Seaver	1.00	.70	.40
39	Ken Singleton	.10	.05	.03
40	Fred Lynn	.20	.10	.05
41	Rich "Goose" Gossage	.20	.10	.05
42	Terry Puhl	.08	.04	.02
43	Larry Bowa	.10	.05	.03
44	Phil Garner	.08	.04	.02
45	Ron Guidry	.20	.10	.05
46	Lee Mazzilli	.08	.04	.02
47	Dave Kingman	.15	.08	.04
48	Carl Yastrzemski	1.00	.70	.40
49	Rick Burleson	.08	.04	.02
50	Steve Carlton	.40	.20	.10
51	Alan Trammell	.30	.15	.08
52	Tommy John	.20	.10	.05
53	Paul Molitor	.20	.10	.05
54	Joe Charboneau	.08	.04	.02
55	Rick Langford	.08	.04	.02
56	Bruce Sutter	.10	.05	.03
57	Robin Yount	1.00	.70	.40
58	Steve Stone	.08	.04	.02
59	Larry Gura	.08	.04	.02
60	Mike Flanagan	.10	.05	.03
61	Bob Horner	.15	.08	.04
62	Bruce Bochte	.08	.04	.02
63	Pete Rose	1.00	.50	.25
64	Buddy Bell	.15	.08	.04
65	Johnny Bench	1.00	.70	.40
66	Mike Hargrove	.08	.04	.02

1982 Kellogg's

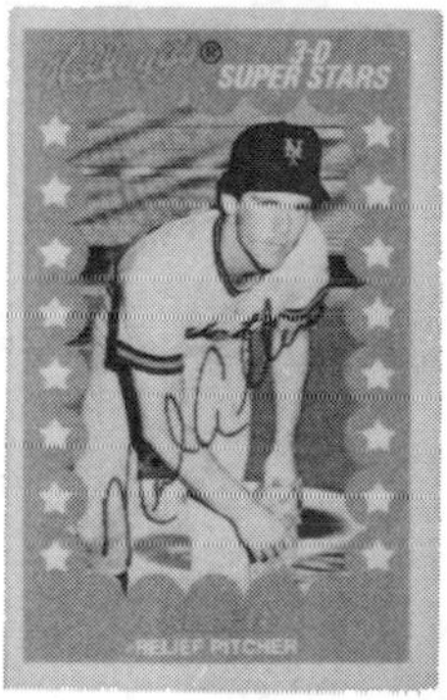

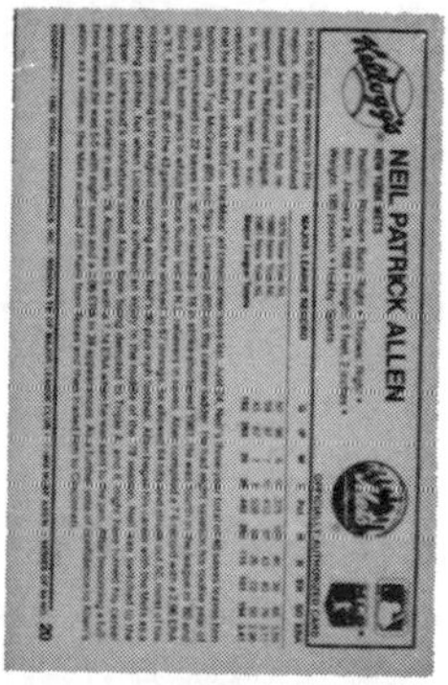

For the second straight year in 1982, Kellogg's cards were not inserted into cereal boxes, but had to be obtained by sending cash and box tops to the company for complete sets. The '82 cards were downsized both in number of cards in the set - 64 - and in physical dimensions, 2-1/8" by 3-1/4".

		MT	NR MT	EX
Complete Set:		16.00	12.00	6.50
Common Player:		.12	.06	.03
1	Richie Zisk	.12	.06	.03
2	Bill Buckner	.12	.06	.03
3	George Brett	1.00	.70	.40
4	Rickey Henderson	1.00	.70	.40
5	Jack Morris	.30	.15	.08
6	Ozzie Smith	.25	.13	.06
7	Rollie Fingers	.25	.13	.06
8	Tom Seaver	.50	.25	.13
9	Fernando Valenzuela	.60	.30	.15
10	Hubie Brooks	.12	.06	.03
11	Nolan Ryan	1.50	1.25	.60
12	Dave Winfield	.60	.30	.15
13	Bob Horner	.20	.10	.05

		MT	NR MT	EX
14	Reggie Jackson	1.00	.70	.40
15	Burt Hooton	.12	.06	.03
16	Mike Schmidt	1.00	.70	.40
17	Bruce Sutter	.20	.10	.05
18	Pete Rose	1.50	.70	.40
19	Dave Kingman	.20	.10	.05
20	Neil Allen	.12	.06	.03
21	Don Sutton	.25	.13	.06
22	Dave Concepcion	.20	.10	.05
23	Keith Hernandez	.50	.25	.13
24	Gary Carter	.70	.35	.20
25	Carlton Fisk	.30	.15	.08
26	Ron Guidry	.25	.13	.06
27	Steve Carlton	.50	.25	.13
28	Robin Yount	.60	.45	.25
29	John Castino	.12	.06	.03
30	Johnny Bench	1.00	.70	.40
31	Bob Knepper	.12	.06	.03
32	Rich "Goose" Gossage	.20	.10	.05
33	Buddy Bell	.20	.10	.05
34	Art Howe	.12	.06	.03
35	Tony Armas	.12	.06	.03
36	Phil Niekro	.30	.15	.08
37	Len Barker	.12	.06	.03
38	Bobby Grich	.20	.10	.05
39	Steve Kemp	.12	.06	.03
40	Kirk Gibson	.35	.20	.09
41	Carney Lansford	.20	.10	.05
42	Jim Palmer	.60	.45	.25
43	Carl Yastrzemski	1.00	.50	.25
44	Rick Burleson	.12	.06	.03
45	Dwight Evans	.25	.13	.06
46	Ron Cey	.20	.10	.05
47	Steve Garvey	.70	.35	.20
48	Dave Parker	.30	.15	.08
49	Mike Easler	.12	.06	.03
50	Dusty Baker	.12	.06	.03
51	Rod Carew	.70	.35	.20
52	Chris Chambliss	.12	.06	.03
53	Tim Raines	.70	.35	.20
54	Chet Lemon	.12	.06	.03
55	Bill Madlock	.20	.10	.05
56	George Foster	.20	.10	.05
57	Dwayne Murphy	.12	.06	.03
58	Ken Singleton	.20	.10	.05
59	Mike Norris	.12	.06	.03
60	Cecil Cooper	.20	.10	.05
61	Al Oliver	.20	.10	.05
62	Willie Wilson	.25	.13	.06
63	Vida Blue	.20	.10	.05
64	Eddie Murray	1.00	.70	.40

1983 Kellogg's

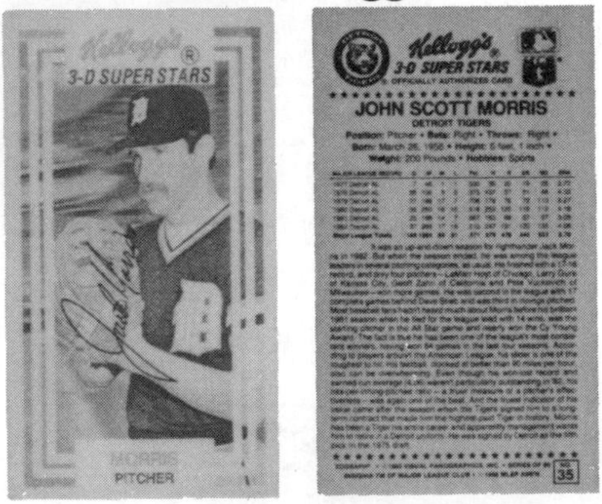

In its 14th and final year of baseball card issue, Kellogg's returned to the policy of inserting single cards into cereal boxes, as well as offering complete sets by a mail-in box top redemption offer. The 3-D cards themselves returned to a narrow - 1-7/8" by 3-1/4" format, while the set size was reduced to 60 cards.

		MT	NR MT	EX
Complete Set:		15.00	11.00	6.00
Common Player:		.10	.08	.04
1	Rod Carew	.80	.60	.30
2	Rollie Fingers	.20	.15	.08
3	Reggie Jackson	.80	.60	.30
4	George Brett	.80	.60	.30
5	Hal McRae	.15	.11	.06
6	Pete Rose	1.25	.90	.50
7	Fernando Valenzuela	.35	.25	.14
8	Rickey Henderson	.80	.60	.30
9	Carl Yastrzemski	.80	.60	.30
10	Rich "Goose" Gossage	.20	.15	.08
11	Eddie Murray	.50	.40	.20
12	Buddy Bell	.15	.11	.06
13	Jim Rice	.40	.30	.15
14	Robin Yount	.80	.60	.30
15	Dave Winfield	.50	.40	.20
16	Harold Baines	.20	.15	.08
17	Garry Templeton	.15	.11	.06
18	Bill Madlock	.25	.20	.10
19	Pete Vuckovich	.10	.08	.04
20	Pedro Guerrero	.25	.20	.10
21	Ozzie Smith	.20	.15	.08
22	George Foster	.20	.15	.08
23	Willie Wilson	.20	.15	.08
24	Johnny Ray	.15	.11	.06
25	George Hendrick	.10	.08	.04
26	Andre Thornton	.10	.08	.04
27	Leon Durham	.10	.08	.04
28	Cecil Cooper	.15	.11	.06
29	Don Baylor	.15	.11	.06
30	Lonnie Smith	.10	.08	.04
31	Nolan Ryan	1.25	.90	.50
32	Dan Quiesenberry (Quisenberry)	.15	.11	.06
33	Len Barker	.10	.08	.04
34	Neil Allen	.10	.08	.04
35	Jack Morris	.30	.25	.12
36	Dave Stieb	.15	.11	.06
37	Bruce Sutter	.15	.11	.06
38	Jim Sundberg	.10	.08	.04
39	Jim Palmer	.35	.25	.14
40	Lance Parrish	.30	.25	.12
41	Floyd Bannister	.15	.11	.06
42	Larry Gura	.10	.08	.04
43	Britt Burns	.10	.08	.04
44	Toby Harrah	.10	.08	.04
45	Steve Carlton	.40	.30	.15
46	Greg Minton	.10	.08	.04
47	Gorman Thomas	.15	.11	.06
48	Jack Clark	.25	.20	.10
49	Keith Hernandez	.40	.30	.15
50	Greg Luzinski	.15	.11	.06
51	Fred Lynn	.25	.20	.10
52	Dale Murphy	.70	.50	.30
53	Kent Hrbek	.35	.25	.14
54	Bob Horner	.15	.11	.06
55	Gary Carter	.50	.40	.20
56	Carlton Fisk	.25	.20	.10
57	Dave Concepcion	.15	.11	.06
58	Mike Schmidt	.70	.50	.30
59	Bill Buckner	.15	.11	.06
60	Bobby Grich	.15	.11	.06

1988 King-B

Created by Mike Schechter Associates, the 1988 King-B set consists of 24 numbered discs that measure 2-3/4" in size. The cards were inserted in specially marked 7/16 ounce tubs of Jerky Stuff (shredded beef jerky). The card fronts feature full-color photos surrounded by a blue border. The King-B logo appears in the upper left portion of the disc. The disc backs are printed in blue on white stock

and carry player personal and playing information. Team insignias have been airbrushed from the players' caps and jerseys.

		MT	NR MT	EX
Complete Set:		25.00	18.50	10.00
Common Player:		.75	.60	.30
1	Mike Schmidt	1.75	1.25	.70
2	Dale Murphy	1.75	1.25	.70
3	Kirby Puckett	1.50	1.25	.60
4	Ozzie Smith	1.00	.70	.40
5	Tony Gwynn	1.50	1.25	.60
6	Mark McGwire	1.50	1.25	.60
7	George Brett	1.75	1.25	.70
8	Darryl Strawberry	1.75	1.25	.70
9	Wally Joyner	1.50	1.25	.60
10	Cory Snyder	1.00	.70	.40
11	Barry Bonds	1.00	.70	.40
12	Darrell Evans	.75	.60	.30
13	Mike Scott	.75	.60	.30
14	Andre Dawson	1.25	.90	.50
15	Don Mattingly	2.50	2.00	1.00
16	Candy Maldonado	.75	.60	.30
17	Alvin Davis	1.00	.70	.40
18	Carlton Fisk	1.00	.70	.40
19	Fernando Valenzuela	1.00	.70	.40
20	Roger Clemens	2.00	1.50	.80
21	Larry Parrish	.75	.60	.30
22	Eric Davis	2.00	1.50	.80
23	Paul Molitor	1.00	.70	.40
24	Cal Ripken, Jr.	1.75	1.25	.70

1989 King-B

The second King-B baseball card set created by Mike Schechter Associates also consists of 24 circular baseball cards measuring 2-3/4" across. The cards were inserted into specially-marked tubs of "Jerky Stuff." The card fronts feature full-color photos bordered in red. The King-B logo appears in the upper left portion of the disc. Like the 1988 set, the team insignias have airbrushed from uniforms and caps. The backs are printed in red and display personal information and stats.

		MT	NR MT	EX
Complete Set:		25.00	18.50	10.00
Common Player:		.75	.60	.30
1	Kirk Gibson	1.00	.70	.40
2	Eddie Murray	1.00	.70	.40
3	Wade Boggs	2.25	1.75	.90
4	Mark McGwire	2.25	1.75	.90
5	Ryne Sandberg	1.75	1.25	.70
6	Ozzie Guillen	.75	.60	.30
7	Chris Sabo	1.25	.90	.50
8	Joe Carter	1.00	.70	.40
9	Alan Trammell	1.00	.70	.40
10	Nolan Ryan	2.50	2.00	1.00
11	Bo Jackson	2.50	2.00	1.00
12	Orel Hershiser	1.00	.70	.40
13	Robin Yount	1.50	1.25	.60
14	Frank Viola	1.00	.70	.40
15	Darryl Strawberry	1.50	1.25	.60
16	Dave Winfield	1.00	.70	.40
17	Jose Canseco	3.00	2.25	1.25
18	Von Hayes	.75	.60	.30
19	Andy Van Slyke	.75	.60	.30
20	Pedro Guerrero	1.00	.70	.40
21	Tony Gwynn	1.75	1.25	.70
22	Will Clark	2.50	2.00	1.00
23	Danny Jackson	.75	.60	.30
24	Pete Incaviglia	.75	.60	.30

1986 Kitty Clover Potato Chips Royals

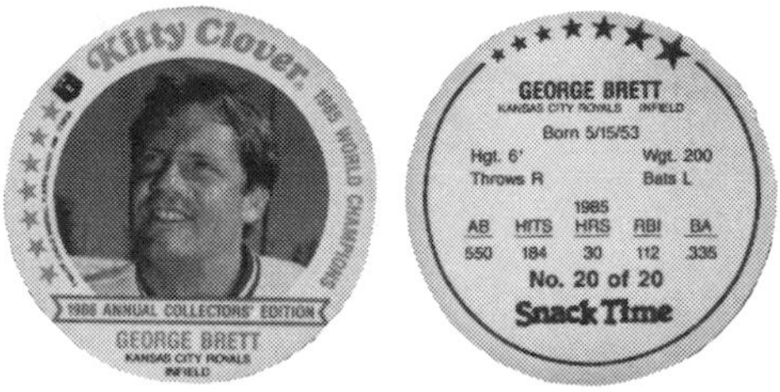

Twenty players of the 1985 World's Champion Kansas City Royals were featured in a round card set inserted into packages of potato chips in the K.C. area. The 2-7/8" discs were similar to a handful of snack issues produced by Mike Schecter Associates in that team logos have been airbrushed off the players' caps, and the photos of some of the players can be found on other regional issues of 1986.

		MT	NR MT	EX
Complete Set:		20.00	15.00	8.00
Common Player:		.70	.50	.30
1	Lonnie Smith	.70	.50	.30
2	Buddy Biancalana	.70	.50	.30
3	Bret Saberhagen	1.75	1.25	.70
4	Hal McRae	1.00	.70	.40
5	Onix Concepcion	.70	.50	.30
6	Jorge Orta	.70	.50	.30
7	Bud Black	.70	.50	.30
8	Dan Quisenberry	1.00	.70	.40
9	Dane Iorg	.70	.50	.30
10	Charlie Leibrandt	.80	.60	.30
11	Pat Sheridan	.70	.50	.30
12	John Wathan	.80	.60	.30
13	Frank White	1.00	.70	.40
14	Darryl Motley	.70	.50	.30
15	Willie Wilson	1.25	.90	.50
16	Danny Jackson	1.25	.90	.50
17	Steve Balboni	.80	.60	.30
18	Jim Sundberg	.70	.50	.30
19	Mark Gubicza	1.25	.90	.50
20	George Brett	3.25	2.50	1.25

1987 Kraft

Kraft Foods, Inc. issued a 48-card set on specially marked packages of their Macaroni & Cheese Dinners. Titled "Home Plate Heroes," 24 two-card panels measuring 3-1/2" by 7-1/8" make up the set. Individual cards measure 2-1/4" by 3-1/2" and are numbered 1 through 48. The blank-backed cards feature fronts with full-color photos, although all team insignias have been erased. In conjunction with the card set, Kraft offered a contest to "Win A Day With A Major Leaguer." Mike Schecter Associates produced the set for Kraft. 120 different panel combinatons can be found.

		MT	NR MT	EX
Complete Set:		35.00	27.50	15.00
Common Player:		.20	.15	.08
1	Eddie Murray	.75	.60	.30
2	Dale Murphy	.60	.45	.25
3	Cal Ripken	.75	.60	.30
4	Mike Scott	.35	.25	.14
5	Jim Rice	.50	.40	.20
6	Jody Davis	.20	.15	.08
7	Wade Boggs	1.00	.70	.40
8	Ryne Sandberg	1.00	.70	.40
9	Wally Joyner	1.00	.70	.40
10	Eric Davis	.80	.60	.30
11	Ozzie Guillen	.20	.15	.08
12	Tony Pena	.20	.15	.08
13	Harold Baines	.35	.25	.14
14	Johnny Ray	.20	.15	.08
15	Joe Carter	.35	.25	.14
16	Ozzie Smith	.35	.25	.14
17	Cory Snyder	.20	.15	.08
18	Vince Coleman	.35	.25	.14
19	Kirk Gibson	.50	.40	.20
20	Steve Garvey	.75	.60	.30
21	George Brett	1.00	.70	.40
22	John Tudor	.20	.15	.08
23	Robin Yount	1.00	.70	.40
24	Von Hayes	.35	.25	.14
25	Kent Hrbek	.50	.40	.20
26	Darryl Strawberry	1.00	.70	.40
27	Kirby Puckett	1.00	.70	.40
28	Ron Darling	.35	.25	.14
29	Don Mattingly	1.50	1.25	.60
30	Mike Schmidt	1.00	.70	.40
31	Rickey Henderson	1.00	.70	.40
32	Fernando Valenzuela	.50	.40	.20
33	Dave Winfield	.60	.45	.25
34	Pete Rose	1.25	.90	.50
35	Jose Canseco	2.00	1.50	.80
36	Glenn Davis	.35	.25	.14
37	Alvin Davis	.35	.25	.14
38	Steve Sax	.35	.25	.14
39	Pete Incaviglia	.30	.25	.12
40	Jeff Reardon	.35	.25	.14
41	Jesse Barfield	.35	.25	.14
42	Hubie Brooks	.20	.15	.08
43	George Bell	.50	.40	.20
44	Tony Gwynn	.75	.60	.30
45	Roger Clemens	1.00	.70	.40
46	Chili Davis	.20	.15	.08
47	Mike Witt	.20	.15	.08
48	Nolan Ryan	2.00	1.50	.80

A player's name in italic type indicates a rookie card. An (FC) indicates a player's first card for that particular card company.

1960 Lake To Lake Dairy Braves

This 28-card set of unnumbered 2-1/2" by 3-1/4" cards offers a special challenge for the condition-conscious collector. Originally issued by being stapled to milk cartons, the cards were redeemable for prizes ranging from pen and pencil sets to Braves tickets. When sent in for redemption, the cards had a hole punched in the corner. Naturally, collectors most desire cards without the staple or punch holes.

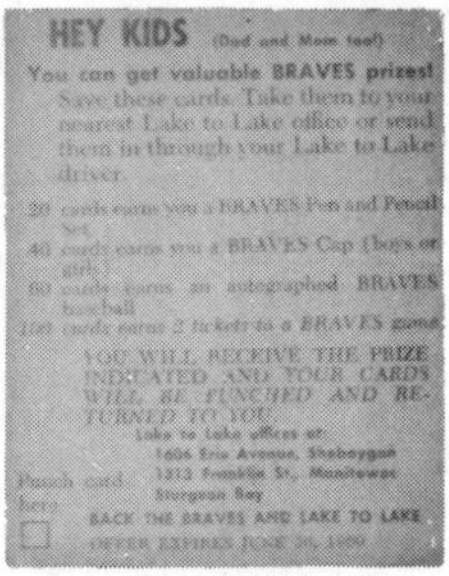

are printed in blue ink on front, red ink on back. Because he was traded in May, and his card withdrawn, the Ray Boone card is scarce; the Billy Bruton card is unaccountably scarcer still.

		NR MT	EX	VG
Complete Set:		1200.00	600.00	360.00
Common Player:		13.00	6.50	4.00
(1)	Henry Aaron	275.00	137.00	82.00
(2)	Joe Adcock	17.50	8.75	5.25
(3)	Ray Boone	125.00	62.00	37.00
(4)	Bill Bruton	275.00	137.00	82.00
(5)	Bob Buhl	17.50	8.75	5.25
(6)	Lou Burdette	20.00	10.00	6.00
(7)	Chuck Cottier	13.00	6.50	4.00
(8)	Wes Covington	15.00	7.50	4.50
(9)	Del Crandall	17.50	8.75	5.25
(10)	Charlie Dressen	15.00	7.50	4.50
(11)	Bob Giggie	13.00	6.50	4.00
(12)	Joey Jay	13.00	6.50	4.00
(13)	Johnny Logan	15.00	7.50	4.50
(14)	Felix Mantilla	13.00	6.50	4.00
(15)	Lee Maye	13.00	6.50	4.00
(16)	Don McMahon	13.00	6.50	4.00
(17)	George Myatt	13.00	6.50	4.00
(18)	Andy Pafko	15.00	7.50	4.50
(19)	Juan Pizarro	13.00	6.50	4.00
(20)	Mel Roach	13.00	6.50	4.00
(21)	Bob Rush	13.00	6.50	4.00
(22)	Bob Scheffing	13.00	6.50	4.00
(23)	Red Schoendienst	20.00	10.00	6.00
(24)	Warren Spahn	75.00	37.00	22.00
(25)	Al Spangler	13.00	6.50	4.00
(26)	Frank Torre	13.00	6.50	4.00
(27)	Carl Willey	13.00	6.50	4.00
(28)	Whitlow Wyatt	13.00	6.50	4.00

A player's name in *italic* indicates a rookie card. An (FC) indicates a player's first card for that particular card company.

1948 Leaf

The first color baseball cards of the post-World War II era were the 98-card, 2-3/8" by 2-7/8", set produced by Chicago's Leaf Gum Company in 1948-1949. The color was crude, probably helping to make the set less popular than the Bowman issues of the same era. One of the toughest post-war sets to complete, exactly half of the Leaf issue - 49 of the cards - are significantly harder to find than the other

1948 Leaf

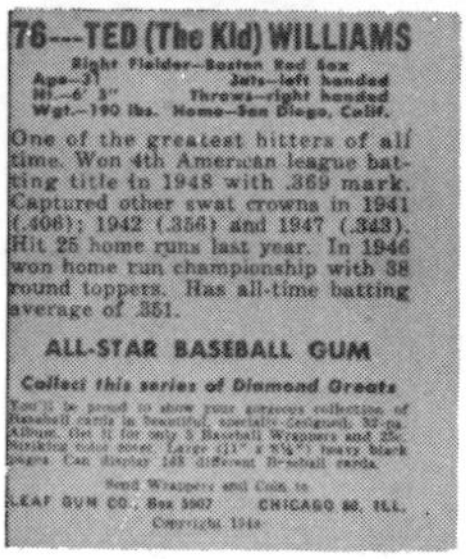

The first color baseball cards of the post-World War II era were the 98-card, 2-3/8" by 2-7/8", set produced by Chicago's Leaf Gum Company in 1948-1949. The color was crude, probably helping to make the set less popular than the Bowman issues of the same era. One of the toughest post-war sets to complete, exactly half of the Leaf issue - 49 of the cards - are significantly harder to find than the other 49. Probably intended to confound bubble gum buyers of the day, the set is skip-numbered between 1-168. Card backs contain offers of felt pennants, an album for the cards or 5-1/2" by 7-1/2" premium photos of Hall of Famers.

		NR MT	EX	VG
Complete Set:		30000.00	15000.00	9000.
Common Player:		25.00	12.50	7.50
Common Scarce Player:		300.00	150.00	90.00
1	Joe DiMaggio	2000.00	1000.00	600.00
3	Babe Ruth	2200.00	1100.00	650.00
4	Stan Musial	700.00	350.00	200.00
5	Virgil Trucks	400.00	200.00	125.00
8	Leroy Paige	2000.00	1000.00	600.00
10	Paul Trout	25.00	12.50	7.50
11	Phil Rizzuto	150.00	75.00	45.00
13	Casimer Michaels	300.00	150.00	90.00
14	Billy Johnson	30.00	15.00	9.00
17	Frank Overmire	25.00	12.50	7.50
19	John Wyrostek	300.00	150.00	90.00
20	Hank Sauer	400.00	200.00	125.00
22	Al Evans	25.00	12.50	7.50
26	Sam Chapman	25.00	12.50	7.50
27	Mickey Harris	25.00	12.50	7.50
28	Jim Hegan	25.00	12.50	7.50
29	Elmer Valo	25.00	12.50	7.50
30	Bill Goodman	300.00	150.00	90.00
31	Lou Brissie	25.00	12.50	7.50
32	Warren Spahn	200.00	100.00	60.00
33	Harry Lowrey	300.00	150.00	90.00
36	Al Zarilla	300.00	150.00	90.00
38	Ted Kluszewski	80.00	40.00	25.00
39	Ewell Blackwell	50.00	25.00	15.00
42	Kent Peterson	25.00	12.50	7.50
43	Eddie Stevens	300.00	150.00	90.00
45	Ken Keltner	300.00	150.00	90.00
46	Johnny Mize	90.00	45.00	27.00
47	George Vico	25.00	12.50	7.50
48	Johnny Schmitz	300.00	150.00	90.00
49	Del Ennis	40.00	20.00	12.00
50	Dick Wakefield	25.00	12.50	7.50
51	Alvin Dark	400.00	200.00	125.00
53	John Vandermeer (Vander Meer)	40.00	20.00	12.00
54	Bobby Adams	300.00	150.00	90.00
55	Tommy Henrich	400.00	200.00	125.00
56	Larry Jensen (Jansen)	25.00	12.50	7.50
57	Bob McCall	25.00	12.50	7.50
59	Lucius Appling	80.00	40.00	25.00
61	Jake Early	25.00	12.50	7.50
62	Eddie Joost	300.00	150.00	90.00
63	Barney McCosky	300.00	150.00	90.00
65	Bob Elliot (Elliott)	25.00	12.50	7.50
66	Orval Grove	300.00	150.00	90.00
68	Ed Miller	300.00	150.00	90.00
70	John Wagner	250.00	125.00	75.00
72	Hank Edwards	25.00	12.50	7.50
73	Pat Seerey	25.00	12.50	7.50
75	Dom DiMaggio	500.00	250.00	150.00
76	Ted Williams	900.00	450.00	275.00
77	Roy Smalley	25.00	12.50	7.50
78	Walter Evers	300.00	150.00	90.00
79	Jackie Robinson	700.00	350.00	210.00
81	George Kurowski	300.00	150.00	90.00
82	Johnny Lindell	25.00	12.50	7.50
83	Bobby Doerr	100.00	50.00	30.00
84	Sid Hudson	25.00	12.50	7.50
85	Dave Philley	300.00	150.00	90.00
86	Ralph Weigel	25.00	12.50	7.50
88	Frank Gustine	300.00	150.00	90.00
91	Ralph Kiner	150.00	75.00	45.00
93	Bob Feller	1200.00	600.00	350.00
95	George Stirnweiss	25.00	12.50	7.50
97	Martin Marion	40.00	20.00	12.00
98	Hal Newhouser	500.00	250.00	150.00
102a	Gene Hermansk (incorrect spelling)	300.00	150.00	90.00
102b	Gene Hermanski (correct spelling)	25.00	12.50	7.50
104	Edward Stewart	300.00	150.00	90.00
106	Lou Boudreau	100.00	50.00	30.00
108	Matthew Batts	300.00	150.00	90.00
111	Gerald Priddy	25.00	12.50	7.50
113	Emil Leonard	300.00	150.00	90.00
117	Joe Gordon	25.00	12.50	7.50
120	George Kell	550.00	275.00	165.00
121	John Pesky	400.00	200.00	120.00
123	Clifford Fannin	300.00	150.00	90.00
125	Andy Pafko	25.00	12.50	7.50
127	Enos Slaughter	600.00	300.00	180.00
128	Warren Rosar	25.00	12.50	7.50
129	Kirby Higbe	300.00	150.00	90.00
131	Sid Gordon	300.00	150.00	90.00
133	Tommy Holmes	400.00	200.00	120.00
136a	Cliff Aberson (full sleeve)	25.00	12.50	7.50
136b	Cliff Aberson (short sleeve)	175.00	87.00	52.00
137	Harry Walker	300.00	150.00	90.00
138	Larry Doby	500.00	250.00	150.00
139	Johnny Hopp	25.00	12.50	7.50
142	Danny Murtaugh	300.00	150.00	90.00
143	Dick Sisler	300.00	150.00	90.00
144	Bob Dillinger	300.00	150.00	90.00
146	Harold Reiser	400.00	200.00	120.00
149	Henry Majeski	300.00	150.00	90.00
153	Floyd Baker	300.00	150.00	90.00
158	Harry Brecheen	400.00	200.00	120.00
159	Mizell Platt	25.00	12.50	7.50
160	Bob Scheffing	400.00	200.00	120.00
161	Vernon Stephens	400.00	200.00	120.00
163	Freddy Hutchinson	400.00	200.00	120.00
165	Dale Mitchell	400.00	200.00	120.00
168	Phil Cavaretta (Cavarretta)	400.00	200.00	120.00

1960 Leaf

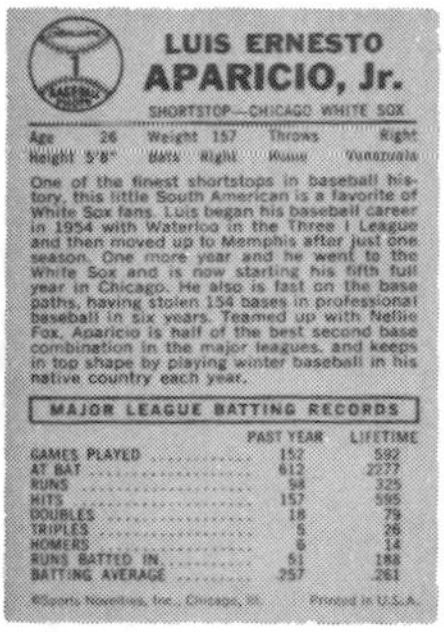

While known to the hobby as "Leaf" cards, this set of 144 cards carries the copyright of Sports Novelties Inc., Chicago. The 2-1/2" by 3-1/2" cards feature black and white player portrait photos, with background airbrushed away. Cards were sold in 5¢ wax packs with a marble, rather than a piece of bubble gum. The second half of the set, cards #73-144, are very scarce and make the set a real challenge for the collector. Card #25, Jim Grant, is found in two versions, with his own picture (black

cap) and with a photo of Brooks Lawrence (white cap). Eight cards (#'s 1, 12, 17, 23, 35, 58, 61 and 72) exist with close-up photos that are much rarer than the normal cap to chest photos. It is believed the scarce "face only" cards are proof cards prepared by Leaf as only a handful are known to exist.

		NR MT	EX	VG
Complete Set:		1800.00	900.00	550.00
Common Player: 1-72		4.00	2.00	1.25
Common Player: 73-144		15.00	7.50	4.50
1	Luis Aparicio	25.00	12.50	7.50
2	Woody Held	4.00	2.00	1.25
3	Frank Lary	3.00	1.50	.90
4	Camilo Pascual	3.00	1.50	.90
5	Frank Herrera	4.00	2.00	1.25
6	Felipe Alou	3.00	1.50	.90
7	Bennie Daniels	4.00	2.00	1.25
8	Roger Craig	3.00	1.50	.90
9	Eddie Kasko	4.00	2.00	1.25
10	Bob Grim	4.00	2.00	1.25
11	Jim Busby	4.00	2.00	1.25
12	Ken Boyer	4.00	2.00	1.25
13	Bob Boyd	4.00	2.00	1.25
14	Sam Jones	4.00	2.00	1.25
15	Larry Jackson	4.00	2.00	1.25
16	Roy Face	4.00	2.00	1.25
17	Walt Moryn	4.00	2.00	1.25
18	Jim Gilliam	4.00	2.00	1.25
19	Don Newcombe	3.00	1.50	.90
20	Glen Hobbie	4.00	2.00	1.25
21	Pedro Ramos	4.00	2.00	1.25
22	Ryne Duren	4.00	2.00	1.25
23	Joe Jay	4.00	2.00	1.25
24	Lou Berberet	4.00	2.00	1.25
25a	Jim Grant (white cap, photo actually Brooks Lawrence)	25.00	12.50	7.50
25b	Jim Grant (dark cap, correct photo)	50.00	25.00	15.00
26	Tom Borland	4.00	2.00	1.25
27	Brooks Robinson	50.00	25.00	15.00
28	Jerry Adair	3.00	1.50	.90
29	Ron Jackson	4.00	2.00	1.25
30	George Strickland	4.00	2.00	1.25
31	Rocky Bridges	4.00	2.00	1.25
32	Bill Tuttle	4.00	2.00	1.25
33	Ken Hunt	3.00	1.50	.90
34	Hal Griggs	4.00	2.00	1.25
35	Jim Coates	3.00	1.50	.90
36	Brooks Lawrence	4.00	2.00	1.25
37	Duke Snider	50.00	25.00	15.00
38	Al Spangler	4.00	2.00	1.25
39	Jim Owens	4.00	2.00	1.25
40	Bill Virdon	4.00	2.00	1.25
41	Ernie Broglio	4.00	2.00	1.25
42	Andre Rodgers	4.00	2.00	1.25
43	Julio Becquer	4.00	2.00	1.25
44	Tony Taylor	4.00	2.00	1.25
45	Jerry Lynch	3.00	1.50	.90
46	Cletis Boyer	4.00	2.00	1.25
47	Jerry Lumpe	3.00	1.50	.90
48	Charlie Maxwell	4.00	2.00	1.25
49	Jim Perry	3.00	1.50	.90
50	Danny McDevitt	4.00	2.00	1.25
51	Juan Pizarro	4.00	2.00	1.25
52	Dallas Green	4.00	2.00	1.25
53	Bob Friend	3.00	1.50	.90
54	Jack Sanford	3.00	1.50	.90
55	Jim Rivera	4.00	2.00	1.25
56	Ted Wills	4.00	2.00	1.25
57	Milt Pappas	3.00	1.50	.90
58a	Hal Smith (team & position on back)	4.00	2.00	1.25
58b	Hal Smith (team blackened out on back)	50.00	25.00	15.00
58c	Hal Smith (team missing on back)	50.00	25.00	15.00
59	Bob Avila	4.00	2.00	1.25
60	Clem Labine	3.00	1.50	.90
61	Vic Rehm	3.00	1.50	.90
62	John Gabler	3.00	1.50	.90
63	John Tsitouris	4.00	2.00	1.25
64	Dave Sisler	4.00	2.00	1.25
65	Vic Power	3.00	1.50	.90
66	Earl Battey	3.00	1.50	.90
67	Bob Purkey	3.00	1.50	.90
68	Moe Drabowsky	4.00	2.00	1.25
69	Hoyt Wilhelm	6.00	3.00	1.75
70	Humberto Robinson	4.00	2.00	1.25
71	Whitey Herzog	4.00	2.00	1.25
72	Dick Donovan	3.00	1.50	.90
73	Gordon Jones	15.00	7.50	4.50
74	Joe Hicks	15.00	7.50	4.50
75	Ray Culp	18.00	9.00	5.50
76	Dick Drott	15.00	7.50	4.50
77	Bob Duliba	15.00	7.50	4.50
78	Art Ditmar	18.00	9.00	5.50
79	Steve Korcheck	15.00	7.50	4.50
80	Henry Mason	15.00	7.50	4.50
81	Harry Simpson	15.00	7.50	4.50
82	Gene Green	15.00	7.50	4.50
83	Bob Shaw	15.00	7.50	4.50
84	Howard Reed	15.00	7.50	4.50
85	Dick Stigman	15.00	7.50	4.50
86	Rip Repulski	15.00	7.50	4.50
87	Seth Morehead	15.00	7.50	4.50
88	Camilo Carreon	15.00	7.50	4.50
89	John Blanchard	18.00	9.00	5.50
90	Billy Hoeft	15.00	7.50	4.50
91	Fred Hopke	18.00	9.00	5.50
92	Joe Martin	15.00	7.50	4.50
93	Wally Shannon	18.00	9.00	5.50
94	Baseball's Two Hal Smiths (Harold Raymond Smith, Harold Wayne Smith)	20.00	10.00	6.00
95	Al Schroll	15.00	7.50	4.50
96	John Kucks	15.00	7.50	4.50
97	Tom Morgan	15.00	7.50	4.50
98	Willie Jones	15.00	7.50	4.50
99	Marshall Renfroe	18.00	9.00	5.50
100	Willie Tasby	15.00	7.50	4.50
101	Irv Noren	15.00	7.50	4.50
102	Russ Snyder	15.00	7.50	4.50
103	Bob Turley	30.00	15.00	9.00
104	Jim Woods	15.00	7.50	4.50
105	Ronnie Kline	15.00	7.50	4.50
106	Steve Bilko	15.00	7.50	4.50
107	Elmer Valo	18.00	9.00	5.50
108	Tom McAvoy	18.00	9.00	5.50
109	Stan Williams	15.00	7.50	4.50
110	Earl Averill	15.00	7.50	4.50
111	Lee Walls	15.00	7.50	4.50
112	Paul Richards	18.00	9.00	5.50
113	Ed Sadowski	15.00	7.50	4.50
114	Stover McIlwain	18.00	9.00	5.50
115	Chuck Tanner (photo actually Ken Kuhn)	20.00	10.00	6.00
116	Lou Klimchock	15.00	7.50	4.50
117	Neil Chrisley	15.00	7.50	4.50
118	John Callison	20.00	10.00	6.00
119	Hal Smith	15.00	7.50	4.50
120	Carl Sawatski	15.00	7.50	4.50
121	Frank Leja	18.00	9.00	5.50
122	Earl Torgeson	15.00	7.50	4.50
123	Art Schult	15.00	7.50	4.50
124	Jim Brosnan	18.00	9.00	5.50
125	George Anderson	40.00	20.00	12.00
126	Joe Pignatano	15.00	7.50	4.50
127	Rocky Nelson	15.00	7.50	4.50
128	Orlando Cepeda	50.00	25.00	15.00
129	Daryl Spencer	15.00	7.50	4.50
130	Ralph Lumenti	15.00	7.50	4.50
131	Sam Taylor	15.00	7.50	4.50
132	Harry Brecheen	18.00	9.00	5.50
133	Johnny Groth	15.00	7.50	4.50
134	Wayne Terwilliger	15.00	7.50	4.50
135	Kent Hadley	18.00	9.00	5.50
136	Faye Throneberry	15.00	7.50	4.50
137	Jack Meyer	15.00	7.50	4.50
138	Chuck Cottier	15.00	7.50	4.50
139	Joe DeMaestri	18.00	9.00	5.50
140	Gene Freese	15.00	7.50	4.50
141	Curt Flood	40.00	20.00	12.00
142	Gino Cimoli	15.00	7.50	4.50
143	Clay Dalrymple	15.00	7.50	4.50
144	Jim Bunning	75.00	38.00	23.00

1990 Leaf

This 528-card set was issued in two 264-card series. The cards were printed on heavy quality stock and both the card fronts and backs have full color player photos. Cards also have an ultra-glossy finish on both the fronts and the backs. A high-tech foil Hall of Fame puzzle featuring former Yankee great Yogi Berra.

		MT	NR MT	EX
Complete Set:		200.00	150.00	80.00
Common Player:		.25	.20	.10
1	Introductory Card	.25	.20	.10
2	Mike Henneman	.25	.20	.10
3	Steve Bedrosian	.25	.20	.10
4	Mike Scott	.35	.25	.14
5	Allan Anderson	.25	.20	.10
6	Rick Sutcliffe	.35	.25	.14

7	Gregg Olson	.50	.40	.20
8	Kevin Elster	.25	.20	.10
9	Pete O'Brien	.30	.25	.12
10	Carlton Fisk	1.00	.70	.40
11	Joe Magrane	.40	.30	.15
12	Roger Clemens	3.00	2.25	1.25
13	Tom Glavine	.80	.60	.30
14	Tom Gordon	.30	.25	.12
15	Todd Benzinger	.25	.20	.10
16	Hubie Brooks	.35	.25	.14
17	Roberto Kelly	.30	.25	.12
18	Barry Larkin	.50	.40	.20
19	Mike Boddicker	.25	.20	.10
20	Roger McDowell	.25	.20	.10
21	Nolan Ryan	6.00	4.50	2.50
22	John Farrell	.30	.25	.12
23	Bruce Hurst	.25	.20	.10
24	Wally Joyner	.40	.30	.15
25	Greg Maddux	.35	.25	.14
26	Chris Bosio	.30	.25	.12
27	John Cerutti	.30	.25	.12
28	Tim Burke	.25	.20	.10
29	Dennis Eckersley	.50	.40	.20
30	Glenn Davis	.40	.30	.15
31	Jim Abbott	1.25	.90	.50
32	Mike LaValliere	.25	.20	.10
33	Andres Thomas	.25	.20	.10
34	Lou Whitaker	.35	.25	.14
35	Alvin Davis	.35	.25	.14
36	Melido Perez	.25	.20	.10
37	Craig Biggio	.80	.60	.30
38	Rick Aguilera	.25	.20	.10
39	Pete Harnisch	.35	.25	.14
40	David Cone	.35	.25	.14
41	Scott Garrelts	.25	.20	.10
42	Jay Howell	.25	.20	.10
43	Eric King	.25	.20	.10
44	Pedro Guerrero	.35	.25	.14
45	Mike Bielecki	.25	.20	.10
46	Bob Boone	.25	.20	.10
47	Kevin Brown	.30	.25	.12
48	Jerry Browne	.25	.20	.10
49	Mike Scioscia	.25	.20	.10
50	Chuck Cary	.30	.25	.12
51	Wade Boggs	1.25	.90	.50
52	Von Hayes	.25	.20	.10
53	Tony Fernandez	.35	.25	.14
54	Dennis Martinez	.35	.25	.14
55	Tom Candiotti	.30	.25	.12
56	Andy Benes	1.25	.90	.50
57	Rob Dibble	.30	.25	.12
58	Chuck Crim	.30	.25	.12
59	John Smoltz	1.25	.90	.50
60	Mike Heath	.30	.25	.12
61	Kevin Gross	.25	.20	.10
62	Mark McGwire	.80	.60	.30
63	Bert Blyleven	.35	.25	.14
64	Bob Walk	.30	.25	.12
65	Mickey Tettleton	.25	.20	.10
66	Sid Fernandez	.35	.25	.14
67	Terry Kennedy	.25	.20	.10
68	Fernando Valenzuela	.40	.30	.15
69	Don Mattingly	1.50	1.25	.60
70	Paul O'Neill	.35	.25	.14
71	Robin Yount	1.00	.70	.40
72	Bret Saberhagen	.30	.25	.12
73	Geno Petralli	.30	.25	.12
74	Brook Jacoby	.25	.20	.10
75	Roberto Alomar	1.00	.70	.40
76	Devon White	.25	.20	.10
77	Jose Lind	.30	.25	.12
78	Pat Combs	.35	.25	.14
79	Dave Steib	.35	.25	.14
80	Tim Wallach	.35	.25	.14
81	Dave Stewart	.30	.25	.12
82	Eric Anthony	.50	.40	.20
83	Randy Bush	.30	.25	.12
84	Checklist	.30	.25	.12
85	Jaime Navarro	.30	.25	.12
86	Tommy Gregg	.30	.25	.12
87	Frank Tanana	.25	.20	.10
88	Omar Vizquel	.30	.25	.12
89	Ivan Calderon	.35	.25	.14
90	Vince Coleman	.35	.25	.14
91	Barry Bonds	1.00	.70	.40
92	Randy Milligan	.35	.25	.14
93	Frank Viola	.35	.25	.14
94	Matt Williams	.60	.45	.25
95	Alfredo Griffin	.30	.25	.12
96	Steve Sax	.35	.25	.14
97	Gary Gaetti	.35	.25	.14
98	Ryne Sandberg	3.00	2.25	1.25
99	Danny Tartabull	.35	.25	.14
100	Rafael Palmeiro	.60	.45	.25
101	Jesse Orosco	.25	.20	.10
102	Garry Templeton	.25	.20	.10
103	Frank DiPino	.25	.20	.10
104	Tony Pena	.25	.20	.10
105	Dickie Thon	.30	.25	.12
106	Kelly Gruber	.30	.25	.12
107	Marquis Grissom	3.00	2.25	1.25
108	Jose Canseco	3.00	2.25	1.25
109	Mike Blowers	.30	.25	.12
110	Tom Browning	.25	.20	.10
111	Greg Vaughn	4.00	3.00	1.50
112	Oddibe McDowell	.25	.20	.10
113	Gary Ward	.25	.20	.10
114	Jay Buhner	.25	.20	.10
115	Eric Show	.30	.25	.12
116	Bryan Harvey	.25	.20	.10
117	Andy Van Slyke	.35	.25	.14
118	Jeff Ballard	.25	.20	.10
119	Barry Lyons	.30	.25	.12
120	Kevin Mitchell	.60	.45	.25
121	Mike Gallego	.30	.25	.12
122	Dave Smith	.25	.20	.10
123	Kirby Puckett	1.50	1.25	.60
124	Jerome Walton	.40	.30	.15
125	Bo Jackson	3.00	2.25	1.25
126	Harold Baines	.35	.25	.14
127	Scott Bankhead	.25	.20	.10
128	Ozzie Guillen	.35	.25	.14
129	Jose Oquendo	.30	.25	.12
130	John Dopson	.30	.25	.12
131	Charlie Hayes	.25	.20	.10
132	Fred McGriff	.80	.60	.30
133	Chet Lemon	.25	.20	.10
134	Gary Carter	.35	.25	.14
135	Rafael Ramirez	.30	.25	.12
136	Shane Mack	.25	.20	.10
137	Mark Grace	.50	.40	.20
138	Phil Bradley	.25	.20	.10
139	Dwight Gooden	.80	.60	.30
140	Harold Reynolds	.35	.25	.14
141	Scott Fletcher	.30	.25	.12
142	Ozzie Smith	.80	.60	.30
143	Mike Greenwell	.80	.60	.30
144	Pete Smith	.25	.20	.10
145	Mark Gubicza	.25	.20	.10
146	Chris Sabo	.25	.20	.10
147	Ramon Martinez	6.00	4.50	2.50
148	Dave Winfield	.40	.30	.15
149	Randy Myers	.35	.25	.14
150	Jody Reed	.25	.20	.10
151	Bruce Ruffin	.30	.25	.12
152	Jeff Russell	.25	.20	.10
153	Doug Jones	.25	.20	.10
154	Tony Gwynn	1.00	.70	.40
155	Mark Langston	.35	.25	.14
156	Mitch Williams	.25	.20	.10
157	Gary Sheffield	.40	.30	.15
158	Tom Henke	.25	.20	.10
159	Oil Can Boyd	.25	.20	.10
160	Rickey Henderson	2.00	1.50	.80
161	Bill Doran	.25	.20	.10
162	Chuck Finley	.40	.30	.15
163	Jeff King	.25	.20	.10
164	Nick Esasky	.25	.20	.10
165	Cecil Fielder	2.50	2.00	1.00
166	Dave Valle	.30	.25	.12
167	Robin Ventura	8.00	6.00	3.00
168	Jim Deshaies	.25	.20	.10
169	Juan Berenguer	.30	.25	.12
170	Craig Worthington	.35	.25	.14
171	Gregg Jefferies	.50	.40	.30
172	Will Clark	3.00	2.25	1.25
173	Kirk Gibson	.35	.25	.14
174	Checklist	.30	.25	.12
175	Bobby Thigpen	.40	.30	.15
176	John Tudor	.25	.20	.10
177	Andre Dawson	.50	.40	.30
178	George Brett	.80	.60	.30
179	Steve Buechele	.30	.25	.12
180	Joey Belle	5.00	3.75	2.00
181	Eddie Murray	.50	.40	.20
182	Bob Geren	.25	.20	.10
183	Rob Murphy	.30	.25	.12
184	Tom Herr	.25	.20	.10
185	George Bell	.50	.40	.20
186	Spike Owen	.25	.20	.10
187	Cory Snyder	.25	.20	.10
188	Fred Lynn	.25	.20	.10
189	Eric Davis	.60	.45	.25
190	Dave Parker	.30	.25	.12

191	Jeff Blauser	.30	.25	.12
192	Matt Nokes	.25	.20	.10
193	Delino DeShields	3.00	2.25	1.25
194	Scott Sanderson	.25	.20	.10
195	Lance Parrish	.25	.20	.10
196	Bobby Bonilla	.80	.60	.30
197	Cal Ripken	3.00	2.25	1.25
198	Kevin McReynolds	.35	.25	.14
199	Robby Thompson	.25	.20	.10
200	Tim Belcher	.25	.20	.10
201	Jesse Barfield	.25	.20	.10
202	Mariano Duncan	.25	.20	.10
203	Bill Spiers	.40	.30	.15
204	Frank White	.25	.20	.10
205	Julio Franco	.35	.25	.14
206	Greg Swindell	.25	.20	.10
207	Benito Santiago	.30	.25	.12
208	Johnny Ray	.30	.25	.12
209	Gary Redus	.30	.25	.12
210	Jeff Parrett	.30	.25	.12
211	Jimmy Key	.25	.20	.10
212	Tim Raines	.35	.25	.14
213	Carney Lansford	.25	.20	.10
214	Gerald Young	.30	.25	.12
215	Gene Larkin	.30	.25	.12
216	Dan Plesac	.25	.20	.10
217	Lonnie Smith	.25	.20	.10
218	Alan Trammell	.40	.30	.15
219	Jeffrey Leonard	.25	.20	.10
220	Sammy Sosa	1.50	1.25	.60
221	Todd Zeile	2.00	1.50	.80
222	Bill Landrum	.25	.20	.10
223	Mike Devereaux	.25	.20	.10
224	Mike Marshall	.25	.20	.10
225	Jose Uribe	.30	.25	.12
226	Juan Samuel	.25	.20	.10
227	Mel Hall	.30	.25	.12
228	Kent Hrbek	.40	.30	.15
229	Shawon Dunston	.40	.30	.15
230	Kevin Seitzer	.35	.25	.14
231	Pete Incaviglia	.25	.20	.10
232	Sandy Alomar	.50	.40	.20
233	Bip Roberts	.25	.20	.10
234	Scott Terry	.25	.20	.10
235	Dwight Evans	.35	.25	.14
236	Ricky Jordan	.35	.25	.14
237	John Olerud	6.00	4.50	2.50
238	Zane Smith	.25	.20	.10
239	Walt Weiss	.25	.20	.10
240	Alvaro Espinoza	.25	.20	.10
241	Billy Hatcher	.25	.20	.10
242	Paul Molitor	.35	.25	.14
243	Dale Murphy	.50	.40	.20
244	Dave Bergman	.30	.25	.12
245	Ken Griffey,Jr.	20.00	15.00	7.50
246	Ed Whitson	.25	.20	.10
247	Kirk McCaskill	.25	.20	.10
248	Jay Bell	.35	.25	.14
249	Ben McDonald	3.00	2.25	1.25
250	Darryl Strawberry	1.75	1.25	.60
251	Brett Butler	.30	.25	.14
252	Terry Steinbach	.25	.20	.10
253	Ken Caminiti	.30	.25	.12
254	Dan Gladden	.25	.20	.10
255	Dwight Smith	.35	.25	.14
256	Kurt Stillwell	.25	.20	.10
257	Ruben Sierra	1.50	1.25	.60
258	Mike Schooler	.25	.20	.10
259	Lance Johnson	.25	.20	.10
260	Terry Pendleton	.30	.25	.14
261	Ellis Burks	.40	.30	.15
262	Len Dykstra	.35	.25	.14
263	Mookie Wilson	.25	.20	.10
264	Checklist	.50	.40	.20
265	No Hit King (Nolan Ryan)	6.00	4.50	2.50
266	Brian DuBois	.35	.25	.14
267	Don Robinson	.30	.25	.12
268	Glenn Wilson	.30	.25	.12
269	Kevin Tapani	2.00	1.50	.80
270	Marvell Wynne	.30	.25	.12
271	Billy Ripken	.30	.25	.12
272	Howard Johnson	.50	.40	.20
273	Brian Holman	.35	.25	.14
274	Dan Pasqua	.30	.25	.12
275	Ken Dayley	.30	.25	.12
276	Jeff Reardon	.25	.20	.10
277	Jim Presley	.25	.20	.10
278	Jim Eisenreich	.30	.25	.12
279	Danny Jackson	.25	.20	.10
280	Orel Hershiser	.35	.25	.14
281	Andy Hawkins	.25	.20	.10
282	Jose Rijo	.35	.25	.14
283	Luis Rivera	.25	.20	.10
284	John Kruk	.25	.20	.10
285	Jeff Huson	.30	.25	.12
286	Joel Skinner	.30	.25	.12
287	Jack Clark	.35	.25	.14
288	Chili Davis	.35	.25	.14
289	Joe Girardi	.25	.20	.10
290	B.J. Surhoff	.25	.20	.10
291	Luis Sojo	.30	.25	.12
292	Tom Foley	.30	.25	.12
293	Mike Moore	.25	.20	.10
294	Ken Oberkfell	.30	.25	.12
295	Luis Polonia	.30	.25	.12
296	Doug Drabek	.35	.25	.14
297	Dave Justice	35.00	26.00	14.00
298	Paul Gibson	.30	.25	.12
299	Edgar Martinez	.50	.40	.20
300	Frank Thomas	60.00	45.00	25.00
301	Eric Yelding	.30	.25	.12
302	Greg Gagne	.30	.25	.12
303	Brad Komminsk	.30	.25	.12
304	Ron Darling	.25	.20	.10
305	Kevin Bass	.25	.20	.10
306	Jeff Hamilton	.30	.25	.12
307	Ron Karkovice	.30	.25	.12
308	Milt Thompson	.30	.25	.12
309	Mike Harkey	.30	.25	.12
310	Mel Stottlemyre	.30	.25	.12
311	Kenny Rogers	.35	.25	.14
312	Mitch Webster	.30	.25	.12
313	Kal Daniels	.35	.25	.14
314	Matt Nokes	.25	.20	.10
315	Dennis Lamp	.30	.25	.12
316	Ken Howell	.30	.25	.12
317	Glenallen Hill	.35	.25	.14
318	Dave Martinez	.30	.25	.12
319	Chris James	.25	.20	.10
320	Mike Pagliarulo	.25	.20	.10
321	Hal Morris	6.00	4.50	2.50
322	Rob Deer	.30	.25	.12
323	Greg Olson	.50	.40	.20
324	Tony Phillips	.30	.25	.12
325	Larry Walker	1.00	.70	.40
326	Ron Hassey	.30	.25	.12
327	Jack Howell	.30	.25	.12
328	John Smiley	.25	.20	.10
329	Steve Finley	.50	.40	.20
330	Dave Magadan	.35	.25	.14
331	Greg Litton	.35	.25	.14
332	Mickey Hatcher	.30	.25	.12
333	Lee Guetterman	.30	.25	.12
334	Norm Charlton	.35	.25	.14
335	Edgar Diaz	.25	.20	.10
336	Willie Wilson	.25	.20	.10
337	Bobby Witt	.35	.25	.14
338	Candy Maldonado	.35	.25	.14
339	Craig Lefferts	.25	.20	.10
340	Dante Bichette	.25	.20	.10
341	Wally Backman	.30	.25	.12
342	Dennis Cook	.25	.20	.10
343	Pat Borders	.25	.20	.10
344	Wallace Johnson	.30	.25	.12
345	Willie Randolph	.25	.20	.10
346	Danny Darwin	.25	.20	.10
347	Al Newman	.30	.25	.12
348	Mark Knudson	.30	.25	.12
349	Joe Boever	.30	.25	.12
350	Larry Sheets	.30	.25	.12
351	Mike Jackson	.30	.25	.12
352	Wayne Edwards	.30	.25	.12
353	Bernard Gilkey	1.50	1.25	.60
354	Don Slaught	.30	.25	.12
355	Joe Orsulak	.30	.25	.12
356	John Franco	.35	.25	.14
357	Jeff Brantley	.25	.20	.10
358	Mike Morgan	.30	.25	.12
359	Deion Sanders	1.50	1.25	.60
360	Terry Leach	.30	.25	.12
361	Les Lancaster	.30	.25	.12
362	Storm Davis	.25	.20	.10
363	Scott Coolbaugh	.30	.25	.12
364	Checklist	.30	.25	.12
365	Cecilio Guante	.30	.25	.12
366	Joey Cora	.30	.25	.12
367	Willie McGee	.35	.25	.14
368	Jerry Reed	.30	.25	.12
369	Darren Daulton	.25	.20	.10
370	Manny Lee	.25	.20	.10
371	Mark Gardner	.30	.25	.12
372	Rick Honeycutt	.30	.25	.12
373	Steve Balboni	.30	.25	.12
374	Jack Armstrong	.30	.25	.12

		MT	NR MT	EX
375	Charlie O'Brien	.30	.25	.12
376	Ron Gant	.30	.25	.12
377	Lloyd Moseby	.25	.20	.10
378	Gene Harris	.30	.25	.12
379	Joe Carter	.35	.25	.14
380	Scott Bailes	.30	.25	.12
381	R.J. Reynolds	.30	.25	.12
382	Bob Melvin	.30	.25	.12
383	Tim Teufel	.30	.25	.12
384	John Burkett	.30	.25	.12
385	Felix Jose	.35	.25	.14
386	Larry Andersen	.30	.25	.12
387	David West	.25	.20	.10
388	Luis Salazar	.30	.25	.12
389	Mike Macfarlane	.30	.25	.12
390	Charlie Hough	.25	.20	.10
391	Greg Briley	.35	.25	.14
392	Donn Pall	.30	.25	.12
393	Bryn Smith	.30	.25	.12
394	Carlos Quintana	.30	.25	.12
395	Steve Lake	.30	.25	.12
396	Mark Whiten	4.00	3.00	1.50
397	Edwin Nunez	.30	.25	.12
398	Rick Parker	.35	.25	.14
399	Mark Portugal	.30	.25	.12
400	Roy Smith	.30	.25	.12
401	Hector Villanueva	.30	.25	.12
402	Bob Milacki	.25	.20	.10
403	Alejandro Pena	.30	.25	.12
404	Scott Bradley	.30	.25	.12
405	Ron Kittle	.25	.20	.10
406	Bob Tewksbury	.30	.25	.12
407	Wes Gardner	.30	.25	.12
408	Ernie Whitt	.30	.25	.12
409	Terry Shumpert	.30	.25	.12
410	Tim Layana	.30	.25	.12
411	Chris Gwynn	.25	.20	.10
412	Jeff Robinson	.30	.25	.12
413	Scott Scudder	.30	.25	.12
414	Kevin Romine	.30	.25	.12
415	Jose DeJesus	.30	.25	.12
416	Mike Jeffcoat	.30	.25	.12
417	Rudy Seanez	.35	.25	.14
418	Mike Dunne	.30	.25	.12
419	Dick Schofield	.30	.25	.12
420	Steve Wilson	.35	.25	.14
421	Bill Krueger	.30	.25	.12
422	Junior Felix	1.00	.70	.40
423	Drew Hall	.30	.25	.12
424	Curt Young	.30	.25	.12
425	Franklin Stubbs	.25	.20	.10
426	Dave Winfield	.30	.25	.12
427	Rick Reed	.30	.25	.12
428	Charlie Leibrandt	.25	.20	.10
429	Jeff Robinson	.30	.25	.12
430	Erik Hanson	.60	.45	.25
431	Barry Jones	.25	.20	.10
432	Alex Trevino	.30	.25	.12
433	John Moses	.30	.25	.12
434	Dave Johnson	.30	.25	.12
435	Mackey Sasser	.25	.20	.10
436	Rick Leach	.30	.25	.12
437	Lenny Harris	.35	.25	.14
438	Carlos Martinez	.25	.20	.10
439	Rex Hudler	.30	.25	.12
440	Domingo Ramos	.30	.25	.12
441	Gerald Perry	.30	.25	.12
442	John Russell	.30	.25	.12
443	Carlos Baerga	3.00	2.25	1.25
444	Checklist	.30	.25	.12
445	Stan Javier	.30	.25	.12
446	Kevin Maas	8.00	6.00	3.25
447	Tom Brunansky	.25	.20	.10
448	Carmelo Martinez	.30	.25	.12
449	Willie Blair	.30	.25	.12
450	Andres Galarraga	.35	.25	.14
451	Bud Black	.30	.25	.12
452	Greg Harris	.30	.25	.12
453	Joe Oliver	.30	.25	.12
454	Greg Brock	.30	.25	.12
455	Jeff Treadway	.25	.20	.10
456	Lance McCullers	.30	.25	.12
457	Dave Schmidt	.30	.25	.12
458	Todd Burns	.30	.25	.12
459	Max Venable	.30	.25	.12
460	Neal Heaton	.30	.25	.12
461	Mark Williamson	.30	.25	.12
462	Keith Miller	.30	.25	.12
463	Mike LaCoss	.30	.25	.12
464	Jose Offerman	3.00	2.25	1.25
465	Jim Leyritz	.60	.45	.25

		MT	NR MT	EX
466	Glenn Braggs	.30	.25	.12
467	Ron Robinson	.30	.25	.12
468	Mark Davis	.30	.25	.12
469	Gary Pettis	.30	.25	.12
470	Keith Hernandez	.25	.20	.10
471	Dennis Rasmussen	.05	.04	.02
472	Mark Eichhorn	.05	.04	.02
473	Ted Power	.05	.04	.02
474	Terry Mulholland	.25	.20	.10
475	Todd Stottlemyre	.25	.20	.10
476	Jerry Goff	.30	.25	.12
477	Gene Nelson	.30	.25	.12
478	Rich Gedman	.30	.25	.12
479	Brian Harper	.25	.20	.10
480	Mike Felder	.30	.25	.12
481	Steve Avery	8.00	6.00	3.25
482	Jack Morris	.25	.20	.10
483	Randy Johnson	.35	.25	.14
484	Scott Radinsky	.30	.25	.12
485	Jose DeLeon	.30	.25	.12
486	Stan Belinda	.30	.25	.12
487	Brain Holton	.30	.25	.12
488	Mark Carreon	.25	.20	.10
489	Trevor Wilson	.30	.25	.12
490	Mike Sharperson	.25	.20	.10
491	Alan Mills	.30	.25	.12
492	John Candelaria	.25	.20	.10
493	Paul Assenmacher	.30	.25	.12
494	Steve Crawford	.30	.25	.12
495	Brad Arnsberg	.25	.20	.10
496	Sergio Valdez	.30	.25	.12
497	Mark Parent	.30	.25	.12
498	Tom Pagnozzi	.30	.25	.12
499	Greg Harris	.30	.25	.12
500	Randy Ready	.30	.25	.12
501	Duane Ward	.30	.25	.12
502	Nelson Santovenia	.30	.25	.12
503	Joe Klink	.25	.20	.10
504	Eric Plunk	.30	.25	.12
505	Jeff Reed	.30	.25	.12
506	Ted Higuera	.35	.25	.14
507	Joe Hesketh	.30	.25	.12
508	Dan Petry	.30	.25	.12
509	Matt Young	.30	.25	.12
510	Jerald Clark	.25	.20	.10
511	John Orton	.35	.25	.14
512	Scott Ruskin	.30	.25	.12
513	Chris Hoiles	.60	.45	.25
514	Daryl Boston	.30	.25	.12
515	Francisco Oliveras	.35	.25	.14
516	Ozzie Canseco	1.00	.70	.40
517	Xavier Hernandez	.35	.25	.14
518	Fred Manrique	.30	.25	.12
519	Shawn Boskie	.60	.45	.25
520	Jeff Montgomery	.25	.20	.10
521	Jack Daugherty	.30	.25	.12
522	Keith Comstock	.30	.25	.12
523	Greg Hibbard	.30	.25	.12
524	Lee Smith	.25	.20	.10
525	Dana Kiecker	.30	.25	.12
526	Darrel Akerfelds	.30	.25	.12
527	Greg Myers	.25	.20	.10
528	Checklist	.30	.25	.12

1991 Leaf Series I

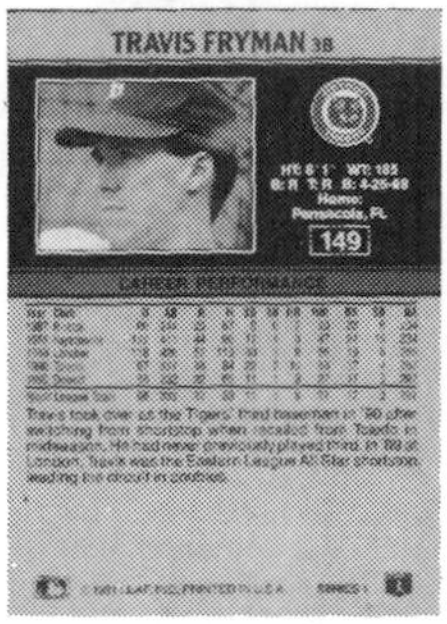

Silver borders and black insets surround the full-color action photos on the 1991 Leaf cards. The set was once again scheduled to be released in two

series. Series I consists of cards 1-264. Card backs feature an additional player photo, biographical information, statistics and career highlights. The 1991 issue is not considered as scarce as the 1990 release. 1991 Leaf promo cards were first introduced in the 1991 Donruss factory sets.

		MT	NR MT	EX
Complete Set:		35.00	27.00	15.00
Common Player:		.08	.06	.03
1	The Leaf Card	.08	.06	.03
2	Kurt Stillwell	.08	.06	.03
3	Bobby Witt	.08	.06	.03
4	Tony Phillips	.08	.06	.03
5	Scott Garrelts	.08	.06	.03
6	Greg Swindell	.10	.08	.04
7	Billy Ripken	.08	.06	.03
8	Dave Martinez	.08	.06	.03
9	Kelly Gruber	.10	.08	.04
10	Juan Samuel	.10	.08	.04
11	Brian Holman	.08	.06	.03
12	Craig Biggio	.20	.15	.08
13	Lonnie Smith	.08	.06	.03
14	Ron Robinson	.08	.06	.03
15	Mike LaValliere	.08	.06	.03
16	Mark Davis	.08	.06	.03
17	Jack Daugherty	.08	.06	.03
18	Mike Henneman	.08	.06	.03
19	Mike Greenwell	.20	.15	.08
20	Dave Magadan	.12	.09	.05
21	Mark Williamson	.08	.06	.03
22	Marquis Grissom	.30	.25	.12
23	Pat Borders	.08	.06	.03
24	Mike Scioscia	.08	.06	.03
25	Shawon Dunston	.15	.11	.06
26	Randy Bush	.08	.06	.03
27	John Smoltz	.30	.25	.12
28	Chuck Crim	.08	.06	.03
29	Don Slaught	.08	.06	.03
30	Mike Macfarlane	.08	.06	.03
31	Wally Joyner	.20	.15	.08
32	Pat Combs	.10	.08	.04
33	Tony Pena	.10	.08	.04
34	Howard Johnson	.25	.20	.10
35	Leo Gomez	.80	.60	.30
36	Spike Owen	.08	.06	.03
37	Eric Davis	.30	.25	.12
38	Roberto Kelly	.20	.15	.08
39	Jerome Walton	.15	.11	.06
40	Shane Mack	.15	.11	.06
41	Kent Mercker	.10	.08	.04
42	B.J. Surhoff	.08	.06	.03
43	Jerry Browne	.08	.06	.03
44	Lee Smith	.10	.08	.04
45	Chuck Finley	.20	.15	.08
46	Terry Mulholland	.10	.08	.04
47	Tom Bolton	.08	.06	.03
48	Tom Herr	.08	.06	.03
49	Jim Deshaies	.08	.06	.03
50	Walt Weiss	.10	.08	.04
51	Hal Morris	.35	.25	.14
52	Lee Guetterman	.08	.06	.03
53	Paul Assenmacher	.08	.06	.03
54	Brian Harper	.10	.08	.04
55	Paul Gibson	.08	.06	.03
56	John Burkett	.08	.06	.03
57	Doug Jones	.08	.06	.03
58	Jose Oquendo	.08	.06	.03
59	Dick Schofield	.08	.06	.03
60	Dickie Thon	.08	.06	.03
61	Ramon Martinez	.80	.60	.30
62	Jay Buhner	.10	.08	.04
63	Mark Portugal	.08	.06	.03
64	Bob Welch	.10	.08	.04
65	Chris Sabo	.20	.15	.08
66	Chuck Cary	.08	.06	.03
67	Mark Langston	.15	.11	.06
68	Joe Boever	.08	.06	.03
69	Jody Reed	.10	.08	.04
70	Alejandro Pena	.08	.06	.03
71	Jeff King	.10	.08	.04
72	Tom Pagnozzi	.08	.06	.03
73	Joe Oliver	.08	.06	.03
74	Mike Witt	.08	.06	.03
75	Hector Villanueva	.15	.11	.06
76	Dan Gladden	.08	.06	.03
77	Dave Justice	3.00	2.25	1.25
78	Mike Gallego	.08	.06	.03
79	Tom Candiotti	.08	.06	.03
80	Ozzie Smith	.30	.25	.12
81	Luis Polonia	.08	.06	.03
82	Randy Ready	.08	.06	.03
83	Greg Harris	.08	.06	.03
84	Checklist (Justice)	.25	.20	.10
85	Kevin Mitchell	.30	.25	.12
86	Mark McLemore	.08	.06	.03
87	Terry Steinbach	.08	.06	.03
88	Tom Browning	.10	.08	.04
89	Matt Nokes	.10	.08	.04
90	Mike Harkey	.12	.09	.05
91	Omar Vizquel	.08	.06	.03
92	Dave Bergman	.08	.06	.03
93	Matt Williams	.30	.25	.12
94	Steve Olin	.08	.06	.03
95	Craig Wilson	.20	.15	.08
96	Dave Stieb	.10	.08	.04
97	Ruben Sierra	.50	.40	.20
98	Jay Howell	.08	.06	.03
99	Scott Bradley	.08	.06	.03
100	Eric Yelding	.08	.06	.03
101	Rickey Henderson	.80	.60	.30
102	Jeff Reed	.08	.06	.03
103	Jimmy Key	.10	.08	.04
104	Terry Shumpert	.08	.06	.03
105	Kenny Rogers	.08	.06	.03
106	Cecil Fielder	.80	.60	.30
107	Robby Thompson	.08	.06	.03
108	Alex Cole	.10	.08	.04
109	Randy Milligan	.10	.08	.04
110	Andres Galarraga	.10	.08	.04
111	Bill Spiers	.08	.06	.03
112	Kal Daniels	.15	.11	.06
113	Henry Cotto	.08	.06	.03
114	Casy Candaele	.08	.06	.03
115	Jeff Blauser	.08	.06	.03
116	Robin Yount	.40	.30	.15
117	Ben McDonald	.30	.25	.12
118	Bret Saberhagen	.15	.11	.06
119	Juan Gonzalez	5.00	3.75	2.00
120	Lou Whitaker	.10	.08	.04
121	Ellis Burks	.20	.15	.08
122	Charlie O'Brien	.08	.06	.03
123	John Smiley	.10	.08	.04
124	Tim Burke	.08	.06	.03
125	John Olerud	.40	.30	.15
126	Eddie Murray	.30	.25	.12
127	Greg Maddux	.10	.08	.04
128	Kevin Tapani	.20	.15	.08
129	Ron Gant	.50	.40	.20
130	Jay Bell	.10	.08	.04
131	Chris Hoiles	.20	.15	.08
132	Tom Gordon	.10	.08	.04
133	Kevin Seitzer	.08	.06	.03
134	Jeff Huson	.10	.08	.04
135	Jerry Don Gleaton	.08	.06	.03
136	Jeff Brantley	.08	.06	.03
137	Felix Fermin	.08	.06	.03
138	Mike Devereaux	.10	.08	.04
139	Delino DeShields	.20	.15	.08
140	David Wells	.08	.06	.03
141	Tim Crews	.08	.06	.03
142	Erik Hanson	.15	.11	.06
143	Mark Davidson	.08	.06	.03
144	Tommy Gregg	.08	.06	.03
145	Jim Gantner	.08	.06	.03
146	Jose Lind	.08	.06	.03
147	Danny Tartabull	.15	.11	.06
148	Geno Petralli	.08	.06	.03
149	Travis Fryman	2.00	1.50	.80
150	Tim Naehring	.20	.15	.08
151	Kevin McReynolds	.12	.09	.05
152	Joe Orsulak	.08	.06	.03
153	Steve Frey	.15	.11	.06
154	Duane Ward	.08	.06	.03
155	Stan Javier	.08	.06	.03
156	Damon Berryhill	.08	.06	.03
157	Gene Larkin	.08	.06	.03
158	Greg Olson	.10	.08	.04
159	Mark Knudson	.08	.06	.03
160	Carmelo Martinez	.08	.06	.03
161	Storm Davis	.08	.06	.03
162	Jim Abbott	.30	.25	.12
163	Len Dykstra	.15	.11	.06
164	Tom Brunansky	.08	.06	.03
165	Dwight Gooden	.25	.20	.10
166	Jose Mesa	.08	.06	.03
167	Oil Can Boyd	.08	.06	.03
168	Barry Larkin	.30	.25	.12
169	Scott Sanderson	.08	.06	.03
170	Mark Grace	.20	.15	.08
171	Mark Guthrie	.08	.06	.03

		MT	NR MT	EX
172	Tom Glavine	.30	.25	.12
173	Gary Sheffield	.15	.11	.06
174	Checklist	.08	.06	.03
175	Chris James	.08	.06	.03
176	Milt Thompson	.08	.06	.03
177	Donnie Hill	.08	.06	.03
178	Wes Chamberlain	1.50	1.25	.60
179	John Marzano	.08	.06	.03
180	Frank Viola	.15	.11	.06
181	Eric Anthony	.15	.11	.06
182	Jose Canseco	1.00	.70	.40
183	Scott Scudder	.10	.08	.04
184	Dave Eiland	.08	.06	.03
185	Luis Salazar	.08	.06	.03
186	Pedro Munoz	.60	.45	.25
187	Steve Searcy	.08	.06	.03
188	Don Robinson	.08	.06	.03
189	Sandy Alomar	.15	.11	.06
190	Jose DeLeon	.08	.06	.03
191	John Orton	.08	.06	.03
192	Darren Daulton	.08	.06	.03
193	Mike Morgan	.08	.06	.03
194	Greg Briley	.08	.06	.03
195	Karl Rhodes	.15	.11	.06
196	Harold Baines	.10	.08	.04
197	Bill Doran	.10	.08	.04
198	Alvaro Espinoza	.08	.06	.03
199	Kirk McCaskill	.10	.08	.04
200	Jose DeJesus	.10	.08	.04
201	Jack Clark	.10	.08	.04
202	Daryl Boston	.08	.06	.03
203	Randy Tomlin	.40	.30	.15
204	Pedro Guerrero	.15	.11	.06
205	Billy Hatcher	.08	.06	.03
206	Tim Leary	.08	.06	.03
207	Ryne Sandberg	.80	.60	.30
208	Kirby Puckett	.50	.40	.20
209	Charlie Leibrandt	.08	.06	.03
210	Rick Honeycutt	.08	.06	.03
211	Joel Skinner	.08	.06	.03
212	Rex Hudler	.08	.06	.03
213	Bryan Harvey	.10	.08	.04
214	Charlie Hayes	.10	.08	.04
215	Matt Young	.08	.06	.03
216	Terry Kennedy	.08	.06	.03
217	Carl Nichols	.08	.06	.03
218	Mike Moore	.08	.06	.03
219	Paul O'Neill	.10	.08	.04
220	Steve Sax	.10	.08	.04
221	Shawn Boskie	.10	.08	.04
222	Rich DeLucia	.30	.25	.12
223	Lloyd Moseby	.08	.06	.03
224	Mike Kingery	.08	.06	.03
225	Carlos Baerga	.25	.20	.10
226	Bryn Smith	.08	.06	.03
227	Todd Stottlemyre	.10	.08	.04
228	Julio Franco	.25	.20	.10
229	Jim Gott	.08	.06	.03
230	Mike Schooler	.10	.08	.04
231	Steve Finley	.10	.08	.04
232	Dave Henderson	.10	.08	.04
233	Luis Quinones	.08	.06	.03
234	Mark Whiten	.40	.30	.15
235	Brian McRae	2.00	1.50	.80
236	Rich Gossage	.10	.08	.04
237	Rob Deer	.08	.06	.03
238	Will Clark	.80	.60	.30
239	Albert Belle	.80	.60	.30
240	Bob Melvin	.08	.06	.03
241	Larry Walker	.15	.11	.06
242	Dante Bichette	.08	.06	.03
243	Orel Hershiser	.15	.11	.06
244	Pete O'Brien	.08	.06	.03
245	Pete Harnisch	.10	.08	.04
246	Jeff Treadway	.08	.06	.03
247	Julio Machado	.08	.06	.03
248	Dave Johnson	.08	.06	.03
249	Kirk Gibson	.12	.09	.05
250	Kevin Brown	.08	.06	.03
251	Milt Cuyler	.50	.40	.20
252	Jeff Reardon	.10	.08	.04
253	David Cone	.15	.11	.06
254	Gary Redus	.08	.06	.03
255	Junior Noboa	.08	.06	.03
256	Greg Myers	.08	.06	.03
257	Dennis Cook	.08	.06	.03
258	Joe Girardi	.08	.06	.03
259	Allan Anderson	.08	.06	.03
260	Paul Marak	.20	.15	.08
261	Barry Bonds	.50	.40	.20
262	Juan Bell	.10	.08	.04
263	Russ Morman	.08	.06	.03
264	Checklist (Brett)	.20	.15	.08

1991 Leaf Gold Rookies Series I

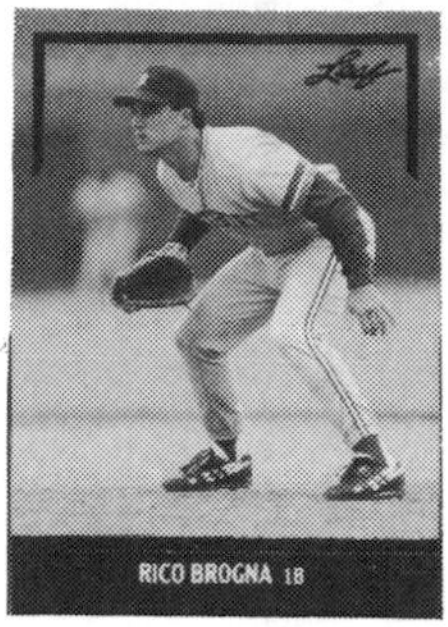

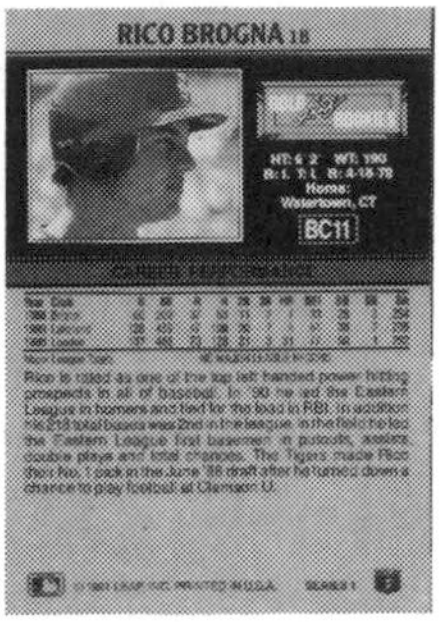

Twelve special gold rookie cards were randomly packed on a limited basis in 1991 Leaf Series I packs. The card backs are designed in the same style as the regular Leaf cards with the exception of a gold back instead of silver. The card fronts feature a partial top inset with a banner on the bottom featuring the player's name and position. Variations of these cards exist. They can be found numbered 265-276 as an extension of the first series. They actually are numbered with a "BC" designation, BC-1-BC12.

		MT	NR MT	EX
Complete Set:		40.00	30.00	15.00
Common Player:		2.00	1.50	.80
1	Scott Leius	2.00	1.50	.80
2	Luis Gonzalez	5.00	3.75	2.00
3	Wil Cordero	3.00	2.25	1.25
4	Gary Scott	2.50	2.00	1.00
5	Willie Banks	3.00	2.25	1.25
6	Arthur Rhodes	3.00	2.25	1.25
7	Mo Vaughn	6.00	4.50	2.50
8	Henry Rodriguez	2.00	1.50	.80
9	Todd Van Poppel	8.00	6.00	3.25
10	Reggie Sanders	5.00	3.75	2.00
11	Rico Brogna	4.00	3.00	1.50
12	Mike Mussina	4.00	3.00	1.50

1986 Lite Beer Astros

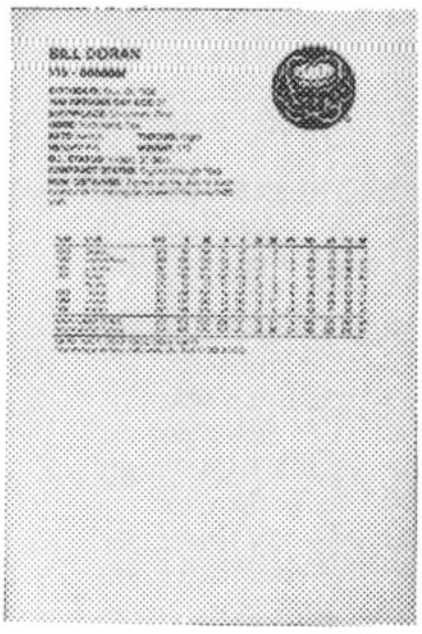

		MT	NR MT	EX
Complete Set:		70.00	52.00	37.00
Common Player:		1.50	1.25	.60
3	Phil Garner	1.50	1.25	.60
6	Mark Bailey	1.50	1.25	.60
10	Dickie Thon	2.00	1.50	.80
11	Frank DiPino	1.50	1.25	.60

		MT	NR MT	EX
12	Craig Reynolds	1.50	1.25	.60
14	Alan Ashby	1.50	1.25	.60
17	Kevin Bass	3.00	2.25	1.25
19	Bill Doran	3.00	2.25	1.25
20	Jim Pankovits	1.50	1.25	.60
21	Terry Puhl	1.50	1.25	.60
22	Hal Lanier	1.50	1.25	.60
25	Jose Cruz	3.00	2.25	1.25
27	Glenn Davis	7.00	5.25	2.75
28	Billy Hatcher	2.50	2.00	1.00
29	Denny Walling	1.50	1.25	.60
33	Mike Scott	4.00	3.00	1.50
34	Nolan Ryan	15.00	11.00	6.00
37	Charlie Kerfeld	2.00	1.50	.80
39	Bob Knepper	2.00	1.50	.80
43	Jim Deshaies	3.00	2.25	1.25
45	Dave Smith	2.00	1.50	.80
53	Mike Madden	1.50	1.25	.60

1986 Lite Beer Rangers

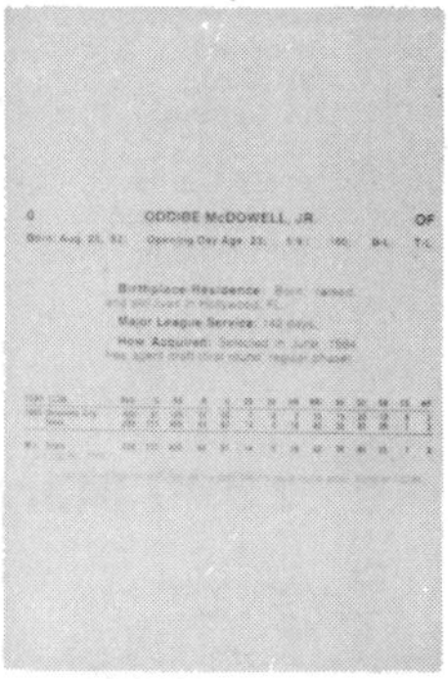

This postcard-size (approximately 4" by 6") regional set of 28 Texas Rangers cards was sponsored by Lite Beer and was available by mail directly from the Rangers. The fronts featured full-color photos surrounded by a wide, white border with the player's name, uniform number and postion appearing below. The Rangers logo is displayed in the lower left corner, while the Lite Beer logo is in the lower right.

		MT	NR MT	EX
Complete Set:		60.00	45.00	24.00
Common Player:		1.50	1.25	.60
0	Oddibe McDowell	3.00	2.25	1.25
1	Scott Fletcher	2.00	1.50	.80
2	Bobby Valentine	2.00	1.50	.80
4	Don Slaught	1.50	1.25	.60
5	Pete Incaviglia	4.00	3.00	1.50
9	Pete O'Brien	3.00	2.25	1.25
10	Art Howe	1.50	1.25	.60
11	Toby Harrah	2.00	1.50	.80
12	Geno Petralli	1.50	1.25	.60
13	Joe Ferguson	1.50	1.25	.60
14	Tim Foli	1.50	1.25	.60
15	Larry Parrish	2.50	2.00	1.00
16	Mike Mason	1.50	1.25	.60
17	Darrell Porter	2.00	1.50	.80
18	Ed Correa	3.00	2.25	1.25
19	Curtis Wilkerson	1.50	1.25	.60
22	Steve Buechele	4.00	3.00	1.50
23	Jose Guzman	4.00	3.00	1.50
24	Ricky Wright	1.50	1.25	.60
27	Greg Harris	1.50	1.25	.60
31	Tom Robson	1.50	1.25	.60
32	Gary Ward	2.00	1.50	.80
35	Tom House	1.50	1.25	.60
44	Tom Paciorek	1.50	1.25	.60
45	Dwayne Henry	2.00	1.50	.80
48	Bobby Witt	5.00	3.75	2.00
49	Charlie Hough	3.00	2.25	1.25
---	Arlington Stadium	1.50	1.25	.60

M

1987 M & M's

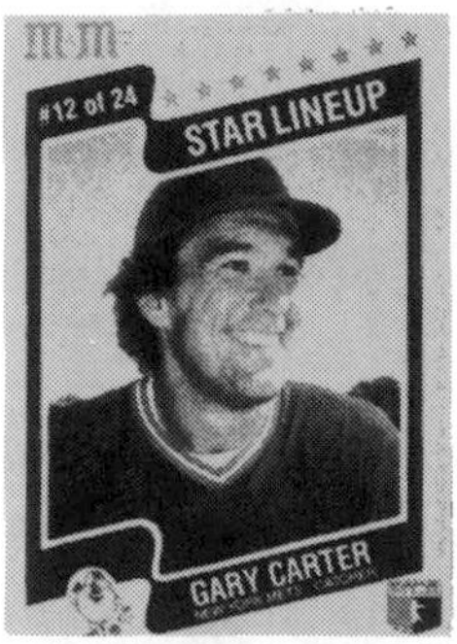

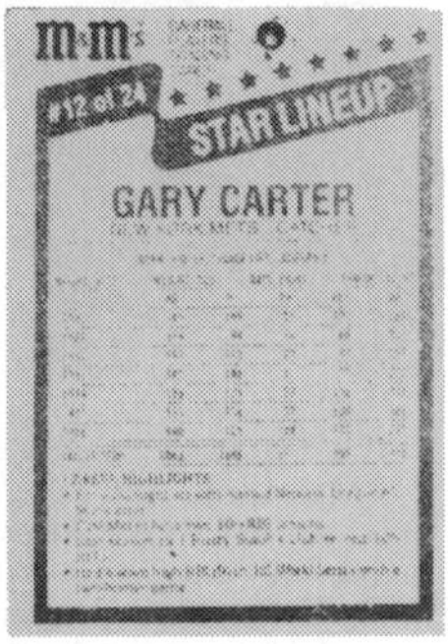

The M&M's "Star Lineup" set consists of 12 two card panels inserted in specially marked packages of large M&M's candy. The two-card panels measure 5" by 3-1/2" with individual cards measuring 2-1/2" by 3-1/2" in size. The full-color photos are enclosed by a wavy blue frame and a white border. Card backs are printed in red ink on white stock and carry the player's career statistics and highlights. All team insignias have been airbrushed away. The set was designed and produced by Mike Schechter and Associates.

		MT	NR MT	EX
Complete Panel Set:		20.00	15.00	8.00
Complete Singles Set:		10.00	7.50	4.00
Common Panel:		1.00	.70	.40
Common Single Player:		.10	.08	.04
	Panel	1.50	1.25	.60
1	Wally Joyner	.50	.40	.20
2	Tony Pena	.10	.08	.04
	Panel	1.50	1.25	.60
3	Mike Schmidt	.40	.30	.15
4	Ryne Sandberg	.40	.30	.15
	Panel	1.50	1.25	.60
5	Wade Boggs	.40	.30	.15
6	Jack Morris	.20	.15	.08
	Panel	1.25	.90	.50
7	Roger Clemens	.40	.30	.15
8	Harold Baines	.15	.11	.06
	Panel	2.75	2.00	1.00
9	Dale Murphy	.30	.25	.12
10	Jose Canseco	1.00	.70	.40
	Panel	3.25	2.50	1.25
11	Don Mattingly	1.25	.90	.50
12	Gary Carter	.20	.15	.08
	Panel	1.50	1.25	.60
13	Cal Ripken, Jr.	1.50	1.25	.60
14	George Brett	.30	.25	.12
	Panel	1.00	.70	.40
15	Kirby Puckett	.20	.15	.08
16	Joe Carter	.20	.15	.08
	Panel	1.00	.70	.40
17	Mike Witt	.15	.11	.06
18	Mike Scott	.15	.11	.06
	Panel	1.25	.90	.50
19	Fernando Valenzuela	.20	.15	.08
20	Steve Garvey	.20	.15	.08
	Panel	1.50	1.25	.60
21	Steve Sax	.15	.11	.06
22	Nolan Ryan	.70	.50	.30
	Panel	1.25	.90	.50
23	Tony Gwynn	.25	.20	.10
24	Ozzie Smith	.15	.11	.06

NOTE: A card number in parentheses ( ) indicates the set is unnumbered.

1989 Marathon Cubs

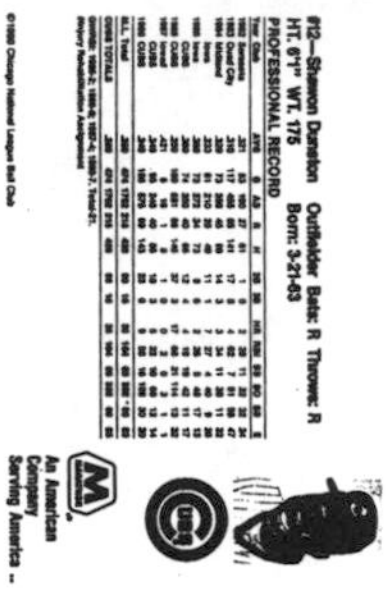

This colorful 25-card Cubs team set was sponsored by Marathon and was distributed as a stadium promotion to fans attending the August 10, 1989, game at Chicago's Wrigley Field. The oversize (2-3/4" by 4-1/4") feature an action photo inside a diagonal box on the card front, with the Chicago Cubs logo at the top and the player's uniform number, name and position along the bottom. The backs include a small black-and-white photo, player data and the Cubs and Marathon logos.

		MT	NR MT	EX
Complete Set:		8.00	6.00	3.25
Common Player:		.10	.08	.04
2	Vance Law	.10	.08	.04
4	Don Zimmer	.15	.11	.06
7	Joe Girardi	.50	.40	.20
8	Andre Dawson	.70	.50	.30
9	Damon Berryhill	.40	.30	.15
10	Lloyd McClendon	.50	.40	.20
12	Shawon Dunston	.50	.40	.20
15	Domingo Ramos	.10	.08	.04
17	Mark Grace	2.00	1.50	.80
18	Dwight Smith	.60	.45	.25
19	Curt Wilkerson	.10	.08	.04
20	Jerome Walton	1.50	1.25	.60
21	Scott Sanderson	.10	.08	.04
23	Ryne Sandberg	3.00	2.25	1.25
28	Mitch Williams	1.00	.70	.40
31	Greg Maddux	.70	.50	.30
32	Calvin Schiraldi	.10	.08	.04
33	Mitch Webster	.10	.08	.04
36	Mike Bielecki	.40	.30	.15
39	Paul Kilgus	.10	.08	.04
40	Rick Sutcliffe	.40	.30	.15
41	Jeff Pico	.25	.20	.10
44	Steve Wilson	.50	.40	.20
50	Les Lancaster	.15	.11	.06
---	Coaches Card	.10	.08	.04

1989 Marathon Tigers

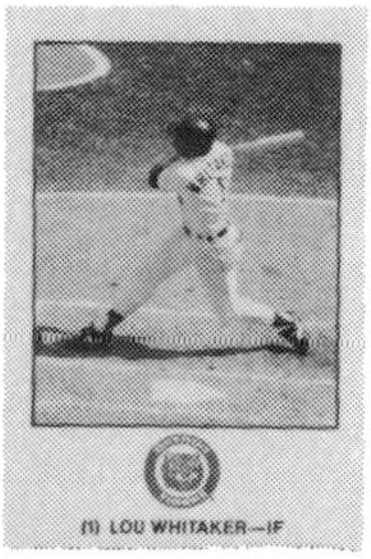

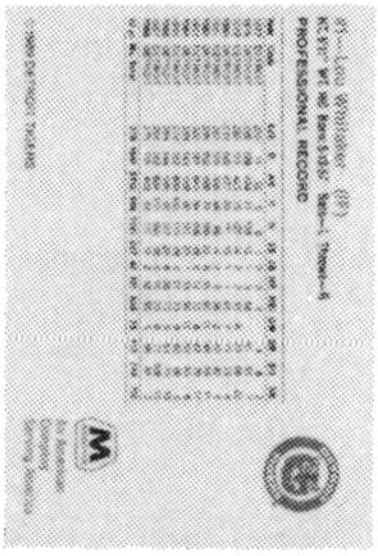

Marathon sponsored this give-away set for a 1989 Tigers home game. The oversized cards feature thin white stock and full-color player photos. The cards are numbered according to uniform number.

		MT	NR MT	EX
Complete Set:		7.00	5.25	2.75
Common Player:		.10	.08	.04
1	Lou Whitaker	.50	.40	.20
3	Alan Trammell	.60	.45	.25
8	Mike Heath	.10	.08	.04
9	Fred Lynn	.30	.25	.12
10	Keith Moreland	.15	.11	.06
11	Sparky Anderson	.40	.30	.15
12	Mike Brumley	.10	.08	.04
14	Dave Bergman	.10	.08	.04
15	Pat Sheridan	.10	.08	.04
17	Al Pedrique	.10	.08	.04
18	Ramon Pena	.15	.11	.06
19	Doyle Alexander	.20	.15	.08
21	Guillermo Hernandez	.20	.15	.08
23	Torey Lovullo	.30	.25	.12
24	Gary Pettis	.20	.15	.08
25	Ken Williams	.10	.08	.04
26	Frank Tanana	.20	.15	.08
27	Charles Hudson	.10	.08	.04
32	Gary Ward	.10	.08	.04
33	Matt Nokes	.40	.30	.15
34	Chet Lemon	.25	.20	.10
35	Rick Schu	.10	.08	.04
36	Frank Williams	.10	.08	.04
39	Mike Henneman	.30	.25	.12
44	Jeff Robinson	.20	.15	.08
47	Jack Morris	.40	.30	.15
48	Paul Gibson	.10	.08	.04
---	Coaches	.10	.08	.04

1990 Marathon Cubs

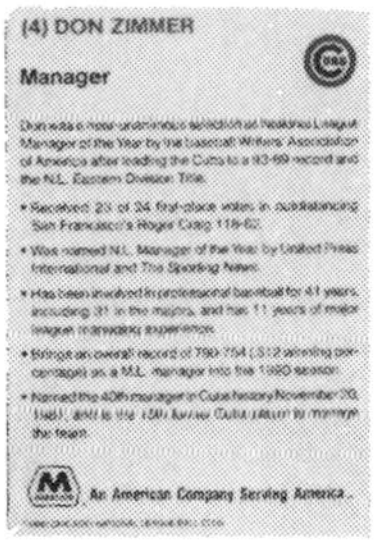

Marathon sponsored its second consecutive Chicago Cubs team set. The oversized cards feature thin white stock and full-color photos. The cards are numbered according to uniform number, and were distributed at a Cubs home game.

		MT	NR MT	EX
Complete Set:		8.00	6.00	3.25
Common Player:		.10	.08	.04
4	Don Zimmer	.15	.11	.06
7	Joe Girardi	.20	.15	.08
8	Andre Dawson	.60	.45	.25
10	Lloyd McClendon	.10	.08	.04
11	Luis Salazar	.10	.08	.04
12	Shawon Dunston	.50	.40	.20
15	Domingo Ramos	.10	.08	.04
17	Mark Grace	1.50	1.25	.60
18	Dwight Smith	.40	.30	.15
19	Curtis Wilkerson	.10	.08	.04
20	Jerome Walton	1.00	.70	.40
22	Mike Harkey	.70	.50	.30
23	Ryne Sandberg	2.00	1.50	.80
25	Marvell Wynne	.10	.08	.04
28	Mitch Williams	.40	.30	.15
29	Doug Dascenzo	.20	.15	.08
30	Dave Clark	.15	.11	.06
31	Greg Maddux	.60	.45	.25
32	Hector Villanueva	.40	.30	.15
36	Mike Bielecki	.20	.15	.08
37	Bill Long	.10	.08	.04

		MT	NR MT	EX
40	Rick Sutcliffe	.30	.25	.12
41	Jeff Pico	.10	.08	.04
44	Steve Wilson	.30	.25	.12
45	Paul Assenmacher	.10	.08	.04
47	Shawn Boskie	.80	.60	.30
50	Les Lancaster	.10	.08	.04
--—	Coaches	.10	.08	.04

1988 Master Bread Twins

This set of 12 cardboard discs (2-3/4" diameter) features full-color photos of Minnesota Twins team members. Disc fronts have a bright blue background with red, yellow and black printing. A thin white line frames the player photo which is centered beneath a "Master Is Good Bread" headliner and a vivid yellow player/team name banner. Disc backs are black and white with five stars printed above the player's name, team, personal data, disc number, stats and "1988 Collector's Edition" banner. The discs were printed in Canada and marketed exclusively in Minnesota in packages of Master Bread, one disc per loaf.

		MT	NR MT	EX
Complete Set:		15.00	11.00	6.00
Common Player:		.50	.40	.20
1	Bert Blyleven	1.00	.70	.40
2	Frank Viola	2.25	1.75	.90
3	Juan Berenguer	.50	.40	.20
4	Jeff Reardon	.80	.60	.30
5	Tim Laudner	.50	.40	.20
6	Steve Lombardozzi	.50	.40	.20
7	Randy Bush	.50	.40	.20
8	Kirby Puckett	4.00	3.00	1.50
9	Gary Gaetti	1.75	1.25	.70
10	Kent Hrbek	1.75	1.25	.70
11	Greg Gagne	.70	.50	.30
12	Tom Brunansky	1.00	.70	.40

1986 Meadow Gold Blank Back Set Of 16

This was the second set to be distributed by Meadow Gold Dairy (Beatrice Foods) in 1986. It was issued on Double Play ice cream cartons, one card per package. Full-color player photos have team logos and insignias airbrushed away. This 16-card set is very similar to the Meadow Gold popsicle set, but the photos are different in some instances. The cards measure 2-3/8" by 3-1/2". The Willie McGee card is reportedly tougher to find than other cards in the set.

		MT	NR MT	EX
Complete Set:		100.00	75.00	40.00
Common Player:		4.00	3.00	1.50
(1)	George Brett	7.00	5.25	2.75
(2)	Wade Boggs	7.00	5.25	2.75
(3)	Carlton Fisk	7.00	5.25	2.75
(4)	Steve Garvey	6.00	4.50	2.50
(5)	Dwight Gooden	6.00	4.50	2.50
(6)	Pedro Guerrero	4.00	3.00	1.50
(7)	Reggie Jackson	8.00	6.00	3.25
(8)	Don Mattingly	10.00	7.50	4.00
(9)	Willie McGee	4.00	3.00	1.50
(10)	Dale Murphy	5.00	3.75	1.50
(11)	Cal Ripken	8.00	6.00	3.25
(12)	Pete Rose	8.00	6.00	3.25
(13)	Ryne Sandberg	8.00	6.00	3.25
(14)	Mike Schmidt	8.00	6.00	3.25
(15)	Fernando Valenzuela	5.00	3.75	2.00
(16)	Dave Winfield	6.50	5.00	2.50

1986 Meadow Gold Statistic Back Set Of 20

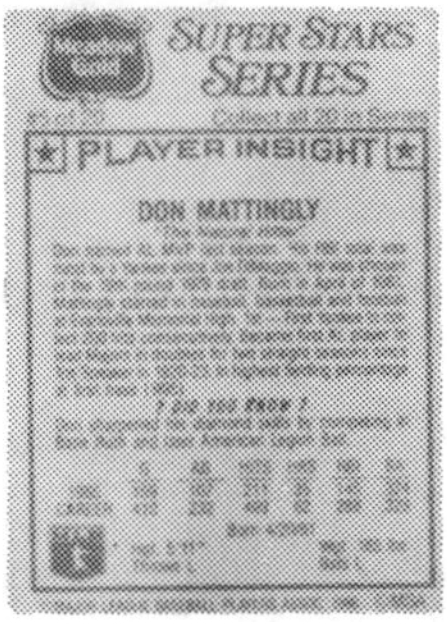

Beatrice Foods produced this set of 20 cards on specially marked boxes of Meadow Gold Double Play popsicles, fudgesicles and bubble gum coolers. They came in two-card panels and have full-color player pictures with player name, team and position printed below the photo. Card backs are printed in red ink and feature player career highlights. The cards measure 2-3/8" by 3-1/2" and were distributed in the West and Midwest. It is considered one of the toughest 1986 regional sets to complete.

		MT	NR MT	EX
Complete Panel Set:		40.00	30.00	15.00
Complete Singles Set:		20.00	15.00	8.00
Common Panel:		2.00	1.50	.80
Common Single Player:		.30	.25	.12
	Panel 1	5.00	3.75	2.00
1	George Brett	1.50	1.25	.60
2	Fernando Valenzuela	.70	.50	.30
	Panel 2	6.50	5.00	2.50
3	Dwight Gooden	2.00	1.50	.80
4	Dale Murphy	1.50	1.25	.60
	Panel 3	8.00	6.00	3.25
5	Don Mattingly	3.00	2.25	1.25
6	Reggie Jackson	2.00	1.50	.80
	Panel 4	6.50	5.00	2.50
7	Dave Winfield	1.00	.70	.40
8	Pete Rose	2.00	1.50	.80
	Panel 5	5.00	3.75	2.00
9	Wade Boggs	2.00	1.50	.80

		MT	NR MT	EX
10	Willie McGee	.50	.40	.20
	Panel 6	6.00	4.50	2.50
11	Cal Ripkin (Ripken)	2.00	1.50	.80
12	Ryne Sandberg	2.00	1.50	.80
	Panel 7	5.00	3.75	2.00
13	Carlton Fisk	.80	.60	.30
14	Jim Rice	1.00	.70	.40
	Panel 8	7.00	5.25	2.75
15	Steve Garvey	1.00	.70	.40
16	Mike Schmidt	2.00	1.50	.80
	Panel 9	4.00	3.00	1.50
17	Bruce Sutter	.60	.45	.25
18	Pedro Guerrero	.60	.45	.25
	Panel 10	4.00	3.00	1.50
19	Rick Sutcliff (Sutcliffe)	.60	.45	.25
20	Rich Gossage	.60	.45	.25

1986 Meadow Gold Milk

The third set from Meadow Gold from 1986 came on milk cartons; on pint, quart and half-gallon size containers. The cards measure 2-1/2" by 3-1/2" and feature drawings instead of photographs. Different dairies distributed the cards in various colors of ink. The cards can be found printed in red, brown or black ink. The crude drawings have prevented this rare set from being higher in price. It was believed that Don Mattingly and Fernando Valenzuela were part of the original set, but it has since been proven they were not.

		MT	NR MT	EX
Complete Set:		50.00	37.00	20.00
Common Player:		2.00	1.50	.80
(1)	Wade Boggs	6.00	4.50	2.50
(2)	George Brett	5.00	3.75	2.00
(3)	Steve Carlton	3.00	2.25	1.25
(4)	Dwight Gooden	6.00	4.50	2.50
(5)	Willie McGee	2.00	1.50	.80
(6)	Dale Murphy	5.00	3.75	2.00
(7)	Cal Ripken, Jr.	6.00	4.50	2.50
(8)	Pete Rose	10.00	7.50	4.00
(9)	Ryne Sandberg	6.00	4.50	2.50
(10)	Mike Schmidt	5.00	3.75	2.00

1971 Milk Duds

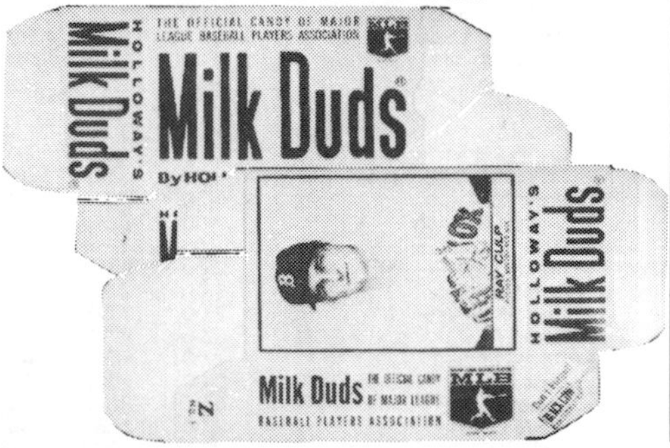

These cards were issued on the backs of five-cent packages of Milk Duds candy. Most collectors prefer to collect complete boxes, rather than cut-out cards, which measure approximately 1-13/16" by 2-5/8" when trimmed tightly. Values quoted below are for complete boxes. The set includes 37 National League and 32 American League players. Card numbers appear on the box flap, with each number from 1 through 24 being shared by three different players. A suffix (a, b and c) has been added for the collector's convenience. Harmon Killebrew, Brooks Robinson and Pete Rose were double-printed.

		NR MT	EX	VG
Complete Set:		1400.00	700.00	420.00
Common Player:		7.00	3.50	2.00
1a	Frank Howard	11.00	5.50	3.25
1b	Fritz Peterson	7.00	3.50	2.00
1c	Pete Rose	80.00	40.00	24.00
2a	Johnny Bench	30.00	15.00	9.00
2b	Rico Carty	9.00	4.50	2.75
2c	Pete Rose	80.00	40.00	24.00
3a	Ken Holtzman	8.00	4.00	2.50
3b	Willie Mays	60.00	30.00	18.00
3c	Cesar Tovar	7.00	3.50	2.00
4a	Willie Davis	9.00	4.50	2.75
4b	Harmon Killebrew	20.00	10.00	6.00
4c	Felix Millan	7.00	3.50	2.00
5a	Billy Grabarkewitz	7.00	3.50	2.00
5b	Andy Messersmith	8.00	4.00	2.50
5c	Thurman Munson	20.00	10.00	6.00
6a	Luis Aparicio	18.00	9.00	5.50
6b	Lou Brock	25.00	12.50	7.50
6c	Bill Melton	7.00	3.50	2.00
7a	Ray Culp	7.00	3.50	2.00
7b	Willie McCovey	25.00	12.50	7.50
7c	Luke Walker	7.00	3.50	2.00
8a	Roberto Clemente	40.00	20.00	12.00
8b	Jim Merritt	7.00	3.50	2.00
8c	Claud Osteen (Claude)	8.00	4.00	2.50
9a	Stan Bahnsen	7.00	3.50	2.00
9b	Sam McDowell	9.00	4.50	2.75
9c	Billy Williams	18.00	9.00	5.50
10a	Jim Hickman	7.00	3.50	2.00
10b	Dave McNally	9.00	4.50	2.75
10c	Tony Perez	13.00	6.50	4.00
11a	Hank Aaron	60.00	30.00	18.00
11b	Glen Beckert (Glenn)	8.00	4.00	2.50
11c	Ray Fosse	7.00	3.50	2.00
12a	Alex Johnson	7.00	3.50	2.00
12b	Gaylord Perry	18.00	9.00	5.50
12c	Wayne Simpson	7.00	3.50	2.00
13a	Dave Johnson	9.00	4.50	2.75
13b	George Scott	8.00	4.00	2.50
13c	Tom Seaver	30.00	15.00	9.00
14a	Bill Freehan	9.00	4.50	2.75
14b	Bud Harrelson	8.00	4.00	2.50
14c	Manny Sanguillen	7.00	3.50	2.00
15a	Bob Gibson	25.00	12.50	7.50
15b	Rusty Staub	11.00	5.50	3.25
15c	Roy White	8.00	4.00	2.50
16a	Jim Fregosi	9.00	4.50	2.75
16b	Jim Hunter	18.00	9.00	5.50
16c	Mel Stottlemyer (Stottlemyre)	8.00	4.00	2.50
17a	Tommy Harper	7.00	3.50	2.00
17b	Frank Robinson	25.00	12.50	7.50
17c	Reggie Smith	9.00	4.50	2.75
18a	Orlando Cepeda	13.00	6.50	4.00
18b	Rico Petrocelli	8.00	4.00	2.50
18c	Brooks Robinson	25.00	12.50	7.50
19a	Tony Oliva	11.00	5.50	3.25
19b	Milt Pappas	8.00	4.00	2.50
19c	Bobby Tolan	7.00	3.50	2.00
20a	Ernie Banks	25.00	12.50	7.50
20b	Don Kessinger	8.00	4.00	2.50
20c	Joe Torre	9.00	4.50	2.75
21a	Fergie Jenkins	13.00	6.50	4.00
21b	Jim Palmer	18.00	9.00	5.50
21c	Ron Santo	9.00	4.50	2.75
22a	Randy Hundley	7.00	3.50	2.00
22b	Dennis Menke (Denis)	7.00	3.50	2.00
22c	Boog Powell	11.00	5.50	3.25
23a	Dick Dietz	7.00	3.50	2.00
23b	Tommy John	13.00	6.50	4.00
23c	Brooks Robinson	25.00	12.50	7.50
24a	Danny Cater	7.00	3.50	2.00
24b	Harmon Killebrew	18.00	9.00	5.50
24c	Jim Perry	8.00	4.00	2.50

1984 Milton Bradley

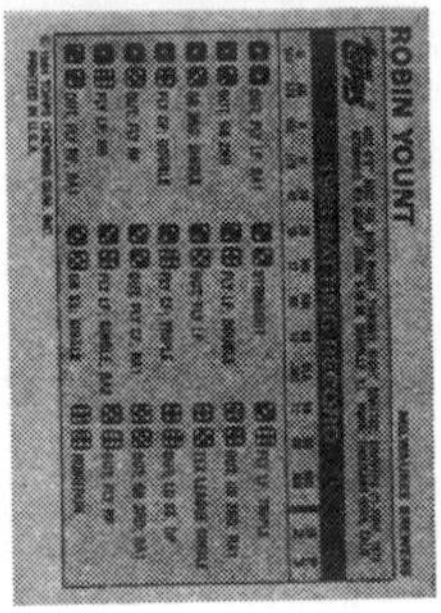

In 1984 Milton Bradley printed their baseball game cards in full-color and adopted the standard baseball card size of 2-1/2" by 3-1/2". A total of 30 cards were in the set. The card fronts show the player photos with the team insignias and logos airbrushed away. The game is called Championship Baseball. Card backs varied in style; some had player statistics plus game information, and others only game information.

		MT	NR MT	EX
Complete Set:		12.00	9.00	4.75
Common Player:		.25	.20	.10
(1)	Wade Boggs	.80	.60	.30
(2)	George Brett	1.00	.70	.40
(3)	Rod Carew	.50	.40	.20
(4)	Steve Carlton	.40	.30	.15
(5)	Gary Carter	.50	.40	.20
(6)	Dave Concepcion	.25	.20	.10
(7)	Cecil Cooper	.25	.20	.10
(8)	Andre Dawson	.50	.40	.20
(9)	Carlton Fisk	.40	.30	.15
(10)	Steve Garvey	.50	.40	.20
(11)	Pedro Guerrero	.35	.25	.14
(12)	Ron Guidry	.25	.20	.10
(13)	Rickey Henderson	1.00	.70	.40
(14)	Reggie Jackson	.50	.40	.20
(15)	Ron Kittle	.25	.20	.10
(16)	Bill Madlock	.25	.20	.10
(17)	Dale Murphy	.80	.60	.30
(18)	Al Oliver	.25	.20	.10
(19)	Darrell Porter	.25	.20	.10
(20)	Cal Ripken	1.00	.70	.40
(21)	Pete Rose	1.25	.90	.50
(22)	Steve Sax	.35	.25	.14
(23)	Mike Schmidt	.80	.60	.30
(24)	Ted Simmons	.25	.20	.10
(25)	Ozzie Smith	.35	.25	.14
(26)	Dave Stieb	.25	.20	.10
(27)	Fernando Valenzuela	.35	.25	.14
(28)	Lou Whitaker	.35	.25	.14
(29)	Dave Winfield	.50	.40	.20
(30)	Robin Yount	.40	.30	.15

1991 Mootown Snackers

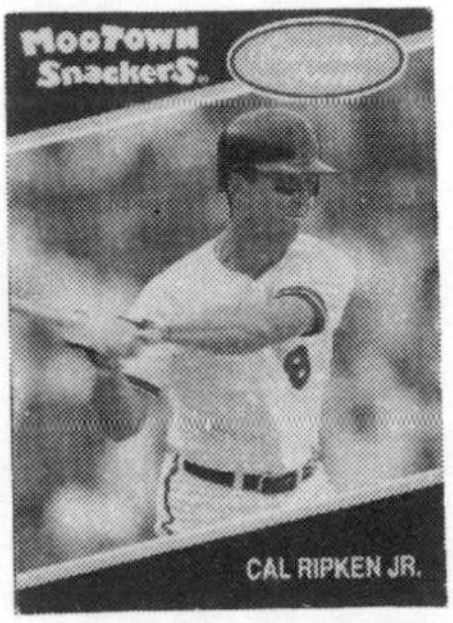

Produced by the Sargento Cheese Co., this 24-card set features the superstars of baseball. Cards were available in Mootown Snacker packages or by sending in a special set redemption coupon from a package to obtain the entire set for $5.95 and three UPC codes. The card fronts feature full-color action photos, but uniform insignias are airbrushed. The backs feature statistics and a facsimile autograph. Sargento is located in Plymouth, Wis.

		MT	NR MT	EX
Complete Set:		8.00	6.00	3.25
Common Player:		.25	.20	.10
1	Jose Canseco	.60	.45	.25
2	Kirby Puckett	.35	.25	.14
3	Barry Bonds	.35	.25	.14
4	Ken Griffey, Jr.	1.25	.90	.50
5	Ryne Sandberg	.50	.40	.20
6	Tony Gwynn	.35	.25	.14
7	Kal Daniels	.25	.20	.10
8	Ozzie Smith	.35	.25	.14
9	Dave Justice	.80	.60	.30
10	Sandy Alomar, Jr.	.30	.25	.12
11	Wade Boggs	.35	.25	.14
12	Ozzie Guillen	.25	.20	.10
13	Dave Magadan	.25	.20	.10
14	Cal Ripken, Jr.	.50	.40	.20
15	Don Mattingly	.50	.40	.20
16	Ruben Sierra	.35	.25	.14
17	Robin Yount	.35	.25	.14
18	Len Dykstra	.25	.20	.10
19	George Brett	.35	.25	.14
20	Lance Parrish	.25	.20	.10
21	Chris Sabo	.25	.20	.10
22	Craig Biggio	.25	.20	.10
23	Kevin Mitchell	.30	.25	.12
24	Cecil Fielder	.50	.40	.20

N

1969 Nabisco Team Flakes

This set of cards is seen in two different sizes: 1-15/16" by 3" and 1-3/4" by 2-15/16". This is explained by the varying widths of the card borders on the backs of Nabisco cereal packages. Cards are action color photos bordered in yellow. Twenty-four of the top players in the game are included in the set, which was issued in three series of eight cards each. No team insignias are visible on any of the cards. Packages described the cards as "Mini Posters."

		NR MT	EX	VG
Complete Set:		650.00	325.00	195.00
Common Player:		4.00	2.00	1.25
(1)	Hank Aaron	60.00	30.00	18.00
(2)	Richie Allen	7.00	3.50	2.00
(3)	Lou Brock	40.00	20.00	12.00
(4)	Paul Casanova	4.00	2.00	1.25
(5)	Roberto Clemente	60.00	30.00	18.00
(6)	Al Ferrara	4.00	2.00	1.25
(7)	Bill Freehan	5.00	2.50	1.50

		NR MT	EX	VG
(8)	Jim Fregosi	5.00	2.50	1.50
(9)	Bob Gibson	25.00	12.50	7.50
(10)	Tony Horton	5.00	2.50	1.50
(11)	Tommy John	10.00	5.00	3.00
(12)	Al Kaline	40.00	20.00	12.00
(13)	Jim Lonborg	4.00	2.00	1.25
(14)	Juan Marichal	25.00	12.50	7.50
(15)	Willie Mays	60.00	30.00	18.00
(16)	Rick Monday	5.00	2.50	1.50
(17)	Tony Oliva	6.00	3.00	1.75
(18)	Brooks Robinson	45.00	22.00	13.50
(19)	Frank Robinson	40.00	20.00	12.00
(20)	Pete Rose	65.00	32.00	19.50
(21)	Ron Santo	6.00	3.00	1.75
(22)	Tom Seaver	50.00	25.00	15.00
(23)	Rusty Staub	6.00	3.00	1.75
(24)	Mel Stottlemyre	5.00	2.50	1.50

1986 National Photo Royals

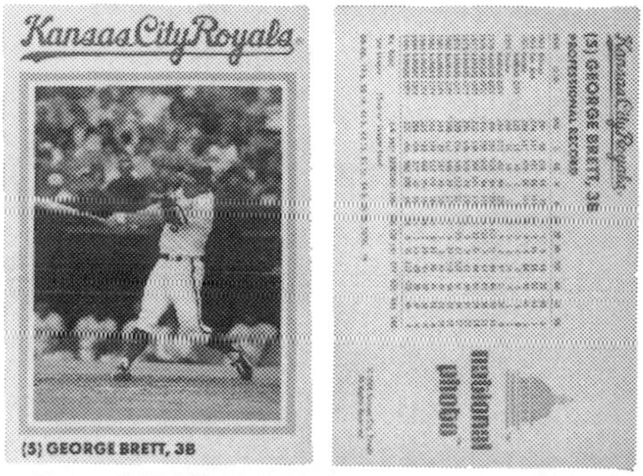

These 2-7/8" by 4-1/4" cards were a team issue produced in conjunction with National Photo. The 24- card set includes 21 players, manager Dick Howser, a card commemorating the Royals' 1985 World Championship and a discount offer card from National Photo. Card fronts feature full-color action photos with a blue "Kansas City Royals" at the top of each card. Each player's name, number and position are also included. Card backs list complete professional career statistics, along with the National Photo logo.

		MT	NR MT	EX
Complete Set:		12.00	9.00	4.75
Common Player:		.25	.20	.10
1	Buddy Biancalana	.25	.20	.10
3	Jorge Orta	.25	.20	.10
4	Greg Pryor	.25	.20	.10
5	George Brett	3.00	2.25	1.25
6	Willie Wilson	.70	.50	.30
8	Jim Sundberg	.25	.20	.10
10	Dick Howser	.35	.25	.14
11	Hal McRae	.50	.40	.20
20	Frank White	.50	.40	.20
21	Lonnie Smith	.40	.30	.15
22	Dennis Leonard	.35	.25	.14
23	Mark Gubicza	.70	.50	.30
24	Darryl Motley	.25	.20	.10
25	Danny Jackson	.70	.50	.30
26	Steve Farr	.25	.20	.10
29	Dan Quisenberry	.50	.40	.20
31	Bret Saberhagen	1.00	.70	.40
35	Lynn Jones	.25	.20	.10
37	Charlie Leibrandt	.35	.25	.14
38	Mark Huismann	.25	.20	.10
40	Buddy Black	.35	.25	.14
45	Steve Balboni	.35	.25	.14
----	Header Card	.25	.20	.10
----	Discount Card	.25	.20	.10

NOTE: A card number in parentheses ( ) indicates the set is unnumbered.

1984 Nestle Dream Team

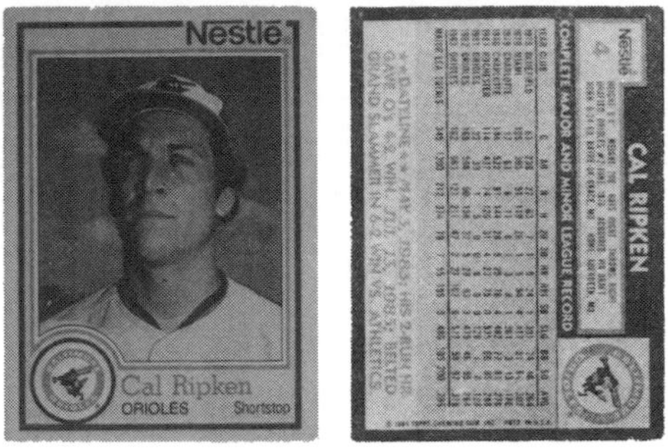

This set was issued by the Nestle candy company in conjunction with Topps. Cards are in standard 2-1/2" by 3-1/2" size and feature the top 22 players of 1984, 11 from each league. This full-color "Dream Team" includes one player at each position, plus right- and left-handed starting pitchers and one reliever. Card fronts have a Nestle logo in the upper-right corner and card backs have the candy company logo in the upper left. An unnumbered checklist was included with the set.

		MT	NR MT	EX
Complete Set:		18.00	13.50	7.25
Common Player:		.60	.45	.25
1	Eddie Murray	1.75	1.25	.70
2	Lou Whitaker	1.00	.70	.40
3	George Brett	2.25	1.75	.90
4	Cal Ripken	2.50	2.00	1.00
5	Jim Rice	1.25	.90	.50
6	Dave Winfield	1.50	1.25	.60
7	Lloyd Moseby	.60	.45	.25
8	Lance Parrish	1.00	.70	.40
9	LaMarr Hoyt	.60	.45	.25
10	Ron Guidry	.80	.60	.30
11	Dan Quisenberry	.60	.45	.25
12	Steve Garvey	1.50	1.25	.60
13	Johnny Ray	.60	.45	.25
14	Mike Schmidt	2.75	2.00	1.00
15	Ozzie Smith	.80	.60	.30
16	Andre Dawson	1.00	.70	.40
17	Tim Raines	1.50	1.25	.60
18	Dale Murphy	2.25	1.75	.90
19	Tony Pena	.60	.45	.25
20	John Denny	.60	.45	.25
21	Steve Carlton	1.25	.90	.50
22	Al Holland	.60	.45	.25
----	Checklist	.30	.25	.12

1987 Nestle

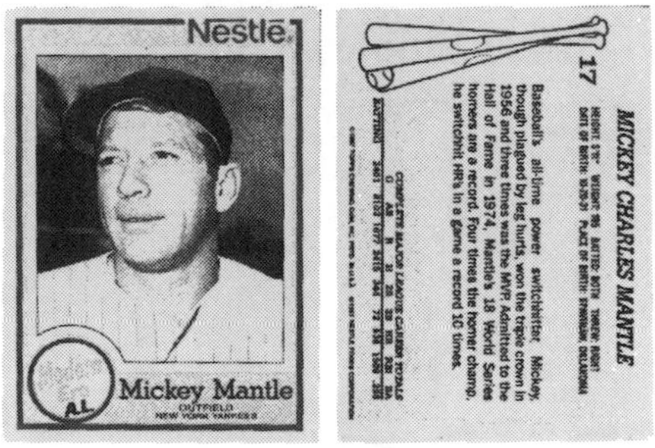

Nestle, in conjunction with Topps, issued a 33-card set in 1987. Card #'s 1-11 feature black and white photos of players from the "Golden Era." Card #'s 12-33 feature full-color photos of American

(12-22.00) and National League (23-33.00) players from the "Modern Era" of baseball. Interestingly, the Feller card is not a photo but rather a color rendering of his 1953 Topps card. The cards measure 2-1/2" by 3-1/2" and have all team emblems airbrushed away. Three cards were inserted in specially marked six-packs of various Nestle candy bars. Two complete sets were available through a mail-in offer for $1.50 and three proof of purchase seals.

		MT	NR MT	EX
Complete Set:		9.00	6.75	3.50
Common Player:		.12	.09	.05
1	Lou Gehrig	.50	.40	.20
2	Rogers Hornsby	.25	.20	.10
3	Pie Traynor	.12	.09	.05
4	Honus Wagner	.30	.25	.12
5	Babe Ruth	1.00	.70	.40
6	Tris Speaker	.20	.15	.08
7	Ty Cobb	.60	.45	.25
8	Mickey Cochrane	.12	.09	.05
9	Walter Johnson	.30	.25	.12
10	Carl Hubbell	.12	.09	.05
11	Jimmie Foxx	.25	.20	.10
12	Rod Carew	.30	.25	.12
13	Nellie Fox	.12	.09	.05
14	Brooks Robinson	.30	.25	.12
15	Luis Aparicio	.12	.09	.05
16	Frank Robinson	.20	.15	.08
17	Mickey Mantle	1.00	.70	.40
18	Ted Williams	.50	.40	.20
19	Yogi Berra	.30	.25	.12
20	Bob Feller	.25	.20	.10
21	Whitey Ford	.25	.20	.10
22	Harmon Killebrew	.20	.15	.08
23	Stan Musial	.50	.40	.20
24	Jackie Robinson	.40	.30	.15
25	Eddie Mathews	.20	.15	.08
26	Ernie Banks	.20	.15	.08
27	Roberto Clemente	.40	.30	.15
28	Willie Mays	.50	.40	.20
29	Hank Aaron	.50	.40	.20
30	Johnny Bench	.30	.25	.12
31	Bob Gibson	.20	.15	.08
32	Warren Spahn	.20	.15	.08
33	Duke Snider	.25	.20	.10

1988 Nestle

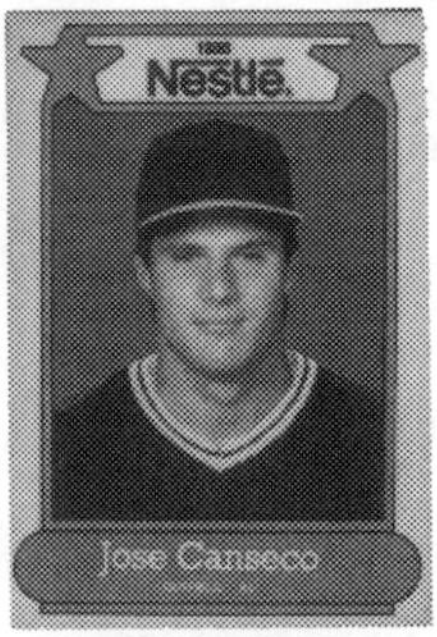

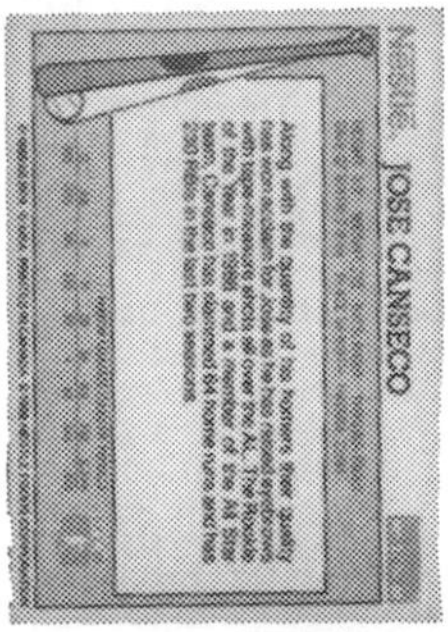

This 44-card set was produced by Mike Schechter Associates for Nestle. "Dream Team" packets of 3 player cards and one checklist card were inserted in 6-packs of Nestle's chocolate candy bars. The 1988 issue, similar to the 33-card Nestle set produced by Topps, features current players divided into four Dream Teams (East and West teams for each league). The "1988 Nestle" header appears at the top of the red and yellow-bordered cards. Below the player closeup (in a plain airbrushed cap) is a blue oval player name banner. Card backs are red, white and blue with card numbers printed upper right above personal stats, career highlights and major league totals. The bright red, blue and yellow checklist card outlines two special offers; one for an uncut sheet of all 44 player cards and one for a 1988 replica autographed baseball.

		MT	NR MT	EX
Complete Set:		20.00	15.00	8.00
Common Player:		.25	.20	.10
1	Roger Clemens	1.00	.70	.40
2	Dale Murphy	.60	.45	.25
3	Eric Davis	.60	.45	.25
4	Gary Gaetti	.30	.25	.12
5	Ozzie Smith	.35	.25	.14
6	Mike Schmidt	1.00	.70	.40
7	Ozzie Guillen	.25	.20	.10
8	John Franco	.25	.20	.10
9	Andre Dawson	.50	.40	.20
10	Mark McGwire	.50	.40	.20
11	Bret Saberhagen	.35	.25	.14
12	Benny Santiago	.35	.25	.14
13	Jose Uribe	.25	.20	.10
14	Will Clark	1.75	1.25	.70
15	Don Mattingly	1.25	.90	.50
16	Juan Samuel	.30	.25	.12
17	Jack Clark	.35	.25	.14
18	Darryl Strawberry	.75	.60	.30
19	Bill Doran	.25	.20	.10
20	Pete Incaviglia	.30	.25	.12
21	Dwight Gooden	.75	.60	.30
22	Willie Randolph	.25	.20	.10
23	Tim Wallach	.25	.20	.10
24	Pedro Guerrero	.35	.25	.14
25	Steve Bedrosian	.25	.20	.10
26	Gary Carter	.50	.40	.20
27	Jeff Reardon	.25	.20	.10
28	Dave Righetti	.35	.25	.14
29	Frank White	.25	.20	.10
30	Buddy Bell	.25	.20	.10
31	Tim Raines	.50	.40	.20
32	Wade Boggs	1.00	.70	.40
33	Dave Winfield	.50	.40	.20
34	George Bell	.40	.30	.15
35	Alan Trammell	.40	.30	.15
36	Joe Carter	.30	.25	.12
37	Jose Canseco	1.50	1.25	.60
38	Carlton Fisk	.60	.45	.25
39	Kirby Puckett	1.00	.70	.40
40	Tony Gwynn	.50	.40	.20
41	Matt Nokes	.40	.30	.15
42	Keith Hernandez	.40	.30	.15
43	Nolan Ryan	2.00	1.50	.80
44	Wally Joyner	.50	.40	.20

1954 N.Y. Journal-American

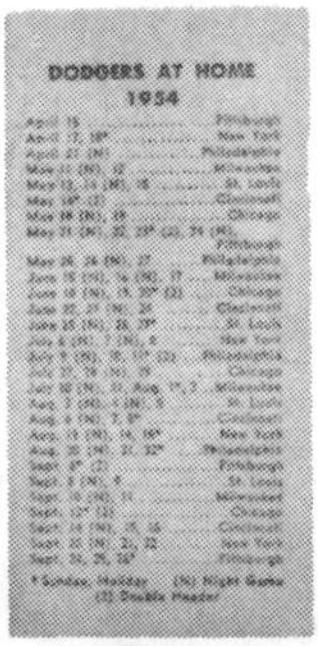

Issued during the Golden Age of baseball in New York City, this 59-card set features only players from the three New York teams of the day - the Giants, Yankees and Dodgers. The 2" by 4" cards were issued at newsstands with the purchase of the now-extinct newspaper. Card fronts have promotional copy and a contest serial number in addition to the player's name and photo. Cards are black and white and unnumbered. Many of the game's top stars are included, such as Mickey Mantle, Willie Mays, Gil Hodges, Duke Snider, Jackie Robinson and Yogi Berra. Card backs featured team schedules. It has been theorized that a 60th Dodgers card should exist. Don Hoak and Bob Milliken have been suggested as the missing card, but the existence of either card has

never been confirmed.

		NR MT	EX	VG
Complete Set:		2250.00	1125.00	675.00
Common Player:		10.00	5.00	3.00
(1)	Johnny Antonelli	12.00	6.00	3.50
(2)	Hank Bauer	20.00	10.00	6.00
(3)	Yogi Berra	100.00	50.00	30.00
(4)	Joe Black	12.00	6.00	3.50
(5)	Harry Byrd	10.00	5.00	3.00
(6)	Roy Campanella	100.00	50.00	30.00
(7)	Andy Carey	10.00	5.00	3.00
(8)	Jerry Coleman	10.00	5.00	3.00
(9)	Joe Collins	10.00	5.00	3.00
(10)	Billy Cox	10.00	5.00	3.00
(11)	Al Dark	12.00	6.00	3.50
(12)	Carl Erskine	20.00	10.00	6.00
(13)	Whitey Ford	40.00	20.00	12.00
(14)	Carl Furillo	20.00	10.00	6.00
(15)	Junior Gilliam	20.00	10.00	6.00
(16)	Ruben Gomez	10.00	5.00	3.00
(17)	Marv Grissom	10.00	5.00	3.00
(18)	Jim Hearn	10.00	5.00	3.00
(19)	Gil Hodges	35.00	17.50	10.50
(20)	Bobby Hofman	10.00	5.00	3.00
(21)	Jim Hughes	10.00	5.00	3.00
(22)	Monte Irvin	25.00	12.50	7.50
(23)	Larry Jansen	10.00	5.00	3.00
(24)	Ray Katt	10.00	5.00	3.00
(25)	Steve Kraly	10.00	5.00	3.00
(26)	Bob Kuzava	10.00	5.00	3.00
(27)	Clem Labine	12.00	6.00	3.50
(28)	Frank Leja	10.00	5.00	3.00
(29)	Don Liddle	10.00	5.00	3.00
(30)	Whitey Lockman	10.00	5.00	3.00
(31)	Billy Loes	10.00	5.00	3.00
(32)	Eddie Lopat	20.00	10.00	6.00
(33)	Gil McDougald	20.00	10.00	6.00
(34)	Sal Maglie	12.00	6.00	3.50
(35)	Mickey Mantle	450.00	225.00	135.00
(36)	Willie Mays	200.00	100.00	60.00
(37)	Russ Meyer	10.00	5.00	3.00
(38)	Bill Miller	10.00	5.00	3.00
(39)	Tom Morgan	10.00	5.00	3.00
(40)	Don Mueller	10.00	5.00	3.00
(41)	Don Newcombe	20.00	10.00	6.00
(42)	Irv Noren	10.00	5.00	3.00
(43)	Erv Palica	10.00	5.00	3.00
(44)	PeeWee Reese	55.00	27.00	16.50
(45)	Allie Reynolds	20.00	10.00	6.00
(46)	Dusty Rhodes	10.00	5.00	3.00
(47)	Phil Rizzuto	35.00	17.50	10.50
(48)	Ed Robinson	10.00	5.00	3.00
(49)	Jackie Robinson	225.00	112.00	67.00
(50)	Preacher Roe	20.00	10.00	6.00
(51)	George Shuba	10.00	5.00	3.00
(52)	Duke Snider	150.00	75.00	45.00
(53)	Hank Thompson	10.00	5.00	3.00
(54)	Wes Westrum	10.00	5.00	3.00
(55)	Hoyt Wilhelm	30.00	15.00	9.00
(56)	Davey Williams	10.00	5.00	3.00
(57)	Dick Williams	12.00	6.00	3.50
(58)	Gene Woodling	12.00	6.00	3.50
(59)	Al Worthington	10.00	5.00	3.00

1986 N.Y. Mets Super Fan Club

This special nine-card panel was issued by the fan club of the 1986 World Champion New York Mets, along with other souvenir items gained with membership in the club. Included in the full-color set are eight top Mets players, with a promotional card in the center of the panel. Individual cards measure 2-1/2" by 3-1/2", and are perforated at the edges to facilitate separation. The full panel measures 70-1/2" by 10-1/2". Card fronts feature posed photos of each player, along with name, position and team logo. Backs feature career and personal data, and are printed in the team's blue and orange colors.

		MT	NR MT	EX
Complete Panel Set:		10.00	7.50	4.00
Complete Singles Set:		4.00	3.00	1.50
Common Single Player:		.15	.11	.06
	Panel	10.00	7.50	4.00
1	Wally Backman	.15	.11	.06
2	Gary Carter	.70	.50	.30
3	Ron Darling	.40	.30	.15
4	Dwight Gooden	1.25	.90	.50
5	Keith Hernandez	.60	.45	.25
6	Howard Johnson	.70	.50	.30
7	Roger McDowell	.40	.30	.15
8	Darryl Strawberry	1.25	.90	.50
----	Membership Card	.05	.04	.02

1960 Nu-Card

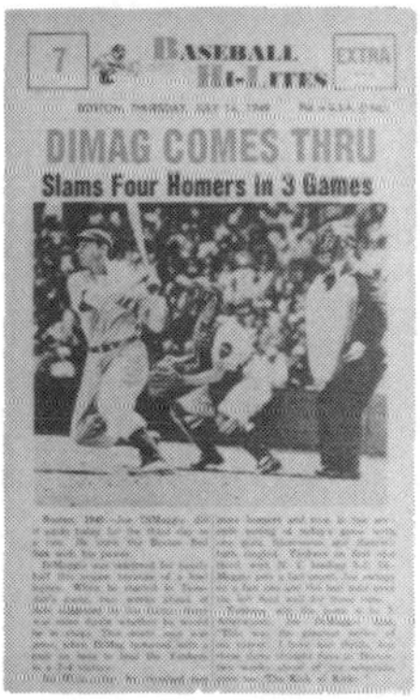

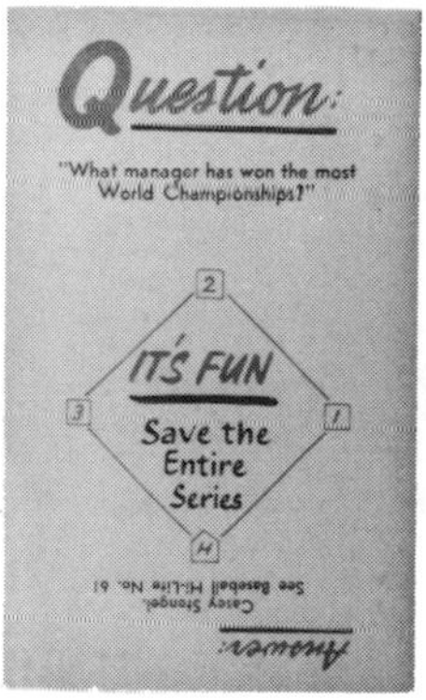

These large, 3-1/4" by 5-3/8" cards are printed in a mock newspaper format, with a headline, picture and story describing one of baseball's greatest events. There are 72 events featured in the set, which is printed in red and black. Each card is numbered in the upper left corner. The card backs offer a quiz question and answer. Certain cards in the set can be found with the fronts printed entirely in black. These cards may command a slight premium.

		NR MT	EX	VG
Complete Set:		225.00	112.00	67.00
Common Player:		1.25	.60	.40
1	Babe Hits 3 Homers In A Series Game	10.00	5.00	3.00
2	Podres Pitching Wins Series	1.25	.60	.40
3	Bevans Pitches No Hitter, Almost	1.25	.60	.40
4	Box Score Devised By Reporter	1.25	.60	.40
5	VanderMeer Pitches 2 No Hitters	1.25	.60	.40
6	Indians Take Bums	1.25	.60	.40
7	DiMag Comes Thru	10.00	5.00	3.00
8	Mathewson Pitches 3 W.S. Shutouts	1.75	.90	.50
9	Haddix Pitches 12 Perfect Innings	1.25	.60	.40
10	Thomson's Homer Sinks Dodgers	1.75	.90	.50
11	Hubbell Strikes Out 5 A.L. Stars	1.50	.70	.45
12	Pickoff Ends Series (Marty Marion)	1.25	.60	.40
13	Cards Take Series From Yanks (Grover Cleveland Alexander)	1.50	.70	.45
14	Dizzy And Daffy Win Series	3.50	1.75	1.00
15	Owen Drops 3rd Strike	1.25	.60	.40
16	Ruth Calls His Shot	8.00	4.00	2.50
17	Merkle Pulls Boner	1.25	.60	.40
18	Larsen Hurls Perfect World Series Game	1.50	.70	.45

		NR MT	EX	VG
19	Bean Ball Ends Career Of Mickey Cochranepremium.	1.25	.60	.40
20	Banks Belts 47 Homers, Earns MVP Honors premium.	2.00	1.00	.60
21	Stan Musial Hits 5 Homers In 1 Day	3.50	1.75	1.00
22	Mickey Mantle Hits Longest Homer	12.00	6.00	3.50
23	Sievers Captures Home Run Title	1.25	.60	.40
24	Gehrig Consecutive Game Record Ends	10.00	5.00	3.00
25	Red Schoendienst Key Player In Victory	1.25	.60	.40
26	Midget Pinch-Hits For St. Louis Browns (Eddie Gaedel)	1.25	.60	.40
27	Willie Mays Makes Greatest Catch	4.00	2.00	1.25
28	Homer By Berra Puts Yanks In 1st Place	3.00	1.50	.90
29	Campy National League's MVP	3.00	1.50	.90
30	Bob Turley Hurls Yanks To Championship	1.25	.60	.40
31	Dodgers Take Series From Sox In Six	1.25	.60	.40
32	Furillo Hero As Dodgers Beat Chicago	1.25	.60	.40
33	Adcock Gets Four Homers And A Double	1.25	.60	.40
34	Dickey Chosen All Star Catcher	1.25	.60	.40
35	Burdette Beats Yanks In 3 Series Games	1.25	.60	.40
36	Umpires Clear White Sox Bench	1.25	.60	.40
37	Reese Honored As Greatest Dodger S.S.	2.50	1.25	.70
38	Joe DiMaggio Hits In 56 Straight Games	10.00	5.00	3.00
39	Ted Williams Hits .406 For Season	5.00	2.50	1.50
40	Johnson Pitches 56 Scoreless Innings	2.25	1.25	.70
41	Hodges Hits 4 Home Runs In Nite Game	1.75	.90	.50
42	Greenberg Returns To Tigers From Army	1.25	.60	.40
43	Ty Cobb Named Best Player Of All Time	10.00	5.00	3.00
44	Robin Roberts Wins 28 Games	1.25	.60	.40
45	Rizzuto's 2 Runs Save 1st Place	1.50	.70	.45
46	Tigers Beat Out Senators For Pennant (Hal Newhouser)	1.25	.60	.40
47	Babe Ruth Hits 60th Home Run	9.00	4.50	2.75
48	Cy Young Honored	1.75	.90	.50
49	Killebrew Starts Spring Training	1.75	.90	.50
50	Mantle Hits Longest Homer At Stadium	12.00	6.00	3.50
51	Braves Take Pennant (Hank Aaron)	3.50	1.75	1.00
52	Ted Williams Hero Of All Star Game	5.00	2.50	1.50
53	Robinson Saves Dodgers For Playoffs (Jackie Robinson)	3.50	1.75	1.00
54	Snodgrass Muffs A Fly Ball	1.25	.60	.40
55	Snider Belts 2 Homers	2.25	1.25	.70
56	New York Giants Win 26 Straight Games (Christy Mathewson)	1.75	.90	.50
57	Ted Kluszewski Stars In 1st Game Win	1.25	.60	.40
58	Ott Walks 5 Times In A Single Game (Mel Ott)	1.25	.60	.40
59	Harvey Kuenn Takes Batting Title	1.25	.60	.40
60	Bob Feller Hurls 3rd No-Hitter Of Careerpremium.	2.25	1.25	.70
61	Yanks Champs Again! (Casey Stengel)	1.50	.70	.45
62	Aaron's Bat Beats Yankees In Series	4.00	2.00	1.25
63	Warren Spahn Beats Yanks in World Seriespremium.	1.50	.70	.45
64	Ump's Wrong Call Helps Dodgers	1.25	.60	.40
65	Kaline Hits 3 Homers, 2 In Same Inning	2.00	1.00	.60
66	Bob Allison Named A.L. Rookie of Year	1.25	.60	.40
67	McCovey Blasts Way Into Giant Lineup	1.75	.90	.50
68	Colavito Hits Four Homers In One Game	1.25	.60	.40
69	Erskine Sets Strike Out Record In W.S.	1.25	.60	.40
70	Sal Maglie Pitches No-Hit Game	1.25	.60	.40
71	Early Wynn Victory Crushes Yanks	1.25	.60	.40
72	Nellie Fox American League's M.V.P.	3.00	1.50	.90

1961 Nu-Card

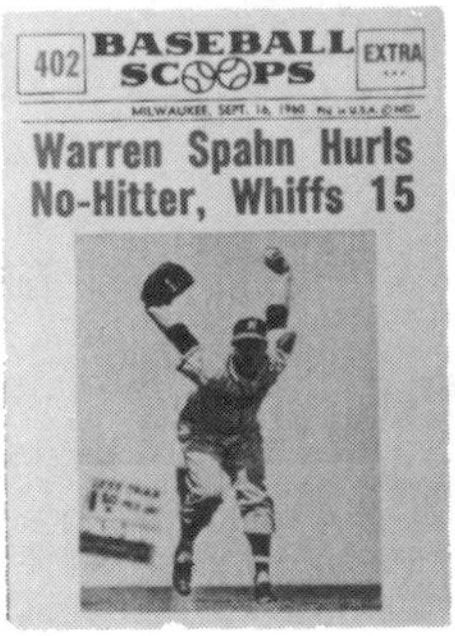

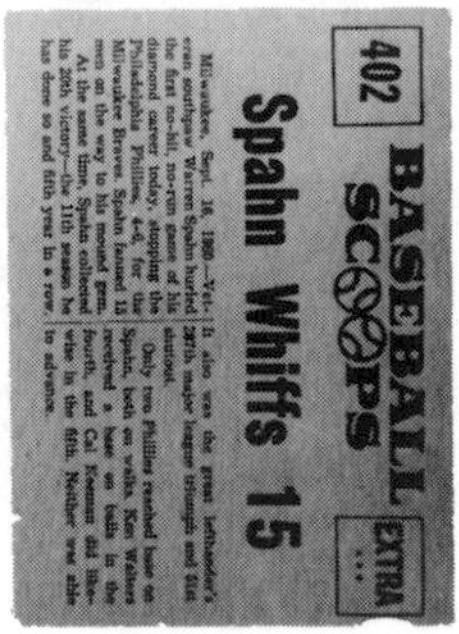

Very similar in style to their set of the year before, the Nu-Card Baseball Scoops were issued in a smaller 2-1/2" by 3-1/2" size, but still featured the mock newspaper card front. This 80-card set is numbered from 401 to 480, with numbers shown on both the card front and back. These cards, which commemorate great moments in individual players' careers, included only the headline and black and white photo on the fronts, with the descriptive story on the card backs. Cards are again printed in red and black. It appears the set may have been counterfeited, though when is not known. These cards can be determined by examining the card photo for unusual blurring and fuzziness.

		NR MT	EX	VG
	Complete Set:	125.00	62.00	37.00
	Common Player:	.50	.25	.15
401	Gentile Powers Birds Into 1st	1.00	.50	.30
402	Warren Spahn Hurls No-Hitter, Whiffs 15	1.00	.50	.30
403	Mazeroski's Homer Wins Series For Bucs	.75	.40	.25
404	Willie Mays' 3 Triples Paces Giants	4.00	2.00	1.25
405	Woodie Held Slugs 2 Homers, 6 RBIs	.50	.25	.15
406	Vern Law Winner Of Cy Young Award	.50	.25	.15
407	Runnels Makes 9 Hits in Twin-Bill	.50	.25	.15
408	Braves' Lew Burdette Wins No-Hitter, 1-0	.70	.35	.20
409	Dick Stuart Hits 3 Homers, Single	.50	.25	.15
410	Don Cardwell Of Cubs Pitches No-Hit Game	.50	.25	.15
411	Camilo Pascual Strikes Out 15 Bosox	.50	.25	.15
412	Eddie Mathews Blasts 300th Big League HR	1.00	.50	.30
413	Groat, NL Bat King, Named Loop's MVP	.70	.35	.20
414	AL Votes To Expand To 10 Teams (Gene Autry)	1.25	.60	.40
415	Bobby Richardson Sets Series Mark	.75	.40	.25
416	Maris Nips Mantle For AL MVP Award	2.50	1.25	.70
417	Merkle Pulls Boner	.50	.25	.15
418	Larsen Hurls Perefect World Series Game	.75	.40	.25
419	Bean Ball Ends Career Of Mickey Cochrane	.70	.35	.20
420	Banks Belts 47 Homers, Earns MVP Award	1.50	.70	.45
421	Stan Musial Hits 5 Homers In 1 Day	2.50	1.25	.70
422	Mickey Mantle Hits Longest Homer	10.00	5.00	3.00
423	Sievers Captures Home Run Title	.50	.25	.15
424	Gehrig Consecutive Game Record Ends	5.00	2.50	1.50
425	Red Schoendienst Key Player In Victory	.70	.35	.20
426	Midget Pinch-Hits For St. Louis Browns (Eddie Gaedel)	.75	.40	.25

		NR MT	EX	VG
427	Willie Mays Makes Greatest Catch	2.50	1.25	.70
428	Robinson Saves Dodgers For Playoffs	2.50	1.25	.70
429	Campy Most Valuable Player	2.50	1.25	.70
430	Turley Hurls Yanks To Championship	.50	.25	.15
431	Dodgers Take Series From Sox In Six (Larry Sherry)	.50	.25	.15
432	Furillo Hero In 3rd World Series Game	.70	.35	.20
433	Adcock Gets Four Homers, Double	.70	.35	.20
434	Dickey Chosen All Star Catcher	1.00	.50	.30
435	Burdette Beats Yanks In 3 Series Games	.75	.40	.25
436	Umpires Clear White Sox Bench	.50	.25	.15
437	Reese Honored As Greatest Dodgers S.S.	1.50	.70	.45
438	Joe DiMaggio Hits In 56 Straight Games	5.00	2.50	1.50
439	Ted Williams Hits .406 For Season	4.00	2.00	1.25
440	Johnson Pitches 56 Scoreless Innings	2.50	1.25	.70
441	Hodges Hits 4 Home Runs In Nite Game	1.50	.70	.45
442	Greenberg Returns To Tigers From Army	1.00	.50	.30
443	Ty Cobb Named Best Player Of All Time	4.00	2.00	1.25
444	Robin Roberts Wins 28 Games	1.00	.50	.30
445	Rizzuto's 2 Runs Save 1st Place	1.25	.60	.40
446	Tigers Beat Out Senators For Pennant (Hal Newhouser)	.50	.25	.15
447	Babe Ruth Hits 60th Home Run	6.00	3.00	1.75
448	Cy Young Honored	1.50	.70	.45
449	Killebrew Starts Spring Training	1.25	.60	.40
450	Mantle Hits Longest Homer At Stadium	9.00	4.50	2.75
451	Braves Take Pennant	.50	.25	.15
452	Ted Williams Hero Of All Star Game	2.50	1.25	.70
453	Homer By Berra Puts Yanks In 1st Place	2.50	1.25	.70
454	Snodgrass Muffs A Fly Ball	.50	.25	.15
455	Babe Hits 3 Homers In A Series Game	8.00	4.00	2.50
456	New York Wins 26 Straight Games	.50	.25	.15
457	Ted Kluszewski Stars In 1st Series Win	.50	.25	.15
458	Ott Walks 5 Times In A Single Game	1.00	.50	.30
459	Harvey Kuenn Takes Batting Title	.50	.25	.15
460	Bob Feller Hurls 3rd No-Hitter Of Career	2.50	1.25	.70
461	Yanks Champs Again! (Casey Stengel)	1.50	.70	.45
462	Aaron's Bat Beats Yankees In Series	2.50	1.25	.70
463	Warren Spahn Beats Yanks In World Series	1.00	.50	.30
464	Ump's Wrong Call Helps Dodgers	.50	.25	.15
465	Kaline Hits 3 Homers, 2 In Same Inning	1.50	.70	.45
466	Bob Allison Named A.L. Rookie Of Year	.50	.25	.15
467	DiMag Comes Thru	5.00	2.50	1.50
468	Colavito Hits Four Homers In One Game	.70	.35	.20
469	Erskine Sets Strike Out Record In W.S.	.70	.35	.20
470	Sal Maglie Pitches No-Hit Game	.70	.35	.20
471	Early Wynn Victory Crushes Yanks	1.00	.50	.30
472	Nellie Fox American League's MVP	.75	.40	.25
473	Pickoff Ends Series (Marty Marion)	.50	.25	.15
474	Podres Pitching Wins Series	.80	.40	.25
475	Owen Drops 3rd Strike	.50	.25	.15
476	Dizzy And Daffy Win Series	2.50	1.25	.70
477	Mathewson Pitches 3 W.S. Shutouts	1.50	.70	.45
478	Haddix Pitches 12 Perfect Innings	.50	.25	.15
479	Hubbell Strike Out 5 A.L. Stars	1.00	.50	.30
480	Homer Sinks Dodgers (Bobby Thomson)	1.25	.60	.40

Definitions for grading conditions are located in the introduction section at the front of this book.

O

1991 O-Pee-Chee Premier

The O-Pee-Chee Co. of London, Ontario, Canada produced this 132-card set. The card fronts feature action photos, while the flip sides display a posed photo and career statistics. The cards were packaged seven cards per pack in a tamper-proof foil wrap. Several Expo and Blue Jay players are featured. Two special cards are included in this set. Card #62 honors Rickey Henderson's stolen base record, while card #102 commemorates Nolan Ryan's seventh no-hitter. Traded players and free agents are featured with their new teams.

		MT	NR MT	EX
Complete Set:		40.00	30.00	15.00
Common Player:		.10	.08	.04
1	Roberto Alomar	.40	.30	.15
2	Sandy Alomar	.20	.15	.08
3	Moises Alou	.12	.09	.05
4	Brian Barnes	.25	.20	.10
5	Steve Bedrosian	.10	.08	.04
6	George Bell	.20	.15	.08
7	Juan Bell	.12	.09	.05
8	Albert Belle	.70	.50	.30
9	Bud Black	.10	.08	.04
10	Mike Boddicker	.10	.08	.04
11	Wade Boggs	.60	.45	.25
12	Barry Bonds	.60	.45	.25
13	Denis Boucher	.25	.20	.10
14	George Brett	.40	.30	.15
15	Hubie Brooks	.10	.08	.04
16	Brett Butler	.12	.09	.05
17	Ivan Calderon	.15	.11	.06
18	Jose Canseco	1.50	1.25	.60
19	Gary Carter	.20	.15	.08
20	Joe Carter	.25	.20	.10
21	Jack Clark	.15	.11	.06
22	Will Clark	1.50	1.25	.60
23	Roger Clemens	1.50	1.25	.60
24	Alex Cole	.15	.11	.06
25	Vince Coleman	.15	.11	.06
26	Jeff Conine	.20	.15	.08
27	Milt Cuyler	.60	.45	.25
28	Danny Darwin	.10	.08	.04
29	Eric Davis	.30	.25	.12
30	Glenn Davis	.15	.11	.06
31	Andre Dawson	.30	.25	.12
32	Ken Dayley	.10	.08	.04
33	Steve Decker	.50	.40	.20
34	Delino DeShields	.30	.25	.12
35	Lance Dickson	.50	.40	.20
36	Kirk Dressendorfer	.80	.60	.30
37	Shawon Dunston	.15	.11	.06
38	Dennis Eckersley	.15	.11	.06
39	Dwight Evans	.12	.09	.05
40	Howard Farmer	.20	.15	.08
41	Junior Felix	.15	.11	.06
42	Alex Fernandez	.50	.40	.20
43	Tony Fernandez	.12	.09	.05
44	Cecil Fielder	1.00	.70	.40
45	Carlton Fisk	.50	.40	.20

		MT	NR MT	EX
46	Willie Fraser	.10	.08	.04
47	Gary Gaetti	.12	.09	.05
48	Andres Galarraga	.10	.08	.04
49	Ron Gant	.60	.45	.25
50	Kirk Gibson	.15	.11	.06
51	Bernard Gilkey	.30	.25	.12
52	Leo Gomez	.80	.60	.30
53	Rene Gonzalez	.10	.08	.04
54	Juan Gonzalez	6.00	4.50	2.50
55	Doc Gooden	.40	.30	.15
56	Ken Griffey,Jr.	8.00	6.00	3.25
57	Kelly Gruber	.20	.15	.08
58	Pedro Guerrero	.15	.11	.06
59	Tony Gwynn	.60	.45	.25
60	Chris Hammond	.20	.15	.08
61	Ron Hassey	.10	.08	.04
62	Rickey Henderson	1.00	.70	.40
63	Tom Henke	.12	.09	.05
64	Orel Hershiser	.20	.15	.08
65	Chris Hoiles	.20	.15	.08
66	Todd Hundley	.30	.25	.12
67	Pete Incaviglia	.10	.08	.04
68	Danny Jackson	.10	.08	.04
69	Barry Jones	.10	.08	.04
70	David Justice	6.00	4.50	2.50
71	Jimmy Key	.12	.09	.05
72	Ray Lankford	1.00	.70	.40
73	Darren Lewis	.80	.60	.30
74	Kevin Maas	1.00	.70	.40
75	Denny Martinez	.12	.09	.05
76	Tino Martinez	.50	.40	.20
77	Don Mattingly	1.00	.70	.40
78	Willie McGee	.15	.11	.06
79	Fred McGriff	.30	.25	.12
80	Hensley Meulens	.20	.15	.08
81	Kevin Mitchell	.30	.25	.12
82	Paul Molitor	.25	.20	.10
83	Mickey Morandini	.25	.20	.10
84	Jack Morris	.25	.20	.10
85	Dale Murphy	.25	.20	.10
86	Eddie Murray	.30	.25	.12
87	Chris Nabholz	.15	.11	.06
88	Tim Naehring	.20	.15	.08
89	Otis Nixon	.12	.09	.05
90	Jose Offerman	.20	.15	.08
91	Bob Ojeda	.10	.08	.04
92	John Olerud	.50	.40	.20
93	Gregg Olson	.15	.11	.06
94	Dave Parker	.15	.11	.06
95	Terry Pendleton	.20	.15	.08
96	Kirby Puckett	.80	.60	.30
97	Rock Raines	.15	.11	.06
98	Jeff Reardon	.12	.09	.05
99	Dave Righetti	.12	.09	.05
100	Cal Ripken	1.50	1.25	.60
101	Mel Rojas	.15	.11	.06
102	Nolan Ryan	5.00	3.75	2.00
103	Ryne Sandberg	1.50	1.25	.60
104	Scott Sanderson	.10	.08	.04
105	Benito Santiago	.15	.11	.06
106	Pete Schourek	.25	.20	.10
107	Gary Scott	.40	.30	.15
108	Terry Shumpert	.10	.08	.04
109	Ruben Sierra	.80	.60	.30
110	Doug Simons	.20	.15	.08
111	Dave Smith	.10	.08	.04
112	Ozzie Smith	.35	.25	.14
113	Cory Snyder	.10	.08	.04
114	Luis Sojo	.10	.08	.04
115	Dave Stewart	.15	.11	.06
116	Dave Stieb	.12	.09	.05
117	Darryl Strawberry	1.25	.90	.50
118	Pat Tabler	.10	.08	.04
119	Wade Taylor	.30	.25	.12
120	Bobby Thigpen	.15	.11	.06
121	Frank Thomas	15.00	11.00	6.00
122	Mike Timlin	.30	.25	.12
123	Alan Trammell	.20	.15	.08
124	Mo Vaughn	2.00	1.50	.80
125	Tim Wallach	.12	.09	.05
126	Devon White	.12	.09	.05
127	Mark Whiten	.60	.45	.25
128	Bernie Williams	1.25	.90	.50
129	Willie Wilson	.10	.08	.04
130	Dave Winfield	.30	.25	.12
131	Robin Yount	.60	.45	.25
132	Checklist	.10	.08	.04

NOTE: A card number in parentheses ( ) indicates the set is unnumbered.

1986 Oh Henry Indians

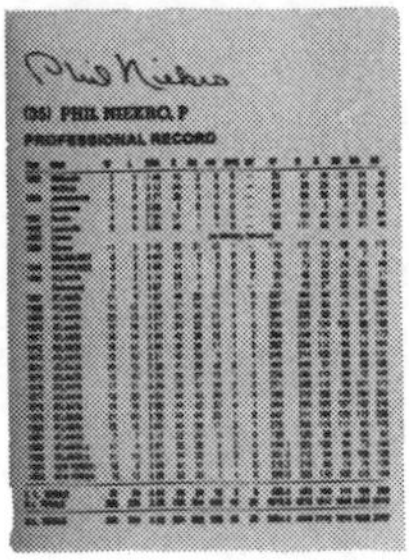

This 30-card set of Cleveland Indians players was distributed by the team at a special Photo/Baseball Card Day at Municipal Stadium. The cards were printed within a special three-panel, perforated fold-out piece which featured four action shots of the Indians on the cover. Unfolded, there are two panels containing the baseball cards and a third which contains a team photo. Cards measure 2-1/4" by 3-1/8" and are full-color studio portraits. Photos are framed in blue with a white border and list player name, number and position. Card fronts also include a picture of the sponsoring candy bar. Card backs include facsimile autograph and professional records. Each card is perforated for separation.

		MT	NR MT	EX
Complete Set:		10.00	7.50	4.00
Common Player:		.15	.11	.06
2	Brett Butler	.70	.50	.30
4	Tony Bernazard	.15	.11	.06
6	Andy Allanson	.25	.20	.10
7	Pat Corrales	.15	.11	.06
8	Carmen Castillo	.15	.11	.06
10	Pat Tabler	.30	.25	.12
13	Ernie Camacho	.15	.11	.06
14	Julio Franco	1.00	.70	.40
15	Dan Rohn	.15	.11	.06
18	Ken Schrom	.15	.11	.06
20	Otis Nixon	.20	.15	.08
22	Fran Mullins	.15	.11	.06
23	Chris Bando	.15	.11	.06
24	Ed Williams	.35	.25	.14
26	Brook Jacoby	.80	.60	.30
27	Mel Hall	.30	.25	.12
29	Andre Thornton	.30	.25	.12
30	Joe Carter	1.00	.70	.40
35	Phil Niekro	.80	.60	.30
36	Jamie Easterly	.15	.11	.06
37	Don Schulze	.15	.11	.06
42	Rich Yett	.20	.15	.08
43	Scott Bailes	.35	.25	.14
44	Neal Heaton	.15	.11	.06
46	Jim Kern	.15	.11	.06
48	Dickie Noles	.15	.11	.06
49	Tom Candiotti	.25	.20	.10
53	Reggie Ritter	.15	.11	.06
54	Tom Waddell	.15	.11	.06
---	Coaching Staff (Jack Aker, Bobby Bonds, Doc Edwards, Johnny Goryl)	.15	.11	.06

P

1988 Pacific Trading Cards Baseball Legends

Pacific Trading Cards rounded up 110 photos of the greatest baseball players from the past 40 years for

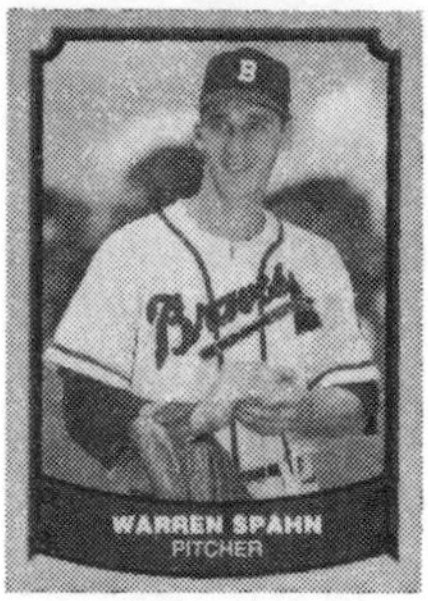

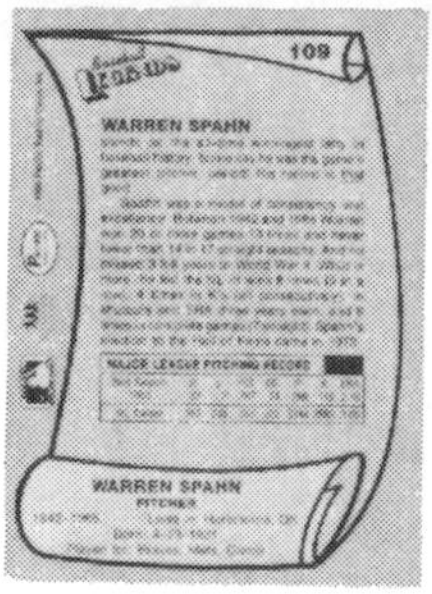

its 1988 "Baseball Legends" set. All players featured in the set are (or were) members of the Major League Baseball Alumni Association. Card fronts feature silver outer borders and large, clear full-color player photos outlined in black against colorful banner-style inner borders of red, blue, green, orange or gold. The player's name and position are printed in white letters on the lower portion of the banner. Card backs are numbered and carry the Baseball Legends logo, player biography, major league career stats, and personal information. The cards were sold in boxed sets via candy wholesalers, with emphasis on Midwest and New England states. Complete collector sets in clear plastic boxes were made available via dealers or directly from Pacific Trading Cards.

	MT	NR MT	EX
Complete Set:	12.00	9.00	4.75
Common Player:	.06	.05	.02

		MT	NR MT	EX
1	Hank Aaron	.50	.40	.20
2	Red Shoendienst (Schoendienst)	.10	.08	.04
3	Brooks Robinson	.30	.25	.12
4	Luke Appling	.15	.11	.06
5	Gene Woodling	.06	.05	.02
6	Stan Musial	.50	.40	.20
7	Mickey Mantle	1.00	.70	.40
8	Richie Ashburn	.10	.08	.04
9	Ralph Kiner	.20	.15	.08
10	Phil Rizzuto	.20	.15	.08
11	Harvey Haddix	.06	.05	.02
12	Ken Boyer	.10	.08	.04
13	Clete Boyer	.06	.05	.02
14	Ken Harrelson	.06	.05	.02
15	Robin Roberts	.20	.15	.08
16	Catfish Hunter	.20	.15	.08
17	Frank Howard	.10	.08	.04
18	Jim Perry	.06	.05	.02
19	Elston Howard	.10	.08	.04
20	Jim Bouton	.10	.08	.04
21	Pee Wee Reese	.25	.20	.10
22	Mel Stottlemyer (Stottlemyre)	.10	.08	.04
23	Hank Sauer	.06	.05	.02
24	Willie Mays	.50	.40	.20
25	Tom Tresh	.06	.05	.02
26	Roy Sievers	.06	.05	.02
27	Leo Durocher	.15	.11	.06
28	Al Dark	.10	.08	.04
29	Tony Kubek	.15	.11	.06
30	Johnny Vander Meer	.10	.08	.04
31	Joe Adcock	.10	.08	.04
32	Bob Lemon	.20	.15	.08
33	Don Newcombe	.15	.11	.06
34	Thurman Munson	.20	.15	.08
35	Earl Battey	.06	.05	.02
36	Ernie Banks	.30	.25	.12
37	Matty Alou	.06	.05	.02
38	Dave McNally	.06	.05	.02
39	Mickey Lolich	.10	.08	.04
40	Jackie Robinson	.50	.40	.20
41	Allie Reynolds	.15	.11	.06
42	Don Larson (Larsen)	.10	.08	.04

A player's name in italic indicates a rookie card. An (FC) indicates a player's first card for that particular card company.

		MT	NR MT	EX
43	Fergie Jenkins	.15	.11	.06
44	Jim Gilliam	.10	.08	.04
45	Bobby Thomson	.10	.08	.04
46	Sparky Anderson	.10	.08	.04
47	Roy Campanella	.30	.25	.12
48	Marv Throneberry	.10	.08	.04
49	Bill Virdon	.06	.05	.02
50	Ted Williams	.50	.40	.20
51	Minnie Minoso	.10	.08	.04
52	Bob Turley	.10	.08	.04
53	Yogi Berra	.30	.25	.12
54	Juan Marichal	.20	.15	.08
55	Duke Snider	.30	.25	.12
56	Harvey Kuenn	.10	.08	.04
57	Nellie Fox	.15	.11	.06
58	Felipe Alou	.06	.05	.02
59	Tony Oliva	.10	.08	.04
60	Bill Mazeroski	.10	.08	.04
61	Bobby Shantz	.10	.08	.04
62	Mark Fidrych	.06	.05	.02
63	Johnny Mize	.15	.11	.06
64	Ralph Terry	.06	.05	.02
65	Gus Bell	.06	.05	.02
66	Jerry Koosman	.10	.08	.04
67	Mike McCormick	.06	.05	.02
68	Lou Burdette	.10	.08	.04
69	George Kell	.15	.11	.06
70	Vic Raschi	.10	.08	.04
71	Chuck Connors	.20	.15	.08
72	Ted Kluszewski	.10	.08	.04
73	Bobby Doerr	.15	.11	.06
74	Bobby Richardson	.15	.11	.06
75	Carl Erskine	.15	.11	.06
76	Hoyt Wilhelm	.20	.15	.08
77	Bob Purkey	.06	.05	.02
78	Bob Friend	.06	.05	.02
79	Monte Irvin	.15	.11	.06
80	Jim Longborg (Lonborg)	.06	.05	.02
81	Wally Moon	.06	.05	.02
82	Moose Skowron	.10	.08	.04
83	Tommy Davis	.10	.08	.04
84	Enos Slaughter	.20	.15	.08
85	Sal Maglie	.10	.08	.04
86	Harmon Killebrew	.25	.20	.10
87	Gil Hodges	.25	.20	.10
88	Jim Kaat	.10	.08	.04
89	Roger Maris	.30	.25	.12
90	Billy Williams	.20	.15	.08
91	Luis Aparicio	.15	.11	.06
92	Jim Bunning	.15	.11	.06
93	Bill Freehan	.06	.05	.02
94	Orlando Cepeda	.10	.08	.04
95	Early Wynn	.20	.15	.08
96	Tug McGraw	.10	.08	.04
97	Ron Santo	.10	.08	.04
98	Del Crandall	.06	.05	.02
99	Sal Bando	.06	.05	.02
100	Joe DiMaggio	.70	.50	.30
101	Bob Feller	.30	.25	.12
102	Larry Doby	.15	.11	.06
103	Rollie Fingers	.15	.11	.06
104	Al Kaline	.30	.25	.12
105	Johnny Podres	.10	.08	.04
106	Lou Boudreau	.15	.11	.06
107	Zoilo Versalles	.06	.05	.02
108	Dick Groat	.06	.05	.02
109	Warren Spahn	.25	.20	.10
110	Johnny Bench	.40	.30	.15

1989 Pacific Trading Cards Legends II

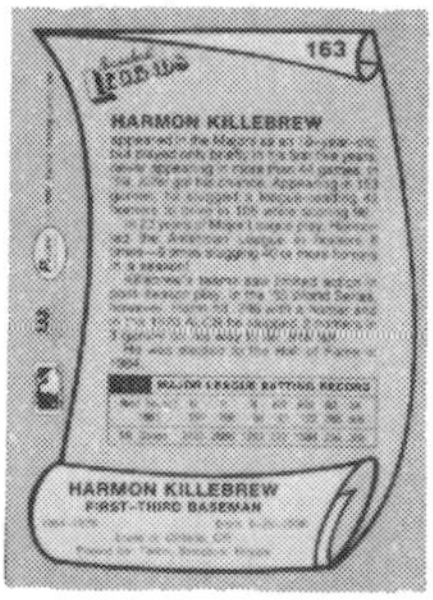

Pacific Trading Cards issued its Baseball Legends II

set as a carry over of its initial set. The photos are printed on silver background and have colorful inner borders of red, blue, orange or gold. Players' names and positions are printed in white letters below the photos. The card backs once again present the "Baseball Legends" logo, player biography, major league career statistics, and personal information. The Baseball Legends II are numbered 110-220 and were available in wax packs at a limited number of retail chains. The complete set was also made available via dealers or could be ordered directly from Pacific Trading Cards.

		MT	NR MT	EX
Complete Set:		10.00	7.50	4.00
Common Player:		.06	.05	.02
111	Reggie Jackson	.30	.25	.12
112	Rich Reese	.06	.05	.02
113	Frankie Frisch	.15	.11	.06
114	Ed Kranepool	.06	.05	.02
115	Al Hrabosky	.06	.05	.02
116	Eddie Mathews	.25	.20	.10
117	Ty Cobb	.50	.40	.20
118	Jim Davenport	.06	.05	.02
119	Buddy Lewis	.06	.05	.02
120	Virgil Trucks	.10	.08	.04
121	Del Ennis	.06	.05	.02
122	Dick Radatz	.06	.05	.02
123	Andy Pafko	.12	.09	.05
124	Wilbur Wood	.10	.08	.04
125	Joe Sewell	.15	.11	.06
126	Herb Score	.06	.05	.02
127	Paul Waner	.06	.05	.02
128	Lloyd Waner	.06	.05	.02
129	Brooks Robinson	.30	.25	.12
130	Bo Belinsky	.10	.08	.04
131	Phil Cavaretta	.06	.05	.02
132	Claude Osteen	.06	.05	.02
133	Tito Francona	.06	.05	.02
134	Billy Pierce	.06	.05	.02
135	Roberto Clemente	.50	.40	.20
136	Spud Chandler	.06	.05	.02
137	Enos Slaughter	.25	.20	.10
138	Ken Holtzman	.06	.05	.02
139	John Hopp	.06	.05	.02
140	Tony LaRussa	.06	.05	.02
141	Ryne Duren	.06	.05	.02
142	Glenn Beckert	.06	.05	.02
143	Ken Keltner	.06	.05	.02
144	Hank Bauer	.15	.11	.06
145	Roger Craig	.10	.08	.04
146	Frank Baker	.10	.08	.04
147	Jim O'Toole	.06	.05	.02
148	Rogers Hornsby	.30	.25	.12
149	Jose Cardenal	.06	.05	.02
150	Bobby Doerr	.10	.08	.04
151	Mickey Cochrane	.10	.08	.04
152	Gaylord Perry	.10	.08	.04
153	Frank Thomas	.06	.05	.02
154	Ted Williams	.40	.30	.15
155	Sam McDowell	.10	.08	.04
156	Bob Feller	.20	.15	.08
157	Bert Campaneris	.06	.05	.02
158	Thornton Lee	.06	.05	.02
159	Gary Peters	.06	.05	.02
160	Joe Medwick	.10	.08	.04
161	Joe Nuxhall	.10	.08	.04
162	Joe Schultz	.06	.05	.02
163	Harmon Killebrew	.25	.20	.10
164	Bucky Walters	.06	.05	.02
165	Bobby Allison	.10	.08	.04
166	Lou Boudreau	.15	.11	.08
167	Joe Cronin	.10	.08	.04
168	Mike Torrez	.10	.08	.04
169	Rich Rollins	.06	.05	.02
170	Tony Cuccinello	.06	.05	.02
171	Hoyt Wilhelm	.20	.15	.08
172	Ernie Harwell	.10	.08	.04
173	George Foster	.06	.05	.02
174	Lou Gehrig	.80	.60	.30
175	Dave Kingman	.06	.05	.02
176	Babe Ruth	1.00	.70	.40
177	Joe Black	.10	.08	.04
178	Roy Face	.10	.08	.04
179	Earl Weaver	.06	.05	.02
180	Johnny Mize	.15	.11	.06
181	Roger Cramer	.06	.05	.02
182	Jim Piersall	.06	.05	.02
183	Ned Garver	.06	.05	.02

NOTE: A card number in parentheses ( ) indicates the set is unnumbered.

		MT	NR MT	EX
184	Billy Williams	.25	.20	.10
185	Lefty Grove	.15	.11	.06
186	Jim Grant	.06	.05	.02
187	Elmer Valo	.06	.05	.02
188	Ewell Blackwell	.10	.08	.04
189	Mel Ott	.20	.15	.08
190	Harry Walker	.06	.05	.02
191	Bill Campbell	.06	.05	.02
192	Walter Johnson	.30	.25	.12
193	Jim "Catfish" Hunter	.10	.08	.04
194	Charlie Keller	.10	.08	.04
195	Hank Greenberg	.15	.11	.06
196	Bobby Murcer	.06	.05	.02
197	Al Lopez	.06	.05	.02
198	Vida Blue	.10	.08	.04
199	Shag Crawford	.06	.05	.02
200	Arky Vaughan	.10	.08	.04
201	Smoky Burgess	.25	.20	.10
202	Rip Sewell	.06	.05	.02
203	Earl Avrerill	.10	.08	.04
204	Milt Pappas	.06	.05	.02
205	Mel Harder	.06	.05	.02
206	Sam Jethroe	.06	.05	.02
207	Randy Hundley	.06	.05	.02
208	Jessie Haines	.10	.08	.04
209	Jack Brickhouse	.10	.08	.04
210	Whitey Ford	.20	.15	.08
211	Honus Wagner	1.00	.70	.40
212	Phil Niekro	.10	.08	.04
213	Gary Bell	.06	.05	.02
214	Jon Matlack	.06	.05	.02
215	Moe Drabowsky	.06	.05	.02
216	Edd Roush	.10	.08	.04
217	Joel Horlen	.06	.05	.02
218	Casey Stengel	.30	.25	.12
219	Burt Hooton	.06	.05	.02
220	Joe Jackson	.80	.60	.30

A player's name in *italic* indicates a rookie card. An (FC) indicates a player's first card for that particular card company.

1990 Pacific Legends

The cards in this 110-card set feature the same style as the previous Pacific Legends releases. The cards were available in wax packs as well as in complete set form. Several players found in the first two legends releases are also found in this issue along with new players.

		MT	NR MT	EX
Complete Set:		10.00	7.50	4.00
Common Player:		.05	.04	.02
1	Hank Aaron	.50	.40	.20
2	Tommie Agee	.05	.04	.02
3	Luke Appling	.15	.11	.06
4	Sal Bando	.05	.04	.02
5	Ernie Banks	.40	.30	.15
6	Don Baylor	.05	.04	.02
7	Yogi Berra	.40	.30	.15
8	Vida Blue	.05	.04	.02
9	Lou Boudreau	.10	.08	.04
10	Clete Boyer	.05	.04	.02
11	George Bamberger	.05	.04	.02
12	Lou Brock	.30	.25	.12
13	Ralph Branca	.05	.04	.02
14	Carl Erskine	.05	.04	.02
15	Bert Campaneris	.05	.04	.02
16	Steve Carlton	.30	.25	.12
17	Rod Carew	.50	.40	.20
18	Rocky Colovito	.15	.11	.06

		MT	NR MT	EX
19	Frank Crosetti	.10	.08	.04
20	Larry Doby	.05	.04	.02
21	Bobby Doerr	.10	.08	.04
22	Walt Dropo	.05	.04	.02
23	Rick Ferrell	.05	.04	.02
24	Joe Garagiola	.25	.20	.10
25	Ralph Garr	.05	.04	.02
26	Dick Groat	.10	.08	.04
27	Steve Garvey	.20	.15	.08
28	Bob Gibson	.25	.20	.10
29	Don Drysdale	.15	.11	.06
30	Billy Herman	.10	.08	.04
31	Bobby Grich	.05	.04	.02
32	Monte Irvin	.15	.11	.06
33	Dave Johnson	.05	.04	.02
34	Don Kessinger	.05	.04	.02
35	Harmon Killebrew	.25	.20	.10
36	Ralph Kiner	.15	.11	.06
37	Vern Law	.05	.04	.02
38	Ed Lopat	.05	.04	.02
39	Bill Mazeroski	.15	.11	.06
40	Rick Monday	.05	.04	.02
41	Manny Mota	.05	.04	.02
42	Don Newcombe	.10	.08	.04
43	Gaylord Perry	.20	.15	.08
44	Jim Piersall	.10	.08	.04
45	Johnny Podres	.05	.04	.02
46	Boog Powell	.10	.08	.04
47	Robin Roberts	.15	.11	.06
48	Ron Santo	.15	.11	.06
49	Herb Score	.10	.08	.04
50	Enos Slaughter	.20	.15	.08
51	Warren Spahn	.35	.25	.14
52	Rusty Staub	.05	.04	.02
53	Frank Torre	.05	.04	.02
54	Bob Horner	.05	.04	.02
55	Lee May	.05	.04	.02
56	Bill White	.10	.08	.04
57	Hoyt Wilhelm	.20	.15	.08
58	Billy Williams	.20	.15	.08
59	Ted Williams	.50	.40	.20
60	Tom Seaver	.35	.25	.14
61	Carl Yaztrzemski	.50	.40	.20
62	Marv Throneberry	.10	.08	.04
63	Steve Stone	.05	.04	.02
64	Rico Petrocelli	.05	.04	.02
65	Orlando Cepeda	.10	.08	.04
66	Eddie Mathews	.25	.20	.10
67	Joe Sewell	.10	.08	.04
68	Jim "Catfish" Hunter	.15	.11	.06
69	Alvin Dark	.05	.04	.02
70	Richie Ashburn	.10	.08	.04
71	Dusty Baker	.05	.04	.02
72	George Foster	.05	.04	.02
73	Eddie Yost	.05	.04	.02
74	Buddy Bell	.05	.04	.02
75	Manny Sanguillen	.05	.04	.02
76	Jim Bunning	.10	.08	.04
77	Smokey Burgess	.10	.08	.04
78	Al Rosen	.10	.08	.04
79	Gene Conley	.05	.04	.02
80	Dave Dravecky	.05	.04	.02
81	Charlie Gehringer	.15	.11	.06
82	Billy Pierce	.05	.04	.02
83	Willie Horton	.05	.04	.02
84	Ron Hunt	.05	.04	.02
85	Bob Feller	.20	.15	.08
86	George Kell	.10	.08	.04
87	Dave Kingman	.10	.08	.04
88	Jerry Koosman	.05	.04	.02
89	Clem Labine	.05	.04	.02
90	Tony LaRussa	.05	.04	.02
91	Dennis Leonard	.05	.04	.02
92	Dale Long	.05	.04	.02
93	Sparky Lyle	.05	.04	.02
94	Gil McDougald	.05	.04	.02
95	Don Mossi	.05	.04	.02
96	Phil Niekro	.15	.11	.06
97	Tom Paciorek	.05	.04	.02
98	Mel Parnell	.05	.04	.02
99	Lou Pinella	.05	.04	.02
100	Bobby Richardson	.10	.08	.04
101	Phil Rizzuto	.20	.15	.08
102	Brooks Robinson	.20	.15	.08
103	Pete Runnels	.05	.04	.02
104	Diego Segui	.05	.04	.02
105	Bobby Shantz	.05	.04	.02
106	Bobby Thomson	.10	.08	.04
107	Joe Torre	.10	.08	.04
108	Earl Weaver	.05	.04	.02
109	Willie Wilson	.05	.04	.02
110	Jesse Barfield	.05	.04	.02

1963 Pepsi-Cola Colt .45'S

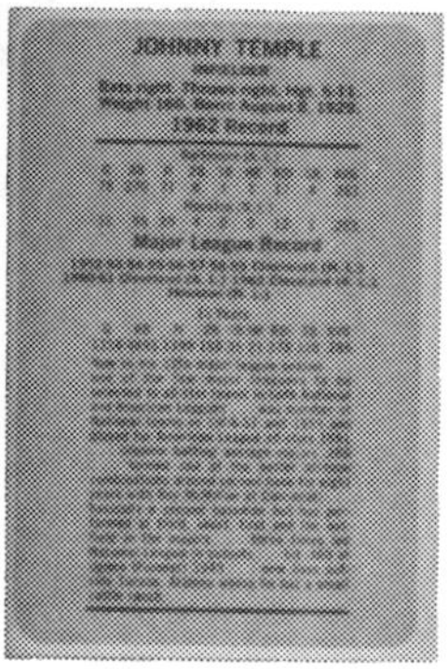

This 16-card set was distributed regionally in Texas in bottled six-packs of Pepsi. The cards were issued on panels 2-3/8" by 9-1/8", which were fit in between the bottles in each carton. Values quoted in the checklist below are for complete panels. A standard 2-3/8" by 3-3/4" card was printed on each panel, which also included promos for Pepsi and the Colt .45's, as well as a team schedule. Card fronts were black and white posed action photos with blue and red trim. Player name and position and Pepsi logo are also included. Card backs offer player statistics and career highlights. The John Bateman card, which was apparently never distributed publicly, is among the rarest collectible baseball cards of the 1960s. The complete set price does not include the Bateman card.

		NR MT	EX	VG
Complete Set:		210.00	105.00	63.00
Common Player:		7.00	3.50	2.00
1	Bob Aspromonte	7.00	3.50	2.00
2	John Bateman	500.00	250.00	150.00
3	Bob Bruce	7.00	3.50	2.00
4	Jim Campbell	7.00	3.50	2.00
5	Dick Farrell	7.00	3.50	2.00
6	Ernie Fazio	7.00	3.50	2.00
7	Carroll Hardy	7.00	3.50	2.00
8	J.C. Hartman	7.00	3.50	2.00
9	Ken Johnson	7.00	3.50	2.00
10	Bob Lillis	7.00	3.50	2.00
11	Don McMahon	7.00	3.50	2.00
12	Pete Runnels	15.00	7.50	4.50
13	Al Spangler	7.00	3.50	2.00
14	Rusty Staub	30.00	15.00	9.00
15	Johnny Temple	7.00	3.50	2.00
16	Carl Warwick	60.00	30.00	18.00

1988 Pepsi-Cola/Kroger Tigers

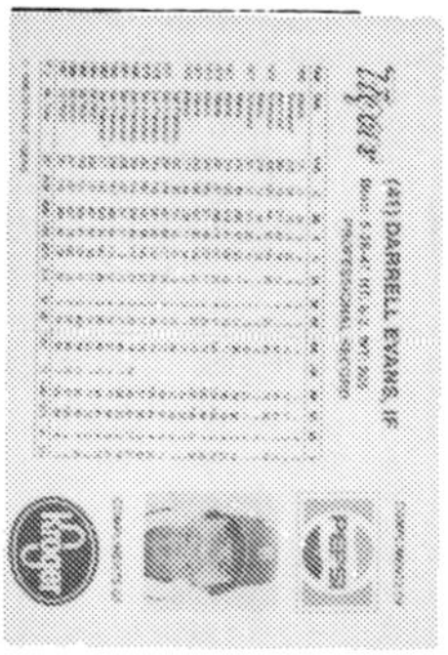

Approximately 38,000 sets of cards were given to fans at Tiger Stadium on July 30th, 1988. The set, sponsored by Pepsi-Cola and Kroger, includes 25 oversized (2-7/8" by 4-1/4") cards printed on glossy white stock with blue and orange borders. The card backs include small black and white close-up photos, the players' professional records and sponsor logos. The numbers in the following checklist refer to the players' uniform.

		MT	NR MT	EX
Complete Set:		8.00	6.00	3.25
Common Player:		.20	.15	.08
1	Lou Whitaker	.70	.50	.30
2	Alan Trammell	.90	.70	.35
8	Mike Heath	.20	.15	.08
11	Sparky Anderson	.40	.30	.15
12	Luis Salazar	.20	.15	.08
14	Dave Bergman	.20	.15	.08
15	Pat Sheridan	.20	.15	.08
16	Tom Brookens	.20	.15	.08
19	Doyle Alexander	.25	.20	.10
21	Guillermo Hernandez	.25	.20	.10
22	Ray Knight	.25	.20	.10
24	Gary Pettis	.20	.15	.08
25	Eric King	.30	.25	.12
26	Frank Tanana	.30	.25	.12
31	Larry Herndon	.20	.15	.08
32	Jim Walewander	.25	.20	.10
33	Matt Nokes	.90	.70	.35
34	Chet Lemon	.25	.20	.10
35	Walt Terrell	.25	.20	.10
39	Mike Henneman	.40	.30	.15
41	Darrell Evans	.40	.30	.15
44	Jeff Robinson	.50	.40	.20
47	Jack Morris	.70	.50	.30
48	Paul Gibson	.30	.25	.12
---	Coaches (Billy Consolo, Alex Grammas, Billy Muffett, Vada Pinson, Dick Tracewski)	.20	.15	.08

1990 Pepsi-Cola Red Sox

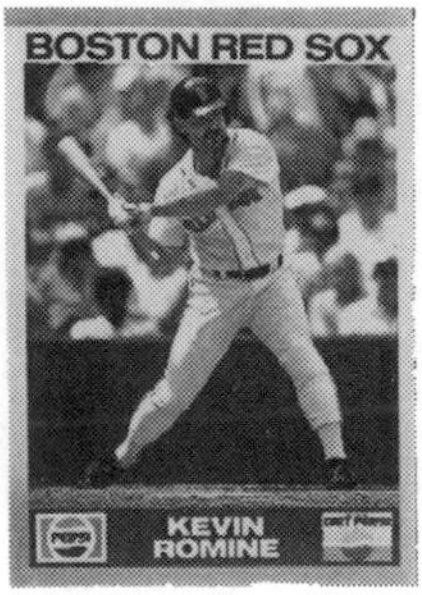

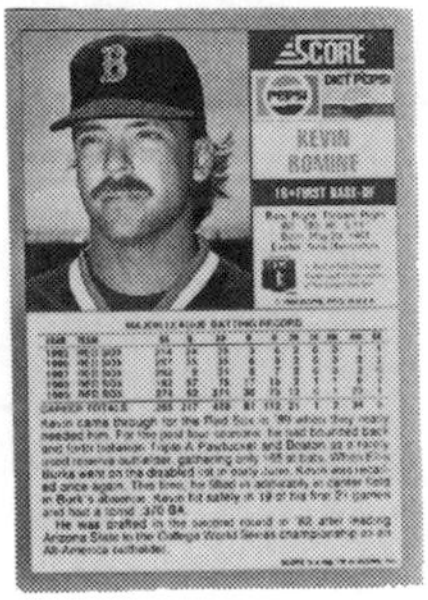

Pepsi combined with Score to produce this special 20-card Boston Red Sox team set. Cards were inserted regionally in 12-packs of Pepsi and Diet Pepsi. The card fronts feature full-color action photos with the team name across the top border and the player's name along the bottom border. The Pepsi and Diet Pepsi logos also appear on the bottom border. The card backs represent standard Score card backs, but are not numbered and also once again feature the Pepsi and Diet Pepsi logos.

		MT	NR MT	EX
Complete Set:		10.00	7.50	4.00
Common Player:		.25	.20	.10
(1)	Marty Barrett	.25	.20	.10
(2)	Mike Boddicker	.35	.25	.14
(3)	Wade Boggs	.80	.60	.30
(4)	Bill Buckner	.25	.20	.10
(5)	Ellis Burks	.80	.60	.30
(6)	Roger Clemens	1.50	1.25	.60
(7)	John Dopson	.25	.20	.10
(8)	Dwight Evans	.50	.40	.20
(9)	Wes Gardner	.25	.20	.10
(10)	Rich Gedman	.25	.20	.10
(11)	Mike Greenwell	.50	.40	.20
(12)	Dennis Lamp	.25	.20	.10
(13)	Rob Murphy	.25	.20	.10
(14)	Tony Pena	.50	.40	.20
(15)	Carlos Quintana	.50	.40	.20
(16)	Jeff Reardon	.40	.30	.15
(17)	Jody Reed	.50	.40	.20
(18)	Luis Rivera	.25	.20	.10
(19)	Kevin Romine	.25	.20	.10
(20)	Lee Smith	.40	.30	.15

1991 Pepsi-Cola Red Sox

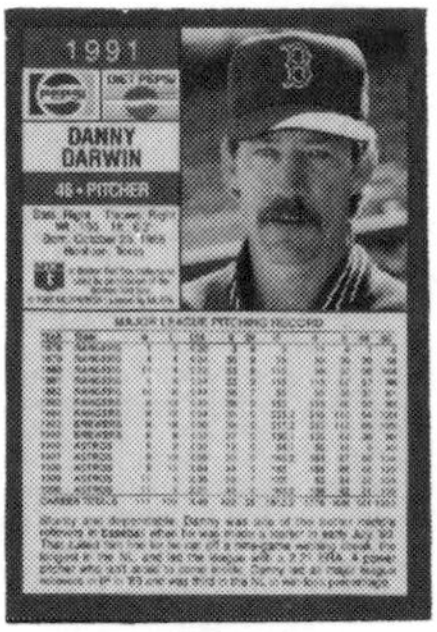

For the second consecutive year, Pepsi/Diet Pepsi sponsored Boston Red Sox trading cards. The cards were inserted in specially marked packs of Pepsi and Diet Pepsi and were made available from July 1 through August 10. A consumer sweepstakes was also included with this promotion. Player jersey numbers are featured on the backs of the cards. Danny Darwin's jersey is incorrectly listed as #46. He actually wears #44 for the BoSox. Wade Boggs is not featured on a 1991 Pepsi-Cola Red Sox card.

		MT	NR MT	EX
Complete Set:		8.00	6.00	3.25
Common Player:		.25	.20	.10
2	Luis Rivera	.25	.20	.10
3	Jody Reed	.40	.30	.15
6	Tony Pena	.40	.30	.15
11	Tim Naehring	.50	.40	.20
12	Ellis Burks	.50	.40	.20
15	Dennis Lamp	.25	.20	.10
18	Carlos Quintana	.30	.25	.12
19	Dana Kiecker	.30	.25	.12
20	John Marzano	.25	.20	.10
21	Roger Clemens	1.00	.70	.40
23	Tom Brunansky	.30	.25	.12
25	Jack Clark	.40	.30	.15
27	Greg Harris	.25	.20	.10
29	Phil Plantier	1.25	.90	.50
30	Matt Young	.25	.20	.10
38	Jeff Gray	.30	.25	.12
39	Mike Greenwell	.50	.40	.20
41	Jeff Reardon	.40	.30	.15
46	Danny Darwin	.25	.20	.10
50	Tom Bolton	.25	.20	.10

1985 Performance Printing Rangers

A local printing company sponsored this 28-card set of the Texas Rangers. The 2-3/8" by 3-1/2" cards are in full color and are numbered on the back by uniform number. Card fronts feature full-color, game-action photos. The 25 players on the Rangers' active roster at press time are included, along with manager Bobby Valentine and unnumbered coaches and trainer cards. The black and white card backs

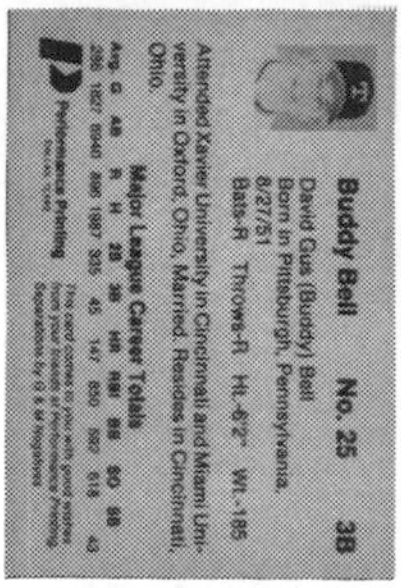

have a smaller portrait photo of each player, as well as biographical information and career statistics.

		MT	NR MT	EX
Complete Set:		5.00	3.75	2.00
Common Player:		.12	.09	.05
0	Oddibe McDowell	.30	.25	.12
1	Bill Stein	.12	.09	.05
2	Bobby Valentine	.15	.11	.06
3	Wayne Tolleson	.12	.09	.05
4	Don Slaught	.12	.09	.05
5	Alan Bannister	.12	.09	.05
6	Bobby Jones	.12	.09	.05
7	Glenn Brummer	.12	.09	.05
8	Luis Pujols	.12	.09	.05
9	Pete O'Brien	.30	.25	.12
11	Toby Harrah	.20	.15	.08
13	Tommy Dunbar	.12	.09	.05
15	Larry Parrish	.30	.25	.12
16	Mike Mason	.12	.09	.05
19	Curtis Wilkerson	.12	.09	.05
24	Dave Schmidt	.15	.11	.06
25	Buddy Bell	.30	.25	.12
27	Greg Harris	.15	.11	.06
30	Dave Rozema	.12	.09	.05
32	Gary Ward	.20	.15	.08
36	Dickie Noles	.12	.09	.05
41	Chris Welsh	.12	.09	.05
44	Cliff Johnson	.12	.09	.05
46	Burt Hooton	.20	.15	.08
48	Dave Stewart	.50	.40	.20
49	Charlie Hough	.30	.25	.12
----	Trainers (Danny Wheat, Bill Ziegler)	.12	.09	.05
----	Rangers Coaches (Rich Donnelly, Glenn Ezell, Tom House, Art Howe, Wayne Terwilliger)	.12	.09	.05

1986 Performance Printing Rangers

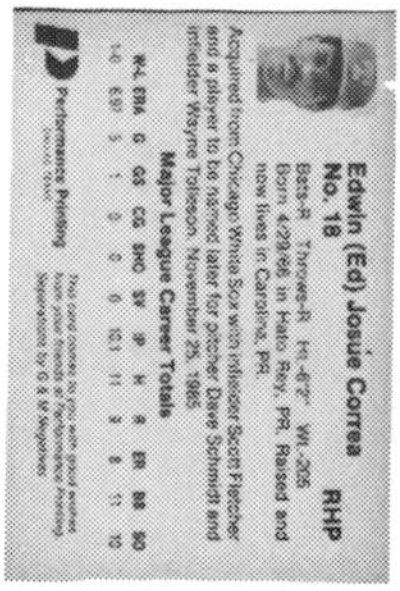

For the second time, the Texas Rangers issued a full-color card set in conjunction with this local printing company. Fronts of the 28-card set include player name, position and team logo beneath the color photo. Backs of the 2-3/8" by 3-1/2" cards in black and white, with a small portrait photo of each player along with personal and professional statistics. Cards were distributed at the August 23 Rangers home game, and the set includes all of the Rangers' fine rookies such as Bobby Witt, Pete Incaviglia, Edwin Correa and Ruben Sierra.

		MT	NR MT	EX
Complete Set:		10.00	7.50	4.00
Common Player:		.10	.08	.04
0	Oddibe McDowell	.20	.15	.08
1	Scott Fletcher	.20	.15	.08
2	Bobby Valentine	.15	.11	.06
3	Ruben Sierra	6.00	4.50	2.50
4	Don Slaught	.10	.08	.04
9	Pete O'Brien	.25	.20	.10
11	Toby Harrah	.20	.15	.08
12	Geno Petralli	.10	.08	.04
15	Larry Parrish	.25	.20	.10
16	Mike Mason	.10	.08	.04
17	Darrell Porter	.15	.11	.06
18	Edwin Correa	.25	.20	.10
19	Curtis Wilkerson	.10	.08	.04
22	Steve Buechele	.30	.25	.12
23	Jose Guzman	.25	.20	.10
24	Ricky Wright	.10	.08	.04
27	Greg Harris	.15	.11	.06
28	Mitch Williams	.30	.25	.12
29	Pete Incaviglia	.60	.45	.25
32	Gary Ward	.15	.11	.06
34	Dale Mohorcic	.30	.25	.12
40	Jeff Russell	.10	.08	.04
44	Tom Paciorek	.10	.08	.04
46	Mike Loynd	.30	.25	.12
48	Bobby Witt	.60	.45	.25
49	Charlie Hough	.25	.20	.10
----	Coaching Staff (Joe Ferguson, Tim Foli, Tom House, Art Howe, Tom Robson)	.10	.08	.04
----	Trainers (Danny Wheat, Bill Zeigler)	.10	.08	.04

1961 Peters Meats Twins

This set, featuring the first-year 1961 Minnesota Twins, is in a large, 4-5/8" by 3-1/2", format. Cards are on thick cardboard and heavily waxed, as they were used as partial packaging for the company's meat products. Card fronts feature full-color photos, team and Peters logos, and biographical information. The cards are blank-backed.

		NR MT	EX	VG
Complete Set:		650.00	325.00	195.00
Common Player:		15.00	7.50	4.50
1	Zoilo Versalles	20.00	10.00	6.00
2	Eddie Lopat	20.00	10.00	6.00
3	Pedro Ramos	15.00	7.50	4.50
4	Charles "Chuck" Stobbs	15.00	7.50	4.50
5	Don Mincher	20.00	10.00	6.00
6	Jack Kralick	15.00	7.50	4.50
7	Jim Kaat	50.00	25.00	15.00
8	Hal Naragon	15.00	7.50	4.50
9	Don Lee	15.00	7.50	4.50
10	Harry "Cookie" Lavagetto	15.00	7.50	4.50
11	Tom "Pete" Whisenant	15.00	7.50	4.50

		NR MT	EX	VG
12	Elmer Valo	15.00	7.50	4.50
13	Ray Moore	15.00	7.50	4.50
14	Billy Gardner	15.00	7.50	4.50
15	Lenny Green	15.00	7.50	4.50
16	Sam Mele	15.00	7.50	4.50
17	Jim Lemon	15.00	7.50	4.50
18	Harmon "Killer" Killebrew	150.00	75.00	45.00
19	Paul Giel	15.00	7.50	4.50
20	Reno Bertoia	15.00	7.50	4.50
21	Clyde McCullough	15.00	7.50	4.50
22	Earl Battey	20.00	10.00	6.00
23	Camilo Pascual	20.00	10.00	6.00
24	Dan Dobbek	15.00	7.50	4.50
25	Joe "Valvy" Valdivielso	15.00	7.50	4.50
26	Billy Consolo	15.00	7.50	4.50

1960 Post Cereal

These cards were issued on the backs of Grape Nuts cereal and measure an oversized 7" by 8-3/4". The nine cards in the set include five baseball players (Al Kaline, Mickey Mantle, Don Drysdale, Harmon Killebrew and Ed Mathews) as well as two football and two basketball players. The full-color photos were placed on a color background and bordered by a wood frame design. The cards covered the entire back of the cereal box and were blank backed. Card fronts also include the player's name and team and a facsimile autograph. A panel on the side of the box contains player biographical information. A scarce set, the cards are very difficult to obtain in mint condition.

		NR MT	EX	VG
Complete Set:		4500.00	2250.00	1350.
Common Player:		350.00	175.00	105.00
(1)	Bob Cousy	350.00	175.00	105.00
(2)	Don Drysdale	400.00	200.00	120.00
(3)	Frank Gifford	400.00	200.00	120.00
(4)	Al Kaline	450.00	225.00	135.00
(5)	Harmon Killebrew	400.00	200.00	120.00
(6)	Ed Mathews	400.00	200.00	120.00
(7)	Mickey Mantle	1500.00	750.00	450.00
(8)	Bob Pettit	350.00	175.00	105.00
(9)	John Unitas	350.00	175.00	105.00

1961 Post Cereal

Two hundred different players are included in this set, but with variations the number of different cards exceeds 350. This was the first large-scale card set by the cereal company and it proved very popular with fans. Cards were issued both singly and in various panel sizes on the thick cardboard stock of cereal boxes, as well on thinner stock, in team sheets issued directly by Post via a mail-in offer. About 10 cards in the set were issued in significantly smaller quantities, making their prices much higher than other comparable players in the set. Individual cards measure a 3-1/2" by 2-1/2", and all cards are numbered in the upper left corner. Card fronts have

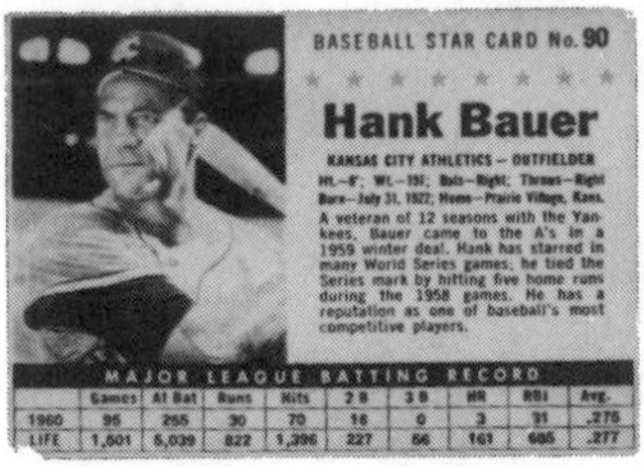

full-color portait photos of the player, along with biographical information and 1960 and career statistics. Card backs are blank. The complete set price includes does not include the scarcer variations.

		NR MT	EX	VG
Complete Set:		1750.00	875.00	525.00
Common Player:		2.00	1.00	.60
1a	Yogi Berra (box)	25.00	12.50	7.50
1b	Yogi Berra (company)	15.00	7.50	4.50
2a	Elston Howard (box)	5.00	2.50	1.50
2b	Elston Howard (company)	3.00	1.50	.90
3a	Bill Skowron (box)	2.50	1.25	.70
3b	Bill Skowron (company)	2.50	1.25	.70
4a	Mickey Mantle (box)	100.00	50.00	30.00
4b	Mickey Mantle (company)	100.00	50.00	30.00
5	Bob Turley (company)	25.00	12.50	7.50
6a	Whitey Ford (box)	8.00	4.00	2.50
6b	Whitey Ford (company)	8.00	4.00	2.50
7a	Roger Maris (box)	25.00	12.50	7.50
7b	Roger Maris (company)	25.00	12.50	7.50
8a	Bobby Richardson (box)	3.00	1.50	.90
8b	Bobby Richardson (company)	3.00	1.50	.90
9a	Tony Kubek (box)	3.00	1.50	.90
9b	Tony Kubek (company)	3.00	1.50	.90
10	Gil McDougald (box)	35.00	17.50	10.50
11	Cletis Boyer (box)	2.00	1.00	.60
12a	Hector Lopez (box)	2.00	1.00	.60
12b	Hector Lopez (company)	2.00	1.00	.60
13	Bob Cerv (box)	2.00	1.00	.60
14	Ryne Duren (box)	2.00	1.00	.60
15	Bobby Shantz (box)	2.00	1.00	.60
16	Art Ditmar (box)	2.00	1.00	.60
17	Jim Coates (box)	2.00	1.00	.60
18	John Blanchard (box)	2.00	1.00	.60
19a	Luis Aparicio (box)	5.00	2.50	1.50
19b	Luis Aparicio (company)	5.00	2.50	1.50
20a	Nelson Fox (box)	4.00	2.00	1.25
20b	Nelson Fox (company)	4.00	2.00	1.25
21a	Bill Pierce (box)	6.00	3.00	1.75
21b	Bill Pierce (company)	3.50	1.75	1.00
22a	Early Wynn (box)	7.00	3.50	2.00
22b	Early Wynn (company)	25.00	12.50	7.50
23	Bob Shaw (box)	100.00	50.00	30.00
24a	Al Smith (box)	3.00	1.50	.90
24b	Al Smith (company)	2.00	1.00	.60
25a	Minnie Minoso (box)	2.50	1.25	.70
25b	Minnie Minoso (company)	2.50	1.25	.70
26a	Roy Sievers (box)	2.25	1.25	.70
26b	Roy Sievers (company)	2.25	1.25	.70
27a	Jim Landis (box)	2.00	1.00	.60
27b	Jim Landis (company)	2.00	1.00	.60
28a	Sherman Lollar (box)	3.00	1.50	.90
28b	Sherman Lollar (company)	2.00	1.00	.60
29	Gerry Staley (box)	2.00	1.00	.60
30a	Gene Freese (box, White Sox)	2.00	1.00	.60
30b	Gene Freese (company, Reds)	6.00	3.00	1.75
31	Ted Kluszewski (box)	3.00	1.50	.90
32	Turk Lown (box)	2.00	1.00	.60
33a	Jim Rivera (box)	2.00	1.00	.60
33b	Jim Rivera (company)	2.00	1.00	.60
34	Frank Baumann (box)	2.00	1.00	.60
35a	Al Kaline (box)	25.00	12.50	7.50
35b	Al Kaline (company)	25.00	12.50	7.50
36a	Rocky Colavito (box)	6.00	3.00	1.75
36b	Rocky Colavito (company)	3.50	1.75	1.00
37a	Charley Maxwell (box)	4.00	2.00	1.25
37b	Charley Maxwell (company)	2.00	1.00	.60
38a	Frank Lary (box)	2.00	1.00	.60
38b	Frank Lary (company)	2.00	1.00	.60

		NR MT	EX	VG
39a	Jim Bunning (box)	4.00	2.00	1.25
39b	Jim Bunning (company)	4.00	2.00	1.25
40a	Norm Cash (box)	2.00	1.00	.60
40b	Norm Cash (company)	2.00	1.00	.60
41a	Frank Bolling (box, Tigers)	8.00	4.00	2.50
41b	Frank Bolling (company, Braves)	5.00	2.50	1.50
42a	Don Mossi (box)	2.00	1.00	.60
42b	Don Mossi (company)	2.00	1.00	.60
43a	Lou Berberet (box)	2.00	1.00	.60
43b	Lou Berberet (company)	2.00	1.00	.60
44	Dave Sisler (box)	2.00	1.00	.60
45	Ed Yost (box)	2.00	1.00	.60
46	Pete Burnside (box)	2.00	1.00	.60
47a	Pete Runnels (box)	3.00	1.50	.90
47b	Pete Runnnels (company)	2.25	1.25	.70
48a	Frank Malzone (box)	2.00	1.00	.60
48b	Frank Malzone (company)	2.00	1.00	.60
49a	Vic Wertz (box)	5.00	2.50	1.50
49b	Vic Wertz (company)	3.00	1.50	.90
50a	Tom Brewer (box)	2.50	1.25	.70
50b	Tom Brewer (company)	2.00	1.00	.60
51a	Willie Tasby (box, no sold line)	8.00	4.00	2.50
51b	Willie Tasby (company, sold line)	2.00	1.00	.60
52a	Russ Nixon (box)	2.00	1.00	.60
52b	Russ Nixon (company)	2.00	1.00	.60
53a	Don Buddin (box)	2.00	1.00	.60
53b	Don Buddin (company)	2.00	1.00	.60
54a	Bill Monbouquette (box)	2.00	1.00	.60
54b	Bill Monbouquette (company)	2.00	1.00	.60
55a	Frank Sullivan (box, Red Sox)	2.00	1.00	.60
55b	Frank Sullivan (company, Phillies)	25.00	12.50	7.50
56a	Haywood Sullivan (box)	2.00	1.00	.60
56b	Haywood Sullivan (company)	2.00	1.00	.60
57a	Harvey Kuenn (box, Indians)	3.00	1.50	.90
57b	Harvey Kuenn (company, Giants)	6.00	3.00	1.75
58a	Gary Bell (box)	5.00	2.50	1.50
58b	Gary Bell (company)	2.25	1.25	.70
59a	Jim Perry (box)	2.25	1.25	.70
59b	Jim Perry (company)	2.25	1.25	.70
60a	Jim Grant (box)	3.00	1.50	.90
60b	Jim Grant (company)	2.25	1.25	.70
61a	Johnny Temple (box)	2.00	1.00	.60
61b	Johnny Temple (company)	2.00	1.00	.60
62a	Paul Foytack (box)	2.00	1.00	.60
62b	Paul Foytack (company)	2.00	1.00	.60
63a	Vic Power (box)	2.00	1.00	.60
63b	Vic Power (company)	2.00	1.00	.60
64a	Tito Francona (box)	2.00	1.00	.60
64b	Tito Francona (company)	2.00	1.00	.60
65a	Ken Aspromonte (box, no sold line)	6.00	3.00	1.75
65b	Ken Aspromonte (company, sold line)	6.00	3.00	1.75
66	Bob Wilson (box)	2.00	1.00	.60
67a	John Romano (box)	2.00	1.00	.60
67b	John Romano (company)	2.00	1.00	.60
68a	Jim Gentile (box)	2.50	1.25	.70
68b	Jim Gentile (company)	2.00	1.00	.60
69a	Gus Triandos (box)	3.00	1.50	.90
69b	Gus Triandos (company)	2.00	1.00	.60
70	Gene Woodling (box)	15.00	7.50	4.50
71a	Milt Pappas (box)	3.00	1.50	.90
71b	Milt Pappas (company)	2.00	1.00	.60
72a	Ron Hansen (box)	3.00	1.50	.90
72b	Ron Hansen (company)	2.00	1.00	.60
73	Chuck Estrada (company)	100.00	50.00	30.00
74a	Steve Barber (box)	2.00	1.00	.60
74b	Steve Barber (company)	2.00	1.00	.60
75a	Brooks Robinson (box)	25.00	12.50	7.50
75b	Brooks Robinson (company)	25.00	12.50	7.50
76a	Jackie Brandt (box)	2.00	1.00	.60
76b	Jackie Brandt (company)	2.00	1.00	.60
77a	Marv Breeding (box)	2.00	1.00	.60
77b	Marv Breedding (company)	2.00	1.00	.60
78	Hal Brown (box)	2.00	1.00	.60
79	Billy Klaus (box)	2.00	1.00	.60
80a	Hoyt Wilhelm (box)	5.00	2.50	1.50
80b	Hoyt Wilhelm (company)	6.00	3.00	1.75
81a	Jerry Lumpe (box)	6.00	3.00	1.75
81b	Jerry Lumpe (company)	4.00	2.00	1.25
82a	Norm Siebern (box)	2.00	1.00	.60
82b	Norm Siebern (company)	2.00	1.00	.60
83a	Bud Daley (box)	2.25	1.25	.70
83b	Bud Daley (company)	2.50	1.25	.70
84a	Bill Tuttle (box)	2.00	1.00	.60
84b	Bill Tuttle (company)	2.00	1.00	.60
85a	Marv Throneberry (box)	2.50	1.25	.70
85b	Marv Throneberry (company)	2.50	1.25	.70
86a	Dick Williams (box)	2.25	1.25	.70
86b	Dick Williams (company)	2.00	1.00	.60

		NR MT	EX	VG
87a	Ray Herbert (box)	2.00	1.00	.60
87b	Ray Herbert (company)	2.00	1.00	.60
88a	Whitey Herzog (box)	2.00	1.00	.60
88b	Whitey Herzog (company)	2.00	1.00	.60
89a	Ken Hamlin (box, no sold line)	2.00	1.00	.60
89b	Ken Hamlin (company, sold line)	8.00	4.00	2.50
90a	Hank Bauer (box)	2.00	1.00	.60
90b	Hank Bauer (company)	2.00	1.00	.60
91a	Bob Allison (box, Minneapolis)	4.00	2.00	1.25
91b	Bob Allison (company, Minnesota)	5.00	2.50	1.50
92a	Harmon Killebrew (box, Minneapolis)	25.00	12.50	7.50
92b	Harmon Killebrew (company, Minnesota)	25.00	12.50	7.50
93a	Jim Lemon (box, Minneapolis)	50.00	25.00	15.00
93b	Jim Lemon (company, Minnesota)	5.00	2.50	1.50
94	Chuck Stobbs (company)	150.00	75.00	45.00
95a	Reno Bertoia (box, Minneapolis)	2.00	1.00	.60
95b	Reno Bertoia (company, Minnesota)	4.00	2.00	1.25
96a	Billy Gardner (box, Minneapolis)	2.00	1.00	.60
96b	Billy Gardner (company, Minnesota)	4.00	2.00	1.25
97a	Earl Battey (box, Minneapolis)	4.00	2.00	1.25
97b	Earl Battey (company, Minnesota)	4.00	2.00	1.25
98a	Pedro Ramos (box, Minneapolis)	2.00	1.00	.60
98b	Pedro Ramos (company, Minnesota)	4.00	2.00	1.25
99a	Camilio Pascual (Camilo) (box, Minneapolis)	2.00	1.00	.60
99b	Camilio Pascual (Camilo) (company, Minnesota)	4.00	2.00	1.25
100a	Billy Consolo (box, Minneapolis)	2.00	1.00	.60
100b	Billy Consolo (company, Minnesota)	4.00	2.00	1.25
101a	Warren Spahn (box)	15.00	7.50	4.50
101b	Warren Spahn (company)	8.00	4.00	2.50
102a	Lew Burdette (box)	2.50	1.25	.70
102b	Lew Burdette (company)	2.50	1.25	.70
103a	Bob Buhl (box)	2.00	1.00	.60
103b	Bob Buhl (company)	2.00	1.00	.60
104a	Joe Adcock (box)	4.00	2.00	1.25
104b	Joe Adcock (company)	2.50	1.25	.70
105a	John Logan (box)	4.00	2.00	1.25
105b	John Logan (company)	2.25	1.25	.70
106	Ed Mathews (company)	35.00	17.50	10.50
107a	Hank Aaron (box)	25.00	12.50	7.50
107b	Hank Aaron (company)	25.00	12.50	7.50
108a	Wes Covington (box)	2.00	1.00	.60
108b	Wes Covington (company)	2.00	1.00	.60
109a	Bill Bruton (box, Braves)	6.00	3.00	1.75
109b	Bill Bruton (company, Tigers)	8.00	4.00	2.50
110a	Del Crandall (box)	4.00	2.00	1.25
110b	Del Crandall (company)	2.25	1.25	.70
111	Red Schoendienst (box)	5.00	2.50	1.50
112	Juan Pizarro (box)	2.00	1.00	.60
113	Chuck Cottier (box)	8.00	4.00	2.50
114	Al Spangler (box)	2.00	1.00	.60
115a	Dick Farrell (box)	6.00	3.00	1.75
115b	Dick Farrell (company)	4.00	2.00	1.25
116a	Jim Owens (box)	6.00	3.00	1.75
116b	Jim Owens (company)	4.00	2.00	1.25
117a	Robin Roberts (box)	6.00	3.00	1.75
117b	Robin Roberts (company)	6.00	3.00	1.75
118a	Tony Taylor (box)	2.00	1.00	.60
118b	Tony Taylor (company)	2.00	1.00	.60
119a	Lee Walls (box)	2.00	1.00	.60
119b	Lee Walls (company)	2.00	1.00	.60
120a	Tony Curry (box)	2.00	1.00	.60
120b	Tony Curry (company)	2.00	1.00	.60
121a	Pancho Herrera (box)	2.00	1.00	.60
121b	Pancho Herrera (company)	2.00	1.00	.60
122a	Ken Walters (box)	2.00	1.00	.60
122b	Ken Walters (company)	2.00	1.00	.60
123a	John Callison (box)	2.00	1.00	.60
123b	John Callison (company)	2.00	1.00	.60
124a	Gene Conley (box, Phillies)	2.00	1.00	.60
124b	Gene Conley (company, Red Sox)	15.00	7.50	4.50
125a	Bob Friend (box)	4.00	2.00	1.25
125b	Bob Friend (company)	2.00	1.00	.60
126a	Vernon Law (box)	4.00	2.00	1.25
126b	Vernon Law (company)	2.00	1.00	.60
127a	Dick Stuart (box)	2.00	1.00	.60
127b	Dick Stuart (company)	2.00	1.00	.60
128a	Bill Mazeroski (box)	2.50	1.25	.70
128b	Bill Mazeroski (company)	2.50	1.25	.70
129a	Dick Groat (box)	3.00	1.50	.90

		NR MT	EX	VG
129b	Dick Groat (company)	2.00	1.00	.60
130a	Don Hoak (box)	2.00	1.00	.60
130b	Don Hoak (company)	2.00	1.00	.60
131a	Bob Skinner (box)	2.00	1.00	.60
131b	Bob Skinner (company)	2.00	1.00	.60
132a	Bob Clemente (box)	25.00	12.50	7.50
132b	Bob Clemente (company)	25.00	12.50	7.50
133	Roy Face (box)	3.00	1.50	.90
134	Harvey Haddix (box)	2.25	1.25	.70
135	Bill Virdon (box)	35.00	17.50	10.50
136a	Gino Cimoli (box)	2.00	1.00	.60
136b	Gino Cimoli (company)	2.00	1.00	.60
137	Rocky Nelson (box)	2.00	1.00	.60
138a	Smoky Burgess (box)	2.25	1.25	.70
138b	Smoky Burgess (company)	2.25	1.25	.70
139	Hal Smith (box)	2.00	1.00	.60
140	Wilmer Mizell (box)	2.00	1.00	.60
141a	Mike McCormick (box)	2.00	1.00	.60
141b	Mike McCormick (company)	2.00	1.00	.60
142a	John Antonelli (box, Giants)	3.00	1.50	.90
142b	John Antonelli (company, Indians)	4.00	2.00	1.25
143a	Sam Jones (box)	4.00	2.00	1.25
143b	Sam Jones (company)	2.00	1.00	.60
144a	Orlando Cepeda (box)	5.00	2.50	1.50
144b	Orlando Cepeda (company)	5.00	2.50	1.50
145a	Willie Mays (box)	25.00	12.50	7.50
145b	Willie Mays (company)	25.00	12.50	7.50
146a	Willie Kirkland (box, Giants)	5.00	2.50	1.50
146b	Willie Kirkland (company, Indians)	5.00	2.50	1.50
147a	Willie McCovey (box)	7.00	3.50	2.00
147b	Willie McCovey (company)	25.00	12.50	7.50
148a	Don Blasingame (box)	2.00	1.00	.60
148b	Don Blasingame (company)	2.00	1.00	.60
149a	Jim Davenport (box)	2.00	1.00	.60
149b	Jim Davenport (company)	2.00	1.00	.60
150a	Hobie Landrith (box)	2.00	1.00	.60
150b	Hobie Landrith (company)	2.00	1.00	.60
151	Bob Schmidt (box)	2.00	1.00	.60
152a	Ed Bressoud (box)	2.00	1.00	.60
152b	Ed Bressoud (company)	2.00	1.00	.60
153a	Andre Rodgers (box, no traded line)	6.00	3.00	1.75
153b	Andre Rodgers (box, traded line)	2.00	1.00	.60
154	Jack Sanford (box)	2.00	1.00	.60
155	Billy O'Dell (box)	2.00	1.00	.60
156a	Norm Larker (box)	2.50	1.25	.70
156b	Norm Larker (company)	2.50	1.25	.70
157a	Charlie Neal (box)	2.00	1.00	.60
157b	Charlie Neal (company)	2.00	1.00	.60
158a	Jim Gilliam (box)	4.00	2.00	1.25
158b	Jim Gilliam (company)	2.50	1.25	.70
159a	Wally Moon (box)	2.00	1.00	.60
159b	Wally Moon (company)	2.00	1.00	.60
160a	Don Drysdale (box)	7.00	3.50	2.00
160b	Don Drysdale (company)	8.00	4.00	2.50
161a	Larry Sherry (box)	2.00	1.00	.60
161b	Larry Sherry (company)	2.00	1.00	.60
162	Stan Williams (box)	5.00	2.50	1.50
163	Mel Roach (box)	50.00	25.00	15.00
164a	Maury Wills (box)	4.00	2.00	1.25
164b	Maury Wills (company)	4.00	2.00	1.25
165	Tom Davis (box)	2.00	1.00	.60
166a	John Roseboro (box)	2.00	1.00	.60
166b	John Roseboro (company)	2.00	1.00	.60
167a	Duke Snider (box)	8.00	4.00	2.50
167b	Duke Snider (company)	25.00	12.50	7.50
168a	Gil Hodges (box)	5.00	2.50	1.50
168b	Gil Hodges (company)	6.00	3.00	1.75
169	John Podres (box)	2.50	1.25	.70
170	Ed Roebuck (box)	2.00	1.00	.60
171a	Ken Boyer (box)	6.00	3.00	1.75
171b	Ken Boyer (company)	4.00	2.00	1.25
172a	Joe Cunningham (box)	2.00	1.00	.60
172b	Joe Cunningham (company)	2.00	1.00	.60
173a	Daryl Spencer (box)	2.00	1.00	.60
173b	Daryl Spencer (company)	2.00	1.00	.60
174a	Larry Jackson (box)	2.00	1.00	.60
174b	Larry Jackson (company)	2.00	1.00	.60
175a	Lindy McDaniel (box)	2.00	1.00	.60
175b	Lindy McDaniel (company)	2.00	1.00	.60
176a	Bill White (box)	2.25	1.25	.70
176b	Bill White (company)	2.25	1.25	.70
177a	Alex Grammas (box)	2.00	1.00	.60
177b	Alex Grammas (company)	2.00	1.00	.60
178a	Curt Flood (box)	2.00	1.00	.60
178b	Curt Flood (company)	2.00	1.00	.60
179a	Ernie Broglio (box)	2.00	1.00	.60
179b	Ernie Broglio (company)	2.00	1.00	.60
180a	Hal Smith (box)	2.00	1.00	.60
180b	Hal Smith (company)	2.00	1.00	.60

		NR MT	EX	VG
181a	Vada Pinson (box)	2.50	1.25	.70
181b	Vada Pinson (company)	2.50	1.25	.70
182a	Frank Robinson (box)	25.00	12.50	7.50
182b	Frank Robinson (company)	25.00	12.50	7.50
183	Roy McMillan (box)	70.00	35.00	21.00
184a	Bob Purkey (box)	2.00	1.00	.60
184b	Bob Purkey (company)	2.00	1.00	.60
185a	Ed Kasko (box)	2.00	1.00	.60
185b	Ed Kasko (company)	2.00	1.00	.60
186a	Gus Bell (box)	2.00	1.00	.60
186b	Gus Bell (company)	2.00	1.00	.60
187a	Jerry Lynch (box)	2.00	1.00	.60
187b	Jerry Lynch (company)	2.00	1.00	.60
188a	Ed Bailey (box)	2.00	1.00	.60
188b	Ed Bailey (company)	2.00	1.00	.60
189a	Jim O'Toole (box)	2.00	1.00	.60
189b	Jim O'Toole (company)	2.00	1.00	.60
190a	Billy Martin (box, no sold line)	3.00	1.50	.90
190b	Billy Martin (company, sold line)	9.00	4.50	2.75
191a	Ernie Banks (box)	9.00	4.50	2.75
191b	Ernie Banks (company)	9.00	4.50	2.75
192a	Richie Ashburn (box)	3.00	1.50	.90
192b	Richie Ashburn (company)	3.00	1.50	.90
193a	Frank Thomas (box)	35.00	17.50	10.50
193b	Frank Thomas (company)	5.00	2.50	1.50
194a	Don Cardwell (box)	2.00	1.00	.60
194b	Don Cardwell (company)	2.00	1.00	.60
195a	George Altman (box)	2.00	1.00	.60
195b	George Altman (company)	2.00	1.00	.60
196a	Ron Santo (box)	3.00	1.50	.90
196b	Ron Santo (company)	3.00	1.50	.90
197a	Glen Hobbie (box)	2.00	1.00	.60
197b	Glen Hobbie (company)	2.00	1.00	.60
198a	Sam Taylor (box)	2.00	1.00	.60
198b	Sam Taylor (company)	2.00	1.00	.60
199a	Jerry Kindall (box)	2.00	1.00	.60
199b	Jerry Kindall (company)	2.00	1.00	.60
200a	Don Elston (box)	3.00	1.50	.90
200b	Don Elston (company)	3.00	1.50	.90

1962 Post Cereal

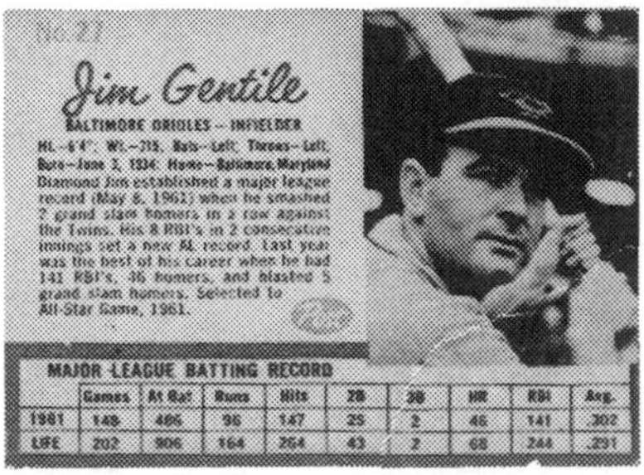

Like the 1961 Post set, there are 200 players pictured in the set of 3-1/2" by 2-1/2" cards. Differences include a Post logo on the card fronts and the player's name in script lettering. Cards are again blank backed and were issued in panels of five to seven cards on cereal boxes. American League players are numbered 1-100 and National League players 101-200. With variations there are 210 of the full-color cards known. A handful of the '62 cards were also issued in smaller quantities. The cards of Mickey Mantle and Roger Maris were reproduced in a special two-card panel for a Life magazine insert. the card stock for this insert is slightly thinner, with white margins. The 1962 Post Canadian and Jell-O sets have virtually the same checklist as this set. The complete set price does not include the scarcer variations.

		NR MT	EX	VG
Complete Set:		1500.00	750.00	450.00
Common Player:		1.50	.70	.45
1	Bill Skowron	4.00	2.00	1.25
2	Bobby Richardson	3.00	1.50	.90

		NR MT	EX	VG
3	Cletis Boyer	2.00	1.00	.60
4	Tony Kubek	3.00	1.50	.90
5a	Mickey Mantle (from box, no printing on back)	80.00	40.00	24.00
5b	Mickey Mantle (from ad, printing on back)	90.00	45.00	27.00
6a	Roger Maris (from box, no printing on back)	15.00	7.50	4.50
6b	Roger Maris (from ad, printing on back)	20.00	10.00	6.00
7	Yogi Berra	15.00	7.50	4.50
8	Elston Howard	3.00	1.50	.90
9	Whitey Ford	7.00	3.50	2.00
10	Ralph Terry	2.00	1.00	.60
11	John Blanchard	2.00	1.00	.60
12	Luis Arroyo	2.00	1.00	.60
13	Bill Stafford	2.00	1.00	.60
14a	Norm Cash (Throws: Right)	2.00	1.00	.60
14b	Norm Cash (Throws: Left)	5.00	2.50	1.50
15	Jake Wood	1.50	.70	.45
16	Steve Boros	1.50	.70	.45
17	Chico Fernandez	1.50	.70	.45
18	Bill Bruton	1.50	.70	.45
19	Rocky Colavito	3.00	1.50	.90
20	Al Kaline	8.00	4.00	2.50
21	Dick Brown	1.50	.70	.45
22	Frank Lary	1.50	.70	.45
23	Don Mossi	1.50	.70	.45
24	Phil Regan	1.50	.70	.45
25	Charley Maxwell	1.50	.70	.45
26	Jim Bunning	3.00	1.50	.90
27a	Jim Gentile (Home: Baltimore)	1.50	.70	.45
27b	Jim Gentile (Home: San Lorenzo)	5.00	2.50	1.50
28	Marv Breeding	1.50	.70	.45
29	Brooks Robinson	8.00	4.00	2.50
30	Ron Hansen	1.50	.70	.45
31	Jackie Brandt	1.50	.70	.45
32	Dick Williams	1.75	.90	.50
33	Gus Triandos	1.50	.70	.45
34	Milt Pappas	1.50	.70	.45
35	Hoyt Wilhelm	4.00	2.00	1.25
36	Chuck Estrada	5.00	2.50	1.50
37	Vic Power	1.50	.70	.45
38	Johnny Temple	1.50	.70	.45
39	Bubba Phillips	1.50	.70	.45
40	Tito Francona	1.50	.70	.45
41	Willie Kirkland	1.50	.70	.45
42	John Romano	1.50	.70	.45
43	Jim Perry	1.75	.90	.50
44	Woodie Held	1.50	.70	.45
45	Chuck Essegian	1.50	.70	.45
46	Roy Sievers	1.75	.90	.50
47	Nellie Fox	3.50	1.75	1.00
48	Al Smith	1.50	.70	.45
49	Luis Aparicio	4.00	2.00	1.25
50	Jim Landis	1.50	.70	.45
51	Minnie Minoso	2.00	1.00	.60
52	Andy Carey	1.50	.70	.45
53	Sherman Lollar	1.50	.70	.45
54	Bill Pierce	1.75	.90	.50
55	Early Wynn	40.00	20.00	12.00
56	Chuck Schilling	1.50	.70	.45
57	Pete Runnels	1.50	.70	.45
58	Frank Malzone	1.50	.70	.45
59	Don Buddin	1.50	.70	.45
60	Gary Geiger	1.50	.70	.45
61	Carl Yastrzemski	45.00	22.00	13.50
62	Jackie Jensen	2.00	1.00	.60
63	Jim Pagliaroni	1.50	.70	.45
64	Don Schwall	1.50	.70	.45
65	Dale Long	1.50	.70	.45
66	Chuck Cottier	1.50	.70	.45
67	Billy Klaus	1.50	.70	.45
68	Coot Veal	1.50	.70	.45
69	Marty Keough	40.00	20.00	12.00
70	Willie Tasby	1.50	.70	.45
71	Gene Woodling	1.50	.70	.45
72	Gene Green	1.50	.70	.45
73	Dick Donovan	1.50	.70	.45
74	Steve Bilko	1.50	.70	.45
75	Rocky Bridges	1.50	.70	.45
76	Eddie Yost	1.50	.70	.45
77	Leon Wagner	1.50	.70	.45
78	Albie Pearson	1.50	.70	.45
79	Ken Hunt	1.50	.70	.45
80	Earl Averill	1.50	.70	.45
81	Ryne Duren	1.50	.70	.45
82	Ted Kluszewski	2.50	1.25	.70
83	Bob Allison	35.00	17.50	10.50
84	Billy Martin	3.50	1.75	1.00
85	Harmon Killebrew	7.00	3.50	2.00
86	Zoilo Versalles	1.50	.70	.45
87	Lenny Green	1.50	.70	.45
88	Bill Tuttle	1.50	.70	.45
89	Jim Lemon	1.50	.70	.45
90	Earl Battey	1.50	.70	.45
91	Camilo Pascual	1.50	.70	.45
92	Norm Siebern	60.00	30.00	18.00
93	Jerry Lumpe	1.50	.70	.45
94	Dick Howser	2.00	1.00	.60
95a	Gene Stephens (Born: Jan. 5)	1.50	.70	.45
95b	Gene Stephens (Born: Jan. 20)	5.00	2.50	1.50
96	Leo Posada	1.50	.70	.45
97	Joe Pignatano	1.50	.70	.45
98	Jim Archer	1.50	.70	.45
99	Haywood Sullivan	1.50	.70	.45
100	Art Ditmar	1.50	.70	.45
101	Gil Hodges	65.00	32.00	19.50
102	Charlie Neal	1.50	.70	.45
103	Daryl Spencer	25.00	12.50	7.50
104	Maury Wills	4.00	2.00	1.25
105	Tommy Davis	2.00	1.00	.60
106	Willie Davis	1.75	.90	.50
107	John Roseboro	1.50	.70	.45
108	John Podres	2.50	1.25	.70
109a	Sandy Koufax (blue lines around stats)	40.00	20.00	12.00
109b	Sandy Koufax (red lines around stats)	25.00	12.50	7.50
110	Don Drysdale	7.00	3.50	2.00
111	Larry Sherry	1.50	.70	.45
112	Jim Gilliam	2.50	1.25	.70
113	Norm Larker	40.00	20.00	12.00
114	Duke Snider	8.00	4.00	2.50
115	Stan Williams	1.50	.70	.45
116	Gordy Coleman	80.00	40.00	24.00
117	Don Blasingame	1.50	.70	.45
118	Gene Freese	1.50	.70	.45
119	Ed Kasko	1.50	.70	.45
120	Gus Bell	1.50	.70	.45
121	Vada Pinson	2.50	1.25	.70
122	Frank Robinson	25.00	12.50	7.50
123	Bob Purkey	1.50	.70	.45
124a	Joey Jay (blue lines around stats)	8.00	4.00	2.50
124b	Joey Jay (red lines around stats)	1.50	.70	.45
125	Jim Brosnan	25.00	12.50	7.50
126	Jim O'Toole	1.50	.70	.45
127	Jerry Lynch	60.00	30.00	18.00
128	Wally Post	1.50	.70	.45
129	Ken Hunt	1.50	.70	.45
130	Jerry Zimmerman	1.50	.70	.45
131	Willie McCovey	80.00	40.00	24.00
132	Jose Pagan	1.50	.70	.45
133	Felipe Alou	1.75	.90	.50
134	Jim Davenport	1.50	.70	.45
135	Harvey Kuenn	2.00	1.00	.60
136	Orlando Cepeda	3.50	1.75	1.00
137	Ed Bailey	1.50	.70	.45
138	Sam Jones	1.50	.70	.45
139	Mike McCormick	1.50	.70	.45
140	Juan Marichal	80.00	40.00	24.00
141	Jack Sanford	1.50	.70	.45
142	Willie Mays	35.00	17.50	10.50
143	Stu Miller (photo actually Chuck Hiller)	6.00	3.00	1.75
144	Joe Amalfitano	15.00	7.50	4.50
145a	Joe Adock (name incorrect)	40.00	20.00	12.00
145b	Joe Adcock (name correct)	2.00	1.00	.60
146	Frank Bolling	1.50	.70	.45
147	Ed Mathews	7.00	3.50	2.00
148	Roy McMillan	1.50	.70	.45
149	Hank Aaron	45.00	22.00	13.50
150	Gino Cimoli	1.50	.70	.45
151	Frank Thomas	1.50	.70	.45
152	Joe Torre	3.00	1.50	.90
153	Lou Burdette	2.50	1.25	.70
154	Bob Buhl	1.50	.70	.45
155	Carlton Willey	1.50	.70	.45
156	Lee Maye	1.50	.70	.45
157	Al Spangler	1.50	.70	.45
158	Bill White	45.00	22.00	13.50
159	Ken Boyer	3.00	1.50	.90
160	Joe Cunningham	1.50	.70	.45
161	Carl Warwick	1.50	.70	.45
162	Carl Sawatski	1.50	.70	.45
163	Lindy McDaniel	1.50	.70	.45
164	Ernie Broglio	1.50	.70	.45
165	Larry Jackson	1.50	.70	.45
166	Curt Flood	2.00	1.00	.60
167	Curt Simmons	1.50	.70	.45
168	Alex Grammas	1.50	.70	.45
169	Dick Stuart	1.50	.70	.45

		NR MT	EX	VG
170	Bill Mazeroski	2.50	1.25	.70
171	Don Hoak	1.50	.70	.45
172	Dick Groat	2.00	1.00	.60
173a	Roberto Clemente (blue lines around stats)	40.00	20.00	12.00
173b	Roberto Clemente (red lines around stats)	25.00	12.50	7.50
174	Bob Skinner	1.50	.70	.45
175	Bill Virdon	1.75	.90	.50
176	Smoky Burgess	1.75	.90	.50
177	Elroy Face	1.75	.90	.50
178	Bob Friend	1.50	.70	.45
179	Vernon Law	1.50	.70	.45
180	Harvey Haddix	1.50	.70	.45
181	Hal Smith	1.50	.70	.45
182	Ed Bouchee	1.50	.70	.45
183	Don Zimmer	1.50	.70	.45
184	Ron Santo	2.50	1.25	.70
185	Andre Rodgers	1.50	.70	.45
186	Richie Ashburn	3.00	1.50	.90
187a	George Altman (last line is "...1955).)	1.50	.70	.45
187b	George Altman (last line is "...1955.")	3.00	1.50	.90
188	Ernie Banks	15.00	7.50	4.50
189	Sam Taylor	1.50	.70	.45
190	Don Elston	1.50	.70	.45
191	Jerry Kindall	1.50	.70	.45
192	Pancho Herrera	1.50	.70	.45
193	Tony Taylor	1.50	.70	.45
194	Ruben Amaro	1.50	.70	.45
195	Don Demeter	1.50	.70	.45
196	Bobby Gene Smith	1.50	.70	.45
197	Clay Dalrymple	1.50	.70	.45
198	Robin Roberts	5.00	2.50	1.50
199	Art Mahaffey	1.50	.70	.45
200	John Buzhardt	2.50	1.25	.70

1962 Post Cereal Canadian

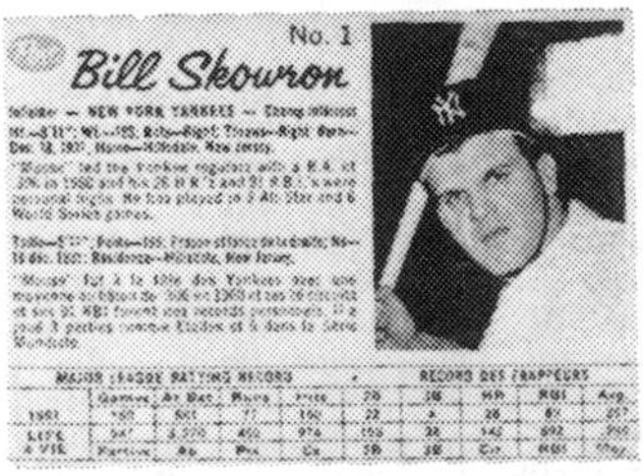

This Canadian set of cards is scarce due to the much more limited distribution in Canada. The cards were printed on the back of the cereal box itself and contains a full-color player photo with biography and statistics given in both French and English. The card backs are blank. Cards measure 3-1/2" by 2-1/2". This 200-card set is very similar to the Post Cereal cards printed in the United States. the Post logo appears at the upper left corner in the Canadian issue. Several cards are scarce because of limited distribution and there are two Whitey Ford cards, the corrected version being the most scarce. The complete set price does not include the scarcer variations.

		NR MT	EX	VG
Complete Set:		2500.00	1250.00	750.00
Common Player:		3.00	1.50	.90
1	Bill Skowron	8.00	4.00	2.50
2	Bobby Richardson	6.00	3.00	1.75
3	Cletis Boyer	3.50	1.75	1.00
4	Tony Kubek	6.00	3.00	1.75
5a	Mickey Mantle (script name large)	200.00	100.00	60.00
5b	Mickey Mantle (script name small)	125.00	62.00	37.00
6	Roger Maris	25.00	12.50	7.50
7	Yogi Berra	25.00	12.50	7.50
8	Elston Howard	4.00	2.00	1.25
9a	Whitey Ford (Dodgers)	30.00	15.00	9.00
9b	Whitey Ford (Yankees)	50.00	25.00	15.00
10	Ralph Terry	35.00	17.50	10.50
11	John Blanchard	3.50	1.75	1.00
12	Luis Arroyo	3.50	1.75	1.00
13	Bill Stafford	3.50	1.75	1.00
14	Norm Cash	4.00	2.00	1.25
15	Jake Wood	3.00	1.50	.90
16	Steve Boros	3.00	1.50	.90
17	Chico Fernandez	3.00	1.50	.90
18	Bill Bruton	3.00	1.50	.90
19a	Rocky Colavito (script name large)	7.00	3.50	2.00
19b	Rocky Colavito (script name small)	7.00	3.50	2.00
20	Al Kaline	25.00	12.50	7.50
21	Dick Brown	7.00	3.50	2.00
22a	Frank Lary (French bio variation)	7.00	3.50	2.00
22b	Frank Lary (French bio variation)	7.00	3.50	2.00
23	Don Mossi	3.00	1.50	.90
24	Phil Regan	3.00	1.50	.90
25	Charley Maxwell	3.00	1.50	.90
26	Jim Bunning	6.00	3.00	1.75
27a	Jim Gentile (French bio variation)	5.00	2.50	1.50
27b	Jim Gentile (French bio variation)	5.00	2.50	1.50
28	Marv Breeding	3.00	1.50	.90
29	Brooks Robinson	35.00	17.50	10.50
30	Ron Hansen	3.00	1.50	.90
31	Jackie Brandt	3.00	1.50	.90
32	Dick Williams	35.00	17.50	10.50
33	Gus Triandos	3.00	1.50	.90
34	Milt Pappas	3.50	1.75	1.00
35	Hoyt Wilhelm	25.00	12.50	7.50
36	Chuck Estrada	3.00	1.50	.90
37	Vic Power	3.00	1.50	.90
38	Johnny Temple	3.00	1.50	.90
39	Bubba Phillips	35.00	17.50	10.50
40	Tito Francona	3.00	1.50	.90
41	Willie Kirkland	7.00	3.50	2.00
42	John Romano	7.00	3.50	2.00
43	Jim Perry	4.00	2.00	1.25
44	Woodie Held	3.00	1.50	.90
45	Chuck Essegian	3.00	1.50	.90
46	Roy Sievers	3.50	1.75	1.00
47	Nellie Fox	6.00	3.00	1.75
48	Al Smith	3.00	1.50	.90
49	Luis Aparicio	25.00	12.50	7.50
50	Jim Landis	3.00	1.50	.90
51	Minnie Minoso	35.00	17.50	10.50
52	Andy Carey	7.00	3.50	2.00
53	Sherman Lollar	3.00	1.50	.90
54	Bill Pierce	3.50	1.75	1.00
55	Early Wynn	20.00	10.00	6.00
56	Chuck Schilling	3.00	1.50	.90
57	Pete Runnels	3.50	1.75	1.00
58	Frank Malzone	3.00	1.50	.90
59	Don Buddin	7.00	3.50	2.00
60	Gary Geiger	3.00	1.50	.90
61	Carl Yastrzemski	50.00	25.00	15.00
62	Jackie Jensen	9.00	4.50	2.75
63	Jim Pagliaroni	3.00	1.50	.90
64	Don Schwall	3.00	1.50	.90
65	Dale Long	3.00	1.50	.90
66	Chuck Cottier	3.00	1.50	.90
67	Billy Klaus	3.00	1.50	.90
68	Coot Veal	3.00	1.50	.90
69	Marty Keough	3.00	1.50	.90
70	Willie Tasby	35.00	17.50	10.50
71	Gene Woodling (photo reversed)	3.50	1.75	1.00
72	Gene Green	3.00	1.50	.90
73	Dick Donovan	3.00	1.50	.90
74	Steve Bilko	3.00	1.50	.90
75	Rocky Bridges	6.00	3.00	1.75
76	Eddie Yost	3.00	1.50	.90
77	Leon Wagner	35.00	17.50	10.50
78	Albie Pearson	7.00	3.50	2.00
79	Ken Hunt	3.00	1.50	.90
80	Earl Averill	3.00	1.50	.90
81	Ryne Duren	4.00	2.00	1.25
82	Ted Kluszewski	4.00	2.00	1.25
83	Bob Allison	3.50	1.75	1.00
84	Billy Martin	6.00	3.00	1.75
85	Harmon Killebrew	20.00	10.00	6.00
86	Zoilo Versalles	3.00	1.50	.90
87	Lenny Green	3.00	1.50	.90
88	Bill Tuttle	3.00	1.50	.90
89	Jim Lemon	3.00	1.50	.90
90	Earl Battey	3.00	1.50	.90

		NR MT	EX	VG
91	Camilo Pascual	3.50	1.75	1.00
92	Norm Siebern	3.00	1.50	.90
93	Jerry Lumpe	3.00	1.50	.90
94	Dick Howser	35.00	17.50	10.50
95	Gene Stephens	3.00	1.50	.90
96	Leo Posada	3.00	1.50	.90
97	Joe Pignatano	3.00	1.50	.90
98	Jim Archer	3.00	1.50	.90
99	Haywood Sullivan	35.00	17.50	10.50
100	Art Ditmar	35.00	17.50	10.50
101	Gil Hodges	20.00	10.00	6.00
102	Charlie Neal	3.00	1.50	.90
103	Daryl Spencer	3.00	1.50	.90
104	Maury Wills	5.00	2.50	1.50
105	Tommy Davis	9.00	4.50	2.75
106	Willie Davis	4.00	2.00	1.25
107	John Roseboro	3.50	1.75	1.00
108	John Podres	4.00	2.00	1.25
109	Sandy Koufax	30.00	15.00	9.00
110	Don Drysdale	25.00	12.50	7.50
111	Larry Sherry	35.00	17.50	10.50
112	Jim Gilliam	35.00	17.50	10.50
113	Norm Larker	3.00	1.50	.90
114	Duke Snider	35.00	17.50	10.50
115	Stan Williams	3.00	1.50	.90
116	Gordy Coleman	3.00	1.50	.90
117	Don Blasingame	35.00	17.50	10.50
118	Gene Freese	7.00	3.50	2.00
119	Ed Kasko	3.00	1.50	.90
120	Gus Bell	3.00	1.50	.90
121	Vada Pinson	5.00	2.50	1.50
122	Frank Robinson	25.00	12.50	7.50
123	Bob Purkey	35.00	17.50	10.50
124	Joey Jay	3.00	1.50	.90
125	Jim Brosnan	3.50	1.75	1.00
126	Jim O'Toole	3.00	1.50	.90
127	Jerry Lynch	3.00	1.50	.90
128	Wally Post	70.00	35.00	21.00
129	Ken Hunt	3.00	1.50	.90
130	Jerry Zimmerman	3.00	1.50	.90
131	Willie McCovey	25.00	12.50	7.50
132	Jose Pagan	3.00	1.50	.90
133	Felipe Alou	3.50	1.75	1.00
134	Jim Davenport	3.00	1.50	.90
135	Harvey Kuenn	4.00	2.00	1.25
136	Orlando Cepeda	6.00	3.00	1.75
137	Ed Bailey	35.00	17.50	10.50
138	Sam Jones	35.00	17.50	10.50
139	Mike McCormick	3.00	1.50	.90
140	Juan Marichal	25.00	12.50	7.50
141	Jack Sanford	3.00	1.50	.90
142a	Willie Mays (big head)	50.00	25.00	15.00
142b	Willie Mays (small head)	60.00	30.00	18.00
143	Stu Miller	3.00	1.50	.90
144	Joe Amalfitano	35.00	17.50	10.50
145	Joe Adcock	4.00	2.00	1.25
146	Frank Bolling	3.00	1.50	.90
147	Ed Mathews	20.00	10.00	6.00
148	Roy McMillan	3.00	1.50	.90
149a	Hank Aaron (script name large)	50.00	25.00	15.00
149b	Hank Aaron (script name small)	50.00	25.00	15.00
150	Gino Cimoli	3.00	1.50	.90
151	Frank Thomas	3.00	1.50	.90
152	Joe Torre	5.00	2.50	1.50
153	Lou Burdette	5.00	2.50	1.50
154	Bob Buhl	3.50	1.75	1.00
155	Carlton Willey	3.00	1.50	.90
156	Lee Maye	3.00	1.50	.90
157	Al Spangler	3.00	1.50	.90
158	Bill White	3.50	1.75	1.00
159	Ken Boyer	30.00	15.00	9.00
160	Joe Cunningham	3.00	1.50	.90
161	Carl Warwick	7.00	3.50	2.00
162	Carl Sawatski	3.00	1.50	.90
163	Lindy McDaniel	3.00	1.50	.90
164	Ernie Broglio	3.00	1.50	.90
165	Larry Jackson	3.00	1.50	.90
166	Curt Flood	4.00	2.00	1.25
167	Curt Simmons	8.00	4.00	2.50
168	Alex Grammas	3.00	1.50	.90
169	Dick Stuart	3.50	1.75	1.00
170	Bill Mazeroski	35.00	17.50	10.50
171	Don Hoak	3.00	1.50	.90
172	Dick Groat	9.00	4.50	2.75
173	Roberto Clemente	30.00	15.00	9.00
174	Bob Skinner	3.00	1.50	.90
175	Bill Virdon	4.00	2.00	1.25
176	Smoky Burgess	8.00	4.00	2.50
177	Elroy Face	8.00	4.00	2.50
178	Bob Friend	3.50	1.75	1.00
179	Vernon Law	3.50	1.75	1.00
180	Harvey Haddix	3.50	1.75	1.00
181	Hal Smith	35.00	17.50	10.50
182	Ed Bouchee	3.00	1.50	.90
183	Don Zimmer	4.00	2.00	1.25
184	Ron Santo	5.00	2.50	1.50
185	Andre Rodgers	3.00	1.50	.90
186	Richie Ashburn	6.00	3.00	1.75
187	George Altman	3.00	1.50	.90
188	Ernie Banks	35.00	17.50	10.50
189	Sam Taylor	3.00	1.50	.90
190	Don Elston	3.00	1.50	.90
191	Jerry Kindall	3.00	1.50	.90
192	Pancho Herrera	3.00	1.50	.90
193	Tony Taylor	3.00	1.50	.90
194	Ruben Amaro	3.00	1.50	.90
195	Don Demeter	35.00	17.50	10.50
196	Bobby Gene Smith	3.00	1.50	.90
197	Clay Dalrymple	3.00	1.50	.90
198	Robin Roberts	20.00	10.00	6.00
199	Art Mahaffey	3.00	1.50	.90
200	John Buzhardt	5.00	2.50	1.50

1963 Post Cereal

Another 200-player, 3-1/2" by 2-1/2" set that, with variations, totals more than 205 cards. Numerous color variations also exist due to the different cereal boxes on which the cards were printed. As many as 25 cards in the set are considered scarce, making it much more difficult to complete than the other major Post sets. Star cards also command higher prices than in the '61 or '62 Post cards. The 1963 Post cards are almost identical to the '63 Jell-O set, which is a slight 1/4" narrower. Cards are still blank backed, with a color player photo, biographies and statistics on the numbered card fronts. No Post logo appears on the '63 cards. The complete set price does not include the scarcer variations.

		NR MT	EX	VG
Complete Set:		3600.00	1800.00	1080.
Common Player:		2.00	1.00	.60
1	Vic Power	3.50	1.75	1.00
2	Bernie Allen	2.00	1.00	.60
3	Zoilo Versalles	2.00	1.00	.60
4	Rich Rollins	2.00	1.00	.60
5	Harmon Killebrew	12.00	6.00	3.50
6	Lenny Green	35.00	17.50	10.50
7	Bob Allison	1.75	.90	.50
8	Earl Battey	2.00	1.00	.60
9	Camilo Pascual	2.00	1.00	.60
10	Jim Kaat	3.00	1.50	.90
11	Jack Kralick	2.00	1.00	.60
12	Bill Skowron	2.50	1.25	.70
13	Bobby Richardson	3.00	1.50	.90
14	Cletis Boyer	2.50	1.25	.70
15	Mickey Mantle	325.00	162.00	97.00
16	Roger Maris	150.00	75.00	45.00
17	Yogi Berra	15.00	7.50	4.50
18	Elston Howard	3.00	1.50	.90
19	Whitey Ford	8.00	4.00	2.50
20	Ralph Terry	2.50	1.25	.70
21	John Blanchard	2.50	1.25	.70
22	Bill Stafford	2.50	1.25	.70
23	Tom Tresh	2.50	1.25	.70

		NR MT	EX	VG
24	Steve Bilko	2.00	1.00	.60
25	Bill Moran	2.00	1.00	.60
26a	Joe Koppe (1962 Avg. is .277)	2.00	1.00	.60
26b	Joe Koppe (1962 Avg. is .227)	12.00	6.00	3.50
27	Felix Torres	2.00	1.00	.60
28a	Leon Wagner (lifetime Avg. is .278)	2.00	1.00	.60
28b	Leon Wagner (lifetime Avg. is .272)	12.00	6.00	3.50
29	Albie Pearson	2.00	1.00	.60
30	Lee Thomas (photo actually George Thomas)	70.00	35.00	21.00
31	Bob Rodgers	2.00	1.00	.60
32	Dean Chance	2.00	1.00	.60
33	Ken McBride	2.00	1.00	.60
34	George Thomas (photo actually Lee Thomas)	2.00	1.00	.60
35	Joe Cunningham	2.00	1.00	.60
36a	Nelson Fox (no bat showing)	3.50	1.75	1.00
36b	Nelson Fox (part of bat showing)	10.00	5.00	3.00
37	Luis Aparicio	4.00	2.00	1.25
38	Al Smith	25.00	12.50	7.50
39	Floyd Robinson	80.00	40.00	24.00
40	Jim Landis	2.00	1.00	.60
41	Charlie Maxwell	2.00	1.00	.60
42	Sherman Lollar	2.00	1.00	.60
43	Early Wynn	6.00	3.00	1.75
44	Juan Pizarro	2.00	1.00	.60
45	Ray Herbert	2.00	1.00	.60
46	Norm Cash	2.50	1.25	.70
47	Steve Boros	2.00	1.00	.60
48	Dick McAuliffe	25.00	12.50	7.50
49	Bill Bruton	2.00	1.00	.60
50	Rocky Colavito	3.00	1.50	.90
51	Al Kaline	10.00	5.00	3.00
52	Dick Brown	2.00	1.00	.60
53	Jim Bunning	110.00	55.00	33.00
54	Hank Aguirre	2.00	1.00	.60
55	Frank Lary	2.00	1.00	.60
56	Don Mossi	2.00	1.00	.60
57	Jim Gentile	2.00	1.00	.60
58	Jackie Brandt	2.00	1.00	.60
59	Brooks Robinson	10.00	5.00	3.00
60	Ron Hansen	2.00	1.00	.60
61	Jerry Adair	150.00	75.00	45.00
62	John Powell	3.00	1.50	.90
63	Russ Snyder	2.00	1.00	.60
64	Steve Barber	2.00	1.00	.60
65	Milt Pappas	2.00	1.00	.60
66	Robin Roberts	4.00	2.00	1.25
67	Tito Francona	2.00	1.00	.60
68	Jerry Kindall	2.00	1.00	.60
69	Woodie Held	2.00	1.00	.60
70	Bubba Phillips	15.00	7.50	4.50
71	Chuck Essegian	2.00	1.00	.60
72	Willie Kirkland	2.00	1.00	.60
73	Al Luplow	2.00	1.00	.60
74	Ty Cline	2.00	1.00	.60
75	Dick Donovan	2.00	1.00	.60
76	John Romano	2.00	1.00	.60
77	Pete Runnels	2.00	1.00	.60
78	Ed Bressoud	2.00	1.00	.60
79	Frank Malzone	2.00	1.00	.60
80	Carl Yastrzemski	325.00	162.00	97.00
81	Gary Geiger	2.00	1.00	.60
82	Lou Clinton	2.00	1.00	.60
83	Earl Wilson	2.00	1.00	.60
84	Bill Monbouquette	2.00	1.00	.60
85	Norm Siebern	2.00	1.00	.60
86	Jerry Lumpe	80.00	40.00	24.00
87	Manny Jimenez	80.00	40.00	24.00
88	Gino Cimoli	2.00	1.00	.60
89	Ed Charles	2.00	1.00	.60
90	Ed Rakow	2.00	1.00	.60
91	Bob Del Greco	2.00	1.00	.60
92	Haywood Sullivan	2.00	1.00	.60
93	Chuck Hinton	2.00	1.00	.60
94	Ken Retzer	2.00	1.00	.60
95	Harry Bright	2.00	1.00	.60
96	Bob Johnson	2.00	1.00	.60
97	Dave Stenhouse	15.00	7.50	4.50
98	Chuck Cottier	25.00	12.50	7.50
99	Tom Cheney	2.00	1.00	.60
100	Claude Osteen	15.00	7.50	4.50
101	Orlando Cepeda	3.00	1.50	.90
102	Charley Hiller	2.00	1.00	.60
103	Jose Pagan	2.00	1.00	.60
104	Jim Davenport	2.00	1.00	.60
105	Harvey Kuenn	2.50	1.25	.70
106	Willie Mays	25.00	12.50	7.50
107	Felipe Alou	1.75	.90	.50
108	Tom Haller	110.00	55.00	33.00

		NR MT	EX	VG
109	Juan Marichal	6.00	3.00	1.75
110	Jack Sanford	2.00	1.00	.60
111	Bill O'Dell	2.00	1.00	.60
112	Willie McCovey	7.00	3.50	2.00
113	Lee Walls	2.00	1.00	.60
114	Jim Gilliam	3.00	1.50	.90
115	Maury Wills	3.00	1.50	.90
116	Ron Fairly	2.00	1.00	.60
117	Tommy Davis	2.50	1.25	.70
118	Duke Snider	8.00	4.00	2.50
119	Willie Davis	150.00	75.00	45.00
120	John Roseboro	2.00	1.00	.60
121	Sandy Koufax	15.00	7.50	4.50
122	Stan Williams	2.00	1.00	.60
123	Don Drysdale	7.00	3.50	2.00
124a	Daryl Spencer (no arm showing)	2.00	1.00	.60
124b	Daryl Spencer (part of arm showing)	10.00	5.00	3.00
125	Gordy Coleman	2.00	1.00	.60
126	Don Blasingame	2.00	1.00	.60
127	Leo Cardenas	2.00	1.00	.60
128	Eddie Kasko	150.00	75.00	45.00
129	Jerry Lynch	15.00	7.50	4.50
130	Vada Pinson	2.50	1.25	.70
131a	Frank Robinson (no stripes on hat)	8.00	4.00	2.50
131b	Frank Robinson (stripes on hat)	15.00	7.50	4.50
132	John Edwards	2.00	1.00	.60
133	Joey Jay	2.00	1.00	.60
134	Bob Purkey	2.00	1.00	.60
135	Marty Keough	15.00	7.50	4.50
136	Jim O'Toole	2.00	1.00	.60
137	Dick Stuart	2.00	1.00	.60
138	Bill Mazeroski	2.50	1.25	.70
139	Dick Groat	2.50	1.25	.70
140	Don Hoak	30.00	15.00	9.00
141	Bob Skinner	15.00	7.50	4.50
142	Bill Virdon	2.50	1.25	.70
143	Roberto Clemente	20.00	10.00	6.00
144	Smoky Burgess	1.75	.90	.50
145	Bob Friend	2.00	1.00	.60
146	Al McBean	2.00	1.00	.60
147	El Roy Face (Elroy)	2.50	1.25	.70
148	Joe Adcock	2.50	1.25	.70
149	Frank Bolling	2.00	1.00	.60
150	Roy McMillan	2.00	1.00	.60
151	Eddie Mathews	6.00	3.00	1.75
152	Hank Aaron	70.00	35.00	21.00
153	Del Crandall	30.00	15.00	9.00
154a	Bob Shaw (third sentence has "In 1959" twice)	10.00	5.00	3.00
154b	Bob Shaw (third sentence has "In 1959" once)	2.00	1.00	.60
155	Lew Burdette	2.50	1.25	.70
156	Joe Torre	3.00	1.50	.90
157	Tony Cloninger	2.00	1.00	.60
158	Bill White	2.50	1.25	.70
159	Julian Javier	2.00	1.00	.60
160	Ken Boyer	3.00	1.50	.90
161	Julio Gotay	2.00	1.00	.60
162	Curt Flood	110.00	55.00	33.00
163	Charlie James	2.00	1.00	.60
164	Gene Oliver	2.00	1.00	.60
165	Ernie Broglio	2.00	1.00	.60
166	Bob Gibson	7.00	3.50	2.00
167a	Lindy McDaniel (asterisk before trade line)	2.00	1.00	.60
167b	Lindy McDaniel (no asterisk before trade line)	5.00	2.50	1.50
168	Ray Washburn	2.00	1.00	.60
169	Ernie Banks	8.00	4.00	2.50
170	Ron Santo	2.50	1.25	.70
171	George Altman	2.00	1.00	.60
172	Billy Williams	110.00	55.00	33.00
173	Andre Rodgers	6.00	3.00	1.75
174	Ken Hubbs	20.00	10.00	6.00
175	Don Landrum	2.00	1.00	.60
176	Dick Bertell	15.00	7.50	4.50
177	Roy Sievers	1.75	.90	.50
178	Tony Taylor	2.00	1.00	.60
179	John Callison	1.75	.90	.50
180	Don Demeter	2.00	1.00	.60
181	Tony Gonzalez	2.00	1.00	.60
182	Wes Covington	20.00	10.00	6.00
183	Art Mahaffey	2.00	1.00	.60
184	Clay Dalrymple	2.00	1.00	.60
185	Al Spangler	2.00	1.00	.60
186	Roman Mejias	2.00	1.00	.60
187	Bob Aspromonte	325.00	162.00	97.00
188	Norm Larker	30.00	15.00	9.00
189	Johnny Temple	2.00	1.00	.60

		NR MT	EX	VG
190	Carl Warwick	2.00	1.00	.60
191	Bob Lillis	2.00	1.00	.60
192	Dick Farrell	2.00	1.00	.60
193	Gil Hodges	7.00	3.50	2.00
194	Marv Throneberry	3.00	1.50	.90
195	Charlie Neal	10.00	5.00	3.00
196	Frank Thomas	150.00	75.00	45.00
197	Richie Ashburn	20.00	10.00	6.00
198	Felix Mantilla	2.00	1.00	.60
199	Rod Kanehl	20.00	10.00	6.00
200	Roger Craig	3.00	1.50	.90

1990 Post Cereal

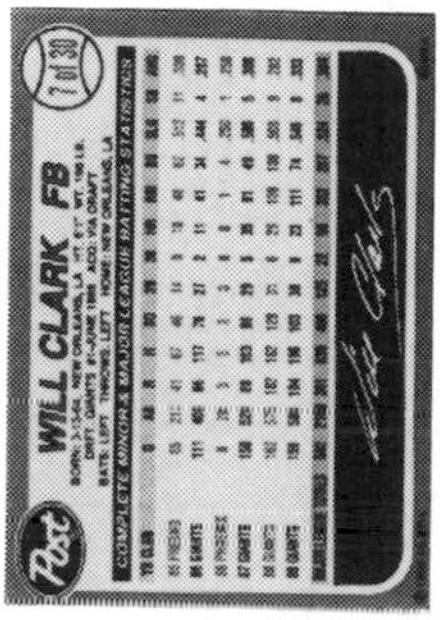

Post Cereal returned in 1990 with a 30-card set. The card fronts feature borders in white, red and blue, with the post logo in the upper left and the Major League Baseball logo in the upper right. Below the full-color shot of the player is his name in red. Backs of the cards show complete major league statistics; underneath is a facsimile autograph. The player photos do not display team logos. Cards were included three per box, inside Alpha-Bits cereal. Considered a difficult set to complete, the insert offer was only available for a limited time.

		MT	NR MT	EX
Complete Set:		30.00	22.00	12.00
Common Player:		.30	.25	.12
1	Don Mattingly	.80	.60	.30
2	Roger Clemens	.80	.60	.30
3	Kirby Puckett	.60	.45	.25
4	George Brett	.60	.45	.25
5	Tony Gwynn	.50	.40	.20
6	Ozzie Smith	.50	.40	.20
7	Will Clark	.80	.60	.30
8	Orel Hershiser	.40	.30	.15
9	Ryne Sandberg	1.00	.70	.40
10	Darryl Strawberry	.80	.60	.30
11	Nolan Ryan	1.50	1.25	.60
12	Mark McGwire	.40	.30	.15
13	Jim Abbott	.30	.25	.12
14	Bo Jackson	1.00	.90	.50
15	Kevin Mitchell	.40	.30	.15
16	Jose Canseco	1.25	.90	.50
17	Wade Boggs	.40	.30	.15
18	Dale Murphy	.40	.30	.15
19	Mark Grace	.40	.30	.15
20	Mike Scott	.30	.25	.12
21	Cal Ripken,Jr.	.80	.60	.30
22	Pedro Guerrero	.30	.25	.12
23	Ken Griffey,Jr.	2.00	1.50	.80
24	Eric Davis	.60	.45	.25
25	Rickey Henderson	.80	.60	.30
26	Robin Yount	.40	.30	.15
27	Von Hayes	.30	.25	.12
28	Alan Trammell	.40	.30	.15
29	Dwight Gooden	.80	.60	.30
30	Joe Carter	.40	.30	.15

1991 Post Cereal

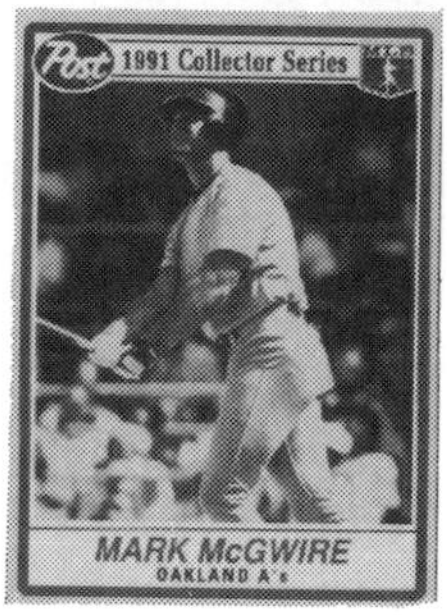

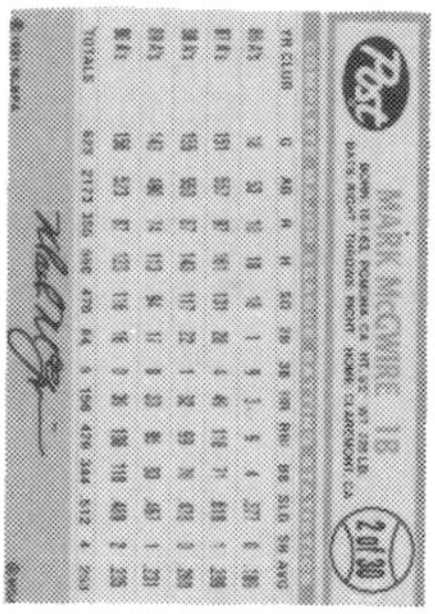

These superstar trading cards were inserted in Post Honeycomb, Super Golden Crisp, Cocoa Pebbles, Fruity Pebbles, Alpha-Bits and Marshmallow Alpha-Bits children's cereals. The complete set features 30 cards of baseball's top players. The cards were produced by Mike Schechter Associates, Inc. and are authorized by The Major League Baseball Players Association. The card fronts feature a player photo, the Post logo and the MLBPA logo. The flip sides feature statistics and a facsimile autograph.

		MT	NR MT	EX
Complete Set:		25.00	20.00	10.00
Common Player:		.30	.25	.12
1	Will Clark	.80	.60	.30
2	Kevin Mitchell	.40	.30	.15
3	Barry Bonds	.50	.40	.20
4	Darryl Strawberry	.50	.40	.20
5	Kirby Puckett	.50	.40	.20
6	Nolan Ryan	1.25	.90	.50
7	Rickey Henderson	.80	.60	.30
8	Ken Griffey,Jr.	2.00	1.50	.80
9	Don Mattingly	.80	.60	.30
10	Jose Canseco	1.00	.70	.40
11	Cecil Fielder	1.00	.70	.40
12	Mark Grace	.40	.30	.15
13	Ryne Sandberg	1.00	.70	.40
14	Sandy Alomar,Jr.	.40	.30	.15
15	Mark McGwire	.40	.30	.15
16	Chris Sabo	.30	.25	.12
17	Roger Clemens	.80	.60	.30
18	Barry Larkin	.50	.40	.20
19	Gary Sheffield	.50	.40	.20
20	Vince Coleman	.30	.25	.12
21	Len Dykstra	.30	.25	.12
22	Gregg Jefferies	.50	.40	.20
23	George Brett	.60	.45	.25
24	Cal Ripken,Jr.	1.00	.70	.40
25	Jim Abbott	.40	.30	.15
26	Bobby Bonilla	.40	.30	.15
27	Tony Gwynn	.40	.30	.15
28	Kevin Maas	.60	.45	.25
29	Todd Zeile	.60	.45	.25
30	Dave Justice	1.75	1.25	.70

1986 Quaker Oats

The Quaker Company, in conjunction with Topps, produced this 33-card set of current baseball stars for packaging in groups of three in Chewy Granola Bars packages. The cards are noted as the "1st Annual Collectors Edition." They are numbered and measure 2-1/2" by 3-1/2". Card fronts feature full-color player photos with the product name at the top and the player name, team and position below

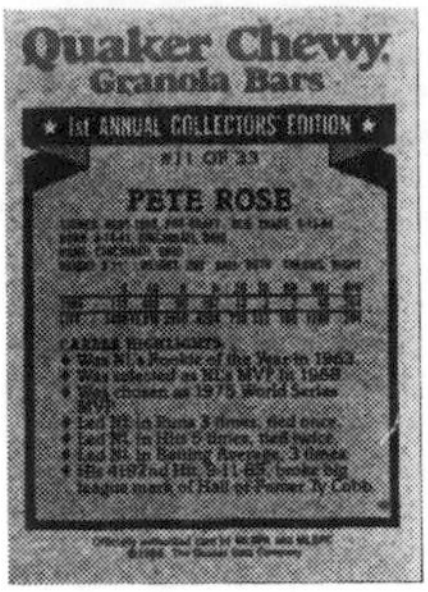

the photo. The complete set was offered via mail order by the Quaker Company.

		MT	NR MT	EX
Complete Set:		8.00	6.00	3.25
Common Player:		.15	.11	.06
1	Willie McGee	.15	.11	.06
2	Dwight Gooden	1.00	.70	.40
3	Vince Coleman	.30	.25	.12
4	Gary Carter	.25	.20	.10
5	Jack Clark	.15	.11	.06
6	Steve Garvey	.25	.20	.10
7	Tony Gwynn	.35	.25	.14
8	Dale Murphy	.40	.30	.15
9	Dave Parker	.15	.11	.06
10	Tim Raines	.25	.20	.10
11	Pete Rose	1.00	.70	.40
12	Nolan Ryan	1.00	.70	.40
13	Ryne Sandberg	1.00	.70	.40
14	Mike Schmidt	.40	.30	.15
15	Ozzie Smith	.15	.11	.06
16	Darryl Strawberry	.40	.30	.15
17	Fernando Valenzuela	.20	.15	.08
18	Don Mattingly	1.00	.70	.40
19	Bret Saberhagen	.20	.15	.08
20	Ozzie Guillen	.15	.11	.06
21	Bert Blyleven	.15	.11	.06
22	Wade Boggs	.80	.60	.30
23	George Brett	.40	.30	.15
24	Darrell Evans	.15	.11	.06
25	Rickey Henderson	1.00	.70	.40
26	Reggie Jackson	.30	.25	.12
27	Eddie Murray	.30	.25	.12
28	Phil Niekro	.20	.15	.08
29	Dan Quisenberry	.15	.11	.06
30	Jim Rice	.25	.20	.10
31	Cal Ripken	.30	.25	.12
32	Tom Seaver	.25	.20	.10
33	Dave Winfield	.25	.20	.10
----	Offer Card	.03	.02	.01

R

1984 Ralston Purina

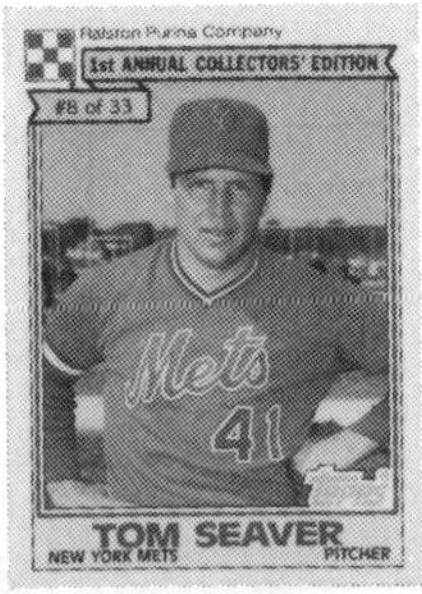

This set, produced in conjunction with Topps, has 33 of the game's top players, and is titled "1st Annual Collector's Edition." The full-color photos on the 2-1/2" by 3-1/2" cards are all close-up poses. Topps' logo appears only on the card fronts, and the backs are completely different from Topps' regular issue of 1984. Card backs feature a checkerboard look, coinciding with the well-known Ralston Purina logo. Cards are numbered 1-33, with odd numbers for American Leaguers and even numbered cards for National League players. Four cards were packed in boxes of Cookie Crisp and Donkey Kong Junior brand cereals, and the complete set was available via a mail-in offer.

		MT	NR MT	EX
Complete Set:		5.00	3.75	2.00
Common Player:		.10	.08	.04
1	Eddie Murray	.30	.25	.12
2	Ozzie Smith	.10	.08	.04
3	Ted Simmons	.10	.08	.04
4	Pete Rose	.80	.60	.30
5	Greg Luzinski	.10	.08	.04
6	Andre Dawson	.15	.11	.06
7	Dave Winfield	.25	.20	.10
8	Tom Seaver	.25	.20	.10
9	Jim Rice	.25	.20	.10
10	Fernando Valenzuela	.20	.15	.08
11	Wade Boggs	.60	.45	.25
12	Dale Murphy	.35	.25	.14
13	George Brett	.35	.25	.14
14	Nolan Ryan	.80	.60	.30
15	Rickey Henderson	.80	.60	.30
16	Steve Carlton	.30	.25	.12
17	Rod Carew	.30	.25	.12
18	Steve Garvey	.25	.20	.10
19	Reggie Jackson	.30	.25	.12
20	Dave Concepcion	.10	.08	.04
21	Robin Yount	.20	.15	.08
22	Mike Schmidt	.35	.25	.14
23	Jim Palmer	.20	.15	.08
24	Bruce Sutter	.10	.08	.04
25	Dan Quisenberry	.10	.08	.04
26	Bill Madlock	.10	.08	.04
27	Cecil Cooper	.10	.08	.04
28	Gary Carter	.25	.20	.10
29	Fred Lynn	.15	.11	.06
30	Pedro Guerrero	.15	.11	.06
31	Ron Guidry	.15	.11	.06
32	Keith Hernandez	.20	.15	.08
33	Carlton Fisk	.20	.15	.08

1987 Ralston Purina

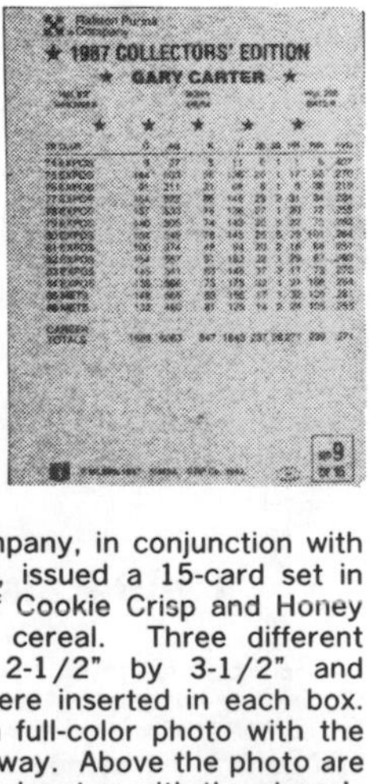

The Ralston Purina Company, in conjunction with Mike Schecter Associates, issued a 15-card set in specially marked boxes of Cookie Crisp and Honey Graham Chex brands of cereal. Three different cards, each measuring 2-1/2" by 3-1/2" and wrapped in cellophane, were inserted in each box. The card fronts contain a full-color photo with the team insignia airbrushed away. Above the photo are two yellow crossed bats and a star, with the player's uniform number inside the star. The card backs are grey with red printing and contain the set name, card

number, player's name, personal information and career major league statistics. As part of the Ralston Purina promotion, the company advertised an uncut sheet of cards which was available by finding an "instant-winner" game card or sending $1 plus two non-winning cards. Cards on the uncut sheet are identical in design to the single cards, save the omission of the words "1987 Collectors Edition" in the upper right corner. A complete uncut sheet in mint condition is valued at $10.

		MT	NR MT	EX
Complete Set:		15.00	11.00	6.00
Common Player:		1.00	.70	.40
1	Nolan Ryan	2.00	1.50	.80
2	Steve Garvey	1.25	.90	.50
3	Wade Boggs	1.25	.90	.50
4	Dave Winfield	1.25	.90	.50
5	Don Mattingly	2.00	1.50	.80
6	Don Sutton	1.00	.70	.40
7	Dave Parker	1.00	.70	.40
8	Eddie Murray	1.25	.90	.50
9	Gary Carter	1.25	.90	.50
10	Roger Clemens	2.00	1.50	.80
11	Fernando Valenzuela	1.25	.90	.50
12	Cal Ripken Jr.	2.00	1.50	.80
13	Ozzie Smith	1.00	.70	.40
14	Mike Schmidt	1.50	1.25	.60
15	Ryne Sandberg	2.00	1.50	.80

1987 Ralston Purina

		MT	NR MT	EX
Complete Panel Set:		10.00	7.50	4.00
Complete Singles Set:		3.50	2.75	1.50
Common Single Player:		.10	.08	.04
1	Nolan Ryan	.20	.15	.08
2	Steve Garvey	.20	.15	.08
3	Wade Boggs	.40	.30	.15
4	Dave Winfield	.20	.15	.08
5	Don Mattingly	.70	.50	.30
6	Don Sutton	.10	.08	.04
7	Dave Parker	.10	.08	.04
8	Eddie Murray	.25	.20	.10
9	Gary Carter	.20	.15	.08
10	Roger Clemens	.30	.25	.12
11	Fernando Valenzuela	.15	.11	.06
12	Cal Ripken Jr.	.25	.20	.10
13	Ozzie Smith	.10	.08	.04
14	Mike Schmidt	.30	.25	.12
15	Ryne Sandberg	.15	.11	.06

1989 Ralston Purina

The Ralston Purina Co., in conjunction with Mike Schechter Associates, issued a 12-card "Superstars" set in 1989. As part of a late-spring and early-summer promotion, the standard-size cards were inserted, two per box, in specially-marked boxes of Crisp Crunch, Honey Nut O's, Fruit Rings and Frosted Flakes in most parts of the country. Ads on cereal

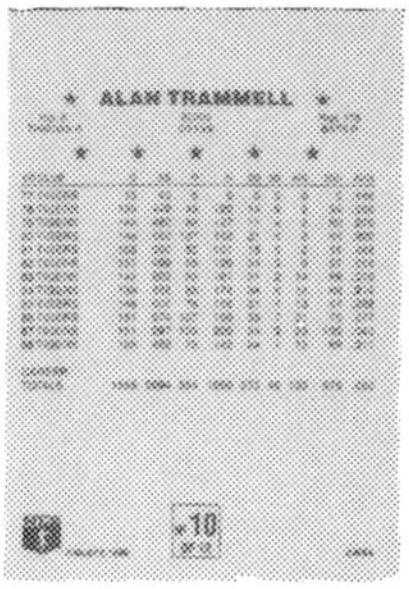

boxes also offered complete sets through a mail-in offer. The fronts of the cards feature full-color player photos flanked by stars in all four corners. "Super Stars" appears at the top; the player's name and position are at the bottom. The backs include player stats and data, the card number and copyright line.

		MT	NR MT	EX
Complete Set:		8.00	6.00	3.25
Common Player:		.80	.60	.30
1	Ozzie Smith	.80	.60	.30
2	Andre Dawson	.80	.60	.30
3	Darryl Strawberry	1.00	.70	.40
4	Mike Schmidt	1.25	.90	.50
5	Orel Hershiser	.90	.70	.35
6	Tim Raines	.80	.60	.30
7	Roger Clemens	1.25	.90	.50
8	Kirby Puckett	1.00	.70	.40
9	George Brett	1.00	.70	.40
10	Alan Trammell	.80	.60	.30
11	Don Mattingly	1.00	.70	.40
12	Jose Canseco	2.00	1.50	.80

1954 Red Heart Dog Food

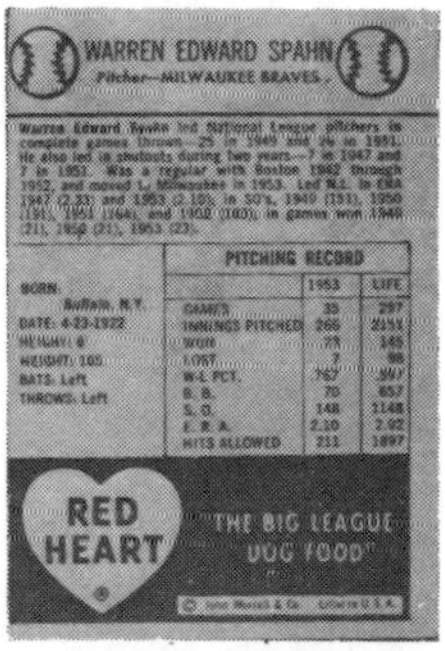

This set of 33 cards was issued in three color-coded series by the Red Heart Dog Food Co. Card fronts feature hand-colored photos on either a blue, green or red background. The 11 red-background cards are scarcer than the 11-card blue or green series. Backs of the 2-5/8" by 3-3/4" cards contain biographical and statistical information along with a Red Heart ad. Each 11-card series was available via a mail-in offer. As late as the early 1970s, the company was still sending cards to collectors who requested them.

		NR MT	EX	VG
Complete Set:		2500.00	1250.00	750.00
Common Player:		25.00	12.50	7.50
(1)	Richie Ashburn	40.00	20.00	12.00
(2)	Frankie Baumholtz	30.00	15.00	9.00
(3)	Gus Bell	25.00	12.50	7.50
(4)	Billy Cox	30.00	15.00	9.00
(5)	Alvin Dark	30.00	15.00	9.00

		NR MT	EX	VG
(6)	Carl Erskine	35.00	17.50	10.50
(7)	Ferris Fain	25.00	12.50	7.50
(8)	Dee Fondy	25.00	12.50	7.50
(9)	Nelson Fox	35.00	17.50	10.50
(10)	Jim Gilliam	35.00	17.50	10.50
(11)	Jim Hegan	30.00	15.00	9.00
(12)	George Kell	35.00	17.50	10.50
(13)	Ted Kluszewski	35.00	17.50	10.50
(14)	Ralph Kiner	55.00	27.00	16.50
(15)	Harvey Kuenn	30.00	15.00	9.00
(16)	Bob Lemon	55.00	27.00	16.50
(17)	Sherman Lollar	25.00	12.50	7.50
(18)	Mickey Mantle	450.00	225.00	135.00
(19)	Billy Martin	55.00	27.00	16.50
(20)	Gil McDougald	35.00	17.50	10.50
(21)	Roy McMillan	25.00	12.50	7.50
(22)	Minnie Minoso	30.00	15.00	9.00
(23)	Stan Musial	300.00	150.00	90.00
(24)	Billy Pierce	30.00	15.00	9.00
(25)	Al Rosen	35.00	17.50	10.50
(26)	Hank Sauer	25.00	12.50	7.50
(27)	Red Schoendienst	35.00	17.50	10.50
(28)	Enos Slaughter	35.00	17.50	10.50
(29)	Duke Snider	100.00	50.00	30.00
(30)	Warren Spahn	60.00	30.00	18.00
(31)	Sammy White	25.00	12.50	7.50
(32)	Eddie Yost	25.00	12.50	7.50
(33)	Gus Zernial	25.00	12.50	7.50

1982 Red Lobster Cubs

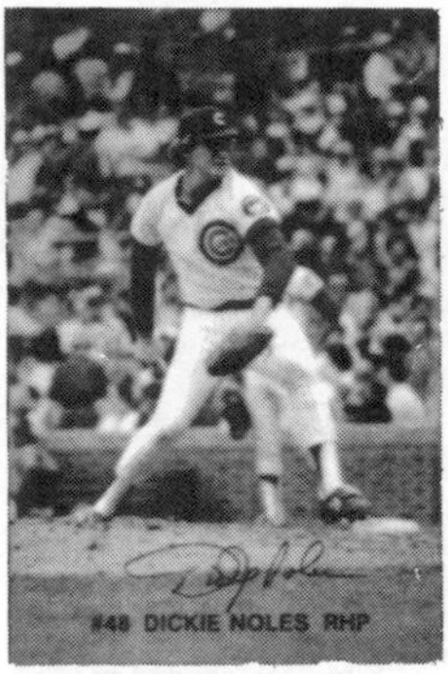

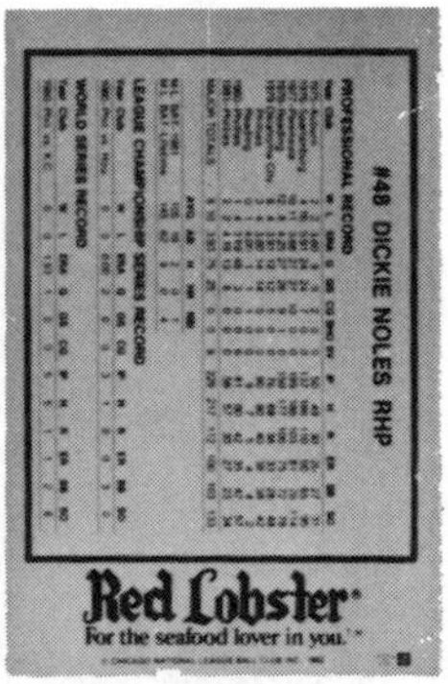

This 28-card set was co-sponsored by the team and a seafood restaurant chain for distribution at a 1982 Cubs promotional game. Card fronts are unbordered color photos, with player name, number, position and a superimposed facsimile autograph. The set includes 25 players on the 2-1/4" by 3-1/2" cards, along with a card for manager Lee Elia, an unnumbered card for the coaching staff and a team picture. Card backs have complete player statistics and a Red Lobster ad.

		MT	NR MT	EX
Complete Set:		12.00	9.00	4.75
Common Player:		.20	.15	.08
1	Larry Bowa	.40	.30	.15
4	Lee Elia	.20	.15	.08
6	Keith Moreland	.40	.30	.15
7	Jody Davis	.40	.30	.15
10	Leon Durham	.40	.30	.15
15	Junior Kennedy	.20	.15	.08
17	Bump Wills	.20	.15	.08
18	Scot Thompson	.20	.15	.08
21	Jay Johnstone	.25	.20	.10
22	Bill Buckner	.40	.30	.15
23	Ryne Sandberg	4.00	3.00	1.50
24	Jerry Morales	.20	.15	.08
25	Gary Woods	.20	.15	.08
28	Steve Henderson	.20	.15	.08
29	Bob Molinaro	.20	.15	.08
31	Fergie Jenkins	1.50	1.25	.60
33	Al Ripley	.20	.15	.08
34	Randy Martz	.20	.15	.08
36	Mike Proly	.20	.15	.08
37	Ken Kravec	.20	.15	.08
38	Willie Hernandez	.30	.25	.12
39	Bill Campbell	.20	.15	.08
41	Dick Tidrow	.20	.15	.08
46	Lee Smith	.50	.40	.20
47	Doug Bird	.20	.15	.08
48	Dickie Noles	.20	.15	.08
----	Team Photo	.20	.15	.08
----	Coaching Staff (Billy Connors, Tom Harmon, Gordy MacKenzie, John Vuckovich, Billy Williams)	.25	.20	.10

1952 Red Man Tobacco

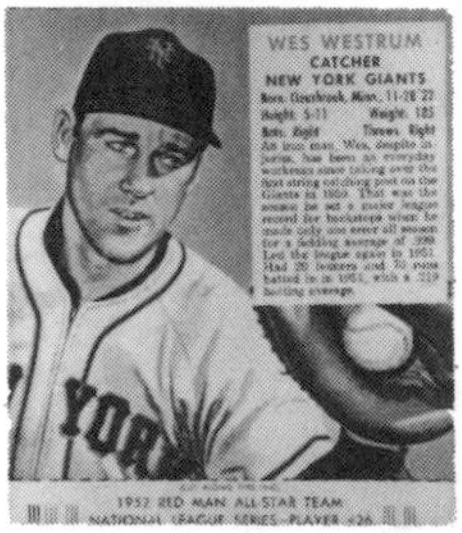

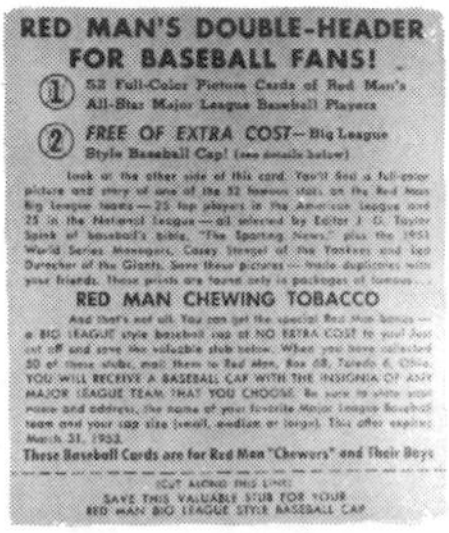

This was the first national set of tobacco cards produced since the golden days of tobacco sets in the early part of the century. There are 52 cards in the set, with 25 top players and one manager from each league. Player selection was made by editor J.G. Taylor Spink of The Sporting News. Cards measure 3-1/2"by 4", including a 1/2" tab at the bottom of each card. These tabs were redeemable for a free baseball cap from Red Man. Cards are harder to find with tabs intact, and thus more valuable in that form. Values quoted here are for cards with tabs. Cards with the tabs removed would be valued about 35-40 percent of the quoted figures. Card fronts are full color paintings of each player with biographical information inset in the portrait area. Card backs contain company advertising. Cards are numbered and dated only on the tabs.

		NR MT	EX	VG
Complete Set:		2000.00	1000.00	600.00
Common Player:		20.00	10.00	6.00
1A	Casey Stengel	55.00	27.00	16.50
1N	Leo Durocher	40.00	20.00	12.00
2A	Roberto Avila	20.00	10.00	6.00
2N	Richie Ashburn	35.00	17.50	10.50
3A	Larry "Yogi" Berra	80.00	40.00	24.00
3N	Ewell Blackwell	25.00	12.50	7.50
4A	Gil Coan	20.00	10.00	6.00
4N	Cliff Chambers	20.00	10.00	6.00
5A	Dom DiMaggio	30.00	15.00	9.00
5N	Murry Dickson	20.00	10.00	6.00
6A	Larry Doby	30.00	15.00	9.00
6N	Sid Gordon	20.00	10.00	6.00
7A	Ferris Fain	25.00	12.50	7.50
7N	Granny Hamner	20.00	10.00	6.00
8A	Bob Feller	80.00	40.00	24.00
8N	Jim Hearn	20.00	10.00	6.00
9A	Nelson Fox	35.00	17.50	10.50
9N	Monte Irvin	50.00	25.00	15.00
10A	Johnny Groth	20.00	10.00	6.00
10N	Larry Jansen	20.00	10.00	6.00
11A	Jim Hegan	20.00	10.00	6.00
11N	Willie Jones	20.00	10.00	6.00
12A	Eddie Joost	20.00	10.00	6.00
12N	Ralph Kiner	50.00	25.00	15.00
13A	George Kell	50.00	25.00	15.00
13N	Whitey Lockman	20.00	10.00	6.00
14A	Gil McDougald	30.00	15.00	9.00
14N	Sal Maglie	25.00	12.50	7.50
15A	Orestes Minoso	25.00	12.50	7.50
15N	Willie Mays	150.00	75.00	45.00
16A	Bill Pierce	25.00	12.50	7.50
16N	Stan Musial	150.00	75.00	45.00
17A	Bob Porterfield	20.00	10.00	6.00

		NR MT	EX	VG
17N	Pee Wee Reese	75.00	37.00	22.00
18A	Eddie Robinson	20.00	10.00	6.00
18N	Robin Roberts	50.00	25.00	15.00
19A	Saul Rogovin	20.00	10.00	6.00
19N	Al Schoendienst	30.00	15.00	9.00
20A	Bobby Shantz	25.00	12.50	7.50
20N	Enos Slaughter	50.00	25.00	15.00
21A	Vern Stephens	20.00	10.00	6.00
21N	Duke Snider	100.00	50.00	30.00
22A	Vic Wertz	20.00	10.00	6.00
22N	Warren Spahn	60.00	30.00	18.00
23A	Ted Williams	175.00	87.00	52.00
23N	Eddie Stanky	25.00	12.50	7.50
24A	Early Wynn	50.00	25.00	15.00
24N	Bobby Thomson	30.00	15.00	9.00
25A	Eddie Yost	20.00	10.00	6.00
25N	Earl Torgeson	20.00	10.00	6.00
26A	Gus Zernial	20.00	10.00	6.00
26N	Wes Westrum	20.00	10.00	6.00

1953 Red Man Tobacco

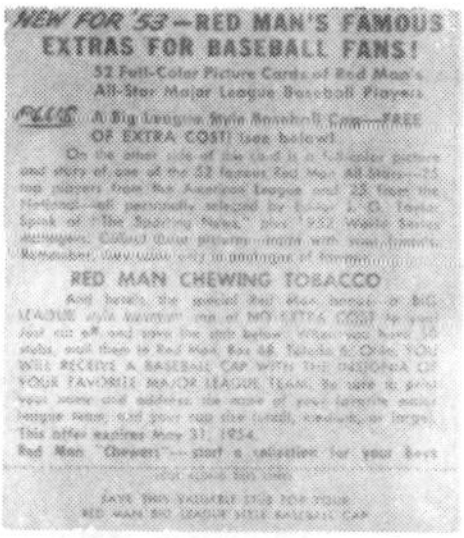

This was the chewing tobacco company's second annual set of 3-1/2" by 4" cards, including the tabs at the bottom of the cards. Formats for both the fronts and backs are similar to the '52 edition. The 1953 Red Man cards, however, include card numbers within the player biographical section, and the card backs are headlined "New for '53." Once again, cards with intact tabs (which were redeemable for a free cap) are more valuable. Prices below are for cards with tabs. Cards with tabs removed are worth about 35-40 percent of the stated values. Each league is represented by 25 players and a manager on the full-color cards, a total of 52.

		NR MT	EX	VG
Complete Set:		1800.00	900.00	540.00
Common Player:		20.00	10.00	6.00
1A	Casey Stengel	55.00	27.00	16.50
1N	Charlie Dressen	25.00	12.50	7.50
2A	Hank Bauer	25.00	12.50	7.50
2N	Bobby Adams	20.00	10.00	6.00
3A	Larry "Yogi" Berra	80.00	40.00	24.00
3N	Richie Ashburn	35.00	17.50	10.50
4A	Walt Dropo	20.00	10.00	6.00
4N	Joe Black	25.00	12.50	7.50
5A	Nelson Fox	35.00	17.50	10.50
5N	Roy Campanella	80.00	40.00	24.00
6A	Jackie Jensen	25.00	12.50	7.50
6N	Ted Kluszewski	30.00	15.00	9.00
7A	Eddie Joost	20.00	10.00	6.00
7N	Whitey Lockman	20.00	10.00	6.00
8A	George Kell	50.00	25.00	15.00
8N	Sal Maglie	25.00	12.50	7.50
9A	Dale Mitchell	20.00	10.00	6.00
9N	Andy Pafko	25.00	12.50	7.50
10A	Phil Rizzuto	60.00	30.00	18.00
10N	Pee Wee Reese	75.00	37.00	22.00
11A	Eddie Robinson	20.00	10.00	6.00
11N	Robin Roberts	50.00	25.00	15.00
12A	Gene Woodling	25.00	12.50	7.50
12N	Al Schoendienst	30.00	15.00	9.00
13A	Gus Zernial	20.00	10.00	6.00
13N	Enos Slaughter	50.00	25.00	15.00
14A	Early Wynn	50.00	25.00	15.00
14N	Edwin "Duke" Snider	100.00	50.00	30.00
15A	Joe Dobson	20.00	10.00	6.00
15N	Ralph Kiner	50.00	25.00	15.00
16A	Billy Pierce	25.00	12.50	7.50
16N	Hank Sauer	20.00	10.00	6.00
17A	Bob Lemon	50.00	25.00	15.00
17N	Del Ennis	20.00	10.00	6.00
18A	Johnny Mize	50.00	25.00	15.00
18N	Granny Hamner	20.00	10.00	6.00
19A	Bob Porterfield	20.00	10.00	6.00
19N	Warren Spahn	60.00	30.00	18.00
20A	Bobby Shantz	25.00	12.50	7.50
20N	Wes Westrum	20.00	10.00	6.00
21A	"Mickey" Vernon	25.00	12.50	7.50
21N	Hoyt Wilhelm	50.00	25.00	15.00
22A	Dom DiMaggio	30.00	15.00	9.00
22N	Murry Dickson	20.00	10.00	6.00
23A	Gil McDougald	30.00	15.00	9.00
23N	Warren Hacker	20.00	10.00	6.00
24A	Al Rosen	30.00	15.00	9.00
24N	Gerry Staley	20.00	10.00	6.00
25A	Mel Parnell	20.00	10.00	6.00
25N	Bobby Thomson	25.00	12.50	7.50
26A	Roberto Avila	20.00	10.00	6.00
26N	Stan Musial	150.00	75.00	45.00

1954 Red Man Tobacco

In 1954, the Red Man set eliminated managers from the set, and issued only 25 player cards for each league. There are, however, four variations which bring the total set size to 54 full-color cards. Two cards exist for Gus Bell and Enos Slaughter, while American Leaguers George Kell, Sam Mele and Dave Philley are each shown with two different teams. Complete set prices quoted below do not include the scarcer of the variation pairs. Cards still measure 3-1/2" by 4" with tabs intact. Cards without tabs are worth about 35-40 per cent of the values quoted below. Formats for the cards remain virtually unchanged, with card numbers included within the player information boxes as well as on the tabs.

		NR MT	EX	VG
Complete Set:		1600.00	800.00	480.00
Common Player:		20.00	10.00	6.00
1A	Bobby Avila	20.00	10.00	6.00
1N	Richie Ashburn	35.00	17.50	10.50
2A	Jim Busby	20.00	10.00	6.00
2N	Billy Cox	25.00	12.50	7.50
3A	Nelson Fox	35.00	17.50	10.50
3N	Del Crandall	25.00	12.50	7.50
4Aa	George Kell (Boston)	65.00	32.00	19.50
4Ab	George Kell (Chicago)	75.00	37.00	22.00
4N	Carl Erskine	30.00	15.00	9.00
5A	Sherman Lollar	20.00	10.00	6.00
5N	Monte Irvin	50.00	25.00	15.00
6Aa	Sam Mele (Baltimore)	50.00	25.00	15.00
6Ab	Sam Mele (Chicago)	75.00	37.00	22.00
6N	Ted Kluszewski	30.00	15.00	9.00
7A	Orestes Minoso	25.00	12.50	7.50
7N	Don Mueller	20.00	10.00	6.00
8A	Mel Parnell	20.00	10.00	6.00
8N	Andy Pafko	25.00	12.50	7.50
9Aa	Dave Philley (Cleveland)	50.00	25.00	15.00
9Ab	Dave Philley (Philadelphia)	75.00	37.00	22.00

		NR MT	EX	VG
9N	Del Rice	20.00	10.00	6.00
10A	Billy Pierce	25.00	12.50	7.50
10N	Al Schoendienst	30.00	15.00	9.00
11A	Jim Piersall	25.00	12.50	7.50
11N	Warren Spahn	60.00	30.00	18.00
12A	Al Rosen	30.00	15.00	9.00
12N	Curt Simmons	25.00	12.50	7.50
13A	"Mickey" Vernon	25.00	12.50	7.50
13N	Roy Campanella	80.00	40.00	24.00
14A	Sammy White	20.00	10.00	6.00
14N	Jim Gilliam	30.00	15.00	9.00
15A	Gene Woodling	25.00	12.50	7.50
15N	"Pee Wee" Reese	75.00	37.00	22.00
16A	Ed "Whitey" Ford	65.00	32.00	19.50
16N	Edwin "Duke" Snider	100.00	50.00	30.00
17A	Phil Rizzuto	60.00	30.00	18.00
17N	Rip Repulski	20.00	10.00	6.00
18A	Bob Porterfield	20.00	10.00	6.00
18N	Robin Roberts	50.00	25.00	15.00
19A	Al "Chico" Carrasquel	20.00	10.00	6.00
19Na	Enos Slaughter	90.00	45.00	27.00
19Nb	Gus Bell	90.00	45.00	27.00
20A	Larry "Yogi" Berra	80.00	40.00	24.00
20N	Johnny Logan	20.00	10.00	6.00
21A	Bob Lemon	50.00	25.00	15.00
21N	Johnny Antonelli	25.00	12.50	7.50
22A	Ferris Fain	25.00	12.50	7.50
22N	Gil Hodges	55.00	27.00	16.50
23A	Hank Bauer	25.00	12.50	7.50
23N	Eddie Mathews	55.00	27.00	16.50
24A	Jim Delsing	20.00	10.00	6.00
24N	Lew Burdette	30.00	15.00	9.00
25A	Gil McDougald	30.00	15.00	9.00
25N	Willie Mays	150.00	75.00	45.00

1955 Red Man Tobacco

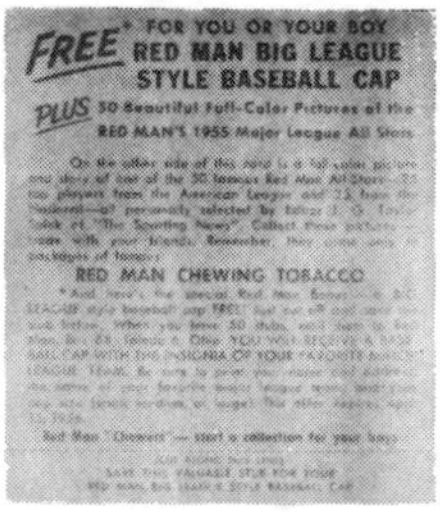

These 50 cards are quite similar to the 1954 edition, with card fronts virtually unchanged except for the data in the biographical box on the color picture area. This set of the 3-1/2" by 4" cards includes 25 players from each league, with no known variations. As with all Red Man sets, those cards complete with the redeemable tabs are more valuable. Values quoted below are for cards with tabs. Cards with the tabs removed are worth about 35-40 percent of those figures.

		NR MT	EX	VG
Complete Set:		1500.00	750.00	450.00
Common Player:		20.00	10.00	6.00
1A	Ray Boone	20.00	10.00	6.00
1N	Richie Ashburn	35.00	17.50	10.50
2A	Jim Busby	20.00	10.00	6.00
2N	Del Crandall	25.00	12.50	7.50
3A	Ed "Whitey" Ford	55.00	27.00	16.50
3N	Gil Hodges	65.00	32.00	19.50
4A	Nelson Fox	35.00	17.50	10.50
4N	Brooks Lawrence	20.00	10.00	6.00
5A	Bob Grim	20.00	10.00	6.00
5N	Johnny Logan	20.00	10.00	6.00
6A	Jack Harshman	20.00	10.00	6.00
6N	Sal Maglie	25.00	12.50	7.50
7A	Jim Hegan	20.00	10.00	6.00
7N	Willie Mays	150.00	75.00	45.00
8A	Bob Lemon	50.00	25.00	15.00

		NR MT	EX	VG
8N	Don Mueller	20.00	10.00	6.00
9A	Irv Noren	20.00	10.00	6.00
9N	Bill Sarni	20.00	10.00	6.00
10A	Bob Porterfield	20.00	10.00	6.00
10N	Warren Spahn	60.00	30.00	18.00
11A	Al Rosen	30.00	15.00	9.00
11N	Henry Thompson	20.00	10.00	6.00
12A	"Mickey" Vernon	25.00	12.50	7.50
12N	Hoyt Wilhelm	50.00	25.00	15.00
13A	Vic Wertz	20.00	10.00	6.00
13N	Johnny Antonelli	25.00	12.50	7.50
14A	Early Wynn	50.00	25.00	15.00
14N	Carl Erskine	30.00	15.00	9.00
15A	Bobby Avila	20.00	10.00	6.00
15N	Granny Hamner	20.00	10.00	6.00
16A	Larry "Yogi" Berra	80.00	40.00	24.00
16N	Ted Kluszewski	30.00	15.00	9.00
17A	Joe Coleman	20.00	10.00	6.00
17N	Pee Wee Reese	75.00	37.00	22.00
18A	Larry Doby	30.00	15.00	9.00
18N	Al Schoendienst	30.00	15.00	9.00
19A	Jackie Jensen	25.00	12.50	7.50
19N	Duke Snider	100.00	50.00	30.00
20A	Pete Runnels	20.00	10.00	6.00
20N	Frank Thomas	20.00	10.00	6.00
21A	Jim Piersall	25.00	12.50	7.50
21N	Ray Jablonski	20.00	10.00	6.00
22A	Hank Bauer	25.00	12.50	7.50
22N	James "Dusty" Rhodes	20.00	10.00	6.00
23A	"Chico" Carrasquel	20.00	10.00	6.00
23N	Gus Bell	20.00	10.00	6.00
24A	Orestes Minoso	25.00	12.50	7.50
24N	Curt Simmons	25.00	12.50	7.50
25A	Sandy Consuegra	20.00	10.00	6.00
25N	Marvin Grissom	20.00	10.00	6.00

1988 Revco

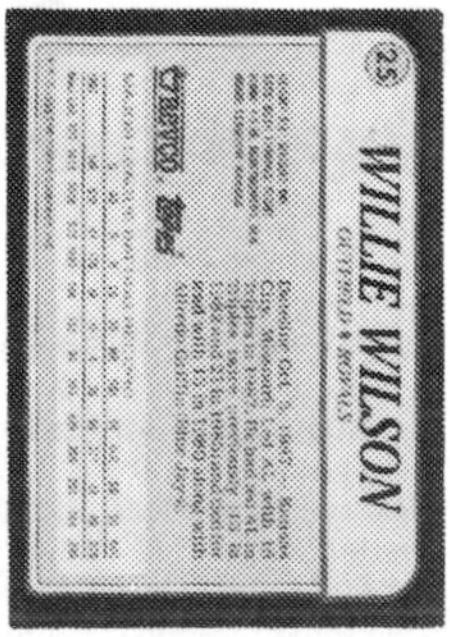

This super-glossy boxed set of 33 standard-size cards was produced by Topps for exclusive distribution by Revco stores east of the Mississippi River. Card fronts feature a large blue Revco logo in the upper left corner opposite a yellow and black boxed "Topps League Leader" label. Player photos are framed in black and orange with a diagonal player name banner in the lower right corner that lists the player's name, team and position on white, orange and gold stripes. The numbered card backs are horizontal, printed in red and black on white stock and include the player name, followed by personal biographical data, batting/pitching stats and a brief career summary.

		MT	NR MT	EX
Complete Set:		5.00	3.75	2.00
Common Player:		.05	.04	.02
1	Tony Gwynn	.25	.20	.10
2	Andre Dawson	.15	.11	.06
3	Vince Coleman	.15	.11	.06
4	Jack Clark	.15	.11	.06
5	Tim Raines	.25	.20	.10
6	Tim Wallach	.10	.08	.04
7	Juan Samuel	.10	.08	.04
8	Nolan Ryan	.80	.60	.30
9	Rick Sutcliffe	.10	.08	.04
10	Kent Tekulve	.05	.04	.02

		MT	NR MT	EX
11	Steve Bedrosian	.10	.08	.04
12	Orel Hershiser	.10	.08	.04
13	Rick Rueschel	.07	.05	.03
14	Fernando Valenzuela	.20	.15	.08
15	Bob Welch	.10	.08	.04
16	Wade Boggs	.50	.40	.20
17	Mark McGwire	.50	.40	.20
18	George Bell	.20	.15	.08
19	Harold Reynolds	.05	.04	.02
20	Paul Molitor	.12	.09	.05
21	Kirby Puckett	.25	.20	.10
22	Kevin Seitzer	.20	.15	.08
23	Brian Downing	.05	.04	.02
24	Dwight Evans	.10	.08	.04
25	Willie Wilson	.07	.05	.03
26	Danny Tartabull	.20	.15	.08
27	Jimmy Key	.07	.05	.03
28	Roger Clemens	.80	.60	.30
29	Dave Stewart	.25	.20	.10
30	Mark Eichhorn	.05	.04	.02
31	Tom Henke	.05	.04	.02
32	Charlie Hough	.05	.04	.02
33	Mark Langston	.10	.08	.04

1988 Rite Aid

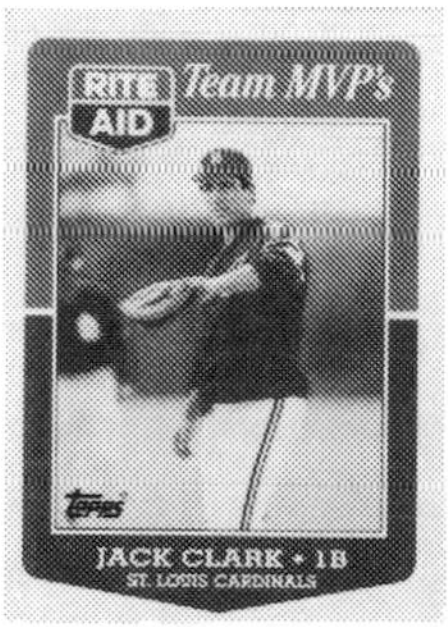

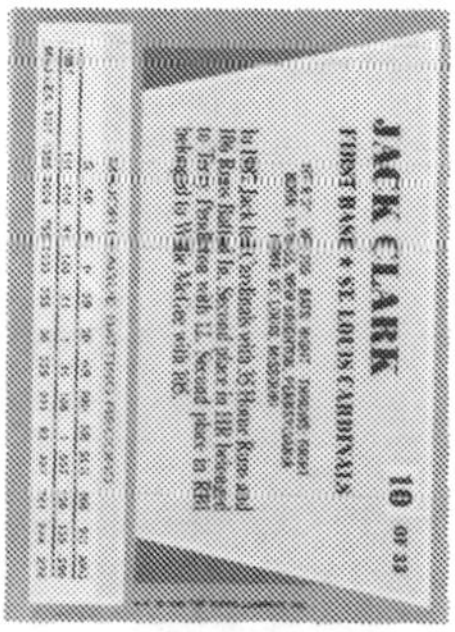

This premiere edition was produced by Topps for distribution by Rite Aid drug and discount stores in the Eastern United States. The boxed set includes 33 standard-size full-color cards with at least one card for each major league team. Four cards in the set highlight MVP's from the 1987 season. Card fronts have white borders and carry a yellow "Team MVP's" header above the player photo which is outlined in red and blue. A large Rite Aid logo appears upper left; the players name appears bottom center. The numbered card backs are black on blue and white card stock in a horizontal layout containing the player name, biography and statistics.

		MT	NR MT	EX
Complete Set:		4.00	3.00	1.50
Common Player:		.05	.04	.02
1	Dale Murphy	.20	.15	.08
2	Andre Dawson	.20	.15	.08
3	Eric Davis	.50	.40	.20
4	Mike Scott	.10	.08	.04
5	Pedro Guerrero	.15	.11	.06
6	Tim Raines	.25	.20	.10
7	Darryl Strawberry	.40	.30	.15
8	Mike Schmidt	.30	.25	.12
9	Mike Dunne	.05	.04	.02
10	Jack Clark	.15	.11	.06
11	Tony Gwynn	.25	.20	.10
12	Will Clark	.30	.25	.12
13	Cal Ripken	.60	.45	.25
14	Wade Boggs	.60	.45	.25
15	Wally Joyner	.30	.25	.12
16	Harold Baines	.12	.09	.05
17	Joe Carter	.12	.09	.05
18	Alan Trammell	.15	.11	.06
19	Kevin Seitzer	.15	.11	.06
20	Paul Molitor	.12	.09	.05
21	Kirby Puckett	.25	.20	.10
22	Don Mattingly	.80	.60	.30
23	Mark McGwire	.50	.40	.20
24	Alvin Davis	.10	.08	.04
25	Ruben Sierra	.35	.25	.14
26	George Bell	.20	.15	.08
27	Jack Morris	.12	.09	.05
28	Jeff Reardon	.07	.05	.03
29	John Tudor	.07	.05	.03
30	Rick Rueschel	.07	.05	.03
31	Gary Gaetti	.12	.09	.05
32	Jeffrey Leonard	.05	.04	.02
33	Frank Viola	.12	.09	.05

1955 Rodeo Meats Athletics

This set of 2-1/2" by 3-1/2" color cards was issued by a local meat company to commemorate the first year of the Athletics in Kansas City. There are 38 different players included in the set, with nine players known to apppear in two different variations for a total of 47 cards in the set. Most variations are in background colors, although Bobby Shantz is also listed incorrectly as "Schantz" on one variation. The cards are unnumbered, with the Rodeo logo and player name on the fronts, and an ad for a scrapbook album listed on the backs.

		NR MT	EX	VG
Complete Set:		4250.00	2125.00	1275.
Common Player:		70.00	35.00	21.00
(1)	Joe Astroth	70.00	35.00	21.00
(2)	Harold Bevan	100.00	50.00	30.00
(3)	Charles Bishop	100.00	50.00	30.00
(4)	Don Bollweg	100.00	50.00	30.00
(5)	Lou Boudreau	250.00	125.00	75.00
(6)	Cloyd Boyer (blue background)	100.00	50.00	30.00
(7)	Cloyd Boyer (pink background)	70.00	35.00	21.00
(8)	Ed Burtschy	100.00	50.00	30.00
(9)	Art Ceccarelli	70.00	35.00	21.00
(10)	Joe DeMaestri (pea green background)	100.00	50.00	30.00
(11)	Joe DeMaestri (light green background)	70.00	35.00	21.00
(12)	Art Ditmar	70.00	35.00	21.00
(13)	John Dixon	100.00	50.00	30.00
(14)	Jim Finigan	70.00	35.00	21.00
(15)	Marion Fricano	100.00	50.00	30.00
(16)	John Gray	100.00	50.00	30.00
(17)	Tom Gorman	70.00	35.00	21.00
(18)	Ray Herbert	70.00	35.00	21.00
(19)	Forest "Spook" Jacobs (Forrest)	100.00	50.00	30.00
(20)	Alex Kellner	100.00	50.00	30.00
(21)	Harry Kraft (Craft)	70.00	35.00	21.00
(22)	Jack Littrell	70.00	35.00	21.00
(23)	Hector Lopez	80.00	40.00	24.00
(24)	Oscar Melillo	70.00	35.00	21.00
(25)	Arnold Portocarrero (purple background)	100.00	50.00	30.00
(26)	Arnold Portocarrero (grey background)	70.00	35.00	21.00
(27)	Vic Power (pink background)	125.00	62.00	37.00
(28)	Vic Power (yellow background)	80.00	40.00	24.00
(29)	Vic Raschi	100.00	50.00	30.00
(30)	Bill Renna (dark pink background)	100.00	50.00	30.00
(31)	Bill Renna (light pink background)	70.00	35.00	21.00

		NR MT	EX	VG
(32)	Al Robertson	100.00	50.00	30.00
(33)	Johnny Sain	125.00	62.00	37.00
(34a)	Bobby Schantz (incorrect spelling)	250.00	125.00	75.00
(34b)	Bobby Shantz (correct spelling)	125.00	62.00	37.00
(35)	Wilmer Shantz (orange background)	100.00	50.00	30.00
(36)	Wilmer Shantz (purple background)	70.00	35.00	21.00
(37)	Harry Simpson	70.00	35.00	21.00
(38)	Enos Slaughter	300.00	150.00	90.00
(39)	Lou Sleater	70.00	35.00	21.00
(40)	George Susce	70.00	35.00	21.00
(41)	Bob Trice	100.00	50.00	30.00
(42)	Elmer Valo (yellow background)	100.00	50.00	30.00
(43)	Elmer Valo (green background)	70.00	35.00	21.00
(44)	Bill Wilson (yellow background)	100.00	50.00	30.00
(45)	Bill Wilson (purple background)	70.00	35.00	21.00
(46)	Gus Zernial	80.00	40.00	24.00

1956 Rodeo Meats Athletics

Rodeo Meats issued another Kansas City Athletics set in 1956, but this one was a much smaller 13-card set. The 2-1/2" by 3-1/2" cards are again unnumbered, with the player name and Rodeo logo on the fronts. Card backs feature some of the same graphics and copy as the 1955 cards, but the album offer is omitted. The full-color cards were only available in packages of Rodeo hot dogs.

		NR MT	EX	VG
Complete Set:		1250.00	625.00	375.00
Common Player:		70.00	35.00	21.00
(1)	Joe Astroth	70.00	35.00	21.00
(2)	Lou Boudreau	250.00	125.00	75.00
(3)	Joe DeMaestri	70.00	35.00	21.00
(4)	Art Ditmar	70.00	35.00	21.00
(5)	Jim Finigan	70.00	35.00	21.00
(6)	Hector Lopez	80.00	40.00	24.00
(7)	Vic Power	80.00	40.00	24.00
(8)	Bobby Shantz	125.00	62.00	37.00
(9)	Harry Simpson	70.00	35.00	21.00
(10)	Enos Slaughter	250.00	125.00	75.00
(11)	Elmer Valo	70.00	35.00	21.00
(12)	Gus Zernial	80.00	40.00	24.00

1970 Rold Gold Pretzels

The 1970 Rold Gold Pretzels set of 15 cards honors the "Greatest Players Ever" in the first 100 years of baseball as chosen by the Baseball Writers of America. The cards, which measure 2-1/4" by 3-1/2" in size, feature a simulated 3-D effect. The set was re-released in 1972 by Kellogg's in packages of Danish-Go-Rounds. Rold Gold cards can be differentiated from the Kellogg's cards of 1972 by the 1970 copyright date found on the card reverse.

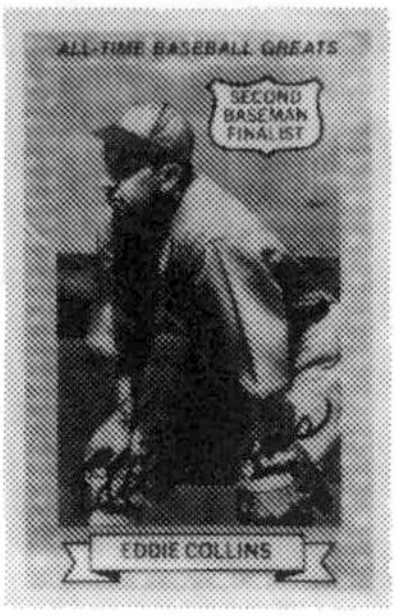

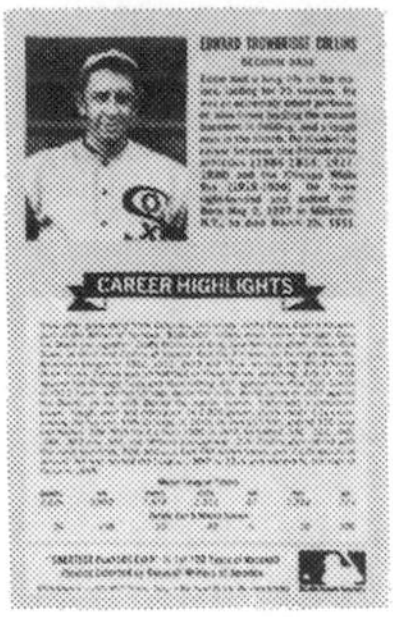

		NR MT	EX	VG
Complete Set:		50.00	25.00	15.00
Common Player:		1.00	.50	.30
1	Walter Johnson	2.50	1.25	.70
2	Rogers Hornsby	1.50	.70	.45
3	John McGraw	1.00	.50	.30
4	Mickey Cochrane	1.00	.50	.30
5	George Sisler	1.00	.50	.30
6	Babe Ruth	15.00	7.50	4.50
7	Robert "Lefty" Grove	1.50	.70	.45
8	Harold "Pie" Traynor	1.00	.50	.30
9	Honus Wagner	1.75	.90	.50
10	Eddie Collins	1.00	.50	.30
11	Tris Speaker	1.50	.70	.45
12	Cy Young	1.00	.50	.30
13	Lou Gehrig	8.00	4.00	2.50
14	Babe Ruth	15.00	7.50	4.50
15	Ty Cobb	8.00	4.00	2.50

1950 Royal Desserts

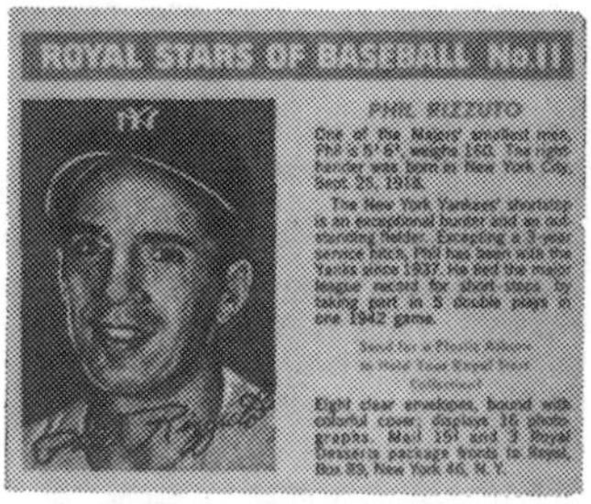

This set of 24 cards was issued one per box on the backs of various Royal Dessert products over a period of three years. The basic set contains 24 players, however a number of variations create the much higher total for the set. In 1950, Royal issued cards with two different tints - black and white with red, or blue and white with red. Over the next two years, various sentences of the cards' biographies were updated up to three times in some cases. Some players from the set left the majors after 1950 and others were apparently never updated, but the 23 biography updates that do exist, added to the original 24 cards issued in 1950, give the set a total of 47 cards. The 2-1/2" by 3-1/2" cards are blank-backed with personal and playing biographies alongside the card front photos.

		NR MT	EX	VG
Complete Set:		1200.00	600.00	360.00
Common Player:		20.00	10.00	6.00
1a	Stan Musial (2nd paragraph begins "Musial's 207...")	125.00	62.00	37.00
1b	Stan Musial (2nd paragraph begins "Musial batted...")	125.00	62.00	37.00
2a	Pee Wee Reese (2nd paragraph begins "Pee Wee's...")	70.00	35.00	21.00

		NR MT	EX	VG
2b	Pee Wee Reese (2nd paragraph begins "Captain...")	70.00	35.00	21.00
3a	George Kell (2nd paragraph ends "...in 1945, '46.")	35.00	17.50	10.50
3b	George Kell (2nd paragraph ends "...two base hits, 56.")	35.00	17.50	10.50
4a	Dom DiMaggio (2nd paragraph ends "...during 1947.")	30.00	15.00	9.00
4b	Dom DiMaggio (2nd paragraph ends "...with 11.")	30.00	15.00	9.00
5a	Warren Spahn (2nd paragraph ends "...shutouts 7.")	50.00	25.00	15.00
5b	Warren Spahn (2nd paragraph ends "...with 191.")	50.00	25.00	15.00
6a	Andy Pafko (2nd paragraph ends "...7 games.")	25.00	12.50	7.50
6b	Andy Pafko (2nd paragraph ends "...National League.")	25.00	12.50	7.50
6c	Andy Pafko (2nd paragraph ends "...weighs 190.")	25.00	12.50	7.50
7a	Andy Seminick (2nd paragraph ends "...as outfield.")	20.00	10.00	6.00
7b	Andy Seminick (2nd paragraph ends "...since 1916.")	20.00	10.00	6.00
7c	Andy Seminick (2nd paragraph ends "...in the outfield.")	20.00	10.00	6.00
7d	Andy Seminick (2nd paragraph ends "...right handed.")	20.00	10.00	6.00
8a	Lou Brissie (2nd paragraph ends "...when pitching.")	20.00	10.00	6.00
8b	Lou Brissie (2nd paragraph ends "...weighs 215.")	20.00	10.00	6.00
9a	Ewell Blackwell (2nd paragraph begins "Despite recent illness...")	25.00	12.50	7.50
9b	Ewell Blackwell (2nd paragraph begins "Blackwell's...")	25.00	12.50	7.50
10a	Bobby Thomson (2nd paragraph begins "In 1949...")	25.00	12.50	7.50
10b	Bobby Thomson (2nd paragraph begins "Thomson is...")	25.00	12.50	7.50
11a	Phil Rizzuto (2nd paragraph ends "...one 1942 game.")	60.00	30.00	18.00
11b	Phil Rizzuto (2nd paragraph ends "...Most Valuable Player.")	60.00	30.00	18.00
12	Tommy Henrich	30.00	15.00	9.00
13	Joe Gordon	25.00	12.50	7.50
14a	Ray Scarborough (Senators)	20.00	10.00	6.00
14b	Ray Scarborough (White Sox, 2nd paragraph ends "...military service.")	20.00	10.00	6.00
14c	Ray Scarborough (White Sox, 2nd paragraph ends "...the season.")	20.00	10.00	6.00
14d	Ray Scarborough (Red Sox)	20.00	10.00	6.00
15a	Stan Rojek (Pirates)	20.00	10.00	6.00
15b	Stan Rojek (Browns)	20.00	10.00	6.00
16	Luke Appling	30.00	15.00	9.00
17	Willard Marshall	20.00	10.00	6.00
18	Alvin Dark	30.00	15.00	9.00
19a	Dick Sisler (2nd paragraph ends "...service record.")	20.00	10.00	6.00
19b	Dick Sisler (2nd paragraph ends "...National League flag.")	20.00	10.00	6.00
19c	Dick Sisler (2nd paragraph ends "...Nov. 2, 1920.")	20.00	10.00	6.00
19d	Dick Sisler (2nd paragraph ends "...from '46 to '48.")	20.00	10.00	6.00
20	Johnny Ostrowski	20.00	10.00	6.00
21a	Virgil Trucks (2nd paragraph ends "...in military service.")	25.00	12.50	7.50
21b	Virgil Trucks (2nd paragraph ends "...that year.")	25.00	12.50	7.50
21c	Virgil Trucks (2nd paragraph ends "...for military service.")	25.00	12.50	7.50
22	Eddie Robinson	20.00	10.00	6.00
23	Nanny Fernandez	20.00	10.00	6.00
24	Ferris Fain	25.00	12.50	7.50

1952 Royal Desserts

This set, issued as a premium by Royal Desserts in 1952, consists of 16 unnumbered black and white cards, each measuring 5" by 7". The cards include the inscription "To A Royal Fan" along with the player's facsimile autograph.

	NR MT	EX	VG
Complete Set:	450.00	225.00	135.00

		NR MT	EX	VG
Common Player:		15.00	7.50	4.50
(1)	Ewell Blackwell	18.00	9.00	5.50
(2)	Leland V. Brissie Jr.	15.00	7.50	4.50
(3)	Alvin Dark	18.00	9.00	5.50
(4)	Dom DiMaggio	25.00	12.50	7.50
(5)	Ferris Fain	15.00	7.50	4.50
(6)	George Kell	28.00	14.00	8.50
(7)	Stan Musial	75.00	37.00	22.00
(8)	Andy Pafko	18.00	9.00	5.50
(9)	Pee Wee Reese	40.00	20.00	12.00
(10)	Phil Rizzuto	40.00	20.00	12.00
(11)	Eddie Robinson	15.00	7.50	4.50
(12)	Ray Scarborough	15.00	7.50	4.50
(13)	Andy Seminick	15.00	7.50	4.50
(14)	Dick Sisler	15.00	7.50	4.50
(15)	Warren Spahn	40.00	20.00	12.00
(16)	Bobby Thomson	25.00	12.50	7.50

S

1988 Score

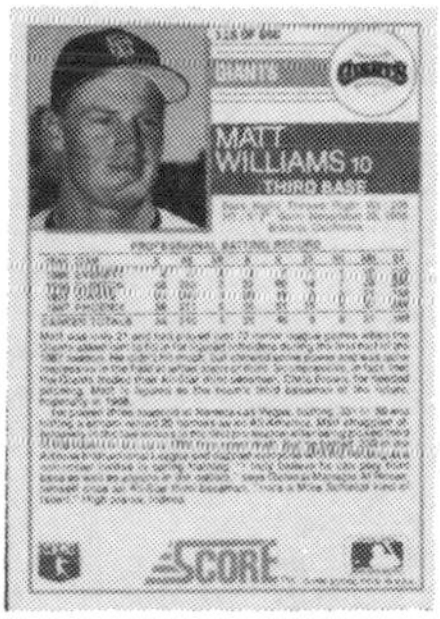

A fifth member joined the group of nationally distributed baseball cards in 1988. Titled "Score," the new cards are characterized by extremely sharp and excellent full-color photography and printing. Card backs are full-color also and carry a player head-shot, along with a brief biography and player personal and statistical information. The 660 cards in the set each measure 2-1/2" by 3-1/2" in size. The fronts come with one of six different border colors - blue, red, green, purple, orange and gold - which are equally divided at 110 cards per color. The Score set was produced by Major League Marketing, the same company that markets the "triple-action" Sportflics card sets.

	MT	NR MT	EX
Complete Set:	20.00	15.00	8.00
Common Player:	.04	.03	.02

1	Don Mattingly	.60	.45	.25
2	Wade Boggs	.40	.30	.15
3	Tim Raines	.20	.15	.08
4	Andre Dawson	.15	.11	.06
5	Mark McGwire	.70	.50	.30
6	Kevin Seitzer	.30	.25	.12
7	Wally Joyner	.35	.25	.14
8	Jesse Barfield	.10	.08	.04
9	Pedro Guerrero	.15	.11	.06
10	Eric Davis	.30	.25	.12
11	George Brett	.30	.25	.12
12	Ozzie Smith	.12	.09	.05
13	Rickey Henderson	.40	.30	.15
14	Jim Rice	.20	.15	.08
15	*Matt Nokes*	.30	.25	.12
16	Mike Schmidt	.40	.30	.15
17	Dave Parker	.12	.09	.05
18	Eddie Murray	.25	.20	.10
19	Andres Galarraga	.12	.09	.05
20	Tony Fernandez	.10	.08	.04
21	Kevin McReynolds	.12	.09	.05
22	B.J. Surhoff	.10	.08	.04
23	Pat Tabler	.06	.05	.02
24	Kirby Puckett	.25	.20	.10
25	Benny Santiago	.25	.20	.10
26	Ryne Sandberg	.40	.30	.15
27	Kelly Downs	.08	.06	.03
28	Jose Cruz	.06	.05	.02
29	Pete O'Brien	.06	.05	.02
30	Mark Langston	.10	.08	.04
31	Lee Smith	.08	.06	.03
32	Juan Samuel	.10	.08	.04
33	Kevin Bass	.06	.05	.02
34	R.J. Reynolds	.04	.03	.02
35	Steve Sax	.12	.09	.05
36	John Kruk	.08	.06	.03
37	Alan Trammell	.15	.11	.06
38	Chris Bosio	.06	.05	.02
39	Brook Jacoby	.08	.06	.03
40	Willie McGee	.10	.08	.04
41	Dave Magadan	.10	.08	.04
42	Fred Lynn	.10	.08	.04
43	Kent Hrbek	.12	.09	.05
44	Brian Downing	.06	.05	.02
45	Jose Canseco	1.00	.70	.40
46	Jim Presley	.08	.06	.03
47	Mike Stanley	.06	.05	.02
48	Tony Pena	.06	.05	.02
49	David Cone	.40	.30	.15
50	Rick Sutcliffe	.08	.06	.03
51	Doug Drabek	.10	.08	.04
52	Bill Doran	.06	.05	.02
53	Mike Scioscia	.06	.05	.02
54	Candy Maldonado	.06	.05	.02
55	Dave Winfield	.20	.15	.08
56	Lou Whitaker	.20	.15	.08
57	Tom Henke	.06	.05	.02
58	Ken Gerhart	.06	.05	.02
59	Glenn Braggs	.08	.06	.03
60	Julio Franco	.08	.06	.03
61	Charlie Leibrandt	.06	.05	.02
62	Gary Gaetti	.10	.08	.04
63	Bob Boone	.06	.05	.02
64	*Luis Polonia*	.35	.25	.14
65	Dwight Evans	.10	.08	.04
66	Phil Bradley	.08	.06	.03
67	Mike Boddicker	.06	.05	.02
68	Vince Coleman	.15	.11	.06
69	Howard Johnson	.08	.06	.03
70	Tim Wallach	.08	.06	.03
71	Keith Moreland	.06	.05	.02
72	Barry Larkin	.40	.30	.15
73	Alan Ashby	.04	.03	.02
74	Rick Rhoden	.06	.05	.02
75	Darrell Evans	.08	.06	.03
76	Dave Stieb	.08	.06	.03
77	Dan Plesac	.08	.06	.03
78	Will Clark	1.00	.70	.40
79	Frank White	.06	.05	.02
80	Joe Carter	.10	.08	.04
81	Mike Witt	.06	.05	.02
82	Terry Steinbach	.10	.08	.04
83	Alvin Davis	.10	.08	.04
84	Tom Herr	.06	.05	.02
85	Vance Law	.06	.05	.02
86	Kal Daniels	.15	.11	.06
87	Rick Honeycutt	.04	.03	.02
88	Alfredo Griffin	.06	.05	.02
89	Bret Saberhagen	.20	.15	.08

		MT	NR MT	EX
90	Bert Blyleven	.10	.08	.04
91	Jeff Reardon	.08	.06	.03
92	Cory Snyder	.15	.11	.06
93	Greg Walker	.06	.05	.02
94	*Joe Magrane*	.30	.25	.12
95	Rob Deer	.06	.05	.02
96	Ray Knight	.06	.05	.02
97	Casey Candaele	.04	.03	.02
98	John Cerutti	.06	.05	.02
99	Buddy Bell	.08	.06	.03
100	Jack Clark	.12	.09	.05
101	Eric Bell	.06	.05	.02
102	Willie Wilson	.08	.06	.03
103	Dave Schmidt	.04	.03	.02
104	Dennis Eckersley	.10	.08	.04
105	Don Sutton	.12	.09	.05
106	Danny Tartabull	.15	.11	.06
107	Fred McGriff	1.00	.70	.40
108	*Les Straker*	.15	.11	.06
109	Lloyd Moseby	.06	.05	.02
110	Roger Clemens	.50	.40	.20
111	Glenn Hubbard	.04	.03	.02
112	*Ken Williams*	.20	.15	.08
113	Ruben Sierra	.35	.25	.14
114	Stan Jefferson	.06	.05	.02
115	Milt Thompson	.04	.03	.02
116	Bobby Bonilla	.40	.30	.15
117	Wayne Tolleson	.04	.03	.02
118	*Matt Williams*	2.50	2.00	1.00
119	Chet Lemon	.06	.05	.02
120	Dale Sveum	.06	.05	.02
121	Dennis Boyd	.06	.05	.02
122	Brett Butler	.06	.05	.02
123	Terry Kennedy	.06	.05	.02
124	Jack Howell	.06	.05	.02
125	Curt Young	.06	.05	.02
126a	Dale Valle (first name incorrect)	.25	.20	.10
126b	Dave Valle (correct spelling)	.06	.05	.02
127	Curt Wilkerson	.04	.03	.02
128	Tim Teufel	.04	.03	.02
129	Ozzie Virgil	.04	.03	.02
130	Brian Fisher	.06	.05	.02
131	Lance Parrish	.12	.09	.05
132	Tom Browning	.08	.06	.03
133a	Larry Anderson (incorrect spelling)	.25	.20	.10
133b	Larry Andersen (correct spelling)	.06	.05	.02
134a	Bob Brenley (incorrect spelling)	.25	.20	.10
134b	Bob Brenly (correct spelling)	.06	.05	.02
135	Mike Marshall	.10	.08	.04
136	Gerald Perry	.08	.06	.03
137	Bobby Meacham	.04	.03	.02
138	Larry Herndon	.04	.03	.02
139	*Fred Manrique*	.12	.09	.05
140	Charlie Hough	.06	.05	.02
141	Ron Darling	.10	.08	.04
142	Herm Winningham	.04	.03	.02
143	Mike Diaz	.06	.05	.02
144	*Mike Jackson*	.15	.11	.06
145	Denny Walling	.04	.03	.02
146	Rob Thompson	.06	.05	.02
147	Franklin Stubbs	.06	.05	.02
148	Albert Hall	.04	.03	.02
149	Bobby Witt	.08	.06	.03
150	Lance McCullers	.06	.05	.02
151	Scott Bradley	.04	.03	.02
152	Mark McLemore	.04	.03	.02
153	Tim Laudner	.04	.03	.02
154	Greg Swindell	.15	.11	.06
155	Marty Barrett	.06	.05	.02
156	Mike Heath	.04	.03	.02
157	Gary Ward	.06	.05	.02
158a	Lee Mazilli (incorrect spelling)	.25	.20	.10
158b	Lee Mazzilli (correct spelling)	.08	.06	.03
159	Tom Foley	.04	.03	.02
160	Robin Yount	.30	.25	.12
161	Steve Bedrosian	.10	.08	.04
162	Bob Walk	.04	.03	.02
163	Nick Esasky	.06	.05	.02
164	*Ken Caminiti*	.25	.20	.10
165	Jose Uribe	.04	.03	.02
166	Dave Anderson	.04	.03	.02
167	Ed Whitson	.04	.03	.02
168	Ernie Whitt	.06	.05	.02
169	Cecil Cooper	.08	.06	.03
170	Mike Pagliarulo	.08	.06	.03
171	Pat Sheridan	.04	.03	.02
172	Chris Bando	.04	.03	.02
173	Lee Lacy	.04	.03	.02
174	Steve Lombardozzi	.04	.03	.02
175	Mike Greenwell	.70	.50	.30
176	Greg Minton	.04	.03	.02

		MT	NR MT	EX
177	Moose Haas	.04	.03	.02
178	Mike Kingery	.04	.03	.02
179	Greg Harris	.04	.03	.02
180	Bo Jackson	1.00	.70	.40
181	Carmelo Martinez	.06	.05	.02
182	Alex Trevino	.04	.03	.02
183	Ron Oester	.04	.03	.02
184	Danny Darwin	.04	.03	.02
185	Mike Krukow	.06	.05	.02
186	Rafael Palmeiro	.50	.40	.20
187	Tim Burke	.04	.03	.02
188	Roger McDowell	.08	.06	.03
189	Garry Templeton	.06	.05	.02
190	Terry Pendleton	.06	.05	.02
191	Larry Parrish	.06	.05	.02
192	Rey Quinones	.04	.03	.02
193	Joaquin Andujar	.06	.05	.02
194	Tom Brunansky	.08	.06	.03
195	Donnie Moore	.04	.03	.02
196	Dan Pasqua	.08	.06	.03
197	Jim Gantner	.04	.03	.02
198	Mark Eichhorn	.06	.05	.02
199	John Grubb	.04	.03	.02
200	*Bill Ripken*	.20	.15	.08
201	*Sam Horn*	.30	.25	.12
202	Todd Worrell	.08	.06	.03
203	Terry Leach	.04	.03	.02
204	Garth Iorg	.04	.03	.02
205	Brian Dayett	.04	.03	.02
206	Bo Diaz	.06	.05	.02
207	Craig Reynolds	.04	.03	.02
208	Brian Holton	.08	.06	.03
209	Marvelle Wynne (Marvell)	.04	.03	.02
210	Dave Concepcion	.06	.05	.02
211	Mike Davis	.06	.05	.02
212	Devon White	.15	.11	.06
213	Mickey Brantley	.04	.03	.02
214	Greg Gagne	.04	.03	.02
215	Oddibe McDowell	.06	.05	.02
216	Jimmy Key	.08	.06	.03
217	Dave Bergman	.04	.03	.02
218	Calvin Schiraldi	.04	.03	.02
219	Larry Sheets	.06	.05	.02
220	Mike Easler	.06	.05	.02
221	Kurt Stillwell	.08	.06	.03
222	*Chuck Jackson*	.15	.11	.06
223	Dave Martinez	.08	.06	.03
224	Tim Leary	.06	.05	.02
225	Steve Garvey	.20	.15	.08
226	Greg Mathews	.06	.05	.02
227	Doug Sisk	.04	.03	.02
228	Dave Henderson	.08	.06	.03
229	Jimmy Dwyer	.04	.03	.02
230	Larry Owen	.04	.03	.02
231	Andre Thornton	.06	.05	.02
232	Mark Salas	.04	.03	.02
233	Tom Brookens	.04	.03	.02
234	Greg Brock	.06	.05	.02
235	Rance Mulliniks	.04	.03	.02
236	Bob Brower	.06	.05	.02
237	Joe Niekro	.06	.05	.02
238	Scott Bankhead	.04	.03	.02
239	Doug DeCinces	.06	.05	.02
240	Tommy John	.12	.09	.05
241	Rich Gedman	.06	.05	.02
242	Ted Power	.04	.03	.02
243	*Dave Meads*	.12	.09	.05
244	Jim Sundberg	.06	.05	.02
245	Ken Oberkfell	.04	.03	.02
246	Jimmy Jones	.08	.06	.03
247	Ken Landreaux	.04	.03	.02
248	Jose Oquendo	.04	.03	.02
249	*John Mitchell*	.15	.11	.06
250	Don Baylor	.08	.06	.03
251	Scott Fletcher	.06	.05	.02
252	Al Newman	.04	.03	.02
253	Carney Lansford	.08	.06	.03
254	Johnny Ray	.06	.05	.02
255	Gary Pettis	.04	.03	.02
256	Ken Phelps	.06	.05	.02
257	Rick Leach	.04	.03	.02
258	Tim Stoddard	.04	.03	.02
259	Ed Romero	.04	.03	.02
260	Sid Bream	.06	.05	.02
261a	Tom Neidenfuer (incorrect spelling)	.25	.20	.10
261b	Tom Niedenfuer (correct spelling)	.06	.05	.02
262	Rick Dempsey	.06	.05	.02
263	Lonnie Smith	.06	.05	.02
264	Bob Forsch	.06	.05	.02
265	Barry Bonds	.40	.30	.15
266	Willie Randolph	.06	.05	.02
267	Mike Ramsey	.04	.03	.02
268	Don Slaught	.04	.03	.02
269	Mickey Tettleton	.04	.03	.02
270	Jerry Reuss	.06	.05	.02
271	Marc Sullivan	.04	.03	.02
272	Jim Morrison	.04	.03	.02
273	Steve Balboni	.06	.05	.02
274	Dick Schofield	.04	.03	.02
275	John Tudor	.08	.06	.03
276	*Gene Larkin*	.20	.15	.08
277	Harold Reynolds	.06	.05	.02
278	Jerry Browne	.06	.05	.02
279	Willie Upshaw	.06	.05	.02
280	Ted Higuera	.08	.06	.03
281	Terry McGriff	.04	.03	.02
282	Terry Puhl	.04	.03	.02
283	*Mark Wasinger*	.12	.09	.05
284	Luis Salazar	.04	.03	.02
285	Ted Simmons	.08	.06	.03
286	John Shelby	.04	.03	.02
287	*John Smiley*	.50	.40	.20
288	Curt Ford	.04	.03	.02
289	Steve Crawford	.04	.03	.02
290	Dan Quisenberry	.06	.05	.02
291	Alan Wiggins	.04	.03	.02
292	Randy Bush	.04	.03	.02
293	John Candelaria	.06	.05	.02
294	Tony Phillips	.04	.03	.02
295	Mike Morgan	.04	.03	.02
296	Bill Wegman	.04	.03	.02
297a	Terry Franconia (incorrect spelling)	.25	.20	.10
297b	Terry Francona (correct spelling)	.06	.05	.02
298	Mickey Hatcher	.04	.03	.02
299	Andres Thomas	.06	.05	.02
300	Bob Stanley	.04	.03	.02
301	*Alfredo Pedrique*	.12	.09	.05
302	Jim Lindeman	.06	.05	.02
303	Wally Backman	.06	.05	.02
304	Paul O'Neill	.06	.05	.02
305	Hubie Brooks	.08	.06	.03
306	Steve Buechele	.04	.03	.02
307	Bobby Thigpen	.08	.06	.03
308	George Hendrick	.06	.05	.02
309	John Moses	.04	.03	.02
310	Ron Guidry	.12	.09	.05
311	Bill Schroeder	.04	.03	.02
312	*Jose Nunez*	.15	.11	.06
313	Bud Black	.04	.03	.02
314	Joe Sambito	.04	.03	.02
315	Scott McGregor	.06	.05	.02
316	Rafael Santana	.04	.03	.02
317	Frank Williams	.04	.03	.02
318	Mike Fitzgerald	.04	.03	.02
319	Rick Mahler	.04	.03	.02
320	Jim Gott	.04	.03	.02
321	Mariano Duncan	.04	.03	.02
322	Jose Guzman	.06	.05	.02
323	Lee Guetterman	.04	.03	.02
324	Dan Gladden	.04	.03	.02
325	Gary Carter	.15	.11	.06
326	Tracy Jones	.10	.08	.04
327	Floyd Youmans	.04	.03	.02
328	Bill Dawley	.04	.03	.02
329	*Paul Noce*	.10	.08	.04
330	Angel Salazar	.04	.03	.02
331	Goose Gossage	.12	.09	.05
332	George Frazier	.04	.03	.02
333	Ruppert Jones	.04	.03	.02
334	Billy Jo Robidoux	.04	.03	.02
335	Mike Scott	.10	.08	.04
336	Randy Myers	.10	.08	.04
337	Bob Sebra	.04	.03	.02
338	Eric Show	.06	.05	.02
339	Mitch Williams	.06	.05	.02
340	Paul Molitor	.10	.08	.04
341	Gus Polidor	.04	.03	.02
342	Steve Trout	.04	.03	.02
343	Jerry Don Gleaton	.04	.03	.02
344	Bob Knepper	.06	.05	.02
345	Mitch Webster	.06	.05	.02
346	John Morris	.04	.03	.02
347	Andy Hawkins	.04	.03	.02
348	Dave Leiper	.04	.03	.02
349	Ernest Riles	.04	.03	.02
350	Dwight Gooden	.40	.30	.15
351	Dave Righetti	.12	.09	.05
352	Pat Dodson	.04	.03	.02
353	John Habyan	.04	.03	.02
354	Jim Deshaies	.06	.05	.02

		MT	NR MT	EX
355	Butch Wynegar	.04	.03	.02
356	Bryn Smith	.04	.03	.02
357	Matt Young	.04	.03	.02
358	*Tom Pagnozzi*	.25	.20	.10
359	Floyd Rayford	.04	.03	.02
360	Darryl Strawberry	.30	.25	.12
361	Sal Butera	.04	.03	.02
362	Domingo Ramos	.04	.03	.02
363	Chris Brown	.06	.05	.02
364	Jose Gonzalez	.04	.03	.02
365	Dave Smith	.06	.05	.02
366	Andy McGaffigan	.04	.03	.02
367	Stan Javier	.04	.03	.02
368	Henry Cotto	.04	.03	.02
369	Mike Birkbeck	.06	.05	.02
370	Len Dykstra	.08	.06	.03
371	Dave Collins	.06	.05	.02
372	Spike Owen	.04	.03	.02
373	Geno Petralli	.04	.03	.02
374	Ron Karkovice	.04	.03	.02
375	Shane Rawley	.06	.05	.02
376	*DeWayne Buice*	.15	.11	.06
377	*Bill Pecota*	.15	.11	.06
378	Leon Durham	.06	.05	.02
379	Ed Olwine	.04	.03	.02
380	Bruce Hurst	.08	.06	.03
381	Bob McClure	.04	.03	.02
382	Mark Thurmond	.04	.03	.02
383	Buddy Biancalana	.04	.03	.02
384	Tim Conroy	.04	.03	.02
385	Tony Gwynn	.25	.20	.10
386	Greg Gross	.04	.03	.02
387	*Barry Lyons*	.12	.09	.05
388	Mike Felder	.04	.03	.02
389	Pat Clements	.04	.03	.02
390	Ken Griffey	.06	.05	.02
391	Mark Davis	.04	.03	.02
392	Jose Rijo	.06	.05	.02
393	Mike Young	.04	.03	.02
394	Willie Fraser	.06	.05	.02
395	Dion James	.06	.05	.02
396	*Steve Shields*	.12	.09	.05
397	Randy St. Claire	.04	.03	.02
398	Danny Jackson	.12	.09	.05
399	Cecil Fielder	.60	.45	.25
400	Keith Hernandez	.15	.11	.06
401	Don Carman	.06	.05	.02
402	*Chuck Crim*	.12	.09	.05
403	Rob Woodward	.04	.03	.02
404	Junior Ortiz	.04	.03	.02
405	Glenn Wilson	.06	.05	.02
406	Ken Howell	.04	.03	.02
407	Jeff Kunkel	.04	.03	.02
408	Jeff Reed	.04	.03	.02
409	Chris James	.10	.08	.04
410	Zane Smith	.06	.05	.02
411	Ken Dixon	.04	.03	.02
412	Ricky Horton	.06	.05	.02
413	Frank DiPino	.04	.03	.02
414	*Shane Mack*	.15	.11	.06
415	Danny Cox	.06	.05	.02
416	Andy Van Slyke	.10	.08	.04
417	Danny Heep	.04	.03	.02
418	John Cangelosi	.04	.03	.02
419a	John Christiansen (incorrect spelling)	.25	.20	.10
419b	John Christensen (correct spelling)	.06	.05	.02
420	*Joey Cora*	.12	.09	.05
421	Mike LaValliere	.06	.05	.02
422	Kelly Gruber	.35	.25	.14
423	Bruce Benedict	.04	.03	.02
424	Len Matuszek	.04	.03	.02
425	Kent Tekulve	.06	.05	.02
426	Rafael Ramirez	.04	.03	.02
427	Mike Flanagan	.06	.05	.02
428	Mike Gallego	.04	.03	.02
429	Juan Castillo	.04	.03	.02
430	Neal Heaton	.04	.03	.02
431	Phil Garner	.04	.03	.02
432	*Mike Dunne*	.12	.09	.05
433	Wallace Johnson	.04	.03	.02
434	Jack O'Connor	.04	.03	.02
435	Steve Jeltz	.04	.03	.02
436	*Donnell Nixon*	.15	.11	.06
437	Jack Lazorko	.04	.03	.02
438	*Keith Comstock*	.12	.09	.05
439	Jeff Robinson	.04	.03	.02
440	Graig Nettles	.08	.06	.03
441	Mel Hall	.06	.05	.02
442	*Gerald Young*	.15	.11	.06
443	Gary Redus	.04	.03	.02

		MT	NR MT	EX
444	Charlie Moore	.04	.03	.02
445	Bill Madlock	.08	.06	.03
446	Mark Clear	.04	.03	.02
447	Greg Booker	.04	.03	.02
448	Rick Schu	.04	.03	.02
449	Ron Kittle	.06	.05	.02
450	Dale Murphy	.30	.25	.12
451	Bob Dernier	.04	.03	.02
452	Dale Mohorcic	.06	.05	.02
453	Rafael Belliard	.04	.03	.02
454	Charlie Puleo	.04	.03	.02
455	Dwayne Murphy	.06	.05	.02
456	Jim Eisenreich	.04	.03	.02
457	David Palmer	.04	.03	.02
458	Dave Stewart	.08	.06	.03
459	Pascual Perez	.06	.05	.02
460	Glenn Davis	.12	.09	.05
461	Dan Petry	.06	.05	.02
462	Jim Winn	.04	.03	.02
463	Darrell Miller	.04	.03	.02
464	Mike Moore	.04	.03	.02
465	Mike LaCoss	.04	.03	.02
466	Steve Farr	.04	.03	.02
467	Jerry Mumphrey	.04	.03	.02
468	Kevin Gross	.06	.05	.02
469	Bruce Bochy	.04	.03	.02
470	Orel Hershiser	.20	.15	.08
471	Eric King	.06	.05	.02
472	*Ellis Burks*	1.00	.70	.40
473	Darren Daulton	.04	.03	.02
474	Mookie Wilson	.06	.05	.02
475	Frank Viola	.12	.09	.05
476	Ron Robinson	.04	.03	.02
477	Bob Melvin	.04	.03	.02
478	Jeff Musselman	.06	.05	.02
479	Charlie Kerfeld	.04	.03	.02
480	Richard Dotson	.06	.05	.02
481	Kevin Mitchell	.50	.40	.20
482	Gary Roenicke	.04	.03	.02
483	Tim Flannery	.04	.03	.02
484	Rich Yett	.04	.03	.02
485	Pete Incaviglia	.12	.09	.05
486	Rick Cerone	.04	.03	.02
487	Tony Armas	.06	.05	.02
488	Jerry Reed	.04	.03	.02
489	Davey Lopes	.06	.05	.02
490	Frank Tanana	.06	.05	.02
491	Mike Loynd	.04	.03	.02
492	Bruce Ruffin	.06	.05	.02
493	Chris Speier	.04	.03	.02
494	Tom Hume	.04	.03	.02
495	Jesse Orosco	.06	.05	.02
496	*Robby Wine, Jr.*	.12	.09	.05
497	*Jeff Montgomery*	.25	.20	.10
498	Jeff Dedmon	.04	.03	.02
499	Luis Aguayo	.04	.03	.02
500	Reggie Jackson (1968-75 Oakland Athletics)	.20	.15	.08
501	Reggie Jackson (1976 Baltimore Orioles)	.20	.15	.08
502	Reggie Jackson (1977-81 New York Yankees)	.20	.15	.08
503	Reggie Jackson (1982-86 California Angels)	.20	.15	.08
504	Reggie Jackson (1987 Oakland Athletics)	.20	.15	.08
505	Billy Hatcher	.06	.05	.02
506	Ed Lynch	.04	.03	.02
507	Willie Hernandez	.06	.05	.02
508	Jose DeLeon	.06	.05	.02
509	Joel Youngblood	.04	.03	.02
510	Bob Welch	.08	.06	.03
511	Steve Ontiveros	.04	.03	.02
512	Randy Ready	.04	.03	.02
513	Juan Nieves	.06	.05	.02
514	Jeff Russell	.04	.03	.02
515	Von Hayes	.06	.05	.02
516	Mark Gubicza	.10	.08	.04
517	Ken Dayley	.04	.03	.02
518	Don Aase	.04	.03	.02
519	Rick Reuschel	.08	.06	.03
520	*Mike Henneman*	.25	.20	.10
521	Rick Aguilera	.04	.03	.02
522	Jay Howell	.06	.05	.02
523	Ed Correa	.04	.03	.02
524	Manny Trillo	.06	.05	.02
525	Kirk Gibson	.15	.11	.06
526	*Wally Ritchie*	.12	.09	.05
527	Al Nipper	.04	.03	.02
528	Atlee Hammaker	.04	.03	.02
529	Shawon Dunston	.08	.06	.03

		MT	NR MT	EX
530	Jim Clancy	.06	.05	.02
531	Tom Paciorek	.04	.03	.02
532	Joel Skinner	.04	.03	.02
533	Scott Garrelts	.04	.03	.02
534	Tom O'Malley	.04	.03	.02
535	John Franco	.08	.06	.03
536	*Paul Kilgus*	.20	.15	.08
537	Darrell Porter	.06	.05	.02
538	Walt Terrell	.06	.05	.02
539	*Bill Long*	.15	.11	.06
540	George Bell	.20	.15	.08
541	Jeff Sellers	.06	.05	.02
542	*Joe Boever*	.12	.09	.05
543	Steve Howe	.06	.05	.02
544	Scott Sanderson	.04	.03	.02
545	Jack Morris	.15	.11	.06
546	*Todd Benzinger*	.30	.25	.12
547	Steve Henderson	.04	.03	.02
548	Eddie Milner	.04	.03	.02
549	*Jeff Robinson*	.25	.20	.10
550	Cal Ripken, Jr.	.25	.20	.10
551	Jody Davis	.06	.05	.02
552	Kirk McCaskill	.06	.05	.02
553	Craig Lefferts	.04	.03	.02
554	Darnell Coles	.06	.05	.02
555	Phil Niekro	.15	.11	.06
556	Mike Aldrete	.06	.05	.02
557	Pat Perry	.04	.03	.02
558	Juan Agosto	.04	.03	.02
559	Rob Murphy	.06	.05	.02
560	Dennis Rasmussen	.08	.06	.03
561	Manny Lee	.04	.03	.02
562	*Jeff Blauser*	.20	.15	.08
563	Bob Ojeda	.06	.05	.02
564	Dave Dravecky	.06	.05	.02
565	Gene Garber	.04	.03	.02
566	Ron Roenicke	.04	.03	.02
567	*Tommy Hinzo*	.12	.09	.05
568	*Eric Nolte*	.12	.09	.05
569	Ed Hearn	.04	.03	.02
570	*Mark Davidson*	.12	.09	.05
571	*Jim Walewander*	.12	.09	.05
572	Donnie Hill	.04	.03	.02
573	Jamie Moyer	.06	.05	.02
574	Ken Schrom	.04	.03	.02
575	Nolan Ryan	.60	.45	.25
576	Jim Acker	.04	.03	.02
577	Jamie Quirk	.04	.03	.02
578	*Jay Aldrich*	.10	.08	.04
579	Claudell Washington	.06	.05	.02
580	Jeff Leonard	.06	.05	.02
581	Carmen Castillo	.04	.03	.02
582	Daryl Boston	.04	.03	.02
583	*Jeff DeWillis*	.15	.11	.06
584	*John Marzano*	.20	.15	.08
585	Bill Gullickson	.06	.05	.02
586	Andy Allanson	.08	.06	.03
587	Lee Tunnell	.04	.03	.02
588	Gene Nelson	.04	.03	.02
589	Dave LaPoint	.06	.05	.02
590	Harold Baines	.10	.08	.04
591	Bill Buckner	.08	.06	.03
592	Carlton Fisk	.20	.15	.08
593	Rick Manning	.04	.03	.02
594	*Doug Jones*	.20	.15	.08
595	Tom Candiotti	.04	.03	.02
596	Steve Lake	.04	.03	.02
597	*Jose Lind*	.25	.20	.10
598	*Ross Jones*	.12	.09	.05
599	Gary Matthews	.06	.05	.02
600	Fernando Valezuela	.15	.11	.06
601	Dennis Martinez	.06	.05	.02
602	*Les Lancaster*	.15	.11	.06
603	Ozzie Guillen	.06	.05	.02
604	Tony Bernazard	.04	.03	.02
605	Chili Davis	.06	.05	.02
606	Roy Smalley	.04	.03	.02
607	Ivan Calderon	.08	.06	.03
608	Jay Tibbs	.04	.03	.02
609	Guy Hoffman	.04	.03	.02
610	Doyle Alexander	.06	.05	.02
611	Mike Bielecki	.04	.03	.02
612	*Shawn Hillegas*	.20	.15	.08
613	Keith Atherton	.04	.03	.02
614	Eric Plunk	.04	.03	.02
615	Sid Fernandez	.08	.06	.03
616	Dennis Lamp	.04	.03	.02
617	Dave Engle	.04	.03	.02
618	Harry Spilman	.04	.03	.02
619	Don Robinson	.06	.05	.02
620	*John Farrell*	.20	.15	.08

		MT	NR MT	EX
621	*Nelson Liriano*	.15	.11	.06
622	Floyd Bannister	.06	.05	.02
623	Rookie Prospect *(Randy Milligan)*	.60	.45	.25
624	Rookie Prospect (Kevin Elster)	.25	.20	.10
625	Rookie Prospect *(Jody Reed)*	.40	.30	.15
626	Rookie Prospect (Shawn Abner)	.20	.15	.08
627	Rookie Prospect *(Kirt Manwaring)*	.20	.15	.08
628	Rookie Prospect *(Pete Stanicek)*	.15	.11	.06
629	Rookie Prospect *(Rob Ducey)*	.12	.09	.05
630	Rookie Prospect (Steve Kiefer)	.04	.03	.02
631	Rookie Prospect *(Gary Thurman)*	.20	.15	.08
632	Rookie Prospect *(Darrel Akerfelds)*	.12	.09	.05
633	Rookie Prospect (Dave Clark)	.10	.08	.04
634	Rookie Prospect *(Roberto Kelly)*	1.00	.70	.40
635	Rookie Prospect *(Keith Hughes)*	.15	.11	.06
636	Rookie Prospect *(John Davis)*	.15	.11	.06
637	Rookie Prospect *(Mike Devereaux)*	.40	.30	.15
638	Rookie Prospect *(Tom Glavine)*	.70	.50	.30
639	Rookie Prospect *(Keith Miller)*	.20	.15	.08
640	Rookie Prospect *(Chris Gwynn)*	.20	.15	.08
641	Rookie Prospect *(Tim Crews)*	.15	.11	.06
642	Rookie Prospect *(Mackey Sasser)*	.20	.15	.08
643	Rookie Prospect *(Vicente Palacios)*	.15	.11	.06
644	Rookie Prospect (Kevin Romine)	.06	.05	.02
645	Rookie Prospect *(Gregg Jefferies)*	1.50	1.15	.60
646	Rookie Prospect *(Jeff Treadway)*	.25	.20	.10
647	Rookie Prospect *(Ronnie Gant)*	2.25	1.75	.90
648	Rookie Sluggers (Mark McGwire, Matt Nokes)	.30	.25	.12
649	Speed and Power (Eric Davis, Tim Raines)	.25	.20	.10
650	Game Breakers (Jack Clark, Don Mattingly)	.40	.30	.15
651	Super Shortstops (Tony Fernandez, Cal Ripken, Jr., Alan Trammell)	.20	.15	.08
652	1987 Highlights (Vince Coleman)	.08	.06	.03
653	1987 Highlights (Kirby Puckett)	.12	.09	.05
654	1987 Highlights (Benito Santiago)	.10	.08	.04
655	1987 Highlights (Juan Nieves)	.06	.05	.02
656	1987 Highlights (Steve Bedrosian)	.06	.05	.02
657	1987 Highlights (Mike Schmidt)	.20	.15	.08
658	1987 Highlights (Don Mattingly)	.30	.25	.12
659	1987 Highlights (Mark McGwire)	.30	.25	.12
660	1987 Highlights (Paul Molitor)	.08	.06	.03

1988 Score Box Panels

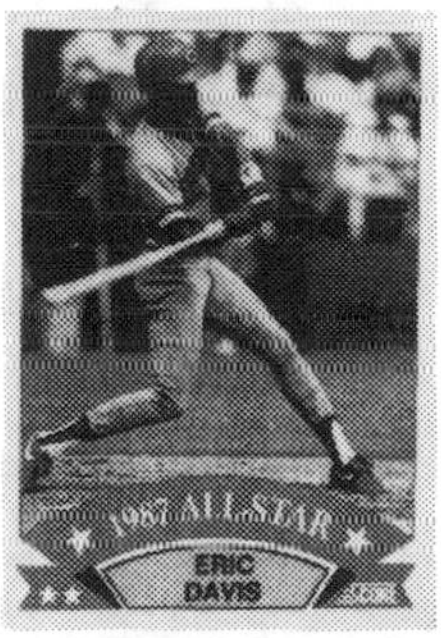

This 18-card set, produced by Major League Marketing and manufactured by Optigraphics, is the premiere box-bottom set issued under the Score trademark. The set features 1987 major league All-star players in full-color action poses, framed by a white border. A "1987 All-Star" banner (red or purple) curves above an orange player name block beneath the player photo. Card backs are printed in red, blue, gold and black and carry the card number, player name and position and league logo. Six colorful "Great Moments in Baseball" trivia cards are also included in this set. Each trivia card highlights an historical event at a famous ballpark.

	MT	NR MT	EX
Complete Panel Set:	8.00	6.00	3.25
Complete Singles Set:	3.00	2.25	1.25
Common Panel:	1.50	1.25	.60
Common Single Player:	.15	.11	.06

		MT	NR MT	EX
	Panel	1.50	1.25	.60
1	Terry Kennedy	.15	.11	.06
3	Willie Randolph	.15	.11	.06
15	Eric Davis	.40	.30	.15
	Panel	1.75	1.25	.70
3	Don Mattingly	.60	.45	.25
5	Cal Ripken, Jr.	.50	.40	.20
11	Jack Clark	.25	.20	.10
	Panel	2.00	1.50	.80
4	Wade Boggs	.50	.40	.20
9	Bret Saberhagen	.20	.15	.08
12	Ryne Sandberg	.60	.45	.25
	Panel	1.50	1.25	.60
6	George Bell	.25	.20	.10
13	Mike Schmidt	.35	.25	.14
18	Mike Scott	.15	.11	.06
	Panel	2.00	1.50	.80
7	Rickey Henderson	.60	.45	.25
16	Andre Dawson	.25	.20	.10
17	Darryl Strawberry	.40	.30	.15
	Panel	1.50	1.25	.60
8	Dave Winfield	.25	.20	.10
10	Gary Carter	.20	.15	.08
14	Ozzie Smith	.25	.20	.10

1988 Score Traded

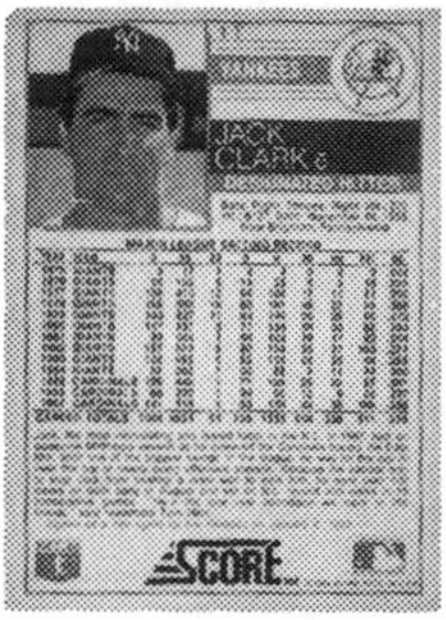

This 110-card set featuring new rookies and traded veterans is similar in design to the 1988 Score set, except for a change in border color. Individual standard-size player cards (2-1/2" by 3-1/2") feature a bright orange border framing full-figure action photos highlighted by a thin white outline. The player name (in white) is centered in the bottom margin, flanked by three yellow stars lower left and a yellow Score logo lower right. The backs carry full-color player close-ups on a cream-colored background, followed by card number, team name and logo, player personal information and a purple stats chart that lists year-by-year and major league totals. A brief player profile follows the stats chart and, on some cards, information is included about the player's trade or acquisition. The update set also includes 10 Magic Motion 3-D trivia cards.

		MT	NR MT	EX
Complete Set:		70.00	52.00	27.00
Common Player:		.08	.06	.03
1T	Jack Clark	.20	.15	.08
2T	Danny Jackson	.20	.15	.08
3T	Brett Butler	.10	.08	.04
4T	Kurt Stillwell	.12	.09	.05
5T	Tom Brunansky	.15	.11	.06
6T	Dennis Lamp	.08	.06	.03
7T	Jose DeLeon	.10	.08	.04
8T	Tom Herr	.12	.09	.05
9T	Keith Moreland	.10	.08	.04
10T	Kirk Gibson	.20	.15	.08
11T	Bud Black	.08	.06	.03
12T	Rafael Ramirez	.08	.06	.03
13T	Luis Salazar	.08	.06	.03
14T	Goose Gossage	.15	.11	.06
15T	Bob Welch	.15	.11	.06
16T	Vance Law	.10	.08	.04
17T	Ray Knight	.10	.08	.04

		MT	NR MT	EX
18T	Dan Quisenberry	.10	.08	.04
19T	Don Slaught	.08	.06	.03
20T	Lee Smith	.12	.09	.05
21T	Rick Cerone	.08	.06	.03
22T	Pat Tabler	.10	.08	.04
23T	Larry McWilliams	.08	.06	.03
24T	Rick Horton	.10	.08	.04
25T	Graig Nettles	.12	.09	.05
26T	Dan Petry	.10	.08	.04
27T	Joe Rijo	.10	.08	.04
28T	Chili Davis	.10	.08	.04
29T	Dickie Thon	.10	.08	.04
30T	Mackey Sasser(FC)	.15	.11	.06
31T	Mickey Tettleton	.08	.06	.03
32T	Rick Dempsey	.08	.06	.03
33T	Ron Hassey	.08	.06	.03
34T	Phil Bradley	.12	.09	.05
35T	Jay Howell	.10	.08	.04
36T	Bill Buckner	.12	.09	.05
37T	Alfredo Griffin	.10	.08	.04
38T	Gary Pettis	.08	.06	.03
39T	Calvin Schiraldi	.08	.06	.03
40T	John Candelaria	.10	.08	.04
41T	Joe Orsulak	.08	.06	.03
42T	Willie Upshaw	.10	.08	.04
43T	Herm Winningham	.08	.06	.03
44T	Ron Kittle	.12	.09	.05
45T	Bob Dernier	.08	.06	.03
46T	Steve Balboni	.10	.08	.04
47T	Steve Shields	.08	.06	.03
48T	Henry Cotto	.08	.06	.03
49T	Dave Henderson	.10	.08	.04
50T	Dave Parker	.15	.11	.06
51T	Mike Young	.08	.06	.03
52T	Mark Salas	.08	.06	.03
53T	Mike Davis	.08	.06	.03
54T	Rafael Santana	.08	.06	.03
55T	Don Baylor	.15	.11	.06
56T	Dan Pasqua	.12	.09	.05
57T	Ernest Riles	.08	.06	.03
58T	Glenn Hubbard	.08	.06	.03
59T	Mike Smithson	.08	.06	.03
60T	Richard Dotson	.10	.08	.04
61T	Jerry Reuss	.10	.08	.04
62T	Mike Jackson	.10	.08	.04
63T	Floyd Bannister	.10	.08	.04
64T	Jesse Orosco	.10	.08	.04
65T	Larry Parrish	.10	.08	.04
66T	Jeff Bittiger(FC)	.20	.15	.08
67T	Ray Hayward(FC)	.10	.08	.04
68T	Ricky Jordan(FC)	1.00	.70	.40
69T	Tommy Gregg(FC)	.12	.09	.05
70T	Brady Anderson(FC)	.35	.25	.14
71T	Jeff Montgomery	.08	.06	.03
72T	Darryl Hamilton(FC)	.50	.40	.20
73T	Cecil Espy(FC)	.10	.08	.04
74T	Greg Briley(FC)	1.00	.70	.40
75T	Joey Meyer(FC)	.20	.15	.08
76T	Mike Macfarlane(FC)	.40	.30	.15
77T	Oswald Peraza(FC)	.20	.15	.08
78T	Jack Armstrong(FC)	1.00	.70	.40
79T	Don Heinkel(FC)	.20	.15	.08
80T	Mark Grace(FC)	25.00	18.00	9.00
81T	Steve Curry(FC)	.20	.15	.08
82T	Damon Berryhill(FC)	.40	.30	.15
83T	Steve Ellsworth(FC)	.20	.15	.08
84T	Pete Smith(FC)	.12	.09	.05
85T	Jack McDowell	5.00	3.75	2.00
86T	Rob Dibble(FC)	4.00	3.00	1.50
87T	Brian Harvey(FC)	1.00	.70	.40
88T	John Dopson(FC)	.25	.20	.10
89T	Dave Gallagher(FC)	.25	.20	.10
90T	Todd Stottlemyre(FC)	3.00	2.25	1.25
91T	Mike Schooler(FC)	1.00	.70	.40
92T	Don Gordon(FC)	.08	.06	.03
93T	Sil Campusano(FC)	.25	.20	.10
94T	Jeff Pico(FC)	.25	.20	.10
95T	Jay Buhner(FC)	1.75	1.25	.70
96T	Nelson Santovenia(FC)	.25	.20	.10
97T	Al Leiter(FC)	.30	.25	.12
98T	Luis Alicea(FC)	.20	.15	.08
99T	Pat Borders(FC)	.60	.45	.25
100T	Chris Sabo(FC)	8.00	6.00	3.25
101T	Tim Belcher(FC)	.70	.50	.30
102T	Walt Weiss(FC)	1.50	1.25	.60
103T	Craig Biggio(FC)	4.00	3.00	1.50
104T	Don August(FC)	.25	.20	.10
105T	Roberto Alomar(FC)	15.00	11.00	6.00
106T	Todd Burns(FC)	.30	.25	.12
107T	John Costello(FC)	.20	.15	.08
108T	Melido Perez(FC)	.60	.45	.25

		MT	NR MT	EX
109T	Darrin Jackson(FC)	.12	.09	.05
110T	Orestes Destrade(FC)	.15	.11	.06

1988 Score Young Superstar - Series I

This 40-card standard-size set (2-1/2" by 3-1/2" cards) from Optigraphics was divided into five separate 8-card sets. Similar to the company's regular issue, these cards are distinguished by excellent full-color photography on both front and back. The glossy player photos, with team logo in the lower right corner, are centered on a white background and framed by a vivid blue and green border. A player name banner beneath the photo includes the name, position and uniform number. The card backs feature ful-color player closeups beneath a hot pink player name/Score logo banner. Hot pink also frames the personal stats (in green), career stats (in black) and career biography (in blue). The backs also include quotes from well-known baseball authorities discussing player performance. This set was distributed via a write-in offer printed on 1988 Score 17-card package wrappers.

		MT	NR MT	EX
Complete Set:		8.00	6.00	3.25
Common Player:		.10	.08	.04
1	Mark McGwire	.70	.50	.30
2	Benito Santiago	.30	.25	.12
3	Sam Horn	.10	.08	.04
4	Chris Bosio	.10	.08	.04
5	Matt Nokes	.25	.20	.10
6	Ken Williams	.10	.08	.04
7	Dion James	.10	.08	.04
8	B.J. Surhoff	.25	.20	.10
9	Joe Margrane	.20	.15	.08
10	Kevin Seitzer	.10	.08	.04
11	Stanley Jefferson	.10	.08	.04
12	Devon White	.30	.25	.12
13	Nelson Liriano	.10	.08	.04
14	Chris James	.10	.08	.04
15	Mike Henneman	.15	.11	.06
16	Terry Steinbach	.20	.15	.08
17	John Kruk	.25	.20	.10
18	Matt Williams	.60	.45	.25
19	Kelly Downs	.10	.08	.04
20	Bill Ripken	.10	.08	.04
21	Ozzie Guillen	.10	.08	.04
22	Luis Polonia	.10	.08	.04
23	Dave Magadan	.40	.30	.15
24	Mike Greenwell	.50	.40	.20
25	Will Clark	1.00	.70	.40
26	Mike Dunne	.10	.08	.04
27	Wally Joyner	.50	.40	.20
28	Robby Thompson	.10	.08	.04
29	Ken Caminiti	.20	.15	.08
30	Jose Canseco	2.00	1.50	.80
31	Todd Benzinger	.30	.25	.12
32	Pete Incaviglia	.20	.15	.08
33	John Farrell	.10	.08	.04
34	Casey Candaele	.10	.08	.04
35	Mike Aldrete	.10	.08	.04
36	Ruben Sierra	.40	.30	.15
37	Ellis Burks	.60	.45	.25
38	Tracy Jones	.10	.08	.04
39	Kal Daniels	.30	.25	.12
40	Cory Snyder	.10	.08	.04

1988 Score Young Superstar - Series II

This set of 40 standard-size cards (2-1/2" by 3-1/2") and five Magic trivia cards is part of a double series issued by Score. Each series is divided into five smaller sets of eight baseball cards and one trivia card. The design on both series is similar, except for border color. Series I has blue and green borders. Series II has red and blue borders framing full-color player photos with the player name and team logo printed beneath the photo. The card backs carry full-color head shots and stats in a variety of colors. Young Superstar series were offered via a write-in offer on the backs of 1988 Score card package wrappers. For each 8-card subset, collectors were instructed to send two Score wrappers and $1. Complete sets were offered by a number of hobby dealers nationwide.

		MT	NR MT	EX
Complete Set:		7.00	5.25	2.75
Common Player:		.10	.08	.04
1	Don Mattingly	1.00	.70	.40
2	Glenn Braggs	.15	.11	.06
3	Dwight Gooden	.50	.40	.20
4	Jose Lind	.10	.08	.04
5	Danny Tartabull	.30	.25	.12
6	Tony Fernandez	.15	.11	.06
7	Julio Franco	.15	.11	.06
8	Andres Galarraga	.15	.11	.06
9	Bobby Bonilla	.40	.30	.15
10	Eric Davis	.40	.30	.15
11	Gerald Young	.10	.08	.04
12	Barry Bonds	.40	.30	.15
13	Jerry Browne	.10	.08	.04
14	Jeff Blauser	.10	.08	.04
15	Mickey Brantley	.10	.08	.04
16	Floyd Youmans	.10	.08	.04
17	Bret Saberhagen	.25	.20	.10
18	Shawon Dunston	.20	.15	.08
19	Len Dykstra	.15	.11	.06
20	Darryl Strawberry	.40	.30	.15
21	Rick Aguilera	.10	.08	.04
22	Ivan Calderon	.10	.08	.04
23	Roger Clemens	.70	.50	.30
24	Vince Coleman	.30	.25	.12
25	Gary Thurman	.10	.08	.04
26	Jeff Treadway	.10	.08	.04
27	Oddibe McDowell	.10	.08	.04
28	Fred McGriff	.40	.30	.15
29	Mark McLemore	.10	.08	.04
30	Jeff Musselman	.10	.08	.04
31	Mitch Williams	.10	.08	.04
32	Dan Plesac	.10	.08	.04
33	Juan Nieves	.10	.08	.04
34	Barry Larkin	.30	.25	.12
35	Greg Mathews	.10	.08	.04
36	Shane Mack	.10	.08	.04
37	Scott Bankhead	.10	.08	.04
38	Eric Bell	.10	.08	.04
39	Greg Swindell	.25	.20	.10
40	Kevin Elster	.10	.08	.04

1989 Score

This set of 660 cards plus 56 Magic Motion trivia cards is the second annual basic issue from Score. Full-color player photos highlight 651 individual players and 9 season highlights, including the first Wrigley Field night game. Action photos are framed by thin brightly colored borders (green, cyan blue, purple, orange, red, royal blue) with a baseball diamond logo/player name beneath the photo. Full-color player close-ups (1-5/16" by 1-5/8") are

printed on the pastel-colored backs, along with the card number, personal information, stats and career highlights. The cards measure 2-1/2" by 3-1/2" in size.

	MT	NR MT	EX
Complete Set:	20.00	15.00	8.00
Common Player:	.03	.02	.01

		MT	NR MT	EX
1	Jose Canseco	.60	.45	.25
2	Andre Dawson	.15	.11	.06
3	Mark McGwire	.40	.30	.15
4	Benny Santiago	.12	.09	.05
5	Rick Reuschel	.08	.06	.03
6	Fred McGriff	.35	.25	.14
7	Kal Daniels	.12	.09	.05
8	Gary Gaetti	.12	.09	.05
9	Ellis Burks	.35	.25	.12
10	Darryl Strawberry	.35	.25	.14
11	Julio Franco	.08	.06	.03
12	Lloyd Moseby	.06	.05	.02
13	*Jeff Pico*	.15	.11	.06
14	Johnny Ray	.06	.05	.02
15	Cal Ripken, Jr.	.30	.25	.12
16	Dick Schofield	.03	.02	.01
17	Mel Hall	.06	.05	.02
18	Bill Ripken	.06	.05	.02
19	Brook Jacoby	.08	.06	.03
20	Kirby Puckett	.35	.25	.14
21	Bill Doran	.06	.05	.02
22	Pete O'Brien	.06	.05	.02
23	Matt Nokes	.15	.11	.06
24	Brian Fisher	.06	.05	.02
25	Jack Clark	.12	.09	.05
26	Gary Pettis	.03	.02	.01
27	Dave Valle	.03	.02	.01
28	Willie Wilson	.08	.06	.03
29	Curt Young	.06	.05	.02
30	Dale Murphy	.30	.25	.12
31	Barry Larkin	.25	.20	.10
32	Dave Stewart	.08	.06	.03
33	Mike LaValliere	.06	.05	.02
34	Glen Hubbard	.03	.02	.01
35	Ryne Sandberg	.30	.25	.12
36	Tony Pena	.06	.05	.02
37	Greg Walker	.06	.05	.02
38	Von Hayes	.08	.06	.03
39	Kevin Mitchell	.30	.25	.12
40	Tim Raines	.25	.20	.10
41	Keith Hernandez	.20	.15	.08
42	Keith Moreland	.06	.05	.02
43	Ruben Sierra	.30	.25	.12
44	Chet Lemon	.06	.05	.02
45	Willie Randolph	.06	.05	.02
46	Andy Allanson	.03	.02	.01
47	Candy Maldonado	.06	.05	.02
48	Sid Bream	.06	.05	.02
49	Denny Walling	.03	.02	.01
50	Dave Winfield	.25	.20	.10
51	Alvin Davis	.10	.08	.04
52	Cory Snyder	.15	.11	.06
53	Hubie Brooks	.08	.06	.03
54	Chili Davis	.06	.05	.02
55	Kevin Seitzer	.12	.09	.05
56	Jose Uribe	.03	.02	.01
57	Tony Fernandez	.10	.08	.04
58	Tim Teufel	.03	.02	.01
59	Oddibe McDowell	.06	.05	.02
60	Les Lancaster	.06	.05	.02
61	Billy Hatcher	.06	.05	.02
62	Dan Gladden	.03	.02	.01
63	Marty Barrett	.06	.05	.02
64	Nick Esasky	.06	.05	.02
65	Wally Joyner	.20	.15	.08
66	Mike Greenwell	.35	.25	.12
67	Ken Williams	.06	.05	.02
68	Bob Horner	.08	.06	.03
69	Steve Sax	.12	.09	.05
70	Rickey Henderson	.30	.25	.12
71	Mitch Webster	.06	.05	.02
72	Rob Deer	.06	.05	.02
73	Jim Presley	.06	.05	.02
74	Albert Hall	.03	.02	.01
75a	George Brett ("...game's top hitters at 33..." on back)	1.00	.70	.40
75b	George Brett ("...game's top hitters at 35..." on back)	.30	.25	.12
76	Brian Downing	.06	.05	.02
77	Dave Martinez	.06	.05	.02
78	Scott Fletcher	.06	.05	.02
79	Phil Bradley	.08	.06	.03
80	Ozzie Smith	.12	.09	.05
81	Larry Sheets	.06	.05	.02
82	Mike Aldrete	.06	.05	.02
83	Darnell Coles	.06	.05	.02
84	Len Dykstra	.08	.06	.03
85	Jim Rice	.20	.15	.08
86	Jeff Treadway	.10	.08	.04
87	Jose Lind	.08	.06	.03
88	Willie McGee	.10	.08	.04
89	Mickey Brantley	.03	.02	.01
90	Tony Gwynn	.20	.15	.08
91	R.J. Reynolds	.03	.02	.01
92	Milt Thompson	.03	.02	.01
93	Kevin McReynolds	.12	.09	.05
94	Eddie Murray	.25	.20	.10
95	Lance Parrish	.12	.09	.05
96	Ron Kittle	.06	.05	.02
97	Gerald Young	.10	.08	.04
98	Ernie Whitt	.06	.05	.02
99	Jeff Reed	.03	.02	.01
100	Don Mattingly	.50	.40	.20
101	Gerald Perry	.08	.06	.03
102	Vance Law	.06	.05	.02
103	John Shelby	.03	.02	.01
104	*Chris Sabo*	.60	.45	.25
105	Danny Tartabull	.15	.11	.06
106	Glenn Wilson	.06	.05	.02
107	Mark Davidson	.06	.05	.02
108	Dave Parker	.10	.08	.04
109	Eric Davis	.35	.25	.14
110	Alan Trammell	.15	.11	.06
111	Ozzie Virgil	.03	.02	.01
112	Frank Tanana	.06	.05	.02
113	Rafael Ramirez	.03	.02	.01
114	Dennis Martinez	.06	.05	.02
115	Jose DeLeon	.06	.05	.02
116	Bob Ojeda	.06	.05	.02
117	Doug Drabek	.06	.05	.02
118	Andy Hawkins	.03	.02	.01
119	Greg Maddux(FC)	.10	.08	.04
120	Cecil Fielder (photo on back reversed)	.60	.45	.25
121	Mike Scioscia	.06	.05	.02
122	Dan Petry	.06	.05	.02
123	Terry Kennedy	.06	.05	.02
124	Kelly Downs	.08	.06	.03
125a	Greg Gross (first name incorrect on card back)	.20	.15	.08
125b	Greg Gross (first name correct on card back)	.08	.06	.03

A player's name in *italic* indicates a rookie card. An (FC) indicates a player's first card for that particular card company.

		MT	NR MT	EX
126	Fred Lynn	.10	.08	.04
127	Barry Bonds	.25	.20	.10
128	Harold Baines	.10	.08	.04
129	Doyle Alexander	.06	.05	.02
130	Kevin Elster	.08	.06	.03
131	Mike Heath	.03	.02	.01
132	Teddy Higuera	.08	.06	.03
133	Charlie Leibrandt	.06	.05	.02
134	Tim Laudner	.03	.02	.01
135a	Ray Knight (photo reversed)	.60	.45	.25
135b	Ray Knight (correct photo)	.08	.06	.03
136	Howard Johnson	.08	.06	.03
137	Terry Pendleton	.08	.06	.03
138	Andy McGaffigan	.03	.02	.01
139	Ken Oberkfell	.03	.02	.01
140	Butch Wynegar	.03	.02	.01
141	Rob Murphy	.03	.02	.01
142	*Rich Renteria*(FC)	.12	.09	.05
143	Jose Guzman	.08	.06	.03
144	Andres Galarraga	.12	.09	.05
145	Rick Horton	.06	.05	.02
146	Frank DiPino	.03	.02	.01
147	Glenn Braggs	.06	.05	.02
148	John Kruk	.06	.05	.02
149	Mike Schmidt	.35	.25	.14
150	Lee Smith	.08	.06	.03
151	Robin Yount	.25	.20	.10
152	Mark Eichhorn	.06	.05	.02
153	DeWayne Buice	.04	.03	.02
154	B.J. Surhoff	.08	.06	.03
155	Vince Coleman	.12	.09	.05
156	Tony Phillips	.03	.02	.01
157	Willie Fraser	.03	.02	.01
158	Lance McCullers	.06	.05	.02
159	Greg Gagne	.03	.02	.01
160	Jesse Barfield	.08	.06	.03
161	Mark Langston	.08	.06	.03
162	Kurt Stillwell	.06	.05	.02
163	Dion James	.03	.02	.01
164	Glenn Davis	.12	.09	.05
165	Walt Weiss	.25	.20	.10
166	Dave Concepcion	.08	.06	.03
167	Alfredo Griffin	.06	.05	.02
168	*Don Heinkel*	.15	.11	.06
169	Luis Rivera(FC)	.03	.02	.01
170	Shane Rawley	.06	.05	.02
171	Darrell Evans	.08	.06	.03
172	Robby Thompson	.06	.05	.02
173	Jody Davis	.06	.05	.02
174	Andy Van Slyke	.12	.09	.05
175	Wade Boggs ("And his .364 career BA..." on back)	.50	.40	.20
176	Garry Templeton	.06	.05	.02
177	Gary Redus	.03	.02	.01
178	Craig Lefferts	.03	.02	.01
179	Carney Lansford	.06	.05	.02
180	Ron Darling	.10	.08	.04
181	Kirk McCaskill	.06	.05	.02
182	Tony Armas	.06	.05	.02
183	Steve Farr	.03	.02	.01
184	Tom Brunansky	.10	.08	.04
185	*Bryan Harvey*	.25	.20	.10
186	Mike Marshall	.10	.08	.04
187	Bo Diaz	.06	.05	.02
188	Willie Upshaw	.06	.05	.02
189	Mike Pagliarulo	.08	.06	.03
190	Mike Krukow	.06	.05	.02
191	Tommy Herr	.06	.05	.02
192	Jim Pankovits	.03	.02	.01
193	Dwight Evans	.10	.08	.04
194	Kelly Gruber	.03	.02	.01
195	Bobby Bonilla	.25	.20	.10
196	Wallace Johnson	.03	.02	.01
197	Dave Stieb	.08	.06	.03
198	*Pat Borders*	.20	.15	.08
199	Rafael Palmeiro	.15	.11	.06
200	Doc Gooden	.40	.30	.15
201	Pete Incaviglia	.08	.06	.03
202	Chris James	.08	.06	.03
203	Marvell Wynne	.03	.02	.01
204	Pat Sheridan	.03	.02	.01
205	Don Baylor	.08	.06	.03
206	Paul O'Neill	.03	.02	.01
207	Pete Smith	.08	.06	.03
208	Mark McLemore	.03	.02	.01
209	Henry Cotto	.03	.02	.01
210	Kirk Gibson	.15	.11	.06
211	Claudell Washington	.06	.05	.02
212	Randy Bush	.03	.02	.01
213	Joe Carter	.10	.08	.04
214	Bill Buckner	.08	.06	.03

		MT	NR MT	EX
215	Bert Blyleven (year of birth is 1957)	.25	.20	.10
216	Brett Butler	.06	.05	.02
217	Lee Mazzilli	.06	.05	.02
218	Spike Owen	.03	.02	.01
219	Bill Swift	.03	.02	.01
220	Tim Wallach	.08	.06	.03
221	David Cone	.20	.15	.08
222	Don Carman	.06	.05	.02
223	Rich Gossage	.10	.08	.04
224	Bob Walk	.03	.02	.01
225	Dave Righetti	.10	.08	.04
226	Kevin Bass	.06	.05	.02
227	Kevin Gross	.06	.05	.02
228	Tim Burke	.03	.02	.01
229	Rick Mahler	.03	.02	.01
230	Lou Whitaker	.15	.11	.06
231	*Luis Alicea*	.15	.11	.06
232	Roberto Alomar	.70	.50	.30
233	Bob Boone	.06	.05	.02
234	Dickie Thon	.03	.02	.01
235	Shawon Dunston	.08	.06	.03
236	Pete Stanicek	.08	.06	.03
237	*Craig Biggio*	.50	.40	.20
238	Dennis Boyd	.06	.05	.02
239	Tom Candiotti	.03	.02	.01
240	Gary Carter	.15	.11	.06
241	Mike Stanley	.03	.02	.01
242	Ken Phelps	.06	.05	.02
243	Chris Bosio	.03	.02	.01
244	Les Straker	.06	.05	.02
245	Dave Smith	.06	.05	.02
246	John Candelaria	.06	.05	.02
247	Joe Orsulak	.03	.02	.01
248	Storm Davis	.08	.06	.03
249	Floyd Bannister	.06	.05	.02
250	Jack Morris	.12	.09	.05
251	Bret Saberhagen	.12	.09	.05
252	Tom Niedenfuer	.06	.05	.02
253	Neal Heaton	.03	.02	.01
254	Eric Show	.06	.05	.02
255	Juan Samuel	.10	.08	.04
256	Dale Sveum	.06	.05	.02
257	Jim Gott	.03	.02	.01
258	Scott Garrelts	.03	.02	.01
259	Larry McWilliams	.03	.02	.01
260	Steve Bedrosian	.08	.06	.03
261	Jack Howell	.06	.05	.02
262	Jay Tibbs	.03	.02	.01
263	Jamie Moyer	.03	.02	.01
264	Doug Sisk	.03	.02	.01
265	Todd Worrell	.08	.06	.03
266	John Farrell	.08	.06	.03
267	Dave Collins	.06	.05	.02
268	Sid Fernandez	.08	.06	.03
269	Tom Brookens	.03	.02	.01
270	Shane Mack	.06	.05	.02
271	Paul Kilgus	.08	.06	.03
272	Chuck Crim	.03	.02	.01
273	Bob Knepper	.06	.05	.02
274	Mike Moore	.03	.02	.01
275	Guillermo Hernandez	.06	.05	.02
276	Dennis Eckersley	.10	.08	.04
277	Graig Nettles	.10	.08	.04
278	Rich Dotson	.06	.05	.02
279	Larry Herndon	.03	.02	.01
280	Gene Larkin	.08	.06	.03
281	Roger McDowell	.08	.06	.03
282	Greg Swindell	.10	.08	.04
283	Juan Agosto	.03	.02	.01
284	Jeff Robinson	.06	.05	.02
285	Mike Dunne	.08	.06	.03
286	Greg Mathews	.06	.05	.02
287	Kent Tekulve	.06	.05	.02
288	Jerry Mumphrey	.03	.02	.01
289	Jack McDowell	.08	.06	.03
290	Frank Viola	.12	.09	.05
291	Mark Gubicza	.08	.06	.03
292	Dave Schmidt	.03	.02	.01
293	Mike Henneman	.08	.06	.03
294	Jimmy Jones	.03	.02	.01
295	Charlie Hough	.06	.05	.02
296	Rafael Santana	.03	.02	.01
297	Chris Speier	.03	.02	.01
298	Mike Witt	.06	.05	.02
299	Pascual Perez	.06	.05	.02
300	Nolan Ryan	.50	.40	.20
301	Mitch Williams	.06	.05	.02
302	Mookie Wilson	.06	.05	.02
303	Mackey Sasser	.06	.05	.02
304	John Cerutti	.06	.05	.02

		MT	NR MT	EX
305	Jeff Reardon	.08	.06	.03
306	Randy Myers	.08	.06	.03
307	Greg Brock	.06	.05	.02
308	Bob Welch	.08	.06	.03
309	Jeff Robinson	.12	.09	.05
310	Harold Reynolds	.06	.05	.02
311	Jim Walewander	.03	.02	.01
312	Dave Magadan	.08	.06	.03
313	Jim Gantner	.03	.02	.01
314	Walt Terrell	.06	.05	.02
315	Wally Backman	.06	.05	.02
316	Luis Salazar	.03	.02	.01
317	Rick Rhoden	.06	.05	.02
318	Tom Henke	.06	.05	.02
319	*Mike Macfarlane*	.20	.15	.08
320	Dan Plesac	.08	.06	.03
321	Calvin Schiraldi	.03	.02	.01
322	Stan Javier	.03	.02	.01
323	Devon White	.10	.08	.04
324	Scott Bradley	.03	.02	.01
325	Bruce Hurst	.08	.06	.03
326	Manny Lee	.03	.02	.01
327	Rick Aguilera	.03	.02	.01
328	Bruce Ruffin	.03	.02	.01
329	Ed Whitson	.03	.02	.01
330	Bo Jackson	.40	.30	.15
331	Ivan Calderon	.06	.05	.02
332	Mickey Hatcher	.03	.02	.01
333	Barry Jones(FC)	.03	.02	.01
334	Ron Hassey	.03	.02	.01
335	Bill Wegman	.03	.02	.01
336	Damon Berryhill	.15	.11	.06
337	Steve Ontiverso	.03	.02	.01
338	Dan Pasqua	.08	.06	.03
339	Bill Pecota	.06	.05	.02
340	Greg Cadaret	.06	.05	.02
341	Scott Bankhead	.03	.02	.01
342	Ron Guidry	.12	.09	.05
343	Danny Heep	.03	.02	.01
344	Bob Brower	.03	.02	.01
345	Rich Gedman	.06	.05	.02
346	*Nelson Santovenia*	.15	.11	.06
347	George Bell	.20	.15	.08
348	Ted Power	.03	.02	.01
349	Mark Grant	.03	.02	.01
350a	Roger Clemens (778 Wins)	4.00	3.00	1.50
350b	Roger Clemens (78 Wins)	.40	.30	.15
351	Bill Long	.06	.05	.02
352	Jay Bell(FC)	.06	.05	.02
353	Steve Balboni	.06	.05	.02
354	Bob Kipper	.03	.02	.01
355	Steve Jeltz	.03	.02	.01
356	Jesse Orosco	.06	.05	.02
357	Bob Dernier	.03	.02	.01
358	Mickey Tettleton	.03	.02	.01
359	Duane Ward(FC)	.03	.02	.01
360	Darrin Jackson(FC)	.08	.06	.03
361	Rey Quinones	.03	.02	.01
362	Mark Grace	.80	.60	.30
363	Steve Lake	.03	.02	.01
364	Pat Perry	.03	.02	.01
365	Terry Steinbach	.08	.06	.03
366	Alan Ashby	.03	.02	.01
367	Jeff Montgomery	.06	.05	.02
368	Steve Buechele	.03	.02	.01
369	Chris Brown	.06	.05	.02
370	Orel Hershiser	.20	.15	.08
371	Todd Benzinger	.10	.08	.04
372	Ron Gant	.30	.25	.12
373	Paul Assenmacher(FC)	.03	.02	.01
374	Joey Meyer	.08	.06	.03
375	Neil Allen	.03	.02	.01
376	Mike Davis	.06	.05	.02
377	Jeff Parrett(FC)	.08	.06	.03
378	Jay Howell	.06	.05	.02
379	Rafael Belliard	.03	.02	.01
380	Luis Polonia	.06	.05	.02
381	Keith Atherton	.03	.02	.01
382	Kent Hrbek	.15	.11	.06
383	Bob Stanley	.03	.02	.01
384	Dave LaPoint	.06	.05	.02
385	Rance Mulliniks	.03	.02	.01
386	Melido Perez	.08	.06	.03
387	Doug Jones	.10	.08	.04
388	Steve Lyons	.03	.02	.01
389	Alejandro Pena	.06	.05	.02
390	Frank White	.06	.05	.02
391	Pat Tabler	.06	.05	.02
392	Eric Plunk(FC)	.03	.02	.01
393	Mike Maddux(FC)	.03	.02	.01
394	Allan Anderson(FC)	.06	.05	.02

		MT	NR MT	EX
395	Bob Brenly	.03	.02	.01
396	Rick Cerone	.03	.02	.01
397	Scott Terry(FC)	.08	.06	.03
398	Mike Jackson	.06	.05	.02
399	Bobby Thigpen	.08	.06	.03
400	Don Sutton	.12	.09	.05
401	Cecil Espy	.06	.05	.02
402	Junior Ortiz	.03	.02	.01
403	Mike Smithson	.03	.02	.01
404	Bud Black	.03	.02	.01
405	Tom Foley	.03	.02	.01
406	Andres Thomas	.06	.05	.02
407	Rick Sutcliffe	.08	.06	.03
408	Brian Harper	.03	.02	.01
409	John Smiley	.10	.08	.04
410	Juan Nieves	.06	.05	.02
411	Shawn Abner	.08	.06	.03
412	Wes Gardner(FC)	.06	.05	.02
413	Darren Daulton	.03	.02	.01
414	Juan Berenguer	.03	.02	.01
415	Charles Hudson	.03	.02	.01
416	Rick Honeycutt	.03	.02	.01
417	Greg Booker	.03	.02	.01
418	Tim Belcher	.08	.06	.03
419	Don August	.08	.06	.03
420	Dale Mohorcic	.03	.02	.01
421	Steve Lombardozzi	.03	.02	.01
422	Atlee Hammaker	.03	.02	.01
423	Jerry Don Gleaton	.03	.02	.01
424	Scott Bailes(FC)	.03	.02	.01
425	Bruce Sutter	.08	.06	.03
426	Randy Ready	.03	.02	.01
427	Jerry Reed	.03	.02	.01
428	Bryn Smith	.03	.02	.01
429	Tim Leary	.06	.05	.02
430	Mark Clear	.03	.02	.01
431	Terry Leach	.03	.02	.01
432	John Moses	.03	.02	.01
433	Ozzie Guillen	.06	.05	.02
434	Gene Nelson	.03	.02	.01
435	Gary Ward	.06	.05	.02
436	Luis Aguayo	.03	.02	.01
437	Fernando Valenzuela	.15	.11	.06
438	Jeff Russell	.03	.02	.01
439	Cecilio Guante	.03	.02	.01
440	Don Robinson	.03	.02	.01
441	Rick Anderson(FC)	.03	.02	.01
442	Tom Glavine	.08	.06	.03
443	Daryl Boston	.03	.02	.01
444	Joe Price	.03	.02	.01
445	Stewart Cliburn	.03	.02	.01
446	Manny Trillo	.03	.02	.01
447	Joel Skinner	.03	.02	.01
448	Charlie Puleo	.03	.02	.01
449	Carlton Fisk	.12	.09	.05
450	Will Clark	.50	.40	.20
451	Otis Nixon	.03	.02	.01
452	Rick Schu	.03	.02	.01
453	Todd Stottlemyre	.15	.11	.06
454	Tim Birtsas	.03	.02	.01
455	*Dave Gallagher*	.20	.15	.08
456	Barry Lyons	.03	.02	.01
457	Fred Manrique	.06	.05	.02
458	Ernest Riles	.03	.02	.01
459	*Doug Jennings*(FC)	.15	.11	.06
460	Joe Magrane	.08	.06	.03
461	Jamie Quirk	.03	.02	.01
462	*Jack Armstrong*	.25	.20	.10
463	Bobby Witt	.08	.06	.03
464	Keith Miller	.06	.05	.02
465	*Todd Burns*	.15	.11	.06
466	*John Dopson*	.15	.11	.06
467	Rich Yett	.03	.02	.01
468	Craig Reynolds	.03	.02	.01
469	Dave Bergman	.03	.02	.01
470	Rex Hudler	.03	.02	.01
471	Eric King	.03	.02	.01
472	Joaquin Andujar	.06	.05	.02
473	*Sil Campusano*	.15	.11	.06
474	Terry Mulholland(FC)	.03	.02	.01
475	Mike Flanagan	.06	.05	.02
476	Greg Harris	.03	.02	.01
477	Tommy John	.10	.08	.04
478	Dave Anderson	.03	.02	.01
479	Fred Toliver	.03	.02	.01
480	Jimmy Key	.08	.06	.03
481	Donell Nixon	.03	.02	.01
482	Mark Portugal(FC)	.03	.02	.01
483	Tom Pagnozzi	.06	.05	.02
484	Jeff Kunkel	.03	.02	.01
485	Frank Williams	.03	.02	.01

		MT	NR MT	EX
486	Jody Reed	.10	.08	.04
487	Roberto Kelly	.25	.20	.10
488	Shawn Hillegas	.06	.05	.02
489	Jerry Reuss	.06	.05	.02
490	Mark Davis	.03	.02	.01
491	Jeff Sellers	.03	.02	.01
492	Zane Smith	.06	.05	.02
493	Al Newman(FC)	.03	.02	.01
494	Mike Young	.03	.02	.01
495	Larry Parrish	.06	.05	.02
496	Herm Winningham	.03	.02	.01
497	Carmen Castillo	.03	.02	.01
498	Joe Hesketh	.03	.02	.01
499	Darrell Miller	.03	.02	.01
500	Mike LaCoss	.03	.02	.01
501	Charlie Lea	.03	.02	.01
502	Bruce Benedict	.03	.02	.01
503	Chuck Finley(FC)	.03	.02	.01
504	Brad Wellman(FC)	.03	.02	.01
505	Tim Crews	.06	.05	.02
506	Ken Gerhart	.06	.05	.02
507	Brian Holton (Born: Jan. 25, 1965 Denver, CO)	.20	.15	.08
508	Dennis Lamp	.03	.02	.01
509	Bobby Meacham (1984 Games is 099)	.20	.15	.08
510	Tracy Jones	.08	.06	.03
511	Mike Fitzgerald	.03	.02	.01
512	*Jeff Bittiger*	.12	.09	.05
513	Tim Flannery	.03	.02	.01
514	Ray Hayward(FC)	.03	.02	.01
515	Dave Leiper	.03	.02	.01
516	Rod Scurry	.03	.02	.01
517	Carmelo Martinez	.03	.02	.01
518	Curtis Wilkerson	.03	.02	.01
519	Stan Jefferson	.03	.02	.01
520	Dan Quisenberry	.06	.05	.02
521	Lloyd McClendon(FC)	.03	.02	.01
522	Steve Trout	.03	.02	.01
523	Larry Andersen	.03	.02	.01
524	Don Aase	.03	.02	.01
525	Bob Forsch	.06	.05	.02
526	Geno Petralli	.03	.02	.01
527	Angel Salazar	.03	.02	.01
528	*Mike Schooler*	.20	.15	.08
529	Jose Oquendo	.03	.02	.01
530	Jay Buhner	.10	.08	.04
531	Tom Bolton(FC)	.06	.05	.02
532	Al Nipper	.03	.02	.01
533	Dave Henderson	.08	.06	.03
534	*John Costello*(FC)	.15	.11	.06
535	Donnie Moore	.03	.02	.01
536	Mike Laga	.03	.02	.01
537	Mike Gallego	.03	.02	.01
538	Jim Clancy	.06	.05	.02
539	Joel Youngblood	.03	.02	.01
540	Rick Leach	.03	.02	.01
541	Kevin Romine	.03	.02	.01
542	Mark Salas	.03	.02	.01
543	Greg Minton	.03	.02	.01
544	Dave Palmer	.03	.02	.01
545	Dwayne Murphy	.06	.05	.02
546	Jim Deshaies	.03	.02	.01
547	Don Gordon(FC)	.03	.02	.01
548	*Ricky Jordan*	.30	.25	.12
549	Mike Boddicker	.06	.05	.02
550	Mike Scott	.10	.08	.04
551	Jeff Ballard(FC)	.08	.06	.03
552a	Jose Rijo (uniform number #24 on card back)	.20	.15	.08
552b	Jose Rijo (uniforn number #27 on card back)	.08	.06	.03
553	Danny Darwin	.03	.02	.01
554	Tom Browning	.08	.06	.03
555	Danny Jackson	.12	.09	.05
556	Rick Dempsey	.06	.05	.02
557	Jeffrey Leonard	.06	.05	.02
558	Jeff Musselman	.06	.05	.02
559	Ron Robinson	.03	.02	.01
560	John Tudor	.08	.06	.03
561	Don Slaught	.03	.02	.01
562	Dennis Rasmussen	.08	.06	.03
563	*Brady Anderson*	.20	.15	.08
564	Pedro Guerrero	.12	.09	.05
565	Paul Molitor	.12	.09	.05
566	*Terry Clark*(FC)	.15	.11	.06
567	Terry Puhl	.03	.02	.01
568	Mike Campbell(FC)	.08	.06	.03
569	Paul Mirabella	.03	.02	.01
570	Jeff Hamilton(FC)	.06	.05	.02
571	*Oswald Peraza*	.15	.11	.06

		MT	NR MT	EX
572	Bob McClure	.03	.02	.01
573	*Jose Bautista*(FC)	.15	.11	.06
574	Alex Trevino	.03	.02	.01
575	John Franco	.08	.06	.03
576	*Mark Parent*(FC)	.15	.11	.06
577	Nelson Liriano	.06	.05	.02
578	Steve Shields	.03	.02	.01
579	Odell Jones	.03	.02	.01
580	Al Leiter	.15	.11	.06
581	Dave Stapleton(FC)	.06	.05	.02
582	1988 World Series (Jose Canseco, Kirk Gibson, Orel Hershiser, Dave Stewart)	.20	.15	.08
583	Donnie Hill	.03	.02	.01
584	Chuck Jackson	.06	.05	.02
585	Rene Gonzales(FC)	.06	.05	.02
586	Tracy Woodson(FC)	.08	.06	.03
587	Jim Adduci(FC)	.03	.02	.01
588	Mario Soto	.06	.05	.02
589	Jeff Blauser	.08	.06	.03
590	Jim Traber	.06	.05	.02
591	Jon Perlman(FC)	.03	.02	.01
592	Mark Williamson(FC)	.06	.05	.02
593	Dave Meads	.03	.02	.01
594	Jim Eisenreich	.03	.02	.01
595	*Paul Gibson*(FC)	.15	.11	.06
596	Mike Birkbeck	.03	.02	.01
597	Terry Francona	.03	.02	.01
598	Paul Zuvella(FC)	.03	.02	.01
599	Franklin Stubbs	.03	.02	.01
600	Gregg Jefferies	.60	.45	.25
601	John Cangelosi	.03	.02	.01
602	Mike Sharperson(FC)	.03	.02	.01
603	Mike Diaz	.06	.05	.02
604	*Gary Varsho*(FC)	.20	.15	.08
605	*Terry Blocker*(FC)	.12	.09	.05
606	Charlie O'Brien(FC)	.03	.02	.01
607	Jim Eppard(FC)	.08	.06	.03
608	John Davis	.03	.02	.01
609	Ken Griffey, Sr.	.08	.06	.03
610	Buddy Bell	.06	.05	.02
611	Ted Simmons	.08	.06	.03
612	Matt Williams	.10	.08	.04
613	Danny Cox	.06	.05	.02
614	Al Pedrique	.03	.02	.01
615	Ron Oester	.03	.02	.01
616	*John Smoltz*(FC)	.40	.30	.15
617	Bob Melvin	.03	.02	.01
618	*Rob Dibble*	.50	.40	.20
619	Kirt Manwaring	.10	.08	.04
620	1989 Rookie (Felix Fermin)(FC)	.06	.05	.02
621	1989 Rookie (*Doug Dascenzo*)(FC)	.20	.15	.08
622	1989 Rookie (*Bill Brennan*)(FC)	.15	.11	.06
623	1989 Rookie (*Carlos Quintana*)(FC)	.40	.30	.15
624	1989 Rookie (*Mike Harkey*)(FC)	.25	.20	.10
625	1989 Rookie (*Gary Sheffield*)(FC)	.70	.50	.30
626	1989 Rookie (Tom Prince)(FC)	.08	.06	.03
627	1989 Rookie (*Steve Searcy*)(FC)	.15	.11	.06
628	1989 Rookie (*Charlie Hayes*)(FC)	.25	.20	.10
629	1989 Rookie (*Felix Jose*)(FC)	1.00	.70	.40
630	1989 Rookie (*Sandy Alomar*)(FC)	.60	.45	.25
631	1989 Rookie (*Derek Lilliquist*)(FC)	.15	.11	.06
632	1989 Rookie (Geronimo Berroa)(FC)	.06	.05	.02
633	1989 Rookie (*Luis Medina*)(FC)	.15	.11	.06
634	1989 Rookie (*Tom Gordon*)(FC)	.40	.30	.15
635	1989 Rookie (*Ramon Martinez*)(FC)	2.00	1.50	.80
636	1989 Rookie (*Craig Worthington*)(FC)	.20	.15	.08
637	1989 Rookie (Edgar Martinez)(FC)	.50	.40	.20
638	1989 Rookie (*Chad Krueter*)(FC)	.15	.11	.06
639	1989 Rookie (*Ron Jones*)(FC)	.20	.15	.08
640	1989 Rookie (*Van Snider*)(FC)	.15	.11	.06
641	1989 Rookie (*Lance Blankenship*)(FC)	.15	.11	.06
642	1989 Rookie (*Dwight Smith*)(FC)	.40	.30	.15
643	1989 Rookie (*Cameron Drew*)(FC)	.15	.11	.06
644	1989 Rookie (*Jerald Clark*)(FC)	.30	.25	.12
645	1989 Rookie (*Randy Johnson*)(FC)	.50	.40	.20
646	1989 Rookie (*Norm Charlton*)(FC)	.20	.15	.08
647	1989 Rookie (Todd Frohwirth)(FC)	.08	.06	.03
648	1989 Rookie (*Luis de los Santos*)(FC)	.15	.11	.06
649	1989 Rookie (*Tim Jones*)(FC)	.15	.11	.06
650	1989 Rookie (*Dave West*)(FC)	.20	.15	.08
651	1989 Rookie (*Bob Milacki*)(FC)	.25	.20	.10
652	1988 Highlight (Wrigley Field)	.06	.05	.02
653	1988 Highlight (Orel Hershiser)	.10	.08	.04
654a	1988 Highlight (Wade Boggs) ("...sixth consecutive seaason..." on back)	4.00	3.00	1.50

		MT	NR MT	EX
654b	1988 Highlight (Wade Boggs) ("...sixth consecutive season..." on back)	.30	.25	.12
655	1988 Highlight (Jose Canseco)	.50	.40	.20
656	1988 Highlight (Doug Jones)	.06	.05	.02
657	1988 Highlight (Rickey Henderson)	.12	.09	.05
658	1988 Highlight (Tom Browning)	.06	.05	.02
659	1988 Highlight (Mike Greenwell)	.15	.11	.06
660	1988 Highlight (A.L. Win Streak)	.06	.05	.02

1989 Score Traded

Score issued its second consecutive traded set in 1989 to supplement and update its regular set. The 110-card traded set features the same basic card design as the regular 1989 Score set. The set consists of rookies and traded players pictured with correct teams. The set was sold by hobby dealers in a special box that included an assortment of "Magic Motion" trivia cards.

		MT	NR MT	EX
Complete Set:		13.00	9.75	5.25
Common Player:		.06	.05	.02
1T	Rafael Palmeiro	.10	.08	.04
2T	Nolan Ryan	1.50	1.25	.60
3T	Jack Clark	.10	.08	.04
4T	Dave LaPoint	.06	.05	.02
5T	Mike Moore	.08	.06	.03
6T	Pete O'Brien	.06	.05	.02
7T	Jeffrey Leonard	.06	.05	.02
8T	Rob Murphy	.06	.05	.02
9T	Tom Herr	.06	.05	.02
10T	Claudell Washington	.06	.05	.02
11T	Mike Pagliarulo	.06	.05	.02
12T	Steve Lake	.06	.05	.02
13T	Spike Owen	.06	.05	.02
14T	Andy Hawkins	.06	.05	.02
15T	Todd Benzinger	.06	.05	.02
16T	Mookie Wilson	.06	.05	.03
17T	Bert Blyleven	.08	.06	.03
18T	Jeff Treadway	.06	.05	.02
19T	Bruce Hurst	.08	.06	.03
20T	Steve Sax	.12	.09	.05
21T	Juan Samuel	.06	.05	.02
22T	Jesse Barfield	.06	.05	.02
23T	Carmelo Castillo	.06	.05	.02
24T	Terry Leach	.06	.05	.02
25T	Mark Langston	.12	.09	.05
26T	Eric King	.06	.05	.02
27T	Steve Balboni	.06	.05	.02
28T	Len Dykstra	.06	.05	.02
29T	Keith Moreland	.06	.05	.02
30T	Terry Kennedy	.06	.05	.02
31T	Eddie Murray	.12	.09	.05
32T	Mitch Williams	.10	.08	.04
33T	Jeff Parrett	.06	.05	.02
34T	Wally Backman	.06	.05	.02
35T	Julio Franco	.10	.08	.04
36T	Lance Parrish	.06	.05	.02
37T	Nick Esasky	.06	.05	.02
38T	Luis Polonia	.06	.05	.02
39T	Kevin Gross	.06	.05	.02
40T	John Dopson	.06	.05	.02
41T	Willie Randolph	.08	.06	.03
42T	Jim Clancy	.06	.05	.02
43T	Tracy Jones	.06	.05	.02
44T	Phil Bradley	.06	.05	.02
45T	Milt Thompson	.06	.05	.02
46T	Chris James	.06	.05	.02
47T	Scott Fletcher	.06	.05	.02
48T	Kal Daniels	.08	.06	.03
49T	Steve Bedrosian	.06	.05	.02
50T	Rickey Henderson	.50	.40	.20
51T	Dion James	.06	.05	.02
52T	Tim Leary	.06	.05	.02
53T	Roger McDowell	.06	.05	.02
54T	Mel Hall	.06	.05	.02
55T	Dickie Thon	.06	.05	.02
56T	Zane Smith	.06	.05	.02
57T	Danny Heep	.06	.05	.02
58T	Bob McClure	.06	.05	.02
59T	Brian Holton	.06	.05	.02
60T	Randy Ready	.06	.05	.02
61T	Bob Melvin	.06	.05	.02
62T	Harold Baines	.08	.06	.03
63T	Lance McCullers	.06	.05	.02
64T	Jody Davis	.06	.05	.02
65T	Darrell Evans	.06	.05	.02
66T	Joel Youngblood	.08	.06	.03
67T	Frank Viola	.08	.06	.03
68T	Mike Aldrete	.06	.05	.02
69T	Greg Cadaret	.06	.05	.02
70T	John Kruk	.06	.05	.02
71T	Pat Sheridan	.06	.05	.02
72T	Oddibe McDowell	.06	.05	.02
73T	Tom Brookens	.06	.05	.02
74T	Bob Boone	.08	.06	.03
75T	Walt Terrell	.06	.05	.02
76T	Joel Skinner	.06	.05	.02
77T	Randy Johnson	.10	.08	.04
78T	Felix Fermin	.06	.05	.03
79T	Rick Mahler	.06	.05	.03
80T	Rich Dotson	.06	.05	.03
81T	Cris Carpenter(FC)	.20	.15	.08
82T	Bill Spiers(FC)	.25	.20	.10
83T	Junior Felix(FC)	.40	.30	.15
84T	Joe Girardi(FC)	.20	.15	.08
85T	Jerome Walton(FC)	.80	.60	.30
86T	Greg Litton(FC)	.25	.20	.10
87T	Greg Harris(FC)	.20	.15	.08
88T	Jim Abbott(FC)	1.00	.70	.40
89T	Kevin Brown(FC)	.20	.15	.08
90T	John Wetteland(FC)	.20	.15	.08
91T	Gary Wayne(FC)	.15	.11	.06
92T	Rich Monteleone(FC)	.15	.11	.06
93T	Bob Geren(FC)	.20	.15	.08
94T	Clay Parker(FC)	.15	.11	.06
95T	Steve Finley(FC)	.40	.30	.15
96T	Gregg Olson(FC)	.80	.60	.30
97T	Ken Patterson(FC)	.15	.11	.06
98T	Ken Hill(FC)	.30	.25	.12
99T	Scott Scudder(FC)	.25	.20	.10
100T	Ken Griffey, Jr.(FC)	7.00	5.25	2.75
101T	Jeff Brantley(FC)	.25	.20	.10
102T	Donn Pall(FC)	.15	.11	.06
103T	Carlos Martinez(FC)	.20	.15	.08
104T	Joe Oliver(FC)	.30	.25	.12
105T	Omar Vizquel(FC)	.15	.11	.06
106T	Joey Belle(FC)	1.75	1.25	.70
107T	Kenny Rogers(FC)	.20	.15	.08
108T	Mark Carreon(FC)	.15	.11	.06
109T	Rolando Roomes(FC)	.15	.11	.06
110T	Pete Harnsisch(FC)	.35	.25	.14

1989 Score Young Superstar-Series I

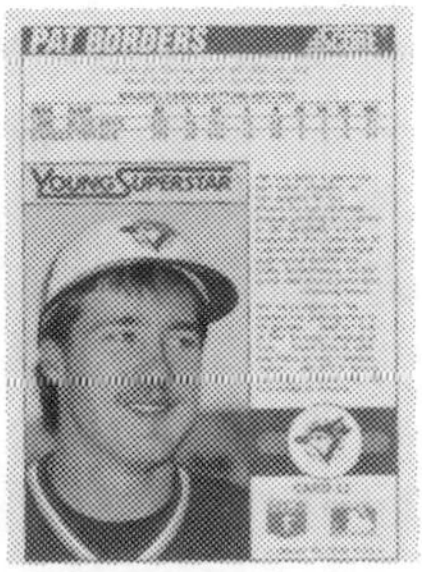

This standard-size card set (2-1/2" by 3-1/2")

displays full-color action photos with a high gloss finish. The card fronts feature a red and blue border surrounding the photo with the team logo in the lower right. A red band beneath the photo provided the setting for the player ID including name, position, and team number. The flip side features a red "Young Superstar" headline above a close-up photo. Above the headline, appears the player's personal information and statistics in orange and black ink respectively. The top of the flip side highlights the player's name and the Score logo in white within a purple band. To the right of the close-up photo a condensed scouting report and career hightlights are revealed. The card number and related logos appear on the bottom portion. Five trivia cards featuring "A Year to Remember" accompanied the series. Each trivia card relates to a highlight from the past 56 years. This set was distributed via a write-in offer with Score card wrappers.

		MT	NR MT	EX
Complete Set:		9.00	6.75	3.50
Common Player:		.10	.08	.04
1	Gregg Jefferies	.40	.30	.15
2	Jody Reed	.10	.08	.04
3	Mark Grace	.40	.30	.15
4	Dave Gallagher	.15	.11	.06
5	Bo Jackson	1.25	.90	.50
6	Jay Buhner	.10	.08	.04
7	Melido Perez	.10	.08	.04
8	Bobby Witt	.10	.08	.04
9	David Cone	.15	.11	.06
10	Chris Sabo	.15	.11	.06
11	Pat Borders	.10	.08	.04
12	Mark Grant	.10	.08	.04
13	Mike Macfarlane	.10	.08	.04
14	Mike Jackson	.10	.08	.04
15	Ricky Jordan	.30	.25	.12
16	Ron Gant	.50	.40	.20
17	Al Leiter	.10	.08	.04
18	Jeff Parrett	.10	.08	.04
19	Pete Smith	.10	.08	.04
20	Walt Weiss	.15	.11	.06
21	Doug Drabek	.12	.09	.05
22	Kirt Manwaring	.15	.11	.06
23	Keith Miller	.10	.08	.04
24	Damon Berryhill	.12	.09	.05
25	Gary Sheffield	.50	.40	.20
26	Brady Anderson	.10	.08	.04
27	Mitch Williams	.15	.11	.06
28	Roberto Alomar	.30	.25	.12
29	Bobby Thigpen	.12	.09	.05
30	Bryan Harvey	.10	.08	.04
31	Jose Rijo	.15	.11	.06
32	Dave West	.10	.08	.04
33	Joey Meyer	.10	.08	.04
34	Allan Anderson	.12	.09	.05
35	Rafael Palmeiro	.20	.15	.08
36	Tim Belcher	.30	.25	.12
37	John Smiley	.15	.11	.06
38	Mackey Sasser	.10	.08	.04
39	Greg Maddux	.30	.25	.12
40	Ramon Martinez	1.00	.70	.40
41	Randy Myers	.12	.09	.05
42	Scott Bankhead	.15	.11	.06

1989 Score Young Superstar-Series II

Score followed up with a second series of Young Superstars in 1989. The second series also included 42 cards and featured the same design as the first series. The set was also distributed via a write-in offer with Score card wrappers.

		MT	NR MT	EX
Complete Set:		5.00	3.75	2.00
Common Player:		.10	.08	.04
1	Sandy Alomar	.40	.30	.15
2	Tom Gordon	.40	.30	.15
3	Ron Jones	.10	.08	.04
4	Todd Burns	.10	.08	.04
5	Paul O'Neill	.10	.08	.04
6	Gene Larkin	.10	.08	.04
7	Eric King	.10	.08	.04
8	Jeff Robinson	.10	.08	.04
9	Bill Wegman	.10	.08	.04
10	Cecil Espy	.10	.08	.04
11	Jose Guzman	.10	.08	.04
12	Kelly Gruber	.20	.15	.08
13	Duane Ward	.10	.08	.04
14	Mark Gubicza	.25	.20	.10
15	Norm Charlton	.20	.15	.08
16	Jose Oquendo	.10	.08	.04
17	Geronimo Berroa	.10	.08	.04
18	Dwight Smith	.20	.15	.08
19	Lance McCullers	.10	.08	.04
20	Jimmy Jones	.10	.08	.04
21	Craig Worthington	.25	.20	.10
22	Mike Devereaux	.12	.09	.05
23	Bob Milacki	.15	.11	.06
24	Dale Sveum	.10	.08	.04
25	Carlos Quintana	.20	.15	.08
26	Luis Medina	.20	.15	.08
27	Steve Searcy	.20	.15	.08
28	Don August	.10	.08	.04
29	Shawn Hillegas	.10	.08	.04
30	Mike Campbell	.10	.08	.04
31	Mike Harkey	.25	.20	.10
32	Randy Johnson	.20	.15	.08
33	Craig Biggio	.35	.25	.12
34	Mike Schooler	.12	.09	.05
35	Andres Thomas	.10	.08	.04
36	Van Snider	.20	.15	.08
37	Cameron Drew	.20	.15	.08
38	Kevin Mitchell	.40	.30	.15
39	Lance Johnson	.15	.11	.06
40	Chad Kreuter	.10	.08	.04
41	Danny Jackson	.10	.08	.04
42	Kurt Stillwell	.10	.08	.04

Definitions for grading conditions are located in the introduction section at the front of this book.

1989 Score Rising Star

Similar in design to the Score Superstar set, this 100-card set showcased a host of rookies including Gary Sheffield and Gregg Jefferies. The full-color action photos are surrounded by a bright blue border with a green inner highlight line. The Score logo appears in the upper left in green and white. The player's name, position and team are found at the bottom. The flip sides display a full-color close-up of the player above his name and career highlights. The card number and player's rookie year are featured to the right. A "Rising Star" headline highlights the top border. Like the "Score Superstar" the Score "Rising Star" set was marketed as a combination with

a related magazine. "1988-89 Baseball's 100 Hottest Rookies" accompanies the set which also includes six Magic Motion baseball trivia cards featuring "Rookies to Remember." The magazine/card sets were available at a select group of retailers.

		MT	NR MT	EX
Complete Set:		10.00	7.50	4.00
Common Player:		.07	.05	.03
1	Gregg Jefferies	.40	.30	.15
2	Vicente Palacios	.15	.11	.06
3	Cameron Drew	.10	.08	.04
4	Doug Dascenzo	.12	.09	.05
5	Luis Medina	.12	.09	.05
6	Craig Worthington	.20	.15	.08
7	Rob Ducey	.08	.06	.04
8	Hal Morris	.60	.45	.25
9	Bill Brennan	.07	.05	.03
10	Gary Sheffield	.40	.30	.15
11	Mike Devereaux	.10	.08	.04
12	Hensley Meulens	.40	.30	.15
13	Carlos Quintana	.20	.15	.08
14	Todd Frohwirth	.07	.05	.03
15	Scott Lusader	.09	.07	.04
16	Mark Carreon	.15	.11	.06
17	Torey Lovullo	.20	.15	.08
18	Randy Velarde	.12	.09	.05
19	Billy Bean	.09	.07	.04
20	Lance Blankenship	.15	.11	.06
21	Chris Gwynn	.15	.11	.06
22	Felix Jose	.20	.15	.08
23	Derek Lilliquist	.20	.15	.08
24	Gary Thurman	.07	.05	.03
25	Ron Jones	.20	.15	.08
26	Dave Justice	1.00	.70	.40
27	Johnny Paredes	.08	.06	.03
28	Tim Jones	.10	.08	.04
29	Jose Gonzalez	.10	.08	.04
30	Geronimo Berroa	.15	.11	.06
31	Trevor Wilson	.12	.09	.05
32	Morris Madden	.10	.08	.04
33	Lance Johnson	.15	.11	.06
34	Marvin Freeman	.07	.05	.03
35	Jose Cecena	.07	.05	.03
36	Jim Corsi	.07	.05	.03
37	Rolando Roomes	.10	.08	.04
38	Scott Medvin	.07	.05	.03
39	Charlie Hayes	.20	.15	.08
40	Edgar Martinez	.15	.11	.06
41	Van Snider	.20	.15	.08
42	John Fishel	.07	.05	.02
43	Bruce Fields	.07	.05	.03
44	Darryl Hamilton	.09	.07	.04
45	Tom Prince	.09	.07	.03
46	Kirt Manwaring	.20	.15	.08
47	Steve Searcy	.12	.09	.05
48	Mike Harkey	.20	.15	.08
49	German Gonzalez	.07	.05	.03
50	Tony Perezchica	.07	.05	.03
51	Chad Kreuter	.15	.11	.06
52	Luis de los Santos	.10	.08	.04
53	Steve Curry	.07	.05	.03
54	Greg Bailey	.10	.08	.04
55	Ramon Martinez	.60	.45	.25
56	Ron Tingley	.07	.05	.03
57	Randy Kramer	.07	.05	.03
58	Alex Madrid	.07	.05	.03
59	Kevin Reimer	.15	.11	.06
60	Dave Otto	.07	.05	.03
61	Ken Patterson	.07	.05	.03
62	Keith Miller	.10	.08	.04
63	Randy Johnson	.10	.08	.04
64	Dwight Smith	.20	.15	.08
65	Eric Yelding	.20	.15	.08
66	Bob Geren	.40	.30	.15
67	Shane Turner	.25	.20	.10
68	Tom Gordon	.40	.30	.15
69	Jeff Huson	.30	.25	.12
70	Marty Brown	.25	.20	.10
71	Nelson Santovenia	.20	.15	.08
72	Roberto Alomar	.40	.30	.15
73	Mike Schooler	.15	.11	.06
74	Pete Smith	.10	.08	.04
75	John Costello	.07	.05	.03
76	Chris Sabo	.20	.15	.08
77	Damon Berryhill	.09	.07	.04
78	Mark Grace	.40	.30	.15
79	Melido Perez	.07	.05	.03
80	Al Leiter	.07	.05	.03
81	Todd Stottlemyre	.20	.15	.08
82	Mackey Sasser	.07	.05	.03
83	Don August	.07	.05	.03
84	Jeff Treadway	.07	.05	.03
85	Jody Reed	.09	.07	.05
86	Mike Campbell	.07	.05	.03
87	Ron Gant	.60	.45	.25
88	Ricky Jordan	.30	.25	.12
89	Terry Clark	.07	.05	.03
90	Roberto Kelly	.20	.15	.08
91	Pat Borders	.20	.15	.08
92	Bryan Harvey	.20	.15	.08
93	Joey Meyer	.10	.08	.04
94	Tim Belcher	.25	.20	.10
95	Walt Weiss	.15	.11	.06
96	Dave Gallagher	.15	.11	.06
97	Mike Macfarlane	.07	.05	.03
98	Craig Biggio	.30	.25	.12
99	Jack Armstrong	.15	.11	.06
100	Todd Burns	.07	.05	.03

1989 Score Superstar

This 100-card set features full-color action photos of baseball's superstars, and also includes six Magic Motion "Rookies to Remember" baseball trivia cards. The card fronts contain a bright red border with a blue line inside highlighting the photo. The Score logo appears in the bottom left corner. The player ID is displayed in unique fashion using overlapping triangles in white, green, and yellow. The flip side features a full-color player close-up directly beneath a bright red "Superstar" headline. The set was marketed along with the magazine "1989 Baseball's 100 Hottest Players". The magazine/card set combo was available at select retailers.

		MT	NR MT	EX
Complete Set:		8.00	6.00	3.25
Common Player:		.06	.05	.02
1	Jose Canseco	1.00	.70	.40
2	David Cone	.15	.11	.06
3	Dave Winfield	.15	.11	.06
4	George Brett	.15	.11	.06
5	Frank Viola	.09	.07	.05
6	Cory Snyder	.06	.05	.02
7	Alan Trammell	.09	.07	.04
8	Dwight Evans	.09	.07	.04
9	Tim Leary	.06	.05	.03
10	Don Mattingly	.80	.60	.30
11	Kirby Puckett	.30	.25	.12
12	Carney Lansford	.06	.05	.02
13	Dennis Martinez	.06	.05	.02
14	Kent Hrbek	.10	.08	.04
15	Doc Gooden	.30	.25	.12
16	Dennis Eckersley	.08	.06	.03
17	Kevin Seitzer	.08	.06	.03
18	Lee Smith	.06	.05	.02
19	Danny Tartabull	.15	.11	.06
20	Gerald Perry	.06	.05	.02
21	Gary Gaetti	.10	.08	.04
22	Rick Reuschel	.08	.06	.03
23	Keith Hernandez	.08	.06	.03
24	Jeff Reardon	.06	.05	.02
25	Mark McGwire	.50	.40	.20
26	Juan Samuel	.06	.05	.02
27	Jack Clark	.06	.05	.02
28	Robin Yount	.15	.11	.06

		MT	NR MT	EX
29	Steve Bedrosian	.06	.05	.02
30	Kirk Gibson	.08	.06	.03
31	Barry Bonds	.08	.06	.03
32	Dan Plesac	.06	.05	.02
33	Steve Sax	.06	.05	.02
34	Jeff Robinson	.06	.05	.02
35	Orel Hershiser	.10	.08	.04
36	Julio Franco	.08	.06	.03
37	Dave Righetti	.06	.05	.02
38	Bob Knepper	.06	.05	.02
39	Carlton Fisk	.08	.06	.03
41	Doug Jones	.06	.05	.02
42	Bobby Bonilla	.20	.15	.08
43	Ellis Burks	.30	.25	.12
44	Pedro Guerrero	.15	.11	.06
45	Rickey Henderson	.25	.20	.12
46	Glenn Davis	.10	.08	.04
47	Benny Santiago	.15	.11	.06
48	Greg Maddux	.20	.15	.08
49	Teddy Higuera	.06	.05	.02
50	Darryl Strawberry	.30	.25	.12
51	Mike Scott	.08	.06	.03
52	Mike Henneman	.06	.05	.02
53	Eric Davis	.35	.25	.12
54	Paul Molitor	.09	.07	.04
55	Rafael Palmeiro	.06	.05	.02
56	Joe Carter	.09	.07	.05
57	Ryne Sandberg	.15	.11	.06
58	Tony Fernandez	.08	.06	.03
59	Barry Larkin	.10	.08	.04
60	Ozzie Guillen	.06	.05	.02
61	Tom Browning	.06	.05	.02
62	Mark Davis	.08	.06	.03
63	Tom Henke	.06	.05	.02
64	Nolan Ryan	.80	.60	.30
65	Fred McGriff	.30	.25	.12
66	Dale Murphy	.10	.08	.06
67	Mark Langston	.10	.08	.06
68	Bobby Thigpen	.06	.05	.02
69	Mark Gubicza	.08	.06	.03
70	Mike Greenwell	.50	.40	.20
71	Ron Darling	.06	.05	.02
72	Gerald Young	.06	.05	.02
73	Wally Joyner	.10	.08	.04
74	Andres Galarraga	.10	.08	.04
75	Danny Jackson	.06	.05	.02
76	Mike Schmidt	.25	.20	.10
77	Cal Ripken, Jr.	.15	.11	.06
78	Alvin Davis	.08	.06	.03
79	Bruce Hurst	.06	.05	.02
80	Andre Dawson	.12	.09	.05
81	Bob Boone	.06	.05	.02
82	Harold Reynolds	.06	.05	.02
83	Eddie Murray	.06	.05	.02
84	Robby Thompson	.06	.05	.02
85	Will Clark	.80	.60	.30
86	Vince Coleman	.09	.07	.04
87	Doug Drabek	.06	.05	.02
88	Ozzie Smith	.08	.06	.03
89	Bob Welch	.06	.05	.02
90	Roger Clemens	.25	.20	.10
91	George Bell	.08	.06	.03
92	Andy Van Slyke	.08	.06	.03
93	Willie McGee	.06	.05	.02
94	Todd Worrell	.06	.05	.02
95	Tim Raines	.06	.05	.02
96	Kevin McReynolds	.10	.08	.04
97	John Franco	.06	.05	.02
98	Jim Gott	.06	.05	.02
99	Johnny Ray	.06	.05	.02
100	Wade Boggs	.50	.40	.20

1989 Score Yankees

This 33-card New York Yankee team set was produced by Score as an in-stadium promotion in 1989 and was distributed to fans attending the July 29 game at Yankee Stadium. The standard-size cards include a full-color player photo with a line drawing of the famous Yankee Stadium facade running along the top of the card. The player's name, "New York Yankees" and position appear below the photo. A second full-color photo is included on the back of the card, along with stats, data and a brief player profile. The set includes a special Thurman Munson commemorative card.

		MT	NR MT	EX
Complete Set:		8.00	6.00	3.25
Common Player:		.15	.11	.06
1	Don Mattingly	1.75	1.25	.70
2	Steve Sax	.30	.25	.12
3	Alvaro Espinoza	.25	.20	.10
4	Luis Polonia	.20	.15	.08
5	Jesse Barfield	.25	.20	.10
6	Dave Righetti	.25	.20	.10
7	Dave Winfield	.50	.40	.20
8	John Candelaria	.15	.11	.06
9	Wayne Tolleson	.15	.11	.06
10	Ken Phelps	.15	.11	.06
11	Rafael Santana	.15	.11	.06
12	Don Slaught	.15	.11	.06
13	Mike Pagliarulo	.20	.15	.08
14	Lance McCullers	.15	.11	.06
15	Dave LaPoint	.15	.11	.06
16	Dale Mohorcic	.15	.11	.06
17	Steve Balboni	.15	.11	.06
18	Roberto Kelly	.50	.40	.20
19	Andy Hawkins	.25	.20	.10
20	Mel Hall	.20	.15	.08
21	Tom Brookens	.15	.11	.06
22	Deion Sanders	.70	.50	.30
23	Richard Dotson	.15	.11	.06
24	Lee Guetterman	.15	.11	.06
25	Bob Geren	.30	.25	.12
26	Jimmy Jones	.15	.11	.06
27	Chuck Cary	.15	.11	.06
28	Ron Guidry	.25	.20	.10
29	Hal Morris	1.00	.70	.40
30	Clay Parker	.25	.20	.10
31	Dallas Green	.20	.15	.08
32	Thurman Munson	.70	.50	.30
33	Sponsor Card	.15	.11	.06

1990 Score

The regular Score set increased to 704 cards in 1990. Included were a series of cards picturing first-round draft picks, an expanded subset of rookie cards, four World Series specials, five Highlight cards, and a 13-card "Dream Team" series featuring the game's top players pictured on old tobacco-style cards. For the first time in a Score set, team logos are displayed on the card fronts in the lower right corner. Card backs again include a full-color portrait photo with player data. A one-paragraph write-up of each player was again provided by former Sports Illustrated editor Les Woodcock. The Score set was again distributed with "Magic Motion" triva cards, this

year using "Baseball's Most Valuable Players" as its theme.

		MT	NR MT	EX
Complete Set:		25.00	20.00	10.00
Common Player:		.04	.03	.02
1	Don Mattingly	.35	.25	.14
2	Cal Ripken, Jr.	.25	.20	.10
3	Dwight Evans	.08	.06	.03
4	Barry Bonds	.12	.09	.05
5	Kevin McReynolds	.12	.09	.05
6	Ozzie Guillen	.05	.04	.02
7	Terry Kennedy	.04	.03	.02
8	Bryan Harvey	.06	.05	.02
9	Alan Trammell	.09	.07	.04
10	Cory Snyder	.09	.07	.04
11	Jody Reed	.05	.04	.02
12	Roberto Alomar	.20	.15	.08
13	Pedro Guerrero	.09	.07	.04
14	Gary Redus	.04	.03	.02
15	Marty Barrett	.05	.04	.02
16	Ricky Jordan	.20	.15	.08
17	Joe Magrane	.07	.05	.03
18	Sid Fernandez	.07	.05	.03
19	Rich Dotson	.04	.03	.02
20	Jack Clark	.09	.07	.04
21	Bob Walk	.05	.04	.02
22	Ron Karkovice	.04	.03	.02
23	Lenny Harris(FC)	.10	.07	.04
24	Phil Bradley	.06	.05	.02
25	Andres Galarraga	.15	.11	.06
26	Brian Downing	.06	.05	.02
27	Dave Martinez	.06	.05	.02
28	Eric King	.04	.03	.02
29	Barry Lyons	.04	.03	.02
30	Dave Schmidt	.04	.03	.02
31	Mike Boddicker	.06	.05	.04
32	Tom Foley	.04	.03	.02
33	Brady Anderson	.07	.05	.03
34	Jim Presley	.05	.04	.02
35	Lance Parrish	.06	.05	.02
36	Von Hayes	.09	.07	.03
37	Lee Smith	.06	.05	.02
38	Herm Winningham	.04	.03	.02
39	Alejandro Pena	.04	.03	.02
40	Mike Scott	.09	.07	.04
41	Joe Orsulak	.04	.03	.02
42	Rafael Ramirez	.05	.04	.02
43	Gerald Young	.05	.04	.02
44	Dick Schofield	.05	.04	.02
45	Dave Smith	.06	.05	.02
46	Dave Magadan	.07	.05	.03
47	Dennis Martinez	.06	.05	.02
48	Greg Minton	.04	.03	.02
49	Milt Thompson	.04	.03	.02
50	Orel Hershiser	.12	.09	.05
51	Bip Roberts(FC)	.09	.07	.04
52	Jerry Browne	.09	.07	.04
53	Bob Ojeda	.05	.04	.02
54	Fernando Valenzuela	.09	.07	.04
55	Matt Nokes	.09	.07	.04
56	Brook Jacoby	.08	.06	.03
57	Frank Tanana	.05	.04	.02
58	Scott Fletcher	.05	.04	.02
59	Ron Oester	.05	.04	.02
60	Bob Boone	.08	.06	.03
61	Dan Gladden	.08	.06	.03
62	Darnell Coles	.04	.03	.02
63	Gregg Olson	.25	.20	.10
64	Todd Burns	.05	.04	.02
65	Todd Benzinger	.07	.05	.03
66	Dale Murphy	.12	.09	.05
67	Mike Flanagan	.06	.05	.02
68	Jose Oquendo	.06	.05	.02
69	Cecil Espy	.08	.06	.03
70	Chris Sabo	.10	.07	.04
71	Shane Rawley	.05	.04	.02
72	Tom Brunansky	.08	.06	.03
73	Vance Law	.05	.04	.02
74	B.J. Surhoff	.08	.06	.03
75	Lou Whitaker	.09	.07	.04
76	Ken Caminiti	.09	.07	.04
77	Nelson Liriano	.04	.03	.02
78	Tommy Gregg	.09	.07	.04
79	Don Slaught	.05	.04	.02
80	Eddie Murray	.12	.09	.05
81	Joe Boever	.08	.06	.02
82	Charlie Leibrandt	.06	.05	.02
83	Jose Lind	.06	.05	.02
84	Tony Phillips	.05	.04	.02

		MT	NR MT	EX
85	Mitch Webster	.04	.03	.02
86	Dan Plesac	.07	.05	.02
87	Rick Mahler	.05	.04	.02
88	Steve Lyons	.05	.04	.02
89	Tony Fernandez	.09	.07	.04
90	Ryne Sandberg	.30	.25	.12
91	Nick Esasky	.09	.07	.04
92	Luis Salazar	.04	.03	.02
93	Pete Incaviglia	.08	.06	.03
94	Ivan Calderon	.06	.05	.02
95	Jeff Treadway	.06	.05	.02
96	Kurt Stillwell	.06	.05	.02
97	Gary Sheffield	.25	.20	.10
98	Jeffrey Leonard	.07	.05	.03
99	Andres Thomas	.05	.04	.02
100	Roberto Kelly	.15	.11	.06
101	Alvaro Espinoza(FC)	.15	.11	.06
102	Greg Gagne	.05	.04	.02
103	John Farrell	.05	.04	.02
104	Willie Wilson	.05	.04	.02
105	Glenn Braggs	.08	.06	.03
106	Chet Lemon	.06	.05	.02
107	Jamie Moyer	.06	.05	.02
108	Chuck Crim	.04	.03	.02
109	Dave Valle	.04	.03	.02
110	Walt Weiss	.10	.07	.04
111	Larry Sheets	.04	.03	.02
112	Don Robinson	.05	.04	.02
113	Danny Heep	.04	.03	.02
114	Carmelo Martinez	.06	.05	.02
115	Dave Gallagher	.08	.06	.03
116	Mike LaValliere	.05	.04	.02
117	Bob McClure	.04	.03	.02
118	Rene Gonzales	.04	.03	.02
119	Mark Parent	.05	.04	.02
120	Wally Joyner	.15	.11	.06
121	Mark Gubicza	.09	.07	.04
122	Tony Pena	.08	.06	.03
123	Carmen Castillo	.04	.03	.02
124	Howard Johnson	.20	.15	.08
125	Steve Sax	.10	.08	.04
126	Tim Belcher	.10	.08	.04
127	Tim Burke	.06	.05	.02
128	Al Newman	.04	.03	.02
129	Dennis Rasmussen	.05	.04	.02
130	Doug Jones	.06	.05	.02
131	Fred Lynn	.09	.07	.04
132	Jeff Hamilton	.06	.05	.02
133	German Gonzalez	.05	.04	.02
134	John Morris	.05	.04	.02
135	Dave Parker	.10	.08	.04
136	Gary Pettis	.05	.04	.02
137	Dennis Boyd	.07	.05	.02
138	Candy Maldonado	.06	.05	.02
139	Rick Cerone	.04	.03	.02
140	George Brett	.15	.11	.06
141	Dave Clark	.05	.04	.02
142	Dickie Thon	.05	.04	.02
143	Junior Ortiz	.04	.03	.02
144	Don August	.06	.05	.02
145	Gary Gaetti	.10	.08	.04
146	Kirt Manwaring	.12	.09	.05
147	Jeff Reed	.04	.03	.02
148	Jose Alvarez(FC)	.08	.06	.03
149	Mike Schooler	.08	.06	.03
150	Mark Grace	.25	.20	.10
151	Geronimo Berroa	.08	.06	.03
152	Barry Jones	.04	.03	.02
153	Geno Petralli	.05	.04	.02
154	Jim Deshaies	.08	.06	.03
155	Barry Larkin	.15	.11	.06
156	Alfredo Griffin	.05	.04	.02
157	Tom Henke	.06	.05	.02
158	Mike Jeffcoat(FC)	.05	.04	.02
159	Bob Welch	.09	.07	.04
160	Julio Franco	.10	.08	.04
161	Henry Cotto	.04	.03	.02
162	Terry Steinbach	.10	.08	.04
163	Damon Berryhill	.08	.06	.03
164	Tim Crews	.04	.03	.02
165	Tom Browning	.09	.07	.04
166	Frd Manrique	.04	.03	.02
167	Harold Reynolds	.09	.07	.04
168	Ron Hassey	.05	.04	.02
169	Shawon Dunston	.08	.06	.03
170	Bobby Bonilla	.15	.11	.06
171	Tom Herr	.07	.05	.03
172	Mike Heath	.04	.03	.02
173	Rich Gedman	.05	.04	.02
174	Bill Ripken	.05	.04	.02
175	Pete O'Brien	.07	.05	.03

		MT	NR MT	EX
176a	Lloyd McClendon (uniform number 1 on back)	1.00	.70	.40
176b	Lloyd McClendon (uniform number 10 on back)	.20	.15	.08
177	Brian Holton	.05	.04	.02
178	Jeff Blauser	.05	.04	.02
179	Jim Eisenreich	.05	.04	.02
180	Bert Blyleven	.09	.07	.04
181	Rob Murphy	.05	.04	.02
182	Bill Doran	.07	.05	.03
183	Curt Ford	.04	.03	.02
184	Mike Henneman	.06	.05	.02
185	Eric Davis	.20	.15	.08
186	Lance McCullers	.06	.05	.03
187	*Steve Davis*(FC)	.15	.11	.06
188	Bill Wegman	.05	.04	.02
189	Brian Harper	.06	.05	.02
190	Mike Moore	.09	.07	.04
191	Dale Mohorcic	.04	.03	.02
192	Tim Wallach	.09	.07	.04
193	Keith Hernandez	.09	.07	.04
194	Dave Righetti	.07	.05	.03
195a	Bret Saberhagen ("joke" on card back)	.25	.20	.10
195b	Bret Saberhagen ("joker" on card back)	.60	.45	.25
196	Paul Kilgus	.04	.03	.02
197	Bud Black	.05	.04	.02
198	Juan Samuel	.09	.07	.04
199	Kevin Seitzer	.15	.11	.06
200	Darryl Strawberry	.30	.25	.12
201	Dave Steib	.09	.07	.04
202	Charlie Hough	.06	.05	.02
203	Jack Morris	.08	.06	.03
204	Rance Mulliniks	.04	.03	.02
205	Alvin Davis	.10	.08	.04
206	Jack Howell	.06	.05	.02
207	Ken Patterson(FC)	.06	.05	.02
208	Terry Pendleton	.09	.07	.03
209	Craig Lefferts	.06	.05	.02
210	Kevin Brown(FC)	.10	.08	.04
211	Dan Petry	.04	.03	.02
212	Dave Leiper	.06	.05	.02
213	Daryl Boston	.04	.03	.02
214	Kevin Hickey(FC)	.08	.06	.03
215	Mike Krukow	.06	.05	.02
216	Terry Francona	.04	.03	.02
217	Kirk McCaskill	.08	.06	.03
218	Scott Bailes	.05	.04	.02
219	Bob Forsch	.04	.03	.02
220	Mike Aldrete	.05	.04	.02
221	Steve Buechele	.06	.05	.02
222	Jesse Barfield	.09	.07	.05
223	Juan Berenguer	.06	.05	.02
224	Andy McGaffigan	.06	.05	.02
225	Pete Smith	.09	.07	.04
226	Mike Witt	.06	.05	.02
227	Jay Howell	.08	.06	.03
228	Scott Bradley	.05	.04	.02
229	*Jerome Walton*	.30	.25	.12
230	Greg Swindell	.15	.11	.06
231	Atlee Hammaker	.04	.03	.02
232	Mike Devereaux	.09	.07	.04
233	Ken Hill	.09	.07	.04
234	Craig Worthington	.15	.11	.06
235	Scott Terry	.08	.06	.03
236	Brett Butler	.09	.07	.04
237	Doyle Alexander	.07	.05	.03
238	Dave Anderson	.04	.03	.02
239	Bob Milacki	.10	.08	.04
240	Dwight Smith	.50	.40	.20
241	Otis Nixon	.04	.03	.02
242	Pat Tabler	.06	.05	.02
243	Derek Lilliquist	.12	.09	.05
244	Danny Tartabull	.15	.11	.06
245	Wade Boggs	.30	.25	.12
246	Scott Garrelts	.08	.06	.03
247	Spike Owen	.04	.03	.02
248	Norm Charlton	.12	.09	.05
249	Gerald Perry	.06	.05	.02
250	Nolan Ryan	.50	.40	.20
251	Kevin Gross	.07	.05	.03
252	Randy Milligan	.07	.05	.03
253	Mike LaCoss	.05	.04	.02
254	Dave Bergman	.04	.03	.02
255	Tony Gwynn	.35	.25	.12
256	Felix Fermin	.04	.03	.02
257	Greg Harris	.10	.08	.04
258	*Junior Felix*	.20	.15	.08
259	Mark Davis	.09	.07	.04
260	Vince Coleman	.15	.11	.06
261	Paul Gibson	.10	.08	.04
262	Mitch Williams	.10	.08	.04
263	Jeff Russell	.08	.06	.03
264	*Omar Vizquel*	.10	.07	.04
265	Andre Dawson	.12	.09	.05
266	Storm Davis	.08	.06	.03
267	Guillermo Hernandez	.04	.03	.02
268	Mike Felder	.05	.04	.02
269	Tom Candiotti	.05	.04	.02
270	Bruce Hurst	.09	.07	.04
271	Fred McGriff	.30	.25	.12
272	Glenn Davis	.15	.11	.60
273	John Franco	.09	.07	.04
274	Rich Yett	.04	.03	.02
275	Craig Biggio	.15	.11	.06
276	Gene Larkin	.05	.04	.02
277	Rob Dibble	.15	.11	.06
278	Randy Bush	.05	.04	.02
279	Kevin Bass	.08	.06	.03
280a	Bo Jackson ("Watham" on card back)	.60	.45	.25
280b	Bo Jackson ("Wathan" on card back)	1.00	.70	.40
281	Wally Backman	.06	.05	.02
282	Larry Andersen	.04	.03	.02
283	Chris Bosio	.09	.07	.04
284	Juan Agosto	.04	.03	.02
285	Ozzie Smith	.10	.08	.04
286	George Bell	.10	.08	.04
287	Rex Hudler	.05	.04	.02
288	Pat Borders	.10	.08	.04
289	Danny Jackson	.07	.05	.03
290	Carlton Fisk	.09	.07	.04
291	Tracy Jones	.05	.04	.02
292	Allan Anderson	.07	.05	.03
293	Johnny Ray	.07	.05	.03
294	Lee Guetterman	.04	.03	.02
295	Paul O'Neill	.09	.07	.05
296	Carney Lansford	.08	.06	.03
297	Tom Brookens	.04	.03	.02
298	Claudell Washington	.08	.06	.03
299	Hubie Brooks	.08	.06	.03
300	Will Clark	.60	.45	.25
301	*Kenny Rogers*	.20	.15	.08
302	Darrell Evans	.07	.05	.03
303	Greg Briley	.25	.20	.10
304	Donn Pall	.09	.07	.04
305	Teddy Higuera	.09	.07	.04
306	Dan Pasqua	.07	.05	.02
307	Dave Winfield	.15	.11	.06
308	Dennis Powell	.04	.03	.02
309	Jose DeLeon	.08	.06	.03
310	Roger Clemens	.25	.20	.10
311	Melido Perez	.09	.07	.04
312	Devon White	.09	.07	.04
313	Doc Gooden	.25	.20	.10
314	*Carlos Martinez*	.20	.15	.08
315	Dennis Eckersley	.10	.08	.04
316	Clay Parker	.12	.09	.05
317	Rick Honeycutt	.05	.04	.02
318	Tim Laudner	.05	.04	.02
319	Joe Carter	.10	.08	.04
320	Robin Yount	.20	.15	.08
321	Felix Jose	.30	.25	.15
322	Mickey Tettleton	.09	.07	.04
323	Mike Gallego	.04	.03	.02
324	Edgar Martinez	.09	.07	.04
325	Dave Henderson	.09	.07	.04
326	Chili Davis	.09	.07	.04
327	Steve Balboni	.05	.04	.02
328	Jody Davis	.04	.03	.02
329	Shawn Hillegas	.04	.03	.02
330	Jim Abbott	.35	.25	.12
331	John Dopson	.10	.08	.04
332	Mark Williamson	.04	.03	.02
333	Jeff Robinson	.08	.06	.03
334	John Smiley	.09	.07	.04
335	Bobby Thigpen	.07	.05	.03
336	Garry Templeton	.05	.04	.02
337	Marvell Wynne	.05	.04	.02
338a	Ken Griffey, Sr. (uniform number 25 on card back)	.25	.20	.10
338b	Ken Griffey, Sr. (uniform number 30 on card back)	3.00	2.25	1.25
339	*Steve Finley*	.25	.20	.10
340	Ellis Burks	.25	.20	.10
341	Frank Williams	.04	.03	.02
342	Mike Morgan	.05	.04	.02
343	Kevin Mitchell	.35	.25	.12
344	Joel Youngblood	.04	.03	.02
345	Mike Greenwell	.25	.20	.10

		MT	NR MT	EX
346	Glenn Wilson	.05	.04	.02
347	John Costello	.05	.04	.02
348	Wes Gardner	.04	.03	.02
349	Jeff Ballard	.09	.07	.04
350	Mark Thurmond	.04	.03	.02
351	Randy Myers	.07	.05	.03
352	Shawn Abner	.07	.05	.03
353	Jesse Orosco	.04	.03	.02
354	Greg Walker	.05	.04	.02
355	Pete Harnisch	.15	.11	.06
356	Steve Farr	.05	.04	.02
357	Dave LaPoint	.05	.04	.02
358	Willie Fraser	.05	.04	.02
359	Mickey Hatcher	.04	.03	.02
360	Rickey Henderson	.30	.25	.12
361	Mike Fitzgerald	.04	.03	.02
362	Bill Schroeder	.04	.03	.02
363	Mark Carreon	.10	.08	.04
364	Ron Jones	.10	.08	.04
365	Jeff Montgomery	.06	.05	.02
366	Bill Krueger(FC)	.04	.03	.02
367	John Cangelosi	.04	.03	.02
368	Jose Gonzalez	.10	.08	.04
369	*Greg Hibbard*(FC)	.30	.25	.12
370	John Smoltz	.15	.11	.06
371	*Jeff Brantley*	.15	.11	.06
372	Frank White	.08	.06	.03
373	Ed Whitson	.06	.05	.02
374	Willie McGee	.09	.07	.04
375	Jose Canseco	.70	.50	.30
376	Randy Ready	.04	.03	.02
377	Don Aase	.04	.03	.02
378	Tony Armas	.05	.04	.02
379	Steve Bedrosian	.07	.05	.03
380	Chuck Finley	.07	.05	.03
381	Kent Hrbek	.12	.09	.05
382	Jim Gantner	.06	.05	.02
383	Mel Hall	.06	.05	.02
384	Mike Marshall	.07	.05	.03
385	Mark McGwire	.20	.15	.08
386	Wayne Tolleson	.04	.03	.02
387	Brian Holton	.05	.04	.02
388	*John Wetteland*	.20	.15	.08
389	Darren Daulton	.04	.03	.02
390	Rob Deer	.07	.05	.03
391	John Moses	.04	.03	.02
392	Todd Worrell	.07	.05	.03
393	Chuck Cary(FC)	.10	.08	.04
394	Stan Javier	.05	.04	.02
395	Willie Randolph	.09	.07	.04
396	Bill Buckner	.06	.05	.02
397	Robby Thompson	.07	.05	.02
398	Mike Scioscia	.07	.05	.03
399	Lonnie Smith	.09	.07	.04
400	Kirby Puckett	.40	.30	.15
401	Mark Langston	.15	.11	.06
402	Danny Darwin	.04	.03	.02
403	Greg Maddux	.15	.11	.06
404	Lloyd Moseby	.07	.05	.02
405	Rafael Palmeiro	.09	.07	.04
406	Chad Kreuter	.10	.08	.04
407	Jimmy Key	.09	.07	.05
408	Tim Birtsas	.04	.03	.02
409	Tim Raines	.10	.08	.04
410	Dave Stewart	.09	.07	.04
411	*Eric Yelding*(FC)	.30	.25	.12
412	*Kent Anderson*(FC)	.15	.11	.06
413	Les Lancaster	.05	.04	.02
414	Rick Dempsey	.04	.03	.02
415	Randy Johnson	.10	.08	.04
416	Gary Carter	.07	.05	.03
417	Rolando Roomes	.15	.11	.06
418	Dan Schatzeder	.04	.03	.02
419	Dryn Smith	.07	.05	.03
420	Ruben Sierra	.20	.15	.08
421	Steve Jeltz	.04	.03	.02
422	Ken Oberkfell	.04	.03	.02
423	Sid Bream	.04	.03	.02
424	Jim Clancy	.04	.03	.02
425	Kelly Gruber	.09	.07	.04
426	Rick Leach	.04	.03	.02
427	Lenny Dykstra	.07	.05	.03
428	Jeff Pico	.06	.05	.02
429	John Cerutti	.06	.05	.02
430	David Cone	.15	.11	.06
431	Jeff Kunkel	.04	.03	.02
432	Luis Aquino	.05	.04	.02
433	Ernie Whitt	.05	.04	.02
434	Bo Diaz	.05	.04	.02
435	Steve Lake	.04	.03	.02
436	Pat Perry	.04	.03	.02
437	Mike Davis	.05	.04	.02
438	Cecilio Guante	.04	.03	.02
439	Duane Ward	.04	.03	.02
440	Andy Van Slyke	.10	.08	.04
441	Gene Nelson	.04	.03	.02
442	Luis Polonia	.06	.05	.02
443	Kevin Elster	.06	.05	.02
444	Keith Moreland	.06	.05	.02
445	Roger McDowell	.06	.05	.02
446	Ron Darling	.08	.06	.03
447	Ernest Riles	.04	.03	.02
448	Mookie Wilson	.08	.06	.03
449a	*Bill Spiers* (66 missing for year of birth)	1.25	.90	.50
449b	*Bill Spiers* (1966 for birth year)	.30	.25	.12
450	Rick Sutcliffe	.07	.05	.03
451	Nelson Santovenia	.10	.08	.04
452	Andy Allanson	.04	.03	.02
453	Bob Melvin	.04	.03	.02
454	Benny Santiago	.12	.09	.05
455	Jose Uribe	.05	.04	.02
456	Bill Landrum(FC)	.08	.06	.03
457	Bobby Witt	.07	.05	.03
458	Kevin Romine	.07	.05	.03
459	Lee Mazzilli	.04	.03	.02
460	Paul Molitor	.10	.08	.04
461	Ramon Martinez(FC)	.60	.45	.25
462	Frank DiPino	.04	.03	.02
463	Walt Terrell	.06	.05	.02
464	*Bob Geren*	.30	.25	.12
465	Rick Reuchel	.09	.07	.04
466	Mark Grant	.06	.05	.02
467	John Kruk	.07	.05	.03
468	Gregg Jefferies	.60	.45	.25
469	R.J. Reynolds	.04	.03	.02
470	Harold Baines	.09	.07	.04
471	Dennis Lamp	.04	.03	.02
472	Tom Gordon	.20	.15	.08
473	Terry Puhl	.04	.03	.02
474	Curtis Wilkerson	.04	.03	.02
475	Dan Quisenberry	.05	.04	.02
476	Oddibe McDowell	.07	.05	.03
477	Zane Smith	.04	.03	.02
478	Franklin Stubbs	.04	.03	.02
479	Wallace Johnson	.04	.03	.02
480	Jay Tibbs	.04	.03	.02
481	Tom Glavine	.09	.07	.03
482	Manny Lee	.05	.04	.02
483	Joe Hesketh	.04	.03	.02
484	Mike Bielecki	.07	.05	.03
485	Greg Brock	.06	.05	.02
486	Pascual Perez	.06	.05	.02
487	Kirk Gibson	.09	.07	.04
488	Scott Sanderson	.05	.04	.02
489	Domingo Ramos	.04	.03	.02
490	Kal Daniels	.10	.08	.04
491a	David Wells (Reverse negative on back photo)	3.00	2.25	1.25
491b	David Wells (Corrected)	.05	.04	.02
492	Jerry Reed	.04	.03	.02
493	Eric Show	.06	.05	.02
494	Mike Pagliarulo	.06	.05	.02
495	Ron Robinson	.05	.04	.02
496	Brad Komminsk	.04	.03	.02
497	*Greg Litton*	.15	.11	.06
498	Chris James	.07	.05	.02
499	Luis Quinones(FC)	.05	.04	.02
500	Frank Viola	.10	.08	.04
501	Tim Teufel	.05	.04	.02
502	Terry Leach	.04	.03	.02
503	Matt Williams	.20	.15	.08
504	Tim Leary	.06	.05	.02
505	Doug Drabek	.06	.05	.02
506	Mariano Duncan	.06	.05	.02
507	Charlie Hayes	.10	.08	.04
508	*Joey Belle*	.60	.45	.25
509	Pat Sheridan	.05	.04	.02
510	Mackey Sasser	.05	.04	.02
511	Jose Rijo	.09	.07	.04
512	Mike Smithson	.04	.03	.02
513	Gary Ward	.04	.03	.02
514	Dion James	.06	.05	.02
515	Jim Gott	.06	.05	.02
516	Drew Hall(FC)	.07	.05	.03
517	Doug Bair	.04	.03	.02
518	*Scott Scudder*	.20	.15	.08
519	Rick Aguilera	.06	.05	.02
520	Rafael Belliard	.05	.04	.02
521	Jay Buhner	.10	.08	.04
522	Jeff Reardon	.06	.05	.02
523	Steve Rosenberg(FC)	.09	.07	.04

		MT	NR MT	EX
524	Randy Velarde(FC)	.09	.07	.04
525	Jeff Musselman	.09	.07	.04
526	Bill Long	.06	.05	.02
527	*Gary Wayne*	.10	.08	.04
528	*Dave Johnson*(FC)	.15	.11	.06
529	Ron Kittle	.08	.06	.03
530	Erik Hanson(FC)	.20	.15	.08
531	Steve Wilson(FC)	.20	.15	.08
532	Joey Meyer	.04	.03	.02
533	Curt Young	.04	.03	.02
534	Kelly Downs	.06	.05	.02
535	Joe Girardi	.20	.15	.08
536	Lance Blankenship	.09	.07	.04
537	Greg Mathews	.05	.04	.02
538	Donell Nixon	.04	.03	.02
539	Mark Knudson(FC)	.09	.07	.04
540	*Jeff Wetherby*(FC)	.15	.11	.06
541	Darrin Jackson	.04	.03	.02
542	Terry Mulholland	.09	.07	.03
543	Eric Hetzel(FC)	.15	.11	.06
544	*Rick Reed*(FC)	.15	.11	.06
545	Dennis Cook(FC)	.20	.15	.08
546	Mike Jackson	.05	.04	.02
547	Brian Fisher	.06	.05	.02
548	*Gene Harris*(FC)	.20	.15	.08
549	Jeff King(FC)	.20	.15	.08
550	Dave Dravecky (Salute)	.10	.08	.04
551	Randy Kutcher(FC)	.08	.06	.03
552	Mark Portugal	.06	.05	.02
553	*Jim Corsi*(FC)	.12	.09	.05
554	Todd Stottlemyre	.12	.09	.05
555	Scott Bankhead	.09	.07	.04
556	Ken Dayley	.05	.04	.02
557	*Rick Wrona*(FC)	.15	.11	.06
558	*Sammy Sosa*(FC)	.40	.30	.15
559	Keith Miller	.08	.06	.03
560	Ken Griffey Jr.	3.00	2.25	1.25
561a	Ryne Sandberg (No Errors- 3B Position designation)	10.00	7.50	4.00
561b	Ryne Sandberg (No Errors- No position designation)	.50	.40	.20
562	Billy Hatcher	.06	.05	.02
563	Jay Bell(FC)	.09	.07	.04
564	*Jack Daugherty*(FC)	.15	.11	.06
565	*Rich Monteleone*	.20	.15	.08
566	Bo Jackson (All-Star MVP)	.30	.25	.12
567	*Tony Fossas*(FC)	.10	.08	.04
568	*Roy Smith*(FC)	.15	.11	.06
569	*Jaime Navarro*(FC)	.25	.20	.10
570	Lance Johnson(FC)	.15	.11	.06
571	*Mike Dyer*(FC)	.25	.20	.10
572	*Kevin Ritz*(FC)	.20	.15	.08
573	Dave West	.15	.11	.06
574	*Gary Mielke*(FC)	.25	.20	.10
575	Scott Lusader(FC)	.09	.07	.04
576	*Joe Oliver*	.30	.25	.12
577	Sandy Alomar, Jr.	.25	.20	.10
578	Andy Benes(FC)	.30	.25	.12
579	Tim Jones	.07	.05	.03
580	*Randy McCament*(FC)	.15	.11	.06
581	Curt Schilling(FC)	.15	.11	.06
582	*John Orton*(FC)	.15	.11	.06
583a	*Milt Cuyler* (played in 998 games)(FC)	2.00	1.50	.80
583b	*Milt Cuyler* (played in 98 games)(FC)	.40	.30	.15
584	*Eric Anthony*(FC)	.25	.20	.10
585	*Greg Vaughn*(FC)	.60	.45	.25
586	*Deion Sanders*(FC)	.50	.40	.20
587	Jose DeJesus(FC)	.15	.11	.06
588	*Chip Hale*(FC)	.15	.11	.06
589	*John Olerud*(FC)	2.00	1.50	.80
590	*Steve Olin*(FC)	.20	.15	.08
591	*Marquis Grissom*(FC)	.60	.45	.25
592	*Moises Alou*(FC)	.50	.40	.20
593	Mark Lemke(FC)	.10	.08	.04
594	*Dean Palmer*(FC)	.80	.60	.30
595	Robin Ventura(FC)	.80	.60	.30
596	*Tino Martinez*(FC)	.90	.70	.35
597	*Mike Huff*(FC)	.25	.20	.10
598	*Scott Hemond*(FC)	.25	.20	.10
599	*Wally Whitehurst*(FC)	.20	.15	.08
600	*Todd Zeile*(FC)	.70	.50	.30
601	Glenallen Hill(FC)	.35	.25	.14
602	Hal Morris(FC)	.15	.11	.06
603	Juan Bell(FC)	.15	.11	.06
604	*Bobby Rose*(FC)	.25	.20	.10
605	*Matt Merullo*(FC)	.20	.15	.08
606	*Kevin Maas*(FC)	2.50	2.00	1.00
607	*Randy Nosek*(FC)	.15	.11	.06
608	*Billy Bates*(FC)	.15	.11	.06

		MT	NR MT	EX
609	*Mike Stanton*(FC)	.25	.20	.10
610	*Goose Gozzo*(FC)	.20	.15	.08
611	*Charles Nagy*(FC)	.30	.25	.12
612	*Scott Coolbaugh*(FC)	.20	.15	.08
613	*Jose Vizcaino*(FC)	.25	.20	.10
614	*Greg Smith*(FC)	.20	.15	.08
615	*Jeff Huson*(FC)	.25	.20	.10
616	*Mickey Weston*(FC)	.15	.11	.06
617	*John Pawlowski*(FC)	.15	.11	.06
618a	*Joe Skalski* (uniform #27)(FC)	.15	.11	.06
618b	*Joe Skalski* (uniform #67)(FC)	2.00	1.50	.80
619	*Bernie Williams*(FC)	.60	.45	.25
620	*Shawn Holman*(FC)	.15	.11	.06
621	*Gary Eave*(FC)	.15	.11	.06
622	*Darrin Fletcher*(FC)	.25	.20	.10
623	*Pat Combs*(FC)	.20	.15	.08
624	*Mike Blowers*(FC)	.25	.20	.10
625	*Kevin Appier*(FC)	.30	.25	.12
626	*Pat Austin*(FC)	.15	.11	.06
627	*Kelly Mann*(FC)	.20	.15	.08
628	*Matt Kinzer*(FC)	.15	.11	.06
629	*Chris Hammond*(FC)	.25	.20	.10
630	*Dean Wilkins*(FC)	.15	.11	.06
631	*Larry Walker*(FC)	.35	.25	.14
632	*Blaine Beatty*(FC)	.20	.15	.08
633a	Tom Barrett (uniform #29)(FC)	.15	.11	.06
633b	Tom Barrett (uniform #14)(FC)	4.00	3.00	1.50
634	*Stan Belinda*(FC)	.35	.25	.14
635	*Tex Smith*(FC)	.15	.11	.06
636	Hensley Meulens(FC)	.40	.30	.15
637	*Juan Gonzalez*(FC)	3.00	2.25	1.25
638	*Lenny Webster*(FC)	.20	.15	.08
639	*Mark Gardner*(FC)	.25	.20	.10
640	*Tommy Greene*(FC)	.35	.25	.14
641	*Mike Hartley*(FC)	.20	.15	.08
642	*Phil Stephenson*(FC)	.15	.11	.06
643	*Kevin Mmahat*(FC)	.15	.11	.06
644	*Ed Whited*(FC)	.15	.11	.06
645	*Delino DeShields*(FC)	.60	.45	.25
646	Kevin Blankenship(FC)	.15	.11	.06
647	*Paul Sorrento*(FC)	.25	.20	.10
648	*Mike Roesler*(FC)	.15	.11	.06
649	*Jason Grimsley*(FC)	.25	.20	.10
650	*Dave Justice*(FC)	3.00	2.25	1.25
651	*Scott Cooper*(FC)	.25	.20	.10
652	Dave Eiland(FC)	.15	.11	.06
653	*Mike Munoz*(FC)	.20	.15	.08
654	*Jeff Fischer*(FC)	.15	.11	.06
655	*Terry Jorgenson*(FC)	.20	.15	.08
656	*George Canale*(FC)	.20	.15	.08
657	*Brian DuBois*(FC)	.15	.11	.06
658	Carlos Quintana	.10	.08	.04
659	Luis De los santos	.10	.08	.04
660	Jerald Clark	.10	.08	.04
661	#1 Draft Pick *(Donald Harris)*(FC)	.30	.25	.12
662	#1 Draft Pick *(Paul Coleman)*(FC)	.40	.30	.15
663	#1 Draft Pick *(Frank Thomas)*(FC)	7.00	5.25	2.75
664	#1 Draft Pick *(Brent Mayne)*(FC)	.30	.25	.12
665	#1 Draft Pick *(Eddie Zosky)*(FC)	.25	.20	.10
666	#1 Draft Pick *(Steve Hosey)*(FC)	.20	.15	.08
667	#1 Draft Pick *(Scott Bryant)*(FC)	.20	.15	.08
668	#1 Draft Pick *(Tom Goodwin)*(FC)	.40	.30	.15
669	#1 Draft Pick *(Cal Eldred)*(FC)	.20	.15	.08
670	#1 Draft Pick *(Earl Cunningham)*(FC)	.25	.20	.10
671	#1 Draft Pick *(Alan Zinter)*(FC)	.25	.20	.10
672	#1 Draft Pick *(Chuck Knoblauch)*(FC)	1.00	.70	.40
673	#1 Draft Pick *(Kyle Abbott)*(FC)	.25	.20	.10
674	#1 Draft Pick *(Roger Salkeld)*(FC)	.60	.45	.25
675	#1 Draft Pick *(Maurice Vaughn)*(FC)	2.00	1.50	.80
676	#1 Draft Pick *(Kiki Jones)*(FC)	.50	.40	.20
677	#1 Draft Pick *(Tyler Houston)*(FC)	.40	.30	.15
678	#1 Draft Pick *(Jeff Jackson)*(FC)	.25	.20	.10
679	#1 Draft Pick *(Greg Gohr)* (#1 Draft Pick)(FC)	.25	.20	.10
680	#1 Draft Pick *(Ben McDonald)* (#1 Draft Pick)(FC)	1.00	.70	.40
681	#1 Draft Pick *(Greg Blosser)* (#1 Draft Pick)(FC)	.50	.40	.20
682	#1 Draft Pick *(Willie Green)* (#1 Draft Pick)(FC)	.25	.20	.10
683	Dream Team (Wade Boggs)	.20	.15	.08
684	Dream Team (Will Clark)	.20	.15	.08
685	Dream Team (Tony Gwynn)	.20	.15	.08
686	Dream Team (Rickey Henderson)	.20	.15	.08
687	Dream Team (Bo Jackson)	.60	.45	.25
688	Dream Team (Mark Langston)	.20	.15	.11
689	Dream Team (Barry Larkin)	.20	.15	.11

1990 Score Rising Stars

For the second consecutive year Score produced a 100-card "Rising Stars" set. The 1990 Score Rising Stars were made available as a boxed set and were also marketed with a related magazine like the 1989 issue. Magic Motion trivia cards featuring past MVP's accompany the card set. The cards feature full- color action photos on the front and posed shots on the flip sides.

		MT	NR MT	EX
Complete Set:		12.00	9.00	4.75
Common Player:		.08	.06	.03
1	Tom Gordon	.25	.20	.10
2	Jerome Walton	.25	.20	.10
3	Ken Griffey,Jr.	3.00	2.25	1.25
4	Dwight Smith	.25	.20	.10
5	Jim Abbott	.25	.20	.10
6	Todd Zeile	.40	.30	.15
7	Donn Pall	.08	.06	.03
8	Rick Reed	.08	.06	.03
9	Joey Belle	.15	.11	.06
10	Gregg Jefferies	.35	.25	.14
11	Kevin Ritz	.10	.08	.04
12	Charlie Hayes	.15	.11	.06
13	Kevin Appier	.30	.25	.12
14	Jeff Huson	.15	.11	.06
15	Gary Wayne	.08	.06	.03
16	Eric Yelding	.15	.11	.06
17	Clay Parker	.08	.06	.03
18	Junior Felix	.30	.25	.12
19	Derek Lilliquist	.08	.06	.03
20	Gary Sheffield	.30	.25	.12
21	Craig Worthington	.08	.06	.03
22	Jeff Brantley	.10	.08	.04
23	Eric Hetzel	.10	.08	.04
24	Greg Harris	.08	.06	.03
25	John Wetteland	.20	.15	.08
26	Joe Oliver	.15	.11	.06
27	Kevin Maas	.80	.60	.30
28	Kevin Brown	.10	.08	.04
29	Mike Stanton	.15	.11	.06
30	Greg Vaughn	.40	.30	.15
31	Ron Jones	.08	.06	.03
32	Gregg Olson	.20	.15	.08
33	Joe Girardi	.10	.08	.04
34	Ken Hill	.08	.06	.03
35	Sammy Sosa	.35	.25	.14
36	Geronimo Berroa	.08	.06	.03
37	Omar Vizquel	.10	.08	.04
38	Dean Palmer	.10	.08	.04
39	John Olerud	.70	.50	.30
40	Deion Sanders	.25	.20	.10
41	Randy Kramer	.08	.06	.03
42	Scott Lusader	.08	.06	.03
43	Dave Johnson	.08	.06	.03
44	Jeff Wetherby	.08	.06	.03
45	Eric Anthony	.40	.30	.15
46	Kenny Rogers	.10	.08	.04
47	Matt Winters	.08	.06	.03
48	Goose Gozzo	.10	.08	.04
49	Carlos Quintana	.15	.11	.06
50	Bob Geren	.10	.08	.04
51	Chad Kreuter	.08	.06	.03
52	Randy Johnson	.10	.08	.04
53	Hensley Meulens	.15	.11	.06
54	Gene Harris	.10	.08	.04
55	Bill Spiers	.10	.08	.04
56	Kelly Mann	.15	.11	.06
57	Tom McCarthy	.08	.06	.03
58	Steve Finley	.10	.08	.04
59	Ramon Martinez	.50	.40	.20
60	Greg Briley	.08	.06	.03
61	Jack Daugherty	.10	.08	.04
62	Tim Jones	.08	.06	.03
63	Doug Strange	.08	.06	.03
64	John Orton	.08	.06	.03
65	Scott Scudder	.15	.11	.06
66	Mark Gardner	.20	.15	.08
67	Mark Carreon	.08	.06	.03
68	Bob Milacki	.08	.06	.03
69	Andy Benes	.10	.08	.04
70	Carlos Martinez	.10	.08	.04
71	Jeff King	.10	.08	.04
72	Brad Arnsberg	.08	.06	.03
73	Rick Wrona	.08	.06	.03
74	Cris Carpenter	.08	.06	.03
75	Dennis Cook	.08	.06	.03
76	Pete Harnisch	.10	.08	.04
77	Greg Hibbard	.15	.11	.06
78	Ed Whited	.08	.06	.03
79	Scott Coolbaugh	.15	.11	.06
80	Billy Bates	.08	.06	.03
81	German Gonzalez	.08	.06	.03
82	Lance Blankenship	.08	.06	.03
83	Lenny Harris	.10	.08	.04
84	Milt Cuyler	.20	.15	.08
85	Erik Hanson	.20	.15	.08
86	Kent Anderson	.08	.06	.03
87	Hal Morris	.40	.30	.15
88	Mike Brumley	.08	.06	.03
89	Ken Patterson	.08	.06	.03
90	Mike Devereaux	.08	.06	.03
91	Greg Litton	.10	.08	.04
92	Rolando Roomes	.08	.06	.03
93	Ben McDonald	.60	.45	.25
94	Curt Schilling	.10	.08	.04
95	Jose DeJesus	.15	.11	.06
96	Robin Ventura	.30	.25	.12
97	Steve Searcy	.08	.06	.03
98	Chip Hale	.10	.08	.04
99	Marquis Grissom	.40	.30	.15
100	Luis de los Santos	.10	.08	.04

1990 Score Superstar

100 of the game's top players are featured in this set. The card fronts feature full-color action photos and are similar in style to the past Score Superstar set. The set was marketed as a boxed set and with a special magazine devoted to baseball's 100 hottest players. Each set includes a series of Magic Motion cards honoring past MVP winners. The player cards measure 2-1/2" by 3-1/2" in size.

		MT	NR MT	EX
Complete Set:		8.00	6.00	3.25
Common Player:		.08	.06	.03
1	Kirby Puckett	.30	.25	.12
2	Steve Sax	.10	.08	.04
3	Tony Gwynn	.15	.11	.06
4	Willie Randolph	.08	.06	.03
5	Jose Canseco	.70	.50	.30
6	Ozzie Smith	.10	.08	.04
7	Rick Reuschel	.08	.06	.03

		MT	NR MT	EX
8	Bill Doran	.08	.06	.03
9	Mickey Tettleton	.08	.06	.03
10	Don Mattingly	.50	.40	.20
11	Greg Swindell	.08	.06	.03
12	Bert Blyleven	.10	.08	.04
13	Dave Stewart	.15	.11	.06
14	Andres Galarraga	.10	.08	.04
15	Darryl Strawberry	.30	.25	.12
16	Ellis Burks	.20	.15	.08
17	Paul O'Neill	.08	.06	.03
18	Bruce Hurst	.08	.06	.03
19	Dave Smith	.08	.06	.03
20	Carney Lansford	.08	.06	.03
21	Robby Thompson	.08	.06	.03
22	Gary Gaetti	.10	.08	.04
23	Jeff Russell	.08	.06	.03
24	Chuck Finley	.10	.08	.04
25	Mark McGwire	.35	.25	.14
26	Alvin Davis	.10	.08	.04
27	George Bell	.10	.08	.04
28	Cory Snyder	.08	.06	.03
29	Keith Hernandez	.08	.06	.03
30	Will Clark	.40	.30	.15
31	Steve Bedrosian	.08	.06	.03
32	Ryne Sandberg	.40	.30	.15
33	Tom Browning	.08	.06	.03
34	Tim Burke	.08	.06	.03
35	John Smoltz	.10	.08	.04
36	Phil Bradley	.08	.06	.03
37	Bobby Bonilla	.15	.11	.06
38	Kirk McCaskill	.08	.06	.03
39	Dave Righetti	.10	.08	.04
40	Bo Jackson	.70	.50	.30
41	Alan Trammell	.10	.08	.04
42	Mike Moore	.08	.06	.03
43	Harold Reynolds	.08	.06	.03
44	Nolan Ryan	.80	.60	.30
45	Fred McGriff	.25	.20	.10
46	Brian Downing	.08	.06	.03
47	Brett Butler	.08	.06	.03
48	Mike Scioscia	.08	.06	.03
49	John Franco	.08	.06	.03
50	Kevin Mitchell	.30	.25	.12
51	Mark Davis	.08	.06	.03
52	Glenn Davis	.15	.11	.06
53	Barry Bonds	.20	.15	.08
54	Dwight Evans	.10	.08	.04
55	Terry Steinbach	.08	.06	.03
56	Dave Gallagher	.08	.06	.03
57	Roberto Kelly	.10	.08	.04
58	Rafael Palmeiro	.10	.08	.04
59	Joe Carter	.10	.08	.04
60	Mark Grace	.20	.15	.08
61	Pedro Guerrero	.10	.08	.04
62	Von Hayes	.08	.06	.03
63	Benny Santiago	.15	.11	.06
64	Dale Murphy	.10	.08	.04
65	John Smiley	.08	.06	.03
66	Cal Ripken,Jr.	.40	.30	.15
67	Mike Greenwell	.25	.20	.10
68	Devon White	.08	.06	.03
69	Ed Whitson	.08	.06	.03
70	Carlton Fisk	.15	.11	.06
71	Lou Whitaker	.10	.08	.04
72	Danny Tartabull	.10	.08	.04
73	Vince Coleman	.10	.08	.04
74	Andre Dawson	.15	.11	.06
75	Tim Raines	.10	.08	.04
76	George Brett	.15	.11	.06
77	Tom Herr	.08	.06	.03
78	Andy Van Slyke	.10	.08	.04
79	Roger Clemens	.30	.25	.12
80	Wade Boggs	.30	.25	.12
81	Wally Joyner	.10	.08	.04
82	Lonnie Smith	.08	.06	.03
83	Howard Johnson	.15	.11	.06
84	Julio Franco	.15	.11	.06
85	Ruben Sierra	.20	.15	.08
86	Dan Plesac	.08	.06	.03
87	Bobby Thigpen	.15	.11	.06
88	Kevin Seitzer	.10	.08	.04
89	Dave Steib	.10	.08	.04
90	Rickey Henderson	.30	.25	.12
91	Jeffrey Leonard	.08	.06	.03
92	Robin Yount	.15	.11	.06
93	Mitch Williams	.10	.08	.04
94	Orel Hershiser	.20	.15	.08
95	Eric Davis	.25	.20	.10
96	Mark Langston	.10	.08	.04
97	Mike Scott	.08	.06	.03
98	Paul Molitor	.10	.08	.04
99	Doc Gooden	.25	.20	.10
100	Kevin Bass	.08	.06	.03

1990 Score Traded

This 110-card set features players with new teams as well as 1990 Major League rookies. The cards feature full-color action photos framed in yellow with an orange border. The player's name and position appear in green print below the photo. The team logo is displayed next to the player's name. The card backs feature posed player photos and follow the style of the regular 1990 Score issue. The cards are numbered 1T-110T. Young hockey phenom Eric Lindros is featured trying out for the Toronto Blue Jays.

		MT	NR MT	EX
Complete Set:		25.00	20.00	10.00
Common Player:		.06	.05	.02
1T	Dave Winfield	.15	.11	.06
2T	Kevin Bass	.06	.05	.02
3T	Nick Esasky	.06	.05	.02
4T	Mitch Webster	.06	.05	.02
5T	Pascual Perez	.06	.05	.02
6T	Gary Pettis	.06	.05	.02
7T	Tony Pena	.08	.06	.03
8T	Candy Maldonado	.08	.06	.03
9T	Cecil Fielder	.60	.45	.25
10T	Carmelo Martinez	.06	.05	.02
11T	Mark Langston	.08	.06	.03
12T	Dave Parker	.15	.11	.06
13T	Don Slaught	.06	.05	.02
14T	Tony Phillips	.06	.05	.02
15T	John Franco	.08	.06	.03
16T	Randy Myers	.08	.06	.03
17T	Jeff Reardon	.08	.06	.03
18T	Sandy Alomar, Jr.	.30	.25	.12
19T	Joe Carter	.10	.08	.04
20T	Fred Lynn	.06	.05	.02
21T	Storm Davis	.06	.05	.02
22T	Craig Lefferts	.06	.05	.02
23T	Pete O'Brien	.06	.05	.02
24T	Dennis Boyd	.06	.05	.02
25T	Lloyd Moseby	.06	.05	.02
26T	Mark Davis	.06	.05	.02
27T	Tim Leary	.06	.05	.02
28T	Gerald Perry	.06	.05	.02
29T	Don Aase	.06	.05	.02
30T	Ernie Whitt	.06	.05	.02
31T	Dale Murphy	.10	.08	.04
32T	Alejandro Pena	.06	.05	.02
33T	Juan Samuel	.08	.06	.03
34T	Hubie Brooks	.08	.06	.03
35T	Gary Carter	.10	.08	.04
36T	Jim Presley	.06	.05	.02
37T	Wally Backman	.06	.05	.02
38T	Matt Nokes	.06	.05	.02
39T	Dan Petry	.06	.05	.02
40T	Franklin Stubbs	.06	.05	.02
41T	Jeff Huson	.15	.11	.06
42T	Billy Hatcher	.06	.05	.02
43T	Terry Leach	.06	.05	.02
44T	Phil Bradley	.06	.05	.02
45T	Claudell Washington	.06	.05	.02
46T	Luis Polonia	.06	.05	.02
47T	Daryl Boston	.06	.05	.02

		MT	NR MT	EX
48T	Lee Smith	.08	.06	.03
49T	Tom Brunansky	.08	.06	.03
50T	Mike Witt	.06	.05	.02
51T	Willie Randolph	.08	.06	.03
52T	Stan Javier	.06	.05	.02
53T	Brad Komminsk	.06	.05	.02
54T	John Candelaria	.06	.05	.02
55T	Bryn Smith	.06	.05	.02
56T	Glenn Braggs	.06	.05	.02
57T	Keith Hernandez	.08	.06	.03
58T	Ken Oberkfell	.06	.05	.02
59T	Steve Jeltz	.06	.05	.02
60T	Chris James	.06	.05	.02
61T	Scott Sanderson	.06	.05	.02
62T	Bill Long	.06	.05	.02
63T	Rick Cerone	.06	.05	.02
64T	Scott Bailes	.06	.05	.02
65T	Larry Sheets	.06	.05	.02
66T	Junior Ortiz	.06	.05	.02
67T	Francisco Cabrera(FC)	.20	.15	.08
68T	Gary DiSarcina(FC)	.15	.11	.06
69T	Greg Olson(FC)	.20	.15	.08
70T	Beau Allred(FC)	.20	.15	.11
71T	Oscar Azocar(FC)	.15	.11	.06
72T	Kent Mercker(FC)	.25	.20	.10
73T	John Burkett(FC)	.20	.15	.08
74T	Carlos Baerga(FC)	.50	.40	.20
75T	Dave Hollins(FC)	.30	.25	.12
76T	Todd Hundley(FC)	.20	.15	.08
77T	Rick Parker(FC)	.15	.11	.06
78T	Steve Cummings(FC)	.15	.11	.06
79T	Bill Sampen(FC)	.25	.20	.10
80T	Jerry Kutzler(FC)	.15	.11	.06
81T	Derek Bell(FC)	1.50	1.25	.60
82T	Kevin Tapani(FC)	.35	.25	.14
83T	Jim Leyritz(FC)	.25	.20	.10
84T	Ray Lankford(FC)	1.25	.90	.50
85T	Wayne Edwards(FC)	.15	.11	.06
86T	Frank Thomas	10.00	7.50	4.00
87T	Tim Naehring(FC)	.40	.30	.15
88T	Willie Blair(FC)	.15	.11	.06
89T	Alan Mills(FC)	.25	.20	.10
90T	Scott Radinsky(FC)	.25	.20	.10
91T	Howard Farmer(FC)	.25	.20	.10
92T	Julio Machado(FC)	.15	.11	.06
93T	Rafael Valdez(FC)	.15	.11	.06
94T	Shawn Boskie(FC)	.25	.20	.10
95T	David Segui(FC)	.50	.40	.20
96T	Chris Hoiles(FC)	.30	.25	.12
97T	D.J. Dozier(FC)	.50	.40	.20
98T	Hector Villanueva(FC)	.25	.20	.10
99T	Eric Gunderson(FC)	.25	.20	.10
100T	Eric Lindros(FC)	8.00	6.00	3.25
101T	Dave Otto(FC)	.12	.09	.05
102T	Dana Kiecker(FC)	.20	.15	.08
103T	Tim Drummond(FC)	.15	.11	.06
104T	Mickey Pina(FC)	.25	.20	.10
105T	Craig Grebeck(FC)	.20	.15	.08
106T	Bernard Gilkey(FC)	.50	.40	.20
107T	Tim Layana(FC)	.25	.20	.10
108T	Scott Chiamparino(FC)	.30	.25	.12
109T	Steve Avery(FC)	1.25	.90	.50
110T	Terry Shumpert(FC)	.20	.15	.08

1991 Score

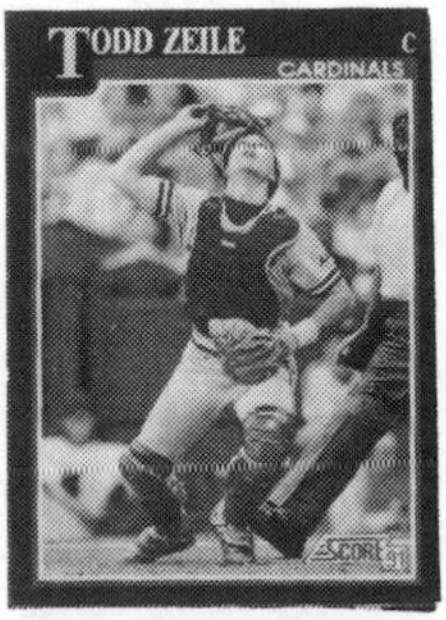

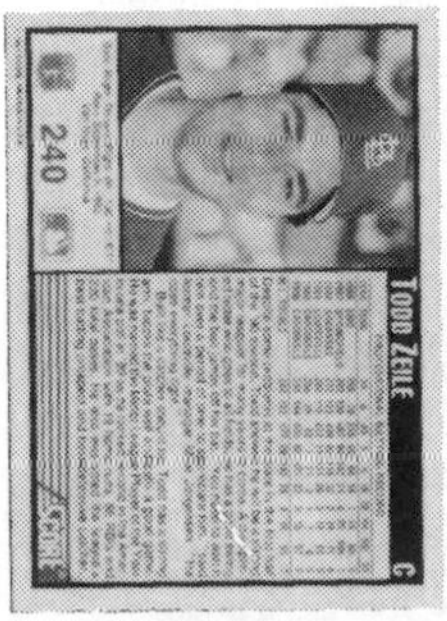

Score introduced a two series format in 1991. The first series includes cards 1-441. Score cards once again feature multiple border colors within the set, several subsets (Master Blaster, K-Man, Highlights and Rifleman), full-color action photos on the front, posed photos on the flip side. Score eliminated providing the player's uniform number on the 1991 cards. Card number 441 of Series I features a Jose Canseco Vanity Fair photo. All of the 1991 Dream Team cards feature this style. The 1991 Score set when complete with Series II will mark its biggest issue. Rookie prospects and #1 Draft Picks highlight the 1991 Score set. The second series was due for release in February of 1991.

	MT	NR MT	EX
Complete Set:	35.00	26.00	14.00
Common Player:	.04	.03	.02

1	Jose Canseco	.35	.25	.14
2	Ken Griffey,Jr.	1.00	.70	.40
3	Ryne Sandberg	.20	.15	.08
4	Nolan Ryan	.30	.25	.12
5	Bo Jackson	.30	.25	.12
6	Bret Saberhagen	.12	.09	.05
7	Will Clark	.20	.15	.08
8	Ellis Burks	.15	.11	.06
9	Joe Carter	.15	.11	.06
10	Rickey Henderson	.25	.20	.10
11	Ozzie Guillen	.10	.08	.04
12	Wade Boggs	.20	.15	.08
13	Jerome Walton	.15	.11	.06
14	John Franco	.10	.08	.04
15	Ricky Jordan	.08	.06	.03
16	Wally Backman	.04	.03	.02
17	Rob Dibble	.10	.08	.04
18	Glenn Braggs	.05	.04	.02
19	Cory Snyder	.10	.08	.04
20	Kal Daniels	.10	.08	.04
21	Mark Langston	.10	.08	.04
22	Kevin Gross	.06	.05	.02
23	Don Mattingly	.25	.20	.10
24	Dave Righetti	.08	.06	.03
25	Roberto Alomar	.25	.20	.10
26	Robby Thompson	.06	.05	.02
27	Jack McDowell	.08	.06	.03
28	Bip Roberts	.08	.06	.03
29	Jay Howell	.05	.04	.02
30	Dave Steib	.08	.06	.03
31	Johnny Ray	.04	.03	.02
32	Steve Sax	.10	.08	.04
33	Terry Mulholland	.08	.06	.03
34	Lee Guetterman	.04	.03	.02
35	Tim Raines	.12	.09	.05
36	Scott Fletcher	.04	.03	.02
37	Lance Parrish	.08	.06	.03
38	Tony Phillips	.05	.04	.02
39	Todd Stottlemyre	.06	.05	.02
40	Alan Trammell	.12	.09	.05
41	Todd Burns	.04	.03	.02
42	Mookie Wilson	.06	.05	.02
43	Chris Bosio	.05	.04	.02
44	Jeffrey Leonard	.06	.05	.02
45	Doug Jones	.08	.06	.03
46	Mike Scott	.08	.06	.03
47	Andy Hawkins	.05	.04	.02
48	Harold Reynolds	.08	.06	.03
49	Paul Molitor	.12	.09	.05
50	John Farrell	.05	.04	.02
51	Danny Darwin	.06	.05	.02
52	Jeff Blauser	.04	.03	.02
53	John Tudor	.05	.04	.02
54	Milt Thompson	.04	.03	.02
55	Dave Justice	.50	.40	.20
56	*Greg Olson*	.12	.09	.05
57	*Willie Blair*	.12	.09	.05
58	*Rick Parker*	.10	.08	.04
59	*Shawn Boskie*	.15	.11	.06
60	Kevin Tapani	.10	.08	.04
61	*Dave Hollins*	.20	.15	.08
62	*Scott Radinsky*	.12	.09	.05
63	Francisco Cabrera	.10	.08	.04
64	*Tim Layana*	.12	.09	.05
65	*Jim Leyritz*	.12	.09	.05
66	Wayne Edwards	.08	.06	.03
67	Lee Stevens(FC)	.15	.11	.06
68	*Bill Sampen*	.15	.11	.06
69	*Craig Grebeck*	.10	.08	.04
70	John Burkett	.15	.11	.06
71	*Hector Villanueva*	.15	.11	.06
72	*Oscar Azocar*	.15	.11	.06
73	*Alan Mills*	.15	.11	.06
74	*Carlos Baerga*	.25	.20	.10

		MT	NR MT	EX
75	Charles Nagy	.08	.06	.03
76	Tim Drummond	.08	.06	.03
77	*Dana Kiecker*	.15	.11	.06
78	*Tom Edens*(FC)	.10	.08	.04
79	Kent Mercker	.10	.08	.04
80	Steve Avery	.20	.15	.08
81	Lee Smith	.08	.06	.03
82	Dave Martinez	.05	.04	.02
83	Dave Winfield	.12	.09	.05
84	Bill Spiers	.06	.05	.02
85	Dan Pasqua	.05	.04	.02
86	Randy Milligan	.06	.05	.02
87	Tracy Jones	.04	.03	.02
88	Greg Myers(FC)	.06	.05	.02
89	Keith Hernandez	.06	.05	.02
90	Todd Benzinger	.06	.05	.02
91	Mike Jackson	.05	.04	.02
92	Mike Stanley	.04	.03	.02
93	Candy Maldonado	.06	.05	.02
94	John Kruk	.05	.04	.02
95	Cal Ripken,Jr.	.15	.11	.06
96	Willie Fraser	.04	.03	.02
97	Mike Felder	.04	.03	.02
98	Bill Landrum	.05	.04	.02
99	Chuck Crim	.04	.03	.02
100	Chuck Finley	.08	.06	.03
101	Kirt Manwaring	.06	.05	.02
102	Jaime Navarro	.08	.06	.03
103	Dickie Thon	.04	.03	.02
104	Brian Downing	.05	.04	.02
105	Jim Abbott	.12	.09	.05
106	Tom Brookens	.04	.03	.02
107	Darryl Hamilton	.06	.05	.02
108	Bryan Harvey	.06	.05	.02
109	Greg Harris	.04	.03	.02
110	Greg Swindell	.08	.06	.03
111	Juan Berenguer	.04	.03	.02
112	Mike Heath	.04	.03	.02
113	Scott Bradley	.04	.03	.02
114	Jack Morris	.08	.06	.03
115	Barry Jones	.05	.04	.02
116	Kevin Romine	.04	.03	.02
117	Garry Templeton	.05	.04	.02
118	Scott Sanderson	.05	.04	.02
119	Roberto Kelly	.08	.06	.03
120	George Brett	.15	.11	.06
121	Oddibe McDowell	.05	.04	.02
122	Jim Acker	.04	.03	.02
123	Bill Swift	.05	.04	.02
124	Eric King	.05	.04	.02
125	Jay Buhner	.06	.05	.02
126	Matt Young	.04	.03	.02
127	Alvaro Espinoza	.05	.04	.02
128	Greg Hibbard	.08	.06	.03
129	Jeff Robinson	.05	.04	.02
130	Mike Greenwell	.15	.11	.06
131	Dion James	.04	.03	.02
132	Donn Pall	.04	.03	.02
133	Lloyd Moseby	.06	.05	.02
134	Randy Velarde	.04	.03	.02
135	Allan Anderson	.05	.04	.02
136	Mark Davis	.06	.05	.02
137	Eric Davis	.15	.11	.06
138	Phil Stephenson	.04	.03	.02
139	Felix Fermin	.04	.03	.02
140	Pedro Guerrero	.08	.06	.03
141	Charlie Hough	.05	.04	.02
142	Mike Henneman	.06	.05	.02
143	Jeff Montgomery	.06	.05	.02
144	Lenny Harris	.06	.05	.02
145	Bruce Hurst	.06	.05	.02
146	Eric Anthony	.15	.11	.06
147	Paul Assenmacher	.04	.03	.02
148	Jesse Barfield	.06	.05	.02
149	Carlos Quintana	.08	.06	.03
150	Dave Stewart	.12	.09	.05
151	Roy Smith	.04	.03	.02
152	Paul Gibson	.04	.03	.02
153	Mickey Hatcher	.04	.03	.02
154	Jim Eisenreich	.04	.03	.02
155	Kenny Rogers	.06	.05	.02
156	Dave Schmidt	.04	.03	.02
157	Lance Johnson	.06	.05	.02
158	Dave West	.05	.04	.02
159	Steve Balboni	.04	.03	.02
160	Jeff Brantley	.08	.06	.03
161	Craig Biggio	.06	.05	.02
162	Brook Jacoby	.06	.05	.02
163	Dan Gladden	.05	.04	.02
164	Jeff Reardon	.08	.06	.03
165	Mark Carreon	.05	.04	.02

		MT	NR MT	EX
166	Mel Hall	.05	.04	.02
167	Gary Mielke	.06	.05	.02
168	Cecil Fielder	.25	.20	.10
169	Darrin Jackson	.04	.03	.02
170	Rick Aguilera	.06	.05	.02
171	Walt Weiss	.06	.05	.02
172	Steve Farr	.05	.04	.02
173	Jody Reed	.06	.05	.02
174	Mike Jeffcoat	.04	.03	.02
175	Mark Grace	.15	.11	.06
176	Larry Sheets	.04	.03	.02
177	Bill Gullickson	.05	.04	.02
178	Chris Gwynn	.06	.05	.02
179	Melido Perez	.06	.05	.02
180	Sid Fernandez	.08	.06	.03
181	Tim Burke	.06	.05	.02
182	Gary Pettis	.05	.04	.02
183	Rob Murphy	.04	.03	.02
184	Craig Lefferts	.06	.05	.02
185	Howard Johnson	.10	.08	.04
186	Ken Caminiti	.05	.04	.02
187	Tim Belcher	.06	.05	.02
188	Greg Cadaret	.04	.03	.02
189	Matt Williams	.15	.11	.06
190	Dave Magadan	.08	.06	.03
191	Geno Petralli	.04	.03	.02
192	Jeff Robinson	.05	.04	.02
193	Jim Deshaies	.05	.04	.02
194	Willie Randolph	.06	.05	.02
195	George Bell	.10	.08	.04
196	Hubie Brooks	.10	.08	.04
197	Tom Gordon	.10	.08	.04
198	Mike Fitzgerald	.04	.03	.02
199	Mike Pagliarulo	.05	.04	.02
200	Kirby Puckett	.15	.11	.06
201	Shawon Dunston	.08	.06	.03
202	Dennis Boyd	.05	.04	.02
203	Junior Felix	.08	.06	.03
204	Alejandro Pena	.04	.03	.02
205	Pete Smith	.05	.04	.02
206	Tom Glavine	.06	.05	.02
207	Luis Salazar	.04	.03	.02
208	John Smoltz	.08	.06	.03
209	Doug Dascenzo	.05	.04	.02
210	Tim Wallach	.08	.06	.03
211	Greg Gagne	.05	.04	.02
212	Mark Gubicza	.08	.06	.03
213	Mark Parent	.04	.03	.02
214	Ken Oberkfell	.04	.03	.02
215	Gary Carter	.08	.06	.03
216	Rafael Palmeiro	.10	.08	.04
217	Tom Niedenfuer	.04	.03	.02
218	Dave LaPoint	.05	.04	.02
219	Jeff Treadway	.05	.04	.02
220	Mitch Williams	.06	.05	.02
221	Jose DeLeon	.05	.04	.02
222	Mike LaValliere	.05	.04	.02
223	Darrel Akerfelds	.04	.03	.02
224	Kent Anderson	.05	.04	.02
225	Dwight Evans	.08	.06	.03
226	Gary Redus	.04	.03	.02
227	Paul O'Neill	.06	.05	.02
228	Marty Barrett	.05	.04	.02
229	Tom Browning	.06	.05	.02
230	Terry Pendleton	.06	.05	.02
231	Jack Armstrong	.08	.06	.03
232	Mike Boddicker	.06	.05	.02
233	Neal Heaton	.05	.04	.02
234	Marquis Grissom	.10	.08	.04
235	Bert Blyleven	.08	.06	.03
236	Curt Young	.05	.04	.02
237	Don Carman	.05	.04	.02
238	Charlie Hayes	.06	.05	.02
239	Mark Knudson	.04	.03	.02
240	Todd Zeile	.20	.15	.08
241	Larry Walker	.10	.08	.04
242	Jerald Clark	.06	.05	.02
243	Jeff Ballard	.05	.04	.02
244	Jeff King	.06	.05	.02
245	Tom Brunansky	.08	.06	.03
246	Darren Daulton	.06	.05	.02
247	Scott Terry	.04	.03	.02
248	Rob Deer	.06	.05	.02
249	Brady Anderson	.04	.03	.02
250	Lenny Dykstra	.08	.06	.03
251	Greg Harris	.06	.05	.02
252	Mike Hartley	.08	.06	.03
253	Joey Cora	.04	.03	.02
254	Ivan Calderon	.08	.06	.03
255	Ted Power	.04	.03	.02
256	Sammy Sosa	.15	.11	.06

		MT	NR MT	EX
257	Steve Buechele	.05	.04	.02
258	Mike Devereaux	.05	.04	.02
259	Brad Komminsk	.04	.03	.02
260	Teddy Higuera	.08	.06	.03
261	Shawn Abner	.05	.04	.02
262	Dave Valle	.05	.04	.02
263	Jeff Huson	.06	.05	.02
264	Edgar Martinez	.06	.05	.02
265	Carlton Fisk	.10	.08	.04
266	Steve Finley	.06	.05	.02
267	John Wetteland	.06	.05	.02
268	Kevin Appier	.08	.06	.03
269	Steve Lyons	.04	.03	.02
270	Mickey Tettleton	.05	.04	.02
271	Luis Rivera	.04	.03	.02
272	Steve Jeltz	.04	.03	.02
273	R.J. Reynolds	.04	.03	.02
274	Carlos Martinez	.05	.04	.02
275	Dan Plesac	.06	.05	.02
276	Mike Morgan	.04	.03	.02
277	Jeff Russell	.06	.05	.02
278	Pete Incaviglia	.06	.05	.02
279	Kevin Seitzer	.08	.06	.03
280	Bobby Thigpen	.08	.06	.03
281	Stan Javier	.04	.03	.02
282	Henry Cotto	.04	.03	.02
283	Gary Wayne	.05	.04	.02
284	Shane Mack	.05	.04	.02
285	Brian Holman	.06	.05	.02
286	Gerald Perry	.05	.04	.02
287	Steve Crawford	.04	.03	.02
288	Nelson Liriano	.04	.03	.02
289	Don Aase	.04	.03	.02
290	Randy Johnson	.06	.05	.02
291	Harold Baines	.08	.06	.03
292	Kent Hrbek	.08	.06	.03
293	Les Lancaster	.04	.03	.02
294	Jeff Musselman	.04	.03	.02
295	Kurt Stillwell	.06	.05	.02
296	Stan Belinda	.06	.05	.02
297	Lou Whitaker	.08	.06	.03
298	Glenn Wilson	.05	.04	.02
299	Omar Vizquel	.04	.03	.02
300	Ramon Martinez	.20	.15	.08
301	Dwight Smith	.06	.05	.02
302	Tim Crews	.04	.03	.02
303	Lance Blankenship	.05	.04	.02
304	Sid Bream	.06	.05	.02
305	Rafael Ramirez	.04	.03	.02
306	Steve Wilson	.06	.05	.02
307	Mackey Sasser	.06	.05	.02
308	Franklin Stubbs	.06	.05	.02
309	Jack Daugherty	.06	.05	.02
310	Eddie Murray	.10	.08	.04
311	Bob Welch	.08	.06	.03
312	Brian Harper	.06	.05	.02
313	Lance McCullers	.04	.03	.02
314	Dave Smith	.06	.05	.02
315	Bobby Bonilla	.15	.11	.06
316	Jerry Don Gleaton	.04	.03	.02
317	Greg Maddux	.08	.06	.03
318	Keith Miller	.05	.04	.03
319	Mark Portugal	.04	.03	.02
320	Robin Ventura	.25	.20	.10
321	Bob Ojeda	.04	.03	.02
322	Mike Harkey	.08	.06	.03
323	Jay Bell	.06	.05	.02
324	Mark McGwire	.20	.15	.08
325	Gary Gaetti	.10	.08	.04
326	Jeff Pico	.04	.03	.02
327	Kevin McReynolds	.08	.06	.03
328	Frank Tanana	.05	.04	.02
329	Eric Yelding	.06	.05	.02
330	Barry Bonds	.20	.15	.08
331	*Brian McRae*(FC)	.60	.45	.25
332	*Pedro Munoz*(FC)	.30	.25	.12
333	*Daryl Irvine*(FC)	.15	.11	.06
334	*Chris Hoiles*	.15	.11	.06
335	*Thomas Howard*(FC)	.20	.15	.08
336	*Jeff Schulz*(FC)	.15	.11	.06
337	Jeff Manto(FC)	.15	.11	.06
338	Beau Allred	.10	.08	.04
339	*Mike Bordick*(FC)	.15	.11	.06
340	*Todd Hundley*	.15	.11	.06
341	*Jim Vatcher*(FC)	.15	.11	.06
342	Luis Sojo(FC)	.10	.08	.04
343	Jose Offerman(FC)	.30	.25	.12
344	*Pete Coachman*(FC)	.15	.11	.06
345	Mike Benjamin(FC)	.10	.08	.04
346	*Ozzie Canseco*(FC)	.15	.11	.06
347	Tim McIntosh(FC)	.15	.11	.06

		MT	NR MT	EX
348	*Phil Plantier*(FC)	.80	.60	.30
349	*Terry Shumpert*	.15	.11	.06
350	*Darren Lewis*(FC)	.30	.25	.12
351	*David Walsh*(FC)	.20	.15	.08
352	*Scott Chiamparino*	.15	.11	.06
353	*Julio Valera*(FC)	.15	.11	.06
354	*Anthony Telford*(FC)	.20	.15	.08
355	Kevin Wickander(FC)	.10	.08	.04
356	*Tim Naehring*	.20	.15	.08
357	*Jim Poole*(FC)	.20	.15	.08
358	*Mark Whiten*(FC)	.40	.30	.15
359	*Terry Wells*(FC)	.20	.15	.08
360	*Rafael Valdez*	.10	.08	.04
361	*Mel Stottlemyre*(FC)	.15	.11	.06
362	*David Segui*	.20	.15	.08
363	Paul Abbott	.15	.11	.06
364	*Steve Howard*(FC)	.15	.11	.06
365	*Karl Rhodes*(FC)	.25	.20	.10
366	*Rafael Novoa*(FC)	.15	.11	.06
367	*Joe Grahe*(FC)	.15	.11	.06
368	*Darren Reed*(FC)	.15	.11	.06
369	Jeff McKnight(FC)	.10	.08	.04
370	Scott Leius(FC)	.10	.08	.04
371	*Mark Dewey*(FC)	.15	.11	.06
372	*Mark Lee*(FC)	.15	.11	.06
373	*Rosario Rodriguez*(FC)	.15	.11	.06
374	Chuck McElroy(FC)	.10	.08	.04
375	*Mike Bell*(FC)	.15	.11	.06
376	Mickey Morandini(FC)	.10	.08	.04
377	*Bill Haselman*(FC)	.15	.11	.06
378	*Dave Pavlas*(FC)	.15	.11	.06
379	Derrick May(FC)	.30	.25	.12
380	*Jeromy Burnitz* (#1 Draft Pick)(FC)	.80	.60	.30
381	*Donald Peters* (#1 Draft Pick)(FC)	.25	.20	.10
382	*Alex Fernandez* (#1 Draft Pick)(FC)	.50	.40	.20
383	*Michael Mussina* (#1 Draft Pick)(FC)	.40	.30	.15
384	*Daniel Smith* (#1 Draft Pick)(FC)	.25	.20	.10
385	*Lance Dickson* (#1 Draft Pick)(FC)	.40	.30	.15
386	*Carl Everett* (#1 Draft Pick)(FC)	.40	.30	.15
387	*Thomas Nevers* (#1 Draft Pick)(FC)	.30	.25	.12
388	*Adam Hyzdu* (#1 Draft Pick)(FC)	.40	.30	.15
389	*Todd Van Poppel* (#1 Draft Pick)(FC)	2.25	1.75	.90
390	*Rondell White* (#1 Draft Pick)(FC)	.60	.45	.25
391	*Marc Newfield* (#1 Draft Pick)(FC)	1.25	.90	.50
392	Julio Franco (AS)	.10	.08	.04
393	Wade Boggs (AS)	.20	.15	.08
394	Ozzie Guillen (AS)	.10	.08	.04
395	Cecil Fielder (AS)	.20	.15	.08
396	Ken Griffey,Jr. (AS)	.40	.30	.15
397	Rickey Henderson (AS)	.20	.15	.08
398	Jose Canseco (AS)	.30	.25	.12
399	Roger Clemens (AS)	.15	.11	.06
400	Sandy Alomar,Jr. (AS)	.10	.08	.04
401	Bobby Thigpen (AS)	.10	.08	.04
402	Bobby Bonilla (Master Blaster)	.10	.08	.04
403	Eric Davis (Master Blaster)	.10	.08	.04
404	Fred McGriff (Master Blaster)	.10	.08	.04
405	Glenn Davis (Master Blaster)	.10	.08	.04
406	Kevin Mitchell (Master Blaster)	.10	.08	.04
407	Rob Dibble (K-Man)	.10	.08	.04
408	Ramon Martinez (K-Man)	.15	.11	.06
409	David Cone (K-Man)	.10	.08	.04
410	Bobby Witt (K-Man)	.10	.08	.04
411	Mark Langston (K-Man)	.10	.08	.04
412	Bo Jackson (Rifleman)	.30	.25	.12
413	Shawon Dunston (Rifleman)	.10	.08	.04
414	Jesse Barfield (Rifleman)	.08	.06	.03
415	Ken Caminiti (Rifleman)	.08	.06	.03
416	Benito Santiago (Rifleman)	.10	.08	.04
417	Nolan Ryan (Highlight)	.30	.25	.12
418	Bobby Thigpen (Highlight)	.10	.08	.04
419	Ramon Martinez (Highlight)	.15	.11	.06
420	Bo Jackson (Highlight)	.20	.15	.08
421	Carlton Fisk (Highlight)	.10	.08	.04
422	Jimmy Key	.06	.05	.02
423	Junior Noboa(FC)	.05	.04	.02
424	Al Newman	.04	.03	.02
425	Pat Borders	.05	.04	.02
426	Von Hayes	.08	.06	.03
427	Tim Teufel	.04	.03	.02
428	Eric Plunk	.04	.03	.02
429	John Moses	.04	.03	.02
430	Mike Witt	.05	.04	.02
431	Otis Nixon	.04	.03	.02
432	Tony Fernandez	.08	.06	.03
433	Rance Mulliniks	.04	.03	.02

		MT	NR MT	EX
434	Dan Petry	.04	.03	.02
435	Bob Geren	.05	.04	.02
436	Steve Frey(FC)	.06	.05	.02
437	Jamie Moyer	.05	.04	.02
438	Junior Ortiz	.04	.03	.02
439	Tom O'Malley	.04	.03	.02
440	Pat Combs	.06	.05	.02
441	Jose Canseco (Dream Team)	3.00	2.25	1.25
442	Alfredo Griffin	.04	.03	.02
443	Andres Galarraga	.08	.06	.03
444	Bryn Smith	.04	.03	.02
445	Andre Dawson	.12	.09	.05
446	Juan Samuel	.06	.05	.02
447	Mike Aldrete	.04	.03	.02
448	Ron Gant	.12	.09	.05
449	Fernando Valenzuela	.08	.06	.03
450	Vince Coleman	.08	.06	.03
451	Kevin Mitchell	.15	.11	.06
452	Spike Owen	.04	.03	.02
453	Mike Bielecki	.04	.03	.02
454	Dennis Martinez	.08	.06	.03
455	Brett Butler	.08	.06	.03
456	Ron Darling	.06	.05	.02
457	Dennis Rasmussen	.04	.03	.02
458	Ken Howell	.04	.03	.02
459	Steve Bedrosian	.05	.04	.02
460	Frank Viola	.12	.09	.05
461	Jose Lind	.04	.03	.02
462	Chris Sabo	.08	.06	.03
463	Dante Bichette	.05	.04	.02
464	Rick Mahler	.04	.03	.02
465	John Smiley	.06	.05	.02
466	Devon White	.06	.05	.02
467	John Orton	.04	.03	.02
468	Mike Stanton	.08	.06	.03
469	Billy Hatcher	.04	.03	.02
470	Wally Joyner	.12	.09	.05
471	Gene Larkin	.05	.04	.02
472	Doug Drabek	.08	.06	.03
473	Gary Sheffield	.15	.11	.06
474	David Wells	.04	.03	.02
475	Andy Van Slyke	.08	.06	.03
476	Mike Gallego	.05	.04	.02
477	B.J. Surhoff	.08	.06	.03
478	Gene Nelson	.04	.03	.02
479	Mariano Duncan	.05	.04	.02
480	Fred McGriff	.12	.09	.05
481	Jerry Browne	.04	.03	.02
482	Alvin Davis	.06	.05	.02
483	Bill Wegman	.05	.04	.02
484	Dave Parker	.08	.06	.03
485	Dennis Eckersley	.12	.09	.05
486	Erik Hanson	.12	.09	.05
487	Bill Ripken	.04	.03	.02
488	Tom Candiotti	.05	.04	.02
489	Mike Schooler	.06	.05	.02
490	Gregg Olson	.12	.09	.05
491	Chris James	.05	.04	.02
492	Pete Harnisch	.06	.05	.02
493	Julio Franco	.10	.08	.04
494	Greg Briley	.05	.04	.02
495	Ruben Sierra	.15	.11	.06
496	Steve Olin	.05	.04	.02
497	Mike Fetters	.05	.04	.02
498	Mark Williamson	.04	.03	.02
499	Bob Tewksbury	.04	.03	.02
500	Tony Gwynn	.15	.11	.06
501	Randy Myers	.08	.06	.03
502	Keith Comstock	.04	.03	.02
503	Craig Worthington	.08	.06	.03
504	Mark Eichhorn	.04	.03	.02
505	Barry Larkin	.12	.09	.05
506	Dave Johnson	.04	.03	.02
507	Bobby Witt	.06	.05	.02
508	Joe Orsulak	.04	.03	.02
509	Pete O'Brien	.04	.03	.02
510	Brad Arnsberg	.05	.04	.02
511	Storm Davis	.05	.04	.02
512	Bob Milacki	.05	.04	.02
513	Bill Pecota	.05	.04	.02
514	Glenallen Hill	.08	.06	.03
515	Danny Tartabull	.10	.08	.04
516	Mike Moore	.05	.04	.02
517	Ron Robinson	.04	.03	.02
518	Mark Gardner	.08	.06	.03
519	Rick Wrona	.04	.03	.02
520	Mike Scioscia	.06	.05	.02
521	Frank Wills	.04	.03	.02
522	Greg Brock	.04	.03	.02
523	Jack Clark	.08	.06	.03
524	Bruce Ruffin	.05	.04	.02
525	Robin Yount	.15	.11	.06
526	Tom Foley	.04	.03	.02
527	Pat Perry	.04	.03	.02
528	Greg Vaughn	.15	.11	.06
529	Wally Whitehurst	.06	.05	.02
530	Norm Charlton	.06	.05	.02
531	Marvell Wynne	.04	.03	.02
532	Jim Gantner	.05	.04	.02
533	Greg Litton	.04	.03	.02
534	Manny Lee	.05	.04	.02
535	Scott Bailes	.04	.03	.02
536	Charlie Leibrandt	.04	.03	.02
537	Roger McDowell	.05	.04	.02
538	Andy Benes	.15	.11	.06
539	Rick Honeycutt	.04	.03	.02
540	Doc Gooden	.15	.11	.06
541	Scott Garrelts	.04	.03	.02
542	Dave Clark	.04	.03	.02
543	Lonnie Smith	.04	.03	.02
544	Rick Rueschel	.05	.04	.02
545	Delino DeShields	.20	.15	.08
546	Mike Sharperson	.04	.03	.02
547	Mike Kingery	.04	.03	.02
548	Terry Kennedy	.04	.03	.02
549	David Cone	.08	.06	.03
550	Orel Hershiser	.12	.09	.05
551	Matt Nokes	.06	.05	.02
552	Eddie Williams	.04	.03	.02
553	Frank DiPino	.04	.03	.02
554	Fred Lynn	.05	.04	.02
555	Alex Cole(FC)	.25	.20	.10
556	Terry Leach	.04	.03	.02
557	Chet Lemon	.04	.03	.02
558	Paul Mirabella	.04	.03	.02
559	Bill Long	.04	.03	.02
560	Phil Bradley	.05	.04	.02
561	Duane Ward	.05	.04	.02
562	Dave Bergman	.04	.03	.02
563	Eric Show	.04	.03	.02
564	Xavier Hernandez(FC)	.08	.06	.03
565	Jeff Parrett	.04	.03	.02
566	Chuck Cary	.04	.03	.02
567	Ken Hill	.06	.05	.02
568	Bob Welch	.08	.06	.03
569	John Mitchell	.04	.03	.02
570	*Travis Fryman*(FC)	.50	.40	.20
571	Derek Lilliquist	.04	.03	.02
572	Steve Lake	.04	.03	.02
573	*John Barfield*(FC)	.10	.08	.04
574	Randy Bush	.04	.03	.02
575	Joe Magrane	.06	.05	.02
576	Edgar Diaz	.04	.03	.02
577	Casy Candaele	.04	.03	.02
578	Jesse Orosco	.04	.03	.02
579	Tom Henke	.06	.05	.02
580	Rick Cerone	.04	.03	.02
581	Drew Hall	.04	.03	.02
582	Tony Castillo	.04	.03	.02
583	Jimmy Jones	.04	.03	.02
584	Rick Reed	.04	.03	.02
585	Joe Girardi	.05	.04	.02
586	*Jeff Gray*(FC)	.15	.11	.06
587	Luis Polonia	.06	.05	.02
588	Joe Klink(FC)	.08	.06	.03
589	Rex Hudler	.05	.04	.02
590	Kirk McCaskill	.06	.05	.02
591	Juan Agosto	.04	.03	.02
592	Wes Gardner	.04	.03	.02
593	*Rich Rodriguez*(FC)	.12	.09	.05
594	Mitch Webster	.04	.03	.02
595	Kelly Gruber	.12	.09	.05
596	Dale Mohorcic	.04	.03	.02
597	Willie McGee	.08	.06	.03
598	Bill Krueger	.05	.04	.02
599	Bob Walk	.04	.03	.02
600	Kevin Maas	.30	.25	.12
601	Danny Jackson	.06	.05	.02
602	Craig McMurtry	.04	.03	.02
603	Curtis Wilkerson	.04	.03	.02
604	Adam Peterson	.04	.03	.02
605	Sam Horn	.06	.05	.02
606	Tommy Gregg	.04	.03	.02
607	Ken Dayley	.04	.03	.02
608	Carmelo Castillo	.04	.03	.02
609	John Shelby	.04	.03	.02
610	Don Slaught	.04	.03	.02
611	Calvin Schiraldi	.04	.03	.02
612	Dennis Lamp	.04	.03	.02
613	Andres Thomas	.04	.03	.02
614	Jose Gonzales	.04	.03	.02
615	Randy Ready	.04	.03	.02

		MT	NR MT	EX
616	Kevin Bass	.06	.05	.02
617	Mike Marshall	.05	.04	.02
618	Daryl Boston	.04	.03	.02
619	Andy McGaffigan	.04	.03	.02
620	Joe Oliver	.06	.05	.02
621	Jim Gott	.04	.03	.02
622	Jose Oquendo	.04	.03	.02
623	Jose DeJesus	.06	.05	.02
624	Mike Brumley	.04	.03	.02
625	John Olerud	.30	.25	.12
626	Ernest Riles	.04	.03	.02
627	Gene Harris	.05	.04	.02
628	Jose Uribe	.04	.03	.02
629	Darnell Coles	.04	.03	.02
630	Carney Lansford	.06	.05	.02
631	Tim Leary	.05	.04	.02
632	Tim Hulett	.04	.03	.02
633	Kevin Elster	.06	.05	.02
634	Tony Fossas	.04	.03	.02
635	Francisco Oliveras	.04	.03	.02
636	Bob Patterson	.04	.03	.02
637	Gary Ward	.04	.03	.02
638	Rene Gonzales	.04	.03	.02
639	Don Robinson	.04	.03	.02
640	Darryl Strawberry	.20	.15	.08
641	Dave Anderson	.04	.03	.02
642	Scott Scudder	.06	.05	.02
643	*Reggie Harris*(FC)	.20	.15	.08
644	Dave Henderson	.08	.06	.03
645	Ben McDonald	.35	.25	.14
646	Bob Kipper	.04	.03	.02
647	Hal Morris	.15	.11	.06
648	Tim Birtsas	.04	.03	.02
649	Steve Searcy	.04	.03	.02
650	Dale Murphy	.12	.09	.05
651	Ron Oester	.04	.03	.02
652	Mike LaCoss	.04	.03	.02
653	Ron Jones	.05	.04	.02
654	Kelly Downs	.04	.03	.02
655	Roger Clemens	.20	.15	.08
656	Herm Winningham	.04	.03	.02
657	Trevor Wilson	.06	.05	.02
658	Jose Rijo	.08	.06	.03
659	Dann Bilardello	.04	.03	.02
660	Gregg Jefferies	.15	.11	.06
661	Doug Drabek (AS)	.08	.06	.03
662	Randy Myers (AS)	.06	.05	.02
663	Benito Santiago (AS)	.08	.06	.03
664	Will Clark (AS)	.15	.11	.06
665	Ryne Sandberg (AS)	.15	.11	.06
666	Barry Larkin (AS)	.08	.06	.03
667	Matt Williams (AS)	.08	.06	.03
668	Barry Bonds (AS)	.12	.09	.05
669	Eric Davis	.12	.09	.05
670	Bobby Bonilla (AS)	.08	.06	.03
671	#1 Draft Pick *(Chipper Jones)*(FC)	.35	.25	.14
672	#1 Draft Pick *(Eric Christopherson)*(FC)	.15	.11	.06
673	#1 Draft Pick *(Robbie Beckett)*(FC)	.15	.11	.06
674	#1 Draft Pick *(Shane Andrews)*(FC)	.20	.15	.08
675	#1 Draft Pick *(Steve Karsay)*(FC)	.40	.30	.15
676	#1 Draft Pick *(Aaron Holbert)*(FC)	.20	.15	.08
677	#1 Draft Pick *(Donovan Osborne)*(FC)	.20	.15	.08
678	#1 Draft Pick *(Todd Ritchie)*(FC)	.15	.11	.06
679	#1 Draft Pick *(Ron Walden)*(FC)	.20	.15	.08
680	#1 Draft Pick *(Tim Costo)*(FC)	.40	.30	.15
681	#1 Draft Pick *(Dan Wilson)*(FC)	.40	.30	.15
682	#1 Draft Pick *(Kurt Miller)*(FC)	.15	.11	.06
683	#1 Draft Pick *(Mike Lieberthal)*(FC)	.25	.20	.10
684	*Roger Clemens* (K-Man)(FC)	.15	.11	.06
685	Doc Gooden (K-Man)	.15	.11	.06
686	Nolan Ryan (K-Man)	.20	.15	.08
687	Frank Viola (K-Man)	.08	.06	.03
688	Erik Hanson (K-Man)	.08	.06	.03
689	Matt Williams (Master Blaster)	.10	.08	.04
690	Jose Canseco (Master Blaster)	.20	.15	.08
691	Darryl Strawberry (Master Blaster)	.15	.11	.06
692	Bo Jackson (Master Blaster)	.30	.25	.12
693	Cecil Fielder (Master Blaster)	.20	.15	.08
694	Sandy Alomar, Jr. (Rifleman)	.08	.06	.03
695	Cory Snyder (Rifleman)	.05	.04	.02
696	Eric Davis, Eric Davis (Rifleman)	.08	.06	.03
697	Ken Griffey,Jr. (Rifleman)	.30	.25	.12
698	Andy Van Slyke (Rifleman)	.08	.06	.03
699	Langston/Witt (No-Hit Club)	.08	.06	.03
700	Randy Johnson (No-Hit Club)	.08	.06	.03
701	Nolan Ryan (No-Hit Club)	.20	.15	.08
702	Dave Stewart (No-Hit Club)	.08	.06	.03
703	Fernando Valenzuela (No-Hit Club)	.06	.05	.02
704	Andy Hawkins (No-Hit Club)	.04	.03	.02
705	Melido Perez (No-Hit Club)	.04	.03	.02
706	Terry Mulholland (No-Hit Club)	.06	.05	.02
707	Dave Stieb (No-Hit Club)	.06	.05	.02
708	*Brian Barnes*(FC)	.20	.15	.08
709	*Bernard Gilkey*	.30	.25	.12
710	*Steve Decker*(FC)	.40	.30	.15
711	*Paul Faries*(FC)	.12	.09	.05
712	*Paul Marak*(FC)	.10	.08	.04
713	*Wes Chamberlain*(FC)	.40	.30	.15
714	*Kevin Belcher*(FC)	.10	.08	.04
715	Dan Boone(FC)	.05	.04	.02
716	*Steve Adkins*(FC)	.10	.08	.04
717	*Geronimo Pena*(FC)	.10	.08	.04
718	*Howard Farmer*	.08	.06	.03
719	*Mark Leonard*(FC)	.25	.20	.10
720	Tom Lampkin	.04	.03	.02
721	*Mike Gardiner*(FC)	.15	.11	.06
722	*Jeff Conine, Jeff Conine*(FC)	.15	.11	.06
723	*Efrain Valdez*(FC)	.10	.08	.04
724	Chuck Malone(FC)	.08	.06	.03
725	*Leo Gomez*(FC)	.50	.40	.20
726	*Paul McClellan*(FC)	.15	.11	.06
727	*Mark Leiter*(FC)	.10	.08	.04
728	*Rich DeLucia*(FC)	.15	.11	.06
729	Mel Rojas(FC)	.08	.06	.03
730	*Hector Wagner*(FC)	.10	.08	.04
731	*Ray Lankford*	.40	.30	.15
732	*Turner Ward*(FC)	.25	.20	.10
733	*Gerald Alexander*(FC)	.10	.08	.04
734	*Scott Anderson*(FC)	.10	.08	.04
735	Tony Perezchica(FC)	.05	.04	.02
736	Jimmy Kremers(FC)	.08	.06	.03
737	American Flag	.50	.40	.20
738	*Mike York*(FC)	.10	.08	.04
739	Mike Rochford(FC)	.06	.05	.02
740	Scott Aldred(FC)	.08	.06	.03
741	*Rico Brogna*(FC)	.25	.20	.10
742	*Dave Burba*(FC)	.10	.08	.04
743	*Ray Stephens*(FC)	.10	.08	.04
744	*Eric Gunderson*	.08	.06	.03
745	*Troy Afenir*(FC)	.08	.06	.03
746	Jeff Shaw(FC)	.08	.06	.03
747	*Orlando Merced*(FC)	.35	.25	.14
748	*Omar Oliveras*(FC)	.10	.08	.04
749	Jerry Kutzler(FC)	.06	.05	.02
750	Maurice Vaughn	.35	.25	.12
751	*Matt Stark*(FC)	.20	.15	.08
752	*Randy Hennis*(FC)	.10	.08	.04
753	*Andujar Cedeno*(FC)	.60	.45	.25
754	Kelvin Torve(FC)	.08	.06	.03
755	Joe Kraemer(FC)	.08	.06	.03
756	*Phil Clark*(FC)	.15	.11	.06
757	*Ed Vosberg*(FC)	.10	.08	.04
758	*Mike Perez*(FC)	.10	.08	.04
759	*Scott Lewis*(FC)	.10	.08	.04
760	*Steve Chitren*(FC)	.10	.08	.04
761	*Ray Young*(FC)	.10	.08	.04
762	*Andres Santana*(FC)	.15	.11	.06
763	*Rodney McCray*(FC)	.10	.08	.04
764	*Sean Berry*(FC)	.10	.08	.04
765	Brent Mayne	.08	.06	.03
766	*Mike Simms*(FC)	.15	.11	.06
767	*Glenn Sutko*(FC)	.10	.08	.04
768	Gary Disarcina	.06	.05	.02
769	George Brett (Highlight)	.08	.06	.03
770	Cecil Fielder (Highlight)	.08	.06	.03
771	Jim Presley	.05	.04	.02
772	John Dopson	.05	.04	.02
773	Bo Jackson (Bo Breaker)	.35	.25	.14
774	Brent Knackert(FC)	.08	.06	.03
775	Bill Doran	.06	.05	.02
776	Dick Schofield	.04	.03	.02
777	Nelson Santovenia	.04	.03	.02
778	Mark Guthrie(FC)	.08	.06	.03
779	Mark Lemke	.08	.06	.03
780	Terry Steinbach	.06	.05	.02
781	Tom Bolton	.05	.04	.02
782	*Randy Tomlin*(FC)	.20	.15	.08
783	Jeff Kunkel	.04	.03	.02
784	Felix Jose	.10	.08	.04
785	Rick Sutcliffe	.05	.04	.02
786	John Cerutti	.04	.03	.02
787	Jose Vizcaino	.05	.04	.02
788	Curt Schilling	.06	.05	.02
789	Ed Whitson	.05	.04	.02
790	Tony Pena	.06	.05	.02
791	John Candelaria	.04	.03	.02
792	Carmelo Martinez	.04	.03	.02

		MT	NR MT	EX
793	Sandy Alomar, Jr.	.08	.06	.03
794	*Jim Neidlinger*(FC)	.08	.06	.03
795	Red's October	.08	.06	.03
796	Paul Sorrento	.05	.04	.02
797	Tom Pagnozzi	.06	.05	.02
798	Tino Martinez	.15	.11	.06
799	Scott Ruskin(FC)	.08	.06	.03
800	Kirk Gibson	.08	.06	.03
801	Walt Terrell	.04	.03	.02
802	John Russell	.04	.03	.02
803	Chili Davis	.08	.06	.03
804	Chris Nabholz(FC)	.08	.06	.03
805	Juan Gonzalez	.30	.25	.12
806	Ron Hassey	.04	.03	.02
807	Todd Worrell	.06	.05	.02
808	Tommy Greene	.06	.05	.02
809	Joel Skinner	.04	.03	.02
810	Benito Santiago	.08	.06	.03
811	Pat Tabler	.04	.03	.02
812	*Scott Erickson*(FC)	1.25	.90	.50
813	Moises Alou	.06	.05	.02
814	Dale Sveum	.04	.03	.02
815	Ryne Sandberg (Man of the Year)	.20	.15	.08
816	Rick Dempsey	.04	.03	.02
817	Scott Bankhead	.05	.04	.02
818	Jason Grimsley	.05	.04	.02
819	Doug Jennings	.04	.03	.02
820	Tom Herr	.05	.04	.02
821	Rob Ducey	.04	.03	.02
822	Luis Quinones	.04	.03	.02
823	Greg Minton	.04	.03	.02
824	Mark Grant	.04	.03	.02
825	Ozzie Smith	.10	.08	.04
826	Dave Eiland	.04	.03	.02
827	Danny Heep	.04	.03	.02
828	Hensley Meulens	.08	.06	.03
829	Charlie O'Brien	.04	.03	.02
830	Glenn Davis	.08	.06	.03
831	John Marzano	.04	.03	.02
832	Steve Ontiveros	.04	.03	.02
833	Ron Karkovice	.04	.03	.02
834	Jerry Goff(FC)	.08	.06	.03
835	Ken Griffey, Sr.	.08	.06	.03
836	Kevin Reimer(FC)	.10	.08	.04
837	Randy Kutcher	.04	.03	.02
838	Mike Blowers	.05	.04	.02
839	Mike Macfarlane	.05	.04	.02
840	Frank Thomas	1.25	.90	.50
841	Ken Griffey, Jr. & Sr. (FS)	1.25	.90	.50
842	Jack Howell	.04	.03	.02
843	Mauro Gozzo(FC)	.06	.05	.02
844	Gerald Young	.04	.03	.02
845	Zane Smith	.05	.04	.02
846	Kevin Brown	.05	.04	.02
847	Sil Campusano	.04	.03	.02
848	Larry Andersen	.04	.03	.02
849	Cal Ripken, Jr. (FR)	.12	.09	.05
850	Roger Clemens (FR)	.12	.09	.05
851	Sandy Alomar, Jr. (FR)	.08	.06	.03
852	Alan Trammell (FR)	.08	.06	.03
853	George Brett (FR)	.08	.06	.03
854	Robin Yount (FR)	.08	.06	.03
855	Kirby Puckett (FR)	.08	.06	.03
856	Don Mattingly (FR)	.15	.11	.06
857	Rickey Henderson (FR)	.15	.11	.06
858	Ken Griffey,Jr. (FR)	1.00	.70	.40
859	Ruben Sierra (FR)	.10	.08	.04
860	John Olerud (FR)	.10	.08	.04
861	Dave Justice (FR)	.50	.40	.20
862	Ryne Sandberg (FR)	.15	.11	.06
863	Eric Davis (FR)	.08	.06	.03
864	Darryl Strawberry (FR)	.10	.08	.04
865	Tim Wallach (FR)	.05	.04	.02
866	Doc Gooden (FR)	.08	.06	.03
867	Lenny Dykstra (FR)	.06	.05	.02
868	Barry Bonds (FR)	.10	.08	.04
869	Todd Zeile (FR)	.10	.08	.04
870	Benito Santiago (FR)	.08	.06	.03
871	Will Clark (FR)	.20	.15	.08
872	Craig Biggio (FR)	.08	.06	.03
873	Wally Joyner (FR)	.08	.06	.03
874	Frank Thomas (FR)	.60	.45	.25
875	Rickey Henderson (MVP)	.10	.08	.04
876	Barry Bonds (MVP)	.10	.08	.04
877	Bob Welch (Cy Young)	.05	.04	.02
878	Doug Drabek (Cy Young)	.06	.05	.03
879	Sandy Alomar, Jr. (ROY)	.08	.06	.03
880	Dave Justice (ROY)	.25	.20	.10
881	Damon Berryhill	.05	.04	.02
882	Frank Viola (Dream Team)	.10	.08	.04
883	Dave Stewart (Dream Team)	.10	.08	.04
884	Doug Jones (Dream Team)	.05	.04	.02
885	Randy Myers (Dream Team)	.06	.05	.02
886	Will Clark (Dream Team)	.30	.25	.12
887	Roberto Alomar (Dream Team)	.08	.06	.03
888	Barry Larkin (Dream Team)	.12	.09	.05
889	Wade Boggs (Dream Team)	.20	.15	.08
890	Rickey Henderson (Dream Team)	.80	.60	.30
891	Kirby Puckett (Dream Team)	.20	.15	.08
892	Ken Griffey,Jr. (Dream Team)	1.50	1.25	.60
893	Benito Santiago (Dream Team)	.10	.08	.04

1991 Score Rising Star

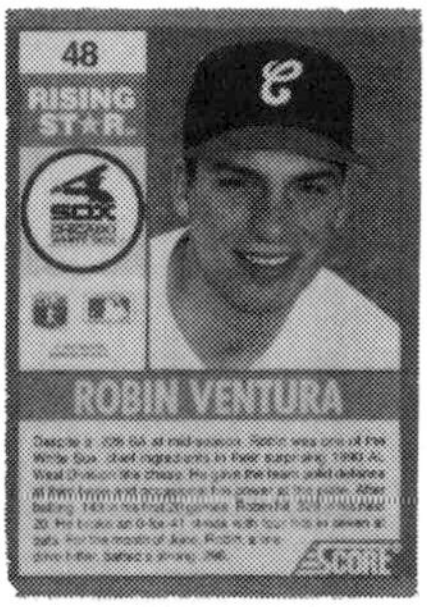

Marketed along with "1990-91 "Baseball's Hottest Rookies" magazine, this 100-card set features top rookies and young players such as Alex Fernandez and Frank Thomas. The cards are similar in design to the Score Superstar set. The magazine/card sets were available to a select group of retailors.

		MT	NR MT	EX
Complete Set:		10.00	7.50	4.00
Common Player:		.08	.06	.03
1	Sandy Alomar,Jr.	.15	.11	.06
2	Tom Edens	.08	.06	.03
3	Terry Shumpert	.15	.11	.06
4	Shawn Boskie	.20	.15	.08
5	Steve Avery	.70	.50	.30
6	Deion Sanders	.10	.08	.04
7	John Burkett	.10	.08	.04
8	Stan Belinda	.08	.06	.03
9	Thomas Howard	.15	.11	.06
10	Wayne Edwards	.08	.06	.03
11	Rick Parker	.08	.06	.03
12	Randy Veres	.08	.06	.03
13	Alex Cole	.15	.11	.06
14	Scott Chaimparino	.10	.08	.04
15	Greg Olson	.08	.06	.03
16	Jose DeJesus	.10	.08	.04
17	Mike Blowers	.08	.06	.03
18	Jeff Huson	.08	.06	.03
19	Willie Blair	.10	.08	.04
20	Howard Farmer	.10	.08	.04
21	Larry Walker	.15	.11	.06
22	Scott Hemond	.08	.06	.03
23	Mel Stottlemyre	.10	.08	.04
24	Mark Whiten	.25	.20	.10
25	Jeff Schulz	.10	.08	.04
26	Gary Disarcina	.08	.06	.03
27	George Canale	.08	.06	.03
28	Dean Palmer	.10	.08	.04
29	Jim Leyritz	.20	.15	.08
30	Carlos Baerga	.20	.15	.08
31	Rafael Valdez	.15	.11	.06
32	Derek Bell	.20	.15	.08
33	Francisco Cabrera	.08	.06	.03
34	Chris Hoiles	.20	.15	.08
35	Craig Grebeck	.08	.06	.03
36	Scott Coolbaugh	.08	.06	.03
37	Kevin Wickander	.10	.08	.04
38	Marquis Grissom	.15	.11	.06
39	Chip Hale	.08	.06	.03
40	Kevin Maas	.50	.40	.20
41	Juan Gonzalez	1.25	.90	.50
42	Eric Anthony	.25	.20	.10
43	Luis Sojo	.10	.08	.04
44	Paul Sorrento	.08	.06	.03

		MT	NR MT	EX
45	Dave Justice	1.00	.70	.40
46	Oscar Azocar	.08	.06	.03
47	Charles Nagy	.08	.06	.03
48	Robin Ventura	.20	.15	.08
49	Reggie Harris	.15	.11	.06
50	Ben McDonald	.50	.40	.20
51	Hector Villanueva	.15	.11	.06
52	Kevin Tapani	.15	.11	.06
53	Brian Bohanon	.08	.06	.03
54	Tim Layana	.10	.08	.04
55	Delino DeShields	.25	.20	.10
56	Beau Allred	.08	.06	.03
57	Eric Gunderson	.20	.15	.08
58	Kent Mercker	.10	.08	.04
59	Juan Bell	.10	.08	.04
60	Glenallen Hill	.10	.08	.04
61	David Segui	.30	.25	.12
62	Alan Mills	.15	.11	.06
63	Mike Harkey	.15	.11	.06
64	Bill Sampen	.15	.11	.06
65	Greg Vaughn	.20	.15	.08
66	Alex Fernandez	.50	.40	.20
67	Mike Hartley	.08	.06	.03
68	Travis Fryman	.40	.30	.15
69	Dave Rohde	.10	.08	.04
70	Tom Lampkin	.08	.06	.03
71	Mark Gardner	.15	.11	.06
72	Pat Combs	.10	.08	.04
73	Kevin Appier	.15	.11	.06
74	Mike Fetters	.08	.06	.03
75	Greg Myers	.08	.06	.03
76	Steve Searcy	.08	.06	.03
77	Tim Naehring	.25	.20	.10
78	Frank Thomas	2.50	2.00	1.00
79	Todd Hundley	.10	.08	.04
80	Ed Vosburg	.15	.11	.06
81	Todd Zeile	.20	.15	.08
82	Lee Stevens	.10	.08	.04
83	Scott Radinsky	.10	.08	.04
84	Hensley Meulens	.10	.08	.04
85	Brian DuBois	.08	.06	.03
86	Steve Olin	.08	.06	.03
87	Julio Machado	.10	.08	.04
88	Jose Vizcaino	.10	.08	.04
89	Mark Lemke	.08	.06	.03
90	Felix Jose	.10	.08	.04
91	Wally Whitehurst	.08	.06	.03
92	Dana Kiecker	.10	.08	.04
93	Mike Munoz	.08	.06	.03
94	Adam Peterson	.08	.06	.03
95	Tim Drummond	.08	.06	.03
96	Dave Hollins	.10	.08	.04
97	Craig Wilson	.10	.08	.04
98	Hal Morris	.20	.15	.08
99	Jose Offerman	.30	.25	.12
100	John Olerud	.30	.25	.12

1991 Score Superstar

This 100-card set features full-color action photos on the card fronts and posed shots on the flip sides. The set was marketed along with the magazine "1991 Baseball's Hottest Players." The cards feature red, white and blue borders and display the player's name and position below the photo on the card front. The backs contain brief career highlights of the player. The magazine/card set combo was available to select retailers.

		MT	NR MT	EX
Complete Set:		10.00	7.50	4.00
Common Player:		.08	.06	.03
1	Jose Canseco	.30	.25	.12
2	Bo Jackson	.30	.25	.12
3	Wade Boggs	.15	.11	.06
4	Will Clark	.35	.25	.14
5	Ken Griffey,Jr.	1.50	1.25	.60
6	Doug Drabek	.10	.08	.04
7	Kirby Puckett	.15	.11	.06
8	Joe Orsulak	.08	.06	.03
9	Eric Davis	.15	.11	.06
10	Rickey Henderson	.20	.15	.08
11	Lenny Dykstra	.10	.08	.04
12	Ruben Sierra	.10	.08	.04
13	Paul Molitor	.10	.08	.04
14	Ron Gant	.35	.25	.14
15	Ozzie Guillen	.10	.08	.04
16	Ramon Martinez	.20	.15	.08
17	Edgar Martinez	.08	.06	.03
18	Ozzie Smith	.10	.08	.04
19	Charlie Hayes	.08	.06	.03
20	Barry Larkin	.15	.11	.06
21	Cal Ripken,Jr.	.30	.25	.12
22	Andy Van Slyke	.10	.08	.04
23	Don Mattingly	.25	.20	.10
24	Dave Stewart	.15	.11	.06
25	Nolan Ryan	.30	.25	.12
26	Barry Bonds	.20	.15	.08
27	Gregg Olson	.10	.08	.04
28	Chris Sabo	.10	.08	.04
29	John Franco	.10	.08	.04
30	Gary Sheffield	.20	.15	.08
31	Jeff Treadway	.08	.06	.03
32	Tom Browning	.08	.06	.03
33	Jose Lind	.08	.06	.03
34	Dave Magadan	.10	.08	.04
35	Dale Murphy	.10	.08	.04
36	Tom Candiotti	.08	.06	.03
37	Willie McGee	.10	.08	.04
38	Robin Yount	.15	.11	.06
39	Mark McGwire	.20	.15	.08
40	George Bell	.10	.08	.04
41	Carlton Fisk	.10	.08	.04
42	Bobby Bonilla	.10	.08	.04
43	Randy Milligan	.08	.06	.03
44	Dave Parker	.15	.11	.06
45	Shawon Dunston	.10	.08	.04
46	Brian Harper	.08	.06	.03
47	John Tudor	.08	.06	.03
48	Ellis Burks	.15	.11	.06
49	Bob Welch	.10	.08	.04
50	Roger Clemens	.20	.15	.08
51	Mike Henneman	.08	.06	.03
52	Eddie Murray	.15	.11	.06
53	Kal Daniels	.10	.08	.04
54	Doug Jones	.10	.08	.04
55	Craig Biggio	.10	.08	.04
56	Rafael Palmeiro	.15	.11	.06
57	Wally Joyner	.10	.08	.04
58	Tim Wallach	.10	.08	.04
59	Bret Saberhagen	.15	.11	.06
60	Ryne Sandberg	.20	.15	.08
61	Benito Santiago	.10	.08	.04
62	Darryl Strawberry	.20	.15	.08
63	Alan Trammell	.10	.08	.04
64	Kelly Gruber	.15	.11	.06
65	Dwight Gooden	.20	.15	.08
66	Dave Winfield	.10	.08	.04
67	Rick Aguilera	.08	.06	.03
68	Dave Righetti	.10	.08	.04
69	Jim Abbott	.10	.08	.04
70	Frank Viola	.15	.11	.06
71	Fred McGriff	.20	.15	.08
72	Steve Sax	.10	.08	.04
73	Dennis Eckersley	.15	.11	.06
74	Cory Snyder	.08	.06	.03
75	Mackey Sasser	.08	.06	.03
76	Candy Maldonado	.10	.08	.04
77	Matt Williams	.15	.11	.06
78	Kent Hrbek	.10	.08	.04
79	Randy Myers	.10	.08	.04
80	Gregg Jefferies	.20	.15	.08
81	Joe Carter	.10	.08	.04
82	Mike Greenwell	.15	.11	.06
83	Jack Armstrong	.10	.08	.04
84	Julio Franco	.10	.08	.04
85	George Brett	.15	.11	.06
86	Howard Johnson	.10	.08	.04

		MT	NR MT	EX
87	Andre Dawson	.15	.11	.06
88	Cecil Fielder	.25	.20	.10
89	Tim Raines	.10	.08	.04
90	Chuck Finley	.10	.08	.04
91	Mark Grace	.15	.11	.06
92	Brook Jacoby	.10	.08	.04
93	Dave Steib	.10	.08	.04
94	Tony Gwynn	.15	.11	.06
95	Bobby Thigpen	.10	.08	.04
96	Roberto Kelly	.10	.08	.04
97	Kevin Seitzer	.10	.08	.04
98	Kevin Mitchell	.15	.11	.06
99	Dwight Evans	.10	.08	.04
100	Roberto Alomar	.10	.08	.04

1991 Score Rookies

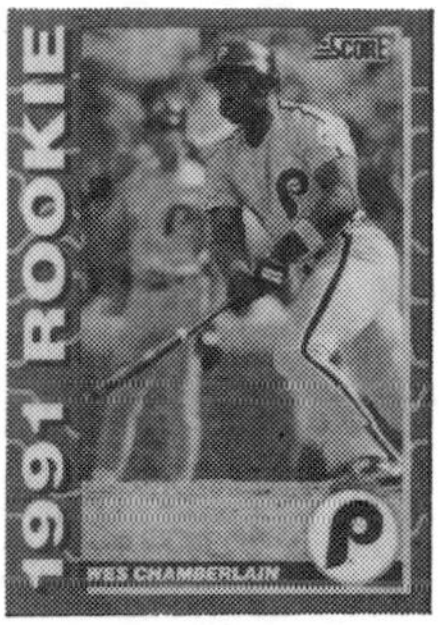

This 40-card boxed set did not receive much attention in the hobby world, but features some of the top young players of 1991. The card fronts feature full-color action photos with a "Rookies" banner along the the side border of the card. The backs feature statistics and a player profile. This set was available through hobby dealers and is Score's first release of its kind.

		MT	NR MT	EX
Complete Set:		8.00	6.00	3.25
Common Player:		.10	.08	.04
1	Mel Rojas	.15	.11	.06
2	Ray Lankford	.30	.25	.12
3	Scott Aldred	.10	.08	.04
4	Turner Ward	.15	.11	.06
5	Omar Olivares	.10	.08	.04
6	Mo Vaughn	.50	.40	.20
7	Phil Clark	.15	.11	.06
8	Brent Mayne	.10	.08	.04
9	Scott Lewis	.15	.11	.06
10	Brian Barnes	.20	.15	.08
11	Bernard Gilkey	.20	.15	.08
12	Steve Decker	.25	.20	.10
13	Paul Marak	.15	.11	.06
14	Wes Chamberlain	.40	.30	.15
15	Kevin Belcher	.10	.08	.04
16	Steve Adkins	.10	.08	.04
17	Geronimo Pena	.20	.15	.08
18	Mark Leonard	.15	.11	.06
19	Jeff Conine	.20	.15	.08
20	Leo Gomez	.25	.20	.10
21	Chuck Malone	.10	.08	.04
22	Beau Allred	.10	.08	.04
23	Todd Hundley	.20	.15	.08
24	Lance Dickson	.20	.15	.08
25	Mike Benjamin	.10	.08	.04
26	Jose Offerman	.25	.20	.10
27	Terry Shumpert	.10	.08	.04
28	Darren Lewis	.25	.20	.10
29	Scott Chiamparino	.10	.08	.04
30	Tim Naehring	.20	.15	.08
31	David Segui	.15	.11	.06
32	Karl Rhodes	.15	.11	.06
33	Mickey Morandini	.15	.11	.06
34	Chuck McElroy	.10	.08	.04
35	Tim McIntosh	.10	.08	.04
36	Derrick May	.30	.25	.12
37	Rich DeLucia	.10	.08	.04
38	Tino Martinez	.20	.15	.08
39	Hensley Meulens	.15	.11	.06
40	Andujar Cedeno	.40	.30	.15

1991 Score Traded

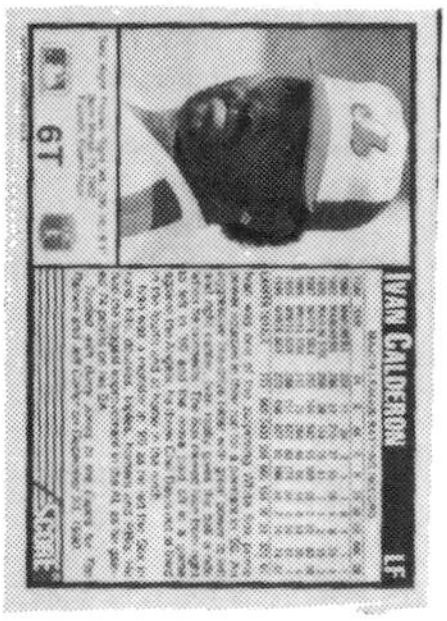

This 110-card set features players with new teams as well as 1991 Major League rookies. The cards are designed in the same style as the regular 1991 Score issue. The cards once again feature a "T" designation along with the card number. The complete set was sold at hobby shops in a special box.

		MT	NR MT	EX
Complete Set:		13.00	9.75	5.25
Common Player:		.06	.05	.02
1	Bo Jackson	1.00	.70	.40
2	Mike Flanagan	.06	.05	.02
3	Pete Incaviglia	.08	.06	.03
4	Jack Clark	.10	.08	.04
5	Hubie Brooks	.08	.06	.03
6	Ivan Calderon	.12	.09	.05
7	Glenn Davis	.12	.09	.05
8	Wally Backman	.06	.05	.02
9	Dave Smith	.08	.06	.03
10	Tim Raines	.15	.11	.06
11	Joe Carter	.15	.11	.06
12	Sid Bream	.08	.06	.03
13	George Bell	.12	.09	.05
14	Steve Bedrosian	.06	.05	.02
15	Willie Wilson	.06	.05	.02
16	Darryl Strawberry	.30	.25	.12
17	Danny Jackson	.06	.05	.02
18	Kirk Gibson	.08	.06	.03
19	Willie McGee	.10	.08	.04
20	Junior Felix	.08	.06	.03
21	Steve Farr	.06	.05	.02
22	Pat Tabler	.06	.05	.02
23	Brett Butler	.10	.08	.04
24	Danny Darwin	.06	.05	.02
25	Mikey Tettleton	.08	.06	.03
26	Gary Carter	.10	.08	.04
27	Mitch Williams	.08	.06	.03
28	Candy Maldonado	.08	.06	.03
29	Otis Nixon	.08	.06	.03
30	Brian Downing	.06	.05	.02
31	Tom Candiotti	.06	.05	.02
32	John Candelaria	.06	.05	.02
33	Rob Murphy	.06	.05	.02
34	Deion Sanders	.20	.15	.08
35	Willie Randolph	.08	.06	.03
36	Pete Harnisch	.08	.06	.03
37	Dante Bichette	.06	.05	.02
38	Garry Templeton	.08	.06	.03
39	Gary Gaetti	.08	.06	.03
40	John Cerutti	.06	.05	.02
41	Rick Cerone	.06	.05	.02
42	Mike Pagliarulo	.06	.05	.02
43	Ron Hassey	.06	.05	.02
44	Roberto Alomar	.25	.20	.10
45	Mike Boddicker	.08	.06	.03
46	Bud Black	.06	.05	.02
47	Rob Deer	.06	.05	.02
48	Devon White	.08	.06	.03
49	Luis Sojo	.06	.05	.02
50	Terry Pendleton	.08	.06	.03
51	Kevin Gross	.06	.05	.02
52	Mike Huff	.08	.06	.03
53	Dave Righetti	.08	.06	.03
54	Matt Young	.06	.05	.02

		MT	NR MT	EX
55	Ernest Riles	.06	.05	.02
56	Bill Gullickson	.08	.06	.03
57	Vince Coleman	.10	.08	.04
58	Fred McGriff	.12	.09	.05
59	Franklin Stubbs	.06	.05	.02
60	Eric King	.06	.05	.02
61	Cory Snyder	.06	.05	.02
62	Dwight Evans	.08	.06	.03
63	Gerald Perry	.06	.05	.02
64	Eric Show	.06	.05	.02
65	Shawn Hillegas	.06	.05	.02
66	Tony Fernandez	.08	.06	.03
67	Tim Teufel	.06	.05	.02
68	Mitch Webster	.06	.05	.02
69	Mike Heath	.06	.05	.02
70	Chili Davis	.08	.06	.03
71	Larry Andersen	.06	.05	.02
72	Gary Varsho	.06	.05	.02
73	Juan Berenguer	.06	.05	.02
74	Jack Morris	.08	.06	.03
75	Barry Jones	.06	.05	.02
76	Rafael Belliard	.06	.05	.02
77	Steve Buechele	.06	.05	.02
78	Scott Sanderson	.06	.05	.02
79	Bob Ojeda	.06	.05	.02
80	Curt Schilling	.06	.05	.02
81	Brian Drahman(FC)	.15	.11	.06
82	Ivan Rodriguez(FC)	2.50	2.00	1.00
83	David Howard(FC)	.20	.15	.08
84	Heath Slocumb(FC)	.15	.11	.06
85	Mike Timlin(FC)	.20	.15	.08
86	Darruyl Kile(FC)	.20	.15	.08
87	Pete Schourek(FC)	.20	.15	.08
88	Bruce Walton(FC)	.12	.09	.05
89	Al Osuna(FC)	.15	.11	.06
90	Gary Scott(FC)	.35	.25	.14
91	Doug Simons(FC)	.15	.11	.06
92	Chris Jones(FC)	.25	.20	.10
93	Chuck Knoblauch	.40	.30	.15
94	Dana Allison(FC)	.15	.11	.06
95	Erik Pappas(FC)	.20	.15	.08
96	Jeff Bagwell(FC)	2.50	2.00	1.00
97	Kirk Dressendorfer(FC)	.35	.25	.14
98	Freddie Benavides(FC)	.20	.15	.08
99	Luis Gonzalez(FC)	.40	.30	.15
100	Wade Taylor(FC)	.20	.15	.08
101	Ed Sprague(FC)	.15	.11	.06
102	Bob Scanlan(FC)	.15	.11	.06
103	Rick Wilkins(FC)	.30	.25	.12
104	Chris Donnels(FC)	.30	.25	.12
105	Joe Slusarski(FC)	.20	.15	.08
106	Mark Lewis(FC)	.30	.25	.12
107	Pat Kelly(FC)	.40	.30	.15
108	John Briscoe(FC)	.15	.11	.06
109	Luis Lopez(FC)	.20	.15	.08
110	Jeff Johnson(FC)	.25	.20	.10

1992 Score Series I

This unique 42-card boxed set from Score was reproduced from original artwork done by sports artist Jeffrey Rubin. The paintings are reproduced on a standard-size, white, glossy stock, and the set includes the top stars of the game, including four key rookies (Walton, Gordon, Jefferies and Griffey Jr.). Score used a two series format for the second consecutive year in 1992. Cards 1-442 are featured in the first series. The card fronts feature full-color game action photos. The player's name, in white lettering, is across the top with the team logo on the upper-right corner. The player's position is across the bottom. Four-color borders are used. Card backs feature color head shots of the players, team logo and career stats on a vertical layout. Several subsets are included in 1992, including a five-card Joe DiMaggio set. DiMaggio autographed cards were also inserted into random packs.

	MT	NR MT	EX
Complete Set:	13.00	9.75	5.25
Common Player:	.04	.03	.02

		MT	NR MT	EX
1	Ken Griffey, Jr.	.50	.40	.20
2	Nolan Ryan	.25	.20	.10
3	Will Clark	.25	.20	.10
4	Dave Justice	.30	.25	.12
5	Dave Henderson	.08	.06	.03
6	Bret Saberhagen	.08	.06	.03
7	Fred McGriff	.08	.06	.03
8	Erik Hanson	.08	.06	.03
9	Darryl Strawberry	.20	.15	.08
10	Doc Gooden	.12	.09	.05
11	Juan Gonzalez	.20	.15	.08
12	Mark Langston	.08	.06	.03
13	Lonnie Smith	.04	.03	.02
14	Jeff Montgomery	.05	.04	.02
15	Roberto Alomar	.12	.09	.05
16	Delino DeShields	.08	.06	.03
17	Steve Bedrosian	.04	.03	.02
18	Terry Pendleton	.08	.06	.03
19	Mark Carreon	.04	.03	.02
20	Mark McGwire	.12	.09	.05
21	Roger Clemens	.15	.11	.06
22	Chuck Crim	.04	.03	.02
23	Don Mattingly	.25	.20	.10
24	Dickie Thon	.04	.03	.02
25	Ron Gant	.15	.11	.06
26	Milt Cuyler	.10	.08	.04
27	Mike Macfarlane	.05	.04	.02
28	Dan Gladden	.04	.03	.02
29	Melido Perez	.04	.03	.02
30	Willie Randolph	.05	.04	.02
31	Albert Belle	.20	.15	.08
32	Dave Winfield	.08	.06	.03
33	Jimmy Jones	.04	.03	.02
34	Kevin Gross	.04	.03	.02
35	Andres Galarraga	.06	.05	.02
36	Mike Devereaux	.05	.04	.02
37	Chris Bosio	.05	.04	.02
38	Mike LaValliere	.05	.04	.02
39	Gary Gaetti	.08	.06	.03
40	Felix Jose	.10	.08	.04
41	Alvaro Espinoza	.04	.03	.02
42	Rick Aguilera	.06	.05	.02
43	Mike Gallego	.04	.03	.02
44	Eric Davis	.12	.09	.05
45	George Bell	.08	.06	.03
46	Tom Brunansky	.06	.05	.02
47	Steve Farr	.04	.03	.02
48	Duane Ward	.05	.04	.02
49	David Wells	.04	.03	.02
50	Cecil Fielder	.20	.15	.08
51	Walt Weiss	.06	.05	.02
52	Todd Zeile	.10	.08	.04
53	Doug Jones	.04	.03	.02
54	Bob Walk	.04	.03	.02
55	Rafael Palmeiro	.08	.06	.03
56	Rob Deer	.04	.03	.02
57	Paul O'Neill	.08	.06	.03
58	Jeff Reardon	.08	.06	.03
59	Randy Ready	.04	.03	.02
60	Scott Erickson	.20	.15	.08
61	Paul Molitor	.08	.06	.03
62	Jack McDowell	.08	.06	.03
63	Jim Acker	.04	.03	.02
64	Jay Buhner	.06	.05	.02
65	Travis Fryman	.20	.15	.08
66	Marquis Grissom	.10	.08	.04
67	Mike Harkey	.05	.04	.02
68	Luis Polonia	.05	.04	.02
69	Ken Caminiti	.05	.04	.02
70	Chris Sabo	.08	.06	.03
71	Gregg Olson	.08	.06	.03
72	Carlton Fisk	.12	.09	.05
73	Juan Samuel	.06	.05	.02
74	Todd Stottlemyre	.06	.05	.02
75	Andre Dawson	.12	.09	.05
76	Alvin Davis	.06	.05	.02
77	Bill Doran	.06	.05	.02

		MT	NR MT	EX
78	B.J. Surhoff	.06	.05	.02
79	Kirk McCaskill	.06	.05	.02
80	Dale Murphy	.12	.09	.05
81	Jose DeLeon	.05	.04	.02
82	Alex Fernandez	.20	.15	.08
83	Ivan Calderon	.08	.06	.03
84	Brent Mayne	.06	.05	.02
85	Jody Reed	.06	.05	.02
86	Randy Tomlin	.06	.05	.02
87	Randy Milligan	.06	.05	.02
88	Pascual Perez	.04	.03	.02
89	Hensley Meulens	.08	.06	.03
90	Joe Carter	.10	.08	.04
91	Mike Moore	.05	.04	.02
92	Ozzie Guillen	.08	.06	.03
93	Shawn Hillegas	.04	.03	.02
94	Chili Davis	.08	.06	.03
95	Vince Coleman	.08	.06	.03
96	Jimmy Key	.06	.05	.02
97	Billy Ripken	.04	.03	.02
98	Dave Smith	.06	.05	.02
99	Tom Bolton	.04	.03	.02
100	Barry Larkin	.12	.09	.05
101	Kenny Rogers	.04	.03	.02
102	Mike Boddicker	.06	.05	.02
103	Kevin Elster	.04	.03	.02
104	Ken Hill	.06	.05	.02
105	Charlie Leibrandt	.04	.03	.02
106	Pat Combs	.06	.05	.02
107	Hubie Brooks	.06	.05	.02
108	Julio Franco	.10	.08	.04
109	Vicente Palacios	.04	.03	.02
110	Kal Daniels	.08	.06	.03
111	Bruce Hurst	.06	.05	.02
112	Willie McGee	.08	.06	.03
113	Ted Power	.04	.03	.02
114	Milt Thompson	.04	.03	.02
115	Doug Drabek	.08	.06	.03
116	Rafael Belliard	.04	.03	.02
117	Scott Garrelts	.04	.03	.02
118	Terry Mulholland	.06	.05	.02
119	Jay Howell	.05	.04	.02
120	Danny Jackson	.05	.04	.02
121	Scott Ruskin	.05	.04	.02
122	Robin Ventura	.15	.11	.06
123	Bip Roberts	.06	.05	.02
124	Jeff Russell	.05	.04	.02
125	Hal Morris	.12	.09	.05
126	Teddy Higuera	.06	.05	.02
127	Luis Sojo	.05	.04	.02
128	Carlos Baerga	.10	.08	.04
129	Jeff Ballard	.04	.03	.02
130	Tom Gordon	.08	.06	.03
131	Sid Bream	.06	.05	.02
132	Rance Mulliniks	.04	.03	.02
133	Andy Benes	.10	.08	.04
134	Mickey Tettleton	.08	.06	.03
135	Rich DeLucia	.06	.05	.02
136	Tom Pagnozzi	.06	.05	.02
137	Harold Baines	.08	.06	.03
138	Danny Darwin	.04	.03	.02
139	Kevin Bass	.06	.05	.02
140	Chris Nabholz	.06	.05	.02
141	Pete O'Brien	.04	.03	.02
142	Jeff Treadway	.05	.04	.02
143	Mickey Morandini	.08	.06	.03
144	Eric King	.04	.03	.02
145	Danny Tartabull	.08	.06	.03
146	Lance Johnson	.04	.03	.02
147	Casey Candaele	.04	.03	.02
148	Felix Fermin	.04	.03	.02
149	Rich Rodriguez	.06	.05	.02
150	Dwight Evans	.08	.06	.03
151	Joe Klink	.04	.03	.02
152	Kevin Reimer	.08	.06	.03
153	Orlando Merced	.20	.15	.08
154	Mel Hall	.05	.04	.02
155	Randy Myers	.06	.05	.02
156	Greg Harris	.04	.03	.02
157	Jeff Brantley	.05	.04	.02
158	Jim Eisenreich	.05	.04	.02
159	Luis Rivera	.04	.03	.02
160	Cris Carpenter	.05	.04	.02
161	Bruce Ruffin	.04	.03	.02
162	Omar Vizquel	.04	.03	.02
163	Gerald Alexander	.05	.04	.02
164	Mark Guthrie	.06	.05	.02
165	Scott Lewis	.06	.05	.02
166	Bill Sampen	.06	.05	.02
167	Dave Anderson	.04	.03	.02
168	Kevin McReynolds	.08	.06	.03

		MT	NR MT	EX
169	Jose Vizcaino	.04	.03	.02
170	Bob Geren	.04	.03	.02
171	Mike Morgan	.05	.04	.02
172	Jim Gott	.04	.03	.02
173	Mike Pagliarulo	.05	.04	.02
174	Mike Jeffcoat	.04	.03	.02
175	Craig Lefferts	.05	.04	.02
176	Steve Finley	.08	.06	.03
177	Wally Backman	.04	.03	.02
178	Kent Mercker	.06	.05	.02
179	John Cerutti	.04	.03	.02
180	Jay Bell	.06	.05	.02
181	Dale Sveum	.04	.03	.02
182	Greg Gagne	.04	.03	.02
183	Donnie Hill	.04	.03	.02
184	Rex Hudler	.04	.03	.02
185	Pat Kelly	.50	.40	.20
186	Jeff Robinson	.04	.03	.02
187	Jeff Gray	.08	.06	.03
188	Jerry Willard	.04	.03	.02
189	Carlos Quintana	.08	.06	.03
190	Dennis Eckersley	.08	.06	.03
191	Kelly Downs	.04	.03	.02
192	Gregg Jefferies	.12	.09	.05
193	Darrin Fletcher	.05	.04	.02
194	Mike Jackson	.05	.04	.02
195	Eddie Murray	.12	.09	.05
196	Billy Landrum	.04	.03	.02
197	Eric Yelding	.04	.03	.02
198	Devon White	.06	.05	.02
199	Larry Walker	.08	.06	.03
200	Ryne Sandberg	.20	.15	.08
201	Dave Magadan	.08	.06	.03
202	Steve Chitren	.06	.05	.02
203	Scott Fletcher	.04	.03	.02
204	Dwayne Henry	.04	.03	.02
205	Scott Coolbaugh	.06	.05	.02
206	Tracy Jones	.04	.03	.02
207	Von Hayes	.06	.05	.02
208	Bob Melvin	.04	.03	.02
209	Scott Scudder	.05	.04	.02
210	Luis Gonzalez	.20	.15	.08
211	Scott Sanderson	.05	.04	.02
212	*Chris Donnels*	.05	.04	.02
213	*Heath Slocumb*	.08	.06	.03
214	Mike Timlin	.12	.09	.05
215	, Brian Harper	.06	.05	.02
216	Juan Berenguer	.04	.03	.02
217	Mike Henneman	.06	.05	.02
218	Bill Spiers	.04	.03	.02
219	Scott Terry	.04	.03	.02
220	Frank Viola	.12	.09	.05
221	Mark Eichhorn	.04	.03	.02
222	Ernest Riles	.04	.03	.02
223	Ray Lankford	.20	.15	.08
224	Pete Harnisch	.06	.05	.02
225	Bobby Bonilla	.12	.09	.05
226	Mike Scioscia	.05	.04	.02
227	Joel Skinner	.04	.03	.02
228	Brian Holman	.05	.04	.02
229	Gilberto Reyes(FC)	.06	.05	.02
230	Matt Williams	.15	.11	.06
231	Jaime Navarro	.06	.05	.02
232	Jose Rijo	.08	.06	.03
233	Atlee Hammaker	.04	.03	.02
234	Tim Teufel	.04	.03	.02
235	John Kruk	.08	.06	.03
236	Kurt Stillwell	.05	.04	.02
237	Dan Pasqua	.05	.04	.02
238	Tim Crews	.04	.03	.02
239	Dave Gallagher	.05	.04	.02
240	Leo Gomez	.15	.11	.06
241	Steve Avery	.25	.20	.10
242	Bill Gullickson	.06	.05	.02
243	Mark Portugal	.04	.03	.02
244	Lee Guetterman	.04	.03	.02
245	Benny Santiago	.08	.06	.03
246	Jim Gantner	.04	.03	.02
247	Robby Thompson	.05	.04	.02
248	Terry Shumpert	.04	.03	.02
249	*Mike Bell*(FC)	.15	.11	.06
250	Harold Reynolds	.06	.05	.02
251	Mike Felder	.04	.03	.02
252	Bill Pecota	.04	.03	.02
253	Bill Krueger	.04	.03	.02
254	Alfredo Griffin	.04	.03	.02
255	Lou Whitaker	.08	.06	.03
256	Roy Smith	.04	.03	.02
257	Jerald Clark	.05	.04	.02
258	Sammy Sosa	.08	.06	.03
259	Tim Naehring	.15	.11	.06

		MT	NR MT	EX
260	Dave Righetti	.08	.06	.03
261	Paul Gibson	.04	.03	.02
262	Chris James	.05	.04	.02
263	Larry Andersen	.04	.03	.02
264	Storm Davis	.05	.04	.02
265	Jose Lind	.04	.03	.02
266	Greg Hibbard	.06	.05	.02
267	Norm Charlton	.06	.05	.02
268	Paul Kilgus	.04	.03	.02
269	Greg Maddux	.06	.05	.02
270	Ellis Burks	.12	.09	.05
271	Frank Tanana	.05	.04	.02
272	Gene Larkin	.05	.04	.02
273	Ron Hassey	.04	.03	.02
274	Jeff Robinson	.04	.03	.02
275	Steve Howe	.05	.04	.02
276	Daryl Boston	.04	.03	.02
277	Mark Lee	.04	.03	.02
278	*Jose Segura*(FC)	.12	.09	.05
279	Lance Blankenship	.04	.03	.02
280	Don Slaught	.04	.03	.02
281	Russ Swan	.08	.06	.03
282	Bob Tewksbury	.04	.03	.02
283	Geno Petralli	.04	.03	.02
284	Shane Mack	.08	.06	.03
285	Bob Scanlan	.25	.20	.10
286	Tim Leary	.05	.04	.02
287	John Smoltz	.15	.11	.06
288	Pat Borders	.05	.04	.02
289	Mark Davidson	.04	.03	.02
290	Sam Horn	.06	.05	.02
291	Lenny Harris	.05	.04	.02
292	Franklin Stubbs	.04	.03	.02
293	Thomas Howard	.05	.04	.02
294	Steve Lyons	.04	.03	.02
295	Francisco Oliveras	.04	.03	.02
296	Terry Leach	.04	.03	.02
297	Barry Jones	.04	.03	.02
298	Lance Parrish	.08	.06	.03
299	Wally Whitehurst	.06	.05	.02
300	Bob Welch	.06	.05	.02
301	Charlie Hayes	.05	.04	.02
302	Charlie Hough	.05	.04	.02
303	Gary Redus	.04	.03	.02
304	Scott Bradley	.04	.03	.02
305	Jose Oquendo	.04	.03	.02
306	Pete Incaviglia	.06	.05	.02
307	Marvin Freeman	.04	.03	.02
308	Gary Pettis	.04	.03	.02
309	Joe Slusarski	.25	.20	.10
310	Kevin Seitzer	.05	.04	.02
311	Jeff Reed	.04	.03	.02
312	Pat Tabler	.04	.03	.02
313	Mike Maddux	.04	.03	.02
314	Bob Milacki	.04	.03	.02
315	Eric Anthony	.10	.08	.04
316	Dante Bichette	.05	.04	.02
317	Steve Decker	.15	.11	.06
318	Jack Clark	.08	.06	.03
319	Doug Dascenzo	.04	.03	.02
320	Scott Leius	.10	.08	.04
321	Jim Lindeman	.04	.03	.02
322	Bryan Harvey	.08	.06	.03
323	Spike Owen	.04	.03	.02
324	Roberto Kelly	.12	.09	.05
325	Stan Belinda	.05	.04	.02
326	Joey Cora	.04	.03	.02
327	Jeff Innis	.04	.03	.02
328	Willie Wilson	.05	.04	.02
329	Juan Agosto	.04	.03	.02
330	Charles Nagy	.10	.08	.04
331	Scott Bailes	.04	.03	.02
332	*Pete Schourek*	.20	.15	.08
333	Mike Flanagan	.04	.03	.02
334	Omar Olivares	.10	.08	.04
335	Dennis Lamp	.04	.03	.02
336	Tommy Greene	.06	.05	.02
337	Randy Velarde	.04	.03	.02
338	Tom Lampkin	.04	.03	.02
339	John Russell	.04	.03	.02
340	Bob Kipper	.04	.03	.02
341	Todd Burns	.04	.03	.02
342	Ron Jones	.05	.04	.02
343	Dave Valle	.04	.03	.02
344	Mike Heath	.04	.03	.02
345	John Olerud	.15	.11	.06
346	Gerald Young	.04	.03	.02
347	Ken Patterson	.04	.03	.02
348	Les Lancaster	.04	.03	.02
349	Steve Crawford	.04	.03	.02
350	John Candelaria	.04	.03	.02

		MT	NR MT	EX
351	Mike Aldrete	.04	.03	.02
352	Mariano Duncan	.05	.04	.02
353	Julio Machado	.04	.03	.02
354	Ken Williams	.04	.03	.02
355	Walt Terrell	.04	.03	.02
356	Mitch Williams	.08	.06	.03
357	Al Newman	.04	.03	.02
358	Bud Black	.05	.04	.02
359	Joe Hesketh	.04	.03	.02
360	Paul Assenmacher	.05	.04	.02
361	Bo Jackson	.50	.40	.20
362	Jeff Blauser	.04	.03	.02
363	Mike Brumley	.04	.03	.02
364	Jim Deshaies	.04	.03	.02
365	Brady Anderson	.04	.03	.02
366	Chuck McElroy	.04	.03	.02
367	Matt Merullo	.04	.03	.02
368	Tim Belcher	.06	.05	.02
369	Luis Aquino	.04	.03	.02
370	Joe Oliver	.05	.04	.02
371	Greg Swindell	.08	.06	.03
372	Lee Stevens	.10	.08	.04
373	Mark Knudson	.04	.03	.02
374	Bill Wegman	.05	.04	.02
375	Jerry Don Gleaton	.04	.03	.02
376	Pedro Guerrero	.10	.08	.04
377	Randy Bush	.04	.03	.02
378	Greg Harris	.04	.03	.02
379	Eric Plunk	.04	.03	.02
380	Jose DeJesus	.08	.06	.03
381	Bobby Witt	.06	.05	.02
382	Curtis Wilkerson	.04	.03	.02
383	Gene Nelson	.04	.03	.02
384	Wes Chamberlain	.20	.15	.08
385	Tom Henke	.06	.05	.02
386	Mark Lemke	.06	.05	.02
387	Greg Briley	.04	.03	.02
388	Rafael Ramirez	.04	.03	.02
389	Tony Fossas	.04	.03	.02
390	Henry Cotto	.04	.03	.02
391	Tim Hulett	.04	.03	.02
392	Dean Palmer	.25	.20	.10
393	Glenn Braggs	.05	.04	.02
394	Mark Salas	.04	.03	.02
395	*Rusty Meacham*(FC)	.20	.15	.08
396	*Andy Ashby*(FC)	.20	.15	.08
397	*Jose Melendez*(FC)	.20	.15	.08
398	*Warren Newson*(FC)	.20	.15	.08
399	*Frank Castillo*(FC)	.15	.11	.06
400	*Chito Martinez*(FC)	.60	.45	.25
401	Bernie Williams	.40	.30	.15
402	Derek Bell(FC)	.40	.30	.15
403	*Javier Ortiz*(FC)	.15	.11	.06
404	*Tim Sherrill*(FC)	.12	.09	.05
405	*Rob MacDonald*(FC)	.15	.11	.06
406	Phil Plantier	.50	.40	.20
407	Troy Afenir	.10	.08	.04
408	*Gino Minutelli*(FC)	.10	.08	.04
409	*Reggie Jefferson*(FC)	.35	.25	.14
410	*Mike Remlinger*(FC)	.15	.11	.06
411	*Carlos Rodriguez*(FC)	.15	.11	.06
412	*Joe Redfield*(FC)	.20	.15	.08
413	Alonzo Powell(FC)	.08	.06	.03
414	*Scott Livingstone*(FC)	.30	.25	.12
415	*Scott Kamieniecki*(FC)	.15	.11	.06
416	*Tim Spehr*(FC)	.20	.15	.08
417	*Brian Hunter*(FC)	.50	.40	.20
418	*Ced Landrum*(FC)	.15	.11	.06
419	*Bret Barberie*(FC)	.15	.11	.06
420	Kevin Morton(FC)	.20	.15	.08
421	*Doug Henry*(FC)	.20	.15	.08
422	*Doug Piatt*(FC)	.15	.11	.06
423	*Pat Rice*(FC)	.15	.11	.06
424	*Juan Guzman*(FC)	.40	.30	.15
425	Nolan Ryan (No-Hit Club)	.30	.25	.12
426	Tommy Greene (No-Hit Club)	.10	.08	.04
427	Milacki/Flanagan/Williamson (No-Hit Club)	.10	.08	.04
428	Wilson Alvarez (No-Hit Club)	.20	.15	.08
429	Otis Nixon (Highlight)	.08	.06	.03
430	Rickey Henderson (Highlight)	.20	.15	.08
431	Cecil Fielder (AS)	.10	.08	.04
432	Julio Franco (AS)	.08	.06	.03
433	Cal Ripken, Jr. (AS)	.15	.11	.06
434	Wade Boggs (AS)	.10	.08	.04
435	Joe Carter (AS)	.10	.08	.04
436	Ken Griffey, Jr. (AS)	.40	.30	.15
437	Ruben Sierra (AS)	.10	.08	.04
438	Scott Erickson (AS)	.15	.11	.06
439	Tom Henke (AS)	.05	.04	.02
440	Terry Steinbach (AS)	.05	.04	.02

		MT	NR MT	EX
441	Rickey Henderson (Dream Team)	.50	.40	.20
442	Ryne Sandberg (Dream Team)	.40	.30	.15

1989 Scoremasters

		MT	NR MT	EX
Complete Set:		12.00	9.00	4.75
Common Player:		.20	.15	.08
1	Bo Jackson	1.00	.70	.40
2	Jerome Walton	.40	.30	.15
3	Cal Ripken, Jr.	1.00	.70	.40
4	Mike Scott	.20	.15	.08
5	Nolan Ryan	1.50	1.25	.60
6	Don Mattingly	1.25	.90	.50
7	Tom Gordon	.50	.40	.20
8	Jack Morris	.20	.15	.08
9	Carlton Fisk	.30	.25	.12
10	Will Clark	1.00	.70	.40
11	George Brett	.40	.30	.15
12	Kevin Mitchell	.40	.30	.15
13	Mark Langston	.30	.25	.12
14	Dave Stewart	.20	.15	.08
15	Dale Murphy	.25	.20	.10
16	Gary Gaetti	.20	.15	.08
17	Wade Boggs	.40	.30	.15
18	Eric Davis	.40	.30	.15
19	Kirby Puckett	.40	.30	.15
20	Roger Clemens	1.00	.70	.40
21	Orel Hershiser	.30	.25	.12
22	Mark Grace	.50	.40	.20
23	Ryne Sandberg	1.00	.70	.40
24	Barry Larkin	.40	.30	.15
25	Ellis Burks	.40	.30	.15
26	Doc Gooden	.40	.30	.15
27	Ozzie Smith	.25	.20	.10
28	Andre Dawson	.40	.30	.15
29	Julio Franco	.40	.30	.15
30	Ken Griffey, Jr.	2.00	1.50	.80
31	Ruben Sierra	.50	.40	.20
32	Mark McGwire	.50	.40	.20
33	Andres Galarraga	.20	.15	.08
34	Joe Carter	.30	.25	.12
35	Vince Coleman	.20	.15	.08
36	Mike Greenwell	.25	.20	.10
37	Tony Gwynn	.40	.30	.15
38	Andy Van Slyke	.25	.20	.10
39	Gregg Jefferies	.50	.40	.20
40	Jose Canseco	1.00	.70	.40
41	Dave Winfield	.25	.20	.10
42	Darryl Strawberry	.40	.30	.15

1985 7-11 Twins

The Minnesota Twins, in co-operation with 7-Eleven and the Fire Marshall's Association, issued this set of 13 baseball fire safety cards. The card fronts feature full-color pictures of Twins players. A fire safety tip and short player history appear on the back. The cards were given out at all 7-Eleven stores in the state and at the Twins June 3 baseball game. Each fan received one baseball card with a poster which told how to collect the other cards in the set. Twelve cards feature players and the 13th card has an

artist's rendering of Twins players on the front and a checklist of the set on the back. A group of 50,000 cards was distributed to fifth graders throughout the state by the fire departments.

		MT	NR MT	EX
Complete Set:		6.00	4.50	2.50
Common Player:		.20	.15	.08
1	Kirby Puckett	2.00	1.50	.80
2	Frank Viola	1.00	.70	.40
3	Mickey Hatcher	.20	.15	.08
4	Kent Hrbek	1.25	.90	.50
5	John Butcher	.20	.15	.08
6	Roy Smalley	.20	.15	.08
7	Tom Brunansky	.50	.40	.20
8	Ron Davis	.20	.15	.08
9	Gary Gaetti	1.00	.70	.40
10	Tim Teufel	.30	.25	.12
11	Mike Smithson	.20	.15	.08
12	Tim Laudner	.30	.25	.12
----	Checklist	.10	.08	.04

1984 7-Up Cubs

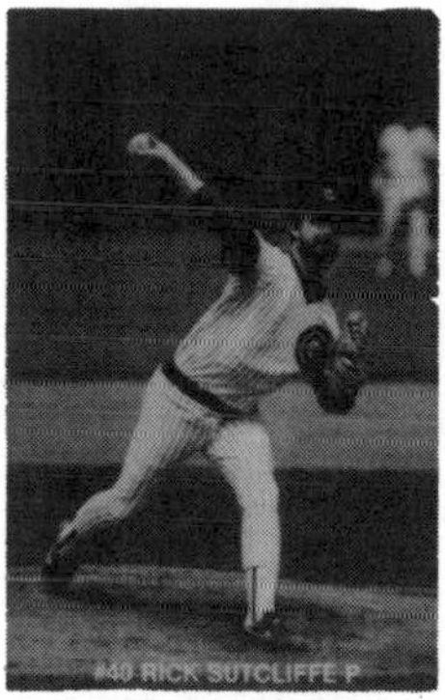

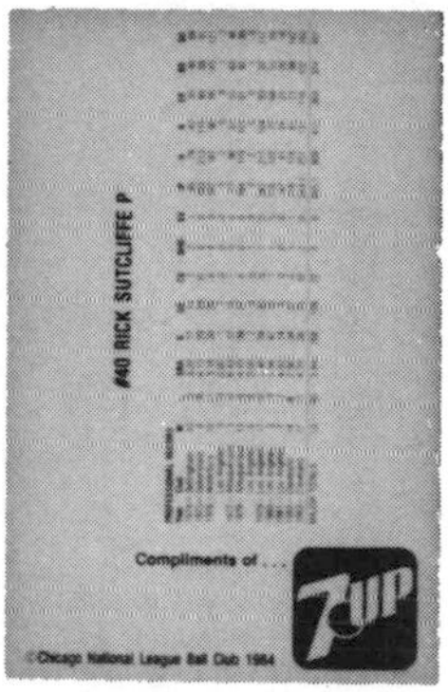

The Chicago Cubs and 7-Up issued this 28-card set featuring full-color game-action photos on a 2-1/4" by 3-1/2" borderless front. The backs have the player's stats and personal information. This was the third consecutive year the Cubs issued this type of set as a giveaway at a "Baseball Card Day" promotional game.

		MT	NR MT	EX
Complete Set:		12.00	9.00	4.75
Common Player:		.20	.15	.08
1	Larry Bowa	.40	.30	.15
6	Keith Moreland	.40	.30	.15
7	Jody Davis	.40	.30	.15
10	Leon Durham	.40	.30	.15
11	Ron Cey	.40	.30	.15
15	Ron Hassey	.20	.15	.08
18	Richie Hebner	.20	.15	.08
19	Dave Owen	.20	.15	.08
20	Bob Dernier	.20	.15	.08
21	Jay Johnstone	.25	.20	.10

		MT	NR MT	EX
23	Ryne Sandberg	3.00	2.25	1.25
24	Scott Sanderson	.25	.20	.10
25	Gary Woods	.20	.15	.08
27	Thad Bosley	.20	.15	.08
28	Henry Cotto	.30	.25	.12
34	Steve Trout	.25	.20	.10
36	Gary Matthews	.40	.30	.15
39	George Frazier	.20	.15	.08
40	Rick Sutcliffe	.80	.60	.30
41	Warren Brusstar	.20	.15	.08
42	Rich Bordi	.20	.15	.08
43	Dennis Eckersley	1.25	.90	.50
44	Dick Ruthven	.20	.15	.08
46	Lee Smith	.50	.40	.20
47	Rick Reuschel	.50	.40	.20
49	Tim Stoddard	.20	.15	.08
---	Jim Frey	.20	.15	.08
---	Cubs Coaches (Ruben Amaro, Billy Connors, Johnny Oates, John Vukovich, Don Zimmer)	.20	.15	.08

1985 7-Up Cubs

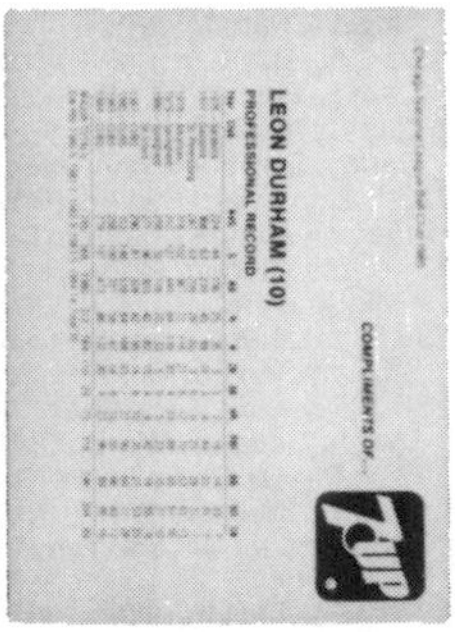

This was the second year a Chicago Cubs card set was released with 7-Up as the sponsor. The set has 28 unnumbered cards in the standard 2-1/2" by 3-1/2" size. They were distributed to fans attending the Cubs game on August 14 at Wrigley Field. They feature full-color game-action photos of the players. Card backs contain the player's professional stats.

		MT	NR MT	EX
Complete Set:		8.00	6.00	3.25
Common Player:		.10	.08	.04
1	Larry Bowa	.25	.20	.10
6	Keith Moreland	.30	.25	.12
7	Jody Davis	.30	.25	.12
10	Leon Durham	.30	.25	.12
11	Ron Cey	.30	.25	.12
15	Davey Lopes	.25	.20	.10
16	Steve Lake	.10	.08	.04
18	Richie Hebner	.10	.08	.04
20	Bob Dernier	.10	.08	.04
21	Scott Sanderson	.15	.11	.06
22	Billy Hatcher	.30	.25	.12
23	Ryne Sandberg	3.00	2.25	1.25
24	Brian Dayett	.10	.08	.04
25	Gary Woods	.10	.08	.04
27	Thad Bosley	.10	.08	.04
28	Chris Speier	.10	.08	.04
31	Ray Fontenot	.10	.08	.04
34	Steve Trout	.20	.15	.08
36	Gary Matthews	.30	.25	.12
39	George Frazier	.10	.08	.04
40	Rick Sutcliffe	.50	.40	.20
41	Warren Brusstar	.10	.08	.04
42	Lary Sorensen	.10	.08	.04
43	Dennis Eckersley	1.00	.70	.40
44	Dick Ruthven	.10	.08	.04
46	Lee Smith	.35	.25	.14
---	Jim Frey	.10	.08	.04
---	Coaching Staff (Ruben Amaro, Billy Connors, Johnny Oates, John Vukovich, Don Zimmer)	.10	.08	.04

1986 Sportflics

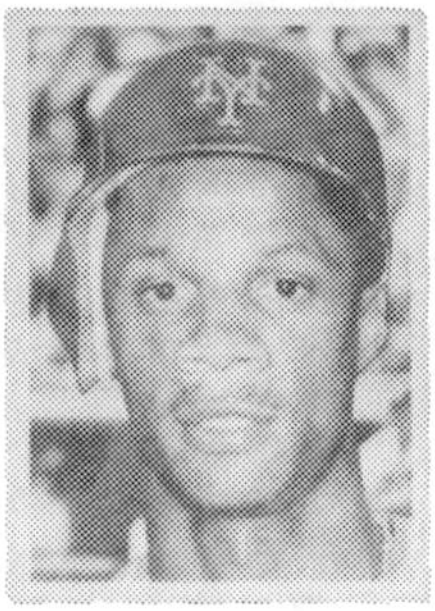

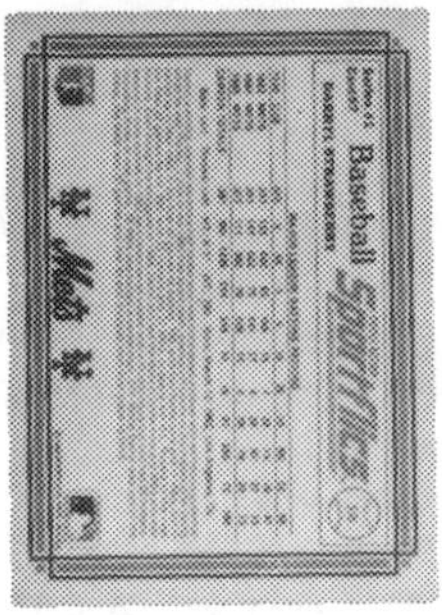

The premiere issue from Sportflics was distributed nationally by Amurol Division of Wrigley Gum Company. These high quality, three-phase "Magic Motion" cards depict three different photos per card, with each visible separately as the card is tilted. The 1986 issue features 200 full-color baseball cards plus 133 trivia cards. The cards come in the standard 2-1/2" by 3-1/2" size with the backs containing player stats and personal information. There are three different types of picture cards: 1) Tri-Star cards - 50 cards feature three players on one card; 2) Big Six cards - 10 cards which have six players in special categories; and 3) the Big Twelve card of 12 World Series players from the Kansas City Royals. The trivia cards are 1-3/4" by 2" and do not have player photos.

		MT	NR MT	EX
Complete Set:		40.00	30.00	16.00
Common Player:		.10	.08	.04
1	George Brett	1.00	.70	.40
2	Don Mattingly	3.00	2.25	1.25
3	Wade Boggs	1.50	1.25	.60
4	Eddie Murray	.60	.45	.25
5	Dale Murphy	.50	.40	.20
6	Rickey Henderson	1.50	1.25	.60
7	Harold Baines	.20	.15	.08
8	Cal Ripken, Jr.	1.00	.70	.40
9	Orel Hershiser	.40	.30	.15
10	Bret Saberhagen	.30	.25	.12
11	Tim Raines	.40	.30	.15
12	Fernando Valenzuela	.30	.25	.12
13	Tony Gwynn	.60	.45	.25
14	Pedro Guerrero	.25	.20	.10
15	Keith Hernandez	.35	.25	.14
16	Ernest Riles	.20	.15	.08
17	Jim Rice	.30	.25	.12
18	Ron Guidry	.25	.20	.10
19	Willie McGee	.25	.20	.10
20	Ryne Sandberg	1.75	1.25	.70
21	Kirk Gibson	.35	.25	.14
22	Ozzie Guillen	.30	.25	.12
23	Dave Parker	.25	.20	.10
24	Vince Coleman	2.00	1.50	.80
25	Tom Seaver	.40	.30	.15
26	Brett Butler	.10	.08	.04
27	Steve Carlton	.50	.40	.20
28	Gary Carter	.35	.25	.14
29	Cecil Cooper	.15	.11	.06
30	Jose Cruz	.10	.08	.04
31	Alvin Davis	.20	.15	.08
32	Dwight Evans	.15	.11	.06
33	Julio Franco	.15	.11	.06
34	Damaso Garcia	.10	.08	.04
35	Steve Garvey	.40	.30	.15
36	Kent Hrbek	.25	.20	.10
37	Reggie Jackson	.70	.50	.30
38	Fred Lynn	.20	.15	.08
39	Paul Molitor	.15	.11	.06
40	Jim Presley	.15	.11	.06
41	Dave Righetti	.20	.15	.08
42a	Robin Yount (Yankees logo on back)	3.00	2.25	1.25
42b	Robin Yount (Brewers logo on back)	.60	.45	.25

		MT	NR MT	EX
43	Nolan Ryan	2.00	1.50	.80
44	Mike Schmidt	1.25	.90	.50
45	Lee Smith	.10	.08	.04
46	Rick Sutcliffe	.15	.11	.06
47	Bruce Sutter	.15	.11	.06
48	Lou Whitaker	.20	.15	.08
49	Dave Winfield	.60	.45	.25
50	Pete Rose	1.50	1.25	.60
51	National League MVPs (Steve Garvey, Pete Rose, Ryne Sandberg)	.70	.50	.30
52	Slugging Stars (Harold Baines, George Brett, Jim Rice)	.35	.25	.14
53	No-Hitters (Phil Niekro, Jerry Reuss, Mike Witt)	.15	.11	.06
54	Big Hitters (Don Mattingly, Cal Ripken, Jr., Robin Yount)	1.25	.90	.50
55	Bullpen Aces (Goose Gossage, Dan Quisenberry, Lee Smith)	.10	.08	.04
56	Rookies of the Year (Pete Rose, Steve Sax, Darryl Strawberry)	.80	.60	.30
57	American League MVPs (Don Baylor, Reggie Jackson, Cal Ripken, Jr.)	.35	.25	.14
58	Repeat Batting Champs (Bill Madlock, Dave Parker, Pete Rose)	.60	.45	.25
59	Cy Young Winners (Mike Flanagan, Ron Guidry, LaMarr Hoyt)	.10	.08	.04
60	Double Award Winners (Tom Seaver, Rick Sutcliffe, Fernando Valenzuela)	.20	.15	.08
61	Home Run Champs (Tony Armas, Reggie Jackson, Jim Rice)	.25	.20	.10
62	National League MVPs (Keith Hernandez, Dale Murphy, Mike Schmidt)	.50	.40	.20
63	American League MVPs (George Brett, Fred Lynn, Robin Yount)	.30	.25	.12
64	Comeback Players (Bert Blyleven, John Denny, Jerry Koosman)	.10	.08	.04
65	Cy Young Relievers (Rollie Fingers, Willie Hernandez, Bruce Sutter)	.15	.11	.06
66	Rookies Of The Year (Andre Dawson, Bob Horner, Gary Matthews)	.15	.11	.06
67	Rookies Of The Year (Carlton Fisk, Ron Kittle, Tom Seaver)	.15	.11	.06
68	Home Run Champs (George Foster, Dave Kingman, Mike Schmidt)	.30	.25	.12
69	Double Award Winners (Rod Carew, Cal Ripken, Jr., Pete Rose)	1.00	.70	.40
70	Cy Young Winners (Steve Carlton, Tom Seaver, Rick Sutcliffe)	.25	.20	.10
71	Top Sluggers (Reggie Jackson, Fred Lynn, Robin Yount)	.30	.25	.12
72	Rookies of the Year (Dave Righetti, Rick Sutcliffe, Fernando Valenzuela)	.15	.11	.06
73	Rookies Of The Year (Fred Lynn, Eddie Murray, Cal Ripken, Jr.)	.25	.20	.10
74	Rookies Of The Year (Rod Carew, Alvin Davis, Lou Whitaker)	.20	.15	.08
75	Batting Champs (Wade Boggs, Carney Lansford, Don Mattingly)	1.50	1.25	.60
76	Jesse Barfield	.20	.15	.08
77	Phil Bradley	.15	.11	.06
78	Chris Brown	.25	.20	.10
79	Tom Browning	.30	.25	.12
80	Tom Brunansky	.15	.11	.06
81	Bill Buckner	.10	.08	.04
82	Chili Davis	.10	.08	.04
83	Mike Davis	.10	.08	.04
84	Rich Gedman	.10	.08	.04
85	Willie Hernandez	.10	.08	.04
86	Ron Kittle	.10	.08	.04
87	Lee Lacy	.10	.08	.04
88	Bill Madlock	.15	.11	.06
89	Mike Marshall	.15	.11	.06
90	Keith Moreland	.10	.08	.04
91	Graig Nettles	.15	.11	.06
92	Lance Parrish	.20	.15	.08
93	Kirby Puckett	2.00	1.50	.80
94	Juan Samuel	.20	.15	.08
95	Steve Sax	.20	.15	.08
96	Dave Stieb	.10	.08	.04
97	Darryl Strawberry	2.00	1.50	.80
98	Willie Upshaw	.10	.08	.04
99	Frank Viola	.50	.40	.20
100	Dwight Gooden	2.00	1.50	.80
101	Joaquin Andujar	.10	.08	.04
102	George Bell	.40	.30	.15
103	Bert Blyleven	.15	.11	.06
104	Mike Boddicker	.10	.08	.04
105	Britt Burns	.10	.08	.04
106	Rod Carew	1.25	.90	.50
107	Jack Clark	.25	.20	.10
108	Danny Cox	.10	.08	.04

		MT	NR MT	EX
109	Ron Darling	.15	.11	.06
110	Andre Dawson	.25	.20	.10
111	Leon Durham	.10	.08	.04
112	Tony Fernandez	.15	.11	.06
113	Tom Herr	.10	.08	.04
114	Teddy Higuera	.80	.60	.30
115	Bob Horner	.15	.11	.06
116	Dave Kingman	.15	.11	.06
117	Jack Morris	.20	.15	.08
118	Dan Quisenberry	.10	.08	.04
119	Jeff Reardon	.15	.11	.06
120	Bryn Smith	.10	.08	.04
121	Ozzie Smith	.25	.20	.10
122	John Tudor	.15	.11	.06
123	Tim Wallach	.15	.11	.06
124	Willie Wilson	.15	.11	.06
125	Carlton Fisk	.25	.20	.10
126	RBI Sluggers (Gary Carter, George Foster, Al Oliver)	.15	.11	.06
127	Run Scorers (Keith Hernandez, Tim Raines, Ryne Sandberg)	.25	.20	.10
128	Run Scorers (Paul Molitor, Cal Ripken, Jr., Willie Wilson)	.20	.15	.08
129	No-Hitters (John Candelaria, Dennis Eckersley, Bob Forsch)	.10	.08	.04
130	World Series MVPs (Ron Cey, Rollie Fingers, Pete Rose)	.50	.40	.20
131	All-Star Game MVPs (Dave Concepcion, George Foster, Bill Madlock)	.10	.08	.04
132	Cy Young Winners (Vida Blue, John Denny, Fernando Valenzuela)	.15	.11	.06
133	Comeback Players (Doyle Alexander, Joaquin Andujar, Richard Dotson)	.10	.08	.04
134	Big Winners (John Denny, Tom Seaver, Rick Sutcliffe)	.15	.11	.06
135	Veteran Pitchers (Phil Niekro, Tom Seaver, Don Sutton)	.25	.20	.10
136	Rookies Of The Year (Vince Coleman, Dwight Gooden, Alfredo Griffin)	.80	.60	.30
137	All-Star Game MVPs (Gary Carter, Steve Garvey, Fred Lynn)	.20	.15	.08
138	Veteran Hitters (Tony Perez, Pete Rose, Rusty Staub)	.50	.40	.20
139	Power Hitters (George Foster, Jim Rice, Mike Schmidt)	.30	.25	.12
140	Batting Champs (Bill Buckner, Tony Gwynn, Al Oliver)	.20	.15	.08
141	No-Hitters (Jack Morris, Dave Righetti, Nolan Ryan)	.20	.15	.08
142	No-Hitters (Vida Blue, Bert Blyleven, Tom Seaver)	.15	.11	.06
143	Strikeout Kings (Dwight Gooden, Nolan Ryan, Fernando Valenzuela)	1.25	.90	.50
144	Base Stealers (Dave Lopes, Tim Raines, Willie Wilson)	.15	.11	.06
145	RBI Sluggers (Tony Armas, Cecil Cooper, Eddie Murray)	.15	.11	.06
146	American League MVPs (Rod Carew, Rollie Fingers, Jim Rice)	.25	.20	.10
147	World Series MVPs (Rick Dempsey, Reggie Jackson, Alan Trammell)	.25	.20	.10
148	World Series MVPs (Pedro Guerrero, Darrell Porter, Mike Schmidt)	.20	.15	.08
149	ERA Leaders (Mike Boddicker, Ron Guidry, Rick Sutcliffe)	.10	.08	.04
150	Comeback Players (Reggie Jackson, Dave Kingman, Fred Lynn)	.20	.15	.08
151	Buddy Bell	.15	.11	.06
152	Dennis Boyd	.10	.08	.04
153	Dave Concepcion	.15	.11	.06
154	Brian Downing	.10	.08	.04
155	Shawon Dunston	.15	.11	.06
156	John Franco	.15	.11	.06
157	Scott Garrelts	.10	.08	.04
158	Bob James	.10	.08	.04
159	Charlie Leibrandt	.10	.08	.04
160	Oddibe McDowell	.30	.25	.12
161	Roger McDowell	.50	.40	.20
162	Mike Moore	.10	.08	.04
163	Phil Niekro	.25	.20	.10
164	Al Oliver	.15	.11	.06
165	Tony Pena	.10	.08	.04
166	Ted Power	.10	.08	.04
167	Mike Scioscia	.10	.08	.04
168	Mario Soto	.10	.08	.04
169	Bob Stanley	.10	.08	.04
170	Garry Templeton	.10	.08	.04
171	Andre Thornton	.10	.08	.04
172	Alan Trammell	.30	.25	.12
173	Doug DeCinces	.10	.08	.04
174	Greg Walker	.10	.08	.04

		MT	NR MT	EX
175	Don Sutton	.25	.20	.10
176	1985 Award Winners (Vince Coleman, Dwight Gooden, Ozzie Guillen, Don Mattingly, Wille McGee, Bret Saberhagen)	1.25	.90	.50
177	1985 Hot Rookies (Stewart Cliburn, Brian Fisher, Joe Hesketh, Joe Orsulak, Mark Salas, Larry Sheets)	.20	.15	.08
178	Future Stars (Jose Canseco, Mark Funderburk, Mike Greenwell, Steve Lombardozzi, Billy Joe Robidoux, Dan Tartabull)	15.00	11.00	6.00
179	1985 Gold Glovers (George Brett, Ron Guidry, Keith Hernandez, Don Mattingly, Willie McGee, Dale Murphy)	1.25	.90	.50
180	Active .300 Hitters (Wade Boggs, George Brett, Rod Carew, Cecil Cooper, Don Mattingly, Willie Wilson)	1.25	.90	.50
181	Active .300 Hitters (Pedro Guerrero, Tony Gwynn, Keith Hernandez, Bill Madlock, Dave Parker, Pete Rose)	.70	.50	.30
182	1985 Milestones (Rod Carew, Phil Niekro, Pete Rose, Nolan Ryan, Tom Seaver, Matt Tallman)	1.50	1.25	.60
183	1985 Triple Crown (Wade Boggs, Darrell Evans, Don Mattingly, Willie McGee, Dale Murphy, Dave Parker)	1.25	.90	.50
184	1985 Highlights (Wade Boggs, Dwight Gooden, Rickey Henderson, Don Mattingly, Willie McGee, John Tudor)	1.50	1.25	.60
185	1985 20-Game Winners (Joaquin Andujar, Tom Browning, Dwight Gooden, Ron Guidry, Bret Saberhagen, John Tudor)	.60	.45	.25
186	Kansas City Royals (Steve Balboni, George Brett, Dane Iorg, Danny Jackson, Charlie Leibrandt, Darryl Motley, Dan Quisenberry, Bret Saberhagen, Lonnie Smith, Jim Sundberg, Frank White, Willie Wilson)	.40	.30	.15
187	Hubie Brooks	.10	.08	.04
188	Glenn Davis	.60	.45	.25
189	Darrell Evans	.10	.08	.04
190	Rich Gossage	.15	.11	.06
191	Andy Hawkins	.10	.08	.04
192	Jay Howell	.10	.08	.04
193	LaMarr Hoyt	.10	.08	.04
194	Davey Lopes	.10	.08	.04
195	Mike Scott	.20	.15	.08
196	Ted Simmons	.15	.11	.06
197	Gary Ward	.10	.08	.04
198	Bob Welch	.15	.11	.06
199	Mike Young	.10	.08	.04
200	Buddy Biancalana	.10	.08	.04

1986 Sportflics Decade Greats

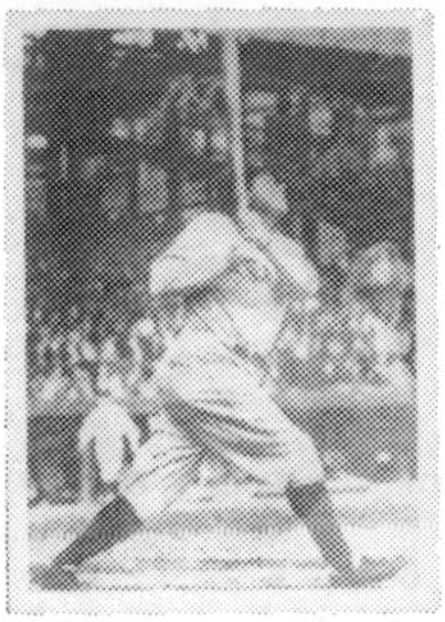

This set, produced by Sportflics, features outstanding players, by position, from the 1930s to the 1980s by decades. The card fronts are printed in sepia-toned photos or full-color with the Sportflics three-phase "Magic Motion" animation. The complete set contains 75 cards with 59 single player cards and 16 multi-player cards. Biographies appear on the card backs which are printed in full-color and color-coded by decade. The set was distributed only through hobby dealers and is in the popular 2-1/2" by 3-1/2" size.

		MT	NR MT	EX
Complete Set:		15.00	11.00	6.00
Common Player:		.15	.11	.06
1	Babe Ruth	3.50	2.75	1.50
2	Jimmie Foxx	.40	.30	.15
3	Lefty Grove	.30	.25	.12
4	Hank Greenberg	.30	.25	.12
5	Al Simmons	.15	.11	.06
6	Carl Hubbell	.30	.25	.12
7	Joe Cronin	.25	.20	.10
8	Mel Ott	.30	.25	.12
9	Lefty Gomez	.30	.25	.12
10	Lou Gehrig	1.50	1.25	.60
11	Pie Traynor	.15	.11	.06
12	Charlie Gehringer	.30	.25	.12
13	Catchers (Mickey Cochrane, Bill Dickey, Gabby Hartnett)	.30	.25	.12
14	Pitchers (Dizzy Dean, Paul Derringer, Red Ruffing)	.30	.25	.12
15	Outfielders (Earl Averill, Joe Medwick, Paul Waner)	.15	.11	.06
16	Bob Feller	.60	.45	.25
17	Lou Boudreau	.15	.11	.06
18	Enos Slaughter	.25	.20	.10
19	Hal Newhouser	.15	.11	.06
20	Joe DiMaggio	1.50	1.25	.60
21	Pee Wee Reese	.40	.30	.15
22	Phil Rizzuto	.30	.25	.12
23	Ernie Lombardi	.15	.11	.06
24	Infielders (Joe Cronin, George Kell, Johnny Mize)	.15	.11	.06
25	Ted Williams	1.25	.90	.50
26	Mickey Mantle	3.50	2.75	1.50
27	Warren Spahn	.30	.25	.12
28	Jackie Robinson	1.00	.70	.40
29	Ernie Banks	.30	.25	.12
30	Stan Musial	1.00	.70	.40
31	Yogi Berra	.60	.45	.25
32	Duke Snider	.70	.50	.30
33	Roy Campanella	.70	.50	.30
34	Eddie Mathews	.30	.25	.12
35	Ralph Kiner	.30	.25	.12
36	Early Wynn	.25	.20	.10
37	Double Play Duo (Luis Aparicio, Nellie Fox)	.25	.20	.10
38	First Basemen (Gil Hodges, Ted Kluszewski, Mickey Vernon)	.25	.20	.10
40	Henry Aaron	1.00	.70	.40
41	Frank Robinson	.30	.25	.12
42	Bob Gibson	.30	.25	.12
43	Roberto Clemente	1.00	.70	.40
44	Whitey Ford	.40	.30	.15
45	Brooks Robinson	.50	.40	.20
46	Juan Marichal	.25	.20	.10
47	Carl Yastrzemski	1.00	.70	.40
48	First Basemen (Orlando Cepeda, Harmon Killebrew, Willie McCovey)	.30	.25	.12
49	Catchers (Bill Freehan, Elston Howard, Joe Torre)	.15	.11	.06
50	Willie Mays	1.00	.70	.40
51	Outfielders (Al Kaline, Tony Oliva, Billy Williams)	.30	.25	.12
52	Tom Seaver	.60	.45	.25
53	Reggie Jackson	.70	.50	.30
54	Steve Carlton	.40	.30	.15
55	Mike Schmidt	.70	.50	.30
56	Joe Morgan	.25	.20	.10
57	Jim Rice	.40	.30	.15
58	Jim Palmer	.30	.25	.12
59	Lou Brock	.30	.25	.12
60	Pete Rose	1.25	.90	.50
61	Steve Garvey	.40	.30	.15
62	Catchers (Carlton Fisk, Thurman Munson, Ted Simmons)	.25	.20	.10
63	Pitchers (Vida Blue, Catfish Hunter, Nolan Ryan)	.30	.25	.12
64	George Brett	.80	.60	.30
65	Don Mattingly	1.25	.90	.50
66	Fernando Valenzuela	.30	.25	.12
67	Dale Murphy	.80	.60	.30
68	Wade Boggs	1.50	1.25	.60
69	Rickey Henderson	.60	.45	.25
70	Eddie Murray	.60	.45	.25
71	Ron Guidry	.25	.20	.10
72	Catchers (Gary Carter, Lance Parrish, Tony Pena)	.30	.25	.12
73	Infielders (Cal Ripken, Jr., Lou Whitaker, Robin Yount)	.30	.25	.12
74	Outfielders (Pedro Guerrero, Tim Raines, Dave Winfield)	.30	.25	.12
75	Dwight Gooden	1.00	.70	.40

1986 Sportflics Rookies

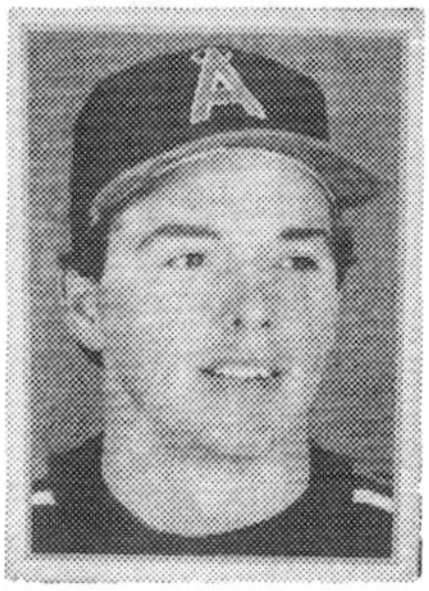

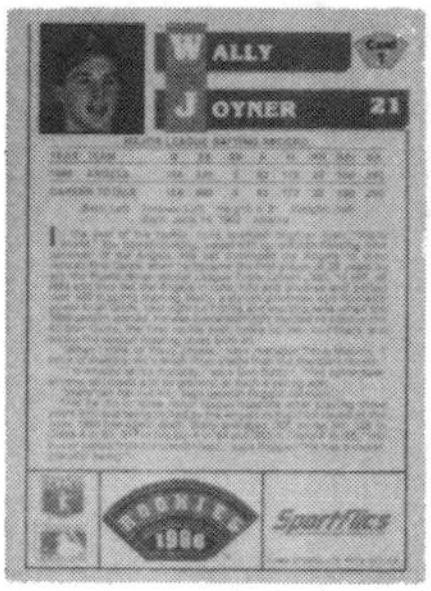

The 1986 Rookies set issued by Sportflics offers 50 cards and features 47 individual rookie players. In addition, there are two Tri-Star cards; one highlights former Rookies of the Year and the other features three prominent players. There is one "Big Six" card featuring six superstars. The full-color photos on the 2-1/2" by 3-1/2" cards use Sportflics three-phase "Magic Motion" animation. The set was packaged in an attractive collector box which also contained 34 trivia cards that measure 1-3/4" by 2". The set was distributed only by hobby dealers.

		MT	NR MT	EX
Complete Set:		18.00	13.50	7.25
Common Player:		.20	.15	.08
1	John Kruk	.80	.60	.30
2	Edwin Correa	.20	.15	.08
3	Pete Incaviglia	.25	.20	.10
4	Dale Sveum	.30	.25	.12
5	Juan Nieves	.30	.25	.12
6	Will Clark	3.00	2.25	1.25
7	Wally Joyner	2.00	1.50	.80
8	Lance McCullers	.20	.15	.08
9	Scott Bailes	.20	.15	.08
10	Dan Plesac	.40	.30	.15
11	Jose Canseco	3.00	2.25	1.25
12	Bobby Witt	.40	.30	.15
13	Barry Bonds	.70	.50	.30
14	Andres Thomas	.20	.15	.08
15	Jim Deshaies	.30	.25	.12
16	Ruben Sierra	2.00	1.50	.80
17	Steve Lombardozzi	.20	.15	.08
18	Cory Snyder	.25	.20	.10
19	Reggie Williams	.20	.15	.08
20	Mitch Williams	.20	.15	.08
21	Glenn Braggs	.30	.25	.12
22	Danny Tartabull	.80	.60	.30
23	Charlie Kerfeld	.20	.15	.08
24	Paul Assenmacher	.20	.15	.08
25	Robby Thompson	.30	.25	.12
26	Bobby Bonilla	.70	.50	.30
27	Andres Galarraga	.70	.50	.30
28	Billy Jo Robidoux	.20	.15	.08
29	Bruce Ruffin	.30	.25	.12
30	Greg Swindell	.60	.45	.25
31	John Cangelosi	.20	.15	.08
32	Jim Traber	.20	.15	.08
33	Russ Morman	.20	.15	.08
34	Barry Larkin	.60	.45	.25
35	Todd Worrell	.25	.20	.10
36	John Cerutti	.20	.15	.08
37	Mike Kingery	.20	.15	.08
38	Mark Eichhorn	.20	.15	.08
39	Scott Bankhead	.20	.15	.08
40	Bo Jackson	2.00	1.50	.80
41	Greg Mathews	.30	.25	.12
42	Eric King	.20	.15	.08
43	Kal Daniels	.80	.60	.30
44	Calvin Schiraldi	.20	.15	.08
45	Mickey Brantley	.20	.15	.08
46	Outstanding Rookie Seasons (Fred Lynn, Willie Mays, Pete Rose)	.80	.60	.30
47	Outstanding Rookie Seasons (Dwight Gooden, Tom Seaver, Fernando Valenzuela)	.80	.60	.30
48	Outstanding Rookie Seasons (Eddie Murray, Dave Righetti, Cal Ripken, Jr., Steve Sax, Darryl Strawberry, Lou Whitaker)	.60	.45	.25
49	Kevin Mitchell	2.00	1.50	.80
50	Mike Diaz	.20	.15	.08

1987 Sportflics

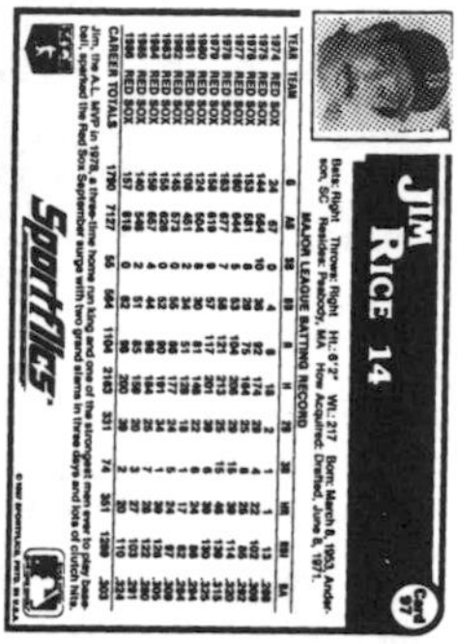

For its second season in the national baseball card market, Sportflics' basic issue was again a 200-card set of 2-1/2" by 3-1/2" "Magic Motion" cards, which offer three different photos on the same card, each visible in turn as the card is moved from top to bottom or side to side. Besides single-player cards, the '87 Sportflics set includes several three- and six-player cards, though not as many as in the 1986 set. The card backs feature a small player portrait photo on the single-player cards, an innovation for 1987.

		MT	NR MT	EX
Complete Set:		30.00	22.00	12.00
Common Player:		.10	.08	.04
1	Don Mattingly	2.00	1.50	.80
2	Wade Boggs	.70	.50	.30
3	Dale Murphy	.50	.40	.20
4	Rickey Henderson	1.00	.70	.40
5	George Brett	.70	.50	.30
6	Eddie Murray	.50	.40	.20
7	Kirby Puckett	.90	.70	.35
8	Ryne Sandberg	1.75	1.25	.70
9	Cal Ripken Jr.	1.00	.70	.40
10	Roger Clemens	1.50	1.25	.60
11	Ted Higuera	.15	.11	.06
12	Steve Sax	.20	.15	.08
13	Chris Brown	.10	.08	.04
14	Jesse Barfield	.15	.11	.06
15	Kent Hrbek	.20	.15	.08
16	Robin Yount	.30	.25	.12
17	Glenn Davis	.25	.20	.10
18	Hubie Brooks	.10	.08	.04
19	Mike Scott	.15	.11	.06
20	Darryl Strawberry	1.50	1.25	.60
21	Alvin Davis	.15	.11	.06
22	Eric Davis	.70	.50	.30
23	Danny Tartabull	.30	.25	.12
24a	Cory Snyder (Pat Tabler photo on back (facing front), 3/4 swing on front)	2.00	1.50	.80
24b	Cory Snyder (Pat Tabler photo on back (facing front), 1/4 swing on front)	2.00	1.50	.80
24c	Cory Snyder (Snyder photo on back (facing to side))	1.00	.70	.40
25	Pete Rose	1.25	.90	.50
26	Wally Joyner	1.00	.70	.40
27	Pedro Guerrero	.20	.15	.08
28	Tom Seaver	.60	.45	.25
29	Bob Knepper	.10	.08	.04
30	Mike Schmidt	1.00	.70	.40
31	Tony Gwynn	.70	.50	.30
32	Don Slaught	.10	.08	.04
33	Todd Worrell	.30	.25	.12
34	Tim Raines	.40	.30	.15
35	Dave Parker	.20	.15	.08
36	Bob Ojeda	.10	.08	.04
37	Pete Incaviglia	.50	.40	.20
38	Bruce Hurst	.15	.11	.06
39	Bobby Witt	.40	.30	.15

		MT	NR MT	EX
40	Steve Garvey	.40	.30	.15
41	Dave Winfield	.40	.30	.15
42	Jose Cruz	.10	.08	.04
43	Orel Hershiser	.40	.30	.15
44	Reggie Jackson	.70	.50	.30
45	Chili Davis	.10	.08	.04
46	Robby Thompson	.30	.25	.12
47	Dennis Boyd	.10	.08	.04
48	Kirk Gibson	.30	.25	.12
49	Fred Lynn	.20	.15	.08
50	Gary Carter	.30	.25	.12
51	George Bell	.40	.30	.15
52	Pete O'Brien	.10	.08	.04
53	Ron Darling	.15	.11	.06
54	Paul Molitor	.15	.11	.06
55	Mike Pagliarulo	.15	.11	.06
56	Mike Boddicker	.10	.08	.04
57	Dave Righetti	.20	.15	.08
58	Len Dykstra(FC)	.15	.11	.06
59	Mike Witt	.10	.08	.04
60	Tony Bernazard	.10	.08	.04
61	John Kruk	.30	.25	.12
62	Mike Krukow	.10	.08	.04
63	Sid Fernandez	.15	.11	.06
64	Gary Gaetti	.20	.15	.08
65	Vince Coleman	.30	.25	.12
66	Pat Tabler	.10	.08	.04
67	Mike Scioscia	.10	.08	.04
68	Scott Garrelts	.10	.08	.04
69	Brett Butler	.10	.08	.04
70	Bill Buckner	.10	.08	.04
71a	Dennis Rasmussen (John Montefusco photo on back)	.25	.20	.10
71b	Dennis Rasmussen (Rasmussen photo on back)	.15	.11	.06
72	Tim Wallach	.15	.11	.06
73	Bob Horner	.15	.11	.06
74	Willie McGee	.15	.11	.06
75	American League First Basemen (Wally Joyner, Don Mattingly, Eddie Murray)	1.00	.70	.40
76	Jesse Orosco	.10	.08	.04
77	National League Relief Pitchers (Jeff Reardon, Dave Smith, Todd Worrell)	.15	.11	.06
78	Candy Maldonado	.10	.08	.04
79	National League Shortstops (Hubie Brooks, Shawon Dunston, Ozzie Smith)	.15	.11	.06
80	American League Left Fielders (George Bell, Jose Canseco, Jim Rice)	1.25	.90	.50
81	Bert Blyleven	.15	.11	.06
82	Mike Marshall	.15	.11	.06
83	Ron Guidry	.20	.15	.08
84	Julio Franco	.15	.11	.06
85	Willie Wilson	.15	.11	.06
86	Lee Lacy	.10	.08	.04
87	Jack Morris	.20	.15	.08
88	Ray Knight	.10	.08	.04
89	Phil Bradley	.15	.11	.06
90	Jose Canseco	2.00	1.50	.80
91	Gary Ward	.10	.08	.04
92	Mike Easler	.10	.08	.04
93	Tony Pena	.10	.08	.04
94	Dave Smith	.10	.08	.04
95	Will Clark	2.50	2.00	1.00
96	Lloyd Moseby	.10	.08	.04
97	Jim Rice	.40	.30	.15
98	Shawon Dunston	.15	.11	.06
99	Don Sutton	.25	.20	.10
100	Dwight Gooden	1.00	.70	.40
101	Lance Parrish	.20	.15	.08
102	Mark Langston	.15	.11	.06
103	Floyd Youmans	.10	.08	.04
104	Lee Smith	.10	.08	.04
105	Willie Hernandez	.10	.08	.04
106	Doug DeCinces	.10	.08	.04
107	Ken Schrom	.10	.08	.04
108	Don Carman	.10	.08	.04
109	Brook Jacoby	.15	.11	.06
110	Steve Bedrosian	.15	.11	.06
111	American League Pitchers (Roger Clemens, Teddy Higuera, Jack Morris)	.50	.40	.20
112	American League Second Basemen (Marty Barrett, Tony Bernazard, Lou Whitaker)	.10	.08	.04
113	American League Shortstops (Tony Fernandez, Scott Fletcher, Cal Ripken)	.25	.20	.10
114	American League Third Basemen (Wade Boggs, George Brett, Gary Gaetti)	.60	.45	.25
115	National League Third Basemen (Chris Brown, Mike Schmidt, Tim Wallach)	.35	.25	.14

		MT	NR MT	EX
116	National League Second Basemen (Bill Doran, Johnny Ray, Ryne Sandberg)	.15	.11	.06
117	National League Right Fielders (Kevin Bass, Tony Gwynn, Dave Parker)	.25	.20	.10
118	Hot Rookie Prospects (David Clark, Pat Dodson, Ty Gainey, Phil Lombardi, Benito Santiago, Terry Steinbach)	1.25	.90	.50
119	1986 Season Highlights (Dave Righetti, Mike Scott, Fernando Valenzuela)	.15	.11	.06
120	National League Pitchers (Dwight Gooden, Mike Scott, Fernando Valenzuela)	.40	.30	.15
121	Johnny Ray	.10	.08	.04
122	Keith Moreland	.10	.08	.04
123	Juan Samuel	.15	.11	.06
124	Wally Backman	.10	.08	.04
125	Nolan Ryan	2.00	1.50	.80
126	Greg Harris	.10	.08	.04
127	Kirk McCaskill	.10	.08	.04
128	Dwight Evans	.15	.11	.06
129	Rick Rhoden	.10	.08	.04
130	Bill Madlock	.15	.11	.06
131	Oddibe McDowell	.10	.08	.04
132	Darrell Evans	.10	.08	.04
133	Keith Hernandez	.30	.25	.12
134	Tom Brunansky	.15	.11	.06
135	Kevin McReynolds	.20	.15	.08
136	Scott Fletcher	.10	.08	.04
137	Lou Whitaker	.20	.15	.08
138	Carney Lansford	.10	.08	.04
139	Andre Dawson	.25	.20	.10
140	Carlton Fisk	.20	.15	.08
141	Buddy Bell	.15	.11	.06
142	Ozzie Smith	.20	.15	.08
143	Dan Pasqua	.15	.11	.06
144	Kevin Mitchell	1.25	.90	.50
145	Bret Saberhagen	.25	.20	.10
146	Charlie Kerfeld	.10	.08	.04
147	Phil Niekro	.25	.20	.10
148	John Candelaria	.10	.08	.04
149	Rich Gedman	.10	.08	.04
150	Fernando Valenzuela	.30	.25	.12
151	National League Catchers (Gary Carter, Tony Pena, Mike Scioscia)	.15	.11	.06
152	National League Left Fielders (Vince Coleman, Jose Cruz, Tim Raines)	.20	.15	.08
153	American League Right Fielders (Harold Baines, Jesse Barfield, Dave Winfield)	.25	.20	.10
154	American League Catchers (Rich Gedman, Lance Parrish, Don Slaught)	.10	.08	.04
155	National League Center Fielders (Eric Davis, Kevin McReynolds, Dale Murphy)	.70	.50	.30
156	1986 Season Highlights (Jim Deshaies, Mike Schmidt, Don Sutton)	.30	.25	.12
157	American League Speedburners (John Cangelosi, Rickey Henderson, Gary Pettis)	.25	.20	.10
158	Hot Rookie Prospects (Randy Asadoor, Casey Candaele, Dave Cochrane, Rafael Palmeiro, Tim Pyznarski, Kevin Seitzer)	1.25	.90	.50
159	The Best of the Best (Roger Clemens, Dwight Gooden, Rickey Henderson, Don Mattingly, Dale Murphy, Eddie Murray)	1.25	.90	.50
160	Roger McDowell	.15	.11	.06
161	Brian Downing	.10	.08	.04
162	Bill Doran	.10	.08	.04
163	Don Baylor	.15	.11	.06
164	Alfredo Griffin	.10	.08	.04
165	Don Aase	.10	.08	.04
166	Glenn Wilson	.10	.08	.04
167	Dan Quisenberry	.10	.08	.04
168	Frank White	.10	.08	.04
169	Cecil Cooper	.15	.11	.06
170	Jody Davis	.10	.08	.04
171	Harold Baines	.20	.15	.08
172	Rob Deer	.10	.08	.04
173	John Tudor	.15	.11	.06
174	Larry Parrish	.10	.08	.04
175	Kevin Bass	.10	.08	.04
176	Joe Carter	.15	.11	.06
177	Mitch Webster	.10	.08	.04
178	Dave Kingman	.15	.11	.06
179	Jim Presley	.15	.11	.06
180	Mel Hall	.10	.08	.04
181	Shane Rawley	.10	.08	.04
182	Marty Barrett	.10	.08	.04
183	Damaso Garcia	.10	.08	.04
184	Bobby Grich	.10	.08	.04

		MT	NR MT	EX
185	Leon Durham	.10	.08	.04
186	Ozzie Guillen	.10	.08	.04
187	Tony Fernandez	.15	.11	.06
188	Alan Trammell	.30	.25	.12
189	Jim Clancy	.10	.08	.04
190	Bo Jackson	2.00	1.50	.80
191	Bob Forsch	.10	.08	.04
192	John Franco	.10	.08	.04
193	Von Hayes	.10	.08	.04
194	American League Relief Pitchers (Don Aase, Mark Eichhorn, Dave Righetti)	.10	.08	.04
195	National League First Basemen (Will Clark, Glenn Davis, Keith Hernandez)	1.00	.70	.40
196	1986 Season Highlights (Roger Clemens, Joe Cowley, Bob Horner)	.35	.25	.14
197	The Best of the Best (Wade Boggs, George Brett, Hubie Brooks, Tony Gwynn, Tim Raines, Ryne Sandberg)	.80	.60	.30
198	American League Center Fielders (Rickey Henderson, Fred Lynn, Kirby Puckett)	.25	.20	.10
199	National League Speedburners (Vince Coleman, Eric Davis, Tim Raines)	.50	.40	.20
200	Steve Carlton	.60	.45	.25

1987 Sportflics Rookie Discs

The 1987 Sportflics Rookie Discs set consists of seven discs which measure 4" in diameter. The front of the discs offer three "Magic Motion" photos in full color, encompassed by a blue border. The disc backs are printed in red, blue, yellow and green and include the team logo, player statistics, player biography and the disc number. The set was issued with Cooperstown Timeless Trivia Cards.

		MT	NR MT	EX
Complete Set:		16.00	12.00	6.50
Common Player:		1.00	.70	.40
1	Casey Candaele	1.00	.70	.40
2	Mark McGwire	3.00	2.25	1.25
3	Kevin Seitzer	1.50	1.25	.60
4	Joe Magrane	2.00	1.50	.80
5	Benito Santiago	2.50	2.00	1.00
6	Dave Magadan	2.00	1.50	.80
7	Devon White	2.50	2.00	1.00

1987 Sportflics Rookie Prospects

The 1987 Sportflics Rookie Prospects set consists of 10 cards that are the standard 2-1/2" by 3-1/2" size. The card fronts feature Sportflics' "Magic Motion" process. Card backs contain a player photo plus a short biography and player personal and statistical information. The set was offered in two separately wrapped mylar packs of five cards to hobby dealers purchasing cases of Sportflics' Team Preview set. Twenty-four packs of "Rookie Prospects" cards were included with each case.

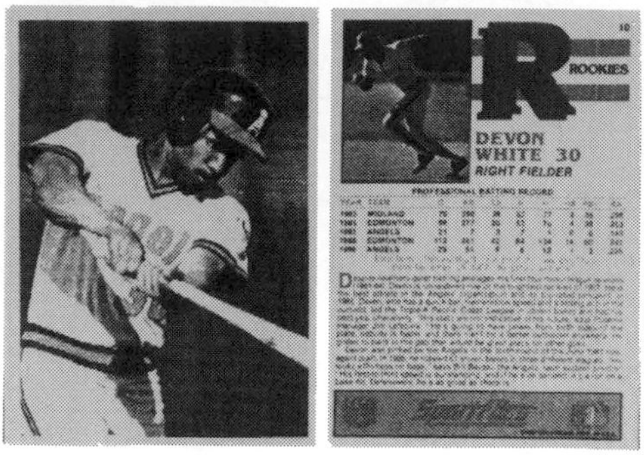

		MT	NR MT	EX
Complete Set:		6.00	4.50	2.50
Common Player:		.50	.40	.20
1	Terry Steinbach	.70	.50	.30
2	Rafael Palmeiro	1.50	1.25	.60
3	Dave Magadan	1.25	.90	.50
4	Marvin Freeman	.50	.40	.20
5	Brick Smith	.50	.40	.20
6	B.J. Surhoff	.70	.50	.30
7	John Smiley	.70	.50	.30
8	Alonzo Powell	.50	.40	.20
9	Benny Santiago	.80	.60	.30
10	Devon White	.70	.50	.30

1987 Sportflics Rookies

The 1987 Sportflics Rookies set was issued in two series of 25 cards. The first was released in July with the second series following in October. The cards, which are the standard 2-1/2" by 3-1/2", feature Sportflics' special "Magic Motion" process. The card fronts contain a full-color photo and present three different pictures, depending on how the card is held. The backs also contain a full-color photo along with player statistics and a biography.

		MT	NR MT	EX
Complete Set:		10.00	7.50	4.00
Common Player:		.20	.15	.08
1	Eric Bell	.20	.15	.08
2	Chris Bosio	.20	.15	.08
3	Bob Brower	.20	.15	.08
4	Jerry Browne	.20	.15	.08
5	Ellis Burks	.80	.60	.30
6	Casey Candaele	.20	.15	.08
7	Joey Cora	.20	.15	.08
8	Ken Gerhart	.30	.25	.12
9	Mike Greenwell	1.00	.70	.40
10	Stan Jefferson	.20	.15	.08
11	Dave Magadan	.70	.50	.30
12	Joe Magrane	.40	.30	.15
13	Fred McGriff	.80	.60	.30
14	Mark McGwire	1.00	.70	.40
15	Mark McLemore	.20	.15	.08
16	Jeff Musselman	.20	.15	.08
17	Matt Nokes	.40	.30	.15

		MT	NR MT	EX
18	Paul O'Neill	.20	.15	.08
19	Luis Polonia	.20	.15	.08
20	Benny Santiago	.80	.60	.30
21	Kevin Seitzer	.80	.60	.30
22	Terry Steinbach	.30	.25	.12
23	B.J. Surhoff	.70	.50	.30
24	Devon White	.40	.30	.15
25	Matt Williams	.70	.50	.30
26	DeWayne Buice	.20	.15	.08
27	Willie Fraser	.20	.15	.08
28	Bill Ripken	.30	.25	.12
29	Mike Henneman	.30	.25	.12
30	Shawn Hillegas	.20	.15	.08
31	Shane Mack	.20	.15	.08
32	Rafael Palmeiro	.70	.50	.30
33	Mike Jackson	.20	.15	.08
34	Gene Larkin	.20	.15	.08
35	Jimmy Jones	.20	.15	.08
36	Gerald Young	.40	.30	.15
37	Ken Caminiti	.20	.15	.08
38	Sam Horn	.60	.45	.25
39	David Cone	.70	.50	.30
40	Mike Dunne	.50	.40	.20
41	Ken Williams	.30	.25	.12
42	John Morris	.20	.15	.08
43	Jim Lindeman	.30	.25	.12
44	Todd Benzinger	.70	.50	.30
45	Mike Stanley	.30	.25	.12
46	Les Straker	.20	.15	.08
47	Jeff Robinson	.50	.40	.20
48	Jeff Blauser	.30	.25	.12
49	John Marzano	.30	.25	.12
50	Keith Miller	.30	.25	.12

1987 Sportflics Superstar Discs

Released in three series of six discs and numbered 1 through 18, the 1987 Sportflics Superstar Disc set features the special "Magic Motion" process. Each disc, which measures 4-1/2" in diameter, contains three different player photos, depending which way it is tilted. A red border, containing eleven stars, the player's name and uniform number, surrounds the photo. The backs have a turquoise border which carries the words "Superstar Disc Collector Series." The backs also include the team logo, player statistics, player biography and the disc number. The discs were issued with eighteen 1-3/4" by 2-1/2" Cooperstown Timeless Trivia Cards.

		MT	NR MT	EX
Complete Set:		55.00	41.00	22.00
Common Player:		2.00	1.50	.80
1	Jose Canseco	5.00	3.75	2.00
2	Mike Scott	2.00	1.50	.80
3	Ryne Sandberg	3.00	2.25	1.25
4	Mike Schmidt	3.00	2.25	1.25
5	Dale Murphy	2.50	2.00	1.00
6	Fernando Valenzuela	2.50	2.00	1.00
7	Tony Gwynn	3.50	2.75	1.50
8	Cal Ripken	3.50	2.75	1.50
9	Gary Carter	2.75	2.00	1.00
10	Cory Snyder	2.75	2.00	1.00
11	Kirby Puckett	3.00	2.25	1.25
12	George Brett	3.00	2.25	1.25
13	Keith Hernandez	2.00	1.50	.80
14	Rickey Henderson	4.00	3.00	1.50
15	Tim Raines	2.75	2.00	1.00
16	Bo Jackson	4.00	3.00	1.50
17	Pete Rose	4.00	3.00	1.50
18	Eric Davis	3.00	2.25	1.25

1987 Sportflics Team Preview

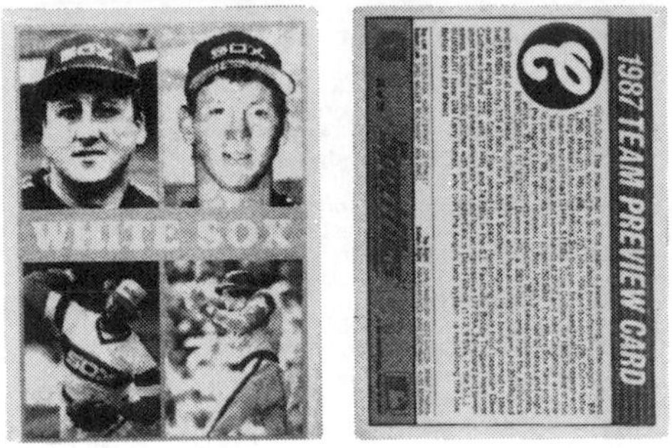

The 1987 Sportflics Team Preview set appeared to be a good idea, but never caught on with collectors. The intent of the set is to provide a pre-season look at each of the 26 major league clubs. The card backs contain three categories of the team preview Outlook, Newcomers to Watch and Summary. Using the "Magic Motion" process, 12 different players are featured on the card fronts. Four of the different player photos can be made visible at once. The cards, which measure 2-1/2" by 3-1/2", were issued with team logo/trivia cards in a specially designed box.

		MT	NR MT	EX
Complete Set:		8.00	6.00	3.25
Common Team:		.40	.30	.15
1	Texas Rangers (Scott Fletcher, Greg Harris, Charlie Hough, Pete Incaviglia, Mike Loynd, Oddibe McDowell, Pete O'Brien, Larry Parrish, Ruben Sierra, Don Slaught, Mitch Williams, Bobby Witt)	.50	.40	.20
2	New York Mets (Wally Backman, Gary Carter, Ron Darling, Lenny Dykstra, Sid Fernandez, Dwight Gooden, Keith Hernandez, Dave Magadan, Kevin McReynolds, Randy Myers, Bob Ojeda, Darryl Strawberry)	.70	.50	.30
3	Cleveland Indians (Tony Bernazard, Brett Butler, Tom Candiotti, Joe Carter, Julio Franco, Mel Hall, Brook Jacoby, Phil Niekro, Ken Schrom, Cory Snyder, Greg Swindell, Pat Tabler)	.50	.40	.20
4	Cincinnati Reds (Buddy Bell, Tom Browning, Kal Daniels, Eric Davis, John Franco, Bill Gullickson, Tracy Jones, Barry Larkin, Rob Murphy, Paul O'Neill, Dave Parker, Pete Rose)	.50	.40	.20
5	Toronto Blue Jays (Jesse Barfield, George Bell, John Cerutti, Mark Eichhorn, Tony Fernandez, Tom Henke, Glenallen Hill, Jimmy Key, Fred McGriff, Lloyd Moseby, Dave Stieb, Willie Upshaw)	.50	.40	.20
6	Philadelphia Phillies (Steve Bedrosian, Don Carman, Marvin Freeman, Kevin Gross, Von Hayes, Shane Rawley, Bruce Ruffin, Juan Samuel, Mike Schmidt, Kent Tekulve, Milt Thompson, Glenn Wilson)	.50	.40	.20
7	New York Yankees (Rickey Henderson, Phil Lombardi, Don Mattingly, Mike Pagliarulo, Dan Pasqua, Willie Randolph, Dennis Rasmussen, Rick Rhoden, Dave Righetti, Joel Skinner, Bob Tewksbury, Dave Winfield)	.80	.60	.30
8	Houston Astros (Kevin Bass, Jose Cruz, Glenn Davis, Jim Deshaies, Bill Doran, Ty Gainey, Charlie Kerfeld, Bob Knepper, Nolan Ryan, Mike Scott, Dave Smith, Robby Wine)	.40	.30	.15
9	Boston Red Sox (Marty Barrett, Don Baylor, Wade Boggs, Dennis Boyd, Roger Clemens, Pat Dodson, Dwight Evans, Mike Greenwell, Dave Henderson, Bruce Hurst, Jim Rice, Calvin Schiraldi)	.50	.40	.20
10	San Francisco Giants (Bob Brenly, Chris Brown, Will Clark, Chili Davis, Kelly Downs, Scott Garrelts, Mark Grant, Mike Krukow, Jeff Leonard, Candy Maldonado, Terry Mulholland, Robby Thompson)	.50	.40	.20

		MT	NR MT	EX
11	California Angels (John Candelaria, Doug DeCinces, Brian Downing, Ruppert Jones, Wally Joyner, Kirk McCaskill, Darrell Miller, Donnie Moore, Gary Pettis, Don Sutton, Devon White, Mike Witt)	.50	.40	.20
12	St. Louis Cardinals (Jack Clark, Vince Coleman, Danny Cox, Bob Forsch, Tom Herr, Joe Magrane, Willie McGee, Terry Pendleton, Ozzie Smith, John Tudor, Andy Van Slyke, Todd Worrell)	.50	.40	.20
13	Kansas City Royals (George Brett, Mark Gubicza, Bo Jackson, Charlie Leibrandt, Hal McRae, Dan Quisenberry, Bret Saberhagen, Kevin Seitzer, Lonnie Smith, Danny Tartabull, Frank White, Willie Wilson)	.50	.40	.20
14	Los Angeles Dodgers (Ralph Bryant, Mariano Duncan, Jose Gonzalez, Pedro Guerrero, Orel Hershiser, Mike Marshall, Steve Sax, Mike Scioscia, Franklin Stubbs, Fernando Valenzuela, Reggie Williams, Matt Young)	.50	.40	.20
15	Detroit Tigers (Darnell Coles, Darrell Evans, Kirk Gibson, Willie Hernandez, Eric King, Chet Lemon, Dwight Lowry, Jack Morris, Dan Petry, Frank Tanana, Alan Trammell, Lou Whitaker)	.50	.40	.20
16	San Diego Padres (Randy Asadoor, Steve Garvey, Tony Gwynn, Andy Hawkins, Jim Jones, John Kruk, Craig Lefferts, Shane Mack, Lance McCullers, Kevin Mitchell, Benny Santiago, Ed Wojna)	.50	.40	.20
17	Minnesota Twins (Bert Blyleven, Tom Brunansky, Gary Gaetti, Greg Gagne, Kent Hrbek, Joe Klink, Steve Lombardozzi, Kirby Puckett, Jeff Reardon, Mark Salas, Roy Smalley, Frank Viola)	.50	.40	.20
18	Pittsburgh Pirates (Barry Bonds, Bobby Bonilla, Sid Bream, Mike Diaz, Brian Fisher, Jim Morrison, Joe Orsulak, Bob Patterson, Tony Pena, Johnny Ray, R.J. Reynolds, John Smiley)	.50	.40	.20
19	Milwaukee Brewers (Glenn Braggs, Rob Deer, Teddy Higuera, Paul Molitor, Juan Nieves, Dan Plesac, Tim Pyznarski, Ernest Riles, Billy Jo Robidoux, B.J. Surhoff, Dale Sveum, Robin Yount)	.50	.40	.20
20	Montreal Expos (Hubie Brooks, Tim Burke, Casey Candaele, Dave Collins, Mike Fitzgerald, Andres Galarraga, Billy Moore, Alonzo Powell, Randy St. Claire, Tim Wallach, Mitch Webster, Floyd Youmans)	.50	.40	.20
21	Baltimore Orioles (Don Aase, Eric Bell, Mike Boddicker, Ken Gerhardt, Terry Kennedy, Ray Knight, Lee Lacy, Fred Lynn, Eddie Murray, Cal Ripken, Jr., Larry Sheets, Jim Traber)	.50	.40	.20
22	Chicago Cubs (Jody Davis, Shawon Dunston, Leon Durham, Dennis Eckersley, Greg Maddux, Dave Martinez, Keith Moreland, Jerry Mumphrey, Rafael Palmeiro, Ryne Sandberg, Scott Sanderson, Lee Smith)	.40	.30	.15
23	Oakland Athletics (Jose Canseco, Mike Davis, Alfredo Griffin, Reggie Jackson, Carney Lansford, Mark McGwire, Dwayne Murphy, Rob Nelson, Tony Phillips, Jose Rijo, Terry Steinbach, Curt Young)	.70	.50	.30
24	Atlanta Braves (Paul Assenmacher, Gene Garber, Tom Glavine, Ken Griffey, Glenn Hubbard, Dion James, Rick Mahler, Dale Murphy, Ken Oberkfell, David Palmer, Zane Smith, Andres Thomas)	.50	.40	.20
25	Seattle Mariners (Scott Bankhead, Phil Bradley, Scott Bradley, Mickey Brantley, Alvin Davis, Steve Fireovid, Mark Langston, Mike Moore, Donell Nixon, Ken Phelps, Jim Presley, Dave Valle)	.40	.30	.15
26	Chicago White Sox (Harold Baines, John Cangelosi, Dave Cochrane, Joe Cowley, Carlton Fisk, Ozzie Guillen, Ron Hassey, Bob James, Ron Karkovice, Russ Mormon, Bobby Thigpen, Greg Walker)	.40	.30	.15

1988 Sportflics

The design of the 1988 Sportflics set differs greatly from the previous two years. Besides increasing the number of cards in the set to 225, Sportflics included the player name, team and uniform number on the card front. The triple-action color photos are surrounded by a red border. The backs are

re-designed, also. Full-color action photos, plus extensive statistics and informative biographies are utilized. Three highlights cards and three rookie prospects card are included in the set. The cards are the standard 2-1/2" by 3-1/2".

		MT	NR MT	EX
Complete Set:		30.00	22.00	12.00
Common Player:		.10	.08	.04
1	Don Mattingly	1.00	.70	.40
2	Tim Raines	.35	.25	.14
3	Andre Dawson	.25	.20	.10
4	George Bell	.30	.25	.12
5	Joe Carter	.15	.11	.06
6	Matt Nokes	.50	.40	.20
7	Dave Winfield	.35	.25	.14
8	Kirby Puckett	.50	.40	.20
9	Will Clark	1.00	.70	.40
10	Eric Davis	.60	.45	.25
11	Rickey Henderson	1.00	.70	.40
12	Ryne Sandberg	1.00	.70	.40
13	Jesse Barfield	.15	.11	.06
14	Ozzie Guillen	.10	.08	.04
15	Bret Saberhagen	.20	.15	.08
16	Tony Gwynn	.40	.30	.15
17	Kevin Seitzer	.30	.25	.12
18	Jack Clark	.20	.15	.08
19	Danny Tartabull	.30	.25	.12
20	Ted Higuera	.15	.11	.06
21	Charlie Leibrandt, Jr.	.10	.08	.04
22	Benny Santiago	.50	.40	.20
23	Fred Lynn	.15	.11	.06
24	Rob Thompson	.10	.08	.04
25	Alan Trammell	.25	.20	.10
26	Tony Fernandez	.15	.11	.06
27	Rick Sutcliffe	.15	.11	.06
28	Gary Carter	.25	.20	.10
29	Cory Snyder	.20	.15	.08
30	Lou Whitaker	.20	.15	.08
31	Keith Hernandez	.25	.20	.10
32	Mike Witt	.10	.08	.04
33	Harold Baines	.15	.11	.06
34	Robin Yount	.25	.20	.10
35	Mike Schmidt	.80	.60	.30
36	Dion James	.10	.08	.04
37	Tom Candiotti	.10	.08	.04
38	Tracy Jones	.15	.11	.06
39	Nolan Ryan	1.00	.70	.40
40	Fernando Valenzuela	.25	.20	.10
41	Vance Law	.10	.08	.04
42	Roger McDowell	.10	.08	.04
43	Carlton Fisk	.15	.11	.06
44	Scott Garrelts	.10	.08	.04
45	Lee Guetterman	.10	.08	.04
46	Mark Langston	.15	.11	.06
47	Willie Randolph	.10	.08	.04
48	Bill Doran	.10	.08	.04
49	Larry Parrish	.10	.08	.04
50	Wade Boggs	.70	.50	.30
51	Shane Rawley	.10	.08	.04
52	Alvin Davis	.15	.11	.06
53	Jeff Reardon	.15	.11	.06
54	Jim Presley	.10	.08	.04
55	Kevin Bass	.10	.08	.04
56	Kevin McReynolds	.20	.15	.08
57	B.J. Surhoff	.15	.11	.06
58	Julio Franco	.15	.11	.06
59	Eddie Murray	.40	.30	.15
60	Jody Davis	.10	.08	.04
61	Todd Worrell	.15	.11	.06
62	Von Hayes	.10	.08	.04
63	Billy Hatcher	.10	.08	.04

		MT	NR MT	EX
64	John Kruk	.15	.11	.06
65	Tom Henke	.10	.08	.04
66	Mike Scott	.15	.11	.06
67	Vince Coleman	.20	.15	.08
68	Ozzie Smith	.20	.15	.08
69	Ken Williams	.20	.15	.08
70	Steve Bedrosian	.15	.11	.06
71	Luis Polonia	.20	.15	.08
72	Brook Jacoby	.15	.11	.06
73	Ron Darling	.15	.11	.06
74	Lloyd Moseby	.10	.08	.04
75	Wally Joyner	.50	.40	.20
76	Dan Quisenberry	.10	.08	.04
77	Scott Fletcher	.10	.08	.04
78	Kirk McCaskill	.10	.08	.04
79	Paul Molitor	.15	.11	.06
80	Mike Aldrete	.10	.08	.04
81	Neal Heaton	.10	.08	.04
82	Jeffrey Leonard	.10	.08	.04
83	Dave Magadan	.15	.11	.06
84	Danny Cox	.10	.08	.04
85	Lance McCullers	.10	.08	.04
86	Jay Howell	.10	.08	.04
87	Charlie Hough	.10	.08	.04
88	Gene Garber	.10	.08	.04
89	Jesse Orosco	.10	.08	.04
90	Don Robinson	.10	.08	.04
91	Willie McGee	.15	.11	.06
92	Bert Blyleven	.15	.11	.06
93	Phil Bradley	.15	.11	.06
94	Terry Kennedy	.10	.08	.04
95	Kent Hrbek	.20	.15	.08
96	Juan Samuel	.15	.11	.06
97	Pedro Guerrero	.20	.15	.08
98	Sid Bream	.10	.08	.04
99	Devon White	.30	.25	.12
100	Mark McGwire	.80	.60	.30
101	Dave Parker	.15	.11	.06
102	Glenn Davis	.20	.15	.08
103	Greg Walker	.10	.08	.04
104	Rick Rhoden	.10	.08	.04
105	Mitch Webster	.10	.08	.04
106	Lenny Dykstra	.10	.08	.04
107	Gene Larkin	.15	.11	.06
108	Floyd Youmans	.10	.08	.04
109	Andy Van Slyke	.15	.11	.06
110	Mike Scioscia	.10	.08	.04
111	Kirk Gibson	.25	.20	.10
112	Kal Daniels	.30	.25	.12
113	Ruben Sierra	.80	.60	.30
114	Sam Horn	.30	.25	.12
115	Ray Knight	.10	.08	.04
116	Jimmy Key	.10	.08	.04
117	Bo Diaz	.10	.08	.04
118	Mike Greenwell	.60	.45	.25
119	Barry Bonds	.70	.50	.30
120	Reggie Jackson	.50	.40	.20
121	Mike Pagliarulo	.15	.11	.06
122	Tommy John	.20	.15	.08
123	Bill Madlock	.15	.11	.06
124	Ken Caminiti	.30	.25	.12
125	Gary Ward	.10	.08	.04
126	Candy Maldonado	.10	.08	.04
127	Harold Reynolds	.10	.08	.04
128	Joe Magrane	.30	.25	.12
129	Mike Henneman	.25	.20	.10
130	Jim Gantner	.10	.08	.04
131	Bobby Bonilla	.15	.11	.06
132	John Farrell	.30	.25	.12
133	Frank Tanana	.10	.08	.04
134	Zane Smith	.10	.08	.04
135	Dave Righetti	.20	.15	.08
136	Rick Reuschel	.10	.08	.04
137	Dwight Evans	.15	.11	.06
138	Howard Johnson	.10	.08	.04
139	Terry Leach	.10	.08	.04
140	Casey Candaele	.10	.08	.04
141	Tom Herr	.10	.08	.04
142	Tony Pena	.10	.08	.04
143	Lance Parrish	.20	.15	.08
144	Ellis Burks	1.00	.70	.40
145	Pete O'Brien	.10	.08	.04
146	Mike Boddicker	.10	.08	.04
147	Buddy Bell	.10	.08	.04
148	Bo Jackson	1.00	.70	.40
149	Frank White	.10	.08	.04
150	George Brett	.60	.45	.25
151	Tim Wallach	.10	.08	.04
152	Cal Ripken, Jr.	.80	.60	.30
153	Brett Butler	.10	.08	.04
154	Gary Gaetti	.15	.11	.06

		MT	NR MT	EX
155	Darryl Strawberry	.80	.60	.30
156	Alfredo Griffin	.10	.08	.04
157	Marty Barrett	.10	.08	.04
158	Jim Rice	.30	.25	.12
159	Terry Pendleton	.10	.08	.04
160	Orel Hershiser	.35	.25	.14
161	Larry Sheets	.10	.08	.04
162	Dave Stewart	.10	.08	.04
163	Shawon Dunston	.15	.11	.06
164	Keith Moreland	.10	.08	.04
165	Ken Oberkfell	.10	.08	.04
166	Ivan Calderon	.10	.08	.04
167	Bob Welch	.15	.11	.06
168	Fred McGriff	.40	.30	.15
169	Pete Incaviglia	.15	.11	.06
170	Dale Murphy	.40	.30	.15
171	Mike Dunne	.25	.20	.10
172	Chili Davis	.10	.08	.04
173	Milt Thompson	.10	.08	.04
174	Terry Steinbach	.15	.11	.06
175	Oddibe McDowell	.10	.08	.04
176	Jack Morris	.20	.15	.08
177	Sid Fernandez	.15	.11	.06
178	Ken Griffey	.10	.08	.04
179	Lee Smith	.10	.08	.04
180	1987 Highlights (Juan Nieves, Kirby Puckett, Mike Schmidt)	.25	.20	.10
181	Brian Downing	.10	.08	.04
182	Andres Galarraga	.20	.15	.08
183	Rob Deer	.10	.08	.04
184	Greg Brock	.10	.08	.04
185	Doug DeCinces	.10	.08	.04
186	Johnny Ray	.10	.08	.04
187	Hubie Brooks	.10	.08	.04
188	Darrell Evans	.10	.08	.04
189	Mel Hall	.10	.08	.04
190	Jim Deshaies	.10	.08	.04
191	Dan Plesac	.15	.11	.06
192	Willie Wilson	.15	.11	.06
193	Mike LaValliere	.10	.08	.04
194	Tom Brunansky	.15	.11	.06
195	John Franco	.15	.11	.06
196	Frank Viola	.20	.15	.08
197	Bruce Hurst	.10	.08	.04
198	John Tudor	.10	.08	.04
199	Bob Forsch	.10	.08	.04
200	Dwight Gooden	.60	.45	.25
201	Jose Canseco	1.00	.70	.40
202	Carney Lansford	.10	.08	.04
203	Kelly Downs	.10	.08	.04
204	Glenn Wilson	.10	.08	.04
205	Pat Tabler	.10	.08	.04
206	Mike Davis	.10	.08	.04
207	Roger Clemens	1.00	.70	.40
208	Dave Smith	.10	.08	.04
209	Curt Young	.10	.08	.04
210	Mark Eichhorn	.10	.08	.04
211	Juan Nieves	.10	.08	.04
212	Bob Boone	.10	.08	.04
213	Don Sutton	.20	.15	.08
214	Willie Upshaw	.10	.08	.04
215	Jim Clancy	.10	.08	.04
216	Bill Ripken	.25	.20	.10
217	Ozzie Virgil	.10	.08	.04
218	Dave Concepcion	.10	.08	.04
219	Alan Ashby	.10	.08	.04
220	Mike Marshall	.15	.11	.06
221	1987 Highlights (Vince Coleman, Mark McGwire, Paul Molitor)	.50	.40	.20
222	1987 Highlights (Steve Bedrosian, Don Mattingly, Benito Santiago)	.50	.40	.20
223	Hot Rookie Prospects (Shawn Abner, Jay Buhner, Gary Thurman)	.40	.30	.15
224	Hot Rookie Prospects (Tim Crews, John Davis, Vincente Palacios)	.30	.25	.12
225	Hot Rookie Prospects (Keith Miller, Jody Reed, Jeff Treadway)	.50	.40	.20

1988 Sportflics Gamewinners

This set of 25 standard-size cards (2-1/2" by 3-1/2"), featuring star players in the Sportflics patented 3-D Magic Motion design, was issued by Weiser Card Co. of Plainsboro, N.J., for use as a youth organizational fundraiser. (Weiser's president is former Yankees outfielder Bobby Murcer.) A limited number of sets was produced for test marketing in the Northwestern U.S., with plans for a 1989 set to be marketed nationwide. A green-and-yellow

Gamewinners logo banner spans the upper border of the cards face, with a matching player name (with uniform number and position) below the full-color triple photo. The card backs carry large full-color player photos (1-3/4" by 1-3/4"), along with stats, personal information and career high-lights.

		MT	NR MT	EX
Complete Set:		10.00	7.50	4.00
Common Player:		.20	.15	.08
1	Don Mattingly	2.00	1.50	.80
2	Mark McGwire	.80	.60	.30
3	Wade Boggs	.80	.60	.30
4	Will Clark	.60	.45	.25
5	Eric Davis	.80	.60	.30
6	Willie Randolph	.20	.15	.08
7	Dave Winfield	.50	.40	.20
8	Rickey Henderson	.60	.45	.25
9	Dwight Gooden	.80	.60	.30
10	Benny Santiago	.40	.30	.15
11	Keith Hernandez	.40	.30	.15
12	Juan Samuel	.30	.25	.12
13	Kevin Seitzer	.60	.45	.25
14	Gary Carter	.50	.40	.20
15	Darryl Strawberry	.80	.60	.30
16	Rick Rhoden	.20	.15	.08
17	Howard Johnson	.20	.15	.08
18	Matt Nokes	.50	.40	.20
19	Dave Righetti	.30	.25	.12
20	Roger Clemens	.80	.60	.30
21	Mike Schmidt	1.00	.70	.40
22	Kevin McReynolds	.30	.25	.12
23	Mike Pagliarulo	.20	.15	.08
24	Kevin Elster	.20	.15	.08
25	Jack Clark	.30	.25	.12

1989 Sportflics

This basic issue includes 225 standard-size player cards (2-1/2" by 3-1/2") and 153 trivia cards, all featuring the patented Magic Motion design. A 5-card sub-set of triple photo cards called "Tri-Star" features a mix of veterans and rookies. The card fronts feature a white outer border and double color inner border in one of six color schemes (i.e. red, blue, purple). The inner border color changes when the card is tilted and the bottom border carries a double stripe of colors. The player name appears in the top border, player postition and uniform number appear, alternately, in the bottom border. The card backs contain crisp 1-7/8" by 1-3/4" player action shots, along with personal information, stats and career highlights. "The Unforgettables" trivia cards in this set salute members of the Hall of Fame.

		MT	NR MT	EX
Complete Set:		30.00	22.00	12.50
Common Player:		.10	.08	.04
1	Jose Canseco	1.50	1.25	.60
2	Wally Joyner	.40	.30	.15
3	Roger Clemens	.60	.45	.25
4	Greg Swindell	.15	.11	.06
5	Jack Morris	.20	.15	.08
6	Mickey Brantley	.10	.08	.04
7	Jim Presley	.15	.11	.06
8	Pete O'Brien	.10	.08	.04
9	Jesse Barfield	.15	.11	.06
10	Frank Viola	.20	.15	.08
11	Kevin Bass	.10	.08	.04
12	Glenn Wilson	.10	.08	.04
13	Chris Sabo	.60	.45	.25
14	Fred McGriff	.50	.40	.20
15	Mark Grace	1.00	.70	.40
16	Devon White	.20	.15	.08
17	Juan Samuel	.15	.11	.06
18	Lou Whitaker	.25	.20	.10
19	Greg Walker	.10	.08	.04
20	Roberto Alomar	.50	.40	.20
21	Mike Schmidt	.60	.45	.25
22	Benny Santiago	.25	.20	.10
23	Dave Stewart	.10	.08	.04
24	Dave Winfield	.35	.25	.14
25	George Bell	.30	.25	.12
26	Jack Clark	.20	.15	.08
27	Doug Drabek	.10	.08	.04
28	Ron Gant	.15	.11	.06
29	Glenn Braggs	.10	.08	.04
30	Rafael Palmeiro	.20	.15	.08
31	Brett Butler	.10	.08	.04
32	Ron Darling	.15	.11	.06
33	Alvin Davis	.15	.11	.06
34	Bob Walk	.10	.08	.04
35	Dave Stieb	.15	.11	.06
36	Orel Hershiser	.40	.30	.15
37	John Farrell	.15	.11	.06
38	Doug Jones	.10	.08	.04
39	Kelly Downs	.10	.08	.04
40	Bob Boone	.10	.08	.04
41	Gary Sheffield	.80	.60	.30
42	Doug Dascenzo	.30	.25	.12
43	Chad Krueter	.20	.15	.08
44	Ricky Jordan	.50	.40	.20
45	Dave West	.30	.25	.12
46	Danny Tartabull	.30	.25	.12
47	Teddy Higuera	.15	.11	.06
48	Gary Gaetti	.15	.11	.06
49	Dave Parker	.15	.11	.06
50	Don Mattingly	.80	.60	.30
51	David Cone	.25	.20	.10
52	Kal Daniels	.25	.20	.10
53	Carney Lansford	.10	.08	.04
54	Mike Marshall	.15	.11	.06
55	Kevin Seitzer	.30	.25	.12
56	Mike Henneman	.10	.08	.04
57	Bill Doran	.10	.08	.04
58	Steve Sax	.20	.15	.08
59	Lance Parrish	.15	.11	.06
60	Keith Hernandez	.25	.20	.10
61	Jose Uribe	.10	.08	.04
62	Jose Lind	.15	.11	.06
63	Steve Bedrosian	.15	.11	.06
64	George Brett	.60	.45	.25
65	Kirk Gibson	.25	.20	.10
66	Cal Ripken, Jr.	.60	.45	.25
67	Mitch Webster	.10	.08	.04
68	Fred Lynn	.15	.11	.06
69	Eric Davis	.50	.40	.20
70	Bo Jackson	1.75	1.25	.70
71	Kevin Elster	.15	.11	.06
72	Rick Reuschel	.10	.08	.04
73	Tim Burke	.10	.08	.04
74	Mark Davis	.10	.08	.04
75	Claudell Washington	.10	.08	.04
76	Lance McCullers	.10	.08	.04
77	Mike Moore	.10	.08	.04
78	Robby Thompson	.10	.08	.04
79	Roger McDowell	.10	.08	.04
80	Danny Jackson	.15	.11	.06
81	Tim Leary	.10	.08	.04
82	Bobby Witt	.15	.11	.06
83	Jim Gott	.10	.08	.04
84	Andy Hawkins	.10	.08	.04
85	Ozzie Guillen	.10	.08	.04
86	John Tudor	.15	.11	.06
87	Todd Burns	.25	.20	.10
88	Dave Gallagher	.25	.20	.10
89	Jay Buhner	.15	.11	.06
90	Gregg Jefferies	.80	.60	.30
91	Bob Welch	.15	.11	.06
92	Charlie Hough	.10	.08	.04
93	Tony Fernandez	.15	.11	.06
94	Ozzie Virgil	.10	.08	.04
95	Andre Dawson	.25	.20	.10
96	Hubie Brooks	.10	.08	.04
97	Kevin McReynolds	.20	.15	.08
98	Mike LaValliere	.10	.08	.04
99	Terry Pendleton	.10	.08	.04
100	Wade Boggs	.80	.60	.30
101	Dennis Eckersley	.15	.11	.06
102	Mark Gubicza	.15	.11	.06
103	Frank Tanana	.10	.08	.04
104	Joe Carter	.15	.11	.06
105	Ozzie Smith	.20	.15	.08
106	Dennis Martinez	.10	.08	.04
107	Jeff Treadway	.15	.11	.06
108	Greg Maddux	.15	.11	.06
109	Bret Saberhagen	.20	.15	.08
110	Dale Murphy	.40	.30	.15
111	Rob Deer	.10	.08	.04
112	Pete Incaviglia	.15	.11	.06
113	Vince Coleman	.20	.15	.08
114	Tim Wallach	.15	.11	.06
115	Nolan Ryan	1.00	.70	.40
116	Walt Weiss	.35	.25	.14
117	Brian Downing	.10	.08	.04
118	Melido Perez	.15	.11	.06

		MT	NR MT	EX
119	Terry Steinbach	.15	.11	.06
120	Mike Scott	.15	.11	.06
121	Tim Belcher	.15	.11	.06
122	Mike Boddicker	.10	.08	.04
123	Len Dykstra	.10	.08	.04
124	Fernando Valenzuela	.25	.20	.10
125	Gerald Young	.15	.11	.06
126	Tom Henke	.10	.08	.04
127	Dave Henderson	.10	.08	.04
128	Dan Plesac	.15	.11	.06
129	Chili Davis	.10	.08	.04
130	Bryan Harvey	.25	.20	.10
131	Don August	.15	.11	.06
132	Mike Harkey	.50	.40	.20
133	Luis Polonia	.10	.08	.04
134	Craig Worthington	.25	.20	.10
135	Joey Meyer	.15	.11	.06
136	Barry Larkin	.25	.20	.10
137	Glenn Davis	.20	.15	.08
138	Mike Scioscia	.10	.08	.04
139	Andres Galarraga	.20	.15	.08
140	Doc Gooden	.60	.45	.25
141	Keith Moreland	.10	.08	.04
142	Kevin Mitchell	.10	.08	.04
143	Mike Greenwell	.40	.30	.15
144	Mel Hall	.10	.08	.04
145	Rickey Henderson	.50	.40	.20
146	Barry Bonds	.20	.15	.08
147	Eddie Murray	.40	.30	.15
148	Lee Smith	.10	.08	.04
149	Julio Franco	.15	.11	.06
150	Tim Raines	.35	.25	.14
151	Mitch Williams	.10	.08	.04
152	Tim Laudner	.10	.08	.04
153	Mike Pagliarulo	.15	.11	.06
154	Floyd Bannister	.10	.08	.04
155	Gary Carter	.25	.20	.10
156	Kirby Puckett	.40	.30	.15
157	Harold Baines	.20	.15	.08
158	Dave Righetti	.20	.15	.08
159	Mark Langston	.15	.11	.06
160	Tony Gwynn	.50	.40	.20
161	Tom Brunansky	.15	.11	.06
162	Vance Law	.10	.08	.04
163	Kelly Gruber	.10	.08	.04
164	Gerald Perry	.15	.11	.06
165	Harold Reynolds	.10	.08	.04
166	Andy Van Slyke	.15	.11	.06
167	Jimmy Key	.15	.11	.06
168	Jeff Reardon	.15	.11	.06
169	Milt Thompson	.10	.08	.04
170	Will Clark	.80	.60	.30
171	Chet Lemon	.10	.08	.04
172	Pat Tabler	.10	.08	.04
173	Jim Rice	.30	.25	.12
174	Billy Hatcher	.10	.08	.04
175	Bruce Hurst	.15	.11	.06
176	John Franco	.15	.11	.06
177	Van Snider	.25	.20	.10
178	Ron Jones	.25	.20	.10
179	Jerald Clark	.30	.25	.12
180	Tom Browning	.15	.11	.06
181	Von Hayes	.10	.08	.04
182	Bobby Bonilla	.15	.11	.06
183	Todd Worrell	.15	.11	.06
184	John Kruk	.15	.11	.06
185	Scott Fletcher	.10	.08	.04
186	Willie Wilson	.15	.11	.06
187	Jody Davis	.10	.08	.04
188	Kent Hrbek	.20	.15	.08
189	Ruben Sierra	.35	.25	.14
190	Shawon Dunston	.15	.11	.06
191	Ellis Burks	.50	.40	.20
192	Brook Jacoby	.15	.11	.06
193	Jeff Robinson	.15	.11	.06
194	Rich Dotson	.10	.08	.04
195	Johnny Ray	.10	.08	.04
196	Cory Snyder	.25	.20	.10
197	Mike Witt	.10	.08	.04
198	Marty Barrett	.10	.08	.04
199	Robin Yount	.30	.25	.12
200	Mark McGwire	.50	.40	.20
201	Ryne Sandberg	.80	.60	.30
202	John Candelaria	.10	.08	.04
203	Matt Nokes	.20	.15	.08
204	Dwight Evans	.15	.11	.06
205	Darryl Strawberry	.60	.45	.25
206	Willie McGee	.15	.11	.06
207	Bobby Thigpen	.15	.11	.06
208	B.J. Surhoff	.15	.11	.06
209	Paul Molitor	.15	.11	.06
210	Jody Reed	.15	.11	.06
211	Doyle Alexander	.10	.08	.04
212	Dennis Rasmussen	.15	.11	.06
213	Kevin Gross	.10	.08	.04
214	Kirk McCaskill	.10	.08	.04
215	Alan Trammell	.30	.25	.12
216	Damon Berryhill	.15	.11	.06
217	Rick Sutcliffe	.15	.11	.06
218	Don Slaught	.10	.08	.04
219	Carlton Fisk	.30	.25	.12
220	Allan Anderson	.10	.08	.04
221	1988 Highlights (Wade Boggs, Jose Canseco, Mike Greenwell)	1.50	1.25	.60
222	1988 Highlights (Tom Browning, Dennis Eckersley, Orel Hershiser)	.25	.20	.10
223	Hot Rookie Prospects (Sandy Alomar, Gregg Jefferies, Gary Sheffield)	4.00	3.00	1.50
224	Hot Rookie Prospects (Randy Johnson, Ramon Martinez, Bob Milacki)	1.50	1.25	.60
225	Hot Rookie Prospects (Geronimo Berroa, Cameron Drew, Ron Jones)	.25	.20	.10

1990 Sportflics

The Sportflics set for 1990 again contained 225 cards. The cards feature the unique "Magic Motion" effect which displays either of two different photos depending on how the card is tilted. (Previous years' sets had used three photos per card.) The two-photo "Magic Motion" sequence is designed to depict sequential game-action, showing a batter following through on his swing, a pitcher completing his motion, etc. Sportflics also added a moving red and yellow "marquee" border on the cards to compliment the animation effect. The player's name, which appears below the animation, remains stationary. The set includes 19 special rookie cards. The backs contain a color player photo, team logo, player information and stats. The cards were distributed in non-transparent mylar packs with small MVP trivia cards.

		MT	NR MT	EX
Complete Set:		25.00	20.00	10.00
Common Player:		.10	.08	.04
1	Kevin Mitchell	.40	.30	.15
2	Wade Boggs	.50	.40	.20
3	Cory Snyder	.10	.08	.04
4	Paul O'Neill	.10	.08	.04
5	Will Clark	.80	.60	.30
6	Tony Fernandez	.10	.08	.04
7	Ken Griffey, Jr.	3.00	2.25	1.25
8	Nolan Ryan	1.00	.70	.40
9	Rafael Palmeiro	.10	.08	.04
10	Jesse Barfield	.10	.08	.04
11	Kirby Puckett	.40	.30	.15
12	Steve Sax	.10	.08	.04
13	Fred McGriff	.40	.30	.15
14	Gregg Jefferies	.50	.40	.20
15	Mark Grace	.90	.70	.35
16	Devon White	.10	.08	.04
17	Juan Samuel	.15	.11	.06
18	Robin Yount	.25	.20	.10
19	Glenn Davis	.10	.08	.04
20	Jeffrey Leonard	.10	.08	.04
21	Chili Davis	.10	.08	.04
22	Craig Biggio	.70	.50	.30
23	Jose Canseco	.50	.40	.20
24	Derek Lilliquist	.20	.15	.08
25	Chris Bosio	.10	.08	.04
26	Dave Steib	.10	.08	.04
27	Bobby Thigpen	.10	.08	.04
28	Jack Clark	.10	.08	.04
29	Kevin Ritz	.20	.15	.08
30	Tom Gordon	.40	.30	.15
31	Bryan Harvey	.10	.08	.04
32	Jim Deshaies	.10	.08	.04
33	Terry Steinbach	.15	.11	.06
34	Tom Glavine	.15	.11	.06
35	Bob Welch	.10	.08	.04
36	Charlie Hayes	.20	.15	.08
37	Jeff Reardon	.10	.08	.04
38	Joe Orsulak	.10	.08	.04
39	Scott Garrelts	.10	.08	.04
40	Bob Boone	.10	.08	.04
41	Scott Bankhead	.10	.08	.04
42	Tom Henke	.10	.08	.04
43	Greg Briley	.40	.30	.15

		MT	NR MT	EX
44	Teddy Higuera	.10	.08	.04
45	Pat Borders	.10	.08	.04
46	Kevin Seitzer	.15	.11	.06
47	Bruce Hurst	.15	.11	.06
48	Ozzie Guillen	.10	.08	.04
49	Wally Joyner	.50	.40	.20
50	Mike Greenwell	.40	.30	.15
51	Gary Gaetti	.12	.09	.05
52	Gary Sheffield	.50	.40	.20
53	Dennis Martinez	.10	.08	.04
54	Ryne Sandberg	.40	.30	.15
55	Mike Scott	.12	.09	.05
56	Todd Benzinger	.10	.08	.04
57	Kelly Gruber	.15	.11	.06
58	Jose Lind	.10	.08	.04
59	Allan Anderson	.10	.08	.04
60	Robby Thompson	.10	.08	.04
61	John Smoltz	.30	.25	.12
62	Mark Davis	.12	.09	.05
63	Tom Herr	.10	.08	.06
64	Randy Johnson	.20	.15	.08
65	Lonnie Smith	.10	.08	.04
66	Pedro Guerrero	.15	.11	.06
67	Jerome Walton	.50	.40	.20
68	Ramon Martinez	.60	.45	.25
69	Tim Raines	.12	.09	.05
70	Matt Williams	.20	.15	.08
71	Joe Oliver	.20	.15	.08
72	Nick Esasky	.12	.09	.05
73	Kevin Brown	.25	.20	.10
74	Walt Weiss	.12	.09	.05
75	Roger McDowell	.10	.08	.04
76	Jose DeLeon	.10	.08	.04
77	Brian Downing	.10	.08	.04
78	Jay Howell	.10	.08	.04
79	Jose Uribe	.10	.08	.04
80	Ellis Burks	.50	.40	.20
81	Sammy Sosa	.50	.40	.20
82	Johnny Ray	.20	.15	.08
83	Danny Darwin	.10	.08	.04
84	Carney Lansford	.12	.09	.05
85	Jose Oquendo	.10	.08	.04
86	John Cerutti	.10	.08	.04
87	Dave Winfield	.15	.11	.08
88	Dave Righetti	.10	.08	.04
89	Danny Jackson	.10	.08	.04
90	Andy Benes	.40	.30	.15
91	Tom Browning	.10	.08	.04
92	Pete O'Brien	.10	.08	.04
93	Roberto Alomar	.15	.11	.06
94	Bret Saberhagen	.15	.11	.06
95	Phil Bradley	.10	.08	.04
96	Doug Jones	.10	.08	.04
97	Eric Davis	.40	.30	.15
98	Tony Gwynn	.40	.30	.15
99	Jim Abbott	.40	.30	.15
100	Cal Ripken, Jr.	.15	.11	.06
101	Andy Van Slyke	.12	.09	.05
102	Dan Plesac	.10	.08	.04
103	Lou Whitaker	.10	.08	.04
104	Steve Bedrosian	.10	.08	.04
105	Dave Gallagher	.10	.08	.04
106	Keith Hernandez	.10	.08	.04
107	Duane Ward	.10	.08	.04
108	Andre Dawson	.15	.11	.08
109	Howard Johnson	.20	.15	.08
110	Mark Langston	.12	.09	.05
111	Jerry Browne	.10	.08	.04
112	Alvin Davis	.10	.08	.04
113	Sid Fernandez	.10	.08	.04
114	Mike Devereaux	.10	.08	.04
115	Benny Santiago	.12	.09	.05
116	Bip Roberts	.10	.08	.04
117	Craig Worthington	.15	.11	.06
118	Kevin Elster	.10	.08	.04
119	Harold Reynolds	.10	.08	.04
120	Joe Carter	.15	.11	.06
121	Brian Harper	.10	.08	.04
122	Frank Viola	.15	.11	.06
123	Jeff Ballard	.10	.08	.04
124	John Kruk	.10	.08	.04
125	Harold Baines	.10	.08	.04
126	Tom Candiotti	.10	.08	.04
127	Kevin McReynolds	.15	.11	.06
128	Mookie Wilson	.10	.08	.04
129	Danny Tartabull	.12	.09	.05
130	Craig Lefferts	.10	.08	.04
131	Jose DeJesus	.15	.11	.06
132	John Orton	.30	.20	.10
133	Curt Schilling	.20	.15	.08
134	Marquis Grissom	.70	.50	.30
135	Greg Vaughn	.80	.60	.30
136	Brett Butler	.10	.08	.04
137	Rob Deer	.10	.08	.04
138	John Franco	.10	.08	.04
139	Keith Moreland	.10	.08	.04
140	Dave Smith	.10	.08	.04
141	Mark McGwire	.60	.45	.25
142	Vince Coleman	.15	.11	.06
143	Barry Bonds	.15	.11	.06
144	Mike Henneman	.10	.08	.04
145	Doc Gooden	.30	.25	.12
146	Darryl Strawberry	.50	.40	.20
147	Von Hayes	.10	.08	.04
148	Andres Galarraga	.12	.09	.05
149	Roger Clemens	.25	.20	.10
150	Don Mattingly	.80	.60	.30
151	Joe Magrane	.10	.08	.04
152	Dwight Smith	.60	.45	.25
153	Ricky Jordan	.30	.25	.12
154	Alan Trammell	.10	.08	.04
155	Brook Jacoby	.10	.08	.04
156	Lenny Dykstra	.10	.08	.04
157	Mike LaValliere	.10	.08	.04
158	Julio Franco	.12	.09	.05
159	Joey Belle	.80	.60	.30
160	Barry Larkin	.15	.11	.06
161	Rick Reuschel	.10	.08	.04
162	Nelson Santovenia	.10	.08	.04
163	Mike Scioscia	.10	.08	.04
164	Damon Berryhill	.10	.08	.04
165	Todd Worrell	.10	.08	.04
166	Jim Eisenreich	.10	.08	.04
167	Ivan Calderon	.10	.08	.04
168	Goose Gozzo	.25	.20	.10
169	Kirk McCaskill	.10	.08	.04
170	Dennis Eckersley	.10	.08	.04
171	Mickey Tettleton	.12	.09	.05
172	Chuck Finley	.10	.08	.04
173	Dave Magadan	.10	.08	.04
174	Terry Pendleton	.10	.08	.04
175	Willie Randolph	.10	.08	.04
176	Jeff Huson	.25	.20	.10
177	Todd Zeile	.70	.50	.30
178	Steve Olin	.40	.30	.15
179	Eric Anthony	.60	.45	.25
180	Scott Coolbaugh	.30	.25	.12
181	Rick Sutcliffe	.10	.08	.04
182	Tim Wallach	.10	.08	.04
183	Paul Molitor	.12	.09	.05
184	Roberto Kelly	.12	.09	.05
185	Mike Moore	.10	.08	.04
186	Junior Felix	.40	.30	.15
187	Mike Schooler	.10	.08	.04
188	Ruben Sierra	.40	.30	.15
189	Dale Murphy	.12	.09	.05
190	Dan Gladden	.10	.08	.04
191	John Smiley	.10	.08	.04
192	Jeff Russell	.10	.08	.04
193	Bert Blyleven	.10	.08	.04
194	Dave Stewart	.12	.09	.05
195	Bobby Bonilla	.12	.09	.05
196	Mitch Williams	.10	.08	.04
197	Orel Hershiser	.20	.15	.08
198	Kevin Bass	.10	.08	.04
199	Tim Burke	.10	.08	.04
200	Bo Jackson	1.00	.70	.40
201	David Cone	.12	.09	.05
202	Gary Pettis	.10	.08	.04
203	Kent Hrbek	.10	.08	.04
204	Carlton Fisk	.10	.08	.04
205	Bob Geren	.20	.15	.08
206	Bill Spiers	.25	.20	.10
207	Oddibe McDowell	.10	.08	.04
208	Rickey Henderson	.40	.30	.15
209	Ken Caminiti	.10	.08	.04
210	Devon White	.10	.08	.04
211	Greg Maddux	.15	.11	.06
212	Ed Whitson	.10	.08	.04
213	Carlos Martinez	.25	.20	.10
214	George Brett	.25	.20	.10
215	Gregg Olson	.50	.40	.20
216	Kenny Rogers	.20	.15	.08
217	Dwight Evans	.10	.08	.04
218	Pat Tabler	.10	.08	.04
219	Jeff Treadway	.10	.08	.04
220	Scott Fletcher	.10	.08	.04
221	Deion Sanders	.70	.50	.30
222	Robin Ventura	1.00	.70	.40
223	Chip Hale	.20	.15	.08
224	Tommy Greene	.40	.30	.15
225	Dean Palmer	.50	.40	.20

T

1948 Topps Magic Photos

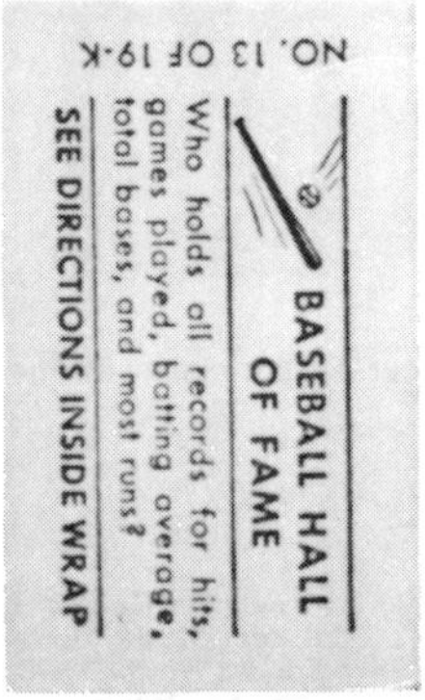

The first Topps baseball cards appeared as a subset of 19 cards from an issue of 252 "Magic Photos." The set takes its name from the self-developing nature of the cards. The cards were blank on the front when first taken from the wrapper. By spitting on the wrapper and holding it to the card while exposing it to light the black and white photo appeared. Measuring 7/8" by 1-1/2," the cards are very similar to Topps 1956 "Hocus Focus" issue.

		NR MT	EX	VG
Complete Set:		750.00	375.00	225.00
Common Player:		10.00	5.00	3.00
1	Lou Boudreau	20.00	10.00	6.00
2	Cleveland Indians	10.00	5.00	3.00
3	Bob Eliott	15.00	7.50	4.50
4	Cleveland Indians 4-3	10.00	5.00	3.00
5	Cleveland Indians 4-1 (Lou Boudreau Scoring)	20.00	10.00	6.00
6	"Babe" Ruth 714	200.00	100.00	60.00
7	Tris Speaker 793	25.00	12.50	7.50
8	Rogers Hornsby	50.00	25.00	15.00
9	Connie Mack	40.00	20.00	12.00
10	Christy Mathewson	50.00	25.00	15.00
11	Hans Wagner	50.00	25.00	15.00
12	Grover Alexander	30.00	15.00	9.00
13	Ty Cobb	100.00	50.00	30.00
14	Lou Gehrig	100.00	50.00	30.00
15	Walter Johnson	50.00	25.00	15.00
16	Cy Young	30.00	15.00	9.00
17	George Sisler 257	20.00	10.00	6.00
18	Tinker and Evers	20.00	10.00	6.00
19	Third Base Cleveland Indians	10.00	5.00	3.00

1951 Topps Blue Backs

Sold two cards in a package with a piece of candy for 1¢, the Topps Blue Backs are more scarce then their Red Back counterparts. The 2" by 2-5/8" cards carry a black and white player photograph on a red, white, yellow and green background along with the player's name and other information including their 1950 record on the front. The back is printed in blue on a white background. The 52-card set has varied baseball situations on them, making the playing of a rather elementary game of baseball possible. Although scarce, Blue Backs were printed on thick cardboard and have survived quite well over the years. There are, however, few stars (Johnny Mize and Enos Slaughter are two) in the set. Despite being a Topps product, Blue Backs do not currently enjoy great popularity.

		NR MT	EX	VG
Complete Set:		2100.00	1050.00	630.00
Common Player:		30.00	15.00	9.00
1	Eddie Yost	30.00	15.00	9.00
2	Henry (Hank) Majeski	30.00	15.00	9.00
3	Richie Ashburn	50.00	25.00	15.00
4	Del Ennis	30.00	15.00	9.00
5	Johnny Pesky	25.00	12.50	7.50
6	Albert (Red) Schoendienst	35.00	17.50	10.50
7	Gerald Staley	30.00	15.00	9.00
8	Dick Sisler	30.00	15.00	9.00
9	Johnny Sain	35.00	17.50	10.50
10	Joe Page	30.00	15.00	9.00
11	Johnny Groth	30.00	15.00	9.00
12	Sam Jethroe	30.00	15.00	9.00
13	James (Mickey) Vernon	25.00	12.50	7.50
14	George Munger	30.00	15.00	9.00
15	Eddie Joost	30.00	15.00	9.00
16	Murry Dickson	30.00	15.00	9.00
17	Roy Smalley	30.00	15.00	9.00
18	Ned Garver	30.00	15.00	9.00
19	Phil Masi	30.00	15.00	9.00
20	Ralph Branca	30.00	15.00	9.00
21	Billy Johnson	30.00	15.00	9.00
22	Bob Kuzava	30.00	15.00	9.00
23	Paul (Dizzy) Trout	30.00	15.00	9.00
24	Sherman Lollar	30.00	15.00	9.00
25	Sam Mele	30.00	15.00	9.00
26	Chico Carresquel (Carrasquel)	30.00	15.00	9.00
27	Andy Pafko	25.00	12.50	7.50
28	Harry (The Cat) Brecheen	30.00	15.00	9.00
29	Granville Hamner	30.00	15.00	9.00
30	Enos (Country) Slaughter	60.00	30.00	18.00
31	Lou Brissie	30.00	15.00	9.00
32	Bob Elliott	30.00	15.00	9.00
33	Don Lenhardt	30.00	15.00	9.00
34	Earl Torgeson	30.00	15.00	9.00
35	Tommy Byrne	30.00	15.00	9.00
36	Cliff Fannin	30.00	15.00	9.00
37	Bobby Doerr	55.00	27.00	16.50
38	Irv Noren	30.00	15.00	9.00
39	Ed Lopat	30.00	15.00	9.00
40	Vic Wertz	25.00	12.50	7.50
41	Johnny Schmitz	30.00	15.00	9.00
42	Bruce Edwards	30.00	15.00	9.00
43	Willie (Puddin' Head) Jones	30.00	15.00	9.00
44	Johnny Wyrostek	30.00	15.00	9.00
45	Bill Pierce	25.00	12.50	7.50
46	Gerry Priddy	30.00	15.00	9.00
47	Herman Wehmeier	30.00	15.00	9.00
48	Billy Cox	30.00	15.00	9.00
49	Henry (Hank) Sauer	30.00	15.00	9.00
50	Johnny Mize	60.00	30.00	18.00
51	Eddie Waitkus	30.00	15.00	9.00
52	Sam Chapman	30.00	15.00	9.00

1951 Topps Red Backs

Like the Blue Backs, the Topps Red Backs which

were sold at the same time, came two to a package for 1¢. Their black and white photographs appear on a red, white, blue and yellow background. The back printing is red on white. Their 2" by 2-5/8" size is the same as Blue Backs. Also identical is the set size (52 cards) and the game situations to be found on the fronts of the cards, for use in playing a card game of baseball. Red Backs are more common than the Blue Backs by virtue of a recent discovery of a large hoard of unopened boxes.

		NR MT	EX	VG
Complete Set:		750.00	375.00	230.00
Common Player:		9.00	4.50	2.75
1	Larry (Yogi) Berra	75.00	38.00	23.50
2	Sid Gordon	5.00	2.50	1.50
3	Ferris Fain	9.00	4.50	2.75
4	Verne Stephens (Vern)	9.00	4.50	2.75
5	Phil Rizzuto	25.00	12.50	7.50
6	Allie Reynolds	10.00	5.00	3.00
7	Howie Pollet	5.00	2.50	1.50
8	Early Wynn	25.00	12.50	7.50
9	Roy Sievers	9.00	4.50	2.75
10	Mel Parnell	9.00	4.50	2.75
11	Gene Hermanski	5.00	2.50	1.50
12	Jim Hegan	5.00	2.50	1.50
13	Dale Mitchell	5.00	2.50	1.50
14	Wayne Terwilliger	5.00	2.50	1.50
15	Ralph Kiner	25.00	12.50	7.50
16	Preacher Roe	8.00	4.00	2.50
17	Dave Bell	8.00	4.00	2.50
18	Gerry Coleman	8.00	4.00	2.50
19	Dick Kokos	5.00	2.50	1.50
20	Dominick DiMaggio (Dominic)	10.00	5.00	3.00
21	Larry Jansen	5.00	2.50	1.50
22	Bob Feller	25.00	12.50	7.50
23	Ray Boone	9.00	4.50	2.75
24	Hank Bauer	10.00	5.00	3.00
25	Cliff Chambers	5.00	2.50	1.50
26	Luke Easter	9.00	4.50	2.75
27	Wally Westlake	5.00	2.50	1.50
28	Elmer Valo	5.00	2.50	1.50
29	Bob Kennedy	5.00	2.50	1.50
30	Warren Spahn	25.00	12.50	7.50
31	Gil Hodges	25.00	12.50	7.50
32	Henry Thompson	5.00	2.50	1.50
33	William Werle	5.00	2.50	1.50
34	Grady Hatton	5.00	2.50	1.50
35	Al Rosen	10.00	5.00	3.00
36a	Gus Zernial (Chicago in bio)	20.00	10.00	6.00
36b	Gus Zernial (Philadelphia in bio)	12.00	6.00	3.50
37	Wes Westrum	9.00	4.50	2.75
38	Ed (Duke) Snider	60.00	30.00	17.50
39	Ted Kluszewski	10.00	5.00	3.00
40	Mike Garcia	9.00	4.50	2.75
41	Whitey Lockman	5.00	2.50	1.50
42	Ray Scarborough	5.00	2.50	1.50
43	Maurice McDermott	5.00	2.50	1.50
44	Sid Hudson	5.00	2.50	1.50
45	Andy Seminick	5.00	2.50	1.50
46	Billy Goodman	5.00	2.50	1.50
47	Tommy Glaviano	5.00	2.50	1.50
48	Eddie Stanky	9.00	4.50	2.75
49	Al Zarilla	5.00	2.50	1.50
50	Monte Irvin	25.00	12.50	7.50
51	Eddie Robinson	5.00	2.50	1.50
52a	Tommy Holmes (Boston in bio)	20.00	10.00	6.00
52b	Tommy Holmes (Hartford in bio)	20.00	10.00	6.00

1951 Topps Connie Mack's All-Stars

A set of die-cut, 2-1/16" by 5-1/4" cards, all eleven players are Hall of Famers. The cards feature a black and white photograph of the player printed on a red background with a red, white, blue, yellow and black plaque underneath. Like the "Current All-Stars," with which they were issued, the background could be removed making it possible for the card to stand up. This practice, however, resulted in the card's mutilation and lowers its condition in the eyes of today's collectors. Connie Mack All-Stars are scarce today and, despite being relatively expensive, retain a

certain popularity as one of Topps first issues.

		NR MT	EX	VG
Complete Set:		9500.00	4500.00	1950.
Common Player:		350.00	150.00	60.00
(1)	Grover Cleveland Alexander	550.00	275.00	100.00
(2)	Gordon Stanley Cochrane	400.00	175.00	75.00
(3)	Edward Trowbridge Collins	350.00	150.00	60.00
(4)	James J. Collins	350.00	150.00	60.00
(5)	Henry Louis Gehrig	2000.00	1000.00	350.00
(6)	Walter Johnson	750.00	325.00	150.00
(7)	Connie Mack	400.00	175.00	75.00
(8)	Christopher Mathewson	750.00	325.00	135.00
(9)	George Herman Ruth	2250.00	1150.00	450.00
(10)	Tristram Speaker	575.00	275.00	100.00
(11)	John Peter Wagner	500.00	225.00	100.00

1951 Topps Current All-Stars

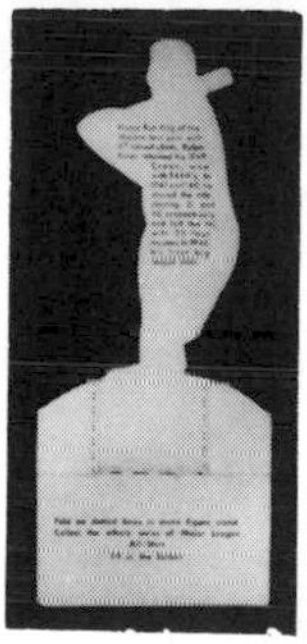

The Topps Current All-Stars are very similar to the Connie Mack All-Stars of the same year. The 2-1/16 by 5-1/4" cards have a black and white photograph on a red die-cut background. Most of the background could be folded over or removed so that the card would stand up. A plaque at the base carries brief biographical information. The set was to contain 11 cards, but only eight were actually issued in gum packs. Those of Jim Konstanty, Robin Roberts and Eddie Stanky were not released and are very rare. A big problem with the set is that if the card was used as it was intended it was folded and, thus, damaged from a collector's viewpoint. That makes top quality examples of any players difficult to find and quite expensive.

		NR MT	EX	VG
Complete Set:		40000.00	20000.00	8500.
Common Player:		500.00	250.00	100.00
(1)	Lawrence (Yogi) Berra	1500.00	750.00	450.00
(2)	Lawrence Eugene Doby	750.00	375.00	150.00
(3)	Walter Dropo	750.00	375.00	150.00
(4)	Walter (Hoot) Evers	500.00	250.00	100.00
(5)	George Clyde Kell	1000.00	500.00	200.00
(6)	Ralph McPherran Kiner	1075.00	525.00	200.00

		NR MT	EX	VG
(7)	James Casimir Konstanty	8500.00	4250.00	2000.
(8)	Robert G. Lemon	1075.00	525.00	200.00
(9)	Phillip Rizzuto	1200.00	600.00	225.00
(10)	Robin Evan Roberts	9500.00	4750.00	2250.
(11)	Edward Raymond Stanky	8500.00	4250.00	2000.

1951 Topps Teams

An innovative issue for 1951, the Topps team cards were a nine-card set, 5-1/4" by 2-1/16," which carried a black and white picture of a major league team surrounded by a yellow border on the front. The back identifies team members with red printing on white cardboard. There are two versions of each card, with and without the date "1950" in the banner that carries the team name. Undated versions are valued slightly higher than the cards with dates. Strangely only nine teams were issued. Scarcity varies, with the Cardinals and Red Sox being the most difficult to obtain. The complete set price does not include the scarcer variations.

		NR MT	EX	VG
Complete Set:		4500.00	2200.00	975.00
Common Team:		150.00	70.00	30.00
(1a)	Boston Red Sox (1950)	250.00	100.00	50.00
(1b)	Boston Red Sox (without 1950)	300.00	125.00	60.00
(2a)	Brooklyn Dodgers (1950)	300.00	125.00	60.00
(2b)	Brooklyn Dodgers (without 1950)	350.00	150.00	70.00
(3a)	Chicago White Sox (1950)	150.00	75.00	45.00
(3b)	Chicago White Sox (without 1950)	200.00	85.00	40.00
(4a)	Cincinnati Reds (1950)	150.00	70.00	30.00
(4b)	Cincinnati Reds (without 1950)	200.00	85.00	40.00
(5a)	New York Giants (1950)	250.00	100.00	50.00
(5b)	New York Giants (without 1950)	300.00	125.00	60.00
(6a)	Philadelphia Athletics (1950)	150.00	70.00	30.00
(6b)	Philadelphia Athletics (without 1950)	200.00	85.00	40.00
(7a)	Philadelphia Phillies (1950)	150.00	70.00	30.00
(7b)	Philadelphia Phillies (without 1950)	200.00	85.00	40.00
(8a)	St. Louis Cardinals (1950)	150.00	70.00	30.00
(8b)	St. Louis Cardinals (without 1950)	200.00	85.00	40.00
(9a)	Washington Senators (1950)	150.00	70.00	30.00
(9b)	Washington Senators (without 1950)	200.00	85.00	40.00

1952 Topps

At 407 cards, the 1952 Topps set was the largest set of its day, both in number of cards and physical dimensions of the cards. Cards are 2-5/8" by 3-3/4" with a hand-colored black and white photo on front. Major baseball card innovations presented in the set include the first-ever use of color team logos as part of the design, and the inclusion of stats for the previous season and overall career on the backs. A

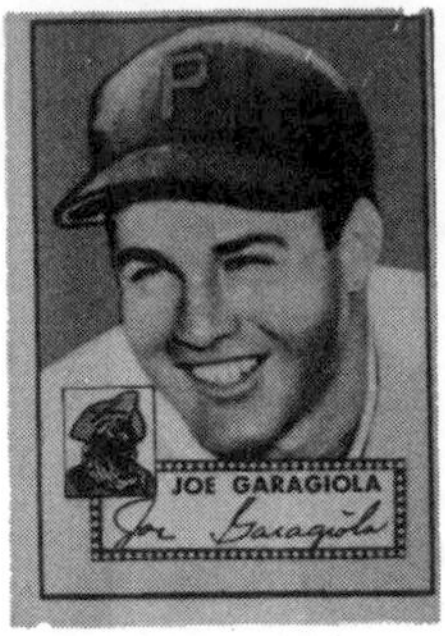

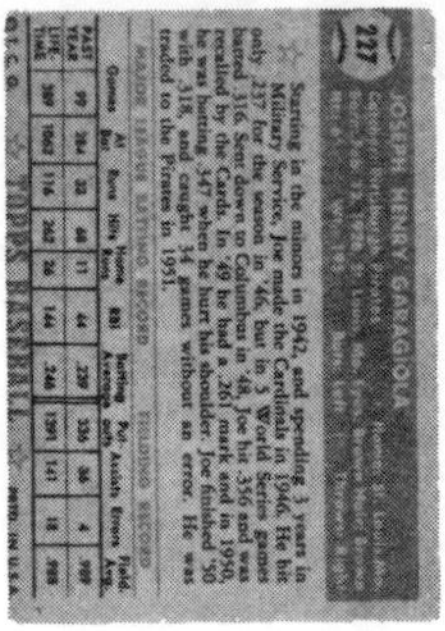

major variety in the set is that first 80 cards can be found with backs printed entirely in black or black and red. Backs entirely in black command a $10-15 premium. Card numbers 311-407 were printed in limited supplies and are extremely rare.

		NR MT	EX	VG
Complete Set:		50000.00	25000.00	15000.
Common Player: 1-80		50.00	25.00	15.00
Common Player: 81-250		25.00	12.50	7.50
Common Player: 251-280		40.00	20.00	12.00
Common Player: 281-300		50.00	25.00	15.00
Common Player: 301-310		40.00	20.00	12.00
Common Player: 311-407		175.00	87.00	52.00
1	Andy Pafko	1200.00	150.00	25.00
2	*James E. Runnels*	80.00	20.00	6.00
3	Hank Thompson	55.00	15.00	5.50
4	Don Lenhardt	55.00	15.00	5.50
5	Larry Jansen	55.00	15.00	5.50
6	Grady Hatton	55.00	15.00	5.50
7	Wayne Terwilliger	60.00	16.00	6.00
8	Fred Marsh	55.00	15.00	5.50
9	Bobby Hogue	65.00	18.00	6.50
10	Al Rosen	80.00	24.00	8.00
11	Phil Rizzuto	175.00	87.00	52.00
12	Monty Basgall	55.00	15.00	5.50
13	Johnny Wyrostek	55.00	15.00	5.50
14	Bob Elliott	55.00	15.00	5.50
15	Johnny Pesky	60.00	16.00	6.00
16	Gene Hermanski	55.00	15.00	5.50
17	Jim Hegan	55.00	15.00	5.50
18	Merrill Combs	55.00	15.00	5.50
19	Johnny Bucha	55.00	15.00	5.50
20	*Billy Loes*	110.00	55.00	32.00
21	Ferris Fain	60.00	16.00	6.00
22	Dom DiMaggio	80.00	40.00	24.00
23	Billy Goodman	55.00	15.00	5.50
24	Luke Easter	60.00	16.00	6.00
25	Johnny Groth	55.00	15.00	5.50
26	Monty Irvin	80.00	40.00	25.00
27	Sam Jethroe	55.00	15.00	5.50
28	Jerry Priddy	55.00	15.00	5.50
29	Ted Kluszewski	75.00	30.00	10.00
30	Mel Parnell	60.00	16.00	6.00
31	Gus Zernial	60.00	16.00	6.00
32	Eddie Robinson	55.00	15.00	5.50
33	Warren Spahn	225.00	112.00	67.00
34	Elmer Valo	55.00	15.00	5.50
35	Hank Sauer	60.00	16.00	6.00
36	Gil Hodges	150.00	75.00	45.00
37	Duke Snider	225.00	100.00	60.00
38	Wally Westlake	55.00	15.00	5.50
39	"Dizzy" Trout	60.00	16.00	6.00
40	Irv Noren	55.00	15.00	5.50
41	Bob Wellman	55.00	15.00	5.50
42	Lou Kretlow	55.00	15.00	5.50
43	Ray Scarborough	55.00	15.00	5.50
44	Con Dempsey	55.00	15.00	5.50
45	Eddie Joost	55.00	15.00	5.50
46	Gordon Goldsberry	55.00	15.00	5.50
47	Willie Jones	55.00	15.00	5.50
48a	Joe Page (Johnny Sain bio)	225.00	68.00	23.00
48b	Joe Page (correct bio)	80.00	24.00	8.00
49a	Johnny Sain (Joe Page bio)	225.00	68.00	23.00
49b	Johnny Sain (correct bio)	80.00	24.00	8.00
50	Marv Rickert	55.00	15.00	5.50
51	Jim Russell	60.00	16.00	6.00
52	Don Mueller	55.00	15.00	5.50
53	Chris Van Cuyk	60.00	16.00	6.00
54	Leo Kiely	55.00	15.00	5.50

		NR MT	EX	VG
55	Ray Boone	60.00	16.00	6.00
56	Tommy Glaviano	55.00	15.00	5.50
57	Ed Lopat	70.00	24.00	8.00
58	Bob Mahoney	55.00	15.00	5.50
59	Robin Roberts	125.00	62.00	37.00
60	Sid Hudson	55.00	15.00	5.50
61	"Tookie" Gilbert	55.00	15.00	5.50
62	Chuck Stobbs	55.00	15.00	5.50
63	Howie Pollet	55.00	15.00	5.50
64	Roy Sievers	65.00	18.00	6.50
65	Enos Slaughter	100.00	50.00	30.00
66	"Preacher" Roe	100.00	50.00	30.00
67	Allie Reynolds	80.00	40.00	25.00
68	Cliff Chambers	55.00	15.00	5.50
69	Virgil Stallcup	55.00	15.00	5.50
70	Al Zarilla	55.00	15.00	5.50
71	Tom Upton	55.00	15.00	5.50
72	Karl Olson	55.00	15.00	5.50
73	William Werle	55.00	15.00	5.50
74	Andy Hansen	55.00	15.00	5.50
75	Wes Westrum	60.00	16.00	6.00
76	Eddie Stanky	65.00	18.00	6.50
77	Bob Kennedy	55.00	15.00	5.50
78	Ellis Kinder	55.00	15.00	5.50
79	Gerald Staley	55.00	15.00	5.50
80	Herman Wehmeier	55.00	15.00	5.50
81	Vernon Law	25.00	11.00	6.25
82	Duane Pillette	25.00	12.50	7.50
83	Billy Johnson	25.00	12.50	7.50
84	Vern Stephens	25.00	12.50	7.50
85	Bob Kuzava	50.00	25.00	15.00
86	Ted Gray	25.00	12.50	7.50
87	Dale Coogan	25.00	12.50	7.50
88	Bob Feller	175.00	87.00	52.00
89	Johnny Lipon	25.00	12.50	7.50
90	Mickey Grasso	25.00	12.50	7.50
91	Al Schoendienst	80.00	20.00	6.00
92	Dale Mitchell	25.00	12.50	7.50
93	Al Sima	25.00	12.50	7.50
94	Sam Mele	25.00	12.50	7.50
95	Ken Holcombe	25.00	12.50	7.50
96	Willard Marshall	25.00	12.50	7.50
97	Earl Torgeson	25.00	12.50	7.50
98	Bill Pierce	25.00	11.00	6.25
99	Gene Woodling	50.00	25.00	15.00
100	Del Rice	25.00	12.50	7.50
101	Max Lanier	25.00	12.50	7.50
102	Bill Kennedy	25.00	12.50	7.50
103	Cliff Mapes	25.00	12.50	7.50
104	Don Kolloway	25.00	12.50	7.50
105	John Pramesa	25.00	12.50	7.50
106	Mickey Vernon	25.00	11.00	6.25
107	Connie Ryan	25.00	12.50	7.50
108	Jim Konstanty	25.00	11.00	6.25
109	Ted Wilks	25.00	12.50	7.50
110	Dutch Leonard	25.00	12.50	7.50
111	Harry Lowrey	25.00	12.50	7.50
112	Henry Majeski	25.00	12.50	7.50
113	Dick Sisler	25.00	12.50	7.50
114	Willard Ramsdell	25.00	12.50	7.50
115	George Munger	25.00	12.50	7.50
116	Carl Scheib	25.00	12.50	7.50
117	Sherman Lollar	25.00	11.00	6.25
118	Ken Raffensberger	25.00	12.50	7.50
119	Maurice McDermott	25.00	12.50	7.50
120	Bob Chakales	25.00	12.50	7.50
121	Gus Niarhos	25.00	12.50	7.50
122	Jack Jensen	70.00	35.00	21.00
123	Eddie Yost	25.00	11.00	6.25
124	Monte Kennedy	25.00	12.50	7.50
125	Bill Rigney	25.00	11.00	6.25
126	Fred Hutchinson	25.00	11.00	6.25
127	Paul Minner	25.00	12.50	7.50
128	Don Bollweg	50.00	25.00	15.00
129	Johnny Mize	70.00	35.00	21.00
130	Sheldon Jones	25.00	12.50	7.50
131	Morrie Martin	25.00	12.50	7.50
132	Clyde Kluttz	25.00	12.50	7.50
133	Al Widmar	25.00	12.50	7.50
134	Joe Tipton	25.00	12.50	7.50
135	Dixie Howell	25.00	12.50	7.50
136	Johnny Schmitz	25.00	11.00	6.25
137	*Roy McMillan*	25.00	11.00	6.25
138	Bill MacDonald	25.00	12.50	7.50
139	Ken Wood	25.00	12.50	7.50
140	John Antonelli	25.00	11.00	6.25
141	Clint Hartung	25.00	12.50	7.50
142	Harry Perkowski	25.00	12.50	7.50
143	Les Moss	25.00	12.50	7.50
144	Ed Blake	25.00	12.50	7.50
145	Joe Haynes	25.00	12.50	7.50

		NR MT	EX	VG
146	Frank House	25.00	12.50	7.50
147	Bob Young	25.00	12.50	7.50
148	Johnny Klippstein	25.00	12.50	7.50
149	Dick Kryhoski	25.00	12.50	7.50
150	Ted Beard	25.00	12.50	7.50
151	Wally Post	25.00	12.50	7.50
152	Al Evans	25.00	12.50	7.50
153	Bob Rush	25.00	12.50	7.50
154	Joe Muir	25.00	12.50	7.50
155	Frank Overmire	50.00	25.00	15.00
156	Frank Hiller	25.00	12.50	7.50
157	Bob Usher	25.00	12.50	7.50
158	Eddie Waitkus	25.00	12.50	7.50
159	Saul Rogovin	25.00	12.50	7.50
160	Owen Friend	25.00	12.50	7.50
161	Bud Byerly	25.00	12.50	7.50
162	Del Crandall	25.00	11.00	6.25
163	Stan Rojek	25.00	12.50	7.50
164	Walt Dubiel	25.00	12.50	7.50
165	Eddie Kazak	25.00	12.50	7.50
166	Paul LaPalme	25.00	12.50	7.50
167	Bill Howerton	25.00	12.50	7.50
168	Charlie Silvera	50.00	25.00	15.00
169	Howie Judson	25.00	12.50	7.50
170	Gus Bell	25.00	11.00	6.25
171	Ed Erautt	25.00	12.50	7.50
172	Eddie Miksis	25.00	12.50	7.50
173	Roy Smalley	25.00	12.50	7.50
174	Clarence Marshall	25.00	12.50	7.50
175	*Billy Martin*	300.00	150.00	90.00
176	Hank Edwards	25.00	12.50	7.50
177	Bill Wight	25.00	12.50	7.50
178	Cass Michaels	25.00	12.50	7.50
179	Frank Smith	25.00	12.50	7.50
180	*Charley Maxwell*	25.00	11.00	6.25
181	Bob Swift	25.00	12.50	7.50
182	Billy Hitchcock	25.00	12.50	7.50
183	Erv Dusak	25.00	12.50	7.50
184	Bob Ramazzotti	25.00	12.50	7.50
185	Bill Nicholson	25.00	12.50	7.50
186	Walt Masterson	25.00	12.50	7.50
187	Bob Miller	25.00	12.50	7.50
188	Clarence Podbielan	25.00	11.00	6.25
189	Pete Reiser	25.00	11.00	6.25
190	Don Johnson	25.00	12.50	7.50
191	Yogi Berra	350.00	175.00	100.00
192	Myron Ginsberg	25.00	12.50	7.50
193	Harry Simpson	25.00	12.50	7.50
194	Joe Hatten	25.00	12.50	7.50
195	*Orestes Minoso*	100.00	50.00	30.00
196	Solly Hemus	25.00	12.50	7.50
197	George Strickland	25.00	12.50	7.50
198	Phil Haugstad	25.00	11.00	6.25
199	George Zuverink	25.00	12.50	7.50
200	Ralph Houk	60.00	30.00	18.00
201	Alex Kellner	25.00	12.50	7.50
202	Joe Collins	50.00	25.00	15.00
203	Curt Simmons	25.00	11.00	6.25
204	Ron Northey	25.00	12.50	7.50
205	Clyde King	25.00	11.00	6.25
206	Joe Ostrowski	50.00	25.00	15.00
207	Mickey Harris	25.00	12.50	7.50
208	Marlin Stuart	25.00	12.50	7.50
209	Howie Fox	25.00	12.50	7.50
210	Dick Fowler	25.00	12.50	7.50
211	Ray Coleman	25.00	12.50	7.50
212	Ned Garver	25.00	12.50	7.50
213	Nippy Jones	25.00	12.50	7.50
214	Johnny Hopp	50.00	25.00	15.00
215	Hank Bauer	40.00	18.00	11.00
216	Richie Ashburn	60.00	30.00	18.00
217	George Stirnweiss	25.00	12.50	7.50
218	Clyde McCullough	25.00	12.50	7.50
219	Bobby Shantz	25.00	11.00	6.25
220	Joe Presko	25.00	12.50	7.50
221	Granny Hamner	25.00	12.50	7.50
222	"Hoot" Evers	25.00	12.50	7.50
223	Del Ennis	25.00	11.00	6.25
224	Bruce Edwards	25.00	12.50	7.50
225	Frank Baumholtz	25.00	12.50	7.50
226	Dave Philley	25.00	11.00	6.25
227	Joe Garagiola	100.00	50.00	30.00
228	Al Brazle	25.00	12.50	7.50
229	Gene Bearden	25.00	12.50	7.50
230	Matt Batts	25.00	12.50	7.50
231	Sam Zoldak	25.00	12.50	7.50
232	Billy Cox	50.00	25.00	15.00
233	*Bob Friend*	25.00	11.00	6.25
234	Steve Souchock	25.00	12.50	7.50
235	Walt Dropo	25.00	11.00	6.25
236	Ed Fitz Gerald	25.00	12.50	7.50

		NR MT	EX	VG
237	Jerry Coleman	50.00	25.00	15.00
238	Art Houtteman	25.00	12.50	7.50
239	Rocky Bridges	25.00	11.00	6.25
240	Jack Phillips	25.00	12.50	7.50
241	Tommy Byrne	25.00	12.50	7.50
242	Tom Poholsky	25.00	12.50	7.50
243	Larry Doby	40.00	18.00	11.00
244	Vic Wertz	25.00	11.00	6.25
245	Sherry Robertson	25.00	12.50	7.50
246	George Kell	60.00	30.00	18.00
247	Randy Gumpert	25.00	12.50	7.50
248	Frank Shea	25.00	12.50	7.50
249	Bobby Adams	25.00	12.50	7.50
250	Carl Erskine	50.00	25.00	15.00
251	Chico Carrasquel	40.00	20.00	12.00
252	Vern Bickford	40.00	20.00	12.00
253	Johnny Berardino	50.00	25.00	15.00
254	Joe Dobson	40.00	20.00	12.00
255	Clyde Vollmer	40.00	20.00	12.00
256	Pete Suder	40.00	20.00	12.00
257	Bobby Avila	40.00	20.00	12.00
258	Steve Gromek	40.00	20.00	12.00
259	Bob Addis	40.00	20.00	12.00
260	Pete Castiglione	40.00	20.00	12.00
261	Willie Mays	1500.00	750.00	450.00
262	Virgil Trucks	50.00	25.00	15.00
263	Harry Brecheen	50.00	25.00	15.00
264	Roy Hartsfield	40.00	20.00	12.00
265	Chuck Diering	40.00	20.00	12.00
266	Murry Dickson	40.00	20.00	12.00
267	Sid Gordon	40.00	20.00	12.00
268	Bob Lemon	200.00	100.00	60.00
269	Willard Nixon	40.00	20.00	12.00
270	Lou Brissie	40.00	20.00	12.00
271	Jim Delsing	40.00	20.00	12.00
272	Mike Garcia	50.00	25.00	15.00
273	Erv Palica	50.00	25.00	15.00
274	Ralph Branca	60.00	25.00	9.00
275	Pat Mullin	40.00	20.00	12.00
276	Jim Wilson	40.00	20.00	12.00
277	Early Wynn	175.00	87.00	52.00
278	Al Clark	40.00	20.00	12.00
279	Ed Stewart	40.00	20.00	12.00
280	Cloyd Boyer	40.00	20.00	12.00
281	Tommy Brown	50.00	25.00	15.00
282	Birdie Tebbetts	50.00	25.00	15.00
283	Phil Masi	50.00	25.00	15.00
284	Hank Arft	50.00	25.00	15.00
285	Cliff Fannin	50.00	25.00	15.00
286	Joe DeMaestri	50.00	25.00	15.00
287	Steve Bilko	50.00	25.00	15.00
288	Chet Nichols	50.00	25.00	15.00
289	Tommy Holmes	55.00	25.00	8.25
290	Joe Astroth	50.00	25.00	15.00
291	Gil Coan	50.00	25.00	15.00
292	Floyd Baker	50.00	25.00	15.00
293	Sibby Sisti	50.00	25.00	15.00
294	Walker Cooper	50.00	25.00	15.00
295	Phil Cavarretta	55.00	22.00	8.25
296	"Red" Rolfe	50.00	25.00	15.00
297	Andy Seminick	50.00	25.00	15.00
298	Bob Ross	50.00	25.00	15.00
299	Ray Murray	50.00	25.00	15.00
300	Barney McCosky	50.00	25.00	15.00
301	Bob Porterfield	40.00	20.00	12.00
302	Max Surkont	40.00	20.00	12.00
303	Harry Dorish	40.00	20.00	12.00
304	Sam Dente	40.00	20.00	12.00
305	Paul Richards	50.00	25.00	15.00
306	Lou Sleater	40.00	20.00	12.00
307	Frank Campos	40.00	20.00	12.00
308	Luis Aloma	40.00	20.00	12.00
309	Jim Busby	40.00	20.00	12.00
310	George Metkovich	40.00	20.00	12.00
311	Mickey Mantle	20000.00	10000.00	6000.
312	Jackie Robinson	875.00	435.00	245.00
313	Bobby Thomson	175.00	87.00	52.00
314	Roy Campanella	1300.00	650.00	375.00
315	Leo Durocher	250.00	100.00	63.00
316	Davey Williams	175.00	87.00	52.00
317	Connie Marrero	175.00	87.00	52.00
318	Hal Gregg	175.00	87.00	52.00
319	Al Walker	175.00	87.00	52.00
320	John Rutherford	175.00	87.00	52.00
321	*Joe Black*	225.00	90.00	56.00
322	Randy Jackson	175.00	87.00	52.00
323	Bubba Church	175.00	87.00	52.00
324	Warren Hacker	175.00	87.00	52.00
325	Bill Serena	175.00	87.00	52.00
326	George Shuba	175.00	87.00	52.00
327	Archie Wilson	175.00	87.00	52.00
328	Bob Borkowski	175.00	87.00	52.00
329	Ivan Delock	175.00	87.00	52.00
330	Turk Lown	175.00	87.00	52.00
331	Tom Morgan	160.00	80.00	48.00
332	Tony Bartirome	175.00	87.00	52.00
333	Pee Wee Reese	800.00	400.00	250.00
334	Wilmer Mizell	175.00	87.00	52.00
335	Ted Lepcio	175.00	87.00	52.00
336	Dave Koslo	175.00	87.00	52.00
337	Jim Hearn	175.00	87.00	52.00
338	Sal Yvars	175.00	87.00	52.00
339	Russ Meyer	175.00	87.00	52.00
340	Bob Hooper	175.00	87.00	52.00
341	Hal Jeffcoat	175.00	87.00	52.00
342	*Clem Labine*	200.00	90.00	52.00
343	Dick Gernert	175.00	87.00	52.00
344	Ewell Blackwell	160.00	80.00	48.00
345	Sam White	175.00	87.00	52.00
346	George Spencer	175.00	87.00	52.00
347	Joe Adcock	200.00	100.00	60.00
348	Bob Kelly	175.00	87.00	52.00
349	Bob Cain	175.00	87.00	52.00
350	Cal Abrams	175.00	87.00	52.00
351	Al Dark	175.00	87.00	52.00
352	Karl Drews	175.00	87.00	52.00
353	Bob Del Greco	175.00	87.00	52.00
354	Fred Hatfield	175.00	87.00	52.00
355	Bobby Morgan	175.00	87.00	52.00
356	Toby Atwell	175.00	87.00	52.00
357	Smoky Burgess	200.00	100.00	60.00
358	John Kucab	175.00	87.00	52.00
359	Dee Fondy	175.00	87.00	52.00
360	George Crowe	175.00	87.00	52.00
361	Bill Posedel	175.00	87.00	52.00
362	Ken Heintzelman	175.00	87.00	52.00
363	Dick Rozek	175.00	87.00	52.00
364	Clyde Sukeforth	175.00	87.00	52.00
365	"Cookie" Lavagetto	175.00	87.00	52.00
366	Dave Madison	175.00	87.00	52.00
367	Bob Thorpe	175.00	87.00	52.00
368	Ed Wright	175.00	87.00	52.00
369	*Dick Groat*	250.00	125.00	60.00
370	Billy Hoeft	175.00	87.00	52.00
371	Bob Hofman	175.00	87.00	52.00
372	*Gil McDougald*	250.00	120.00	67.00
373	Jim Turner	160.00	80.00	48.00
374	Al Benton	175.00	87.00	52.00
375	Jack Merson	175.00	87.00	52.00
376	Faye Throneberry	175.00	87.00	52.00
377	Chuck Dressen	175.00	90.00	52.00
378	Les Fusselman	175.00	87.00	52.00
379	Joe Rossi	175.00	87.00	52.00
380	Clem Koshorek	175.00	87.00	52.00
381	Milton Stock	175.00	87.00	52.00
382	Sam Jones	175.00	87.00	52.00
383	Del Wilber	175.00	87.00	52.00
384	Frank Crosetti	250.00	125.00	67.00
385	Herman Franks	175.00	87.00	52.00
386	Eddie Yuhas	175.00	87.00	52.00
387	Billy Meyer	175.00	87.00	52.00
388	Bob Chipman	175.00	87.00	52.00
389	Ben Wade	175.00	87.00	52.00
390	Glenn Nelson	175.00	87.00	52.00
391	Ben Chapman (photo actually Sam Chapman)	175.00	87.00	52.00
392	*Hoyt Wilhelm*	500.00	250.00	150.00
393	Ebba St. Claire	175.00	87.00	52.00
394	Billy Herman	250.00	125.00	75.00
395	Jake Pitler	175.00	87.00	52.00
396	*Dick Williams*	250.00	125.00	75.00
397	Forrest Main	175.00	87.00	52.00
398	Hal Rice	175.00	87.00	52.00
399	Jim Fridley	175.00	87.00	52.00
400	Bill Dickey	500.00	225.00	135.00
401	Bob Schultz	175.00	87.00	52.00
402	Earl Harrist	175.00	87.00	52.00
403	Bill Miller	160.00	80.00	48.00
404	Dick Brodowski	175.00	87.00	52.00
405	Eddie Pellagrini	175.00	87.00	52.00
406	*Joe Nuxhall*	175.00	87.00	52.00
407	*Ed Mathews*	2000.00	1000.00	600.00

1953 Topps

The 1953 Topps set reflects the company's continuing legal battles with Bowman. The set, originally intended to consist of 280 cards, is lacking six numbers (#'s 253, 261, 267, 268, 271 and 275)

which probably represent players whose contracts were lost to the competition. The 2-5/8" by 3-3/4" cards feature painted player pictures. A color team logo appears at a bottom panel (red for American Leauge and black for National.) Card backs contain the first baseball trivia questions along with brief statistics and player biographies. In the red panel at the top which lists the player's personal data, cards from the 2nd Series (#'s 86-165 plus 10, 44, 61, 72 and 81) can be found with that data printed in either black or white, black being the scarcer variety. Card numbers 221-280 are the scarce high numbers.

	NR MT	EX	VG
Complete Set:	13000.00	6500.00	3750.
Common Player Singleprint: 1-165	25.00	12.50	7.50
Common Player: 1-165	16.00	8.00	4.75
Common Player: 166-220	16.00	8.00	4.75
Common Player Singleprint: 221-280	90.00	45.00	27.00
Common Player: 221-280	50.00	25.00	15.00

		NR MT	EX	VG
1	Jackie Robinson	650.00	275.00	175.00
2	Luke Easter	25.00	12.50	7.50
3	George Crowe	25.00	12.50	7.50
4	Ben Wade	25.00	12.50	7.50
5	Joe Dobson	25.00	12.50	7.50
6	Sam Jones	25.00	12.50	7.50
7	Bob Borkowski	16.00	8.00	4.75
8	Clem Koshorek	16.00	8.00	4.75
9	Joe Collins	30.00	15.00	9.00
10	Smoky Burgess	30.00	15.00	9.00
11	Sal Yvars	25.00	12.50	7.50
12	Howie Judson	16.00	8.00	4.75
13	Connie Marrero	16.00	8.00	4.75
14	Clem Labine	25.00	12.50	7.50
15	Bobo Newsom	25.00	12.50	7.50
16	Harry Lowrey	16.00	8.00	4.75
17	Billy Hitchcock	25.00	12.50	7.50
18	Ted Lepcio	16.00	8.00	4.75
19	Mel Parnell	16.00	8.00	4.75
20	Hank Thompson	25.00	12.50	7.50
21	Billy Johnson	25.00	12.50	7.50
22	Howie Fox	25.00	12.50	7.50
23	Toby Atwell	16.00	8.00	4.75
24	Ferris Fain	25.00	12.50	7.50
25	Ray Boone	25.00	12.50	7.50
26	Dale Mitchell	16.00	8.00	4.75
27	Roy Campanella	250.00	125.00	75.00
28	Eddie Pellagrini	25.00	12.50	7.50
29	Hal Jeffcoat	25.00	12.50	7.50
30	Willard Nixon	25.00	12.50	7.50
31	Ewell Blackwell	40.00	20.00	12.00
32	Clyde Vollmer	25.00	12.50	7.50
33	Bob Kennedy	16.00	8.00	4.75
34	George Shuba	25.00	12.50	7.50
35	Irv Noren	25.00	12.50	7.50
36	Johnny Groth	16.00	8.00	4.75
37	Ed Mathews	110.00	55.00	33.00
38	Jim Hearn	16.00	8.00	4.75
39	Eddie Miksis	25.00	12.50	7.50
40	John Lipon	25.00	12.50	7.50
41	Enos Slaughter	80.00	40.00	25.00
42	Gus Zernial	16.00	8.00	4.75
43	Gil McDougald	40.00	20.00	12.00
44	Ellis Kinder	30.00	15.00	9.00
45	Grady Hatton	16.00	8.00	4.75
46	Johnny Klippstein	16.00	8.00	4.75
47	Bubba Church	16.00	8.00	4.75
48	Bob Del Greco	16.00	8.00	4.75
49	Faye Throneberry	16.00	8.00	4.75
50	Chuck Dressen	25.00	12.50	7.50
51	Frank Campos	16.00	8.00	4.75
52	Ted Gray	16.00	8.00	4.75
53	Sherman Lollar	16.00	8.00	4.75
54	Bob Feller	100.00	50.00	30.00
55	Maurice McDermott	16.00	8.00	4.75
56	Gerald Staley	16.00	8.00	4.75
57	Carl Scheib	25.00	12.50	7.50
58	George Metkovich	25.00	12.50	7.50
59	Karl Drews	16.00	8.00	4.75
60	Cloyd Boyer	16.00	8.00	4.75
61	Early Wynn	75.00	38.00	23.00
62	Monte Irvin	45.00	23.00	13.50
63	Gus Niarhos	16.00	8.00	4.75
64	Dave Philley	25.00	12.50	7.50
65	Earl Harrist	25.00	12.50	7.50
66	Orestes Minoso	30.00	15.00	9.00
67	Roy Sievers	25.00	12.50	7.50
68	Del Rice	25.00	12.50	7.50
69	Dick Brodowski	25.00	12.50	7.50
70	Ed Yuhas	25.00	12.50	7.50
71	Tony Bartirome	25.00	12.50	7.50
72	Fred Hutchinson	25.00	12.50	7.50
73	Eddie Robinson	25.00	12.50	7.50
74	Joe Rossi	25.00	12.50	7.50
75	Mike Garcia	25.00	12.50	7.50
76	Pee Wee Reese	175.00	87.00	52.00
77	John Mize	70.00	35.00	21.00
78	Al Schoendienst	65.00	33.00	20.00
79	Johnny Wyrostek	25.00	12.50	7.50
80	Jim Hegan	25.00	12.50	7.50
82	Mickey Mantle	2000.00	1000.00	600.00
83	Howie Pollet	25.00	12.50	7.50
84	Bob Hooper	16.00	8.00	4.75
85	Bobby Morgan	25.00	12.50	7.50
86	Billy Martin	125.00	67.00	37.00
87	Ed Lopat	35.00	17.50	10.50
88	Willie Jones	16.00	8.00	4.75
89	Chuck Stobbs	16.00	8.00	4.75
90	Hank Edwards	16.00	8.00	4.75
91	Ebba St. Claire	16.00	8.00	4.75
92	Paul Minner	16.00	8.00	4.75
93	Hal Rice	16.00	8.00	4.75
94	William Kennedy	16.00	8.00	4.75
95	Willard Marshall	16.00	8.00	4.75
96	Virgil Trucks	25.00	12.50	7.50
97	Don Kolloway	16.00	8.00	4.75
98	Cal Abrams	16.00	8.00	4.75
99	Dave Madison	16.00	8.00	4.75
100	Bill Miller	25.00	12.50	7.50
101	Ted Wilks	16.00	8.00	4.75
102	Connie Ryan	16.00	8.00	4.75
103	Joe Astroth	16.00	8.00	4.75
104	Yogi Berra	200.00	100.00	60.00
105	Joe Nuxhall	25.00	12.50	7.50
106	Johnny Antonelli	25.00	12.50	7.50
107	Danny O'Connell	16.00	8.00	4.75
108	Bob Porterfield	16.00	8.00	4.75
109	Alvin Dark	30.00	15.00	9.00
110	Herman Wehmeier	16.00	8.00	4.75
111	Hank Sauer	16.00	8.00	4.75
112	Ned Garver	16.00	8.00	4.75
113	Jerry Priddy	16.00	8.00	4.75
114	Phil Rizzuto	100.00	50.00	30.00
115	George Spencer	16.00	8.00	4.75
116	Frank Smith	16.00	8.00	4.75
117	Sid Gordon	16.00	8.00	4.75
118	Gus Bell	16.00	8.00	4.75
119	John Sain	40.00	20.00	12.00
120	Davey Williams	16.00	8.00	4.75
121	Walt Dropo	16.00	8.00	4.75
122	Elmer Valo	16.00	8.00	4.75
123	Tommy Byrne	16.00	8.00	4.75
124	Sibby Sisti	16.00	8.00	4.75
125	Dick Williams	25.00	12.50	7.50
126	Bill Connelly	16.00	8.00	4.75
127	Clint Courtney	16.00	8.00	4.75
128	Wilmer Mizell	16.00	8.00	4.75
129	Keith Thomas	16.00	8.00	4.75
130	Turk Lown	16.00	8.00	4.75
131	Harry Byrd	16.00	8.00	4.75
132	Tom Morgan	25.00	12.50	7.50
133	Gil Coan	16.00	8.00	4.75
134	Rube Walker	25.00	12.50	7.50
135	Al Rosen	35.00	17.50	10.50
136	Ken Heintzelman	16.00	8.00	4.75
137	John Rutherford	25.00	12.50	7.50
138	George Kell	60.00	30.00	18.00
139	Sammy White	16.00	8.00	4.75
140	Tommy Glaviano	16.00	8.00	4.75

		NR MT	EX	VG
141	Allie Reynolds	35.00	17.50	10.50
142	Vic Wertz	25.00	12.50	7.50
143	Billy Pierce	25.00	12.50	7.50
144	Bob Schultz	16.00	8.00	4.75
145	Harry Dorish	16.00	8.00	4.75
146	Granville Hamner	16.00	8.00	4.75
147	Warren Spahn	110.00	50.00	28.00
148	Mickey Grasso	16.00	8.00	4.75
149	Dom DiMaggio	30.00	15.00	9.00
150	Harry Simpson	16.00	8.00	4.75
151	Hoyt Wilhelm	70.00	35.00	20.00
152	Bob Adams	16.00	8.00	4.75
153	Andy Seminick	16.00	8.00	4.75
154	Dick Groat	25.00	12.50	7.50
155	Dutch Leonard	16.00	8.00	4.75
156	Jim Rivera	16.00	8.00	4.75
157	Bob Addis	16.00	8.00	4.75
158	*John Logan*	25.00	12.50	7.50
159	Wayne Terwilliger	16.00	8.00	4.75
160	Bob Young	16.00	8.00	4.75
161	Vern Bickford	16.00	8.00	4.75
162	Ted Kluszewski	40.00	20.00	12.00
163	Fred Hatfield	16.00	8.00	4.75
164	Frank Shea	16.00	8.00	4.75
165	Billy Hoeft	16.00	8.00	4.75
166	Bill Hunter	16.00	8.00	4.75
167	Art Schult	16.00	8.00	4.75
168	Willard Schmidt	16.00	8.00	4.75
169	Dizzy Trout	16.00	8.00	4.75
170	Bill Werle	16.00	8.00	4.75
171	Bill Glynn	16.00	8.00	4.75
172	Rip Repulski	16.00	8.00	4.75
173	Preston Ward	16.00	8.00	4.75
174	Billy Loes	16.00	8.00	4.75
175	Ron Kline	16.00	8.00	4.75
176	*Don Hoak*	16.00	8.00	4.75
177	Jim Dyck	16.00	8.00	4.75
178	Jim Waugh	16.00	8.00	4.75
179	Gene Hermanski	16.00	8.00	4.75
180	Virgil Stallcup	16.00	8.00	4.75
181	Al Zarilla	16.00	8.00	4.75
182	Bob Hofman	16.00	8.00	4.75
183	*Stu Miller*	16.00	8.00	4.75
184	*Hal Brown*	16.00	8.00	4.75
185	Jim Pendleton	16.00	8.00	4.75
186	Charlie Bishop	16.00	8.00	4.75
187	Jim Fridley	16.00	8.00	4.75
188	*Andy Carey*	16.00	8.00	4.75
189	Ray Jablonski	16.00	8.00	4.75
190	Dixie Walker	16.00	8.00	4.75
191	Ralph Kiner	50.00	25.00	15.00
192	Wally Westlake	16.00	8.00	4.75
193	Mike Clark	16.00	8.00	4.75
194	Eddie Kazak	16.00	8.00	4.75
195	Ed McGhee	16.00	8.00	4.75
196	Bob Keegan	16.00	8.00	4.75
197	Del Crandall	16.00	8.00	4.75
198	Forrest Main	16.00	8.00	4.75
199	Marion Fricano	16.00	8.00	4.75
200	Gordon Goldsberry	16.00	8.00	4.75
201	Paul LaPalme	16.00	8.00	4.75
202	Carl Sawatski	16.00	8.00	4.75
203	Cliff Fannin	16.00	8.00	4.75
204	Dick Bokelmann	16.00	8.00	4.75
205	Vern Benson	16.00	8.00	4.75
206	*Ed Bailey*	16.00	8.00	4.75
207	Whitey Ford	150.00	75.00	45.00
208	Jim Wilson	16.00	8.00	4.75
209	Jim Greengrass	16.00	8.00	4.75
210	*Bob Cerv*	16.00	8.00	4.75
211	J.W. Porter	16.00	8.00	4.75
212	Jack Dittmer	16.00	8.00	4.75
213	Ray Scarborough	16.00	8.00	4.75
214	*Bill Bruton*	16.00	8.00	4.75
215	*Gene Conley*	16.00	8.00	4.75
216	Jim Hughes	16.00	8.00	4.75
217	Murray Wall	16.00	8.00	4.75
218	Les Fusselman	16.00	8.00	4.75
219	Pete Runnels (photo actually Don Johnson)	16.00	8.00	4.75
220	Satchell Paige	400.00	200.00	120.00
221	Bob Milliken	90.00	45.00	27.00
222	Vic Janowicz	50.00	25.00	15.00
223	John O'Brien	50.00	25.00	15.00
224	Lou Sleater	50.00	25.00	15.00
225	Bobby Shantz	90.00	45.00	27.00
226	Ed Erautt	90.00	45.00	27.00
227	Morris Martin	50.00	25.00	15.00
228	Hal Newhouser	100.00	45.00	27.00
229	Rocky Krsnich	90.00	45.00	27.00
230	Johnny Lindell	50.00	25.00	15.00
231	Solly Hemus	50.00	25.00	15.00
232	Dick Kokos	90.00	45.00	27.00
233	Al Aber	90.00	45.00	27.00
234	Ray Murray	50.00	25.00	15.00
235	John Hetki	50.00	25.00	15.00
236	Harry Perkowski	90.00	45.00	27.00
237	Clarence Podbielan	50.00	25.00	15.00
238	Cal Hogue	50.00	25.00	15.00
239	Jim Delsing	90.00	45.00	27.00
240	Freddie Marsh	50.00	25.00	15.00
241	Al Sima	50.00	25.00	15.00
242	Charlie Silvera	90.00	45.00	27.00
243	Carlos Bernier	50.00	25.00	15.00
244	Willie Mays	1800.00	900.00	550.00
245	Bill Norman	90.00	45.00	27.00
246	*Roy Face*	80.00	40.00	25.00
247	Mike Sandlock	50.00	25.00	15.00
248	Gene Stephens	50.00	25.00	15.00
249	Ed O'Brien	50.00	25.00	15.00
250	Bob Wilson	90.00	45.00	27.00
251	Sid Hudson	90.00	45.00	27.00
252	Henry Foiles	90.00	45.00	27.00
253	Not Issued			
254	Preacher Roe	80.00	40.00	24.00
255	Dixie Howell	90.00	45.00	27.00
256	Les Peden	90.00	45.00	27.00
257	Bob Boyd	90.00	45.00	27.00
258	*Jim Gilliam*	325.00	162.00	98.00
259	Roy McMillan	90.00	45.00	27.00
260	Sam Calderone	90.00	45.00	27.00
261	Not Issued			
262	Bob Oldis	90.00	45.00	27.00
263	*John Podres*	250.00	125.00	70.00
264	Gene Woodling	70.00	35.00	20.00
265	Jackie Jensen	100.00	50.00	30.00
266	Bob Cain	90.00	45.00	27.00
267	Not Issued			
268	Not Issued			
269	Duane Pillette	90.00	45.00	27.00
270	Vern Stephens	90.00	45.00	27.00
271	Not Issued			
272	Bill Antonello	90.00	45.00	27.00
273	*Harvey Haddix*	125.00	62.00	37.00
274	John Riddle	90.00	45.00	27.00
275	Not Issued			
276	Ken Raffensberger	50.00	25.00	15.00
277	Don Lund	90.00	45.00	27.00
278	Willie Miranda	90.00	45.00	27.00
279	Joe Coleman	50.00	25.00	15.00
280	Milt Bolling	350.00	150.00	60.00

1954 Topps

The first issue to use two player pictures on the front, the 1954 Topps set is very popular today. Solid color backgrounds frame both color head- and-shoulders and black and white action pictures of the player. The player's name, position, team and team logo appear at the top. Backs include an "Inside Baseball" cartoon regarding the player as well as statistics and biography. The 250-card, 2-5/8" by 3-3/4", set includes manager and coaches cards, and the first use of two players together on a modern card; the players were, appropriately, the O'Brien twins.

		NR MT	EX	VG
Complete Set:		7500.00	3750.00	2250.
Common Player: 1-50		13.00	6.50	4.00
Common Player: 51-75		30.00	15.00	9.00
Common Player: 76-250		13.00	6.50	4.00
1	Ted Williams	600.00	150.00	90.00
2	Gus Zernial	13.00	6.50	4.00
3	Monte Irvin	35.00	17.50	10.50
4	Hank Sauer	15.00	7.50	4.50
5	Ed Lopat	20.00	10.00	6.00
6	Pete Runnels	13.00	6.50	4.00
7	Ted Kluszewski	30.00	15.00	9.00
8	Bobby Young	13.00	6.50	4.00
9	Harvey Haddix	13.00	6.50	4.00
10	Jackie Robinson	300.00	150.00	90.00
11	Paul Smith	13.00	6.50	4.00
12	Del Crandall	13.00	6.50	4.00
13	Billy Martin	80.00	40.00	25.00
14	Preacher Roe	40.00	20.00	12.00
15	Al Rosen	20.00	10.00	6.00
16	Vic Janowicz	13.00	6.50	4.00
17	Phil Rizzuto	70.00	35.00	20.00
18	Walt Dropo	13.00	6.50	4.00
19	Johnny Lipon	13.00	6.50	4.00
20	Warren Spahn	100.00	50.00	30.00
21	Bobby Shantz	13.00	6.50	4.00
22	Jim Greengrass	13.00	6.50	4.00
23	Luke Easter	13.00	6.50	4.00
24	Granny Hamner	13.00	6.50	4.00
25	*Harvey Kuenn*	35.00	17.50	10.50
26	Ray Jablonski	13.00	6.50	4.00
27	Ferris Fain	13.00	6.50	4.00
28	Paul Minner	13.00	6.50	4.00
29	Jim Hegan	13.00	6.50	4.00
30	Ed Mathews	90.00	45.00	27.00
31	Johnny Klippstein	13.00	6.50	4.00
32	Duke Snider	150.00	75.00	45.00
33	Johnny Schmitz	13.00	6.50	4.00
34	Jim Rivera	13.00	6.50	4.00
35	Junior Gilliam	20.00	10.00	6.00
36	Hoyt Wilhelm	40.00	20.00	12.00
37	Whitey Ford	90.00	45.00	25.00
38	Eddie Stanky	13.00	6.50	4.00
39	Sherm Lollar	13.00	6.50	4.00
40	Mel Parnell	13.00	6.50	4.00
41	Willie Jones	13.00	6.50	4.00
42	Don Mueller	13.00	6.50	4.00
43	Dick Groat	13.00	6.50	4.00
44	Ned Garver	13.00	6.50	4.00
45	Richie Ashburn	30.00	15.00	9.00
46	Ken Raffensberger	13.00	6.50	4.00
47	Ellis Kinder	13.00	6.50	4.00
48	Billy Hunter	13.00	6.50	4.00
49	Ray Murray	13.00	6.50	4.00
50	Yogi Berra	250.00	125.00	75.00
51	Johnny Lindell	30.00	15.00	9.00
52	Vic Power	30.00	15.00	9.00
53	Jack Dittmer	30.00	15.00	9.00
54	Vern Stephens	30.00	15.00	9.00
55	Phil Cavarretta	30.00	15.00	9.00
56	Willie Miranda	30.00	15.00	9.00
57	Luis Aloma	30.00	15.00	9.00
58	Bob Wilson	30.00	15.00	9.00
59	Gene Conley	30.00	15.00	9.00
60	Frank Baumholtz	30.00	15.00	9.00
61	Bob Cain	30.00	15.00	9.00
62	Eddie Robinson	30.00	15.00	9.00
63	Johnny Pesky	30.00	15.00	9.00
64	Hank Thompson	30.00	15.00	9.00
65	Bob Swift	30.00	15.00	9.00
66	Ted Lepcio	30.00	15.00	9.00
67	Jim Willis	30.00	15.00	9.00
68	Sammy Calderone	30.00	15.00	9.00
69	Bud Podbielan	30.00	15.00	9.00
70	Larry Doby	50.00	25.00	15.00
71	Frank Smith	30.00	15.00	9.00
72	Preston Ward	30.00	15.00	9.00
73	Wayne Terwilliger	30.00	15.00	9.00
74	Bill Taylor	30.00	15.00	9.00
75	Fred Haney	30.00	15.00	9.00
76	Bob Scheffing	13.00	6.50	4.00
77	Ray Boone	13.00	6.50	4.00
78	Ted Kazanski	13.00	6.50	4.00
79	Andy Pafko	13.00	6.50	4.00
80	Jackie Jensen	13.00	6.50	4.00
81	Dave Hoskins	13.00	6.50	4.00
82	Milt Bolling	13.00	6.50	4.00
83	Joe Collins	13.00	6.50	4.00
84	Dick Cole	13.00	6.50	4.00
85	*Bob Turley*	13.00	6.50	4.00
86	Billy Herman	30.00	15.00	9.00

		NR MT	EX	VG
87	Roy Face	13.00	6.50	4.00
88	Matt Batts	13.00	6.50	4.00
89	Howie Pollet	13.00	6.50	4.00
90	Willie Mays	400.00	200.00	120.00
91	Bob Oldis	13.00	6.50	4.00
92	Wally Westlake	13.00	6.50	4.00
93	Sid Hudson	13.00	6.50	4.00
94	*Ernie Banks*	650.00	325.00	200.00
95	Hal Rice	13.00	6.50	4.00
96	Charlie Silvera	13.00	6.50	4.00
97	Jerry Lane	13.00	6.50	4.00
98	Joe Black	13.00	6.50	4.00
99	Bob Hofman	13.00	6.50	4.00
100	Bob Keegan	13.00	6.50	4.00
101	Gene Woodling	20.00	10.00	6.00
102	Gil Hodges	75.00	38.00	23.00
103	*Jim Lemon*	13.00	6.50	4.00
104	Mike Sandlock	13.00	6.50	4.00
105	Andy Carey	13.00	6.50	4.00
106	Dick Kokos	13.00	6.50	4.00
107	Duane Pillette	13.00	6.50	4.00
108	Thornton Kipper	13.00	6.50	4.00
109	Bill Bruton	13.00	6.50	4.00
110	Harry Dorish	13.00	6.50	4.00
111	Jim Delsing	13.00	6.50	4.00
112	Bill Renna	13.00	6.50	4.00
113	Bob Boyd	13.00	6.50	4.00
114	Dean Stone	13.00	6.50	4.00
115	"Rip" Repulski	13.00	6.50	4.00
116	Steve Bilko	13.00	6.50	4.00
117	Solly Hemus	13.00	6.50	4.00
118	Carl Scheib	13.00	6.50	4.00
119	Johnny Antonelli	13.00	6.50	4.00
120	Roy McMillan	13.00	6.50	4.00
121	Clem Labine	13.00	6.50	4.00
122	Johnny Logan	13.00	6.50	4.00
123	Bobby Adams	13.00	6.50	4.00
124	Marion Fricano	13.00	6.50	4.00
125	Harry Perkowski	13.00	6.50	4.00
126	Ben Wade	13.00	6.50	4.00
127	Steve O'Neill	13.00	6.50	4.00
128	*Henry Aaron*	1200.00	600.00	350.00
129	Forrest Jacobs	13.00	6.50	4.00
130	Hank Bauer	30.00	15.00	9.00
131	Reno Bertoia	13.00	6.50	4.00
132	*Tom Lasorda*	175.00	87.00	50.00
133	Del Baker	13.00	6.50	4.00
134	Cal Hogue	13.00	6.50	4.00
135	Joe Presko	13.00	6.50	4.00
136	Connie Ryan	13.00	6.50	4.00
137	*Wally Moon*	13.00	6.50	4.00
138	Bob Borkowski	13.00	6.50	4.00
139	Ed & Johnny O'Brien	30.00	15.00	9.00
140	Tom Wright	13.00	6.50	4.00
141	*Joe Jay*	13.00	6.50	4.00
142	Tom Poholsky	13.00	6.50	4.00
143	Rollie Hemsley	13.00	6.50	4.00
144	Bill Werle	13.00	6.50	4.00
145	Elmer Valo	13.00	6.50	4.00
146	Don Johnson	13.00	6.50	4.00
147	John Riddle	13.00	6.50	4.00
148	Bob Trice	13.00	6.50	4.00
149	Jim Robertson	13.00	6.50	4.00
150	Dick Kryhoski	13.00	6.50	4.00
151	Alex Grammas	13.00	6.50	4.00
152	Mike Blyzka	13.00	6.50	4.00
153	"Rube" Walker	13.00	6.50	4.00
154	Mike Fornieles	13.00	6.50	4.00
155	Bob Kennedy	13.00	6.50	4.00
156	Joe Coleman	13.00	6.50	4.00
157	Don Lenhardt	13.00	6.50	4.00
158	"Peanuts" Lowrey	13.00	6.50	4.00
159	Dave Philley	13.00	6.50	4.00
160	"Red" Kress	13.00	6.50	4.00
161	John Hetki	13.00	6.50	4.00
162	Herman Wehmeier	13.00	6.50	4.00
163	Frank House	13.00	6.50	4.00
164	Stu Miller	13.00	6.50	4.00
165	Jim Pendleton	13.00	6.50	4.00
166	Johnny Podres	30.00	15.00	9.00
167	Don Lund	13.00	6.50	4.00
168	Morrie Martin	13.00	6.50	4.00
169	Jim Hughes	13.00	6.50	4.00
170	*Jim Rhodes*	13.00	6.50	4.00
171	Leo Kiely	13.00	6.50	4.00
172	Hal Brown	13.00	6.50	4.00
173	Jack Harshman	13.00	6.50	4.00
174	Tom Qualters	13.00	6.50	4.00
175	Frank Leja	13.00	6.50	4.00
176	Bob Keely	13.00	6.50	4.00
177	Bob Milliken	13.00	6.50	4.00

		NR MT	EX	VG
178	Bill Gylnn (Glynn)	13.00	6.50	4.00
179	Gair Allie	13.00	6.50	4.00
180	Wes Westrum	13.00	6.50	4.00
181	Mel Roach	13.00	6.50	4.00
182	Chuck Harmon	13.00	6.50	4.00
183	Earle Combs	35.00	17.50	10.50
184	Ed Bailey	13.00	6.50	4.00
185	Chuck Stobbs	13.00	6.50	4.00
186	Karl Olson	13.00	6.50	4.00
187	"Heinie" Manush	35.00	17.50	10.50
188	Dave Jolly	13.00	6.50	4.00
189	Bob Ross	13.00	6.50	4.00
190	Ray Herbert	13.00	6.50	4.00
191	*Dick Schofield*	13.00	6.50	4.00
192	"Cot" Deal	13.00	6.50	4.00
193	Johnny Hopp	13.00	6.50	4.00
194	Bill Sarni	13.00	6.50	4.00
195	Bill Consolo	13.00	6.50	4.00
196	Stan Jok	13.00	6.50	4.00
197	"Schoolboy" Rowe	13.00	6.50	4.00
198	Carl Sawatski	13.00	6.50	4.00
199	"Rocky" Nelson	13.00	6.50	4.00
200	Larry Jansen	13.00	6.50	4.00
201	*Al Kaline*	650.00	330.00	200.00
202	*Bob Purkey*	13.00	6.50	4.00
203	Harry Brecheen	13.00	6.50	4.00
204	Angel Scull	13.00	6.50	4.00
205	Johnny Sain	35.00	17.50	10.50
206	Ray Crone	13.00	6.50	4.00
207	Tom Oliver	13.00	6.50	4.00
208	Grady Hatton	13.00	6.50	4.00
209	Charlie Thompson	13.00	6.50	4.00
210	*Bob Buhl*	13.00	6.50	4.00
211	Don Hoak	13.00	6.50	4.00
212	Mickey Micelotta	13.00	6.50	4.00
213	John Fitzpatrick	13.00	6.50	4.00
214	Arnold Portocarrero	13.00	6.50	4.00
215	Ed McGhee	13.00	6.50	4.00
216	Al Sima	13.00	6.50	4.00
217	Paul Schreiber	13.00	6.50	4.00
218	Fred Marsh	13.00	6.50	4.00
219	Charlie Kress	13.00	6.50	4.00
220	Ruben Gomez	13.00	6.50	4.00
221	Dick Brodowski	13.00	6.50	4.00
222	Bill Wilson	13.00	6.50	4.00
223	Joe Haynes	13.00	6.50	4.00
224	Dick Weik	13.00	6.50	4.00
225	Don Liddle	13.00	6.50	4.00
226	Jehosie Heard	13.00	6.50	4.00
227	Buster Mills	13.00	6.50	4.00
228	Gene Hermanski	13.00	6.50	4.00
229	Bob Talbot	13.00	6.50	4.00
230	Bob Kuzava	13.00	6.50	4.00
231	Roy Smalley	13.00	6.50	4.00
232	Lou Limmer	13.00	6.50	4.00
233	Augie Galan	13.00	6.50	4.00
234	*Jerry Lynch*	13.00	6.50	4.00
235	Vern Law	13.00	6.50	4.00
236	Paul Penson	13.00	6.50	4.00
237	Mike Ryba	13.00	6.50	4.00
238	Al Aber	13.00	6.50	4.00
239	*Bill Skowron*	80.00	40.00	25.00
240	Sam Mele	13.00	6.50	4.00
241	Bob Miller	13.00	6.50	4.00
242	Curt Roberts	13.00	6.50	4.00
243	Ray Blades	13.00	6.50	4.00
244	Leroy Wheat	13.00	6.50	4.00
245	Roy Sievers	13.00	6.50	4.00
246	Howie Fox	13.00	6.50	4.00
247	Eddie Mayo	13.00	6.50	4.00
248	*Al Smith*	13.00	6.50	4.00
249	Wilmer Mizell	13.00	6.50	4.00
250	Ted Williams	700.00	200.00	100.00

1955 Topps

The 1955 Topps set is numerically the smallest of the regular issue Topps sets. The 3-3/4" by 2-5/8" cards mark the first time that Topps used a horizontal format. While that format was new, the design was not; they are very similar to the 1954 cards to the point many pictures appeared in both years. Although it was slated for a 210-card set, the 1955 Topps set turned out to be only 206 cards with numbers 175, 186, 203 and 209 never being released. The scarce high numbers in this set begin with #161.

		NR MT	EX	VG
Complete Set:		7000.00	3500.00	2100.
Common Player: 1-150		8.00	4.00	2.50
Common Player: 151-160		17.00	8.50	5.00
Common Player: 161-210		25.00	12.50	7.50
1	"Dusty" Rhodes	50.00	15.00	9.00
2	Ted Williams	350.00	150.00	100.00
3	Art Fowler	8.00	4.00	2.50
4	Al Kaline	200.00	100.00	60.00
5	Jim Gilliam	10.00	5.00	3.00
6	Stan Hack	8.00	4.00	2.50
7	Jim Hegan	8.00	4.00	2.50
8	Hal Smith	8.00	4.00	2.50
9	Bob Miller	8.00	4.00	2.50
10	Bob Keegan	8.00	4.00	2.50
11	Ferris Fain	8.00	4.00	2.50
12	"Jake" Thies	8.00	4.00	2.50
13	Fred Marsh	8.00	4.00	2.50
14	Jim Finigan	8.00	4.00	2.50
15	Jim Pendleton	8.00	4.00	2.50
16	Roy Sievers	15.00	7.50	4.50
17	Bobby Hofman	8.00	4.00	2.50
18	Russ Kemmerer	8.00	4.00	2.50
19	Billy Herman	12.00	6.00	3.50
20	Andy Carey	9.00	4.50	2.75
21	Alex Grammas	8.00	4.00	2.50
22	Bill Skowron	15.00	7.50	4.50
23	Jack Parks	8.00	4.00	2.50
24	Hal Newhouser	8.00	4.00	2.50
25	Johnny Podres	20.00	10.00	6.00
26	Dick Groat	15.00	7.50	4.50
27	Billy Gardner	8.00	4.00	2.50
28	Ernie Banks	200.00	100.00	60.00
29	Herman Wehmeier	8.00	4.00	2.50
30	Vic Power	8.00	4.00	2.50
31	Warren Spahn	70.00	35.00	20.00
32	Ed McGhee	8.00	4.00	2.50
33	Tom Qualters	8.00	4.00	2.50
34	Wayne Terwilliger	8.00	4.00	2.50
35	Dave Jolly	8.00	4.00	2.50
36	Leo Kiely	8.00	4.00	2.50
37	*Joe Cunningham*	10.00	5.00	3.00
38	Bob Turley	17.00	8.50	5.00
39	Bill Glynn	8.00	4.00	2.50
40	Don Hoak	10.00	5.00	3.00
41	Chuck Stobbs	8.00	4.00	2.50
42	"Windy" McCall	8.00	4.00	2.50
43	Harvey Haddix	8.00	4.00	2.50
44	"Corky" Valentine	8.00	4.00	2.50
45	Hank Sauer	8.00	4.00	2.50
46	Ted Kazanski	8.00	4.00	2.50
47	Hank Aaron	350.00	175.00	105.00
48	Bob Kennedy	8.00	4.00	2.50
49	J.W. Porter	8.00	4.00	2.50
50	Jackie Robinson	225.00	100.00	60.00
51	Jim Hughes	8.00	4.00	2.50
52	Bill Tremel	8.00	4.00	2.50
53	Bill Taylor	8.00	4.00	2.50
54	Lou Limmer	8.00	4.00	2.50
55	"Rip" Repulski	8.00	4.00	2.50
56	Ray Jablonski	8.00	4.00	2.50
57	*Billy O'Dell*	8.00	4.00	2.50
58	Jim Rivera	8.00	4.00	2.50
59	Gair Allie	8.00	4.00	2.50
60	Dean Stone	8.00	4.00	2.50
61	"Spook" Jacobs	8.00	4.00	2.50
62	Thornton Kipper	8.00	4.00	2.50
63	Joe Collins	9.00	4.50	2.75
64	*Gus Triandos*	10.00	5.00	3.00
65	Ray Boone	8.00	4.00	2.50
66	Ron Jackson	8.00	4.00	2.50

		NR MT	EX	VG
67	Wally Moon	8.00	4.00	2.50
68	Jim Davis	8.00	4.00	2.50
69	Ed Bailey	8.00	4.00	2.50
70	Al Rosen	17.00	8.50	5.00
71	Ruben Gomez	8.00	4.00	2.50
72	Karl Olson	8.00	4.00	2.50
73	Jack Shepard	8.00	4.00	2.50
74	Bob Borkowski	8.00	4.00	2.50
75	Sandy Amoros	8.00	4.00	2.50
76	Howie Pollet	8.00	4.00	2.50
77	Arnold Portocarrero	8.00	4.00	2.50
78	Gordon Jones	8.00	4.00	2.50
79	Danny Schell	8.00	4.00	2.50
80	Bob Grim	9.00	4.50	2.75
81	Gene Conley	8.00	4.00	2.50
82	Chuck Harmon	8.00	4.00	2.50
83	Tom Brewer	8.00	4.00	2.50
84	*Camilo Pascual*	8.00	4.00	2.50
85	*Don Mossi*	8.00	4.00	2.50
86	Bill Wilson	8.00	4.00	2.50
87	Frank House	8.00	4.00	2.50
88	*Bob Skinner*	8.00	4.00	2.50
89	Joe Frazier	8.00	4.00	2.50
90	Karl Spooner	9.00	4.50	2.75
91	Milt Bolling	8.00	4.00	2.50
92	*Don Zimmer*	30.00	15.00	9.00
93	Steve Bilko	8.00	4.00	2.50
94	Reno Bertoia	8.00	4.00	2.50
95	Preston Ward	8.00	4.00	2.50
96	Charlie Bishop	8.00	4.00	2.50
97	Carlos Paula	8.00	4.00	2.50
98	Johnny Riddle	8.00	4.00	2.50
99	Frank Leja	9.00	4.50	2.75
100	Monte Irvin	25.00	12.50	7.50
101	Johnny Gray	8.00	4.00	2.50
102	Wally Westlake	8.00	4.00	2.50
103	Charlie White	8.00	4.00	2.50
104	Jack Harshman	8.00	4.00	2.50
105	Chuck Diering	8.00	4.00	2.50
106	*Frank Sullivan*	8.00	4.00	2.50
107	Curt Roberts	8.00	4.00	2.50
108	"Rube" Walker	8.00	4.00	2.50
109	Ed Lopat	10.00	5.00	3.00
110	Gus Zernial	8.00	4.00	2.50
111	Bob Milliken	8.00	4.00	2.50
112	Nelson King	8.00	4.00	2.50
113	Harry Brecheen	8.00	4.00	2.50
114	Lou Ortiz	8.00	4.00	2.50
115	Ellis Kinder	8.00	4.00	2.50
116	Tom Hurd	8.00	4.00	2.50
117	Mel Roach	8.00	4.00	2.50
118	Bob Purkey	8.00	4.00	2.50
119	Bob Lennon	8.00	4.00	2.50
120	Ted Kluszewski	25.00	12.50	7.50
121	Bill Renna	8.00	4.00	2.50
122	Carl Sawatski	8.00	4.00	2.50
123	*Sandy Koufax*	1000.00	500.00	300.00
124	*Harmon Killebrew*	300.00	150.00	90.00
125	*Ken Boyer*	60.00	30.00	17.50
126	*Dick Hall*	8.00	4.00	2.50
127	*Dale Long*	8.00	4.00	2.50
128	Ted Lepcio	8.00	4.00	2.50
129	Elvin Tappe	8.00	4.00	2.50
130	Mayo Smith	8.00	4.00	2.50
131	Grady Hatton	8.00	4.00	2.50
132	Bob Trice	8.00	4.00	2.50
133	Dave Hoskins	8.00	4.00	2.50
134	Joe Jay	8.00	4.00	2.50
135	Johnny O'Brien	8.00	4.00	2.50
136	"Bunky" Stewart	8.00	4.00	2.50
137	Harry Elliott	8.00	4.00	2.50
138	Ray Herbert	8.00	4.00	2.50
139	Steve Kraly	9.00	4.50	2.75
140	Mel Parnell	8.00	4.00	2.50
141	Tom Wright	8.00	4.00	2.50
142	Jerry Lynch	8.00	4.00	2.50
143	Dick Schofield	8.00	4.00	2.50
144	Joe Amalfitano	8.00	4.00	2.50
145	Elmer Valo	8.00	4.00	2.50
146	*Dick Donovan*	8.00	4.00	2.50
147	Laurin Pepper	8.00	4.00	2.50
148	Hal Brown	8.00	4.00	2.50
149	Ray Crone	8.00	4.00	2.50
150	Mike Higgins	8.00	4.00	2.50
151	"Red" Kress	17.00	8.50	5.00
152	*Harry Agganis*	75.00	38.00	23.00
153	"Bud" Podbielan	17.00	8.50	5.00
154	Willie Miranda	17.00	8.50	5.00
155	Ed Mathews	100.00	50.00	30.00
156	Joe Black	20.00	10.00	6.00
157	Bob Miller	17.00	8.50	5.00

		NR MT	EX	VG
158	Tom Carroll	20.00	10.00	6.00
159	Johnny Schmitz	17.00	8.50	5.00
160	Ray Narleski	17.00	8.50	5.00
161	*Chuck Tanner*	30.00	15.00	9.00
162	Joe Coleman	25.00	12.50	7.50
163	Faye Throneberry	25.00	12.50	7.50
164	*Roberto Clemente*	1500.00	750.00	450.00
165	Don Johnson	25.00	12.50	7.50
166	Hank Bauer	35.00	17.50	10.50
167	Tom Casagrande	25.00	12.50	7.50
168	Duane Pillette	25.00	12.50	7.50
169	Bob Oldis	25.00	12.50	7.50
170	Jim Pearce	25.00	12.50	7.50
171	Dick Brodowski	25.00	12.50	7.50
172	Frank Baumholtz	25.00	12.50	7.50
173	Bob Kline	25.00	12.50	7.50
174	Rudy Minarcin	25.00	12.50	7.50
175	Not Issued			
176	Norm Zauchin	25.00	12.50	7.50
177	Jim Robertson	25.00	12.50	7.50
178	Bobby Adams	25.00	12.50	7.50
179	Jim Bolger	25.00	12.50	7.50
180	Clem Labine	25.00	12.50	7.50
181	Roy McMillan	25.00	12.50	7.50
182	Humberto Robinson	25.00	12.50	7.50
183	Tony Jacobs	25.00	12.50	7.50
184	Harry Perkowski	25.00	12.50	7.50
185	Don Ferrarese	25.00	12.50	7.50
186	Not Issued			
187	Gil Hodges	150.00	75.00	45.00
188	Charlie Silvera	25.00	12.50	7.50
189	Phil Rizzuto	150.00	75.00	45.00
190	Gene Woodling	25.00	12.50	7.50
191	Ed Stanky	25.00	12.50	7.50
192	Jim Delsing	25.00	12.50	7.50
193	Johnny Sain	35.00	17.50	10.50
194	Willie Mays	500.00	250.00	150.00
195	Ed Roebuck	25.00	12.50	7.50
196	Gale Wade	25.00	12.50	7.50
197	Al Smith	25.00	12.50	7.50
198	Yogi Berra	225.00	112.00	67.00
199	Bert Hamric	25.00	12.50	7.50
200	Jack Jensen	50.00	25.00	15.00
201	Sherm Lollar	25.00	12.50	7.50
202	Jim Owens	25.00	12.50	7.50
203	Not Issued			
204	Frank Smith	25.00	12.50	7.50
205	Gene Freese	25.00	12.50	7.50
206	Pete Daley	25.00	12.50	7.50
207	Bill Consolo	25.00	12.50	7.50
208	Ray Moore	25.00	12.50	7.50
209	Not Issued			
210	Duke Snider	500.00	200.00	110.00

1955 Topps Doubleheaders

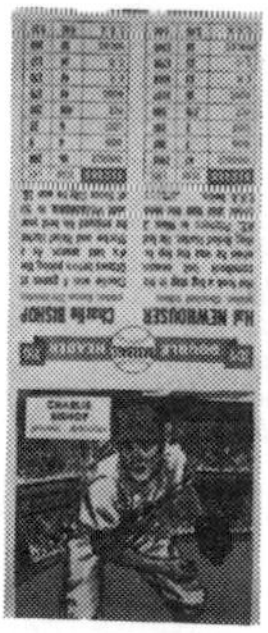

This set is a throwback to the 1911 T201 Mecca Double Folders. The cards were perforated allowing them to be folded. Open, there is a color painting of a player set against a ballpark background. When folded , a different stadium and player appears, although both share the same lower legs and feet. Back gives abbreviated career histories. Placed side by side in reverse numerical order, the backgrounds form a continuous stadium scene. When open, the cards measure 2-1/16" by 4-7/8." The 66 cards in the set mean 132 total players, all of whom also appeared in the lower number regular 1955 Topps

set.

		NR MT	EX	VG
Complete Set:		3750.00	1875.00	1125.
Common Player:		30.00	15.00	9.00
1	Al Rosen			
2	Chuck Diering	30.00	15.00	9.00
3	Monte Irvin			
4	Russ Kemmerer	30.00	15.00	9.00
5	Ted Kazanski			
6	Gordon Jones	30.00	15.00	9.00
7	Bill Taylor			
8	Billy O'Dell	30.00	15.00	9.00
9	J.W. Porter			
10	Thornton Kipper	30.00	15.00	9.00
11	Curt Roberts			
12	Arnie Portocarrero	30.00	15.00	9.00
13	Wally Westlake			
14	Frank House	30.00	15.00	9.00
15	"Rube" Walker			
16	Lou Limmer	30.00	15.00	9.00
17	Dean Stone			
18	Charlie White	30.00	15.00	9.00
19	Karl Spooner			
20	Jim Hughes	30.00	15.00	9.00
21	Bill Skowron			
22	Frank Sullivan	30.00	15.00	9.00
23	Jack Shepard			
24	Stan Hack	30.00	15.00	9.00
25	Jackie Robinson			
26	Don Hoak	275.00	137.00	80.00
27	"Dusty" Rhodes			
28	Jim Davis	30.00	15.00	9.00
29	Vic Power			
30	Ed Bailey	30.00	15.00	9.00
31	Howie Pollet			
32	Ernie Banks	150.00	75.00	45.00
33	Jim Pendleton			
34	Gene Conley	30.00	15.00	9.00
35	Karl Olson	30.00	15.00	9.00
36	Andy Carey	30.00	15.00	9.00
37	Wally Moon	30.00	15.00	9.00
38	Joe Cunningham	30.00	15.00	9.00
39	Fred Marsh			
40	"Jake" Thies	30.00	15.00	9.00
41	Ed Lopat			
42	Harvey Haddix	30.00	15.00	9.00
43	Leo Kiely			
44	Chuck Stobbs	30.00	15.00	9.00
45	Al Kaline			
46	"Corky" Valentine	300.00	150.00	90.00
47	"Spook" Jacobs			
48	Johnny Gray	30.00	15.00	9.00
49	Ron Jackson			
50	Jim Finigan	30.00	15.00	9.00
51	Ray Jablonski			
52	Bob Keegan	30.00	15.00	9.00
53	Billy Herman			
54	Sandy Amoros	30.00	15.00	9.00
55	Chuck Harmon			
56	Bob Skinner	30.00	15.00	9.00
57	Dick Hall			
58	Bob Grim	30.00	15.00	9.00
59	Billy Glynn			
60	Bob Miller	30.00	15.00	9.00
61	Billy Gardner			
62	John Hetki	30.00	15.00	9.00
63	Bob Borkowski			
64	Bob Turley	30.00	15.00	9.00
65	Joe Collins			
66	Jack Harshman	30.00	15.00	9.00
67	Jim Hegan			
68	Jack Parks	30.00	15.00	9.00
69	Ted Williams			
70	Hal Smith	300.00	150.00	90.00
71	Gair Allie			
72	Grady Hatton	30.00	15.00	9.00
73	Jerry Lynch			
74	Harry Brecheen	30.00	15.00	9.00
75	Tom Wright			
76	"Bunky" Stewart	30.00	15.00	9.00
77	Dave Hoskins			
78	Ed McGhee	30.00	15.00	9.00
79	Roy Sievers			
80	Art Fowler	30.00	15.00	9.00
81	Danny Schell			
82	Gus Triandos	30.00	15.00	9.00
83	Joe Frazier			
84	Don Mossi	30.00	15.00	9.00
85	Elmer Valo			
86	Hal Brown	30.00	15.00	9.00
87	Bob Kennedy			
88	"Windy" McCall	30.00	15.00	9.00
89	Ruben Gomez			
90	Jim Rivera	30.00	15.00	9.00
91	Lou Ortiz			
92	Milt Bolling	30.00	15.00	9.00
93	Carl Sawatski			
94	Elvin Tappe	30.00	15.00	9.00
95	Dave Jolly			
96	Bobby Hofman	30.00	15.00	9.00
97	Preston Ward			
98	Don Zimmer	30.00	15.00	9.00
99	Bill Renna			
100	Dick Groat	30.00	15.00	9.00
101	Bill Wilson			
102	Bill Tremel	30.00	15.00	9.00
103	Hank Sauer			
104	Camilo Pascual	30.00	15.00	9.00
105	Hank Aaron			
106	Ray Herbert	450.00	225.00	135.00
107	Alex Grammas			
108	Tom Qualters	30.00	15.00	9.00
109	Hal Newhouser			
110	Charlie Bishop	30.00	15.00	9.00
111	Harmon Killebrew			
112	John Podres	250.00	125.00	75.00
113	Ray Boone			
114	Bob Purkey	30.00	15.00	9.00
115	Dale Long			
116	Ferris Fain	30.00	15.00	9.00
117	Steve Bilko			
118	Bob Milliken	30.00	15.00	9.00
119	Mel Parnell			
120	Tom Hurd	30.00	15.00	9.00
121	Ted Kluszewski			
122	Jim Owens	30.00	15.00	9.00
123	Gus Zernial			
124	Bob Trice	30.00	15.00	9.00
125	"Rip" Repulski			
126	Ted Lepcio	30.00	15.00	9.00
127	Warren Spahn			
128	Tom Brewer	200.00	100.00	60.00
129	Jim Gilliam			
130	Ellis Kinder	30.00	15.00	9.00
131	Herm Wehmeier			
132	Wayne Terwilliger	30.00	15.00	9.00

1956 Topps

This 340-card set is quite similar in design to the 1955 Topps set, again using both a portrait and an "action" picture. Some portraits are the same as those used in 1955 (and even 1954). Innovations found in the 1956 Topps set of 2-5/8" by 3-3/4" cards include team cards introduced as part of a regular set. Additionally, there are two unnumbered checklist cards (the complete set price quoted below does not include the checklist cards). Finally, there are cards of the two league presidents, William Harridge and Warren Giles. On the backs, a three-panel cartoon depicts big moments from the player's career while biographical information appears above the cartoon and the statistics below. Card backs for numbers 1-180 can be found with either white or grey cardboard. Some dealers charge a premium for grey backs (#'s 1-100) and white

backs (#'s 101-180).

		NR MT	EX	VG
Complete Set:		6500.00	3250.00	2000.
Common Player: 1-100		7.00	3.50	2.00
Common Player: 101-180		9.00	4.50	2.75
Common Player: 181-260		15.00	7.50	4.50
Common Player: 261-340		9.00	4.50	2.75
1	William Harridge	110.00	25.00	3.75
2	Warren Giles	15.00	7.50	4.50
3	Elmer Valo	7.00	3.50	2.00
4	Carlos Paula	7.00	3.50	2.00
5	Ted Williams	300.00	150.00	90.00
6	Ray Boone	9.00	4.50	2.75
7	Ron Negray	7.00	3.50	2.00
8	Walter Alston	30.00	15.00	9.00
9	Ruben Gomez	7.00	3.50	2.00
10	Warren Spahn	60.00	45.00	25.00
11a	Cubs Team (with date)	50.00	25.00	15.00
11b	Cubs Team (no date, name centered)	15.00	7.50	4.50
11c	Cubs Team (no date, name at left)	15.00	7.50	4.50
12	Andy Carey	10.00	5.00	3.00
13	Roy Face	10.00	5.00	3.00
14	Ken Boyer	15.00	7.50	4.50
15	Ernie Banks	90.00	45.00	25.00
16	*Hector Lopez*	10.00	5.00	3.00
17	Gene Conley	9.00	4.50	2.75
18	Dick Donovan	7.00	3.50	2.00
19	Chuck Diering	7.00	3.50	2.00
20	Al Kaline	90.00	45.00	25.00
21	Joe Collins	10.00	5.00	3.00
22	Jim Finigan	7.00	3.50	2.00
23	Freddie Marsh	7.00	3.50	2.00
24	Dick Groat	10.00	5.00	3.00
25	Ted Kluszewski	15.00	7.50	4.50
26	Grady Hatton	7.00	3.50	2.00
27	Nelson Burbrink	7.00	3.50	2.00
28	Bobby Hofman	7.00	3.50	2.00
29	Jack Harshman	7.00	3.50	2.00
30	Jackie Robinson	150.00	60.00	38.00
31	Hank Aaron	200.00	100.00	60.00
32	Frank House	7.00	3.50	2.00
33	Roberto Clemente	300.00	150.00	90.00
34	Tom Brewer	7.00	3.50	2.00
35	Al Rosen	15.00	7.50	4.50
36	Rudy Minarcin	7.00	3.50	2.00
37	Alex Grammas	7.00	3.50	2.00
38	Bob Kennedy	7.00	3.50	2.00
39	Don Mossi	9.00	4.50	2.75
40	Bob Turley	15.00	7.50	4.50
41	Hank Sauer	7.00	3.50	2.00
42	Sandy Amoros	9.00	4.50	2.75
43	Ray Moore	7.00	3.50	2.00
44	"Windy" McCall	7.00	3.50	2.00
45	Gus Zernial	9.00	4.50	2.75
46	Gene Freese	7.00	3.50	2.00
47	Art Fowler	7.00	3.50	2.00
48	Jim Hegan	7.00	3.50	2.00
49	*Pedro Ramos*	9.00	4.50	2.75
50	"Dusty" Rhodes	9.00	4.50	2.75
51	Ernie Oravetz	7.00	3.50	2.00
52	Bob Grim	10.00	5.00	3.00
53	Arnold Portocarrero	7.00	3.50	2.00
54	Bob Keegan	7.00	3.50	2.00
55	Wally Moon	9.00	4.50	2.75
56	Dale Long	9.00	4.50	2.75
57	"Duke" Maas	7.00	3.50	2.00
58	Ed Roebuck	9.00	4.50	2.75
59	Jose Santiago	7.00	3.50	2.00
60	Mayo Smith	7.00	3.50	2.00
61	Bill Skowron	15.00	7.50	4.50
62	Hal Smith	7.00	3.50	2.00
63	*Roger Craig*	30.00	15.00	9.00
64	Luis Arroyo	7.00	3.50	2.00
65	Johnny O'Brien	7.00	3.50	2.00
66	Bob Speake	7.00	3.50	2.00
67	Vic Power	7.00	3.50	2.00
68	Chuck Stobbs	7.00	3.50	2.00
69	Chuck Tanner	10.00	5.00	3.00
70	Jim Rivera	7.00	3.50	2.00
71	Frank Sullivan	7.00	3.50	2.00
72a	Phillies Team (with date)	50.00	25.00	15.00
72b	Phillies Team (no date, name centered)	15.00	7.50	4.50
72c	Philadelphia Phillies (no date, name at left)	15.00	7.50	4.50
73	Wayne Terwilliger	7.00	3.50	2.00
74	Jim King	7.00	3.50	2.00

		NR MT	EX	VG
75	Roy Sievers	9.00	4.50	2.75
76	Ray Crone	7.00	3.50	2.00
77	Harvey Haddix	9.00	4.50	2.75
78	Herman Wehmeier	7.00	3.50	2.00
79	Sandy Koufax	300.00	150.00	90.00
80	Gus Triandos	9.00	4.50	2.75
81	Wally Westlake	7.00	3.50	2.00
82	Bill Renna	7.00	3.50	2.00
83	Karl Spooner	9.00	4.50	2.75
84	"Babe" Birrer	7.00	3.50	2.00
85a	Indians Team (with date)	50.00	25.00	15.00
85b	Indians Team (no date, name centered)	15.00	7.50	4.50
85c	Indians Team (no date, name at left)	15.00	7.50	4.50
86	Ray Jablonski	7.00	3.50	2.00
87	Dean Stone	7.00	3.50	2.00
88	Johnny Kucks	10.00	5.00	3.00
89	Norm Zauchin	7.00	3.50	2.00
90a	Redlegs Team (with date)	50.00	25.00	15.00
90b	Redlegs Team (no date, name centered)	15.00	7.50	4.50
90c	Redlegs Team (no date, name at left)	15.00	7.50	4.50
91	Gail Harris	7.00	3.50	2.00
92	"Red" Wilson	7.00	3.50	2.00
93	George Susce, Jr.	7.00	3.50	2.00
94	Ronnie Kline	7.00	3.50	2.00
95a	Braves Team (with date)	50.00	25.00	15.00
95b	Braves Team (no date, name centered)	15.00	7.50	4.50
95c	Braves Team (no date, name at left)	15.00	7.50	4.50
96	Bill Tremel	7.00	3.50	2.00
97	Jerry Lynch	7.00	3.50	2.00
98	Camilo Pascual	9.00	4.50	2.75
99	Don Zimmer	15.00	7.50	4.50
100a	Orioles Team (with date)	40.00	20.00	12.00
100b	Orioles Team (no date, name centered)	15.00	7.50	4.50
100c	Orioles Team (no date, name at left)	15.00	7.50	4.50
101	Roy Campanella	150.00	75.00	45.00
102	Jim Davis	9.00	4.50	2.75
103	Willie Miranda	9.00	4.50	2.75
104	Bob Lennon	9.00	4.50	2.75
105	Al Smith	9.00	4.50	2.75
106	Joe Astroth	9.00	4.50	2.75
107	Ed Mathews	50.00	25.00	15.00
108	Laurin Pepper	9.00	4.50	2.75
109	Enos Slaughter	25.00	12.50	7.50
110	Yogi Berra	125.00	56.00	35.00
111	Red Sox Team	9.00	4.50	2.75
112	Dee Fondy	9.00	4.50	2.75
113	Phil Rizzuto	50.00	25.00	15.00
114	Jim Owens	9.00	4.50	2.75
115	Jackie Jensen	10.00	5.00	3.00
116	Eddie O'Brien	9.00	4.50	2.75
117	Virgil Trucks	9.00	4.50	2.75
118	"Nellie" Fox	25.00	12.50	7.50
119	*Larry Jackson*	9.00	4.50	2.75
120	Richie Ashburn	30.00	15.00	9.00
121	Pirates Team	15.00	7.50	4.50
122	Willard Nixon	9.00	4.50	2.75
123	Roy McMillan	9.00	4.50	2.75
124	Don Kaiser	9.00	4.50	2.75
125	"Minnie" Minoso	15.00	7.50	4.50
126	Jim Brady	9.00	4.50	2.75
127	Willie Jones	9.00	4.50	2.75
128	Eddie Yost	9.00	4.50	2.75
129	"Jake" Martin	9.00	4.50	2.75
130	Willie Mays	250.00	125.00	75.00
131	Bob Roselli	9.00	4.50	2.75
132	Bobby Avila	9.00	4.50	2.75
133	Ray Narleski	9.00	4.50	2.75
134	Cardinals Team	15.00	7.50	4.50
135	Mickey Mantle	750.00	375.00	225.00
136	Johnny Logan	9.00	4.50	2.75
137	Al Silvera	9.00	4.50	2.75
138	Johnny Antonelli	9.00	4.50	2.75
139	Tommy Carroll	9.00	4.50	2.75
140	*Herb Score*	20.00	10.00	6.00
141	Joe Frazier	9.00	4.50	2.75
142	Gene Baker	9.00	4.50	2.75
143	Jim Piersall	9.00	4.50	2.75
144	Leroy Powell	9.00	4.50	2.75
145	Gil Hodges	45.00	23.00	13.50
146	Senators Team	15.00	7.50	4.50
147	Earl Torgeson	9.00	4.50	2.75
148	Alvin Dark	9.00	4.50	2.75
149	"Dixie" Howell	9.00	4.50	2.75

		NR MT	EX	VG
150	"Duke" Snider	100.00	45.00	27.00
151	"Spook" Jacobs	9.00	4.50	2.75
152	Billy Hoeft	9.00	4.50	2.75
153	Frank Thomas	9.00	4.50	2.75
154	Dave Pope	9.00	4.50	2.75
155	Harvey Kuenn	15.00	7.50	4.50
156	Wes Westrum	9.00	4.50	2.75
157	Dick Brodowski	9.00	4.50	2.75
158	Wally Post	9.00	4.50	2.75
159	Clint Courtney	9.00	4.50	2.75
160	Billy Pierce	15.00	7.50	4.50
161	Joe DeMaestri	9.00	4.50	2.75
162	"Gus" Bell	9.00	4.50	2.75
163	Gene Woodling	9.00	4.50	2.75
164	Harmon Killebrew	110.00	55.00	33.00
165	"Red" Schoendienst	25.00	12.50	7.50
166	Dodgers Team	200.00	100.00	60.00
167	Harry Dorish	9.00	4.50	2.75
168	Sammy White	9.00	4.50	2.75
169	Bob Nelson	9.00	4.50	2.75
170	Bill Virdon	15.00	7.50	4.50
171	Jim Wilson	9.00	4.50	2.75
172	*Frank Torre*	9.00	4.50	2.75
173	Johnny Podres	15.00	7.50	4.50
174	Glen Gorbous	9.00	4.50	2.75
175	Del Crandall	15.00	7.50	4.50
176	Alex Kellner	9.00	4.50	2.75
177	Hank Bauer	15.00	7.50	4.50
178	Joe Black	9.00	4.50	2.75
179	Harry Chiti	9.00	4.50	2.75
180	Robin Roberts	25.00	12.50	7.50
181	Billy Martin	80.00	40.00	25.00
182	Paul Minner	15.00	7.50	4.50
183	Stan Lopata	15.00	7.50	4.50
184	Don Bessent	15.00	7.50	4.50
185	Bill Bruton	15.00	7.50	4.50
186	Ron Jackson	15.00	7.50	4.50
187	Early Wynn	30.00	15.00	9.00
188	White Sox Team	15.00	7.50	4.50
189	Ned Garver	15.00	7.50	4.50
190	Carl Furillo	20.00	10.00	6.00
191	Frank Lary	15.00	7.50	4.50
192	"Smoky" Burgess	15.00	7.50	4.50
193	Wilmer Mizell	15.00	7.50	4.50
194	Monte Irvin	30.00	15.00	9.00
195	George Kell	30.00	15.00	9.00
196	Tom Poholsky	15.00	7.50	4.50
197	Granny Hamner	15.00	7.50	4.50
198	Ed Fitzgerald (Fitz Gerald)	15.00	7.50	4.50
199	Hank Thompson	15.00	7.50	4.50
200	Bob Feller	100.00	50.00	30.00
201	"Rip" Repulski	15.00	7.50	4.50
202	Jim Hearn	15.00	7.50	4.50
203	Bill Tuttle	15.00	7.50	4.50
204	Art Swanson	15.00	7.50	4.50
205	"Whitey" Lockman	15.00	7.50	4.50
206	Erv Palica	15.00	7.50	4.50
207	Jim Small	15.00	7.50	4.50
208	Elston Howard	30.00	15.00	9.00
209	Max Surkont	15.00	7.50	4.50
210	Mike Garcia	15.00	7.50	4.50
211	Murry Dickson	15.00	7.50	4.50
212	Johnny Temple	15.00	7.50	4.50
213	Tigers Team	35.00	17.50	10.50
214	Bob Rush	15.00	7.50	4.50
215	Tommy Byrne	15.00	7.50	4.50
216	Jerry Schoonmaker	15.00	7.50	4.50
217	Billy Klaus	15.00	7.50	4.50
218	Joe Nuxall (Nuxhall)	15.00	7.50	4.50
219	Lew Burdette	15.00	7.50	4.50
220	Del Ennis	15.00	7.50	4.50
221	Bob Friend	15.00	7.50	4.50
222	Dave Philley	15.00	7.50	4.50
223	Randy Jackson	15.00	7.50	4.50
224	"Bud" Podbielan	15.00	7.50	4.50
225	Gil McDougald	25.00	12.50	7.50
226	Giants Team	60.00	30.00	18.00
227	Russ Meyer	15.00	7.50	4.50
228	"Mickey" Vernon	15.00	7.50	4.50
229	Harry Brecheen	15.00	7.50	4.50
230	"Chico" Carrasquel	15.00	7.50	4.50
231	Bob Hale	15.00	7.50	4.50
232	"Toby" Atwell	15.00	7.50	4.50
233	Carl Erskine	20.00	10.00	6.00
234	"Pete" Runnels	15.00	7.50	4.50
235	Don Newcombe	30.00	15.00	9.00
236	Athletics Team	15.00	7.50	4.50
237	Jose Valdivielso	15.00	7.50	4.50
238	Walt Dropo	15.00	7.50	4.50
239	Harry Simpson	15.00	7.50	4.50
240	"Whitey" Ford	100.00	50.00	30.00

		NR MT	EX	VG
241	Don Mueller	15.00	7.50	4.50
242	Hershell Freeman	15.00	7.50	4.50
243	Sherm Lollar	15.00	7.50	4.50
244	Bob Buhl	15.00	7.50	4.50
245	Billy Goodman	15.00	7.50	4.50
246	Tom Gorman	15.00	7.50	4.50
247	Bill Sarni	15.00	7.50	4.50
248	Bob Porterfield	15.00	7.50	4.50
249	Johnny Klippstein	15.00	7.50	4.50
250	Larry Doby	20.00	10.00	6.00
251	Yankees Team	225.00	112.00	67.00
252	Vernon Law	15.00	7.50	4.50
253	Irv Noren	15.00	7.50	4.50
254	George Crowe	15.00	7.50	4.50
255	Bob Lemon	25.00	12.50	7.50
256	Tom Hurd	15.00	7.50	4.50
257	Bobby Thomson	15.00	7.50	4.50
258	Art Ditmar	15.00	7.50	4.50
259	Sam Jones	15.00	7.50	4.50
260	"Pee Wee" Reese	125.00	62.00	37.00
261	Bobby Shantz	9.00	4.50	2.75
262	Howie Pollet	9.00	4.50	2.75
263	Bob Miller	9.00	4.50	2.75
264	Ray Monzant	9.00	4.50	2.75
265	Sandy Consuegra	9.00	4.50	2.75
266	Don Ferrarese	9.00	4.50	2.75
267	Bob Nieman	9.00	4.50	2.75
268	Dale Mitchell	9.00	4.50	2.75
269	Jack Meyer	9.00	4.50	2.75
270	Billy Loes	9.00	4.50	2.75
271	Foster Castleman	9.00	4.50	2.75
272	Danny O'Connell	9.00	4.50	2.75
273	Walker Cooper	9.00	4.50	2.75
274	Frank Baumholtz	9.00	4.50	2.75
275	Jim Greengrass	9.00	4.50	2.75
276	George Zuverink	9.00	4.50	2.75
277	Daryl Spencer	9.00	4.50	2.75
278	Chet Nichols	9.00	4.50	2.75
279	Johnny Groth	9.00	4.50	2.75
280	Jim Gilliam	9.00	4.50	2.75
281	Art Houtteman	9.00	4.50	2.75
282	Warren Hacker	9.00	4.50	2.75
283	Hal Smith	9.00	4.50	2.75
284	Ike Delock	9.00	4.50	2.75
285	Eddie Miksis	9.00	4.50	2.75
286	Bill Wight	9.00	4.50	2.75
287	Bobby Adams	9.00	4.50	2.75
288	Bob Cerv	20.00	10.00	6.00
289	Hal Jeffcoat	9.00	4.50	2.75
290	Curt Simmons	9.00	4.50	2.75
291	Frank Kellert	9.00	4.50	2.75
292	*Luis Aparicio*	125.00	62.00	37.00
293	Stu Miller	9.00	4.50	2.75
294	Ernie Johnson	9.00	4.50	2.75
295	Clem Labine	9.00	4.50	2.75
296	Andy Seminick	9.00	4.50	2.75
297	Bob Skinner	9.00	4.50	2.75
298	Johnny Schmitz	9.00	4.50	2.75
299	Charley Neal	25.00	12.50	7.50
300	Vic Wertz	9.00	4.50	2.75
301	Marv Grissom	9.00	4.50	2.75
302	Eddie Robinson	15.00	7.50	4.50
303	Jim Dyck	9.00	4.50	2.75
304	Frank Malzone	9.00	4.50	2.75
305	Brooks Lawrence	9.00	4.50	2.75
306	Curt Roberts	9.00	4.50	2.75
307	Hoyt Wilhelm	35.00	17.50	10.50
308	"Chuck" Harmon	9.00	4.50	2.75
309	*Don Blasingame*	9.00	4.50	2.75
310	Steve Gromek	9.00	4.50	2.75
311	Hal Naragon	9.00	4.50	2.75
312	Andy Pafko	9.00	4.50	2.75
313	Gene Stephens	9.00	4.50	2.75
314	Hobie Landrith	9.00	4.50	2.75
315	Milt Bolling	9.00	4.50	2.75
316	Jerry Coleman	9.00	4.50	2.75
317	Al Aber	9.00	4.50	2.75
318	Fred Hatfield	9.00	4.50	2.75
319	Jack Crimian	9.00	4.50	2.75
320	Joe Adcock	9.00	4.50	2.75
321	Jim Konstanty	15.00	7.50	4.50
322	Karl Olson	9.00	4.50	2.75
323	Willard Schmidt	9.00	4.50	2.75
324	"Rocky" Bridges	9.00	4.50	2.75
325	Don Liddle	9.00	4.50	2.75
326	Connie Johnson	9.00	4.50	2.75
327	Bob Wiesler	9.00	4.50	2.75
328	Preston Ward	9.00	4.50	2.75
329	Lou Berberet	9.00	4.50	2.75
330	Jim Busby	9.00	4.50	2.75
331	Dick Hall	9.00	4.50	2.75

		NR MT	EX	VG
332	Don Larsen	30.00	15.00	9.00
333	Rube Walker	9.00	4.50	2.75
334	Bob Miller	9.00	4.50	2.75
335	Don Hoak	9.00	4.50	2.75
336	Ellis Kinder	9.00	4.50	2.75
337	Bobby Morgan	9.00	4.50	2.75
338	Jim Delsing	9.00	4.50	2.75
339	Rance Pless	9.00	4.50	2.75
340	Mickey McDermott	30.00	15.00	9.00
----	Checklist 1/3	200.00	75.00	45.00
----	Checklist 2/4	200.00	75.00	45.00

1956 Topps Hocus Focus Large

These sets are a direct descendant of the 1948 Topps Magic Photo" issue. Again, the baseball players were part of a larger overall series covering several topical areas. There are two distinct issues of Hocus Focus cards in 1956. The "large" cards, measuring 1" by 1-5/8," consists of 18 players. The "small" cards, 7/8 by 1-3/8," state on the back that they are a series of 23, though only 13 are known. Besides players on the cards themselves, the easiest way to distinguish Hocus Focus cards of 1956 from the Magic Photos series of 1948 is to remember that the 1956 cards actually have the words "Hocus Focus" on the back. The photos on these cards were developed by wetting the cards surface and exposing to light. Prices below are for cards with well-developed pictures. Cards with poorly developed photos are worth significantly less.

		NR MT	EX	VG
Complete Set:		525.00	262.00	157.00
Common Player:		12.00	6.00	3.50
1	Dick Groat	25.00	12.50	7.50
2	Ed Lopat	25.00	12.50	7.50
3	Hank Sauer	12.00	6.00	3.50
4	"Dusty" Rhodes	12.00	6.00	3.50
5	Ted Williams	125.00	62.00	37.00
6	Harvey Haddix	12.00	6.00	3.50
7	Ray Boone	12.00	6.00	3.50
8	Al Rosen	25.00	12.50	7.50
9	Mayo Smith	12.00	6.00	3.50
10	Warren Spahn	70.00	35.00	21.00
11	Jim Rivera	12.00	6.00	3.50
12	Ted Kluszewski	25.00	12.50	7.50
13	Gus Zernial	12.00	6.00	3.50
14	Jackie Robinson	125.00	62.00	37.00
15	Hal Smith	12.00	6.00	3.50
16	Johnny Schmitz	12.00	6.00	3.50
17	"Spook" Jacobs	12.00	6.00	3.50
18	Mel Parnell	12.00	6.00	3.50

1956 Topps Pins

One of Topps first specialty issues, the 60-pin set of ballplayers issued in 1956 contains a high percentage of big-name stars which, combined with the scarcity of the pins, makes collecting a complete set extremely challenging. Compounding the situation is the fact that some pins are seen far less often than others, though the reason is unknown. Chuck Stobbs, Hector Lopez and Chuck Diering are unaccountably scarce. Measuring 1-1/8" in diameter, the pins utilize the same portraits found on 1956 Topps baseball cards. The photos are set against a solid color background.

		NR MT	EX	VG
Complete Set:		2500.00	1250.00	750.00
Common Player:		15.00	7.50	4.50
(1)	Hank Aaron	100.00	50.00	30.00
(2)	Sandy Amoros	15.00	7.50	4.50
(3)	Luis Arroyo	15.00	7.50	4.50
(4)	Ernie Banks	50.00	25.00	15.00
(5)	Yogi Berra	70.00	35.00	21.00
(6)	Joe Black	15.00	7.50	4.50
(7)	Ray Boone	15.00	7.50	4.50
(8)	Ken Boyer	20.00	10.00	6.00
(9)	Joe Collins	15.00	7.50	4.50
(10)	Gene Conley	15.00	7.50	4.50
(11)	Chuck Diering	225.00	112.00	67.00
(12)	Dick Donovan	15.00	7.50	4.50
(13)	Jim Finigan	15.00	7.50	4.50
(14)	Art Fowler	15.00	7.50	4.50
(15)	Ruben Gomez	15.00	7.50	4.50
(16)	Dick Groat	20.00	10.00	6.00
(17)	Harvey Haddix	15.00	7.50	4.50
(18)	Jack Harshman	15.00	7.50	4.50
(19)	Grady Hatton	15.00	7.50	4.50
(20)	Jim Hegan	15.00	7.50	4.50
(21)	Gil Hodges	40.00	20.00	12.00
(22)	Bobby Hofman	15.00	7.50	4.50
(23)	Frank House	15.00	7.50	4.50
(24)	Jackie Jensen	20.00	10.00	6.00
(25)	Al Kaline	60.00	30.00	18.00
(26)	Bob Kennedy	15.00	7.50	4.50
(27)	Ted Kluszewski	25.00	12.50	7.50
(28)	Dale Long	15.00	7.50	4.50
(29)	Hector Lopez	200.00	100.00	60.00
(30)	Ed Mathews	40.00	20.00	12.00
(31)	Willie Mays	100.00	50.00	30.00
(32)	Roy McMillan	15.00	7.50	4.50
(33)	Willie Miranda	15.00	7.50	4.50
(34)	Wally Moon	15.00	7.50	4.50
(35)	Don Mossi	15.00	7.50	4.50
(36)	Ron Negray	15.00	7.50	4.50
(37)	Johnny O'Brien	15.00	7.50	4.50
(38)	Carlos Paula	15.00	7.50	4.50
(39)	Vic Power	15.00	7.50	4.50
(40)	Jim Rivera	15.00	7.50	4.50
(41)	Phil Rizzuto	40.00	20.00	12.00
(42)	Jackie Robinson	100.00	50.00	30.00
(43)	Al Rosen	25.00	12.50	7.50
(44)	Hank Sauer	15.00	7.50	4.50
(45)	Roy Sievers	15.00	7.50	4.50
(46)	Bill Skowron	20.00	10.00	6.00
(47)	Al Smith	15.00	7.50	4.50
(48)	Hal Smith	15.00	7.50	4.50
(49)	Mayo Smith	15.00	7.50	4.50
(50)	Duke Snider	70.00	35.00	21.00
(51)	Warren Spahn	50.00	25.00	15.00
(52)	Karl Spooner	15.00	7.50	4.50
(53)	Chuck Stobbs	175.00	87.00	52.00
(54)	Frank Sullivan	15.00	7.50	4.50
(55)	Bill Tremel	15.00	7.50	4.50
(56)	Gus Triandos	15.00	7.50	4.50
(57)	Bob Turley	20.00	10.00	6.00
(58)	Herman Wehmeier	15.00	7.50	4.50
(59)	Ted Williams	110.00	55.00	33.00
(60)	Gus Zernial	15.00	7.50	4.50

1957 Topps

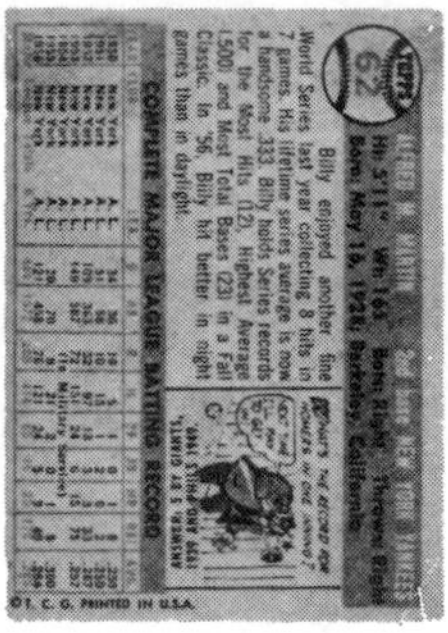

For 1957, Topps reduced the size of its cards to the now-standard 2-1/2" by 3-1/2." Set size was increased to 407 cards. Another change came in the form of the use of real color photographs as opposed to the hand-colored black and whites of previous years. For the first time since 1954, there were also cards with more than one player. The two, "Dodger Sluggers" and "Yankees' Power Hitters" began a trend toward the increased use of mulitple-player cards. Another first-time innovation, found on the backs, is complete players statistics. The scarce cards in the set are not the highest numbers, but rather numbers 265-352. Four unnumbered checklist cards were issued along with the set. They are quite expensive and are not included in the complete set prices quoted below.

	NR MT	EX	VG
Complete Set:	7000.00	3500.00	2100.
Common Player: 1-264	7.00	3.50	2.00
Common Player: 265-352	18.00	9.00	5.50
Common Player: 353-407	7.00	3.50	2.00

		NR MT	EX	VG
1	Ted Williams	425.00	100.00	38.00
2	Yogi Berra	150.00	70.00	45.00
3	Dale Long	7.00	3.50	2.00
4	Johnny Logan	7.00	3.50	2.00
5	Sal Maglie	8.00	4.00	2.50
6	Hector Lopez	7.00	3.50	2.00
7	Luis Aparicio	30.00	15.00	9.00
8	Don Mossi	7.00	3.50	2.00
9	Johnny Temple	7.00	3.50	2.00
10	Willie Mays	225.00	112.00	67.00
11	George Zuverink	7.00	3.50	2.00
12	Dick Groat	6.00	3.00	1.75
13	Wally Burnette	7.00	3.50	2.00
14	Bob Nieman	7.00	3.50	2.00
15	Robin Roberts	20.00	10.00	6.00
16	Walt Moryn	7.00	3.50	2.00
17	Billy Gardner	7.00	3.50	2.00
18	*Don Drysdale*	180.00	90.00	55.00
19	Bob Wilson	7.00	3.50	2.00
20	Hank Aaron (photo reversed)	225.00	112.00	67.00
21	Frank Sullivan	7.00	3.50	2.00
22	Jerry Snyder (photo actually Ed Fitz Gerald)	7.00	3.50	2.00
23	Sherm Lollar	7.00	3.50	2.00
24	*Bill Mazeroski*	50.00	25.00	15.00
25	Whitey Ford	50.00	25.00	15.00
26	Bob Boyd	7.00	3.50	2.00
27	Ted Kazanski	7.00	3.50	2.00
28	Gene Conley	7.00	3.50	2.00
29	*Whitey Herzog*	25.00	12.50	7.50
30	Pee Wee Reese	60.00	30.00	18.00
31	Ron Northey	7.00	3.50	2.00
32	Hersh Freeman	7.00	3.50	2.00
33	Jim Small	7.00	3.50	2.00
34	Tom Sturdivant	6.00	3.00	1.75
35	*Frank Robinson*	250.00	125.00	75.00
36	Bob Grim	6.00	3.00	1.75
37	Frank Torre	7.00	3.50	2.00
38	Nellie Fox	18.00	9.00	5.50
39	Al Worthington	7.00	3.50	2.00
40	Early Wynn	18.00	9.00	5.50
41	Hal Smith	7.00	3.50	2.00
42	Dee Fondy	7.00	3.50	2.00
43	Connie Johnson	7.00	3.50	2.00
44	Joe DeMaestri	7.00	3.50	2.00
45	Carl Furillo	9.00	4.50	2.75
46	Bob Miller	7.00	3.50	2.00
47	Don Blasingame	7.00	3.50	2.00
48	Bill Bruton	7.00	3.50	2.00
49	Daryl Spencer	7.00	3.50	2.00
50	Herb Score	6.00	3.00	1.75
51	Clint Courtney	7.00	3.50	2.00
52	Lee Walls	7.00	3.50	2.00
53	Clem Labine	6.00	3.00	1.75
54	Elmer Valo	7.00	3.50	2.00
55	Ernie Banks	80.00	40.00	25.00
56	Dave Sisler	7.00	3.50	2.00
57	Jim Lemon	7.00	3.50	2.00
58	Ruben Gomez	7.00	3.50	2.00
59	Dick Williams	6.00	3.00	1.75
60	Billy Hoeft	7.00	3.50	2.00
61	Dusty Rhodes	7.00	3.50	2.00
62	Billy Martin	50.00	25.00	15.00
63	Ike Delock	7.00	3.50	2.00
64	Pete Runnels	6.00	3.00	1.75
65	Wally Moon	7.00	3.50	2.00
66	Brooks Lawrence	7.00	3.50	2.00
67	Chico Carrasquel	7.00	3.50	2.00
68	Ray Crone	7.00	3.50	2.00
69	Roy McMillan	7.00	3.50	2.00
70	Richie Ashburn	20.00	10.00	6.00
71	Murry Dickson	7.00	3.50	2.00
72	Bill Tuttle	7.00	3.50	2.00
73	George Crowe	7.00	3.50	2.00
74	Vito Valentinetti	7.00	3.50	2.00
75	Jim Piersall	6.00	3.00	1.75
76	Bob Clemente	200.00	100.00	60.00
77	Paul Foytack	7.00	3.50	2.00
78	Vic Wertz	6.00	3.00	1.75
79	*Lindy McDaniel*	6.00	3.00	1.75
80	Gil Hodges	50.00	30.00	15.00
81	Herm Wehmeier	7.00	3.50	2.00
82	Elston Howard	15.00	7.50	4.50
83	Lou Skizas	7.00	3.50	2.00
84	Moe Drabowsky	7.00	3.50	2.00
85	Larry Doby	10.00	5.00	3.00
86	Bill Sarni	7.00	3.50	2.00
87	Tom Gorman	7.00	3.50	2.00
88	Harvey Kuenn	6.00	3.00	1.75
89	Roy Sievers	7.00	3.50	2.00
90	Warren Spahn	75.00	38.00	23.00
91	Mack Burk	7.00	3.50	2.00
92	Mickey Vernon	6.00	3.00	1.75
93	Hal Jeffcoat	7.00	3.50	2.00
94	Bobby Del Greco	7.00	3.50	2.00
95	Mickey Mantle	650.00	325.00	200.00
96	*Hank Aguirre*	6.00	3.00	1.75
97	Yankees Team	40.00	20.00	12.00
98	Al Dark	8.00	4.00	2.50
99	Bob Keegan	7.00	3.50	2.00
100	League Presidents (Warren Giles, William Harridge)	6.00	3.00	1.75
101	Chuck Stobbs	7.00	3.50	2.00
102	Ray Boone	7.00	3.50	2.00
103	Joe Nuxhall	6.00	3.00	1.75
104	Hank Foiles	7.00	3.50	2.00
105	Johnny Antonelli	7.00	3.50	2.00
106	Ray Moore	7.00	3.50	2.00
107	Jim Rivera	7.00	3.50	2.00
108	Tommy Byrne	6.00	3.00	1.75
109	Hank Thompson	7.00	3.50	2.00
110	Bill Virdon	6.00	3.00	1.75
111	Hal Smith	7.00	3.50	2.00
112	Tom Brewer	7.00	3.50	2.00
113	Wilmer Mizell	7.00	3.50	2.00
114	Braves Team	10.00	5.00	3.00
115	Jim Gilliam	10.00	5.00	3.00
116	Mike Fornieles	7.00	3.50	2.00
117	Joe Adcock	6.00	3.00	1.75
118	Bob Porterfield	7.00	3.50	2.00
119	Stan Lopata	7.00	3.50	2.00
120	Bob Lemon	15.00	7.50	4.50
121	*Cletis Boyer*	15.00	7.50	4.50
122	Ken Boyer	8.00	4.00	2.50
123	Steve Ridzik	7.00	3.50	2.00
124	Dave Philley	7.00	3.50	2.00
125	Al Kaline	70.00	35.00	21.00
126	Bob Wiesler	7.00	3.50	2.00
127	Bob Buhl	7.00	3.50	2.00
128	Ed Bailey	7.00	3.50	2.00
129	Saul Rogovin	7.00	3.50	2.00
130	Don Newcombe	10.00	5.00	3.00
131	Milt Bolling	7.00	3.50	2.00
132	Art Ditmar	6.00	3.00	1.75

		NR MT	EX	VG
133	Del Crandall	6.00	3.00	1.75
134	Don Kaiser	7.00	3.50	2.00
135	Bill Skowron	12.00	6.00	3.50
136	Jim Hegan	7.00	3.50	2.00
137	Bob Rush	7.00	3.50	2.00
138	Minnie Minoso	8.00	4.00	2.50
139	Lou Kretlow	7.00	3.50	2.00
140	Frank Thomas	7.00	3.50	2.00
141	Al Aber	7.00	3.50	2.00
142	Charley Thompson	7.00	3.50	2.00
143	Andy Pafko	6.00	3.00	1.75
144	Ray Narleski	7.00	3.50	2.00
145	Al Smith	7.00	3.50	2.00
146	Don Ferrarese	7.00	3.50	2.00
147	Al Walker	6.00	3.00	1.75
148	Don Mueller	7.00	3.50	2.00
149	Bob Kennedy	7.00	3.50	2.00
150	Bob Friend	6.00	3.00	1.75
151	Willie Miranda	7.00	3.50	2.00
152	Jack Harshman	7.00	3.50	2.00
153	Karl Olson	7.00	3.50	2.00
154	Red Schoendienst	20.00	10.00	6.00
155	Jim Brosnan	7.00	3.50	2.00
156	Gus Triandos	7.00	3.50	2.00
157	Wally Post	7.00	3.50	2.00
158	Curt Simmons	6.00	3.00	1.75
159	Solly Drake	7.00	3.50	2.00
160	Billy Pierce	6.00	3.00	1.75
161	Pirates Team	8.00	4.00	2.50
162	Jack Meyer	7.00	3.50	2.00
163	Sammy White	7.00	3.50	2.00
164	Tommy Carroll	6.00	3.00	1.75
165	Ted Kluszewski	25.00	12.50	7.50
166	Roy Face	6.00	3.00	1.75
167	Vic Power	7.00	3.50	2.00
168	Frank Lary	6.00	3.00	1.75
169	Herb Plews	7.00	3.50	2.00
170	Duke Snider	100.00	50.00	30.00
171	Red Sox Team	9.00	4.50	2.75
172	Gene Woodling	6.00	3.00	1.75
173	Roger Craig	8.00	4.00	2.50
174	Willie Jones	7.00	3.50	2.00
175	Don Larsen	8.00	4.00	2.50
176	Gene Baker	7.00	3.50	2.00
177	Eddie Yost	7.00	3.50	2.00
178	Don Bessent	7.00	3.50	2.00
179	Ernie Oravetz	7.00	3.50	2.00
180	Gus Bell	7.00	3.50	2.00
181	Dick Donovan	7.00	3.50	2.00
182	Hobie Landrith	7.00	3.50	2.00
183	Cubs Team	8.00	4.00	2.50
184	*Tito Francona*	6.00	3.00	1.75
185	Johnny Kucks	6.00	3.00	1.75
186	Jim King	7.00	3.50	2.00
187	Virgil Trucks	7.00	3.50	2.00
188	Felix Mantilla	7.00	3.50	2.00
189	Willard Nixon	7.00	3.50	2.00
190	Randy Jackson	7.00	3.50	2.00
191	Joe Margoneri	7.00	3.50	2.00
192	Jerry Coleman	6.00	3.00	1.75
193	Del Rice	7.00	3.50	2.00
194	Hal Brown	7.00	3.50	2.00
195	Bobby Avila	7.00	3.50	2.00
196	Larry Jackson	7.00	3.50	2.00
197	Hank Sauer	7.00	3.50	2.00
198	Tigers Team	9.00	4.50	2.75
199	Vernon Law	6.00	3.00	1.75
200	Gil McDougald	12.00	6.00	3.50
201	Sandy Amoros	7.00	3.50	2.00
202	Dick Gernert	7.00	3.50	2.00
203	Hoyt Wilhelm	18.00	9.00	5.50
204	Athletics Team	8.00	4.00	2.50
205	Charley Maxwell	7.00	3.50	2.00
206	Willard Schmidt	7.00	3.50	2.00
207	Billy Hunter	7.00	3.50	2.00
208	Lew Burdette	6.00	3.00	1.75
209	Bob Skinner	7.00	3.50	2.00
210	Roy Campanella	80.00	40.00	24.00
211	Camilo Pascual	7.00	3.50	2.00
212	*Rocco Colavito*	100.00	50.00	30.00
213	Les Moss	7.00	3.50	2.00
214	Phillies Team	8.00	4.00	2.50
215	Enos Slaughter	20.00	10.00	6.00
216	Marv Grissom	7.00	3.50	2.00
217	Gene Stephens	7.00	3.50	2.00
218	Ray Jablonski	7.00	3.50	2.00
219	Tom Acker	7.00	3.50	2.00
220	Jackie Jensen	6.00	3.00	1.75
221	Dixie Howell	7.00	3.50	2.00
222	Alex Grammas	7.00	3.50	2.00
223	Frank House	7.00	3.50	2.00

		NR MT	EX	VG
224	Marv Blaylock	7.00	3.50	2.00
225	Harry Simpson	7.00	3.50	2.00
226	Preston Ward	7.00	3.50	2.00
227	Jerry Staley	7.00	3.50	2.00
228	Smoky Burgess	6.00	3.00	1.75
229	George Susce	7.00	3.50	2.00
230	George Kell	18.00	9.00	5.50
231	Solly Hemus	7.00	3.50	2.00
232	Whitey Lockman	7.00	3.50	2.00
233	Art Fowler	7.00	3.50	2.00
234	Dick Cole	7.00	3.50	2.00
235	Tom Poholsky	7.00	3.50	2.00
236	Joe Ginsberg	7.00	3.50	2.00
237	Foster Castleman	7.00	3.50	2.00
238	Eddie Robinson	7.00	3.50	2.00
239	Tom Morgan	7.00	3.50	2.00
240	Hank Bauer	10.00	5.00	3.00
241	Joe Lonnett	7.00	3.50	2.00
242	Charley Neal	7.00	3.50	2.00
243	Cardinals Team	8.00	4.00	2.50
244	Billy Loes	7.00	3.50	2.00
245	Rip Repulski	7.00	3.50	2.00
246	Jose Valdivielso	7.00	3.50	2.00
247	Turk Lown	7.00	3.50	2.00
248	Jim Finigan	7.00	3.50	2.00
249	Dave Pope	7.00	3.50	2.00
250	Ed Mathews	35.00	17.50	10.50
251	Orioles Team	8.00	4.00	2.50
252	Carl Erskine	10.00	5.00	3.00
253	Gus Zernial	7.00	3.50	2.00
254	Ron Negray	7.00	3.50	2.00
255	Charlie Silvera	7.00	3.50	2.00
256	Ronnie Kline	7.00	3.50	2.00
257	Walt Dropo	7.00	3.50	2.00
258	Steve Gromek	7.00	3.50	2.00
259	Eddie O'Brien	7.00	3.50	2.00
260	Del Ennis	7.00	3.50	2.00
261	Bob Chakales	7.00	3.50	2.00
262	Bobby Thomson	6.00	3.00	1.75
263	George Strickland	7.00	3.50	2.00
264	Bob Turley	8.00	4.00	2.50
265	Harvey Haddix	20.00	10.00	6.00
266	Ken Kuhn	18.00	9.00	5.50
267	Danny Kravitz	18.00	9.00	5.50
268	Jackie Collum	18.00	9.00	5.50
269	Bob Cerv	18.00	9.00	5.50
270	Senators Team	25.00	12.50	7.50
271	Danny O'Connell	18.00	9.00	5.50
272	Bobby Shantz	25.00	12.50	7.50
273	Jim Davis	18.00	9.00	5.50
274	Don Hoak	18.00	9.00	5.50
275	Indians Team	35.00	17.50	10.50
276	Jim Pyburn	18.00	9.00	5.50
277	Johnny Podres	50.00	25.00	15.00
278	Fred Hatfield	18.00	9.00	5.50
279	Bob Thurman	18.00	9.00	5.50
280	Alex Kellner	18.00	9.00	5.50
281	Gail Harris	18.00	9.00	5.50
282	Jack Dittmer	18.00	9.00	5.50
283	*Wes Covington*	18.00	9.00	5.50
284	Don Zimmer	20.00	10.00	6.00
285	Ned Garver	18.00	9.00	5.50
286	*Bobby Richardson*	100.00	50.00	30.00
287	Sam Jones	18.00	9.00	5.50
288	Ted Lepcio	18.00	9.00	5.50
289	Jim Bolger	18.00	9.00	5.50
290	Andy Carey	18.00	9.00	5.50
291	Windy McCall	18.00	9.00	5.50
292	Billy Klaus	18.00	9.00	5.50
293	Ted Abernathy	18.00	9.00	5.50
294	Rocky Bridges	18.00	9.00	5.50
295	Joe Collins	18.00	9.00	5.50
296	Johnny Klippstein	18.00	9.00	5.50
297	Jack Crimian	18.00	9.00	5.50
298	Irv Noren	18.00	9.00	5.50
299	Chuck Harmon	18.00	9.00	5.50
300	Mike Garcia	18.00	9.00	5.50
301	Sam Esposito	18.00	9.00	5.50
302	Sandy Koufax	400.00	200.00	125.00
303	Billy Goodman	18.00	9.00	5.50
304	Joe Cunningham	18.00	9.00	5.50
305	Chico Fernandez	18.00	9.00	5.50
306	Darrell Johnson	18.00	9.00	5.50
307	Jack Phillips	18.00	9.00	5.50
308	Dick Hall	18.00	9.00	5.50
309	Jim Busby	18.00	9.00	5.50
310	Max Surkont	18.00	9.00	5.50
311	Al Pilarcik	18.00	9.00	5.50
312	*Tony Kubek*	100.00	50.00	30.00
313	Mel Parnell	18.00	9.00	5.50
314	Ed Bouchee	18.00	9.00	5.50

		NR MT	EX	VG
315	Lou Berberet	18.00	9.00	5.50
316	Billy O'Dell	18.00	9.00	5.50
317	Giants Team	50.00	25.00	15.00
318	Mickey McDermott	18.00	9.00	5.50
319	Gino Cimoli	18.00	9.00	5.50
320	Neil Chrisley	18.00	9.00	5.50
321	Red Murff	18.00	9.00	5.50
322	Redlegs Team	50.00	25.00	15.00
323	Wes Westrum	18.00	9.00	5.50
324	Dodgers Team	90.00	45.00	27.00
325	Frank Bolling	18.00	9.00	5.50
326	Pedro Ramos	18.00	9.00	5.50
327	Jim Pendleton	18.00	9.00	5.50
328	*Brooks Robinson*	350.00	175.00	105.00
329	White Sox Team	35.00	17.50	10.50
330	Jim Wilson	18.00	9.00	5.50
331	Ray Katt	18.00	9.00	5.50
332	Bob Bowman	18.00	9.00	5.50
333	Ernie Johnson	18.00	9.00	5.50
334	Jerry Schoonmaker	18.00	9.00	5.50
335	Granny Hamner	18.00	9.00	5.50
336	*Haywood Sullivan*	18.00	9.00	5.50
337	Rene Valdes	18.00	9.00	5.50
338	*Jim Bunning*	125.00	62.00	37.00
339	Bob Speake	18.00	9.00	5.50
340	Bill Wight	18.00	9.00	5.50
341	Don Gross	18.00	9.00	5.50
342	Gene Mauch	18.00	9.00	5.50
343	Taylor Phillips	18.00	9.00	5.50
344	Paul LaPalme	18.00	9.00	5.50
345	Paul Smith	18.00	9.00	5.50
346	Dick Littlefield	18.00	9.00	5.50
347	Hal Naragon	18.00	9.00	5.50
348	Jim Hearn	18.00	9.00	5.50
349	Nelson King	18.00	9.00	5.50
350	Eddie Miksis	18.00	9.00	5.50
351	Dave Hillman	18.00	9.00	5.50
352	Ellis Kinder	18.00	9.00	5.50
353	Cal Neeman	7.00	3.50	2.00
354	Rip Coleman	7.00	3.50	2.00
355	Frank Malzone	7.00	3.50	2.00
356	Faye Throneberry	7.00	3.50	2.00
357	Earl Torgeson	7.00	3.50	2.00
358	Jerry Lynch	7.00	3.50	2.00
359	Tom Cheney	7.00	3.50	2.00
360	Johnny Groth	7.00	3.50	2.00
361	Curt Barclay	7.00	3.50	2.00
362	Roman Mejias	7.00	3.50	2.00
363	Eddie Kasko	7.00	3.50	2.00
364	Cal McLish	7.00	3.50	2.00
365	Ossie Virgil	7.00	3.50	2.00
366	Ken Lehman	7.00	3.50	2.00
367	Ed Fitz Gerald	7.00	3.50	2.00
368	Bob Purkey	7.00	3.50	2.00
369	Milt Graff	7.00	3.50	2.00
370	Warren Hacker	7.00	3.50	2.00
371	Bob Lennon	7.00	3.50	2.00
372	Norm Zauchin	7.00	3.50	2.00
373	Pete Whisenant	7.00	3.50	2.00
374	Don Cardwell	7.00	3.50	2.00
375	*Jim Landis*	6.00	3.00	1.75
376	Don Elston	7.00	3.50	2.00
377	Andre Rodgers	7.00	3.50	2.00
378	Elmer Singleton	7.00	3.50	2.00
379	Don Lee	7.00	3.50	2.00
380	Walker Cooper	7.00	3.50	2.00
381	Dean Stone	7.00	3.50	2.00
382	Jim Brideweser	7.00	3.50	2.00
383	*Juan Pizarro*	6.00	3.00	1.75
384	Bobby Gene Smith	7.00	3.50	2.00
385	Art Houtteman	7.00	3.50	2.00
386	Lyle Luttrell	7.00	3.50	2.00
387	*Jack Sanford*	6.00	3.00	1.75
388	Pete Daley	7.00	3.50	2.00
389	Dave Jolly	7.00	3.50	2.00
390	Reno Bertoia	7.00	3.50	2.00
391	*Ralph Terry*	10.00	5.00	3.00
392	Chuck Tanner	6.00	3.00	1.75
393	Raul Sanchez	7.00	3.50	2.00
394	Luis Arroyo	7.00	3.50	2.00
395	Bubba Phillips	7.00	3.50	2.00
396	Casey Wise	7.00	3.50	2.00
397	Roy Smalley	7.00	3.50	2.00
398	Al Cicotte	6.00	3.00	1.75
399	Billy Consolo	7.00	3.50	2.00
400	Dodgers' Sluggers (Roy Campanella, Carl Furillo, Gil Hodges, Duke Snider)	150.00	60.00	38.00
401	*Earl Battey*	6.00	3.00	1.75
402	Jim Pisoni	7.00	3.50	2.00
403	Dick Hyde	7.00	3.50	2.00
404	Harry Anderson	7.00	3.50	2.00
405	Duke Maas	7.00	3.50	2.00
406	Bob Hale	7.00	3.50	2.00
407	Yankees' Power Hitters (Yogi Berra, Mickey Mantle)	350.00	140.00	88.00
---a	Checklist Series 1-2 (Big Blony ad on back)	175.00	87.00	52.00
---b	Checklist Series 1-2 (Bazooka ad on back)	175.00	87.00	52.00
---a	Checklist Series 2-3 (Big Blony ad on back)	300.00	150.00	90.00
---b	Checklist Series 2-3 (Bazooka ad on back)	300.00	150.00	90.00
---a	Checklist Series 3-4 (Big Blony ad on back)	500.00	250.00	150.00
---b	Checklist Series 3-4 (Bazooka ad on back)	500.00	250.00	150.00
---a	Checklist Series 4-5 (Big Blony ad on back)	750.00	325.00	225.00
---b	Checklist Series 4-5 (Bazooka ad on back)	750.00	325.00	225.00
——	Contest Card (Saturday, May 4th)	15.00	7.50	4.50
——	Contest Card (Saturday, May 25th)	15.00	7.50	4.50
——	Contest Card (Saturday, June 22nd)	15.00	7.50	4.50
——	Contest Card (Friday, July 19)	15.00	7.50	4.50
——	Lucky Penny Insert Card	15.00	7.50	4.50

1958 Topps

Topps continued to expand its set size in 1958 with the release of a 494-card set. One card (#145) was not issued after Ed Bouchee was suspended from baseball. Cards retained the 2-1/2" by 3-1/2" size. There are a number of variations, including yellow or white lettering on 33 cards between numbers 2-108 (higher priced yellow letter variations checklisted below are not included in the complete set prices). The number of multiple-player cards was increased. A major innovation is the addition of 20 "All-Star" cards. For the first time, checklists were incorporated into the numbered series, as the backs of team cards.

	NR MT	EX	VG
Complete Set:	4500.00	2250.00	1350.
Common Player: 1-110	7.00	3.50	2.00
Common Player: 111-440	5.00	2.50	1.50
Common Player: 441-495	4.00	2.00	1.25

		NR MT	EX	VG
1	Ted Williams	375.00	80.00	35.00
2a	Bob Lemon (yellow team letters)	35.00	17.50	10.50
2b	Bob Lemon (white team letters)	12.00	6.00	3.50
3	Alex Kellner	7.00	3.50	2.00
4	Hank Foiles	7.00	3.50	2.00
5	Willie Mays	150.00	75.00	45.00
6	George Zuverink	7.00	3.50	2.00
7	Dale Long	7.00	3.50	2.00
8a	Eddie Kasko (yellow name letters)	20.00	10.00	6.00
8b	Eddie Kasko (white name letters)	7.00	3.50	2.00
9	Hank Bauer	10.00	5.00	3.00
10	Lou Burdette	8.00	4.00	2.50
11a	Jim Rivera (yellow team letters)	20.00	10.00	6.00
11b	Jim Rivera (white team letters)	7.00	3.50	2.00
12	George Crowe	7.00	3.50	2.00

		NR MT	EX	VG
13a	Billy Hoeft (yellow name letters)	20.00	10.00	6.00
13b	Billy Hoeft (white name, orange triangle by foot)	7.00	3.50	2.00
13c	Billy Hoeft (white name, red triangle by foot)	7.00	3.50	2.00
14	Rip Repulski	7.00	3.50	2.00
15	Jim Lemon	7.00	3.50	2.00
16	Charley Neal	7.00	3.50	2.00
17	Felix Mantilla	7.00	3.50	2.00
18	Frank Sullivan	7.00	3.50	2.00
19	Giants Team/Checklist 1-88	10.00	5.00	3.00
20a	Gil McDougald (yellow name letters)	25.00	12.50	7.50
20b	Gil McDougald (white name letters)	9.00	4.50	2.75
21	Curt Barclay	7.00	3.50	2.00
22	Hal Naragon	7.00	3.50	2.00
23a	Bill Tuttle (yellow name letters)	20.00	10.00	6.00
23b	Bill Tuttle (white name letters)	7.00	3.50	2.00
24a	Hobie Landrith (yellow name letters)	20.00	10.00	6.00
24b	Hobie Landrith (white name letters)	7.00	3.50	2.00
25	Don Drysdale	60.00	30.00	18.00
26	Ron Jackson	7.00	3.50	2.00
27	Bud Freeman	7.00	3.50	2.00
28	Jim Busby	7.00	3.50	2.00
29	Ted Lepcio	7.00	3.50	2.00
30a	Hank Aaron (yellow name letters)	350.00	140.00	88.00
30b	Hank Aaron (white name letters)	150.00	60.00	38.00
31	Tex Clevenger	7.00	3.50	2.00
32a	J.W. Porter (yellow name letters)	20.00	10.00	6.00
32b	J.W. Porter (white name letters)	7.00	3.50	2.00
33a	Cal Neeman (yellow team letters)	20.00	10.00	6.00
33b	Cal Neeman (white team letters)	7.00	3.50	2.00
34	Bob Thurman	7.00	3.50	2.00
35a	Don Mossi (yellow team letters)	20.00	10.00	6.00
35b	Don Mossi (white team letters)	7.00	3.50	2.00
36	Ted Kazanski	7.00	3.50	2.00
37	*Mike McCormick* (photo actually Ray Monzant)	7.00	3.50	2.00
38	Dick Gernert	7.00	3.50	2.00
39	Bob Martyn	7.00	3.50	2.00
40	George Kell	15.00	7.50	4.50
41	Dave Hillman	7.00	3.50	2.00
42	*John Roseboro*	7.00	3.50	2.00
43	Sal Maglie	10.00	5.00	3.00
44	Senators Team/Checklist 1-88	10.00	5.00	3.00
45	Dick Groat	7.00	3.50	2.00
46a	Lou Sleater (yellow name letters)	20.00	10.00	6.00
46b	Lou Sleater (white name letters)	7.00	3.50	2.00
47	*Roger Maris*	350.00	175.00	105.00
48	Chuck Harmon	7.00	3.50	2.00
49	Smoky Burgess	7.00	3.50	2.00
50a	Billy Pierce (yellow team letters)	20.00	10.00	6.00
50b	Billy Pierce (white team letters)	7.00	3.50	2.00
51	Del Rice	7.00	3.50	2.00
52a	Bob Clemente (yellow team letters)	250.00	100.00	63.00
52b	Bob Clemente (white team letters)	175.00	87.00	52.00
53a	Morrie Martin (yellow name letters)	20.00	10.00	6.00
53b	Morrie Martin (white name letters)	7.00	3.50	2.00
54	*Norm Siebern*	7.00	3.50	2.00
55	Chico Carrasquel	7.00	3.50	2.00
56	Bill Fischer	7.00	3.50	2.00
57a	Tim Thompson (yellow name letters)	20.00	10.00	6.00
57b	Tim Thompson (white name letters)	7.00	3.50	2.00
58a	Art Schult (yellow team letters)	20.00	10.00	6.00
58b	Art Schult (white team letters)	7.00	3.50	2.00
59	Dave Sisler	7.00	3.50	2.00
60a	Del Ennis (yellow name letters)	20.00	10.00	6.00
60b	Del Ennis (white name letters)	7.00	3.50	2.00
61a	Darrell Johnson (yellow name letters)	20.00	10.00	6.00
61b	Darrell Johnson (white name letters)	7.00	3.50	2.00
62	Joe DeMaestri	7.00	3.50	2.00
63	Joe Nuxhall	7.00	3.50	2.00
64	Joe Lonnett	7.00	3.50	2.00
65a	Von McDaniel (yellow name letters)	20.00	10.00	6.00
65b	Von McDaniel (white name letters)	7.00	3.50	2.00

		NR MT	EX	VG
66	Lee Walls	7.00	3.50	2.00
67	Joe Ginsberg	7.00	3.50	2.00
68	Daryl Spencer	7.00	3.50	2.00
69	Wally Burnette	7.00	3.50	2.00
70a	Al Kaline (yellow name letters)	175.00	87.00	52.00
70b	Al Kaline (white name letters)	75.00	38.00	23.00
71	Dodgers Team/Checklist 1-88	20.00	10.00	6.00
72	Bud Byerly	7.00	3.50	2.00
73	Pete Daley	7.00	3.50	2.00
74	Roy Face	7.00	3.50	2.00
75	Gus Bell	7.00	3.50	2.00
76a	Dick Farrell (yellow team letters)	20.00	10.00	6.00
76b	Dick Farrell (white team letters)	7.00	3.50	2.00
77a	Don Zimmer (yellow team letters)	20.00	10.00	6.00
77b	Don Zimmer (white team letters)	7.00	3.50	2.00
78a	Ernie Johnson (yellow name letters)	20.00	10.00	6.00
78b	Ernie Johnson (white name letters)	7.00	3.50	2.00
79a	Dick Williams (yellow team letters)	20.00	10.00	6.00
79b	Dick Williams (white team letters)	7.00	3.50	2.00
80	Dick Drott	7.00	3.50	2.00
81a	*Steve Boros* (yellow team letters)	20.00	10.00	6.00
81b	*Steve Boros* (white team letters)	7.00	3.50	2.00
82	Ronnie Kline	7.00	3.50	2.00
83	Bob Hazle	7.00	3.50	2.00
84	Billy O'Dell	7.00	3.50	2.00
85a	Luis Aparicio (yellow team letters)	50.00	25.00	15.00
85b	Luis Aparicio (white team letters)	15.00	7.50	4.50
86	Valmy Thomas	7.00	3.50	2.00
87	Johnny Kucks	7.00	3.50	2.00
88	Duke Snider	70.00	35.00	20.00
89	Billy Klaus	7.00	3.50	2.00
90	Robin Roberts	15.00	7.50	4.50
91	Chuck Tanner	7.00	3.50	2.00
92a	Clint Courtney (yellow name letters)	20.00	10.00	6.00
92b	Clint Courtney (white name letters)	7.00	3.50	2.00
93	Sandy Amoros	7.00	3.50	2.00
94	Bob Skinner	7.00	3.50	2.00
95	Frank Bolling	7.00	3.50	2.00
96	Joe Durham	7.00	3.50	2.00
97a	Larry Jackson (yellow name letters)	20.00	10.00	6.00
97b	Larry Jackson (white name letters)	7.00	3.50	2.00
98a	Billy Hunter (yellow name letters)	20.00	10.00	6.00
98b	Billy Hunter (white name letters)	7.00	3.50	2.00
99	Bobby Adams	7.00	3.50	2.00
100a	Early Wynn (yellow team letters)	30.00	15.00	9.00
100b	Early Wynn (white team letters)	15.00	7.50	4.50
101a	Bobby Richardson (yellow name letters)	30.00	15.00	9.00
101b	Bobby Richardson (white name letters)	15.00	7.50	4.50
102	George Strickland	7.00	3.50	2.00
103	Jerry Lynch	7.00	3.50	2.00
104	Jim Pendleton	7.00	3.50	2.00
105	Billy Gardner	7.00	3.50	2.00
106	Dick Schofield	7.00	3.50	2.00
107	Ossie Virgil	7.00	3.50	2.00
108a	Jim Landis (yellow team letters)	20.00	10.00	6.00
108b	Jim Landis (white team letters)	7.00	3.50	2.00
109	Herb Plews	7.00	3.50	2.00
110	Johnny Logan	7.00	3.50	2.00
111	Stu Miller	5.00	2.50	1.50
112	Gus Zernial	5.50	2.75	1.75
113	Jerry Walker	5.00	2.50	1.50
114	Irv Noren	5.00	2.50	1.50
115	Jim Bunning	15.00	7.50	4.50
116	Dave Philley	5.50	2.75	1.75
117	Frank Torre	5.00	2.50	1.50
118	Harvey Haddix	5.00	2.50	1.50
119	Harry Chiti	5.00	2.50	1.50
120	Johnny Podres	7.00	3.50	2.00
121	Eddie Miksis	5.00	2.50	1.50
122	Walt Moryn	5.00	2.50	1.50
123	Dick Tomanek	5.00	2.50	1.50
124	Bobby Usher	5.00	2.50	1.50
125	Al Dark	7.00	3.50	2.00
126	Stan Palys	5.00	2.50	1.50
127	Tom Sturdivant	7.00	3.50	2.00
128	*Willie Kirkland*	5.50	2.75	1.75

		NR MT	EX	VG
129	Jim Derrington	5.00	2.50	1.50
130	Jackie Jensen	7.00	3.50	2.00
131	Bob Henrich	5.00	2.50	1.50
132	Vernon Law	6.00	3.00	1.75
133	Russ Nixon	5.00	2.50	1.50
134	Phillies Team/Checklist 89-176	8.00	4.00	2.50
135	Mike Drabowsky	5.00	2.50	1.50
136	Jim Finigan	5.00	2.50	1.50
137	Russ Kemmerer	5.00	2.50	1.50
138	Earl Torgeson	5.00	2.50	1.50
139	George Brunet	5.00	2.50	1.50
140	Wes Covington	5.50	2.75	1.75
141	Ken Lehman	5.00	2.50	1.50
142	Enos Slaughter	20.00	10.00	6.00
143	Billy Muffett	5.00	2.50	1.50
144	Bobby Morgan	5.00	2.50	1.50
145	Not Issued			
146	Dick Gray	5.00	2.50	1.50
147	*Don McMahon*	6.00	3.00	1.75
148	Billy Consolo	5.00	2.50	1.50
149	Tom Acker	5.00	2.50	1.50
150	Mickey Mantle	450.00	225.00	140.00
151	Buddy Pritchard	5.00	2.50	1.50
152	Johnny Antonelli	6.00	3.00	1.75
153	Les Moss	5.00	2.50	1.50
154	Harry Byrd	5.00	2.50	1.50
155	Hector Lopez	5.00	2.50	1.50
156	Dick Hyde	5.00	2.50	1.50
157	Dee Fondy	5.00	2.50	1.50
158	Indians Team/Checklist 177-264	7.00	3.50	2.00
159	Taylor Phillips	5.00	2.50	1.50
160	Don Hoak	5.50	2.75	1.75
161	Don Larsen	7.00	3.50	2.00
162	Gil Hodges	20.00	10.00	6.00
163	Jim Wilson	5.00	2.50	1.50
164	Bob Taylor	5.00	2.50	1.50
165	Bob Nieman	5.00	2.50	1.50
166	Danny O'Connell	5.00	2.50	1.50
167	Frank Baumann	5.00	2.50	1.50
168	Joe Cunningham	5.50	2.75	1.75
169	Ralph Terry	5.50	2.75	1.75
170	Vic Wertz	6.00	3.00	1.75
171	Harry Anderson	5.00	2.50	1.50
172	Don Gross	5.00	2.50	1.50
173	Eddie Yost	5.50	2.75	1.75
174	A's Team/Checklist 89-176	8.00	4.00	2.50
175	*Marv Throneberry*	12.00	6.00	3.50
176	Bob Buhl	5.50	2.75	1.75
177	Al Smith	5.00	2.50	1.50
178	Ted Kluszewski	5.00	2.50	1.50
179	Willy Miranda	5.00	2.50	1.50
180	Lindy McDaniel	5.00	2.50	1.50
181	Willie Jones	5.00	2.50	1.50
182	Joe Caffie	5.00	2.50	1.50
183	Dave Jolly	5.00	2.50	1.50
184	Elvin Tappe	5.00	2.50	1.50
185	Ray Boone	5.50	2.75	1.75
186	Jack Meyer	5.00	2.50	1.50
187	Sandy Koufax	125.00	62.00	37.00
188	Milt Bolling (photo actually Lou Berberet)	5.00	2.50	1.50
189	George Susce	5.00	2.50	1.50
190	Red Schoendienst	15.00	7.50	4.50
191	Art Ceccarelli	5.00	2.50	1.50
192	Milt Graff	5.00	2.50	1.50
193	*Jerry Lumpe*	5.00	2.50	1.50
194	Roger Craig	6.00	3.00	1.75
195	Whitey Lockman	5.00	2.50	1.50
196	Mike Garcia	5.50	2.75	1.75
197	Haywood Sullivan	5.50	2.75	1.75
198	Bill Virdon	6.00	3.00	1.75
199	Don Blasingame	5.00	2.50	1.50
200	Bob Keegan	5.00	2.50	1.50
201	Jim Bolger	5.00	2.50	1.50
202	*Woody Held*	6.00	3.00	1.75
203	Al Walker	5.00	2.50	1.50
204	Leo Kiely	5.00	2.50	1.50
205	Johnny Temple	5.00	2.50	1.50
206	Bob Shaw	6.00	3.00	1.75
207	Solly Hemus	5.00	2.50	1.50
208	Cal McLish	5.00	2.50	1.50
209	Bob Anderson	5.00	2.50	1.50
210	Wally Moon	5.50	2.75	1.75
211	Pete Burnside	5.00	2.50	1.50
212	Bubba Phillips	5.00	2.50	1.50
213	Red Wilson	5.00	2.50	1.50
214	Willard Schmidt	5.00	2.50	1.50
215	Jim Gilliam	5.00	2.50	1.50
216	Cards Team/Checklist 177-264	7.00	3.50	2.00
217	Jack Harshman	5.00	2.50	1.50
218	Dick Rand	5.00	2.50	1.50
219	Camilo Pascual	5.50	2.75	1.75
220	Tom Brewer	5.00	2.50	1.50
221	Jerry Kindall	5.00	2.50	1.50
222	Bud Daley	5.00	2.50	1.50
223	Andy Pafko	6.00	3.00	1.75
224	Bob Grim	7.00	3.50	2.00
225	Billy Goodman	5.00	2.50	1.50
226	Bob Smith (photo actually Bobby Gene Smith)	5.00	2.50	1.50
227	Gene Stephens	5.00	2.50	1.50
228	Duke Maas	5.00	2.50	1.50
229	Frank Zupo	5.00	2.50	1.50
230	Richie Ashburn	8.00	4.00	2.50
231	Lloyd Merritt	5.00	2.50	1.50
232	Reno Bertoia	5.00	2.50	1.50
233	Mickey Vernon	5.50	2.75	1.75
234	Carl Sawatski	5.00	2.50	1.50
235	Tom Gorman	5.00	2.50	1.50
236	Ed Fitz Gerald	5.00	2.50	1.50
237	Bill Wight	5.00	2.50	1.50
238	Bill Mazeroski	7.00	3.50	2.00
239	Chuck Stobbs	5.00	2.50	1.50
240	Moose Skowron	7.00	3.50	2.00
241	Dick Littlefield	5.00	2.50	1.50
242	Johnny Klippstein	5.00	2.50	1.50
243	Larry Raines	5.00	2.50	1.50
244	*Don Demeter*	5.50	2.75	1.75
245	*Frank Lary*	5.50	2.75	1.75
246	Yankees Team/Checklist 177-264	40.00	20.00	12.00
247	Casey Wise	5.00	2.50	1.50
248	Herm Wehmeier	5.00	2.50	1.50
249	Ray Moore	5.00	2.50	1.50
250	Roy Sievers	6.00	3.00	1.75
251	Warren Hacker	5.00	2.50	1.50
252	Bob Trowbridge	5.00	2.50	1.50
253	Don Mueller	5.00	2.50	1.50
254	Alex Grammas	5.00	2.50	1.50
255	Bob Turley	5.00	2.50	1.50
256	White Sox Team/Checklist 265-352	8.00	4.00	2.50
257	Hal Smith	5.00	2.50	1.50
258	Carl Erskine	5.00	2.50	1.50
259	Al Pilarcik	5.00	2.50	1.50
260	Frank Malzone	5.50	2.75	1.75
261	Turk Lown	5.00	2.50	1.50
262	Johnny Groth	5.00	2.50	1.50
263	Eddie Bressoud	5.50	2.75	1.75
264	Jack Sanford	5.50	2.75	1.75
265	Pete Runnels	5.50	2.75	1.75
266	Connie Johnson	5.00	2.50	1.50
267	Sherm Lollar	5.50	2.75	1.75
268	Granny Hamner	5.00	2.50	1.50
269	Paul Smith	5.00	2.50	1.50
270	Warren Spahn	40.00	20.00	12.00
271	Billy Martin	15.00	7.50	4.50
272	Ray Crone	5.00	2.50	1.50
273	Hal Smith	5.00	2.50	1.50
274	Rocky Bridges	5.00	2.50	1.50
275	Elston Howard	8.00	4.00	2.50
276	Bobby Avila	5.00	2.50	1.50
277	Virgil Trucks	5.50	2.75	1.75
278	Mack Burk	5.00	2.50	1.50
279	Bob Boyd	5.00	2.50	1.50
280	Jim Piersall	6.00	3.00	1.75
281	Sam Taylor	5.00	2.50	1.50
282	Paul Foytack	5.00	2.50	1.50
283	Ray Shearer	5.00	2.50	1.50
284	Ray Katt	5.00	2.50	1.50
285	Frank Robinson	65.00	33.00	20.00
286	Gino Cimoli	5.00	2.50	1.50
287	Sam Jones	5.00	2.50	1.50
288	Harmon Killebrew	50.00	30.00	15.00
289	Series Hurling Rivals (Lou Burdette, Bobby Shantz)	4.00	2.00	1.25
290	Dick Donovan	5.00	2.50	1.50
291	Don Landrum	5.00	2.50	1.50
292	Ned Garver	5.00	2.50	1.50
293	Gene Freese	5.00	2.50	1.50
294	Hal Jeffcoat	5.00	2.50	1.50
295	Minnie Minoso	4.00	2.00	1.25
296	*Ryne Duren*	10.00	5.00	3.00
297	Don Buddin	5.00	2.50	1.50
298	Jim Hearn	5.00	2.50	1.50
299	Harry Simpson	7.00	3.50	2.00
300	League Presidents (Warren Giles, William Harridge)	7.00	3.50	2.00
301	Randy Jackson	5.00	2.50	1.50
302	Mike Baxes	5.00	2.50	1.50
303	Neil Chrisley	5.00	2.50	1.50
304	Tigers' Big Bats (Al Kaline, Harvey Kuenn)	10.00	5.00	3.00

		NR MT	EX	VG
305	Clem Labine	5.50	2.75	1.75
306	Whammy Douglas	5.00	2.50	1.50
307	Brooks Robinson	90.00	45.00	27.00
308	Paul Giel	5.00	2.50	1.50
309	Gail Harris	5.00	2.50	1.50
310	Ernie Banks	70.00	35.00	20.00
311	Bob Purkey	5.00	2.50	1.50
312	Red Sox Team/Checklist 353-440	8.00	4.00	2.50
313	Bob Rush	5.00	2.50	1.50
314	Dodgers' Boss & Power (Walter Alston, Duke Snider)	15.00	7.50	4.50
315	Bob Friend	6.00	3.00	1.75
316	Tito Francona	5.50	2.75	1.75
317	*Albie Pearson*	6.00	3.00	1.75
318	Frank House	5.00	2.50	1.50
319	Lou Skizas	5.00	2.50	1.50
320	Whitey Ford	35.00	17.50	10.50
321	Sluggers Supreme (Ted Kluszewski, Ted Williams)	20.00	10.00	6.00
322	Harding Peterson	5.00	2.50	1.50
323	Elmer Valo	5.00	2.50	1.50
324	Hoyt Wilhelm	15.00	7.50	4.50
325	Joe Adcock	6.00	3.00	1.75
326	Bob Miller	5.00	2.50	1.50
327	Cubs Team/Checklist 265-352	8.00	4.00	2.50
328	Ike Delock	5.00	2.50	1.50
329	Bob Cerv	5.00	2.50	1.50
330	Ed Bailey	5.00	2.50	1.50
331	Pedro Ramos	5.00	2.50	1.50
332	Jim King	5.00	2.50	1.50
333	Andy Carey	7.00	3.50	2.00
334	Mound Aces (Bob Friend, Billy Pierce)	6.00	3.00	1.75
335	Ruben Gomez	5.00	2.50	1.50
336	Bert Hamric	5.00	2.50	1.50
337	Hank Aguirre	5.00	2.50	1.50
338	Walt Dropo	5.50	2.75	1.75
339	Fred Hatfield	5.00	2.50	1.50
340	Don Newcombe	7.00	3.50	2.00
341	Pirates Team/Checklist 265-352	8.00	4.00	2.50
342	Jim Brosnan	5.50	2.75	1.75
343	*Orlando Cepeda*	80.00	40.00	25.00
344	Bob Porterfield	5.00	2.50	1.50
345	Jim Hegan	5.00	2.50	1.50
346	Steve Bilko	5.00	2.50	1.50
347	Don Rudolph	5.00	2.50	1.50
348	Chico Fernandez	5.00	2.50	1.50
349	Murry Dickson	5.00	2.50	1.50
350	Ken Boyer	5.00	2.50	1.50
351	Braves' Fence Busters (Hank Aaron, Joe Adcock, Del Crandall, Ed Mathews)	20.00	10.00	6.00
352	Herb Score	7.00	3.50	2.00
353	Stan Lopata	5.00	2.50	1.50
354	Art Ditmar	7.00	3.50	2.00
355	Bill Bruton	5.50	2.75	1.75
356	Bob Malkmus	5.00	2.50	1.50
357	Danny McDevitt	5.00	2.50	1.50
358	Gene Baker	5.00	2.50	1.50
359	Billy Loes	5.00	2.50	1.50
360	Roy McMillan	5.00	2.50	1.50
361	Mike Fornieles	5.00	2.50	1.50
362	Ray Jablonski	5.00	2.50	1.50
363	Don Elston	5.00	2.50	1.50
364	Earl Battey	5.50	2.75	1.75
365	Tom Morgan	5.00	2.50	1.50
366	Gene Green	5.00	2.50	1.50
367	Jack Urban	5.00	2.50	1.50
368	Rocky Colavito	25.00	12.50	7.50
369	Ralph Lumenti	5.00	2.50	1.50
370	Yogi Berra	80.00	40.00	25.00
371	Marty Keough	5.00	2.50	1.50
372	Don Cardwell	5.00	2.50	1.50
373	Joe Pignatano	5.00	2.50	1.50
374	Brooks Lawrence	5.00	2.50	1.50
375	Pee Wee Reese	50.00	30.00	15.00
376	Charley Rabe	5.00	2.50	1.50
377a	Braves Team (alphabetical checklist on back)	9.00	4.50	2.75
377b	Braves Team (numerical checklist on back)	60.00	30.00	18.00
378	Hank Sauer	5.50	2.75	1.75
379	Ray Herbert	5.00	2.50	1.50
380	Charley Maxwell	5.00	2.50	1.50
381	Hal Brown	5.00	2.50	1.50
382	Al Cicotte	7.00	3.50	2.00
383	Lou Berberet	5.00	2.50	1.50
384	John Goryl	5.00	2.50	1.50
385	Wilmer Mizell	5.00	2.50	1.50
386	Birdie's Young Sluggers (Ed Bailey, Frank Robinson, Birdie Tebbetts)	7.00	3.50	2.00

		NR MT	EX	VG
387	Wally Post	5.00	2.50	1.50
388	Billy Moran	5.00	2.50	1.50
389	Bill Taylor	5.00	2.50	1.50
390	Del Crandall	6.00	3.00	1.75
391	Dave Melton	5.00	2.50	1.50
392	Bennie Daniels	5.00	2.50	1.50
393	Tony Kubek	15.00	7.50	4.50
394	*Jim Grant*	6.00	3.00	1.75
395	Willard Nixon	5.00	2.50	1.50
396	Dutch Dotterer	5.00	2.50	1.50
397a	Tigers Team (alphabetical checklist on back)	9.00	4.50	2.75
397b	Tigers Team (numerical checklist on back)	60.00	30.00	18.00
398	Gene Woodling	5.50	2.75	1.75
399	Marv Grissom	5.00	2.50	1.50
400	Nellie Fox	10.00	5.00	3.00
401	Don Bessent	5.00	2.50	1.50
402	Bobby Gene Smith	5.00	2.50	1.50
403	Steve Korcheck	5.00	2.50	1.50
404	Curt Simmons	6.00	3.00	1.75
405	Ken Aspromonte	5.00	2.50	1.50
406	Vic Power	5.00	2.50	1.50
407	Carlton Willey	5.00	2.50	1.50
408a	Orioles Team (alphabetical checklist on back)	8.00	4.00	2.50
408b	Orioles Team (numerical checklist on back)	60.00	30.00	18.00
409	Frank Thomas	5.00	2.50	1.50
410	Murray Wall	5.00	2.50	1.50
411	*Tony Taylor*	5.50	2.75	1.75
412	Jerry Staley	5.00	2.50	1.50
413	*Jim Davenport*	5.50	2.75	1.75
414	Sammy White	5.00	2.50	1.50
415	Bob Bowman	5.00	2.50	1.50
416	Foster Castleman	5.00	2.50	1.50
417	Carl Furillo	7.00	3.50	2.00
418	World Series Batting Foes (Hank Aaron, Mickey Mantle)	100.00	45.00	27.00
419	Bobby Shantz	7.00	3.50	2.00
420	*Vada Pinson*	25.00	12.50	7.50
421	Dixie Howell	5.00	2.50	1.50
422	Norm Zauchin	5.00	2.50	1.50
423	Phil Clark	5.00	2.50	1.50
424	Larry Doby	5.00	2.50	1.50
425	Sam Esposito	5.00	2.50	1.50
426	Johnny O'Brien	5.00	2.50	1.50
427	Al Worthington	5.00	2.50	1.50
428a	Redlegs Team (alphabetical checklist on back)	8.00	4.00	2.50
428b	Redlegs Team (numerical checklist on back)	50.00	25.00	15.00
429	Gus Triandos	5.50	2.75	1.75
430	Bobby Thomson	6.00	3.00	1.75
431	Gene Conley	5.50	2.75	1.75
432	John Powers	5.00	2.50	1.50
433	Pancho Herrera	5.00	2.50	1.50
434	Harvey Kuenn	6.00	3.00	1.75
435	Ed Roebuck	5.00	2.50	1.50
436	Rival Fence Busters (Willie Mays, Duke Snider)	50.00	25.00	15.00
437	Bob Speake	5.00	2.50	1.50
438	Whitey Herzog	7.00	3.50	2.00
439	Ray Narleski	5.00	2.50	1.50
440	Ed Mathews	30.00	15.00	9.00
441	Jim Marshall	4.00	2.00	1.25
442	Phil Paine	4.00	2.00	1.25
443	Billy Harrell	7.00	3.50	2.00
444	Danny Kravitz	4.00	2.00	1.25
445	Bob Smith	4.00	2.00	1.25
446	Carroll Hardy	7.00	3.50	2.00
447	Ray Monzant	4.00	2.00	1.25
448	*Charlie Lau*	5.50	2.75	1.75
449	Gene Fodge	4.00	2.00	1.25
450	Preston Ward	7.00	3.50	2.00
451	Joe Taylor	4.00	2.00	1.25
452	Roman Mejias	4.00	2.00	1.25
453	Tom Qualters	4.00	2.00	1.25
454	Harry Hanebrink	4.00	2.00	1.25
455	Hal Griggs	4.00	2.00	1.25
456	Dick Brown	4.00	2.00	1.25
457	*Milt Pappas*	5.50	2.75	1.75
458	Julio Becquer	4.00	2.00	1.25
459	Ron Blackburn	4.00	2.00	1.25
460	Chuck Essegian	4.00	2.00	1.25
461	Ed Mayer	4.00	2.00	1.25
462	Gary Geiger	7.00	3.50	2.00
463	Vito Valentinetti	4.00	2.00	1.25
464	*Curt Flood*	15.00	7.50	4.50
465	Arnie Portocarrero	4.00	2.00	1.25
466	Pete Whisenant	4.00	2.00	1.25

		NR MT	EX	VG
467	Glen Hobbie	4.00	2.00	1.25
468	Bob Schmidt	4.00	2.00	1.25
469	Don Ferrarese	4.00	2.00	1.25
470	R.C. Stevens	4.00	2.00	1.25
471	Lenny Green	4.00	2.00	1.25
472	Joe Jay	4.00	2.00	1.25
473	Bill Renna	4.00	2.00	1.25
474	Roman Semproch	4.00	2.00	1.25
475	All-Star Managers (Fred Haney, Casey Stengel)	15.00	7.50	4.50
476	Stan Musial AS	30.00	15.00	9.00
477	Bill Skowron AS	4.00	2.00	1.25
478	Johnny Temple AS	5.00	2.50	1.50
479	Nellie Fox AS	5.00	2.50	1.50
480	Eddie Mathews AS	10.00	5.00	3.00
481	Frank Malzone AS	5.00	2.50	1.50
482	Ernie Banks AS	15.00	7.50	4.50
483	Luis Aparicio AS	8.00	4.00	2.50
484	Frank Robinson AS	15.00	7.50	4.50
485	Ted Williams AS	40.00	20.00	12.00
486	Willie Mays AS	30.00	15.00	9.00
487	Mickey Mantle AS	90.00	45.00	27.00
488	Hank Aaron AS	30.00	15.00	9.00
489	Jackie Jensen AS	6.00	3.00	1.75
490	Ed Bailey AS	5.00	2.50	1.50
491	Sherm Lollar AS	5.00	2.50	1.50
492	Bob Friend AS	6.00	3.00	1.75
493	Bob Turley AS	7.00	3.50	2.00
494	Warren Spahn AS	15.00	7.50	4.50
495	Herb Score AS	7.00	3.50	2.00
----	Contest Card (All-Star Game, July 8)	15.00	7.50	4.50
----	Felt Emblems Insert Card	15.00	7.50	4.50

1959 Topps

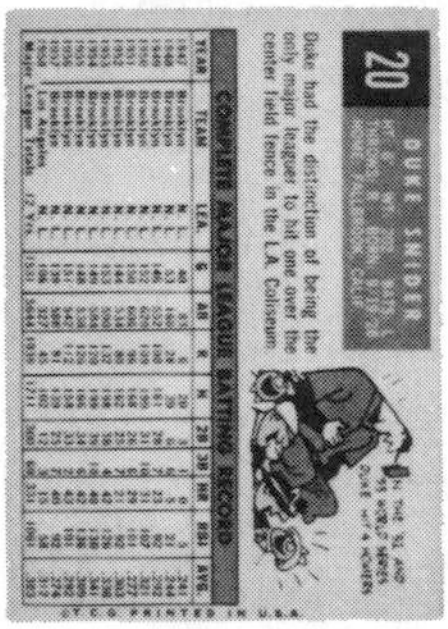

These 2-1/2" by 3-1/2" cards have a round photograph at the center of the front with a solid-color background and white border. A facsimile autograph is found across the photo. The 572- card set marks the largest set issued to that time. Card numbers below 507 have red and green printing with the card number in white in a green box. On high number cards beginning with #507, the printing is black and red and the card number is in a black box. Specialty cards include multiple-player cards, team cards with checklists, "All-Star" cards, highlights from previous season, and 31 "Rookie Stars." There is also a card of the commissioner, Ford Frick, and one Roy Campanella in a wheelchair. A handful of cards can be found with and without lines added to the biographies on back indicating trades or demotions; those without the added lines are considerably more rare and valuable and are not included in the complete set price. Card numbers 199-286 can be found with either white or grey backs, with the grey stock being the less common.

	NR MT	EX	VG
Complete Set:	4500.00	2250.00	1350.
Common Player: 1-110	5.00	2.50	1.50
Common Player: 111-506	3.00	1.50	.90
Common Player: 507-572	15.00	7.50	4.50

		NR MT	EX	VG
1	Ford Frick	60.00	3.75	1.50
2	Eddie Yost	5.00	2.00	1.25
3	Don McMahon	5.00	2.50	1.50
4	Albie Pearson	5.00	2.50	1.50
5	Dick Donovan	5.00	2.50	1.50
6	Alex Grammas	5.00	2.50	1.50
7	Al Pilarcik	5.00	2.50	1.50
8	Phillies Team/Checklist 1-88	20.00	10.00	6.00
9	Paul Giel	5.00	2.50	1.50
10	Mickey Mantle	350.00	140.00	88.00
11	Billy Hunter	5.00	2.50	1.50
12	Vern Law	5.00	2.50	1.50
13	Dick Gernert	5.00	2.50	1.50
14	Pete Whisenant	5.00	2.50	1.50
15	Dick Drott	5.00	2.50	1.50
16	Joe Pignatano	5.00	2.50	1.50
17	Danny's All-Stars (Ted Kluszewski, Danny Murtaugh, Frank Thomas)	5.00	2.50	1.50
18	Jack Urban	5.00	2.50	1.50
19	Ed Bressoud	5.00	2.50	1.50
20	Duke Snider	60.00	30.00	18.00
21	Connie Johnson	5.00	2.50	1.50
22	Al Smith	5.00	2.50	1.50
23	Murry Dickson	5.00	2.50	1.50
24	Red Wilson	5.00	2.50	1.50
25	Don Hoak	6.00	3.00	1.75
26	Chuck Stobbs	5.00	2.50	1.50
27	Andy Pafko	6.00	3.00	1.75
28	Red Worthington	5.00	2.50	1.50
29	Jim Bolger	5.00	2.50	1.50
30	Nellie Fox	18.00	9.00	5.50
31	Ken Lehman	5.00	2.50	1.50
32	Don Buddin	5.00	2.50	1.50
33	Ed Fitz Gerald	5.00	2.50	1.50
34	Pitchers Beware (Al Kaline, Charlie Maxwell)	9.00	4.50	2.75
35	Ted Kluszewski	7.00	3.50	2.00
36	Hank Aguirre	5.00	2.50	1.50
37	Gene Green	5.00	2.50	1.50
38	Morrie Martin	5.00	2.50	1.50
39	Ed Bouchee	5.00	2.50	1.50
40	Warren Spahn	40.00	20.00	12.00
41	Bob Martyn	5.00	2.50	1.50
42	Murray Wall	5.00	2.50	1.50
43	Steve Bilko	5.00	2.50	1.50
44	Vito Valentinetti	5.00	2.50	1.50
45	Andy Carey	5.00	2.50	1.50
46	Bill Henry	5.00	2.50	1.50
47	Jim Finigan	5.00	2.50	1.50
48	Orioles Team/Checklist 1-88	15.00	7.50	4.50
49	Bill Hall	5.00	2.50	1.50
50	Willie Mays	125.00	56.00	35.00
51	Rip Coleman	5.00	2.50	1.50
52	Coot Veal	5.00	2.50	1.50
53	Stan Williams	5.00	2.50	1.50
54	Mel Roach	5.00	2.50	1.50
55	Tom Brewer	5.00	2.50	1.50
56	Carl Sawatski	5.00	2.50	1.50
57	Al Cicotte	5.00	2.50	1.50
58	Eddie Miksis	5.00	2.50	1.50
59	Irv Noren	5.00	2.50	1.50
60	Bob Turley	6.00	3.00	1.75
61	Dick Brown	5.00	2.50	1.50
62	Tony Taylor	5.00	2.50	1.50
63	Jim Hearn	5.00	2.50	1.50
64	Joe DeMaestri	5.00	2.50	1.50
65	Frank Torre	5.00	2.50	1.50
66	Joe Ginsberg	5.00	2.50	1.50
67	Brooks Lawrence	5.00	2.50	1.50
68	Dick Schofield	5.00	2.50	1.50
69	Giants Team/Checklist 89-176	18.00	9.00	5.50
70	Harvey Kuenn	5.00	2.50	1.50
71	Don Bessent	5.00	2.50	1.50
72	Bill Renna	5.00	2.50	1.50
73	Ron Jackson	5.00	2.50	1.50
74	Directing the Power (Cookie Lavagetto, Jim Lemon, Roy Sievers)	6.00	3.00	1.75
75	Sam Jones	5.00	2.50	1.50
76	Bobby Richardson	15.00	7.50	4.50
77	John Goryl	5.00	2.50	1.50
78	Pedro Ramos	5.00	2.50	1.50
79	Harry Chiti	5.00	2.50	1.50
80	Minnie Minoso	5.00	2.50	1.50
81	Hal Jeffcoat	5.00	2.50	1.50
82	Bob Boyd	5.00	2.50	1.50
83	Bob Smith	5.00	2.50	1.50
84	Reno Bertoia	5.00	2.50	1.50
85	Harry Anderson	5.00	2.50	1.50
86	Bob Keegan	5.00	2.50	1.50
87	Danny O'Connell	5.00	2.50	1.50
88	Herb Score	6.00	3.00	1.75
89	Billy Gardner	5.00	2.50	1.50
90	Bill Skowron	15.00	7.50	4.50
91	Herb Moford	5.00	2.50	1.50

		NR MT	EX	VG
92	Dave Philley	5.00	2.50	1.50
93	Julio Becquer	5.00	2.50	1.50
94	W. Sox Team/Checklist 89-176	15.00	7.50	4.50
95	Carl Willey	5.00	2.50	1.50
96	Lou Berberet	5.00	2.50	1.50
97	Jerry Lynch	5.00	2.50	1.50
98	Arnie Portocarrero	5.00	2.50	1.50
99	Ted Kazanski	5.00	2.50	1.50
100	Bob Cerv	5.00	2.50	1.50
101	Alex Kellner	5.00	2.50	1.50
102	*Felipe Alou*	15.00	7.50	4.50
103	Billy Goodman	5.00	2.50	1.50
104	Del Rice	5.00	2.50	1.50
105	Lee Walls	5.00	2.50	1.50
106	Hal Woodeshick	5.00	2.50	1.50
107	Norm Larker	5.00	2.50	1.50
108	Zack Monroe	5.00	2.50	1.50
109	Bob Schmidt	5.00	2.50	1.50
110	George Witt	5.00	2.50	1.50
111	Redlegs Team/Checklist 89-176	8.00	4.00	2.50
112	Billy Consolo	3.00	1.50	.90
113	Taylor Phillips	3.00	1.50	.90
114	Earl Battey	3.25	1.75	1.00
115	Mickey Vernon	3.25	1.75	1.00
116	*Bob Allison*	5.00	2.50	1.50
117	*John Blanchard*	3.25	1.75	1.00
118	John Buzhardt	3.00	1.50	.90
119	*John Callison*	5.00	2.50	1.50
120	Chuck Coles	3.00	1.50	.90
121	Bob Conley	3.00	1.50	.90
122	Bennie Daniels	3.00	1.50	.90
123	Don Dillard	3.00	1.50	.90
124	Dan Dobbek	3.00	1.50	.90
125	*Ron Fairly*	3.50	1.75	1.00
126	Eddie Haas	3.00	1.50	.90
127	Kent Hadley	3.00	1.50	.90
128	Bob Hartman	3.00	1.50	.90
129	Frank Herrera	3.00	1.50	.90
130	Lou Jackson	3.00	1.50	.90
131	*Deron Johnson*	3.25	1.75	1.00
132	Don Lee	3.00	1.50	.90
133	*Bob Lillis*	3.25	1.75	1.00
134	Jim McDaniel	3.00	1.50	.90
135	Gene Oliver	3.00	1.50	.90
136	*Jim O'Toole*	3.25	1.75	1.00
137	Dick Ricketts	3.00	1.50	.90
138	John Romano	3.00	1.50	.90
139	Ed Sadowski	3.00	1.50	.90
140	Charlie Secrest	3.00	1.50	.90
141	Joe Shipley	3.00	1.50	.90
142	Dick Stigman	3.00	1.50	.90
143	Willie Tasby	3.00	1.50	.90
144	Jerry Walker	3.00	1.50	.90
145	Dom Zanni	3.00	1.50	.90
146	Jerry Zimmerman	3.00	1.50	.90
147	Cub's Clubbers (Ernie Banks, Dale Long, Walt Moryn)	9.00	4.50	2.75
148	Mike McCormick	3.25	1.75	1.00
149	Jim Bunning	15.00	7.50	4.50
150	Stan Musial	150.00	75.00	45.00
151	Bob Malkmus	3.00	1.50	.90
152	Johnny Klippstein	3.00	1.50	.90
153	Jim Marshall	3.00	1.50	.90
154	Ray Herbert	3.00	1.50	.90
155	Enos Slaughter	18.00	9.00	5.50
156	Ace Hurlers (Billy Pierce, Robin Roberts)	3.50	1.75	1.00
157	Felix Mantilla	3.00	1.50	.90
158	Walt Dropo	3.25	1.75	1.00
159	Bob Shaw	3.00	1.50	.90
160	Dick Groat	3.00	1.50	.90
161	Frank Baumann	3.00	1.50	.90
162	Bobby G. Smith	3.00	1.50	.90
163	Sandy Koufax	150.00	75.00	45.00
164	Johnny Groth	3.00	1.50	.90
165	Bill Bruton	3.25	1.75	1.00
166	Destruction Crew (Rocky Colavito, Larry Doby, Minnie Minoso)	3.25	1.75	1.00
167	Duke Maas	3.00	1.50	.90
168	Carroll Hardy	3.00	1.50	.90
169	Ted Abernathy	3.00	1.50	.90
170	Gene Woodling	3.25	1.75	1.00
171	Willard Schmidt	3.00	1.50	.90
172	A's Team/Checklist 177-242	7.00	3.50	2.00
173	*Bill Monbouquette*	3.25	1.75	1.00
174	Jim Pendleton	3.00	1.50	.90
175	Dick Farrell	3.00	1.50	.90
176	Preston Ward	3.00	1.50	.90
177	Johnny Briggs	3.00	1.50	.90
178	Ruben Amaro	3.00	1.50	.90
179	Don Rudolph	3.00	1.50	.90
180	Yogi Berra	60.00	30.00	18.00
181	Bob Porterfield	3.00	1.50	.90
182	Milt Graff	3.00	1.50	.90
183	Stu Miller	3.00	1.50	.90
184	Harvey Haddix	3.25	1.75	1.00
185	Jim Busby	3.00	1.50	.90
186	Mudcat Grant	3.25	1.75	1.00
187	Bubba Phillips	3.00	1.50	.90
188	Juan Pizarro	3.00	1.50	.90
189	Neil Chrisley	3.00	1.50	.90
190	Bill Virdon	3.25	1.75	1.00
191	Russ Kemmerer	3.00	1.50	.90
192	Charley Beamon	3.00	1.50	.90
193	Sammy Taylor	3.00	1.50	.90
194	Jim Brosnan	3.25	1.75	1.00
195	Rip Repulski	3.00	1.50	.90
196	Billy Moran	3.00	1.50	.90
197	Ray Semproch	3.00	1.50	.90
198	Jim Davenport	3.00	1.50	.90
199	Leo Kiely	3.00	1.50	.90
200	Warren Giles	3.25	1.75	1.00
201	Tom Acker	3.00	1.50	.90
202	Roger Maris	150.00	75.00	45.00
203	Ozzie Virgil	3.00	1.50	.90
204	Casey Wise	3.00	1.50	.90
205	Don Larsen	7.00	3.50	2.00
206	Carl Furillo	5.00	2.50	1.50
207	George Strickland	3.00	1.50	.90
208	Willie Jones	3.00	1.50	.90
209	Lenny Green	3.00	1.50	.90
210	Ed Bailey	3.00	1.50	.90
211	Bob Blaylock	3.00	1.50	.90
212	Fence Busters (Hank Aaron, Eddie Mathews)	50.00	25.00	15.00
213	Jim Rivera	3.00	1.50	.90
214	Marcelino Solis	3.00	1.50	.90
215	Jim Lemon	3.00	1.50	.90
216	Andre Rodgers	3.00	1.50	.90
217	Carl Erskine	5.00	2.50	1.50
218	Roman Mejias	3.00	1.50	.90
219	George Zuverink	3.00	1.50	.90
220	Frank Malzone	3.25	1.75	1.00
221	Bob Bowman	3.00	1.50	.90
222	Bobby Shantz	3.50	1.75	1.00
223	Cards Team/Checklist 265-352	7.00	3.50	2.00
224	*Claude Osteen*	3.00	1.50	.90
225	Johnny Logan	3.25	1.75	1.00
226	Art Ceccarelli	3.00	1.50	.90
227	Hal Smith	3.00	1.50	.90
228	Don Gross	3.00	1.50	.90
229	Vic Power	3.00	1.50	.90
230	Bill Fischer	3.00	1.50	.90
231	Ellis Burton	3.00	1.50	.90
232	Eddie Kasko	3.00	1.50	.90
233	Paul Foytack	3.00	1.50	.90
234	Chuck Tanner	3.00	1.50	.90
235	Valmy Thomas	3.00	1.50	.90
236	Ted Bowsfield	3.00	1.50	.90
237	Run Preventers (Gil McDougald, Bobby Richardson, Bob Turley)	5.00	2.50	1.50
238	Gene Baker	3.00	1.50	.90
239	Bob Trowbridge	3.00	1.50	.90
240	Hank Bauer	7.00	3.50	2.00
241	Billy Muffett	3.00	1.50	.90
242	Ron Samford	3.00	1.50	.90
243	Marv Grissom	3.00	1.50	.90
244	Dick Gray	3.00	1.50	.90
245	Ned Garver	3.00	1.50	.90
246	J.W. Porter	3.00	1.50	.90
247	Don Ferrarese	3.00	1.50	.90
248	Red Sox Team/Checklist 177-264	8.00	4.00	2.50
249	Bobby Adams	3.00	1.50	.90
250	Billy O'Dell	3.00	1.50	.90
251	Cletis Boyer	6.00	3.00	1.75
252	Ray Boone	3.25	1.75	1.00
253	Seth Morehead	3.00	1.50	.90
254	Zeke Bella	3.00	1.50	.90
255	Del Ennis	3.25	1.75	1.00
256	Jerry Davie	3.00	1.50	.90
257	*Leon Wagner*	3.00	1.50	.90
258	Fred Kipp	3.00	1.50	.90
259	Jim Pisoni	3.00	1.50	.90
260	Early Wynn	15.00	7.50	4.50
261	Gene Stephens	3.00	1.50	.90
262	Hitters' Foes (Don Drysdale, Clem Labine, Johnny Podres)	8.00	4.00	2.50
263	Buddy Daley	3.00	1.50	.90
264	Chico Carrasquel	3.00	1.50	.90
265	Ron Kline	3.00	1.50	.90
266	Woody Held	3.25	1.75	1.00

		NR MT	EX	VG
267	John Romonosky	3.00	1.50	.90
268	Tito Francona	3.25	1.75	1.00
269	Jack Meyer	3.00	1.50	.90
270	Gil Hodges	18.00	9.00	5.50
271	*Orlando Pena*	3.25	1.75	1.00
272	Jerry Lumpe	3.25	1.75	1.00
273	Joe Jay	3.00	1.50	.90
274	Jerry Kindall	3.00	1.50	.90
275	Jack Sanford	3.00	1.50	.90
276	Pete Daley	3.00	1.50	.90
277	Turk Lown	3.00	1.50	.90
278	Chuck Essegian	3.00	1.50	.90
279	Ernie Johnson	3.00	1.50	.90
280	Frank Bolling	3.00	1.50	.90
281	Walt Craddock	3.00	1.50	.90
282	R.C. Stevens	3.00	1.50	.90
283	Russ Heman	3.00	1.50	.90
284	Steve Korcheck	3.00	1.50	.90
285	Joe Cunningham	3.25	1.75	1.00
286	Dean Stone	3.00	1.50	.90
287	Don Zimmer	3.25	1.75	1.00
288	Dutch Dotterer	3.00	1.50	.90
289	Johnny Kucks	3.00	1.50	.90
290	Wes Covington	3.25	1.75	1.00
291	Pitching Partners (Camilo Pascual, Pedro Ramos)	3.25	1.75	1.00
292	Dick Williams	3.25	1.75	1.00
293	Ray Moore	3.00	1.50	.90
294	Hank Foiles	3.00	1.50	.90
295	Billy Martin	15.00	7.50	4.50
296	*Ernie Broglio*	3.25	1.75	1.00
297	*Jackie Brandt*	3.25	1.75	1.00
298	Tex Clevenger	3.00	1.50	.90
299	Billy Klaus	3.00	1.50	.90
300	Richie Ashburn	18.00	9.00	5.50
301	Earl Averill	3.00	1.50	.90
302	Don Mossi	3.25	1.75	1.00
303	Marty Keough	3.00	1.50	.90
304	Cubs Team/Checklist 265-352	7.00	3.50	2.00
305	Curt Raydon	3.00	1.50	.90
306	Jim Gilliam	5.00	2.50	1.50
307	Curt Barclay	3.00	1.50	.90
308	Norm Siebern	3.50	1.75	1.00
309	Sal Maglie	3.00	1.50	.90
310	Luis Aparicio	15.00	7.50	4.50
311	Norm Zauchin	3.00	1.50	.90
312	Don Newcombe	6.00	3.00	1.75
313	Frank House	3.00	1.50	.90
314	Don Cardwell	3.00	1.50	.90
315	Joe Adcock	3.00	1.50	.90
316a	Ralph Lumenti (without option statement)	80.00	40.00	24.00
316b	Ralph Lumenti (with option statement)	3.00	1.50	.90
317	N.L. Hitting Kings (Richie Ashburn, Willie Mays)	15.00	7.50	4.50
318	Rocky Bridges	3.00	1.50	.90
319	Dave Hillman	3.00	1.50	.90
320	Bob Skinner	3.25	1.75	1.00
321a	Bob Giallombardo (without option statement)	80.00	40.00	24.00
321b	Bob Giallombardo (with option statement)	3.00	1.50	.90
322a	Harry Hanebrink (without trade statement)	65.00	33.00	18.00
322b	Harry Hanebrink (with trade statement)	3.00	1.50	.90
323	Frank Sullivan	3.00	1.50	.90
324	Don Demeter	3.00	1.50	.90
325	Ken Boyer	5.00	2.50	1.50
326	Marv Throneberry	5.00	2.50	1.50
327	*Gary Bell*	3.25	1.75	1.00
328	Lou Skizas	3.00	1.50	.90
329	Tigers Team/Checklist 353-429	8.00	4.00	2.50
330	Gus Triandos	3.25	1.75	1.00
331	Steve Boros	3.25	1.75	1.00
332	Ray Monzant	3.00	1.50	.90
333	Harry Simpson	3.00	1.50	.90
334	Glen Hobbie	3.00	1.50	.90
335	Johnny Temple	3.00	1.50	.90
336a	Billy Loes (without trade statement)	65.00	33.00	18.00
336b	Billy Loes (with trade statement)	3.00	1.50	.90
337	George Crowe	3.00	1.50	.90
338	*George Anderson*	25.00	12.50	7.50
339	Roy Face	3.00	1.50	.90
340	Roy Sievers	3.25	1.75	1.00
341	Tom Qualters	3.00	1.50	.90
342	Ray Jablonski	3.00	1.50	.90
343	Billy Hoeft	3.00	1.50	.90
344	Russ Nixon	3.00	1.50	.90

		NR MT	EX	VG
345	Gil McDougald	8.00	4.00	2.50
346	Batter Bafflers (Tom Brewer, Dave Sisler)	3.25	1.75	1.00
347	Bob Buhl	3.25	1.75	1.00
348	Ted Lepcio	3.00	1.50	.90
349	Hoyt Wilhelm	15.00	7.50	4.50
350	Ernie Banks	60.00	30.00	18.00
351	Earl Torgeson	3.00	1.50	.90
352	Robin Roberts	15.00	7.50	4.50
353	Curt Flood	3.00	1.50	.90
354	Pete Burnside	3.00	1.50	.90
355	Jim Piersall	3.00	1.50	.90
356	Bob Mabe	3.00	1.50	.90
357	*Dick Stuart*	6.00	3.00	1.75
358	Ralph Terry	3.25	1.75	1.00
359	*Bill White*	20.00	10.00	6.00
360	Al Kaline	50.00	25.00	15.00
361	Willard Nixon	3.00	1.50	.90
362a	Dolan Nichols (without option statement)	80.00	40.00	24.00
362b	Dolan Nichols (with option statement)	3.00	1.50	.90
363	Bobby Avila	3.00	1.50	.90
364	Danny McDevitt	3.00	1.50	.90
365	Gus Bell	3.25	1.75	1.00
366	Humberto Robinson	3.00	1.50	.90
367	Cal Neeman	3.00	1.50	.90
368	Don Mueller	3.00	1.50	.90
369	Dick Tomanek	3.00	1.50	.90
370	Pete Runnels	3.25	1.75	1.00
371	Dick Brodowski	3.00	1.50	.90
372	Jim Hegan	3.00	1.50	.90
373	Herb Plews	3.00	1.50	.90
374	Art Ditmar	3.00	1.50	.90
375	Bob Nieman	3.00	1.50	.90
376	Hal Naragon	3.00	1.50	.90
377	Johnny Antonelli	3.25	1.75	1.00
378	Gail Harris	3.00	1.50	.90
379	Bob Miller	3.00	1.50	.90
380	Hank Aaron	125.00	62.00	37.00
381	Mike Baxes	3.00	1.50	.90
382	Curt Simmons	3.25	1.75	1.00
383	Words of Wisdom (Don Larsen, Casey Stengel)	5.00	2.50	1.50
384	Dave Sisler	3.00	1.50	.90
385	Sherm Lollar	3.25	1.75	1.00
386	Jim Delsing	3.00	1.50	.90
387	Don Drysdale	30.00	15.00	9.00
388	Bob Will	3.00	1.50	.90
389	Joe Nuxhall	3.25	1.75	1.00
390	Orlando Cepeda	18.00	9.00	5.50
391	Milt Pappas	3.25	1.75	1.00
392	Whitey Herzog	6.00	3.00	1.75
393	Frank Lary	3.25	1.75	1.00
394	Randy Jackson	3.00	1.50	.90
395	Elston Howard	7.00	3.50	2.00
396	Bob Rush	3.00	1.50	.90
397	Senators Team/Checklist 430-495	7.00	3.50	2.00
398	Wally Post	3.00	1.50	.90
399	Larry Jackson	3.00	1.50	.90
400	Jackie Jensen	5.00	2.50	1.50
401	Ron Blackburn	3.00	1.50	.90
402	Hector Lopez	3.00	1.50	.90
403	Clem Labine	3.25	1.75	1.00
404	Hank Sauer	3.25	1.75	1.00
405	Roy McMillan	3.00	1.50	.90
406	Solly Drake	3.00	1.50	.90
407	Moe Drabowsky	3.00	1.50	.90
408	Keystone Combo (Luis Aparicio, Nellie Fox)	7.00	3.50	2.00
409	Gus Zernial	3.25	1.75	1.00
410	Billy Pierce	3.25	1.75	1.00
411	Whitey Lockman	3.00	1.50	.90
412	Stan Lopata	3.00	1.50	.90
413	Camillo Pascual (Camilo)	3.25	1.75	1.00
414	Dale Long	3.25	1.75	1.00
415	Bill Mazeroski	3.50	1.75	1.00
416	Haywood Sullivan	3.00	1.50	.90
417	Virgil Trucks	3.00	1.50	.90
418	Gino Cimoli	3.00	1.50	.90
419	Braves Team/Checklist 353-429	8.00	4.00	2.50
420	Rocco Colavito	15.00	7.50	4.50
421	Herm Wehmeier	3.00	1.50	.90
422	Hobie Landrith	3.00	1.50	.90
423	Bob Grim	3.00	1.50	.90
424	Ken Aspromonte	3.00	1.50	.90
425	Del Crandall	3.25	1.75	1.00
426	Jerry Staley	3.00	1.50	.90
427	Charlie Neal	3.00	1.50	.90
428	Buc Hill Aces (Roy Face, Bob Friend, Ron Kline, Vern Law)	3.25	1.75	1.00

		NR MT	EX	VG
429	Bobby Thomson	3.25	1.75	1.00
430	Whitey Ford	30.00	15.00	9.00
431	Whammy Douglas	3.00	1.50	.90
432	Smoky Burgess	3.00	1.50	.90
433	Billy Harrell	3.00	1.50	.90
434	Hal Griggs	3.00	1.50	.90
435	Frank Robinson	40.00	20.00	12.00
436	Granny Hamner	3.00	1.50	.90
437	Ike Delock	3.00	1.50	.90
438	Sam Esposito	3.00	1.50	.90
439	Brooks Robinson	40.00	20.00	12.00
440	Lou Burdette	8.00	4.00	2.50
441	John Roseboro	3.25	1.75	1.00
442	Ray Narleski	3.00	1.50	.90
443	Daryl Spencer	3.00	1.50	.90
444	*Ronnie Hansen*	3.25	1.75	1.00
445	Cal McLish	3.00	1.50	.90
446	Rocky Nelson	3.00	1.50	.90
447	Bob Anderson	3.00	1.50	.90
448	Vada Pinson	5.00	2.50	1.50
449	Tom Gorman	3.00	1.50	.90
450	Ed Mathews	30.00	15.00	9.00
451	Jimmy Constable	3.00	1.50	.90
452	Chico Fernandez	3.00	1.50	.90
453	Les Moss	3.00	1.50	.90
454	Phil Clark	3.00	1.50	.90
455	Larry Doby	3.25	1.75	1.00
456	Jerry Casale	3.00	1.50	.90
457	Dodgers Team/Checklist 430-495	15.00	7.50	4.50
458	Gordon Jones	3.00	1.50	.90
459	Bill Tuttle	3.00	1.50	.90
460	Bob Friend	3.25	1.75	1.00
461	Mantle Hits 42nd Homer For Crown	35.00	17.50	10.50
462	Colavito's Great Catch Saves Game	3.00	1.50	.90
463	Kaline Becomes Youngest Bat Champ	8.00	4.00	2.50
464	Mays' Catch Makes Series History	18.00	9.00	5.50
465	Sievers Sets Homer Mark	3.25	1.75	1.00
466	Pierce All Star Starter	3.25	1.75	1.00
467	Aaron Clubs World Series Homer	15.00	7.50	4.50
468	Snider's Play Brings L.A. Victory	9.00	4.50	2.75
469	Hustler Banks Wins M.V.P. Award	8.00	4.00	2.50
470	Musial Raps Out 3,000th Hit	18.00	9.00	5.50
471	Tom Sturdivant	3.00	1.50	.90
472	Gene Freese	3.00	1.50	.90
473	Mike Fornieles	3.00	1.50	.90
474	Moe Thacker	3.00	1.50	.90
475	Jack Harshman	3.00	1.50	.90
476	Indians Team/Checklist 496-572	7.00	3.50	2.00
477	Barry Latman	3.00	1.50	.90
478	Bob Clemente	100.00	50.00	30.00
479	Lindy McDaniel	3.00	1.50	.90
480	Red Schoendienst	18.00	9.00	5.50
481	Charley Maxwell	3.00	1.50	.90
482	Russ Meyer	3.00	1.50	.90
483	Clint Courtney	3.00	1.50	.90
484	Willie Kirkland	3.00	1.50	.90
485	Ryne Duren	3.50	1.75	1.00
486	Sammy White	3.00	1.50	.90
487	Hal Brown	3.00	1.50	.90
488	Walt Moryn	3.00	1.50	.90
489	John C. Powers	3.00	1.50	.90
490	Frank Thomas	3.00	1.50	.90
491	Don Blasingame	3.00	1.50	.90
492	Gene Conley	3.25	1.75	1.00
493	Jim Landis	3.00	1.50	.90
494	Don Pavletich	3.00	1.50	.90
495	Johnny Podres	5.00	2.50	1.50
496	Wayne Terwilliger	3.00	1.50	.90
497	Hal R. Smith	3.00	1.50	.90
498	Dick Hyde	3.00	1.50	.90
499	Johnny O'Brien	3.00	1.50	.90
500	Vic Wertz	3.25	1.75	1.00
501	Bobby Tiefenauer	3.00	1.50	.90
502	Al Dark	3.25	1.75	1.00
503	Jim Owens	3.00	1.50	.90
504	Ossie Alvarez	3.00	1.50	.90
505	Tony Kubek	8.00	4.00	2.50
506	Bob Purkey	3.00	1.50	.90
507	Bob Hale	15.00	7.50	4.50
508	Art Fowler	15.00	7.50	4.50
509	*Norm Cash*	40.00	20.00	12.00
510	Yankees Team/Checklist 496-572	60.00	30.00	18.00
511	George Susce	15.00	7.50	4.50
512	George Altman	15.00	7.50	4.50
513	Tom Carroll	15.00	7.50	4.50

		NR MT	EX	VG
514	*Bob Gibson*	350.00	175.00	105.00
515	Harmon Killebrew	125.00	62.00	37.00
516	Mike Garcia	16.00	8.00	4.75
517	Joe Koppe	15.00	7.50	4.50
518	*Mike Cueller (Cuellar)*	15.00	7.50	4.50
519	Infield Power (Dick Gernert, Frank Malzone, Pete Runnels)	18.00	9.00	5.50
520	Don Elston	15.00	7.50	4.50
521	Gary Geiger	15.00	7.50	4.50
522	Gene Snyder	15.00	7.50	4.50
523	Harry Bright	15.00	7.50	4.50
524	Larry Osborne	15.00	7.50	4.50
525	Jim Coates	16.00	8.00	4.75
526	Bob Speake	15.00	7.50	4.50
527	Solly Hemus	15.00	7.50	4.50
528	Pirates Team/Checklist 496-572	25.00	12.50	7.50
529	*George Bamberger*	16.00	8.00	4.75
530	Wally Moon	16.00	8.00	4.75
531	Ray Webster	15.00	7.50	4.50
532	Mark Freeman	15.00	7.50	4.50
533	Darrell Johnson	16.00	8.00	4.75
534	Faye Throneberry	15.00	7.50	4.50
535	Ruben Gomez	15.00	7.50	4.50
536	Dan Kravitz	15.00	7.50	4.50
537	Rodolfo Arias	15.00	7.50	4.50
538	Chick King	15.00	7.50	4.50
539	Gary Blaylock	15.00	7.50	4.50
540	Willy Miranda	15.00	7.50	4.50
541	Bob Thurman	15.00	7.50	4.50
542	*Jim Perry*	15.00	7.50	4.50
543	Corsair Outfield Trio (Bob Clemente, Bob Skinner, Bill Virdon)	40.00	20.00	12.00
544	Lee Tate	15.00	7.50	4.50
545	Tom Morgan	15.00	7.50	4.50
546	Al Schroll	15.00	7.50	4.50
547	Jim Baxes	15.00	7.50	4.50
548	Elmer Singleton	15.00	7.50	4.50
549	Howie Nunn	15.00	7.50	4.50
550	Roy Campanella	125.00	62.00	37.00
551	Fred Haney AS	16.00	8.00	4.75
552	Casey Stengel AS	25.00	12.50	7.50
553	Orlando Cepeda AS	18.00	9.00	5.50
554	Bill Skowron AS	18.00	9.00	5.50
555	Bill Mazeroski AS	18.00	9.00	5.50
556	Nellie Fox AS	15.00	7.50	4.50
557	Ken Boyer AS	18.00	9.00	5.50
558	Frank Malzone AS	16.00	8.00	4.75
559	Ernie Banks AS	30.00	15.00	9.00
560	Luis Aparicio AS	20.00	10.00	6.00
561	Hank Aaron AS	125.00	62.00	37.00
562	Al Kaline AS	35.00	17.50	10.50
563	Willie Mays AS	125.00	62.00	37.00
564	Mickey Mantle AS	200.00	100.00	60.00
565	Wes Covington AS	16.00	8.00	4.75
566	Roy Sievers AS	16.00	8.00	4.75
567	Del Crandall AS	16.00	8.00	4.75
568	Gus Triandos AS	16.00	8.00	4.75
569	Bob Friend AS	16.00	8.00	4.75
570	Bob Turley AS	16.00	8.00	4.75
571	Warren Spahn AS	30.00	15.00	9.00
572	Billy Pierce AS	25.00	12.50	7.50
----	Elect Your Favorite Rookie Insert (paper stock, September 29 date on back)	15.00	7.50	4.50
----	Felt Pennants Insert (paper stock)	15.00	7.50	4.50

1960 Topps

In 1960, Topps returned to a horizontal format

(3-1/2" by 2-1/2") with a color portrait and a black and white "action" photograph on the front. The backs returned to the use of just the previous year and lifetime statistics along with a cartoon and short career summary or previous season highlights. Specialty cards in the 572-card set are multi-player cards, managers and coaches cards, and highlights of the 1959 World Series. Two groups of rookie cards are included. The first are numbers 117-148, which are the Sport Magazine rookies. The second group is called "Topps All-Star Rookies." Finally, there is a continuation of the All-Star cards to close out the set in the scarcer high numbers. Card #'s 375-440 can be found with backs printed on either white or grey cardboard, with the white stock being the less common.

	NR MT	EX	VG
Complete Set:	3400.00	1700.00	1020.
Common Player: 1-286	3.00	1.50	.90
Common Player: 287-440	3.00	1.50	.90
Common Player: 441-506	4.00	2.00	1.25
Common Player: 507-572	10.00	5.00	3.00

		NR MT	EX	VG
1	Early Wynn	35.00	10.00	5.00
2	Roman Mejias	3.25	1.75	1.00
3	Joe Adcock	3.25	1.75	1.00
4	Bob Purkey	3.00	1.50	.90
5	Wally Moon	3.00	1.50	.90
6	Lou Berberet	3.00	1.50	.90
7	Master & Mentor (Willie Mays, Bill Rigney)	12.00	6.00	3.50
8	Bud Daley	3.00	1.50	.90
9	Faye Throneberry	3.00	1.50	.90
10	Ernie Banks	50.00	25.00	15.00
11	Norm Siebern	3.00	1.50	.90
12	Milt Pappas	3.00	1.50	.90
13	Wally Post	3.00	1.50	.90
14	Jim Grant	3.00	1.50	.90
15	Pete Runnels	3.00	1.50	.90
16	Ernie Broglio	3.00	1.50	.90
17	Johnny Callison	3.00	1.50	.90
18	Dodgers Team/Checklist 1-88	10.00	5.00	3.00
19	Felix Mantilla	3.00	1.50	.90
20	Roy Face	3.00	1.50	.90
21	Dutch Dotterer	3.00	1.50	.90
22	Rocky Bridges	3.00	1.50	.90
23	Eddie Fisher	3.00	1.50	.90
24	Dick Gray	3.00	1.50	.90
25	Roy Sievers	4.00	2.00	1.25
26	Wayne Terwilliger	3.00	1.50	.90
27	Dick Drott	3.00	1.50	.90
28	Brooks Robinson	40.00	20.00	12.00
29	Clem Labine	3.00	1.50	.90
30	Tito Francona	3.00	1.50	.90
31	Sammy Esposito	3.00	1.50	.90
32	Sophomore Stalwarts (Jim O'Toole, Vada Pinson)	4.00	2.00	1.25
33	Tom Morgan	3.00	1.50	.90
34	George Anderson	2.50	1.25	.70
35	Whitey Ford	30.00	15.00	9.00
36	Russ Nixon	3.00	1.50	.90
37	Bill Bruton	3.00	1.50	.90
38	Jerry Casale	3.00	1.50	.90
39	Earl Averill	3.00	1.50	.90
40	Joe Cunningham	3.00	1.50	.90
41	Barry Latman	3.00	1.50	.90
42	Hobie Landrith	3.00	1.50	.90
43	Senators Team/Checklist 1-88	6.00	3.00	1.75
44	Bobby Locke	3.00	1.50	.90
45	Roy McMillan	3.00	1.50	.90
46	Jack Fisher	3.00	1.50	.90
47	Don Zimmer	3.25	1.75	1.00
48	Hal Smith	3.00	1.50	.90
49	Curt Raydon	3.00	1.50	.90
50	Al Kaline	40.00	20.00	12.00
51	Jim Coates	3.00	1.50	.90
52	Dave Philley	3.00	1.50	.90
53	Jackie Brandt	3.00	1.50	.90
54	Mike Fornieles	3.00	1.50	.90
55	Bill Mazeroski	3.00	1.50	.90
56	Steve Korcheck	3.00	1.50	.90
57	Win - Savers (Turk Lown, Gerry Staley)	3.00	1.50	.90
58	Gino Cimoli	3.00	1.50	.90
59	Juan Pizarro	3.00	1.50	.90
60	Gus Triandos	3.00	1.50	.90
61	Eddie Kasko	3.00	1.50	.90
62	Roger Craig	3.25	1.75	1.00

		NR MT	EX	VG
63	George Strickland	3.00	1.50	.90
64	Jack Meyer	3.00	1.50	.90
65	Elston Howard	6.00	3.00	1.75
66	Bob Trowbridge	3.00	1.50	.90
67	*Jose Pagan*	3.00	1.50	.90
68	Dave Hillman	3.00	1.50	.90
69	Billy Goodman	3.00	1.50	.90
70	Lou Burdette	3.25	1.75	1.00
71	Marty Keough	3.00	1.50	.90
72	Tigers Team/Checklist 89-176	10.00	5.00	3.00
73	Bob Gibson	40.00	20.00	12.00
74	Walt Moryn	3.00	1.50	.90
75	Vic Power	3.00	1.50	.90
76	Bill Fischer	3.00	1.50	.90
77	Hank Foiles	3.00	1.50	.90
78	Bob Grim	3.00	1.50	.90
79	Walt Dropo	3.00	1.50	.90
80	Johnny Antonelli	3.00	1.50	.90
81	Russ Snyder	3.00	1.50	.90
82	Ruben Gomez	3.00	1.50	.90
83	Tony Kubek	4.50	2.25	1.25
84	Hal Smith	3.00	1.50	.90
85	Frank Lary	3.00	1.50	.90
86	Dick Gernert	3.00	1.50	.90
87	John Romonosky	3.00	1.50	.90
88	John Roseboro	3.00	1.50	.90
89	Hal Brown	3.00	1.50	.90
90	Bobby Avila	3.00	1.50	.90
91	Bennie Daniels	3.00	1.50	.90
92	Whitey Herzog	3.25	1.75	1.00
93	Art Schult	3.00	1.50	.90
94	Leo Kiely	3.00	1.50	.90
95	Frank Thomas	3.00	1.50	.90
96	Ralph Terry	2.50	1.25	.70
97	Ted Lepcio	3.00	1.50	.90
98	Gordon Jones	3.00	1.50	.90
99	Lenny Green	3.00	1.50	.90
100	Nellie Fox	7.00	3.50	2.00
101	Bob Miller	3.00	1.50	.90
102	Kent Hadley	3.00	1.50	.90
103	Dick Farrell	3.00	1.50	.90
104	Dick Schofield	3.00	1.50	.90
105	Larry Sherry	3.00	1.50	.90
106	Billy Gardner	3.00	1.50	.90
107	Carl Willey	3.00	1.50	.90
108	Pete Daley	3.00	1.50	.90
109	Cletis Boyer	3.00	1.50	.90
110	Cal McLish	3.00	1.50	.90
111	Vic Wertz	3.00	1.50	.90
112	Jack Harshman	3.00	1.50	.90
113	Bob Skinner	3.00	1.50	.90
114	Ken Aspromonte	3.00	1.50	.90
115	Fork & Knuckler (Roy Face, Hoyt Wilhelm)	4.00	2.00	1.25
116	Jim Rivera	3.00	1.50	.90
117	Tom Borland	3.00	1.50	.90
118	Bob Bruce	3.00	1.50	.90
119	*Chico Cardenas*	3.00	1.50	.90
120	Duke Carmel	3.00	1.50	.90
121	Camilo Carreon	3.00	1.50	.90
122	Don Dillard	3.00	1.50	.90
123	Dan Dobbek	3.00	1.50	.90
124	Jim Donohue	3.00	1.50	.90
125	*Dick Ellsworth*	3.00	1.50	.90
126	*Chuck Estrada*	3.00	1.50	.90
127	Ronnie Hansen	3.00	1.50	.90
128	Bill Harris	3.00	1.50	.90
129	Bob Hartman	3.00	1.50	.90
130	Frank Herrera	3.00	1.50	.90
131	Ed Hobaugh	3.00	1.50	.90
132	*Frank Howard*	12.00	6.00	3.50
133	*Manuel Javier*	3.00	1.50	.90
134	Deron Johnson	3.00	1.50	.90
135	Ken Johnson	3.00	1.50	.90
136	*Jim Kaat*	30.00	15.00	9.00
137	Lou Klimchock	3.00	1.50	.90
138	*Art Mahaffey*	3.00	1.50	.90
139	Carl Mathias	3.00	1.50	.90
140	Julio Navarro	3.00	1.50	.90
141	Jim Proctor	3.00	1.50	.90
142	Bill Short	3.00	1.50	.90
143	Al Spangler	3.00	1.50	.90
144	Al Stieglitz	3.00	1.50	.90
145	Jim Umbricht	3.00	1.50	.90
146	Ted Wieand	3.00	1.50	.90
147	Bob Will	3.00	1.50	.90
148	*Carl Yastrzemski*	350.00	140.00	88.00
149	Bob Nieman	3.00	1.50	.90
150	Billy Pierce	3.25	1.75	1.00
151	Giants Team/Checklist 177-264	6.00	3.00	1.75
152	Gail Harris	3.00	1.50	.90

		NR MT	EX	VG
153	Bobby Thomson	3.00	1.50	.90
154	Jim Davenport	3.00	1.50	.90
155	Charlie Neal	3.00	1.50	.90
156	Art Ceccarelli	3.00	1.50	.90
157	Rocky Nelson	3.00	1.50	.90
158	Wes Covington	3.00	1.50	.90
159	Jim Piersall	3.00	1.50	.90
160	Rival All Stars (Ken Boyer, Mickey Mantle)	30.00	15.00	9.00
161	Ray Narleski	3.00	1.50	.90
162	Sammy Taylor	3.00	1.50	.90
163	Hector Lopez	3.00	1.50	.90
164	Reds Team/Checklist 89-176	7.00	3.50	2.00
165	Jack Sanford	3.00	1.50	.90
166	Chuck Essegian	3.00	1.50	.90
167	Valmy Thomas	3.00	1.50	.90
168	Alex Grammas	3.00	1.50	.90
169	Jake Striker	3.00	1.50	.90
170	Del Crandall	3.00	1.50	.90
171	Johnny Groth	3.00	1.50	.90
172	Willie Kirkland	3.00	1.50	.90
173	Billy Martin	10.00	5.00	3.00
174	Indians Team/Checklist 89-176	6.00	3.00	1.75
175	Pedro Ramos	3.00	1.50	.90
176	Vada Pinson	3.25	1.75	1.00
177	Johnny Kucks	3.00	1.50	.90
178	Woody Held	3.00	1.50	.90
179	Rip Coleman	3.00	1.50	.90
180	Harry Simpson	3.00	1.50	.90
181	Billy Loes	3.00	1.50	.90
182	Glen Hobbie	3.00	1.50	.90
183	Eli Grba	3.00	1.50	.90
184	Gary Geiger	3.00	1.50	.90
185	Jim Owens	3.00	1.50	.90
186	Dave Sisler	3.00	1.50	.90
187	Jay Hook	3.00	1.50	.90
188	Dick Williams	3.00	1.50	.90
189	Don McMahon	3.00	1.50	.90
190	Gene Woodling	3.00	1.50	.90
191	Johnny Klippstein	3.00	1.50	.90
192	Danny O'Connell	3.00	1.50	.90
193	Dick Hyde	3.00	1.50	.90
194	Bobby Gene Smith	3.00	1.50	.90
195	Lindy McDaniel	3.00	1.50	.90
196	Andy Carey	3.00	1.50	.90
197	Ron Kline	3.00	1.50	.90
198	Jerry Lynch	3.00	1.50	.90
199	Dick Donovan	3.00	1.50	.90
200	Willie Mays	100.00	50.00	30.00
201	Larry Osborne	3.00	1.50	.90
202	Fred Kipp	3.00	1.50	.90
203	Sammy White	3.00	1.50	.90
204	Ryne Duren	2.50	1.25	.70
205	Johnny Logan	3.00	1.50	.90
206	Claude Osteen	3.00	1.50	.90
207	Bob Boyd	3.00	1.50	.90
208	White Sox Team/Checklist 177-264	6.00	3.00	1.75
209	Ron Blackburn	3.00	1.50	.90
210	Harmon Killebrew	25.00	12.50	7.50
211	Taylor Phillips	3.00	1.50	.90
212	Walt Alston	6.00	3.00	1.75
213	Chuck Dressen	3.00	1.50	.90
214	Jimmie Dykes	3.00	1.50	.90
215	Bob Elliott	3.00	1.50	.90
216	Joe Gordon	3.00	1.50	.90
217	Charley Grimm	3.00	1.50	.90
218	Solly Hemus	3.00	1.50	.90
219	Fred Hutchinson	3.00	1.50	.90
220	Billy Jurges	3.00	1.50	.90
221	Cookie Lavagetto	3.00	1.50	.90
222	Al Lopez	5.00	2.50	1.50
223	Danny Murtaugh	3.00	1.50	.90
224	Paul Richards	3.00	1.50	.90
225	Bill Rigney	3.00	1.50	.90
226	Eddie Sawyer	3.00	1.50	.90
227	Casey Stengel	15.00	7.50	4.50
228	Ernie Johnson	3.00	1.50	.90
229	Joe Morgan	3.00	1.50	.90
230	Mound Magicians (Bob Buhl, Lou Burdette, Warren Spahn)	6.00	3.00	1.75
231	Hal Naragon	3.00	1.50	.90
232	Jim Busby	3.00	1.50	.90
233	Don Elston	3.00	1.50	.90
234	Don Demeter	3.00	1.50	.90
235	Gus Bell	3.00	1.50	.90
236	Dick Ricketts	3.00	1.50	.90
237	Elmer Valo	3.00	1.50	.90
238	Danny Kravitz	3.00	1.50	.90
239	Joe Shipley	3.00	1.50	.90
240	Luis Aparicio	10.00	5.00	3.00

		NR MT	EX	VG
241	Albie Pearson	3.00	1.50	.90
242	Cards Team/Checklist 265-352	6.00	3.00	1.75
243	Bubba Phillips	3.00	1.50	.90
244	Hal Griggs	3.00	1.50	.90
245	Eddie Yost	3.00	1.50	.90
246	Lee Maye	3.00	1.50	.90
247	Gil McDougald	4.50	2.25	1.25
248	Del Rice	3.00	1.50	.90
249	*Earl Wilson*	3.00	1.50	.90
250	Stan Musial	100.00	50.00	30.00
251	Bobby Malkmus	3.00	1.50	.90
252	Ray Herbert	3.00	1.50	.90
253	Eddie Bressoud	3.00	1.50	.90
254	Arnie Portocarrero	3.00	1.50	.90
255	Jim Gilliam	3.25	1.75	1.00
256	Dick Brown	3.00	1.50	.90
257	Gordy Coleman	3.00	1.50	.90
258	Dick Groat	4.00	2.00	1.25
259	George Altman	3.00	1.50	.90
260	Power Plus (Rocky Colavito, Tito Francona)	3.00	1.50	.90
261	Pete Burnside	3.00	1.50	.90
262	Hank Bauer	3.00	1.50	.90
263	Darrell Johnson	3.00	1.50	.90
264	Robin Roberts	12.00	6.00	3.50
265	Rip Repulski	3.00	1.50	.90
266	Joe Jay	3.00	1.50	.90
267	Jim Marshall	3.00	1.50	.90
268	Al Worthington	3.00	1.50	.90
269	Gene Green	3.00	1.50	.90
270	Bob Turley	3.25	1.75	1.00
271	Julio Becquer	3.00	1.50	.90
272	Fred Green	3.00	1.50	.90
273	Neil Chrisley	3.00	1.50	.90
274	Tom Acker	3.00	1.50	.90
275	Curt Flood	3.00	1.50	.90
276	Ken McBride	3.00	1.50	.90
277	Harry Bright	3.00	1.50	.90
278	Stan Williams	3.00	1.50	.90
279	Chuck Tanner	2.50	1.25	.70
280	Frank Sullivan	3.00	1.50	.90
281	Ray Boone	3.00	1.50	.90
282	Joe Nuxhall	3.00	1.50	.90
283	John Blanchard	2.75	1.50	.80
284	Don Gross	3.00	1.50	.90
285	Harry Anderson	3.00	1.50	.90
286	Ray Semproch	3.00	1.50	.90
287	Felipe Alou	2.50	1.25	.70
288	Bob Mabe	3.00	1.50	.90
289	Willie Jones	3.00	1.50	.90
290	Jerry Lumpe	3.00	1.50	.90
291	Bob Keegan	3.00	1.50	.90
292	Dodger Backstops (Joe Pignatano, John Roseboro)	3.00	1.50	.90
293	Gene Conley	3.00	1.50	.90
294	Tony Taylor	3.00	1.50	.90
295	Gil Hodges	18.00	9.00	5.50
296	Nelson Chittum	3.00	1.50	.90
297	Reno Bertoia	3.00	1.50	.90
298	George Witt	3.00	1.50	.90
299	Earl Torgeson	3.00	1.50	.90
300	Hank Aaron	100.00	50.00	30.00
301	Jerry Davie	3.00	1.50	.90
302	Phillies Team/Checklist 353-429	7.00	3.50	2.00
303	Billy O'Dell	3.00	1.50	.90
304	Joe Ginsberg	3.00	1.50	.90
305	Richie Ashburn	7.00	3.50	2.00
306	Frank Baumann	3.00	1.50	.90
307	Gene Oliver	3.00	1.50	.90
308	Dick Hall	3.00	1.50	.90
309	Bob Hale	3.00	1.50	.90
310	Frank Malzone	3.00	1.50	.90
311	Raul Sanchez	3.00	1.50	.90
312	Charlie Lau	3.00	1.50	.90
313	Turk Lown	3.00	1.50	.90
314	Chico Fernandez	3.00	1.50	.90
315	Bobby Shantz	3.25	1.75	1.00
316	*Willie McCovey*	150.00	75.00	45.00
317	Pumpsie Green	3.00	1.50	.90
318	Jim Baxes	3.00	1.50	.90
319	Joe Koppe	3.00	1.50	.90
320	Bob Allison	3.25	1.75	1.00
321	Ron Fairly	3.00	1.50	.90
322	Willie Tasby	3.00	1.50	.90
323	Johnny Romano	3.00	1.50	.90
324	Jim Perry	2.50	1.25	.70
325	Jim O'Toole	3.00	1.50	.90
326	Bob Clemente	100.00	50.00	30.00
327	*Ray Sadecki*	3.25	1.75	1.00
328	Earl Battey	3.00	1.50	.90
329	Zack Monroe	3.25	1.75	1.00

		NR MT	EX	VG
330	Harvey Kuenn	3.00	1.50	.90
331	Henry Mason	3.00	1.50	.90
332	Yankees Team/Checklist 265-352	20.00	10.00	6.00
333	Danny McDevitt	3.00	1.50	.90
334	Ted Abernathy	3.00	1.50	.90
335	Red Schoendienst	15.00	7.50	4.50
336	Ike Delock	3.00	1.50	.90
337	Cal Neeman	3.00	1.50	.90
338	Ray Monzant	3.00	1.50	.90
339	Harry Chiti	3.00	1.50	.90
340	Harvey Haddix	3.25	1.75	1.00
341	Carroll Hardy	3.00	1.50	.90
342	Casey Wise	3.00	1.50	.90
343	Sandy Koufax	90.00	45.00	27.00
344	Clint Courtney	3.00	1.50	.90
345	Don Newcombe	2.50	1.25	.70
346	J.C. Martin (photo actually Gary Peters)	3.00	1.50	.90
347	Ed Bouchee	3.00	1.50	.90
348	Barry Shetrone	3.00	1.50	.90
349	Moe Drabowsky	3.00	1.50	.90
350	Mickey Mantle	350.00	175.00	105.00
351	Don Nottebart	3.00	1.50	.90
352	Cincy Clouters (Gus Bell, Jerry Lynch, Frank Robinson)	5.00	2.50	1.50
353	Don Larsen	3.25	1.75	1.00
354	Bob Lillis	3.00	1.50	.90
355	Bill White	3.00	1.50	.90
356	Joe Amalfitano	3.00	1.50	.90
357	Al Schroll	3.00	1.50	.90
358	Joe DeMaestri	3.25	1.75	1.00
359	Buddy Gilbert	3.00	1.50	.90
360	Herb Score	2.50	1.25	.70
361	Bob Oldis	3.00	1.50	.90
362	Russ Kemmerer	3.00	1.50	.90
363	Gene Stephens	3.00	1.50	.90
364	Paul Foytack	3.00	1.50	.90
365	Minnie Minoso	3.00	1.50	.90
366	*Dallas Green*	3.25	1.75	1.00
367	Bill Tuttle	3.00	1.50	.90
368	Daryl Spencer	3.00	1.50	.90
369	Billy Hoeft	3.00	1.50	.90
370	Bill Skowron	6.00	3.00	1.75
371	Bud Byerly	3.00	1.50	.90
372	Frank House	3.00	1.50	.90
373	Don Hoak	3.00	1.50	.90
374	Bob Buhl	3.00	1.50	.90
375	Dale Long	3.00	1.50	.90
376	Johnny Briggs	3.00	1.50	.90
377	Roger Maris	100.00	50.00	30.00
378	Stu Miller	3.00	1.50	.90
379	Red Wilson	3.00	1.50	.90
380	Bob Shaw	3.00	1.50	.90
381	Braves Team/Checklist 353-429	7.00	3.50	2.00
382	Ted Bowsfield	3.00	1.50	.90
383	Leon Wagner	3.00	1.50	.90
384	Don Cardwell	3.00	1.50	.90
385	World Series Game 1 (Neal Steals Second)	4.00	2.00	1.25
386	World Series Game 2 (Neal Belts 2nd Homer)	4.00	2.00	1.25
387	World Series Game 3 (Furillo Breaks Up Game)	4.00	2.00	1.25
388	World Series Game 4 (Hodges' Winning Homer)	5.00	2.50	1.50
389	World Series Game 5 (Luis Swipes Base)	5.00	2.50	1.50
390	World Series Game 6 (Scrambling After Ball)	4.00	2.00	1.25
391	World Series Summary (The Champs Celebrate)	4.00	2.00	1.25
392	Tex Clevenger	3.00	1.50	.90
393	Smoky Burgess	2.50	1.25	.70
394	Norm Larker	3.00	1.50	.90
395	Hoyt Wilhelm	15.00	7.50	4.50
396	Steve Bilko	3.00	1.50	.90
397	Don Blasingame	3.00	1.50	.90
398	Mike Cuellar	3.25	1.75	1.00
399	Young Hill Stars (Jack Fisher, Milt Pappas, Jerry Walker)	3.25	1.75	1.00
400	Rocky Colavito	10.00	5.00	3.00
401	Bob Duliba	3.00	1.50	.90
402	Dick Stuart	3.00	1.50	.90
403	Ed Sadowski	3.00	1.50	.90
404	Bob Rush	3.00	1.50	.90
405	Bobby Richardson	6.00	3.00	1.75
406	Billy Klaus	3.00	1.50	.90
407	*Gary Peters* (photo actually J.C. Martin)	3.25	1.75	1.00
408	Carl Furillo	4.00	2.00	1.25
409	Ron Samford	3.00	1.50	.90
410	Sam Jones	3.00	1.50	.90
411	Ed Bailey	3.00	1.50	.90
412	Bob Anderson	3.00	1.50	.90
413	A's Team/Checklist 430-495	7.00	3.50	2.00
414	Don Williams	3.00	1.50	.90
415	Bob Cerv	3.00	1.50	.90
416	Humberto Robinson	3.00	1.50	.90
417	Chuck Cottier	3.00	1.50	.90
418	Don Mossi	3.00	1.50	.90
419	George Crowe	3.00	1.50	.90
420	Ed Mathews	30.00	15.00	9.00
421	Duke Maas	3.25	1.75	1.00
422	Johnny Powers	3.00	1.50	.90
423	Ed Fitz Gerald	3.00	1.50	.90
424	Pete Whisenant	3.00	1.50	.90
425	Johnny Podres	3.00	1.50	.90
426	Ron Jackson	3.00	1.50	.90
427	Al Grunwald	3.00	1.50	.90
428	Al Smith	3.00	1.50	.90
429	American League Kings (Nellie Fox, Harvey Kuenn)	3.25	1.75	1.00
430	Art Ditmar	3.00	1.50	.90
431	Andre Rodgers	3.00	1.50	.90
432	Chuck Stobbs	3.00	1.50	.90
433	Irv Noren	3.00	1.50	.90
434	Brooks Lawrence	3.00	1.50	.90
435	Gene Freese	3.00	1.50	.90
436	Marv Throneberry	3.25	1.75	1.00
437	Bob Friend	2.50	1.25	.70
438	Jim Coker	3.00	1.50	.90
439	Tom Brewer	3.00	1.50	.90
440	Jim Lemon	3.00	1.50	.90
441	Gary Bell	4.00	2.00	1.25
442	Joe Pignatano	4.00	2.00	1.25
443	Charlie Maxwell	4.00	2.00	1.25
444	Jerry Kindall	4.00	2.00	1.25
445	Warren Spahn	40.00	20.00	12.00
446	Ellis Burton	4.00	2.00	1.25
447	Ray Moore	4.00	2.00	1.25
448	*Jim Gentile*	4.00	2.00	1.25
449	Jim Brosnan	5.00	2.50	1.50
450	Orlando Cepeda	10.00	5.00	3.00
451	Curt Simmons	4.00	2.00	1.25
452	Ray Webster	4.00	2.00	1.25
453	Vern Law	4.50	2.25	1.25
454	Hal Woodeshick	4.00	2.00	1.25
455	Orioles Coaches (Harry Brecheen, Lum Harris, Eddie Robinson)	5.00	2.50	1.50
456	Red Sox Coaches (Del Baker, Billy Herman, Sal Maglie, Rudy York)	4.00	2.00	1.25
457	Cubs Coaches (Lou Klein, Charlie Root, Elvin Tappe)	5.00	2.50	1.50
458	White Sox Coaches (Ray Berres, Johnny Cooney, Tony Cuccinello, Don Gutteridge)	5.00	2.50	1.50
459	Reds Coaches (Cot Deal, Wally Moses, Reggie Otero)	5.00	2.50	1.50
460	Indians Coaches (Mel Harder, Red Kress, Bob Lemon, Jo-Jo White)	4.00	2.00	1.25
461	Tigers Coaches (Luke Appling, Tom Ferrick, Billy Hitchcock)	4.00	2.00	1.25
462	A's Coaches (Walker Cooper, Fred Fitzsimmons, Don Heffner)	5.00	2.50	1.50
463	Dodgers Coaches (Joe Becker, Bobby Bragan, Greg Mulleavy, Pete Reiser)	4.00	2.00	1.25
464	Braves Coaches (George Myatt, Andy Pafko, Bob Scheffing, Whitlow Wyatt)	5.00	2.50	1.50
465	Yankees Coaches (Frank Crosetti, Bill Dickey, Ralph Houk, Ed Lopat)	11.00	5.50	3.25
466	Phillies Coaches (Dick Carter, Andy Cohen, Ken Silvestri)	5.00	2.50	1.50
467	Pirates Coaches (Bill Burwell, Sam Narron, Frank Oceak, Mickey Vernon)	4.00	2.00	1.25
468	Cardinals Coaches (Ray Katt, Johnny Keane, Howie Pollet, Harry Walker)	5.00	2.50	1.50
469	Giants Coaches (Salty Parker, Bill Posedel, Wes Westrum)	5.00	2.50	1.50
470	Senators Coaches (Ellis Clary, Sam Mele, Bob Swift)	5.00	2.50	1.50
471	Ned Garver	4.00	2.00	1.25
472	Al Dark	4.50	2.25	1.25
473	Al Cicotte	4.00	2.00	1.25
474	Haywood Sullivan	5.00	2.50	1.50
475	Don Drysdale	30.00	15.00	9.00
476	Lou Johnson	4.00	2.00	1.25
477	Don Ferrarese	4.00	2.00	1.25
478	Frank Torre	4.00	2.00	1.25
479	Georges Maranda	4.00	2.00	1.25
480	Yogi Berra	60.00	30.00	18.00

		NR MT	EX	VG
481	Wes Stock	4.00	2.00	1.25
482	Frank Bolling	4.00	2.00	1.25
483	Camilo Pascual	5.00	2.50	1.50
484	Pirates Team/Checklist 430-495	15.00	7.50	4.50
485	Ken Boyer	4.50	2.25	1.25
486	Bobby Del Greco	4.00	2.00	1.25
487	Tom Sturdivant	4.00	2.00	1.25
488	Norm Cash	5.00	2.50	1.50
489	Steve Ridzik	4.00	2.00	1.25
490	Frank Robinson	45.00	23.00	13.50
491	Mel Roach	4.00	2.00	1.25
492	Larry Jackson	4.00	2.00	1.25
493	Duke Snider	45.00	23.00	13.50
494	Orioles Team/Checklist 496-572	7.00	3.50	2.00
495	Sherm Lollar	4.00	2.00	1.25
496	Bill Virdon	4.00	2.00	1.25
497	John Tsitouris	4.00	2.00	1.25
498	Al Pilarcik	4.00	2.00	1.25
499	Johnny James	4.00	2.00	1.25
500	Johnny Temple	4.00	2.00	1.25
501	Bob Schmidt	4.00	2.00	1.25
502	Jim Bunning	10.00	5.00	3.00
503	Don Lee	4.00	2.00	1.25
504	Seth Morehead	4.00	2.00	1.25
505	Ted Kluszewski	6.00	3.00	1.75
506	Lee Walls	4.00	2.00	1.25
507	Dick Stigman	10.00	5.00	3.00
508	Billy Consolo	10.00	5.00	3.00
509	*Tommy Davis*	18.00	9.00	5.50
510	Jerry Staley	10.00	5.00	3.00
511	Ken Walters	10.00	5.00	3.00
512	Joe Gibbon	10.00	5.00	3.00
513	Cubs Team/Checklist 496-572	25.00	12.50	7.50
514	*Steve Barber*	11.00	5.50	3.25
515	Stan Lopata	10.00	5.00	3.00
516	Marty Kutyna	10.00	5.00	3.00
517	Charley James	10.00	5.00	3.00
518	*Tony Gonzalez*	11.00	5.50	3.25
519	Ed Roebuck	10.00	5.00	3.00
520	Don Buddin	10.00	5.00	3.00
521	Mike Lee	10.00	5.00	3.00
522	Ken Hunt	11.00	5.50	3.25
523	*Clay Dalrymple*	11.00	5.50	3.25
524	Bill Henry	10.00	5.00	3.00
525	Marv Breeding	10.00	5.00	3.00
526	Paul Giel	10.00	5.00	3.00
527	Jose Valdivielso	10.00	5.00	3.00
528	Ben Johnson	10.00	5.00	3.00
529	Norm Sherry	10.00	5.00	3.00
530	Mike McCormick	11.00	5.50	3.25
531	Sandy Amoros	10.00	5.00	3.00
532	Mike Garcia	10.00	5.00	3.00
533	Lu Clinton	10.00	5.00	3.00
534	Ken MacKenzie	10.00	5.00	3.00
535	Whitey Lockman	10.00	5.00	3.00
536	Wynn Hawkins	10.00	5.00	3.00
537	Red Sox Team/Checklist 496-572	25.00	12.50	7.50
538	Frank Barnes	10.00	5.00	3.00
539	Gene Baker	10.00	5.00	3.00
540	Jerry Walker	10.00	5.00	3.00
541	Tony Curry	10.00	5.00	3.00
542	Ken Hamlin	10.00	5.00	3.00
543	Elio Chacon	10.00	5.00	3.00
544	Bill Monbouquette	11.00	5.50	3.25
545	Carl Sawatski	10.00	5.00	3.00
546	Hank Aguirre	10.00	5.00	3.00
547	*Bob Aspromonte*	11.00	5.50	3.25
548	*Don Mincher*	11.00	5.50	3.25
549	John Buzhardt	10.00	5.00	3.00
550	Jim Landis	10.00	5.00	3.00
551	Ed Rakow	10.00	5.00	3.00
552	Walt Bond	10.00	5.00	3.00
553	Bill Skowron AS	12.00	6.00	3.50
554	Willie McCovey AS	45.00	22.00	13.50
555	Nellie Fox AS	15.00	7.50	4.50
556	Charlie Neal AS	11.00	5.50	3.25
557	Frank Malzone AS	11.00	5.50	3.25
558	Eddie Mathews AS	25.00	12.50	7.50
559	Luis Aparicio AS	18.00	9.00	5.50
560	Ernie Banks AS	40.00	20.00	12.00
561	Al Kaline AS	40.00	20.00	12.00
562	Joe Cunningham AS	11.00	5.50	3.25
563	Mickey Mantle AS	175.00	87.00	50.00
564	Willie Mays AS	90.00	45.00	27.00
565	Roger Maris AS	70.00	35.00	20.00
566	Hank Aaron AS	100.00	50.00	30.00
567	Sherm Lollar AS	11.00	5.50	3.25
568	Del Crandall AS	11.00	5.50	3.25
569	Camilo Pascual AS	11.00	5.50	3.25
570	Don Drysdale AS	20.00	10.00	6.00
571	Billy Pierce AS	11.00	5.50	3.25
572	Johnny Antonelli AS	20.00	7.00	3.00
----	Elect Your Favorite Rookie Insert (paper stock, no date on back)	15.00	7.50	4.50
----	Hot Iron Transfer Insert (paper stock)	15.00	7.50	4.50

1960 Topps Baseball Tattoos

Probably the least popular of all Topps products among parents and teachers, the Topps Tattoos were delightful little items on the reverse of the wrappers of Topps "Tattoo Bubble Gum." The entire wrapper was 1-9/16" by 3-1/2." The happy owner simply moistened his skin and applied the back of the wrapper to the wet spot. Presto, out came a "tattoo" in color (although often blurred by running colors). The set offered 96 tattoo possibilities of which 55 were players, 16 teams, 15 action shots and 10 autographed balls. Surviving specimens are very rare today.

		NR MT	EX	VG
Complete Set:		675.00	337.00	202.00
Common Player:		3.00	1.50	.90
(1)	Hank Aaron	25.00	12.50	7.50
(2)	Bob Allison	5.00	2.50	1.50
(3)	John Antonelli	5.00	2.50	1.50
(4)	Richie Ashburn	7.00	3.50	2.00
(5)	Ernie Banks	15.00	7.50	4.50
(6)	Yogi Berra	18.00	9.00	5.50
(7)	Lew Burdette	6.00	3.00	1.75
(8)	Orlando Cepeda	7.00	3.50	2.00
(9)	Rocky Colavito	6.00	3.00	1.75
(10)	Joe Cunningham	3.00	1.50	.90
(11)	Buddy Daley	3.00	1.50	.90
(12)	Don Drysdale	12.00	6.00	3.50
(13)	Ryne Duren	5.00	2.50	1.50
(14)	Roy Face	5.00	2.50	1.50
(15)	Whitey Ford	15.00	7.50	4.50
(16)	Nellie Fox	7.00	3.50	2.00
(17)	Tito Francona	3.00	1.50	.90
(18)	Gene Freese	3.00	1.50	.90
(19)	Jim Gilliam	6.00	3.00	1.75
(20)	Dick Groat	6.00	3.00	1.75
(21)	Ray Herbert	3.00	1.50	.90
(22)	Glen Hobbie	3.00	1.50	.90
(23)	Jackie Jensen	6.00	3.00	1.75
(24)	Sam Jones	3.00	1.50	.90
(25)	Al Kaline	15.00	7.50	4.50
(26)	Harmon Killebrew	12.00	6.00	3.50
(27)	Harvy Kuenn (Harvey)	6.00	3.00	1.75
(28)	Frank Lary	3.00	1.50	.90
(29)	Vernon Law	5.00	2.50	1.50
(30)	Frank Malzone	3.00	1.50	.90
(31)	Mickey Mantle	75.00	37.00	22.00
(32)	Roger Maris	15.00	7.50	4.50
(33)	Ed Mathews	12.00	6.00	3.50
(34)	Willie Mays	25.00	12.50	7.50
(35)	Cal Mclish	3.00	1.50	.90
(36)	Wally Moon	5.00	2.50	1.50
(37)	Walt Moryn	3.00	1.50	.90
(38)	Don Mossi	3.00	1.50	.90
(39)	Stan Musial	25.00	12.50	7.50
(40)	Charlie Neal	3.00	1.50	.90

		NR MT	EX	VG
(41)	Don Newcombe	5.00	2.50	1.50
(42)	Milt Pappas	5.00	2.50	1.50
(43)	Camilo Pascual	5.00	2.50	1.50
(44)	Billie Pierce (Billy)	5.00	2.50	1.50
(45)	Robin Roberts	12.00	6.00	3.50
(46)	Frank Robinson	15.00	7.50	4.50
(47)	Pete Runnels	5.00	2.50	1.50
(48)	Herb Score	5.00	2.50	1.50
(49)	Warren Spahn	12.00	6.00	3.50
(50)	Johnny Temple	3.00	1.50	.90
(51)	Gus Triandos	3.00	1.50	.90
(52)	Jerry Walker	3.00	1.50	.90
(53)	Bill White	5.00	2.50	1.50
(54)	Gene Woodling	5.00	2.50	1.50
(55)	Early Wynn	12.00	6.00	3.50
(56)	Chicago Cubs Logo	3.00	1.50	.90
(57)	Cincinnati Reds Logo	3.00	1.50	.90
(58)	Los Angeles Dodgers Logo	3.00	1.50	.90
(59)	Milwaukee Braves Logo	3.00	1.50	.90
(60)	Philadelphia Phillies Logo	3.00	1.50	.90
(61)	Pittsburgh Pirates Logo	5.00	2.50	1.50
(62)	San Francisco Giants Logo	3.00	1.50	.90
(63)	St. Louis Cardinals Logo	3.00	1.50	.90
(64)	Baltimore Orioles Logo	3.00	1.50	.90
(65)	Boston Red Sox Logo	3.00	1.50	.90
(66)	Chicago White Sox Logo	3.00	1.50	.90
(67)	Cleveland Indians Logo	3.00	1.50	.90
(68)	Detroit Tigers Logo	3.00	1.50	.90
(69)	Kansas City Athletics Logo	3.00	1.50	.90
(70)	New York Yankees Logo	6.00	3.00	1.75
(71)	Washington Senators Logo	3.00	1.50	.90
(72)	Autograph (Richie Ashburn)	3.00	1.50	.90
(73)	Autograph (Rocky Colavito)	3.00	1.50	.90
(74)	Autograph (Roy Face)	3.00	1.50	.90
(75)	Autograph (Jackie Jensen)	3.00	1.50	.90
(76)	Autograph (Harmon Killebrew)	5.00	2.50	1.50
(77)	Autograph (Mickey Mantle)	25.00	12.50	7.50
(78)	Autograph (Willie Mays)	10.00	5.00	3.00
(79)	Autograph (Stan Musial)	10.00	5.00	3.00
(80)	Autograph (Billy Pierce)	3.00	1.50	.90
(81)	Autograph (Jerry Walker)	3.00	1.50	.90
(82)	Run-Down	3.00	1.50	.90
(83)	Out At First	3.00	1.50	.90
(84)	The Final Word	3.00	1.50	.90
(85)	Twisting Foul	3.00	1.50	.90
(86)	Out At Home	3.00	1.50	.90
(87)	Circus Catch	3.00	1.50	.90
(88)	Great Catch	3.00	1.50	.90
(89)	Stolen Base	3.00	1.50	.90
(90)	Grand Slam Homer	3.00	1.50	.90
(91)	Double Play	3.00	1.50	.90
(92)	Right-Handed Follow-Thru (no caption)	3.00	1.50	.90
(93)	Right-Handed High Leg Kick (no caption)	3.00	1.50	.90
(94)	Left-Handed Pitcher (no caption)	3.00	1.50	.90
(95)	Right-Handed Batter (no caption)	3.00	1.50	.90
(96)	Left-Handed Batter (no caption)	3.00	1.50	.90

1961 Topps

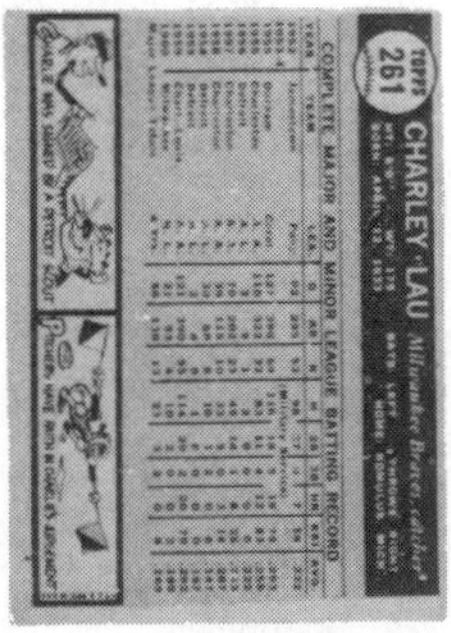

Except for some of the specialty cards, Topps returned to a vertical format with their 1961 cards. The set is numbered through 598, however only 587 cards were printed. No numbers 426, 587 and 588 were issued. Two cards numbered 463 exist (one a Braves team card and one a player card of Jack Fisher). Actually, the Braves team card is checklisted as #426. Designs for 1961 are basically large color portraits; the backs return to extensive statistics. A three-panel cartoon highlighting the player's career appears on the card backs. Innovations include numbered checklists, cards for statistical leaders, and 10 "Baseball Thrills" cards. The scarce high numbers are card numbers 523-589.

		NR MT	EX	VG
Complete Set:		5200.00	2600.00	1560.
Common Player: 1-370		2.00	1.00	.60
Common Player: 371-522		4.00	2.00	1.25
Common Player: 523-589		25.00	12.50	7.50
1	Dick Groat	20.00	5.00	3.00
2	Roger Maris	150.00	75.00	45.00
3	John Buzhardt	2.00	1.00	.60
4	Lenny Green	2.00	1.00	.60
5	Johnny Romano	2.00	1.00	.60
6	Ed Roebuck	2.00	1.00	.60
7	White Sox Team	4.00	2.00	1.25
8	Dick Williams	4.00	2.00	1.25
9	Bob Purkey	2.00	1.00	.60
10	Brooks Robinson	30.00	15.00	9.00
11	Curt Simmons	2.25	1.25	.70
12	Moe Thacker	2.00	1.00	.60
13	Chuck Cottier	2.00	1.00	.60
14	Don Mossi	2.25	1.25	.70
15	Willie Kirkland	2.00	1.00	.60
16	Billy Muffett	2.00	1.00	.60
17	Checklist 1-88	5.00	2.50	1.50
18	Jim Grant	2.00	1.00	.60
19	Cletis Boyer	2.25	1.25	.70
20	Robin Roberts	10.00	5.00	3.00
21	*Zorro Versalles*	4.00	2.00	1.25
22	Clem Labine	2.25	1.25	.70
23	Don Demeter	2.00	1.00	.60
24	Ken Johnson	2.00	1.00	.60
25	Red's Heavy Artillery (Gus Bell, Vada Pinson, Frank Robinson)	6.00	3.00	1.75
26	Wes Stock	2.00	1.00	.60
27	Jerry Kindall	2.00	1.00	.60
28	Hector Lopez	4.00	2.00	1.25
29	Don Nottebart	2.00	1.00	.60
30	Nellie Fox	6.00	3.00	1.75
31	Bob Schmidt	2.00	1.00	.60
32	Ray Sadecki	2.00	1.00	.60
33	Gary Geiger	2.00	1.00	.60
34	Wynn Hawkins	2.00	1.00	.60
35	*Ron Santo*	35.00	17.50	10.50
36	Jack Kralick	2.00	1.00	.60
37	Charlie Maxwell	2.00	1.00	.60
38	Bob Lillis	2.00	1.00	.60
39	Leo Posada	2.00	1.00	.60
40	Bob Turley	4.00	2.00	1.25
41	N.L. Batting Leaders (Bob Clemente, Dick Groat, Norm Larker, Willie Mays)	4.00	2.00	1.25
42	A.L. Batting Leaders (Minnie Minoso, Pete Runnels, Bill Skowron, Al Smith)	4.00	2.00	1.25
43	N.L. Home Run Leaders (Hank Aaron, Ernie Banks, Ken Boyer, Eddie Mathews)	4.00	2.00	1.25
44	A.L. Home Run Leaders (Rocky Colavito, Jim Lemon, Mickey Mantle, Roger Maris)	30.00	15.00	9.00
45	N.L. E.R.A. Leaders (Ernie Broglio, Don Drysdale, Bob Friend, Mike McCormick, Stan Williams)	3.25	1.75	1.00
46	A.L. E.R.A. Leaders (Frank Baumann, Hal Brown, Jim Bunning, Art Ditmar)	4.00	2.00	1.25
47	N.L. Pitching Leaders (Ernie Broglio, Lou Burdette, Vern Law, Warren Spahn)	3.25	1.75	1.00
48	A.L. Pitching Leaders (Bud Daley, Art Ditmar, Chuck Estrada, Frank Lary, Milt Pappas, Jim Perry)	4.00	2.00	1.25
49	N.L. Strikeout Leaders (Ernie Broglio, Don Drysdale, Sam Jones, Sandy Koufax)	4.00	2.00	1.25
50	A.L. Strikeout Leaders (Jim Bunning, Frank Lary, Pedro Ramos, Early Wynn)	5.00	2.50	1.50
51	Tigers Team	5.00	2.50	1.50
52	George Crowe	2.00	1.00	.60
53	Russ Nixon	2.00	1.00	.60
54	Earl Francis	2.00	1.00	.60
55	Jim Davenport	2.00	1.00	.60
56	Russ Kemmerer	2.00	1.00	.60
57	Marv Throneberry	4.00	2.00	1.25
58	Joe Schaffernoth	2.00	1.00	.60
59	Jim Woods	2.00	1.00	.60
60	Woodie Held	2.00	1.00	.60
61	Ron Piche	2.00	1.00	.60
62	Al Pilarcik	2.00	1.00	.60

		NR MT	EX	VG
63	Jim Kaat	8.00	4.00	2.50
64	Alex Grammas	2.00	1.00	.60
65	Ted Kluszewski	4.00	2.00	1.25
66	Bill Henry	2.00	1.00	.60
67	Ossie Virgil	2.00	1.00	.60
68	Deron Johnson	4.00	2.00	1.25
69	Earl Wilson	2.00	1.00	.60
70	Bill Virdon	4.00	2.00	1.25
71	Jerry Adair	2.25	1.25	.70
72	Stu Miller	2.00	1.00	.60
73	Al Spangler	2.00	1.00	.60
74	Joe Pignatano	2.00	1.00	.60
75	Lindy Shows Larry (Larry Jackson, Lindy McDaniel)	4.00	2.00	1.25
76	Harry Anderson	2.00	1.00	.60
77	Dick Stigman	2.00	1.00	.60
78	Lee Walls	2.00	1.00	.60
79	Joe Ginsberg	2.00	1.00	.60
80	Harmon Killebrew	25.00	12.50	7.50
81	Tracy Stallard	2.00	1.00	.60
82	Joe Christopher	2.00	1.00	.60
83	Bob Bruce	2.00	1.00	.60
84	Lee Maye	2.00	1.00	.60
85	Jerry Walker	2.00	1.00	.60
86	Dodgers Team	5.00	2.50	1.50
87	Joe Amalfitano	2.00	1.00	.60
88	Richie Ashburn	6.00	3.00	1.75
89	Billy Martin	7.00	3.50	2.00
90	Jerry Staley	2.00	1.00	.60
91	Walt Moryn	2.00	1.00	.60
92	Hal Naragon	2.00	1.00	.60
93	Tony Gonzalez	2.00	1.00	.60
94	Johnny Kucks	2.00	1.00	.60
95	Norm Cash	5.00	2.50	1.50
96	Billy O'Dell	2.00	1.00	.60
97	Jerry Lynch	2.00	1.00	.60
98a	Checklist 89-176 (word "Checklist" in red on front)	7.00	3.50	2.00
98b	Checklist 89-176 ("Checklist" in yellow, 98 on back in black)	5.00	2.50	1.50
98c	Checklist 89-176 ("Checklist" in yellow, 98 on back in white)	7.00	3.50	2.00
99	Don Buddin	2.00	1.00	.60
100	Harvey Haddix	4.00	2.00	1.25
101	Bubba Phillips	2.00	1.00	.60
102	Gene Stephens	2.00	1.00	.60
103	Ruben Amaro	2.00	1.00	.60
104	John Blanchard	4.00	2.00	1.25
105	Carl Willey	2.00	1.00	.60
106	Whitey Herzog	2.25	1.25	.70
107	Seth Morehead	2.00	1.00	.60
108	Dan Dobbek	2.00	1.00	.60
109	Johnny Podres	2.25	1.25	.70
110	Vada Pinson	5.00	2.50	1.50
111	Jack Meyer	2.00	1.00	.60
112	Chico Fernandez	2.00	1.00	.60
113	Mike Fornieles	2.00	1.00	.60
114	Hobie Landrith	2.00	1.00	.60
115	Johnny Antonelli	2.25	1.25	.70
116	Joe DeMaestri	4.00	2.00	1.25
117	Dale Long	2.25	1.25	.70
118	Chris Cannizzaro	2.00	1.00	.60
119	A's Big Armor (Hank Bauer, Jerry Lumpe, Norm Siebern)	4.00	2.00	1.25
120	Ed Mathews	25.00	12.50	7.50
121	Eli Grba	2.00	1.00	.60
122	Cubs Team	4.00	2.00	1.25
123	Billy Gardner	2.00	1.00	.60
124	J.C. Martin	2.00	1.00	.60
125	Steve Barber	2.00	1.00	.60
126	Dick Stuart	2.25	1.25	.70
127	Ron Kline	2.00	1.00	.60
128	Rip Repulski	2.00	1.00	.60
129	Ed Hobaugh	2.00	1.00	.60
130	Norm Larker	2.00	1.00	.60
131	Paul Richards	2.25	1.25	.70
132	Al Lopez	5.00	2.50	1.50
133	Ralph Houk	5.00	2.50	1.50
134	Mickey Vernon	2.25	1.25	.70
135	Fred Hutchinson	2.25	1.25	.70
136	Walt Alston	4.00	2.00	1.25
137	Chuck Dressen	2.25	1.25	.70
138	Danny Murtaugh	2.25	1.25	.70
139	Solly Hemus	2.00	1.00	.60
140	Gus Triandos	2.25	1.25	.70
141	*Billy Williams*	125.00	62.00	37.00
142	Luis Arroyo	4.00	2.00	1.25
143	Russ Snyder	2.00	1.00	.60
144	Jim Coker	2.00	1.00	.60
145	Bob Buhl	2.25	1.25	.70
146	Marty Keough	2.00	1.00	.60
147	Ed Rakow	2.00	1.00	.60
148	Julian Javier	2.25	1.25	.70
149	Bob Oldis	2.00	1.00	.60
150	Willie Mays	100.00	50.00	30.00
151	Jim Donohue	2.00	1.00	.60
152	Earl Torgeson	2.00	1.00	.60
153	Don Lee	2.00	1.00	.60
154	Bobby Del Greco	2.00	1.00	.60
155	Johnny Temple	2.00	1.00	.60
156	Ken Hunt	2.00	1.00	.60
157	Cal McLish	2.00	1.00	.60
158	Pete Daley	2.00	1.00	.60
159	Orioles Team	4.00	2.00	1.25
160	Whitey Ford	35.00	17.50	10.50
161	Sherman Jones (photo actually Eddie Fisher)	2.00	1.00	.60
162	Jay Hook	2.00	1.00	.60
163	Ed Sadowski	2.00	1.00	.60
164	Felix Mantilla	2.00	1.00	.60
165	Gino Cimoli	2.00	1.00	.60
166	Danny Kravitz	2.00	1.00	.60
167	Giants Team	4.00	2.00	1.25
168	Tommy Davis	5.00	2.50	1.50
169	Don Elston	2.00	1.00	.60
170	Al Smith	2.00	1.00	.60
171	Paul Foytack	2.00	1.00	.60
172	Don Dillard	2.00	1.00	.60
173	Beantown Bombers (Jackie Jensen, Frank Malzone, Vic Wertz)	4.00	2.00	1.25
174	Ray Semproch	2.00	1.00	.60
175	Gene Freese	2.00	1.00	.60
176	Ken Aspromonte	2.00	1.00	.60
177	Don Larsen	4.00	2.00	1.25
178	Bob Nieman	2.00	1.00	.60
179	Joe Koppe	2.00	1.00	.60
180	Bobby Richardson	5.00	2.50	1.50
181	Fred Green	2.00	1.00	.60
182	Dave Nicholson	2.00	1.00	.60
183	Andre Rodgers	2.00	1.00	.60
184	Steve Bilko	2.00	1.00	.60
185	Herb Score	4.00	2.00	1.25
186	Elmer Valo	2.00	1.00	.60
187	Billy Klaus	2.00	1.00	.60
188	Jim Marshall	2.00	1.00	.60
189	Checklist 177-264	5.00	2.50	1.50
190	Stan Williams	2.00	1.00	.60
191	Mike de la Hoz	2.00	1.00	.60
192	Dick Brown	2.00	1.00	.60
193	Gene Conley	2.25	1.25	.70
194	Gordy Coleman	2.00	1.00	.60
195	Jerry Casale	2.00	1.00	.60
196	Ed Bouchee	2.00	1.00	.60
197	Dick Hall	2.00	1.00	.60
198	Carl Sawatski	2.00	1.00	.60
199	Bob Boyd	2.00	1.00	.60
200	Warren Spahn	30.00	15.00	9.00
201	Pete Whisenant	2.00	1.00	.60
202	Al Neiger	2.00	1.00	.60
203	Eddie Bressoud	2.00	1.00	.60
204	Bob Skinner	2.25	1.25	.70
205	Bill Pierce	4.00	2.00	1.25
206	Gene Green	2.00	1.00	.60
207	Dodger Southpaws (Sandy Koufax, Johnny Podres)	15.00	7.50	4.50
208	Larry Osborne	2.00	1.00	.60
209	Ken McBride	2.00	1.00	.60
210	Pete Runnels	2.25	1.25	.70
211	Bob Gibson	35.00	17.50	10.50
212	Haywood Sullivan	2.25	1.25	.70
213	*Bill Stafford*	4.00	2.00	1.25
214	Danny Murphy	2.00	1.00	.60
215	Gus Bell	2.25	1.25	.70
216	Ted Bowsfield	2.00	1.00	.60
217	Mel Roach	2.00	1.00	.60
218	Hal Brown	2.00	1.00	.60
219	Gene Mauch	4.00	2.00	1.25
220	Al Dark	2.25	1.25	.70
221	Mike Higgins	2.00	1.00	.60
222	Jimmie Dykes	2.00	1.00	.60
223	Bob Scheffing	2.00	1.00	.60
224	Joe Gordon	2.25	1.25	.70
225	Bill Rigney	2.00	1.00	.60
226	Harry Lavagetto	2.00	1.00	.60
227	Juan Pizarro	2.00	1.00	.60
228	Yankees Team	18.00	9.00	5.50
229	Rudy Hernandez	2.00	1.00	.60
230	Don Hoak	2.25	1.25	.70
231	Dick Drott	2.00	1.00	.60
232	Bill White	4.00	2.00	1.25
233	Joe Jay	2.00	1.00	.60
234	Ted Lepcio	2.00	1.00	.60

		NR MT	EX	VG
235	Camilo Pascual	2.25	1.25	.70
236	Don Gile	2.00	1.00	.60
237	Billy Loes	2.00	1.00	.60
238	Jim Gilliam	4.00	2.00	1.25
239	Dave Sisler	2.00	1.00	.60
240	Ron Hansen	2.00	1.00	.60
241	Al Cicotte	2.00	1.00	.60
242	Hal W. Smith	2.00	1.00	.60
243	Frank Lary	2.25	1.25	.70
244	Chico Cardenas	2.25	1.25	.70
245	Joe Adcock	4.00	2.00	1.25
246	Bob Davis	2.00	1.00	.60
247	Billy Goodman	2.00	1.00	.60
248	Ed Keegan	2.00	1.00	.60
249	Reds Team	4.00	2.00	1.25
250	Buc Hill Aces (Roy Face, Vern Law)	4.00	2.00	1.25
251	Bill Bruton	2.00	1.00	.60
252	Bill Short	4.00	2.00	1.25
253	Sammy Taylor	2.00	1.00	.60
254	Ted Sadowski	2.00	1.00	.60
255	Vic Power	2.00	1.00	.60
256	Billy Hoeft	2.00	1.00	.60
257	Carroll Hardy	2.00	1.00	.60
258	Jack Sanford	2.00	1.00	.60
259	John Schaive	2.00	1.00	.60
260	Don Drysdale	25.00	12.50	7.50
261	Charlie Lau	2.25	1.25	.70
262	Tony Curry	2.00	1.00	.60
263	Ken Hamlin	2.00	1.00	.60
264	Glen Hobbie	2.00	1.00	.60
265	Tony Kubek	5.00	2.50	1.50
266	Lindy McDaniel	2.00	1.00	.60
267	Norm Siebern	2.25	1.25	.70
268	Ike DeLock (Delock)	2.00	1.00	.60
269	Harry Chiti	2.00	1.00	.60
270	Bob Friend	4.00	2.00	1.25
271	Jim Landis	2.00	1.00	.60
272	Tom Morgan	2.00	1.00	.60
273	Checklist 265-352	5.00	2.50	1.50
274	Gary Bell	2.00	1.00	.60
275	Gene Woodling	2.25	1.25	.70
276	Ray Rippelmeyer	2.00	1.00	.60
277	Hank Foiles	2.00	1.00	.60
278	Don McMahon	2.00	1.00	.60
279	Jose Pagan	2.00	1.00	.60
280	Frank Howard	4.00	2.00	1.25
281	Frank Sullivan	2.00	1.00	.60
282	Faye Throneberry	2.00	1.00	.60
283	Bob Anderson	2.00	1.00	.60
284	Dick Gernert	2.00	1.00	.60
285	Sherm Lollar	2.25	1.25	.70
286	George Witt	2.00	1.00	.60
287	Carl Yastrzemski	175.00	87.00	52.00
288	Albie Pearson	2.00	1.00	.60
289	Ray Moore	2.00	1.00	.60
290	Stan Musial	75.00	37.00	23.00
291	Tex Clevenger	2.00	1.00	.60
292	Jim Baumer	2.00	1.00	.60
293	Tom Sturdivant	2.00	1.00	.60
294	Don Blasingame	2.00	1.00	.60
295	Milt Pappas	2.25	1.25	.70
296	Wes Covington	2.00	1.00	.60
297	Athletics Team	4.00	2.00	1.25
298	Jim Golden	2.00	1.00	.60
299	Clay Dalrymple	2.00	1.00	.60
300	Mickey Mantle	350.00	175.00	105.00
301	Chet Nichols	2.00	1.00	.60
302	Al Heist	2.00	1.00	.60
303	Gary Peters	2.25	1.25	.70
304	Rocky Nelson	2.00	1.00	.60
305	Mike McCormick	2.25	1.25	.70
306	World Series Game 1 (Virdon Saves Game)	5.00	2.50	1.50
307	World Series Game 2 (Mantle Slams 2 Homers)	30.00	15.00	9.00
308	World Series Game 3 (Richardson Is Hero)	4.00	2.00	1.25
309	World Series Game 4 (Cimoli Is Safe In Crucial Play)	5.00	2.50	1.50
310	World Series Game 5 (Face Saves the Day)	5.00	2.50	1.50
311	World Series Game 6 (Ford Pitches Second Shutout)	5.00	2.50	1.50
312	World Series Game 7 (Mazeroski's Homer Wins It!)	5.00	2.50	1.50
313	World Series Summary (The Winners Celebrate)	5.00	2.50	1.50
314	Bob Miller	2.00	1.00	.60
315	Earl Battey	2.25	1.25	.70
316	Bobby Gene Smith	2.00	1.00	.60

		NR MT	EX	VG
317	*Jim Brewer*	2.25	1.25	.70
318	Danny O'Connell	2.00	1.00	.60
319	Valmy Thomas	2.00	1.00	.60
320	Lou Burdette	4.00	2.00	1.25
321	Marv Breeding	2.00	1.00	.60
322	Bill Kunkel	2.00	1.00	.60
323	Sammy Esposito	2.00	1.00	.60
324	Hank Aguirre	2.00	1.00	.60
325	Wally Moon	2.25	1.25	.70
326	Dave Hillman	2.00	1.00	.60
327	*Matty Alou*	4.00	2.00	1.25
328	Jim O'Toole	2.00	1.00	.60
329	Julio Becquer	2.00	1.00	.60
330	Rocky Colavito	5.00	2.50	1.50
331	Ned Garver	2.00	1.00	.60
332	Dutch Dotterer (photo actually Tommy Dotterer)	2.00	1.00	.60
333	Fritz Brickell	4.00	2.00	1.25
334	Walt Bond	2.00	1.00	.60
335	Frank Bolling	2.00	1.00	.60
336	Don Mincher	2.25	1.25	.70
337	Al's Aces (Al Lopez, Herb Score, Early Wynn)	5.00	2.50	1.50
338	Don Landrum	2.00	1.00	.60
339	Gene Baker	2.00	1.00	.60
340	Vic Wertz	2.25	1.25	.70
341	Jim Owens	2.00	1.00	.60
342	Clint Courtney	2.00	1.00	.60
343	Earl Robinson	2.00	1.00	.60
344	Sandy Koufax	80.00	40.00	24.00
345	Jim Piersall	4.00	2.00	1.25
346	Howie Nunn	2.00	1.00	.60
347	Cardinals Team	4.00	2.00	1.25
348	Steve Boros	2.00	1.00	.60
349	Danny McDevitt	4.00	2.00	1.25
350	Ernie Banks	30.00	15.00	9.00
351	Jim King	2.00	1.00	.60
352	Bob Shaw	2.00	1.00	.60
353	Howie Bedell	2.00	1.00	.60
354	Billy Harrell	2.00	1.00	.60
355	Bob Allison	2.25	1.25	.70
356	Ryne Duren	2.25	1.25	.70
357	Daryl Spencer	2.00	1.00	.60
358	Earl Averill	2.00	1.00	.60
359	Dallas Green	2.25	1.25	.70
360	Frank Robinson	30.00	15.00	9.00
361a	Checklist 353-429 ("Topps Baseball" in black on front)	5.00	2.50	1.50
361b	Checklist 353-429 ("Topps Baseball" in yellow)	6.00	3.00	1.75
362	Frank Funk	2.00	1.00	.60
363	John Roseboro	2.25	1.25	.70
364	Moe Drabowsky	2.00	1.00	.60
365	Jerry Lumpe	2.25	1.25	.70
366	Eddie Fisher	2.00	1.00	.60
367	Jim Rivera	2.00	1.00	.60
368	Bennie Daniels	2.00	1.00	.60
369	Dave Philley	2.25	1.25	.70
370	Roy Face	4.00	2.00	1.25
371	Bill Skowron	5.00	2.50	1.50
372	Bob Hendley	4.00	2.00	1.25
373	Red Sox Team	5.00	2.50	1.50
374	Paul Giel	4.00	2.00	1.25
375	Ken Boyer	4.00	2.00	1.25
376	Mike Roarke	4.00	2.00	1.25
377	Ruben Gomez	4.00	2.00	1.25
378	Wally Post	4.00	2.00	1.25
379	Bobby Shantz	4.00	2.00	1.25
380	Minnie Minoso	5.00	2.50	1.50
381	Dave Wickersham	4.00	2.00	1.25
382	Frank Thomas	4.00	2.00	1.25
383	Frisco First Liners (Mike McCormick, Billy O'Dell, Jack Sanford)	4.00	2.00	1.25
384	Chuck Essegian	4.00	2.00	1.25
385	Jim Perry	4.00	2.00	1.25
386	Joe Hicks	4.00	2.00	1.25
387	Duke Maas	4.00	2.00	1.25
388	Bob Clemente	80.00	40.00	25.00
389	Ralph Terry	5.00	2.50	1.50
390	Del Crandall	4.00	2.00	1.25
391	Winston Brown	4.00	2.00	1.25
392	Reno Bertoia	4.00	2.00	1.25
393	Batter Bafflers (Don Cardwell, Glen Hobbie)	4.00	2.00	1.25
394	Ken Walters	4.00	2.00	1.25
395	Chuck Estrada	4.00	2.00	1.25
396	Bob Aspromonte	4.00	2.00	1.25
397	Hal Woodeshick	4.00	2.00	1.25
398	Hank Bauer	4.00	2.00	1.25
399	Cliff Cook	4.00	2.00	1.25
400	Vern Law	4.00	2.00	1.25

		NR MT	EX	VG
401	Babe Ruth Hits 60th Homer	25.00	12.50	7.50
402	Larsen Pitches Perfect Game	12.00	6.00	3.50
403	Brooklyn-Boston Play 26-Inning Tie	4.00	2.00	1.25
404	Hornsby Tops N.L. With .424 Average	5.00	2.50	1.50
405	Gehrig Benched After 2,130 Games	15.00	7.50	4.50
406	Mantle Blasts 565 ft. Home Run	40.00	20.00	12.00
407	Jack Chesbro Wins 41st Game	4.00	2.00	1.25
408	Mathewson Strikes Out 267 Batters	5.00	2.50	1.50
409	Johnson Hurls 3rd Shutout in 4 Days	4.00	2.00	1.25
410	Haddix Pitches 12 Perfect Innings	4.00	2.00	1.25
411	Tony Taylor	4.00	2.00	1.25
412	Larry Sherry	4.00	2.00	1.25
413	Eddie Yost	4.00	2.00	1.25
414	Dick Donovan	4.00	2.00	1.25
415	Hank Aaron	100.00	50.00	30.00
416	*Dick Howser*	8.00	4.00	2.50
417	*Juan Marichal*	110.00	55.00	33.00
418	Ed Bailey	4.00	2.00	1.25
419	Tom Borland	4.00	2.00	1.25
420	Ernie Broglio	4.00	2.00	1.25
421	Ty Cline	4.00	2.00	1.25
422	Bud Daley	4.00	2.00	1.25
423	Charlie Neal	4.00	2.00	1.25
424	Turk Lown	4.00	2.00	1.25
425	Yogi Berra	60.00	30.00	18.00
426	Not Issued			
427	Dick Ellsworth	4.00	2.00	1.25
428	Ray Barker	4.00	2.00	1.25
429	Al Kaline	40.00	20.00	12.00
430	Bill Mazeroski	10.00	5.00	3.00
431	Chuck Stobbs	4.00	2.00	1.25
432	Coot Veal	4.00	2.00	1.25
433	Art Mahaffey	4.00	2.00	1.25
434	Tom Brewer	4.00	2.00	1.25
435	Orlando Cepeda	7.00	3.50	2.00
436	*Jim Maloney*	4.00	2.00	1.25
437a	Checklist 430-506 (#440 is Louis Aparicio)	6.00	3.00	1.75
437b	Checklist 430-506 (#440 is Luis Aparicio)	6.50	3.25	2.00
438	Curt Flood	4.00	2.00	1.25
439	*Phil Regan*	4.00	2.00	1.25
440	Luis Aparicio	12.00	6.00	3.50
441	Dick Bertell	4.00	2.00	1.25
442	Gordon Jones	4.00	2.00	1.25
443	Duke Snider	40.00	20.00	12.00
444	Joe Nuxhall	4.00	2.00	1.25
445	Frank Malzone	4.00	2.00	1.25
446	Bob "Hawk" Taylor	4.00	2.00	1.25
447	Harry Bright	4.00	2.00	1.25
448	Del Rice	4.00	2.00	1.25
449	*Bobby Bolin*	4.00	2.00	1.25
450	Jim Lemon	4.00	2.00	1.25
451	Power For Ernie (Ernie Broglio, Daryl Spencer, Bill White)	4.00	2.00	1.25
452	Bob Allen	4.00	2.00	1.25
453	Dick Schofield	4.00	2.00	1.25
454	Pumpsie Green	4.00	2.00	1.25
455	Early Wynn	15.00	7.50	4.50
456	Hal Bevan	4.00	2.00	1.25
457	Johnny James	4.00	2.00	1.25
458	Willie Tasby	4.00	2.00	1.25
459	Terry Fox	4.00	2.00	1.25
460	Gil Hodges	18.00	9.00	5.50
461	Smoky Burgess	4.00	2.00	1.25
462	Lou Klimchock	4.00	2.00	1.25
463a	Braves Team (should be card #426)	4.00	2.00	1.25
463b	Jack Fisher	4.00	2.00	1.25
464	*Leroy Thomas*	4.00	2.00	1.25
465	Roy McMillan	4.00	2.00	1.25
466	Ron Moeller	4.00	2.00	1.25
467	Indians Team	5.00	2.50	1.50
468	Johnny Callison	4.00	2.00	1.25
469	Ralph Lumenti	4.00	2.00	1.25
470	Roy Sievers	4.00	2.00	1.25
471	Phil Rizzuto MVP	12.00	6.00	3.50
472	Yogi Berra MVP	40.00	20.00	12.00
473	Bobby Shantz MVP	5.00	2.50	1.50
474	Al Rosen MVP	5.00	2.50	1.50
475	Mickey Mantle MVP	90.00	45.00	27.00
476	Jackie Jensen MVP	5.00	2.50	1.50
477	Nellie Fox MVP	4.00	2.00	1.25
478	Roger Maris MVP	40.00	20.00	12.00
479	Jim Konstanty MVP	4.00	2.00	1.25
480	Roy Campanella MVP	25.00	12.50	7.50

		NR MT	EX	VG
481	Hank Sauer MVP	4.00	2.00	1.25
482	Willie Mays MVP	40.00	20.00	12.00
483	Don Newcombe MVP	5.00	2.50	1.50
484	Hank Aaron MVP	40.00	20.00	12.00
485	Ernie Banks MVP	25.00	12.50	7.50
486	Dick Groat MVP	5.00	2.50	1.50
487	Gene Oliver	4.00	2.00	1.25
488	Joe McClain	4.00	2.00	1.25
489	Walt Dropo	4.00	2.00	1.25
490	Jim Bunning	8.00	4.00	2.50
491	Phillies Team	5.00	2.50	1.50
492	Ron Fairly	4.00	2.00	1.25
493	Don Zimmer	4.00	2.00	1.25
494	Tom Cheney	4.00	2.00	1.25
495	Elston Howard	6.00	3.00	1.75
496	Ken MacKenzie	4.00	2.00	1.25
497	Willie Jones	4.00	2.00	1.25
498	Ray Herbert	4.00	2.00	1.25
499	Chuck Schilling	4.00	2.00	1.25
500	Harvey Kuenn	5.00	2.50	1.50
501	John DeMerit	4.00	2.00	1.25
502	Clarence Coleman	4.00	2.00	1.25
503	Tito Francona	4.00	2.00	1.25
504	Billy Consolo	4.00	2.00	1.25
505	Red Schoendienst	12.00	6.00	3.50
506	*Willie Davis*	10.00	5.00	3.00
507	Pete Burnside	4.00	2.00	1.25
508	Rocky Bridges	4.00	2.00	1.25
509	Camilo Carreon	4.00	2.00	1.25
510	Art Ditmar	4.00	2.00	1.25
511	Joe Morgan	4.00	2.00	1.25
512	Bob Will	4.00	2.00	1.25
513	Jim Brosnan	4.00	2.00	1.25
514	Jake Wood	4.00	2.00	1.25
515	Jackie Brandt	4.00	2.00	1.25
516	Checklist 507-587	6.00	3.00	1.75
517	Willie McCovey	60.00	30.00	18.00
518	Andy Carey	4.00	2.00	1.25
519	Jim Pagliaroni	4.00	2.00	1.25
520	Joe Cunningham	4.00	2.00	1.25
521	Brother Battery (Larry Sherry, Norm Sherry)	4.00	2.00	1.25
522	Dick Farrell	4.00	2.00	1.25
523	Joe Gibbon	25.00	12.50	7.50
524	Johnny Logan	27.00	13.50	8.00
525	*Ron Perranoski*	27.00	13.50	8.00
526	R.C. Stevens	25.00	12.50	7.50
527	Gene Leek	25.00	12.50	7.50
528	Pedro Ramos	25.00	12.50	7.50
529	Bob Roselli	25.00	12.50	7.50
530	Bobby Malkmus	25.00	12.50	7.50
531	Jim Coates	27.00	13.50	8.00
532	Bob Hale	25.00	12.50	7.50
533	Jack Curtis	25.00	12.50	7.50
534	Eddie Kasko	25.00	12.50	7.50
535	Larry Jackson	25.00	12.50	7.50
536	Bill Tuttle	25.00	12.50	7.50
537	Bobby Locke	25.00	12.50	7.50
538	Chuck Hiller	25.00	12.50	7.50
539	Johnny Klippstein	25.00	12.50	7.50
540	Jackie Jensen	30.00	15.00	9.00
541	Roland Sheldon	27.00	13.50	8.00
542	Twins Team	50.00	25.00	15.00
543	Roger Craig	35.00	17.50	10.50
544	George Thomas	25.00	12.50	7.50
545	Hoyt Wilhelm	55.00	28.00	16.50
546	Marty Kutyna	25.00	12.50	7.50
547	Leon Wagner	27.00	13.50	8.00
548	Ted Wills	25.00	12.50	7.50
549	Hal R. Smith	25.00	12.50	7.50
550	Frank Baumann	25.00	12.50	7.50
551	George Altman	25.00	12.50	7.50
552	Jim Archer	25.00	12.50	7.50
553	Bill Fischer	25.00	12.50	7.50
554	Pirates Team	40.00	20.00	12.00
555	Sam Jones	25.00	12.50	7.50
556	Ken R. Hunt	25.00	12.50	7.50
557	Jose Valdivielso	25.00	12.50	7.50
558	Don Ferrarese	25.00	12.50	7.50
559	Jim Gentile	27.00	13.50	8.00
560	Barry Latman	25.00	12.50	7.50
561	Charley James	25.00	12.50	7.50
562	Bill Monbouquette	27.00	13.50	8.00
563	Bob Cerv	27.00	13.50	8.00
564	Don Cardwell	25.00	12.50	7.50
565	Felipe Alou	25.00	12.50	7.50
566	Paul Richards AS	25.00	12.50	7.50
567	Danny Murtaugh AS	25.00	12.50	7.50
568	Bill Skowron AS	35.00	17.50	10.50
569	Frank Herrera AS	25.00	12.50	7.50
570	Nellie Fox AS	40.00	20.00	12.00

		NR MT	EX	VG
571	Bill Mazeroski AS	35.00	17.50	10.50
572	Brooks Robinson AS	75.00	38.00	23.00
573	Ken Boyer AS	35.00	17.50	10.50
574	Luis Aparicio AS	45.00	23.00	13.50
575	Ernie Banks AS	80.00	40.00	25.00
576	Roger Maris AS	100.00	50.00	30.00
577	Hank Aaron AS	150.00	75.00	45.00
578	Mickey Mantle AS	300.00	150.00	90.00
579	Willie Mays AS	150.00	75.00	45.00
580	Al Kaline AS	75.00	38.00	23.00
581	Frank Robinson AS	80.00	40.00	25.00
582	Earl Battey AS	25.00	12.50	7.50
583	Del Crandall AS	30.00	15.00	9.00
584	Jim Perry AS	30.00	15.00	9.00
585	Bob Friend AS	30.00	15.00	9.00
586	Whitey Ford AS	75.00	38.00	23.00
587	Not Issued			
588	Not Issued			
589	Warren Spahn AS	125.00	56.00	35.00

1961 Topps Dice Game

One of the more obscure Topps test issues that may have never actually been issued is the 1961 Topps Dice Game. Eighteen black and white cards, each measuring 2-1/2" by 3-1/2" in size, comprise the set. Interestingly, there are no identifying marks, such as copyrights or trademarks, to indicate the set was produced by Topps. The card backs contain various baseball plays that occur when a certain pitch is called and a specific number of the dice is rolled.

		NR MT	EX	VG
Complete Set:		7500.00	3750.00	2250.
Common Player:		100.00	50.00	30.00
(1)	Earl Battey	100.00	50.00	30.00
(2)	Del Crandall	100.00	50.00	30.00
(3)	Jim Davenport	100.00	50.00	30.00
(4)	Don Drysdale	350.00	175.00	105.00
(5)	Dick Groat	150.00	75.00	45.00
(6)	Al Kaline	600.00	300.00	175.00
(7)	Tony Kubek	150.00	75.00	45.00
(8)	Mickey Mantle	2500.00	1250.00	750.00
(9)	Willie Mays	1000.00	500.00	300.00
(10)	Bill Mazeroski	150.00	75.00	45.00
(11)	Stan Musial	800.00	400.00	240.00
(12)	Camilo Pascual	100.00	50.00	30.00
(13)	Bobby Richardson	150.00	75.00	45.00
(14)	Brooks Robinson	400.00	200.00	120.00
(15)	Frank Robinson	350.00	175.00	105.00
(16)	Norm Siebern	100.00	50.00	30.00
(17)	Leon Wagner	100.00	50.00	30.00
(18)	Bill White	100.00	50.00	30.00

1961 Topps Magic Rub-Offs

Not too different in concept from the tattoos of the previous year, the Topps Magic Rub-Off was designed to leave impressions of team themes or individual players when properly applied. Measuring 2-1/16" by 3-1/16," the Magic Rub-Off was not designed specifically for application to the owner's skin. The set of 36 Rub-Offs seems to almost be a tongue-in-cheek product as the team themes were a far cry from official logos, and the players seem to have been included for their nicknames. Among the players (one representing each team) the best known and most valuable are Yogi Berra and Ernie Banks.

		NR MT	EX	VG
Complete Set:		85.00	42.00	25.00
Common Player:		1.00	.50	.30
(1)	Baltimore Orioles Pennant	1.00	.50	.30
(2)	Ernie "Bingo" Banks	12.00	6.00	3.50
(3)	Yogi Berra	20.00	10.00	6.00
(4)	Boston Red Sox Pennant	1.00	.50	.30
(5)	Jackie "Ozark" Brandt	1.25	.60	.40
(6)	Jim "Professor" Brosnan	1.25	.60	.40
(7)	Chicago Cubs Pennant	1.00	.50	.30
(8)	Chicago White Sox Pennant	1.00	.50	.30
(9)	Cincinnati Red Legs Pennan'	1.00	.50	.30
(10)	Cleveland Indians Pennant	1.00	.50	.30
(11)	Detroit Tigers Pennant	1.25	.60	.40
(12)	Henry "Dutch" Dotterer	1.25	.60	.40
(13)	Joe "Flash" Gordon	1.50	.70	.45
(14)	Harvey "The Kitten" Haddix	1.50	.70	.45
(15)	Frank "Pancho" Hererra	1.25	.60	.40
(16)	Frank "Tower" Howard	3.50	1.75	1.00
(17)	"Sad" Sam Jones	1.25	.60	.40
(18)	Kansas City Athletics Pennant	1.00	.50	.30
(19)	Los Angeles Angels Pennant	1.00	.50	.30
(20)	Los Angeles Dodgers Pennant	1.25	.60	.40
(21)	Omar "Turk" Lown	1.25	.60	.40
(22)	Billy "The Kid" Martin	8.00	4.00	2.50
(23)	Duane "Duke" Mass (Maas)	1.25	.60	.40
(24)	Charlie "Paw Paw" Maxwell	1.25	.60	.40
(25)	Milwaukee Braves Pennant	1.00	.50	.30
(26)	Minnesota Twins Pennant	1.00	.50	.30
(27)	"Farmer" Ray Moore	1.00	.50	.30
(28)	Walt "Moose" Moryn	1.00	.50	.30
(29)	New York Yankees Pennant	2.50	1.25	.70
(30)	Philadelphia Phillies Pennant	1.00	.50	.30
(31)	Pittsburgh Pirates Pennant	1.00	.50	.30
(32)	John "Honey" Romano	1.25	.60	.40
(33)	"Pistol Pete" Runnels	1.50	.70	.45
(34)	St. Louis Cardinals Pennant	1.00	.50	.30
(35)	San Francisco Giants Pennant	1.00	.50	.30
(36)	Washington Senators Pennant	1.00	.50	.30

1961 Topps Stamps

Issued as an added insert to 1961 Topps wax

packs these 1-3/8" by 1-3/16" stamps were desigend to be collected and placed in an album which could be bought for an additional 10¢. Packs of cards contained two stamps. There are 208 stamps in a complete set which depict 207 different players (Al Kaline appears twice). There are 104 players on brown stamps and 104 on green. While there are many Hall of Famers on the stamps, prices remain low because there is relatively little interest in what is a non-card set.

		NR MT	EX	VG
Complete Set:		225.00	112.00	70.00
Stamp Album:		35.00	17.50	10.50
Common Player:		.40	.20	.12
(1)	Hank Aaron	10.00	5.00	3.00
(2)	Joe Adcock	.50	.25	.15
(3)	Hank Aguirre	.40	.20	.12
(4)	Bob Allison	.50	.25	.15
(5)	George Altman	.40	.20	.12
(6)	Bob Anderson	.40	.20	.12
(7)	Johnny Antonelli	.50	.25	.15
(8)	Luis Aparicio	1.50	.70	.45
(9)	Luis Arroyo	.50	.25	.15
(10)	Richie Ashburn	.80	.40	.25
(11)	Ken Aspromonte	.40	.20	.12
(12)	Ed Bailey	.40	.20	.12
(13)	Ernie Banks	6.00	3.00	1.75
(14)	Steve Barber	.40	.20	.12
(15)	Earl Battey	.50	.25	.15
(16)	Hank Bauer	.50	.25	.15
(17)	Gus Bell	.50	.25	.15
(18)	Yogi Berra	5.00	2.50	1.50
(19)	Reno Bertoia	.40	.20	.12
(20)	John Blanchard	.50	.25	.15
(21)	Don Blasingame	.40	.20	.12
(22)	Frank Bolling	.40	.20	.12
(23)	Steve Boros	.40	.20	.12
(24)	Ed Bouchee	.40	.20	.12
(25)	Bob Boyd	.40	.20	.12
(26)	Cletis Boyer	.50	.25	.15
(27)	Ken Boyer	.50	.25	.15
(28)	Jackie Brandt	.40	.20	.12
(29)	Marv Breeding	.40	.20	.12
(30)	Eddie Bressoud	.40	.20	.12
(31)	Jim Brewer	.40	.20	.12
(32)	Tom Brewer	.40	.20	.12
(33)	Jim Brosnan	.50	.25	.15
(34)	Bill Bruton	.40	.20	.12
(35)	Bob Buhl	.50	.25	.15
(36)	Jim Bunning	1.00	.50	.30
(37)	Smoky Burgess	.50	.25	.15
(38)	John Buzhardt	.40	.20	.12
(39)	Johnny Callison	.50	.25	.15
(40)	Chico Cardenas	.40	.20	.12
(41)	Andy Carey	.40	.20	.12
(42)	Jerry Casale	.40	.20	.12
(43)	Norm Cash	.50	.25	.15
(44)	Orlando Cepeda	1.25	.60	.40
(45)	Bob Cerv	.40	.20	.12
(46)	Harry Chiti	.40	.20	.12
(47)	Gene Conley	.50	.25	.15
(48)	Wes Covington	.40	.20	.12
(49)	Del Crandall	.50	.25	.15
(50)	Tony Curry	.40	.20	.12
(51)	Bud Daley	.40	.20	.12
(52)	Pete Daley	.40	.20	.12
(53)	Clay Dalrymple	.40	.20	.12
(54)	Jim Davenport	.40	.20	.12
(55)	Tommy Davis	.50	.25	.15
(56)	Bobby Del Greco	.40	.20	.12
(57)	Ike Delock	.40	.20	.12
(58)	Art Ditmar	.50	.25	.15
(59)	Dick Donovan	.40	.20	.12
(60)	Don Drysdale	6.00	3.00	1.75
(61)	Dick Ellsworth	.40	.20	.12
(62)	Don Elston	.40	.20	.12
(63)	Chuck Estrada	.40	.20	.12
(64)	Roy Face	.50	.25	.15
(65)	Dick Farrell	.40	.20	.12
(66)	Chico Fernandez	.40	.20	.12
(67)	Curt Flood	.50	.25	.15
(68)	Whitey Ford	4.00	2.00	1.25
(69)	Tito Francona	.40	.20	.12
(70)	Gene Freese	.40	.20	.12
(71)	Bob Friend	.50	.25	.15
(72)	Billy Gardner	.40	.20	.12
(73)	Ned Garver	.40	.20	.12
(74)	Gary Geiger	.40	.20	.12

		NR MT	EX	VG
(75)	Jim Gentile	.40	.20	.12
(76)	Dick Gernert	.40	.20	.12
(77)	Tony Gonzalez	.40	.20	.12
(78)	Alex Grammas	.40	.20	.12
(79)	Jim Grant	.40	.20	.12
(80)	Dick Groat	.50	.25	.15
(81)	Dick Hall	.40	.20	.12
(82)	Ron Hansen	.40	.20	.12
(83)	Bob Hartman	.40	.20	.12
(84)	Woodie Held	.40	.20	.12
(85)	Ray Herbert	.40	.20	.12
(86)	Frank Herrera	.40	.20	.12
(87)	Whitey Herzog	.50	.25	.15
(88)	Don Hoak	.50	.25	.15
(89)	Elston Howard	.80	.40	.25
(90)	Frank Howard	.50	.25	.15
(91)	Ken Hunt	.40	.20	.12
(92)	Larry Jackson	.40	.20	.12
(93)	Julian Javier	.40	.20	.12
(94)	Joe Jay	.40	.20	.12
(95)	Jackie Jensen	.50	.25	.15
(96)	Jim Kaat	1.00	.50	.30
(97a)	Al Kaline (green)	7.00	3.50	2.00
(97b)	Al Kaline (brown)	7.00	3.50	2.00
(98)	Eddie Kasko	.40	.20	.12
(99)	Russ Kemmerer	.40	.20	.12
(100)	Harmon Killebrew	5.00	2.50	1.50
(101)	Billy Klaus	.40	.20	.12
(102)	Ron Kline	.40	.20	.12
(103)	Johnny Klippstein	.40	.20	.12
(104)	Ted Kluszewski	.40	.20	.12
(105)	Tony Kubek	.80	.40	.25
(106)	Harvey Kuenn	.50	.25	.15
(107)	Jim Landis	.40	.20	.12
(108)	Hobie Landrith	.40	.20	.12
(109)	Norm Larker	.40	.20	.12
(110)	Frank Lary	.40	.20	.12
(111)	Barry Latman	.40	.20	.12
(112)	Vern Law	.50	.25	.15
(113)	Jim Lemon	.40	.20	.12
(114)	Sherm Lollar	.50	.25	.15
(115)	Dale Long	.50	.25	.15
(116)	Jerry Lumpe	.40	.20	.12
(117)	Jerry Lynch	.40	.20	.12
(118)	Art Mahaffey	.40	.20	.12
(119)	Frank Malzone	.40	.20	.12
(120)	Felix Mantilla	.40	.20	.12
(121)	Mickey Mantle	50.00	25.00	15.00
(122)	Juan Marichal	5.00	2.50	1.50
(123)	Roger Maris	12.00	6.00	3.50
(124)	Billy Martin	1.00	.50	.30
(125)	J.C. Martin	.40	.20	.12
(126)	Ed Mathews	3.00	1.50	.90
(127)	Charlie Maxwell	.40	.20	.12
(128)	Willie Mays	7.00	3.50	2.00
(129)	Bill Mazeroski	.50	.25	.15
(130)	Mike McCormick	.40	.20	.12
(131)	Willie McCovey	3.00	1.50	.90
(132)	Lindy McDaniel	.40	.20	.12
(133)	Roy McMillan	.40	.20	.12
(134)	Minnie Minoso	.50	.25	.15
(135)	Bill Monbouquette	.40	.20	.12
(136)	Wally Moon	.50	.25	.15
(137)	Stan Musial	7.00	3.50	2.00
(138)	Charlie Neal	.40	.20	.12
(139)	Rocky Nelson	.40	.20	.12
(140)	Russ Nixon	.40	.20	.12
(141)	Billy O'Dell	.40	.20	.12
(142)	Jim O'Toole	.40	.20	.12
(143)	Milt Pappas	.50	.25	.15
(144)	Camilo Pascual	.50	.25	.15
(145)	Jim Perry	.50	.25	.15
(146)	Bubba Phillips	.40	.20	.12
(147)	Bill Pierce	.50	.25	.15
(148)	Jim Piersall	.50	.25	.15
(149)	Vada Pinson	.50	.25	.15
(150)	Johnny Podres	.50	.25	.15
(151)	Wally Post	.40	.20	.12
(152)	Vic Powers (Power)	.40	.20	.12
(153)	Pedro Ramos	.40	.20	.12
(154)	Robin Roberts	1.50	.70	.45
(155)	Brooks Robinson	3.75	2.00	1.25
(156)	Frank Robinson	3.50	1.75	1.00
(157)	Ed Roebuck	.40	.20	.12
(158)	John Romano	.40	.20	.12
(159)	John Roseboro	.50	.25	.15
(160)	Pete Runnels	.50	.25	.15
(161)	Ed Sadowski	.40	.20	.12
(162)	Jack Sanford	.40	.20	.12
(163)	Ron Santo	.50	.25	.15
(164)	Ray Semproch	.40	.20	.12

	NR MT	EX	VG
(165) Bobby Shantz	.50	.25	.15
(166) Bob Shaw	.40	.20	.12
(167) Larry Sherry	.40	.20	.12
(168) Norm Siebern	.40	.20	.12
(169) Roy Sievers	.50	.25	.15
(170) Curt Simmons	.50	.25	.15
(171) Dave Sisler	.40	.20	.12
(172) Bob Skinner	.40	.20	.12
(173) Al Smith	.40	.20	.12
(174) Hal Smith	.40	.20	.12
(175) Hal Smith	.40	.20	.12
(176) Duke Snider	3.75	2.00	1.25
(177) Warren Spahn	3.00	1.50	.90
(178) Daryl Spencer	.40	.20	.12
(179) Bill Stafford	.50	.25	.15
(180) Jerry Staley	.40	.20	.12
(181) Gene Stephens	.40	.20	.12
(182) Chuck Stobbs	.40	.20	.12
(183) Dick Stuart	.50	.25	.15
(184) Willie Tasby	.40	.20	.12
(185) Sammy Taylor	.40	.20	.12
(186) Tony Taylor	.40	.20	.12
(187) Johnny Temple	.40	.20	.12
(188) Marv Throneberry	.50	.25	.15
(189) Gus Triandos	.50	.25	.15
(190) Bob Turley	.50	.25	.15
(191) Bill Tuttle	.40	.20	.12
(192) Zorro Versalles	.40	.20	.12
(193) Bill Virdon	.50	.25	.15
(194) Lee Walls	.40	.20	.12
(195) Vic Wertz	.50	.25	.15
(196) Pete Whisenant	.40	.20	.12
(197) Bill White	.50	.25	.15
(198) Hoyt Wilhelm	1.50	.70	.45
(199) Bob Will	.40	.20	.12
(200) Carl Willey	.40	.20	.12
(201) Billy Williams	2.50	1.25	.70
(202) Dick Williams	.50	.25	.15
(203) Stan Williams	.40	.20	.12
(204) Gene Woodling	.50	.25	.15
(205) Early Wynn	2.00	1.00	.60
(206) Carl Yastrzemski	12.00	6.00	3.50
(207) Eddie Yost	.40	.20	.12

1962 Topps

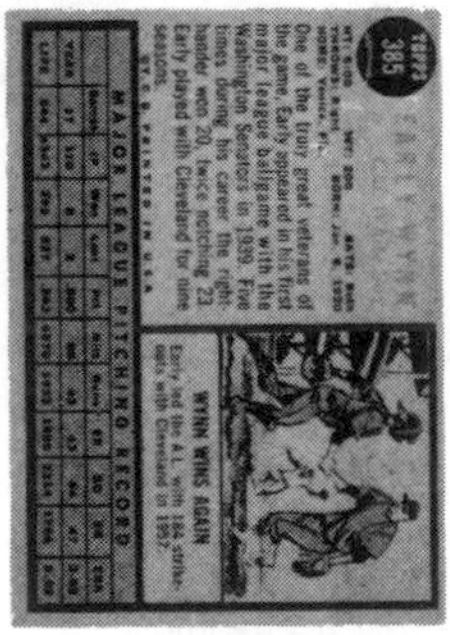

The 1962 Topps set established another plateau for set size with 598 cards. The 2-1/2" by 3-1/2" cards feature a photograph set against a woodgrain background. The lower righthand corner has been made to look like it is curling away. Many established specialty cards dot the set including statistical leaders, multi-player cards, team cards, checklists, World Series cards and All-Stars. Of note is that 1962 was the first year of the multi-player rookie card. There is a 9-card "In Action" subset and a 10-card run of special Babe Ruth cards. Photo variations of several cards in the 2nd Series (#'s 110-196) exist. All cards in the 2nd Series can be found with two distinct printing variations, an early printing with the cards containing a very noticeable greenish tint, having been corrected to clear photos in subsequent print runs. The complete set price in the checklist that follows does not include the higher-priced variations.

		NR MT	EX	VG
Complete Set:		4500.00	2000.00	1200.
Common Player: 1-370		2.00	1.00	.60
Common Player: 371-522		4.00	2.00	1.25
Common Player: 523-598		12.00	5.50	3.00
1	Roger Maris	225.00	45.00	27.00
2	Jim Brosnan	2.25	1.25	.70
3	Pete Runnels	2.00	1.00	.60
4	John DeMerit	2.00	.90	.50
5	Sandy Koufax	100.00	50.00	30.00
6	Marv Breeding	2.00	1.00	.60
7	Frank Thomas	2.00	.90	.50
8	Ray Herbert	2.00	1.00	.60
9	Jim Davenport	2.00	1.00	.60
10	Bob Clemente	100.00	40.00	25.00
11	Tom Morgan	2.00	1.00	.60
12	Harry Craft	2.00	1.00	.60
13	Dick Howser	2.25	1.25	.70
14	Bill White	2.00	1.00	.60
15	Dick Donovan	2.00	1.00	.60
16	Darrell Johnson	2.00	1.00	.60
17	Johnny Callison	2.25	1.25	.70
18	Managers' Dream (Mickey Mantle, Willie Mays)	100.00	50.00	30.00
19	*Ray Washburn*	2.00	1.00	.60
20	Rocky Colavito	6.00	3.00	1.75
21	Jim Kaat	5.00	2.00	1.25
22a	Checklist 1-88 (numbers 121 - 176 on back)	5.00	2.25	1.25
22b	Checklist 1-88 (numbers 33-88 on back)	4.00	1.75	1.00
23	Norm Larker	2.00	1.00	.60
24	Tigers Team	5.00	2.50	1.50
25	Ernie Banks	35.00	15.00	9.00
26	Chris Cannizzaro	2.00	.90	.50
27	Chuck Cottier	2.00	1.00	.60
28	Minnie Minoso	4.00	2.00	1.25
29	Casey Stengel	15.00	6.75	3.75
30	Ed Mathews	18.00	7.50	4.50
31	*Tom Tresh*	7.00	3.25	1.75
32	John Roseboro	2.25	1.25	.70
33	Don Larsen	2.25	1.25	.70
34	Johnny Temple	2.00	1.00	.60
35	*Don Schwall*	2.25	1.25	.70
36	Don Leppert	2.00	1.00	.60
37	Tribe Hill Trio (Barry Latman, Jim Perry, Dick Stigman)	2.25	1.25	.70
38	Gene Stephens	2.00	1.00	.60
39	Joe Koppe	2.00	1.00	.60
40	Orlando Cepeda	5.00	2.25	1.25
41	Cliff Cook	2.00	1.00	.60
42	Jim King	2.00	1.00	.60
43	Dodgers Team	5.00	2.50	1.50
44	Don Taussig	2.00	1.00	.60
45	Brooks Robinson	30.00	12.50	7.50
46	*Jack Baldschun*	2.00	1.00	.60
47	Bob Will	2.00	1.00	.60
48	Ralph Terry	4.00	2.00	1.25
49	Hal Jones	2.00	1.00	.60
50	Stan Musial	80.00	35.00	18.00
51	A.L. Batting Leaders (Norm Cash, Elston Howard, Al Kaline, Jim Piersall)	5.00	2.50	1.50
52	N.L. Batting Leaders (Ken Boyer, Bob Clemente, Wally Moon, Vada Pinson)	5.00	2.50	1.50
53	A.L. Home Run Leaders (Jim Gentile, Harmon Killebrew, Mickey Mantle, Roger Maris)	35.00	15.00	9.00
54	N.L. Home Run Leaders (Orlando Cepeda, Willie Mays, Frank Robinson)	5.00	2.50	1.50
55	A.L. E.R.A. Leaders (Dick Donovan, Don Mossi, Milt Pappas, Bill Stafford)	4.00	2.00	1.25
56	N.L. E.R.A. Leaders (Mike McCormick, Jim O'Toole, Curt Simmons, Warren Spahn)	5.00	2.50	1.50
57	A.L. Win Leaders (Steve Barber, Jim Bunning, Whitey Ford, Frank Lary)	5.00	2.50	1.50
58	N.L. Win Leaders (Joe Jay, Jim O'Toole, Warren Spahn)	5.00	2.50	1.50
59	A.L. Strikeout Leaders (Jim Bunning, Whitey Ford, Camilo Pascual, Juan Pizzaro)	5.00	2.50	1.50
60	N.L. Strikeout Leaders (Don Drysdale, Sandy Koufax, Jim O'Toole, Stan Williams)	5.00	2.50	1.50
61	Cardinals Team	4.00	2.00	1.25
62	Steve Boros	2.00	1.00	.60
63	*Tony Cloninger*	2.00	.90	.50
64	Russ Snyder	2.00	1.00	.60
65	Bobby Richardson	6.00	2.75	1.50
66	Cuno Barragon (Barragan)	2.00	1.00	.60
67	Harvey Haddix	2.25	1.25	.70

		NR MT	EX	VG
68	Ken L. Hunt	2.00	1.00	.60
69	Phil Ortega	2.00	1.00	.60
70	Harmon Killebrew	20.00	10.00	6.00
71	Dick LeMay	2.00	1.00	.60
72	Bob's Pupils (Steve Boros, Bob Scheffing, Jake Wood)	2.25	1.25	.70
73	Nellie Fox	7.00	3.25	1.75
74	Bob Lillis	2.00	1.00	.60
75	Milt Pappas	2.25	1.25	.70
76	Howie Bedell	2.00	1.00	.60
77	Tony Taylor	2.00	1.00	.60
78	Gene Green	2.00	1.00	.60
79	Ed Hobaugh	2.00	1.00	.60
80	Vada Pinson	4.00	2.00	1.25
81	Jim Pagliaroni	2.00	1.00	.60
82	Deron Johnson	2.00	1.00	.60
83	Larry Jackson	2.00	1.00	.60
84	Lenny Green	2.00	1.00	.60
85	Gil Hodges	12.00	6.00	3.50
86	*Donn Clendenon*	2.25	1.25	.70
87	Mike Roarke	2.00	1.00	.60
88	Ralph Houk	4.00	2.00	1.25
89	Barney Schultz	2.00	1.00	.60
90	Jim Piersall	2.00	.90	.50
91	J.C. Martin	2.00	1.00	.60
92	Sam Jones	2.00	1.00	.60
93	John Blanchard	2.00	.90	.50
94	Jay Hook	2.00	.90	.50
95	Don Hoak	2.25	1.25	.70
96	Eli Grba	2.00	1.00	.60
97	Tito Francona	2.00	1.00	.60
98	Checklist 89-176	4.00	1.75	1.00
99	*John Powell*	15.00	6.75	4.00
100	Warren Spahn	30.00	12.50	7.50
101	Carroll Hardy	2.00	1.00	.60
102	Al Schroll	2.00	1.00	.60
103	Don Blasingame	2.00	1.00	.60
104	Ted Savage	2.00	1.00	.60
105	Don Mossi	2.00	1.00	.60
106	Carl Sawatski	2.00	1.00	.60
107	Mike McCormick	2.00	1.00	.60
108	Willie Davis	4.00	2.00	1.25
109	Bob Shaw	2.00	1.00	.60
110	Bill Skowron	5.00	2.25	1.25
111	Dallas Green	2.25	1.25	.70
112	Hank Foiles	2.00	1.00	.60
113	White Sox Team	4.00	2.00	1.25
114	Howie Koplitz	2.00	1.00	.60
115	Bob Skinner	2.00	1.00	.60
116	Herb Score	2.00	.90	.50
117	Gary Geiger	2.00	1.00	.60
118	Julian Javier	2.00	1.00	.60
119	Danny Murphy	2.00	1.00	.60
120	Bob Purkey	2.00	1.00	.60
121	Billy Hitchcock	2.00	1.00	.60
122	Norm Bass	2.00	1.00	.60
123	Mike de la Hoz	2.00	1.00	.60
124	Bill Pleis	2.00	1.00	.60
125	Gene Woodling	2.25	1.25	.70
126	Al Cicotte	2.00	1.00	.60
127	Pride of the A's (Hank Bauer, Jerry Lumpe, Norm Siebern)	2.25	1.25	.70
128	Art Fowler	2.00	1.00	.60
129a	Lee Walls (facing left)	15.00	7.50	4.50
129b	Lee Walls (facing right)	2.00	1.00	.60
130	Frank Bolling	2.00	1.00	.60
131	*Pete Richert*	2.25	1.25	.70
132a	Angels Team (with inset photos)	10.00	4.50	2.50
132b	Angels Team (without inset photos)	5.00	2.50	1.50
133	Felipe Alou	2.25	1.25	.70
134a	Billy Hoeft (green sky in background)	15.00	7.50	4.50
134b	Billy Hoeft (blue sky in background)	2.00	1.00	.60
135	Babe As A Boy	7.00	3.25	1.75
136	Babe Joins Yanks	7.00	3.25	1.75
137	Babe and Mgr. Huggins	7.00	3.25	1.75
138	The Famous Slugger	7.00	3.25	1.75
139a	Hal Reniff (pitching)	40.00	20.00	12.00
139b	Hal Reniff (portrait)	18.00	9.00	5.50
139c	Babe Hits 60	10.00	4.00	2.50
140	Gehrig and Ruth	9.00	4.00	2.25
141	Twilight Years	7.00	3.25	1.75
142	Coaching for the Dodgers	7.00	3.25	1.75
143	Greatest Sports Hero	7.00	3.25	1.75
144	Farewell Speech	7.00	3.25	1.75
145	Barry Latman	2.00	1.00	.60
146	Don Demeter	2.00	1.00	.60
147a	Bill Kunkel (pitching)	15.00	7.50	4.50
147b	Bill Kunkel (portrait)	2.00	1.00	.60
148	Wally Post	2.00	1.00	.60
149	Bob Duliba	2.00	1.00	.60
150	Al Kaline	30.00	15.00	9.00
151	Johnny Klippstein	2.00	1.00	.60
152	Mickey Vernon	2.00	1.00	.60
153	Pumpsie Green	2.00	1.00	.60
154	Lee Thomas	2.00	1.00	.60
155	Stu Miller	2.00	1.00	.60
156	Merritt Ranew	2.00	1.00	.60
157	Wes Covington	2.00	1.00	.60
158	Braves Team	5.00	2.50	1.50
159	Hal Reniff	2.00	.90	.50
160	Dick Stuart	2.00	1.00	.60
161	Frank Baumann	2.00	1.00	.60
162	Sammy Drake	2.00	.90	.50
163	Hot Corner Guardians (Cletis Boyer, Billy Gardner)	5.00	2.50	1.50
164	Hal Naragon	2.00	1.00	.60
165	Jackie Brandt	2.00	1.00	.60
166	Don Lee	2.00	1.00	.60
167	*Tim McCarver*	25.00	12.50	7.50
168	Leo Posada	2.00	1.00	.60
169	Bob Cerv	2.00	.90	.50
170	Ron Santo	5.00	2.50	1.50
171	Dave Sisler	2.00	1.00	.60
172	Fred Hutchinson	2.00	1.00	.60
173	Chico Fernandez	2.00	1.00	.60
174a	Carl Willey (with cap)	15.00	7.50	4.50
174b	Carl Willey (no cap)	2.00	1.00	.60
175	Frank Howard	5.00	2.50	1.50
176a	Eddie Yost (batting)	15.00	7.50	4.50
176b	Eddie Yost (portrait)	2.00	1.00	.60
177	Bobby Shantz	2.25	1.25	.70
178	Camilo Carreon	2.00	1.00	.60
179	Tom Sturdivant	2.00	1.00	.60
180	Bob Allison	2.25	1.25	.70
181	Paul Brown	2.00	1.00	.60
182	Bob Nieman	2.00	1.00	.60
183	Roger Craig	5.00	2.50	1.50
184	Haywood Sullivan	2.00	1.00	.60
185	Roland Sheldon	2.00	.90	.50
186	*Mack Jones*	2.00	1.00	.60
187	Gene Conley	2.00	1.00	.60
188	Chuck Hiller	2.00	1.00	.60
189	Dick Hall	2.00	1.00	.60
190a	Wally Moon (with cap)	9.00	4.00	2.25
190b	Wally Moon (no cap)	2.25	1.25	.70
191	Jim Brewer	2.00	1.00	.60
192a	Checklist 177-264 (192 is Check List, 3)	6.00	2.75	1.50
192b	Checklist 177-264 (192 is Check List 3)	4.00	1.75	1.00
193	Eddie Kasko	2.00	1.00	.60
194	*Dean Chance*	5.00	2.50	1.50
195	Joe Cunningham	2.00	1.00	.60
196	Terry Fox	2.00	1.00	.60
197	Daryl Spencer	2.00	1.00	.60
198	Johnny Keane	2.00	1.00	.60
199	*Gaylord Perry*	150.00	60.00	38.50
200	Mickey Mantle	400.00	175.00	105.00
201	Ike Delock	2.00	1.00	.60
202	Carl Warwick	2.00	1.00	.60
203	Jack Fisher	2.00	1.00	.60
204	Johnny Weekly	2.00	1.00	.60
205	Gene Freese	2.00	1.00	.60
206	Senators Team	4.00	2.00	1.25
207	Pete Burnside	2.00	1.00	.60
208	Billy Martin	6.00	2.75	1.50
209	*Jim Fregosi*	6.00	2.50	1.50
210	Roy Face	2.00	.90	.50
211	Midway Masters (Frank Bolling, Roy McMillan)	2.25	1.25	.70
212	Jim Owens	2.00	1.00	.60
213	Richie Ashburn	6.00	2.75	1.50
214	Dom Zanni	2.00	1.00	.60
215	Woody Held	2.00	1.00	.60
216	Ron Kline	2.00	1.00	.60
217	Walt Alston	4.00	1.75	1.00
218	*Joe Torre*	18.00	9.00	5.50
219	*Al Downing*	4.00	1.75	1.00
220	Roy Sievers	2.25	1.25	.70
221	Bill Short	2.00	1.00	.60
222	Jerry Zimmerman	2.00	1.00	.60
223	Alex Grammas	2.00	1.00	.60
224	Don Rudolph	2.00	1.00	.60
225	Frank Malzone	2.00	1.00	.60
226	Giants Team	4.00	1.75	1.00
227	Bobby Tiefenauer	2.00	1.00	.60
228	Dale Long	2.00	1.00	.60
229	Jesus McFarlane	2.00	1.00	.60
230	Camlio Pascual	2.25	1.25	.70

		NR MT	EX	VG
231	Ernie Bowman	2.00	1.00	.60
232	World Series Game 1 (Yanks Win Opener)	5.00	2.50	1.50
233	World Series Game 2 (Jay Ties It Up)	5.00	2.50	1.50
234	World Series Game 3 (Maris Wins It In The 9th)	8.00	3.50	2.00
235	World Series Game 4 (Ford Sets New Mark)	7.00	3.25	1.75
236	World Series Game 5 (Yanks Crush Reds In Finale)	5.00	2.50	1.50
237	World Series Summary (The Winners Celebrate)	5.00	2.50	1.50
238	Norm Sherry	2.00	1.00	.60
239	Cecil Butler	2.00	1.00	.60
240	George Altman	2.00	1.00	.60
241	Johnny Kucks	2.00	1.00	.60
242	Mel McGaha	2.00	1.00	.60
243	Robin Roberts	12.00	5.50	3.00
244	Don Gile	2.00	1.00	.60
245	Ron Hansen	2.00	1.00	.60
246	Art Ditmar	2.00	1.00	.60
247	Joe Pignatano	2.00	1.00	.60
248	Bob Aspromonte	2.00	1.00	.60
249	Ed Keegan	2.00	1.00	.60
250	Norm Cash	5.00	2.50	1.50
251	Yankees Team	15.00	7.50	4.50
252	Earl Francis	2.00	1.00	.60
253	Harry Chiti	2.00	1.00	.60
254	Gordon Windhorn	2.00	1.00	.60
255	Juan Pizarro	2.00	1.00	.60
256	Elio Chacon	2.00	.90	.50
257	Jack Spring	2.00	1.00	.60
258	Marty Keough	2.00	1.00	.60
259	Lou Klimchock	2.00	1.00	.60
260	Bill Pierce	2.00	.90	.50
261	George Alusik	2.00	1.00	.60
262	Bob Schmidt	2.00	1.00	.60
263	The Right Pitch (Joe Jay, Bob Purkey, Jim Turner)	2.25	1.25	.70
264	Dick Ellsworth	2.00	1.00	.60
265	Joe Adcock	2.00	.90	.50
266	John Anderson	2.00	1.00	.60
267	Dan Dobbek	2.00	1.00	.60
268	Ken McBride	2.00	1.00	.60
269	Bob Oldis	2.00	1.00	.60
270	Dick Groat	2.00	.90	.50
271	Ray Rippelmeyer	2.00	1.00	.60
272	Earl Robinson	2.00	1.00	.60
273	Gary Bell	2.00	1.00	.60
274	Sammy Taylor	2.00	1.00	.60
275	Norm Siebern	2.00	1.00	.60
276	Hal Kostad	2.00	1.00	.60
277	Checklist 265-352	4.00	1.75	1.00
278	Ken Johnson	2.00	1.00	.60
279	Hobie Landrith	2.00	.90	.50
280	Johnny Podres	4.00	2.00	1.25
281	*Jake Gibbs*	2.25	1.00	.60
282	Dave Hillman	2.00	1.00	.60
283	Charlie Smith	2.00	1.00	.60
284	Ruben Amaro	2.00	1.00	.60
285	Curt Simmons	2.00	.90	.50
286	Al Lopez	5.00	2.50	1.50
287	George Witt	2.00	1.00	.60
288	Billy Williams	30.00	15.00	9.00
289	Mike Krsnich	2.00	1.00	.60
290	Jim Gentile	2.00	1.00	.60
291	Hal Stowe	2.00	.90	.50
292	Jerry Kindall	2.00	1.00	.60
293	Bob Miller	2.00	.90	.50
294	Phillies Team	4.00	2.00	1.25
295	Vern Law	2.00	.90	.50
296	Ken Hamlin	2.00	1.00	.60
297	Ron Perranoski	2.00	1.00	.60
298	Bill Tuttle	2.00	1.00	.60
299	*Don Wert*	2.00	1.00	.60
300	Willie Mays	125.00	62.00	37.00
301	Galen Cisco	2.00	1.00	.60
302	*John Edwards*	2.00	1.00	.60
303	Frank Torre	2.00	1.00	.60
304	Dick Farrell	2.00	1.00	.60
305	Jerry Lumpe	2.00	1.00	.60
306	Redbird Rippers (Larry Jackson, Lindy McDaniel)	2.25	1.25	.70
307	Jim Grant	2.00	1.00	.60
308	Neil Chrisley	2.00	.90	.50
309	Moe Morhardt	2.00	1.00	.60
310	Whitey Ford	25.00	12.50	7.50
311	Kubek Makes The Double Play	5.00	2.50	1.50
312	Spahn Shows No-Hit Form	7.00	3.50	2.00
313	Maris Blasts 61st	20.00	10.00	6.00

		NR MT	EX	VG
314	Colavito's Power	5.00	2.50	1.50
315	Ford Tosses A Curve	6.00	2.75	1.50
316	Killebrew Sends One Into Orbit	5.00	2.25	1.25
317	Musial Plays 21st Season	12.00	5.50	3.00
318	The Switch Hitter Connects (Mickey Mantle)	40.00	16.00	9.00
319	McCormick Shows His Stuff	2.25	1.25	.70
320	Hank Aaron	125.00	62.00	37.00
321	Lee Stange	2.00	1.00	.60
322	Al Dark	2.25	1.25	.70
323	Don Landrum	2.00	1.00	.60
324	Joe McClain	2.00	1.00	.60
325	Luis Aparicio	15.00	7.50	4.50
326	Tom Parsons	2.00	1.00	.60
327	Ozzie Virgil	2.00	1.00	.60
328	Ken Walters	2.00	1.00	.60
329	Bob Bolin	2.00	1.00	.60
330	Johnny Romano	2.00	1.00	.60
331	Moe Drabowsky	2.00	1.00	.60
332	Don Buddin	2.00	1.00	.60
333	Frank Cipriani	2.00	1.00	.60
334	Red Sox Team	5.00	2.50	1.50
335	Bill Bruton	2.00	1.00	.60
336	Billy Muffett	2.00	1.00	.60
337	Jim Marshall	2.00	.90	.50
338	Billy Gardner	2.25	1.00	.60
339	Jose Valdivielso	2.00	1.00	.60
340	Don Drysdale	30.00	15.00	9.00
341	Mike Hershberger	2.00	1.00	.60
342	Ed Rakow	2.00	1.00	.60
343	Albie Pearson	2.00	1.00	.60
344	Ed Bauta	2.00	1.00	.60
345	Chuck Schilling	2.00	1.00	.60
346	Jack Kralick	2.00	1.00	.60
347	Chuck Hinton	2.00	1.00	.60
348	Larry Burright	2.00	1.00	.60
349	Paul Foytack	2.00	1.00	.60
350	Frank Robinson	50.00	25.00	15.00
351	Braves' Backstops (Del Crandall, Joe Torre)	5.00	2.50	1.50
352	Frank Sullivan	2.00	1.00	.60
353	Bill Mazeroski	5.00	2.50	1.50
354	Roman Mejias	2.00	1.00	.60
355	Steve Barber	2.00	1.00	.60
356	Tom Haller	2.25	1.25	.70
357	Jerry Walker	2.00	1.00	.60
358	Tommy Davis	4.00	2.00	1.25
359	Bobby Locke	2.00	1.00	.60
360	Yogi Berra	70.00	35.00	21.00
361	Bob Hendley	2.00	1.00	.60
362	Ty Cline	2.00	1.00	.60
363	Bob Roselli	2.00	1.00	.60
364	Ken Hunt	2.00	1.00	.60
365	Charley Neal	2.00	.90	.50
366	Phil Regan	2.00	1.00	.60
367	Checklist 353-429	4.00	1.75	1.00
368	Bob Tillman	2.00	1.00	.60
369	Ted Bowsfield	2.00	1.00	.60
370	Ken Boyer	4.00	1.75	1.00
371	Earl Battey	4.00	2.00	1.25
372	Jack Curtis	4.00	2.00	1.25
373	Al Heist	4.00	2.00	1.25
374	Gene Mauch	4.00	2.00	1.25
375	Ron Fairly	4.00	2.00	1.25
376	Bud Daley	5.00	2.50	1.50
377	Johnny Orsino	4.00	2.00	1.25
378	Bennie Daniels	4.00	2.00	1.25
379	Chuck Essegian	4.00	2.00	1.25
380	Lou Burdette	4.00	1.75	1.00
381	Chico Cardenas	4.00	2.00	1.25
382	Dick Williams	5.00	2.50	1.50
383	Ray Sadecki	4.00	2.00	1.25
384	Athletics Team	5.00	2.50	1.50
385	Early Wynn	20.00	10.00	6.00
386	Don Mincher	4.00	2.00	1.25
387	Lou Brock	200.00	100.00	60.00
388	Ryne Duren	4.00	2.00	1.25
389	Smoky Burgess	5.00	2.50	1.50
390	Orlando Cepeda AS	5.00	2.25	1.25
391	Bill Mazeroski AS	5.00	2.50	1.50
392	Ken Boyer AS	5.00	2.50	1.50
393	Roy McMillan AS	4.00	2.00	1.25
394	Hank Aaron AS	30.00	15.00	9.00
395	Willie Mays AS	30.00	15.00	9.00
396	Frank Robinson AS	12.00	5.50	3.00
397	John Roseboro AS	4.00	2.00	1.25
398	Don Drysdale AS	10.00	4.50	2.50
399	Warren Spahn AS	10.00	4.50	2.50
400	Elston Howard	7.00	3.25	1.75
401	AL & NL Homer Kings (Orlando Cepeda, Roger Maris)	25.00	10.00	6.00

		NR MT	EX	VG
402	Gino Cimoli	4.00	2.00	1.25
403	Chet Nichols	4.00	2.00	1.25
404	Tim Harkness	4.00	2.00	1.25
405	Jim Perry	5.00	2.50	1.50
406	Bob Taylor	4.00	2.00	1.25
407	Hank Aguirre	4.00	2.00	1.25
408	Gus Bell	5.00	2.50	1.50
409	Pirates Team	5.00	2.50	1.50
410	Al Smith	4.00	2.00	1.25
411	Danny O'Connell	4.00	2.00	1.25
412	Charlie James	4.00	2.00	1.25
413	Matty Alou	5.00	2.50	1.50
414	Joe Gaines	4.00	2.00	1.25
415	Bill Virdon	5.00	2.50	1.50
416	Bob Scheffing	4.00	2.00	1.25
417	Joe Azcue	4.00	2.00	1.25
418	Andy Carey	4.00	2.00	1.25
419	Bob Bruce	4.00	2.00	1.25
420	Gus Triandos	4.00	2.00	1.25
421	Ken MacKenzie	5.00	2.50	1.50
422	Steve Bilko	4.00	2.00	1.25
423	Rival League Relief Aces (Roy Face, Hoyt Wilhelm)	5.00	2.25	1.25
424	Al McBean	4.00	2.00	1.25
425	Carl Yastrzemski	175.00	87.00	52.00
426	Bob Farley	4.00	2.00	1.25
427	Jake Wood	4.00	2.00	1.25
428	Joe Hicks	4.00	2.00	1.25
429	Bill O'Dell	4.00	2.00	1.25
430	Tony Kubek	7.00	3.25	1.75
431	*Bob Rodgers*	5.00	2.50	1.50
432	Jim Pendleton	4.00	2.00	1.25
433	Jim Archer	4.00	2.00	1.25
434	Clay Dalrymple	4.00	2.00	1.25
435	Larry Sherry	4.00	2.00	1.25
436	Felix Mantilla	5.00	2.50	1.50
437	Ray Moore	4.00	2.00	1.25
438	Dick Brown	4.00	2.00	1.25
439	Jerry Buchek	4.00	2.00	1.25
440	Joe Jay	4.00	2.00	1.25
441	Checklist 430-506	5.00	2.25	1.25
442	Wes Stock	4.00	2.00	1.25
443	Del Crandall	5.00	2.50	1.50
444	Ted Wills	4.00	2.00	1.25
445	Vic Power	4.00	2.00	1.25
446	Don Elston	4.00	2.00	1.25
447	Willie Kirkland	4.00	2.00	1.25
448	Joe Gibbon	4.00	2.00	1.25
449	Jerry Adair	4.00	2.00	1.25
450	Jim O'Toole	4.00	2.00	1.25
451	*Jose Tartabull*	4.00	2.00	1.25
452	Earl Averill	4.00	2.00	1.25
453	Cal McLish	4.00	2.00	1.25
454	Floyd Robinson	4.00	2.00	1.25
455	Luis Arroyo	5.00	2.50	1.50
456	Joe Amalfitano	4.00	2.00	1.25
457	Lou Clinton	4.00	2.00	1.25
458a	Bob Buhl ("M" on cap)	4.00	2.00	1.25
458b	Bob Buhl (plain cap)	60.00	30.00	18.00
459	Ed Bailey	4.00	2.00	1.25
460	Jim Bunning	9.00	4.00	2.50
461	*Ken Hubbs*	10.00	4.00	2.50
462a	Willie Tasby ("W" on cap)	4.00	2.00	1.25
462b	Willie Tasby (plain cap)	60.00	30.00	18.00
463	Hank Bauer	5.00	2.50	1.50
464	*Al Jackson*	5.00	2.50	1.50
465	Reds Team	4.00	1.75	1.00
466	Norm Cash AS	4.00	1.75	1.00
467	Chuck Schilling AS	5.00	2.50	1.50
468	Brooks Robinson AS	12.00	5.50	3.00
469	Luis Aparicio AS	8.00	3.50	2.00
470	Al Kaline AS	10.00	4.50	2.50
471	Mickey Mantle AS	80.00	40.00	25.00
472	Rocky Colavito AS	5.00	2.25	1.25
473	Elston Howard AS	5.00	2.25	1.25
474	Frank Lary AS	5.00	2.50	1.50
475	Whitey Ford AS	10.00	4.50	2.50
476	Orioles Team	5.00	2.50	1.50
477	Andre Rodgers	4.00	2.00	1.25
478	Don Zimmer	5.00	2.50	1.50
479	*Joel Horlen*	4.00	2.00	1.25
480	Harvey Kuenn	5.00	2.50	1.50
481	Vic Wertz	4.00	2.00	1.25
482	Sam Mele	4.00	2.00	1.25
483	Don McMahon	4.00	2.00	1.25
484	Dick Schofield	4.00	2.00	1.25
485	Pedro Ramos	4.00	2.00	1.25
486	Jim Gilliam	4.00	1.75	1.00
487	Jerry Lynch	4.00	2.00	1.25
488	Hal Brown	4.00	2.00	1.25
489	Julio Gotay	4.00	2.00	1.25

		NR MT	EX	VG
490	Clete Boyer	4.00	1.75	1.00
491	Leon Wagner	4.00	2.00	1.25
492	Hal Smith	4.00	2.00	1.25
493	Danny McDevitt	4.00	2.00	1.25
494	Sammy White	4.00	2.00	1.25
495	Don Cardwell	4.00	2.00	1.25
496	Wayne Causey	4.00	2.00	1.25
497	Ed Bouchee	5.00	2.50	1.50
498	Jim Donohue	4.00	2.00	1.25
499	Zoilo Versalles	4.00	2.00	1.25
500	Duke Snider	40.00	20.00	12.00
501	Claude Osteen	4.00	2.00	1.25
502	Hector Lopez	5.00	2.50	1.50
503	Danny Murtaugh	4.00	2.00	1.25
504	Eddie Bressoud	4.00	2.00	1.25
505	Juan Marichal	35.00	17.50	10.50
506	Charley Maxwell	4.00	2.00	1.25
507	Ernie Broglio	4.00	2.00	1.25
508	Gordy Coleman	4.00	2.00	1.25
509	*Dave Giusti*	4.00	2.00	1.25
510	Jim Lemon	4.00	2.00	1.25
511	Bubba Phillips	4.00	2.00	1.25
512	Mike Fornieles	4.00	2.00	1.25
513	Whitey Herzog	4.00	1.75	1.00
514	Sherm Lollar	4.00	2.00	1.25
515	Stan Williams	4.00	2.00	1.25
516	Checklist 507-598	8.00	3.50	2.00
517	Dave Wickersham	4.00	2.00	1.25
518	Lee Maye	4.00	2.00	1.25
519	Bob Johnson	4.00	2.00	1.25
520	Bob Friend	5.00	2.50	1.50
521	Jacke Davis	4.00	2.00	1.25
522	Lindy McDaniel	4.00	2.00	1.25
523	Russ Nixon	12.00	5.50	3.00
524	Howie Nunn	12.00	5.50	3.00
525	George Thomas	12.00	5.50	3.00
526	Hal Woodeshick	12.00	5.50	3.00
527	*Dick McAuliffe*	15.00	5.00	2.75
528	Turk Lown	12.00	5.50	3.00
529	John Schaive	12.00	5.50	3.00
530	Bob Gibson	175.00	87.00	52.00
531	Bobby G. Smith	12.00	5.50	3.00
532	Dick Stigman	12.00	5.50	3.00
533	Charley Lau	13.00	5.75	3.25
534	Tony Gonzalez	12.00	5.50	3.00
535	Ed Roebuck	12.00	5.50	3.00
536	Dick Gernert	12.00	5.50	3.00
537	Indians Team	15.00	6.75	3.75
538	Jack Sanford	12.00	5.50	3.00
539	Billy Moran	12.00	5.50	3.00
540	Jim Landis	12.00	5.50	3.00
541	Don Nottebart	12.00	5.50	3.00
542	Dave Philley	12.00	5.50	3.00
543	Bob Allen	12.00	5.50	3.00
544	Willie McCovey	125.00	62.00	37.00
545	Hoyt Wilhelm	55.00	25.00	14.00
546	Moe Thacker	12.00	5.50	3.00
547	Don Ferrarese	12.00	5.50	3.00
548	Bobby Del Greco	12.00	5.50	3.00
549	Bill Rigney	12.00	5.50	3.00
550	Art Mahaffey	12.00	5.50	3.00
551	Harry Bright	12.00	5.50	3.00
552	Cubs Team	15.00	6.75	3.75
553	Jim Coates	15.00	6.75	3.75
554	Bubba Morton	12.00	5.50	3.00
555	John Buzhardt	12.00	5.50	3.00
556	Al Spangler	12.00	5.50	3.00
557	Bob Anderson	12.00	5.50	3.00
558	John Goryl	12.00	5.50	3.00
559	Mike Higgins	12.00	5.50	3.00
560	Chuck Estrada	12.00	5.50	3.00
561	Gene Oliver	12.00	5.50	3.00
562	Bill Henry	12.00	5.50	3.00
563	Ken Aspromonte	12.00	5.50	3.00
564	Bob Grim	12.00	5.50	3.00
565	Jose Pagan	12.00	5.50	3.00
566	Marty Kutyna	12.00	5.50	3.00
567	Tracy Stallard	12.00	5.50	3.00
568	Jim Golden	12.00	5.50	3.00
569	Ed Sadowski	12.00	5.50	3.00
570	Bill Stafford	15.00	6.75	3.75
571	Billy Klaus	12.00	5.50	3.00
572	Bob Miller	13.00	5.75	3.25
573	Johnny Logan	13.00	5.75	3.25
574	Dean Stone	12.00	5.50	3.00
575	Red Schoendienst	35.00	15.00	9.00
576	Russ Kemmerer	12.00	5.50	3.00
577	Dave Nicholson	12.00	5.50	3.00
578	Jim Duffalo	12.00	5.50	3.00
579	Jim Schaffer	12.00	5.50	3.00
580	Bill Monbouquette	13.00	5.75	3.25

		NR MT	EX	VG
581	Mel Roach	12.00	5.50	3.00
582	Ron Piche	12.00	5.50	3.00
583	Larry Osborne	12.00	5.50	3.00
584	Twins Team	15.00	6.75	3.75
585	Glen Hobbie	12.00	5.50	3.00
586	Sammy Esposito	12.00	5.50	3.00
587	Frank Funk	12.00	5.50	3.00
588	Birdie Tebbetts	12.00	5.50	3.00
589	Bob Turley	18.00	8.00	4.50
590	Curt Flood	18.00	8.00	4.50
591	Rookie Parade Pitchers *(Sam McDowell,* Ron Nischwitz, Art Quirk, *Dick Radatz, Ron Taylor)*	60.00	30.00	18.00
592	Rookie Parade Pitchers *(Bo Belinsky,* Joe Bonikowski, *Jim Bouton,* Dan Pfister, Dave Stenhouse)	45.00	20.00	11.25
593	Rookie Parade Pitchers (Craig Anderson, *Jack Hamilton,* Jack Lamabe, Bob Moorhead, *Bob Veale)*	25.00	11.25	6.25
594	Rookie Parade Catchers (Doug Camilli, *Doc Edwards,* Don Pavletich, Ken Retzer, *Bob Uecker)*	110.00	55.00	33.00
595	Rookie Parade Infielders *(Ed Charles,* Marlin Coughtry, Bob Sadowski, Felix Torres)	25.00	11.25	6.25
596	Rookie Parade Infielders *(Bernie Allen, Phil Linz, Joe Pepitone, Rich Rollins)*	50.00	25.00	15.00
597	Rookie Parade Infielders (Rod Kanehl, Jim McKnight, *Denis Menke,* Amado Samuel)	25.00	11.25	6.25
598	Rookie Parade Outfielders (Howie Goss, *Jim Hickman,* Manny Jimenez, Al Luplow, Ed Olivares)	50.00	25.00	12.00

1962 Topps Baseball Bucks

Issued in their own 1¢ package, the 1962 Topps "Baseball Bucks" were another in the growing list of specialty Topps items. The 96 Baseball Bucks in the set measure 4-1/8" by 1-3/4," and were designed to look vaguely like dollar bills. The center player portrait has a banner underneath with the player's name. His home park is shown on the right and there is some biographical information on the left. The back features a large denomination, with the player's league and team logo on either side.

		NR MT	EX	VG
Complete Set:		750.00	375.00	225.00
Common Player:		2.00	1.00	.60
(1)	Hank Aaron	30.00	15.00	9.00
(2)	Joe Adcock	3.00	1.50	.90
(3)	George Altman	2.00	1.00	.60
(4)	Jim Archer	2.00	1.00	.60
(5)	Richie Ashburn	5.00	2.50	1.50
(6)	Ernie Banks	20.00	10.00	8.00
(7)	Earl Battey	2.50	1.25	.70
(8)	Gus Bell	2.50	1.25	.70
(9)	Yogi Berra	18.00	9.00	5.50
(10)	Ken Boyer	3.00	1.50	.90
(11)	Jackie Brandt	2.00	1.00	.60
(12)	Jim Bunning	4.00	2.00	1.25
(13)	Lou Burdette	3.00	1.50	.90
(14)	Don Cardwell	2.00	1.00	.60
(15)	Norm Cash	3.00	1.50	.90
(16)	Orlando Cepeda	4.50	2.25	1.25
(17)	Bob Clemente	40.00	20.00	12.50
(18)	Rocky Colavito	3.00	1.50	.90
(19)	Chuck Cottier	2.00	1.00	.60
(20)	Roger Craig	2.50	1.25	.70
(21)	Bennie Daniels	2.00	1.00	.60
(22)	Don Demeter	2.00	1.00	.60
(23)	Don Drysdale	15.00	7.50	4.50
(24)	Chuck Estrada	2.00	1.00	.60
(25)	Dick Farrell	2.00	1.00	.60
(26)	Whitey Ford	12.00	6.00	3.50
(27)	Nellie Fox	4.00	2.00	1.25
(28)	Tito Francona	2.00	1.00	.60
(29)	Bob Friend	2.50	1.25	.70
(30)	Jim Gentile	2.00	1.00	.60
(31)	Dick Gernert	2.00	1.00	.60
(32)	Lenny Green	2.00	1.00	.60
(33)	Dick Groat	3.00	1.50	.90
(34)	Woody Held	2.00	1.00	.60
(35)	Don Hoak	2.50	1.25	.70
(36)	Gil Hodges	10.00	5.00	3.00
(37)	Frank Howard	3.00	1.50	.90
(38)	Elston Howard	4.00	2.00	1.25
(39)	Dick Howser	3.00	1.50	.90
(40)	Ken Hunt	2.00	1.00	.60
(41)	Larry Jackson	2.00	1.00	.60
(42)	Joe Jay	4.00	2.00	1.25
(43)	Al Kaline	12.00	6.00	3.50
(44)	Harmon Killebrew	12.00	6.00	3.50
(45)	Sandy Koufax	35.00	17.50	10.50
(46)	Harvey Kuenn	4.00	2.00	1.25
(47)	Jim Landis	2.00	1.00	.60
(48)	Norm Larker	2.00	1.00	.60
(49)	Frank Lary	2.00	1.00	.60
(50)	Jerry Lumpe	2.00	1.00	.60
(51)	Art Mahaffey	2.00	1.00	.60
(52)	Frank Malzone	2.00	1.00	.60
(53)	Felix Mantilla	2.50	1.25	.70
(54)	Mickey Mantle	125.00	62.00	37.00
(55)	Roger Maris	12.00	6.00	3.50
(56)	Ed Mathews	10.00	5.00	3.00
(57)	Willie Mays	35.00	17.50	10.50
(58)	Ken McBride	2.00	1.00	.60
(59)	Mike McCormick	2.00	1.00	.60
(60)	Minnie Minoso	4.00	2.00	1.25
(61)	Wally Moon	2.50	1.25	.70
(62)	Stu Miller	2.00	1.00	.60
(63)	Stan Musial	30.00	15.00	9.00
(64)	Danny O'Connell	2.00	1.00	.60
(65)	Jim O'Toole	4.00	2.00	1.25
(66)	Camilo Pascual	2.50	1.25	.70
(67)	Jim Perry	3.00	1.50	.90
(68)	Jimmy Piersall	4.00	2.00	1.25
(69)	Vada Pinson	6.00	3.00	1.75
(70)	Juan Pizarro	2.00	1.00	.60
(71)	Johnny Podres	3.00	1.50	.90
(72)	Vic Power	2.00	1.00	.60
(73)	Bob Purkey	12.00	6.00	3.50
(74)	Pedro Ramos	2.00	1.00	.60
(75)	Brooks Robinson	15.00	7.50	4.50
(76)	Floyd Robinson	2.00	1.00	.60
(77)	Frank Robinson	15.00	7.50	4.50
(78)	Johnny Romano	2.00	1.00	.60
(79)	Pete Runnels	2.50	1.25	.70
(80)	Don Schwall	2.00	1.00	.60
(81)	Bobby Shantz	3.00	1.50	.90
(82)	Norm Siebern	2.00	1.00	.60
(83)	Roy Sievers	2.50	1.25	.70
(84)	Hal (W.) Smith	2.00	1.00	.60
(85)	Warren Spahn	10.00	5.00	3.00
(86)	Dick Stuart	2.50	1.25	.70
(87)	Tony Taylor	2.00	1.00	.60
(88)	Lee Thomas	2.00	1.00	.60
(89)	Gus Triandos	2.50	1.25	.70
(90)	Leon Wagner	2.00	1.00	.60
(91)	Jerry Walker	2.00	1.00	.60
(92)	Bill White	2.50	1.25	.70
(93)	Billy Williams	9.00	4.50	2.75
(94)	Gene Woodling	2.50	1.25	.70
(95)	Early Wynn	9.00	4.50	2.75
(96)	Carl Yastrzemski	30.00	15.00	9.00

1962 Topps Stamps

An artistic improvement over the somewhat drab Topps stamps of the previous year, the 1962 stamps, 1-3/8" by 1-7/8," had color player photographs set on red or yellow backgrounds. As in 1961, they were

1962 Topps Stamps

An artistic improvement over the somewhat drab Topps stamps of the previous year, the 1962 stamps, 1-3/8" by 1-7/8," had color player photographs set on red or yellow backgrounds. As in 1961, they were issued in two-stamp panels as insert with Topps baseball cards. A change from 1961 was the inclusion of team emblems in the set. A complete set consists of 201 stamps; Roy Sievers was originally portrayed on the wrong team - Athletics - and was later corrected to the Phillies.

	NR MT	EX	VG
Complete Set:	220.00	110.00	67.00
Stamp Album:	35.00	17.50	10.50
Common Player:	.25	.13	.08

		NR MT	EX	VG
(1)	Hank Aaron	10.00	5.00	3.00
(2)	Jerry Adair	.25	.13	.08
(3)	Joe Adcock	.35	.20	.11
(4)	Bob Allison	.30	.15	.09
(5)	Felipe Alou	.35	.20	.11
(6)	George Altman	.25	.13	.08
(7)	Joe Amalfitano	.25	.13	.08
(8)	Ruben Amaro	.25	.13	.08
(9)	Luis Aparicio	1.50	.70	.45
(10)	Jim Archer	.25	.13	.08
(11)	Bob Aspromonte	.25	.13	.08
(12)	Ed Bailey	.25	.13	.08
(13)	Jack Baldschun	.25	.13	.08
(14)	Ernie Banks	6.00	3.00	1.75
(15)	Earl Battey	.30	.15	.09
(16)	Gus Bell	.35	.20	.11
(17)	Yogi Berra	5.00	2.50	1.50
(18)	Dick Bertell	.25	.13	.08
(19)	Steve Bilko	.25	.13	.08
(20)	Frank Bolling	.25	.13	.08
(21)	Steve Boros	.25	.13	.08
(22)	Ted Bowsfield	.25	.13	.08
(23)	Clete Boyer	.35	.20	.11
(24)	Ken Boyer	.50	.25	.15
(25)	Jackie Brandt	.25	.13	.08
(26)	Bill Bruton	.25	.13	.08
(27)	Jim Bunning	1.00	.50	.30
(28)	Lou Burdette	.35	.20	.11
(29)	Smoky Burgess	.30	.15	.09
(30)	Johnny Callizon (Callison)	.30	.15	.09
(31)	Don Cardwell	.25	.13	.08
(32)	Camilo Carreon	.25	.13	.08
(33)	Norm Cash	.50	.25	.15
(34)	Orlando Cepeda	1.00	.50	.30
(35)	Bob Clemente	15.00	7.50	4.50
(36)	Ty Cline	.25	.13	.08
(37)	Rocky Colavito	.80	.40	.25
(38)	Gordon Coleman	.25	.13	.08
(39)	Chuck Cottier	.25	.13	.08
(40)	Roger Craig	.35	.20	.11
(41)	Del Crandall	.35	.20	.11
(42)	Pete Daley	.25	.13	.08
(43)	Clay Dalrymple	.25	.13	.08
(44)	Bennie Daniels	.25	.13	.08
(45)	Jim Davenport	.25	.13	.08
(46)	Don Demeter	.25	.13	.08
(47)	Dick Donovan	.25	.13	.08
(48)	Don Drysdale	7.00	3.50	2.00
(49)	John Edwards	.25	.13	.08
(50)	Dick Ellsworth	.25	.13	.08
(51)	Chuck Estrada	.25	.13	.08
(52)	Roy Face	.35	.20	.11
(53)	Ron Fairly	.30	.15	.09
(54)	Dick Farrell	.25	.13	.08
(55)	Whitey Ford	5.00	2.50	1.50
(56)	Mike Fornieles	.25	.13	.08
(57)	Nellie Fox	.80	.40	.25
(58)	Tito Francona	.25	.13	.08
(59)	Gene Freese	.25	.13	.08
(60)	Bob Friend	.35	.20	.11
(61)	Gary Geiger	.25	.13	.08
(62)	Jim Gentile	.25	.13	.08
(63)	Tony Gonzalez	.25	.13	.08
(64)	Lenny Green	.25	.13	.08
(65)	Dick Groat	.35	.20	.11
(66)	Ron Hansen	.25	.13	.08
(67)	Al Heist	.25	.13	.08
(68)	Woody Held	.25	.13	.08
(69)	Ray Herbert	.25	.13	.08
(70)	Chuck Hinton	.25	.13	.08
(71)	Don Hoak	.30	.15	.09
(72)	Glen Hobbie	.25	.13	.08
(73)	Gil Hodges	5.00	2.50	1.50
(74)	Jay Hook	.35	.20	.11
(75)	Elston Howard	.80	.40	.25
(76)	Frank Howard	.50	.25	.15
(77)	Dick Howser	.35	.20	.11
(78)	Ken Hunt	.25	.13	.08
(79)	Larry Jackson	.25	.13	.08
(80)	Julian Javier	.25	.13	.08
(81)	Joe Jay	.25	.13	.08
(82)	Bob Johnson	.25	.13	.08
(83)	Sam Jones	.25	.13	.08
(84)	Al Kaline	7.00	3.50	2.00
(85)	Eddie Kasko	.25	.13	.08
(86)	Harmon Killebrew	5.00	2.50	1.50
(87)	Sandy Koufax	10.00	5.00	3.00
(88)	Jack Kralick	.25	.13	.08
(89)	Tony Kubek	.80	.40	.25
(90)	Harvey Kuenn	.50	.25	.15
(91)	Jim Landis	.25	.13	.08
(92)	Hobie Landrith	.35	.20	.11
(93)	Frank Lary	.25	.13	.08
(94)	Barry Latman	.25	.13	.08
(95)	Jerry Lumpe	.25	.13	.08
(96)	Art Mahaffey	.25	.13	.08
(97)	Frank Malzone	.25	.13	.08
(98)	Felix Mantilla	.35	.20	.11
(99)	Mickey Mantle	45.00	22.00	13.50
(100)	Juan Marichal	2.00	1.00	.60
(101)	Roger Maris	5.00	2.50	1.50
(102)	J.C. Martin	.25	.13	.08
(103)	Ed Mathews	3.00	1.50	.90
(104)	Willie Mays	7.00	3.50	2.00
(105)	Bill Mazeroski	.50	.25	.15
(106)	Ken McBride	.25	.13	.08
(107)	Tim McCarver	.50	.25	.15
(108)	Joe McClain	.25	.13	.08
(109)	Mike McCormick	.25	.13	.08
(110)	Lindy McDaniel	.25	.13	.08
(111)	Roy McMillan	.25	.13	.08
(112)	Bob L. Miller	.35	.20	.11
(113)	Stu Miller	.25	.13	.08
(114)	Minnie Minoso	.50	.25	.15
(115)	Bill Monbouquette	.25	.13	.08
(116)	Wally Moon	.30	.15	.09
(117)	Don Mossi	.30	.15	.09
(118)	Stan Musial	7.00	3.50	2.00
(119)	Russ Nixon	.25	.13	.08
(120)	Danny O'Connell	.25	.13	.08
(121)	Jim O'Toole	.25	.13	.08
(122)	Milt Pappas	.30	.15	.09
(123)	Camilo Pascual	.30	.15	.09
(124)	Albie Pearson	.25	.13	.08
(125)	Jim Perry	.35	.20	.11
(126)	Bubba Phillips	.25	.13	.08
(127)	Jimmy Piersall	.35	.20	.11
(128)	Vada Pinson	.50	.25	.15
(129)	Juan Pizarro	.25	.13	.08
(130)	Johnny Podres	.35	.20	.11
(131)	Leo Posada	.25	.13	.08
(132)	Vic Power	.25	.13	.08
(133)	Bob Purkey	.25	.13	.08
(134)	Pedro Ramos	.25	.13	.08
(135)	Bobby Richardson	.80	.40	.25
(136)	Brooks Robinson	3.75	2.00	1.25
(137)	Floyd Robinson	.25	.13	.08
(138)	Frank Robinson	3.50	1.75	1.00
(139)	Bob Rodgers	.30	.15	.09
(140)	Johnny Romano	.25	.13	.08
(141)	John Roseboro	.30	.15	.09
(142)	Pete Runnels	.30	.15	.09

	NR MT	EX	VG
(150) Norm Siebern	.25	.13	.08
(151a) Roy Sievers (Kansas City)	1.00	.50	.30
(151b) Roy Sievers (Philadelphia)	.30	.15	.09
(152) Bill Skowron	.50	.25	.15
(153) Hal (W.) Smith	.25	.13	.08
(154) Duke Snider	3.75	2.00	1.25
(155) Warren Spahn	3.00	1.50	.90
(156) Al Spangler	.25	.13	.08
(157) Daryl Spencer	.25	.13	.08
(158) Gene Stephens	.25	.13	.08
(159) Dick Stuart	.30	.15	.09
(160) Haywood Sullivan	.25	.13	.08
(161) Tony Taylor	.25	.13	.08
(162) George Thomas	.25	.13	.08
(163) Lee Thomas	.25	.13	.08
(164) Bob Tiefenauer	.25	.13	.08
(165) Joe Torre	.50	.25	.15
(166) Gus Triandos	.30	.15	.09
(167) Bill Tuttle	.25	.13	.08
(168) Zoilo Versalles	.25	.13	.08
(169) Bill Virdon	.35	.20	.11
(170) Leon Wagner	.25	.13	.08
(171) Jerry Walker	.25	.13	.08
(172) Lee Walls	.25	.13	.08
(173) Bill White	.30	.15	.09
(174) Hoyt Wilhelm	1.50	.70	.45
(175) Billy Williams	2.00	1.00	.60
(176) Jake Wood	.25	.13	.08
(177) Gene Woodling	.35	.20	.11
(178) Early Wynn	2.00	1.00	.60
(179) Carl Yastrzemski	12.00	6.00	3.50
(180) Don Zimmer	.35	.20	.11
(181) Baltimore Orioles Logo	.25	.13	.08
(182) Boston Red Sox Logo	.25	.13	.08
(183) Chicago Cubs Logo	.25	.13	.08
(184) Chicago White Sox Logo	.25	.13	.08
(185) Cincinnati Reds Logo	.25	.13	.08
(186) Cleveland Indians Logo	.25	.13	.08
(187) Detroit Tigers Logo	.25	.13	.08
(188) Houston Colts Logo	.25	.13	.08
(189) Kansas City Athletics Logo	.25	.13	.08
(190) Los Angeles Angels Logo	.25	.13	.08
(191) Los Angeles Dodgers Logo	.25	.13	.08
(192) Milwaukee Braves Logo	.25	.13	.08
(193) Minnesota Twins Logo	.25	.13	.08
(194) New York Mets Logo	.35	.20	.11
(195) New York Yankees Logo	.35	.20	.11
(196) Philadelphia Phillies Logo	.25	.13	.08
(197) Pittsburgh Pirates Logo	.25	.13	.08
(198) St. Louis Cardinals Logo	.25	.13	.08
(199) San Francisco Giants Logo	.25	.13	.08
(200) Washington Senators Logo	.25	.13	.08

1963 Topps

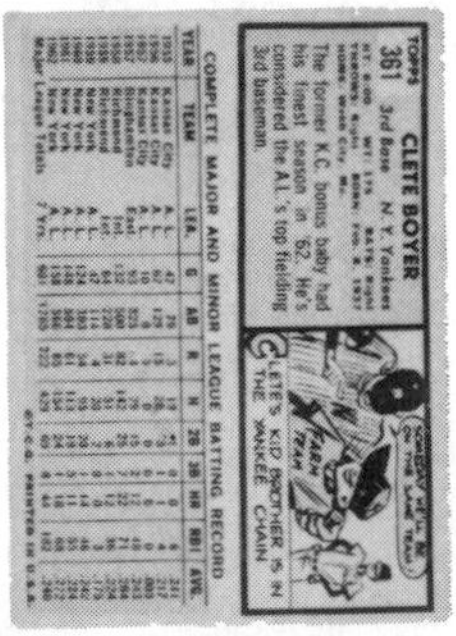

Although the number of cards dropped to 576, the 1963 Topps set is among the most popular of the 1960s. A color photo dominates the 2-1/2" by 3-1/2" card, but a colored circle at the bottom carries a black and white portrait as well. A colored band gives the player's name, team and position. The backs again feature career statistics and a cartoon, career summary and brief biographical details. The set is somewhat unlike those immediately preceding it in that there are fewer specialty cards. The major groupings are statistical leaders, World Series highlights and rookies. It is one rookie which makes the set special - Pete Rose. As one of most avidly sought cards in history and a high-numbered card at that, the Rose rookie card accounts for much of the value of a complete set.

	NR MT	EX	VG
Complete Set:	4500.00	2250.00	1350.
Common Player: 1-283	1.50	.70	.45
Common Player: 284-446	3.00	1.50	.90
Common Player: 447-506	10.00	5.00	3.00
Common Player: 507-576	7.00	3.50	2.00

		NR MT	EX	VG
1	N.L. Batting Leaders (Hank Aaron, Tommy Davis, Stan Musial, Frank Robinson, Bill White)	40.00	6.00	3.50
2	A.L. Batting Leaders (Chuck Hinton, Mickey Mantle, Floyd Robinson, Pete Runnels, Norm Siebern)	25.00	12.50	7.50
3	N.L. Home Run Leaders (Hank Aaron, Ernie Banks, Orlando Cepeda, Willie Mays, Frank Robinson)	12.00	6.00	3.50
4	A.L. Home Run Leaders (Norm Cash, Rocky Colavito, Jim Gentile, Harmon Killebrew, Roger Maris, Leon Wagner)	4.00	2.00	1.25
5	N.L. E.R.A. Leaders (Don Drysdale, Bob Gibson, Sandy Koufax, Bob Purkey, Bob Shaw)	4.00	2.00	1.25
6	A.L. E.R.A. Leaders (Hank Aguirre, Dean Chance, Eddie Fisher, Whitey Ford, Robin Roberts)	3.50	1.75	1.00
7	N.L. Pitching Leaders (Don Drysdale, Joe Jay, Art Mahaffey, Billy O'Dell, Bob Purkey, Jack Sanford)	3.50	1.75	1.00
8	A.L. Pitching Leaders (Jim Bunning, Dick Donovan, Ray Herbert, Camilo Pascual, Ralph Terry)	3.00	1.50	.90
9	N.L. Strikeout Leaders (Don Drysdale, Dick Farrell, Bob Gibson, Sandy Koufax, Billy O'Dell)	4.00	2.00	1.25
10	A.L. Strikeout Leaders (Jim Bunning, Jim Kaat, Camilo Pascual, Juan Pizarro, Ralph Terry)	3.00	1.50	.90
11	Lee Walls	1.50	.70	.45
12	Steve Barber	1.50	.70	.45
13	Phillies Team	3.25	1.75	1.00
14	Pedro Ramos	1.50	.70	.45
15	Ken Hubbs	3.00	1.50	.90
16	Al Smith	1.50	.70	.45
17	Ryne Duren	1.75	.90	.50
18	Buc Blasters (Smoky Burgess, Bob Clemente, Bob Skinner, Dick Stuart)	10.00	5.00	3.00
19	Pete Burnside	1.50	.70	.45
20	Tony Kubek	7.00	3.50	2.00
21	Marty Keough	1.50	.70	.45
22	Curt Simmons	1.75	.90	.50
23	Ed Lopat	2.00	1.00	.60
24	Bob Bruce	1.50	.70	.45
25	Al Kaline	35.00	17.50	10.50
26	Ray Moore	1.50	.70	.45
27	Choo Choo Coleman	2.00	1.00	.60
28	Mike Fornieles	1.50	.70	.45
29a	1962 Rookie Stars (John Boozer, *Ray Culp, Sammy Ellis,* Jesse Gonder)	7.00	3.50	2.00
29b	1963 Rookie Stars (John Boozer, *Ray Culp, Sammy Ellis,* Jesse Gonder)	2.00	1.00	.60
30	Harvey Kuenn	1.50	.70	.45
31	Cal Koonce	1.50	.70	.45
32	Tony Gonzalez	1.50	.70	.45
33	Bo Belinsky	3.00	1.50	.90
34	Dick Schofield	1.50	.70	.45
35	John Buzhardt	1.50	.70	.45
36	Jerry Kindall	1.50	.70	.45
37	Jerry Lynch	1.50	.70	.45
38	Bud Daley	2.00	1.00	.60
39	Angels Team	3.25	1.75	1.00
40	Vic Power	1.50	.70	.45
41	Charlie Lau	1.75	.90	.50
42	Stan Williams	2.00	1.00	.60
43	Veteran Masters (Casey Stengel, Gene Woodling)	4.00	2.00	1.25
44	Terry Fox	1.50	.70	.45
45	Bob Aspromonte	1.50	.70	.45
46	*Tommie Aaron*	2.00	1.00	.60
47	Don Lock	1.50	.70	.45
48	Birdie Tebbetts	1.50	.70	.45
49	*Dal Maxvill*	2.00	1.00	.60
50	Bill Pierce	2.00	1.00	.60
51	George Alusik	1.50	.70	.45
52	Chuck Schilling	1.50	.70	.45
53	Joe Moeller	1.50	.70	.45

		NR MT	EX	VG
54a	1962 Rookie Stars (Jack Cullen, *Dave DeBusschere*, Harry Fanok, Nelson Mathews)	12.00	6.00	3.50
54b	1963 Rookie Stars (Jack Cullen, *Dave DeBusschere*, Harry Fanok, Nelson Mathews)	4.00	2.00	1.25
55	Bill Virdon	1.50	.70	.45
56	Dennis Bennett	1.50	.70	.45
57	Billy Moran	1.50	.70	.45
58	Bob Will	1.50	.70	.45
59	Craig Anderson	1.75	.90	.50
60	Elston Howard	8.00	4.00	2.50
61	Ernie Bowman	1.50	.70	.45
62	Bob Hendley	1.50	.70	.45
63	Reds Team	2.50	1.25	.70
64	Dick McAuliffe	1.75	.90	.50
65	Jackie Brandt	1.50	.70	.45
66	Mike Joyce	1.50	.70	.45
67	Ed Charles	1.50	.70	.45
68	Friendly Foes (Gil Hodges, Duke Snider)	6.50	3.25	2.00
69	Bud Zipfel	1.50	.70	.45
70	Jim O'Toole	1.50	.70	.45
71	*Bobby Wine*	1.75	.90	.50
72	Johnny Romano	1.50	.70	.45
73	Bobby Bragan	1.75	.90	.50
74	*Denver Lemaster*	1.75	.90	.50
75	Bob Allison	2.00	1.00	.60
76	Earl Wilson	1.50	.70	.45
77	Al Spangler	1.50	.70	.45
78	Marv Throneberry	3.50	1.75	1.00
79	Checklist 1-88	2.50	1.25	.70
80	Jim Gilliam	3.00	1.50	.90
81	Jimmie Schaffer	1.50	.70	.45
82	Ed Rakow	1.50	.70	.45
83	Charley James	1.50	.70	.45
84	Ron Kline	1.50	.70	.45
85	Tom Haller	1.75	.90	.50
86	Charley Maxwell	1.50	.70	.45
87	Bob Veale	1.75	.90	.50
88	Ron Hansen	1.50	.70	.45
89	Dick Stigman	1.50	.70	.45
90	Gordy Coleman	1.50	.70	.45
91	Dallas Green	1.75	.90	.50
92	Hector Lopez	2.00	1.00	.60
93	Galen Cisco	1.75	.90	.50
94	Bob Schmidt	1.50	.70	.45
95	Larry Jackson	1.50	.70	.45
96	Lou Clinton	1.50	.70	.45
97	Bob Duliba	1.50	.70	.45
98	George Thomas	1.50	.70	.45
99	Jim Umbricht	1.50	.70	.45
100	Joe Cunningham	1.75	.90	.50
101	Joe Gibbon	1.50	.70	.45
102a	Checklist 89-176 ("Checklist" in red on front)	3.00	1.50	.90
102b	Checklist 89-176 ("Checklist" in white)	8.00	4.00	2.50
103	Chuck Esseglan	1.50	.70	.45
104	Lew Krausse	1.50	.70	.45
105	Ron Fairly	1.75	.90	.50
106	Bob Bolin	1.50	.70	.45
107	Jim Hickman	1.75	.90	.50
108	Hoyt Wilhelm	11.00	5.50	3.25
109	Lee Maye	1.50	.70	.45
110	Rich Rollins	1.75	.90	.50
111	Al Jackson	1.75	.90	.50
112	Dick Brown	1.50	.70	.45
113	Don Landrum (photo actally Ron Santo)	1.75	.90	.50
114	Dan Osinski	1.50	.70	.45
115	Carl Yastrzemski	100.00	50.00	30.00
116	Jim Brosnan	1.75	.90	.50
117	Jacke Davis	1.50	.70	.45
118	Sherm Lollar	1.75	.90	.50
119	Bob Lillis	1.50	.70	.45
120	Roger Maris	60.00	30.00	18.00
121	Jim Hannan	1.50	.70	.45
122	Julio Gotay	1.50	.70	.45
123	Frank Howard	2.50	1.25	.70
124	Dick Howser	1.50	.70	.45
125	Robin Roberts	8.00	4.00	2.50
126	Bob Uecker	40.00	20.00	12.00
127	Bill Tuttle	1.50	.70	.45
128	Matty Alou	1.75	.90	.50
129	Gary Bell	1.50	.70	.45
130	Dick Groat	1.50	.70	.45
131	Senators Team	3.25	1.75	1.00
132	Jack Hamilton	1.50	.70	.45
133	Gene Freese	1.50	.70	.45
134	Bob Scheffing	1.50	.70	.45
135	Richie Ashburn	8.00	4.00	2.50
136	Ike Delock	1.50	.70	.45
137	Mack Jones	1.50	.70	.45
138	Pride of N.L. (Willie Mays, Stan Musial)	30.00	15.00	9.00
139	Earl Averill	1.50	.70	.45
140	Frank Lary	1.75	.90	.50
141	*Manny Mota*	7.00	3.50	2.00
142	World Series Game 1 (Yanks' Ford Wins Series Opener)	3.50	1.75	1.00
143	World Series Game 2 (Sanford Flashes Shutout Magic)	3.25	1.75	1.00
144	World Series Game 3 (Maris Sparks Yankee Rally)	4.00	2.00	1.25
145	World Series Game 4 (Hiller Blasts Grand Slammer)	3.25	1.75	1.00
146	World Series Game 5 (Tresh's Homer Defeats Giants)	3.00	1.50	.90
147	World Series Game 6 (Pierce Stars In 3 Hit Victory)	3.00	1.50	.90
148	World Series Game 7 (Yanks Celebrate As Terry Wins)	3.00	1.50	.90
149	Marv Breeding	1.50	.70	.45
150	Johnny Podres	3.00	1.50	.90
151	Pirates Team	3.25	1.75	1.00
152	Ron Nischwitz	1.50	.70	.45
153	Hal Smith	1.50	.70	.45
154	Walt Alston	3.00	1.50	.90
155	Bill Stafford	2.00	1.00	.60
156	Roy McMillan	1.50	.70	.45
157	*Diego Segui*	1.75	.90	.50
158	1963 Rookie Stars (Rogelio Alvarez, *Tommy Harper*, Dave Roberts, Bob Saverine)	1.75	.90	.50
159	Jim Pagliaroni	1.50	.70	.45
160	Juan Pizarro	1.50	.70	.45
161	Frank Torre	1.50	.70	.45
162	Twins Team	3.25	1.75	1.00
163	Don Larsen	2.00	1.00	.60
164	Bubba Morton	1.50	.70	.45
165	Jim Kaat	7.00	3.50	2.00
166	Johnny Keane	1.50	.70	.45
167	Jim Fregosi	1.50	.70	.45
168	Russ Nixon	1.50	.70	.45
169	1963 Rookie Stars (Dick Egan, Julio Navarro, Gaylord Perry, Tommie Sisk)	30.00	15.00	9.00
170	Joe Adcock	1.50	.70	.45
171	Steve Hamilton	1.50	.70	.45
172	Gene Oliver	1.50	.70	.45
173	Bomber's Best (Mickey Mantle, Bobby Richardson, Tom Tresh)	45.00	23.00	13.50
174	Larry Burright	1.75	.90	.50
175	Bob Buhl	1.75	.90	.50
176	Jim King	1.50	.70	.45
177	Bubba Phillips	1.50	.70	.45
178	Johnny Edwards	1.50	.70	.45
179	Ron Piche	1.50	.70	.45
180	Bill Skowron	1.50	.70	.45
181	Sammy Esposito	1.50	.70	.45
182	Albie Pearson	1.50	.70	.45
183	Joe Pepitone	4.00	2.00	1.25
184	Vern Law	2.00	1.00	.60
185	Chuck Hiller	1.50	.70	.45
186	Jerry Zimmerman	1.50	.70	.45
187	Willie Kirkland	1.50	.70	.45
188	Eddie Bressoud	1.50	.70	.45
189	Dave Giusti	1.50	.70	.45
190	Minnie Minoso	1.50	.70	.45
191	Checklist 177-264	3.00	1.50	.90
192	Clay Dalrymple	1.50	.70	.45
193	Andre Rodgers	1.50	.70	.45
194	Joe Nuxhall	1.75	.90	.50
195	Manny Jimenez	1.50	.70	.45
196	Doug Camilli	1.50	.70	.45
197	Roger Craig	3.00	1.50	.90
198	Lenny Green	1.50	.70	.45
199	Joe Amalfitano	1.50	.70	.45
200	Mickey Mantle	325.00	182.00	97.00
201	Cecil Butler	1.50	.70	.45
202	Red Sox Team	2.50	1.25	.70
203	Chico Cardenas	1.50	.70	.45
204	Don Nottebart	1.50	.70	.45
205	Luis Aparicio	10.00	5.00	3.00
206	Ray Washburn	1.50	.70	.45
207	Ken Hunt	1.50	.70	.45
208	1963 Rookie Stars (Ron Herbel, John Miller, Ron Taylor, Wally Wolf)	1.50	.70	.45
209	Hobie Landrith	1.50	.70	.45
210	Sandy Koufax	125.00	67.00	37.00
211	Fred Whitfield	1.50	.70	.45

		NR MT	EX	VG
212	Glen Hobbie	1.50	.70	.45
213	Billy Hitchcock	1.50	.70	.45
214	Orlando Pena	1.50	.70	.45
215	Bob Skinner	1.75	.90	.50
216	Gene Conley	1.75	.90	.50
217	Joe Christopher	1.75	.90	.50
218	Tiger Twirlers (Jim Bunning, Frank Lary, Don Mossi)	3.00	1.50	.90
219	Chuck Cottier	1.50	.70	.45
220	Camilo Pascual	1.75	.90	.50
221	*Cookie Rojas*	1.75	.90	.50
222	Cubs Team	3.25	1.75	1.00
223	Eddie Fisher	1.50	.70	.45
224	Mike Roarke	1.50	.70	.45
225	Joe Jay	1.50	.70	.45
226	Julian Javier	1.75	.90	.50
227	Jim Grant	1.50	.70	.45
228	1963 Rookie Stars *(Max Alvis, Bob Bailey, Ed Kranepool, Pedro Oliva)*	35.00	17.50	10.50
229	Willie Davis	1.50	.70	.45
230	Pete Runnels	1.75	.90	.50
231	Eli Grba (photo actually Ryne Duren)	1.75	.90	.50
232	Frank Malzone	1.75	.90	.50
233	Casey Stengel	12.00	6.00	3.50
234	Dave Nicholson	1.50	.70	.45
235	Billy O'Dell	1.50	.70	.45
236	Bill Bryan	1.50	.70	.45
237	Jim Coates	2.00	1.00	.60
238	Lou Johnson	1.50	.70	.45
239	Harvey Haddix	1.75	.90	.50
240	Rocky Colavito	7.00	3.50	2.00
241	Billy Smith	1.50	.70	.45
242	Power Plus (Hank Aaron, Ernie Banks)	35.00	17.50	10.50
243	Don Leppert	1.50	.70	.45
244	John Tsitouris	1.50	.70	.45
245	Gil Hodges	12.00	6.00	3.50
246	Lee Stange	1.50	.70	.45
247	Yankees Team	10.00	5.00	3.00
248	Tito Francona	1.75	.90	.50
249	Leo Burke	1.50	.70	.45
250	Stan Musial	100.00	45.00	27.00
251	Jack Lamabe	1.50	.70	.45
252	Ron Santo	3.00	1.50	.90
253	1963 Rookie Stars (Len Gabrielson, Pete Jernigan, Deacon Jones, John Wojcik)	1.50	.70	.45
254	Mike Hershberger	1.50	.70	.45
255	Bob Shaw	1.50	.70	.45
256	Jerry Lumpe	1.75	.90	.50
257	Hank Aguirre	1.50	.70	.45
258	Alvin Dark	1.75	.90	.50
259	Johnny Logan	1.75	.90	.50
260	Jim Gentile	1.75	.90	.50
261	Bob Miller	1.50	.70	.45
262	Ellis Burton	1.50	.70	.45
263	Dave Stenhouse	1.50	.70	.45
264	Phil Linz	1.50	.70	.45
265	Vada Pinson	2.50	1.25	.70
266	Bob Allen	1.50	.70	.45
267	Carl Sawatski	1.50	.70	.45
268	Don Demeter	1.50	.70	.45
269	Don Mincher	1.75	.90	.50
270	Felipe Alou	1.75	.90	.50
271	Dean Stone	1.50	.70	.45
272	Danny Murphy	1.50	.70	.45
273	Sammy Taylor	1.75	.90	.50
274	Checklist 265-352	3.00	1.50	.90
275	Ed Mathews	20.00	10.00	6.00
276	Barry Shetrone	1.50	.70	.45
277	Dick Farrell	1.50	.70	.45
278	Chico Fernandez	1.50	.70	.45
279	Wally Moon	1.75	.90	.50
280	Bob Rodgers	1.75	.90	.50
281	Tom Sturdivant	1.50	.70	.45
282	Bob Del Greco	1.50	.70	.45
283	Roy Sievers	1.75	.90	.50
284	Dave Sisler	3.00	1.50	.90
285	Dick Stuart	3.25	1.75	1.00
286	Stu Miller	3.00	1.50	.90
287	Dick Bertell	3.00	1.50	.90
288	White Sox Team	3.50	1.75	1.00
289	Hal Brown	3.50	1.75	1.00
290	Bill White	3.25	1.75	1.00
291	Don Rudolph	3.00	1.50	.90
292	Pumpsie Green	3.25	1.75	1.00
293	Bill Pleis	3.00	1.50	.90
294	Bill Rigney	3.00	1.50	.90
295	Ed Roebuck	3.00	1.50	.90
296	Doc Edwards	3.25	1.75	1.00

		NR MT	EX	VG
297	Jim Golden	3.00	1.50	.90
298	Don Dillard	3.00	1.50	.90
299	1963 Rookie Stars (Tom Butters, Bob Dustal, Dave Morehead, Dan Schneider)	3.00	1.50	.90
300	Willie Mays	125.00	56.00	35.00
301	Bill Fischer	3.00	1.50	.90
302	Whitey Herzog	3.50	1.75	1.00
303	Earl Francis	3.00	1.50	.90
304	Harry Bright	3.00	1.50	.90
305	Don Hoak	3.25	1.75	1.00
306	Star Receivers (Earl Battey, Elston Howard)	3.50	1.75	1.00
307	Chet Nichols	3.00	1.50	.90
308	Camilo Carreon	3.00	1.50	.90
309	Jim Brewer	3.00	1.50	.90
310	Tommy Davis	3.00	1.50	.90
311	Joe McClain	3.00	1.50	.90
312	Colt .45s Team	12.00	6.00	3.50
313	Ernie Broglio	3.00	1.50	.90
314	John Goryl	3.00	1.50	.90
315	Ralph Terry	3.00	1.50	.90
316	Norm Sherry	2.00	1.00	.60
317	Sam McDowell	3.00	1.50	.90
318	Gene Mauch	3.25	1.75	1.00
319	Joe Gaines	3.00	1.50	.90
320	Warren Spahn	25.00	12.50	7.50
321	Gino Cimoli	3.00	1.50	.90
322	Bob Turley	3.25	1.75	1.00
323	Bill Mazeroski	3.50	1.75	1.00
324	1963 Rookie Stars *(Vic Davalillo,* Phil Roof, *Pete Ward,* George Williams)	2.50	1.25	.70
325	Jack Sanford	3.00	1.50	.90
326	Hank Foiles	3.00	1.50	.90
327	Paul Foytack	3.00	1.50	.90
328	Dick Williams	3.50	1.75	1.00
329	Lindy McDaniel	3.00	1.50	.90
330	Chuck Hinton	3.00	1.50	.90
331	Series Foes (Bill Pierce, Bill Stafford)	3.00	1.50	.90
332	Joel Horlen	3.00	1.50	.90
333	Carl Warwick	3.00	1.50	.90
334	Wynn Hawkins	3.25	1.75	1.00
335	Leon Wagner	3.25	1.75	1.00
336	Ed Bauta	3.00	1.50	.90
337	Dodgers Team	10.00	5.00	3.00
338	Russ Kemmerer	3.00	1.50	.90
339	Ted Bowsfield	3.00	1.50	.90
340	Yogi Berra	60.00	30.00	18.00
341	Jack Baldschun	3.00	1.50	.90
342	Gene Woodling	2.50	1.25	.70
343	Johnny Pesky	3.25	1.75	1.00
344	Don Schwall	3.00	1.50	.90
345	Brooks Robinson	30.00	15.00	9.00
346	Billy Hoeft	3.00	1.50	.90
347	Joe Torre	4.50	2.25	1.25
348	Vic Wertz	3.25	1.75	1.00
349	Zoilo Versalles	3.25	1.75	1.00
350	Bob Purkey	3.00	1.50	.90
351	Al Luplow	3.00	1.50	.90
352	Ken Johnson	3.00	1.50	.90
353	Billy Williams	20.00	10.00	6.00
354	Dom Zanni	3.00	1.50	.90
355	Dean Chance	3.25	1.75	1.00
356	John Schaive	3.00	1.50	.90
357	George Altman	3.00	1.50	.90
358	Milt Pappas	3.25	1.75	1.00
359	Haywood Sullivan	3.25	1.75	1.00
360	Don Drysdale	30.00	15.00	9.00
361	Clete Boyer	3.50	1.75	1.00
362	Checklist 353-429	4.00	2.00	1.25
363	Dick Radatz	3.25	1.75	1.00
364	Howie Goss	3.00	1.50	.90
365	Jim Bunning	10.00	5.00	3.00
366	Tony Taylor	3.00	1.50	.90
367	Tony Cloninger	3.25	1.75	1.00
368	Ed Bailey	3.00	1.50	.90
369	Jim Lemon	3.00	1.50	.90
370	Dick Donovan	3.00	1.50	.90
371	Rod Kanehl	3.25	1.75	1.00
372	Don Lee	3.00	1.50	.90
373	Jim Campbell	3.00	1.50	.90
374	Claude Osteen	3.25	1.75	1.00
375	Ken Boyer	4.00	2.00	1.25
376	Johnnie Wyatt	3.00	1.50	.90
377	Orioles Team	3.50	1.75	1.00
378	Bill Henry	3.00	1.50	.90
379	Bob Anderson	3.00	1.50	.90
380	Ernie Banks	40.00	20.00	12.00
381	Frank Baumann	3.00	1.50	.90
382	Ralph Houk	3.50	1.75	1.00

		NR MT	EX	VG
383	Pete Richert	3.00	1.50	.90
384	Bob Tillman	3.00	1.50	.90
385	Art Mahaffey	3.00	1.50	.90
386	1963 Rookie Stars (*John Bateman*, Larry Bearnarth, *Ed Kirkpatrick*, Garry Roggenburk)	3.25	1.75	1.00
387	Al McBean	3.00	1.50	.90
388	Jim Davenport	3.00	1.50	.90
389	Frank Sullivan	3.00	1.50	.90
390	Hank Aaron	125.00	62.00	37.00
391	Bill Dailey	3.00	1.50	.90
392	Tribe Thumpers (Tito Francona, Johnny Romano)	3.25	1.75	1.00
393	Ken MacKenzie	3.25	1.75	1.00
394	Tim McCarver	4.00	2.00	1.25
395	Don McMahon	3.00	1.50	.90
396	Joe Koppe	3.00	1.50	.90
397	Athletics Team	3.50	1.75	1.00
398	Boog Powell	7.00	3.50	2.00
399	Dick Ellsworth	3.00	1.50	.90
400	Frank Robinson	45.00	23.00	13.50
401	Jim Bouton	10.00	5.00	3.00
402	Mickey Vernon	3.25	1.75	1.00
403	Ron Perranoski	3.25	1.75	1.00
404	Bob Oldis	3.00	1.50	.90
405	Floyd Robinson	3.00	1.50	.90
406	Howie Koplitz	3.00	1.50	.90
407	1963 Rookie Stars (Larry Elliot, Frank Kostro, Chico Ruiz, Dick Simpson)	3.00	1.50	.90
408	Billy Gardner	3.00	1.50	.90
409	Roy Face	3.50	1.75	1.00
410	Earl Battey	3.25	1.75	1.00
411	Jim Constable	3.00	1.50	.90
412	Dodgers' Big Three (Don Drysdale, Sandy Koufax, Johnny Podres)	30.00	15.00	9.00
413	Jerry Walker	3.00	1.50	.90
414	Ty Cline	3.00	1.50	.90
415	Bob Gibson	30.00	15.00	9.00
416	Alex Grammas	3.00	1.50	.90
417	Giants Team	3.50	1.75	1.00
418	Johnny Orsino	3.00	1.50	.90
419	Tracy Stallard	3.25	1.75	1.00
420	Bobby Richardson	10.00	5.00	3.00
421	Tom Morgan	3.00	1.50	.90
422	Fred Hutchinson	3.25	1.75	1.00
423	Ed Hobaugh	3.00	1.50	.90
424	Charley Smith	3.00	1.50	.90
425	Smoky Burgess	2.50	1.25	.70
426	Barry Latman	3.00	1.50	.90
427	Bernie Allen	3.00	1.50	.90
428	Carl Boles	3.00	1.50	.90
429	Lou Burdette	3.00	1.50	.90
430	Norm Siebern	3.25	1.75	1.00
431a	Checklist 430-506 ("Checklist" in black on front)	4.50	2.25	1.25
431b	Checklist 430-506 ("Checklist" in white)	7.00	3.50	2.00
432	Roman Mejias	3.00	1.50	.90
433	Denis Menke	3.25	1.75	1.00
434	Johnny Callison	2.50	1.25	.70
435	Woody Held	3.00	1.50	.90
436	Tim Harkness	3.25	1.75	1.00
437	Bill Bruton	3.00	1.50	.90
438	Wes Stock	3.00	1.50	.90
439	Don Zimmer	3.50	1.75	1.00
440	Juan Marichal	20.00	10.00	6.00
441	Lee Thomas	3.00	1.50	.90
442	J.C. Hartman	3.00	1.50	.90
443	Jim Piersall	3.50	1.75	1.00
444	Jim Maloney	3.25	1.75	1.00
445	Norm Cash	3.00	1.50	.90
446	Whitey Ford	35.00	17.50	10.50
447	Felix Mantilla	10.00	5.00	3.00
448	Jack Kralick	10.00	5.00	3.00
449	Jose Tartabull	10.00	5.00	3.00
450	Bob Friend	11.00	5.50	3.25
451	Indians Team	10.00	5.00	3.00
452	Barney Schultz	10.00	5.00	3.00
453	Jake Wood	10.00	5.00	3.00
454a	Art Fowler (card # on orange background)	10.00	5.00	3.00
454b	Art Fowler (card # on white background)	10.00	5.00	3.00
455	Ruben Amaro	10.00	5.00	3.00
456	Jim Coker	10.00	5.00	3.00
457	Tex Clevenger	11.00	5.50	3.25
458	Al Lopez	15.00	7.50	4.50
459	Dick LeMay	10.00	5.00	3.00
460	Del Crandall	11.00	5.50	3.25
461	Norm Bass	10.00	5.00	3.00
462	Wally Post	10.00	5.00	3.00

		NR MT	EX	VG
463	Joe Schaffernoth	10.00	5.00	3.00
464	Ken Aspromonte	10.00	5.00	3.00
465	Chuck Estrada	10.00	5.00	3.00
466	1963 Rookie Stars (*Bill Freehan*, Tony Martinez, Nate Oliver, Jerry Robinson)	30.00	15.00	9.00
467	Phil Ortega	10.00	5.00	3.00
468	Carroll Hardy	10.00	5.00	3.00
469	Jay Hook	11.00	5.50	3.25
470	Tom Tresh	20.00	10.00	6.00
471	Ken Retzer	10.00	5.00	3.00
472	Lou Brock	125.00	62.00	37.00
473	Mets Team	100.00	50.00	30.00
474	Jack Fisher	10.00	5.00	3.00
475	Gus Triandos	10.00	5.00	3.00
476	Frank Funk	10.00	5.00	3.00
477	Donn Clendenon	11.00	5.50	3.25
478	Paul Brown	10.00	5.00	3.00
479	*Ed Brinkman*	11.00	5.50	3.25
480	Bill Monbouquette	11.00	5.50	3.25
481	Bob Taylor	10.00	5.00	3.00
482	Felix Torres	10.00	5.00	3.00
483	Jim Owens	10.00	5.00	3.00
484	Dale Long	11.00	5.50	3.25
485	Jim Landis	10.00	5.00	3.00
486	Ray Sadecki	10.00	5.00	3.00
487	John Roseboro	11.00	5.50	3.25
488	Jerry Adair	10.00	5.00	3.00
489	Paul Toth	10.00	5.00	3.00
490	Willie McCovey	110.00	55.00	33.00
491	Harry Craft	10.00	5.00	3.00
492	Dave Wickersham	10.00	5.00	3.00
493	Walt Bond	10.00	5.00	3.00
494	Phil Regan	10.00	5.00	3.00
495	Frank Thomas	11.00	5.50	3.25
496	1963 Rookie Stars (Carl Bouldin, *Steve Dalkowski*, *Fred Newman*, Jack Smith)	11.00	5.50	3.25
497	Bennie Daniels	10.00	5.00	3.00
498	Eddie Kasko	10.00	5.00	3.00
499	J.C. Martin	10.00	5.00	3.00
500	Harmon Killebrew	100.00	50.00	30.00
501	Joe Azcue	10.00	5.00	3.00
502	Daryl Spencer	10.00	5.00	3.00
503	Braves Team	10.00	5.00	3.00
504	Bob Johnson	10.00	5.00	3.00
505	Curt Flood	12.00	6.00	3.50
506	Gene Green	11.00	5.50	3.25
507	Roland Sheldon	8.00	4.00	2.50
508	Ted Savage	7.00	3.50	2.00
509a	Checklist 507-576 (copyright centered)	15.00	7.50	4.50
509b	Checklist 509-576 (copyright to right)	12.00	6.00	3.50
510	Ken McBride	7.00	3.50	2.00
511	Charlie Neal	7.50	3.75	2.25
512	Cal McLish	7.00	3.50	2.00
513	Gary Geiger	7.00	3.50	2.00
514	Larry Osborne	7.00	3.50	2.00
515	Don Elston	7.00	3.50	2.00
516	Purnal Goldy	7.00	3.50	2.00
517	Hal Woodeshick	7.00	3.50	2.00
518	Don Blasingame	7.00	3.50	2.00
519	Claude Raymond	7.00	3.50	2.00
520	Orlando Cepeda	15.00	7.50	4.50
521	Dan Pfister	7.00	3.50	2.00
522	1963 Rookie Stars (Mel Nelson, Gary Peters, Art Quirk, Jim Roland)	7.50	3.75	2.25
523	Bill Kunkel	8.00	4.00	2.50
524	Cardinals Team	10.00	5.00	3.00
525	Nellie Fox	12.00	6.00	3.50
526	Dick Hall	7.00	3.50	2.00
527	Ed Sadowski	7.00	3.50	2.00
528	Carl Willey	7.50	3.75	2.25
529	Wes Covington	7.00	3.50	2.00
530	Don Mossi	7.50	3.75	2.25
531	Sam Mele	7.00	3.50	2.00
532	Steve Boros	7.00	3.50	2.00
533	Bobby Shantz	8.00	4.00	2.50
534	Ken Walters	7.00	3.50	2.00
535	Jim Perry	8.00	4.00	2.50
536	Norm Larker	7.00	3.50	2.00
537	1963 Rookie Stars (Pedro Gonzalez, *Ken McMullen*, *Pete Rose*, *Al Weis*)	550.00	225.00	165.00
538	George Brunet	7.00	3.50	2.00
539	Wayne Causey	7.00	3.50	2.00
540	Bob Clemente	200.00	100.00	60.00
541	Ron Moeller	7.00	3.50	2.00
542	Lou Klimchock	7.00	3.50	2.00
543	Russ Snyder	7.00	3.50	2.00
544	1963 Rookie Stars (Duke Carmel, Bill Haas, Dick Phillips, *Rusty Staub*)	30.00	15.00	9.00

		NR MT	EX	VG
545	Jose Pagan	7.00	3.50	2.00
546	Hal Reniff	8.00	4.00	2.50
547	Gus Bell	7.50	3.75	2.25
548	Tom Satriano	7.00	3.50	2.00
549	1963 Rookie Stars *(Marcelino Lopez,* Pete Lovrich, Elmo Plaskett, Paul Ratliff)	7.50	3.75	2.25
550	Duke Snider	50.00	25.00	15.00
551	Billy Klaus	7.00	3.50	2.00
552	Tigers Team	12.00	6.00	3.50
553	1963 Rookie Stars (Brock Davis, Jim Gosger, John Herrnstein, *Willie Stargell)*	200.00	100.00	60.00
554	Hank Fischer	7.00	3.50	2.00
555	John Blanchard	8.00	4.00	2.50
556	Al Worthington	7.00	3.50	2.00
557	Cuno Barragan	7.00	3.50	2.00
558	1963 Rookie Stars (Bill Faul, *Ron Hunt,* Bob Lipski, Al Moran)	8.00	4.00	2.50
559	Danny Murtaugh	7.50	3.75	2.25
560	Ray Herbert	7.00	3.50	2.00
561	Mike de la Hoz	7.00	3.50	2.00
562	1963 Rookie Stars (Randy Cardinal, *Dave McNally,* Don Rowe, Ken Rowe)	10.00	5.00	3.00
563	Mike McCormick	7.50	3.75	2.25
564	George Banks	7.00	3.50	2.00
565	Larry Sherry	7.00	3.50	2.00
566	Cliff Cook	7.50	3.75	2.25
567	Jim Duffalo	7.00	3.50	2.00
568	Bob Sadowski	7.00	3.50	2.00
569	Luis Arroyo	8.00	4.00	2.50
570	Frank Bolling	7.00	3.50	2.00
571	Johnny Klippstein	7.00	3.50	2.00
572	Jack Spring	7.00	3.50	2.00
573	Coot Veal	7.00	3.50	2.00
574	Hal Kolstad	7.00	3.50	2.00
575	Don Cardwell	7.50	3.75	2.25
576	Johnny Temple	10.00	5.00	3.00

1963 Topps Peel-Offs

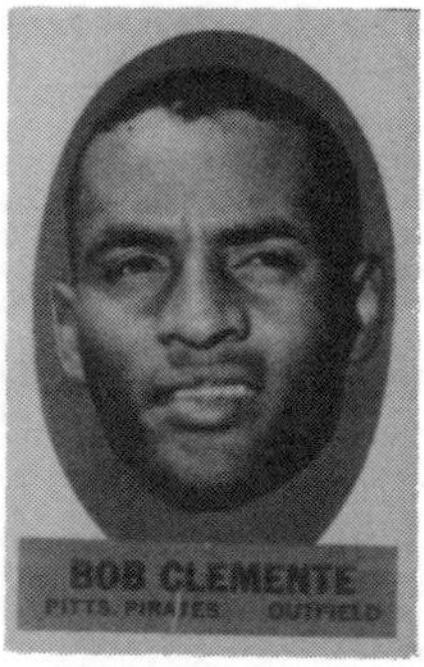

Measuring 1-1/4" by 2-3/4," Topps Peel-Offs were an insert with 1963 Topps baseball cards. There are 46 players in the unnumbered set, each pictured in a color photo inside an oval with the player's name, team and position in a band below. The back of the Peel-Off is removable, leaving a sticky surface that made the Peel-Off a popular decorative item among youngsters of the day. Naturally, that makes them quite scarce today, but as a non-card Topps issue, demand is not particularly strong.

		NR MT	EX	VG
Complete Set:		175.00	87.00	52.00
Common Player:		1.00	.50	.30
(1)	Hank Aaron	10.00	5.00	3.00
(2)	Luis Aparicio	3.00	1.50	.90
(3)	Richie Ashburn	2.00	1.00	.60
(4)	Bob Aspromonte	1.00	.50	.30
(5)	Ernie Banks	5.00	2.50	1.50
(6)	Ken Boyer	1.50	.70	.45
(7)	Jim Bunning	1.75	.90	.50
(8)	Johnny Callison	1.25	.60	.40
(9)	Orlando Cepeda	1.75	.90	.50
(10)	Bob Clemente	8.00	4.00	2.50
(11)	Rocky Colavito	1.75	.90	.50
(12)	Tommy Davis	1.50	.70	.45
(13)	Dick Donovan	1.00	.50	.30
(14)	Don Drysdale	4.00	2.00	1.25
(15)	Dick Farrell	1.00	.50	.30
(16)	Jim Gentile	1.00	.50	.30
(17)	Ray Herbert	1.00	.50	.30
(18)	Chuck Hinton	1.00	.50	.30
(19)	Ken Hubbs	1.50	.70	.45
(20)	Al Jackson	1.00	.50	.30
(21)	Al Kaline	5.00	2.50	1.50
(22)	Harmon Killebrew	5.00	2.50	1.50
(23)	Sandy Koufax	8.00	4.00	2.50
(24)	Jerry Lumpe	1.00	.50	.30
(25)	Art Mahaffey	1.00	.50	.30
(26)	Mickey Mantle	50.00	25.00	15.00
(27)	Willie Mays	10.00	5.00	3.00
(28)	Bill Mazeroski	1.50	.70	.45
(29)	Bill Monbouquette	1.00	.50	.30
(30)	Stan Musial	10.00	5.00	3.00
(31)	Camilo Pascual	1.25	.60	.40
(32)	Bob Purkey	1.00	.50	.30
(33)	Bobby Richardson	1.75	.90	.50
(34)	Brooks Robinson	6.00	3.00	1.75
(35)	Floyd Robinson	1.00	.50	.30
(36)	Frank Robinson	5.00	2.50	1.50
(37)	Bob Rodgers	1.00	.50	.30
(38)	Johnny Romano	1.00	.50	.30
(39)	Jack Sanford	1.00	.50	.30
(40)	Norm Siebern	1.00	.50	.30
(41)	Warren Spahn	5.00	2.50	1.50
(42)	Dave Stenhouse	1.00	.50	.30
(43)	Ralph Terry	1.25	.60	.40
(44)	Lee Thomas	1.00	.50	.30
(45)	Bill White	1.25	.60	.40
(46)	Carl Yastrzemski	12.00	6.00	3.50

1964 Topps

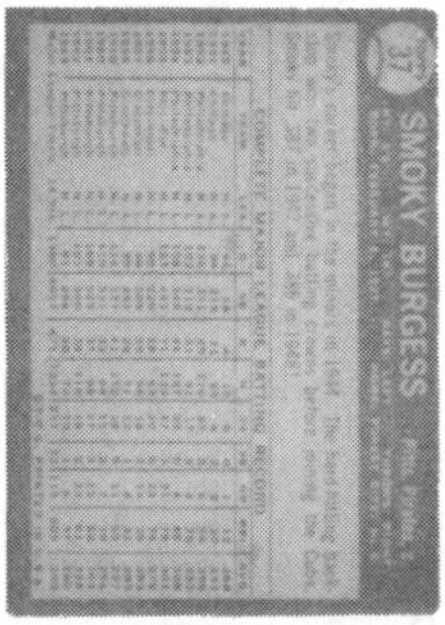

The 1964 Topps set is a 587-card issue of 2-1/2" by 3-1/2" cards which is considered by many as being among the company's best efforts. Card fronts feature a large color photo which blends into a top panel which contains the team name, while a panel below the picture carries the player's name and position. An interesting innovation on the back is a baseball quiz question which required the rubbing of a white panel to reveal the answer. As in 1963, specialty cards remained modest in number with a 12-card set of statistical leaders, a few multi-player cards, rookies and World Series highlights. An interesting card is an "In Memoriam" card for Ken Hubbs who was killed in an airplane crash.

		NR MT	EX	VG
Complete Set:		2600.00	1300.00	800.00
Common Player: 1-370		2.00	1.00	.60
Common Player: 371-522		3.00	1.50	.90
Common Player: 523-587		7.00	3.50	2.00
1	N.L. E.R.A. Leaders (Dick Ellsworth, Bob Friend, Sandy Koufax)	10.00	3.00	1.50
2	A.L. E.R.A. Leaders (Camilo Pascual, Gary Peters, Juan Pizarro)	3.00	1.50	.90
3	N.L. Pitching Leaders (Sandy Koufax, Jim Maloney, Juan Marichal, Warren Spahn)	7.00	3.50	2.00
4a	A.L. Pitching Leaders (Jim Bouton, Whitey Ford, Camilo Pascual) (apostrophe after "Pitching" on back)	7.00	3.50	2.00

		NR MT	EX	VG
4b	A.L. Pitching Leaders (Jim Bouton, Whitey Ford, Camilo Pascual) (no apostrophe)	3.50	1.75	1.00
5	N.L. Strikeout Leaders (Don Drysdale, Sandy Koufax, Jim Maloney)	7.00	3.50	2.00
6	A.L. Strikeout Leaders (Jim Bunning, Camilo Pascual, Dick Stigman)	3.00	1.50	.90
7	N.L. Batting Leaders (Hank Aaron, Bob Clemente, Tommy Davis, Dick Groat)	7.00	3.50	2.00
8	A.L. Batting Leaders (Al Kaline, Rich Rollins, Carl Yastrzemski)	7.00	3.50	2.00
9	N.L. Home Run Leaders (Hank Aaron, Orlando Cepeda, Willie Mays, Willie McCovey)	7.00	3.50	2.00
10	A.L. Home Run Leaders (Bob Allison, Harmon Killebrew, Dick Stuart)	3.50	1.75	1.00
11	N.L. R.B.I. Leaders (Hank Aaron, Ken Boyer, Bill White)	7.50	3.75	2.25
12	A.L. R.B.I. Leaders (Al Kaline, Harmon Killebrew, Dick Stuart)	7.50	3.75	2.25
13	Hoyt Wilhelm	8.00	4.00	2.50
14	Dodgers Rookies (Dick Nen, Nick Willhite)	2.00	1.00	.60
15	Zoilo Versalles	2.00	1.00	.60
16	John Boozer	2.00	1.00	.60
17	Willie Kirkland	2.00	1.00	.60
18	Billy O'Dell	2.00	1.00	.60
19	Don Wert	2.00	1.00	.60
20	Bob Friend	3.75	2.00	1.25
21	Yogi Berra	35.00	17.50	10.50
22	Jerry Adair	2.00	1.00	.60
23	Chris Zachary	2.00	1.00	.60
24	Carl Sawatski	2.00	1.00	.60
25	Bill Monbouquette	2.00	1.00	.60
26	Gino Cimoli	2.00	1.00	.60
27	Mets Team	3.50	1.75	1.00
28	Claude Osteen	2.00	1.00	.60
29	Lou Brock	35.00	17.50	10.50
30	Ron Perranoski	2.00	1.00	.60
31	Dave Nicholson	2.00	1.00	.60
32	Dean Chance	3.75	2.00	1.25
33	Reds Rookies (Sammy Ellis, Mel Queen)	2.00	1.00	.60
34	Jim Perry	3.75	2.00	1.25
35	Ed Mathews	18.00	9.00	5.50
36	Hal Reniff	3.00	1.50	.90
37	Smoky Burgess	3.75	2.00	1.25
38	*Jim Wynn*	3.25	1.75	1.00
39	Hank Aguirre	2.00	1.00	.60
40	Dick Groat	3.25	1.75	1.00
41	Friendly Foes (Willie McCovey, Leon Wagner)	3.00	1.50	.90
42	Moe Drabowsky	2.00	1.00	.60
43	Roy Sievers	2.25	1.25	.70
44	Duke Carmel	2.00	1.00	.60
45	Milt Pappas	2.25	1.25	.70
46	Ed Brinkman	2.00	1.00	.60
47	Giants Rookies (*Jesus Alou*, Ron Herbel)	3.75	2.00	1.25
48	Bob Perry	2.00	1.00	.60
49	Bill Henry	2.00	1.00	.60
50	Mickey Mantle	250.00	125.00	75.00
51	Pete Richert	2.00	1.00	.60
52	Chuck Hinton	2.00	1.00	.60
53	Denis Menke	2.00	1.00	.60
54	Sam Mele	2.00	1.00	.60
55	Ernie Banks	30.00	15.00	9.00
56	Hal Brown	2.00	1.00	.60
57	Tim Harkness	2.00	1.00	.60
58	Don Demeter	2.00	1.00	.60
59	Ernie Broglio	2.00	1.00	.60
60	Frank Malzone	2.00	1.00	.60
61	Angel Backstops (Bob Rodgers, Ed Sadowski)	2.00	1.00	.60
62	Ted Savage	2.00	1.00	.60
63	Johnny Orsino	2.00	1.00	.60
64	Ted Abernathy	2.00	1.00	.60
65	Felipe Alou	3.75	2.00	1.25
66	Eddie Fisher	2.00	1.00	.60
67	Tigers Team	3.50	1.75	1.00
68	Willie Davis	3.25	1.75	1.00
69	Clete Boyer	3.25	1.75	1.00
70	Joe Torre	2.50	1.25	.70
71	Jack Spring	2.00	1.00	.60
72	Chico Cardenas	2.00	1.00	.60
73	*Jimmie Hall*	2.00	1.00	.60
74	Pirates Rookies (Tom Butters, Bob Priddy)	2.00	1.00	.60
75	Wayne Causey	2.00	1.00	.60
76	Checklist 1-88	3.00	1.50	.90
77	Jerry Walker	2.00	1.00	.60
78	Merritt Ranew	2.00	1.00	.60

		NR MT	EX	VG
79	Bob Heffner	2.00	1.00	.60
80	Vada Pinson	2.50	1.25	.70
81	All-Star Vets (Nellie Fox, Harmon Killebrew)	7.00	3.50	2.00
82	Jim Davenport	2.00	1.00	.60
83	Gus Triandos	2.00	1.00	.60
84	Carl Willey	2.00	1.00	.60
85	Pete Ward	2.00	1.00	.60
86	Al Downing	3.25	1.75	1.00
87	Cardinals Team	7.00	3.50	2.00
88	John Roseboro	2.00	1.00	.60
89	Boog Powell	2.50	1.25	.70
90	Earl Battey	2.00	1.00	.60
91	Bob Bailey	2.00	1.00	.60
92	Steve Ridzik	2.00	1.00	.60
93	Gary Geiger	2.00	1.00	.60
94	Braves Rookies (Jim Britton, Larry Maxie)	2.00	1.00	.60
95	George Altman	2.00	1.00	.60
96	Bob Buhl	2.00	1.00	.60
97	Jim Fregosi	3.75	2.00	1.25
98	Bill Bruton	2.00	1.00	.60
99	Al Stanek	2.00	1.00	.60
100	Elston Howard	7.00	3.50	2.00
101	Walt Alston	3.00	1.50	.90
102	Checklist 89-176	3.00	1.50	.90
103	Curt Flood	3.00	1.50	.90
104	Art Mahaffey	2.00	1.00	.60
105	Woody Held	2.00	1.00	.60
106	Joe Nuxhall	2.00	1.00	.60
107	White Sox Rookies (Bruce Howard, Frank Kreutzer)	2.00	1.00	.60
108	John Wyatt	2.00	1.00	.60
109	Rusty Staub	9.00	4.50	2.75
110	Albie Pearson	2.00	1.00	.60
111	Don Elston	2.00	1.00	.60
112	Bob Tillman	2.00	1.00	.60
113	Grover Powell	2.00	1.00	.60
114	Don Lock	2.00	1.00	.60
115	Frank Bolling	2.00	1.00	.60
116	Twins Rookies (Tony Oliva, Jay Ward)	8.00	4.00	2.50
117	Earl Francis	2.00	1.00	.60
118	John Blanchard	3.00	1.50	.90
119	Gary Kolb	2.00	1.00	.60
120	Don Drysdale	18.00	9.00	5.50
121	Pete Runnels	2.00	1.00	.60
122	Don McMahon	2.00	1.00	.60
123	Jose Pagan	2.00	1.00	.60
124	Orlando Pena	2.00	1.00	.60
125	Pete Rose	150.00	75.00	45.00
126	Russ Snyder	2.00	1.00	.60
127	Angels Rookies (Aubrey Gatewood, Dick Simpson)	2.00	1.00	.60
128	*Mickey Lolich*	12.00	6.00	3.50
129	Amado Samuel	2.00	1.00	.60
130	Gary Peters	2.00	1.00	.60
131	Steve Boros	2.00	1.00	.60
132	Braves Team	3.75	2.00	1.25
133	Jim Grant	2.00	1.00	.60
134	Don Zimmer	3.25	1.75	1.00
135	Johnny Callison	3.25	1.75	1.00
136	World Series Game 1 (Koufax Strikes Out 15)	7.00	3.50	2.00
137	World Series Game 2 (Davis Sparks Rally)	2.50	1.25	.70
138	World Series Game 3 (L.A. Takes 3rd Straight)	2.50	1.25	.70
139	World Series Game 4 (Sealing Yanks' Doom)	2.50	1.25	.70
140	World Series Summary (The Dodgers Celebrate)	2.50	1.25	.70
141	Danny Murtaugh	2.00	1.00	.60
142	John Bateman	2.00	1.00	.60
143	Bubba Phillips	2.00	1.00	.60
144	Al Worthington	2.00	1.00	.60
145	Norm Siebern	2.00	1.00	.60
146	Indians Rookies (Bob Chance, *Tommy John*)	70.00	35.00	20.00
147	Ray Sadecki	2.00	1.00	.60
148	J.C. Martin	2.00	1.00	.60
149	Paul Foytack	2.00	1.00	.60
150	Willie Mays	90.00	45.00	27.00
151	Athletics Team	3.75	2.00	1.25
152	Denver Lemaster	2.00	1.00	.60
153	Dick Williams	3.25	1.75	1.00
154	Dick Tracewski	2.00	1.00	.60
155	Duke Snider	25.00	12.50	7.50
156	Bill Dailey	2.00	1.00	.60
157	Gene Mauch	2.25	1.25	.70
158	Ken Johnson	2.00	1.00	.60

		NR MT	EX	VG
159	Charlie Dees	2.00	1.00	.60
160	Ken Boyer	7.00	3.50	2.00
161	Dave McNally	3.75	2.00	1.25
162	Hitting Area (Vada Pinson, Dick Sisler)	2.00	1.00	.60
163	Donn Clendenon	3.00	1.50	.90
164	Bud Daley	3.00	1.50	.90
165	Jerry Lumpe	2.00	1.00	.60
166	Marty Keough	2.00	1.00	.60
167	Senators Rookies (Mike Brumley, *Lou Piniella*)	25.00	12.50	7.50
168	Al Weis	2.00	1.00	.60
169	Del Crandall	3.75	2.00	1.25
170	Dick Radatz	2.00	1.00	.60
171	Ty Cline	2.00	1.00	.60
172	Indians Team	3.75	2.00	1.25
173	Ryne Duren	2.25	1.25	.70
174	Doc Edwards	2.00	1.00	.60
175	Billy Williams	12.00	6.00	3.50
176	Tracy Stallard	2.00	1.00	.60
177	Harmon Killebrew	20.00	10.00	6.00
178	Hank Bauer	2.25	1.25	.70
179	Carl Warwick	2.00	1.00	.60
180	Tommy Davis	3.25	1.75	1.00
181	Dave Wickersham	2.00	1.00	.60
182	Sox Sockers (Chuck Schilling, Carl Yastrzemski)	7.00	3.50	2.00
183	Ron Taylor	2.00	1.00	.60
184	Al Luplow	2.00	1.00	.60
185	Jim O'Toole	2.00	1.00	.60
186	Roman Mejias	2.00	1.00	.60
187	Ed Roebuck	2.00	1.00	.60
188	Checklist 177-264	3.00	1.50	.90
189	Bob Hendley	2.00	1.00	.60
190	Bobby Richardson	7.50	3.75	2.25
191	Clay Dalrymple	2.00	1.00	.60
192	Cubs Rookies (John Boccabella, Billy Cowan)	2.00	1.00	.60
193	Jerry Lynch	2.00	1.00	.60
194	John Goryl	2.00	1.00	.60
195	Floyd Robinson	2.00	1.00	.60
196	Jim Gentile	2.00	1.00	.60
197	Frank Lary	2.00	1.00	.60
198	Len Gabrielson	2.00	1.00	.60
199	Joe Azcue	2.00	1.00	.60
200	Sandy Koufax	90.00	45.00	27.00
201	Orioles Rookies (Sam Bowens, *Wally Bunker*)	2.00	1.00	.60
202	Galen Cisco	2.00	1.00	.60
203	John Kennedy	2.00	1.00	.60
204	Matty Alou	2.25	1.25	.70
205	Nellie Fox	7.00	3.50	2.00
206	Steve Hamilton	3.00	1.50	.90
207	Fred Hutchinson	2.00	1.00	.60
208	Wes Covington	2.00	1.00	.60
209	Bob Allen	2.00	1.00	.60
210	Carl Yastrzemski	80.00	40.00	25.00
211	Jim Coker	2.00	1.00	.60
212	Pete Lovrich	2.00	1.00	.60
213	Angels Team	3.75	2.00	1.25
214	Ken McMullen	2.00	1.00	.60
215	Ray Herbert	2.00	1.00	.60
216	Mike de la Hoz	2.00	1.00	.60
217	Jim King	2.00	1.00	.60
218	Hank Fischer	2.00	1.00	.60
219	Young Aces (Jim Bouton, Al Downing)	3.00	1.50	.90
220	Dick Ellsworth	2.00	1.00	.60
221	Bob Saverine	2.00	1.00	.60
222	Bill Pierce	2.25	1.25	.70
223	George Banks	2.00	1.00	.60
224	Tommie Sisk	2.00	1.00	.60
225	Roger Maris	45.00	23.00	13.50
226	Colts Rookies (*Gerald Grote*, Larry Yellen)	3.75	2.00	1.25
227	Barry Latman	2.00	1.00	.60
228	Felix Mantilla	2.00	1.00	.60
229	Charley Lau	2.00	1.00	.60
230	Brooks Robinson	20.00	10.00	6.00
231	Dick Calmus	2.00	1.00	.60
232	Al Lopez	3.00	1.50	.90
233	Hal Smith	2.00	1.00	.60
234	Gary Bell	2.00	1.00	.60
235	Ron Hunt	2.00	1.00	.60
236	Bill Faul	2.00	1.00	.60
237	Cubs Team	3.75	2.00	1.25
238	Roy McMillan	2.00	1.00	.60
239	Herm Starrette	2.00	1.00	.60
240	Bill White	3.25	1.75	1.00
241	Jim Owens	2.00	1.00	.60
242	Harvey Kuenn	3.25	1.75	1.00
243	Phillies Rookies (*Richie Allen*, John Herrnstein)	10.00	5.00	3.00
244	*Tony LaRussa*	12.00	6.00	3.50
245	Dick Stigman	2.00	1.00	.60
246	Manny Mota	3.75	2.00	1.25
247	Dave DeBusschere	3.00	1.50	.90
248	Johnny Pesky	2.00	1.00	.60
249	Doug Camilli	2.00	1.00	.60
250	Al Kaline	30.00	15.00	9.00
251	Choo Choo Coleman	2.00	1.00	.60
252	Ken Aspromonte	2.00	1.00	.60
253	Wally Post	2.00	1.00	.60
254	Don Hoak	2.00	1.00	.60
255	Lee Thomas	2.00	1.00	.60
256	Johnny Weekly	2.00	1.00	.60
257	Giants Team	3.75	2.00	1.25
258	Garry Roggenburk	2.00	1.00	.60
259	Harry Bright	3.00	1.50	.90
260	Frank Robinson	25.00	12.50	7.50
261	Jim Hannan	2.00	1.00	.60
262	Cardinals Rookie Stars (Harry Fanok, *Mike Shannon*)	3.25	1.75	1.00
263	Chuck Estrada	2.00	1.00	.60
264	Jim Landis	2.00	1.00	.60
265	Jim Bunning	7.00	3.50	2.00
266	Gene Freese	2.00	1.00	.60
267	*Wilbur Wood*	3.25	1.75	1.00
268	Bill's Got It (Danny Murtaugh, Bill Virdon)	2.25	1.25	.70
269	Ellis Burton	2.00	1.00	.60
270	Rich Rollins	2.00	1.00	.60
271	Bob Sadowski	2.00	1.00	.60
272	Jake Wood	2.00	1.00	.60
273	Mel Nelson	2.00	1.00	.60
274	Checklist 265-352	3.00	1.50	.90
275	John Tsitouris	2.00	1.00	.60
276	Jose Tartabull	2.00	1.00	.60
277	Ken Retzer	2.00	1.00	.60
278	Bobby Shantz	3.25	1.75	1.00
279	Joe Koppe	2.00	1.00	.60
280	Juan Marichal	10.00	5.00	3.00
281	Yankees Rookies (Jake Gibbs, Tom Metcalf)	3.00	1.50	.90
282	Bob Bruce	2.00	1.00	.60
283	*Tommy McCraw*	2.00	1.00	.60
284	Dick Schofield	2.00	1.00	.60
285	Robin Roberts	10.00	5.00	3.00
286	Don Landrum	2.00	1.00	.60
287	Red Sox Rookies (*Tony Conigliaro*, Bill Spanswick)	25.00	12.50	7.50
288	Al Moran	2.00	1.00	.60
289	Frank Funk	2.00	1.00	.60
290	Bob Allison	2.25	1.25	.70
291	Phil Ortega	2.00	1.00	.60
292	Mike Roarke	2.00	1.00	.60
293	Phillies Team	3.75	2.00	1.25
294	Ken Hunt	2.00	1.00	.60
295	Roger Craig	3.25	1.75	1.00
296	Ed Kirkpatrick	2.00	1.00	.60
297	Ken MacKenzie	2.00	1.00	.60
298	Harry Craft	2.00	1.00	.60
299	Bill Stafford	3.00	1.50	.90
300	Hank Aaron	100.00	50.00	30.00
301	Larry Brown	2.00	1.00	.60
302	Dan Pfister	2.00	1.00	.60
303	Jim Campbell	2.00	1.00	.60
304	Bob Johnson	2.00	1.00	.60
305	Jack Lamabe	2.00	1.00	.60
306	Giant Gunners (Orlando Cepeda, Willie Mays)	18.00	9.00	5.50
307	Joe Gibbon	2.00	1.00	.60
308	Gene Stephens	2.00	1.00	.60
309	Paul Toth	2.00	1.00	.60
310	Jim Gilliam	3.00	1.50	.90
311	Tom Brown	2.00	1.00	.60
312	Tigers Rookies (Fritz Fisher, Fred Gladding)	2.00	1.00	.60
313	Chuck Hiller	2.00	1.00	.60
314	Jerry Buchek	2.00	1.00	.60
315	Bo Belinsky	2.25	1.25	.70
316	Gene Oliver	2.00	1.00	.60
317	Al Smith	2.00	1.00	.60
318	Twins Team	3.75	2.00	1.25
319	Paul Brown	2.00	1.00	.60
320	Rocky Colavito	3.00	1.50	.90
321	Bob Lillis	2.00	1.00	.60
322	George Brunet	2.00	1.00	.60
323	John Buzhardt	2.00	1.00	.60
324	Casey Stengel	15.00	7.50	4.50
325	Hector Lopez	3.00	1.50	.90
326	Ron Brand	2.00	1.00	.60

		NR MT	EX	VG
327	Don Blasingame	2.00	1.00	.60
328	Bob Shaw	2.00	1.00	.60
329	Russ Nixon	2.00	1.00	.60
330	Tommy Harper	2.00	1.00	.60
331	A.L. Bombers (Norm Cash, Al Kaline, Mickey Mantle, Roger Maris)	70.00	35.00	21.00
332	Ray Washburn	2.00	1.00	.60
333	Billy Moran	2.00	1.00	.60
334	Lew Krausse	2.00	1.00	.60
335	Don Mossi	2.00	1.00	.60
336	Andre Rodgers	2.00	1.00	.60
337	Dodgers Rookies *(Al Ferrara, Jeff Torborg)*	2.00	1.00	.60
338	Jack Kralick	2.00	1.00	.60
339	Walt Bond	2.00	1.00	.60
340	Joe Cunningham	2.00	1.00	.60
341	Jim Roland	2.00	1.00	.60
342	Willie Stargell	40.00	20.00	12.00
343	Senators Team	3.75	2.00	1.25
344	Phil Linz	3.00	1.50	.90
345	Frank Thomas	2.00	1.00	.60
346	Joe Jay	2.00	1.00	.60
347	Bobby Wine	2.00	1.00	.60
348	Ed Lopat	2.25	1.25	.70
349	Art Fowler	2.00	1.00	.60
350	Willie McCovey	20.00	10.00	6.00
351	Dan Schneider	2.00	1.00	.60
352	Eddie Bressoud	2.00	1.00	.60
353	Wally Moon	2.25	1.25	.70
354	Dave Giusti	2.00	1.00	.60
355	Vic Power	2.00	1.00	.60
356	Reds Rookies (Bill McCool, Chico Ruiz)	2.00	1.00	.60
357	Charley James	2.00	1.00	.60
358	Ron Kline	2.00	1.00	.60
359	Jim Schaffer	2.00	1.00	.60
360	Joe Pepitone	2.50	1.25	.70
361	Jay Hook	2.00	1.00	.60
362	Checklist 353-429	3.00	1.50	.90
363	Dick McAuliffe	2.00	1.00	.60
364	Joe Gaines	2.00	1.00	.60
365	Cal McLish	2.00	1.00	.60
366	Nelson Mathews	2.00	1.00	.60
367	Fred Whitfield	2.00	1.00	.60
368	White Sox Rookies (Fritz Ackley, *Don Buford*)	2.25	1.25	.70
369	Jerry Zimmerman	2.00	1.00	.60
370	Hal Woodeshick	2.00	1.00	.60
371	Frank Howard	3.00	1.50	.90
372	Howie Koplitz	3.00	1.50	.90
373	Pirates Team	3.00	1.50	.90
374	Bobby Bolin	3.00	1.50	.90
375	Ron Santo	2.50	1.25	.70
376	Dave Morehead	3.00	1.50	.90
377	Bob Skinner	3.00	1.50	.90
378	Braves Rookies (Jack Smith, *Woody Woodward*)	3.75	2.00	1.25
379	Tony Gonzalez	3.00	1.50	.90
380	Whitey Ford	25.00	12.50	7.50
381	Bob Taylor	3.75	2.00	1.25
382	Wes Stock	3.00	1.50	.90
383	Bill Rigney	3.00	1.50	.90
384	Ron Hansen	3.00	1.50	.90
385	Curt Simmons	3.75	2.00	1.25
386	Lenny Green	3.00	1.50	.90
387	Terry Fox	3.00	1.50	.90
388	Athletics Rookies (John O'Donoghue, George Williams)	3.00	1.50	.90
389	Jim Umbricht	3.00	1.50	.90
390	Orlando Cepeda	9.00	4.50	2.75
391	Sam McDowell	3.75	2.00	1.25
392	Jim Pagliaroni	3.00	1.50	.90
393	Casey Teaches (Ed Kranepool, Casey Stengel)	7.00	3.50	2.00
394	Bob Miller	3.00	1.50	.90
395	Tom Tresh	3.00	1.50	.90
396	Dennis Bennett	3.00	1.50	.90
397	Chuck Cottier	3.00	1.50	.90
398	Mets Rookies (Bill Haas, Dick Smith)	3.75	2.00	1.25
399	Jackie Brandt	3.00	1.50	.90
400	Warren Spahn	25.00	12.50	7.50
401	Charlie Maxwell	3.00	1.50	.90
402	Tom Sturdivant	3.00	1.50	.90
403	Reds Team	3.50	1.75	1.00
404	Tony Martinez	3.00	1.50	.90
405	Ken McBride	3.00	1.50	.90
406	Al Spangler	3.00	1.50	.90
407	Bill Freehan	3.00	1.50	.90
408	Cubs Rookies (Fred Burdette, Jim Stewart)	3.00	1.50	.90

		NR MT	EX	VG
409	Bill Fischer	3.00	1.50	.90
410	Dick Stuart	3.75	2.00	1.25
411	Lee Walls	3.00	1.50	.90
412	Ray Culp	3.00	1.50	.90
413	Johnny Keane	3.00	1.50	.90
414	Jack Sanford	3.00	1.50	.90
415	Tony Kubek	7.00	3.50	2.00
416	Lee Maye	3.00	1.50	.90
417	Don Cardwell	3.00	1.50	.90
418	Orioles Rookies *(Darold Knowles*, Les Narum)	3.75	2.00	1.25
419	*Ken Harrelson*	7.00	3.50	2.00
420	Jim Maloney	3.75	2.00	1.25
421	Camilo Carreon	3.00	1.50	.90
422	Jack Fisher	3.75	2.00	1.25
423	Tops In NL (Hank Aaron, Willie Mays)	80.00	40.00	25.00
424	Dick Bertell	3.00	1.50	.90
425	Norm Cash	2.50	1.25	.70
426	Bob Rodgers	3.75	2.00	1.25
427	Don Rudolph	3.00	1.50	.90
428	Red Sox Rookies (Archie Skeen, Pete Smith)	3.00	1.50	.90
429	Tim McCarver	3.00	1.50	.90
430	Juan Pizarro	3.00	1.50	.90
431	George Alusik	3.00	1.50	.90
432	Ruben Amaro	3.00	1.50	.90
433	Yankees Team	10.00	5.00	3.00
434	Don Nottebart	3.00	1.50	.90
435	Vic Davalillo	3.00	1.50	.90
436	Charlie Neal	3.00	1.50	.90
437	Ed Bailey	3.00	1.50	.90
438	Checklist 430-506	7.00	3.50	2.00
439	Harvey Haddix	3.25	1.75	1.00
440	Bob Clemente	100.00	50.00	30.00
441	Bob Duliba	3.00	1.50	.90
442	Pumpsie Green	3.75	2.00	1.25
443	Chuck Dressen	3.75	2.00	1.25
444	Larry Jackson	3.00	1.50	.90
445	Bill Skowron	2.50	1.25	.70
446	Julian Javier	3.75	2.00	1.25
447	Ted Bowsfield	3.00	1.50	.90
448	Cookie Rojas	3.75	2.00	1.25
449	Deron Johnson	3.00	1.50	.90
450	Steve Barber	3.00	1.50	.90
451	Joe Amalfitano	3.00	1.50	.90
452	Giants Rookies (Gil Garrido, *Jim Hart)*	3.75	2.00	1.25
453	Frank Baumann	3.00	1.50	.90
454	Tommie Aaron	3.75	2.00	1.25
455	Bernie Allen	3.00	1.50	.90
456	Dodgers Rookies *(Wes Parker*, John Werhas)	3.00	1.50	.90
457	Jesse Gonder	3.75	2.00	1.25
458	Ralph Terry	3.00	1.50	.90
459	Red Sox Rookies (Pete Charton, Dalton Jones)	3.00	1.50	.90
460	Bob Gibson	20.00	10.00	6.00
461	George Thomas	3.00	1.50	.90
462	Birdie Tebbetts	3.00	1.50	.90
463	Don Leppert	3.00	1.50	.90
464	Dallas Green	3.75	2.00	1.25
465	Mike Hershberger	3.00	1.50	.90
466	Athletics Rookies *(Dick Green*, Aurelio Monteagudo)	3.75	2.00	1.25
467	Bob Aspromonte	3.00	1.50	.90
468	Gaylord Perry	40.00	20.00	12.00
469	Cubs Rookies (Fred Norman, Sterling Slaughter)	3.00	1.50	.90
470	Jim Bouton	3.00	1.50	.90
471	*Gates Brown*	3.75	2.00	1.25
472	Vern Law	3.25	1.75	1.00
473	Orioles Team	3.00	1.50	.90
474	Larry Sherry	3.00	1.50	.90
475	Ed Charles	3.00	1.50	.90
476	Braves Rookies *(Rico Carty*, Dick Kelley)	7.00	3.50	2.00
477	Mike Joyce	2.25	1.25	.70
478	Dick Howser	3.00	1.50	.90
479	Cardinals Rookies (Dave Bakenhaster, Johnny Lewis)	3.00	1.50	.90
480	Bob Purkey	3.00	1.50	.90
481	Chuck Schilling	3.00	1.50	.90
482	Phillies Rookies *(John Briggs, Danny Cater)*	3.75	2.00	1.25
483	Fred Valentine	3.00	1.50	.90
484	Bill Pleis	3.00	1.50	.90
485	Tom Haller	3.75	2.00	1.25
486	Bob Kennedy	3.00	1.50	.90
487	Mike McCormick	3.75	2.00	1.25
488	Yankees Rookies (Bob Meyer, Pete Mikkelsen)	3.25	1.75	1.00

		NR MT	EX	VG
489	Julio Navarro	3.00	1.50	.90
490	Ron Fairly	3.25	1.75	1.00
491	Ed Rakow	3.00	1.50	.90
492	Colts Rookies (Jim Beauchamp, Mike White)	3.00	1.50	.90
493	Don Lee	3.00	1.50	.90
494	Al Jackson	3.75	2.00	1.25
495	Bill Virdon	3.00	1.50	.90
496	White Sox Team	3.00	1.50	.90
497	Jeoff Long	3.00	1.50	.90
498	Dave Stenhouse	3.00	1.50	.90
499	Indians Rookies (Chico Salmon, Gordon Seyfried)	3.00	1.50	.90
500	Camilo Pascual	3.75	2.00	1.25
501	Bob Veale	3.75	2.00	1.25
502	Angels Rookies (*Bobby Knoop*, Bob Lee)	3.75	2.00	1.25
503	Earl Wilson	3.00	1.50	.90
504	Claude Raymond	3.00	1.50	.90
505	Stan Williams	3.25	1.75	1.00
506	Bobby Bragan	3.75	2.00	1.25
507	John Edwards	3.00	1.50	.90
508	Diego Segui	3.00	1.50	.90
509	Pirates Rookies (*Gene Alley*, Orlando McFarlane)	3.75	2.00	1.25
510	Lindy McDaniel	3.00	1.50	.90
511	Lou Jackson	3.00	1.50	.90
512	Tigers Rookies (*Willie Horton, Joe Sparma*)	7.00	3.50	2.00
513	Don Larsen	3.25	1.75	1.00
514	Jim Hickman	3.75	2.00	1.25
515	Johnny Romano	3.00	1.50	.90
516	Twins Rookies (Jerry Arrigo, Dwight Siebler)	3.00	1.50	.90
517a	Checklist 507-587 (wrong numbering on back)	7.00	3.50	2.00
517b	Checklist 507-587 (correct numbering on back)	7.50	3.75	2.25
518	Carl Bouldin	3.00	1.50	.90
519	Charlie Smith	3.75	2.00	1.25
520	Jack Baldschun	3.00	1.50	.90
521	Tom Satriano	3.00	1.50	.90
522	Bobby Tiefenauer	3.00	1.50	.90
523	Lou Burdette	9.00	4.50	2.75
524	Reds Rookies (Jim Dickson, Bobby Klaus)	7.00	3.50	2.00
525	Al McBean	7.00	3.50	2.00
526	Lou Clinton	7.00	3.50	2.00
527	Larry Bearnarth	7.50	3.75	2.25
528	Athletics Rookies (*Dave Duncan*, Tom Reynolds)	7.50	3.75	2.25
529	Al Dark	7.50	3.75	2.25
530	Leon Wagner	7.50	3.75	2.25
531	Dodgers Team	8.00	4.00	2.50
532	Twins Rookies (Bud Bloomfield, Joe Nossek)	7.00	3.50	2.00
533	Johnny Klippstein	7.00	3.50	2.00
534	Gus Bell	7.50	3.75	2.25
535	Phil Regan	7.00	3.50	2.00
536	Mets Rookies (Larry Elliot, John Stephenson)	7.50	3.75	2.25
537	Dan Osinski	7.00	3.50	2.00
538	Minnie Minoso	8.00	4.00	2.50
539	Roy Face	7.00	3.50	2.00
540	Luis Aparicio	15.00	7.50	4.50
541	Braves Rookies (*Phil Niekro*, Phil Roof)	150.00	60.00	38.00
542	Don Mincher	7.50	3.75	2.25
543	Bob Uecker	75.00	38.00	23.00
544	Colts Rookies (Steve Hertz, Joe Hoerner)	7.00	3.50	2.00
545	Max Alvis	7.50	3.75	2.25
546	Joe Christopher	7.50	3.75	2.25
547	Gil Hodges	12.00	6.00	3.50
548	N.L. Rookies (Wayne Schurr, Paul Speckenbach)	7.00	3.50	2.00
549	Joe Moeller	7.00	3.50	2.00
550	Ken Hubbs	10.00	5.00	3.00
551	Billy Hoeft	7.00	3.50	2.00
552	Indians Rookies (Tom Kelley, *Sonny Siebert*)	7.50	3.75	2.25
553	Jim Brewer	7.00	3.50	2.00
554	Hank Foiles	7.00	3.50	2.00
555	Lee Stange	7.00	3.50	2.00
556	Mets Rookies (Steve Dillon, Ron Locke)	7.50	3.75	2.25
557	Leo Burke	7.00	3.50	2.00
558	Don Schwall	7.00	3.50	2.00
559	Dick Phillips	7.00	3.50	2.00
560	Dick Farrell	7.00	3.50	2.00
561	Phillies Rookies (Dave Bennett, *Rick Wise*)	7.50	3.75	2.25
562	Pedro Ramos	7.00	3.50	2.00
563	Dal Maxvill	7.50	3.75	2.25
564	A.L. Rookies (Joe McCabe, Jerry McNertney)	7.00	3.50	2.00
565	Stu Miller	7.00	3.50	2.00
566	Ed Kranepool	7.00	3.50	2.00
567	Jim Kaat	12.00	6.00	3.50
568	N.L. Rookies (Phil Gagliano, Cap Peterson)	7.00	3.50	2.00
569	Fred Newman	7.00	3.50	2.00
570	Bill Mazeroski	8.00	4.00	2.50
571	Gene Conley	3.50	1.75	1.00
572	A.L. Rookies (Dick Egan, Dave Gray)	7.00	3.50	2.00
573	Jim Duffalo	7.00	3.50	2.00
574	Manny Jimenez	7.00	3.50	2.00
575	Tony Cloninger	7.50	3.75	2.25
576	Mets Rookies (Jerry Hinsley, Bill Wakefield)	7.50	3.75	2.25
577	Gordy Coleman	7.00	3.50	2.00
578	Glen Hobbie	7.00	3.50	2.00
579	Red Sox Team	15.00	7.50	4.50
580	Johnny Podres	9.00	4.50	2.75
581	Yankees Rookies (Pedro Gonzalez, Archie Moore)	7.00	3.50	2.00
582	Rod Kanehl	7.50	3.75	2.25
583	Tito Francona	7.50	3.75	2.25
584	Joel Horlen	7.00	3.50	2.00
585	Tony Taylor	7.00	3.50	2.00
586	Jim Piersall	9.00	4.50	2.75
587	Bennie Daniels	8.00	2.50	1.25

1964 Topps Coins

The 164 metal coins in this set were issued by Topps as inserts in the company's baseball card wax packs. The series is divided into two principal types, 120 "regular" coins and 44 All-Star coins. The 1-1/2" diameter coins feature a full-color background for the player photos in the "regular" series, while the players in the All-Star series are featured against plain red or blue backgrounds. There are two variations each of the Mantle, Causey and Hinton coins among the All-Star subset.

		NR MT	EX	VG
Complete Set:		700.00	350.00	210.00
Common Player:		1.00	.50	.30
1	Don Zimmer	1.00	.50	.30
2	Jim Wynn	1.00	.50	.30
3	Johnny Orsino	1.00	.50	.30
4	Jim Bouton	1.25	.60	.40
5	Dick Groat	1.25	.60	.40
6	Leon Wagner	1.00	.50	.30
7	Frank Malzone	1.00	.50	.30
8	Steve Barber	1.00	.50	.30
9	Johnny Romano	1.00	.50	.30
10	Tom Tresh	1.25	.60	.40
11	Felipe Alou	1.00	.50	.30
12	Dick Stuart	1.00	.50	.30
13	Claude Osteen	1.00	.50	.30
14	Juan Pizarro	1.00	.50	.30
15	Donn Clendenon	1.00	.50	.30
16	Jimmie Hall	1.00	.50	.30
17	Larry Jackson	1.00	.50	.30
18	Brooks Robinson	12.00	6.00	3.50

		NR MT	EX	VG
9	Johnny Romano	1.00	.50	.30
10	Tom Tresh	1.25	.60	.40
11	Felipe Alou	1.00	.50	.30
12	Dick Stuart	1.00	.50	.30
13	Claude Osteen	1.00	.50	.30
14	Juan Pizarro	1.00	.50	.30
15	Donn Clendenon	1.00	.50	.30
16	Jimmie Hall	1.00	.50	.30
17	Larry Jackson	1.00	.50	.30
18	Brooks Robinson	12.00	6.00	3.50
19	Bob Allison	1.00	.50	.30
20	Ed Roebuck	1.00	.50	.30
21	Pete Ward	1.00	.50	.30
22	Willie McCovey	8.00	4.00	2.50
23	Elston Howard	1.50	.70	.45
24	Diego Segui	1.00	.50	.30
25	Ken Boyer	1.50	.70	.45
26	Carl Yastrzemski	20.00	10.00	6.00
27	Bill Mazeroski	1.50	.70	.45
28	Jerry Lumpe	1.00	.50	.30
29	Woody Held	1.00	.50	.30
30	Dick Radatz	1.00	.50	.30
31	Luis Aparicio	5.00	2.50	1.50
32	Dave Nicholson	1.00	.50	.30
33	Ed Mathews	8.00	4.00	2.50
34	Don Drysdale	10.00	5.00	3.00
35	Ray Culp	1.00	.50	.30
36	Juan Marichal	8.00	4.00	2.50
37	Frank Robinson	8.00	4.00	2.50
38	Chuck Hinton	1.00	.50	.30
39	Floyd Robinson	1.00	.50	.30
40	Tommy Harper	1.00	.50	.30
41	Ron Hansen	1.00	.50	.30
42	Ernie Banks	10.00	5.00	3.00
43	Jesse Gonder	1.00	.50	.30
44	Billy Williams	7.00	3.50	2.00
45	Vada Pinson	1.50	.70	.45
46	Rocky Colavito	1.50	.70	.45
47	Bill Monbouquette	1.00	.50	.30
48	Max Alvis	1.00	.50	.30
49	Norm Siebern	1.00	.50	.30
50	John Callison	1.00	.50	.30
51	Rich Rollins	1.00	.50	.30
52	Ken McBride	1.00	.50	.30
53	Don Lock	1.00	.50	.30
54	Ron Fairly	1.00	.50	.30
55	Bob Clemente	20.00	10.00	6.00
56	Dick Ellsworth	1.00	.50	.30
57	Tommy Davis	1.25	.60	.40
58	Tony Gonzalez	1.00	.50	.30
59	Bob Gibson	10.00	5.00	3.00
60	Jim Maloney	1.00	.50	.30
61	Frank Howard	1.50	.70	.45
62	Jim Pagliaroni	1.00	.50	.30
63	Orlando Cepeda	2.00	1.00	.60
64	Ron Perranoski	1.00	.50	.30
65	Curt Flood	1.25	.60	.40
66	Al McBean	1.00	.50	.30
67	Dean Chance	1.00	.50	.30
68	Ron Santo	1.25	.60	.40
69	Jack Baldschun	1.00	.50	.30
70	Milt Pappas	1.00	.50	.30
71	Gary Peters	1.00	.50	.30
72	Bobby Richardson	1.50	.70	.45
73	Lee Thomas	1.00	.50	.30
74	Hank Aguirre	1.00	.50	.30
75	Carl Willey	1.00	.50	.30
76	Camilo Pascual	1.00	.50	.30
77	Bob Friend	1.00	.50	.30
78	Bill White	1.00	.50	.30
79	Norm Cash	1.25	.60	.40
80	Willie Mays	18.00	9.00	5.50
81	Duke Carmel	1.00	.50	.30
82	Pete Rose	25.00	12.50	7.50
83	Hank Aaron	20.00	10.00	6.00
84	Bob Aspromonte	1.00	.50	.30
85	Jim O'Toole	1.00	.50	.30
86	Vic Davalillo	1.00	.50	.30
87	Bill Freehan	1.00	.50	.30
88	Warren Spahn	8.00	4.00	2.50
89	Ron Hunt	1.00	.50	.30
90	Denis Menke	1.00	.50	.30
91	Turk Farrell	1.00	.50	.30
92	Jim Hickman	1.00	.50	.30
93	Jim Bunning	2.00	1.00	.60
94	Bob Hendley	1.00	.50	.30
95	Ernie Broglio	1.00	.50	.30
96	Rusty Staub	1.50	.70	.45
97	Lou Brock	8.00	4.00	2.50
98	Jim Fregosi	1.00	.50	.30
99	Jim Grant	1.00	.50	.30
100	Al Kaline	15.00	7.50	4.50
101	Earl Battey	1.00	.50	.30
102	Wayne Causey	1.00	.50	.30
103	Chuck Schilling	1.00	.50	.30
104	Boog Powell	1.50	.70	.45
105	Dave Wickersham	1.00	.50	.30
106	Sandy Koufax	15.00	7.50	4.50
107	John Bateman	1.00	.50	.30
108	Ed Brinkman	1.00	.50	.30
109	Al Downing	1.00	.50	.30
110	Joe Azcue	1.00	.50	.30
111	Albie Pearson	1.00	.50	.30
112	Harmon Killebrew	10.00	5.00	3.00
113	Tony Taylor	1.00	.50	.30
114	Alvin Jackson	1.00	.50	.30
115	Billy O'Dell	1.00	.50	.30
116	Don Demeter	1.00	.50	.30
117	Ed Charles	1.00	.50	.30
118	Joe Torre	1.50	.70	.45
119	Don Nottebart	1.00	.50	.30
120	Mickey Mantle	40.00	20.00	12.00
121	Joe Pepitone	1.25	.60	.40
122	Dick Stuart	1.00	.50	.30
123	Bobby Richardson	1.50	.70	.45
124	Jerry Lumpe	1.00	.50	.30
125	Brooks Robinson	10.00	5.00	3.00
126	Frank Malzone	1.00	.50	.30
127	Luis Aparicio	5.00	2.50	1.50
128	Jim Fregosi	1.00	.50	.30
129	Al Kaline	15.00	7.50	4.50
130	Leon Wagner	1.00	.50	.30
131a	Mickey Mantle (batting lefthanded)	45.00	23.00	13.50
131b	Mickey Mantle (batting righthanded)	45.00	23.00	13.50
132	Albie Pearson	1.00	.50	.30
133	Harmon Killebrew	10.00	5.00	3.00
134	Carl Yastrzemski	20.00	10.00	6.00
135	Elston Howard	1.50	.70	.45
136	Earl Battey	1.00	.50	.30
137	Camilo Pascual	1.00	.50	.30
138	Jim Bouton	1.25	.60	.40
139	Whitey Ford	8.00	4.00	2.50
140	Gary Peters	1.00	.50	.30
141	Bill White	1.00	.50	.30
142	Orlando Cepeda	2.00	1.00	.60
143	Bill Mazeroski	1.50	.70	.45
144	Tony Taylor	1.00	.50	.30
145	Ken Boyer	1.50	.70	.45
146	Ron Santo	1.25	.60	.40
147	Dick Groat	1.25	.60	.40
148	Roy McMillan	1.00	.50	.30
149	Hank Aaron	18.00	9.00	4.50
150	Bob Clemente	20.00	10.00	6.00
151	Willie Mays	18.00	9.00	5.50
152	Vada Pinson	1.50	.70	.45
153	Tommy Davis	1.25	.60	.40
154	Frank Robinson	8.00	4.00	2.50
155	Joe Torre	1.50	.70	.45
156	Tim McCarver	1.25	.60	.40
157	Juan Marichal	7.00	3.50	2.00
158	Jim Maloney	1.00	.50	.30
159	Sandy Koufax	15.00	7.50	4.50
160	Warren Spahn	8.00	4.00	2.50
161a	Wayne Causey (N.L. on back)	15.00	7.50	4.50
161b	Wayne Causey (A.L. on back)	1.00	.50	.30
162a	Chuck Hinton (N.L. on back)	15.00	7.50	4.50
162b	Chuck Hinton (A.L. on back)	1.00	.50	.30
163	Bob Aspromonte	1.00	.50	.30
164	Ron Hunt	1.00	.50	.30

1964 Topps Giants

Measuring 3-1/8" by 5-1/4" the Topps Giants were

the company's first postcard-size issue. The cards feature large color photographs surrounded by white borders with a white baseball containing the player's name, position and team. Card backs carry another photo of the player surrounded by a newspaper-style explanation of the depicted career highlight. The 60-card set contains primarily stars which means it's an excellent place to find inexpensive cards of Hall of Famers. The '64 Giants were not printed in equal quantity and seven of the cards, including Sandy Koufax and Willie Mays, are significantly scarcer than the remainder of the set.

		NR MT	EX	VG
Complete Set:		110.00	55.00	33.00
Common Player:		.12	.06	.04
1	Gary Peters	.12	.06	.04
2	Ken Johnson	.12	.06	.04
3	Sandy Koufax	18.00	9.00	5.50
4	Bob Bailey	.12	.06	.04
5	Milt Pappas	.25	.13	.08
6	Ron Hunt	.12	.06	.04
7	Whitey Ford	1.75	.90	.50
8	Roy McMillan	.12	.06	.04
9	Rocky Colavito	.40	.20	.12
10	Jim Bunning	.50	.25	.15
11	Bob Clemente	5.00	2.50	1.50
12	Al Kaline	3.00	1.50	.90
13	Nellie Fox	.60	.30	.20
14	Tony Gonzalez	.12	.06	.04
15	Jim Gentile	.12	.06	.04
16	Dean Chance	.12	.06	.04
17	Dick Ellsworth	.12	.06	.04
18	Jim Fregosi	.25	.13	.08
19	Dick Groat	.40	.20	.12
20	Chuck Hinton	.12	.06	.04
21	Elston Howard	.50	.25	.15
22	Dick Farrell	.12	.06	.04
23	Albie Pearson	.12	.06	.04
24	Frank Howard	.50	.25	.15
25	Mickey Mantle	18.00	9.00	5.50
26	Joe Torre	.40	.20	.12
27	Ed Brinkman	.12	.06	.04
28	Bob Friend	4.00	2.00	1.25
29	Frank Robinson	1.75	.90	.50
30	Bill Freehan	.25	.13	.08
31	Warren Spahn	1.25	.60	.40
32	Camilo Pascual	.12	.06	.04
33	Pete Ward	.12	.06	.04
34	Jim Maloney	.12	.06	.04
35	Dave Wickersham	.12	.06	.04
36	Johnny Callison	.25	.13	.08
37	Juan Marichal	3.00	1.50	.90
38	Harmon Killebrew	3.00	1.50	.90
39	Luis Aparicio	1.25	.60	.40
40	Dick Radatz	.12	.06	.04
41	Bob Gibson	3.00	1.50	.90
42	Dick Stuart	4.00	2.00	1.25
43	Tommy Davis	.40	.20	.12
44	Tony Oliva	.50	.25	.15
45	Wayne Causey	4.00	2.00	1.25
46	Max Alvis	.12	.06	.04
47	Galen Cisco	4.00	2.00	1.25
48	Carl Yastrzemski	3.00	1.50	.90
49	Hank Aaron	5.00	2.50	1.50
50	Brooks Robinson	3.00	1.50	.90
51	Willie Mays	18.00	9.00	5.50
52	Billy Williams	1.25	.60	.40
53	Juan Pizarro	.12	.06	.04
54	Leon Wagner	.12	.06	.04
55	Orlando Cepeda	.70	.35	.20
56	Vada Pinson	.50	.25	.15
57	Ken Boyer	.60	.30	.20
58	Ron Santo	.40	.20	.12
59	John Romano	.12	.06	.04
60	Bill Skowron	4.00	2.00	1.25

1964 Topps Photo Tatoos

Apparently not content to leave the skin of American children without adornment, Topps jumped back into the tattoo field in 1964 with the release of a new series. Measuring 1-9/16" by 3-1/2," there were 75 tattoos in a complete set. The picture side for the 20 team tattoos gives the team logo and

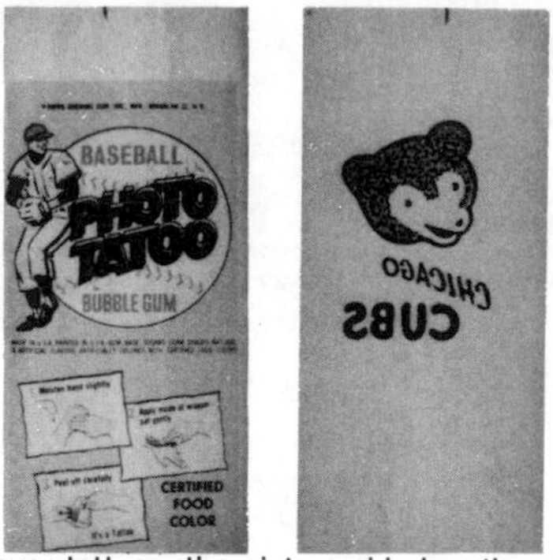

the player tattoos, the picture side has the player's face, name and team.

		NR MT	EX	VG
Complete Set:		600.00	300.00	180.00
Common Player:		3.00	1.50	.90
(1)	Hank Aaron	40.00	20.00	12.50
(2)	H. Aguirre	3.00	1.50	.90
(3)	Max Alvis	3.00	1.50	.90
(4)	Ernie Banks	25.00	12.50	7.50
(5)	S. Barber	3.00	1.50	.90
(6)	K. Boyer	5.00	2.50	1.50
(7)	J. Callison	4.00	2.00	1.25
(8)	Norm Cash	5.00	2.50	1.50
(9)	W. Causey	3.00	1.50	.90
(10)	O. Cepeda	7.00	3.50	2.00
(11)	R. Colavito	7.00	3.50	2.00
(12)	Ray Culp	3.00	1.50	.90
(13)	Davalillo	3.00	1.50	.90
(14)	Drabowsky	3.00	1.50	.90
(15)	Ellsworth	3.00	1.50	.90
(16)	Curt Flood	5.00	2.50	1.50
(17)	B. Freehan	4.00	2.00	1.25
(18)	J. Fregosi	4.00	2.00	1.25
(19)	Bob Friend	4.00	2.00	1.25
(20)	D. Groat	4.00	2.00	1.25
(21)	Woody Held	3.00	1.50	.90
(22)	F. Howard	5.00	2.50	1.50
(23)	Al Jackson	3.00	1.50	.90
(24)	L. Jackson	3.00	1.50	.90
(25)	K. Johnson	3.00	1.50	.90
(26)	Al Kaline	25.00	12.50	7.50
(27a)	Killebrew (green background)	25.00	12.50	7.50
(27b)	Killebrew (red background)	25.00	12.50	7.50
(28)	S. Koufax	35.00	17.50	10.50
(29)	Lock	3.00	1.50	.90
(30)	F. Malzone	3.00	1.50	.90
(31)	M. Mantle	100.00	45.00	27.00
(32)	E. Mathews	15.00	7.50	4.50
(33a)	Willie Mays (yellow background encompasses entire head)	40.00	20.00	12.50
(33b)	Willie Mays (yellow background covers one-half of head)	40.00	20.00	12.50
(34)	Mazeroski	5.00	2.50	1.50
(35)	K. McBride	3.00	1.50	.90
(36)	Monbouquette	3.00	1.50	.90
(37)	Nicholson	3.00	1.50	.90
(38)	C. Osteen	4.00	2.00	1.25
(39)	M. Pappas	4.00	2.00	1.25
(40)	C. Pascual	4.00	2.00	1.25
(41)	A. Pearson	3.00	1.50	.90
(42)	Perranoski	3.00	1.50	.90
(43)	G. Peters	3.00	1.50	.90
(44)	B. Powell	5.00	2.50	1.50
(45)	F. Robinson	20.00	10.00	6.00
(46)	J. Romano	3.00	1.50	.90
(47)	N. Siebern	3.00	1.50	.90
(48)	W. Spahn	15.00	7.50	4.50
(49)	D. Stuart	4.00	2.00	1.25
(50)	Lee Thomas	3.00	1.50	.90
(51)	Joe Torre	5.00	2.50	1.50
(52)	Pete Ward	3.00	1.50	.90
(53)	C. Willey	3.00	1.50	.90
(54)	B. Williams	25.00	12.50	7.50
(55)	Yastrzemski	50.00	25.00	15.00
(56)	Baltimore Orioles Logo	3.00	1.50	.90
(57)	Boston Red Sox Logo	3.00	1.50	.90
(58)	Chicago Cubs Logo	3.00	1.50	.90
(59)	Chicago White Sox Logo	3.00	1.50	.90
(60)	Cincinnati Reds Logo	3.00	1.50	.90

		NR MT	EX	VG
(66)	Los Angeles Dodgers Logo	2.50	1.25	.70
(67)	Milwaukee Braves Logo	3.00	1.50	.90
(68)	Minnesota Twins Logo	3.00	1.50	.90
(69)	New York Mets Logo	2.50	1.25	.70
(70)	New York Yankees Logo	4.00	2.00	1.25
(71)	Philadelphia Phillies Logo	3.00	1.50	.90
(72)	Pittsburgh Pirates Logo	3.00	1.50	.90
(73)	St. Louis Cardinals Logo	2.50	1.25	.70
(74)	San Francisco Giants Logo	3.00	1.50	.90
(75)	Washington Senators Logo	3.00	1.50	.90

1964 Topps Stand-Ups

These 2-1/2" by 3-1/2" cards were the first since the All-Star sets of 1951 to be die-cut. This made it possible for a folded card to stand on display. The 77-cards in the set feature color photographs of the player with yellow and green backgrounds. Directions for folding are on the yellow top background, and when folded only the green background remains. Of the 77 cards, 55 were double-printed while 22 were single-printed, making them twice as scarce. Included in the single-printed group are Warren Spahn, Don Drysdale, Juan Marichal, Willie McCovey and Carl Yastrzemski.

		NR MT	EX	VG
Complete Set:		2400.00	1200.00	720.00
Common Player:		3.50	1.75	1.00
(1)	Hank Aaron	110.00	55.00	33.00
(2)	Hank Aguirre	3.50	1.75	1.00
(3)	George Altman	3.50	1.75	1.00
(4)	Max Alvis	3.50	1.75	1.00
(5)	Bob Aspromonte	3.50	1.75	1.00
(6)	Jack Baldschun	20.00	10.00	6.00
(7)	Ernie Banks	40.00	20.00	12.00
(8)	Steve Barber	3.50	1.75	1.00
(9)	Earl Battey	3.50	1.75	1.00
(10)	Ken Boyer	6.00	3.00	1.75
(11)	Ernie Broglio	3.50	1.75	1.00
(12)	Johnny Callison	4.00	2.00	1.25
(13)	Norm Cash	25.00	12.50	7.50
(14)	Wayne Causey	3.50	1.75	1.00
(15)	Orlando Cepeda	8.00	4.00	2.50
(16)	Ed Charles	3.50	1.75	1.00
(17)	Bob Clemente	55.00	27.00	16.50
(18)	Donn Clendenon	20.00	10.00	6.00
(19)	Rocky Colavito	6.00	3.00	1.75
(20)	Ray Culp	20.00	10.00	6.00
(21)	Tommy Davis	6.00	3.00	1.75
(22)	Don Drysdale	125.00	62.00	37.00
(23)	Dick Ellsworth	3.50	1.75	1.00
(24)	Dick Farrell	3.50	1.75	1.00
(25)	Jim Fregosi	4.00	2.00	1.25
(26)	Bob Friend	4.00	2.00	1.25
(27)	Jim Gentile	3.50	1.75	1.00
(28)	Jesse Gonder	20.00	10.00	6.00
(29)	Tony Gonzalez	20.00	10.00	6.00
(30)	Dick Groat	6.00	3.00	1.75
(31)	Woody Held	3.50	1.75	1.00
(32)	Chuck Hinton	3.50	1.75	1.00
(33)	Elston Howard	7.00	3.50	2.00
(34)	Frank Howard	25.00	12.50	7.50
(35)	Ron Hunt	3.50	1.75	1.00
(36)	Al Jackson	3.50	1.75	1.00
(37)	Ken Johnson	3.50	1.75	1.00
(38)	Al Kaline	40.00	20.00	12.00
(39)	Harmon Killebrew	40.00	20.00	12.00
(40)	Sandy Koufax	40.00	20.00	12.00
(41)	Don Lock	20.00	10.00	6.00
(42)	Jerry Lumpe	20.00	10.00	6.00
(43)	Jim Maloney	3.50	1.75	1.00
(44)	Frank Malzone	3.50	1.75	1.00
(45)	Mickey Mantle	400.00	200.00	120.00
(46)	Juan Marichal	125.00	62.00	37.00
(47)	Ed Mathews	125.00	62.00	37.00
(48)	Willie Mays	110.00	55.00	33.00
(49)	Bill Mazeroski	6.00	3.00	1.75
(50)	Ken McBride	3.50	1.75	1.00
(51)	Willie McCovey	125.00	62.00	37.00
(52)	Claude Osteen	3.50	1.75	1.00
(53)	Jim O'Toole	3.50	1.75	1.00
(54)	Camilo Pascual	3.50	1.75	1.00
(55)	Albie Pearson	20.00	10.00	6.00
(56)	Gary Peters	3.50	1.75	1.00
(57)	Vada Pinson	6.00	3.00	1.75
(58)	Juan Pizarro	3.50	1.75	1.00
(59)	Boog Powell	6.00	3.00	1.75
(60)	Bobby Richardson	7.00	3.50	2.00
(61)	Brooks Robinson	50.00	25.00	15.00
(62)	Floyd Robinson	3.50	1.75	1.00
(63)	Frank Robinson	40.00	20.00	12.00
(64)	Ed Roebuck	20.00	10.00	6.00
(65)	Rich Rollins	3.50	1.75	1.00
(66)	Johnny Romano	3.50	1.75	1.00
(67)	Ron Santo	25.00	12.50	7.50
(68)	Norm Siebern	3.50	1.75	1.00
(69)	Warren Spahn	125.00	62.00	37.00
(70)	Dick Stuart	20.00	10.00	6.00
(71)	Lee Thomas	3.50	1.75	1.00
(72)	Joe Torre	7.00	3.50	2.00
(73)	Pete Ward	3.50	1.75	1.00
(74)	Bill White	20.00	10.00	6.00
(75)	Billy Williams	125.00	62.00	37.00
(76)	Hal Woodeshick	20.00	10.00	6.00
(77)	Carl Yastrzemski	400.00	200.00	120.00

1965 Topps

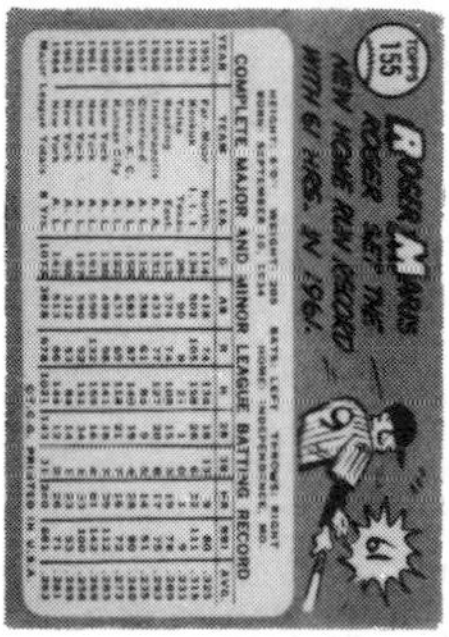

The 1965 Topps set features a large color photograph of the player which was surrounded by a colored, round-cornered frame and a white border. The bottom of the 2-1/2" by 3-1/2" cards include a pennant with a color team logo and name over the left side of a rectangle which features the player's name and position. Backs feature statistics and, if space allowed, a cartoon and headline about the player. There are no multi-player cards in the 1965 set other than the usual team cards and World Series highlights. Rookie cards include team, as well as league groupings from two to four players per card. Also present in the 598-card set are statistical leaders.

	NR MT	EX	VG
Complete Set:	3500.00	1750.00	1050.
Common Player: 1-198	2.00	1.00	.60
Common Player: 199-446	2.00	1.00	.60
Common Player: 447-522	2.00	1.00	.60
Common Player: 523-598	5.00	2.50	1.50
1 A.L. Batting Leaders (Elston Howard, Tony Oliva, Brooks Robinson)	10.00	4.00	2.50

		NR MT	EX	VG
2	N.L. Batting Leaders (Hank Aaron, Rico Carty, Bob Clemente)	5.00	2.50	1.50
3	A.L. Home Run Leaders (Harmon Killebrew, Mickey Mantle, Boog Powell)	20.00	10.00	6.00
4	N.L. Home Run Leaders (Johnny Callison, Orlando Cepeda, Jim Hart, Willie Mays, Billy Williams)	6.00	3.00	1.75
5	A.L. RBI Leaders (Harmon Killebrew, Mickey Mantle, Brooks Robinson, Dick Stuart)	20.00	10.00	6.00
6	N.L. RBI Leaders (Ken Boyer, Willie Mays, Ron Santo)	6.00	3.00	1.75
7	A.L. ERA Leaders (Dean Chance, Joel Horlen)	5.00	2.50	1.50
8	N.L. ERA Leaders (Don Drysdale, Sandy Koufax)	6.00	3.00	1.75
9	A.L. Pitching Leaders (Wally Bunker, Dean Chance, Gary Peters, Juan Pizarro, Dave Wickersham)	5.00	2.50	1.50
10	N.L. Pitching Leaders (Larry Jackson, Juan Marichal, Ray Sadecki)	3.50	1.75	1.00
11	A.L. Strikeout Leaders (Dean Chance, Al Downing, Camilo Pascual)	5.00	2.50	1.50
12	N.L. Strikeout Leaders (Don Drysdale, Bob Gibson, Bob Veale)	3.50	1.75	1.00
13	Pedro Ramos	2.00	1.00	.60
14	Len Gabrielson	2.00	1.00	.60
15	Robin Roberts	8.00	4.00	2.50
16	Astros Rookies *(Sonny Jackson, Joe Morgan)*	200.00	100.00	60.00
17	Johnny Romano	2.00	1.00	.60
18	Bill McCool	2.00	1.00	.60
19	Gates Brown	2.00	1.00	.60
20	Jim Bunning	5.00	2.50	1.50
21	Don Blasingame	2.00	1.00	.60
22	Charlie Smith	2.00	1.00	.60
23	Bob Tiefenauer	2.00	1.00	.60
24	Twins Team	5.00	2.50	1.50
25	Al McBean	2.00	1.00	.60
26	Bobby Knoop	2.00	1.00	.60
27	Dick Bertell	2.00	1.00	.60
28	Barney Schultz	2.00	1.00	.60
29	Felix Mantilla	2.00	1.00	.60
30	Jim Bouton	5.00	2.50	1.50
31	Mike White	2.00	1.00	.60
32	Herman Franks	2.00	1.00	.60
33	Jackie Brandt	2.00	1.00	.60
34	Cal Koonce	2.00	1.00	.60
35	Ed Charles	2.00	1.00	.60
36	Bobby Wine	2.00	1.00	.60
37	Fred Gladding	2.00	1.00	.60
38	Jim King	2.00	1.00	.60
39	Gerry Arrigo	2.00	1.00	.60
40	Frank Howard	5.00	2.50	1.50
41	White Sox Rookies (Bruce Howard, Marv Staehle)	2.00	1.00	.60
42	Earl Wilson	2.00	1.00	.60
43	Mike Shannon	2.00	1.00	.60
44	Wade Blasingame	2.00	1.00	.60
45	Roy McMillan	2.00	1.00	.60
46	Bob Lee	2.00	1.00	.60
47	Tommy Harper	2.00	1.00	.60
48	Claude Raymond	2.00	1.00	.60
49	Orioles Rookies *(Curt Blefary,* John Miller)	2.00	1.00	.60
50	Juan Marichal	9.00	4.50	2.75
51	Billy Bryan	2.00	1.00	.60
52	Ed Roebuck	2.00	1.00	.60
53	Dick McAuliffe	2.00	1.00	.60
54	Joe Gibbon	2.00	1.00	.60
55	Tony Conigliaro	6.00	3.00	1.75
56	Ron Kline	2.00	1.00	.60
57	Cardinals Team	2.25	1.25	.70
58	Fred Talbot	2.00	1.00	.60
59	Nate Oliver	2.00	1.00	.60
60	Jim O'Toole	2.00	1.00	.60
61	Chris Cannizzaro	2.00	1.00	.60
62	Jim Katt (Kaat)	5.00	2.50	1.50
63	Ty Cline	2.00	1.00	.60
64	Lou Burdette	2.00	1.00	.60
65	Tony Kubek	6.00	3.00	1.75
66	Bill Rigney	2.00	1.00	.60
67	Harvey Haddix	2.00	1.00	.60
68	Del Crandall	2.00	1.00	.60
69	Bill Virdon	2.00	1.00	.60
70	Bill Skowron	2.00	1.00	.60
71	John O'Donoghue	2.00	1.00	.60
72	Tony Gonzalez	2.00	1.00	.60
73	Dennis Ribant	2.00	1.00	.60
74	Red Sox Rookies *(Rico Petrocelli,* Jerry Stephenson)	5.00	2.50	1.50
75	Deron Johnson	2.00	1.00	.60
76	Sam McDowell	2.00	1.00	.60
77	Doug Camilli	2.00	1.00	.60
78	Dal Maxvill	2.00	1.00	.60
79a	Checklist 1-88 (61 is C. Cannizzaro)	2.00	1.00	.60
79b	Checklist 1-88 (61 is Cannizzaro)	5.00	2.50	1.50
80	Turk Farrell	2.00	1.00	.60
81	Don Buford	2.00	1.00	.60
82	Braves Rookies *(Santos Alomar,* John Braun)	2.00	1.00	.60
83	George Thomas	2.00	1.00	.60
84	Ron Herbel	2.00	1.00	.60
85	Willie Smith	2.00	1.00	.60
86	Les Narum	2.00	1.00	.60
87	Nelson Mathews	2.00	1.00	.60
88	Jack Lamabe	2.00	1.00	.60
89	Mike Hershberger	2.00	1.00	.60
90	Rich Rollins	2.00	1.00	.60
91	Cubs Team	2.25	1.25	.70
92	Dick Howser	2.00	1.00	.60
93	Jack Fisher	2.00	1.00	.60
94	Charlie Lau	2.00	1.00	.60
95	Bill Mazeroski	5.00	2.50	1.50
96	Sonny Siebert	2.00	1.00	.60
97	Pedro Gonzalez	2.00	1.00	.60
98	Bob Miller	2.00	1.00	.60
99	Gil Hodges	6.00	3.00	1.75
100	Ken Boyer	5.00	2.50	1.50
101	Fred Newman	2.00	1.00	.60
102	Steve Boros	2.00	1.00	.60
103	Harvey Kuenn	2.00	1.00	.60
104	Checklist 89-176	2.00	1.00	.60
105	Chico Salmon	2.00	1.00	.60
106	Gene Oliver	2.00	1.00	.60
107	Phillies Rookies *(Pat Corrales,* Costen Shockley)	2.00	1.00	.60
108	Don Mincher	2.00	1.00	.60
109	Walt Bond	2.00	1.00	.60
110	Ron Santo	2.25	1.25	.70
111	Lee Thomas	2.00	1.00	.60
112	Derrell Griffith	2.00	1.00	.60
113	Steve Barber	2.00	1.00	.60
114	Jim Hickman	2.00	1.00	.60
115	Bobby Richardson	6.00	3.00	1.75
116	Cardinals Rookies (Dave Dowling, *Bob Tolan)*	2.00	1.00	.60
117	Wes Stock	2.00	1.00	.60
118	*Hal Lanier*	2.25	1.25	.70
119	John Kennedy	2.00	1.00	.60
120	Frank Robinson	25.00	12.50	7.50
121	Gene Alley	2.00	1.00	.60
122	Bill Pleis	2.00	1.00	.60
123	Frank Thomas	2.00	1.00	.60
124	Tom Satriano	2.00	1.00	.60
125	Juan Pizarro	2.00	1.00	.60
126	Dodgers Team	5.00	2.50	1.50
127	Frank Lary	2.00	1.00	.60
128	Vic Davalillo	2.00	1.00	.60
129	Bennie Daniels	2.00	1.00	.60
130	Al Kaline	25.00	12.50	7.50
131	Johnny Keane	2.25	1.25	.70
132	World Series Game 1 (Cards Take Opener)	5.00	2.50	1.50
133	World Series Game 2 (Stottlemyre Wins)	2.00	1.00	.60
134	World Series Game 3 (Mantle's Clutch HR)	25.00	12.50	7.50
135	World Series Game 4 (Boyer's Grand Slam)	5.00	2.50	1.50
136	World Series Game 5 (10th Inning Triumph)	5.00	2.50	1.50
137	World Series Game 6 (Bouton Wins Again)	2.00	1.00	.60
138	World Series Game 7 (Gibson Wins Finale)	3.50	1.75	1.00
139	World Series Summary (The Cards Celebrate)	5.00	2.50	1.50
140	Dean Chance	2.00	1.00	.60
141	Charlie James	2.00	1.00	.60
142	Bill Monbouquette	2.00	1.00	.60
143	Pirates Rookies (John Gelnar, Jerry May)	2.00	1.00	.60
144	Ed Kranepool	2.00	1.00	.60
145	*Luis Tiant*	10.00	5.00	3.00
146	Ron Hansen	2.00	1.00	.60
147	Dennis Bennett	2.00	1.00	.60
148	Willie Kirkland	2.00	1.00	.60
149	Wayne Schurr	2.00	1.00	.60
150	Brooks Robinson	25.00	12.50	7.50
151	Athletics Team	2.25	1.25	.70

		NR MT	EX	VG
152	Phil Ortega	2.00	1.00	.60
153	Norm Cash	2.00	1.00	.60
154	Bob Humphreys	2.00	1.00	.60
155	Roger Maris	40.00	20.00	12.00
156	Bob Sadowski	2.00	1.00	.60
157	Zoilo Versalles	2.25	1.25	.70
158	Dick Sisler	2.00	1.00	.60
159	Jim Duffalo	2.00	1.00	.60
160	Bob Clemente	75.00	38.00	23.00
161	Frank Baumann	2.00	1.00	.60
162	Russ Nixon	2.00	1.00	.60
163	John Briggs	2.00	1.00	.60
164	Al Spangler	2.00	1.00	.60
165	Dick Ellsworth	2.00	1.00	.60
166	Indians Rookies (*Tommie Agee*, George Culver)	2.25	1.25	.70
167	Bill Wakefield	2.00	1.00	.60
168	Dick Green	2.00	1.00	.60
169	Dave Vineyard	2.00	1.00	.60
170	Hank Aaron	80.00	40.00	25.00
171	Jim Roland	2.00	1.00	.60
172	Jim Piersall	2.25	1.25	.70
173	Tigers Team	3.25	1.75	1.00
174	Joe Jay	2.00	1.00	.60
175	Bob Aspromonte	2.00	1.00	.60
176	Willie McCovey	20.00	10.00	6.00
177	Pete Mikkelsen	2.00	1.00	.60
178	Dalton Jones	2.00	1.00	.60
179	Hal Woodeshick	2.00	1.00	.60
180	Bob Allison	2.00	1.00	.60
181	Senators Rookies (Don Loun, Joe McCabe)	2.00	1.00	.60
182	Mike de la Hoz	2.00	1.00	.60
183	Dave Nicholson	2.00	1.00	.60
184	John Boozer	2.00	1.00	.60
185	Max Alvis	2.00	1.00	.60
186	Billy Cowan	2.00	1.00	.60
187	Casey Stengel	18.00	9.00	5.00
188	Sam Bowens	2.00	1.00	.60
189	Checklist 177-264	2.00	1.00	.60
190	Bill White	2.00	1.00	.60
191	Phil Regan	2.00	1.00	.60
192	Jim Coker	2.00	1.00	.60
193	Gaylord Perry	18.00	9.00	5.50
194	Angels Rookies (Bill Kelso, *Rick Reichardt*)	2.00	1.00	.60
195	Bob Veale	2.00	1.00	.60
196	Ron Fairly	2.00	1.00	.60
197	Diego Segui	2.00	1.00	.60
198	Smoky Burgess	2.00	1.00	.60
199	Bob Heffner	2.00	1.00	.60
200	Joe Torre	5.00	2.50	1.50
201	Twins Rookies (*Cesar Tovar*, Sandy Valdespino)	2.00	1.00	.60
202	Leo Burke	2.00	1.00	.60
203	Dallas Green	2.00	1.00	.60
204	Russ Snyder	2.00	1.00	.60
205	Warren Spahn	20.00	10.00	6.00
206	Willie Horton	2.00	1.00	.60
207	Pete Rose	150.00	60.00	38.00
208	Tommy John	10.00	5.00	3.00
209	Pirates Team	5.00	2.50	1.50
210	Jim Fregosi	2.25	1.25	.70
211	Steve Ridzik	2.00	1.00	.60
212	Ron Brand	2.00	1.00	.60
213	Jim Davenport	2.00	1.00	.60
214	Bob Purkey	2.00	1.00	.60
215	Pete Ward	2.00	1.00	.60
216	Al Worthington	2.00	1.00	.60
217	Walt Alston	3.50	1.75	1.00
218	Dick Schofield	2.00	1.00	.60
219	Bob Meyer	2.00	1.00	.60
220	Billy Williams	10.00	5.00	3.00
221	John Tsitouris	2.00	1.00	.60
222	Bob Tillman	2.00	1.00	.60
223	Dan Osinski	2.00	1.00	.60
224	Bob Chance	2.00	1.00	.60
225	Bo Belinsky	2.00	1.00	.60
226	Yankees Rookies (Jake Gibbs, Elvio Jimenez)	2.25	1.25	.70
227	Bobby Klaus	2.00	1.00	.60
228	Jack Sanford	2.00	1.00	.60
229	Lou Clinton	2.00	1.00	.60
230	Ray Sadecki	2.00	1.00	.60
231	Jerry Adair	2.00	1.00	.60
232	*Steve Blass*	2.00	1.00	.60
233	Don Zimmer	2.25	1.25	.70
234	White Sox Team	5.00	2.50	1.50
235	Chuck Hinton	2.00	1.00	.60
236	*Dennis McLain*	18.00	9.00	5.50
237	Bernie Allen	2.00	1.00	.60
238	Joe Moeller	2.00	1.00	.60
239	Doc Edwards	2.00	1.00	.60
240	Bob Bruce	2.00	1.00	.60
241	Mack Jones	2.00	1.00	.60
242	George Brunet	2.00	1.00	.60
243	Reds Rookies (Ted Davidson, *Tommy Helms*)	2.00	1.00	.60
244	Lindy McDaniel	2.00	1.00	.60
245	Joe Pepitone	2.00	1.00	.60
246	Tom Butters	2.00	1.00	.60
247	Wally Moon	2.00	1.00	.60
248	Gus Triandos	2.00	1.00	.60
249	Dave McNally	2.00	1.00	.60
250	Willie Mays	100.00	50.00	30.00
251	Billy Herman	2.00	1.00	.60
252	Pete Richert	2.00	1.00	.60
253	Danny Cater	2.00	1.00	.60
254	Roland Sheldon	2.25	1.25	.70
255	Camilo Pascual	2.00	1.00	.60
256	Tito Francona	2.00	1.00	.60
257	Jim Wynn	2.00	1.00	.60
258	Larry Bearnarth	2.00	1.00	.60
259	Tigers Rookies (*Jim Northrup, Ray Oyler*)	2.00	1.00	.60
260	Don Drysdale	18.00	9.00	5.50
261	Duke Carmel	2.25	1.25	.70
262	Bud Daley	2.00	1.00	.60
263	Marty Keough	2.00	1.00	.60
264	Bob Buhl	2.00	1.00	.60
265	Jim Pagliaroni	2.00	1.00	.60
266	*Bert Campaneris*	5.00	2.50	1.50
267	Senators Team	5.00	2.50	1.50
268	Ken McBride	2.00	1.00	.60
269	Frank Bolling	2.00	1.00	.60
270	Milt Pappas	2.00	1.00	.60
271	Don Wert	2.00	1.00	.60
272	Chuck Schilling	2.00	1.00	.60
273	Checklist 265-352	3.25	1.75	1.00
274	Lum Harris	2.00	1.00	.60
275	Dick Groat	3.25	1.75	1.00
276	Hoyt Wilhelm	8.00	4.00	2.50
277	Johnny Lewis	2.00	1.00	.60
278	Ken Retzer	2.00	1.00	.60
279	Dick Tracewski	2.00	1.00	.60
280	Dick Stuart	2.00	1.00	.60
281	Bill Stafford	2.25	1.25	.70
282	Giants Rookies (Dick Estelle, *Masanori Murakami*)	2.00	1.00	.60
283	Fred Whitfield	2.00	1.00	.60
284	Nick Willhite	2.00	1.00	.60
285	Ron Hunt	2.00	1.00	.60
286	Athletics Rookies (Jim Dickson, Aurelio Monteagudo)	2.00	1.00	.60
287	Gary Kolb	2.00	1.00	.60
288	Jack Hamilton	2.00	1.00	.60
289	Gordy Coleman	2.00	1.00	.60
290	Wally Bunker	2.00	1.00	.60
291	Jerry Lynch	2.00	1.00	.60
292	Larry Yellen	2.00	1.00	.60
293	Angels Team	5.00	2.50	1.50
294	Tim McCarver	2.75	1.50	.80
295	Dick Radatz	2.00	1.00	.60
296	Tony Taylor	2.00	1.00	.60
297	Dave DeBusschere	3.50	1.75	1.00
298	Jim Stewart	2.00	1.00	.60
299	Jerry Zimmerman	2.00	1.00	.60
300	Sandy Koufax	110.00	55.00	33.00
301	Birdie Tebbetts	2.00	1.00	.60
302	Al Stanek	2.00	1.00	.60
303	Johnny Orsino	2.00	1.00	.60
304	Dave Stenhouse	2.00	1.00	.60
305	Rico Carty	2.25	1.25	.70
306	Bubba Phillips	2.00	1.00	.60
307	Barry Latman	2.00	1.00	.60
308	Mets Rookies (*Cleon Jones*, Tom Parsons)	2.00	1.00	.60
309	Steve Hamilton	2.25	1.25	.70
310	Johnny Callison	2.00	1.00	.60
311	Orlando Pena	2.00	1.00	.60
312	Joe Nuxhall	2.00	1.00	.60
313	Jimmie Schaffer	2.00	1.00	.60
314	Sterling Slaughter	2.00	1.00	.60
315	Frank Malzone	2.00	1.00	.60
316	Reds Team	2.75	1.50	.80
317	Don McMahon	2.00	1.00	.60
318	Matty Alou	2.00	1.00	.60
319	Ken McMullen	2.00	1.00	.60
320	Bob Gibson	20.00	10.00	6.00
321	Rusty Staub	5.00	2.50	1.50
322	Rick Wise	2.00	1.00	.60
323	Hank Bauer	2.00	1.00	.60

		NR MT	EX	VG
324	Bobby Locke	2.00	1.00	.60
325	Donn Clendenon	2.00	1.00	.60
326	Dwight Siebler	2.00	1.00	.60
327	Denis Menke	2.00	1.00	.60
328	Eddie Fisher	2.00	1.00	.60
329	Hawk Taylor	2.00	1.00	.60
330	Whitey Ford	20.00	10.00	6.00
331	Dodgers Rookies (Al Ferrara, John Purdin)	2.00	1.00	.60
332	Ted Abernathy	2.00	1.00	.60
333	Tommie Reynolds	2.00	1.00	.60
334	Vic Roznovsky	2.00	1.00	.60
335	Mickey Lolich	3.50	1.75	1.00
336	Woody Held	2.00	1.00	.60
337	Mike Cuellar	2.25	1.25	.70
338	Phillies Team	5.00	2.50	1.50
339	Ryne Duren	2.00	1.00	.60
340	Tony Oliva	3.50	1.75	1.00
341	Bobby Bolin	2.00	1.00	.60
342	Bob Rodgers	2.00	1.00	.60
343	Mike McCormick	2.00	1.00	.60
344	Wes Parker	2.00	1.00	.60
345	Floyd Robinson	2.00	1.00	.60
346	Bobby Bragan	2.00	1.00	.60
347	Roy Face	2.25	1.25	.70
348	George Banks	2.00	1.00	.60
349	Larry Miller	2.00	1.00	.60
350	Mickey Mantle	400.00	200.00	120.00
351	Jim Perry	2.00	1.00	.60
352	*Alex Johnson*	2.00	1.00	.60
353	Jerry Lumpe	2.00	1.00	.60
354	Cubs Rookies (Billy Ott, Jack Warner)	2.00	1.00	.60
355	Vada Pinson	5.00	2.50	1.50
356	Bill Spanswick	2.00	1.00	.60
357	Carl Warwick	2.00	1.00	.60
358	Albie Pearson	2.00	1.00	.60
359	Ken Johnson	2.00	1.00	.60
360	Orlando Cepeda	5.00	2.50	1.50
361	Checklist 353-429	3.25	1.75	1.00
362	Don Schwall	2.00	1.00	.60
363	Bob Johnson	2.00	1.00	.60
364	Galen Cisco	2.00	1.00	.60
365	Jim Gentile	2.00	1.00	.60
366	Dan Schneider	2.00	1.00	.60
367	Leon Wagner	2.00	1.00	.60
368	White Sox Rookies (*Ken Berry*, Joel Gibson)	2.00	1.00	.60
369	Phil Linz	2.25	1.25	.70
370	Tommy Davis	2.25	1.25	.70
371	Frank Kreutzer	2.00	1.00	.60
372	Clay Dalrymple	2.00	1.00	.60
373	Curt Simmons	2.00	1.00	.60
374	Angels Rookies (*Jose Cardenal*, Dick Simpson)	2.00	1.00	.60
375	Dave Wickersham	2.00	1.00	.60
376	Jim Landis	2.00	1.00	.60
377	Willie Stargell	20.00	10.00	6.00
378	Chuck Estrada	2.00	1.00	.60
379	Giants Team	5.00	2.50	1.50
380	Rocky Colavito	2.00	1.00	.60
381	Al Jackson	2.00	1.00	.60
382	J.C. Martin	2.00	1.00	.60
383	Felipe Alou	2.00	1.00	.60
384	Johnny Klippstein	2.00	1.00	.60
385	Carl Yastrzemski	75.00	38.00	23.00
386	Cubs Rookies (Paul Jaeckel, Fred Norman)	2.00	1.00	.60
387	Johnny Podres	2.00	1.00	.60
388	John Blanchard	2.25	1.25	.70
389	Don Larsen	2.00	1.00	.60
390	Bill Freehan	2.00	1.00	.60
391	Mel McGaha	2.00	1.00	.60
392	Bob Friend	2.25	1.25	.70
393	Ed Kirkpatrick	2.00	1.00	.60
394	Jim Hannan	2.00	1.00	.60
395	Jim Hart	2.00	1.00	.60
396	Frank Bertaina	2.00	1.00	.60
397	Jerry Buchek	2.00	1.00	.60
398	Reds Rookies (Dan Neville, *Art Shamsky*)	2.00	1.00	.60
399	Ray Herbert	2.00	1.00	.60
400	Harmon Killebrew	15.00	7.50	4.50
401	Carl Willey	2.00	1.00	.60
402	Joe Amalfitano	2.00	1.00	.60
403	Red Sox Team	2.00	1.00	.60
404	Stan Williams	2.00	1.00	.60
405	John Roseboro	2.00	1.00	.60
406	Ralph Terry	2.00	1.00	.60
407	Lee Maye	2.00	1.00	.60
408	Larry Sherry	2.00	1.00	.60
409	Astros Rookies (Jim Beauchamp, *Larry Dierker*)	2.00	1.00	.60
410	Luis Aparicio	9.00	4.50	2.75
411	Roger Craig	2.00	1.00	.60
412	Bob Bailey	2.00	1.00	.60
413	Hal Reniff	2.25	1.25	.70
414	Al Lopez	2.00	1.00	.60
415	Curt Flood	2.25	1.25	.70
416	Jim Brewer	2.00	1.00	.60
417	Ed Brinkman	2.00	1.00	.60
418	Johnny Edwards	2.00	1.00	.60
419	Ruben Amaro	2.00	1.00	.60
420	Larry Jackson	2.00	1.00	.60
421	Twins Rookies (Gary Dotter, Jay Ward)	2.00	1.00	.60
422	Aubrey Gatewood	2.00	1.00	.60
423	Jesse Gonder	2.00	1.00	.60
424	Gary Bell	2.00	1.00	.60
425	Wayne Causey	2.00	1.00	.60
426	Braves Team	5.00	2.50	1.50
427	Bob Saverine	2.00	1.00	.60
428	Bob Shaw	2.00	1.00	.60
429	Don Demeter	2.00	1.00	.60
430	Gary Peters	2.00	1.00	.60
431	Cardinals Rookies (*Nelson Briles*, Wayne Spiezio)	2.00	1.00	.60
432	Jim Grant	2.00	1.00	.60
433	John Bateman	2.00	1.00	.60
434	Dave Morehead	2.00	1.00	.60
435	Willie Davis	2.25	1.25	.70
436	Don Elston	2.00	1.00	.60
437	Chico Cardenas	2.00	1.00	.60
438	Harry Walker	2.00	1.00	.60
439	Moe Drabowsky	2.00	1.00	.60
440	Tom Tresh	5.00	2.50	1.50
441	Denver Lemaster	2.00	1.00	.60
442	Vic Power	2.00	1.00	.60
443	Checklist 430-506	3.25	1.75	1.00
444	Bob Hendley	2.00	1.00	.60
445	Don Lock	2.00	1.00	.60
446	Art Mahaffey	2.00	1.00	.60
447	Julian Javier	2.00	1.00	.60
448	Lee Stange	2.00	1.00	.60
449	Mets Rookies (Jerry Hinsley, Gary Kroll)	2.25	1.25	.70
450	Elston Howard	5.00	2.50	1.50
451	Jim Owens	2.00	1.00	.60
452	Gary Geiger	2.00	1.00	.60
453	Dodgers Rookies (*Willie Crawford*, John Werhas)	2.25	1.25	.70
454	Ed Rakow	2.00	1.00	.60
455	Norm Siebern	2.25	1.25	.70
456	Bill Henry	2.00	1.00	.60
457	Bob Kennedy	2.00	1.00	.60
458	John Buzhardt	2.00	1.00	.60
459	Frank Kostro	2.00	1.00	.60
460	Richie Allen	10.00	5.00	3.00
461	Braves Rookies (*Clay Carroll*, Phil Niekro)	45.00	23.00	13.50
462	Lew Krausse (photo actually Pete Lovrich)	2.00	1.00	.60
463	Manny Mota	2.25	1.25	.70
464	Ron Piche	2.00	1.00	.60
465	Tom Haller	2.00	1.00	.60
466	Senators Rookies (Pete Craig, Dick Nen)	2.00	1.00	.60
467	Ray Washburn	2.00	1.00	.60
468	Larry Brown	2.00	1.00	.60
469	Don Nottebart	2.00	1.00	.60
470	Yogi Berra	50.00	30.00	15.00
471	Billy Hoeft	2.00	1.00	.60
472	Don Pavletich	2.00	1.00	.60
473	Orioles Rookies (*Paul Blair, Dave Johnson*)	15.00	7.50	4.50
474	Cookie Rojas	2.00	1.00	.60
475	Clete Boyer	2.00	1.00	.60
476	Billy O'Dell	2.00	1.00	.60
477	Cardinals Rookies (Fritz Ackley, *Steve Carlton*)	500.00	250.00	150.00
478	Wilbur Wood	2.00	1.00	.60
479	Ken Harrelson	5.00	2.50	1.50
480	Joel Horlen	2.00	1.00	.60
481	Indians Team	2.00	1.00	.60
482	Bob Priddy	2.00	1.00	.60
483	George Smith	2.00	1.00	.60
484	Ron Perranoski	2.25	1.25	.70
485	Nellie Fox	6.00	3.00	1.75
486	Angels Rookies (Tom Egan, Pat Rogan)	2.00	1.00	.60
487	Woody Woodward	2.25	1.25	.70
488	Ted Wills	2.00	1.00	.60

		NR MT	EX	VG
489	Gene Mauch	2.25	1.25	.70
490	Earl Battey	2.25	1.25	.70
491	Tracy Stallard	2.00	1.00	.60
492	Gene Freese	2.00	1.00	.60
493	Tigers Rookies (Bruce Brubaker, Bill Roman)	2.00	1.00	.60
494	Jay Ritchie	2.00	1.00	.60
495	Joe Christopher	2.25	1.25	.70
496	Joe Cunningham	2.00	1.00	.60
497	Giants Rookies (*Ken Henderson*, Jack Hiatt)	2.25	1.25	.70
498	Gene Stephens	2.00	1.00	.60
499	Stu Miller	2.00	1.00	.60
500	Ed Mathews	30.00	15.00	9.00
501	Indians Rookies (Ralph Gagliano, Jim Rittwage)	2.00	1.00	.60
502	Don Cardwell	2.00	1.00	.60
503	Phil Gagliano	2.00	1.00	.60
504	Jerry Grote	2.25	1.25	.70
505	Ray Culp	2.00	1.00	.60
506	Sam Mele	2.00	1.00	.60
507	Sammy Ellis	2.00	1.00	.60
508a	Checklist 507-598 (large print on front)	6.00	3.00	1.75
508b	Checklist 507-598 (small print on front)	5.00	2.50	1.50
509	Red Sox Rookies (Bob Guindon, Gerry Vezendy)	2.00	1.00	.60
510	Ernie Banks	60.00	30.00	18.00
511	Ron Locke	2.25	1.25	.70
512	Cap Peterson	2.00	1.00	.60
513	Yankees Team	10.00	5.00	3.00
514	Joe Azcue	2.00	1.00	.60
515	Vern Law	2.00	1.00	.60
516	Al Weis	2.00	1.00	.60
517	Angels Rookies (Paul Schaal, Jack Warner)	2.00	1.00	.60
518	Ken Rowe	2.00	1.00	.60
519	Bob Uecker	45.00	22.00	13.50
520	Tony Cloninger	2.25	1.25	.70
521	Phillies Rookies (Dave Bennett, Morrie Stevens)	2.00	1.00	.60
522	Hank Aguirre	2.00	1.00	.60
523	Mike Brumley	5.00	2.50	1.50
524	Dave Giusti	5.00	2.50	1.50
525	Eddie Bressoud	5.00	2.50	1.50
526	Athletics Rookies *(Jim Hunter, Rene Lachemann, Skip Lockwood, Johnny Odom)*	150.00	75.00	45.00
527	Jeff Torborg	6.00	3.00	1.75
528	George Altman	5.00	2.50	1.50
529	Jerry Fosnow	5.00	2.50	1.50
530	Jim Maloney	6.00	3.00	1.75
531	Chuck Hiller	5.00	2.50	1.50
532	Hector Lopez	5.00	2.50	1.50
533	Mets Rookies (Jim Bethke, *Tug McGraw*, Dan Napolean, *Ron Swoboda*)	20.00	10.00	6.00
534	John Herrnstein	5.00	2.50	1.50
535	Jack Kralick	5.00	2.50	1.50
536	Andre Rodgers	5.00	2.50	1.50
537	Angels Rookies (Marcelino Lopez, *Rudy May*, Phil Roof)	5.00	2.50	1.50
538	Chuck Dressen	6.00	3.00	1.75
539	Herm Starrette	5.00	2.50	1.50
540	Lou Brock	50.00	25.00	15.00
541	White Sox Rookies (Greg Bollo, Bob Locker)	5.00	2.50	1.50
542	Lou Klimchock	5.00	2.50	1.50
543	Ed Connolly	5.00	2.50	1.50
544	Howie Reed	5.00	2.50	1.50
545	Jesus Alou	6.00	3.00	1.75
546	Indians Rookies (Ray Barker, Bill Davis, Mike Hedlund, Floyd Weaver)	5.00	2.50	1.50
547	Jake Wood	5.00	2.50	1.50
548	Dick Stigman	5.00	2.50	1.50
549	Cubs Rookies *(Glenn Beckert*, Roberto Pena)	5.00	2.50	1.50
550	*Mel Stottlemyre*	20.00	10.00	6.00
551	Mets Team	15.00	7.50	4.50
552	Julio Gotay	5.00	2.50	1.50
553	Astros Rookies (Dan Coombs, Jack McClure, Gene Ratliff)	5.00	2.50	1.50
554	Chico Ruiz	5.00	2.50	1.50
555	Jack Baldschun	5.00	2.50	1.50
556	Red Schoendienst	10.00	5.00	3.00
557	Jose Santiago	5.00	2.50	1.50
558	Tommie Sisk	5.00	2.50	1.50
559	Ed Bailey	5.00	2.50	1.50
560	Boog Powell	10.00	5.00	3.00
561	Dodgers Rookies (Dennis Daboll, *Mike Kekich, Jim Lefebvre,* Hector Valle)	6.00	3.00	1.75
562	Billy Moran	5.00	2.50	1.50
563	Julio Navarro	5.00	2.50	1.50
564	Mel Nelson	5.00	2.50	1.50
565	Ernie Broglio	5.00	2.50	1.50
566	Yankees Rookies (Gil Blanco, Art Lopez, Ross Moschitto)	5.00	2.50	1.50
567	Tommie Aaron	6.00	3.00	1.75
568	Ron Taylor	5.00	2.50	1.50
569	Gino Cimoli	5.00	2.50	1.50
570	Claude Osteen	6.00	3.00	1.75
571	Ossie Virgil	5.00	2.50	1.50
572	Orioles Team	6.00	3.00	1.75
573	Red Sox Rookies *(Jim Lonborg*, Gerry Moses, Mike Ryan, Bill Schlesinger)	10.00	5.00	3.00
574	Roy Sievers	6.00	3.00	1.75
575	Jose Pagan	5.00	2.50	1.50
576	Terry Fox	5.00	2.50	1.50
577	A.L. Rookies (Jim Buschhorn, Darold Knowles, Richie Scheinblum)	5.00	2.50	1.50
578	Camilo Carreon	5.00	2.50	1.50
579	Dick Smith	5.00	2.50	1.50
580	Jimmie Hall	5.00	2.50	1.50
581	N.L. Rookies (Kevin Collins, *Tony Perez*, Dave Ricketts)	150.00	75.00	45.00
582	Bob Schmidt	5.00	2.50	1.50
583	Wes Covington	5.00	2.50	1.50
584	Harry Bright	5.00	2.50	1.50
585	Hank Fischer	5.00	2.50	1.50
586	Tommy McCraw	5.00	2.50	1.50
587	Joe Sparma	5.00	2.50	1.50
588	Lenny Green	5.00	2.50	1.50
589	Giants Rookies (Frank Linzy, Bob Schroder)	5.00	2.50	1.50
590	Johnnie Wyatt	5.00	2.50	1.50
591	Bob Skinner	6.00	3.00	1.75
592	Frank Bork	5.00	2.50	1.50
593	Tigers Rookies (Jackie Moore, John Sullivan)	5.00	2.50	1.50
594	Joe Gaines	5.00	2.50	1.50
595	Don Lee	5.00	2.50	1.50
596	Don Landrum	5.00	2.50	1.50
597	Twins Rookies (Joe Nossek, Dick Reese, John Sevcik)	6.00	3.00	1.75
598	Al Downing	10.00	3.00	1.75

1965 Topps Embossed

Inserted in regular packs, the 2-1/8" by 3-1/2" Topps Embossed cards are one of the more fascinating issues of the company. The fronts feature an embossed profile portrait on gold foil-like cardboard (some collectors report finding the cards with silver cardboard). The player's name, team and position are below the portrait - which is good, because most of the embossed portraits are otherwise unrecognizeable. There is a gold border with American players framed in blue and National Leaguers in red. The set contains 72 cards divided equally bewteen the leagues. The set provides an inexpensive way to add some interesting cards to a collection. Being special cards, many stars appear in the set.

	NR MT	EX	VG
Complete Set:	100.00	50.00	30.00
Common Player:	.50	.25	.15

		NR MT	EX	VG
1	Carl Yastrzemski	5.00	2.50	1.50
2	Ron Fairly	.50	.25	.15
3	Max Alvis	.50	.25	.15
4	Jim Ray Hart	.50	.25	.15
5	Bill Skowron	.60	.30	.20
6	Ed Kranepool	.50	.25	.15
7	Tim McCarver	.60	.30	.20
8	Sandy Koufax	5.00	2.50	1.50
9	Donn Clendenon	.50	.25	.15
10	John Romano	.50	.25	.15
11	Mickey Mantle	15.00	7.50	4.50
12	Joe Torre	.70	.35	.20
13	Al Kaline	5.00	2.50	1.50
14	Al McBean	.50	.25	.15
15	Don Drysdale	1.50	.70	.45
16	Brooks Robinson	2.00	1.00	.60
17	Jim Bunning	1.00	.50	.30
18	Gary Peters	.50	.25	.15
19	Bob Clemente	5.00	2.50	1.50
20	Milt Pappas	.50	.25	.15
21	Wayne Causey	.50	.25	.15
22	Frank Robinson	2.00	1.00	.60
23	Bill Mazeroski	.60	.30	.20
24	Diego Segui	.50	.25	.15
25	Jim Bouton	.60	.30	.20
26	Ed Mathews	1.50	.70	.45
27	Willie Mays	6.00	3.00	1.75
28	Ron Santo	.60	.30	.20
29	Boog Powell	.60	.30	.20
30	Ken McBride	.50	.25	.15
31	Leon Wagner	.50	.25	.15
32	John Callison	.50	.25	.15
33	Zoilo Versalles	.50	.25	.15
34	Jack Baldschun	.50	.25	.15
35	Ron Hunt	.50	.25	.15
36	Richie Allen	.70	.35	.20
37	Frank Malzone	.50	.25	.15
38	Bob Allison	.50	.25	.15
39	Jim Fregosi	.60	.30	.20
40	Billy Williams	1.50	.70	.45
41	Bill Freehan	.50	.25	.15
42	Vada Pinson	.70	.35	.20
43	Bill White	.50	.25	.15
44	Roy McMillan	.50	.25	.15
45	Orlando Cepeda	1.00	.50	.30
46	Rocky Colavito	.70	.35	.20
47	Ken Boyer	.70	.35	.20
48	Dick Radatz	.50	.25	.15
49	Tommy Davis	.60	.30	.20
50	Walt Bond	.50	.25	.15
51	John Orsino	.50	.25	.15
52	Joe Christopher	.50	.25	.15
53	Al Spangler	.50	.25	.15
54	Jim King	.50	.25	.15
55	Mickey Lolich	.70	.35	.20
56	Harmon Killebrew	2.00	1.00	.60
57	Bob Shaw	.50	.25	.15
58	Ernie Banks	4.00	2.00	1.25
59	Hank Aaron	5.00	2.50	1.50
60	Chuck Hinton	.50	.25	.15
61	Bob Aspromonte	.50	.25	.15
62	Lee Maye	.50	.25	.15
63	Joe Cunningham	.50	.25	.15
64	Pete Ward	.50	.25	.15
65	Bobby Richardson	1.00	.50	.30
66	Dean Chance	.50	.25	.15
67	Dick Ellsworth	.50	.25	.15
68	Jim Maloney	.50	.25	.15
69	Bob Gibson	1.50	.70	.45
70	Earl Battey	.50	.25	.15
71	Tony Kubek	1.00	.50	.30
72	Jack Kralick	.50	.25	.15

1965 Topps Transfers

Issued as strips of three players each as inserts in 1965, the Topps Transfers were 2" by 3" portraits of players. The transfers have blue or red bands at the top and bottom with the team name and position in the top band and the player's name in the bottom. As is so often the case, the superstars in the transfer set can be quite expensive, but like many of Topps non-card products, the transfers are neither terribly expensive or popular today.

		NR MT	EX	VG
Complete Set:		225.00	112.00	67.00
Common Player:		.60	.30	.20
(1)	Hank Aaron	15.00	7.50	4.50
(2)	Richie Allen	.80	.40	.25
(3)	Bob Allison	.70	.35	.20
(4)	Max Alvis	.60	.30	.20
(5)	Luis Aparicio	2.50	1.25	.70
(6)	Bob Aspromonte	.60	.30	.20
(7)	Walt Bond	.60	.30	.20
(8)	Jim Bouton	.80	.40	.25
(9)	Ken Boyer	.80	.40	.25
(10)	Jim Bunning	1.00	.50	.30
(11)	John Callison	.70	.35	.20
(12)	Rico Carty	.70	.35	.20
(13)	Wayne Causey	.60	.30	.20
(14)	Orlando Cepeda	1.00	.50	.30
(15)	Bob Chance	.60	.30	.20
(16)	Dean Chance	.60	.30	.20
(17)	Joe Christopher	.60	.30	.20
(18)	Bob Clemente	15.00	7.50	4.50
(19)	Rocky Colavito	.80	.40	.25
(20)	Tony Conigliaro	.70	.35	.20
(21)	Tommy Davis	.80	.40	.25
(22)	Don Drysdale	4.00	2.00	1.25
(23)	Bill Freehan	.70	.35	.20
(24)	Jim Fregosi	.70	.35	.20
(25)	Bob Gibson	4.00	2.00	1.25
(26)	Dick Groat	.70	.35	.20
(27)	Tom Haller	.60	.30	.20
(28)	Chuck Hinton	.60	.30	.20
(29)	Elston Howard	1.00	.50	.30
(30)	Ron Hunt	.60	.30	.20
(31)	Al Jackson	.60	.30	.20
(32)	Al Kaline	5.00	2.50	1.50
(33)	Harmon Killebrew	5.00	2.50	1.50
(34)	Jim King	.60	.30	.20
(35)	Ron Kline	.60	.30	.20
(36)	Bobby Knoop	.60	.30	.20
(37)	Sandy Koufax	10.00	5.00	3.00
(38)	Ed Kranepool	.60	.30	.20
(39)	Jim Maloney	.60	.30	.20
(40)	Mickey Mantle	60.00	30.00	18.00
(41)	Juan Marichal	4.00	2.00	1.25
(42)	Lee Maye	.60	.30	.20
(43)	Willie Mays	15.00	7.50	4.50
(44)	Bill Mazeroski	.80	.40	.25
(45)	Tony Oliva	.80	.40	.25
(46)	Jim O'Toole	.60	.30	.20
(47)	Milt Pappas	.70	.35	.20
(48)	Camilo Pascual	.70	.35	.20
(49)	Gary Peters	.60	.30	.20
(50)	Vada Pinson	.80	.40	.25
(51)	Juan Pizarro	.60	.30	.20
(52)	Boog Powell	.80	.40	.25
(53)	Dick Radatz	.60	.30	.20
(54)	Bobby Richardson	1.00	.50	.30
(55)	Brooks Robinson	6.00	3.00	1.75
(56)	Frank Robinson	5.00	2.50	1.50
(57)	Bob Rodgers	.70	.35	.20
(58)	John Roseboro	.70	.35	.20
(59)	Ron Santo	.80	.40	.25
(60)	Diego Segui	.60	.30	.20
(61)	Bill Skowron	.70	.35	.20
(62)	Al Spangler	.60	.30	.20
(63)	Dick Stuart	.70	.35	.20
(64)	Luis Tiant	.80	.40	.25
(65)	Joe Torre	.80	.40	.25
(66)	Bob Veale	.60	.30	.20
(67)	Leon Wagner	.60	.30	.20
(68)	Pete Ward	.60	.30	.20
(69)	Bill White	.70	.35	.20
(70)	Dave Wickersham	.60	.30	.20
(71)	Billy Williams	3.00	1.50	.90
(72)	Carl Yastrzemski	25.00	12.50	7.50

1966 Topps

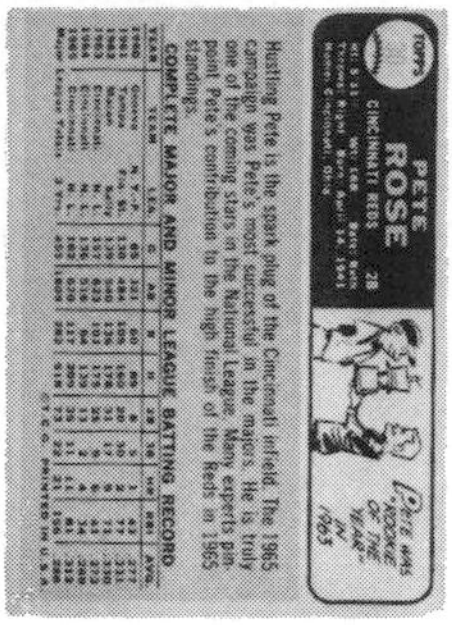

In 1966, Topps produced another 598-card set. The 2-1/2" by 3-1/2" cards feature the almost traditional color photograph with a diagonal strip in the upper left-hand corner carrying the team name. A band at the bottom carries the player's name and position. Multi-player cards returned in 1966 after having had a year's hiatus. The statistical leader cards feature the categorical leader and two runners-up. Most team managers have cards as well. The 1966 set features a handful of cards found with without a notice of the player's sale or trade to another team. Cards without the notice bring higher prices not included in the complete set prices below.

	NR MT	EX	VG
Complete Set:	4500.00	2250.00	1350.
Common Player: 1-110	1.00	.50	.30
Common Player: 111-446	1.25	.60	.40
Common Player: 447-522	5.00	2.50	1.50
Common Player Singleprint: 523-598	20.00	10.00	6.00
Common Player: 523-598	15.00	7.50	4.50

		NR MT	EX	VG
1	Willie Mays	150.00	50.00	25.00
2	Ted Abernathy	1.25	.60	.40
3	Sam Mele	1.00	.50	.30
4	Ray Culp	1.00	.50	.30
5	Jim Fregosi	1.50	.70	.45
6	Chuck Schilling	1.00	.50	.30
7	Tracy Stallard	1.00	.50	.30
8	Floyd Robinson	1.00	.50	.30
9	Clete Boyer	5.00	2.50	1.50
10	Tony Cloninger	1.25	.60	.40
11	Senators Rookies (Brant Alyea, Pete Craig)	1.00	.50	.30
12	John Tsitouris	1.00	.50	.30
13	Lou Johnson	1.00	.50	.30
14	Norm Siebern	1.25	.60	.40
15	Vern Law	1.50	.70	.45
16	Larry Brown	1.25	.60	.40
17	Johnny Stephenson	1.25	.60	.40
18	Roland Sheldon	1.00	.50	.30
19	Giants Team	5.00	2.50	1.50
20	Willie Horton	1.25	.60	.40
21	Don Nottebart	1.00	.50	.30
22	Joe Nossek	1.00	.50	.30
23	Jack Sanford	1.00	.50	.30
24	*Don Kessinger*	1.25	.60	.40
25	Pete Ward	1.00	.50	.30
26	Ray Sadecki	1.00	.50	.30
27	Orioles Rookies *(Andy Etchebarren,* Darold Knowles)	1.25	.60	.40
28	Phil Niekro	12.00	6.00	3.50
29	Mike Brumley	1.00	.50	.30
30	Pete Rose	60.00	30.00	18.00
31	Jack Cullen	1.25	.60	.40
32	Adolfo Phillips	1.00	.50	.30
33	Jim Pagliaroni	1.00	.50	.30
34	Checklist 1-88	5.00	2.50	1.50
35	Ron Swoboda	1.25	.60	.40
36	Jim Hunter	30.00	15.00	9.00
37	Billy Herman	5.00	2.50	1.50
38	Ron Nischwitz	1.00	.50	.30
39	Ken Henderson	1.00	.50	.30
40	Jim Grant	1.00	.50	.30
41	Don LeJohn	1.00	.50	.30
42	Aubrey Gatewood	1.00	.50	.30
43	Don Landrum	1.00	.50	.30
44	Indians Rookies (Bill Davis, Tom Kelley)	1.00	.50	.30
45	Jim Gentile	1.25	.60	.40
46	Howie Koplitz	1.00	.50	.30
47	J.C. Martin	1.00	.50	.30
48	Paul Blair	1.25	.60	.40
49	Woody Woodward	1.25	.60	.40
50	Mickey Mantle	200.00	100.00	60.00
51	Gordon Richardson	1.25	.60	.40
52	Power Plus (Johnny Callison, Wes Covington)	1.50	.70	.45
53	Bob Duliba	1.00	.50	.30
54	Jose Pagan	1.00	.50	.30
55	Ken Harrelson	5.00	2.50	1.50
56	Sandy Valdespino	1.00	.50	.30
57	Jim Lefebvre	1.25	.60	.40
58	Dave Wickersham	1.00	.50	.30
59	Reds Team	2.25	1.25	.70
60	Curt Flood	5.00	2.50	1.50
61	Bob Bolin	1.00	.50	.30
62a	Merritt Ranew (no sold statement)	15.00	7.50	4.50
62b	Merritt Ranew (with sold statement)	1.00	.50	.30
63	Jim Stewart	1.00	.50	.30
64	Bob Bruce	1.00	.50	.30
65	Leon Wagner	1.25	.60	.40
66	Al Weis	1.00	.50	.30
67	Mets Rookies (Cleon Jones, Dick Selma)	1.25	.60	.40
68	Hal Reniff	1.25	.60	.40
69	Ken Hamlin	1.00	.50	.30
70	Carl Yastrzemski	55.00	28.00	16.50
71	Frank Carpin	1.00	.50	.30
72	Tony Perez	20.00	10.00	6.00
73	Jerry Zimmerman	1.00	.50	.30
74	Don Mossi	1.25	.60	.40
75	Tommy Davis	5.00	2.50	1.50
76	Red Schoendienst	3.00	1.50	.90
77	Johnny Orsino	1.00	.50	.30
78	Frank Linzy	1.00	.50	.30
79	Joe Pepitone	5.00	2.50	1.50
80	Richie Allen	2.50	1.25	.70
81	Ray Oyler	1.00	.50	.30
82	Bob Hendley	1.00	.50	.30
83	Albie Pearson	1.00	.50	.30
84	Braves Rookies (Jim Beauchamp, Dick Kelley)	1.00	.50	.30
85	Eddie Fisher	1.00	.50	.30
86	John Bateman	1.00	.50	.30
87	Dan Napoleon	1.25	.60	.40
88	Fred Whitfield	1.00	.50	.30
89	Ted Davidson	1.00	.50	.30
90	Luis Aparicio	9.00	4.50	2.75
91a	Bob Uecker (no trade statement)	80.00	40.00	25.00
91b	Bob Uecker (with trade statement)	20.00	10.00	6.00
92	Yankees Team	5.00	2.50	1.50
93	Jim Lonborg	1.50	.70	.45
94	Matty Alou	1.50	.70	.45
95	Pete Richert	1.00	.50	.30
96	Felipe Alou	1.50	.70	.45
97	Jim Merritt	1.00	.50	.30
98	Don Demeter	1.00	.50	.30
99	Buc Belters (Donn Clendenon, Willie Stargell)	5.00	2.50	1.50
100	Sandy Koufax	90.00	45.00	27.00
101a	Checklist 89-176 (115 is Spahn)	7.00	3.50	2.00
101b	Checklist 89-176 (115 is Henry)	3.00	1.50	.90
102	Ed Kirkpatrick	1.00	.50	.30
103a	Dick Groat (no trade statement)	20.00	10.00	6.00
103b	Dick Groat (with trade statement)	5.00	2.50	1.50
104a	Alex Johnson (no trade statement)	15.00	7.50	4.50
104b	Alex Johnson (with trade statement)	1.25	.60	.40
105	Milt Pappas	1.25	.60	.40
106	Rusty Staub	2.50	1.25	.70
107	Athletics Rookies (Larry Stahl, Ron Tompkins)	1.00	.50	.30
108	Bobby Klaus	1.25	.60	.40
109	Ralph Terry	1.25	.60	.40
110	Ernie Banks	25.00	12.50	7.50
111	Gary Peters	1.25	.60	.40
112	Manny Mota	1.25	.60	.40
113	Hank Aguirre	1.25	.60	.40
114	Jim Gosger	1.25	.60	.40
115	Bill Henry	1.25	.60	.40
116	Walt Alston	2.50	1.25	.70
117	Jake Gibbs	1.50	.70	.45

		NR MT	EX	VG
118	Mike McCormick	1.25	.60	.40
119	Art Shamsky	1.25	.60	.40
120	Harmon Killebrew	15.00	7.50	4.50
121	Ray Herbert	1.25	.60	.40
122	Joe Gaines	1.25	.60	.40
123	Pirates Rookies (Frank Bork, Jerry May)	1.25	.60	.40
124	Tug McGraw	3.00	1.50	.90
125	Lou Brock	20.00	10.00	6.00
126	*Jim Palmer*	250.00	125.00	75.00
127	Ken Berry	1.25	.60	.40
128	Jim Landis	1.25	.60	.40
129	Jack Kralick	1.25	.60	.40
130	Joe Torre	2.25	1.25	.70
131	Angels Team	2.25	1.25	.70
132	Orlando Cepeda	5.00	2.50	1.50
133	Don McMahon	1.25	.60	.40
134	Wes Parker	1.25	.60	.40
135	Dave Morehead	1.25	.60	.40
136	Woody Held	1.25	.60	.40
137	Pat Corrales	1.50	.70	.45
138	Roger Repoz	1.50	.70	.45
139	Cubs Rookies (Byron Browne, Don Young)	1.25	.60	.40
140	Jim Maloney	1.25	.60	.40
141	Tom McCraw	1.25	.60	.40
142	Don Dennis	1.25	.60	.40
143	Jose Tartabull	1.25	.60	.40
144	Don Schwall	1.25	.60	.40
145	Bill Freehan	1.25	.60	.40
146	George Altman	1.25	.60	.40
147	Lum Harris	1.25	.60	.40
148	Bob Johnson	1.25	.60	.40
149	Dick Nen	1.25	.60	.40
150	Rocky Colavito	2.50	1.25	.70
151	Gary Wagner	1.25	.60	.40
152	Frank Malzone	1.25	.60	.40
153	Rico Carty	5.00	2.50	1.50
154	Chuck Hiller	1.25	.60	.40
155	Marcelino Lopez	1.25	.60	.40
156	DP Combo (Hal Lanier, Dick Schofield)	1.50	.70	.45
157	Rene Lachemann	1.25	.60	.40
158	Jim Brewer	1.25	.60	.40
159	Chico Ruiz	1.25	.60	.40
160	Whitey Ford	25.00	12.50	7.50
161	Jerry Lumpe	1.25	.60	.40
162	Lee Maye	1.25	.60	.40
163	Tito Francona	1.25	.60	.40
164	White Sox Rookies (Tommie Agee, Marv Staehle)	1.25	.60	.40
165	Don Lock	1.25	.60	.40
166	Chris Krug	1.25	.60	.40
167	Boog Powell	2.50	1.25	.70
168	Dan Osinski	1.25	.60	.40
169	Duke Sims	1.25	.60	.40
170	Cookie Rojas	1.25	.60	.40
171	Nick Willhite	1.25	.60	.40
172	Mets Team	3.00	1.50	.90
173	Al Spangler	1.25	.60	.40
174	Ron Taylor	1.25	.60	.40
175	Bert Campaneris	5.00	2.50	1.50
176	Jim Davenport	1.25	.60	.40
177	Hector Lopez	1.50	.70	.45
178	Bob Tillman	1.25	.60	.40
179	Cardinals Rookies (Dennis Aust, Bob Tolan)	1.25	.60	.40
180	Vada Pinson	2.50	1.25	.70
181	Al Worthington	1.25	.60	.40
182	Jerry Lynch	1.25	.60	.40
183a	Checklist 177-264 (large print on front)	2.50	1.25	.70
183b	Checklist 177-264 (small print on front)	6.00	3.00	1.75
184	Denis Menke	1.25	.60	.40
185	Bob Buhl	1.25	.60	.40
186	Ruben Amaro	1.50	.70	.45
187	Chuck Dressen	1.25	.60	.40
188	Al Luplow	1.25	.60	.40
189	John Roseboro	1.25	.60	.40
190	Jimmie Hall	1.25	.60	.40
191	Darrell Sutherland	1.25	.60	.40
192	Vic Power	1.25	.60	.40
193	Dave McNally	1.50	.70	.45
194	Senators Team	2.25	1.25	.70
195	Joe Morgan	40.00	20.00	12.00
196	Don Pavletich	1.25	.60	.40
197	Sonny Siebert	1.25	.60	.40
198	*Mickey Stanley*	1.50	.70	.45
199	Chisox Clubbers (Floyd Robinson, Johnny Romano, Bill Skowron)	1.50	.70	.45

		NR MT	EX	VG
200	Ed Mathews	15.00	7.50	4.50
201	Jim Dickson	1.25	.60	.40
202	Clay Dalrymple	1.25	.60	.40
203	Jose Santiago	1.25	.60	.40
204	Cubs Team	2.25	1.25	.70
205	Tom Tresh	5.00	2.50	1.50
206	Alvin Jackson	1.25	.60	.40
207	Frank Quilici	1.25	.60	.40
208	Bob Miller	1.25	.60	.40
209	Tigers Rookies (Fritz Fisher, *John Hiller*)	1.25	.60	.40
210	Bill Mazeroski	2.50	1.25	.70
211	Frank Kreutzer	1.25	.60	.40
212	Ed Kranepool	1.50	.70	.45
213	Fred Newman	1.25	.60	.40
214	Tommy Harper	1.25	.60	.40
215	N.L. Batting Leaders (Hank Aaron, Bob Clemente, Willie Mays)	10.00	5.00	3.00
216	A.L. Batting Leaders (Vic Davalillo, Tony Oliva, Carl Yastrzemski)	6.00	3.00	1.75
217	N.L. Home Run Leaders (Willie Mays, Willie McCovey, Billy Williams)	5.00	2.50	1.50
218	A.L. Home Run Leaders (Norm Cash, Tony Conigliaro, Willie Horton)	2.50	1.25	.70
219	N.L. RBI Leaders (Deron Johnson, Willie Mays, Frank Robinson)	6.00	3.00	1.75
220	A.L. RBI Leaders (Rocky Colavito, Willie Horton, Tony Oliva)	2.50	1.25	.70
221	N.L. ERA Leaders (Sandy Koufax, Vern Law, Juan Marichal)	6.00	3.00	1.75
222	A.L. ERA Leaders (Eddie Fisher, Sam McDowell, Sonny Siebert)	2.50	1.25	.70
223	N.L. Pitching Leaders (Tony Cloninger, Don Drysdale, Sandy Koufax)	6.00	3.00	1.75
224	A.L. Pitching Leaders (Jim Grant, Jim Kaat, Mel Stottlemyre)	3.00	1.50	.90
225	N.L. Strikeout Leaders (Bob Gibson, Sandy Koufax, Bob Veale)	6.00	3.00	1.75
226	A.L. Strikeout Leaders (Mickey Lolich, Sam McDowell, Denny McLain, Sonny Siebert)	2.50	1.25	.70
227	Russ Nixon	1.25	.60	.40
228	Larry Dierker	1.25	.60	.40
229	Hank Bauer	1.25	.60	.40
230	Johnny Callison	1.25	.60	.40
231	Floyd Weaver	1.25	.60	.40
232	Glenn Beckert	1.50	.70	.45
233	Dom Zanni	1.25	.60	.40
234	Yankees Rookies (Rich Beck, *Roy White*)	5.00	2.50	1.50
235	Don Cardwell	1.25	.60	.40
236	Mike Hershberger	1.25	.60	.40
237	Billy O'Dell	1.25	.60	.40
238	Dodgers Team	5.00	2.50	1.50
239	Orlando Pena	1.25	.60	.40
240	Earl Battey	1.25	.60	.40
241	Dennis Ribant	1.25	.60	.40
242	Jesus Alou	1.25	.60	.40
243	Nelson Briles	1.25	.60	.40
244	Astros Rookies (Chuck Harrison, Sonny Jackson)	1.25	.60	.40
245	John Buzhardt	1.25	.60	.40
246	Ed Bailey	1.25	.60	.40
247	Carl Warwick	1.25	.60	.40
248	Pete Mikkelsen	1.25	.60	.40
249	Bill Rigney	1.25	.60	.40
250	Sam Ellis	1.25	.60	.40
251	Ed Brinkman	1.25	.60	.40
252	Denver Lemaster	1.25	.60	.40
253	Don Wert	1.25	.60	.40
254	Phillies Rookies (*Ferguson Jenkins*, Bill Sorrell)	110.00	55.00	33.00
255	Willie Stargell	15.00	7.50	4.50
256	Lew Krausse	1.25	.60	.40
257	Jeff Torborg	1.25	.60	.40
258	Dave Giusti	1.25	.60	.40
259	Red Sox Team	2.50	1.25	.70
260	Bob Shaw	1.25	.60	.40
261	Ron Hansen	1.25	.60	.40
262	Jack Hamilton	1.25	.60	.40
263	Tom Egan	1.25	.60	.40
264	Twins Rookies (Andy Kosco, Ted Uhlaender)	1.25	.60	.40
265	Stu Miller	1.25	.60	.40
266	Pedro Gonzalez	1.25	.60	.40
267	Joe Sparma	1.25	.60	.40
268	John Blanchard	1.25	.60	.40
269	Don Heffner	1.25	.60	.40
270	Claude Osteen	1.25	.60	.40
271	Hal Lanier	1.50	.70	.45
272	Jack Baldschun	1.25	.60	.40

		NR MT	EX	VG
273	Astro Aces (Bob Aspromonte, Rusty Staub)	5.00	2.50	1.50
274	Buster Narum	1.25	.60	.40
275	Tim McCarver	2.50	1.25	.70
276	Jim Bouton	2.50	1.25	.70
277	George Thomas	1.25	.60	.40
278	Calvin Koonce	1.25	.60	.40
279a	Checklist 265-352 (player's cap black)	6.00	3.00	1.75
279b	Checklist 265-352 (player's cap red)	3.00	1.50	.90
280	Bobby Knoop	1.25	.60	.40
281	Bruce Howard	1.25	.60	.40
282	Johnny Lewis	1.25	.60	.40
283	Jim Perry	1.50	.70	.45
284	Bobby Wine	1.25	.60	.40
285	Luis Tiant	2.50	1.25	.70
286	Gary Geiger	1.25	.60	.40
287	Jack Aker	1.25	.60	.40
288	Dodgers Rookies *(Bill Singer, Don Sutton)*	125.00	56.00	35.00
289	Larry Sherry	1.25	.60	.40
290	Ron Santo	5.00	2.50	1.50
291	Moe Drabowsky	1.25	.60	.40
292	Jim Coker	1.25	.60	.40
293	Mike Shannon	1.25	.60	.40
294	Steve Ridzik	1.25	.60	.40
295	Jim Hart	1.25	.60	.40
296	Johnny Keane	1.25	.60	.40
297	Jim Owens	1.25	.60	.40
298	Rico Petrocelli	1.25	.60	.40
299	Lou Burdette	5.00	2.50	1.50
300	Bob Clemente	80.00	40.00	25.00
301	Greg Bollo	1.25	.60	.40
302	Ernie Bowman	1.25	.60	.40
303	Indians Team	2.25	1.25	.70
304	John Herrnstein	1.25	.60	.40
305	Camilo Pascual	1.25	.60	.40
306	Ty Cline	1.25	.60	.40
307	Clay Carroll	1.25	.60	.40
308	Tom Haller	1.25	.60	.40
309	Diego Segui	1.25	.60	.40
310	Frank Robinson	30.00	15.00	9.00
311	Reds Rookies (Tommy Helms, Dick Simpson)	1.25	.60	.40
312	Bob Saverine	1.25	.60	.40
313	Chris Zachary	1.25	.60	.40
314	Hector Valle	1.25	.60	.40
315	Norm Cash	5.00	2.50	1.50
316	Jack Fisher	1.25	.60	.40
317	Dalton Jones	1.25	.60	.40
318	Harry Walker	1.25	.60	.40
319	Gene Freese	1.25	.60	.40
320	Bob Gibson	20.00	10.00	6.00
321	Rick Reichardt	1.25	.60	.40
322	Bill Faul	1.25	.60	.40
323	Ray Barker	1.50	.70	.45
324	John Boozer	1.25	.60	.40
325	Vic Davalillo	1.25	.60	.40
326	Braves Team	2.25	1.25	.70
327	Bernie Allen	1.25	.60	.40
328	Jerry Grote	1.25	.60	.40
329	Pete Charton	1.25	.60	.40
330	Ron Fairly	1.25	.60	.40
331	Ron Herbel	1.25	.60	.40
332	Billy Bryan	1.25	.60	.40
333	Senators Rookies *(Joe Coleman,* Jim French)	1.25	.60	.40
334	Marty Keough	1.25	.60	.40
335	Juan Pizarro	1.25	.60	.40
336	Gene Alley	1.25	.60	.40
337	Fred Gladding	1.25	.60	.40
338	Dal Maxvill	1.25	.60	.40
339	Del Crandall	1.50	.70	.45
340	Dean Chance	1.25	.60	.40
341	Wes Westrum	1.25	.60	.40
342	Bob Humphreys	1.25	.60	.40
343	Joe Christopher	1.25	.60	.40
344	Steve Blass	1.25	.60	.40
345	Bob Allison	1.50	.70	.45
346	Mike de la Hoz	1.25	.60	.40
347	Phil Regan	1.25	.60	.40
348	Orioles Team	5.00	2.50	1.50
349	Cap Peterson	1.25	.60	.40
350	Mel Stottlemyre	3.00	1.50	.90
351	Fred Valentine	1.25	.60	.40
352	Bob Aspromonte	1.25	.60	.40
353	Al McBean	1.25	.60	.40
354	Smoky Burgess	1.50	.70	.45
355	Wade Blasingame	1.25	.60	.40
356	Red Sox Rookies (Owen Johnson, Ken Sanders)	1.25	.60	.40

		NR MT	EX	VG
357	Gerry Arrigo	1.25	.60	.40
358	Charlie Smith	1.25	.60	.40
359	Johnny Briggs	1.25	.60	.40
360	Ron Hunt	1.25	.60	.40
361	Tom Satriano	1.25	.60	.40
362	Gates Brown	1.25	.60	.40
363	Checklist 353-429	3.00	1.50	.90
364	Nate Oliver	1.25	.60	.40
365	Roger Maris	60.00	30.00	18.00
366	Wayne Causey	1.25	.60	.40
367	Mel Nelson	1.25	.60	.40
368	Charlie Lau	1.25	.60	.40
369	Jim King	1.25	.60	.40
370	Chico Cardenas	1.25	.60	.40
371	Lee Stange	1.25	.60	.40
372	Harvey Kuenn	5.00	2.50	1.50
373	Giants Rookies (Dick Estelle, Jack Hiatt)	1.25	.60	.40
374	Bob Locker	1.25	.60	.40
375	Donn Clendenon	1.25	.60	.40
376	Paul Schaal	1.25	.60	.40
377	Turk Farrell	1.25	.60	.40
378	Dick Tracewski	1.25	.60	.40
379	Cardinals Team	2.25	1.25	.70
380	Tony Conigliaro	5.00	2.50	1.50
381	Hank Fischer	1.25	.60	.40
382	Phil Roof	1.25	.60	.40
383	Jackie Brandt	1.25	.60	.40
384	Al Downing	5.00	2.50	1.50
385	Ken Boyer	2.50	1.25	.70
386	Gil Hodges	6.00	3.00	1.75
387	Howie Reed	1.25	.60	.40
388	Don Mincher	1.25	.60	.40
389	Jim O'Toole	1.25	.60	.40
390	Brooks Robinson	20.00	10.00	6.00
391	Chuck Hinton	1.25	.60	.40
392	Cubs Rookies *(Bill Hands, Randy Hundley)*	1.25	.60	.40
393	George Brunet	1.25	.60	.40
394	Ron Brand	1.25	.60	.40
395	Len Gabrielson	1.25	.60	.40
396	Jerry Stephenson	1.25	.60	.40
397	Bill White	1.50	.70	.45
398	Danny Cater	1.25	.60	.40
399	Ray Washburn	1.25	.60	.40
400	Zoilo Versalles	1.25	.60	.40
401	Ken McMullen	1.25	.60	.40
402	Jim Hickman	1.25	.60	.40
403	Fred Talbot	1.25	.60	.40
404	Pirates Team	2.25	1.25	.70
405	Elston Howard	6.00	3.00	1.75
406	Joe Jay	1.25	.60	.40
407	John Kennedy	1.25	.60	.40
408	Lee Thomas	1.25	.60	.40
409	Billy Hoeft	1.25	.60	.40
410	Al Kaline	25.00	12.50	7.50
411	Gene Mauch	1.25	.60	.40
412	Sam Bowens	1.25	.60	.40
413	John Romano	1.25	.60	.40
414	Dan Coombs	1.25	.60	.40
415	Max Alvis	1.25	.60	.40
416	Phil Ortega	1.25	.60	.40
417	Angels Rookies (Jim McGlothlin, Ed Sukla)	1.25	.60	.40
418	Phil Gagliano	1.25	.60	.40
419	Mike Ryan	1.25	.60	.40
420	Juan Marichal	8.00	4.00	2.50
421	Roy McMillan	1.25	.60	.40
422	Ed Charles	1.25	.60	.40
423	Ernie Broglio	1.25	.60	.40
424	Reds Rookies *(Lee May,* Darrell Osteen)	2.25	1.25	.70
425	Bob Veale	1.25	.60	.40
426	White Sox Team	2.25	1.25	.70
427	John Miller	1.25	.60	.40
428	Sandy Alomar	1.25	.60	.40
429	Bill Monbouquette	1.25	.60	.40
430	Don Drysdale	15.00	7.50	4.50
431	Walt Bond	1.25	.60	.40
432	Bob Heffner	1.25	.60	.40
433	Alvin Dark	1.25	.60	.40
434	Willie Kirkland	1.25	.60	.40
435	Jim Bunning	6.00	3.00	1.75
436	Julian Javier	1.25	.60	.40
437	Al Stanek	1.25	.60	.40
438	Willie Smith	1.25	.60	.40
439	Pedro Ramos	1.50	.70	.45
440	Deron Johnson	1.25	.60	.40
441	Tommie Sisk	1.25	.60	.40
442	Orioles Rookies (Ed Barnowski, Eddie Watt)	1.25	.60	.40

		NR MT	EX	VG
443	Bill Wakefield	1.25	.60	.40
444a	Checklist 430-506 (456 is R. Sox Rookies)	3.00	1.50	.90
444b	Checklist 430-506 (456 is Red Sox Rookies)	5.00	2.50	1.50
445	Jim Kaat	6.00	3.00	1.75
446	Mack Jones	1.25	.60	.40
447	Dick Ellsworth (photo actually Ken Hubbs)	5.00	2.50	1.50
448	Eddie Stanky	6.00	3.00	1.75
449	Joe Moeller	5.00	2.50	1.50
450	Tony Oliva	7.00	3.50	2.00
451	Barry Latman	5.00	2.50	1.50
452	Joe Azcue	5.00	2.50	1.50
453	Ron Kline	5.00	2.50	1.50
454	Jerry Buchek	5.00	2.50	1.50
455	Mickey Lolich	6.00	3.00	1.75
456	Red Sox Rookies (Darrell Brandon, Joe Foy)	5.00	2.50	1.50
457	Joe Gibbon	5.00	2.50	1.50
458	Manny Jiminez (Jimenez)	5.00	2.50	1.50
459	Bill McCool	5.00	2.50	1.50
460	Curt Blefary	5.00	2.50	1.50
461	Roy Face	6.00	3.00	1.75
462	Bob Rodgers	2.50	1.25	.70
463	Phillies Team	6.00	3.00	1.75
464	Larry Bearnarth	6.00	3.00	1.75
465	Don Buford	6.00	3.00	1.75
466	Ken Johnson	5.00	2.50	1.50
467	Vic Roznovsky	5.00	2.50	1.50
468	Johnny Podres	6.00	3.00	1.75
469	Yankees Rookies (*Bobby Murcer*, Dooley Womack)	15.00	7.50	4.50
470	Sam McDowell	6.00	3.00	1.75
471	Bob Skinner	5.00	2.50	1.50
472	Terry Fox	5.00	2.50	1.50
473	Rich Rollins	5.00	2.50	1.50
474	Dick Schofield	5.00	2.50	1.50
475	Dick Radatz	6.00	3.00	1.75
476	Bobby Bragan	6.00	3.00	1.75
477	Steve Barber	5.00	2.50	1.50
478	Tony Gonzalez	5.00	2.50	1.50
479	Jim Hannan	5.00	2.50	1.50
480	Dick Stuart	6.00	3.00	1.75
481	Bob Lee	5.00	2.50	1.50
482	Cubs Rookies (John Boccabella, Dave Dowling)	5.00	2.50	1.50
483	Joe Nuxhall	6.00	3.00	1.75
484	Wes Covington	5.00	2.50	1.50
485	Bob Bailey	5.00	2.50	1.50
486	Tommy John	15.00	7.50	4.50
487	Al Ferrara	5.00	2.50	1.50
488	George Banks	5.00	2.50	1.50
489	Curt Simmons	6.00	3.00	1.75
490	Bobby Richardson	12.00	6.00	3.50
491	Dennis Bennett	5.00	2.50	1.50
492	Athletics Team	5.00	2.50	1.50
493	Johnny Klippstein	5.00	2.50	1.50
494	Gordon Coleman	5.00	2.50	1.50
495	Dick McAuliffe	6.00	3.00	1.75
496	Lindy McDaniel	5.00	2.50	1.50
497	Chris Cannizzaro	5.00	2.50	1.50
498	Pirates Rookies (*Woody Fryman*, Luke Walker)	6.00	3.00	1.75
499	Wally Bunker	5.00	2.50	1.50
500	Hank Aaron	90.00	45.00	27.00
501	John O'Donoghue	5.00	2.50	1.50
502	Lenny Green	5.00	2.50	1.50
503	Steve Hamilton	6.00	3.00	1.75
504	Grady Hatton	5.00	2.50	1.50
505	Jose Cardenal	5.00	2.50	1.50
506	Bo Belinsky	6.00	3.00	1.75
507	John Edwards	5.00	2.50	1.50
508	*Steve Hargan*	6.00	3.00	1.75
509	Jake Wood	5.00	2.50	1.50
510	Hoyt Wilhelm	15.00	7.50	4.50
511	Giants Rookies (Bob Barton, *Tito Fuentes*)	6.00	3.00	1.75
512	Dick Stigman	5.00	2.50	1.50
513	Camilo Carreon	5.00	2.50	1.50
514	Hal Woodeshick	5.00	2.50	1.50
515	Frank Howard	7.00	3.50	2.00
516	Eddie Bressoud	5.00	2.50	1.50
517a	Checklist 507-598 (529 is W. Sox Rookies)	9.00	4.50	2.75
517b	Checklist 506-598 (529 is White Sox Rookies)	10.00	5.00	3.00
518	Braves Rookies (Herb Hippauf, Arnie Umbach)	5.00	2.50	1.50
519	Bob Friend	6.00	3.00	1.75
520	Jim Wynn	6.00	3.00	1.75

		NR MT	EX	VG
521	John Wyatt	5.00	2.50	1.50
522	Phil Linz	5.00	2.50	1.50
523	Bob Sadowski	15.00	7.50	4.50
524	Giants Rookies (Ollie Brown, Don Mason)	20.00	10.00	6.00
525	Gary Bell	15.00	7.50	4.50
526	Twins Team	60.00	30.00	18.00
527	Julio Navarro	15.00	7.50	4.50
528	Jesse Gonder	20.00	10.00	6.00
529	White Sox Rookies (*Lee Elia*, Dennis Higgins, Bill Voss)	18.00	9.00	5.50
530	Robin Roberts	35.00	17.50	10.50
531	Joe Cunningham	15.00	7.50	4.50
532	Aurelio Monteagudo	15.00	7.50	4.50
533	Jerry Adair	15.00	7.50	4.50
534	Mets Rookies (Dave Eilers, Rob Gardner)	18.00	9.00	5.50
535	Willie Davis	25.00	12.50	7.50
536	Dick Egan	15.00	7.50	4.50
537	Herman Franks	15.00	7.50	4.50
538	Bob Allen	15.00	7.50	4.50
539	Astros Rookies (Bill Heath, Carroll Sembera)	15.00	7.50	4.50
540	Denny McLain	35.00	17.50	10.50
541	Gene Oliver	15.00	7.50	4.50
542	George Smith	15.00	7.50	4.50
543	Roger Craig	20.00	10.00	6.00
544	Cardinals Rookies (Joe Hoerner, George Kernek, Jimmy Williams)	20.00	10.00	6.00
545	Dick Green	20.00	10.00	6.00
546	Dwight Siebler	15.00	7.50	4.50
547	*Horace Clarke*	20.00	10.00	6.00
548	Gary Kroll	20.00	10.00	6.00
549	Senators Rookies (Al Closter, Casey Cox)	15.00	7.50	4.50
550	Willie McCovey	100.00	50.00	30.00
551	Bob Purkey	20.00	10.00	6.00
552	Birdie Tebbetts	15.00	7.50	4.50
553	Major League Rookies (Pat Garrett, Jackie Warner)	15.00	7.50	4.50
554	Jim Northrup	18.00	9.00	5.50
555	Ron Perranoski	18.00	9.00	5.50
556	Mel Queen	20.00	10.00	6.00
557	Felix Mantilla	15.00	7.50	4.50
558	Red Sox Rookies (Guido Grilli, Pete Magrini, *George Scott*)	20.00	10.00	6.00
559	Roberto Pena	15.00	7.50	4.50
560	Joel Horlen	15.00	7.50	4.50
561	Choo Choo Coleman	20.00	10.00	6.00
562	Russ Snyder	15.00	7.50	4.50
563	Twins Rookies (Pete Cimino, Cesar Tovar)	18.00	9.00	5.50
564	Bob Chance	15.00	7.50	4.50
565	Jimmy Piersall	35.00	17.50	10.50
566	Mike Cuellar	18.00	9.00	5.50
567	Dick Howser	20.00	10.00	6.00
568	Athletics Rookies (Paul Lindblad, Ron Stone)	15.00	7.50	4.50
569	Orlando McFarlane	15.00	7.50	4.50
570	Art Mahaffey	20.00	10.00	6.00
571	Dave Roberts	15.00	7.50	4.50
572	Bob Priddy	15.00	7.50	4.50
573	Derrell Griffith	15.00	7.50	4.50
574	Mets Rookies (Bill Hepler, Bill Murphy)	18.00	9.00	5.50
575	Earl Wilson	15.00	7.50	4.50
576	Dave Nicholson	20.00	10.00	6.00
577	Jack Lamabe	15.00	7.50	4.50
578	Chi Chi Olivo	15.00	7.50	4.50
579	Orioles Rookies (Frank Bertaina, Gene Brabender, Dave Johnson)	20.00	10.00	6.00
580	Billy Williams	80.00	40.00	25.00
581	Tony Martinez	15.00	7.50	4.50
582	Garry Roggenburk	15.00	7.50	4.50
583	Tigers Team	125.00	62.00	37.00
584	Yankees Rookies (Frank Fernandez, *Fritz Peterson*)	18.00	9.00	5.50
585	Tony Taylor	15.00	7.50	4.50
586	Claude Raymond	15.00	7.50	4.50
587	Dick Bertell	15.00	7.50	4.50
588	Athletics Rookies (Chuck Dobson, Ken Suarez)	15.00	7.50	4.50
589	Lou Klimchock	18.00	9.00	5.50
590	Bill Skowron	35.00	17.50	10.50
591	N.L. Rookies (*Grant Jackson*, Bart Shirley)	20.00	10.00	6.00
592	Andre Rodgers	15.00	7.50	4.50
593	Doug Camilli	20.00	10.00	6.00
594	Chico Salmon	15.00	7.50	4.50
595	Larry Jackson	15.00	7.50	4.50
596	Astros Rookies (*Nate Colbert*, Greg Sims)	18.00	9.00	5.50

		NR MT	EX	VG
597	John Sullivan	15.00	7.50	4.50
598	Gaylord Perry	300.00	150.00	90.00

1966 Topps Rub-Offs

Returning to a concept last tried in 1961, Topps tried an expanded version of Rub-Offs in 1966. Measuring 2-1/16" by 3," the Rub-Offs are in vertical format for the 100 players and horizontal for the 20 team pennants. The player Rub-Offs feature a color photo.

		NR MT	EX	VG
Complete Set:		225.00	112.00	67.00
Common Player:		.60	.30	.20
(1)	Hank Aaron	8.00	4.00	2.50
(2)	Jerry Adair	.60	.30	.20
(3)	Richie Allen	1.00	.50	.30
(4)	Jesus Alou	.60	.30	.20
(5)	Max Alvis	.60	.30	.20
(6)	Bob Aspromonte	.60	.30	.20
(7)	Ernie Banks	3.50	1.75	1.00
(8)	Earl Battey	.70	.35	.20
(9)	Curt Blefary	.60	.30	.20
(10)	Ken Boyer	1.00	.50	.30
(11)	Bob Bruce	.60	.30	.20
(12)	Jim Bunning	1.50	.70	.45
(13)	Johnny Callison	.70	.35	.20
(14)	Bert Campaneris	.70	.35	.20
(15)	Jose Cardenal	.60	.30	.20
(16)	Dean Chance	.60	.30	.20
(17)	Ed Charles	.60	.30	.20
(18)	Bob Clemente	7.00	3.50	2.00
(19)	Tony Cloninger	.60	.30	.20
(20)	Rocky Colavito	1.00	.50	.30
(21)	Tony Conigliaro	1.00	.50	.30
(22)	Vic Davalillo	.60	.30	.20
(23)	Willie Davis	.70	.35	.20
(24)	Don Drysdale	3.00	1.50	.90
(25)	Sammy Ellis	.60	.30	.20
(26)	Dick Ellsworth	.60	.30	.20
(27)	Ron Fairly	.70	.35	.20
(28)	Dick Farrell	.60	.30	.20
(29)	Eddie Fisher	.60	.30	.20
(30)	Jack Fisher	.60	.30	.20
(31)	Curt Flood	.70	.35	.20
(32)	Whitey Ford	3.50	1.75	1.00
(33)	Bill Freehan	.70	.35	.20
(34)	Jim Fregosi	.70	.35	.20
(35)	Bob Gibson	3.00	1.50	.90
(36)	Jim Grant	.60	.30	.20
(37)	Jimmie Hall	.60	.30	.20
(38)	Ken Harrelson	.70	.35	.20
(39)	Jim Hart	.60	.30	.20
(40)	Joel Horlen	.60	.30	.20
(41)	Willie Horton	.70	.35	.20
(42)	Frank Howard	1.00	.50	.30
(43)	Deron Johnson	.60	.30	.20
(44)	Al Kaline	4.00	2.00	1.25
(45)	Harmon Killebrew	4.00	2.00	1.25
(46)	Bobby Knoop	.60	.30	.20
(47)	Sandy Koufax	7.00	3.50	2.00
(48)	Ed Kranepool	.60	.30	.20
(49)	Gary Kroll	.60	.30	.20
(50)	Don Landrum	.60	.30	.20
(51)	Vernon Law	.70	.35	.20
(52)	Johnny Lewis	.60	.30	.20
(53)	Don Lock	.60	.30	.20
(54)	Mickey Lolich	1.00	.50	.30
(55)	Jim Maloney	.60	.30	.20
(56)	Felix Mantilla	.60	.30	.20
(57)	Mickey Mantle	40.00	20.00	12.00
(58)	Juan Marichal	3.00	1.50	.90
(59)	Ed Mathews	3.00	1.50	.90
(60)	Willie Mays	8.00	4.00	2.50
(61)	Bill Mazeroski	1.00	.50	.30
(62)	Dick McAuliffe	.60	.30	.20
(63)	Tim McCarver	.70	.35	.20
(64)	Willie McCovey	3.00	1.50	.90
(65)	Sammy McDowell	.70	.35	.20
(66)	Ken McMullen	.60	.30	.20
(67)	Denis Menke	.60	.30	.20
(68)	Bill Monbouquette	.60	.30	.20
(69)	Joe Morgan	2.00	1.00	.60
(70)	Fred Newman	.60	.30	.20
(71)	John O'Donoghue	.60	.30	.20
(72)	Tony Oliva	1.00	.50	.30
(73)	Johnny Orsino	.60	.30	.20
(74)	Phil Ortega	.60	.30	.20
(75)	Milt Pappas	.70	.35	.20
(76)	Dick Radatz	.60	.30	.20
(77)	Bobby Richardson	1.50	.70	.45
(78)	Pete Richert	.60	.30	.20
(79)	Brooks Robinson	4.00	2.00	1.25
(80)	Floyd Robinson	.60	.30	.20
(81)	Frank Robinson	3.50	1.75	1.00
(82)	Cookie Rojas	.60	.30	.20
(83)	Pete Rose	20.00	10.00	6.00
(84)	John Roseboro	.60	.30	.20
(85)	Ron Santo	1.00	.50	.30
(86)	Bill Skowron	.70	.35	.20
(87)	Willie Stargell	3.00	1.50	.90
(88)	Mel Stottlemyre	.70	.35	.20
(89)	Dick Stuart	.60	.30	.20
(90)	Ron Swoboda	.60	.30	.20
(91)	Fred Talbot	.60	.30	.20
(92)	Ralph Terry	.60	.30	.20
(93)	Joe Torre	1.00	.50	.30
(94)	Tom Tresh	.70	.35	.20
(95)	Bob Veale	.60	.30	.20
(96)	Pete Ward	.60	.30	.20
(97)	Bill White	.70	.35	.20
(98)	Billy Williams	2.00	1.00	.60
(99)	Jim Wynn	.70	.35	.20
(100)	Carl Yastrzemski	12.00	6.00	3.50
(101)	Angels Pennant	.60	.30	.20
(102)	Astros Pennant	.60	.30	.20
(103)	Athletics Pennant	.60	.30	.20
(104)	Braves Pennant	.60	.30	.20
(105)	Cards Pennant	.60	.30	.20
(106)	Cubs Pennant	.60	.30	.20
(107)	Dodgers Pennant	.60	.30	.20
(108)	Giants Pennant	.60	.30	.20
(109)	Indians Pennant	.60	.30	.20
(110)	Mets Pennant	.60	.30	.20
(111)	Orioles Pennant	.60	.30	.20
(112)	Phillies Pennant	.60	.30	.20
(113)	Pirates Pennant	.60	.30	.20
(114)	Red Sox Pennant	.60	.30	.20
(115)	Reds Pennant	.60	.30	.20
(116)	Senators Pennant	.60	.30	.20
(117)	Tigers Pennant	.60	.30	.20
(118)	Twins Pennant	.60	.30	.20
(119)	White Sox Pennant	.60	.30	.20
(120)	Yankees Pennant	.60	.30	.20

1967 Topps

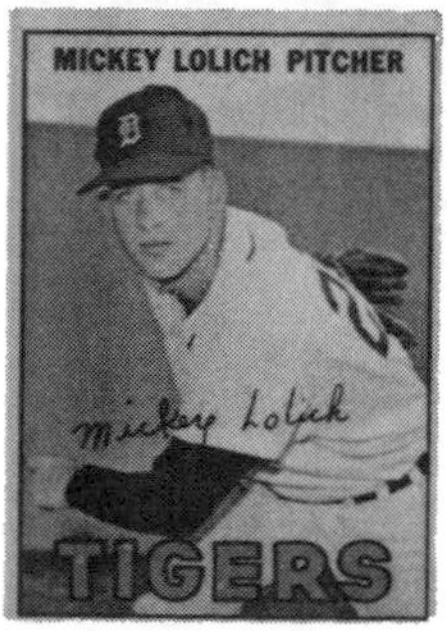

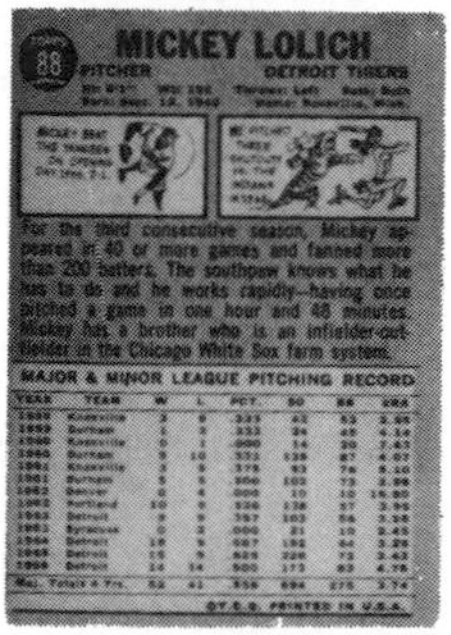

This 609-card set of 2-1/2" by 3-1/2" cards

marked the largest set up to that time for Topps. Card fronts feature large color photographs bordered by white. The player's name and position are printed at the top with the team at the bottom. Across the front of the card with the exception of #254 (Milt Pappas) there is a facsimile autograph. The backs were the first to be done vertically, although they continued to carry familiar statistical and biographical information. The only subsets are statistical leaders and World Series highlights. Rookie cards are done by team or league with two players per card. The high numbers (#'s 534-609) in '67 are quite scarce, and while it is known that some are even scarcer, by virtue of having been short-printed in relation to the rest of the series, there is no general agreement on which cards are involved.

	NR MT	EX	VG
Complete Set:	5000.00	2500.00	1500.
Common Player: 1-110	1.00	.50	.30
Common Player: 111-370	1.50	.70	.45
Common Player: 371-457	1.25	.60	.40
Common Player: 458-533	5.00	2.50	1.50
Common Player: 534-609	12.00	6.00	3.50

		NR MT	EX	VG
1	The Champs (Hank Bauer, Brooks Robinson, Frank Robinson)	20.00	9.00	5.50
2	Jack Hamilton	1.25	.60	.40
3	Duke Sims	1.00	.50	.30
4	Hal Lanier	1.25	.60	.40
5	Whitey Ford	20.00	10.00	6.00
6	Dick Simpson	1.00	.50	.30
7	Don McMahon	1.00	.50	.30
8	Chuck Harrison	1.00	.50	.30
9	Ron Hansen	1.00	.50	.30
10	Matty Alou	1.25	.60	.40
11	Barry Moore	1.00	.50	.30
12	Dodgers Rookies (Jimmy Campanis, Bill Singer)	1.50	.70	.45
13	Joe Sparma	1.00	.50	.30
14	Phil Linz	1.00	.50	.30
15	Earl Battey	1.50	.70	.45
16	Bill Hands	1.00	.50	.30
17	Jim Gosger	1.00	.50	.30
18	Gene Oliver	1.00	.50	.30
19	Jim McGlothlin	1.00	.50	.30
20	Orlando Cepeda	12.00	6.00	3.50
21	Dave Bristol	1.00	.50	.30
22	Gene Brabender	1.00	.50	.30
23	Larry Elliot	1.50	.70	.45
24	Bob Allen	1.00	.50	.30
25	Elston Howard	5.00	2.50	1.50
26a	Bob Priddy (no trade statement)	15.00	7.50	4.50
26b	Bob Priddy (with trade statement)	1.00	.50	.30
27	Bob Saverine	1.00	.50	.30
28	Barry Latman	1.00	.50	.30
29	Tommy McCraw	1.00	.50	.30
30	Al Kaline	20.00	10.00	6.00
31	Jim Brewer	1.00	.50	.30
32	Bob Bailey	1.00	.50	.30
33	Athletics Rookies (*Sal Bando*, Randy Schwartz)	1.75	.90	.50
34	Pete Cimino	1.00	.50	.30
35	Rico Carty	1.25	.60	.40
36	Bob Tillman	1.00	.50	.30
37	Rick Wise	1.50	.70	.45
38	Bob Johnson	1.00	.50	.30
39	Curt Simmons	1.25	.60	.40
40	Rick Reichardt	1.00	.50	.30
41	Joe Hoerner	1.00	.50	.30
42	Mets Team	5.00	2.50	1.50
43	Chico Salmon	1.00	.50	.30
44	Joe Nuxhall	1.25	.60	.40
45	Roger Maris	40.00	20.00	12.00
46	Lindy McDaniel	1.00	.50	.30
47	Ken McMullen	1.00	.50	.30
48	Bill Freehan	1.25	.60	.40
49	Roy Face	1.50	.70	.45
50	Tony Oliva	2.50	1.25	.70
51	Astros Rookies (Dave Adlesh, Wes Bales)	1.00	.50	.30
52	Dennis Higgins	1.00	.50	.30
53	Clay Dalrymple	1.00	.50	.30
54	Dick Green	1.00	.50	.30
55	Don Drysdale	12.00	6.00	3.50
56	Jose Tartabull	1.00	.50	.30
57	*Pat Jarvis*	1.50	.70	.45
58	Paul Schaal	1.00	.50	.30
59	Ralph Terry	1.25	.60	.40
60	Luis Aparicio	5.00	2.50	1.50
61	Gordy Coleman	1.00	.50	.30
62	Checklist 1-109 (Frank Robinson)	5.00	2.50	1.50
63	Cards' Clubbers (Lou Brock, Curt Flood)	13.00	6.50	4.00
64	Fred Valentine	1.00	.50	.30
65	Tom Haller	1.50	.70	.45
66	Manny Mota	1.25	.60	.40
67	Ken Berry	1.00	.50	.30
68	Bob Buhl	1.50	.70	.45
69	Vic Davalillo	1.50	.70	.45
70	Ron Santo	1.75	.90	.50
71	Camilo Pascual	1.50	.70	.45
72	Tigers Rookies (George Korince, John Matchick)	1.00	.50	.30
73	Rusty Staub	2.50	1.25	.70
74	Wes Stock	1.00	.50	.30
75	George Scott	1.25	.60	.40
76	Jim Barbieri	1.00	.50	.30
77	Dooley Womack	1.25	.60	.40
78	Pat Corrales	1.25	.60	.40
79	Bubba Morton	1.00	.50	.30
80	Jim Maloney	1.50	.70	.45
81	Eddie Stanky	1.50	.70	.45
82	Steve Barber	1.00	.50	.30
83	Ollie Brown	1.00	.50	.30
84	Tommie Sisk	1.00	.50	.30
85	Johnny Callison	1.25	.60	.40
86a	Mike McCormick (no trade statement)	9.00	4.50	2.75
86b	Mike McCormick (with trade statement)	1.50	.70	.45
87	George Altman	1.00	.50	.30
88	Mickey Lolich	2.25	1.25	.70
89	*Felix Millan*	1.25	.60	.40
90	Jim Nash	1.00	.50	.30
91	Johnny Lewis	1.50	.70	.45
92	Ray Washburn	1.00	.50	.30
93	Yankees Rookies (*Stan Bahnsen*, Bobby Murcer)	2.50	1.25	.70
94	Ron Fairly	1.25	.60	.40
95	Sonny Siebert	1.50	.70	.45
96	Art Shamsky	1.00	.50	.30
97	Mike Cuellar	1.25	.60	.40
98	Rich Rollins	1.00	.50	.30
99	Lee Stange	1.00	.50	.30
100	Frank Robinson	20.00	10.00	6.00
101	Ken Johnson	1.00	.50	.30
102	Phillies Team	2.00	1.00	.60
103a	Checklist 110-196 (Mickey Mantle) (170 is D McAuliffe)	15.00	7.50	4.50
103b	Checklist 110-196 (Mickey Mantle) (170 is D. McAuliffe)	12.00	6.00	3.50
104	Minnie Rojas	1.00	.50	.30
105	Ken Boyer	2.00	1.00	.60
106	Randy Hundley	1.50	.70	.45
107	Joel Horlen	1.00	.50	.30
108	Alex Johnson	1.00	.50	.30
109	Tribe Thumpers (Rocky Colavito, Leon Wagner)	1.50	.70	.45
110	Jack Aker	1.00	.50	.30
111	John Kennedy	1.50	.70	.45
112	Dave Wickersham	1.50	.70	.45
113	Dave Nicholson	1.50	.70	.45
114	Jack Baldschun	1.50	.70	.45
115	Paul Casanova	1.50	.70	.45
116	Herman Franks	1.50	.70	.45
117	Darrell Brandon	1.50	.70	.45
118	Bernie Allen	1.50	.70	.45
119	Wade Blasingame	1.50	.70	.45
120	Floyd Robinson	1.50	.70	.45
121	Ed Bressoud	1.25	.60	.40
122	George Brunet	1.50	.70	.45
123	Pirates Rookies (Jim Price, Luke Walker)	1.50	.70	.45
124	Jim Stewart	1.50	.70	.45
125	Moe Drabowsky	1.50	.70	.45
126	Tony Taylor	1.50	.70	.45
127	John O'Donoghue	1.50	.70	.45
128	Ed Spiezio	1.50	.70	.45
129	Phil Roof	1.50	.70	.45
130	Phil Regan	1.50	.70	.45
131	Yankees Team	5.00	2.50	1.50
132	Ozzie Virgil	1.50	.70	.45
133	Ron Kline	1.50	.70	.45
134	Gates Brown	1.50	.70	.45
135	Deron Johnson	1.50	.70	.45
136	Carroll Sembera	1.50	.70	.45
137	Twins Rookies (Ron Clark, Jim Ollom)	1.50	.70	.45

		NR MT	EX	VG
138	Dick Kelley	1.50	.70	.45
139	Dalton Jones	1.50	.70	.45
140	Willie Stargell	20.00	10.00	6.00
141	John Miller	1.50	.70	.45
142	Jackie Brandt	1.50	.70	.45
143	Sox Sockers (Don Buford, Pete Ward)	1.25	.60	.40
144	Bill Hepler	1.25	.60	.40
145	Larry Brown	1.50	.70	.45
146	Steve Carlton	100.00	50.00	30.00
147	Tom Egan	1.50	.70	.45
148	Adolfo Phillips	1.50	.70	.45
149	Joe Moeller	1.50	.70	.45
150	Mickey Mantle	200.00	80.00	50.00
151	World Series Game 1 (Moe Mows Down 11)	2.00	1.00	.60
152	World Series Game 2 (Palmer Blanks Dodgers)	3.50	1.75	1.00
153	World Series Game 3 (Blair's Homer Defeats L.A.)	2.00	1.00	.60
154	World Series Game 4 (Orioles Win 4th Straight)	2.00	1.00	.60
155	World Series Summary (The Winners Celebrate)	2.00	1.00	.60
156	Ron Herbel	1.50	.70	.45
157	Danny Cater	1.50	.70	.45
158	Jimmy Coker	1.50	.70	.45
159	Bruce Howard	1.50	.70	.45
160	Willie Davis	1.50	.70	.45
161	Dick Williams	1.50	.70	.45
162	Billy O'Dell	1.50	.70	.45
163	Vic Roznovsky	1.50	.70	.45
164	Dwight Siebler	1.50	.70	.45
165	Cleon Jones	1.25	.60	.40
166	Ed Mathews	12.00	6.00	3.50
167	Senators Rookies (Joe Coleman, Tim Cullen)	1.25	.60	.40
168	Ray Culp	1.50	.70	.45
169	Horace Clarke	1.25	.60	.40
170	Dick McAuliffe	1.25	.60	.40
171	Calvin Koonce	1.50	.70	.45
172	Bill Heath	1.50	.70	.45
173	Cardinals Team	2.00	1.00	.60
174	Dick Radatz	1.25	.60	.40
175	Bobby Knoop	1.50	.70	.45
176	Sammy Ellis	1.50	.70	.45
177	Tito Fuentes	1.50	.70	.45
178	John Buzhardt	1.50	.70	.45
179	Braves Rookies (Cecil Upshaw, Chas. Vaughn)	1.50	.70	.45
180	Curt Blefary	1.50	.70	.45
181	Terry Fox	1.50	.70	.45
182	Ed Charles	1.50	.70	.45
183	Jim Pagliaroni	1.50	.70	.45
184	George Thomas	1.50	.70	.45
185	*Ken Holtzman*	2.75	1.50	.80
186	Mets Maulers (Ed Kranepool, Ron Swoboda)	1.50	.70	.45
187	Pedro Ramos	1.50	.70	.45
188	Ken Harrelson	1.50	.70	.45
189	Chuck Hinton	1.50	.70	.45
190	Turk Farrell	1.50	.70	.45
191a	Checklist 197-283 (Willie Mays) (214 is Dick Kelley)	12.00	6.00	3.50
191b	Checklist 197-283 (Willie Mays) (214 is Tom Kelley)	12.00	6.00	3.50
192	Fred Gladding	1.50	.70	.45
193	Jose Cardenal	1.25	.60	.40
194	Bob Allison	1.50	.70	.45
195	Al Jackson	1.50	.70	.45
196	Johnny Romano	1.50	.70	.45
197	Ron Perranoski	1.25	.60	.40
198	Chuck Hiller	1.25	.60	.40
199	Billy Hitchcock	1.50	.70	.45
200	Willie Mays	75.00	38.00	23.00
201	Hal Reniff	1.25	.60	.40
202	Johnny Edwards	1.50	.70	.45
203	Al McBean	1.50	.70	.45
204	Orioles Rookies (*Mike Epstein,* Tom Phoebus)	1.50	.70	.45
205	Dick Groat	1.50	.70	.45
206	Dennis Bennett	1.50	.70	.45
207	John Orsino	1.50	.70	.45
208	Jack Lamabe	1.50	.70	.45
209	Joe Nossek	1.50	.70	.45
210	Bob Gibson	18.00	9.00	5.50
211	Twins Team	2.00	1.00	.60
212	Chris Zachary	1.50	.70	.45
213	*Jay Johnstone*	1.75	.90	.50
214	Tom Kelley	1.50	.70	.45
215	Ernie Banks	18.00	9.00	5.50

		NR MT	EX	VG
216	Bengal Belters (Norm Cash, Al Kaline)	5.00	2.50	1.50
217	Rob Gardner	1.25	.60	.40
218	Wes Parker	1.25	.60	.40
219	Clay Carroll	1.25	.60	.40
220	Jim Hart	1.25	.60	.40
221	Woody Fryman	1.25	.60	.40
222	Reds Rookies (Lee May, Darrell Osteen)	1.25	.60	.40
223	Mike Ryan	1.50	.70	.45
224	Walt Bond	1.50	.70	.45
225	Mel Stottlemyre	2.25	1.25	.70
226	Julian Javier	1.25	.60	.40
227	Paul Lindblad	1.50	.70	.45
228	Gil Hodges	5.00	2.50	1.50
229	Larry Jackson	1.50	.70	.45
230	Boog Powell	2.50	1.25	.70
231	John Bateman	1.50	.70	.45
232	Don Buford	1.25	.60	.40
233	A.L. ERA Leaders (Steve Hargan, Joel Horlen, Gary Peters)	2.00	1.00	.60
234	N.L. ERA Leaders (Mike Cuellar, Sandy Koufax, Juan Marichal)	12.00	6.00	3.50
235	A.L. Pitching Leaders (Jim Kaat, Denny McLain, Earl Wilson)	2.50	1.25	.70
236	N.L. Pitching Leaders (Bob Gibson, Sandy Koufax, Juan Marichal, Gaylord Perry)	12.00	6.00	3.50
237	A.L. Strikeout Leaders (Jim Kaat, Sam McDowell, Earl Wilson)	2.50	1.25	.70
238	N.L. Strikeout Leaders (Jim Bunning, Sandy Koufax, Bob Veale)	12.00	6.00	3.50
239	AL 1966 Batting Leaders (Al Kaline, Tony Oliva, Frank Robinson)	12.00	6.00	3.50
240	N.L. Batting Leaders (Felipe Alou, Matty Alou, Rico Carty)	2.00	1.00	.60
241	A.L. RBI Leaders (Harmon Killebrew, Boog Powell, Frank Robinson)	3.50	1.75	1.00
242	N.L. RBI Leaders (Hank Aaron, Richie Allen, Bob Clemente)	12.00	6.00	3.50
243	A.L. Home Run Leaders (Harmon Killebrew, Boog Powell, Frank Robinson)	3.50	1.75	1.00
244	N.L. Home Run Leaders (Hank Aaron, Richie Allen, Willie Mays)	12.00	6.00	3.50
245	Curt Flood	2.50	1.25	.70
246	Jim Perry	1.25	.60	.40
247	Jerry Lumpe	1.25	.60	.40
248	Gene Mauch	1.25	.60	.40
249	Nick Willhite	1.50	.70	.45
250	Hank Aaron	80.00	40.00	25.00
251	Woody Held	1.50	.70	.45
252	Bob Bolin	1.50	.70	.45
253	Indians Rookies (Bill Davis, Gus Gil)	1.50	.70	.45
254	Milt Pappas	1.25	.60	.40
255	Frank Howard	2.50	1.25	.70
256	Bob Hendley	1.50	.70	.45
257	Charley Smith	1.25	.60	.40
258	Lee Maye	1.50	.70	.45
259	Don Dennis	1.50	.70	.45
260	Jim Lefebvre	1.25	.60	.40
261	John Wyatt	1.50	.70	.45
262	Athletics Team	2.00	1.00	.60
263	Hank Aguirre	1.50	.70	.45
264	Ron Swoboda	1.25	.60	.40
265	Lou Burdette	2.50	1.25	.70
266	Pitt Power (Donn Clendenon, Willie Stargell)	3.50	1.75	1.00
267	Don Schwall	1.50	.70	.45
268	John Briggs	1.50	.70	.45
269	Don Nottebart	1.50	.70	.45
270	Zoilo Versalles	1.25	.60	.40
271	Eddie Watt	1.50	.70	.45
272	Cubs Rookies (Bill Connors, Dave Dowling)	1.50	.70	.45
273	Dick Lines	1.50	.70	.45
274	Bob Aspromonte	1.50	.70	.45
275	Fred Whitfield	1.50	.70	.45
276	Bruce Brubaker	1.50	.70	.45
277	Steve Whitaker	1.25	.60	.40
278	Checklist 284-370 (Jim Kaat)	5.00	2.50	1.50
279	Frank Linzy	1.50	.70	.45
280	Tony Conigliaro	2.00	1.00	.60
281	Bob Rodgers	1.50	.70	.45
282	Johnny Odom	1.25	.60	.40
283	Gene Alley	1.25	.60	.40
284	Johnny Podres	5.00	2.50	1.50
285	Lou Brock	20.00	10.00	6.00
286	Wayne Causey	1.50	.70	.45
287	Mets Rookies (Greg Goossen, Bart Shirley)	1.25	.60	.40

		NR MT	EX	VG
288	Denver Lemaster	1.50	.70	.45
289	Tom Tresh	1.75	.90	.50
290	Bill White	1.25	.60	.40
291	Jim Hannan	1.50	.70	.45
292	Don Pavletich	1.50	.70	.45
293	Ed Kirkpatrick	1.50	.70	.45
294	Walt Alston	3.25	1.75	1.00
295	Sam McDowell	1.25	.60	.40
296	Glenn Beckert	1.25	.60	.40
297	Dave Morehead	1.50	.70	.45
298	Ron Davis	1.50	.70	.45
299	Norm Siebern	1.25	.60	.40
300	Jim Kaat	13.00	6.50	4.00
301	Jesse Gonder	1.50	.70	.45
302	Orioles Team	2.00	1.00	.60
303	Gil Blanco	1.50	.70	.45
304	Phil Gagliano	1.50	.70	.45
305	Earl Wilson	1.50	.70	.45
306	*Bud Harrelson*	1.75	.90	.50
307	Jim Beauchamp	1.50	.70	.45
308	Al Downing	1.50	.70	.45
309	Hurlers Beware (Richie Allen, Johnny Callison)	2.00	1.00	.60
310	Gary Peters	1.25	.60	.40
311	Ed Brinkman	1.25	.60	.40
312	Don Mincher	1.25	.60	.40
313	Bob Lee	1.50	.70	.45
314	Red Sox Rookies *(Mike Andrews, Reggie Smith)*	5.00	2.50	1.50
315	Billy Williams	12.00	6.00	3.50
316	Jack Kralick	1.50	.70	.45
317	Cesar Tovar	1.50	.70	.45
318	Dave Giusti	1.50	.70	.45
319	Paul Blair	1.25	.60	.40
320	Gaylord Perry	12.00	6.00	3.50
321	Mayo Smith	1.50	.70	.45
322	Jose Pagan	1.50	.70	.45
323	Mike Hershberger	1.50	.70	.45
324	Hal Woodeshick	1.50	.70	.45
325	Chico Cardenas	1.50	.70	.45
326	Bob Uecker	20.00	10.00	6.00
327	Angels Team	2.00	1.00	.60
328	Clete Boyer	1.50	.70	.45
329	Charlie Lau	1.25	.60	.40
330	Claude Osteen	1.25	.60	.40
331	Joe Foy	1.50	.70	.45
332	Jesus Alou	1.50	.70	.45
333	Ferguson Jenkins	25.00	12.50	7.50
334	Twin Terrors (Bob Allison, Harmon Killebrew)	3.50	1.75	1.00
335	Bob Veale	1.25	.60	.40
336	Joe Azcue	1.50	.70	.45
337	Joe Morgan	25.00	12.50	7.50
338	Bob Locker	1.50	.70	.45
339	Chico Ruiz	1.50	.70	.45
340	Joe Pepitone	2.00	1.00	.60
341	Giants Rookies *(Dick Dietz,* Bill Sorrell)	1.25	.60	.40
342	Hank Fischer	1.50	.70	.45
343	Tom Satriano	1.50	.70	.45
344	Ossie Chavarria	1.50	.70	.45
345	Stu Miller	1.50	.70	.45
346	Jim Hickman	1.25	.60	.40
347	Grady Hatton	1.50	.70	.45
348	Tug McGraw	2.25	1.25	.70
349	Bob Chance	1.50	.70	.45
350	Joe Torre	2.00	1.00	.60
351	Vern Law	1.50	.70	.45
352	Ray Oyler	1.50	.70	.45
353	Bill McCool	1.50	.70	.45
354	Cubs Team	2.00	1.00	.60
355	Carl Yastrzemski	80.00	40.00	25.00
356	Larry Jaster	1.50	.70	.45
357	Bill Skowron	1.50	.70	.45
358	Ruben Amaro	1.25	.60	.40
359	Dick Ellsworth	1.50	.70	.45
360	Leon Wagner	1.25	.60	.40
361	Checklist 371-457 (Bob Clemente)	13.00	6.50	4.00
362	Darold Knowles	1.50	.70	.45
363	Dave Johnson	2.00	1.00	.60
364	Claude Raymond	1.50	.70	.45
365	John Roseboro	1.25	.60	.40
366	Andy Kosco	1.50	.70	.45
367	Angels Rookies (Bill Kelso, Don Wallace)	1.50	.70	.45
368	Jack Hiatt	1.50	.70	.45
369	Jim Hunter	18.00	9.00	5.50
370	Tommy Davis	1.50	.70	.45
371	Jim Lonborg	1.50	.70	.45
372	Mike de la Hoz	1.25	.60	.40

		NR MT	EX	VG
373	White Sox Rookies (Duane Josephson, Fred Klages)	1.25	.60	.40
374	Mel Queen	1.25	.60	.40
375	Jake Gibbs	1.25	.60	.40
376	Don Lock	1.25	.60	.40
377	Luis Tiant	2.25	1.25	.70
378	Tigers Team	5.00	2.50	1.50
379	Jerry May	1.25	.60	.40
380	Dean Chance	1.50	.70	.45
381	Dick Schofield	1.25	.60	.40
382	Dave McNally	1.25	.60	.40
383	Ken Henderson	1.25	.60	.40
384	Cardinals Rookies (Jim Cosman, Dick Hughes)	1.25	.60	.40
385	Jim Fregosi	1.50	.70	.45
386	Dick Selma	1.50	.70	.45
387	Cap Peterson	1.25	.60	.40
388	Arnold Earley	1.25	.60	.40
389	Al Dark	1.50	.70	.45
390	Jim Wynn	1.25	.60	.40
391	Wilbur Wood	1.50	.70	.45
392	Tommy Harper	1.50	.70	.45
393	Jim Bouton	2.25	1.25	.70
394	Jake Wood	1.25	.60	.40
395	Chris Short	1.25	.60	.40
396	Atlanta Aces (Tony Cloninger, Denis Menke)	1.25	.60	.40
397	Willie Smith	1.25	.60	.40
398	Jeff Torborg	1.50	.70	.45
399	Al Worthington	1.25	.60	.40
400	Bob Clemente	75.00	38.00	23.00
401	Jim Coates	1.25	.60	.40
402	Phillies Rookies (Grant Jackson, Billy Wilson)	1.25	.60	.40
403	Dick Nen	1.25	.60	.40
404	Nelson Briles	1.50	.70	.45
405	Russ Snyder	1.25	.60	.40
406	Lee Elia	1.50	.70	.45
407	Reds Team	2.50	1.25	.70
408	Jim Northrup	1.50	.70	.45
409	Ray Sadecki	1.25	.60	.40
410	Lou Johnson	1.25	.60	.40
411	Dick Howser	1.50	.70	.45
412	Astros Rookies (Norm Miller, *Doug Rader*)	1.25	.60	.40
413	Jerry Grote	1.50	.70	.45
414	Casey Cox	1.25	.60	.40
415	Sonny Jackson	1.25	.60	.40
416	Roger Repoz	1.25	.60	.40
417	Bob Bruce	1.25	.60	.40
418	Sam Mele	1.25	.60	.40
419	Don Kessinger	1.50	.70	.45
420	Denny McLain	5.00	2.50	1.50
421	Dal Maxvill	1.50	.70	.45
422	Hoyt Wilhelm	15.00	7.50	4.50
423	Fence Busters (Willie Mays, Willie McCovey)	20.00	10.00	6.00
424	Pedro Gonzalez	1.25	.60	.40
425	Pete Mikkelsen	1.25	.60	.40
426	Lou Clinton	1.25	.60	.40
427	Ruben Gomez	1.25	.60	.40
428	Dodgers Rookies (Tom Hutton, *Gene Michael)*	1.25	.60	.40
429	Garry Roggenburk	1.25	.60	.40
430	Pete Rose	75.00	38.00	23.00
431	Ted Uhlaender	1.25	.60	.40
432	Jimmie Hall	1.25	.60	.40
433	Al Luplow	1.50	.70	.45
434	Eddie Fisher	1.25	.60	.40
435	Mack Jones	1.25	.60	.40
436	Pete Ward	1.25	.60	.40
437	Senators Team	2.25	1.25	.70
438	Chuck Dobson	1.25	.60	.40
439	Byron Browne	1.25	.60	.40
440	Steve Hargan	1.25	.60	.40
441	Jim Davenport	1.25	.60	.40
442	Yankees Rookies *(Bill Robinson,* Joe Verbanic)	1.50	.70	.45
443	Tito Francona	1.50	.70	.45
444	George Smith	1.25	.60	.40
445	Don Sutton	18.00	9.00	5.50
446	Russ Nixon	1.25	.60	.40
447	Bo Belinsky	1.25	.60	.40
448	Harry Walker	1.50	.70	.45
449	Orlando Pena	1.25	.60	.40
450	Richie Allen	5.00	2.50	1.50
451	Fred Newman	1.25	.60	.40
452	Ed Kranepool	1.25	.60	.40
453	Aurelio Monteagudo	1.25	.60	.40
454a	Checklist 458-533 (Juan Marichal) (left ear shows)	12.00	6.00	3.50

		NR MT	EX	VG
454b	Checklist 458-533 (Juan Marichal) (no left ear)	12.00	6.00	3.50
455	Tommie Agee	1.50	.70	.45
456	Phil Niekro	12.00	6.00	3.50
457	Andy Etchebarren	1.25	.60	.40
458	Lee Thomas	5.00	2.50	1.50
459	Senators Rookies (*Dick Bosman*, Pete Craig)	12.00	6.00	3.50
460	Harmon Killebrew	45.00	23.00	13.50
461	Bob Miller	5.00	2.50	1.50
462	Bob Barton	5.00	2.50	1.50
463	Tribe Hill Aces (Sam McDowell, Sonny Siebert)	12.00	6.00	3.50
464	Dan Coombs	5.00	2.50	1.50
465	Willie Horton	12.00	6.00	3.50
466	Bobby Wine	5.00	2.50	1.50
467	Jim O'Toole	5.00	2.50	1.50
468	Ralph Houk	13.00	6.50	4.00
469	Len Gabrielson	5.00	2.50	1.50
470	Bob Shaw	5.00	2.50	1.50
471	Rene Lachemann	5.00	2.50	1.50
472	Pirates Rookies (John Gelnar, George Spriggs)	5.00	2.50	1.50
473	Jose Santiago	5.00	2.50	1.50
474	Bob Tolan	12.00	6.00	3.50
475	Jim Palmer	75.00	38.00	23.00
476	Tony Perez	70.00	35.00	20.00
477	Braves Team	5.50	2.75	1.75
478	Bob Humphreys	5.00	2.50	1.50
479	Gary Bell	5.00	2.50	1.50
480	Willie McCovey	30.00	15.00	9.00
481	Leo Durocher	13.00	6.50	4.00
482	Bill Monbouquette	12.00	6.00	3.50
483	Jim Landis	5.00	2.50	1.50
484	Jerry Adair	5.00	2.50	1.50
485	Tim McCarver	13.00	6.50	4.00
486	Twins Rookies (Rich Reese, Bill Whitby)	5.00	2.50	1.50
487	Tom Reynolds	5.00	2.50	1.50
488	Gerry Arrigo	5.00	2.50	1.50
489	Doug Clemens	5.00	2.50	1.50
490	Tony Cloninger	12.00	6.00	3.50
491	Sam Bowens	5.00	2.50	1.50
492	Pirates Team	5.50	2.75	1.75
493	Phil Ortega	5.00	2.50	1.50
494	Bill Rigney	5.00	2.50	1.50
495	Fritz Peterson	12.00	6.00	3.50
496	Orlando McFarlane	5.00	2.50	1.50
497	Ron Campbell	5.00	2.50	1.50
498	Larry Dierker	12.00	6.00	3.50
499	Indians Rookies (George Culver, Jose Vidal)	5.00	2.50	1.50
500	Juan Marichal	20.00	10.00	6.00
501	Jerry Zimmerman	5.00	2.50	1.50
502	Derrell Griffith	5.00	2.50	1.50
503	Dodgers Team	13.00	6.50	4.00
504	Orlando Martinez	5.00	2.50	1.50
505	Tommy Helms	5.00	2.50	1.50
506	Smoky Burgess	12.00	6.00	3.50
507	Orioles Rookies (Ed Barnowski, Larry Haney)	5.00	2.50	1.50
508	Dick Hall	5.00	2.50	1.50
509	Jim King	5.00	2.50	1.50
510	Bill Mazeroski	13.00	6.50	4.00
511	Don Wert	5.00	2.50	1.50
512	Red Schoendienst	15.00	7.50	4.50
513	Marcelino Lopez	5.00	2.50	1.50
514	John Werhas	5.00	2.50	1.50
515	Bert Campaneris	12.00	6.00	3.50
516	Giants Team	5.50	2.75	1.75
517	Fred Talbot	12.00	6.00	3.50
518	Denis Menke	5.00	2.50	1.50
519	Ted Davidson	5.00	2.50	1.50
520	Max Alvis	5.00	2.50	1.50
521	Bird Bombers (Curt Blefary, Boog Powell)	13.00	6.50	4.00
522	John Stephenson	5.00	2.50	1.50
523	Jim Merritt	5.00	2.50	1.50
524	Felix Mantilla	5.00	2.50	1.50
525	Ron Hunt	12.00	6.00	3.50
526	Tigers Rookies (*Pat Dobson*, George Korince)	12.00	6.00	3.50
527	Dennis Ribant	5.00	2.50	1.50
528	Rico Petrocelli	12.00	6.00	3.50
529	Gary Wagner	5.00	2.50	1.50
530	Felipe Alou	12.00	6.00	3.50
531	Checklist 534-609 (Brooks Robinson)	12.00	6.00	3.50
532	Jim Hicks	5.00	2.50	1.50
533	Jack Fisher	5.00	2.50	1.50
534	Hank Bauer	15.00	7.50	4.50
535	Donn Clendenon	12.00	6.00	3.50
536	Cubs Rookies (*Joe Niekro*, Paul Popovich)	30.00	15.00	9.00
537	Chuck Estrada	12.00	6.00	3.50
538	J.C. Martin	15.00	7.50	4.50
539	Dick Egan	12.00	6.00	3.50
540	Norm Cash	35.00	17.50	10.50
541	Joe Gibbon	15.00	7.50	4.50
542	Athletics Rookies (*Rick Monday*, Tony Pierce)	12.00	6.00	3.50
543	Dan Schneider	15.00	7.50	4.50
544	Indians Team	12.00	6.00	3.50
545	Jim Grant	15.00	7.50	4.50
546	Woody Woodward	15.00	7.50	4.50
547	Red Sox Rookies (Russ Gibson, Bill Rohr)	15.00	7.50	4.50
548	Tony Gonzalez	12.00	6.00	3.50
549	Jack Sanford	12.00	6.00	3.50
550	Vada Pinson	12.00	6.00	3.50
551	Doug Camilli	12.00	6.00	3.50
552	Ted Savage	12.00	6.00	3.50
553	Yankees Rookies (Mike Hegan, Thad Tillotson)	18.00	9.00	5.50
554	Andre Rodgers	12.00	6.00	3.50
555	Don Cardwell	15.00	7.50	4.50
556	Al Weis	12.00	6.00	3.50
557	Al Ferrara	12.00	6.00	3.50
558	Orioles Rookies (*Mark Belanger*, Bill Dillman)	35.00	17.50	10.50
559	Dick Tracewski	12.00	6.00	3.50
560	Jim Bunning	40.00	20.00	12.00
561	Sandy Alomar	15.00	7.50	4.50
562	Steve Blass	12.00	6.00	3.50
563	Joe Adcock	18.00	9.00	5.50
564	Astros Rookies (Alonzo Harris, Aaron Pointer)	15.00	7.50	4.50
565	Lew Krausse	15.00	7.50	4.50
566	Gary Geiger	12.00	6.00	3.50
567	Steve Hamilton	15.00	7.50	4.50
568	John Sullivan	15.00	7.50	4.50
569	A.L. Rookies (Hank Allen, *Rod Carew*)	475.00	237.00	142.00
570	Maury Wills	80.00	40.00	25.00
571	Larry Sherry	12.00	6.00	3.50
572	Don Demeter	12.00	6.00	3.50
573	White Sox Team	18.00	9.00	5.50
574	Jerry Buchek	12.00	6.00	3.50
575	*Dave Boswell*	12.00	6.00	3.50
576	N.L. Rookies (Norm Gigon, Ramon Hernandez)	18.00	9.00	5.50
577	Bill Short	15.00	7.50	4.50
578	John Boccabella	15.00	7.50	4.50
579	Bill Henry	15.00	7.50	4.50
580	Rocky Colavito	70.00	35.00	21.00
581	Mets Rookies (Bill Denehy, *Tom Seaver*)	1200.00	600.00	350.00
582	Jim Owens	12.00	6.00	3.50
583	Ray Barker	15.00	7.50	4.50
584	Jim Piersall	20.00	10.00	6.00
585	Wally Bunker	15.00	7.50	4.50
586	Manny Jimenez	15.00	7.50	4.50
587	N.L. Rookies (Don Shaw, Gary Sutherland)	18.00	9.00	5.50
588	Johnny Klippstein	12.00	6.00	3.50
589	Dave Ricketts	12.00	6.00	3.50
590	Pete Richert	15.00	7.50	4.50
591	Ty Cline	12.00	6.00	3.50
592	N.L. Rookies (Jim Shellenback, Ron Willis)	13.00	6.50	4.00
593	Wes Westrum	15.00	7.50	4.50
594	Dan Osinski	15.00	7.50	4.50
595	Cookie Rojas	12.00	6.00	3.50
596	Galen Cisco	12.00	6.00	3.50
597	Ted Abernathy	12.00	6.00	3.50
598	White Sox Rookies (Ed Stroud, Walt Williams)	13.00	6.50	4.00
599	Bob Duliba	12.00	6.00	3.50
600	Brooks Robinson	225.00	112.00	67.00
601	Bill Bryan	15.00	7.50	4.50
602	Juan Pizarro	15.00	7.50	4.50
603	Athletics Rookies (Tim Talton, Ramon Webster)	15.00	7.50	4.50
604	Red Sox Team	100.00	50.00	30.00
605	Mike Shannon	30.00	15.00	9.00
606	Ron Taylor	15.00	7.50	4.50
607	Mickey Stanley	12.00	6.00	3.50
608	Cubs Rookies (Rich Nye, John Upham)	12.00	6.00	3.50
609	Tommy John	125.00	62.00	37.00

1967 Topps Pin-Ups

The 5" by 7" "All Star Pin-ups" were inserts to regular 1967 Topps baseball cards. They feature a full color picture with the player's name, position and team in a circle on the lower left side of the front. The numbered set consists of 32 players (generally big names). Even so, they are rather inexpensive. Because the large paper pin-ups had to be folded several times to fit into the wax packs, they are almost never found in true "Mint" condition.

		NR MT	EX	VG
Complete Set:		60.00	30.00	18.00
Common Player:		.25	.13	.08
1	Boog Powell	.40	.20	.12
2	Bert Campaneris	.30	.15	.09
3	Brooks Robinson	3.00	1.50	.90
4	Tommie Agee	.25	.13	.08
5	Carl Yastrzemski	3.50	1.75	1.00
6	Mickey Mantle	12.00	6.00	3.50
7	Frank Howard	.50	.25	.15
8	Sam McDowell	.25	.13	.08
9	Orlando Cepeda	.60	.30	.20
10	Chico Cardenas	.25	.13	.08
11	Bob Clemente	5.00	2.50	1.50
12	Willie Mays	5.00	2.50	1.50
13	Cleon Jones	.25	.13	.08
14	John Callison	.25	.13	.08
15	Hank Aaron	5.00	2.50	1.50
16	Don Drysdale	3.00	1.50	.90
17	Bobby Knoop	.25	.13	.08
18	Tony Oliva	.50	.25	.15
19	Frank Robinson	2.00	1.00	.60
20	Denny McLain	.50	.25	.15
21	Al Kaline	5.00	2.50	1.50
22	Joe Pepitone	.40	.20	.12
23	Harmon Killebrew	5.00	2.50	1.50
24	Leon Wagner	.25	.13	.08
25	Joe Morgan	5.00	2.50	1.50
26	Ron Santo	.40	.20	.12
27	Joe Torre	.60	.30	.20
28	Juan Marichal	2.00	1.00	.60
29	Matty Alou	.25	.13	.08
30	Felipe Alou	.25	.13	.08
31	Ron Hunt	.25	.13	.08
32	Willie McCovey	2.00	1.00	.60

1967 Topps Stand-Ups

Never actually issued, no more than a handful of each of these rare test issues has made their way into the hobby market. Designed so that the color photo of the player's head could be popped out of the black background, and the top folded over to create a stand-up display, examples of these 3-1/8" by 5-1/4" cards can be found either die-cut around the portrait or without the cutting. Blank-backed, there are 24 cards in the set, numbered on the front at bottom left. The cards are popular with advanced superstar collectors.

		NR MT	EX	VG
Complete Set:		6750.00	3375.00	2025.
Common Player:		65.00	32.00	19.50
1	Pete Rose	700.00	350.00	210.00
2	Gary Peters	65.00	32.00	19.50
3	Frank Robinson	200.00	100.00	60.00
4	Jim Lonborg	65.00	32.00	19.50
5	Ron Swoboda	65.00	32.00	19.50
6	Harmon Killebrew	200.00	100.00	60.00
7	Bob Clemente	800.00	400.00	240.00
8	Mickey Mantle	1500.00	750.00	450.00
9	Jim Fregosi	75.00	37.00	22.00
10	Al Kaline	300.00	150.00	90.00
11	Don Drysdale	250.00	125.00	75.00
12	Dean Chance	65.00	32.00	19.50
13	Orlando Cepeda	75.00	37.00	22.00
14	Tim McCarver	75.00	37.00	22.00
15	Frank Howard	75.00	37.00	22.00
16	Max Alvis	65.00	32.00	19.50
17	Rusty Staub	75.00	37.00	22.00
18	Richie Allen	75.00	37.00	22.00
19	Willie Mays	600.00	300.00	175.00
20	Hank Aaron	600.00	300.00	175.00
21	Carl Yastrzemski	600.00	300.00	180.00
22	Ron Santo	75.00	37.00	22.00
23	Jim Hunter	200.00	100.00	60.00
24	Jim Wynn	65.00	32.00	19.50

1967 Topps Stickers Pirates

Considered a "test" issue, this 33-sticker set of 2-1/2" by 3-1/2" stickers is very similar to the Red Sox stickers which were produced the same year. Player stickers have a color picture (often just the player's head) and the player's name in large "comic book" letters. Besides the players, there are other topics such as "I Love the Pirates," "Bob Clemente for Mayor," and a number of similar sentiments. The stickers have blank backs and are rather scarce.

		NR MT	EX	VG
Complete Set:		250.00	125.00	75.00
Common Player:		3.00	1.50	.90
1	Gene Alley	5.00	2.50	1.50
2	Matty Alou	7.00	3.50	2.00
3	Dennis Ribant	3.00	1.50	.90
4	Steve Blass	5.00	2.50	1.50
5	Juan Pizarro	3.00	1.50	.90
6	Bob Clemente	75.00	38.00	23.00
7	Donn Clendenon	5.00	2.50	1.50
8	Roy Face	7.00	3.50	2.00
9	Woody Fryman	3.00	1.50	.90

		NR MT	EX	VG
10	Jesse Gonder	3.00	1.50	.90
11	Vern Law	7.00	3.50	2.00
12	Al McBean	3.00	1.50	.90
13	Jerry May	3.00	1.50	.90
14	Bill Mazeroski	12.00	6.00	3.50
15	Pete Mikkelsen	3.00	1.50	.90
16	Manny Mota	5.00	2.50	1.50
17	Billy O'Dell	3.00	1.50	.90
18	Jose Pagan	3.00	1.50	.90
19	Jim Pagliaroni	3.00	1.50	.90
20	Johnny Pesky	3.00	1.50	.90
21	Tommie Sisk	3.00	1.50	.90
22	Willie Stargell	40.00	20.00	12.50
23	Bob Veale	5.00	2.50	1.50
24	Harry Walker	3.00	1.50	.90
25	I Love The Pirates	3.00	1.50	.90
26	Let's Go Pirates	3.00	1.50	.90
27	Bob Clemente For Mayor	35.00	17.50	10.50
28	National League Batting Champion (Matty Alou)	4.00	2.00	1.25
29	Happiness Is A Pirate Win	3.00	1.50	.90
30	Donn Clendenon Is My Hero	4.00	2.00	1.25
31	Pirates' Home Run Champion (Willie Stargell)	15.00	7.50	4.50
32	Pirates Logo	3.00	1.50	.90
33	Pirates Pennant	3.00	1.50	.90

1967 Topps Stickers Red Sox

Like the 1967 Pirates Stickers, the Red Sox Stickers were part of the same test procedure. The Red Sox Stickers have the same 2-1/2" by 3-1/2" dimensions, color picture and large player's name on the front. A set is complete at 33 stickers. The majority are players, but themes such as "Let's Go Red Sox" are also included.

		NR MT	EX	VG
Complete Set:		225.00	112.00	67.00
Common Player:		3.00	1.50	.90
1	Dennis Bennett	3.00	1.50	.90
2	Darrell Brandon	3.00	1.50	.90
3	Tony Conigliaro	15.00	7.50	4.50
4	Don Demeter	3.00	1.50	.90
5	Hank Fischer	3.00	1.50	.90
6	Joe Foy	3.00	1.50	.90
7	Mike Andrews	3.00	1.50	.90
8	Dalton Jones	3.00	1.50	.90
9	Jim Lonborg	9.00	4.50	2.75
10	Don McMahon	3.00	1.50	.90
11	Dave Morehead	3.00	1.50	.90
12	George Smith	3.00	1.50	.90
13	Rico Petrocelli	6.00	3.00	1.75
14	Mike Ryan	3.00	1.50	.90
15	Jose Santiago	3.00	1.50	.90
16	George Scott	6.00	3.00	1.75
17	Sal Maglie	5.00	2.50	1.50
18	Reggie Smith	10.00	5.00	3.00
19	Lee Stange	3.00	1.50	.90
20	Jerry Stephenson	3.00	1.50	.90
21	Jose Tartabull	3.00	1.50	.90
22	George Thomas	3.00	1.50	.90
23	Bob Tillman	3.00	1.50	.90
24	Johnnie Wyatt	3.00	1.50	.90
25	Carl Yastrzemski	75.00	37.00	22.00
26	Dick Williams	6.00	3.00	1.75
27	I Love The Red Sox	3.00	1.50	.90

		NR MT	EX	VG
28	Let's Go Red Sox	3.00	1.50	.90
29	Carl Yastrzemski For Mayor	35.00	17.50	10.50
30	Tony Conigliaro Is My Hero	7.00	3.50	2.00
31	Happiness Is A Boston Win	3.00	1.50	.90
32	Red Sox Logo	3.00	1.50	.90
33	Red Sox Pennant	3.00	1.50	.90

1968 Topps

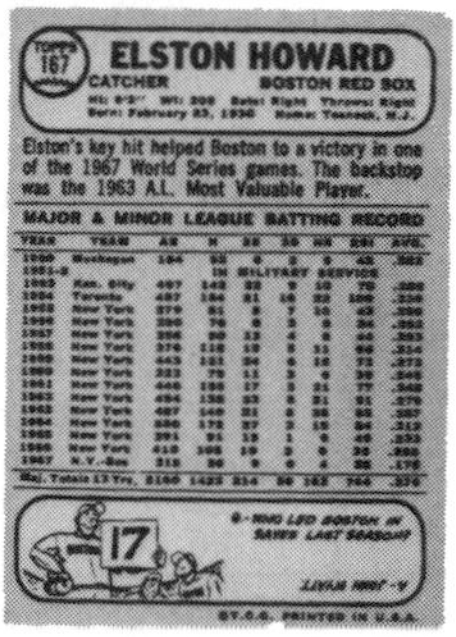

In 1968, Topps returned to a 598-card set of 2-1/2" by 3-1/2" cards. It is not, however, more of the same by way of appearance as the cards feature a color photograph on a background of what appears to be a burlap fabric. The player's name is below the photo but on the unusual background. A colored circle on the lower right carries the team and position. Backs were also changed. While retaining the vertical format introduced the previous year, with stats in the middle and cartoon at the bottom. The set features many of the old favorite subsets, including statistical leaders, World Series highlights, multi-player cards, checklists, rookie cards and the return of All-Star cards.

		NR MT	EX	VG
Complete Set:		3000.00	1500.00	900.00
Common Player: 1-533		1.00	.50	.30
Common Player: 534-598		2.50	1.25	.70
1	N.L. Batting Leaders (Matty Alou, Bob Clemente, Tony Gonzalez)	12.00	6.00	3.50
2	A.L. Batting Leaders (Al Kaline, Frank Robinson, Carl Yastrzemski)	4.00	2.00	1.25
3	N.L. RBI Leaders (Hank Aaron, Orlando Cepeda, Bob Clemente)	4.00	2.00	1.25
4	A.L. RBI Leaders (Harmon Killebrew, Frank Robinson, Carl Yastrzemski)	4.00	2.00	1.25
5	N.L. Home Run Leaders (Hank Aaron, Willie McCovey, Ron Santo, Jim Wynn)	4.00	2.00	1.25
6	A.L. Home Run Leaders (Frank Howard, Harmon Killebrew, Carl Yastrzemski)	4.00	2.00	1.25
7	N.L. ERA Leaders (Jim Bunning, Phil Niekro, Chris Short)	2.50	1.25	.70
8	A.L. ERA Leaders (Joe Horlen, Gary Peters, Sonny Siebert)	2.50	1.25	.70
9	N.L. Pitching Leaders (Jim Bunning, Ferguson Jenkins, Mike McCormick, Claude Osteen)	2.50	1.25	.70
10a	A.L. Pitching Leaders (Dean Chance, Jim Lonborg, Earl Wilson) ("Lonberg" on back)	3.50	1.75	1.00
10b	A.L. Pitching Leaders (Dean Chance, Jim Lonborg, Earl Wilson) ("Lonborg" on back)	2.50	1.25	.70
11	N.L. Strikeout Leaders (Jim Bunning, Ferguson Jenkins, Gaylord Perry)	3.00	1.50	.90
12	A.L. Strikeout Leaders (Dean Chance, Jim Lonborg, Sam McDowell)	2.50	1.25	.70
13	Chuck Hartenstein	1.00	.50	.30
14	Jerry McNertney	1.00	.50	.30
15	Ron Hunt	1.00	.50	.30
16	Indians Rookies (Lou Piniella, Richie Scheinblum)	2.50	1.25	.70
17	Dick Hall	1.00	.50	.30
18	Mike Hershberger	1.00	.50	.30
19	Juan Pizarro	1.00	.50	.30

		NR MT	EX	VG
20	Brooks Robinson	18.00	9.00	5.50
21	Ron Davis	1.00	.50	.30
22	Pat Dobson	1.00	.50	.30
23	Chico Cardenas	1.00	.50	.30
24	Bobby Locke	1.00	.50	.30
25	Julian Javier	1.00	.50	.30
26	Darrell Brandon	1.00	.50	.30
27	Gil Hodges	6.00	3.00	1.75
28	Ted Uhlaender	1.00	.50	.30
29	Joe Verbanic	1.00	.50	.30
30	Joe Torre	3.00	1.50	.90
31	Ed Stroud	1.00	.50	.30
32	Joe Gibbon	1.00	.50	.30
33	Pete Ward	1.00	.50	.30
34	Al Ferrara	1.00	.50	.30
35	Steve Hargan	1.00	.50	.30
36	Pirates Rookies (Bob Moose, *Bob Robertson*)	1.00	.50	.30
37	Billy Williams	7.00	3.50	2.00
38	Tony Pierce	1.00	.50	.30
39	Cookie Rojas	1.00	.50	.30
40	Denny McLain	3.75	2.00	1.25
41	Julio Gotay	1.00	.50	.30
42	Larry Haney	1.00	.50	.30
43	Gary Bell	1.00	.50	.30
44	Frank Kostro	1.00	.50	.30
45	Tom Seaver	170.00	85.00	47.00
46	Dave Ricketts	1.00	.50	.30
47	Ralph Houk	3.00	1.50	.90
48	Ted Davidson	1.00	.50	.30
49a	Ed Brinkman (yellow team letters)	60.00	30.00	18.00
49b	Ed Brinkman (white team letters)	1.00	.50	.30
50	Willie Mays	60.00	30.00	18.00
51	Bob Locker	1.00	.50	.30
52	Hawk Taylor	1.00	.50	.30
53	Gene Alley	1.00	.50	.30
54	Stan Williams	1.00	.50	.30
55	Felipe Alou	2.50	1.25	.70
56	Orioles Rookies (Dave Leonhard, Dave May)	1.00	.50	.30
57	Dan Schneider	1.00	.50	.30
58	Ed Mathews	10.00	5.00	3.00
59	Don Lock	1.00	.50	.30
60	Ken Holtzman	2.50	1.25	.70
61	Reggie Smith	2.50	1.25	.70
62	Chuck Dobson	1.00	.50	.30
63	Dick Kenworthy	1.00	.50	.30
64	Jim Merritt	1.00	.50	.30
65	John Roseboro	1.00	.50	.30
66a	Casey Cox (yellow team letters)	60.00	30.00	18.00
66b	Casey Cox (white team letters)	1.00	.50	.30
67	Checklist 1-109 (Jim Kaat)	3.00	1.50	.90
68	Ron Willis	1.00	.50	.30
69	Tom Tresh	3.00	1.50	.90
70	Bob Veale	1.00	.50	.30
71	Vern Fuller	1.00	.50	.30
72	Tommy John	5.00	2.50	1.50
73	Jim Hart	1.00	.50	.30
74	Milt Pappas	1.00	.50	.30
75	Don Mincher	1.00	.50	.30
76	Braves Rookies (Jim Britton, *Ron Reed*)	2.50	1.25	.70
77	*Don Wilson*	1.00	.50	.30
78	Jim Northrup	1.00	.50	.30
79	Ted Kubiak	1.00	.50	.30
80	Rod Carew	150.00	75.00	45.00
81	Larry Jackson	1.00	.50	.30
82	Sam Bowens	1.00	.50	.30
83	John Stephenson	1.00	.50	.30
84	Bob Tolan	1.00	.50	.30
85	Gaylord Perry	10.00	5.00	3.00
86	Willie Stargell	8.00	4.00	2.50
87	Dick Williams	2.50	1.25	.70
88	Phil Regan	1.00	.50	.30
89	Jake Gibbs	1.00	.50	.30
90	Vada Pinson	3.00	1.50	.90
91	Jim Ollom	1.00	.50	.30
92	Ed Kranepool	1.00	.50	.30
93	Tony Cloninger	1.00	.50	.30
94	Lee Maye	1.00	.50	.30
95	Bob Aspromonte	1.00	.50	.30
96	Senators Rookies (Frank Coggins, Dick Nold)	1.00	.50	.30
97	Tom Phoebus	1.00	.50	.30
98	Gary Sutherland	1.00	.50	.30
99	Rocky Colavito	2.25	1.25	.70
100	Bob Gibson	18.00	9.00	5.50
101	Glenn Beckert	1.00	.50	.30
102	Jose Cardenal	1.00	.50	.30
103	Don Sutton	8.00	4.00	2.50
104	Dick Dietz	1.00	.50	.30
105	Al Downing	2.50	1.25	.70
106	Dalton Jones	1.00	.50	.30
107	Checklist 110-196 (Juan Marichal)	3.50	1.75	1.00
108	Don Pavletich	1.00	.50	.30
109	Bert Campaneris	2.50	1.25	.70
110	Hank Aaron	80.00	40.00	25.00
111	Rich Reese	1.00	.50	.30
112	Woody Fryman	1.00	.50	.30
113	Tigers Rookies (Tom Matchick, Daryl Patterson)	1.00	.50	.30
114	Ron Swoboda	1.00	.50	.30
115	Sam McDowell	1.00	.50	.30
116	Ken McMullen	1.00	.50	.30
117	Larry Jaster	1.00	.50	.30
118	Mark Belanger	2.50	1.25	.70
119	Ted Savage	1.00	.50	.30
120	Mel Stottlemyre	3.00	1.50	.90
121	Jimmie Hall	1.00	.50	.30
122	Gene Mauch	1.00	.50	.30
123	Jose Santiago	1.00	.50	.30
124	Nate Oliver	1.00	.50	.30
125	Joe Horlen	1.00	.50	.30
126	Bobby Etheridge	1.00	.50	.30
127	Paul Lindblad	1.00	.50	.30
128	Astros Rookies (Tom Dukes, Alonzo Harris)	1.00	.50	.30
129	Mickey Stanley	1.00	.50	.30
130	Tony Perez	6.00	3.00	1.75
131	Frank Bertaina	1.00	.50	.30
132	Bud Harrelson	2.50	1.25	.70
133	Fred Whitfield	1.00	.50	.30
134	Pat Jarvis	1.00	.50	.30
135	Paul Blair	1.00	.50	.30
136	Randy Hundley	1.00	.50	.30
137	Twins Team	3.00	1.50	.90
138	Ruben Amaro	1.00	.50	.30
139	Chris Short	1.00	.50	.30
140	Tony Conigliaro	2.50	1.25	.70
141	Dal Maxvill	1.00	.50	.30
142	White Sox Rookies (Buddy Bradford, Bill Voss)	1.00	.50	.30
143	Pete Cimino	1.00	.50	.30
144	Joe Morgan	15.00	7.50	4.50
145	Don Drysdale	8.00	4.00	2.50
146	Sal Bando	2.50	1.25	.70
147	Frank Linzy	1.00	.50	.30
148	Dave Bristol	1.00	.50	.30
149	Bob Saverine	1.00	.50	.30
150	Bob Clemente	50.00	25.00	15.00
151	World Series Game 1 (Brock Socks 4-Hits In Opener)	3.50	1.75	1.00
152	World Series Game 2 (Yaz Smashes Two Homers)	5.00	2.50	1.50
153	World Series Game 3 (Briles Cools Off Boston)	3.00	1.50	.90
154	World Series Game 4 (Gibson Hurls Shutout!)	3.50	1.75	1.00
155	World Series Game 5 (Lonborg Wins Again!)	2.50	1.25	.70
156	World Series Game 6 (Petrocelli Socks Two Homers)	2.50	1.25	.70
157	World Series Game 7 (St. Louis Wins It!)	3.00	1.50	.90
158	World Series Summary (The Cardinals Celebrate!)	3.00	1.50	.90
159	Don Kessinger	1.00	.50	.30
160	Earl Wilson	1.00	.50	.30
161	Norm Miller	1.00	.50	.30
162	Cardinals Rookies (Hal Gilson, *Mike Torrez*)	2.50	1.25	.70
163	Gene Brabender	1.00	.50	.30
164	Ramon Webster	1.00	.50	.30
165	Tony Oliva	2.50	1.25	.70
166	Claude Raymond	1.00	.50	.30
167	Elston Howard	3.00	1.50	.90
168	Dodgers Team	2.50	1.25	.70
169	Bob Bolin	1.00	.50	.30
170	Jim Fregosi	2.50	1.25	.70
171	Don Nottebart	1.00	.50	.30
172	Walt Williams	1.00	.50	.30
173	John Boozer	1.00	.50	.30
174	Bob Tillman	1.00	.50	.30
175	Maury Wills	3.50	1.75	1.00
176	Bob Allen	1.00	.50	.30
177	Mets Rookies *(Jerry Koosman, Nolan Ryan)*	1200.00	600.00	350.00
178	Don Wert	1.00	.50	.30
179	Bill Stoneman	1.00	.50	.30
180	Curt Flood	2.50	1.25	.70

		NR MT	EX	VG
181	Jerry Zimmerman	1.00	.50	.30
182	Dave Giusti	1.00	.50	.30
183	Bob Kennedy	1.00	.50	.30
184	Lou Johnson	1.00	.50	.30
185	Tom Haller	1.00	.50	.30
186	Eddie Watt	1.00	.50	.30
187	Sonny Jackson	1.00	.50	.30
188	Cap Peterson	1.00	.50	.30
189	Bill Landis	1.00	.50	.30
190	Bill White	2.50	1.25	.70
191	Dan Frisella	1.00	.50	.30
192a	Checklist 197-283 (Carl Yastrzemski) ("To increase the..." on back)	4.50	2.25	1.25
192b	Checklist 197-283 (Carl Yastrzemski) ("To increase your..." on back)	6.00	3.00	1.75
193	Jack Hamilton	1.00	.50	.30
194	Don Buford	1.00	.50	.30
195	Joe Pepitone	3.00	1.50	.90
196	Gary Nolan	1.00	.50	.30
197	Larry Brown	1.00	.50	.30
198	Roy Face	2.50	1.25	.70
199	A's Rookies (Darrell Osteen, Roberto Rodriguez)	1.00	.50	.30
200	Orlando Cepeda	4.00	2.00	1.25
201	*Mike Marshall*	3.00	1.50	.90
202	Adolfo Phillips	1.00	.50	.30
203	Dick Kelley	1.00	.50	.30
204	Andy Etchebarren	1.00	.50	.30
205	Juan Marichal	8.00	4.00	2.50
206	Cal Ermer	1.00	.50	.30
207	Carroll Sembera	1.00	.50	.30
208	Willie Davis	2.50	1.25	.70
209	Tim Cullen	1.00	.50	.30
210	Gary Peters	1.00	.50	.30
211	J.C. Martin	1.00	.50	.30
212	Dave Morehead	1.00	.50	.30
213	Chico Ruiz	1.00	.50	.30
214	Yankees Rookies (Stan Bahnsen, Frank Fernandez)	2.50	1.25	.70
215	Jim Bunning	4.50	2.25	1.25
216	Bubba Morton	1.00	.50	.30
217	Turk Farrell	1.00	.50	.30
218	Ken Suarez	1.00	.50	.30
219	Rob Gardner	1.00	.50	.30
220	Harmon Killebrew	12.00	6.00	3.50
221	Braves Team	3.00	1.50	.90
222	Jim Hardin	1.00	.50	.30
223	Ollie Brown	1.00	.50	.30
224	Jack Aker	1.00	.50	.30
225	Richie Allen	2.25	1.25	.70
226	Jimmie Price	1.00	.50	.30
227	Joe Hoerner	1.00	.50	.30
228	Dodgers Rookies (*Jack Billingham*, Jim Fairey)	.80	.40	.25
229	Fred Klages	1.00	.50	.30
230	Pete Rose	50.00	25.00	15.00
231	Dave Baldwin	1.00	.50	.30
232	Denis Menke	1.00	.50	.30
233	George Scott	1.00	.50	.30
234	Bill Monbouquette	1.00	.50	.30
235	Ron Santo	2.50	1.25	.70
236	Tug McGraw	3.00	1.50	.90
237	Alvin Dark	1.00	.50	.30
238	Tom Satriano	1.00	.50	.30
239	Bill Henry	1.00	.50	.30
240	Al Kaline	18.00	9.00	5.50
241	Felix Millan	1.00	.50	.30
242	Moe Drabowsky	1.00	.50	.30
243	Rich Rollins	1.00	.50	.30
244	John Donaldson	1.00	.50	.30
245	Tony Gonzalez	1.00	.50	.30
246	Fritz Peterson	2.50	1.25	.70
247	Red Rookies (*Johnny Bench*, Ron Tompkins)	325.00	162.00	97.00
248	Fred Valentine	1.00	.50	.30
249	Bill Singer	.80	.40	.25
250	Carl Yastrzemski	35.00	17.50	10.50
251	*Manny Sanguillen*	2.50	1.25	.70
252	Angels Team	3.00	1.50	.90
253	Dick Hughes	1.00	.50	.30
254	Cleon Jones	1.00	.50	.30
255	Dean Chance	1.00	.50	.30
256	Norm Cash	3.00	1.50	.90
257	Phil Niekro	5.00	2.50	1.50
258	Cubs Rookies (Jose Arcia, Bill Schlesinger)	1.00	.50	.30
259	Ken Boyer	3.00	1.50	.90
260	Jim Wynn	1.00	.50	.30
261	Dave Duncan	1.00	.50	.30
262	Rick Wise	1.00	.50	.30
263	Horace Clarke	1.00	.50	.30

		NR MT	EX	VG
264	Ted Abernathy	1.00	.50	.30
265	Tommy Davis	2.50	1.25	.70
266	Paul Popovich	1.00	.50	.30
267	Herman Franks	1.00	.50	.30
268	Bob Humphreys	1.00	.50	.30
269	Bob Tiefenauer	1.00	.50	.30
270	Matty Alou	2.50	1.25	.70
271	Bobby Knoop	1.00	.50	.30
272	Ray Culp	1.00	.50	.30
273	Dave Johnson	3.00	1.50	.90
274	Mike Cuellar	1.00	.50	.30
275	Tim McCarver	3.00	1.50	.90
276	Jim Roland	1.00	.50	.30
277	Jerry Buchek	1.00	.50	.30
278a	Checklist 284-370 (Orlando Cepeda) (copyright at right)	3.00	1.50	.90
278b	Checklist 284-370 (Orlando Cepeda) (copyright at left)	5.00	2.50	1.50
279	Bill Hands	1.00	.50	.30
280	Mickey Mantle	175.00	87.00	52.00
281	Jim Campanis	1.00	.50	.30
282	Rick Monday	2.50	1.25	.70
283	Mel Queen	1.00	.50	.30
284	John Briggs	1.00	.50	.30
285	Dick McAuliffe	.80	.40	.25
286	Cecil Upshaw	1.00	.50	.30
287	White Sox Rookies (Mickey Abarbanel, Cisco Carlos)	1.00	.50	.30
288	Dave Wickersham	1.00	.50	.30
289	Woody Held	1.00	.50	.30
290	Willie McCovey	10.00	5.00	3.00
291	Dick Lines	1.00	.50	.30
292	Art Shamsky	.80	.40	.25
293	Bruce Howard	1.00	.50	.30
294	Red Schoendienst	2.50	1.25	.70
295	Sonny Siebert	1.00	.50	.30
296	Byron Browne	1.00	.50	.30
297	Russ Gibson	1.00	.50	.30
298	Jim Brewer	1.00	.50	.30
299	Gene Michael	2.50	1.25	.70
300	Rusty Staub	3.00	1.50	.90
301	Twins Rookies (George Mitterwald, Rick Renick)	1.00	.50	.30
302	Gerry Arrigo	1.00	.50	.30
303	Dick Green	1.00	.50	.30
304	Sandy Valdespino	1.00	.50	.30
305	Minnie Rojas	1.00	.50	.30
306	Mike Ryan	1.00	.50	.30
307	John Hiller	1.00	.50	.30
308	Pirates Team	3.00	1.50	.90
309	Ken Henderson	1.00	.50	.30
310	Luis Aparicio	5.00	2.50	1.50
311	Jack Lamabe	1.00	.50	.30
312	Curt Blefary	1.00	.50	.30
313	Al Weis	1.00	.50	.30
314	Red Sox Rookies (Bill Rohr, George Spriggs)	1.00	.50	.30
315	Zoilo Versalles	1.00	.50	.30
316	Steve Barber	1.00	.50	.30
317	Ron Brand	1.00	.50	.30
318	Chico Salmon	1.00	.50	.30
319	George Culver	1.00	.50	.30
320	Frank Howard	3.00	1.50	.90
321	Leo Durocher	2.25	1.25	.70
322	Dave Boswell	1.00	.50	.30
323	Deron Johnson	1.00	.50	.30
324	Jim Nash	1.00	.50	.30
325	Manny Mota	1.00	.50	.30
326	Dennis Ribant	1.00	.50	.30
327	Tony Taylor	1.00	.50	.30
328	Angels Rookies (Chuck Vinson, Jim Weaver)	1.00	.50	.30
329	Duane Josephson	1.00	.50	.30
330	Roger Maris	35.00	17.50	10.50
331	Dan Osinski	1.00	.50	.30
332	Doug Rader	1.00	.50	.30
333	Ron Herbel	1.00	.50	.30
334	Orioles Team	3.00	1.50	.90
335	Bob Allison	2.50	1.25	.70
336	John Purdin	1.00	.50	.30
337	Bill Robinson	1.00	.50	.30
338	Bob Johnson	1.00	.50	.30
339	Rich Nye	1.00	.50	.30
340	Max Alvis	1.00	.50	.30
341	Jim Lemon	1.00	.50	.30
342	Ken Johnson	1.00	.50	.30
343	Jim Gosger	1.00	.50	.30
344	Donn Clendenon	1.00	.50	.30
345	Bob Hendley	1.00	.50	.30
346	Jerry Adair	1.00	.50	.30
347	George Brunet	1.00	.50	.30

		NR MT	EX	VG
348	Phillies Rookies (Larry Colton, Dick Thoenen)	1.00	.50	.30
349	Ed Spiezio	1.00	.50	.30
350	Hoyt Wilhelm	6.00	3.00	1.75
351	Bob Barton	1.00	.50	.30
352	Jackie Hernandez	1.00	.50	.30
353	Mack Jones	1.00	.50	.30
354	Pete Richert	1.00	.50	.30
355	Ernie Banks	20.00	10.00	6.00
356	Checklist 371-457 (Ken Holtzman)	2.50	1.25	.70
357	Len Gabrielson	1.00	.50	.30
358	Mike Epstein	1.00	.50	.30
359	Joe Moeller	1.00	.50	.30
360	Willie Horton	1.00	.50	.30
361	Harmon Killebrew AS	5.00	2.50	1.50
362	Orlando Cepeda AS	2.75	1.50	.80
363	Rod Carew AS	12.00	6.00	3.50
364	Joe Morgan AS	3.00	1.50	.90
365	Brooks Robinson AS	6.00	3.00	1.75
366	Ron Santo AS	3.00	1.50	.90
367	Jim Fregosi AS	2.50	1.25	.70
368	Gene Alley AS	2.50	1.25	.70
369	Carl Yastrzemski AS	15.00	7.50	4.50
370	Hank Aaron AS	15.00	7.50	4.50
371	Tony Oliva AS	3.00	1.50	.90
372	Lou Brock AS	6.00	3.00	1.75
373	Frank Robinson AS	5.00	2.50	1.50
374	Bob Clemente AS	15.00	7.50	4.50
375	Bill Freehan AS	2.50	1.25	.70
376	Tim McCarver AS	2.50	1.25	.70
377	Joe Horlen AS	2.50	1.25	.70
378	Bob Gibson AS	7.00	3.50	2.00
379	Gary Peters AS	2.50	1.25	.70
380	Ken Holtzman AS	2.50	1.25	.70
381	Boog Powell	2.50	1.25	.70
382	Ramon Hernandez	1.00	.50	.30
383	Steve Whitaker	1.00	.50	.30
384	Reds Rookies (Bill Henry, *Hal McRae*)	7.00	3.50	2.00
385	Jim Hunter	10.00	5.00	3.00
386	Greg Goossen	1.00	.50	.30
387	Joe Foy	1.00	.50	.30
388	Ray Washburn	1.00	.50	.30
389	Jay Johnstone	1.00	.50	.30
390	Bill Mazeroski	3.00	1.50	.90
391	Bob Priddy	1.00	.50	.30
392	Grady Hatton	1.00	.50	.30
393	Jim Perry	2.50	1.25	.70
394	Tommie Aaron	1.00	.50	.30
395	Camilo Pascual	1.00	.50	.30
396	Bobby Wine	1.00	.50	.30
397	Vic Davalillo	1.00	.50	.30
398	Jim Grant	1.00	.50	.30
399	Ray Oyler	1.00	.50	.30
400a	Mike McCormick (white team letters)	40.00	20.00	12.00
400b	Mike McCormick (yellow team letters)	1.00	.50	.30
401	Mets Team	3.25	1.75	1.00
402	Mike Hegan	2.50	1.25	.70
403	John Buzhardt	1.00	.50	.30
404	Floyd Robinson	1.00	.50	.30
405	Tommy Helms	1.00	.50	.30
406	Dick Ellsworth	1.00	.50	.30
407	Gary Kolb	1.00	.50	.30
408	Steve Carlton	50.00	25.00	15.00
409	Orioles Rookies (Frank Peters, Ron Stone)	1.00	.50	.30
410	Ferguson Jenkins	15.00	7.50	4.50
411	Ron Hansen	1.00	.50	.30
412	Clay Carroll	1.00	.50	.30
413	Tommy McCraw	1.00	.50	.30
414	Mickey Lolich	2.75	1.50	.80
415	Johnny Callison	2.50	1.25	.70
416	Bill Rigney	1.00	.50	.30
417	Willie Crawford	1.00	.50	.30
418	Eddie Fisher	1.00	.50	.30
419	Jack Hiatt	1.00	.50	.30
420	Cesar Tovar	1.00	.50	.30
421	Ron Taylor	1.00	.50	.30
422	Rene Lachemann	1.00	.50	.30
423	Fred Gladding	1.00	.50	.30
424	White Sox Team	3.00	1.50	.90
425	Jim Maloney	1.00	.50	.30
426	Hank Allen	1.00	.50	.30
427	Dick Calmus	1.00	.50	.30
428	Vic Roznovsky	1.00	.50	.30
429	Tommie Sisk	1.00	.50	.30
430	Rico Petrocelli	1.00	.50	.30
431	Dooley Womack	1.00	.50	.30

		NR MT	EX	VG
432	Indians Rookies (Bill Davis, Jose Vidal)	1.00	.50	.30
433	Bob Rodgers	1.00	.50	.30
434	Ricardo Joseph	1.00	.50	.30
435	Ron Perranoski	1.00	.50	.30
436	Hal Lanier	1.00	.50	.30
437	Don Cardwell	1.00	.50	.30
438	Lee Thomas	1.00	.50	.30
439	Luman Harris	1.00	.50	.30
440	Claude Osteen	1.00	.50	.30
441	Alex Johnson	1.00	.50	.30
442	Dick Bosman	1.00	.50	.30
443	Joe Azcue	1.00	.50	.30
444	Jack Fisher	1.00	.50	.30
445	Mike Shannon	1.00	.50	.30
446	Ron Kline	1.00	.50	.30
447	Tigers Rookies (George Korince, Fred Lasher)	1.00	.50	.30
448	Gary Wagner	1.00	.50	.30
449	Gene Oliver	1.00	.50	.30
450	Jim Kaat	6.00	3.00	1.75
451	Al Spangler	1.00	.50	.30
452	Jesús Alou	1.00	.50	.30
453	Sammy Ellis	1.00	.50	.30
454	Checklist 458-533 (Frank Robinson)	4.00	2.00	1.25
455	Rico Carty	2.50	1.25	.70
456	John O'Donoghue	1.00	.50	.30
457	Jim Lefebvre	1.00	.50	.30
458	Lew Krausse	1.00	.50	.30
459	Dick Simpson	1.00	.50	.30
460	Jim Lonborg	2.50	1.25	.70
461	Chuck Hiller	1.00	.50	.30
462	Barry Moore	1.00	.50	.30
463	Jimmie Schaffer	1.00	.50	.30
464	Don McMahon	1.00	.50	.30
465	Tommie Agee	1.00	.50	.30
466	Bill Dillman	1.00	.50	.30
467	Dick Howser	2.50	1.25	.70
468	Larry Sherry	1.00	.50	.30
469	Ty Cline	1.00	.50	.30
470	Bill Freehan	2.50	1.25	.70
471	Orlando Pena	1.00	.50	.30
472	Walt Alston	2.50	1.25	.70
473	Al Worthington	1.00	.50	.30
474	Paul Schaal	1.00	.50	.30
475	Joe Niekro	2.25	1.25	.70
476	Woody Woodward	1.00	.50	.30
477	Phillies Team	3.00	1.50	.90
478	Dave McNally	2.50	1.25	.70
479	Phil Gagliano	1.00	.50	.30
480	Manager's Dream (Chico Cardenas, Bob Clemente, Tony Oliva)	18.00	9.00	5.50
481	John Wyatt	1.00	.50	.30
482	Jose Pagan	1.00	.50	.30
483	Darold Knowles	1.00	.50	.30
484	Phil Roof	1.00	.50	.30
485	Ken Berry	1.00	.50	.30
486	Cal Koonce	1.00	.50	.30
487	Lee May	2.50	1.25	.70
488	Dick Tracewski	1.00	.50	.30
489	Wally Bunker	1.00	.50	.30
490	Super Stars (Harmon Killebrew, Mickey Mantle, Willie Mays)	80.00	40.00	24.00
491	Denny Lemaster	1.00	.50	.30
492	Jeff Torborg	1.00	.50	.30
493	Jim McGlothlin	1.00	.50	.30
494	Ray Sadecki	1.00	.50	.30
495	Leon Wagner	1.00	.50	.30
496	Steve Hamilton	1.00	.50	.30
497	Cards Team	3.50	1.75	1.00
498	Bill Bryan	1.00	.50	.30
499	Steve Blass	1.00	.50	.30
500	Frank Robinson	20.00	10.00	6.00
501	John Odom	1.00	.50	.30
502	Mike Andrews	1.00	.50	.30
503	Al Jackson	1.00	.50	.30
504	Russ Snyder	1.00	.50	.30
505	Joe Sparma	1.00	.50	.30
506	Clarence Jones	1.00	.50	.30
507	Wade Blasingame	1.00	.50	.30
508	Duke Sims	1.00	.50	.30
509	Dennis Higgins	1.00	.50	.30
510	Ron Fairly	1.00	.50	.30
511	Bill Kelso	1.00	.50	.30
512	Grant Jackson	1.00	.50	.30
513	Hank Bauer	1.00	.50	.30
514	Al McBean	1.00	.50	.30
515	Russ Nixon	1.00	.50	.30
516	Pete Mikkelsen	1.00	.50	.30
517	Diego Segui	1.00	.50	.30

		NR MT	EX	VG
518a	Checklist 534-598 (Clete Boyer) (539 is Maj. L. Rookies)	3.00	1.50	.90
518b	Checklist 534-598 (Clete Boyer) (539 is Amer. L. Rookies)	5.00	2.50	1.50
519	Jerry Stephenson	1.00	.50	.30
520	Lou Brock	20.00	10.00	6.00
521	Don Shaw	1.00	.50	.30
522	Wayne Causey	1.00	.50	.30
523	John Tsitouris	1.00	.50	.30
524	Andy Kosco	1.00	.50	.30
525	Jim Davenport	1.00	.50	.30
526	Bill Denehy	1.00	.50	.30
527	Tito Francona	1.00	.50	.30
528	Tigers Team	50.00	25.00	15.00
529	Bruce Von Hoff	1.00	.50	.30
530	Bird Belters (Brooks Robinson, Frank Robinson)	7.00	3.50	2.00
531	Chuck Hinton	1.00	.50	.30
532	Luis Tiant	3.00	1.50	.90
533	Wes Parker	1.00	.50	.30
534	Bob Miller	2.50	1.25	.70
535	Danny Cater	2.50	1.25	.70
536	Bill Short	2.50	1.25	.70
537	Norm Siebern	2.50	1.25	.70
538	Manny Jimenez	2.50	1.25	.70
539	Major League Rookies (Mike Ferraro, Jim Ray)	2.50	1.25	.70
540	Nelson Briles	2.50	1.25	.70
541	Sandy Alomar	2.50	1.25	.70
542	John Boccabella	2.50	1.25	.70
543	Bob Lee	2.50	1.25	.70
544	Mayo Smith	2.50	1.25	.70
545	Lindy McDaniel	2.50	1.25	.70
546	Roy White	2.50	1.25	.70
547	Dan Coombs	2.50	1.25	.70
548	Bernie Allen	2.50	1.25	.70
549	Orioles Rookies (Curt Motton, Roger Nelson)	2.50	1.25	.70
550	Clete Boyer	2.50	1.25	.70
551	Darrell Sutherland	2.50	1.25	.70
552	Ed Kirkpatrick	2.50	1.25	.70
553	Hank Aguirre	2.50	1.25	.70
554	A's Team	3.00	1.50	.90
555	Jose Tartabull	2.50	1.25	.70
556	Dick Selma	2.50	1.25	.70
557	Frank Quilici	2.50	1.25	.70
558	John Edwards	2.50	1.25	.70
559	Pirates Rookies (Carl Taylor, Luke Walker)	2.50	1.25	.70
560	Paul Casanova	2.50	1.25	.70
561	Lee Elia	2.50	1.25	.70
562	Jim Bouton	2.50	1.25	.70
563	Ed Charles	2.50	1.25	.70
564	Eddie Stanky	2.50	1.25	.70
565	Larry Dierker	2.50	1.25	.70
566	Ken Harrelson	3.00	1.50	.90
567	Clay Dalrymple	2.50	1.25	.70
568	Willie Smith	2.50	1.25	.70
569	N.L. Rookies (Ivan Murrell, Les Rohr)	2.50	1.25	.70
570	Rick Reichardt	2.50	1.25	.70
571	Tony LaRussa	3.00	1.50	.90
572	Don Bosch	2.50	1.25	.70
573	Joe Coleman	2.50	1.25	.70
574	Reds Team	3.00	1.50	.90
575	Jim Palmer	50.00	25.00	15.00
576	Dave Adlesh	2.50	1.25	.70
577	Fred Talbot	2.50	1.25	.70
578	Orlando Martinez	2.50	1.25	.70
579	N.L. Rookies *(Larry Hisle, Mike Lum)*	3.00	1.50	.90
580	Bob Bailey	2.50	1.25	.70
581	Garry Roggenburk	2.50	1.25	.70
582	Jerry Grote	2.50	1.25	.70
583	Gates Brown	2.50	1.25	.70
584	Larry Shepard	2.50	1.25	.70
585	Wilbur Wood	2.50	1.25	.70
586	Jim Pagliaroni	2.50	1.25	.70
587	Roger Repoz	2.50	1.25	.70
588	Dick Schofield	2.50	1.25	.70
589	Twins Rookies (Ron Clark, Moe Ogier)	2.50	1.25	.70
590	Tommy Harper	2.50	1.25	.70
591	Dick Nen	2.50	1.25	.70
592	John Bateman	2.50	1.25	.70
593	Lee Stange	2.50	1.25	.70
594	Phil Linz	2.50	1.25	.70
595	Phil Ortega	2.50	1.25	.70
596	Charlie Smith	2.50	1.25	.70
597	Bill McCool	2.50	1.25	.70
598	Jerry May	3.00	1.50	.90

1968 Topps Action All-Star Stickers

Still another of the many Topps test issues of the late 1960s, the Action All-Star stickers were sold in a strip of three, with bubblegum, for 10¢. The strip is comprised of three 3-1/4" by 5-1/4" panels, perforated at the joints for separation. The central panel which is numbered, contains a large color picture of a star player. The top and bottom panels contains smaller pictures of three players each. While there are 16 numbered center panels, only 12 of them are different; panels 13-16 show players previously used. Similarly, the triple-player panels at top and bottom of stickers 13-16 repeat panels from #'s 1-4. Prices below are for stickers which have all three panels still joined. Individual panels are priced signicantly lower.

	NR MT	EX	VG
Complete Set:	1300.00	650.00	390.00
Common Player:	18.00	9.00	5.50

		NR MT	EX	VG
1	Orlando Cepeda, Joe Horlen, Al Kaline, Bill Mazeroski, Claude Osteen, Mel Stottlemyre, Carl Yastrzemski	100.00	50.00	30.00
2	Don Drysdale, Harmon Killebrew, Mike McCormick, Tom Phoebus, George Scott, Ron Swoboda, Pete Ward	30.00	15.00	9.00
3	Hank Aaron, Paul Casanova, Jim Maloney, Joe Pepitone, Rick Reichardt, Frank Robinson, Tom Seaver	35.00	17.50	10.50
4	Bob Aspromonte, Johnny Callison, Dean Chance, Jim Lefebvre, Jim Lonborg, Frank Robinson, Ron Santo	25.00	12.50	7.50
5	Bert Campaneris, Al Downing, Willie Horton, Ed Kranepool, Willie Mays, Pete Rose, Ron Santo	200.00	100.00	60.00
6	Max Alvis, Ernie Banks, Al Kaline, Tim McCarver, Rusty Staub, Walt Williams, Carl Yastrzemski	70.00	35.00	21.00
7	Rod Carew, Tony Gonzalez, Steve Hargan, Mickey Mantle, Willie McCovey, Rick Monday, Billy Williams	300.00	150.00	90.00
8	Clete Boyer, Jim Bunning, Tony Conigliaro, Mike Cuellar, Joe Horlen, Ken McMullen, Don Mincher	18.00	9.00	5.50
9	Orlando Cepeda, Bob Clemente, Jim Fregosi, Harmon Killebrew, Willie Mays, Chris Short, Earl Wilson	40.00	20.00	12.00
10	Hank Aaron, Bob Gibson, Bud Harrelson, Jim Hunter, Mickey Mantle, Gary Peters, Vada Pinson	100.00	50.00	30.00
11	Don Drysdale, Bill Freehan, Frank Howard, Ferguson Jenkins, Tony Oliva, Bob Veale, Jim Wynn	30.00	15.00	9.00
12	Richie Allen, Bob Clemente, Sam McDowell, Jim McGlothlin, Tony Perez, Brooks Robinson, Joe Torre	100.00	50.00	30.00
13	Dean Chance, Don Drysdale, Jim Lefebvre, Tom Phoebus, Frank Robinson, George Scott, Carl Yastrzemski	100.00	50.00	30.00
14	Paul Casanova, Orlando Cepeda, Joe Horlen, Harmon Killebrew, Bill Mazeroski, Rick Reichardt, Tom Seaver	35.00	17.50	10.50

15	Bob Aspromonte, Johnny Callison, Jim Lonborg, Mike McCormick, Frank Robinson, Ron Swoboda, Pete Ward	30.00	15.00	9.00
16	Hank Aaron, Al Kaline, Jim Maloney, Claude Osteen, Joe Pepitone, Ron Santo, Mel Stottlemyre	30.00	15.00	9.00

1968 Topps Discs

One of the scarcest of all Topps collectibles, this 28-player set was apparently a never-completed test issue. These full-color, cardboard discs, which measure approximately 2-1/8" in diameter, were apparently intended to be made into a "pin" set, but for some reason, production was never completed and no actual "pins" are known to exist. Uncut sheets of the player discs have been found, however. The discs include a player portrait photo with the name beneath and the city and team nickname along the sides. The set includes eight Hall of Famers.

		NR MT	EX	VG
Complete Set:		3500.00	1750.00	1050.
Common Player:		35.00	17.50	10.50
(1)	Hank Aaron	250.00	125.00	75.00
(2)	Richie Allen	60.00	30.00	18.00
(3)	Gene Alley	35.00	17.50	10.50
(4)	Rod Carew	300.00	150.00	90.00
(5)	Orlando Cepeda	60.00	30.00	18.00
(6)	Dean Chance	35.00	17.50	10.50
(7)	Bob Clemente	350.00	175.00	100.00
(8)	Tommy Davis	35.00	17.50	10.50
(9)	Bill Freehan	35.00	17.50	10.50
(10)	Jim Fregosi	35.00	17.50	10.50
(11)	Steve Hargan	35.00	17.50	10.50
(12)	Frank Howard	60.00	30.00	18.00
(13)	Al Kaline	200.00	100.00	60.00
(14)	Harmon Killebrew	150.00	75.00	45.00
(15)	Mickey Mantle	600.00	300.00	175.00
(16)	Willie Mays	300.00	150.00	90.00
(17)	Mike McCormick	35.00	17.50	10.50
(18)	Rick Monday	35.00	17.50	10.50
(19)	Claude Osteen	35.00	17.50	10.50
(20)	Gary Peters	35.00	17.50	10.50
(21)	Brooks Robinson	200.00	100.00	60.00
(22)	Frank Robinson	150.00	75.00	45.00
(23)	Pete Rose	400.00	200.00	125.00
(24)	Ron Santo	60.00	30.00	18.00
(25)	Rusty Staub	60.00	30.00	18.00
(26)	Joe Torre	60.00	30.00	18.00
(27)	Carl Yastrzemski	150.00	75.00	45.00
(28)	Bob Veale	35.00	17.50	10.50

1968 Topps Game

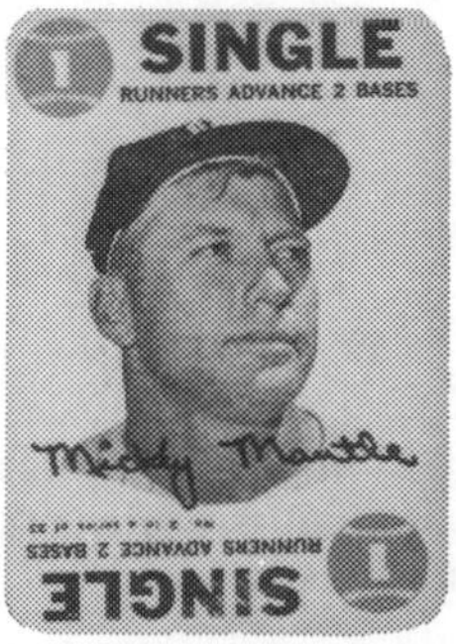

A throwback to the Red and Blue Back sets of 1951, the 33-cards in the 1968 Topps Game set, inserted into packs of regular '68 Topps cards or purchases as a complete boxed set, enable the owner to play a game of baseball based on the game situations on each card. Also on the 2-1/4" by 3-1/4" cards were a color photograph of a player and his facsimile autograph. One redeeming social value of the set (assuming you're not mesmerized by the game) is that it affords an inexpensive way to get big-name cards as the set is loaded with stars, but not at all popular with collectors.

		NR MT	EX	VG
Complete Set:		70.00	35.00	21.00
Common Player:		.30	.15	.09
1	Mateo Alou	.50	.25	.15
2	Mickey Mantle	15.00	7.50	4.50
3	Carl Yastrzemski	3.25	1.75	1.00
4	Henry Aaron	3.00	1.50	.90
5	Harmon Killebrew	1.75	.90	.50
6	Roberto Clemente	3.00	1.50	.90
7	Frank Robinson	1.75	.90	.50
8	Willie Mays	3.00	1.50	.90
9	Brooks Robinson	2.00	1.00	.60
10	Tommy Davis	.50	.25	.15
11	Bill Freehan	.50	.25	.15
12	Claude Osteen	.40	.20	.12
13	Gary Peters	.30	.15	.09
14	Jim Lonborg	.40	.20	.12
15	Steve Hargan	.30	.15	.09
16	Dean Chance	.40	.20	.12
17	Mike McCormick	.30	.15	.09
18	Tim McCarver	.60	.30	.20
19	Ron Santo	.60	.30	.20
20	Tony Gonzalez	.30	.15	.09
21	Frank Howard	.70	.35	.20
22	George Scott	.40	.20	.12
23	Rich Allen	.70	.35	.20
24	Jim Wynn	.40	.20	.12
25	Gene Alley	.40	.20	.12
26	Rick Monday	.40	.20	.12
27	Al Kaline	2.00	1.00	.60
28	Rusty Staub	.70	.35	.20
29	Rod Carew	2.75	1.50	.80
30	Pete Rose	7.50	3.75	2.25
31	Joe Torre	.70	.35	.20
32	Orlando Cepeda	1.00	.50	.30
33	Jim Fregosi	.50	.25	.15

1968 Topps Plaks

Among the scarcest of the Topps test issues of the late 1960s, the "All Star Baseball Plaks" were plastic busts of two dozen stars of the era which came packaged like model airplane parts. The busts had to

be snapped off a sprue and could be inserted into a base which carried the player's name. Packed with the plastic plaks was one of two checklist cards which featured six color photos per side. The 2-1/8" by 4" checklist cards are popular with superstar collectors and are considerably easier to find today than the actual plaks.

		NR MT	EX	VG
Complete Set:		2300.00	1150.00	690.00
Common Player:		20.00	10.00	6.00
1	Max Alvis	20.00	10.00	6.00
2	Frank Howard	30.00	15.00	9.00
3	Dean Chance	20.00	10.00	6.00
4	Jim Hunter	50.00	25.00	15.00
5	Jim Fregosi	25.00	12.50	7.50
6	Al Kaline	60.00	30.00	18.00
7	Harmon Killebrew	60.00	30.00	18.00
8	Gary Peters	20.00	10.00	6.00
9	Jim Lonborg	20.00	10.00	6.00
10	Frank Robinson	60.00	30.00	18.00
11	Mickey Mantle	800.00	400.00	240.00
12	Carl Yastrzemski	175.00	87.00	52.00
13	Hank Aaron	100.00	50.00	30.00
14	Bob Clemente	100.00	50.00	30.00
15	Richie Allen	30.00	15.00	9.00
16	Tommy Davis	25.00	12.50	7.50
17	Orlando Cepeda	30.00	15.00	9.00
18	Don Drysdale	50.00	25.00	15.00
19	Willie Mays	100.00	50.00	30.00
20	Rusty Staub	30.00	15.00	9.00
21	Tim McCarver	30.00	15.00	9.00
22	Pete Rose	250.00	125.00	75.00
23	Ron Santo	30.00	15.00	9.00
24	Jim Wynn	20.00	10.00	6.00
---	Checklist Card 1-12	250.00	125.00	75.00
---	Checklist Card 13-24	250.00	125.00	75.00

1968 Topps Posters

Yet another innovation from the creative minds at Topps appeared in 1968; a set of color player posters. Measuring 9-3/4" by 18-1/8," each poster was sold separately with its own piece of gum, rather than as an insert. The posters feature a large color photograph with a star at the bottom containing the player's name, position and team. There are 24 different posters which were folded numerous times to fit into the package they were sold in.

		NR MT	EX	VG
Complete Set:		325.00	162.00	97.00
Common Player:		3.00	1.50	.90
1	Dean Chance	3.00	1.50	.90
2	Max Alvis	3.00	1.50	.90
3	Frank Howard	8.00	4.00	2.50
4	Jim Fregosi	7.00	3.50	2.00
5	Jim Hunter	12.00	6.00	3.50
6	Bob Clemente	25.00	12.50	7.50
7	Don Drysdale	12.00	6.00	3.50
8	Jim Wynn	3.00	1.50	.90
9	Al Kaline	25.00	12.50	7.50
10	Harmon Killebrew	20.00	10.00	6.00
11	Jim Lonborg	3.00	1.50	.90
12	Orlando Cepeda	8.00	4.00	2.50
13	Gary Peters	3.00	1.50	.90
14	Hank Aaron	25.00	12.50	7.50
15	Richie Allen	8.00	4.00	2.50
16	Carl Yastrzemski	20.00	10.00	6.00
17	Ron Swoboda	3.00	1.50	.90
18	Mickey Mantle	50.00	25.00	15.00
19	Tim McCarver	7.00	3.50	2.00
20	Willie Mays	25.00	12.50	7.50
21	Ron Santo	7.00	3.50	2.00
22	Rusty Staub	7.00	3.50	2.00
23	Pete Rose	40.00	20.00	12.00
24	Frank Robinson	15.00	7.50	4.50

1968 Topps 3-D

These are very rare pioneer issues on the part of Topps. The cards measure 2-1/4" by 3-1/2" and were specially printed to simulate a three-dimensional effect. Backgrounds are a purposely blurred stadium scene, in front of which was a normally sharp color player photograph. The outer layer is a thin coating of ribbed plastic. The special process gives the picture the illusion of depth when the card is moved or tilted. As this was done two years before Kellogg's began its 3-D cards, this 12-card test issue really was breaking new ground. Unfortunately, production and distribution were limited making the cards very tough to find.

		NR MT	EX	VG
Complete Set:		9000.00	4500.00	2500.
Common Player:		350.00	175.00	105.00
(1)	Bob Clemente	2500.00	1250.00	750.00
(2)	Willie Davis	400.00	200.00	125.00
(3)	Ron Fairly	400.00	200.00	125.00
(4)	Curt Flood	400.00	200.00	125.00
(5)	Jim Lonborg	400.00	200.00	125.00
(6)	Jim Maloney	350.00	175.00	105.00
(7)	Tony Perez	600.00	300.00	175.00
(8)	Boog Powell	500.00	250.00	150.00
(9)	Bill Robinson	350.00	175.00	105.00
(10)	Rusty Staub	450.00	230.00	135.00
(11)	Mel Stottlemyre	400.00	200.00	120.00
(12)	Ron Swoboda	350.00	175.00	105.00

1969 Topps

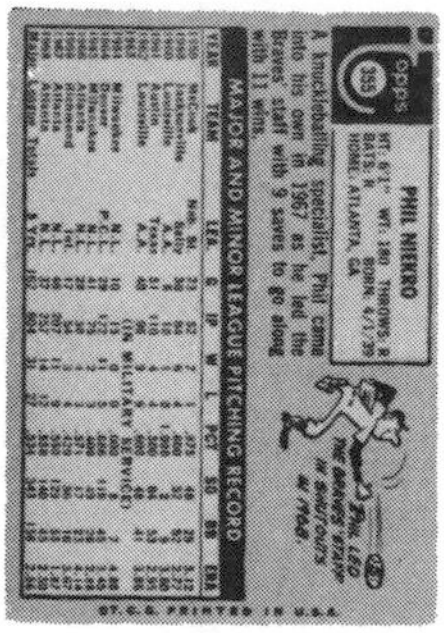

A player's name in italic type indicates a rookie card. An (FC) indicates a player's first card for that particular card company.

The 1969 Topps set broke yet another record for quantity as the issue is officially a whopping 664 cards. With substantial numbers of variations, the number of possible cards runs closer to 700. The design of the 2-1/2" by 3-1/2" cards in the set feature a color photo with the team name printed in block letters underneath. A circle contains the player's name and position. Card backs returned to a horizontal format. Despite the size of the set, it contains no teamcards. It does, however, have multi-player cards, All-Stars, statistical leaders, and World Series highlights. Most significant among the varieties are white and yellow letter cards from the run of #'s 440-511. The complete set prices below do not include the scarcer and more expensive "white letter" variations.

	NR MT	EX	VG
Complete Set:	2200.00	1100.00	650.00
Common Player: 1-218	1.00	.50	.30
Common Player: 219-327	1.50	.70	.45
Common Player: 328-512	1.00	.50	.30
Common Player: 513-664	1.00	.50	.30

		NR MT	EX	VG
1	A.L. Batting Leaders (Danny Cater, Tony Oliva, Carl Yastrzemski)	9.00	4.50	2.75
2	N.L. Batting Leaders (Felipe Alou, Matty Alou, Pete Rose)	4.00	2.00	1.25
3	A.L. RBI Leaders (Ken Harrelson, Frank Howard, Jim Northrup)	2.00	1.00	.60
4	N.L. RBI Leaders (Willie McCovey, Ron Santo, Billy Williams)	3.50	1.75	1.00
5	A.L. Home Run Leaders (Ken Harrelson, Willie Horton, Frank Howard)	2.00	1.00	.60
6	N.L. Home Run Leaders (Richie Allen, Ernie Banks, Willie McCovey)	3.50	1.75	1.00
7	A.L. ERA Leaders (Sam McDowell, Dave McNally, Luis Tiant)	2.00	1.00	.60
8	N.L. ERA Leaders (Bobby Bolin, Bob Gibson, Bob Veale)	3.00	1.50	.90
9	A.L. Pitching Leaders (Denny McLain, Dave McNally, Mel Stottlemyre, Luis Tiant)	2.00	1.00	.60
10	N.L. Pitching Leaders (Bob Gibson, Fergie Jenkins, Juan Marichal)	3.50	1.75	1.00
11	A.L. Strikeout Leaders (Sam McDowell, Denny McLain, Luis Tiant)	2.00	1.00	.60
12	N.L. Strikeout Leaders (Bob Gibson, Fergie Jenkins, Bill Singer)	3.00	1.50	.90
13	Mickey Stanley	1.00	.50	.30
14	Al McBean	1.00	.50	.30
15	Boog Powell	2.50	1.25	.70
16	Giants Rookies (Cesar Gutierrez, Rich Robertson)	1.00	.50	.30
17	Mike Marshall	1.50	.70	.45
18	Dick Schofield	1.00	.50	.30
19	Ken Suarez	1.00	.50	.30
20	Ernie Banks	15.00	7.50	4.50
21	Jose Santiago	1.00	.50	.30
22	Jesus Alou	1.00	.50	.30
23	Lew Krausse	1.00	.50	.30
24	Walt Alston	3.00	1.50	.90
25	Roy White	1.50	.70	.45
26	Clay Carroll	1.00	.50	.30
27	Bernie Allen	1.00	.50	.30
28	Mike Ryan	1.00	.50	.30
29	Dave Morehead	1.00	.50	.30
30	Bob Allison	1.00	.50	.30
31	Mets Rookies (*Gary Gentry, Amos Otis*)	1.50	.70	.45
32	Sammy Ellis	1.00	.50	.30
33	Wayne Causey	1.00	.50	.30
34	Gary Peters	1.00	.50	.30
35	Joe Morgan	12.00	6.00	3.50
36	Luke Walker	1.00	.50	.30
37	Curt Motton	1.00	.50	.30
38	Zoilo Versalles	1.00	.50	.30
39	Dick Hughes	1.00	.50	.30
40	Mayo Smith	1.00	.50	.30
41	Bob Barton	1.00	.50	.30
42	Tommy Harper	1.00	.50	.30
43	Joe Niekro	1.50	.70	.45
44	Danny Cater	1.00	.50	.30
45	Maury Wills	2.50	1.25	.70
46	Fritz Peterson	1.00	.50	.30
47a	Paul Popovich (emblem visible thru airbrush)	4.00	2.00	1.25
47b	Paul Popovich (helmet emblem completely airbrushed)	1.00	.50	.30
48	Brant Alyea	1.00	.50	.30
49a	Royals Rookies (Steve Jones, Eliseo Rodriquez) (Rodriquez on front)	6.00	3.00	1.75
49b	Royals Rookies (Steve Jones, Eliseo Rodriguez) (Rodriguez on front)	1.00	.50	.30
50	Bob Clemente	45.00	23.00	13.50
51	Woody Fryman	1.00	.50	.30
52	Mike Andrews	1.00	.50	.30
53	Sonny Jackson	1.00	.50	.30
54	Cisco Carlos	1.00	.50	.30
55	Jerry Grote	1.00	.50	.30
56	Rich Reese	1.00	.50	.30
57	Checklist 1-109 (Denny McLain)	3.00	1.50	.90
58	Fred Gladding	1.00	.50	.30
59	Jay Johnstone	1.00	.50	.30
60	Nelson Briles	1.00	.50	.30
61	Jimmie Hall	1.00	.50	.30
62	Chico Salmon	1.25	.60	.40
63	Jim Hickman	1.00	.50	.30
64	Bill Monbouquette	1.00	.50	.30
65	Willie Davis	1.00	.50	.30
66	Orioles Rookies (Mike Adamson, *Merv Rettenmund*)	1.00	.50	.30
67	Bill Stoneman	1.00	.50	.30
68	Dave Duncan	1.00	.50	.30
69	Steve Hamilton	1.00	.50	.30
70	Tommy Helms	1.00	.50	.30
71	Steve Whitaker	1.00	.50	.30
72	Ron Taylor	1.00	.50	.30
73	Johnny Briggs	1.00	.50	.30
74	Preston Gomez	1.00	.50	.30
75	Luis Aparicio	5.00	2.50	1.50
76	Norm Miller	1.00	.50	.30
77a	Ron Perranoski (LA visible thru airbrush)	4.50	2.25	1.25
77b	Ron Perranoski (cap emblem completely airbrushed)	1.00	.50	.30
78	Tom Satriano	1.00	.50	.30
79	Milt Pappas	1.00	.50	.30
80	Norm Cash	1.75	.90	.50
81	Mel Queen	1.00	.50	.30
82	Pirates Rookies (*Rich Hebner, Al Oliver*)	12.00	6.00	3.50
83	Mike Ferraro	1.25	.60	.40
84	Bob Humphreys	1.00	.50	.30
85	Lou Brock	15.00	7.50	4.50
86	Pete Richert	1.00	.50	.30
87	Horace Clarke	1.00	.50	.30
88	Rich Nye	1.00	.50	.30
89	Russ Gibson	1.00	.50	.30
90	Jerry Koosman	2.50	1.25	.70
91	Al Dark	1.00	.50	.30
92	Jack Billingham	1.00	.50	.30
93	Joe Foy	1.00	.50	.30
94	Hank Aguirre	1.00	.50	.30
95	Johnny Bench	175.00	87.00	52.00
96	Denver Lemaster	1.00	.50	.30
97	Buddy Bradford	1.00	.50	.30
98	Dave Giusti	1.00	.50	.30
99a	Twins Rookies (Danny Morris, *Graig Nettles*) (black loop above "Twins")	20.00	10.00	6.00
99b	Twins Rookies (Danny Morris, *Graig Nettles*) (no black loop)	12.00	6.00	3.50
100	Hank Aaron	60.00	30.00	18.00
101	Daryl Patterson	1.00	.50	.30
102	Jim Davenport	1.00	.50	.30
103	Roger Repoz	1.00	.50	.30
104	Steve Blass	1.00	.50	.30
105	Rick Monday	1.25	.60	.40
106	Jim Hannan	1.00	.50	.30
107a	Checklist 110-218 (Bob Gibson) (161 is Jim Purdin)	3.00	1.50	.90
107b	Checklist 110-218 (Bob Gibson) (161 is John Purdin)	6.00	3.00	1.75
108	Tony Taylor	1.00	.50	.30
109	Jim Lonborg	1.25	.60	.40
110	Mike Shannon	1.00	.50	.30
111	Johnny Morris	1.25	.60	.40
112	J.C. Martin	1.00	.50	.30
113	Dave May	1.00	.50	.30
114	Yankees Rookies (Alan Closter, John Cumberland)	1.00	.50	.30
115	Bill Hands	1.00	.50	.30
116	Chuck Harrison	1.00	.50	.30
117	Jim Fairey	1.00	.50	.30
118	Stan Williams	1.00	.50	.30
119	Doug Rader	1.00	.50	.30
120	Pete Rose	35.00	17.50	10.50
121	Joe Grzenda	1.00	.50	.30
122	Ron Fairly	1.25	.60	.40
123	Wilbur Wood	1.25	.60	.40

		NR MT	EX	VG
124	Hank Bauer	1.25	.60	.40
125	Ray Sadecki	1.00	.50	.30
126	Dick Tracewski	1.00	.50	.30
127	Kevin Collins	1.00	.50	.30
128	Tommie Aaron	1.00	.50	.30
129	Bill McCool	1.00	.50	.30
130	Carl Yastrzemski	30.00	15.00	9.00
131	Chris Cannizzaro	1.00	.50	.30
132	Dave Baldwin	1.00	.50	.30
133	Johnny Callison	1.00	.50	.30
134	Jim Weaver	1.00	.50	.30
135	Tommy Davis	1.50	.70	.45
136	Cards Rookies (Steve Huntz, Mike Torrez)	1.00	.50	.30
137	Wally Bunker	1.00	.50	.30
138	John Bateman	1.00	.50	.30
139	Andy Kosco	1.00	.50	.30
140	Jim Lefebvre	1.00	.50	.30
141	Bill Dillman	1.00	.50	.30
142	Woody Woodward	1.00	.50	.30
143	Joe Nossek	1.00	.50	.30
144	Bob Hendley	1.00	.50	.30
145	Max Alvis	1.00	.50	.30
146	Jim Perry	1.00	.50	.30
147	Leo Durocher	2.25	1.25	.70
148	Lee Stange	1.00	.50	.30
149	Ollie Brown	1.00	.50	.30
150	Denny McLain	3.00	1.50	.90
151a	Clay Dalrymple (Phillies)	7.00	3.50	2.00
151b	Clay Dalrymple (Orioles)	1.00	.50	.30
152	Tommie Sisk	1.00	.50	.30
153	Ed Brinkman	1.00	.50	.30
154	Jim Britton	1.00	.50	.30
155	Pete Ward	1.00	.50	.30
156	Astros Rookies (Hal Gilson, Leon McFadden)	1.00	.50	.30
157	Bob Rodgers	1.00	.50	.30
158	Joe Gibbon	1.00	.50	.30
159	Jerry Adair	1.00	.50	.30
160	Vada Pinson	2.00	1.00	.60
161	John Purdin	1.00	.50	.30
162	World Series Game 1 (Gibson Fans 17; Sets New Record)	3.50	1.75	1.00
163	World Series Game 2 (Tiger Homers Deck The Cards)	2.50	1.25	.70
164	World Series Game 3 (McCarver's Homer Puts St. Louis Ahead)	2.50	1.25	.70
165	World Series Game 4 (Brock's Lead-Off Homer Starts Cards' Romp)	3.50	1.75	1.00
166	World Series Game 5 (Kaline's Key Hit Sparks Tiger Rally)	3.50	1.75	1.00
167	World Series Game 6 (Tiger 10-Run Inning Ties Mark)	2.50	1.25	.70
168	World Series Game 7 (Lolich Series Hero, Outduels Gibson)	2.75	1.50	.80
169	World Series Summary (Tigers Celebrate Their Victory)	2.50	1.25	.70
170	Frank Howard	2.00	1.00	.60
171	Glenn Beckert	1.25	.60	.40
172	Jerry Stephenson	1.00	.50	.30
173	White Sox Rookies (Bob Christian, Gerry Nyman)	1.00	.50	.30
174	Grant Jackson	1.00	.50	.30
175	Jim Bunning	4.00	2.00	1.25
176	Joe Azcue	1.00	.50	.30
177	Ron Reed	1.00	.50	.30
178	Ray Oyler	1.25	.60	.40
179	Don Pavletich	1.00	.50	.30
180	Willie Horton	1.25	.60	.40
181	Mel Nelson	1.00	.50	.30
182	Bill Rigney	1.00	.50	.30
183	Don Shaw	1.00	.50	.30
184	Roberto Pena	1.00	.50	.30
185	Tom Phoebus	1.00	.50	.30
186	John Edwards	1.00	.50	.30
187	Leon Wagner	1.00	.50	.30
188	Rick Wise	1.00	.50	.30
189	Red Sox Rookies (Joe Lahoud, John Thibdeau)	1.00	.50	.30
190	Willie Mays	50.00	25.00	15.00
191	Lindy McDaniel	1.00	.50	.30
192	Jose Pagan	1.00	.50	.30
193	Don Cardwell	1.00	.50	.30
194	Ted Uhlaender	1.00	.50	.30
195	John Odom	1.00	.50	.30
196	Lum Harris	1.00	.50	.30
197	Dick Selma	1.00	.50	.30
198	Willie Smith	1.00	.50	.30
199	Jim French	1.00	.50	.30
200	Bob Gibson	12.00	6.00	3.50
201	Russ Snyder	1.00	.50	.30
202	Don Wilson	1.00	.50	.30
203	Dave Johnson	1.50	.70	.45
204	Jack Hiatt	1.00	.50	.30
205	Rick Reichardt	1.00	.50	.30
206	Phillies Rookies (Larry Hisle, Barry Lersch)	1.25	.60	.40
207	Roy Face	1.50	.70	.45
208a	Donn Clendenon (Expos)	7.00	3.50	2.00
208b	Donn Clendenon (Houston)	1.00	.50	.30
209	Larry Haney (photo reversed)	1.25	.60	.40
210	Felix Millan	1.00	.50	.30
211	Galen Cisco	1.00	.50	.30
212	Tom Tresh	1.50	.70	.45
213	Gerry Arrigo	1.00	.50	.30
214	Checklist 219-327	2.50	1.25	.70
215	Rico Petrocelli	1.25	.60	.40
216	Don Sutton	5.00	2.50	1.50
217	John Donaldson	1.00	.50	.30
218	John Roseboro	1.00	.50	.30
219	*Freddie Patek*	2.00	1.00	.60
220	Sam McDowell	1.50	.70	.45
221	Art Shamsky	1.50	.70	.45
222	Duane Josephson	1.50	.70	.45
223	Tom Dukes	1.50	.70	.45
224	Angels Rookies (Bill Harrelson, Steve Kealey)	1.50	.70	.45
225	Don Kessinger	1.50	.70	.45
226	Bruce Howard	1.50	.70	.45
227	Frank Johnson	1.50	.70	.45
228	Dave Leonhard	1.50	.70	.45
229	Don Lock	1.50	.70	.45
230	Rusty Staub	2.50	1.25	.70
231	Pat Dobson	1.50	.70	.45
232	Dave Ricketts	1.50	.70	.45
233	Steve Barber	1.50	.70	.45
234	Dave Bristol	1.50	.70	.45
235	Jim Hunter	10.00	5.00	3.00
236	Manny Mota	1.50	.70	.45
237	*Bobby Cox*	1.50	.70	.45
238	Ken Johnson	1.50	.70	.45
239	Bob Taylor	1.50	.70	.45
240	Ken Harrelson	2.00	1.00	.60
241	Jim Brewer	1.50	.70	.45
242	Frank Kostro	1.50	.70	.45
243	Ron Kline	1.50	.70	.45
244	Indians Rookies (*Ray Fosse*, George Woodson)	1.50	.70	.45
245	Ed Charles	1.50	.70	.45
246	Joe Coleman	1.50	.70	.45
247	Gene Oliver	1.50	.70	.45
248	Bob Priddy	1.50	.70	.45
249	Ed Spiezio	1.50	.70	.45
250	Frank Robinson	20.00	10.00	6.00
251	Ron Herbel	1.50	.70	.45
252	Chuck Cottier	1.50	.70	.45
253	Jerry Johnson	1.50	.70	.30
254	Joe Schultz	1.50	.70	.30
255	Steve Carlton	50.00	25.00	15.00
256	Gates Brown	1.50	.70	.30
257	Jim Ray	1.50	.70	.30
258	Jackie Hernandez	1.50	.70	.30
259	Bill Short	1.50	.70	.30
260	*Reggie Jackson*	450.00	225.00	135.00
261	Bob Johnson	1.50	.70	.30
262	Mike Kekich	1.50	.70	.30
263	Jerry May	1.50	.70	.30
264	Bill Landis	1.50	.70	.30
265	Chico Cardenas	1.50	.70	.30
266	Dodgers Rookies (Alan Foster, Tom Hutton)	1.50	.70	.30
267	Vicente Romo	1.50	.70	.30
268	Al Spangler	1.50	.70	.30
269	Al Weis	1.50	.70	.30
270	Mickey Lolich	3.50	1.75	1.00
271	Larry Stahl	1.50	.70	.30
272	Ed Stroud	1.50	.70	.30
273	Ron Willis	1.50	.70	.30
274	Clyde King	1.50	.70	.30
275	Vic Davalillo	1.50	.70	.30
276	Gary Wagner	1.50	.70	.30
277	*Rod Hendricks*	1.50	.70	.30
278	Gary Geiger	1.50	.70	.30
279	Roger Nelson	1.50	.70	.30
280	Alex Johnson	1.50	.70	.30
281	Ted Kubiak	1.50	.70	.30
282	Pat Jarvis	1.50	.70	.30
283	Sandy Alomar	1.50	.70	.30
284	Expos Rookies (Jerry Robertson, Mike Wegener)	1.50	.70	.30
285	Don Mincher	1.50	.70	.30
286	*Dock Ellis*	1.50	.70	.30

		NR MT	EX	VG
287	Jose Tartabull	1.50	.70	.30
288	Ken Holtzman	1.50	.70	.30
289	Bart Shirley	1.50	.70	.30
290	Jim Kaat	4.50	2.25	1.25
291	Vern Fuller	1.50	.70	.30
292	Al Downing	1.50	.70	.45
293	Dick Dietz	1.50	.70	.30
294	Jim Lemon	1.50	.70	.30
295	Tony Perez	10.00	5.00	3.00
296	*Andy Messersmith*	1.50	.70	.45
297	Deron Johnson	1.50	.70	.30
298	Dave Nicholson	1.50	.70	.30
299	Mark Belanger	1.50	.70	.30
300	Felipe Alou	1.50	.70	.45
301	Darrell Brandon	1.50	.70	.30
302	Jim Pagliaroni	1.50	.70	.30
303	Cal Koonce	1.50	.70	.30
304	Padres Rookies (Bill Davis, *Clarence Gaston*)	1.50	.70	.30
305	Dick McAuliffe	1.50	.70	.30
306	Jim Grant	1.50	.70	.30
307	Gary Kolb	1.50	.70	.30
308	Wade Blasingame	1.50	.70	.30
309	Walt Williams	1.50	.70	.30
310	Tom Haller	1.50	.70	.30
311	*Sparky Lyle*	10.00	5.00	3.00
312	Lee Elia	1.50	.70	.30
313	Bill Robinson	1.50	.70	.30
314	Checklist 328-425 (Don Drysdale)	3.50	1.75	1.00
315	Eddie Fisher	1.50	.70	.30
316	Hal Lanier	1.50	.70	.30
317	Bruce Look	1.50	.70	.30
318	Jack Fisher	1.50	.70	.30
319	Ken McMullen	1.50	.70	.30
320	Dal Maxvill	1.50	.70	.30
321	Jim McAndrew	1.50	.70	.30
322	Jose Vidal	1.50	.70	.30
323	Larry Miller	1.50	.70	.30
324	Tigers Rookies (Les Cain, Dave Campbell)	1.50	.70	.30
325	Jose Cardenal	1.50	.70	.30
326	Gary Sutherland	1.50	.70	.30
327	Willie Crawford	1.50	.70	.30
328	Joe Horlen	1.00	.50	.30
329	Rick Joseph	1.00	.50	.30
330	Tony Conigliaro	1.50	.70	.45
331	Braves Rookies (Gil Garrido, *Tom House*)	1.00	.50	.30
332	Fred Talbot	1.25	.60	.40
333	Ivan Murrell	1.00	.50	.30
334	Phil Roof	1.00	.50	.30
335	Bill Mazeroski	1.75	.90	.50
336	Jim Roland	1.00	.50	.30
337	Marty Martinez	1.00	.50	.30
338	*Del Unser*	1.00	.50	.30
339	Reds Rookies (Steve Mingori, Jose Pena)	1.00	.50	.30
340	Dave McNally	1.25	.60	.40
341	Dave Adlesh	1.00	.50	.30
342	Bubba Morton	1.00	.50	.30
343	Dan Frisella	1.00	.50	.30
344	Tom Matchick	1.00	.50	.30
345	Frank Linzy	1.00	.50	.30
346	Wayne Comer	1.25	.60	.40
347	Randy Hundley	1.00	.50	.30
348	Steve Hargan	1.00	.50	.30
349	Dick Williams	1.25	.60	.40
350	Richie Allen	2.00	1.00	.60
351	Carroll Sembera	1.00	.50	.30
352	Paul Schaal	1.00	.50	.30
353	Jeff Torborg	1.00	.50	.30
354	Nate Oliver	1.25	.60	.40
355	Phil Niekro	7.00	3.50	2.00
356	Frank Quilici	1.00	.50	.30
357	Carl Taylor	1.00	.50	.30
358	Athletics Rookies (George Lauzerique, Roberto Rodriguez)	1.00	.50	.30
359	Dick Kelley	1.00	.50	.30
360	Jim Wynn	1.25	.60	.40
361	Gary Holman	1.00	.50	.30
362	Jim Maloney	1.00	.50	.30
363	Russ Nixon	1.00	.50	.30
364	Tommie Agee	1.25	.60	.40
365	Jim Fregosi	1.00	.50	.30
366	Bo Belinsky	1.00	.50	.30
367	Lou Johnson	1.00	.50	.30
368	Vic Roznovsky	1.00	.50	.30
369	Bob Skinner	1.00	.50	.30
370	Juan Marichal	7.00	3.50	2.00
371	Sal Bando	1.25	.60	.40
372	Adolfo Phillips	1.00	.50	.30
373	Fred Lasher	1.00	.50	.30
374	Bob Tillman	1.00	.50	.30
375	Harmon Killebrew	15.00	7.50	4.50
376	Royals Rookies (Mike Fiore, *Jim Rooker*)	1.00	.50	.30
377	Gary Bell	1.25	.60	.40
378	Jose Herrera	1.00	.50	.30
379	Ken Boyer	1.75	.90	.50
380	Stan Bahnsen	1.25	.60	.40
381	Ed Kranepool	1.25	.60	.40
382	Pat Corrales	1.25	.60	.40
383	Casey Cox	1.00	.50	.30
384	Larry Shepard	1.00	.50	.30
385	Orlando Cepeda	3.50	1.75	1.00
386	Jim McGlothlin	1.00	.50	.30
387	Bobby Klaus	1.00	.50	.30
388	Tom McCraw	1.00	.50	.30
389	Dan Coombs	1.00	.50	.30
390	Bill Freehan	1.00	.50	.30
391	Ray Culp	1.00	.50	.30
392	Bob Burda	1.00	.50	.30
393	Gene Brabender	1.00	.50	.30
394	Pilots Rookies (Lou Piniella, Marv Staehle)	3.00	1.50	.90
395	Chris Short	1.00	.50	.30
396	Jim Campanis	1.00	.50	.30
397	Chuck Dobson	1.00	.50	.30
398	Tito Francona	1.00	.50	.30
399	Bob Bailey	1.00	.50	.30
400	Don Drysdale	8.00	4.00	2.50
401	Jake Gibbs	1.25	.60	.40
402	Ken Boswell	1.00	.50	.30
403	Bob Miller	1.00	.50	.30
404	Cubs Rookies (Vic LaRose, Gary Ross)	1.00	.50	.30
405	Lee May	1.00	.50	.30
406	Phil Ortega	1.00	.50	.30
407	Tom Egan	1.00	.50	.30
408	Nate Colbert	1.00	.50	.30
409	Bob Moose	1.00	.50	.30
410	Al Kaline	12.00	6.00	3.50
411	Larry Dierker	1.00	.50	.30
412	Checklist 426-512 (Mickey Mantle)	7.00	3.50	2.00
413	Roland Sheldon	1.25	.60	.40
414	Duke Sims	1.00	.50	.30
415	Ray Washburn	1.00	.50	.30
416	Willie McCovey AS	3.50	1.75	1.00
417	Ken Harrelson AS	1.00	.50	.30
418	Tommy Helms AS	1.00	.50	.30
419	Rod Carew AS	10.00	7.50	4.50
420	Ron Santo AS	1.00	.50	.30
421	Brooks Robinson AS	4.00	2.00	1.25
422	Don Kessinger AS	1.00	.50	.30
423	Bert Campaneris AS	1.25	.60	.40
424	Pete Rose AS	12.00	6.00	3.50
425	Carl Yastrzemski AS	6.00	3.00	1.75
426	Curt Flood AS	1.00	.50	.30
427	Tony Oliva AS	1.50	.70	.45
428	Lou Brock AS	3.50	1.75	1.00
429	Willie Horton AS	1.25	.60	.40
430	Johnny Bench AS	12.00	6.00	3.50
431	Bill Freehan AS	1.00	.50	.30
432	Bob Gibson AS	5.00	2.50	1.50
433	Denny McLain AS	1.50	.70	.45
434	Jerry Koosman AS	1.00	.50	.30
435	Sam McDowell AS	1.25	.60	.40
436	Gene Alley	1.00	.50	.30
437	Luis Alcaraz	1.00	.50	.30
438	Gary Waslewski	1.00	.50	.30
439	White Sox Rookies (Ed Herrmann, Dan Lazar)	1.00	.50	.30
440a	Willie McCovey (last name in white)	90.00	45.00	27.00
440b	Willie McCovey (last name in yellow)	18.00	9.00	5.50
441a	Dennis Higgins (last name in white)	10.00	5.00	3.00
441b	Dennis Higgins (last name in yellow)	1.00	.50	.30
442	Ty Cline	1.00	.50	.30
443	Don Wert	1.00	.50	.30
444a	Joe Moeller (last name in white)	10.00	5.00	3.00
444b	Joe Moeller (last name in yellow)	1.00	.50	.30
445	Bobby Knoop	1.00	.50	.30
446	Claude Raymond	1.00	.50	.30
447a	Ralph Houk (last name in white)	15.00	7.50	4.50
447b	Ralph Houk (last name in yellow)	1.50	.70	.45
448	Bob Tolan	1.00	.50	.30
449	Paul Lindblad	1.00	.50	.30
450	Billy Williams	6.00	3.00	1.75

		NR MT	EX	VG
451a	Rich Rollins (first name in white)	10.00	5.00	3.00
451b	Rich Rollins (first name in yellow)	1.25	.60	.40
452a	Al Ferrara (first name in white)	10.00	5.00	3.00
452b	Al Ferrara (first name in yellow)	1.00	.50	.30
453	Mike Cuellar	1.25	.60	.40
454a	Phillies Rookies (Larry Colton, *Don Money*) (names in white)	10.00	5.00	3.00
454b	Phillies Rookies (Larry Colton, *Don Money*) (names in yellow)	1.25	.60	.40
455	Sonny Siebert	1.00	.50	.30
456	Bud Harrelson	1.00	.50	.30
457	Dalton Jones	1.00	.50	.30
458	Curt Blefary	1.00	.50	.30
459	Dave Boswell	1.00	.50	.30
460	Joe Torre	1.75	.90	.50
461a	Mike Epstein (last name in white)	10.00	5.00	3.00
461b	Mike Epstein (last name in yellow)	1.00	.50	.30
462	Red Schoendienst	1.50	.70	.45
463	Dennis Ribant	1.00	.50	.30
464a	Dave Marshall (last name in white)	10.00	5.00	3.00
464b	Dave Marshall (last name in yellow)	1.00	.50	.30
465	Tommy John	4.50	2.25	1.25
466	John Boccabella	1.00	.50	.30
467	Tom Reynolds	1.00	.50	.30
468a	Pirates Rookies (Bruce Dal Canton, Bob Robertson) (names in white)	10.00	5.00	3.00
468b	Pirates Rookies (Bruce Dal Canton, Bob Robertson) (names in yellow)	1.00	.50	.30
469	Chico Ruiz	1.00	.50	.30
470a	Mel Stottlemyre (last name in white)	15.00	7.50	4.50
470b	Mel Stottlemyre (last name in yellow)	1.50	.70	.45
471a	Ted Savage (last name in white)	10.00	5.00	3.00
471b	Ted Savage (last name in yellow)	1.00	.50	.30
472	Jim Price	1.00	.50	.30
473a	Jose Arcia (first name in white)	10.00	5.00	3.00
473b	Jose Arcia (first name in yellow)	1.00	.50	.30
474	Tom Murphy	1.00	.50	.30
475	Tim McCarver	1.50	.70	.45
476a	Red Sox Rookies *(Ken Brett*, Gerry Moses) (names in white)	10.00	5.00	3.00
476b	Red Sox Rookies *(Ken Brett*, Gerry Moses) (names in yellow)	1.00	.50	.30
477	Jeff James	1.00	.50	.30
478	Don Buford	1.00	.50	.30
479	Richie Scheinblum	1.00	.50	.30
480	Tom Seaver	100.00	50.00	30.00
481	*Bill Melton*	1.25	.60	.40
482a	Jim Gosger (first name in white)	10.00	5.00	3.00
482b	Jim Gosger (first name in yellow)	1.25	.60	.40
483	Ted Abernathy	1.00	.50	.30
484	Joe Gordon	1.00	.50	.30
485a	Gaylord Perry (last name in white)	75.00	38.00	23.00
485b	Gaylord Perry (last name in yellow)	10.00	5.00	3.00
486a	Paul Casanova (last name in white)	10.00	5.00	3.00
486b	Paul Casanova (last name in yellow)	1.00	.50	.30
487	Denis Menke	1.00	.50	.30
488	Joe Sparma	1.00	.50	.30
489	Clete Boyer	1.25	.60	.40
490	Matty Alou	1.00	.50	.30
491a	Twins Rookies (Jerry Crider, George Mitterwald) (names in white)	10.00	5.00	3.00
491b	Twins Rookies (Jerry Crider, George Mitterwald) (names in yellow)	1.00	.50	.30
492	Tony Cloninger	1.00	.50	.30
493a	Wes Parker (last name in white)	10.00	5.00	3.00
493b	Wes Parker (last name in yellow)	1.00	.50	.30
494	Ken Berry	1.00	.50	.30
495	Bert Campaneris	1.50	.70	.45
496	Larry Jaster	1.00	.50	.30
497	Julian Javier	1.00	.50	.30
498	Juan Pizarro	1.00	.50	.30
499	Astros Rookies (Don Bryant, Steve Shea)	1.00	.50	.30
500a	Mickey Mantle (last name in white)	475.00	190.00	119.00
500b	Mickey Mantle (last name in yellow)	190.00	80.00	50.00
501a	Tony Gonzalez (first name in white)	10.00	5.00	3.00
501b	Tony Gonzalez (first name in yellow)	1.00	.50	.30
502	Minnie Rojas	1.00	.50	.30

		NR MT	EX	VG
503	Larry Brown	1.00	.50	.30
504	Checklist 513-588 (Brooks Robinson)	4.00	2.00	1.25
505a	Bobby Bolin (last name in white)	10.00	5.00	3.00
505b	Bobby Bolin (last name in yellow)	1.00	.50	.30
506	Paul Blair	1.00	.50	.30
507	Cookie Rojas	1.00	.50	.30
508	Moe Drabowsky	1.00	.50	.30
509	Manny Sanguillen	1.00	.50	.30
510	Rod Carew	60.00	30.00	18.00
511a	Diego Segui (first name in white)	10.00	5.00	3.00
511b	Diego Segui (first name in yellow)	1.25	.60	.40
512	Cleon Jones	1.25	.60	.40
513	Camilo Pascual	1.00	.50	.30
514	Mike Lum	1.00	.50	.30
515	Dick Green	1.00	.50	.30
516	Earl Weaver	5.00	2.50	1.50
517	Mike McCormick	1.25	.60	.40
518	Fred Whitfield	1.00	.50	.30
519	Yankees Rookies (Len Boehmer, Gerry Kenney)	1.00	.50	.30
520	Bob Veale	1.25	.60	.40
521	George Thomas	1.00	.50	.30
522	Joe Hoerner	1.00	.50	.30
523	Bob Chance	1.00	.50	.30
524	Expos Rookies (Jose Laboy, Floyd Wicker)	1.00	.50	.30
525	Earl Wilson	1.00	.50	.30
526	Hector Torres	1.00	.50	.30
527	Al Lopez	3.00	1.50	.90
528	Claude Osteen	1.00	.50	.30
529	Ed Kirkpatrick	1.00	.50	.30
530	Cesar Tovar	1.00	.50	.30
531	Dick Farrell	1.00	.50	.30
532	Bird Hill Aces (Mike Cuellar, Jim Hardin, Dave McNally, Tom Phoebus)	1.50	.70	.45
533	Nolan Ryan	375.00	187.00	112.00
534	Jerry McNertney	1.00	.50	.30
535	Phil Regan	1.00	.50	.30
536	Padres Rookies (Danny Breeden, *Dave Roberts)*	1.25	.60	.40
537	Mike Paul	1.00	.50	.30
538	Charlie Smith	1.00	.50	.30
539	Ted Shows How (Mike Epstein, Ted Williams)	3.25	1.75	1.00
540	Curt Flood	1.50	.70	.45
541	Joe Verbanic	1.00	.50	.30
542	Bob Aspromonte	1.00	.50	.30
543	Fred Newman	1.00	.50	.30
544	Tigers Rookies (Mike Kilkenny, Ron Woods)	1.00	.50	.30
545	Willie Stargell	10.00	5.00	3.00
546	Jim Nash	1.00	.50	.30
547	Billy Martin	5.00	2.50	1.50
548	Bob Locker	1.00	.50	.30
549	Ron Brand	1.00	.50	.30
550	Brooks Robinson	15.00	7.50	4.50
551	Wayne Granger	1.00	.50	.30
552	Dodgers Rookies *(Ted Sizemore, Bill Sudakis)*	1.25	.60	.40
553	Ron Davis	1.00	.50	.30
554	Frank Bertaina	1.00	.50	.30
555	Jim Hart	1.25	.60	.40
556	A's Stars (Sal Bando, Bert Campaneris, Danny Cater)	1.50	.70	.45
557	Frank Fernandez	1.00	.50	.30
558	*Tom Burgmeier*	1.25	.60	.40
559	Cards Rookies (Joe Hague, Jim Hicks)	1.00	.50	.30
560	Luis Tiant	1.50	.70	.45
561	Ron Clark	1.00	.50	.30
562	*Bob Watson*	1.00	.50	.30
563	Marty Pattin	1.00	.50	.30
564	Gil Hodges	6.00	3.00	1.75
565	Hoyt Wilhelm	6.00	3.00	1.75
566	Ron Hansen	1.00	.50	.30
567	Pirates Rookies (Elvio Jimenez, Jim Shellenback)	1.00	.50	.30
568	Cecil Upshaw	1.00	.50	.30
569	Billy Harris	1.00	.50	.30
570	Ron Santo	1.75	.90	.50
571	Cap Peterson	1.00	.50	.30
572	Giants Heroes (Juan Marichal, Willie McCovey)	7.00	3.50	2.00
573	Jim Palmer	30.00	15.00	9.00
574	George Scott	1.00	.50	.30
575	Bill Singer	1.25	.60	.40
576	Phillies Rookies (Ron Stone, Bill Wilson)	1.00	.50	.30
577	Mike Hegan	1.00	.50	.30
578	Don Bosch	1.00	.50	.30

		NR MT	EX	VG
579	*Dave Nelson*	1.25	.60	.40
580	Jim Northrup	1.25	.60	.40
581	Gary Nolan	1.00	.50	.30
582a	Checklist 589-664 (Tony Oliva) (red circle on back)	3.50	1.75	1.00
582b	Checklist 589-664 (Tony Oliva) (white circle on back)	2.50	1.25	.70
583	*Clyde Wright*	1.25	.60	.40
584	Don Mason	1.00	.50	.30
585	Ron Swoboda	1.00	.50	.30
586	Tim Cullen	1.00	.50	.30
587	*Joe Rudi*	1.75	.90	.50
588	Bill White	1.00	.50	.30
589	Joe Pepitone	2.00	1.00	.60
590	Rico Carty	1.00	.50	.30
591	Mike Hedlund	1.00	.50	.30
592	Padres Rookies (Rafael Robles, Al Santorini)	1.00	.50	.30
593	Don Nottebart	1.00	.50	.30
594	Dooley Womack	1.00	.50	.30
595	Lee Maye	1.00	.50	.30
596	Chuck Hartenstein	1.00	.50	.30
597	A.L. Rookies (Larry Burchart, *Rollie Fingers*, Bob Floyd)	80.00	40.00	25.00
598	Ruben Amaro	1.00	.50	.30
599	John Boozer	1.00	.50	.30
600	Tony Oliva	2.25	1.25	.70
601	Tug McGraw	2.00	1.00	.60
602	Cubs Rookies (Alec Distaso, Jim Qualls, Don Young)	1.00	.50	.30
603	Joe Keough	1.00	.50	.30
604	Bobby Etheridge	1.00	.50	.30
605	Dick Ellsworth	1.00	.50	.30
606	Gene Mauch	1.00	.50	.30
607	Dick Bosman	1.00	.50	.30
608	Dick Simpson	1.00	.50	.30
609	Phil Gagliano	1.00	.50	.30
610	Jim Hardin	1.00	.50	.30
611	Braves Rookies (Bob Didier, Walt Hriniak, Gary Neibauer)	1.00	.50	.30
612	Jack Aker	1.00	.50	.30
613	Jim Beauchamp	1.00	.50	.30
614	Astros Rookies (Tom Griffin, Skip Guinn)	1.00	.50	.30
615	Len Gabrielson	1.00	.50	.30
616	Don McMahon	1.00	.50	.30
617	Jesse Gonder	1.00	.50	.30
618	Ramon Webster	1.00	.50	.30
619	Royals Rookies (Bill Butler, *Pat Kelly*, Juan Rios)	1.25	.60	.40
620	Dean Chance	1.25	.60	.40
621	Bill Voss	1.00	.50	.30
622	Dan Osinski	1.00	.50	.30
623	Hank Allen	1.00	.50	.30
624	N.L. Rookies (Darrel Chaney, Duffy Dyer, Terry Harmon)	1.25	.60	.40
625	Mack Jones	1.00	.50	.30
626	Gene Michael	1.00	.50	.30
627	George Stone	1.00	.50	.30
628	Red Sox Rookies (*Bill Conigliaro*, Syd O'Brien, Fred Wenz)	1.00	.50	.30
629	Jack Hamilton	1.00	.50	.30
630	*Bobby Bonds*	30.00	15.00	9.00
631	John Kennedy	1.00	.50	.30
632	Jon Warden	1.00	.50	.30
633	Harry Walker	1.25	.60	.40
634	Andy Etchebarren	1.00	.50	.30
635	George Culver	1.00	.50	.30
636	Woodie Held	1.00	.50	.30
637	Padres Rookies (Jerry DaVanon, *Clay Kirby*, Frank Reberger)	1.25	.60	.40
638	Ed Sprague	1.00	.50	.30
639	Barry Moore	1.00	.50	.30
640	Fergie Jenkins	15.00	7.50	4.50
641	N.L. Rookies (Bobby Darwin, Tommy Dean, John Miller)	1.00	.50	.30
642	John Hiller	1.25	.60	.40
643	Billy Cowan	1.00	.50	.30
644	Chuck Hinton	1.00	.50	.30
645	George Brunet	1.00	.50	.30
646	Expos Rookies (Dan McGinn, *Carl Morton*)	1.00	.50	.30
647	Dave Wickersham	1.00	.50	.30
648	Bobby Wine	1.00	.50	.30
649	Al Jackson	1.00	.50	.30
650	Ted Williams	10.00	5.00	3.00
651	Gus Gil	1.00	.50	.30
652	Eddie Watt	1.00	.50	.30
653	*Aurelio Rodriguez* (photo actually batboy Leonard Garcia)	1.50	.70	.45
654	White Sox Rookies (*Carlos May*, Rich Morales, Don Secrist)	1.00	.50	.30
655	Mike Hershberger	1.00	.50	.30
656	Dan Schneider	1.00	.50	.30
657	Bobby Murcer	2.25	1.25	.70
658	A.L. Rookies (Bill Burbach, Tom Hall, Jim Miles)	1.00	.50	.30
659	Johnny Podres	1.75	.90	.50
660	Reggie Smith	1.75	.90	.50
661	Jim Merritt	1.00	.50	.30
662	Royals Rookies (Dick Drago, Bob Oliver George Spriggs)	1.25	.60	.40
663	Dick Radatz	1.00	.50	.30
664	Ron Hunt	2.00	.50	.25

1969 Topps Decals

Designed as an insert for 1969 regular issue card packs, these decals are virtually identical in format to the '69 cards. The 48 decals in the set measure 1" by 2-1/2," although they are mounted on white paper backing which measures 1-3/4" by 2-1/8."

		NR MT	EX	VG
Complete Set:		350.00	175.00	105.00
Common Player:		4.00	2.00	1.25
(1)	Hank Aaron	40.00	20.00	12.00
(2)	Richie Allen	4.00	2.00	1.25
(3)	Felipe Alou	4.00	2.00	1.25
(4)	Matty Alou	4.00	2.00	1.25
(5)	Luis Aparicio	4.50	2.25	1.25
(6)	Bob Clemente	50.00	25.00	15.00
(7)	Donn Clendenon	4.00	2.00	1.25
(8)	Tommy Davis	4.00	2.00	1.25
(9)	Don Drysdale	7.00	3.50	2.00
(10)	Joe Foy	4.00	2.00	1.25
(11)	Jim Fregosi	4.00	2.00	1.25
(12)	Bob Gibson	7.00	3.50	2.00
(13)	Tony Gonzalez	4.00	2.00	1.25
(14)	Tom Haller	4.00	2.00	1.25
(15)	Ken Harrelson	4.00	2.00	1.25
(16)	Tommy Helms	4.00	2.00	1.25
(17)	Willie Horton	4.00	2.00	1.25
(18)	Frank Howard	4.00	2.00	1.25
(19)	Reggie Jackson	100.00	50.00	30.00
(20)	Fergie Jenkins	6.00	3.00	1.75
(21)	Harmon Killebrew	6.00	3.00	1.75
(22)	Jerry Koosman	4.00	2.00	1.25
(23)	Mickey Mantle	75.00	38.00	23.00
(24)	Willie Mays	35.00	17.50	10.50
(25)	Tim McCarver	4.00	2.00	1.25
(26)	Willie McCovey	7.00	3.50	2.00
(27)	Sam McDowell	4.00	2.00	1.25
(28)	Denny McLain	4.00	2.00	1.25
(29)	Dave McNally	4.00	2.00	1.25
(30)	Don Mincher	4.00	2.00	1.25
(31)	Rick Monday	4.00	2.00	1.25
(32)	Tony Oliva	4.00	2.00	1.25
(33)	Camilo Pascual	4.00	2.00	1.25
(34)	Rick Reichardt	4.00	2.00	1.25
(35)	Pete Rose	25.00	12.50	7.50
(36)	Frank Robinson	7.00	3.50	2.00
(37)	Ron Santo	4.00	2.00	1.25
(38)	Dick Selma	4.00	2.00	1.25
(39)	Tom Seaver	50.00	25.00	15.00
(40)	Chris Short	4.00	2.00	1.25
(41)	Rusty Staub	4.00	2.00	1.25
(42)	Mel Stottlemyre	4.00	2.00	1.25
(43)	Luis Tiant	4.00	2.00	1.25

		NR MT	EX	VG
(21)	Harmon Killebrew	6.00	3.00	1.75
(22)	Jerry Koosman	4.00	2.00	1.25
(23)	Mickey Mantle	75.00	38.00	23.00
(24)	Willie Mays	35.00	17.50	10.50
(25)	Tim McCarver	4.00	2.00	1.25
(26)	Willie McCovey	7.00	3.50	2.00
(27)	Sam McDowell	4.00	2.00	1.25
(28)	Denny McLain	4.00	2.00	1.25
(29)	Dave McNally	4.00	2.00	1.25
(30)	Don Mincher	4.00	2.00	1.25
(31)	Rick Monday	4.00	2.00	1.25
(32)	Tony Oliva	4.00	2.00	1.25
(33)	Camilo Pascual	4.00	2.00	1.25
(34)	Rick Reichardt	4.00	2.00	1.25
(35)	Pete Rose	25.00	12.50	7.50
(36)	Frank Robinson	7.00	3.50	2.00
(37)	Ron Santo	4.00	2.00	1.25
(38)	Dick Selma	4.00	2.00	1.25
(39)	Tom Seaver	50.00	25.00	15.00
(40)	Chris Short	4.00	2.00	1.25
(41)	Rusty Staub	4.00	2.00	1.25
(42)	Mel Stottlemyre	4.00	2.00	1.25
(43)	Luis Tiant	4.00	2.00	1.25
(44)	Pete Ward	4.00	2.00	1.25
(45)	Hoyt Wilhelm	6.00	3.00	1.75
(46)	Maury Wills	4.00	2.00	1.25
(47)	Jim Wynn	4.00	2.00	1.25
(48)	Carl Yastrzemski	30.00	15.00	9.00

1969 Topps Deckle Edge

These 2-1/4" by 3-1/4" inch cards take their name from their interesting borders which have a scalloped effect. The fronts have a black and white picture of the player along with a blue facsimile autograph. Backs have the player's name and the card number in light blue ink in a small box at the bottom of the card. Technically, there are only 33 numbered cards, but there are actually 35 possible players; both Jim Wynn and Hoyt Wilhelm cards are found as #11 while cards of Joe Foy and Rusty Staub can be found as #22. Many of the players in the set are stars.

		NR MT	EX	VG
Complete Set:		100.00	50.00	30.00
Common Player:		1.00	.50	.30
1	Brooks Robinson	15.00	7.50	4.50
2	Boog Powell	1.00	.50	.30
3	Ken Harrelson	1.00	.50	.30
4	Carl Yastrzemski	15.00	7.50	4.50
5	Jim Fregosi	1.00	.50	.30
6	Luis Aparicio	1.25	.60	.40
7	Luis Tiant	1.00	.50	.30
8	Denny McLain	1.00	.50	.30
9	Willie Horton	1.00	.50	.30
10	Bill Freehan	1.00	.50	.30
11a	Hoyt Wilhelm	10.00	5.00	3.00
11b	Jim Wynn	10.00	5.00	3.00
12	Rod Carew	15.00	7.50	4.50
13	Mel Stottlemyre	1.00	.50	.30
14	Rick Monday	1.00	.50	.30
15	Tommy Davis	1.00	.50	.30
16	Frank Howard	1.00	.50	.30
17	Felipe Alou	1.00	.50	.30
18	Don Kessinger	1.00	.50	.30
19	Ron Santo	1.00	.50	.30
20	Tommy Helms	1.00	.50	.30
21	Pete Rose	10.00	5.00	3.00
22a	Rusty Staub	2.25	1.25	.70
22b	Joe Foy	7.00	3.50	2.00
23	Tom Haller	1.00	.50	.30
24	Maury Wills	1.00	.50	.30
25	Jerry Koosman	1.00	.50	.30
26	Richie Allen	1.00	.50	.30
27	Bob Clemente	15.00	7.50	4.50
28	Curt Flood	1.00	.50	.30
29	Bob Gibson	10.00	5.00	3.00
30	Al Ferrara	1.00	.50	.30
31	Willie McCovey	10.00	5.00	3.00
32	Juan Marichal	7.00	3.50	2.00
33	Willie Mays, Willie Mays	15.00	7.50	4.50

1969 Topps 4-On-1 Mini Stickers

Another in the long line of Topps test issues, the 4-on-1s are 2-1/2" by 3-1/2" cards with blank backs featuring a quartet of miniature stickers in the design of the same cards from the 1969 Topps regular set. There are 25 different cards, for a total of 100 different stickers. As they are not common, Mint cards bring fairly strong prices on today's market. As the set was drawn from the 3rd Series of the regular cards, it includes some rookie stickers and World Series highlight stickers.

	NR MT	EX	VG
Complete Set:	950.00	475.00	285.00
Common Player:	15.00	7.50	4.50
(1) Jerry Adair, Willie Mays, Johnny Morris, Don Wilson	100.00	50.00	30.00
(2) Tommie Aaron, Jim Britton, Donn Clendenon, Woody Woodward	15.00	7.50	4.50
(3) World Series Game 4, Tommy Davis, Don Pavletich, Vada Pinson	20.00	10.00	6.00
(4) Max Alvis, Glenn Beckert, Ron Fairly, Rick Wise	15.00	7.50	4.50
(5) Johnny Callison, Jim French, Lum Harris, Dick Selma	15.00	7.50	4.50
(6) World Series Game 3, Bob Gibson, Larry Haney, Rick Reichardt	40.00	20.00	12.00
(7) Houston Rookie Stars, Wally Bunker, Don Cardwell, Joe Gibbon	15.00	7.50	4.50
(8) Ollie Brown, Jim Bunning, Andy Kosco, Ron Reed	20.00	10.00	6.00
(9) Bill Dillman, Jim Lefebvre, John Purdin, John Roseboro	15.00	7.50	4.50
(10) Bill Hands, Chuck Harrison, Lindy McDaniel, Felix Millan	15.00	7.50	4.50
(11) Jack Hiatt, Dave Johnson, Mel Nelson, Tommie Sisk	18.00	9.00	5.50
(12) Clay Dalrymple, Leo Durocher, John Odom, Wilbur Wood	18.00	9.00	5.50
(13) Hank Bauer, Kevin Collins, Ray Oyler, Russ Snyder	15.00	7.50	4.50
(14) Red Sox Rookie Stars, World Series Game 7, Gerry Arrigo, Jim Perry	18.00	9.00	5.50
(15) World Series Game 2, Bill McCool, Roberto Pena, Doug Rader	15.00	7.50	4.50
(16) Ed Brinkman, Roy Face, Willie Horton, Bob Rodgers	18.00	9.00	5.50

	NR MT	EX	VG
(17) Dave Baldwin, J.C. Martin, Dave May, Ray Sadecki	15.00	7.50	4.50
(18) World Series Game 1, Jose Pagan, Tom Phoebus, Mike Shannon	15.00	7.50	4.50
(19) Pete Rose, Lee Stange, Don Sutton, Ted Uhlaender	275.00	137.00	82.00
(20) Joe Grzenda, Frank Howard, Dick Tracewski, Jim Weaver	20.00	10.00	6.00
(21) White Sox Rookie Stars, Joe Azcue, Grant Jackson, Denny McLain	20.00	10.00	6.00
(22) John Edwards, Jim Fairey, Phillies Rookies, Stan Williams	15.00	7.50	4.50
(23) World Series Summary, John Bateman, Willie Smith, Leon Wagner	15.00	7.50	4.50
(24) World Series Game 5, Yankees Rookies, Chris Cannizzaro, Bob Hendley	15.00	7.50	4.50
(25) Cardinals Rookie Stars, Joe Nossek, Rico Petrocelli, Carl Yastrzemski	175.00	87.00	52.00

1969 Topps Stamps

Topps continued to refine its efforts at baseball stamps in 1969 with the release of 240 player stamps, each measuring 1" by 1-7/16." Each stamp jsd s color photo along with the player's name, position and team. Unlike prior stamp issues, the 1969 stamps have 24 separate albums (one per team). The stamps were issued in strips of 12.

	NR MT	EX	VG
Complete Sheet Set:	250.00	125.00	75.00
Common Sheet:	1.25	.60	.40
Complete Stamp Album Set:	14.00	7.00	4.25
Single Stamp Album:	.50	.25	.15

	NR MT	EX	VG
(1) Tommie Agee, Sandy Alomar, Jose Cardenal, Dean Chance, Joe Foy, Jim Grant, Don Kessinger, Mickey Mantle, Jerry May, Bob Rodgers, Cookie Rojas, Gary Sutherland	18.00	9.00	5.50
(2) Jesus Alou, Mike Andrews, Larry Brown, Moe Drabowsky, Alex Johnson, Lew Krausse, Jim Lefebvre, Dal Maxvill, John Odom, Claude Osteen, Rick Reichardt, Luis Tiant	1.50	.70	.45
(3) Hank Aaron, Matty Alou, Max Alvis, Nelson Briles, Eddie Fisher, Bud Harrelson, Willie Horton, Randy Hundley, Larry Jaster, Jim Kaat, Gary Peters, Pete Ward	7.00	3.50	2.00
(4) Don Buford, John Callison, Tommy Davis, Jackie Hernandez, Fergie Jenkins, Lee May, Denny McLain, Bob Oliver, Roberto Pena, Tony Perez, Joe Torre, Tom Tresh	3.00	1.50	.90
(5) Jim Bunning, Dean Chance, Joe Foy, Sonny Jackson, Don Kessinger, Rick Monday, Gaylord Perry, Roger Repoz, Cookie Rojas, Mel Stottlemyre, Leon Wagner, Jim Wynn	3.00	1.50	.90
(6) Felipe Alou, Gerry Arrigo, Bob Aspromonte, Gary Bell, Clay Dalrymple, Jim Fregosi, Tony Gonzalez, Duane Josephson, Dick McAuliffe, Tony Oliva, Brooks Robinson, Willie Stargell	6.00	3.00	1.75
(7) Steve Barber, Donn Clendenon, Joe Coleman, Vic Davalillo, Russ Gibson, Jerry Grote, Tom Haller, Andy Kosco, Willie McCovey, Don Mincher, Joe Morgan, Don Wilson	4.00	2.00	1.25
(8) George Brunet, Don Buford, John Callison, Danny Cater, Tommy Davis, Willie Davis, John Edwards, Jim Hart, Mickey Lolich, Willie Mays, Roberto Pena, Mickey Stanley	7.00	3.50	2.00
(9) Ernie Banks, Glenn Beckert, Ken Berry, Horace Clarke, Bob Clemente, Larry Dierker, Len Gabrielson, Jake Gibbs, Jerry Koosman, Sam McDowell, Tom Satriano, Bill Singer	3.50	1.75	1.00
(10) Gene Alley, Lou Brock, Larry Brown, Moe Drabowsky, Frank Howard, Tommie John, Roger Nelson, Claude Osteen, Phil Regan, Rick Reichardt, Tony Taylor, Roy White	4.00	2.00	1.25
(11) Bob Allison, John Bateman, Don Drysdale, Dave Johnson, Harmon Killebrew, Jim Maloney, Bill Mazeroski, Gerry McNertney, Ron Perranoski, Rico Petrocelli, Pete Rose, Billy Williams	18.00	9.00	5.50
(12) Bernie Allen, Jose Arcia, Stan Bahnsen, Sal Bando, Jim Davenport, Tito Francona, Dick Green, Ron Hunt, Mack Jones, Vada Pinson, George Scott, Don Wert	1.50	.70	.45
(13) Gerry Arrigo, Bob Aspromonte, Joe Azcue, Curt Blefary, Orlando Cepeda, BIll Freehan, Jim Fregosi, Dave Giusti, Duane Josephson, Tim McCarver, Jose Santiago, Bob Tolan	2.00	1.00	.60
(14) Jerry Adair, Johnny Bench, Clete Boyer, John Briggs, Bert Campaneris, Woody Fryman, Ron Kline, Bobby Knoop, Ken McMullen, Adolfo Phillips, John Roseboro, Tom Seaver	7.00	3.50	2.00
(15) Norm Cash, Ron Fairly, Bob Gibson, Bill Hands, Cleon Jones, Al Kaline, Paul Schaal, Mike Shannon, Duke Sims, Reggie Smith, Steve Whitaker, Carl Yastrzemski	12.00	6.00	3.50
(16) Steve Barber, Paul Casanova, Dick Dietz, Russ Gibson, Jerry Grote, Tom Haller, Ed Kranepool, Juan Marichal, Denis Menke, Jim Nash, Bill Robinson, Frank Robinson	4.00	2.00	1.25
(17) Bobby Bolin, Ollie Brown, Rod Carew, Mike Epstein, Bud Harrelson, Larry Jaster, Dave McNally, Willie Norton, Milt Pappas, Gary Peters, Paul Popovich, Stan Williams	6.00	3.00	1.75
(18) Ted Abernathy, Bob Allison, Ed Brinkman, Don Drysdale, Jim Hardin, Julian Javier, Hal Lanier, Jim McGlothlin, Ron Perranoski, Rich Rollins, Ron Santo, Billy Williams	3.00	1.50	.90
(19) Richie Allen, Luis Aparicio, Wally Bunker, Curt Flood, Ken Harrelson, Jim Hunter, Denver Lemaster, Felix Millan, Jim Northrop (Northrup), Art Shamsky, Larry Stahl, Ted Uhlaender	3.00	1.50	.90
(20) Bob Bailey, Johnny Bench, Woody Fryman, Jim Hannan, Ron Kline, Al McBean, Camilo Pascual, Joe Pepitone, Doug Rader, Ron Reed, John Roseboro, Sonny Siebert	3.00	1.50	.90
(21) Jack Aker, Tommy Harper, Tommy Helms, Dennis Higgins, Jim Hunter, Don Lock, Lee Maye, Felix Millan, Jim Northrop (Northrup), Larry Stahl, Don Sutton, Zoilo Versalles	3.00	1.50	.90
(22) Norm Cash, Ed Charles, Joe Horlen, Pat Jarvis, Jim Lonborg, Manny Mota, Boog Powell, Dick Selma, Mike Shannon, Duke Sims, Steve Whitaker, Hoyt Wilhelm	3.00	1.50	.90
(23) Bernie Allen, Ray Culp, Al Ferrara, Tito Francona, Dick Green, Ron Hunt, Ray Oyler, Tom Phoebus, Rusty Staub, Bob Veale, Maury Wills, Wilbur Wood	2.00	1.00	.60
(24) Ernie Banks, Mark Belanger, Steve Blass, Horace Clarke, Bob Clemente, Larry Dierker, Dave Duncan, Chico Salmon, Chris Short, Ron Swoboda, Cesar Tovar, Rick Wise	3.50	1.75	1.00

1969 Topps Super

These 2-1/4" by 3-1/4" cards are not the bigger "Super" cards which would be seen in following years. Rather, what enabled Topps to dub them "Super Baseball Cards" is their high-gloss finish which enhances the bright color photograph used on their fronts. The only other design element on the front is

a facsimile autograph. The backs contain a box at the the bottom which carries the player's name, team, position, a copyright line and the card number. Another unusual feature is that the cards have rounded corners. The 66-card set saw limited production, meaning supplies are tight today. Considering the quality of the cards and the fact that many big names are represented, it's easy to understand why the set is quite expensive and desirable.

		NR MT	EX	VG
Complete Set:		6000.00	3000.00	1800.
Common Player:		25.00	12.50	7.50
1	Dave McNally	25.00	12.50	7.50
2	Frank Robinson	350.00	175.00	105.00
3	Brooks Robinson	350.00	175.00	105.00
4	Ken Harrelson	25.00	12.50	7.50
5	Carl Yastrzemski	700.00	350.00	210.00
6	Ray Culp	25.00	12.50	7.50
7	James Fregosi	25.00	12.50	7.50
8	Rick Reichardt	25.00	12.50	7.50
9	V. Davalillo	25.00	12.50	7.50
10	Luis Aparicio	35.00	17.50	10.50
11	Pete Ward	25.00	12.50	7.50
12	Joe Horlen	25.00	12.50	7.50
13	Luis Tiant	25.00	12.50	7.50
14	Sam McDowell	25.00	12.50	7.50
15	Jose Cardenal	25.00	12.50	7.50
16	Willie Horton	25.00	12.50	7.50
17	Denny McLain	25.00	12.50	7.50
18	Bill Freehan	25.00	12.50	7.50
19	Harmon Killebrew	275.00	137.00	82.00
20	Tony Oliva	25.00	12.50	7.50
21	Dean Chance	25.00	12.50	7.50
22	Joe Foy	25.00	12.50	7.50
23	Roger Nelson	25.00	12.50	7.50
24	Mickey Mantle	1500.00	750.00	450.00
25	Mel Stottlemyre	25.00	12.50	7.50
26	Roy White	25.00	12.50	7.50
27	Rick Monday	25.00	12.50	7.50
28	Reginald Jackson	750.00	375.00	225.00
29	Dagoberto Campaneris	25.00	12.50	7.50
30	Frank Howard	25.00	12.50	7.50
31	Camilo Pascual	25.00	12.50	7.50
32	Tommy Davis	25.00	12.50	7.50
33	Don Mincher	25.00	12.50	7.50
34	Henry Aaron	500.00	250.00	150.00
35	Felipe Rojas Alou	25.00	12.50	7.50
36	Joseph Torre	25.00	12.50	7.50
37	Fergie Jenkins	25.00	12.50	7.50
38	Ronald Santo	25.00	12.50	7.50
39	Billy Williams	40.00	20.00	12.00
40	Tommy Helms	25.00	12.50	7.50
41	Pete Rose	500.00	250.00	150.00
42	Joe Morgan	275.00	137.00	82.00
43	Jim Wynn	25.00	12.50	7.50
44	Curt Blefary	25.00	12.50	7.50
45	Willie Davis	25.00	12.50	7.50
46	Donald Drysdale	275.00	137.00	82.00
47	Tom Haller	25.00	12.50	7.50
48	Rusty Staub	25.00	12.50	7.50
49	Maurice Wills	25.00	12.50	7.50
50	Cleon Jones	25.00	12.50	7.50
51	Jerry Koosman	25.00	12.50	7.50
52	Tom Seaver	700.00	350.00	210.00
53	Rich Allen	25.00	12.50	7.50
54	Chris Short	25.00	12.50	7.50
55	Cookie Rojas	25.00	12.50	7.50
56	Mateo Alou	25.00	12.50	7.50
57	Steve Blass	25.00	12.50	7.50
58	Roberto Clemente	700.00	350.00	210.00
59	Curt Flood	25.00	12.50	7.50
60	Robert Gibson	90.00	45.00	27.00
61	Tim McCarver	25.00	12.50	7.50
62	Dick Selma	25.00	12.50	7.50
63	Ollie Brown	25.00	12.50	7.50
64	Juan Marichal	90.00	45.00	27.00
65	Willie Mays	500.00	250.00	150.00
66	Willie McCovey	90.00	45.00	27.00

1969 Topps Team Posters

Picking up where the 1968 posters left off, the 1969 poster is larger at about 12" by 20." The posters, 24 in number like the previous year, are very different in style. Each has a team focus with a large pennant carrying the team name, along with nine or ten photos of players. Each of the photos carries a name and a facsimile autograph. Unfortunately, the bigger size of 1969 posters meant they had to be folded to fit in their packages as was the case in 1968. That means that collectors today will have a tough job finding them without fairly heavy creases from the folding.

		NR MT	EX	VG
Complete Set:		900.00	450.00	270.00
Common Poster:		17.00	8.50	5.00
1	Detroit Tigers (Norm Cash, Bill Freehan, Willie Horton, Al Kaline, Mickey Lolich, Dick McAuliffe, Denny McLain, Jim Northrup, Mickey Stanley, Don Wert, Earl Wilson)	40.00	20.00	12.00
2	Atlanta Braves (Hank Aaron, Felipe Alou, Clete Boyer, Rico Carty, Tito Francona, Sonny Jackson, Pat Jarvis, Felix Millan, Phil Niekro, Milt Pappas, Joe Torre)	40.00	20.00	12.00
3	Boston Red Sox (Mike Andrews, Tony Conigliaro, Ray Culp, Russ Gibson, Ken Harrelson, Jim Lonborg, Rico Petrocelli, Jose Santiago, George Scott, Reggie Smith, Carl Yastrzemski)	60.00	30.00	18.00
4	Chicago Cubs (Ernie Banks, Glenn Beckert, Bill Hands, Jim Hickman, Ken Holtzman, Randy Hundley, Fergie Jenkins, Don Kessinger, Adolfo Phillips, Ron Santo, Billy Williams)	35.00	17.50	10.50
5	Baltimore Orioles (Mark Belanger, Paul Blair, Don Buford, Andy Etchebarren, Jim Hardin, Dave Johnson, Dave McNally, Tom Phoebus, Boog Powell, Brooks Robinson, Frank Robinson)	50.00	25.00	15.00
6	Houston Astros (Curt Blefary, Donn Clendenon, Larry Dierker, John Edwards, Denny Lemaster, Denis Menke, Norm Miller, Joe Morgan, Doug Rader, Don Wilson, Jim Wynn)	17.00	8.50	5.00
7	Kansas City Royals (Jerry Adair, Wally Bunker, Mike Fiore, Joe Foy, Jackie Hernandez, Pat Kelly, Dave Morehead, Roger Nelson, Dave Nicholson, Eliseo Rodriguez, Steve Whitaker)	17.00	8.50	5.00
8	Philadelphia Phillies (Richie Allen, Johnny Callison, Woody Fryman, Larry Hisle, Don Money, Cookie Rojas, Mike Ryan, Chris Short, Tony Taylor, Bill White, Rick Wise)	17.00	8.50	5.00

		NR MT	EX	VG
13	Cleveland Indians (Max Alvis, Joe Azcue, Jose Cardenal, Vern Fuller, Lou Johnson, Sam McDowell, Sonny Siebert, Duke Sims, Russ Snyder, Luis Tiant, Zoilo Versalles)	17.00	8.50	5.00
14	San Francisco Giants (Bobby Bolin, Jim Davenport, Dick Dietz, Jim Hart, Ron Hunt, Hal Lanier, Juan Marichal, Willie Mays, Willie McCovey, Gaylord Perry, Charlie Smith)	40.00	20.00	12.00
15	Minnesota Twins (Bob Allison, Chico Cardenas, Rod Carew, Dean Chance, Jim Kaat, Harmon Killebrew, Tony Oliva, Jim Perry, John Roseboro, Cesar Tovar, Ted Uhlaender)	40.00	20.00	12.00
16	Pittsburgh Pirates (Gene Alley, Matty Alou, Steve Blass, Jim Bunning, Bob Clemente, Rich Hebner, Jerry May, Bill Mazeroski, Bob Robertson, Willie Stargell, Bob Veale)	40.00	20.00	12.00
17	California Angels (Ruben Amaro, George Brunet, Bob Chance, Vic Davalillo, Jim Fregosi, Bobby Knoop, Jim McGlothlin, Rick Reichardt, Roger Repoz, Bob Rodgers, Hoyt Wilhelm)	20.00	10.00	6.00
18	St. Louis Cardinals (Nelson Briles, Lou Brock, Orlando Cepeda, Curt Flood, Bob Gibson, Julian Javier, Dal Maxvill, Tim McCarver, Vada Pinson, Mike Shannon, Ray Washburn)	35.00	17.50	10.50
19	New York Yankees (Stan Bahnsen, Horace Clarke, Bobby Cox, Jake Gibbs, Mickey Mantle, Joe Pepitone, Fritz Peterson, Bill Robinson, Mel Stottlemyre, Tom Tresh, Roy White)	90.00	45.00	27.00
20	Cincinnati Reds (Gerry Arrigo, Johnny Bench, Tommy Helms, Alex Johnson, Jim Maloney, Lee May, Gary Nolan, Tony Perez, Pete Rose, Bob Tolan, Woody Woodward)	90.00	45.00	27.00
21	Oakland Athletics (Sal Bando, Bert Campaneris, Danny Cater, Dick Green, Mike Hershberger, Jim Hunter, Reggie Jackson, Rick Monday, Jim Nash, John Odom, Jim Pagliaroni)	60.00	30.00	18.00
22	Los Angeles Dodgers (Willie Crawford, Willie Davis, Don Drysdale, Ron Fairly, Tom Haller, Andy Kosco, Jim Lefebvre, Claude Osteen, Paul Popovich, Bill Singer, Bill Sudakis)	35.00	17.50	10.50
23	Washington Senators (Bernie Allen, Brant Alyea, Ed Brinkman, Paul Casanova, Joe Coleman, Mike Epstein, Jim Hannan, Frank Howard, Ken McMullen, Camilo Pascual, Del Unser)	17.00	8.50	5.00
24	New York Mets (Tommie Agee, Ken Boswell, Ed Charles, Jerry Grote, Bud Harrelson, Cleon Jones, Jerry Koosman, Ed Kranepool, Jim McAndrew, Tom Seaver, Ron Swoboda)	100.00	50.00	30.00

1970 Topps

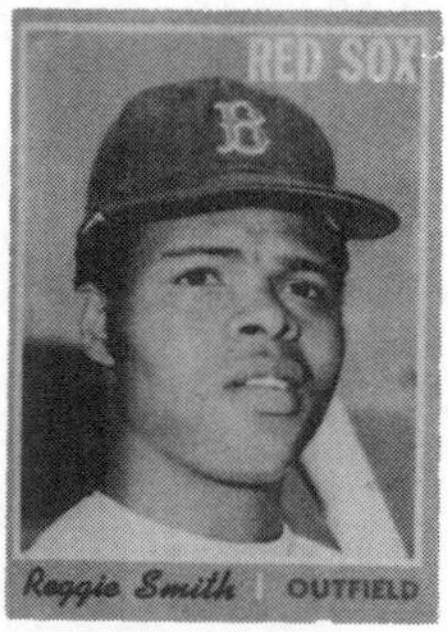

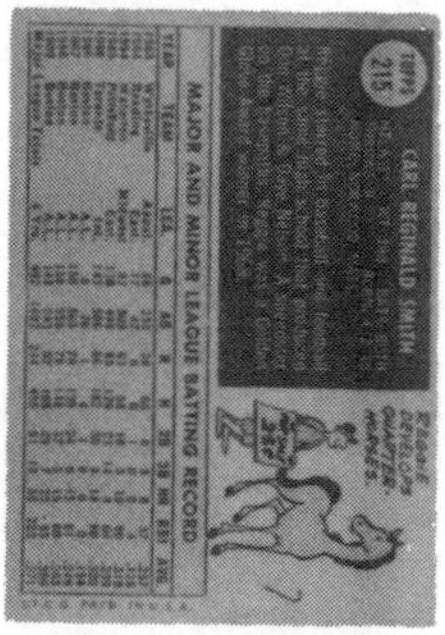

Topps established another set size record by coming out with 720 cards in 1970. The 2-1/2" by 3-1/2" cards have a color photo with a thin white frame. The photo have the player's team overprinted at the top, while the player's name in script and his position are at the bottom. A gray border surrounds the front. Card backs follows the normal design pattern, although they are more readable than some issues of the past. Team cards returned and were joined with many of the usual specialty cards. The World Series highlights were joined by cards with playoff highlights. Statistical leaders and All-Stars are also included in the set. High-numbered cards provide the most expensive cards in the set.

	NR MT	EX	VG
Complete Set:	2000.00	1000.00	600.00
Common Player: 1-546	.80	.40	.25
Common Player: 547-633	1.50	.70	.45
Common Player: 634-720	3.00	1.50	.90

		NR MT	EX	VG
1	World Champions (Mets Team)	10.00	3.00	1.00
2	Diego Segui	1.00	.50	.30
3	Darrel Chaney	.80	.40	.25
4	Tom Egan	.80	.40	.25
5	Wes Parker	.90	.45	.25
6	Grant Jackson	.80	.40	.25
7	Indians Rookies (Gary Boyd, Russ Nagelson)	.80	.40	.25
8	Jose Martinez	.80	.40	.25
9	Checklist 1-132	3.50	1.75	1.00
10	Carl Yastrzemski	30.00	15.00	9.00
11	Nate Colbert	.80	.40	.25
12	John Hiller	.90	.45	.25
13	Jack Hiatt	.80	.40	.25
14	Hank Allen	.80	.40	.25
15	Larry Dierker	.90	.45	.25
16	Charlie Metro	.80	.40	.25
17	Hoyt Wilhelm	4.00	2.00	1.25
18	Carlos May	.80	.40	.25
19	John Boccabella	.80	.40	.25
20	Dave McNally	1.00	.50	.30
21	Athletics Rookies *(Vida Blue, Gene Tenace)*	4.00	2.00	1.25
22	Ray Washburn	.80	.40	.25
23	Bill Robinson	.80	.40	.25
24	Dick Selma	.80	.40	.25
25	Cesar Tovar	.80	.40	.25
26	Tug McGraw	1.75	.90	.50
27	Chuck Hinton	.80	.40	.25
28	Billy Wilson	.80	.40	.25
29	Sandy Alomar	.80	.40	.25
30	Matty Alou	1.50	.70	.45
31	Marty Pattin	.80	.40	.25
32	Harry Walker	.90	.45	.25
33	Don Wert	.80	.40	.25
34	Willie Crawford	.80	.40	.25
35	Joe Horlen	.80	.40	.25
36	Reds Rookies (Danny Breeden, *Bernie Carbo*)	.80	.40	.25
37	Dick Drago	.80	.40	.25
38	Mack Jones	.80	.40	.25
39	Mike Nagy	.80	.40	.25
40	Rich Allen	3.00	1.50	.90
41	George Lauzerique	.80	.40	.25
42	Tito Fuentes	.80	.40	.25
43	Jack Aker	.80	.40	.25
44	Roberto Pena	.80	.40	.25
45	Dave Johnson	1.50	.70	.45
46	Ken Rudolph	.80	.40	.25
47	Bob Miller	.80	.40	.25
48	Gill Garrido (Gil)	.80	.40	.25
49	Tim Cullen	.80	.40	.25
50	Tommie Agee	.90	.45	.25
51	Bob Christian	.80	.40	.25
52	Bruce Dal Canton	.80	.40	.25
53	John Kennedy	.80	.40	.25
54	Jeff Torborg	.90	.45	.25
55	John Odom	.90	.45	.25
56	Phillies Rookies (Joe Lis, Scott Reid)	.80	.40	.25
57	Pat Kelly	.80	.40	.25
58	Dave Marshall	.80	.40	.25
59	Dick Ellsworth	.80	.40	.25
60	Jim Wynn	1.00	.50	.30
61	N.L. Batting Leaders (Bob Clemente, Cleon Jones, Pete Rose)	5.00	2.50	1.50
62	A.L. Batting Leaders (Rod Carew, Tony Oliva, Reggie Smith)	3.50	1.75	1.00
63	N.L. RBI Leaders (Willie McCovey, Tony Perez, Ron Santo)	3.50	1.75	1.00
64	A.L. RBI Leaders (Reggie Jackson, Harmon Killebrew, Boog Powell)	3.50	1.75	1.00
65	N.L. Home Run Leaders (Hank Aaron, Lee May, Willie McCovey)	3.00	1.50	.90
66	A.L. Home Run Leaders (Frank Howard, Reggie Jackson, Harmon Killebrew)	3.50	1.75	1.00

		NR MT	EX	VG
67	N.L. ERA Leaders (Steve Carlton, Bob Gibson, Juan Marichal)	3.00	1.50	.90
68	A.L. ERA Leaders (Dick Bosman, Mike Cuellar, Jim Palmer)	3.00	1.50	.90
69	N.L. Pitching Leaders (Fergie Jenkins, Juan Marichal, Phil Niekro, Tom Seaver)	3.50	1.75	1.00
70	A.L. Pitching Leaders (Dave Boswell, Mike Cuellar, Dennis McLain, Dave McNally, Jim Perry, Mel Stottlemyre)	3.00	1.50	.90
71	N.L. Strikeout Leaders (Bob Gibson, Fergie Jenkins, Bill Singer)	3.50	1.75	1.00
72	A.L. Strikeout Leaders (Mickey Lolich, Sam McDowell, Andy Messersmith)	3.00	1.50	.90
73	Wayne Granger	.80	.40	.25
74	Angels Rookies (Greg Washburn, Wally Wolf)	.80	.40	.25
75	Jim Kaat	3.50	1.75	1.00
76	Carl Taylor	.80	.40	.25
77	Frank Linzy	.80	.40	.25
78	Joe Lahoud	.80	.40	.25
79	Clay Kirby	.80	.40	.25
80	Don Kessinger	.90	.45	.25
81	Dave May	.80	.40	.25
82	Frank Fernandez	.80	.40	.25
83	Don Cardwell	.80	.40	.25
84	Paul Casanova	.80	.40	.25
85	Max Alvis	.80	.40	.25
86	Lum Harris	.80	.40	.25
87	Steve Renko	.80	.40	.25
88	Pilots Rookies (Dick Baney, Miguel Fuentes)	.80	.40	.25
89	Juan Rios	.80	.40	.25
90	Tim McCarver	1.50	.70	.45
91	Rich Morales	.80	.40	.25
92	George Culver	.80	.40	.25
93	Rick Renick	.80	.40	.25
94	Fred Patek	.90	.45	.25
95	Earl Wilson	.80	.40	.25
96	Cards Rookies (Leron Lee, *Jerry Reuss*)	3.00	1.50	.90
97	Joe Moeller	.80	.40	.25
98	Gates Brown	.80	.40	.25
99	Bobby Pfeil	.80	.40	.25
100	Mel Stottlemyre	1.50	.70	.45
101	Bobby Floyd	.80	.40	.25
102	Joe Rudi	1.50	.70	.45
103	Frank Reberger	.80	.40	.25
104	Gerry Moses	.80	.40	.25
105	Tony Gonzalez	.80	.40	.25
106	Darold Knowles	.80	.40	.25
107	Bobby Etheridge	.80	.40	.25
108	Tom Burgmeier	.90	.45	.25
109	Expos Rookies (Garry Jestadt, Carl Morton)	.90	.45	.25
110	Bob Moose	.80	.40	.25
111	Mike Hegan	.80	.40	.25
112	Dave Nelson	.80	.40	.25
113	Jim Ray	.80	.40	.25
114	Gene Michael	1.00	.50	.30
115	Alex Johnson	.90	.45	.25
116	Sparky Lyle	1.50	.70	.45
117	Don Young	.80	.40	.25
118	George Mitterwald	.80	.40	.25
119	Chuck Taylor	.80	.40	.25
120	Sal Bando	1.50	.70	.45
121	Orioles Rookies (Fred Beene, *Terry Crowley*)	.90	.45	.25
122	George Stone	.80	.40	.25
123	Don Gutteridge	.80	.40	.25
124	Larry Jaster	.80	.40	.25
125	Deron Johnson	.80	.40	.25
126	Marty Martinez	.80	.40	.25
127	Joe Coleman	.90	.45	.25
128a	Checklist 133-263 (226 is R Perranoski)	3.00	1.50	.90
128b	Checklist 133-263 (226 is R. Perranoski)	3.50	1.75	1.00
129	Jimmie Price	.80	.40	.25
130	Ollie Brown	.80	.40	.25
131	Dodgers Rookies (Ray Lamb, Bob Stinson)	.80	.40	.25
132	Jim McGlothlin	.80	.40	.25
133	Clay Carroll	.90	.45	.25
134	Danny Walton	.80	.40	.25
135	Dick Dietz	.80	.40	.25
136	Steve Hargan	.80	.40	.25
137	Art Shamsky	.80	.40	.25
138	Joe Foy	.80	.40	.25
139	Rich Nye	.80	.40	.25
140	Reggie Jackson	150.00	75.00	45.00
141	Pirates Rookies (*Dave Cash*, Johnny Jeter)	.80	.40	.25
142	Fritz Peterson	.80	.40	.25
143	Phil Gagliano	.80	.40	.25
144	Ray Culp	.80	.40	.25
145	Rico Carty	1.50	.70	.45
146	Danny Murphy	.80	.40	.25
147	Angel Hermoso	.80	.40	.25
148	Earl Weaver	1.75	.90	.50
149	Billy Champion	.80	.40	.25
150	Harmon Killebrew	7.00	3.50	2.00
151	Dave Roberts	.80	.40	.25
152	Ike Brown	.80	.40	.25
153	Gary Gentry	.80	.40	.25
154	Senators Rookies (Jan Dukes, Jim Miles)	.80	.40	.25
155	Denis Menke	.80	.40	.25
156	Eddie Fisher	.80	.40	.25
157	Manny Mota	.80	.40	.25
158	Jerry McNertney	.80	.40	.25
159	Tommy Helms	.90	.45	.25
160	Phil Niekro	3.50	1.75	1.00
161	Richie Scheinblum	.80	.40	.25
162	Jerry Johnson	.80	.40	.25
163	Syd O'Brien	.80	.40	.25
164	Ty Cline	.80	.40	.25
165	Ed Kirkpatrick	.80	.40	.25
166	Al Oliver	3.00	1.50	.90
167	Bill Burbach	.80	.40	.25
168	Dave Watkins	.80	.40	.25
169	Tom Hall	.80	.40	.25
170	Billy Williams	4.50	2.25	1.25
171	Jim Nash	.80	.40	.25
172	Braves Rookies (*Ralph Garr*, Garry Hill)	1.50	.70	.45
173	Jim Hicks	.80	.40	.25
174	Ted Sizemore	.80	.40	.25
175	Dick Bosman	.80	.40	.25
176	Jim Hart	.90	.45	.25
177	Jim Northrup	.90	.45	.25
178	Denny Lemaster	.80	.40	.25
179	Ivan Murrell	.80	.40	.25
180	Tommy John	4.00	2.00	1.25
181	Sparky Anderson	1.75	.90	.50
182	Dick Hall	.80	.40	.25
183	Jerry Grote	.90	.45	.25
184	Ray Fosse	.90	.45	.25
185	Don Mincher	.80	.40	.25
186	Rick Joseph	.80	.40	.25
187	Mike Hedlund	.80	.40	.25
188	Manny Sanguillen	.90	.45	.25
189	Yankees Rookies (Dave McDonald, *Thurman Munson*)	100.00	50.00	30.00
190	Joe Torre	1.75	.90	.50
191	Vicente Romo	.80	.40	.25
192	Jim Qualls	.80	.40	.25
193	Mike Wegener	.80	.40	.25
194	Chuck Manuel	.80	.40	.25
195	N.L. Playoff Game 1 (Seaver Wins Opener!)	4.00	2.00	1.25
196	N.L. Playoff Game 2 (Mets Show Muscle!)	3.50	1.75	1.00
197	N.L. Playoff Game 3 (Ryan Saves The Day!)	6.00	3.00	1.75
198	N.L. Playoffs Summary (We're Number One!)	3.50	1.75	1.00
199	A.L. Playoff Game 1 (Orioles Win A Squeaker!)	3.00	1.50	.90
200	A.L. Playoff Game 2 (Powell Scores Winning Run!)	3.50	1.75	1.00
201	A.L. Playoff Game 3 (Birds Wrap It Up!)	3.00	1.50	.90
202	A.L. Playoffs Summary (Sweep Twins In Three!)	3.00	1.50	.90
203	Rudy May	.90	.45	.25
204	Len Gabrielson	.80	.40	.25
205	Bert Campaneris	1.50	.70	.45
206	Clete Boyer	.90	.45	.25
207	Tigers Rookies (Norman McRae, Bob Reed)	.80	.40	.25
208	Fred Gladding	.80	.40	.25
209	Ken Suarez	.80	.40	.25
210	Juan Marichal	8.00	4.00	2.50
211	Ted Williams	7.00	3.50	2.00
212	Al Santorini	.80	.40	.25
213	Andy Etchebarren	.80	.40	.25
214	Ken Boswell	.80	.40	.25
215	Reggie Smith	1.00	.50	.30
216	Chuck Hartenstein	.80	.40	.25
217	Ron Hansen	.80	.40	.25
218	Ron Stone	.80	.40	.25
219	Jerry Kenney	.80	.40	.25
220	Steve Carlton	30.00	15.00	9.00

		NR MT	EX	VG
221	Ron Brand	.80	.40	.25
222	Jim Rooker	.80	.40	.25
223	Nate Oliver	.80	.40	.25
224	Steve Barber	.80	.40	.25
225	Lee May	1.00	.50	.30
226	Ron Perranoski	.90	.45	.25
227	Astros Rookies (*John Mayberry*, Bob Watkins)	1.50	.70	.45
228	Aurelio Rodriguez	.90	.45	.25
229	Rich Robertson	.80	.40	.25
230	Brooks Robinson	12.00	6.00	3.50
231	Luis Tiant	1.75	.90	.50
232	Bob Didier	.80	.40	.25
233	Lew Krausse	.80	.40	.25
234	Tommy Dean	.80	.40	.25
235	Mike Epstein	.90	.45	.25
236	Bob Veale	.90	.45	.25
237	Russ Gibson	.80	.40	.25
238	Jose Laboy	.80	.40	.25
239	Ken Berry	.80	.40	.25
240	Fergie Jenkins	10.00	5.00	3.00
241	Royals Rookies (Al Fitzmorris, Scott Northey)	.80	.40	.25
242	Walter Alston	3.50	1.75	1.00
243	Joe Sparma	.80	.40	.25
244a	Checklist 264-372 (red bat on front)	3.00	1.50	.90
244b	Checklist 264-372 (brown bat on front)	3.50	1.75	1.00
245	Leo Cardenas	.80	.40	.25
246	Jim McAndrew	.80	.40	.25
247	Lou Klimchock	.80	.40	.25
248	Jesus Alou	.90	.45	.25
249	Bob Locker	.80	.40	.25
250	Willie McCovey	6.00	3.00	1.75
251	Dick Schofield	.80	.40	.25
252	Lowell Palmer	.80	.40	.25
253	Ron Woods	.80	.40	.25
254	Camilo Pascual	.80	.40	.25
255	*Jim Spencer*	.80	.40	.25
256	Vic Davalillo	.90	.45	.25
257	Dennis Higgins	.80	.40	.25
258	Paul Popovich	.80	.40	.25
259	Tommie Reynolds	.80	.40	.25
260	Claude Osteen	.80	.40	.25
261	Curt Motton	.80	.40	.25
262	Padres Rookies (Jerry Morales, Jim Williams)	.80	.40	.25
263	Duane Josephson	.80	.40	.25
264	Rich Hebner	.90	.45	.25
265	Randy Hundley	.80	.40	.25
266	Wally Bunker	.80	.40	.25
267	Twins Rookies (Herman Hill, Paul Ratliff)	.80	.40	.25
268	Claude Raymond	.80	.40	.25
269	Cesar Gutierrez	.80	.40	.25
270	Chris Short	.90	.45	.25
271	Greg Goossen	.80	.40	.25
272	Hector Torres	.80	.40	.25
273	Ralph Houk	1.50	.70	.45
274	Gerry Arrigo	.80	.40	.25
275	Duke Sims	.80	.40	.25
276	Ron Hunt	.90	.45	.25
277	Paul Doyle	.80	.40	.25
278	Tommie Aaron	.80	.40	.25
279	*Bill Lee*	.80	.40	.25
280	Donn Clendenon	.90	.45	.25
281	Casey Cox	.80	.40	.25
282	Steve Huntz	.80	.40	.25
283	Angel Bravo	.80	.40	.25
284	Jack Baldschun	.80	.40	.25
285	Paul Blair	.90	.45	.25
286	Dodgers Rookies (*Bill Buckner*, Jack Jenkins)	6.00	3.00	1.75
287	Fred Talbot	.80	.40	.25
288	Larry Hisle	.90	.45	.25
289	Gene Brabender	.80	.40	.25
290	Rod Carew	60.00	30.00	18.00
291	Leo Durocher	1.75	.90	.50
292	Eddie Leon	.80	.40	.25
293	Bob Bailey	.80	.40	.25
294	Jose Azcue	.80	.40	.25
295	Cecil Upshaw	.80	.40	.25
296	Woody Woodward	.90	.45	.25
297	Curt Blefary	.80	.40	.25
298	Ken Henderson	.80	.40	.25
299	Buddy Bradford	.80	.40	.25
300	Tom Seaver	70.00	35.00	21.00
301	Chico Salmon	.80	.40	.25
302	Jeff James	.80	.40	.25
303	Brant Alyea	.80	.40	.25

		NR MT	EX	VG
304	*Bill Russell*	3.00	1.50	.90
305	World Series Game 1 (Buford Belts Leadoff Homer!)	3.50	1.75	1.00
306	World Series Game 2 (Clendenon's Homer Breaks Ice!)	3.50	1.75	1.00
307	World Series Game 3 (Agee's Catch Saves The Day!)	3.50	1.75	1.00
308	World Series Game 4 (Martin's Bunt Ends Deadlock!)	3.50	1.75	1.00
309	World Series Game 5 (Koosman Shuts The Door!)	3.50	1.75	1.00
310	World Series Summary (Mets Whoop It Up!)	3.50	1.75	1.00
311	Dick Green	.80	.40	.25
312	Mike Torrez	.90	.45	.25
313	Mayo Smith	.80	.40	.25
314	Bill McCool	.80	.40	.25
315	Luis Aparicio	4.50	2.25	1.25
316	Skip Guinn	.80	.40	.25
317	Red Sox Rookies (Luis Alvarado, Billy Conigliaro)	.90	.45	.25
318	Willie Smith	.80	.40	.25
319	Clayton Dalrymple	.80	.40	.25
320	Jim Maloney	.90	.45	.25
321	Lou Piniella	3.00	1.50	.90
322	Luke Walker	.80	.40	.25
323	Wayne Comer	.80	.40	.25
324	Tony Taylor	.80	.40	.25
325	Dave Boswell	.80	.40	.25
326	Bill Voss	.80	.40	.25
327	Hal King	.80	.40	.25
328	George Brunet	.80	.40	.25
329	Chris Cannizzaro	.80	.40	.25
330	Lou Brock	6.00	3.00	1.75
331	Chuck Dobson	.80	.40	.25
332	Bobby Wine	.80	.40	.25
333	Bobby Murcer	1.75	.90	.50
334	Phil Regan	.80	.40	.25
335	Bill Freehan	.90	.45	.25
336	Del Unser	.80	.40	.25
337	Mike McCormick	.90	.45	.25
338	Paul Schaal	.80	.40	.25
339	Johnny Edwards	.80	.40	.25
340	Tony Conigliaro	1.75	.90	.50
341	Bill Sudakis	.80	.40	.25
342	Wilbur Wood	.90	.45	.25
343a	Checklist 373-459 (red bat on front)	3.50	1.75	1.00
343b	Checklist 373-459 (brown bat on front)	3.00	1.50	.90
344	Marcelino Lopez	.80	.40	.25
345	Al Ferrara	.80	.40	.25
346	Red Schoendienst	1.75	.90	.50
347	Russ Snyder	.80	.40	.25
348	Mets Rookies (Jesse Hudson, Mike Jorgensen)	.90	.45	.25
349	Steve Hamilton	.80	.40	.25
350	Roberto Clemente	40.00	20.00	12.50
351	Tom Murphy	.80	.40	.25
352	Bob Barton	.80	.40	.25
353	Stan Williams	.80	.40	.25
354	Amos Otis	.80	.40	.25
355	Doug Rader	.80	.40	.25
356	Fred Lasher	.80	.40	.25
357	Bob Burda	.80	.40	.25
358	*Pedro Borbon*	.90	.45	.25
359	Phil Roof	.80	.40	.25
360	Curt Flood	1.50	.70	.45
361	Ray Jarvis	.80	.40	.25
362	Joe Hague	.80	.40	.25
363	Tom Shopay	.80	.40	.25
364	Dan McGinn	.80	.40	.25
365	Zoilo Versalles	.90	.45	.25
366	Barry Moore	.80	.40	.25
367	Mike Lum	.80	.40	.25
368	Ed Herrmann	.80	.40	.25
369	Alan Foster	.80	.40	.25
370	Tommy Harper	.70	.35	.20
371	Rod Gaspar	.80	.40	.25
372	Dave Giusti	.80	.40	.25
373	Roy White	1.50	.70	.45
374	Tommie Sisk	.80	.40	.25
375	Johnny Callison	1.50	.70	.45
376	Lefty Phillips	.80	.40	.25
377	Bill Butler	.80	.40	.25
378	Jim Davenport	.80	.40	.25
379	Tom Tischinski	.80	.40	.25
380	Tony Perez	3.00	1.50	.90
381	Athletics Rookies (Bobby Brooks, Mike Olivo)	.80	.40	.25
382	Jack DiLauro	.80	.40	.25

		NR MT	EX	VG
383	Mickey Stanley	.90	.45	.25
384	Gary Neibauer	.80	.40	.25
385	George Scott	.90	.45	.25
386	Bill Dillman	.80	.40	.25
387	Orioles Team	3.00	1.50	.90
388	Byron Browne	.80	.40	.25
389	Jim Shellenback	.80	.40	.25
390	Willie Davis	1.50	.70	.45
391	Larry Brown	.80	.40	.25
392	Walt Hriniak	.80	.40	.25
393	John Gelnar	.80	.40	.25
394	Gil Hodges	4.00	2.00	1.25
395	Walt Williams	.80	.40	.25
396	Steve Blass	.90	.45	.25
397	Roger Repoz	.80	.40	.25
398	Bill Stoneman	.80	.40	.25
399	Yankees Team	3.00	1.50	.90
400	Denny McLain	3.00	1.50	.90
401	Giants Rookies (John Harrell, Bernie Williams)	.80	.40	.25
402	Ellie Rodriguez	.80	.40	.25
403	Jim Bunning	3.25	1.75	1.00
404	Rich Reese	.80	.40	.25
405	Bill Hands	.80	.40	.25
406	Mike Andrews	.80	.40	.25
407	Bob Watson	.90	.45	.25
408	Paul Lindblad	.80	.40	.25
409	Bob Tolan	.90	.45	.25
410	Boog Powell	3.00	1.50	.90
411	Dodgers Team	3.00	1.50	.90
412	Larry Burchart	.80	.40	.25
413	Sonny Jackson	.80	.40	.25
414	Paul Edmondson	.80	.40	.25
415	Julian Javier	.80	.40	.25
416	Joe Verbanic	.80	.40	.25
417	John Bateman	.80	.40	.25
418	John Donaldson	.80	.40	.25
419	Ron Taylor	.80	.40	.25
420	Ken McMullen	.80	.40	.25
421	Pat Dobson	.90	.45	.25
422	Royals Team	1.75	.90	.50
423	Jerry May	.80	.40	.25
424	Mike Kilkenny	.80	.40	.25
425	Bobby Bonds	1.75	.90	.50
426	Bill Rigney	.80	.40	.25
427	Fred Norman	.80	.40	.25
428	Don Buford	.90	.45	.25
429	Cubs Rookies (Randy Bobb, Jim Cosman)	.80	.40	.25
430	Andy Messersmith	.80	.40	.25
431	Ron Swoboda	.90	.45	.25
432a	Checklist 460-546 ("Baseball" on front in yellow)	4.00	2.00	1.25
432b	Checklist 460-546 ("Baseball" on front in white)	3.50	1.75	1.00
433	Ron Bryant	.80	.40	.25
434	Felipe Alou	.70	.35	.20
435	Nelson Briles	.80	.40	.25
436	Phillies Team	1.75	.90	.50
437	Danny Cater	.80	.40	.25
438	Pat Jarvis	.80	.40	.25
439	Lee Maye	.80	.40	.25
440	Bill Mazeroski	1.50	.70	.45
441	John O'Donoghue	.80	.40	.25
442	Gene Mauch	.70	.35	.20
443	Al Jackson	.80	.40	.25
444	White Sox Rookies (Bill Farmer, John Matias)	.80	.40	.25
445	Vada Pinson	1.75	.90	.50
446	*Billy Grabarkewitz*	.90	.45	.25
447	Lee Stange	.80	.40	.25
448	Astros Team	1.75	.90	.50
449	Jim Palmer	20.00	10.00	6.00
450	Willie McCovey AS	3.50	1.75	1.00
451	Boog Powell AS	1.50	.70	.45
452	Felix Millan AS	.80	.40	.25
453	Rod Carew AS	4.00	2.00	1.25
454	Ron Santo AS	1.50	.70	.45
455	Brooks Robinson AS	3.50	1.75	1.00
456	Don Kessinger AS	.80	.40	.25
457	Rico Petrocelli AS	.80	.40	.25
458	Pete Rose AS	8.00	4.00	2.50
459	Reggie Jackson AS	12.00	6.00	3.50
460	Matty Alou AS	.70	.35	.20
461	Carl Yastrzemski AS	8.00	4.00	2.50
462	Hank Aaron AS	8.00	4.00	2.50
463	Frank Robinson AS	5.00	2.50	1.50
464	Johnny Bench AS	10.00	5.00	3.00
465	Bill Freehan AS	.80	.40	.25
466	Juan Marichal AS	4.00	2.00	1.25
467	Denny McLain AS	1.50	.70	.45
468	Jerry Koosman AS	1.00	.50	.30
469	Sam McDowell AS	1.00	.50	.30
470	Willie Stargell	7.00	3.50	2.00
471	Chris Zachary	.80	.40	.25
472	Braves Team	1.75	.90	.50
473	Don Bryant	.80	.40	.25
474	Dick Kelley	.80	.40	.25
475	Dick McAuliffe	.90	.45	.25
476	Don Shaw	.80	.40	.25
477	Orioles Rookies (Roger Freed, Al Severinsen)	.80	.40	.25
478	Bob Heise	.80	.40	.25
479	Dick Woodson	.80	.40	.25
480	Glenn Beckert	.90	.45	.25
481	Jose Tartabull	.80	.40	.25
482	Tom Hilgendorf	.80	.40	.25
483	Gail Hopkins	.80	.40	.25
484	Gary Nolan	.80	.40	.25
485	Jay Johnstone	.80	.40	.25
486	Terry Harmon	.80	.40	.25
487	Cisco Carlos	.80	.40	.25
488	J.C. Martin	.80	.40	.25
489	Eddie Kasko	.80	.40	.25
490	Bill Singer	.90	.45	.25
491	Graig Nettles	4.00	2.00	1.25
492	Astros Rookies (Keith Lampard, Scipio Spinks)	.80	.40	.25
493	Lindy McDaniel	.80	.40	.25
494	Larry Stahl	.80	.40	.25
495	Dave Morehead	.80	.40	.25
496	Steve Whitaker	.80	.40	.25
497	Eddie Watt	.80	.40	.25
498	Al Weis	.80	.40	.25
499	Skip Lockwood	.80	.40	.25
500	Hank Aaron	35.00	17.50	10.50
501	White Sox Team	1.75	.90	.50
502	Rollie Fingers	20.00	10.00	6.00
503	Dal Maxvill	.90	.45	.25
504	Don Pavletich	.80	.40	.25
505	Ken Holtzman	.90	.45	.25
506	Ed Stroud	.80	.40	.25
507	Pat Corrales	.80	.40	.25
508	Joe Niekro	.70	.35	.20
509	Expos Team	1.75	.90	.50
510	Tony Oliva	3.50	1.75	1.00
511	Joe Hoerner	.80	.40	.25
512	Billy Harris	.80	.40	.25
513	Preston Gomez	.80	.40	.25
514	Steve Hovley	.80	.40	.25
515	Don Wilson	.80	.40	.25
516	Yankees Rookies (John Ellis, Jim Lyttle)	.80	.40	.25
517	Joe Gibbon	.80	.40	.25
518	Bill Melton	.90	.45	.25
519	Don McMahon	.80	.40	.25
520	Willie Horton	.70	.35	.20
521	Cal Koonce	.80	.40	.25
522	Angels Team	1.75	.90	.50
523	Jose Pena	.80	.40	.25
524	Alvin Dark	1.00	.50	.30
525	Jerry Adair	.80	.40	.25
526	Ron Herbel	.80	.40	.25
527	Don Bosch	.80	.40	.25
528	Elrod Hendricks	.80	.40	.25
529	Bob Aspromonte	.80	.40	.25
530	Bob Gibson	10.00	5.00	3.00
531	Ron Clark	.80	.40	.25
532	Danny Murtaugh	.80	.40	.25
533	Buzz Stephen	.80	.40	.25
534	Twins Team	3.00	1.50	.90
535	Andy Kosco	.80	.40	.25
536	Mike Kekich	.80	.40	.25
537	Joe Morgan	10.00	5.00	3.00
538	Bob Humphreys	.80	.40	.25
539	Phillies Rookies (*Larry Bowa*, Dennis Doyle)	3.00	1.50	.90
540	Gary Peters	.90	.45	.25
541	Bill Heath	.80	.40	.25
542a	Checklist 547-633 (grey bat on front)	3.50	1.75	1.00
542b	Checklist 547-633 (brown bat on front)	3.50	1.75	1.00
543	Clyde Wright	.80	.40	.25
544	Reds Team	1.75	.90	.50
545	Ken Harrelson	1.75	.90	.50
546	Ron Reed	.90	.45	.25
547	Rick Monday	1.50	.70	.45
548	Howie Reed	1.50	.70	.45
549	Cardinals Team	3.50	1.75	1.00
550	Frank Howard	3.50	1.75	1.00
551	Dock Ellis	1.50	.70	.45

		NR MT	EX	VG
552	Royals Rookies (Don O'Riley, Dennis Paepke, Fred Rico)	1.50	.70	.45
553	Jim Lefebvre	1.50	.70	.45
554	Tom Timmermann	1.50	.70	.45
555	Orlando Cepeda	3.50	1.75	1.00
556	Dave Bristol	1.50	.70	.45
557	Ed Kranepool	1.50	.70	.45
558	Vern Fuller	1.50	.70	.45
559	Tommy Davis	1.75	.90	.50
560	Gaylord Perry	8.00	4.00	2.50
561	Tom McCraw	1.50	.70	.45
562	Ted Abernathy	1.50	.70	.45
563	Red Sox Team	3.00	1.50	.90
564	Johnny Briggs	1.50	.70	.45
565	Jim Hunter	7.00	3.50	2.00
566	Gene Alley	1.50	.70	.45
567	Bob Oliver	1.50	.70	.45
568	Stan Bahnsen	1.50	.70	.45
569	Cookie Rojas	1.50	.70	.45
570	Jim Fregosi	1.50	.70	.45
571	Jim Brewer	1.50	.70	.45
572	Frank Quilici	1.50	.70	.45
573	Padres Rookies (Mike Corkins, Rafael Robles, Ron Slocum)	1.50	.70	.45
574	Bobby Bolin	1.50	.70	.45
575	Cleon Jones	1.50	.70	.45
576	Milt Pappas	1.50	.70	.45
577	Bernie Allen	1.50	.70	.45
578	Tom Griffin	1.50	.70	.45
579	Tigers Team	3.50	1.75	1.00
580	Pete Rose	75.00	37.00	22.00
581	Tom Satriano	1.50	.70	.45
582	Mike Paul	1.50	.70	.45
583	Hal Lanier	1.50	.70	.45
584	Al Downing	1.50	.70	.45
585	Rusty Staub	3.00	1.50	.90
586	Rickey Clark	1.50	.70	.45
587	Jose Arcia	1.50	.70	.45
588a	Checklist 634-720 (666 is Adolpho Phillips)	4.50	2.25	1.25
588b	Checklist 634-720 (666 is Adolfo Phillips)	3.00	1.50	.90
589	Joe Keough	1.50	.70	.45
590	Mike Cuellar	1.50	.70	.45
591	Mike Ryan	1.50	.70	.45
592	Daryl Patterson	1.50	.70	.45
593	Cubs Team	3.50	1.75	1.00
594	Jake Gibbs	1.50	.70	.45
595	Maury Wills	3.50	1.75	1.00
596	Mike Hershberger	1.50	.70	.45
597	Sonny Siebert	1.50	.70	.45
598	Joe Pepitone	1.75	.90	.50
599	Senators Rookies (Gene Martin, Dick Stelmaszek, Dick Such)	1.50	.70	.45
600	Willie Mays	50.00	25.00	15.00
601	Pete Richert	1.50	.70	.45
602	Ted Savage	1.50	.70	.45
603	Ray Oyler	1.50	.70	.45
604	Clarence Gaston	1.50	.70	.45
605	Rick Wise	1.50	.70	.45
606	Chico Ruiz	1.50	.70	.45
607	Gary Waslewski	1.50	.70	.45
608	Pirates Team	3.50	1.75	1.00
609	*Buck Martinez*	1.50	.70	.45
610	Jerry Koosman	1.75	.90	.50
611	Norm Cash	3.00	1.50	.90
612	Jim Hickman	1.50	.70	.45
613	Dave Baldwin	1.50	.70	.45
614	Mike Shannon	1.50	.70	.45
615	Mark Belanger	1.50	.70	.45
616	Jim Merritt	1.50	.70	.45
617	Jim French	1.50	.70	.45
618	Billy Wynne	1.50	.70	.45
619	Norm Miller	1.50	.70	.45
620	Jim Perry	1.50	.70	.45
621	Braves Rookies (*Darrell Evans*, Rick Kester, Mike McQueen)	18.00	9.00	5.50
622	Don Sutton	7.00	3.50	2.00
623	Horace Clarke	1.50	.70	.45
624	Clyde King	1.50	.70	.45
625	Dean Chance	1.50	.70	.45
626	Dave Ricketts	1.50	.70	.45
627	Gary Wagner	1.50	.70	.45
628	Wayne Garrett	1.50	.70	.45
629	Merv Rettenmund	1.50	.70	.45
630	Ernie Banks	20.00	10.00	6.00
631	Athletics Team	3.50	1.75	1.00
632	Gary Sutherland	1.50	.70	.45
633	Roger Nelson	1.50	.70	.45
634	Bud Harrelson	3.50	1.75	1.00
635	Bob Allison	3.50	1.75	1.00

		NR MT	EX	VG
636	Jim Stewart	3.00	1.50	.90
637	Indians Team	3.00	1.50	.90
638	Frank Bertaina	3.00	1.50	.90
639	Dave Campbell	3.00	1.50	.90
640	Al Kaline	35.00	17.50	10.50
641	Al McBean	3.00	1.50	.90
642	Angels Rookies (Greg Garrett, Gordon Lund, Jarvis Tatum)	3.00	1.50	.90
643	Jose Pagan	3.00	1.50	.90
644	Gerry Nyman	3.00	1.50	.90
645	Don Money	3.00	1.50	.90
646	Jim Britton	3.00	1.50	.90
647	Tom Matchick	3.00	1.50	.90
648	Larry Haney	3.00	1.50	.90
649	Jimmie Hall	3.00	1.50	.90
650	Sam McDowell	3.50	1.75	1.00
651	Jim Gosger	3.00	1.50	.90
652	Rich Rollins	3.50	1.75	1.00
653	Moe Drabowsky	3.00	1.50	.90
654	N.L. Rookies (Boots Day, *Oscar Gamble*, Angel Mangual)	3.50	1.75	1.00
655	John Roseboro	3.50	1.75	1.00
656	Jim Hardin	3.00	1.50	.90
657	Padres Team	4.00	2.00	1.25
658	Ken Tatum	3.00	1.50	.90
659	Pete Ward	3.50	1.75	1.00
660	Johnny Bench	175.00	87.00	52.00
661	Jerry Robertson	3.00	1.50	.90
662	Frank Lucchesi	3.00	1.50	.90
663	Tito Francona	3.50	1.75	1.00
664	Bob Robertson	3.00	1.50	.90
665	Jim Lonborg	3.50	1.75	1.00
666	Adolfo Phillips	3.00	1.50	.90
667	Bob Meyer	3.50	1.75	1.00
668	Bob Tillman	3.00	1.50	.90
669	White Sox Rookies (Bart Johnson, Dan Lazar, Mickey Scott)	3.00	1.50	.90
670	Ron Santo	3.25	1.75	1.00
671	Jim Campanis	3.00	1.50	.90
672	Leon McFadden	3.00	1.50	.90
673	Ted Uhlaender	3.00	1.50	.90
674	Dave Leonhard	3.00	1.50	.90
675	Jose Cardenal	3.50	1.75	1.00
676	Senators Team	3.25	1.75	1.00
677	Woodie Fryman	3.50	1.75	1.00
678	Dave Duncan	3.00	1.50	.90
679	Ray Sadecki	3.00	1.50	.90
680	Rico Petrocelli	3.50	1.75	1.00
681	Bob Garibaldi	3.00	1.50	.90
682	Dalton Jones	3.00	1.50	.90
683	Reds Rookies (Vern Geishert, Hal McRae, Wayne Simpson)	4.00	2.00	1.25
684	Jack Fisher	3.00	1.50	.90
685	Tom Haller	3.50	1.75	1.00
686	Jackie Hernandez	3.00	1.50	.90
687	Bob Priddy	3.00	1.50	.90
688	Ted Kubiak	3.50	1.75	1.00
689	Frank Tepedino	3.50	1.75	1.00
690	Ron Fairly	3.50	1.75	1.00
691	Joe Grzenda	3.00	1.50	.90
692	Duffy Dyer	3.00	1.50	.90
693	Bob Johnson	3.00	1.50	.90
694	Gary Ross	3.00	1.50	.90
695	Bobby Knoop	3.00	1.50	.90
696	Giants Team	3.25	1.75	1.00
697	Jim Hannan	3.00	1.50	.90
698	Tom Tresh	4.00	2.00	1.25
699	Hank Aguirre	3.00	1.50	.90
700	Frank Robinson	40.00	20.00	12.00
701	Jack Billingham	3.00	1.50	.90
702	A.L. Rookies (Bob Johnson, Ron Klimkowski, Bill Zepp)	3.50	1.75	1.00
703	Lou Marone	3.00	1.50	.90
704	Frank Baker	3.00	1.50	.90
705	Tony Cloninger	3.50	1.75	1.00
706	John McNamara	3.50	1.75	1.00
707	Kevin Collins	3.00	1.50	.90
708	Jose Santiago	3.00	1.50	.90
709	Mike Fiore	3.00	1.50	.90
710	Felix Millan	3.00	1.50	.90
711	Ed Brinkman	3.50	1.75	1.00
712	Nolan Ryan	350.00	175.00	105.00
713	Pilots Team	15.00	7.50	4.50
714	Al Spangler	3.00	1.50	.90
715	Mickey Lolich	5.00	2.50	1.50
716	Cards Rookies (Sal Campisi, *Reggie Cleveland*, Santiago Guzman)	3.50	1.75	1.00
717	Tom Phoebus	3.00	1.50	.90
718	Ed Spiezio	3.00	1.50	.90
719	Jim Roland	3.50	1.75	1.00
720	Rick Reichardt	4.00	1.00	.50

1970 Topps Candy Lids

The 1970 Topps Candy Lids are a test issue that was utilized again in 1973. The set is made up of 24 lids that measure 1-7/8" in diameter and were the tops of small 1.1 oz. tubs of "Baseball Stars Candy." Unlike the 1973 versions, the 1970 lids have no border surrounding the full-color photos. Frank Howard, Tom Seaver and Carl Yastrzemski photos are found on the bottom (inside) of the candy lid.

		NR MT	EX	VG
Complete Set:		2000.00	1000.00	600.00
Common Player:		30.00	15.00	9.00
(1)	Hank Aaron	200.00	100.00	60.00
(2)	Rich Allen	50.00	25.00	15.00
(3)	Luis Aparicio	80.00	40.00	24.00
(4)	Johnny Bench	200.00	100.00	60.00
(5)	Ollie Brown	30.00	15.00	9.00
(6)	Willie Davis	30.00	15.00	9.00
(7)	Jim Fregosi	30.00	15.00	9.00
(8)	Mike Hegan	30.00	15.00	9.00
(9)	Frank Howard	50.00	25.00	15.00
(10)	Reggie Jackson	200.00	100.00	60.00
(11)	Fergie Jenkins	60.00	30.00	18.00
(12)	Harmon Killebrew	100.00	50.00	30.00
(13)	Juan Marichal	100.00	50.00	30.00
(14)	Bill Mazeroski	50.00	25.00	15.00
(15)	Tim McCarver	50.00	25.00	15.00
(16)	Sam McDowell	30.00	15.00	9.00
(17)	Denny McLain	50.00	25.00	15.00
(18)	Lou Piniella	50.00	25.00	15.00
(19)	Frank Robinson	100.00	50.00	30.00
(20)	Tom Seaver	175.00	87.00	52.00
(21)	Rusty Staub	50.00	25.00	15.00
(22)	Mel Stottlemyre	50.00	25.00	15.00
(23)	Jim Wynn	30.00	15.00	9.00
(24)	Carl Yastrzemski	150.00	75.00	45.00

1970 Topps Posters

Helping to ease a price increase, Topps included extremely fragile 8-11/16" by 9-5/8" posters in packs of regular cards. The posters feature color portraits and a smaller black and white "action" pose as well as the player's name, team and position at the top. Although there are Hall of Famers in the 24-poster set, all the top names are not represented. Once again, due to folding, heavy creases are a fact of life for today's collector.

		NR MT	EX	VG
Complete Set:		30.00	15.00	9.00
Common Player:		.40	.20	.12
1	Joe Horlen	.40	.20	.12
2	Phil Niekro	1.50	.70	.45
3	Willie Davis	.50	.25	.15
4	Lou Brock	2.00	1.00	.60
5	Ron Santo	.60	.30	.20
6	Ken Harrelson	.50	.25	.15
7	Willie McCovey	2.00	1.00	.60
8	Rick Wise	.40	.20	.12
9	Andy Messersmith	.40	.20	.12
10	Ron Fairly	.50	.25	.15
11	Johnny Bench	3.25	1.75	1.00
12	Frank Robinson	2.50	1.25	.70
13	Tommie Agee	.40	.20	.12
14	Roy White	.50	.25	.15
15	Larry Dierker	.40	.20	.12
16	Rod Carew	3.00	1.50	.90
17	Don Mincher	.40	.20	.12
18	Ollie Brown	.40	.20	.12
19	Ed Kirkpatrick	.40	.20	.12
20	Reggie Smith	.50	.25	.15
21	Bob Clemente	5.00	2.50	1.50
22	Frank Howard	.60	.30	.20
23	Bert Campaneris	.50	.25	.15
24	Denny McLain	.60	.30	.20

1970 Topps Scratch-Offs

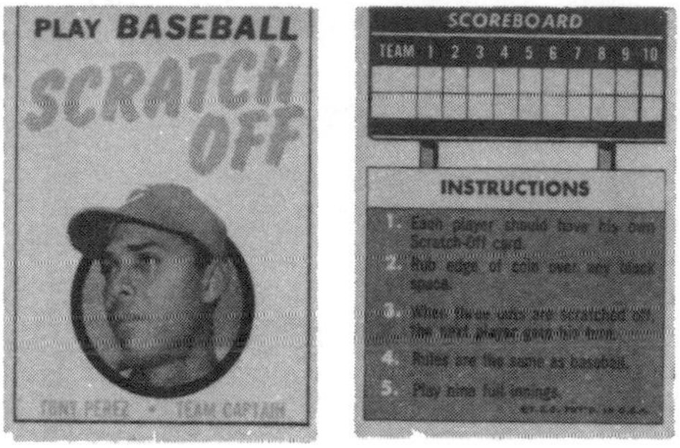

Needing inserts, and having not given up on the idea of a game which could be played with baseball cards, Topps provided a new game - the baseball scratch-off. The set consists of 24 cards. Unfolded, they measure 3-3/8" by 5," and reveal a baseball game of sorts which was played by rubbing the black ink off playing squares which then determined the "action." Fronts of the cards have a player picture as "captain," while backs have instructions and a scoreboard. Inserts with white centers are from 1970 while those with red centers are from 1971.

		NR MT	EX	VG
Complete Set:		20.00	10.00	6.00
Common Player:		.30	.15	.09
(1)	Hank Aaron	2.00	1.00	.60
(2)	Rich Allen	.50	.25	.15
(3)	Luis Aparicio	1.00	.50	.30
(4)	Sal Bando	.30	.15	.09
(5)	Glenn Beckert	.30	.15	.09
(6)	Dick Bosman	.30	.15	.09
(7)	Nate Colbert	.30	.15	.09
(8)	Mike Hegan	.30	.15	.09
(9)	Mack Jones	.30	.15	.09
(10)	Al Kaline	1.50	.70	.45
(11)	Harmon Killebrew	1.50	.70	.45
(12)	Juan Marichal	1.25	.60	.40
(13)	Tim McCarver	.40	.20	.12
(14)	Sam McDowell	.30	.15	.09

they measure 3-3/8" by 5," and reveal a baseball game of sorts which was played by rubbing the black ink off playing squares which then determined the "action." Fronts of the cards have a player picture as "captain," while backs have instructions and a scoreboard. Inserts with white centers are from 1970 while those with red centers are from 1971.

		NR MT	EX	VG
Complete Set:		20.00	10.00	6.00
Common Player:		.30	.15	.09
(1)	Hank Aaron	2.00	1.00	.60
(2)	Rich Allen	.50	.25	.15
(3)	Luis Aparicio	1.00	.50	.30
(4)	Sal Bando	.30	.15	.09
(5)	Glenn Beckert	.30	.15	.09
(6)	Dick Bosman	.30	.15	.09
(7)	Nate Colbert	.30	.15	.09
(8)	Mike Hegan	.30	.15	.09
(9)	Mack Jones	.30	.15	.09
(10)	Al Kaline	1.50	.70	.45
(11)	Harmon Killebrew	1.50	.70	.45
(12)	Juan Marichal	1.25	.60	.40
(13)	Tim McCarver	.40	.20	.12
(14)	Sam McDowell	.30	.15	.09
(15)	Claude Osteen	.30	.15	.09
(16)	Tony Perez	.60	.30	.20
(17)	Lou Piniella	.40	.20	.12
(18)	Boog Powell	.50	.25	.15
(19)	Tom Seaver	2.00	1.00	.60
(20)	Jim Spencer	.30	.15	.09
(21)	Willie Stargell	1.25	.60	.40
(22)	Mel Stottlemyre	.30	.15	.09
(23)	Jim Wynn	.30	.15	.09
(24)	Carl Yastrzemski	2.25	1.25	.70

1970 Topps Story Booklets

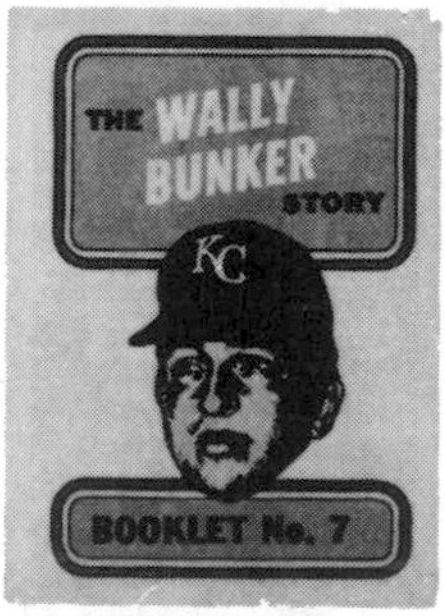

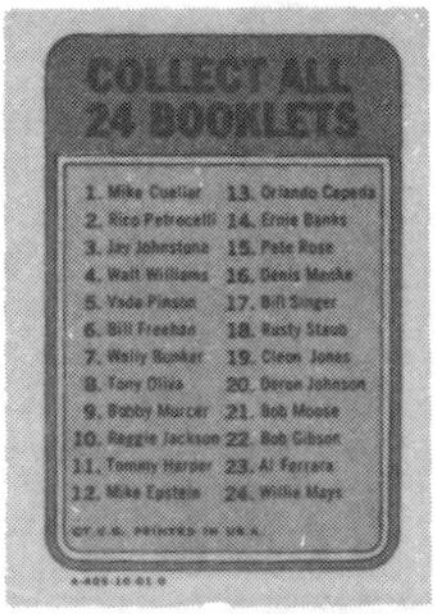

Measuring 2-1/2" by 3-7/16," the Topps Story Booklet was a 1970 regular pack insert. The booklet feature a photo, title and booklet number on the "cover." Inside are six pages of comic book story. The backs give a checklist of other available booklets. Not every star had a booklet as the set is only 24 in number.

		NR MT	EX	VG
Complete Set:		30.00	15.00	9.00
Common Player:		.30	.15	.09
1	Mike Cuellar	.40	.20	.12
2	Rico Petrocelli	.40	.20	.12
3	Jay Johnstone	.40	.20	.12
4	Walt Williams	.30	.15	.09
5	Vada Pinson	.50	.25	.15
6	Bill Freehan	.40	.20	.12
7	Wally Bunker	.30	.15	.09
8	Tony Oliva	.50	.25	.15
9	Bobby Murcer	.40	.20	.12
10	Reggie Jackson	5.00	2.50	1.50
11	Tommy Harper	.30	.15	.09
12	Mike Epstein	.30	.15	.09
13	Orlando Cepeda	.90	.45	.25
14	Ernie Banks	3.00	1.50	.90
15	Pete Rose	8.00	4.00	2.50
16	Denis Menke	.30	.15	.09
17	Bill Singer	.30	.15	.09
18	Rusty Staub	.50	.25	.15
19	Cleon Jones	.30	.15	.09
20	Deron Johnson	.30	.15	.09
21	Bob Moose	.30	.15	.09
22	Bob Gibson	4.00	2.00	1.25
23	Al Ferrara	.30	.15	.09
24	Willie Mays	7.00	3.50	2.00

1970 Topps Super

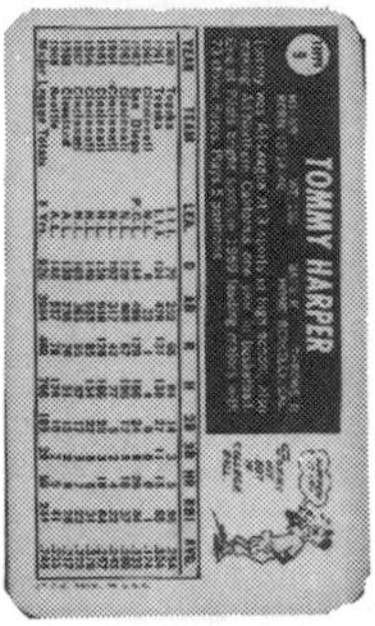

Representing a refinement of the concept begun in 1969, the 1970 Topps Supers had a new 3-1/8" by 5-1/4" postcard size. Printed on heavy stock with rounded corners, card fronts feature a borderless color photograph and facsimile autograph. Card backs are simply an enlarged back from the player's regular 1970 Topps card. The Topps Supers set numbers 42 cards. Probably due to the press sheet configuration eight of the 42 had smaller printings. The most elusive is card #38 (Boog Powell). The set was more widely produced than was the case in 1969, meaning collectors stand a much better chance of affording it.

		NR MT	EX	VG
Complete Set:		250.00	125.00	75.00
Common Player:		.75	.40	.25
1	Claude Osteen	3.00	1.50	.90
2	Sal Bando	3.50	1.75	1.00
3	Luis Aparicio	2.50	1.25	.70
4	Harmon Killebrew	4.00	2.00	1.25
5	Tom Seaver	25.00	12.50	7.50
6	Larry Dierker	.90	.45	.25
7	Bill Freehan	1.00	.50	.30
8	Johnny Bench	15.00	7.50	4.50
9	Tommy Harper	.90	.45	.25
10	Sam McDowell	1.00	.50	.30
11	Louis Brock	4.00	2.00	1.25
12	Roberto Clemente	15.00	7.50	4.50
13	Willie McCovey	4.00	2.00	1.25
14	Rico Petrocelli	.90	.45	.25
15	Philip Niekro	2.25	1.25	.70
16	Frank Howard	1.50	.70	.45
17	Denny McLain	1.25	.60	.40
18	Willie Mays	15.00	7.50	4.50
19	Wilver Stargell	3.50	1.75	1.00
20	Joe Horlen	.90	.45	.25
21	Ronald Santo	1.00	.50	.30
22	Dick Bosman	.90	.45	.25
23	Tim McCarver	1.00	.50	.30
24	Henry Aaron	15.00	7.50	4.50
25	Andy Messersmith	.90	.45	.25
26	Tony Oliva	1.25	.60	.40
27	Mel Stottlemyre	1.00	.50	.30
28	Reginald M. Jackson	18.00	9.00	5.50
29	Carl Yastrzemski	12.00	6.00	3.50
30	James Fregosi	1.00	.50	.30
31	Vada Pinson	1.25	.60	.40
32	Lou Piniella	1.25	.60	.40
33	Robert Gibson	4.00	2.00	1.25
34	Pete Rose	25.00	12.50	7.50
35	Jim Wynn	1.00	.50	.30
36	Ollie Brown	3.00	1.50	.90
37	Frank Robinson	18.00	9.00	5.50
38	John "Boog" Powell	60.00	30.00	18.00

Topps once again produced baseball tattoos in 1971. This time, the tattoos came in a variety of sizes, shapes and themes. The sheets of tattoos measure 3-1/2" by 14-1/4." Each sheet contains an assortment of tattoos in two sizes, 1-3/4" by 2-3/8," or 1-3/16" by 1-3/4." There are players, facsimile autographed baseballs, team pennants and assorted baseball cartoon figures carried on the 16 different sheets. Listings below are for complete sheets; with the exception of the biggest-name stars, individual tattoos have little or no collector value.

	NR MT	EX	VG
Complete Sheet Set:	175.00	87.00	52.00
Common Sheet:	4.00	2.00	1.25

		NR MT	EX	VG
1	Brooks Robinson Autograph, Montreal Expos Pennant, San Francisco Giants Pennant, Sal Bando, Dick Bosman, Nate Colbert, Cleon Jones, Juan Marichal, B. Robinson	10.00	5.00	3.00
2	Boston Red Sox Pennant, Carl Yastrzemski Autograph, New York Mets Pennant, Glenn Beckert, Tommy Harper, Ken Henderson, Fritz Peterson, Bob Robertson, C. Yastrzemski	18.00	9.00	5.50
3	Jim Fregosi Autograph, New York Yankees Pennant, Philadelphia Phillies Pennant ector value., Orlando Cepeda, Jim Fregosi, Randy Hundley, Reggie Jackson, Jerry Koosman, Jim Palmer	15.00	7.50	4.50
4	Kansas City Royals Pennant, Oakland Athletics Pennant, Sam McDowell Autograph, Dick Dietz, C. Gaston, Dave Johnson, Sam McDowell, Gary Nolan, Amos Otis	3.50	1.75	1.00
5	Al Kaline Autograph, Atlanta Braves Pennant, L.A. Dodgers Pennant, B. Grabarkewitz, Al Kaline, Lee May, Tom Murphy, Vada Pinson, M. Sanguillen	10.00	5.00	3.00
6	Chicago Cubs Pennant, Cincinnati Reds Pennant, Harmon Killebrew Autograph, Luis Aparicio, Paul Blair, C. Cannizzaro, D. Clendenon, Larry Dieker, H. Killebrew	10.00	5.00	3.00
7	Boog Powell Autograph, Cleveland Indians Pennant, Milwaukee Brewers Pennant, Rich Allen, B. Campaneris, Don Money, Boog Powell, Ted Savage, Rusty Staub	5.00	2.50	1.50
8	Chicago White Sox Pennant, Frank Howard Autograph, San Diego Padres Pennant, Leo Cardenas, Bill Hands, Frank Howard, Wes Parker, Reggie Smith, W. Stargell	5.00	2.50	1.50
9	Detroit Tigers Pennant, Henry Aaron Autograph, Hank Aaron, Tommy Agee, Jim Hunter, Dick McAuliffe, Tony Perez, Lou Piniella	15.00	7.50	4.50
10	Baltimore Orioles Pennant, Fergie Jenkins Autograph, R. Clemente, T. Conigliaro, Fergie Jenkins, T. Munson, Gary Peters, Joe Torre	12.00	6.00	3.50
11	Johnny Bench Autograph, Washington Senators Pennant, Johnny Bench, Rico Carty, B. Mazeroski, Bob Oliver, R. Petrocelli, F. Robinson	10.00	5.00	3.00
12	Billy Williams Autograph, Houston Astros Pennant, Bill Freehan, Dave McNally, Felix Millan, M. Stottlemyre, Bob Tolan, Billy Williams	6.00	3.00	1.75
13	Pittsburgh Pirates Pennant, Willie McCovey Autograph, Ray Culp, Bud Harrelson, Mickey Lolich, W. McCovey, Ron Santo, Roy White	9.00	4.50	2.75
14	Minnesota Twins Pennant, Tom Seaver Autograph, Bill Melton, Jim Perry, Pete Rose, Tom Seaver, Maury Wills, Clyde Wright	25.00	12.50	7.50
15	Robert Gibson Autograph, St. Louis Cardinals Pennant, Rod Carew, Bob Gibson, Alex Johnson, Don Kessinger, Jim Merritt, Rick Monday	9.00	4.50	2.75
16	California Angels Pennant, Willie Mays Autograph, Larry Bowa, Mike Cuellar, Ray Fosse, Willie Mays, Carl Morton, Tony Oliva	15.00	7.50	4.50

1971 Topps

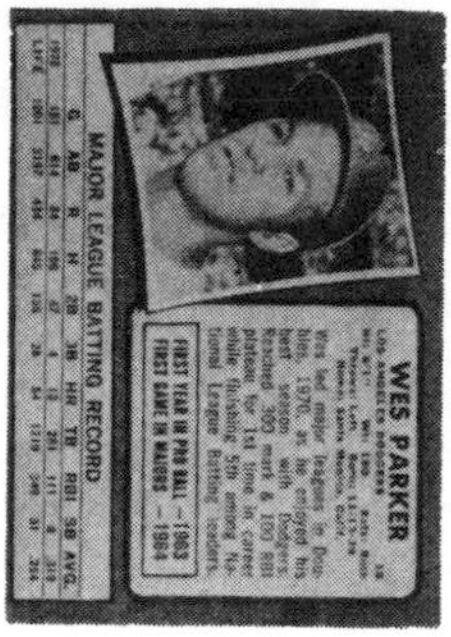

In 1971, Topps again increased the size of its set to 752 cards. These well-liked cards, measuring 2-1/2" by 3-1/2," feature a large color photo which has a thin white frame. Above the picture, in the card's overall black border, is the player's name, team and position. A facsimile autograph completes the front. Backs feature a major change as a black and white "snapshot" of the player appears. Abbreviated statistics, a line giving the player's first pro and major league games and a short biography complete the back of these innovative cards. Specialty cards in this issue are limited. There are statistical leaders as well as World Series and playoff highlights. High numbered cards #644-752 are scarce.

	NR MT	EX	VG
Complete Set:	2000.00	1000.00	600.00
Common Player: 1-523	.70	.35	.20
Common Player: 524-643	1.75	.90	.50
Common Player: 644-752	3.00	1.50	.90

		NR MT	EX	VG
1	World Champions (Orioles Team)	12.00	6.00	3.50
2	Dock Ellis	.80	.40	.25
3	Dick McAuliffe	.80	.40	.25
4	Vic Davalillo	.80	.40	.25
5	Thurman Munson	30.00	15.00	9.00
6	Ed Spiezio	.70	.35	.20
7	Jim Holt	.70	.35	.20
8	Mike McQueen	.70	.35	.20
9	George Scott	.80	.40	.25
10	Claude Osteen	.80	.40	.25
11	*Elliott Maddox*	.80	.40	.25
12	Johnny Callison	2.00	1.00	.60
13	White Sox Rookies (Charlie Brinkman, Dick Moloney)	.70	.35	.20
14	*Dave Concepcion*	10.00	5.00	3.00
15	Andy Messersmith	.80	.40	.25
16	*Ken Singleton*	2.25	1.25	.70
17	Billy Sorrell	.70	.35	.20
18	Norm Miller	.70	.35	.20
19	Skip Pitlock	.70	.35	.20
20	Reggie Jackson	70.00	35.00	21.00
21	Dan McGinn	.70	.35	.20
22	Phil Roof	.70	.35	.20
23	Oscar Gamble	.80	.40	.25
24	Rich Hand	.70	.35	.20
25	Clarence Gaston	.70	.35	.20
26	*Bert Blyleven*	60.00	30.00	18.00
27	Pirates Rookies (Fred Cambria, Gene Clines)	.70	.35	.20
28	Ron Klimkowski	.80	.40	.25
29	Don Buford	.80	.40	.25
30	Phil Niekro	3.25	1.75	1.00
31	Eddie Kasko	.70	.35	.20
32	Jerry DaVanon	.70	.35	.20
33	Del Unser	.70	.35	.20
34	Sandy Vance	.70	.35	.20
35	Lou Piniella	1.25	.60	.40
36	Dean Chance	.80	.40	.25
37	Rich McKinney	.70	.35	.20
38	*Jim Colborn*	.80	.40	.25
39	Tigers Rookies (Gene Lamont, *Lerrin LaGrow*)	.80	.40	.25
40	Lee May	2.00	1.00	.60
41	Rick Austin	.70	.35	.20
42	Boots Day	.70	.35	.20

		NR MT	EX	VG
43	Steve Kealey	.70	.35	.20
44	Johnny Edwards	.70	.35	.20
45	Jim Hunter	5.00	2.50	1.50
46	Dave Campbell	.70	.35	.20
47	Johnny Jeter	.70	.35	.20
48	Dave Baldwin	.70	.35	.20
49	Don Money	.80	.40	.25
50	Willie McCovey	7.00	3.50	2.00
51	Steve Kline	.80	.40	.25
52	Braves Rookies (Oscar Brown, *Earl Williams*)	.80	.40	.25
53	Paul Blair	.80	.40	.25
54	Checklist 1-132	3.25	1.75	1.00
55	Steve Carlton	25.00	12.50	7.50
56	Duane Josephson	.70	.35	.20
57	Von Joshua	.70	.35	.20
58	Bill Lee	.80	.40	.25
59	Gene Mauch	2.00	1.00	.60
60	Dick Bosman	.70	.35	.20
61	A.L. Batting Leaders (Alex Johnson, Tony Oliva, Carl Yastrzemski)	3.00	1.50	.90
62	N.L. Batting Leaders (Rico Carty, Manny Sanguillen, Joe Torre)	1.25	.60	.40
63	A.L. RBI Leaders (Tony Conigliaro, Frank Howard, Boog Powell)	1.25	.60	.40
64	N.L. RBI Leaders (Johnny Bench, Tony Perez, Billy Williams)	3.00	1.50	.90
65	A.L. Home Run Leaders (Frank Howard, Harmon Killebrew, Carl Yastrzemski)	3.00	1.50	.90
66	N.L. Home Run Leaders (Johnny Bench, Tony Perez, Billy Williams)	3.00	1.50	.90
67	A.L. ERA Leaders (Jim Palmer, Diego Segui, Clyde Wright)	1.25	.60	.40
68	N.L. ERA Leaders (Tom Seaver, Wayne Simpson, Luke Walker)	1.50	.70	.45
69	A.L. Pitching Leaders (Mike Cuellar, Dave McNally, Jim Perry)	1.25	.60	.40
70	N.L. Pitching Leaders (Bob Gibson, Fergie Jenkins, Gaylord Perry)	2.00	1.00	.60
71	A.L. Strikeout Leaders (Bob Johnson, Mickey Lolich, Sam McDowell)	1.25	.60	.40
72	N.L. Strikeout Leaders (Bob Gibson, Fergie Jenkins, Tom Seaver)	3.00	1.50	.90
73	George Brunet	.70	.35	.20
74	Twins Rookies (Pete Hamm, Jim Nettles)	.70	.35	.20
75	Gary Nolan	.70	.35	.20
76	Ted Savage	.70	.35	.20
77	Mike Compton	.70	.35	.20
78	Jim Spencer	.80	.40	.25
79	Wade Blasingame	.70	.35	.20
80	Bill Melton	.80	.40	.25
81	Felix Millan	.70	.35	.20
82	Casey Cox	.70	.35	.20
83	Mets Rookies (Randy Bobb, *Tim Foli*)	.80	.40	.25
84	Marcel Lachemann	.70	.35	.20
85	Billy Grabarkewitz	.70	.35	.20
86	Mike Kilkenny	.70	.35	.20
87	Jack Heidemann	.70	.35	.20
88	Hal King	.70	.35	.20
89	Ken Brett	.70	.35	.20
90	Joe Pepitone	.70	.35	.20
91	Bob Lemon	1.25	.60	.40
92	Fred Wenz	.70	.35	.20
93	Senators Rookies (Norm McRae, Denny Riddleberger)	.70	.35	.20
94	Don Hahn	.70	.35	.20
95	Luis Tiant	1.50	.70	.45
96	Joe Hague	.70	.35	.20
97	Floyd Wicker	.70	.35	.20
98	Joe Decker	.70	.35	.20
99	Mark Belanger	.80	.40	.25
100	Pete Rose	45.00	23.00	13.50
101	Les Cain	.70	.35	.20
102	Astros Rookies (*Ken Forsch*, Larry Howard)	.80	.40	.25
103	Rich Severson	.70	.35	.20
104	Dan Frisella	.70	.35	.20
105	Tony Conigliaro	1.25	.60	.40
106	Tom Dukes	.70	.35	.20
107	Roy Foster	.70	.35	.20
108	John Cumberland	.70	.35	.20
109	Steve Hovley	.70	.35	.20
110	Bill Mazeroski	1.25	.60	.40
111	Yankees Rookies (Loyd Colson, Bobby Mitchell)	.80	.40	.25
112	Manny Mota	2.00	1.00	.60
113	Jerry Crider	.70	.35	.20
114	Billy Conigliaro	.80	.40	.25
115	Donn Clendenon	.80	.40	.25
116	Ken Sanders	.70	.35	.20
117	*Ted Simmons*	12.00	6.00	3.50
118	Cookie Rojas	.70	.35	.20
119	Frank Lucchesi	.70	.35	.20
120	Willie Horton	2.00	1.00	.60
121	1971 Rookie Stars (Jim Dunegan, Roe Skidmore)	.70	.35	.20
122	Eddie Watt	.70	.35	.20
123a	Checklist 133-263 (card # on right, orange helmet)	3.25	1.75	1.00
123b	Checklist 133-263 (card # on right, red helmet)	3.25	1.75	1.00
123c	Checklist 133-263 (card # centered)	3.50	1.75	1.00
124	*Don Gullett*	.70	.35	.20
125	Ray Fosse	.70	.35	.20
126	Danny Coombs	.70	.35	.20
127	*Danny Thompson*	.80	.40	.25
128	Frank Johnson	.70	.35	.20
129	Aurelio Monteagudo	.70	.35	.20
130	Denis Menke	.70	.35	.20
131	Curt Blefary	.80	.40	.25
132	Jose Laboy	.70	.35	.20
133	Mickey Lolich	1.25	.60	.40
134	Jose Arcia	.70	.35	.20
135	Rick Monday	.80	.40	.25
136	Duffy Dyer	.70	.35	.20
137	Marcelino Lopez	.70	.35	.20
138	Phillies Rookies (Joe Lis, *Willie Montanez*)	.80	.40	.25
139	Paul Casanova	.70	.35	.20
140	Gaylord Perry	7.00	3.50	2.00
141	Frank Quilici	.70	.35	.20
142	Mack Jones	.70	.35	.20
143	Steve Blass	.80	.40	.25
144	Jackie Hernandez	.70	.35	.20
145	Bill Singer	.80	.40	.25
146	Ralph Houk	1.75	.90	.50
147	Bob Priddy	.70	.35	.20
148	John Mayberry	.80	.40	.25
149	Mike Hershberger	.70	.35	.20
150	Sam McDowell	.70	.35	.20
151	Tommy Davis	.70	.35	.20
152	Angels Rookies (Lloyd Allen, Winston Llenas)	.70	.35	.20
153	Gary Ross	.70	.35	.20
154	Cesar Gutierrez	.70	.35	.20
155	Ken Henderson	.70	.35	.20
156	Bart Johnson	.70	.35	.20
157	Bob Bailey	.70	.35	.20
158	Jerry Reuss	2.00	1.00	.60
159	Jarvis Tatum	.70	.35	.20
160	Tom Seaver	50.00	25.00	15.00
161	Coins Checklist	3.25	1.75	1.00
162	Jack Billingham	.70	.35	.20
163	Buck Martinez	.70	.35	.20
164	Reds Rookies (Frank Duffy, *Milt Wilcox*)	2.00	1.00	.60
165	Cesar Tovar	.70	.35	.20
166	Joe Hoerner	.70	.35	.20
167	Tom Grieve	.70	.35	.20
168	Bruce Dal Canton	.70	.35	.20
169	Ed Herrmann	.70	.35	.20
170	Mike Cuellar	2.00	1.00	.60
171	Bobby Wine	.70	.35	.20
172	Duke Sims	.70	.35	.20
173	Gil Garrido	.70	.35	.20
174	*Dave LaRoche*	.80	.40	.25
175	Jim Hickman	.80	.40	.25
176	Red Sox Rookies (Doug Griffin, Bob Montgomery)	.70	.35	.20
177	Hal McRae	.70	.35	.20
178	Dave Duncan	.70	.35	.20
179	Mike Corkins	.70	.35	.20
180	Al Kaline	15.00	7.50	4.50
181	Hal Lanier	2.00	1.00	.60
182	Al Downing	.80	.40	.25
183	Gil Hodges	4.00	2.00	1.25
184	Stan Bahnsen	.80	.40	.25
185	Julian Javier	.80	.40	.25
186	Bob Spence	.70	.35	.20
187	Ted Abernathy	.70	.35	.20
188	Dodgers Rookies (Mike Strahler, *Bob Valentine*)	2.25	1.25	.70
189	George Mitterwald	.70	.35	.20
190	Bob Tolan	.80	.40	.25
191	Mike Andrews	.70	.35	.20
192	Billy Wilson	.70	.35	.20
193	*Bob Grich*	2.25	1.25	.70
194	Mike Lum	.70	.35	.20
195	A.L. Playoff Game 1 (Powell Muscles Twins!)	1.25	.60	.40

		NR MT	EX	VG
196	A.L. Playoff Game 2 (McNally Makes It Two Straight!)	1.25	.60	.40
197	A.L. Playoff Game 3 (Palmer Mows 'Em Down!)	2.25	1.25	.70
198	A.L. Playoffs Summary (A Team Effort!)	1.25	.60	.40
199	N.L. Playoff Game 1 (Cline Pinch-Triple Decides It!)	1.25	.60	.40
200	N.L. Playoff Game 2 (Tolan Scores For Third Time!)	1.25	.60	.40
201	N.L. Playoff Game 3 (Cline Scores Winning Run!)	1.25	.60	.40
202	N.L. Playoffs Summary (World Series Bound!)	1.25	.60	.40
203	*Larry Gura*	.70	.35	.20
204	Brewers Rookies (George Kopacz, Bernie Smith)	.70	.35	.20
205	Gerry Moses	.70	.35	.20
206a	Checklist 264-393 (orange helmet)	3.25	1.75	1.00
206b	Checklist 264-393 (red helmet)	3.25	1.75	1.00
207	Alan Foster	.70	.35	.20
208	Billy Martin	2.25	1.25	.70
209	Steve Renko	.70	.35	.20
210	Rod Carew	35.00	17.50	10.50
211	Phil Hennigan	.70	.35	.20
212	Rich Hebner	.80	.40	.25
213	Frank Baker	.80	.40	.25
214	Al Ferrara	.70	.35	.20
215	Diego Segui	.70	.35	.20
216	Cards Rookies (Reggie Cleveland, Luis Melendez)	.70	.35	.20
217	Ed Stroud	.70	.35	.20
218	Tony Cloninger	.80	.40	.25
219	Elrod Hendricks	.70	.35	.20
220	Ron Santo	1.75	.90	.50
221	Dave Morehead	.70	.35	.20
222	Bob Watson	.80	.40	.25
223	Cecil Upshaw	.70	.35	.20
224	Alan Gallagher	.70	.35	.20
225	Gary Peters	.80	.40	.25
226	Bill Russell	2.00	1.00	.60
227	Floyd Weaver	.70	.35	.20
228	Wayne Garrett	.70	.35	.20
229	Jim Hannan	.70	.35	.20
230	Willie Stargell	8.00	4.00	2.50
231	Indians Rookies (Vince Colbert, *John Lowenstein*)	.80	.40	.25
232	John Strohmayer	.70	.35	.20
233	Larry Bowa	2.25	1.25	.70
234	Jim Lyttle	.80	.40	.25
235	Nate Colbert	.70	.35	.20
236	Bob Humphreys	.70	.35	.20
237	*Cesar Cedeno*	1.50	.70	.45
238	Chuck Dobson	.70	.35	.20
239	Red Schoendienst	2.00	1.00	.60
240	Clyde Wright	.70	.35	.20
241	Dave Nelson	.70	.35	.20
242	Jim Ray	.70	.35	.20
243	Carlos May	.80	.40	.25
244	Bob Tillman	.70	.35	.20
245	Jim Kaat	3.25	1.75	1.00
246	Tony Taylor	.70	.35	.20
247	Royals Rookies (Jerry Cram, *Paul Splittorff*)	.70	.35	.20
248	Hoyt Wilhelm	3.75	2.00	1.25
249	Chico Salmon	.70	.35	.20
250	Johnny Bench	40.00	20.00	12.00
251	Frank Reberger	.70	.35	.20
252	Eddie Leon	.70	.35	.20
253	Bill Sudakis	.70	.35	.20
254	Cal Koonce	.70	.35	.20
255	Bob Robertson	.70	.35	.20
256	Tony Gonzalez	.70	.35	.20
257	Nelson Briles	.70	.35	.20
258	Dick Green	.70	.35	.20
259	Dave Marshall	.70	.35	.20
260	Tommy Harper	.80	.40	.25
261	Darold Knowles	.70	.35	.20
262	Padres Rookies (Dave Robinson, Jim Williams)	.70	.35	.20
263	John Ellis	.80	.40	.25
264	Joe Morgan	10.00	5.00	3.00
265	Jim Northrup	.80	.40	.25
266	Bill Stoneman	.70	.35	.20
267	Rich Morales	.70	.35	.20
268	Phillies Team	1.25	.60	.40
269	Gail Hopkins	.70	.35	.20
270	Rico Carty	.70	.35	.20
271	Bill Zepp	.70	.35	.20
272	Tommy Helms	.80	.40	.25

		NR MT	EX	VG
273	Pete Richert	.70	.35	.20
274	Ron Slocum	.70	.35	.20
275	Vada Pinson	1.25	.60	.40
276	Giants Rookies (Mike Davison, *George Foster*)	6.00	3.00	1.75
277	Gary Waslewski	.80	.40	.25
278	Jerry Grote	.80	.40	.25
279	Lefty Phillips	.70	.35	.20
280	Fergie Jenkins	10.00	5.00	3.00
281	Danny Walton	.70	.35	.20
282	Jose Pagan	.70	.35	.20
283	Dick Such	.70	.35	.20
284	Jim Gosger	.70	.35	.20
285	Sal Bando	2.00	1.00	.60
286	Jerry McNertney	.70	.35	.20
287	Mike Fiore	.70	.35	.20
288	Joe Moeller	.70	.35	.20
289	White Sox Team	1.25	.60	.40
290	Tony Oliva	1.50	.70	.45
291	George Culver	.70	.35	.20
292	Jay Johnstone	2.00	1.00	.60
293	Pat Corrales	.80	.40	.25
294	Steve Dunning	.70	.35	.20
295	Bobby Bonds	1.25	.60	.40
296	Tom Timmermann	.70	.35	.20
297	Johnny Briggs	.70	.35	.20
298	Jim Nelson	.70	.35	.20
299	Ed Kirkpatrick	.70	.35	.20
300	Brooks Robinson	12.00	6.00	3.50
301	Earl Wilson	.70	.35	.20
302	Phil Gagliano	.70	.35	.20
303	Lindy McDaniel	.80	.40	.25
304	Ron Brand	.70	.35	.20
305	Reggie Smith	2.00	1.00	.60
306	Jim Nash	.70	.35	.20
307	Don Wert	.70	.35	.20
308	Cards Team	1.25	.60	.40
309	Dick Ellsworth	.70	.35	.20
310	Tommie Agee	.80	.40	.25
311	Lee Stange	.70	.35	.20
312	Harry Walker	.80	.40	.25
313	Tom Hall	.70	.35	.20
314	Jeff Torborg	.80	.40	.25
315	Ron Fairly	.80	.40	.25
316	Fred Scherman	.70	.35	.20
317	Athletics Rookies (Jim Driscoll, Angel Mangual)	.70	.35	.20
318	Rudy May	.80	.40	.25
319	Ty Cline	.70	.35	.20
320	Dave McNally	.80	.40	.25
321	Tom Matchick	.70	.35	.20
322	Jim Beauchamp	.70	.35	.20
323	Billy Champion	.70	.35	.20
324	Graig Nettles	3.25	1.75	1.00
325	Juan Marichal	5.00	2.50	1.50
326	Richie Scheinblum	.70	.35	.20
327	World Series Game 1 (Powell Homers To Opposite Field!)	1.25	.60	.40
328	World Series Game 2 (Buford Goes 2-For 4!)	1.25	.60	.40
329	World Series Game 3 (F. Robinson Shows Muscle!)	2.00	1.00	.60
330	World Series Game 4 (Reds Stay Alive!)	1.25	.60	.40
331	World Series Game 5 (B. Robinson Commits Robbery!)	2.00	1.00	.60
332	World Series Summary (Clinching Performance!)	1.25	.60	.40
333	Clay Kirby	.70	.35	.20
334	Roberto Pena	.70	.35	.20
335	Jerry Koosman	2.00	1.00	.60
336	Tigers Team	2.25	1.25	.70
337	Jesus Alou	.80	.40	.25
338	Gene Tenace	.80	.40	.25
339	Wayne Simpson	.70	.35	.20
340	Rico Petrocelli	.80	.40	.25
341	*Steve Garvey*	80.00	40.00	25.00
342	Frank Tepedino	.80	.40	.25
343	Pirates Rookies (Ed Acosta, *Milt May*)	.80	.40	.25
344	Ellie Rodriguez	.70	.35	.20
345	Joe Horlen	.70	.35	.20
346	Lum Harris	.70	.35	.20
347	Ted Uhlaender	.70	.35	.20
348	Fred Norman	.70	.35	.20
349	Rich Reese	.70	.35	.20
350	Billy Williams	4.50	2.25	1.25
351	Jim Shellenback	.70	.35	.20
352	Denny Doyle	.70	.35	.20
353	Carl Taylor	.70	.35	.20
354	Don McMahon	.70	.35	.20

		NR MT	EX	VG
355	Bud Harrelson	.80	.40	.25
356	Bob Locker	.70	.35	.20
357	Reds Team	1.25	.60	.40
358	Danny Cater	.80	.40	.25
359	Ron Reed	.80	.40	.25
360	Jim Fregosi	1.75	.90	.50
361	Don Sutton	3.50	1.75	1.00
362	Orioles Rookies (Mike Adamson, Roger Freed)	.70	.35	.20
363	Mike Nagy	.70	.35	.20
364	Tommy Dean	.70	.35	.20
365	Bob Johnson	.70	.35	.20
366	Ron Stone	.70	.35	.20
367	Dalton Jones	.70	.35	.20
368	Bob Veale	.80	.40	.25
369a	Checklist 394-523 (orange helmet)	3.25	1.75	1.00
369b	Checklist 394-523 (red helmet, black line above ear)	3.25	1.75	1.00
369c	Checklist 394-523 (red helmet, no line)	3.25	1.75	1.00
370	Joe Torre	3.00	1.50	.90
371	Jack Hiatt	.70	.35	.20
372	Lew Krausse	.70	.35	.20
373	Tom McCraw	.70	.35	.20
374	Clete Boyer	.80	.40	.25
375	Steve Hargan	.70	.35	.20
376	Expos Rookies (Clyde Mashore, Ernie McAnally)	.70	.35	.20
377	Greg Garrett	.70	.35	.20
378	Tito Fuentes	.70	.35	.20
379	Wayne Granger	.70	.35	.20
380	Ted Williams	5.00	2.50	1.50
381	Fred Gladding	.70	.35	.20
382	Jake Gibbs	.80	.40	.25
383	Rod Gaspar	.70	.35	.20
384	Rollie Fingers	4.00	2.00	1.25
385	Maury Wills	1.25	.60	.40
386	Red Sox Team	1.50	.70	.45
387	Ron Herbel	.70	.35	.20
388	Al Oliver	2.25	1.25	.70
389	Ed Brinkman	.80	.40	.25
390	Glenn Beckert	.80	.40	.25
391	Twins Rookies (Steve Brye, Cotton Nash)	.70	.35	.20
392	Grant Jackson	.70	.35	.20
393	Merv Rettenmund	.80	.40	.25
394	Clay Carroll	.80	.40	.25
395	Roy White	.70	.35	.20
396	Dick Schofield	.70	.35	.20
397	Alvin Dark	.80	.40	.25
398	Howie Reed	.70	.35	.20
399	Jim French	.70	.35	.20
400	Hank Aaron	40.00	20.00	12.00
401	Tom Murphy	.70	.35	.20
402	Dodgers Team	1.50	.70	.45
403	Joe Coleman	.80	.40	.25
404	Astros Rookies (Buddy Harris, Roger Metzger)	.70	.35	.20
405	Leo Cardenas	.70	.35	.20
406	Ray Sadecki	.70	.35	.20
407	Joe Rudi	2.00	1.00	.60
408	Rafael Robles	.70	.35	.20
409	Don Pavletich	.70	.35	.20
410	Ken Holtzman	.80	.40	.25
411	George Spriggs	.70	.35	.20
412	Jerry Johnson	.70	.35	.20
413	Pat Kelly	.70	.35	.20
414	Woodie Fryman	.80	.40	.25
415	Mike Hegan	.70	.35	.20
416	Gene Alley	.80	.40	.25
417	Dick Hall	.70	.35	.20
418	Adolfo Phillips	.70	.35	.20
419	Ron Hansen	.80	.40	.25
420	Jim Merritt	.70	.35	.20
421	John Stephenson	.70	.35	.20
422	Frank Bertaina	.70	.35	.20
423	Tigers Rookies (Tim Marting, Dennis Saunders)	.70	.35	.20
424	Roberto Rodriquez (Rodriguez)	.70	.35	.20
425	Doug Rader	.70	.35	.20
426	Chris Cannizzaro	.70	.35	.20
427	Bernie Allen	.70	.35	.20
428	Jim McAndrew	.70	.35	.20
429	Chuck Hinton	.70	.35	.20
430	Wes Parker	.80	.40	.25
431	Tom Burgmeier	.70	.35	.20
432	Bob Didier	.70	.35	.20
433	Skip Lockwood	.70	.35	.20
434	Gary Sutherland	.70	.35	.20
435	Jose Cardenal	.80	.40	.25
436	Wilbur Wood	.80	.40	.25
437	Danny Murtaugh	.80	.40	.25
438	Mike McCormick	.80	.40	.25
439	Phillies Rookies (*Greg Luzinski*, Scott Reid)	2.00	1.00	.60
440	Bert Campaneris	.70	.35	.20
441	Milt Pappas	.80	.40	.25
442	Angels Team	1.25	.60	.40
443	Rich Robertson	.70	.35	.20
444	Jimmie Price	.70	.35	.20
445	Art Shamsky	.70	.35	.20
446	Bobby Bolin	.70	.35	.20
447	*Cesar Geronimo*	2.00	1.00	.60
448	Dave Roberts	.70	.35	.20
449	Brant Alyea	.70	.35	.20
450	Bob Gibson	10.00	5.00	3.00
451	Joe Keough	.70	.35	.20
452	John Boccabella	.70	.35	.20
453	Terry Crowley	.70	.35	.20
454	Mike Paul	.70	.35	.20
455	Don Kessinger	.80	.40	.25
456	Bob Meyer	.70	.35	.20
457	Willie Smith	.70	.35	.20
458	White Sox Rookies (Dave Lemonds, Ron Lolich)	.70	.35	.20
459	Jim Lefebvre	.80	.40	.25
460	Fritz Peterson	.80	.40	.25
461	Jim Hart	.80	.40	.25
462	Senators Team	1.50	.70	.45
463	Tom Kelley	.70	.35	.20
464	Aurelio Rodriguez	.80	.40	.25
465	Tim McCarver	1.75	.90	.50
466	Ken Berry	.70	.35	.20
467	Al Santorini	.70	.35	.20
468	Frank Fernandez	.70	.35	.20
469	Bob Aspromonte	.70	.35	.20
470	Bob Oliver	.70	.35	.20
471	Tom Griffin	.70	.35	.20
472	Ken Rudolph	.70	.35	.20
473	Gary Wagner	.70	.35	.20
474	Jim Fairey	.70	.35	.20
475	Ron Perranoski	.80	.40	.25
476	Dal Maxvill	.80	.40	.25
477	Earl Weaver	2.00	1.00	.60
478	Bernie Carbo	.80	.40	.25
479	Dennis Higgins	.70	.35	.20
480	Manny Sanguillen	.80	.40	.25
481	Daryl Patterson	.70	.35	.20
482	Padres Team	1.25	.60	.40
483	Gene Michael	.80	.40	.25
484	Don Wilson	.70	.35	.20
485	Ken McMullen	.70	.35	.20
486	Steve Huntz	.70	.35	.20
487	Paul Schaal	.70	.35	.20
488	Jerry Stephenson	.70	.35	.20
489	Luis Alvarado	.70	.35	.20
490	Deron Johnson	.70	.35	.20
491	Jim Hardin	.70	.35	.20
492	Ken Boswell	.70	.35	.20
493	Dave May	.70	.35	.20
494	Braves Rookies (Ralph Garr, Rick Kester)	.80	.40	.25
495	Felipe Alou	2.00	1.00	.60
496	Woody Woodward	.80	.40	.25
497	Horacio Pina	.70	.35	.20
498	John Kennedy	.70	.35	.20
499	Checklist 524-643	3.25	1.75	1.00
500	Jim Perry	2.00	1.00	.60
501	Andy Etchebarren	.70	.35	.20
502	Cubs Team	1.25	.60	.40
503	Gates Brown	.70	.35	.20
504	Ken Wright	.70	.35	.20
505	Ollie Brown	.70	.35	.20
506	Bobby Knoop	.70	.35	.20
507	George Stone	.70	.35	.20
508	Roger Repoz	.70	.35	.20
509	Jim Grant	.70	.35	.20
510	Ken Harrelson	1.25	.60	.40
511	Chris Short	.80	.40	.25
512	Red Sox Rookies (Mike Garman, Dick Mills)	.70	.35	.20
513	Nolan Ryan	175.00	87.00	52.00
514	Ron Woods	.80	.40	.25
515	Carl Morton	.70	.35	.20
516	Ted Kubiak	.70	.35	.20
517	Charlie Fox	.70	.35	.20
518	Joe Grzenda	.70	.35	.20
519	Willie Crawford	.70	.35	.20
520	Tommy John	3.00	1.50	.90
521	Leron Lee	.70	.35	.20
522	Twins Team	1.25	.60	.40

		NR MT	EX	VG
523	John Odom	.80	.40	.25
524	Mickey Stanley	2.00	1.00	.60
525	Ernie Banks	30.00	15.00	9.00
526	Ray Jarvis	1.75	.90	.50
527	Cleon Jones	2.00	1.00	.60
528	Wally Bunker	1.75	.90	.50
529	N.L. Rookies (Bill Buckner, Enzo Hernandez, Marty Perez)	4.00	2.00	1.25
530	Carl Yastrzemski	40.00	20.00	12.00
531	Mike Torrez	2.00	1.00	.60
532	Bill Rigney	1.75	.90	.50
533	Mike Ryan	1.75	.90	.50
534	Luke Walker	1.75	.90	.50
535	Curt Flood	2.25	1.25	.70
536	Claude Raymond	1.75	.90	.50
537	Tom Egan	1.75	.90	.50
538	Angel Bravo	1.75	.90	.50
539	Larry Brown	1.75	.90	.50
540	Larry Dierker	2.00	1.00	.60
541	Bob Burda	1.75	.90	.50
542	Bob Miller	1.75	.90	.50
543	Yankees Team	3.50	1.75	1.00
544	Vida Blue	3.25	1.75	1.00
545	Dick Dietz	1.75	.90	.50
546	John Matias	1.75	.90	.50
547	Pat Dobson	2.00	1.00	.60
548	Don Mason	1.75	.90	.50
549	Jim Brewer	1.75	.90	.50
550	Harmon Killebrew	15.00	7.50	4.50
551	Frank Linzy	1.75	.90	.50
552	Buddy Bradford	1.75	.90	.50
553	Kevin Collins	1.75	.90	.50
554	Lowell Palmer	1.75	.90	.50
555	Walt Williams	1.75	.90	.50
556	Jim McGlothlin	1.75	.90	.50
557	Tom Satriano	1.75	.90	.50
558	Hector Torres	1.75	.90	.50
559	A.L. Rookies (Terry Cox, Bill Gogolewski, Gary Jones)	2.00	1.00	.60
560	Rusty Staub	3.00	1.50	.90
561	Syd O'Brien	1.75	.90	.50
562	Dave Giusti	1.75	.90	.50
563	Giants Team	2.00	1.00	.60
564	Al Fitzmorris	1.75	.90	.50
565	Jim Wynn	2.00	1.00	.60
566	Tim Cullen	1.75	.90	.50
567	Walt Alston	3.25	1.75	1.00
568	Sal Campisi	1.75	.90	.50
569	Ivan Murrell	1.75	.90	.50
570	Jim Palmer	30.00	15.00	9.00
571	Ted Sizemore	1.75	.90	.50
572	Jerry Kenney	2.00	1.00	.60
573	Ed Kranepool	2.00	1.00	.60
574	Jim Bunning	4.00	2.00	1.25
575	Bill Freehan	2.00	1.00	.60
576	Cubs Rookies (Brock Davis, Adrian Garrett, Garry Jestadt)	1.75	.90	.50
577	Jim Lonborg	2.00	1.00	.60
578	Ron Hunt	2.00	1.00	.60
579	Marty Pattin	1.75	.90	.50
580	Tony Perez	6.00	3.00	1.75
581	Roger Nelson	1.75	.90	.50
582	Dave Cash	1.75	.90	.50
583	Ron Cook	1.75	.90	.50
584	Indians Team	2.00	1.00	.60
585	Willie Davis	3.00	1.50	.90
586	Dick Woodson	1.75	.90	.50
587	Sonny Jackson	1.75	.90	.50
588	Tom Bradley	1.75	.90	.50
589	Bob Barton	1.75	.90	.50
590	Alex Johnson	1.75	.90	.50
591	Jackie Brown	1.75	.90	.50
592	Randy Hundley	1.75	.90	.50
593	Jack Aker	2.00	1.00	.60
594	Cards Rookies (Bob Chlupsa, *Al Hrabosky*, Bob Stinson)	3.00	1.50	.90
595	Dave Johnson	2.25	1.25	.70
596	Mike Jorgensen	1.75	.90	.50
597	Ken Suarez	1.75	.90	.50
598	Rick Wise	2.00	1.00	.60
599	Norm Cash	2.00	1.00	.60
600	Willie Mays	70.00	35.00	21.00
601	Ken Tatum	1.75	.90	.50
602	Marty Martinez	1.75	.90	.50
603	Pirates Team	3.00	1.50	.90
604	John Gelnar	1.75	.90	.50
605	Orlando Cepeda	3.25	1.75	1.00
606	Chuck Taylor	1.75	.90	.50
607	Paul Ratliff	1.75	.90	.50
608	Mike Wegener	1.75	.90	.50
609	Leo Durocher	3.00	1.50	.90

		NR MT	EX	VG
610	Amos Otis	2.00	1.00	.60
611	Tom Phoebus	1.75	.90	.50
612	Indians Rookies (Lou Camilli, Ted Ford, Steve Mingori)	1.75	.90	.50
613	Pedro Borbon	2.00	1.00	.60
614	Billy Cowan	1.75	.90	.50
615	Mel Stottlemyre	2.25	1.25	.70
616	Larry Hisle	2.00	1.00	.60
617	Clay Dalrymple	1.75	.90	.50
618	Tug McGraw	3.00	1.50	.90
619a	Checklist 644-752 (no copyright on back)	4.50	2.25	1.25
619b	Checklist 644-752 (with copyright, no wavy line on helmet brim)	3.00	1.50	.90
619c	Checklist 644-752 (with copyright, wavy line on helmet brim)	3.00	1.50	.90
620	Frank Howard	3.00	1.50	.90
621	Ron Bryant	1.75	.90	.50
622	Joe Lahoud	1.75	.90	.50
623	Pat Jarvis	1.75	.90	.50
624	Athletics Team	2.00	1.00	.60
625	Lou Brock	20.00	10.00	6.00
626	Freddie Patek	2.00	1.00	.60
627	Steve Hamilton	1.75	.90	.50
628	John Bateman	1.75	.90	.50
629	John Hiller	2.00	1.00	.60
630	Roberto Clemente	50.00	25.00	15.00
631	Eddie Fisher	1.75	.90	.50
632	Darrel Chaney	1.75	.90	.50
633	A.L. Rookies (Bobby Brooks, Pete Koegel, Scott Northey)	1.75	.90	.50
634	Phil Regan	1.75	.90	.50
635	Bobby Murcer	2.00	1.00	.60
636	Denny Lemaster	1.75	.90	.50
637	Dave Bristol	1.75	.90	.50
638	Stan Williams	1.75	.90	.50
639	Tom Haller	2.00	1.00	.60
640	Frank Robinson	35.00	17.50	10.50
641	Mets Team	6.00	3.00	1.75
642	Jim Roland	1.75	.90	.50
643	Rick Reichardt	1.75	.90	.50
644	Jim Stewart	3.00	1.50	.90
645	Jim Maloney	3.25	1.75	1.00
646	Bobby Floyd	3.00	1.50	.90
647	Juan Pizarro	3.00	1.50	.90
648	Mets Rookies (Rich Folkers, Ted Martinez, *Jon Matlack*)	3.50	1.75	1.00
649	Sparky Lyle	3.00	1.50	.90
650	Rich Allen	9.00	4.50	2.75
651	Jerry Robertson	3.00	1.50	.90
652	Braves Team	3.25	1.75	1.00
653	Russ Snyder	3.00	1.50	.90
654	Don Shaw	3.00	1.50	.90
655	Mike Epstein	3.25	1.75	1.00
656	Gerry Nyman	3.00	1.50	.90
657	Jose Azcue	3.00	1.50	.90
658	Paul Lindblad	3.00	1.50	.90
659	Byron Browne	3.00	1.50	.90
660	Ray Culp	3.00	1.50	.90
661	Chuck Tanner	3.00	1.50	.90
662	Mike Hedlund	3.00	1.50	.90
663	Marv Staehle	3.00	1.50	.90
664	Major League Rookies (Archie Reynolds, Bob Reynolds, Ken Reynolds)	3.00	1.50	.90
665	Ron Swoboda	3.00	1.50	.90
666	Gene Brabender	3.00	1.50	.90
667	Pete Ward	3.25	1.75	1.00
668	Gary Neibauer	3.00	1.50	.90
669	Ike Brown	3.00	1.50	.90
670	Bill Hands	3.00	1.50	.90
671	Bill Voss	3.00	1.50	.90
672	Ed Crosby	3.00	1.50	.90
673	Gerry Janeski	3.00	1.50	.90
674	Expos Team	3.25	1.75	1.00
675	Dave Boswell	3.00	1.50	.90
676	Tommie Reynolds	3.00	1.50	.90
677	Jack DiLauro	3.00	1.50	.90
678	George Thomas	3.00	1.50	.90
679	Don O'Riley	3.00	1.50	.90
680	Don Mincher	3.25	1.75	1.00
681	Bill Butler	3.00	1.50	.90
682	Terry Harmon	3.00	1.50	.90
683	Bill Burbach	3.25	1.75	1.00
684	Curt Motton	3.00	1.50	.90
685	Moe Drabowsky	3.00	1.50	.90
686	Chico Ruiz	3.00	1.50	.90
687	Ron Taylor	3.00	1.50	.90
688	Sparky Anderson	3.50	1.75	1.00
689	Frank Baker	3.00	1.50	.90
690	Bob Moose	3.00	1.50	.90
691	Bob Heise	3.00	1.50	.90

		NR MT	EX	VG
692	A.L. Rookies (Hal Haydel, Rogelio Moret, Wayne Twitchell)	3.00	1.50	.90
693	Jose Pena	3.00	1.50	.90
694	Rick Renick	3.00	1.50	.90
695	Joe Niekro	3.25	1.75	1.00
696	Jerry Morales	3.00	1.50	.90
697	Rickey Clark	3.00	1.50	.90
698	Brewers Team	3.50	1.75	1.00
699	Jim Britton	3.00	1.50	.90
700	Boog Powell	4.00	2.00	1.25
701	Bob Garibaldi	3.00	1.50	.90
702	Milt Ramirez	3.00	1.50	.90
703	Mike Kekich	3.25	1.75	1.00
704	J.C. Martin	3.00	1.50	.90
705	Dick Selma	3.00	1.50	.90
706	Joe Foy	3.00	1.50	.90
707	Fred Lasher	3.00	1.50	.90
708	Russ Nagelson	3.00	1.50	.90
709	Major League Rookies *(Dusty Baker, Don Baylor, Tom Paciorek)*	40.00	20.00	12.00
710	Sonny Siebert	3.00	1.50	.90
711	Larry Stahl	3.00	1.50	.90
712	Jose Martinez	3.00	1.50	.90
713	Mike Marshall	3.50	1.75	1.00
714	Dick Williams	3.50	1.75	1.00
715	Horace Clarke	3.25	1.75	1.00
716	Dave Leonhard	3.00	1.50	.90
717	Tommie Aaron	3.25	1.75	1.00
718	Billy Wynne	3.00	1.50	.90
719	Jerry May	3.00	1.50	.90
720	Matty Alou	3.50	1.75	1.00
721	John Morris	3.00	1.50	.90
722	Astros Team	3.25	1.75	1.00
723	Vicente Romo	3.00	1.50	.90
724	Tom Tischinski	3.00	1.50	.90
725	Gary Gentry	3.00	1.50	.90
726	Paul Popovich	3.00	1.50	.90
727	Ray Lamb	3.00	1.50	.90
728	N.L. Rookies (Keith Lampard, Wayne Redmond, Bernie Williams)	3.00	1.50	.90
729	Dick Billings	3.00	1.50	.90
730	Jim Rooker	3.00	1.50	.90
731	Jim Qualls	3.00	1.50	.90
732	Bob Reed	3.00	1.50	.90
733	Lee Maye	3.00	1.50	.90
734	Rob Gardner	3.25	1.75	1.00
735	Mike Shannon	3.25	1.75	1.00
736	Mel Queen	3.00	1.50	.90
737	Preston Gomez	3.00	1.50	.90
738	Russ Gibson	3.00	1.50	.90
739	Barry Lersch	3.00	1.50	.90
740	Luis Aparicio	15.00	7.50	4.50
741	Skip Guinn	3.00	1.50	.90
742	Royals Team	3.25	1.75	1.00
743	John O'Donoghue	3.00	1.50	.90
744	Chuck Manuel	3.00	1.50	.90
745	Sandy Alomar	3.00	1.50	.90
746	Andy Kosco	3.00	1.50	.90
747	N.L. Rookies (Balor Moore, Al Severinsen, Scipio Spinks)	3.00	1.50	.90
748	John Purdin	3.00	1.50	.90
749	Ken Szotkiewicz	3.00	1.50	.90
750	Denny McLain	6.00	3.00	1.75
751	Al Weis	3.25	1.75	1.00
752	Dick Drago	3.75	1.25	.70

1971 Topps Coins

Measuring 1-1/2" in diameter, the latest edition of the Topps coins was a 153-piece set. The coins feature a color photograph surrounded by a colored band on the front. The band carries the player's name, team, position and several stars. Backs have a short biography, the coin number and encouragement to collect the entire set. Back colors differ, with #'s 1-51 having a brass back, #'s 52-102 chrome backs, and the rest have blue backs. Most of the stars of the period are included in the set.

		NR MT	EX	VG
Complete Set:		400.00	200.00	120.00
Common Player:		.90	.45	.25
1	Clarence Gaston	.90	.45	.25
2	Dave Johnson	1.25	.60	.40
3	Jim Bunning	2.00	1.00	.60
4	Jim Spencer	.90	.45	.25
5	Felix Millan	.90	.45	.25
6	Gerry Moses	.90	.45	.25
7	Fergie Jenkins	2.00	1.00	.60
8	Felipe Alou	1.00	.50	.30
9	Jim McGlothlin	.90	.45	.25
10	Dick McAuliffe	.90	.45	.25
11	Joe Torre	1.50	.70	.45
12	Jim Perry	1.25	.60	.40
13	Bobby Bonds	1.25	.60	.40
14	Danny Cater	.90	.45	.25
15	Bill Mazeroski	1.50	.70	.45
16	Luis Aparicio	5.00	2.50	1.50
17	Doug Rader	.90	.45	.25
18	Vada Pinson	1.50	.70	.45
19	John Bateman	.90	.45	.25
20	Lew Krausse	.90	.45	.25
21	Billy Grabarkewitz	.90	.45	.25
22	Frank Howard	1.50	.70	.45
23	Jerry Koosman	1.25	.60	.40
24	Rod Carew	8.00	4.00	2.50
25	Al Ferrara	.90	.45	.25
26	Dave McNally	1.00	.50	.30
27	Jim Hickman	.90	.45	.25
28	Sandy Alomar	.90	.45	.25
29	Lee May	1.00	.50	.30
30	Rico Petrocelli	1.00	.50	.30
31	Don Money	.90	.45	.25
32	Jim Rooker	.90	.45	.25
33	Dick Dietz	.90	.45	.25
34	Roy White	1.00	.50	.30
35	Carl Morton	.90	.45	.25
36	Walt Williams	.90	.45	.25
37	Phil Niekro	3.25	1.75	1.00
38	Bill Freehan	1.00	.50	.30
39	Julian Javier	.90	.45	.25
40	Rick Monday	1.00	.50	.30
41	Don Wilson	.90	.45	.25
42	Ray Fosse	.90	.45	.25
43	Art Shamsky	.90	.45	.25
44	Ted Savage	.90	.45	.25
45	Claude Osteen	1.00	.50	.30
46	Ed Brinkman	.90	.45	.25
47	Matty Alou	1.00	.50	.30
48	Bob Oliver	.90	.45	.25
49	Danny Coombs	.90	.45	.25
50	Frank Robinson	7.00	3.50	2.00
51	Randy Hundley	.90	.45	.25
52	Cesar Tovar	.90	.45	.25
53	Wayne Simpson	.90	.45	.25
54	Bobby Murcer	1.25	.60	.40
55	Tony Taylor	.90	.45	.25
56	Tommy John	2.50	1.25	.70
57	Willie McCovey	7.00	3.50	2.00
58	Carl Yastrzemski	15.00	7.50	4.50
59	Bob Bailey	.90	.45	.25
60	Clyde Wright	.90	.45	.25
61	Orlando Cepeda	2.00	1.00	.60
62	Al Kaline	7.00	3.50	2.00
63	Bob Gibson	7.00	3.50	2.00
64	Bert Campaneris	1.25	.60	.40
65	Ted Sizemore	.90	.45	.25
66	Duke Sims	.90	.45	.25
67	Bud Harrelson	.90	.45	.25
68	Jerry McNertney	.90	.45	.25
69	Jim Wynn	1.00	.50	.30
70	Dick Bosman	.90	.45	.25
71	Roberto Clemente	15.00	7.50	4.50
72	Rich Reese	.90	.45	.25
73	Gaylord Perry	4.00	2.00	1.25
74	Boog Powell	1.50	.70	.45
75	Billy Williams	5.00	2.50	1.50
76	Bill Melton	.90	.45	.25
77	Nate Colbert	.90	.45	.25

		NR MT	EX	VG
49	Danny Coombs	.90	.45	.25
50	Frank Robinson	7.00	3.50	2.00
51	Randy Hundley	.90	.45	.25
52	Cesar Tovar	.90	.45	.25
53	Wayne Simpson	.90	.45	.25
54	Bobby Murcer	1.25	.60	.40
55	Tony Taylor	.90	.45	.25
56	Tommy John	2.50	1.25	.70
57	Willie McCovey	7.00	3.50	2.00
58	Carl Yastrzemski	15.00	7.50	4.50
59	Bob Bailey	.90	.45	.25
60	Clyde Wright	.90	.45	.25
61	Orlando Cepeda	2.00	1.00	.60
62	Al Kaline	7.00	3.50	2.00
63	Bob Gibson	7.00	3.50	2.00
64	Bert Campaneris	1.25	.60	.40
65	Ted Sizemore	.90	.45	.25
66	Duke Sims	.90	.45	.25
67	Bud Harrelson	.90	.45	.25
68	Jerry McNertney	.90	.45	.25
69	Jim Wynn	1.00	.50	.30
70	Dick Bosman	.90	.45	.25
71	Roberto Clemente	15.00	7.50	4.50
72	Rich Reese	.90	.45	.25
73	Gaylord Perry	4.00	2.00	1.25
74	Boog Powell	1.50	.70	.45
75	Billy Williams	5.00	2.50	1.50
76	Bill Melton	.90	.45	.25
77	Nate Colbert	.90	.45	.25
78	Reggie Smith	1.25	.60	.40
79	Deron Johnson	.90	.45	.25
80	Jim Hunter	5.00	2.50	1.50
81	Bob Tolan	.90	.45	.25
82	Jim Northrup	.90	.45	.25
83	Ron Fairly	1.00	.50	.30
84	Alex Johnson	.90	.45	.25
85	Pat Jarvis	.90	.45	.25
86	Sam McDowell	1.00	.50	.30
87	Lou Brock	7.00	3.50	2.00
88	Danny Walton	.90	.45	.25
89	Denis Menke	.90	.45	.25
90	Jim Palmer	7.00	3.50	2.00
91	Tommie Agee	.90	.45	.25
92	Duane Josephson	.90	.45	.25
93	Willie Davis	1.00	.50	.30
94	Mel Stottlemyre	1.00	.50	.30
95	Ron Santo	1.25	.60	.40
96	Amos Otis	1.00	.50	.30
97	Ken Henderson	.90	.45	.25
98	George Scott	1.00	.50	.30
99	Dock Ellis	.90	.45	.25
100	Harmon Killebrew	7.00	3.50	2.00
101	Pete Rose	30.00	15.00	9.00
102	Rick Reichardt	.90	.45	.25
103	Cleon Jones	.90	.45	.25
104	Ron Perranoski	.90	.45	.25
105	Tony Perez	2.50	1.25	.70
106	Mickey Lolich	1.25	.60	.40
107	Tim McCarver	1.25	.60	.40
108	Reggie Jackson	12.00	6.00	3.50
109	Chris Cannizzaro	.90	.45	.25
110	Steve Hargan	.90	.45	.25
111	Rusty Staub	2.50	1.25	.70
112	Andy Messersmith	1.00	.50	.30
113	Rico Carty	1.25	.60	.40
114	Brooks Robinson	7.00	3.50	2.00
115	Steve Carlton	7.00	3.50	2.00
116	Mike Hegan	.90	.45	.25
117	Joe Morgan	4.50	2.25	1.25
118	Thurman Munson	5.00	2.50	1.50
119	Don Kessinger	1.00	.50	.30
120	Joe Horlen	.90	.45	.25
121	Wes Parker	1.00	.50	.30
122	Sonny Siebert	.90	.45	.25
123	Willie Stargell	5.00	2.50	1.50
124	Ellie Rodriguez	.90	.45	.25
125	Juan Marichal	5.00	2.50	1.50
126	Mike Epstein	.90	.45	.25
127	Tom Seaver	8.00	4.00	2.50
128	Tony Oliva	2.50	1.25	.70
129	Jim Merritt	.90	.45	.25
130	Willie Horton	1.00	.50	.30
131	Rick Wise	.90	.45	.25
132	Sal Bando	1.00	.50	.30
133	Ollie Brown	.90	.45	.25
134	Ken Harrelson	1.00	.50	.30
135	Mack Jones	.90	.45	.25
136	Jim Fregosi	1.00	.50	.30
137	Hank Aaron	15.00	7.50	4.50
138	Fritz Peterson	.90	.45	.25
139	Joe Hague	.90	.45	.25
140	Tommy Harper	.90	.45	.25
141	Larry Dierker	.90	.45	.25
142	Tony Conigliaro	1.50	.70	.45
143	Glenn Beckert	1.00	.50	.30
144	Carlos May	.90	.45	.25
145	Don Sutton	3.25	1.75	1.00
146	Paul Casanova	.90	.45	.25
147	Bob Moose	.90	.45	.25
148	Leo Cardenas	.90	.45	.25
149	Johnny Bench	8.00	4.00	2.50
150	Mike Cuellar	1.00	.50	.30
151	Donn Clendenon	.90	.45	.25
152	Lou Piniella	1.25	.60	.40
153	Willie Mays	15.00	7.50	4.50

1971 Topps Greatest Moments

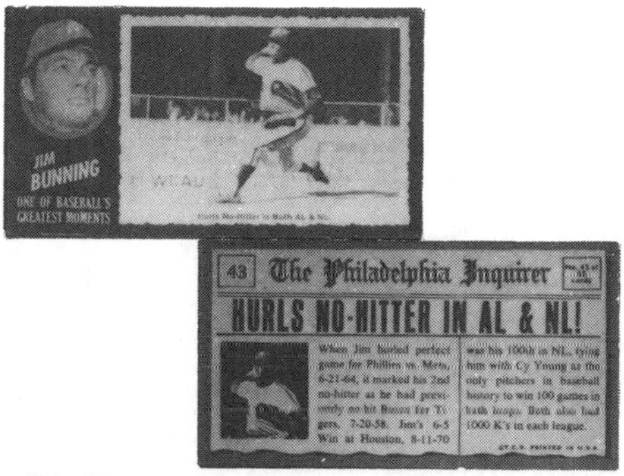

This 55-card set features a great moment from the careers of top players at the time. The front of the 2-1/2" by 4-3/4" cards features a portrait photo of the player at the left and deckle-edge action photo at the right. There is a small headline on the white border of the action photo. The player's name and "One of Baseball's Greatest Moments" along with a black border complete the front. The back features a detail from the front photo and the story of the event. The newspaper style presentation includes the name of real newspapers. Relatively scarce, virtually every card in this set is a star or at least an above-average player.

		NR MT	EX	VG
Complete Set:		1650.00	825.00	495.00
Common Player:		4.00	2.00	1.25
1	Thurman Munson	60.00	30.00	18.00
2	Hoyt Wilhelm	30.00	15.00	9.00
3	Rico Carty	15.00	7.50	4.50
4	Carl Morton	4.00	2.00	1.25
5	Sal Bando	5.00	2.50	1.50
6	Bert Campaneris	5.00	2.50	1.50
7	Jim Kaat	20.00	10.00	6.00
8	Harmon Killebrew	60.00	30.00	18.00
9	Brooks Robinson	75.00	37.00	22.00
10	Jim Perry	15.00	7.50	4.50
11	Tony Oliva	20.00	10.00	6.00
12	Vada Pinson	20.00	10.00	6.00
13	Johnny Bench	175.00	87.00	52.00
14	Tony Perez	25.00	12.50	7.50
15	Pete Rose	90.00	45.00	27.00
16	Jim Fregosi	4.00	2.00	1.25
17	Alex Johnson	4.00	2.00	1.25
18	Clyde Wright	4.00	2.00	1.25
19	Al Kaline	25.00	12.50	7.50
20	Denny McLain	20.00	10.00	6.00
21	Jim Northrup	15.00	7.50	4.50
22	Bill Freehan	15.00	7.50	4.50
23	Mickey Lolich	20.00	10.00	6.00
24	Bob Gibson	18.00	9.00	5.50
25	Tim McCarver	5.00	2.50	1.50
26	Orlando Cepeda	7.00	3.50	2.00
27	Lou Brock	18.00	9.00	5.50
28	Nate Colbert	4.00	2.00	1.25
29	Maury Wills	20.00	10.00	6.00
30	Wes Parker	15.00	7.50	4.50
31	Jim Wynn	15.00	7.50	4.50
32	Larry Dierker	15.00	7.50	4.50

		NR MT	EX	VG
33	Bill Melton	15.00	7.50	4.50
34	Joe Morgan	40.00	20.00	12.00
35	Rusty Staub	20.00	10.00	6.00
36	Ernie Banks	25.00	12.50	7.50
37	Billy Williams	50.00	25.00	15.00
38	Lou Piniella	20.00	10.00	6.00
39	Rico Petrocelli	4.00	2.00	1.25
40	Carl Yastrzemski	60.00	30.00	18.00
41	Willie Mays	45.00	22.00	13.50
42	Tommy Harper	15.00	7.50	4.50
43	Jim Bunning	7.00	3.50	2.00
44	Fritz Peterson	15.00	7.50	4.50
45	Roy White	15.00	7.50	4.50
46	Bobby Murcer	15.00	7.50	4.50
47	Reggie Jackson	250.00	125.00	75.00
48	Frank Howard	20.00	10.00	6.00
49	Dick Bosman	15.00	7.50	4.50
50	Sam McDowell	4.00	2.00	1.25
51	Luis Aparicio	12.00	6.00	3.50
52	Willie McCovey	15.00	7.50	4.50
53	Joe Pepitone	15.00	7.50	4.50
54	Jerry Grote	15.00	7.50	4.50
55	Bud Harrelson	15.00	7.50	4.50

1971 Topps Super

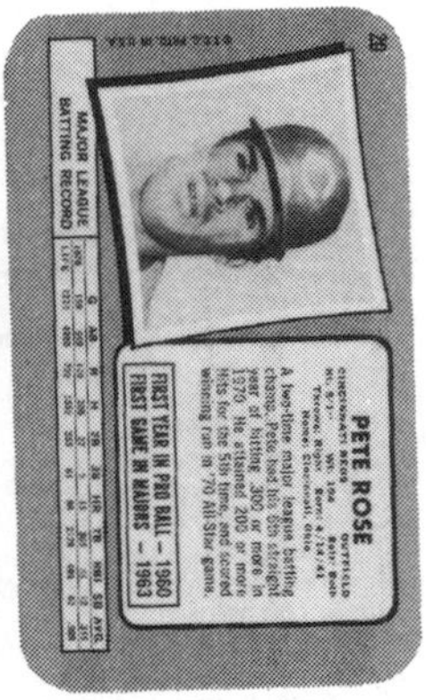

Topps continued to produce its special oversized cards in 1971. The cards, measuring 3-1/8" by 5-1/4," carry a large color photograph with a facsimile autograph on the front. Backs are basically enlargements of the player's regular Topps card. The set size was enlarged to 63 cards in 1971, so there are no short-printed cards as in 1970. Again, Topps included almost every major star who was active at the time, so the set of oversized cards with rounded corners remains an interesting source for those seeking the big names of the era.

	NR MT	EX	VG
Complete Set:	200.00	100.00	60.00
Common Player:	.80	.40	.25

		NR MT	EX	VG
1	Reggie Smith	1.00	.50	.30
2	Gaylord Perry	3.00	1.50	.90
3	Ted Savage	.80	.40	.25
4	Donn Clendenon	.80	.40	.25
5	John "Boog" Powell	1.25	.60	.40
6	Tony Perez	1.75	.90	.50
7	Dick Bosman	.80	.40	.25
8	Alex Johnson	.80	.40	.25
9	Rusty Staub	1.25	.60	.40
10	Mel Stottlemyre	1.00	.50	.30
11	Tony Oliva	1.50	.70	.45
12	Bill Freehan	1.00	.50	.30
13	Fritz Peterson	.80	.40	.25
14	Wes Parker	.80	.40	.25
15	Cesar Cedeno	1.25	.60	.40
16	Sam McDowell	1.00	.50	.30
17	Frank Howard	1.50	.70	.45
18	Dave McNally	1.00	.50	.30
19	Rico Petrocelli	.80	.40	.25
20	Pete Rose	25.00	12.50	7.50
21	Luke Walker	.80	.40	.25
22	Nate Colbert	.80	.40	.25
23	Luis Aparicio	2.50	1.25	.70
24	Jim Perry	1.00	.50	.30
25	Louis Brock	4.50	2.25	1.25
26	Roy White	1.00	.50	.30
27	Claude Osteen	.80	.40	.25
28	Carl W. Morton	.80	.40	.25
29	Ricardo A. Jacabo Carty	1.00	.50	.30
30	Larry Dierker	.80	.40	.25
31	Dagoberto Campaneris	1.00	.50	.30
32	Johnny Bench	8.00	4.00	2.50
33	Felix Millan	.80	.40	.25
34	Tim McCarver	1.25	.60	.40
35	Ronald Santo	1.25	.60	.40
36	Tommie Agee	.80	.40	.25
37	Roberto Clemente	10.00	5.00	3.00
38	Reggie Jackson	15.00	7.50	4.50
39	Clyde Wright	.80	.40	.25
40	Rich Allen	1.50	.70	.45
41	Curt Flood	1.25	.60	.40
42	Fergie Jenkins	1.75	.90	.50
43	Willie Stargell	3.00	1.50	.90
44	Henry Aaron	10.00	5.00	3.00
45	Amos Otis	1.00	.50	.30
46	Willie McCovey	4.50	2.25	1.25
47	William Melton	.80	.40	.25
48	Robert Gibson	3.50	1.75	1.00
49	Carl Yastrzemski	15.00	7.50	4.50
50	Glenn Beckert	1.00	.50	.30
51	Ray Fosse	.80	.40	.25
52	Clarence Gaston	.80	.40	.25
53	Tom Seaver	8.00	4.00	2.50
54	Al Kaline	6.00	3.00	1.75
55	Jim Northrup	.80	.40	.25
56	Willie Mays	10.00	5.00	3.00
57	Sal Bando	1.00	.50	.30
58	Deron Johnson	.80	.40	.25
59	Brooks Robinson	7.00	3.50	2.00
60	Harmon Killebrew	6.00	3.00	1.75
61	Joseph Torre	1.75	.90	.50
62	Lou Piniella	1.25	.60	.40
63	Tommy Harper	.80	.40	.25

1972 Topps

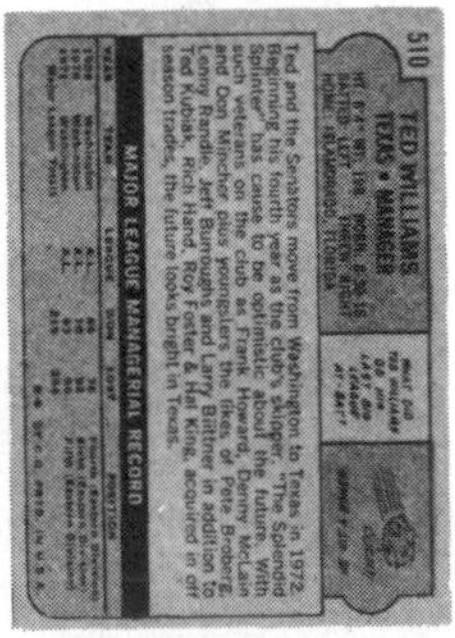

The largest Topps issue of its time appeared in 1972, with the set size reaching the 787 mark. The 2-1/2" by 3-1/2" cards are something special as well. Their fronts have a color photo which is shaped into an arch and surrounded by two different color borders, all of which is inside the overall white border. The player's name is in a white panel below the picture while the team name is above the picture in what might best be described as "superhero" type in a variety of colors. No mention of the player's position appears on the front. Cards backs are tame by comparison, featuring statistics and a trivia question. The set features a record number of specialty card including more than six dozen "In Action" (shown as "IA" in checklists below) cards featuring action shots of popular players. There are the usual statistical leaders, playoff and World Series highlights. Other innovations are 16 "Boyhood Photo" cards which depict scrapbook black and white photos of 1972's top players, and a group of cards depicting the trophies which comprise baseball's major awards. Finally, a group of seven "Traded" cards was included which feature a large "Traded" across the front of the card.

		NR MT	EX	VG
18a	Juan Pizarro (green under "C" and "S")	3.50	1.75	1.00
18b	Juan Pizarro (yellow under "C" and "S")	.40	.20	.12
19	Billy Cowan	.40	.20	.12
20	Don Wilson	.40	.20	.12
21	Braves Team	1.25	.60	.40
22	Rob Gardner	.40	.20	.12
23	Ted Kubiak	.40	.20	.12
24	Ted Ford	.40	.20	.12
25	Bill Singer	.40	.20	.12
26	Andy Etchebarren	.40	.20	.12
27	Bob Johnson	.40	.20	.12
28	Twins Rookies (Steve Brye, Bob Gebhard, Hal Haydel)	.40	.20	.12
29a	Bill Bonham (green under "C" and "S")	3.50	1.75	1.00
29b	Bill Bonham (yellow under "C" and "S")	.40	.20	.12
30	Rico Petrocelli	.70	.35	.20
31	Cleon Jones	.40	.20	.12
32	Cleon Jones IA	.40	.20	.12
33	Billy Martin	3.00	1.50	.90
34	Billy Martin IA	1.00	.50	.30
35	Jerry Johnson	.40	.20	.12
36	Jerry Johnson IA	.40	.20	.12
37	Carl Yastrzemski	18.00	9.00	5.50
38	Carl Yastrzemski IA	8.00	4.00	2.50
39	Bob Barton	.40	.20	.12
40	Bob Barton IA	.40	.20	.12
41	Tommy Davis	.80	.40	.25
42	Tommy Davis IA	.40	.20	.12
43	Rick Wise	.40	.20	.12
44	Rick Wise IA	.40	.20	.12
45a	Glenn Beckert (green under "C" and "S")	3.50	1.75	1.00
45b	Glenn Beckert (yellow under "C" and "S")	.60	.30	.20
46	Glenn Beckert IA	.40	.20	.12
47	John Ellis	.40	.20	.12
48	John Ellis IA	.40	.20	.12
49	Willie Mays	25.00	12.50	7.50
50	Willie Mays IA	10.00	5.00	3.00
51	Harmon Killebrew	5.00	2.50	1.50
52	Harmon Killebrew IA	2.00	1.00	.60
53	Bud Harrelson	.60	.30	.20
54	Bud Harrelson IA	.40	.20	.12
55	Clyde Wright	.40	.20	.12
56	Rich Chiles	.40	.20	.12
57	Bob Oliver	.40	.20	.12
58	Ernie McAnally	.40	.20	.12
59	*Fred Stanley*	.60	.30	.20
60	Manny Sanguillen	.40	.20	.12
61	Cubs Rookies (Gene Hiser, *Burt Hooton*, Earl Stephenson)	1.00	.50	.30
62	Angel Mangual	.40	.20	.12
63	Duke Sims	.40	.20	.12
64	Pete Broberg	.40	.20	.12
65	Cesar Cedeno	1.00	.50	.30
66	Ray Corbin	.40	.20	.12
67	Red Schoendienst	1.00	.50	.30
68	Jim York	.40	.20	.12
69	Roger Freed	.40	.20	.12
70	Mike Cuellar	.70	.35	.20
71	Angels Team	1.25	.60	.40
72	*Bruce Kison*	1.00	.50	.30
73	Steve Huntz	.40	.20	.12
74	Cecil Upshaw	.40	.20	.12
75	Bert Campaneris	.80	.40	.25
76	Don Carrithers	.40	.20	.12
77	Ron Theobald	.40	.20	.12
78	Steve Arlin	.40	.20	.12
79	Red Sox Rookies (*Cecil Cooper, Carlton Fisk*, Mike Garman)	150.00	75.00	45.00
80	Tony Perez	3.00	1.50	.90
81	Mike Hedlund	.40	.20	.12
82	Ron Woods	.40	.20	.12
83	Dalton Jones	.40	.20	.12
84	Vince Colbert	.40	.20	.12
85	N.L. Batting Leaders (Glenn Beckert, Ralph Garr, Joe Torre)	1.25	.60	.40
86	A.L. Batting Leaders (Bobby Murcer, Tony Oliva, Merv Rettenmund)	1.25	.60	.40
87	N.L. RBI Leaders (Hank Aaron, Willie Stargell, Joe Torre)	3.00	1.50	.90
88	A.L. RBI Leaders (Harmon Killebrew, Frank Robinson, Reggie Smith)	3.00	1.50	.90
89	N.L. Home Run Leaders (Hank Aaron, Lee May, Willie Stargell)	3.00	1.50	.90
90	A.L. Home Run Leaders (Norm Cash, Reggie Jackson, Bill Melton)	1.75	.90	.50

		NR MT	EX	VG
91	N.L. ERA Leaders (Dave Roberts, Tom Seaver, Don Wilson)	1.75	.90	.50
92	A.L. ERA Leaders (Vida Blue, Jim Palmer, Wilbur Wood)	1.50	.70	.45
93	N.L. Pitching Leaders (Steve Carlton, Al Downing, Fergie Jenkins, Tom Seaver)	2.00	1.00	.60
94	A.L. Pitching Leaders (Vida Blue, Mickey Lolich, Wilbur Wood)	1.25	.60	.40
95	N.L. Strikeout Leaders (Fergie Jenkins, Tom Seaver, Bill Stoneman)	1.75	.90	.50
96	A.L. Strikeout Leaders (Vida Blue, Joe Coleman, Mickey Lolich)	1.25	.60	.40
97	Tom Kelley	.40	.20	.12
98	Chuck Tanner	.70	.35	.20
99	*Ross Grimsley*	.80	.40	.25
100	Frank Robinson	5.00	2.50	1.50
101	Astros Rookies (Ray Busse, Bill Grief, *J.R. Richard*)	1.00	.50	.30
102	Lloyd Allen	.40	.20	.12
103	Checklist 133-263	3.00	1.50	.90
104	*Toby Harrah*	1.00	.50	.30
105	Gary Gentry	.40	.20	.12
106	Brewers Team	1.25	.60	.40
107	*Jose Cruz*	1.75	.90	.50
108	Gary Waslewski	.40	.20	.12
109	Jerry May	.40	.20	.12
110	Ron Hunt	.40	.20	.12
111	Jim Grant	.40	.20	.12
112	Greg Luzinski	1.00	.50	.30
113	Rogelio Moret	.40	.20	.12
114	Bill Buckner	1.25	.60	.40
115	Jim Fregosi	1.00	.50	.30
116	*Ed Farmer*	.40	.20	.12
117a	Cleo James (green under "C" and "S")	3.50	1.75	1.00
117b	Cleo James (yellow under "C" and "S")	.40	.20	.12
118	Skip Lockwood	.40	.20	.12
119	Marty Perez	.40	.20	.12
120	Bill Freehan	.80	.40	.25
121	Ed Sprague	.40	.20	.12
122	Larry Biittner	.40	.20	.12
123	Ed Acosta	.40	.20	.12
124	Yankees (Alan Closter, Roger Hambright, Rusty Torres)	.40	.20	.12
125	Dave Cash	.40	.20	.12
126	Bart Johnson	.40	.20	.12
127	Duffy Dyer	.40	.20	.12
128	Eddie Watt	.40	.20	.12
129	Charlie Fox	.40	.20	.12
130	Bob Gibson	5.00	2.50	1.50
131	Jim Nettles	.40	.20	.12
132	Joe Morgan	5.00	2.50	1.50
133	Joe Keough	.40	.20	.12
134	Carl Morton	.40	.20	.12
135	Vada Pinson	1.00	.50	.30
136	Darrel Chaney	.40	.20	.12
137	Dick Williams	.70	.35	.20
138	Mike Kekich	.40	.20	.12
139	Tim McCarver	1.00	.50	.30
140	Pat Dobson	.40	.20	.12
141	Mets Rookies (Buzz Capra, Jon Matlack, Leroy Stanton)	.60	.30	.20
142	*Chris Chambliss*	1.25	.60	.40
143	Garry Jestadt	.40	.20	.12
144	Marty Pattin	.40	.20	.12
145	Don Kessinger	.60	.30	.20
146	Steve Kealey	.40	.20	.12
147	*Dave Kingman*	6.00	3.00	1.75
148	Dick Billings	.40	.20	.12
149	Gary Neibauer	.40	.20	.12
150	Norm Cash	1.00	.50	.30
151	Jim Brewer	.40	.20	.12
152	Gene Clines	.40	.20	.12
153	Rick Auerbach	.40	.20	.12
154	Ted Simmons	2.00	1.00	.60
155	Larry Dierker	.40	.20	.12
156	Twins Team	1.25	.60	.40
157	Don Gullett	.60	.30	.20
158	Jerry Kenney	.40	.20	.12
159	John Boccabella	.40	.20	.12
160	Andy Messersmith	.60	.30	.20
161	Brock Davis	.40	.20	.12
162	Brewers Rookies (Jerry Bell, *Darrell Porter*, Bob Reynolds) (Bell & Porter photos transposed)	1.00	.50	.30
163	Tug McGraw	1.00	.50	.30
164	Tug McGraw IA	.60	.30	.20
165	*Chris Speier*	1.00	.50	.30
166	Chris Speier IA	.60	.30	.20

		NR MT	EX	VG
167	Deron Johnson	.40	.20	.12
168	Deron Johnson IA	.40	.20	.12
169	Vida Blue	1.00	.50	.30
170	Vida Blue IA	.60	.30	.20
171	Darrell Evans	1.50	.70	.45
172	Darrell Evans IA	1.00	.50	.30
173	Clay Kirby	.40	.20	.12
174	Clay Kirby IA	.40	.20	.12
175	Tom Haller	.40	.20	.12
176	Tom Haller IA	.40	.20	.12
177	Paul Schaal	.40	.20	.12
178	Paul Schaal IA	.40	.20	.12
179	Dock Ellis	.40	.20	.12
180	Dock Ellis IA	.40	.20	.12
181	Ed Kranepool	.60	.30	.20
182	Ed Kranepool IA	.40	.20	.12
183	Bill Melton	.40	.20	.12
184	Bill Melton IA	.40	.20	.12
185	Ron Bryant	.40	.20	.12
186	Ron Bryant IA	.40	.20	.12
187	Gates Brown	.40	.20	.12
188	Frank Lucchesi	.40	.20	.12
189	Gene Tenace	.60	.30	.20
190	Dave Giusti	.40	.20	.12
191	*Jeff Burroughs*	1.00	.50	.30
192	Cubs Team	1.25	.60	.40
193	*Kurt Bevacqua*	.60	.30	.20
194	Fred Norman	.40	.20	.12
195	Orlando Cepeda	2.00	1.00	.60
196	Mel Queen	.40	.20	.12
197	Johnny Briggs	.40	.20	.12
198	Dodgers Rookies *(Charlie Hough,* Bob O'Brien, Mike Strahler)	3.00	1.50	.90
199	Mike Fiore	.40	.20	.12
200	Lou Brock	5.00	2.50	1.50
201	Phil Roof	.40	.20	.12
202	Scipio Spinks	.40	.20	.12
203	*Ron Blomberg*	.70	.35	.20
204	Tommy Helms	.40	.20	.12
205	Dick Drago	.40	.20	.12
206	Dal Maxvill	.40	.20	.12
207	Tom Egan	.40	.20	.12
208	Milt Pappas	.60	.30	.20
209	Joe Rudi	.80	.40	.25
210	Denny McLain	1.25	.60	.40
211	Gary Sutherland	.40	.20	.12
212	Grant Jackson	.40	.20	.12
213	Angels Rookies (Art Kusnyer, Billy Parker, Tom Silverio)	.40	.20	.12
214	Mike McQueen	.40	.20	.12
215	Alex Johnson	.40	.20	.12
216	Joe Niekro	.70	.35	.20
217	Roger Metzger	.40	.20	.12
218	Eddie Kasko	.40	.20	.12
219	*Rennie Stennett*	.60	.30	.20
220	Jim Perry	.80	.40	.25
221	N.L. Playoffs (Bucs Champs!)	1.25	.60	.40
222	A.L. Playoffs (Orioles Champs!)	1.25	.60	.40
223	World Series Game 1	1.25	.60	.40
224	World Series Game 2	1.25	.60	.40
225	World Series Game 3	1.25	.60	.40
226	World Series Game 4	1.50	.70	.45
227	World Series Game 5	1.25	.60	.40
228	World Series Game 6	1.25	.60	.40
229	World Series Game 7	1.25	.60	.40
230	World Series Summary (Series Celebration)	1.25	.60	.40
231	Casey Cox	.40	.20	.12
232	Giants Rookies (Chris Arnold, Jim Barr, Dave Rader)	.40	.20	.12
233	Jay Johnstone	.60	.30	.20
234	Ron Taylor	.40	.20	.12
235	Merv Rettenmund	.40	.20	.12
236	Jim McGlothlin	.40	.20	.12
237	Yankees Team	1.25	.60	.40
238	Leron Lee	.40	.20	.12
239	Tom Timmermann	.40	.20	.12
240	Rich Allen	1.75	.90	.50
241	Rollie Fingers	4.00	2.00	1.25
242	Don Mincher	.40	.20	.12
243	Frank Linzy	.40	.20	.12
244	Steve Braun	.40	.20	.12
245	Tommie Agee	.40	.20	.12
246	Tom Burgmeier	.40	.20	.12
247	Milt May	.40	.20	.12
248	Tom Bradley	.40	.20	.12
249	Harry Walker	.40	.20	.12
250	Boog Powell	1.25	.60	.40
251a	Checklist 264-394 (small print on front)	3.00	1.50	.90
251b	Checklist 264-394 (large print on front)	3.00	1.50	.90

		NR MT	EX	VG
252	Ken Reynolds	.40	.20	.12
253	Sandy Alomar	.40	.20	.12
254	Boots Day	.40	.20	.12
255	Jim Lonborg	.60	.30	.20
256	George Foster	1.50	.70	.45
257	Tigers Rookies (Jim Foor, Tim Hosley, Paul Jata)	.40	.20	.12
258	Randy Hundley	.40	.20	.12
259	Sparky Lyle	1.00	.50	.30
260	Ralph Garr	.60	.30	.20
261	Steve Mingori	.40	.20	.12
262	Padres Team	1.25	.60	.40
263	Felipe Alou	.70	.35	.20
264	Tommy John	2.00	1.00	.60
265	Wes Parker	.40	.20	.12
266	Bobby Bolin	.40	.20	.12
267	Dave Concepcion	1.75	.90	.50
268	A's Rookies (Dwain Anderson, Chris Floethe)	.40	.20	.12
269	Don Hahn	.40	.20	.12
270	Jim Palmer	12.00	6.00	3.50
271	Ken Rudolph	.40	.20	.12
272	*Mickey Rivers*	1.00	.50	.30
273	Bobby Floyd	.40	.20	.12
274	Al Severinsen	.40	.20	.12
275	Cesar Tovar	.40	.20	.12
276	Gene Mauch	.70	.35	.20
277	Elliott Maddox	.40	.20	.12
278	Dennis Higgins	.40	.20	.12
279	Larry Brown	.40	.20	.12
280	Willie McCovey	4.00	2.00	1.25
281	Bill Parsons	.40	.20	.12
282	Astros Team	1.25	.60	.40
283	Darrell Brandon	.40	.20	.12
284	Ike Brown	.40	.20	.12
285	Gaylord Perry	5.00	2.50	1.50
286	Gene Alley	.40	.20	.12
287	Jim Hardin	.40	.20	.12
288	Johnny Jeter	.40	.20	.12
289	Syd O'Brien	.40	.20	.12
290	Sonny Siebert	.40	.20	.12
291	Hal McRae	.80	.40	.25
292	Hal McRae IA	.40	.20	.12
293	Danny Frisella	.40	.20	.12
294	Danny Frisella IA	.40	.20	.12
295	Dick Dietz	.40	.20	.12
296	Dick Dietz IA	.40	.20	.12
297	Claude Osteen	.60	.30	.20
298	Claude Osteen IA	.40	.20	.12
299	Hank Aaron	25.00	12.50	7.50
300	Hank Aaron IA	10.00	5.00	3.00
301	George Mitterwald	.40	.20	.12
302	George Mitterwald IA	.40	.20	.12
303	Joe Pepitone	.70	.35	.20
304	Joe Pepitone IA	.40	.20	.12
305	Ken Boswell	.40	.20	.12
306	Ken Boswell IA	.40	.20	.12
307	Steve Renko	.40	.20	.12
308	Steve Renko IA	.40	.20	.12
309	Roberto Clemente	25.00	12.50	7.50
310	Roberto Clemente IA	10.00	5.00	3.00
311	Clay Carroll	.40	.20	.12
312	Clay Carroll IA	.40	.20	.12
313	Luis Aparicio	4.00	2.00	1.25
314	Luis Aparicio IA	2.00	1.00	.60
315	Paul Splittorff	.40	.20	.12
316	Cardinals Rookies *(Jim Bibby,* Santiago Guzman, Jorge Roque)	.70	.35	.20
317	Rich Hand	.40	.20	.12
318	Sonny Jackson	.40	.20	.12
319	Aurelio Rodriguez	.40	.20	.12
320	Steve Blass	.40	.20	.12
321	Joe Lahoud	.40	.20	.12
322	Jose Pena	.40	.20	.12
323	Earl Weaver	1.00	.50	.30
324	Mike Ryan	.40	.20	.12
325	Mel Stottlemyre	1.00	.50	.30
326	Pat Kelly	.40	.20	.12
327	*Steve Stone*	1.00	.50	.30
328	Red Sox Team	1.00	.50	.30
329	Roy Foster	.40	.20	.12
330	Jim Hunter	3.50	1.75	1.00
331	Stan Swanson	.40	.20	.12
332	Buck Martinez	.40	.20	.12
333	Steve Barber	.40	.20	.12
334	Rangers Rookies (Bill Fahey, Jim Mason, Tom Ragland)	.40	.20	.12
335	Bill Hands	.40	.20	.12
336	Marty Martinez	.40	.20	.12
337	Mike Kilkenny	.40	.20	.12
338	Bob Grich	1.00	.50	.30

		NR MT	EX	VG
339	Ron Cook	.40	.20	.12
340	Roy White	1.00	.50	.30
341	Boyhood Photo (Joe Torre)	.70	.35	.20
342	Boyhood Photo (Wilbur Wood)	.60	.30	.20
343	Boyhood Photo (Willie Stargell)	1.50	.70	.45
344	Boyhood Photo (Dave McNally)	.60	.30	.20
345	Boyhood Photo (Rick Wise)	.40	.20	.12
346	Boyhood Photo (Jim Fregosi)	.60	.30	.20
347	Boyhood Photo (Tom Seaver)	2.00	1.00	.60
348	Boyhood Photo (Sal Bando)	.60	.30	.20
349	Al Fitzmorris	.40	.20	.12
350	Frank Howard	1.25	.60	.40
351	Braves Rookies (Jimmy Britton, Tom House, Rick Kester)	.40	.20	.12
352	Dave LaRoche	.40	.20	.12
353	Art Shamsky	.40	.20	.12
354	Tom Murphy	.40	.20	.12
355	Bob Watson	.40	.20	.12
356	Gerry Moses	.40	.20	.12
357	Woodie Fryman	.40	.20	.12
358	Sparky Anderson	1.00	.50	.30
359	Don Pavletich	.40	.20	.12
360	Dave Roberts	.40	.20	.12
361	Mike Andrews	.40	.20	.12
362	Mets Team	1.25	.60	.40
363	Ron Klimkowski	.40	.20	.12
364	Johnny Callison	.70	.35	.20
365	Dick Bosman	.40	.20	.12
366	Jimmy Rosario	.40	.20	.12
367	Ron Perranoski	.40	.20	.12
368	Danny Thompson	.40	.20	.12
369	Jim Lefebvre	.40	.20	.12
370	Don Buford	.40	.20	.12
371	Denny Lemaster	.40	.20	.12
372	Royals Rookies (Lance Clemons, Monty Montgomery)	.40	.20	.12
373	John Mayberry	.60	.30	.20
374	Jack Heidemann	.40	.20	.12
375	Reggie Cleveland	.40	.20	.12
376	Andy Kosco	.40	.20	.12
377	Terry Harmon	.40	.20	.12
378	Checklist 395-525	3.00	1.50	.90
379	Ken Berry	.40	.20	.12
380	Earl Williams	.40	.20	.12
381	White Sox Team	1.25	.60	.40
382	Joe Gibbon	.40	.20	.12
383	Brant Alyea	.40	.20	.12
384	Dave Campbell	.40	.20	.12
385	Mickey Stanley	.40	.20	.12
386	Jim Colborn	.40	.20	.12
387	Horace Clarke	.40	.20	.12
388	Charlie Williams	.40	.20	.12
389	Bill Rigney	.40	.20	.12
390	Willie Davis	.70	.35	.20
391	Ken Sanders	.40	.20	.12
392	Pirates Rookies (Fred Cambria, *Richie Zisk*)	1.00	.50	.30
393	Curt Motton	.40	.20	.12
394	Ken Forsch	.40	.20	.12
395	Matty Alou	.80	.40	.25
396	Paul Lindblad	.40	.20	.12
397	Phillies Team	1.25	.60	.40
398	Larry Hisle	.60	.30	.20
399	Milt Wilcox	.60	.30	.20
400	Tony Oliva	1.50	.70	.45
401	Jim Nash	.40	.20	.12
402	Bobby Heise	.40	.20	.12
403	John Cumberland	.40	.20	.12
404	Jeff Torborg	.60	.30	.20
405	Ron Fairly	.70	.35	.20
406	*George Hendrick*	1.00	.50	.30
407	Chuck Taylor	.40	.20	.12
408	Jim Northrup	.60	.30	.20
409	Frank Baker	.60	.30	.20
410	Fergie Jenkins	5.00	2.50	1.50
411	Bob Montgomery	.40	.20	.12
412	Dick Kelley	.40	.20	.12
413	White Sox Rookies (Don Eddy, Dave Lemonds)	.40	.20	.12
414	Bob Miller	.40	.20	.12
415	Cookie Rojas	.40	.20	.12
416	Johnny Edwards	.40	.20	.12
417	Tom Hall	.40	.20	.12
418	Tom Shopay	.40	.20	.12
419	Jim Spencer	.40	.20	.12
420	Steve Carlton	18.00	9.00	5.50
421	Ellie Rodriguez	.40	.20	.12
422	Ray Lamb	.40	.20	.12
423	Oscar Gamble	.60	.30	.20
424	Bill Gogolewski	.40	.20	.12
425	Ken Singleton	1.00	.50	.30

		NR MT	EX	VG
426	Ken Singleton IA	.60	.30	.20
427	Tito Fuentes	.40	.20	.12
428	Tito Fuentes IA	.40	.20	.12
429	Bob Robertson	.40	.20	.12
430	Bob Robertson IA	.40	.20	.12
431	Clarence Gaston	.40	.20	.12
432	Clarence Gaston IA	.40	.20	.12
433	Johnny Bench	35.00	17.50	10.50
434	Johnny Bench IA	15.00	7.50	4.50
435	Reggie Jackson	35.00	17.50	10.50
436	Reggie Jackson IA	10.00	5.00	3.00
437	Maury Wills	1.50	.70	.45
438	Maury Wills IA	1.00	.50	.30
439	Billy Williams	4.00	2.00	1.25
440	Billy Williams IA	2.00	1.00	.60
441	Thurman Munson	15.00	7.50	4.50
442	Thurman Munson IA	10.00	5.00	3.00
443	Ken Henderson	.40	.20	.12
444	Ken Henderson IA	.40	.20	.12
445	Tom Seaver	25.00	12.50	7.50
446	Tom Seaver IA	10.00	5.00	3.00
447	Willie Stargell	4.00	2.00	1.25
448	Willie Stargell IA	2.00	1.00	.60
449	Bob Lemon	1.25	.60	.40
450	Mickey Lolich	1.25	.60	.40
451	Tony LaRussa	.80	.40	.25
452	Ed Herrmann	.40	.20	.12
453	Barry Lersch	.40	.20	.12
454	A's Team	2.00	1.00	.60
455	Tommy Harper	.60	.30	.20
456	Mark Belanger	.60	.30	.20
457	Padres Rookies (Darcy Fast, Mike Ivie, *Derrel Thomas*)	.60	.30	.20
458	Aurelio Monteagudo	.40	.20	.12
459	Rick Renick	.40	.20	.12
460	Al Downing	.60	.30	.20
461	Tim Cullen	.40	.20	.12
462	Rickey Clark	.40	.20	.12
463	Bernie Carbo	.40	.20	.12
464	Jim Roland	.40	.20	.12
465	Gil Hodges	3.00	1.50	.90
466	Norm Miller	.40	.20	.12
467	Steve Kline	.60	.30	.20
468	Richie Scheinblum	.40	.20	.12
469	Ron Herbel	.40	.20	.12
470	Ray Fosse	.40	.20	.12
471	Luke Walker	.40	.20	.12
472	Phil Gagliano	.40	.20	.12
473	Dan McGinn	.40	.20	.12
474	Orioles Rookies (Don Baylor, Roric Harrison, Johnny Oates)	3.25	1.75	1.00
475	Gary Nolan	.40	.20	.12
476	Lee Richard	.40	.20	.12
477	Tom Phoebus	.40	.20	.12
478a	Checklist 526-656 (small print on front)	3.00	1.50	.90
478b	Checklist 526-656 (large printing on front)	3.00	1.50	.90
479	Don Shaw	.40	.20	.12
480	Lee May	.80	.40	.25
481	Billy Conigliaro	.40	.20	.12
482	Joe Hoerner	.40	.20	.12
483	Ken Suarez	.40	.20	.12
484	Lum Harris	.40	.20	.12
485	Phil Regan	.40	.20	.12
486	John Lowenstein	.40	.20	.12
487	Tigers Team	1.50	.70	.45
488	Mike Nagy	.40	.20	.12
489	Expos Rookies (Terry Humphrey, Keith Lampard)	.40	.20	.12
490	Dave McNally	.70	.35	.20
491	Boyhood Photo (Lou Piniella)	.80	.40	.25
492	Boyhood Photo (Mel Stottlemyre)	.60	.30	.20
493	Boyhood Photo (Bob Bailey)	.40	.20	.12
494	Boyhood Photo (Willie Horton)	.60	.30	.20
495	Boyhood Photo (Bill Melton)	.40	.20	.12
496	Boyhood Photo (Bud Harrelson)	.60	.30	.20
497	Boyhood Photo (Jim Perry)	.60	.30	.20
498	Boyhood Photo (Brooks Robinson)	2.00	1.00	.60
499	Vicente Romo	.40	.20	.12
500	Joe Torre	1.25	.60	.40
501	Pete Hamm	.40	.20	.12
502	Jackie Hernandez	.40	.20	.12
503	Gary Peters	.40	.20	.12
504	Ed Spiezio	.40	.20	.12
505	Mike Marshall	.70	.35	.20
506	Indians Rookies (Terry Ley, Jim Moyer, *Dick Tidrow*)	.80	.40	.25
507	Fred Gladding	.40	.20	.12
508	Ellie Hendricks	.40	.20	.12

		NR MT	EX	VG
509	Don McMahon	.40	.20	.12
510	Ted Williams	6.00	3.00	1.75
511	Tony Taylor	.40	.20	.12
512	Paul Popovich	.40	.20	.12
513	Lindy McDaniel	.60	.30	.20
514	Ted Sizemore	.40	.20	.12
515	Bert Blyleven	10.00	5.00	3.00
516	Oscar Brown	.40	.20	.12
517	Ken Brett	.60	.30	.20
518	Wayne Garrett	.40	.20	.12
519	Ted Abernathy	.40	.20	.12
520	Larry Bowa	1.25	.60	.40
521	Alan Foster	.40	.20	.12
522	Dodgers Team	1.25	.60	.40
523	Chuck Dobson	.40	.20	.12
524	Reds Rookies (Ed Armbrister, Mel Behney)	.40	.20	.12
525	Carlos May	.60	.30	.20
526	Bob Bailey	1.00	.50	.30
527	Dave Leonhard	1.00	.50	.30
528	Ron Stone	1.00	.50	.30
529	Dave Nelson	1.00	.50	.30
530	Don Sutton	4.00	2.00	1.25
531	Freddie Patek	1.00	.50	.30
532	Fred Kendall	1.00	.50	.30
533	Ralph Houk	1.25	.60	.40
534	Jim Hickman	1.00	.50	.30
535	Ed Brinkman	1.00	.50	.30
536	Doug Rader	1.00	.50	.30
537	Bob Locker	1.00	.50	.30
538	Charlie Sands	1.00	.50	.30
539	*Terry Forster*	2.00	1.00	.60
540	Felix Millan	1.00	.50	.30
541	Roger Repoz	1.00	.50	.30
542	Jack Billingham	1.00	.50	.30
543	Duane Josephson	1.00	.50	.30
544	Ted Martinez	1.00	.50	.30
545	Wayne Granger	1.00	.50	.30
546	Joe Hague	1.00	.50	.30
547	Indians Team	1.50	.70	.45
548	Frank Reberger	1.00	.50	.30
549	Dave May	1.00	.50	.30
550	Brooks Robinson	15.00	7.50	4.50
551	Ollie Brown	1.00	.50	.30
552	Ollie Brown IA	1.00	.50	.30
553	Wilbur Wood	1.25	.60	.40
554	Wilbur Wood IA	1.00	.50	.30
555	Ron Santo	1.50	.70	.45
556	Ron Santo IA	1.00	.50	.30
557	John Odom	1.00	.50	.30
558	John Odom IA	1.00	.50	.30
559	Pete Rose	60.00	30.00	18.00
560	Pete Rose IA	30.00	15.00	9.00
561	Leo Cardenas	1.00	.50	.30
562	Leo Cardenas IA	1.00	.50	.30
563	Ray Sadecki	1.00	.50	.30
564	Ray Sadecki IA	1.00	.50	.30
565	Reggie Smith	1.25	.60	.40
566	Reggie Smith IA	1.00	.50	.30
567	Juan Marichal	6.00	3.00	1.75
568	Juan Marichal IA	3.00	1.50	.90
569	Ed Kirkpatrick	1.00	.50	.30
570	Ed Kirkpatrick IA	1.00	.50	.30
571	Nate Colbert	1.00	.50	.30
572	Nate Colbert IA	1.00	.50	.30
573	Fritz Peterson	1.00	.50	.30
574	Fritz Peterson IA	1.00	.50	.30
575	Al Oliver	2.00	1.00	.60
576	Leo Durocher	1.25	.60	.40
577	Mike Paul	1.00	.50	.30
578	Billy Grabarkewitz	1.00	.50	.30
579	*Doyle Alexander*	3.25	1.75	1.00
580	Lou Piniella	1.75	.90	.50
581	Wade Blasingame	1.00	.50	.30
582	Expos Team	3.00	1.50	.90
583	Darold Knowles	1.00	.50	.30
584	Jerry McNertney	1.00	.50	.30
585	George Scott	1.00	.50	.30
586	Denis Menke	1.00	.50	.30
587	Billy Wilson	1.00	.50	.30
588	Jim Holt	1.00	.50	.30
589	Hal Lanier	1.00	.50	.30
590	Graig Nettles	3.25	1.75	1.00
591	Paul Casanova	1.00	.50	.30
592	Lew Krausse	1.00	.50	.30
593	Rich Morales	1.00	.50	.30
594	Jim Beauchamp	1.00	.50	.30
595	Nolan Ryan	150.00	75.00	45.00
596	Manny Mota	1.25	.60	.40
597	Jim Magnuson	1.00	.50	.30
598	Hal King	1.00	.50	.30

		NR MT	EX	VG
599	Billy Champion	1.00	.50	.30
600	Al Kaline	12.00	6.00	3.50
601	George Stone	1.00	.50	.30
602	Dave Bristol	1.00	.50	.30
603	Jim Ray	1.00	.50	.30
604a	Checklist 657-787 (copyright on right)	3.50	1.75	1.00
604b	Checklist 657-787 (copyright on left)	5.00	2.50	1.50
605	Nelson Briles	1.00	.50	.30
606	Luis Melendez	1.00	.50	.30
607	Frank Duffy	1.00	.50	.30
608	Mike Corkins	1.00	.50	.30
609	Tom Grieve	1.00	.50	.30
610	Bill Stoneman	1.00	.50	.30
611	Rich Reese	1.00	.50	.30
612	Joe Decker	1.00	.50	.30
613	Mike Ferraro	1.00	.50	.30
614	Ted Uhlaender	1.00	.50	.30
615	Steve Hargan	1.00	.50	.30
616	*Joe Ferguson*	1.00	.50	.30
617	Royals Team	3.00	1.50	.90
618	Rich Robertson	1.00	.50	.30
619	Rich McKinney	1.00	.50	.30
620	Phil Niekro	4.50	2.25	1.25
621	Commissioners Award	1.25	.60	.40
622	MVP Award	1.25	.60	.40
623	Cy Young Award	1.25	.60	.40
624	Minor League Player Of The Year Award	1.25	.60	.40
625	Rookie Of The Year Award	1.25	.60	.40
626	Babe Ruth Award	1.00	.50	.30
627	Moe Drabowsky	1.00	.50	.30
628	Terry Crowley	1.00	.50	.30
629	Paul Doyle	1.00	.50	.30
630	Rich Hebner	1.00	.50	.30
631	John Strohmayer	1.00	.50	.30
632	Mike Hegan	1.00	.50	.30
633	Jack Hiatt	1.00	.50	.30
634	Dick Woodson	1.00	.50	.30
635	Don Money	1.00	.50	.30
636	Bill Lee	1.25	.60	.40
637	Preston Gomez	1.00	.50	.30
638	Ken Wright	1.00	.50	.30
639	J.C. Martin	1.00	.50	.30
640	Joe Coleman	1.00	.50	.30
641	Mike Lum	1.00	.50	.30
642	Denny Riddleberger	1.00	.50	.30
643	Russ Gibson	1.00	.50	.30
644	Bernie Allen	1.00	.50	.30
645	Jim Maloney	1.00	.50	.30
646	Chico Salmon	1.00	.50	.30
647	Bob Moose	1.00	.50	.30
648	Jim Lyttle	1.00	.50	.30
649	Pete Richert	1.00	.50	.30
650	Sal Bando	1.00	.50	.30
651	Reds Team	2.00	1.00	.60
652	Marcelino Lopez	1.00	.50	.30
653	Jim Fairey	1.00	.50	.30
654	Horacio Pina	1.00	.50	.30
655	Jerry Grote	1.00	.50	.30
656	Rudy May	1.00	.50	.30
657	Bobby Wine	3.00	1.50	.90
658	Steve Dunning	3.00	1.50	.90
659	Bob Aspromonte	3.00	1.50	.90
660	Paul Blair	3.25	1.75	1.00
661	Bill Virdon	3.25	1.75	1.00
662	Stan Bahnsen	3.25	1.75	1.00
663	Fran Healy	3.00	1.50	.90
664	Bobby Knoop	3.00	1.50	.90
665	Chris Short	3.25	1.75	1.00
666	Hector Torres	3.00	1.50	.90
667	Ray Newman	3.00	1.50	.90
668	Rangers Team	3.25	1.75	1.00
669	Willie Crawford	3.00	1.50	.90
670	Ken Holtzman	3.50	1.75	1.00
671	Donn Clendenon	3.25	1.75	1.00
672	Archie Reynolds	3.00	1.50	.90
673	Dave Marshall	3.00	1.50	.90
674	John Kennedy	3.00	1.50	.90
675	Pat Jarvis	3.00	1.50	.90
676	Danny Cater	3.00	1.50	.90
677	Ivan Murrell	3.00	1.50	.90
678	Steve Luebber	3.00	1.50	.90
679	Astros Rookies (Bob Fenwick, Bob Stinson)	3.00	1.50	.90
680	Dave Johnson	3.50	1.75	1.00
681	Bobby Pfeil	3.00	1.50	.90
682	Mike McCormick	3.25	1.75	1.00
683	Steve Hovley	3.00	1.50	.90
684	Hal Breeden	3.00	1.50	.90

		NR MT	EX	VG
685	Joe Horlen	3.00	1.50	.90
686	Steve Garvey	75.00	38.00	23.00
687	Del Unser	3.00	1.50	.90
688	Cardinals Team	3.25	1.75	1.00
689	Eddie Fisher	3.00	1.50	.90
690	Willie Montanez	3.25	1.75	1.00
691	Curt Blefary	3.00	1.50	.90
692	Curt Blefary IA	3.00	1.50	.90
693	Alan Gallagher	3.00	1.50	.90
694	Alan Gallagher IA	3.00	1.50	.90
695	Rod Carew	100.00	50.00	30.00
696	Rod Carew IA	40.00	20.00	12.00
697	Jerry Koosman	4.50	2.25	1.25
698	Jerry Koosman IA	3.25	1.75	1.00
699	Bobby Murcer	4.00	2.00	1.25
700	Bobby Murcer IA	3.25	1.75	1.00
701	Jose Pagan	3.00	1.50	.90
702	Jose Pagan IA	3.00	1.50	.90
703	Doug Griffin	3.00	1.50	.90
704	Doug Griffin IA	3.00	1.50	.90
705	Pat Corrales	3.25	1.75	1.00
706	Pat Corrales IA	3.00	1.50	.90
707	Tim Foli	3.00	1.50	.90
708	Tim Foli IA	3.00	1.50	.90
709	Jim Kaat	9.00	4.50	2.75
710	Jim Kaat IA	5.00	2.50	1.50
711	Bobby Bonds	10.00	5.00	3.00
712	Bobby Bonds IA	3.25	1.75	1.00
713	Gene Michael	3.25	1.75	1.00
714	Gene Michael IA	3.25	1.75	1.00
715	Mike Epstein	3.25	1.75	1.00
716	Jesus Alou	3.25	1.75	1.00
717	Bruce Dal Canton	3.00	1.50	.90
718	Del Rice	3.00	1.50	.90
719	Cesar Geronimo	3.25	1.75	1.00
720	Sam McDowell	3.00	1.50	.90
721	Eddie Leon	3.00	1.50	.90
722	Bill Sudakis	3.00	1.50	.90
723	Al Santorini	3.00	1.50	.90
724	A.L. Rookies (John Curtis, Rich Hinton, Mickey Scott)	3.25	1.75	1.00
725	Dick McAuliffe	3.25	1.75	1.00
726	Dick Selma	3.00	1.50	.90
727	Jose Laboy	3.00	1.50	.90
728	Gail Hopkins	3.00	1.50	.90
729	Bob Veale	3.25	1.75	1.00
730	Rick Monday	3.50	1.75	1.00
731	Orioles Team	3.25	1.75	1.00
732	George Culver	3.00	1.50	.90
733	Jim Hart	3.25	1.75	1.00
734	Bob Burda	3.00	1.50	.90
735	Diego Segui	3.00	1.50	.90
736	Bill Russell	3.00	1.50	.90
737	*Lenny Randle*	3.25	1.75	1.00
738	Jim Merritt	3.00	1.50	.90
739	Don Mason	3.00	1.50	.90
740	Rico Carty	3.25	1.75	1.00
741	Major League Rookies (Tom Hutton, *Rick Miller, John Milner*)	3.25	1.75	1.00
742	Jim Rooker	3.00	1.50	.90
743	Cesar Gutierrez	3.00	1.50	.90
744	*Jim Slaton*	3.25	1.75	1.00
745	Julian Javier	3.00	1.50	.90
746	Lowell Palmer	3.00	1.50	.90
747	Jim Stewart	3.00	1.50	.90
748	Phil Hennigan	3.00	1.50	.90
749	Walter Alston	5.00	2.50	1.50
750	Willie Horton	3.50	1.75	1.00
751	Steve Carlton Traded	35.00	17.50	10.50
752	Joe Morgan Traded	30.00	15.00	9.00
753	Denny McLain Traded	8.00	4.00	2.50
754	Frank Robinson Traded	25.00	12.50	7.50
755	Jim Fregosi Traded	3.50	1.75	1.00
756	Rick Wise Traded	3.25	1.75	1.00
757	Jose Cardenal Traded	3.25	1.75	1.00
758	Gil Garrido	3.00	1.50	.90
759	Chris Cannizzaro	3.00	1.50	.90
760	Bill Mazeroski	6.00	3.00	1.75
761	Major League Rookies *(Ron Cey, Ben Oglivie,* Bernie Williams)	12.00	6.00	3.50
762	Wayne Simpson	3.00	1.50	.90
763	Ron Hansen	3.00	1.50	.90
764	Dusty Baker	3.00	1.50	.90
765	Ken McMullen	3.00	1.50	.90
766	Steve Hamilton	3.00	1.50	.90
767	Tom McCraw	3.00	1.50	.90
768	Denny Doyle	3.00	1.50	.90
769	Jack Aker	3.25	1.75	1.00
770	Jim Wynn	3.50	1.75	1.00
771	Giants Team	3.25	1.75	1.00
772	Ken Tatum	3.00	1.50	.90
773	Ron Brand	3.00	1.50	.90
774	Luis Alvarado	3.00	1.50	.90
775	Jerry Reuss	3.50	1.75	1.00
776	Bill Voss	3.00	1.50	.90
777	Hoyt Wilhelm	18.00	9.00	5.50
778	Twins Rookies (Vic Albury, *Rick Dempsey,* Jim Strickland)	3.25	1.75	1.00
779	Tony Cloninger	3.25	1.75	1.00
780	Dick Green	3.00	1.50	.90
781	Jim McAndrew	3.00	1.50	.90
782	Larry Stahl	3.00	1.50	.90
783	Les Cain	3.00	1.50	.90
784	Ken Aspromonte	3.00	1.50	.90
785	Vic Davalillo	3.00	1.50	.90
786	Chuck Brinkman	3.25	1.75	1.00
787	Ron Reed	4.50	1.25	.70

1972 Topps Cloth Stickers

Despite the fact they were never actually issued, examples of this test issue can readily be found within the hobby. The set of 33 contains stickers with designs identical to cards found in three contiguous rows of a regular Topps card sheet that year; thus the inclusion of a meaningless checklist card. Sometimes found in complete 33-sticker strips, individual stickers nominally measure 2-1/2" by 3-1/2," though dimensions vary according to the care with which they were cut. Stickers are unnumbered and blank-backed, and do not contain glue.

		NR MT	EX	VG
Complete Set:		200.00	100.00	60.00
Common Player:		3.00	1.50	.90
(1)	Hank Aaron	50.00	25.00	15.00
(2)	Luis Aparicio IA	10.00	5.00	3.00
(3)	Ike Brown	3.00	1.50	.90
(4)	Johnny Callison	5.00	2.50	1.50
(5)	Checklist 264-319	3.00	1.50	.90
(6)	Roberto Clemente IA	25.00	12.50	7.50
(7)	Dave Concepcion	8.00	4.00	2.50
(8)	Ron Cook	3.00	1.50	.90
(9)	Willie Davis	5.00	2.50	1.50
(10)	Al Fitzmorris	3.00	1.50	.90
(11)	Bobby Floyd	3.00	1.50	.90
(12)	Roy Foster	3.00	1.50	.90
(13)	Jim Fregosi Boyhood Photo	4.00	2.00	1.25
(14)	Danny Frisella IA	3.00	1.50	.90
(15)	Woody Fryman	3.50	1.75	1.00
(16)	Terry Harmon	3.00	1.50	.90
(17)	Frank Howard	7.00	3.50	2.00
(18)	Ron Klimkowski	3.00	1.50	.90
(19)	Joe Lahoud	3.00	1.50	.90
(20)	Jim Lefebvre	3.50	1.75	1.00
(21)	Elliott Maddox	3.00	1.50	.90
(22)	Marty Martinez	3.00	1.50	.90
(23)	Willie McCovey	25.00	12.50	7.50
(24)	Hal McRae	6.00	3.00	1.75
(25)	Syd O'Brien	3.00	1.50	.90
(26)	Red Sox Team	4.00	2.00	1.25
(27)	Aurelio Rodriguez	3.50	1.75	1.00
(28)	Al Severinsen	3.00	1.50	.90
(29)	Art Shamsky	3.00	1.50	.90
(30)	Steve Stone	4.00	2.00	1.25
(31)	Stan Swanson	3.00	1.50	.90
(32)	Bob Watson	3.50	1.75	1.00

		NR MT	EX	VG
(33)	Roy White	6.00	3.00	1.75

1972 Topps Posters

Issued as a separate set, rather than as a wax pack insert, the twenty-four 9-7/16" by 18" posters of 1972 feature a borderless full-color picture on the front with the player's name, team and position. Printed on very thin paper, the posters, as happened with earlier issues, were folded for packaging, causing large creases which cannot be removed. Even so, they are good display items for they feature many of stars of the period.

		NR MT	EX	VG
Complete Set:		300.00	150.00	90.00
Common Player:		5.00	2.50	1.50
1	Dave McNally	5.00	2.50	1.50
2	Carl Yastrzemski	30.00	15.00	9.00
3	Bill Melton	5.00	2.50	1.50
4	Ray Fosse	5.00	2.50	1.50
5	Mickey Lolich	6.00	3.00	1.75
6	Amos Otis	5.00	2.50	1.50
7	Tony Oliva	6.00	3.00	1.75
8	Vida Blue	6.00	3.00	1.75
9	Hank Aaron	20.00	10.00	6.00
10	Fergie Jenkins	8.00	4.00	2.50
11	Pete Rose	50.00	25.00	15.00
12	Willie Davis	6.00	3.00	1.75
13	Tom Seaver	20.00	10.00	6.00
14	Rick Wise	5.00	2.50	1.50
15	Willie Stargell	12.00	6.00	3.50
16	Joe Torre	7.00	3.50	2.00
17	Willie Mays	20.00	10.00	6.00
18	Andy Messersmith	5.00	2.50	1.50
19	Wilbur Wood	5.00	2.50	1.50
20	Harmon Killebrew	15.00	7.50	4.50
21	Billy Williams	12.00	6.00	3.50
22	Bud Harrelson	5.00	2.50	1.50
23	Roberto Clemente	20.00	10.00	6.00
24	Willie McCovey	15.00	7.50	4.50

1973 Topps

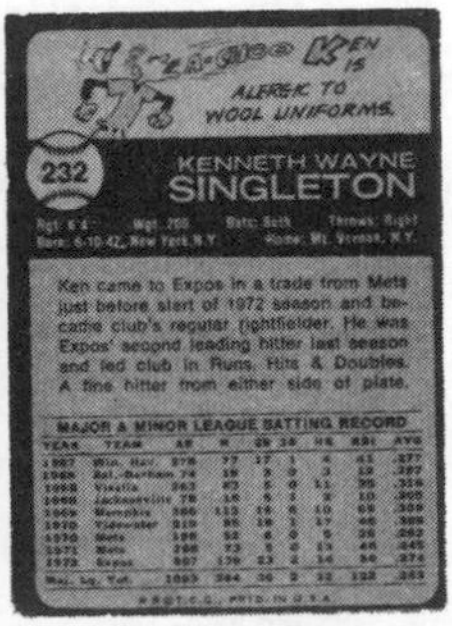

Topps cut back to 660 cards in 1973. The set is interesting for it marks the last time cards were issued by series, a procedure which had produced many a scarce high number card over the years. These 2-1/2" by 3-1/2" cards have a color photo, accented by a silhouette of a player on the front, indicative of his position. Card backs are vertical for the first time since 1968, with the usual statistical and biographical information. Specialty cards begin with card number 1, which depicted Ruth, Mays and Aaron as the all-time home run leaders. It was followed by statistical leaders, although there also were additional all-time leader cards. Also present are playoff and World Series highlights. From the age-and-youth department, the 1973 Topps set has coaches and managers as well as more "Boyhood Photos."

		NR MT	EX	VG
Complete Set:		1000.00	450.00	275.00
Common Player: 1-396		.40	.20	.12
Common Player: 397-528		.70	.35	.20
Common Player: 529-660		2.00	1.00	.60
1	All Time Home Run Leaders (Hank Aaron, Willie Mays, Babe Ruth)	20.00	10.00	6.00
2	Rich Hebner	.50	.25	.15
3	Jim Lonborg	.70	.35	.20
4	John Milner	.40	.20	.12
5	Ed Brinkman	.50	.25	.15
6	Mac Scarce	.40	.20	.12
7	Rangers Team	1.25	.60	.40
8	Tom Hall	.40	.20	.12
9	Johnny Oates	.40	.20	.12
10	Don Sutton	2.00	1.00	.60
11	Chris Chambliss	.90	.45	.25
12a	Padres Mgr./Coaches (Dave Garcia, Johnny Podres, Bob Skinner, Whitey Wietelmann, Don Zimmer) (Coaches background brown)	.70	.35	.20
12b	Padres Mgr./Coaches (Dave Garcia, Johnny Podres, Bob Skinner, Whitey Wietelmann, Don Zimmer) (Coaches background orange)	.70	.35	.20
13	George Hendrick	.90	.45	.25
14	Sonny Siebert	.40	.20	.12
15	Ralph Garr	.50	.25	.15
16	Steve Braun	.40	.20	.12
17	Fred Gladding	.40	.20	.12
18	Leroy Stanton	.40	.20	.12
19	Tim Foli	.40	.20	.12
20a	Stan Bahnsen (small gap in left border)	.70	.35	.20
20b	Stan Bahnsen (no gap)	.40	.20	.12
21	Randy Hundley	.40	.20	.12
22	Ted Abernathy	.40	.20	.12
23	Dave Kingman	2.00	1.00	.60
24	Al Santorini	.40	.20	.12
25	Roy White	.70	.35	.20
26	Pirates Team	1.25	.60	.40
27	Bill Gogolewski	.40	.20	.12
28	Hal McRae	.70	.35	.20
29	Tony Taylor	.40	.20	.12
30	Tug McGraw	.80	.40	.25
31	*Buddy Bell*	4.00	2.00	1.25
32	Fred Norman	.40	.20	.12
33	Jim Breazeale	.40	.20	.12
34	Pat Dobson	.50	.25	.15
35	Willie Davis	.70	.35	.20
36	Steve Barber	.40	.20	.12
37	Bill Robinson	.40	.20	.12
38	Mike Epstein	.50	.25	.15
39	Dave Roberts	.40	.20	.12
40	Reggie Smith	.70	.35	.20
41	Tom Walker	.40	.20	.12
42	Mike Andrews	.40	.20	.12
43	*Randy Moffitt*	.50	.25	.15
44	Rick Monday	.70	.35	.20
45	Ellie Rodriguez (photo actually Paul Ratliff)	.40	.20	.12
46	Lindy McDaniel	.50	.25	.15
47	Luis Melendez	.40	.20	.12
48	Paul Splittorff	.50	.25	.15
49a	Twins Mgr./Coaches (Vern Morgan, Frank Quilici, Bob Rodgers, Ralph Rowe, Al Worthington) (Coaches background brown)	.70	.35	.20
49b	Twins Mgr./Coaches (Vern Morgan, Frank Quilici, Bob Rodgers, Ralph Rowe, Al Worthington) (Coaches background orange)	.50	.25	.15

		NR MT	EX	VG
50	Roberto Clemente	30.00	15.00	9.00
51	Chuck Seelbach	.40	.20	.12
52	Denis Menke	.40	.20	.12
53	Steve Dunning	.40	.20	.12
54	Checklist 1-132	2.00	1.00	.60
55	Jon Matlack	.70	.35	.20
56	Merv Rettenmund	.50	.25	.15
57	Derrel Thomas	.40	.20	.12
58	Mike Paul	.40	.20	.12
59	*Steve Yeager*	.80	.40	.25
60	Ken Holtzman	.70	.35	.20
61	Batting Leaders (Rod Carew, Billy Williams)	2.25	1.25	.70
62	Home Run Leaders (Dick Allen, Johnny Bench)	2.25	1.25	.70
63	Runs Batted In Leaders (Dick Allen, Johnny Bench)	2.25	1.25	.70
64	Stolen Base Leaders (Lou Brock, Bert Campaneris)	2.00	1.00	.60
65	Earned Run Average Leaders (Steve Carlton, Luis Tiant)	2.00	1.00	.60
66	Victory Leaders (Steve Carlton, Gaylord Perry, Wilbur Wood)	2.00	1.00	.60
67	Strikeout Leaders (Steve Carlton, Nolan Ryan)	5.00	2.50	1.50
68	Leading Firemen (Clay Carroll, Sparky Lyle)	1.00	.50	.30
69	Phil Gagliano	.40	.20	.12
70	Milt Pappas	.70	.35	.20
71	Johnny Briggs	.40	.20	.12
72	Ron Reed	.50	.25	.15
73	Ed Herrmann	.40	.20	.12
74	Billy Champion	.40	.20	.12
75	Vada Pinson	1.00	.50	.30
76	Doug Rader	.40	.20	.12
77	Mike Torrez	.50	.25	.15
78	Richie Scheinblum	.40	.20	.12
79	Jim Willoughby	.40	.20	.12
80	Tony Oliva	2.00	1.00	.60
81a	Cubs Mgr./Coaches (Hank Aguirre, Ernie Banks, Larry Jansen, Whitey Lockman, Pete Reiser) (trees in Coaches background)	.90	.45	.25
81b	Cubs Mgr./Coaches (Hank Aguirre, Ernie Banks, Larry Jansen, Whitey Lockman, Pete Reiser) (orange, solid background)	.70	.35	.20
82	Fritz Peterson	.50	.25	.15
83	Leron Lee	.40	.20	.12
84	Rollie Fingers	4.00	2.00	1.25
85	Ted Simmons	2.00	1.00	.60
86	Tom McCraw	.40	.20	.12
87	Ken Boswell	.40	.20	.12
88	Mickey Stanley	.50	.25	.15
89	Jack Billingham	.40	.20	.12
90	Brooks Robinson	5.00	2.50	1.50
91	Dodgers Team	2.25	1.25	.70
92	Jerry Bell	.40	.20	.12
93	Jesus Alou	.50	.25	.15
94	Dick Billings	.40	.20	.12
95	Steve Blass	.50	.25	.15
96	Doug Griffin	.40	.20	.12
97	Willie Montanez	.50	.25	.15
98	Dick Woodson	.40	.20	.12
99	Carl Taylor	.40	.20	.12
100	Hank Aaron	20.00	10.00	6.00
101	Ken Henderson	.40	.20	.12
102	Rudy May	.50	.25	.15
103	Celerino Sanchez	.50	.25	.15
104	Reggie Cleveland	.40	.20	.12
105	Carlos May	.50	.25	.15
106	Terry Humphrey	.40	.20	.12
107	Phil Hennigan	.40	.20	.12
108	Bill Russell	.70	.35	.20
109	Doyle Alexander	2.25	1.25	.70
110	Bob Watson	.50	.25	.15
111	Dave Nelson	.40	.20	.12
112	Gary Ross	.40	.20	.12
113	Jerry Grote	.50	.25	.15
114	Lynn McGlothen	.40	.20	.12
115	Ron Santo	1.00	.50	.30
116a	Yankees Mgr./Coaches (Jim Hegan, Ralph Houk, Elston Howard, Dick Howser, Jim Turner) (Coaches background brown)	2.25	1.25	.70
116b	Yankees Mgr./Coaches (Jim Hegan, Ralph Houk, Elston Howard, Dick Howser, Jim Turner) (Coaches background orange)	.90	.45	.25
117	Ramon Hernandez	.40	.20	.12
118	John Mayberry	.70	.35	.20
119	Larry Bowa	1.00	.50	.30
120	Joe Coleman	.50	.25	.15
121	Dave Rader	.40	.20	.12

		NR MT	EX	VG
122	Jim Strickland	.40	.20	.12
123	Sandy Alomar	.40	.20	.12
124	Jim Hardin	.40	.20	.12
125	Ron Fairly	.70	.35	.20
126	Jim Brewer	.40	.20	.12
127	Brewers Team	1.25	.60	.40
128	Ted Sizemore	.40	.20	.12
129	Terry Forster	.70	.35	.20
130	Pete Rose	20.00	10.00	6.00
131a	Red Sox Mgr./Coaches (Doug Camilli, Eddie Kasko, Don Lenhardt, Eddie Popowski, Lee Stange) (Coaches background brown)	.70	.35	.20
131b	Red Sox Mgr./Coaches (Doug Camilli, Eddie Kasko, Don Lenhardt, Eddie Popowski, Lee Stange) (Coaches background orange)	.50	.25	.15
132	Matty Alou	.80	.40	.25
133	Dave Roberts	.40	.20	.12
134	Milt Wilcox	.50	.25	.15
135	Lee May	.70	.35	.20
136a	Orioles Mgr./Coaches (George Bamberger, Jim Frey, Billy Hunter, George Staller, Earl Weaver) (Coaches background brown)	2.25	1.25	.70
136b	Orioles Mgr./Coaches (George Bamberger, Jim Frey, Billy Hunter, George Staller, Earl Weaver) (Coaches background orange)	.90	.45	.25
137	Jim Beauchamp	.40	.20	.12
138	Horacio Pina	.40	.20	.12
139	Carmen Fanzone	.40	.20	.12
140	Lou Piniella	1.00	.50	.30
141	Bruce Kison	.50	.25	.15
142	Thurman Munson	9.00	4.50	2.75
143	John Curtis	.40	.20	.12
144	Marty Perez	.40	.20	.12
145	Bobby Bonds	.90	.45	.25
146	Woodie Fryman	.50	.25	.15
147	Mike Anderson	.40	.20	.12
148	*Dave Goltz*	.80	.40	.25
149	Ron Hunt	.50	.25	.15
150	Wilbur Wood	.70	.35	.20
151	Wes Parker	.50	.25	.15
152	Dave May	.40	.20	.12
153	Al Hrabosky	.70	.35	.20
154	Jeff Torborg	.50	.25	.15
155	Sal Bando	.90	.45	.25
156	Cesar Geronimo	.50	.25	.15
157	Denny Riddleberger	.40	.20	.12
158	Astros Team	1.25	.60	.40
159	Clarence Gaston	.40	.20	.12
160	Jim Palmer	10.00	5.00	3.00
161	Ted Martinez	.40	.20	.12
162	Pete Broberg	.40	.20	.12
163	Vic Davalillo	.50	.25	.15
164	Monty Montgomery	.40	.20	.12
165	Luis Aparicio	2.75	1.50	.80
166	Terry Harmon	.40	.20	.12
167	Steve Stone	.70	.35	.20
168	Jim Northrup	.50	.25	.15
169	Ron Schueler	.40	.20	.12
170	Harmon Killebrew	4.00	2.00	1.25
171	Bernie Carbo	.40	.20	.12
172	Steve Kline	.50	.25	.15
173	Hal Breeden	.40	.20	.12
174	*Rich Gossage*	12.00	6.00	3.50
175	Frank Robinson	5.00	2.50	1.50
176	Chuck Taylor	.40	.20	.12
177	Bill Plummer	.40	.20	.12
178	Don Rose	.40	.20	.12
179a	A's Mgr./Coaches (Jerry Adair, Vern Hoscheit, Irv Noren, Wes Stock, Dick Williams) (Coaches background brown)	1.00	.50	.30
179b	A's Mgr./Coaches (Jerry Adair, Vern Hoscheit, Irv Noren, Wes Stock, Dick Williams) (Coaches background orange)	.70	.35	.20
180	Fergie Jenkins	3.00	1.50	.90
181	Jack Brohamer	.40	.20	.12
182	*Mike Caldwell*	.70	.35	.20
183	Don Buford	.50	.25	.15
184	Jerry Koosman	.70	.35	.20
185	Jim Wynn	.70	.35	.20
186	Bill Fahey	.40	.20	.12
187	Luke Walker	.40	.20	.12
188	Cookie Rojas	.40	.20	.12
189	Greg Luzinski	.90	.45	.25
190	Bob Gibson	5.00	2.50	1.50
191	Tigers Team	2.00	1.00	.60

#	Card	NR MT	EX	VG
192	Pat Jarvis	.40	.20	.12
193	Carlton Fisk	40.00	20.00	12.00
194	*Jorge Orta*	.70	.35	.20
195	Clay Carroll	.50	.25	.15
196	Ken McMullen	.40	.20	.12
197	Ed Goodson	.40	.20	.12
198	Horace Clarke	.50	.25	.15
199	Bert Blyleven	2.25	1.25	.70
200	Billy Williams	2.75	1.50	.80
201	A.L. Playoffs (Hendrick Scores Winning Run.)	2.25	1.25	.70
202	N.L. Playoffs (Foster's Run Decides It.)	2.25	1.25	.70
203	World Series Game 1 (Tenace The Menace.)	2.25	1.25	.70
204	World Series Game 2 (A's Make It Two Straight.)	2.25	1.25	.70
205	World Series Game 3 (Reds Win Squeeker.)	2.25	1.25	.70
206	World Series Game 4 (Tenace Singles In Ninth.)	2.25	1.25	.70
207	World Series Game 5 (Odom Out At Plate.)	2.25	1.25	.70
208	World Series Game 6 (Reds' Slugging Ties Series.)	2.25	1.25	.70
209	World Series Game 7 (Campy Starts Winning Rally.)	2.25	1.25	.70
210	World Series Summary (World Champions.)	2.25	1.25	.70
211	Balor Moore	.40	.20	.12
212	Joe Lahoud	.40	.20	.12
213	Steve Garvey	15.00	7.50	4.50
214	Dave Hamilton	.40	.20	.12
215	Dusty Baker	.70	.35	.20
216	Toby Harrah	.70	.35	.20
217	Don Wilson	.40	.20	.12
218	Aurelio Rodriguez	.50	.25	.15
219	Cardinals Team	1.25	.60	.40
220	Nolan Ryan	70.00	35.00	20.00
221	Fred Kendall	.40	.20	.12
222	Rob Gardner	.40	.20	.12
223	Bud Harrelson	.50	.25	.15
224	Bill Lee	.50	.25	.15
225	Al Oliver	2.00	1.00	.60
226	Ray Fosse	.40	.20	.12
227	Wayne Twitchell	.40	.20	.12
228	Bobby Darwin	.40	.20	.12
229	Roric Harrison	.40	.20	.12
230	Joe Morgan	5.00	2.50	1.50
231	Bill Parsons	.40	.20	.12
232	Ken Singleton	.70	.35	.20
233	Ed Kirkpatrick	.40	.20	.12
234	*Bill North*	.70	.35	.20
235	Jim Hunter	4.00	2.00	1.25
236	Tito Fuentes	.40	.20	.12
237a	Braves Mgr./Coaches (Lew Burdette, Jim Busby, Roy Hartsfield, Eddie Mathews, Ken Silvestri) (Coaches background brown)	2.00	1.00	.60
237b	Braves Mgr./Coaches (Lew Burdette, Jim Busby, Roy Hartsfield, Eddie Mathews, Ken Silvestri) (Coaches background orange)	2.25	1.25	.70
238	Tony Muser	.40	.20	.12
239	Pete Richert	.40	.20	.12
240	Bobby Murcer	.80	.40	.25
241	Dwain Anderson	.40	.20	.12
242	George Culver	.40	.20	.12
243	Angels Team	1.25	.60	.40
244	Ed Acosta	.40	.20	.12
245	Carl Yastrzemski	15.00	7.50	4.50
246	Ken Sanders	.40	.20	.12
247	Del Unser	.40	.20	.12
248	Jerry Johnson	.40	.20	.12
249	Larry Biittner	.40	.20	.12
250	Manny Sanguillen	.50	.25	.15
251	Roger Nelson	.40	.20	.12
252a	Giants Mgr./Coaches (Joe Amalfitano, Charlie Fox, Andy Gilbert, Don McMahon, John McNamara) (Coaches background brown)	.70	.35	.20
252b	Giants Mgr./Coaches (Joe Amalfitano, Charlie Fox, Andy Gilbert, Don McMahon, John McNamara) (Coaches background orange)	.50	.25	.15
253	Mark Belanger	.50	.25	.15
254	Bill Stoneman	.40	.20	.12
255	Reggie Jackson	25.00	12.50	7.50
256	Chris Zachary	.40	.20	.12
257a	Mets Mgr./Coaches (Yogi Berra, Roy McMillan, Joe Pignatano, Rube Walker, Eddie Yost) (Coaches background brown)	2.25	1.25	.70
257b	Mets Mgr./Coaches (Yogi Berra, Roy McMillan, Joe Pignatano, Rube Walker, Eddie Yost) (Coaches background orange)	2.00	1.00	.60
258	Tommy John	2.25	1.25	.70
259	Jim Holt	.40	.20	.12
260	Gary Nolan	.40	.20	.12
261	Pat Kelly	.40	.20	.12
262	Jack Aker	.40	.20	.12
263	George Scott	.50	.25	.15
264	Checklist 133-264	2.00	1.00	.60
265	Gene Michael	.70	.35	.20
266	Mike Lum	.40	.20	.12
267	Lloyd Allen	.40	.20	.12
268	Jerry Morales	.40	.20	.12
269	Tim McCarver	.90	.45	.25
270	Luis Tiant	1.00	.50	.30
271	Tom Hutton	.40	.20	.12
272	Ed Farmer	.40	.20	.12
273	Chris Speier	.50	.25	.15
274	Darold Knowles	.40	.20	.12
275	Tony Perez	2.00	1.00	.60
276	Joe Lovitto	.40	.20	.12
277	Bob Miller	.40	.20	.12
278	Orioles Team	1.25	.60	.40
279	Mike Strahler	.40	.20	.12
280	Al Kaline	5.00	2.50	1.50
281	Mike Jorgensen	.40	.20	.12
282	Steve Hovley	.40	.20	.12
283	Ray Sadecki	.40	.20	.12
284	Glenn Borgmann	.40	.20	.12
285	Don Kessinger	.50	.25	.15
286	Frank Linzy	.40	.20	.12
287	Eddie Leon	.40	.20	.12
288	Gary Gentry	.40	.20	.12
289	Bob Oliver	.40	.20	.12
290	Cesar Cedeno	.70	.35	.20
291	Rogelio Moret	.40	.20	.12
292	Jose Cruz	1.00	.50	.30
293	Bernie Allen	.50	.25	.15
294	Steve Arlin	.40	.20	.12
295	Bert Campaneris	.80	.40	.25
296	Reds Mgr./Coaches (Sparky Anderson, Alex Grammas, Ted Kluszewski, George Scherger, Larry Shepard)	.90	.45	.25
297	Walt Williams	.40	.20	.12
298	Ron Bryant	.40	.20	.12
299	Ted Ford	.40	.20	.12
300	Steve Carlton	12.00	6.00	3.50
301	Billy Grabarkewitz	.40	.20	.12
302	Terry Crowley	.40	.20	.12
303	Nelson Briles	.40	.20	.12
304	Duke Sims	.40	.20	.12
305	Willie Mays	30.00	15.00	9.00
306	Tom Burgmeier	.40	.20	.12
307	Boots Day	.40	.20	.12
308	Skip Lockwood	.40	.20	.12
309	Paul Popovich	.40	.20	.12
310	Dick Allen	1.00	.50	.30
311	Joe Decker	.40	.20	.12
312	Oscar Brown	.40	.20	.12
313	Jim Ray	.40	.20	.12
314	Ron Swoboda	.50	.25	.15
315	John Odom	.50	.25	.15
316	Padres Team	1.25	.60	.40
317	Danny Cater	.40	.20	.12
318	Jim McGlothlin	.40	.20	.12
319	Jim Spencer	.40	.20	.12
320	Lou Brock	5.00	2.50	1.50
321	Rich Hinton	.40	.20	.12
322	*Garry Maddox*	1.00	.50	.30
323	Tigers Mgr./Coaches (Art Fowler, Billy Martin, Joe Schultz, Charlie Silvera, Dick Tracewski)	2.25	1.25	.70
324	Al Downing	.50	.25	.15
325	Boog Powell	2.25	1.25	.70
326	Darrell Brandon	.40	.20	.12
327	John Lowenstein	.40	.20	.12
328	Bill Bonham	.40	.20	.12
329	Ed Kranepool	.50	.25	.15
330	Rod Carew	18.00	9.00	5.50
331	Carl Morton	.40	.20	.12
332	*John Felske*	.50	.25	.15
333	Gene Clines	.40	.20	.12
334	Freddie Patek	.40	.20	.12
335	Bob Tolan	.50	.25	.15
336	Tom Bradley	.40	.20	.12
337	Dave Duncan	.40	.20	.12
338	Checklist 265-396	2.00	1.00	.60
339	Dick Tidrow	.50	.25	.15
340	Nate Colbert	.50	.25	.15
341	Boyhood Photo (Jim Palmer)	2.00	1.00	.60

		NR MT	EX	VG
342	Boyhood Photo (Sam McDowell)	.70	.35	.20
343	Boyhood Photo (Bobby Murcer)	.70	.35	.20
344	Boyhood Photo (Jim Hunter)	2.00	1.00	.60
345	Boyhood Photo (Chris Speier)	.50	.25	.15
346	Boyhood Photo (Gaylord Perry)	2.00	1.00	.60
347	Royals Team	1.25	.60	.40
348	Rennie Stennett	.50	.25	.15
349	Dick McAuliffe	.50	.25	.15
350	Tom Seaver	20.00	10.00	6.00
351	Jimmy Stewart	.40	.20	.12
352	*Don Stanhouse*	.70	.35	.20
353	Steve Brye	.40	.20	.12
354	Billy Parker	.40	.20	.12
355	Mike Marshall	.70	.35	.20
356	White Sox Mgr./Coaches (Joe Lonnett, Jim Mahoney, Al Monchak, Johnny Sain, Chuck Tanner)	.70	.35	.20
357	Ross Grimsley	.50	.25	.15
358	Jim Nettles	.40	.20	.12
359	Cecil Upshaw	.40	.20	.12
360	Joe Rudi (photo actually Gene Tenace)	.70	.35	.20
361	Fran Healy	.40	.20	.12
362	Eddie Watt	.40	.20	.12
363	Jackie Hernandez	.40	.20	.12
364	Rick Wise	.50	.25	.15
365	Rico Petrocelli	.70	.35	.20
366	Brock Davis	.40	.20	.12
367	Burt Hooton	.70	.35	.20
368	Bill Buckner	.90	.45	.25
369	Lerrin LaGrow	.40	.20	.12
370	Willie Stargell	4.00	2.00	1.25
371	Mike Kekich	.50	.25	.15
372	Oscar Gamble	.50	.25	.15
373	Clyde Wright	.40	.20	.12
374	Darrell Evans	.90	.45	.25
375	Larry Dierker	.50	.25	.15
376	Frank Duffy	.40	.20	.12
377	Expos Mgr./Coaches (Dave Bristol, Larry Doby, Gene Mauch, Cal McLish, Jerry Zimmerman)	.70	.35	.20
378	Lenny Randle	.40	.20	.12
379	Cy Acosta	.40	.20	.12
380	Johnny Bench	20.00	10.00	6.00
381	Vicente Romo	.40	.20	.12
382	Mike Hegan	.40	.20	.12
383	Diego Segui	.40	.20	.12
384	Don Baylor	2.25	1.25	.70
385	Jim Perry	.70	.35	.20
386	Don Money	.50	.25	.15
387	Jim Barr	.40	.20	.12
388	Ben Oglivie	.70	.35	.20
389	Mets Team	2.00	1.00	.60
390	Mickey Lolich	.90	.45	.25
391	*Lee Lacy*	1.00	.50	.30
392	Dick Drago	.40	.20	.12
393	Jose Cardenal	.50	.25	.15
394	Sparky Lyle	.90	.45	.25
395	Roger Metzger	.40	.20	.12
396	Grant Jackson	.40	.20	.12
397	Dave Cash	.70	.35	.20
398	Rich Hand	.70	.35	.20
399	George Foster	2.25	1.25	.70
400	Gaylord Perry	4.00	2.00	1.25
401	Clyde Mashore	.70	.35	.20
402	Jack Hiatt	.70	.35	.20
403	Sonny Jackson	.70	.35	.20
404	Chuck Brinkman	.70	.35	.20
405	Cesar Tovar	.70	.35	.20
406	Paul Lindblad	.70	.35	.20
407	Felix Millan	.70	.35	.20
408	Jim Colborn	.70	.35	.20
409	Ivan Murrell	.70	.35	.20
410	Willie McCovey	5.00	2.50	1.50
411	Ray Corbin	.70	.35	.20
412	Manny Mota	.80	.40	.25
413	Tom Timmermann	.70	.35	.20
414	Ken Rudolph	.70	.35	.20
415	Marty Pattin	.70	.35	.20
416	Paul Schaal	.70	.35	.20
417	Scipio Spinks	.70	.35	.20
418	Bobby Grich	.80	.40	.25
419	Casey Cox	.70	.35	.20
420	Tommie Agee	.70	.35	.20
421	Angels Mgr./Coaches (Tom Morgan, Salty Parker, Jimmie Reese, John Roseboro, Bobby Winkles)	.70	.35	.20
422	Bob Robertson	.70	.35	.20
423	Johnny Jeter	.70	.35	.20
424	Denny Doyle	.70	.35	.20
425	Alex Johnson	.70	.35	.20

		NR MT	EX	VG
426	Dave LaRoche	.70	.35	.20
427	Rick Auerbach	.70	.35	.20
428	Wayne Simpson	.70	.35	.20
429	Jim Fairey	.70	.35	.20
430	Vida Blue	1.00	.50	.30
431	Gerry Moses	.70	.35	.20
432	Dan Frisella	.70	.35	.20
433	Willie Horton	.80	.40	.25
434	Giants Team	2.25	1.25	.70
435	Rico Carty	.80	.40	.25
436	Jim McAndrew	.70	.35	.20
437	John Kennedy	.70	.35	.20
438	Enzo Hernandez	.70	.35	.20
439	Eddie Fisher	.70	.35	.20
440	Glenn Beckert	.70	.35	.20
441	Gail Hopkins	.70	.35	.20
442	Dick Dietz	.70	.35	.20
443	Danny Thompson	.70	.35	.20
444	Ken Brett	.70	.35	.20
445	Ken Berry	.70	.35	.20
446	Jerry Reuss	.80	.40	.25
447	Joe Hague	.70	.35	.20
448	John Hiller	.70	.35	.20
449a	Indians Mgr./Coaches (Ken Aspromonte, Rocky Colavito, Joe Lutz, Warren Spahn) (Spahn's ear pointed)	.70	.35	.20
449b	Indians Mgr./Coaches (Ken Aspromonte, Rocky Colavito, Joe Lutz, Warren Spahn) (Spahn's ear round)	1.00	.50	.30
450	Joe Torre	2.25	1.25	.70
451	John Vukovich	.70	.35	.20
452	Paul Casanova	.70	.35	.20
453	Checklist 397-528	2.25	1.25	.70
454	Tom Haller	.70	.35	.20
455	Bill Melton	.70	.35	.20
456	Dick Green	.70	.35	.20
457	John Strohmayer	.70	.35	.20
458	Jim Mason	.70	.35	.20
459	Jimmy Howarth	.70	.35	.20
460	Bill Freehan	.80	.40	.25
461	Mike Corkins	.70	.35	.20
462	Ron Blomberg	.70	.35	.20
463	Ken Tatum	.70	.35	.20
464	Cubs Team	2.25	1.25	.70
465	Dave Giusti	.70	.35	.20
466	Jose Arcia	.70	.35	.20
467	Mike Ryan	.70	.35	.20
468	Tom Griffin	.70	.35	.20
469	Dan Monzon	.70	.35	.20
470	Mike Cuellar	.80	.40	.25
471	Hit Leader (Ty Cobb)	4.00	2.00	1.25
472	Grand Slam Leader (Lou Gehrig)	4.00	2.00	1.25
473	Total Base Leader (Hank Aaron)	4.00	2.00	1.25
474	R.B.I. Leader (Babe Ruth)	6.00	3.00	1.75
475	Batting Leader (Ty Cobb)	4.00	2.00	1.25
476	Shutout Leader (Walter Johnson)	2.00	1.00	.60
477	Victory Leader (Cy Young)	2.00	1.00	.60
478	Strikeout Leader (Walter Johnson)	2.00	1.00	.60
479	Hal Lanier	.80	.40	.25
480	Juan Marichal	3.50	1.75	1.00
481	White Sox Team	2.00	1.00	.60
482	*Rick Reuschel*	4.00	2.00	1.25
483	Dal Maxvill	.70	.35	.20
484	Ernie McAnally	.70	.35	.20
485	Norm Cash	1.00	.50	.30
486a	Phillies Mgr./Coaches (Carroll Berringer, Billy DeMars, Danny Ozark, Ray Rippelmeyer, Bobby Wine) (Coaches background brown red)	.90	.45	.25
486b	Phillies Mgr./Coaches (Carroll Beringer, Billy DeMars, Danny Ozark, Ray Rippelmeyer, Bobby Wine) (Coaches background orange)	.70	.35	.20
487	Bruce Dal Canton	.70	.35	.20
488	Dave Campbell	.70	.35	.20
489	Jeff Burroughs	.80	.40	.25
490	Claude Osteen	.80	.40	.25
491	Bob Montgomery	.70	.35	.20
492	Pedro Borbon	.70	.35	.20
493	Duffy Dyer	.70	.35	.20
494	Rich Morales	.70	.35	.20
495	Tommy Helms	.70	.35	.20
496	Ray Lamb	.70	.35	.20
497	Cardinals Mgr./Coaches (Vern Benson, George Kissell, Red Schoendienst, Barney Schultz)	1.25	.60	.40
498	Graig Nettles	2.50	1.25	.70
499	Bob Moose	.70	.35	.20
500	A's Team	2.25	1.25	.70
501	Larry Gura	.70	.35	.20

		NR MT	EX	VG
502	Bobby Valentine	.80	.40	.25
503	Phil Niekro	3.25	1.75	1.00
504	Earl Williams	.70	.35	.20
505	Bob Bailey	.70	.35	.20
506	Bart Johnson	.70	.35	.20
507	Darrel Chaney	.70	.35	.20
508	Gates Brown	.70	.35	.20
509	Jim Nash	.70	.35	.20
510	Amos Otis	.80	.40	.25
511	Sam McDowell	.80	.40	.25
512	Dalton Jones	.70	.35	.20
513	Dave Marshall	.70	.35	.20
514	Jerry Kenney	.70	.35	.20
515	Andy Messersmith	.70	.35	.20
516	Danny Walton	.70	.35	.20
517a	Pirates Mgr./Coaches (Don Leppert, Bill Mazeroski, Dave Ricketts, Bill Virdon, Mel Wright) (Coaches background brown)	2.25	1.25	.70
517b	Pirates Mgr./Coaches (Don Leppert, Bill Mazeroski, Dave Ricketts, Bill Virdon, Mel Wright) (Coaches background orange)	.70	.35	.20
518	Bob Veale	.70	.35	.20
519	John Edwards	.70	.35	.20
520	Mel Stottlemyre	.80	.40	.25
521	Braves Team	2.25	1.25	.70
522	Leo Cardenas	.70	.35	.20
523	Wayne Granger	.70	.35	.20
524	Gene Tenace	.70	.35	.20
525	Jim Fregosi	.90	.45	.25
526	Ollie Brown	.70	.35	.20
527	Dan McGinn	.70	.35	.20
528	Paul Blair	.70	.35	.20
529	Milt May	2.00	1.00	.60
530	Jim Kaat	4.00	2.00	1.25
531	Ron Woods	2.00	1.00	.60
532	Steve Mingori	2.00	1.00	.60
533	Larry Stahl	2.00	1.00	.60
534	Dave Lemonds	2.00	1.00	.60
535	John Callison	2.25	1.25	.70
536	Phillies Team	2.50	1.25	.70
537	Bill Slayback	2.00	1.00	.60
538	Jim Hart	2.25	1.25	.70
539	Tom Murphy	2.00	1.00	.60
540	Cleon Jones	2.25	1.25	.70
541	Bob Bolin	2.00	1.00	.60
542	Pat Corrales	2.25	1.25	.70
543	Alan Foster	2.00	1.00	.60
544	Von Joshua	2.00	1.00	.60
545	Orlando Cepeda	4.00	2.00	1.25
546	Jim York	2.00	1.00	.60
547	Bobby Heise	2.00	1.00	.60
548	Don Durham	2.00	1.00	.60
549	Rangers Mgr./Coaches (Chuck Estrada, Whitey Herzog, Chuck Hiller, Jackie Moore)	2.00	1.00	.60
550	Dave Johnson	2.75	1.50	.80
551	Mike Kilkenny	2.00	1.00	.60
552	J.C. Martin	2.00	1.00	.60
553	Mickey Scott	2.00	1.00	.60
554	Dave Concepcion	2.50	1.25	.70
555	Bill Hands	2.00	1.00	.60
556	Yankees Team	6.00	3.00	1.75
557	Bernie Williams	2.00	1.00	.60
558	Jerry May	2.00	1.00	.60
559	Barry Lersch	2.00	1.00	.60
560	Frank Howard	2.25	1.25	.70
561	Jim Geddes	2.00	1.00	.60
562	Wayne Garrett	2.00	1.00	.60
563	Larry Haney	2.00	1.00	.60
564	Mike Thompson	2.00	1.00	.60
565	Jim Hickman	2.25	1.25	.70
566	Lew Krausse	2.00	1.00	.60
567	Bob Fenwick	2.00	1.00	.60
568	Ray Newman	2.00	1.00	.60
569	Dodgers Mgr./Coaches (Red Adams, Walt Alston, Monty Basgall, Jim Gillam, Tom Lasorda)	3.00	1.50	.90
570	Bill Singer	2.25	1.25	.70
571	Rusty Torres	2.00	1.00	.60
572	Gary Sutherland	2.00	1.00	.60
573	Fred Beene	2.25	1.25	.70
574	Bob Didier	2.00	1.00	.60
575	Dock Ellis	2.25	1.25	.70
576	Expos Team	2.50	1.25	.70
577	*Eric Soderholm*	2.25	1.25	.70
578	Ken Wright	2.00	1.00	.60
579	Tom Grieve	2.00	1.00	.60
580	Joe Pepitone	2.00	1.00	.60
581	Steve Kealey	2.00	1.00	.60
582	Darrell Porter	2.25	1.25	.70
583	Bill Greif	2.00	1.00	.60
584	Chris Arnold	2.00	1.00	.60
585	Joe Niekro	2.00	1.00	.60
586	Bill Sudakis	2.25	1.25	.70
587	Rich McKinney	2.00	1.00	.60
588	Checklist 529-660	18.00	9.00	5.50
589	Ken Forsch	2.25	1.25	.70
590	Deron Johnson	2.00	1.00	.60
591	Mike Hedlund	2.00	1.00	.60
592	John Boccabella	2.00	1.00	.60
593	Royals Mgr./Coaches (Galen Cisco, Harry Dunlop, Charlie Lau, Jack McKeon)	2.25	1.25	.70
594	Vic Harris	2.00	1.00	.60
595	Don Gullett	2.25	1.25	.70
596	Red Sox Team	2.75	1.50	.80
597	Mickey Rivers	2.25	1.25	.70
598	Phil Roof	2.00	1.00	.60
599	Ed Crosby	2.00	1.00	.60
600	Dave McNally	2.25	1.25	.70
601	Rookie Catchers (George Pena, Sergio Robles, Rick Stelmaszek)	2.00	1.00	.60
602	Rookie Pitchers (Mel Behney, Ralph Garcia, *Doug Rau*)	2.25	1.25	.70
603	Rookie Third Basemen (Terry Hughes, Bill McNulty, *Ken Reitz*)	2.25	1.25	.70
604	Rookie Pitchers (Jesse Jefferson, Dennis O'Toole, Bob Strampe)	2.00	1.00	.60
605	Rookie First Basemen (Pat Bourque, *Enos Cabell*, Gonzalo Marquez)	2.25	1.25	.70
606	Rookie Outfielders (*Gary Matthews*, Tom Paciorek, Jorge Roque)	2.25	1.25	.70
607	Rookie Shortstops (Ray Busse, Pepe Frias, Mario Guerrero)	2.00	1.00	.60
608	Rookie Pitchers (*Steve Busby*, Dick Colpaert, *George Medich*)	2.25	1.25	.70
609	Rookie Second Basemen (Larvell Blanks, Pedro Garcia, *Dave Lopes*)	4.00	2.00	1.25
610	Rookie Pitchers (Jimmy Freeman, Charlie Hough, Hank Webb)	2.25	1.25	.70
611	Rookie Outfielders (Rich Coggins, Jim Wohlford, Richie Zisk)	2.25	1.25	.70
612	Rookie Pitchers (Steve Lawson, Bob Reynolds, Brent Strom)	2.00	1.00	.60
613	Rookie Catchers (*Bob Boone*, Mike Ivie, Skip Jutze)	30.00	15.00	9.00
614	Rookie Outfielders (*Alonza Bumbry*, *Dwight Evans*, Charlie Spikes)	70.00	35.00	21.00
615	Rookie Third Basemen (Ron Cey, John Hilton, *Mike Schmidt*)	450.00	225.00	135.00
616	Rookie Pitchers (Norm Angelini, Steve Blateric, Mike Garman)	2.25	1.25	.70
617	Rich Chiles	2.00	1.00	.60
618	Andy Etchebarren	2.00	1.00	.60
619	Billy Wilson	2.00	1.00	.60
620	Tommy Harper	2.25	1.25	.70
621	Joe Ferguson	2.00	1.00	.60
622	Larry Hisle	2.25	1.25	.70
623	Steve Renko	2.00	1.00	.60
624	Astros Mgr./Coaches (Leo Durocher, Preston Gomez, Grady Hatton, Hub Kittle, Jim Owens)	2.25	1.25	.70
625	Angel Mangual	2.00	1.00	.60
626	Bob Barton	2.00	1.00	.60
627	Luis Alvarado	2.00	1.00	.60
628	Jim Slaton	2.25	1.25	.70
629	Indians Team	2.50	1.25	.70
630	Denny McLain	3.00	1.50	.90
631	Tom Matchick	2.00	1.00	.60
632	Dick Selma	2.00	1.00	.60
633	Ike Brown	2.00	1.00	.60
634	Alan Closter	2.25	1.25	.70
635	Gene Alley	2.25	1.25	.70
636	Rick Clark	2.00	1.00	.60
637	Norm Niller	2.00	1.00	.60
638	Ken Reynolds	2.00	1.00	.60
639	Willie Crawford	2.00	1.00	.60
640	Dick Bosman	2.00	1.00	.60
641	Reds Team	2.75	1.50	.80
642	Jose Laboy	2.00	1.00	.60
643	Al Fitzmorris	2.00	1.00	.60
644	Jack Heidemann	2.00	1.00	.60
645	Bob Locker	2.00	1.00	.60
646	Brewers Mgr./Coaches (Del Crandall, Harvey Kuenn, Joe Nossek, Bob Shaw, Jim Walton)	2.25	1.25	.70
647	George Stone	2.00	1.00	.60
648	Tom Egan	2.00	1.00	.60
649	Rich Folkers	2.00	1.00	.60
650	Felipe Alou	2.25	1.25	.70
651	Don Carrithers	2.00	1.00	.60
652	Ted Kubiak	2.00	1.00	.60

		NR MT	EX	VG
628	Jim Slaton	1.50	.70	.45
629	Indians Team	2.50	1.25	.70
630	Denny McLain	3.00	1.50	.90
631	Tom Matchick	2.00	1.00	.60
632	Dick Selma	2.00	1.00	.60
633	Ike Brown	2.00	1.00	.60
634	Alan Closter	1.50	.70	.45
635	Gene Alley	1.50	.70	.45
636	Rick Clark	2.00	1.00	.60
637	Norm Niller	2.00	1.00	.60
638	Ken Reynolds	2.00	1.00	.60
639	Willie Crawford	2.00	1.00	.60
640	Dick Bosman	2.00	1.00	.60
641	Reds Team	2.75	1.50	.80
642	Jose Laboy	2.00	1.00	.60
643	Al Fitzmorris	2.00	1.00	.60
644	Jack Heidemann	2.00	1.00	.60
645	Bob Locker	2.00	1.00	.60
646	Brewers Mgr./Coaches (Del Crandall, Harvey Kuenn, Joe Nossek, Bob Shaw, Jim Walton)	2.25	1.25	.70
647	George Stone	2.00	1.00	.60
648	Tom Egan	2.00	1.00	.60
649	Rich Folkers	2.00	1.00	.60
650	Felipe Alou	2.25	1.25	.70
651	Don Carrithers	2.00	1.00	.60
652	Ted Kubiak	2.00	1.00	.60
653	Joe Hoerner	2.00	1.00	.60
654	Twins Team	2.50	1.25	.70
655	Clay Kirby	2.00	1.00	.60
656	John Ellis	2.00	1.00	.60
657	Bob Johnson	2.00	1.00	.60
658	Elliott Maddox	2.25	1.25	.70
659	Jose Pagan	2.25	1.25	.70
660	Fred Scherman	2.25	.70	.45

1973 Topps Candy Lids

A bit out of the ordinary, the Topps Candy Lids were the top of a product called "Baseball Stars Bubble Gum." The bottom (inside) of the lids carry a color photo of a player with a ribbon which contains the name, position and team. The lids are 1-7/8" in diameter. A total of 55 different lids were made, featuring most of the stars of the day.

		NR MT	EX	VG
Complete Set:		450.00	225.00	135.00
Common Player:		2.00	1.00	.60
(1)	Hank Aaron	30.00	15.00	9.00
(2)	Dick Allen	4.00	2.00	1.25
(3)	Dusty Baker	2.00	1.00	.60
(4)	Sal Bando	3.00	1.50	.90
(5)	Johnny Bench	20.00	10.00	6.00
(6)	Bobby Bonds	3.00	1.50	.90
(7)	Dick Bosman	2.00	1.00	.60
(8)	Lou Brock	15.00	7.50	4.50
(9)	Rod Carew	20.00	10.00	6.00
(10)	Steve Carlton	20.00	10.00	6.00
(11)	Nate Colbert	2.00	1.00	.60
(12)	Willie Davis	3.00	1.50	.90
(13)	Larry Dierker	2.00	1.00	.60
(14)	Mike Epstein	2.00	1.00	.60
(15)	Carlton Fisk	7.00	3.50	2.00
(16)	Tim Foli	2.00	1.00	.60
(17)	Ray Fosse	2.00	1.00	.60
(18)	Bill Freehan	3.00	1.50	.90
(19)	Bob Gibson	15.00	7.50	4.50
(20)	Bud Harrelson	2.00	1.00	.60
(21)	Jim Hunter	12.00	6.00	3.50
(22)	Reggie Jackson	25.00	12.50	7.50
(23)	Fergie Jenkins	7.00	3.50	2.00
(24)	Al Kaline	15.00	7.50	4.50
(25)	Harmon Killebrew	15.00	7.50	4.50
(26)	Clay Kirby	2.00	1.00	.60
(27)	Mickey Lolich	4.00	2.00	1.25
(28)	Greg Luzinski	3.00	1.50	.90
(29)	Mike Marshall	2.00	1.00	.60
(30)	Lee May	2.00	1.00	.60
(31)	John Mayberry	2.00	1.00	.60
(32)	Willie Mays	30.00	15.00	9.00
(33)	Willie McCovey	15.00	7.50	4.50
(34)	Thurman Munson	15.00	7.50	4.50
(35)	Bobby Murcer	3.00	1.50	.90
(36)	Gary Nolan	2.00	1.00	.60
(37)	Amos Otis	2.00	1.00	.60
(38)	Jim Palmer	12.00	6.00	3.50
(39)	Gaylord Perry	12.00	6.00	3.50
(40)	Lou Piniella	3.00	1.50	.90
(41)	Brooks Robinson	18.00	9.00	5.50
(42)	Frank Robinson	15.00	7.50	4.50
(43)	Ellie Rodriguez	2.00	1.00	.60
(44)	Pete Rose	65.00	32.00	19.50
(45)	Nolan Ryan	18.00	9.00	5.50
(46)	Manny Sanguillen	2.00	1.00	.60
(47)	George Scott	2.00	1.00	.60
(48)	Tom Seaver	20.00	10.00	6.00
(49)	Chris Speier	2.00	1.00	.60
(50)	Willie Stargell	15.00	7.50	4.50
(51)	Don Sutton	12.00	6.00	3.50
(52)	Joe Torre	4.00	2.00	1.25
(53)	Billy Williams	12.00	6.00	3.50
(54)	Wilbur Wood	2.00	1.00	.60
(55)	Carl Yastrzemski	25.00	12.50	7.50

1973 Topps Comics

Strictly a test issue, if ever publicly distributed at all (most are found without any folding which would have occurred had they actually been used to wrap a piece of bubblegum), the 24 players in the 1973 Topps Comics issue appear on 4-5/8" by 3-7/16" waxed paper wrappers. The inside of the wrapper combines a color photo and facsimile autograph with a comic-style presentation of the player's career highlights. The Comics share a checklist with the 1973 Topps Pin-Ups, virtually all star players.

		NR MT	EX	VG
Complete Set:		3000.00	1500.00	900.00
Common Player:		70.00	35.00	21.00
(1)	Hank Aaron	200.00	100.00	60.00
(2)	Dick Allen	80.00	40.00	24.00
(3)	Johnny Bench	150.00	75.00	45.00
(4)	Steve Carlton	125.00	62.00	37.00
(5)	Nate Colbert	70.00	35.00	21.00
(6)	Willie Davis	80.00	40.00	24.00
(7)	Mike Epstein	70.00	35.00	21.00
(8)	Reggie Jackson	200.00	100.00	60.00
(9)	Harmon Killebrew	125.00	62.00	37.00
(10)	Mickey Lolich	80.00	40.00	24.00
(11)	Mike Marshall	70.00	35.00	21.00
(12)	Lee May	70.00	35.00	21.00

		NR MT	EX	VG
(13)	Willie McCovey	125.00	62.00	37.00
(14)	Bobby Murcer	80.00	40.00	24.00
(15)	Gaylord Perry	100.00	50.00	30.00
(16)	Lou Piniella	80.00	40.00	24.00
(17)	Brooks Robinson	125.00	62.00	37.00
(18)	Nolan Ryan	125.00	62.00	37.00
(19)	George Scott	70.00	35.00	21.00
(20)	Tom Seaver	150.00	75.00	45.00
(21)	Willie Stargell	100.00	50.00	30.00
(22)	Joe Torre	80.00	40.00	24.00
(23)	Billy Williams	100.00	50.00	30.00
(24)	Carl Yastrzemski	250.00	125.00	75.00

1973 Topps Pin-Ups

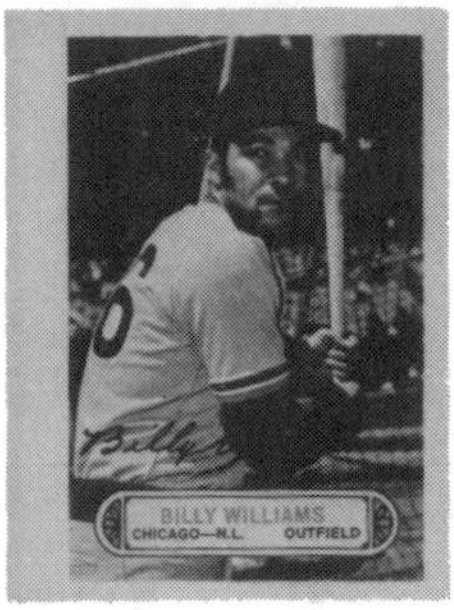

Another test issue of 1973, the 24 Topps Pin-Ups include the same basic format and the same checklist of star-caliber players as the Comics test issue of the same year. The 3-7/16" by 4-5/8" Pin-Ups are actually the inside of a wrapper for a piece of bubblegum. The color player photo features a decorative lozenge inserted at bottom with the player's name, team and position. There is also a facsimile autograph. Curiously, neither the Pin-Ups nor the Comics of 1973 bear team logos on the players' caps.

		NR MT	EX	VG
Complete Set:		1250.00	625.00	375.00
Common Player:		30.00	15.00	9.00
(1)	Hank Aaron	90.00	45.00	27.00
(2)	Dick Allen	35.00	17.50	10.50
(3)	Johnny Bench	70.00	35.00	21.00
(4)	Steve Carlton	60.00	30.00	18.00
(5)	Nate Colbert	30.00	15.00	9.00
(6)	Willie Davis	35.00	17.50	10.50
(7)	Mike Epstein	30.00	15.00	9.00
(8)	Reggie Jackson	90.00	45.00	27.00
(9)	Harmon Killebrew	50.00	25.00	15.00
(10)	Mickey Lolich	35.00	17.50	10.50
(11)	Mike Marshall	30.00	15.00	9.00
(12)	Lee May	30.00	15.00	9.00
(13)	Willie McCovey	50.00	25.00	15.00
(14)	Bobby Murcer	35.00	17.50	10.50
(15)	Gaylord Perry	45.00	22.00	13.50
(16)	Lou Piniella	35.00	17.50	10.50
(17)	Brooks Robinson	55.00	27.00	16.50
(18)	Nolan Ryan	55.00	27.00	16.50
(19)	George Scott	30.00	15.00	9.00
(20)	Tom Seaver	75.00	37.00	22.00
(21)	Willie Stargell	45.00	22.00	13.50
(22)	Joe Torre	35.00	17.50	10.50
(23)	Billy Williams	45.00	22.00	13.50
(24)	Carl Yastrzemski	110.00	55.00	33.00

1973 Topps Team Checklists

This is a 24-card unnumbered set of 2-1/2" by 3-1/2" cards that is generally believed to have been included with the high-numbered series in 1973, while also being made available in a mail-in offer. The front of the cards have the team name at the top and a white panel with various facsimile autographs takes

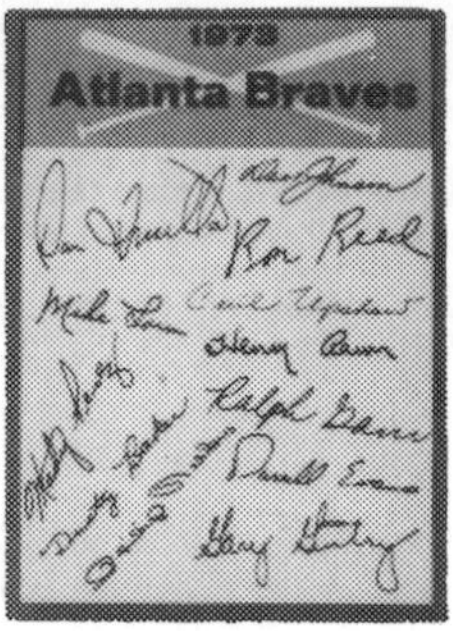

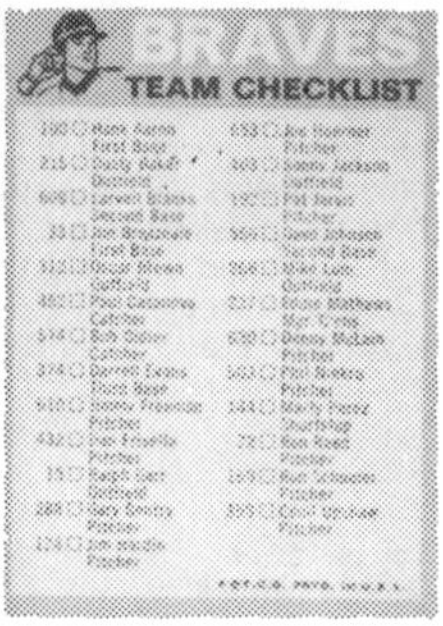

up the rest of the space except for a blue border. Backs feature the team name and checklist. Relatively scarce, these somewhat mysterious cards are not included by many in their collections despite their obvious relationship to the regular set.

		NR MT	EX	VG
Complete Set:		75.00	37.00	22.00
Common Checklist:		3.00	1.50	.90
(1)	Atlanta Braves	3.00	1.50	.90
(2)	Baltimore Orioles	3.00	1.50	.90
(3)	Boston Red Sox	3.00	1.50	.90
(4)	California Angels	3.00	1.50	.90
(5)	Chicago Cubs	3.00	1.50	.90
(6)	Chicago White Sox	3.00	1.50	.90
(7)	Cincinnati Reds	3.00	1.50	.90
(8)	Cleveland Indians	3.00	1.50	.90
(9)	Detroit Tigers	3.50	1.75	1.00
(10)	Houston Astros	3.00	1.50	.90
(11)	Kansas City Royals	3.00	1.50	.90
(12)	Los Angeles Dodgers	3.00	1.50	.90
(13)	Milwaukee Brewers	3.00	1.50	.90
(14)	Minnesota Twins	3.00	1.50	.90
(15)	Montreal Expos	3.00	1.50	.90
(16)	New York Mets	3.50	1.75	1.00
(17)	New York Yankees	3.50	1.75	1.00
(18)	Oakland A's	3.50	1.75	1.00
(19)	Philadelphia Phillies	3.00	1.50	.90
(20)	Pittsburgh Pirates	3.00	1.50	.90
(21)	St. Louis Cardinals	3.00	1.50	.90
(22)	San Diego Padres	3.00	1.50	.90
(23)	San Francisco Giants	3.00	1.50	.90
(24)	Texas Rangers	3.00	1.50	.90

1974 Topps

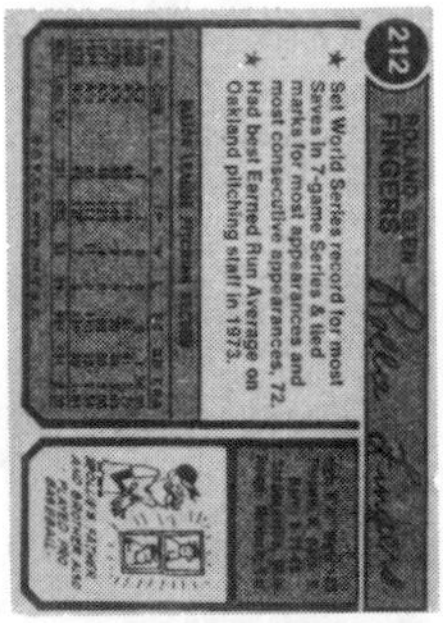

Issued all at once at the beginning of the year, rather than by series throughout the baseball season as had been done since 1952, this 660-card '74 Topps set features a famous group of error cards. At the time the cards were printed, it was uncertain whether the San Diego Padres would move to Washington, D.C., and by the time a decision was made some Padres cards had appeared with a "Washington, Nat'l League" designation on the front. A total of 15 cards were affected, and those with the

Washington designation bring prices well in excess of regular cards of the same players (the Washington variations are not included in the complete set prices quoted below). The 2-1/2" by 3-1/2" cards feature color photos (frequently game-action shots) along with the player's name, team and position. Specialty cards abound, starting with a Hank Aaron tribute and running through the usual managers, statistical leaders, playoff and World Series highlights, multi-player rookie cards and All-Stars.

		NR MT	EX	VG
Complete Set:		550.00	275.00	165.00
Common Player:		.30	.15	.09
1	Hank Aaron	30.00	15.00	9.00
2	Aaron Special 1954-57	3.00	1.50	.90
3	Aaron Special 1958-61	3.00	1.50	.90
4	Aaron Special 1962-65	3.00	1.50	.90
5	Aaron Special 1966-69	3.00	1.50	.90
6	Aaron Special 1970-73	3.00	1.50	.90
7	Jim Hunter	3.00	1.50	.90
8	George Theodore	.30	.15	.09
9	Mickey Lolich	.60	.30	.20
10	Johnny Bench	15.00	7.50	4.50
11	Jim Bibby	.30	.15	.09
12	Dave May	.30	.15	.09
13	Tom Hilgendorf	.30	.15	.09
14	Paul Popovich	.30	.15	.09
15	Joe Torre	.80	.40	.25
16	Orioles Team	.80	.40	.25
17	Doug Bird	.30	.15	.09
18	Gary Thomasson	.30	.15	.09
19	Gerry Moses	.30	.15	.09
20	Nolan Ryan	40.00	20.00	12.00
21	Bob Gallagher	.30	.15	.09
22	Cy Acosta	.30	.15	.09
23	Craig Robinson	.30	.15	.09
24	John Hiller	.30	.15	.09
25	Ken Singleton	.30	.15	.09
26	*Bill Campbell*	.40	.20	.12
27	George Scott	.30	.15	.09
28	Manny Sanguillen	.30	.15	.09
29	Phil Niekro	2.00	1.00	.60
30	Bobby Bonds	.50	.25	.15
31	Astros Mgr./Coaches (Roger Craig, Preston Gomez, Grady Hatton, Hub Kittle, Bob Lillis)	.30	.15	.09
32a	John Grubb (Washington)	3.50	1.75	1.00
32b	John Grubb (San Diego)	.30	.15	.09
33	Don Newhauser	.30	.15	.09
34	Andy Kosco	.30	.15	.09
35	Gaylord Perry	3.00	1.50	.90
36	Cardinals Team	.80	.40	.25
37	Dave Sells	.30	.15	.09
38	Don Kessinger	.30	.15	.09
39	Ken Suarez	.30	.15	.09
40	Jim Palmer	8.00	4.00	2.50
41	Bobby Floyd	.30	.15	.09
42	Claude Osteen	.30	.15	.09
43	Jim Wynn	.30	.15	.09
44	Mel Stottlemyre	.40	.20	.12
45	Dave Johnson	.70	.35	.20
46	Pat Kelly	.30	.15	.09
47	*Dick Ruthven*	.30	.15	.09
48	Dick Sharon	.30	.15	.09
49	Steve Renko	.30	.15	.09
50	Rod Carew	15.00	7.50	4.50
51	Bobby Heise	.30	.15	.09
52	Al Oliver	1.00	.50	.30
53a	Fred Kendall (Washington)	3.50	1.75	1.00
53b	Fred Kendall (San Diego)	.30	.15	.09
54	*Elias Sosa*	.30	.15	.09
55	Frank Robinson	5.00	2.50	1.50
56	Mets Team	1.00	.50	.30
57	Darold Knowles	.30	.15	.09
58	Charlie Spikes	.30	.15	.09
59	Ross Grimsley	.30	.15	.09
60	Lou Brock	5.00	2.50	1.50
61	Luis Aparicio	2.50	1.25	.70
62	Bob Locker	.30	.15	.09
63	Bill Sudakis	.30	.15	.09
64	Doug Rau	.30	.15	.09
65	Amos Otis	.30	.15	.09
66	Sparky Lyle	.50	.25	.15
67	Tommy Helms	.30	.15	.09
68	Grant Jackson	.30	.15	.09
69	Del Unser	.30	.15	.09
70	Dick Allen	.80	.40	.25
71	Danny Frisella	.30	.15	.09
72	Aurleio Rodriguez	.30	.15	.09
73	Mike Marshall	.70	.35	.20
74	Twins Team	.80	.40	.25
75	Jim Colborn	.30	.15	.09
76	Mickey Rivers	.30	.15	.09
77a	Rich Troedson (Washington)	3.50	1.75	1.00
77b	Rich Troedson (San Diego)	.30	.15	.09
78	Giants Mgr./Coaches (Joe Amalfitano, Charlie Fox, Andy Gilbert, Don McMahon, John McNamara)	.30	.15	.09
79	Gene Tenace	.30	.15	.09
80	Tom Seaver	15.00	7.50	4.50
81	Frank Duffy	.30	.15	.09
82	Dave Giusti	.30	.15	.09
83	Orlando Cepeda	1.00	.50	.30
84	Rick Wise	.30	.15	.09
85	Joe Morgan	5.00	2.50	1.50
86	Joe Ferguson	.30	.15	.09
87	Fergie Jenkins	3.00	1.50	.90
88	Freddie Patek	.30	.15	.09
89	Jackie Brown	.30	.15	.09
90	Bobby Murcer	.40	.20	.12
91	Ken Forsch	.30	.15	.09
92	Paul Blair	.30	.15	.09
93	Rod Gilbreath	.30	.15	.09
94	Tigers Team	.90	.45	.25
95	Steve Carlton	9.00	4.50	2.75
96	*Jerry Hairston*	.40	.20	.12
97	Bob Bailey	.30	.15	.09
98	Bert Blyleven	1.00	.50	.30
99	Brewers Mgr./Coaches (Del Crandall, Harvey Kuenn, Joe Nossek, Jim Walton, Al Widmar)	.30	.15	.09
100	Willie Stargell	3.00	1.50	.90
101	Bobby Valentine	.30	.15	.09
102a	Bill Greif (Washington)	3.50	1.75	1.00
102b	Bill Greif (San Diego)	.30	.15	.09
103	Sal Bando	.40	.20	.12
104	Ron Bryant	.30	.15	.09
105	Carlton Fisk	20.00	10.00	6.00
106	Harry Parker	.30	.15	.09
107	Alex Johnson	.30	.15	.09
108	Al Hrabosky	.30	.15	.09
109	Bob Grich	.40	.20	.12
110	Billy Williams	3.00	1.50	.90
111	Clay Carroll	.30	.15	.09
112	Dave Lopes	.40	.20	.12
113	Dick Drago	.30	.15	.09
114	Angels Team	.80	.40	.25
115	Willie Horton	.30	.15	.09
116	Jerry Reuss	.30	.15	.09
117	Ron Blomberg	.30	.15	.09
118	Bill Lee	.30	.15	.09
119	Phillies Mgr./Coaches (Carroll Beringer, Bill DeMars, Danny Ozark, Ray Ripplemeyer, Bobby Wine)	.30	.15	.09
120	Wilbur Wood	.30	.15	.09
121	Larry Lintz	.30	.15	.09
122	Jim Holt	.30	.15	.09
123	Nelson Briles	.30	.15	.09
124	Bob Coluccio	.30	.15	.09
125a	Nate Colbert (Washington)	3.50	1.75	1.00
125b	Nate Colbert (San Diego)	.30	.15	.09
126	Checklist 1-132	1.50	.70	.45
127	Tom Paciorek	.30	.15	.09
128	John Ellis	.30	.15	.09
129	Chris Speier	.30	.15	.09
130	Reggie Jackson	15.00	7.50	4.50
131	Bob Boone	2.00	1.00	.60
132	Felix Millan	.30	.15	.09
133	*David Clyde*	.30	.15	.09
134	Denis Menke	.30	.15	.09
135	Roy White	.40	.20	.12
136	Rick Reuschel	.80	.40	.25
137	Al Bumbry	.30	.15	.09
138	Ed Brinkman	.30	.15	.09
139	Aurelio Monteagudo	.30	.15	.09
140	Darrell Evans	.60	.30	.20
141	Pat Bourque	.30	.15	.09
142	Pedro Garcia	.30	.15	.09
143	Dick Woodson	.30	.15	.09
144	Dodgers Mgr./Coaches (Red Adams, Walter Alston, Monty Basgall, Jim Gilliam, Tom Lasorda)	1.25	.60	.40
145	Dock Ellis	.30	.15	.09
146	Ron Fairly	.30	.15	.09
147	Bart Johnson	.30	.15	.09
148a	Dave Hilton (Washington)	3.50	1.75	1.00
148b	Dave Hilton (San Diego)	.30	.15	.09
149	Mac Scarce	.30	.15	.09

		NR MT	EX	VG
150	John Mayberry	.30	.15	.09
151	Diego Segui	.30	.15	.09
152	Oscar Gamble	.30	.15	.09
153	Jon Matlack	.30	.15	.09
154	Astros Team	.80	.40	.25
155	Bert Campaneris	.40	.20	.12
156	Randy Moffitt	.30	.15	.09
157	Vic Harris	.30	.15	.09
158	Jack Billingham	.30	.15	.09
159	Jim Ray Hart	.30	.15	.09
160	Brooks Robinson	3.50	1.75	1.00
161	*Ray Burris*	.40	.20	.12
162	Bill Freehan	.40	.20	.12
163	Ken Berry	.30	.15	.09
164	Tom House	.30	.15	.09
165	Willie Davis	.40	.20	.12
166	Royals Mgr./Coaches (Galen Cisco, Harry Dunlop, Charlie Lau, Jack McKeon)	.30	.15	.09
167	Luis Tiant	.50	.25	.15
168	Danny Thompson	.30	.15	.09
169	*Steve Rogers*	.70	.35	.20
170	Bill Melton	.30	.15	.09
171	Eduardo Rodriguez	.30	.15	.09
172	Gene Clines	.30	.15	.09
173a	*Randy Jones* (Washington)	5.00	2.50	1.50
173b	*Randy Jones* (San Diego)	.40	.20	.12
174	Bill Robinson	.30	.15	.09
175	Reggie Cleveland	.30	.15	.09
176	John Lowenstein	.30	.15	.09
177	Dave Roberts	.30	.15	.09
178	Garry Maddox	.40	.20	.12
179	Mets Mgr./Coaches (Yogi Berra, Roy McMillan, Joe Pignatano, Rube Walker, Eddie Yost)	1.25	.60	.40
180	Ken Holtzman	.30	.15	.09
181	Cesar Geronimo	.30	.15	.09
182	Lindy McDaniel	.30	.15	.09
183	Johnny Oates	.30	.15	.09
184	Rangers Team	.80	.40	.25
185	Jose Cardenal	.30	.15	.09
186	Fred Scherman	.30	.15	.09
187	Don Baylor	.70	.35	.20
188	Rudy Meoli	.30	.15	.09
189	Jim Brewer	.30	.15	.09
190	Tony Oliva	.80	.40	.25
191	Al Fitzmorris	.30	.15	.09
192	Mario Guerrero	.30	.15	.09
193	Tom Walker	.30	.15	.09
194	Darrell Porter	.30	.15	.09
195	Carlos May	.30	.15	.09
196	Jim Fregosi	.40	.20	.12
197a	Vicente Romo (Washington)	3.50	1.75	1.00
197b	Vicente Romo (San Diego)	.30	.15	.09
198	Dave Cash	.30	.15	.09
199	Mike Kekich	.30	.15	.09
200	Cesar Cedeno	.40	.20	.12
201	Batting Leaders (Rod Carew, Pete Rose)	4.00	2.00	1.25
202	Home Run Leaders (Reggie Jackson, Willie Stargell)	2.00	1.00	.60
203	Runs Batted In Leaders (Reggie Jackson, Willie Stargell)	2.00	1.00	.60
204	Stolen Base Leaders (Lou Brock, Tommy Harper)	1.25	.60	.40
205	Victory Leaders (Ron Bryant, Wilbur Wood)	.50	.25	.15
206	Earned Run Average Leaders (Jim Palmer, Tom Seaver)	2.00	1.00	.60
207	Strikeout Leaders (Nolan Ryan, Tom Seaver)	5.00	2.50	1.50
208	Leading Firemen (John Hiller, Mike Marshall)	.50	.25	.15
209	Ted Sizemore	.30	.15	.09
210	Bill Singer	.30	.15	.09
211	Cubs Team	.80	.40	.25
212	Rollie Fingers	4.00	2.00	1.25
213	Dave Rader	.30	.15	.09
214	Billy Grabarkewitz	.30	.15	.09
215	Al Kaline	5.00	2.50	1.50
216	Ray Sadecki	.30	.15	.09
217	Tim Foli	.30	.15	.09
218	Johnny Briggs	.30	.15	.09
219	Doug Griffin	.30	.15	.09
220	Don Sutton	2.00	1.00	.60
221	White Sox Mgr./Coaches (Joe Lonnett, Jim Mahoney, Alex Monchak, Johnny Sain, Chuck Tanner)	.30	.15	.09
222	Ramon Hernandez	.30	.15	.09
223	Jeff Burroughs	.50	.25	.15
224	Roger Metzger	.30	.15	.09
225	Paul Splittorff	.30	.15	.09

		NR MT	EX	VG
226a	Washington Nat'l. Team	6.00	3.00	1.75
226b	Padres Team	1.00	.50	.30
227	Mike Lum	.30	.15	.09
228	Ted Kubiak	.30	.15	.09
229	Fritz Peterson	.30	.15	.09
230	Tony Perez	1.25	.60	.40
231	Dick Tidrow	.30	.15	.09
232	Steve Brye	.30	.15	.09
233	Jim Barr	.30	.15	.09
234	John Milner	.30	.15	.09
235	Dave McNally	.30	.15	.09
236	Cardinals Mgr./Coaches (Vern Benson, George Kissell, Johnny Lewis, Red Schoendienst, Barney Schultz)	.40	.20	.12
237	Ken Brett	.30	.15	.09
238	Fran Healy	.30	.15	.09
239	Bill Russell	.30	.15	.09
240	Joe Coleman	.30	.15	.09
241a	Glenn Beckert (Washington)	4.00	2.00	1.25
241b	Glenn Beckert (San Diego)	.30	.15	.09
242	Bill Gogolewski	.30	.15	.09
243	Bob Oliver	.30	.15	.09
244	Carl Morton	.30	.15	.09
245	Cleon Jones	.30	.15	.09
246	A's Team	1.25	.60	.40
247	Rick Miller	.30	.15	.09
248	Tom Hall	.30	.15	.09
249	George Mitterwald	.30	.15	.09
250a	Willie McCovey (Washington)	25.00	12.50	7.50
250b	Willie McCovey (San Diego)	4.00	2.00	1.25
251	Graig Nettles	1.50	.70	.45
252	*Dave Parker*	45.00	23.00	13.50
253	John Boccabella	.30	.15	.09
254	Stan Bahnsen	.30	.15	.09
255	Larry Bowa	.40	.20	.12
256	Tom Griffin	.30	.15	.09
257	Buddy Bell	1.25	.60	.40
258	Jerry Morales	.30	.15	.09
259	Bob Reynolds	.30	.15	.09
260	Ted Simmons	.80	.40	.25
261	Jerry Bell	.30	.15	.09
262	Ed Kirkpatrick	.30	.15	.09
263	Checklist 133-264	1.50	.70	.45
264	Joe Rudi	.40	.20	.12
265	Tug McGraw	.60	.30	.20
266	Jim Northrup	.30	.15	.09
267	Andy Messersmith	.30	.15	.09
268	Tom Grieve	.30	.15	.09
269	Bob Johnson	.30	.15	.09
270	Ron Santo	.50	.25	.15
271	Bill Hands	.30	.15	.09
272	Paul Casanova	.30	.15	.09
273	Checklist 265-396	1.50	.70	.45
274	Fred Beene	.30	.15	.09
275	Ron Hunt	.30	.15	.09
276	Angels Mgr./Coaches (Tom Morgan, Salty Parker, Jimmie Reese, John Roseboro, Bobby Winkles)	.30	.15	.09
277	Gary Nolan	.30	.15	.09
278	Cookie Rojas	.30	.15	.09
279	Jim Crawford	.30	.15	.09
280	Carl Yastrzemski	15.00	7.50	4.50
281	Giants Team	.80	.40	.25
282	Doyle Alexander	.40	.20	.12
283	Mike Schmidt	125.00	62.00	37.00
284	Dave Duncan	.30	.15	.09
285	Reggie Smith	.40	.20	.12
286	Tony Muser	.30	.15	.09
287	Clay Kirby	.30	.15	.09
288	*Gorman Thomas*	2.00	1.00	.60
289	Rick Auerbach	.30	.15	.09
290	Vida Blue	.60	.30	.20
291	Don Hahn	.30	.15	.09
292	Chuck Seelbach	.30	.15	.09
293	Milt May	.30	.15	.09
294	Steve Foucault	.30	.15	.09
295	Rick Monday	.30	.15	.09
296	Ray Corbin	.30	.15	.09
297	Hal Breeden	.30	.15	.09
298	Roric Harrison	.30	.15	.09
299	Gene Michael	.30	.15	.09
300	Pete Rose	15.00	7.50	4.50
301	Bob Montgomery	.30	.15	.09
302	Rudy May	.30	.15	.09
303	George Hendrick	.30	.15	.09
304	Don Wilson	.30	.15	.09
305	Tito Fuentes	.30	.15	.09
306	Orioles Mgr./Coaches (George Bamberger, Jim Frey, Billy Hunter, George Staller, Earl Weaver)	.70	.35	.20
307	Luis Melendez	.30	.15	.09

		NR MT	EX	VG
308	Bruce Dal Canton	.30	.15	.09
309a	Dave Roberts (Washington)	3.50	1.75	1.00
309b	Dave Roberts (San Diego)	.30	.15	.09
310	Terry Forster	.30	.15	.09
311	Jerry Grote	.30	.15	.09
312	Deron Johnson	.30	.15	.09
313	Berry Lersch	.30	.15	.09
314	Brewers Team	.80	.40	.25
315	Ron Cey	.60	.30	.20
316	Jim Perry	.40	.20	.12
317	Richie Zisk	.30	.15	.09
318	Jim Merritt	.30	.15	.09
319	Randy Hundley	.30	.15	.09
320	Dusty Baker	.40	.20	.12
321	Steve Braun	.30	.15	.09
322	Ernie McAnally	.30	.15	.09
323	Richie Scheinblum	.30	.15	.09
324	Steve Kline	.30	.15	.09
325	Tommy Harper	.30	.15	.09
326	Reds Mgr./Coaches (Sparky Anderson, Alex Grammas, Ted Kluszewski, George Scherger, Larry Shepard)	.50	.25	.15
327	Tom Timmermann	.30	.15	.09
328	Skip Jutze	.30	.15	.09
329	Mark Belanger	.30	.15	.09
330	Juan Marichal	2.75	1.50	.80
331	All Star Catchers (Johnny Bench, Carlton Fisk)	2.00	1.00	.60
332	All Star First Basemen (Hank Aaron, Dick Allen)	2.00	1.00	.60
333	All Star Second Basemen (Rod Carew, Joe Morgan)	2.00	1.00	.60
334	All Star Third Basemen (Brooks Robinson, Ron Santo)	1.25	.60	.40
335	All Star Shortstops (Bert Campaneris, Chris Speier)	.40	.20	.12
336	All Star Left Fielders (Bobby Murcer, Pete Rose)	2.50	1.25	.70
337	All Star Center Fielders (Cesar Cedeno, Amos Otis)	.40	.20	.12
338	All Star Right Fielders (Reggie Jackson, Billy Williams)	2.00	1.00	.60
339	All Star Pitchers (Jim Hunter, Rick Wise)	.80	.40	.25
340	Thurman Munson	8.00	4.00	2.50
341	*Dan Driessen*	.80	.40	.25
342	Jim Lonborg	.30	.15	.09
343	Royals Team	.80	.40	.25
344	Mike Caldwell	.30	.15	.09
345	Bill North	.30	.15	.09
346	Ron Reed	.30	.15	.09
347	Sandy Alomar	.30	.15	.09
348	Pete Richert	.30	.15	.09
349	John Vukovich	.30	.15	.09
350	Bob Gibson	4.00	2.00	1.25
351	Dwight Evans	15.00	7.50	4.50
352	Bill Stoneman	.30	.15	.09
353	Rich Coggins	.30	.15	.09
354	Cubs Mgr./Coaches (Hank Aguirre, Whitey Lockman, Jim Marshall, J.C. Martin, Al Spangler)	.30	.15	.09
355	Dave Nelson	.30	.15	.09
356	Jerry Koosman	.40	.20	.12
357	Buddy Bradford	.30	.15	.09
358	Dal Maxvill	.30	.15	.09
359	Brent Strom	.30	.15	.09
360	Greg Luzinski	.70	.35	.20
361	Don Carrithers	.30	.15	.09
362	Hal King	.30	.15	.09
363	Yankees Team	1.25	.60	.40
364a	Clarence Gaston (Washington)	3.50	1.75	1.00
364b	Clarence Gaston (San Diego)	.30	.15	.09
365	Steve Busby	.30	.15	.09
366	Larry Hisle	.30	.15	.09
367	Norm Cash	.50	.25	.15
368	Manny Mota	.40	.20	.12
369	Paul Lindblad	.30	.15	.09
370	Bob Watson	.30	.15	.09
371	Jim Slaton	.30	.15	.09
372	Ken Reitz	.30	.15	.09
373	John Curtis	.30	.15	.09
374	Marty Perez	.30	.15	.09
375	Earl Williams	.30	.15	.09
376	Jorge Orta	.30	.15	.09
377	Ron Woods	.30	.15	.09
378	Burt Hooton	.30	.15	.09
379	Rangers Mgr./Coaches (Art Fowler, Frank Lucchesi, Billy Martin, Jackie Moore, Charlie Silvera)	.80	.40	.25
380	Bud Harrelson	.30	.15	.09
381	Charlie Sands	.30	.15	.09
382	Bob Moose	.30	.15	.09
383	Phillies Team	.80	.40	.25
384	Chris Chambliss	.40	.20	.12
385	Don Gullett	.30	.15	.09
386	Gary Matthews	.60	.30	.20
387a	Rich Morales (Washington)	3.50	1.75	1.00
387b	Rich Morales (San Diego)	.30	.15	.09
388	Phil Roof	.30	.15	.09
389	Gates Brown	.30	.15	.09
390	Lou Piniella	.70	.35	.20
391	Billy Champion	.30	.15	.09
392	Dick Green	.30	.15	.09
393	Orlando Pena	.30	.15	.09
394	Ken Henderson	.30	.15	.09
395	Doug Rader	.30	.15	.09
396	Tommy Davis	.40	.20	.12
397	George Stone	.30	.15	.09
398	Duke Sims	.30	.15	.09
399	Mike Paul	.30	.15	.09
400	Harmon Killebrew	4.00	2.00	1.25
401	Elliott Maddox	.30	.15	.09
402	Jim Rooker	.30	.15	.09
403	Red Sox Mgr./Coaches (Don Bryant, Darrell Johnson, Eddie Popowski, Lee Stange, Don Zimmer)	.30	.15	.09
404	Jim Howarth	.30	.15	.09
405	Ellie Rodriguez	.30	.15	.09
406	Steve Arlin	.30	.15	.09
407	Jim Wohlford	.30	.15	.09
408	Charlie Hough	.40	.20	.12
409	Ike Brown	.30	.15	.09
410	Pedro Borbon	.30	.15	.09
411	Frank Baker	.30	.15	.09
412	Chuck Taylor	.30	.15	.09
413	Don Money	.30	.15	.09
414	Checklist 397-528	1.50	.70	.45
415	Gary Gentry	.30	.15	.09
416	White Sox Team	.80	.40	.25
417	Rich Folkers	.30	.15	.09
418	Walt Williams	.30	.15	.09
419	Wayne Twitchell	.30	.15	.09
420	Ray Fosse	.30	.15	.09
421	Dan Fife	.30	.15	.09
422	Gonzalo Marquez	.30	.15	.09
423	Fred Stanley	.30	.15	.09
424	Jim Beauchamp	.30	.15	.09
425	Pete Broberg	.30	.15	.09
426	Rennie Stennett	.30	.15	.09
427	Bobby Bolin	.30	.15	.09
428	Gary Sutherland	.30	.15	.09
429	Dick Lange	.30	.15	.09
430	Matty Alou	.40	.20	.12
431	*Gene Garber*	.50	.25	.15
432	Chris Arnold	.30	.15	.09
433	Lerrin LaGrow	.30	.15	.09
434	Ken McMullen	.30	.15	.09
435	Dave Concepcion	.70	.35	.20
436	Don Hood	.30	.15	.09
437	Jim Lyttle	.30	.15	.09
438	Ed Herrmann	.30	.15	.09
439	Norm Miller	.30	.15	.09
440	Jim Kaat	1.25	.60	.40
441	Tom Ragland	.30	.15	.09
442	Alan Foster	.30	.15	.09
443	Tom Hutton	.30	.15	.09
444	Vic Davalillo	.30	.15	.09
445	George Medich	.30	.15	.09
446	Len Randle	.30	.15	.09
447	Twins Mgr./Coaches (Vern Morgan, Frank Quilici, Bob Rodgers, Ralph Rowe)	.30	.15	.09
448	Ron Hodges	.30	.15	.09
449	Tom McCraw	.30	.15	.09
450	Rich Hebner	.30	.15	.09
451	Tommy John	1.50	.70	.45
452	Gene Hiser	.30	.15	.09
453	Balor Moore	.30	.15	.09
454	Kurt Bevacqua	.30	.15	.09
455	Tom Bradley	.30	.15	.09
456	*Dave Winfield*	75.00	38.00	23.00
457	Chuck Goggin	.30	.15	.09
458	Jim Ray	.30	.15	.09
459	Reds Team	.90	.45	.25
460	Boog Powell	.90	.45	.25
461	John Odom	.30	.15	.09
462	Luis Alvarado	.30	.15	.09
463	Pat Dobson	.30	.15	.09
464	Jose Cruz	.80	.40	.25
465	Dick Bosman	.30	.15	.09
466	Dick Billings	.30	.15	.09
467	Winston Llenas	.30	.15	.09
468	Pepe Frias	.30	.15	.09

		NR MT	EX	VG
469	Joe Decker	.30	.15	.09
470	A.L. Playoffs	3.00	1.50	.90
471	N.L. Playoffs	.80	.40	.25
472	World Series Game 1	.80	.40	.25
473	World Series Game 2	3.00	1.50	.90
474	World Series Game 3	.80	.40	.25
475	World Series Game 4	.80	.40	.25
476	World Series Game 5	.80	.40	.25
477	World Series Game 6	3.00	1.50	.90
478	World Series Game 7	.80	.40	.25
479	World Series Summary	.80	.40	.25
480	Willie Crawford	.30	.15	.09
481	Jerry Terrell	.30	.15	.09
482	Bob Didier	.30	.15	.09
483	Braves Team	.80	.40	.25
484	Carmen Fanzone	.30	.15	.09
485	Felipe Alou	.40	.20	.12
486	Steve Stone	.40	.20	.12
487	Ted Martinez	.30	.15	.09
488	Andy Etchebarren	.30	.15	.09
489	Pirates Mgr./Coaches (Don Leppert, Bill Mazeroski, Danny Murtaugh, Don Osborn, Bob Skinner)	.30	.15	.09
490	Vada Pinson	.70	.35	.20
491	Roger Nelson	.30	.15	.09
492	Mike Rogodzinski	.30	.15	.09
493	Joe Hoerner	.30	.15	.09
494	Ed Goodson	.30	.15	.09
495	Dick McAuliffe	.30	.15	.09
496	Tom Murphy	.30	.15	.09
497	Bobby Mitchell	.30	.15	.09
498	Pat Corrales	.40	.20	.12
499	Rusty Torres	.30	.15	.09
500	Lee May	.40	.20	.12
501	Eddie Leon	.30	.15	.09
502	Dave LaRoche	.30	.15	.09
503	Eric Soderholm	.30	.15	.09
504	Joe Niekro	.40	.20	.12
505	Bill Buckner	.50	.25	.15
506	Ed Farmer	.30	.15	.09
507	Larry Stahl	.30	.15	.09
508	Expos Team	.80	.40	.25
509	Jesse Jefferson	.30	.15	.09
510	Wayne Garrett	.30	.15	.09
511	Toby Harrah	.30	.15	.09
512	Joe Lahoud	.30	.15	.09
513	Jim Campanis	.30	.15	.09
514	Paul Schaal	.30	.15	.09
515	Willie Montanez	.30	.15	.09
516	Horacio Pina	.30	.15	.09
517	Mike Hegan	.30	.15	.09
518	Derrel Thomas	.30	.15	.09
519	Bill Sharp	.30	.15	.09
520	Tim McCarver	.60	.30	.20
521	Indians Mgr./Coaches (Ken Aspromonte, Clay Bryant, Tony Pacheco)	.30	.15	.09
522	J.R. Richard	.30	.15	.09
523	Cecil Cooper	1.50	.70	.45
524	Bill Plummer	.30	.15	.09
525	Clyde Wright	.30	.15	.09
526	Frank Tepedino	.30	.15	.09
527	Bobby Darwin	.30	.15	.09
528	Bill Bonham	.30	.15	.09
529	Horace Clarke	.30	.15	.09
530	Mickey Stanley	.30	.15	.09
531	Expos Mgr./Coaches (Dave Bristol, Larry Doby, Gene Mauch, Cal McLish, Jerry Zimmerman)	.40	.20	.12
532	Skip Lockwood	.30	.15	.09
533	Mike Phillips	.30	.15	.09
534	Eddie Watt	.30	.15	.09
535	Bob Tolan	.30	.15	.09
536	Duffy Dyer	.30	.15	.09
537	Steve Mingori	.30	.15	.09
538	Cesar Tovar	.30	.15	.09
539	Lloyd Allen	.30	.15	.09
540	Bob Robertson	.30	.15	.09
541	Indians Team	.80	.40	.25
542	Rich Gossage	2.00	1.00	.60
543	Danny Cater	.30	.15	.09
544	Ron Schueler	.30	.15	.09
545	Billy Conigliaro	.30	.15	.09
546	Mike Corkins	.30	.15	.09
547	Glenn Borgmann	.30	.15	.09
548	Sonny Siebert	.30	.15	.09
549	Mike Jorgensen	.30	.15	.09
550	Sam McDowell	.40	.20	.12
551	Von Joshua	.30	.15	.09
552	Denny Doyle	.30	.15	.09
553	Jim Willoughby	.30	.15	.09
554	Tim Johnson	.30	.15	.09

		NR MT	EX	VG
555	Woodie Fryman	.30	.15	.09
556	Dave Campbell	.30	.15	.09
557	Jim McGlothlin	.30	.15	.09
558	Bill Fahey	.30	.15	.09
559	Darrel Chaney	.30	.15	.09
560	Mike Cuellar	.40	.20	.12
561	Ed Kranepool	.30	.15	.09
562	Jack Aker	.30	.15	.09
563	Hal McRae	.40	.20	.12
564	Mike Ryan	.30	.15	.09
565	Milt Wilcox	.30	.15	.09
566	Jackie Hernandez	.30	.15	.09
567	Red Sox Team	.90	.45	.25
568	Mike Torrez	.30	.15	.09
569	Rick Dempsey	.40	.20	.12
570	Ralph Garr	.30	.15	.09
571	Rich Hand	.30	.15	.09
572	Enzo Hernandez	.30	.15	.09
573	Mike Adams	.30	.15	.09
574	Bill Parsons	.30	.15	.09
575	Steve Garvey	12.00	6.00	3.50
576	Scipio Spinks	.30	.15	.09
577	Mike Sadek	.30	.15	.09
578	Ralph Houk	.40	.20	.12
579	Cecil Upshaw	.30	.15	.09
580	Jim Spencer	.30	.15	.09
581	Fred Norman	.30	.15	.09
582	*Bucky Dent*	.90	.45	.25
583	Marty Pattin	.30	.15	.09
584	Ken Rudolph	.30	.15	.09
585	Merv Rettenmund	.30	.15	.09
586	Jack Brohamer	.30	.15	.09
587	*Larry Christenson*	.30	.15	.09
588	Hal Lanier	.40	.20	.12
589	Boots Day	.30	.15	.09
590	Rogelio Moret	.30	.15	.09
591	Sonny Jackson	.30	.15	.09
592	Ed Bane	.30	.15	.09
593	Steve Yeager	.30	.15	.09
594	Leroy Stanton	.30	.15	.09
595	Steve Blass	.30	.15	.09
596	Rookie Pitchers (*Wayne Garland*, Fred Holdsworth, *Mark Littell*, Dick Pole)	.30	.15	.09
597	Rookie Shortstops (Dave Chalk, John Gamble, Pete Mackanin, *Manny Trillo*)	.80	.40	.25
598	Rookie Outfielders (Dave Augustine, *Ken Griffey*, Steve Ontiveros, Jim Tyrone)	20.00	10.00	6.00
599a	Rookie Pitchers (Ron Diorio, Dave Freisleben, Frank Riccelli, Greg Shanahan) (Freisleben- Washington)	.80	.40	.25
599b	Rookie Pitchers (Ron Diorio, Dave Freisleben, Frank Riccelli, Greg Shanahan) (Freisleben- San Diego large print)	3.50	1.75	1.00
599c	Rookie Pitchers (Ron Diorio, Dave Freisleben, Frank Riccelli, Greg Shanahan) (Freisleben- San Diego small print)	6.00	3.00	1.75
600	Rookie Infielders (Ron Cash, Jim Cox, *Bill Madlock*, Reggie Sanders)	5.00	2.50	1.50
601	Rookie Outfielders (Ed Armbrister, Rich Bladt, *Brian Downing*, *Bake McBride*)	3.00	1.50	.90
602	Rookie Pitchers (Glenn Abbott, Rick Henninger, Craig Swan, Dan Vossler)	.30	.15	.09
603	Rookie Catchers (Barry Foote, Tom Lundstedt, *Charlie Moore*, Sergio Robles)	.30	.15	.09
604	Rookie Infielders (Terry Hughes, John Knox, *Andy Thornton*, *Frank White*)	5.00	2.50	1.50
605	Rookie Pitchers (Vic Albury, Ken Frailing, Kevin Kobel, *Frank Tanana*)	2.00	1.00	.60
606	Rookie Outfielders (Jim Fuller, Wilbur Howard, Tommy Smith, Otto Velez)	.30	.15	.09
607	Rookie Shortstops (Leo Foster, Tom Heintzelman, Dave Rosello, *Frank Taveras*)	.30	.15	.09
608a	Rookie Pitchers (Bob Apodaco, Dick Baney, John D'Acquisto, Mike Wallace)	2.50	1.25	.70
608b	Rookie Pitchers (Bob Apodaca, Dick Baney, John D'Acquisto, Mike Wallace)	.30	.15	.09
609	Rico Petrocelli	.30	.15	.09
610	Dave Kingman	.90	.45	.25
611	Rick Stelmaszek	.30	.15	.09
612	Luke Walker	.30	.15	.09
613	Dan Monzon	.30	.15	.09
614	Adrian Devine	.30	.15	.09
615	Johnny Jeter	.30	.15	.09
616	Larry Gura	.30	.15	.09
617	Ted Ford	.30	.15	.09
618	Jim Mason	.30	.15	.09

		NR MT	EX	VG
619	Mike Anderson	.30	.15	.09
620	Al Downing	.30	.15	.09
621	Bernie Carbo	.30	.15	.09
622	Phil Gagliano	.30	.15	.09
623	Celerino Sanchez	.30	.15	.09
624	Bob Miller	.30	.15	.09
625	Ollie Brown	.30	.15	.09
626	Pirates Team	.80	.40	.25
627	Carl Taylor	.30	.15	.09
628	Ivan Murrell	.30	.15	.09
629	Rusty Staub	.70	.35	.20
630	Tommie Agee	.30	.15	.09
631	Steve Barber	.30	.15	.09
632	George Culver	.30	.15	.09
633	Dave Hamilton	.30	.15	.09
634	Braves Mgr./Coaches (Jim Busby, Eddie Mathews, Connie Ryan, Ken Silvestri, Herm Starrette)	.90	.45	.25
635	John Edwards	.30	.15	.09
636	Dave Goltz	.30	.15	.09
637	Checklist 529-660	1.50	.70	.45
638	Ken Sanders	.30	.15	.09
639	Joe Lovitto	.30	.15	.09
640	Milt Pappas	.40	.20	.12
641	Chuck Brinkman	.30	.15	.09
642	Terry Harmon	.30	.15	.09
643	Dodgers Team	.90	.45	.25
644	Wayne Granger	.30	.15	.09
645	Ken Boswell	.30	.15	.09
646	George Foster	1.25	.60	.40
647	*Juan Beniquez*	.70	.35	.20
648	Terry Crowley	.30	.15	.09
649	Fernando Gonzalez	.30	.15	.09
650	Mike Epstein	.30	.15	.09
651	Leron Lee	.30	.15	.09
652	Gail Hopkins	.30	.15	.09
653	Bob Stinson	.30	.15	.09
654a	Jesus Alou (no position listed)	5.00	2.50	1.50
654b	Jesus Alou (Outfield)	.40	.20	.12
655	Mike Tyson	.30	.15	.09
656	Adrian Garrett	.30	.15	.09
657	Jim Shellenback	.30	.15	.09
658	Lee Lacy	.30	.15	.09
659	Joe Lis	.30	.15	.09
660	Larry Dierker	.50	.15	.09

1974 Topps Deckle Edge

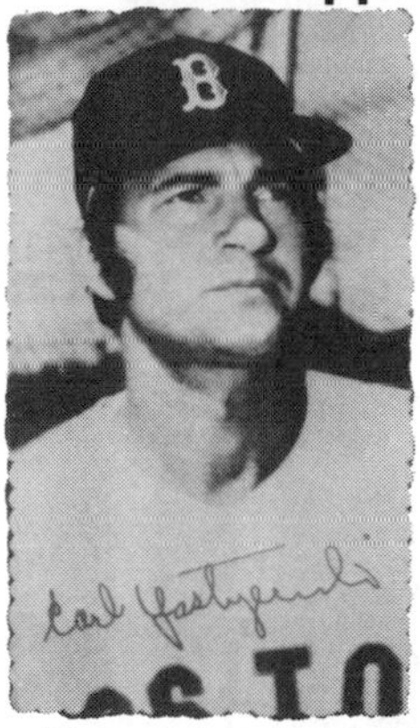

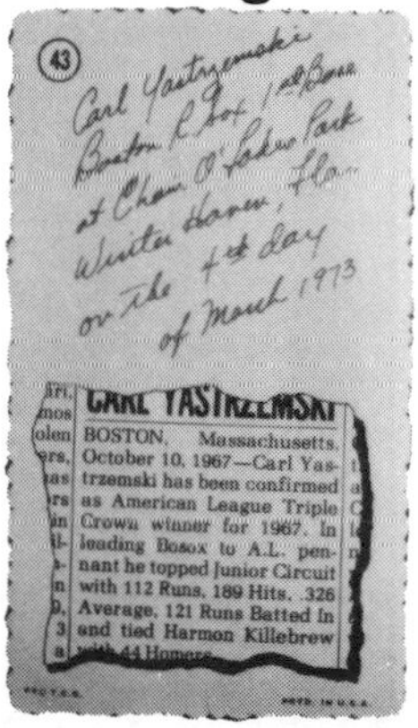

These borderless 2-7/8" by 5" cards feature a black and white photograph with a facsimile autograph on the front. The backs have in handwritten script the player's name, team, position and the date and location of the picture. Below is a mock newspaper clipping providing a detail from the player's career. The cards take their names from their specially cut edges which give them a scalloped appearance. The 72-card set was a test issue and received rather limited distribution.

		NR MT	EX	VG
Complete Set:		2000.00	1000.00	600.00
Common Player:		10.00	5.00	3.00
1	Amos Otis	10.00	5.00	3.00
2	Darrell Evans	15.00	7.50	4.50
3	Robert Gibson	50.00	25.00	15.00
4	David Nelson	10.00	5.00	3.00
5	Steven N. Carlton	80.00	40.00	25.00
6	Jim "Catfish" Hunter	40.00	20.00	12.00
7	Thurman Munson	50.00	25.00	15.00
8	Bob Grich	15.00	7.50	4.50
9	Tom Seaver	100.00	50.00	30.00
10	Ted L. Simmons	20.00	10.00	6.00
11	Robert J. Valentine	10.00	5.00	3.00
12	Don Sutton	25.00	12.50	7.50
13	Wilbur Wood	10.00	5.00	3.00
14	Douglas Lee Rader	10.00	5.00	3.00
15	Chris Chambliss	10.00	5.00	3.00
16	Pete Rose	200.00	100.00	60.00
17	John F. Hiller	10.00	5.00	3.00
18	Burt Hooton	10.00	5.00	3.00
19	Tim Foli	10.00	5.00	3.00
20	Louis Brock	60.00	30.00	20.00
21	Ron Bryant	10.00	5.00	3.00
22	Manuel Sanguillen	10.00	5.00	3.00
23	Bobby Tolan	10.00	5.00	3.00
24	Greg Luzinski	15.00	7.50	4.50
25	Brooks Robinson	60.00	30.00	18.00
26	Felix Millan	10.00	5.00	3.00
27	Luis Tiant	15.00	7.50	4.50
28	Willie McCovey	60.00	30.00	20.00
29	Chris Speier	10.00	5.00	3.00
30	George Scott	10.00	5.00	3.00
31	Willie Stargell	50.00	25.00	15.00
32	Rod Carew	100.00	50.00	30.00
33	Leslie Charles Spikes	10.00	5.00	3.00
34	Nate Colbert	10.00	5.00	3.00
35	Richie Hebner	10.00	5.00	3.00
36	Bobby Lee Bonds	15.00	7.50	4.50
37	Buddy Bell	15.00	7.50	4.50
38	Claude Osteen	10.00	5.00	3.00
39	Richard A. Allen	15.00	7.50	4.50
40	Bill Russell	10.00	5.00	3.00
41	Nolan Ryan	175.00	87.00	52.00
42	Willie Davis	15.00	7.50	4.50
43	Carl Yastrzemski	125.00	62.00	37.00
44	Jonathon T. Matlack	10.00	5.00	3.00
45	Jim Palmer	30.00	15.00	9.00
46	Dagoberto Campaneris	15.00	7.50	4.50
47	Bert Blyleven	20.00	10.00	6.00
48	Jeff Burroughs	10.00	5.00	3.00
49	James W. Colborn	10.00	5.00	3.00
50	Dave Johnson	15.00	7.50	4.50
51	John Mayberry	10.00	5.00	3.00
52	Don Kessinger	10.00	5.00	3.00
53	Joseph H. Coleman	10.00	5.00	3.00
54	Tony Perez	20.00	10.00	6.00
55	Jose Cardenal	10.00	5.00	3.00
56	Paul Splittorff	10.00	5.00	3.00
57	Henry Aaron	150.00	75.00	45.00
58	David May	10.00	5.00	3.00
59	Fergie Jenkins	30.00	15.00	9.00
60	Ron Blomberg	10.00	5.00	3.00
61	Reggie Jackson	150.00	75.00	45.00
62	Tony Oliva	15.00	7.50	4.50
63	Bobby Ray Murcer	15.00	7.50	4.50
64	Carlton Fisk	20.00	10.00	6.00
65	Stephen Rogers	10.00	5.00	3.00
66	Frank Robinson	40.00	20.00	12.00
67	Joe Ferguson	10.00	5.00	3.00
68	Bill Melton	10.00	5.00	3.00
69	Robert Watson	10.00	5.00	3.00
70	Larry Bowa	15.00	7.50	4.50
71	Johnny Bench	90.00	45.00	27.00
72	Willie Horton	10.00	5.00	3.00

1974 Topps Puzzles

One of many test issues by Topps in the mid-1970s,

the 12-player jigsaw puzzle set was an innovation which never caught on with collectors. The 40-piece puzzles (4-3/4" by 7-1/2") feature color photos with a decorative lozenge at bottom naming the player, team and position. The puzzles came in individual wrappers.

		NR MT	EX	VG
Complete Set:		600.00	300.00	200.00
Common Player:		12.00	6.00	3.50
(1)	Hank Aaron	80.00	40.00	25.00
(2)	Dick Allen	12.00	6.00	3.50
(3)	Johnny Bench	75.00	38.00	23.00
(4)	Bobby Bonds	12.00	6.00	3.50
(5)	Bob Gibson	35.00	17.50	10.50
(6)	Reggie Jackson	60.00	30.00	18.00
(7)	Bobby Murcer	12.00	6.00	3.50
(8)	Jim Palmer	50.00	25.00	15.00
(9)	Nolan Ryan	80.00	40.00	24.00
(10)	Tom Seaver	80.00	40.00	24.00
(11)	Willie Stargell	30.00	15.00	9.00
(12)	Carl Yastrzemski	70.00	35.00	21.00

1974 Topps Stamps

Topps continued to market baseball stamps in 1974 through the release of 240 unnumbered stamps featuring color player portraits. The player's name, team and position are found in an oval at the bottom of the 1" by 1-1/2" stamps. The stamps, sold separately rather than issued as an insert, came in strips of six which were then pasted in an appropriate team album designed to hold 10 stamps.

	NR MT	EX	VG
Complete Sheet Set:	100.00	50.00	30.00
Common Sheet:	1.00	.50	.30
Complete Stamp Album Set:	75.00	37.00	22.00
Single Stamp Album:	2.50	1.25	.70
(1) Hank Aaron, Luis Aparicio, Bob Bailey, Johnny Bench, Ron Blomberg, Bob Boone, Lou Brock, Bud Harrelson, Randy Jones, Dave Rader, Nolan Ryan, Joe Torre	6.00	3.00	1.75
(2) Buddy Bell, Steve Braun, Jerry Grote, Tommy Helms, Bill Lee, Mike Lum, Dave May, Brooks Robinson, Bill Russell, Del Unser, Wilbur Wood, Carl Yastrzemski	10.00	5.00	3.00
(3) Jerry Bell, Jerry Bell, Jim Colborn, Toby Harrah, Ken Henderson, John Hiller, Randy Hundley, Don Kessinger, Jerry Koosman, Dave Lopes, Felix Millan, Thurman Munson, Ted Simmons	3.50	1.75	1.00
(4) Jerry Bell, Bill Buckner, Jim Colborn, Ken Henderson, Don Kessinger, Felix Millan, George Mitterwald, Dave Roberts, Ted Simmons, Jim Slaton, Charlie Spikes, Paul Splittorff	1.00	.50	.30
(5) Glenn Beckert, Jim Bibby, Bill Buckner, Jim Lonborg, George Mitterwald, Dave Parker, Dave Roberts, Jim Slaton, Reggie Smith, Charlie Spikes, Paul Splittorff, Bob Watson	3.50	1.75	1.00
(6) Paul Blair, Bobby Bonds, Ed Brinkman, Norm Cash, Mike Epstein, Tommy Harper, Mike Marshall, Phil Niekro, Cookie Rojas, George Scott, Mel Stottlemyre, Jim Wynn	3.50	1.75	1.00
(7) Jack Billingham, Reggie Cleveland, Bobby Darwin, Dave Duncan, Tim Foli, Ed Goodson, Cleon Jones, Mickey Lolich, George Medich, John Milner, Rick Monday, Bobby Murcer	1.00	.50	.30
(8) Steve Carlton, Orlando Cepeda, Joe Decker, Reggie Jackson, Dave Johnson, John Mayberry, Bill Melton, Roger Metzger, Dave Nelson, Jerry Reuss, Jim Spencer, Bobby Valentine	6.00	3.00	1.75
(9) Dan Driessen, Pedro Garcia, Grant Jackson, Al Kaline, Clay Kirby, Carlos May, Willie Montanez, Rogelio Moret, Jim Palmer, Doug Rader, J. R. Richard, Frank Robinson	3.50	1.75	1.00
(10) Pedro Garcia, Ralph Garr, Wayne Garrett, Ron Hunt, Al Kaline, Fred Kendall, Carlos May, Jim Palmer, Doug Rader, Frank Robinson, Rick Wise, Richie Zisk	3.50	1.75	1.00
(11) Dusty Baker, Larry Bowa, Steve Busby, Chris Chambliss, Dock Ellis, Cesar Geronimo, Fran Healy, Deron Johnson, Jorge Orta, Joe Rudi, Mickey Stanley, Rennie Stennett	3.50	1.75	1.00
(12) Bob Coluccio, Ray Corbin, John Ellis, Oscar Gamble, Dave Giusti, Bill Greif, Alex Johnson, Mike Jorgensen, Andy Messersmith, Elias Sosa, Willie Stargell	3.50	1.75	1.00
(13) Ron Bryant, Nate Colbert, Jose Cruz, Dan Driessen, Billy Grabarkewitz, Don Gullett, Willie Horton, Grant Jackson, Clay Kirby, Willie Montanez, Rogelio Moret, J. R. Richard	1.00	.50	.30
(14) Carlton Fisk, Bill Freehan, Bobby Grich, Vic Harris, George Hendrick, Ed Herrmann, Jim Holt, Ken Holtzman, Fergie Jenkins, Lou Piniella, Steve Rogers, Ken Singleton	3.50	1.75	1.00
(15) Stan Bahnsen, Sal Bando, Mark Belanger, David Clyde, Willie Crawford, Burt Hooton, Jon Matlack, Tim McCarver, Joe Morgan, Gene Tenace, Dick Tidrow, Dave Winfield	5.00	2.50	1.50
(16) Hank Aaron, Stan Bahnsen, Bob Bailey, Johnny Bench, Bob Boone, Joe Matlack, Tim McCarver, Joe Morgan, Dave Rader, Gene Tenace, Dick Tidrow, Joe Torre	5.00	2.50	1.50
(17) John Boccabella, Frank Duffy, Darrell Evans, Sparky Lyle, Lee May, Don Money, Bill North, Ted Sizemore, Chris Speier, Wayne Twitchell, Billy Williams, Earl Williams	1.00	.50	.30
(18) John Boccabella, Bobby Darwin, Frank Duffy, Dave Duncan, Tim Foli, Cleon Jones, Mickey Lolich, Sparky Lyle, Lee May, Rick Monday, Bill North, Billy Williams	1.00	.50	.30
(19) Don Baylor, Vida Blue, Tom Bradley, Jose Cardenal, Ron Cey, Greg Luzinski, Johnny Oates, Tony Oliva, Al Oliver, Tony Perez, Darrell Porter, Roy White	3.50	1.75	1.00
(20) Pedro Borbon, Rod Carew, Roric Harrison, Jim Hunter, Ed Kirkpatrick, Garry Maddox, Gene Michael, Rick Miller, Claude Osteen, Amos Otis, Rich Reuschel, Mike Tyson	5.00	2.50	1.50
(21) Sandy Alomar, Bert Campaneris, Tommy Davis, Joe Ferguson, Tito Fuentes, Jerry Morales, Carl Morton, Gaylord Perry, Vada Pinson, Dave Roberts, Ellie Rodriguez	3.50	1.75	1.00
(22) Dick Allen, Jeff Burroughs, Joe Coleman, Terry Forster, Bob Gibson, Harmon Killebrew, Tug McGraw, Bob Oliver, Steve Renko, Pete Rose, Luis Tiant, Otto Velez	13.00	6.50	4.00
(23) Johnny Briggs, Willie Davis, Jim Fregosi, Rich Hebner, Pat Kelly, Dave Kingman, Willie McCovey, Graig Nettles, Freddie Patek, Marty Pattin, Manny Sanguillen, Richie Scheinblum	5.00	2.50	1.50
(24) Bert Blyleven, Nelson Briles, Cesar Cedeno, Ron Fairly, Johnny Grubb, Dave McNally, Aurelio Rodriguez, Ron Santo, Tom Seaver, Bill Singer, Bill Sudakis, Don Sutton	6.00	3.00	1.75

A player's name in *italic* type indicates a rookie card. An (FC) indicates a player's first card for that particular card company.

1974 Topps Team Checklists

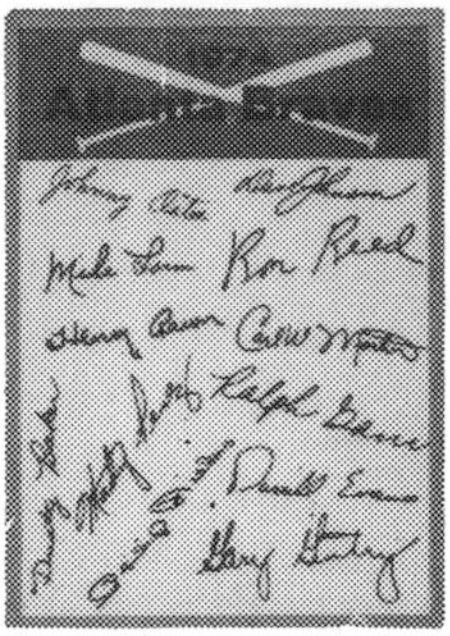

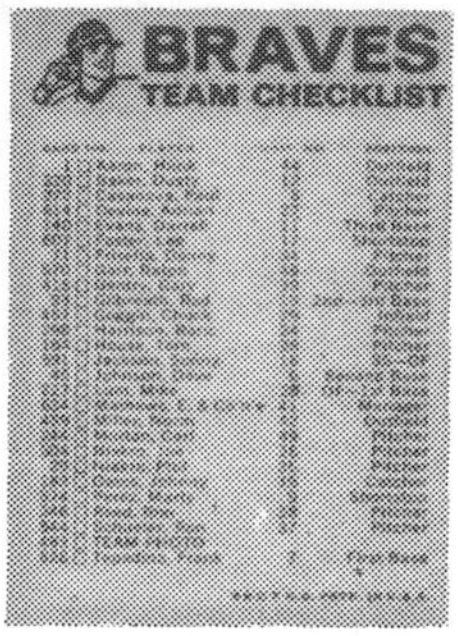

This set is a repeat of the 1973 mystery set in the form of 24 unnumbered 2-1/2" by 3-1/2" checklist cards. As with the 1973 set, the 1974s feature a team name on the front at the top with a white panel and a number of facsimile autographs below. Backs feature the team name and a checklist. The big difference between the 1973 and 1974 checklists is that the 1973s have blue borders while the 1974s have a red border. The 1974s were inserted into packages of the regular issue Topps cards.

		NR MT	EX	VG
Complete Set:		12.00	6.00	3.50
Common Checklist:		.50	.25	.15
(1)	Atlanta Braves	.50	.25	.15
(2)	Baltimore Orioles	.50	.25	.15
(3)	Boston Red Sox	.50	.25	.15
(4)	California Angels	.50	.25	.15
(5)	Chicago Cubs	.50	.25	.15
(6)	Chicago White Sox	.50	.25	.15
(7)	Cincinnati Reds	.50	.25	.15
(8)	Cleveland Indians	.50	.25	.15
(9)	Detroit Tigers	.50	.25	.15
(10)	Houston Astros	.50	.25	.15
(11)	Kansas City Royals	.50	.25	.15
(12)	Los Angeles Dodgers	.50	.25	.15
(13)	Milwaukee Brewers	.50	.25	.15
(14)	Minnesota Twins	.50	.25	.15
(15)	Montreal Expos	.50	.25	.15
(16)	New York Mets	.50	.25	.15
(17)	New York Yankees	.50	.25	.15
(18)	Oakland A's	.50	.25	.15
(19)	Philadelphia Phillies	.50	.25	.15
(20)	Pittsburgh Pirates	.50	.25	.15
(21)	St. Louis Cardinals	.50	.25	.15
(22)	San Diego Padres	.50	.25	.15
(23)	San Francisco Giants	.50	.25	.15
(24)	Texas Rangers	.50	.25	.15

1974 Topps Traded

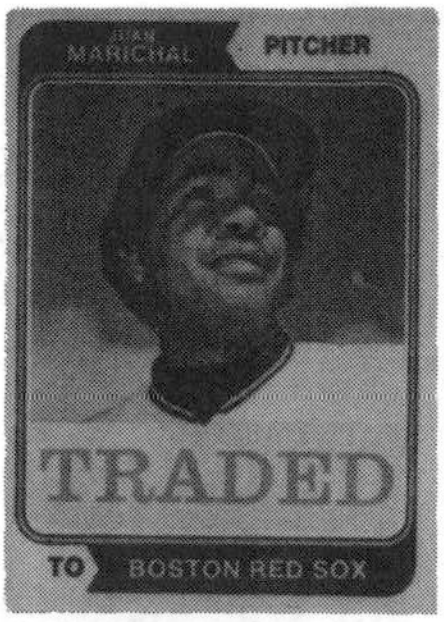

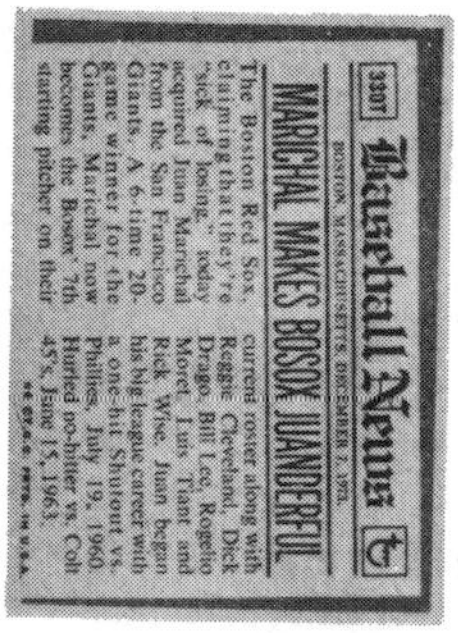

Appearing late in the season, these 2-1/2" by 3-1/2" cards are basically the same as the regular issue Topps cards. The major change was that a big red panel with the word "Traded" was added below the player photo. Backs feature a "Baseball News" newspaper which contains the details of the trade. Card numbers correspond to the player's regular card number in 1974 except that the suffix "T" is added after the number. The set consists of 43 player cards and a checklist. In most cases, Topps did not obtain pictures of the players in their new uniforms. Instead the Topps artists simply provided the needed changes to existing photos.

		NR MT	EX	VG
Complete Set:		8.00	4.00	2.50
Common Player:		.12	.06	.04
23T	Craig Robinson	.12	.06	.04
42T	Claude Osteen	.15	.08	.05
43T	Jim Wynn	.20	.10	.06
51T	Bobby Heise	.12	.06	.04
59T	Ross Grimsley	.15	.08	.05
62T	Bob Locker	.12	.06	.04
63T	Bill Sudakis	.12	.06	.04
73T	Mike Marshall	.20	.10	.06
123T	Nelson Briles	.12	.06	.04
139T	Aurelio Monteagudo	.12	.06	.04
151T	Diego Segui	.12	.06	.04
165T	Willie Davis	.20	.10	.06
175T	Reggie Cleveland	.12	.06	.04
182T	Lindy McDaniel	.12	.06	.04
186T	Fred Scherman	.12	.06	.04
249T	George Mitterwald	.12	.06	.04
262T	Ed Kirkpatrick	.12	.06	.04
269T	Bob Johnson	.12	.06	.04
270T	Ron Santo	.30	.15	.09
313T	Barry Lersch	.12	.06	.04
319T	Randy Hundley	.12	.06	.04
330T	Juan Marichal	1.50	.70	.45
348T	Pete Richert	.12	.06	.04
373T	John Curtis	.12	.06	.04
390T	Lou Piniella	.50	.25	.15
428T	Gary Sutherland	.12	.06	.04
454T	Kurt Bevacqua	.12	.06	.04
458T	Jim Ray	.12	.06	.04
485T	Felipe Alou	.20	.10	.06
486T	Steve Stone	.20	.10	.06
496T	Tom Murphy	.12	.06	.04
516T	Horacio Pina	.12	.06	.04
534T	Eddie Watt	.12	.06	.04
538T	Cesar Tovar	.12	.06	.04
544T	Ron Schueler	.12	.06	.04
579T	Cecil Upshaw	.12	.06	.04
585T	Merv Rettenmund	.15	.08	.05
612T	Luke Walker	.12	.06	.04
616T	Larry Gura	.15	.08	.05
618T	Jim Mason	.12	.06	.04
630T	Tommie Agee	.15	.08	.05
648T	Terry Crowley	.12	.06	.04
649T	Fernando Gonzalez	.12	.06	.04
——	Traded Checklist	.70	.35	.20

1975 Topps

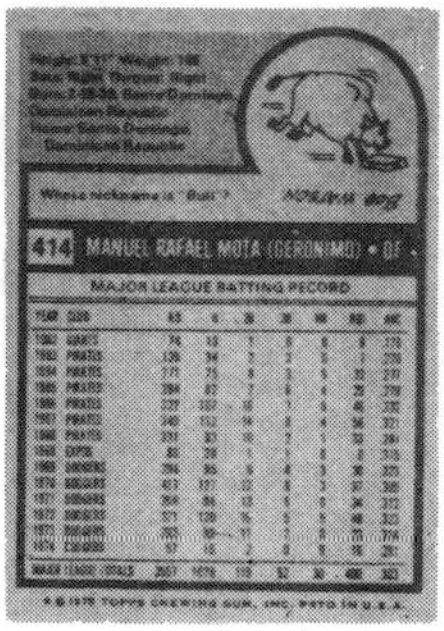

This year Topps produced another 660-card set, one which collectors either seem to like or despise. The 2-1/2" by 3-1/2" cards have a color photo which is framed by a round-cornered white frame. Around that is an eye-catching two-color border in bright colors. The team name appears at the top in bright

letters while the player name is at the bottom and his position a baseball at the lower right. A facsimile autograph runs across the picture. The card backs are vertical feature normal statistical and biographical information along with a trivia quiz. Specialty cards include a new 24-card series on MVP winners going back to 1951. Other specialty cards include statistical leaders and post-season highlights. The real highlight of the set, however, are the rookie cards which include their numbers such names as George Brett, Gary Carter, Robin Yount, Jim Rice, Keith Hernandez and Fred Lynn. While the set was released at one time, card numbers 1-132 were printed in somewhat shorter supply than the remainder of the issue.

	NR MT	EX	VG
Complete Set:	750.00	375.00	225.00
Common Player: 1-132	.35	.20	.11
Common Player: 133-660	.30	.15	.09
Complete Mini Set:	1400.00	700.00	400.00
Common Mini Player:	.40	.20	.12

		NR MT	EX	VG
1	'74 Highlights (Hank Aaron)	30.00	15.00	9.00
2	'74 Highlights (Lou Brock)	2.00	1.00	.60
3	'74 Highlights (Bob Gibson)	1.75	.90	.50
4	'74 Highlights (Al Kaline)	1.75	.90	.50
5	'74 Highlights (Nolan Ryan)	10.00	5.00	3.00
6	'74 Highlights (Mike Marshall)	.40	.20	.12
7	'74 Highlights (Dick Bosman, Steve Busby, Nolan Ryan)	1.00	.50	.30
8	Rogelio Moret	.35	.20	.11
9	Frank Tepedino	.35	.20	.11
10	Willie Davis	.35	.20	.11
11	Bill Melton	.35	.20	.11
12	David Clyde	.35	.20	.11
13	Gene Locklear	.35	.20	.11
14	Milt Wilcox	.35	.20	.11
15	Jose Cardenal	.35	.20	.11
16	Frank Tanana	.40	.20	.12
17	Dave Concepcion	.60	.30	.20
18	Tigers Team (Ralph Houk)	.90	.45	.25
19	Jerry Koosman	.40	.20	.12
20	Thurman Munson	6.00	3.00	1.75
21	Rollie Fingers	4.00	2.00	1.25
22	Dave Cash	.35	.20	.11
23	Bill Russell	.35	.20	.11
24	Al Fitzmorris	.35	.20	.11
25	Lee May	.40	.20	.12
26	Dave McNally	.35	.20	.11
27	Ken Reitz	.35	.20	.11
28	Tom Murphy	.35	.20	.11
29	Dave Parker	15.00	7.50	4.50
30	Bert Blyleven	1.00	.50	.30
31	Dave Rader	.35	.20	.11
32	Reggie Cleveland	.35	.20	.11
33	Dusty Baker	.40	.20	.12
34	Steve Renko	.35	.20	.11
35	Ron Santo	.50	.25	.15
36	Joe Lovitto	.35	.20	.11
37	Dave Freisleben	.35	.20	.11
38	Buddy Bell	.80	.40	.25
39	Andy Thornton	.70	.35	.20
40	Bill Singer	.35	.20	.11
41	Cesar Geronimo	.35	.20	.11
42	Joe Coleman	.35	.20	.11
43	Cleon Jones	.35	.20	.11
44	Pat Dobson	.35	.20	.11
45	Joe Rudi	.40	.20	.12
46	Phillies Team (Danny Ozark)	.80	.40	.25
47	Tommy John	1.25	.60	.40
48	Freddie Patek	.35	.20	.11
49	Larry Dierker	.35	.20	.11
50	Brooks Robinson	5.00	2.50	1.50
51	*Bob Forsch*	.80	.40	.25
52	Darrell Porter	.35	.20	.11
53	Dave Giusti	.35	.20	.11
54	Eric Soderholm	.35	.20	.11
55	Bobby Bonds	.50	.25	.15
56	Rick Wise	.35	.20	.11
57	Dave Johnson	.80	.40	.25
58	Chuck Taylor	.35	.20	.11
59	Ken Henderson	.35	.20	.11
60	Fergie Jenkins	2.50	1.25	.70
61	Dave Winfield	20.00	10.00	6.00
62	Fritz Peterson	.35	.20	.11
63	Steve Swisher	.35	.20	.11
64	Dave Chalk	.35	.20	.11
65	Don Gullett	.35	.20	.11
66	Willie Horton	.35	.20	.11
67	Tug McGraw	.50	.25	.15
68	Ron Blomberg	.35	.20	.11
69	John Odom	.35	.20	.11
70	Mike Schmidt	60.00	30.00	18.00
71	Charlie Hough	.35	.20	.11
72	Royals Team (Jack McKeon)	.80	.40	.25
73	J.R. Richard	.35	.20	.11
74	Mark Belanger	.35	.20	.11
75	Ted Simmons	.70	.35	.20
76	Ed Sprague	.35	.20	.11
77	Richie Zisk	.35	.20	.11
78	Ray Corbin	.35	.20	.11
79	Gary Matthews	.40	.20	.12
80	Carlton Fisk	12.00	6.00	3.50
81	Ron Reed	.35	.20	.11
82	Pat Kelly	.35	.20	.11
83	Jim Merritt	.35	.20	.11
84	Enzo Hernandez	.35	.20	.11
85	Bill Bonham	.35	.20	.11
86	Joe Lis	.35	.20	.11
87	George Foster	1.25	.60	.40
88	Tom Egan	.35	.20	.11
89	Jim Ray	.35	.20	.11
90	Rusty Staub	.60	.30	.20
91	Dick Green	.35	.20	.11
92	Cecil Upshaw	.35	.20	.11
93	Dave Lopes	.40	.20	.12
94	Jim Lonborg	.35	.20	.11
95	John Mayberry	.35	.20	.11
96	Mike Cosgrove	.35	.20	.11
97	Earl Williams	.35	.20	.11
98	Rich Folkers	.35	.20	.11
99	Mike Hegan	.35	.20	.11
100	Willie Stargell	2.50	1.25	.70
101	Expos Team (Gene Mauch)	.80	.40	.25
102	Joe Decker	.35	.20	.11
103	Rick Miller	.35	.20	.11
104	Bill Madlock	1.25	.60	.40
105	Buzz Capra	.35	.20	.11
106	*Mike Hargrove*	.40	.20	.12
107	Jim Barr	.35	.20	.11
108	Tom Hall	.35	.20	.11
109	George Hendrick	.35	.20	.11
110	Wilbur Wood	.35	.20	.11
111	Wayne Garrett	.35	.20	.11
112	Larry Hardy	.35	.20	.11
113	Elliott Maddox	.35	.20	.11
114	Dick Lange	.35	.20	.11
115	Joe Ferguson	.35	.20	.11
116	Lerrin LaGrow	.35	.20	.11
117	Orioles Team (Earl Weaver)	.90	.45	.25
118	Mike Anderson	.35	.20	.11
119	Tommy Helms	.35	.20	.11
120	Steve Busby (photo actually Fran Healy)	.35	.20	.11
121	Bill North	.35	.20	.11
122	Al Hrabosky	.35	.20	.11
123	Johnny Briggs	.35	.20	.11
124	Jerry Reuss	.40	.20	.12
125	Ken Singleton	.40	.20	.12
126	Checklist 1-132	1.50	.70	.45
127	Glen Borgmann	.35	.20	.11
128	Bill Lee	.35	.20	.11
129	Rick Monday	.35	.20	.11
130	Phil Niekro	2.00	1.00	.60
131	Toby Harrah	.35	.20	.11
132	Randy Moffitt	.35	.20	.11
133	Dan Driessen	.35	.20	.11
134	Ron Hodges	.30	.15	.09
135	Charlie Spikes	.30	.15	.09
136	Jim Mason	.30	.15	.09
137	Terry Forster	.35	.20	.11
138	Del Unser	.30	.15	.09
139	Horacio Pina	.30	.15	.09
140	Steve Garvey	7.00	3.50	2.00
141	Mickey Stanley	.30	.15	.09
142	Bob Reynolds	.30	.15	.09
143	*Cliff Johnson*	.40	.20	.12
144	Jim Wohlford	.30	.15	.09
145	Ken Holtzman	.35	.20	.11
146	Padres Team (John McNamara)	.80	.40	.25
147	Pedro Garcia	.30	.15	.09
148	Jim Rooker	.30	.15	.09
149	Tim Foli	.30	.15	.09
150	Bob Gibson	3.00	1.50	.90
151	Steve Brye	.30	.15	.09
152	Mario Guerrero	.30	.15	.09
153	Rick Reuschel	.40	.20	.12
154	Mike Lum	.30	.15	.09
155	Jim Bibby	.30	.15	.09

		NR MT	EX	VG
156	Dave Kingman	.90	.45	.25
157	Pedro Borbon	.30	.15	.09
158	Jerry Grote	.30	.15	.09
159	Steve Arlin	.30	.15	.09
160	Graig Nettles	1.50	.70	.45
161	Stan Bahnsen	.30	.15	.09
162	Willie Montanez	.30	.15	.09
163	Jim Brewer	.30	.15	.09
164	Mickey Rivers	.30	.15	.09
165	Doug Rader	.30	.15	.09
166	Woodie Fryman	.30	.15	.09
167	Rich Coggins	.30	.15	.09
168	Bill Greif	.30	.15	.09
169	Cookie Rojas	.30	.15	.09
170	Bert Campaneris	.40	.20	.12
171	Ed Kirkpatrick	.30	.15	.09
172	Red Sox Team (Darrell Johnson)	1.25	.60	.40
173	Steve Rogers	.35	.20	.11
174	Bake McBride	.30	.15	.09
175	Don Money	.30	.15	.09
176	Burt Hooton	.35	.20	.11
177	Vic Correll	.30	.15	.09
178	Cesar Tovar	.30	.15	.09
179	Tom Bradley	.30	.15	.09
180	Joe Morgan	6.00	3.00	1.75
181	Fred Beene	.30	.15	.09
182	Don Hahn	.30	.15	.09
183	Mel Stottlemyre	.40	.20	.12
184	Jorge Orta	.30	.15	.09
185	Steve Carlton	8.00	4.00	2.50
186	Willie Crawford	.30	.15	.09
187	Denny Doyle	.30	.15	.09
188	Tom Griffin	.30	.15	.09
189	1951 - MVPs (Larry (Yogi) Berra, Roy Campanella)	1.50	.70	.45
190	1952 - MVPs (Hank Sauer, Bobby Shantz)	.40	.20	.12
191	1953 - MVPs (Roy Campanella, Al Rosen)	.90	.45	.25
192	1954 - MVPs (Yogi Berra, Willie Mays)	1.50	.70	.45
193	1955 - MVPs (Yogi Berra, Roy Campanella)	1.50	.70	.45
194	1956 - MVPs (Mickey Mantle, Don Newcombe)	12.00	6.00	3.50
195	1957 - MVPs (Hank Aaron, Mickey Mantle)	12.00	6.00	3.50
196	1958 - MVPs (Ernie Banks, Jackie Jensen)	.90	.45	.25
197	1959 - MVPs (Ernie Banks, Nellie Fox)	.90	.45	.25
198	1960 - MVPs (Dick Groat, Roger Maris)	1.25	.60	.40
199	1961 - MVPs (Roger Maris, Frank Robinson)	1.50	.70	.45
200	1962 - MVPs (Mickey Mantle, Maury Wills)	12.00	6.00	3.50
201	1963 - MVPs (Elston Howard, Sandy Koufax)	1.50	.70	.45
202	1964 - MVPs (Ken Boyer, Brooks Robinson)	1.25	.60	.40
203	1965 - MVPs (Willie Mays, Zoilo Versalles)	1.25	.60	.40
204	1966 - MVPs (Bob Clemente, Frank Robinson)	1.50	.70	.45
205	1967 - MVPs (Orlando Cepeda, Carl Yastrzemski)	1.25	.60	.40
206	1968 - MVPs (Bob Gibson, Denny McLain)	1.25	.60	.40
207	1969 - MVPs (Harmon Killebrew, Willie McCovey)	1.50	.70	.45
208	1970 - MVPs (Johnny Bench, Boog Powell)	1.25	.60	.40
209	1971 - MVPs (Vida Blue, Joe Torre)	.50	.25	.15
210	1972 - MVPs (Rich Allen, Johnny Bench)	1.25	.60	.40
211	1973 - MVPs (Reggie Jackson, Pete Rose)	4.00	2.00	1.25
212	1974 - MVPs (Jeff Burroughs, Steve Garvey)	.90	.45	.25
213	Oscar Gamble	.30	.15	.09
214	Harry Parker	.30	.15	.09
215	Bobby Valentine	.35	.20	.11
216	Giants Team (Wes Westrum)	.80	.40	.25
217	Lou Piniella	.70	.35	.20
218	Jerry Johnson	.30	.15	.09
219	Ed Herrmann	.30	.15	.09
220	Don Sutton	2.00	1.00	.60
221	Aurelio Rodriquez (Rodriguez)	.30	.15	.09
222	Dan Spillner	.30	.15	.09
223	*Robin Yount*	225.00	112.00	67.00
224	Ramon Hernandez	.30	.15	.09
225	Bob Grich	.40	.20	.12
226	Bill Campbell	.30	.15	.09
227	Bob Watson	.30	.15	.09
228	*George Brett*	225.00	112.00	67.00
229	Barry Foote	.30	.15	.09
230	Jim Hunter	2.00	1.00	.60
231	Mike Tyson	.30	.15	.09
232	Diego Segui	.30	.15	.09
233	Billy Grabarkewitz	.30	.15	.09
234	Tom Grieve	.30	.15	.09
235	Jack Billingham	.30	.15	.09
236	Angels Team (Dick Williams)	.80	.40	.25
237	Carl Morton	.30	.15	.09
238	Dave Duncan	.30	.15	.09
239	George Stone	.30	.15	.09
240	Garry Maddox	.30	.15	.09
241	Dick Tidrow	.30	.15	.09
242	Jay Johnstone	.30	.15	.09
243	Jim Kaat	1.25	.60	.40
244	Bill Buckner	.50	.25	.15
245	Mickey Lolich	.50	.25	.15
246	Cardinals Team (Red Schoendienst)	.80	.40	.25
247	Enos Cabell	.30	.15	.09
248	Randy Jones	.30	.15	.09
249	Danny Thompson	.30	.15	.09
250	Ken Brett	.30	.15	.09
251	Fran Healy	.30	.15	.09
252	Fred Scherman	.30	.15	.09
253	Jesus Alou	.30	.15	.09
254	Mike Torrez	.30	.15	.09
255	Dwight Evans	6.00	3.00	1.75
256	Billy Champion	.30	.15	.09
257	Checklist 133-264	1.50	.70	.45
258	Dave LaRoche	.30	.15	.09
259	Len Randle	.30	.15	.09
260	Johnny Bench	12.00	6.00	3.50
261	Andy Hassler	.30	.15	.09
262	Rowland Office	.30	.15	.09
263	Jim Perry	.40	.20	.12
264	John Milner	.30	.15	.09
265	Ron Bryant	.30	.15	.09
266	Sandy Alomar	.30	.15	.09
267	Dick Ruthven	.30	.15	.09
268	Hal McRae	.40	.20	.12
269	Doug Rau	.30	.15	.09
270	Ron Fairly	.35	.20	.11
271	Jerry Moses	.30	.15	.09
272	Lynn McGlothen	.30	.15	.09
273	Steve Braun	.30	.15	.09
274	Vicente Romo	.30	.15	.09
275	Paul Blair	.30	.15	.09
276	White Sox Team (Chuck Tanner)	.80	.40	.25
277	Frank Taveras	.30	.15	.09
278	Paul Lindblad	.30	.15	.09
279	Milt May	.30	.15	.09
280	Carl Yastrzemski	12.00	6.00	3.50
281	Jim Slaton	.30	.15	.09
282	Jerry Morales	.30	.15	.09
283	Steve Foucault	.30	.15	.09
284	Ken Griffey	.70	.35	.20
285	Ellie Rodriguez	.30	.15	.09
286	Mike Jorgensen	.30	.15	.09
287	Roric Harrison	.30	.15	.09
288	Bruce Ellingsen	.30	.15	.09
289	Ken Rudolph	.30	.15	.09
290	Jon Matlack	.30	.15	.09
291	Bill Sudakis	.30	.15	.09
292	Ron Schueler	.30	.15	.09
293	Dick Sharon	.30	.15	.09
294	*Geoff Zahn*	.40	.20	.12
295	Vada Pinson	.60	.30	.20
296	Alan Foster	.30	.15	.09
297	Craig Kusick	.30	.15	.09
298	Johnny Grubb	.30	.15	.09
299	Bucky Dent	.40	.20	.12
300	Reggie Jackson	15.00	7.50	4.50
301	Dave Roberts	.30	.15	.09
302	*Rick Burleson*	.50	.25	.15
303	Grant Jackson	.30	.15	.09
304	Pirates Team (Danny Murtaugh)	.80	.40	.25
305	Jim Colborn	.30	.15	.09
306	Batting Leaders (Rod Carew, Ralph Garr)	.80	.40	.25
307	Home Run Leaders (Dick Allen, Mike Schmidt)	.90	.45	.25
308	Runs Batted In Leaders (Johnny Bench, Jeff Burroughs)	.90	.45	.25
309	Stolen Base Leaders (Lou Brock, Bill North)	.80	.40	.25

	NR MT	EX	VG
310 Victory Leaders (Jim Hunter, Fergie Jenkins, Andy Messersmith, Phil Niekro)	.80	.40	.25
311 Earned Run Average Leaders (Buzz Capra, Jim Hunter)	.50	.25	.15
312 Strikeout Leaders (Steve Carlton, Nolan Ryan)	4.00	2.00	1.25
313 Leading Firemen (Terry Forster, Mike Marshall)	.50	.25	.15
314 Buck Martinez	.30	.15	.09
315 Don Kessinger	.30	.15	.09
316 Jackie Brown	.30	.15	.09
317 Joe Lahoud	.30	.15	.09
318 Ernie McAnally	.30	.15	.09
319 Johnny Oates	.30	.15	.09
320 Pete Rose	18.00	9.00	5.50
321 Rudy May	.30	.15	.09
322 Ed Goodson	.30	.15	.09
323 Fred Holdsworth	.30	.15	.09
324 Ed Kranepool	.35	.20	.11
325 Tony Oliva	.80	.40	.25
326 Wayne Twitchell	.30	.15	.09
327 Jerry Hairston	.30	.15	.09
328 Sonny Siebert	.30	.15	.09
329 Ted Kubiak	.30	.15	.09
330 Mike Marshall	.35	.20	.11
331 Indians Team (Frank Robinson)	.90	.45	.25
332 Fred Kendall	.30	.15	.09
333 Dick Drago	.30	.15	.09
334 *Greg Gross*	.35	.20	.11
335 Jim Palmer	10.00	5.00	3.00
336 Rennie Stennett	.30	.15	.09
337 Kevin Kobel	.30	.15	.09
338 Rick Stelmaszek	.30	.15	.09
339 Jim Fregosi	.40	.20	.12
340 Paul Splittorff	.30	.15	.09
341 Hal Breeden	.30	.15	.09
342 Leroy Stanton	.30	.15	.09
343 Danny Frisella	.30	.15	.09
344 Ben Oglivie	.35	.20	.11
345 Clay Carroll	.30	.15	.09
346 Bobby Darwin	.30	.15	.09
347 Mike Caldwell	.30	.15	.09
348 Tony Muser	.30	.15	.09
349 Ray Sadecki	.30	.15	.09
350 Bobby Murcer	.40	.20	.12
351 Bob Boone	.40	.20	.12
352 Darold Knowles	.30	.15	.09
353 Luis Melendez	.30	.15	.09
354 Dick Bosman	.30	.15	.09
355 Chris Cannizzaro	.30	.15	.09
356 Rico Petrocelli	.35	.20	.11
357 Ken Forsch	.30	.15	.09
358 Al Bumbry	.30	.15	.09
359 Paul Popovich	.30	.15	.09
360 George Scott	.35	.20	.11
361 Dodgers Team (Walter Alston)	1.00	.50	.30
362 Steve Hargan	.30	.15	.09
363 Carmen Fanzone	.30	.15	.09
364 Doug Bird	.30	.15	.09
365 Bob Bailey	.30	.15	.09
366 Ken Sanders	.30	.15	.09
367 Craig Robinson	.30	.15	.09
368 Vic Albury	.30	.15	.09
369 Merv Rettenmund	.30	.15	.09
370 Tom Seaver	12.00	6.00	3.50
371 Gates Brown	.30	.15	.09
372 John D'Acquisto	.30	.15	.09
373 Bill Sharp	.30	.15	.09
374 Eddie Watt	.30	.15	.09
375 Roy White	.40	.20	.12
376 Steve Yeager	.30	.15	.09
377 Tom Hilgendorf	.30	.15	.09
378 Derrel Thomas	.30	.15	.09
379 Bernie Carbo	.30	.15	.09
380 Sal Bando	.40	.20	.12
381 John Curtis	.30	.15	.09
382 Don Baylor	.60	.30	.20
383 Jim York	.30	.15	.09
384 Brewers Team (Del Crandall)	.80	.40	.25
385 Dock Ellis	.30	.15	.09
386 Checklist 265-396	1.50	.70	.45
387 Jim Spencer	.30	.15	.09
388 Steve Stone	.35	.20	.11
389 Tony Solaita	.30	.15	.09
390 Ron Cey	.40	.20	.12
391 Don DeMola	.30	.15	.09
392 Bruce Bochte	.40	.20	.12
393 Gary Gentry	.30	.15	.09
394 Larvell Blanks	.30	.15	.09
395 Bud Harrelson	.30	.15	.09

	NR MT	EX	VG
396 Fred Norman	.30	.15	.09
397 Bill Freehan	.40	.20	.12
398 Elias Sosa	.30	.15	.09
399 Terry Harmon	.30	.15	.09
400 Dick Allen	.80	.40	.25
401 Mike Wallace	.30	.15	.09
402 Bob Tolan	.30	.15	.09
403 Tom Buskey	.30	.15	.09
404 Ted Sizemore	.30	.15	.09
405 John Montague	.30	.15	.09
406 Bob Gallagher	.30	.15	.09
407 *Herb Washington*	.35	.20	.11
408 Clyde Wright	.30	.15	.09
409 Bob Robertson	.30	.15	.09
410 Mike Cueller (Cuellar)	.40	.20	.12
411 George Mitterwald	.30	.15	.09
412 Bill Hands	.30	.15	.09
413 Marty Pattin	.30	.15	.09
414 Manny Mota	.35	.20	.11
415 John Hiller	.30	.15	.09
416 Larry Lintz	.30	.15	.09
417 Skip Lockwood	.30	.15	.09
418 Leo Foster	.30	.15	.09
419 Dave Goltz	.30	.15	.09
420 Larry Bowa	.40	.20	.12
421 Mets Team (Yogi Berra)	1.00	.50	.30
422 Brian Downing	.35	.20	.11
423 Clay Kirby	.30	.15	.09
424 John Lowenstein	.30	.15	.09
425 Tito Fuentes	.30	.15	.09
426 George Medich	.30	.15	.09
427 Clarence Gaston	.30	.15	.09
428 Dave Hamilton	.30	.15	.09
429 *Jim Dwyer*	.35	.20	.11
430 Luis Tiant	.50	.25	.15
431 Rod Gilbreath	.30	.15	.09
432 Ken Berry	.30	.15	.09
433 Larry Demery	.30	.15	.09
434 Bob Locker	.30	.15	.09
435 Dave Nelson	.30	.15	.09
436 Ken Frailing	.30	.15	.09
437 *Al Cowens*	.40	.20	.12
438 Don Carrithers	.30	.15	.09
439 Ed Brinkman	.30	.15	.09
440 Andy Messersmith	.35	.20	.11
441 Bobby Heise	.30	.15	.09
442 Maximino Leon	.30	.15	.09
443 Twins Team (Frank Quilici)	.80	.40	.25
444 Gene Garber	.30	.15	.09
445 Felix Millan	.30	.15	.09
446 Bart Johnson	.30	.15	.09
447 Terry Crowley	.30	.15	.09
448 Frank Duffy	.30	.15	.09
449 Charlie Williams	.30	.15	.09
450 Willie McCovey	3.00	1.50	.90
451 Rick Dempsey	.40	.20	.12
452 Angel Mangual	.30	.15	.09
453 Claude Osteen	.35	.20	.11
454 Doug Griffin	.30	.15	.09
455 Don Wilson	.30	.15	.09
456 Bob Coluccio	.30	.15	.09
457 Mario Mendoza	.30	.15	.09
458 Ross Grimsley	.30	.15	.09
459 A.L. Championships	.80	.40	.25
460 N.L. Championships	.80	.40	.25
461 World Series Game 1	2.00	1.00	.60
462 World Series Game 2	.80	.40	.25
463 World Series Game 3	1.00	.50	.30
464 World Series Game 4	.80	.40	.25
465 World Series Game 5	.80	.40	.25
466 World Series Summary	.80	.40	.25
467 Ed Halicki	.30	.15	.09
468 Bobby Mitchell	.30	.15	.09
469 Tom Dettore	.30	.15	.09
470 Jeff Burroughs	.35	.20	.11
471 Bob Stinson	.30	.15	.09
472 Bruce Dal Canton	.30	.15	.09
473 Ken McMullen	.30	.15	.09
474 Luke Walker	.30	.15	.09
475 Darrell Evans	.60	.30	.20
476 *Ed Figueroa*	.35	.20	.11
477 Tom Hutton	.30	.15	.09
478 Tom Burgmeier	.30	.15	.09
479 Ken Boswell	.30	.15	.09
480 Carlos May	.30	.15	.09
481 *Will McEnaney*	.35	.20	.11
482 Tom McCraw	.30	.15	.09
483 Steve Ontiveros	.30	.15	.09
484 Glenn Beckert	.35	.20	.11
485 Sparky Lyle	.40	.20	.12
486 Ray Fosse	.30	.15	.09

		NR MT	EX	VG
487	Astros Team (Preston Gomez)	.80	.40	.25
488	Bill Travers	.30	.15	.09
489	Cecil Cooper	1.00	.50	.30
490	Reggie Smith	.35	.20	.11
491	Doyle Alexander	.40	.20	.12
492	Rich Hebner	.30	.15	.09
493	Don Stanhouse	.30	.15	.09
494	*Pete LaCock*	.30	.15	.09
495	Nelson Briles	.30	.15	.09
496	Pepe Frias	.30	.15	.09
497	Jim Nettles	.30	.15	.09
498	Al Downing	.30	.15	.09
499	Marty Perez	.30	.15	.09
500	Nolan Ryan	40.00	20.00	12.00
501	Bill Robinson	.30	.15	.09
502	Pat Bourque	.30	.15	.09
503	Fred Stanley	.30	.15	.09
504	Buddy Bradford	.30	.15	.09
505	Chris Speier	.30	.15	.09
506	Leron Lee	.30	.15	.09
507	Tom Carroll	.30	.15	.09
508	Bob Hansen	.30	.15	.09
509	Dave Hilton	.30	.15	.09
510	Vida Blue	.50	.25	.15
511	Rangers Team (Billy Martin)	.90	.45	.25
512	Larry Milbourne	.30	.15	.09
513	Dick Pole	.30	.15	.09
514	Jose Cruz	.50	.25	.15
515	Manny Sanguillen	.30	.15	.09
516	Don Hood	.30	.15	.09
517	Checklist 397-528	1.25	.60	.40
518	Leo Cardenas	.30	.15	.09
519	Jim Todd	.30	.15	.09
520	Amos Otis	.35	.20	.11
521	Dennis Blair	.30	.15	.09
522	Gary Sutherland	.30	.15	.09
523	Tom Paciorek	.30	.15	.09
524	John Doherty	.30	.15	.09
525	Tom House	.30	.15	.09
526	Larry Hisle	.30	.15	.09
527	Mac Scarce	.30	.15	.09
528	Eddie Leon	.30	.15	.09
529	Gary Thomasson	.30	.15	.09
530	Gaylord Perry	3.00	1.50	.90
531	Reds Team (Sparky Anderson)	.90	.45	.25
532	Gorman Thomas	.60	.30	.20
533	Rudy Meoli	.30	.15	.09
534	Alex Johnson	.30	.15	.09
535	Gene Tenace	.30	.15	.09
536	Bob Moose	.30	.15	.09
537	Tommy Harper	.30	.15	.09
538	Duffy Dyer	.30	.15	.09
539	Jesse Jefferson	.30	.15	.09
540	Lou Brock	4.00	2.00	1.25
541	Roger Metzger	.30	.15	.09
542	Pete Broberg	.30	.15	.09
543	Larry Biittner	.30	.15	.09
544	Steve Mingori	.30	.15	.09
545	Billy Williams	3.00	1.50	.90
546	John Knox	.30	.15	.09
547	Von Joshua	.30	.15	.09
548	Charlie Sands	.30	.15	.09
549	Bill Butler	.30	.15	.09
550	Ralph Garr	.30	.15	.09
551	Larry Christenson	.30	.15	.09
552	Jack Brohamer	.30	.15	.09
553	John Boccabella	.30	.15	.09
554	Rich Gossage	1.50	.70	.45
555	Al Oliver	.80	.40	.25
556	Tim Johnson	.30	.15	.09
557	Larry Gura	.30	.15	.09
558	Dave Roberts	.30	.15	.09
559	Bob Montgomery	.30	.15	.09
560	Tony Perez	1.50	.70	.45
561	A's Team (Alvin Dark)	.90	.45	.25
562	Gary Nolan	.30	.15	.09
563	Wilbur Howard	.30	.15	.09
564	Tommy Davis	.40	.20	.12
565	Joe Torre	.70	.35	.20
566	Ray Burris	.30	.15	.09
567	*Jim Sundberg*	.70	.35	.20
568	Dale Murray	.30	.15	.09
569	Frank White	.40	.20	.12
570	Jim Wynn	.35	.20	.11
571	Dave Lemanczyk	.30	.15	.09
572	Roger Nelson	.30	.15	.09
573	Orlando Pena	.30	.15	.09
574	Tony Taylor	.30	.15	.09
575	Gene Clines	.30	.15	.09
576	Phil Roof	.30	.15	.09
577	John Morris	.30	.15	.09

		NR MT	EX	VG
578	Dave Tomlin	.30	.15	.09
579	Skip Pitlock	.30	.15	.09
580	Frank Robinson	4.00	2.00	1.25
581	Darrel Chaney	.30	.15	.09
582	Eduardo Rodriguez	.30	.15	.09
583	Andy Etchebarren	.30	.15	.09
584	Mike Garman	.30	.15	.09
585	Chris Chambliss	.40	.20	.12
586	Tim McCarver	.60	.30	.20
587	Chris Ward	.30	.15	.09
588	Rick Auerbach	.30	.15	.09
589	Braves Team (Clyde King)	.80	.40	.25
590	Cesar Cedeno	.40	.20	.12
591	Glenn Abbott	.30	.15	.09
592	Balor Moore	.30	.15	.09
593	Gene Lamont	.30	.15	.09
594	Jim Fuller	.30	.15	.09
595	Joe Niekro	.40	.20	.12
596	Ollie Brown	.30	.15	.09
597	Winston Llenas	.30	.15	.09
598	Bruce Kison	.30	.15	.09
599	Nate Colbert	.30	.15	.09
600	Rod Carew	12.00	6.00	3.50
601	Juan Beniquez	.35	.20	.11
602	John Vukovich	.30	.15	.09
603	Lew Krausse	.30	.15	.09
604	Oscar Zamora	.30	.15	.09
605	John Ellis	.30	.15	.09
606	Bruce Miller	.30	.15	.09
607	Jim Holt	.30	.15	.09
608	Gene Michael	.35	.20	.11
609	Ellie Hendricks	.30	.15	.09
610	Ron Hunt	.30	.15	.09
611	Yankees Team (Bill Virdon)	1.25	.60	.40
612	Terry Hughes	.30	.15	.09
613	Bill Parsons	.30	.15	.09
614	Rookie Pitchers (Jack Kucek, Dyar Miller, Vern Ruhle, Paul Siebert)	.30	.15	.09
615	Rookie Pitchers (Pat Darcy, *Dennis Leonard, Tom Underwood*, Hank Webb)	.60	.30	.20
616	Rookie Outfielders (Dave Augustine, Pepe Mangual, *Jim Rice*, John Scott)	30.00	15.00	9.00
617	Rookie Infielders (Mike Cubbage, *Doug DeCinces*, Reggie Sanders, Manny Trillo)	1.25	.60	.40
618	Rookie Pitchers (*Jamie Easterly*, Tom Johnson, *Scott McGregor, Rick Rhoden*)	2.25	1.25	.70
619	Rookie Outfielders (Benny Ayala, Nyls Nyman, Tommy Smith, Jerry Turner)	.30	.15	.09
620	Rookie Catchers-Outfielders (*Gary Carter*, Marc Hill, Danny Meyer, Leon Roberts)	35.00	17.50	10.50
621	Rookie Pitchers (*John Denny, Rawly Eastwick, Jim Kern*, Juan Veintidos)	.60	.30	.20
622	Rookie Outfielders (Ed Armbrister, *Fred Lynn*, Tom Poquette, Terry Whitfield)	12.00	6.00	3.50
623	Rookie Infielders (*Phil Garner, Keith Hernandez*, Bob Sheldon, Tom Veryzer)	20.00	10.00	6.00
624	Rookie Pitchers (Doug Konieczny, *Gary Lavelle*, Jim Otten, Eddie Solomon)	.35	.20	.11
625	Boog Powell	.70	.35	.20
626	Larry Haney	.30	.15	.09
627	Tom Walker	.30	.15	.09
628	*Ron LeFlore*	.80	.40	.25
629	Joe Hoerner	.30	.15	.09
630	Greg Luzinski	.70	.35	.20
631	Lee Lacy	.30	.15	.09
632	Morris Nettles	.30	.15	.09
633	Paul Casanova	.30	.15	.09
634	Cy Acosta	.30	.15	.09
635	Chuck Dobson	.30	.15	.09
636	Charlie Moore	.30	.15	.09
637	Ted Martinez	.30	.15	.09
638	Cubs Team (Jim Marshall)	.80	.40	.25
639	Steve Kline	.30	.15	.09
640	Harmon Killebrew	4.00	2.00	1.25
641	Jim Northrup	.30	.15	.09
642	Mike Phillips	.30	.15	.09
643	Brent Strom	.30	.15	.09
644	Bill Fahey	.30	.15	.09
645	Danny Cater	.30	.15	.09
646	Checklist 529-660	1.50	.70	.45
647	*Claudell Washington*	2.50	1.25	.70
648	Dave Pagan	.30	.15	.09
649	Jack Heidemann	.30	.15	.09
650	Dave May	.30	.15	.09
651	John Morlan	.30	.15	.09

		NR MT	EX	VG
652	Lindy McDaniel	.30	.15	.09
653	Lee Richards	.30	.15	.09
654	Jerry Terrell	.30	.15	.09
655	Rico Carty	.40	.20	.12
656	Bill Plummer	.30	.15	.09
657	Bob Oliver	.30	.15	.09
658	Vic Harris	.30	.15	.09
659	Bob Apodaca	.30	.15	.09
660	Hank Aaron	25.00	12.50	7.50

1976 Topps

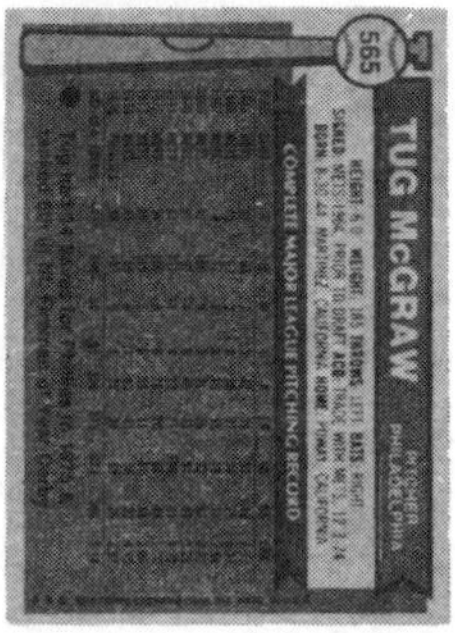

These 2-1/2" by 3-1/2" cards begin a design trend for Topps. The focus was more on the photo quality than in past years with a corresponding trend toward simplicity in the borders. The front of the cards has the player's name and team in two strips while his position is in the lower left corner under a drawing of a player representing that position. The backs have a bat and ball with the card number on the left; statistics and personal information and career highlights on the right. The 660-card set features a number of specialty sets including record-setting performances, statistical leaders, playoff and World Series highlights, the Sporting News All-Time All-Stars and father and son combinations.

	NR MT	EX	VG
Complete Set:	450.00	225.00	135.00
Commmon Player:	.25	.13	.08

		NR MT	EX	VG
1	'75 Record Breaker (Hank Aaron)	12.00	6.00	3.50
2	'75 Record Breaker (Bobby Bonds)	.40	.20	.12
3	'75 Record Breaker (Mickey Lolich)	.35	.20	.11
4	'75 Record Breaker (Dave Lopes)	.35	.20	.11
5	'75 Record Breaker (Tom Seaver)	2.00	1.00	.60
6	'75 Record Breaker (Rennie Stennett)	.30	.15	.09
7	Jim Umbarger	.25	.13	.08
8	Tito Fuentes	.25	.13	.08
9	Paul Lindblad	.25	.13	.08
10	Lou Brock	3.00	1.50	.90
11	Jim Hughes	.25	.13	.08
12	Richie Zisk	.25	.13	.08
13	Johnny Wockenfuss	.25	.13	.08
14	Gene Garber	.25	.13	.08
15	George Scott	.25	.13	.08
16	Bob Apodaca	.25	.13	.08
17	Yankees Team (Billy Martin)	1.25	.60	.40
18	Dale Murray	.25	.13	.08
19	George Brett	40.00	20.00	12.00
20	Bob Watson	.25	.13	.08
21	Dave LaRoche	.25	.13	.08
22	Bill Russell	.25	.13	.08
23	Brian Downing	.25	.13	.08
24	Cesar Geronimo	.25	.13	.08
25	Mike Torrez	.25	.13	.08
26	Andy Thornton	.25	.13	.08
27	Ed Figueroa	.25	.13	.08
28	Dusty Baker	.25	.13	.08
29	Rick Burleson	.30	.15	.09
30	*John Montefusco*	.35	.20	.11
31	Len Randle	.25	.13	.08
32	Danny Frisella	.25	.13	.08
33	Bill North	.25	.13	.08
34	Mike Garman	.25	.13	.08
35	Tony Oliva	.60	.30	.20
36	Frank Taveras	.25	.13	.08
37	John Hiller	.25	.13	.08
38	Garry Maddox	.25	.13	.08
39	Pete Broberg	.25	.13	.08
40	Dave Kingman	.80	.40	.25
41	*Tippy Martinez*	.40	.20	.12
42	Barry Foote	.25	.13	.08
43	Paul Splittorff	.25	.13	.08
44	Doug Rader	.25	.13	.08
45	Boog Powell	.60	.30	.20
46	Dodgers Team (Walter Alston)	1.00	.50	.30
47	Jesse Jefferson	.25	.13	.08
48	Dave Concepcion	.40	.20	.12
49	Dave Duncan	.25	.13	.08
50	Fred Lynn	2.00	1.00	.60
51	Ray Burris	.25	.13	.08
52	Dave Chalk	.25	.13	.08
53	Mike Beard	.25	.13	.08
54	Dave Rader	.25	.13	.08
55	Gaylord Perry	3.00	1.50	.90
56	Bob Tolan	.25	.13	.08
57	Phil Garner	.30	.15	.09
58	Ron Reed	.25	.13	.08
59	Larry Hisle	.25	.13	.08
60	Jerry Reuss	.30	.15	.09
61	Ron LeFlore	.30	.15	.09
62	Johnny Oates	.25	.13	.08
63	Bobby Darwin	.25	.13	.08
64	Jerry Koosman	.30	.15	.09
65	Chris Chambliss	.30	.15	.09
66	Father & Son (Buddy Bell, Gus Bell)	.50	.25	.15
67	Father & Son (Bob Boone, Ray Boone)	.40	.20	.12
68	Father & Son (Joe Coleman, Joe Coleman, Jr.)	.25	.13	.08
69	Father & Son (Jim Hegan, Mike Hegan)	.25	.13	.08
70	Father & Son (Roy Smalley, Roy Smalley, Jr.)	.25	.13	.08
71	Steve Rogers	.25	.13	.08
72	Hal McRae	.25	.13	.08
73	Orioles Team (Earl Weaver)	.80	.40	.25
74	Oscar Gamble	.25	.13	.08
75	Larry Dierker	.25	.13	.08
76	Willie Crawford	.25	.13	.08
77	Pedro Borbon	.25	.13	.08
78	Cecil Cooper	1.00	.50	.30
79	Jerry Morales	.25	.13	.08
80	Jim Kaat	.90	.45	.25
81	Darrell Evans	.50	.25	.15
82	Von Joshua	.25	.13	.08
83	Jim Spencer	.25	.13	.08
84	Brent Strom	.25	.13	.08
85	Mickey Rivers	.25	.13	.08
86	Mike Tyson	.25	.13	.08
87	Tom Burgmeier	.25	.13	.08
88	Duffy Dyer	.25	.13	.08
89	Vern Ruhle	.25	.13	.08
90	Sal Bando	.30	.15	.09
91	Tom Hutton	.25	.13	.08
92	Eduardo Rodriguez	.25	.13	.08
93	Mike Phillips	.25	.13	.08
94	Jim Dwyer	.30	.15	.09
95	Brooks Robinson	4.00	2.00	1.25
96	Doug Bird	.25	.13	.08
97	Wilbur Howard	.25	.13	.08
98	*Dennis Eckersley*	35.00	17.50	10.50
99	Lee Lacy	.25	.13	.08
100	Jim Hunter	3.00	1.50	.90
101	Pete LaCock	.25	.13	.08
102	Jim Willoughby	.25	.13	.08
103	Biff Pocoroba	.25	.13	.08
104	Reds Team (Sparky Anderson)	.90	.45	.25
105	Gary Lavelle	.25	.13	.08
106	Tom Grieve	.25	.13	.08
107	Dave Roberts	.25	.13	.08
108	Don Kirkwood	.25	.13	.08
109	Larry Lintz	.25	.13	.08
110	Carlos May	.25	.13	.08
111	Danny Thompson	.25	.13	.08
112	*Kent Tekulve*	.80	.40	.25
113	Gary Sutherland	.25	.13	.08
114	Jay Johnstone	.25	.13	.08
115	Ken Holtzman	.25	.13	.08
116	Charlie Moore	.25	.13	.08
117	Mike Jorgensen	.25	.13	.08
118	Red Sox Team (Darrell Johnson)	.90	.45	.25
119	Checklist 1-132	1.25	.60	.40

		NR MT	EX	VG
120	Rusty Staub	.35	.20	.11
121	Tony Solaita	.25	.13	.08
122	Mike Cosgrove	.25	.13	.08
123	Walt Williams	.25	.13	.08
124	Doug Rau	.25	.13	.08
125	Don Baylor	.50	.25	.15
126	Tom Dettore	.25	.13	.08
127	Larvell Blanks	.25	.13	.08
128	Ken Griffey	.35	.20	.11
129	Andy Etchebarren	.25	.13	.08
130	Luis Tiant	.40	.20	.12
131	Bill Stein	.25	.13	.08
132	Don Hood	.25	.13	.08
133	Gary Matthews	.25	.13	.08
134	Mike Ivie	.25	.13	.08
135	Bake McBride	.25	.13	.08
136	Dave Goltz	.25	.13	.08
137	Bill Robinson	.25	.13	.08
138	Lerrin LaGrow	.25	.13	.08
139	Gorman Thomas	.35	.20	.11
140	Vida Blue	.40	.20	.12
141	*Larry Parrish*	.80	.40	.25
142	Dick Drago	.25	.13	.08
143	Jerry Grote	.25	.13	.08
144	Al Fitzmorris	.25	.13	.08
145	Larry Bowa	.35	.20	.11
146	George Medich	.25	.13	.08
147	Astros Team (Bill Virdon)	.80	.40	.25
148	Stan Thomas	.25	.13	.08
149	Tommy Davis	.30	.15	.09
150	Steve Garvey	5.00	2.50	1.50
151	Bill Bonham	.25	.13	.08
152	Leroy Stanton	.25	.13	.08
153	Buzz Capra	.25	.13	.08
154	Bucky Dent	.30	.15	.09
155	Jack Billingham	.25	.13	.08
156	Rico Carty	.25	.13	.08
157	Mike Caldwell	.25	.13	.08
158	Ken Reitz	.25	.13	.08
159	Jerry Terrell	.25	.13	.08
160	Dave Winfield	12.00	6.00	3.50
161	Bruce Kison	.25	.13	.08
162	Jack Pierce	.25	.13	.08
163	Jim Slaton	.25	.13	.08
164	Pepe Mangual	.25	.13	.08
165	Gene Tenace	.25	.13	.08
166	Skip Lockwood	.25	.13	.08
167	Freddie Patek	.25	.13	.08
168	Tom Hilgendorf	.25	.13	.08
169	Graig Nettles	1.00	.50	.30
170	Rick Wise	.25	.13	.08
171	Greg Gross	.25	.13	.08
172	Rangers Team (Frank Lucchesi)	.80	.40	.25
173	Steve Swisher	.25	.13	.08
174	Charlie Hough	.25	.13	.08
175	Ken Singleton	.30	.15	.09
176	Dick Lange	.25	.13	.08
177	Marty Perez	.25	.13	.08
178	Tom Buskey	.25	.13	.08
179	George Foster	1.00	.50	.30
180	Rich Gossage	1.50	.70	.45
181	Willie Montanez	.25	.13	.08
182	Harry Rasmussen	.25	.13	.08
183	Steve Braun	.25	.13	.08
184	Bill Greif	.25	.13	.08
185	Dave Parker	7.00	3.50	2.00
186	Tom Walker	.25	.13	.08
187	Pedro Garcia	.25	.13	.08
188	Fred Scherman	.25	.13	.08
189	Claudell Washington	.40	.20	.12
190	Jon Matlack	.25	.13	.08
191	N.L. Batting Leaders (Bill Madlock, Manny Sanguillen, Ted Simmons)	.60	.30	.20
192	A.L. Batting Leaders (Rod Carew, Fred Lynn, Thurman Munson)	1.75	.90	.50
193	N.L. Home Run Leaders (Dave Kingman, Greg Luzinski, Mike Schmidt)	1.25	.60	.40
194	A.L. Home Run Leaders (Reggie Jackson, John Mayberry, George Scott)	1.25	.60	.40
195	N.L. Runs Batted In Ldrs. (Johnny Bench, Greg Luzinski, Tony Perez)	1.25	.60	.40
196	A.L. Runs Batted In Ldrs. (Fred Lynn, John Mayberry, George Scott)	.60	.30	.20
197	N.L. Stolen Base Leaders (Lou Brock, Dave Lopes, Joe Morgan)	.90	.45	.25
198	A.L. Stolen Base Leaders (Amos Otis, Mickey Rivers, Claudell Washington)	.50	.25	.15
199	N.L. Victory Leaders (Randy Jones, Andy Messersmith, Tom Seaver)	.80	.40	.25
200	A.L. Victory Leaders (Vida Blue, Jim Hunter, Jim Palmer)	.90	.45	.25

		NR MT	EX	VG
201	N.L. Earned Run Avg. Ldrs. (Randy Jones, Andy Messersmith, Tom Seaver)	.80	.40	.25
202	A.L. Earned Run Avg. Ldrs. (Dennis Eckersley, Jim Hunter, Jim Palmer)	.90	.45	.25
203	N.L. Strikeout Leaders (Andy Messersmith, John Montefusco, Tom Seaver)	.80	.40	.25
204	A.L. Strikeout Leaders (Bert Blyleven, Gaylord Perry, Frank Tanana)	.70	.35	.20
205	Major League Leading Firemen (Rich Gossage, Al Hrabosky)	.50	.25	.15
206	Manny Trillo	.25	.13	.08
207	Andy Hassler	.25	.13	.08
208	Mike Lum	.25	.13	.08
209	Alan Ashby	.35	.20	.11
210	Lee May	.25	.13	.08
211	Clay Carroll	.25	.13	.08
212	Pat Kelly	.25	.13	.08
213	Dave Heaverlo	.25	.13	.08
214	Eric Soderholm	.25	.13	.08
215	Reggie Smith	.25	.13	.08
216	Expos Team (Karl Kuehl)	.80	.40	.25
217	Dave Freisleben	.25	.13	.08
218	John Knox	.25	.13	.08
219	Tom Murphy	.25	.13	.08
220	Manny Sanguillen	.25	.13	.08
221	Jim Todd	.25	.13	.08
222	Wayne Garrett	.25	.13	.08
223	Ollie Brown	.25	.13	.08
224	Jim York	.25	.13	.08
225	Roy White	.25	.13	.08
226	Jim Sundberg	.25	.13	.08
227	Oscar Zamora	.25	.13	.08
228	John Hale	.25	.13	.08
229	*Jerry Remy*	.30	.15	.09
230	Carl Yastrzemski	9.00	4.50	2.75
231	Tom House	.25	.13	.08
232	Frank Duffy	.25	.13	.08
233	Grant Jackson	.25	.13	.08
234	Mike Sadek	.25	.13	.08
235	Bert Blyleven	1.00	.50	.30
236	Royals Team (Whitey Herzog)	.80	.40	.25
237	Dave Hamilton	.25	.13	.08
238	Larry Biittner	.25	.13	.08
239	John Curtis	.25	.13	.08
240	Pete Rose	15.00	7.50	4.50
241	Hector Torres	.25	.13	.08
242	Dan Meyer	.25	.13	.08
243	Jim Rooker	.25	.13	.08
244	Bill Sharp	.25	.13	.08
245	Felix Millan	.25	.13	.08
246	Cesar Tovar	.25	.13	.08
247	Terry Harmon	.25	.13	.08
248	Dick Tidrow	.25	.13	.08
249	Cliff Johnson	.25	.13	.08
250	Fergie Jenkins	2.00	1.00	.60
251	Rick Monday	.30	.15	.09
252	Tim Nordbrook	.25	.13	.08
253	Bill Buckner	.50	.25	.15
254	Rudy Meoli	.25	.13	.08
255	Fritz Peterson	.25	.13	.08
256	Rowland Office	.25	.13	.08
257	Ross Grimsley	.25	.13	.08
258	Nyls Nyman	.25	.13	.08
259	Darrel Chaney	.25	.13	.08
260	Steve Busby	.25	.13	.08
261	Gary Thomasson	.25	.13	.08
262	Checklist 133-264	1.50	.70	.45
263	*Lyman Bostock*	.80	.40	.25
264	Steve Renko	.25	.13	.08
265	Willie Davis	.30	.15	.09
266	Alan Foster	.25	.13	.08
267	Aurelio Rodriguez	.25	.13	.08
268	Del Unser	.25	.13	.08
269	Rick Austin	.25	.13	.08
270	Willie Stargell	3.00	1.50	.90
271	Jim Lonborg	.25	.13	.08
272	Rick Dempsey	.25	.13	.08
273	Joe Niekro	.30	.15	.09
274	Tommy Harper	.25	.13	.08
275	*Rick Manning*	.40	.20	.12
276	Mickey Scott	.25	.13	.08
277	Cubs Team (Jim Marshall)	.80	.40	.25
278	Bernie Carbo	.25	.13	.08
279	Roy Howell	.25	.13	.08
280	Burt Hooton	.25	.13	.08
281	Dave May	.25	.13	.08
282	Dan Osborn	.25	.13	.08
283	Merv Rettenmund	.25	.13	.08
284	Steve Ontiveros	.25	.13	.08
285	Mike Cuellar	.25	.13	.08

		NR MT	EX	VG
286	Jim Wohlford	.25	.13	.08
287	Pete Mackanin	.25	.13	.08
288	Bill Campbell	.25	.13	.08
289	Enzo Hernandez	.25	.13	.08
290	Ted Simmons	.60	.30	.20
291	Ken Sanders	.25	.13	.08
292	Leon Roberts	.25	.13	.08
293	Bill Castro	.25	.13	.08
294	Ed Kirkpatrick	.25	.13	.08
295	Dave Cash	.25	.13	.08
296	Pat Dobson	.25	.13	.08
297	Roger Metzger	.25	.13	.08
298	Dick Bosman	.25	.13	.08
299	Champ Summers	.25	.13	.08
300	Johnny Bench	10.00	5.00	3.00
301	Jackie Brown	.25	.13	.08
302	Rick Miller	.25	.13	.08
303	Steve Foucault	.25	.13	.08
304	Angels Team (Dick Williams)	.80	.40	.25
305	Andy Messersmith	.25	.13	.08
306	Rod Gilbreath	.25	.13	.08
307	Al Bumbry	.25	.13	.08
308	Jim Barr	.25	.13	.08
309	Bill Melton	.25	.13	.08
310	Randy Jones	.30	.15	.09
311	Cookie Rojas	.25	.13	.08
312	Don Carrithers	.25	.13	.08
313	*Dan Ford*	.25	.13	.08
314	Ed Kranepool	.25	.13	.08
315	Al Hrabosky	.25	.13	.08
316	Robin Yount	40.00	20.00	12.00
317	*John Candelaria*	2.00	1.00	.60
318	Bob Boone	.30	.15	.09
319	Larry Gura	.25	.13	.08
320	Willie Horton	.25	.13	.08
321	Jose Cruz	.35	.20	.11
322	Glenn Abbott	.25	.13	.08
323	Rob Sperring	.25	.13	.08
324	Jim Bibby	.25	.13	.08
325	Tony Perez	1.25	.60	.40
326	Dick Pole	.25	.13	.08
327	Dave Moates	.25	.13	.08
328	Carl Morton	.25	.13	.08
329	Joe Ferguson	.25	.13	.08
330	Nolan Ryan	35.00	17.50	10.50
331	Padres Team (John McNamara)	.80	.40	.25
332	Charlie Williams	.25	.13	.08
333	Bob Coluccio	.25	.13	.08
334	Dennis Leonard	.25	.13	.08
335	Bob Grich	.25	.13	.08
336	Vic Albury	.25	.13	.08
337	Bud Harrelson	.25	.13	.08
338	Bob Bailey	.25	.13	.08
339	John Denny	.25	.13	.08
340	Jim Rice	8.00	4.00	2.50
341	All Time All-Stars (Lou Gehrig)	4.00	2.00	1.25
342	All Time All-Stars (Rogers Hornsby)	1.25	.60	.40
343	All Time All-Stars (Pie Traynor)	.80	.40	.25
344	All Time All-Stars (Honus Wagner)	1.25	.60	.40
345	All Time All-Stars (Babe Ruth)	6.00	3.00	1.75
346	All Time All-Stars (Ty Cobb)	6.00	3.00	1.75
347	All Time All-Stars (Ted Williams)	6.00	3.00	1.75
348	All Time All-Stars (Mickey Cochrane)	.80	.40	.25
349	All Time All-Stars (Walter Johnson)	1.25	.60	.40
350	All Time All-Stars (Lefty Grove)	1.00	.50	.30
351	Randy Hundley	.25	.13	.08
352	Dave Giusti	.25	.13	.08
353	*Sixto Lezcano*	.30	.15	.09
354	Ron Blomberg	.25	.13	.08
355	Steve Carlton	7.00	3.50	2.00
356	Ted Martinez	.25	.13	.08
357	Ken Forsch	.25	.13	.08
358	Buddy Bell	.50	.25	.15
359	Rick Reuschel	.30	.15	.09
360	Jeff Burroughs	.25	.13	.08
361	Tigers Team (Ralph Houk)	1.00	.50	.30
362	Will McEnaney	.25	.13	.08
363	*Dave Collins*	.40	.20	.12
364	Elias Sosa	.25	.13	.08
365	Carlton Fisk	10.00	5.00	3.00
366	Bobby Valentine	.30	.15	.09
367	Bruce Miller	.25	.13	.08
368	Wilbur Wood	.25	.13	.08
369	Frank White	.30	.15	.09
370	Ron Cey	.40	.20	.12
371	Ellie Hendricks	.25	.13	.08
372	Rick Baldwin	.25	.13	.08
373	Johnny Briggs	.25	.13	.08

		NR MT	EX	VG
374	Dan Warthen	.25	.13	.08
375	Ron Fairly	.25	.13	.08
376	Rich Hebner	.25	.13	.08
377	Mike Hegan	.25	.13	.08
378	Steve Stone	.25	.13	.08
379	Ken Boswell	.25	.13	.08
380	Bobby Bonds	.35	.20	.11
381	Denny Doyle	.25	.13	.08
382	Matt Alexander	.25	.13	.08
383	John Ellis	.25	.13	.08
384	Phillies Team (Danny Ozark)	.80	.40	.25
385	Mickey Lolich	.40	.20	.12
386	Ed Goodson	.25	.13	.08
387	Mike Miley	.25	.13	.08
388	Stan Perzanowski	.25	.13	.08
389	Glenn Adams	.25	.13	.08
390	Don Gullett	.25	.13	.08
391	Jerry Hairston	.25	.13	.08
392	Checklist 265-396	1.50	.70	.45
393	Paul Mitchell	.25	.13	.08
394	Fran Healy	.25	.13	.08
395	Jim Wynn	.30	.15	.09
396	Bill Lee	.25	.13	.08
397	Tim Foli	.25	.13	.08
398	Dave Tomlin	.25	.13	.08
399	Luis Melendez	.25	.13	.08
400	Rod Carew	8.00	4.00	2.50
401	Ken Brett	.25	.13	.08
402	Don Money	.25	.13	.08
403	Geoff Zahn	.25	.13	.08
404	Enos Cabell	.25	.13	.08
405	Rollie Fingers	5.00	2.50	1.50
406	Ed Herrmann	.25	.13	.08
407	Tom Underwood	.25	.13	.08
408	Charlie Spikes	.25	.13	.08
409	Dave Lemanczyk	.25	.13	.08
410	Ralph Garr	.25	.13	.08
411	Bill Singer	.25	.13	.08
412	Toby Harrah	.25	.13	.08
413	Pete Varney	.25	.13	.08
414	Wayne Garland	.25	.13	.08
415	Vada Pinson	.50	.25	.15
416	Tommy John	1.25	.60	.40
417	Gene Clines	.25	.13	.08
418	Jose Morales	.25	.13	.08
419	Reggie Cleveland	.25	.13	.08
420	Joe Morgan	5.00	2.50	1.50
421	A's Team	.80	.40	.25
422	Johnny Grubb	.25	.13	.08
423	Ed Halicki	.25	.13	.08
424	Phil Roof	.25	.13	.08
425	Rennie Stennett	.25	.13	.08
426	Bob Forsch	.25	.13	.08
427	Kurt Bevacqua	.25	.13	.08
428	Jim Crawford	.25	.13	.08
429	Fred Stanley	.25	.13	.08
430	Jose Cardenal	.25	.13	.08
431	Dick Ruthven	.25	.13	.08
432	Tom Veryzer	.25	.13	.08
433	Rick Waits	.25	.13	.08
434	Morris Nettles	.25	.13	.08
435	Phil Niekro	2.00	1.00	.60
436	Bill Fahey	.25	.13	.08
437	Terry Forster	.25	.13	.08
438	Doug DeCinces	.50	.25	.15
439	Rick Rhoden	.60	.30	.20
440	John Mayberry	.25	.13	.08
441	Gary Carter	10.00	5.00	3.00
442	Hank Webb	.25	.13	.08
443	Giants Team	.80	.40	.25
444	Gary Nolan	.25	.13	.08
445	Rico Petrocelli	.25	.13	.08
446	Larry Haney	.25	.13	.08
447	Gene Locklear	.25	.13	.08
448	Tom Johnson	.25	.13	.08
449	Bob Robertson	.25	.13	.08
450	Jim Palmer	6.00	3.00	1.75
451	Buddy Bradford	.25	.13	.08
452	Tom Hausman	.25	.13	.08
453	Lou Piniella	.60	.30	.20
454	Tom Griffin	.25	.13	.08
455	Dick Allen	.50	.25	.15
456	Joe Coleman	.25	.13	.08
457	Ed Crosby	.25	.13	.08
458	Earl Williams	.25	.13	.08
459	Jim Brewer	.25	.13	.08
460	Cesar Cedeno	.30	.15	.09
461	NL & AL Championships	.80	.40	.25
462	1975 World Series	.80	.40	.25
463	Steve Hargan	.25	.13	.08
464	Ken Henderson	.25	.13	.08

		NR MT	EX	VG
465	Mike Marshall	.30	.15	.09
466	Bob Stinson	.25	.13	.08
467	Woodie Fryman	.25	.13	.08
468	Jesus Alou	.25	.13	.08
469	Rawly Eastwick	.25	.13	.08
470	Bobby Murcer	.35	.20	.11
471	Jim Burton	.25	.13	.08
472	Bob Davis	.25	.13	.08
473	Paul Blair	.25	.13	.08
474	Ray Corbin	.25	.13	.08
475	Joe Rudi	.30	.15	.09
476	Bob Moose	.25	.13	.08
477	Indians Team (Frank Robinson)	.80	.40	.25
478	Lynn McGlothen	.25	.13	.08
479	Bobby Mitchell	.25	.13	.08
480	Mike Schmidt	30.00	15.00	9.00
481	Rudy May	.25	.13	.08
482	Tim Hosley	.25	.13	.08
483	Mickey Stanley	.25	.13	.08
484	Eric Raich	.25	.13	.08
485	Mike Hargrove	.25	.13	.08
486	Bruce Dal Canton	.25	.13	.08
487	Leron Lee	.25	.13	.08
488	Claude Osteen	.25	.13	.08
489	Skip Jutze	.25	.13	.08
490	Frank Tanana	.30	.15	.09
491	Terry Crowley	.25	.13	.08
492	Marty Pattin	.25	.13	.08
493	Derrel Thomas	.25	.13	.08
494	Craig Swan	.25	.13	.08
495	Nate Colbert	.25	.13	.08
496	Juan Beniquez	.25	.13	.08
497	Joe McIntosh	.25	.13	.08
498	Glenn Borgmann	.25	.13	.08
499	Mario Guerrero	.25	.13	.08
500	Reggie Jackson	15.00	7.50	4.50
501	Billy Champion	.25	.13	.08
502	Tim McCarver	.50	.25	.15
503	Elliott Maddox	.25	.13	.08
504	Pirates Team (Danny Murtaugh)	.80	.40	.25
505	Mark Belanger	.25	.13	.08
506	George Mitterwald	.25	.13	.08
507	Ray Bare	.25	.13	.08
508	*Duane Kuiper*	.25	.13	.08
509	Bill Hands	.25	.13	.08
510	Amos Otis	.25	.13	.08
511	Jamie Easterly	.25	.13	.08
512	Ellie Rodriguez	.25	.13	.08
513	Bart Johnson	.25	.13	.08
514	Dan Driessen	.30	.15	.09
515	Steve Yeager	.25	.13	.08
516	Wayne Granger	.25	.13	.08
517	John Milner	.25	.13	.08
518	*Doug Flynn*	.25	.13	.08
519	Steve Brye	.25	.13	.08
520	Willie McCovey	2.50	1.25	.70
521	Jim Colborn	.25	.13	.08
522	Ted Sizemore	.25	.13	.08
523	Bob Montgomery	.25	.13	.08
524	Pete Falcone	.25	.13	.08
525	Billy Williams	2.25	1.25	.70
526	Checklist 397-528	1.50	.70	.45
527	Mike Anderson	.25	.13	.08
528	Dock Ellis	.25	.13	.08
529	Deron Johnson	.25	.13	.08
530	Don Sutton	1.50	.70	.45
531	Mets Team (Joe Frazier)	.90	.45	.25
532	Milt May	.25	.13	.08
533	Lee Richard	.25	.13	.08
534	Stan Bahnsen	.25	.13	.08
535	Dave Nelson	.25	.13	.08
536	Mike Thompson	.25	.13	.08
537	Tony Muser	.25	.13	.08
538	Pat Darcy	.25	.13	.08
539	John Balaz	.25	.13	.08
540	Bill Freehan	.25	.13	.08
541	Steve Mingori	.25	.13	.08
542	Keith Hernandez	6.00	3.00	1.75
543	Wayne Twitchell	.25	.13	.08
544	Pepe Frias	.25	.13	.08
545	Sparky Lyle	.35	.20	.11
546	Dave Rosello	.25	.13	.08
547	Roric Harrison	.25	.13	.08
548	Manny Mota	.25	.13	.08
549	Randy Tate	.25	.13	.08
550	Hank Aaron	15.00	7.50	4.50
551	Jerry DaVanon	.25	.13	.08
552	Terry Humphrey	.25	.13	.08
553	Randy Moffitt	.25	.13	.08
554	Ray Fosse	.25	.13	.08
555	Dyar Miller	.25	.13	.08
556	Twins Team (Gene Mauch)	.80	.40	.25
557	Dan Spillner	.25	.13	.08
558	Clarence Gaston	.25	.13	.08
559	Clyde Wright	.25	.13	.08
560	Jorge Orta	.25	.13	.08
561	Tom Carroll	.25	.13	.08
562	Adrian Garrett	.25	.13	.08
563	Larry Demery	.25	.13	.08
564	Bubble Gum Blowing Champ (Kurt Bevacqua)	.30	.15	.09
565	Tug McGraw	.35	.20	.11
566	Ken McMullen	.25	.13	.08
567	George Stone	.25	.13	.08
568	Rob Andrews	.25	.13	.08
569	Nelson Briles	.25	.13	.08
570	George Hendrick	.25	.13	.08
571	Don DeMola	.25	.13	.08
572	Rich Coggins	.25	.13	.08
573	Bill Travers	.25	.13	.08
574	Don Kessinger	.25	.13	.08
575	Dwight Evans	3.00	1.50	.90
576	Maximino Leon	.25	.13	.08
577	Marc Hill	.25	.13	.08
578	Ted Kubiak	.25	.13	.08
579	Clay Kirby	.25	.13	.08
580	Bert Campaneris	.30	.15	.09
581	Cardinals Team (Red Schoendienst)	.80	.40	.25
582	Mike Kekich	.25	.13	.08
583	Tommy Helms	.25	.13	.08
584	Stan Wall	.25	.13	.08
585	Joe Torre	.50	.25	.15
586	Ron Schueler	.25	.13	.08
587	Leo Cardenas	.25	.13	.08
588	Kevin Kobel	.25	.13	.08
589	Rookie Pitchers (Santo Alcala, *Mike Flanagan*, Joe Pactwa, Pablo Torrealba)	2.00	1.00	.60
590	Rookie Outfielders (Henry Cruz, *Chet Lemon, Ellis Valentine*, Terry Whitfield)	1.00	.50	.30
591	Rookie Pitchers (Steve Grilli, Craig Mitchell, Jose Sosa, George Throop)	.25	.13	.08
592	Rookie Infielders (Dave McKay, *Willie Randolph, Jerry Royster*, Roy Staiger)	5.00	2.50	1.50
593	Rookie Pitchers (Larry Anderson, Ken Crosby, Mark Littell, *Butch Metzger*)	.25	.13	.08
594	Rookie Catchers & Outfielders (Andy Merchant, Ed Ott, Royle Stillman, Jerry White)	.25	.13	.08
595	Rookie Pitchers (Steve Barr, Art DeFilippis, Randy Lerch, Sid Monge)	.25	.13	.08
596	Rookie Infielders (Lamar Johnson, *Johnny LeMaster*, Jerry Manuel, *Craig Reynolds*)	.35	.20	.11
597	Rookie Pitchers (*Don Aase*, Jack Kucek, Frank LaCorte, Mike Pazik)	.50	.25	.15
598	Rookie Outfielders (Hector Cruz, *Jamie Quirk*, Jerry Turner, Joe Wallis)	.25	.13	.08
599	Rookie Pitchers (Rob Dressler, *Ron Guidry, Bob McClure*, Pat Zachry)	10.00	5.00	3.00
600	Tom Seaver	10.00	5.00	3.00
601	Ken Rudolph	.25	.13	.08
602	Doug Konieczny	.25	.13	.08
603	Jim Holt	.25	.13	.08
604	Joe Lovitto	.25	.13	.08
605	Al Downing	.25	.13	.08
606	Brewers Team (Alex Grammas)	.80	.40	.25
607	Rich Hinton	.25	.13	.08
608	Vic Correll	.25	.13	.08
609	Fred Norman	.25	.13	.08
610	Greg Luzinski	.40	.20	.12
611	Rich Folkers	.25	.13	.08
612	Joe Lahoud	.25	.13	.08
613	Tim Johnson	.25	.13	.08
614	Fernando Arroyo	.25	.13	.08
615	Mike Cubbage	.25	.13	.08
616	Buck Martinez	.25	.13	.08
617	Darold Knowles	.25	.13	.08
618	Jack Brohamer	.25	.13	.08
619	Bill Butler	.25	.13	.08
620	Al Oliver	.70	.35	.20
621	Tom Hall	.25	.13	.08
622	Rick Auerbach	.25	.13	.08
623	Bob Allietta	.25	.13	.08
624	Tony Taylor	.25	.13	.08
625	J.R. Richard	.25	.13	.08
626	Bob Sheldon	.25	.13	.08
627	Bill Plummer	.25	.13	.08
628	John D'Acquisto	.25	.13	.08

		NR MT	EX	VG
629	Sandy Alomar	.25	.13	.08
630	Chris Speier	.25	.13	.08
631	Braves Team (Dave Bristol)	.80	.40	.25
632	Rogelio Moret	.25	.13	.08
633	*John Stearns*	.30	.15	.09
634	Larry Christenson	.25	.13	.08
635	Jim Fregosi	.25	.13	.08
636	Joe Decker	.25	.13	.08
637	Bruce Bochte	.25	.13	.08
638	Doyle Alexander	.30	.15	.09
639	Fred Kendall	.25	.13	.08
640	Bill Madlock	1.00	.50	.30
641	Tom Paciorek	.25	.13	.08
642	Dennis Blair	.25	.13	.08
643	Checklist 529-660	1.50	.70	.45
644	Tom Bradley	.25	.13	.08
645	Darrell Porter	.25	.13	.08
646	John Lowenstein	.25	.13	.08
648	Al Cowens	.25	.13	.08
649	Dave Roberts	.25	.13	.08
650	Thurman Munson	7.00	3.50	2.00
651	John Odom	.25	.13	.08
652	Ed Armbrister	.25	.13	.08
653	*Mike Norris*	.30	.15	.09
654	Doug Griffin	.25	.13	.08
655	Mike Vail	.25	.13	.08
656	White Sox Team (Chuck Tanner)	.80	.40	.25
657	*Roy Smalley*	.40	.20	.12
658	Jerry Johnson	.25	.13	.08
659	Ben Oglivie	.25	.13	.08
660	Dave Lopes	.60	.13	.08

1976 Topps Traded

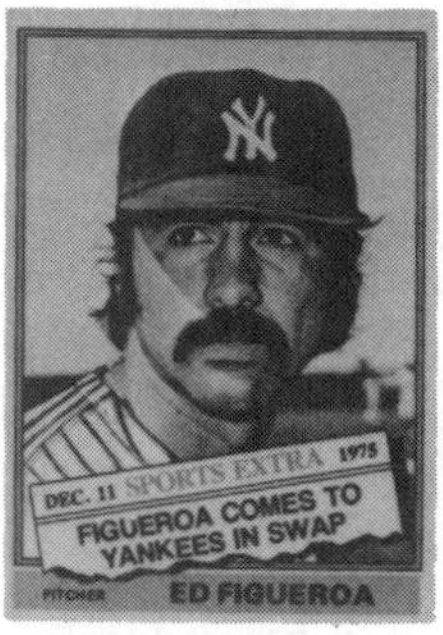

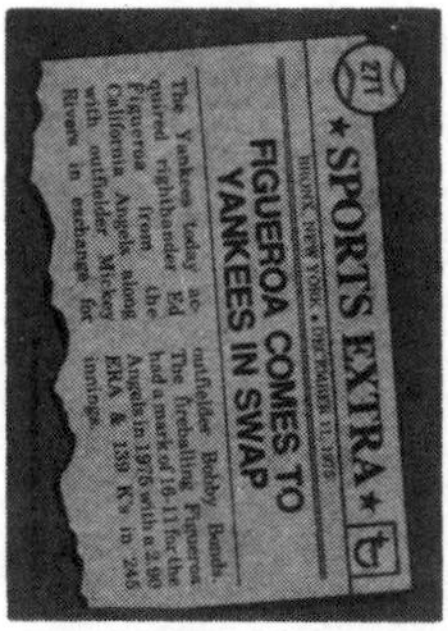

Similar to the Topps Traded set of 1974, the 2-1/2" by 3-1/2" cards feature photos of players traded after the printing deadline. The style of the cards is essentially the same as the regular issue but with a large "Sports Extra" headline announcing the trade and its date. The backs continue in newspaper style to detail the specifics of the trade. There are 43 player cards and one checklist in the set. Numbers remain the same as the player's regular card, with the addition of a "T" suffix.

	NR MT	EX	VG
Complete Set:	10.00	5.00	3.00
Common Player:	.15	.08	.05

		NR MT	EX	VG
27T	Ed Figueroa	.20	.10	.06
28T	Dusty Baker	.35	.20	.11
44T	Doug Rader	.15	.08	.05
58T	Ron Reed	.20	.10	.06
74T	Oscar Gamble	.25	.13	.08
80T	Jim Kaat	.60	.30	.20
83T	Jim Spencer	.15	.08	.05
85T	Mickey Rivers	.30	.15	.09
99T	Lee Lacy	.20	.10	.06
120T	Rusty Staub	.50	.25	.15
127T	Larvell Blanks	.15	.08	.05
146T	George Medich	.15	.08	.05
158T	Ken Reitz	.15	.08	.05
208T	Mike Lum	.15	.08	.05
211T	Clay Carroll	.20	.10	.06
231T	Tom House	.15	.08	.05
250T	Fergie Jenkins	1.00	.50	.30
259T	Darrel Chaney	.15	.08	.05
292T	Leon Roberts	.15	.08	.05
296T	Pat Dobson	.20	.10	.06
309T	Bill Melton	.20	.10	.06
338T	Bob Bailey	.15	.08	.05
380T	Bobby Bonds	.35	.20	.11
383T	John Ellis	.15	.08	.05
385T	Mickey Lolich	.50	.25	.15
401T	Ken Brett	.20	.10	.06
410T	Ralph Garr	.20	.10	.06
411T	Bill Singer	.20	.10	.06
428T	Jim Crawford	.15	.08	.05
434T	Morris Nettles	.15	.08	.05
464T	Ken Henderson	.15	.08	.05
497T	Joe McIntosh	.15	.08	.05
524T	Pete Falcone	.15	.08	.05
527T	Mike Anderson	.15	.08	.05
528T	Dock Ellis	.20	.10	.06
532T	Milt May	.15	.08	.05
554T	Ray Fosse	.15	.08	.05
579T	Clay Kirby	.15	.08	.05
583T	Tommy Helms	.15	.08	.05
592T	Willie Randolph	1.00	.50	.30
618T	Jack Brohamer	.15	.08	.05
632T	Rogelio Moret	.15	.08	.05
649T	Dave Roberts	.15	.08	.05
----	Traded Checklist	.80	.40	.25

1977 Topps

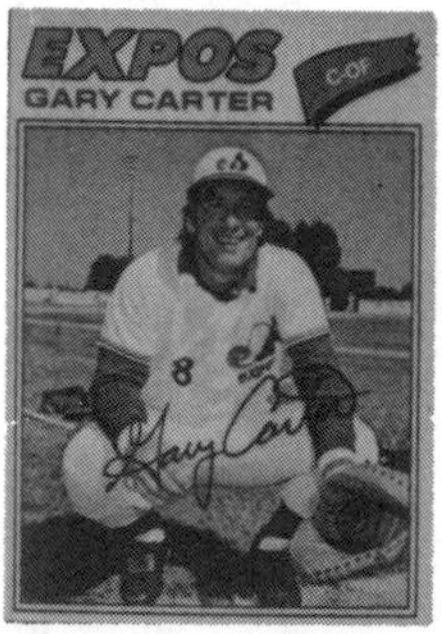

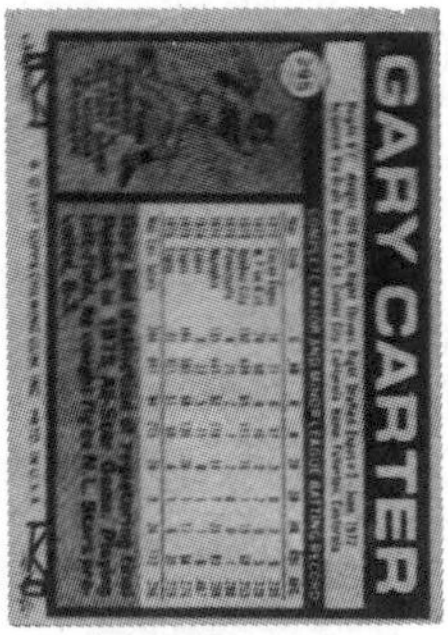

The 1977 Topps Set is a 660-card effort featuring front designs dominated by a color photograph on which there is a facsimile autograph. Above the picture are the player's name, team and position. The backs of the 2-1/2" by 3-1/2" cards include personal and career statistics along with newspaper-style highlights and a cartoon. Specialty cards include statistical leaders, record performances, a new "Turn Back The Clock" feature which highlighted great past moments and a "Big League Brothers" feature.

	NR MT	EX	VG
Complete Set:	400.00	200.00	125.00
Common Player:	.20	.10	.06

		NR MT	EX	VG
1	Batting Leaders (George Brett, Bill Madlock)	3.50	1.75	1.00
2	Home Run Leaders (Graig Nettles, Mike Schmidt)	1.25	.60	.40
3	Runs Batted In Leaders (George Foster, Lee May)	.50	.25	.15
4	Stolen Base Leaders (Dave Lopes, Bill North)	.30	.15	.09
5	Victory Leaders (Randy Jones, Jim Palmer)	.80	.40	.25
6	Strikeout Leaders (Nolan Ryan, Tom Seaver)	5.00	2.50	1.50
7	Earned Run Avg. Ldrs. (John Denny, Mark Fidrych)	.30	.15	.09
8	Leading Firemen (Bill Campbell, Rawly Eastwick)	.30	.15	.09
9	Doug Rader	.20	.10	.06
10	Reggie Jackson	10.00	5.00	3.00
11	Rob Dressler	.20	.10	.06
12	Larry Haney	.20	.10	.06
13	Luis Gomez	.20	.10	.06
14	Tommy Smith	.20	.10	.06
15	Don Gullett	.20	.10	.06

		NR MT	EX	VG
16	Bob Jones	.20	.10	.06
17	Steve Stone	.25	.13	.08
18	Indians Team (Frank Robinson)	.80	.40	.25
19	John D'Acquisto	.20	.10	.06
20	Graig Nettles	.90	.45	.25
21	Ken Forsch	.20	.10	.06
22	Bill Freehan	.25	.13	.08
23	Dan Driessen	.25	.13	.08
24	Carl Morton	.20	.10	.06
25	Dwight Evans	2.50	1.25	.70
26	Ray Sadecki	.20	.10	.06
27	Bill Buckner	.35	.20	.11
28	Woodie Fryman	.20	.10	.06
29	Bucky Dent	.25	.13	.08
30	Greg Luzinski	.40	.20	.12
31	Jim Todd	.20	.10	.06
32	Checklist 1-132	1.25	.60	.40
33	Wayne Garland	.20	.10	.06
34	Angels Team (Norm Sherry)	.70	.35	.20
35	Rennie Stennett	.20	.10	.06
36	John Ellis	.20	.10	.06
37	Steve Hargan	.20	.10	.06
38	Craig Kusick	.20	.10	.06
39	Tom Griffin	.20	.10	.06
40	Bobby Murcer	.30	.15	.09
41	Jim Kern	.20	.10	.06
42	Jose Cruz	.30	.15	.09
43	Ray Bare	.20	.10	.06
44	Bud Harrelson	.20	.10	.06
45	Rawly Eastwick	.20	.10	.06
46	Buck Martinez	.20	.10	.06
47	Lynn McGlothen	.20	.10	.06
48	Tom Paciorek	.20	.10	.06
49	Grant Jackson	.20	.10	.06
50	Ron Cey	.35	.20	.11
51	Brewers Team (Alex Grammas)	.70	.35	.20
52	Ellis Valentine	.20	.10	.06
53	Paul Mitchell	.20	.10	.06
54	Sandy Alomar	.20	.10	.06
55	Jeff Burroughs	.25	.13	.08
56	Rudy May	.20	.10	.06
57	Marc Hill	.20	.10	.06
58	Chet Lemon	.30	.15	.09
59	Larry Christenson	.20	.10	.06
60	Jim Rice	4.50	2.25	1.25
61	Manny Sanguillen	.20	.10	.06
62	Eric Raich	.20	.10	.06
63	Tito Fuentes	.20	.10	.06
64	Larry Biittner	.20	.10	.06
65	Skip Lockwood	.20	.10	.06
66	Roy Smalley	.20	.10	.06
67	*Joaquin Andujar*	.60	.30	.20
68	Bruce Bochte	.20	.10	.06
69	Jim Crawford	.20	.10	.06
70	Johnny Bench	8.00	4.00	2.50
71	Dock Ellis	.20	.10	.06
72	Mike Anderson	.20	.10	.06
73	Charlie Williams	.20	.10	.06
74	A's Team (Jack McKeon)	.70	.35	.20
75	Dennis Leonard	.20	.10	.06
76	Tim Foli	.20	.10	.06
77	Dyar Miller	.20	.10	.06
78	Bob Davis	.20	.10	.06
79	Don Money	.20	.10	.06
80	Andy Messersmith	.25	.13	.08
81	Juan Beniquez	.20	.10	.06
82	Jim Rooker	.20	.10	.06
83	Kevin Bell	.20	.10	.06
84	Ollie Brown	.20	.10	.06
85	Duane Kuiper	.20	.10	.06
86	Pat Zachry	.20	.10	.06
87	Glenn Borgmann	.20	.10	.06
88	Stan Wall	.20	.10	.06
89	*Butch Hobson*	.20	.10	.06
90	Cesar Cedeno	.30	.15	.09
91	John Verhoeven	.20	.10	.06
92	Dave Rosello	.20	.10	.06
93	Tom Poquette	.20	.10	.06
94	Craig Swan	.20	.10	.06
95	Keith Hernandez	3.00	1.50	.90
96	Lou Piniella	.40	.20	.12
97	Dave Heaverlo	.20	.10	.06
98	Milt May	.20	.10	.06
99	Tom Hausman	.20	.10	.06
100	Joe Morgan	4.00	2.00	1.25
101	Dick Bosman	.20	.10	.06
102	Jose Morales	.20	.10	.06
103	Mike Bacsik	.20	.10	.06
104	*Omar Moreno*	.25	.13	.08
105	Steve Yeager	.20	.10	.06
106	Mike Flanagan	.35	.20	.11
107	Bill Melton	.20	.10	.06
108	Alan Foster	.20	.10	.06
109	Jorge Orta	.20	.10	.06
110	Steve Carlton	6.00	3.00	1.75
111	Rico Petrocelli	.25	.13	.08
112	Bill Greif	.20	.10	.06
113	Blue Jays Mgr./Coaches (Roy Hartsfield, Don Leppert, Bob Miller, Jackie Moore, Harry Warner)	.25	.13	.08
114	Bruce Dal Canton	.20	.10	.06
115	Rick Manning	.20	.10	.06
116	Joe Niekro	.30	.15	.09
117	Frank White	.25	.13	.08
118	Rick Jones	.20	.10	.06
119	John Stearns	.20	.10	.06
120	Rod Carew	8.00	4.00	2.50
121	Gary Nolan	.20	.10	.06
122	Ben Oglivie	.20	.10	.06
123	Fred Stanley	.20	.10	.06
124	George Mitterwald	.20	.10	.06
125	Bill Travers	.20	.10	.06
126	Rod Gilbreath	.20	.10	.06
127	Ron Fairly	.25	.13	.08
128	Tommy John	1.25	.60	.40
129	Mike Sadek	.20	.10	.06
130	Al Oliver	.60	.30	.20
131	Orlando Ramirez	.20	.10	.06
132	Chip Lang	.20	.10	.06
133	Ralph Garr	.20	.10	.06
134	Padres Team (John McNamara)	.70	.35	.20
135	Mark Belanger	.20	.10	.06
136	*Jerry Mumphrey*	.20	.10	.06
137	Jeff Terpko	.20	.10	.06
138	Bob Stinson	.20	.10	.06
139	Fred Norman	.20	.10	.06
140	Mike Schmidt	20.00	10.00	6.00
141	Mark Littell	.20	.10	.06
142	Steve Dillard	.20	.10	.06
143	Ed Herrmann	.20	.10	.06
144	*Bruce Sutter*	3.00	1.50	.90
145	Tom Veryzer	.20	.10	.06
146	Dusty Baker	.25	.13	.08
147	Jackie Brown	.20	.10	.06
148	Fran Healy	.20	.10	.06
149	Mike Cubbage	.20	.10	.06
150	Tom Seaver	8.00	4.00	2.50
151	Johnnie LeMaster	.20	.10	.06
152	Gaylord Perry	2.50	1.25	.70
153	Ron Jackson	.20	.10	.06
154	Dave Giusti	.20	.10	.06
155	Joe Rudi	.25	.13	.08
156	Pete Mackanin	.20	.10	.06
157	Ken Brett	.20	.10	.06
158	Ted Kubiak	.20	.10	.06
159	Bernie Carbo	.20	.10	.06
160	Will McEnaney	.20	.10	.06
161	*Garry Templeton*	1.50	.70	.45
162	Mike Cuellar	.25	.13	.08
163	Dave Hilton	.20	.10	.06
164	Tug McGraw	.35	.20	.11
165	Jim Wynn	.25	.13	.08
166	Bill Campbell	.20	.10	.06
167	Rich Hebner	.20	.10	.06
168	Charlie Spikes	.20	.10	.06
169	Darold Knowles	.20	.10	.06
170	Thurman Munson	5.00	2.50	1.50
171	Ken Sanders	.20	.10	.06
172	John Milner	.20	.10	.06
173	Chuck Scrivener	.20	.10	.06
174	Nelson Briles	.20	.10	.06
175	*Butch Wynegar*	.40	.20	.12
176	Bob Robertson	.20	.10	.06
177	Bart Johnson	.20	.10	.06
178	Bombo Rivera	.20	.10	.06
179	Paul Hartzell	.20	.10	.06
180	Dave Lopes	.25	.13	.08
181	Ken McMullen	.20	.10	.06
182	Dan Spillner	.20	.10	.06
183	Cardinals Team (Vern Rapp)	.70	.35	.20
184	Bo McLaughlin	.20	.10	.06
185	Sixto Lezcano	.20	.10	.06
186	Doug Flynn	.20	.10	.06
187	Dick Pole	.20	.10	.06
188	Bob Tolan	.20	.10	.06
189	Rick Dempsey	.20	.10	.06
190	Ray Burris	.20	.10	.06
191	Doug Griffin	.20	.10	.06
192	Clarence Gaston	.20	.10	.06
193	Larry Gura	.20	.10	.06
194	Gary Matthews	.25	.13	.08
195	Ed Figueroa	.20	.10	.06

		NR MT	EX	VG
196	Len Randle	.20	.10	.06
197	Ed Ott	.20	.10	.06
198	Wilbur Wood	.20	.10	.06
199	Pepe Frias	.20	.10	.06
200	Frank Tanana	.30	.15	.09
201	Ed Kranepool	.25	.13	.08
202	Tom Johnson	.20	.10	.06
203	Ed Armbrister	.20	.10	.06
204	Jeff Newman	.20	.10	.06
205	Pete Falcone	.20	.10	.06
206	Boog Powell	.50	.25	.15
207	Glenn Abbott	.20	.10	.06
208	Checklist 133-264	1.25	.60	.40
209	Rob Andrews	.20	.10	.06
210	Fred Lynn	1.50	.70	.45
211	Giants Team (Joe Altobelli)	.70	.35	.20
212	Jim Mason	.20	.10	.06
213	Maximino Leon	.20	.10	.06
214	Darrell Porter	.20	.10	.06
215	Butch Metzger	.20	.10	.06
216	Doug DeCinces	.25	.13	.08
217	Tom Underwood	.20	.10	.06
218	*John Wathan*	.60	.30	.20
219	Joe Coleman	.20	.10	.06
220	Chris Chambliss	.30	.15	.09
221	Bob Bailey	.20	.10	.06
222	Francisco Barrios	.20	.10	.06
223	Earl Williams	.20	.10	.06
224	Rusty Torres	.20	.10	.06
225	Bob Apodaca	.20	.10	.06
226	Leroy Stanton	.20	.10	.06
227	*Joe Sambito*	.25	.13	.08
228	Twins Team (Gene Mauch)	.80	.40	.25
229	Don Kessinger	.20	.10	.06
230	Vida Blue	.40	.20	.12
231	Record Breaker (George Brett)	5.00	2.50	1.50
232	Record Breaker (Minnie Minoso)	.35	.20	.11
233	Record Breaker (Jose Morales)	.20	.10	.06
234	Record Breaker (Nolan Ryan)	7.00	3.50	2.00
235	Cecil Cooper	.60	.30	.20
236	Tom Buskey	.20	.10	.06
237	Gene Clines	.20	.10	.06
238	Tippy Martinez	.20	.10	.06
239	Bill Plummer	.20	.10	.06
240	Ron LeFlore	.25	.13	.08
241	Dave Tomlin	.20	.10	.06
242	Ken Henderson	.20	.10	.06
243	Ron Reed	.20	.10	.06
244	John Mayberry	.20	.10	.06
245	Rick Rhoden	.30	.15	.09
246	Mike Vail	.20	.10	.06
247	Chris Knapp	.20	.10	.06
248	Wilbur Howard	.20	.10	.06
249	Pete Redfern	.20	.10	.06
250	Bill Madlock	.40	.20	.12
251	Tony Muser	.20	.10	.06
252	Dale Murray	.20	.10	.06
253	John Hale	.20	.10	.06
254	Doyle Alexander	.30	.15	.09
255	George Scott	.20	.10	.06
256	Joe Hoerner	.20	.10	.06
257	Mike Miley	.20	.10	.06
258	Luis Tiant	.35	.20	.11
259	Mets Team (Joe Frazier)	.80	.40	.25
260	J.R. Richard	.25	.13	.08
261	Phil Garner	.20	.10	.06
262	Al Cowens	.20	.10	.06
263	Mike Marshall	.25	.13	.08
264	Tom Hutton	.20	.10	.06
265	*Mark Fidrych*	.70	.35	.20
266	Derrel Thomas	.20	.10	.06
267	Ray Fosse	.20	.10	.06
268	Rick Sawyer	.20	.10	.06
269	Joe Lis	.20	.10	.06
270	Dave Parker	5.00	2.50	1.50
271	Terry Forster	.20	.10	.06
272	Lee Lacy	.20	.10	.06
273	Eric Soderholm	.20	.10	.06
274	Don Stanhouse	.20	.10	.06
275	Mike Hargrove	.20	.10	.06
276	A.L. Championship (Chambliss' Dramatic Homer Decides It)	.70	.35	.20
277	N.L. Championship (Reds Sweep Phillies 3 In Row)	.70	.35	.20
278	Danny Frisella	.20	.10	.06
279	Joe Wallis	.20	.10	.06
280	Jim Hunter	2.00	1.00	.60
281	Roy Staiger	.20	.10	.06
282	Sid Monge	.20	.10	.06
283	Jerry DaVanon	.20	.10	.06
284	Mike Norris	.20	.10	.06
285	Brooks Robinson	2.50	1.25	.70
286	Johnny Grubb	.20	.10	.06
287	Reds Team (Sparky Anderson)	.80	.40	.25
288	Bob Montgomery	.20	.10	.06
289	Gene Garber	.20	.10	.06
290	Amos Otis	.20	.10	.06
291	*Jason Thompson*	.35	.20	.11
292	Rogelio Moret	.20	.10	.06
293	Jack Brohamer	.20	.10	.06
294	George Medich	.20	.10	.06
295	Gary Carter	6.00	3.00	1.75
296	Don Hood	.20	.10	.06
297	Ken Reitz	.20	.10	.06
298	Charlie Hough	.25	.13	.08
299	Otto Velez	.20	.10	.06
300	Jerry Koosman	.30	.15	.09
301	Toby Harrah	.20	.10	.06
302	Mike Garman	.20	.10	.06
303	Gene Tenace	.20	.10	.06
304	Jim Hughes	.20	.10	.06
305	Mickey Rivers	.25	.13	.08
306	Rick Waits	.20	.10	.06
307	Gary Sutherland	.20	.10	.06
308	Gene Pentz	.20	.10	.06
309	Red Sox Team (Don Zimmer)	.80	.40	.25
310	Larry Bowa	.30	.15	.09
311	Vern Ruhle	.20	.10	.06
312	Rob Belloir	.20	.10	.06
313	Paul Blair	.20	.10	.06
314	Steve Mingori	.20	.10	.06
315	Dave Chalk	.20	.10	.06
316	Steve Rogers	.20	.10	.06
317	Kurt Bevacqua	.20	.10	.06
318	Duffy Dyer	.20	.10	.06
319	Rich Gossage	1.00	.50	.30
320	Ken Griffey	.30	.15	.09
321	Dave Goltz	.20	.10	.06
322	Bill Russell	.20	.10	.06
323	Larry Lintz	.20	.10	.06
324	John Curtis	.20	.10	.06
325	Mike Ivie	.20	.10	.06
326	Jesse Jefferson	.20	.10	.06
327	Astros Team (Bill Virdon)	.70	.35	.20
328	Tommy Boggs	.20	.10	.06
329	Ron Hodges	.20	.10	.06
330	George Hendrick	.20	.10	.06
331	Jim Colborn	.20	.10	.06
332	Elliott Maddox	.20	.10	.06
333	Paul Reuschel	.20	.10	.06
334	Bill Stein	.20	.10	.06
335	Bill Robinson	.20	.10	.06
336	Denny Doyle	.20	.10	.06
337	Ron Schueler	.20	.10	.06
338	Dave Duncan	.20	.10	.06
339	Adrian Devine	.20	.10	.06
340	Hal McRae	.30	.15	.09
341	Joe Kerrigan	.20	.10	.06
342	Jerry Remy	.20	.10	.06
343	Ed Halicki	.20	.10	.06
344	Brian Downing	.25	.13	.08
345	Reggie Smith	.25	.13	.08
346	Bill Singer	.20	.10	.06
347	George Foster	1.25	.60	.40
348	Brent Strom	.20	.10	.06
349	Jim Holt	.20	.10	.06
350	Larry Dierker	.20	.10	.06
351	Jim Sundberg	.20	.10	.06
352	Mike Phillips	.20	.10	.06
353	Stan Thomas	.20	.10	.06
354	Pirates Team (Chuck Tanner)	.80	.40	.25
355	Lou Brock	3.00	1.50	.90
356	Checklist 265-396	1.25	.60	.40
357	Tim McCarver	.40	.20	.12
358	Tom House	.20	.10	.06
359	Willie Randolph	1.00	.50	.30
360	Rick Monday	.25	.13	.08
361	Eduardo Rodriguez	.20	.10	.06
362	Tommy Davis	.30	.15	.09
363	Dave Roberts	.20	.10	.06
364	Vic Correll	.20	.10	.06
365	Mike Torrez	.20	.10	.06
366	Ted Sizemore	.20	.10	.06
367	Dave Hamliton	.20	.10	.06
368	Mike Jorgensen	.20	.10	.06
369	Terry Humphrey	.20	.10	.06
370	John Montefusco	.20	.10	.06
371	Royals Team (Whitey Herzog)	.80	.40	.25
372	Rich Folkers	.20	.10	.06
373	Bert Campaneris	.30	.15	.09
374	Kent Tekulve	.30	.15	.09
375	Larry Hisle	.20	.10	.06

		NR MT	EX	VG
376	Nino Espinosa	.20	.10	.06
377	Dave McKay	.20	.10	.06
378	Jim Umbarger	.20	.10	.06
379	Larry Cox	.20	.10	.06
380	Lee May	.25	.13	.08
381	Bob Forsch	.20	.10	.06
382	Charlie Moore	.20	.10	.06
383	Stan Bahnsen	.20	.10	.06
384	Darrel Chaney	.20	.10	.06
385	Dave LaRoche	.20	.10	.06
386	Manny Mota	.25	.13	.08
387	Yankees Team (Billy Martin)	1.25	.60	.40
388	Terry Harmon	.20	.10	.06
389	Ken Kravec	.20	.10	.06
390	Dave Winfield	7.00	3.50	2.00
391	Dan Warthen	.20	.10	.06
392	Phil Roof	.20	.10	.06
393	John Lowenstein	.20	.10	.06
394	Bill Laxton	.20	.10	.06
395	Manny Trillo	.20	.10	.06
396	Tom Murphy	.20	.10	.06
397	*Larry Herndon*	.40	.20	.12
398	Tom Burgmeier	.20	.10	.06
399	Bruce Boisclair	.20	.10	.06
400	Steve Garvey	5.00	2.50	1.50
401	Mickey Scott	.20	.10	.06
402	Tommy Helms	.20	.10	.06
403	Tom Grieve	.20	.10	.06
404	Eric Rasmussen	.20	.10	.06
405	Claudell Washington	.25	.13	.08
406	Tim Johnson	.20	.10	.06
407	Dave Freisleben	.20	.10	.06
408	Cesar Tovar	.20	.10	.06
409	Pete Broberg	.20	.10	.06
410	Willie Montanez	.20	.10	.06
411	World Series Games 1 & 2	.70	.35	.20
412	World Series Games 3 & 4	.70	.35	.20
413	World Series Summary	.70	.35	.20
414	Tommy Harper	.20	.10	.06
415	Jay Johnstone	.20	.10	.06
416	Chuck Hartenstein	.20	.10	.06
417	Wayne Garrett	.20	.10	.06
418	White Sox Team (Bob Lemon)	.80	.40	.25
419	Steve Swisher	.20	.10	.06
420	Rusty Staub	.35	.20	.11
421	Doug Rau	.20	.10	.06
422	Freddie Patek	.20	.10	.06
423	Gary Lavelle	.20	.10	.06
424	Steve Brye	.20	.10	.06
425	Joe Torre	.40	.20	.12
426	Dick Drago	.20	.10	.06
427	Dave Rader	.20	.10	.06
428	Rangers Team (Frank Lucchesi)	.70	.35	.20
429	Ken Boswell	.20	.10	.06
430	Fergie Jenkins	1.75	.90	.50
431	Dave Collins	.25	.13	.08
432	Buzz Capra	.20	.10	.06
433	Turn Back The Clock (Nate Colbert)	.20	.10	.06
434	Turn Back The Clock (Carl Yastrzemski)	2.00	1.00	.60
435	Turn Back The Clock (Maury Wills)	.35	.20	.11
436	Turn Back The Clock (Bob Keegan)	.20	.10	.06
437	Turn Back The Clock (Ralph Kiner)	.50	.25	.15
438	Marty Perez	.20	.10	.06
439	Gorman Thomas	.30	.15	.09
440	Jon Matlack	.20	.10	.06
441	Larvell Blanks	.20	.10	.06
442	Braves Team (Dave Bristol)	.70	.35	.20
443	Lamar Johnson	.20	.10	.06
444	Wayne Twitchell	.20	.10	.06
445	Ken Singleton	.25	.13	.08
446	Bill Bonham	.20	.10	.06
447	Jerry Turner	.20	.10	.06
448	Ellie Rodriguez	.20	.10	.06
449	Al Fitzmorris	.20	.10	.06
450	Pete Rose	9.00	4.50	2.75
451	Checklist 397-528	1.25	.60	.40
452	Mike Caldwell	.20	.10	.06
453	Pedro Garcia	.20	.10	.06
454	Andy Etchebarren	.20	.10	.06
455	Rick Wise	.20	.10	.06
456	Leon Roberts	.20	.10	.06
457	Steve Luebber	.20	.10	.06
458	Leo Foster	.20	.10	.06
459	Steve Foucault	.20	.10	.06
460	Willie Stargell	2.50	1.25	.70
461	Dick Tidrow	.20	.10	.06
462	Don Baylor	.35	.20	.11
463	Jamie Quirk	.20	.10	.06
464	Randy Moffitt	.20	.10	.06
465	Rico Carty	.25	.13	.08
466	Fred Holdsworth	.20	.10	.06
467	Phillies Team (Danny Ozark)	.70	.35	.20
468	Ramon Hernandez	.20	.10	.06
469	Pat Kelly	.20	.10	.06
470	Ted Simmons	.60	.30	.20
471	Del Unser	.20	.10	.06
472	Rookie Pitchers (Don Aase, Bob McClure, Gil Patterson, Dave Wehrmeister)	.25	.13	.08
473	Rookie Outfielders (*Andre Dawson*, Gene Richards, John Scott, *Denny Walling*)	60.00	30.00	18.00
474	Rookie Shortstops (Bob Bailor, Kiko Garcia, Craig Reynolds, Alex Taveras)	.20	.10	.06
475	Rookie Pitchers (Chris Batton, Rick Camp, Scott McGregor, Manny Sarmiento)	.30	.15	.09
476	Rookie Catchers (Gary Alexander, *Rick Cerone, Dale Murphy*, Kevin Pasley)	50.00	25.00	15.00
477	Rookie Infielders (Doug Ault, *Rich Dauer*, Orlando Gonzalez, Phil Mankowski)	.25	.13	.08
478	Rookie Pitchers (Jim Gideon, Leon Hooten, Dave Johnson, Mark Lemongello)	.20	.10	.06
479	Rookie Outfielders (Brian Asselstine, *Wayne Gross*, Sam Mejias, Alvis Woods)	.25	.13	.08
480	Carl Yastrzemski	7.00	3.50	2.00
481	Roger Metzger	.20	.10	.06
482	Tony Solaita	.20	.10	.06
483	Richie Zisk	.20	.10	.06
484	Burt Hooton	.20	.10	.06
485	Roy White	.30	.15	.09
486	Ed Bane	.20	.10	.06
487	Rookie Pitchers (Larry Anderson, Ed Glynn, Joe Henderson, Greg Terlecky)	.20	.10	.06
488	Rookie Outfielders (*Jack Clark, Ruppert Jones, Lee Mazzilli*, Dan Thomas)	18.00	9.00	5.50
489	Rookie Pitchers (*Len Barker*, Randy Lerch, *Greg Minton*, Mike Overy)	.40	.20	.12
490	Rookie Shortstops (*Billy Almon*, Mickey Klutts, Tommy McMillan, Mark Wagner)	.25	.13	.08
491	Rookie Pitchers (Mike Dupree, *Denny Martinez*, Craig Mitchell, Bob Sykes)	5.00	2.50	1.50
492	Rookie Outfielders (*Tony Armas, Steve Kemp*, Carlos Lopez, Gary Woods)	1.00	.50	.30
493	Rookie Pitchers (*Mike Krukow*, Jim Otten, Gary Wheelock, Mike Willis)	.50	.25	.15
494	Rookie Infielders (Juan Bernhardt, Mike Champion, *Jim Gantner, Bump Wills*)	.50	.25	.15
495	Al Hrabosky	.20	.10	.06
496	Gary Thomasson	.20	.10	.06
497	Clay Carroll	.20	.10	.06
498	Sal Bando	.25	.13	.08
499	Pablo Torrealba	.20	.10	.06
500	Dave Kingman	.60	.30	.20
501	Jim Bibby	.20	.10	.06
502	Randy Hundley	.20	.10	.06
503	Bill Lee	.20	.10	.06
504	Dodgers Team (Tom Lasorda)	1.00	.50	.30
505	Oscar Gamble	.20	.10	.06
506	Steve Grilli	.20	.10	.06
507	Mike Hegan	.20	.10	.06
508	Dave Pagan	.20	.10	.06
509	Cookie Rojas	.20	.10	.06
510	John Candelaria	.80	.40	.25
511	Bill Fahey	.20	.10	.06
512	Jack Billingham	.20	.10	.06
513	Jerry Terrell	.20	.10	.06
514	Cliff Johnson	.20	.10	.06
515	Chris Speier	.20	.10	.06
516	Bake McBride	.20	.10	.06
517	*Pete Vuckovich*	.50	.25	.15
518	Cubs Team (Herman Franks)	.70	.35	.20
519	Don Kirkwood	.20	.10	.06
520	Garry Maddox	.20	.10	.06
521	Bob Grich	.25	.13	.08
522	Enzo Hernandez	.20	.10	.06
523	Rollie Fingers	2.50	1.25	.70
524	Rowland Office	.20	.10	.06
525	Dennis Eckersley	8.00	4.00	2.50
526	Larry Parrish	.35	.20	.11
527	Dan Meyer	.20	.10	.06
528	Bill Castro	.20	.10	.06
529	Jim Essian	.20	.10	.06
530	Rick Reuschel	.30	.15	.09
531	Lyman Bostock	.25	.13	.08
532	Jim Willoughby	.20	.10	.06
533	Mickey Stanley	.20	.10	.06

		NR MT	EX	VG
534	Paul Splittorff	.20	.10	.06
535	Cesar Geronimo	.20	.10	.06
536	Vic Albury	.20	.10	.06
537	Dave Roberts	.20	.10	.06
538	Frank Taveras	.20	.10	.06
539	Mike Wallace	.20	.10	.06
540	Bob Watson	.20	.10	.06
541	John Denny	.20	.10	.06
542	Frank Duffy	.20	.10	.06
543	Ron Blomberg	.20	.10	.06
544	Gary Ross	.20	.10	.06
545	Bob Boone	.25	.13	.08
546	Orioles Team (Earl Weaver)	.80	.40	.25
547	Willie McCovey	2.75	1.50	.80
548	*Joel Youngblood*	.30	.15	.09
549	Jerry Royster	.20	.10	.06
550	Randy Jones	.20	.10	.06
551	Bill North	.20	.10	.06
552	Pepe Mangual	.20	.10	.06
553	Jack Heidemann	.20	.10	.06
554	Bruce Kimm	.20	.10	.06
555	Dan Ford	.20	.10	.06
556	Doug Bird	.20	.10	.06
557	Jerry White	.20	.10	.06
558	Elias Sosa	.20	.10	.06
559	Alan Bannister	.20	.10	.06
560	Dave Concepcion	.35	.20	.11
561	Pete LaCock	.20	.10	.06
562	Checklist 529-660	1.25	.60	.40
563	Bruce Kison	.20	.10	.06
564	Alan Ashby	.20	.10	.06
565	Mickey Lolich	.50	.25	.15
566	Rick Miller	.20	.10	.06
567	Enos Cabell	.20	.10	.06
568	Carlos May	.20	.10	.06
569	Jim Lonborg	.20	.10	.06
570	Bobby Bonds	.35	.20	.11
571	Darrell Evans	.40	.20	.12
572	Ross Grimsley	.20	.10	.06
573	Joe Ferguson	.20	.10	.06
574	Aurelio Rodriguez	.20	.10	.06
575	Dick Ruthven	.20	.10	.06
576	Fred Kendall	.20	.10	.06
577	Jerry Augustine	.20	.10	.06
578	Bob Randall	.20	.10	.06
579	Don Carrithers	.20	.10	.06
580	George Brett	20.00	10.00	6.00
581	Pedro Borbon	.20	.10	.06
582	Ed Kirkpatrick	.20	.10	.06
583	Paul Lindblad	.20	.10	.06
584	Ed Goodson	.20	.10	.06
585	Rick Burleson	.20	.10	.06
586	Steve Renko	.20	.10	.06
587	Rick Baldwin	.20	.10	.06
588	Dave Moates	.20	.10	.06
589	Mike Cosgrove	.20	.10	.06
590	Buddy Bell	.30	.15	.09
591	Chris Arnold	.20	.10	.06
592	Dan Briggs	.20	.10	.06
593	Dennis Blair	.20	.10	.06
594	Biff Pocoroba	.20	.10	.06
595	John Hiller	.20	.10	.06
596	*Jerry Martin*	.25	.13	.08
597	Mariners Mgr./Coaches (Don Bryant, Jim Busby, Darrell Johnson, Vada Pinson, Wes Stock)	.25	.13	.08
598	Sparky Lyle	.35	.20	.11
599	Mike Tyson	.20	.10	.06
600	Jim Palmer	5.00	2.50	1.50
601	Mike Lum	.20	.10	.06
602	Andy Hassler	.20	.10	.06
603	Willie Davis	.25	.13	.08
604	Jim Slaton	.20	.10	.06
605	Felix Millan	.20	.10	.06
606	Steve Braun	.20	.10	.06
607	Larry Demery	.20	.10	.06
608	Roy Howell	.20	.10	.06
609	Jim Barr	.20	.10	.06
610	Jose Cardenal	.20	.10	.06
611	Dave Lemanczyk	.20	.10	.06
612	Barry Foote	.20	.10	.06
613	Reggie Cleveland	.20	.10	.06
614	Greg Gross	.20	.10	.06
615	Phil Niekro	1.50	.70	.45
616	Tommy Sandt	.20	.10	.06
617	Bobby Darwin	.20	.10	.06
618	Pat Dobson	.20	.10	.06
619	Johnny Oates	.20	.10	.06
620	Don Sutton	1.50	.70	.45
621	Tigers Team (Ralph Houk)	.80	.40	.25
622	Jim Wohlford	.20	.10	.06

		NR MT	EX	VG
623	Jack Kucek	.20	.10	.06
624	Hector Cruz	.20	.10	.06
625	Ken Holtzman	.25	.13	.08
626	Al Bumbry	.20	.10	.06
627	Bob Myrick	.20	.10	.06
628	Mario Guerrero	.20	.10	.06
629	Bobby Valentine	.25	.13	.08
630	Bert Blyleven	1.25	.60	.40
631	Big League Brothers (George Brett, Ken Brett)	2.00	1.00	.60
632	Big League Brothers (Bob Forsch, Ken Forsch)	.30	.15	.09
633	Big League Brothers (Carlos May, Lee May)	.30	.15	.09
634	Big League Brothers (Paul Reuschel, Rick Reuschel) (names switched)	.30	.15	.09
635	Robin Yount	20.00	10.00	6.00
636	Santo Alcala	.20	.10	.06
637	Alex Johnson	.20	.10	.06
638	Jim Kaat	.80	.40	.25
639	Jerry Morales	.20	.10	.06
640	Carlton Fisk	6.00	3.00	1.75
641	Dan Larson	.20	.10	.06
642	Willie Crawford	.20	.10	.06
643	Mike Pazik	.20	.10	.06
644	Matt Alexander	.20	.10	.06
645	Jerry Reuss	.25	.13	.08
646	Andres Mora	.20	.10	.06
647	Expos Team (Dick Williams)	.80	.40	.25
648	Jim Spencer	.20	.10	.06
649	Dave Cash	.20	.10	.06
650	Nolan Ryan	25.00	12.50	7.50
651	Von Joshua	.20	.10	.06
652	Tom Walker	.20	.10	.06
653	Diego Segui	.20	.10	.06
654	Ron Pruitt	.20	.10	.06
655	Tony Perez	1.00	.50	.30
656	Ron Guidry	2.75	1.50	.80
657	Mick Kelleher	.20	.10	.06
658	Marty Pattin	.20	.10	.06
659	Merv Rettenmund	.20	.10	.06
660	Willie Horton	.40	.13	.08

1977 Topps Cloth Stickers

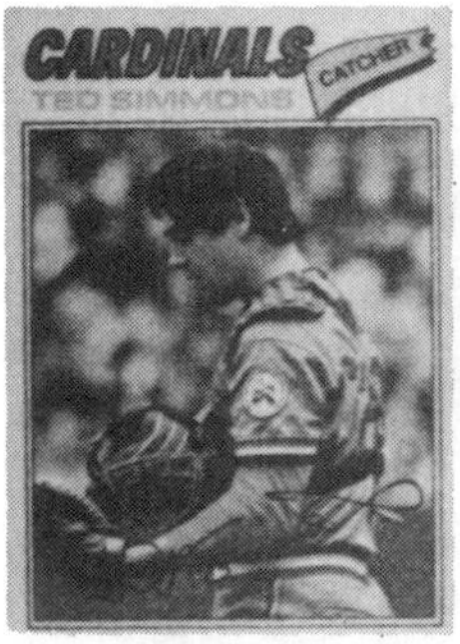

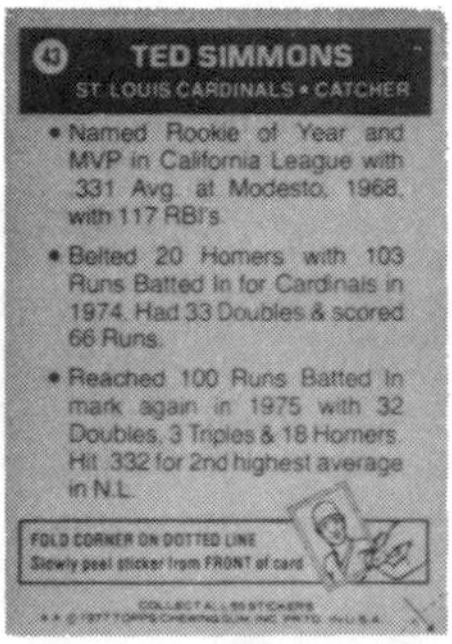

One of the few Topps specialty issues of the late 1970s, the 73-piece set of cloth stickers issued in 1977 includes 55 player stickers and 18 puzzle cards which could be joined to form a photo of the American League or National League All-Star teams. Issued as a separate issue, the 2-1/2" by 3-1/2" stickers have a paper backing which could be removed to allow the cloth to be adhered to a jacket, notebook, etc.

	NR MT	EX	VG
Complete Set:	300.00	150.00	90.00
Common Player:	.20	.10	.06

		NR MT	EX	VG
1	Alan Ashby	.20	.10	.06
2	Buddy Bell	1.00	.50	.30
3	Johnny Bench	5.00	2.50	1.50
4	Vida Blue	.50	.25	.15
5	Bert Blyleven	1.00	.50	.30
6	Steve Braun	.50	.25	.15
7	George Brett	15.00	7.50	4.50
8	Lou Brock	6.00	3.00	1.75
9	Jose Cardenal	.20	.10	.06

		NR MT	EX	VG
10	Rod Carew	15.00	7.50	4.50
11	Steve Carlton	12.00	6.00	3.50
12	Dave Cash	.20	.10	.06
13	Cesar Cedeno	1.00	.50	.30
14	Ron Cey	.50	.25	.15
15	Mark Fidrych	.50	.25	.15
16	Dan Ford	.20	.10	.06
17	Wayne Garland	.20	.10	.06
18	Ralph Garr	.20	.10	.06
19	Steve Garvey	4.00	2.00	1.25
20	Mike Hargrove	.20	.10	.06
21	Jim Hunter	6.00	3.00	1.75
22	Reggie Jackson	12.00	6.00	3.50
23	Randy Jones	.20	.10	.06
24	Dave Kingman	1.00	.50	.30
25	Bill Madlock	.70	.35	.20
26	Lee May	.50	.25	.15
27	John Mayberry	.20	.10	.06
28	Andy Messersmith	.20	.10	.06
29	Willie Montanez	.20	.10	.06
30	John Montefusco	.50	.25	.15
31	Joe Morgan	6.00	3.00	1.75
32	Thurman Munson	6.00	3.00	1.75
33	Bobby Murcer	.50	.25	.15
34	Al Oliver	1.25	.60	.40
35	Dave Pagan	.20	.10	.06
36	Jim Palmer	15.00	7.50	4.50
37	Tony Perez	.70	.35	.20
38	Pete Rose	30.00	15.00	9.00
39	Joe Rudi	.50	.25	.15
40	Nolan Ryan	40.00	20.00	12.00
41	Mike Schmidt	30.00	15.00	9.00
42	Tom Seaver	25.00	12.50	7.50
43	Ted Simmons	.70	.35	.20
44	Bill Singer	.20	.10	.06
45	Willie Stargell	1.50	.70	.45
46	Rusty Staub	.50	.25	.15
47	Don Sutton	1.25	.60	.40
48	Luis Tiant	.70	.35	.20
49	Bill Travers	.20	.10	.06
50	Claudell Washington	.50	.25	.15
51	Bob Watson	.20	.10	.06
52	Dave Winfield	6.00	3.00	1.75
53	Carl Yastrzemski	4.50	2.25	1.25
54	Robin Yount	25.00	12.50	7.50
55	Richie Zisk	.20	.10	.06

NOTE: A card number in parentheses ( ) indicates the set is unnumbered.

1978 Topps

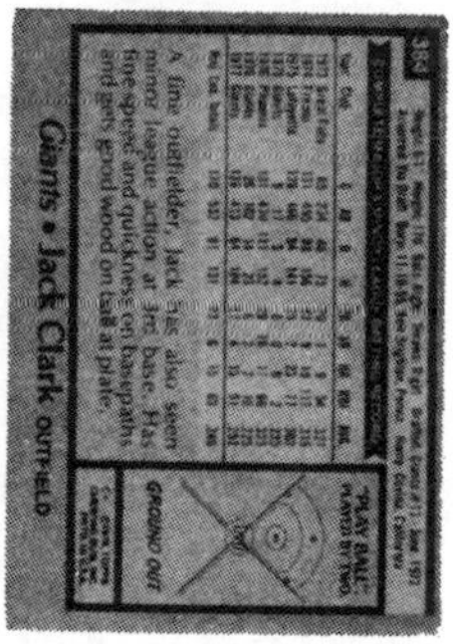

At 726 cards, this was the largest issue from Topps since 1972. In design, the color player photo is slightly larger than usual, with the player's name and team at the bottom. In the upper right-hand corner of the 2-1/2" by 3-1/2" cards there is a small white baseball with the player's position. Most of the starting All-Stars from the previous year had a red, white and blue shield instead of the baseball. Backs feature statistics and a baseball situation which made a card game of baseball possible. Specialty cards include baseball records, statistical leaders and the World Series and playoffs. As one row of cards per sheet had to be double-printed to accommodate the 726-card set size, some cards are more common, yet that seems to have no serious impact on their prices.

		NR MT	EX	VG
	Complete Set:	325.00	162.00	97.00
	Common Player:	.12	.06	.04
1	Record Breaker (Lou Brock)	3.00	1.50	.90
2	Record Breaker (Sparky Lyle)	.25	.13	.08
3	Record Breaker (Willie McCovey)	.70	.35	.20
4	Record Breaker (Brooks Robinson)	.90	.45	.25
5	Record Breaker (Pete Rose)	2.00	1.00	.60
6	Record Breaker (Nolan Ryan)	5.00	2.50	1.50
7	Record Breaker (Reggie Jackson)	3.00	1.50	.90
8	Mike Sadek	.12	.06	.04
9	Doug DeCinces	.25	.13	.08
10	Phil Niekro	1.25	.60	.40
11	Rick Manning	.12	.06	.04
12	Don Aase	.20	.10	.06
13	Art Howe	.12	.06	.04
14	Lerrin LaGrow	.12	.06	.04
15	Tony Perez	.25	.13	.08
16	Roy White	.25	.13	.08
17	Mike Krukow	.25	.13	.08
18	Bob Grich	.25	.13	.08
19	Darrell Porter	.20	.10	.06
20	Pete Rose	4.00	2.00	1.25
21	Steve Kemp	.25	.13	.08
22	Charlie Hough	.20	.10	.06
23	Bump Wills	.12	.06	.04
24	Don Money	.12	.06	.04
25	Jon Matlack	.20	.10	.06
26	Rich Hebner	.12	.06	.04
27	Geoff Zahn	.12	.06	.04
28	Ed Ott	.12	.06	.04
29	Bob Lacey	.12	.06	.04
30	George Hendrick	.20	.10	.06
31	Glenn Abbott	.12	.06	.04
32	Garry Templeton	.30	.15	.09
33	Dave Lemanczyk	.12	.06	.04
34	Willie McCovey	2.50	1.25	.70
35	Sparky Lyle	.30	.15	.09
36	*Eddie Murray*	70.00	35.00	21.00
37	Rick Waits	.12	.06	.04
38	Willie Montanez	.12	.06	.04
39	*Floyd Bannister*	.70	.35	.20
40	Carl Yastrzemski	5.00	2.50	1.50
41	Burt Hooton	.20	.10	.06
42	Jorge Orta	.12	.06	.04
43	Bill Atkinson	.12	.06	.04
44	Toby Harrah	.20	.10	.06
45	Mark Fidrych	.25	.13	.08
46	Al Cowens	.12	.06	.04
47	Jack Billingham	.12	.06	.04
48	Don Baylor	.35	.20	.11
49	Ed Kranepool	.20	.10	.06
50	Rick Reuschel	.40	.20	.12
51	Charlie Moore	.12	.06	.04
52	Jim Lonborg	.20	.10	.06
53	Phil Garner	.12	.06	.04
54	Tom Johnson	.12	.06	.04
55	Mitchell Page	.12	.06	.04
56	Randy Jones	.20	.10	.06
57	Dan Meyer	.12	.06	.04
58	Bob Forsch	.20	.10	.06
59	Otto Velez	.12	.06	.04
60	Thurman Munson	4.00	2.00	1.25
61	Larvell Blanks	.12	.06	.04
62	Jim Barr	.12	.06	.04
63	Don Zimmer	.20	.10	.06
64	Gene Pentz	.12	.06	.04
65	Ken Singleton	.25	.13	.08
66	White Sox Team	.50	.25	.15
67	Claudell Washington	.25	.13	.08
68	Steve Foucault	.12	.06	.04
69	Mike Vail	.12	.06	.04
70	Rich Gossage	1.00	.50	.30
71	Terry Humphrey	.12	.06	.04
72	Andre Dawson	15.00	7.50	4.50
73	Andy Hassler	.12	.06	.04
74	Checklist 1-121	.90	.45	.25
75	Dick Ruthven	.12	.06	.04
76	Steve Ontiveros	.12	.06	.04
77	Ed Kirkpatrick	.12	.06	.04
78	Pablo Torrealba	.12	.06	.04
79	Darrell Johnson	.12	.06	.04
80	Ken Griffey	.25	.13	.08
81	Pete Redfern	.12	.06	.04
82	Giants Team	.50	.25	.15
83	Bob Montgomery	.12	.06	.04
84	Kent Tekulve	.25	.13	.08
85	Ron Fairly	.20	.10	.06
86	Dave Tomlin	.12	.06	.04
87	John Lowenstein	.12	.06	.04
88	Mike Phillips	.12	.06	.04

		NR MT	EX	VG
89	Ken Clay	.20	.10	.06
90	Larry Bowa	.30	.15	.09
91	Oscar Zamora	.12	.06	.04
92	Adrian Devine	.12	.06	.04
93	Bobby Cox	.12	.06	.04
94	Chuck Scrivener	.12	.06	.04
95	Jamie Quirk	.12	.06	.04
96	Orioles Team	.50	.25	.15
97	Stan Bahnsen	.12	.06	.04
98	Jim Essian	.12	.06	.04
99	*Willie Hernandez*	.70	.35	.20
100	George Brett	12.00	6.00	3.50
101	Sid Monge	.12	.06	.04
102	Matt Alexander	.12	.06	.04
103	Tom Murphy	.12	.06	.04
104	Lee Lacy	.12	.06	.04
105	Reggie Cleveland	.12	.06	.04
106	Bill Plummer	.12	.06	.04
107	Ed Halicki	.12	.06	.04
108	Von Joshua	.12	.06	.04
109	Joe Torre	.30	.15	.09
110	Richie Zisk	.20	.10	.06
111	Mike Tyson	.12	.06	.04
112	Astros Team	.50	.25	.15
113	Don Carrithers	.12	.06	.04
114	Paul Blair	.20	.10	.06
115	Gary Nolan	.12	.06	.04
116	Tucker Ashford	.12	.06	.04
117	John Montague	.12	.06	.04
118	Terry Harmon	.12	.06	.04
119	Denny Martinez	.25	.13	.08
120	Gary Carter	4.00	2.00	1.25
121	Alvis Woods	.12	.06	.04
122	Dennis Eckersley	5.00	2.50	1.50
123	Manny Trillo	.20	.10	.06
124	*Dave Rozema*	.25	.13	.08
125	George Scott	.20	.10	.06
126	Paul Moskau	.12	.06	.04
127	Chet Lemon	.20	.10	.06
128	Bill Russell	.20	.10	.06
129	Jim Colborn	.12	.06	.04
130	Jeff Burroughs	.20	.10	.06
131	Bert Blyleven	.90	.45	.25
132	Enos Cabell	.20	.10	.06
133	Jerry Augustine	.12	.06	.04
134	*Steve Henderson*	.25	.13	.08
135	Ron Guidry	.70	.35	.20
136	Ted Sizemore	.12	.06	.04
137	Craig Kusick	.12	.06	.04
138	Larry Demery	.12	.06	.04
139	Wayne Gross	.12	.06	.04
140	Rollie Fingers	2.00	1.00	.60
141	Ruppert Jones	.20	.10	.06
142	John Montefusco	.20	.10	.06
143	Keith Hernandez	2.00	1.00	.60
144	Jesse Jefferson	.12	.06	.04
145	Rick Monday	.20	.10	.06
146	Doyle Alexander	.30	.15	.09
147	Lee Mazzilli	.25	.13	.08
148	Andre Thornton	.25	.13	.08
149	Dale Murray	.12	.06	.04
150	Bobby Bonds	.35	.20	.11
151	Milt Wilcox	.12	.06	.04
152	*Ivan DeJesus*	.20	.10	.06
153	Steve Stone	.25	.13	.08
154	Cecil Cooper	.20	.10	.06
155	Butch Hobson	.12	.06	.04
156	Andy Messersmith	.20	.10	.06
157	Pete LaCock	.12	.06	.04
158	Joaquin Andujar	.25	.13	.08
159	Lou Piniella	.35	.20	.11
160	Jim Palmer	4.00	2.00	1.25
161	Bob Boone	.25	.13	.08
162	Paul Thormodsgard	.12	.06	.04
163	Bill North	.12	.06	.04
164	Bob Owchinko	.12	.06	.04
165	Rennie Stennett	.12	.06	.04
166	Carlos Lopez	.12	.06	.04
167	Tim Foli	.12	.06	.04
168	Reggie Smith	.25	.13	.08
169	Jerry Johnson	.12	.06	.04
170	Lou Brock	2.50	1.25	.70
171	Pat Zachry	.12	.06	.04
172	Mike Hargrove	.20	.10	.06
173	Robin Yount	12.00	6.00	3.50
174	Wayne Garland	.12	.06	.04
175	Jerry Morales	.12	.06	.04
176	Milt May	.12	.06	.04
177	Gene Garber	.12	.06	.04
178	Dave Chalk	.12	.06	.04
179	Dick Tidrow	.20	.10	.06

		NR MT	EX	VG
180	Dave Concepcion	.35	.20	.11
181	Ken Forsch	.20	.10	.06
182	Jim Spencer	.12	.06	.04
183	Doug Bird	.12	.06	.04
184	Checklist 122-242	.90	.45	.25
185	Ellis Valentine	.20	.10	.06
186	*Bob Stanley*	.25	.13	.08
187	Jerry Royster	.12	.06	.04
188	Al Bumbry	.20	.10	.06
189	Tom Lasorda	.30	.15	.09
190	John Candelaria	.25	.13	.08
191	Rodney Scott	.12	.06	.04
192	Padres Team	.50	.25	.15
193	Rich Chiles	.12	.06	.04
194	Derrel Thomas	.12	.06	.04
195	Larry Dierker	.20	.10	.06
196	Bob Bailor	.12	.06	.04
197	Nino Espinosa	.12	.06	.04
198	Ron Pruitt	.12	.06	.04
199	Craig Reynolds	.12	.06	.04
200	Reggie Jackson	7.00	3.50	2.00
201	Batting Leaders (Rod Carew, Dave Parker)	1.00	.50	.30
202	Home Run Leaders (George Foster, Jim Rice)	.25	.13	.08
203	Runs Batted In Ldrs. (George Foster, Larry Hisle)	.25	.13	.08
204	Stolen Base Leaders (Freddie Patek, Frank Taveras)	.12	.06	.04
205	Victory Leaders (Steve Carlton, Dave Goltz, Dennis Leonard, Jim Palmer)	.60	.30	.20
206	Strikeout Leaders (Phil Niekro, Nolan Ryan)	.35	.20	.11
207	Earned Run Avg. Ldrs. (John Candelaria, Frank Tanana)	.12	.06	.04
208	Leading Firemen (Bill Campbell, Rollie Fingers)	.35	.20	.11
209	Dock Ellis	.12	.06	.04
210	Jose Cardenal	.12	.06	.04
211	Earl Weaver	.20	.10	.06
212	Mike Caldwell	.12	.06	.04
213	Alan Bannister	.12	.06	.04
214	Angels Team	.50	.25	.15
215	Darrell Evans	.35	.20	.11
216	Mike Paxton	.12	.06	.04
217	Rod Gilbreath	.12	.06	.04
218	Marty Pattin	.12	.06	.04
219	Mike Cubbage	.12	.06	.04
220	Pedro Borbon	.12	.06	.04
221	Chris Speier	.20	.10	.06
222	Jerry Martin	.12	.06	.04
223	Bruce Kison	.12	.06	.04
224	Jerry Tabb	.12	.06	.04
225	Don Gullett	.12	.06	.04
226	Joe Ferguson	.12	.06	.04
227	Al Fitzmorris	.12	.06	.04
228	Manny Mota	.12	.06	.04
229	Leo Foster	.12	.06	.04
230	Al Hrabosky	.20	.10	.06
231	Wayne Nordhagen	.12	.06	.04
232	Mickey Stanley	.20	.10	.06
233	Dick Pole	.12	.06	.04
234	Herman Franks	.12	.06	.04
235	Tim McCarver	.35	.20	.11
236	Terry Whitfield	.12	.06	.04
237	Rich Dauer	.12	.06	.04
238	Juan Beniquez	.20	.10	.06
239	Dyar Miller	.12	.06	.04
240	Gene Tenace	.20	.10	.06
241	Pete Vuckovich	.20	.10	.06
242	Barry Bonnell	.12	.06	.04
243	Bob McClure	.12	.06	.04
244	Expos Team	.20	.10	.06
245	Rick Burleson	.20	.10	.06
246	Dan Driessen	.20	.10	.06
247	Larry Christenson	.12	.06	.04
248	Frank White	.12	.06	.04
249	Dave Goltz	.12	.06	.04
250	Graig Nettles	.30	.15	.09
251	Don Kirkwood	.12	.06	.04
252	Steve Swisher	.12	.06	.04
253	Jim Kern	.12	.06	.04
254	Dave Collins	.20	.10	.06
255	Jerry Reuss	.20	.10	.06
256	Joe Altobelli	.12	.06	.04
257	Hector Cruz	.12	.06	.04
258	John Hiller	.20	.10	.06
259	Dodgers Team	.80	.40	.25
260	Bert Campaneris	.25	.13	.08
261	Tim Hosley	.12	.06	.04
262	Rudy May	.12	.06	.04

		NR MT	EX	VG
263	Danny Walton	.12	.06	.04
264	Jamie Easterly	.12	.06	.04
265	Sal Bando	.12	.06	.04
266	*Bob Shirley*	.20	.10	.06
267	Doug Ault	.12	.06	.04
268	Gil Flores	.12	.06	.04
269	Wayne Twitchell	.12	.06	.04
270	Carlton Fisk	5.00	2.50	1.50
271	Randy Lerch	.12	.06	.04
272	Royle Stillman	.12	.06	.04
273	Fred Norman	.12	.06	.04
274	Freddie Patek	.12	.06	.04
275	Dan Ford	.12	.06	.04
276	Bill Bonham	.12	.06	.04
277	Bruce Boisclair	.12	.06	.04
278	Enrique Romo	.12	.06	.04
279	Bill Virdon	.20	.10	.06
280	Buddy Bell	.30	.15	.09
281	Eric Rasmussen	.12	.06	.04
282	Yankees Team	1.00	.50	.30
283	Omar Moreno	.12	.06	.04
284	Randy Moffitt	.12	.06	.04
285	Steve Yeager	.12	.06	.04
286	Ben Oglivie	.20	.10	.06
287	Kiko Garcia	.12	.06	.04
288	Dave Hamilton	.12	.06	.04
289	Checklist 243-363	.90	.45	.25
290	Willie Horton	.20	.10	.06
291	Gary Ross	.12	.06	.04
292	Gene Richard	.12	.06	.04
293	Mike Willis	.12	.06	.04
294	Larry Parrish	.25	.13	.08
295	Bill Lee	.20	.10	.06
296	Biff Pocoroba	.12	.06	.04
297	Warren Brusstar	.12	.06	.04
298	Tony Armas	.25	.13	.08
299	Whitey Herzog	.30	.15	.09
300	Joe Morgan	3.00	1.50	.90
301	Buddy Schultz	.12	.06	.04
302	Cubs Team	.50	.25	.15
303	Sam Hinds	.12	.06	.04
304	John Milner	.12	.06	.04
305	Rico Carty	.20	.10	.06
306	Joe Niekro	.25	.13	.08
307	Glenn Borgmann	.12	.06	.04
308	Jim Rooker	.12	.06	.04
309	Cliff Johnson	.20	.10	.06
310	Don Sutton	2.00	1.00	.60
311	Jose Baez	.12	.06	.04
312	Greg Minton	.12	.06	.04
313	Andy Etchebarren	.12	.06	.04
314	Paul Lindblad	.12	.06	.04
315	Mark Belanger	.20	.10	.06
316	Henry Cruz	.12	.06	.04
317	Dave Johnson	.30	.15	.09
318	Tom Griffin	.12	.06	.04
319	Alan Ashby	.12	.06	.04
320	Fred Lynn	.90	.45	.25
321	Santo Alcala	.12	.06	.04
322	Tom Paciorek	.12	.06	.04
323	Jim Fregosi	.12	.06	.04
324	Vern Rapp	.12	.06	.04
325	Bruce Sutter	.50	.25	.15
326	Mike Lum	.12	.06	.04
327	Rick Langford	.12	.06	.04
328	Brewers Team	.50	.25	.15
329	John Verhoeven	.12	.06	.04
330	Bob Watson	.20	.10	.06
331	Mark Littell	.12	.06	.04
332	Duane Kuiper	.12	.06	.04
333	Jim Todd	.12	.06	.04
334	John Stearns	.12	.06	.04
335	Bucky Dent	.30	.15	.09
336	Steve Busby	.20	.10	.06
337	Tom Grieve	.12	.06	.04
338	Dave Heaverlo	.12	.06	.04
339	Mario Guerrero	.12	.06	.04
340	Bake McBride	.12	.06	.04
341	Mike Flanagan	.25	.13	.08
342	Aurelio Rodriguez	.20	.10	.06
343	John Wathan	.12	.06	.04
344	Sam Ewing	.12	.06	.04
345	Luis Tiant	.35	.20	.11
346	Larry Biittner	.12	.06	.04
347	Terry Forster	.20	.10	.06
348	Del Unser	.12	.06	.04
349	Rick Camp	.12	.06	.04
350	Steve Garvey	4.00	2.00	1.25
351	Jeff Torborg	.20	.10	.06
352	Tony Scott	.12	.06	.04
353	Doug Bair	.12	.06	.04

		NR MT	EX	VG
354	Cesar Geronimo	.20	.10	.06
355	Bill Travers	.12	.06	.04
356	Mets Team	.70	.35	.20
357	Tom Poquette	.12	.06	.04
358	Mark Lemongello	.12	.06	.04
359	Marc Hill	.12	.06	.04
360	Mike Schmidt	15.00	7.50	4.50
361	Chris Knapp	.12	.06	.04
362	Dave May	.12	.06	.04
363	Bob Randall	.12	.06	.04
364	Jerry Turner	.12	.06	.04
365	Ed Figueroa	.20	.10	.06
366	Larry Milbourne	.12	.06	.04
367	Rick Dempsey	.20	.10	.06
368	Balor Moore	.12	.06	.04
369	Tim Nordbrook	.12	.06	.04
370	Rusty Staub	.30	.15	.09
371	Ray Burris	.12	.06	.04
372	Brian Asselstine	.12	.06	.04
373	Jim Willoughby	.12	.06	.04
374	Jose Morales	.12	.06	.04
375	Tommy John	.90	.45	.25
376	Jim Wohlford	.12	.06	.04
377	Manny Sarmiento	.12	.06	.04
378	Bobby Winkles	.12	.06	.04
379	Skip Lockwood	.12	.06	.04
380	Ted Simmons	.40	.20	.12
381	Phillies Team	.70	.35	.20
382	Joe Lahoud	.12	.06	.04
383	Mario Mendoza	.12	.06	.04
384	Jack Clark	4.00	2.00	1.25
385	Tito Fuentes	.12	.06	.04
386	Bob Gorinski	.12	.06	.04
387	Ken Holtzman	.25	.13	.08
388	Bill Fahey	.12	.06	.04
389	Julio Gonzalez	.12	.06	.04
390	Oscar Gamble	.20	.10	.06
391	Larry Haney	.12	.06	.04
392	Billy Almon	.12	.06	.04
393	Tippy Martinez	.12	.06	.04
394	Roy Howell	.12	.06	.04
395	Jim Hughes	.12	.06	.04
396	Bob Stinson	.12	.06	.04
397	Greg Gross	.12	.06	.04
398	Don Hood	.12	.06	.04
399	Pete Mackanin	.12	.06	.04
400	Nolan Ryan	20.00	10.00	6.00
401	Sparky Anderson	.30	.15	.09
402	Dave Campbell	.12	.06	.04
403	Bud Harrelson	.20	.10	.06
404	Tigers Team	.60	.30	.20
405	Rawly Eastwick	.12	.06	.04
406	Mike Jorgensen	.12	.06	.04
407	Odell Jones	.12	.06	.04
408	Joe Zdeb	.12	.06	.04
409	Ron Schueler	.12	.06	.04
410	Bill Madlock	.50	.25	.15
411	A.L. Championships (Yankees Rally To Defeat Royals)	.70	.35	.20
412	N.L. Championships (Dodgers Overpower Phillies In Four)	.50	.25	.15
413	World Series (Reggie & Yankees Reign Supreme)	2.00	1.00	.60
414	Darold Knowles	.12	.06	.04
415	Ray Fosse	.12	.06	.04
416	Jack Brohamer	.12	.06	.04
417	Mike Garman	.12	.06	.04
418	Tony Muser	.12	.06	.04
419	Jerry Garvin	.12	.06	.04
420	Greg Luzinski	.35	.20	.11
421	Junior Moore	.12	.06	.04
422	Steve Braun	.12	.06	.04
423	Dave Rosello	.12	.06	.04
424	Red Sox Team	.70	.35	.20
425	Steve Rogers	.12	.06	.04
426	Fred Kendall	.12	.06	.04
427	*Mario Soto*	.40	.20	.12
428	Joel Youngblood	.20	.10	.06
429	Mike Barlow	.12	.06	.04
430	Al Oliver	.40	.20	.12
431	Butch Metzger	.12	.06	.04
432	Terry Bulling	.12	.06	.04
433	Fernando Gonzalez	.12	.06	.04
434	Mike Norris	.12	.06	.04
435	Checklist 364-484	.90	.45	.25
436	Vic Harris	.12	.06	.04
437	Bo McLaughlin	.12	.06	.04
438	John Ellis	.12	.06	.04
439	Ken Kravec	.12	.06	.04
440	Dave Lopes	.25	.13	.08
441	Larry Gura	.12	.06	.04

		NR MT	EX	VG
442	Elliott Maddox	.12	.06	.04
443	Darrel Chaney	.12	.06	.04
444	Roy Hartsfield	.12	.06	.04
445	Mike Ivie	.12	.06	.04
446	Tug McGraw	.35	.20	.11
447	Leroy Stanton	.12	.06	.04
448	Bill Castro	.12	.06	.04
449	Tim Blackwell	.12	.06	.04
450	Tom Seaver	6.00	3.00	1.75
451	Twins Team	.50	.25	.15
452	Jerry Mumphrey	.20	.10	.06
453	Doug Flynn	.12	.06	.04
454	Dave LaRoche	.12	.06	.04
455	Bill Robinson	.12	.06	.04
456	Vern Ruhle	.12	.06	.04
457	Bob Bailey	.12	.06	.04
458	Jeff Newman	.12	.06	.04
459	Charlie Spikes	.12	.06	.04
460	Jim Hunter	2.00	1.00	.60
461	Rob Andrews	.12	.06	.04
462	Rogelio Moret	.12	.06	.04
463	Kevin Bell	.12	.06	.04
464	Jerry Grote	.20	.10	.06
465	Hal McRae	.30	.15	.09
466	Dennis Blair	.12	.06	.04
467	Alvin Dark	.20	.10	.06
468	*Warren Cromartie*	.20	.10	.06
469	Rick Cerone	.20	.10	.06
470	J.R. Richard	.25	.13	.08
471	Roy Smalley	.20	.10	.06
472	Ron Reed	.20	.10	.06
473	Bill Buckner	.30	.15	.09
474	Jim Slaton	.12	.06	.04
475	Gary Matthews	.20	.10	.06
476	Bill Stein	.12	.06	.04
477	Doug Capilla	.12	.06	.04
478	Jerry Remy	.12	.06	.04
479	Cardinals Team	.50	.25	.15
480	Ron LeFlore	.25	.13	.08
481	Jackson Todd	.12	.06	.04
482	Rick Miller	.12	.06	.04
483	Ken Macha	.12	.06	.04
484	Jim Norris	.12	.06	.04
485	Chris Chambliss	.30	.15	.09
486	John Curtis	.12	.06	.04
487	Jim Tyrone	.12	.06	.04
488	Dan Spillner	.12	.06	.04
489	Rudy Meoli	.12	.06	.04
490	Amos Otis	.20	.10	.06
491	Scott McGregor	.20	.10	.06
492	Jim Sundberg	.20	.10	.06
493	Steve Renko	.12	.06	.04
494	Chuck Tanner	.20	.10	.06
495	Dave Cash	.12	.06	.04
496	*Jim Clancy*	.30	.15	.09
497	Glenn Adams	.12	.06	.04
498	Joe Sambito	.12	.06	.04
499	Mariners Team	.50	.25	.15
500	George Foster	.70	.35	.20
501	Dave Roberts	.12	.06	.04
502	Pat Rockett	.12	.06	.04
503	Ike Hampton	.12	.06	.04
504	Roger Freed	.12	.06	.04
505	Felix Millan	.12	.06	.04
506	Ron Blomberg	.12	.06	.04
507	Willie Crawford	.12	.06	.04
508	Johnny Oates	.12	.06	.04
509	Brent Strom	.12	.06	.04
510	Willie Stargell	3.00	1.50	.90
511	Frank Duffy	.12	.06	.04
512	Larry Herndon	.20	.10	.06
513	Barry Foote	.12	.06	.04
514	Rob Sperring	.12	.06	.04
515	Tim Corcoran	.12	.06	.04
516	Gary Beare	.12	.06	.04
517	Andres Mora	.12	.06	.04
518	Tommy Boggs	.12	.06	.04
519	Brian Downing	.25	.13	.08
520	Larry Hisle	.20	.10	.06
521	Steve Staggs	.12	.06	.04
522	Dick Williams	.20	.10	.06
523	*Donnie Moore*	.25	.13	.08
524	Bernie Carbo	.12	.06	.04
525	Jerry Terrell	.12	.06	.04
526	Reds Team	.60	.30	.20
527	Vic Correll	.12	.06	.04
528	Rob Picciolo	.12	.06	.04
529	Paul Hartzell	.12	.06	.04
530	Dave Winfield	6.00	3.00	1.75
531	Tom Underwood	.12	.06	.04
532	Skip Jutze	.12	.06	.04

		NR MT	EX	VG
533	Sandy Alomar	.12	.06	.04
534	Wilbur Howard	.12	.06	.04
535	Checklist 485-605	.90	.45	.25
536	Roric Harrison	.12	.06	.04
537	Bruce Bochte	.20	.10	.06
538	Johnnie LeMaster	.12	.06	.04
539	Vic Davalillo	.12	.06	.04
540	Steve Carlton	4.00	2.00	1.25
541	Larry Cox	.12	.06	.04
542	Tim Johnson	.12	.06	.04
543	Larry Harlow	.12	.06	.04
544	Len Randle	.12	.06	.04
545	Bill Campbell	.12	.06	.04
546	Ted Martinez	.12	.06	.04
547	John Scott	.12	.06	.04
548	Billy Hunter	.12	.06	.04
549	Joe Kerrigan	.12	.06	.04
550	John Mayberry	.20	.10	.06
551	Braves Team	.50	.25	.15
552	Francisco Barrios	.12	.06	.04
553	*Terry Puhl*	.35	.20	.11
554	Joe Coleman	.20	.10	.06
555	Butch Wynegar	.20	.10	.06
556	Ed Armbrister	.12	.06	.04
557	Tony Solaita	.12	.06	.04
558	Paul Mitchell	.12	.06	.04
559	Phil Mankowski	.12	.06	.04
560	Dave Parker	4.00	2.00	1.25
561	Charlie Williams	.12	.06	.04
562	Glenn Burke	.12	.06	.04
563	Dave Rader	.12	.06	.04
564	Mick Kelleher	.12	.06	.04
565	Jerry Koosman	.25	.13	.08
566	Merv Rettenmund	.12	.06	.04
567	Dick Drago	.12	.06	.04
568	Tom Hutton	.12	.06	.04
569	*Lary Sorensen*	.20	.10	.06
570	Dave Kingman	.60	.30	.20
571	Buck Martinez	.12	.06	.04
572	Rick Wise	.20	.10	.06
573	Luis Gomez	.12	.06	.04
574	Bob Lemon	.30	.15	.09
575	Pat Dobson	.20	.10	.06
576	Sam Mejias	.12	.06	.04
577	A's Team	.50	.25	.15
578	Buzz Capra	.12	.06	.04
579	*Rance Mulliniks*	.35	.20	.11
580	Rod Carew	6.00	3.00	1.75
581	Lynn McGlothen	.12	.06	.04
582	Fran Healy	.20	.10	.06
583	George Medich	.12	.06	.04
584	John Hale	.12	.06	.04
585	Woodie Fryman	.12	.06	.04
586	Ed Goodson	.12	.06	.04
587	John Urrea	.12	.06	.04
588	Jim Mason	.12	.06	.04
589	*Bob Knepper*	.70	.35	.20
590	Bobby Murcer	.30	.15	.09
591	George Zeber	.20	.10	.06
592	Bob Apodaca	.12	.06	.04
593	Dave Skaggs	.12	.06	.04
594	Dave Freisleben	.12	.06	.04
595	Sixto Lezcano	.12	.06	.04
596	Gary Wheelock	.12	.06	.04
597	Steve Dillard	.12	.06	.04
598	Eddie Solomon	.12	.06	.04
599	Gary Woods	.12	.06	.04
600	Frank Tanana	.25	.13	.08
601	Gene Mauch	.25	.13	.08
602	Eric Soderholm	.12	.06	.04
603	Will McEnaney	.12	.06	.04
604	Earl Williams	.12	.06	.04
605	Rick Rhoden	.25	.13	.08
606	Pirates Team	.50	.25	.15
607	Fernando Arroyo	.12	.06	.04
608	Johnny Grubb	.12	.06	.04
609	John Denny	.12	.06	.04
610	Garry Maddox	.20	.10	.06
611	Pat Scanlon	.12	.06	.04
612	Ken Henderson	.12	.06	.04
613	Marty Perez	.12	.06	.04
614	Joe Wallis	.12	.06	.04
615	Clay Carroll	.20	.10	.06
616	Pat Kelly	.12	.06	.04
617	Joe Nolan	.12	.06	.04
618	Tommy Helms	.12	.06	.04
619	*Thad Bosley*	.20	.10	.06
620	Willie Randolph	.30	.15	.09
621	Craig Swan	.12	.06	.04
622	Champ Summers	.12	.06	.04
623	Eduardo Rodriguez	.12	.06	.04

		NR MT	EX	VG
624	Gary Alexander	.12	.06	.04
625	Jose Cruz	.25	.13	.08
626	Blue Jays Team	.25	.13	.08
627	Dave Johnson	.12	.06	.04
628	Ralph Garr	.20	.10	.06
629	Don Stanhouse	.12	.06	.04
630	Ron Cey	.25	.13	.08
631	Danny Ozark	.20	.10	.06
632	Rowland Office	.12	.06	.04
633	Tom Veryzer	.12	.06	.04
634	Len Barker	.20	.10	.06
635	Joe Rudi	.25	.13	.08
636	Jim Bibby	.12	.06	.04
637	Duffy Dyer	.12	.06	.04
638	Paul Splittorff	.20	.10	.06
639	Gene Clines	.12	.06	.04
640	Lee May	.12	.06	.04
641	Doug Rau	.12	.06	.04
642	Denny Doyle	.12	.06	.04
643	Tom House	.12	.06	.04
644	Jim Dwyer	.12	.06	.04
645	Mike Torrez	.20	.10	.06
646	Rick Auerbach	.12	.06	.04
647	Steve Dunning	.12	.06	.04
648	Gary Thomasson	.12	.06	.04
649	*Moose Haas*	.25	.13	.08
650	Cesar Cedeno	.25	.13	.08
651	Doug Rader	.12	.06	.04
652	Checklist 606-726	.90	.45	.25
653	Ron Hodges	.12	.06	.04
654	Pepe Frias	.12	.06	.04
655	Lyman Bostock	.20	.10	.06
656	Dave Garcia	.12	.06	.04
657	Bombo Rivera	.12	.06	.04
658	Manny Sanguillen	.12	.06	.04
659	Rangers Team	.50	.25	.15
660	Jason Thompson	.20	.10	.06
661	Grant Jackson	.12	.06	.04
662	Paul Dade	.12	.06	.04
663	Paul Reuschel	.12	.06	.04
664	Fred Stanley	.20	.10	.06
665	Dennis Leonard	.20	.10	.06
666	Billy Smith	.12	.06	.04
667	Jeff Byrd	.12	.06	.04
668	Dusty Baker	.25	.13	.08
669	Pete Falcone	.12	.06	.04
670	Jim Rice	3.50	1.75	1.00
671	Gary Lavelle	.12	.06	.04
672	Don Kessinger	.20	.10	.06
673	Steve Brye	.12	.06	.04
674	*Ray Knight*	1.50	.70	.45
675	Jay Johnstone	.20	.10	.06
676	Bob Myrick	.12	.06	.04
677	Ed Herrmann	.12	.06	.04
678	Tom Burgmeier	.12	.06	.04
679	Wayne Garrett	.12	.06	.04
680	Vida Blue	.30	.15	.09
681	Rob Belloir	.12	.06	.04
682	Ken Brett	.20	.10	.06
683	Mike Champion	.12	.06	.04
684	Ralph Houk	.20	.10	.06
685	Frank Taveras	.12	.06	.04
686	Gaylord Perry	2.00	1.00	.60
687	*Julio Cruz*	.25	.13	.08
688	George Mitterwald	.12	.06	.04
689	Indians Team	.50	.25	.15
690	Mickey Rivers	.25	.13	.08
691	Ross Grimsley	.20	.10	.06
692	Ken Reitz	.12	.06	.04
693	Lamar Johnson	.12	.06	.04
694	Elias Sosa	.12	.06	.04
695	Dwight Evans	2.00	1.00	.60
696	Steve Mingori	.12	.06	.04
697	Roger Metzger	.12	.06	.04
698	Juan Bernhardt	.12	.06	.04
699	Jackie Brown	.12	.06	.04
700	Johnny Bench	5.00	2.50	1.50
701	Rookie Pitchers (*Tom Hume*, Larry Landreth, *Steve McCatty*, Bruce Taylor)	.25	.13	.08
702	Rookie Catchers (Bill Nahorodny, Kevin Pasley, Rick Sweet, Don Werner)	.12	.06	.04
703	Rookie Pitchers (*Larry Andersen*, Tim Jones, Mickey Mahler, *Jack Morris*)	10.00	5.00	3.00
704	Rookie 2nd Basemen (*Garth Iorg*, Dave Oliver, Sam Perlozzo, *Lou Whitaker*)	15.00	7.50	4.50
705	Rookie Outfielders (*Dave Bergman*, Miguel Dilone, *Clint Hurdle*, Willie Norwood)	.25	.13	.08
706	Rookie 1st Basemen (Wayne Cage, Ted Cox, *Pat Putnam, Dave Revering*)	.20	.10	.06
707	Rookie Shortstops (Mickey Klutts, *Paul Molitor, Alan Trammell, U.L. Washington*)	60.00	30.00	18.00
708	Rookie Catchers (*Bo Diaz*, Dale Murphy, *Lance Parrish, Ernie Whitt*)	25.00	12.50	7.50
709	Rookie Pitchers (Steve Burke, *Matt Keough*, Lance Rautzhan, *Dan Schatzeder*)	.20	.10	.06
710	Rookie Outfielders (Dell Alston, Rick Bosetti, *Mike Easler*, Keith Smith)	.50	.25	.15
711	Rookie Pitchers (Cardell Camper, Dennis Lamp, Craig Mitchell, Roy Thomas)	.12	.06	.04
712	Bobby Valentine	.25	.13	.08
713	Bob Davis	.12	.06	.04
714	Mike Anderson	.12	.06	.04
715	Jim Kaat	.60	.30	.20
716	Clarence Gaston	.12	.06	.04
717	Nelson Briles	.12	.06	.04
718	Ron Jackson	.12	.06	.04
719	Randy Elliott	.12	.06	.04
720	Fergie Jenkins	2.00	1.00	.60
721	Billy Martin	1.00	.50	.30
722	Pete Broberg	.12	.06	.04
723	Johnny Wockenfuss	.12	.06	.04
724	Royals Team	.70	.35	.20
725	Kurt Bevacqua	.12	.06	.04
726	Wilbur Wood	.40	.10	.06

1979 Topps

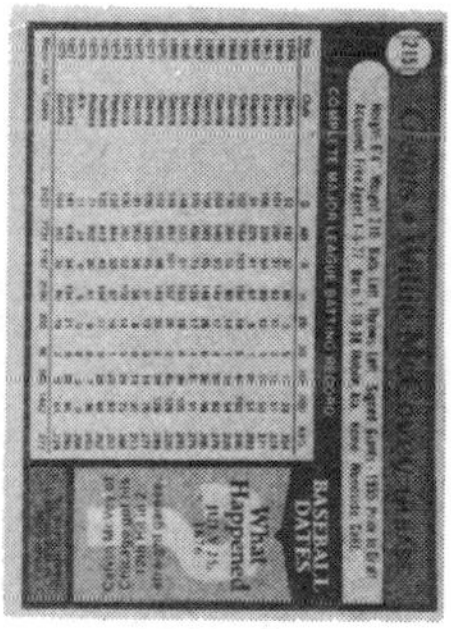

The size of this issue remained the same as in 1978 with 726 cards making their appearance. Actually, the 2-1/2" by 3-1/2" cards have a relatively minor design change from the previous year. The large color photo still dominates the front, with the player's name, team and position below it. The baseball with the player's position was moved to the lower left and the position replaced by a Topps logo. On the back, the printing color was changed and the game situation was replaced by a quiz called "Baseball Dates". Specialty cards include statistical leaders, major league records set during the season and eight cards devoted to career records. For the first time, rookies were arranged by teams under the heading of "Prospects."

		NR MT	EX	VG
	Complete Set:	250.00	125.00	75.00
	Common Player:	.12	.06	.04
1	Batting Leaders (Rod Carew, Dave Parker)	2.00	1.00	.60
2	Home Run Leaders (George Foster, Jim Rice)	.50	.25	.15
3	Runs Batted In Leaders (George Foster, Jim Rice)	.50	.25	.15
4	Stolen Base Leaders (Ron LeFlore, Omar Moreno)	.25	.13	.08
5	Victory Leaders (Ron Guidry, Gaylord Perry)	.50	.25	.15
6	Strikeout Leaders (J.R. Richard, Nolan Ryan)	.50	.25	.15
7	Earned Run Avg. Leaders (Ron Guidry, Craig Swan)	.25	.13	.08
8	Leading Firemen (Rollie Fingers, Rich Gossage)	.40	.20	.12
9	Dave Campbell	.12	.06	.04

		NR MT	EX	VG
10	Lee May	.20	.10	.06
11	Marc Hill	.12	.06	.04
12	Dick Drago	.12	.06	.04
13	Paul Dade	.12	.06	.04
14	Rafael Landestoy	.12	.06	.04
15	Ross Grimsley	.20	.10	.06
16	Fred Stanley	.20	.10	.06
17	Donnie Moore	.20	.10	.06
18	Tony Solaita	.12	.06	.04
19	Larry Gura	.12	.06	.04
20	Joe Morgan	.40	.20	.12
21	Kevin Kobel	.12	.06	.04
22	Mike Jorgensen	.12	.06	.04
23	Terry Forster	.20	.10	.06
24	Paul Molitor	5.00	2.50	1.50
25	Steve Carlton	3.50	1.75	1.00
26	Jamie Quirk	.12	.06	.04
27	Dave Goltz	.20	.10	.06
28	Steve Brye	.12	.06	.04
29	Rick Langford	.12	.06	.04
30	Dave Winfield	5.00	2.50	1.50
31	Tom House	.12	.06	.04
32	Jerry Mumphrey	.12	.06	.04
33	Dave Rozema	.12	.06	.04
34	Rob Andrews	.12	.06	.04
35	Ed Figueroa	.20	.10	.06
36	Alan Ashby	.12	.06	.04
37	Joe Kerrigan	.12	.06	.04
38	Bernie Carbo	.12	.06	.04
39	Dale Murphy	7.00	3.50	2.00
40	Dennis Eckersley	2.00	1.00	.60
41	Twins Team (Gene Mauch)	.50	.25	.15
42	Ron Blomberg	.12	.06	.04
43	Wayne Twitchell	.12	.06	.04
44	Kurt Bevacqua	.12	.06	.04
45	Al Hrabosky	.20	.10	.06
46	Ron Hodges	.12	.06	.04
47	Fred Norman	.12	.06	.04
48	Merv Rettenmund	.12	.06	.04
49	Vern Ruhle	.12	.06	.04
50	Steve Garvey	1.25	.60	.40
51	Ray Fosse	.12	.06	.04
52	Randy Lerch	.12	.06	.04
53	Mick Kelleher	.12	.06	.04
54	Dell Alston	.12	.06	.04
55	Willie Stargell	2.00	1.00	.60
56	John Hale	.12	.06	.04
57	Eric Rasmussen	.12	.06	.04
58	Bob Randall	.12	.06	.04
59	John Denny	.12	.06	.04
60	Mickey Rivers	.20	.10	.06
61	Bo Diaz	.20	.10	.06
62	Randy Moffitt	.12	.06	.04
63	Jack Brohamer	.12	.06	.04
64	Tom Underwood	.12	.06	.04
65	Mark Belanger	.20	.10	.06
66	Tigers Team (Les Moss)	.60	.30	.20
67	Jim Mason	.12	.06	.04
68	Joe Niekro	.12	.06	.04
69	Elliott Maddox	.12	.06	.04
70	John Candelaria	.25	.13	.08
71	Brian Downing	.20	.10	.06
72	Steve Mingori	.12	.06	.04
73	Ken Henderson	.12	.06	.04
74	*Shane Rawley*	.30	.15	.09
75	Steve Yeager	.12	.06	.04
76	Warren Cromartie	.12	.06	.04
77	Dan Briggs	.12	.06	.04
78	Elias Sosa	.12	.06	.04
79	Ted Cox	.12	.06	.04
80	Jason Thompson	.20	.10	.06
81	Roger Erickson	.12	.06	.04
82	Mets Team (Joe Torre)	.60	.30	.20
83	Fred Kendall	.12	.06	.04
84	Greg Minton	.12	.06	.04
85	Gary Matthews	.20	.10	.06
86	Rodney Scott	.12	.06	.04
87	Pete Falcone	.12	.06	.04
88	Bob Molinaro	.12	.06	.04
89	Dick Tidrow	.20	.10	.06
90	Bob Boone	.25	.13	.08
91	Terry Crowley	.12	.06	.04
92	Jim Bibby	.12	.06	.04
93	Phil Mankowski	.12	.06	.04
94	Len Barker	.12	.06	.04
95	Robin Yount	9.00	4.50	2.75
96	Indians Team (Jeff Torborg)	.50	.25	.15
97	Sam Mejias	.12	.06	.04
98	Ray Burris	.12	.06	.04
99	John Wathan	.20	.10	.06
100	Tom Seaver	4.00	2.00	1.25
101	Roy Howell	.12	.06	.04
102	Mike Anderson	.12	.06	.04
103	Jim Todd	.12	.06	.04
104	Johnny Oates	.12	.06	.04
105	Rick Camp	.12	.06	.04
106	Frank Duffy	.12	.06	.04
107	Jesus Alou	.20	.10	.06
108	Eduardo Rodriguez	.12	.06	.04
109	Joel Youngblood	.12	.06	.04
110	Vida Blue	.30	.15	.09
111	Roger Freed	.12	.06	.04
112	Phillies Team (Danny Ozark)	.50	.25	.15
113	Pete Redfern	.12	.06	.04
114	Cliff Johnson	.20	.10	.06
115	Nolan Ryan	18.00	9.00	5.50
116	*Ozzie Smith*	60.00	30.00	17.50
117	Grant Jackson	.12	.06	.04
118	Bud Harrelson	.20	.10	.06
119	Don Stanhouse	.12	.06	.04
120	Jim Sundberg	.20	.10	.06
121	Checklist 1-121	.25	.13	.08
122	Mike Paxton	.12	.06	.04
123	Lou Whitaker	3.00	1.50	.90
124	Dan Schatzeder	.12	.06	.04
125	Rick Burleson	.20	.10	.06
126	Doug Bair	.12	.06	.04
127	Thad Bosley	.12	.06	.04
128	Ted Martinez	.12	.06	.04
129	Marty Pattin	.12	.06	.04
130	Bob Watson	.12	.06	.04
131	Jim Clancy	.25	.13	.08
132	Rowland Office	.12	.06	.04
133	Bill Castro	.12	.06	.04
134	Alan Bannister	.12	.06	.04
135	Bobby Murcer	.25	.13	.08
136	Jim Kaat	.60	.30	.20
137	Larry Wolfe	.12	.06	.04
138	Mark Lee	.12	.06	.04
139	Luis Pujols	.12	.06	.04
140	Don Gullett	.20	.10	.06
141	Tom Paciorek	.12	.06	.04
142	Charlie Williams	.12	.06	.04
143	Tony Scott	.12	.06	.04
144	Sandy Alomar	.12	.06	.04
145	Rick Rhoden	.25	.13	.08
146	Duane Kuiper	.12	.06	.04
147	Dave Hamilton	.12	.06	.04
148	Bruce Boisclair	.12	.06	.04
149	Manny Sarmiento	.12	.06	.04
150	Wayne Cage	.12	.06	.04
151	John Hiller	.20	.10	.06
152	Rick Cerone	.20	.10	.06
153	Dennis Lamp	.12	.06	.04
154	Jim Gantner	.12	.06	.04
155	Dwight Evans	1.25	.60	.40
156	Buddy Solomon	.12	.06	.04
157	U.L. Washington	.12	.06	.04
158	Joe Sambito	.12	.06	.04
159	Roy White	.25	.13	.08
160	Mike Flanagan	.30	.15	.09
161	Barry Foote	.12	.06	.04
162	Tom Johnson	.12	.06	.04
163	Glenn Burke	.12	.06	.04
164	Mickey Lolich	.40	.20	.12
165	Frank Taveras	.12	.06	.04
166	Leon Roberts	.12	.06	.04
167	Roger Metzger	.12	.06	.04
168	Dave Freisleben	.12	.06	.04
169	Bill Nahorodny	.12	.06	.04
170	Don Sutton	1.25	.60	.40
171	Gene Clines	.12	.06	.04
172	Mike Bruhert	.12	.06	.04
173	John Lowenstein	.12	.06	.04
174	Rick Auerbach	.12	.06	.04
175	George Hendrick	.20	.10	.06
176	Aurelio Rodriguez	.20	.10	.06
177	Ron Reed	.20	.10	.06
178	Alvis Woods	.12	.06	.04
179	Jim Beattie	.12	.06	.04
180	Larry Hisle	.20	.10	.06
181	Mike Garman	.12	.06	.04
182	Tim Johnson	.12	.06	.04
183	Paul Splittorff	.20	.10	.06
184	Darrel Chaney	.12	.06	.04
185	Mike Torrez	.20	.10	.06
186	Eric Soderholm	.12	.06	.04
187	Mark Lemongello	.12	.06	.04
188	Pat Kelly	.12	.06	.04
189	*Eddie Whitson*	.50	.25	.15
190	Ron Cey	.25	.13	.08
191	Mike Norris	.12	.06	.04
192	Cardinals Team (Ken Boyer)	.50	.25	.15

		NR MT	EX	VG
193	Glenn Adams	.12	.06	.04
194	Randy Jones	.20	.10	.06
195	Bill Madlock	.40	.20	.12
196	Steve Kemp	.12	.06	.04
197	Bob Apodaca	.12	.06	.04
198	Johnny Grubb	.12	.06	.04
199	Larry Milbourne	.12	.06	.04
200	Johnny Bench	2.00	1.00	.60
201	Record Breaker (Mike Edwards)	.12	.06	.04
202	Record Breaker (Ron Guidry)	.35	.20	.11
203	Record Breaker (J.R. Richard)	.20	.10	.06
204	Record Breaker (Pete Rose)	1.50	.70	.45
205	Record Breaker (John Stearns)	.12	.06	.04
206	Record Breaker (Sammy Stewart)	.12	.06	.04
207	Dave Lemanczyk	.12	.06	.04
208	Clarence Gaston	.12	.06	.04
209	Reggie Cleveland	.12	.06	.04
210	Larry Bowa	.30	.15	.09
211	Denny Martinez	.20	.10	.06
212	*Carney Lansford*	6.00	3.00	1.75
213	Bill Travers	.12	.06	.04
214	Red Sox Team (Don Zimmer)	.60	.30	.20
215	Willie McCovey	2.00	1.00	.60
216	Wilbur Wood	.20	.10	.06
217	Steve Dillard	.12	.06	.04
218	Dennis Leonard	.20	.10	.06
219	Roy Smalley	.20	.10	.06
220	Cesar Geronimo	.20	.10	.06
221	Jesse Jefferson	.12	.06	.04
222	Bob Beall	.12	.06	.04
223	Kent Tekulve	.25	.13	.08
224	Dave Revering	.12	.06	.04
225	Rich Gossage	.70	.35	.20
226	Ron Pruitt	.12	.06	.04
227	Steve Stone	.20	.10	.06
228	Vic Davalillo	.12	.06	.04
229	Doug Flynn	.12	.06	.04
230	Bob Forsch	.20	.10	.06
231	Johnny Wockenfuss	.12	.06	.04
232	Jimmy Sexton	.12	.06	.04
233	Paul Mitchell	.12	.06	.04
234	Toby Harrah	.20	.10	.06
235	Steve Rogers	.20	.10	.06
236	Jim Dwyer	.12	.06	.04
237	Billy Smith	.12	.06	.04
238	Balor Moore	.12	.06	.04
239	Willie Horton	.20	.10	.06
240	Rick Reuschel	.25	.13	.08
241	Checklist 122-242	.25	.13	.08
242	Pablo Torrealba	.12	.06	.04
243	Buck Martinez	.12	.06	.04
244	Pirates Team (Chuck Tanner)	.80	.40	.25
245	Jeff Burroughs	.20	.10	.06
246	Darrell Jackson	.12	.06	.04
247	Tucker Ashford	.12	.06	.04
248	Pete LaCock	.12	.06	.04
249	Paul Thormodsgard	.12	.06	.04
250	Willie Randolph	.30	.15	.09
251	Jack Morris	2.50	1.25	.70
252	Bob Stinson	.12	.06	.04
253	Rick Wise	.20	.10	.06
254	Luis Gomez	.12	.06	.04
255	Tommy John	.80	.40	.25
256	Mike Sadek	.12	.06	.04
257	Adrian Devine	.12	.06	.04
258	Mike Phillips	.12	.06	.04
259	Reds Team (Sparky Anderson)	.60	.30	.20
260	Richie Zisk	.20	.10	.06
261	Mario Guerrero	.12	.06	.04
262	Nelson Briles	.12	.06	.04
263	Oscar Gamble	.20	.10	.06
264	*Don Robinson*	.50	.25	.15
265	Don Money	.12	.06	.04
266	Jim Willoughby	.12	.06	.04
267	Joe Rudi	.20	.10	.06
268	Julio Gonzalez	.12	.06	.04
269	Woodie Fryman	.20	.10	.06
270	Butch Hobson	.12	.06	.04
271	Rawly Eastwick	.12	.06	.04
272	Tim Corcoran	.12	.06	.04
273	Jerry Terrell	.12	.06	.04
274	Willie Norwood	.12	.06	.04
275	Junior Moore	.12	.06	.04
276	Jim Colborn	.12	.06	.04
277	Tom Grieve	.12	.06	.04
278	Andy Messersmith	.25	.13	.08
279	Jerry Grote	.12	.06	.04
280	Andre Thornton	.25	.13	.08
281	Vic Correll	.12	.06	.04
282	Blue Jays Team (Roy Hartsfield)	.50	.25	.15
283	Ken Kravec	.12	.06	.04
284	Johnnie LeMaster	.12	.06	.04
285	Bobby Bonds	.30	.15	.09
286	Duffy Dyer	.12	.06	.04
287	Andres Mora	.12	.06	.04
288	Milt Wilcox	.20	.10	.06
289	Jose Cruz	.25	.13	.08
290	Dave Lopes	.25	.13	.08
291	Tom Griffin	.12	.06	.04
292	Don Reynolds	.12	.06	.04
293	Jerry Garvin	.12	.06	.04
294	Pepe Frias	.12	.06	.04
295	Mitchell Page	.12	.06	.04
296	Preston Hanna	.12	.06	.04
297	Ted Sizemore	.12	.06	.04
298	Rich Gale	.12	.06	.04
299	Steve Ontiveros	.12	.06	.04
300	Rod Carew	4.00	2.00	1.25
301	Tom Hume	.12	.06	.04
302	Braves Team (Bobby Cox)	.50	.25	.15
303	Lary Sorensen	.12	.06	.04
304	Steve Swisher	.12	.06	.04
305	Willie Montanez	.12	.06	.04
306	Floyd Bannister	.30	.15	.09
307	Larvell Blanks	.12	.06	.04
308	Bert Blyleven	.60	.30	.20
309	Ralph Garr	.20	.10	.06
310	Thurman Munson	5.00	2.50	1.50
311	Gary Lavelle	.12	.06	.04
312	Bob Robertson	.12	.06	.04
313	Dyar Miller	.12	.06	.04
314	Larry Harlow	.12	.06	.04
315	Jon Matlack	.20	.10	.06
316	Milt May	.12	.06	.04
317	Jose Cardenal	.12	.06	.04
318	*Bob Welch*	12.00	6.00	3.50
319	Wayne Garrett	.12	.06	.04
320	Carl Yastrzemski	4.00	2.00	1.25
321	Gaylord Perry	2.00	1.00	.60
322	Danny Goodwin	.12	.06	.04
323	Lynn McGlothen	.12	.06	.04
324	Mike Tyson	.12	.06	.04
325	Cecil Cooper	.40	.20	.12
326	Pedro Borbon	.12	.06	.04
327	Art Howe	.12	.06	.04
328	A's Team (Jack McKeon)	.50	.25	.15
329	Joe Coleman	.20	.10	.06
330	George Brett	10.00	5.00	3.00
331	Mickey Mahler	.12	.06	.04
332	Gary Alexander	.12	.06	.04
333	Chet Lemon	.20	.10	.06
334	Craig Swan	.12	.06	.04
335	Chris Chambliss	.25	.13	.08
336	Bobby Thompson	.12	.06	.04
337	John Montague	.12	.06	.04
338	Vic Harris	.12	.06	.04
339	Ron Jackson	.12	.06	.04
340	Jim Palmer	4.00	2.00	1.25
341	*Willie Upshaw*	.40	.20	.12
342	Dave Roberts	.12	.06	.04
343	Ed Glynn	.12	.06	.04
344	Jerry Royster	.12	.06	.04
345	Tug McGraw	.30	.15	.09
346	Bill Buckner	.30	.15	.09
347	Doug Rau	.12	.06	.04
348	Andre Dawson	10.00	5.00	3.00
349	Jim Wright	.12	.06	.04
350	Garry Templeton	.20	.10	.06
351	Wayne Nordhagen	.12	.06	.04
352	Steve Renko	.12	.06	.04
353	Checklist 243-363	.60	.30	.20
354	Bill Bonham	.12	.06	.04
355	Lee Mazzilli	.20	.10	.06
356	Giants Team (Joe Altobelli)	.50	.25	.15
357	Jerry Augustine	.12	.06	.04
358	Alan Trammell	10.00	5.00	3.00
359	Dan Spillner	.12	.06	.04
360	Amos Otis	.20	.10	.06
361	Tom Dixon	.12	.06	.04
362	Mike Cubbage	.12	.06	.04
363	Craig Skok	.12	.06	.04
364	Gene Richards	.12	.06	.04
365	Sparky Lyle	.30	.15	.09
366	Juan Bernhardt	.12	.06	.04
367	Dave Skaggs	.12	.06	.04
368	Don Aase	.20	.10	.06
369a	Bump Wills (Blue Jays)	3.00	1.50	.90
369b	Bump Wills (Rangers)	3.50	1.75	1.00
370	Dave Kingman	.35	.20	.11
371	Jeff Holly	.12	.06	.04
372	Lamar Johnson	.12	.06	.04
373	Lance Rautzhan	.12	.06	.04

		NR MT	EX	VG
374	Ed Herrmann	.12	.06	.04
375	Bill Campbell	.12	.06	.04
376	Gorman Thomas	.25	.13	.08
377	Paul Moskau	.12	.06	.04
378	Rob Picciolo	.12	.06	.04
379	Dale Murray	.12	.06	.04
380	John Mayberry	.20	.10	.06
381	Astros Team (Bill Virdon)	.50	.25	.15
382	Jerry Martin	.12	.06	.04
383	Phil Garner	.20	.10	.06
384	Tommy Boggs	.12	.06	.04
385	Dan Ford	.12	.06	.04
386	Francisco Barrios	.12	.06	.04
387	Gary Thomasson	.12	.06	.04
388	Jack Billingham	.12	.06	.04
389	Joe Zdeb	.12	.06	.04
390	Rollie Fingers	2.50	1.25	.70
391	Al Oliver	.40	.20	.12
392	Doug Ault	.12	.06	.04
393	Scott McGregor	.20	.10	.06
394	Randy Stein	.12	.06	.04
395	Dave Cash	.12	.06	.04
396	Bill Plummer	.12	.06	.04
397	Sergio Ferrer	.12	.06	.04
398	Ivan DeJesus	.12	.06	.04
399	David Clyde	.12	.06	.04
400	Jim Rice	2.00	1.00	.60
401	Ray Knight	.25	.13	.08
402	Paul Hartzell	.12	.06	.04
403	Tim Foli	.12	.06	.04
404	White Sox Team (Don Kessinger)	.50	.25	.15
405	Butch Wynegar	.20	.10	.06
406	Joe Wallis	.12	.06	.04
407	Pete Vuckovich	.20	.10	.06
408	Charlie Moore	.12	.06	.04
409	*Willie Wilson*	2.00	1.00	.60
410	Darrell Evans	.30	.15	.09
411	Hits Record Holders (Ty Cobb, George Sisler)	.70	.35	.20
412	Runs Batted In Record Holders (Hank Aaron, Hack Wilson)	.70	.35	.20
413	Home Run Record Holders (Hank Aaron, Roger Maris)	1.00	.50	.30
414	Batting Avg. Record Holders (Ty Cobb, Roger Hornsby)	.70	.35	.20
415	Stolen Bases Record Holders (Lou Brock)	.70	.35	.20
416	Wins Record Holders (Jack Chesbro, Cy Young)	.40	.20	.12
417	Strikeouts Record Holders (Walter Johnson, Nolan Ryan)	.40	.20	.12
418	Earned Run Avg. Record Holders (Walter Johnson, Dutch Leonard)	.20	.10	.06
419	Dick Ruthven	.12	.06	.04
420	Ken Griffey	.25	.13	.08
421	Doug DeCinces	.25	.13	.08
422	Ruppert Jones	.12	.06	.04
423	Bob Montgomery	.12	.06	.04
424	Angels Team (Jim Fregosi)	.60	.30	.20
425	Rick Manning	.12	.06	.04
426	Chris Speier	.20	.10	.06
427	Andy Replogle	.12	.06	.04
428	Bobby Valentine	.25	.13	.08
429	John Urrea	.12	.06	.04
430	Dave Parker	3.00	1.50	.90
431	Glenn Borgmann	.12	.06	.04
432	Dave Heaverlo	.12	.06	.04
433	Larry Biittner	.12	.06	.04
434	Ken Clay	.20	.10	.06
435	Gene Tenace	.20	.10	.06
436	Hector Cruz	.12	.06	.04
437	Rick Williams	.12	.06	.04
438	Horace Speed	.12	.06	.04
439	Frank White	.25	.13	.08
440	Rusty Staub	.30	.15	.09
441	Lee Lacy	.12	.06	.04
442	Doyle Alexander	.25	.13	.08
443	Bruce Bochte	.12	.06	.04
444	*Aurelio Lopez*	.20	.10	.06
445	Steve Henderson	.12	.06	.04
446	Jim Lonborg	.20	.10	.06
447	Manny Sanguillen	.12	.06	.04
448	Moose Haas	.12	.06	.04
449	Bombo Rivera	.12	.06	.04
450	Dave Concepcion	.30	.15	.09
451	Royals Team (Whitey Herzog)	.50	.25	.15
452	Jerry Morales	.12	.06	.04
453	Chris Knapp	.12	.06	.04
454	Len Randle	.12	.06	.04
455	Bill Lee	.12	.06	.04
456	Chuck Baker	.12	.06	.04

		NR MT	EX	VG
457	Bruce Sutter	.60	.30	.20
458	Jim Essian	.12	.06	.04
459	Sid Monge	.12	.06	.04
460	Graig Nettles	.50	.25	.15
461	Jim Barr	.12	.06	.04
462	Otto Velez	.12	.06	.04
463	Steve Comer	.12	.06	.04
464	Joe Nolan	.12	.06	.04
465	Reggie Smith	.25	.13	.08
466	Mark Littell	.12	.06	.04
467	Don Kessinger	.12	.06	.04
468	Stan Bahnsen	.12	.06	.04
469	Lance Parrish	3.00	1.50	.90
470	Garry Maddox	.12	.06	.04
471	Joaquin Andujar	.20	.10	.06
472	Craig Kusick	.12	.06	.04
473	Dave Roberts	.12	.06	.04
474	Dick Davis	.12	.06	.04
475	Dan Driessen	.20	.10	.06
476	Tom Poquette	.12	.06	.04
477	Bob Grich	.25	.13	.08
478	Juan Beniquez	.12	.06	.04
479	Padres Team (Roger Craig)	.50	.25	.15
480	Fred Lynn	.70	.35	.20
481	Skip Lockwood	.12	.06	.04
482	Craig Reynolds	.12	.06	.04
483	Checklist 364-484	.25	.13	.08
484	Rick Waits	.12	.06	.04
485	Bucky Dent	.25	.13	.08
486	Bob Knepper	.25	.13	.08
487	Miguel Dilone	.12	.06	.04
488	Bob Owchinko	.12	.06	.04
489	Larry Cox (photo actually Dave Rader)	.12	.06	.04
490	Al Cowens	.12	.06	.04
491	Tippy Martinez	.12	.06	.04
492	Bob Bailor	.12	.06	.04
493	Larry Christenson	.12	.06	.04
494	Jerry White	.12	.06	.04
495	Tony Perez	.60	.30	.20
496	Barry Bonnell	.12	.06	.04
497	Glenn Abbott	.12	.06	.04
498	Rich Chiles	.12	.06	.04
499	Rangers Team (Pat Corrales)	.50	.25	.15
500	Ron Guidry	.90	.45	.25
501	Junior Kennedy	.12	.06	.04
502	Steve Braun	.12	.06	.04
503	Terry Humphrey	.12	.06	.04
504	*Larry McWilliams*	.20	.10	.06
505	Ed Kranepool	.20	.10	.06
506	John D'Acquisto	.12	.06	.04
507	Tony Armas	.20	.10	.06
508	Charlie Hough	.20	.10	.06
509	Mario Mendoza	.12	.06	.04
510	Ted Simmons	.40	.20	.12
511	Paul Reuschel	.12	.06	.04
512	Jack Clark	1.50	.70	.45
513	Dave Johnson	.30	.15	.09
514	Mike Proly	.12	.06	.04
515	Enos Cabell	.12	.06	.04
516	Champ Summers	.12	.06	.04
517	Al Bumbry	.20	.10	.06
518	Jim Umbarger	.12	.06	.04
519	Ben Oglivie	.20	.10	.06
520	Gary Carter	3.00	1.50	.90
521	Sam Ewing	.12	.06	.04
522	Ken Holtzman	.20	.10	.06
523	John Milner	.12	.06	.04
524	Tom Burgmeier	.12	.06	.04
525	Freddie Patek	.12	.06	.04
526	Dodgers Team (Tom Lasorda)	.60	.30	.20
527	Lerrin LaGrow	.12	.06	.04
528	Wayne Gross	.12	.06	.04
529	Brian Asselstine	.12	.06	.04
530	Frank Tanana	.25	.13	.08
531	Fernando Gonzalez	.12	.06	.04
532	Buddy Schultz	.12	.06	.04
533	Leroy Stanton	.12	.06	.04
534	Ken Forsch	.12	.06	.04
535	Ellis Valentine	.12	.06	.04
536	Jerry Reuss	.20	.10	.06
537	Tom Veryzer	.12	.06	.04
538	Mike Ivie	.12	.06	.04
539	John Ellis	.12	.06	.04
540	Greg Luzinski	.30	.15	.09
541	Jim Slaton	.12	.06	.04
542	Rick Bosetti	.12	.06	.04
543	Kiko Garcia	.12	.06	.04
544	Fergie Jenkins	1.25	.60	.40
545	John Stearns	.12	.06	.04
546	Bill Russell	.20	.10	.06

		NR MT	EX	VG
547	Clint Hurdle	.12	.06	.04
548	Enrique Romo	.12	.06	.04
549	Bob Bailey	.12	.06	.04
550	Sal Bando	.20	.10	.06
551	Cubs Team (Herman Franks)	.50	.25	.15
552	Jose Morales	.12	.06	.04
553	Denny Walling	.12	.06	.04
554	Matt Keough	.12	.06	.04
555	Biff Pocoroba	.12	.06	.04
556	Mike Lum	.12	.06	.04
557	Ken Brett	.20	.10	.06
558	Jay Johnstone	.20	.10	.06
559	Greg Pryor	.12	.06	.04
560	John Montefusco	.12	.06	.04
561	Ed Ott	.12	.06	.04
562	Dusty Baker	.25	.13	.08
563	Roy Thomas	.12	.06	.04
564	Jerry Turner	.12	.06	.04
565	Rico Carty	.25	.13	.08
566	Nino Espinosa	.12	.06	.04
567	Rich Hebner	.12	.06	.04
568	Carlos Lopez	.12	.06	.04
569	Bob Sykes	.12	.06	.04
570	Cesar Cedeno	.25	.13	.08
571	Darrell Porter	.20	.10	.06
572	Rod Gilbreath	.12	.06	.04
573	Jim Kern	.12	.06	.04
574	Claudell Washington	.20	.10	.06
575	Luis Tiant	.30	.15	.09
576	Mike Parrott	.12	.06	.04
577	Brewers Team (George Bamberger)	.50	.25	.15
578	Pete Broberg	.12	.06	.04
579	Greg Gross	.12	.06	.04
580	Ron Fairly	.20	.10	.06
581	Darold Knowles	.12	.06	.04
582	Paul Blair	.20	.10	.06
583	Julio Cruz	.12	.06	.04
584	Jim Rooker	.12	.06	.04
585	Hal McRae	.25	.13	.08
586	*Bob Horner*	.90	.45	.25
587	Ken Reitz	.12	.06	.04
588	Tom Murphy	.12	.06	.04
589	Terry Whitfield	.12	.06	.04
590	J.R. Richard	.20	.10	.06
591	Mike Hargrove	.20	.10	.06
592	Mike Krukow	.20	.10	.06
593	Rick Dempsey	.20	.10	.06
594	Bob Shirley	.12	.06	.04
595	Phil Niekro	1.25	.60	.40
596	Jim Wohlford	.12	.06	.04
597	Bob Stanley	.20	.10	.06
598	Mark Wagner	.12	.06	.04
599	Jim Spencer	.20	.10	.06
600	George Foster	.60	.30	.20
601	Dave LaRoche	.12	.06	.04
602	Checklist 485-605	.60	.30	.20
603	Rudy May	.12	.06	.04
604	Jeff Newman	.12	.06	.04
605	Rick Monday	.12	.06	.04
606	Expos Team (Dick Williams)	.50	.25	.15
607	Omar Moreno	.12	.06	.04
608	Dave McKay	.12	.06	.04
609	Silvio Martinez	.12	.06	.04
610	Mike Schmidt	12.00	6.00	3.50
611	Jim Norris	.12	.06	.04
612	*Rick Honeycutt*	.30	.15	.09
613	Mike Edwards	.12	.06	.04
614	Willie Hernandez	.20	.10	.06
615	Ken Singleton	.20	.10	.06
616	Billy Almon	.12	.06	.04
617	Terry Puhl	.12	.06	.04
618	Jerry Remy	.12	.06	.04
619	*Ken Landreaux*	.25	.13	.08
620	Bert Campaneris	.25	.13	.08
621	Pat Zachry	.12	.06	.04
622	Dave Collins	.20	.10	.06
623	Bob McClure	.12	.06	.04
624	Larry Herndon	.20	.10	.06
625	Mark Fidrych	.25	.13	.08
626	Yankees Team (Bob Lemon)	.80	.40	.25
627	Gary Serum	.12	.06	.04
628	Del Unser	.12	.06	.04
629	Gene Garber	.12	.06	.04
630	Bake McBride	.12	.06	.04
631	Jorge Orta	.12	.06	.04
632	Don Kirkwood	.12	.06	.04
633	Rob Wilfong	.12	.06	.04
634	Paul Lindblad	.20	.10	.06
635	Don Baylor	.80	.40	.25
636	Wayne Garland	.12	.06	.04
637	Bill Robinson	.12	.06	.04
638	Al Fitzmorris	.12	.06	.04
639	Manny Trillo	.20	.10	.06
640	Eddie Murray	15.00	7.50	4.50
641	*Bobby Castillo*	.12	.06	.04
642	Wilbur Howard	.12	.06	.04
643	Tom Hausman	.12	.06	.04
644	Manny Mota	.20	.10	.06
645	George Scott	.12	.06	.04
646	Rick Sweet	.12	.06	.04
647	Bob Lacey	.12	.06	.04
648	Lou Piniella	.35	.20	.11
649	John Curtis	.12	.06	.04
650	Pete Rose	4.50	2.25	1.25
651	Mike Caldwell	.12	.06	.04
652	Stan Papi	.12	.06	.04
653	Warren Brusstar	.12	.06	.04
654	Rick Miller	.12	.06	.04
655	Jerry Koosman	.30	.15	.09
656	Hosken Powell	.12	.06	.04
657	George Medich	.12	.06	.04
658	Taylor Duncan	.12	.06	.04
659	Mariners Team (Darrell Johnson)	.50	.25	.15
660	Ron LeFlore	.12	.06	.04
661	Bruce Kison	.12	.06	.04
662	Kevin Bell	.12	.06	.04
663	Mike Vail	.12	.06	.04
664	Doug Bird	.12	.06	.04
665	Lou Brock	2.00	1.00	.60
666	Rich Dauer	.12	.06	.04
667	Don Hood	.12	.06	.04
668	Bill North	.12	.06	.04
669	Checklist 606-726	.60	.30	.20
670	Jim Hunter	1.25	.60	.40
671	Joe Ferguson	.12	.06	.04
672	Ed Halicki	.12	.06	.04
673	Tom Hutton	.12	.06	.04
674	Dave Tomlin	.12	.06	.04
675	Tim McCarver	.30	.15	.09
676	Johnny Sutton	.12	.06	.04
677	Larry Parrish	.25	.13	.08
678	Geoff Zahn	.12	.06	.04
679	Derrel Thomas	.12	.06	.04
680	Carlton Fisk	3.00	1.50	.90
681	*John Henry Johnson*	.12	.06	.04
682	Dave Chalk	.12	.06	.04
683	Dan Meyer	.12	.06	.04
684	Jamie Easterly	.12	.06	.04
685	Sixto Lezcano	.12	.06	.04
686	Ron Schueler	.12	.06	.04
687	Rennie Stennett	.12	.06	.04
688	Mike Willis	.12	.06	.04
689	Orioles Team (Earl Weaver)	.70	.35	.20
690	Buddy Bell	.12	.06	.04
691	Dock Ellis	.12	.06	.04
692	Mickey Stanley	.20	.10	.06
693	Dave Rader	.12	.06	.04
694	Burt Hooton	.20	.10	.06
695	Keith Hernandez	2.00	1.00	.60
696	Andy Hassler	.12	.06	.04
697	Dave Bergman	.12	.06	.04
698	Bill Stein	.12	.06	.04
699	Hal Dues	.12	.06	.04
700	Reggie Jackson	4.00	2.00	1.25
701	Orioles Prospects (Mark Corey, John Flinn, *Sammy Stewart*)	.20	.10	.06
702	Red Sox Prospects (Joel Finch, Garry Hancock, Allen Ripley)	.12	.06	.04
703	Angels Prospects (Jim Anderson, Dave Frost, Bob Slater)	.12	.06	.04
704	White Sox Prospects (Ross Baumgarten, Mike Colbern, *Mike Squires*)	.20	.10	.06
705	Indians Prospects (*Alfredo Griffin*, Tim Norrid, Dave Oliver)	.70	.35	.20
706	Tigers Prospects (Dave Stegman, Dave Tobik, Kip Young)	.12	.06	.04
707	Royals Prospects (Randy Bass, Jim Gaudet, Randy McGilberry)	.12	.06	.04
708	Brewers Prospects (*Kevin Bass, Eddie Romero*, Ned Yost)	1.00	.50	.30
709	Twins Prospects (Sam Perlozzo, Rick Sofield, Kevin Stanfield)	.12	.06	.04
710	Yankees Prospects (Brian Doyle, *Mike Heath*, Dave Rajsich)	.30	.15	.09
711	A's Prospects (*Dwayne Murphy*, Bruce Robinson, Alan Wirth)	.50	.25	.15
712	Mariners Prospects (Bud Anderson, Greg Biercevicz, Byron McLaughlin)	.12	.06	.04
713	Rangers Prospects (*Danny Darwin*, Pat Putnam, *Billy Sample*)	.70	.35	.20
714	Blue Jays Prospects (Victor Cruz, Pat Kelly, Ernie Whitt)	.20	.10	.06

		NR MT	EX	VG
715	Braves Prospects *(Bruce Benedict, Glenn Hubbard,* Larry Whisenton)	.40	.20	.12
716	Cubs Prospects (Dave Geisel, Karl Pagel, *Scot Thompson)*	.12	.06	.04
717	Reds Prospects *(Mike LaCoss, Ron Oester, Harry Spilman)*	.40	.20	.12
718	Astros Prospects (Bruce Bochy, Mike Fischlin, Don Pisker)	.12	.06	.04
719	Dodgers Prospects *(Pedro Guerrero, Rudy Law,* Joe Simpson)	10.00	5.00	3.00
720	Expos Prospects (Jerry Fry, Jerry Pirtle, *Scott Sanderson)*	.90	.45	.25
721	Mets Prospects *(Juan Berenguer,* Dwight Bernard, Dan Norman)	.30	.15	.09
722	Phillies Prospects *(Jim Morrison, Lonnie Smith,* Jim Wright)	2.00	1.00	.60
723	Pirates Prospects *(Dale Berra,* Eugenio Cotes, Ben Wiltbank)	.20	.10	.06
724	Cardinals Prospects (Tom Bruno, *George Frazier, Terry Kennedy)*	.50	.25	.15
725	Padres Prospects (Jim Beswick, Steve Mura, Broderick Perkins)	.12	.06	.04
726	Giants Prospects (Greg Johnston, Joe Strain, John Tamargo)	.25	.06	.04

1979 Topps Comics

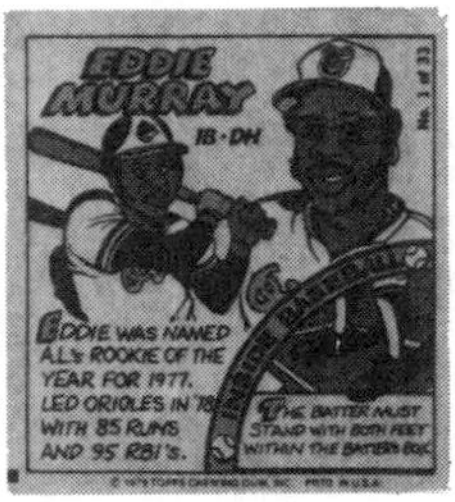

Issued as the 3" by 3-3/4" wax wrapper for a piece of bubblegum, this "test" issue was bought up in great quantities by speculators and remains rather common. It is also inexpensive, because the comic-style player representations were not popular with collectors. The set is complete at 33 pieces.

		NR MT	EX	VG
Complete Set:		8.00	4.00	2.50
Common Player:		.10	.05	.03
1	Eddie Murray	.40	.20	.12
2	Jim Rice	.30	.15	.09
3	Carl Yastrzemski	.60	.30	.20
4	Nolan Ryan	.30	.15	.09
5	Chet Lemon	.10	.05	.03
6	Andre Thornton	.10	.05	.03
7	Rusty Staub	.15	.08	.05
8	Ron LeFlore	.10	.05	.03
9	George Brett	.50	.25	.15
10	Larry Hisle	.10	.05	.03
11	Rod Carew	.35	.20	.11
12	Reggie Jackson	.40	.20	.12
13	Ron Guidry	.20	.10	.06
14	Mitchell Page	.10	.05	.03
15	Leon Roberts	.10	.05	.03
16	Al Oliver	.15	.08	.05
17	John Mayberry	.10	.05	.03
18	Bob Horner	.20	.10	.06
19	Phil Niekro	.25	.13	.08
20	Dave Kingman	.15	.08	.05
21	John Bench	.40	.20	.12
22	Tom Seaver	.40	.20	.12
23	J.R. Richard	.10	.05	.03
24	Steve Garvey	.35	.20	.11
25	Reggie Smith	.15	.08	.05
26	Ross Grimsley	.10	.05	.03
27	Craig Swan	.10	.05	.03
28	Pete Rose	.90	.45	.25
29	Dave Parker	.20	.10	.06
30	Ted Simmons	.15	.08	.05
31	Dave Winfield	.30	.15	.09
32	Jack Clark	.20	.10	.06
33	Vida Blue	.15	.08	.05

1980 Topps

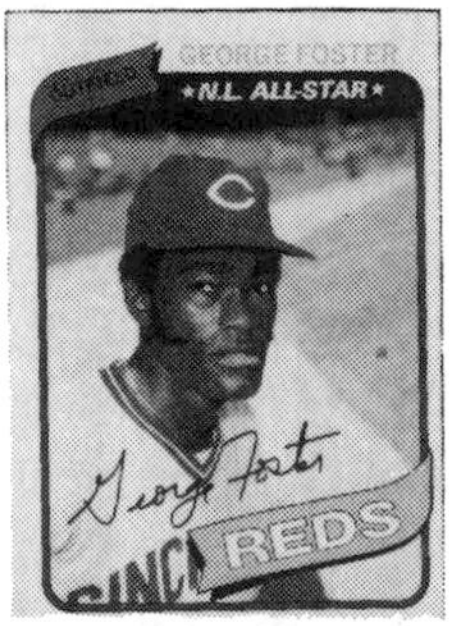

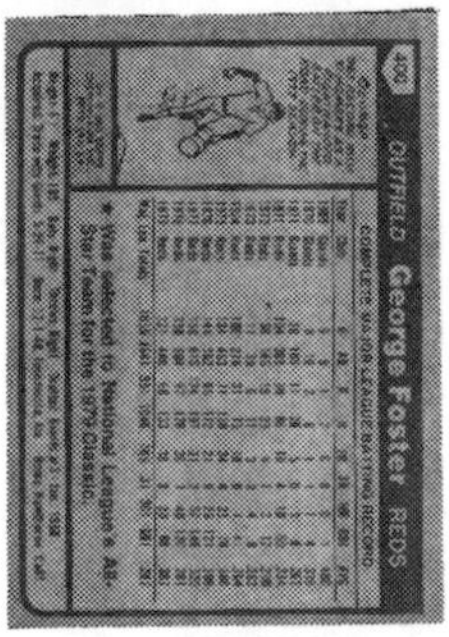

Again numbering 726 cards measuring 2-1/2" by 3-1/2", Topps did make some design changes in 1980. Fronts have the usual color picture with a facsimile autograph. The player's name appears above the picture, while his position is on a pennant at the upper left and his team on another pennant in the lower right. Backs no longer feature games, returning instead to statistics, personal information, a few headlines and a cartoon about the player. Specialty cards include statistical leaders, and previous season highlights. Many rookies again appear in team threesomes.

		NR MT	EX	VG
Complete Set:		300.00	150.00	90.00
Common Player:		.12	.06	.04
1	1979 Highlights (Lou Brock, Carl Yastrzemski)	2.00	1.00	.60
2	1979 Highlights (Willie McCovey)	.80	.40	.25
3	1979 Highlights (Manny Mota)	.20	.10	.06
4	1979 Highlights (Pete Rose)	2.00	1.00	.60
5	1979 Highlights (Garry Templeton)	.20	.10	.06
6	1979 Highlights (Del Unser)	.12	.06	.04
7	Mike Lum	.12	.06	.04
8	Craig Swan	.12	.06	.04
9	Steve Braun	.12	.06	.04
10	Denny Martinez	.20	.10	.06
11	Jimmy Sexton	.12	.06	.04
12	John Curtis	.12	.06	.04
13	Ron Pruitt	.12	.06	.04
14	Dave Cash	.12	.06	.04
15	Bill Campbell	.12	.06	.04
16	Jerry Narron	.20	.10	.06
17	Bruce Sutter	.35	.25	.14
18	Ron Jackson	.12	.06	.04
19	Balor Moore	.12	.06	.04
20	Dan Ford	.12	.06	.04
21	Manny Sarmiento	.12	.06	.04
22	Pat Putnam	.12	.06	.04
23	Derrel Thomas	.12	.06	.04
24	Jim Slaton	.12	.06	.04
25	Lee Mazzilli	.20	.10	.06
26	Marty Pattin	.12	.06	.04
27	Del Unser	.12	.06	.04
28	Bruce Kison	.12	.06	.04
29	Mark Wagner	.12	.06	.04
30	Vida Blue	.30	.15	.09
31	Jay Johnstone	.20	.10	.06
32	Julio Cruz	.12	.06	.04
33	Tony Scott	.12	.06	.04
34	Jeff Newman	.12	.06	.04
35	Luis Tiant	.30	.15	.09
36	Rusty Torres	.12	.06	.04
37	Kiko Garcia	.12	.06	.04
38	Dan Spillner	.12	.06	.04
39	Rowland Office	.12	.06	.04
40	Carlton Fisk	4.00	2.00	1.25
41	Rangers Team (Pat Corrales)	.50	.25	.15
42	*Dave Palmer*	.20	.10	.06
43	Bombo Rivera	.12	.06	.04

		NR MT	EX	VG
44	Bill Fahey	.12	.06	.04
45	Frank White	.25	.13	.08
46	Rico Carty	.20	.10	.06
47	Bill Bonham	.12	.06	.04
48	Rick Miller	.12	.06	.04
49	Mario Guerrero	.12	.06	.04
50	J.R. Richard	.20	.10	.06
51	Joe Ferguson	.12	.06	.04
52	Warren Brusstar	.12	.06	.04
53	Ben Oglivie	.20	.10	.06
54	Dennis Lamp	.12	.06	.04
55	Bill Madlock	.40	.20	.12
56	Bobby Valentine	.20	.10	.06
57	Pete Vuckovich	.20	.10	.06
58	Doug Flynn	.12	.06	.04
59	Eddy Putman	.12	.06	.04
60	Bucky Dent	.25	.13	.08
61	Gary Serum	.12	.06	.04
62	Mike Ivie	.12	.06	.04
63	Bob Stanley	.20	.10	.06
64	Joe Nolan	.12	.06	.04
65	Al Bumbry	.20	.10	.06
66	Royals Team (Jim Frey)	.60	.30	.20
67	Doyle Alexander	.25	.13	.08
68	Larry Harlow	.12	.06	.04
69	Rick Williams	.12	.06	.04
70	Gary Carter	2.25	1.25	.70
71	John Milner	.12	.06	.04
72	Fred Howard	.12	.06	.04
73	Dave Collins	.20	.10	.06
74	Sid Monge	.12	.06	.04
75	Bill Russell	.20	.10	.06
76	John Stearns	.12	.06	.04
77	*Dave Stieb*	7.00	3.50	2.00
78	Ruppert Jones	.12	.06	.04
79	Bob Owchinko	.12	.06	.04
80	Ron LeFlore	.20	.10	.06
81	Ted Sizemore	.12	.06	.04
82	Astros Team (Bill Virdon)	.50	.25	.15
83	*Steve Trout*	.30	.15	.09
84	Gary Lavelle	.12	.06	.04
85	Ted Simmons	.40	.20	.12
86	Dave Hamilton	.12	.06	.04
87	Pepe Frias	.12	.06	.04
88	Ken Landreaux	.20	.10	.06
89	Don Hood	.20	.10	.06
90	Manny Trillo	.20	.10	.06
91	Rick Dempsey	.20	.10	.06
92	Rick Rhoden	.25	.13	.08
93	Dave Roberts	.12	.06	.04
94	*Neil Allen*	.30	.15	.09
95	Cecil Cooper	.35	.20	.11
96	A's Team (Jim Marshall)	.50	.25	.15
97	Bill Lee	.20	.10	.06
98	Jerry Terrell	.12	.06	.04
99	Victor Cruz	.12	.06	.04
100	Johnny Bench	3.00	1.50	.90
101	Aurelio Lopez	.12	.06	.04
102	Rich Dauer	.12	.06	.04
103	*Bill Caudill*	.20	.10	.06
104	Manny Mota	.20	.10	.06
105	Frank Tanana	.20	.10	.06
106	*Jeff Leonard*	.80	.40	.25
107	Francisco Barrios	.12	.06	.04
108	Bob Horner	.40	.30	.15
109	Bill Travers	.12	.06	.04
110	Fred Lynn	.35	.20	.11
111	Bob Knepper	.20	.10	.06
112	White Sox Team (Tony LaRussa)	.50	.25	.15
113	Geoff Zahn	.12	.06	.04
114	Juan Beniquez	.12	.06	.04
115	Sparky Lyle	.25	.13	.08
116	Larry Cox	.12	.06	.04
117	Dock Ellis	.12	.06	.04
118	Phil Garner	.20	.10	.06
119	Sammy Stewart	.12	.06	.04
120	Greg Luzinski	.30	.15	.09
121	Checklist 1-121	.50	.25	.15
122	Dave Rosello	.12	.06	.04
123	Lynn Jones	.12	.06	.04
124	Dave Lemanczyk	.12	.06	.04
125	Tony Perez	.60	.30	.20
126	Dave Tomlin	.12	.06	.04
127	Gary Thomasson	.12	.06	.04
128	Tom Burgmeier	.12	.06	.04
129	Craig Reynolds	.12	.06	.04
130	Amos Otis	.20	.10	.06
131	Paul Mitchell	.12	.06	.04
132	Biff Pocoroba	.12	.06	.04
133	Jerry Turner	.12	.06	.04
134	Matt Keough	.12	.06	.04
135	Bill Buckner	.30	.15	.09
136	Dick Ruthven	.12	.06	.04
137	*John Castino*	.20	.10	.06
138	Ross Baumgarten	.12	.06	.04
139	*Dane Iorg*	.20	.10	.06
140	Rich Gossage	.60	.30	.20
141	Gary Alexander	.12	.06	.04
142	Phil Huffman	.12	.06	.04
143	Bruce Bochte	.12	.06	.04
144	Steve Comer	.12	.06	.04
145	Darrell Evans	.30	.15	.09
146	Bob Welch	2.00	1.00	.60
147	Terry Puhl	.12	.06	.04
148	Manny Sanguillen	.12	.06	.04
149	Tom Hume	.12	.06	.04
150	Jason Thompson	.20	.10	.06
151	Tom Hausman	.12	.06	.04
152	John Fulgham	.12	.06	.04
153	Tim Blackwell	.12	.06	.04
154	Lary Sorensen	.12	.06	.04
155	Jerry Remy	.12	.06	.04
156	Tony Brizzolara	.12	.06	.04
157	Willie Wilson	.20	.10	.06
158	Rob Picciolo	.12	.06	.04
159	Ken Clay	.20	.10	.06
160	Eddie Murray	7.00	3.50	2.00
161	Larry Christenson	.12	.06	.04
162	Bob Randall	.12	.06	.04
163	Steve Swisher	.12	.06	.04
164	Greg Pryor	.12	.06	.04
165	Omar Moreno	.12	.06	.04
166	Glenn Abbott	.12	.06	.04
167	Jack Clark	1.00	.50	.30
168	Rick Waits	.12	.06	.04
169	Luis Gomez	.12	.06	.04
170	Burt Hooton	.20	.10	.06
171	Fernando Gonzalez	.12	.06	.04
172	Ron Hodges	.12	.06	.04
173	John Henry Johnson	.12	.06	.04
174	Ray Knight	.20	.10	.06
175	Rick Reuschel	.25	.13	.08
176	Champ Summers	.12	.06	.04
177	Dave Heaverlo	.12	.06	.04
178	Tim McCarver	.30	.15	.09
179	*Ron Davis*	.20	.10	.06
180	Warren Cromartie	.12	.06	.04
181	Moose Haas	.12	.06	.04
182	Ken Reitz	.12	.06	.04
183	Jim Anderson	.12	.06	.04
184	Steve Renko	.12	.06	.04
185	Hal McRae	.25	.13	.08
186	Junior Moore	.12	.06	.04
187	Alan Ashby	.12	.06	.04
188	Terry Crowley	.12	.06	.04
189	Kevin Kobel	.12	.06	.04
190	Buddy Bell	.25	.13	.08
191	Ted Martinez	.12	.06	.04
192	Braves Team (Bobby Cox)	.50	.25	.15
193	Dave Goltz	.20	.10	.06
194	Mike Easler	.20	.10	.06
195	John Montefusco	.20	.10	.06
196	Lance Parrish	1.50	.70	.45
197	Byron McLaughlin	.12	.06	.04
198	Dell Alston	.12	.06	.04
199	Mike LaCoss	.20	.10	.06
200	Jim Rice	2.00	1.00	.60
201	Batting Leaders (Keith Hernandez, Fred Lynn)	.50	.25	.15
202	Home Run Leaders (Dave Kingman, Gorman Thomas)	.25	.13	.08
203	Runs Batted In Leaders (Don Baylor, Dave Winfield)	.50	.25	.15
204	Stolen Base Leaders (Omar Moreno, Willie Wilson)	.20	.10	.06
205	Victory Leaders (Mike Flanagan, Joe Niekro, Phil Niekro)	.40	.20	.12
206	Strikeout Leaders (J.R. Richard, Nolan Ryan)	.50	.25	.15
207	Earned Run Avg. Leaders (Ron Guidry, J.R. Richard)	.25	.13	.08
208	Wayne Cage	.12	.06	.04
209	Von Joshua	.12	.06	.04
210	Steve Carlton	3.00	1.50	.90
211	Dave Skaggs	.12	.06	.04
212	Dave Roberts	.12	.06	.04
213	Mike Jorgensen	.12	.06	.04
214	Angels Team (Jim Fregosi)	.50	.25	.15
215	Sixto Lezcano	.12	.06	.04
216	Phil Mankowski	.12	.06	.04
217	Ed Halicki	.12	.06	.04
218	Jose Morales	.12	.06	.04

		NR MT	EX	VG
219	Steve Mingori	.12	.06	.04
220	Dave Concepcion	.30	.15	.09
221	Joe Cannon	.12	.06	.04
222	*Ron Hassey*	.50	.25	.15
223	Bob Sykes	.12	.06	.04
224	Willie Montanez	.12	.06	.04
225	Lou Piniella	.30	.15	.09
226	Bill Stein	.12	.06	.04
227	Len Barker	.12	.06	.04
228	Johnny Oates	.12	.06	.04
229	Jim Bibby	.12	.06	.04
230	Dave Winfield	4.00	2.00	1.25
231	Steve McCatty	.12	.06	.04
232	Alan Trammell	4.00	2.00	1.25
233	LaRue Washington	.12	.06	.04
234	Vern Ruhle	.12	.06	.04
235	Andre Dawson	6.00	3.00	1.75
236	Marc Hill	.12	.06	.04
237	Scott McGregor	.20	.10	.06
238	Rob Wilfong	.12	.06	.04
239	Don Aase	.12	.06	.04
240	Dave Kingman	.40	.20	.12
241	Checklist 122-242	.50	.25	.15
242	Lamar Johnson	.12	.06	.04
243	Jerry Augustine	.12	.06	.04
244	Cardinals Team (Ken Boyer)	.50	.25	.15
245	Phil Niekro	1.00	.50	.30
246	Tim Foli	.12	.06	.04
247	Frank Riccelli	.12	.06	.04
248	Jamie Quirk	.12	.06	.04
249	Jim Clancy	.20	.10	.06
250	Jim Kaat	.50	.25	.15
251	Kip Young	.12	.06	.04
252	Ted Cox	.12	.06	.04
253	John Montague	.12	.06	.04
254	Paul Dade	.12	.06	.04
255	Dusty Baker	.12	.06	.04
256	Roger Erickson	.12	.06	.04
257	Larry Herndon	.20	.10	.06
258	Paul Moskau	.12	.06	.04
259	Mets Team (Joe Torre)	.60	.30	.20
260	Al Oliver	.35	.20	.11
261	Dave Chalk	.12	.06	.04
262	Benny Ayala	.12	.06	.04
263	Dave LaRoche	.12	.06	.04
264	Bill Robinson	.12	.06	.04
265	Robin Yount	8.00	4.00	2.50
266	Bernie Carbo	.12	.06	.04
267	Dan Schatzeder	.12	.06	.04
268	Rafael Landestoy	.12	.06	.04
269	Dave Tobik	.12	.06	.04
270	Mike Schmidt	6.00	3.00	1.75
271	Dick Drago	.12	.06	.04
272	Ralph Garr	.20	.10	.06
273	Eduardo Rodriguez	.12	.06	.04
274	Dale Murphy	5.50	2.75	1.75
275	Jerry Koosman	.25	.13	.08
276	Tom Veryzer	.12	.06	.04
277	Rick Bosetti	.12	.06	.04
278	Jim Spencer	.20	.10	.06
279	Rob Andrews	.12	.06	.04
280	Gaylord Perry	1.50	.70	.45
281	Paul Blair	.20	.10	.06
282	Mariners Team (Darrell Johnson)	.50	.25	.15
283	John Ellis	.12	.06	.04
284	Larry Murray	.12	.06	.04
285	Don Baylor	.35	.20	.11
286	Darold Knowles	.12	.06	.04
287	John Lowenstein	.12	.06	.04
288	Dave Rozema	.12	.06	.04
289	Bruce Bochy	.12	.06	.04
290	Steve Garvey	2.00	1.00	.60
291	Randy Scarbery	.12	.06	.04
292	Dale Berra	.12	.06	.04
293	Elias Sosa	.12	.06	.04
294	Charlie Spikes	.12	.06	.04
295	Larry Gura	.12	.06	.04
296	Dave Rader	.12	.06	.04
297	Tim Johnson	.12	.06	.04
298	Ken Holtzman	.20	.10	.06
299	Steve Henderson	.12	.06	.04
300	Ron Guidry	.70	.35	.20
301	Mike Edwards	.12	.06	.04
302	Dodgers Team (Tom Lasorda)	.60	.30	.20
303	Bill Castro	.12	.06	.04
304	Butch Wynegar	.20	.10	.06
305	Randy Jones	.20	.10	.06
306	Denny Walling	.12	.06	.04
307	Rick Honeycutt	.20	.10	.06
308	Mike Hargrove	.20	.10	.06
309	Larry McWilliams	.12	.06	.04

		NR MT	EX	VG
310	Dave Parker	2.00	1.00	.60
311	Roger Metzger	.12	.06	.04
312	Mike Barlow	.12	.06	.04
313	Johnny Grubb	.12	.06	.04
314	*Tim Stoddard*	.20	.10	.06
315	Steve Kemp	.25	.13	.08
316	Bob Lacey	.12	.06	.04
317	Mike Anderson	.12	.06	.04
318	Jerry Reuss	.20	.10	.06
319	Chris Speier	.12	.06	.04
320	Dennis Eckersley	1.50	.70	.45
321	Keith Hernandez	1.50	.70	.45
322	Claudell Washington	.20	.10	.06
323	Mick Kelleher	.12	.06	.04
324	Tom Underwood	.12	.06	.04
325	Dan Driessen	.20	.10	.06
326	Bo McLaughlin	.12	.06	.04
327	Ray Fosse	.12	.06	.04
328	Twins Team (Gene Mauch)	.50	.25	.15
329	Bert Roberge	.12	.06	.04
330	Al Cowens	.12	.06	.04
331	Rich Hebner	.12	.06	.04
332	Enrique Romo	.12	.06	.04
333	Jim Norris	.12	.06	.04
334	Jim Beattie	.20	.10	.06
335	Willie McCovey	1.50	.70	.45
336	George Medich	.12	.06	.04
337	Carney Lansford	.30	.15	.09
338	Johnny Wockenfuss	.12	.06	.04
339	John D'Acquisto	.12	.06	.04
340	Ken Singleton	.20	.10	.06
341	Jim Essian	.12	.06	.04
342	Odell Jones	.12	.06	.04
343	Mike Vail	.12	.06	.04
344	Randy Lerch	.12	.06	.04
345	Larry Parrish	.20	.10	.06
346	Buddy Solomon	.12	.06	.04
347	*Harry Chappas*	.20	.10	.06
348	Checklist 243-363	.50	.25	.15
349	Jack Brohamer	.12	.06	.04
350	George Hendrick	.20	.10	.06
351	Bob Davis	.12	.06	.04
352	Dan Briggs	.12	.06	.04
353	Andy Hassler	.12	.06	.04
354	Rick Auerbach	.12	.06	.04
355	Gary Matthews	.20	.10	.06
356	Padres Team (Jerry Coleman)	.50	.25	.15
357	Bob McClure	.12	.06	.04
358	Lou Whitaker	1.25	.60	.40
359	Randy Moffitt	.12	.06	.04
360	Darrell Porter	.12	.06	.04
361	Wayne Garland	.12	.06	.04
362	Danny Goodwin	.12	.06	.04
363	Wayne Gross	.12	.06	.04
364	Ray Burris	.12	.06	.04
365	Bobby Murcer	.25	.13	.08
366	Rob Dressler	.12	.06	.04
367	Billy Smith	.12	.06	.04
368	*Willie Aikens*	.20	.10	.06
369	Jim Kern	.12	.06	.04
370	Cesar Cedeno	.25	.13	.08
371	Jack Morris	1.50	.70	.45
372	Joel Youngblood	.12	.06	.04
373	*Dan Petry*	.30	.15	.09
374	Jim Gantner	.20	.10	.06
375	Ross Grimsley	.12	.06	.04
376	Gary Allenson	.12	.06	.04
377	Junior Kennedy	.12	.06	.04
378	Jerry Mumphrey	.12	.06	.04
379	Kevin Bell	.12	.06	.04
380	Garry Maddox	.20	.10	.06
381	Cubs Team (Preston Gomez)	.50	.25	.15
382	Dave Freisleben	.12	.06	.04
383	Ed Ott	.12	.06	.04
384	Joey McLaughlin	.12	.06	.04
385	Enos Cabell	.12	.06	.04
386	Darrell Jackson	.12	.06	.04
387a	Fred Stanley (name in red)	.20	.10	.06
387b	Fred Stanley (name in yellow)	3.00	1.50	.90
388	Mike Paxton	.12	.06	.04
389	Pete LaCock	.12	.06	.04
390	Fergie Jenkins	.40	.20	.12
391	Tony Armas	.12	.06	.04
392	Milt Wilcox	.12	.06	.04
393	Ozzie Smith	12.00	6.00	3.50
394	Reggie Cleveland	.12	.06	.04
395	Ellis Valentine	.12	.06	.04
396	Dan Meyer	.12	.06	.04
397	Roy Thomas	.12	.06	.04
398	Barry Foote	.12	.06	.04
399	Mike Proly	.12	.06	.04

		NR MT	EX	VG
400	George Foster	.50	.25	.15
401	Pete Falcone	.12	.06	.04
402	Merv Rettenmund	.12	.06	.04
403	Pete Redfern	.12	.06	.04
404	Orioles Team (Earl Weaver)	.60	.30	.20
405	Dwight Evans	1.00	.50	.30
406	Paul Molitor	2.00	1.00	.60
407	Tony Solaita	.12	.06	.04
408	Bill North	.12	.06	.04
409	Paul Splittorff	.20	.10	.06
410	Bobby Bonds	.25	.13	.08
411	Frank LaCorte	.12	.06	.04
412	Thad Bosley	.12	.06	.04
413	Allen Ripley	.12	.06	.04
414	George Scott	.20	.10	.06
415	Bill Atkinson	.12	.06	.04
416	*Tom Brookens*	.35	.20	.11
417	Craig Chamberlain	.12	.06	.04
418	Roger Freed	.12	.06	.04
419	Vic Correll	.12	.06	.04
420	Butch Hobson	.12	.06	.04
421	Doug Bird	.12	.06	.04
422	Larry Milbourne	.12	.06	.04
423	Dave Frost	.12	.06	.04
424	Yankees Team (Dick Howser)	.70	.35	.20
425	Mark Belanger	.20	.10	.06
426	Grant Jackson	.12	.06	.04
427	Tom Hutton	.12	.06	.04
428	Pat Zachry	.12	.06	.04
429	Duane Kuiper	.12	.06	.04
430	Larry Hisle	.12	.06	.04
431	Mike Krukow	.20	.10	.06
432	Willie Norwood	.12	.06	.04
433	Rich Gale	.12	.06	.04
434	Johnnie LeMaster	.12	.06	.04
435	Don Gullett	.20	.10	.06
436	Billy Almon	.12	.06	.04
437	Joe Niekro	.20	.10	.06
438	Dave Revering	.12	.06	.04
439	Mike Phillips	.12	.06	.04
440	Don Sutton	1.00	.50	.30
441	Eric Soderholm	.12	.06	.04
442	Jorge Orta	.12	.06	.04
443	Mike Parrott	.12	.06	.04
444	Alvis Woods	.12	.06	.04
445	Mark Fidrych	.20	.10	.06
446	Duffy Dyer	.12	.06	.04
447	Nino Espinosa	.12	.06	.04
448	Jim Wohlford	.12	.06	.04
449	Doug Bair	.12	.06	.04
450	George Brett	8.00	4.00	2.50
451	Indians Team (Dave Garcia)	.50	.25	.15
452	Steve Dillard	.12	.06	.04
453	Mike Bacsik	.12	.06	.04
454	Tom Donohue	.12	.06	.04
455	Mike Torrez	.20	.10	.06
456	Frank Taveras	.12	.06	.04
457	Bert Blyleven	.50	.25	.15
458	Billy Sample	.12	.06	.04
459	Mickey Lolich	.12	.06	.04
460	Willie Randolph	.25	.13	.08
461	Dwayne Murphy	.20	.10	.06
462	Mike Sadek	.12	.06	.04
463	Jerry Royster	.12	.06	.04
464	John Denny	.12	.06	.04
465	Rick Monday	.20	.10	.06
466	Mike Squires	.12	.06	.04
467	Jesse Jefferson	.12	.06	.04
468	Aurelio Rodriguez	.20	.10	.06
469	Randy Niemann	.12	.06	.04
470	Bob Boone	.20	.10	.06
471	Hosken Powell	.12	.06	.04
472	Willie Hernandez	.20	.10	.06
473	Bump Wills	.12	.06	.04
474	Steve Busby	.12	.06	.04
475	Cesar Geronimo	.12	.06	.04
476	Bob Shirley	.12	.06	.04
477	Buck Martinez	.12	.06	.04
478	Gil Flores	.12	.06	.04
479	Expos Team (Dick Williams)	.50	.25	.15
480	Bob Watson	.20	.10	.06
481	Tom Paciorek	.12	.06	.04
482	*Rickey Henderson*	180.00	90.00	55.00
483	Bo Diaz	.20	.10	.06
484	Checklist 364-484	.50	.25	.15
485	Mickey Rivers	.20	.10	.06
486	Mike Tyson	.12	.06	.04
487	Wayne Nordhagen	.12	.06	.04
488	Roy Howell	.12	.06	.04
489	Preston Hanna	.12	.06	.04
490	Lee May	.20	.10	.06

		NR MT	EX	VG
491	Steve Mura	.12	.06	.04
492	Todd Cruz	.12	.06	.04
493	Jerry Martin	.12	.06	.04
494	Craig Minetto	.12	.06	.04
495	Bake McBride	.12	.06	.04
496	Silvio Martinez	.12	.06	.04
497	Jim Mason	.12	.06	.04
498	Danny Darwin	.20	.10	.06
499	Giants Team (Dave Bristol)	.50	.25	.15
500	Tom Seaver	3.00	1.50	.90
501	Rennie Stennett	.12	.06	.04
502	Rich Wortham	.12	.06	.04
503	Mike Cubbage	.12	.06	.04
504	Gene Garber	.12	.06	.04
505	Bert Campaneris	.20	.10	.06
506	Tom Buskey	.12	.06	.04
507	Leon Roberts	.12	.06	.04
508	U.L. Washington	.12	.06	.04
509	Ed Glynn	.12	.06	.04
510	Ron Cey	.25	.13	.08
511	Eric Wilkins	.12	.06	.04
512	Jose Cardenal	.12	.06	.04
513	Tom Dixon	.12	.06	.04
514	Steve Ontiveros	.12	.06	.04
515	Mike Caldwell	.12	.06	.04
516	Hector Cruz	.12	.06	.04
517	Don Stanhouse	.12	.06	.04
518	Nelson Norman	.12	.06	.04
519	Steve Nicosia	.12	.06	.04
520	Steve Rogers	.20	.10	.06
521	Ken Brett	.12	.06	.04
522	Jim Morrison	.12	.06	.04
523	Ken Henderson	.12	.06	.04
524	Jim Wright	.12	.06	.04
525	Clint Hurdle	.12	.06	.04
526	Phillies Team (Dallas Green)	.70	.35	.20
527	Doug Rau	.12	.06	.04
528	Adrian Devine	.12	.06	.04
529	Jim Barr	.12	.06	.04
530	Jim Sundberg	.12	.06	.04
531	Eric Rasmussen	.12	.06	.04
532	Willie Horton	.20	.10	.06
533	Checklist 485-605	.50	.25	.15
534	Andre Thornton	.25	.13	.08
535	Bob Forsch	.20	.10	.06
536	Lee Lacy	.12	.06	.04
537	*Alex Trevino*	.20	.10	.06
538	Joe Strain	.12	.06	.04
539	Rudy May	.12	.06	.04
540	Pete Rose	4.00	2.00	1.25
541	Miguel Dilone	.12	.06	.04
542	Joe Coleman	.12	.06	.04
543	Pat Kelly	.12	.06	.04
544	*Rick Sutcliffe*	2.00	1.00	.60
545	Jeff Burroughs	.20	.10	.06
546	Rick Langford	.12	.06	.04
547	John Wathan	.20	.10	.06
548	Dave Rajsich	.12	.06	.04
549	Larry Wolfe	.12	.06	.04
550	Ken Griffey	.25	.13	.08
551	Pirates Team (Chuck Tanner)	.50	.25	.15
552	Bill Nahorodny	.12	.06	.04
553	Dick Davis	.12	.06	.04
554	Art Howe	.12	.06	.04
555	Ed Figueroa	.20	.10	.06
556	Joe Rudi	.20	.10	.06
557	Mark Lee	.12	.06	.04
558	Alfredo Griffin	.25	.13	.08
559	Dale Murray	.12	.06	.04
560	Dave Lopes	.25	.13	.08
561	Eddie Whitson	.20	.10	.06
562	Joe Wallis	.12	.06	.04
563	Will McEnaney	.12	.06	.04
564	Rick Manning	.12	.06	.04
565	Dennis Leonard	.20	.10	.06
566	Bud Harrelson	.20	.10	.06
567	Skip Lockwood	.12	.06	.04
568	*Gary Roenicke*	.25	.13	.08
569	Terry Kennedy	.25	.13	.08
570	Roy Smalley	.20	.10	.06
571	Joe Sambito	.12	.06	.04
572	Jerry Morales	.12	.06	.04
573	Kent Tekulve	.20	.10	.06
574	Scot Thompson	.12	.06	.04
575	Ken Kravec	.12	.06	.04
576	Jim Dwyer	.12	.06	.04
577	Blue Jays Team (Bobby Mattick)	.50	.25	.15
578	Scott Sanderson	.20	.10	.06
579	Charlie Moore	.12	.06	.04
580	Nolan Ryan	15.00	7.50	4.50
581	Bob Bailor	.12	.06	.04

		NR MT	EX	VG
582	Brian Doyle	.20	.10	.06
583	Bob Stinson	.12	.06	.04
584	Kurt Bevacqua	.12	.06	.04
585	Al Hrabosky	.20	.10	.06
586	Mitchell Page	.12	.06	.04
587	Garry Templeton	.20	.10	.06
588	Greg Minton	.12	.06	.04
589	Chet Lemon	.20	.10	.06
590	Jim Palmer	3.00	1.50	.90
591	Rick Cerone	.12	.06	.04
592	Jon Matlack	.20	.10	.06
593	Jesus Alou	.12	.06	.04
594	Dick Tidrow	.12	.06	.04
595	Don Money	.12	.06	.04
596	Rick Matula	.12	.06	.04
597	Tom Poquette	.12	.06	.04
598	Fred Kendall	.12	.06	.04
599	Mike Norris	.12	.06	.04
600	Reggie Jackson	7.00	3.50	2.00
601	Buddy Schultz	.12	.06	.04
602	Brian Downing	.20	.10	.06
603	Jack Billingham	.12	.06	.04
604	Glenn Adams	.12	.06	.04
605	Terry Forster	.20	.10	.06
606	Reds Team (John McNamara)	.50	.25	.15
607	Woodie Fryman	.20	.10	.06
608	Alan Bannister	.12	.06	.04
609	Ron Reed	.20	.10	.06
610	Willie Stargell	1.50	.70	.45
611	Jerry Garvin	.12	.06	.04
612	Cliff Johnson	.12	.06	.04
613	Randy Stein	.12	.06	.04
614	John Hiller	.20	.10	.06
615	Doug DeCinces	.20	.10	.06
616	Gene Richards	.12	.06	.04
617	Joaquin Andujar	.20	.10	.06
618	Bob Montgomery	.12	.06	.04
619	Sergio Ferrer	.12	.06	.04
620	Richie Zisk	.20	.10	.06
621	Bob Grich	.20	.10	.06
622	Mario Soto	.20	.10	.06
623	Gorman Thomas	.20	.10	.06
624	Lerrin LaGrow	.12	.06	.04
625	Chris Chambliss	.25	.13	.08
626	Tigers Team (Sparky Anderson)	.60	.30	.20
627	Pedro Borbon	.12	.06	.04
628	Doug Capilla	.12	.06	.04
629	Jim Todd	.12	.06	.04
630	Larry Bowa	.25	.13	.08
631	Mark Littell	.12	.06	.04
632	Barry Bonnell	.12	.06	.04
633	Bob Apodaca	.12	.06	.04
634	Glenn Borgmann	.12	.06	.04
635	John Candelaria	.20	.10	.06
636	Toby Harrah	.20	.10	.06
637	Joe Simpson	.12	.06	.04
638	*Mark Clear*	.20	.10	.06
639	Larry Biittner	.12	.06	.04
640	Mike Flanagan	.25	.13	.08
641	Ed Kranepool	.20	.10	.06
642	Ken Forsch	.12	.06	.04
643	John Mayberry	.20	.10	.06
644	Charlie Hough	.20	.10	.06
645	Rick Burleson	.20	.10	.06
646	Checklist 606-726	.50	.25	.15
647	Milt May	.12	.06	.04
648	Roy White	.20	.10	.06
649	Tom Griffin	.12	.06	.04
650	Joe Morgan	3.00	1.50	.90
651	Rollie Fingers	.80	.40	.25
652	Mario Mendoza	.12	.06	.04
653	Stan Bahnsen	.12	.06	.04
654	Bruce Boisclair	.12	.06	.04
655	Tug McGraw	.25	.13	.08
656	Larvell Blanks	.12	.06	.04
657	Dave Edwards	.12	.06	.04
658	Chris Knapp	.12	.06	.04
659	Brewers Team (George Bamberger)	.50	.25	.15
660	Rusty Staub	.30	.15	.09
661	Orioles Future Stars (Mark Corey, Dave Ford, Wayne Krenchicki)	.12	.06	.04
662	Red Sox Future Stars (Joel Finch, Mike O'Berry, Chuck Rainey)	.12	.06	.04
663	Angels Future Stars (Ralph Botting, Bob Clark, *Dickie Thon*)	.30	.15	.09
664	White Sox Future Stars (Mike Colbern, *Guy Hoffman*, Dewey Robinson)	.20	.10	.06
665	Indians Future Stars (Larry Andersen, Bobby Cuellar, Sandy Wihtol)	.12	.06	.04
666	Tigers Future Stars (Mike Chris, Al Greene, Bruce Robbins)	.12	.06	.04
667	Royals Future Stars (Renie Martin, Bill Paschall, *Dan Quisenberry*)	1.00	.50	.30
668	Brewers Future Stars (Danny Boitano, Willie Mueller, Lenn Sakata)	.12	.06	.04
669	Twins Future Stars (Dan Graham, Rick Sofield, *Gary Ward*)	.35	.20	.11
670	Yankees Future Stars (Bobby Brown, Brad Gulden, Darryl Jones)	.20	.10	.06
671	A's Future Stars (Derek Bryant, Brian Kingman, *Mike Morgan*)	.80	.60	.30
672	Mariners Future Stars (Charlie Beamon, Rodney Craig, Rafael Vasquez)	.12	.06	.04
673	Rangers Future Stars (Brian Allard, Jerry Don Gleaton, Greg Mahlberg)	.12	.06	.04
674	Blue Jays Future Stars (Butch Edge, Pat Kelly, Ted Wilborn)	.12	.06	.04
675	Braves Future Stars (Bruce Benedict, Larry Bradford, Eddie Miller)	.12	.06	.04
676	Cubs Future Stars (Dave Geisel, Steve Macko, Karl Pagel)	.12	.06	.04
677	Reds Future Stars (Art DeFreites, *Frank Pastore*, Harry Spilman)	.12	.06	.04
678	Astros Future Stars (Reggie Baldwin, Alan Knicely, *Pete Ladd*)	.12	.06	.04
679	Dodgers Future Stars (Joe Beckwith, *Mickey Hatcher*, Dave Patterson)	.50	.25	.15
680	Expos Future Stars (*Tony Bernazard*, Randy Miller, John Tâmargo)	.20	.10	.06
681	Mets Future Stars (Dan Norman, *Jesse Orosco, Mike Scott*)	5.00	2.50	1.50
682	Phillies Future Stars (Ramon Aviles, *Dickie Noles*, Kevin Saucier)	.20	.10	.06
683	Pirates Future Stars (Dorian Boyland, Alberto Lois, Harry Saferight)	.12	.06	.04
684	Cardinals Future Stars (George Frazier, *Tom Herr*, Dan O'Brien)	1.50	.70	.45
685	Padres Future Stars (Tim Flannery, Brian Greer, Jim Wilhelm)	.12	.06	.04
686	Giants Future Stars (Greg Johnston, Dennis Littlejohn, Phil Nastu)	.12	.06	.04
687	Mike Heath	.12	.06	.04
688	Steve Stone	.20	.10	.06
689	Red Sox Team (Don Zimmer)	.60	.30	.20
690	Tommy John	.60	.30	.20
691	Ivan DeJesus	.12	.06	.04
692	Rawly Eastwick	.12	.06	.04
693	Craig Kusick	.12	.06	.04
694	Jim Rooker	.12	.06	.04
695	Reggie Smith	.20	.10	.06
696	Julio Gonzalez	.12	.06	.04
697	David Clyde	.12	.06	.04
698	Oscar Gamble	.20	.10	.06
699	Floyd Bannister	.20	.10	.06
700	Rod Carew	2.00	1.00	.60
701	*Ken Oberkfell*	.30	.15	.09
702	Ed Farmer	.12	.06	.04
703	Otto Velez	.12	.06	.04
704	Gene Tenace	.20	.10	.06
705	Freddie Patek	.12	.06	.04
706	Tippy Martinez	.12	.06	.04
707	Elliott Maddox	.12	.06	.04
708	Bob Tolan	.12	.06	.04
709	Pat Underwood	.12	.06	.04
710	Graig Nettles	.35	.20	.11
711	Bob Galasso	.12	.06	.04
712	Rodney Scott	.12	.06	.04
713	Terry Whitfield	.12	.06	.04
714	Fred Norman	.12	.06	.04
715	Sal Bando	.20	.10	.06
716	Lynn McGlothen	.12	.06	.04
717	Mickey Klutts	.12	.06	.04
718	Greg Gross	.12	.06	.04
719	Don Robinson	.20	.10	.06
720	Carl Yastrzemski	1.50	.70	.45
721	Paul Hartzell	.12	.06	.04
722	Jose Cruz	.20	.10	.06
723	Shane Rawley	.20	.10	.06
724	Jerry White	.12	.06	.04
725	Rick Wise	.20	.10	.06
726	Steve Yeager	.20	.06	.04

A player's name in italic indicates a rookie card. An (FC) indicates a player's first card for that particular card company.

1980 Topps Superstar 5X7 Photos

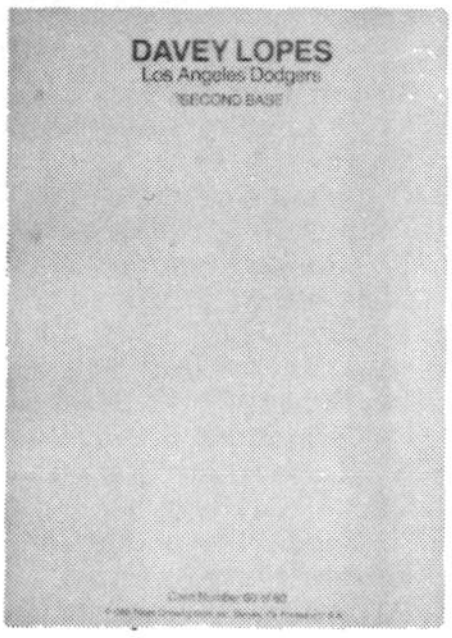

In actuality, these cards measure 4-7/8" by 6-7/8". These were another Topps "test" issue that was bought out almost entirely by investors. The 60 cards have a color photo on the front and a blue ink facsimile autograph. Backs have the player's name, team position and card number. The issue was printed on different cardboard stocks, with the first on thick cardboard with a white back and the second on thinner cardboard with a gray back. Prices below are for the more common gray backs; white backs are valued about three times the figures shown. The issue was distributed in selected geographical areas, but they were hoarded quickly. Those who hoarded them still probably have much of their supply as the set has never taken off, despite the presence of many big-name stars.

		NR MT	EX	VG
Complete Set:		9.00	4.50	2.75
Common Player:		.10	.05	.03
1	Willie Stargell	.30	.15	.09
2	Mike Schmidt	.30	.15	.09
3	Johnny Bench	.50	.25	.15
4	Jim Palmer	.35	.20	.11
5	Jim Rice	.40	.20	.12
6	Reggie Jackson	.25	.13	.08
7	Ron Guidry	.20	.10	.06
8	Lee Mazzilli	.10	.05	.03
9	Don Baylor	.15	.08	.05
10	Fred Lynn	.20	.10	.06
11	Ken Singleton	.10	.05	.03
12	Rod Carew	.25	.13	.08
13	Steve Garvey	.25	.13	.08
14	George Brett	.30	.15	.09
15	Tom Seaver	.40	.20	.12
16	Dave Kingman	.15	.08	.05
17	Dave Parker	.10	.05	.03
18	Dave Winfield	.40	.20	.12
19	Pete Rose	1.00	.50	.30
20	Nolan Ryan	1.00	.50	.30
21	Graig Nettles	.15	.08	.05
22	Carl Yastrzemski	.60	.30	.20
23	Tommy John	.25	.13	.08
24	George Foster	.15	.08	.05
25	James Rodney Richard	.10	.05	.03
26	Keith Hernandez	.30	.15	.09
27	Bob Horner	.15	.08	.05
28	Eddie Murray	.40	.20	.12
29	Steve Kemp	.10	.05	.03
30	Gorman Thomas	.10	.05	.03
31	Sixto Lezcano	.10	.05	.03
32	Bruce Sutter	.15	.08	.05
33	Cecil Cooper	.15	.08	.05
34	Larry Bowa	.10	.05	.03
35	Al Oliver	.15	.08	.05
36	Ted Simmons	.15	.08	.05
37	Garry Templeton	.10	.05	.03
38	Jerry Koosman	.10	.05	.03
39	Darrell Porter	.10	.05	.03
40	Roy Smalley	.10	.05	.03
41	Craig Swan	.10	.05	.03
42	Jason Thompson	.10	.05	.03
43	Andre Thornton	.10	.05	.03
44	Rick Manning	.10	.05	.03
45	Kent Tekulve	.10	.05	.03
46	Phil Niekro	.30	.15	.09
47	Buddy Bell	.15	.08	.05
48	Randy Jones	.10	.05	.03
49	Brian Downing	.10	.05	.03
50	Amos Otis	.10	.05	.03
51	Rick Bosetti	.10	.05	.03
52	Gary Carter	.40	.20	.12
53	Larry Parrish	.15	.08	.05
54	Jack Clark	.20	.10	.06
55	Bruce Bochte	.10	.05	.03
56	Cesar Cedeno	.15	.08	.05
57	Chet Lemon	.10	.05	.03
58	Dave Revering	.10	.05	.03
59	Vida Blue	.15	.08	.05
60	Davey Lopes	.15	.08	.05

1981 Topps

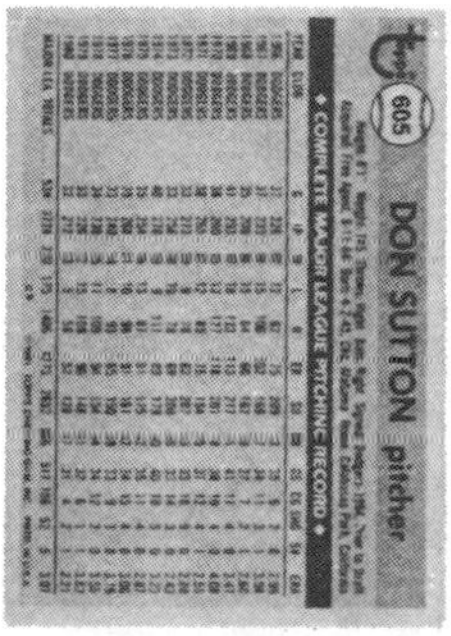

This is another 726-card set of 2-1/2" by 3-1/2" cards from Topps. The cards have the usual color photo with all cards from the same team sharing the same color borders. The player's name appears under the photo with his team and position appearing on a baseball cap at the lower left. The Topps logo returned in a small baseball in the lower right corner. Card backs include the usual stats along with a headline and a cartoon if there was room. Specialty cards include previous season record-breakers, highlights of the playoffs and World Series, along with the final appearance of team cards.

		MT	NR MT	EX
Complete Set:		100.00	75.00	40.00
Common Player:		.08	.06	.03
1	Batting Leaders (George Brett, Bill Buckner)	1.00	.70	.40
2	Home Run Leaders (Reggie Jackson, Ben Oglivie, Mike Schmidt)	.40	.30	.15
3	Runs Batted In Leaders (Cecil Cooper, Mike Schmidt)	.30	.25	.12
4	Stolen Base Leaders (Rickey Henderson, Ron LeFlore)	1.00	.70	.40
5	Victory Leaders (Steve Carlton, Steve Stone)	.20	.15	.08
6	Strikeout Leaders (Len Barker, Steve Carlton)	.20	.15	.08
7	Earned Run Avg. Leaders (Rudy May, Don Sutton)	.15	.11	.06
8	Leading Firemen (Rollie Fingers, Tom Hume, Dan Quisenberry)	.10	.08	.04
9	Pete LaCock	.08	.06	.03
10	Mike Flanagan	.12	.09	.05
11	Jim Wohlford	.08	.06	.03
12	Mark Clear	.08	.06	.03
13	*Joe Charboneau*	.15	.11	.06
14	*John Tudor*	1.75	1.25	.70
15	Larry Parrish	.15	.11	.06
16	Ron Davis	.10	.08	.04
17	Cliff Johnson	.08	.06	.03
18	Glenn Adams	.08	.06	.03
19	Jim Clancy	.12	.09	.05
20	Jeff Burroughs	.10	.08	.04
21	Ron Oester	.08	.06	.03
22	Danny Darwin	.08	.06	.03

		MT	NR MT	EX
23	Alex Trevino	.08	.06	.03
24	Don Stanhouse	.08	.06	.03
25	Sixto Lezcano	.08	.06	.03
26	U.L. Washington	.08	.06	.03
27	Champ Summers	.08	.06	.03
28	Enrique Romo	.08	.06	.03
29	Gene Tenace	.10	.08	.04
30	Jack Clark	.50	.40	.20
31	Checklist 1-121	.08	.06	.03
32	Ken Oberkfell	.08	.06	.03
33	Rick Honeycutt	.08	.06	.03
34	Aurelio Rodriguez	.10	.08	.04
35	Mitchell Page	.08	.06	.03
36	Ed Farmer	.08	.06	.03
37	Gary Roenicke	.08	.06	.03
38	Win Remmerswaal	.08	.06	.03
39	Tom Veryzer	.08	.06	.03
40	Tug McGraw	.20	.15	.08
41	Rangers Future Stars (Bob Babcock, John Butcher, Jerry Don Gleaton)	.10	.08	.04
42	Jerry White	.08	.06	.03
43	Jose Morales	.08	.06	.03
44	Larry McWilliams	.08	.06	.03
45	Enos Cabell	.08	.06	.03
46	Rick Bosetti	.08	.06	.03
47	Ken Brett	.10	.08	.04
48	Dave Skaggs	.08	.06	.03
49	Bob Shirley	.08	.06	.03
50	Dave Lopes	.12	.09	.05
51	Bill Robinson	.08	.06	.03
52	Hector Cruz	.08	.06	.03
53	Kevin Saucier	.08	.06	.03
54	Ivan DeJesus	.08	.06	.03
55	Mike Norris	.08	.06	.03
56	Buck Martinez	.08	.06	.03
57	Dave Roberts	.08	.06	.03
58	Joel Youngblood	.08	.06	.03
59	Dan Petry	.12	.09	.05
60	Willie Randolph	.15	.11	.06
61	Butch Wynegar	.08	.06	.03
62	Joe Pettini	.08	.06	.03
63	Steve Renko	.08	.06	.03
64	Brian Asselstine	.08	.06	.03
65	Scott McGregor	.10	.08	.04
66	Royals Future Stars (Manny Castillo, Tim Ireland, Mike Jones)	.08	.06	.03
67	Ken Kravec	.08	.06	.03
68	Matt Alexander	.08	.06	.03
69	Ed Halicki	.08	.06	.03
70	Al Oliver	.15	.11	.06
71	Hal Dues	.08	.06	.03
72	Barry Evans	.08	.06	.03
73	Doug Bair	.08	.06	.03
74	Mike Hargrove	.08	.06	.03
75	Reggie Smith	.15	.11	.06
76	Mario Mendoza	.08	.06	.03
77	Mike Barlow	.08	.06	.03
78	Steve Dillard	.08	.06	.03
79	Bruce Robbins	.08	.06	.03
80	Rusty Staub	.15	.11	.06
81	Dave Stapleton	.08	.06	.03
82	Astros Future Stars (Danny Heep, Alan Knicely, Bobby Sprowl)	.08	.06	.03
83	Mike Proly	.08	.06	.03
84	Johnnie LeMaster	.08	.06	.03
85	Mike Caldwell	.08	.06	.03
86	Wayne Gross	.08	.06	.03
87	Rick Camp	.08	.06	.03
88	Joe Lefebvre	.08	.06	.03
89	Darrell Jackson	.08	.06	.03
90	Bake McBride	.08	.06	.03
91	Tim Stoddard	.08	.06	.03
92	Mike Easler	.10	.08	.04
93	Ed Glynn	.08	.06	.03
94	Harry Spilman	.08	.06	.03
95	Jim Sundberg	.10	.08	.04
96	A's Future Stars (Dave Beard, *Ernie Camacho*, Pat Dempsey)	.12	.09	.05
97	Chris Speier	.08	.06	.03
98	Clint Hurdle	.08	.06	.03
99	Eric Wilkins	.08	.06	.03
100	Rod Carew	3.00	2.25	1.25
101	Benny Ayala	.08	.06	.03
102	Dave Tobik	.08	.06	.03
103	Jerry Martin	.08	.06	.03
104	Terry Forster	.10	.08	.04
105	Jose Cruz	.15	.11	.06
106	Don Money	.08	.06	.03
107	Rich Wortham	.08	.06	.03
108	Bruce Benedict	.08	.06	.03
109	Mike Scott	.80	.60	.30

		MT	NR MT	EX
110	Carl Yastrzemski	2.00	1.50	.80
111	Greg Minton	.08	.06	.03
112	White Sox Future Stars (Rusty Kuntz, Fran Mullins, Leo Sutherland)	.08	.06	.03
113	Mike Phillips	.08	.06	.03
114	Tom Underwood	.08	.06	.03
115	Roy Smalley	.08	.06	.03
116	Joe Simpson	.08	.06	.03
117	Pete Falcone	.08	.06	.03
118	Kurt Bevacqua	.08	.06	.03
119	Tippy Martinez	.08	.06	.03
120	Larry Bowa	.20	.15	.08
121	Larry Harlow	.08	.06	.03
122	John Denny	.08	.06	.03
123	Al Cowens	.08	.06	.03
124	Jerry Garvin	.08	.06	.03
125	Andre Dawson	2.50	2.00	1.00
126	*Charlie Leibrandt*	.50	.40	.20
127	Rudy Law	.08	.06	.03
128	Gary Allenson	.08	.06	.03
129	Art Howe	.08	.06	.03
130	Larry Gura	.08	.06	.03
131	*Keith Moreland*	.35	.25	.14
132	Tommy Boggs	.08	.06	.03
133	Jeff Cox	.08	.06	.03
134	Steve Mura	.08	.06	.03
135	Gorman Thomas	.12	.09	.05
136	Doug Capilla	.08	.06	.03
137	Hosken Powell	.08	.06	.03
138	*Rich Dotson*	.20	.15	.08
139	Oscar Gamble	.10	.08	.04
140	Bob Forsch	.10	.08	.04
141	Miguel Dilone	.08	.06	.03
142	Jackson Todd	.08	.06	.03
143	Dan Meyer	.08	.06	.03
144	Allen Ripley	.08	.06	.03
145	Mickey Rivers	.10	.08	.04
146	Bobby Castillo	.08	.06	.03
147	Dale Berra	.08	.06	.03
148	Randy Niemann	.08	.06	.03
149	Joe Nolan	.08	.06	.03
150	Mark Fidrych	.12	.09	.05
151	Claudell Washington	.12	.09	.05
152	John Urrea	.08	.06	.03
153	Tom Poquette	.08	.06	.03
154	Rick Langford	.08	.06	.03
155	Chris Chambliss	.12	.09	.05
156	Bob McClure	.08	.06	.03
157	John Wathan	.12	.09	.05
158	Fergie Jenkins	1.00	.70	.40
159	Brian Doyle	.08	.06	.03
160	Garry Maddox	.12	.09	.05
161	Dan Graham	.08	.06	.03
162	Doug Corbett	.08	.06	.03
163	Billy Almon	.08	.06	.03
164	*Lamarr Hoyt (LaMarr)*	.20	.15	.08
165	Tony Scott	.08	.06	.03
166	Floyd Bannister	.12	.09	.05
167	Terry Whitfield	.08	.06	.03
168	Don Robinson	.08	.06	.03
169	John Mayberry	.10	.08	.04
170	Ross Grimsley	.08	.06	.03
171	Gene Richards	.08	.06	.03
172	Gary Woods	.08	.06	.03
173	Bump Wills	.08	.06	.03
174	Doug Rau	.08	.06	.03
175	Dave Collins	.10	.08	.04
176	Mike Krukow	.10	.08	.04
177	Rick Peters	.08	.06	.03
178	Jim Essian	.08	.06	.03
179	Rudy May	.08	.06	.03
180	Pete Rose	3.00	2.25	1.25
181	Elias Sosa	.08	.06	.03
182	Bob Grich	.15	.11	.06
183	Dick Davis	.08	.06	.03
184	Jim Dwyer	.08	.06	.03
185	Dennis Leonard	.10	.08	.04
186	Wayne Nordhagen	.08	.06	.03
187	Mike Parrott	.08	.06	.03
188	Doug DeCinces	.15	.11	.06
189	Craig Swan	.08	.06	.03
190	Cesar Cedeno	.15	.11	.06
191	Rick Sutcliffe	.40	.30	.15
192	Braves Future Stars (*Terry Harper*, Ed Miller, *Rafael Ramirez*)	.25	.20	.10
193	Pete Vuckovich	.10	.08	.04
194	*Rod Scurry*	.10	.08	.04
195	Rich Murray	.08	.06	.03
196	Duffy Dyer	.08	.06	.03
197	Jim Kern	.08	.06	.03
198	Jerry Dybzinski	.08	.06	.03

		MT	NR MT	EX
199	Chuck Rainey	.08	.06	.03
200	George Foster	.25	.20	.10
201	Record Breaker (Johnny Bench)	.40	.30	.15
202	Record Breaker (Steve Carlton)	.40	.30	.15
203	Record Breaker (Bill Gullickson)	.08	.06	.03
204	Record Breaker (Ron LeFlore, Rodney Scott)	.10	.08	.04
205	Record Breaker (Pete Rose)	.80	.60	.30
206	Record Breaker (Mike Schmidt)	.80	.60	.30
207	Record Breaker (Ozzie Smith)	.20	.15	.08
208	Record Breaker (Willie Wilson)	.20	.15	.08
209	Dickie Thon	.10	.08	.04
210	Jim Palmer	2.00	1.50	.80
211	Derrel Thomas	.08	.06	.03
212	Steve Nicosia	.08	.06	.03
213	*Al Holland*	.10	.08	.04
214	Angels Future Stars (Ralph Botting, Jim Dorsey, John Harris)	.08	.06	.03
215	Larry Hisle	.10	.08	.04
216	John Henry Johnson	.08	.06	.03
217	Rich Hebner	.08	.06	.03
218	Paul Splittorff	.08	.06	.03
219	Ken Landreaux	.08	.06	.03
220	Tom Seaver	2.50	2.00	1.00
221	Bob Davis	.08	.06	.03
222	Jorge Orta	.08	.06	.03
223	Roy Lee Jackson	.08	.06	.03
224	Pat Zachry	.08	.06	.03
225	Ruppert Jones	.08	.06	.03
226	Manny Sanguillen	.08	.06	.03
227	Fred Martinez	.08	.06	.03
228	Tom Paciorek	.08	.06	.03
229	Rollie Fingers	1.00	.70	.40
230	George Hendrick	.10	.08	.04
231	Joe Beckwith	.08	.06	.03
232	Mickey Klutts	.08	.06	.03
233	Skip Lockwood	.08	.06	.03
234	Lou Whitaker	.60	.45	.25
235	Scott Sanderson	.08	.06	.03
236	Mike Ivie	.08	.06	.03
237	Charlie Moore	.08	.06	.03
238	Willie Hernandez	.12	.09	.05
239	Rick Miller	.08	.06	.03
240	Nolan Ryan	7.00	5.25	2.75
241	Checklist 122-242	.08	.06	.03
242	Chet Lemon	.10	.08	.04
243	Sal Butera	.08	.06	.03
244	Cardinals Future Stars (*Tito Landrum*, Al Olmsted, Andy Rincon)	.15	.11	.06
245	Ed Figueroa	.08	.06	.03
246	Ed Ott	.08	.06	.03
247	Glenn Hubbard	.10	.08	.04
248	Joey McLaughlin	.08	.06	.03
249	Larry Cox	.08	.06	.03
250	Ron Guidry	.50	.40	.20
251	Tom Brookens	.10	.08	.04
252	Victor Cruz	.08	.06	.03
253	Dave Bergman	.08	.06	.03
254	Ozzie Smith	3.00	2.25	1.25
255	Mark Littell	.08	.06	.03
256	Bombo Rivera	.08	.06	.03
257	Rennie Stennett	.08	.06	.03
258	*Joe Price*	.12	.09	.05
259	Mets Future Stars (Juan Berenguer, *Hubie Brooks, Mookie Wilson*)	2.50	2.00	1.00
260	Ron Cey	.15	.11	.06
261	Rickey Henderson	30.00	22.00	12.00
262	Sammy Stewart	.08	.06	.03
263	Brian Downing	.12	.09	.05
264	Jim Norris	.08	.06	.03
265	John Candelaria	.12	.09	.05
266	Tom Herr	.15	.11	.06
267	Stan Bahnsen	.08	.06	.03
268	Jerry Royster	.08	.06	.03
269	Ken Forsch	.08	.06	.03
270	Greg Luzinski	.20	.15	.08
271	Bill Castro	.08	.06	.03
272	Bruce Kimm	.08	.06	.03
273	Stan Papi	.08	.06	.03
274	Craig Chamberlain	.08	.06	.03
275	Dwight Evans	.25	.20	.10
276	Dan Spillner	.08	.06	.03
277	Alfredo Griffin	.12	.09	.05
278	Rick Sofield	.08	.06	.03
279	Bob Knepper	.12	.09	.05
280	Ken Griffey	.15	.11	.06
281	Fred Stanley	.08	.06	.03
282	Mariners Future Stars (Rick Anderson, Greg Biercevicz, Rodney Craig)	.08	.06	.03
283	Billy Sample	.08	.06	.03
284	Brian Kingman	.08	.06	.03
285	Jerry Turner	.08	.06	.03
286	Dave Frost	.08	.06	.03
287	Lenn Sakata	.08	.06	.03
288	Bob Clark	.08	.06	.03
289	Mickey Hatcher	.10	.08	.04
290	Bob Boone	.08	.06	.03
291	Aurelio Lopez	.08	.06	.03
292	Mike Squires	.08	.06	.03
293	*Charlie Lea*	.15	.11	.06
294	Mike Tyson	.08	.06	.03
295	Hal McRae	.15	.11	.06
296	Bill Nahorodny	.08	.06	.03
297	Bob Bailor	.08	.06	.03
298	Buddy Solomon	.08	.06	.03
299	Elliott Maddox	.08	.06	.03
300	Paul Molitor	.40	.30	.15
301	Matt Keough	.08	.06	.03
302	Dodgers Future Stars (Jack Perconte, *Mike Scioscia, Fernando Valenzuela*)	6.00	4.50	2.50
303	Johnny Oates	.08	.06	.03
304	John Castino	.08	.06	.03
305	Ken Clay	.08	.06	.03
306	Juan Beniquez	.08	.06	.03
307	Gene Garber	.08	.06	.03
308	Rick Manning	.08	.06	.03
309	*Luis Salazar*	.20	.15	.08
310	Vida Blue	.08	.06	.03
311	Freddie Patek	.08	.06	.03
312	Rick Rhoden	.12	.09	.05
313	Luis Pujols	.08	.06	.03
314	Rich Dauer	.08	.06	.03
315	*Kirk Gibson*	7.00	5.25	2.75
316	Craig Minetto	.08	.06	.03
317	Lonnie Smith	.10	.08	.04
318	Steve Yeager	.08	.06	.03
319	Rowland Office	.08	.06	.03
320	Tom Burgmeier	.08	.06	.03
321	*Leon Durham*	.25	.20	.10
322	Neil Allen	.10	.08	.04
323	Jim Morrison	.08	.06	.03
324	Mike Willis	.08	.06	.03
325	Ray Knight	.12	.09	.05
326	Biff Pocoroba	.08	.06	.03
327	Moose Haas	.08	.06	.03
328	Twins Future Stars (*Dave Engle*, Greg Johnston, Gary Ward)	.12	.09	.05
329	Joaquin Andujar	.12	.09	.05
330	Frank White	.12	.09	.05
331	Dennis Lamp	.08	.06	.03
332	Lee Lacy	.08	.06	.03
333	Sid Monge	.08	.06	.03
334	Dane Iorg	.08	.06	.03
335	Rick Cerone	.08	.06	.03
336	Eddie Whitson	.08	.06	.03
337	Lynn Jones	.08	.06	.03
338	Checklist 243-363	.25	.20	.10
339	John Ellis	.08	.06	.03
340	Bruce Kison	.08	.06	.03
341	Dwayne Murphy	.10	.08	.04
342	Eric Rasmussen	.08	.06	.03
343	Frank Taveras	.08	.06	.03
344	Byron McLaughlin	.08	.06	.03
345	Warren Cromartie	.08	.06	.03
346	Larry Christenson	.08	.06	.03
347	*Harold Baines*	5.00	3.75	2.00
348	Bob Sykes	.08	.06	.03
349	Glenn Hoffman	.08	.06	.03
350	J.R. Richard	.12	.09	.05
351	Otto Velez	.08	.06	.03
352	Dick Tidrow	.08	.06	.03
353	Terry Kennedy	.12	.09	.05
354	Mario Soto	.10	.08	.04
355	Bob Horner	.25	.20	.10
356	Padres Future Stars (George Stablein, Craig Stimac, Tom Tellmann)	.08	.06	.03
357	Jim Slaton	.08	.06	.03
358	Mark Wagner	.08	.06	.03
359	Tom Hausman	.08	.06	.03
360	Willie Wilson	.30	.25	.12
361	Joe Strain	.08	.06	.03
362	Bo Diaz	.10	.08	.04
363	Geoff Zahn	.08	.06	.03
364	*Mike Davis*	.25	.20	.10
365	Graig Nettles	.12	.09	.05
366	Mike Ramsey	.08	.06	.03
367	Denny Martinez	.10	.08	.04
368	Leon Roberts	.08	.06	.03
369	Frank Tanana	.12	.09	.05
370	Dave Winfield	1.50	1.25	.60
371	Charlie Hough	.15	.11	.06

#	Player	MT	NR MT	EX
372	Jay Johnstone	.10	.08	.04
373	Pat Underwood	.08	.06	.03
374	Tom Hutton	.08	.06	.03
375	Dave Concepcion	.20	.15	.08
376	Ron Reed	.08	.06	.03
377	Jerry Morales	.08	.06	.03
378	Dave Rader	.08	.06	.03
379	Lary Sorensen	.08	.06	.03
380	Willie Stargell	1.00	.70	.40
381	Cubs Future Stars (Carlos Lezcano, Steve Macko, Randy Martz)	.08	.06	.03
382	*Paul Mirabella*(FC)	.12	.09	.05
383	Eric Soderholm	.08	.06	.03
384	Mike Sadek	.08	.06	.03
385	Joe Sambito	.08	.06	.03
386	Dave Edwards	.08	.06	.03
387	Phil Niekro	.80	.60	.30
388	Andre Thornton	.12	.09	.05
389	Marty Pattin	.08	.06	.03
390	Cesar Geronimo	.08	.06	.03
391	Dave Lemanczyk	.08	.06	.03
392	Lance Parrish	.70	.50	.30
393	Broderick Perkins	.08	.06	.03
394	Woodie Fryman	.10	.08	.04
395	Scot Thompson	.08	.06	.03
396	Bill Campbell	.08	.06	.03
397	Julio Cruz	.08	.06	.03
398	Ross Baumgarten	.08	.06	.03
399	Orioles Future Stars (*Mike Boddicker*, Mark Corey, *Floyd Rayford*)	2.00	1.50	.80
400	Reggie Jackson	2.00	1.50	.80
401	A.L. Championships (Royals Sweep Yankees)	.50	.40	.20
402	N.L. Championships (Phillies Squeak Past Astros)	.40	.30	.15
403	World Series (Phillies Beat Royals In 6)	.25	.20	.10
404	World Series Summary (Phillies Win First World Series)	.25	.20	.10
405	Nino Espinosa	.08	.06	.03
406	Dickie Noles	.08	.06	.03
407	Ernie Whitt	.10	.08	.04
408	Fernando Arroyo	.08	.06	.03
409	Larry Herndon	.10	.08	.04
410	Bert Campaneris	.12	.09	.05
411	Terry Puhl	.08	.06	.03
412	*Britt Burns*	.12	.09	.05
413	Tony Bernazard	.08	.06	.03
414	John Pacella	.08	.06	.03
415	Ben Oglivie	.10	.08	.04
416	Gary Alexander	.08	.06	.03
417	Dan Schatzeder	.08	.06	.03
418	Bobby Brown	.08	.06	.03
419	Tom Hume	.08	.06	.03
420	Keith Hernandez	.50	.40	.20
421	Bob Stanley	.08	.06	.03
422	Dan Ford	.08	.06	.03
423	Shane Rawley	.15	.11	.06
424	Yankees Future Stars (Tim Lollar, Bruce Robinson, Dennis Werth)	.08	.06	.03
425	Al Bumbry	.10	.08	.04
426	Warren Brusstar	.08	.06	.03
427	John D'Acquisto	.08	.06	.03
428	John Stearns	.08	.06	.03
429	Mick Kelleher	.08	.06	.03
430	Jim Bibby	.08	.06	.03
431	Dave Roberts	.08	.06	.03
432	Len Barker	.10	.08	.04
433	Rance Mulliniks	.08	.06	.03
434	Roger Erickson	.08	.06	.03
435	Jim Spencer	.08	.06	.03
436	Gary Lucas	.08	.06	.03
437	Mike Heath	.08	.06	.03
438	John Montefusco	.10	.08	.04
439	Denny Walling	.08	.06	.03
440	Jerry Reuss	.12	.09	.05
441	Ken Reitz	.08	.06	.03
442	Ron Pruitt	.08	.06	.03
443	Jim Beattie	.08	.06	.03
444	Garth Iorg	.08	.06	.03
445	Ellis Valentine	.08	.06	.03
446	Checklist 364-484	.25	.20	.10
447	Junior Kennedy	.08	.06	.03
448	Tim Corcoran	.08	.06	.03
449	Paul Mitchell	.08	.06	.03
450	Dave Kingman	.10	.08	.04
451	Indians Future Stars (Chris Bando, Tom Brennan, Sandy Wihtol)	.12	.09	.05
452	Renie Martin	.08	.06	.03
453	Rob Wilfong	.08	.06	.03
454	Andy Hassler	.08	.06	.03
455	Rick Burleson	.10	.08	.04
456	*Jeff Reardon*	4.00	3.00	1.50
457	Mike Lum	.08	.06	.03
458	Randy Jones	.10	.08	.04
459	Greg Gross	.08	.06	.03
460	Rich Gossage	.40	.30	.15
461	Dave McKay	.08	.06	.03
462	Jack Brohamer	.08	.06	.03
463	Milt May	.08	.06	.03
464	Adrian Devine	.08	.06	.03
465	Bill Russell	.12	.09	.05
466	Bob Molinaro	.08	.06	.03
467	Dave Stieb	.80	.60	.30
468	Johnny Wockenfuss	.08	.06	.03
469	Jeff Leonard	.20	.15	.08
470	Manny Trillo	.10	.08	.04
471	Mike Vail	.08	.06	.03
472	Dyar Miller	.08	.06	.03
473	Jose Cardenal	.08	.06	.03
474	Mike LaCoss	.08	.06	.03
475	Buddy Bell	.15	.11	.06
476	Jerry Koosman	.15	.11	.06
477	Luis Gomez	.08	.06	.03
478	Juan Eichelberger	.08	.06	.03
479	Expos Future Stars (Bobby Pate, *Tim Raines*, Roberto Ramos)	12.00	9.00	4.75
480	Carlton Fisk	2.00	1.50	.80
481	Bob Lacey	.08	.06	.03
482	Jim Gantner	.10	.08	.04
483	Mike Griffin	.08	.06	.03
484	Max Venable	.08	.06	.03
485	Garry Templeton	.12	.09	.05
486	Marc Hill	.08	.06	.03
487	Dewey Robinson	.08	.06	.03
488	*Damaso Garcia*	.12	.09	.05
489	John Littlefield (photo actually Mark Riggins)	.08	.06	.03
490	Eddie Murray	3.00	2.25	1.25
491	Gordy Pladson	.08	.06	.03
492	Barry Foote	.08	.06	.03
493	Dan Quisenberry	.20	.15	.08
494	*Bob Walk*	.50	.40	.20
495	Dusty Baker	.12	.09	.05
496	Paul Dade	.08	.06	.03
497	Fred Norman	.08	.06	.03
498	Pat Putnam	.08	.06	.03
499	Frank Pastore	.08	.06	.03
500	Jim Rice	1.00	.70	.40
501	Tim Foli	.08	.06	.03
502	Giants Future Stars (Chris Bourjos, Al Hargesheimer, Mike Rowland)	.08	.06	.03
503	Steve McCatty	.08	.06	.03
504	Dale Murphy	2.50	2.00	1.00
505	Jason Thompson	.08	.06	.03
506	Phil Huffman	.08	.06	.03
507	Jamie Quirk	.08	.06	.03
508	Rob Dressler	.08	.06	.03
509	Pete Mackanin	.08	.06	.03
510	Lee Mazzilli	.10	.08	.04
511	Wayne Garland	.08	.06	.03
512	Gary Thomasson	.08	.06	.03
513	Frank LaCorte	.08	.06	.03
514	George Riley	.08	.06	.03
515	Robin Yount	3.00	2.25	1.25
516	Doug Bird	.08	.06	.03
517	Richie Zisk	.10	.08	.04
518	Grant Jackson	.08	.06	.03
519	John Tamargo	.08	.06	.03
520	Steve Stone	.12	.09	.05
521	Sam Mejias	.08	.06	.03
522	Mike Colbern	.08	.06	.03
523	John Fulgham	.08	.06	.03
524	Willie Aikens	.08	.06	.03
525	Mike Torrez	.10	.08	.04
526	Phillies Future Stars (Marty Bystrom, Jay Loviglio, Jim Wright)	.08	.06	.03
527	Danny Goodwin	.08	.06	.03
528	Gary Matthews	.12	.09	.05
529	Dave LaRoche	.08	.06	.03
530	Steve Garvey	1.25	.90	.50
531	John Curtis	.08	.06	.03
532	Bill Stein	.08	.06	.03
533	Jesus Figueroa	.08	.06	.03
534	*Dave Smith*	.60	.45	.25
535	Omar Moreno	.08	.06	.03
536	Bob Owchinko	.08	.06	.03
537	Ron Hodges	.08	.06	.03
538	Tom Griffin	.08	.06	.03
539	Rodney Scott	.08	.06	.03
540	Mike Schmidt	4.00	3.00	1.50
541	Steve Swisher	.08	.06	.03

		MT	NR MT	EX
542	Larry Bradford	.08	.06	.03
543	Terry Crowley	.08	.06	.03
544	Rich Gale	.08	.06	.03
545	Johnny Grubb	.08	.06	.03
546	Paul Moskau	.08	.06	.03
547	Mario Guerrero	.08	.06	.03
548	Dave Goltz	.10	.08	.04
549	Jerry Remy	.08	.06	.03
550	Tommy John	.50	.40	.20
551	Pirates Future Stars *(Vance Law, Tony Pena, Pascual Perez)*	2.50	2.00	1.00
552	Steve Trout	.08	.06	.03
553	Tim Blackwell	.08	.06	.03
554	Bert Blyleven	.25	.20	.10
555	Cecil Cooper	.20	.15	.08
556	Jerry Mumphrey	.08	.06	.03
557	Chris Knapp	.08	.06	.03
558	Barry Bonnell	.08	.06	.03
559	Willie Montanez	.08	.06	.03
560	Joe Morgan	.70	.50	.30
561	Dennis Littlejohn	.08	.06	.03
562	Checklist 485-605	.25	.20	.10
563	Jim Kaat	.30	.25	.12
564	Ron Hassey	.08	.06	.03
565	Burt Hooton	.10	.08	.04
566	Del Unser	.08	.06	.03
567	Mark Bomback	.08	.06	.03
568	Dave Revering	.08	.06	.03
569	Al Williams	.08	.06	.03
570	Ken Singleton	.12	.09	.05
571	Todd Cruz	.08	.06	.03
572	Jack Morris	.60	.45	.25
573	Phil Garner	.10	.08	.04
574	Bill Caudill	.08	.06	.03
575	Tony Perez	.50	.40	.20
576	Reggie Cleveland	.08	.06	.03
577	Blue Jays Future Stars (Luis Leal, Brian Milner, *Ken Schrom)*	.20	.15	.08
578	*Bill Gullickson*	.20	.15	.08
579	Tim Flannery	.08	.06	.03
580	Don Baylor	.15	.11	.06
581	Roy Howell	.08	.06	.03
582	Gaylord Perry	.70	.50	.30
583	Larry Milbourne	.08	.06	.03
584	Randy Lerch	.08	.06	.03
585	Amos Otis	.10	.08	.04
586	Silvio Martinez	.08	.06	.03
587	Jeff Newman	.08	.06	.03
588	Gary Lavelle	.08	.06	.03
589	Lamar Johnson	.08	.06	.03
590	Bruce Sutter	.25	.20	.10
591	John Lowenstein	.08	.06	.03
592	Steve Comer	.08	.06	.03
593	Steve Kemp	.12	.09	.05
594	Preston Hanna	.08	.06	.03
595	Butch Hobson	.08	.06	.03
596	Jerry Augustine	.08	.06	.03
597	Rafael Landestoy	.08	.06	.03
598	George Vukovich	.08	.06	.03
599	Dennis Kinney	.08	.06	.03
600	Johnny Bench	2.00	1.50	.80
601	Don Aase	.08	.06	.03
602	Bobby Murcer	.15	.11	.06
603	John Verhoeven	.08	.06	.03
604	Rob Picciolo	.08	.06	.03
605	Don Sutton	.70	.50	.30
606	Reds Future Stars (Bruce Berenyi, Geoff Combe, Paul Householder)	.08	.06	.03
607	Dave Palmer	.08	.06	.03
608	Greg Pryor	.08	.06	.03
609	Lynn McGlothen	.08	.06	.03
610	Darrell Porter	.10	.08	.04
611	Rick Matula	.08	.06	.03
612	Duane Kuiper	.08	.06	.03
613	Jim Anderson	.08	.06	.03
614	Dave Rozema	.08	.06	.03
615	Rick Dempsey	.12	.09	.05
616	Rick Wise	.10	.08	.04
617	Craig Reynolds	.08	.06	.03
618	John Milner	.08	.06	.03
619	Steve Henderson	.08	.06	.03
620	Dennis Eckersley	1.00	.70	.40
621	Tom Donohue	.08	.06	.03
622	Randy Moffitt	.08	.06	.03
623	Sal Bando	.12	.09	.05
624	Bob Welch	.70	.50	.30
625	Bill Buckner	.15	.11	.06
626	Tigers Future Stars (Dave Steffen, Jerry Ujdur, Roger Weaver)	.08	.06	.03
627	Luis Tiant	.20	.15	.08
628	Vic Correll	.08	.06	.03

		MT	NR MT	EX
629	Tony Armas	.12	.09	.05
630	Steve Carlton	1.50	1.25	.60
631	Ron Jackson	.08	.06	.03
632	Alan Bannister	.08	.06	.03
633	Bill Lee	.10	.08	.04
634	Doug Flynn	.08	.06	.03
635	Bobby Bonds	.15	.11	.06
636	Al Hrabosky	.10	.08	.04
637	Jerry Narron	.08	.06	.03
638	Checklist 606	.25	.20	.10
639	Carney Lansford	.15	.11	.06
640	Dave Parker	.60	.45	.25
641	Mark Belanger	.10	.08	.04
642	Vern Ruhle	.08	.06	.03
643	*Lloyd Moseby*	1.25	.90	.50
644	Ramon Aviles	.08	.06	.03
645	Rick Reuschel	.15	.11	.06
646	Marvis Foley	.08	.06	.03
647	Dick Drago	.08	.06	.03
648	Darrell Evans	.25	.20	.10
649	Manny Sarmiento	.08	.06	.03
650	Bucky Dent	.12	.09	.05
651	Pedro Guerrero	1.25	.90	.50
652	John Montague	.08	.06	.03
653	Bill Fahey	.08	.06	.03
654	Ray Burris	.08	.06	.03
655	Dan Driessen	.12	.09	.05
656	Jon Matlack	.10	.08	.04
657	Mike Cubbage	.08	.06	.03
658	Milt Wilcox	.08	.06	.03
659	Brewers Future Stars (John Flinn, Ed Romero, Ned Yost)	.08	.06	.03
660	Gary Carter	1.00	.70	.40
661	Orioles Team (Earl Weaver)	.30	.25	.12
662	Red Sox Team (Ralph Houk)	.30	.25	.12
663	Angels Team (Jim Fregosi)	.25	.20	.10
664	White Sox Team (Tony LaRussa)	.25	.20	.10
665	Indians Team (Dave Garcia)	.25	.20	.10
666	Tigers Team (Sparky Anderson)	.30	.25	.12
667	Royals Team (Jim Frey)	.25	.20	.10
668	Brewers Team (Bob Rodgers)	.25	.20	.10
669	Twins Team (John Goryl)	.25	.20	.10
670	Yankees Team (Gene Michael)	.35	.25	.14
671	A's Team (Billy Martin)	.30	.25	.12
672	Mariners Team (Maury Wills)	.25	.20	.10
673	Rangers Team (Don Zimmer)	.25	.20	.10
674	Blue Jays Team (Bobby Mattick)	.25	.20	.10
675	Braves Team (Bobby Cox)	.25	.20	.10
676	Cubs Team (Joe Amalfitano)	.25	.20	.10
677	Reds Team (John McNamara)	.25	.20	.10
678	Astros Team (Bill Virdon)	.25	.20	.10
679	Dodgers Team (Tom Lasorda)	.35	.25	.14
680	Expos Team (Dick Williams)	.25	.20	.10
681	Mets Team (Joe Torre)	.30	.25	.12
682	Phillies Team (Dallas Green)	.25	.20	.10
683	Pirates Team (Chuck Tanner)	.25	.20	.10
684	Cardinals Team (Whitey Herzog)	.30	.25	.12
685	Padres Team (Frank Howard)	.25	.20	.10
686	Giants Team (Dave Bristol)	.25	.20	.10
687	Jeff Jones	.08	.06	.03
688	Kiko Garcia	.08	.06	.03
689	Red Sox Future Stars *(Bruce Hurst,* Keith MacWhorter, *Reid Nichols)*	2.00	1.50	.80
690	Bob Watson	.10	.08	.04
691	Dick Ruthven	.08	.06	.03
692	Lenny Randle	.08	.06	.03
693	*Steve Howe*	.20	.15	.08
694	Bud Harrelson	.08	.06	.03
695	Kent Tekulve	.10	.08	.04
696	Alan Ashby	.08	.06	.03
697	Rick Waits	.08	.06	.03
698	Mike Jorgensen	.08	.06	.03
699	Glenn Abbott	.08	.06	.03
700	George Brett	4.00	3.00	1.50
701	Joe Rudi	.12	.09	.05
702	George Medich	.08	.06	.03
703	Alvis Woods	.08	.06	.03
704	Bill Travers	.08	.06	.03
705	Ted Simmons	.25	.20	.10
706	Dave Ford	.08	.06	.03
707	Dave Cash	.08	.06	.03
708	Doyle Alexander	.12	.09	.05
709	Alan Trammell	.30	.25	.12
710	Ron LeFlore	.08	.06	.03
711	Joe Ferguson	.08	.06	.03
712	Bill Bonham	.08	.06	.03
713	Bill North	.08	.06	.03
714	Pete Redfern	.08	.06	.03
715	Bill Madlock	.25	.20	.10
716	Glenn Borgmann	.08	.06	.03
717	Jim Barr	.08	.06	.03

		MT	NR MT	EX
718	Larry Biittner	.08	.06	.03
719	Sparky Lyle	.12	.09	.05
720	Fred Lynn	.35	.25	.14
721	Toby Harrah	.10	.08	.04
722	Joe Niekro	.20	.15	.08
723	Bruce Bochte	.08	.06	.03
724	Lou Piniella	.20	.15	.08
725	Steve Rogers	.10	.08	.04
726	Rick Monday	.15	.11	.06

1981 Topps Home Team 5 X 7 Photos

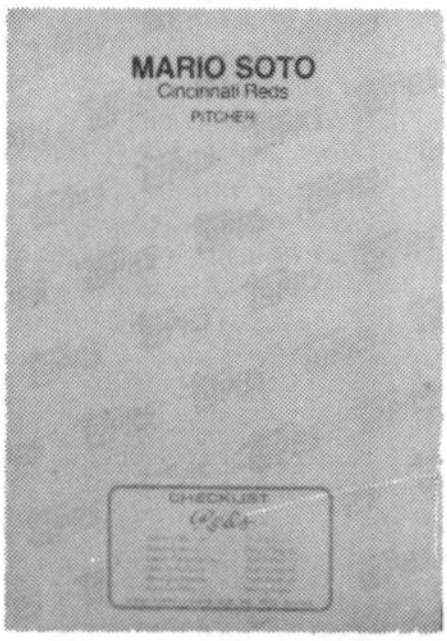

Once again testing the popularity of large cards, Topps issued 4-7/8" by 6-7/8" cards in two different sets. The Home Team cards feature a large color photo, facsimile autograph and white border on the front. Backs have the player's name, team, position and a checklist at the bottom. The 102 cards were sold in limited areas corresponding to the teams' geographic home. It was also possible to order the whole set by mail. Eleven teams are involved in the issue, with the number of players from each team ranging from 6 to 12. Although it is an attractive set featuring many stars, ready availability and many collectors' aversion to large cards keep prices relatively low today.

		MT	NR MT	EX
Complete Set:		40.00	30.00	16.00
Common Player:		.20	.15	.08
(1)	Dusty Baker	.25	.20	.10
(2)	Don Baylor	.40	.30	.15
(3)	Rick Burleson	.20	.15	.08
(4)	Rod Carew	.90	.70	.35
(5)	Ron Cey	.30	.25	.12
(6)	Steve Garvey	.90	.70	.35
(7)	Bobby Grich	.30	.25	.12
(8)	Butch Hobson	.20	.15	.08
(9)	Burt Hooton	.20	.15	.08
(10)	Steve Howe	.20	.15	.08
(11)	Dave Lopes	.25	.20	.10
(12)	Fred Lynn	.50	.40	.20
(13)	Rick Monday	.25	.20	.10
(14)	Jerry Reuss	.25	.20	.10
(15)	Bill Russell	.25	.20	.10
(16)	Reggie Smith	.30	.25	.12
(17)	Bob Welch	.40	.30	.15
(18)	Steve Yeager	.20	.15	.08
(19)	Buddy Bell	.30	.25	.12
(20)	Cesar Cedeno	.30	.25	.12
(21)	Jose Cruz	.30	.25	.12
(22)	Art Howe	.20	.15	.08
(23)	Jon Matlack	.20	.15	.08
(24)	Al Oliver	.40	.30	.15
(25)	Terry Puhl	.20	.15	.08
(26)	Mickey Rivers	.25	.20	.10
(27)	Nolan Ryan	.70	.50	.30
(28)	Jim Sundberg	.25	.20	.10
(29)	Don Sutton	.60	.45	.25
(30)	Bump Wills	.20	.15	.08
(31)	Tim Blackwell	.20	.15	.08
(32)	Bill Buckner	.40	.30	.15
(33)	Britt Burns	.20	.15	.08
(34)	Ivan DeJesus	.20	.15	.08
(35)	Rich Dotson	.25	.20	.10
(36)	Leon Durham	.25	.20	.10
(37)	Ed Farmer	.20	.15	.08
(38)	Lamar Johnson	.20	.15	.08
(39)	Dave Kingman	.40	.30	.15
(40)	Mike Krukow	.25	.20	.10
(41)	Ron LeFlore	.25	.20	.10
(42)	Chet Lemon	.25	.20	.10
(43)	Bob Molinaro	.20	.15	.08
(44)	Jim Morrison	.20	.15	.08
(45)	Wayne Nordhagen	.20	.15	.08
(46)	Ken Reitz	.20	.15	.08
(47)	Rick Reuschel	.30	.25	.12
(48)	Mike Tyson	.20	.15	.08
(49)	Neil Allen	.20	.15	.08
(50)	Rick Cerone	.20	.15	.08
(51)	Bucky Dent	.25	.20	.10
(52)	Doug Flynn	.20	.15	.08
(53)	Rich Gossage	.60	.45	.25
(54)	Ron Guidry	.60	.45	.25
(55)	Reggie Jackson	.90	.70	.35
(56)	Tommy John	.50	.40	.20
(57)	Ruppert Jones	.20	.15	.08
(58)	Rudy May	.20	.15	.08
(59)	Lee Mazzilli	.25	.20	.10
(60)	Graig Nettles	.40	.30	.15
(61)	Willie Randolph	.30	.25	.12
(62)	Rusty Staub	.40	.30	.15
(63)	Frank Taveras	.20	.15	.08
(64)	Alex Trevino	.20	.15	.08
(65)	Bob Watson	.25	.20	.10
(66)	Dave Winfield	.90	.70	.35
(67)	Bob Boone	.25	.20	.10
(68)	Larry Bowa	.40	.30	.15
(69)	Steve Carlton	.70	.50	.30
(70)	Greg Luzinski	.40	.30	.15
(71)	Garry Maddox	.25	.20	.10
(72)	Bake McBride	.20	.15	.08
(73)	Tug McGraw	.40	.30	.15
(74)	Pete Rose	1.75	1.25	.70
(75)	Dick Ruthven	.20	.15	.08
(76)	Mike Schmidt	.90	.70	.35
(77)	Manny Trillo	.25	.20	.10
(78)	Del Unser	.20	.15	.08
(79)	Tom Burgmeier	.20	.15	.08
(80)	Dennis Eckersley	.40	.30	.15
(81)	Dwight Evans	.50	.40	.20
(82)	Carlton Fisk	.60	.45	.25
(83)	Glenn Hoffman	.20	.15	.08
(84)	Carney Lansford	.30	.25	.12
(85)	Tony Perez	.50	.40	.20
(86)	Jim Rice	.70	.50	.30
(87)	Bob Stanley	.20	.15	.08
(88)	Dave Stapleton	.20	.15	.08
(89)	Frank Tanana	.25	.20	.10
(90)	Carl Yastrzemski	1.25	.90	.50
(91)	Johnny Bench	.90	.70	.35
(92)	Dave Collins	.25	.20	.10
(93)	Dave Concepcion	.40	.30	.15
(94)	Dan Driessen	.25	.20	.10
(95)	George Foster	.50	.40	.20
(96)	Ken Griffey	.30	.25	.12
(97)	Tom Hume	.20	.15	.08
(98)	Ray Knight	.25	.20	.10
(99)	Joe Nolan	.20	.15	.08
(100)	Ron Oester	.20	.15	.08
(101)	Tom Seaver	.70	.50	.30
(102)	Mario Soto	.25	.20	.10

1981 Topps National 5X7 Photos

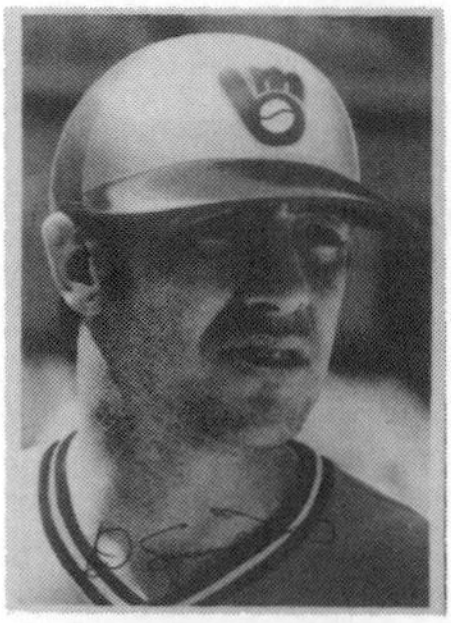

This set is the other half of Topps' efforts with large

cards in 1981. Measuring 4-7/8" by 6-7/8", the National photo issue was limited to 15 cards. They were sold in areas not covered by the Home Team sets and feature ten cards which carry the same photos as found in the Home Team set, but with no checklist on the backs. Five cards are unique to the National set: George Brett, Cecil Cooper, Jim Palmer, Dave Parker and Ted Simmons. With their wide distribution and a limited demand, there are currently plenty of these cards to meet the demand, thus keeping prices fairly low.

		MT	NR MT	EX
Complete Set:		8.00	6.00	3.25
Common Player:		.30	.25	.12
(1)	Buddy Bell	.30	.25	.12
(2)	Johnny Bench	.60	.45	.25
(3)	George Brett	.90	.70	.35
(4)	Rod Carew	.60	.45	.25
(5)	Cecil Cooper	.40	.30	.15
(6)	Steve Garvey	.70	.50	.30
(7)	Rich Gossage	.40	.30	.15
(8)	Reggie Jackson	.70	.50	.30
(9)	Jim Palmer	.70	.50	.30
(10)	Dave Parker	.60	.45	.25
(11)	Jim Rice	.50	.40	.20
(12)	Pete Rose	1.25	.90	.50
(13)	Mike Schmidt	.70	.50	.30
(14)	Tom Seaver	.60	.45	.25
(15)	Ted Simmons	.50	.40	.20

1981 Topps Scratchoffs

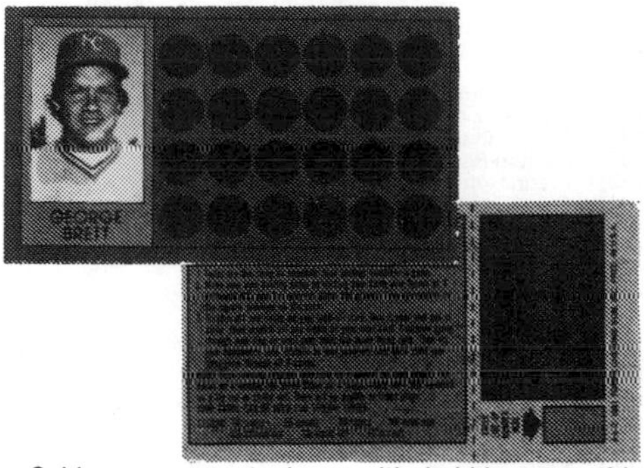

Sold as a separate issue with bubble gum, this 108-card set was issued in three-card panels that measure 3-1/4" by 5-1/4". Each individual card measures 1-13/16" by 3-1/4" and contains a small player photo alongside a series of black dots designed to be scratched off as part of a baseball game. Cards of National League players have a green back-grounds, while American League players have a red background. While there are 108 different players in the set, there are 144 possible panel combinations. An intact panel of three cards is valued approximately 20-25 percent more the sum of the individual cards.

		MT	NR MT	EX
Complete Set:		4.00	3.00	1.50
Common Player:		.02	.02	.01
1	George Brett	.12	.09	.05
2	Cecil Cooper	.04	.03	.02
3	Reggie Jackson	.12	.09	.05
4	Al Oliver	.04	.03	.02
5	Fred Lynn	.06	.05	.02
6	Tony Armas	.02	.02	.01
7	Ben Oglivie	.02	.02	.01
8	Tony Perez	.06	.05	.02
9	Eddie Murray	.10	.08	.04
10	Robin Yount	.08	.06	.03
11	Steve Kemp	.04	.03	.02
12	Joe Charboneau	.04	.03	.02
13	Jim Rice	.10	.08	.04
14	Lance Parrish	.08	.06	.03
15	John Mayberry	.02	.02	.01
16	Richie Zisk	.02	.02	.01
17	Ken Singleton	.04	.03	.02
18	Rod Carew	.10	.08	.04
19	Rick Manning	.02	.02	.01
20	Willie Wilson	.04	.03	.02
21	Buddy Bell	.04	.03	.02
22	Dave Revering	.02	.02	.01
23	Tom Paciorek	.02	.02	.01
24	Champ Summers	.02	.02	.01
25	Carney Lansford	.04	.03	.02
26	Lamar Johnson	.02	.02	.01
27	Willie Aikens	.02	.02	.01
28	Rick Cerone	.02	.02	.01
29	Al Bumbry	.02	.02	.01
30	Bruce Bochte	.02	.02	.01
31	Mickey Rivers	.02	.02	.01
32	Mike Hargrove	.02	.02	.01
33	John Castino	.02	.02	.01
34	Chet Lemon	.04	.03	.02
35	Paul Molitor	.06	.05	.02
36	Willie Randolph	.04	.03	.02
37	Rick Burleson	.02	.02	.01
38	Alan Trammell	.08	.06	.03
39	Rickey Henderson	.10	.08	.04
40	Dan Meyer	.02	.02	.01
41	Ken Landreaux	.02	.02	.01
42	Damaso Garcia	.02	.02	.01
43	Roy Smalley	.02	.02	.01
44	Otto Velez	.02	.02	.01
45	Sixto Lezcano	.02	.02	.01
46	Toby Harrah	.02	.02	.01
47	Frank White	.04	.03	.02
48	Dave Stapleton	.02	.02	.01
49	Steve Stone	.04	.03	.02
50	Jim Palmer	.08	.06	.03
51	Larry Gura	.02	.02	.01
52	Tommy John	.06	.05	.02
53	Mike Norris	.02	.02	.01
54	Ed Farmer	.02	.02	.01
55	Bill Buckner	.04	.03	.02
56	Steve Garvey	.10	.08	.04
57	Reggie Smith	.04	.03	.02
58	Bake McBride	.02	.02	.01
59	Dave Parker	.06	.05	.02
60	Mike Schmidt	.12	.09	.05
61	Bob Horner	.04	.03	.02
62	Pete Rose	.20	.15	.08
63	Ted Simmons	.06	.05	.02
64	Johnny Bench	.12	.09	.05
65	George Foster	.06	.05	.02
66	Gary Carter	.10	.08	.04
67	Keith Hernandez	.08	.06	.03
68	Ozzie Smith	.06	.05	.02
69	Dave Kingman	.06	.05	.02
70	Jack Clark	.06	.05	.02
71	Dusty Baker	.04	.03	.02
72	Dale Murphy	.12	.09	.05
73	Ron Cey	.04	.03	.02
74	Greg Luzinski	.04	.03	.02
75	Lee Mazzilli	.02	.02	.01
76	Gary Matthews	.04	.03	.02
77	Cesar Cedeno	.04	.03	.02
78	Warren Cromartie	.02	.02	.01
79	Steve Henderson	.02	.02	.01
80	Ellis Valentine	.02	.02	.01
81	Mike Easler	.02	.02	.01
82	Garry Templeton	.04	.03	.02
83	Jose Cruz	.04	.03	.02
84	Dave Collins	.02	.02	.01
85	George Hendrick	.02	.02	.01
86	Gene Richards	.02	.02	.01
87	Terry Whitfield	.02	.02	.01
88	Terry Puhl	.02	.02	.01
89	Larry Parrish	.04	.03	.02
90	Andre Dawson	.08	.06	.03
91	Ken Griffey	.04	.03	.02
92	Dave Lopes	.02	.02	.01
93	Doug Flynn	.02	.02	.01
94	Ivan DeJesus	.02	.02	.01
95	Dave Concepcion	.04	.03	.02
96	John Stearns	.02	.02	.01
97	Jerry Mumphrey	.02	.02	.01
98	Jerry Martin	.02	.02	.01
99	Art Howe	.02	.02	.01
100	Omar Moreno	.02	.02	.01
101	Ken Reitz	.02	.02	.01
102	Phil Garner	.02	.02	.01
103	Jerry Reuss	.04	.03	.02
104	Steve Carlton	.10	.08	.04
105	Jim Bibby	.02	.02	.01
106	Steve Rogers	.02	.02	.01
107	Tom Seaver	.10	.08	.04

		MT	NR MT	EX
108	Vida Blue	.04	.03	.02

1981 Topps Stickers

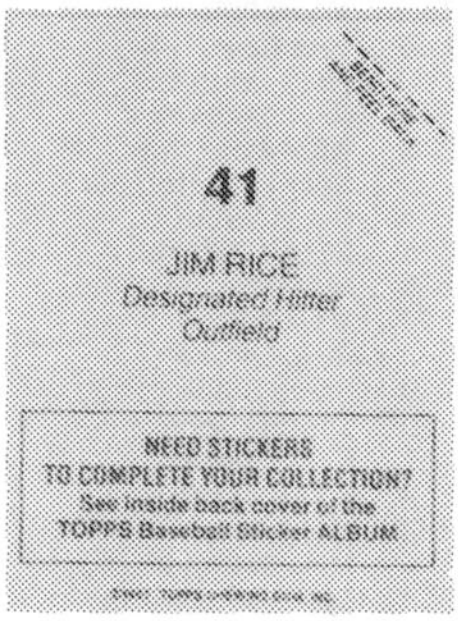

The 262 stickers in this full-color set measure 1-15/16" by 2-9/16" and are numbered on both the front and back. They were produced for Topps by the Panini Company of Italy. The set includes a series of "All-Star" stickers printed on silver or gold "foil". An album to house the stickers was also available.

	MT	NR MT	EX
Complete Set:	17.00	12.50	6.75
Common Player:	.03	.02	.01
Sticker Album:	.80	.60	.30

		MT	NR MT	EX
1	Steve Stone	.06	.05	.02
2	Tommy John, Mike Norris	.06	.05	.02
3	Rudy May	.03	.02	.01
4	Mike Norris	.03	.02	.01
5	Len Barker	.03	.02	.01
6	Mike Norris	.03	.02	.01
7	Dan Quisenberry	.06	.05	.02
8	Rich Gossage	.10	.08	.04
9	George Brett	.25	.20	.10
10	Cecil Cooper	.08	.06	.03
11	Reggie Jackson, Ben Oglivie	.06	.05	.02
12	Gorman Thomas	.06	.05	.02
13	Cecil Cooper	.08	.06	.03
14	George Brett, Ben Oglivie	.20	.15	.08
15	Rickey Henderson	.25	.20	.10
16	Willie Wilson	.08	.06	.03
17	Bill Buckner	.06	.05	.02
18	Keith Hernandez	.12	.09	.05
19	Mike Schmidt	.25	.20	.10
20	Bob Horner	.10	.08	.04
21	Mike Schmidt	.25	.20	.10
22	George Hendrick	.06	.05	.02
23	Ron LeFlore	.04	.03	.02
24	Omar Moreno	.03	.02	.01
25	Steve Carlton	.20	.15	.08
26	Joe Niekro	.06	.05	.02
27	Don Sutton	.10	.08	.04
28	Steve Carlton	.20	.15	.08
29	Steve Carlton	.20	.15	.08
30	Nolan Ryan	.20	.15	.08
31	Rollie Fingers, Tom Hume	.08	.06	.03
32	Bruce Sutter	.08	.06	.03
33	Ken Singleton	.06	.05	.02
34	Eddie Murray	.20	.15	.08
35	Al Bumbry	.03	.02	.01
36	Rich Dauer	.03	.02	.01
37	Scott McGregor	.04	.03	.02
38	Rick Dempsey	.04	.03	.02
39	Jim Palmer	.15	.11	.06
40	Steve Stone	.06	.05	.02
41	Jim Rice	.20	.15	.08
42	Fred Lynn	.10	.08	.04
43	Carney Lansford	.06	.05	.02
44	Tony Perez	.10	.08	.04
45	Carl Yastrzemski	.30	.25	.12
46	Carlton Fisk	.12	.09	.05
47	Dave Stapleton	.03	.02	.01
48	Dennis Eckersley	.06	.05	.02
49	Rod Carew	.20	.15	.08
50	Brian Downing	.04	.03	.02
51	Don Baylor	.08	.06	.03
52	Rick Burleson	.04	.03	.02
53	Bobby Grich	.06	.05	.02
54	Butch Hobson	.03	.02	.01
55	Andy Hassler	.03	.02	.01
56	Frank Tanana	.04	.03	.02
57	Chet Lemon	.04	.03	.02
58	Lamar Johnson	.03	.02	.01
59	Wayne Nordhagen	.03	.02	.01
60	Jim Morrison	.03	.02	.01
61	Bob Molinaro	.03	.02	.01
62	Rich Dotson	.04	.03	.02
63	Britt Burns	.03	.02	.01
64	Ed Farmer	.03	.02	.01
65	Toby Harrah	.04	.03	.02
66	Joe Charboneau	.04	.03	.02
67	Miguel Dilone	.03	.02	.01
68	Mike Hargrove	.04	.03	.02
69	Rick Manning	.03	.02	.01
70	Andre Thornton	.06	.05	.02
71	Ron Hassey	.03	.02	.01
72	Len Barker	.03	.02	.01
73	Lance Parrish	.12	.09	.05
74	Steve Kemp	.04	.03	.02
75	Alan Trammell	.15	.11	.06
76	Champ Summers	.03	.02	.01
77	Rick Peters	.03	.02	.01
78	Kirk Gibson	.15	.11	.06
79	Johnny Wockenfuss	.03	.02	.01
80	Jack Morris	.12	.09	.05
81	Willie Wilson	.08	.06	.03
82	George Brett	.25	.20	.10
83	Frank White	.06	.05	.02
84	Willie Aikens	.03	.02	.01
85	Clint Hurdle	.03	.02	.01
86	Hal McRae	.06	.05	.02
87	Dennis Leonard	.04	.03	.02
88	Larry Gura	.03	.02	.01
89	American League Pennant Winner (Kansas City Royals Team)	.04	.03	.02
90	American League Pennant Winner (Kansas City Royals Team)	.04	.03	.02
91	Paul Molitor	.10	.08	.04
92	Ben Oglivie	.04	.03	.02
93	Cecil Cooper	.08	.06	.03
94	Ted Simmons	.08	.06	.03
95	Robin Yount	.15	.11	.06
96	Gorman Thomas	.06	.05	.02
97	Mike Caldwell	.03	.02	.01
98	Moose Haas	.03	.02	.01
99	John Castino	.03	.02	.01
100	Roy Smalley	.03	.02	.01
101	Ken Landreaux	.03	.02	.01
102	Butch Wynegar	.04	.03	.02
103	Ron Jackson	.03	.02	.01
104	Jerry Koosman	.04	.03	.02
105	Roger Erickson	.03	.02	.01
106	Doug Corbett	.03	.02	.01
107	Reggie Jackson	.25	.20	.10
108	Willie Randolph	.04	.03	.02
109	Rick Cerone	.03	.02	.01
110	Bucky Dent	.04	.03	.02
111	Dave Winfield	.20	.15	.08
112	Ron Guidry	.12	.09	.05
113	Rich Gossage	.10	.08	.04
114	Tommy John	.10	.08	.04
115	Rickey Henderson	.25	.20	.10
116	Tony Armas	.04	.03	.02
117	Dave Revering	.03	.02	.01
118	Wayne Gross	.03	.02	.01
119	Dwayne Murphy	.04	.03	.02
120	Jeff Newman	.03	.02	.01
121	Rick Langford	.03	.02	.01
122	Mike Norris	.03	.02	.01
123	Bruce Bochte	.03	.02	.01
124	Tom Paciorek	.03	.02	.01
125	Dan Meyer	.03	.02	.01
126	Julio Cruz	.03	.02	.01
127	Richie Zisk	.04	.03	.02
128	Floyd Bannister	.04	.03	.02
129	Shane Rawley	.04	.03	.02
130	Buddy Bell	.06	.05	.02
131	Al Oliver	.06	.05	.02
132	Mickey Rivers	.04	.03	.02
133	Jim Sundberg	.03	.02	.01
134	Bump Wills	.03	.02	.01
135	Jon Matlack	.04	.03	.02
136	Danny Darwin	.03	.02	.01
137	Damaso Garcia	.04	.03	.02
138	Otto Velez	.03	.02	.01
139	John Mayberry	.04	.03	.02
140	Alfredo Griffin	.04	.03	.02
141	Alvis Woods	.03	.02	.01

		MT	NR MT	EX
142	Dave Stieb	.06	.05	.02
143	Jim Clancy	.04	.03	.02
144	Gary Matthews	.06	.05	.02
145	Bob Horner	.08	.06	.03
146	Dale Murphy	.25	.20	.10
147	Chris Chambliss	.04	.03	.02
148	Phil Niekro	.12	.09	.05
149	Glenn Hubbard	.03	.02	.01
150	Rick Camp	.03	.02	.01
151	Dave Kingman	.08	.06	.03
152	Bill Caudill	.03	.02	.01
153	Bill Buckner	.06	.05	.02
154	Barry Foote	.03	.02	.01
155	Mike Tyson	.03	.02	.01
156	Ivan DeJesus	.03	.02	.01
157	Rick Reuschel	.06	.05	.02
158	Ken Reitz	.03	.02	.01
159	George Foster	.08	.06	.03
160	Johnny Bench	.25	.20	.10
161	Dave Concepcion	.06	.05	.02
162	Dave Collins	.04	.03	.02
163	Ken Griffey	.06	.05	.02
164	Dan Driessen	.04	.03	.02
165	Tom Seaver	.20	.15	.08
166	Tom Hume	.03	.02	.01
167	Cesar Cedeno	.06	.05	.02
168	Rafael Landestoy	.03	.02	.01
169	Jose Cruz	.06	.05	.02
170	Art Howe	.03	.02	.01
171	Terry Puhl	.03	.02	.01
172	Joe Sambito	.03	.02	.01
173	Nolan Ryan	.20	.15	.08
174	Joe Niekro	.06	.05	.02
175	Dave Lopes	.04	.03	.02
176	Steve Garvey	.20	.15	.08
177	Ron Cey	.06	.05	.02
178	Reggie Smith	.06	.05	.02
179	Bill Russell	.04	.03	.02
180	Burt Hooton	.03	.02	.01
181	Jerry Reuss	.06	.05	.02
182	Dusty Baker	.04	.03	.02
183	Larry Parrish	.04	.03	.02
184	Gary Carter	.20	.15	.08
185	Rodney Scott	.03	.02	.01
186	Ellis Valentine	.03	.02	.01
187	Andre Dawson	.12	.09	.05
188	Warren Cromartie	.03	.02	.01
189	Chris Speier	.03	.02	.01
190	Steve Rogers	.03	.02	.01
191	Lee Mazzilli	.04	.03	.02
192	Doug Flynn	.03	.02	.01
193	Steve Henderson	.03	.02	.01
194	John Stearns	.03	.02	.01
195	Joel Youngblood	.03	.02	.01
196	Frank Taveras	.03	.02	.01
197	Pat Zachry	.03	.02	.01
198	Neil Allen	.03	.02	.01
199	Mike Schmidt	.25	.20	.10
200	Pete Rose	.40	.30	.15
201	Larry Bowa	.06	.05	.02
202	Bake McBride	.03	.02	.01
203	Bob Boone	.04	.03	.02
204	Garry Maddox	.04	.03	.02
205	Tug McGraw	.06	.05	.02
206	Steve Carlton	.20	.15	.08
207	National League Pennant Winner (Philadelphia Phillies Team)	.04	.03	.02
208	National League Pennant Winner (Philadelphia Phillies Team)	.04	.03	.02
209	Phil Garner	.04	.03	.02
210	Dave Parker	.12	.09	.05
211	Omar Moreno	.03	.02	.01
212	Mike Easler	.04	.03	.02
213	Bill Madlock	.06	.05	.02
214	Ed Ott	.03	.02	.01
215	Willie Stargell	.20	.15	.08
216	Jim Bibby	.03	.02	.01
217	Garry Templeton	.06	.05	.02
218	Sixto Lezcano	.03	.02	.01
219	Keith Hernandez	.12	.09	.05
220	George Hendrick	.04	.03	.02
221	Bruce Sutter	.08	.06	.03
222	Ken Oberkfell	.03	.02	.01
223	Tony Scott	.03	.02	.01
224	Darrell Porter	.04	.03	.02
225	Gene Richards	.03	.02	.01
226	Broderick Perkins	.03	.02	.01
227	Jerry Mumphrey	.03	.02	.01
228	Luis Salazar	.03	.02	.01
229	Jerry Turner	.03	.02	.01
230	Ozzie Smith	.10	.08	.04
231	John Curtis	.03	.02	.01
232	Rick Wise	.03	.02	.01
233	Terry Whitfield	.03	.02	.01
234	Jack Clark	.10	.08	.04
235	Darrell Evans	.08	.06	.03
236	Larry Herndon	.03	.02	.01
237	Milt May	.03	.02	.01
238	Greg Minton	.03	.02	.01
239	Vida Blue	.06	.05	.02
240	Eddie Whitson	.03	.02	.01
241	Cecil Cooper	.20	.15	.08
242	Willie Randolph	.20	.15	.08
243	George Brett	.40	.30	.15
244	Robin Yount	.30	.25	.12
245	Reggie Jackson	.40	.30	.15
246	Al Oliver	.20	.15	.08
247	Willie Wilson	.20	.15	.08
248	Rick Cerone	.15	.11	.06
249	Steve Stone	.15	.11	.06
250	Tommy John	.25	.20	.10
251	Rich Gossage	.25	.20	.10
252	Steve Garvey	.30	.25	.12
253	Phil Garner	.15	.11	.06
254	Mike Schmidt	.40	.30	.15
255	Garry Templeton	.20	.15	.08
256	George Hendrick	.15	.11	.06
257	Dave Parker	.25	.20	.10
258	Cesar Cedeno	.20	.15	.08
259	Gary Carter	.30	.25	.12
260	Jim Bibby	.15	.11	.06
261	Steve Carlton	.30	.25	.12
262	Tug McGraw	.20	.15	.08

1981 Topps Traded

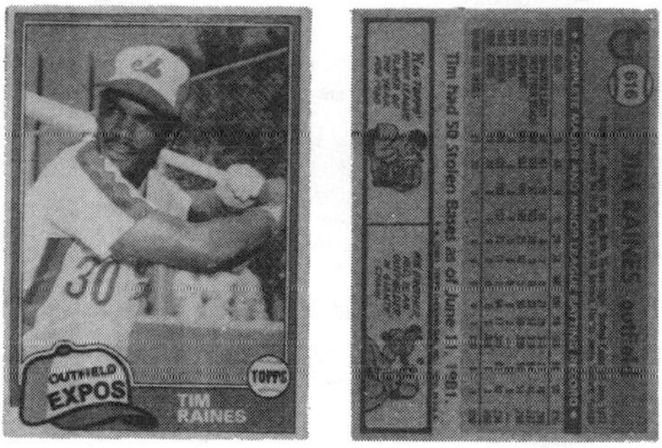

The 132 cards in this extension set are numbered from 727 to 858, technically making them a high-numbered series of the regular Topps set. The set was not packaged in gum packs, but rather placed in a specially designed red box and sold through baseball card dealers only. While many complained about the method, the fact remains, even at higher prices, the set has done well for its owners as it features not only mid-season trades, but also single-player rookie cards of some of the hottest prospects. The cards measure 2-1/2" by 3-1/2".

		MT	NR MT	EX
Complete Set:		30.00	22.00	12.00
Common Player:		.10	.08	.04
727	Danny Ainge(FC)	1.25	.90	.50
728	Doyle Alexander	.20	.15	.08
729	Gary Alexander	.10	.08	.04
730	Billy Almon	.10	.08	.04
731	Joaquin Andujar	.15	.11	.06
732	Bob Bailor	.10	.08	.04
733	Juan Beniquez	.10	.08	.04
734	Dave Bergman	.10	.08	.04
735	Tony Bernazard	.10	.08	.04
736	Larry Biittner	.10	.08	.04
737	Doug Bird	.10	.08	.04
738	Bert Blyleven	1.00	.70	.40
739	Mark Bomback	.10	.08	.04
740	Bobby Bonds	.20	.15	.08
741	Rick Bosetti	.10	.08	.04
742	Hubie Brooks	1.75	1.25	.70

		MT	NR MT	EX
743	Rick Burleson	.15	.11	.06
744	Ray Burris	.10	.08	.04
745	Jeff Burroughs	.15	.11	.06
746	Enos Cabell	.10	.08	.04
747	Ken Clay	.10	.08	.04
748	Mark Clear	.10	.08	.04
749	Larry Cox	.10	.08	.04
750	Hector Cruz	.10	.08	.04
751	Victor Cruz	.10	.08	.04
752	Mike Cubbage	.10	.08	.04
753	Dick Davis	.10	.08	.04
754	Brian Doyle	.10	.08	.04
755	Dick Drago	.10	.08	.04
756	Leon Durham	.25	.20	.10
757	Jim Dwyer	.10	.08	.04
758	Dave Edwards	.10	.08	.04
759	Jim Essian	.10	.08	.04
760	Bill Fahey	.10	.08	.04
761	Rollie Fingers	1.75	1.25	.70
762	Carlton Fisk	5.00	3.75	2.00
763	Barry Foote	.10	.08	.04
764	Ken Forsch	.10	.08	.04
765	Kiko Garcia	.10	.08	.04
766	Cesar Geronimo	.10	.08	.04
767	Gary Gray	.10	.08	.04
768	Mickey Hatcher	.15	.11	.06
769	Steve Henderson	.10	.08	.04
770	Marc Hill	.10	.08	.04
771	Butch Hobson	.10	.08	.04
772	Rick Honeycutt	.10	.08	.04
773	Roy Howell	.10	.08	.04
774	Mike Ivie	.10	.08	.04
775	Roy Lee Jackson	.10	.08	.04
776	Cliff Johnson	.10	.08	.04
777	Randy Jones	.15	.11	.06
778	Ruppert Jones	.10	.08	.04
779	Mick Kelleher	.10	.08	.04
780	Terry Kennedy	.20	.15	.08
781	Dave Kingman	.40	.30	.15
782	Bob Knepper	.15	.11	.06
783	Ken Kravec	.10	.08	.04
784	Bob Lacey	.10	.08	.04
785	Dennis Lamp	.10	.08	.04
786	Rafael Landestoy	.10	.08	.04
787	Ken Landreaux	.10	.08	.04
788	Carney Lansford	.80	.60	.30
789	Dave LaRoche	.10	.08	.04
790	Joe Lefebvre	.10	.08	.04
791	Ron LeFlore	.15	.11	.06
792	Randy Lerch	.10	.08	.04
793	Sixto Lezcano	.10	.08	.04
794	John Littlefield	.10	.08	.04
795	Mike Lum	.10	.08	.04
796	Greg Luzinski	.25	.20	.10
797	Fred Lynn	.50	.40	.20
798	Jerry Martin	.10	.08	.04
799	Buck Martinez	.10	.08	.04
800	Gary Matthews	.20	.15	.08
801	Mario Mendoza	.10	.08	.04
802	Larry Milbourne	.10	.08	.04
803	Rick Miller	.10	.08	.04
804	John Montefusco	.10	.08	.04
805	Jerry Morales	.10	.08	.04
806	Jose Morales	.10	.08	.04
807	Joe Morgan	2.00	1.50	.80
808	Jerry Mumphrey	.10	.08	.04
809	Gene Nelson(FC)	.30	.25	.12
810	Ed Ott	.10	.08	.04
811	Bob Owchinko	.10	.08	.04
812	Gaylord Perry	1.75	1.25	.60
813	Mike Phillips	.10	.08	.04
814	Darrell Porter	.15	.11	.06
815	Mike Proly	.10	.08	.04
816	Tim Raines	12.00	9.00	4.75
817	Lenny Randle	.10	.08	.04
818	Doug Rau	.10	.08	.04
819	Jeff Reardon	3.00	2.25	1.25
820	Ken Reitz	.10	.08	.04
821	Steve Renko	.10	.08	.04
822	Rick Reuschel	.25	.20	.10
823	Dave Revering	.10	.08	.04
824	Dave Roberts	.10	.08	.04
825	Leon Roberts	.10	.08	.04
826	Joe Rudi	.20	.15	.08
827	Kevin Saucier	.10	.08	.04
828	Tony Scott	.10	.08	.04
829	Bob Shirley	.10	.08	.04
830	Ted Simmons	.40	.30	.15
831	Lary Sorensen	.10	.08	.04
832	Jim Spencer	.10	.08	.04
833	Harry Spilman	.10	.08	.04
834	Fred Stanley	.10	.08	.04
835	Rusty Staub	.30	.25	.12
836	Bill Stein	.10	.08	.04
837	Joe Strain	.10	.08	.04
838	Bruce Sutter	.50	.40	.20
839	Don Sutton	1.50	1.25	.60
840	Steve Swisher	.10	.08	.04
841	Frank Tanana	.20	.15	.08
842	Gene Tenace	.15	.11	.06
843	Jason Thompson	.10	.08	.04
844	Dickie Thon	.15	.11	.06
845	Bill Travers	.10	.08	.04
846	Tom Underwood	.10	.08	.04
847	John Urrea	.10	.08	.04
848	Mike Vail	.10	.08	.04
849	Ellis Valentine	.10	.08	.04
850	Fernando Valenzuela	4.00	3.00	1.50
851	Pete Vuckovich	.15	.11	.06
852	Mark Wagner	.10	.08	.04
853	Bob Walk	.50	.40	.20
854	Claudell Washington	.15	.11	.06
855	Dave Winfield	4.00	3.00	1.50
856	Geoff Zahn	.10	.08	.04
857	Richie Zisk	.15	.11	.06
858	Checklist 727-858	.10	.08	.04

1982 Topps

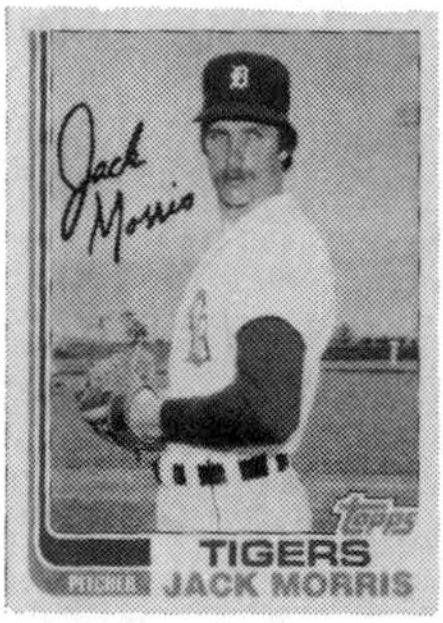

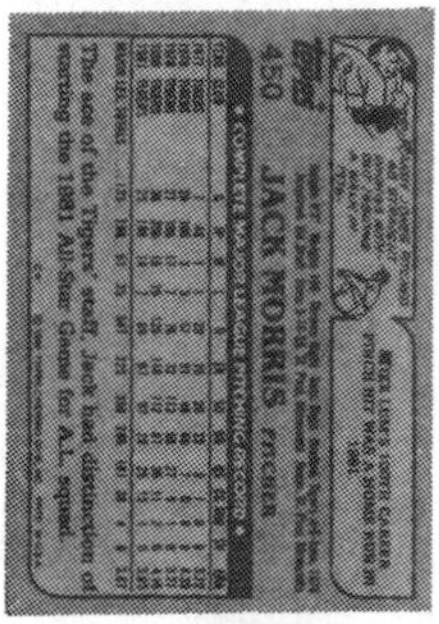

At 792 cards, this was the largest issue produced up to that time, eliminating the need for double-printed cards. The 2-1/2" by 3-1/2" cards feature a front color photo with a pair of stripes down the left side. Under the player's photo are found his name, team and position. A facsimile autograph runs across the front of the picture. Specialty cards include great performances of the previous season, All-Stars, statistical leaders and "In Action" cards (indicated by "IA" in listings below). Managers and hitting/pitching leaders have cards, while rookies are shown as "Future Stars" on group cards.

		MT	NR MT	EX
Complete Set:		125.00	90.00	50.00
Common Player:		.08	.06	.03
1	1981 Highlight (Steve Carlton)	.50	.40	.20
2	1981 Highlight (Ron Davis)	.08	.06	.03
3	1981 Highlight (Tim Raines)	.30	.25	.12
4	1981 Highlight (Pete Rose)	.70	.50	.30
5	1981 Highlight (Nolan Ryan)	1.00	.70	.40
6	1981 Highlight (Fernando Valenzuela)	.30	.25	.12
7	Scott Sanderson	.08	.06	.03
8	Rich Dauer	.08	.06	.03
9	Ron Guidry	.35	.25	.14
10	Ron Guidry IA	.15	.11	.06
11	Gary Alexander	.08	.06	.03
12	Moose Haas	.08	.06	.03
13	Lamar Johnson	.08	.06	.03
14	Steve Howe	.10	.08	.04
15	Ellis Valentine	.08	.06	.03
16	Steve Comer	.08	.06	.03
17	Darrell Evans	.25	.20	.10
18	Fernando Arroyo	.08	.06	.03
19	Ernie Whitt	.10	.08	.04
20	Garry Maddox	.12	.09	.05
21	Orioles Future Stars (Bob Bonner, *Cal Ripken*, Jeff Schneider)	70.00	52.00	27.00

		MT	NR MT	EX
22	Jim Beattie	.08	.06	.03
23	Willie Hernandez	.10	.08	.04
24	Dave Frost	.08	.06	.03
25	Jerry Remy	.08	.06	.03
26	Jorge Orta	.08	.06	.03
27	Tom Herr	.12	.09	.05
28	John Urrea	.08	.06	.03
29	Dwayne Murphy	.10	.08	.04
30	Tom Seaver	1.25	.90	.50
31	Tom Seaver IA	.30	.25	.12
32	Gene Garber	.08	.06	.03
33	Jerry Morales	.08	.06	.03
34	Joe Sambito	.08	.06	.03
35	Willie Aikens	.08	.06	.03
36	Rangers Batting & Pitching Ldrs. (George Medich, Al Oliver)	.12	.09	.05
37	Dan Graham	.08	.06	.03
38	Charlie Lea	.08	.06	.03
39	Lou Whitaker	.40	.30	.15
40	Dave Parker	.35	.25	.14
41	Dave Parker IA	.15	.11	.06
42	Rick Sofield	.08	.06	.03
43	Mike Cubbage	.08	.06	.03
44	Britt Burns	.08	.06	.03
45	Rick Cerone	.08	.06	.03
46	Jerry Augustine	.08	.06	.03
47	Jeff Leonard	.15	.11	.06
48	Bobby Castillo	.08	.06	.03
49	Alvis Woods	.08	.06	.03
50	Buddy Bell	.15	.11	.06
51	Cubs Future Stars (*Jay Howell*, Carlos Lezcano, Ty Waller)	.40	.30	.15
52	Larry Andersen	.08	.06	.03
53	Greg Gross	.08	.06	.03
54	Ron Hassey	.08	.06	.03
55	Rick Burleson	.10	.08	.04
56	Mark Littell	.08	.06	.03
57	Craig Reynolds	.08	.06	.03
58	John D'Acquisto	.08	.06	.03
59	*Rich Gedman*(FC)	.50	.40	.20
60	Tony Armas	.12	.09	.05
61	Tommy Boggs	.08	.06	.03
62	Mike Tyson	.08	.06	.03
63	Mario Soto	.10	.08	.04
64	Lynn Jones	.08	.06	.03
65	Terry Kennedy	.12	.09	.05
66	Astros Batting & Pitching Ldrs. (Art Howe, Nolan Ryan)	.25	.20	.10
67	Rich Gale	.08	.06	.03
68	Roy Howell	.08	.06	.03
69	Al Williams	.08	.06	.03
70	Tim Raines	3.00	2.25	1.25
71	Roy Lee Jackson	.08	.06	.03
72	Rick Auerbach	.08	.06	.03
73	Buddy Solomon	.08	.06	.03
74	Bob Clark	.08	.06	.03
75	Tommy John	.30	.25	.12
76	Greg Pryor	.08	.06	.03
77	Miguel Dilone	.08	.06	.03
78	George Medich	.08	.06	.03
79	Bob Bailor	.08	.06	.03
80	Jim Palmer	1.00	.70	.40
81	Jim Palmer IA	.30	.25	.12
82	Bob Welch	.60	.45	.25
83	Yankees Future Stars (*Steve Balboni, Andy McGaffigan, Andre Robertson*)(FC)	.25	.20	.10
84	Rennie Stennett	.08	.06	.03
85	Lynn McGlothen	.08	.06	.03
86	Dane Iorg	.08	.06	.03
87	Matt Keough	.08	.06	.03
88	Biff Pocoroba	.08	.06	.03
89	Steve Henderson	.08	.06	.03
90	Nolan Ryan	5.00	3.75	2.00
91	Carney Lansford	.12	.09	.05
92	Brad Havens	.08	.06	.03
93	Larry Hisle	.10	.08	.04
94	Andy Hassler	.08	.06	.03
95	Ozzie Smith	2.00	1.50	.80
96	Royals Batting & Pitching Ldrs. (George Brett, Larry Gura)	.35	.25	.14
97	Paul Moskau	.08	.06	.03
98	Terry Bulling	.08	.06	.03
99	Barry Bonnell	.08	.06	.03
100	Mike Schmidt	2.50	2.00	1.00
101	Mike Schmidt IA	.70	.50	.30
102	Dan Briggs	.08	.06	.03
103	Bob Lacey	.08	.06	.03
104	Rance Mulliniks	.08	.06	.03
105	Kirk Gibson	1.25	.90	.50
106	Enrique Romo	.08	.06	.03
107	Wayne Krenchicki	.08	.06	.03
108	Bob Sykes	.08	.06	.03
109	Dave Revering	.08	.06	.03
110	Carlton Fisk	.50	.40	.20
111	Carlton Fisk IA	.15	.11	.06
112	Billy Sample	.08	.06	.03
113	Steve McCatty	.08	.06	.03
114	Ken Landreaux	.08	.06	.03
115	Gaylord Perry	.50	.40	.20
116	Jim Wohlford	.08	.06	.03
117	Rawly Eastwick	.08	.06	.03
118	Expos Future Stars (*Terry Francona*, Brad Mills, *Bryn Smith*)(FC)	.40	.30	.15
119	Joe Pittman	.08	.06	.03
120	Gary Lucas	.08	.06	.03
121	Ed Lynch	.08	.06	.03
122	Jamie Easterly	.08	.06	.03
123	Danny Goodwin	.08	.06	.03
124	Reid Nichols	.08	.06	.03
125	Danny Ainge	.20	.15	.08
126	Braves Batting & Pitching Ldrs. (Rick Mahler, Claudell Washington)	.10	.08	.04
127	Lonnie Smith	.10	.08	.04
128	Frank Pastore	.08	.06	.03
129	Checklist 1-132	.12	.09	.05
130	Julio Cruz	.08	.06	.03
131	Stan Bahnsen	.08	.06	.03
132	Lee May	.10	.08	.04
133	Pat Underwood	.08	.06	.03
134	Dan Ford	.08	.06	.03
135	Andy Rincon	.08	.06	.03
136	Lenn Sakata	.08	.06	.03
137	George Cappuzzello	.08	.06	.03
138	Tony Pena	.20	.15	.08
139	Jeff Jones	.08	.06	.03
140	Ron LeFlore	.10	.08	.04
141	Indians Future Stars (Chris Bando, Tom Brennan, *Von Hayes*)(FC)	1.50	1.25	.60
142	Dave LaRoche	.08	.06	.03
143	Mookie Wilson	.12	.09	.05
144	Fred Breining	.08	.06	.03
145	Bob Horner	.20	.15	.08
146	Mike Griffin	.08	.06	.03
147	Denny Walling	.08	.06	.03
148	Mickey Klutts	.08	.06	.03
149	Pat Putnam	.08	.06	.03
150	Ted Simmons	.20	.15	.08
151	Dave Edwards	.08	.06	.03
152	Ramon Aviles	.08	.06	.03
153	Roger Erickson	.08	.06	.03
154	Dennis Werth	.08	.06	.03
155	Otto Velez	.08	.06	.03
156	A's Batting & Pitching Ldrs. (Rickey Henderson, Steve McCatty)	.25	.20	.10
157	Steve Crawford	.08	.06	.03
158	Brian Downing	.12	.09	.05
159	Larry Biittner	.08	.06	.03
160	Luis Tiant	.15	.11	.06
161	Batting Leaders (Carney Lansford, Bill Madlock)	.20	.15	.08
162	Home Run Leaders (Tony Armas, Dwight Evans, Bobby Grich, Eddie Murray, Mike Schmidt)	.35	.25	.14
163	Runs Batted In Leaders (Eddie Murray, Mike Schmidt)	.40	.30	.15
164	Stolen Base Leaders (Rickey Henderson, Tim Raines)	.35	.25	.14
165	Victory Leaders (Denny Martinez, Steve McCatty, Jack Morris, Tom Seaver, Pete Vuckovich)	.20	.15	.08
166	Strikeout Leaders (Len Barker, Fernando Valenzuela)	.20	.15	.08
167	Earned Run Avg. Leaders (Steve McCatty, Nolan Ryan)	.20	.15	.08
168	Leading Relievers (Rollie Fingers, Bruce Sutter)	.20	.15	.08
169	Charlie Leibrandt	.12	.09	.05
170	Jim Bibby	.08	.06	.03
171	Giants Future Stars (*Bob Brenly, Chili Davis*, Bob Tufts)	2.50	2.00	1.00
172	Bill Gullickson	.10	.08	.04
173	Jamie Quirk	.08	.06	.03
174	Dave Ford	.08	.06	.03
175	Jerry Mumphrey	.08	.06	.03
176	Dewey Robinson	.08	.06	.03
177	John Ellis	.08	.06	.03
178	Dyar Miller	.08	.06	.03
179	Steve Garvey	.80	.60	.30
180	Steve Garvey IA	.40	.30	.15
181	Silvio Martinez	.08	.06	.03
182	Larry Herndon	.10	.08	.04
183	Mike Proly	.08	.06	.03

		MT	NR MT	EX
184	Mick Kelleher	.08	.06	.03
185	Phil Niekro	.50	.40	.20
186	Cardinals Batting & Pitching Ldrs. (Bob Forsch, Keith Hernandez)	.25	.20	.10
187	Jeff Newman	.08	.06	.03
188	Randy Martz	.08	.06	.03
189	Glenn Hoffman	.08	.06	.03
190	J.R. Richard	.12	.09	.05
191	*Tim Wallach*(FC)	2.00	1.50	.80
192	Broderick Perkins	.08	.06	.03
193	Darrell Jackson	.08	.06	.03
194	Mike Vail	.08	.06	.03
195	Paul Molitor	.35	.25	.14
196	Willie Upshaw	.12	.09	.05
197	Shane Rawley	.15	.11	.06
198	Chris Speier	.08	.06	.03
199	Don Aase	.08	.06	.03
200	George Brett	2.00	1.50	.80
201	George Brett IA	1.00	.70	.40
202	Rick Manning	.08	.06	.03
203	Blue Jays Future Stars *(Jesse Barfield,* Brian Milner, Boomer Wells)	3.00	2.25	1.25
204	Gary Roenicke	.08	.06	.03
205	Neil Allen	.08	.06	.03
206	Tony Bernazard	.08	.06	.03
207	Rod Scurry	.08	.06	.03
208	Bobby Murcer	.15	.11	.06
209	Gary Lavelle	.08	.06	.03
210	Keith Hernandez	.60	.45	.25
211	Dan Petry	.10	.08	.04
212	Mario Mendoza	.08	.06	.03
213	*Dave Stewart*(FC)	8.00	6.00	3.25
214	Brian Asselstine	.08	.06	.03
215	Mike Krukow	.10	.08	.04
216	White Sox Batting & Pitching Ldrs. (Dennis Lamp, Chet Lemon)	.10	.08	.04
217	Bo McLaughlin	.08	.06	.03
218	Dave Roberts	.08	.06	.03
219	John Curtis	.08	.06	.03
220	Manny Trillo	.10	.08	.04
221	Jim Slaton	.08	.06	.03
222	Butch Wynegar	.08	.06	.03
223	Lloyd Moseby	.20	.15	.08
224	Bruce Bochte	.08	.06	.03
225	Mike Torrez	.10	.08	.04
226	Checklist 133-264	.12	.09	.05
227	Ray Burris	.08	.06	.03
228	Sam Mejias	.08	.06	.03
229	Geoff Zahn	.08	.06	.03
230	Willie Wilson	.20	.15	.08
231	Phillies Future Stars *(Mark Davis, Bob Dernier, Ozzie Virgil)*(FC)	.60	.45	.25
232	Terry Crowley	.08	.06	.03
233	Duane Kuiper	.08	.06	.03
234	Ron Hodges	.08	.06	.03
235	Mike Easler	.10	.08	.04
236	John Martin	.08	.06	.03
237	Rusty Kuntz	.08	.06	.03
238	Kevin Saucier	.08	.06	.03
239	Jon Matlack	.10	.08	.04
240	Bucky Dent	.12	.09	.05
241	Bucky Dent IA	.10	.08	.04
242	Milt May	.08	.06	.03
243	Bob Owchinko	.08	.06	.03
244	Rufino Linares	.08	.06	.03
245	Ken Reitz	.08	.06	.03
246	Mets Batting & Pitching Ldrs. (Hubie Brooks, Mike Scott)	.20	.15	.08
247	Pedro Guerrero	.90	.70	.35
248	Frank LaCorte	.08	.06	.03
249	Tim Flannery	.08	.06	.03
250	Tug McGraw	.15	.11	.06
251	Fred Lynn	.30	.25	.12
252	Fred Lynn IA	.15	.11	.06
253	Chuck Baker	.08	.06	.03
254	*Jorge Bell*(FC)	12.00	9.00	4.75
255	Tony Perez	.30	.25	.12
256	Tony Perez IA	.15	.11	.06
257	Larry Harlow	.08	.06	.03
258	Bo Diaz	.10	.08	.04
259	Rodney Scott	.08	.06	.03
260	Bruce Sutter	.20	.15	.08
261	Tigers Future Stars (Howard Bailey, Marty Castillo, Dave Rucker)	.08	.06	.03
262	Doug Bair	.08	.06	.03
263	Victor Cruz	.08	.06	.03
264	Dan Quisenberry	.20	.15	.08
265	Al Bumbry	.10	.08	.04
266	Rick Leach	.15	.11	.06
267	Kurt Bevacqua	.08	.06	.03
268	Rickey Keeton	.08	.06	.03

		MT	NR MT	EX
269	Jim Essian	.08	.06	.03
270	Rusty Staub	.15	.11	.06
271	Larry Bradford	.08	.06	.03
272	Bump Wills	.08	.06	.03
273	Doug Bird	.08	.06	.03
274	*Bob Ojeda*(FC)	.70	.50	.30
275	Bob Watson	.10	.08	.04
276	Angels Batting & Pitching Ldrs. (Rod Carew, Ken Forsch)	.25	.20	.10
277	Terry Puhl	.08	.06	.03
278	John Littlefield	.08	.06	.03
279	Bill Russell	.10	.08	.04
280	Ben Oglivie	.10	.08	.04
281	John Verhoeven	.08	.06	.03
282	Ken Macha	.08	.06	.03
283	Brian Allard	.08	.06	.03
284	Bob Grich	.15	.11	.06
285	Sparky Lyle	.12	.09	.05
286	Bill Fahey	.08	.06	.03
287	Alan Bannister	.08	.06	.03
288	Garry Templeton	.12	.09	.05
289	Bob Stanley	.08	.06	.03
290	Ken Singleton	.12	.09	.05
291	Pirates Future Stars (Vance Law, Bob Long, *Johnny Ray*)(FC)	.60	.45	.25
292	Dave Palmer	.08	.06	.03
293	Rob Picciolo	.08	.06	.03
294	Mike LaCoss	.08	.06	.03
295	Jason Thompson	.08	.06	.03
296	Bob Walk	.12	.09	.05
297	Clint Hurdle	.08	.06	.03
298	Danny Darwin	.08	.06	.03
299	Steve Trout	.08	.06	.03
300	Reggie Jackson	1.00	.70	.40
301	Reggie Jackson IA	.50	.40	.20
302	Doug Flynn	.08	.06	.03
303	Bill Caudill	.08	.06	.03
304	Johnnie LeMaster	.08	.06	.03
305	Don Sutton	.50	.40	.20
306	Don Sutton IA	.25	.20	.10
307	Randy Bass	.08	.06	.03
308	Charlie Moore	.08	.06	.03
309	Pete Redfern	.08	.06	.03
310	Mike Hargrove	.08	.06	.03
311	Dodgers Batting & Pitching Leaders (Dusty Baker, Burt Hooton)	.12	.09	.05
312	Lenny Randle	.08	.06	.03
313	John Harris	.08	.06	.03
314	Buck Martinez	.08	.06	.03
315	Burt Hooton	.10	.08	.04
316	Steve Braun	.08	.06	.03
317	Dick Ruthven	.08	.06	.03
318	Mike Heath	.08	.06	.03
319	Dave Rozema	.08	.06	.03
320	Chris Chambliss	.10	.08	.04
321	Chris Chambliss IA	.10	.08	.04
322	Garry Hancock	.08	.06	.03
323	Bill Lee	.10	.08	.04
324	Steve Dillard	.08	.06	.03
325	Jose Cruz	.15	.11	.06
326	Pete Falcone	.08	.06	.03
327	Joe Nolan	.08	.06	.03
328	Ed Farmer	.08	.06	.03
329	U.L. Washington	.08	.06	.03
330	Rick Wise	.10	.08	.04
331	Benny Ayala	.08	.06	.03
332	Don Robinson	.10	.08	.04
333	Brewers Future Stars *(Frank DiPino,* Marshall Edwards, Chuck Porter)	.12	.09	.05
334	Aurelio Rodriguez	.10	.08	.04
335	Jim Sundberg	.10	.08	.04
336	Mariners Batting & Pitching Ldrs. (Glenn Abbott, Tom Paciorek)	.10	.08	.04
337	Pete Rose AS	.80	.60	.30
338	Dave Lopes AS	.12	.09	.05
339	Mike Schmidt AS	.60	.45	.25
340	Dave Concepcion AS	.12	.09	.05
341	Andre Dawson AS	.25	.20	.10
342a	George Foster AS (no autograph)	2.25	1.75	.90
342b	George Foster AS (autograph on front)	.40	.30	.15
343	Dave Parker AS	.20	.15	.08
344	Gary Carter AS	.35	.25	.14
345	Fernando Valenzuela AS	.35	.25	.14
346	Tom Seaver AS	.35	.25	.14
347	Bruce Sutter AS	.12	.09	.05
348	Derrel Thomas	.08	.06	.03
349	George Frazier	.08	.06	.03
350	Thad Bosley	.08	.06	.03
351	Reds Future Stars (Scott Brown, Geoff Combe, Paul Householder)	.08	.06	.03

		MT	NR MT	EX
352	Dick Davis	.08	.06	.03
353	Jack O'Connor	.08	.06	.03
354	Roberto Ramos	.08	.06	.03
355	Dwight Evans	.25	.20	.10
356	Denny Lewallyn	.08	.06	.03
357	Butch Hobson	.08	.06	.03
358	Mike Parrott	.08	.06	.03
359	Jim Dwyer	.08	.06	.03
360	Len Barker	.10	.08	.04
361	Rafael Landestoy	.08	.06	.03
362	Jim Wright	.08	.06	.03
363	Bob Molinaro	.08	.06	.03
364	Doyle Alexander	.12	.09	.05
365	Bill Madlock	.20	.15	.08
366	Padres Batting & Pitching Ldrs. (Juan Eichelberger, Luis Salazar)	.10	.08	.04
367	Jim Kaat	.25	.20	.10
368	Alex Trevino	.08	.06	.03
369	Champ Summers	.08	.06	.03
370	Mike Norris	.08	.06	.03
371	Jerry Don Gleaton	.08	.06	.03
372	Luis Gomez	.08	.06	.03
373	*Gene Nelson*	.15	.11	.06
374	Tim Blackwell	.08	.06	.03
375	Dusty Baker	.12	.09	.05
376	Chris Welsh	.08	.06	.03
377	Kiko Garcia	.08	.06	.03
378	Mike Caldwell	.08	.06	.03
379	Rob Wilfong	.08	.06	.03
380	Dave Stieb	.25	.20	.10
381	Red Sox Future Stars (Bruce Hurst, Dave Schmidt, Julio Valdez)	.25	.20	.10
382	Joe Simpson	.08	.06	.03
383a	Pascual Perez (no position on front)	30.00	22.00	12.00
383b	Pascual Perez (position on front)	.12	.09	.05
384	Keith Moreland	.12	.09	.05
385	Ken Forsch	.08	.06	.03
386	Jerry White	.08	.06	.03
387	Tom Veryzer	.08	.06	.03
388	Joe Rudi	.12	.09	.05
389	George Vukovich	.08	.06	.03
390	Eddie Murray	1.25	.90	.50
391	Dave Tobik	.08	.06	.03
392	Rick Bosetti	.08	.06	.03
393	Al Hrabosky	.10	.08	.04
394	Checklist 265-396	.12	.09	.05
395	Omar Moreno	.08	.06	.03
396	Twins Batting & Pitching Ldrs. (Fernando Arroyo, John Castino)	.10	.08	.04
397	Ken Brett	.10	.08	.04
398	Mike Squires	.08	.06	.03
399	Pat Zachry	.08	.06	.03
400	Johnny Bench	1.50	1.25	.60
401	Johnny Bench IA	.40	.30	.15
402	Bill Stein	.08	.06	.03
403	Jim Tracy	.08	.06	.03
404	Dickie Thon	.10	.08	.04
405	Rick Reuschel	.15	.11	.06
406	Al Holland	.08	.06	.03
407	Danny Boone	.08	.06	.03
408	Ed Romero	.08	.06	.03
409	Don Cooper	.08	.06	.03
410	Ron Cey	.15	.11	.06
411	Ron Cey IA	.10	.08	.04
412	Luis Leal	.08	.06	.03
413	Dan Meyer	.08	.06	.03
414	Elias Sosa	.08	.06	.03
415	Don Baylor	.15	.11	.06
416	Marty Bystrom	.08	.06	.03
417	Pat Kelly	.08	.06	.03
418	Rangers Future Stars (John Butcher, Bobby Johnson, *Dave Schmidt*)(FC)	.20	.15	.08
419	Steve Stone	.12	.09	.05
420	George Hendrick	.10	.08	.04
421	Mark Clear	.08	.06	.03
422	Cliff Johnson	.08	.06	.03
423	Stan Papi	.08	.06	.03
424	Bruce Benedict	.08	.06	.03
425	John Candelaria	.12	.09	.05
426	Orioles Batting & Pitching Ldrs. (Eddie Murray, Sammy Stewart)	.35	.25	.14
427	Ron Oester	.08	.06	.03
428	Lamarr Hoyt (LaMarr)	.08	.06	.03
429	John Wathan	.10	.08	.04
430	Vida Blue	.15	.11	.06
431	Vida Blue IA	.10	.08	.04
432	Mike Scott	.25	.20	.10
433	Alan Ashby	.08	.06	.03
434	Joe Lefebvre	.08	.06	.03
435	Robin Yount	2.00	1.50	.80

		MT	NR MT	EX
436	Joe Strain	.08	.06	.03
437	Juan Berenguer	.08	.06	.03
438	Pete Mackanin	.08	.06	.03
439	*Dave Righetti*(FC)	2.50	2.00	1.00
440	Jeff Burroughs	.10	.08	.04
441	Astros Future Stars (Danny Heep, Billy Smith, Bobby Sprowl)	.08	.06	.03
442	Bruce Kison	.08	.06	.03
443	Mark Wagner	.08	.06	.03
444	Terry Forster	.10	.08	.04
445	Larry Parrish	.12	.09	.05
446	Wayne Garland	.08	.06	.03
447	Darrell Porter	.10	.08	.04
448	Darrell Porter IA	.10	.08	.04
449	*Luis Aguayo*(FC)	.12	.09	.05
450	Jack Morris	.50	.40	.20
451	Ed Miller	.08	.06	.03
452	*Lee Smith*(FC)	1.25	.90	.50
453	Art Howe	.08	.06	.03
454	Rick Langford	.08	.06	.03
455	Tom Burgmeier	.08	.06	.03
456	Cubs Batting & Pitching Ldrs. (Bill Buckner, Randy Martz)	.15	.11	.06
457	Tim Stoddard	.08	.06	.03
458	Willie Montanez	.08	.06	.03
459	Bruce Berenyi	.08	.06	.03
460	Jack Clark	.30	.25	.12
461	Rich Dotson	.12	.09	.05
462	Dave Chalk	.08	.06	.03
463	Jim Kern	.08	.06	.03
464	Juan Bonilla	.08	.06	.03
465	Lee Mazzilli	.10	.08	.04
466	Randy Lerch	.08	.06	.03
467	Mickey Hatcher	.10	.08	.04
468	Floyd Bannister	.12	.09	.05
469	Ed Ott	.08	.06	.03
470	John Mayberry	.10	.08	.04
471	Royals Future Stars (*Atlee Hammaker*, Mike Jones, Darryl Motley)	.25	.20	.10
472	Oscar Gamble	.10	.08	.04
473	Mike Stanton	.08	.06	.03
474	Ken Oberkfell	.08	.06	.03
475	Alan Trammell	.50	.40	.20
476	Brian Kingman	.08	.06	.03
477	Steve Yeager	.08	.06	.03
478	Ray Searage	.08	.06	.03
479	Rowland Office	.08	.06	.03
480	Steve Carlton	1.00	.70	.40
481	Steve Carlton IA	.40	.30	.15
482	Glenn Hubbard	.10	.08	.04
483	Gary Woods	.08	.06	.03
484	Ivan DeJesus	.08	.06	.03
485	Kent Tekulve	.10	.08	.04
486	Yankees Batting & Pitching Ldrs. (Tommy John, Jerry Mumphrey)	.20	.15	.08
487	Bob McClure	.08	.06	.03
488	Ron Jackson	.08	.06	.03
489	Rick Dempsey	.10	.08	.04
490	Dennis Eckersley	.20	.15	.08
491	Checklist 397-528	.12	.09	.05
492	Joe Price	.08	.06	.03
493	Chet Lemon	.10	.08	.04
494	Hubie Brooks	.20	.15	.08
495	Dennis Leonard	.10	.08	.04
496	Johnny Grubb	.08	.06	.03
497	Jim Anderson	.08	.06	.03
498	Dave Bergman	.08	.06	.03
499	Paul Mirabella	.08	.06	.03
500	Rod Carew	1.00	.70	.40
501	Rod Carew IA	.40	.30	.15
502	Braves Future Stars (*Steve Bedrosian, Brett Butler*, Larry Owen)	3.00	2.25	1.25
503	Julio Gonzalez	.08	.06	.03
504	Rick Peters	.08	.06	.03
505	Graig Nettles	.25	.20	.10
506	Graig Nettles IA	.12	.09	.05
507	Terry Harper	.08	.06	.03
508	*Jody Davis*(FC)	.25	.20	.10
509	Harry Spilman	.08	.06	.03
510	Fernando Valenzuela	1.50	1.25	.60
511	Ruppert Jones	.08	.06	.03
512	Jerry Dybzinski	.08	.06	.03
513	Rick Rhoden	.12	.09	.05
514	Joe Ferguson	.08	.06	.03
515	Larry Bowa	.20	.15	.08
516	Larry Bowa IA	.12	.09	.05
517	Mark Brouhard	.08	.06	.03
518	Garth Iorg	.08	.06	.03
519	Glenn Adams	.08	.06	.03
520	Mike Flanagan	.12	.09	.05
521	Billy Almon	.08	.06	.03

		MT	NR MT	EX
522	Chuck Rainey	.08	.06	.03
523	Gary Gray	.08	.06	.03
524	Tom Hausman	.08	.06	.03
525	Ray Knight	.12	.09	.05
526	Expos Batting & Pitching Ldrs. (Warren Cromartie, Bill Gullickson)	.10	.08	.04
527	John Henry Johnson	.08	.06	.03
528	Matt Alexander	.08	.06	.03
529	Allen Ripley	.08	.06	.03
530	Dickie Noles	.08	.06	.03
531	A's Future Stars (Rich Bordi, Mark Budaska, Kelvin Moore)	.08	.06	.03
532	Toby Harrah	.10	.08	.04
533	Joaquin Andujar	.10	.08	.04
534	Dave McKay	.08	.06	.03
535	Lance Parrish	.50	.40	.20
536	Rafael Ramirez	.10	.08	.04
537	Doug Capilla	.08	.06	.03
538	Lou Piniella	.15	.11	.06
539	Vern Ruhle	.08	.06	.03
540	Andre Dawson	2.00	1.50	.80
541	Barry Evans	.08	.06	.03
542	Ned Yost	.08	.06	.03
543	Bill Robinson	.08	.06	.03
544	Larry Christenson	.08	.06	.03
545	Reggie Smith	.15	.11	.06
546	Reggie Smith IA	.10	.08	.04
547	Rod Carew AS	.35	.25	.14
548	Willie Randolph AS	.12	.09	.05
549	George Brett AS	.60	.45	.25
550	Bucky Dent AS	.12	.09	.05
551	Reggie Jackson AS	.50	.40	.20
552	Ken Singleton AS	.12	.09	.05
553	Dave Winfield AS	.40	.30	.15
554	Carlton Fisk AS	.20	.15	.08
555	Scott McGregor AS	.12	.09	.05
556	Jack Morris AS	.20	.15	.08
557	Rich Gossage AS	.20	.15	.08
558	John Tudor	.30	.25	.12
559	Indians Batting & Pitching Ldrs. (Bert Blyleven, Mike Hargrove)	.15	.11	.06
560	Doug Corbett	.08	.06	.03
561	Cardinals Future Stars (Glenn Brummer, Luis DeLeon, Gene Roof)	.08	.06	.03
562	Mike O'Berry	.08	.06	.03
563	Ross Baumgarten	.08	.06	.03
564	Doug DeCinces	.15	.11	.06
565	Jackson Todd	.08	.06	.03
566	Mike Jorgensen	.08	.06	.03
567	Bob Babcock	.08	.06	.03
568	Joe Pettini	.08	.06	.03
569	Willie Randolph	.15	.11	.06
570	Willie Randolph IA	.10	.08	.04
571	Glenn Abbott	.08	.06	.03
572	Juan Beniquez	.08	.06	.03
573	Rick Waits	.08	.06	.03
574	Mike Ramsey	.08	.06	.03
575	Al Cowens	.08	.06	.03
576	Giants Batting & Pitching Ldrs. (Vida Blue, Milt May)	.15	.11	.06
577	Rick Monday	.12	.09	.05
578	Shooty Babitt	.08	.06	.03
579	*Rick Mahler*(FC)	.30	.25	.12
580	Bobby Bonds	.15	.11	.06
581	Ron Reed	.08	.06	.03
582	Luis Pujols	.08	.06	.03
583	Tippy Martinez	.08	.06	.03
584	Hosken Powell	.08	.06	.03
585	Rollie Fingers	.30	.25	.12
586	Rollie Fingers IA	.15	.11	.06
587	Tim Lollar	.08	.06	.03
588	Dale Berra	.08	.06	.03
589	Dave Stapleton	.08	.06	.03
590	Al Oliver	.20	.15	.08
591	Al Oliver IA	.10	.08	.04
592	Craig Swan	.08	.06	.03
593	Billy Smith	.08	.06	.03
594	Renie Martin	.08	.06	.03
595	Dave Collins	.10	.08	.04
596	Damaso Garcia	.08	.06	.03
597	Wayne Nordhagen	.08	.06	.03
598	Bob Galasso	.08	.06	.03
599	White Sox Future Stars (Jay Loviglio, Reggie Patterson, Leo Sutherland)	.08	.06	.03
600	Dave Winfield	.60	.45	.25
601	Sid Monge	.08	.06	.03
602	Freddie Patek	.08	.06	.03
603	Rich Hebner	.08	.06	.03
604	Orlando Sanchez	.08	.06	.03
605	Steve Rogers	.10	.08	.04
606	Blue Jays Batting & Pitching Ldrs. (John Mayberry, Dave Stieb)	.15	.11	.06

		MT	NR MT	EX
607	Leon Durham	.10	.08	.04
608	Jerry Royster	.08	.06	.03
609	Rick Sutcliffe	.25	.20	.10
610	Rickey Henderson	8.00	6.00	3.25
611	Joe Niekro	.20	.15	.08
612	Gary Ward	.10	.08	.04
613	Jim Gantner	.10	.08	.04
614	Juan Eichelberger	.08	.06	.03
615	Bob Boone	.12	.09	.05
616	Bob Boone IA	.10	.08	.04
617	Scott McGregor	.10	.08	.04
618	Tim Foli	.08	.06	.03
619	Bill Campbell	.08	.06	.03
620	Ken Griffey	.15	.11	.06
621	Ken Griffey IA	.10	.08	.04
622	Dennis Lamp	.08	.06	.03
623	Mets Future Stars (Ron Gardenhire, *Terry Leach, Tim Leary*)(FC)	.50	.40	.20
624	Fergie Jenkins	.60	.45	.25
625	Hal McRae	.15	.11	.06
626	Randy Jones	.10	.08	.04
627	Enos Cabell	.08	.06	.03
628	Bill Travers	.08	.06	.03
629	Johnny Wockenfuss	.08	.06	.03
630	Joe Charboneau	.10	.08	.04
631	Gene Tenace	.10	.08	.04
632	Bryan Clark	.08	.06	.03
633	Mitchell Page	.08	.06	.03
634	Checklist 529-660	.12	.09	.05
635	Ron Davis	.10	.08	.04
636	Phillies Batting & Pitching Ldrs. (Steve Carlton, Pete Rose)	.50	.40	.20
637	Rick Camp	.08	.06	.03
638	John Milner	.08	.06	.03
639	Ken Kravec	.08	.06	.03
640	Cesar Cedeno	.15	.11	.06
641	Steve Mura	.08	.06	.03
642	Mike Scioscia	.10	.08	.04
643	Pete Vuckovich	.10	.08	.04
644	John Castino	.08	.06	.03
645	Frank White	.12	.09	.05
646	Frank White IA	.10	.08	.04
647	Warren Brusstar	.08	.06	.03
648	Jose Morales	.08	.06	.03
649	Ken Clay	.08	.06	.03
650	Carl Yastrzemski	1.50	1.25	.60
651	Carl Yastrzemski IA	.60	.45	.25
652	Steve Nicosia	.08	.06	.03
653	Angels Future Stars (*Tom Brunansky*, Luis Sanchez, Daryl Sconiers)	2.00	1.50	.80
654	Jim Morrison	.08	.06	.03
655	Joel Youngblood	.08	.06	.03
656	Eddie Whitson	.08	.06	.03
657	Tom Poquette	.08	.06	.03
658	Tito Landrum	.08	.06	.03
659	Fred Martinez	.08	.06	.03
660	Dave Concepcion	.15	.11	.06
661	Dave Concepcion IA	.10	.08	.04
662	Luis Salazar	.08	.06	.03
663	Hector Cruz	.08	.06	.03
664	Dan Spillner	.08	.06	.03
665	Jim Clancy	.12	.09	.05
666	Tigers Batting & Pitching Ldrs. (Steve Kemp, Dan Petry)	.15	.11	.06
667	Jeff Reardon	.25	.20	.10
668	Dale Murphy	2.00	1.50	.80
669	Larry Milbourne	.08	.06	.03
670	Steve Kemp	.12	.09	.05
671	Mike Davis	.10	.08	.04
672	Bob Knepper	.12	.09	.05
673	Keith Drumright	.08	.06	.03
674	Dave Goltz	.10	.08	.04
675	Cecil Cooper	.20	.15	.08
676	Sal Butera	.08	.06	.03
677	Alfredo Griffin	.12	.09	.05
678	Tom Paciorek	.08	.06	.03
679	Sammy Stewart	.08	.06	.03
680	Gary Matthews	.12	.09	.05
681	Dodgers Future Stars (*Mike Marshall*, Ron Roenicke, *Steve Sax*)(FC)	5.00	3.75	2.00
682	Jesse Jefferson	.08	.06	.03
683	Phil Garner	.10	.08	.04
684	Harold Baines	.70	.50	.30
685	Bert Blyleven	.20	.15	.08
686	Gary Allenson	.08	.06	.03
687	Greg Minton	.08	.06	.03
688	Leon Roberts	.08	.06	.03
689	Lary Sorensen	.08	.06	.03
690	Dave Kingman	.20	.15	.08
691	Dan Schatzeder	.08	.06	.03
692	Wayne Gross	.08	.06	.03

		MT	NR MT	EX
693	Cesar Geronimo	.08	.06	.03
694	Dave Wehrmeister	.08	.06	.03
695	Warren Cromartie	.08	.06	.03
696	Pirates Batting & Pitching Ldrs. (Bill Madlock, Buddy Solomon)	.15	.11	.06
697	John Montefusco	.08	.06	.03
698	Tony Scott	.08	.06	.03
699	Dick Tidrow	.08	.06	.03
700	George Foster	.25	.20	.10
701	George Foster IA	.12	.09	.05
702	Steve Renko	.08	.06	.03
703	Brewers Batting & Pitching Ldrs. (Cecil Cooper, Pete Vuckovich)	.15	.11	.06
704	Mickey Rivers	.10	.08	.04
705	Mickey Rivers IA	.10	.08	.04
706	Barry Foote	.08	.06	.03
707	Mark Bomback	.08	.06	.03
708	Gene Richards	.08	.06	.03
709	Don Money	.08	.06	.03
710	Jerry Reuss	.12	.09	.05
711	Mariners Future Stars (Dave Edler, *Dave Henderson*, Reggie Walton)	5.00	3.75	2.00
712	Denny Martinez	.10	.08	.04
713	Del Unser	.08	.06	.03
714	Jerry Koosman	.12	.09	.05
715	Willie Stargell	.70	.50	.30
716	Willie Stargell IA	.30	.25	.12
717	Rick Miller	.08	.06	.03
718	Charlie Hough	.12	.09	.05
719	Jerry Narron	.08	.06	.03
720	Greg Luzinski	.20	.15	.08
721	Greg Luzinski IA	.12	.09	.05
722	Jerry Martin	.08	.06	.03
723	Junior Kennedy	.08	.06	.03
724	Dave Rosello	.08	.06	.03
725	Amos Otis	.10	.08	.04
726	Amos Otis IA	.10	.08	.04
727	Sixto Lezcano	.08	.06	.03
728	Aurelio Lopez	.08	.06	.03
729	Jim Spencer	.08	.06	.03
730	Gary Carter	.70	.50	.30
731	Padres Future Stars (Mike Armstrong, Doug Gwosdz, Fred Kuhaulua)	.08	.06	.03
732	Mike Lum	.08	.06	.03
733	Larry McWilliams	.08	.06	.03
734	Mike Ivie	.08	.06	.03
735	Rudy May	.08	.06	.03
736	Jerry Turner	.08	.06	.03
737	Reggie Cleveland	.08	.06	.03
738	Dave Engle	.08	.06	.03
739	Joey McLaughlin	.08	.06	.03
740	Dave Lopes	.12	.09	.05
741	Dave Lopes IA	.10	.08	.04
742	Dick Drago	.08	.06	.03
743	John Stearns	.08	.06	.03
744	*Mike Witt*(FC)	.80	.60	.30
745	Bake McBride	.08	.06	.03
746	Andre Thornton	.12	.09	.05
747	John Lowenstein	.08	.06	.03
748	Marc Hill	.08	.06	.03
749	Bob Shirley	.08	.06	.03
750	Jim Rice	.70	.50	.30
751	Rick Honeycutt	.08	.06	.03
752	Lee Lacy	.08	.06	.03
753	Tom Brookens	.08	.06	.03
754	Joe Morgan	.70	.50	.30
755	Joe Morgan IA	.20	.15	.08
756	Reds Batting & Pitching Ldrs. (Ken Griffey, Tom Seaver)	.30	.25	.12
757	Tom Underwood	.08	.06	.03
758	Claudell Washington	.12	.09	.05
759	Paul Splittorff	.08	.06	.03
760	Bill Buckner	.15	.11	.06
761	Dave Smith	.12	.09	.05
762	Mike Phillips	.08	.06	.03
763	Tom Hume	.08	.06	.03
764	Steve Swisher	.08	.06	.03
765	Gorman Thomas	.12	.09	.05
766	Twins Future Stars (Lenny Faedo, *Kent Hrbek, Tim Laudner*)(FC)	5.00	3.75	2.00
767	Roy Smalley	.08	.06	.03
768	Jerry Garvin	.08	.06	.03
769	Richie Zisk	.10	.08	.04
770	Rich Gossage	.35	.25	.14
771	Rich Gossage IA	.15	.11	.06
772	Bert Campaneris	.12	.09	.05
773	John Denny	.08	.06	.03
774	Jay Johnstone	.10	.08	.04
775	Bob Forsch	.10	.08	.04
776	Mark Belanger	.10	.08	.04
777	Tom Griffin	.08	.06	.03
778	Kevin Hickey	.08	.06	.03
779	Grant Jackson	.08	.06	.03
780	Pete Rose	2.25	1.75	.90
781	Pete Rose IA	1.00	.70	.40
782	Frank Taveras	.08	.06	.03
783	*Greg Harris*(FC)	.15	.11	.06
784	Milt Wilcox	.08	.06	.03
785	Dan Driessen	.10	.08	.04
786	Red Sox Batting & Pitching Ldrs. (Carney Lansford, Mike Torrez)	.12	.09	.05
787	Fred Stanley	.08	.06	.03
788	Woodie Fryman	.10	.08	.04
789	Checklist 661-792	.12	.09	.05
790	Larry Gura	.08	.06	.03
791	Bobby Brown	.08	.06	.03
792	Frank Tanana	.12	.09	.05

1982 Topps Insert Stickers

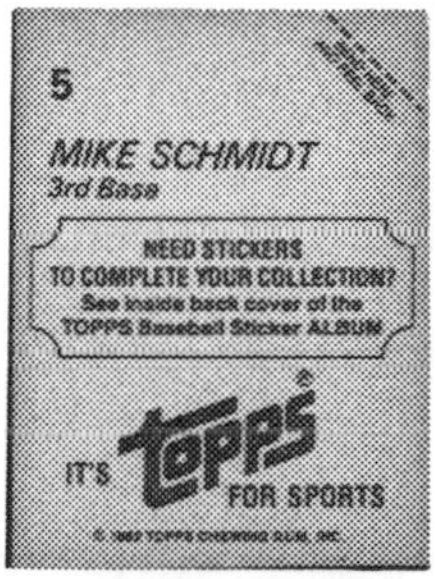

This 48-player set is actually an abbreviated version of the regular 1982 Topps sticker set with different backs. Used to promote the 1982 sticker set, Topps inserted these stickers in its baseball card wax packs. They are identical to the regular 1982 stickers, except for the backs, which advertise that the Topps sticker album will be "Coming Soon." The 48 stickers retain the same numbers used in the regular sticker set, resulting in the smaller set being skip-numbered.

		MT	NR MT	EX
Complete Set:		2.00	1.50	.80
Common Player:		.03	.02	.01
17	Chris Chambliss	.04	.03	.02
21	Bruce Benedict	.03	.02	.01
25	Leon Durham	.06	.05	.02
29	Bill Buckner	.06	.05	.02
33	Dave Collins	.04	.03	.02
37	Dave Concepcion	.06	.05	.02
41	Nolan Ryan	.15	.11	.06
45	Bob Knepper	.04	.03	.02
49	Ken Landreaux	.03	.02	.01
53	Burt Hooton	.03	.02	.01
57	Andre Dawson	.12	.09	.05
61	Gary Carter	.20	.15	.08
65	Joel Youngblood	.03	.02	.01
69	Ellis Valentine	.03	.02	.01
73	Garry Maddox	.04	.03	.02
77	Bob Boone	.04	.03	.02
81	Omar Moreno	.03	.02	.01
85	Willie Stargell	.20	.15	.08
89	Ken Oberkfell	.03	.02	.01
93	Darrell Porter	.04	.03	.02
97	Juan Eichelberger	.03	.02	.01
101	Luis Salazar	.03	.02	.01
105	Enos Cabell	.03	.02	.01
109	Larry Herndon	.03	.02	.01
143	Scott McGregor	.04	.03	.02
148	Mike Flanagan	.06	.05	.02
151	Mike Torrez	.04	.03	.02
156	Carney Lansford	.06	.05	.02
161	Fred Lynn	.10	.08	.04
166	Rich Dotson	.04	.03	.02
171	Tony Bernazard	.03	.02	.01
176	Bo Diaz	.04	.03	.02
181	Alan Trammell	.15	.11	.06

		MT	NR MT	EX
186	Milt Wilcox	.03	.02	.01
191	Dennis Leonard	.04	.03	.02
196	Willie Aikens	.03	.02	.01
201	Ted Simmons	.08	.06	.03
206	Hosken Powell	.03	.02	.01
211	Roger Erickson	.03	.02	.01
215	Graig Nettles	.06	.05	.02
216	Reggie Jackson	.25	.20	.10
221	Rickey Henderson	.25	.20	.10
226	Cliff Johnson	.03	.02	.01
231	Jeff Burroughs	.04	.03	.02
236	Tom Paciorek	.03	.02	.01
241	Pat Putnam	.03	.02	.01
246	Lloyd Moseby	.06	.05	.02
251	Barry Bonnell	.03	.02	.01

A player's name in *italic* indicates a rookie card. An (FC) indicates a player's first card for that particular card company.

1982 Topps Stickers

The 1982 Topps sticker set is complete at 260 stickers and includes another series of "foil" All-Stars. The stickers measure 1-15/16" by 2-9/16" and feature full-color photos surrounded by a red border for American League players or a blue border for National League players. They are numbered on both the front and back and were designed to be mounted in a special album.

		MT	NR MT	EX
Complete Set:		15.00	11.00	6.00
Common Player:		.03	.02	.01
Sticker Album:		.80	.60	.30
1	Bill Madlock	.06	.05	.02
2	Carney Lansford	.06	.05	.02
3	Mike Schmidt	.25	.20	.10
4	Tony Armas, Dwight Evans, Bobby Grich, Eddie Murray	.12	.09	.05
5	Mike Schmidt	.25	.20	.10
6	Eddie Murray	.20	.15	.08
7	Tim Raines	.03	.02	.01
8	Rickey Henderson	.25	.20	.10
9	Tom Seaver	.20	.15	.08
10	Denny Martinez, Steve McCatty, Jack Morris, Pete Vuckovich	.06	.05	.02
11	Fernando Valenzuela	.15	.11	.06
12	Len Barker	.03	.02	.01
13	Nolan Ryan	.20	.15	.08
14	Steve McCatty	.03	.02	.01
15	Bruce Sutter	.08	.06	.03
16	Rollie Fingers	.10	.08	.04
17	Chris Chambliss	.04	.03	.02
18	Bob Horner	.08	.06	.03
19	Dale Murphy	.25	.20	.10
20	Phil Niekro	.12	.09	.05
21	Bruce Benedict	.03	.02	.01
22	Claudell Washington	.04	.03	.02
23	Glenn Hubbard	.03	.02	.01
24	Rick Camp	.03	.02	.01
25	Leon Durham	.06	.05	.02
26	Ken Reitz	.03	.02	.01
27	Dick Tidrow	.03	.02	.01
28	Tim Blackwell	.03	.02	.01
29	Bill Buckner	.06	.05	.02
30	Steve Henderson	.03	.02	.01
31	Mike Krukow	.04	.03	.02
32	Ivan DeJesus	.03	.02	.01
33	Dave Collins	.04	.03	.02
34	Ron Oester	.03	.02	.01

		MT	NR MT	EX
35	Johnny Bench	.25	.20	.10
36	Tom Seaver	.20	.15	.08
37	Dave Concepcion	.06	.05	.02
38	Ken Griffey	.06	.05	.02
39	Ray Knight	.06	.05	.02
40	George Foster	.08	.06	.03
41	Nolan Ryan	.20	.15	.08
42	Terry Puhl	.03	.02	.01
43	Art Howe	.03	.02	.01
44	Jose Cruz	.06	.05	.02
45	Bob Knepper	.06	.05	.02
46	Craig Reynolds	.03	.02	.01
47	Cesar Cedeno	.06	.05	.02
48	Alan Ashby	.03	.02	.01
49	Ken Landreaux	.03	.02	.01
50	Fernando Valenzuela	.15	.11	.06
51	Ron Cey	.06	.05	.02
52	Dusty Baker	.04	.03	.02
53	Burt Hooton	.04	.03	.02
54	Steve Garvey	.20	.15	.08
55	Pedro Guerrero	.12	.09	.05
56	Jerry Reuss	.06	.05	.02
57	Andre Dawson	.12	.09	.05
58	Chris Speier	.03	.02	.01
59	Steve Rogers	.03	.02	.01
60	Warren Cromartie	.03	.02	.01
61	Gary Carter	.20	.15	.08
62	Tim Raines	.20	.15	.08
63	Scott Sanderson	.03	.02	.01
64	Larry Parrish	.06	.05	.02
65	Joel Youngblood	.03	.02	.01
66	Neil Allen	.03	.02	.01
67	Lee Mazzilli	.04	.03	.02
68	Hubie Brooks	.06	.05	.02
69	Ellis Valentine	.03	.02	.01
70	Doug Flynn	.03	.02	.01
71	Pat Zachry	.03	.02	.01
72	Dave Kingman	.08	.06	.03
73	Garry Maddox	.04	.03	.02
74	Mike Schmidt	.25	.20	.10
75	Steve Carlton	.20	.15	.08
76	Manny Trillo	.04	.03	.02
77	Bob Boone	.04	.03	.02
78	Pete Rose	.40	.30	.15
79	Gary Matthews	.04	.03	.02
80	Larry Bowa	.06	.05	.02
81	Omar Moreno	.03	.02	.01
82	Rick Rhoden	.04	.03	.02
83	Bill Madlock	.06	.05	.02
84	Mike Easler	.04	.03	.02
85	Willie Stargell	.20	.15	.08
86	Jim Bibby	.03	.02	.01
87	Dave Parker	.12	.09	.05
88	Tim Foli	.03	.02	.01
89	Ken Oberkfell	.03	.02	.01
90	Bob Forsch	.04	.03	.02
91	George Hendrick	.04	.03	.02
92	Keith Hernandez	.12	.09	.05
93	Darrell Porter	.04	.03	.02
94	Bruce Sutter	.08	.06	.03
95	Sixto Lezcano	.03	.02	.01
96	Garry Templeton	.04	.03	.02
97	Juan Eichelberger	.03	.02	.01
98	Broderick Perkins	.03	.02	.01
99	Ruppert Jones	.03	.02	.01
100	Terry Kennedy	.04	.03	.02
101	Luis Salazar	.03	.02	.01
102	Gary Lucas	.03	.02	.01
103	Gene Richards	.03	.02	.01
104	Ozzie Smith	.10	.08	.04
105	Enos Cabell	.03	.02	.01
106	Jack Clark	.10	.08	.04
107	Greg Minton	.03	.02	.01
108	Johnnie LeMaster	.03	.02	.01
109	Larry Herndon	.03	.02	.01
110	Milt May	.03	.02	.01
111	Vida Blue	.06	.05	.02
112	Darrell Evans	.08	.06	.03
113	Len Barker	.03	.02	.01
114	Julio Cruz	.03	.02	.01
115	Billy Martin	.08	.06	.03
116	Tim Raines	.20	.15	.08
117	Pete Rose	.40	.30	.15
118	Bill Stein	.03	.02	.01
119	Fernando Valenzuela	.15	.11	.06
120	Carl Yastrzemski	.25	.20	.10
121	Pete Rose	.50	.40	.20
122	Manny Trillo	.15	.11	.06
123	Mike Schmidt	.40	.30	.15
124	Dave Concepcion	.20	.15	.08
125	Andre Dawson	.25	.20	.10

		MT	NR MT	EX
126	George Foster	.20	.15	.08
127	Dave Parker	.25	.20	.10
128	Gary Carter	.30	.25	.12
129	Steve Carlton	.30	.25	.12
130	Bruce Sutter	.25	.20	.10
131	Rod Carew	.40	.30	.15
132	Jerry Remy	.15	.11	.06
133	George Brett	.40	.30	.15
134	Rick Burleson	.15	.11	.06
135	Dwight Evans	.25	.20	.10
136	Ken Singleton	.20	.15	.08
137	Dave Winfield	.30	.25	.12
138	Carlton Fisk	.25	.20	.10
139	Jack Morris	.25	.20	.10
140	Rich Gossage	.25	.20	.10
141	Al Bumbry	.04	.03	.02
142	Doug DeCinces	.06	.05	.02
143	Scott McGregor	.04	.03	.02
144	Ken Singleton	.06	.05	.02
145	Eddie Murray	.20	.15	.08
146	Jim Palmer	.15	.11	.06
147	Rich Dauer	.03	.02	.01
148	Mike Flanagan	.04	.03	.02
149	Jerry Remy	.03	.02	.01
150	Jim Rice	.20	.15	.08
151	Mike Torrez	.04	.03	.02
152	Tony Perez	.10	.08	.04
153	Dwight Evans	.10	.08	.04
154	Mark Clear	.03	.02	.01
155	Carl Yastrzemski	.25	.20	.10
156	Carney Lansford	.06	.05	.02
157	Rick Burleson	.04	.03	.02
158	Don Baylor	.08	.06	.03
159	Ken Forsch	.03	.02	.01
160	Rod Carew	.20	.15	.08
161	Fred Lynn	.10	.08	.04
162	Bob Grich	.06	.05	.02
163	Dan Ford	.03	.02	.01
164	Butch Hobson	.03	.02	.01
165	Greg Luzinski	.08	.06	.03
166	Rich Dotson	.04	.03	.02
167	Billy Almon	.03	.02	.01
168	Chet Lemon	.04	.03	.02
169	Steve Trout	.03	.02	.01
170	Carlton Fisk	.12	.09	.05
171	Tony Bernazard	.03	.02	.01
172	Ron LeFlore	.04	.03	.02
173	Bert Blyleven	.08	.06	.03
174	Andre Thornton	.06	.05	.02
175	Jorge Orta	.03	.02	.01
176	Bo Diaz	.04	.03	.02
177	Toby Harrah	.04	.03	.02
178	Len Barker	.03	.02	.01
179	Rick Manning	.03	.02	.01
180	Mike Hargrove	.04	.03	.02
181	Alan Trammell	.15	.11	.06
182	Al Cowens	.03	.02	.01
183	Jack Morris	.12	.09	.05
184	Kirk Gibson	.15	.11	.06
185	Steve Kemp	.04	.03	.02
186	Milt Wilcox	.03	.02	.01
187	Lou Whitaker	.12	.09	.05
188	Lance Parrish	.12	.09	.05
189	Willie Wilson	.08	.06	.03
190	George Brett	.25	.20	.10
191	Dennis Leonard	.04	.03	.02
192	John Wathan	.04	.03	.02
193	Frank White	.06	.05	.02
194	Amos Otis	.04	.03	.02
195	Larry Gura	.03	.02	.01
196	Willie Aikens	.03	.02	.01
197	Ben Oglivie	.06	.05	.02
198	Rollie Fingers	.10	.08	.04
199	Cecil Cooper	.08	.06	.03
200	Paul Molitor	.10	.08	.04
201	Ted Simmons	.08	.06	.03
202	Pete Vuckovich	.04	.03	.02
203	Robin Yount	.15	.11	.06
204	Gorman Thomas	.04	.03	.02
205	Rob Wilfong	.03	.02	.01
206	Hosken Powell	.03	.02	.01
207	Roy Smalley	.03	.02	.01
208	Butch Wynegar	.04	.03	.02
209	John Castino	.03	.02	.01
210	Doug Corbett	.03	.02	.01
211	Roger Erickson	.03	.02	.01
212	Mickey Hatcher	.03	.02	.01
213	Dave Winfield	.20	.15	.08
214	Tommy John	.10	.08	.04
215	Graig Nettles	.06	.05	.02
216	Reggie Jackson	.25	.20	.10
217	Rich Gossage	.10	.08	.04
218	Rick Cerone	.03	.02	.01
219	Willie Randolph	.06	.05	.02
220	Jerry Mumphrey	.03	.02	.01
221	Rickey Henderson	.20	.15	.08
222	Mike Norris	.03	.02	.01
223	Jim Spencer	.03	.02	.01
224	Tony Armas	.04	.03	.02
225	Matt Keough	.03	.02	.01
226	Cliff Johnson	.03	.02	.01
227	Dwayne Murphy	.04	.03	.02
228	Steve McCatty	.03	.02	.01
229	Richie Zisk	.04	.03	.02
230	Lenny Randle	.03	.02	.01
231	Jeff Burroughs	.04	.03	.02
232	Bruce Bochte	.03	.02	.01
233	Gary Gray	.03	.02	.01
234	Floyd Bannister	.04	.03	.02
235	Julio Cruz	.03	.02	.01
236	Tom Paciorek	.03	.02	.01
237	Danny Darwin	.03	.02	.01
238	Buddy Bell	.06	.05	.02
239	Al Oliver	.06	.05	.02
240	Jim Sundberg	.04	.03	.02
241	Pat Putnam	.03	.02	.01
242	Steve Comer	.03	.02	.01
243	Mickey Rivers	.04	.03	.02
244	Bump Wills	.03	.02	.01
245	Damaso Garcia	.04	.03	.02
246	Lloyd Moseby	.06	.05	.02
247	Ernie Whitt	.03	.02	.01
248	John Mayberry	.03	.02	.01
249	Otto Velez	.03	.02	.01
250	Dave Stieb	.06	.05	.02
251	Barry Bonnell	.03	.02	.01
252	Alfredo Griffin	.04	.03	.02
253	1981 N.L. Championship (Gary Carter)	.10	.08	.04
254	1981 A.L. Championship (Mike Heath, Larry Milbourne)	.03	.02	.01
255	1981 World Champions (Los Angeles Dodgers Team)	.04	.03	.02
256	1981 World Champions (Los Angeles Dodgers Team)	.04	.03	.02
257	1981 World Series - Game 3 (Fernando Valenzuela)	.10	.08	.04
258	1981 World Series - Game 4 (Steve Garvey)	.10	.08	.04
259	1981 World Series - Game 5 (Jerry Reuss, Steve Yeager)	.03	.02	.01
260	1981 World Series - Game 6 (Pedro Guerrero)	.08	.06	.03

1982 Topps Traded

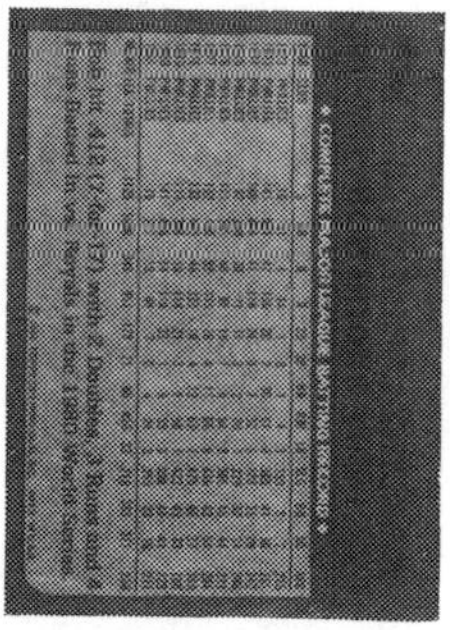

Topps released its second straight 132-card Traded set in September of 1982. Again, the 2-1/2" by 3-1/2" cards feature not only players who had been traded during the season, but also promising rookies who were given their first individual cards. The cards follow the basic design of the regular issues, but have their backs printed in red rather than the regular-issue green. As in 1981, the cards were not available in normal retail outlets and could only be purchased through regular baseball card dealers. Unlike the previous year, the cards are numbered 1-132 with the letter "T" following the number.

		MT	NR MT	EX
Complete Set:		175.00	130.00	70.00
Common Player:		.10	.08	.04
1T	Doyle Alexander	.20	.15	.08
2T	Jesse Barfield	2.00	1.50	.80
3T	Ross Baumgarten	.10	.08	.04
4T	Steve Bedrosian	.80	.60	.30
5T	Mark Belanger	.15	.11	.06
6T	Kurt Bevacqua	.10	.08	.04
7T	Tim Blackwell	.10	.08	.04
8T	Vida Blue	.25	.20	.10
9T	Bob Boone	.20	.15	.08
10T	Larry Bowa	.25	.20	.10
11T	Dan Briggs	.10	.08	.04
12T	Bobby Brown	.10	.08	.04
13T	Tom Brunansky	2.00	1.50	.80
14T	Jeff Burroughs	.15	.11	.06
15T	Enos Cabell	.10	.08	.04
16T	Bill Campbell	.10	.08	.04
17T	Bobby Castillo	.10	.08	.04
18T	Bill Caudill	.10	.08	.04
19T	Cesar Cedeno	.20	.15	.08
20T	Dave Collins	.15	.11	.06
21T	Doug Corbett	.10	.08	.04
22T	Al Cowens	.10	.08	.04
23T	Chili Davis	2.00	1.50	.80
24T	Dick Davis	.10	.08	.04
25T	Ron Davis	.10	.08	.04
26T	Doug DeCinces	.20	.15	.08
27T	Ivan DeJesus	.10	.08	.04
28T	Bob Dernier	.20	.15	.08
29T	Bo Diaz	.15	.11	.06
30T	Roger Erickson	.10	.08	.04
31T	Jim Essian	.10	.08	.04
32T	Ed Farmer	.10	.08	.04
33T	Doug Flynn	.10	.08	.04
34T	Tim Foli	.10	.08	.04
35T	Dan Ford	.10	.08	.04
36T	George Foster	.40	.30	.15
37T	Dave Frost	.10	.08	.04
38T	Rich Gale	.10	.08	.04
39T	Ron Gardenhire	.10	.08	.04
40T	Ken Griffey	.25	.20	.10
41T	Greg Harris	.15	.11	.06
42T	Von Hayes	1.25	.90	.50
43T	Larry Herndon	.15	.11	.06
44T	Kent Hrbek	6.00	4.50	2.50
45T	Mike Ivie	.10	.08	.04
46T	Grant Jackson	.10	.08	.04
47T	Reggie Jackson	6.00	4.50	2.50
48T	Ron Jackson	.10	.08	.04
49T	Fergie Jenkins	1.25	.90	.50
50T	Lamar Johnson	.10	.08	.04
51T	Randy Johnson	.10	.08	.04
52T	Jay Johnstone	.15	.11	.06
53T	Mick Kelleher	.10	.08	.04
54T	Steve Kemp	.15	.11	.06
55T	Junior Kennedy	.10	.08	.04
56T	Jim Kern	.10	.08	.04
57T	Ray Knight	.20	.15	.08
58T	Wayne Krenchicki	.10	.08	.04
59T	Mike Krukow	.15	.11	.06
60T	Duane Kuiper	.10	.08	.04
61T	Mike LaCoss	.10	.08	.04
62T	Chet Lemon	.15	.11	.06
63T	Sixto Lezcano	.10	.08	.04
64T	Dave Lopes	.15	.11	.06
65T	Jerry Martin	.10	.08	.04
66T	Renie Martin	.10	.08	.04
67T	John Mayberry	.15	.11	.06
68T	Lee Mazzilli	.15	.11	.06
69T	Bake McBride	.10	.08	.04
70T	Dan Meyer	.10	.08	.04
71T	Larry Milbourne	.10	.08	.04
72T	Eddie Milner(FC)	.20	.15	.08
73T	Sid Monge	.10	.08	.04
74T	Jose Morales	.10	.08	.04
75T	Keith Moreland	.20	.15	.08
76T	John Montefusco	.10	.08	.04
77T	Jim Morrison	.10	.08	.04
78T	Rance Mulliniks	.10	.08	.04
79T	Steve Mura	.10	.08	.04
80T	Gene Nelson	.10	.08	.04
81T	Joe Nolan	.10	.08	.04
82T	Dickie Noles	.10	.08	.04
83T	Al Oliver	.30	.25	.12
84T	Jorge Orta	.10	.08	.04
85T	Tom Paciorek	.10	.08	.04
86T	Larry Parrish	.20	.15	.08
87T	Jack Perconte	.10	.08	.04
88T	Gaylord Perry	2.00	1.50	.80
89T	Rob Picciolo	.10	.08	.04
90T	Joe Pittman	.10	.08	.04
91T	Hosken Powell	.10	.08	.04
92T	Mike Proly	.10	.08	.04
93T	Greg Pryor	.10	.08	.04
94T	Charlie Puleo(FC)	.15	.11	.06
95T	Shane Rawley	.20	.15	.08
96T	Johnny Ray	.80	.60	.30
97T	Dave Revering	.10	.08	.04
98T	Cal Ripken	150.00	110.00	60.00
99T	Allen Ripley	.10	.08	.04
100T	Bill Robinson	.10	.08	.04
101T	Aurelio Rodriguez	.15	.11	.06
102T	Joe Rudi	.20	.15	.08
103T	Steve Sax	6.00	4.50	2.50
104T	Dan Schatzeder	.10	.08	.04
105T	Bob Shirley	.10	.08	.04
106T	Eric Show(FC)	.50	.40	.20
107T	Roy Smalley	.15	.11	.06
108T	Lonnie Smith	.15	.11	.06
109T	Ozzie Smith	10.00	7.50	4.00
110T	Reggie Smith	.20	.15	.08
111T	Lary Sorensen	.10	.08	.04
112T	Elias Sosa	.10	.08	.04
113T	Mike Stanton	.10	.08	.04
114T	Steve Stroughter	.10	.08	.04
115T	Champ Summers	.10	.08	.04
116T	Rick Sutcliffe	.50	.40	.20
117T	Frank Tanana	.20	.15	.08
118T	Frank Taveras	.10	.08	.04
119T	Garry Templeton	.20	.15	.08
120T	Alex Trevino	.10	.08	.04
121T	Jerry Turner	.10	.08	.04
122T	Ed Vande Berg(FC)	.15	.11	.06
123T	Tom Veryzer	.10	.08	.04
124T	Ron Washington	.10	.08	.04
125T	Bob Watson	.15	.11	.06
126T	Dennis Werth	.10	.08	.04
127T	Eddie Whitson	.15	.11	.06
128T	Rob Wilfong	.10	.08	.04
129T	Bump Wills	.10	.08	.04
130T	Gary Woods	.10	.08	.04
131T	Butch Wynegar	.15	.11	.06
132T	Checklist 1-132	.10	.08	.04

1983 Topps

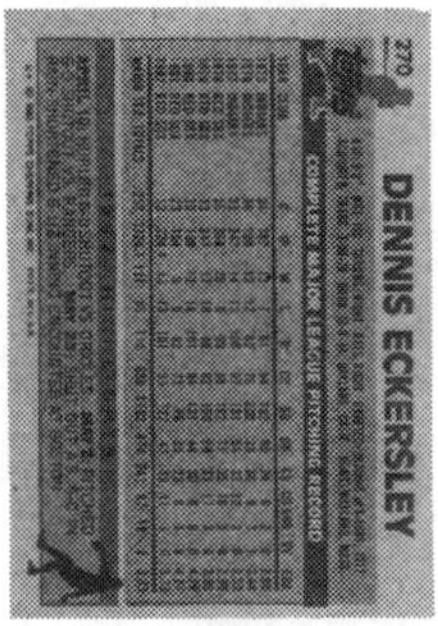

The 1983 Topps set totals 792 cards. Missing among the regular 2-1/2" by 3-1/2" cards are some form of future stars cards, as Topps was saving them for the now-established late season "Traded" set. The 1983 cards carry a large color photo as well as a smaller color photo on the front, quite similar in design to the 1963 set. Team colors frame the card, which, at the bottom, have the player's name, position and team. At the upper right-hand corner is a Topps Logo. The backs are horizontal and include statistics, personal information and 1982 highlights. Specialty cards include record-breaking performances, league leaders, All-Stars, numbered checklists "Team Leaders" and "Super Veteran" cards which are horizontal with a current and first-season picture of the honored player.

	MT	NR MT	EX
Complete Set:	150.00	110.00	60.00
Common Player:	.08	.06	.03

		MT	NR MT	EX
1	Record Breaker (Tony Armas)	.12	.09	.05
2	Record Breaker (Rickey Henderson)	1.00	.70	.40
3	Record Breaker (Greg Minton)	.08	.06	.03
4	Record Breaker (Lance Parrish)	.20	.15	.08
5	Record Breaker (Manny Trillo)	.08	.06	.03
6	Record Breaker (John Wathan)	.08	.06	.03
7	Gene Richards	.08	.06	.03
8	Steve Balboni	.10	.08	.04
9	Joey McLaughlin	.08	.06	.03
10	Gorman Thomas	.12	.09	.05
11	Billy Gardner	.08	.06	.03
12	Paul Mirabella	.08	.06	.03
13	Larry Herndon	.10	.08	.04
14	Frank LaCorte	.08	.06	.03
15	Ron Cey	.15	.11	.06
16	George Vukovich	.08	.06	.03
17	Kent Tekulve	.10	.08	.04
18	Super Veteran (Kent Tekulve)	.10	.08	.04
19	Oscar Gamble	.10	.08	.04
20	Carlton Fisk	1.00	.70	.40
21	Orioles Batting & Pitching Ldrs. (Eddie Murray, Jim Palmer)	.35	.25	.14
22	Randy Martz	.08	.06	.03
23	Mike Heath	.08	.06	.03
24	Steve Mura	.08	.06	.03
25	Hal McRae	.15	.11	.06
26	Jerry Royster	.08	.06	.03
27	Doug Corbett	.08	.06	.03
28	Bruce Bochte	.08	.06	.03
29	Randy Jones	.10	.08	.04
30	Jim Rice	.70	.50	.30
31	Bill Gullickson	.08	.06	.03
32	Dave Bergman	.08	.06	.03
33	Jack O'Connor	.08	.06	.03
34	Paul Householder	.08	.06	.03
35	Rollie Fingers	.30	.25	.12
36	Super Veteran (Rollie Fingers)	.15	.11	.06
37	Darrell Johnson	.08	.06	.03
38	Tim Flannery	.08	.06	.03
39	Terry Puhl	.08	.06	.03
40	Fernando Valenzuela	.50	.40	.20
41	Jerry Turner	.08	.06	.03
42	Dale Murray	.08	.06	.03
43	Bob Dernier	.08	.06	.03
44	Don Robinson	.10	.08	.04
45	John Mayberry	.10	.08	.04
46	Richard Dotson	.12	.09	.05
47	Dave McKay	.08	.06	.03
48	Lary Sorensen	.08	.06	.03
49	*Willie McGee*(FC)	6.00	4.50	2.50
50	Bob Horner	.20	.15	.08
51	Cubs Batting & Pitching Ldrs. (Leon Durham, Fergie Jenkins)	.15	.11	.06
52	*Onix Concepcion*(FC)	.08	.06	.03
53	Mike Witt	.30	.25	.12
54	Jim Maler	.08	.06	.03
55	Mookie Wilson	.12	.09	.05
56	Chuck Rainey	.08	.06	.03
57	Tim Blackwell	.08	.06	.03
58	Al Holland	.08	.06	.03
59	Benny Ayala	.08	.06	.03
60	Johnny Bench	1.25	.90	.50
61	Super Veteran (Johnny Bench)	.30	.25	.12
62	Bob McClure	.08	.06	.03
63	Rick Monday	.12	.09	.05
64	Bill Stein	.08	.06	.03
65	Jack Morris	.35	.25	.14
66	Bob Lillis	.08	.06	.03
67	Sal Butera	.08	.06	.03
68	*Eric Show*	.30	.25	.12
69	Lee Lacy	.08	.06	.03
70	Steve Carlton	1.25	.90	.50
71	Super Veteran (Steve Carlton)	.30	.25	.12
72	Tom Paciorek	.08	.06	.03
73	Allen Ripley	.08	.06	.03
74	Julio Gonzalez	.08	.06	.03
75	Amos Otis	.10	.08	.04
76	Rick Mahler	.12	.09	.05
77	Hosken Powell	.08	.06	.03
78	Bill Caudill	.08	.06	.03
79	Mick Kelleher	.08	.06	.03
80	George Foster	.20	.15	.08
81	Yankees Batting & Pitching Ldrs. (Jerry Mumphrey, Dave Righetti)	.15	.11	.06
82	Bruce Hurst	.15	.11	.06
83	*Ryne Sandberg*(FC)	50.00	37.00	20.00
84	Milt May	.08	.06	.03
85	Ken Singleton	.12	.09	.05
86	Tom Hume	.08	.06	.03
87	Joe Rudi	.12	.09	.05
88	Jim Gantner	.10	.08	.04
89	Leon Roberts	.08	.06	.03
90	Jerry Reuss	.12	.09	.05
91	Larry Milbourne	.08	.06	.03
92	Mike LaCoss	.08	.06	.03
93	John Castino	.08	.06	.03
94	Dave Edwards	.08	.06	.03
95	Alan Trammell	.50	.40	.20
96	Dick Howser	.08	.06	.03
97	Ross Baumgarten	.08	.06	.03
98	Vance Law	.10	.08	.04
99	Dickie Noles	.08	.06	.03
100	Pete Rose	1.75	1.25	.70
101	Super Veteran (Pete Rose)	.80	.60	.30
102	Dave Beard	.08	.06	.03
103	Darrell Porter	.10	.08	.04
104	Bob Walk	.08	.06	.03
105	Don Baylor	.15	.11	.06
106	Gene Nelson	.08	.06	.03
107	Mike Jorgensen	.08	.06	.03
108	Glenn Hoffman	.08	.06	.03
109	Luis Leal	.08	.06	.03
110	Ken Griffey	.15	.11	.06
111	Expos Batting & Pitching Ldrs. (Al Oliver, Steve Rogers)	.15	.11	.06
112	Bob Shirley	.08	.06	.03
113	Ron Roenicke	.08	.06	.03
114	Jim Slaton	.08	.06	.03
115	Chili Davis	.20	.15	.08
116	Dave Schmidt	.10	.08	.04
117	Alan Knicely	.08	.06	.03
118	Chris Welsh	.08	.06	.03
119	Tom Brookens	.08	.06	.03
120	Len Barker	.10	.08	.04
121	Mickey Hatcher	.10	.08	.04
122	Jimmy Smith	.08	.06	.03
123	George Frazier	.08	.06	.03
124	Marc Hill	.08	.06	.03
125	Leon Durham	.10	.08	.04
126	Joe Torre	.10	.08	.04
127	Preston Hanna	.08	.06	.03
128	Mike Ramsey	.08	.06	.03
129	Checklist 1-132	.12	.09	.05
130	Dave Stieb	.20	.15	.08
131	Ed Ott	.08	.06	.03
132	Todd Cruz	.08	.06	.03
133	Jim Barr	.08	.06	.03
134	Hubie Brooks	.15	.11	.06
135	Dwight Evans	.25	.20	.10
136	Willie Aikens	.08	.06	.03
137	Woodie Fryman	.10	.08	.04
138	Rick Dempsey	.10	.08	.04
139	Bruce Berenyi	.08	.06	.03
140	Willie Randolph	.12	.09	.05
141	Indians Batting & Pitching Ldrs. (Toby Harrah, Rick Sutcliffe)	.12	.09	.05
142	Mike Caldwell	.08	.06	.03
143	Joe Pettini	.08	.06	.03
144	Mark Wagner	.08	.06	.03
145	Don Sutton	.40	.30	.15
146	Super Veteran (Don Sutton)	.20	.15	.08
147	Rick Leach	.08	.06	.03
148	Dave Roberts	.08	.06	.03
149	Johnny Ray	.15	.11	.06
150	Bruce Sutter	.20	.15	.08
151	Super Veteran (Bruce Sutter)	.12	.09	.05
152	Jay Johnstone	.10	.08	.04
153	Jerry Koosman	.12	.09	.05
154	Johnnie LeMaster	.08	.06	.03
155	Dan Quisenberry	.20	.15	.08
156	Billy Martin	.12	.09	.05
157	Steve Bedrosian	.25	.20	.10
158	Rob Wilfong	.08	.06	.03
159	Mike Stanton	.08	.06	.03
160	Dave Kingman	.20	.15	.08
161	Super Veteran (Dave Kingman)	.10	.08	.04
162	Mark Clear	.08	.06	.03
163	Cal Ripken	20.00	15.00	8.00
164	Dave Palmer	.08	.06	.03
165	Dan Driessen	.10	.08	.04
166	John Pacella	.08	.06	.03
167	Mark Brouhard	.08	.06	.03
168	Juan Eichelberger	.08	.06	.03
169	Doug Flynn	.08	.06	.03
170	Steve Howe	.10	.08	.04
171	Giants Batting & Pitching Ldrs. (Bill Laskey, Joe Morgan)	.15	.11	.06
172	Vern Ruhle	.08	.06	.03
173	Jim Morrison	.08	.06	.03
174	Jerry Ujdur	.08	.06	.03
175	Bo Diaz	.10	.08	.04
176	Dave Righetti	.35	.25	.14

		MT	NR MT	EX
177	Harold Baines	.25	.20	.10
178	Luis Tiant	.15	.11	.06
179	Super Veteran (Luis Tiant)	.10	.08	.04
180	Rickey Henderson	8.00	6.00	3.25
181	Terry Felton	.08	.06	.03
182	Mike Fischlin	.08	.06	.03
183	*Ed Vande Berg*	.12	.09	.05
184	Bob Clark	.08	.06	.03
185	Tim Lollar	.08	.06	.03
186	Whitey Herzog	.10	.08	.04
187	Terry Leach	.12	.09	.05
188	Rick Miller	.08	.06	.03
189	Dan Schatzeder	.08	.06	.03
190	Cecil Cooper	.20	.15	.08
191	Joe Price	.08	.06	.03
192	Floyd Rayford	.08	.06	.03
193	Harry Spilman	.08	.06	.03
194	Cesar Geronimo	.08	.06	.03
195	Bob Stoddard	.08	.06	.03
196	Bill Fahey	.08	.06	.03
197	*Jim Eisenreich*(FC)	.15	.11	.06
198	Kiko Garcia	.08	.06	.03
199	Marty Bystrom	.08	.06	.03
200	Rod Carew	.70	.50	.30
201	Super Veteran (Rod Carew)	.35	.25	.14
202	Blue Jays Batting & Pitching Ldrs. (Damaso Garcia, Dave Stieb)	.12	.09	.05
203	Mike Morgan	.15	.11	.06
204	Junior Kennedy	.08	.06	.03
205	Dave Parker	.40	.30	.15
206	Ken Oberkfell	.08	.06	.03
207	Rick Camp	.08	.06	.03
208	Dan Meyer	.08	.06	.03
209	*Mike Moore*(FC)	1.25	.90	.50
210	Jack Clark	.30	.25	.12
211	John Denny	.08	.06	.03
212	John Stearns	.08	.06	.03
213	Tom Burgmeier	.08	.06	.03
214	Jerry White	.08	.06	.03
215	Mario Soto	.10	.08	.04
216	Tony LaRussa	.10	.08	.04
217	Tim Stoddard	.08	.06	.03
218	Roy Howell	.08	.06	.03
219	Mike Armstrong	.08	.06	.03
220	Dusty Baker	.12	.09	.05
221	Joe Niekro	.15	.11	.06
222	Damaso Garcia	.08	.06	.03
223	John Montefusco	.08	.06	.03
224	Mickey Rivers	.10	.08	.04
225	Enos Cabell	.08	.06	.03
226	Enrique Romo	.08	.06	.03
227	Chris Bando	.08	.06	.03
228	Joaquin Andujar	.10	.08	.04
229	Phillies Batting & Pitching Ldrs. (Steve Carlton, Bo Diaz)	.20	.15	.08
230	Fergie Jenkins	.50	.40	.20
231	Super Veteran (Fergie Jenkins)	.12	.09	.05
232	Tom Brunansky	.30	.25	.12
233	Wayne Gross	.08	.06	.03
234	Larry Andersen	.08	.06	.03
235	Claudell Washington	.10	.08	.04
236	Steve Renko	.08	.06	.03
237	Dan Norman	.08	.06	.03
238	*Bud Black*(FC)	.70	.50	.30
239	Dave Stapleton	.08	.06	.03
240	Rich Gossage	.30	.25	.12
241	Super Veteran (Rich Gossage)	.15	.11	.06
242	Joe Nolan	.08	.06	.03
243	Duane Walker	.08	.06	.03
244	Dwight Bernard	.08	.06	.03
245	Steve Sax	.35	.25	.14
246	George Bamberger	.08	.06	.03
247	Dave Smith	.12	.09	.05
248	Bake McBride	.08	.06	.03
249	Checklist 133-264	.12	.09	.05
250	Bill Buckner	.15	.11	.06
251	*Alan Wiggins*(FC)	.08	.06	.03
252	Luis Aguayo	.08	.06	.03
253	Larry McWilliams	.08	.06	.03
254	Rick Cerone	.08	.06	.03
255	Gene Garber	.08	.06	.03
256	Super Veteran (Gene Garber)	.08	.06	.03
257	Jesse Barfield	.50	.40	.20
258	Manny Castillo	.08	.06	.03
259	Jeff Jones	.08	.06	.03
260	Steve Kemp	.12	.09	.05
261	Tigers Batting & Pitching Ldrs. (Larry Herndon, Dan Petry)	.10	.08	.04
262	Ron Jackson	.08	.06	.03
263	Renie Martin	.08	.06	.03
264	Jamie Quirk	.08	.06	.03
265	Joel Youngblood	.08	.06	.03
266	Paul Boris	.08	.06	.03
267	Terry Francona	.08	.06	.03
268	*Storm Davis*(FC)	.50	.40	.20
269	Ron Oester	.08	.06	.03
270	Dennis Eckersley	.20	.15	.08
271	Ed Romero	.08	.06	.03
272	Frank Tanana	.12	.09	.05
273	Mark Belanger	.10	.08	.04
274	Terry Kennedy	.12	.09	.05
275	Ray Knight	.12	.09	.05
276	Gene Mauch	.10	.08	.04
277	Rance Mulliniks	.08	.06	.03
278	Kevin Hickey	.08	.06	.03
279	Greg Gross	.08	.06	.03
280	Bert Blyleven	.20	.15	.08
281	Andre Robertson	.08	.06	.03
282	Reggie Smith	.12	.09	.05
283	Super Veteran (Reggie Smith)	.10	.08	.04
284	Jeff Lahti	.08	.06	.03
285	Lance Parrish	.40	.30	.15
286	Rick Langford	.08	.06	.03
287	Bobby Brown	.08	.06	.03
288	*Joe Cowley*(FC)	.12	.09	.05
289	Jerry Dybzinski	.08	.06	.03
290	Jeff Reardon	.15	.11	.06
291	Pirates Batting & Pitching Ldrs. (John Candelaria, Bill Madlock)	.15	.11	.06
292	Craig Swan	.08	.06	.03
293	Glenn Gulliver	.08	.06	.03
294	Dave Engle	.08	.06	.03
295	Jerry Remy	.08	.06	.03
296	Greg Harris	.08	.06	.03
297	Ned Yost	.08	.06	.03
298	Floyd Chiffer	.08	.06	.03
299	George Wright	.08	.06	.03
300	Mike Schmidt	2.25	1.75	.90
301	Super Veteran (Mike Schmidt)	.60	.45	.25
302	Ernie Whitt	.10	.08	.04
303	Miguel Dilone	.08	.06	.03
304	Dave Rucker	.08	.06	.03
305	Larry Bowa	.15	.11	.06
306	Tom Lasorda	.12	.09	.05
307	Lou Piniella	.15	.11	.06
308	Jesus Vega	.08	.06	.03
309	Jeff Leonard	.12	.09	.05
310	Greg Luzinski	.15	.11	.06
311	Glenn Brummer	.08	.06	.03
312	Brian Kingman	.08	.06	.03
313	Gary Gray	.08	.06	.03
314	Ken Dayley(FC)	.15	.11	.06
315	Rick Burleson	.10	.08	.04
316	Paul Splittorff	.08	.06	.03
317	Gary Rajsich	.08	.06	.03
318	John Tudor	.15	.11	.06
319	Lenn Sakata	.08	.06	.03
320	Steve Rogers	.10	.08	.04
321	Brewers Batting & Pitching Ldrs. (Pete Vuckovich, Robin Yount)	.20	.15	.08
322	Dave Van Gorder	.08	.06	.03
323	Luis DeLeon	.08	.06	.03
324	Mike Marshall	.30	.25	.12
325	Von Hayes	.20	.15	.08
326	Garth Iorg	.08	.06	.03
327	Bobby Castillo	.08	.06	.03
328	Craig Reynolds	.08	.06	.03
329	Randy Niemann	.08	.06	.03
330	Buddy Bell	.15	.11	.06
331	Mike Krukow	.10	.08	.04
332	*Glenn Wilson*(FC)	.30	.25	.12
333	Dave LaRoche	.08	.06	.03
334	Super Veteran (Dave LaRoche)	.08	.06	.03
335	Steve Henderson	.08	.06	.03
336	Rene Lachemann	.08	.06	.03
337	Tito Landrum	.08	.06	.03
338	Bob Owchinko	.08	.06	.03
339	Terry Harper	.08	.06	.03
340	Larry Gura	.08	.06	.03
341	Doug DeCinces	.15	.11	.06
342	Atlee Hammaker	.10	.08	.04
343	Bob Bailor	.08	.06	.03
344	Roger LaFrancois	.08	.06	.03
345	Jim Clancy	.10	.08	.04
346	Joe Pittman	.08	.06	.03
347	Sammy Stewart	.08	.06	.03
348	Alan Bannister	.08	.06	.03
349	Checklist 265-396	.12	.09	.05
350	Robin Yount	1.75	1.25	.70
351	Reds Batting & Pitching Ldrs. (Cesar Cedeno, Mario Soto)	.12	.09	.05
352	Mike Scioscia	.10	.08	.04

		MT	NR MT	EX
353	Steve Comer	.08	.06	.03
354	Randy Johnson	.08	.06	.03
355	Jim Bibby	.08	.06	.03
356	Gary Woods	.08	.06	.03
357	*Len Matuszek*(FC)	.08	.06	.03
358	Jerry Garvin	.08	.06	.03
359	Dave Collins	.10	.08	.04
360	Nolan Ryan	6.00	4.50	2.50
361	Super Veteran (Nolan Ryan)	.30	.25	.12
362	Bill Almon	.08	.06	.03
363	*John Stuper*(FC)	.08	.06	.03
364	Brett Butler	.20	.15	.08
365	Dave Lopes	.12	.09	.05
366	Dick Williams	.08	.06	.03
367	Bud Anderson	.08	.06	.03
368	Richie Zisk	.10	.08	.04
369	Jesse Orosco	.15	.11	.06
370	Gary Carter	.50	.40	.20
371	Mike Richardt	.08	.06	.03
372	Terry Crowley	.08	.06	.03
373	Kevin Saucier	.08	.06	.03
374	Wayne Krenchicki	.08	.06	.03
375	Pete Vuckovich	.10	.08	.04
376	Ken Landreaux	.08	.06	.03
377	Lee May	.10	.08	.04
378	Super Veteran (Lee May)	.10	.08	.04
379	Guy Sularz	.08	.06	.03
380	Ron Davis	.08	.06	.03
381	Red Sox Batting & Pitching Ldrs. (Jim Rice, Bob Stanley)	.25	.20	.10
382	Bob Knepper	.12	.09	.05
383	Ozzie Virgil	.10	.08	.04
384	*Dave Dravecky*(FC)	1.00	.70	.40
385	Mike Easler	.10	.08	.04
386	Rod Carew AS	.50	.40	.20
387	Bob Grich AS	.10	.08	.04
388	George Brett AS	.50	.40	.20
389	Robin Yount AS	.25	.20	.10
390	Reggie Jackson AS	.50	.40	.20
391	Rickey Henderson AS	1.75	1.25	.70
392	Fred Lynn AS	.15	.11	.06
393	Carlton Fisk AS	.15	.11	.06
394	Pete Vuckovich AS	.10	.08	.04
395	Larry Gura AS	.08	.06	.03
396	Dan Quisenberry AS	.12	.09	.05
397	Pete Rose AS	.70	.50	.30
398	Manny Trillo AS	.10	.08	.04
399	Mike Schmidt AS	.60	.45	.25
400	Dave Concepcion AS	.12	.09	.05
401	Dale Murphy AS	.70	.50	.30
402	Andre Dawson AS	.20	.15	.08
403	Tim Raines AS	.35	.25	.14
404	Gary Carter AS	.35	.25	.14
405	Steve Rogers AS	.10	.08	.04
406	Steve Carlton AS	.35	.25	.14
407	Bruce Sutter AS	.12	.09	.05
408	Rudy May	.08	.06	.03
409	Marvis Foley	.08	.06	.03
410	Phil Niekro	.40	.30	.15
411	Super Veteran (Phil Niekro)	.20	.15	.08
412	Rangers Batting & Pitching Ldrs. (Buddy Bell, Charlie Hough)	.15	.11	.06
413	Matt Keough	.08	.06	.03
414	Julio Cruz	.08	.06	.03
415	Bob Forsch	.10	.08	.04
416	Joe Ferguson	.08	.06	.03
417	Tom Hausman	.08	.06	.03
418	Greg Pryor	.08	.06	.03
419	Steve Crawford	.08	.06	.03
420	Al Oliver	.20	.15	.08
421	Super Veteran (Al Oliver)	.12	.09	.05
422	George Cappuzzello	.08	.06	.03
423	*Tom Lawless*(FC)	.10	.08	.04
424	Jerry Augustine	.08	.06	.03
425	Pedro Guerrero	.35	.25	.14
426	Earl Weaver	.10	.08	.04
427	Roy Lee Jackson	.08	.06	.03
428	Champ Summers	.08	.06	.03
429	Eddie Whitson	.08	.06	.03
430	Kirk Gibson	.50	.40	.20
431	*Gary Gaetti*(FC)	3.00	2.25	1.25
432	Porfirio Altamirano	.08	.06	.03
433	Dale Berra	.08	.06	.03
434	Dennis Lamp	.08	.06	.03
435	Tony Armas	.12	.09	.05
436	Bill Campbell	.08	.06	.03
437	Rick Sweet	.08	.06	.03
438	*Dave LaPoint*(FC)	.40	.30	.15
439	Rafael Ramirez	.08	.06	.03
440	Ron Guidry	.30	.25	.12
441	Astros Batting & Pitching Ldrs. (Ray Knight, Joe Niekro)	.12	.09	.05

		MT	NR MT	EX
442	Brian Downing	.12	.09	.05
443	Don Hood	.08	.06	.03
444	Wally Backman(FC)	.25	.20	.10
445	Mike Flanagan	.12	.09	.05
446	Reid Nichols	.08	.06	.03
447	Bryn Smith	.10	.08	.04
448	Darrell Evans	.20	.15	.08
449	*Eddie Milner*	.12	.09	.05
450	Ted Simmons	.20	.15	.08
451	Super Veteran (Ted Simmons)	.12	.09	.05
452	Lloyd Moseby	.15	.11	.06
453	Lamar Johnson	.08	.06	.03
454	Bob Welch	.15	.11	.06
455	Sixto Lezcano	.08	.06	.03
456	Lee Elia	.08	.06	.03
457	Milt Wilcox	.08	.06	.03
458	Ron Washington	.08	.06	.03
459	Ed Farmer	.08	.06	.03
460	Roy Smalley	.08	.06	.03
461	Steve Trout	.08	.06	.03
462	Steve Nicosia	.08	.06	.03
463	Gaylord Perry	.40	.30	.15
464	Super Veteran (Gaylord Perry)	.20	.15	.08
465	Lonnie Smith	.10	.08	.04
466	Tom Underwood	.08	.06	.03
467	Rufino Linares	.08	.06	.03
468	Dave Goltz	.10	.08	.04
469	Ron Gardenhire	.08	.06	.03
470	Greg Minton	.08	.06	.03
471	Royals Batting & Pitching Ldrs. (Vida Blue, Willie Wilson)	.15	.11	.06
472	Gary Allenson	.08	.06	.03
473	John Lowenstein	.08	.06	.03
474	Ray Burris	.08	.06	.03
475	Cesar Cedeno	.12	.09	.05
476	Rob Picciolo	.08	.06	.03
477	Tom Niedenfuer(FC)	.15	.11	.06
478	Phil Garner	.10	.08	.04
479	Charlie Hough	.12	.09	.05
480	Toby Harrah	.10	.08	.04
481	Scot Thompson	.08	.06	.03
482	*Tony Gwynn*(FC)	30.00	22.00	12.00
483	Lynn Jones	.08	.06	.03
484	Dick Ruthven	.08	.06	.03
485	Omar Moreno	.08	.06	.03
486	Clyde King	.08	.06	.03
487	Jerry Hairston	.08	.06	.03
488	Alfredo Griffin	.10	.08	.04
489	Tom Herr	.12	.09	.05
490	Jim Palmer	.80	.60	.30
491	Super Veteran (Jim Palmer)	.20	.15	.08
492	Paul Serna	.08	.06	.03
493	Steve McCatty	.08	.06	.03
494	Bob Brenly	.10	.08	.04
495	Warren Cromartie	.08	.06	.03
496	Tom Veryzer	.08	.06	.03
497	Rick Sutcliffe	.20	.15	.08
498	*Wade Boggs*(FC)	35.00	27.00	15.00
499	Jeff Little	.10	.08	.04
500	Reggie Jackson	.70	.50	.30
501	Super Veteran (Reggie Jackson)	.35	.25	.14
502	Braves Batting & Pitching Ldrs. (Dale Murphy, Phil Niekro)	.50	.40	.20
503	Moose Haas	.08	.06	.03
504	Don Werner	.08	.06	.03
505	Garry Templeton	.12	.09	.05
506	*Jim Gott*(FC)	.25	.20	.10
507	Tony Scott	.08	.06	.03
508	Tom Filer	.15	.11	.06
509	Lou Whitaker	.40	.30	.20
510	Tug McGraw	.15	.11	.06
511	Super Veteran (Tug McGraw)	.10	.08	.04
512	Doyle Alexander	.12	.09	.05
513	Fred Stanley	.08	.06	.03
514	Rudy Law	.08	.06	.03
515	Gene Tenace	.10	.08	.04
516	Bill Virdon	.08	.06	.03
517	Gary Ward	.10	.08	.04
518	Bill Laskey	.08	.06	.03
519	Terry Bulling	.08	.06	.03
520	Fred Lynn	.25	.20	.10
521	Bruce Benedict	.08	.06	.03
522	Pat Zachry	.08	.06	.03
523	Carney Lansford	.12	.09	.05
524	Tom Brennan	.08	.06	.03
525	Frank White	.12	.09	.05
526	Checklist 397-528	.12	.09	.05
527	Larry Biittner	.08	.06	.03
528	Jamie Easterly	.08	.06	.03
529	Tim Laudner	.10	.08	.04
530	Eddie Murray	.80	.60	.30

		MT	NR MT	EX
531	Athletics Batting & Pitching Ldrs. (Rickey Henderson, Rick Langford)	.30	.25	.12
532	Dave Stewart	2.00	1.50	.80
533	Luis Salazar	.08	.06	.03
534	John Butcher	.08	.06	.03
535	Manny Trillo	.10	.08	.04
536	Johnny Wockenfuss	.08	.06	.03
537	Rod Scurry	.08	.06	.03
538	Danny Heep	.08	.06	.03
539	Roger Erickson	.08	.06	.03
540	Ozzie Smith	.30	.25	.12
541	Britt Burns	.08	.06	.03
542	Jody Davis	.12	.09	.05
543	Alan Fowlkes	.08	.06	.03
544	Larry Whisenton	.08	.06	.03
545	Floyd Bannister	.12	.09	.05
546	Dave Garcia	.08	.06	.03
547	Geoff Zahn	.08	.06	.03
548	Brian Giles	.08	.06	.03
549	*Charlie Puleo*	.15	.11	.06
550	Carl Yastrzemski	1.00	.70	.40
551	Super Veteran (Carl Yastrzemski)	.40	.30	.15
552	Tim Wallach	.30	.25	.12
553	Denny Martinez	.10	.08	.04
554	Mike Vail	.08	.06	.03
555	Steve Yeager	.08	.06	.03
556	Willie Upshaw	.10	.08	.04
557	Rick Honeycutt	.08	.06	.03
558	Dickie Thon	.10	.08	.04
559	Pete Redfern	.08	.06	.03
560	Ron LeFlore	.10	.08	.04
561	Cardinals Batting & Pitching Ldrs. (Joaquin Andujar, Lonnie Smith)	.12	.09	.05
562	Dave Rozema	.08	.06	.03
563	Juan Bonilla	.08	.06	.03
564	Sid Monge	.08	.06	.03
565	Bucky Dent	.12	.09	.05
566	Manny Sarmiento	.08	.06	.03
567	Joe Simpson	.08	.06	.03
568	Willie Hernandez	.12	.09	.05
569	Jack Perconte	.08	.06	.03
570	Vida Blue	.15	.11	.06
571	Mickey Klutts	.08	.06	.03
572	Bob Watson	.10	.08	.04
573	Andy Hassler	.08	.06	.03
574	Glenn Adams	.08	.06	.03
575	Neil Allen	.08	.06	.03
576	Frank Robinson	.12	.09	.05
577	Luis Aponte	.08	.06	.03
578	David Green	.08	.06	.03
579	Rich Dauer	.08	.06	.03
580	Tom Seaver	1.25	.90	.50
581	Super Veteran (Tom Seaver)	.30	.25	.12
582	Marshall Edwards	.08	.06	.03
583	Terry Forster	.10	.08	.04
584	Dave Hostetler	.08	.06	.03
585	Jose Cruz	.15	.11	.06
586	*Frank Viola*(FC)	7.00	5.25	2.75
587	Ivan DeJesus	.08	.06	.03
588	Pat Underwood	.08	.06	.03
589	Alvis Woods	.08	.06	.03
590	Tony Pena	.12	.09	.05
591	White Sox Batting & Pitching Ldrs. (LaMarr Hoyt, Greg Luzinski)	.15	.11	.06
592	Shane Rawley	.12	.09	.05
593	Broderick Perkins	.08	.06	.03
594	Eric Rasmussen	.08	.06	.03
595	Tim Raines	1.00	.70	.40
596	Randy Johnson	.08	.06	.03
597	Mike Proly	.08	.06	.03
598	Dwayne Murphy	.10	.08	.04
599	Don Aase	.08	.06	.03
600	George Brett	1.75	1.25	.70
601	Ed Lynch	.08	.06	.03
602	Rich Gedman	.12	.09	.05
603	Joe Morgan	.40	.30	.15
604	Super Veteran (Joe Morgan)	.15	.11	.06
605	Gary Roenicke	.08	.06	.03
606	Bobby Cox	.08	.06	.03
607	Charlie Leibrandt	.10	.08	.04
608	Don Money	.08	.06	.03
609	Danny Darwin	.08	.06	.03
610	Steve Garvey	.70	.50	.30
611	Bert Roberge	.08	.06	.03
612	Steve Swisher	.08	.06	.03
613	Mike Ivie	.08	.06	.03
614	Ed Glynn	.08	.06	.03
615	Garry Maddox	.12	.09	.05
616	Bill Nahorodny	.08	.06	.03
617	Butch Wynegar	.08	.06	.03
618	LaMarr Hoyt	.08	.06	.03
619	Keith Moreland	.10	.08	.04
620	Mike Norris	.08	.06	.03
621	Mets Batting & Pitching Ldrs. (Craig Swan, Mookie Wilson)	.12	.09	.05
622	Dave Edler	.08	.06	.03
623	Luis Sanchez	.08	.06	.03
624	Glenn Hubbard	.10	.08	.04
625	Ken Forsch	.08	.06	.03
626	Jerry Martin	.08	.06	.03
627	Doug Bair	.08	.06	.03
628	Julio Valdez	.08	.06	.03
629	Charlie Lea	.08	.06	.03
630	Paul Molitor	.30	.25	.12
631	Tippy Martinez	.08	.06	.03
632	Alex Trevino	.08	.06	.03
633	Vicente Romo	.08	.06	.03
634	Max Venable	.08	.06	.03
635	Graig Nettles	.20	.15	.08
636	Super Veteran (Graig Nettles)	.12	.09	.05
637	Pat Corrales	.08	.06	.03
638	Dan Petry	.10	.08	.04
639	Art Howe	.08	.06	.03
640	Andre Thornton	.12	.09	.05
641	Billy Sample	.08	.06	.03
642	Checklist 529-660	.12	.09	.05
643	Bump Wills	.08	.06	.03
644	Joe Lefebvre	.08	.06	.03
645	Bill Madlock	.15	.11	.06
646	Jim Essian	.08	.06	.03
647	Bobby Mitchell	.08	.06	.03
648	Jeff Burroughs	.10	.08	.04
649	Tommy Boggs	.08	.06	.03
650	George Hendrick	.10	.08	.04
651	Angels Batting & Pitching Ldrs. (Rod Carew, Mike Witt)	.30	.25	.12
652	Butch Hobson	.08	.06	.03
653	Ellis Valentine	.08	.06	.03
654	Bob Ojeda	.15	.11	.06
655	Al Bumbry	.10	.08	.04
656	Dave Frost	.08	.06	.03
657	Mike Gates	.08	.06	.03
658	Frank Pastore	.08	.06	.03
659	Charlie Moore	.08	.06	.03
660	Mike Hargrove	.08	.06	.03
661	Bill Russell	.10	.08	.04
662	Joe Sambito	.08	.06	.03
663	Tom O'Malley	.08	.06	.03
664	Bob Molinaro	.08	.06	.03
665	Jim Sundberg	.10	.08	.04
666	Sparky Anderson	.12	.09	.05
667	Dick Davis	.08	.06	.03
668	Larry Christenson	.08	.06	.03
669	Mike Squires	.08	.06	.03
670	Jerry Mumphrey	.08	.06	.03
671	Lenny Faedo	.08	.06	.03
672	Jim Kaat	.20	.15	.08
673	Super Veteran (Jim Kaat)	.12	.09	.05
674	Kurt Bevacqua	.08	.06	.03
675	Jim Beattie	.08	.06	.03
676	Biff Pocoroba	.08	.06	.03
677	Dave Revering	.08	.06	.03
678	Juan Beniquez	.08	.06	.03
679	Mike Scott	.20	.15	.08
680	Andre Dawson	1.25	.90	.50
681	Dodgers Batting & Pitching Ldrs. (Pedro Guerrero, Fernando Valenzuela)	.25	.20	.10
682	Bob Stanley	.08	.06	.03
683	Dan Ford	.08	.06	.03
684	Rafael Landestoy	.08	.06	.03
685	Lee Mazzilli	.10	.08	.04
686	Randy Lerch	.08	.06	.03
687	U.L. Washington	.08	.06	.03
688	Jim Wohlford	.08	.06	.03
689	Ron Hassey	.08	.06	.03
690	Kent Hrbek	.70	.50	.30
691	Dave Tobik	.08	.06	.03
692	Denny Walling	.08	.06	.03
693	Sparky Lyle	.12	.09	.05
694	Super Veteran (Sparky Lyle)	.10	.08	.04
695	Ruppert Jones	.08	.06	.03
696	Chuck Tanner	.08	.06	.03
697	Barry Foote	.08	.06	.03
698	Tony Bernazard	.08	.06	.03
699	Lee Smith	.20	.15	.08
700	Keith Hernandez	.50	.40	.20
701	Batting Leaders (Al Oliver, Willie Wilson)	.15	.11	.06
702	Home Run Leaders (Reggie Jackson, Dave Kingman, Gorman Thomas)	.25	.20	.10
703	Runs Batted In Leaders (Hal McRae, Dale Murphy, Al Oliver)	.35	.25	.14

		MT	NR MT	EX
704	Stolen Base Leaders (Rickey Henderson, Tim Raines)	.35	.25	.14
705	Victory Leaders (Steve Carlton, LaMarr Hoyt)	.20	.15	.08
706	Strikeout Leaders (Floyd Bannister, Steve Carlton)	.20	.15	.08
707	Earned Run Average Leaders (Steve Rogers, Rick Sutcliffe)	.12	.09	.05
708	Leading Firemen (Dan Quisenberry, Bruce Sutter)	.15	.11	.06
709	Jimmy Sexton	.08	.06	.03
710	Willie Wilson	.20	.15	.08
711	Mariners Batting & Pitching Ldrs. (Jim Beattie, Bruce Bochte)	.12	.09	.05
712	Bruce Kison	.08	.06	.03
713	Ron Hodges	.08	.06	.03
714	Wayne Nordhagen	.08	.06	.03
715	Tony Perez	.25	.20	.10
716	Super Veteran (Tony Perez)	.12	.09	.05
717	Scott Sanderson	.08	.06	.03
718	Jim Dwyer	.08	.06	.03
719	Rich Gale	.08	.06	.03
720	Dave Concepcion	.15	.11	.06
721	John Martin	.08	.06	.03
722	Jorge Orta	.08	.06	.03
723	Randy Moffitt	.08	.06	.03
724	Johnny Grubb	.08	.06	.03
725	Dan Spillner	.08	.06	.03
726	Harvey Kuenn	.10	.08	.04
727	Chet Lemon	.10	.08	.04
728	Ron Reed	.08	.06	.03
729	Jerry Morales	.08	.06	.03
730	Jason Thompson	.08	.06	.03
731	Al Williams	.08	.06	.03
732	Dave Henderson	.15	.11	.06
733	Buck Martinez	.08	.06	.03
734	Steve Braun	.08	.06	.03
735	Tommy John	.25	.20	.10
736	Super Veteran (Tommy John)	.12	.09	.05
737	Mitchell Page	.08	.06	.03
738	Tim Foli	.08	.06	.03
739	Rick Ownbey	.08	.06	.03
740	Rusty Staub	.15	.11	.06
741	Super Veteran (Rusty Staub)	.10	.08	.04
742	Padres Batting & Pitching Ldrs. (Terry Kennedy, Tim Lollar)	.12	.09	.05
743	Mike Torrez	.10	.08	.04
744	Brad Mills	.08	.06	.03
745	Scott McGregor	.10	.08	.04
746	John Wathan	.10	.08	.04
747	Fred Breining	.08	.06	.03
748	Derrel Thomas	.08	.06	.03
749	Jon Matlack	.10	.08	.04
750	Ben Oglivie	.10	.08	.04
751	Brad Havens	.08	.06	.03
752	Luis Pujols	.08	.06	.03
753	Elias Sosa	.08	.06	.03
754	Bill Robinson	.08	.06	.03
755	John Candelaria	.12	.09	.05
756	Russ Nixon	.08	.06	.03
757	Rick Manning	.08	.06	.03
758	Aurelio Rodriguez	.10	.08	.04
759	Doug Bird	.08	.06	.03
760	Dale Murphy	1.50	1.25	.60
761	Gary Lucas	.08	.06	.03
762	Cliff Johnson	.08	.06	.03
763	Al Cowens	.08	.06	.03
764	Pete Falcone	.08	.06	.03
765	Bob Boone	.12	.09	.05
766	Barry Bonnell	.08	.06	.03
767	Duane Kuiper	.08	.06	.03
768	Chris Speier	.08	.06	.03
769	Checklist 661-792	.12	.09	.05
770	Dave Winfield	.80	.60	.30
771	Twins Batting & Pitching Ldrs. (Bobby Castillo, Kent Hrbek)	.20	.15	.08
772	Jim Kern	.08	.06	.03
773	Larry Hisle	.10	.08	.04
774	Alan Ashby	.08	.06	.03
775	Burt Hooton	.10	.08	.04
776	Larry Parrish	.12	.09	.05
777	John Curtis	.08	.06	.03
778	Rich Hebner	.08	.06	.03
779	Rick Waits	.08	.06	.03
780	Gary Matthews	.12	.09	.05
781	Rick Rhoden	.12	.09	.05
782	Bobby Murcer	.12	.09	.05
783	Super Veteran (Bobby Murcer)	.10	.08	.04
784	Jeff Newman	.08	.06	.03
785	Dennis Leonard	.10	.08	.04
786	Ralph Houk	.10	.08	.04
787	Dick Tidrow	.08	.06	.03
788	Dane Iorg	.08	.06	.03
789	Bryan Clark	.08	.06	.03
790	Bob Grich	.12	.09	.05
791	Gary Lavelle	.08	.06	.03
792	Chris Chambliss	.10	.08	.04

1983 Topps All-Star Glossy Set Of 40

This set was a "consolation prize" in a scratch-off contest in regular packs of 1983 cards. The 2-1/2" by 3-1/2" cards have a large color photo surrounded by a yellow frame on the front. In very small type on a white border is printed the player's name. Backs carry the player's name, team, position and the card number along with a Topps identification. A major feature is that the surface of the front is glossy, which most collectors find very attractive. With many top stars, the set is a popular one, but the price has not moved too far above the issue price.

		MT	NR MT	EX
Complete Set:		13.00	9.75	5.25
Common Player:		.15	.11	.06
1	Carl Yastrzemski	1.00	.70	.40
2	Mookie Wilson	.15	.11	.06
3	Andre Thornton	.15	.11	.06
4	Keith Hernandez	.40	.30	.15
5	Robin Yount	.40	.30	.15
6	Terry Kennedy	.15	.11	.06
7	Dave Winfield	.60	.45	.25
8	Mike Schmidt	1.00	.70	.40
9	Buddy Bell	.20	.15	.08
10	Fernando Valenzuela	.50	.40	.20
11	Rich Gossage	.25	.20	.10
12	Bob Horner	.20	.15	.08
13	Toby Harrah	.15	.11	.06
14	Pete Rose	1.25	.90	.50
15	Cecil Cooper	.20	.15	.08
16	Dale Murphy	1.00	.70	.40
17	Carlton Fisk	.30	.25	.12
18	Ray Knight	.15	.11	.06
19	Jim Palmer	.40	.30	.15
20	Gary Carter	.50	.40	.20
21	Richard Zisk	.15	.11	.06
22	Dusty Baker	.15	.11	.06
23	Willie Wilson	.20	.15	.08
24	Bill Buckner	.15	.11	.06
25	Dave Stieb	.20	.15	.08
26	Bill Madlock	.20	.15	.08
27	Lance Parrish	.30	.25	.12
28	Nolan Ryan	1.00	.70	.40
29	Rod Carew	.60	.45	.25
30	Al Oliver	.20	.15	.08
31	George Brett	1.00	.70	.40
32	Jack Clark	.25	.20	.10
33	Rickey Henderson	.70	.50	.30
34	Dave Concepcion	.20	.15	.08
35	Kent Hrbek	.30	.25	.12
36	Steve Carlton	.50	.40	.20
37	Eddie Murray	.60	.45	.25
38	Ruppert Jones	.15	.11	.06
39	Reggie Jackson	.70	.50	.30
40	Bruce Sutter	.20	.15	.08

1983 Topps Foldouts

Another Topps test issue, these 3-1/2" by 5-5/16" cards were printed in booklets like souvenier postcards. Each of the booklets have a theme of currently playing statistical leaders in a specific category such as home runs. The cards feature a color player photo on each side. A black strip at the bottom gives the player's name, position and team along with statistics in the particular category. A facsimile autograph crosses the photograph. Booklets carry nine cards, with eight having players on both sides and one doubling as the back cover, for a total of 17 cards per booklet. There are 85 cards in the set, although some players appear in more than one category. Naturally, most of the players pictured are stars. Even so, the set is a problem as it seems to be most valuable when complete and unseparated, so the cards are difficult to display.

	MT	NR MT	EX
Complete Set:	10.00	7.50	4.00
Common Folder:	1.25	.90	.50

		MT	NR MT	EX
1	Pitching Leaders (Vida Blue, Bert Blyleven, Steve Carlton, Fergie Jenkins, Tommy John, Jim Kaat, Jerry Koosman, Joe Niekro, Phil Niekro, Jim Palmer, Gaylord Perry, Jerry Reuss, Nolan Ryan, Tom Seaver, Paul Splittorff, Don Sutton, Mike Torrez)	1.75	1.25	.70
2	Home Run Leaders (Johnny Bench, Ron Cey, Darrell Evans, George Foster, Reggie Jackson, Dave Kingman, Greg Luzinski, John Mayberry, Rick Monday, Joe Morgan, Bobby Murcer, Graig Nettles, Tony Perez, Jim Rice, Mike Schmidt, Rusty Staub, Carl Yastrzemski)	2.50	2.00	1.00
3	Batting Leaders (George Brett, Rod Carew, Cecil Cooper, Steve Garvey, Ken Griffey, Pedro Guerrero, Keith Hernandez, Dane Iorg, Fred Lynn, Bill Madlock, Bake McBride, Al Oliver, Dave Parker, Jim Rice, Pete Rose, Lonnie Smith, Willie Wilson)	2.50	2.00	1.00
4	Relief Aces (Tom Burgmeier, Bill Campbell, Ed Farmer, Rollie Fingers, Terry Forster, Gene Garber, Rich Gossage, Jim Kern, Gary Lavelle, Tug McGraw, Greg Minton, Randy Moffitt, Dan Quisenberry, Ron Reed, Elias Sosa, Bruce Sutter, Kent Tekulve)	1.25	.90	.50
5	Stolen Base Leaders (Don Baylor, Larry Bowa, Al Bumbry, Rod Carew, Cesar Cedeno, Dave Concepcion, Jose Cruz, Julio Cruz, Rickey Henderson, Ron LeFlore, Davey Lopes, Garry Maddox, Omar Moreno, Joe Morgan, Amos Otis, Mickey Rivers, Willie Wilson)	1.25	.90	.50

NOTE: A card number in parentheses ( ) indicates the set is unnumbered.

1983 Topps Stickers

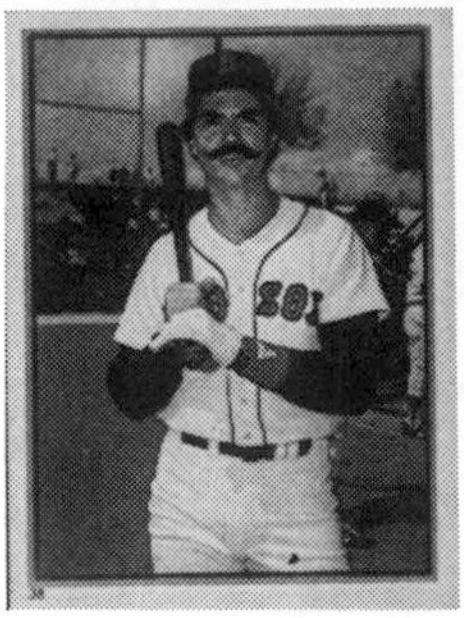

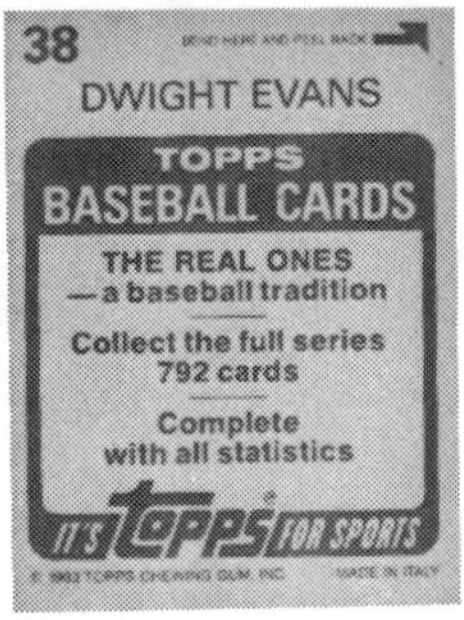

Topps increased the number of stickers in its set to 220 in 1983, but retained the same 1-15/16" by 2-9/16" size. The stickers are again numbered on both the front and back. Similar in style to previous sticker issues, the set includes 28 "foil" stickers, and various special stickers highlighting the 1982 season, playoffs and World Series. An album was also available.

	MT	NR MT	EX
Complete Set:	15.00	11.00	6.00
Common Player:	.03	.02	.01
Sticker Album:	.80	.60	.30

		MT	NR MT	EX
1	Hank Aaron	.40	.30	.15
2	Babe Ruth	.60	.45	.25
3	Willie Mays	.40	.30	.15
4	Frank Robinson	.30	.25	.12
5	Reggie Jackson	.20	.15	.08
6	Carl Yastrzemski	.25	.20	.10
7	Johnny Bench	.20	.15	.08
8	Tony Perez	.10	.08	.04
9	Lee May	.06	.05	.02
10	Mike Schmidt	.25	.20	.10
11	Dave Kingman	.08	.06	.03
12	Reggie Smith	.06	.05	.02
13	Graig Nettles	.06	.05	.02
14	Rusty Staub	.06	.05	.02
15	Willie Wilson	.06	.05	.02
16	LaMarr Hoyt	.03	.02	.01
17	Reggie Jackson, Gorman Thomas	.15	.11	.06
18	Floyd Bannister	.04	.03	.02
19	Hal McRae	.06	.05	.02
20	Rick Sutcliffe	.08	.06	.03
21	Rickey Henderson	.25	.20	.10
22	Dan Quisenberry	.06	.05	.02
23	Jim Palmer	.30	.25	.12
24	John Lowenstein	.03	.02	.01
25	Mike Flanagan	.04	.03	.02
26	Cal Ripken	.20	.15	.08
27	Rich Dauer	.03	.02	.01
28	Ken Singleton	.06	.05	.02
29	Eddie Murray	.20	.15	.08
30	Rick Dempsey	.04	.03	.02
31	Carl Yastrzemski	.40	.30	.15
32	Carney Lansford	.06	.05	.02
33	Jerry Remy	.03	.02	.01
34	Dennis Eckersley	.06	.05	.02
35	Dave Stapleton	.03	.02	.01
36	Mark Clear	.03	.02	.01
37	Jim Rice	.20	.15	.08
38	Dwight Evans	.08	.06	.03
39	Rod Carew	.20	.15	.08
40	Don Baylor	.08	.06	.03
41	Reggie Jackson	.40	.30	.15
42	Geoff Zahn	.03	.02	.01
43	Bobby Grich	.06	.05	.02
44	Fred Lynn	.10	.08	.04
45	Bob Boone	.04	.03	.02
46	Doug DeCinces	.06	.05	.02
47	Tom Paciorek	.03	.02	.01
48	Britt Burns	.03	.02	.01
49	Tony Bernazard	.03	.02	.01
50	Steve Kemp	.04	.03	.02
51	Greg Luzinski	.20	.15	.08
52	Harold Baines	.10	.08	.04
53	LaMarr Hoyt	.03	.02	.01
54	Carlton Fisk	.12	.09	.05
55	Andre Thornton	.15	.11	.06

		MT	NR MT	EX
56	Mike Hargrove	.04	.03	.02
57	Len Barker	.03	.02	.01
58	Toby Harrah	.04	.03	.02
59	Dan Spillner	.03	.02	.01
60	Rick Manning	.03	.02	.01
61	Rick Sutcliffe	.08	.06	.03
62	Ron Hassey	.03	.02	.01
63	Lance Parrish	.30	.25	.12
64	John Wockenfuss	.03	.02	.01
65	Lou Whitaker	.12	.09	.05
66	Alan Trammell	.15	.11	.06
67	Kirk Gibson	.15	.11	.06
68	Larry Herndon	.03	.02	.01
69	Jack Morris	.12	.09	.05
70	Dan Petry	.04	.03	.02
71	Frank White	.06	.05	.02
72	Amos Otis	.04	.03	.02
73	Willie Wilson	.25	.20	.10
74	Dan Quisenberry	.06	.05	.02
75	Hal McRae	.06	.05	.02
76	George Brett	.25	.20	.10
77	Larry Gura	.03	.02	.01
78	John Wathan	.04	.03	.02
79	Rollie Fingers	.10	.08	.04
80	Cecil Cooper	.08	.06	.03
81	Robin Yount	.30	.25	.12
82	Ben Oglivie	.06	.05	.02
83	Paul Molitor	.10	.08	.04
84	Gorman Thomas	.06	.05	.02
85	Ted Simmons	.06	.05	.02
86	Pete Vuckovich	.04	.03	.02
87	Gary Gaetti	.08	.06	.03
88	Kent Hrbek	.30	.25	.12
89	John Castino	.03	.02	.01
90	Tom Brunansky	.06	.05	.02
91	Bobby Mitchell	.03	.02	.01
92	Gary Ward	.04	.03	.02
93	Tim Laudner	.03	.02	.01
94	Ron Davis	.03	.02	.01
95	Willie Randolph	.06	.05	.02
96	Roy Smalley	.03	.02	.01
97	Jerry Mumphrey	.03	.02	.01
98	Ken Griffey	.06	.05	.02
99	Dave Winfield	.30	.25	.12
100	Rich Gossage	.10	.08	.04
101	Butch Wynegar	.04	.03	.02
102	Ron Guidry	.12	.09	.05
103	Rickey Henderson	.40	.30	.15
104	Mike Heath	.03	.02	.01
105	Dave Lopes	.06	.05	.02
106	Rick Langford	.03	.02	.01
107	Dwayne Murphy	.04	.03	.02
108	Tony Armas	.06	.05	.02
109	Matt Keough	.03	.02	.01
110	Dan Meyer	.03	.02	.01
111	Bruce Bochte	.03	.02	.01
112	Julio Cruz	.03	.02	.01
113	Floyd Bannister	.04	.03	.02
114	Gaylord Perry	.30	.25	.12
115	Al Cowens	.03	.02	.01
116	Richie Zisk	.04	.03	.02
117	Jim Essian	.03	.02	.01
118	Bill Caudill	.03	.02	.01
119	Buddy Bell	.20	.15	.08
120	Larry Parrish	.06	.05	.02
121	Danny Darwin	.03	.02	.01
122	Bucky Dent	.04	.03	.02
123	Johnny Grubb	.03	.02	.01
124	George Wright	.03	.02	.01
125	Charlie Hough	.06	.05	.02
126	Jim Sundberg	.04	.03	.02
127	Dave Stieb	.20	.15	.08
128	Willie Upshaw	.06	.05	.02
129	Alfredo Griffin	.04	.03	.02
130	Lloyd Moseby	.06	.05	.02
131	Ernie Whitt	.03	.02	.01
132	Jim Clancy	.04	.03	.02
133	Barry Bonnell	.03	.02	.01
134	Damaso Garcia	.04	.03	.02
135	Jim Kaat	.08	.06	.03
136	Jim Kaat	.06	.05	.02
137	Greg Minton	.03	.02	.01
138	Greg Minton	.03	.02	.01
139	Paul Molitor	.10	.08	.04
140	Paul Molitor	.08	.06	.03
141	Manny Trillo	.04	.03	.02
142	Manny Trillo	.04	.03	.02
143	Joel Youngblood	.03	.02	.01
144	Joel Youngblood	.03	.02	.01
145	Robin Yount	.15	.11	.06
146	Robin Yount	.12	.09	.05

		MT	NR MT	EX
147	Willie McGee	.08	.06	.03
148	Darrell Porter	.04	.03	.02
149	Darrell Porter	.04	.03	.02
150	Robin Yount	.15	.11	.06
151	Bruce Benedict	.03	.02	.01
152	Bruce Benedict	.03	.02	.01
153	George Hendrick	.04	.03	.02
154	Bruce Benedict	.03	.02	.01
155	Doug DeCinces	.06	.05	.02
156	Paul Molitor	.10	.08	.04
157	Charlie Moore	.03	.02	.01
158	Fred Lynn	.10	.08	.04
159	Rickey Henderson	.20	.15	.08
160	Dale Murphy	.25	.20	.10
161	Willie Wilson	.08	.06	.03
162	Jack Clark	.10	.08	.04
163	Reggie Jackson	.20	.15	.08
164	Andre Dawson	.15	.11	.06
165	Dan Quisenberry	.06	.05	.02
166	Bruce Sutter	.08	.06	.03
167	Robin Yount	.15	.11	.06
168	Ozzie Smith	.10	.08	.04
169	Frank White	.06	.05	.02
170	Phil Garner	.04	.03	.02
171	Doug DeCinces	.06	.05	.02
172	Mike Schmidt	.25	.20	.10
173	Cecil Cooper	.06	.05	.02
174	Al Oliver	.06	.05	.02
175	Jim Palmer	.15	.11	.06
176	Steve Carlton	.15	.11	.06
177	Carlton Fisk	.12	.09	.05
178	Gary Carter	.20	.15	.08
179	Joaquin Andujar	.04	.03	.02
180	Ozzie Smith	.10	.08	.04
181	Cecil Cooper	.06	.05	.02
182	Darrell Porter	.04	.03	.02
183	Darrell Porter	.04	.03	.02
184	Mike Caldwell	.03	.02	.01
185	Mike Caldwell	.03	.02	.01
186	Ozzie Smith	.10	.08	.04
187	Bruce Sutter	.08	.06	.03
188	Keith Hernandez	.12	.09	.05
189	Dane Iorg	.03	.02	.01
190	Dane Iorg	.03	.02	.01
191	Tony Armas	.04	.03	.02
192	Tony Armas	.04	.03	.02
193	Lance Parrish	.12	.09	.05
194	Lance Parrish	.12	.09	.05
195	John Wathan	.04	.03	.02
196	John Wathan	.04	.03	.02
197	Rickey Henderson	.12	.09	.05
198	Rickey Henderson	.12	.09	.05
199	Rickey Henderson	.12	.09	.05
200	Rickey Henderson	.12	.09	.05
201	Rickey Henderson	.12	.09	.05
202	Rickey Henderson	.12	.09	.05
203	Steve Carlton	.15	.11	.06
204	Steve Carlton	.12	.09	.05
205	Al Oliver	.06	.05	.02
206	Dale Murphy, Al Oliver	.20	.15	.08
207	Dave Kingman	.08	.06	.03
208	Steve Rogers			
209	Bruce Sutter	.08	.06	.03
210	Tim Raines	.20	.15	.08
211	Dale Murphy	.40	.30	.15
212	Chris Chambliss	.04	.03	.02
213	Gene Garber	.03	.02	.01
214	Bob Horner	.08	.06	.03
215	Glenn Hubbard	.03	.02	.01
216	Claudell Washington	.04	.03	.02
217	Bruce Benedict	.03	.02	.01
218	Phil Niekro	.12	.09	.05
219	Leon Durham	.20	.15	.08
220	Jay Johnstone	.04	.03	.02
221	Larry Bowa	.06	.05	.02
222	Keith Moreland	.06	.05	.02
223	Bill Buckner	.06	.05	.02
224	Fergie Jenkins	.08	.06	.03
225	Dick Tidrow	.03	.02	.01
226	Jody Davis	.06	.05	.02
227	Dave Concepcion	.06	.05	.02
228	Dan Driessen	.04	.03	.02
229	Johnny Bench	.20	.15	.08
230	Ron Oester	.03	.02	.01
231	Cesar Cedeno	.06	.05	.02
232	Alex Trevino	.03	.02	.01
233	Tom Seaver	.20	.15	.08
234	Mario Soto	.20	.15	.08
235	Nolan Ryan	.30	.25	.12
236	Art Howe	.03	.02	.01
237	Phil Garner	.04	.03	.02

		MT	NR MT	EX
238	Ray Knight	.06	.05	.02
239	Terry Puhl	.03	.02	.01
240	Joe Niekro	.06	.05	.02
241	Alan Ashby	.03	.02	.01
242	Jose Cruz	.06	.05	.02
243	Steve Garvey	.20	.15	.08
244	Ron Cey	.06	.05	.02
245	Dusty Baker	.04	.03	.02
246	Ken Landreaux	.03	.02	.01
247	Jerry Reuss	.06	.05	.02
248	Pedro Guerrero	.12	.09	.05
249	Bill Russell	.04	.03	.02
250	Fernando Valenzuela	.30	.25	.12
251	Al Oliver	.25	.20	.10
252	Andre Dawson	.15	.11	.06
253	Tim Raines	.20	.15	.08
254	Jeff Reardon	.08	.06	.03
255	Gary Carter	.20	.15	.08
256	Steve Rogers	.03	.02	.01
257	Tim Wallach	.08	.06	.03
258	Chris Speier	.03	.02	.01
259	Dave Kingman	.08	.06	.03
260	Bob Bailor	.03	.02	.01
261	Hubie Brooks	.06	.05	.02
262	Craig Swan	.03	.02	.01
263	George Foster	.08	.06	.03
264	John Stearns	.03	.02	.01
265	Neil Allen	.03	.02	.01
266	Mookie Wilson	.20	.15	.08
267	Steve Carlton	.30	.25	.12
268	Manny Trillo	.04	.03	.02
269	Gary Matthews	.06	.05	.02
270	Mike Schmidt	.25	.20	.10
271	Ivan DeJesus	.03	.02	.01
272	Pete Rose	.40	.30	.15
273	Bo Diaz	.04	.03	.02
274	Sid Monge	.03	.02	.01
275	Bill Madlock	.25	.20	.10
276	Jason Thompson	.03	.02	.01
277	Don Robinson	.03	.02	.01
278	Omar Moreno	.03	.02	.01
279	Dale Berra	.03	.02	.01
280	Dave Parker	.10	.08	.04
281	Tony Pena	.06	.05	.02
282	John Candelaria	.06	.05	.02
283	Lonnie Smith	.04	.03	.02
284	Bruce Sutter	.25	.20	.10
285	George Hendrick	.04	.03	.02
286	Tom Herr	.06	.05	.02
287	Ken Oberkfell	.03	.02	.01
288	Ozzie Smith	.10	.08	.04
289	Bob Forsch	.04	.03	.02
290	Keith Hernandez	.15	.11	.06
291	Garry Templeton	.06	.05	.02
292	Broderick Perkins	.03	.02	.01
293	Terry Kennedy	.20	.15	.08
294	Gene Richards	.03	.02	.01
295	Ruppert Jones	.03	.02	.01
296	Tim Lollar	.03	.02	.01
297	John Montefusco	.03	.02	.01
298	Sixto Lezcano	.03	.02	.01
299	Greg Minton	.03	.02	.01
300	Jack Clark	.25	.20	.10
301	Milt May	.03	.02	.01
302	Reggie Smith	.06	.05	.02
303	Joe Morgan	.10	.08	.04
304	John LeMaster	.03	.02	.01
305	Darrell Evans	.08	.06	.03
306	Al Holland	.03	.02	.01
307	Jesse Barfield	.08	.06	.03
308	Wade Boggs	.60	.45	.25
309	Tom Brunansky	.06	.05	.02
310	Storm Davis	.04	.03	.02
311	Von Hayes	.06	.05	.02
312	Dave Hostetler	.03	.02	.01
313	Kent Hrbek	.12	.09	.05
314	Tim Laudner	.03	.02	.01
315	Cal Ripken	.20	.15	.08
316	Andre Robertson	.03	.02	.01
317	Ed Vande Berg	.03	.02	.01
318	Glenn Wilson	.04	.03	.02
319	Chili Davis	.06	.05	.02
320	Bob Dernier	.03	.02	.01
321	Terry Francona	.03	.02	.01
322	Brian Giles	.03	.02	.01
323	David Green	.03	.02	.01
324	Atlee Hammaker	.03	.02	.01
325	Bill Laskey	.03	.02	.01
326	Willie McGee	.12	.09	.05
327	Johnny Ray	.06	.05	.02
328	Ryne Sandberg	.25	.20	.10
329	Steve Sax	.10	.08	.04
330	Eric Show	.04	.03	.02

1983 Topps Stickers Boxes

These eight cards were printed on the back panels of 1983 Topps sticker boxes, on card per box. The blank- backed cards measure the standard 2-1/2" by 3-1/2" and feature a full-color photo with the player's name at the top. The rest of the back panel advertises the sticker album, while the front of the box has an action photo of Reggie Jackson. The boxes are numbered on the front. Prices in the checklist that follows are for complete boxes.

		MT	NR MT	EX
Complete Set:		6.50	5.00	2.50
Common Player:		.75	.60	.30
1	Fernando Valenzuela	1.00	.70	.40
2	Gary Carter	1.25	.90	.50
3	Mike Schmidt	1.25	.90	.50
4	Reggie Jackson	1.25	.90	.50
5	Jim Palmer	1.00	.70	.40
6	Rollie Fingers	.75	.60	.30
7	Pete Rose	1.50	1.25	.60
8	Rickey Henderson	1.25	.90	.50

1983 Topps Traded

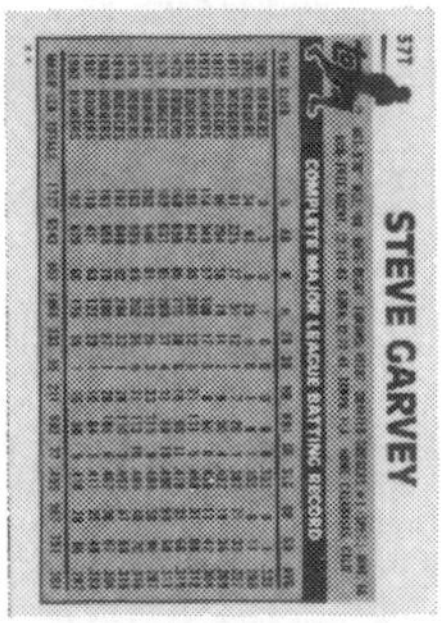

These 2-1/2" by 3-1/2" cards mark a continuation of the traded set introduced in 1981. The 132 cards retain the basic design of the year's regular issue, with their numbering being 1-132 with the "T" suffix. Cards in the set include traded players, new managers and promising rookies. Sold only through dealers, the set was in heavy demand as it contained the first cards of Darryl Strawberry, Ron Kittle, Julio Franco and Mel Hall. While some of those cards were very hot in 1983, it seems likely that some of the rookies may not live up to their initial promise.

	MT	NR MT	EX
Complete Set:	125.00	90.00	50.00

		MT	NR MT	EX
Common Player:		.10	.08	.04
1T	Neil Allen	.10	.08	.04
2T	Bill Almon	.10	.08	.04
3T	Joe Altobelli	.10	.08	.04
4T	Tony Armas	.20	.15	.08
5T	Doug Bair	.10	.08	.04
6T	Steve Baker	.10	.08	.04
7T	Floyd Bannister	.20	.15	.08
8T	Don Baylor	.30	.25	.12
9T	Tony Bernazard	.10	.08	.04
10T	Larry Biittner	.10	.08	.04
11T	Dann Bilardello	.10	.08	.04
12T	Doug Bird	.10	.08	.04
13T	Steve Boros	.10	.08	.04
14T	Greg Brock(FC)	.30	.25	.12
15T	Mike Brown	.10	.08	.04
16T	Tom Burgmeier	.10	.08	.04
17T	Randy Bush(FC)	.20	.15	.08
18T	Bert Campaneris	.20	.15	.08
19T	Ron Cey	.25	.20	.10
20T	Chris Codiroli(FC)	.15	.11	.06
21T	Dave Collins	.15	.11	.06
22T	Terry Crowley	.10	.08	.04
23T	Julio Cruz	.10	.08	.04
24T	Mike Davis	.15	.11	.06
25T	Frank DiPino	.10	.08	.04
26T	Bill Doran(FC)	2.00	1.50	.80
27T	Jerry Dybzinski	.10	.08	.04
28T	Jamie Easterly	.10	.08	.04
29T	Juan Eichelberger	.10	.08	.04
30T	Jim Essian	.10	.08	.04
31T	Pete Falcone	.10	.08	.04
32T	Mike Ferraro	.10	.08	.04
33T	Terry Forster	.15	.11	.06
34T	Julio Franco(FC)	10.00	7.50	4.00
35T	Rich Gale	.10	.08	.04
36T	Kiko Garcia	.10	.08	.04
37T	Steve Garvey	1.50	1.25	.60
38T	Johnny Grubb	.10	.08	.04
39T	Mel Hall(FC)	1.25	.90	.50
40T	Von Hayes	1.00	.70	.40
41T	Danny Heep	.10	.08	.04
42T	Steve Henderson	.10	.08	.04
43T	Keith Hernandez	1.00	.70	.40
44T	Leo Hernandez	.10	.08	.04
45T	Willie Hernandez	.25	.20	.10
46T	Al Holland	.10	.08	.04
47T	Frank Howard	.15	.11	.06
48T	Bobby Johnson	.10	.08	.04
49T	Cliff Johnson	.10	.08	.04
50T	Odell Jones	.10	.08	.04
51T	Mike Jorgensen	.10	.08	.04
52T	Bob Kearney	.10	.08	.04
53T	Steve Kemp	.15	.11	.06
54T	Matt Keough	.10	.08	.04
55T	Ron Kittle(FC)	.80	.60	.30
56T	Mickey Klutts	.10	.08	.04
57T	Alan Knicely	.10	.08	.04
58T	Mike Krukow	.15	.11	.06
59T	Rafael Landestoy	.10	.08	.04
60T	Carney Lansford	.50	.40	.20
61T	Joe Lefebvre	.10	.08	.04
62T	Bryan Little	.10	.08	.04
63T	Aurelio Lopez	.10	.08	.04
64T	Mike Madden	.10	.08	.04
65T	Rick Manning	.10	.08	.04
66T	Billy Martin	.20	.15	.08
67T	Lee Mazzilli	.15	.11	.06
68T	Andy McGaffigan	.10	.08	.04
69T	Craig McMurtry(FC)	.20	.15	.08
70T	John McNamara	.10	.08	.04
71T	Orlando Mercado	.10	.08	.04
72T	Larry Milbourne	.10	.08	.04
73T	Randy Moffitt	.10	.08	.04
74T	Sid Monge	.10	.08	.04
75T	Jose Morales	.10	.08	.04
76T	Omar Moreno	.10	.08	.04
77T	Joe Morgan	2.00	1.50	.80
78T	Mike Morgan	.10	.08	.04
79T	Dale Murray	.10	.08	.04
80T	Jeff Newman	.10	.08	.04
81T	Pete O'Brien(FC)	1.00	.70	.40
82T	Jorge Orta	.10	.08	.04
83T	Alejandro Pena(FC)	.60	.45	.25
84T	Pascual Perez	.20	.15	.08
85T	Tony Perez	.80	.60	.30
86T	Broderick Perkins	.10	.08	.04
87T	Tony Phillips(FC)	1.00	.70	.40
88T	Charlie Puleo	.10	.08	.04
89T	Pat Putnam	.10	.08	.04
90T	Jamie Quirk	.10	.08	.04
91T	Doug Rader	.10	.08	.04
92T	Chuck Rainey	.10	.08	.04
93T	Bobby Ramos	.10	.08	.04
94T	Gary Redus(FC)	.30	.25	.12
95T	Steve Renko	.10	.08	.04
96T	Leon Roberts	.10	.08	.04
97T	Aurelio Rodriguez	.15	.11	.06
98T	Dick Ruthven	.10	.08	.04
99T	Daryl Sconiers	.10	.08	.04
100T	Mike Scott	.70	.50	.30
101T	Tom Seaver	6.00	4.50	2.50
102T	John Shelby(FC)	.25	.20	.10
103T	Bob Shirley	.10	.08	.04
104T	Joe Simpson	.10	.08	.04
105T	Doug Sisk(FC)	.15	.11	.06
106T	Mike Smithson(FC)	.20	.15	.08
107T	Elias Sosa	.10	.08	.04
108T	Darryl Strawberry(FC)	100.00	75.00	40.00
109T	Tom Tellmann	.10	.08	.04
110T	Gene Tenace	.15	.11	.06
111T	Gorman Thomas	.25	.20	.10
112T	Dick Tidrow	.10	.08	.04
113T	Dave Tobik	.10	.08	.04
114T	Wayne Tolleson(FC)	.20	.15	.08
115T	Mike Torrez	.15	.11	.06
116T	Manny Trillo	.15	.11	.06
117T	Steve Trout	.10	.08	.04
118T	Lee Tunnell(FC)	.15	.11	.06
119T	Mike Vail	.10	.08	.04
120T	Ellis Valentine	.10	.08	.04
121T	Tom Veryzer	.10	.08	.04
122T	George Vukovich	.10	.08	.04
123T	Rick Waits	.10	.08	.04
124T	Greg Walker(FC)	.20	.15	.08
125T	Chris Welsh	.10	.08	.04
126T	Len Whitehouse	.10	.08	.04
127T	Eddie Whitson	.15	.11	.06
128T	Jim Wohlford	.10	.08	.04
129T	Matt Young(FC)	.20	.15	.08
130T	Joel Youngblood	.10	.08	.04
131T	Pat Zachry	.10	.08	.04
132T	Checklist 1-132	.10	.08	.04

1984 Topps

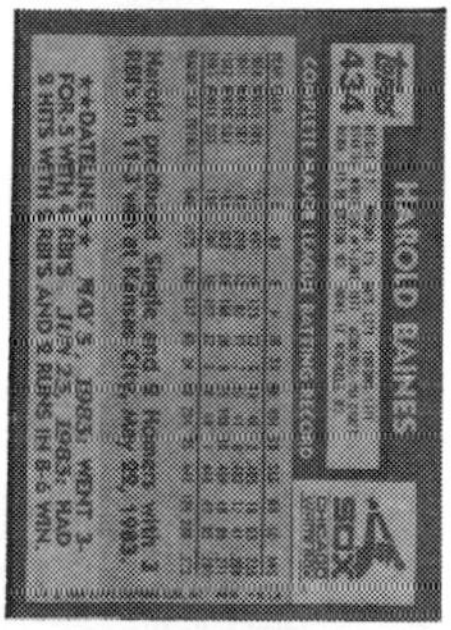

Another 792-card regular set from Topps. For the second straight year, the 2-1/2" by 3-1/2" cards featured a color action photo on the front along with a small portrait photo in the lower left. The team name runs in big letters down the left side, while the player's name and position runs under the large action photo. In the upper right-hand corner is the Topps logo. Backs have a team logo in the upper right corner, along with statistics, personal information and a few highlights. The backs have an unusual and hard-to-read red and purple coloring. Specialty cards include past season highlights, team leaders, major league statistical leaders, All-Stars, active career leaders and numbered checklists. Again, promising rookies were saved for the traded set. Late in 1984, Topps introduced a specially boxed "Tiffany" edition of the 1984 set, with the cards printed on white cardboard with a glossy finish. A total of 10,000 sets were produced. Prices for Tiffany edition super- stars can run from six to eight times the value of the "regular" edition, while common cards sell in the 40¢ range.

		MT	NR MT	EX
Complete Set:		110.00	83.00	45.00
Common Player:		.08	.06	.03
1	1983 Highlight (Steve Carlton)	.30	.25	.12
2	1983 Highlight (Rickey Henderson)	.80	.60	.30
3	1983 Highlight (Dan Quisenberry)	.10	.08	.04
4	1983 Highlight (Steve Carlton, Gaylord Perry, Nolan Ryan)	.30	.25	.12
5	1983 Highlight (Bob Forsch, Dave Righetti, Mike Warren)	.15	.11	.06
6	1983 Highlight (Johnny Bench, Gaylord Perry, Carl Yastrzemski)	.40	.30	.15
7	Gary Lucas	.08	.06	.03
8	*Don Mattingly*(FC)	25.00	20.00	10.00
9	Jim Gott	.10	.08	.04
10	Robin Yount	1.00	.70	.40
11	Twins Batting & Pitching Leaders (Kent Hrbek, Ken Schrom)	.20	.15	.08
12	Billy Sample	.08	.06	.03
13	Scott Holman	.08	.06	.03
14	Tom Brookens	.08	.06	.03
15	Burt Hooton	.10	.08	.04
16	Omar Moreno	.08	.06	.03
17	John Denny	.08	.06	.03
18	Dale Berra	.08	.06	.03
19	*Ray Fontenot*(FC)	.10	.08	.04
20	Greg Luzinski	.12	.09	.05
21	Joe Altobelli	.08	.06	.03
22	Bryan Clark	.08	.06	.03
23	Keith Moreland	.10	.08	.04
24	John Martin	.08	.06	.03
25	Glenn Hubbard	.10	.08	.04
26	Bud Black	.10	.08	.04
27	Daryl Sconiers	.08	.06	.03
28	Frank Viola	1.00	.70	.40
29	Danny Heep	.08	.06	.03
30	Wade Boggs	5.00	3.75	2.00
31	Andy McGaffigan	.08	.06	.03
32	Bobby Ramos	.08	.06	.03
33	Tom Burgmeier	.08	.06	.03
34	Eddie Milner	.08	.06	.03
35	Don Sutton	.30	.25	.12
36	Denny Walling	.08	.06	.03
37	Rangers Batting & Pitching Leaders (Buddy Bell, Rick Honeycutt)	.12	.09	.05
38	Luis DeLeon	.08	.06	.03
39	Garth Iorg	.08	.06	.03
40	Dusty Baker	.12	.09	.05
41	Tony Bernazard	.08	.06	.03
42	Johnny Grubb	.08	.06	.03
43	Ron Reed	.10	.08	.04
44	Jim Morrison	.08	.06	.03
45	Jerry Mumphrey	.08	.06	.03
46	Ray Smith	.08	.06	.03
47	Rudy Law	.08	.06	.03
48	Julio Franco(FC)	2.25	1.75	.90
49	John Stuper	.08	.06	.03
50	Chris Chambliss	.10	.08	.04
51	Jim Frey	.08	.06	.03
52	Paul Splittorff	.08	.06	.03
53	Juan Beniquez	.08	.06	.03
54	Jesse Orosco	.10	.08	.04
55	Dave Concepcion	.15	.11	.06
56	Gary Allenson	.08	.06	.03
57	Dan Schatzeder	.08	.06	.03
58	Max Venable	.08	.06	.03
59	Sammy Stewart	.08	.06	.03
60	Paul Molitor	.20	.15	.08
61	*Chris Codiroli*	.10	.08	.04
62	Dave Hostetler	.08	.06	.03
63	Ed Vande Berg	.08	.06	.03
64	Mike Scioscia	.08	.06	.03
65	Kirk Gibson	.40	.30	.15
66	Astros Batting & Pitching Leaders (Jose Cruz, Nolan Ryan)	.25	.20	.10
67	Gary Ward	.10	.08	.04
68	Luis Salazar	.08	.06	.03
69	Rod Scurry	.08	.06	.03
70	Gary Matthews	.12	.09	.05
71	Leo Hernandez	.08	.06	.03
72	Mike Squires	.08	.06	.03
73	Jody Davis	.10	.08	.04
74	Jerry Martin	.08	.06	.03
75	Bob Forsch	.10	.08	.04
76	Alfredo Griffin	.10	.08	.04
77	Brett Butler	.10	.08	.04
78	Mike Torrez	.10	.08	.04
79	Rob Wilfong	.08	.06	.03
80	Steve Rogers	.10	.08	.04

		MT	NR MT	EX
81	Billy Martin	.12	.09	.05
82	Doug Bird	.08	.06	.03
83	Richie Zisk	.10	.08	.04
84	Lenny Faedo	.08	.06	.03
85	Atlee Hammaker	.08	.06	.03
86	*John Shelby*(FC)	.25	.20	.10
87	Frank Pastore	.08	.06	.03
88	Rob Picciolo	.08	.06	.03
89	*Mike Smithson*(FC)	.15	.11	.06
90	Pedro Guerrero	.35	.25	.14
91	Dan Spillner	.08	.06	.03
92	Lloyd Moseby	.12	.09	.05
93	Bob Knepper	.10	.08	.04
94	Mario Ramirez	.08	.06	.03
95	Aurelio Lopez	.08	.06	.03
96	Royals Batting & Pitching Leaders (Larry Gura, Hal McRae)	.10	.08	.04
97	LaMarr Hoyt	.08	.06	.03
98	Steve Nicosia	.08	.06	.03
99	*Craig Lefferts*(FC)	.30	.25	.12
100	Reggie Jackson	.80	.60	.30
101	Porfirio Altamirano	.08	.06	.03
102	Ken Oberkfell	.08	.06	.03
103	Dwayne Murphy	.10	.08	.04
104	Ken Dayley	.08	.06	.03
105	Tony Armas	.12	.09	.05
106	Tim Stoddard	.08	.06	.03
107	Ned Yost	.08	.06	.03
108	Randy Moffitt	.08	.06	.03
109	Brad Wellman	.08	.06	.03
110	Ron Guidry	.30	.25	.12
111	Bill Virdon	.08	.06	.03
112	Tom Niedenfuer	.10	.08	.04
113	Kelly Paris	.08	.06	.03
114	Checklist 1-132	.08	.06	.03
115	Andre Thornton	.12	.09	.05
116	George Bjorkman	.08	.06	.03
117	Tom Veryzer	.08	.06	.03
118	Charlie Hough	.12	.09	.05
119	Johnny Wockenfuss	.08	.06	.03
120	Keith Hernandez	.40	.30	.15
121	*Pat Sheridan*(FC)	.15	.11	.06
122	Cecilio Guante(FC)	.10	.08	.04
123	Butch Wynegar	.08	.06	.03
124	Damaso Garcia	.08	.06	.03
125	Britt Burns	.08	.06	.03
126	Braves Batting & Pitching Leaders (Craig McMurtry, Dale Murphy)	.25	.20	.10
127	Mike Madden	.08	.06	.03
128	Rick Manning	.08	.06	.03
129	Bill Laskey	.08	.06	.03
130	Ozzie Smith	.70	.50	.30
131	Batting Leaders (Wade Boggs, Bill Madlock)	.50	.40	.20
132	Home Run Leaders (Jim Rice, Mike Schmidt)	.50	.40	.20
133	Runs Batted In Leaders (Cecil Cooper, Dale Murphy, Jim Rice)	.40	.30	.15
134	Stolen Base Leaders (Rickey Henderson, Tim Raines)	.30	.25	.12
135	Victory Leaders (John Denny, LaMarr Hoyt)	.10	.08	.04
136	Strikeout Leaders (Steve Carlton, Jack Morris)	.25	.20	.10
137	Earned Run Average Leaders (Atlee Hammaker, Rick Honeycutt)	.10	.08	.04
138	Leading Firemen (Al Holland, Dan Quisenberry)	.12	.09	.05
139	Bert Campaneris	.12	.09	.05
140	Storm Davis	.12	.09	.05
141	Pat Corrales	.08	.06	.03
142	Rich Gale	.08	.06	.03
143	Jose Morales	.08	.06	.03
144	Brian Harper	.08	.06	.03
145	Gary Lavelle	.08	.06	.03
146	Ed Romero	.08	.06	.03
147	Dan Petry	.10	.08	.04
148	Joe Lefebvre	.08	.06	.03
149	Jon Matlack	.10	.08	.04
150	Dale Murphy	.70	.50	.30
151	Steve Trout	.08	.06	.03
152	Glenn Brummer	.08	.06	.03
153	Dick Tidrow	.08	.06	.03
154	Dave Henderson	.12	.09	.05
155	Frank White	.12	.09	.05
156	Athletics Batting & Pitching Leaders (Tim Conroy, Rickey Henderson)	.25	.20	.10
157	Gary Gaetti	.70	.50	.30
158	John Curtis	.08	.06	.03
159	Darryl Cias	.08	.06	.03
160	Mario Soto	.10	.08	.04

		MT	NR MT	EX
161	*Junior Ortiz*(FC)	.10	.08	.04
162	Bob Ojeda	.12	.09	.05
163	Lorenzo Gray	.08	.06	.03
164	Scott Sanderson	.08	.06	.03
165	Ken Singleton	.12	.09	.05
166	Jamie Nelson	.08	.06	.03
167	Marshall Edwards	.08	.06	.03
168	Juan Bonilla	.08	.06	.03
169	Larry Parrish	.12	.09	.05
170	Jerry Reuss	.12	.09	.05
171	Frank Robinson	.12	.09	.05
172	Frank DiPino	.08	.06	.03
173	*Marvell Wynne*(FC)	.20	.15	.08
174	Juan Berenguer	.08	.06	.03
175	Graig Nettles	.20	.15	.08
176	Lee Smith	.15	.11	.06
177	Jerry Hairston	.08	.06	.03
178	Bill Krueger	.08	.06	.03
179	Buck Martinez	.08	.06	.03
180	Manny Trillo	.10	.08	.04
181	Roy Thomas	.08	.06	.03
182	*Darryl Strawberry*	20.00	15.00	8.00
183	Al Williams	.08	.06	.03
184	Mike O'Berry	.08	.06	.03
185	Sixto Lezcano	.08	.06	.03
186	Cardinals Batting & Pitching Leaders (Lonnie Smith, John Stuper)	.10	.08	.04
187	Luis Aponte	.08	.06	.03
188	Bryan Little	.08	.06	.03
189	*Tim Conroy*(FC)	.12	.09	.05
190	Ben Oglivie	.10	.08	.04
191	Mike Boddicker	.12	.09	.05
192	*Nick Esasky*(FC)	.40	.30	.15
193	Darrell Brown	.08	.06	.03
194	Domingo Ramos	.08	.06	.03
195	Jack Morris	.30	.25	.12
196	Don Slaught(FC)	.12	.09	.05
197	Garry Hancock	.08	.06	.03
198	*Bill Doran*	.80	.60	.30
199	Willie Hernandez	.12	.09	.05
200	Andre Dawson	.80	.60	.30
201	Bruce Kison	.08	.06	.03
202	Bobby Cox	.08	.06	.03
203	Matt Keough	.08	.06	.03
204	*Bobby Meacham*(FC)	.15	.11	.06
205	Greg Minton	.08	.06	.03
206	*Andy Van Slyke*(FC)	3.00	2.25	1.25
207	Donnie Moore	.08	.06	.03
208	*Jose Oquendo*(FC)	.15	.11	.06
209	Manny Sarmiento	.08	.06	.03
210	Joe Morgan	.30	.25	.12
211	Rick Sweet	.08	.06	.03
212	Broderick Perkins	.08	.06	.03
213	Bruce Hurst	.15	.11	.06
214	Paul Householder	.08	.06	.03
215	Tippy Martinez	.08	.06	.03
216	White Sox Batting & Pitching Leaders (Richard Dotson, Carlton Fisk)	.15	.11	.06
217	Alan Ashby	.08	.06	.03
218	Rick Waits	.08	.06	.03
219	Joe Simpson	.08	.06	.03
220	Fernando Valenzuela	.40	.30	.15
221	Cliff Johnson	.08	.06	.03
222	Rick Honeycutt	.08	.06	.03
223	Wayne Krenchicki	.08	.06	.03
224	Sid Monge	.08	.06	.03
225	Lee Mazzilli	.10	.08	.04
226	Juan Eichelberger	.08	.06	.03
227	Steve Braun	.08	.06	.03
228	John Rabb	.08	.06	.03
229	Paul Owens	.08	.06	.03
230	Rickey Henderson	5.00	3.75	2.00
231	Gary Woods	.08	.06	.03
232	Tim Wallach	.15	.11	.06
233	Checklist 133-264	.08	.06	.03
234	Rafael Ramirez	.08	.06	.03
235	*Matt Young*	.15	.11	.06
236	Ellis Valentine	.08	.06	.03
237	John Castino	.08	.06	.03
238	Reid Nichols	.08	.06	.03
239	Jay Howell	.10	.08	.04
240	Eddie Murray	.80	.60	.30
241	Billy Almon	.08	.06	.03
242	Alex Trevino	.08	.06	.03
243	Pete Ladd	.08	.06	.03
244	Candy Maldonado(FC)	.50	.40	.20
245	Rick Sutcliffe	.15	.11	.06
246	Mets Batting & Pitching Leaders (Tom Seaver, Mookie Wilson)	.25	.20	.10
247	Onix Concepcion	.08	.06	.03
248	*Bill Dawley*(FC)	.10	.08	.04
249	Jay Johnstone	.10	.08	.04
250	Bill Madlock	.12	.09	.05
251	Tony Gwynn	3.50	2.75	1.50
252	Larry Christenson	.08	.06	.03
253	Jim Wohlford	.08	.06	.03
254	Shane Rawley	.12	.09	.05
255	Bruce Benedict	.08	.06	.03
256	Dave Geisel	.08	.06	.03
257	Julio Cruz	.08	.06	.03
258	Luis Sanchez	.08	.06	.03
259	Sparky Anderson	.12	.09	.05
260	Scott McGregor	.10	.08	.04
261	Bobby Brown	.08	.06	.03
262	*Tom Candiotti*(FC)	.25	.20	.10
263	Jack Fimple	.08	.06	.03
264	Doug Frobel	.08	.06	.03
265	*Donnie Hill*(FC)	.15	.11	.06
266	Steve Lubratich	.08	.06	.03
267	*Carmelo Martinez*(FC)	.25	.20	.10
268	Jack O'Connor	.08	.06	.03
269	Aurelio Rodriguez	.10	.08	.04
270	*Jeff Russell*(FC)	.20	.15	.08
271	Moose Haas	.08	.06	.03
272	Rick Dempsey	.10	.08	.04
273	Charlie Puleo	.08	.06	.03
274	Rick Monday	.10	.08	.04
275	Len Matuszek	.08	.06	.03
276	Angels Batting & Pitching Leaders (Rod Carew, Geoff Zahn)	.20	.15	.08
277	Eddie Whitson	.08	.06	.03
278	Jorge Bell	1.25	.90	.50
279	Ivan DeJesus	.08	.06	.03
280	Floyd Bannister	.12	.09	.05
281	Larry Milbourne	.08	.06	.03
282	Jim Barr	.08	.06	.03
283	Larry Biittner	.08	.06	.03
284	Howard Bailey	.08	.06	.03
285	Darrell Porter	.10	.08	.04
286	Lary Sorensen	.08	.06	.03
287	Warren Cromartie	.08	.06	.03
288	Jim Beattie	.08	.06	.03
289	Randy Johnson	.08	.06	.03
290	Dave Dravecky	.10	.08	.04
291	Chuck Tanner	.08	.06	.03
292	Tony Scott	.08	.06	.03
293	Ed Lynch	.08	.06	.03
294	U.L. Washington	.08	.06	.03
295	Mike Flanagan	.12	.09	.05
296	Jeff Newman	.08	.06	.03
297	Bruce Berenyi	.08	.06	.03
298	Jim Gantner	.10	.08	.04
299	John Butcher	.08	.06	.03
300	Pete Rose	1.50	1.25	.60
301	Frank LaCorte	.08	.06	.03
302	Barry Bonnell	.08	.06	.03
303	Marty Castillo	.08	.06	.03
304	Warren Brusstar	.08	.06	.03
305	Roy Smalley	.08	.06	.03
306	Dodgers Batting & Pitching Leaders (Pedro Guerrero, Bob Welch)	.15	.11	.06
307	Bobby Mitchell	.08	.06	.03
308	Ron Hassey	.08	.06	.03
309	*Tony Phillips*	.15	.11	.06
310	Willie McGee	.35	.25	.14
311	Jerry Koosman	.12	.09	.05
312	Jorge Orta	.08	.06	.03
313	Mike Jorgensen	.08	.06	.03
314	Orlando Mercado	.08	.06	.03
315	Bob Grich	.12	.09	.05
316	Mark Bradley	.08	.06	.03
317	Greg Pryor	.08	.06	.03
318	Bill Gullickson	.08	.06	.03
319	Al Bumbry	.10	.08	.04
320	Bob Stanley	.08	.06	.03
321	Harvey Kuenn	.10	.08	.04
322	Ken Schrom	.08	.06	.03
323	Alan Knicely	.08	.06	.03
324	*Alejandro Pena*	.30	.25	.12
325	Darrell Evans	.15	.11	.06
326	Bob Kearney	.08	.06	.03
327	Ruppert Jones	.08	.06	.03
328	Vern Ruhle	.08	.06	.03
329	Pat Tabler(FC)	.20	.15	.08
330	John Candelaria	.12	.09	.05
331	Bucky Dent	.12	.09	.05
332	*Kevin Gross*(FC)	.40	.30	.15
333	Larry Herndon	.10	.08	.04
334	Chuck Rainey	.08	.06	.03
335	Don Baylor	.15	.11	.06
336	Mariners Batting & Pitching Leaders (Pat Putnam, Matt Young)	.10	.08	.04

		MT	NR MT	EX
337	Kevin Hagen	.08	.06	.03
338	Mike Warren	.08	.06	.03
339	Roy Lee Jackson	.08	.06	.03
340	Hal McRae	.12	.09	.05
341	Dave Tobik	.08	.06	.03
342	Tim Foli	.08	.06	.03
343	Mark Davis	.08	.06	.03
344	Rick Miller	.08	.06	.03
345	Kent Hrbek	.40	.30	.15
346	Kurt Bevacqua	.08	.06	.03
347	Allan Ramirez	.08	.06	.03
348	Toby Harrah	.10	.08	.04
349	Bob Gibson	.08	.06	.03
350	George Foster	.20	.15	.08
351	Russ Nixon	.08	.06	.03
352	Dave Stewart	.70	.50	.30
353	Jim Anderson	.08	.06	.03
354	Jeff Burroughs	.10	.08	.04
355	Jason Thompson	.08	.06	.03
356	Glenn Abbott	.08	.06	.03
357	Ron Cey	.12	.09	.05
358	Bob Dernier	.08	.06	.03
359	*Jim Acker*(FC)	.12	.09	.05
360	Willie Randolph	.12	.09	.05
361	Dave Smith	.10	.08	.04
362	David Green	.08	.06	.03
363	Tim Laudner	.08	.06	.03
364	Scott Fletcher(FC)	.15	.11	.06
365	Steve Bedrosian	.12	.09	.05
366	Padres Batting & Pitching Leaders (Dave Dravecky, Terry Kennedy)	.12	.09	.05
367	Jamie Easterly	.08	.06	.03
368	Hubie Brooks	.15	.11	.06
369	Steve McCatty	.08	.06	.03
370	Tim Raines	.50	.40	.20
371	Dave Gumpert	.08	.06	.03
372	Gary Roenicke	.08	.06	.03
373	Bill Scherrer	.08	.06	.03
374	Don Money	.08	.06	.03
375	Dennis Leonard	.10	.08	.04
376	*Dave Anderson*(FC)	.15	.11	.06
377	Danny Darwin	.08	.06	.03
378	Bob Brenly	.08	.06	.03
379	Checklist 265-396	.08	.06	.03
380	Steve Garvey	.50	.40	.20
381	Ralph Houk	.10	.08	.04
382	Chris Nyman	.08	.06	.03
383	Terry Puhl	.08	.06	.03
384	*Lee Tunnell*	.10	.08	.04
385	Tony Perez	.20	.15	.08
386	George Hendrick AS	.10	.08	.04
387	Johnny Ray AS	.12	.09	.05
388	Mike Schmidt AS	.35	.25	.14
389	Ozzie Smith AS	.15	.11	.06
390	Tim Raines AS	.25	.20	.10
391	Dale Murphy AS	.40	.30	.15
392	Andre Dawson AS	.20	.15	.08
393	Gary Carter AS	.30	.25	.12
394	Steve Rogers AS	.10	.08	.04
395	Steve Carlton AS	.25	.20	.10
396	Jesse Orosco AS	.10	.08	.04
397	Eddie Murray AS	.35	.25	.14
398	Lou Whitaker AS	.20	.15	.08
399	George Brett AS	.35	.25	.14
400	Cal Ripken AS	.35	.25	.14
401	Jim Rice AS	.30	.25	.12
402	Dave Winfield AS	.30	.25	.12
403	Lloyd Moseby AS	.12	.09	.05
404	Ted Simmons AS	.15	.11	.06
405	LaMarr Hoyt AS	.10	.08	.04
406	Ron Guidry AS	.20	.15	.08
407	Dan Quisenberry AS	.12	.09	.05
408	Lou Piniella	.15	.11	.06
409	*Juan Agosto*(FC)	.15	.11	.06
410	Claudell Washington	.10	.08	.04
411	Houston Jimenez	.08	.06	.03
412	Doug Rader	.08	.06	.03
413	*Spike Owen*(FC)	.20	.15	.08
414	Mitchell Page	.08	.06	.03
415	Tommy John	.25	.20	.10
416	Dane Iorg	.08	.06	.03
417	Mike Armstrong	.08	.06	.03
418	Ron Hodges	.08	.06	.03
419	John Henry Johnson	.08	.06	.03
420	Cecil Cooper	.15	.11	.06
421	Charlie Lea	.08	.06	.03
422	Jose Cruz	.12	.09	.05
423	Mike Morgan	.08	.06	.03
424	Dann Bilardello	.08	.06	.03
425	Steve Howe	.10	.08	.04
426	Orioles Batting & Pitching Leaders (Mike Boddicker, Cal Ripken)	.25	.20	.10

		MT	NR MT	EX
427	Rick Leach	.08	.06	.03
428	Fred Breining	.08	.06	.03
429	*Randy Bush*	.15	.11	.06
430	Rusty Staub	.12	.09	.05
431	Chris Bando	.08	.06	.03
432	*Charlie Hudson*(FC)	.20	.15	.08
433	Rich Hebner	.08	.06	.03
434	Harold Baines	.25	.20	.10
435	Neil Allen	.08	.06	.03
436	Rick Peters	.08	.06	.03
437	Mike Proly	.08	.06	.03
438	Biff Pocoroba	.08	.06	.03
439	Bob Stoddard	.08	.06	.03
440	Steve Kemp	.10	.08	.04
441	Bob Lillis	.08	.06	.03
442	Byron McLaughlin	.08	.06	.03
443	Benny Ayala	.08	.06	.03
444	Steve Renko	.08	.06	.03
445	Jerry Remy	.08	.06	.03
446	Luis Pujols	.08	.06	.03
447	Tom Brunansky	.20	.15	.08
448	Ben Hayes	.08	.06	.03
449	Joe Pettini	.08	.06	.03
450	Gary Carter	.40	.30	.15
451	Bob Jones	.08	.06	.03
452	Chuck Porter	.08	.06	.03
453	Willie Upshaw	.10	.08	.04
454	Joe Beckwith	.08	.06	.03
455	Terry Kennedy	.10	.08	.04
456	Cubs Batting & Pitching Leaders (Fergie Jenkins, Keith Moreland)	.15	.11	.06
457	Dave Rozema	.08	.06	.03
458	Kiko Garcia	.08	.06	.03
459	Kevin Hickey	.08	.06	.03
460	Dave Winfield	.40	.30	.15
461	Jim Maler	.08	.06	.03
462	Lee Lacy	.08	.06	.03
463	Dave Engle	.08	.06	.03
464	Jeff Jones	.08	.06	.03
465	Mookie Wilson	.12	.09	.05
466	Gene Garber	.08	.06	.03
467	Mike Ramsey	.08	.06	.03
468	Geoff Zahn	.08	.06	.03
469	Tom O'Malley	.08	.06	.03
470	Nolan Ryan	5.00	3.75	2.00
471	Dick Howser	.08	.06	.03
472	Mike Brown	.08	.06	.03
473	Jim Dwyer	.08	.06	.03
474	Greg Bargar	.08	.06	.03
475	*Gary Redus*	.25	.20	.10
476	Tom Tellmann	.08	.06	.03
477	Rafael Landestoy	.08	.06	.03
478	Alan Bannister	.08	.06	.03
479	Frank Tanana	.12	.09	.05
480	Ron Kittle(FC)	.40	.30	.15
481	*Mark Thurmond*(FC)	.10	.08	.04
482	Enos Cabell	.08	.06	.03
483	Fergie Jenkins	.20	.15	.08
484	Ozzie Virgil	.08	.06	.03
485	Rick Rhoden	.12	.09	.05
486	Yankees Batting & Pitching Leaders (Don Baylor, Ron Guidry)	.15	.11	.06
487	Ricky Adams	.08	.06	.03
488	Jesse Barfield	.25	.20	.10
489	Dave Von Ohlen	.08	.06	.03
490	Cal Ripken	6.00	4.50	2.50
491	Bobby Castillo	.08	.06	.03
492	Tucker Ashford	.08	.06	.03
493	Mike Norris	.08	.06	.03
494	Chili Davis	.12	.09	.05
495	Rollie Fingers	.25	.20	.10
496	Terry Francona	.08	.06	.03
497	Bud Anderson	.08	.06	.03
498	Rich Gedman	.10	.08	.04
499	Mike Witt	.15	.11	.06
500	George Brett	1.00	.70	.40
501	Steve Henderson	.08	.06	.03
502	Joe Torre	.08	.06	.03
503	Elias Sosa	.08	.06	.03
504	Mickey Rivers	.10	.08	.04
505	Pete Vuckovich	.10	.08	.04
506	Ernie Whitt	.10	.08	.04
507	Mike LaCoss	.08	.06	.03
508	Mel Hall	.20	.15	.08
509	Brad Havens	.08	.06	.03
510	Alan Trammell	.40	.30	.15
511	Marty Bystrom	.08	.06	.03
512	Oscar Gamble	.10	.08	.04
513	Dave Beard	.08	.06	.03
514	Floyd Rayford	.08	.06	.03
515	Gorman Thomas	.10	.08	.04

		MT	NR MT	EX
516	Expos Batting & Pitching Leaders (Charlie Lea, Al Oliver)	.12	.09	.05
517	John Moses	.12	.09	.05
518	*Greg Walker*	.25	.20	.10
519	Ron Davis	.08	.06	.03
520	Bob Boone	.10	.08	.04
521	Pete Falcone	.08	.06	.03
522	Dave Bergman	.08	.06	.03
523	Glenn Hoffman	.08	.06	.03
524	Carlos Diaz	.08	.06	.03
525	Willie Wilson	.15	.11	.06
526	Ron Oester	.08	.06	.03
527	Checklist 397-528	.08	.06	.03
528	Mark Brouhard	.08	.06	.03
529	*Keith Atherton*(FC)	.20	.15	.08
530	Dan Ford	.08	.06	.03
531	Steve Boros	.08	.06	.03
532	Eric Show	.12	.09	.05
533	Ken Landreaux	.08	.06	.03
534	*Pete O'Brien*	.70	.50	.30
535	Bo Diaz	.10	.08	.04
536	Doug Bair	.08	.06	.03
537	Johnny Ray	.12	.09	.05
538	Kevin Bass	.15	.11	.06
539	George Frazier	.08	.06	.03
540	George Hendrick	.10	.08	.04
541	Dennis Lamp	.08	.06	.03
542	Duane Kuiper	.08	.06	.03
543	*Craig McMurtry*	.12	.09	.05
544	Cesar Geronimo	.08	.06	.03
545	Bill Buckner	.15	.11	.06
546	Indians Batting & Pitching Leaders (Mike Hargrove, Lary Sorensen)	.10	.08	.04
547	Mike Moore	.10	.08	.04
548	Ron Jackson	.08	.06	.03
549	*Walt Terrell*	.50	.40	.20
550	Jim Rice	.40	.30	.15
551	Scott Ullger	.08	.06	.03
552	Ray Burris	.08	.06	.03
553	Joe Nolan	.08	.06	.03
554	Ted Power(FC)	.12	.09	.05
555	Greg Brock	.15	.11	.06
556	Joey McLaughlin	.08	.06	.03
557	Wayne Tolleson	.10	.08	.04
558	Mike Davis	.10	.08	.04
559	Mike Scott	.20	.15	.08
560	Carlton Fisk	.50	.40	.20
561	Whitey Herzog	.10	.08	.04
562	Manny Castillo	.08	.06	.03
563	Glenn Wilson	.10	.08	.04
564	Al Holland	.08	.06	.03
565	Leon Durham	.10	.08	.04
566	Jim Bibby	.08	.06	.03
567	Mike Heath	.08	.06	.03
568	Pete Filson	.08	.06	.03
569	Bake McBride	.08	.06	.03
570	Dan Quisenberry	.12	.09	.05
571	Bruce Bochy	.08	.06	.03
572	Jerry Royster	.08	.06	.03
573	Dave Kingman	.15	.11	.06
574	Brian Downing	.12	.09	.05
575	Jim Clancy	.10	.08	.04
576	Giants Batting & Pitching Leaders (Atlee Hammaker, Jeff Leonard)	.10	.08	.04
577	Mark Clear	.08	.06	.03
578	Lenn Sakata	.08	.06	.03
579	Bob James	.08	.06	.03
580	Lonnie Smith	.10	.08	.04
581	*Jose DeLeon*(FC)	.60	.45	.25
582	Bob McClure	.08	.06	.03
583	Derrel Thomas	.08	.06	.03
584	Dave Schmidt	.08	.06	.03
585	Dan Driessen	.10	.08	.04
586	Joe Niekro	.15	.11	.06
587	Von Hayes	.15	.11	.06
588	Milt Wilcox	.08	.06	.03
589	Mike Easler	.10	.08	.04
590	Dave Stieb	.15	.11	.06
591	Tony LaRussa	.10	.08	.04
592	Andre Robertson	.08	.06	.03
593	Jeff Lahti	.08	.06	.03
594	Gene Richards	.08	.06	.03
595	Jeff Reardon	.15	.11	.06
596	Ryne Sandberg	10.00	7.50	4.50
597	Rick Camp	.08	.06	.03
598	Rusty Kuntz	.08	.06	.03
599	*Doug Sisk*	.10	.08	.04
600	Rod Carew	.50	.40	.20
601	John Tudor	.12	.09	.05
602	John Wathan	.10	.08	.04
603	Renie Martin	.08	.06	.03

		MT	NR MT	EX
604	John Lowenstein	.08	.06	.03
605	Mike Caldwell	.08	.06	.03
606	Blue Jays Batting & Pitching Leaders (Lloyd Moseby, Dave Stieb)	.15	.11	.06
607	Tom Hume	.08	.06	.03
608	Bobby Johnson	.08	.06	.03
609	Dan Meyer	.08	.06	.03
610	Steve Sax	.30	.25	.12
611	Chet Lemon	.10	.08	.04
612	Harry Spilman	.08	.06	.03
613	Greg Gross	.08	.06	.03
614	Len Barker	.10	.08	.04
615	Garry Templeton	.12	.09	.05
616	Don Robinson	.10	.08	.04
617	Rick Cerone	.08	.06	.03
618	Dickie Noles	.08	.06	.03
619	Jerry Dybzinski	.08	.06	.03
620	Al Oliver	.20	.15	.08
621	Frank Howard	.10	.08	.04
622	Al Cowens	.08	.06	.03
623	Ron Washington	.08	.06	.03
624	Terry Harper	.08	.06	.03
625	Larry Gura	.10	.08	.04
626	Bob Clark	.08	.06	.03
627	Dave LaPoint	.10	.08	.04
628	Ed Jurak	.08	.06	.03
629	Rick Langford	.08	.06	.03
630	Ted Simmons	.15	.11	.06
631	Denny Martinez	.10	.08	.04
632	Tom Foley	.08	.06	.03
633	Mike Krukow	.10	.08	.04
634	Mike Marshall	.15	.11	.06
635	Dave Righetti	.25	.20	.10
636	Pat Putnam	.08	.06	.03
637	Phillies Batting & Pitching Leaders (John Denny, Gary Matthews)	.10	.08	.04
638	George Vukovich	.08	.06	.03
639	Rick Lysander	.08	.06	.03
640	Lance Parrish	.35	.25	.14
641	Mike Richardt	.08	.06	.03
642	Tom Underwood	.08	.06	.03
643	Mike Brown	.08	.06	.03
644	Tim Lollar	.08	.06	.03
645	Tony Pena	.12	.09	.05
646	Checklist 529-660	.08	.06	.03
647	Ron Roenicke	.08	.06	.03
648	Len Whitehouse	.08	.06	.03
649	Tom Herr	.12	.09	.05
650	Phil Niekro	.30	.25	.12
651	John McNamara	.08	.06	.03
652	Rudy May	.08	.06	.03
653	Dave Stapleton	.08	.06	.03
654	Bob Bailor	.08	.06	.03
655	Amos Otis	.10	.08	.04
656	Bryn Smith	.08	.06	.03
657	Thad Bosley	.08	.06	.03
658	Jerry Augustine	.08	.06	.03
659	Duane Walker	.08	.06	.03
660	Ray Knight	.12	.09	.05
661	Steve Yeager	.08	.06	.03
662	Tom Brennan	.08	.06	.03
663	Johnnie LeMaster	.08	.06	.03
664	Dave Stegman	.08	.06	.03
665	Buddy Bell	.15	.11	.06
666	Tigers Batting & Pitching Leaders (Jack Morris, Lou Whitaker)	.15	.11	.06
667	Vance Law	.10	.08	.04
668	Larry McWilliams	.08	.06	.03
669	Dave Lopes	.10	.08	.04
670	Rich Gossage	.25	.20	.10
671	Jamie Quirk	.08	.06	.03
672	Ricky Nelson	.08	.06	.03
673	Mike Walters	.08	.06	.03
674	Tim Flannery	.08	.06	.03
675	Pascual Perez	.10	.08	.04
676	Brian Giles	.08	.06	.03
677	Doyle Alexander	.12	.09	.05
678	Chris Speier	.08	.06	.03
679	Art Howe	.08	.06	.03
680	Fred Lynn	.25	.20	.10
681	Tom Lasorda	.12	.09	.05
682	Dan Morogiello	.08	.06	.03
683	*Marty Barrett*(FC)	.35	.25	.14
684	Bob Shirley	.08	.06	.03
685	Willie Aikens	.08	.06	.03
686	Joe Price	.08	.06	.03
687	Roy Howell	.08	.06	.03
688	George Wright	.08	.06	.03
689	Mike Fischlin	.08	.06	.03
690	Jack Clark	.25	.20	.10
691	*Steve Lake*(FC)	.10	.08	.04

		MT	NR MT	EX
692	Dickie Thon	.10	.08	.04
693	Alan Wiggins	.08	.06	.03
694	Mike Stanton	.08	.06	.03
695	Lou Whitaker	.40	.30	.15
696	Pirates Batting & Pitching Leaders (Bill Madlock, Rick Rhoden)	.15	.11	.06
697	Dale Murray	.08	.06	.03
698	Marc Hill	.08	.06	.03
699	Dave Rucker	.08	.06	.03
700	Mike Schmidt	1.75	1.25	.70
701	NL Active Career Batting Leaders (Bill Madlock, Dave Parker, Pete Rose)	.35	.25	.14
702	NL Active Career Hit Leaders (Tony Perez, Pete Rose, Rusty Staub)	.35	.25	.14
703	NL Active Career Home Run Leaders (Dave Kingman, Tony Perez, Mike Schmidt)	.30	.25	.12
704	NL Active Career RBI Leaders (Al Oliver, Tony Perez, Rusty Staub)	.15	.11	.06
705	NL Active Career Stolen Bases Leaders (Larry Bowa, Cesar Cedeno, Joe Morgan)	.12	.09	.05
706	NL Active Career Victory Leaders (Steve Carlton, Fergie Jenkins, Tom Seaver)	.30	.25	.12
707	NL Active Career Strikeout Leaders (Steve Carlton, Nolan Ryan, Tom Seaver)	.35	.25	.14
708	NL Active Career ERA Leaders (Steve Carlton, Steve Rogers, Tom Seaver)	.25	.20	.10
709	NL Active Career Save Leaders (Gene Garber, Tug McGraw, Bruce Sutter)	.12	.09	.05
710	AL Active Career Batting Leaders (George Brett, Rod Carew, Cecil Cooper)	.30	.25	.12
711	AL Active Career Hit Leaders (Bert Campaneris, Rod Carew, Reggie Jackson)	.30	.25	.12
712	AL Active Career Home Run Leaders (Reggie Jackson, Greg Luzinski, Graig Nettles)	.20	.15	.08
713	AL Active Career RBI Leaders (Reggie Jackson, Graig Nettles, Ted Simmons)	.20	.15	.08
714	AL Active Career Stolen Bases Leaders (Bert Campaneris, Dave Lopes, Omar Moreno)	.10	.08	.04
715	AL Active Career Victory Leaders (Tommy John, Jim Palmer, Don Sutton)	.25	.20	.10
716	AL Active Strikeout Leaders (Bert Blyleven, Jerry Koosman, Don Sutton)	.15	.11	.06
717	AL Active Career ERA Leaders (Rollie Fingers, Ron Guidry, Jim Palmer)	.15	.11	.06
718	AL Active Career Save Leaders (Rollie Fingers, Rich Gossage, Dan Quisenberry)	.15	.11	.06
719	Andy Hassler	.08	.06	.03
720	Dwight Evans	.20	.15	.08
721	Del Crandall	.08	.06	.03
722	Bob Welch	.15	.11	.06
723	Rich Dauer	.08	.06	.03
724	Eric Rasmussen	.08	.06	.03
725	Cesar Cedeno	.12	.09	.05
726	Brewers Batting & Pitching Leaders (Moose Haas, Ted Simmons)	.12	.09	.05
727	Joel Youngblood	.08	.06	.03
728	Tug McGraw	.12	.09	.05
729	Gene Tenace	.10	.08	.04
730	Bruce Sutter	.20	.15	.08
731	Lynn Jones	.08	.06	.03
732	Terry Crowley	.08	.06	.03
733	Dave Collins	.10	.08	.04
734	Odell Jones	.08	.06	.03
735	Rick Burleson	.10	.08	.04
736	Dick Ruthven	.08	.06	.03
737	Jim Essian	.08	.06	.03
738	*Bill Schroeder*(FC)	.20	.15	.08
739	Bob Watson	.10	.08	.04
740	Tom Seaver	1.00	.70	.40
741	Wayne Gross	.08	.06	.03
742	Dick Williams	.08	.06	.03
743	Don Hood	.08	.06	.03
744	Jamie Allen	.08	.06	.03
745	Dennis Eckersley	.15	.11	.06
746	Mickey Hatcher	.10	.08	.04
747	Pat Zachry	.08	.06	.03
748	Jeff Leonard	.12	.09	.05
749	Doug Flynn	.08	.06	.03
750	Jim Palmer	.70	.50	.30
751	Charlie Moore	.08	.06	.03
752	Phil Garner	.10	.08	.04
753	Doug Gwosdz	.08	.06	.03
754	Kent Tekulve	.10	.08	.04
755	Garry Maddox	.10	.08	.04
756	Reds Batting & Pitching Leaders (Ron Oester, Mario Soto)	.10	.08	.04
757	Larry Bowa	.15	.11	.06
758	Bill Stein	.08	.06	.03
759	Richard Dotson	.12	.09	.05
760	Bob Horner	.15	.11	.06
761	John Montefusco	.08	.06	.03
762	Rance Mulliniks	.08	.06	.03
763	Craig Swan	.08	.06	.03
764	Mike Hargrove	.08	.06	.03
765	Ken Forsch	.08	.06	.03
766	Mike Vail	.08	.06	.03
767	Carney Lansford	.12	.09	.05
768	Champ Summers	.08	.06	.03
769	Bill Caudill	.08	.06	.03
770	Ken Griffey	.12	.09	.05
771	Billy Gardner	.08	.06	.03
772	Jim Slaton	.08	.06	.03
773	Todd Cruz	.08	.06	.03
774	Tom Gorman	.08	.06	.03
775	Dave Parker	.30	.25	.12
776	Craig Reynolds	.08	.06	.03
777	Tom Paciorek	.08	.06	.03
778	*Andy Hawkins*(FC)	.25	.20	.10
779	Jim Sundberg	.10	.08	.04
780	Steve Carlton	.60	.45	.25
781	Checklist 661-792	.08	.06	.03
782	Steve Balboni	.10	.08	.04
783	Luis Leal	.08	.06	.03
784	Leon Roberts	.08	.06	.03
785	Joaquin Andujar	.10	.08	.04
786	Red Sox Batting & Pitching Leaders (Wade Boggs, Bob Ojeda)	.40	.30	.15
787	Bill Campbell	.08	.06	.03
788	Milt May	.08	.06	.03
789	Bert Blyleven	.20	.15	.08
790	Doug DeCinces	.12	.09	.05
791	Terry Forster	.10	.08	.04
792	Bill Russell	.10	.08	.04

1984 Topps All-Star Glossy Set Of 22

These 2-1/2" by 3-1/2" cards were a result of the success of Topps' efforts the previous year with glossy cards on a mail-in basis. A 22-card set, the cards are divided evenly between the two leagues. Each All-Star Game starter for both leagues, the managers and the honorary team captains have an All-Star Glossy card. The cards feature a large color photo on the front with an All-Star banner across the top and the league emblem in the lower left. The player's name and position appear below the photo. Backs have a name, team, position and card number along with the phrase "1983 All-Star Game Commemorative Set". The '84 Glossy All-Stars were distributed one card per pack in Topps rack packs that year.

		MT	NR MT	EX
Complete Set:		6.00	4.50	2.50
Common Player:		.20	.15	.08
1	Harvey Kuenn	.20	.15	.08
2	Rod Carew	.50	.40	.20

		MT	NR MT	EX
3	Manny Trillo	.20	.15	.08
4	George Brett	.80	.60	.30
5	Robin Yount	.40	.30	.15
6	Jim Rice	.50	.40	.20
7	Fred Lynn	.25	.20	.10
8	Dave Winfield	.50	.40	.20
9	Ted Simmons	.25	.20	.10
10	Dave Stieb	.25	.20	.10
11	Carl Yastrzemski	.80	.60	.30
12	Whitey Herzog	.20	.15	.08
13	Al Oliver	.25	.20	.10
14	Steve Sax	.30	.25	.12
15	Mike Schmidt	.80	.60	.30
16	Ozzie Smith	.30	.25	.12
17	Tim Raines	.50	.40	.20
18	Andre Dawson	.35	.25	.14
19	Dale Murphy	.80	.60	.30
20	Gary Carter	.50	.40	.20
21	Mario Soto	.20	.15	.08
22	Johnny Bench	.60	.45	.25

1984 Topps All-Star Glossy Set Of 40

For the second straight year in 1984, Topps produced a 40-card All-Star "Collector's Edition" set as a "consolation prize" for its sweepstakes game. By collecting game cards and sending them in with a bit of cash, the collector could receive one of eight different five-card series. As the previous year, the 2-1/2" by 3-1/2" cards feature a nearly full-frame color photo on its glossy finish front. Backs are printed in red and blue.

		MT	NR MT	EX
Complete Set:		16.00	12.00	6.50
Common Player:		.15	.11	.06
1	Pete Rose	1.25	.90	.50
2	Lance Parrish	.30	.25	.12
3	Steve Rogers	.15	.11	.06
4	Eddie Murray	.60	.45	.25
5	Johnny Ray	.20	.15	.08
6	Rickey Henderson	.70	.50	.30
7	Atlee Hammaker	.15	.11	.06
8	Wade Boggs	3.00	2.25	1.25
9	Gary Carter	.50	.40	.20
10	Jack Morris	.30	.25	.12
11	Darrell Evans	.20	.15	.08
12	George Brett	1.00	.70	.40
13	Bob Horner	.20	.15	.08
14	Ron Guidry	.30	.25	.12
15	Nolan Ryan	.50	.40	.20
16	Dave Winfield	.60	.45	.25
17	Ozzie Smith	.25	.20	.10
18	Ted Simmons	.20	.15	.08
19	Bill Madlock	.20	.15	.08
20	Tony Armas	.15	.11	.06
21	Al Oliver	.20	.15	.08
22	Jim Rice	.50	.40	.20
23	George Hendrick	.15	.11	.06
24	Dave Stieb	.20	.15	.08
25	Pedro Guerrero	.25	.20	.10
26	Rod Carew	.60	.45	.25
27	Steve Carlton	.50	.40	.20
28	Dave Righetti	.30	.25	.12
29	Darryl Strawberry	3.00	2.25	1.25
30	Lou Whitaker	.30	.25	.12
31	Dale Murphy	1.00	.70	.40
32	LaMarr Hoyt	.15	.11	.06
33	Jesse Orosco	.15	.11	.06
34	Cecil Cooper	.20	.15	.08
35	Andre Dawson	.35	.25	.14
36	Robin Yount	.40	.30	.15
37	Tim Raines	.50	.40	.20
38	Dan Quisenberry	.15	.11	.06
39	Mike Schmidt	1.00	.70	.40
40	Carlton Fisk	.30	.25	.12

1984 Topps Gallery of Immortals

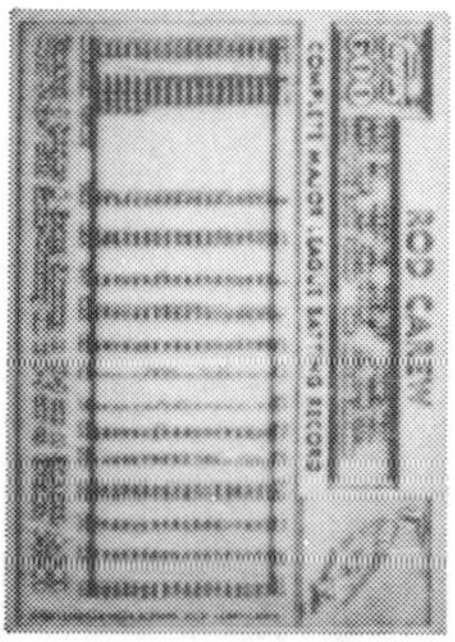

The Gallery of Immortals set of aluminum, bronze and silver replicas was the first miniature set of 12 from Topps and the start of an annual tradition (in 1985, the name was changed to Gallery of Champions) .Each mini is an exact replica (one-quarter scale) of the featured player's official Topps baseball card card, both front and back, in minute detail. The bronze and silver sets include a dozen three-dimensional raised metal cards packaged in a velvet-lined case that bears the title of the set in gold-embossed letters. A certificate of authenticity is included with each set. A Tom Seaver pewter metal mini-card was given as a premium to dealers who purchsed bronze and silver sets (value $75). A Darryl Strawberry bronze was given as a premium to dealers who purchased cases of the 1984 Topps Traded sets (value $12). Additionally, a Steve Carlton bronze was issued as a premium in 1983 to dealers who purchased 1983 Topps Traded sets (value $50).

		MT	NR MT	EX
Complete Aluminum Set:		30.00	22.00	12.00
Complete Bronze Set:		175.00	131.00	70.00
Complete Silver Set:		600.00	450.00	240.00
(1a)	George Brett (aluminum)	1.50	1.25	.60
(1b)	George Brett (bronze)	15.00	11.00	6.00
(1c)	George Brett (silver)	80.00	60.00	32.00
(2a)	Rod Carew (aluminum)	1.50	1.25	.60
(2b)	Rod Carew (bronze)	12.50	9.50	5.00
(2c)	Rod Carew (silver)	50.00	37.00	20.00
(3a)	Steve Carlton (aluminum)	1.50	1.25	.60
(3b)	Steve Carlton (bronze)	12.50	9.50	5.00
(3c)	Steve Carlton (silver)	50.00	37.00	20.00
(4a)	Rollie Fingers (aluminum)	1.25	.90	.50
(4b)	Rollie Fingers (bronze)	10.00	7.50	4.00
(4c)	Rollie Fingers (silver)	20.00	15.00	8.00
(5a)	Steve Garvey (aluminum)	1.50	1.25	.60
(5b)	Steve Garvey (bronze)	12.50	9.50	5.00
(5c)	Steve Garvey (silver)	50.00	37.00	20.00
(6a)	Reggie Jackson (aluminum)	1.50	1.25	.60
(6b)	Reggie Jackson (bronze)	15.00	11.00	6.00
(6c)	Reggie Jackson (silver)	80.00	60.00	32.00
(7a)	Joe Morgan (aluminum)	1.25	.90	.50
(7b)	Joe Morgan (bronze)	10.00	7.50	4.00
(7c)	Joe Morgan (silver)	20.00	15.00	8.00
(8a)	Jim Palmer (aluminum)	1.25	.90	.50
(8b)	Jim Palmer (bronze)	10.00	7.50	4.00
(8c)	Jim Palmer (silver)	20.00	15.00	8.00

	MT	NR MT	EX
(9a) Pete Rose (aluminum)	2.50	2.00	1.00
(9b) Pete Rose (bronze)	25.00	18.50	10.00
(9c) Pete Rose (silver)	110.00	82.00	44.00
(10a) Nolan Ryan (aluminum)	1.50	1.25	.60
(10b) Nolan Ryan (bronze)	12.50	9.50	5.00
(10c) Nolan Ryan (silver)	80.00	60.00	33.00
(11a) Mike Schmidt (aluminum)	1.50	1.25	.60
(11b) Mike Schmidt (bronze)	15.00	11.00	6.00
(11c) Mike Schmidt (silver)	80.00	60.00	32.00
(12a) Tom Seaver (aluminum)	1.50	1.25	.60
(12b) Tom Seaver (bronze)	12.50	9.50	5.00
(12c) Tom Seaver (silver)	50.00	37.00	20.00

1984 Topps Rub Downs

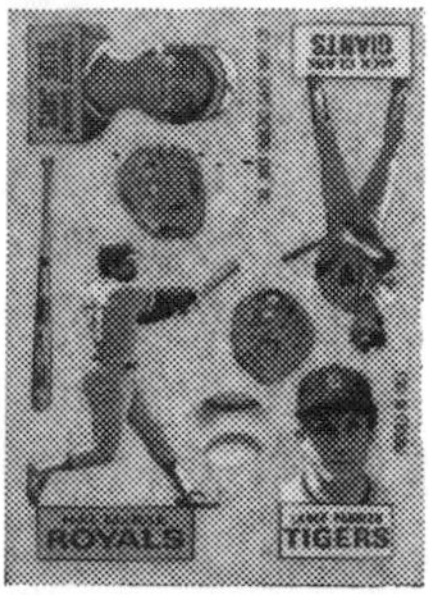

This set, produced by Topps in 1984, consists of 32 "Rub Down" sheets featuring 112 different players. Each sheet measures 2-3/8" by 3-15/16" and includes small, color baseball player figures along with bats, balls and gloves. The pictures can be transferred to another surface by rubbing the paper backing. The sheets, which were sold as a separate issue, are somewhat reminiscent of earlier tattoo sets issued by Topps. The sheets are not numbered.

	MT	NR MT	EX
Complete Set:	9.00	6.75	3.50
Common Player:	.10	.08	.04
(1) Tony Armas, Harold Baines, Lonnie Smith	.10	.08	.04
(2) Don Baylor, George Hendrick, Ron Kittle, Johnnie LeMaster	.10	.08	.04
(3) Buddy Bell, Ray Knight, Lloyd Moseby	.10	.08	.04
(4) Bruce Benedict, Atlee Hammaker, Frank White	.10	.08	.04
(5) Wade Boggs, Rick Dempsey, Keith Hernandez	.60	.45	.25
(6) George Brett, Andre Dawson, Paul Molitor, Alan Wiggins	.30	.25	.12
(7) Tom Brunansky, Pedro Guerrero, Darryl Strawberry	.40	.30	.15
(8) Bill Buckner, Rich Gossage, Dave Stieb, Rick Sutcliffe	.15	.11	.06
(9) Rod Carew, Carlton Fisk, Johnny Ray, Matt Young	.25	.20	.10
(10) Steve Carlton, Bob Horner, Dan Quisenberry	.25	.20	.10
(11) Gary Carter, Phil Garner, Ron Guidry	.25	.20	.10
(12) Ron Cey, Steve Kemp, Greg Luzinski, Kent Tekulve	.10	.08	.04
(13) Chris Chambliss, Dwight Evans, Julio Franco	.15	.11	.06
(14) Jack Clark, Damaso Garcia, Hal McRae, Lance Parrish	.20	.15	.08
(15) Dave Concepcion, Cecil Cooper, Fred Lynn, Jesse Orosco	.15	.11	.06
(16) Jose Cruz, Gary Matthews, Jack Morris, Jim Rice	.20	.15	.08
(17) Ron Davis, Kent Hrbek, Tom Seaver	.25	.20	.10
(18) John Denny, Carney Lansford, Mario Soto, Lou Whitaker	.10	.08	.04
(19) Leon Durham, Dave Lopes, Steve Sax	.15	.11	.06
(20) George Foster, Gary Gaetti, Bobby Grich, Gary Redus	.15	.11	.06
(21) Steve Garvey, Bill Russell, Jerry REmy, George Wright	.20	.15	.08
(22) Moose Haas, Bruce Sutter, Dickie Thon, Andre Thornton	.10	.08	.04
(23) Toby Harrah, Pat Putnam, Tim Raines, Mike Schmidt	.30	.25	.12
(24) Rickey Henderson, Dave Righetti, Pete Rose	.70	.50	.30
(25) Steve Henderson, Bill Madlock, Alan Trammell	.20	.15	.08
(26) LaMarr Hoyt, Larry Parrish, Nolan Ryan	.25	.20	.10
(27) Reggie Jackson, Eric Show, Jason Thompson	.30	.25	.12
(28) Tommy John, Terry Kennedy, Eddie Murray, Ozzie Smith	.25	.20	.10
(29) Jeff Leonard, Dale Murphy, Ken Singleton, Dave Winfield	.30	.25	.12
(30) Craig McMurtry, Cal Ripken, Steve Rogers, Willie Upshaw	.25	.20	.10
(31) Ben Oglivie, Jim Palmer, Darrell Porter	.20	.15	.08
(32) Tony Pena, Fernando Valenzuela, Robin Yount	.20	.15	.08

1984 Topps Stickers

The largest sticker set issued by Topps, the 1984 set consists of 386 stickers, each measuring 1-15/16" by 2-9/16". The full color photos have stars in each of the corners and are numbered on both the front and the back. The back includes information about the sticker album and a promotion to order stickers through the mail.

		MT	NR MT	EX
Complete Set:		15.00	11.00	6.00
Common Player:		.03	.02	.01
Sticker Album:		.80	.60	.30
1	Steve Carlton	.15	.11	.06
2	Steve Carlton	.12	.09	.05
3	Rickey Henderson	.20	.15	.08
4	Rickey Henderson	.15	.11	.06
5	Fred Lynn	.12	.09	.05
6	Fred Lynn	.10	.08	.04
7	Greg Luzinski	.08	.06	.03
8	Greg Luzinski	.06	.05	.02
9	Dan Quisenberry	.08	.06	.03
10	Dan Quisenberry	.06	.05	.02
11	1983 Championship (LaMarr Hoyt)	.03	.02	.01
12	1983 Championship (Mike Flanagan)	.04	.03	.02
13	1983 Championship (Mike Boddicker)	.04	.03	.02
14	1983 Championship (Tito Landrum)	.03	.02	.01
15	1983 Championship (Steve Carlton)	.12	.09	.05
16	1983 Championship (Fernando Valenzuela)	.12	.09	.05
17	1983 Championship (Charlie Hudson)	.03	.02	.01
18	1983 Championship (Gary Matthews)	.04	.03	.02
19	1983 World Series (John Denny)	.03	.02	.01
20	1983 World Series (John Lowenstein)	.03	.02	.01

		MT	NR MT	EX
21	1983 World Series (Jim Palmer)	.10	.08	.04
22	1983 World Series (Benny Ayala)	.03	.02	.01
23	1983 World Series (Rick Dempsey)	.03	.02	.01
24	1983 World Series (Cal Ripken)	.15	.11	.06
25	1983 World Series (Sammy Stewart)	.03	.02	.01
26	1983 World Series (Eddie Murray)	.15	.11	.06
27	Dale Murphy	.25	.20	.10
28	Chris Chambliss	.04	.03	.02
29	Glenn Hubbard	.04	.03	.02
30	Bob Horner	.08	.06	.03
31	Phil Niekro	.12	.09	.05
32	Claudell Washington	.04	.03	.02
33	Rafael Ramirez	.03	.02	.01
34	Bruce Benedict	.04	.03	.02
35	Gene Garber	.03	.02	.01
36	Pascual Perez	.04	.03	.02
37	Jerry Royster	.03	.02	.01
38	Steve Bedrosian	.06	.05	.02
39	Keith Moreland	.06	.05	.02
40	Leon Durham	.06	.05	.02
41	Ron Cey	.06	.05	.02
42	Bill Buckner	.06	.05	.02
43	Jody Davis	.06	.05	.02
44	Lee Smith	.06	.05	.02
45	Ryne Sandberg	.10	.08	.04
46	Larry Bowa	.04	.03	.02
47	Chuck Rainey	.04	.03	.02
48	Fergie Jenkins	.06	.05	.02
49	Dick Ruthven	.03	.02	.01
50	Jay Johnstone	.04	.03	.02
51	Mario Soto	.06	.05	.02
52	Gary Redus	.04	.03	.02
53	Ron Oester	.04	.03	.02
54	Cesar Cedeno	.06	.05	.02
55	Dan Driessen	.04	.03	.02
56	Dave Concepcion	.06	.05	.02
57	Dann Bilardello	.03	.02	.01
58	Joe Price	.03	.02	.01
59	Tom Hume	.03	.02	.01
60	Eddie Milner	.03	.02	.01
61	Paul Householder	.04	.03	.02
62	Bill Scherrer	.04	.03	.02
63	Phil Garner	.04	.03	.02
64	Dickie Thon	.04	.03	.02
65	Jose Cruz	.06	.05	.02
66	Nolan Ryan	.15	.11	.06
67	Terry Puhl	.03	.02	.01
68	Ray Knight	.06	.05	.02
69	Joe Niekro	.06	.05	.02
70	Jerry Mumphrey	.10	.08	.04
71	Bill Dawley	.03	.02	.01
72	Alan Ashby	.04	.03	.02
73	Denny Walling	.04	.03	.02
74	Frank DiPino	.04	.03	.02
75	Pedro Guerrero	.12	.09	.05
76	Ken Landreaux	.03	.02	.01
77	Bill Russell	.04	.03	.02
78	Steve Sax	.10	.08	.04
79	Fernando Valenzuela	.15	.11	.06
80	Dusty Baker	.04	.03	.02
81	Jerry Reuss	.04	.03	.02
82	Alejandro Pena	.04	.03	.02
83	Rick Monday	.06	.05	.02
84	Rick Honeycutt	.03	.02	.01
85	Mike Marshall	.06	.05	.02
86	Steve Yeager	.04	.03	.02
87	Al Oliver	.06	.05	.02
88	Steve Rogers	.03	.02	.01
89	Jeff Reardon	.08	.06	.03
90	Gary Carter	.20	.15	.08
91	Tim Raines	.15	.11	.06
92	Andre Dawson	.12	.09	.05
93	Manny Trillo	.04	.03	.02
94	Tim Wallach	.06	.05	.02
95	Chris Speier	.03	.02	.01
96	Bill Gullickson	.04	.03	.02
97	Doug Flynn	.04	.03	.02
98	Charlie Lea	.03	.02	.01
99	Bill Madlock	.06	.05	.02
100	Wade Boggs	.25	.20	.10
101	Mike Schmidt	.15	.11	.06
102a	Jim Rice	.06	.05	.02
102b	Reggie Jackson	.06	.05	.02
103	Hubie Brooks	.06	.05	.02
104	Jesse Orosco	.04	.03	.02
105	George Foster	.08	.06	.03
106	Tom Seaver	.20	.15	.08
107	Keith Hernandez	.15	.11	.06
108	Mookie Wilson	.06	.05	.02
109	Bob Bailor	.03	.02	.01
110	Walt Terrell	.04	.03	.02
111	Brian Giles	.06	.05	.02
112	Jose Oquendo	.06	.05	.02
113	Mike Torrez	.03	.02	.01
114	Junior Ortiz	.03	.02	.01
115	Pete Rose	.40	.30	.15
116	Joe Morgan	.12	.09	.05
117	Mike Schmidt	.25	.20	.10
118	Gary Matthews	.06	.05	.02
119	Steve Carlton	.15	.11	.06
120	Bo Diaz	.04	.03	.02
121	Ivan DeJesus	.04	.03	.02
122	John Denny	.03	.02	.01
123	Garry Maddox	.03	.02	.01
124	Von Hayes	.08	.06	.03
125	Al Holland	.03	.02	.01
126	Tony Perez	.06	.05	.02
127	John Candelaria	.06	.05	.02
128	Jason Thompson	.03	.02	.01
129	Tony Pena	.06	.05	.02
130	Dave Parker	.12	.09	.05
131	Bill Madlock	.08	.06	.03
132	Kent Tekulve	.04	.03	.02
133	larry McWilliams	.03	.02	.01
134	Johnny Ray	.04	.03	.02
135	Marvell Wynne	.03	.02	.01
136	Dale Berra	.03	.02	.01
137	Mike Easler	.03	.02	.01
138	Lee Lacy	.03	.02	.01
139	George Hendrick	.04	.03	.02
140	Lonnie Smith	.04	.03	.02
141	Willie McGee	.08	.06	.03
142	Tom Herr	.06	.05	.02
143	Darrell Porter	.04	.03	.02
144	Ozzie Smith	.10	.08	.04
145	Bruce Sutter	.06	.05	.02
146	Dave LaPoint	.03	.02	.01
147	Neil Allen	.03	.02	.01
148	Ken Oberkfell	.04	.03	.02
149	David Green	.03	.02	.01
150	Andy Van Slyke	.04	.03	.02
151	Garry Templeton	.06	.05	.02
152	Juan Bonilla	.03	.02	.01
153	Alan Wiggins	.03	.02	.01
154	Terry Kennedy	.04	.03	.02
155	Dave Dravecky	.04	.03	.02
156	Steve Garvey	.15	.11	.06
157	Bobby Brown	.04	.03	.02
158	Ruppert Jones	.03	.02	.01
159	Luis Salazar	.03	.02	.01
160	Tony Gwynn	.12	.09	.05
161	Gary Lucas	.10	.08	.04
162	Eric Show	.04	.03	.02
163	Darrell Evans	.08	.06	.03
164	Gary Lavelle	.03	.02	.01
165	Atlee Hammaker	.03	.02	.01
166	Jeff Leonard	.06	.05	.02
167	Jack Clark	.10	.08	.04
168	Johnny LeMaster	.03	.02	.01
169	Duane Kuiper	.03	.02	.01
170	Tom O'Malley	.06	.05	.02
171	Chili Davis	.06	.05	.02
172	Bill Laskey	.03	.02	.01
173	Joel Youngblood	.06	.05	.02
174	Bob Brenly	.06	.05	.02
175	Atlee Hammaker	.15	.11	.06
176	Rick Honeycutt	.15	.11	.06
177	John Denny	.06	.05	.02
178	LaMarr Hoyt	.03	.02	.01
179	Tim Raines	.30	.25	.12
180	Dale Murphy	.40	.30	.15
181	Andre Dawson	.25	.20	.10
182	Steve Rogers	.15	.11	.06
183	Gary Carter	.30	.25	.12
184	Steve Carlton	.25	.20	.10
185	George Hendrick	.15	.11	.06
186	Johnny Ray	.15	.11	.06
187	Ozzie Smith	.20	.15	.08
188	Mike Schmidt	.40	.30	.15
189	Jim Rice	.30	.25	.12
190	Dave Winfield	.30	.25	.12
191	Lloyd Moseby	.15	.11	.06
192	LaMarr Hoyt	.15	.11	.06
193	Ted Simmons	.15	.11	.06
194	Ron Guidry	.20	.15	.08
195	Eddie Murray	.40	.30	.15
196	Lou Whitaker	.25	.20	.10
197	Cal Ripken	.40	.30	.15
198	George Brett	.40	.30	.15
199	Dale Murphy	.15	.11	.06
200a	Cecil Cooper	.03	.02	.01

		MT	NR MT	EX
200b	Jim Rice	.25	.20	.10
201	Tim Raines	.10	.08	.04
202	Rickey Henderson	.15	.11	.06
203	Eddie Murray	.20	.15	.08
204	Cal Ripken	.20	.15	.08
205	Gary Roenicke	.03	.02	.01
206	Ken Singleton	.06	.05	.02
207	Scott McGregor	.04	.03	.02
208	Tippy Martinez	.03	.02	.01
209	John Lowenstein	.04	.03	.02
210	Mike Flanagan	.04	.03	.02
211	Jim Palmer	.10	.08	.04
212	Dan Ford	.12	.09	.05
213	Rick Dempsey	.04	.03	.02
214	Rich Dauer	.03	.02	.01
215	Jerry Remy	.03	.02	.01
216	Wade Boggs	.50	.40	.20
217	Jim Rice	.20	.15	.08
218	Tony Armas	.06	.05	.02
219	Dwight Evans	.08	.06	.03
220	Bob Stanley	.04	.03	.02
221	Dave Stapleton	.06	.05	.02
222	Rich Gedman	.04	.03	.02
223	Glenn Hoffman	.06	.05	.02
224	Dennis Eckersley	.08	.06	.03
225	John Tudor	.06	.05	.02
226	Bruce Hurst	.04	.03	.02
227	Rod Carew	.20	.15	.08
228	Bobby Grich	.06	.05	.02
229	Doug DeCinces	.06	.05	.02
230	Fred Lynn	.10	.08	.04
231	Reggie Jackson	.20	.15	.08
232	Tommy John	.10	.08	.04
233	Luis Sanchez	.03	.02	.01
234	Bob Boone	.04	.03	.02
235	Bruce Kison	.04	.03	.02
236	Brian Downing	.04	.03	.02
237	Ken Forsch	.03	.02	.01
238	Rick Burleson	.04	.03	.02
239	Dennis Lamp	.03	.02	.01
240	LaMarr Hoyt	.03	.02	.01
241	Richard Dotson	.04	.03	.02
242	Harold Baines	.10	.08	.04
243	Carlton Fisk	.12	.09	.05
244	Greg Luzinski	.08	.06	.03
245	Rudy Law	.06	.05	.02
246	Tom Paciorek	.03	.02	.01
247	Floyd Bannister	.04	.03	.02
248	Julio Cruz	.04	.03	.02
249	Vance Law	.03	.02	.01
250	Scott Fletcher	.04	.03	.02
251	Toby Harrah	.04	.03	.02
252	Pat Tabler	.04	.03	.02
253	Gorman Thomas	.06	.05	.02
254	Rick Sutcliffe	.08	.06	.03
255	Andre Thornton	.06	.05	.02
256	Bake McBride	.03	.02	.01
257	Alan Bannister	.03	.02	.01
258	Jamie Easterly	.03	.02	.01
259	Lary Sorenson	.03	.02	.01
260	Mike Hargrove	.03	.02	.01
261	Bert Blyleven	.06	.05	.02
262	Ron Hassey	.04	.03	.02
263	Jack Morris	.12	.09	.05
264	Larry Herndon	.03	.02	.01
265	Lance Parrish	.12	.09	.05
266	Alan Trammell	.15	.11	.06
267	Lou Whitaker	.12	.09	.05
268	Aurelio Lopez	.03	.02	.01
269	Dan Petry	.04	.03	.02
270	Glenn Wilson	.04	.03	.02
271	Chet Lemon	.04	.03	.02
272	Kirk Gibson	.06	.05	.02
273	Enos Cabell	.04	.03	.02
274	Johnny Wockenfuss	.03	.02	.01
275	George Brett	.25	.20	.10
276	Willie Aikens	.03	.02	.01
277	Frank White	.04	.03	.02
278	Hal McRae	.06	.05	.02
279	Dan Quisenberry	.06	.05	.02
280	Willie Wilson	.08	.06	.03
281	Paul Splitorff	.03	.02	.01
282	U.L. Washington	.03	.02	.01
283	Bud Black	.06	.05	.02
284	John Wathan	.04	.03	.02
285	Larry Gura	.03	.02	.01
286	Pat Sheridan	.03	.02	.01
287a	Rusty Staub	.06	.05	.02
287b	Dave Righetti	.25	.20	.10
288a	Bob Forsch	.03	.02	.01
288b	Mike Warren	.06	.05	.02

		MT	NR MT	EX
289	Al Holland	.10	.08	.04
290	Dan Quisenberry	.15	.11	.06
291	Cecil Cooper	.06	.05	.02
292	Moose Haas	.03	.02	.01
293	Ted Simmons	.08	.06	.03
294	Paul Molitor	.10	.08	.04
295	Robin Yount	.15	.11	.06
296	Ben Oglivie	.04	.03	.02
297	Tom Tellmann	.50	.40	.20
298	Jim Gantner	.04	.03	.02
299	Rick Manning	.03	.02	.01
300	Don Sutton	.06	.05	.02
301	Charlie Moore	.04	.03	.02
302	Jim Slaton	.03	.02	.01
303	Gary Ward	.04	.03	.02
304	Tom Brunansky	.08	.06	.03
305	Kent Hrbek	.12	.09	.05
306	Gary Gaetti	.10	.08	.04
307	John Castino	.03	.02	.01
308	Ken Schrom	.03	.02	.01
309	Ron Davis	.03	.02	.01
310	Lenny Faedo	.03	.02	.01
311	Darrell Brown	.06	.05	.02
312	Frank Viola	.06	.05	.02
313	Dave Engle	.03	.02	.01
314	Randy Bush	.03	.02	.01
315	Dave Righetti	.12	.09	.05
316	Rich Gossage	.12	.09	.05
317	Ken Griffey	.06	.05	.02
318	Ron Guidry	.12	.09	.05
319	Dave Winfield	.15	.11	.06
320	Don Baylor	.08	.06	.03
321	Butch Wynegar	.03	.02	.01
322	Omar Moreno	.03	.02	.01
323	Andre Robertson	.03	.02	.01
324	Willie Randolph	.04	.03	.02
325	Don Mattingly	.50	.40	.20
326	Graig Nettles	.06	.05	.02
327	Rickey Henderson	.25	.20	.10
328	Carney Lansford	.08	.06	.03
329	Jeff Burroughs	.04	.03	.02
330	Chris Codiroli	.03	.02	.01
331	Dave Lopes	.06	.05	.02
332	Dwayne Murphy	.04	.03	.02
333	Wayne Gross	.03	.02	.01
334	Bill Almon	.03	.02	.01
335	Tom Underwood	.04	.03	.02
336	Dave Beard	.03	.02	.01
337	Mike Heath	.03	.02	.01
338	Mike Davis	.04	.03	.02
339	Pat Putnam	.03	.02	.01
340	Tony Bernazard	.03	.02	.01
341	Steve Henderson	.03	.02	.01
342	Richie Zisk	.04	.03	.02
343	Dave Henderson	.06	.05	.02
344	Al Cowens	.03	.02	.01
345	Bill Caudill	.03	.02	.01
346	Jim Beattie	.06	.05	.02
347	Ricky Nelson	.04	.03	.02
348	Roy Thomas	.06	.05	.02
349	Spike Owen	.04	.03	.02
350	Jamie Allen	.03	.02	.01
351	Buddy Bell	.06	.05	.02
352	Billy Sample	.03	.02	.01
353	George Wright	.03	.02	.01
354	Larry Parrish	.06	.05	.02
355	Jim Sundberg	.04	.03	.02
356	Charlie Hough	.06	.05	.02
357	Pete O'Brien	.06	.05	.02
358	Wayne Tolleson	.03	.02	.01
359	Danny Darwin	.03	.02	.01
360	Dave Stewart	.04	.03	.02
361	Mickey Rivers	.04	.03	.02
362	Bucky Dent	.04	.03	.02
363	Willie Upshaw	.06	.05	.02
364	Damaso Garcia	.04	.03	.02
365	Lloyd Moseby	.06	.05	.02
366	Cliff Johnson	.03	.02	.01
367	Jim Clancy	.04	.03	.02
368	Dave Stieb	.06	.05	.02
369	Alfredo Griffin	.04	.03	.02
370	Barry Bonnell	.04	.03	.02
371	Luis Leal	.03	.02	.01
372	Jesse Barfield	.06	.05	.02
373	Ernie Whitt	.03	.02	.01
374	Rance Mulliniks	.06	.05	.02
375	Mike Boddicker	.06	.05	.02
376	Greg Brock	.06	.05	.02
377	Bill Doran	.06	.05	.02
378	Nick Esasky	.06	.05	.02
379	Julio Franco	.08	.06	.03

		MT	NR MT	EX
380	Mel Hall	.06	.05	.02
381	Bob Kearney	.03	.02	.01
382	Ron Kittle	.06	.05	.02
383	Carmelo Martinez	.06	.05	.02
384	Craig McMurtry	.03	.02	.01
385	Darryl Strawberry	.30	.25	.12
386	Matt Young	.04	.03	.02

1984 Topps Stickers Boxes

For the second straight year, Topps printed baseball cards on the back of its sticker boxes. The 1984 set, titled "The Super Bats" features 24 hitting leaders. The cards are blank-backed and measure 2-1/2" by 3-1/2". Two cards were printed on each of 12 different boxes. The player's name appears inside a bat above his photo. Prices listed are for complete boxes.

		MT	NR MT	EX
Complete Set:		8.50	6.50	3.50
Common Player:		.75	.60	.30
1	Al Oliver, Lou Whitaker	1.00	.70	.40
2	Ken Oberkfell, Ted Simmons	.75	.60	.30
3	Hal McRae, Alan Wiggins	.75	.60	.30
4	Lloyd Moseby, Tim Raines	1.00	.70	.40
5	Lonnie Smith, Willie Wilson	.75	.60	.30
6	Keith Hernandez, Robin Yount	.75	.60	.30
7	Wade Boggs, Johnny Ray	1.50	1.25	.60
8	Willie McGee, Ken Singleton	.75	.60	.30
9	Ray Knight, Alan Trammell	1.00	.70	.40
11	Rod Carew, George Hendrick	1.25	.90	.50
12	Bill Madlock, Eddie Murray	1.25	.90	.50
13	Jose Cruz, Cal Ripken, Jr.	1.25	.90	.50

1984 Topps Super

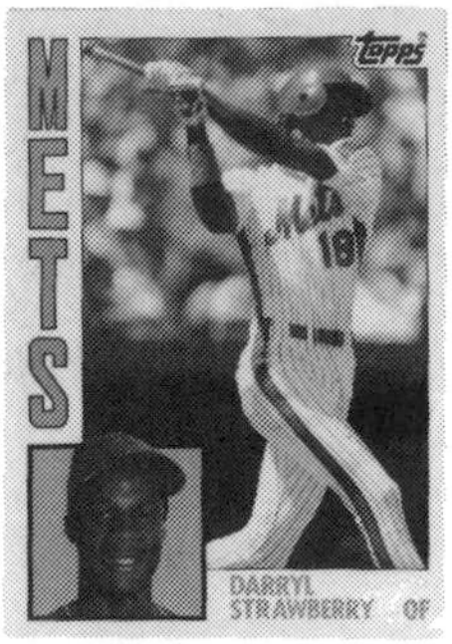

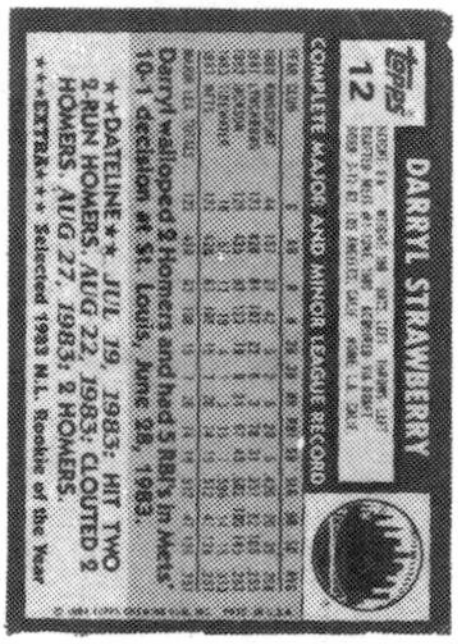

The next installment in Topps' continuing production of large-format cards, these 4-7/8" by 6-7/8" cards were sold in cellophane packs with a complete set being 30 cards. Other than their size and the change in card number on the back, there is nothing to distinguish the Supers from the regular 1984 Topps cards of the same players. One plus is that the players are all big name stars, and are likely to remain in demand.

		MT	NR MT	EX
Complete Set:		12.00	9.00	4.75
Common Player:		.20	.15	.08
1	Cal Ripken	.70	.50	.30
2	Dale Murphy	.90	.70	.35
3	LaMarr Hoyt	.20	.15	.08
4	John Denny	.20	.15	.08
5	Jim Rice	.50	.40	.20
6	Mike Schmidt	.90	.70	.35
7	Wade Boggs	1.25	.90	.50
8	Bill Madlock	.20	.15	.08
9	Dan Quisenberry	.20	.15	.08
10	Al Holland	.20	.15	.08
11	Ron Kittle	.20	.15	.08
12	Darryl Strawberry	1.25	.90	.50
13	George Brett	.90	.70	.35
14	Bill Buckner	.25	.20	.10
15	Carlton Fisk	.30	.25	.12
16	Steve Carlton	.50	.40	.20
17	Ron Guidry	.35	.25	.14
18	Gary Carter	.50	.40	.20
19	Rickey Henderson	1.00	.70	.40
20	Andre Dawson	.35	.25	.14
21	Reggie Jackson	.60	.45	.25
22	Steve Garvey	.50	.40	.20
23	Fred Lynn	.30	.25	.12
24	Pedro Guerrero	.25	.20	.10
25	Eddie Murray	.60	.45	.25
26	Keith Hernandez	.50	.40	.20
27	Dave Winfield	.50	.40	.20
28	Nolan Ryan	1.00	.70	.40
29	Robin Yount	.40	.30	.15
30	Fernando Valenzuela	.40	.30	.15

1984 Topps Traded

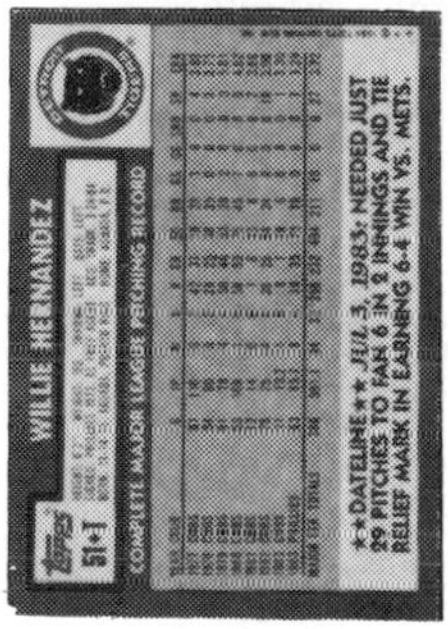

The popular Topps Traded set returned for its fourth year in 1984 with another 132-card set. The 2-1/2" by 3-1/2" cards have an identical design to the regular Topps cards except that the back cardboard is white and the card numbers carry a "T" suffix. As before, the set was sold only through hobby dealers. Also as before, players who changed teams, new managers and promising rookies are included in the set. The presence of several promising young rookies in especially high demand from investors and speculators had made this one of the most expensive Topps issues of recent years. A glossy-finish "Tiffany" version of the set was also issued, valued at four to five times the price of the normal Traded cards.

		MT	NR MT	EX
Complete Set:		110.00	82.00	45.00
Common Player:		.10	.08	.04
1T	Willie Aikens	.10	.08	.04
2T	Luis Aponte	.10	.08	.04
3T	Mike Armstrong	.10	.08	.04
4T	Bob Bailor	.10	.08	.04
5T	Dusty Baker	.20	.15	.08
6T	Steve Balboni	.20	.15	.08
7T	Alan Bannister	.10	.08	.04
8T	Dave Beard	.10	.08	.04
9T	Joe Beckwith	.10	.08	.04

		MT	NR MT	EX
10T	Bruce Berenyi	.10	.08	.04
11T	Dave Bergman	.10	.08	.04
12T	Tony Bernazard	.10	.08	.04
13T	Yogi Berra	.20	.15	.08
14T	Barry Bonnell	.10	.08	.04
15T	Phil Bradley(FC)	1.25	.90	.50
16T	Fred Breining	.10	.08	.04
17T	Bill Buckner	.25	.20	.10
18T	Ray Burris	.10	.08	.04
19T	John Butcher	.10	.08	.04
20T	Brett Butler	.20	.15	.08
21T	Enos Cabell	.10	.08	.04
22T	Bill Campbell	.10	.08	.04
23T	Bill Caudill	.10	.08	.04
24T	Bob Clark	.10	.08	.04
25T	Bryan Clark	.10	.08	.04
26T	Jaime Cocanower	.10	.08	.04
27T	Ron Darling(FC)	4.00	3.00	1.50
28T	Alvin Davis(FC)	5.00	3.75	2.00
29T	Ken Dayley	.10	.08	.04
30T	Jeff Dedmon(FC)	.15	.11	.06
31T	Bob Dernier	.10	.08	.04
32T	Carlos Diaz	.10	.08	.04
33T	Mike Easler	.15	.11	.06
34T	Dennis Eckersley	2.00	1.50	.80
35T	Jim Essian	.10	.08	.04
36T	Darrell Evans	.25	.20	.10
37T	Mike Fitzgerald(FC)	.15	.11	.06
38T	Tim Foli	.10	.08	.04
39T	George Frazier	.10	.08	.04
40T	Rich Gale	.10	.08	.04
41T	Barbaro Garbey	.15	.11	.06
42T	Dwight Gooden(FC)	40.00	30.00	15.00
43T	Rich Gossage	.40	.30	.15
44T	Wayne Gross	.10	.08	.04
45T	Mark Gubicza(FC)	3.00	2.25	1.25
46T	Jackie Gutierrez	.10	.08	.04
47T	Mel Hall	.20	.15	.08
48T	Toby Harrah	.15	.11	.06
49T	Ron Hassey	.10	.08	.04
50T	Rich Hebner	.10	.08	.04
51T	Willie Hernandez	.30	.25	.12
52T	Ricky Horton(FC)	.40	.30	.15
53T	Art Howe	.10	.08	.04
54T	Dane Iorg	.10	.08	.04
55T	Brook Jacoby(FC)	2.50	2.00	1.00
56T	Mike Jeffcoat(FC)	.15	.11	.06
57T	Dave Johnson	.15	.11	.06
58T	Lynn Jones	.10	.08	.04
59T	Ruppert Jones	.10	.08	.04
60T	Mike Jorgensen	.10	.08	.04
61T	Bob Kearney	.10	.08	.04
62T	Jimmy Key(FC)	5.00	3.75	2.00
63T	Dave Kingman	.40	.30	.15
64T	Jerry Koosman	.25	.20	.10
65T	Wayne Krenchicki	.10	.08	.04
66T	Rusty Kuntz	.10	.08	.04
67T	Rene Lachemann	.10	.08	.04
68T	Frank LaCorte	.10	.08	.04
69T	Dennis Lamp	.10	.08	.04
70T	Mark Langston(FC)	10.00	7.50	4.00
71T	Rick Leach	.10	.08	.04
72T	Craig Lefferts	.15	.11	.06
73T	Gary Lucas	.10	.08	.04
74T	Jerry Martin	.10	.08	.04
75T	Carmelo Martinez	.25	.20	.10
76T	Mike Mason(FC)	.15	.11	.06
77T	Gary Matthews	.25	.20	.10
78T	Andy McGaffigan	.10	.08	.04
79T	Larry Milbourne	.10	.08	.04
80T	Sid Monge	.10	.08	.04
81T	Jackie Moore	.10	.08	.04
82T	Joe Morgan	2.50	2.00	1.00
83T	Graig Nettles	.50	.40	.20
84T	Phil Niekro	1.00	.70	.40
85T	Ken Oberkfell	.10	.08	.04
86T	Mike O'Berry	.10	.08	.04
87T	Al Oliver	.30	.25	.12
88T	Jorge Orta	.10	.08	.04
89T	Amos Otis	.15	.11	.06
90T	Dave Parker	2.00	1.50	.80
91T	Tony Perez	.70	.50	.30
92T	Gerald Perry(FC)	.80	.60	.30
93T	Gary Pettis(FC)	.25	.20	.10
94T	Rob Picciolo	.10	.08	.04
95T	Vern Rapp	.10	.08	.04
96T	Floyd Rayford	.10	.08	.04
97T	Randy Ready(FC)	.25	.20	.10
98T	Ron Reed	.15	.11	.06
99T	Gene Richards	.10	.08	.04
100T	Jose Rijo(FC)	6.00	4.50	2.50
101T	Jeff Robinson(FC)	.50	.40	.20
102T	Ron Romanick(FC)	.20	.15	.08
103T	Pete Rose	8.00	6.00	3.25
104T	Bret Saberhagen(FC)	15.00	11.00	6.00
105T	Juan Samuel(FC)	4.00	3.00	1.50
106T	Scott Sanderson	.10	.08	.04
107T	Dick Schofield(FC)	.35	.25	.14
108T	Tom Seaver	8.00	6.00	3.25
109T	Jim Slaton	.10	.08	.04
110T	Mike Smithson	.10	.08	.04
111T	Lary Sorensen	.10	.08	.04
112T	Tim Stoddard	.10	.08	.04
113T	Champ Summers	.10	.08	.04
114T	Jim Sundberg	.15	.11	.06
115T	Rick Sutcliffe	.50	.40	.20
116T	Craig Swan	.10	.08	.04
117T	Tim Teufel(FC)	.30	.25	.12
118T	Derrel Thomas	.10	.08	.04
119T	Gorman Thomas	.25	.20	.10
120T	Alex Trevino	.10	.08	.04
121T	Manny Trillo	.15	.11	.06
122T	John Tudor	.25	.20	.10
123T	Tom Underwood	.10	.08	.04
124T	Mike Vail	.10	.08	.04
125T	Tom Waddell	.10	.08	.04
126T	Gary Ward	.10	.08	.04
127T	Curt Wilkerson	.10	.08	.04
128T	Frank Williams(FC)	.25	.20	.10
129T	Glenn Wilson	.20	.15	.08
130T	Johnny Wockenfuss	.10	.08	.04
131T	Ned Yost	.10	.08	.04
132T	Checklist 1-132	.10	.08	.04

1985 Topps

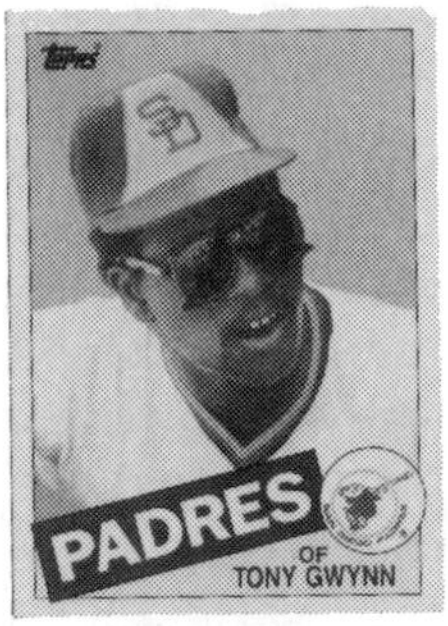

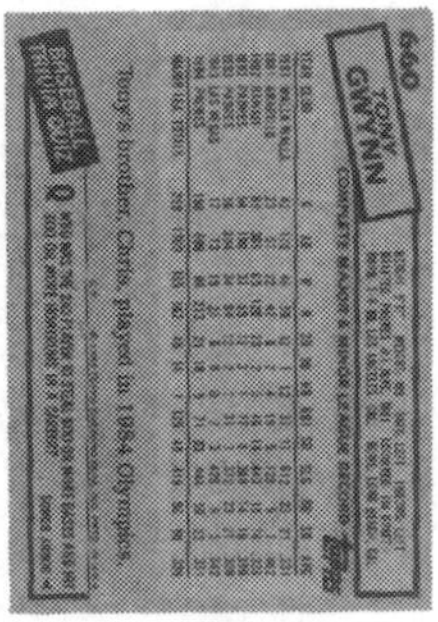

Holding the line at 792 cards, Topps did initiate some major design changes in its 2-1/2" by 3-1/2" cards in 1985. The use of two photos on the front was discontinued in favor of one large color photo. The Topps logo appears in the upper left-hand corner. At the bottom runs a diagonal rectangular box with the team name. It joins a team logo, and below that point runs the player's position and name. The backs feature statistics, biographical information and a trivia question. Some interesting specialty sets were introduced in 1985, including the revival of the father/son theme from 1976, a subset of the 1984 U.S. Olympic Baseball Team members and a set featuring #1 draft choices since the inception of the baseball draft in 1965. Again in 1985, a glossy-finish "Tiffany" edition of the regular set was produced, though the number was cut back to 5,000 sets. Values range from four times regular value for common cards to five-six times for high-demand stars and rookie cards.

	MT	NR MT	EX
Complete Set:	110.00	82.00	44.00
Common Player:	.06	.05	.02

		MT	NR MT	EX
1	Record Breaker (Carlton Fisk)	.15	.11	.06
2	Record Breaker (Steve Garvey)	.20	.15	.08
3	Record Breaker (Dwight Gooden)	1.00	.70	.40
4	Record Breaker (Cliff Johnson)	.08	.06	.03
5	Record Breaker (Joe Morgan)	.15	.11	.06
6	Record Breaker (Pete Rose)	.60	.45	.25
7	Record Breaker (Nolan Ryan)	1.00	.70	.40

		MT	NR MT	EX
8	Record Breaker (Juan Samuel)(FC)	.20	.15	.08
9	Record Breaker (Bruce Sutter)	.12	.09	.05
10	Record Breaker (Don Sutton)	.20	.15	.08
11	Ralph Houk	.08	.06	.03
12	Dave Lopes	.08	.06	.03
13	Tim Lollar	.06	.05	.02
14	Chris Bando	.06	.05	.02
15	Jerry Koosman	.10	.08	.04
16	Bobby Meacham	.06	.05	.02
17	Mike Scott	.15	.11	.06
18	Mickey Hatcher	.06	.05	.02
19	George Frazier	.06	.05	.02
20	Chet Lemon	.08	.06	.03
21	Lee Tunnell	.06	.05	.02
22	Duane Kuiper	.06	.05	.02
23	*Bret Saberhagen*	4.00	3.00	1.50
24	Jesse Barfield	.25	.20	.10
25	Steve Bedrosian	.12	.09	.05
26	Roy Smalley	.06	.05	.02
27	Bruce Berenyi	.06	.05	.02
28	Dann Bilardello	.06	.05	.02
29	Odell Jones	.06	.05	.02
30	Cal Ripken	3.00	2.25	1.25
31	Terry Whitfield	.06	.05	.02
32	Chuck Porter	.06	.05	.02
33	Tito Landrum	.06	.05	.02
34	Ed Nunez(FC)	.08	.06	.03
35	Graig Nettles	.15	.11	.06
36	Fred Breining	.06	.05	.02
37	Reid Nichols	.06	.05	.02
38	Jackie Moore	.06	.05	.02
39	Johnny Wockenfuss	.06	.05	.02
40	Phil Niekro	.25	.20	.10
41	Mike Fischlin	.06	.05	.02
42	Luis Sanchez	.06	.05	.02
43	Andre David	.06	.05	.02
44	Dickie Thon	.08	.06	.03
45	Greg Minton	.06	.05	.02
46	Gary Woods	.06	.05	.02
47	Dave Rozema	.06	.05	.02
48	Tony Fernandez(FC)	1.25	.90	.50
49	Butch Davis	.06	.05	.02
50	John Candelaria	.10	.08	.04
51	Bob Watson	.08	.06	.03
52	Jerry Dybzinski	.06	.05	.02
53	Tom Gorman	.06	.05	.02
54	Cesar Cedeno	.10	.08	.04
55	Frank Tanana	.10	.08	.04
56	Jim Dwyer	.06	.05	.02
57	Pat Zachry	.06	.05	.02
58	Orlando Mercado	.06	.05	.02
59	Rick Waits	.06	.05	.02
60	George Hendrick	.08	.06	.03
61	Curt Kaufman	.06	.05	.02
62	Mike Ramsey	.06	.05	.02
63	Steve McCatty	.06	.05	.02
64	*Mark Bailey*(FC)	.10	.08	.04
65	Bill Buckner	.12	.09	.05
66	Dick Williams	.06	.05	.02
67	*Rafael Santana*(FC)	.20	.15	.08
68	Von Hayes	.10	.08	.04
69	*Jim Winn*(FC)	.10	.08	.04
70	Don Baylor	.12	.09	.05
71	Tim Laudner	.06	.05	.02
72	Rick Sutcliffe	.12	.09	.05
73	Rusty Kuntz	.06	.05	.02
74	Mike Krukow	.08	.06	.03
75	Willie Upshaw	.08	.06	.03
76	Alan Bannister	.06	.05	.02
77	Joe Beckwith	.06	.05	.02
78	Scott Fletcher	.08	.06	.03
79	Rick Mahler	.06	.05	.02
80	Keith Hernandez	.30	.25	.12
81	Lenn Sakata	.06	.05	.02
82	Joe Price	.06	.05	.02
83	Charlie Moore	.06	.05	.02
84	Spike Owen	.08	.06	.03
85	Mike Marshall	.15	.11	.06
86	Don Aase	.06	.05	.02
87	David Green	.06	.05	.02
88	Bryn Smith	.06	.05	.02
89	Jackie Gutierrez	.06	.05	.02
90	Rich Gossage	.20	.15	.08
91	Jeff Burroughs	.08	.06	.03
92	Paul Owens	.06	.05	.02
93	*Don Schulze*(FC)	.10	.08	.04
94	Toby Harrah	.08	.06	.03
95	Jose Cruz	.10	.08	.04
96	Johnny Ray	.12	.09	.05
97	Pete Filson	.06	.05	.02
98	Steve Lake	.06	.05	.02

		MT	NR MT	EX
99	Milt Wilcox	.06	.05	.02
100	George Brett	.50	.40	.20
101	Jim Acker	.06	.05	.02
102	Tommy Dunbar	.06	.05	.02
103	Randy Lerch	.06	.05	.02
104	Mike Fitzgerald	.08	.06	.03
105	Ron Kittle	.10	.08	.04
106	Pascual Perez	.08	.06	.03
107	Tom Foley	.06	.05	.02
108	Darnell Coles(FC)	.15	.11	.06
109	Gary Roenicke	.06	.05	.02
110	Alejandro Pena	.08	.06	.03
111	Doug DeCinces	.10	.08	.04
112	Tom Tellmann	.06	.05	.02
113	Tom Herr	.10	.08	.04
114	Bob James	.06	.05	.02
115	Rickey Henderson	2.00	1.50	.80
116	Dennis Boyd(FC)	.15	.11	.06
117	Greg Gross	.06	.05	.02
118	Eric Show	.08	.06	.03
119	Pat Corrales	.06	.05	.02
120	Steve Kemp	.08	.06	.03
121	Checklist 1-132	.06	.05	.02
122	Tom Brunansky	.12	.09	.05
123	Dave Smith	.08	.06	.03
124	Rich Hebner	.06	.05	.02
125	Kent Tekulve	.08	.06	.03
126	Ruppert Jones	.06	.05	.02
127	*Mark Gubicza*	1.00	.70	.40
128	Ernie Whitt	.08	.06	.03
129	Gene Garber	.06	.05	.02
130	Al Oliver	.12	.09	.05
131	Father - Son (Buddy Bell, Gus Bell)	.12	.09	.05
132	Father - Son (Dale Berra, Yogi Berra)	.20	.15	.08
133	Father - Son (Bob Boone, Ray Boone)	.12	.09	.05
134	Father - Son (Terry Francona, Tito Francona)	.08	.06	.03
135	Father - Son (Bob Kennedy, Terry Kennedy)	.08	.06	.03
136	Father - Son (Bill Kunkel, Jeff Kunkel)(FC)	.08	.06	.03
137	Father - Son (Vance Law, Vern Law)	.10	.08	.04
138	Father - Son (Dick Schofield, Dick Schofield)	.08	.06	.03
139	Father - Son (Bob Skinner, Joel Skinner)	.08	.06	.03
140	Father - Son (Roy Smalley, Roy Smalley)	.08	.06	.03
141	Father - Son (Dave Stenhouse, Mike Stenhouse)	.08	.06	.03
142	Father - Son (Dizzy Trout, Steve Trout)	.08	.06	.03
143	Father - Son (Ossie Virgil, Ozzie Virgil)	.08	.06	.03
144	Ron Gardenhire	.06	.05	.02
145	*Alvin Davis*	1.25	.90	.50
146	Gary Redus	.08	.06	.03
147	Bill Swaggerty	.06	.05	.02
148	Steve Yeager	.06	.05	.02
149	Dickie Noles	.06	.05	.02
150	Jim Rice	.35	.25	.14
151	Moose Haas	.06	.05	.02
152	Steve Braun	.06	.05	.02
153	Frank LaCorte	.06	.05	.02
154	Argenis Salazar(FC)	.06	.05	.02
155	Yogi Berra	.12	.09	.05
156	Craig Reynolds	.06	.05	.02
157	Tug McGraw	.10	.08	.04
158	Pat Tabler	.08	.06	.03
159	Carlos Diaz	.06	.05	.02
160	Lance Parrish	.25	.20	.10
161	Ken Schrom	.06	.05	.02
162	*Benny Distefano*(FC)	.10	.08	.04
163	Dennis Eckersley	.12	.09	.05
164	Jorge Orta	.06	.05	.02
165	Dusty Baker	.08	.06	.03
166	Keith Atherton	.06	.05	.02
167	Rufino Linares	.06	.05	.02
168	Garth Iorg	.06	.05	.02
169	Dan Spillner	.06	.05	.02
170	George Foster	.15	.11	.06
171	Bill Stein	.06	.05	.02
172	Jack Perconte	.06	.05	.02
173	Mike Young(FC)	.12	.09	.05
174	Rick Honeycutt	.06	.05	.02
175	Dave Parker	.25	.20	.10
176	Bill Schroeder	.06	.05	.02
177	Dave Von Ohlen	.06	.05	.02

		MT	NR MT	EX
178	Miguel Dilone	.06	.05	.02
179	Tommy John	.20	.15	.08
180	Dave Winfield	.35	.25	.14
181	*Roger Clemens*(FC)	20.00	15.00	8.00
182	Tim Flannery	.06	.05	.02
183	Larry McWilliams	.06	.05	.02
184	Carmen Castillo(FC)	.10	.08	.04
185	Al Holland	.06	.05	.02
186	Bob Lillis	.06	.05	.02
187	Mike Walters	.06	.05	.02
188	Greg Pryor	.06	.05	.02
189	Warren Brusstar	.06	.05	.02
190	Rusty Staub	.12	.09	.05
191	Steve Nicosia	.08	.06	.03
192	Howard Johnson(FC)	4.00	3.00	1.50
193	*Jimmy Key*	1.00	.70	.40
194	Dave Stegman	.06	.05	.02
195	Glenn Hubbard	.06	.05	.02
196	Pete O'Brien	.12	.09	.05
197	Mike Warren	.06	.05	.02
198	Eddie Milner	.06	.05	.02
199	Denny Martinez	.08	.06	.03
200	Reggie Jackson	.60	.45	.25
201	Burt Hooton	.08	.06	.03
202	Gorman Thomas	.10	.08	.04
203	Bob McClure	.06	.05	.02
204	Art Howe	.06	.05	.02
205	Steve Rogers	.08	.06	.03
206	Phil Garner	.08	.06	.03
207	Mark Clear	.06	.05	.02
208	Champ Summers	.06	.05	.02
209	Bill Campbell	.06	.05	.02
210	Gary Matthews	.10	.08	.04
211	Clay Christiansen	.06	.05	.02
212	George Vukovich	.06	.05	.02
213	Billy Gardner	.06	.05	.02
214	John Tudor	.10	.08	.04
215	Bob Brenly	.06	.05	.02
216	Jerry Don Gleaton	.06	.05	.02
217	Leon Roberts	.06	.05	.02
218	Doyle Alexander	.10	.08	.04
219	Gerald Perry	.35	.25	.14
220	Fred Lynn	.20	.15	.08
221	Ron Reed	.06	.05	.02
222	Hubie Brooks	.10	.08	.04
223	Tom Hume	.06	.05	.02
224	Al Cowens	.06	.05	.02
225	Mike Boddicker	.10	.08	.04
226	Juan Beniquez	.06	.05	.02
227	Danny Darwin	.06	.05	.02
228	Dion James(FC)	.20	.15	.08
229	Dave LaPoint	.08	.06	.03
230	Gary Carter	.35	.25	.14
231	Dwayne Murphy	.08	.06	.03
232	Dave Beard	.06	.05	.02
233	Ed Jurak	.06	.05	.02
234	Jerry Narron	.06	.05	.02
235	Garry Maddox	.10	.08	.04
236	Mark Thurmond	.06	.05	.02
237	Julio Franco	.50	.40	.20
238	*Jose Rijo*	1.25	.90	.50
239	Tim Teufel	.12	.09	.05
240	Dave Stieb	.12	.09	.05
241	Jim Frey	.06	.05	.02
242	Greg Harris	.06	.05	.02
243	Barbaro Garbey	.10	.08	.04
244	Mike Jones	.06	.05	.02
245	Chili Davis	.10	.08	.04
246	Mike Norris	.06	.05	.02
247	Wayne Tolleson	.06	.05	.02
248	Terry Forster	.08	.06	.03
249	Harold Baines	.15	.11	.06
250	Jesse Orosco	.08	.06	.03
251	Brad Gulden	.06	.05	.02
252	Dan Ford	.06	.05	.02
253	*Sid Bream*(FC)	.50	.40	.20
254	Pete Vuckovich	.08	.06	.03
255	Lonnie Smith	.08	.06	.03
256	Mike Stanton	.06	.05	.02
257	Brian Little (Bryan)	.06	.05	.02
258	Mike Brown	.06	.05	.02
259	Gary Allenson	.06	.05	.02
260	Dave Righetti	.20	.15	.08
261	Checklist 133-264	.06	.05	.02
262	*Greg Booker*(FC)	.12	.09	.05
263	Mel Hall	.08	.06	.03
264	Joe Sambito	.06	.05	.02
265	Juan Samuel(FC)	.50	.40	.20
266	Frank Viola	.20	.15	.08
267	*Henry Cotto*(FC)	.15	.11	.06
268	Chuck Tanner	.06	.05	.02

		MT	NR MT	EX
269	*Doug Baker*(FC)	.10	.08	.04
270	Dan Quisenberry	.10	.08	.04
271	1968 #1 Draft Pick (Tim Foli)	.08	.06	.03
272	1969 #1 Draft Pick (Jeff Burroughs)	.08	.06	.03
273	1974 #1 Draft Pick (Bill Almon)	.08	.06	.03
274	1976 #1 Draft Pick (Floyd Bannister)	.10	.08	.04
275	1977 #1 Draft Pick (Harold Baines)	.15	.11	.06
276	1978 #1 Draft Pick (Bob Horner)	.15	.11	.06
277	1979 #1 Draft Pick (Al Chambers)	.08	.06	.03
278	1980 #1 Draft Pick (Darryl Strawberry)	2.00	1.50	.80
279	1981 #1 Draft Pick (Mike Moore)(FC)	.20	.15	.08
280	1982 #1 Draft Pick *(Shawon Dunston)*(FC)	3.00	2.25	1.25
281	1983 #1 Draft Pick (Tim Belcher)(FC)	1.25	.90	.50
282	1984 #1 Draft Pick *(Shawn Abner)*(FC)	.60	.45	.25
283	Fran Mullins	.06	.05	.02
284	Marty Bystrom	.06	.05	.02
285	Dan Driessen	.08	.06	.03
286	Rudy Law	.06	.05	.02
287	Walt Terrell	.08	.06	.03
288	*Jeff Kunkel*(FC)	.10	.08	.04
289	Tom Underwood	.06	.05	.02
290	Cecil Cooper	.12	.09	.05
291	Bob Welch	.12	.09	.05
292	Brad Komminsk(FC)	.08	.06	.03
293	*Curt Young*(FC)	.35	.25	.14
294	*Tom Nieto*(FC)	.10	.08	.04
295	Joe Niekro	.10	.08	.04
296	Ricky Nelson	.06	.05	.02
297	Gary Lucas	.06	.05	.02
298	Marty Barrett	.15	.11	.06
299	Andy Hawkins	.08	.06	.03
300	Rod Carew	.50	.40	.20
301	John Montefusco	.06	.05	.02
302	Tim Corcoran	.06	.05	.02
303	*Mike Jeffcoat*	.08	.06	.03
304	Gary Gaetti	.25	.20	.10
305	Dale Berra	.06	.05	.02
306	Rick Reuschel	.10	.08	.04
307	Sparky Anderson	.08	.06	.03
308	John Wathan	.08	.06	.03
309	Mike Witt	.12	.09	.05
310	Manny Trillo	.08	.06	.03
311	Jim Gott	.06	.05	.02
312	Marc Hill	.06	.05	.02
313	Dave Schmidt	.06	.05	.02
314	Ron Oester	.06	.05	.02
315	Doug Sisk	.06	.05	.02
316	John Lowenstein	.06	.05	.02
317	*Jack Lazorko*(FC)	.10	.08	.04
318	Ted Simmons	.12	.09	.05
319	Jeff Jones	.06	.05	.02
320	Dale Murphy	.60	.45	.25
321	*Ricky Horton*	.30	.25	.12
322	Dave Stapleton	.06	.05	.02
323	Andy McGaffigan	.06	.05	.02
324	Bruce Bochy	.06	.05	.02
325	John Denny	.06	.05	.02
326	Kevin Bass	.10	.08	.04
327	Brook Jacoby	.30	.25	.12
328	Bob Shirley	.06	.05	.02
329	Ron Washington	.06	.05	.02
330	Leon Durham	.08	.06	.03
331	Bill Laskey	.06	.05	.02
332	Brian Harper	.06	.05	.02
333	Willie Hernandez	.08	.06	.03
334	Dick Howser	.06	.05	.02
335	Bruce Benedict	.06	.05	.02
336	Rance Mulliniks	.06	.05	.02
337	Billy Sample	.06	.05	.02
338	Britt Burns	.06	.05	.02
339	Danny Heep	.06	.05	.02
340	Robin Yount	.60	.45	.25
341	Floyd Rayford	.06	.05	.02
342	Ted Power	.06	.05	.02
343	Bill Russell	.08	.06	.03
344	Dave Henderson	.10	.08	.04
345	Charlie Lea	.06	.05	.02
346	*Terry Pendleton*(FC)	1.50	1.25	.60
347	Rick Langford	.06	.05	.02
348	Bob Boone	.08	.06	.03
349	Domingo Ramos	.06	.05	.02
350	Wade Boggs	3.00	2.25	1.25
351	Juan Agosto	.06	.05	.02

		MT	NR MT	EX
352	Joe Morgan	.30	.25	.12
353	Julio Solano	.06	.05	.02
354	Andre Robertson	.06	.05	.02
355	Bert Blyleven	.12	.09	.05
356	Dave Meier	.06	.05	.02
357	Rich Bordi	.06	.05	.02
358	Tony Pena	.10	.08	.04
359	Pat Sheridan	.06	.05	.02
360	Steve Carlton	.40	.30	.15
361	Alfredo Griffin	.08	.06	.03
362	Craig McMurtry	.06	.05	.02
363	Ron Hodges	.06	.05	.02
364	Richard Dotson	.10	.08	.04
365	Danny Ozark	.06	.05	.02
366	Todd Cruz	.06	.05	.02
367	Keefe Cato	.06	.05	.02
368	Dave Bergman	.06	.05	.02
369	*R.J. Reynolds*(FC)	.25	.20	.10
370	Bruce Sutter	.12	.09	.05
371	Mickey Rivers	.08	.06	.03
372	Roy Howell	.06	.05	.02
373	Mike Moore	.06	.05	.02
374	Brian Downing	.10	.08	.04
375	Jeff Reardon	.12	.09	.05
376	Jeff Newman	.06	.05	.02
377	Checklist 265-396	.06	.05	.02
378	Alan Wiggins	.06	.05	.02
379	Charles Hudson	.08	.06	.03
380	Ken Griffey	.10	.08	.04
381	Roy Smith	.06	.05	.02
382	Denny Walling	.06	.05	.02
383	Rick Lysander	.06	.05	.02
384	Jody Davis	.10	.08	.04
385	Jose DeLeon	.08	.06	.03
386	*Dan Gladden*(FC)	.30	.25	.12
387	*Buddy Biancalana*(FC)	.12	.09	.05
388	Bert Roberge	.06	.05	.02
389	1984 United States Baseball Team (Rod Dedeaux)	.06	.05	.02
390	1984 United States Baseball Team (Sid Akins)(FC)	.10	.08	.04
391	1984 United States Baseball Team (Flavio Alfaro)	.06	.05	.02
392	1984 United States Baseball Team (Don August)(FC)	.20	.15	.08
393	1984 United States Baseball Team (Scott Bankhead)(FC)	.60	.45	.25
394	1984 United States Baseball Team (Bob Caffrey)(FC)	.08	.06	.03
395	1984 United States Baseball Team (Mike Dunne)(FC)	.20	.15	.08
396	1984 United States Baseball Team (Gary Green)(FC)	.08	.06	.03
397	1984 United States Baseball Team (John Hoover)	.06	.05	.02
398	1984 United States Baseball Team (Shane Mack)(FC)	1.25	.90	.50
399	1984 United States Baseball Team (John Marzano)(FC)	.25	.20	.10
400	1984 United States Baseball Team (Oddibe McDowell)(FC)	.30	.25	.12
401	1984 United States Baseball Team (Mark McGwire)(FC)	12.00	9.00	4.75
402	1984 United States Baseball Team (Pat Pacillo)(FC)	.20	.15	.08
403	1984 United States Baseball Team (Cory Snyder)(FC)	1.00	.70	.40
404	1984 United States Baseball Team (Billy Swift)(FC)	.30	.25	.12
405	Tom Veryzer	.06	.05	.02
406	Len Whitehouse	.06	.05	.02
407	Bobby Ramos	.06	.05	.02
408	Sid Monge	.06	.05	.02
409	Brad Wellman	.06	.05	.02
410	Bob Horner	.15	.11	.06
411	Bobby Cox	.06	.05	.02
412	Bud Black	.06	.05	.02
413	Vance Law	.08	.06	.03
414	Gary Ward	.08	.06	.03
415	Ron Darling	.60	.45	.25
416	Wayne Gross	.06	.05	.02
417	*John Franco*(FC)	1.50	1.25	.70
418	Ken Landreaux	.06	.05	.02
419	Mike Caldwell	.06	.05	.02
420	Andre Dawson	.30	.25	.12
421	Dave Rucker	.06	.05	.02
422	Carney Lansford	.10	.08	.04
423	Barry Bonnell	.06	.05	.02
424	*Al Nipper*(FC)	.15	.11	.06
425	Mike Hargrove	.06	.05	.02
426	Verne Ruhle	.06	.05	.02

		MT	NR MT	EX
427	Mario Ramirez	.06	.05	.02
428	Larry Andersen	.06	.05	.02
429	Rick Cerone	.06	.05	.02
430	Ron Davis	.06	.05	.02
431	U.L. Washington	.06	.05	.02
432	Thad Bosley	.06	.05	.02
433	Jim Morrison	.06	.05	.02
434	Gene Richards	.06	.05	.02
435	Dan Petry	.08	.06	.03
436	Willie Aikens	.06	.05	.02
437	Al Jones	.06	.05	.02
438	Joe Torre	.08	.06	.03
439	Junior Ortiz	.06	.05	.02
440	Fernando Valenzuela	.30	.25	.12
441	Duane Walker	.06	.05	.02
442	Ken Forsch	.06	.05	.02
443	George Wright	.06	.05	.02
444	Tony Phillips	.06	.05	.02
445	Tippy Martinez	.06	.05	.02
446	Jim Sundberg	.08	.06	.03
447	Jeff Lahti	.06	.05	.02
448	Derrel Thomas	.06	.05	.02
449	*Phil Bradley*	.80	.60	.30
450	Steve Garvey	.40	.30	.15
451	Bruce Hurst	.12	.09	.05
452	John Castino	.06	.05	.02
453	Tom Waddell	.06	.05	.02
454	Glenn Wilson	.08	.06	.03
455	Bob Knepper	.08	.06	.03
456	Tim Foli	.06	.05	.02
457	Cecilio Guante	.06	.05	.02
458	Randy Johnson	.06	.05	.02
459	Charlie Leibrandt	.08	.06	.03
460	Ryne Sandberg	2.75	2.00	1.00
461	Marty Castillo	.06	.05	.02
462	Gary Lavelle	.06	.05	.02
463	Dave Collins	.08	.06	.03
464	*Mike Mason*(FC)	.10	.08	.04
465	Bob Grich	.10	.08	.04
466	Tony LaRussa	.08	.06	.03
467	Ed Lynch	.06	.05	.02
468	Wayne Krenchicki	.06	.05	.02
469	Sammy Stewart	.06	.05	.02
470	Steve Sax	.20	.15	.08
471	Pete Ladd	.06	.05	.02
472	Jim Essian	.06	.05	.02
473	Tim Wallach	.12	.09	.05
474	Kurt Kepshire	.06	.05	.02
475	Andre Thornton	.10	.08	.04
476	*Jeff Stone*(FC)	.12	.09	.05
477	Bob Ojeda	.10	.08	.04
478	Kurt Bevacqua	.06	.05	.02
479	Mike Madden	.06	.05	.02
480	Lou Whitaker	.30	.25	.12
481	Dale Murray	.06	.05	.02
482	Harry Spilman	.06	.05	.02
483	Mike Smithson	.06	.05	.02
484	Larry Bowa	.10	.08	.04
485	Matt Young	.06	.05	.02
486	Steve Balboni	.08	.06	.03
487	*Frank Williams*	.15	.11	.06
488	Joel Skinner(FC)	.08	.06	.03
489	Bryan Clark	.06	.05	.02
490	Jason Thompson	.06	.05	.02
491	Rick Camp	.06	.05	.02
492	Dave Johnson	.08	.06	.03
493	*Orel Hershiser*(FC)	3.50	2.75	1.50
494	Rich Dauer	.06	.05	.02
495	Mario Soto	.08	.06	.03
496	Donnie Scott	.06	.05	.02
497	Gary Pettis	.15	.11	.06
498	Ed Romero	.06	.05	.02
499	Danny Cox(FC)	.20	.20	.10
500	Mike Schmidt	1.00	.70	.40
501	Dan Schatzeder	.06	.05	.02
502	Rick Miller	.06	.05	.02
503	Tim Conroy	.06	.05	.02
504	Jerry Willard	.06	.05	.02
505	Jim Beattie	.06	.05	.02
506	*Franklin Stubbs*(FC)	.40	.30	.15
507	Ray Fontenot	.06	.05	.02
508	John Shelby	.08	.06	.03
509	Milt May	.06	.05	.02
510	Kent Hrbek	.25	.20	.10
511	Lee Smith	.10	.08	.04
512	Tom Brookens	.06	.05	.02
513	Lynn Jones	.06	.05	.02
514	Jeff Cornell	.06	.05	.02
515	Dave Concepcion	.12	.09	.05
516	Roy Lee Jackson	.06	.05	.02
517	Jerry Martin	.06	.05	.02

		MT	NR MT	EX
518	Chris Chambliss	.08	.06	.03
519	Doug Rader	.06	.05	.02
520	LaMarr Hoyt	.06	.05	.02
521	Rick Dempsey	.08	.06	.03
522	Paul Molitor	.15	.11	.06
523	Candy Maldonado	.10	.08	.04
524	Rob Wilfong	.06	.05	.02
525	Darrell Porter	.08	.06	.03
526	Dave Palmer	.06	.05	.02
527	Checklist 397-528	.06	.05	.02
528	Bill Krueger	.06	.05	.02
529	Rich Gedman	.10	.08	.04
530	Dave Dravecky	.08	.06	.03
531	Joe Lefebvre	.06	.05	.02
532	Frank DiPino	.06	.05	.02
533	Tony Bernazard	.06	.05	.02
534	Brian Dayett(FC)	.06	.05	.02
535	Pat Putnam	.06	.05	.02
536	*Kirby Puckett*(FC)	18.00	13.50	7.25
537	Don Robinson	.08	.06	.03
538	Keith Moreland	.08	.06	.03
539	Aurelio Lopez	.06	.05	.02
540	Claudell Washington	.08	.06	.03
541	Mark Davis	.06	.05	.02
542	Don Slaught	.06	.05	.02
543	Mike Squires	.06	.05	.02
544	Bruce Kison	.06	.05	.02
545	Lloyd Moseby	.10	.08	.04
546	Brent Gaff	.06	.05	.02
547	Pete Rose	.60	.45	.25
548	Larry Parrish	.10	.08	.04
549	Mike Scioscia	.08	.06	.03
550	Scott McGregor	.08	.06	.03
551	Andy Van Slyke	.35	.25	.14
552	Chris Codiroli	.06	.05	.02
553	Bob Clark	.06	.05	.02
554	Doug Flynn	.06	.05	.02
555	Bob Stanley	.06	.05	.02
556	Sixto Lezcano	.06	.05	.02
557	Len Barker	.08	.06	.03
558	Carmelo Martinez	.08	.06	.03
559	Jay Howell	.08	.06	.03
560	Bill Madlock	.12	.09	.05
561	Darryl Motley	.06	.05	.02
562	Houston Jimenez	.06	.05	.02
563	Dick Ruthven	.06	.05	.02
564	Alan Ashby	.06	.05	.02
565	Kirk Gibson	.35	.25	.14
566	Ed Vande Berg	.06	.05	.02
567	Joel Youngblood	.06	.05	.02
568	Cliff Johnson	.06	.05	.02
569	Ken Oberkfell	.06	.05	.02
570	Darryl Strawberry	5.00	3.75	2.00
571	Charlie Hough	.08	.06	.03
572	Tom Paciorek	.06	.05	.02
573	*Jay Tibbs*(FC)	.15	.11	.06
574	Joe Altobelli	.06	.05	.02
575	Pedro Guerrero	.25	.20	.10
576	Jaime Cocanower	.06	.05	.02
577	Chris Speier	.06	.05	.02
578	Terry Francona	.06	.05	.02
579	*Ron Romanick*	.10	.08	.04
580	Dwight Evans	.12	.09	.05
581	Mark Wagner	.06	.05	.02
582	Ken Phelps(FC)	.20	.15	.08
583	Bobby Brown	.06	.05	.02
584	Kevin Gross	.10	.08	.04
585	Butch Wynegar	.06	.05	.02
586	Bill Scherrer	.06	.05	.02
587	Doug Frobel	.06	.05	.02
588	Bobby Castillo	.06	.05	.02
589	Bob Dernier	.06	.05	.02
590	Ray Knight	.10	.08	.04
591	Larry Herndon	.08	.06	.03
592	*Jeff Robinson*	.30	.25	.12
593	Rick Leach	.06	.05	.02
594	Curt Wilkerson(FC)	.08	.06	.03
595	Larry Gura	.06	.05	.02
596	Jerry Hairston	.06	.05	.02
597	Brad Lesley	.06	.05	.02
598	Jose Oquendo	.06	.05	.02
599	Storm Davis	.10	.08	.04
600	Pete Rose	1.00	.70	.40
601	Tom Lasorda	.10	.08	.04
602	*Jeff Dedmon*	.12	.09	.05
603	Rick Manning	.06	.05	.02
604	Daryl Sconiers	.06	.05	.02
605	Ozzie Smith	.15	.11	.06
606	Rich Gale	.06	.05	.02
607	Bill Almon	.06	.05	.02
608	Craig Lefferts	.08	.06	.03
609	Broderick Perkins	.06	.05	.02
610	Jack Morris	.25	.20	.10
611	Ozzie Virgil	.06	.05	.02
612	Mike Armstrong	.06	.05	.02
613	Terry Puhl	.06	.05	.02
614	Al Williams	.06	.05	.02
615	Marvell Wynne	.06	.05	.02
616	Scott Sanderson	.06	.05	.02
617	Willie Wilson	.12	.09	.05
618	Pete Falcone	.06	.05	.02
619	Jeff Leonard	.10	.08	.04
620	*Dwight Gooden*	9.00	6.75	3.50
621	Marvis Foley	.06	.05	.02
622	Luis Leal	.06	.05	.02
623	Greg Walker	.12	.09	.05
624	Benny Ayala	.06	.05	.02
625	*Mark Langston*	2.25	1.75	.90
626	German Rivera	.06	.05	.02
627	*Eric Davis*(FC)	10.00	7.50	4.00
628	Rene Lachemann	.06	.05	.02
629	Dick Schofield	.12	.09	.05
630	Tim Raines	.35	.25	.14
631	Bob Forsch	.08	.06	.03
632	Bruce Bochte	.06	.05	.02
633	Glenn Hoffman	.06	.05	.02
634	Bill Dawley	.06	.05	.02
635	Terry Kennedy	.08	.06	.03
636	Shane Rawley	.10	.08	.04
637	Brett Butler	.08	.06	.03
638	*Mike Pagliarulo*(FC)	.80	.60	.30
639	Ed Hodge	.06	.05	.02
640	Steve Henderson	.06	.05	.02
641	Rod Scurry	.06	.05	.02
642	Dave Owen	.06	.05	.02
643	Johnny Grubb	.06	.05	.02
644	Mark Huismann(FC)	.06	.05	.02
645	Damaso Garcia	.06	.05	.02
646	Scot Thompson	.06	.05	.02
647	Rafael Ramirez	.06	.05	.02
648	Bob Jones	.06	.05	.02
649	Sid Fernandez(FC)	.90	.70	.35
650	Greg Luzinski	.10	.08	.04
651	Jeff Russell	.08	.06	.03
652	Joe Nolan	.06	.05	.02
653	Mark Brouhard	.06	.05	.02
654	Dave Anderson	.06	.05	.02
655	Joaquin Andujar	.08	.06	.03
656	Chuck Cottier	.06	.05	.02
657	Jim Slaton	.06	.05	.02
658	Mike Stenhouse	.06	.05	.02
659	Checklist 529-660	.06	.05	.02
660	Tony Gwynn	.80	.60	.30
661	Steve Crawford	.06	.05	.02
662	Mike Heath	.06	.05	.02
663	Luis Aguayo	.06	.05	.02
664	*Steve Farr*(FC)	.30	.25	.12
665	Don Mattingly	5.00	3.75	2.00
666	Mike LaCoss	.06	.05	.02
667	Dave Engle	.06	.05	.02
668	Steve Trout	.06	.05	.02
669	Lee Lacy	.06	.05	.02
670	Tom Seaver	.30	.25	.12
671	Dane Iorg	.06	.05	.02
672	Juan Berenguer	.06	.05	.02
673	Buck Martinez	.06	.05	.02
674	Atlee Hammaker	.06	.05	.02
675	Tony Perez	.15	.11	.06
676	*Albert Hall*(FC)	.15	.11	.06
677	Wally Backman	.08	.06	.03
678	Joey McLaughlin	.06	.05	.02
679	Bob Kearney	.06	.05	.02
680	Jerry Reuss	.08	.06	.03
681	Ben Oglivie	.08	.06	.03
682	Doug Corbett	.06	.05	.02
683	Whitey Herzog	.08	.06	.03
684	Bill Doran	.12	.09	.05
685	Bill Caudill	.06	.05	.02
686	Mike Easler	.08	.06	.03
687	Bill Gullickson	.06	.05	.02
688	Len Matuszek	.06	.05	.02
689	Luis DeLeon	.06	.05	.02
690	Alan Trammell	.35	.25	.14
691	Dennis Rasmussen(FC)	.30	.25	.12
692	Randy Bush	.06	.05	.02
693	Tim Stoddard	.06	.05	.02
694	Joe Carter(FC)	4.00	3.00	1.50
695	Rick Rhoden	.10	.08	.04
696	John Rabb	.06	.05	.02
697	Onix Concepcion	.06	.05	.02
698	Jorge Bell	.40	.30	.15
699	Donnie Moore	.06	.05	.02

		MT	NR MT	EX
700	Eddie Murray	.50	.40	.20
701	Eddie Murray AS	.30	.25	.12
702	Damaso Garcia AS	.08	.06	.03
703	George Brett AS	.35	.25	.14
704	Cal Ripken AS	.30	.25	.12
705	Dave Winfield AS	.20	.15	.08
706	Rickey Henderson AS	.30	.25	.12
707	Tony Armas AS	.08	.06	.03
708	Lance Parrish AS	.15	.11	.06
709	Mike Boddicker AS	.08	.06	.03
710	Frank Viola AS	.12	.09	.05
711	Dan Quisenberry AS	.10	.08	.04
712	Keith Hernandez AS	.20	.15	.08
713	Ryne Sandberg AS	.20	.15	.08
714	Mike Schmidt AS	.30	.25	.12
715	Ozzie Smith AS	.12	.09	.05
716	Dale Murphy AS	.35	.25	.14
717	Tony Gwynn AS	.35	.25	.14
718	Jeff Leonard AS	.10	.08	.04
719	Gary Carter AS	.20	.15	.08
720	Rick Sutcliffe AS	.12	.09	.05
721	Bob Knepper AS	.08	.06	.03
722	Bruce Sutter AS	.10	.08	.04
723	Dave Stewart	.12	.09	.05
724	Oscar Gamble	.08	.06	.03
725	Floyd Bannister	.10	.08	.04
726	Al Bumbry	.08	.06	.03
727	Frank Pastore	.06	.05	.02
728	Bob Bailor	.06	.05	.02
729	Don Sutton	.30	.25	.12
730	Dave Kingman	.15	.11	.06
731	Neil Allen	.06	.05	.02
732	John McNamara	.06	.05	.02
733	Tony Scott	.06	.05	.02
734	John Henry Johnson	.06	.05	.02
735	Garry Templeton	.08	.06	.03
736	Jerry Mumphrey	.06	.05	.02
737	Bo Diaz	.08	.06	.03
738	Omar Moreno	.06	.05	.02
739	Ernie Camacho	.06	.05	.02
740	Jack Clark	.20	.15	.08
741	John Butcher	.06	.05	.02
742	Ron Hassey	.06	.05	.02
743	Frank White	.10	.08	.04
744	Doug Bair	.06	.05	.02
745	Buddy Bell	.12	.09	.05
746	Jim Clancy	.08	.06	.03
747	Alex Trevino	.06	.05	.02
748	Lee Mazzilli	.08	.06	.03
749	Julio Cruz	.06	.05	.02
750	Rollie Fingers	.20	.15	.08
751	Kelvin Chapman	.06	.05	.02
752	Bob Owchinko	.06	.05	.02
753	Greg Brock	.08	.06	.03
754	Larry Milbourne	.06	.05	.02
755	Ken Singleton	.08	.06	.03
756	Rob Picciolo	.06	.05	.02
757	Willie McGee	.30	.25	.12
758	Ray Burris	.06	.05	.02
759	Jim Fanning	.06	.05	.02
760	Nolan Ryan	3.00	2.25	1.25
761	Jerry Remy	.06	.05	.02
762	Eddie Whitson	.06	.05	.02
763	Kiko Garcia	.06	.05	.02
764	Jamie Easterly	.06	.05	.02
765	Willie Randolph	.10	.08	.04
766	Paul Mirabella	.06	.05	.02
767	Darrell Brown	.06	.05	.02
768	Ron Cey	.10	.08	.04
769	Joe Cowley	.06	.05	.02
770	Carlton Fisk	.40	.30	.15
771	Geoff Zahn	.06	.05	.02
772	Johnnie LeMaster	.06	.05	.02
773	Hal McRae	.10	.08	.04
774	Dennis Lamp	.06	.05	.02
775	Mookie Wilson	.10	.08	.04
776	Jerry Royster	.06	.05	.02
777	Ned Yost	.06	.05	.02
778	Mike Davis	.08	.06	.03
779	Nick Esasky	.08	.06	.03
780	Mike Flanagan	.10	.08	.04
781	Jim Gantner	.08	.06	.03
782	Tom Niedenfuer	.08	.06	.03
783	Mike Jorgensen	.06	.05	.02
784	Checklist 661-792	.06	.05	.02
785	Tony Armas	.10	.08	.04
786	Enos Cabell	.06	.05	.02
787	Jim Wohlford	.06	.05	.02
788	Steve Comer	.06	.05	.02
789	Luis Salazar	.06	.05	.02
790	Ron Guidry	.25	.20	.10
791	Ivan DeJesus	.06	.05	.02
792	Darrell Evans	.12	.09	.05

1985 Topps All-Star Glossy Set Of 22

This was the second straight year for this set of 22 cards featuring the starting players, the honorary captains and the managers in the All-Star Game. The set is virtually identical to that of the previous year in design with a color photo, All-Star banner, league emblem, and player's name and position on the front. What makes the cards special is their high gloss finish. The cards were available as inserts in Topps rack packs. With their combination of attractive appearance and big-name stars, these 2-1/2" by 3-1/2" cards will probably continue to enjoy a great deal of popularity.

		MT	NR MT	EX
Complete Set:		7.00	5.25	2.75
Common Player:		.20	.15	.08
1	Paul Owens	.20	.15	.08
2	Steve Garvey	.50	.40	.20
3	Ryne Sandberg	.40	.30	.15
4	Mike Schmidt	.60	.45	.25
5	Ozzie Smith	.30	.25	.12
6	Tony Gwynn	.60	.45	.25
7	Dale Murphy	.80	.60	.30
8	Darryl Strawberry	1.00	.70	.40
9	Gary Carter	.50	.40	.20
10	Charlie Lea	.20	.15	.08
11	Willie McCovey	.40	.30	.15
12	Joe Altobelli	.20	.15	.08
13	Rod Carew	.50	.40	.20
14	Lou Whitaker	.30	.25	.12
15	George Brett	.80	.60	.30
16	Cal Ripken	.60	.45	.25
17	Dave Winfield	.50	.40	.20
18	Chet Lemon	.20	.15	.08
19	Reggie Jackson	.60	.45	.25
20	Lance Parrish	.30	.25	.12
21	Dave Stieb	.25	.20	.10
22	Hank Greenberg	.20	.15	.08

1985 Topps All-Star Glossy Set Of 40

Similar to previous years' glossy sets, the 1985 All-Star "Collector's Edition" glossy set of 40 could be obtained through the mail in eight five-card subsets. To obtain the 2-1/2" by 3-1/2" cards, collectors had to accumulate sweepstakes insert cards from Topps packs, and pay 75¢ postage and handling. Under the circumstances, the complete set of 40 cards was not inexpensive. They are however, rather attractive and popular cards, and the set size enabled Topps to include some players who didn't make their 22-card set.

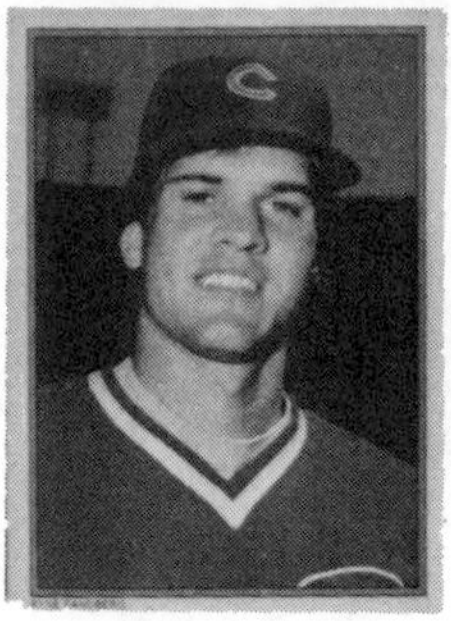

		MT	NR MT	EX
Complete Set:		18.00	13.50	7.25
Common Player:		.15	.11	.06
1	Dale Murphy	1.00	.70	.40
2	Jesse Orosco	.15	.11	.06
3	Bob Brenly	.15	.11	.06
4	Mike Boddicker	.15	.11	.06
5	Dave Kingman	.25	.20	.10
6	Jim Rice	.50	.40	.20
7	Frank Viola	.30	.25	.12
8	Alvin Davis	.35	.25	.14
9	Rick Sutcliffe	.20	.15	.08
10	Pete Rose	1.25	.90	.50
11	Leon Durham	.15	.11	.06
12	Joaquin Andujar	.15	.11	.06
13	Keith Hernandez	.40	.30	.15
14	Dave Winfield	.60	.45	.25
15	Reggie Jackson	.70	.50	.30
16	Alan Trammell	.35	.25	.14
17	Bert Blyleven	.20	.15	.08
18	Tony Armas	.15	.11	.06
19	Rich Gossage	.25	.20	.10
20	Jose Cruz	.15	.11	.06
21	Ryne Sandberg	.40	.30	.15
22	Bruce Sutter	.20	.15	.08
23	Mike Schmidt	1.00	.70	.40
24	Cal Ripken	.70	.50	.30
25	Dan Petry	.15	.11	.06
26	Jack Morris	.30	.25	.12
27	Don Mattingly	3.50	2.75	1.50
28	Eddie Murray	.60	.45	.25
29	Tony Gwynn	.60	.45	.25
30	Charlie Lea	.15	.11	.06
31	Juan Samuel	.30	.25	.12
32	Phil Niekro	.35	.25	.14
33	Alejandro Pena	.15	.11	.06
34	Harold Baines	.25	.20	.10
35	Dan Quisenberry	.15	.11	.06
36	Gary Carter	.50	.40	.20
37	Mario Soto	.15	.11	.06
38	Dwight Gooden	2.50	2.00	1.00
39	Tom Brunansky	.20	.15	.08
40	Dave Stieb	.20	.15	.08

1985 Topps All-Time Record Holders

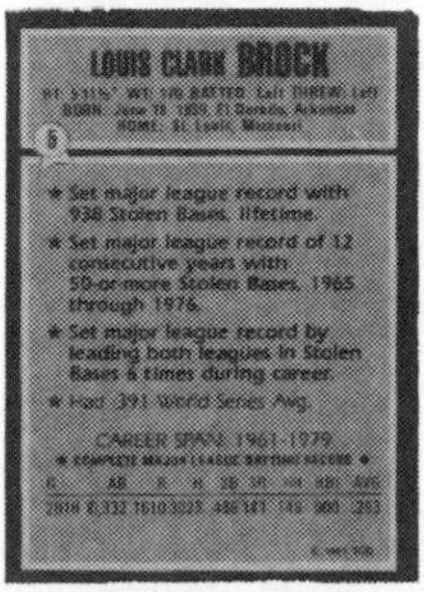

This 44-card boxed set was produced by Topps for the Woolworth's chain stores. Many hobbyists refer to this as the "Woolworth's" set, but that name does not appear anywhere on the cards. Featuring a combination of black and white and color photos of baseball record holders from all eras, the set is in the standard 2-1/2" by 3-1/2" format. Backs, printed in blue and orange, give career details and personal data. Because it combined old-timers with current players, the set did not achieve a great deal of collector popularity.

		MT	NR MT	EX
Complete Set:		5.00	3.75	2.00
Common Player:		.05	.04	.02
1	Hank Aaron	.25	.20	.10
2	Grover Alexander	.10	.08	.04
3	Ernie Banks	.12	.09	.05
4	Yogi Berra	.15	.11	.06
5	Lou Brock	.12	.09	.05
6	Steve Carlton	.12	.09	.05
7	Jack Chesbro	.07	.05	.03
8	Ty Cobb	.30	.25	.12
9	Sam Crawford	.07	.05	.03
10	Rollie Fingers	.07	.05	.03
11	Whitey Ford	.12	.09	.05
12	Johnny Frederick	.05	.04	.02
13	Frankie Frisch	.07	.05	.03
14	Lou Gehrig	.30	.25	.12
15	Jim Gentile	.05	.04	.02
16	Dwight Gooden	.60	.45	.25
17	Rickey Henderson	.15	.11	.06
18	Rogers Hornsby	.12	.09	.05
19	Frank Howard	.07	.05	.03
20	Cliff Johnson	.05	.04	.02
21	Walter Johnson	.15	.11	.06
22	Hub Leonard	.05	.04	.02
23	Mickey Mantle	1.00	.70	.40
24	Roger Maris	.12	.09	.05
25	Christy Mathewson	.12	.09	.05
26	Willie Mays	.20	.15	.08
27	Stan Musial	.20	.15	.08
28	Dan Quisenberry	.05	.04	.02
29	Frank Robinson	.12	.09	.05
30	Pete Rose	.40	.30	.15
31	Babe Ruth	.60	.45	.25
32	Nolan Ryan	.12	.09	.05
33	George Sisler	.10	.08	.04
34	Tris Speaker	.10	.08	.04
35	Ed Walsh	.07	.05	.03
36	Lloyd Waner	.07	.05	.03
37	Earl Webb	.05	.04	.02
38	Ted Williams	.30	.25	.12
39	Maury Wills	.07	.05	.03
40	Hack Wilson	.07	.05	.03
41	Owen Wilson	.05	.04	.02
42	Willie Wilson	.07	.05	.03
43	Rudy York	.05	.04	.02
44	Cy Young	.12	.09	.05

1985 Topps Gallery of Champions

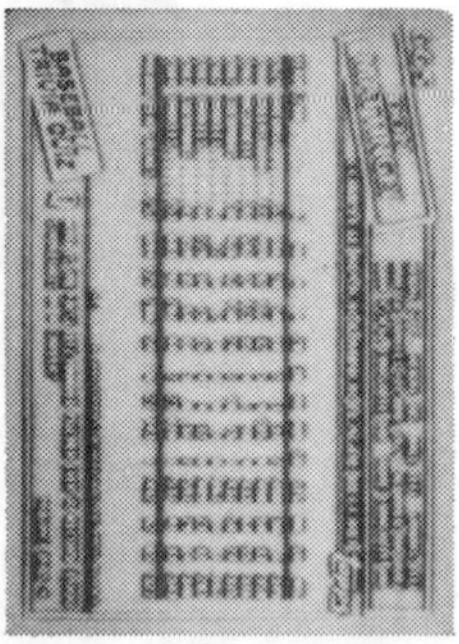

This second annual aluminum, bronze, and silver miniature issues honors 12 award winners from the previous season (MVP, Cy Young, Rookie of Year, Fireman, etc.). Each mini is an exact reproduction, at

one-quarter scale of the player's official Topps baseball card, both front and back. The bronze and silver sets were issued in a specially-designed velvet-like case. Aluminum sets came cello-wrapped. A Dwight Gooden pewter replica was given as a premium to dealers who bought bronze and silver sets (value $75). A Pete Rose bronze was issued as a premium to dealers purchasing cases of 1985 Topps Traded sets (value $12).

	MT	NR MT	EX
Complete Aluminum Set:	30.00	22.00	12.00
Complete Bronze Set:	175.00	131.00	70.00
Complete Silver Set:	600.00	450.00	240.00

		MT	NR MT	EX
(1a)	Tony Armas (aluminum)	.70	.50	.30
(1b)	Tony Armas (bronze)	7.50	5.75	3.00
(1c)	Tony Armas (silver)	20.00	15.00	8.00
(2a)	Alvin Davis (aluminum)	1.00	.70	.40
(2b)	Alvin Davis (bronze)	10.00	7.50	4.00
(2c)	Alvin Davis (silver)	30.00	22.00	12.00
(3a)	Dwight Gooden (aluminum)	3.00	2.25	1.25
(3b)	Dwight Gooden (bronze)	25.00	18.50	10.00
(3c)	Dwight Gooden (silver)	125.00	94.00	50.00
(4a)	Tony Gwynn (aluminum)	1.25	.90	.50
(4b)	Tony Gwynn (bronze)	12.00	9.00	4.75
(4c)	Tony Gwynn (silver)	50.00	37.00	20.00
(5a)	Willie Hernandez (aluminum)	.70	.50	.30
(5b)	Willie Hernandez (bronze)	7.50	5.75	3.00
(5c)	Willie Hernandez (silver)	20.00	15.00	8.00
(6a)	Don Mattingly (aluminum)	8.00	6.00	3.25
(6b)	Don Mattingly (bronze)	50.00	37.00	20.00
(6c)	Don Mattingly (silver)	200.00	150.00	80.00
(7a)	Dale Murphy (aluminum)	1.50	1.25	.60
(7b)	Dale Murphy (bronze)	15.00	11.00	6.00
(7c)	Dale Murphy (silver)	80.00	60.00	32.00
(8a)	Dan Quisenberry (aluminum)	.70	.50	.30
(8b)	Dan Quisenberry (bronze)	7.50	5.75	3.00
(8c)	Dan Quisenberry (silver)	20.00	15.00	8.00
(9a)	Ryne Sandberg (aluminum)	1.25	.90	.50
(9b)	Ryne Sandberg (bronze)	12.50	9.50	5.00
(9c)	Ryne Sandberg (silver)	70.00	52.00	27.00
(10a)	Mike Schmidt (aluminum)	1.50	1.25	.60
(10b)	Mike Schmidt (bronze)	15.00	11.00	6.00
(10c)	Mike Schmidt (silver)	80.00	60.00	32.00
(11a)	Rick Sutcliffe (aluminum)	.70	.50	.30
(11b)	Rick Sutcliffe (bronze)	7.50	5.75	3.00
(11c)	Rick Sutcliffe (silver)	20.00	15.00	8.00
(12a)	Bruce Sutter (aluminum)	.70	.50	.30
(12b)	Bruce Sutter (bronze)	7.50	5.75	3.00
(12c)	Bruce Sutter (silver)	20.00	15.00	8.00

1985 Topps Rub Downs

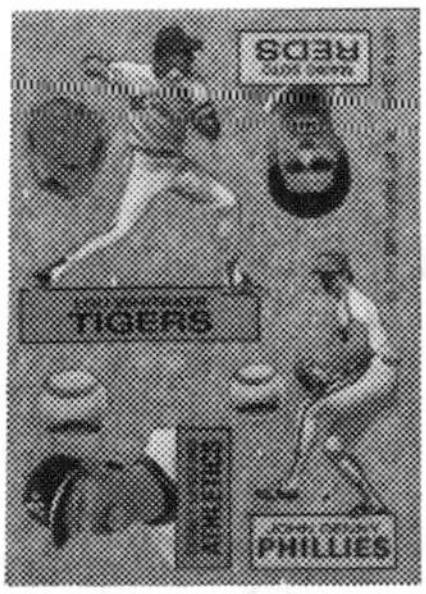

Similar in size and design to the Rub Downs of the previous year, the 1985 set again consisted of 32 unnumbered sheets featuring 112 different players. The set was sold by Topps as a separate issue.

	MT	NR MT	EX
Complete Set:	6.00	4.50	2.50
Common Player:	.10	.08	.04

		MT	NR MT	EX
(1)	Tony Armas, Harold Baines, Lonnie Smith	.10	.08	.04
(2)	Don Baylor, George Hendrick, Ron Kittle, Johnnie LeMaster	.10	.08	.04
(3)	Buddy Bell, Tony Gwynn, Lloyd Moseby	.25	.20	.10
(4)	Bruce Benedict, Atlee Hammaker, Frank White	.10	.08	.04
(5)	Mike Boddicker, Rod Carew, Carlton Fisk, Johnny Ray	.25	.20	.10
(6)	Wade Boggs, Rick Dempsey, Keith Hernandez	.60	.45	.25
(7)	George Brett, Andre Dawson, Paul Molitor, Alan Wiggins	.30	.25	.12
(8)	Tom Brunansky, Pedro Guerrero, Darryl Strawberry	.40	.30	.15
(9)	Bill Buckner, Tim Raines, Ryne Sandberg, Mike Schmidt	.30	.25	.12
(10)	Steve Carlton, Bob Horner, Dan Quisenberry	.25	.20	.10
(11)	Gary Carter, Phil Garner, Ron Guidry	.25	.20	.10
(12)	Jack Clark, Damaso Garcia, Hal McRae, Lance Parrish	.20	.15	.08
(13)	Dave Concepcion, Cecil Cooper, Fred Lynn, Jesse Orosco	.15	.11	.06
(14)	Jose Cruz, Jack Morris, Jim Rice, Rick Sutcliffe	.20	.15	.08
(15)	Alvin Davis, Steve Kemp, Greg Luzinski, Kent Tekulve	.20	.15	.08
(16)	Ron Davis, Kent Hrbek, Juan Samuel	.20	.15	.08
(17)	John Denny, Carney Lansford, Mario Soto, Lou Whitaker	.15	.11	.06
(18)	Leon Durham, Willie Hernandez, Steve Sax	.15	.11	.06
(19)	Dwight Evans, Julio Franco, Dwight Gooden	.40	.30	.15
(20)	George Foster, Gary Gaetti, Bobby Grich, Gary Redus	.15	.11	.06
(21)	Steve Garvey, Jerry Remy, Bill Russell, George Wright	.20	.15	.08
(22)	Kirk Gibson, Rich Gossage, Don Mattingly, Dave Stieb	.90	.70	.35
(23)	Moose Haas, Bruce Sutter, Dickie Thon, Andre Thornton	.10	.08	.04
(24)	Rickey Henderson, Dave Righetti, Pete Rose	.70	.50	.30
(25)	Steve Henderson, Bill Madlock, Alan Trammell	.15	.11	.06
(26)	LaMarr Hoyt, Larry Parrish, Nolan Ryan	.25	.20	.10
(27)	Reggie Jackson, Eric Show, Jason Thompson	.30	.25	.12
(28)	Terry Kennedy, Eddie Murray, Tom Seaver, Ozzie Smith	.25	.20	.10
(29)	Mark Langston, Ben Oglivie, Darrell Porter	.15	.11	.06
(30)	Jeff Leonard, Gary Matthews, Dale Murphy, Dave Winfield	.30	.25	.12
(31)	Craig McMurtry, Cal Ripken, Steve Rogers, Willie Upshaw	.25	.20	.10
(32)	Tony Pena, Fernando Valenzuela, Robin Yount	.20	.15	.08

1985 Topps Stickers

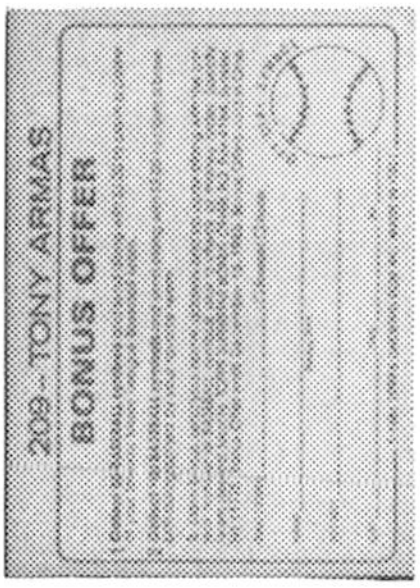

Topps went to a larger size for its stickers in 1985. Each of the 376 stickers measures 2-1/8" by 3" and is numbered on both the front and the back. The backs contain either an offer to obtain an autographed team ball or a poster. An album was also available.

		MT	NR MT	EX
Complete Set:		16.00	12.00	6.50
Common Player:		.03	.02	.01
Sticker Album:		.80	.60	.30
1	Steve Garvey	.25	.20	.10
2	Steve Garvey	.25	.20	.10
3	Dwight Gooden	.25	.20	.10
4	Dwight Gooden	.25	.20	.10
5	Joe Morgan	.10	.08	.04
6	Joe Morgan	.10	.08	.04
7	Don Sutton	.10	.08	.04
8	Don Sutton	.10	.08	.04
9	1984 A.L. Championships (Jack Morris)	.06	.05	.02
10	1984 A.L. Championships (Milt Wilcox)	.03	.02	.01
11	1984 A.L. Championships (Kirk Gibson)	.08	.06	.03
12	1984 N.L. Championships (Gary Matthews)	.04	.03	.02
13	1984 N.L. Championships (Steve Garvey)	.10	.08	.04
14	1984 N.L. Championships (Steve Garvey)	.15	.11	.06
15	1984 World Series (Jack Morris)	.06	.05	.02
16	1984 World Series (Kurt Bevacqua)	.03	.02	.01
17	1984 World Series (Milt Wilcox)	.03	.02	.01
18	1984 World Series (Alan Trammell)	.08	.06	.03
19	1984 World Series (Kirk Gibson)	.08	.06	.03
20	1984 World Series (Alan Trammell)	.12	.09	.05
21	1984 World Series (Chet Lemon)	.03	.02	.01
22	Dale Murphy	.25	.20	.10
23	Steve Bedrosian	.10	.08	.04
24	Bob Horner	.10	.08	.04
25	Claudell Washington	.06	.05	.02
26	Rick Mahler	.06	.05	.02
27	Rafael Ramirez	.04	.03	.02
28	Craig McMurtry	.04	.03	.02
29	Chris Chambliss	.04	.03	.02
30	Alex Trevino	.03	.02	.01
31	Bruce Benedict	.04	.03	.02
32	Ken Oberkfell	.03	.02	.01
33	Glenn Hubbard	.04	.03	.02
34	Ryne Sandberg	.15	.11	.06
35	Rick Sutcliffe	.08	.06	.03
36	Leon Durham	.06	.05	.02
37	Jody Davis	.06	.05	.02
38	Bob Dernier	.04	.03	.02
39	Keith Moreland	.06	.05	.02
40	Scott Sanderson	.04	.03	.02
41	Lee Smith	.06	.05	.02
42	Ron Cey	.06	.05	.02
43	Steve Trout	.06	.05	.02
44	Gary Matthews	.06	.05	.02
45	Larry Bowa	.04	.03	.02
46	Mario Soto	.06	.05	.02
47	Dave Parker	.12	.09	.05
48	Dave Concepcion	.06	.05	.02
49	Gary Redus	.06	.05	.02
50	Ted Power	.06	.05	.02
51	Nick Esasky	.04	.03	.02
52	Duane Walker	.06	.05	.02
53	Eddie Milner	.03	.02	.01
54	Ron Oester	.03	.02	.01
55	Cesar Cedeno	.04	.03	.02
56	Joe Price	.03	.02	.01
57	Pete Rose	.20	.15	.08
58	Nolan Ryan	.15	.11	.06
59	Jose Cruz	.06	.05	.02
60	Jerry Mumphrey	.04	.03	.02
61	Enos Cabell	.03	.02	.01
62	Bob Knepper	.04	.03	.02
63	Dickie Thon	.04	.03	.02
64	Phil Garner	.04	.03	.02
65	Craig Reynolds	.06	.05	.02
66	Frank DiPino	.03	.02	.01
67	Terry Puhl	.03	.02	.01
68	Bill Doran	.06	.05	.02
69	Joe Niekro	.04	.03	.02
70	Pedro Guerrero	.12	.09	.05
71	Fernando Valenzuela	.15	.11	.06
72	Mike Marshall	.08	.06	.03
73	Alejandro Pena	.04	.03	.02
74	Orel Hershiser	.10	.08	.04
75	Ken Landreaux	.06	.05	.02
76	Bill Russell	.06	.05	.02
77	Steve Sax	.06	.05	.02
78	Rick Honeycutt	.03	.02	.01
79	Mike Scioscia	.03	.02	.01
80	Tom Niedenfuer	.06	.05	.02

		MT	NR MT	EX
81	Candy Maldonado	.03	.02	.01
82	Tim Raines	.15	.11	.06
83	Gary Carter	.20	.15	.08
84	Charlie Lea	.03	.02	.01
85	Jeff Reardon	.08	.06	.03
86	Andre Dawson	.06	.05	.02
87	Tim Wallach	.04	.03	.02
88	Terry Francona	.04	.03	.02
89	Steve Rogers	.03	.02	.01
90	Bryn Smith	.03	.02	.01
91	Bill Gullickson	.04	.03	.02
92	Dan Driessen	.03	.02	.01
93	Doug Flynn	.03	.02	.01
94	Mike Schmidt	.20	.15	.08
95	Tony Armas	.30	.25	.12
96	Dale Murphy	.15	.11	.06
97	Rick Sutcliffe	.10	.08	.04
98	Keith Hernandez	.12	.09	.05
99	George Foster	.08	.06	.03
100	Darryl Strawberry	.30	.25	.12
101	Jesse Orosco	.04	.03	.02
102	Mookie Wilson	.04	.03	.02
103	Doug Sisk	.03	.02	.01
104	Hubie Brooks	.06	.05	.02
105	Ron Darling	.04	.03	.02
106	Wally Backman	.04	.03	.02
107	Dwight Gooden	.15	.11	.06
108	Mike Fitzgerald	.04	.03	.02
109	Walt Terrell	.03	.02	.01
110	Ozzie Virgil	.04	.03	.02
111	Mike Schmidt	.25	.20	.10
112	Steve Carlton	.15	.11	.06
113	Al Holland	.03	.02	.01
114	Juan Samuel	.06	.05	.02
115	Von Hayes	.04	.03	.02
116	Jeff Stone	.06	.05	.02
117	Jerry Koosman	.04	.03	.02
118	Al Oliver	.04	.03	.02
119	John Denny	.03	.02	.01
120	Charles Hudson	.03	.02	.01
121	Garry Maddox	.06	.05	.02
122	Bill Madlock	.06	.05	.02
123	John Candelaria	.06	.05	.02
124	Tony Pena	.06	.05	.02
125	Jason Thompson	.03	.02	.01
126	Lee Lacy	.04	.03	.02
127	Rick Rhoden	.06	.05	.02
128	Doug Frobel	.06	.05	.02
129	Kent Tekulve	.04	.03	.02
130	Johnny Ray	.04	.03	.02
131	Marvell Wynne	.08	.06	.03
132	Larry McWilliams	.03	.02	.01
133	Dale Berra	.03	.02	.01
134	George Hendrick	.06	.05	.02
135	Bruce Sutter	.08	.06	.03
136	Joaquin Andujar	.04	.03	.02
137	Ozzie Smith	.10	.08	.04
138	Andy Van Slyke	.04	.03	.02
139	Lonnie Smith	.06	.05	.02
140	Darrell Porter	.03	.02	.01
141	Willie McGee	.06	.05	.02
142	Tom Herr	.04	.03	.02
143	Dave LaPoint	.03	.02	.01
144	Neil Allen	.04	.03	.02
145	David Green	.03	.02	.01
146	Tony Gwynn	.20	.15	.08
147	Rich Gossage	.12	.09	.05
148	Terry Kennedy	.04	.03	.02
149	Steve Garvey	.15	.11	.06
150	Alan Wiggins	.03	.02	.01
151	Garry Templeton	.08	.06	.03
152	Ed Whitson	.04	.03	.02
153	Tim Lollar	.03	.02	.01
154	Dave Dravecky	.04	.03	.02
155	Graig Nettles	.04	.03	.02
156	Eric Show	.03	.02	.01
157	Carmelo Martinez	.03	.02	.01
158	Bob Brenly	.03	.02	.01
159	Gary Lavelle	.03	.02	.01
160	Jack Clark	.10	.08	.04
161	Jeff Leonard	.04	.03	.02
162	Chili Davis	.06	.05	.02
163	Mike Krukow	.03	.02	.01
164	Johnnie LeMaster	.03	.02	.01
165	Atlee Hammaker	.03	.02	.01
166	Dan Gladden	.06	.05	.02
167	Greg Minton	.03	.02	.01
168	Joel Youngblood	.03	.02	.01
169	Frank Williams	.04	.03	.02
170	Tony Gwynn	.20	.15	.08
171	Don Mattingly	.30	.25	.12

		MT	NR MT	EX
172	Bruce Sutter	.15	.11	.06
173	Dan Quisenberry	.10	.08	.04
174	Tony Gwynn	.40	.30	.15
175	Ryne Sandberg	.35	.25	.14
176	Steve Garvey	.30	.25	.12
177	Dale Murphy	.40	.30	.15
178	Mike Schmidt	.40	.30	.15
179	Darryl Strawberry	.50	.40	.20
180	Gary Carter	.30	.25	.12
181	Ozzie Smith	.20	.15	.08
182	Charlie Lea	.15	.11	.06
183	Lou Whitaker	.25	.20	.10
184	Rod Carew	.30	.25	.12
185	Cal Ripken	.40	.30	.15
186	Dave Winfield	.30	.25	.12
187	Reggie Jackson	.40	.30	.15
188	George Brett	.40	.30	.15
189	Lance Parrish	.25	.20	.10
190	Chet Lemon	.15	.11	.06
191	Dave Stieb	.15	.11	.06
192	Gary Carter	.20	.15	.08
193	Mike Schmidt	.30	.25	.12
194	Tony Armas	.15	.11	.06
195	Mike Witt	.10	.08	.04
196	Eddie Murray	.20	.15	.08
197	Cal Ripken	.20	.15	.08
198	Scott McGregor	.04	.03	.02
199	Rick Dempsey	.04	.03	.02
200	Tippy Martinez	.08	.06	.03
201	Ken Singleton	.04	.03	.02
202	Mike Boddicker	.06	.05	.02
203	Rich Dauer	.03	.02	.01
204	John Shelby	.04	.03	.02
205	Al Bumbry	.04	.03	.02
206	John Lowenstein	.04	.03	.02
207	Mike Flanagan	.04	.03	.02
209	Tony Armas	.04	.03	.02
210	Wade Boggs	.60	.45	.25
211	Bruce Hurst	.06	.05	.02
212	Dwight Evans	.06	.05	.02
213	Mike Easler	.04	.03	.02
214	Bill Buckner	.04	.03	.02
215	Bob Stanley	.04	.03	.02
216	Jackie Gutierrez	.03	.02	.01
217	Rich Gedman	.04	.03	.02
218	Jerry Remy	.03	.02	.01
219	Marty Barrett	.04	.03	.02
220	Reggie Jackson	.20	.15	.08
221	Geoff Zahn	.03	.02	.01
222	Doug DeCinces	.06	.05	.02
223	Rod Carew	.20	.15	.08
224	Brian Downing	.04	.03	.02
225	Fred Lynn	.06	.05	.02
226	Gary Pettis	.04	.03	.02
227	Mike Witt	.06	.05	.02
228	Bob Boone	.06	.05	.02
229	Tommy John	.06	.05	.02
230	Bobby Grich	.06	.05	.02
231	Ron Romanick	.04	.03	.02
232	Ron Kittle	.06	.05	.02
233	Richard Dotson	.06	.05	.02
234	Harold Baines	.08	.06	.03
235	Tom Seaver	.15	.11	.06
236	Greg Walker	.06	.05	.02
237	Roy Smalley	.04	.03	.02
238	Greg Luzinski	.06	.05	.02
239	Julio Cruz	.03	.02	.01
240	Scott Fletcher	.03	.02	.01
241	Rudy Law	.04	.03	.02
242	Vance Law	.03	.02	.01
243	Carlton Fisk	.20	.15	.08
244	Andre Thornton	.06	.05	.02
245	Julio Franco	.08	.06	.03
246	Brett Butler	.06	.05	.02
247	Bert Blyleven	.08	.06	.03
248	Mike Hargrove	.04	.03	.02
249	George Vukovich	.04	.03	.02
250	Pat Tabler	.04	.03	.02
251	Brook Jacoby	.06	.05	.02
252	Tony Bernazard	.03	.02	.01
253	Ernie Camacho	.03	.02	.01
254	Mel Hall	.06	.05	.02
255	Carmen Castillo	.04	.03	.02
256	Jack Morris	.12	.09	.05
257	Willie Hernandez	.06	.05	.02
258	Alan Trammell	.15	.11	.06
259	Lance Parrish	.12	.09	.05
260	Chet Lemon	.10	.08	.04
261	Lou Whitaker	.06	.05	.02
262	Howard Johnson	.06	.05	.02
263	Barbaro Garbey	.06	.05	.02

		MT	NR MT	EX
264	Dan Petry	.03	.02	.01
265	Aurelio Lopez	.03	.02	.01
266	Larry Herndon	.03	.02	.01
267	Kirk Gibson	.06	.05	.02
268	George Brett	.25	.20	.10
269	Dan Quisenberry	.06	.05	.02
270	Hal McRae	.06	.05	.02
271	Steve Balboni	.06	.05	.02
272	Pat Sheridan	.06	.05	.02
273	Jorge Orta	.04	.03	.02
274	Frank White	.04	.03	.02
275	Bud Black	.03	.02	.01
276	Darryl Motley	.03	.02	.01
277	Willie Wilson	.04	.03	.02
278	Larry Gura	.03	.02	.01
279	Don Slaught	.03	.02	.01
280	Dwight Gooden	.20	.15	.08
281	Mark Langston	.30	.25	.12
282	Tim Raines	.15	.11	.06
283	Rickey Henderson	.10	.08	.04
284	Robin Yount	.15	.11	.06
285	Rollie Fingers	.10	.08	.04
286	Jim Sundberg	.03	.02	.01
287	Cecil Cooper	.06	.05	.02
288	Jaime Cocanower	.04	.03	.02
289	Mike Caldwell	.03	.02	.01
290	Don Sutton	.06	.05	.02
291	Rick Manning	.04	.03	.02
292	Ben Oglivie	.04	.03	.02
293	Moose Haas	.15	.11	.06
294	Ted Simmons	.04	.03	.02
295	Jim Gantner	.03	.02	.01
296	Kent Hrbek	.12	.09	.05
297	Ron Davis	.03	.02	.01
298	Dave Engle	.03	.02	.01
299	Tom Brunansky	.06	.05	.02
300	Frank Viola	.06	.05	.02
301	Mike Smithson	.04	.03	.02
302	Gary Gaetti	.06	.05	.02
303	Tim Teufel	.04	.03	.02
304	Mickey Hatcher	.04	.03	.02
305	John Butcher	.03	.02	.01
306	Darrell Brown	.03	.02	.01
307	Kirby Puckett	.06	.05	.02
308	Dave Winfield	.15	.11	.06
309	Phil Niekro	.12	.09	.05
310	Don Mattingly	.70	.50	.30
311	Don Baylor	.08	.06	.03
312	Willie Randolph	.04	.03	.02
313	Ron Guidry	.06	.05	.02
314	Dave Righetti	.06	.05	.02
315	Bobby Meacham	.04	.03	.02
316	Butch Wynegar	.04	.03	.02
317	Mike Pagliarulo	.08	.06	.03
318	Joe Cowley	.03	.02	.01
319	John Montefusco	.03	.02	.01
320	Dave Kingman	.08	.06	.03
321	Rickey Henderson	.20	.15	.08
322	Bill Caudill	.03	.02	.01
323	Dwayne Murphy	.04	.03	.02
324	Steve McCatty	.04	.03	.02
325	Joe Morgan	.06	.05	.02
326	Mike Heath	.03	.02	.01
327	Chris Codiroli	.06	.05	.02
328	Ray Burris	.04	.03	.02
329	Tony Phillips	.03	.02	.01
330	Carney Lansford	.04	.03	.02
331	Bruce Bochte	.03	.02	.01
332	Alvin Davis	.15	.11	.06
333	Al Cowens	.03	.02	.01
334	Jim Beattie	.03	.02	.01
335	Bob Kearney	.03	.02	.01
336	Ed Vande Berg	.03	.02	.01
337	Mark Langston	.08	.06	.03
338	Dave Henderson	.04	.03	.02
339	Spike Owen	.03	.02	.01
340	Matt Young	.04	.03	.02
341	Jack Perconte	.04	.03	.02
342	Barry Bonnell	.03	.02	.01
343	Mike Stanton	.03	.02	.01
344	Pete O'Brien	.08	.06	.03
345	Charlie Hough	.06	.05	.02
346	Larry Parrish	.06	.05	.02
347	Buddy Bell	.08	.06	.03
348	Frank Tanana	.06	.05	.02
349	Curt Wilkerson	.03	.02	.01
350	Jeff Kunkel	.03	.02	.01
351	Billy Sample	.03	.02	.01
352	Danny Darwin	.03	.02	.01
353	Gary Ward	.03	.02	.01
354	Mike Mason	.03	.02	.01

		MT	NR MT	EX
355	Mickey Rivers	.04	.03	.02
356	Dave Stieb	.08	.06	.03
357	Damaso Garcia	.04	.03	.02
358	Willie Upshaw	.06	.05	.02
359	Lloyd Moseby	.08	.06	.03
360	George Bell	.08	.06	.03
361	Luis Leal	.04	.03	.02
362	Jesse Barfield	.06	.05	.02
363	Dave Collins	.03	.02	.01
364	Roy Lee Jackson	.04	.03	.02
365	Doyle Alexander	.04	.03	.02
366	Alfredo Griffin	.04	.03	.02
367	Cliff Johnson	.04	.03	.02
368	Alvin Davis	.15	.11	.06
369	Juan Samuel	.10	.08	.04
370	Brook Jacoby	.08	.06	.03
371	Dwight Gooden, Mark Langston	.30	.25	.12
372	Mike Fitzgerald	.04	.03	.02
373	Jackie Gutierrez	.03	.02	.01
374	Dan Gladden	.08	.06	.03
375	Carmelo Martinez	.06	.05	.02
376	Kirby Puckett	.20	.15	.08

1985 Topps Super

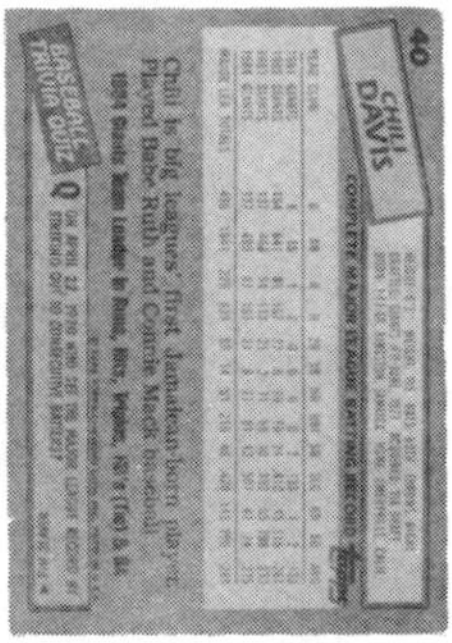

Still trying to sell collectors on the idea of jumbo-sized cards, Topps returned for a second year with its 4-7/8" by 6-7/8" "Super" set. In fact, the set size was doubled from the previous year, to 60 cards. The Supers are identical to the regular-issue 1985 cards of the same players, only the card numbers on back were changed. The cards were again sold three per pack for 50¢.

		MT	NR MT	EX
Complete Set:		14.00	10.50	5.50
Common Player:		.20	.15	.08
1	Ryne Sandberg	.50	.40	.20
2	Willie Hernandez	.20	.15	.08
3	Rick Sutcliffe	.25	.20	.10
4	Don Mattingly	2.25	1.75	.90
5	Tony Gwynn	.70	.50	.30
6	Alvin Davis	.35	.25	.14
7	Dwight Gooden	2.00	1.50	.80
8	Dan Quisenberry	.20	.15	.08
9	Bruce Sutter	.25	.20	.10
10	Tony Armas	.20	.15	.08
11	Dale Murphy	.90	.70	.35
12	Mike Schmidt	.90	.70	.35
13	Gary Carter	.50	.40	.20
14	Rickey Henderson	.70	.50	.30
15	Tim Raines	.50	.40	.20
16	Mike Boddicker	.20	.15	.08
17	Alejandro Pena	.20	.15	.08
18	Eddie Murray	.60	.45	.25
19	Gary Matthews	.20	.15	.08
20	Mark Langston	.30	.25	.12
21	Mario Soto	.20	.15	.08
22	Dave Stieb	.20	.15	.08
23	Nolan Ryan	.50	.40	.20
24	Steve Carlton	.50	.40	.20
25	Alan Trammell	.40	.30	.15
26	Steve Garvey	.50	.40	.20
27	Kirk Gibson	.35	.25	.14
28	Juan Samuel	.35	.25	.14
29	Reggie Jackson	.60	.45	.25
30	Darryl Strawberry	.90	.70	.35

		MT	NR MT	EX
31	Tom Seaver	.50	.40	.20
32	Pete Rose	1.25	.90	.50
33	Dwight Evans	.30	.25	.12
34	Jose Cruz	.20	.15	.08
35	Bert Blyleven	.25	.20	.10
36	Keith Hernandez	.50	.40	.20
37	Robin Yount	.40	.30	.15
38	Joaquin Andujar	.20	.15	.08
39	Lloyd Moseby	.20	.15	.08
40	Chili Davis	.20	.15	.08
41	Kent Hrbek	.35	.25	.14
42	Dave Parker	.30	.25	.12
43	Jack Morris	.35	.25	.14
44	Pedro Guerrero	.30	.25	.12
45	Mike Witt	.20	.15	.08
46	George Brett	.90	.70	.35
47	Ozzie Smith	.30	.25	.12
48	Cal Ripken	.70	.50	.30
49	Rich Gossage	.25	.20	.10
50	Jim Rice	.50	.40	.20
51	Harold Baines	.25	.20	.10
52	Fernando Valenzuela	.40	.30	.15
53	Buddy Bell	.25	.20	.10
54	Jesse Orosco	.20	.15	.08
55	Lance Parrish	.35	.25	.14
56	Jason Thompson	.20	.15	.08
57	Tom Brunansky	.25	.20	.10
58	Dave Righetti	.30	.25	.12
59	Dave Kingman	.25	.20	.10
60	Dave Winfield	.50	.40	.20

1985 Topps 3-D

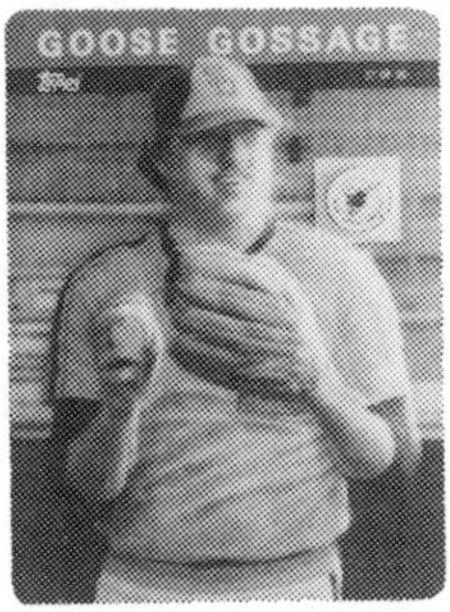

These 4-1/4" by 6" cards were something new. Printed on plastic, rather than paper, the player picture on the card is actually raised above the surface much like might be found on a relief map; a true 3-D baseball card. The plastic cards include the player's name, a Topps logo and card number across the top, and a team logo on the side. The backs are blank but have two peel-off adhesive strips so that the card may be attached to a flat surface. There are 30 cards in the set, the bulk of whom are stars.

		MT	NR MT	EX
Complete Set:		16.00	12.00	6.50
Common Player:		.20	.15	.08
1	Mike Schmidt	.90	.70	.35
2	Eddie Murray	.70	.50	.30
3	Dale Murphy	.90	.70	.35
4	George Brett	.90	.70	.35
5	Pete Rose	1.25	.90	.50
6	Jim Rice	.60	.45	.25
7	Ryne Sandberg	.50	.40	.20
8	Don Mattingly	2.50	2.00	1.00
9	Darryl Strawberry	.90	.70	.35
10	Rickey Henderson	.80	.60	.30
11	Keith Hernandez	.50	.40	.20
12	Dave Kingman	.20	.15	.08
13	Tony Gwynn	.80	.60	.30
14	Reggie Jackson	.70	.50	.30
15	Gary Carter	.60	.45	.25
16	Cal Ripken	.80	.60	.30
17	Tim Raines	.50	.40	.20
18	Dave Winfield	.60	.45	.25
19	Dwight Gooden	2.00	1.50	.80

		MT	NR MT	EX
20	Dave Stieb	.20	.15	.08
21	Fernando Valenzuela	.50	.40	.20
22	Mark Langston	.30	.25	.12
23	Bruce Sutter	.25	.20	.10
24	Dan Quisenberry	.20	.15	.08
25	Steve Carlton	.60	.45	.25
26	Mike Boddicker	.20	.15	.08
27	Goose Gossage	.30	.25	.12
28	Jack Morris	.40	.30	.15
29	Rick Sutcliffe	.25	.20	.10
30	Tom Seaver	.60	.45	.25

1985 Topps Traded

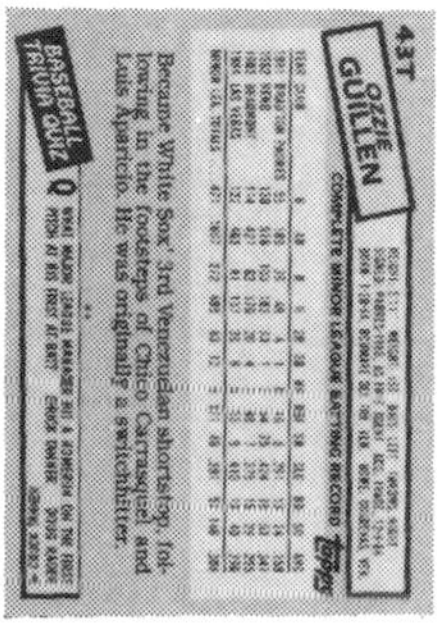

By 1985, the Topps Traded set had become a yearly feature, and Topps continued the tradition with another 132-card set. The 2-1/2" by 3-1/2" cards followed the pattern of being virtually identical in design to the regular cards issued by Topps. Sold only through established hobby dealers, the set features traded veterans and promising rookies. A glossy-finish "Tiffany" edition of the set is valued at four times normal Traded card value for commons, up to five or six times normal value for superstars and hot rookies.

		MT	NR MT	EX
Complete Set:		25.00	18.00	10.00
Common Player:		.10	.08	.04
1T	Don Aase	.10	.08	.04
2T	Bill Almon	.10	.08	.04
3T	Benny Ayala	.10	.08	.04
4T	Dusty Baker	.15	.11	.06
5T	George Bamberger	.10	.08	.04
6T	Dale Berra	.10	.08	.04
7T	Rich Bordi	.10	.08	.04
8T	Daryl Boston(FC)	.20	.15	.08
9T	Hubie Brooks	.25	.20	.10
10T	Chris Brown(FC)	.25	.20	.10
11T	Tom Browning(FC)	1.25	.90	.50
12T	Al Bumbry	.10	.08	.04
13T	Ray Burris	.10	.08	.04
14T	Jeff Burroughs	.15	.11	.06
15T	Bill Campbell	.10	.08	.04
16T	Don Carman(FC)	.15	.11	.06
17T	Gary Carter	.70	.50	.30
18T	Bobby Castillo	.10	.08	.04
19T	Bill Caudill	.10	.08	.04
20T	Rick Cerone	.10	.08	.04
21T	Bryan Clark	.10	.08	.04
22T	Jack Clark	.35	.25	.14
23T	Pat Clements(FC)	.20	.15	.08
24T	Vince Coleman(FC)	12.00	9.00	4.75
25T	Dave Collins	.15	.11	.06
26T	Danny Darwin	.15	.11	.06
27T	Jim Davenport	.10	.08	.04
28T	Jerry Davis	.10	.08	.04
29T	Brian Dayett	.10	.08	.04
30T	Ivan DeJesus	.10	.08	.04
31T	Ken Dixon	.10	.08	.04
32T	Mariano Duncan(FC)	.20	.15	.08
33T	John Felske	.10	.08	.04
34T	Mike Fitzgerald	.10	.08	.04
35T	Ray Fontenot	.10	.08	.04
36T	Greg Gagne(FC)	.35	.25	.14
37T	Oscar Gamble	.15	.11	.06
38T	Scott Garrelts(FC)	.50	.40	.20
39T	Bob Gibson	.10	.08	.04
40T	Jim Gott	.10	.08	.04
41T	David Green	.10	.08	.04
42T	Alfredo Griffin	.15	.11	.06
43T	Ozzie Guillen(FC)	2.50	2.00	1.00
44T	Eddie Haas	.10	.08	.04
45T	Terry Harper	.10	.08	.04
46T	Toby Harrah	.15	.11	.06
47T	Greg Harris	.10	.08	.04
48T	Ron Hassey	.10	.08	.04
49T	Rickey Henderson	5.00	3.75	2.00
50T	Steve Henderson	.10	.08	.04
51T	George Hendrick	.15	.11	.06
52T	Joe Hesketh(FC)	.20	.15	.08
53T	Teddy Higuera(FC)	1.00	.70	.40
54T	Donnie Hill	.10	.08	.04
55T	Al Holland	.10	.08	.04
56T	Burt Hooton	.15	.11	.06
57T	Jay Howell	.15	.11	.06
58T	Ken Howell(FC)	.15	.11	.06
59T	LaMarr Hoyt	.10	.08	.04
60T	Tim Hulett(FC)	.15	.11	.06
61T	Bob James	.10	.08	.04
62T	Steve Jeltz(FC)	.15	.11	.06
63T	Cliff Johnson	.10	.08	.04
64T	Howard Johnson	2.50	2.00	1.00
65T	Ruppert Jones	.10	.08	.04
66T	Steve Kemp	.15	.11	.06
67T	Bruce Kison	.10	.08	.04
68T	Alan Knicely	.10	.08	.04
69T	Mike LaCoss	.10	.08	.04
70T	Lee Lacy	.10	.08	.04
71T	Dave LaPoint	.20	.15	.08
72T	Gary Lavelle	.10	.08	.04
73T	Vance Law	.15	.11	.06
74T	Johnnie LeMaster	.10	.08	.04
75T	Sixto Lezcano	.10	.08	.04
76T	Tim Lollar	.10	.08	.04
77T	Fred Lynn	.30	.25	.12
78T	Billy Martin	.20	.15	.08
79T	Ron Mathis	.10	.08	.04
80T	Len Matuszek	.10	.08	.04
81T	Gene Mauch	.15	.11	.06
82T	Oddibe McDowell	.25	.20	.10
83T	Roger McDowell(FC)	.50	.40	.20
84T	John McNamara	.10	.08	.04
85T	Donnie Moore	.10	.08	.04
86T	Gene Nelson	.10	.08	.04
87T	Steve Nicosia	.10	.08	.04
88T	Al Oliver	.30	.25	.12
89T	Joe Orsulak(FC)	.20	.15	.08
90T	Rob Picciolo	.10	.08	.04
91T	Chris Pittaro	.10	.08	.04
92T	Jim Presley(FC)	.60	.45	.25
93T	Rick Reuschel	.25	.20	.10
94T	Bert Roberge	.10	.08	.04
95T	Bob Rodgers	.10	.08	.04
96T	Jerry Royster	.10	.08	.04
97T	Dave Rozema	.10	.08	.04
98T	Dave Rucker	.10	.08	.04
99T	Vern Ruhle	.10	.08	.04
100T	Paul Runge(FC)	.15	.11	.06
101T	Mark Salas(FC)	.15	.11	.06
102T	Luis Salazar	.10	.08	.04
103T	Joe Sambito	.10	.08	.04
104T	Rick Schu(FC)	.20	.15	.08
105T	Donnie Scott	.10	.08	.04
106T	Larry Sheets(FC)	.50	.40	.20
107T	Don Slaught	.10	.08	.04
108T	Roy Smalley	.15	.11	.06
109T	Lonnie Smith	.15	.11	.06
110T	Nate Snell	.10	.08	.04
111T	Chris Speier	.10	.08	.04
112T	Mike Stenhouse	.10	.08	.04
113T	Tim Stoddard	.10	.08	.04
114T	Jim Sundberg	.15	.11	.06
115T	Bruce Sutter	.25	.20	.10
116T	Don Sutton	.60	.45	.25
117T	Kent Tekulve	.15	.11	.06
118T	Tom Tellmann	.10	.08	.04
119T	Walt Terrell	.15	.11	.06
120T	Mickey Tettleton(FC)	1.50	1.25	.60
121T	Derrel Thomas	.10	.08	.04
122T	Rich Thompson	.10	.08	.04
123T	Alex Trevino	.10	.08	.04
124T	John Tudor	.25	.20	.10
125T	Jose Uribe(FC)	.25	.20	.10
126T	Bobby Valentine	.10	.08	.04
127T	Dave Von Ohlen	.10	.08	.04
128T	U.L. Washington	.10	.08	.04

		MT	NR MT	EX
129T	Earl Weaver	.15	.11	.06
130T	Eddie Whitson	.10	.08	.04
131T	Herm Winningham(FC)	.20	.15	.08
132T	Checklist 1-132	.10	.08	.04

1986 Topps

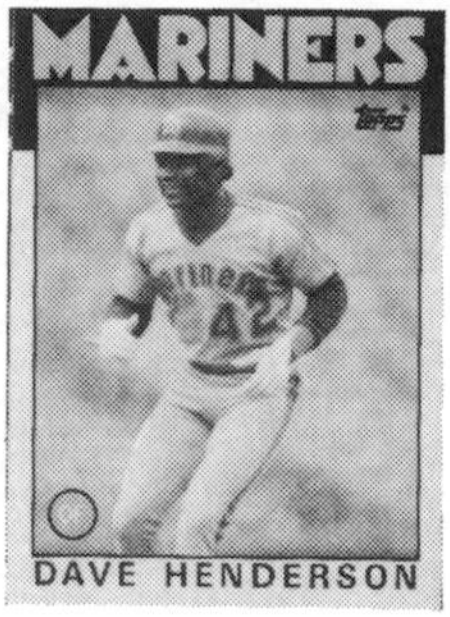

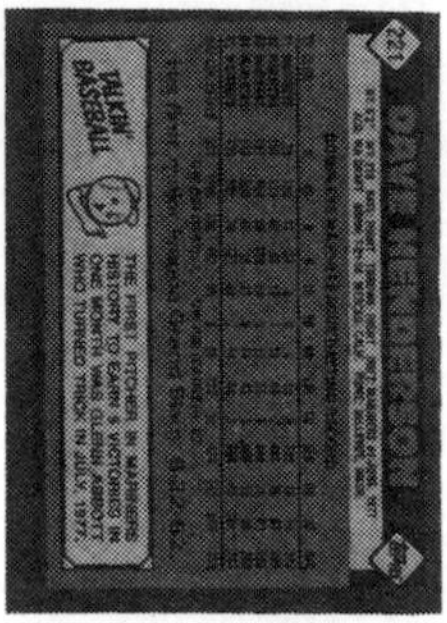

The 1986 Topps set consists of 792 cards. Fronts of the 2-1/2" by 3-1/2" cards feature color photos with the Topps logo in the upper right-hand corner while the player's position is in the lower left-hand corner. Above the picture is the team name, while below it is the player's name. The borders are a departure from previous practice, as the top 7/8" is black, while the remainder was white. There are no card numbers 51 and 171 in the set; the card that should have been #51, Bobby Wine, shares #57 with Bill Doran, while #171, Bob Rodgers, shares #141 with Chuck Cottier. Once again, a 5,000-set glossy-finish "Tiffany" edition was produced. Values are four to six times higher than the same card in the regular issue.

		MT	NR MT	EX
Complete Set:		45.00	33.00	18.00
Common Player:		.05	.04	.02
1	Pete Rose	.90	.70	.35
2	Rose Special 1963-66	.30	.25	.12
3	Rose Special 1967-70	.30	.25	.12
4	Rose Special 1971-74	.30	.25	.12
5	Rose Special 1975-78	.30	.25	.12
6	Rose Special 1979-82	.30	.25	.12
7	Rose Special 1983-85	.30	.25	.12
8	Dwayne Murphy	.07	.05	.03
9	Roy Smith	.05	.04	.02
10	Tony Gwynn	.60	.45	.25
11	Bob Ojeda	.07	.05	.03
12	*Jose Uribe*(FC)	.20	.15	.08
13	Bob Kearney	.05	.04	.02
14	Julio Cruz	.05	.04	.02
15	Eddie Whitson	.05	.04	.02
16	Rick Schu(FC)	.07	.05	.03
17	Mike Stenhouse	.05	.04	.02
18	Brent Gaff	.05	.04	.02
19	Rich Hebner	.05	.04	.02
20	Lou Whitaker	.25	.20	.10
21	George Bamberger	.05	.04	.02
22	Duane Walker	.05	.04	.02
23	*Manny Lee*(FC)	.15	.11	.06
24	Len Barker	.07	.05	.03
25	Willie Wilson	.12	.09	.05
26	Frank DiPino	.05	.04	.02
27	Ray Knight	.07	.05	.03
28	Eric Davis	1.00	.70	.40
29	Tony Phillips	.05	.04	.02
30	Eddie Murray	.40	.30	.15
31	Jamie Easterly	.05	.04	.02
32	Steve Yeager	.05	.04	.02
33	Jeff Lahti	.05	.04	.02
34	Ken Phelps(FC)	.07	.05	.03
35	Jeff Reardon	.12	.09	.05
36	Tigers Leaders (Lance Parrish)	.12	.09	.05
37	Mark Thurmond	.05	.04	.02
38	Glenn Hoffman	.05	.04	.02
39	Dave Rucker	.05	.04	.02
40	Ken Griffey	.10	.08	.04
41	Brad Wellman	.05	.04	.02
42	Geoff Zahn	.05	.04	.02
43	Dave Engle	.05	.04	.02
44	*Lance McCullers*(FC)	.25	.20	.10
45	Damaso Garcia	.05	.04	.02
46	Billy Hatcher(FC)	.20	.15	.08
47	Juan Berenguer	.05	.04	.02
48	Bill Almon	.05	.04	.02
49	Rick Manning	.05	.04	.02
50	Dan Quisenberry	.07	.05	.03
51	Not Issued			
52	Chris Welsh	.05	.04	.02
53	*Len Dykstra*(FC)	2.00	1.50	.80
54	John Franco	.12	.09	.05
55	Fred Lynn	.15	.11	.06
56	Tom Niedenfuer	.07	.05	.03
57a	Bobby Wine	.05	.04	.02
57b	Bill Doran	.10	.08	.04
58	Bill Krueger	.05	.04	.02
59	Andre Thornton	.07	.05	.03
60	Dwight Evans	.12	.09	.05
61	Karl Best	.05	.04	.02
62	Bob Boone	.07	.05	.03
63	Ron Roenicke	.05	.04	.02
64	Floyd Bannister	.10	.08	.04
65	Dan Driessen	.07	.05	.03
66	Cardinals Leaders (Bob Forsch)	.07	.05	.03
67	Carmelo Martinez	.07	.05	.03
68	Ed Lynch	.05	.04	.02
69	Luis Aguayo	.05	.04	.02
70	Dave Winfield	.30	.25	.12
71	Ken Schrom	.05	.04	.02
72	Shawon Dunston	.20	.15	.08
73	Randy O'Neal(FC)	.07	.05	.03
74	Rance Mulliniks	.05	.04	.02
75	Jose DeLeon	.07	.05	.03
76	Dion James	.07	.05	.03
77	Charlie Leibrandt	.07	.05	.03
78	Bruce Benedict	.05	.04	.02
79	Dave Schmidt	.07	.05	.03
80	Darryl Strawberry	1.50	1.25	.60
81	Gene Mauch	.07	.05	.03
82	Tippy Martinez	.05	.04	.02
83	Phil Garner	.07	.05	.03
84	Curt Young	.07	.05	.03
85	Tony Perez	.15	.11	.06
86	Tom Waddell	.05	.04	.02
87	Candy Maldonado	.10	.08	.04
88	Tom Nieto	.05	.04	.02
89	Randy St. Claire(FC)	.07	.05	.03
90	Garry Templeton	.07	.05	.03
91	Steve Crawford	.05	.04	.02
92	Al Cowens	.05	.04	.02
93	Scot Thompson	.05	.04	.02
94	Rick Bordi	.05	.04	.02
95	Ozzie Virgil	.05	.04	.02
96	Blue Jay Leaders (Jim Clancy)	.07	.05	.03
97	Gary Gaetti	.20	.15	.08
98	Dick Ruthven	.05	.04	.02
99	Buddy Biancalana	.05	.04	.02
100	Nolan Ryan	2.00	1.50	.80
101	Dave Bergman	.05	.04	.02
102	*Joe Orsulak*	.15	.11	.06
103	Luis Salazar	.05	.04	.02
104	Sid Fernandez	.12	.09	.05
105	Gary Ward	.07	.05	.03
106	Ray Burris	.05	.04	.02
107	Rafael Ramirez	.05	.04	.02
108	Ted Power	.05	.04	.02
109	Len Matuszek	.05	.04	.02
110	Scott McGregor	.07	.05	.03
111	Roger Craig	.07	.05	.03
112	Bill Campbell	.05	.04	.02
113	U.L. Washington	.05	.04	.02
114	Mike Brown	.05	.04	.02
115	Jay Howell	.07	.05	.03
116	Brook Jacoby	.10	.08	.04
117	Bruce Kison	.05	.04	.02
118	Jerry Royster	.05	.04	.02
119	Barry Bonnell	.05	.04	.02
120	Steve Carlton	.30	.25	.12
121	Nelson Simmons	.05	.04	.02
122	Pete Filson	.05	.04	.02
123	Greg Walker	.10	.08	.04
124	Luis Sanchez	.05	.04	.02
125	Dave Lopes	.07	.05	.03
126	Mets Leaders (Mookie Wilson)	.07	.05	.03
127	*Jack Howell*(FC)	.30	.25	.12
128	John Wathan	.07	.05	.03
129	Jeff Dedmon(FC)	.05	.04	.02
130	Alan Trammell	.30	.25	.12
131	Checklist 1-132	.05	.04	.02

		MT	NR MT	EX
132	Razor Shines	.05	.04	.02
133	Andy McGaffigan	.05	.04	.02
134	Carney Lansford	.10	.08	.04
135	Joe Niekro	.10	.08	.04
136	Mike Hargrove	.05	.04	.02
137	Charlie Moore	.05	.04	.02
138	Mark Davis	.05	.04	.02
139	Daryl Boston	.10	.08	.04
140	John Candelaria	.10	.08	.04
141a	Bob Rodgers	.05	.04	.02
141b	Chuck Cottier	.05	.04	.02
142	Bob Jones	.05	.04	.02
143	Dave Van Gorder	.05	.04	.02
144	Doug Sisk	.05	.04	.02
145	Pedro Guerrero	.20	.15	.08
146	Jack Perconte	.05	.04	.02
147	Larry Sheets	.20	.15	.08
148	Mike Heath	.05	.04	.02
149	Brett Butler	.07	.05	.03
150	Joaquin Andujar	.07	.05	.03
151	Dave Stapleton	.05	.04	.02
152	Mike Morgan	.05	.04	.02
153	Ricky Adams	.05	.04	.02
154	Bert Roberge	.05	.04	.02
155	Bob Grich	.10	.08	.04
156	White Sox Leaders (Richard Dotson)	.07	.05	.03
157	Ron Hassey	.05	.04	.02
158	Derrel Thomas	.05	.04	.02
159	Orel Hershiser	.70	.50	.30
160	Chet Lemon	.07	.05	.03
161	Lee Tunnell	.05	.04	.02
162	Greg Gagne	.10	.08	.04
163	Pete Ladd	.05	.04	.02
164	Steve Balboni	.07	.05	.03
165	Mike Davis	.07	.05	.03
166	Dickie Thon	.07	.05	.03
167	Zane Smith(FC)	.15	.11	.06
168	Jeff Burroughs	.07	.05	.03
169	George Wright	.05	.04	.02
170	Gary Carter	.25	.20	.10
171	Not Issued			
172	Jerry Reed	.05	.04	.02
173	Wayne Gross	.05	.04	.02
174	Brian Snyder	.05	.04	.02
175	Steve Sax	.15	.11	.06
176	Jay Tibbs	.05	.04	.02
177	Joel Youngblood	.05	.04	.02
178	Ivan DeJesus	.05	.04	.02
179	*Stu Cliburn*(FC)	.10	.08	.04
180	Don Mattingly	2.50	2.00	1.00
181	Al Nipper	.05	.04	.02
182	Bobby Brown	.05	.04	.02
183	Larry Andersen	.05	.04	.02
184	Tim Laudner	.05	.04	.02
185	Rollie Fingers	.20	.15	.08
186	Astros Leaders (Jose Cruz)	.07	.05	.03
187	Scott Fletcher	.07	.05	.03
188	Bob Dernier	.05	.04	.02
189	Mike Mason	.05	.04	.02
190	George Hendrick	.07	.05	.03
191	Wally Backman	.07	.05	.03
192	Milt Wilcox	.05	.04	.02
193	Daryl Sconiers	.05	.04	.02
194	Craig McMurtry	.05	.04	.02
195	Dave Concepcion	.12	.09	.05
196	Doyle Alexander	.10	.08	.04
197	Enos Cabell	.05	.04	.02
198	Ken Dixon	.05	.04	.02
199	Dick Howser	.05	.04	.02
200	Mike Schmidt	.80	.60	.30
201	Record Breaker (Vince Coleman)(FC)	.30	.25	.12
202	Record Breaker (Dwight Gooden)	.40	.30	.15
203	Record Breaker (Keith Hernandez)	.20	.15	.08
204	Record Breaker (Phil Niekro)	.15	.11	.06
205	Record Breaker (Tony Perez)	.10	.08	.04
206	Record Breaker (Pete Rose)	.50	.40	.20
207	Record Breaker (Fernando Valenzuela)	.20	.15	.08
208	Ramon Romero	.05	.04	.02
209	Randy Ready	.10	.08	.04
210	Calvin Schiraldi(FC)	.10	.08	.04
211	Ed Wojna	.05	.04	.02
212	Chris Speier	.05	.04	.02
213	Bob Shirley	.05	.04	.02
214	Randy Bush	.05	.04	.02
215	Frank White	.10	.08	.04
216	A's Leaders (Dwayne Murphy)	.07	.05	.03
217	Bill Scherrer	.05	.04	.02
218	Randy Hunt	.05	.04	.02
219	Dennis Lamp	.05	.04	.02
220	Bob Horner	.10	.08	.04
221	Dave Henderson	.10	.08	.04
222	Craig Gerber	.05	.04	.02
223	Atlee Hammaker	.05	.04	.02
224	Cesar Cedeno	.10	.08	.04
225	Ron Darling	.15	.11	.06
226	Lee Lacy	.05	.04	.02
227	Al Jones	.05	.04	.02
228	Tom Lawless	.05	.04	.02
229	Bill Gullickson	.05	.04	.02
230	Terry Kennedy	.07	.05	.03
231	Jim Frey	.05	.04	.02
232	Rick Rhoden	.10	.08	.04
233	Steve Lyons(FC)	.07	.05	.03
234	Doug Corbett	.05	.04	.02
235	Butch Wynegar	.05	.04	.02
236	Frank Eufemia	.05	.04	.02
237	Ted Simmons	.12	.09	.05
238	Larry Parrish	.10	.08	.04
239	Joel Skinner	.05	.04	.02
240	Tommy John	.20	.15	.08
241	Tony Fernandez	.20	.15	.08
242	Rich Thompson	.05	.04	.02
243	Johnny Grubb	.05	.04	.02
244	Craig Lefferts	.05	.04	.02
245	Jim Sundberg	.07	.05	.03
246	Phillies Leaders (Steve Carlton)	.15	.11	.06
247	Terry Harper	.05	.04	.02
248	Spike Owen	.05	.04	.02
249	Rob Deer(FC)	.40	.30	.15
250	Dwight Gooden	1.50	1.25	.60
251	Rich Dauer	.05	.04	.02
252	Bobby Castillo	.05	.04	.02
253	Dann Bilardello	.05	.04	.02
254	*Ozzie Guillen*	1.00	.70	.40
255	Tony Armas	.07	.05	.03
256	Kurt Kepshire	.05	.04	.02
257	Doug DeCinces	.10	.08	.04
258	*Tim Burke*(FC)	.25	.20	.10
259	Dan Pasqua(FC)	.20	.15	.08
260	Tony Pena	.10	.08	.04
261	Bobby Valentine	.05	.04	.02
262	Mario Ramirez	.05	.04	.02
263	Checklist 133-264	.05	.04	.02
264	*Darren Daulton*(FC)	.12	.09	.05
265	Ron Davis	.05	.04	.02
266	Keith Moreland	.07	.05	.03
267	Paul Molitor	.15	.11	.06
268	Mike Scott	.15	.11	.06
269	Dane Iorg	.05	.04	.02
270	Jack Morris	.20	.15	.08
271	Dave Collins	.07	.05	.03
272	Tim Tolman	.05	.04	.02
273	Jerry Willard	.05	.04	.02
274	Ron Gardenhire	.05	.04	.02
275	Charlie Hough	.08	.06	.03
276	Yankees Leaders (Willie Randolph)	.07	.05	.03
277	Jaime Cocanower	.05	.04	.02
278	Sixto Lezcano	.05	.04	.02
279	Al Pardo	.05	.04	.02
280	Tim Raines	.30	.25	.12
281	Steve Mura	.05	.04	.02
282	Jerry Mumphrey	.05	.04	.02
283	Mike Fischlin	.05	.04	.02
284	Brian Dayett	.05	.04	.02
285	Buddy Bell	.10	.08	.04
286	Luis DeLeon	.05	.04	.02
287	*John Christensen*(FC)	.10	.08	.04
288	Don Aase	.05	.04	.02
289	Johnnie LeMaster	.05	.04	.02
290	Carlton Fisk	.40	.30	.15
291	Tom Lasorda	.07	.05	.03
292	Chuck Porter	.05	.04	.02
293	Chris Chambliss	.07	.05	.03
294	Danny Cox	.10	.08	.04
295	Kirk Gibson	.30	.25	.12
296	Geno Petralli(FC)	.07	.05	.03
297	Tim Lollar	.05	.04	.02
298	Craig Reynolds	.05	.04	.02
299	Bryn Smith	.05	.04	.02
300	George Brett	.50	.40	.20
301	Dennis Rasmussen	.12	.09	.05
302	Greg Gross	.05	.04	.02
303	Curt Wardle	.05	.04	.02
304	*Mike Gallego*(FC)	.12	.09	.05
305	Phil Bradley	.15	.11	.06
306	Padres Leaders (Terry Kennedy)	.07	.05	.03
307	Dave Sax	.05	.04	.02
308	Ray Fontenot	.05	.04	.02
309	John Shelby	.05	.04	.02

		MT	NR MT	EX
310	Greg Minton	.05	.04	.02
311	Dick Schofield	.05	.04	.02
312	Tom Filer	.05	.04	.02
313	Joe DeSa	.05	.04	.02
314	Frank Pastore	.05	.04	.02
315	Mookie Wilson	.10	.08	.04
316	Sammy Khalifa	.05	.04	.02
317	Ed Romero	.05	.04	.02
318	Terry Whitfield	.05	.04	.02
319	Rick Camp	.05	.04	.02
320	Jim Rice	.30	.25	.12
321	Earl Weaver	.07	.05	.03
322	Bob Forsch	.07	.05	.03
323	Jerry Davis	.05	.04	.02
324	Dan Schatzeder	.05	.04	.02
325	Juan Beniquez	.05	.04	.02
326	Kent Tekulve	.07	.05	.03
327	Mike Pagliarulo	.20	.15	.08
328	Pete O'Brien	.10	.08	.04
329	Kirby Puckett	3.00	2.25	1.25
330	Rick Sutcliffe	.12	.09	.05
331	Alan Ashby	.05	.04	.02
332	Darryl Motley	.05	.04	.02
333	Tom Henke(FC)	.15	.11	.06
334	Ken Oberkfell	.05	.04	.02
335	Don Sutton	.25	.20	.10
336	Indians Leaders (Andre Thornton)	.07	.05	.03
337	Darnell Coles	.07	.05	.03
338	Jorge Bell	.25	.20	.10
339	Bruce Berenyi	.05	.04	.02
340	Cal Ripken	.80	.60	.30
341	Frank Williams	.05	.04	.02
342	Gary Redus	.05	.04	.02
343	Carlos Diaz	.05	.04	.02
344	Jim Wohlford	.05	.04	.02
345	Donnie Moore	.05	.04	.02
346	Bryan Little	.05	.04	.02
347	*Teddy Higuera*	.70	.50	.30
348	Cliff Johnson	.05	.04	.02
349	Mark Clear	.05	.04	.02
350	Jack Clark	.20	.15	.08
351	Chuck Tanner	.05	.04	.02
352	Harry Spilman	.05	.04	.02
353	Keith Atherton	.05	.04	.02
354	Tony Bernazard	.05	.04	.02
355	Lee Smith	.10	.08	.04
356	Mickey Hatcher	.05	.04	.02
357	Ed Vande Berg	.05	.04	.02
358	Rick Dempsey	.07	.05	.03
359	Mike LaCoss	.05	.04	.02
360	Lloyd Moseby	.10	.08	.04
361	Shane Rawley	.10	.08	.04
362	Tom Paciorek	.05	.04	.02
363	Terry Forster	.07	.05	.03
364	Reid Nichols	.05	.04	.02
365	Mike Flanagan	.10	.08	.04
366	Reds Leaders (Dave Concepcion)	.07	.05	.03
367	Aurelio Lopez	.05	.04	.02
368	Greg Brock	.07	.05	.03
369	Al Holland	.05	.04	.02
370	*Vince Coleman*	2.50	2.00	1.00
371	Bill Stein	.05	.04	.02
372	Ben Oglivie	.07	.05	.03
373	*Urbano Lugo*(FC)	.07	.05	.03
374	Terry Francona	.05	.04	.02
375	Rich Gedman	.10	.08	.04
376	Bill Dawley	.05	.04	.02
377	Joe Carter	.70	.50	.30
378	Bruce Bochte	.05	.04	.02
379	Bobby Meacham	.05	.04	.02
380	LaMarr Hoyt	.05	.04	.02
381	Ray Miller	.05	.04	.02
382	*Ivan Calderon*(FC)	1.25	.90	.50
383	*Chris Brown*	.15	.11	.06
384	Steve Trout	.05	.04	.02
385	Cecil Cooper	.10	.08	.04
386	*Cecil Fielder*(FC)	8.00	6.00	3.25
387	Steve Kemp	.07	.05	.03
388	Dickie Noles	.05	.04	.02
389	Glenn Davis(FC)	2.00	1.50	.80
390	Tom Seaver	.40	.30	.15
391	Julio Franco	.10	.08	.04
392	John Russell(FC)	.10	.08	.04
393	Chris Pittaro	.05	.04	.02
394	Checklist 265-396	.05	.04	.02
395	Scott Garrelts	.07	.05	.03
396	Red Sox Leaders (Dwight Evans)	.07	.05	.03
397	*Steve Buechele*(FC)	.20	.15	.08
398	*Earnie Riles*(FC)	.15	.11	.06
399	Bill Swift	.12	.09	.05
400	Rod Carew	.30	.25	.12

		MT	NR MT	EX
401	Turn Back The Clock (Fernando Valenzuela)	.15	.11	.06
402	Turn Back The Clock (Tom Seaver)	.15	.11	.06
403	Turn Back The Clock (Willie Mays)	.20	.15	.08
404	Turn Back The Clock (Frank Robinson)	.15	.11	.06
405	Turn Back The Clock (Roger Maris)	.20	.15	.08
406	Scott Sanderson	.05	.04	.02
407	Sal Butera	.05	.04	.02
408	Dave Smith	.07	.05	.03
409	*Paul Runge*	.07	.05	.03
410	Dave Kingman	.15	.11	.06
411	Sparky Anderson	.07	.05	.03
412	Jim Clancy	.07	.05	.03
413	Tim Flannery	.05	.04	.02
414	Tom Gorman	.05	.04	.02
415	Hal McRae	.10	.08	.04
416	Denny Martinez	.07	.05	.03
417	R.J. Reynolds	.07	.05	.03
418	Alan Knicely	.05	.04	.02
419	Frank Wills	.05	.04	.02
420	Von Hayes	.10	.08	.04
421	Dave Palmer	.05	.04	.02
422	Mike Jorgensen	.05	.04	.02
423	Dan Spillner	.05	.04	.02
424	Rick Miller	.05	.04	.02
425	Larry McWilliams	.05	.04	.02
426	Brewers Leaders (Charlie Moore)	.07	.05	.03
427	Joe Cowley	.05	.04	.02
428	Max Venable	.05	.04	.02
429	Greg Booker	.05	.04	.02
430	Kent Hrbek	.20	.15	.08
431	George Frazier	.05	.04	.02
432	Mark Bailey	.05	.04	.02
433	Chris Codiroli	.05	.04	.02
434	Curt Wilkerson	.05	.04	.02
435	Bill Caudill	.05	.04	.02
436	Doug Flynn	.05	.04	.02
437	Rick Mahler	.05	.04	.02
438	Clint Hurdle	.05	.04	.02
439	Rick Honeycutt	.05	.04	.02
440	Alvin Davis	.30	.25	.12
441	Whitey Herzog	.07	.05	.03
442	Ron Robinson(FC)	.12	.09	.05
443	Bill Buckner	.10	.08	.04
444	Alex Trevino	.05	.04	.02
445	Bert Blyleven	.12	.09	.05
446	Lenn Sakata	.05	.04	.02
447	Jerry Don Gleaton	.05	.04	.02
448	*Herm Winningham*	.15	.11	.06
449	Rod Scurry	.05	.04	.02
450	Graig Nettles	.15	.11	.06
451	Mark Brown	.05	.04	.02
452	Bob Clark	.05	.04	.02
453	Steve Jeltz	.07	.05	.03
454	Burt Hooton	.07	.05	.03
455	Willie Randolph	.10	.08	.04
456	Braves Leaders (Dale Murphy)	.25	.20	.10
457	*Mickey Tettleton*	.60	.45	.25
458	Kevin Bass	.10	.08	.04
459	Luis Leal	.05	.04	.02
460	Leon Durham	.07	.05	.03
461	Walt Terrell	.07	.05	.03
462	Domingo Ramos	.05	.04	.02
463	Jim Gott	.05	.04	.02
464	Ruppert Jones	.05	.04	.02
465	Jesse Orosco	.07	.05	.03
466	Tom Foley	.05	.04	.02
467	Bob James	.05	.04	.02
468	Mike Scioscia	.07	.05	.03
469	Storm Davis	.10	.08	.04
470	Bill Madlock	.12	.09	.05
471	Bobby Cox	.05	.04	.02
472	Joe Hesketh	.07	.05	.03
473	Mark Brouhard	.05	.04	.02
474	John Tudor	.10	.08	.04
475	Juan Samuel	.12	.09	.05
476	Ron Mathis	.05	.04	.02
477	Mike Easler	.07	.05	.03
478	Andy Hawkins	.05	.04	.02
479	*Bob Melvin*(FC)	.12	.09	.05
480	*Oddibe McDowell*	.15	.11	.06
481	Scott Bradley(FC)	.10	.08	.04
482	Rick Lysander	.05	.04	.02
483	George Vukovich	.05	.04	.02
484	Donnie Hill	.05	.04	.02
485	Gary Matthews	.10	.08	.04
486	Angels Leaders (Bob Grich)	.07	.05	.03
487	Bret Saberhagen	.70	.50	.30
488	Lou Thornton	.05	.04	.02
489	Jim Winn	.05	.04	.02

		MT	NR MT	EX
490	Jeff Leonard	.07	.05	.03
491	Pascual Perez	.07	.05	.03
492	Kelvin Chapman	.05	.04	.02
493	Gene Nelson	.05	.04	.02
494	Gary Roenicke	.05	.04	.02
495	Mark Langston	.20	.15	.08
496	Jay Johnstone	.07	.05	.03
497	John Stuper	.05	.04	.02
498	Tito Landrum	.05	.04	.02
499	Bob Gibson	.05	.04	.02
500	Rickey Henderson	1.25	.90	.50
501	Dave Johnson	.07	.05	.03
502	Glen Cook	.05	.04	.02
503	Mike Fitzgerald	.05	.04	.02
504	Denny Walling	.05	.04	.02
505	Jerry Koosman	.10	.08	.04
506	Bill Russell	.07	.05	.03
507	*Steve Ontiveros*(FC)	.12	.09	.05
508	Alan Wiggins	.05	.04	.02
509	Ernie Camacho	.05	.04	.02
510	Wade Boggs	1.25	.90	.50
511	Ed Nunez	.05	.04	.02
512	Thad Bosley	.05	.04	.02
513	Ron Washington	.05	.04	.02
514	Mike Jones	.05	.04	.02
515	Darrell Evans	.12	.09	.05
516	Giants Leaders (Greg Minton)	.07	.05	.03
517	*Milt Thompson*(FC)	.25	.20	.10
518	Buck Martinez	.05	.04	.02
519	Danny Darwin	.05	.04	.02
520	Keith Hernandez	.30	.25	.12
521	Nate Snell	.05	.04	.02
522	Bob Bailor	.05	.04	.02
523	Joe Price	.05	.04	.02
524	Darrell Miller(FC)	.07	.05	.03
525	Marvell Wynne	.05	.04	.02
526	Charlie Lea	.05	.04	.02
527	Checklist 397-528	.05	.04	.02
528	Terry Pendleton	.15	.11	.06
529	Marc Sullivan	.05	.04	.02
530	Rich Gossage	.20	.15	.08
531	Tony LaRussa	.07	.05	.03
532	*Don Carman*	.25	.20	.10
533	Billy Sample	.05	.04	.02
534	Jeff Calhoun	.05	.04	.02
535	Toby Harrah	.07	.05	.03
536	Jose Rijo	.10	.08	.04
537	Mark Salas	.07	.05	.03
538	Dennis Eckersley	.12	.09	.05
539	Glenn Hubbard	.05	.04	.02
540	Dan Petry	.07	.05	.03
541	Jorge Orta	.05	.04	.02
542	Don Schulze	.05	.04	.02
543	Jerry Narron	.05	.04	.02
544	Eddie Milner	.05	.04	.02
545	Jimmy Key	.15	.11	.06
546	Mariners Leaders (Dave Henderson)	.07	.05	.03
547	*Roger McDowell*	.40	.30	.15
548	Mike Young	.05	.04	.02
549	Bob Welch	.12	.09	.05
550	Tom Herr	.10	.08	.04
551	Dave LaPoint	.07	.05	.03
552	Marc Hill	.05	.04	.02
553	Jim Morrison	.05	.04	.02
554	Paul Householder	.05	.04	.02
555	Hubie Brooks	.10	.08	.04
556	John Denny	.05	.04	.02
557	Gerald Perry	.12	.09	.05
558	Tim Stoddard	.05	.04	.02
559	Tommy Dunbar	.05	.04	.02
560	Dave Righetti	.20	.15	.08
561	Bob Lillis	.05	.04	.02
562	Joe Beckwith	.05	.04	.02
563	Alejandro Sanchez	.05	.04	.02
564	Warren Brusstar	.05	.04	.02
565	Tom Brunansky	.12	.09	.05
566	Alfredo Griffin	.07	.05	.03
567	Jeff Barkley	.05	.04	.02
568	Donnie Scott	.05	.04	.02
569	Jim Acker	.05	.04	.02
570	Rusty Staub	.10	.08	.04
571	Mike Jeffcoat	.05	.04	.02
572	Paul Zuvella	.05	.04	.02
573	Tom Hume	.05	.04	.02
574	Ron Kittle	.10	.08	.04
575	Mike Boddicker	.07	.05	.03
576	Expos Leaders (Andre Dawson)	.12	.09	.05
577	Jerry Reuss	.07	.05	.03
578	Lee Mazzilli	.07	.05	.03
579	Jim Slaton	.05	.04	.02

		MT	NR MT	EX
580	Willie McGee	.15	.11	.06
581	Bruce Hurst	.12	.09	.05
582	Jim Gantner	.07	.05	.03
583	Al Bumbry	.05	.04	.02
584	*Brian Fisher*(FC)	.12	.09	.05
585	Garry Maddox	.07	.05	.03
586	Greg Harris	.05	.04	.02
587	Rafael Santana	.05	.04	.02
588	Steve Lake	.05	.04	.02
589	Sid Bream	.10	.08	.04
590	Bob Knepper	.07	.05	.03
591	Jackie Moore	.05	.04	.02
592	Frank Tanana	.10	.08	.04
593	Jesse Barfield	.20	.15	.08
594	Chris Bando	.05	.04	.02
595	Dave Parker	.20	.15	.08
596	Onix Concepcion	.05	.04	.02
597	Sammy Stewart	.05	.04	.02
598	Jim Presley	.25	.20	.10
599	*Rick Aguilera*(FC)	.40	.30	.15
600	Dale Murphy	.50	.40	.20
601	Gary Lucas	.05	.04	.02
602	*Mariano Duncan*	.15	.11	.06
603	Bill Laskey	.05	.04	.02
604	Gary Pettis	.05	.04	.02
605	Dennis Boyd	.07	.05	.03
606	Royals Leaders (Hal McRae)	.07	.05	.03
607	Ken Dayley	.05	.04	.02
608	Bruce Bochy	.05	.04	.02
609	Barbaro Garbey	.05	.04	.02
610	Ron Guidry	.15	.11	.06
611	Gary Woods	.05	.04	.02
612	Richard Dotson	.10	.08	.04
613	Roy Smalley	.05	.04	.02
614	Rick Waits	.05	.04	.02
615	Johnny Ray	.10	.08	.04
616	Glenn Brummer	.05	.04	.02
617	Lonnie Smith	.07	.05	.03
618	Jim Pankovits	.05	.04	.02
619	Danny Heep	.05	.04	.02
620	Bruce Sutter	.12	.09	.05
621	John Felske	.05	.04	.02
622	Gary Lavelle	.05	.04	.02
623	Floyd Rayford	.05	.04	.02
624	Steve McCatty	.05	.04	.02
625	Bob Brenly	.05	.04	.02
626	Roy Thomas	.05	.04	.02
627	Ron Oester	.05	.04	.02
628	*Kirk McCaskill*(FC)	.35	.25	.14
629	*Mitch Webster*(FC)	.25	.20	.10
630	Fernando Valenzuela	.30	.25	.12
631	Steve Braun	.05	.04	.02
632	Dave Von Ohlen	.05	.04	.02
633	Jackie Gutierrez	.05	.04	.02
634	Roy Lee Jackson	.05	.04	.02
635	Jason Thompson	.05	.04	.02
636	Cubs Leaders (Lee Smith)	.07	.05	.03
637	Rudy Law	.05	.04	.02
638	John Butcher	.05	.04	.02
639	Bo Diaz	.07	.05	.03
640	Jose Cruz	.10	.08	.04
641	Wayne Tolleson	.05	.04	.02
642	Ray Searage	.05	.04	.02
643	Tom Brookens	.05	.04	.02
644	Mark Gubicza	.12	.09	.05
645	Dusty Baker	.07	.05	.03
646	Mike Moore	.05	.04	.02
647	Mel Hall	.07	.05	.03
648	Steve Bedrosian	.10	.08	.04
649	Ronn Reynolds	.05	.04	.02
650	Dave Stieb	.12	.09	.05
651	Billy Martin	.12	.09	.05
652	Tom Browning	.25	.20	.10
653	Jim Dwyer	.05	.04	.02
654	Ken Howell	.07	.05	.03
655	Manny Trillo	.07	.05	.03
656	Brian Harper	.05	.04	.02
657	Juan Agosto	.05	.04	.02
658	Rob Wilfong	.05	.04	.02
659	Checklist 529-660	.05	.04	.02
660	Steve Garvey	.30	.25	.12
661	Roger Clemens	3.00	2.25	1.25
662	Bill Schroeder	.05	.04	.02
663	Neil Allen	.05	.04	.02
664	Tim Corcoran	.05	.04	.02
665	Alejandro Pena	.07	.05	.03
666	Rangers Leaders (Charlie Hough)	.07	.05	.03
667	Tim Teufel	.05	.04	.02
668	Cecilio Guante	.05	.04	.02
669	Ron Cey	.10	.08	.04
670	Willie Hernandez	.07	.05	.03

		MT	NR MT	EX
671	Lynn Jones	.05	.04	.02
672	Rob Picciolo	.05	.04	.02
673	Ernie Whitt	.07	.05	.03
674	Pat Tabler	.07	.05	.03
675	Claudell Washington	.07	.05	.03
676	Matt Young	.05	.04	.02
677	Nick Esasky	.07	.05	.03
678	Dan Gladden	.07	.05	.03
679	Britt Burns	.05	.04	.02
680	George Foster	.15	.11	.06
681	Dick Williams	.05	.04	.02
682	Junior Ortiz	.05	.04	.02
683	Andy Van Slyke	.15	.11	.06
684	Bob McClure	.05	.04	.02
685	Tim Wallach	.12	.09	.05
686	Jeff Stone	.05	.04	.02
687	Mike Trujillo	.05	.04	.02
688	Larry Herndon	.07	.05	.03
689	Dave Stewart	.12	.09	.05
690	Ryne Sandberg	1.75	1.25	.70
691	Mike Madden	.05	.04	.02
692	Dale Berra	.05	.04	.02
693	Tom Tellmann	.05	.04	.02
694	Garth Iorg	.05	.04	.02
695	Mike Smithson	.05	.04	.02
696	Dodgers Leaders (Bill Russell)	.07	.05	.03
697	Bud Black	.05	.04	.02
698	Brad Komminsk	.05	.04	.02
699	Pat Corrales	.05	.04	.02
700	Reggie Jackson	.35	.25	.14
701	Keith Hernandez AS	.15	.11	.06
702	Tom Herr AS	.07	.05	.03
703	Tim Wallach AS	.07	.05	.03
704	Ozzie Smith AS	.10	.08	.04
705	Dale Murphy AS	.30	.25	.12
706	Pedro Guerrero AS	.12	.09	.05
707	Willie McGee AS	.12	.09	.05
708	Gary Carter AS	.20	.15	.08
709	Dwight Gooden AS	.40	.30	.15
710	John Tudor AS	.07	.05	.03
711	Jeff Reardon AS	.07	.05	.03
712	Don Mattingly AS	.60	.45	.25
713	Damaso Garcia AS	.05	.04	.02
714	George Brett AS	.30	.25	.12
715	Cal Ripken AS	.25	.20	.10
716	Rickey Henderson AS	.25	.20	.10
717	Dave Winfield AS	.20	.15	.08
718	Jorge Bell AS	.20	.15	.08
719	Carlton Fisk AS	.12	.09	.05
720	Bret Saberhagen AS	.15	.11	.06
721	Ron Guidry AS	.10	.08	.04
722	Dan Quisenberry AS	.07	.05	.03
723	Marty Bystrom	.05	.04	.02
724	Tim Hulett	.07	.05	.03
725	Mario Soto	.07	.05	.03
726	Orioles Leaders (Rick Dempsey)	.07	.05	.03
727	David Green	.05	.04	.02
728	Mike Marshall	.12	.09	.05
729	Jim Beattie	.05	.04	.02
730	Ozzie Smith	.15	.11	.06
731	Don Robinson	.07	.05	.03
732	*Floyd Youmans*(FC)	.12	.09	.05
733	Ron Romanick	.05	.04	.02
734	Marty Barrett	.10	.08	.04
735	Dave Dravecky	.07	.05	.03
736	Glenn Wilson	.07	.05	.03
737	Pete Vuckovich	.07	.05	.03
738	Andre Robertson	.05	.04	.02
739	Dave Rozema	.05	.04	.02
740	Lance Parrish	.20	.15	.08
741	Pete Rose	.40	.30	.15
742	Frank Viola	.15	.11	.06
743	Pat Sheridan	.05	.04	.02
744	Lary Sorensen	.05	.04	.02
745	Willie Upshaw	.07	.05	.03
746	Denny Gonzalez	.05	.04	.02
747	Rick Cerone	.05	.04	.02
748	Steve Henderson	.05	.04	.02
749	Ed Jurak	.05	.04	.02
750	Gorman Thomas	.10	.08	.04
751	Howard Johnson	.12	.09	.05
752	Mike Krukow	.07	.05	.03
753	Dan Ford	.05	.04	.02
754	*Pat Clements*	.12	.09	.05
755	Harold Baines	.15	.11	.06
756	Pirates Leaders (Rick Rhoden)	.07	.05	.03
757	Darrell Porter	.07	.05	.03
758	Dave Anderson	.05	.04	.02
759	Moose Haas	.05	.04	.02
760	Andre Dawson	.20	.15	.08
761	Don Slaught	.05	.04	.02

		MT	NR MT	EX
762	Eric Show	.07	.05	.03
763	Terry Puhl	.05	.04	.02
764	Kevin Gross	.07	.05	.03
765	Don Baylor	.12	.09	.05
766	Rick Langford	.05	.04	.02
767	Jody Davis	.10	.08	.04
768	Vern Ruhle	.05	.04	.02
769	*Harold Reynolds*(FC)	.60	.45	.25
770	Vida Blue	.10	.08	.04
771	John McNamara	.05	.04	.02
772	Brian Downing	.07	.05	.03
773	Greg Pryor	.05	.04	.02
774	Terry Leach	.05	.04	.02
775	Al Oliver	.10	.08	.04
776	Gene Garber	.05	.04	.02
777	Wayne Krenchicki	.05	.04	.02
778	Jerry Hairston	.05	.04	.02
779	Rick Reuschel	.10	.08	.04
780	Robin Yount	.50	.40	.20
781	Joe Nolan	.05	.04	.02
782	Ken Landreaux	.05	.04	.02
783	Ricky Horton	.07	.05	.03
784	Alan Bannister	.05	.04	.02
785	Bob Stanley	.05	.04	.02
786	Twins Leaders (Mickey Hatcher)	.07	.05	.03
787	Vance Law	.07	.05	.03
788	Marty Castillo	.05	.04	.02
789	Kurt Bevacqua	.05	.04	.02
790	Phil Niekro	.25	.20	.10
791	Checklist 661-792	.05	.04	.02
792	Charles Hudson	.06	.05	.02

1986 Topps All-Star Glossy Set Of 22

As in previous years, Topps continued to make the popular glossy-surfaced cards as an insert in rack packs. The All-Star Glossy set of 22 2-1/2" by 3-1/2" cards shows little design change from previous years. Cards feature a front color photo and All-Star banner at the top. The bottom has the player's name and position. The set includes the All-Star starting teams as well as the managers and honorary captains.

		MT	NR MT	EX
Complete Set:		6.00	4.50	2.50
Common Player:		.20	.15	.08
1	Sparky Anderson	.20	.15	.08
2	Eddie Murray	.50	.40	.20
3	Lou Whitaker	.30	.25	.12
4	George Brett	.80	.60	.30
5	Cal Ripken	.60	.45	.25
6	Jim Rice	.50	.40	.20
7	Rickey Henderson	.60	.45	.25
8	Dave Winfield	.50	.40	.20
9	Carlton Fisk	.30	.25	.12
10	Jack Morris	.30	.25	.12
11	A.L. All-Star Team	.20	.15	.08
12	Dick Williams	.20	.15	.08
13	Steve Garvey	.50	.40	.20
14	Tom Herr	.20	.15	.08
15	Graig Nettles	.20	.15	.08
16	Ozzie Smith	.30	.25	.12
17	Tony Gwynn	.60	.45	.25
18	Dale Murphy	.80	.60	.30

		MT	NR MT	EX
19	Darryl Strawberry	.80	.60	.30
20	Terry Kennedy	.20	.15	.08
21	LaMarr Hoyt	.20	.15	.08
22	N.L. All-Star Team	.20	.15	.08

1986 Topps All-Star Glossy Set Of 60

The Topps All-Star & Hot Prospects Glossy Set of 60 cards represents an expansion of a good idea. The 2-1/2" by 3-1/2" cards had a good following when they were limited to stars, but Topps realized that the addition of top young players would spice up the set even further, so in 1986 it was expanded from 40 to 60 cards. The cards themselves are basically all color glossy pictures with the player's name in very small print in the lower left-hand corner. To obtain the set, it was necessary to send $1 plus six special offer cards from wax packs to Topps for each series. At 60 cards, that meant the process had to be repeated six times as there were 10 cards in each series, making the set quite expensive from the outset.

		MT	NR MT	EX
Complete Set:		15.00	11.00	6.00
Common Player:		.15	.11	.06
1	Oddibe McDowell	.25	.20	.10
2	Reggie Jackson	.70	.50	.30
3	Fernando Valenzuela	.35	.25	.14
4	Jack Clark	.25	.20	.10
5	Rickey Henderson	.70	.50	.30
6	Steve Balboni	.15	.11	.06
7	Keith Hernandez	.40	.30	.15
8	Lance Parrish	.30	.25	.12
9	Willie McGee	.25	.20	.10
10	Chris Brown	.40	.30	.15
11	Darryl Strawberry	.90	.70	.35
12	Ron Guidry	.30	.25	.12
13	Dave Parker	.25	.20	.10
14	Cal Ripken	.70	.50	.30
15	Tim Raines	.50	.40	.20
16	Rod Carew	.60	.45	.25
17	Mike Schmidt	.90	.70	.35
18	George Brett	.90	.70	.35
19	Joe Hesketh	.15	.11	.06
20	Dan Pasqua	.20	.15	.08
21	Vince Coleman	1.00	.70	.40
22	Tom Seaver	.50	.40	.20
23	Gary Carter	.50	.40	.20
24	Orel Hershiser	.40	.30	.15
25	Pedro Guerrero	.30	.25	.12
26	Wade Boggs	1.25	.90	.50
27	Bret Saberhagen	.30	.25	.12
28	Carlton Fisk	.25	.20	.10
29	Kirk Gibson	.35	.25	.14
30	Brian Fisher	.20	.15	.08
31	Don Mattingly	3.00	2.25	1.25
32	Tom Herr	.15	.11	.06
33	Eddie Murray	.60	.45	.25
34	Ryne Sandberg	.40	.30	.15
35	Dan Quisenberry	.15	.11	.06
36	Jim Rice	.50	.40	.20
37	Dale Murphy	.90	.70	.35
38	Steve Garvey	.50	.40	.20
39	Roger McDowell	.25	.20	.10
40	Earnie Riles	.15	.11	.06
41	Dwight Gooden	1.25	.90	.50
42	Dave Winfield	.50	.40	.20
43	Dave Stieb	.20	.15	.08
44	Bob Horner	.20	.15	.08
45	Nolan Ryan	.50	.40	.20
46	Ozzie Smith	.25	.20	.10
47	Jorge Bell	.50	.40	.20
48	Gorman Thomas	.15	.11	.06
49	Tom Browning	.25	.20	.10
50	Larry Sheets	.20	.15	.08
51	Pete Rose	1.25	.90	.50
52	Brett Butler	.15	.11	.06
53	John Tudor	.20	.15	.08
54	Phil Bradley	.20	.15	.08
55	Jeff Reardon	.20	.15	.08
56	Rich Gossage	.25	.20	.10
57	Tony Gwynn	.60	.45	.25
58	Ozzie Guillen	.25	.20	.10
59	Glenn Davis	.35	.25	.14
60	Darrell Evans	.15	.11	.06

1986 Topps Box Panels

Following the lead of Donruss, which introduced the concept in 1985, Topps produced special cards on the bottom panels of wax boxes. Individual cards measure 2-1/2" by 3-1/2", the same as regular cards. Design of the cards is virtually identical with regular '86 Topps, though the top border is in red, rather than black. The cards are lettered "A" through "P", rather than numbered on the back.

		MT	NR MT	EX
Complete Panel Set:		10.00	7.50	4.00
Complete Singles Set:		5.00	3.75	2.00
Common Panel:		2.00	1.50	.80
Common Single Player:		.15	.11	.06
	Panel	3.50	2.75	1.50
A	Jorge Bell	.20	.15	.08
B	Wade Boggs	.60	.45	.25
C	George Brett	.35	.25	.14
D	Vince Coleman	.35	.25	.14
	Panel	2.00	1.50	.80
E	Carlton Fisk	.15	.11	.06
F	Dwight Gooden	.40	.30	.15
G	Pedro Guerrero	.15	.11	.06
H	Ron Guidry	.15	.11	.06
	Panel	3.50	2.75	1.50
I	Reggie Jackson	.30	.25	.12
J	Don Mattingly	.90	.70	.35
K	Oddibe McDowell	.15	.11	.06
L	Willie McGee	.15	.11	.06
	Panel	3.00	2.25	1.25
M	Dale Murphy	.35	.25	.14
N	Pete Rose	.50	.40	.20
O	Bret Saberhagen	.15	.11	.06
P	Fernando Valenzuela	.20	.15	.08

A player's name in italic type indicates a rookie card. An (FC) indicates a player's first card for that particular card company.

1986 Topps Gallery Of Champions

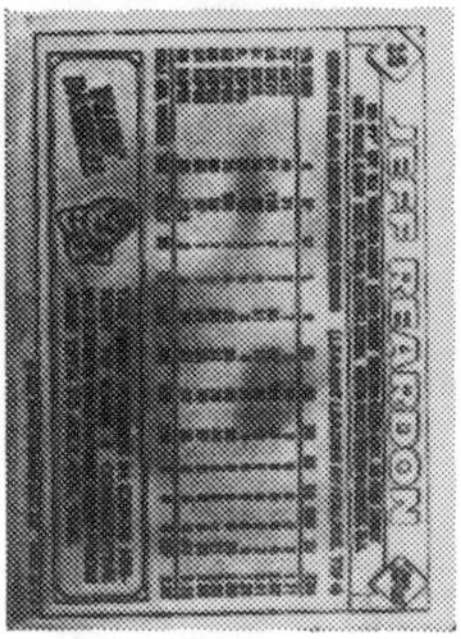

For the third consecutive year Topps issued 12 "metal mini-cards" as a dealer-ordering incentive. The metal replicas were minted 1/4-size (approximately 1-1/4" by 1-3/4") of the regular cards and come in silver, aluminum and bronze. The bronze and silver sets were issued in leather-like velvet-lined display cases. A bronze 1952 Topps Mickey Mantle was given as a premium for dealers purchasing 1986 Traded sets, while a pewter Don Mattingly was issued as a premium to those ordering the aluminum, bronze and silver sets. The Mantle bronze is valued at $12 and the Mattingly pewter at $100.

		MT	NR MT	EX
Complete Aluminum Set:		30.00	22.00	12.00
Complete Bronze Set:		175.00	131.00	70.00
Complete Silver Set:		650.00	487.00	260.00
(1a)	Wade Boggs (aluminum)	3.00	2.25	1.25
(1b)	Wade Boggs (bronze)	25.00	18.50	10.00
(1c)	Wade Boggs (silver)	125.00	94.00	50.00
(2a)	Vince Coleman (aluminum)	1.25	.90	.50
(2b)	Vince Coleman (bronze)	12.00	9.00	4.75
(2c)	Vince Coleman (silver)	50.00	37.00	20.00
(3a)	Darrell Evans (aluminum)	.70	.50	.30
(3b)	Darrell Evans (bronze)	7.50	5.75	3.00
(3c)	Darrell Evans (silver)	20.00	15.00	8.00
(4a)	Dwight Gooden (aluminum)	2.00	1.50	.80
(4b)	Dwight Gooden (bronze)	20.00	15.00	8.00
(4c)	Dwight Gooden (silver)	100.00	75.00	40.00
(5a)	Ozzie Guillen (aluminum)	.70	.50	.30
(5b)	Ozzie Guillen (bronze)	7.50	5.75	3.00
(5c)	Ozzie Guillen (silver)	20.00	15.00	8.00
(6a)	Don Mattingly (aluminum)	8.00	6.00	3.25
(6b)	Don Mattingly (bronze)	50.00	37.00	20.00
(6c)	Don Mattingly (silver)	200.00	150.00	80.00
(7a)	Willie McGee (aluminum)	1.00	.70	.40
(7b)	Willie McGee (bronze)	10.00	7.50	4.00
(7c)	Willie McGee (silver)	30.00	22.00	12.00
(8a)	Dale Murphy (aluminum)	1.50	1.25	.60
(8b)	Dale Murphy (bronze)	15.00	11.00	6.00
(8c)	Dale Murphy (silver)	80.00	60.00	32.00
(9a)	Dan Quisenberry (aluminum)	.70	.50	.30
(9b)	Dan Quisenberry (bronze)	7.50	5.75	3.00
(9c)	Dan Quisenberry (silver)	20.00	15.00	8.00
(10a)	Jeff Reardon (aluminum)	.70	.50	.30
(10b)	Jeff Reardon (bronze)	7.50	5.75	3.00
(10c)	Jeff Reardon (silver)	20.00	15.00	8.00
(11a)	Pete Rose (aluminum)	2.50	2.00	1.00
(11b)	Pete Rose (bronze)	25.00	18.50	10.00
(11c)	Pete Rose (silver)	110.00	82.00	44.00
(12a)	Bret Saberhagen (aluminum)	1.00	.70	.40
(12b)	Bret Saberhagen (bronze)	10.00	7.50	4.00
(12c)	Bret Saberhagen (silver)	30.00	22.00	12.00

A baseball card history feature, definitions for grading conditions and tips on how to use this catalog are located in the introduction section at the front of this book.

1986 Topps Mini League Leaders

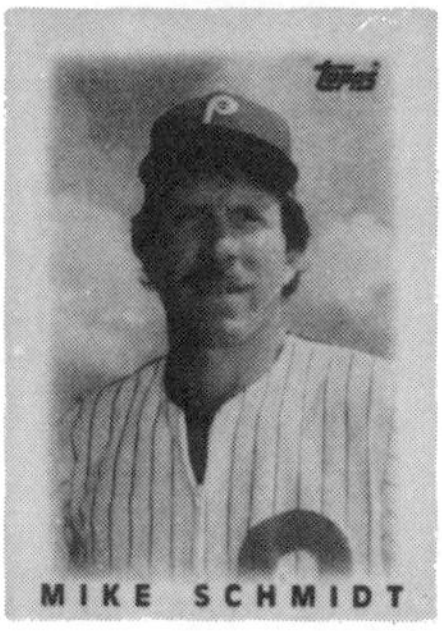

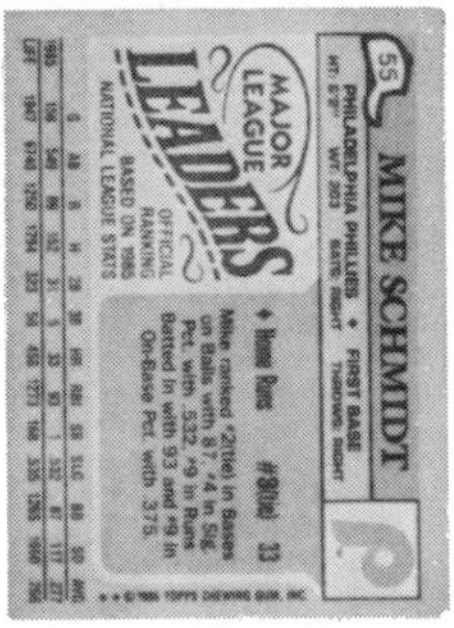

Topps had long experimented with bigger cards, but in 1986, they also decided to try smaller ones. These 2-1/8" by 2-15/16" cards feature top players in a number of categories. Sold in plastic packs as a regular Topps issue, the 66-card set is attractive as well as innovative. The cards feature color photos and a minimum of added information on the fronts where only the player's name and Topps logo appear. Backs limited information as well, but do feature whatever information was required to justify the player's inclusion in a set of league leaders.

		MT	NR MT	EX
Complete Set:		8.00	6.00	3.25
Common Player:		.09	.07	.04
1	Eddie Murray	.40	.30	.15
2	Cal Ripken	.40	.30	.15
3	Wade Boggs	.80	.60	.30
4	Dennis Boyd	.09	.07	.04
5	Dwight Evans	.15	.11	.06
6	Bruce Hurst	.15	.11	.06
7	Gary Pettis	.09	.07	.04
8	Harold Baines	.15	.11	.06
9	Floyd Bannister	.09	.07	.04
10	Britt Burns	.09	.07	.04
11	Carlton Fisk	.20	.15	.08
12	Brett Butler	.15	.11	.06
13	Darrell Evans	.15	.11	.06
14	Jack Morris	.25	.20	.10
15	Lance Parrish	.25	.20	.10
16	Walt Terrell	.09	.07	.04
17	Steve Balboni	.09	.07	.04
18	George Brett	.50	.40	.20
19	Charlie Leibrandt	.09	.07	.04
20	Bret Saberhagen	.20	.15	.08
21	Lonnie Smith	.09	.07	.04
22	Willie Wilson	.15	.11	.06
23	Bert Blyleven	.15	.11	.06
24	Mike Smithson	.09	.07	.04
25	Frank Viola	.20	.15	.08
26	Ron Guidry	.20	.15	.08
27	Rickey Henderson	.40	.30	.15
28	Don Mattingly	1.25	.90	.50
29	Dave Winfield	.30	.25	.12
30	Mike Moore	.09	.07	.04
31	Gorman Thomas	.09	.07	.04
32	Toby Harrah	.09	.07	.04
33	Charlie Hough	.09	.07	.04
34	Doyle Alexander	.09	.07	.04
35	Jimmy Key	.15	.11	.06
36	Dave Stieb	.15	.11	.06
37	Dale Murphy	.50	.40	.20
38	Keith Moreland	.09	.07	.04
39	Ryne Sandberg	.30	.25	.12
40	Tom Browning	.15	.11	.06
41	Dave Parker	.20	.15	.08
42	Mario Soto	.09	.07	.04
43	Nolan Ryan	.30	.25	.12
44	Pedro Guerrero	.20	.15	.08
45	Orel Hershiser	.30	.25	.12
46	Mike Scioscia	.09	.07	.04
47	Fernando Valenzuela	.25	.20	.10
48	Bob Welch	.15	.11	.06
49	Tim Raines	.30	.25	.12

		MT	NR MT	EX
50	Gary Carter	.30	.25	.12
51	Sid Fernandez	.15	.11	.06
52	Dwight Gooden	.70	.50	.30
53	Keith Hernandez	.25	.20	.10
54	Juan Samuel	.20	.15	.08
55	Mike Schmidt	.50	.40	.20
56	Glenn Wilson	.09	.07	.04
57	Rick Reuschel	.15	.11	.06
58	Joaquin Andujar	.09	.07	.04
59	Jack Clark	.20	.15	.08
60	Vince Coleman	.60	.45	.25
61	Danny Cox	.09	.07	.04
62	Tom Herr	.09	.07	.04
63	Willie McGee	.15	.11	.06
64	John Tudor	.15	.11	.06
65	Tony Gwynn	.40	.30	.15
66	Checklist	.09	.07	.04

1986 Topps Stickers

The 1986 Topps stickers are 2-1/8" by 3". The 200- piece set features 316 different subjects, with some stickers including two or three players. Numbers run only to 315, however. The set includes some specialty stickers such as League Championships and World Series themes. Stickers are numbered both front and back and included a chance to win a trip to spring training as well as an offer to buy a complete 1986 Topps regular set. An album for the stickers was available in stores.

		MT	NR MT	EX
	Complete Set:	15.00	11.00	6.00
	Common Player:	.03	.02	.01
	Sticker Album:	.70	.50	.30
1	Pete Rose	.25	.20	.10
2	Pete Rose	.25	.20	.10
3	George Brett	.12	.09	.05
4	Rod Carew	.10	.08	.04
5	Vince Coleman	.12	.09	.05
6	Dwight Gooden	.15	.11	.06
7	Phil Niekro	.08	.06	.03
8	Tony Perez	.06	.05	.02
9	Nolan Ryan	.10	.08	.04
10	Tom Seaver	.10	.08	.04
11	N.L. Championship Series (Ozzie Smith)	.06	.05	.02
12	N.L. Championship Series (Bill Madlock)	.04	.03	.02
13	N.L. Championship Series (Cardinals Celebrate)	.03	.02	.01
14	A.L. Championship Series (Al Oliver)	.04	.03	.02
15	A.L. Championship Series (Jim Sundberg)	.03	.02	.01
16	A.L. Championship Series (George Brett)	.10	.08	.04
17	World Series (Bret Saberhagen)	.06	.05	.02
18	World Series (Dane Iorg)	.03	.02	.01
19	World Series (Tito Landrum)	.03	.02	.01
20	World Series (John Tudor)	.04	.03	.02
21	World Series (Buddy Biancalana)	.03	.02	.01
22	World Series (Darryl Motley, Darrell Porter)	.03	.02	.01
23	World Series (George Brett, Frank White)	.10	.08	.04

		MT	NR MT	EX
24	Nolan Ryan	.15	.11	.06
25	Bill Doran	.08	.06	.03
26	Jose Cruz	.04	.03	.02
27	Mike Scott	.08	.06	.03
28	Kevin Bass	.04	.03	.02
29	Glenn Davis	.10	.08	.04
30	Mark Bailey	.06	.05	.02
31	Dave Smith	.10	.08	.04
32	Phil Garner	.03	.02	.01
33	Dickie Thon	.06	.05	.02
34	Bob Horner	.12	.09	.05
35	Dale Murphy	.25	.20	.10
36	Glenn Hubbard	.04	.03	.02
37	Bruce Sutter	.08	.06	.03
38	Ken Oberkfell	.04	.03	.02
39	Claudell Washington	.04	.03	.02
40	Steve Bedrosian	.04	.03	.02
41	Terry Harper	.03	.02	.01
42	Rafael Ramirez	.06	.05	.02
43	Rick Mahler	.03	.02	.01
44	Joaquin Andujar	.06	.05	.02
45	Willie McGee	.10	.08	.04
46	Ozzie Smith	.06	.05	.02
47	Vince Coleman	.12	.09	.05
48	Danny Cox	.04	.03	.02
49	Tom Herr	.04	.03	.02
50	Jack Clark	.08	.06	.03
51	Andy Van Slyke	.04	.03	.02
52	John Tudor	.08	.06	.03
53	Terry Pendleton	.03	.02	.01
54	Keith Moreland	.06	.05	.02
55	Ryne Sandberg	.15	.11	.06
56	Lee Smith	.04	.03	.02
57	Steve Trout	.06	.05	.02
58	Jody Davis	.08	.06	.03
59	Gary Matthews	.04	.03	.02
60	Leon Durham	.04	.03	.02
61	Rick Sutcliffe	.06	.05	.02
62	Dennis Eckersley	.04	.03	.02
63	Bob Dernier	.03	.02	.01
64	Fernando Valenzuela	.15	.11	.06
65	Pedro Guerrero	.12	.09	.05
66	Jerry Reuss	.06	.05	.02
67	Greg Brock	.06	.05	.02
68	Mike Scioscia	.03	.02	.01
69	Ken Howell	.04	.03	.02
70	Bill Madlock	.04	.03	.02
71	Mike Marshall	.06	.05	.02
72	Steve Sax	.06	.05	.02
73	Orel Hershiser	.06	.05	.02
74	Andre Dawson	.12	.09	.05
75	Tim Raines	.12	.09	.05
76	Jeff Reardon	.06	.05	.02
77	Hubie Brooks	.04	.03	.02
78	Bill Gullickson	.04	.03	.02
79	Bryn Smith	.04	.03	.02
80	Terry Francona	.04	.03	.02
81	Vance Law	.03	.02	.01
82	Tim Wallach	.04	.03	.02
83	Herm Winningham	.04	.03	.02
84	Jeff Leonard	.06	.05	.02
85	Chris Brown	.20	.15	.08
86	Scott Garrelts	.03	.02	.01
87	Jose Uribe	.04	.03	.02
88	Manny Trillo	.04	.03	.02
89	Dan Driessen	.04	.03	.02
90	Dan Gladden	.06	.05	.02
91	Mark Davis	.04	.03	.02
92	Bob Brenly	.03	.02	.01
93	Mike Krukow	.04	.03	.02
94	Dwight Gooden	.35	.25	.14
95	Darryl Strawberry	.25	.20	.10
96	Gary Carter	.10	.08	.04
97	Wally Backman	.06	.05	.02
98	Ron Darling	.06	.05	.02
99	Keith Hernandez	.12	.09	.05
100	George Foster	.06	.05	.02
101	Howard Johnson	.06	.05	.02
102	Rafael Santana	.04	.03	.02
103	Roger McDowell	.06	.05	.02
104	Steve Garvey	.15	.11	.06
105	Tony Gwynn	.20	.15	.08
106	Graig Nettles	.06	.05	.02
107	Rich Gossage	.10	.08	.04
108	Andy Hawkins	.04	.03	.02
109	Carmelo Martinez	.04	.03	.02
110	Garry Templeton	.04	.03	.02
111	Terry Kennedy	.06	.05	.02
112	Tim Flannery	.08	.06	.03
113	LaMarr Hoyt	.03	.02	.01
114	Mike Schmidt	.25	.20	.10

		MT	NR MT	EX
115	Ozzie Virgil	.06	.05	.02
116	Steve Carlton	.10	.08	.04
117	Garry Maddox	.03	.02	.01
118	Glenn Wilson	.06	.05	.02
119	Kevin Gross	.03	.02	.01
120	Von Hayes	.04	.03	.02
121	Juan Samuel	.06	.05	.02
122	Rick Schu	.08	.06	.03
123	Shane Rawley	.06	.05	.02
124	Johnny Ray	.06	.05	.02
125	Tony Pena	.06	.05	.02
126	Rick Reuschel	.12	.09	.05
127	Sammy Khalifa	.06	.05	.02
128	Marvell Wynne	.04	.03	.02
129	Jason Thompson	.03	.02	.01
130	Rick Rhoden	.04	.03	.02
131	Bill Almon	.03	.02	.01
132	Joe Orsulak	.06	.05	.02
133	Jim Morrison	.06	.05	.02
134	Pete Rose	.40	.30	.15
135	Dave Parker	.12	.09	.05
136	Mario Soto	.03	.02	.01
137	Dave Concepcion	.10	.08	.04
138	Ron Oester	.03	.02	.01
139	Buddy Bell	.06	.05	.02
140	Ted Power	.03	.02	.01
141	Tom Browning	.06	.05	.02
142	John Franco	.08	.06	.03
143	Tony Perez	.06	.05	.02
144	Willie McGee	.08	.06	.03
145	Dale Murphy	.15	.11	.06
146	Tony Gwynn	.40	.30	.15
147	Tom Herr	.15	.11	.06
148	Steve Garvey	.30	.25	.12
149	Dale Murphy	.40	.30	.15
150	Darryl Strawberry	.40	.30	.15
151	Graig Nettles	.15	.11	.06
152	Terry Kennedy	.15	.11	.06
153	Ozzie Smith	.20	.15	.08
154	LaMarr Hoyt	.15	.11	.06
155	Rickey Henderson	.40	.30	.15
156	Lou Whitaker	.25	.20	.10
157	George Brett	.40	.30	.15
158	Eddie Murray	.40	.30	.15
159	Cal Ripken	.40	.30	.15
160	Dave Winfield	.30	.25	.12
161	Jim Rice	.30	.25	.12
162	Carlton Fisk	.25	.20	.10
163	Jack Morris	.25	.20	.10
164	Wade Boggs	.15	.11	.06
165	Darrell Evans	.06	.05	.02
166	Mike Davis	.06	.05	.02
167	Dave Kingman	.08	.06	.03
168	Alfredo Griffin	.04	.03	.02
169	Carney Lansford	.04	.03	.02
170	Bruce Bochte	.10	.08	.04
171	Dwayne Murphy	.08	.06	.03
172	Dave Collins	.04	.03	.02
173	Chris Codiroli	.10	.08	.04
174	Mike Heath	.03	.02	.01
175	Jay Howell	.12	.09	.05
176	Rod Carew	.20	.15	.08
177	Reggie Jackson	.20	.15	.08
178	Doug DeCinces	.10	.08	.04
179	Bob Boone	.12	.09	.05
180	Ron Romanick	.15	.11	.06
181	Bob Grich	.08	.06	.03
182	Donnie Moore	.06	.05	.02
183	Brian Downing	.10	.08	.04
184	Ruppert Jones	.10	.08	.04
185	Juan Beniquez	.04	.03	.02
186	Dave Stieb	.06	.05	.02
187	Jorge Bell	.20	.15	.08
188	Willie Upshaw	.08	.06	.03
189	Tom Henke	.04	.03	.02
190	Damaso Garcia	.10	.08	.04
191	Jimmy Key	.06	.05	.02
192	Jesse Barfield	.10	.08	.04
193	Dennis Lamp	.03	.02	.01
194	Tony Fernandez	.06	.05	.02
195	Lloyd Moseby	.04	.03	.02
196	Cecil Cooper	.08	.06	.03
197	Robin Yount	.15	.11	.06
198	Rollie Fingers	.08	.06	.03
199	Ted Simmons	.04	.03	.02
200	Ben Oglivie	.04	.03	.02
201	Moose Haas	.04	.03	.02
202	Jim Gantner	.03	.02	.01
203	Paul Molitor	.06	.05	.02
204	Charlie Moore	.03	.02	.01
205	Danny Darwin	.06	.05	.02

		MT	NR MT	EX
206	Brett Butler	.06	.05	.02
207	Brook Jacoby	.08	.06	.03
208	Andre Thornton	.12	.09	.05
209	Tom Waddell	.04	.03	.02
210	Tony Bernazard	.04	.03	.02
211	Julio Franco	.08	.06	.03
212	Pat Tabler	.04	.03	.02
213	Joe Carter	.08	.06	.03
214	George Vukovich	.03	.02	.01
215	Rich Thompson	.04	.03	.02
216	Gorman Thomas	.06	.05	.02
217	Phil Bradley	.10	.08	.04
218	Alvin Davis	.06	.05	.02
219	Jim Presley	.08	.06	.03
220	Matt Young	.04	.03	.02
221	Mike Moore	.04	.03	.02
222	Dave Henderson	.06	.05	.02
223	Ed Nunez	.04	.03	.02
224	Spike Owen	.03	.02	.01
225	Mark Langston	.06	.05	.02
226	Cal Ripken	.20	.15	.08
227	Eddie Murray	.20	.15	.08
228	Fred Lynn	.06	.05	.02
229	Lee Lacy	.03	.02	.01
230	Scott McGregor	.04	.03	.02
231	Storm Davis	.04	.03	.02
232	Rick Dempsey	.06	.05	.02
233	Mike Boddicker	.06	.05	.02
234	Mike Young	.06	.05	.02
235	Sammy Stewart	.06	.05	.02
236	Pete O'Brien	.08	.06	.03
237	Oddibe McDowell	.15	.11	.06
238	Toby Harrah	.04	.03	.02
239	Gary Ward	.04	.03	.02
240	Larry Parrish	.04	.03	.02
241	Charlie Hough	.04	.03	.02
242	Burt Hooton	.03	.02	.01
243	Don Slaught	.04	.03	.02
244	Curt Wilkerson	.04	.03	.02
245	Greg Harris	.03	.02	.01
246	Jim Rice	.15	.11	.06
247	Wade Boggs	.60	.45	.25
248	Rich Gedman	.04	.03	.02
249	Dennis Boyd	.04	.03	.02
250	Marty Barrett	.04	.03	.02
251	Dwight Evans	.06	.05	.02
252	Bill Buckner	.04	.03	.02
253	Bob Stanley	.03	.02	.01
254	Tony Armas	.04	.03	.02
255	Mike Easler	.10	.08	.04
256	George Brett	.25	.20	.10
257	Dan Quisenberry	.06	.05	.02
258	Willie Wilson	.06	.05	.02
259	Jim Sundberg	.06	.05	.02
260	Bret Saberhagen	.12	.09	.05
261	Bud Black	.06	.05	.02
262	Charlie Leibrandt	.06	.05	.02
263	Frank White	.04	.03	.02
264	Lonnie Smith	.06	.05	.02
265	Steve Balboni	.06	.05	.02
266	Kirk Gibson	.15	.11	.06
267	Alan Trammell	.15	.11	.06
268	Jack Morris	.10	.08	.04
269	Darrell Evans	.04	.03	.02
270	Dan Petry	.04	.03	.02
271	Larry Herndon	.04	.03	.02
272	Lou Whitaker	.06	.05	.02
273	Lance Parrish	.08	.06	.03
274	Chet Lemon	.03	.02	.01
275	Willie Hernandez	.10	.08	.04
276	Tom Brunansky	.08	.06	.03
277	Kent Hrbek	.12	.09	.05
278	Mark Salas	.03	.02	.01
279	Bert Blyleven	.06	.05	.02
280	Tim Teufel	.03	.02	.01
281	Ron Davis	.04	.03	.02
282	Mike Smithson	.06	.05	.02
283	Gary Gaetti	.08	.06	.03
284	Frank Viola	.06	.05	.02
285	Kirby Puckett	.12	.09	.05
286	Carlton Fisk	.12	.09	.05
287	Tom Seaver	.15	.11	.06
288	Harold Baines	.06	.05	.02
289	Ron Kittle	.04	.03	.02
290	Bob James	.03	.02	.01
291	Rudy Law	.04	.03	.02
292	Britt Burns	.03	.02	.01
293	Greg Walker	.06	.05	.02
294	Ozzie Guillen	.06	.05	.02
295	Tim Hulett	.03	.02	.01
296	Don Mattingly	.70	.50	.30

		MT	NR MT	EX
297	Rickey Henderson	.20	.15	.08
298	Dave Winfield	.10	.08	.04
299	Butch Wynegar	.03	.02	.01
300	Don Baylor	.06	.05	.02
301	Eddie Whitson	.03	.02	.01
302	Ron Guidry	.06	.05	.02
303	Dave Righetti	.08	.06	.03
304	Bobby Meacham	.06	.05	.02
305	Willie Randolph	.08	.06	.03
306	Vince Coleman	.15	.11	.06
307	Oddibe McDowell	.15	.11	.06
308	Larry Sheets	.06	.05	.02
309	Ozzie Guillen	.06	.05	.02
310	Earnie Riles	.04	.03	.02
311	Chris Brown	.10	.08	.04
312	Brian Fisher, Roger McDowell	.08	.06	.03
313	Tom Browning	.04	.03	.02
314	Glenn Davis	.10	.08	.04
315	Mark Salas	.03	.02	.01

1986 Topps Super

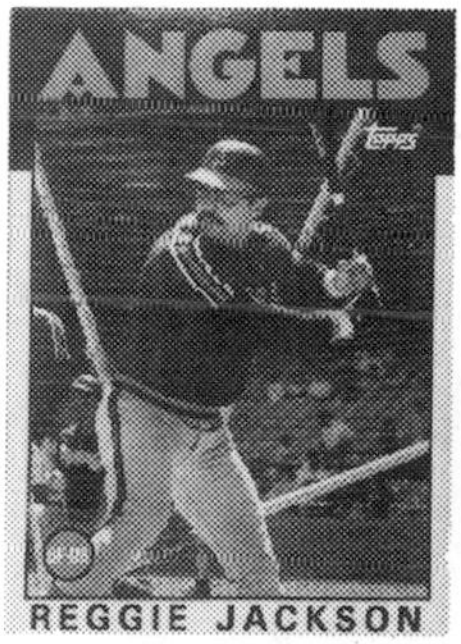

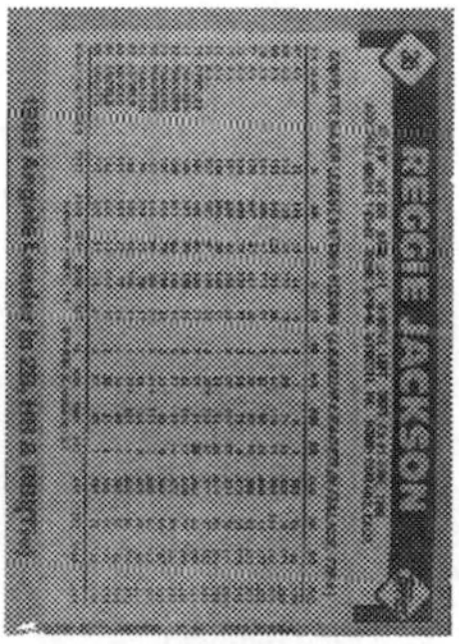

A third year of oversize, 4-7/8" by 6-7/8", versions of Topps' regular issue cards saw the set once again hit the 60-card mark. Besides being four times the size of a normal card, the Supers differ only in the number on the back of the card.

		MT	NR MT	EX
Complete Set:		12.00	9.00	4.75
Common Player:		.20	.15	.08
1	Don Mattingly	2.25	1.75	.90
2	Willie McGee	.35	.25	.14
3	Bret Saberhagen	.35	.25	.14
4	Dwight Gooden	1.50	1.25	.60
5	Dan Quisenberry	.20	.15	.08
6	Jeff Reardon	.25	.20	.10
7	Ozzie Guillen	.25	.20	.10
8	Vince Coleman	.70	.50	.30
9	Harold Baines	.25	.20	.10
10	Jorge Bell	.50	.40	.20
11	Bert Blyleven	.25	.20	.10
12	Wade Boggs	1.25	.90	.50
13	Phil Bradley	.25	.20	.10
14	George Brett	.80	.60	.30
15	Hubie Brooks	.20	.15	.08
16	Tom Browning	.25	.20	.10
17	Bill Buckner	.20	.15	.08
18	Brett Butler	.20	.15	.08
19	Gary Carter	.50	.40	.20
20	Cecil Cooper	.25	.20	.10
21	Darrell Evans	.25	.20	.10
22	Dwight Evans	.20	.15	.08
23	Carlton Fisk	.30	.25	.12
24	Steve Garvey	.50	.40	.20
25	Kirk Gibson	.35	.25	.14
26	Rich Gossage	.25	.20	.10
27	Pedro Guerrero	.30	.25	.12
28	Ron Guidry	.30	.25	.12
29	Tony Gwynn	.70	.50	.30
30	Rickey Henderson	.70	.50	.30
31	Keith Hernandez	.50	.40	.20
32	Tom Herr	.20	.15	.08
33	Orel Hershiser	.50	.40	.20
34	Jay Howell	.20	.15	.08
35	Reggie Jackson	.60	.45	.25
36	Bob James	.20	.15	.08
37	Charlie Leibrandt	.20	.15	.08
38	Jack Morris	.35	.25	.14
39	Dale Murphy	.80	.60	.30
40	Eddie Murray	.60	.45	.25
41	Dave Parker	.35	.25	.14
42	Tim Raines	.50	.40	.20
43	Jim Rice	.50	.40	.20
44	Dave Righetti	.30	.25	.12
45	Cal Ripken	.70	.50	.30
46	Pete Rose	1.00	.70	.40
47	Nolan Ryan	.50	.40	.20
48	Ryne Sandberg	.50	.40	.20
49	Mike Schmidt	.80	.60	.30
50	Tom Seaver	.50	.40	.20
51	Bryn Smith	.20	.15	.08
52	Lee Smith	.20	.15	.08
53	Ozzie Smith	.30	.25	.12
54	Dave Stieb	.20	.15	.08
55	Darryl Strawberry	.80	.60	.30
56	Gorman Thomas	.20	.15	.08
57	John Tudor	.20	.15	.08
58	Fernando Valenzuela	.40	.30	.15
59	Willie Wilson	.25	.20	.10
60	Dave Winfield	.50	.40	.20

1986 Topps Super Star

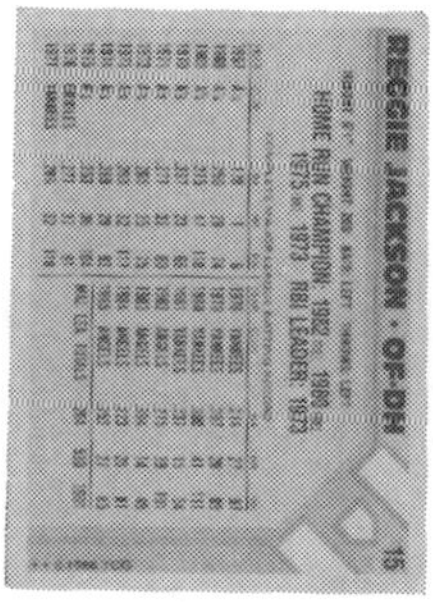

Labeled "Topps' Collector Series" in a red band at the top of the front, this set marked the second year of Topps' production of a special boxed set for the Woolworth chain of stores, though Woolworth's name does not appear anywhere on the card. The cards, which measure 2-1/2" by 3-1/2", feature a color photo with its lower right corner rolled up to reveal the words "Super Star" on a bright yellow border. The player's name appears in the lower left corner. The 66-card set features stars and retains a certain measure of popularity on that basis.

		MT	NR MT	EX
Complete Set:		5.00	3.75	2.00
Common Player:		.09	.07	.04
1	Tony Armas	.09	.07	.04
2	Don Baylor	.12	.09	.05
3	Wade Boggs	.80	.60	.30
4	George Brett	.40	.30	.15
5	Bill Buckner	.09	.07	.04
6	Rod Carew	.30	.25	.12
7	Gary Carter	.30	.25	.12
8	Cecil Cooper	.12	.09	.05
9	Darrell Evans	.12	.09	.05
10	Dwight Evans	.15	.11	.06
11	George Foster	.12	.09	.05
12	Bobby Grich	.09	.07	.04
13	Tony Gwynn	.35	.25	.14
14	Keith Hernandez	.25	.20	.10
15	Reggie Jackson	.30	.25	.12
16	Dave Kingman	.12	.09	.05
17	Carney Lansford	.09	.07	.04
18	Fred Lynn	.12	.09	.05
19	Bill Madlock	.12	.09	.05
20	Don Mattingly	1.50	1.25	.60
21	Willie McGee	.20	.15	.08
22	Hal McRae	.09	.07	.04
23	Dale Murphy	.40	.30	.15
24	Eddie Murray	.35	.25	.14

		MT	NR MT	EX
25	Ben Oglivie	.09	.07	.04
26	Al Oliver	.12	.09	.05
27	Dave Parker	.20	.15	.08
28	Jim Rice	.30	.25	.12
29	Pete Rose	.90	.70	.35
30	Mike Schmidt	.40	.30	.15
31	Gorman Thomas	.09	.07	.04
32	Willie Wilson	.12	.09	.05
33	Dave Winfield	.30	.25	.12

1986 Topps Tattoos

Topps returned to tattoos in 1986, marketing a set of 24 different tattoo sheets. Each sheet of tattoos measures 3-7/16" by 14" and includes both player and smaller action tattoos. As the action tattoos were uniform and not of any particular player, they add little value to the sheet. The player tattoos measure 1-3/16" by 2-3/8". With 24 sheets, eight players per sheet, there are 192 players represented in the set. The sheets are numbered.

	MT	NR MT	EX
Complete Set:	5.00	3.75	2.00
Common Player:	.20	.15	.08

		MT	NR MT	EX
1	Julio Franco, Rich Gossage, Keith Hernandez, Charlie Leibrandt, Jack Perconte, Lee Smith, Dickie Thon, Dave Winfield	.25	.20	.10
2	Jesse Barfield, Shawon Dunston, Dennis Eckersley, Brian Fisher, Moose Haas, Mike Moore, Dale Murphy, Bret Saberhagen	.30	.25	.12
3	George Bell, Bob Brenly, Steve Carlton, Jose DeLeon, Bob Horner, Bob James, Dan Quisenberry, Andre Thornton	.25	.20	.10
4	Mike Davis, Leon Durham, Darrell Evans, Glenn Hubbard, Johnny Ray, Cal Ripken, Ted Simmons	.25	.20	.10
5	John Candelaria, Rick Dempsey, Steve Garvey, Ozzie Guillen, Gary Matthews, Jesse Orosco, Tony Pena	.25	.20	.10
6	Bruce Bochte, George Brett, Cecil Cooper, Sammy Khalifa, Ron Kittle, Scott McGregor, Pete Rose, Mookie Wilson	.45	.35	.20
7	John Franco, Carney Lansford, Don Mattingly, Graig Nettles, Rick Reuschel, Mike Schmidt, Larry Sheets, Don Sutton	.45	.35	.20
8	Cecilio Guante, Willie Hernandez, Mike Krukow, Fred Lynn, Phil Niekro, Ed Nunez, Ryne Sandberg, Pat Tabler	.25	.20	.10
9	Brett Butler, Chris Codiroli, Jim Gantner, Charlie Hough, Dave Parker, Rick Rhoden, Glenn Wilson, Robin Yount	.20	.15	.08
10	Tom Browning, Ron Darling, Von Hayes, Chet Lemon, Tom Seaver, Mike Smithson, Bruce Sutter, Alan Trammell	.25	.20	.10
11	Tony Armas, Jose Cruz, Jay Howell, Rick Mahler, Jack Morris, Rafael Ramirez, Dave Righetti, Mike Young	.20	.15	.08
12	Alvin Davis, Doug DeCinces, Andy Hawkins, Dennis Lamp, Keith Moreland, Jim Presley, Mario Soto, John Tudor	.20	.15	.08
13	Hubie Brooks, Jody Davis, Dwight Evans, Ron Hassey, Charles Hudson, Kirby Puckett, Jose Uribe	.20	.15	.08
14	Tony Bernazard, Phil Bradley, Bill Buckner, Brian Downing, Dan Driessen, Ron Guidry, LaMarr Hoyt, Garry Maddox	.20	.15	.08
15	Buddy Bell, Joe Carter, Tony Fernandez, Tito Landrum, Jeff Leonard, Hal McRae, Willie Randolph, Juan Samuel	.20	.15	.08
16	Dennis Boyd, Vince Coleman, Scott Garrelts, Alfredo Griffin, Donnie Moore, Tony Perez, Ozzie Smith, Frank White	.25	.20	.10
17	Rich Gedman, Kent Hrbek, Reggie Jackson, Mike Marshall, Terry Pendleton, Tim Raines, Mark Salas, Claudell Washington	.25	.20	.10
18	Chris Brown, Tom Brunansky, Glenn Davis, Ron Davis, Burt Hooton, Darryl Strawberry, Frank Viola, Tim Wallach	.30	.25	.12
19	Jack Clark, Bill Doran, Toby Harrah, Bill Madlock, Pete O'Brien, Larry Parrish, Mike Scioscia, Garry Templeton	.20	.15	.08
20	Gary Carter, Andre Dawson, Dwight Gooden, Orel Hershiser, Oddibe McDowell, Roger McDowell, Dwayne Murphy, Jim Rice	.40	.30	.15
21	Steve Balboni, Mike Easler, Charlie Lea, Lloyd Moseby, Steve Sax, Rick Sutcliffe, Gary Ward, Willie Wilson	.20	.15	.08
22	Wade Boggs, Dave Concepcion, Kirk Gibson, Tom Herr, Lance Parrish, Jeff Reardon, Bryn Smith, Gorman Thomas	.30	.25	.12
23	Carlton Fisk, Bob Grich, Pedro Guerrero, Willie McGee, Paul Molitor, Mike Scott, Dave Stieb, Lou Whitaker	.20	.15	.08
24	Bert Blyleven, Damaso Garcia, Phil Garner, Tony Gwynn, Rickey Henderson, Ben Oglivie, Nolan Ryan, Fernando Valenzuela	.30	.25	.12

1986 Topps Traded

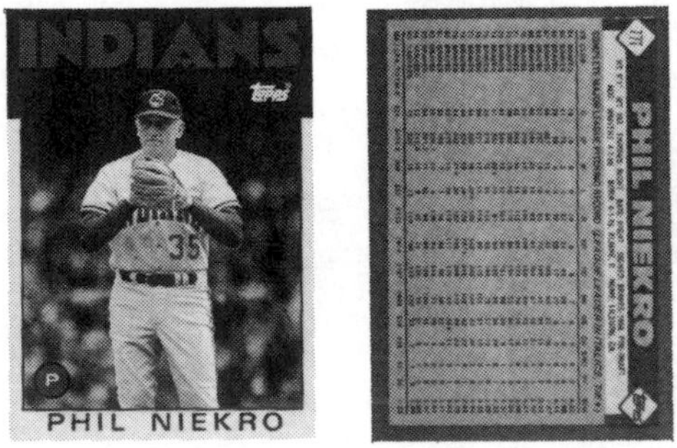

This 132-card set of 2-1/2" by 3-1/2" cards is one of the most popular sets of recent times. As always, the set features traded veterans, including such players as Phil Niekro and Tom Seaver. They are not, however, the reason for the excitement. The demand is there because of a better than usual crop of rookies who also appear in the sets. Among those are Jose Canseco, Wally Joyner, Pete Incaviglia, Todd Worrell and the first card of Bo Jackson. As in the previous two years, a glossy-finish "Tiffany" edition of 5,000 Traded sets was produced. The "Tiffany" cards are worth four to six times the value of the regular Traded cards.

	MT	NR MT	EX
Complete Set:	30.00	22.00	12.00
Common Player:	.08	.06	.03

		MT	NR MT	EX
1T	Andy Allanson(FC)	.20	.15	.08
2T	Neil Allen	.08	.06	.03
3T	Joaquin Andujar	.10	.08	.04
4T	Paul Assenmacher(FC)	.20	.15	.08
5T	Scott Bailes(FC)	.20	.15	.08
6T	Don Baylor	.15	.11	.06
7T	Steve Bedrosian	.15	.11	.06
8T	Juan Beniquez	.08	.06	.03
9T	Juan Berenguer	.08	.06	.03
10T	Mike Bielecki(FC)	.20	.15	.08
11T	Barry Bonds(FC)	4.00	3.00	1.50
12T	Bobby Bonilla(FC)	3.00	2.25	1.25

		MT	NR MT	EX
13T	Juan Bonilla	.08	.06	.03
14T	Rich Bordi	.08	.06	.03
15T	Steve Boros	.08	.06	.03
16T	Rick Burleson	.10	.08	.04
17T	Bill Campbell	.08	.06	.03
18T	Tom Candiotti	.08	.06	.03
19T	John Cangelosi(FC)	.20	.15	.08
20T	Jose Canseco(FC)	9.00	6.75	3.50
21T	Carmen Castillo	.08	.06	.03
22T	Rick Cerone	.08	.06	.03
23T	John Cerutti(FC)	.20	.15	.08
24T	Will Clark(FC)	9.00	6.75	3.50
25T	Mark Clear	.08	.06	.03
26T	Darnell Coles	.12	.09	.05
27T	Dave Collins	.10	.08	.04
28T	Tim Conroy	.08	.06	.03
29T	Joe Cowley	.08	.06	.03
30T	Joel Davis(FC)	.12	.09	.05
31T	Rob Deer	.15	.11	.06
32T	John Denny	.08	.06	.03
33T	Mike Easler	.10	.08	.04
34T	Mark Eichhorn(FC)	.20	.15	.08
35T	Steve Farr	.08	.06	.03
36T	Scott Fletcher	.15	.11	.06
37T	Terry Forster	.10	.08	.04
38T	Terry Francona	.08	.06	.03
39T	Jim Fregosi	.08	.06	.03
40T	Andres Galarraga(FC)	.35	.25	.14
41T	Ken Griffey	.12	.09	.05
42T	Bill Gullickson	.08	.06	.03
43T	Jose Guzman(FC)	.35	.25	.14
44T	Moose Haas	.08	.06	.03
45T	Billy Hatcher	.20	.15	.08
46T	Mike Heath	.08	.06	.03
47T	Tom Hume	.08	.06	.03
48T	Pete Incaviglia(FC)	.40	.30	.15
49T	Dane Iorg	.08	.06	.03
50T	Bo Jackson(FC)	8.00	6.00	3.25
51T	Wally Joyner(FC)	2.00	1.50	.80
52T	Charlie Kerfeld(FC)	.15	.11	.06
53T	Eric King(FC)	.20	.15	.08
54T	Bob Kipper(FC)	.12	.09	.05
55T	Wayne Krenchicki	.08	.06	.03
56T	John Kruk(FC)	.50	.40	.20
57T	Mike LaCoss	.08	.06	.03
58T	Pete Ladd	.08	.06	.03
59T	Mike Laga	.08	.06	.03
60T	Hal Lanier	.08	.06	.03
61T	Dave LaPoint	.12	.09	.05
62T	Rudy Law	.08	.06	.03
63T	Rick Leach	.08	.06	.03
64T	Tim Leary	.08	.06	.03
65T	Dennis Leonard	.10	.08	.04
66T	Jim Leyland	.08	.06	.03
67T	Steve Lyons	.12	.09	.05
68T	Mickey Mahler	.08	.06	.03
69T	Candy Maldonado	.15	.11	.06
70T	Roger Mason(FC)	.10	.08	.04
71T	Bob McClure	.08	.06	.03
72T	Andy McGaffigan	.08	.06	.03
73T	Gene Michael	.08	.06	.03
74T	Kevin Mitchell(FC)	3.00	2.25	1.25
75T	Omar Moreno	.08	.06	.03
76T	Jerry Mumphrey	.08	.06	.03
77T	Phil Niekro	.40	.30	.15
78T	Randy Niemann	.08	.06	.03
79T	Juan Nieves(FC)	.15	.11	.06
80T	Otis Nixon(FC)	.12	.09	.05
81T	Bob Ojeda	.12	.09	.05
82T	Jose Oquendo	.08	.06	.03
83T	Tom Paciorek	.08	.06	.03
84T	Dave Palmer	.08	.06	.03
85T	Frank Pastore	.08	.06	.03
86T	Lou Piniella	.12	.09	.05
87T	Dan Plesac(FC)	.20	.15	.08
88T	Darrell Porter	.10	.08	.04
89T	Rey Quinones(FC)	.20	.15	.08
90T	Gary Redus	.10	.08	.04
91T	Bip Roberts	.60	.45	.25
92T	Billy Jo Robidoux(FC)	.15	.11	.06
93T	Jeff Robinson	.12	.09	.05
94T	Gary Roenicke	.08	.06	.03
95T	Ed Romero	.08	.06	.03
96T	Argenis Salazar	.08	.06	.03
97T	Joe Sambito	.08	.06	.03
98T	Billy Sample	.08	.06	.03
99T	Dave Schmidt	.08	.06	.03
100T	Ken Schrom	.08	.06	.03
101T	Tom Seaver	.60	.45	.25
102T	Ted Simmons	.20	.15	.08
103T	Sammy Stewart	.08	.06	.03
104T	Kurt Stillwell(FC)	.20	.15	.08
105T	Franklin Stubbs	.12	.09	.05
106T	Dale Sveum(FC)	.20	.15	.08
107T	Chuck Tanner	.08	.06	.03
108T	Danny Tartabull(FC)	1.25	.90	.50
109T	Tim Teufel	.08	.06	.03
110T	Bob Tewksbury(FC)	.15	.11	.06
111T	Andres Thomas(FC)	.12	.09	.05
112T	Milt Thompson	.12	.09	.05
113T	Robby Thompson(FC)	.50	.40	.20
114T	Jay Tibbs	.08	.06	.03
115T	Wayne Tolleson	.08	.06	.03
116T	Alex Trevino	.08	.06	.03
117T	Manny Trillo	.10	.08	.04
118T	Ed Vande Berg	.08	.06	.03
119T	Ozzie Virgil	.08	.06	.03
120T	Bob Walk	.08	.06	.03
121T	Gene Walter(FC)	.12	.09	.05
122T	Claudell Washington	.12	.09	.05
123T	Bill Wegman(FC)	.20	.15	.08
124T	Dick Williams	.08	.06	.03
125T	Mitch Williams(FC)	.50	.40	.20
126T	Bobby Witt(FC)	.50	.40	.20
127T	Todd Worrell(FC)	.60	.45	.25
128T	George Wright	.08	.06	.03
129T	Ricky Wright	.08	.06	.03
130T	Steve Yeager	.08	.06	.03
131T	Paul Zuvella	.08	.06	.03
132T	Checklist	.08	.06	.03

1986 Topps 3-D

This set is a second effort in the production of over-size (4-1/2" by 6") plastic cards on which the player figure is embossed. Cards were sold one per pack for approximately 50¢. The 30 players in the set are among the game's top stars. The embossed color photo is bordered at bottom by a strip of contrasting color on which the player name appears. At the top, a row of white baseballs each contain a letter of the team nickname. Backs have no printing, and contain two self-adhesive strips with which the cards can be attached to a hard surface.

		MT	NR MT	EX
Complete Set:		10.00	7.50	4.00
Common Player:		.20	.15	.08
1	Bert Blyleven	.30	.25	.12
2	Gary Carter	.60	.45	.25
3	Wade Boggs	1.00	.70	.40
4	Dwight Gooden	1.00	.70	.40
5	George Brett	.80	.60	.30
6	Rich Gossage	.30	.25	.12
7	Darrell Evans	.20	.15	.08
8	Pedro Guerrero	.30	.25	.12
9	Ron Guidry	.30	.25	.12
10	Keith Hernandez	.50	.40	.20
11	Rickey Henderson	.70	.50	.30
12	Orel Hershiser	.50	.40	.20
13	Reggie Jackson	.60	.45	.25
14	Willie McGee	.30	.25	.12
15	Don Mattingly	1.75	1.25	.70
16	Dale Murphy	.40	.30	.15
17	Jack Morris	.30	.25	.12
18	Dave Parker	.30	.25	.12
19	Eddie Murray	.60	.45	.25

		MT	NR MT	EX
20	Jeff Reardon	.30	.25	.12
21	Dan Quisenberry	.20	.15	.08
22	Pete Rose	1.00	.70	.40
23	Jim Rice	.50	.40	.20
24	Mike Schmidt	.80	.60	.30
25	Bret Saberhagen	.30	.25	.12
26	Darryl Strawberry	.80	.60	.30
27	Dave Stieb	.20	.15	.08
28	John Tudor	.20	.15	.08
29	Dave Winfield	.50	.40	.20
30	Fernando Valenzuela	.40	.30	.15

1987 Topps

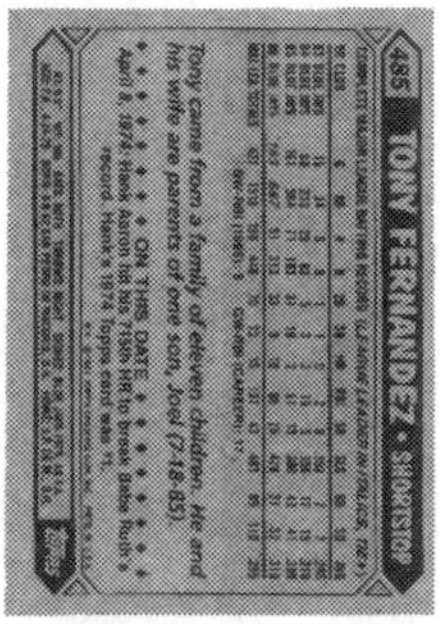

Many collectors feel that Topps' 1987 set of 792 card is a future classic. The 2-1/2" by 3-1/2" design is closely akin to the 1962 set in that the player photo is set against a woodgrain border. Instead of a rolling corner, as in 1962, the player photos in '87 feature a couple of clipped corners at top left and bottom right, where the team logo and player name appear. The player's position is not given on the front of the card. For the first time in several years, the trophy which designates members of Topps All-Star Rookie Team returned to the card design. As in the previous three years, Topps issued a glossy-finish "Tiffany" edition of their 792-card set. However, it was speculated that as many as 50,000 sets were produced as opposed to the 5,000 sets printed in 1985 and 1986. Because of the large print run, the values for the Tiffany cards are only 3-4 times higher than the same card in the regular issue.

		MT	NR MT	EX
	Complete Set:	40.00	30.00	15.00
	Common Player:	.05	.04	.02
1	Record Breaker (Roger Clemens)	.35	.25	.14
2	Record Breaker (Jim Deshaies)	.07	.05	.03
3	Record Breaker (Dwight Evans)	.07	.05	.03
4	Record Breaker (Dave Lopes)	.07	.05	.03
5	Record Breaker (Dave Righetti)	.07	.05	.03
6	Record Breaker (Ruben Sierra)	.25	.20	.10
7	Record Breaker (Todd Worrell)	.07	.05	.03
8	Terry Pendleton	.07	.05	.03
9	Jay Tibbs	.05	.04	.02
10	Cecil Cooper	.10	.08	.04
11	Indians Leaders (Jack Aker, Chris Bando, Phil Niekro)	.07	.05	.03
12	*Jeff Sellers*(FC)	.15	.11	.06
13	Nick Esasky	.07	.05	.03
14	Dave Stewart	.12	.09	.05
15	Claudell Washington	.07	.05	.03
16	Pat Clements	.05	.04	.02
17	Pete O'Brien	.10	.08	.04
18	Dick Howser	.05	.04	.02
19	Matt Young	.05	.04	.02
20	Gary Carter	.20	.15	.08
21	Mark Davis	.05	.04	.02
22	Doug DeCinces	.07	.05	.03
23	Lee Smith	.10	.08	.04
24	Tony Walker	.05	.04	.02
25	Bert Blyleven	.12	.09	.05
26	Greg Brock	.07	.05	.03
27	Joe Cowley	.05	.04	.02
28	Rick Dempsey	.07	.05	.03
29	Jimmy Key	.10	.08	.04
30	Tim Raines	.25	.20	.10
31	Braves Leaders (Glenn Hubbard, Rafael Ramirez)	.07	.05	.03
32	Tim Leary	.07	.05	.03
33	Andy Van Slyke	.12	.09	.05
34	Jose Rijo	.07	.05	.03
35	Sid Bream	.07	.05	.03
36	*Eric King*	.25	.20	.10
37	Marvell Wynne	.05	.04	.02
38	Dennis Leonard	.07	.05	.03
39	Marty Barrett	.07	.05	.03
40	Dave Righetti	.12	.09	.05
41	Bo Diaz	.07	.05	.03
42	Gary Redus	.05	.04	.02
43	Gene Michael	.05	.04	.02
44	Greg Harris	.05	.04	.02
45	Jim Presley	.10	.08	.04
46	Danny Gladden	.05	.04	.02
47	Dennis Powell	.07	.05	.03
48	Wally Backman	.07	.05	.03
49	Terry Harper	.05	.04	.02
50	Dave Smith	.07	.05	.03
51	Mel Hall	.07	.05	.03
52	Keith Atherton	.05	.04	.02
53	Ruppert Jones	.05	.04	.02
54	Bill Dawley	.05	.04	.02
55	Tim Wallach	.10	.08	.04
56	Brewers Leaders (Jamie Cocanower, Paul Molitor, Charlie Moore, Herm Starrette)	.07	.05	.03
57	*Scott Nielsen*(FC)	.10	.08	.04
58	Thad Bosley	.05	.04	.02
59	Ken Dayley	.05	.04	.02
60	Tony Pena	.07	.05	.03
61	*Bobby Thigpen*(FC)	.70	.50	.30
62	Bobby Meacham	.05	.04	.02
63	Fred Toliver(FC)	.07	.05	.03
64	Harry Spilman	.05	.04	.02
65	Tom Browning	.10	.08	.04
66	Marc Sullivan	.05	.04	.02
67	Bill Swift	.05	.04	.02
68	Tony LaRussa	.07	.05	.03
69	Lonnie Smith	.07	.05	.03
70	Charlie Hough	.07	.05	.03
71	*Mike Aldrete*(FC)	.15	.11	.06
72	Walt Terrell	.07	.05	.03
73	Dave Anderson	.05	.04	.02
74	Dan Pasqua	.10	.08	.04
75	Ron Darling	.12	.09	.05
76	Rafael Ramirez	.05	.04	.02
77	Bryan Oelkers	.05	.04	.02
78	Tom Foley	.05	.04	.02
79	Juan Nieves	.10	.08	.04
80	*Wally Joyner*	1.00	.70	.40
81	Padres Leaders (Andy Hawkins, Terry Kennedy)	.07	.05	.03
82	*Rob Murphy*(FC)	.15	.11	.06
83	Mike Davis	.07	.05	.03
84	Steve Lake	.05	.04	.02
85	Kevin Bass	.07	.05	.03
86	Nate Snell	.05	.04	.02
87	Mark Salas	.05	.04	.02
88	Ed Wojna	.05	.04	.02
89	Ozzie Guillen	.25	.20	.10
90	Dave Stieb	.10	.08	.04
91	Harold Reynolds	.10	.08	.04
92a	Urbano Lugo (no trademark on front)	.30	.25	.12
92b	Urbano Lugo (trademark on front)	.07	.05	.03
93	Jim Leyland	.05	.04	.02
94	Calvin Schiraldi	.05	.04	.02
95	Oddibe McDowell	.07	.05	.03
96	Frank Williams	.05	.04	.02
97	Glenn Wilson	.07	.05	.03
98	Bill Scherrer	.05	.04	.02
99	Darryl Motley	.05	.04	.02
100	Steve Garvey	.20	.15	.08
101	*Carl Willis*(FC)	.10	.08	.04
102	Paul Zuvella	.05	.04	.02
103	Rick Aguilera	.06	.05	.02
104	Billy Sample	.05	.04	.02
105	Floyd Youmans	.07	.05	.03
106	Blue Jays Leaders (George Bell, Willie Upshaw)	.07	.05	.03
107	John Butcher	.05	.04	.02
108	Jim Gantner (photo reversed)	.07	.05	.03
109	R.J. Reynolds	.05	.04	.02
110	John Tudor	.10	.08	.04
111	Alfredo Griffin	.07	.05	.03
112	Alan Ashby	.05	.04	.02

		MT	NR MT	EX
113	Neil Allen	.05	.04	.02
114	Billy Beane	.05	.04	.02
115	Donnie Moore	.05	.04	.02
116	Bill Russell	.07	.05	.03
117	Jim Beattie	.05	.04	.02
118	Bobby Valentine	.05	.04	.02
119	Ron Robinson	.05	.04	.02
120	Eddie Murray	.30	.25	.12
121	*Kevin Romine*(FC)	.12	.09	.05
122	Jim Clancy	.07	.05	.03
123	*John Kruk*	.40	.30	.15
124	Ray Fontenot	.05	.04	.02
125	Bob Brenly	.05	.04	.02
126	*Mike Loynd*(FC)	.15	.11	.06
127	Vance Law	.07	.05	.03
128	Checklist 1-132	.05	.04	.02
129	Rick Cerone	.05	.04	.02
130	Dwight Gooden	.60	.45	.25
131	Pirates Leaders (Sid Bream, Tony Pena)	.07	.05	.03
132	*Paul Assenmacher*	.15	.11	.06
133	Jose Oquendo	.05	.04	.02
134	*Rich Yett*(FC)	.12	.09	.05
135	Mike Easler	.07	.05	.03
136	Ron Romanick	.05	.04	.02
137	Jerry Willard	.05	.04	.02
138	Roy Lee Jackson	.05	.04	.02
139	*Devon White*(FC)	.60	.45	.25
140	Bret Saberhagen	.15	.11	.06
141	Herm Winningham	.05	.04	.02
142	Rick Sutcliffe	.10	.08	.04
143	Steve Boros	.05	.04	.02
144	Mike Scioscia	.07	.05	.03
145	Charlie Kerfeld	.07	.05	.03
146	*Tracy Jones*(FC)	.25	.20	.10
147	Randy Niemann	.05	.04	.02
148	Dave Collins	.07	.05	.03
149	Ray Searage	.05	.04	.02
150	Wade Boggs	.70	.50	.30
151	Mike LaCoss	.05	.04	.02
152	Toby Harrah	.07	.05	.03
153	*Duane Ward*(FC)	.12	.09	.05
154	Tom O'Malley	.05	.04	.02
155	Eddie Whitson	.05	.04	.02
156	Mariners Leaders (Bob Kearney, Phil Regan, Matt Young)	.07	.05	.03
157	Danny Darwin	.05	.04	.02
158	Tim Teufel	.05	.04	.02
159	Ed Olwine	.05	.04	.02
160	Julio Franco	.10	.08	.04
161	Steve Ontiveros	.05	.04	.02
162	*Mike LaValliere*	.25	.20	.10
163	Kevin Gross	.07	.05	.03
164	Sammy Khalifa	.05	.04	.02
165	Jeff Reardon	.10	.08	.04
166	Bob Boone	.07	.05	.03
167	*Jim Deshaies*	.25	.20	.10
168	Lou Piniella	.07	.05	.03
169	Ron Washington	.05	.04	.02
170	Future Stars *(Bo Jackson)*	3.50	2.75	1.50
171	*Chuck Cary*(FC)	.10	.08	.04
172	Ron Oester	.05	.04	.02
173	Alex Trevino	.05	.04	.02
174	Henry Cotto	.05	.04	.02
175	Bob Stanley	.05	.04	.02
176	Steve Buechele	.07	.05	.03
177	Keith Moreland	.07	.05	.03
178	Cecil Fielder	1.75	1.25	.70
179	Bill Wegman	.10	.08	.04
180	Chris Brown	.07	.05	.03
181	Cardinals Leaders (Mike LaValliere, Ozzie Smith, Ray Soff)	.07	.05	.03
182	Lee Lacy	.05	.04	.02
183	Andy Hawkins	.05	.04	.02
184	*Bobby Bonilla*	2.00	1.50	.80
185	Roger McDowell	.10	.08	.04
186	Bruce Benedict	.05	.04	.02
187	Mark Huismann	.05	.04	.02
188	Tony Phillips	.05	.04	.02
189	Joe Hesketh	.05	.04	.02
190	Jim Sundberg	.07	.05	.03
191	Charles Hudson	.05	.04	.02
192	Cory Snyder(FC)	.40	.30	.15
193	Roger Craig	.07	.05	.03
194	Kirk McCaskill	.07	.05	.03
195	Mike Pagliarulo	.10	.08	.04
196	Randy O'Neal	.05	.04	.02
197	Mark Bailey	.05	.04	.02
198	Lee Mazzilli	.07	.05	.03
199	Mariano Duncan	.05	.04	.02
200	Pete Rose	.60	.45	.25
201	*John Cangelosi*	.12	.09	.05
202	Ricky Wright	.05	.04	.02
203	*Mike Kingery*(FC)	.15	.11	.06
204	Sammy Stewart	.05	.04	.02
205	Graig Nettles	.10	.08	.04
206	Twins Leaders (Tim Laudner, Frank Viola)	.07	.05	.03
207	George Frazier	.05	.04	.02
208	John Shelby	.05	.04	.02
209	Rick Schu	.05	.04	.02
210	Lloyd Moseby	.07	.05	.03
211	John Morris(FC)	.07	.05	.03
212	Mike Fitzgerald	.05	.04	.02
213	*Randy Myers*(FC)	.30	.25	.12
214	Omar Moreno	.05	.04	.02
215	Mark Langston	.12	.09	.05
216	Future Stars *(B.J. Surhoff)*(FC)	.30	.25	.12
217	Chris Codiroli	.05	.04	.02
218	Sparky Anderson	.07	.05	.03
219	Cecilio Guante	.05	.04	.02
220	Joe Carter	.12	.09	.05
221	Vern Ruhle	.05	.04	.02
222	Denny Walling	.05	.04	.02
223	Charlie Leibrandt	.07	.05	.03
224	Wayne Tolleson	.05	.04	.02
225	Mike Smithson	.05	.04	.02
226	Max Venable	.05	.04	.02
227	*Jamie Moyer*(FC)	.20	.15	.08
228	Curt Wilkerson	.05	.04	.02
229	*Mike Birkbeck*(FC)	.15	.11	.06
230	Don Baylor	.10	.08	.04
231	Giants Leaders (Bob Brenly, Mike Krukow)	.07	.05	.03
232	*Reggie Williams*	.10	.08	.04
233	*Russ Morman*(FC)	.10	.08	.04
234	Pat Sheridan	.05	.04	.02
235	Alvin Davis	.10	.08	.04
236	Tommy John	.15	.11	.06
237	Jim Morrison	.05	.04	.02
238	Bill Krueger	.05	.04	.02
239	Juan Espino	.05	.04	.02
240	Steve Balboni	.07	.05	.03
241	Danny Heep	.05	.04	.02
242	Rick Mahler	.05	.04	.02
243	Whitey Herzog	.07	.05	.03
244	Dickie Noles	.05	.04	.02
245	Willie Upshaw	.07	.05	.03
246	Jim Dwyer	.05	.04	.02
247	Jeff Reed(FC)	.07	.05	.03
248	Gene Walter	.07	.05	.03
249	Jim Pankovits	.05	.04	.02
250	Teddy Higuera	.15	.11	.06
251	Rob Wilfong	.05	.04	.02
252	Denny Martinez	.05	.04	.02
253	Eddie Milner	.05	.04	.02
254	*Bob Tewksbury*	.12	.09	.05
255	Juan Samuel	.10	.08	.04
256	Royals Leaders (George Brett, Frank White)	.10	.08	.04
257	Bob Forsch	.07	.05	.03
258	Steve Yeager	.05	.04	.02
259	*Mike Greenwell*(FC)	2.00	1.50	.80
260	Vida Blue	.07	.05	.03
261	*Ruben Sierra*(FC)	2.75	2.00	1.00
262	Jim Winn	.05	.04	.02
263	Stan Javier(FC)	.07	.05	.03
264	Checklist 133-264	.05	.04	.02
265	Darrell Evans	.10	.08	.04
266	*Jeff Hamilton*(FC)	.25	.20	.10
267	Howard Johnson	.10	.08	.04
268	Pat Corrales	.05	.04	.02
269	Cliff Speck	.05	.04	.02
270	Jody Davis	.07	.05	.03
271	Mike Brown	.05	.04	.02
272	Andres Galarraga	.35	.25	.14
273	Gene Nelson	.05	.04	.02
274	*Jeff Hearron*(FC)	.05	.04	.02
275	LaMarr Hoyt	.05	.04	.02
276	Jackie Gutierrez	.05	.04	.02
277	Juan Agosto	.05	.04	.02
278	Gary Pettis	.05	.04	.02
279	*Dan Plesac*	.30	.25	.12
280	Jeffrey Leonard	.07	.05	.03
281	Reds Leaders (Bo Diaz, Bill Gullickson, Pete Rose)	.10	.08	.04
282	Jeff Calhoun	.05	.04	.02
283	*Doug Drabek*(FC)	.80	.60	.30
284	John Moses	.05	.04	.02
285	Dennis Boyd	.07	.05	.03
286	Mike Woodard(FC)	.07	.05	.03
287	Dave Von Ohlen	.05	.04	.02

		MT	NR MT	EX
288	Tito Landrum	.05	.04	.02
289	Bob Kipper	.07	.05	.03
290	Leon Durham	.07	.05	.03
291	*Mitch Williams*(FC)	.40	.30	.15
292	Franklin Stubbs	.07	.05	.03
293	Bob Rodgers	.05	.04	.02
294	Steve Jeltz	.05	.04	.02
295	Len Dykstra	.12	.09	.05
296	*Andres Thomas*	.15	.11	.06
297	Don Schulze	.05	.04	.02
298	Larry Herndon	.05	.04	.02
299	Joel Davis	.07	.05	.03
300	Reggie Jackson	.30	.25	.12
301	*Luis Aquino*(FC)	.10	.08	.04
302	Bill Schroeder	.05	.04	.02
303	Juan Berenguer	.05	.04	.02
304	Phil Garner	.05	.04	.02
305	John Franco	.10	.08	.04
306	Red Sox Leaders (Rich Gedman, John McNamara, Tom Seaver)	.07	.05	.03
307	*Lee Guetterman*(FC)	.15	.11	.06
308	Don Slaught	.05	.04	.02
309	Mike Young	.05	.04	.02
310	Frank Viola	.15	.11	.06
311	Turn Back The Clock (Rickey Henderson)	.10	.08	.04
312	Turn Back The Clock (Reggie Jackson)	.10	.08	.04
313	Turn Back The Clock (Roberto Clemente)	.15	.11	.06
314	Turn Back The Clock (Carl Yastrzemski)	.10	.08	.04
315	Turn Back The Clock (Maury Wills)	.07	.05	.03
316	Brian Fisher	.07	.05	.03
317	Clint Hurdle	.05	.04	.02
318	Jim Fregosi	.05	.04	.02
319	*Greg Swindell*(FC)	.60	.45	.25
320	*Barry Bonds*	3.00	2.25	1.25
321	Mike Laga	.05	.04	.02
322	Chris Bando	.05	.04	.02
323	*Al Newman*	.07	.05	.03
324	Dave Palmer	.05	.04	.02
325	Garry Templeton	.07	.05	.03
326	Mark Gubicza	.10	.08	.04
327	*Dale Sveum*	.20	.15	.08
328	Bob Welch	.10	.08	.04
329	Ron Roenicke	.05	.04	.02
330	Mike Scott	.12	.09	.05
331	Mets Leaders (Gary Carter, Keith Hernandez, Dave Johnson, Darryl Strawberry)	.10	.08	.04
332	Joe Price	.05	.04	.02
333	Ken Phelps	.07	.05	.03
334	*Ed Correa*	.15	.11	.06
335	Candy Maldonado	.07	.05	.03
336	*Allan Anderson*(FC)	.25	.20	.10
337	Darrell Miller	.05	.04	.02
338	Tim Conroy	.05	.04	.02
339	Donnie Hill	.05	.04	.02
340	Roger Clemens	1.00	.70	.40
341	Mike Brown	.05	.04	.02
342	Bob James	.05	.04	.02
343	Hal Lanier	.05	.04	.02
344a	Joe Niekro (copyright outside yellow on back)	.30	.25	.12
344b	Joe Niekro (copyright inside yellow on back)	.07	.05	.03
345	Andre Dawson	.20	.15	.08
346	Shawon Dunston	.07	.05	.03
347	Mickey Brantley(FC)	.07	.05	.03
348	Carmelo Martinez	.07	.05	.03
349	Storm Davis	.10	.08	.04
350	Keith Hernandez	.20	.15	.08
351	Gene Garber	.05	.04	.02
352	Mike Felder(FC)	.07	.05	.03
353	Ernie Camacho	.05	.04	.02
354	Jamie Quirk	.05	.04	.02
355	Don Carman	.07	.05	.03
356	White Sox Leaders (Ed Brinkman, Julio Cruz)	.07	.05	.03
357	*Steve Fireovid*(FC)	.07	.05	.03
358	Sal Butera	.05	.04	.02
359	Doug Corbett	.05	.04	.02
360	Pedro Guerrero	.15	.11	.06
361	Mark Thurmond	.05	.04	.02
362	*Luis Quinones*(FC)	.12	.09	.05
363	Jose Guzman	.12	.09	.05
364	Randy Bush	.05	.04	.02
365	Rick Rhoden	.07	.05	.03
366	*Mark McGwire*	2.00	1.50	.80
367	Jeff Lahti	.05	.04	.02
368	John McNamara	.05	.04	.02
369	Brian Dayett	.05	.04	.02
370	Fred Lynn	.15	.11	.06
371	*Mark Eichhorn*	.15	.11	.06
372	Jerry Mumphrey	.05	.04	.02
373	Jeff Dedmon	.05	.04	.02
374	Glenn Hoffman	.05	.04	.02
375	Ron Guidry	.12	.09	.05
376	Scott Bradley	.05	.04	.02
377	John Henry Johnson	.05	.04	.02
378	Rafael Santana	.05	.04	.02
379	John Russell	.05	.04	.02
380	Rich Gossage	.15	.11	.06
381	Expos Leaders (Mike Fitzgerald, Bob Rodgers)	.07	.05	.03
382	Rudy Law	.05	.04	.02
383	Ron Davis	.05	.04	.02
384	Johnny Grubb	.05	.04	.02
385	Orel Hershiser	.30	.25	.12
386	Dickie Thon	.07	.05	.03
387	*T.R. Bryden*(FC)	.10	.08	.04
388	Geno Petralli	.05	.04	.02
389	Jeff Robinson	.07	.05	.03
390	Gary Matthews	.07	.05	.03
391	Jay Howell	.07	.05	.03
392	Checklist 265-396	.05	.04	.02
393	Pete Rose	.40	.30	.15
394	Mike Bielecki	.07	.05	.03
395	Damaso Garcia	.05	.04	.02
396	Tim Lollar	.05	.04	.02
397	Greg Walker	.07	.05	.03
398	Brad Havens	.05	.04	.02
399	Curt Ford(FC)	.07	.05	.03
400	George Brett	.35	.25	.14
401	Billy Jo Robidoux	.07	.05	.03
402	Mike Trujillo	.05	.04	.02
403	Jerry Royster	.05	.04	.02
404	Doug Sisk	.05	.04	.02
405	Brook Jacoby	.10	.08	.04
406	Yankees Leaders (Rickey Henderson, Don Mattingly)	.25	.20	.10
407	Jim Acker	.05	.04	.02
408	John Mizerock	.05	.04	.02
409	Milt Thompson	.07	.05	.03
410	Fernando Valenzuela	.25	.20	.10
411	Darnell Coles	.07	.05	.03
412	Eric Davis	.90	.70	.35
413	Moose Haas	.05	.04	.02
414	Joe Orsulak	.05	.04	.02
415	*Bobby Witt*	.50	.40	.20
416	Tom Nieto	.05	.04	.02
417	Pat Perry(FC)	.07	.05	.03
418	Dick Williams	.05	.04	.02
419	*Mark Portugal*(FC)	.10	.08	.04
420	*Will Clark*	3.50	2.75	1.50
421	Jose DeLeon	.07	.05	.03
422	Jack Howell	.07	.05	.03
423	Jaime Cocanower	.05	.04	.02
424	Chris Speier	.05	.04	.02
425	Tom Seaver	.30	.25	.12
426	Floyd Rayford	.05	.04	.02
427	Ed Nunez	.05	.04	.02
428	Bruce Bochy	.05	.04	.02
429	Future Stars *(Tim Pyznarski)*(FC)	.10	.08	.04
430	Mike Schmidt	.40	.30	.15
431	Dodgers Leaders (Tom Niedenfuer, Ron Perranoski, Alex Trevino)	.07	.05	.03
432	Jim Slaton	.05	.04	.02
433	*Ed Hearn*(FC)	.10	.08	.04
434	Mike Fischlin	.05	.04	.02
435	Bruce Sutter	.12	.09	.05
436	*Andy Allanson*	.15	.11	.06
437	Ted Power	.05	.04	.02
438	*Kelly Downs*(FC)	.30	.25	.12
439	Karl Best	.05	.04	.02
440	Willie McGee	.10	.08	.04
441	*Dave Leiper*(FC)	.10	.08	.04
442	Mitch Webster	.07	.05	.03
443	John Felske	.05	.04	.02
444	Jeff Russell	.05	.04	.02
445	Dave Lopes	.07	.05	.03
446	*Chuck Finley*(FC)	1.00	.70	.40
447	Bill Almon	.05	.04	.02
448	*Chris Bosio*(FC)	.25	.20	.10
449	Future Stars *(Pat Dodson)*(FC)	.10	.08	.04
450	Kirby Puckett	.30	.25	.12
451	Joe Sambito	.05	.04	.02
452	Dave Henderson	.10	.08	.04
453	*Scott Terry*(FC)	.12	.09	.05
454	Luis Salazar	.05	.04	.02
455	Mike Boddicker	.07	.05	.03

		MT	NR MT	EX
456	A's Leaders (Carney Lansford, Tony LaRussa, Mickey Tettleton, Dave Von Ohlen)	.07	.05	.03
457	Len Matuszek	.05	.04	.02
458	Kelly Gruber(FC)	1.25	.90	.50
459	Dennis Eckersley	.10	.08	.04
460	Darryl Strawberry	.35	.25	.14
461	Craig McMurtry	.05	.04	.02
462	Scott Fletcher	.07	.05	.03
463	Tom Candiotti	.05	.04	.02
464	Butch Wynegar	.05	.04	.02
465	Todd Worrell	.30	.25	.12
466	Kal Daniels(FC)	.80	.60	.30
467	Randy St. Claire	.05	.04	.02
468	George Bamberger	.05	.04	.02
469	*Mike Diaz*(FC)	.15	.11	.06
470	Dave Dravecky	.07	.05	.03
471	Ronn Reynolds	.05	.04	.02
472	Bill Doran	.07	.05	.03
473	Steve Farr	.05	.04	.02
474	Jerry Narron	.05	.04	.02
475	Scott Garrelts	.05	.04	.02
476	Danny Tartabull	.90	.70	.35
477	Ken Howell	.05	.04	.02
478	Tim Laudner	.05	.04	.02
479	*Bob Sebra*(FC)	.10	.08	.04
480	Jim Rice	.25	.20	.10
481	Phillies Leaders (Von Hayes, Juan Samuel, Glenn Wilson)	.07	.05	.03
482	Daryl Boston	.05	.04	.02
483	Dwight Lowry	.05	.04	.02
484	Jim Traber(FC)	.15	.11	.06
485	Tony Fernandez	.10	.08	.04
486	Otis Nixon	.05	.04	.02
487	Dave Gumpert	.05	.04	.02
488	Ray Knight	.07	.05	.03
489	Bill Gullickson	.05	.04	.02
490	Dale Murphy	.40	.30	.15
491	*Ron Karkovice*(FC)	.10	.08	.04
492	Mike Heath	.05	.04	.02
493	Tom Lasorda	.07	.05	.03
494	*Barry Jones*(FC)	.12	.09	.05
495	Gorman Thomas	.10	.08	.04
496	Bruce Bochte	.05	.04	.02
497	*Dale Mohorcic*(FC)	.15	.11	.06
498	Bob Kearney	.05	.04	.02
499	*Bruce Ruffin*(FC)	.20	.15	.08
500	Don Mattingly	.80	.60	.30
501	Craig Lefferts	.05	.04	.02
502	Dick Schofield	.05	.04	.02
503	Larry Andersen	.05	.04	.02
504	Mickey Hatcher	.05	.04	.02
505	Bryn Smith	.05	.04	.02
506	Orioles Leaders (Rich Bordi, Rick Dempsey, Earl Weaver)	.07	.05	.03
507	Dave Stapleton	.05	.04	.02
508	*Scott Bankhead*	.25	.20	.10
509	Enos Cabell	.05	.04	.02
510	Tom Henke	.07	.05	.03
511	Steve Lyons	.05	.04	.02
512	*Dave Magadan*(FC)	.80	.60	.30
513	Carmen Castillo	.05	.04	.02
514	Orlando Mercado	.05	.04	.02
515	Willie Hernandez	.07	.05	.03
516	Ted Simmons	.10	.08	.04
517	Mario Soto	.07	.05	.03
518	Gene Mauch	.07	.05	.03
519	Curt Young	.07	.05	.03
520	Jack Clark	.15	.11	.06
521	Rick Reuschel	.10	.08	.04
522	Checklist 397-528	.05	.04	.02
523	Earnie Riles	.05	.04	.02
524	Bob Shirley	.05	.04	.02
525	Phil Bradley	.10	.08	.04
526	Roger Mason	.05	.04	.02
527	Jim Wohlford	.05	.04	.02
528	Ken Dixon	.05	.04	.02
529	*Alvaro Espinoza*(FC)	.07	.05	.03
530	Tony Gwynn	.35	.25	.14
531	Astros Leaders (Yogi Berra, Hal Lanier, Denis Menke, Gene Tenace)	.07	.05	.03
532	Jeff Stone	.05	.04	.02
533	Argenis Salazar	.05	.04	.02
534	Scott Sanderson	.05	.04	.02
535	Tony Armas	.07	.05	.03
536	*Terry Mulholland*(FC)	.10	.08	.04
537	Rance Mulliniks	.05	.04	.02
538	Tom Niedenfuer	.07	.05	.03
539	Reid Nichols	.05	.04	.02
540	Terry Kennedy	.07	.05	.03
541	*Rafael Belliard*(FC)	.10	.08	.04

		MT	NR MT	EX
542	Ricky Horton	.07	.05	.03
543	Dave Johnson	.07	.05	.03
544	Zane Smith	.07	.05	.03
545	Buddy Bell	.07	.05	.03
546	Mike Morgan	.05	.04	.02
547	Rob Deer	.10	.08	.04
548	*Bill Mooneyham*(FC)	.10	.08	.04
549	Bob Melvin	.05	.04	.02
550	*Pete Incaviglia*	.40	.30	.15
551	Frank Wills	.05	.04	.02
552	Larry Sheets	.07	.05	.03
553	*Mike Maddux*(FC)	.15	.11	.06
554	Buddy Biancalana	.05	.04	.02
555	Dennis Rasmussen	.10	.08	.04
556	Angels Leaders (Bob Boone, Marcel Lachemann, Mike Witt)	.07	.05	.03
557	*John Cerutti*	.15	.11	.06
558	Greg Gagne	.05	.04	.02
559	Lance McCullers	.07	.05	.03
560	Glenn Davis	.25	.20	.10
561	*Rey Quinones*	.15	.11	.06
562	*Bryan Clutterbuck*(FC)	.10	.08	.04
563	John Stefero	.05	.04	.02
564	Larry McWilliams	.05	.04	.02
565	Dusty Baker	.07	.05	.03
566	Tim Hulett	.05	.04	.02
567	*Greg Mathews*(FC)	.20	.15	.08
568	Earl Weaver	.07	.05	.03
569	Wade Rowdon(FC)	.07	.05	.03
570	Sid Fernandez	.10	.08	.04
571	Ozzie Virgil	.05	.04	.02
572	Pete Ladd	.05	.04	.02
573	Hal McRae	.07	.05	.03
574	Manny Lee	.05	.04	.02
575	Pat Tabler	.07	.05	.03
576	Frank Pastore	.05	.04	.02
577	Dann Bilardello	.05	.04	.02
578	Billy Hatcher	.07	.05	.03
579	Rick Burleson	.07	.05	.03
580	Mike Krukow	.07	.05	.03
581	Cubs Leaders (Ron Cey, Steve Trout)	.07	.05	.03
582	Bruce Berenyi	.05	.04	.02
583	Junior Ortiz	.05	.04	.02
584	Ron Kittle	.07	.05	.03
585	*Scott Bailes*	.15	.11	.06
586	Ben Oglivie	.07	.05	.03
587	Eric Plunk(FC)	.10	.08	.04
588	Wallace Johnson	.05	.04	.02
589	Steve Crawford	.05	.04	.02
590	Vince Coleman	.30	.25	.12
591	Spike Owen	.05	.04	.02
592	Chris Welsh	.05	.04	.02
593	Chuck Tanner	.05	.04	.02
594	Rick Anderson	.05	.04	.02
595	Keith Hernandez AS	.12	.09	.05
596	Steve Sax AS	.07	.05	.03
597	Mike Schmidt AS	.20	.15	.08
598	Ozzie Smith AS	.07	.05	.03
599	Tony Gwynn AS	.20	.15	.08
600	Dave Parker AS	.10	.08	.04
601	Darryl Strawberry AS	.20	.15	.08
602	Gary Carter AS	.15	.11	.06
603a	Dwight Gooden AS (no trademark on front)	.80	.60	.30
603b	Dwight Gooden AS (trademark on front)	.30	.25	.12
604	Fernando Valenzuela AS	.12	.09	.05
605	Todd Worrell AS	.10	.08	.04
606a	Don Mattingly AS (no trademark on front)	1.25	.90	.50
606b	Don Mattingly AS (trademark on front)	.70	.50	.30
607	Tony Bernazard AS	.05	.04	.02
608	Wade Boggs AS	.40	.30	.15
609	Cal Ripken AS	.20	.15	.08
610	Jim Rice AS	.15	.11	.06
611	Kirby Puckett AS	.15	.11	.06
612	George Bell AS	.12	.09	.05
613	Lance Parrish AS	.10	.08	.04
614	Roger Clemens AS	.30	.25	.12
615	Teddy Higuera AS	.10	.08	.04
616	Dave Righetti AS	.10	.08	.04
617	Al Nipper	.05	.04	.02
618	Tom Kelly	.05	.04	.02
619	Jerry Reed	.05	.04	.02
620	Jose Canseco	4.00	3.00	1.50
621	Danny Cox	.07	.05	.03
622	*Glenn Braggs*(FC)	.30	.25	.12
623	*Kurt Stillwell*(FC)	.30	.25	.12
624	Tim Burke	.05	.04	.02

		MT	NR MT	EX
625	Mookie Wilson	.07	.05	.03
626	Joel Skinner	.05	.04	.02
627	Ken Oberkfell	.05	.04	.02
628	Bob Walk	.05	.04	.02
629	Larry Parrish	.07	.05	.03
630	John Candelaria	.07	.05	.03
631	Tigers Leaders (Sparky Anderson, Mike Heath, Willie Hernandez)	.07	.05	.03
632	Rob Woodward(FC)	.07	.05	.03
633	Jose Uribe	.07	.05	.03
634	Future Stars (*Rafael Palmeiro*)(FC)	1.75	1.25	.70
635	Ken Schrom	.05	.04	.02
636	Darren Daulton	.05	.04	.02
637	*Bip Roberts*	.40	.30	.15
638	Rich Bordi	.05	.04	.02
639	Gerald Perry	.10	.08	.04
640	Mark Clear	.05	.04	.02
641	Domingo Ramos	.05	.04	.02
642	Al Pulido	.05	.04	.02
643	Ron Shepherd	.05	.04	.02
644	John Denny	.05	.04	.02
645	Dwight Evans	.12	.09	.05
646	Mike Mason	.05	.04	.02
647	Tom Lawless	.05	.04	.02
648	*Barry Larkin*	2.25	1.75	.90
649	Mickey Tettleton	.05	.04	.02
650	Hubie Brooks	.07	.05	.03
651	Benny Distefano	.05	.04	.02
652	Terry Forster	.07	.05	.03
653	*Kevin Mitchell*	2.25	1.75	.90
654	Checklist 529-660	.05	.04	.02
655	Jesse Barfield	.15	.11	.06
656	Rangers Leaders (Bobby Valentine, Rickey Wright)	.07	.05	.03
657	Tom Waddell	.05	.04	.02
658	*Robby Thompson*	.30	.25	.12
659	Aurelio Lopez	.05	.04	.02
660	Bob Horner	.10	.08	.04
661	Lou Whitaker	.15	.11	.06
662	Frank DiPino	.05	.04	.02
663	Cliff Johnson	.05	.04	.02
664	Mike Marshall	.10	.08	.04
665	Rod Scurry	.05	.04	.02
666	Von Hayes	.07	.05	.03
667	Ron Hassey	.05	.04	.02
668	Juan Bonilla	.05	.04	.02
669	Bud Black	.05	.04	.02
670	Jose Cruz	.07	.05	.03
671a	Ray Soff (no "D*" before copyright line)	.20	.15	.08
671b	Ray Soff ("D*" before copyright line)	.05	.04	.02
672	Chili Davis	.07	.05	.03
673	Don Sutton	.15	.11	.06
674	Bill Campbell	.05	.04	.02
675	Ed Romero	.05	.04	.02
676	Charlie Moore	.05	.04	.02
677	Bob Grich	.07	.05	.03
678	Carney Lansford	.07	.05	.03
679	Kent Hrbek	.15	.11	.06
680	Ryne Sandberg	.70	.50	.30
681	George Bell	.25	.20	.10
682	Jerry Reuss	.07	.05	.03
683	Gary Roenicke	.05	.04	.02
684	Kent Tekulve	.07	.05	.03
685	Jerry Hairston	.05	.04	.02
686	Doyle Alexander	.07	.05	.03
687	Alan Trammell	.25	.20	.10
688	Juan Beniquez	.05	.04	.02
689	Darrell Porter	.07	.05	.03
690	Dane Iorg	.05	.04	.02
691	Dave Parker	.20	.15	.08
692	Frank White	.07	.05	.03
693	Terry Puhl	.05	.04	.02
694	Phil Niekro	.20	.15	.08
695	Chico Walker	.05	.04	.02
696	Gary Lucas	.05	.04	.02
697	Ed Lynch	.05	.04	.02
698	Ernie Whitt	.07	.05	.03
699	Ken Landreaux	.05	.04	.02
700	Dave Bergman	.05	.04	.02
701	Willie Randolph	.07	.05	.03
702	Greg Gross	.05	.04	.02
703	Dave Schmidt	.05	.04	.02
704	Jesse Orosco	.07	.05	.03
705	Bruce Hurst	.10	.08	.04
706	Rick Manning	.05	.04	.02
707	Bob McClure	.05	.04	.02
708	Scott McGregor	.07	.05	.03
709	Dave Kingman	.10	.08	.04
710	Gary Gaetti	.15	.11	.06
711	Ken Griffey	.07	.05	.03
712	Don Robinson	.07	.05	.03
713	Tom Brookens	.05	.04	.02
714	Dan Quisenberry	.07	.05	.03
715	Bob Dernier	.05	.04	.02
716	Rick Leach	.05	.04	.02
717	Ed Vande Berg	.05	.04	.02
718	Steve Carlton	.25	.20	.10
719	Tom Hume	.05	.04	.02
720	Richard Dotson	.07	.05	.03
721	Tom Herr	.07	.05	.03
722	Bob Knepper	.07	.05	.03
723	Brett Butler	.07	.05	.03
724	Greg Minton	.05	.04	.02
725	George Hendrick	.07	.05	.03
726	Frank Tanana	.07	.05	.03
727	Mike Moore	.05	.04	.02
728	Tippy Martinez	.05	.04	.02
729	Tom Paciorek	.05	.04	.02
730	Eric Show	.07	.05	.03
731	Dave Concepcion	.10	.08	.04
732	Manny Trillo	.07	.05	.03
733	Bill Caudill	.05	.04	.02
734	Bill Madlock	.10	.08	.04
735	Rickey Henderson	.70	.50	.30
736	Steve Bedrosian	.10	.08	.04
737	Floyd Bannister	.07	.05	.03
738	Jorge Orta	.05	.04	.02
739	Chet Lemon	.07	.05	.03
740	Rich Gedman	.07	.05	.03
741	Paul Molitor	.12	.09	.05
742	Andy McGaffigan	.05	.04	.02
743	Dwayne Murphy	.07	.05	.03
744	Roy Smalley	.05	.04	.02
745	Glenn Hubbard	.05	.04	.02
746	Bob Ojeda	.07	.05	.03
747	Johnny Ray	.07	.05	.03
748	Mike Flanagan	.07	.05	.03
749	Ozzie Smith	.15	.11	.06
750	Steve Trout	.07	.05	.03
751	Garth Iorg	.05	.04	.02
752	Dan Petry	.07	.05	.03
753	Rick Honeycutt	.05	.04	.02
754	Dave LaPoint	.07	.05	.03
755	Luis Aguayo	.05	.04	.02
756	Carlton Fisk	.25	.20	.10
757	Nolan Ryan	.80	.60	.30
758	Tony Bernazard	.05	.04	.02
759	Joel Youngblood	.05	.04	.02
760	Mike Witt	.07	.05	.03
761	Greg Pryor	.05	.04	.02
762	Gary Ward	.07	.05	.03
763	Tim Flannery	.05	.04	.02
764	Bill Buckner	.07	.05	.03
765	Kirk Gibson	.20	.15	.08
766	Don Aase	.05	.04	.02
767	Ron Cey	.07	.05	.03
768	Dennis Lamp	.05	.04	.02
769	Steve Sax	.15	.11	.06
770	Dave Winfield	.25	.20	.10
771	Shane Rawley	.07	.05	.03
772	Harold Baines	.12	.09	.05
773	Robin Yount	.35	.25	.14
774	Wayne Krenchicki	.05	.04	.02
775	Joaquin Andujar	.07	.05	.03
776	Tom Brunansky	.10	.08	.04
777	Chris Chambliss	.07	.05	.03
778	Jack Morris	.20	.15	.08
779	Craig Reynolds	.05	.04	.02
780	Andre Thornton	.07	.05	.03
781	Atlee Hammaker	.05	.04	.02
782	Brian Downing	.07	.05	.03
783	Willie Wilson	.10	.08	.04
784	Cal Ripken	.80	.60	.30
785	Terry Francona	.05	.04	.02
786	Jimy Williams	.05	.04	.02
787	Alejandro Pena	.07	.05	.03
788	Tim Stoddard	.05	.04	.02
789	Dan Schatzeder	.05	.04	.02
790	Julio Cruz	.05	.04	.02
791	Lance Parrish	.15	.11	.06
792	Checklist 661-792	.05	.04	.02

A player's name in *italic* type indicates a rookie card. An (FC) indicates a player's first card for that particular card company.

1987 Topps All-Star Glossy Set Of 22

For the fourth consecutive year, Topps produced an All-Star Game commemorative set of 22 cards. The glossy cards, which measure 2-1/2" by 3-1/2", were included in rack packs. Using the same basic card design as in previous efforts with a few minor changes, the 1987 edition features American and National League logos on the card fronts. Card #'s 1-12 feature representatives from the American League, while #'s 13-22 are National Leaguers.

		MT	NR MT	EX
Complete Set:		5.00	3.75	2.00
Common Player:		.15	.11	.06
1	Whitey Herzog	.15	.11	.06
2	Keith Hernandez	.40	.30	.15
3	Ryne Sandberg	.40	.30	.15
4	Mike Schmidt	.70	.50	.30
5	Ozzie Smith	.30	.25	.12
6	Tony Gwynn	.50	.40	.20
7	Dale Murphy	.50	.40	.20
8	Darryl Strawberry	.80	.60	.30
9	Gary Carter	.40	.30	.15
10	Dwight Gooden	.60	.45	.25
11	Fernando Valenzuela	.30	.25	.12
12	Dick Howser	.15	.11	.06
13	Wally Joyner	.70	.50	.30
14	Lou Whitaker	.30	.25	.12
15	Wade Boggs	.70	.50	.30
16	Cal Ripken	.50	.40	.20
17	Dave Winfield	.40	.30	.15
18	Rickey Henderson	.80	.60	.30
19	Kirby Puckett	.40	.30	.15
20	Lance Parrish	.30	.25	.12
21	Roger Clemens	.60	.45	.25
22	Teddy Higuera	.30	.25	.12

1987 Topps All-Star Glossy Set Of 60

Using the same design as the previous year, the 1987 Topps All-Star Glossy set includes 48 All-Star performers plus 12 potential superstars branded as "Hot Prospects". The card fronts are uncluttered, save the player's name found in very small print at the bottom. The set was available via a mail-in offer. Six subsets make up the 60-card set, with each subset being available for $1.00 plus six special offer cards that were found in wax packs.

		MT	NR MT	EX
Complete Set:		12.00	9.00	4.75
Common Player:		.15	.11	.06
1	Don Mattingly	2.50	2.00	1.00
2	Tony Gwynn	.60	.45	.25
3	Gary Gaetti	.25	.20	.10
4	Glenn Davis	.30	.25	.12
5	Roger Clemens	.70	.50	.30
6	Dale Murphy	.90	.70	.35
7	Lou Whitaker	.30	.25	.12
8	Roger McDowell	.15	.11	.06
9	Cory Snyder	.50	.40	.20
10	Todd Worrell	.20	.15	.08
11	Gary Carter	.50	.40	.20
12	Eddie Murray	.60	.45	.25
13	Bob Knepper	.15	.11	.06
14	Harold Baines	.20	.15	.08
15	Jeff Reardon	.20	.15	.08
16	Joe Carter	.25	.20	.10
17	Dave Parker	.25	.20	.10
18	Wade Boggs	1.25	.90	.50
19	Danny Tartabull	.35	.25	.14
20	Jim Deshaies	.20	.15	.08
21	Rickey Henderson	.70	.50	.30
22	Rob Deer	.15	.11	.06
23	Ozzie Smith	.25	.20	.10
24	Dave Righetti	.25	.20	.10
25	Kent Hrbek	.30	.25	.12
26	Keith Hernandez	.40	.30	.15
27	Don Baylor	.15	.11	.06
28	Mike Schmidt	.90	.70	.35
29	Pete Incaviglia	.50	.40	.20
30	Barry Bonds	.50	.40	.20
31	George Brett	.90	.70	.35
32	Darryl Strawberry	.90	.70	.35
33	Mike Witt	.15	.11	.06
34	Kevin Bass	.15	.11	.06
35	Jesse Barfield	.20	.15	.08
36	Bob Ojeda	.15	.11	.06
37	Cal Ripken	.70	.50	.30
38	Vince Coleman	.25	.20	.10
39	Wally Joyner	1.75	1.25	.70
40	Robby Thompson	.20	.15	.08
41	Pete Rose	1.25	.90	.50
42	Jim Rice	.50	.40	.20
43	Tony Bernazard	.15	.11	.06
44	Eric Davis	1.00	.70	.40
45	George Bell	.50	.40	.20
46	Hubie Brooks	.15	.11	.06
47	Jack Morris	.30	.25	.12
48	Tim Raines	.50	.40	.20
49	Mark Eichhorn	.20	.15	.08
50	Kevin Mitchell	.25	.20	.10
51	Dwight Gooden	.80	.60	.30
52	Doug DeCinces	.15	.11	.06
53	Fernando Valenzuela	.35	.25	.14
54	Reggie Jackson	.70	.50	.30
55	Johnny Ray	.15	.11	.06
56	Mike Pagliarulo	.20	.15	.08
57	Kirby Puckett	.50	.40	.20
58	Lance Parrish	.30	.25	.12
59	Jose Canseco	2.50	2.00	1.00
60	Greg Mathews	.25	.20	.10

1987 Topps Baseball Highlights

The "Baseball Highlights" boxed set of 33 cards was prepared by Topps for distribution at stores in the Woolworth's chain. Each card measures 2-1/2" by 3-1/2" in size and features a memorable baseball event that occurred during the 1986 season. The glossy set sold for $1.99 in Woolworth's stores.

	MT	NR MT	EX
Complete Set:	5.00	3.75	2.00

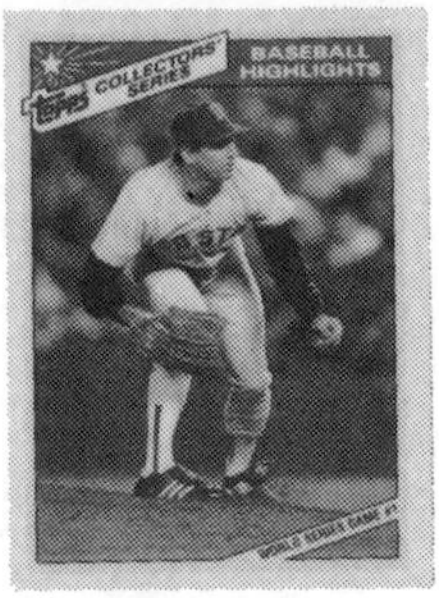

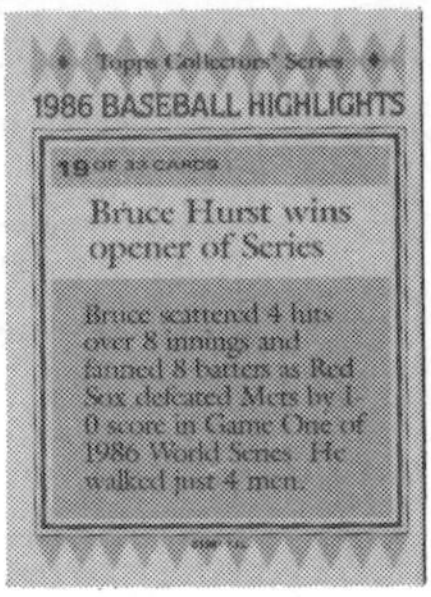

Common Player:		.09	.07	.04
1	Steve Carlton	.30	.25	.12
2	Cecil Cooper	.12	.09	.05
3	Rickey Henderson	.50	.40	.20
4	Reggie Jackson	.30	.25	.12
5	Jim Rice	.25	.20	.10
6	Don Sutton	.20	.15	.08
7	Roger Clemens	.50	.40	.20
8	Mike Schmidt	.35	.25	.14
9	Jesse Barfield	.15	.11	.06
10	Wade Boggs	.70	.50	.30
11	Tim Raines	.30	.25	.12
12	Jose Canseco	1.00	.70	.40
13	Todd Worrell	.15	.11	.06
14	Dave Righetti	.15	.11	.06
15	Don Mattingly	1.25	.90	.50
16	Tony Gwynn	.35	.25	.14
17	Marty Barrett	.09	.07	.04
18	Mike Scott	.12	.09	.05
19	World Series Game #1 (Bruce Hurst)	.12	.09	.05
20	World Series Game #1 (Calvin Schiraldi)	.09	.07	.04
21	World Series Game #2 (Dwight Evans)	.12	.09	.05
22	World Series Game #2 (Dave Henderson)	.09	.07	.04
23	World Series Game #3 (Len Dykstra)	.12	.09	.05
24	World Series Game #3 (Bob Ojeda)	.09	.07	.04
25	World Series Game #4 (Gary Carter)	.30	.25	.12
26	World Series Game #4 (Ron Darling)	.15	.11	.06
27	Jim Rice	.30	.25	.12
28	Bruce Hurst	.09	.07	.04
29	World Series Game #6 (Darryl Strawberry)	.35	.25	.14
30	World Series Game #6 (Ray Knight)	.09	.07	.04
31	World Series Game #6 (Keith Hernandez)	.25	.20	.10
32	World Series Games #7 (Mets Celebrate)	.12	.09	.05
33	Ray Knight	.09	.07	.04

1987 Topps Box Panels

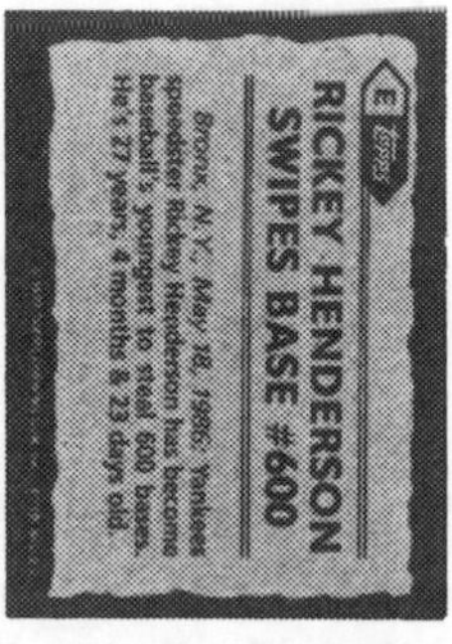

Offering baseball cards on retail boxes for a second straight year, Topps reduced the size of the cards to 2-1/8" by 3". Four different wax pack boxes were available, each featuring two cards that were placed on the sides of the boxes. The card fronts are identical in design to the regular issue cards. The backs are printed in blue and yellow and carry a commentary imitating a newspaper format. The cards are numbered A through H.

		MT	NR MT	EX
Complete Panel Set:		5.00	3.75	2.00
Complete Singles Set:		2.00	1.50	.80
Common Panel:		.75	.60	.30
Common Single Player:		.15	.11	.06
	Panel	1.25	.90	.50
A	Don Baylor	.15	.11	.06
B	Steve Carlton	.30	.25	.12
	Panel	.75	.60	.30
C	Ron Cey	.15	.11	.06
D	Cecil Cooper	.15	.11	.06
	Panel	1.75	1.25	.70
E	Rickey Henderson	.40	.30	.15
F	Jim Rice	.25	.20	.10
	Panel	1.25	.90	.50
G	Don Sutton	.20	.15	.08
H	Dave Winfield	.30	.25	.12

1987 Topps Coins

For the first time since 1971, Topps issued a set of baseball "coins". Similar in design to the 1964 edition of Topps coins, the metal discs measure 1-1/2" in diameter. The aluminum coins were sold on a limited basis in retail outlets. Three coins and three sticks of gum were found in a pack. The coin fronts feature a full-color photo along with the player's name, team ans position in a white band at the bottom of the coin. Gold-colored rims are found for American League players; National League players have silver-colored rims. Backs are silver in color and carry the coin number, player's name and personal and statistical information.

		MT	NR MT	EX
Complete Set:		10.00	7.50	4.00
Common Player:		.15	.11	.06
1	Harold Baines	.15	.11	.06
2	Jesse Barfield	.15	.11	.06
3	George Bell	.20	.15	.08
4	Wade Boggs	.70	.50	.30
5	George Brett	.30	.25	.12
6	Jose Canseco	1.00	.70	.40
7	Joe Carter	.15	.11	.06
8	Roger Clemens	.40	.30	.15
9	Alvin Davis	.15	.11	.06
10	Rob Deer	.15	.11	.06
11	Kirk Gibson	.20	.15	.08
12	Rickey Henderson	.25	.20	.10
13	Kent Hrbek	.20	.15	.08
14	Pete Incaviglia	.20	.15	.08
15	Reggie Jackson	.25	.20	.10
16	Wally Joyner	.60	.45	.25
17	Don Mattingly	1.25	.90	.50
18	Jack Morris	.20	.15	.08

		MT	NR MT	EX
19	Eddie Murray	.25	.20	.10
20	Kirby Puckett	.30	.25	.12
21	Jim Rice	.25	.20	.10
22	Dave Righetti	.20	.15	.08
23	Cal Ripken	.25	.20	.10
24	Cory Snyder	.25	.20	.10
25	Danny Tartabull	.20	.15	.08
26	Dave Winfield	.25	.20	.10
27	Hubie Brooks	.15	.11	.06
28	Gary Carter	.25	.20	.10
29	Vince Coleman	.20	.15	.08
30	Eric Davis	.70	.50	.30
31	Glenn Davis	.15	.11	.06
32	Steve Garvey	.25	.20	.10
33	Dwight Gooden	.40	.30	.15
34	Tony Gwynn	.30	.25	.12
35	Von Hayes	.15	.11	.06
36	Keith Hernandez	.20	.15	.08
37	Dale Murphy	.30	.25	.12
38	Dave Parker	.20	.15	.08
39	Tony Pena	.15	.11	.06
40	Nolan Ryan	.25	.20	.10
41	Ryne Sandberg	.20	.15	.08
42	Steve Sax	.15	.11	.06
43	Mike Schmidt	.30	.25	.12
44	Mike Scott	.15	.11	.06
45	Ozzie Smith	.15	.11	.06
46	Darryl Strawberry	.40	.30	.15
47	Fernando Valenzuela	.20	.15	.08
48	Todd Worrell	.15	.11	.06

1987 Topps Gallery Of Champions

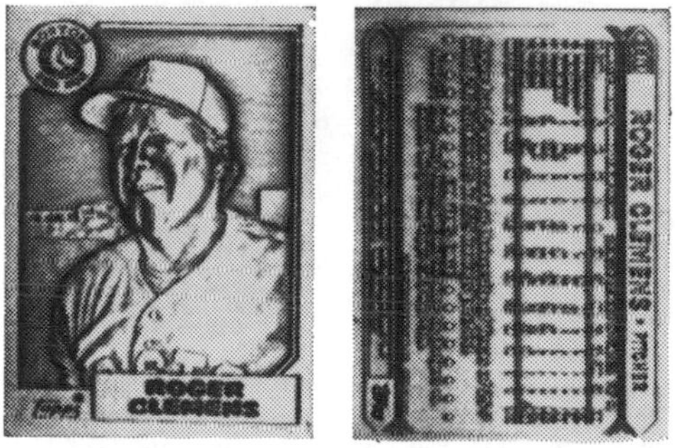

Designed as a tribute to the 1986 season's winners of baseball's most prestigious awards, the Gallery of Champions are metal "cards" that are one-quarter size replicas of the regular issue Topps cards. The bronze and silver sets were issued in leather-like velvet-lined display cases; the aluminum sets came cello-wrapped. Hobby dealers who purchased one bronze set or a 16-set case of aluminum "cards" received one free Jose Canseco pewter metal mini-card (value $60). The purchase of a silver set included five Canseco pewters. A 1953 Willie Mays bronze was given to dealers who brought cases of 1987 Topps Traded sets (value $10).

		MT	NR MT	EX
Complete Aluminum Set:		30.00	22.00	12.00
Complete Bronze Set:		175.00	131.00	70.00
Complete Silver Set:		700.00	525.00	280.00
(1a)	Jesse Barfield (aluminum)	.70	.50	.30
(1b)	Jesse Barfield (bronze)	7.50	5.75	3.00
(1c)	Jesse Barfield (silver)	20.00	15.00	8.00
(2a)	Wade Boggs (aluminum)	3.00	2.25	1.25
(2b)	Wade Boggs (bronze)	25.00	18.50	10.00
(2c)	Wade Boggs (silver)	125.00	94.00	50.00
(3a)	Jose Canseco (aluminum)	3.00	2.25	1.25
(3b)	Jose Canseco (bronze)	25.00	18.50	10.00
(3c)	Jose Canseco (silver)	125.00	94.00	50.00
(4a)	Joe Carter (aluminum)	.70	.50	.30
(4b)	Joe Carter (bronze)	7.50	5.75	3.00
(4c)	Joe Carter (silver)	20.00	15.00	8.00
(5a)	Roger Clemens (aluminum)	2.00	1.50	.80
(5b)	Roger Clemens (bronze)	20.00	15.00	8.00
(5c)	Roger Clemens (silver)	90.00	67.00	36.00
(6a)	Tony Gwynn (aluminum)	1.25	.90	.50
(6b)	Tony Gwynn (bronze)	12.00	9.00	4.75
(6c)	Tony Gwynn (silver)	50.00	37.00	20.00
(7a)	Don Mattingly (aluminum)	8.00	6.00	3.25
(7b)	Don Mattingly (bronze)	50.00	37.00	20.00
(7c)	Don Mattingly (silver)	200.00	150.00	80.00
(8a)	Tim Raines (aluminum)	1.00	.70	.40
(8b)	Tim Raines (bronze)	10.00	7.50	4.00
(8c)	Tim Raines (silver)	30.00	22.00	12.00
(9a)	Dave Righetti (aluminum)	1.00	.70	.40
(9b)	Dave Righetti (bronze)	10.00	7.50	4.00
(9c)	Dave Righetti (silver)	30.00	22.00	12.00
(10a)	Mike Schmidt (aluminum)	1.50	1.25	.60
(10b)	Mike Schmidt (bronze)	15.00	11.00	6.00
(10c)	Mike Schmidt (silver)	80.00	60.00	32.00
(11a)	Mike Scott (aluminum)	.70	.50	.30
(11b)	Mike Scott (bronze)	7.50	5.75	3.00
(11c)	Mike Scott (silver)	20.00	15.00	8.00
(12a)	Todd Worrell (aluminum)	.70	.50	.30
(12b)	Todd Worrell (bronze)	10.00	7.50	4.00
(12c)	Todd Worrell (silver)	20.00	15.00	8.00

1987 Topps Glossy Rookies

The 1987 Topps Glossy Rookies set of 22 cards was introduced with Topps' new 100-card "Jumbo Packs". Intended for sale in supermarkets, the jumbo packs contained one glossy card. Measuring the standard 2-1/2" by 3-1/2" size, the special insert cards feature the top rookies from the previous season.

		MT	NR MT	EX
Complete Set:		12.00	9.00	4.75
Common Player:		.20	.15	.08
1	Andy Allanson	.20	.15	.08
2	John Cangelosi	.20	.15	.08
3	Jose Canseco	3.00	2.25	1.25
4	Will Clark	3.00	1.50	.90
5	Mark Eichhorn	.40	.30	.15
6	Pete Incaviglia	.70	.50	.30
7	Wally Joyner	1.00	.70	.40
8	Eric King	.30	.25	.12
9	Dave Magadan	.60	.45	.25
10	John Morris	.20	.15	.08
11	Juan Nieves	.40	.30	.15
12	Rafael Palmeiro	1.00	.70	.40
13	Billy Jo Robidoux	.20	.15	.08
14	Bruce Ruffin	.40	.30	.15
15	Ruben Sierra	1.25	.90	.50
16	Cory Snyder	.80	.60	.30
17	Kurt Stillwell	.60	.45	.25
18	Dale Sveum	.40	.30	.15
19	Danny Tartabull	.80	.60	.30
20	Andres Thomas	.40	.30	.15
21	Robby Thompson	.40	.30	.15
22	Todd Worrell	.40	.30	.15

A player's name in *italic* type indicates a rookie card. An (FC) indicates a player's first card for that particular card company.

1987 Topps Mini League Leaders

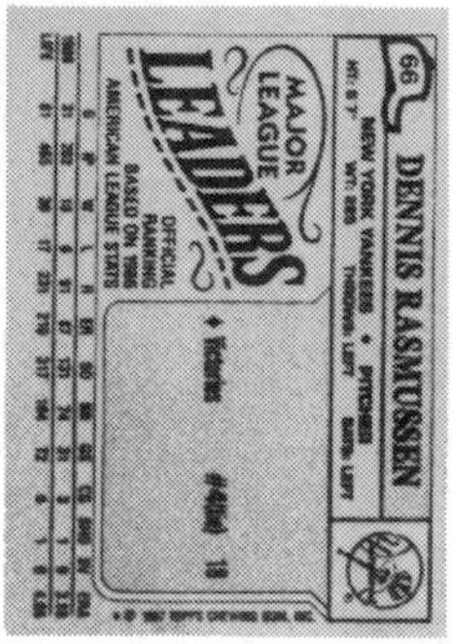

Returning for 1987, the Topps "Major League Leaders" set was increased in size from 66 to 76 cards. The 2-1/8" by 3" cards feature wood grain borders that encompass a white-bordered full-color photo. The card backs are printed in yellow, orange and brown and list the player's official ranking based on his 1986 American or National League statistics. The players featured are those who finished the top five in their leagues' various batting and pitching statistics. The cards were sold in plastic-wrapped packs, seven cards plus a game card per pack.

		MT	NR MT	EX
Complete Set:		8.00	6.00	3.25
Common Player:		.09	.07	.04
1	Bob Horner	.20	.15	.08
2	Dale Murphy	.50	.40	.20
3	Lee Smith	.09	.07	.04
4	Eric Davis	.60	.45	.25
5	John Franco	.15	.11	.06
6	Dave Parker	.20	.15	.08
7	Kevin Bass	.09	.07	.04
8	Glenn Davis	.20	.15	.08
9	Bill Doran	.15	.11	.06
10	Bob Knepper	.09	.07	.04
11	Mike Scott	.20	.15	.08
12	Dave Smith	.09	.07	.04
13	Mariano Duncan	.09	.07	.04
14	Orel Hershiser	.30	.25	.12
15	Steve Sax	.20	.15	.08
16	Fernando Valenzuela	.25	.20	.10
17	Tim Raines	.30	.25	.12
18	Jeff Reardon	.15	.11	.06
19	Floyd Youmans	.09	.07	.04
20	Gary Carter	.30	.25	.12
21	Ron Darling	.20	.15	.08
22	Sid Fernandez	.15	.11	.06
23	Dwight Gooden	.60	.45	.25
24	Keith Hernandez	.25	.20	.10
25	Bob Ojeda	.09	.07	.04
26	Darryl Strawberry	.50	.40	.20
27	Steve Bedrosian	.15	.11	.06
28	Von Hayes	.15	.11	.06
29	Juan Samuel	.20	.15	.08
30	Mike Schmidt	.50	.40	.20
31	Rick Rhoden	.09	.07	.04
32	Vince Coleman	.20	.15	.08
33	Danny Cox	.09	.07	.04
34	Todd Worrell	.15	.11	.06
35	Tony Gwynn	.40	.30	.15
36	Mike Krukow	.09	.07	.04
37	Candy Maldonado	.09	.07	.04
38	Don Aase	.09	.07	.04
39	Eddie Murray	.40	.30	.15
40	Cal Ripken	.40	.30	.15
41	Wade Boggs	.80	.60	.30
42	Roger Clemens	.60	.45	.25
43	Bruce Hurst	.15	.11	.06
44	Jim Rice	.30	.25	.12
45	Wally Joyner	.80	.60	.30
46	Donnie Moore	.09	.07	.04
47	Gary Pettis	.09	.07	.04
48	Mike Witt	.09	.07	.04
49	John Cangelosi	.09	.07	.04
50	Tom Candiotti	.09	.07	.04
51	Joe Carter	.20	.15	.08
52	Pat Tabler	.09	.07	.04
53	Kirk Gibson	.25	.20	.10
54	Willie Hernandez	.09	.07	.04
55	Jack Morris	.25	.20	.10
56	Alan Trammell	.30	.25	.12
57	George Brett	.50	.40	.20
58	Willie Wilson	.15	.11	.06
59	Rob Deer	.09	.07	.04
60	Teddy Higuera	.15	.11	.06
61	Bert Blyleven	.15	.11	.06
62	Gary Gaetti	.20	.15	.08
63	Kirby Puckett	.35	.25	.14
64	Rickey Henderson	.40	.30	.15
65	Don Mattingly	1.25	.90	.50
66	Dennis Rasmussen	.15	.11	.06
67	Dave Righetti	.20	.15	.08
68	Jose Canseco	1.00	.70	.40
69	Dave Kingman	.15	.11	.06
70	Phil Bradley	.15	.11	.06
71	Mark Langston	.15	.11	.06
72	Pete O'Brien	.09	.07	.04
73	Jesse Barfield	.15	.11	.06
74	George Bell	.25	.20	.10
75	Tony Fernandez	.15	.11	.06
76	Tom Henke	.09	.07	.04
77	Checklist	.09	.07	.04

1987 Topps Stickers

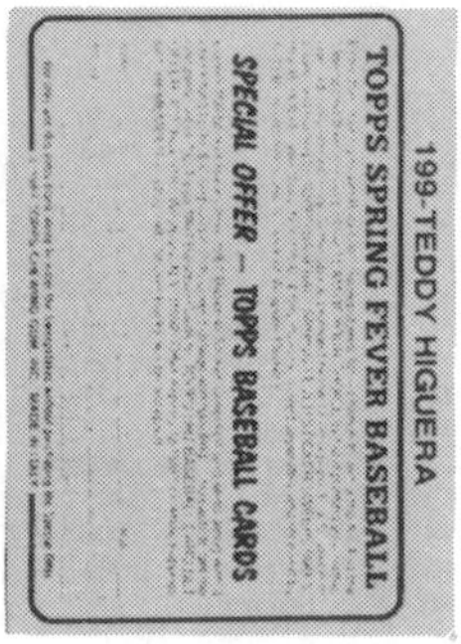

For the seventh consecutive year, Topps issued stickers to be housed in a specially designed yearbook. The stickers, which measure 2-1/8" by 3", offer a full-color front with a peel-off back printed in blue ink on white stock. The sticker fronts feature either one full-size player picture or two half-size individual stickers. The sticker yearbook measures 9" by 10-3/4" and contains 36 glossy, magazine-style pages, all printed in full color. Mike Schmidt, 1986 National League MVP, is featured on the cover. The yearbook sold in retail outlets for 35¢, while stickers were sold five in a pack for 25¢. The number in parentheses in the following checklist is the sticker number the player shares the sticker with.

		MT	NR MT	EX
Complete Set:		18.00	13.50	7.25
Common Player:		.03	.02	.01
Sticker Album:		.70	.50	.30
1	1986 Highlights (Jim Deshaies) (172)	.04	.03	.02
2	1986 Highlights (Roger Clemens) (175)	.15	.11	.06
3	1986 Highlights (Roger Clemens) (176)	.15	.11	.06
4	1986 Highlights (Dwight Evans) (177)	.06	.05	.02
5	1986 Highlights (Dwight Gooden) (178)	.15	.11	.06
6	1986 Highlights (Dwight Gooden) (180)	.15	.11	.06
7	1986 Highlights (Dave Lopes) (181)	.03	.02	.01
8	1986 Highlights (Dave Righetti) (182)	.06	.05	.02

		MT	NR MT	EX
9	1986 Highlights (Dave Righetti) (183)	.10	.08	.04
10	1986 Highlights (Ruben Sierra) (185)	.15	.11	.06
11	1986 Highlights (Todd Worrell) (186)	.06	.05	.02
12	1986 Highlights (Todd Worrell) (187)	.06	.05	.02
13	N.L. Championship Series (Lenny Dykstra)	.06	.05	.02
14	N.L. Championship Series (Gary Carter)	.08	.06	.03
15	N.L. Championship Series (Mike Scott)	.06	.05	.02
16	A.L. Championship Series (Gary Pettis)	.03	.02	.01
17	A.L. Championship Series (Jim Rice)	.08	.06	.03
18	A.L. Championship Series (Bruce Hurst)	.04	.03	.02
19	1986 World Series (Bruce Hurst)	.04	.03	.02
20	1986 World Series (Wade Boggs)	.15	.11	.06
21	1986 World Series (Lenny Dykstra)	.06	.05	.02
22	1986 World Series (Gary Carter)	.08	.06	.03
23	1986 World Series (Dave Henderson)	.04	.03	.02
24	1986 World Series (Howard Johnson)	.04	.03	.02
25	1986 World Series (Mets Celebrate)	.08	.06	.03
26	Glenn Davis	.15	.11	.06
27	Nolan Ryan (188)	.10	.08	.04
28	Charlie Kerfeld (189)	.03	.02	.01
29	Jose Cruz (190)	.04	.03	.02
30	Phil Garner (191)	.06	.05	.02
31	Bill Doran (192)	.06	.05	.02
32	Bob Knepper (195)	.03	.02	.01
33	Denny Walling (196)	.10	.08	.04
34	Kevin Bass (197)	.04	.03	.02
35	Mike Scott	.10	.08	.04
36	Dale Murphy	.25	.20	.10
37	Paul Assenmacher (198)	.06	.05	.02
38	Ken Oberkfell (200)	.06	.05	.02
39	Andres Thomas (201)	.08	.06	.03
40	Gene Garber (202)	.03	.02	.01
41	Bob Horner	.08	.06	.03
42	Rafael Ramirez (203)	.03	.02	.01
43	Rick Mahler (204)	.03	.02	.01
44	Omar Moreno (205)	.03	.02	.01
45	Dave Palmer (206)	.03	.02	.01
46	Ozzie Smith	.12	.09	.05
47	Bob Forsch (207)	.03	.02	.01
48	Willie McGee (209)	.06	.05	.02
49	Tom Herr (210)	.06	.05	.02
50	Vince Coleman (211)	.08	.06	.03
51	Andy Van Slyke (212)	.06	.05	.02
52	Jack Clark (215)	.08	.06	.03
53	John Tudor (216)	.04	.03	.02
54	Terry Pendleton (217)	.03	.02	.01
55	Todd Worrell	.10	.08	.04
56	Lee Smith	.06	.05	.02
57	Leon Durham (218)	.03	.02	.01
58	Jerry Mumphrey (219)	.06	.05	.02
59	Shawon Dunston (220)	.06	.05	.02
60	Scott Sanderson (221)	.06	.05	.02
61	Ryne Sandberg	.15	.11	.06
62	Gary Matthews (222)	.04	.03	.02
63	Dennis Eckersley (225)	.06	.05	.02
64	Jody Davis (226)	.06	.05	.02
65	Keith Moreland (227)	.04	.03	.02
66	Mike Marshall (228)	.06	.05	.02
67	Bill Madlock (229)	.06	.05	.02
68	Greg Brock (230)	.04	.03	.02
69	Pedro Guerrero (231)	.08	.06	.03
70	Steve Sax	.12	.09	.05
71	Rick Honeycutt (232)	.03	.02	.01
72	Franklin Stubbs (235)	.03	.02	.01
73	Mike Scioscia (236)	.10	.08	.04
74	Mariano Duncan (237)	.03	.02	.01
75	Fernando Valenzuela	.15	.11	.06
76	Hubie Brooks	.06	.05	.02
77	Andre Dawson (238)	.08	.06	.03
78	Tim Burke (240)	.04	.03	.02
79	Floyd Youmans (241)	.03	.02	.01
80	Tim Wallach (242)	.04	.03	.02
81	Jeff Reardon (243)	.06	.05	.02
82	Mitch Webster (244)	.15	.11	.06
83	Bryn Smith (245)	.03	.02	.01
84	Andres Galarraga (246)	.12	.09	.05
85	Tim Raines	.15	.11	.06
86	Chris Brown	.08	.06	.03

		MT	NR MT	EX
87	Bob Brenly (247)	.03	.02	.01
88	Will Clark (249)	.25	.20	.10
89	Scott Garrelts (250)	.04	.03	.02
90	Jeffrey Leonard (251)	.06	.05	.02
91	Robby Thompson (252)	.06	.05	.02
92	Mike Krukow (255)	.03	.02	.01
93	Danny Gladden (256)	.03	.02	.01
94	Candy Maldonado (257)	.04	.03	.02
95	Chili Davis	.04	.03	.02
96	Dwight Gooden	.30	.25	.12
97	Sid Fernandez (258)	.04	.03	.02
98	Len Dykstra (259)	.06	.05	.02
99	Bob Ojeda (260)	.04	.03	.02
100	Wally Backman (261)	.04	.03	.02
101	Gary Carter	.15	.11	.06
102	Keith Hernandez (262)	.10	.08	.04
103	Darryl Strawberry (265)	.15	.11	.06
104	Roger McDowell (266)	.08	.06	.03
105	Ron Darling (267)	.08	.06	.03
106	Tony Gwynn	.20	.15	.08
107	Dave Dravecky (268)	.04	.03	.02
108	Terry Kennedy (269)	.08	.06	.03
109	Rich Gossage (270)	.10	.08	.04
110	Garry Templeton (271)	.04	.03	.02
111	Lance McCullers (272)	.04	.03	.02
112	Eric Show (275)	.04	.03	.02
113	John Kruk (276)	.12	.09	.05
114	Tim Flannery (277)	.06	.05	.02
115	Steve Garvey	.15	.11	.06
116	Mike Schmidt	.25	.20	.10
117	Glenn Wilson (278)	.06	.05	.02
118	Kent Tekulve (280)	.06	.05	.02
119	Gary Redus (281)	.08	.06	.03
120	Shane Rawley (282)	.03	.02	.01
121	Von Hayes	.06	.05	.02
122	Don Carman (283)	.04	.03	.02
123	Bruce Ruffin (285)	.04	.03	.02
124	Steve Bedrosian (286)	.06	.05	.02
125	Juan Samuel (287)	.06	.05	.02
126	Sid Bream (288)	.06	.05	.02
127	Cecilio Guante (289)	.03	.02	.01
128	Rick Reuschel (290)	.04	.03	.02
129	Tony Pena (291)	.04	.03	.02
130	Rick Rhoden	.06	.05	.02
131	Barry Bonds (292)	.10	.08	.04
132	Joe Orsulak (295)	.03	.02	.01
133	Jim Morrison (296)	.12	.09	.05
134	R.J. Reynolds (297)	.04	.03	.02
135	Johnny Ray	.06	.05	.02
136	Eric Davis	.30	.25	.12
137	Tom Browning (298)	.10	.08	.04
138	John Franco (300)	.06	.05	.02
139	Pete Rose (301)	.20	.15	.08
140	Bill Gullickson (302)	.04	.03	.02
141	Ron Oester (303)	.04	.03	.02
142	Bo Diaz (304)	.40	.30	.15
143	Buddy Bell (305)	.04	.03	.02
144	Eddie Milner (306)	.08	.06	.03
145	Dave Parker	.10	.08	.04
146	Kirby Puckett	.35	.25	.14
147	Rickey Henderson	.40	.30	.15
148	Wade Boggs	.60	.45	.25
149	Lance Parrish	.25	.20	.10
150	Wally Joyner	.70	.50	.30
151	Cal Ripken	.40	.30	.15
152	Dave Winfield	.30	.25	.12
153	Lou Whitaker	.25	.20	.10
154	Roger Clemens	.50	.40	.20
155	Tony Gwynn	.40	.30	.15
156	Ryne Sandberg	.25	.20	.10
157	Keith Hernandez	.25	.20	.10
158	Gary Carter	.30	.25	.12
159	Darryl Strawberry	.50	.40	.20
160	Mike Schmidt	.40	.30	.15
161	Dale Murphy	.40	.30	.15
162	Ozzie Smith	.20	.15	.08
163	Dwight Gooden	.50	.40	.20
164	Jose Canseco	.80	.60	.30
165	Curt Young (307)	.04	.03	.02
166	Alfredo Griffin (308)	.12	.09	.05
167	Dave Stewart (309)	.06	.05	.02
168	Mike Davis (310)	.06	.05	.02
169	Bruce Bochte (311)	.03	.02	.01
170	Dwayne Murphy (312)	.04	.03	.02
171	Carney Lansford (313)	.20	.15	.08
172	Joaquin Andujar (1)	.04	.03	.02
173	Dave Kingman	.08	.06	.03
174	Wally Joyner	.40	.30	.15
175	Gary Pettis (2)	.15	.11	.06
176	Dick Schofield (3)	.15	.11	.06
177	Donnie Moore (4)	.06	.05	.02

		MT	NR MT	EX
178	Brian Downing (5)	.15	.11	.06
179	Mike Witt	.06	.05	.02
180	Bob Boone (6)	.15	.11	.06
181	Kirk McCaskill (7)	.03	.02	.01
182	Doug DeCinces (8)	.06	.05	.02
183	Don Sutton (9)	.10	.08	.04
184	Jessie Barfield	.10	.08	.04
185	Tom Henke (10)	.15	.11	.06
186	Willie Upshaw (11)	.06	.05	.02
187	Mark Eichhorn (12)	.06	.05	.02
188	Damaso Garcia (27)	.10	.08	.04
189	Jim Clancy (28)	.03	.02	.01
190	Lloyd Moseby (29)	.04	.03	.02
191	Tony Fernandez (30)	.06	.05	.02
192	Jimmy Key (31)	.06	.05	.02
193	George Bell	.20	.15	.08
194	Rob Deer	.06	.05	.02
195	Mark Clear (32)	.03	.02	.01
196	Robin Yount (33)	.10	.08	.04
197	Jim Gantner (34)	.04	.03	.02
198	Cecil Cooper (37)	.06	.05	.02
199	Teddy Higuera	.08	.06	.03
200	Paul Molitor (38)	.08	.06	.03
201	Dan Plesac (39)	.08	.06	.03
202	Billy Jo Robidoux (40)	.03	.02	.01
203	Earnie Riles (42)	.03	.02	.01
204	Ken Schrom (43)	.03	.02	.01
205	Pat Tabler (44)	.03	.02	.01
206	Mel Hall (45)	.03	.02	.01
207	Tony Bernazard (47)	.03	.02	.01
208	Joe Carter	.10	.08	.04
209	Ernie Camacho (48)	.06	.05	.02
210	Julio Franco (49)	.06	.05	.02
211	Tom Candiotti (50)	.08	.06	.03
212	Brook Jacoby (51)	.06	.05	.02
213	Cory Snyder	.30	.25	.12
214	Jim Presley	.08	.06	.03
215	Mike Moore (52)	.08	.06	.03
216	Harold Reynolds (53)	.04	.03	.02
217	Scott Bradley (54)	.03	.02	.01
218	Matt Young (57)	.03	.02	.01
219	Mark Langston (58)	.06	.05	.02
220	Alvin Davis (59)	.06	.05	.02
221	Phil Bradley (60)	.06	.05	.02
222	Ken Phelps (62)	.04	.03	.02
223	Danny Tartabull	.20	.15	.08
224	Eddie Murray	.20	.15	.08
225	Rick Dempsey (63)	.06	.05	.02
226	Fred Lynn (64)	.06	.05	.02
227	Mike Boddicker (65)	.04	.03	.02
228	Don Aase (66)	.06	.05	.02
229	Larry Sheets (67)	.06	.05	.02
230	Storm Davis (68)	.04	.03	.02
231	Lee Lacy (69)	.08	.06	.03
232	Jim Traber (71)	.03	.02	.01
233	Cal Ripken	.20	.15	.08
234	Larry Parrish	.06	.05	.02
235	Gary Ward (72)	.03	.02	.01
236	Pete Incaviglia (73)	.10	.08	.04
237	Scott Fletcher (74)	.03	.02	.01
238	Greg Harris (77)	.08	.06	.03
239	Pete O'Brien	.06	.05	.02
240	Charlie Hough (78)	.04	.03	.02
241	Don Slaught (79)	.03	.02	.01
242	Steve Buechele (80)	.04	.03	.02
243	Oddibe McDowell (81)	.06	.05	.02
244	Roger Clemens (82)	.15	.11	.06
245	Bob Stanley (83)	.03	.02	.01
246	Tom Seaver (84)	.12	.09	.05
247	Rich Gedman (87)	.03	.02	.01
248	Jim Rice	.15	.11	.06
249	Dennis Boyd (88)	.25	.20	.10
250	Bill Buckner (89)	.04	.03	.02
251	Dwight Evans (90)	.06	.05	.02
252	Don Baylor (91)	.06	.05	.02
253	Wade Boggs	.40	.30	.15
254	George Brett	.25	.20	.10
255	Steve Farr (92)	.03	.02	.01
256	Jim Sundberg (93)	.03	.02	.01
257	Dan Quisenberry (94)	.04	.03	.02
258	Charlie Leibrandt (97)	.04	.03	.02
259	Argenis Salazar (98)	.06	.05	.02
260	Frank White (99)	.04	.03	.02
261	Willie Wilson (100)	.04	.03	.02
262	Lonnie Smith (102)	.10	.08	.04
263	Steve Balboni	.04	.03	.02
264	Darrell Evans	.06	.05	.02
265	Johnny Grubb (103)	.15	.11	.06
266	Jack Morris (104)	.08	.06	.03
267	Lou Whitaker (105)	.08	.06	.03
268	Chet Lemon (107)	.04	.03	.02
269	Lance Parrish (108)	.08	.06	.03
270	Alan Trammell (109)	.10	.08	.04
271	Darnell Coles (110)	.04	.03	.02
272	Willie Hernandez (111)	.04	.03	.02
273	Kirk Gibson	.15	.11	.06
274	Kirby Puckett	.20	.15	.08
275	Mike Smithson (112)	.04	.03	.02
276	Mickey Hatcher (113)	.12	.09	.05
277	Frank Viola (114)	.06	.05	.02
278	Bert Blyleven (117)	.06	.05	.02
279	Gary Gaetti	.10	.08	.04
280	Tom Brunansky (118)	.06	.05	.02
281	Kent Hrbek (119)	.08	.06	.03
282	Roy Smalley (120)	.03	.02	.01
283	Greg Gagne (122)	.04	.03	.02
284	Harold Baines	.10	.08	.04
285	Ron Hassey (123)	.04	.03	.02
286	Floyd Bannister (124)	.06	.05	.02
287	Ozzie Guillen (125)	.06	.05	.02
288	Carlton Fisk (126)	.06	.05	.02
289	Tim Hulett (127)	.03	.02	.01
290	Joe Cowley (128)	.04	.03	.02
291	Greg Walker (129)	.04	.03	.02
292	Neil Allen (131)	.10	.08	.04
293	John Cangelosi	.04	.03	.02
294	Don Mattingly	.90	.70	.35
295	Mike Easler (132)	.03	.02	.01
296	Rickey Henderson (133)	.12	.09	.05
297	Dan Pasqua (134)	.04	.03	.02
298	Dave Winfield (137)	.10	.08	.04
299	Dave Righetti	.12	.09	.05
300	Mike Pagliarulo (138)	.06	.05	.02
301	Ron Guidry (139)	.20	.15	.08
302	Willie Randolph (140)	.04	.03	.02
303	Dennis Rasmussen (141)	.04	.03	.02
304	Jose Canseco (142)	.40	.30	.15
305	Andres Thomas (143)	.04	.03	.02
306	Danny Tartabull (144)	.08	.06	.03
307	Robby Thompson (165)	.04	.03	.02
308	Pete Incaviglia, Cory Snyder (166)	.12	.09	.05
309	Dale Sveum (167)	.06	.05	.02
310	Todd Worrell (168)	.06	.05	.02
311	Andy Allanson (169)	.03	.02	.01
312	Bruce Ruffin (170)	.04	.03	.02
313	Wally Joyner (171)	.20	.15	.08

1987 Topps Traded

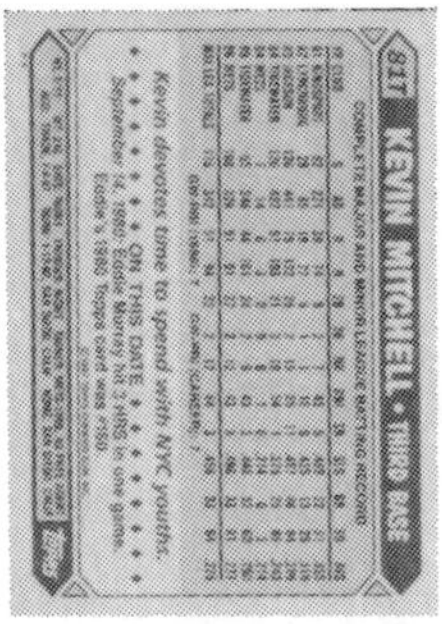

The Topps Traded set consists of 132 cards as have all Traded sets issued by Topps since 1981. The cards measure the standard 2 1/2" by 3 1/2" and are identical in design to the regular edition set. The purpose of the set is to update player trades and feature rookies not included in the regular issue. As they had done the previous three years, Topps produced a glossy-coated "Tiffany" edition of the Traded set. The Tiffany edition cards are valued at two to three times greater than the regular Traded cards.

		MT	NR MT	EX
Complete Set:		10.00	7.50	4.00
Common Player:		.06	.05	.02
1T	Bill Almon	.06	.05	.02
2T	Scott Bankhead	.08	.06	.03
3T	Eric Bell(FC)	.15	.11	.06

		MT	NR MT	EX
4T	Juan Beniquez	.06	.05	.02
5T	Juan Berenguer	.06	.05	.02
6T	Greg Booker	.06	.05	.02
7T	Thad Bosley	.06	.05	.02
8T	Larry Bowa	.10	.08	.04
9T	Greg Brock	.10	.08	.04
10T	Bob Brower(FC)	.15	.11	.06
11T	Jerry Browne(FC)	.30	.25	.12
12T	Ralph Bryant(FC)	.12	.09	.05
13T	DeWayne Buice(FC)	.15	.11	.06
14T	Ellis Burks(FC)	2.00	1.50	.80
15T	Ivan Calderon	.25	.20	.10
16T	Jeff Calhoun	.06	.05	.02
17T	Casey Candaele(FC)	.10	.08	.04
18T	John Cangelosi	.06	.05	.02
19T	Steve Carlton	.30	.25	.12
20T	Juan Castillo(FC)	.06	.05	.02
21T	Rick Cerone	.06	.05	.02
22T	Ron Cey	.10	.08	.04
23T	John Christensen	.06	.05	.02
24T	Dave Cone(FC)	1.25	.90	.50
25T	Chuck Crim(FC)	.15	.11	.06
26T	Storm Davis	.06	.05	.02
27T	Andre Dawson	.40	.30	.15
28T	Rick Dempsey	.08	.06	.03
29T	Doug Drabek	.40	.30	.15
30T	Mike Dunne	.30	.25	.12
31T	Dennis Eckersley	.30	.25	.12
32T	Lee Elia	.06	.05	.02
33T	Brian Fisher	.10	.08	.04
34T	Terry Francona	.06	.05	.02
35T	Willie Fraser(FC)	.15	.11	.06
36T	Billy Gardner	.06	.05	.02
37T	Ken Gerhart(FC)	.15	.11	.06
38T	Danny Gladden	.06	.05	.02
39T	Jim Gott	.06	.05	.02
40T	Cecilio Guante	.06	.05	.02
41T	Albert Hall	.06	.05	.02
42T	Terry Harper	.06	.05	.02
43T	Mickey Hatcher	.06	.05	.02
44T	Brad Havens	.06	.05	.02
45T	Neal Heaton	.06	.05	.02
46T	Mike Henneman(FC)	.30	.25	.12
47T	Donnie Hill	.06	.05	.02
48T	Guy Hoffman	.06	.05	.02
49T	Brian Holton(FC)	.15	.11	.06
50T	Charles Hudson	.06	.05	.02
51T	Danny Jackson(FC)	.30	.25	.12
52T	Reggie Jackson	.50	.40	.20
53T	Chris James(FC)	.40	.30	.15
54T	Dion James	.10	.08	.04
55T	Stan Jefferson(FC)	.20	.15	.08
56T	Joe Johnson(FC)	.08	.06	.03
57T	Terry Kennedy	.08	.06	.03
58T	Mike Kingery	.08	.06	.03
59T	Ray Knight	.10	.08	.04
60T	Gene Larkin(FC)	.30	.25	.12
61T	Mike LaValliere	.10	.08	.04
62T	Jack Lazorko	.06	.05	.02
63T	Terry Leach	.06	.05	.02
64T	Tim Leary	.06	.05	.02
65T	Jim Lindeman(FC)	.15	.11	.06
66T	Steve Lombardozzi(FC)	.06	.05	.02
67T	Bill Long(FC)	.20	.15	.08
68T	Barry Lyons(FC)	.15	.11	.06
69T	Shane Mack	.40	.30	.15
70T	Greg Maddux(FC)	.70	.50	.30
71T	Bill Madlock	.15	.11	.06
72T	Joe Magrane(FC)	.50	.40	.20
73T	Dave Martinez(FC)	.25	.20	.10
74T	Fred McGriff(FC)	2.50	2.00	1.00
75T	Mark McLemore(FC)	.10	.08	.04
76T	Kevin McReynolds(FC)	.40	.30	.15
77T	Dave Meads(FC)	.15	.11	.06
78T	Eddie Milner	.06	.05	.02
79T	Greg Minton	.06	.05	.02
80T	John Mitchell(FC)	.15	.11	.06
81T	Kevin Mitchell	1.00	.70	.40
82T	Charlie Moore	.06	.05	.02
83T	Jeff Musselman(FC)	.12	.09	.05
84T	Gene Nelson	.06	.05	.02
85T	Graig Nettles	.12	.09	.05
86T	Al Newman	.06	.05	.02
87T	Reid Nichols	.06	.05	.02
88T	Tom Niedenfuer	.08	.06	.03
89T	Joe Niekro	.10	.08	.04
90T	Tom Nieto	.06	.05	.02
91T	Matt Nokes(FC)	.40	.30	.15
92T	Dickie Noles	.06	.05	.02
93T	Pat Pacillo	.15	.11	.06
94T	Lance Parrish	.20	.15	.08
95T	Tony Pena	.10	.08	.04
96T	Luis Polonia(FC)	.40	.30	.15
97T	Randy Ready	.06	.05	.02
98T	Jeff Reardon	.12	.09	.05
99T	Gary Redus	.08	.06	.03
100T	Jeff Reed	.06	.05	.02
101T	Rick Rhoden	.10	.08	.04
102T	Cal Ripken, Sr.	.06	.05	.02
103T	Wally Ritchie(FC)	.15	.11	.06
104T	Jeff Robinson(FC)	.40	.30	.15
105T	Gary Roenicke	.06	.05	.02
106T	Jerry Royster	.06	.05	.02
107T	Mark Salas	.06	.05	.02
108T	Luis Salazar	.06	.05	.02
109T	Benny Santiago(FC)	.80	.60	.30
110T	Dave Schmidt	.08	.06	.03
111T	Kevin Seitzer(FC)	.50	.40	.20
112T	John Shelby	.06	.05	.02
113T	Steve Shields(FC)	.08	.06	.03
114T	John Smiley(FC)	.60	.45	.25
115T	Chris Speier	.06	.05	.02
116T	Mike Stanley(FC)	.20	.15	.08
117T	Terry Steinbach(FC)	.40	.30	.15
118T	Les Straker(FC)	.20	.15	.08
119T	Jim Sundberg	.08	.06	.03
120T	Danny Tartabull	.35	.25	.14
121T	Tom Trebelhorn	.08	.06	.03
122T	Dave Valle(FC)	.12	.09	.05
123T	Ed Vande Berg	.06	.05	.02
124T	Andy Van Slyke	.20	.15	.08
125T	Gary Ward	.06	.05	.02
126T	Alan Wiggins	.06	.05	.02
127T	Bill Wilkinson(FC)	.15	.11	.06
128T	Frank Williams	.08	.06	.03
129T	Matt Williams(FC)	3.00	2.25	1.25
130T	Jim Winn	.06	.05	.02
131T	Matt Young	.06	.05	.02
132T	Checklist 1T-132T	.06	.05	.02

1988 Topps

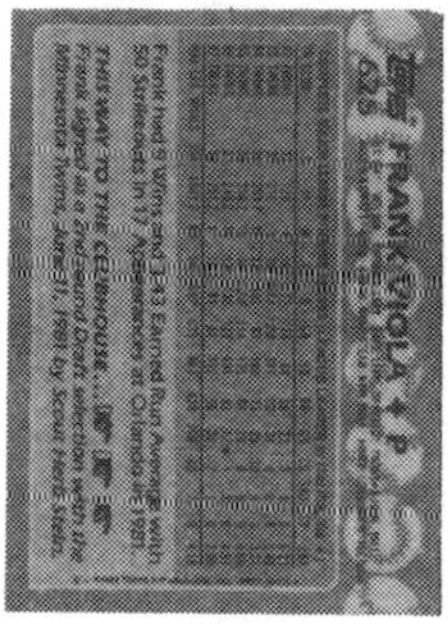

The 1988 Topps set features a clean, attractive design that should prove to be very popular with collectors for many years to come. The full-color player photo is surrounded by a thin yellow frame which is encompassed by a white border. The player's name appears in the lower right corner in a colored band which appears to wrap around the player photo. The player's team nickname is located in large letters at the top of the card. The Topps logo is placed in the lower left corner of the card. The card backs feature black print on orange and gray stock and includes the usual player personal and career statistics. Many of the cards contain a new feature entitled "This Way To The Clubhouse", which explains how the player joined his current team, be it by trade, free agency, etc. The 792-card set includes a number of special subsets including "Future Stars", "Turn Back The Clock", All-Star teams, All-Star rookie selections, and Record Breakers. All cards measure 2-1/2" by 3-1/2". For the fifth consecutive year, Topps issued a glossy "Tiffany" edition of its 792-card regular-issue set. The Tiffany cards have a value of 3-4 times greater than the same card in the regular issue. The Tiffany edition could be purchased by collectors directly from Topps for $99. The company

placed ads for the Tiffany set in publications such as USA Today and The Sporting News.

		MT	NR MT	EX
Complete Set:		20.00	15.00	8.00
Common Player:		.04	.03	.02
1	'87 Record Breakers (Vince Coleman)	.08	.06	.03
2	'87 Record Breakers (Don Mattingly)	.40	.30	.15
3a	'87 Record Breakers (Mark McGwire) (white triangle by left foot)	.40	.30	.15
3b	'87 Record Breakers (Mark McGwire) (no triangle by left foot)	.25	.20	.10
4a	'87 Record Breakers (Eddie Murray) (no mention of record on front)	.10	.08	.04
4b	'87 Record Breakers (Eddie Murray) (record stated on card front)	1.25	.90	.50
5	'87 Record Breakers (Joe Niekro, Phil Niekro)	.10	.08	.04
6	'87 Record Breakers (Nolan Ryan)	.10	.08	.04
7	'87 Record Breakers (Benito Santiago)	.15	.11	.06
8	Kevin Elster(FC)	.25	.20	.10
9	Andy Hawkins	.04	.03	.02
10	Ryne Sandberg	.35	.25	.12
11	Mike Young	.04	.03	.02
12	Bill Schroeder	.04	.03	.02
13	Andres Thomas	.06	.05	.02
14	Sparky Anderson	.06	.05	.02
15	Chili Davis	.06	.05	.02
16	Kirk McCaskill	.06	.05	.02
17	Ron Oester	.04	.03	.02
18a	*Al Leiter* (no "NY" on shirt, photo actually Steve George)(FC)	.40	.30	.15
18b	*Al Leiter* ("NY" on shirt, correct photo)(FC)	.20	.15	.08
19	*Mark Davidson*(FC)	.12	.09	.05
20	Kevin Gross	.06	.05	.02
21	Red Sox Leaders (Wade Boggs, Spike Owen)	.15	.11	.06
22	Greg Swindell	.15	.11	.06
23	Ken Landreaux	.04	.03	.02
24	Jim Deshaies	.06	.05	.02
25	Andres Galarraga	.12	.09	.05
26	Mitch Williams	.06	.05	.02
27	R.J. Reynolds	.04	.03	.02
28	*Jose Nunez*(FC)	.10	.08	.04
29	Argenis Salazar	.04	.03	.02
30	Sid Fernandez	.08	.06	.03
31	Bruce Bochy	.04	.03	.02
32	Mike Morgan	.04	.03	.02
33	Rob Deer	.06	.05	.02
34	Ricky Horton	.06	.05	.02
35	Harold Baines	.10	.08	.04
36	Jamie Moyer	.06	.05	.02
37	Ed Romero	.04	.03	.02
38	Jeff Calhoun	.04	.03	.02
39	Gerald Perry	.08	.06	.03
40	Orel Hershiser	.20	.15	.08
41	Bob Melvin	.04	.03	.02
42	*Bill Landrum*(FC)	.10	.08	.04
43	Dick Schofield	.04	.03	.02
44	Lou Piniella	.06	.05	.02
45	Kent Hrbek	.12	.09	.05
46	Darnell Coles	.06	.05	.02
47	Joaquin Andujar	.06	.05	.02
48	Alan Ashby	.04	.03	.02
49	Dave Clark(FC)	.10	.08	.04
50	Hubie Brooks	.08	.06	.03
51	Orioles Leaders (Eddie Murray, Cal Ripken)	.12	.09	.05
52	Don Robinson	.06	.05	.02
53	Curt Wilkerson	.04	.03	.02
54	Jim Clancy	.06	.05	.02
55	Phil Bradley	.08	.06	.03
56	Ed Hearn	.04	.03	.02
57	*Tim Crews*(FC)	.15	.11	.06
58	Dave Magadan	.10	.08	.04
59	Danny Cox	.06	.05	.02
60	Rickey Henderson	.35	.25	.14
61	*Mark Knudson*(FC)	.10	.08	.04
62	Jeff Hamilton	.08	.06	.03
63	Jimmy Jones(FC)	.10	.08	.04
64	*Ken Caminiti*(FC)	.30	.25	.12
65	Leon Durham	.06	.05	.02
66	Shane Rawley	.06	.05	.02
67	Ken Oberkfell	.04	.03	.02
68	Dave Dravecky	.06	.05	.02
69	*Mike Hart*(FC)	.10	.08	.04

		MT	NR MT	EX
70	Roger Clemens	.50	.40	.20
71	Gary Pettis	.04	.03	.02
72	Dennis Eckersley	.10	.08	.04
73	Randy Bush	.04	.03	.02
74	Tom Lasorda	.06	.05	.02
75	Joe Carter	.10	.08	.04
76	Denny Martinez	.04	.03	.02
77	Tom O'Malley	.04	.03	.02
78	Dan Petry	.06	.05	.02
79	Ernie Whitt	.06	.05	.02
80	Mark Langston	.10	.08	.04
81	Reds Leaders (John Franco, Ron Robinson)	.06	.05	.02
82	*Darrel Akerfelds*(FC)	.12	.09	.05
83	Jose Oquendo	.04	.03	.02
84	Cecilio Guante	.04	.03	.02
85	Howard Johnson	.08	.06	.03
86	Ron Karkovice	.04	.03	.02
87	Mike Mason	.04	.03	.02
88	Earnie Riles	.04	.03	.02
89	*Gary Thurman*(FC)	.20	.15	.08
90	Dale Murphy	.30	.25	.12
91	*Joey Cora*(FC)	.12	.09	.05
92	Len Matuszek	.04	.03	.02
93	Bob Sebra	.04	.03	.02
94	*Chuck Jackson*(FC)	.15	.11	.06
95	Lance Parrish	.12	.09	.05
96	*Todd Benzinger*(FC)	.25	.20	.10
97	Scott Garrelts	.04	.03	.02
98	*Rene Gonzales*(FC)	.15	.11	.06
99	Chuck Finley	.06	.05	.02
100	Jack Clark	.12	.09	.05
101	Allan Anderson	.06	.05	.02
102	Barry Larkin	.35	.25	.14
103	Curt Young	.06	.05	.02
104	Dick Williams	.04	.03	.02
105	Jesse Orosco	.06	.05	.02
106	*Jim Walewander*(FC)	.12	.09	.05
107	Scott Bailes	.06	.05	.02
108	Steve Lyons	.04	.03	.02
109	Joel Skinner	.04	.03	.02
110	Teddy Higuera	.08	.06	.03
111	Expos Leaders (Hubie Brooks, Vance Law)	.06	.05	.02
112	*Les Lancaster*(FC)	.15	.11	.06
113	Kelly Gruber	.04	.03	.02
114	Jeff Russell	.04	.03	.02
115	Johnny Ray	.06	.05	.02
116	Jerry Don Gleaton	.04	.03	.02
117	*James Steels*(FC)	.10	.08	.04
118	Bob Welch	.08	.06	.03
119	*Robbie Wine*(FC)	.12	.09	.05
120	Kirby Puckett	.40	.30	.15
121	Checklist 1-132	.04	.03	.02
122	Tony Bernazard	.04	.03	.02
123	Tom Candiotti	.04	.03	.02
124	Ray Knight	.06	.05	.02
125	Bruce Hurst	.08	.06	.03
126	Steve Jeltz	.04	.03	.02
127	Jim Gott	.04	.03	.02
128	Johnny Grubb	.04	.03	.02
129	Greg Minton	.04	.03	.02
130	Buddy Bell	.08	.06	.03
131	Don Schulze	.04	.03	.02
132	Donnie Hill	.04	.03	.02
133	Greg Mathews	.06	.05	.02
134	Chuck Tanner	.04	.03	.02
135	Dennis Rasmussen	.08	.06	.03
136	Brian Dayett	.04	.03	.02
137	Chris Bosio	.06	.05	.02
138	Mitch Webster	.06	.05	.02
139	Jerry Browne	.06	.05	.02
140	Jesse Barfield	.10	.08	.04
141	Royals Leaders (George Brett, Bret Saberhagen)	.12	.09	.05
142	Andy Van Slyke	.10	.08	.04
143	Mickey Tettleton	.04	.03	.02
144	*Don Gordon*(FC)	.08	.06	.03
145	Bill Madlock	.08	.06	.03
146	*Donell Nixon*(FC)	.15	.11	.06
147	Bill Buckner	.08	.06	.03
148	Carmelo Martinez	.06	.05	.02
149	Ken Howell	.04	.03	.02
150	Eric Davis	.40	.30	.15
151	Bob Knepper	.06	.05	.02
152	*Jody Reed*(FC)	.50	.40	.20
153	John Habyan	.04	.03	.02
154	Jeff Stone	.04	.03	.02
155	Bruce Sutter	.10	.08	.04
156	Gary Matthews	.06	.05	.02
157	Atlee Hammaker	.04	.03	.02

		MT	NR MT	EX
158	Tim Hulett	.04	.03	.02
159	*Brad Arnsberg*(FC)	.12	.09	.05
160	Willie McGee	.10	.08	.04
161	Bryn Smith	.06	.05	.02
162	Mark McLemore	.06	.05	.02
163	Dale Mohorcic	.04	.03	.02
164	Dave Johnson	.06	.05	.02
165	Robin Yount	.20	.15	.08
166	*Rick Rodriguez*(FC)	.10	.08	.04
167	Rance Mulliniks	.04	.03	.02
168	Barry Jones	.04	.03	.02
169	*Ross Jones*(FC)	.12	.09	.05
170	Rich Gossage	.12	.09	.05
171	Cubs Leaders (Shawon Dunston, Manny Trillo)	.06	.05	.02
172	*Lloyd McClendon*(FC)	.10	.08	.04
173	Eric Plunk	.04	.03	.02
174	Phil Garner	.04	.03	.02
175	Kevin Bass	.06	.05	.02
176	Jeff Reed	.04	.03	.02
177	Frank Tanana	.06	.05	.02
178	Dwayne Henry(FC)	.06	.05	.02
179	Charlie Puleo	.04	.03	.02
180	Terry Kennedy	.06	.05	.02
181	Dave Cone	.50	.40	.20
182	Ken Phelps	.06	.05	.02
183	Tom Lawless	.04	.03	.02
184	Ivan Calderon	.08	.06	.03
185	Rick Rhoden	.06	.05	.02
186	Rafael Palmeiro	.35	.25	.14
187	Steve Kiefer(FC)	.06	.05	.02
188	John Russell	.04	.03	.02
189	*Wes Gardner*(FC)	.20	.15	.08
190	Candy Maldonado	.06	.05	.02
191	John Cerutti	.06	.05	.02
192	Devon White	.20	.15	.08
193	Brian Fisher	.06	.05	.02
194	Tom Kelly	.04	.03	.02
195	Dan Quisenberry	.06	.05	.02
196	Dave Engle	.04	.03	.02
197	Lance McCullers	.06	.05	.02
198	Franklin Stubbs	.06	.05	.02
199	*Dave Meads*	.12	.09	.05
200	Wade Boggs	.50	.40	.20
201	Rangers Leaders (Steve Buechele, Pete Incaviglia, Pete O'Brien, Bobby Valentine)	.06	.05	.02
202	Glenn Hoffman	.04	.03	.02
203	Fred Toliver	.04	.03	.02
204	Paul O'Neill(FC)	.12	.09	.05
205	*Nelson Liriano*(FC)	.12	.09	.05
206	Domingo Ramos	.04	.03	.02
207	*John Mitchell, John Mitchell*(FC)	.20	.15	.08
208	Steve Lake	.04	.03	.02
209	Richard Dotson	.06	.05	.02
210	Willie Randolph	.06	.05	.02
211	Frank DiPino	.04	.03	.02
212	Greg Brock	.06	.05	.02
213	Albert Hall	.04	.03	.02
214	Dave Schmidt	.04	.03	.02
215	Von Hayes	.06	.05	.02
216	Jerry Reuss	.06	.05	.02
217	Harry Spilman	.04	.03	.02
218	Dan Schatzeder	.04	.03	.02
219	Mike Stanley	.08	.06	.03
220	Tom Henke	.06	.05	.02
221	Rafael Belliard	.04	.03	.02
222	Steve Farr	.04	.03	.02
223	Stan Jefferson	.08	.06	.03
224	Tom Trebelhorn	.04	.03	.02
225	Mike Scioscia	.06	.05	.02
226	Dave Lopes	.06	.05	.02
227	Ed Correa	.04	.03	.02
228	Wallace Johnson	.04	.03	.02
229	Jeff Musselman	.08	.06	.03
230	Pat Tabler	.06	.05	.02
231	Pirates Leaders (Barry Bonds, Bobby Bonilla)	.10	.08	.04
232	Bob James	.04	.03	.02
233	Rafael Santana	.04	.03	.02
234	Ken Dayley	.04	.03	.02
235	Gary Ward	.06	.05	.02
236	Ted Power	.04	.03	.02
237	Mike Heath	.04	.03	.02
238	*Luis Polonia*	.20	.15	.08
239	Roy Smalley	.04	.03	.02
240	Lee Smith	.08	.06	.03
241	Damaso Garcia	.04	.03	.02
242	Tom Niedenfuer	.06	.05	.02
243	Mark Ryal(FC)	.04	.03	.02
244	Jeff Robinson	.04	.03	.02
245	Rich Gedman	.06	.05	.02
246	*Mike Campbell*(FC)	.10	.08	.04
247	Thad Bosley	.04	.03	.02
248	Storm Davis	.08	.06	.03
249	Mike Marshall	.10	.08	.04
250	Nolan Ryan	.60	.45	.25
251	Tom Foley	.04	.03	.02
252	Bob Brower	.06	.05	.02
253	Checklist 133-264	.04	.03	.02
254	Lee Elia	.04	.03	.02
255	Mookie Wilson	.06	.05	.02
256	Ken Schrom	.04	.03	.02
257	Jerry Royster	.04	.03	.02
258	Ed Nunez	.04	.03	.02
259	Ron Kittle	.06	.05	.02
260	Vince Coleman	.15	.11	.06
261	Giants Leaders (Will Clark, Candy Maldonado, Kevin Mitchell, Robby Thompson, Jose Uribe)	.10	.08	.04
262	Drew Hall(FC)	.12	.09	.05
263	Glenn Braggs	.08	.06	.03
264	*Les Straker*	.15	.11	.06
265	Bo Diaz	.06	.05	.02
266	Paul Assenmacher	.04	.03	.02
267	*Billy Bean*(FC)	.10	.08	.04
268	Bruce Ruffin	.06	.05	.02
269	*Ellis Burks*	1.00	.70	.40
270	Mike Witt	.06	.05	.02
271	Ken Gerhart	.06	.05	.02
272	Steve Ontiveros	.04	.03	.02
273	Garth Iorg	.04	.03	.02
274	Junior Ortiz	.04	.03	.02
275	Kevin Seitzer	.30	.25	.12
276	Luis Salazar	.04	.03	.02
277	Alejandro Pena	.06	.05	.02
278	Jose Cruz	.06	.05	.02
279	Randy St. Claire	.04	.03	.02
280	Pete Incaviglia	.12	.09	.05
281	Jerry Hairston	.04	.03	.02
282	Pat Perry	.04	.03	.02
283	Phil Lombardi(FC)	.06	.05	.02
284	Larry Bowa	.06	.05	.02
285	Jim Presley	.08	.06	.03
286	*Chuck Crim*	.12	.09	.05
287	Manny Trillo	.06	.05	.02
288	*Pat Pacillo*	.15	.11	.06
289	Dave Bergman	.04	.03	.02
290	Tony Fernandez	.10	.08	.04
291	Astros Leaders (Kevin Bass, Billy Hatcher)	.06	.05	.02
292	Carney Lansford	.08	.06	.03
293	*Doug Jones*(FC)	.25	.20	.10
294	*Al Pedrique*(FC)	.12	.09	.05
295	Bert Blyleven	.10	.08	.04
296	Floyd Rayford	.04	.03	.02
297	Zane Smith	.06	.05	.02
298	Milt Thompson	.04	.03	.02
299	Steve Crawford	.04	.03	.02
300	Don Mattingly	.60	.45	.25
301	Bud Black	.04	.03	.02
302	Jose Uribe	.04	.03	.02
303	Eric Show	.06	.05	.02
304	George Hendrick	.06	.05	.02
305	Steve Sax	.12	.09	.05
306	Billy Hatcher	.06	.05	.02
307	Mike Trujillo	.04	.03	.02
308	Lee Mazzilli	.06	.05	.02
309	*Bill Long*	.15	.11	.06
310	Tom Herr	.06	.05	.02
311	Scott Sanderson	.04	.03	.02
312	Joey Meyer(FC)	.20	.15	.08
313	Bob McClure	.04	.03	.02
314	Jimy Williams	.04	.03	.02
315	Dave Parker	.12	.09	.05
316	Jose Rijo	.06	.05	.02
317	Tom Nieto	.04	.03	.02
318	Mel Hall	.06	.05	.02
319	Mike Loynd	.04	.03	.02
320	Alan Trammell	.15	.11	.06
321	White Sox Leaders (Harold Baines, Carlton Fisk)	.08	.06	.03
322	*Vicente Palacios*(FC)	.15	.11	.06
323	Rick Leach	.04	.03	.02
324	Danny Jackson	.20	.15	.08
325	Glenn Hubbard	.04	.03	.02
326	Al Nipper	.04	.03	.02
327	Larry Sheets	.06	.05	.02
328	*Greg Cadaret*(FC)	.15	.11	.06
329	Chris Speier	.04	.03	.02
330	Eddie Whitson	.04	.03	.02

		MT	NR MT	EX
331	Brian Downing	.06	.05	.02
332	Jerry Reed	.04	.03	.02
333	Wally Backman	.06	.05	.02
334	Dave LaPoint	.06	.05	.02
335	Claudell Washington	.06	.05	.02
336	Ed Lynch	.04	.03	.02
337	Jim Gantner	.04	.03	.02
338	Brian Holton	.08	.06	.03
339	Kurt Stillwell	.08	.06	.03
340	Jack Morris	.15	.11	.06
341	Carmen Castillo	.04	.03	.02
342	Larry Andersen	.04	.03	.02
343	Greg Gagne	.04	.03	.02
344	Tony LaRussa	.04	.03	.02
345	Scott Fletcher	.06	.05	.02
346	Vance Law	.06	.05	.02
347	Joe Johnson	.04	.03	.02
348	Jim Eisenreich	.04	.03	.02
349	Bob Walk	.04	.03	.02
350	Will Clark	1.00	.70	.40
351	Cardinals Leaders (Tony Pena, Red Schoendienst)	.06	.05	.02
352	*Billy Ripken*(FC)	.20	.15	.08
353	Ed Olwine	.04	.03	.02
354	Marc Sullivan	.04	.03	.02
355	Roger McDowell	.08	.06	.03
356	Luis Aguayo	.04	.03	.02
357	Floyd Bannister	.06	.05	.02
358	Rey Quinones	.04	.03	.02
359	Tim Stoddard	.04	.03	.02
360	Tony Gwynn	.25	.20	.10
361	Greg Maddux	.35	.25	.14
362	Juan Castillo	.04	.03	.02
363	Willie Fraser	.06	.05	.02
364	Nick Esasky	.06	.05	.02
365	Floyd Youmans	.04	.03	.02
366	Chet Lemon	.06	.05	.02
367	Tim Leary	.06	.05	.02
368	*Gerald Young*(FC)	.15	.11	.06
369	Greg Harris	.04	.03	.02
370	Jose Canseco	1.25	.90	.50
371	Joe Hesketh	.04	.03	.02
372	*Matt Williams*	2.00	1.50	.80
373	Checklist 265-396	.04	.03	.02
374	Doc Edwards	.04	.03	.02
375	Tom Brunansky	.08	.06	.03
376	*Bill Wilkinson*	.12	.09	.05
377	*Sam Horn*(FC)	.20	.15	.08
378	*Todd Frohwirth*(FC)	.15	.11	.06
379	Rafael Ramirez	.04	.03	.02
380	*Joe Magrane*	.30	.25	.12
381	Angels Leaders (Jack Howell, Wally Joyner)	.12	.09	.05
382	*Keith Miller*(FC)	.15	.11	.06
383	Eric Bell	.06	.05	.02
384	Neil Allen	.04	.03	.02
385	Carlton Fisk	.30	.25	.12
386	Don Mattingly AS	.40	.30	.15
387	Willie Randolph AS	.06	.05	.02
388	Wade Boggs AS	.35	.25	.14
389	Alan Trammell AS	.08	.06	.03
390	George Bell AS	.10	.08	.04
391	Kirby Puckett AS	.12	.09	.05
392	Dave Winfield AS	.12	.09	.05
393	Matt Nokes AS	.15	.11	.06
394	Roger Clemens AS	.15	.11	.06
395	Jimmy Key AS	.06	.05	.02
396	Tom Henke AS	.06	.05	.02
397	Jack Clark AS	.06	.05	.02
398	Juan Samuel AS	.06	.05	.02
399	Tim Wallach AS	.06	.05	.02
400	Ozzie Smith AS	.08	.06	.03
401	Andre Dawson AS	.10	.08	.04
402	Tony Gwynn AS	.15	.11	.06
403	Tim Raines AS	.12	.09	.05
404	Benny Santiago AS	.10	.08	.04
405	Dwight Gooden AS	.15	.11	.06
406	Shane Rawley AS	.06	.05	.02
407	Steve Bedrosian AS	.08	.06	.03
408	Dion James	.06	.05	.02
409	Joel McKeon(FC)	.04	.03	.02
410	Tony Pena	.06	.05	.02
411	Wayne Tolleson	.04	.03	.02
412	Randy Myers	.10	.08	.04
413	John Christensen	.04	.03	.02
414	John McNamara	.04	.03	.02
415	Don Carman	.06	.05	.02
416	Keith Moreland	.06	.05	.02
417	*Mark Ciardi*(FC)	.10	.08	.04
418	Joel Youngblood	.04	.03	.02
419	Scott McGregor	.06	.05	.02

		MT	NR MT	EX
420	Wally Joyner	.25	.20	.10
421	Ed Vande Berg	.04	.03	.02
422	Dave Concepcion	.06	.05	.02
423	*John Smiley*	.50	.40	.20
424	Dwayne Murphy	.06	.05	.02
425	Jeff Reardon	.08	.06	.03
426	Randy Ready	.04	.03	.02
427	*Paul Kilgus*(FC)	.20	.15	.08
428	John Shelby	.04	.03	.02
429	Tigers Leaders (Kirk Gibson, Alan Trammell)	.08	.06	.03
430	Glenn Davis	.12	.09	.05
431	Casey Candaele	.04	.03	.02
432	Mike Moore	.04	.03	.02
433	*Bill Pecota*(FC)	.15	.11	.06
434	Rick Aguilera	.04	.03	.02
435	Mike Pagliarulo	.08	.06	.03
436	Mike Bielecki	.04	.03	.02
437	*Fred Manrique*(FC)	.12	.09	.05
438	*Rob Ducey*(FC)	.12	.09	.05
439	Dave Martinez	.08	.06	.03
440	Steve Bedrosian	.10	.08	.04
441	Rick Manning	.04	.03	.02
442	*Tom Bolton*(FC)	.15	.11	.06
443	Ken Griffey	.06	.05	.02
444	Cal Ripken, Sr.	.04	.03	.02
445	Mike Krukow	.06	.05	.02
446	Doug DeCinces	.06	.05	.02
447	*Jeff Montgomery*(FC)	.30	.25	.12
448	Mike Davis	.06	.05	.02
449	*Jeff Robinson*	.15	.11	.06
450	Barry Bonds	.40	.30	.15
451	Keith Atherton	.04	.03	.02
452	Willie Wilson	.08	.06	.03
453	Dennis Powell	.04	.03	.02
454	Marvell Wynne	.04	.03	.02
455	*Shawn Hillegas*(FC)	.15	.11	.06
456	Dave Anderson	.04	.03	.02
457	Terry Leach	.04	.03	.02
458	Ron Hassey	.04	.03	.02
459	Yankees Leaders (Willie Randolph, Dave Winfield)	.08	.06	.03
460	Ozzie Smith	.12	.09	.05
461	Danny Darwin	.04	.03	.02
462	Don Slaught	.04	.03	.02
463	*Fred McGriff*	1.00	.70	.40
464	Jay Tibbs	.04	.03	.02
465	Paul Molitor	.10	.08	.04
466	Jerry Mumphrey	.04	.03	.02
467	Don Aase	.04	.03	.02
468	Darren Daulton	.04	.03	.02
469	Jeff Dedmon	.04	.03	.02
470	Dwight Evans	.10	.08	.04
471	Donnie Moore	.04	.03	.02
472	Robby Thompson	.06	.05	.02
473	Joe Niekro	.06	.05	.02
474	Tom Brookens	.04	.03	.02
475	Pete Rose	.20	.15	.08
476	Dave Stewart	.08	.06	.03
477	Jamie Quirk	.04	.03	.02
478	Sid Bream	.06	.05	.02
479	Brett Butler	.06	.05	.02
480	Dwight Gooden	.40	.30	.15
481	Mariano Duncan	.04	.03	.02
482	Mark Davis	.04	.03	.02
483	*Rod Booker*(FC)	.12	.09	.05
484	Pat Clements	.04	.03	.02
485	Harold Reynolds	.06	.05	.02
486	*Pat Keedy*(FC)	.10	.08	.04
487	Jim Pankovits	.04	.03	.02
488	Andy McGaffigan	.04	.03	.02
489	Dodgers Leaders (Pedro Guerrero, Fernando Valenzuela)	.08	.06	.03
490	Larry Parrish	.06	.05	.02
491	B.J. Surhoff	.10	.08	.04
492	Doyle Alexander	.06	.05	.02
493	Mike Greenwell	.50	.40	.20
494	*Wally Ritchie*	.12	.09	.05
495	Eddie Murray	.25	.20	.10
496	Guy Hoffman	.04	.03	.02
497	Kevin Mitchell	.30	.25	.12
498	Bob Boone	.06	.05	.02
499	Eric King	.06	.05	.02
500	Andre Dawson	.15	.11	.06
501	Tim Birtsas(FC)	.06	.05	.02
502	Danny Gladden	.04	.03	.02
503	*Junior Noboa*(FC)	.10	.08	.04
504	Bob Rodgers	.04	.03	.02
505	Willie Upshaw	.06	.05	.02
506	John Cangelosi	.04	.03	.02
507	Mark Gubicza	.10	.08	.04

		MT	NR MT	EX
508	Tim Teufel	.04	.03	.02
509	Bill Dawley	.04	.03	.02
510	Dave Winfield	.20	.15	.08
511	Joel Davis	.04	.03	.02
512	Alex Trevino	.04	.03	.02
513	Tim Flannery	.04	.03	.02
514	Pat Sheridan	.04	.03	.02
515	Juan Nieves	.06	.05	.02
516	Jim Sundberg	.06	.05	.02
517	Ron Robinson	.04	.03	.02
518	Greg Gross	.04	.03	.02
519	Mariners Leaders (Phil Bradley, Harold Reynolds)	.06	.05	.02
520	Dave Smith	.06	.05	.02
521	Jim Dwyer	.04	.03	.02
522	*Bob Patterson*(FC)	.12	.09	.05
523	Gary Roenicke	.04	.03	.02
524	Gary Lucas	.04	.03	.02
525	Marty Barrett	.06	.05	.02
526	Juan Berenguer	.04	.03	.02
527	Steve Henderson	.04	.03	.02
528a	Checklist 397-528 (#455 is Steve Carlton)	.80	.60	.30
528b	Checklist 397-528 (#455 is Shawn Hillegas)	.06	.05	.02
529	Tim Burke	.04	.03	.02
530	Gary Carter	.15	.11	.06
531	Rich Yett	.04	.03	.02
532	Mike Kingery	.04	.03	.02
533	*John Farrell*(FC)	.15	.11	.06
534	John Wathan	.06	.05	.02
535	Ron Guidry	.12	.09	.05
536	John Morris	.04	.03	.02
537	Steve Buechele	.04	.03	.02
538	Bill Wegman	.04	.03	.02
539	Mike LaValliere	.06	.05	.02
540	Bret Saberhagen	.25	.20	.10
541	Juan Beniquez	.04	.03	.02
542	*Paul Noce*(FC)	.10	.08	.04
543	Kent Tekulve	.06	.05	.02
544	Jim Traber	.06	.05	.02
545	Don Baylor	.08	.06	.03
546	John Candelaria	.06	.05	.02
547	*Felix Fermin*(FC)	.12	.09	.05
548	*Shane Mack*	.15	.11	.06
549	Braves Leaders (Ken Griffey, Dion James, Dale Murphy, Gerald Perry)	.08	.06	.03
550	Pedro Guerrero	.15	.11	.06
551	Terry Steinbach	.15	.11	.06
552	Mark Thurmond	.04	.03	.02
553	Tracy Jones	.10	.08	.04
554	Mike Smithson	.04	.03	.02
555	Brook Jacoby	.08	.06	.03
556	*Stan Clarke*(FC)	.12	.09	.05
557	Craig Reynolds	.04	.03	.02
558	Bob Ojeda	.06	.05	.02
559	*Ken Williams*(FC)	.20	.15	.08
560	Tim Wallach	.08	.06	.03
561	Rick Cerone	.04	.03	.02
562	Jim Lindeman	.10	.08	.04
563	Jose Guzman	.06	.05	.02
564	Frank Lucchesi	.04	.03	.02
565	Lloyd Moseby	.06	.05	.02
566	*Charlie O'Brien*(FC)	.12	.09	.05
567	Mike Diaz	.06	.05	.02
568	Chris Brown	.06	.05	.02
569	Charlie Leibrandt	.06	.05	.02
570	Jeffrey Leonard	.06	.05	.02
571	*Mark Williamson*(FC)	.12	.09	.05
572	Chris James	.15	.11	.06
573	Bob Stanley	.04	.03	.02
574	Graig Nettles	.08	.06	.03
575	Don Sutton	.12	.09	.05
576	*Tommy Hinzo*(FC)	.12	.09	.05
577	Tom Browning	.08	.06	.03
578	Gary Gaetti	.10	.08	.04
579	Mets Leaders (Gary Carter, Kevin McReynolds)	.08	.06	.03
580	Mark McGwire	.60	.45	.25
581	Tito Landrum	.04	.03	.02
582	*Mike Henneman*	.25	.20	.10
583	Dave Valle(FC)	.06	.05	.02
584	Steve Trout	.04	.03	.02
585	Ozzie Guillen	.06	.05	.02
586	Bob Forsch	.06	.05	.02
587	Terry Puhl	.04	.03	.02
588	*Jeff Parrett*(FC)	.20	.15	.08
589	Geno Petralli	.04	.03	.02
590	George Bell	.20	.15	.08
591	Doug Drabek	.06	.05	.02
592	Dale Sveum	.06	.05	.02

		MT	NR MT	EX
593	Bob Tewksbury	.04	.03	.02
594	Bobby Valentine	.04	.03	.02
595	Frank White	.06	.05	.02
596	John Kruk	.08	.06	.03
597	Gene Garber	.04	.03	.02
598	Lee Lacy	.04	.03	.02
599	Calvin Schiraldi	.04	.03	.02
600	Mike Schmidt	.40	.30	.15
601	Jack Lazorko	.04	.03	.02
602	Mike Aldrete	.06	.05	.02
603	Rob Murphy	.06	.05	.02
604	Chris Bando	.04	.03	.02
605	Kirk Gibson	.15	.11	.06
606	Moose Haas	.04	.03	.02
607	Mickey Hatcher	.04	.03	.02
608	Charlie Kerfeld	.04	.03	.02
609	Twins Leaders (Gary Gaetti, Kent Hrbek)	.08	.06	.03
610	Keith Hernandez	.15	.11	.06
611	Tommy John	.12	.09	.05
612	Curt Ford	.04	.03	.02
613	Bobby Thigpen	.08	.06	.03
614	Herm Winningham	.04	.03	.02
615	Jody Davis	.06	.05	.02
616	*Jay Aldrich*(FC)	.10	.08	.04
617	Oddibe McDowell	.06	.05	.02
618	Cecil Fielder	.60	.45	.25
619	*Mike Dunne*	.15	.11	.06
620	Cory Snyder	.15	.11	.06
621	Gene Nelson	.04	.03	.02
622	Kal Daniels	.15	.11	.06
623	Mike Flanagan	.06	.05	.02
624	Jim Leyland	.04	.03	.02
625	Frank Viola	.12	.09	.05
626	Glenn Wilson	.06	.05	.02
627	*Joe Boever*(FC)	.12	.09	.05
628	Dave Henderson	.08	.06	.03
629	Kelly Downs	.08	.06	.03
630	Darrell Evans	.08	.06	.03
631	Jack Howell	.06	.05	.02
632	*Steve Shields*	.12	.09	.05
633	*Barry Lyons*	.12	.09	.05
634	Jose DeLeon	.06	.05	.02
635	Terry Pendleton	.06	.05	.02
636	Charles Hudson	.04	.03	.02
637	*Jay Bell*(FC)	.35	.25	.14
638	Steve Balboni	.06	.05	.02
639	Brewers Leaders (Glenn Braggs, Tony Muser)	.06	.05	.02
640	Garry Templeton	.06	.05	.02
641	Rick Honeycutt	.04	.03	.02
642	Bob Dernier	.04	.03	.02
643	*Rocky Childress*(FC)	.12	.09	.05
644	Terry McGriff(FC)	.06	.05	.02
645	*Matt Nokes*	.30	.25	.12
646	Checklist 529-660	.04	.03	.02
647	Pascual Perez	.06	.05	.02
648	Al Newman	.04	.03	.02
649	*DeWayne Buice*	.15	.11	.06
650	Cal Ripken	.25	.20	.10
651	*Mike Jackson*(FC)	.15	.11	.06
652	Bruce Benedict	.04	.03	.02
653	Jeff Sellers	.06	.05	.02
654	Roger Craig	.06	.05	.02
655	Len Dykstra	.08	.06	.03
656	Lee Guetterman	.04	.03	.02
657	Gary Redus	.04	.03	.02
658	Tim Conroy	.04	.03	.02
659	Bobby Meacham	.04	.03	.02
660	Rick Reuschel	.08	.06	.03
661	Turn Back The Clock (Nolan Ryan)	.08	.06	.03
662	Turn Back The Clock (Jim Rice)	.08	.06	.03
663	Turn Back The Clock (Ron Blomberg)	.04	.03	.02
664	Turn Back The Clock (Bob Gibson)	.08	.06	.03
665	Turn Back The Clock (Stan Musial)	.12	.09	.05
666	Mario Soto	.06	.05	.02
667	Luis Quinones	.04	.03	.02
668	Walt Terrell	.06	.05	.02
669	Phillies Leaders (Lance Parrish, Mike Ryan)	.06	.05	.02
670	Dan Plesac	.08	.06	.03
671	Tim Laudner	.04	.03	.02
672	*John Davis*(FC)	.15	.11	.06
673	Tony Phillips	.04	.03	.02
674	Mike Fitzgerald	.04	.03	.02
675	Jim Rice	.20	.15	.08
676	Ken Dixon	.04	.03	.02
677	Eddie Milner	.04	.03	.02
678	Jim Acker	.04	.03	.02
679	Darrell Miller	.04	.03	.02

		MT	NR MT	EX
680	Charlie Hough	.06	.05	.02
681	Bobby Bonilla	.40	.30	.15
682	Jimmy Key	.08	.06	.03
683	Julio Franco	.08	.06	.03
684	Hal Lanier	.04	.03	.02
685	Ron Darling	.10	.08	.04
686	Terry Francona	.04	.03	.02
687	Mickey Brantley	.04	.03	.02
688	Jim Winn	.04	.03	.02
689	*Tom Pagnozzi*(FC)	.20	.15	.08
690	Jay Howell	.06	.05	.02
691	Dan Pasqua	.08	.06	.03
692	Mike Birkbeck	.06	.05	.02
693	Benny Santiago	.30	.25	.12
694	*Eric Nolte*(FC)	.12	.09	.05
695	Shawon Dunston	.08	.06	.03
696	Duane Ward	.04	.03	.02
697	Steve Lombardozzi	.08	.06	.03
698	Brad Havens	.04	.03	.02
699	Padres Leaders (Tony Gwynn, Benny Santiago)	.12	.09	.05
700	George Brett	.30	.25	.12
701	Sammy Stewart	.04	.03	.02
702	Mike Gallego	.04	.03	.02
703	Bob Brenly	.04	.03	.02
704	Dennis Boyd	.06	.05	.02
705	Juan Samuel	.10	.08	.04
706	Rick Mahler	.04	.03	.02
707	Fred Lynn	.10	.08	.04
708	Gus Polidor(FC)	.06	.05	.02
709	George Frazier	.04	.03	.02
710	Darryl Strawberry	.30	.25	.12
711	Bill Gullickson	.04	.03	.02
712	John Moses	.04	.03	.02
713	Willie Hernandez	.06	.05	.02
714	Jim Fregosi	.04	.03	.02
715	Todd Worrell	.08	.06	.03
716	Lenn Sakata	.04	.03	.02
717	Jay Baller(FC)	.06	.05	.02
718	Mike Felder	.04	.03	.02
719	Denny Walling	.04	.03	.02
720	Tim Raines	.20	.15	.08
721	Pete O'Brien	.06	.05	.02
722	Manny Lee	.04	.03	.02
723	Bob Kipper	.04	.03	.02
724	Danny Tartabull	.15	.11	.06
725	Mike Boddicker	.06	.05	.02
726	Alfredo Griffin	.06	.05	.02
727	Greg Booker	.04	.03	.02
728	Andy Allanson	.06	.05	.02
729	Blue Jays Leaders (George Bell, Fred McGriff)	.10	.08	.04
730	John Franco	.08	.06	.03
731	Rick Schu	.04	.03	.02
732	Dave Palmer	.04	.03	.02
733	Spike Owen	.04	.03	.02
734	Craig Lefferts	.04	.03	.02
735	Kevin McReynolds	.20	.15	.08
736	Matt Young	.04	.03	.02
737	Butch Wynegar	.04	.03	.02
738	Scott Bankhead	.04	.03	.02
739	Daryl Boston	.04	.03	.02
740	Rick Sutcliffe	.08	.06	.03
741	Mike Easler	.06	.05	.02
742	Mark Clear	.04	.03	.02
743	Larry Herndon	.04	.03	.02
744	Whitey Herzog	.06	.05	.02
745	Bill Doran	.06	.05	.02
746	*Gene Larkin*	.25	.20	.10
747	Bobby Witt	.08	.06	.03
748	Reid Nichols	.04	.03	.02
749	Mark Eichhorn	.06	.05	.02
750	Bo Jackson	1.00	.70	.40
751	Jim Morrison	.04	.03	.02
752	Mark Grant	.04	.03	.02
753	Danny Heep	.04	.03	.02
754	Mike LaCoss	.04	.03	.02
755	Ozzie Virgil	.04	.03	.02
756	Mike Maddux	.06	.05	.02
757	*John Marzano*	.15	.11	.06
758	*Eddie Williams*(FC)	.15	.11	.06
759	A's Leaders (Jose Canseco, Mark McGwire)	.40	.30	.15
760	Mike Scott	.10	.08	.04
761	Tony Armas	.06	.05	.02
762	Scott Bradley	.04	.03	.02
763	Doug Sisk	.04	.03	.02
764	Greg Walker	.06	.05	.02
765	Neal Heaton	.06	.05	.02
766	Henry Cotto	.04	.03	.02
767	*Jose Lind*(FC)	.25	.20	.10

		MT	NR MT	EX
768	Dickie Noles	.04	.03	.02
769	Cecil Cooper	.08	.06	.03
770	Lou Whitaker	.20	.15	.08
771	Ruben Sierra	.50	.40	.20
772	Sal Butera	.04	.03	.02
773	Frank Williams	.04	.03	.02
774	Gene Mauch	.06	.05	.02
775	Dave Stieb	.08	.06	.03
776	Checklist 661-792	.04	.03	.02
777	Lonnie Smith	.06	.05	.02
778a	*Keith Comstock* (white team letters)(FC)	3.00	2.25	1.25
778b	*Keith Comstock* (blue team letters)(FC)	.25	.20	.10
779	*Tom Glavine*(FC)	.60	.45	.25
780	Fernando Valenzuela	.15	.11	.06
781	*Keith Hughes*(FC)	.15	.11	.06
782	*Jeff Ballard*(FC)	.15	.11	.06
783	Ron Roenicke	.04	.03	.02
784	Joe Sambito	.04	.03	.02
785	Alvin Davis	.10	.08	.04
786	Joe Price	.04	.03	.02
787	Bill Almon	.04	.03	.02
788	Ray Searage	.04	.03	.02
789	Indians Leaders (Joe Carter, Cory Snyder)	.08	.06	.03
790	Dave Righetti	.12	.09	.05
791	Ted Simmons	.08	.06	.03
792	John Tudor	.08	.06	.03

1988 Topps All-Star Glossy Set Of 22

The fifth edition of Topps' special All-Star inserts (22 cards) was included in the company's 1988 rack packs. The 1987 American and National League All-Star lineup, plus honorary captains Jim Hunter and Billy Williams, are featured on the standard-size All-Star inserts. The glossy full-color card fronts contain player photos centered between a red and yellow "1987 All-Star" logo printed across the card top and the player name (also red and yellow) which is printed across the bottom margin. A National or American League logo appears in the lower left corner. Card backs are printed in red and blue on a white background, with the title and All-Star logo emblem printed above the player name and card number.

		MT	NR MT	EX
Complete Set:		4.00	3.00	1.50
Common Player:		.15	.11	.06
1	John McNamara	.15	.11	.06
2	Don Mattingly	1.00	.70	.40
3	Willie Randolph	.15	.11	.06
4	Wade Boggs	.80	.60	.30
5	Cal Ripken	.50	.40	.20
6	George Bell	.30	.25	.12
7	Rickey Henderson	.50	.40	.20
8	Dave Winfield	.40	.30	.15
9	Terry Kennedy	.15	.11	.06
10	Bret Saberhagen	.25	.20	.10
11	Jim Hunter	.25	.20	.10
12	Davey Johnson	.15	.11	.06

		MT	NR MT	EX
13	Jack Clark	.25	.20	.10
14	Ryne Sandberg	.40	.30	.15
15	Mike Schmidt	.60	.45	.25
16	Ozzie Smith	.25	.20	.10
17	Eric Davis	.60	.45	.25
18	Andre Dawson	.25	.20	.10
19	Darryl Strawberry	.60	.45	.25
20	Gary Carter	.40	.30	.15
21	Mike Scott	.15	.11	.06
22	Billy Williams	.25	.20	.10

1988 Topps All-Star Glossy Set Of 60

This standard-size collectors set includes 60 full-color glossy cards featuring All-Stars and Prospects in six separate 10-card sets. In 1986, Topps issued a similar set that included only All-Stars. Card fronts have a white border and a thin red line framing the player photo, with the player's name in the lower left corner. Card backs, in red and blue, include very basic player information (name, team and position), along with the card set logo and card number. Topps glossy collector sets were marketed via a special offer printed on a card packaged in all Topps wax packs. For six special offer cards and $1.25, collectors received one of the six 10-card sets; 18 special offer cards and $7.50 earned the entire 60-card collection.

		MT	NR MT	EX
Complete Set:		14.00	10.50	5.50
Common Player:		.15	.11	.06
1	Andre Dawson	.30	.25	.12
2	Jesse Barfield	.20	.15	.08
3	Mike Schmidt	.70	.50	.30
4	Ruben Sierra	.40	.30	.15
5	Mike Scott	.20	.15	.08
6	Cal Ripken	.70	.50	.30
7	Gary Carter	.50	.40	.20
8	Kent Hrbek	.30	.25	.12
9	Kevin Seitzer	.70	.50	.30
10	Mike Henneman	.25	.20	.10
11	Don Mattingly	2.00	1.50	.80
12	Tim Raines	.40	.30	.15
13	Roger Clemens	.80	.60	.30
14	Ryne Sandberg	.40	.30	.15
15	Tony Fernandez	.20	.15	.08
16	Eric Davis	.80	.60	.30
17	Jack Morris	.30	.25	.12
18	Tim Wallach	.20	.15	.08
19	Mike Dunne	.25	.20	.10
20	Mike Greenwell	1.00	.70	.40
21	Dwight Evans	.20	.15	.08
22	Darryl Strawberry	.80	.60	.30
23	Cory Snyder	.30	.25	.12
24	Pedro Guerrero	.25	.20	.10
25	Rickey Henderson	.60	.45	.25
26	Dale Murphy	.70	.50	.30
27	Kirby Puckett	.50	.40	.20
28	Steve Bedrosian	.20	.15	.08
29	Devon White	.25	.20	.10
30	Benny Santiago	.25	.20	.10
31	George Bell	.40	.30	.15
32	Keith Hernandez	.40	.30	.15
33	Dave Stewart	.15	.11	.06
34	Dave Parker	.25	.20	.10
35	Tom Henke	.15	.11	.06
36	Willie McGee	.20	.15	.08
37	Alan Trammell	.30	.25	.12
38	Tony Gwynn	.60	.45	.25
39	Mark McGwire	.80	.60	.30
40	Joe Magrane	.25	.20	.10
41	Jack Clark	.25	.20	.10
42	Willie Randolph	.15	.11	.06
43	Juan Samuel	.25	.20	.10
44	Joe Carter	.25	.20	.10
45	Shane Rawley	.15	.11	.06
46	Dave Winfield	.50	.40	.20
47	Ozzie Smith	.25	.20	.10
48	Wally Joyner	.70	.50	.30
49	B.J. Surhoff	.20	.15	.08
50	Ellis Burks	.80	.60	.30
51	Wade Boggs	.80	.60	.30
52	Howard Johnson	.20	.15	.08
53	George Brett	.70	.50	.30
54	Dwight Gooden	.80	.60	.30
55	Jose Canseco	2.00	1.50	.80
56	Lee Smith	.15	.11	.06
57	Paul Molitor	.20	.15	.08
58	Andres Galarraga	.30	.25	.12
59	Matt Nokes	.40	.30	.15
60	Casey Candaele	.15	.11	.06

1988 Topps American Baseball

This 88-card set, unlike Topps' United Kingdom football cards, was made available for distribution by U.S. hobby dealers. The cards were packaged in checklist-backed boxes with an American flag on the top flap. The 2-1/4" by 3" cards feature full-color player photos printed on white stock with a red line framing the photo. The team name, printed in individual team colors, intersects the red frame at the top of the card. A bright yellow name banner appears below the photo. Card backs have bright blue borders and cartoon-style horizontal layouts. The card number appears within a circle of red stars upper left, beside the player's name and team logo. A red banner containing the player career stats runs the length of the card back. The lower half of the flip side features a caricature of the player and a one-line caption. Below the cartoon, a short "Talkin' Baseball" paragraph provides elementary baseball information, obviously designed to acquaint soccer-playing European collectors with American baseball rules and terminology. A glossy edition of the set was issued and is valued at 2-3 times greater than the regular issue.

		MT	NR MT	EX
Complete Set:		10.00	7.50	4.00
Common Player:		.08	.06	.03
1	Harold Baines	.15	.11	.06
2	Steve Bedrosian	.10	.08	.04
3	George Bell	.25	.20	.10
4	Wade Boggs	.70	.50	.30
5	Barry Bonds	.20	.15	.08

		MT	NR MT	EX
6	Bob Boone	.08	.06	.03
7	George Brett	.40	.30	.15
8	Hubie Brooks	.08	.06	.03
9	Ivan Calderon	.10	.08	.04
10	Jose Canseco	1.25	.90	.50
11	Gary Carter	.30	.25	.12
12	Joe Carter	.15	.11	.06
13	Jack Clark	.20	.15	.08
14	Will Clark	.50	.40	.20
15	Roger Clemens	.60	.45	.25
16	Vince Coleman	.20	.15	.08
17	Alvin Davis	.15	.11	.06
18	Eric Davis	.70	.50	.30
19	Glenn Davis	.20	.15	.08
20	Andre Dawson	.25	.20	.10
21	Mike Dunne	.15	.11	.06
22	Dwight Evans	.10	.08	.04
23	Tony Fernandez	.15	.11	.06
24	John Franco	.10	.08	.04
25	Gary Gaetti	.20	.15	.08
26	Kirk Gibson	.25	.20	.10
27	Dwight Gooden	.60	.45	.25
28	Pedro Guerrero	.20	.15	.08
29	Tony Gwynn	.35	.25	.14
30	Billy Hatcher	.08	.06	.03
31	Rickey Henderson	.35	.25	.14
32	Tom Henke	.08	.06	.03
33	Keith Hernandez	.25	.20	.10
34	Orel Hershiser	.30	.25	.12
35	Teddy Higuera	.10	.08	.04
36	Charlie Hough	.08	.06	.03
37	Kent Hrbek	.25	.20	.10
38	Brook Jacoby	.10	.08	.04
39	Dion James	.08	.06	.03
40	Wally Joyner	.50	.40	.20
41	John Kruk	.15	.11	.06
42	Mark Langston	.15	.11	.06
43	Jeffrey Leonard	.08	.06	.03
44	Candy Maldonaldo	.08	.06	.03
45	Don Mattingly	1.25	.90	.50
46	Willie McGee	.15	.11	.06
47	Mark McGwire	.80	.60	.30
48	Kevin Mitchell	.08	.06	.03
49	Paul Molitor	.15	.11	.06
50	Jack Morris	.15	.11	.06
51	Lloyd Moseby	.10	.08	.04
52	Dale Murphy	.40	.30	.15
53	Eddie Murray	.30	.25	.12
54	Matt Nokes	.40	.30	.15
55	Dave Parker	.20	.15	.08
56	Larry Parrish	.08	.06	.03
57	Kirby Puckett	.35	.25	.14
58	Tim Raines	.30	.25	.12
59	Willie Randolph	.08	.06	.03
60	Harold Reynolds	.08	.06	.03
61	Cal Ripken	.35	.25	.14
62	Nolan Ryan	.80	.60	.30
63	Bret Saberhagen	.20	.15	.08
64	Juan Samuel	.15	.11	.06
65	Ryne Sandberg	.25	.20	.10
66	Benny Santiago	.15	.11	.06
67	Mike Schmidt	.40	.30	.15
68	Mike Scott	.10	.08	.04
69	Kevin Seitzer	.40	.30	.15
70	Larry Sheets	.08	.06	.03
71	Ruben Sierra	.15	.11	.06
72	Ozzie Smith	.15	.11	.06
73	Zane Smith	.08	.06	.03
74	Cory Snyder	.15	.11	.06
75	Dave Stewart	.10	.08	.04
76	Darryl Strawberry	.50	.40	.20
77	Rick Sutcliffe	.15	.11	.06
78	Danny Tartabull	.20	.15	.08
79	Alan Trammell	.25	.20	.10
80	Fernando Valenzuela	.20	.15	.08
81	Andy Van Slyke	.15	.11	.06
82	Frank Viola	.15	.11	.06
83	Greg Walker	.10	.08	.04
84	Tim Wallach	.10	.08	.04
85	Dave Winfield	.30	.25	.12
86	Mike Witt	.08	.06	.03
87	Robin Yount	.25	.20	.10
88	Checklist	.08	.06	.03

Definitions for grading conditions are located in the introduction section at the front of this book.

1988 Topps Big Baseball

1988 Topps Big Baseball cards (2-5/8" by 3-3/4") were issued in three series, 88 cards per series (a total set of 264 cards). Each series features current star players, sold in 7-card packages. The glossy cards are similar in format, both front and back, to the 1956 Topps 340-card set. Each card features a posed head shot and a close-up action photo on the front, framed by a wide white border and a dark blue inner border. A white outlines highlights the player closeup. The player's name appears below his head shot, in reversed type on a splash of color that fades from yellow to orange to red to pink. On the card back, the player's name is printed in large red letters across the top, followed by his team name and position in black. Personal info is printed in a red rectangle beside a Topps baseball logo bearing the card number. A triple cartoon strip, in full-color, illustrates career highlights, performance, personal background, etc. A red, white and blue statistics box (pitching, batting, fielding) is printed across the bottom.

		MT	NR MT	EX
Complete Set:		20.00	15.00	8.00
Common Player:		.05	.04	.02
1	Paul Molitor	.12	.09	.05
2	Milt Thompson	.05	.04	.02
3	Billy Hatcher	.05	.04	.02
4	Mike Witt	.05	.04	.02
5	Vince Coleman	.12	.09	.05
6	Dwight Evans	.10	.08	.04
7	Tim Wallach	.10	.08	.04
8	Alan Trammell	.15	.11	.06
9	Will Clark	.80	.60	.30
10	Jeff Reardon	.08	.06	.03
11	Dwight Gooden	.50	.40	.20
12	Benny Santiago	.12	.09	.05
13	Jose Canseco	1.25	.90	.50
14	Dale Murphy	.30	.25	.12
15	George Bell	.20	.15	.08
16	Ryne Sandberg	.20	.15	.08
17	Brook Jacoby	.08	.06	.03
18	Fernando Valenzuela	.15	.11	.06
19	Scott Fletcher	.05	.04	.02
20	Eric Davis	.60	.45	.25
21	Willie Wilson	.10	.08	.04
22	B.J. Surhoff	.10	.08	.04
23	Steve Bedrosian	.08	.06	.03
24	Dave Winfield	.25	.20	.10
25	Bobby Bonilla	.15	.11	.06
26	Larry Sheets	.08	.06	.03
27	Ozzie Guillen	.08	.06	.03
28	Checklist 1-88	.05	.04	.02
29	Nolan Ryan	.80	.60	.30
30	Bob Boone	.05	.04	.02
31	Tom Herr	.08	.06	.03
32	Wade Boggs	.90	.70	.35
33	Neal Heaton	.05	.04	.02
34	Doyle Alexander	.05	.04	.02
35	Candy Maldonado	.08	.06	.03
36	Kirby Puckett	.25	.20	.10
37	Gary Carter	.20	.15	.08

		MT	NR MT	EX
38	Lance McCullers	.08	.06	.03
39a	Terry Steinbach (black Topps logo on front)	.12	.09	.05
39b	Terry Steinbach (white Topps logo on front)	.12	.09	.05
40	Gerald Perry	.10	.08	.04
41	Tom Henke	.05	.04	.02
42	Leon Durham	.05	.04	.02
43	Cory Snyder	.12	.09	.05
44	Dale Sveum	.05	.04	.02
45	Lance Parrish	.12	.09	.05
46	Steve Sax	.12	.09	.05
47	Charlie Hough	.05	.04	.02
48	Kal Daniels	.15	.11	.06
49	Bo Jackson	1.00	.70	.40
50	Ron Guidry	.10	.08	.04
51	Bill Doran	.08	.06	.03
52	Wally Joyner	.40	.30	.15
53	Terry Pendleton	.08	.06	.03
54	Marty Barrett	.08	.06	.03
55	Andres Galarraga	.15	.11	.06
56	Larry Herndon	.05	.04	.02
57	Kevin Mitchell	.08	.06	.03
58	Greg Gagne	.05	.04	.02
59	Keith Hernandez	.15	.11	.06
60	John Kruk	.10	.08	.04
61	Mike LaValliere	.08	.06	.03
62	Cal Ripken	.30	.25	.12
63	Ivan Calderon	.08	.06	.03
64	Alvin Davis	.10	.08	.04
65	Luis Polonia	.08	.06	.03
66	Robin Yount	.20	.15	.08
67	Juan Samuel	.12	.09	.05
68	Andres Thomas	.05	.04	.02
69	Jeff Musselman	.05	.04	.02
70	Jerry Mumphrey	.05	.04	.02
71	Joe Carter	.12	.09	.05
72	Mike Scioscia	.05	.04	.02
73	Pete Incaviglia	.10	.08	.04
74	Barry Larkin	.15	.11	.06
75	Frank White	.08	.06	.03
76	Willie Randolph	.08	.06	.03
77	Kevin Bass	.05	.04	.02
78	Brian Downing	.08	.06	.03
79	Willie McGee	.10	.08	.04
80	Ellis Burks	.40	.30	.15
81	Hubie Brooks	.08	.06	.03
82	Darrell Evans	.08	.06	.03
83	Robby Thompson	.05	.04	.02
84	Kent Hrbek	.15	.11	.06
85	Ron Darling	.12	.09	.05
86	Stan Jefferson	.05	.04	.02
87	Teddy Higuera	.10	.08	.04
88	Mike Schmidt	.30	.25	.12
89	Barry Bonds	.15	.11	.06
90	Jim Presley	.08	.06	.03
91	Orel Hershiser	.25	.20	.10
92	Jesse Barfield	.10	.08	.04
93	Tom Candiotti	.05	.04	.02
94	Bret Saberhagen	.12	.09	.05
95	Jose Uribe	.05	.04	.02
96	Tom Browning	.10	.08	.04
97	Johnny Ray	.08	.06	.03
98	Mike Morgan	.05	.04	.02
100	Jim Sundberg	.05	.04	.02
101	Roger McDowell	.08	.06	.03
102	Randy Ready	.05	.04	.02
103	Mike Gallego	.05	.04	.02
104	Steve Buechele	.05	.04	.02
105	Greg Walker	.08	.06	.03
106	Jose Lind	.12	.09	.05
107	Steve Trout	.05	.04	.02
108	Rick Rhoden	.08	.06	.03
109	Jim Pankovits	.05	.04	.02
110	Ken Griffey	.08	.06	.03
111	Danny Cox	.08	.06	.03
112	Franklin Stubbs	.05	.04	.02
113	Lloyd Moseby	.08	.06	.03
114	Mel Hall	.08	.06	.03
115	Kevin Seitzer	.25	.20	.10
116	Tim Raines	.25	.20	.10
117	Juan Castillo	.05	.04	.02
118	Roger Clemens	.50	.40	.20
119	Mike Aldrete	.08	.06	.03
120	Mario Soto	.05	.04	.02
121	Jack Howell	.05	.04	.02
122	Rick Schu	.05	.04	.02
123	Jeff Robinson	.10	.08	.04
124	Doug Drabek	.08	.06	.03
125	Henry Cotto	.05	.04	.02
126	Checklist 89-176	.05	.04	.02

		MT	NR MT	EX
127	Gary Gaetti	.12	.09	.05
128	Rick Sutcliffe	.10	.08	.04
129	Howard Johnson	.08	.06	.03
130	Chris Brown	.08	.06	.03
131	Dave Henderson	.08	.06	.03
132	Curt Wilkerson	.05	.04	.02
133	Mike Marshall	.10	.08	.04
134	Kelly Gruber	.05	.04	.02
135	Julio Franco	.10	.08	.04
136	Kurt Stillwell	.12	.09	.05
137	Donnie Hill	.05	.04	.02
138	Mike Pagliarulo	.10	.08	.04
139	Von Hayes	.08	.06	.03
140	Mike Scott	.10	.08	.04
141	Bob Kipper	.05	.04	.02
142	Harold Reynolds	.08	.06	.03
143	Bob Brenly	.05	.04	.02
144	Dave Concepcion	.08	.06	.03
145	Devon White	.12	.09	.05
146	Jeff Stone	.05	.04	.02
147	Chet Lemon	.05	.04	.02
148	Ozzie Virgil	.05	.04	.02
149	Todd Worrell	.10	.08	.04
150	Mitch Webster	.05	.04	.02
151	Rob Deer	.08	.06	.03
152	Rich Gedman	.08	.06	.03
153	Andre Dawson	.15	.11	.06
154	Mike Davis	.05	.04	.02
155	Nelson Liriano	.08	.06	.03
156	Greg Swindell	.10	.08	.04
157	George Brett	.30	.25	.12
158	Kevin McReynolds	.15	.11	.06
159	Brian Fisher	.08	.06	.03
160	Mike Kingery	.05	.04	.02
161	Tony Gwynn	.25	.20	.10
162	Don Baylor	.10	.08	.04
163	Jerry Browne	.05	.04	.02
164	Dan Pasqua	.08	.06	.03
165	Rickey Henderson	.25	.20	.10
166	Brett Butler	.08	.06	.03
167	Nick Esasky	.05	.04	.02
168	Kirk McCaskill	.05	.04	.02
169	Fred Lynn	.10	.08	.04
170	Jack Morris	.12	.09	.05
171	Pedro Guerrero	.12	.09	.05
172	Dave Stieb	.10	.08	.04
173	Pat Tabler	.08	.06	.03
174	Floyd Bannister	.05	.04	.02
175	Rafael Belliard	.05	.04	.02
176	Mark Langston	.10	.08	.04
177	Greg Mathews	.08	.06	.03
178	Claudell Washington	.05	.04	.02
179	Mark McGwire	1.00	.70	.40
180	Bert Blyleven	.10	.08	.04
181	Jim Rice	.20	.15	.08
182	Mookie Wilson	.08	.06	.03
183	Willie Fraser	.05	.04	.02
184	Andy Van Slyke	.10	.08	.04
185	Matt Nokes	.10	.08	.04
186	Eddie Whitson	.05	.04	.02
187	Tony Fernandez	.10	.08	.04
188	Rick Reuschel	.08	.06	.03
189	Ken Phelps	.05	.04	.02
190	Juan Nieves	.08	.06	.03
191	Kirk Gibson	.20	.15	.08
192	Glenn Davis	.15	.11	.06
193	Zane Smith	.05	.04	.02
194	Jose DeLeon	.08	.06	.03
195	Gary Ward	.05	.04	.02
196	Pascual Perez	.05	.04	.02
197	Carlton Fisk	.12	.09	.05
198	Oddibe McDowell	.08	.06	.03
199	Mark Gubicza	.10	.08	.04
200	Glenn Hubbard	.05	.04	.02
201	Frank Viola	.15	.11	.06
202	Jody Reed	.12	.09	.05
203	Len Dykstra	.08	.06	.03
204	Dick Schofield	.05	.04	.02
205	Sid Bream	.05	.04	.02
206	Guillermo Hernandez	.05	.04	.02
207	Keith Moreland	.05	.04	.02
208	Mark Eichhorn	.05	.04	.02
209	Rene Gonzales	.08	.06	.03
210	Dave Valle	.05	.04	.02
211	Tom Brunansky	.10	.08	.04
212	Charles Hudson	.05	.04	.02
213	John Farrell	.10	.08	.04
214	Jeff Treadway	.12	.09	.05
215	Eddie Murray	.25	.20	.10
216	Checklist 177-264	.05	.04	.02
217	Greg Brock	.08	.06	.03

		MT	NR MT	EX
218	John Shelby	.05	.04	.02
219	Craig Reynolds	.05	.04	.02
220	Dion James	.05	.04	.02
221	Carney Lansford	.08	.06	.03
222	Juan Berenguer	.05	.04	.02
223	Luis Rivera	.08	.06	.03
224	Harold Baines	.12	.09	.05
225	Shawon Dunston	.08	.06	.03
226	Luis Aguayo	.05	.04	.02
227	Pete O'Brien	.08	.06	.03
228	Ozzie Smith	.12	.09	.05
229	Don Mattingly	1.50	1.25	.60
230	Danny Tartabull	.15	.11	.06
231	Andy Allanson	.05	.04	.02
232	John Franco	.08	.06	.03
233	Mike Greenwell	.80	.60	.30
234	Bob Ojeda	.08	.06	.03
235	Chili Davis	.08	.06	.03
236	Mike Dunne	.12	.09	.05
237	Jim Morrison	.05	.04	.02
238	Carmelo Martinez	.05	.04	.02
239	Ernie Whitt	.05	.04	.02
240	Scott Garrelts	.05	.04	.02
241	Mike Moore	.05	.04	.02
242	Dave Parker	.10	.08	.04
243	Tim Laudner	.05	.04	.02
244	Bill Wegman	.05	.04	.02
245	Bob Horner	.08	.06	.03
246	Rafael Santana	.05	.04	.02
247	Alfredo Griffin	.05	.04	.02
248	Mark Bailey	.05	.04	.02
249	Ron Gant	.12	.09	.05
250	Bryn Smith	.05	.04	.02
251	Lance Johnson	.10	.08	.04
252	Sam Horn	.10	.08	.04
253	Darryl Strawberry	.40	.30	.15
254	Chuck Finley	.05	.04	.02
255	Darnell Coles	.08	.06	.03
256	Mike Henneman	.10	.08	.04
257	Andy Hawkins	.08	.06	.03
258	Jim Clancy	.08	.06	.03
259	Atlee Hammaker	.05	.04	.02
260	Glenn Wilson	.05	.04	.02
261	Larry McWilliams	.05	.04	.02
262	Jack Clark	.12	.09	.05
263	Walt Weiss	.80	.60	.30
264	Gene Larkin	.08	.06	.03

1988 Topps Box Panels

After a one-year hiatus during which they appeared on the sides of Topps wax pack display boxes, Topps retail box cards returned to box bottoms in 1988. Topps first issued box-bottom cards in 1986, following the introduction of the concept by Donruss in 1985. Topps 1988 box-bottom series includes 16 standard-size baseball cards, four cards per each of four different display boxes. Card fronts follow the same design as the 1988 Topps basic issue; full-color player photos, framed in yellow, surrounded by a white border; diagonal player name lower right; team name in large letters at the top of the card front. Card backs are "numbered" A through P and are printed in black and orange.

		MT	NR MT	EX
Complete Panel Set:		7.00	5.25	2.75
Complete Singles Set:		3.00	2.25	1.25
Common Panel:		1.00	.70	.40
Common Single Player:		.08	.06	.03
	Panel	1.00	.70	.40
A	Don Baylor	.12	.09	.05
B	Steve Bedrosian	.12	.09	.05
C	Juan Beniquez	.08	.06	.03
D	Bob Boone	.08	.06	.03
	Panel	1.75	1.25	.70
E	Darrell Evans	.12	.09	.05
F	Tony Gwynn	.30	.25	.12
G	John Kruk	.15	.11	.06
H	Marvell Wynne	.08	.06	.03
	Panel	2.75	2.00	1.00
I	Joe Carter	.15	.11	.06
J	Eric Davis	.50	.40	.20
K	Howard Johnson	.12	.09	.05
L	Darryl Strawberry	.35	.25	.14
	Panel	2.50	2.00	1.00
M	Rickey Henderson	.50	.40	.20
N	Nolan Ryan	.35	.25	.14
O	Mike Schmidt	.08	.06	.03
P	Kent Tekulve	.08	.06	.03

1988 Topps Coins

This edition of 60 lightweight metal coins is similar in design to Topps' 1964 set. The 1988 coins are 1-1/2" in diameter and feature full-color player closeups under crimped edges in silver, gold and pink. Curved under the photo is a red and white player name banner pinned by two gold stars. Coin backs list the coin number, player name, personal information and career summary in black letters on a silver background.

		MT	NR MT	EX
Complete Set:		8.00	6.00	3.25
Common Player:		.10	.08	.04
1	George Bell	.25	.20	.10
2	Roger Clemens	.40	.30	.15
3	Mark McGwire	.60	.45	.25
4	Wade Boggs	.70	.50	.30
5	Harold Baines	.15	.11	.06
6	Ivan Calderon	.10	.08	.04
7	Jose Canseco	.80	.60	.30
8	Joe Carter	.15	.11	.06
9	Jack Clark	.15	.11	.06
10	Alvin Davis	.15	.11	.06
11	Dwight Evans	.15	.11	.06
12	Tony Fernandez	.15	.11	.06
13	Gary Gaetti	.15	.11	.06
14	Mike Greenwell	.40	.30	.15
15	Charlie Hough	.10	.08	.04
16	Wally Joyner	.30	.25	.12
17	Jimmy Key	.10	.08	.04
18	Mark Langston	.15	.11	.06
19	Don Mattingly	1.00	.70	.40
20	Paul Molitor	.15	.11	.06
21	Jack Morris	.15	.11	.06
22	Eddie Murray	.20	.15	.08
23	Kirby Puckett	.25	.20	.10
24	Cal Ripken	.25	.20	.10
25	Bret Saberhagen	.15	.11	.06
26	Ruben Sierra	.15	.11	.06
27	Cory Snyder	.15	.11	.06

		MT	NR MT	EX
28	Terry Steinbach	.15	.11	.06
29	Danny Tartabull	.15	.11	.06
30	Alan Trammell	.15	.11	.06
31	Devon White	.15	.11	.06
32	Robin Yount	.15	.11	.06
33	Andre Dawson	.15	.11	.06
34	Steve Bedrosian	.15	.11	.06
35	Benny Santiago	.15	.11	.06
36	Tony Gwynn	.25	.20	.10
37	Bobby Bonilla	.15	.11	.06
38	Will Clark	.30	.25	.12
39	Eric Davis	.40	.30	.15
40	Mike Dunne	.15	.11	.06
41	John Franco	.10	.08	.04
42	Dwight Gooden	.40	.30	.15
43	Pedro Guerrero	.15	.11	.06
44	Dion James	.10	.08	.04
45	John Kruk	.15	.11	.06
46	Jeffrey Leonard	.10	.08	.04
47	Carmelo Martinez	.10	.08	.04
48	Dale Murphy	.30	.25	.12
49	Tim Raines	.20	.15	.08
50	Nolan Ryan	.20	.15	.08
51	Juan Samuel	.15	.11	.06
52	Ryne Sandberg	.20	.15	.08
53	Mike Schmidt	.30	.25	.12
54	Mike Scott	.15	.11	.06
55	Ozzie Smith	.15	.11	.06
56	Darryl Strawberry	.40	.30	.15
57	Rick Sutcliffe	.15	.11	.06
58	Fernando Valenzuela	.15	.11	.06
59	Tim Wallach	.15	.11	.06
60	Todd Worrell	.15	.11	.06

1988 Topps Gallery Of Champions

These bronze replicas are exact reproductions at one-quarter scale of Topps official 1988 cards, both front and back. The set includes 12 three-dimensional raised metal cards packaged in a velvet-lined case that bears the title of the set in gold embossed letters. A deluxe limited edition of the set (1,000) was produced in sterling silver and an economy version in aluminum. Topps first issued the metal mini-cards in 1984 (the initial set was called Gallery of Immortals). Since 1985, the metal cards have honored award-winning players from the previous season. A Mark McGwire pewter replica was given as a premium to dealers ordering the aluminum, bronze and silver sets ($50 value). The special pewter card is distinguished from the regular issue by a diagonal name banner in the lower right corner (regular) replicas have a rectangular name banner printer parallel to the lower edge of the card). A 1955 Topps Duke Snider bronze (value $10) was available to dealers purchasing cases of the 1988 Topps Traded sets.

		MT	NR MT	EX
Complete Aluminum Set:		20.00	15.00	8.00
Complete Bronze Set:		125.00	94.00	50.00
Complete Silver Set:		500.00	375.00	200.00
(1a)	Steve Bedrosian (aluminum)	.70	.50	.30
(1b)	Steve Bedrosian (bronze)	7.50	5.75	3.00
(1c)	Steve Bedrosian (silver)	20.00	15.00	8.00
(2a)	George Bell (aluminum)	1.00	.70	.40
(2b)	George Bell (bronze)	10.00	7.50	4.00
(2c)	George Bell (silver)	20.00	15.00	8.00
(3a)	Wade Boggs (aluminum)	3.00	2.25	1.25
(3b)	Wade Boggs (bronze)	25.00	18.50	10.00
(3c)	Wade Boggs (silver)	125.00	94.00	50.00
(4a)	Jack Clark (aluminum)	1.00	.70	.40
(4b)	Jack Clark (bronze)	10.00	7.50	4.00
(4c)	Jack Clark (silver)	20.00	15.00	8.00
(5a)	Roger Clemens (aluminum)	2.00	1.50	.80
(5b)	Roger Clemens (bronze)	20.00	15.00	8.00
(5c)	Roger Clemens (silver)	90.00	67.00	36.00
(6a)	Andre Dawson (aluminum)	1.00	.70	.40
(6b)	Andre Dawson (bronze)	10.00	7.50	4.00
(6c)	Andre Dawson (silver)	20.00	15.00	8.00
(7a)	Tony Gwynn (aluminum)	1.25	.90	.50
(7b)	Tony Gwynn (bronze)	12.00	9.00	4.75
(7c)	Tony Gwynn (silver)	50.00	37.00	20.00
(8a)	Mark Langston (aluminum)	.70	.50	.30
(8b)	Mark Langston (bronze)	7.50	5.75	3.00
(8c)	Mark Langston (silver)	20.00	15.00	8.00
(9a)	Mark McGwire (aluminum)	3.00	2.25	1.25
(9b)	Mark McGwire (bronze)	25.00	18.50	10.00
(9c)	Mark McGwire (silver)	125.00	94.00	50.00
(10a)	Dave Righetti (aluminum)	1.00	.70	.40
(10b)	Dave Righetti (bronze)	10.00	7.50	4.00
(10c)	Dave Righetti (silver)	20.00	15.00	8.00
(11a)	Nolan Ryan (aluminum)	1.00	.70	.40
(11b)	Nolan Ryan (bronze)	10.00	7.50	4.00
(11c)	Nolan Ryan (silver)	20.00	15.00	8.00
(12a)	Benny Santiago (aluminum)	1.00	.70	.40
(12b)	Benny Santiago (bronze)	10.00	7.50	4.00
(12c)	Benny Santiago (silver)	20.00	15.00	8.00

1988 Topps Glossy Rookies

The Topps 1988 Rookies special insert cards follow the same basic design as the All-Star inserts. The set consists of 22 standard-size cards. Large, glossy color player photos are printed on a white background below a red, yellow and blue "1987 Rookies" banner. A red and yellow player name appears beneath the photo. Red, white and blue card backs bear the title of the special insert set, the Rookies logo emblem, player name and card number.

		MT	NR MT	EX
Complete Set:		10.00	7.50	4.00
Common Player:		.20	.15	.08
1	Billy Ripken	.30	.25	.12
2	Ellis Burks	1.50	1.25	.60
3	Mike Greenwell	2.00	1.50	.80
4	DeWayne Buice	.20	.15	.08
5	Devon White	.40	.30	.15
6	Fred Manrique	.20	.15	.08
7	Mike Henneman	.40	.30	.15
8	Matt Nokes	.60	.45	.25
9	Kevin Seitzer	.80	.60	.30
10	B.J. Surhoff	.40	.30	.15
11	Casey Candaele	.20	.15	.08
12	Randy Myers	.60	.45	.25
13	Mark McGwire	1.50	1.25	.60
14	Luis Polonia	.25	.20	.10

		MT	NR MT	EX
15	Terry Steinbach	.40	.30	.15
16	Mike Dunne	.40	.30	.15
17	Al Pedrique	.20	.15	.08
18	Benny Santiago	.70	.50	.30
19	Kelly Downs	.40	.30	.15
20	Joe Magrane	.40	.30	.15
21	Jerry Browne	.20	.15	.08
22	Jeff Musselman	.25	.20	.10

1988 Topps Mini League Leaders

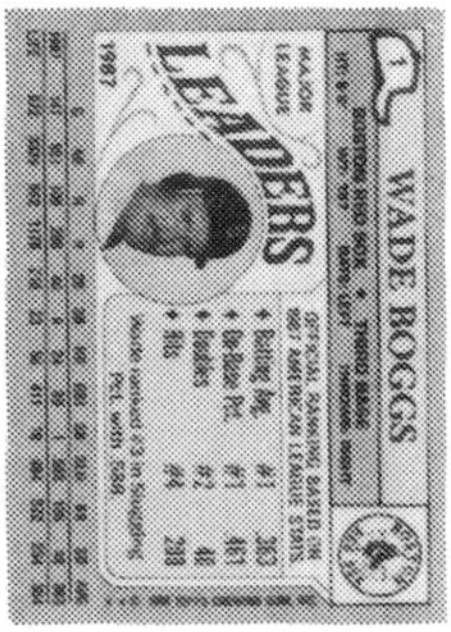

The third consecutive issue of Topps mini-cards (2-1/8" by 3") includes 77 cards spotlighting the top five ranked pitchers and batters. This set is unique in that it was the first time Topps included full-color player photos on both the front and back. Glossy action shots on the card fronts fade into a white border with a Topps logo in an upper corner. The player's name is printed in bold black letters beneath the photo. Horizontal reverses feature circular player photos on a blue and white background with the card number, player name, personal information, 1987 ranking and lifetime/1987 stats printed in red, black and yellow lettering.

		MT	NR MT	EX
Complete Set:		6.00	4.50	2.50
Common Player:		.09	.07	.04
1	Wade Boggs	.80	.60	.30
2	Roger Clemens	.60	.45	.25
3	Dwight Evans	.15	.11	.06
4	DeWayne Buice	.09	.07	.04
5	Brian Downing	.09	.07	.04
6	Wally Joyner	.60	.45	.25
7	Ivan Calderon	.15	.11	.06
8	Carlton Fisk	.20	.15	.08
9	Gary Redus	.09	.07	.04
10	Darrell Evans	.15	.11	.06
11	Jack Morris	.25	.20	.10
12	Alan Trammell	.30	.25	.12
13	Lou Whitaker	.20	.15	.08
14	Bret Saberhagen	.20	.15	.08
15	Kevin Seitzer	.50	.40	.20
16	Danny Tartabull	.25	.20	.10
17	Willie Wilson	.15	.11	.06
18	Teddy Higuera	.15	.11	.06
19	Paul Molitor	.20	.15	.08
20	Dan Plesac	.15	.11	.06
21	Robin Yount	.25	.20	.10
22	Kent Hrbek	.25	.20	.10
23	Kirby Puckett	.35	.25	.14
24	Jeff Reardon	.15	.11	.06
25	Frank Viola	.20	.15	.08
26	Rickey Henderson	.60	.45	.25
27	Don Mattingly	1.25	.90	.50
28	Willie Randolph	.15	.11	.06
29	Dave Righetti	.20	.15	.08
30	Jose Canseco	1.00	.70	.40
31	Mark McGwire	.90	.70	.35
32	Dave Stewart	.09	.07	.04
33	Phil Bradley	.15	.11	.06
34	Mark Langston	.15	.11	.06
35	Harold Reynolds	.09	.07	.04
36	Charlie Hough	.09	.07	.04
37	George Bell	.25	.20	.10
38	Tom Henke	.09	.07	.04
39	Jimmy Key	.15	.11	.06
40	Dion James	.09	.07	.04
41	Dale Murphy	.50	.40	.20
42	Zane Smith	.09	.07	.04
43	Andre Dawson	.25	.20	.10
44	Lee Smith	.09	.07	.04
45	Rick Sutcliffe	.15	.11	.06
46	Eric Davis	.60	.45	.25
47	John Franco	.15	.11	.06
48	Dave Parker	.20	.15	.08
49	Billy Hatcher	.09	.07	.04
50	Nolan Ryan	.60	.45	.25
51	Mike Scott	.20	.15	.08
52	Pedro Guerrero	.20	.15	.08
53	Orel Hershiser	.30	.25	.12
54	Fernando Valenzuela	.25	.20	.10
55	Bob Welch	.15	.11	.06
56	Andres Galarraga	.25	.20	.10
57	Tim Raines	.30	.25	.12
58	Tim Wallach	.15	.11	.06
59	Len Dykstra	.15	.11	.06
60	Dwight Gooden	.60	.45	.25
61	Howard Johnson	.15	.11	.06
62	Roger McDowell	.15	.11	.06
63	Darryl Strawberry	.50	.40	.20
64	Steve Bedrosian	.15	.11	.06
65	Shane Rawley	.09	.07	.04
66	Juan Samuel	.20	.15	.08
67	Mike Schmidt	.50	.40	.20
68	Mike Dunne	.15	.11	.06
69	Jack Clark	.25	.20	.10
70	Vince Coleman	.20	.15	.08
71	Willie McGee	.15	.11	.06
72	Ozzie Smith	.20	.15	.08
73	Todd Worrell	.15	.11	.06
74	Tony Gwynn	.40	.30	.15
75	John Kruk	.20	.15	.08
76	Rick Rueschel	.15	.11	.06
77	Checklist	.09	.07	.04

1988 Topps Stickercards

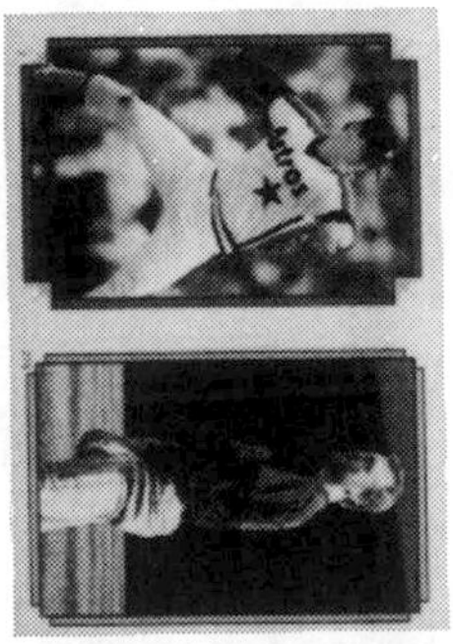

Actually a part of the 1988 Topps Stickers issue, this set consists of 67 cards. The cards are the backs of the peel-off stickers and measure 2-1/8" by 3". To determine total value, combine the prices of the stickers (found in the 1988 Topps Stickers checklist) on the stickercard front with the value assigned to the stickercard in the following checklist.

		MT	NR MT	EX
Complete Set:		2.00	1.50	.80
Common Player:		.02	.02	.01
1	Jack Clark	.03	.02	.01
2	Andres Galarraga	.03	.02	.01
3	Keith Hernandez	.04	.03	.02
4	Tom Herr	.02	.02	.01
5	Juan Samuel	.03	.02	.01
6	Ryne Sandberg	.04	.03	.02
7	Terry Pendleton	.02	.02	.01
8	Mike Schmidt	.06	.05	.02
9	Tim Wallach	.02	.02	.01
10	Hubie Brooks	.02	.02	.01
11	Shawon Dunston	.02	.02	.01
12	Ozzie Smith	.03	.02	.01

		MT	NR MT	EX
13	Andre Dawson	.04	.03	.02
14	Eric Davis	.06	.05	.02
15	Pedro Guerrero	.03	.02	.01
16	Tony Gwynn	.05	.04	.02
17	Jeffrey Leonard	.02	.02	.01
18	Dale Murphy	.06	.05	.02
19	Dave Parker	.03	.02	.01
20	Tim Raines	.04	.03	.02
21	Darryl Strawberry	.06	.05	.02
22	Gary Carter	.04	.03	.02
23	Jody Davis	.02	.02	.01
24	Ozzie Virgil	.02	.02	.01
25	Dwight Gooden	.08	.06	.03
26	Mike Scott	.02	.02	.01
27	Rick Sutcliffe	.02	.02	.01
28	Sid Fernandez	.02	.02	.01
29	Neal Heaton	.02	.02	.01
30	Fernando Valenzuela	.03	.02	.01
31	Steve Bedrosian	.02	.02	.01
32	John Franco	.02	.02	.01
33	Lee Smith	.02	.02	.01
34	Wally Joyner	.06	.05	.02
35	Don Mattingly	.12	.09	.05
36	Mark McGwire	.08	.06	.03
37	Willie Randolph	.02	.02	.01
38	Lou Whitaker	.03	.02	.01
39	Frank White	.02	.02	.01
40	Wade Boggs	.10	.08	.04
41	George Brett	.06	.05	.02
42	Paul Molitor	.02	.02	.01
43	Tony Fernandez	.02	.02	.01
44	Cal Ripken	.06	.05	.02
45	Alan Trammell	.04	.03	.02
46	Jesse Barfield	.03	.02	.01
47	George Bell	.04	.03	.02
48	Jose Canseco	.10	.08	.04
49	Joe Carter	.03	.02	.01
50	Dwight Evans	.02	.02	.01
51	Rickey Henderson	.05	.04	.02
52	Kirby Puckett	.05	.04	.02
53	Cory Snyder	.03	.02	.01
54	Dave Winfield	.04	.03	.02
55	Terry Kennedy	.02	.02	.01
56	Matt Nokes	.03	.02	.01
57	B.J. Surhoff	.02	.02	.01
58	Roger Clemens	.08	.06	.03
59	Jack Morris	.03	.02	.01
60	Bret Saberhagen	.03	.02	.01
61	Ron Guidry	.03	.02	.01
62	Bruce Hurst	.02	.02	.01
63	Mark Langston	.02	.02	.01
64	Tom Henke	.02	.02	.01
65	Dan Plesac	.02	.02	.01
66	Dave Righetti	.03	.02	.01
67	Checklist	.02	.02	.01

1988 Topps Stickers

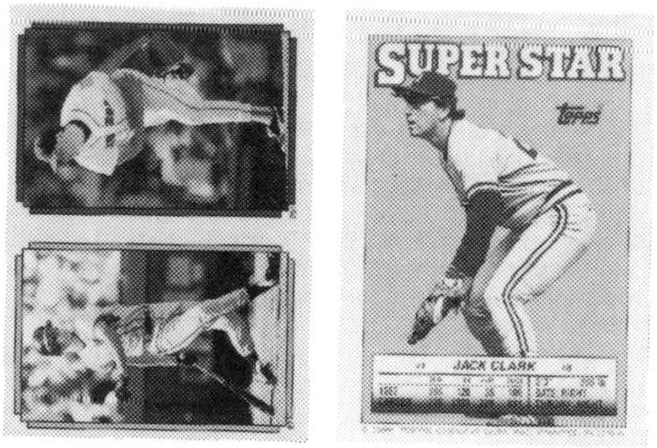

This set of 313 stickers (on 198 cards) offers a new addition for 1988 - 66 different players are pictured on the reverse of the sticker cards. The stickers come in two sizes (2-1/8" by 3" or 1-1/2" by 2-1/8"). Larger stickers fill an entire card, smaller ones are attached in pairs. A 36-page sticker yearbook produced by Topps has a designated space inside for each sticker,with one page per team and special pages of 1987 Highlights, World Series, All-Stars and Future Stars. No printing appears on the full-color action shot stickers except for a small black number in the lower left corner. Sticker card backs carry a Super Star header, player close-up and stats. Stickers were sold in packages of five (with gum) for 25 cents per pack. Unlike the 1987 Topps Stickers set, different pairings can be found, rather than the same two players/numbers always sharing the same sticker. To determine total value, combine the value of the stickercard (found in the 1988 Topps Stickercard checklist) with the values assigned the stickers in the following checklist.

	MT	NR MT	EX
Complete Set:	15.00	11.00	6.00
Common Player:	.02	.02	.01
Sticker Album:	.60	.45	.25

		MT	NR MT	EX
1	1987 Highlights (Mark McGwire)	.20	.15	.08
2	1987 Highlights (Benny Santiago)	.04	.03	.02
3	1987 Highlights (Don Mattingly)	.25	.20	.10
4	1987 Highlights (Vince Coleman)	.04	.03	.02
5	1987 Highlights (Bob Boone)	.02	.02	.01
6	1987 Highlights (Steve Bedrosian)	.02	.02	.01
7	1987 Highlights (Nolan Ryan)	.08	.06	.03
8	1987 Highlights (Darrell Evans)	.02	.02	.01
9	1987 Highlights (Mike Schmidt)	.10	.08	.04
10	1987 Highlights (Don Baylor)	.04	.03	.02
11	1987 Highlights (Eddie Murray)	.08	.06	.03
12	1987 Highlights (Juan Beniquez)	.02	.02	.01
13	1987 Championship Series (John Tudor)	.04	.03	.02
14	1987 Championship Series (Jeff Reardon)	.04	.03	.02
15	1987 Championship Series (Tom Brunansky)	.06	.05	.02
16	1987 Championship Series (Jeffrey Leonard)	.04	.03	.02
17	1987 Championship Series (Gary Gaetti)	.10	.08	.04
18	1987 Championship Series (Cardinals Celebrate)	.04	.03	.02
19	1987 World Series (Danny Gladden)	.04	.03	.02
20	1987 World Series (Bert Blyleven)	.08	.06	.03
21	1987 World Series (John Tudor)	.06	.05	.02
22	1987 World Series (Tom Lawless)	.04	.03	.02
23	1987 World Series (Curt Ford)	.04	.03	.02
24	1987 World Series (Kent Hrbek)	.12	.09	.05
25	1987 World Series (Frank Viola)	.10	.08	.04
26	Dave Smith	.02	.02	.01
27	Jim Deshaies	.02	.02	.01
28	Billy Hatcher	.02	.02	.01
29	Kevin Bass	.02	.02	.01
30	Mike Scott	.04	.03	.02
31	Danny Walling	.02	.02	.01
32	Alan Ashby	.02	.02	.01
33	Ken Caminiti	.02	.02	.01
34	Bill Doran	.02	.02	.01
35	Glenn Davis	.12	.09	.05
36	Ozzie Virgil	.02	.02	.01
37	Ken Oberkfell	.02	.02	.01
38	Ken Griffey	.02	.02	.01
39	Albert Hall	.02	.02	.01
40	Zane Smith	.02	.02	.01
41	Andres Thomas	.02	.02	.01
42	Dion James	.02	.02	.01
43	Jim Acker	.02	.02	.01
44	Tom Glavine	.04	.03	.02
45	Dale Murphy	.25	.20	.10
46	Jack Clark	.10	.08	.04
47	Vince Coleman	.04	.03	.02
48	Ricky Horton	.02	.02	.01
49	Terry Pendleton	.02	.02	.01
50	Tom Herr	.02	.02	.01
51	Joe Magrane	.04	.03	.02
52	Tony Pena	.02	.02	.01
53	Ozzie Smith	.04	.03	.02
54	Todd Worrell	.04	.03	.02
55	Willie McGee	.10	.08	.04
56	Andre Dawson	.15	.11	.06
57	Ryne Sandberg	.06	.05	.02
58	Keith Moreland	.02	.02	.01
59	Greg Maddux	.04	.03	.02
60	Jody Davis	.02	.02	.01
61	Rick Sutcliffe	.08	.06	.03
62	Jamie Moyer	.02	.02	.01
63	Leon Durham	.02	.02	.01
64	Lee Smith	.02	.02	.01
65	Shawon Dunston	.02	.02	.01
66	Franklin Stubbs	.02	.02	.01

		MT	NR MT	EX
67	Mike Scioscia	.02	.02	.01
68	Orel Hershiser	.06	.05	.02
69	Mike Marshall	.04	.03	.02
70	Fernando Valenzuela	.15	.11	.06
71	Mickey Hatcher	.02	.02	.01
72	Matt Young	.02	.02	.01
73	Bob Welch	.04	.03	.02
74	Steve Sax	.04	.03	.02
75	Pedro Guerrero	.12	.09	.05
76	Tim Raines	.15	.11	.06
77	Casey Candaele	.02	.02	.01
78	Mike Fitzgerald	.02	.02	.01
79	Andres Galarraga	.04	.03	.02
80	Neal Heaton	.02	.02	.01
81	Hubie Brooks	.02	.02	.01
82	Floyd Youmans	.02	.02	.01
83	Herm Winningham	.02	.02	.01
84	Denny Martinez	.02	.02	.01
85	Tim Wallach	.08	.06	.03
86	Jeffrey Leonard	.04	.03	.02
87	Will Clark	.10	.08	.04
88	Kevin Mitchell	.04	.03	.02
89	Mike Aldrete	.02	.02	.01
90	Scott Garrelts	.02	.02	.01
91	Jose Uribe	.02	.02	.01
92	Bob Brenly	.02	.02	.01
93	Robby Thompson	.02	.02	.01
94	Don Robinson	.02	.02	.01
95	Candy Maldonado	.04	.03	.02
96	Darryl Strawberry	.25	.20	.10
97	Keith Hernandez	.06	.05	.02
98	Ron Darling	.04	.03	.02
99	Howard Johnson	.04	.03	.02
100	Roger McDowell	.02	.02	.01
101	Dwight Gooden	.30	.25	.12
102	Kevin McReynolds	.04	.03	.02
103	Sid Fernandez	.02	.02	.01
104	Dave Magadan	.04	.03	.02
105	Gary Carter	.08	.06	.03
106	Carmelo Martinez	.02	.02	.01
107	Eddie Whitson	.02	.02	.01
108	Tim Flannery	.02	.02	.01
109	Stan Jefferson	.02	.02	.01
110	John Kruk	.10	.08	.04
111	Chris Brown	.04	.03	.02
112	Benny Santiago	.04	.03	.02
113	Garry Templeton	.02	.02	.01
114	Lance McCullers	.02	.02	.01
115	Tony Gwynn	.20	.15	.08
116	Steve Bedrosian	.06	.05	.02
117	Von Hayes	.02	.02	.01
118	Kevin Gross	.02	.02	.01
119	Bruce Ruffin	.02	.02	.01
120	Juan Samuel	.04	.03	.02
121	Shane Rawley	.02	.02	.01
122	Chris James	.04	.03	.02
123	Lance Parrish	.04	.03	.02
124	Glenn Wilson	.02	.02	.01
125	Mike Schmidt	.25	.20	.10
126	Andy Van Slyke	.08	.06	.03
127	Jose Lind	.04	.03	.02
128	Al Pedrique	.02	.02	.01
129	Bobby Bonilla	.04	.03	.02
130	Sed Bream	.02	.02	.01
131	Mike LaValliere	.02	.02	.01
132	Mike Dunne	.04	.03	.02
133	Jeff Robinson	.02	.02	.01
134	Doug Drabek	.02	.02	.01
135	Barry Bonds	.10	.08	.04
136	Dave Parker	.08	.06	.03
137	Nick Esasky	.02	.02	.01
138	Buddy Bell	.02	.02	.01
139	Kal Daniels	.04	.03	.02
140	Barry Larkin	.04	.03	.02
141	Eric Davis	.25	.20	.10
142	John Franco	.02	.02	.01
143	Bo Diaz	.02	.02	.01
144	Ron Oester	.02	.02	.01
145	Dennis Rasmussen	.02	.02	.01
146	Eric Davis	.40	.30	.15
147	Ryne Sandberg	.30	.25	.12
148	Andre Dawson	.20	.15	.08
149	Mike Schmidt	.40	.30	.15
150	Jack Clark	.20	.15	.08
151	Darryl Strawberry	.40	.30	.15
152	Gary Carter	.30	.25	.12
153	Ozzie Smith	.20	.15	.08
154	Mike Scott	.20	.15	.08
155	Rickey Henderson	.40	.30	.15
156	Don Mattingly	.90	.70	.35
157	Wade Boggs	.60	.45	.25
158	George Bell	.30	.25	.12
159	Dave Winfield	.30	.25	.12
160	Cal Ripken	.40	.30	.15
161	Terry Kennedy	.15	.11	.06
162	Willie Randolph	.15	.11	.06
163	Bret Saberhagen	.25	.20	.10
164	Mark McGwire	.35	.25	.14
165	Tony Phillips	.02	.02	.01
166	Jay Howell	.02	.02	.01
167	Carney Lansford	.02	.02	.01
168	Dave Stewart	.02	.02	.01
169	Alfredo Griffin	.02	.02	.01
170	Dennis Eckersley	.04	.03	.02
171	Mike Davis	.02	.02	.01
172	Luis Polonia	.02	.02	.01
173	Jose Canseco	.60	.45	.25
174	Mike Witt	.06	.05	.02
175	Jack Howell	.02	.02	.01
176	Greg Minton	.02	.02	.01
177	Dick Schofield	.02	.02	.01
178	Gary Pettis	.02	.02	.01
179	Wally Joyner	.25	.20	.10
180	DeWayne Buice	.02	.02	.01
181	Brian Downing	.02	.02	.01
182	Bob Boone	.02	.02	.01
183	Devon White	.04	.03	.02
184	Jim Clancy	.02	.02	.01
185	Willie Upshaw	.02	.02	.01
186	Tom Henke	.02	.02	.01
187	Ernie Whitt	.02	.02	.01
188	George Bell	.20	.15	.08
189	Lloyd Moseby	.02	.02	.01
190	Jimmy Key	.02	.02	.01
191	Dave Stieb	.02	.02	.01
192	Jesse Barfield	.04	.03	.02
193	Tony Fernandez	.10	.08	.04
194	Paul Molitor	.06	.05	.02
195	Jim Gantner	.02	.02	.01
196	Teddy Higuera	.04	.03	.02
197	Glenn Braggs	.02	.02	.01
198	Rob Deer	.02	.02	.01
199	Dale Sveum	.02	.02	.01
200	Bill Wegman	.02	.02	.01
201	Robin Yount	.06	.05	.02
202	B.J. Surhoff	.04	.03	.02
203	Dan Plesac	.06	.05	.02
204	Pat Tabler	.04	.03	.02
205	Mel Hall	.02	.02	.01
206	Scott Bailes	.02	.02	.01
207	Julio Franco	.04	.03	.02
208	Cory Snyder	.06	.05	.02
209	Chris Bando	.02	.02	.01
210	Greg Swindell	.04	.03	.02
211	Brook Jacoby	.02	.02	.01
212	Brett Butler	.02	.02	.01
213	Joe Carter	.10	.08	.04
214	Mark Langston	.08	.06	.03
215	Rey Quinones	.02	.02	.01
216	Ed Nunez	.02	.02	.01
217	Jim Presley	.02	.02	.01
218	Phil Bradley	.04	.03	.02
219	Alvin Davis	.10	.08	.04
220	Dave Valle	.02	.02	.01
221	Harold Reynolds	.02	.02	.01
222	Scott Bradley	.02	.02	.01
223	Gary Matthews	.02	.02	.01
224	Eric Bell	.02	.02	.01
225	Terry Kennedy	.02	.02	.01
226	Dave Schmidt	.02	.02	.01
227	Billy Ripken	.04	.03	.02
228	Cal Ripken	.20	.15	.08
229	Ray Knight	.02	.02	.01
230	Larry Sheets	.02	.02	.01
231	Mike Boddicker	.02	.02	.01
232	Tom Niedenfuer	.02	.02	.01
233	Eddie Murray	.20	.15	.08
234	Ruben Sierra	.12	.09	.05
235	Steve Buechele	.02	.02	.01
236	Charlie Hough	.02	.02	.01
237	Oddibe McDowell	.02	.02	.01
238	Mike Stanley	.02	.02	.01
239	Pete Incaviglia	.04	.03	.02
240	Pete O'Brien	.02	.02	.01
241	Scott Fletcher	.02	.02	.01
242	Dale Mohorcic	.02	.02	.01
243	Larry Parrish	.04	.03	.02
244	Wade Boggs	.35	.25	.14
245	Dwight Evans	.04	.03	.02
246	Sam Horn	.04	.03	.02
247	Jim Rice	.06	.05	.02
248	Marty Barrett	.02	.02	.01

		MT	NR MT	EX
249	Mike Greenwell	.15	.11	.06
250	Ellis Burks	.10	.08	.04
251	Roger Clemens	.12	.09	.05
252	Rich Gedman	.02	.02	.01
253	Bruce Hurst	.06	.05	.02
254	Bret Saberhagen	.15	.11	.06
255	Frank White	.02	.02	.01
256	Dan Quisenberry	.02	.02	.01
257	Danny Tartabull	.06	.05	.02
258	Bo Jackson	.08	.06	.03
259	George Brett	.25	.20	.10
260	Charlie Leibrandt	.02	.02	.01
261	Kevin Seitzer	.10	.08	.04
262	Mark Gubicza	.04	.03	.02
263	Willie Wilson	.04	.03	.02
264	Frank Tanana	.02	.02	.01
265	Darrell Evans	.02	.02	.01
266	Bill Madlock	.04	.03	.02
267	Kirk Gibson	.06	.05	.02
268	Jack Morris	.12	.09	.05
269	Matt Nokes	.06	.05	.02
270	Lou Whitaker	.04	.03	.02
271	Eric King	.02	.02	.01
272	Jim Morrison	.02	.02	.01
273	Alan Trammell	.20	.15	.08
274	Kent Hrbek	.12	.09	.05
275	Tom Brunansky	.04	.03	.02
276	Bert Blyleven	.04	.03	.02
277	Gary Gaetti	.04	.03	.02
278	Tim Laudner	.04	.03	.02
279	Gene Larkin	.02	.02	.01
280	Jeff Reardon	.02	.02	.01
281	Danny Gladden	.02	.02	.01
282	Frank Viola	.04	.03	.02
283	Kirby Puckett	.20	.15	.08
284	Ozzie Guillen	.06	.05	.02
285	Ivan Calderon	.02	.02	.01
286	Donnie Hill	.02	.02	.01
287	Ken Williams	.04	.03	.02
288	Jim Winn	.02	.02	.01
289	Bob James	.02	.02	.01
290	Carlton Fisk	.04	.03	.02
291	Richard Dotson	.02	.02	.01
292	Greg Walker	.02	.02	.01
293	Harold Baines	.10	.08	.04
294	Willie Randolph	.06	.05	.02
295	Mike Pagliarulo	.04	.03	.02
296	Ron Guidry	.04	.03	.02
297	Rickey Henderson	.10	.08	.04
298	Rick Rhoden	.02	.02	.01
299	Don Mattingly	.70	.50	.30
300	Dave Righetti	.04	.03	.02
301	Claudell Washington	.02	.02	.01
302	Dave Winfield	.08	.06	.03
303	Gary Ward	.02	.02	.01
304	Al Pedrique	.02	.02	.01
305	Casey Candaele	.02	.02	.01
306	Kevin Seitzer	.10	.08	.04
307	Mike Dunne	.04	.03	.02
308	Jeff Musselman	.02	.02	.01
309	Mark McGwire	.20	.15	.08
310	Ellis Burks	.10	.08	.04
311	Matt Nokes	.06	.05	.02
312	Mike Greenwell	.15	.11	.06
313	Devon White	.04	.03	.02

1988 Topps Traded

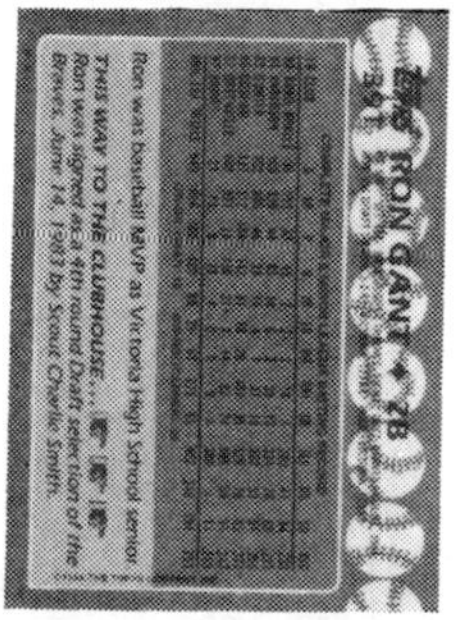

In addition to new players and traded veterans, 21 members of the U.S.A. Olympic Baseball team are showcased in this 132-card set, numbered 1T-132T. The standard-size (2-1/2" by 3-1/2") set follows the same design as the basic Topps issue - white borders, large full-color photos, team name (or U.S.A.) in large bold letters at the top of the card face, player name on a diagonal stripe across the lower right corner. Topps has issued its traded series each year since 1981 in boxed complete sets available through hobby dealers.

		MT	NR MT	EX
Complete Set:		30.00	22.00	12.00
Common Player:		.06	.05	.02
1T	Jim Abbott (U.S.A.)(FC)	4.00	3.00	1.50
2T	Juan Agosto	.06	.05	.02
3T	Luis Alicea(FC)	.15	.11	.06
4T	Roberto Alomar(FC)	3.00	2.25	1.25
5T	Brady Anderson(FC)	.30	.25	.12
6T	Jack Armstrong(FC)	.50	.40	.20
7T	Don August	.15	.11	.06
8T	Floyd Bannister	.08	.06	.03
9T	Bret Barberie (U.S.A.)(FC)	.30	.25	.12
10T	Jose Bautista(FC)	.15	.11	.06
11T	Don Baylor	.10	.08	.04
12T	Tim Belcher	.20	.15	.08
13T	Buddy Bell	.10	.08	.04
14T	Andy Benes (U.S.A.)(FC)	3.00	2.25	1.25
15T	Damon Berryhill(FC)	.25	.20	.10
16T	Bud Black	.06	.05	.02
17T	Pat Borders(FC)	.30	.25	.12
18T	Phil Bradley	.10	.08	.04
19T	Jeff Branson (U.S.A.)(FC)	.20	.15	.08
20T	Tom Brunansky	.12	.09	.05
21T	Jay Buhner(FC)	.40	.30	.15
22T	Brett Butler	.08	.06	.03
23T	Jim Campanis (U.S.A.)(FC)	.20	.15	.08
24T	Sil Campusano(FC)	.20	.15	.08
25T	John Candelaria	.08	.06	.03
26T	Jose Cecena(FC)	.15	.11	.06
27T	Rick Cerone	.06	.05	.02
28T	Jack Clark	.15	.11	.06
29T	Kevin Coffman(FC)	.10	.08	.04
30T	Pat Combs (U.S.A.)(FC)	.60	.45	.25
31T	Henry Cotto	.06	.05	.02
32T	Chili Davis	.08	.06	.03
33T	Mike Davis	.08	.06	.03
34T	Jose DeLeon	.08	.06	.03
35T	Richard Dotson	.10	.08	.04
36T	Cecil Espy(FC)	.08	.06	.03
37T	Tom Filer	.06	.05	.02
38T	Mike Fiore (U.S.A.)(FC)	.20	.15	.08
39T	Ron Gant(FC)	2.50	2.00	1.00
40T	Kirk Gibson	.20	.15	.08
41T	Rich Gossage	.15	.11	.06
42T	Mark Grace(FC)	4.00	3.00	1.50
43T	Alfredo Griffin	.08	.06	.03
44T	Ty Griffin (U.S.A.)(FC)	.30	.25	.12
45T	Bryan Harvey(FC)	.40	.30	.15
46T	Ron Hassey	.06	.05	.02
47T	Ray Hayward(FC)	.08	.06	.03
48T	Dave Henderson	.20	.15	.08
49T	Tom Herr	.10	.08	.04
50T	Bob Horner	.10	.08	.04
51T	Ricky Horton	.08	.06	.03
52T	Jay Howell	.08	.06	.03
53T	Glenn Hubbard	.06	.05	.02
54T	Jeff Innis(FC)	.15	.11	.06
55T	Danny Jackson	.15	.11	.06
56T	Darrin Jackson(FC)	.10	.08	.04
57T	Roberto Kelly(FC)	1.00	.70	.40
58T	Ron Kittle	.10	.08	.04
59T	Ray Knight	.08	.06	.03
60T	Vance Law	.08	.06	.03
61T	Jeffrey Leonard	.08	.06	.03
62T	Mike Macfarlane(FC)	.25	.20	.10
63T	Scotti Madison(FC)	.15	.11	.06
64T	Kirt Manwaring(FC)	.20	.15	.08
65T	Mark Marquess (U.S.A.)	.06	.05	.02
66T	Tino Martinez (U.S.A.)(FC)	4.00	3.00	1.50
67T	Billy Masse (U.S.A.)(FC)	.30	.25	.12
68T	Jack McDowell(FC)	2.50	2.00	1.00
69T	Jack McKeon	.06	.05	.02
70T	Larry McWilliams	.06	.05	.02
71T	Mickey Morandini (U.S.A.)(FC)	.50	.40	.20
72T	Keith Moreland	.08	.06	.03
73T	Mike Morgan	.06	.05	.02
74T	Charles Nagy (U.S.A.)(FC)	.70	.50	.30
75T	Al Nipper	.06	.05	.02
76T	Russ Nixon	.06	.05	.02

		MT	NR MT	EX
77T	Jesse Orosco	.08	.06	.03
78T	Joe Orsulak	.06	.05	.02
79T	Dave Palmer	.06	.05	.02
80T	Mark Parent(FC)	.20	.15	.08
81T	Dave Parker	.12	.09	.05
82T	Dan Pasqua	.10	.08	.04
83T	Melido Perez(FC)	.40	.30	.15
84T	Steve Peters(FC)	.15	.11	.06
85T	Dan Petry	.08	.06	.03
86T	Gary Pettis	.08	.06	.03
87T	Jeff Pico(FC)	.20	.15	.08
88T	Jim Poole (U.S.A.)(FC)	.20	.15	.08
89T	Ted Power	.06	.05	.02
90T	Rafael Ramirez	.06	.05	.02
91T	Dennis Rasmussen	.10	.08	.04
92T	Jose Rijo	.08	.06	.03
93T	Earnie Riles	.06	.05	.02
94T	Luis Rivera(FC)	.08	.06	.03
95T	Doug Robbins (U.S.A.)(FC)	.20	.15	.08
96T	Frank Robinson	.10	.08	.04
97T	Cookie Rojas	.06	.05	.02
98T	Chris Sabo(FC)	2.00	1.50	.80
99T	Mark Salas	.06	.05	.02
100T	Luis Salazar	.06	.05	.02
101T	Rafael Santana	.06	.05	.02
102T	Nelson Santovenia(FC)	.20	.15	.08
103T	Mackey Sasser(FC)	.25	.20	.10
104T	Calvin Schiraldi	.06	.05	.02
105T	Mike Schooler(FC)	.30	.25	.12
106T	Scott Servais (U.S.A.)(FC)	.30	.25	.12
107T	Dave Silvestri (U.S.A.)(FC)	.20	.15	.08
108T	Don Slaught	.06	.05	.02
109T	Joe Slusarski (U.S.A.)(FC)	.35	.25	.14
110T	Lee Smith	.10	.08	.04
111T	Pete Smith(FC)	.10	.08	.04
112T	Jim Snyder	.06	.05	.02
113T	Ed Sprague (U.S.A.)(FC)	.60	.45	.25
114T	Pete Stanicek(FC)	.15	.11	.06
115T	Kurt Stillwell	.10	.08	.04
116T	Todd Stottlemyre(FC)	.90	.70	.35
117T	Bill Swift	.06	.05	.02
118T	Pat Tabler	.08	.06	.03
119T	Scott Terry(FC)	.10	.08	.04
120T	Mickey Tettleton	.06	.05	.02
121T	Dickie Thon	.08	.06	.03
122T	Jeff Treadway(FC)	.20	.15	.08
123T	Willie Upshaw	.08	.06	.03
124T	Robin Ventura(FC)	7.00	5.25	2.75
125T	Ron Washington	.06	.05	.02
126T	Walt Weiss(FC)	.60	.45	.25
127T	Bob Welch	.10	.08	.04
128T	David Wells(FC)	.15	.11	.06
129T	Glenn Wilson	.08	.06	.03
130T	Ted Wood (U.S.A.)(FC)	.30	.25	.12
131T	Don Zimmer	.06	.05	.02
132T	Checklist 1T-132T	.06	.05	.02

1989 Topps

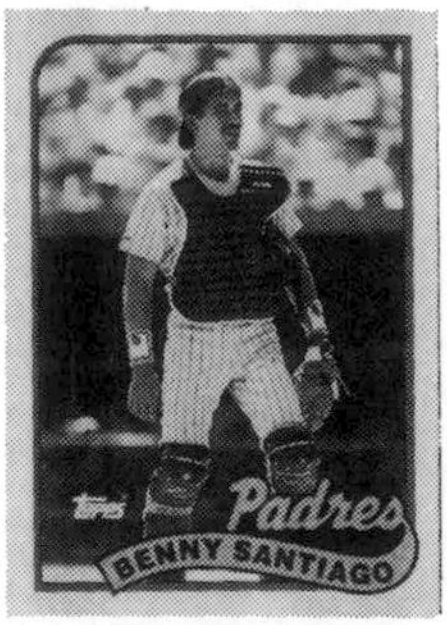

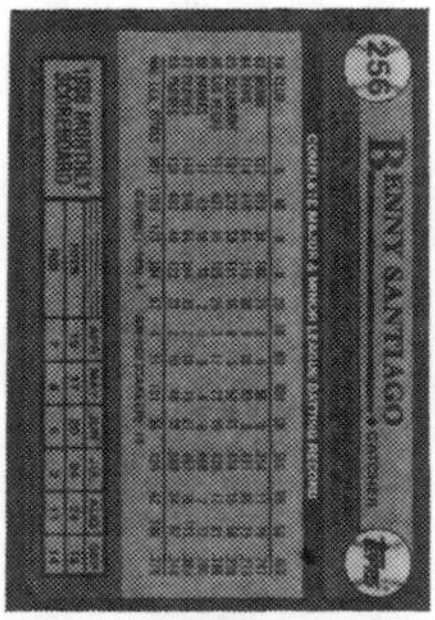

Ten top young players who led the June 1988 draft picks are featured on "#1 Draft Pick" cards in this full-color basic set of 792 standard-size baseball cards. An additional five cards salute 1989 Future Stars, 22 cards highlight All-Stars, seven contain Record Breakers, five are designated Turn Back The Clock, and six contain checklists. This set features the familiar white borders, but two inner photo corners (upper left and lower right) have been rounded off and the rectangular player name was replaced by a curved name banner in bright red or blue that leads to the team name in large script in the lower right corner. The card backs are printed in black on a red background and include personal information and complete minor and major league stats. Another new addition in this set is the special Monthly Scoreboard chart that lists monthly stats (April through September) in two of several categories (hits, run, home runs, stolen bases, RBIs, wins, strikeouts, games or saves).

	MT	NR MT	EX
Complete Set:	22.00	16.50	8.75
Common Player:	.03	.02	.01

		MT	NR MT	EX
1	Record Breaker (George Bell)	.08	.06	.03
2	Record Breaker (Wade Boggs)	.35	.25	.14
3	Record Breaker (Gary Carter)	.10	.08	.04
4	Record Breaker (Andre Dawson)	.08	.06	.03
5	Record Breaker (Orel Hershiser)	.10	.08	.04
6	Record Breaker (Doug Jones)	.06	.05	.02
7	Record Breaker (Kevin McReynolds)	.08	.06	.03
8	*Dave Eiland*(FC)	.20	.15	.08
9	Tim Teufel	.03	.02	.01
10	Andre Dawson	.15	.11	.06
11	Bruce Sutter	.08	.06	.03
12	Dale Sveum	.06	.05	.02
13	Doug Sisk	.03	.02	.01
14	Tom Kelly	.03	.02	.01
15	Robby Thompson	.06	.05	.02
16	Ron Robinson	.03	.02	.01
17	Brian Downing	.06	.05	.02
18	Rick Rhoden	.06	.05	.02
19	Greg Gagne	.03	.02	.01
20	Steve Bedrosian	.08	.06	.03
21	White Sox Leaders (Greg Walker)	.06	.05	.02
22	Tim Crews	.06	.05	.02
23	Mike Fitzgerald	.03	.02	.01
24	Larry Andersen	.03	.02	.01
25	Frank White	.06	.05	.02
26	Dale Mohorcic	.03	.02	.01
27	*Orestes Destrade*(FC)	.12	.09	.05
28	Mike Moore	.03	.02	.01
29	Kelly Gruber	.03	.02	.01
30	Doc Gooden	.40	.30	.15
31	Terry Francona	.03	.02	.01
32	Dennis Rasmussen	.08	.06	.03
33	B.J. Surhoff	.08	.06	.03
34	Ken Williams	.06	.05	.02
35	John Tudor	.08	.06	.03
36	Mitch Webster	.06	.05	.02
37	Bob Stanley	.03	.02	.01
38	Paul Runge	.03	.02	.01
39	Mike Maddux	.03	.02	.01
40	Steve Sax	.12	.09	.05
41	Terry Mulholland	.03	.02	.01
42	Jim Eppard(FC)	.08	.06	.03
43	Guillermo Hernandez	.06	.05	.02
44	Jim Snyder	.03	.02	.01
45	Kal Daniels	.12	.09	.05
46	Mark Portugal	.03	.02	.01
47	Carney Lansford	.06	.05	.02
48	Tim Burke	.03	.02	.01
49	*Craig Biggio*(FC)	.35	.25	.12
50	George Bell	.20	.15	.08
51	Angels Leaders (Mark McLemore)	.06	.05	.02
52	Bob Brenly	.03	.02	.01
53	Ruben Sierra	.30	.25	.12
54	Steve Trout	.03	.02	.01
55	Julio Franco	.08	.06	.03
56	Pat Tabler	.06	.05	.02
57	Alejandro Pena	.06	.05	.02
58	Lee Mazzilli	.06	.05	.02
59	Mark Davis	.03	.02	.01
60	Tom Brunansky	.10	.08	.04
61	Neil Allen	.03	.02	.01
62	Alfredo Griffin	.06	.05	.02
63	Mark Clear	.03	.02	.01
64	Alex Trevino	.03	.02	.01
65	Rick Reuschel	.08	.06	.03
66	Manny Trillo	.03	.02	.01
67	Dave Palmer	.03	.02	.01
68	Darrell Miller	.03	.02	.01
69	Jeff Ballard	.06	.05	.02
70	Mark McGwire	.30	.25	.12
71	Mike Boddicker	.06	.05	.02
72	John Moses	.03	.02	.01
73	Pascual Perez	.06	.05	.02

		MT	NR MT	EX
74	Nick Leyva	.03	.02	.01
75	Tom Henke	.06	.05	.02
76	*Terry Blocker*(FC)	.12	.09	.05
77	Doyle Alexander	.06	.05	.02
78	Jim Sundberg	.06	.05	.02
79	Scott Bankhead	.03	.02	.01
80	Cory Snyder	.15	.11	.06
81	Expos Leaders (Tim Raines)	.08	.06	.03
82	Dave Leiper	.03	.02	.01
83	Jeff Blauser(FC)	.15	.11	.06
84	#1 Draft Pick *(Bill Bene)*(FC)	.15	.11	.06
85	Kevin McReynolds	.12	.09	.05
86	Al Nipper	.03	.02	.01
87	Larry Owen	.03	.02	.01
88	*Darryl Hamilton*(FC)	.20	.15	.08
89	Dave LaPoint	.06	.05	.02
90	Vince Coleman	.12	.09	.05
91	Floyd Youmans	.03	.02	.01
92	Jeff Kunkel	.03	.02	.01
93	Ken Howell	.03	.02	.01
94	Chris Speier	.03	.02	.01
95	Gerald Young	.10	.08	.04
96	Rick Cerone	.03	.02	.01
97	Greg Mathews	.06	.05	.02
98	Larry Sheets	.06	.05	.02
99	*Sherman Corbett*(FC)	.12	.09	.05
100	Mike Schmidt	.35	.25	.14
101	Les Straker	.06	.05	.02
102	Mike Gallego	.03	.02	.01
103	Tim Birtsas	.03	.02	.01
104	Dallas Green	.03	.02	.01
105	Ron Darling	.10	.08	.04
106	Willie Upshaw	.06	.05	.02
107	Jose DeLeon	.06	.05	.02
108	Fred Manrique	.06	.05	.02
109	*Hipolito Pena*(FC)	.12	.09	.05
110	Paul Molitor	.12	.09	.05
111	Reds Leaders (Eric Davis)	.10	.08	.04
112	Jim Presley	.06	.05	.02
113	Lloyd Moseby	.06	.05	.02
114	Bob Kipper	.03	.02	.01
115	Jody Davis	.06	.05	.02
116	Jeff Montgomery	.06	.05	.02
117	Dave Anderson	.03	.02	.01
118	Checklist 1-132	.03	.02	.01
119	Terry Puhl	.03	.02	.01
120	Frank Viola	.12	.09	.05
121	Garry Templeton	.06	.05	.02
122	Lance Johnson(FC)	.10	.08	.04
123	Spike Owen	.03	.02	.01
124	Jim Traber	.06	.05	.02
125	Mike Krukow	.06	.05	.02
126	Sid Bream	.06	.05	.02
127	Walt Terrell	.06	.05	.02
128	Milt Thompson	.03	.02	.01
129	*Terry Clark*(FC)	.12	.09	.05
130	Gerald Perry	.08	.06	.03
131	Dave Otto(FC)	.08	.06	.03
132	Curt Ford	.03	.02	.01
133	Bill Long	.06	.05	.02
134	Don Zimmer	.03	.02	.01
135	Jose Rijo	.06	.05	.02
136	Joey Meyer	.08	.06	.03
137	Geno Petralli	.03	.02	.01
138	Wallace Johnson	.03	.02	.01
139	Mike Flanagan	.06	.05	.02
140	Shawon Dunston	.08	.06	.03
141	Indians Leaders (Brook Jacoby)	.06	.05	.02
142	Mike Diaz	.06	.05	.02
143	Mike Campbell	.08	.06	.03
144	Jay Bell	.06	.05	.02
145	Dave Stewart	.08	.06	.03
146	Gary Pettis	.03	.02	.01
147	DeWayne Buice	.03	.02	.01
148	Bill Pecota	.06	.05	.02
149	*Doug Dascenzo*(FC)	.20	.15	.08
150	Fernando Valenzuela	.15	.11	.06
151	Terry McGriff	.03	.02	.01
152	Mark Thurmond	.03	.02	.01
153	Jim Pankovits	.03	.02	.01
154	Don Carman	.06	.05	.02
155	Marty Barrett	.06	.05	.02
156	*Dave Gallagher*(FC)	.15	.11	.06
157	Tom Glavine	.08	.06	.03
158	Mike Aldrete	.06	.05	.02
159	Pat Clements	.03	.02	.01
160	Jeffrey Leonard	.06	.05	.02
161	#1 Draft Pick *(Gregg Olson)*(FC)	.60	.45	.25
162	John Davis	.03	.02	.01
163	Bob Forsch	.06	.05	.02
164	Hal Lanier	.03	.02	.01

		MT	NR MT	EX
165	Mike Dunne	.08	.06	.03
166	*Doug Jennings*(FC)	.12	.09	.05
167	Future Star *(Steve Searcy)*(FC)	.25	.20	.10
168	Willie Wilson	.08	.06	.03
169	Mike Jackson	.06	.05	.02
170	Tony Fernandez	.10	.08	.04
171	Braves Leaders (Andres Thomas)	.06	.05	.02
172	Frank Williams	.03	.02	.01
173	Mel Hall	.06	.05	.02
174	*Todd Burns*(FC)	.12	.09	.05
175	John Shelby	.03	.02	.01
176	Jeff Parrett	.08	.06	.03
177	#1 Draft Pick *(Monty Fariss)*(FC)	.25	.20	.10
178	Mark Grant	.03	.02	.01
179	Ozzie Virgil	.03	.02	.01
180	Mike Scott	.10	.08	.04
181	*Craig Worthington*(FC)	.20	.15	.08
182	Bob McClure	.03	.02	.01
183	Oddibe McDowell	.06	.05	.02
184	*John Costello*	.20	.15	.08
185	Claudell Washington	.06	.05	.02
186	Pat Perry	.03	.02	.01
187	Darren Daulton	.03	.02	.01
188	Dennis Lamp	.03	.02	.01
189	Kevin Mitchell	.50	.40	.20
190	Mike Witt	.06	.05	.02
191	*Sil Campusano*	.20	.15	.08
192	Paul Mirabella	.03	.02	.01
193	Sparky Anderson	.06	.05	.02
194	*Greg Harris*(FC)	.25	.20	.10
195	Ozzie Guillen	.06	.05	.02
196	Denny Walling	.03	.02	.01
197	Neal Heaton	.03	.02	.01
198	Danny Heep	.03	.02	.01
199	*Mike Schooler*	.30	.25	.12
200	George Brett	.30	.25	.12
201	Blue Jays Leaders (Kelly Gruber)	.06	.05	.02
202	*Brad Moore*(FC)	.12	.09	.05
203	Rob Ducey	.03	.02	.01
204	Brad Havens	.03	.02	.01
205	Dwight Evans	.10	.08	.04
206	Roberto Alomar	.50	.40	.20
207	Terry Leach	.03	.02	.01
208	Tom Pagnozzi	.06	.05	.02
209	*Jeff Bittiger*(FC)	.12	.09	.05
210	Dale Murphy	.30	.25	.12
211	Mike Pagliarulo	.08	.06	.03
212	Scott Sanderson	.03	.02	.01
213	Rene Gonzales	.06	.05	.02
214	Charlie O'Brien	.03	.02	.01
215	Kevin Gross	.06	.05	.02
216	Jack Howell	.06	.05	.02
217	Joe Price	.03	.02	.01
218	Mike LaValliere	.06	.05	.02
219	Jim Clancy	.06	.05	.02
220	Gary Gaetti	.12	.09	.05
221	Cecil Espy	.08	.06	.03
222	#1 Draft Pick *(Mark Lewis)*(FC)	.70	.50	.30
223	Jay Buhner	.10	.08	.04
224	Tony LaRussa	.06	.05	.02
225	*Ramon Martinez*(FC)	1.50	1.25	.60
226	Bill Doran	.06	.05	.02
227	John Farrell	.08	.06	.03
228	*Nelson Santovenia*	.15	.11	.06
229	Jimmy Key	.08	.06	.03
230	Ozzie Smith	.12	.09	.05
231	Padres Leaders (Roberto Alomar)	.10	.08	.04
232	Ricky Horton	.06	.05	.02
233	Future Star (Gregg Jefferies)(FC)	1.00	.70	.40
234	Tom Browning	.08	.06	.03
235	John Kruk	.06	.05	.02
236	Charles Hudson	.03	.02	.01
237	Glenn Hubbard	.03	.02	.01
238	Eric King	.03	.02	.01
239	Tim Laudner	.03	.02	.01
240	Greg Maddux	.10	.08	.04
241	Brett Butler	.06	.05	.02
242	Ed Vande Berg	.03	.02	.01
243	Bob Boone	.06	.05	.02
244	Jim Acker	.03	.02	.01
245	Jim Rice	.20	.15	.08
246	Rey Quinones	.03	.02	.01
247	Shawn Hillegas	.06	.05	.02
248	Tony Phillips	.03	.02	.01
249	Tim Leary	.06	.05	.02
250	Cal Ripken	.30	.25	.12
251	*John Dopson*(FC)	.20	.15	.08
252	Billy Hatcher	.06	.05	.02
253	*Jose Alvarez*(FC)	.12	.09	.05
254	Tom LaSorda	.06	.05	.02
255	Ron Guidry	.12	.09	.05

		MT	NR MT	EX
256	Benny Santiago	.12	.09	.05
257	Rick Aguilera	.03	.02	.01
258	Checklist 133-264	.03	.02	.01
259	Larry McWilliams	.03	.02	.01
260	Dave Winfield	.25	.20	.10
261	Cardinals Leaders (Tom Brunansky)	.06	.05	.02
262	*Jeff Pico*	.15	.11	.06
263	Mike Felder	.03	.02	.01
264	*Rob Dibble*(FC)	.40	.30	.15
265	Kent Hrbek	.15	.11	.06
266	Luis Aquino	.03	.02	.01
267	Jeff Robinson	.06	.05	.02
268	Keith Miller	.06	.05	.02
269	Tom Bolton	.06	.05	.02
270	Wally Joyner	.20	.15	.08
271	Jay Tibbs	.03	.02	.01
272	Ron Hassey	.03	.02	.01
273	Jose Lind	.08	.06	.03
274	Mark Eichhorn	.06	.05	.02
275	Danny Tartabull	.15	.11	.06
276	Paul Kilgus	.08	.06	.03
277	Mike Davis	.06	.05	.02
278	Andy McGaffigan	.03	.02	.01
279	Scott Bradley	.03	.02	.01
280	Bob Knepper	.06	.05	.02
281	Gary Redus	.03	.02	.01
282	*Cris Carpenter*(FC)	.15	.11	.06
283	Andy Allanson	.03	.02	.01
284	Jim Leyland	.03	.02	.01
285	John Candelaria	.06	.05	.02
286	Darrin Jackson	.08	.06	.03
287	Juan Nieves	.06	.05	.02
288	Pat Sheridan	.03	.02	.01
289	Ernie Whitt	.06	.05	.02
290	John Franco	.08	.06	.03
291	Mets Leaders (Darryl Strawberry)	.12	.09	.05
292	*Jim Corsi*(FC)	.15	.11	.06
293	Glenn Wilson	.06	.05	.02
294	Juan Berenguer	.03	.02	.01
295	Scott Fletcher	.06	.05	.02
296	Ron Gant	.40	.30	.15
297	*Oswald Peraza*(FC)	.15	.11	.06
298	Chris James	.08	.06	.03
299	*Steve Ellsworth*(FC)	.12	.09	.05
300	Darryl Strawberry	.35	.25	.14
301	Charlie Leibrandt	.06	.05	.02
302	Gary Ward	.06	.05	.02
303	Felix Fermin	.06	.05	.02
304	Joel Youngblood	.03	.02	.01
305	Dave Smith	.06	.05	.02
306	Tracy Woodson(FC)	.10	.08	.04
307	Lance McCullers	.06	.05	.02
308	Ron Karkovice	.03	.02	.01
309	Mario Diaz(FC)	.10	.08	.04
310	Rafael Palmeiro	.20	.15	.08
311	Chris Bosio	.03	.02	.01
312	Tom Lawless	.03	.02	.01
313	Denny Martinez	.06	.05	.02
314	Bobby Valentine	.03	.02	.01
315	Greg Swindell	.10	.08	.04
316	Walt Weiss	.20	.15	.08
317	*Jack Armstrong*	.35	.25	.14
318	Gene Larkin	.08	.06	.03
319	Greg Booker	.03	.02	.01
320	Lou Whitaker	.15	.11	.06
321	Red Sox Leaders (Jody Reed)	.06	.05	.02
322	John Smiley	.10	.08	.04
323	Gary Thurman	.10	.08	.04
324	*Bob Milacki*(FC)	.25	.20	.10
325	Jesse Barfield	.08	.06	.03
326	Dennis Boyd	.06	.05	.02
327	*Mark Lemke*(FC)	.20	.15	.08
328	Rick Honeycutt	.03	.02	.01
329	Bob Melvin	.03	.02	.01
330	Eric Davis	.35	.25	.14
331	Curt Wilkerson	.03	.02	.01
332	Tony Armas	.06	.05	.02
333	Bob Ojeda	.06	.05	.02
334	Steve Lyons	.03	.02	.01
335	Dave Righetti	.10	.08	.04
336	Steve Balboni	.06	.05	.02
337	Calvin Schiraldi	.03	.02	.01
338	Jim Adduci(FC)	.06	.05	.02
339	Scott Bailes	.03	.02	.01
340	Kirk Gibson	.15	.11	.06
341	Jim Deshaies	.03	.02	.01
342	Tom Brookens	.03	.02	.01
343	Future Star (*Gary Sheffield*)(FC)	.60	.45	.25
344	Tom Trebelhorn	.03	.02	.01
345	Charlie Hough	.06	.05	.02

		MT	NR MT	EX
346	Rex Hudler(FC)	.06	.05	.02
347	John Cerutti	.06	.05	.02
348	Ed Hearn	.03	.02	.01
349	*Ron Jones*(FC)	.15	.11	.06
350	Andy Van Slyke	.12	.09	.05
351	Giants Leaders (Bob Melvin)	.06	.05	.02
352	Rick Schu	.03	.02	.01
353	Marvell Wynne	.03	.02	.01
354	Larry Parrish	.06	.05	.02
355	Mark Langston	.08	.06	.03
356	Kevin Elster	.08	.06	.03
357	Jerry Reuss	.06	.05	.02
358	*Ricky Jordan*(FC)	.40	.30	.15
359	Tommy John	.10	.08	.04
360	Ryne Sandberg	.30	.25	.12
361	Kelly Downs	.08	.06	.03
362	Jack Lazorko	.03	.02	.01
363	Rich Yett	.03	.02	.01
364	Rob Deer	.06	.05	.02
365	Mike Henneman	.08	.06	.03
366	Herm Winningham	.03	.02	.01
367	*Johnny Paredes*(FC)	.15	.11	.06
368	Brian Holton	.06	.05	.02
369	Ken Caminiti	.06	.05	.02
370	Dennis Eckersley	.10	.08	.04
371	Manny Lee	.03	.02	.01
372	Craig Lefferts	.03	.02	.01
373	Tracy Jones	.08	.06	.03
374	John Wathan	.06	.05	.02
375	Terry Pendleton	.08	.06	.03
376	Steve Lombardozzi	.03	.02	.01
377	Mike Smithson	.03	.02	.01
378	Checklist 265-396	.03	.02	.01
379	Tim Flannery	.03	.02	.01
380	Rickey Henderson	.30	.25	.12
381	Orioles Leaders (Larry Sheets)	.06	.05	.02
382	*John Smoltz*(FC)	.40	.30	.15
383	Howard Johnson	.08	.06	.03
384	Mark Salas	.03	.02	.01
385	Von Hayes	.08	.06	.03
386	Andres Galarraga AS	.08	.06	.03
387	Ryne Sandberg AS	.10	.08	.04
388	Bobby Bonilla AS	.08	.06	.03
389	Ozzie Smith AS	.08	.06	.03
390	Darryl Strawberry AS	.15	.11	.06
391	Andre Dawson AS	.10	.08	.04
392	Andy Van Slyke AS	.08	.06	.03
393	Gary Carter AS	.10	.08	.04
394	Orel Hershiser AS	.12	.09	.05
395	Danny Jackson AS	.08	.06	.03
396	Kirk Gibson AS	.08	.06	.03
397	Don Mattingly AS	.30	.25	.12
398	Julio Franco AS	.06	.05	.02
399	Wade Boggs AS	.20	.15	.08
400	Alan Trammell AS	.08	.06	.03
401	Jose Canseco AS	.30	.25	.12
402	Mike Greenwell AS	.15	.11	.06
403	Kirby Puckett AS	.12	.09	.05
404	Bob Boone AS	.06	.05	.02
405	Roger Clemens AS	.15	.11	.06
406	Frank Viola AS	.08	.06	.03
407	Dave Winfield AS	.12	.09	.05
408	Greg Walker	.06	.05	.02
409	Ken Dayley	.03	.02	.01
410	Jack Clark	.12	.09	.05
411	Mitch Williams	.06	.05	.02
412	Barry Lyons	.03	.02	.01
413	Mike Kingery	.03	.02	.01
414	Jim Fregosi	.03	.02	.01
415	Rich Gossage	.10	.08	.04
416	Fred Lynn	.10	.08	.04
417	Mike LaCoss	.03	.02	.01
418	Bob Dernier	.03	.02	.01
419	Tom Filer	.03	.02	.01
420	Joe Carter	.10	.08	.04
421	Kirk McCaskill	.06	.05	.02
422	Bo Diaz	.06	.05	.02
423	Brian Fisher	.06	.05	.02
424	Luis Polonia	.06	.05	.02
425	Jay Howell	.06	.05	.02
426	Danny Gladden	.03	.02	.01
427	Eric Show	.06	.05	.02
428	Craig Reynolds	.03	.02	.01
429	Twins Leaders (Greg Gagne)	.06	.05	.02
430	Mark Gubicza	.08	.06	.03
431	Luis Rivera	.06	.05	.02
432	*Chad Kreuter*(FC)	.15	.11	.06
433	Albert Hall	.03	.02	.01
434	*Ken Patterson*(FC)	.15	.11	.06
435	Len Dykstra	.08	.06	.03
436	Bobby Meacham	.03	.02	.01

		MT	NR MT	EX
437	#1 Draft Pick *(Andy Benes)*	1.00	.70	.40
438	Greg Gross	.03	.02	.01
439	Frank DiPino	.03	.02	.01
440	Bobby Bonilla	.25	.20	.10
441	Jerry Reed	.03	.02	.01
442	Jose Oquendo	.03	.02	.01
443	*Rod Nichols*(FC)	.15	.11	.06
444	Moose Stubing	.03	.02	.01
445	Matt Nokes	.15	.11	.06
446	Rob Murphy	.03	.02	.01
447	Donell Nixon	.03	.02	.01
448	Eric Plunk	.03	.02	.01
449	Carmelo Martinez	.03	.02	.01
450	Roger Clemens	.40	.30	.15
451	Mark Davidson	.06	.05	.02
452	*Israel Sanchez*	.12	.09	.05
453	Tom Prince(FC)	.08	.06	.03
454	Paul Assenmacher	.03	.02	.01
455	Johnny Ray	.06	.05	.02
456	Tim Belcher	.08	.06	.03
457	Mackey Sasser	.06	.05	.02
458	*Donn Pall*(FC)	.12	.09	.05
459	Mariners Leaders (Dave Valle)	.06	.05	.02
460	Dave Stieb	.08	.06	.03
461	Buddy Bell	.06	.05	.02
462	Jose Guzman	.08	.06	.03
463	Steve Lake	.03	.02	.01
464	Bryn Smith	.03	.02	.01
465	Mark Grace	.70	.50	.30
466	Chuck Crim	.03	.02	.01
467	Jim Walewander	.03	.02	.01
468	Henry Cotto	.03	.02	.01
469	*Jose Bautista*	.20	.15	.08
470	Lance Parrish	.12	.09	.05
471	*Steve Curry*(FC)	.15	.11	.06
472	Brian Harper	.03	.02	.01
473	Don Robinson	.03	.02	.01
474	Bob Rodgers	.03	.02	.01
475	Dave Parker	.10	.08	.04
476	Jon Perlman(FC)	.06	.05	.02
477	Dick Schofield	.03	.02	.01
478	Doug Drabek	.06	.05	.02
479	*Mike Macfarlane*	.25	.20	.10
480	Keith Hernandez	.15	.11	.06
481	Chris Brown	.06	.05	.02
482	*Steve Peters*	.12	.09	.05
483	Mickey Hatcher	.03	.02	.01
484	Steve Shields	.03	.02	.01
485	Hubie Brooks	.08	.06	.03
486	Jack McDowell	.20	.15	.08
487	Scott Lusader(FC)	.08	.06	.03
488	Kevin Coffman	.06	.05	.02
489	Phillies Leaders (Mike Schmidt)	.12	.09	.05
490	*Chris Sabo*	.60	.45	.25
491	Mike Birkbeck	.03	.02	.01
492	Alan Ashby	.03	.02	.01
493	Todd Benzinger	.10	.08	.04
494	Shane Rawley	.06	.05	.02
495	Candy Maldonado	.06	.05	.02
496	Dwayne Henry	.03	.02	.01
497	Pete Stanicek	.12	.09	.05
498	Dave Valle	.03	.02	.01
499	*Don Heinkel*(FC)	.15	.11	.06
500	Jose Canseco	1.00	.70	.40
501	Vance Law	.06	.05	.02
502	Duane Ward	.03	.02	.01
503	Al Newman	.03	.02	.01
504	Bob Walk	.03	.02	.01
505	Pete Rose	.20	.15	.08
506	Kirt Manwaring	.10	.08	.04
507	Steve Farr	.03	.02	.01
508	Wally Backman	.06	.05	.02
509	Bud Black	.03	.02	.01
510	Bob Horner	.08	.06	.03
511	Richard Dotson	.06	.05	.02
512	Donnie Hill	.03	.02	.01
513	Jesse Orosco	.06	.05	.02
514	Chet Lemon	.06	.05	.02
515	Barry Larkin	.20	.15	.08
516	Eddie Whitson	.03	.02	.01
517	Greg Brock	.06	.05	.02
518	Bruce Ruffin	.03	.02	.01
519	Yankees Leaders (Willie Randolph)	.03	.02	.01
520	Rick Sutcliffe	.08	.06	.03
521	Mickey Tettleton	.03	.02	.01
522	*Randy Kramer*(FC)	.12	.09	.05
523	Andres Thomas	.06	.05	.02
524	Checklist 397-528	.03	.02	.01
525	Chili Davis	.06	.05	.02
526	Wes Gardner	.06	.05	.02
527	Dave Henderson	.08	.06	.03

		MT	NR MT	EX
528	*Luis Medina*(FC)	.15	.11	.06
529	Tom Foley	.03	.02	.01
530	Nolan Ryan	.50	.40	.20
531	Dave Hengel(FC)	.08	.06	.03
532	Jerry Browne	.03	.02	.01
533	Andy Hawkins	.03	.02	.01
534	Doc Edwards	.03	.02	.01
535	Todd Worrell	.08	.06	.03
536	Joel Skinner	.03	.02	.01
537	Pete Smith	.08	.06	.03
538	Juan Castillo	.03	.02	.01
539	Barry Jones	.03	.02	.01
540	Bo Jackson	.50	.40	.20
541	Cecil Fielder	.30	.25	.12
542	Todd Frohwirth	.06	.05	.02
543	Damon Berryhill	.15	.11	.06
544	Jeff Sellers	.03	.02	.01
545	Mookie Wilson	.06	.05	.02
546	Mark Williamson	.06	.05	.02
547	Mark McLemore	.03	.02	.01
548	Bobby Witt	.08	.06	.03
549	Cubs Leaders (Jamie Moyer)	.03	.02	.01
550	Orel Hershiser	.20	.15	.08
551	Randy Ready	.03	.02	.01
552	Greg Cadaret	.06	.05	.02
553	Luis Salazar	.03	.02	.01
554	Nick Esasky	.06	.05	.02
555	Bert Blyleven	.10	.08	.04
556	Bruce Fields(FC)	.06	.05	.02
557	*Keith Miller*(FC)	.15	.11	.06
558	Dan Pasqua	.08	.06	.03
559	Juan Agosto	.03	.02	.01
560	Rock Raines	.15	.11	.06
561	Luis Aguayo	.03	.02	.01
562	Danny Cox	.06	.05	.02
563	Bill Schroeder	.03	.02	.01
564	Russ Nixon	.03	.02	.01
565	Jeff Russell	.03	.02	.01
566	Al Pedrique	.03	.02	.01
567	David Wells	.08	.06	.03
568	Mickey Brantley	.03	.02	.01
569	*German Jimenez*(FC)	.08	.06	.03
570	Tony Gwynn	.30	.25	.12
571	Billy Ripken	.06	.05	.02
572	Atlee Hammaker	.03	.02	.01
573	#1 Draft Pick *(Jim Abbott)*	1.25	.90	.50
574	Dave Clark	.06	.05	.02
575	Juan Samuel	.10	.08	.04
576	Greg Minton	.03	.02	.01
577	Randy Bush	.03	.02	.01
578	John Morris	.03	.02	.01
579	Astros Leaders (Glenn Davis)	.08	.06	.03
580	Harold Reynolds	.06	.05	.02
581	Gene Nelson	.03	.02	.01
582	Mike Marshall	.10	.08	.04
583	*Paul Gibson*(FC)	.15	.11	.06
584	Randy Velarde(FC)	.10	.08	.04
585	Harold Baines	.10	.08	.04
586	Joe Boever	.03	.02	.01
587	Mike Stanley	.03	.02	.01
588	*Luis Alicea*	.15	.11	.06
589	Dave Meads	.03	.02	.01
590	Andres Galarraga	.12	.09	.05
591	Jeff Musselman	.06	.05	.02
592	John Cangelosi	.03	.02	.01
593	Drew Hall	.10	.08	.04
594	Jimy Williams	.03	.02	.01
595	Teddy Higuera	.08	.06	.03
596	Kurt Stillwell	.06	.05	.02
597	*Terry Taylor*(FC)	.12	.09	.05
598	Ken Gerhart	.06	.05	.02
599	Tom Candiotti	.03	.02	.01
600	Wade Boggs	.40	.30	.15
601	Dave Dravecky	.06	.05	.02
602	Devon White	.10	.08	.04
603	Frank Tanana	.06	.05	.02
604	Paul O'Neill	.03	.02	.01
605a	Bob Welch (missing Complete Major League Pitching Record line)	4.00	3.00	1.50
605b	Bob Welch (contains Complete Major League Pitching Record line)	.08	.06	.03
606	Rick Dempsey	.06	.05	.02
607	#1 Draft Pick *(Willie Ansley)*(FC)	.30	.25	.12
608	Phil Bradley	.08	.06	.03
609	Tigers Leaders (Frank Tanana)	.06	.05	.02
610	Randy Myers	.08	.06	.03
611	Don Slaught	.03	.02	.01
612	Dan Quisenberry	.06	.05	.02
613	*Gary Varsho*(FC)	.15	.11	.06
614	Joe Hesketh	.03	.02	.01
615	Robin Yount	.25	.20	.10

		MT	NR MT	EX
616	*Steve Rosenberg*(FC)	.15	.11	.06
617	*Mark Parent*	.15	.11	.06
618	Rance Mulliniks	.03	.02	.01
619	Checklist 529-660	.03	.02	.01
620	Barry Bonds	.20	.15	.08
621	Rick Mahler	.03	.02	.01
622	Stan Javier	.03	.02	.01
623	Fred Toliver	.03	.02	.01
624	Jack McKeon	.03	.02	.01
625	Eddie Murray	.25	.20	.10
626	Jeff Reed	.03	.02	.01
627	Greg Harris	.03	.02	.01
628	Matt Williams	.10	.08	.04
629	Pete O'Brien	.06	.05	.02
630	Mike Greenwell	.30	.25	.12
631	Dave Bergman	.03	.02	.01
632	*Bryan Harvey*	.25	.20	.10
633	Daryl Boston	.03	.02	.01
634	Marvin Freeman(FC)	.08	.06	.03
635	Willie Randolph	.06	.05	.02
636	Bill Wilkinson	.06	.05	.02
637	Carmen Castillo	.03	.02	.01
638	Floyd Bannister	.06	.05	.02
639	Athletics Leaders (Walt Weiss)	.15	.11	.06
640	Willie McGee	.10	.08	.04
641	Curt Young	.06	.05	.02
642	Argenis Salazar	.03	.02	.01
643	*Louie Meadows*(FC)	.12	.09	.05
644	Lloyd McClendon	.03	.02	.01
645	Jack Morris	.12	.09	.05
646	Kevin Bass	.06	.05	.02
647	*Randy Johnson*(FC)	.30	.25	.12
648	Future Star *(Sandy Alomar)*(FC)	.80	.60	.30
649	Stewart Cliburn	.03	.02	.01
650	Kirby Puckett	.25	.20	.10
651	Tom Niedenfuer	.06	.05	.02
652	Rich Gedman	.06	.05	.02
653	*Tommy Barrett*(FC)	.12	.09	.05
654	Whitey Herzog	.06	.05	.02
655	Dave Magadan	.08	.06	.03
656	Ivan Calderon	.06	.05	.02
657	Joe Magrane	.08	.06	.03
658	R.J. Reynolds	.03	.02	.01
659	Al Leiter	.15	.11	.06
660	Will Clark	.50	.40	.20
661	Turn Back The Clock (Dwight Gooden)	.20	.15	.08
662	Turn Back The Clock (Lou Brock)	.08	.06	.03
663	Turn Back The Clock (Hank Aaron)	.15	.11	.06
664	Turn Back The Clock (Gil Hodges)	.06	.05	.02
665	Turn Back The Clock (Tony Oliva)	.06	.05	.02
666	Randy St. Claire	.03	.02	.01
667	Dwayne Murphy	.06	.05	.02
668	Mike Bielecki	.03	.02	.01
669	Dodgers Leaders (Orel Hershiser)	.12	.09	.05
670	Kevin Seitzer	.12	.09	.05
671	Jim Gantner	.03	.02	.01
672	Allan Anderson	.06	.05	.02
673	Don Baylor	.08	.06	.03
674	Otis Nixon	.03	.02	.01
675	Bruce Hurst	.08	.06	.03
676	Ernie Riles	.03	.02	.01
677	Dave Schmidt	.03	.02	.01
678	Dion James	.03	.02	.01
679	Willie Fraser	.03	.02	.01
680	Gary Carter	.15	.11	.06
681	Jeff Robinson	.10	.08	.04
682	Rick Leach	.03	.02	.01
683	*Jose Cecena*	.15	.11	.06
684	Dave Johnson	.06	.05	.02
685	Jeff Treadway	.10	.08	.04
686	Scott Terry	.08	.06	.03
687	Alvin Davis	.10	.08	.04
688	Zane Smith	.06	.05	.02
689	Stan Jefferson	.03	.02	.01
690	Doug Jones	.10	.08	.04
691	Roberto Kelly	.25	.20	.10
692	Steve Ontiveros	.03	.02	.01
693	*Pat Borders*	.20	.15	.08
694	Les Lancaster	.06	.05	.02
695	Carlton Fisk	.20	.15	.08
696	Don August	.08	.06	.03
697	Franklin Stubbs	.03	.02	.01
698	Keith Atherton	.03	.02	.01
699	Pirates Leaders (Al Pedrique)	.06	.05	.02
700	Don Mattingly	.60	.45	.25
701	Storm Davis	.08	.06	.03
702	Jamie Quirk	.03	.02	.01
703	Scott Garrelts	.03	.02	.01
704	*Carlos Quintana*(FC)	.40	.30	.15
705	Terry Kennedy	.06	.05	.02
706	Pete Incaviglia	.08	.06	.03
707	Steve Jeltz	.03	.02	.01
708	Chuck Finley	.03	.02	.01
709	Tom Herr	.06	.05	.02
710	Dave Cone	.20	.15	.08
711	*Candy Sierra*(FC)	.12	.09	.05
712	Bill Swift	.03	.02	.01
713	#1 Draft Pick *(Ty Griffin)*	.20	.15	.08
714	Joe Morgan	.03	.02	.01
715	Tony Pena	.06	.05	.02
716	Wayne Tolleson	.03	.02	.01
717	Jamie Moyer	.03	.02	.01
718	Glenn Braggs	.06	.05	.02
719	Danny Darwin	.03	.02	.01
720	Tim Wallach	.08	.06	.03
721	*Ron Tingley*(FC)	.12	.09	.05
722	Todd Stottlemyre	.15	.11	.06
723	Rafael Belliard	.03	.02	.01
724	Jerry Don Gleaton	.03	.02	.01
725	Terry Steinbach	.08	.06	.03
726	Dickie Thon	.03	.02	.01
727	Joe Orsulak	.03	.02	.01
728	Charlie Puleo	.03	.02	.01
729	Rangers Leaders (Steve Buechele)	.06	.05	.02
730	Danny Jackson	.12	.09	.05
731	Mike Young	.03	.02	.01
732	Steve Buechele	.03	.02	.01
733	*Randy Bockus*(FC)	.06	.05	.02
734	Jody Reed	.10	.08	.04
735	Roger McDowell	.08	.06	.03
736	Jeff Hamilton	.06	.05	.02
737	*Norm Charlton*(FC)	.30	.25	.12
738	Darnell Coles	.06	.05	.02
739	Brook Jacoby	.08	.06	.03
740	Dan Plesac	.08	.06	.03
741	Ken Phelps	.06	.05	.02
742	Future Star *(Mike Harkey)*(FC)	.30	.25	.12
743	Mike Heath	.03	.02	.01
744	Roger Craig	.06	.05	.02
745	Fred McGriff	.30	.25	.12
746	*German Gonzalez*(FC)	.15	.11	.06
747	Wil Tejada(FC)	.06	.05	.02
748	Jimmy Jones	.03	.02	.01
749	Rafael Ramirez	.03	.02	.01
750	Bret Saberhagen	.12	.09	.05
751	Ken Oberkfell	.03	.02	.01
752	Jim Gott	.03	.02	.01
753	Jose Uribe	.03	.02	.01
754	Bob Brower	.03	.02	.01
755	Mike Scioscia	.06	.05	.02
756	*Scott Medvin*(FC)	.12	.09	.05
757	*Brady Anderson*	.20	.15	.08
758	Gene Walter	.03	.02	.01
759	Brewers Leaders (Rob Deer)	.06	.05	.02
760	Lee Smith	.08	.06	.03
761	*Dante Bichette*(FC)	.25	.20	.10
762	Bobby Thigpen	.08	.06	.03
763	Dave Martinez	.06	.05	.02
764	#1 Draft Pick *(Robin Ventura)*	2.00	1.50	.80
765	Glenn Davis	.15	.11	.06
766	Cecilio Guante	.03	.02	.01
767	*Mike Capel*(FC)	.15	.11	.06
768	Bill Wegman	.03	.02	.01
769	Junior Ortiz	.03	.02	.01
770	Alan Trammell	.15	.11	.06
771	Ron Kittle	.06	.05	.02
772	Ron Oester	.03	.02	.01
773	Keith Moreland	.06	.05	.02
774	Frank Robinson	.08	.06	.03
775	Jeff Reardon	.08	.06	.03
776	Nelson Liriano	.06	.05	.02
777	Ted Power	.03	.02	.01
778	Bruce Benedict	.03	.02	.01
779	Craig McMurtry	.03	.02	.01
780	Pedro Guerrero	.12	.09	.05
781	*Greg Briley*(FC)	.30	.25	.12
782	Checklist 661-792	.03	.02	.01
783	*Trevor Wilson*(FC)	.20	.15	.08
784	#1 Draft Pick *(Steve Avery)*(FC)	2.00	1.50	.80
785	Ellis Burks	.40	.30	.15
786	Melido Perez	.08	.06	.03
787	*Dave West*(FC)	.20	.15	.08
788	Mike Morgan	.03	.02	.01
789	Royals Leaders (Bo Jackson)	.15	.11	.06
790	Sid Fernandez	.08	.06	.03
791	Jim Lindeman	.03	.02	.01
792	Rafael Santana	.03	.02	.01

NOTE: A card number in parentheses ( ) indicates the set is unnumbered.

1989 Topps Traded

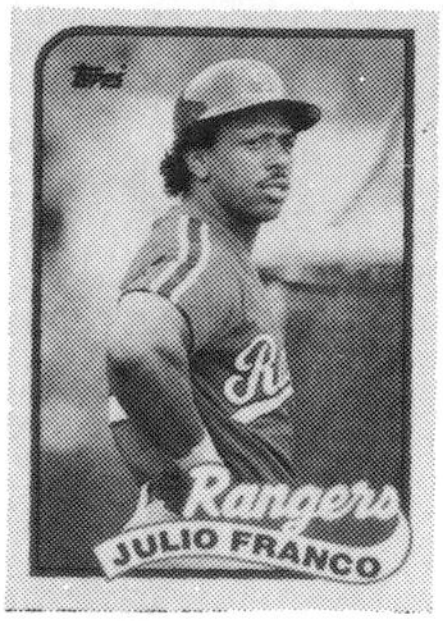

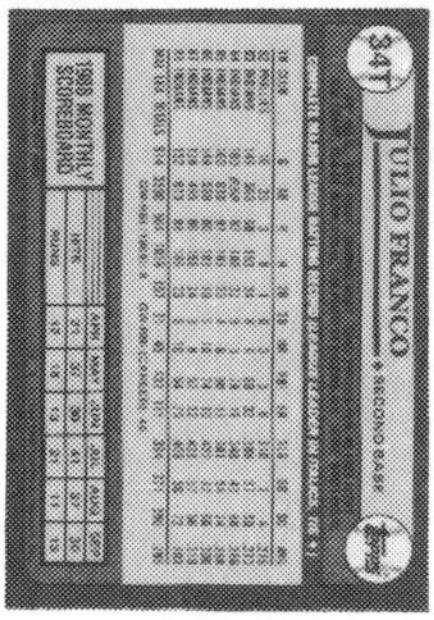

For the ninth straight year, Topps issued its annual 132-card "Traded" set at the end of the 1989 baseball season. The set, which was packaged in a special box and sold by hobby dealers, includes traded players and rookies who were not in the regular 1989 Topps set.

		MT	NR MT	EX
Complete Set:		10.00	7.50	4.00
Common Player:		.05	.04	.02
1T	Don Aase	.05	.04	.02
2T	Jim Abbott	.70	.50	.30
3T	Kent Anderson(FC)	.15	.11	.06
4T	Keith Atherton	.05	.04	.02
5T	Wally Backman	.05	.04	.02
6T	Steve Balboni	.05	.04	.02
7T	Jesse Barfield	.05	.04	.02
8T	Steve Bedrosian	.05	.04	.02
9T	Todd Benzinger	.05	.04	.02
10T	Geronimo Berroa(FC)	.10	.08	.04
11T	Bert Blyleven	.05	.04	.02
12T	Bob Boone	.05	.04	.02
13T	Phil Bradley	.08	.06	.03
14T	Jeff Brantley(FC)	.25	.20	.10
15T	Kevin Brown(FC)	.20	.15	.08
16T	Jerry Browne	.05	.04	.02
17T	Chuck Cary	.20	.15	.08
18T	Carmen Castillo	.05	.04	.02
19T	Jim Clancy	.05	.04	.02
20T	Jack Clark	.10	.08	.04
21T	Bryan Clutterbuck	.05	.04	.02
22T	Jody Davis	.05	.04	.02
23T	Mike Devereaux(FC)	.10	.08	.04
24T	Frank DiPino	.05	.04	.02
25T	Benny Distefano	.05	.04	.02
26T	John Dopson	.20	.15	.08
27T	Len Dykstra	.10	.08	.04
28T	Jim Eisenreich	.05	.04	.02
29T	Nick Esasky	.08	.06	.03
30T	Alvaro Espinoza	.25	.20	.10
31T	Darrell Evans	.08	.06	.03
32T	Junior Felix(FC)	.30	.25	.12
33T	Felix Fermin	.05	.04	.02
34T	Julio Franco	.15	.11	.06
35T	Terry Francona	.05	.04	.02
36T	Cito Gaston	.05	.04	.02
37T	Bob Geren (incorrect photo)(FC)	.30	.25	.12
38T	Tom Gordon(FC)	.60	.45	.25
39T	Tommy Gregg(FC)	.25	.20	.10
40T	Ken Griffey	.15	.11	.06
41T	Ken Griffey, Jr.(FC)	7.00	5.25	2.75
42T	Kevin Gross	.05	.04	.02
43T	Lee Guetterman	.05	.04	.02
44T	Mel Hall	.05	.04	.02
45T	Erik Hanson(FC)	.80	.60	.30
46T	Gene Harris(FC)	.20	.15	.08
47T	Andy Hawkins	.05	.04	.02
48T	Rickey Henderson	.50	.40	.20
49T	Tom Herr	.05	.04	.02
50T	Ken Hill(FC)	.20	.15	.08
51T	Brian Holman(FC)	.30	.25	.12
52T	Brian Holton	.10	.08	.04
53T	Art Howe	.05	.04	.03
54T	Ken Howell	.05	.04	.02
55T	Bruce Hurst	.05	.04	.02
56T	Chris James	.05	.04	.02
57T	Randy Johnson	.30	.25	.12
58T	Jimmy Jones	.05	.04	.02
59T	Terry Kennedy	.05	.04	.02
60T	Paul Kilgus	.05	.04	.02
61T	Eric King	.08	.06	.03
62T	Ron Kittle	.08	.06	.03
63T	John Kruk	.08	.06	.03
64T	Randy Kutcher(FC)	.08	.06	.03
65T	Steve Lake	.05	.04	.02
66T	Mark Langston	.25	.20	.10
67T	Dave LaPoint	.05	.04	.02
68T	Rick Leach	.05	.04	.02
69T	Terry Leach	.05	.04	.02
70T	Jim Levebvre	.05	.04	.02
71T	Al Leiter	.05	.04	.02
72T	Jeffrey Leonard	.05	.04	.02
73T	Derek Lilliquist(FC)	.15	.11	.06
74T	Rick Mahler	.05	.04	.02
75T	Tom McCarthy(FC)	.15	.11	.06
76T	Lloyd McClendon	.20	.15	.08
77T	Lance McCullers	.05	.04	.02
78T	Oddibe McDowell	.05	.04	.02
79T	Roger McDowell	.05	.04	.02
80T	Larry McWilliams	.05	.04	.02
81T	Randy Milligan	.30	.25	.12
82T	Mike Moore	.15	.11	.06
83T	Keith Moreland	.05	.04	.02
84T	Mike Morgan	.05	.04	.02
85T	Jamie Moyer	.05	.04	.02
86T	Rob Murphy	.05	.04	.02
87T	Eddie Murray	.30	.25	.12
88T	Pete O'Brien	.05	.04	.02
89T	Gregg Olson	.40	.30	.15
90T	Steve Ontiveros	.05	.04	.02
91T	Jesse Orosco	.05	.04	.02
92T	Spike Owen	.05	.04	.02
93T	Rafael Palmeiro	.08	.06	.03
94T	Clay Parker(FC)	.20	.15	.08
95T	Jeff Parrett	.05	.04	.02
96T	Lance Parrish	.05	.04	.02
97T	Dennis Powell	.05	.04	.02
98T	Rey Quinones	.05	.04	.02
99T	Doug Rader	.05	.04	.02
100T	Willie Randolph	.08	.06	.03
101T	Shane Rawley	.05	.04	.02
102T	Randy Ready	.05	.04	.02
103T	Bip Roberts	.05	.04	.02
104T	Kenny Rogers(FC)	.25	.20	.10
105T	Ed Romero	.05	.04	.02
106T	Nolan Ryan	1.50	1.25	.60
107T	Luis Salazar	.05	.04	.02
108T	Juan Samuel	.08	.06	.03
109T	Alex Sanchez(FC)	.20	.15	.08
110T	Deion Sanders(FC)	.60	.45	.25
111T	Steve Sax	.15	.11	.06
112T	Rick Schu	.05	.04	.02
113T	Dwight Smith(FC)	.40	.30	.15
114T	Lonnie Smith	.05	.04	.02
115T	Billy Spiers(FC)	.30	.25	.12
116T	Kent Tekulve	.05	.04	.02
117T	Walt Terrell	.05	.04	.02
118T	Milt Thompson	.05	.04	.02
119T	Dickie Thon	.05	.04	.02
120T	Jeff Torborg	.05	.04	.02
121T	Jeff Treadway	.05	.04	.02
122T	Omar Vizquel(FC)	.15	.11	.06
123T	Jerome Walton(FC)	.70	.50	.30
124T	Gary Ward	.05	.04	.02
125T	Claudell Washington	.05	.04	.02
126T	Curt Wilkerson	.05	.04	.02
127T	Eddie Williams	.05	.04	.02
128T	Frank Williams	.05	.04	.02
129T	Ken Williams	.05	.04	.02
130T	Mitch Williams	.20	.15	.08
131T	Steve Wilson(FC)	.20	.15	.08
132T	Checklist	.05	.04	.02

1989 Topps All-Star Glossy Set Of 22

Bearing the same design and style of the past two years, Topps featured the top first-year players from the 1988 season in this glossy set. The full-color player photos appears beneath the "1988 Rookies" banner. The player's name is displayed beneath the photo. The flip side features the "1988 Rookies Commemorative Set" logo followed by the player's name, position, team, and card

GRADING GUIDE

Mint (MT): A perfect card. Well-centered with all corners sharp and square. No creases, stains, edge nicks, surface marks, yellowing or fading.
Near Mint (NM): A nearly perfect card. At first glance may appear to be perfect. May have one corner not perfectly sharp. May be slightly off-center. No surface marks, creases or loss of gloss.
Excellent (EX): Corners are still fairly sharp with only moderate wear. Borders may be off-center. No creases or stains on front or back, but may show slight loss of surface luster.
Very Good (VG): Shows obvious handling. May have rounded corners, minor creases, major gum or wax stains. No major creases, tape marks, writing, etc.
Good (G): A well-worn card but exhibits no intentional damage. Corners may be rounded beyond card border. May have major or multiple creases.

number. The glossy All-Stars are included in the Topps 1989 Jumbo Paks.

		MT	NR MT	EX
Complete Set:		3.50	2.75	1.50
Common Player:		.15	.11	.06
1	Roberto Alomar	.25	.20	.10
2	Brady Anderson	.20	.15	.08
3	Tim Belcher	.20	.15	.08
4	Damon Berryhill	.15	.11	.06
5	Jay Buhner	.20	.15	.11
6	Kevin Elster	.15	.11	.06
7	Cecil Espy	.15	.11	.06
8	Dave Gallagher	.15	.11	.06
9	Ron Gant	.15	.11	.06
10	Paul Gibson	.15	.11	.06
11	Mark Grace	.60	.45	.25
12	Darrin Jackson	.15	.11	.06
13	Gregg Jefferies	.70	.50	.30
14	Ricky Jordan	.50	.40	.20
15	Al Leiter	.15	.11	.06
16	Melido Perez	.15	.11	.06
17	Chris Sabo	.35	.25	.14
18	Nelson Santovenia	.20	.15	.08
19	Mackey Sasser			

1989 Topps All-Star Glossy Set Of 60

For the seventh straight year Topps issued this "send-away" glossy set. Divided into six 10-card sets, it was available only by sending in special offer cards from the 1989 Topps wax packs. The 2-1/2" by 3-1/2" cards feature full-color photos bordered in white with a thin yellow frame. The player's name appears in small print in the lower right corner. Red-and-blue-printed flip sides provide basic information including player's name, team, and position. Any of the six 10-card sets were available for $1.25 and six special offer cards. The set was also made available in its complete 60-card set form for $7.50 and 18 special offer cards.

		MT	NR MT	EX
Complete Set:		10.00	7.50	4.00
Common Player:		.15	.11	.06
1	Kirby Puckett	.50	.40	.20
2	Eric Davis	.70	.50	.30
3	Joe Carter	.20	.15	.08
4	Andy Van Slyke	.20	.15	.08
5	Wade Boggs	.70	.50	.30
6	Dave Cone	.25	.20	.10
7	Kent Hrbek	.15	.11	.06
8	Darryl Strawberry	.70	.50	.30
9	Jay Buhner	.15	.11	.06
10	Ron Gant	.30	.25	.12
11	Will Clark	1.00	.70	.40
12	Jose Canseco	1.25	.90	.50
13	Juan Samuel	.15	.11	.06
14	George Brett	.25	.20	.10
15	Benny Santiago	.20	.15	.08
16	Dennis Eckersley	.15	.11	.06
17	Gary Carter	.15	.11	.06
18	Frank Viola	.20	.15	.08
19	Roberto Alomar	.30	.25	.12
20	Paul Gibson	.15	.11	.06
21	Dave Winfield	.20	.15	.08
22	Howard Johnson	.35	.25	.14
23	Roger Clemens	.40	.30	.15
24	Bobby Bonilla	.25	.20	.10
25	Alan Trammell	.20	.15	.08
26	Kevin McReynolds	.20	.15	.08
27	George Bell	.20	.15	.08
28	Bruce Hurst	.15	.11	.06
29	Mark Grace	.70	.50	.30
30	Tim Belcher	.20	.15	.08
31	Mike Greenwell	.70	.50	.30
32	Glenn Davis	.15	.11	.06
33	Gary Gaetti	.15	.11	.06
34	Ryne Sandberg	.70	.50	.30
35	Rickey Henderson	.70	.50	.30
36	Dwight Evans	.15	.11	.06
37	Doc Gooden	.50	.40	.20
38	Robin Yount	.25	.20	.10
39	Damon Berryhill	.15	.11	.06
40	Chris Sabo	.20	.15	.11
41	Mark McGwire	.70	.50	.30
42	Ozzie Smith	.25	.20	.10
43	Paul Molitor	.20	.15	.08
44	Andres Galarraga	.30	.25	.12
45	Dave Stewart	.15	.11	.06
46	Tom Browning	.15	.11	.06
47	Cal Ripken	.50	.40	.20
48	Orel Hershiser	.40	.30	.15
49	Dave Gallagher	.15	.11	.06
50	Walt Weiss	.20	.15	.08
51	Don Mattingly	1.50	1.25	.60
52	Tony Fernandez	.20	.15	.08
53	Rock Raines	.20	.15	.08
54	Jeff Reardon	.15	.11	.06
55	Kirk Gibson	.20	.15	.08
56	Jack Clark	.20	.15	.08
57	Danny Jackson	.15	.11	.06
58	Tony Gwynn	.60	.45	.25
59	Cecil Espy	.15	.11	.06
60	Jody Reed	.15	.11	.06

Note: All values listed in this guide are intended to serve only as an aid in evaluating your cards. Actual market conditions are constantly changing, especially for current players, whose on-field performance during the course of a season can affect affect the value of their cards — either up or down.

GRADING GUIDE

Mint (MT): A perfect card. Well-centered with all corners sharp and square. No creases, stains, edge nicks, surface marks, yellowing or fading.
Near Mint (NM): A nearly perfect card. At first glance may appear to be perfect. May have one corner not perfectly sharp. May be slightly off-center. No surface marks, creases or loss of gloss.
Excellent (EX): Corners are still fairly sharp with only moderate wear. Borders may be off-center. No creases or stains on front or back, but may show slight loss of surface luster.
Very Good (VG): Shows obvious handling. May have rounded corners, minor creases, major gum or wax stains. No major creases, tape marks, writing, etc.
Good (G): A well-worn card but exhibits no intentional damage. Corners may be rounded beyond card border. May have major or multiple creases.

1989 Topps Big Baseball

Known by collectors as Topps "Big Baseball," the cards in this 330-card set measure 2-5/8" by 3-3/4" and are patterned after the 1956 Topps cards. The glossy card fronts are horizontally-designed and include two photos of each player, a posed head shot alongside an action photo. The backs include 1988 and career stats, but are dominated by a color cartoon featuring the player. The set was issued in three series of 110 cards each.

		MT	NR MT	EX
Complete Set:		20.00	15.00	8.00
1	Common Player:, Orel Hershiser	.15	.11	.06
2	Harold Reynolds	.08	.06	.03
3	Jody Davis	.05	.04	.02
4	Greg Walker	.05	.04	.02
5	Barry Bonds	.08	.06	.03
6	Bret Saberhagen	.12	.09	.05
7	Johnny Ray	.05	.04	.02
8	Mike Fiore	.20	.15	.08
9	Juan Castillo	.05	.04	.02
10	Todd Burns	.05	.04	.02
11	Carmelo Martinez	.05	.04	.02
12	Geno Petralli	.05	.04	.02
13	Mel Hall	.05	.04	.02
14	Tom Browning	.08	.06	.03
15	Fred McGriff	.15	.11	.06
16	Kevin Elster	.05	.04	.02

		MT	NR MT	EX
17	Tim Leary	.05	.04	.02
18	Jim Rice	.05	.04	.02
19	Bret Barberie	.15	.11	.06
20	Jay Buhner	.05	.04	.02
21	Atlee Hammaker	.05	.04	.02
22	Lou Whitaker	.05	.04	.02
23	Paul Runge	.05	.04	.02
24	Carlton Fisk	.08	.06	.03
25	Jose Lind	.05	.04	.02
26	Mark Gubicza	.08	.06	.03
27	Billy Ripken	.05	.04	.02
28	Mike Pagliarulo	.05	.04	.02
29	Jim Deshaies	.05	.04	.02
30	Mark McLemore	.05	.04	.02
31	Scott Terry	.05	.04	.02
32	Franklin Stubbs	.05	.04	.02
33	Don August	.05	.04	.02
34	Mark McGwire	1.00	.70	.40
35	Eric Show	.05	.04	.02
36	Cecil Espy	.05	.04	.02
37	Ron Tingley	.05	.04	.02
38	Mickey Brantley	.05	.04	.02
39	Paul O'Neill	.05	.04	.02
40	Ed Sprague	.35	.25	.14
41	Len Dykstra	.05	.04	.02
42	Roger Clemens	.25	.20	.10
43	Ron Gant	.05	.04	.02
44	Dan Pasqua	.05	.04	.02
45	Jeff Robinson	.05	.04	.02
46	George Brett	.15	.11	.06
47	Bryn Smith	.05	.04	.02
48	Mike Marshall	.05	.04	.02
49	Doug Robbins	.15	.11	.06
50	Don Mattingly	1.50	1.25	.60
51	Mike Scott	.08	.06	.03
52	Steve Jeltz	.05	.04	.02
53	Dick Schofield	.05	.04	.02
54	Tom Brunansky	.08	.06	.03
55	Gary Sheffield	1.00	.70	.40
56	Dave Valle	.05	.04	.02
57	Carney Lansford	.08	.06	.03
58	Tony Gwynn	.15	.11	.06
59	Checklist	.05	.04	.02
60	Damon Berryhill	.05	.04	.02
61	Jack Morris	.05	.04	.02
62	Brett Butler	.05	.04	.02
63	Mickey Hatcher	.05	.04	.02
64	Bruce Sutter	.05	.04	.02
65	Robin Ventura	.80	.60	.30
66	Junior Oritiz	.05	.04	.02
67	Pat Tabler	.05	.04	.02
68	Greg Swindell	.08	.06	.03
69	Jeff Branson	.20	.15	.08
70	Manny Lee	.05	.04	.02
71	Dave Magadan	.05	.04	.02
72	Rich Gedman	.05	.04	.02
73	Rock Raines	.08	.06	.03
74	Mike Maddux	.05	.04	.02
75	Jim Presley	.05	.04	.02
76	Chuck Finley	.05	.04	.02
77	Jose Oquendo	.05	.04	.02
78	Rob Deer	.05	.04	.02
79	Jay Howell	.05	.04	.02
80	Terry Steinbach	.08	.06	.03
81	Eddie Whitson	.05	.04	.02
82	Ruben Sierra	.20	.15	.08
83	Bruce Benedict	.05	.04	.02
84	Fred Manrique	.05	.04	.02
85	John Smiley	.05	.04	.02
86	Mike Macfarlane	.05	.04	.02
87	Rene Gonzales	.05	.04	.02
88	Charles Hudson	.05	.04	.02
90	Les Straker	.05	.04	.02
91	Carmen Castillo	.05	.04	.02
92	Tracy Woodson	.05	.04	.02
93	Tino Martinez	.70	.50	.30
94	Herm Winningham	.05	.04	.02
95	Kelly Gruber	.05	.04	.02
96	Terry Leach	.05	.04	.02
97	Jody Reed	.05	.04	.02
98	Nelson Santovenia	.05	.04	.02
99	Tony Armas	.05	.04	.02
100	Greg Brock	.05	.04	.02
101	Dave Stewart	.05	.04	.02
102	Roberto Alomar	.08	.06	.03
103	Jim Sundberg	.05	.04	.02
104	Albert Hall	.05	.04	.02
105	Steve Lyons	.05	.04	.02
106	Sid Bream	.05	.04	.02
107	Danny Tartabull	.08	.06	.03
108	Rick Dempsey	.05	.04	.02
109	Rich Renteria	.05	.04	.02
110	Ozzie Smith	.08	.06	.03

		MT	NR MT	EX
111	Steve Sax	.08	.06	.03
112	Kelly Downs	.05	.04	.02
113	Larry Sheets	.05	.04	.02
114	Andy Benes	.50	.40	.20
115	Pete O'Brien	.05	.04	.02
116	Kevin McReynolds	.08	.06	.03
117	Juan Berenguer	.05	.04	.02
118	Billy Hatcher	.05	.04	.02
119	Rick Cerone	.05	.04	.02
120	Andre Dawson	.08	.06	.03
121	Storm Davis	.05	.04	.02
122	Devon White	.05	.04	.02
123	Alan Trammell	.08	.06	.03
124	Vince Coleman	.08	.06	.03
125	Al Leiter	.05	.04	.02
126	Dale Sveum	.05	.04	.02
127	Pete Incaviglia	.05	.04	.02
128	Dave Stieb	.08	.06	.03
129	Kevin Mitchell	.30	.25	.12
130	Dave Schmidt	.05	.04	.02
131	Gary Redus	.05	.04	.02
132	Ron Robinson	.05	.04	.02
133	Darnell Coles	.05	.04	.02
134	Benny Santiago	.08	.06	.03
135	John Farrell	.05	.04	.02
136	Willie Wilson	.05	.04	.02
137	Steve Bedrosian	.05	.04	.02
138	Don Slaught	.05	.04	.02
139	Darryl Strawberry	.25	.20	.10
140	Frank Viola	.10	.08	.04
141	Dave Silvestri	.20	.15	.08
142	Carlos Quintana	.05	.04	.02
143	Vance Law	.05	.04	.02
144	Dave Parker	.05	.04	.02
145	Tim Belcher	.05	.04	.02
146	Will Clark	.90	.70	.35
147	Mark Williamson	.05	.04	.02
148	Ozzie Guillen	.05	.04	.02
149	Kirk McCaskill	.05	.04	.02
150	Pat Sheridan	.05	.04	.02
151	Terry Pendleton	.05	.04	.02
152	Roberto Kelly	.05	.04	.02
153	Joey Meyer	.05	.04	.02
154	Mark Grant	.05	.04	.02
155	Joe Carter	.08	.06	.03
156	Steve Buechele	.05	.04	.02
157	Tony Fernandez	.08	.06	.03
158	Jeff Reed	.05	.04	.02
159	Bobby Bonilla	.08	.06	.03
160	Henry Cotto	.05	.04	.02
161	Kurt Stillwell	.05	.04	.02
162	Mickey Morandini	.25	.20	.10
163	Robby Thompson	.05	.04	.02
164	Rick Schu	.05	.04	.02
165	Stan Jefferson	.05	.04	.02
166	Ron Darling	.05	.04	.02
167	Kirby Puckett	.25	.20	.10
168	Bill Doran	.05	.04	.02
169	Dennis Lamp	.05	.04	.02
170	Ty Griffin	.60	.45	.25
171	Ron Hassey	.05	.04	.02
172	Dale Murphy	.08	.06	.03
173	Andres Galarraga	.08	.06	.03
174	Tim Flannery	.05	.04	.02
175	Cory Snyder	.05	.04	.02
176	Checklist	.05	.04	.02
177	Tommy Barrett	.05	.04	.02
178	Dan Petry	.05	.04	.02
179	Billy Masse	.20	.15	.08
180	Terry Kennedy	.05	.04	.02
181	Joe Orsulak	.05	.04	.02
182	Doyle Alexander	.05	.04	.02
183	Willie McGee	.05	.04	.02
184	Jim Gantner	.05	.04	.02
185	Keith Hernandez	.05	.04	.02
186	Greg Gagne	.05	.04	.02
187	Kevin Bass	.05	.04	.02
188	Mark Eichhorn	.05	.04	.02
189	Mark Grace	.25	.20	.10
190	Jose Canseco	1.00	.70	.40
191	Bobby Witt	.05	.04	.02
192	Rafael Santana	.05	.04	.02
193	Dwight Evans	.05	.04	.02
194	Greg Booker	.05	.04	.02
195	Brook Jacoby	.05	.04	.02
196	Rafael Belliard	.05	.04	.02
197	Candy Maldonado	.05	.04	.02
198	Mickey Tettleton	.08	.06	.03
199	Barry Larkin	.08	.06	.03
200	Frank White	.05	.04	.02
201	Wally Joyner	.15	.11	.06

		MT	NR MT	EX
202	Chet Lemon	.05	.04	.02
203	Joe Magrane	.05	.04	.02
204	Glenn Braggs	.05	.04	.02
205	Scott Fletcher	.05	.04	.02
206	Gary Ward	.05	.04	.02
207	Nelson Liriano	.05	.04	.02
208	Howard Johnson	.15	.11	.06
209	Kent Hrbek	.08	.06	.03
210	Ken Caminiti	.05	.04	.02
211	Mike Greenwell	.50	.40	.20
212	Ryne Sandberg	.25	.20	.10
213	Joe Slusarski	.25	.20	.10
214	Donnell Nixon	.05	.04	.02
215	Tim Wallach	.05	.04	.02
216	John Kruk	.05	.04	.02
217	Charles Nagy	.25	.20	.10
218	Alvin Davis	.08	.06	.03
219	Oswald Peraza	.05	.04	.02
220	Mike Schmidt	.30	.25	.12
221	Spike Owen	.05	.04	.02
222	Mike Smithson	.05	.04	.02
223	Dion James	.05	.04	.02
224	Ernie Whitt	.05	.04	.02
225	Mike Davis	.05	.04	.02
226	Gene Larkin	.05	.04	.02
227	Pat Combs	.50	.40	.20
228	Jack Howell	.05	.04	.02
229	Ron Oester	.05	.04	.02
230	Paul Gibson	.05	.04	.02
231	Mookie Wilson	.05	.04	.02
232	Glenn Hubbard	.05	.04	.02
233	Shawon Dunston	.05	.04	.02
234	Otis Nixon	.05	.04	.02
235	Melido Perez	.05	.04	.02
236	Jerry Browne	.05	.04	.02
237	Rick Rhoden	.05	.04	.02
238	Bo Jackson	.50	.40	.20
239	Randy Velarde	.05	.04	.02
240	Jack Clark	.05	.04	.02
241	Wade Boggs	.80	.60	.30
242	Lonnie Smith	.05	.04	.02
243	Mike Flanagan	.05	.04	.02
244	Willie Randolph	.05	.04	.02
245	Oddibe McDowell	.05	.04	.02
246	Ricky Jordan	.35	.25	.14
247	Greg Briley	.20	.15	.08
248	Rex Hudler	.05	.04	.02
249	Robin Yount	.20	.15	.08
250	Lance Parrish	.05	.04	.02
251	Chris Sabo	.20	.15	.08
252	Mike Henneman	.05	.04	.02
253	Gregg Jefferies	1.00	.70	.40
254	Curt Young	.05	.04	.02
255	Andy Van Slyke	.08	.06	.03
256	Rod Booker	.05	.04	.02
257	Rafael Palmeiro	.05	.04	.02
258	Jose Uribe	.05	.04	.02
259	Ellis Burks	.20	.15	.08
260	John Smoltz	.10	.08	.04
261	Tom Foley	.05	.04	.02
262	Lloyd Moseby	.05	.04	.02
263	Jim Poole	.15	.11	.06
264	Gary Gaetti	.08	.06	.03
265	Bob Dernier	.05	.04	.02
266	Harold Baines	.08	.06	.03
267	Tom Candiotti	.05	.04	.02
268	Rafael Ramirez	.05	.04	.02
269	Bob Boone	.05	.04	.02
270	Buddy Bell	.05	.04	.02
271	Rickey Henderson	.15	.11	.06
272	Willie Fraser	.05	.04	.02
273	Eric Davis	.25	.20	.10
274	Jeff Robinson	.05	.04	.02
275	Damaso Garcia	.05	.04	.02
276	Sid Fernandez	.05	.04	.02
277	Stan Javier	.05	.04	.02
278	Marty Barrett	.05	.04	.02
279	Gerald Perry	.05	.04	.02
280	Rob Ducey	.05	.04	.02
281	Mike Scioscia	.05	.04	.02
282	Randy Bush	.05	.04	.02
283	Tom Herr	.05	.04	.02
284	Glenn Wilson	.05	.04	.02
285	Pedro Guerrero	.10	.08	.04
286	Cal Ripken	.10	.08	.04
287	Randy Johnson	.15	.11	.06
288	Julio Franco	.08	.06	.03
289	Ivan Calderon	.05	.04	.02
290	Rich Yett	.05	.04	.02
291	Scott Servais	.20	.15	.08
292	Bill Pecota	.05	.04	.02

		MT	NR MT	EX
293	Ken Phelps	.05	.04	.02
294	Chili Davis	.05	.04	.02
295	Manny Trillo	.05	.04	.02
296	Mike Boddicker	.05	.04	.02
297	Geronimo Berroa	.05	.04	.02
298	Todd Stottlemyre	.05	.04	.02
299	Kirk Gibson	.05	.04	.02
300	Wally Backman	.05	.04	.02
301	Hubie Brooks	.05	.04	.02
302	Von Hayes	.05	.04	.02
303	Matt Nokes	.05	.04	.02
304	Doc Gooden	.20	.15	.08
305	Walt Weiss	.10	.08	.04
306	Mike LaValliere	.05	.04	.02
307	Cris Carpenter	.10	.08	.04
308	Ted Wood	.20	.15	.08
309	Jeff Russell	.05	.04	.02
310	Dave Gallagher	.05	.04	.02
311	Andy Allanson	.05	.04	.02
312	Craig Reynolds	.05	.04	.02
313	Kevin Seitzer	.08	.06	.03
314	Dave Winfield	.10	.08	.04
315	Andy McGaffigan	.05	.04	.02
316	Nick Esasky	.05	.04	.02
317	Jeff Blauser	.05	.04	.02
318	George Bell	.10	.08	.04
319	Eddie Murray	.10	.08	.04
320	Mark Davidson	.05	.04	.02
321	Juan Samuel	.05	.04	.02
322	Jim Abbott	.50	.40	.20
323	Kal Daniels	.05	.04	.02
324	Mike Brumley	.05	.04	.02
325	Gary Carter	.05	.04	.02
326	Dave Henderson	.05	.04	.02
327	Checklist	.05	.04	.02
328	Garry Templeton	.05	.04	.02
329	Pat Perry	.05	.04	.02
330	Paul Molitor	.08	.06	.03

1989 Topps Box Panels

Continuing its practice of printing baseball cards on the bottom panels of its wax pack boxes, Topps in 1989 issued a special 16-card set, printing four cards on each of four different box-bottom panels. The cards are identical in design to the regular 1989 Topps cards. They are designated by letter (from A through P) rather than by number.

	MT	NR MT	EX
Complete Panel Set:	5.00	3.75	2.00
Complete Singles Set:	2.00	1.50	.80
Common Panel:	.50	.40	.20
Common Single Player:	.08	.06	.03

		MT	NR MT	EX
	Panel	.50	.40	.20
A	George Brett	.25	.20	.10
B	Bill Buckner	.08	.06	.03
C	Darrell Evans	.08	.06	.03
D	Rich Gossage	.08	.06	.03
	Panel	1.00	.70	.40
E	Greg Gross	.08	.06	.03
F	Rickey Henderson	.30	.25	.12
G	Keith Hernandez	.15	.11	.06
H	Tom Lasorda	.08	.06	.03
	Panel	2.50	2.00	1.00
I	Jim Rice	.15	.11	.06
J	Cal Ripken	.35	.25	.14
K	Nolan Ryan	.50	.40	.20
L	Mike Schmidt	.25	.20	.10
	Panel	1.00	.70	.40
M	Bruce Sutter	.15	.11	.06
N	Don Sutton	.10	.08	.04
O	Kent Tekulve	.08	.06	.03
P	Dave Winfield	.25	.20	.10

1989 Topps Major League Debut

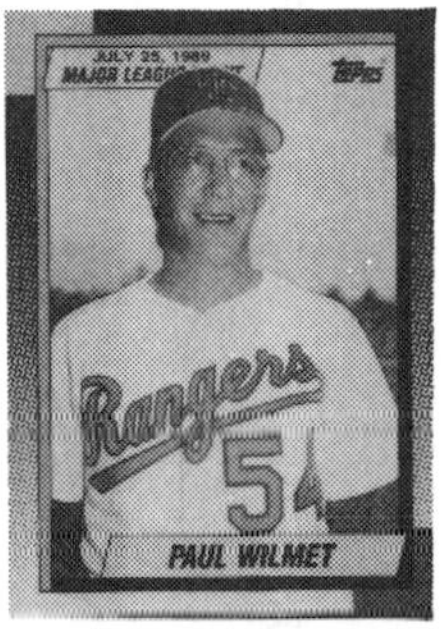

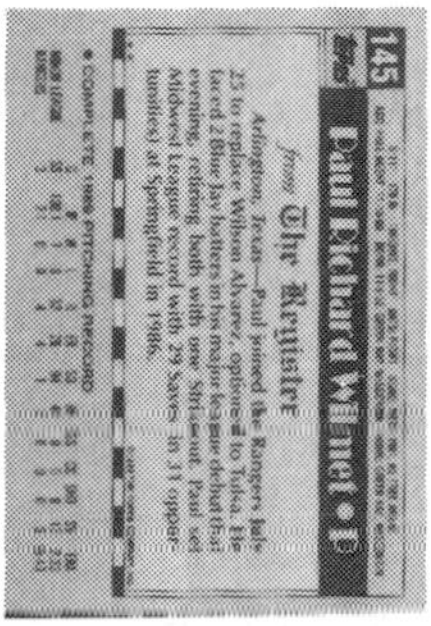

This 150-card set highlights the debut date of 1989 Major League rookies. Two checklist cards are also included in this boxed set. The checklist cards list the players in order of debut date, but the cards are numbered alphabetically. The card fronts resemble the 1990 Topps cards in style. A debut banner appears in an upper corner of the card. The flip sides are horizontal and are printed in black on yellow stock. An overview of the player's first game is provided on the card back. The set is packaged in an attractive red, blue, green and yellow collectors box. The set was available through select hobby dealers.

	MT	NR MT	EX
Complete Set:	18.00	13.50	7.25
Common Player:	.08	.06	.03

		MT	NR MT	EX
1	Jim Abbott	.30	.25	.12
2	Beau Allred	.15	.11	.06
3	Wilson Alvarez	.25	.20	.10
4	Kent Anderson	.08	.06	.03
5	Eric Anthony	.40	.30	.15
6	Kevin Appier	.25	.20	.10
7	Larry Arndt	.08	.06	.03
8	John Barfield	.08	.06	.03
9	Billy Bates	.08	.06	.03
10	Kevin Batiste	.10	.08	.04
11	Blaine Beatty	.20	.15	.08
12	Stan Belinda	.15	.11	.06
13	Juan Bell	.15	.11	.06
14	Joey Belle	.20	.15	.08
15	Andy Benes	.30	.25	.12
16	Mike Benjamin	.20	.15	.08
17	Geronimo Berroa	.08	.06	.03
18	Mike Blowers	.10	.08	.04
19	Brian Brady	.08	.06	.03
20	Francisco Cabrera	.25	.20	.10
21	George Canale	.08	.06	.03
22	Jose Cano	.08	.06	.03
23	Steve Carter	.10	.08	.04
24	Pat Combs	.30	.25	.12
25	Scott Coolbaugh	.15	.11	.06
26	Steve Cummings	.10	.08	.04
27	Pete Dalena	.08	.06	.03
28	Jeff Datz	.08	.06	.03
29	Bobby Davidson	.08	.06	.03
30	Drew Denson	.08	.06	.03
31	Gary DiSarcina	.20	.15	.08
32	Brian DuBois	.15	.11	.06
33	Mike Dyer	.10	.08	.04
34	Wayne Edwards	.10	.08	.04
35	Junior Felix	.30	.25	.12
36	Mike Fetters	.15	.11	.06
37	Steve Finley	.15	.11	.06

		MT	NR MT	EX
38	Darren Fletcher	.15	.11	.06
39	LaVel Freeman	.08	.06	.03
40	Steve Frey	.10	.08	.04
41	Mark Gardner	.20	.15	.08
42	Joe Girardi	.20	.15	.08
43	Juan Gonzalez	2.00	1.50	.80
44	Goose Gozzo	.15	.11	.06
45	Tommy Greene	.15	.11	.06
46	Ken Griffey,Jr.	3.50	2.75	1.50
47	Jason Grimsley	.20	.15	.08
48	Marquis Grissom	.40	.30	.15
49	Mark Guthrie	.10	.08	.04
50	Chip Hale	.08	.06	.03
51	John Hardy	.08	.06	.03
52	Gene Harris	.10	.08	.04
53	Mike Hartley	.10	.08	.04
54	Scott Hemond	.10	.08	.04
55	Xavier Hernandez	.10	.08	.04
56	Eric Hetzel	.15	.11	.06
57	Greg Hibbard	.25	.20	.10
58	Mark Higgins	.08	.06	.03
59	Glenallen Hill	.20	.15	.08
60	Chris Hoiles	.30	.25	.12
61	Shawn Holman	.10	.08	.04
62	Dann Howitt	.10	.08	.04
63	Mike Huff	.10	.08	.04
64	Terry Jorgenson	.10	.08	.04
65	Dave Justice	2.00	1.50	.80
66	Jeff King	.20	.15	.08
67	Matt Kinzer	.08	.06	.03
68	Joe Kraemer	.08	.06	.03
69	Marcus Lawton	.08	.06	.03
70	Derek Lilliquist	.15	.11	.06
71	Scott Little	.08	.06	.03
72	Greg Litton	.15	.11	.06
73	Rick Lueken	.10	.08	.04
74	Julio Machado	.15	.11	.06
75	Tom Magrann	.08	.06	.03
76	Kelly Mann	.20	.15	.08
77	Randy McCament	.08	.06	.03
78	Ben McDonald	.50	.40	.20
79	Chuck McElroy	.20	.15	.08
80	Jeff McKnight	.10	.08	.04
81	Kent Mercker	.25	.20	.10
82	Matt Merullo	.08	.06	.03
83	Hensley Meulens	.15	.11	.06
84	Kevin Mmahat	.08	.06	.03
85	Mike Munoz	.08	.06	.03
86	Dan Murphy	.08	.06	.03
87	Jaime Navarro	.20	.15	.08
88	Randy Nosek	.10	.08	.04
89	John Olerud	.50	.40	.20
90	Steve Olin	.10	.08	.04
91	Joe Oliver	.20	.15	.08
92	Francisco Oliveras	.10	.08	.04
93	Greg Olson	.15	.11	.06
94	John Orton	.10	.08	.04
95	Dean Palmer	.20	.15	.08
96	Ramon Pena	.08	.06	.03
97	Jeff Peterek	.08	.06	.03
98	Marty Pevey	.08	.06	.03
99	Rusty Richards	.08	.06	.03
100	Jeff Richardson	.08	.06	.03
101	Rob Richie	.08	.06	.03
102	Kevin Ritz	.10	.08	.04
103	Rosario Rodriguez	.25	.20	.10
104	Mike Roesler	.10	.08	.04
105	Kenny Rogers	.15	.11	.06
106	Bobby Rose	.20	.15	.08
107	Alex Sanchez	.15	.11	.06
108	Deion Sanders	.25	.20	.10
109	Jeff Schaefer	.08	.06	.03
110	Jeff Schulz	.10	.08	.04
111	Mike Schwabe	.10	.08	.04
112	Dick Scott	.08	.06	.03
113	Scott Scudder	.25	.20	.10
114	Rudy Seanez	.15	.11	.06
115	Joe Skalski	.08	.06	.03
116	Dwight Smith	.20	.15	.08
117	Greg Smith	.15	.11	.06
118	Mike Smith	.10	.08	.04
119	Paul Sorrento	.15	.11	.06
120	Sammy Sosa	.50	.40	.20
121	Billy Spiers	.15	.11	.06
122	Mike Stanton	.20	.15	.08
123	Phil Stephenson	.08	.06	.03
124	Doug Strange	.08	.06	.03
125	Russ Swan	.10	.08	.04
126	Kevin Tapani	.35	.25	.14
127	Stu Tate	.08	.06	.03
128	Greg Vaughn	.40	.30	.15
129	Robin Ventura	.25	.20	.10
130	Randy Veres	.08	.06	.03
131	Jose Vizcaino	.15	.11	.06
132	Omar Vizquel	.10	.08	.04
133	Larry Walker	.40	.30	.15
134	Jerome Walton	.50	.40	.20
135	Gary Wayne	.10	.08	.04
136	Lenny Webster	.10	.08	.04
137	Mickey Weston	.10	.08	.04
138	Jeff Wetherby	.08	.06	.03
139	John Wetteland	.25	.20	.10
140	Ed Whited	.08	.06	.03
141	Wally Whitehurst	.10	.08	.04
142	Kevin Wickander	.15	.11	.06
143	Dean Wilkins	.10	.08	.04
144	Dana Williams	.10	.08	.04
145	Paul Wilmet	.08	.06	.03
146	Craig Wilson	.15	.11	.06
147	Matt Winters	.08	.06	.03
148	Eric Yelding	.25	.20	.10
149	Clint Zavaras	.15	.11	.06
150	Todd Zeile	.50	.40	.20
---	Checklist (1 of 2)	.08	.06	.03
---	Checklist (2 of 2)	.08	.06	.03

1989 Topps Mini League Leaders

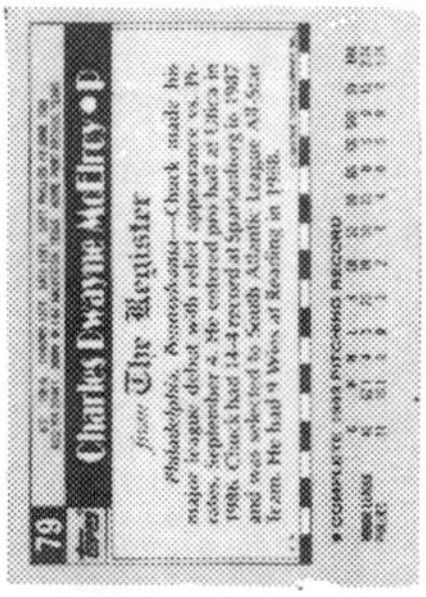

This 77-card set from Topps features baseball's statistical leaders from the 1988 season, and is referred to as a "mini" set because of the cards' small (2-1/8" by 3") size. The glossy cards feature action photos that have a soft focus on all edges. The player's team and name appear along the bottom of the card. The back features a head- shot of the player along with his 1988 season ranking and stats.

		MT	NR MT	EX
Complete Set:		6.00	4.50	2.50
Common Player:		.09	.07	.04
1	Dale Murphy	.35	.25	.14
2	Gerald Perry	.09	.07	.04
3	Andre Dawson	.20	.15	.08
4	Greg Maddux	.20	.15	.08
5	Rafael Palmeiro	.15	.11	.06
6	Tom Browning	.12	.09	.05
7	Kal Daniels	.15	.11	.06
8	Eric Davis	.60	.45	.25
9	John Franco	.09	.07	.04
10	Danny Jackson	.09	.07	.04
11	Barry Larkin	.15	.11	.06
12	Jose Rijo	.12	.09	.05
13	Chris Sabo	.20	.15	.08
14	Mike Scott	.09	.07	.04
15	Nolan Ryan	.50	.40	.20
16	Gerald Young	.09	.07	.04
17	Kirk Gibson	.12	.09	.05
18	Orel Hershiser	.25	.20	.10
19	Steve Sax	.12	.09	.05
20	John Tudor	.09	.07	.04
21	Hubie Brooks	.09	.07	.04
22	Andres Galarraga	.15	.11	.06
23	Otis Nixon	.09	.07	.04
24	Dave Cone	.15	.11	.06

		MT	NR MT	EX
25	Sid Fernandez	.12	.09	.05
26	Doc Gooden	.30	.25	.12
27	Kevin McReynolds	.20	.15	.08
28	Darryl Strawberry	.35	.25	.14
29	Juan Samuel	.09	.07	.04
30	Bobby Bonilla	.12	.09	.05
31	Sid Bream	.09	.07	.04
32	Andy Van Slyke	.12	.09	.05
33	Vince Coleman	.12	.09	.05
34	Jose DeLeon	.09	.07	.04
35	Joe Magrane	.12	.09	.05
36	Ozzie Smith	.12	.09	.05
37	Todd Worrell	.09	.07	.04
38	Tony Gwynn	.30	.25	.12
39	Brett Butler	.12	.09	.05
40	Will Clark	.80	.60	.30
41	Jim Gott	.09	.07	.04
42	Rick Reuschel	.12	.09	.05
43	Checklist	.09	.07	.04
44	Eddie Murray	.20	.15	.08
45	Wade Boggs	.80	.60	.30
46	Roger Clemens	.30	.25	.12
47	Dwight Evans	.12	.09	.05
48	Mike Greenwell	.70	.50	.30
49	Bruce Hurst	.12	.09	.05
50	Johnny Ray	.09	.07	.04
51	Doug Jones	.09	.07	.04
52	Greg Swindell	.15	.11	.06
53	Gary Pettis	.09	.07	.04
54	George Brett	.15	.11	.06
55	Mark Gubicza	.15	.11	.06
56	Willie Wilson	.09	.07	.04
57	Teddy Higuera	.12	.09	.05
58	Paul Molitor	.15	.11	.06
59	Robin Yount	.25	.20	.10
60	Allan Anderson	.09	.07	.04
61	Gary Gaetti	.12	.09	.04
62	Kirby Puckett	.40	.30	.15
63	Jeff Reardon	.09	.07	.04
64	Frank Viola	.12	.09	.05
65	Jack Clark	.12	.09	.05
66	Rickey Henderson	.25	.20	.10
67	Dave Winfield	.15	.11	.06
68	Jose Canseco	.80	.60	.30
69	Dennis Eckersley	.12	.09	.05
70	Mark McGwire	.80	.60	.30
71	Dave Stewart	.12	.09	.05
72	Alvin Davis	.12	.09	.05
73	Mark Langston	.12	.09	.05
74	Harold Reynolds	.12	.09	.05
75	George Bell	.15	.11	.06
76	Tony Fernandez	.15	.11	.06
77	Fred McGriff	.25	.20	.10

1989 Topps American Baseball

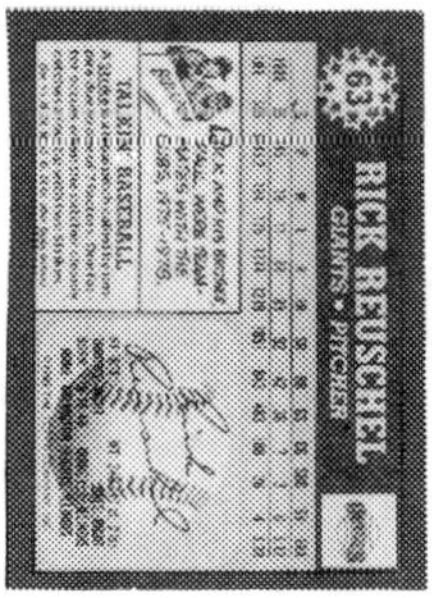

For the second consecutive year Topps released an 88-card set of baseball cards available in both the United States and the United Kingdom. The mini-sized cards (2-1/4" by 3") feature full-color photos on the card fronts. The cards are printed on white stock with a low gloss finish. The player action photo is outlined in red, white, and blue and framed in white. The card backs are printed horizontally and include a characterization cartoon along with biographical information and statistics. The cards are sold in packs of five cards with a stick of bubble gum.

		MT	NR MT	EX
Complete Set:		8.00	6.00	3.25
Common Player:		.08	.06	.03
1	Brady Anderson	.08	.06	.03
2	Harold Baines	.15	.11	.06
3	George Bell	.15	.11	.06
4	Wade Boggs	1.00	.70	.40
5	Barry Bonds	.20	.15	.08
6	Bobby Bonilla	.20	.15	.08
7	George Brett	.15	.11	.06
8	Hubie Brooks	.08	.06	.03
9	Tom Brunansky	.08	.06	.03
10	Jay Buhner	.08	.06	.03
11	Brett Butler	.08	.06	.03
12	Jose Canseco	1.25	.90	.50
13	Joe Carter	.15	.11	.06
14	Jack Clark	.08	.06	.03
15	Will Clark	.80	.60	.30
16	Roger Clemens	.30	.25	.12
17	Dave Cone	.08	.06	.03
18	Alvin Davis	.08	.06	.03
19	Eric Davis	.30	.25	.12
20	Glenn Davis	.08	.06	.03
21	Andre Dawson	.12	.09	.05
22	Bill Doran	.08	.06	.03
23	Dennis Eckersley	.08	.06	.03
24	Dwight Evans	.08	.06	.03
25	Tony Fernandez	.08	.06	.03
26	Carlton Fisk	.08	.06	.03
27	John Franco	.08	.06	.03
28	Andres Galarraga	.15	.11	.06
29	Ron Gant	.08	.06	.03
30	Kirk Gibson	.08	.06	.03
31	Doc Gooden	.25	.20	.10
32	Mike Greenwell	.50	.40	.20
33	Mark Gubicza	.08	.06	.03
34	Pedro Gurrero	.12	.09	.05
35	Ozzie Guillen	.08	.06	.03
36	Tony Gwynn	.15	.11	.06
37	Rickey Henderson	.15	.11	.06
38	Orel Hershiser	.15	.11	.06
39	Teddy Higuera	.08	.06	.03
40	Charlie Hough	.08	.06	.03
41	Kent Hrbek	.12	.09	.05
42	Bruce Hurst	.08	.06	.03
43	Bo Jackson	.50	.40	.20
44	Gregg Jefferies	.60	.45	.25
45	Ricky Jordan	.25	.20	.10
46	Wally Joyner	.15	.11	.06
47	Mark Langston	.12	.09	.05
48	Mike Marshall	.08	.06	.03
49	Don Mattingly	2.00	1.50	.80
50	Fred McGriff	.35	.25	.14
51	Mark McGwire	1.00	.70	.40
52	Kevin McReynolds	.15	.11	.06
53	Paul Molitor	.08	.06	.03
54	Jack Morris	.08	.06	.03
55	Dale Murphy	.15	.11	.06
56	Eddie Murray	.10	.08	.04
57	Pete O'Brien	.08	.06	.03
58	Rafael Palmeiro	.08	.06	.03
59	Gerald Perry	.08	.06	.03
60	Kirby Puckett	.30	.25	.12
61	Rock Raines	.15	.11	.06
62	Johnny Ray	.08	.06	.03
63	Rick Reuschel	.08	.06	.03
64	Cal Ripken	.15	.11	.06
65	Chris Sabo	.15	.11	.06
66	Juan Samuel	.08	.06	.03
67	Ryane Sandberg	.15	.11	.06
68	Benny Santiago	.15	.11	.06
69	Steve Sax	.08	.06	.03
70	Mike Schmidt	.20	.15	.11
71	Ruben Sierra	.20	.15	.11
72	Ozzie Smith	.15	.11	.06
73	Cory Snyder	.08	.06	.03
74	Dave Stewart	.08	.06	.03
75	Darryl Strawberry	.25	.20	.10
76	Greg Swindell	.15	.11	.06
77	Alan Trammell	.15	.11	.06
78	Fernando Valenzuela	.08	.06	.03
79	Andy Van Slyke	.20	.15	.08
80	Frank Viola	.20	.15	.08
81	Claudell Washington	.08	.06	.03
82	Walt Weiss	.08	.06	.03
83	Lou Whitaker	.08	.06	.03
84	Dave Winfield	.20	.15	.08
85	Mike Witt	.08	.06	.03
86	Gerald Young	.08	.06	.03

		MT	NR MT	EX
87	Robin Yount	.20	.15	.08
88	Checklist	.08	.06	.03

1990 Topps

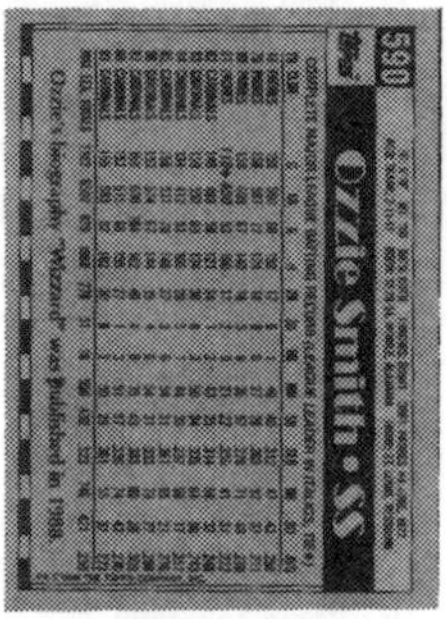

The 1990 Topps set again included 792 cards, and sported a newly-designed front that featured six different color schemes. The set led off with a special four-card salute to Nolan Ryan, and featured various other specials, including All-Stars, Number 1 Draft Picks, Record Breakers, manager cards, rookies, and "Turn Back the Clock" cards. The set also includes a special card commemorating A. Bartlett Giamatti, the late Baseball Commissioner. The backs are printed in black on a chartreuse background with the card number in the upper left corner. The set features 725 different individual player cards, the most ever, including 138 players making their first appearance in a regular Topps set.

		MT	NR MT	EX
Complete Set:		25.00	20.00	10.00
Common Player:		.03	.02	.01
1	Nolan Ryan	.35	.25	.14
2	Nolan Ryan (The Mets Years)	.20	.15	.08
3	Nolan Ryan (The Angels Years)	.20	.15	.08
4	Nolan Ryan (The Astros Years)	.20	.15	.08
5	Nolan Ryan (The Rangers)	.20	.15	.08
6	1989 Record Breaker (Vince Coleman)	.10	.08	.04
7	1989 Record Breaker (Rickey Henderson)	.20	.15	.08
8	1989 Record Breaker (Cal Ripken)	.15	.11	.06
9	Eric Plunk	.03	.02	.01
10	Barry Larkin	.15	.11	.06
11	Paul Gibson	.04	.03	.02
12	Joe Girardi(FC)	.15	.11	.06
13	Mark Williamson	.03	.02	.01
14	*Mike Fetters*(FC)	.20	.15	.08
15	Teddy Higuera	.06	.05	.02
16	*Kent Anderson*	.10	.08	.04
17	Kelly Downs	.05	.04	.02
18	Carlos Quintana	.09	.07	.04
19	Al Newman	.03	.02	.01
20	Mark Gubicza	.12	.09	.05
21	Jeff Torborg	.03	.02	.01
22	Bruce Ruffin	.03	.02	.01
23	Randy Velarde	.07	.05	.03
24	Joe Hesketh	.03	.02	.01
25	Willie Randolph	.08	.06	.03
26	Don Slaught	.03	.02	.01
27	Rick Leach	.03	.02	.01
28	Duane Ward	.04	.03	.02
29	John Cangelosi	.03	.02	.01
30	David Cone	.10	.08	.04
31	Henry Cotto	.03	.02	.01
32	John Farrell	.05	.04	.02
33	Greg Walker	.05	.04	.02
34	*Tony Fossas*(FC)	.07	.05	.03
35	Benito Santiago	.12	.09	.05
36	John Costello	.04	.03	.02
37	Domingo Ramos	.03	.02	.01
38	Wes Gardner	.04	.03	.02
39	Curt Ford	.04	.03	.02
40	Jay Howell	.06	.05	.02
41	Matt Williams	.15	.11	.06
42	Jeff Robinson	.05	.04	.02
43	Dante Bichette	.07	.05	.03
44	#1 Draft Pick *(Roger Salkeld)*(FC)	.50	.40	.20
45	Dave Parker	.09	.07	.04
46	Rob Dibble	.07	.05	.03
47	Brian Harper	.04	.03	.02
48	Zane Smith	.03	.02	.01
49	Tom Lawless	.03	.02	.01
50	Glenn Davis	.08	.06	.03
51	Doug Rader	.03	.02	.01
52	*Jack Daugherty*(FC)	.20	.15	.08
53	Mike LaCoss	.04	.03	.02
54	Joel Skinner	.04	.03	.02
55	Darrell Evans	.05	.04	.02
56	Franklin Stubbs	.04	.03	.02
57	*Greg Vaughn*(FC)	.60	.45	.25
58	Keith Miller	.10	.08	.04
59	Ted Power	.03	.02	.01
60	George Brett	.15	.11	.06
61	*Deion Sanders*	.30	.25	.12
62	Ramon Martinez	.30	.25	.12
63	Mike Pagliarulo	.04	.03	.02
64	Danny Darwin	.03	.02	.01
65	Devon White	.07	.05	.03
66	*Greg Litton*(FC)	.15	.11	.06
67	Scott Sanderson	.04	.03	.02
68	Dave Henderson	.06	.05	.02
69	Todd Frohwirth	.03	.02	.01
70	Mike Greenwell	.30	.25	.12
71	Allan Anderson	.05	.04	.02
72	*Jeff Huson*(FC)	.25	.20	.10
73	Bob Milacki	.05	.04	.02
74	#1 Draft Pick *(Jeff Jackson)*(FC)	.30	.25	.12
75	Doug Jones	.05	.04	.02
76	Dave Valle	.03	.02	.01
77	Dave Bergman	.03	.02	.01
78	Mike Flanagan	.04	.03	.02
79	Ron Kittle	.05	.04	.02
80	Jeff Russell	.05	.04	.02
81	Bob Rodgers	.03	.02	.01
82	Scott Terry	.04	.03	.02
83	Hensley Meulens	.30	.25	.12
84	Ray Searage	.03	.02	.01
85	Juan Samuel	.05	.04	.02
86	Paul Kilgus	.03	.02	.01
87	*Rick Luecken*(FC)	.15	.11	.06
88	Glenn Braggs	.05	.04	.02
89	*Clint Zavaras*(FC)	.15	.11	.06
90	Jack Clark	.06	.05	.02
91	*Steve Frey*(FC)	.20	.15	.08
92	Mike Stanley	.03	.02	.01
93	Shawn Hillegas	.03	.02	.01
94	Herm Winningham	.03	.02	.01
95	Todd Worrell	.05	.04	.02
96	Jody Reed	.04	.03	.02
97	Curt Schilling(FC)	.10	.08	.04
98	Jose Gonzalez(FC)	.10	.08	.04
99	*Rich Monteleone*(FC)	.15	.11	.06
100	Will Clark	.50	.40	.20
101	Shane Rawley	.04	.03	.02
102	Stan Javier	.04	.03	.02
103	Marvin Freeman	.09	.07	.04
104	Bob Knepper	.03	.02	.01
105	Randy Myers	.05	.04	.02
106	Charlie O'Brien	.03	.02	.01
107	Fred Lynn	.05	.04	.02
108	Rod Nichols	.04	.03	.02
109	Roberto Kelly	.08	.06	.03
110	Tommy Helms	.03	.02	.01
111	Ed Whited	.20	.15	.08
112	Glenn Wilson	.03	.02	.01
113	Manny Lee	.03	.02	.01
114	Mike Bielecki	.05	.04	.02
115	Tony Pena	.06	.05	.02
116	Floyd Bannister	.04	.03	.02
117	Mike Sharperson(FC)	.09	.07	.04
118	Erik Hanson	.10	.08	.04
119	Billy Hatcher	.04	.03	.02
120	John Franco	.05	.04	.02
121	Robin Ventura	.60	.45	.25
122	Shawn Abner	.03	.02	.01
123	Rich Gedman	.04	.03	.02
124	Dave Dravecky	.04	.03	.02
125	Kent Hrbek	.07	.05	.03
126	Randy Kramer	.03	.02	.01
127	Mike Devereaux	.06	.05	.02
128	Checklist 1-132	.03	.02	.01
129	Ron Jones	.10	.08	.04
130	Bert Blyleven	.05	.04	.02
131	Matt Nokes	.06	.05	.02
132	Lance Blankenship(FC)	.10	.08	.04

		MT	NR MT	EX
133	Ricky Horton	.03	.02	.01
134	#1 Draft Pick *(Earl Cunningham)*(FC)	.20	.15	.08
135	Dave Magadan	.05	.04	.02
136	Kevin Brown	.06	.05	.02
137	*Marty Pevey*(FC)	.15	.11	.06
138	Al Leiter	.04	.03	.02
139	Greg Brock	.04	.03	.02
140	Andre Dawson	.12	.09	.05
141	John Hart	.05	.04	.02
142	*Jeff Wetherby*(FC)	.15	.11	.06
143	Rafael Belliard	.03	.02	.01
144	Bud Black	.03	.02	.01
145	Terry Steinbach	.07	.05	.03
146	*Rob Richie*(FC)	.15	.11	.06
147	Chuck Finley	.04	.03	.02
148	Edgar Martinez(FC)	.09	.07	.04
149	Steve Farr	.04	.03	.02
150	Kirk Gibson	.09	.07	.04
151	Rick Mahler	.03	.02	.01
152	Lonnie Smith	.05	.04	.02
153	Randy Milligan	.05	.04	.02
154	Mike Maddux	.05	.04	.02
155	Ellis Burks	.25	.20	.10
156	Ken Patterson	.04	.03	.02
157	Craig Biggio	.15	.11	.06
158	Craig Lefferts	.04	.03	.02
159	Mike Felder	.03	.02	.01
160	Dave Righetti	.06	.05	.02
161	Harold Reynolds	.06	.05	.02
162	*Todd Zeile*(FC)	.60	.45	.25
163	Phil Bradley	.05	.04	.02
164	#1 Draft Pick *(Jeff Juden)*(FC)	.50	.40	.20
165	Walt Weiss	.08	.06	.03
166	Bobby Witt	.04	.03	.02
167	*Kevin Appier*(FC)	.35	.25	.14
168	Jose Lind	.04	.03	.02
169	Richard Dotson	.03	.02	.01
170	George Bell	.12	.09	.05
171	Russ Nixon	.03	.02	.01
172	Tom Lampkin(FC)	.10	.08	.04
173	Tim Belcher	.12	.09	.05
174	Jeff Kunkel	.03	.02	.01
175	Mike Moore	.07	.05	.02
176	Luis Quinones	.03	.02	.01
177	Mike Henneman	.05	.04	.02
178	Chris James	.06	.05	.02
179	Brian Holton	.04	.03	.02
180	Rock Raines	.10	.08	.04
181	Juan Agosto	.03	.02	.01
182	Mookie Wilson	.05	.04	.02
183	Steve Lake	.03	.02	.01
184	Danny Cox	.04	.03	.02
185	Ruben Sierra	.20	.15	.08
186	Dave LaPoint	.03	.02	.01
187	*Rick Wrona*(FC)	.12	.09	.05
188	Mike Smithson	.03	.02	.01
189	Dick Schofield	.04	.03	.02
190	Rick Reuschel	.06	.05	.02
191	Pat Borders	.08	.06	.03
192	Don August	.04	.03	.02
193	Andy Benes	.25	.20	.10
194	Glenallen Hill(FC)	.25	.20	.10
195	Tim Burke	.05	.04	.02
196	Gerald Young	.04	.03	.02
197	Doug Drabek	.07	.05	.03
198	Mike Marshall	.06	.05	.02
199	*Sergio Valdez*(FC)	.20	.15	.08
200	Don Mattingly	.40	.30	.15
201	Cito Gaston	.03	.02	.01
202	Mike Macfarlane	.03	.02	.01
203	*Mike Roesler*(FC)	.15	.11	.06
204	Bob Dernier	.03	.02	.01
205	Mark Davis	.09	.07	.04
206	Nick Esasky	.07	.05	.03
207	Bob Ojeda	.04	.03	.02
208	Brook Jacoby	.04	.03	.02
209	Greg Mathews	.04	.03	.02
210	Ryne Sandberg	.30	.25	.12
211	John Cerutti	.04	.03	.02
212	Joe Orsulak	.03	.02	.01
213	Scott Bankhead	.05	.04	.02
214	Terry Francona	.03	.02	.01
215	Kirk McCaskill	.04	.03	.02
216	Ricky Jordan	.20	.15	.08
217	Don Robinson	.04	.03	.02
218	Wally Backman	.04	.03	.02
219	Donn Pall	.03	.02	.01
220	Barry Bonds	.10	.08	.04
221	*Gary Mielke*(FC)	.15	.11	.06
222	Kurt Stillwell	.05	.04	.02

		MT	NR MT	EX
223	Tommy Gregg	.06	.05	.02
224	*Delino DeShields*(FC)	.60	.45	.25
225	Jim Deshaies	.05	.04	.02
226	Mickey Hatcher	.03	.02	.01
227	*Kevin Tapani*(FC)	.30	.25	.12
228	Dave Martinez	.03	.02	.01
229	David Wells	.03	.02	.01
230	Keith Hernandez	.07	.05	.03
231	Jack McKeon	.03	.02	.01
232	Darnell Coles	.04	.03	.02
233	Ken Hill	.10	.08	.06
234	Mariano Duncan	.05	.04	.02
235	Jeff Reardon	.04	.03	.02
236	Hal Morris(FC)	.50	.40	.20
237	*Kevin Ritz*(FC)	.15	.11	.06
238	Felix Jose(FC)	.10	.08	.04
239	Eric Show	.04	.03	.02
240	Mark Grace	.40	.30	.15
241	Mike Krukow	.04	.03	.02
242	Fred Manrique	.03	.02	.01
243	Barry Jones	.03	.02	.01
244	Bill Schroeder	.03	.02	.01
245	Roger Clemens	.25	.20	.10
246	Jim Eisenreich	.03	.02	.01
247	Jerry Reed	.03	.02	.01
248	Dave Anderson	.03	.02	.01
249	*Mike Smith*(FC)	.12	.09	.05
250	Jose Canseco	.70	.50	.30
251	Jeff Blauser	.05	.04	.02
252	Otis Nixon	.03	.02	.01
253	Mark Portugal	.03	.02	.01
254	Francisco Cabrera	.25	.20	.10
255	Bobby Thigpen	.07	.05	.03
256	Marvell Wynne	.03	.02	.01
257	Jose DeLeon	.07	.05	.03
258	Barry Lyons	.03	.02	.01
259	Lance McCullers	.05	.04	.02
260	Eric Davis	.30	.25	.12
261	Whitey Herzog	.03	.02	.01
262	Checklist 133-264	.03	.02	.01
263	*Mel Stottlemyre, Jr.*(FC)	.12	.09	.05
264	Bryan Clutterbuck	.03	.02	.01
265	Pete O'Brien	.06	.05	.02
266	German Gonzalez	.04	.03	.02
267	Mark Davidson	.03	.02	.01
268	Rob Murphy	.03	.02	.01
269	Dickie Thon	.03	.02	.01
270	Dave Stewart	.08	.06	.03
271	Chet Lemon	.05	.04	.02
272	Bryan Harvey	.04	.03	.02
273	Bobby Bonilla	.15	.11	.06
274	*Goose Gozzo*(FC)	.15	.11	.06
275	Mickey Tettleton	.07	.05	.03
276	Gary Thurman	.03	.02	.01
277	Lenny Harris(FC)	.12	.09	.05
278	Pascual Perez	.04	.03	.02
279	Steve Buechele	.04	.03	.02
280	Lou Whitaker	.07	.05	.03
281	Kevin Bass	.05	.04	.02
282	Derek Lilliquist	.10	.08	.04
283	*Joey Belle*(FC)	.60	.45	.25
284	*Mark Gardner*(FC)	.30	.25	.12
285	Willie McGee	.06	.05	.02
286	Lee Guetterman	.03	.02	.01
287	Vance Law	.03	.02	.01
288	Greg Briley	.15	.11	.06
289	Norm Charlton	.10	.08	.04
290	Robin Yount	.20	.15	.08
291	Dave Johnson	.03	.02	.01
292	Jim Gott	.04	.03	.02
293	Mike Gallego	.04	.03	.02
294	Craig McMurtry	.03	.02	.01
295	Fred McGriff	.25	.20	.10
296	Jeff Ballard	.07	.05	.03
297	Tom Herr	.06	.05	.02
298	Danny Gladden	.05	.04	.02
299	Adam Peterson(FC)	.09	.07	.04
300	Bo Jackson	.60	.45	.25
301	Don Aase	.03	.02	.01
302	*Marcus Lawton*(FC)	.08	.06	.03
303	Rick Cerone	.03	.02	.01
304	Marty Clary(FC)	.08	.06	.03
305	Eddie Murray	.15	.11	.06
306	Tom Niedenfuer	.03	.02	.01
307	Bip Roberts	.08	.06	.03
308	Jose Guzman	.05	.04	.02
309	*Eric Yelding*(FC)	.20	.15	.08
310	Steve Bedrosian	.05	.04	.02
311	Dwight Smith	.25	.20	.10
312	Dan Quisenberry	.05	.04	.02
313	Gus Polidor	.03	.02	.01

		MT	NR MT	EX
314	#1 Draft Pick *(Donald Harris)*(FC)	.20	.15	.08
315	Bruce Hurst	.06	.05	.02
316	Carney Lansford	.06	.05	.02
317	*Mark Guthrie*(FC)	.20	.15	.08
318	Wallace Johnson	.03	.02	.01
319	Dion James	.04	.03	.02
320	Dave Steib	.07	.05	.03
321	Joe Morgan	.03	.02	.01
322	Junior Ortiz	.03	.02	.01
323	Willie Wilson	.04	.03	.02
324	Pete Harnisch(FC)	.10	.08	.04
325	Robby Thompson	.06	.05	.02
326	*Tom McCarthy*	.10	.08	.04
327	Ken Williams	.03	.02	.01
328	Curt Young	.03	.02	.01
329	Oddibe McDowell	.06	.05	.02
330	Ron Darling	.09	.07	.04
331	*Juan Gonzalez*(FC)	2.00	1.50	.80
332	Paul O'Neill	.07	.05	.03
333	Bill Wegman	.03	.02	.01
334	Johnny Ray	.05	.04	.02
335	Andy Hawkins	.05	.04	.02
336	Ken Griffey, Jr.	2.50	2.00	1.00
337	Lloyd McClendon	.06	.05	.02
338	Dennis Lamp	.03	.02	.01
339	Dave Clark	.04	.03	.02
340	Fernando Valenzuela	.06	.05	.02
341	Tom Foley	.03	.02	.01
342	Alex Trevino	.03	.02	.01
343	Frank Tanana	.04	.03	.02
344	*George Canale*(FC)	.15	.11	.06
345	Harold Baines	.09	.07	.04
346	Jim Presley	.04	.03	.02
347	*Junior Felix*	.20	.15	.08
348	*Gary Wayne*(FC)	.12	.09	.05
349	*Steve Finley*(FC)	.30	.25	.12
350	Bret Saberhagen	.10	.08	.04
351	Roger Craig	.03	.02	.01
352	Bryn Smith	.05	.04	.02
353	Sandy Alomar	.25	.20	.10
354	*Stan Belinda*(FC)	.20	.15	.08
355	Marty Barrett	.05	.04	.02
356	Randy Ready	.03	.02	.01
357	Dave West	.20	.15	.08
358	Andres Thomas	.04	.03	.02
359	Jimmy Jones	.03	.02	.01
360	Paul Molitor	.09	.07	.04
361	*Randy McCament*(FC)	.15	.11	.06
362	Damon Berryhill	.06	.05	.02
363	Dan Petry	.03	.02	.01
364	Rolando Roomes(FC)	.15	.11	.06
365	Ozzie Guillen	.05	.04	.02
366	Mike Heath	.03	.02	.01
367	Mike Morgan	.03	.02	.01
368	Bill Doran	.06	.05	.02
369	Todd Burns	.04	.03	.02
370	Tim Wallach	.07	.05	.03
371	Jimmy Key	.08	.06	.03
372	Terry Kennedy	.03	.02	.01
373	Alvin Davis	.08	.06	.03
374	*Steve Cummings*(FC)	.15	.11	.06
375	Dwight Evans	.08	.06	.03
376	Checklist 265-396	.03	.02	.01
377	*Mickey Weston*(FC)	.15	.11	.06
378	Luis Salazar	.03	.02	.01
379	Steve Rosenberg	.03	.02	.01
380	Dave Winfield	.15	.11	.06
381	Frank Robinson	.03	.02	.01
382	Jeff Musselman	.03	.02	.01
383	John Morris	.04	.03	.02
384	*Pat Combs*	.20	.15	.08
385	Fred McGriff AS	.20	.15	.08
386	Julio Franco AS	.10	.08	.04
387	Wade Boggs AS	.20	.15	.08
388	Cal Ripken AS	.15	.11	.06
389	Robin Yount AS	.20	.15	.08
390	Ruben Sierra AS	.20	.15	.08
391	Kirby Puckett AS	.20	.15	.08
392	Carlton Fisk AS	.08	.06	.03
393	Bret Saberhagen AS	.10	.08	.04
394	Jeff Ballard AS	.08	.06	.03
395	Jeff Russell AS	.08	.06	.03
396	A. Bartlett Giamatti	.30	.25	.12
397	Will Clark AS	.25	.20	.10
398	Ryne Sandberg AS	.15	.11	.06
399	Howard Johnson AS	.15	.11	.06
400	Ozzie Smith AS	.10	.08	.04
401	Kevin Mitchell AS	.20	.15	.08
402	Eric Davis AS	.20	.15	.08
403	Tony Gwynn AS	.15	.11	.06
404	Craig Biggio AS	.15	.11	.06

		MT	NR MT	EX
405	Mike Scott AS	.08	.06	.03
406	Joe Magrane AS	.08	.06	.03
407	Mark Davis AS	.08	.06	.03
408	Trevor Wilson	.06	.05	.02
409	Tom Brunansky	.09	.07	.04
410	Joe Boever	.06	.05	.02
411	Ken Phelps	.03	.02	.01
412	Jamie Moyer	.04	.03	.02
413	*Brian DuBois*(FC)	.15	.11	.06
414	#1 Draft Pick *(Frank Thomas)*(FC)	4.00	3.00	1.50
415	Shawon Dunston	.06	.05	.02
416	*Dave Johnson*(FC)	.12	.09	.05
417	Jim Gantner	.06	.05	.02
418	Tom Browning	.08	.06	.03
419	*Beau Allred*(FC)	.20	.15	.08
420	Carlton Fisk	.08	.06	.03
421	Greg Minton	.03	.02	.01
422	Pat Sheridan	.03	.02	.01
423	Fred Toliver	.03	.02	.01
424	Jerry Reuss	.05	.04	.02
425	Bill Landrum	.05	.04	.02
426	Jeff Hamilton	.05	.04	.02
427	Carmem Castillo	.03	.02	.01
428	*Steve Davis*(FC)	.12	.09	.05
429	Tom Kelly	.03	.02	.01
430	Pete Incaviglia	.06	.05	.02
431	Randy Johnson	.10	.08	.04
432	Damaso Garcia	.03	.02	.01
433	*Steve Olin*(FC)	.12	.08	.04
434	Mark Carreon(FC)	.09	.07	.04
435	Kevin Seitzer	.09	.07	.04
436	Mel Hall	.05	.04	.02
437	Les Lancaster	.05	.04	.02
438	Greg Myers(FC)	.10	.08	.04
439	Jeff Parrett	.06	.05	.02
440	Alan Trammell	.09	.07	.04
441	Bob Kipper	.03	.02	.01
442	Jerry Browne	.07	.05	.02
443	Cris Carpenter	.09	.07	.04
444	*Kyle Abbott* (Number 1 Daft Pick)(FC)	.30	.25	.12
445	Danny Jackson	.05	.04	.02
446	Dan Pasqua	.05	.04	.02
447	Atlee Hammaker	.03	.02	.01
448	Greg Gagne	.04	.03	.02
449	Dennis Rasmussen	.04	.03	.02
450	Rickey Henderson	.25	.20	.10
451	Mark Lemke(FC)	.10	.08	.04
452	Luis de los Santos(FC)	.10	.08	.04
453	Jody Davis	.03	.02	.01
454	Jeff King(FC)	.15	.11	.06
455	Jeffrey Leonard	.06	.05	.02
456	Chris Gwynn(FC)	.09	.07	.03
457	Gregg Jefferies	.30	.25	.12
458	Bob McClure	.03	.02	.01
459	Jim Lefebvre	.03	.02	.01
460	Mike Scott	.09	.07	.03
461	*Carlos Martinez*(FC)	.15	.11	.06
462	Denny Walling	.03	.02	.01
463	Drew Hall	.03	.02	.01
464	*Jerome Walton*	.25	.20	.10
465	Kevin Gross	.06	.05	.02
466	Rance Mulliniks	.03	.02	.01
467	Juan Nieves	.04	.03	.02
468	Billy Ripken	.04	.03	.02
469	John Kruk	.07	.05	.02
470	Frank Viola	.09	.07	.04
471	Mike Brumley	.03	.02	.01
472	Jose Uribe	.04	.03	.02
473	Joe Price	.03	.02	.01
474	Rich Thompson	.04	.03	.02
475	Bob Welch	.06	.05	.02
476	Brad Komminsk	.03	.02	.02
477	Willie Fraser	.03	.02	.02
478	Mike LaValliere	.04	.03	.02
479	Frank White	.06	.05	.02
480	Sid Fernandez	.09	.07	.04
481	Garry Templeton	.05	.04	.02
482	*Steve Carter*(FC)	.15	.11	.06
483	Alejandro Pena	.04	.03	.02
484	Mike Fitzgerald	.03	.02	.01
485	John Candelaria	.05	.04	.02
486	Jeff Treadway	.05	.04	.02
487	Steve Searcy	.05	.04	.02
488	Ken Oberkfell	.03	.02	.01
489	Nick Leyva	.03	.02	.01
490	Dan Plesac	.07	.05	.03
491	*Dave Cochrane*(FC)	.15	.11	.06
492	Ron Oester	.04	.03	.02
493	*Jason Grimsley*(FC)	.25	.20	.10

		MT	NR MT	EX
494	Terry Puhl	.03	.02	.01
495	Lee Smith	.06	.05	.02
496	Cecil Espy	.06	.05	.02
497	Dave Schmidt	.03	.02	.01
498	Rick Schu	.03	.02	.01
499	Bill Long	.04	.03	.02
500	Kevin Mitchell	.35	.25	.14
501	Matt Young	.03	.02	.01
502	Mitch Webster	.04	.03	.02
503	Randy St. Claire	.03	.02	.01
504	Tom O'Malley	.03	.02	.01
505	Kelly Gruber	.08	.06	.03
506	Tom Glavine	.10	.08	.04
507	Gary Redus	.04	.03	.02
508	Terry Leach	.03	.02	.01
509	Tom Pagnozzi	.03	.02	.01
510	Doc Gooden	.25	.20	.10
511	Clay Parker	.07	.05	.03
512	Gary Pettis	.03	.02	.01
513	Mark Eichhorn	.03	.02	.01
514	Andy Allanson	.03	.02	.01
515	Len Dykstra	.06	.05	.02
516	Tim Leary	.05	.04	.02
517	Roberto Alomar	.15	.11	.06
518	Bill Krueger	.03	.02	.01
519	Bucky Dent	.03	.02	.01
520	Mitch Williams	.09	.07	.03
521	Craig Worthington	.15	.11	.06
522	Mike Dunne	.04	.03	.02
523	Jay Bell	.03	.02	.01
524	Daryl Boston	.03	.02	.01
525	Wally Joyner	.20	.15	.08
526	Checklist 397-528	.03	.02	.01
527	Ron Hassey	.03	.02	.01
528	*Kevin Wickander*(FC)	.20	.15	.08
529	Greg Harris	.03	.02	.01
530	Mark Langston	.10	.08	.04
531	Ken Caminiti	.06	.05	.02
532	Cecilio Guante	.03	.02	.01
533	Tim Jones(FC)	.07	.05	.03
534	Louie Meadows	.07	.05	.03
535	John Smoltz	.15	.11	.06
536	*Bob Geren*	.15	.11	.06
537	Mark Grant	.03	.02	.01
538	*Billy Spiers*	.20	.15	.08
539	Neal Heaton	.03	.02	.01
540	Danny Tartabull	.09	.07	.03
541	Pat Perry	.03	.02	.01
542	Darren Daulton	.03	.02	.01
543	Nelson Liriano	.03	.02	.01
544	Dennis Boyd	.05	.04	.02
545	Kevin McReynolds	.09	.07	.04
546	Kevin Hickey	.05	.04	.02
547	Jack Howell	.05	.04	.02
548	Pat Clements	.03	.02	.01
549	Don Zimmer	.03	.02	.01
550	Julio Franco	.09	.07	.04
551	Tim Crews	.03	.02	.01
552	*Mike Smith*(FC)	.12	.09	.05
553	*Scott Scudder*(FC)	.20	.15	.11
554	Jay Buhner	.08	.06	.03
555	Jack Morris	.07	.05	.03
556	Gene Larkin	.03	.02	.01
557	*Jeff Innis*	.15	.11	.08
558	Rafael Ramirez	.04	.03	.02
559	Andy McGaffigan	.04	.03	.02
560	Steve Sax	.08	.06	.03
561	Ken Dayley	.03	.02	.01
562	Chad Kreuter	.10	.08	.04
563	Alex Sanchez	.10	.08	.04
564	#1 Draft Pick *(Tyler Houston)*(FC)	.20	.15	.08
565	Scott Fletcher	.05	.04	.02
566	Mark Knudson	.06	.05	.02
567	Ron Gant	.10	.08	.04
568	John Smiley	.07	.05	.03
569	Ivan Calderon	.05	.04	.02
570	Cal Ripken	.20	.15	.08
571	Brett Butler	.06	.05	.02
572	Greg Harris	.09	.07	.04
573	Danny Heep	.03	.02	.01
574	Bill Swift	.04	.03	.02
575	Lance Parrish	.07	.05	.03
576	*Mike Dyer*(FC)	.20	.15	.08
577	Charlie Hayes(FC)	.10	.08	.04
578	Joe Magrane	.09	.07	.04
579	Art Howe	.03	.02	.01
580	Joe Carter	.15	.11	.06
581	Ken Griffey	.05	.04	.02
582	Rick Honeycutt	.03	.02	.01
583	Bruce Benedict	.03	.02	.01
584	*Phil Stephenson*(FC)	.09	.07	.04
585	Kal Daniels	.10	.08	.04
586	Ed Nunez	.03	.02	.01
587	Lance Johnson	.08	.06	.03
588	Rick Rhoden	.03	.02	.01
589	Mike Aldrete	.03	.02	.01
590	Ozzie Smith	.10	.08	.04
591	Todd Stottlemyre	.08	.06	.03
592	R.J. Reynolds	.03	.02	.01
593	Scott Bradley	.03	.02	.01
594	*Luis Sojo*(FC)	.20	.15	.08
595	Greg Swindell	.10	.08	.04
596	Jose DeJesus(FC)	.10	.08	.04
597	Chris Bosio	.07	.05	.03
598	Brady Anderson	.05	.04	.02
599	Frank Williams	.03	.02	.01
600	Darryl Strawberry	.30	.15	.08
601	Luis Rivera	.04	.03	.02
602	Scott Garrelts	.07	.05	.03
603	Tony Armas	.03	.02	.01
604	Ron Robinson	.03	.02	.01
605	Mike Scioscia	.07	.05	.03
606	Storm Davis	.07	.05	.03
607	Steve Jeltz	.03	.02	.01
608	*Eric Anthony*(FC)	.40	.30	.15
609	Sparky Anderson	.03	.02	.01
610	Pedro Guererro	.12	.09	.05
611	Walt Terrell	.05	.04	.02
612	Dave Gallagher	.07	.05	.02
613	Jeff Pico	.04	.03	.02
614	Nelson Santovenia	.09	.07	.04
615	Rob Deer	.07	.05	.03
616	Brian Holman	.10	.08	.04
617	Geronimo Berroa	.08	.06	.03
618	Eddie Whitson	.05	.04	.02
619	Rob Ducey	.08	.06	.03
620	*Tony Castillo*(FC)	.20	.15	.08
621	Melido Perez	.07	.05	.03
622	Sid Bream	.05	.04	.02
623	Jim Corsi	.05	.04	.02
624	Darrin Jackson	.04	.03	.02
625	Roger McDowell	.07	.05	.03
626	Bob Melvin	.03	.02	.01
627	Jose Rijo	.07	.05	.03
628	Candy Maldonado	.04	.03	.02
629	Eric Hetzel(FC)	.10	.08	.04
630	Gary Gaetti	.10	.08	.04
631	*John Wetteland*(FC)	.20	.15	.08
632	Scott Lusader	.06	.05	.02
633	Dennis Cook(FC)	.25	.20	.10
634	Luis Polonia	.06	.05	.02
635	Brian Downing	.06	.05	.02
636	Jesse Orosco	.03	.02	.01
637	Craig Reynolds	.03	.02	.01
638	Jeff Montgomery	.07	.05	.03
639	Tony LaRussa	.03	.02	.01
640	Rick Sutcliffe	.06	.05	.02
641	*Doug Strange*(FC)	.15	.11	.06
642	Jack Armstrong	.04	.03	.02
643	Alfredo Griffin	.04	.03	.02
644	Paul Assenmacher	.04	.03	.02
645	Jose Oquendo	.06	.05	.02
646	Checklist 529-660	.03	.02	.01
647	Rex Hudler	.03	.02	.01
648	Jim Clancy	.03	.02	.01
649	*Dan Murphy*(FC)	.15	.11	.06
650	Mike Witt	.06	.05	.02
651	Rafael Santana	.06	.05	.02
652	Mike Boddicker	.06	.05	.02
653	John Moses	.03	.02	.01
654	#1 Draft Pick *(Paul Coleman)*(FC)	.30	.25	.12
655	Gregg Olson	.30	.25	.12
656	Mackey Sasser	.05	.04	.02
657	Terry Mulholland	.06	.05	.02
658	Donell Nixon	.03	.02	.01
659	Greg Cadaret	.03	.02	.01
660	Vince Coleman	.10	.08	.04
661	Turn Back The Clock - 1985 (Dick Howser)	.07	.05	.03
662	Turn Back The Clock - 1980 (Mike Schmidt)	.07	.05	.03
663	Turn Back The Clock - 1975 (Fred Lynn)	.07	.05	.03
664	Turn Back The Clock - 1970 (Johnny Bench)	.07	.05	.03
665	Turn Back The Clock - 1965 (Sandy Koufax)	.07	.05	.03
666	Brian Fisher	.05	.04	.02
667	Curt Wilkerson	.03	.02	.01
668	*Joe Oliver*(FC)	.30	.25	.12
669	Tom Lasorda	.03	.02	.01
670	Dennis Eckersley	.09	.07	.04

		MT	NR MT	EX
671	Bob Boone	.09	.07	.04
672	Roy Smith	.03	.02	.01
673	Joey Meyer	.03	.02	.01
674	Spike Owen	.05	.04	.02
675	Jim Abbott	.35	.25	.12
676	Randy Kutcher(FC)	.07	.05	.03
677	Jay Tibbs	.03	.02	.01
678	Kirt Manwaring	.10	.08	.04
679	Gary Ward	.04	.03	.02
680	Howard Johnson	.15	.11	.06
681	Mike Schooler	.07	.05	.03
682	Dann Bilardello	.03	.02	.01
683	*Kenny Rogers*	.10	.08	.04
684	*Julio Machado*(FC)	.20	.15	.08
685	Tony Fernandez	.09	.07	.04
686	Carmelo Martinez	.06	.05	.02
687	Tim Birtsas	.03	.02	.01
688	Milt Thompson	.06	.05	.02
689	Rich Yett	.03	.02	.01
690	Mark McGwire	.30	.25	.12
691	Chuck Cary	.03	.02	.01
692	Sammy Sosa	.35	.25	.14
693	Calvin Schiraldi	.03	.02	.01
694	*Mike Stanton*(FC)	.15	.11	.06
695	Tom Henke	.06	.05	.02
696	B.J. Surhoff	.07	.05	.03
697	Mike Davis	.03	.02	.01
698	*Omar Vizquel*	.10	.08	.04
699	Jim Leyland	.03	.02	.01
700	Kirby Puckett	.25	.20	.10
701	*Bernie Williams*(FC)	.40	.30	.15
702	Tony Phillips	.04	.03	.02
703	*Jeff Brantley*	.12	.09	.05
704	*Chip Hale*(FC)	.15	.11	.06
705	Claudell Washington	.07	.05	.03
706	Geno Petralli	.03	.02	.01
707	Luis Aquino	.03	.02	.01
708	Larry Sheets	.03	.02	.01
709	Juan Berneguer	.03	.02	.01
710	Von Hayes	.09	.07	.04
711	Rick Aguilera	.05	.04	.02
712	Todd Benzinger	.09	.07	.04
713	*Tim Drummond*(FC)	.15	.11	.06
714	*Marquis Grissom*(FC)	.50	.40	.20
715	Greg Maddux	.15	.11	.06
716	Steve Balboni	.03	.02	.01
717	Ron Kakovice	.03	.02	.01
718	Gary Sheffield	.30	.25	.12
719	*Wally Whitehurst*(FC)	.15	.11	.06
720	Andres Galarraga	.15	.11	.06
721	Lee Mazzilli	.03	.02	.01
722	Felix Fermin	.03	.02	.01
723	Jeff Robinson	.05	.04	.02
724	Juan Bell(FC)	.10	.08	.04
725	Terry Pendleton	.07	.05	.03
726	Gene Nelson	.03	.02	.01
727	Pat Tabler	.05	.04	.02
728	Jim Acker	.03	.02	.01
729	Bobby Valentine	.03	.02	.01
730	Tony Gwynn	.20	.15	.08
731	Don Carman	.05	.04	.02
732	Ernie Riles	.03	.02	.01
733	John Dopson	.09	.07	.04
734	Kevin Elster	.06	.05	.02
735	Charlie Hough	.06	.05	.02
736	Rick Dempsey	.03	.02	.01
737	Chris Sabo	.15	.11	.06
738	*Gene Harris*	.10	.08	.04
739	Dale Sveum	.04	.03	.02
740	Jesse Barfield	.08	.06	.03
741	Steve Wilson	.10	.08	.04
742	Ernie Whitt	.05	.04	.02
743	Tom Candiotti	.05	.04	.02
744	*Kelly Mann*(FC)	.20	.15	.08
745	Hubie Brooks	.06	.05	.02
746	Dave Smith	.06	.05	.02
747	Randy Bush	.03	.02	.01
748	Doyle Alexander	.06	.05	.02
749	Mark Parent	.04	.03	.02
750	Dale Murphy	.10	.08	.04
751	Steve Lyons	.04	.03	.02
752	Tom Gordon	.25	.20	.10
753	Chris Speier	.03	.02	.01
754	Bob Walk	.05	.04	.02
755	Rafael Palmeiro	.08	.06	.03
756	Ken Howell	.03	.02	.01
757	*Larry Walker*(FC)	.40	.30	.15
758	Mark Thurmond	.03	.02	.01
759	Tom Trebelhorn	.03	.02	.01
760	Wade Boggs	.40	.30	.15
761	Mike Jackson	.05	.04	.02

		MT	NR MT	EX
762	Doug Dascenzo	.07	.05	.03
763	Denny Martinez	.07	.05	.03
764	Tim Teufel	.05	.04	.02
765	Chili Davis	.07	.05	.03
766	Brian Meyer(FC)	.10	.08	.04
767	Tracy Jones	.06	.05	.02
768	Chuck Crim	.04	.03	.02
769	*Greg Hibbard*(FC)	.30	.25	.12
770	Cory Snyder	.09	.07	.04
771	Pete Smith	.06	.05	.02
772	Jeff Reed	.03	.02	.01
773	Dave Leiper	.03	.02	.01
774	*Ben McDonald*(FC)	.80	.60	.30
775	Andy Van Slyke	.09	.07	.04
776	Charlie Leibrandt	.04	.03	.02
777	Tim Laudner	.03	.02	.01
778	Mike Jeffcoat	.03	.02	.01
779	Lloyd Moseby	.06	.05	.02
780	Orel Hershiser	.15	.11	.06
781	Mario Diaz	.03	.02	.01
782	Jose Alvarez	.03	.02	.01
783	Checklist 661-792	.03	.02	.01
784	Scott Bailes	.03	.02	.01
785	Jim Rice	.07	.05	.03
786	Eric King	.04	.03	.02
787	Rene Gonzales	.03	.02	.01
788	Frank DiPino	.03	.02	.01
789	John Wathan	.03	.02	.01
790	Gary Carter	.07	.05	.03
791	Alvaro Espinoza	.15	.11	.06
792	Gerald Perry	.06	.05	.02

1990 Topps All-Star Glossy Set of 22

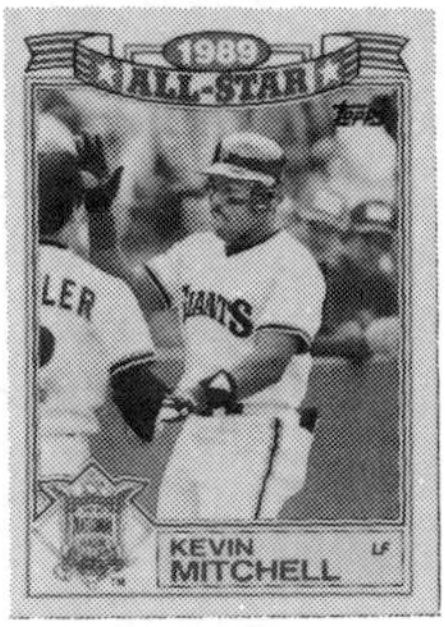

One glossy All-Star card was included in each 1990 Topps rack pack. The cards measure 2-1/2" by 3-1/2" and feature a similar style to past glossy All-Star cards. Special cards of All-Star team captains Carl Yastrzemski and Don Drysdale are included in the set.

		MT	NR MT	EX
Complete Set:		3.50	2.75	1.50
Common Player:		.12	.09	.05
1	Tom Lasorda	.12	.09	.05
2	Will Clark	.35	.25	.14
3	Ryne Sandberg	.30	.25	.12
4	Howard Johnson	.15	.11	.06
5	Ozzie Smith	.15	.11	.06
6	Kevin Mitchell	.25	.20	.10
7	Eric Davis	.25	.20	.10
8	Tony Gwynn	.20	.15	.08
9	Benny Santiago	.15	.11	.06
10	Rick Rueschel	.12	.09	.05
11	Don Drysdale	.12	.09	.05
12	Tony LaRussa	.12	.09	.05
13	Mark McGwire	.30	.25	.12
14	Julio Franco	.15	.11	.06
15	Wade Boggs	.25	.20	.10
16	Cal Ripken	.20	.15	.08
17	Bo Jackson	.60	.45	.25
18	Kirby Puckett	.25	.20	.10
19	Ruben Sierra	.25	.20	.10
20	Terry Steinbach	.12	.09	.05
21	Dave Stewart	.15	.11	.06
22	Carl Yastrzemski	.15	.11	.06

1990 Topps All Star Glossy Set of 60

Sharp color photographs and a clutter-free design are features of the cards in this 60-card send away set. Topps initiated the redemption series in 1983 and increased the size of the set to 60 in 1986. Six special offer cards, which were included in Topps baseball wax packs, are necessary to obtain each of the six 10-card sets in the series.

		MT	NR MT	EX
Complete Set:		9.00	6.75	3.50
Common Player:		.10	.08	.04
1	Ryne Sandberg	.70	.50	.30
2	Nolan Ryan	.70	.50	.30
3	Glenn Davis	.15	.11	.06
4	Dave Stewart	.15	.11	.06
5	Barry Larkin	.15	.11	.06
6	Carney Lansford	.15	.11	.06
7	Darryl Strawberry	.60	.45	.25
8	Steve Sax	.15	.11	.06
9	Carlos Martinez	.10	.08	.04
10	Gary Sheffield	.40	.30	.15
11	Don Mattingly	.80	.60	.30
12	Mark Grace	.40	.30	.15
13	Bret Saberhagen	.20	.15	.08
14	Mike Scott	.10	.08	.04
15	Robin Yount	.20	.15	.08
16	Ozzie Smith	.15	.11	.06
17	Jeff Ballard	.10	.08	.04
18	Rick Reuschel	.10	.08	.04
19	Greg Briley	.10	.08	.04
20	Ken Griffey,Jr.	1.75	1.25	.70
21	Kevin Mitchell	.30	.25	.12
22	Wade Boggs	.60	.45	.25
23	Doc Gooden	.50	.40	.20
24	George Bell	.15	.11	.06
25	Eric Davis	.40	.30	.15
26	Ruben Sierra	.25	.20	.10
27	Roberto Alomar	.20	.15	.08
28	Gary Gaetti	.15	.11	.06
29	Gregg Olson	.20	.15	.08
30	Tom Gordon	.20	.15	.08
31	Jose Canseco	.80	.60	.30
32	Pedro Guerrero	.15	.11	.06
33	Joe Carter	.15	.11	.06
34	Mike Scioscia	.10	.08	.04
35	Julio Franco	.15	.11	.06
36	Joe Magrane	.10	.08	.04
37	Rickey Henderson	.40	.30	.15
38	Rock Raines	.15	.11	.06
39	Jerome Walton	.35	.25	.14
40	Bob Geren	.10	.08	.04
41	Andre Dawson	.20	.15	.08
42	Mark McGwire	.60	.45	.25
43	Howard Johnson	.20	.15	.08
44	Bo Jackson	.80	.60	.30
45	Shawon Dunston	.20	.15	.08
46	Carlton Fisk	.20	.15	.08
47	Mitch Williams	.15	.11	.06
48	Kirby Puckett	.35	.25	.14
49	Craig Worthington	.10	.08	.04
50	Jim Abbott	.20	.15	.08
51	Cal Ripken	.25	.20	.10
52	Will Clark	.70	.50	.30
53	Dennis Eckersley	.20	.15	.08
54	Craig Biggio	.15	.11	.06
55	Fred McGriff	.20	.15	.08
56	Tony Gwynn	.20	.15	.08
57	Mickey Tettleton	.10	.08	.04
58	Mark Davis	.10	.08	.04
59	Omar Vizquel	.10	.08	.04
60	Gregg Jefferies	.30	.25	.12

Remember: All values quoted in this guide reflect the retail price of a card — the price a collector can expect to pay when buying a card from a dealer. The wholesale price — that which a collector can expect to receive from a dealer when selling a card — will be significantly lower, depending on desirability and condition of the particular card or cards.

1990 Topps Big Baseball

For the third consecutive year, Topps issued a 330-card set of the oversized cards (2-5/8" by 3-3/4"). The cards were issued in three 110-card series. The cards are reminiscent of Topps cards from the mid-1950s in that they feature players in portrait and action shots. The 1990 set has action photos in freeze frames. As in previous years, the cards are printed on white card stock with a glossy finish on the front. The card backs include 1989 and career hitting, fielding and pitching stats and a player cartoon.

		MT	NR MT	EX
Complete Set:		18.00	13.50	7.25
Common Player:		.05	.04	.02
1	Dwight Evans	.08	.06	.03
2	Kirby Puckett	.25	.20	.10
3	Kevin Gross	.06	.05	.02
4	Ron Hassey	.05	.04	.02
5	Lloyd McClendon	.05	.04	.02
6	Bo Jackson	1.00	.70	.40
7	Lonnie Smith	.06	.05	.02
8	Alvaro Espinoza	.06	.05	.02
9	Roberto Alomar	.15	.11	.06
10	Glenn Braggs	.06	.05	.02
11	David Cone	.10	.08	.04
12	Claudell Washington	.05	.04	.02
13	Pedro Guerrero	.10	.08	.04
14	Todd Benzinger	.06	.05	.02
15	Jeff Russell	.06	.05	.02
16	Terry Kennedy	.05	.04	.02

		MT	NR MT	EX
17	Kelly Gruber	.15	.11	.06
18	Alfredo Griffin	.05	.04	.02
19	Mark Grace	.20	.15	.08
20	Dave Winfield	.12	.09	.05
21	Bret Saberhagen	.15	.11	.06
22	Roger Clemens	.30	.25	.12
23	Bob Walk	.05	.04	.02
24	Dave Magadan	.15	.11	.06
25	Spike Owen	.06	.05	.02
26	Jody Davis	.05	.04	.02
27	Kent Hrbek	.12	.09	.05
28	Mark McGwire	.50	.40	.20
29	Eddie Murray	.15	.11	.06
30	Paul O'Neill	.06	.05	.02
31	Jose DeLeon	.06	.05	.02
32	Steve Lyons	.05	.04	.02
33	Dan Plesac	.06	.05	.02
34	Jack Howell	.05	.04	.02
35	Greg Briley	.06	.05	.02
36	Andy Hawkins	.06	.05	.02
37	Cecil Espy	.05	.04	.02
38	Rick Sutcliffe	.08	.06	.03
39	Jack Clark	.12	.09	.05
40	Dale Murphy	.12	.09	.05
41	Mike Henneman	.06	.05	.02
42	Rick Honeycutt	.05	.04	.02
43	Willie Randolph	.06	.05	.02
44	Marty Barrett	.06	.05	.02
45	Willie Wilson	.06	.05	.02
46	Wallace Johnson	.05	.04	.02
47	Greg Brock	.06	.05	.02
48	Tom Browning	.06	.05	.02
49	Gerald Young	.05	.04	.02
50	Dennis Eckersley	.15	.11	.06
51	Scott Garrelts	.06	.05	.02
52	Gary Redus	.05	.04	.02
53	Al Newman	.05	.04	.02
54	Darryl Boston	.05	.04	.02
55	Ron Oester	.05	.04	.02
56	Danny Tartabull	.08	.06	.03
57	Gregg Jefferies	.30	.25	.12
58	Tom Foley	.05	.04	.02
59	Robin Yount	.20	.15	.08
60	Pat Borders	.06	.05	.02
61	Mike Greenwell	.30	.25	.12
62	Shawon Dunston	.10	.08	.04
63	Steve Buechele	.05	.04	.02
64	Dave Stewart	.12	.09	.05
65	Jose Oquendo	.05	.04	.02
66	Ron Gant	.20	.15	.08
67	Mike Scioscia	.06	.05	.02
68	Randy Velarde	.05	.04	.02
69	Charlie Hayes	.06	.05	.02
70	Tim Wallach	.08	.06	.03
71	Eric Show	.06	.05	.02
72	Eric Davis	.25	.20	.10
73	Mike Gallego	.05	.04	.02
74	Rob Deer	.06	.05	.02
75	Ryne Sandberg	.40	.30	.15
76	Kevin Seitzer	.08	.06	.03
77	Wade Boggs	.50	.40	.20
78	Greg Gagne	.06	.05	.02
79	John Smiley	.06	.05	.02
80	Ivan Calderon	.08	.06	.03
81	Pete Incaviglia	.06	.05	.02
82	Orel Hershiser	.12	.09	.05
83	Carney Lansford	.08	.06	.03
84	Mike Fitzgerald	.05	.04	.02
85	Don Mattingly	.60	.45	.25
86	Chet Lemon	.06	.05	.02
87	Rolando Roomes	.05	.04	.02
88	Bill Spiers	.06	.05	.02
89	Pat Tabler	.06	.05	.02
90	Danny Heep	.05	.04	.02
91	Andre Dawson	.15	.11	.06
92	Randy Bush	.05	.04	.02
93	Tony Gwynn	.15	.11	.06
94	Tom Brunansky	.08	.06	.03
95	Johnny Ray	.06	.05	.02
96	Matt Williams	.15	.11	.06
97	Barry Lyons	.05	.04	.02
98	Jeff Hamilton	.05	.04	.02
99	Tom Glavine	.06	.05	.02
100	Ken Griffey,Sr.	.06	.05	.02
101	Tom Henke	.06	.05	.02
102	Dave Righetti	.08	.06	.03
103	Paul Molitor	.12	.09	.05
104	Mike LaValliere	.06	.05	.02
105	Frank White	.06	.05	.02
106	Bob Welch	.08	.06	.03
107	Ellis Burks	.25	.20	.10
108	Andres Galarraga	.08	.06	.03

		MT	NR MT	EX
109	Mitch Williams	.08	.06	.03
110	Checklist	.05	.04	.02
111	Craig Biggio	.08	.06	.03
112	Dave Steib	.08	.06	.03
113	Ron Darling	.06	.05	.02
114	Bert Blyleven	.10	.08	.04
115	Dickie Thon	.05	.04	.02
116	Carlos Martinez	.06	.05	.02
117	Jeff King	.06	.05	.02
118	Terry Steinbach	.06	.05	.02
119	Frank Tanana	.06	.05	.02
120	Mark Lemke	.06	.05	.02
121	Chris Sabo	.10	.08	.04
122	Glenn Davis	.15	.11	.06
123	Mel Hall	.06	.05	.02
124	Jim Gantner	.06	.05	.02
125	Benito Santiago	.10	.08	.04
126	Milt Thompson	.06	.05	.02
127	Rafael Palmeiro	.12	.09	.05
128	Barry Bonds	.20	.15	.08
129	Mike Bielecki	.06	.05	.02
130	Lou Whitaker	.10	.08	.04
131	Bob Ojeda	.05	.04	.02
132	Dion James	.05	.04	.02
133	Denny Martinez	.06	.05	.02
134	Fred McGriff	.20	.15	.08
135	Terry Pendleton	.06	.05	.02
136	Pat Combs	.10	.08	.04
137	Kevin Mitchell	.30	.25	.12
138	Marquis Grissom	.50	.40	.20
139	Chris Bosio	.06	.05	.02
140	Omar Vizquel	.05	.04	.02
141	Steve Sax	.10	.08	.04
142	Nelson Liriano	.05	.04	.02
143	Kevin Elster	.06	.05	.02
144	Dan Pasqua	.06	.05	.02
145	Dave Smith	.06	.05	.02
146	Craig Worthington	.06	.05	.02
147	Dan Gladden	.06	.05	.02
148	Oddibe McDowell	.05	.04	.02
149	Bip Roberts	.06	.05	.02
150	Randy Ready	.05	.04	.02
151	Dwight Smith	.10	.08	.04
152	Ed Whitson	.06	.05	.02
153	George Bell	.12	.09	.05
154	Tim Raines	.15	.11	.06
155	Sid Fernandez	.08	.06	.03
156	Henry Cotto	.05	.04	.02
157	Harold Baines	.12	.09	.05
158	Willie McGee	.10	.08	.04
159	Bill Doran	.06	.05	.02
160	Steve Balboni	.05	.04	.02
161	Pete Smith	.06	.05	.02
162	Frank Viola	.12	.09	.05
163	Gary Sheffield	.25	.20	.10
164	Bill Landrum	.06	.05	.02
165	Tony Fernandez	.08	.06	.03
166	Mike Heath	.05	.04	.02
167	Jody Reed	.08	.06	.03
168	Wally Joyner	.08	.06	.03
169	Robby Thompson	.06	.05	.02
170	Ken Caminiti	.06	.05	.02
171	Nolan Ryan	.40	.30	.15
172	Ricky Jordan	.08	.06	.03
173	Lance Blankenship	.05	.04	.02
174	Dwight Gooden	.30	.25	.12
175	Ruben Sierra	.20	.15	.08
176	Carlton Fisk	.15	.11	.06
177	Garry Templeton	.06	.05	.02
178	Mike Devereaux	.06	.05	.02
179	Mookie Wilson	.06	.05	.02
180	Jeff Blauser	.06	.05	.02
181	Scott Bradley	.05	.04	.02
182	Luis Salazar	.05	.04	.02
183	Rafael Ramirez	.06	.05	.02
184	Vince Coleman	.08	.06	.03
185	Doug Drabek	.10	.08	.04
186	Darryl Strawberry	.30	.25	.12
187	Tim Burke	.06	.05	.02
188	Jesse Barfield	.08	.06	.03
189	Barry Larkin	.15	.11	.06
190	Alan Trammell	.10	.08	.04
191	Steve Lake	.05	.04	.02
192	Derek Lilliquist	.06	.05	.02
193	Don Robinson	.06	.05	.02
194	Kevin McReynolds	.08	.06	.03
195	Melido Perez	.06	.05	.02
196	Jose Lind	.06	.05	.02
197	Eric Anthony	.50	.40	.20
198	B.J. Surhoff	.06	.05	.02
199	John Olerud	1.00	.70	.40

		MT	NR MT	EX
200	Mike Moore	.06	.05	.02
201	Mark Gubicza	.08	.06	.03
202	Phil Bradley	.06	.05	.02
203	Ozzie Smith	.12	.09	.05
204	Greg Maddux	.08	.06	.03
205	Julio Franco	.12	.09	.05
206	Tom Herr	.06	.05	.02
207	Scott Fletcher	.05	.04	.02
208	Bobby Bonilla	.15	.11	.06
209	Bob Geren	.06	.05	.02
210	Junior Felix	.20	.15	.08
211	Dick Schofield	.05	.04	.02
212	Jim Deshaies	.06	.05	.02
213	Jose Uribe	.06	.05	.02
214	John Kruk	.06	.05	.02
215	Ozzie Guillen	.08	.06	.03
216	Howard Johnson	.10	.08	.04
217	Andy Van Slyke	.08	.06	.03
218	Tim Laudner	.05	.04	.02
219	Manny Lee	.06	.05	.02
220	Checklist	.05	.04	.02
221	Cory Snyder	.08	.06	.03
222	Billy Hatcher	.06	.05	.02
223	Bud Black	.05	.04	.02
224	Will Clark	.40	.30	.15
225	Kevin Tapani	.20	.15	.08
226	Mike Pagliarulo	.06	.05	.02
227	Dave Parker	.12	.09	.05
228	Ben McDonald	1.00	.70	.40
229	Carlos Baerga	.50	.40	.20
230	Roger McDowell	.06	.05	.02
231	Delino DeShields	.50	.40	.20
232	Mark Langston	.10	.08	.04
233	Wally Backman	.06	.05	.02
234	Jim Eisenreich	.06	.05	.02
235	Mike Schooler	.06	.05	.02
236	Kevin Bass	.06	.05	.02
237	John Farrell	.05	.04	.02
238	Kal Daniels	.10	.08	.04
239	Tony Phillips	.06	.05	.02
240	Todd Stottlemyre	.06	.05	.02
241	Greg Olson	.15	.11	.06
242	Charlie Hough	.06	.05	.02
243	Mariano Duncan	.06	.05	.02
244	Billy Ripken	.05	.04	.02
245	Joe Carter	.12	.09	.05
246	Tim Belcher	.08	.06	.03
247	Roberto Kelly	.08	.06	.03
248	Candy Maldonado	.08	.06	.03
249	Mike Scott	.08	.06	.03
250	Ken Griffey,Jr.	1.25	.90	.50
251	Nick Esasky	.06	.05	.02
252	Tom Gordon	.15	.11	.06
253	John Tudor	.06	.05	.02
254	Gary Gaetti	.10	.08	.04
255	Neal Heaton	.06	.05	.02
256	Jerry Browne	.06	.05	.02
257	Joe Rijo	.06	.05	.02
258	Mike Boddicker	.06	.05	.02
259	Brett Butler	.06	.05	.02
260	Andy Benes	.10	.08	.04
261	Kevin Brown	.08	.06	.03
262	Hubie Brooks	.08	.06	.03
263	Randy Milligan	.06	.05	.02
264	John Franco	.10	.08	.04
265	Sandy Alomar	.30	.25	.12
266	Dave Valle	.06	.05	.02
267	Jerome Walton	.25	.20	.10
268	Bob Boone	.08	.06	.03
269	Ken Howell	.06	.05	.02
270	Jose Canseco	1.00	.70	.40
271	Joe Magrane	.08	.06	.03
272	Brian DuBois	.08	.06	.03
273	Carlos Quintana	.08	.06	.03
274	Lance Johnson	.06	.05	.02
275	Steve Bedrosian	.06	.05	.02
276	Brook Jacoby	.08	.06	.03
277	Fred Lynn	.06	.05	.02
278	Jeff Ballard	.06	.05	.02
279	Otis Nixon	.05	.04	.02
280	Chili Davis	.06	.05	.02
281	Joe Oliver	.12	.09	.05
282	Brian Holman	.08	.06	.03
283	Juan Samuel	.08	.06	.03
284	Rick Aguilera	.06	.05	.02
285	Jeff Reardon	.08	.06	.03
286	Sammy Sosa	.30	.25	.12
287	Carmelo Martinez	.06	.05	.02
288	Greg Swindell	.08	.06	.03
289	Erik Hanson	.15	.11	.06
290	Tony Pena	.08	.06	.03
291	Pascual Perez	.06	.05	.02
292	Rickey Henderson	.35	.25	.14
293	Kurt Stillwell	.06	.05	.02
294	Todd Zeile	.50	.40	.20
295	Bobby Thigpen	.10	.08	.04
296	Larry Walker	.30	.25	.12
297	Rob Murphy	.05	.04	.02
298	Mitch Webster	.05	.04	.02
299	Devon White	.06	.05	.02
300	Len Dykstra	.10	.08	.04
301	Keith Hernandez	.06	.05	.02
302	Gene Larkin	.06	.05	.02
303	Jeffrey Leonard	.06	.05	.02
304	Jim Presley	.06	.05	.02
305	Lloyd Moseby	.08	.06	.03
306	John Smoltz	.08	.06	.03
307	Sam Horn	.06	.05	.02
308	Greg Litton	.06	.05	.02
309	Dave Henderson	.08	.06	.03
310	Mark McLemore	.05	.04	.02
311	Gary Pettis	.06	.05	.02
312	Mark Davis	.05	.04	.02
313	Cecil Fielder	.50	.40	.20
314	Jack Armstrong	.08	.06	.03
315	Alvin Davis	.08	.06	.03
316	Doug Jones	.08	.06	.03
317	Eric Yelding	.08	.06	.03
318	Joe Orsulak	.06	.05	.02
319	Chuck Finley	.08	.06	.03
320	Glenn Wilson	.06	.05	.02
321	Harold Reynolds	.08	.06	.03
322	Teddy Higuera	.08	.06	.03
323	Lance Parrish	.08	.06	.03
324	Bruce Hurst	.06	.05	.02
325	Dave West	.06	.05	.02
326	Kirk Gibson	.10	.08	.04
327	Cal Ripken	.15	.11	.06
328	Rick Reuschel	.06	.05	.02
329	Jim Abbott	.15	.11	.06
330	Checklist	.05	.04	.02

1990 Topps Box Panels

This special 16-card set features four cards on four different box-bottom panels. The cards are identical in design to the regular 1990 Topps cards. The cards are designated by letter.

		MT	NR MT	EX
Complete Panel Set:		3.00	2.25	1.25
Complete Singles Set:		1.50	1.25	.60
Common Panel:		.40	.30	.15
Common Single Player:		.06	.05	.02
	Panel	.60	.45	.25
A	Wade Boggs	.25	.20	.10
B	George Brett	.20	.15	.08
C	Andre Dawson	.15	.11	.06
D	Darrell Evans	.06	.05	.02
	Panel	.60	.45	.25
E	Doc Gooden	.25	.20	.10
F	Rickey Henderson	.25	.20	.10
G	Tom Lasorda	.06	.05	.02
H	Fred Lynn	.06	.05	.02
	Panel	.40	.30	.15
I	Mark McGwire	.25	.20	.10
J	Dave Parker	.10	.08	.04
K	Jeff Reardon	.06	.05	.02

		MT	NR MT	EX
L	Rick Reuschel	.06	.05	.02
	Panel	.60	.45	.25
M	Jim Rice	.06	.05	.02
N	Cal Ripken	.10	.08	.04
O	Nolan Ryan	.25	.20	.10
P	Ryne Sandberg	.25	.20	.10

1990 Topps Traded

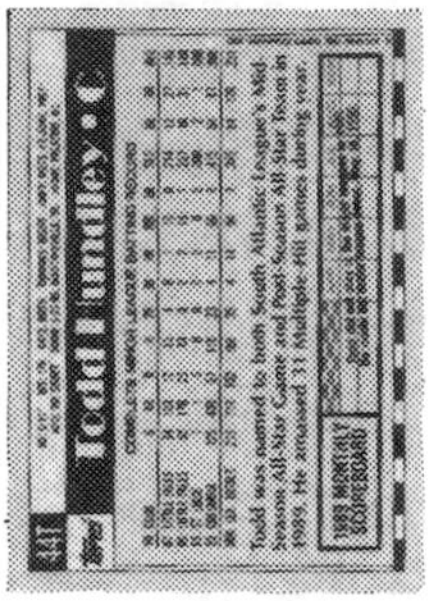

For the first time, Topps "Traded" series cards were made available nationwide in retail wax packs. The 132-card set was also sold in complete boxed form as it has been in recent years. The wax pack traded cards feature gray backs, while the boxed set cards feature white backs. The cards are numbered 1T-132T and showcase rookies, players who changed teams and new managers.

		MT	NR MT	EX
Complete Set:		16.00	12.00	6.50
Common Player:		.05	.04	.02
1T	Darrel Akerfelds	.05	.04	.02
2T	Sandy Alomar,Jr.	.20	.15	.08
3T	Brad Arnsberg	.05	.04	.02
4T	Steve Avery	.50	.40	.20
5T	Wally Backman	.05	.04	.02
6T	Carlos Baerga(FC)	.40	.30	.15
7T	Kevin Bass	.06	.05	.02
8T	Willie Blair(FC)	.10	.08	.04
9T	Mike Blowers(FC)	.20	.15	.08
10T	Shawn Boskie(FC)	.20	.15	.08
11T	Daryl Boston	.05	.04	.02
12T	Dennis Boyd	.06	.05	.02
13T	Glenn Braggs	.06	.05	.02
14T	Hubie Brooks	.08	.06	.03
15T	Tom Brunansky	.08	.06	.03
16T	John Burkett(FC)	.25	.20	.10
17T	Casey Candaele	.05	.04	.02
18T	John Candelaria	.06	.05	.02
19T	Gary Carter	.10	.08	.04
20T	Joe Carter	.10	.08	.04
21T	Rick Cerone	.05	.04	.02
22T	Scott Coolbaugh(FC)	.15	.11	.06
23T	Bobby Cox	.05	.04	.02
24T	Mark Davis	.06	.05	.02
25T	Storm Davis	.06	.05	.02
26T	Edgar Diaz(FC)	.10	.08	.04
27T	Wayne Edwards(FC)	.20	.15	.08
28T	Mark Eichhorn	.05	.04	.02
29T	Scott Erickson(FC)	4.00	3.00	1.50
30T	Nick Esasky	.06	.05	.02
31T	Cecil Fielder	.50	.40	.20
32T	John Franco	.08	.06	.03
33T	Travis Fryman(FC)	1.25	.90	.50
34T	Bill Gullickson	.05	.04	.02
35T	Darryl Hamilton	.15	.11	.06
36T	Mike Harkey	.20	.15	.08
37T	Bud Harrelson	.05	.04	.02
38T	Billy Hatcher	.06	.05	.02
39T	Keith Hernandez	.08	.06	.03
40T	Joe Hesketh	.05	.04	.02
41T	Dave Hollins(FC)	.25	.20	.10
42T	Sam Horn	.08	.06	.03
43T	Steve Howard(FC)	.20	.15	.08
44T	Todd Hundley(FC)	.25	.20	.10
45T	Jeff Huson	.10	.08	.04
46T	Chris James	.05	.04	.02
47T	Stan Javier	.05	.04	.02
48T	Dave Justice(FC)	2.50	2.00	1.00
49T	Jeff Kaiser(FC)	.12	.09	.05
50T	Dana Kiecker(FC)	.20	.15	.08
51T	Joe Klink(FC)	.10	.08	.04
52T	Brent Knackert(FC)	.12	.09	.05
53T	Brad Komminsk	.05	.04	.02
54T	Mark Langston	.10	.08	.04
55T	Tim Layana(FC)	.25	.20	.10
56T	Rick Leach	.05	.04	.02
57T	Terry Leach	.05	.04	.02
58T	Tim Leary	.05	.04	.02
59T	Craig Lefferts	.05	.04	.02
60T	Charlie Leibrandt	.05	.04	.02
61T	Jim Leyritz(FC)	.20	.15	.08
62T	Fred Lynn	.06	.05	.02
63T	Kevin Maas(FC)	2.00	1.50	.80
64T	Shane Mack	.08	.06	.03
65T	Candy Maldonado	.06	.05	.02
66T	Fred Manrique	.05	.04	.02
67T	Mike Marshall	.05	.04	.02
68T	Carmelo Martinez	.05	.04	.02
69T	John Marzano	.06	.05	.02
70T	Ben McDonald	1.00	.70	.40
71T	Jack McDowell	.08	.06	.03
72T	John McNamara	.05	.04	.02
73T	Orlando Mercado	.05	.04	.02
74T	Stump Merrill	.05	.04	.02
75T	Alan Mills(FC)	.20	.15	.08
76T	Hal Morris	.40	.30	.15
77T	Lloyd Moseby	.06	.05	.02
78T	Randy Myers	.08	.06	.03
79T	Tim Naehring(FC)	.35	.25	.14
80T	Junior Noboa	.06	.05	.02
81T	Matt Nokes	.06	.05	.02
82T	Pete O'Brien	.05	.04	.02
83T	John Olerud(FC)	1.25	.90	.50
84T	Greg Olson(FC)	.15	.11	.06
85T	Junior Ortiz	.05	.04	.02
86T	Dave Parker	.15	.11	.06
87T	Rick Parker(FC)	.15	.11	.06
88T	Bob Patterson	.05	.04	.02
89T	Alejandro Pena	.05	.04	.02
90T	Tony Pena	.08	.06	.03
91T	Pascual Perez	.05	.04	.02
92T	Gerald Perry	.05	.04	.02
93T	Dan Petry	.05	.04	.02
94T	Gary Pettis	.06	.05	.02
95T	Tony Phillips	.05	.04	.02
96T	Lou Pinella	.05	.04	.02
97T	Luis Polonia	.05	.04	.02
98T	Jim Presley	.06	.05	.02
99T	Scott Radinsky(FC)	.25	.20	.10
100T	Willie Randolph	.08	.06	.03
101T	Jeff Reardon	.08	.06	.03
102T	Greg Riddoch	.05	.04	.02
103T	Jeff Robinson	.05	.04	.02
104T	Ron Robinson	.05	.04	.02
105T	Kevin Romine	.05	.04	.02
106T	Scott Ruskin(FC)	.20	.15	.08
107T	John Russell	.05	.04	.02
108T	Bill Sampen(FC)	.20	.15	.08
109T	Juan Samuel	.08	.06	.03
110T	Scott Sanderson	.06	.05	.02
111T	Jack Savage(FC)	.10	.08	.04
112T	Dave Schmidt	.05	.04	.02
113T	Red Schoendienst	.05	.04	.02
114T	Terry Shumpert(FC)	.20	.15	.08
115T	Matt Sinatro	.05	.04	.02
116T	Don Slaught	.05	.04	.02
117T	Bryn Smith	.05	.04	.02
118T	Lee Smith	.08	.06	.03
119T	Paul Sorrento(FC)	.20	.15	.08
120T	Franklin Stubbs	.05	.04	.02
121T	Russ Swan(FC)	.20	.15	.08
122T	Bob Tewksbury	.05	.04	.02
123T	Wayne Tolleson	.05	.04	.02
124T	John Tudor	.06	.05	.02
125T	Randy Veres(FC)	.10	.08	.04
126T	Hector Villanueva(FC)	.20	.15	.08
127T	Mitch Webster	.05	.04	.02
128T	Ernie Whitt	.06	.05	.02
129T	Frank Wills	.06	.05	.02
130T	Dave Winfield	.15	.11	.06
131T	Matt Young	.05	.04	.02
132T	Checklist	.05	.04	.02

NOTE: A card number in parentheses ( ) indicates the set is unnumbered.

1991 Topps

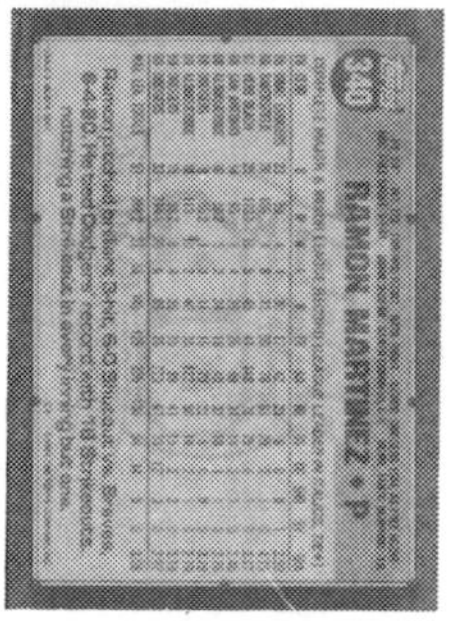

Topps celebrated its 40th anniversary in 1991 with the biggest promotional campaign in baseball card history. More than 300,000 vintage Topps cards (or certificates which can be redeemed for valuable older cards) produced from 1952 to present were randomly inserted in packs. Also a grand prize winner will receive one complete set from each year, and others will receive a single set from 1952-present. The 1991 Topps card fronts feature the "Topps 40 Years of Baseball" logo in the upper left corner. Card borders frame the player photos. All players of the same team have cards with the same frame/border colors. Both action and posed shots appear in full-color on the card fronts. The flip sides are printed horizontally and feature complete statistics. Record Breakers and other special cards were once again included in the set. The cards measure 2-1/2" by 3-1/2". Several cards feature horizontal fronts.

		MT	NR MT	EX
Complete Set:		22.00	16.50	8.75
Common Player:		.03	.02	.01
1	Nolan Ryan	.30	.25	.12
2	Record Breaker (George Brett)	.08	.06	.03
3	Record Breaker (Carlton Fisk)	.08	.06	.03
4	Record Breaker (Kevin Maas)	.10	.08	.04
5	Record Breaker (Cal Ripken)	.08	.04	.02
6	Record Breaker (Nolan Ryan)	.20	.15	.08
7	Record Breaker (Ryne Sandberg)	.10	.08	.04
8	Record Breaker (Bobby Thigpen)	.08	.06	.03
9	Darrin Fletcher(FC)	.10	.08	.04
10	Gregg Olson	.08	.06	.03
11	Roberto Kelly	.08	.06	.03
12	Paul Assenmacher	.04	.03	.02
13	Mariano Duncan	.06	.05	.02
14	Dennis Lamp	.03	.02	.01
15	Von Hayes	.08	.06	.03
16	Mike Heath	.04	.03	.02
17	Jeff Brantley	.06	.05	.02
18	Nelson Liriano	.03	.02	.01
19	Jeff Robinson	.04	.03	.02
20	Pedro Guerrero	.08	.06	.03
21	Joe Morgan	.03	.02	.01
22	Storm Davis	.06	.05	.02
23	Jim Gantner	.04	.03	.02
24	Dave Martinez	.05	.04	.02
25	Tim Belcher	.08	.06	.03
26	Luis Sojo	.06	.05	.02
27	Bobby Witt	.08	.06	.03
28	Alvaro Espinoza	.05	.04	.02
29	Bob Walk	.03	.02	.01
30	Gregg Jefferies	.15	.11	.06
31	*Colby Ward*(FC)	.15	.11	.06
32	*Mike Simms*(FC)	.20	.15	.08
33	Barry Jones	.05	.04	.02
34	Atlee Hammaker	.03	.02	.01
35	Greg Maddux	.08	.06	.03
36	Donnie Hill	.03	.02	.01
37	Tom Bolton	.05	.04	.02
38	Scott Bradley	.03	.02	.01
39	*Jim Neidlinger*(FC)	.15	.11	.06
40	Kevin Mitchell	.20	.15	.08
41	Ken Dayley	.04	.03	.02
42	*Chris Hoiles*(FC)	.15	.11	.06
43	Roger McDowell	.06	.05	.02

		MT	NR MT	EX
44	Mike Felder	.04	.03	.02
45	Chris Sabo	.10	.08	.04
46	Tim Drummond	.06	.05	.02
47	Brook Jacoby	.06	.05	.02
48	Dennis Boyd	.05	.04	.02
49a	Pat Borders (40 stolen bases in 1986)	.20	.15	.06
49b	Pat Borders (0 stolen bases in 1986)	.15	.11	.06
50	Bob Welch	.08	.06	.03
51	Art Howe	.03	.02	.01
52	*Francisco Oliveras*(FC)	.10	.08	.04
53	Mike Sahrperson	.06	.05	.02
54	Gary Mielke	.05	.04	.02
55	Jeffrey Leonard	.05	.04	.02
56	Jeff Parrett	.04	.03	.02
57	Jack Howell	.04	.03	.02
58	Mel Stottlemyre	.08	.06	.03
59	Eric Yelding	.06	.05	.02
60	Frank Viola	.12	.09	.05
61	Stan Javier	.04	.03	.02
62	Lee Guetterman	.03	.02	.01
63	Milt Thompson	.04	.03	.02
64	Tom Herr	.05	.04	.02
65	Bruce Hurst	.06	.05	.02
66	Terry Kennedy	.03	.02	.01
67	Rick Honeycutt	.03	.02	.01
68	Gary Sheffield	.15	.11	.06
69	Steve Wilson	.06	.05	.02
70	Ellis Burks	.15	.11	.06
71	Jim Acker	.03	.02	.01
72	Junior Ortiz	.03	.02	.01
73	Craig Worthington	.06	.05	.02
74	#1 Draft Pick *(Shane Andrews)*(FC)	.30	.25	.12
75	Jack Morris	.08	.06	.03
76	Jerry Browne	.05	.04	.02
77	Drew Hall	.03	.02	.01
78	Geno Petralli	.03	.02	.01
79	Frank Thomas	1.00	.70	.40
80a	Fernando Valenzuela (italics error)	.25	.20	.10
80b	Fernando Valenzuela (correct italics)	.15	.11	.06
81	Cito Gaston	.03	.02	.01
82	Tom Glavine	.05	.04	.02
83	Daryl Boston	.03	.02	.01
84	Bob McClure	.03	.02	.01
85	Jesse Barfield	.08	.06	.03
86	Les Lancaster	.04	.03	.02
87	Tracy Jones	.03	.02	.01
88	Bob Tewksbury	.04	.03	.02
89	Darren Daulton	.06	.05	.02
90	Danny Tartabull	.08	.06	.03
91	*Greg Colbrunn*(FC)	.15	.11	.06
92	Danny Jackson	.06	.05	.02
93	Ivan Calderon	.08	.06	.03
94	John Dopson	.05	.04	.02
95	Paul Molitor	.10	.08	.04
96	Trevor Wilson	.04	.03	.02
97	Brady Anderson	.04	.03	.02
98	Sergio Valdez	.05	.04	.02
99	Chris Gwynn	.05	.04	.02
100a	Don Mattingly (10 hits in 1990)	1.00	.70	.40
100b	Don Mattingly (101 hits in 1990)	.40	.30	.15
101	Rob Ducey	.04	.03	.02
102	Gene Larkin	.06	.05	.02
103	#1 Draft Pick *(Tim Costo)*(FC)	.35	.25	.14
104	Don Robinson	.04	.03	.02
105	Keith Miller	.05	.04	.02
106	Ed Nunez	.03	.02	.01
107	Luis Polonia	.04	.03	.02
108	Matt Young	.04	.03	.02
109	Greg Riddoch	.03	.02	.01
110	Tom Henke	.06	.05	.02
111	Andres Thomas	.03	.02	.01
112	Frank DiPino	.03	.02	.01
113	#1 Draft Pick *(Carl Everett)*(FC)	.35	.25	.14
114	*Lance Dickson*(FC)	.40	.30	.15
115	Hubie Brooks	.08	.06	.03
116	Mark Davis	.05	.04	.02
117	Dion James	.03	.02	.01
118	*Tom Edens*(FC)	.10	.08	.04
119	Carl Nichols(FC)	.05	.04	.02
120	Joe Carter	.08	.06	.03
121	Eric King	.05	.04	.02
122	Paul O'Neill	.06	.05	.02
123	Greg Harris	.05	.04	.02
124	Randy Bush	.04	.03	.02
125	Steve Bedrosian	.06	.05	.02
126	*Bernard Gilkey*(FC)	.20	.15	.08
127	Joe Price	.03	.02	.01

		MT	NR MT	EX
128	*Travis Fryman*	.50	.40	.20
129	Mark Eichhorn	.03	.02	.01
130	Ozzie Smith	.08	.06	.03
131	Checklist 1	.03	.02	.01
132	Jamie Quirk	.03	.02	.01
133	Greg Briley	.08	.06	.03
134	Kevin Elster	.04	.03	.02
135	Jerome Walton	.08	.06	.03
136	Dave Schmidt	.03	.02	.01
137	Randy Ready	.03	.02	.01
138	Jamie Moyer	.04	.03	.02
139	Jeff Treadway	.05	.04	.02
140	Fred McGriff	.10	.08	.04
141	Nick Leyva	.03	.02	.01
142	Curtis Wilkerson	.04	.03	.02
143	John Smiley	.04	.03	.02
144	Dave Henderson	.06	.05	.02
145	Lou Whitaker	.08	.06	.03
146	Dan Plesac	.06	.05	.02
147	*Carlos Baerga*	.20	.15	.08
148	Rey Palacios	.04	.03	.02
149	*Al Osuna*(FC)	.15	.11	.06
150	Cal Ripken	.12	.09	.05
151	Tom Browning	.06	.05	.02
152	Mickey Hatcher	.04	.03	.02
153	Bryan Harvey	.06	.05	.02
154	Jay Buhner	.06	.05	.02
155	Dwight Evans	.08	.06	.03
156	Carlos Martinez	.06	.05	.02
157	John Smoltz	.08	.06	.03
158	Jose Uribe	.04	.03	.02
159	Joe Boever	.03	.02	.01
160	Vince Coleman	.08	.06	.03
161	Tim Leary	.04	.03	.02
162	*Ozzie Canseco*(FC)	.15	.11	.06
163	Dave Johnson	.04	.03	.02
164	Edgar Diaz	.05	.04	.02
165	Sandy Alomar	.15	.11	.06
166	Harold Baines	.08	.06	.03
167	*Randy Tomlin*(FC)	.25	.20	.10
168	John Olerud	.30	.25	.12
169	Luis Aquino	.04	.03	.02
170	Carlton Fisk	.10	.08	.04
171	Tony LaRussa	.04	.03	.02
172	Pete Incaviglia	.06	.05	.02
173	Jason Grimsley	.06	.05	.02
174	Ken Caminiti	.05	.04	.02
175	Jack Armstrong	.08	.06	.03
176	John Orton(FC)	.06	.05	.02
177	*Reggie Harris*(FC)	.15	.11	.06
178	Dave Valle	.04	.03	.02
179	Pete Harnisch	.06	.05	.02
180	Tony Gwynn	.12	.09	.05
181	Duane Ward	.04	.03	.02
182	Junior Noboa	.04	.03	.02
183	Clay Parker	.04	.03	.02
184	Gary Green	.10	.08	.04
185	Joe Magrane	.06	.05	.02
186	Rod Booker	.03	.02	.01
187	Greg Cadaret	.03	.02	.01
188	Damon Berryhill	.06	.05	.02
189	*Daryl Irvine*(FC)	.15	.11	.06
190	Matt Williams	.15	.11	.06
191	*Willie Blair*	.10	.08	.04
192	Rob Deer	.06	.05	.02
193	Felix Fermin	.03	.02	.01
194	Xavier Hernandez(FC)	.08	.06	.03
195	Wally Joyner	.10	.08	.04
196	*Jim Vatcher*(FC)	.12	.09	.05
197	*Chris Nabholz*(FC)	.20	.15	.08
198	R.J. Reynolds	.04	.03	.02
199	Mike Hartley(FC)	.15	.11	.06
200	Darryl Strawberry	.20	.15	.08
201	Tom Kelly	.03	.02	.01
202	*Jim Leyritz*	.12	.09	.05
203	Gene Harris	.05	.04	.02
204	Herm Winningham	.04	.03	.02
205	*Mike Perez*(FC)	.15	.11	.06
206	Carlos Quintana	.08	.06	.03
207	Gary Wayne	.05	.04	.02
208	Willie Wilson	.06	.05	.02
209	Ken Howell	.05	.04	.02
210	Lance Parrish	.08	.06	.03
211	*Brian Barnes*(FC)	.20	.15	.08
212	Steve Finley	.06	.05	.02
213	Frank Wills	.06	.05	.02
214	Joe Girardi	.06	.05	.02
215	Dave Smith	.06	.05	.02
216	Greg Gagne	.04	.03	.02
217	Chris Bosio	.05	.04	.02
218	*Rick Parker*	.03	.02	.01

		MT	NR MT	EX
219	Jack McDowell	.06	.05	.02
220	Tim Wallach	.08	.06	.03
221	Don Slaught	.04	.03	.02
222	*Brian McRae*(FC)	.60	.45	.25
223	Allan Anderson	.04	.03	.02
224	Juan Gonzalez	.35	.25	.14
225	Randy Johnson	.06	.05	.02
226	Alfredo Griffin	.04	.03	.02
227	Steve Avery	.15	.11	.06
228	Rex Hudler	.04	.03	.02
229	Rance Mulliniks	.03	.02	.01
230	Sid Fernandez	.08	.06	.03
231	Doug Rader	.03	.02	.01
232	Jose DeJesus	.08	.06	.03
233	Al Leiter	.03	.02	.01
234	*Scott Erickson*	.80	.60	.30
235	Dave Parker	.10	.08	.04
236	Frank Tanana	.06	.05	.02
237	Rick Cerone	.03	.02	.01
238	Mike Dunne	.03	.02	.01
239	*Darren Lewis*(FC)	.30	.25	.12
240	Mike Scott	.08	.06	.03
241	Dave Clark	.04	.03	.02
242	Mike LaCoss	.03	.02	.01
243	Lance Johnson	.06	.05	.02
244	Mike Jeffcoat	.03	.02	.01
245	Kal Daniels	.08	.06	.03
246	Kevin Wickander	.05	.04	.02
247	Jody Reed	.08	.06	.03
248	Tom Gordon	.08	.06	.03
249	Bob Melvin	.03	.02	.01
250	Dennis Eckersley	.10	.08	.04
251	Mark Lemke	.05	.04	.02
252	*Mel Rojas*(FC)	.15	.11	.06
253	Garry Templeton	.04	.03	.02
254	*Shawn Boskie*	.15	.11	.06
255	Brian Downing	.05	.04	.02
256	Greg Hibbard	.08	.06	.03
257	Tom O'Malley	.03	.02	.01
258	Chris Hammond(FC)	.15	.11	.06
259	Hensley Meulens	.08	.06	.03
260	Harold Reynolds	.06	.05	.02
261	Bud Harrelson	.03	.02	.01
262	Tim Jones	.04	.03	.02
263	Checklist 2	.03	.02	.01
264	*Dave Hollins*	.15	.11	.06
265	Mark Gubicza	.06	.05	.02
266	Carmen Castillo	.03	.02	.01
267	Mark Knudson	.03	.02	.01
268	Tom Brookens	.04	.03	.02
269	Joe Hesketh	.03	.02	.01
270	Mark McGwire	.25	.20	.10
271	*Omar Olivares*(FC)	.15	.11	.06
272	Jeff King	.06	.05	.02
273	Johnny Ray	.05	.04	.02
274	Ken Williams	.03	.02	.01
275	Alan Trammell	.10	.08	.04
276	Bill Swift	.05	.04	.02
277	Scott Coolbaugh	.06	.05	.02
278	*Alex Fernandez*(FC)	.60	.45	.25
279a	Jose Gonzalez (photo of Billy Bean)	.20	.15	.08
279b	Jose Gonzalez (correct photo)	.12	.09	.05
280	Bret Saberhagen	.08	.06	.03
281	Larry Sheets	.04	.03	.02
282	Don Carman	.04	.03	.02
283	Marquis Grissom	.10	.08	.04
284	Bill Spiers	.06	.05	.02
285	Jim Abbott	.10	.08	.04
286	Ken Oberkfell	.04	.03	.02
287	Mark Grant	.03	.02	.01
288	Derrick May(FC)	.40	.30	.15
289	Tim Birtsas	.03	.02	.01
290	Steve Sax	.08	.06	.03
291	John Wathan	.03	.02	.01
292	Bud Black	.04	.03	.02
293	Jay Bell	.06	.05	.02
294	Mike Moore	.06	.05	.02
295	Rafael Palmeiro	.08	.06	.03
296	Mark Williamson	.04	.03	.02
297	Manny Lee	.04	.03	.02
298	Omar Vizquel	.04	.03	.02
299	*Scott Radinsky*	.15	.11	.06
300	Kirby Puckett	.15	.11	.06
301	Steve Farr	.04	.03	.02
302	Tim Teufel	.03	.02	.01
303	Mike Boddicker	.06	.05	.02
304	Kevin Reimer(FC)	.10	.08	.04
305	Mike Scioscia	.06	.05	.02
306	Lonnie Smith	.06	.05	.02
307	Andy Benes	.08	.06	.03

		MT	NR MT	EX
308	Tom Pagnozzi	.04	.03	.02
309	Norm Charlton	.08	.06	.03
310	Gary Carter	.08	.06	.03
311	Jeff Pico	.03	.02	.01
312	Charlie Hayes	.06	.05	.02
313	Ron Robinson	.06	.05	.02
314	Gary Pettis	.04	.03	.02
315	Roberto Alomar	.10	.08	.04
316	Gene Nelson	.03	.02	.01
317	Mike Fitzgerald	.03	.02	.01
318	Rick Aguilera	.06	.05	.02
319	Jeff McKnight(FC)	.06	.05	.02
320	Tony Fernandez	.08	.06	.03
321	Bob Rodgers	.03	.02	.01
322	*Terry Shumpert*	.15	.11	.06
323	Cory Snyder	.08	.06	.03
324	Ron Kittle	.08	.06	.03
325	Brett Butler	.06	.05	.02
326	Ken Patterson	.04	.03	.02
327	Ron Hassey	.03	.02	.01
328	Walt Terrell	.04	.03	.02
329	Dave Justice	.80	.60	.30
330	Doc Gooden	.20	.15	.08
331	Eric Anthony	.10	.08	.04
332	Kenny Rogers	.06	.05	.02
333	#1 Draft Pick *(Chipper Jones)*(FC)	.30	.25	.12
334	Todd Benzinger	.05	.04	.02
335	Mitch Williams	.08	.06	.03
336	Matt Nokes	.06	.05	.02
337	Keith Comstock	.03	.02	.01
338	Luis Rivera	.04	.03	.02
339	Larry Walker	.08	.06	.03
340	Ramon Martinez	.15	.11	.06
341	John Moses	.03	.02	.01
342	*Mickey Morandini*	.15	.11	.06
343	Jose Oquendo	.04	.03	.02
344	Jeff Russell	.06	.05	.02
345	Jose DeJesus	.06	.05	.02
346	Jesse Orosco	.04	.03	.02
347	Greg Vaughn	.10	.08	.04
348	Todd Stottlemyre	.06	.05	.02
349	Dave Gallagher	.04	.03	.02
350	Glenn Davis	.12	.09	.05
351	Joe Torre	.03	.02	.01
352	Frank White	.06	.05	.02
353	Tony Castillo	.05	.04	.02
354	Sid Bream	.05	.04	.02
355	Chili Davis	.06	.05	.02
356	Mike Marshall	.06	.05	.02
357	Jack Savage	.10	.08	.04
358	Mark Parent	.03	.02	.01
359	Chuck Cary	.04	.03	.02
360	Rock Raines	.15	.11	.06
361	Scott Garrelts	.05	.04	.02
362	*Hector Villanueva*	.15	.11	.06
363	Rick Mahler	.04	.03	.02
364	Dan Pasqua	.06	.05	.02
365	Mike Schooler	.06	.05	.02
366	Checklist 3	.03	.02	.01
367	*Dave Walsh*(FC)	.15	.11	.06
368	Felix Jose	.06	.05	.02
369	Steve Searcy	.06	.05	.02
370	Kelly Gruber	.12	.09	.05
371	Jeff Montgomery	.06	.05	.02
372	Spike Owen	.05	.04	.02
373	Darrin Jackson	.04	.03	.02
374	*Larry Casian*(FC)	.15	.11	.06
375	Tony Pena	.06	.05	.02
376	Mike Harkey	.08	.06	.03
377	Rene Gonzales	.03	.02	.01
378	*Wilson Alvarez*(FC)	.40	.30	.15
379	Randy Velarde	.04	.03	.02
380	Willie McGee	.08	.06	.03
381	Jose Lind	.05	.04	.02
382	Mackey Sasser	.05	.04	.02
383	Pete Smith	.06	.05	.02
384	Gerald Perry	.05	.04	.02
385	Mickey Tettleton	.05	.04	.02
386	Cecil Fielder (AS)	.10	.08	.04
387	Julio Franco (AS)	.08	.06	.03
388	Kelly Gruber (AS)	.08	.06	.03
389	Alan Trammell (AS)	.06	.05	.02
390	Jose Canseco (AS)	.10	.08	.04
391	Rickey Henderson (AS)	.10	.08	.04
392	Ken Griffey,Jr. (AS)	.30	.25	.12
393	Carlton Fisk (AS)	.08	.06	.03
394	Bob Welch (AS)	.06	.05	.02
395	Chuck Finley (AS)	.06	.05	.02
396	Bobby Thigpen (AS)	.08	.06	.03
397	Eddie Murray (AS)	.08	.06	.03
398	Ryne Sandberg (AS)	.10	.08	.04

		MT	NR MT	EX
399	Matt Williams (AS)	.08	.06	.03
400	Barry Larkin (AS)	.08	.06	.03
401	Barry Bonds (AS)	.10	.08	.04
402	Darryl Strawberry (AS)	.10	.08	.04
403	Bobby Bonilla (AS)	.10	.08	.04
404	Mike Scoscia (AS)	.06	.05	.02
405	Doug Drabek (AS)	.08	.06	.03
406	Frank Viola (AS)	.08	.06	.03
407	John Franco (AS)	.06	.05	.02
408	Ernie Riles	.04	.03	.02
409	Mike Stanley	.03	.02	.01
410	Dave Righetti	.08	.06	.03
411	Lance Blankenship	.04	.03	.02
412	Dave Bergman	.03	.02	.01
413	Terry Mulholland	.06	.05	.02
414	Sammy Sosa	.15	.11	.06
415	Rick Sutcliffe	.08	.06	.03
416	Randy Milligan	.06	.05	.02
417	Bill Krueger	.03	.02	.01
418	Nick Esasky	.06	.05	.02
419	Jeff Reed	.03	.02	.01
420	Bobby Thigpen	.08	.06	.03
421	Alex Cole(FC)	.20	.15	.08
422	Rick Rueschel	.06	.05	.02
423	Rafael Ramirez	.04	.03	.02
424	Calvin Schiraldi	.03	.02	.01
425	Andy Van Slyke	.08	.06	.03
426	*Joe Grahe*(FC)	.15	.11	.06
427	Rick Dempsey	.03	.02	.01
428	*John Barfield*(FC)	.10	.08	.04
429	Stump Merrill	.03	.02	.01
430	Gary Gaetti	.08	.06	.03
431	Paul Gibson	.03	.02	.01
432	Delino DeShields	.20	.15	.08
433	Pat Tabler	.04	.03	.02
434	Julio Machado(FC)	.10	.08	.04
435	Kevin Maas	.40	.30	.15
436	Scott Bankhead	.05	.04	.02
437	Doug Dascenzo	.04	.03	.02
438	Vicente Palacios	.05	.04	.02
439	Dickie Thon	.03	.02	.01
440	George Bell	.08	.06	.03
441	Zane Smith	.04	.03	.02
442	Charlie O'Brien	.04	.03	.02
443	Jeff Innis	.05	.04	.02
444	Glenn Braggs	.05	.04	.02
445	Greg Swindell	.06	.05	.02
446	*Craig Grebeck*(FC)	.15	.11	.06
447	John Burkett	.12	.09	.05
448	Craig Lefferts	.05	.04	.02
449	Juan Berenguer	.03	.02	.01
450	Wade Boggs	.15	.11	.06
451	Neal Heaton	.05	.04	.02
452	Bill Schroeder	.03	.02	.01
453	Lenny Harris	.05	.04	.02
454	Kevin Appier	.08	.06	.03
455	Walt Weiss	.06	.05	.02
456	Charlie Leibrandt	.05	.04	.02
457	*Todd Hundley*	.20	.15	.08
458	Brian Holman	.06	.05	.02
459	Tom Trebelhorn	.03	.02	.01
460	Dave Steib	.08	.06	.03
461	Robin Ventura	.08	.06	.03
462	Steve Frey	.06	.05	.02
463	Dwight Smith	.06	.05	.02
464	Steve Buechele	.04	.03	.02
465	Ken Griffey	.05	.04	.02
466	Charles Nagy(FC)	.10	.08	.04
467	Dennis Cook	.06	.05	.02
468	Tim Hulett	.04	.03	.02
469	Chet Lemon	.05	.04	.02
470	Howard Johnson	.10	.08	.04
471	#1 Draft Pick *(Mike Lieberthal)*(FC)	.30	.25	.12
472	Kirt Manwaring	.05	.04	.02
473	Curt Young	.04	.03	.02
474	*Phil Plantier*(FC)	.50	.40	.20
475	Teddy Higuera	.08	.06	.03
476	Glenn Wilson	.05	.04	.02
477	Mike Fetters	.06	.05	.02
478	Kurt Stillwell	.05	.04	.02
479	Bob Patterson	.03	.02	.01
480	Dave Magadan	.10	.08	.04
481	Eddie Whitson	.05	.04	.02
482	Tino Martinez	.40	.30	.15
483	Mike Aldrete	.04	.03	.02
484	Dave LaPoint	.04	.03	.02
485	Terry Pendleton	.06	.05	.02
486	Tommy Greene(FC)	.10	.08	.04
487	Rafael Belliard	.03	.02	.01
488	Jeff Manto(FC)	.15	.11	.06

		MT	NR MT	EX
489	Bobby Valentine	.03	.02	.01
490	Kirk Gibson	.08	.06	.03
491	#1 Draft Pick *(Kurt Miller)*(FC)	.30	.25	.12
492	Ernie Whitt	.05	.04	.02
493	Jose Rijo	.08	.06	.03
494	Chris James	.06	.05	.02
495	Charlie Hough	.04	.03	.02
496	Marty Barrett	.05	.04	.02
497	Ben McDonald	.30	.25	.12
498	Mark Salas	.03	.02	.01
499	Melido Perez	.06	.05	.02
500	Will Clark	.30	.25	.12
501	Mike Bielecki	.05	.04	.02
502	Carney Lansford	.06	.05	.02
503	Roy Smith	.04	.03	.02
504	*Julio Valera*(FC)	.15	.11	.06
505	Chuck Finley	.08	.06	.03
506	Darnell Coles	.04	.03	.02
507	Steve Jeltz	.03	.02	.01
508	*Mike York*(FC)	.15	.11	.06
509	Glenallen Hill	.06	.05	.02
510	John Franco	.08	.06	.03
511	Steve Balboni	.03	.02	.01
512	Jose Mesa(FC)	.05	.04	.02
513	Jerald Clark	.05	.04	.02
514	Mike Stanton	.08	.06	.03
515	Alvin Davis	.08	.06	.03
516	*Karl Rhodes*(FC)	.20	.15	.08
517	Joe Oliver	.06	.05	.02
518	Cris Carpenter	.05	.04	.02
519	Sparky Anderson	.04	.03	.02
520	Mark Grace	.15	.11	.06
521	Joe Orsulak	.05	.04	.02
522	Stan Belinda	.06	.05	.02
523	*Rodney McCray*(FC)	.15	.11	.06
524	Darrel Akerfelds	.04	.03	.02
525	Willie Randolph	.06	.05	.02
526	Moises Alou(FC)	.15	.11	.06
527	Checklist 4	.03	.02	.01
528	Denny Martinez	.06	.05	.02
529	#1 Draft Pick *(Mark Newfield)*(FC)	.80	.60	.30
530	Roger Clemens	.20	.15	.08
531	*Dave Rhode*(FC)	.15	.11	.06
532	Kirk McCaskill	.06	.05	.02
533	Oddibe McDowell	.05	.04	.02
534	Mike Jackson	.04	.03	.02
535	Ruben Sierra	.15	.11	.06
536	Mike Witt	.04	.03	.02
537	Mike LaValliere	.05	.04	.02
538	Bip Roberts	.05	.04	.02
539	Scott Terry	.03	.02	.01
540	George Brett	.12	.09	.05
541	Domingo Ramos	.03	.02	.01
542	Rob Murphy	.03	.02	.01
543	Junior Felix	.08	.06	.03
544	Alejandro Pena	.03	.02	.01
545	Dale Murphy	.10	.08	.04
546	Jeff Ballard	.05	.04	.02
547	Mike Pagliarulo	.04	.03	.02
548	Jaime Navarro	.10	.08	.04
549	John McNamara	.03	.02	.01
550	Eric Davis	.15	.11	.06
551	Bob Kipper	.03	.02	.01
552	Jeff Hamilton	.04	.03	.02
553	*Joe Klink*	.10	.08	.04
554	Brian Harper	.06	.05	.02
555	*Turner Ward*(FC)	.20	.15	.08
556	Gary Ward	.04	.03	.02
557	Wally Whitehurst	.06	.05	.02
558	Otis Nixon	.03	.02	.01
559	Adam Peterson	.06	.05	.02
560	Greg Smith(FC)	.15	.11	.06
561	Tim McIntosh(FC)	.15	.11	.06
562	Jeff Kunkel	.03	.02	.01
563	*Brent Knackert*	.10	.08	.04
564	Dante Bichette	.08	.06	.03
565	Craig Biggio	.08	.06	.03
566	*Craig Wilson*(FC)	.15	.11	.06
567	Dwayne Henry	.03	.02	.01
568	Ron Karkovice	.04	.03	.02
569	Curt Schilling	.05	.04	.02
570	Barry Bonds	.15	.11	.06
571	Pat Combs	.08	.06	.03
572	Dave Anderson	.03	.02	.01
573	*Rich Rodriguez*(FC)	.15	.11	.06
574	John Marzano	.04	.03	.02
575	Robin Yount	.15	.11	.06
576	Jeff Kaiser(FC)	.10	.08	.04
577	Bill Doran	.06	.05	.02
578	Dave West	.06	.05	.02
579	Roger Craig	.03	.02	.01

		MT	NR MT	EX
580	Dave Stewart	.12	.09	.05
581	Luis Quinones	.03	.02	.01
582	Marty Clary	.03	.02	.01
583	Tony Phillips	.04	.03	.02
584	Kevin Brown	.06	.05	.02
585	Pete O'Brien	.04	.03	.02
586	Fred Lynn	.05	.04	.02
587	Jose Offerman(FC)	.25	.20	.10
588	*Mark Whiten*(FC)	.35	.25	.14
589	*Scott Ruskin*	.10	.08	.04
590	Eddie Murray	.12	.09	.05
591	Ken Hill	.05	.04	.02
592	B.J. Surhoff	.06	.05	.02
593	*Mike Walker*(FC)	.15	.11	.06
594	*Rich Garces*(FC)	.15	.11	.06
595	Bill Landrum	.05	.04	.02
596	#1 Draft Pick *(Ronnie Walden)*(FC)	.30	.25	.12
597	Jerry Don Gleaton	.03	.02	.01
598	Sam Horn	.05	.04	.02
599	Greg Myers	.04	.03	.02
600	Bo Jackson	.40	.30	.15
601	Bob Ojeda	.04	.03	.02
602	Casey Candaele	.04	.03	.02
603a	*Wes Chamberlain* (photo of Louie Meadows)(FC)	1.25	.90	.50
603b	*Wes Chamberlain* (correct photo)(FC)	.40	.30	.15
604	Billy Hatcher	.05	.04	.02
605	Jeff Reardon	.08	.06	.03
606	Jim Gott	.04	.03	.02
607	Edgar Martinez	.06	.05	.02
608	Todd Burns	.03	.02	.01
609	Jeff Torborg	.03	.02	.01
610	Andres Galarraga	.08	.06	.03
611	Dave Eiland	.04	.03	.02
612	Steve Lyons	.04	.03	.02
613	Eric Show	.04	.03	.02
614	Luis Salazar	.04	.03	.02
615	Bert Blyleven	.08	.06	.03
616	Todd Zeile	.15	.11	.06
617	Bill Wegman	.04	.03	.02
618	Sil Campusano	.04	.03	.02
619	David Wells	.04	.03	.02
620	Ozzie Guillen	.08	.06	.03
621	Ted Power	.03	.02	.01
622	Jack Daugherty	.05	.04	.02
623	Jeff Blauser	.04	.03	.02
624	Tom Candiotti	.04	.03	.02
625	Terry Steinbach	.06	.05	.02
626	Gerald Young	.03	.02	.01
627	*Tim Layana*	.15	.11	.06
628	Greg Litton	.05	.04	.02
629	Wes Gardner	.04	.03	.02
630	Dave Winfield	.10	.08	.04
631	Mike Morgan	.04	.03	.02
632	Lloyd Moseby	.06	.05	.02
633	Kevin Tapani	.10	.08	.04
634	Henry Cotto	.03	.02	.01
635	Andy Hawkins	.04	.03	.02
636	*Geronimo Pena*(FC)	.20	.15	.08
637	Bruce Ruffin	.04	.03	.02
638	Mike Macfarlane	.04	.03	.02
639	Frank Robinson	.05	.04	.02
640	Andre Dawson	.10	.08	.04
641	Mike Henneman	.06	.05	.02
642	Hal Morris	.15	.11	.06
643	Jim Presley	.06	.05	.02
644	Chuck Crim	.04	.03	.02
645	Juan Samuel	.06	.05	.02
646	*Andujar Cedeno*(FC)	.50	.40	.20
647	Mark Portugal	.04	.03	.02
648	Lee Stevens(FC)	.15	.11	.06
649	*Bill Sampen*	.15	.11	.06
650	Jack Clark	.08	.06	.03
651	*Alan Mills*	.12	.09	.05
652	Kevin Romine	.03	.02	.01
653	*Anthony Telford*(FC)	.20	.15	.08
654	Paul Sorrento(FC)	.15	.11	.06
655	Erik Hanson	.08	.06	.03
656	Checklist 5	.03	.02	.01
657	Mike Kingery	.03	.02	.01
658	*Scott Aldred*(FC)	.15	.11	.06
659	*Oscar Azocar*(FC)	.15	.11	.06
660	Lee Smith	.06	.05	.02
661	Steve Lake	.03	.02	.01
662	Rob Dibble	.08	.06	.03
663	Greg Brock	.05	.04	.02
664	John Farrell	.04	.03	.02
665	Jim Leyland	.03	.02	.01
666	Danny Darwin	.06	.05	.02
667	Kent Anderson	.04	.03	.02

		MT	NR MT	EX
668	Bill Long	.04	.03	.02
669	Lou Pinella	.04	.03	.02
670	Rickey Henderson	.35	.25	.14
671	Andy McGaffigan	.03	.02	.01
672	Shane Mack	.06	.05	.02
673	*Greg Olson*	.20	.15	.08
674	Kevin Gross	.06	.05	.02
675	Tom Brunansky	.08	.06	.03
676	*Scott Chiamparino*(FC)	.20	.15	.08
677	Billy Ripken	.04	.03	.02
678	Mark Davidson	.03	.02	.01
679	Bill Bathe(FC)	.04	.03	.02
680	David Cone	.06	.05	.02
681	*Jeff Schaefer*(FC)	.10	.08	.04
682	*Ray Lankford*(FC)	.50	.40	.20
683	Derek Lilliquist	.05	.04	.02
684	Milt Cuyler(FC)	.25	.20	.10
685	Doug Drabek	.08	.06	.03
686	Mike Gallego	.03	.02	.01
687	John Cerutti	.03	.02	.01
688	*Rosario Rodriguez*(FC)	.15	.11	.06
689	John Kruk	.06	.05	.02
690	Orel Hershiser	.10	.08	.04
691	Mike Blowers	.10	.08	.04
692	*Efrain Valdez*(FC)	.15	.11	.06
693	Francisco Cabrera	.08	.06	.03
694	Randy Veres	.03	.02	.01
695	Kevin Seitzer	.08	.06	.03
696	Steve Olin	.05	.04	.02
697	Shawn Abner	.04	.03	.02
698	Mark Guthrie	.05	.04	.02
699	Jim Lefebvre	.03	.02	.01
700	Jose Canseco	.40	.30	.15
701	Pascual Perez	.05	.04	.02
702	*Tim Naehring*	.25	.20	.10
703	Juan Agosto	.03	.02	.01
704	Devon White	.06	.05	.02
705	Robby Thompson	.05	.04	.02
706	Brad Arnsberg	.04	.03	.02
707	Jim Eisenreich	.04	.03	.02
708	John Mitchell(FC)	.12	.09	.05
709	Matt Sinatro	.03	.02	.01
710	Kent Hrbek	.08	.06	.03
711	Gary Redus, Jose DeLeon	.05	.04	.02
712	Ricky Jordan	.06	.05	.02
713	Scott Scudder	.08	.06	.03
714	Marvell Wynne	.04	.03	.02
715	Tim Burke	.06	.05	.02
716	Bob Geren	.06	.05	.02
717	Phil Bradley	.06	.05	.02
718	Steve Crawford	.03	.02	.01
719	Kevin McReynolds	.06	.05	.02
720	Cecil Fielder	.20	.15	.08
721	*Mark Lee*(FC)	.15	.11	.06
722	Wally Backman	.04	.03	.02
723	Candy Maldonado	.08	.06	.03
724	*David Segui*(FC)	.25	.20	.10
725	Ron Gant	.15	.11	.06
726	Phil Stephenson	.04	.03	.02
727	Mookie Wilson	.06	.05	.02
728	Scott Sanderson	.04	.03	.02
729	Don Zimmer	.04	.03	.02
730	Barry Larkin	.12	.09	.05
731	*Jeff Gray*(FC)	.15	.11	.06
732	Franklin Stubbs	.05	.04	.02
733	Kelly Downs	.04	.03	.02
734	John Russell	.03	.02	.01
735	Ron Darling	.06	.05	.02
736	Dick Schofield	.04	.03	.02
737	Tim Crews	.03	.02	.01
738	Mel Hall	.04	.03	.02
739	*Russ Swan*	.10	.08	.04
740	Ryne Sandberg	.20	.15	.08
741	Jimmy Key	.06	.05	.02
742	Tommy Gregg	.04	.03	.02
743	Bryn Smith	.04	.03	.02
744	Nelson Santovenia	.05	.04	.02
745	Doug Jones	.08	.06	.03
746	John Shelby	.03	.02	.01
747	Tony Fossas	.03	.02	.01
748	Al Newman	.03	.02	.01
749	Greg Harris	.04	.03	.02
750	Bobby Bonilla	.12	.09	.05
751	*Wayne Edwards*	.10	.08	.04
752	Kevin Bass	.05	.04	.02
753	*Paul Marak*(FC)	.15	.11	.06
754	Bill Pecota	.04	.03	.02
755	Mark Langston	.10	.08	.04
756	Jeff Huson	.05	.04	.02
757	Mark Gardner	.06	.05	.02
758	Mike Devereaux	.06	.05	.02

		MT	NR MT	EX
759	Bobby Cox	.03	.02	.01
760	Benny Santiago	.08	.06	.03
761	Larry Andersen	.04	.03	.02
762	Mitch Webster	.04	.03	.02
763	*Dana Kiecker*	.10	.08	.04
764	Mark Carreon	.05	.04	.02
765	Shawon Dunston	.08	.06	.03
766	Jeff Robinson	.05	.04	.02
767	#1 Draft Pick *(Dan Wilson)*(FC)	.30	.25	.12
768	Donn Pall	.04	.03	.02
769	*Tim Sherrill*(FC)	.15	.11	.06
770	Jay Howell	.06	.05	.02
772	Kent Mercker(FC)	.10	.08	.04
773	Tom Foley	.03	.02	.01
774	Dennis Rasmussen	.04	.03	.02
775	Julio Franco	.08	.06	.03
776	Brent Mayne(FC)	.15	.11	.06
777	John Candelaria	.05	.04	.02
778	Dan Gladden	.05	.04	.02
779	Carmelo Martinez	.04	.03	.02
780	Randy Myers	.08	.06	.03
781	Darryl Hamilton	.05	.04	.02
782	Jim Deshaies	.05	.04	.02
783	Joel Skinner	.03	.02	.01
784	Willie Fraser	.04	.03	.02
785	Scott Fletcher	.04	.03	.02
786	Eric Plunk	.03	.02	.01
787	Checklist 6	.03	.02	.01
788	Bob Milacki	.06	.05	.02
789	Tom Lasorda	.04	.03	.02
790	Ken Griffey,Jr.	1.00	.70	.40
791	Mike Benjamin(FC)	.15	.11	.06
792	Mike Greenwell	.15	.11	.06

1991 Topps

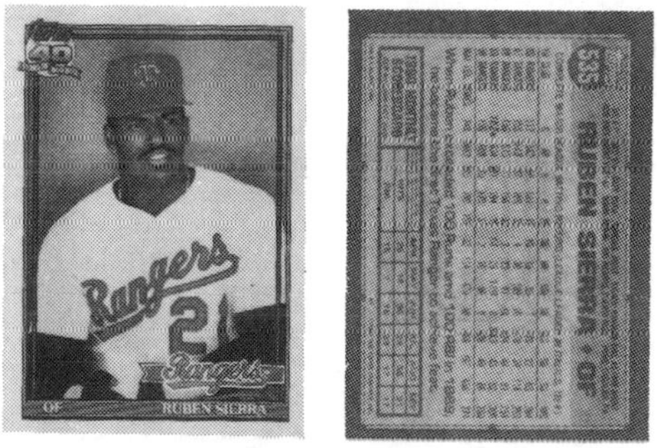

Styled like the standard 1991 Topps cards, this 16-card set honors milestones of the featured players. The cards were found on the bottom of wax pack boxes. The cards are designated in alphabetical order by (A-P) and are not numbered.

		MT	NR MT	EX
Complete Set:		2.50	2.00	1.00
Common Player:		.08	.06	.03
(1)	Bert Blyleven	.08	.06	.03
(2)	George Brett	.20	.15	.08
(3)	Brett Butler	.10	.08	.04
(4)	Andre Dawson	.15	.11	.06
(5)	Dwight Evans	.10	.08	.04
(6)	Carlton Fisk	.20	.15	.08
(7)	Alfredo Griffin	.08	.06	.03
(8)	Rickey Henderson	.30	.25	.12
(9)	Willie McGee	.15	.11	.06
(10)	Dale Murphy	.20	.15	.08
(11)	Eddie Murray	.20	.15	.08
(12)	Dave Parker	.15	.11	.06
(13)	Jeff Reardon	.15	.11	.06
(14)	Nolan Ryan	.40	.30	.15
(15)	Juan Samuel	.08	.06	.03
(16)	Robin Yount	.20	.15	.08

1991 Topps Major League Debut

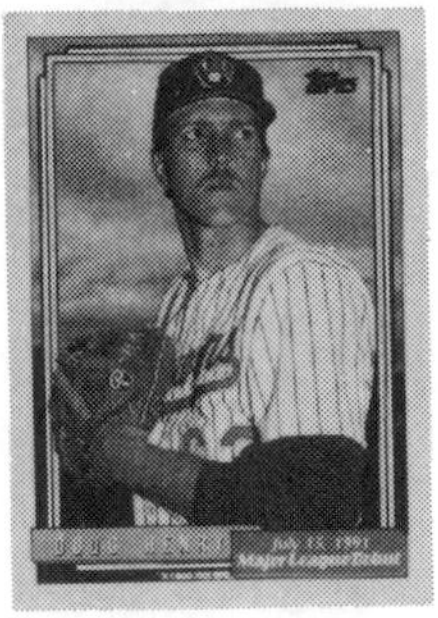
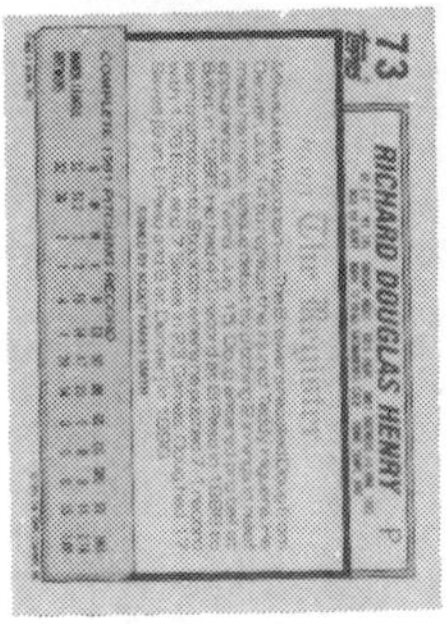

This 194-card set highlights the debut date of 1991 Major League rookies. Two checklist cards are also included in this boxed set. The card fronts resemble the 1992 Topps cards. A debut banner appears in the lower right hand corner of the card front. The set is packaged in an attractive collector box and the cards are numbered alphabetically. This set was available through select hobby dealers.

		MT	NR MT	EX
Complete Set:		15.00	11.00	6.00
Common Player:		.08	.06	.03
1	Kyle Abbott	.20	.15	.08
2	Dana Allison	.15	.11	.06
3	Rich Amaral	.08	.06	.03
4	Ruben Amaro	.10	.08	.04
5	Andy Ashby	.15	.11	.06
6	Jim Austin	.08	.06	.03
7	Jeff Bagwell	1.50	1.25	.60
8	Jeff Banister	.10	.08	.04
9	Willie Banks	.25	.20	.10
10	Bret Barberie	.20	.15	.08
11	Kim Batiste	.10	.08	.04
12	Chris Beasley	.10	.08	.04
13	Rodd Beck	.08	.06	.03
14	Derek Bell	.50	.40	.20
15	Esteban Beltre	.08	.06	.03
16	Freddie Benavides	.10	.08	.04
17	Rickey Bones	.10	.08	.04
18	Denis Boucher	.15	.11	.06
19	Ryan Bowen	.20	.15	.08
20	Cliff Brantley	.10	.08	.04
21	John Briscoe	.10	.08	.04
22	Scott Brosius	.10	.08	.04
23	Terry Bross	.08	.06	.03
24	Jarvis Brown	.10	.08	.04
25	Scott Bullett	.10	.08	.04
26	Kevin Campbell	.08	.06	.03
27	Amalio Carreno	.08	.06	.03
28	Matias Carrillo	.10	.08	.04
29	Jeff Carter	.08	.06	.03
30	Vinny Castilla	.10	.08	.04
31	Braulio Castillo	.10	.08	.04
32	Frank Castillo	.25	.20	.10
33	Darrin Chapin	.10	.08	.04
34	Mike Christopher	.08	.06	.03
35	Mark Clark	.15	.11	.06
36	Royce Clayton	.25	.20	.10
37	Stu Cole	.10	.08	.04
38	Gary Cooper	.08	.06	.03
39	Archie Corbin	.10	.08	.04
40	Rheal Cormier	.20	.15	.08
41	Chris Cron	.08	.06	.03
42	Mike Dalton	.08	.06	.03
43	Mark Davis	.08	.06	.03
44	Francisco de la Rosa	.08	.06	.03
45	Chris Donnels	.35	.25	.14
46	Brian Drahman	.25	.20	.10
47	Tom Drees	.15	.11	.06
48	Kirk Dressendorfer	.40	.30	.15
49	Bruce Egloff	.30	.25	.12
50	Cal Eldred	.30	.25	.12
51	Jose Escobar	.30	.25	.12
52	Tony Eusebio	.08	.06	.03
53	Hector Fajardo	.10	.08	.04
54	Monty Farriss	.10	.08	.04
55	Jeff Fassero	.15	.11	.06
56	Dave Fleming	.10	.08	.04
57	Kevin Flora	.10	.08	.04
58	Steve Foster	.10	.08	.04
59	Dan Gakeler	.08	.06	.03
60	Ramon Garcia	.15	.11	.06
61	Chris Gardner	.10	.08	.04
62	Jeff Gardner	.15	.11	.06
63	Chris George	.15	.11	.06
64	Ray Giannelli	.08	.06	.03
65	Tom Goodwin	.20	.15	.08
66	Mark Grater	.08	.06	.03
67	Johnny Guzman	.15	.11	.06
68	Juan Guzman	.60	.45	.25
69	Dave Haas	.08	.06	.03
70	Chris Haney	.25	.20	.10
71	Shawn Hare	.08	.06	.03
72	Donald Harris	.20	.15	.08
73	Doug Henry	.20	.15	.08
74	Pat Hentgen	.10	.08	.04
75	Gil Heredia	.20	.15	.08
76	Jeremy Hernandez	.20	.15	.08
77	Jose Hernandez	.08	.06	.03
78	Roberto Hernandez	.10	.08	.04
79	Bryan Hickerson	.15	.11	.06
80	Milt Hill	.08	.06	.03
81	Vince Horsman	.08	.06	.03
82	Wayne Housie	.08	.06	.03
83	Chris Howard	.15	.11	.06
84	David Howard	.20	.15	.08
85	Mike Humphreys	.15	.11	.06
86	Brian Hunter	.70	.50	.30
87	Jim Hunter	.08	.06	.03
88	Mike Ignasiak	.08	.06	.03
89	Reggie Jefferson	.35	.25	.14
90	Jeff Johnson	.20	.15	.08
91	Joel Johnson	.10	.08	.04
92	Calvin Jones	.15	.11	.06
93	Chris Jones	.25	.20	.10
94	Stacy Jones	.08	.06	.03
95	Jeff Juden	.25	.20	.10
96	Scott Kamieniecki	.20	.15	.08
97	Eric Karros	.60	.45	.25
98	Pat Kelly	.50	.40	.20
99	John Kiely	.08	.06	.03
100	Darryl Kile	.20	.15	.08
101	Wayne Kirby	.08	.06	.03
102	Garland Kiser	.10	.08	.04
103	Chuck Knoblauch	.60	.45	.25
104	Randy Knorr	.08	.06	.03
105	Tom Kramer	.08	.06	.03
106	Ced Landrum	.20	.15	.08
107	Patrick Lennon	.20	.15	.08
108	Jim Lewis	.08	.06	.03
109	Mark Lewis	.35	.25	.14
110	Doug Lindsey	.08	.06	.03
111	Scott Livingstone	.30	.25	.12
112	Kenny Lofton	.40	.30	.15
113	Ever Magallanes	.10	.08	.04
114	Mike Magnante	.10	.08	.04
115	Barry Manuel	.10	.08	.04
116	Josias Manzanillo	.10	.08	.04
117	Chito Martinez	.60	.45	.25
118	Terry Mathews	.08	.06	.03
119	Rob Mauer	.10	.08	.04
120	Tim Mauser	.08	.06	.03
121	Terry McDaniel	.20	.15	.08
122	Rusty Meacham	.15	.11	.06
123	Luis Mercedes	.25	.20	.10
124	Paul Miller	.15	.11	.06
125	Keith Mitchell	.25	.20	.10
126	Bobby Moore	.08	.06	.03
127	Kevin Morton	.30	.25	.12
128	Andy Mota	.25	.20	.10
129	Jose Mota	.15	.11	.06
130	Mike Mussina	.25	.20	.10
131	Jeff Mutis	.08	.06	.03
132	Denny Neagle	.40	.30	.15
133	Warren Newson	.15	.11	.06
134	Jim Olander	.08	.06	.03
135	Erik Pappas	.15	.11	.06
136	Jorge Pedre	.10	.08	.04
137	Yorkis Perez	.15	.11	.06
138	Mark Petkovsek	.15	.11	.06
139	Doug Piatt	.15	.11	.06
140	Jeff Plympton	.15	.11	.06
141	Harvey Pulliam	.15	.11	.06
142	John Ramos	.15	.11	.06
143	Mike Remlinger	.10	.08	.04
144	Laddie Renfroe	.10	.08	.04
145	Armando Reynoso	.10	.08	.04
146	Arthur Rhodes	.20	.15	.08
147	Pat Rice	.15	.11	.06

		MT	NR MT	EX
148	Nikco Riesgo	.10	.08	.04
149	Carlos Rodriguez	.10	.08	.04
150	Ivan Rodriguez	1.50	1.25	.60
151	Wayne Rosenthal	.10	.08	.04
152	Rico Rossy	.08	.06	.03
153	Stan Royer	.15	.11	.06
154	Rey Sanchez	.08	.06	.03
155	Reggie Sanders	.40	.30	.15
156	Mo Sanford	.35	.25	.14
157	Bob Scanlan	.15	.11	.06
158	Pete Schourek	.15	.11	.06
159	Gary Scott	.25	.20	.10
160	Tim Scott	.08	.06	.03
161	Tony Scruggs	.10	.08	.04
162	Scott Servais	.10	.08	.04
163	Doug Simons	.15	.11	.06
164	Heathcliff Slocumb	.10	.08	.04
165	Joe Slusarski	.10	.08	.04
166	Tim Spehr	.15	.11	.06
167	Ed Sprague	.10	.08	.04
168	Jeff Tackett	.08	.06	.03
169	Eddie Taubensee	.15	.11	.06
170	Wade Taylor	.15	.11	.06
171	Jim Thome	.60	.45	.25
172	Mike Timlin	.25	.20	.10
173	Jose Tolentino	.10	.08	.04
174	John Vander Wal	.08	.06	.03
175	Todd Van Poppel	.80	.60	.30
176	Mo Vaughn	.50	.40	.20
177	Dave Wainhouse	.15	.11	.06
178	Don Wakamatsu	.10	.08	.04
179	Bruce Walton	.08	.06	.03
180	Kevin Ward	.08	.06	.03
181	Dave Weathers	.08	.06	.03
182	Eric Wedge	.08	.06	.03
183	John Wehner	.25	.20	.10
184	Rick Wilkins	.30	.25	.12
185	Bernie Williams	.35	.25	.14
186	Brian Williams	.15	.11	.06
187	Ron Witmeyer	.08	.06	.03
188	Mark Wohlers	.25	.20	.10
189	Ted Wood	.20	.15	.08
190	Anthony Young	.50	.40	.20
191	Eddie Zosky	.20	.15	.08
192	Bob Zupcic	.15	.11	.06
193	Checklist	.08	.06	.03
194	Checklist	.08	.06	.03

1991 Topps Stadium Club

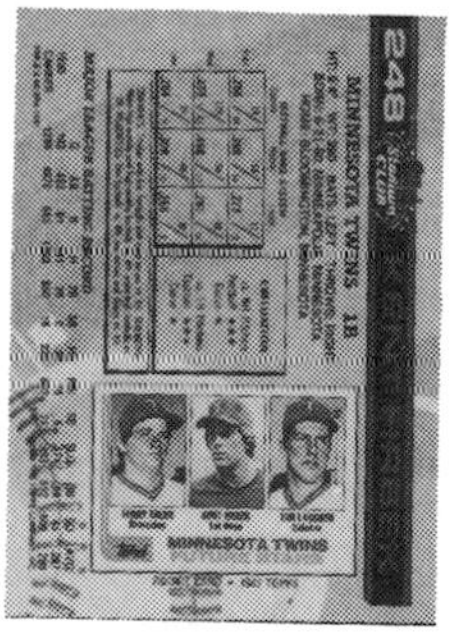

One of the most popular sets of 1991, this 600-card issue was released in two 300-card series. The cards were available in foil packs only. No factory sets were available. The cards feature orderless high gloss photos on the front and a player evaluation and card photo on the back. Stadium Club cards were considered scarce in many areas, thus driving up the price per pack. A special Stadium Club membership package was made available for $29.95 with 10 proof of purchase seals from wrappers.

		MT	NR MT	EX
Complete Set:		250.00	188.00	100.00
Common Player:		.20	.15	.08
1	Dave Stewart	1.00	.70	.40
2	Wally Joyner	.30	.25	.12
3	Shawon Dunston	.25	.20	.10
4	Darren Daulton	.20	.15	.08
5	Will Clark	3.00	2.25	1.25
6	Sammy Sosa	.25	.20	.10
7	Dan Plesac	.20	.15	.08
8	Marquis Grissom	.80	.60	.30
9	Erik Hanson	.30	.25	.12
10	Geno Petralli	.20	.15	.08
11	Jose Rijo	.25	.20	.10
12	Carlos Quintana	.20	.15	.08
13	Junior Ortiz	.20	.15	.08
14	Bob Walk	.20	.15	.08
15	Mike Macfarlane	.20	.15	.08
16	Eric Yelding	.20	.15	.08
17	Bryn Smith	.20	.15	.08
18	Bip Roberts	.20	.15	.08
19	Mike Scioscia	.20	.15	.08
20	Mark Williamson	.20	.15	.08
21	Don Mattingly	1.50	1.25	.60
22	John Franco	.20	.15	.08
23	Chet Lemon	.20	.15	.08
24	Tom Henke	.20	.15	.08
25	Jerry Browne	.20	.15	.08
26	Dave Justice	10.00	7.50	4.00
27	Mark Langston	.30	.25	.12
28	Damon Berryhill	.20	.15	.08
29	Kevin Bass	.20	.15	.08
30	Scott Fletcher	.20	.15	.08
31	Moises Alou	.25	.20	.10
32	Dave Valle	.20	.15	.08
33	Jody Reed	.20	.15	.08
34	Dave West	.20	.15	.08
35	Kevin McReynolds	.25	.20	.10
36	Pat Combs	.20	.15	.08
37	Eric Davis	.50	.40	.20
38	Bret Saberhagen	.30	.25	.12
39	Stan Javier	.20	.15	.08
40	Chuck Cary	.20	.15	.08
41	Tony Phillips	.20	.15	.08
42	Lee Smith	.25	.20	.10
43	Tim Teufel	.20	.15	.08
44	Lance Dickson	.80	.60	.30
45	Greg Litton	.20	.15	.08
46	Teddy Higuera	.25	.20	.10
47	Edgar Martinez	.30	.25	.12
48	Steve Avery	6.00	4.50	2.50
49	Walt Weiss	.20	.15	.08
50	David Segui	.30	.25	.12
51	Andy Benes	.30	.25	.12
52	Karl Rhodes	.30	.25	.12
53	Neal Heaton	.20	.15	.08
54	Danny Gladden	.20	.15	.08
55	Luis Rivera	.20	.15	.08
56	Kevin Brown	.20	.15	.08
57	Frank Thomas	30.00	22.00	12.50
58	Terry Mulholland	.25	.20	.10
59	Dick Schofield	.20	.15	.08
60	Ron Darling	.20	.15	.08
61	Sandy Alomar, Jr.	.35	.25	.14
62	Dave Stieb	.20	.15	.08
63	Alan Trammell	.40	.30	.15
64	Matt Nokes	.20	.15	.08
65	Lenny Harris	.20	.15	.08
66	Milt Thompson	.20	.15	.08
67	Storm Davis	.20	.15	.08
68	Joe Oliver	.20	.15	.08
69	Andres Galarraga	.20	.15	.08
70	Ozzie Guillen	.25	.20	.10
71	Ken Howell	.20	.15	.08
72	Garry Templeton	.20	.15	.08
73	Derrick May	.35	.25	.14
74	Xavier Hernandez	.20	.15	.08
75	Dave Parker	.25	.20	.10
76	Rick Aguilera	.20	.15	.08
77	Robby Thompson	.20	.15	.08
78	Pete Incaviglia	.20	.15	.08
79	Bob Welch	.25	.20	.10
80	Randy Milligan	.25	.20	.10
81	Chuck Finley	.35	.25	.14
82	Alvin Davis	.20	.15	.08
83	Tim Naehring	.35	.25	.14
84	Jay Bell	.25	.20	.10
85	Joe Magrane	.25	.20	.10
86	Howard Johnson	.40	.30	.15
87	Jack McDowell	.40	.30	.15
88	Kevin Seitzer	.20	.15	.08
89	Bruce Ruffin	.20	.15	.08
90	Fernando Valenzuela	.30	.25	.12
91	Terry Kennedy	.20	.15	.08
92	Barry Larkin	.80	.60	.30
93	Larry Walker	.30	.25	.12
94	Luis Salazar	.20	.15	.08
95	Gary Sheffield	.30	.25	.12
96	Bobby Witt	.20	.15	.08

		MT	NR MT	EX
97	Lonnie Smith	.20	.15	.08
98	Bryan Harvey	.25	.20	.10
99	Mookie Wilson	.25	.20	.10
100	Doc Gooden	.70	.50	.30
101	Lou Whitaker	.25	.20	.10
102	Ron Karkovice	.20	.15	.08
103	Jesse Barfield	.25	.20	.10
104	Jose DeJesus	.25	.20	.10
105	Benito Santiago	.25	.20	.10
106	Brian Holman	.20	.15	.08
107	Rafael Ramirez	.20	.15	.08
108	Ellis Burks	.50	.40	.20
109	Mike Bielecki	.20	.15	.08
110	Kirby Puckett	1.50	1.25	.60
111	Terry Shumpert	.25	.20	.10
112	Chuck Crim	.20	.15	.08
113	Todd Benzinger	.20	.15	.08
114	Brian Barnes	.40	.30	.15
115	Carlos Baerga	.60	.45	.25
116	Kal Daniels	.25	.20	.10
117	Dave Johnson	.20	.15	.08
118	Andy Van Slyke	.35	.25	.14
119	John Burkett	.20	.15	.08
120	Rickey Henderson	2.50	2.00	1.00
121	Tim Jones	.20	.15	.08
122	Daryl Irvine	.30	.20	.10
123	Ruben Sierra	1.50	1.25	.60
124	Jim Abbott	.80	.60	.30
125	Daryl Boston	.20	.15	.08
126	Greg Maddux	.25	.20	.10
127	Von Hayes	.20	.15	.08
128	Mike Fitzgerald	.20	.15	.08
129	Wayne Edwards	.20	.15	.08
130	Greg Briley	.20	.15	.08
131	Rob Dibble	.30	.25	.12
132	Gene Larkin	.20	.15	.08
133	David Wells	.20	.15	.08
134	Steve Balboni	.20	.15	.08
135	Greg Vaughn	1.25	.90	.50
136	Mark Davis	.20	.15	.08
137	Dave Rohde	.20	.15	.08
138	Eric Show	.20	.15	.08
139	Bobby Bonilla	1.00	.70	.40
140	Dana Kiecker	.25	.20	.10
141	Gary Pettis	.20	.15	.08
142	Dennis Boyd	.20	.15	.08
143	Mike Benjamin	.20	.15	.08
144	Luis Polonia	.20	.15	.08
145	Doug Jones	.20	.15	.08
146	Al Newman	.20	.15	.08
147	Alex Fernandez	.80	.60	.30
148	Bill Doran	.20	.15	.08
149	Kevin Elster	.20	.15	.08
150	Len Dykstra	.30	.25	.12
151	Mike Gallego	.20	.15	.08
152	Tim Belcher	.20	.15	.08
153	Jay Buhner	.20	.15	.08
154	Ozzie Smith	.70	.50	.30
155	Jose Canseco	4.00	3.00	1.50
156	Gregg Olson	.30	.25	.12
157	Charlie O'Brien	.20	.15	.08
158	Frank Tanana	.20	.15	.08
159	George Brett	.80	.60	.30
160	Jeff Huson	.20	.15	.08
161	Kevin Tapani	.35	.25	.14
162	Jerome Walton	.25	.20	.10
163	Charlie Hayes	.20	.15	.08
164	Chris Bosio	.20	.15	.08
165	Chris Sabo	.40	.30	.15
166	Lance Parrish	.20	.15	.08
167	Don Robinson	.20	.15	.08
168	Manuel Lee	.20	.15	.08
169	Dennis Rasmussen	.20	.15	.08
170	Wade Boggs	1.50	1.25	.60
171	Bob Geren	.20	.15	.08
172	Mackey Sasser	.20	.15	.08
173	Julio Franco	.50	.40	.20
174	Otis Nixon	.20	.15	.08
175	Bert Blyleven	.20	.15	.08
176	Craig Biggio	.40	.30	.15
177	Eddie Murray	.60	.45	.25
178	Randy Tomlin	.80	.60	.30
179	Tino Martinez	.80	.60	.30
180	Carlton Fisk	.80	.60	.30
181	Dwight Smith	.20	.15	.08
182	Scott Garrelts	.20	.15	.08
183	Jim Gantner	.20	.15	.08
184	Dickie Thon	.20	.15	.08
185	John Farrell	.20	.15	.08
186	Cecil Fielder	2.00	1.50	.80
187	Glenn Braggs	.20	.15	.08

		MT	NR MT	EX
188	Allan Anderson	.20	.15	.08
189	Kurt Stillwell	.20	.15	.08
190	Jose Oquendo	.20	.15	.08
191	Joe Orsulak	.20	.15	.08
192	Ricky Jordan	.20	.15	.08
193	Kelly Downs	.20	.15	.08
194	Delino DeShields	.60	.45	.25
195	Omar Vizquel	.20	.15	.08
196	Mark Carreon	.20	.15	.08
197	Mike Harkey	.20	.15	.08
198	Jack Howell	.20	.15	.08
199	Lance Johnson	.20	.15	.08
200	Nolan Ryan	15.00	11.00	6.00
201	John Marzano	.20	.15	.08
202	Doug Drabek	.30	.25	.12
203	Mark Lemke	.30	.25	.12
204	Steve Sax	.30	.25	.12
205	Greg Harris	.20	.15	.08
206	B.J. Surhoff	.20	.15	.08
207	Todd Burns	.20	.15	.08
208	Jose Gonzalez	.20	.15	.08
209	Mike Scott	.20	.15	.08
210	Dave Magadan	.30	.25	.12
211	Dante Bichette	.20	.15	.08
212	Trevor Wilson	.20	.15	.08
213	Hector Villanueva	.20	.15	.08
214	Dan Pasqua	.20	.15	.08
215	Greg Colbrunn	.30	.25	.12
216	Mike Jeffcoat	.20	.15	.08
217	Harold Reynolds	.25	.20	.10
218	Paul O'Neill	.25	.20	.10
219	Mark Guthrie	.25	.20	.10
220	Barry Bonds	1.00	.70	.40
221	Jimmy Key	.25	.20	.10
222	Billy Ripken	.20	.15	.08
223	Tom Pagnozzi	.20	.15	.08
224	Bo Jackson	4.00	3.00	1.50
225	Sid Fernandez	.20	.15	.08
226	Mike Marshall	.20	.15	.08
227	John Kruk	.25	.20	.10
228	Mike Fetters	.20	.15	.08
229	Eric Anthony	.20	.15	.08
230	Ryne Sandberg	3.00	2.25	1.25
231	Carney Lansford	.20	.15	.08
232	Melido Perez	.20	.15	.08
233	Jose Lind	.20	.15	.08
234	Darryl Hamilton	.20	.15	.08
235	Tom Browning	.20	.15	.08
236	Spike Owen	.20	.15	.08
237	Juan Gonzalez	12.00	9.00	5.00
238	Felix Fermin	.20	.15	.08
239	Keith Miller	.20	.15	.08
240	Mark Gubicza	.20	.15	.08
241	Kent Anderson	.20	.15	.08
242	Alvaro Espinoza	.20	.15	.08
243	Dale Murphy	.50	.40	.20
244	Orel Hershiser	.30	.25	.12
245	Paul Molitor	.30	.25	.12
246	Eddie Whitson	.20	.15	.08
247	Joe Girardi	.20	.15	.08
248	Kent Hrbek	.25	.20	.10
249	Bill Sampen	.20	.15	.08
250	Kevin Mitchell	.50	.40	.20
251	Mariano Duncan	.20	.15	.08
252	Scott Bradley	.20	.15	.08
253	Mike Greenwell	.50	.40	.20
254	Tom Gordon	.25	.20	.10
255	Todd Zeile	.80	.60	.30
256	Bobby Thigpen	.25	.20	.10
257	Gregg Jefferies	.40	.30	.15
258	Kenny Rogers	.20	.15	.08
259	Shane Mack	.30	.25	.12
260	Zane Smith	.20	.15	.08
261	Mitch Williams	.25	.20	.10
262	Jim DeShaies	.20	.15	.08
263	Dave Winfield	.50	.40	.20
264	Ben McDonald	1.00	.70	.40
265	Randy Ready	.20	.15	.08
266	Pat Borders	.20	.15	.08
267	Jose Uribe	.20	.15	.08
268	Derek Lilliquist	.20	.15	.08
269	Greg Brock	.20	.15	.08
270	Ken Griffey, Jr.	15.00	11.00	6.00
271	Jeff Gray	.25	.20	.10
272	Danny Tartabull	.40	.30	.15
273	Dennis Martinez	.20	.15	.08
274	Robin Ventura	3.00	2.25	1.25
275	Randy Myers	.20	.15	.08
276	Jack Daugherty	.20	.15	.08
277	Greg Gagne	.20	.15	.08
278	Jay Howell	.20	.15	.08

		MT	NR MT	EX
279	Mike LaValliere	.20	.15	.08
280	Rex Hudler	.20	.15	.08
281	Mike Simms	.50	.40	.20
282	Kevin Maas	2.50	2.00	1.00
283	Jeff Ballard	.20	.15	.08
284	Dave Henderson	.30	.25	.14
285	Pete O'Brien	.20	.15	.08
286	Brook Jacoby	.20	.15	.08
287	Mike Henneman	.20	.15	.08
288	Greg Olson	.20	.15	.08
289	Greg Myers	.20	.15	.08
290	Mark Grace	.50	.40	.20
291	Shawn Abner	.20	.15	.08
292	Frank Viola	.30	.25	.12
293	Lee Stevens	.30	.25	.12
294	Jason Grimsley	.20	.15	.08
295	Matt Williams	.70	.50	.30
296	Ron Robinson	.20	.15	.08
297	Tom Brunansky	.20	.15	.08
298	Checklist	.20	.15	.08
299	Checklist	.20	.15	.08
300	Checklist	.20	.15	.08
301	Darryl Strawberry	2.00	1.50	.80
302	Bud Black	.20	.15	.08
303	Harold Baines	.30	.25	.12
304	Roberto Alomar	.50	.40	.20
305	Norm Charlton	.20	.15	.08
306	Gary Thurman	.20	.15	.08
307	Mike Felder	.20	.15	.08
308	Tony Gwynn	.70	.50	.30
309	Roger Clemens	2.00	1.50	.80
310	Andre Dawson	.50	.40	.20
311	Scott Radinsky	.20	.15	.08
312	Bob Melvin	.20	.15	.08
313	Kirk McCaskill	.20	.15	.08
314	Pedro Guerrero	.35	.25	.14
315	Walt Terrell	.20	.15	.08
316	Sam Horn	.20	.15	.08
317	Wes Chamberlain	3.00	2.25	1.25
318	Pedro Munoz	.80	.60	.30
319	Roberto Kelly	.35	.25	.14
320	Mark Portugal	.20	.15	.08
321	Tim McIntosh	.20	.15	.08
322	Jesse Orosco	.20	.15	.08
323	Gary Green	.20	.15	.08
324	Greg Harris	.20	.15	.08
325	Hubie Brooks	.20	.15	.08
326	Chris Nabholz	.20	.15	.08
327	Terry Pendleton	.35	.25	.14
328	Eric King	.20	.15	.08
329	Chili Davis	.20	.15	.08
330	Anthony Telford	.20	.15	.08
331	Kelly Gruber	.35	.25	.14
332	Dennis Eckersley	.35	.25	.14
333	Mel Hall	.20	.15	.08
334	Bob Kipper	.20	.15	.08
335	Willie McGee	.30	.25	.12
336	Steve Olin	.20	.15	.08
337	Steve Buechele	.20	.15	.08
338	Scott Leius	.35	.25	.14
339	Hal Morris	1.00	.70	.40
340	Jose Offerman	.40	.30	.15
341	Kent Mercker	.30	.25	.14
342	Ken Griffey	.20	.15	.08
343	Pete Harnisch	.20	.15	.08
344	Kirk Gibson	.30	.25	.12
345	Dave Smith	.20	.15	.08
346	Dave Martinez	.20	.15	.08
347	Atlee Hammaker	.20	.15	.08
348	Brian Downing	.20	.15	.08
349	Todd Hundley	.35	.25	.14
350	Candy Maldonado	.20	.15	.08
351	Dwight Evans	.30	.25	.12
352	Steve Searcy	.20	.15	.08
353	Gary Gaetti	.25	.20	.10
354	Jeff Reardon	.25	.20	.10
355	Travis Fryman	3.00	2.25	1.25
356	Dave Righetti	.20	.15	.08
357	Fred McGriff	.50	.40	.20
358	Don Slaught	.20	.15	.08
359	Gene Nelson	.20	.15	.08
360	Billy Spiers	.20	.15	.08
361	Lee Guetterman	.20	.15	.08
362	Darren Lewis	1.00	.70	.40
363	Duane Ward	.20	.15	.08
364	Lloyd Moseby	.20	.15	.08
365	John Smoltz	.50	.40	.20
366	Felix Jose	.80	.60	.30
367	David Cone	.30	.25	.12
368	Wally Backman	.20	.15	.08
369	Jeff Montgomery	.20	.15	.08
370	Rich Garces	.35	.25	.14
371	Billy Hatcher	.20	.15	.08
372	Bill Swift	.20	.15	.08
373	Jim Eisenreich	.20	.15	.08
374	Rob Ducey	.20	.15	.08
375	Tim Crews	.20	.15	.08
376	Steve Finley	.20	.15	.08
377	Jeff Blauser	.20	.15	.08
378	Willie Wilson	.20	.15	.08
379	Gerald Perry	.20	.15	.08
380	Jose Mesa	.20	.15	.08
381	Pat Kelly	2.00	1.50	.80
382	Matt Merullo	.20	.15	.08
383	Ivan Calderon	.30	.25	.12
384	Scott Chiamparino	.20	.15	.08
385	Lloyd McClendon	.20	.15	.08
386	Dave Bergman	.20	.15	.08
387	Ed Sprague	.40	.30	.15
388	Jeff Bagwell	15.00	11.00	6.00
389	Brett Butler	.25	.20	.10
390	Larry Andersen	.20	.15	.08
391	Glenn Davis	.30	.25	.12
392	Alex Cole (photo of Otis Nixon)	.30	.25	.12
393	Mike Heath	.20	.15	.08
394	Danny Darwin	.20	.15	.08
395	Steve Lake	.20	.15	.08
396	Tim Layana	.20	.15	.08
397	Terry Leach	.20	.15	.08
398	Bill Wegman	.20	.15	.08
399	Mark McGwire	.50	.40	.20
400	Mike Boddicker	.20	.15	.08
401	Steve Howe	.20	.15	.08
402	Bernard Gilkey	.40	.30	.15
403	Thomas Howard	.20	.15	.08
404	Rafael Belliard	.20	.15	.08
405	Tom Candiotti	.20	.15	.08
406	Rene Gonzalez	.25	.20	.10
407	Chuck McElroy	.25	.20	.10
408	Paul Sorrento	.25	.20	.10
409	Randy Johnson	.25	.20	.10
410	Brady Anderson	.20	.15	.08
411	Dennis Cook	.20	.15	.08
412	Mickey Tettleton	.25	.20	.10
413	Mike Stanton	.20	.15	.08
414	Ken Oberkfell	.20	.15	.08
415	Rick Honeycutt	.20	.15	.08
416	Nelson Santovenia	.20	.15	.08
417	Bob Tewksbury	.20	.15	.08
418	Brent Mayne	.20	.15	.08
419	Steve Farr	.20	.15	.08
420	Phil Stephenson	.20	.15	.08
421	Jeff Russell	.20	.15	.08
422	Chris James	.20	.15	.08
423	Tim Leary	.20	.15	.08
424	Gary Carter	.30	.25	.12
425	Glenallen Hill	.30	.25	.12
426	Matt Young	.20	.15	.08
427	Sid Bream	.20	.15	.08
428	Greg Swindell	.30	.25	.12
429	Scott Aldred	.30	.25	.12
430	Cal Ripken	2.50	2.00	1.00
431	Bill Landrum	.20	.15	.08
432	Ernie Riles	.20	.15	.08
433	Danny Jackson	.20	.15	.08
434	Casey Candaele	.20	.15	.08
435	Ken Hill	.20	.15	.08
436	Jaime Navarro	.20	.15	.08
437	Lance Blankenship	.20	.15	.08
438	Randy Velarde	.20	.15	.08
439	Frank DiPino	.20	.15	.08
440	Carl Nichols	.20	.15	.08
441	Jeff Robinson	.20	.15	.08
442	Deion Sanders	.35	.25	.14
443	Vincente Palacios	.20	.15	.08
444	Devon White	.30	.25	.12
445	John Cerutti	.20	.15	.08
446	Tracy Jones	.20	.15	.08
447	Jack Morris	.30	.25	.12
448	Mitch Webster	.20	.15	.08
449	Bob Ojeda	.20	.15	.08
450	Oscar Azocar	.20	.15	.08
451	Luis Aquino	.20	.15	.08
452	Mark Whiten	.60	.45	.25
453	Stan Belinda	.20	.15	.08
454	Ron Gant	1.00	.70	.40
455	Jose DeLeon	.20	.15	.08
456	Mark Salas	.20	.15	.08
457	Junior Felix	.20	.15	.08
458	Wally Whitehurst	.20	.15	.08
459	Phil Plantier	10.00	7.50	4.00
460	Juan Berenguer	.20	.15	.08

		MT	NR MT	EX
461	Franklin Stubbs	.20	.15	.08
462	Joe Boever	.20	.15	.08
463	Tim Wallach	.30	.25	.12
464	Mike Moore	.20	.15	.08
465	Albert Belle	1.25	.90	.50
466	Mike Witt	.20	.15	.08
467	Craig Worthington	.20	.15	.08
468	Jerald Clark	.20	.15	.08
469	Scott Terry	.20	.15	.08
470	Milt Cuyler	.60	.45	.25
471	John Smiley	.25	.20	.10
472	Charles Nagy	.25	.20	.10
473	Alan Mills	.20	.15	.08
474	John Russell	.20	.15	.08
475	Bruce Hurst	.20	.15	.08
476	Andujar Cedeno	3.00	2.25	1.25
477	Dave Eiland	.20	.15	.08
478	Brian McRae	3.00	2.25	1.25
479	Mike LaCoss	.20	.15	.08
480	Chris Gwynn	.20	.15	.08
481	Jamie Moyer	.20	.15	.08
482	John Olerud	.80	.60	.30
483	Efrain Valdez	.20	.15	.08
484	Sil Campusano	.20	.15	.08
485	Pascual Perez	.20	.15	.08
486	Gary Redus	.20	.15	.08
487	Andy Hawkins	.20	.15	.08
488	Cory Snyder	.20	.15	.08
489	Chris Hoiles	.25	.20	.10
490	Ron Hassey	.20	.15	.08
491	Gary Wayne	.20	.15	.08
492	Mark Lewis	.80	.60	.30
493	Scott Coolbaugh	.20	.15	.08
494	Gerald Young	.20	.15	.08
495	Juan Samuel	.20	.15	.08
496	Willie Fraser	.20	.15	.08
497	Jeff Treadway	.20	.15	.08
498	Vince Coleman	.30	.25	.12
499	Cris Carpenter	.20	.15	.08
500	Jack Clark	.30	.25	.12
501	Kevin Appier	.25	.20	.10
502	Rafael Palmeiro	.60	.45	.25
503	Hensley Meulens	.30	.25	.12
504	George Bell	.30	.25	.12
505	Tony Pena	.30	.25	.12
506	Roger McDowell	.20	.15	.08
507	Luis Sojo	.20	.15	.08
508	Mike Schooler	.20	.15	.08
509	Robin Yount	1.00	.70	.40
510	Jack Armstrong	.20	.15	.08
511	Rick Cerone	.20	.15	.08
512	Curt Wilkerson	.20	.15	.08
513	Joe Carter	.60	.45	.25
514	Tim Burke	.20	.15	.08
515	Tony Fernandez	.25	.20	.10
516	Ramon Martinez	2.00	1.50	.80
517	Tim Hulett	.20	.15	.08
518	Terry Steinbach	.20	.15	.08
519	Pete Smith	.20	.15	.08
520	Ken Caminiti	.20	.15	.08
521	Shawn Boskie	.20	.15	.08
522	Mike Pagliarulo	.20	.15	.08
523	Tim Raines	.35	.25	.14
524	Alfredo Griffin	.20	.15	.08
525	Henry Cotto	.20	.15	.08
526	Mike Stanley	.20	.15	.08
527	Charlie Leibrandt	.20	.15	.08
528	Jeff King	.20	.15	.08
529	Eric Plunk	.20	.15	.08
530	Tom Lampkin	.20	.15	.08
531	Steve Bedrosian	.20	.15	.08
532	Tom Herr	.20	.15	.08
533	Craig Lefferts	.20	.15	.08
534	Jeff Reed	.20	.15	.08
535	Mickey Morandini	.35	.25	.14
536	Greg Cadaret	.20	.15	.08
537	Ray Lankford	2.00	1.50	.80
538	John Candelaria	.20	.15	.08
539	Rob Deer	.20	.15	.08
540	Brad Arnsberg	.20	.15	.08
541	Mike Sharperson	.20	.15	.08
542	Jeff Robinson	.20	.15	.08
543	Mo Vaughn	2.50	2.00	1.00
544	Jeff Parrett	.20	.15	.08
545	Willie Randolph	.20	.15	.08
546	Herm Winningham	.20	.15	.08
547	Jeff Innis	.20	.15	.08
548	Chuck Knoblauch	3.00	2.25	1.25
549	Tommy Greene	.25	.20	.10
550	Jeff Hamilton	.20	.15	.08
551	Barry Jones	.20	.15	.08
552	Ken Dayley	.20	.15	.08
553	Rick Dempsey	.20	.15	.08
554	Greg Smith	.20	.15	.08
555	Mike Devereaux	.20	.15	.08
556	Keith Comstock	.20	.15	.08
557	Paul Faries	.20	.15	.08
558	Tom Glavine	.50	.40	.20
559	Craig Grebeck	.20	.15	.08
560	Scott Erickson	5.00	3.75	2.00
561	Joel Skinner	.20	.15	.08
562	Mike Morgan	.20	.15	.08
563	Dave Gallagher	.20	.15	.08
564	Todd Stottlemyre	.25	.20	.10
565	Rich Rodriguez	.25	.20	.10
566	Craig Wilson	.25	.20	.10
567	Jeff Brantley	.25	.20	.10
568	Scott Kamieniecki	.30	.25	.12
569	Steve Decker	.80	.60	.30
570	Juan Agosto	.20	.15	.08
571	Tommy Gregg	.20	.15	.08
572	Kevin Wickander	.20	.15	.08
573	Jamie Quirk	.20	.15	.08
574	Jerry Don Gleaton	.20	.15	.08
575	Chris Hammond	.20	.15	.08
576	Luis Gonzalez	3.00	2.25	1.25
577	Russ Swan	.20	.15	.08
578	Jeff Conine	.40	.30	.15
579	Charlie Hough	.20	.15	.08
580	Jeff Kunkel	.20	.15	.08
581	Darrel Akerfelds	.20	.15	.08
582	Jeff Manto	.25	.20	.10
583	Alejandro Pena	.20	.15	.08
584	Mark Davidson	.20	.15	.08
585	Bob MacDonald	.25	.20	.10
586	Paul Assenmacher	.20	.15	.08
587	Dan Wilson	.60	.45	.25
588	Tom Bolton	.20	.15	.08
589	Brian Harper	.20	.15	.08
590	John Habyan	.20	.15	.08
591	John Orton	.20	.15	.08
592	Mark Gardner	.20	.15	.08
593	Turner Ward	.40	.30	.15
594	Bob Patterson	.20	.15	.08
595	Edwin Nunez	.20	.15	.08
596	Gary Scott	.40	.30	.15
597	Scott Bankhead	.20	.15	.08
598	Checklist	.20	.15	.08
599	Checklist	.20	.15	.08
600	Checklist	.20	.15	.08

1991 Topps Traded

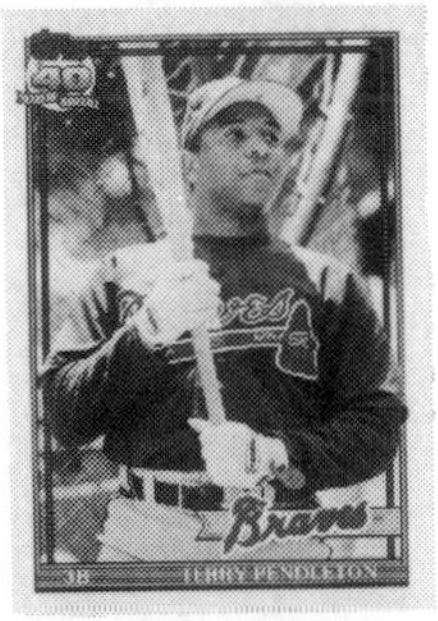

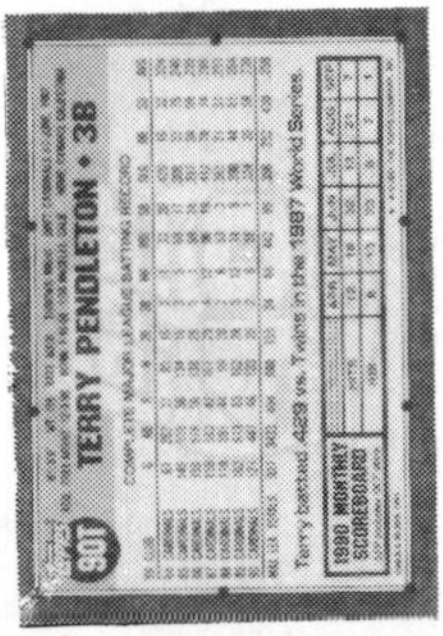

"Team USA" is featured in the 1991 Topps Traded set. The cards feature the same style as the regular 1991 issue, including the 40th anniversary logo. The set includes 132 cards and showcases rookies and traded players along with "Team USA." The cards are numbered with a "T" designation in alphabetical order.

		MT	NR MT	EX
Complete Set:		12.00	9.00	4.75
Common Player:		.05	.04	.02
1	Juan Agosto	.05	.04	.02
2	Roberto Alomar	.20	.15	.08
3	Wally Backman	.05	.04	.02
4	Jeff Bagwell(FC)	2.00	1.50	.80
5	Skeeter Barnes(FC)	.15	.11	.06

		MT	NR MT	EX
6	Steve Bedrosian	.06	.05	.02
7	Derek Bell(FC)	.35	.25	.14
8	George Bell	.10	.08	.04
9	Rafael Belliard	.05	.04	.02
10	Dante Bichette	.06	.05	.02
11	Bud Black	.05	.04	.02
12	Mike Boddicker	.06	.05	.02
13	Sid Bream	.06	.05	.02
14	Hubie Brooks	.06	.05	.02
15	Brett Butler	.08	.06	.03
16	Ivan Calderon	.08	.06	.03
17	John Candelaria	.05	.04	.02
18	Tom Candiotti	.06	.05	.02
19	Gary Carter	.08	.06	.03
20	Joe Carter	.12	.09	.05
21	Rick Cerone	.05	.04	.02
22	Jack Clark	.08	.06	.03
23	Vince Coleman	.15	.11	.06
24	Scott Coolbaugh	.10	.08	.04
25	Danny Cox	.05	.04	.02
26	Danny Darwin	.05	.04	.02
27	Chili Davis	.08	.06	.03
28	Glenn Davis	.08	.06	.03
29	Steve Decker(FC)	.40	.30	.15
30	Rob Deer	.06	.05	.02
31	Rich DeLucia(FC)	.15	.11	.06
32	John Dettmer (U.S.A.)(FC)	.20	.15	.08
33	Brian Downing	.05	.04	.02
34	Darren Dreifort (U.S.A.)(FC)	.20	.15	.08
35	Kirk Dressendorfer(FC)	.40	.30	.15
36	Jim Essian	.05	.04	.02
37	Dwight Evans	.08	.06	.03
38	Steve Farr	.06	.05	.02
39	Jeff Fassero(FC)	.20	.15	.08
40	Junior Felix	.08	.06	.03
41	Tony Fernandez	.08	.06	.03
42	Steve Finley	.08	.06	.03
43	Jim Fregosi	.05	.04	.02
44	Gary Gaetti	.06	.05	.02
45	Jason Giambi (U.S.A.)(FC)	.30	.25	.12
46	Kirk Gibson	.08	.06	.03
47	Leo Gomez(FC)	.40	.30	.15
48	Luis Gonzalez(FC)	.30	.25	.12
49	Jeff Granger (U.S.A.)(FC)	.20	.15	.08
50	Todd Greene (U.S.A.)(FC)	.20	.15	.08
51	Jeffrey Hammonds (U.S.A.)(FC)	.20	.15	.08
52	Mike Hargrove	.05	.04	.02
53	Pete Harnisch	.08	.06	.03
54	Rick Helling (U.S.A.)(FC)	.20	.15	.08
55	Glenallen Hill	.08	.06	.03
56	Charlie Hough	.06	.05	.02
57	Pete Incaviglia	.08	.06	.03
58	Bo Jackson	.80	.60	.30
59	Danny Jackson	.06	.05	.02
60	Reggie Jefferson(FC)	.50	.40	.20
61	Charles Johnson (U.S.A.)(FC)	.25	.20	.10
62	Jeff Johnson(FC)	.20	.15	.08
63	Todd Johnson (U.S.A.)(FC)	.20	.15	.08
64	Barry Jones	.05	.04	.02
65	Chris Jones(FC)	.20	.15	.08
66	Scott Kamieniecki(FC)	.20	.15	.08
67	Pat Kelly(FC)	.50	.40	.20
68	Darryl Kile(FC)	.20	.15	.08
69	Chuck Knoblauch(FC)	.40	.30	.15
70	Bill Krueger	.05	.04	.02
71	Scott Leius(FC)	.15	.11	.06
72	Donnie Leshnock (U.S.A.)(FC)	.20	.15	.08
73	Mark Lewis	.30	.25	.12
74	Candy Maldonado	.06	.05	.02
75	Jason McDonald (U.S.A.)(FC)	.25	.20	.10
76	Willie McGee	.08	.06	.03
77	Fred McGriff	.10	.08	.04
78	Billy McMillon (U.S.A.)(FC)	.20	.15	.08
79	Hal McRae	.06	.05	.02
80	Dan Melendez (U.S.A.)(FC)	.20	.15	.08
81	Orlando Merced(FC)	.40	.30	.15
82	Jack Morris	.08	.06	.03
83	Phil Nevin (U.S.A.)(FC)	.25	.20	.10
84	Otis Nixon	.06	.05	.02
85	Johnny Oates	.05	.04	.02
86	Bob Ojeda	.05	.04	.02
87	Mike Pagliarulo	.05	.04	.02
88	Dean Palmer(FC)	.35	.25	.14
89	Dave Parker	.08	.06	.03
90	Terry Pendleton	.08	.06	.03
91	Tony Phillips (U.S.A.)(FC)	.20	.15	.08
92	Doug Piatt(FC)	.20	.15	.08
93	Ron Polk (U.S.A.)	.06	.05	.02
94	Rock Raines	.12	.09	.05
95	Willie Randolph	.06	.05	.02
96	Dave Righetti	.06	.05	.02

		MT	NR MT	EX
97	Ernie Riles	.05	.04	.02
98	Chris Roberts (U.S.A.)(FC)	.20	.15	.08
99	Jeff Robinson (Angels)	.05	.04	.02
100	Jeff Robinson (Orioles)	.05	.04	.02
101	Ivan Rodriguez(FC)	2.00	1.50	.80
102	Steve Rodriguez (U.S.A.)(FC)	.20	.15	.08
103	Tom Runnells	.05	.04	.02
104	Scott Sanderson	.06	.05	.02
105	Bob Scanlan(FC)	.15	.11	.06
106	Pete Schourek(FC)	.15	.11	.06
107	Gary Scott(FC)	.35	.25	.14
108	Paul Shuey (U.S.A.)(FC)	.20	.15	.08
109	Doug Simons(FC)	.20	.15	.08
110	Dave Smith	.06	.05	.02
111	Cory Snyder	.05	.04	.02
112	Luis Sojo	.06	.05	.02
113	Kennie Steenstra (U.S.A.)(FC)	.20	.15	.08
114	Darryl Strawberry	.30	.25	.12
115	Franklin Stubbs	.05	.04	.02
116	Todd Taylor (U.S.A.)(FC)	.20	.15	.08
117	Wade Taylor(FC)	.20	.15	.08
118	Garry Templeton	.06	.05	.02
119	Mickey Tettleton	.06	.05	.02
120	Tim Teufel	.05	.04	.02
121	Mike Timlin(FC)	.20	.15	.08
122	David Tuttle (U.S.A.)(FC)	.20	.15	.08
123	Mo Vaughn(FC)	.50	.40	.20
124	Jeff Ware (U.S.A.)(FC)	.20	.15	.08
125	Devon White	.08	.06	.03
126	Mark Whiten	.20	.15	.08
127	Mitch Williams	.08	.06	.03
128	Craig Wilson (U.S.A.)(FC)	.20	.15	.08
129	Willie Wilson	.06	.05	.02
130	Chris Wimmer (U.S.A.)(FC)	.25	.20	.10
131	Ivan Zweig (U.S.A.)(FC)	.20	.15	.08
132	Checklist	.05	.04	.02

1992 Topps

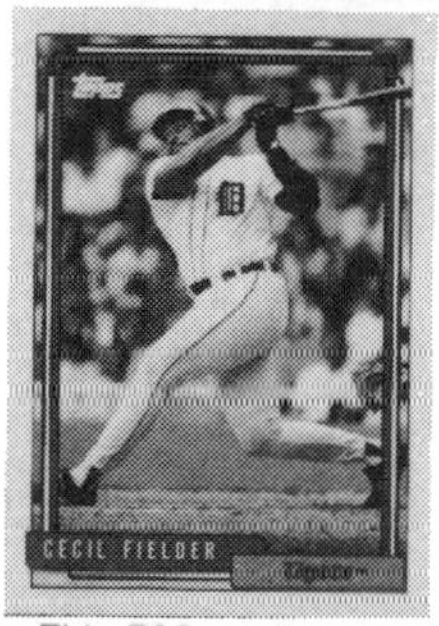

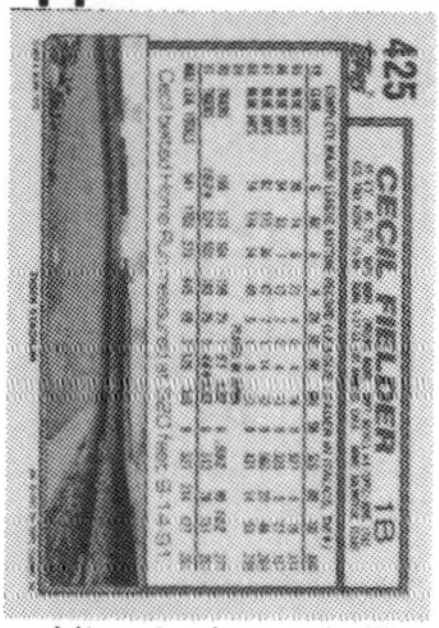

This 792-card set features white stock much like the 1991 issue. The card fronts feature full-color action and posed photos with a gray inner frame and the player name and position on the bottom. The backs feature biographical information, statistics and stadium photos on player cards where space is available. All-Star cards and #1 Draft Pick cards are once again included. Topps brought back four-player rookie cards in 1992. Nine Top Prospect cards of this nature can be found within the set. Several cards can once again be found with horizontal fronts. "Match the Stats" game cards were inserted into packs of 1992 Topps cards. Special bonus cards were given away to winners of this insert game. Record Breaker cards are also featured in this set.

	MT	NR MT	EX
Complete Set:	20.00	15.00	8.00
Common Player:	.03	.02	.01

		MT	NR MT	EX
1	Nolan Ryan	.30	.25	.12
2	Record Breaker (Rickey Henderson)	.10	.08	.04
3	Record Breaker (Jeff Reardon)	.05	.04	.02
4	Record Breaker (Nolan Ryan)	.10	.08	.04
5	Record Breaker (Dave Winfield)	.06	.05	.02
6	#1 Draft Pick *(Brien Taylor)*(FC)	2.00	1.50	.80
7	*Jim Olander*(FC)	.10	.08	.04
8	*Bryan Hickerson*(FC)	.10	.08	.04
9	John Farrell	.03	.02	.01

		MT	NR MT	EX
10	Wade Boggs	.15	.11	.06
11	Jack McDowell	.08	.06	.03
12	Luis Gonzalez	.15	.11	.06
13	Mike Scioscia	.04	.03	.02
14	Wes Chamberlain	.20	.15	.08
15	Denny Martinez	.04	.03	.02
16	Jeff Montgomery	.04	.03	.02
17	Randy Milligan	.06	.05	.02
18	Greg Cadaret	.03	.02	.01
19	Jamie Quirk	.03	.02	.01
20	Bip Roberts	.05	.04	.02
21	Buck Rogers	.03	.02	.01
22	Bill Wegman	.04	.03	.02
23	Chuck Knoblauch	.20	.15	.08
24	Randy Myers	.05	.04	.02
25	Ron Gant	.12	.09	.05
26	Mike Bielecki	.03	.02	.01
27	Juan Gonzalez	.20	.15	.08
28	Mike Schooler	.04	.03	.02
29	Mickey Tettleton	.05	.04	.02
30	John Kruk	.06	.05	.02
31	Bryn Smith	.03	.02	.01
32	Chris Nabholz	.06	.05	.02
33	Carlos Baerga	.08	.06	.03
34	Jeff Juden	.15	.11	.06
35	Dave Righetti	.06	.05	.02
36	#1 Draft Pick *(Scott Ruffcorn)*(FC)	.25	.20	.10
37	Luis Polonia	.04	.03	.02
38	Tom Candiotti	.04	.03	.02
39	Greg Olson	.04	.03	.02
40	Cal Ripken	.20	.15	.08
41	Craig Lefferts	.04	.03	.02
42	Mike Macfarlane	.04	.03	.02
43	Jose Lind	.04	.03	.02
44	Rick Aguilera	.05	.04	.02
45	Gary Carter	.08	.06	.03
46	Steve Farr	.04	.03	.02
47	Rex Hudler	.04	.03	.02
48	Scott Scudder	.05	.04	.02
49	Damon Berryhill	.04	.03	.02
50	Ken Griffey, Jr.	.40	.30	.15
51	Tom Runnells	.03	.02	.01
52	Juan Bell	.05	.04	.02
53	Tommy Gregg	.03	.02	.01
54	David Wells	.04	.03	.02
55	Rafael Palmeiro	.10	.08	.04
56	Charlie O'Brien	.03	.02	.01
57	Donn Pall	.03	.02	.01
58	Top Prospects-Catchers *(Brad Ausmus, Jim Campanis, Dave Nilsson, Doug Robbins)*(FC)	.40	.30	.15
59	Mo Vaughn	.25	.20	.10
60	Tony Fernandez	.05	.04	.02
61	Paul O'Neill	.06	.05	.02
62	Gene Nelson	.03	.02	.01
63	Randy Ready	.03	.02	.01
64	Bob Kipper	.03	.02	.01
65	Willie McGee	.08	.06	.03
66	#1 Draft Pick *(Scott Stahoviak)*(FC)	.30	.25	.12
67	Luis Salazar	.03	.02	.01
68	Marvin Freeman	.03	.02	.01
69	*Kenny Lofton*(FC)	.20	.15	.08
70	Gary Gaetti	.06	.05	.02
71	Erik Hanson	.08	.06	.03
72	Eddie Zosky(FC)	.10	.08	.04
73	Brian Barnes	.10	.08	.04
74	Scott Leius	.10	.08	.04
75	Bret Saberhagen	.08	.06	.03
76	Mike Gallego	.03	.02	.01
77	Jack Armstrong	.05	.04	.02
78	*Ivan Rodriguez*	1.00	.70	.40
79	Jesse Orosco	.03	.02	.01
80	David Justice	.20	.15	.08
81	*Ced Landrum*(FC)	.15	.11	.06
82	*Doug Simons*	.10	.08	.04
83	Tommy Greene	.06	.05	.02
84	Leo Gomez	.15	.11	.06
85	Jose DeLeon	.04	.03	.02
86	Steve Finley	.06	.05	.02
87	*Bob MacDonald*(FC)	.15	.11	.06
88	Darrin Jackson	.04	.03	.02
89	Neal Heaton	.03	.02	.01
90	Robin Yount	.12	.09	.05
91	Jeff Reed	.03	.02	.01
92	Lenny Harris	.04	.03	.02
93	Reggie Jefferson	.15	.11	.06
94	Sammy Sosa	.08	.06	.03
95	Scott Bailes	.03	.02	.01
96	#1 Draft Pick *(Tom McKinnon)*(FC)	.15	.11	.06
97	Luis Rivera	.03	.02	.01
98	Mike Harkey	.06	.05	.02
99	Jeff Treadway	.04	.03	.02
100	Jose Canseco	.20	.15	.08
101	Omar Vizquel	.03	.02	.01
102	*Scott Kamieniecki*	.12	.09	.05
103	Ricky Jordan	.06	.05	.02
104	Jeff Ballard	.04	.03	.02
105	Felix Jose	.10	.08	.04
106	Mike Boddicker	.05	.04	.02
107	Dan Pasqua	.04	.03	.02
108	*Mike Timlin*	.12	.09	.05
109	Roger Craig	.04	.03	.02
110	Ryne Sandberg	.20	.15	.08
111	Mark Carreon	.03	.02	.01
112	Oscar Azocar	.04	.03	.02
113	Mike Greenwell	.10	.08	.04
114	Mark Portugal	.03	.02	.01
115	Terry Pendleton	.08	.06	.03
116	Willie Randolph	.05	.04	.02
117	Scott Terry	.03	.02	.01
118	Chili Davis	.08	.06	.03
119	Mark Gardner	.05	.04	.02
120	Alan Trammell	.10	.08	.04
121	Derek Bell	.25	.20	.10
122	Gary Varsho	.03	.02	.01
123	Bob Ojeda	.04	.03	.02
124	#1 Draft Pick *(Shawn Livsey)*(FC)	.15	.11	.06
125	Chris Hoiles	.08	.06	.03
126	Top Prospects-1st Baseman (Rico Brogna, *John Jaha, Ryan Klesko*, Dave Staton)(FC)	1.25	.90	.50
127	Carlos Quintana	.06	.05	.02
128	Kurt Stillwell	.04	.03	.02
129	Melido Perez	.04	.03	.02
130	Alvin Davis	.06	.05	.02
131	Checklist 1	.03	.02	.01
132	Eric Show	.03	.02	.01
133	Rance Mulliniks	.03	.02	.01
134	Darryl Kile	.08	.06	.03
135	Von Hayes	.05	.04	.02
136	Bill Doran	.05	.04	.02
137	Jeff Robinson	.03	.02	.01
138	Monty Fariss	.08	.06	.03
139	Jeff Innis	.05	.04	.03
140	Mark Grace	.12	.09	.05
141	Jim Leyland	.03	.02	.01
142	Todd Van Poppel(FC)	.50	.40	.20
143	Paul Gibson	.03	.02	.01
144	Bill Swift	.04	.03	.02
145	Danny Tartabull	.08	.06	.03
146	Al Newman	.03	.02	.01
147	Cris Carpenter	.04	.03	.02
148	*Anthony Young*(FC)	.25	.20	.10
149	*Brian Bohanon*(FC)	.15	.11	.06
150	Roger Clemens	.15	.11	.06
151	Jeff Hamilton	.03	.02	.01
152	Charlie Leibrandt	.04	.03	.02
153	Ron Karkovice	.04	.03	.02
154	Hensley Meulens	.08	.06	.03
155	Scott Bankhead	.04	.03	.02
156	#1 Draft Pick *(Manny Ramirez)*(FC)	.35	.25	.14
157	Keith Miller	.03	.02	.01
158	Todd Frohwirth	.03	.02	.01
159	Darrin Fletcher	.05	.04	.02
160	Bobby Bonilla	.12	.09	.05
161	Casey Candaele	.03	.02	.01
162	Paul Faries(FC)	.10	.08	.04
163	Dana Kiecker	.03	.02	.01
164	Shane Mack	.08	.06	.03
165	Mark Langston	.10	.08	.04
166	Geronimo Pena	.06	.05	.02
167	Andy Allanson	.03	.02	.01
168	Dwight Smith	.04	.03	.02
169	Chuck Crim	.03	.02	.01
170	Alex Cole	.05	.04	.02
171	Bill Plummer	.03	.02	.01
172	Juan Berenguer	.03	.02	.01
173	Brian Downing	.04	.03	.02
174	Steve Frey	.03	.02	.01
175	Orel Hershiser	.08	.06	.03
176	*Ramon Garcia*(FC)	.15	.11	.06
177	Danny Gladden	.04	.03	.02
178	Jim Acker	.03	.02	.01
179	Top Prospects-2nd Baseman *(Cesar Bernhardt, Bobby DeJardin, Armando Moreno, Andy Stankiewicz)*(FC)	.25	.20	.10
180	Kevin Mitchell	.10	.08	.04
181	Hector Villanueva	.06	.05	.02
182	Jeff Reardon	.06	.05	.02
183	Brent Mayne	.06	.05	.02

		MT	NR MT	EX
184	Jimmy Jones	.03	.02	.01
185	Benny Santiago	.08	.06	.03
186	#1 Draft Pick *(Cliff Floyd)*(FC)	.25	.20	.10
187	Ernie Riles	.03	.02	.01
188	Jose Guzman	.05	.04	.02
189	Junior Felix	.06	.05	.02
190	Glenn Davis	.08	.06	.03
191	Charlie Hough	.04	.03	.02
192	*Dave Fleming*(FC)	.15	.11	.06
193	Omar Oliveras(FC)	.08	.06	.03
194	Eric Karros(FC)	.20	.15	.08
195	David Cone	.08	.06	.03
196	*Frank Castillo*(FC)	.12	.09	.05
197	Glenn Braggs	.04	.03	.02
198	Scott Aldred	.06	.05	.02
199	Jeff Blauser	.04	.03	.02
200	Len Dykstra	.08	.06	.03
201	Buck Showalter	.03	.02	.01
202	Rick Honeycutt	.03	.02	.01
203	Greg Myers	.03	.02	.01
204	Trevor Wilson	.05	.04	.02
205	Jay Howell	.04	.03	.02
206	Luis Sojo	.05	.04	.02
207	Jack Clark	.08	.06	.03
208	Julio Machado	.03	.02	.01
209	Lloyd McClendon	.03	.02	.01
210	Ozzie Guillen	.06	.05	.02
211	*Jeremy Hernandez*(FC)	.15	.11	.06
212	Randy Velarde	.03	.02	.01
213	Les Lancaster	.03	.02	.01
214	*Andy Mota*(FC)	.15	.11	.06
215	Rich Gossage	.05	.04	.02
216	#1 Draft Pick *(Brent Gates)*(FC)	.25	.20	.10
217	Brian Harper	.05	.04	.02
218	Mike Flanagan	.03	.02	.01
219	Jerry Browne	.04	.03	.02
220	Jose Rijo	.08	.06	.03
221	Skeeter Barnes	.04	.03	.02
222	Jaime Navarro	.04	.03	.02
223	Mel Hall	.04	.03	.02
224	*Brett Barberie*	.20	.15	.08
225	Roberto Alomar	.10	.08	.04
226	Pete Smith	.03	.02	.01
227	Daryl Boston	.03	.02	.01
228	Eddie Whitson	.04	.03	.02
229	Shawn Boskie	.04	.03	.02
230	Dick Schofield	.03	.02	.01
231	*Brian Drahman*(FC)	.10	.08	.04
232	John Smiley	.05	.04	.02
233	Mitch Webster	.04	.03	.02
234	Terry Steinbach	.05	.04	.02
235	Jack Morris	.08	.06	.03
236	Bill Pecota	.04	.03	.02
237	*Jose Hernandez*(FC)	.10	.08	.04
238	Greg Litton	.03	.02	.01
239	Brian Holman	.05	.04	.02
240	Andres Galarraga	.06	.05	.02
241	Gerald Young	.03	.02	.01
242	Mike Mussina(FC)	.25	.20	.10
243	Alvaro Espinoza	.03	.02	.01
244	Darren Daulton	.04	.03	.02
245	John Smoltz	.08	.06	.03
246	#1 Draft Pick *(Jason Pruitt)*(FC)	.15	.11	.06
247	Chuck Finley	.08	.06	.03
248	Jim Gantner	.04	.03	.02
249	Tony Fossas	.03	.02	.01
250	Ken Griffey	.05	.04	.02
251	Kevin Elster	.04	.03	.02
252	Dennis Rasmussen	.03	.02	.01
253	Terry Kennedy	.03	.02	.01
254	*Ryan Bowen*(FC)	.15	.11	.06
255	Robin Ventura	.15	.11	.06
256	Mike Aldrete	.03	.02	.01
257	Jeff Russell	.04	.03	.02
258	Jim Lindeman	.03	.02	.01
259	Ron Darling	.05	.04	.02
260	Devon White	.06	.05	.02
261	Tom Lasorda	.04	.03	.02
262	Terry Lee(FC)	.10	.08	.04
263	Bob Patterson	.03	.02	.01
264	Checklist 2	.03	.02	.01
265	Teddy Higuera	.05	.04	.02
266	Roberto Kelly	.08	.06	.03
267	Steve Bedrosian	.04	.03	.02
268	Brady Anderson	.03	.02	.01
269	*Ruben Amaro*(FC)	.15	.11	.06
270	Tony Gwynn	.12	.09	.05
271	Tracy Jones	.03	.02	.01
272	Jerry Don Gleaton	.03	.02	.01
273	Craig Grebeck	.04	.03	.02
274	*Bob Scanlan*	.10	.08	.04
275	Todd Zeile	.10	.08	.04
276	#1 Draft Pick *(Shawn Green)*(FC)	.20	.15	.08
277	Scott Chiamparino	.04	.03	.02
278	Darryl Hamilton	.04	.03	.02
279	Jim Clancy	.03	.02	.01
280	Carlos Martinez	.04	.03	.02
281	Kevin Appier	.05	.04	.02
282	*John Wehner*(FC)	.15	.11	.06
283	*Reggie Sanders*(FC)	.25	.20	.10
284	Gene Larkin	.04	.03	.02
285	Bob Welch	.06	.05	.02
286	Gilberto Reyes(FC)	.05	.04	.02
287	*Pete Schourek*	.15	.11	.06
288	Andujar Cedeno	.15	.11	.06
289	Mike Morgan	.04	.03	.02
290	Bo Jackson	.20	.15	.08
291	Phil Garner	.03	.02	.01
292	Ray Lankford	.15	.11	.06
293	Mike Henneman	.05	.04	.02
294	Dave Valle	.03	.02	.01
295	Alonzo Powell(FC)	.08	.06	.03
296	Tom Brunansky	.05	.04	.02
297	Kevin Brown	.05	.04	.02
298	Kelly Gruber	.08	.06	.03
299	Charles Nagy	.06	.05	.02
300	Don Mattingly	.15	.11	.06
301	Kirk McCaskill	.04	.03	.02
302	Joey Cora	.04	.03	.02
303	Dan Plesac	.04	.03	.02
304	Joe Oliver	.04	.03	.02
305	Tom Glavine	.08	.06	.03
306	#1 Draft Pick *(Al Shirley)*(FC)	.25	.20	.10
307	Bruce Ruffin	.03	.02	.01
308	*Craig Shipley*(FC)	.08	.06	.03
309	Dave Martinez	.04	.03	.02
310	Jose Mesa	.03	.02	.01
311	Henry Cotto	.03	.02	.01
312	Mike LaValliere	.04	.03	.02
313	Kevin Tapani	.08	.06	.03
314	Jeff Huson	.04	.03	.02
315	Juan Samuel	.06	.05	.02
316	Curt Schilling	.06	.05	.02
317	Mike Bordick(FC)	.06	.05	.02
318	Steve Howe	.04	.03	.02
319	Tony Phillips	.04	.03	.02
320	George Bell	.10	.08	.04
321	Lou Pinella	.03	.02	.01
322	Tim Burke	.04	.03	.02
323	Milt Thompson	.04	.03	.02
324	Danny Darwin	.04	.03	.02
325	Joe Orsulak	.03	.02	.01
326	Eric King	.04	.03	.02
327	Jay Buhner	.05	.04	.02
328	*Joel Johnson*(FC)	.15	.11	.06
329	Franklin Stubbs	.03	.02	.01
330	Will Clark	.20	.15	.08
331	Steve Lake	.03	.02	.01
332	*Chris Jones*	.10	.08	.04
333	Pat Tabler	.03	.02	.01
334	Kevin Gross	.03	.02	.01
335	Dave Henderson	.08	.06	.03
336	#1 Draft Pick *(Greg Anthony)*(FC)	.15	.11	.06
337	Alejandro Pena	.04	.03	.02
338	Shawn Abner	.03	.02	.01
339	Tom Browning	.06	.05	.02
340	Otis Nixon	.04	.03	.02
341	Bob Geren	.03	.02	.01
342	*Tim Spehr*(FC)	.10	.08	.04
343	*Jon Vander Wal*(FC)	.15	.11	.06
344	Jack Daugherty	.03	.02	.01
345	Zane Smith	.04	.03	.02
346	*Rheal Cormier*(FC)	.15	.11	.06
347	Kent Hrbek	.06	.05	.02
348	*Rick Wilkins*(FC)	.15	.11	.06
349	Steve Lyons	.03	.02	.01
350	Gregg Olson	.08	.06	.03
351	Greg Riddoch	.03	.02	.01
352	Ed Nunez	.03	.02	.01
353	*Braulio Castillo*(FC)	.08	.06	.03
354	Dave Bergman	.03	.02	.01
355	*Warren Newson*(FC)	.15	.11	.06
356	Luis Quinones	.03	.02	.01
357	Mike Witt	.04	.03	.02
358	*Ted Wood*	.15	.11	.06
359	Mike Moore	.04	.03	.02
360	Lance Parrish	.06	.05	.02
361	Barry Jones	.03	.02	.01
362	*Javier Ortiz*(FC)	.10	.08	.04
363	John Candelaria	.04	.03	.02
364	Glenallen Hill	.06	.05	.02
365	Duane Ward	.04	.03	.02

		MT	NR MT	EX
366	Checklist 3	.03	.02	.01
367	Rafael Belliard	.03	.02	.01
368	Bill Krueger	.03	.02	.01
369	#1 Draft Pick *(Steve Whitaker)*(FC)	.20	.15	.08
370	Shawon Dunston	.06	.05	.02
371	Dante Bichette	.04	.03	.02
372	*Kip Gross*(FC)	.10	.08	.04
373	Don Robinson	.03	.02	.01
374	Bernie Williams	.03	.02	.01
375	Bert Blyleven	.05	.04	.02
376	*Chris Donnels*(FC)	.15	.11	.06
377	*Bob Zupcic*(FC)	.15	.11	.06
378	Joel Skinner	.03	.02	.01
379	Steve Chitren	.06	.05	.02
380	Barry Bonds	.15	.11	.06
381	Sparky Anderson	.03	.02	.01
382	Sid Fernandez	.05	.04	.02
383	Dave Hollins	.06	.05	.02
384	Mark Lee	.03	.02	.01
385	Tim Wallach	.05	.04	.02
386	Will Clark (AS)	.10	.08	.04
387	Ryne Sandberg (AS)	.10	.08	.04
388	Howard Johnson (AS)	.05	.04	.02
389	Barry Larkin (AS)	.05	.04	.02
390	Barry Bonds (AS)	.10	.08	.04
391	Ron Gant (AS)	.08	.06	.03
392	Bobby Bonilla (AS)	.08	.06	.03
393	Craig Biggio (AS)	.05	.04	.02
394	Denny Martinez (AS)	.04	.03	.02
395	Tom Glavine (AS)	.05	.04	.02
396	Ozzie Smith (AS)	.08	.06	.03
397	Cecil Fielder (AS)	.10	.08	.04
398	Julio Franco (AS)	.08	.06	.03
399	Wade Boggs (AS)	.10	.08	.04
400	Cal Ripken (AS)	.15	.11	.06
401	Jose Canseco (AS)	.15	.11	.06
402	Joe Carter (AS)	.08	.06	.03
403	Ruben Sierra (AS)	.10	.08	.04
404	Matt Nokes (AS)	.04	.03	.02
405	Roger Clemens (AS)	.12	.09	.05
406	Jim Abbott (AS)	.08	.06	.03
407	Bryan Harvey (AS)	.05	.04	.02
408	Bob Milacki	.03	.02	.01
409	Geno Petralli	.03	.02	.01
410	Dave Stewart	.08	.06	.03
411	Mike Jackson	.03	.02	.01
412	Luis Aquino	.03	.02	.01
413	Tim Teufel	.03	.02	.01
414	#1 Draft Pick *(Jeff Ware)*(FC)	.15	.11	.06
415	Jim Deshaies	.04	.03	.02
416	Ellis Burks	.10	.08	.04
417	Allan Anderson	.03	.02	.01
418	Alfredo Griffin	.03	.02	.01
419	Wally Whitehurst	.05	.04	.02
420	Sandy Alomar	.08	.06	.03
421	Juan Agosto	.03	.02	.01
422	Sam Horn	.03	.02	.01
423	*Jeff Fassero*	.10	.08	.04
424	*Paul McClellan*(FC)	.10	.08	.04
425	Cecil Fielder	.15	.11	.06
426	Rock Raines	.10	.08	.04
427	*Eddie Taubensee*(FC)	.15	.11	.06
428	Dennis Boyd	.05	.04	.02
429	Tony LaRussa	.03	.02	.01
430	Steve Sax	.06	.05	.02
431	Tom Gordon	.08	.06	.03
432	Billy Hatcher	.04	.03	.02
433	Cal Eldred(FC)	.10	.08	.04
434	Wally Backman	.03	.02	.01
435	Mark Eichhorn	.03	.02	.01
436	Mookie Wilson	.03	.02	.01
437	*Scott Servais*	.10	.08	.04
438	Mike Maddux	.03	.02	.01
439	*Chico Walker*(FC)	.10	.08	.04
440	Doug Drabek	.08	.06	.03
441	Rob Deer	.04	.03	.02
442	Dave West	.04	.03	.02
443	Spike Owen	.03	.02	.01
444	#1 Draft Pick *(Tyrone Hill)*(FC)	.15	.11	.06
445	Matt Williams	.12	.09	.05
446	Mark Lewis	.12	.09	.05
447	David Segui	.08	.06	.03
448	Tom Pagnozzi	.04	.03	.02
449	*Jeff Johnson*	.12	.09	.05
450	Mark McGwire	.12	.09	.05
451	Tom Henke	.05	.04	.02
452	Wilson Alvarez	.08	.06	.03
453	Gary Redus	.03	.02	.01
454	Darren Holmes	.03	.02	.01
455	Pete O'Brien	.03	.02	.01
456	Pat Combs	.04	.03	.02

		MT	NR MT	EX
457	Hubie Brooks	.04	.03	.02
458	Frank Tanana	.03	.02	.01
459	Tom Kelly	.03	.02	.01
460	Andre Dawson	.12	.09	.05
461	Doug Jones	.04	.03	.02
462	Rich Rodriguez	.04	.03	.02
463	*Mike Simms*	.10	.08	.04
464	Mike Jeffcoat	.03	.02	.01
465	Barry Larkin	.12	.09	.05
466	Stan Belinda	.04	.03	.02
467	Lonnie Smith	.04	.03	.02
468	Greg Harris	.03	.02	.01
469	Jim Eisenreich	.03	.02	.01
470	Pedro Guerrero	.08	.06	.03
471	Jose DeJesus	.04	.03	.02
472	*Rich Rowland*(FC)	.15	.11	.06
473	Top Prospects-3rd Baseman *(Frank Bolick, Craig Paquette, Tom Redington, Paul Russo)*(FC)	.35	.25	.14
474	#1 Draft Pick *(Mike Rossiter)*(FC)	.25	.20	.10
475	Robby Thompson	.04	.03	.02
476	Randy Bush	.03	.02	.01
477	Greg Hibbard	.04	.03	.02
478	Dale Sveum	.03	.02	.01
479	*Chito Martinez*(FC)	.20	.15	.08
480	Scott Sanderson	.04	.03	.02
481	Tino Martinez	.10	.08	.04
482	Jimmy Key	.05	.04	.02
483	Terry Shumpert	.03	.02	.01
484	Mike Hartley	.03	.02	.01
485	Chris Sabo	.08	.06	.03
486	Bob Walk	.03	.02	.01
487	John Cerutti	.03	.02	.01
488	Scott Cooper(FC)	.10	.08	.04
489	Bobby Cox	.03	.02	.01
490	Julio Franco	.10	.08	.04
491	Jeff Brantley	.04	.03	.02
492	Mike Devereaux	.04	.03	.02
493	Jose Offerman	.10	.08	.04
494	Gary Thurman	.03	.02	.01
495	Carney Lansford	.06	.05	.02
496	Joe Grahe	.04	.03	.02
497	*Andy Ashby*(FC)	.15	.11	.06
498	Gerald Perry	.03	.02	.01
499	Dave Otto	.03	.02	.01
500	Vince Coleman	.08	.06	.03
501	*Rob Mallicoat*(FC)	.15	.11	.06
502	Greg Briley	.03	.02	.01
503	Pascual Perez	.03	.02	.01
504	#1 Draft Pick *(Aaron Sele)*(FC)	.25	.20	.10
505	Bobby Thigpen	.08	.06	.03
506	Todd Benzinger	.04	.03	.02
507	Candy Maldonado	.04	.03	.02
508	Bill Gullickson	.05	.04	.02
509	Doug Dascenzo	.03	.02	.01
510	Frank Viola	.08	.06	.03
511	Kenny Rogers	.04	.03	.02
512	Mike Heath	.03	.02	.01
513	Kevin Bass	.04	.03	.02
514	*Kim Batiste*(FC)	.15	.11	.06
515	Delino DeShields	.08	.06	.03
516	*Ed Sprague*	.10	.08	.04
517	Jim Gott	.03	.02	.01
518	*Jose Melendez*(FC)	.10	.08	.04
519	Hal McRae	.03	.02	.01
520	*Jeff Bagwell*	.40	.30	.15
521	Joe Hesketh	.03	.02	.01
522	Milt Cuyler	.12	.09	.05
523	Shawn Hillegas	.03	.02	.01
524	Don Slaught	.03	.02	.01
525	Randy Johnson	.06	.05	.02
526	*Doug Piatt*	.10	.08	.04
527	Checklist 4	.03	.02	.01
528	*Steve Foster*(FC)	.15	.11	.06
529	Joe Girardi	.04	.03	.02
530	Jim Abbott	.10	.08	.04
531	Larry Walker	.08	.06	.03
532	Mike Huff	.04	.03	.02
533	Mackey Sasser	.03	.02	.01
534	#1 Draft Pick *(Benji Gil)*(FC)	.15	.11	.06
535	Dave Stieb	.06	.05	.02
536	Willie Wilson	.04	.03	.02
537	*Mark Leiter*(FC)	.10	.08	.04
538	Jose Uribe	.03	.02	.01
539	Thomas Howard	.03	.02	.01
540	Ben McDonald	.12	.09	.05
541	*Jose Tolentino*(FC)	.15	.11	.06
542	*Keith Mitchell*(FC)	.20	.15	.08
543	Jerome Walton	.08	.06	.03
544	*Cliff Brantley*(FC)	.15	.11	.06
545	Andy Van Slyke	.08	.06	.03

		MT	NR MT	EX
546	Paul Sorrento	.04	.03	.02
547	Herm Winningham	.03	.02	.01
548	Mark Guthrie	.04	.03	.02
549	Joe Torre	.03	.02	.01
550	Darryl Strawberry	.12	.09	.05
551	Top Prospects-Shortstops *(Manny Alexander, Alex Arias,* Wil Cordero, Chipper Jones)	.60	.45	.25
552	Dave Gallagher	.04	.03	.02
553	Edgar Martinez	.06	.05	.02
554	Donald Harris	.15	.11	.06
555	Frank Thomas	.50	.40	.20
556	Storm Davis	.04	.03	.02
557	Dickie Thon	.03	.02	.01
558	Scott Garrelts	.03	.02	.01
559	Steve Olin	.03	.02	.01
560	Rickey Henderson	.15	.11	.06
561	Jose Vizcaino	.04	.03	.02
562	*Wade Taylor*	.10	.08	.04
563	Pat Borders	.04	.03	.02
564	#1 Draft Pick *(Jimmy Gonzalez)*(FC)	.20	.15	.08
565	Lee Smith	.05	.04	.02
566	Bill Sampen	.05	.04	.02
567	Dean Palmer	.12	.09	.05
568	Bryan Harvey	.05	.04	.02
569	Tony Pena	.05	.04	.02
570	Lou Whitaker	.06	.05	.02
571	Randy Tomlin	.06	.05	.02
572	Greg Vaughn	.12	.09	.05
573	Kelly Downs	.03	.02	.01
574	Steve Avery	.15	.11	.06
575	Kirby Puckett	.15	.11	.06
576	*Heathcliff Slocumb*(FC)	.10	.08	.04
577	Kevin Seitzer	.04	.03	.02
578	Lee Guetterman	.03	.02	.01
579	Johnny Oates	.03	.02	.01
580	Greg Maddux	.05	.04	.02
581	Stan Javier	.03	.02	.01
582	Vicente Palacios	.03	.02	.01
583	Mel Rojas	.03	.02	.01
584	*Wayne Rosenthal*(FC)	.10	.08	.04
585	Lenny Webster(FC)	.10	.08	.04
586	Rod Nichols	.03	.02	.01
587	Mickey Morandini	.08	.06	.03
588	Russ Swan	.03	.02	.01
589	Mariano Duncan	.04	.03	.02
590	Howard Johnson	.10	.08	.04
591	Top Prospects-Outfielders *(Jacob Brumfield,* Jeromy Burnitz, *Alan Cockrell,* D.J. Dozier)(FC)	.70	.50	.30
592	*Denny Neagle*(FC)	.15	.11	.06
593	Steve Decker	.10	.08	.04
594	#1 Draft Pick *(Brian Barber)*(FC)	.15	.11	.06
595	Bruce Hurst	.04	.03	.02
596	Kent Mercker	.04	.03	.02
597	*Mike Magnante*(FC)	.10	.08	.04
598	Jody Reed	.04	.03	.02
599	Steve Searcy	.03	.02	.01
600	Paul Molitor	.10	.08	.04
601	Dave Smith	.05	.04	.02
602	Mike Fetters	.04	.03	.02
603	*Luis Mercedes*(FC)	.25	.20	.10
604	Chris Gwynn	.03	.02	.01
605	Scott Erickson	.20	.15	.08
606	Brook Jacoby	.04	.03	.02
607	Todd Stottlemyre	.05	.04	.02
608	Scott Bradley	.03	.02	.01
609	Mike Hargrove	.03	.02	.01
610	Eric Davis	.12	.09	.05
611	*Brian Hunter*(FC)	.35	.25	.14
612	Pat Kelly	.10	.08	.04
613	Pedro Munoz(FC)	.15	.11	.06
614	Al Osuna	.04	.03	.02
615	Matt Merullo	.03	.02	.01
616	Larry Andersen	.03	.02	.01
617	Junior Ortiz	.03	.02	.01
618	Top Prospects-Outfielders *(Cesar Hernandez,* Steve Hosey, Dan Peltier, *Jeff McNeely)*(FC)	.60	.45	.25
619	Danny Jackson	.04	.03	.02
620	George Brett	.12	.09	.05
621	*Dan Gakeler*(FC)	.10	.08	.04
622	Steve Buechele	.04	.03	.02
623	Bob Tewksbury	.03	.02	.01
624	#1 Draft Pick *(Shawn Estes)*(FC)	.15	.11	.06
625	Kevin McReynolds	.08	.06	.03
626	*Chris Haney*(FC)	.15	.11	.06
627	Mike Sharperson	.03	.02	.01
628	Mark Williamson	.03	.02	.01
629	Wally Joyner	.10	.08	.04

		MT	NR MT	EX
630	Carlton Fisk	.12	.09	.05
631	*Armando Reynoso*(FC)	.10	.08	.04
632	Felix Fermin	.03	.02	.01
633	Mitch Williams	.05	.04	.02
634	Manuel Lee	.04	.03	.02
635	Harold Baines	.08	.06	.03
636	Greg Harris	.05	.04	.02
637	Orlando Merced	.12	.09	.05
638	Chris Bosio	.04	.03	.02
639	*Wayne Housie*(FC)	.10	.08	.04
640	Xavier Hernandez	.04	.03	.02
641	*David Howard*(FC)	.10	.08	.04
642	Tim Crews	.03	.02	.01
643	Rick Cerone	.03	.02	.01
644	Terry Leach	.03	.02	.01
645	Deion Sanders	.12	.09	.05
646	Craig Wilson	.04	.03	.02
647	Marquis Grissom	.12	.09	.05
648	Scott Fletcher	.03	.02	.01
649	Norm Charlton	.04	.03	.02
650	Jesse Barfield	.06	.05	.02
651	*Joe Slusarski*	.10	.08	.04
652	Bobby Rose	.04	.03	.02
653	Dennis Lamp	.03	.02	.01
654	#1 Draft Pick *(Allen Watson)*(FC)	.15	.11	.06
655	Brett Butler	.06	.05	.02
656	Top Prospects-Outfielders *(Rudy Pemberton,* Henry Rodriguez, *Lee Tinsley, Gerald Williams)*(FC)	.60	.45	.25
657	Dave Johnson	.03	.02	.01
658	Checklist 5	.03	.02	.01
659	Brian McRae	.12	.09	.05
660	Fred McGriff	.10	.08	.04
661	Bill Landrum	.03	.02	.01
662	*Juan Guzman*(FC)	.25	.20	.10
663	Greg Gagne	.03	.02	.01
664	Ken Hill	.04	.03	.02
665	*Dave Haas*(FC)	.15	.11	.06
666	Tom Foley	.03	.02	.01
667	*Roberto Hernandez*(FC)	.10	.08	.04
668	Dwayne Henry	.03	.02	.01
669	Jim Fregosi	.03	.02	.01
670	Harold Reynolds	.05	.04	.02
671	Mark Whiten	.10	.08	.04
672	Eric Plunk	.03	.02	.01
673	Todd Hundley	.10	.08	.04
674	*Mo Sanford*(FC)	.25	.20	.10
675	Bobby Witt	.04	.03	.02
676	Top Prospects-Pitchers *(Pat Mahomes, Sam Militello,* Roger Salkeld, *Turk Wendell)*(FC)	.60	.45	.25
677	John Marzano	.03	.02	.01
678	Joe Klink	.03	.02	.01
679	Pete Incaviglia	.04	.03	.02
680	Dale Murphy	.08	.06	.03
681	Rene Gonzales	.03	.02	.01
682	Andy Benes	.08	.06	.03
683	Jim Poole(FC)	.08	.06	.03
684	#1 Draft Pick *(Trever Miller)*(FC)	.15	.11	.06
685	*Scott Livingstone*(FC)	.12	.09	.05
686	Rich DeLucia	.04	.03	.02
687	*Harvey Pulliam*(FC)	.15	.11	.06
688	Tim Belcher	.04	.03	.02
689	Mark Lemke	.05	.04	.02
690	John Franco	.06	.05	.02
691	Walt Weiss	.06	.05	.02
692	Scott Ruskin	.04	.03	.02
693	Jeff King	.04	.03	.02
694	Mike Gardiner(FC)	.06	.05	.02
695	Gary Sheffield	.12	.09	.05
696	Joe Boever	.03	.02	.01
697	Mike Felder	.03	.02	.01
698	John Habyan	.03	.02	.01
699	Cito Gaston	.03	.02	.01
700	Ruben Sierra	.15	.11	.06
701	Scott Radinsky	.03	.02	.01
702	Lee Stevens	.06	.05	.02
703	*Mark Wohlers*(FC)	.15	.11	.06
704	Curt Young	.03	.02	.01
705	Dwight Evans	.06	.05	.02
706	Rob Murphy	.03	.02	.01
707	Gregg Jefferies	.12	.09	.05
708	Tom Bolton	.03	.02	.01
709	Chris James	.03	.02	.01
710	Kevin Maas	.12	.09	.05
711	*Ricky Bones*(FC)	.10	.08	.04
712	Curt Wilkerson	.03	.02	.01
713	Roger McDowell	.04	.03	.02
714	#1 Draft Pick *(Calvin Reese)*(FC)	.50	.40	.20
715	Craig Biggio	.08	.06	.03
716	*Kirk Dressendorfer*	.15	.11	.06

		MT	NR MT	EX
717	Ken Dayley	.03	.02	.01
718	B.J. Surhoff	.05	.04	.02
719	Terry Mulholland	.05	.04	.02
720	Kirk Gibson	.06	.05	.02
721	Mike Pagliarulo	.04	.03	.02
722	Walt Terrell	.03	.02	.01
723	Jose Oquendo	.03	.02	.01
724	Kevin Morton(FC)	.08	.06	.03
725	Doc Gooden	.12	.09	.05
726	Kirt Manwaring	.04	.03	.02
727	Chuck McElroy	.03	.02	.01
728	Dave Burba(FC)	.06	.05	.02
729	Art Howe	.03	.02	.01
730	Ramon Martinez	.15	.11	.06
731	Donnie Hill	.03	.02	.01
732	Nelson Santovenia	.03	.02	.01
733	Bob Melvin	.03	.02	.01
734	#1 Draft Pick *(Scott Hatteberg)*(FC)	.15	.11	.06
735	Greg Swindell	.05	.04	.02
736	Lance Johnson	.03	.02	.01
737	Kevin Reimer	.05	.04	.02
738	Dennis Eckersley	.08	.06	.03
739	Rob Ducey	.03	.02	.01
740	Ken Caminiti	.04	.03	.02
741	Mark Gubicza	.04	.03	.02
742	Billy Spiers	.04	.03	.02
743	Darren Lewis	.15	.11	.06
744	Chris Hammond	.05	.04	.02
745	Dave Magadan	.05	.04	.02
746	Bernard Gilkey	.10	.08	.04
747	Willie Banks(FC)	.15	.11	.06
748	Matt Nokes	.04	.03	.02
749	Jerald Clark	.04	.03	.02
750	Travis Fryman	.15	.11	.06
751	Steve Wilson	.03	.02	.01
752	Billy Ripken	.03	.02	.01
753	Paul Assenmacher	.03	.02	.01
754	Charlie Hayes	.04	.03	.02
755	Alex Fernandez	.15	.11	.06
756	Gary Pettis	.03	.02	.01
757	Rob Dibble	.08	.06	.03
758	Tim Naehring	.08	.06	.03
759	Jeff Torborg	.03	.02	.01
760	Ozzie Smith	.10	.08	.04
761	Mike Fitzgerald	.03	.02	.01
762	John Burkett	.04	.03	.02
763	Kyle Abbott	.06	.05	.02
764	#1 Draft Pick *(Tyler Green)*(FC)	.35	.25	.14
765	Pete Harnisch	.06	.05	.02
766	Mark Davis	.03	.02	.01
767	Kal Daniels	.06	.05	.02
768	*Jim Thome*(FC)	.30	.25	.12
769	Jack Howell	.03	.02	.01
770	Sid Bream	.05	.04	.02
771	*Arthur Rhodes*(FC)	.20	.15	.08
772	Garry Templeton	.04	.03	.02
773	Hal Morris	.12	.09	.05
774	Bud Black	.04	.03	.02
775	Ivan Calderon	.06	.05	.02
776	*Doug Henry*(FC)	.15	.11	.06
777	John Olerud	.12	.09	.05
778	Tim Leary	.04	.03	.02
779	Jay Bell	.05	.04	.02
780	Eddie Murray	.10	.08	.04
781	Paul Abbott(FC)	.08	.06	.03
782	Phil Plantier	.30	.25	.12
783	Joe Magrane	.05	.04	.02
784	Ken Patterson	.03	.02	.01
785	Albert Belle	.15	.11	.06
786	Royce Clayton(FC)	.25	.20	.10
787	Checklist 6	.03	.02	.01
788	Mike Stanton	.04	.03	.02
789	Bobby Valentine	.03	.02	.01
790	Joe Carter	.10	.08	.04
791	Danny Cox	.03	.02	.01
792	Dave Winfield	.12	.09	.05

1987 Toys "R" Us

Marked as a collectors' edition set and titled "Baseball Rookies," the 1987 Toys "R" Us issue was produced by Topps for the toy store chain. The set is comprised of 33 glossy-coated cards, each measur ing 2-1/2" by 3-1/2". The card fronts are very colorful, employing nine different colors including deep black borders. The backs, printed in blue and

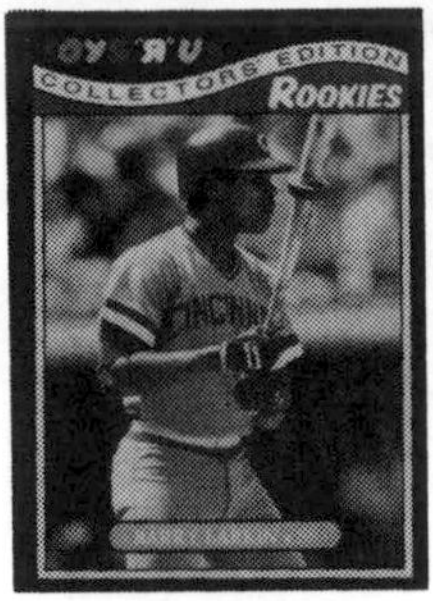

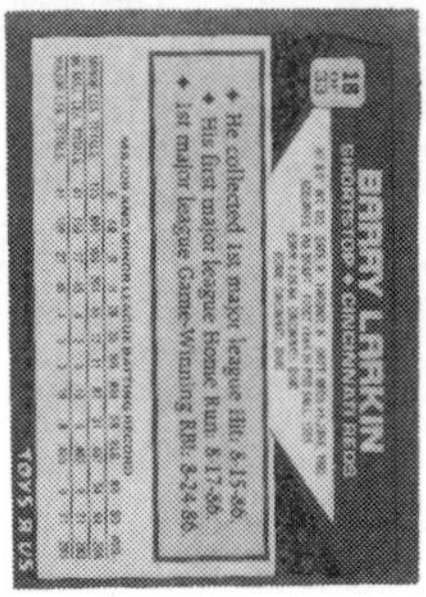

orange, contain career highlights and composite minor and major league statistics. The set was distributed in a specially designed box and sold for $1.99 in retail outlets.

		MT	NR MT	EX
Complete Set:		6.00	4.50	2.50
Common Player:		.09	.07	.04
1	Andy Allanson	.09	.07	.04
2	Paul Assenmacher	.09	.07	.04
3	Scott Bailes	.09	.07	.04
4	Barry Bonds	.40	.30	.15
5	Jose Canseco	1.50	1.25	.60
6	John Cerutti	.09	.07	.04
7	Will Clark	.90	.70	.35
8	Kal Daniels	.25	.20	.10
9	Jim Deshaies	.09	.07	.04
10	Mark Eichhorn	.09	.07	.04
11	Ed Hearn	.09	.07	.04
12	Pete Incaviglia	.12	.09	.05
13	Bo Jackson	.60	.45	.25
14	Wally Joyner	.60	.45	.25
15	Charlie Kerfeld	.09	.07	.04
16	Eric King	.12	.09	.05
17	John Kruk	.40	.30	.15
18	Barry Larkin	.50	.40	.20
19	Mike LaValliere	.15	.11	.06
20	Greg Mathews	.09	.07	.04
21	Kevin Mitchell	.20	.15	.08
22	Dan Plesac	.20	.15	.08
23	Bruce Ruffin	.15	.11	.06
24	Ruben Sierra	.50	.40	.20
25	Cory Snyder	.10	.08	.04
26	Kurt Stillwell	.20	.15	.08
27	Dale Sveum	.12	.09	.05
28	Danny Tartabull	.30	.25	.12
29	Andres Thomas	.09	.07	.04
30	Robby Thompson	.15	.11	.06
31	Jim Traber	.09	.07	.04
32	Mitch Williams	.15	.11	.06
33	Todd Worrell	.15	.11	.06

1988 Toys "R" Us Rookies

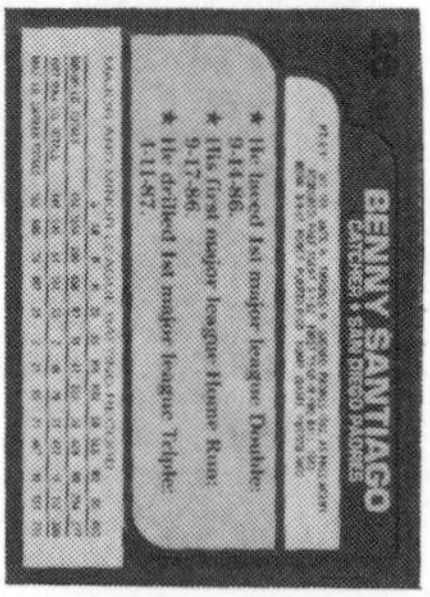

This 33-card boxed edition was produced by Topps for exclusive distribution at Toys "R" Us stores. The

glossy standard-size cards spotlight rookies in both closeups and action photos on a bright blue background inlaid with yellow. The Toys "R" Us logo frames the top left corner, above a curving white banner that reads "Topps 1988 Collectors' Edition Rookies". A black Topps logo hugs the upper right-hand edge of the photo. The player name, red-lettered on a tube of yellow, frames the bottom. Card backs are horizontal, blue and pink on a bright pink background and include the player name, personal information and career highlights and stats.

		MT	NR MT	EX
Complete Set:		5.00	3.75	2.00
Common Player:		.09	.07	.04
1	Todd Benzinger	.20	.15	.08
2	Bob Brower	.09	.07	.04
3	Jerry Browne	.09	.07	.04
4	DeWayne Buice	.09	.07	.04
5	Ellis Burks	.70	.50	.30
6	Ken Caminiti	.12	.09	.05
7	Casey Candaele	.09	.07	.04
8	Dave Cone	.50	.40	.20
9	Kelly Downs	.20	.15	.08
10	Mike Dunne	.15	.11	.06
11	Ken Gerhart	.12	.09	.05
12	Mike Greenwell	.40	.30	.15
13	Mike Henneman	.12	.09	.05
14	Sam Horn	.20	.15	.08
15	Joe Magrane	.20	.15	.08
16	Fred Manrique	.12	.09	.05
17	John Marzano	.12	.09	.05
18	Fred McGriff	.15	.11	.06
19	Mark McGwire	.50	.40	.20
20	Jeff Musselman	.12	.09	.05
21	Randy Myers	.20	.15	.08
22	Matt Nokes	.40	.30	.15
23	Al Pedrique	.12	.09	.05
24	Luis Polonia	.15	.11	.06
25	Billy Ripken	.25	.20	.10
26	Benny Santiago	.25	.20	.10
27	Kevin Seitzer	.10	.08	.04
28	John Smiley	.20	.15	.08
29	Mike Stanley	.09	.07	.04
30	Terry Steinbach	.20	.15	.08
31	B.J. Surhoff	.25	.20	.10
32	Bobby Thigpen	.25	.20	.10
33	Devon White	.25	.20	.10

1989 Toys "R" Us Rookies

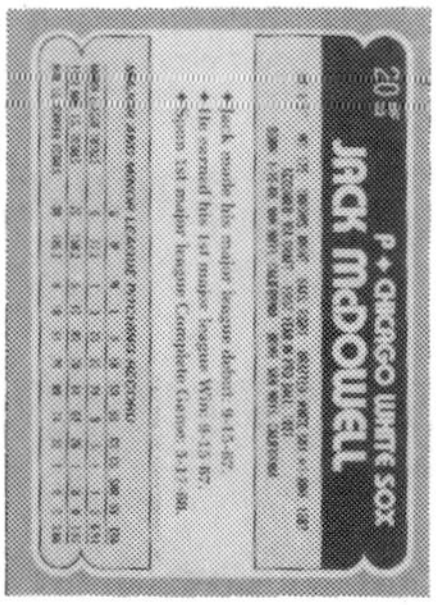

This glossy set of 33 top rookies was produced by Topps for the Toys 'R' Us chain and was sold in a special box. Each player's name and position appear below the full-color photo, while the Toys 'R' Us logo and "Topps 1989 Collector's Edition" appear along the top. Major and minor league stats are on the back. The set is numbered alphabetically.

		MT	NR MT	EX
Complete Set:		4.00	3.00	1.50
Common Player:		.09	.07	.04
1	Roberto Alomar	.50	.40	.20
2	Brady Anderson	.09	.07	.04
3	Tim Belcher	.20	.15	.08
4	Damon Berryhill	.12	.09	.05
5	Jay Buhner	.12	.09	.05
6	Sherman Corbett	.09	.07	.04
7	Kevin Elster	.12	.09	.05
8	Cecil Espy	.12	.09	.05
9	Dave Gallagher	.12	.09	.05
10	Ron Gant	.12	.09	.05
11	Paul Gibson	.09	.07	.04
12	Mark Grace	.90	.70	.35
13	Bryan Harvey	.12	.09	.05
14	Darrin Jackson	.09	.07	.04
15	Gregg Jefferies	.70	.50	.30
16	Ron Jones	.15	.11	.06
17	Ricky Jordan	.35	.25	.14
18	Roberto Kelly	.25	.20	.10
19	Al Leiter	.09	.07	.04
20	Jack McDowell	.09	.07	.04
21	Melido Perez	.12	.09	.05
22	Jeff Pico	.09	.07	.04
23	Jody Reed	.12	.09	.05
24	Chris Sabo	.25	.20	.10
25	Nelson Santovenia	.15	.11	.06
26	Mackey Sasser	.09	.07	.04
27	Mike Schooler	.12	.09	.05
28	Gary Sheffield	.60	.45	.25
29	Pete Smith	.12	.09	.05
30	Pete Stanicek	.09	.07	.04
31	Jeff Treadway	.09	.07	.04
32	Walt Weiss	.25	.20	.10
33	Dave West	.10	.08	.04

1990 Toys "R" Us Rookies

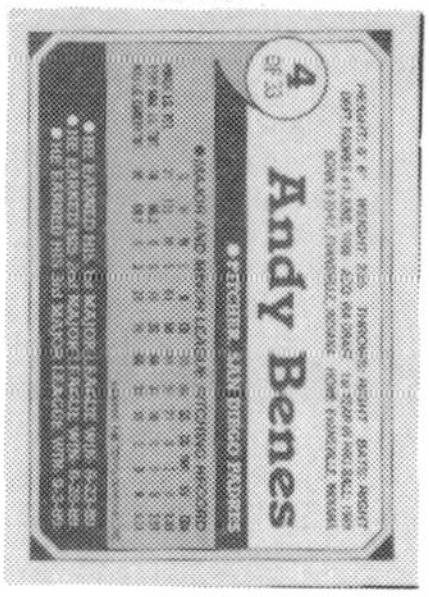

This 33-card set marks the fourth straigh year that Topps has produced a set to be sold exclusively at Toys "R" Us stores. The card fronts contain full- color photos of 1989 rookies. The flip sides are horizontal and provide both minor and major league totals. The complete set is packaged in a special box which features a checklist uon the back.

		MT	NR MT	EX
Complete Set:		5.00	3.75	2.00
Common Player:		.08	.06	.03
1	Jim Abbott	.15	.11	.06
2	Eric Anthony	.40	.30	.15
3	Joey Belle	.15	.11	.06
4	Andy Benes	.20	.15	.08
5	Greg Briley	.08	.06	.03
6	Kevin Brown	.10	.08	.04
7	Mark Carreon	.08	.06	.03
8	Mike Devereaux	.08	.06	.03
9	Junior Felix	.25	.20	.10
10	Mark Gardner	.15	.11	.06
11	Bob Geren	.08	.06	.03
12	Tom Gordon	.20	.15	.08
13	Ken Griffey,Jr.	2.00	1.50	.80
14	Pete Harnisch	.10	.08	.04
15	Ken Hill	.08	.06	.03
16	Gregg Jefferies	.30	.25	.12
17	Derek Lilliquist	.08	.06	.03
18	Carlos Martinez	.10	.08	.04
19	Ramon Martinez	.60	.45	.25
20	Bob Milacki	.08	.06	.03

		MT	NR MT	EX
21	Gregg Olson	.15	.11	.06
22	Kenny Rogers	.10	.08	.04
23	Alex Sanchez	.10	.08	.04
24	Gary Sheffield	.30	.25	.12
25	Dwight Smith	.10	.08	.04
26	Billy Spiers	.08	.06	.03
27	Greg Vaughn	.40	.30	.15
28	Robin Ventura	.25	.20	.10
29	Jerome Walton	.40	.30	.15
30	Dave West	.08	.06	.03
31	John Wetteland	.15	.11	.06
32	Craig Worthington	.10	.08	.04
33	Todd Zeile	.40	.30	.15

1969 Transogram

Produced by the Transogram toy company, the 2-1/2" by 3-1/2" cards were printed on the bottom of toy baseball player statue boxes. The cards feature a color photo of the player surrounded by a rounded white border. Below the photo is the player's name in red and his team and other personal details all printed in black. The overall background is yellow. The cards were designed to be cut off the box, but collectors prefer to find the box intact and better still, with the statue inside. Although the 60-card set features a lot of stars, and is fairly scarce, it does not not have a lot of popularity today.

		NR MT	EX	VG
Complete Set:		650.00	325.00	195.00
Common Player:		.80	.40	.25
(1)	Hank Aaron	30.00	15.00	9.00
(2)	Richie Allen	4.00	2.00	1.25
(3)	Felipe Alou	3.00	1.50	.90
(4)	Matty Alou	3.00	1.50	.90
(5)	Luis Aparicio	20.00	10.00	6.00
(6)	Joe Azcue	2.00	1.00	.60
(7)	Ernie Banks	20.00	10.00	6.00
(8)	Lou Brock	20.00	10.00	6.00
(9)	John Callison	3.00	1.50	.90
(10)	Jose Cardenal	2.00	1.00	.60
(11)	Danny Cater	2.00	1.00	.60
(12)	Roberto Clemente	30.00	15.00	9.00
(13)	Willie Davis	1.00	.50	.30
(14)	Mike Epstein	2.00	1.00	.60
(15)	Jim Fregosi	1.00	.50	.30
(16)	Bob Gibson	8.00	4.00	2.50
(17)	Tom Haller	2.00	1.00	.60
(18)	Ken Harrelson	3.00	1.50	.90
(19)	Willie Horton	3.00	1.50	.90
(20)	Frank Howard	1.50	.70	.45
(21)	Tommy John	8.00	4.00	2.50
(22)	Al Kaline	20.00	10.00	6.00
(23)	Harmon Killebrew	20.00	10.00	6.00
(24)	Bobby Knoop	2.00	1.00	.60
(25)	Jerry Koosman	.80	.40	.25
(26)	Jim Lefebvre	2.00	1.00	.60
(27)	Mickey Mantle	125.00	62.00	37.00
(28)	Juan Marichal	8.00	4.00	2.50
(29)	Lee May	3.00	1.50	.90
(30)	Willie Mays	30.00	15.00	9.00
(31)	Bill Mazeroski	4.00	2.00	1.25
(32)	Tim McCarver	4.00	2.00	1.25
(33)	Willie McCovey	20.00	10.00	6.00
(34)	Denny McLain	1.50	.70	.45
(35)	Dave McNally	3.00	1.50	.90
(36)	Rick Monday	3.00	1.50	.90
(37)	Blue Moon Odom	.80	.40	.25
(38)	Tony Oliva	1.50	.70	.45
(39)	Camilo Pascual	3.00	1.50	.90
(40)	Tony Perez	7.00	3.50	2.00
(41)	Rico Petrocelli	1.00	.50	.30
(42)	Rick Reichardt	.80	.40	.25
(43)	Brooks Robinson	30.00	15.00	9.00
(44)	Frank Robinson	8.00	4.00	2.50
(45)	Cookie Rojas	2.00	1.00	.60
(46)	Pete Rose	30.00	15.00	9.00
(47)	Ron Santo	1.50	.70	.45
(48)	Tom Seaver	20.00	10.00	6.00
(49)	Rusty Staub	4.00	2.00	1.25
(50)	Mel Stottlemyre	1.00	.50	.30
(51)	Ron Swoboda	.80	.40	.25
(52)	Luis Tiant	3.00	1.50	.90
(53)	Joe Torre	4.00	2.00	1.25
(54)	Cesar Tovar	2.00	1.00	.60
(55)	Pete Ward	2.00	1.00	.60
(56)	Roy White	3.00	1.50	.90
(57)	Billy Williams	20.00	10.00	6.00
(58)	Don Wilson	2.00	1.00	.60
(59)	Jim Wynn	.80	.40	.25
(60)	Carl Yastrzemski	30.00	15.00	9.00

1970 Transogram

Like the 1969 cards, the 1970 Transogram cards were available on boxes of Transogram baseball statues. The cards are slightly larger at 2-9/16" by 3- 1/2". The 30-card set has the same pictures as the 1969 set except for Joe Torre. All players in the '70 set were included in the '69 Transogram issue except for Reggie Jackson, Sam McDowell and Boog Powell. Three cards and three statues were part of each Transogram box in 1970. When available, most collectors prefer to find the cards as uncut panels of three, better yet, as complete boxes.

		NR MT	EX	VG
Complete Set:		325.00	162.00	97.00
Common Player:		.80	.40	.25
(1)	Hank Aaron	30.00	15.00	9.00
(2)	Ernie Banks	8.00	4.00	2.50
(3)	Roberto Clemente	30.00	15.00	9.00
(4)	Willie Davis	1.00	.50	.30
(5)	Jim Fregosi	1.00	.50	.30
(6)	Bob Gibson	8.00	4.00	2.50
(7)	Frank Howard	1.50	.70	.45
(8)	Reggie Jackson	40.00	20.00	12.00
(9)	Cleon Jones	.80	.40	.25
(10)	Al Kaline	18.00	9.00	5.50
(11)	Harmon Killebrew	18.00	9.00	5.50
(12)	Jerry Koosman	.80	.40	.25
(13)	Willie McCovey	18.00	9.00	5.50
(14)	Sam McDowell	3.00	1.50	.90
(15)	Denny McLain	1.50	.70	.45
(16)	Juan Marichal	8.00	4.00	2.50
(17)	Willie Mays	30.00	15.00	9.00
(18)	Blue Moon Odom	.80	.40	.25
(19)	Tony Oliva	1.50	.70	.45
(20)	Rico Petrocelli	1.00	.50	.30
(21)	Boog Powell	4.00	2.00	1.25
(22)	Rick Reichardt	.80	.40	.25

		NR MT	EX	VG
(23)	Frank Robinson	18.00	9.00	5.50
(24)	Pete Rose	30.00	15.00	9.00
(25)	Ron Santo	1.50	.70	.45
(26)	Tom Seaver	18.00	9.00	5.50
(27)	Mel Stottlemyre	1.00	.50	.30
(28)	Joe Torre	4.00	2.00	1.25
(29)	Jim Wynn	.80	.40	.25
(30)	Carl Yastrzemski	30.00	15.00	9.00

1970 Transogram Mets

The Transogram Mets set is a second set that the company produced in 1970. The cards are 2-9/16" by 3-1/2" and feature members of the World Champions Mets team. There are 15 cards in the set which retains the basic color picture with player's names in red and team, position and biographical details in ablack format. As with the other Transogram sets, the cards are most valuable when they are still part of their original box with the statues. Values decrease for them if the cards are removed from the box. While the Mets set does not have the attraction of many Hall of Famers as was the case with the regular set, it does make a very nice item for the Mets team collector.

		NR MT	EX	VG
Complete Set:		200.00	100.00	60.00
Common Player:		.80	.40	.25
(1)	Tommie Agee	3.00	1.50	.90
(2)	Ken Boswell	2.00	1.00	.60
(3)	Donn Clendenon	3.00	1.50	.90
(4)	Gary Gentry	2.00	1.00	.60
(5)	Jerry Grote	3.00	1.50	.90
(6)	Bud Harrelson	3.00	1.50	.90
(7)	Cleon Jones	.80	.40	.25
(8)	Jerry Koosman	.80	.40	.25
(9)	Ed Kranepool	3.00	1.50	.90
(10)	Tug McGraw	7.00	3.50	2.00
(11)	Nolan Ryan	125.00	62.00	37.00
(12)	Art Shamsky	2.00	1.00	.60
(13)	Tom Seaver	40.00	20.00	12.00
(14)	Ron Swoboda	.80	.40	.25
(15)	Al Weis	2.00	1.00	.60

1983 True Value White Sox

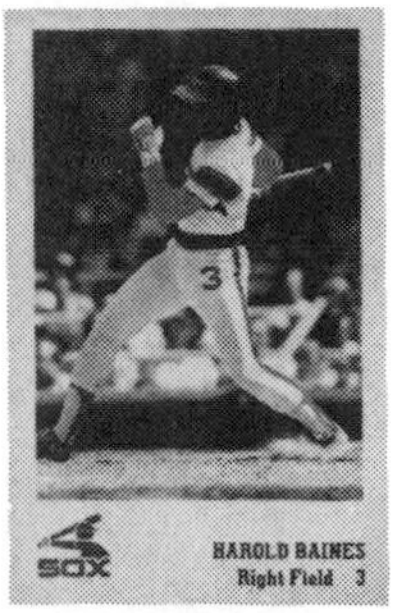

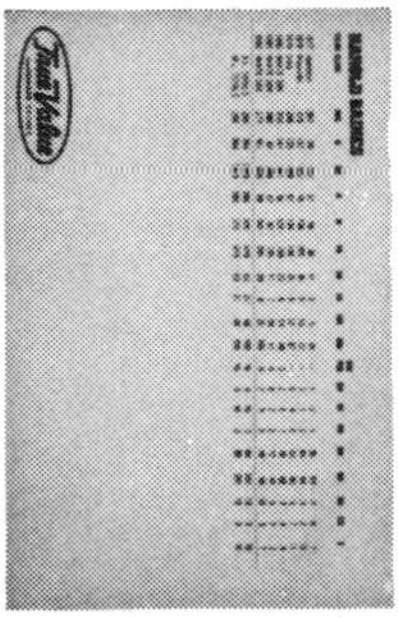

Issued by the Chicago White Sox and True Value hardware stores, these 2-5/8" by 4-1/8" cards are a rather expensive and scarce regional set. The 23-card set was originally scheduled as part of a promotion in which cards were given out at special Tuesday night games. The idea was sound, but rainouts forced the cancellation of some games so those scheduled cards were never given out. They were, however, smuggled out to hobby channels making it possible, although not easy, to assemble complete sets. The cards feature a large color photo with a wide white border. A red and blue White Sox logo is in the lower left corner, while the player's name, position and team number are in the lower right. Backs feature a True Value ad along with statistics. The three cards which were never given out through the normal channels are considered more scarce than the others. They are Marc Hill, Harold Baines and Salome Barojas.

		MT	NR MT	EX
Complete Set:		30.00	22.00	12.00
Common Player:		.40	.30	.15
1	Scott Fletcher	.60	.45	.25
2	Harold Baines	7.00	5.25	2.75
5	Vance Law	.50	.40	.20
7	Marc Hill	3.25	2.50	1.25
10	Tony LaRussa	.50	.40	.20
11	Rudy Law	.40	.30	.15
14	Tony Bernazard	.40	.30	.15
17	Jerry Hairston	.40	.30	.15
19	Greg Luzinski	1.00	.70	.40
24	Floyd Bannister	.60	.45	.25
25	Mike Squires	.40	.30	.15
30	Salome Barojas	3.25	2.50	1.25
31	LaMarr Hoyt	.50	.40	.20
34	Richard Dotson	.70	.50	.30
36	Jerry Koosman	.70	.50	.30
40	Britt Burns	.50	.40	.20
41	Dick Tidrow	.40	.30	.15
42	Ron Kittle	1.75	1.25	.70
44	Tom Paciorek	.40	.30	.15
45	Kevin Hickey	.40	.30	.15
53	Dennis Lamp	.40	.30	.15
67	Jim Kern	.40	.30	.15
72	Carlton Fisk	3.00	2.25	1.25

1984 True Value White Sox

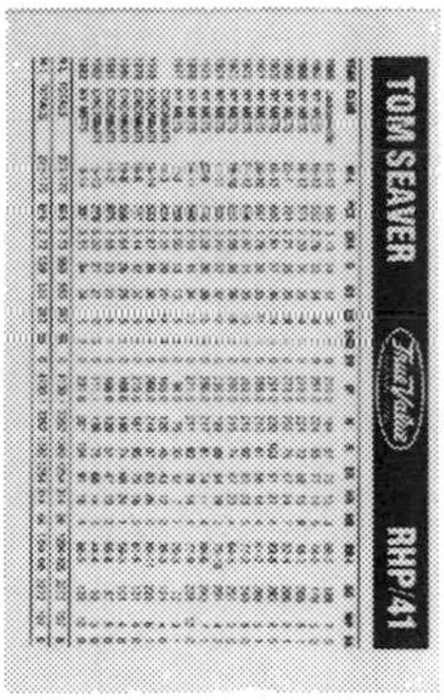

True Value hardware stores and the Chicago White Sox gave their Tuesday night baseball card promotion at Comiskey Park another try in 1984. The cards measure 2-5/8" by 4-1/8" with 30 cards comprising the set. In addition to the players, there are cards for manager Tony LaRussa, the coaching staff, and former Sox greats Luis Aparicio and Minnie Minoso. Cards designs are very similar to the 1983 cards. As the cards were given out two at a time, it was very difficult to acquire a complete set. Additionally, as numbers available vary because of attendance, some cards are scarcer than others.

	MT	NR MT	EX
Complete Set:	25.00	18.50	10.00
Common Player:	.40	.30	.15

1	Scott Fletcher	.60	.45	.25
3	Harold Baines	2.25	1.75	.90
5	Vance Law	.50	.40	.20
7	Marc Hill	.40	.30	.15
8	Dave Stegman	.40	.30	.15
10	Tony LaRussa	.50	.40	.20
11	Rudy Law	.40	.30	.15
16	Julio Cruz	.40	.30	.15
17	Jerry Hairston	.40	.30	.15
19	Greg Luzinski	.90	.70	.35
20	Jerry Dybzinski	.40	.30	.15
24	Floyd Bannister	.60	.45	.25
25	Mike Squires	.40	.30	.15
27	Ron Reed	.40	.30	.15
29	Greg Walker	.50	.40	.20
30	Salome Barojas	.40	.30	.15
31	LaMarr Hoyt	.50	.40	.20
32	Tim Hulett	1.00	.70	.40
34	Richard Dotson	.70	.50	.30
40	Britt Burns	.40	.30	.15
41	Tom Seaver	4.00	3.00	1.50
42	Ron Kittle	1.00	.70	.40
44	Tom Paciorek	.40	.30	.15
50	Juan Agosto	.40	.30	.15
59	Tom Brennan	1.00	.70	.40
72	Carlton Fisk	2.00	1.50	.80
----	Minnie Minoso	2.00	1.50	.80
----	Luis Aparicio	2.00	1.50	.80
----	Nancy Faust (organist)	1.00	.70	.40
----	The Coaching Staff (Ed Brinkman, Dave Duncan, Art Kusnyer, Tony LaRussa, Jim Leyland, Dave Nelson, Joe Nossek)	.40	.30	.15

1986 True Value

A 30-card set of 2-1/2" by 3-1/2" cards was available in three-card packets at True Value hardware stores with a purchase of $5 or more. Cards feature a photo enclosed by stars and a ball and bat at the bottom. The player's name and team are in the lower left while his position and a Major League Baseball logo are in the lower right. The True Value logo is in the upper left. Above the picture runs the phrase "Collector Series." Backs feature some personal information and brief 1985 statistics. Along with the player cards, the folders contained a sweepstakes card offering trips to post-season games and other prizes.

		MT	NR MT	EX
Complete Panel Set:		12.00	9.00	4.75
Complete Singles Set:		6.00	4.50	2.50
Common Panel:		.40	.30	.15
Common Single Player:		.05	.04	.02
	Panel	1.00	.70	.40
1	Pedro Guerrero	.08	.06	.03
2	Steve Garvey	.15	.11	.06
3	Eddie Murray	.20	.15	.08
	Panel	3.25	2.50	1.25
4	Pete Rose	.30	.25	.12
5	Don Mattingly	.80	.60	.30
6	Fernando Valenzuela	.10	.08	.04
	Panel	.60	.45	.25
7	Jim Rice	.15	.11	.06
8	Kirk Gibson	.10	.08	.04
9	Ozzie Smith	.15	.11	.06
	Panel	1.00	.70	.40
10	Dale Murphy	.20	.15	.08
11	Robin Yount	.15	.11	.06
12	Tom Seaver	.15	.11	.06
	Panel	.80	.60	.30
13	Reggie Jackson	.15	.11	.06
14	Ryne Sandberg	.15	.11	.06
15	Bruce Sutter	.05	.04	.02
	Panel	1.00	.70	.40
16	Gary Carter	.15	.11	.06
17	George Brett	.20	.15	.08
18	Rick Sutcliffe	.05	.04	.02
	Panel	.40	.30	.15
19	Dave Stieb	.05	.04	.02
20	Buddy Bell	.05	.04	.02
21	Alvin Davis	.08	.06	.03
	Panel	.60	.45	.25
22	Cal Ripken, Jr.	.20	.15	.08
23	Bill Madlock	.05	.04	.02
24	Kent Hrbek	.10	.08	.04
	Panel	1.50	1.25	.60
25	Lou Whitaker	.08	.06	.03
26	Nolan Ryan	.40	.30	.15
27	Dwayne Murphy	.05	.04	.02
	Panel	2.00	1.50	.80
28	Mike Schmidt	.20	.15	.08
29	Andre Dawson	.10	.08	.04
30	Wade Boggs	.50	.40	.20

U

1989 Upper Deck

This premiere "Collector's Choice' issue from Upper Deck contains 700 cards (2-1/2" by 3-1/2") with full-color photos on both sides. The first 26 cards feature Star Rookies. The set also includes 26 special portrait cards with team checklist backs and seven numberical checklist cards (one for each 100 numbers). Team Checklist cards feature individual player portraits by artist Vernon Wells. Major 1988 award winners (Cy Young, Rookie of Year, MVP) are honored on 10 cards in the set, in addition to their individual player cards. There are also special cards for the Most Valuable Players in both League Championship series and the World Series. The card fronts feature head-and-shoulder poses framed by a white border. A vertical brown and green artist's rendition of the runner's lane that leads from home plate to first base is found along the right margin. The backs carry full-color action poses that fill the card back, except for a compact (yet complete) stats chart. A high-number series, cards 701-800, featuring rookies and traded players, was released in mid-season in foil packs mixed within the complete set, in boxed complete sets and in high number set boxes.

	MT	NR MT	EX
Complete Set: 1-700	150.00	125.00	60.00
Common Player: 1-700	.08	.06	.03

		MT	NR MT	EX
Complete Set: 1-800		200.00	150.00	75.00
Common Player: 701-800		.10	.08	.04
1	Star Rookie *(Ken Griffey, Jr.)*	60.00	45.00	25.00
2	Star Rookie *(Luis Medina)*	.30	.25	.12
3	Star Rookie *(Tony Chance)*	.15	.11	.06
4	Star Rookie (Dave Otto)	.08	.06	.03
5	Star Rookie *(Sandy Alomar, Jr.)*	3.00	2.25	1.25
6	Star Rookie *(Rolando Roomes)*	.20	.15	.08
7	Star Rookie *(David West)*	.25	.20	.10
8	Star Rookie *(Cris Carpenter)*	.30	.25	.12
9	Star Rookie (Gregg Jefferies)	2.00	1.50	.80
10	Star Rookie *(Doug Dascenzo)*	.25	.20	.10
11	Star Rookie *(Ron Jones)*	.20	.15	.08
12	Star Rookie *(Luis de los Santos)*	.25	.20	.10
13a	Star Rookie *(Gary Sheffield)* (SS position on front is upside down)	5.00	3.75	2.00
13b	Star Rookie *(Gary Sheffield)* (SS position on front is correct)	3.00	2.25	1.25
14	Star Rookie *(Mike Harkey)*	.60	.45	.25
15	Star Rookie *(Lance Blankenship)*	.25	.20	.10
16	Star Rookie *(William Brennan)*	.15	.11	.06
17	Star Rookie *(John Smoltz)*	2.00	1.50	.80
18	Star Rookie *(Ramon Martinez)*	10.00	7.50	4.00
19	Star Rookie *(Mark Lemke)*	.30	.25	.12
20	Star Rookie *(Juan Bell)*	.25	.20	.10
21	Star Rookie *(Rey Palacios)*	.15	.11	.06
22	Star Rookie *(Felix Jose)*	4.00	3.00	1.50
23	Star Rookie *(Van Snider)*	.25	.20	.10
24	Star Rookie *(Dante Bichette)*	.40	.30	.15
25	Star Rookie *(Randy Johnson)*	.70	.50	.30
26	Star Rookie *(Carlos Quintana)*	.70	.50	.30
27	Star Rookie Checklist 1-26	.08	.06	.03
28	*Mike Schooler*	.40	.30	.15
29	Randy St. Claire	.08	.06	.03
30	*Jerald Clark*	.35	.25	.14
31	Kevin Gross	.08	.06	.03
32	*Dan Firova*	.20	.15	.08
33	Jeff Calhoun	.08	.06	.03
34	Tommy Hinzo	.08	.06	.03
35	*Ricky Jordan*	.60	.45	.25
36	Larry Parrish	.08	.06	.03
37	Bret Saberhagen	.15	.11	.06
38	Mike Smithson	.08	.06	.03
39	Dave Dravecky	.08	.06	.03
40	Ed Romero	.08	.06	.03
41	Jeff Musselman	.08	.06	.03
42	Ed Hearn	.08	.06	.03
43	Rance Mulliniks	.08	.06	.03
44	Jim Eisenreich	.08	.06	.03
45	*Sil Campusano*	.20	.15	.08
46	Mike Krukow	.08	.06	.03
47	*Paul Gibson*	.20	.15	.08
48	Mike LaCoss	.08	.06	.03
49	Larry Herndon	.08	.06	.03
50	Scott Garrelts	.08	.06	.03
51	Dwayne Henry	.08	.06	.03
52	Jim Acker	.08	.06	.03
53	Steve Sax	.15	.11	.06
54	Pete O'Brien	.08	.06	.03
55	Paul Runge	.08	.06	.03
56	Rick Rhoden	.08	.06	.03
57	*John Dopson*	.25	.20	.10
58	Casey Candaele	.08	.06	.03
59	Dave Righetti	.12	.09	.05
60	Joe Hesketh	.08	.06	.03
61	Frank DiPino	.08	.06	.03
62	Tim Laudner	.08	.06	.03
63	Jamie Moyer	.08	.06	.03
64	Fred Toliver	.08	.06	.03
65	Mitch Webster	.08	.06	.03
66	John Tudor	.10	.08	.04
67	John Cangelosi	.08	.06	.03
68	Mike Devereaux	.15	.11	.06
69	Brian Fisher	.08	.06	.03
70	Mike Marshall	.12	.09	.05
71	Zane Smith	.08	.06	.03
72a	Brian Holton (ball not visible on card front, photo actually Shawn Hillegas)	1.50	1.25	.60
72b	Brian Holton (ball visible, correct photo)	.15	.11	.06
73	Jose Guzman	.10	.08	.04
74	Rick Mahler	.08	.06	.03
75	John Shelby	.08	.06	.03
76	Jim Deshaies	.08	.06	.03
77	Bobby Meacham	.08	.06	.03
78	Bryn Smith	.08	.06	.03
79	Joaquin Andujar	.08	.06	.03
80	Richard Dotson	.08	.06	.03
81	Charlie Lea	.08	.06	.03
82	Calvin Schiraldi	.08	.06	.03
83	Les Straker	.08	.06	.03

		MT	NR MT	EX
84	Les Lancaster	.08	.06	.03
85	Allan Anderson	.08	.06	.03
86	Junior Ortiz	.08	.06	.03
87	Jesse Orosco	.08	.06	.03
88	Felix Fermin	.08	.06	.03
89	Dave Anderson	.08	.06	.03
90	Rafael Belliard	.08	.06	.03
91	Franklin Stubbs	.08	.06	.03
92	Cecil Espy	.08	.06	.03
93	Albert Hall	.08	.06	.03
94	Tim Leary	.08	.06	.03
95	Mitch Williams	.08	.06	.03
96	Tracy Jones	.10	.08	.04
97	Danny Darwin	.08	.06	.03
98	Gary Ward	.08	.06	.03
99	Neal Heaton	.08	.06	.03
100	Jim Pankovits	.08	.06	.03
101	Bill Doran	.08	.06	.03
102	Tim Wallach	.10	.08	.04
103	Joe Magrane	.10	.08	.04
104	Ozzie Virgil	.08	.06	.03
105	Alvin Davis	.12	.09	.05
106	Tom Brookens	.08	.06	.03
107	Shawon Dunston	.10	.08	.04
108	Tracy Woodson	.10	.08	.04
109	Nelson Liriano	.08	.06	.03
110	Devon White	.12	.09	.05
111	Steve Balboni	.08	.06	.03
112	Buddy Bell	.08	.06	.03
113	*German Jimenez*	.08	.06	.03
114	Ken Dayley	.08	.06	.03
115	Andres Galarraga	.15	.11	.06
116	Mike Scioscia	.08	.06	.03
117	Gary Pettis	.08	.06	.03
118	Ernie Whitt	.08	.06	.03
119	Bob Boone	.08	.06	.03
120	Ryne Sandberg	.80	.60	.30
121	Bruce Benedict	.08	.06	.03
122	Hubie Brooks	.10	.08	.04
123	Mike Moore	.08	.06	.03
124	Wallace Johnson	.08	.06	.03
125	Bob Horner	.10	.08	.04
126	Chili Davis	.08	.06	.03
127	Manny Trillo	.08	.06	.03
128	Chet Lemon	.08	.06	.03
129	John Cerutti	.08	.06	.03
130	Orel Hershiser	.25	.20	.10
131	Terry Pendleton	.10	.08	.04
132	Jeff Blauser	.10	.08	.04
133	Mike Fitzgerald	.08	.06	.03
134	Henry Cotto	.08	.06	.03
135	Gerald Young	.12	.09	.05
136	Luis Salazar	.08	.06	.03
137	Alejandro Pena	.08	.06	.03
138	Jack Howell	.08	.06	.03
139	Tony Fernandez	.12	.09	.05
140	Mark Grace	1.75	1.25	.70
141	Ken Caminiti	.08	.06	.03
142	Mike Jackson	.08	.06	.03
143	Larry McWilliams	.08	.06	.03
144	Andres Thomas	.08	.06	.03
145	Nolan Ryan	2.75	2.00	1.00
146	Mike Davis	.08	.06	.03
147	DeWayne Buice	.08	.06	.03
148	Jody Davis	.08	.06	.03
149	Jesse Barfield	.10	.08	.04
150	Matt Nokes	.15	.11	.06
151	Jerry Reuss	.08	.06	.03
152	Rick Cerone	.08	.06	.03
153	Storm Davis	.10	.08	.04
154	Marvell Wynne	.08	.06	.03
155	Will Clark	1.50	1.25	.60
156	Luis Aguayo	.08	.06	.03
157	Willie Upshaw	.08	.06	.03
158	Randy Bush	.08	.06	.03
159	Ron Darling	.12	.09	.05
160	Kal Daniels	.15	.11	.06
161	Spike Owen	.08	.06	.03
162	Luis Polonia	.08	.06	.03
163	Kevin Mitchell	.50	.40	.20
164	*Dave Gallagher*	.25	.20	.10
165	Benito Santiago	.15	.11	.06
166	Greg Gagne	.08	.06	.03
167	Ken Phelps	.08	.06	.03
168	Sid Fernandez	.10	.08	.04
169	Bo Diaz	.08	.06	.03
170	Cory Snyder	.15	.11	.06
171	Eric Show	.08	.06	.03
172	Rob Thompson	.08	.06	.03
173	Marty Barrett	.08	.06	.03
174	Dave Henderson	.10	.08	.04

		MT	NR MT	EX
175	Ozzie Guillen	.08	.06	.03
176	Barry Lyons	.08	.06	.03
177	*Kelvin Torve*(FC)	.20	.15	.08
178	Don Slaught	.08	.06	.03
179	Steve Lombardozzi	.08	.06	.03
180	*Chris Sabo*	2.00	1.50	.80
181	Jose Uribe	.08	.06	.03
182	Shane Mack	.08	.06	.03
183	Ron Karkovice	.08	.06	.03
184	Todd Benzinger	.12	.09	.05
185	Dave Stewart	.10	.08	.04
186	Julio Franco	.10	.08	.04
187	Ron Robinson	.08	.06	.03
188	Wally Backman	.08	.06	.03
189	Randy Velarde	.08	.06	.03
190	Joe Carter	.12	.09	.05
191	Bob Welch	.10	.08	.04
192	Kelly Paris	.08	.06	.03
193	Chris Brown	.08	.06	.03
194	Rick Reuschel	.10	.08	.04
195	Roger Clemens	.50	.40	.20
196	Dave Concepcion	.10	.08	.04
197	Al Newman	.08	.06	.03
198	Brook Jacoby	.10	.08	.04
199	Mookie Wilson	.08	.06	.03
200	Don Mattingly	1.00	.70	.40
201	Dick Schofield	.08	.06	.03
202	Mark Gubicza	.10	.08	.04
203	Gary Gaetti	.15	.11	.06
204	Dan Pasqua	.10	.08	.04
205	Andre Dawson	.20	.15	.08
206	Chris Speier	.08	.06	.03
207	Kent Tekulve	.08	.06	.03
208	Rod Scurry	.08	.06	.03
209	Scott Bailes	.08	.06	.03
210	Rickey Henderson	.60	.45	.25
211	Harold Baines	.12	.09	.05
212	Tony Armas	.08	.06	.03
213	Kent Hrbek	.20	.15	.08
214	Darrin Jackson	.08	.06	.03
215	George Brett	.35	.25	.14
216	Rafael Santana	.08	.06	.03
217	Andy Allanson	.08	.06	.03
218	Brett Butler	.08	.06	.03
219	Steve Jeltz	.08	.06	.03
220	Jay Buhner	.10	.08	.04
221	Bo Jackson	2.00	1.50	.80
222	Angel Salazar	.08	.06	.03
223	Kirk McCaskill	.08	.06	.03
224	Steve Lyons	.08	.06	.03
225	Bert Blyleven	.10	.08	.04
226	Scott Bradley	.08	.06	.03
227	Bob Melvin	.08	.06	.03
228	Ron Kittle	.08	.06	.03
229	Phil Bradley	.10	.08	.04
230	Tommy John	.12	.09	.05
231	Greg Walker	.08	.06	.03
232	Juan Berenguer	.08	.06	.03
233	Pat Tabler	.08	.06	.03
234	*Terry Clark*	.20	.15	.08
235	Rafael Palmeiro	.25	.20	.10
236	Paul Zuvella	.08	.06	.03
237	Willie Randolph	.08	.06	.03
238	Bruce Fields	.08	.06	.03
239	Mike Aldrete	.08	.06	.03
240	Lance Parrish	.15	.11	.06
241	Greg Maddux	.12	.09	.05
242	John Moses	.08	.06	.03
243	Melido Perez	.10	.08	.04
244	Willie Wilson	.10	.08	.04
245	Mark McLemore	.08	.06	.03
246	Von Hayes	.10	.08	.04
247	Matt Williams	.12	.09	.05
248	John Candelaria	.08	.06	.03
249	Harold Reynolds	.08	.06	.03
250	Greg Swindell	.12	.09	.05
251	Juan Agosto	.08	.06	.03
252	Mike Felder	.08	.06	.03
253	Vince Coleman	.15	.11	.06
254	Larry Sheets	.08	.06	.03
255	George Bell	.25	.20	.10
256	Terry Steinbach	.10	.08	.04
257	*Jack Armstrong*	.40	.30	.15
258	Dickie Thon	.08	.06	.03
259	Ray Knight	.08	.06	.03
260	Darryl Strawberry	.40	.30	.15
261	Doug Sisk	.08	.06	.03
262	Alex Trevino	.08	.06	.03
263	Jeff Leonard	.08	.06	.03
264	Tom Henke	.08	.06	.03
265	Ozzie Smith	.15	.11	.06

		MT	NR MT	EX
266	Dave Bergman	.08	.06	.03
267	Tony Phillips	.08	.06	.03
268	Mark Davis	.08	.06	.03
269	Kevin Elster	.10	.08	.04
270	Barry Larkin	.20	.15	.08
271	Manny Lee	.08	.06	.03
272	Tom Brunansky	.12	.09	.05
273	*Craig Biggio*	1.00	.70	.40
274	Jim Gantner	.08	.06	.03
275	Eddie Murray	.25	.20	.10
276	Jeff Reed	.08	.06	.03
277	Tim Teufel	.08	.06	.03
278	Rick Honeycutt	.08	.06	.03
279	Guillermo Hernandez	.08	.06	.03
280	John Kruk	.10	.08	.04
281	*Luis Alicea*	.20	.15	.08
282	Jim Clancy	.08	.06	.03
283	Billy Ripken	.08	.06	.03
284	Craig Reynolds	.08	.06	.03
285	Robin Yount	.35	.25	.14
286	Jimmy Jones	.08	.06	.03
287	Ron Oester	.08	.06	.03
288	Terry Leach	.08	.06	.03
289	Dennis Eckersley	.12	.09	.05
290	Alan Trammell	.20	.15	.08
291	Jimmy Key	.10	.08	.04
292	Chris Bosio	.08	.06	.03
293	Jose DeLeon	.08	.06	.03
294	Jim Traber	.08	.06	.03
295	Mike Scott	.12	.09	.05
296	Roger McDowell	.10	.08	.04
297	Garry Templeton	.08	.06	.03
298	Doyle Alexander	.08	.06	.03
299	Nick Esasky	.08	.06	.03
300	Mark McGwire	.70	.50	.30
301	*Darryl Hamilton*	.35	.25	.14
302	Dave Smith	.08	.06	.03
303	Rick Sutcliffe	.10	.08	.04
304	Dave Stapleton	.08	.06	.03
305	Alan Ashby	.08	.06	.03
306	Pedro Guerrero	.15	.11	.06
307	Ron Guidry	.12	.09	.05
308	Steve Farr	.08	.06	.03
309	Curt Ford	.08	.06	.03
310	Claudell Washington	.08	.06	.03
311	Tom Prince	.08	.06	.03
312	*Chad Kreuter*	.15	.11	.06
313	Ken Oberkfell	.08	.06	.03
314	Jerry Browne	.08	.06	.03
315	R.J. Reynolds	.08	.06	.03
316	Scott Bankhead	.08	.06	.03
317	Milt Thompson	.08	.06	.03
318	Mario Diaz	.10	.08	.04
319	Bruce Ruffin	.08	.06	.03
320	Dave Valle	.08	.06	.03
321a	*Gary Varsho* (batting righty on card back, photo actually Mike Bielecki)	2.00	1.50	.80
321b	*Gary Varsho* (batting lefty on card back, correct photo)	.30	.25	.12
322	Paul Mirabella	.08	.06	.03
323	Chuck Jackson	.08	.06	.03
324	Drew Hall	.10	.08	.04
325	Don August	.10	.08	.04
326	*Israel Sanchez*	.15	.11	.06
327	Denny Walling	.08	.06	.03
328	Joel Skinner	.08	.06	.03
329	Danny Tartabull	.15	.11	.06
330	Tony Pena	.08	.06	.03
331	Jim Sundberg	.08	.06	.03
332	Jeff Robinson	.12	.09	.05
333	Odibbe McDowell	.08	.06	.03
334	Jose Lind	.10	.08	.04
335	Paul Kilgus	.10	.08	.04
336	Juan Samuel	.12	.09	.05
337	Mike Campbell	.10	.08	.04
338	Mike Maddux	.08	.06	.03
339	Darnell Coles	.08	.06	.03
340	Bob Dernier	.08	.06	.03
341	Rafael Ramirez	.08	.06	.03
342	Scott Sanderson	.08	.06	.03
343	B.J. Surhoff	.10	.08	.04
344	Billy Hatcher	.08	.06	.03
345	Pat Perry	.08	.06	.03
346	Jack Clark	.15	.11	.06
347	Gary Thurman	.12	.09	.05
348	*Timmy Jones*	.20	.15	.08
349	Dave Winfield	.30	.25	.12
350	Frank White	.08	.06	.03
351	Dave Collins	.08	.06	.03
352	Jack Morris	.15	.11	.06
353	Eric Plunk	.08	.06	.03

		MT	NR MT	EX
354	Leon Durham	.08	.06	.03
355	Ivan DeJesus	.08	.06	.03
356	*Brian Holman*	.40	.30	.15
357a	Dale Murphy (photo on card front reversed)	60.00	45.00	25.00
357b	Dale Murphy (correct photo)	.35	.25	.14
358	Mark Portugal	.08	.06	.03
359	Andy McGaffigan	.08	.06	.03
360	Tom Glavine	.10	.08	.04
361	Keith Moreland	.08	.06	.03
362	Todd Stottlemyre	.15	.11	.06
363	Dave Leiper	.08	.06	.03
364	Cecil Fielder	.80	.60	.30
365	Carmelo Martinez	.08	.06	.03
366	Dwight Evans	.10	.08	.04
367	Kevin McReynolds	.15	.11	.06
368	Rich Gedman	.08	.06	.03
369	Len Dykstra	.10	.08	.04
370	Jody Reed	.12	.09	.05
371	Jose Canseco	2.00	1.50	.80
372	Rob Murphy	.08	.06	.03
373	Mike Henneman	.10	.08	.04
374	Walt Weiss	.40	.30	.15
375	*Rob Dibble*	1.00	.70	.40
376	Kirby Puckett	.30	.25	.12
377	Denny Martinez	.08	.06	.03
378	Ron Gant	2.00	1.50	.80
379	Brian Harper	.08	.06	.03
380	*Nelson Santovenia*	.20	.15	.08
381	Lloyd Moseby	.08	.06	.03
382	Lance McCullers	.08	.06	.03
383	Dave Stieb	.10	.08	.04
384	Tony Gwynn	.30	.25	.12
385	Mike Flanagan	.08	.06	.03
386	Bob Ojeda	.08	.06	.03
387	Bruce Hurst	.10	.08	.04
388	Dave Magadan	.10	.08	.04
389	Wade Boggs	.60	.45	.25
390	Gary Carter	.25	.20	.10
391	Frank Tanana	.08	.06	.03
392	Curt Young	.08	.06	.03
393	Jeff Treadway	.10	.08	.04
394	Darrell Evans	.10	.08	.04
395	Glenn Hubbard	.08	.06	.03
396	Chuck Cary	.08	.06	.03
397	Frank Viola	.15	.11	.06
398	Jeff Parrett	.10	.08	.04
399	*Terry Blocker*	.15	.11	.06
400	Dan Gladden	.08	.06	.03
401	*Louie Meadows*	.15	.11	.06
402	Tim Raines	.25	.20	.10
403	Joey Meyer	.10	.08	.04
404	Larry Andersen	.08	.06	.03
405	Rex Hudler	.08	.06	.03
406	Mike Schmidt	1.50	1.25	.60
407	John Franco	.10	.08	.04
408	*Brady Anderson*	.20	.15	.08
409	Don Carman	.08	.06	.03
410	Eric Davis	.40	.30	.15
411	Bob Stanley	.08	.06	.03
412	Pete Smith	.10	.08	.04
413	Jim Rice	.25	.20	.10
414	Bruce Sutter	.10	.08	.04
415	Oil Can Boyd	.08	.06	.03
416	Ruben Sierra	.50	.40	.20
417	Mike LaValliere	.08	.06	.03
418	Steve Buechele	.08	.06	.03
419	Gary Redus	.08	.06	.03
420	Scott Fletcher	.08	.06	.03
421	Dale Sveum	.08	.06	.03
422	Bob Knepper	.08	.06	.03
423	Luis Rivera	.08	.06	.03
424	Ted Higuera	.10	.08	.04
425	Kevin Bass	.08	.06	.03
426	Ken Gerhart	.08	.06	.03
427	Shane Rawley	.08	.06	.03
428	Paul O'Neill	.08	.06	.03
429	Joe Orsulak	.08	.06	.03
430	Jackie Gutierrez	.08	.06	.03
431	Gerald Perry	.10	.08	.04
432	Mike Greenwell	.60	.45	.25
433	Jerry Royster	.08	.06	.03
434	Ellis Burks	.60	.45	.25
435	Ed Olwine	.08	.06	.03
436	Dave Rucker	.08	.06	.03
437	Charlie Hough	.08	.06	.03
438	Bob Walk	.08	.06	.03
439	Bob Brower	.08	.06	.03
440	Barry Bonds	.12	.09	.05
441	Tom Foley	.08	.06	.03
442	Rob Deer	.08	.06	.03

		MT	NR MT	EX
443	Glenn Davis	.15	.11	.06
444	Dave Martinez	.08	.06	.03
445	Bill Wegman	.08	.06	.03
446	Lloyd McClendon	.08	.06	.03
447	Dave Schmidt	.08	.06	.03
448	Darren Daulton	.08	.06	.03
449	Frank Williams	.08	.06	.03
450	Don Aase	.08	.06	.03
451	Lou Whitaker	.15	.11	.06
452	Goose Gossage	.12	.09	.05
453	Ed Whitson	.08	.06	.03
454	Jim Walewander	.08	.06	.03
455	Damon Berryhill	.12	.09	.05
456	Tim Burke	.08	.06	.03
457	Barry Jones	.08	.06	.03
458	Joel Youngblood	.08	.06	.03
459	Floyd Youmans	.08	.06	.03
460	Mark Salas	.08	.06	.03
461	Jeff Russell	.08	.06	.03
462	Darrell Miller	.08	.06	.03
463	Jeff Kunkel	.08	.06	.03
464	*Sherman Corbett*	.20	.15	.08
465	Curtis Wilkerson	.08	.06	.03
466	Bud Black	.08	.06	.03
467	Cal Ripken, Jr.	.80	.60	.30
468	John Farrell	.10	.08	.04
469	Terry Kennedy	.08	.06	.03
470	Tom Candiotti	.08	.06	.03
471	Roberto Alomar	1.25	.90	.50
472	Jeff Robinson	.12	.09	.05
473	Vance Law	.08	.06	.03
474	Randy Ready	.08	.06	.03
475	Walt Terrell	.08	.06	.03
476	Kelly Downs	.10	.08	.04
477	*Johnny Paredes*	.15	.11	.06
478	Shawn Hillegas	.08	.06	.03
479	Bob Brenly	.08	.06	.03
480	Otis Nixon	.08	.06	.03
481	Johnny Ray	.08	.06	.03
482	Geno Petralli	.08	.06	.03
483	Stu Cliburn	.08	.06	.03
484	Pete Incaviglia	.10	.08	.04
485	Brian Downing	.08	.06	.03
486	Jeff Stone	.08	.06	.03
487	Carmen Castillo	.08	.06	.03
488	Tom Niedenfuer	.08	.06	.03
489	Jay Bell	.08	.06	.03
490	Rick Schu	.08	.06	.03
491	*Jeff Pico*	.15	.11	.06
492	*Mark Parent*	.20	.15	.08
493	Eric King	.08	.06	.03
494	Al Nipper	.08	.06	.03
495	Andy Hawkins	.08	.06	.03
496	Daryl Boston	.08	.06	.03
497	Ernie Riles	.08	.06	.03
498	Pascual Perez	.08	.06	.03
499	Bill Long	.08	.06	.03
500	Kirt Manwaring	.10	.08	.04
501	Chuck Crim	.08	.06	.03
502	Candy Maldonado	.08	.06	.03
503	Dennis Lamp	.08	.06	.03
504	Glenn Braggs	.08	.06	.03
505	Joe Price	.08	.06	.03
506	Ken Williams	.08	.06	.03
507	Bill Pecota	.08	.06	.03
508	Rey Quinones	.08	.06	.03
509	*Jeff Bittiger*	.15	.11	.06
510	Kevin Seitzer	.30	.25	.12
511	Steve Bedrosian	.10	.08	.04
512	Todd Worrell	.10	.08	.04
513	Chris James	.10	.08	.04
514	Jose Oquendo	.08	.06	.03
515	David Palmer	.08	.06	.03
516	John Smiley	.12	.09	.05
517	Dave Clark	.08	.06	.03
518	Mike Dunne	.10	.08	.04
519	Ron Washington	.08	.06	.03
520	Bob Kipper	.08	.06	.03
521	Lee Smith	.10	.08	.04
522	Juan Castillo	.08	.06	.03
523	Don Robinson	.08	.06	.03
524	Kevin Romine	.08	.06	.03
525	Paul Molitor	.15	.11	.06
526	Mark Langston	.10	.08	.04
527	Donnie Hill	.08	.06	.03
528	Larry Owen	.08	.06	.03
529	Jerry Reed	.08	.06	.03
530	Jack McDowell	.10	.08	.04
531	Greg Mathews	.08	.06	.03
532	John Russell	.08	.06	.03
533	Don Quisenberry	.08	.06	.03

		MT	NR MT	EX
534	Greg Gross	.08	.06	.03
535	Danny Cox	.08	.06	.03
536	Terry Francona	.08	.06	.03
537	Andy Van Slyke	.15	.11	.06
538	Mel Hall	.08	.06	.03
539	Jim Gott	.08	.06	.03
540	Doug Jones	.10	.08	.04
541	Criag Lefferts	.08	.06	.03
542	Mike Boddicker	.08	.06	.03
543	Greg Brock	.08	.06	.03
544	Atlee Hammaker	.08	.06	.03
545	Tom Bolton	.08	.06	.03
546	*Mike Macfarlane*	.20	.15	.08
547	*Rich Renteria*	.15	.11	.06
548	John Davis	.08	.06	.03
549	Floyd Bannister	.08	.06	.03
550	Mickey Brantley	.08	.06	.03
551	Duane Ward	.08	.06	.03
552	Dan Petry	.08	.06	.03
553	Mickey Tettleton	.08	.06	.03
554	Rick Leach	.08	.06	.03
555	Mike Witt	.08	.06	.03
556	Sid Bream	.08	.06	.03
557	Bobby Witt	.10	.08	.04
558	Tommy Herr	.08	.06	.03
559	Randy Milligan	.08	.06	.03
560	*Jose Cecena*	.20	.15	.08
561	Mackey Sasser	.08	.06	.03
562	Carney Lansford	.08	.06	.03
563	Rick Aguilera	.08	.06	.03
564	Ron Hassey	.08	.06	.03
565	Dwight Gooden	.50	.40	.20
566	Paul Assenmacher	.08	.06	.03
567	Neil Allen	.08	.06	.03
568	Jim Morrison	.08	.06	.03
569	Mike Pagliarulo	.10	.08	.04
570	Ted Simmons	.10	.08	.04
571	Mark Thurmond	.08	.06	.03
572	Fred McGriff	.40	.30	.15
573	Wally Joyner	.25	.20	.10
574	*Jose Bautista*	.20	.15	.08
575	Kelly Gruber	.08	.06	.03
576	Cecilio Guante	.08	.06	.03
577	Mark Davidson	.08	.06	.03
578	Bobby Bonilla	.12	.09	.05
579	Mike Stanley	.08	.06	.03
580	Gene Larkin	.10	.08	.04
581	Stan Javier	.08	.06	.03
582	Howard Johnson	.10	.08	.04
583a	Mike Gallego (photo on card back reversed)	1.50	1.25	.60
583b	Mike Gallego (correct photo)	.15	.11	.06
584	David Cone	.35	.25	.14
585	*Doug Jennings*	.20	.15	.08
586	Charlie Hudson	.08	.06	.03
587	Dion James	.08	.06	.03
588	Al Leiter	.15	.11	.06
589	Charlie Puleo	.08	.06	.03
590	Roberto Kelly	.25	.20	.10
591	Thad Bosley	.08	.06	.03
592	Pete Stanicek	.10	.08	.04
593	*Pat Borders*	.25	.20	.10
594	*Bryan Harvey*	.60	.45	.25
595	Jeff Ballard	.10	.08	.04
596	Jeff Reardon	.10	.08	.04
597	Doug Drabek	.08	.06	.03
598	Edwin Correa	.08	.06	.03
599	Keith Atherton	.08	.06	.03
600	Dave LaPoint	.08	.06	.03
601	Don Baylor	.10	.08	.04
602	Tom Pagnozzi	.08	.06	.03
603	Tim Flannery	.08	.06	.03
604	Gene Walter	.08	.06	.03
605	Dave Parker	.12	.09	.05
606	Mike Diaz	.08	.06	.03
607	Chris Gwynn	.10	.08	.04
608	Odell Jones	.08	.06	.03
609	Carlton Fisk	.30	.25	.12
610	Jay Howell	.08	.06	.03
611	Tim Crews	.08	.06	.03
612	Keith Hernandez	.20	.15	.08
613	Willie Fraser	.08	.06	.03
614	Jim Eppard	.08	.06	.03
615	Jeff Hamilton	.08	.06	.03
616	Kurt Stillwell	.08	.06	.03
617	Tom Browning	.10	.08	.04
618	Jeff Montgomery	.08	.06	.03
619	Jose Rijo	.08	.06	.03
620	Jamie Quirk	.08	.06	.03
621	Willie McGee	.12	.09	.05
622	Mark Grant	.08	.06	.03
623	Bill Swift	.08	.06	.03
624	Orlando Mercado	.08	.06	.03
625	*John Costello*	.15	.11	.06
626	Jose Gonzalez	.08	.06	.03
627a	Bill Schroeder (putting on shin guards on card back, photo actually Ronn Reynolds)	1.25	.90	.50
627b	Bill Schroeder (arms crossed on card back, correct photo)	.15	.11	.06
628a	Fred Manrique (throwing on card back, photo actually Ozzie Guillen)	1.25	.90	.50
628b	Fred Manrique (batting on card back, correct photo)	.15	.11	.06
629	Ricky Horton	.08	.06	.03
630	Dan Plesac	.10	.08	.04
631	Alfredo Griffin	.08	.06	.03
632	Chuck Finley	.08	.06	.03
633	Kirk Gibson	.20	.15	.08
634	Randy Myers	.10	.08	.04
635	Greg Minton	.08	.06	.03
636	Herm Winningham	.08	.06	.03
637	Charlie Leibrandt	.08	.06	.03
638	Tim Birtsas	.08	.06	.03
639	Bill Buckner	.10	.08	.04
640	Danny Jackson	.15	.11	.06
641	Greg Booker	.08	.06	.03
642	Jim Presley	.08	.06	.03
643	Gene Nelson	.08	.06	.03
644	Rod Booker	.08	.06	.03
645	Dennis Rasmussen	.10	.08	.04
646	Juan Nieves	.08	.06	.03
647	Bobby Thigpen	.10	.08	.04
648	Tim Belcher	.10	.08	.04
649	Mike Young	.08	.06	.03
650	Ivan Calderon	.08	.06	.03
651	*Oswaldo Peraza*	.20	.15	.08
652a	Pat Sheridan (no position on front)	30.00	22.00	12.00
652b	Pat Sheridan (position on front)	.08	.06	.03
653	Mike Morgan	.08	.06	.03
654	Mike Heath	.08	.06	.03
655	Jay Tibbs	.08	.06	.03
656	Fernando Valenzuela	.20	.15	.08
657	Lee Mazzilli	.08	.06	.03
658	Frank Viola	.08	.06	.03
659	Jose Canseco	.08	.06	.03
660	Walt Weiss	.08	.06	.03
661	Orel Hershiser	.08	.06	.03
662	Kirk Gibson	.08	.06	.03
663	Chris Sabo	.08	.06	.03
664	Dennis Eckersley	.08	.06	.03
665	Orel Hershiser	.08	.06	.03
666	Kirk Gibson	.08	.06	.03
667	Orel Hershiser	.08	.06	.03
668	Angels Checklist (Wally Joyner)	.08	.06	.03
669	Astros Checklist (Nolan Ryan)	.40	.30	.15
670	Athletics Checklist (Jose Canseco)	.08	.06	.03
671	Blue Jays Checklist (Fred McGriff)	.08	.06	.03
672	Braves Checklist (Dale Murphy)	.08	.06	.03
673	Brewers Checklist (Paul Molitor)	.08	.06	.03
674	Cardinals Checklist (Ozzie Smith)	.08	.06	.03
675	Cubs Checklist (Ryne Sandberg)	.08	.06	.03
676	Dodgers Checklist (Kirk Gibson)	.08	.06	.03
677	Expos Checklist (Andres Galarraga)	.08	.06	.03
678	Giants Checklist (Will Clark)	.08	.06	.03
679	Indians Checklist (Cory Snyder)	.08	.06	.03
680	Mariners Checklist (Alvin Davis)	.08	.06	.03
681	Mets Checklist (Darryl Strawberry)	.08	.06	.03
682	Orioles Checklist (Cal Ripken, Jr.)	.08	.06	.03
683	Padres Checklist (Tony Gwynn)	.08	.06	.03
684	Phillies Checklist (Mike Schmidt)	.08	.06	.03
685	Pirates Checklist (Andy Van Slyke)	.08	.06	.03
686	Rangers Checklist (Ruben Sierra)	.08	.06	.03
687	Red Sox Checklist (Wade Boggs)	.08	.06	.03
688	Reds Checklist (Eric Davis)	.08	.06	.03
689	Royals Checklist (George Brett)	.08	.06	.03
690	Tigers Checklist (Alan Trammell)	.08	.06	.03
691	Twins Checklist (Frank Viola)	.08	.06	.03
692	White Sox Checklist (Harold Baines)	.08	.06	.03
693	Yankees Checklist (Don Mattingly)	.08	.06	.03
694	Checklist 1-100	.08	.06	.03
695	Checklist 101-200	.08	.06	.03
696	Checklist 201-300	.08	.06	.03
697	Checklist 301-400	.08	.06	.03
698	Checklist 401-500	.08	.06	.03
699	Checklist 501-600	.08	.06	.03
700	Checklist 601-700	.08	.06	.03
701	Checklist 701-800	.20	.15	.08
702	Jessie Barfield	.10	.08	.04

		MT	NR MT	EX
703	Walt Terrell	.10	.08	.04
704	Dickie Thon	.10	.08	.04
705	Al Leiter	.10	.08	.04
706	Dave LaPoint	.10	.08	.04
707	Charlie Hayes(FC)	.20	.15	.08
708	Andy Hawkins	.10	.08	.04
709	Mickey Hatcher	.10	.08	.04
710	Lance McCullers	.10	.08	.04
711	Ron Kittle	.10	.08	.04
712	Bert Blyleven	.10	.08	.04
713	Rick Dempsey	.10	.08	.04
714	Ken Williams	.10	.08	.04
715	Steve Rosenberg(FC)	.15	.11	.06
716	Joe Skalski(FC)	.20	.15	.08
717	Spike Owen	.10	.08	.04
718	Todd Burns	.10	.08	.04
719	Kevin Gross	.10	.08	.04
720	Tommy Herr	.10	.08	.04
721	Rob Ducey	.10	.08	.04
722	Gary Green(FC)	.15	.11	.06
723	Gregg Olson(FC)	2.00	1.50	.80
724	Greg Harris(FC)	.15	.11	.06
725	Craig Worthington(FC)	.50	.40	.20
726	Tom Howard(FC)	.25	.20	.10
727	Dale Mohorcic	.10	.08	.04
728	Rich Yett	.10	.08	.04
729	Mel Hall	.10	.08	.04
730	Floyd Youmans	.10	.08	.04
731	Lonnie Smith	.15	.11	.06
732	Wally Backman	.10	.08	.04
733	Trevor Wilson	.10	.08	.04
734	Jose Alvarez	.10	.08	.04
735	Bob Milacki(FC)	.15	.11	.06
736	Tom Gordon(FC)	1.25	.90	.50
737	Wally Whitehurst(FC)	.25	.20	.10
738	Mike Aldrete	.10	.08	.04
739	Keith Miller	.10	.08	.04
740	Randy Milligan	.10	.08	.04
741	Jeff Parrett	.10	.08	.04
742	Steve Finley(FC)	.60	.45	.25
743	Junior Felix(FC)	.80	.60	.30
744	Pete Harnisch(FC)	.50	.40	.20
745	Bill Spiers(FC)	.40	.30	.15
746	Hensley Meulens(FC)	1.50	1.25	.60
747	Juan Bell	.20	.15	.08
748	Steve Sax	.15	.11	.06
749	Phil Bradley	.10	.08	.04
750	Rey Quinones	.10	.08	.04
751	Tommy Gregg(FC)	.15	.11	.06
752	Kevin Brown(FC)	.10	.08	.04
753	Derek Lilliquist(FC)	.15	.11	.06
754	Todd Zeile(FC)	3.00	2.25	1.25
755	Jim Abbott(FC)	3.00	2.25	1.25
756	Ozzie Canseco(FC)	.30	.25	.12
757	Nick Esasky	.10	.08	.04
758	Mike Moore	.15	.11	.06
759	Rob Murphy	.10	.08	.04
760	Rick Mahler	.10	.08	.04
761	Fred Lynn	.10	.08	.04
762	Kevin Blankenship(FC)	.10	.08	.04
763	Eddie Murray	.15	.11	.06
764	Steve Searcy(FC)	.10	.08	.04
765	Jerome Walton(FC)	2.00	1.50	.80
766	Erik Hanson(FC)	2.00	1.50	.80
767	Bob Boone	.15	.11	.06
768	Edgar Martinez(FC)	1.25	.90	.50
769	Jose DeJesus(FC)	.10	.08	.04
770	Greg Briley(FC)	.60	.45	.25
771	Steve Peters(FC)	.10	.08	.04
772	Rafael Palmeiro	.40	.30	.15
773	Jack Clark	.15	.11	.06
774	Nolan Ryan	4.00	3.00	1.50
775	Lance Parrish	.10	.08	.04
776	Joe Girardi(FC)	.25	.20	.10
777	Willie Randolph	.10	.08	.04
778	Mitch Williams	.30	.25	.12
779	Dennis Cook(FC)	.40	.30	.15
780	Dwight Smith(FC)	.50	.40	.20
781	Lenny Harris(FC)	.40	.30	.15
782	Torey Lovullo(FC)	.15	.11	.06
783	Norm Charlton(FC)	.10	.08	.04
784	Chris Brown	.10	.08	.04
785	Todd Benzinger	.10	.08	.04
786	Shane Rawley	.10	.08	.04
787	Omar Vizquel(FC)	.25	.20	.10
788	LaVel Freeman(FC)	.25	.20	.10
789	Jeffrey Leonard	.10	.08	.04
790	Eddie Williams(FC)	.10	.08	.04
791	Jamie Moyer	.10	.08	.04
792	Bruce Hurst	.10	.08	.04
793	Julio Franco	.15	.11	.06
794	Claudell Washington	.10	.08	.04
795	Jody Davis	.10	.08	.04
796	Odibbe McDowell	.10	.08	.04
797	Paul Kilgus	.10	.08	.04
798	Tracy Jones	.10	.08	.04
799	Steve Wilson(FC)	.20	.15	.08
800	Pete O'Brien,			

1990 Upper Deck

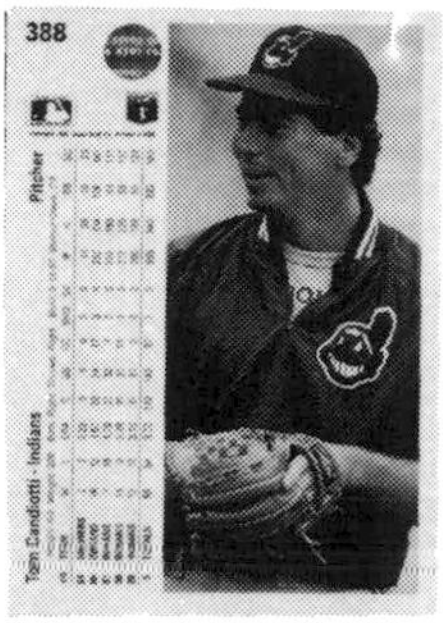

Following the success of its first issue, Upper Deck released another 800-card set in 1990. The cards contain full-color photos on both sides and are 2-1/2" by 3-1/2" in size. The artwork of Vernon Wells is featured on the front of all team checklist cards. The 1990 set also introduces two new Wells illustrations - a tribute to Mike Schmidt upon his retirement and one commemorating Nolan Ryan's 5,000 career strikeouts. The cards are similar in design to the 1989 issue. The Wade Boggs card depicts the Red Sox star in four stages of his batting swing via a quad-action photograph, much like the Jim Abbott card of 1989. The high- number series (701-800) was released as a boxed set, in factory sets and in wax packs at mid-season.

	MT	NR MT	EX
Complete Set: 1-700	40.00	30.00	15.00
Common Player: 1-700	.06	.05	.02
Complete Set: 1-800	50.00	37.00	20.00
Common Player: 701-800	.10	.08	.04

1	Star Rookie Checklist	.06	.05	.02
2	*Randy Nosek*(FC)	.15	.11	.06
3	*Tom Dress*(FC)	.15	.11	.06
4	Curt Young	.06	.05	.02
5	Angels Checklist	.06	.05	.02
6	Luis Salazar	.06	.05	.02
7	Phillies Checklist	.06	.05	.02
8	Jose Bautista	.08	.06	.03
9	*Marquis Grissom*(FC)	1.00	.70	.40
10	Dodgers Checklist	.06	.05	.02
11	Rick Aguilera	.08	.06	.03
12	Padres Checklist	.06	.05	.02
13	*Deion Sanders*(FC)	.40	.30	.15
14	Marvell Wynne	.06	.05	.02
15	David West	.15	.11	.06
16	Pirates Checklist	.06	.05	.02
17	*Sammy Sosa*(FC)	.70	.50	.30
18	Yankees Checklist	.06	.05	.02
19	Jack Howell	.06	.05	.02
20	Mike Schmidt (Special Card)	1.00	.70	.40
21	Robin Ventura(FC)	2.00	1.50	.80
22	Brian Meyer(FC)	.20	.15	.08
23	*Blaine Beatty*(FC)	.20	.15	.08
24	Mariners Checklist	.06	.05	.02
25	*Greg Vaughn*(FC)	1.00	.70	.40
26	*Xavier Hernandez*(FC)	.15	.11	.06
27	*Jason Grimsley*(FC)	.25	.20	.10
28	*Eric Anthony*(FC)	.50	.40	.20
29	Expos Checklist	.06	.05	.02
30	David Wells	.06	.05	.02
31	Hal Morris(FC)	1.25	.90	.50
32	Royals Checklist	.25	.20	.10
33	*Kelly Mann*(FC)	.15	.11	.06
34	Nolan Ryan (Special Card)	1.25	.90	.50
35	*Scott Service*(FC)	.20	.15	.08

		MT	NR MT	EX
36	Athletics Checklist	.06	.05	.02
37	*Tino Martinez*(FC)	1.50	1.25	.60
38	Chili Davis	.09	.07	.04
39	Scott Sanderson	.06	.05	.02
40	Giants Checklist	.06	.05	.02
41	Tigers Checklist	.06	.05	.02
42	*Scott Coolbaugh*(FC)	.40	.30	.15
43	*Jose Cano*(FC)	.15	.11	.06
44	*Jose Vizcaino*(FC)	.30	.25	.12
45	*Bob Hamelin*(FC)	.30	.25	.12
46	*Jose Offerman*(FC)	1.00	.70	.40
47	Kevin Blankenship	.10	.08	.04
48	Twins Checklist	.06	.05	.02
49	*Tommy Greene*(FC)	.50	.40	.20
50	Will Clark (Special Card)	.40	.30	.15
51	Rob Nelson(FC)	.09	.07	.04
52	*Chris Hammond*(FC)	.30	.25	.12
53	Indians Checklist	.06	.05	.02
54a	*Ben McDonald* (Orioles Logo)(FC)	20.00	15.00	8.00
54b	*Ben McDonald* (Rookies Logo)(FC)	3.00	2.25	1.25
55	Andy Benes(FC)	.40	.30	.15
56	*John Olerud*(FC)	3.00	2.25	1.25
57	Red Sox Checklist	.06	.05	.02
58	Tony Armas	.06	.05	.02
59	*George Canale*(FC)	.20	.15	.08
60a	Orioles Checklist (Jamie Weston)	4.00	3.00	1.50
60b	Orioles Checklist (Mickey Weston)	.08	.06	.03
61	*Mike Stanton*(FC)	.15	.11	.06
62	Mets Checklist	.06	.05	.02
63	*Kent Mercker*(FC)	.50	.40	.20
64	*Francisco Cabrera*(FC)	.30	.25	.20
65	Steve Avery(FC)	1.75	1.25	.70
66	Jose Canseco	.90	.70	.50
67	*Matt Merullo*(FC)	.15	.11	.06
68	Cardinals Checklist	.06	.05	.02
69	Ron Karkovice	.06	.05	.02
70	*Kevin Maas*(FC)	4.00	3.00	1.50
71	Dennis Cook	.10	.08	.04
72	*Juan Gonzalez*(FC)	9.00	6.75	3.50
73	Cubs Checklist	.06	.05	.02
74	*Dean Palmer*(FC)	3.00	2.25	1.25
75	Bo Jackson (Special Card)	.60	.45	.25
76	*Rob Richie*(FC)	.20	.15	.08
77	*Bobby Rose*(FC)	.20	.15	.08
78	*Brian DuBois*(FC)	.15	.11	.06
79	White Sox Checklist	.06	.05	.02
80	Gene Nelson	.06	.05	.02
81	Bob McClure	.06	.05	.02
82	Rangers Checklist	.06	.05	.02
83	Greg Minton	.06	.05	.02
84	Braves Checklist	.06	.05	.02
85	Willie Fraser	.06	.05	.02
86	Neal Heaton	.06	.05	.02
87	*Kevin Tapani*(FC)	.30	.25	.12
88	Astros Checklist	.06	.05	.02
89a	Jim Gott (Incorrect Photo)	5.00	3.75	2.00
89b	Jim Gott (Photo of Gott)	.10	.08	.04
90	Lance Johnson(FC)	.09	.07	.04
91	Brewers Checklist	.06	.05	.02
92	Jeff Parrett	.08	.06	.03
93	*Julio Machado*(FC)	.25	.20	.10
94	Ron Jones	.10	.08	.04
95	Blue Jays Checklist	.06	.05	.02
96	Jerry Reuss	.06	.05	.02
97	Brian Fisher	.06	.05	.02
98	*Kevin Ritz*(FC)	.25	.20	.10
99	Reds Checklist	.06	.05	.02
100	Checklist 1-100	.06	.05	.02
101	Gerald Perry	.06	.05	.02
102	*Kevin Appier*(FC)	.30	.15	.08
103	Julio Franco	.10	.08	.04
104	Craig Biggio	.20	.15	.08
105	Bo Jackson	1.00	.70	.40
106	*Junior Felix*	.30	.25	.12
107	Mike Harkey(FC)	.30	.25	.12
108	Fred McGriff	.25	.20	.10
109	Rick Sutcliffe	.08	.06	.03
110	Pete O'Brien	.08	.06	.03
111	Kelly Gruber	.10	.08	.04
112	Pat Borders	.10	.08	.04
113	Dwight Evans	.10	.08	.04
114	Dwight Gooden	.20	.15	.08
115	*Kevin Batiste*(FC)	.15	.11	.06
116	Eric Davis	.25	.20	.10
117	Kevin Mitchell	.40	.30	.15
118	Ron Oester	.06	.05	.02
119	Brett Butler	.09	.07	.04
120	Danny Jackson	.06	.05	.02
121	Tommy Gregg	.06	.05	.02
122	Ken Caminiti	.08	.06	.03

		MT	NR MT	EX
123	Kevin Brown	.10	.08	.04
124	George Brett	.15	.11	.06
125	Mike Scott	.10	.08	.04
126	Cory Snyder	.10	.08	.04
127	George Bell	.15	.11	.06
128	Mark Grace	.50	.40	.20
129	Devon White	.10	.08	.04
130	Tony Fernandez	.15	.11	.06
131	Dan Aase	.06	.05	.02
132	Rance Mulliniks	.06	.05	.02
133	Marty Barrett	.08	.06	.03
134	Nelson Liriano	.07	.05	.03
135	Mark Carreon(FC)	.15	.11	.06
136	Candy Maldonado	.06	.05	.02
137	Tim Birtsas	.06	.05	.02
138	Tom Brookens	.06	.05	.02
139	John Franco	.08	.06	.03
140	Mike LaCoss	.06	.05	.02
141	Jeff Treadway	.07	.05	.03
142	Pat Tabler	.07	.05	.03
143	Darrell Evans	.06	.05	.02
144	Rafael Ramirez	.06	.05	.02
145	Oddibe McDowell	.09	.07	.04
146	Brian Downing	.09	.07	.04
147	Curtis Wilkerson	.06	.05	.02
148	Ernie Whitt	.07	.05	.02
149	Bill Schroeder	.06	.05	.02
150	Domingo Ramos	.06	.05	.02
151	Rick Honeycutt	.06	.05	.02
152	Don Slaught	.06	.05	.02
153	Mitch Webster	.06	.05	.02
154	Tony Phillips	.07	.05	.02
155	Paul Kilgus	.06	.05	.02
156	Ken Griffey, Jr.	6.00	4.50	2.50
157	Gary Sheffield	.50	.40	.20
158	Wally Backman	.06	.05	.02
159	B.J. Surhoff	.08	.06	.03
160	Louie Meadows	.08	.06	.03
161	Paul O'Neill	.09	.07	.04
162	*Jeff McKnight*(FC)	.15	.11	.06
163	Alvaro Espinoza(FC)	.15	.11	.06
164	*Scott Scudder*(FC)	.20	.15	.08
165	Jeff Reed	.06	.05	.02
166	Gregg Jefferies	.30	.25	.12
167	Barry Larkin	.15	.11	.06
168	Gary Carter	.10	.08	.04
169	Robby Thompson	.09	.07	.04
170	Rolando Roomes	.15	.11	.06
171	Mark McGwire	.50	.40	.20
172	Steve Sax	.10	.08	.04
173	Mark Williamson	.06	.05	.02
174	Mitch Williams	.15	.11	.06
175	Brian Holton	.06	.05	.02
176	Rob Deer	.08	.06	.03
177	Tim Raines	.12	.09	.05
178	Mike Felder	.06	.05	.02
179	Harold Reynolds	.10	.08	.04
180	Terry Francona	.06	.05	.02
181	Chris Sabo	.15	.11	.06
182	Darryl Strawberry	.30	.25	.14
183	Willie Randolph	.10	.08	.04
184	Billy Ripken	.06	.05	.02
185	Mackey Sasser	.08	.06	.03
186	Todd Benzinger	.08	.06	.03
187	Kevin Elster	.07	.05	.03
188	Jose Uribe	.06	.05	.02
189	Tom Browning	.10	.08	.04
190	Keith Miller	.09	.07	.04
191	Don Mattingly	.60	.45	.25
192	Dave Parker	.12	.09	.05
193	Roberto Kelly	.12	.09	.05
194	Phil Bradley	.09	.07	.04
195	Ron Hassey	.07	.05	.03
196	Gerald Young	.06	.05	.02
197	Hubie Brooks	.08	.06	.03
198	Bill Doran	.09	.07	.04
199	Al Newman	.06	.05	.02
200	Checklist 101-200	.06	.05	.02
201	Terry Puhl	.06	.05	.02
202	Frank DiPino	.06	.05	.02
203	Jim Clancy	.06	.05	.02
204	Bob Ojeda	.07	.05	.03
205	Alex Trevino	.06	.05	.02
206	Dave Henderson	.10	.08	.04
207	Henry Cotto	.06	.05	.02
208	Rafael Belliard	.06	.05	.02
209	Stan Javier	.07	.05	.03
210	Jerry Reed	.06	.05	.02
211	Doug Dascenzo	.08	.06	.03
212	Andres Thomas	.07	.05	.03
213	Greg Maddux	.20	.15	.08

		MT	NR MT	EX
214	Mike Schooler	.09	.07	.04
215	Lonnie Smith	.09	.07	.04
216	Jose Rijo	.10	.08	.04
217	Greg Gagne	.08	.06	.03
218	Jim Gantner	.08	.06	.03
219	Allan Anderson	.09	.07	.04
220	Rick Mahler	.06	.05	.02
221	Jim Deshaies	.09	.07	.04
222	Keith Hernandez	.10	.08	.04
223	Vince Coleman	.12	.09	.05
224	David Cone	.20	.15	.08
225	Ozzie Smith	.20	.15	.08
226	Matt Nokes	.10	.08	.04
227	Barry Bonds	.10	.08	.04
228	Felix Jose	.10	.08	.04
229	Dennis Powell	.06	.05	.02
230	Mike Gallego	.06	.05	.02
231	Shawon Dunston	.09	.07	.04
232	Ron Gant	.10	.08	.04
233	*Omar Vizquel*	.10	.08	.04
234	Derek Lilliquist	.10	.08	.04
235	Erik Hanson	.10	.08	.04
236	Kirby Puckett	.35	.25	.14
237	*Bill Spiers*	.25	.20	.10
238	Dan Gladden	.07	.05	.03
239	Bryan Clutterbuck(FC)	.07	.05	.03
240	John Moses	.06	.05	.02
241	Ron Darling	.12	.09	.05
242	Joe Magrane	.12	.09	.05
243	Dave Magadan	.09	.07	.03
244	Pedro Guererro	.15	.11	.06
245	Glenn Davis	.10	.08	.04
246	Terry Steinbach	.12	.09	.05
247	Fred Lynn	.09	.07	.04
248	Gary Redus	.06	.05	.02
249	Kenny Williams	.06	.05	.02
250	Sid Bream	.06	.05	.02
251	Bob Welch	.08	.06	.03
252	Bill Buckner	.07	.05	.03
253	Carney Lansford	.09	.07	.04
254	Paul Molitor	.12	.09	.05
255	Jose DeJesus	.15	.11	.06
256	Orel Hershiser	.25	.20	.10
257	Tom Brunansky	.10	.08	.04
258	Mike Davis	.06	.05	.02
259	Jeff Ballard	.12	.09	.05
260	Scott Terry	.09	.07	.04
261	Sid Fernandez	.10	.08	.04
262	Mike Marshall	.08	.06	.03
263	Howard Johnson	.20	.15	.08
264	Kirk Gibson	.09	.07	.04
265	Kevin McReynolds	.15	.11	.06
266	Cal Ripken, Jr.	.30	.25	.12
267	Ozzie Guillen	.07	.05	.03
268	Jim Traber	.06	.05	.02
269	Bobby Thigpen	.09	.07	.04
270	Joe Orsulak	.06	.05	.02
271	Bob Boone	.09	.07	.04
272	Dave Stewart	.09	.07	.04
273	Tim Wallach	.09	.07	.04
274	Luis Aquino	.06	.05	.02
275	Mike Moore	.10	.08	.04
276	Tony Pena	.08	.06	.03
277	Eddie Murray	.15	.11	.06
278	Milt Thompson	.07	.05	.03
279	Alejandro Pena	.06	.05	.02
280	Ken Dayley	.06	.05	.02
281	Carmen Castillo	.06	.05	.02
282	Tom Henke	.08	.06	.03
283	Mickey Hatcher	.06	.05	.02
284	Roy Smith(FC)	.06	.05	.02
285	Manny Lee	.06	.05	.02
286	Dan Pasqua	.07	.05	.02
287	Larry Sheets	.06	.05	.02
288	Garry Templeton	.07	.05	.03
289	Eddie Williams	.07	.05	.03
290	Brady Anderson	.07	.05	.03
291	Spike Owen	.07	.05	.03
292	Storm Davis	.09	.07	.04
293	Chris Bosio	.09	.07	.04
294	Jim Eisenreich	.07	.05	.03
295	Don August	.07	.05	.03
296	Jeff Hamilton	.07	.05	.03
297	Mickey Tettleton	.10	.08	.04
298	Mike Scioscia	.09	.07	.04
299	Kevin Hickey(FC)	.06	.05	.02
300	Checklist 201-300	.06	.05	.02
301	Shawn Abner	.06	.05	.02
302	Kevin Bass	.08	.06	.03
303	Bip Roberts(FC)	.08	.06	.03
304	Joe Girardi	.10	.08	.04
305	Danny Darwin	.06	.05	.02
306	Mike Heath	.06	.05	.02
307	Mike Macfarlane	.06	.05	.02
308	Ed Whitson	.08	.06	.03
309	Tracy Jones	.07	.05	.02
310	Scott Fletcher	.07	.05	.02
311	Darnell Coles	.07	.05	.02
312	Mike Brumley	.06	.05	.02
313	Bill Swift	.06	.05	.02
314	Charlie Hough	.07	.05	.03
315	Jim Presley	.08	.06	.03
316	Luis Polonia	.07	.05	.03
317	Mike Morgan	.06	.05	.02
318	Lee Guetterman	.06	.05	.02
319	Jose Oquendo	.08	.06	.03
320	Wayne Tollenson	.06	.05	.02
321	Jody Reed	.07	.05	.03
322	Damon Berryhill	.09	.07	.04
323	Roger Clemens	.40	.30	.15
324	Ryne Sandberg	.30	.25	.12
325	Benito Santiago	.10	.08	.04
326	Bret Saberhagen	.15	.11	.06
327	Lou Whitaker	.10	.08	.04
328	Dave Gallagher	.10	.08	.04
329	Mike Pagliarulo	.07	.05	.03
330	Doyle Alexander	.07	.05	.03
331	Jeffrey Leonard	.09	.07	.04
332	Torey Lovullo	.20	.15	.08
333	Pete Incaviglia	.09	.07	.04
334	Rickey Henderson	.30	.25	.12
335	Rafael Palmeiro	.10	.08	.04
336	Ken Hill	.10	.08	.04
337	Dave Winfield	.12	.09	.05
338	Alfredo Griffin	.07	.05	.03
339	Andy Hawkins	.07	.05	.03
340	Ted Power	.06	.05	.02
341	Steve Wilson	.10	.08	.04
342	Jack Clark	.10	.08	.04
343	Ellis Burks	.25	.20	.10
344	Tony Gwynn	.20	.15	.08
345	*Jerome Walton*	.40	.30	.15
346	Roberto Alomar	.10	.08	.04
347	*Carlos Martinez*(FC)	.15	.11	.06
348	Chet Lemon	.07	.05	.03
349	Willie Wilson	.07	.05	.03
350	Greg Walker	.07	.05	.03
351	Tom Bolton	.06	.05	.02
352	German Gonzalez(FC)	.08	.06	.03
353	Harold Baines	.10	.08	.04
354	Mike Greenwell	.30	.25	.12
355	Ruben Sierra	.20	.15	.08
356	Anres Galarraga	.12	.09	.05
357	Andre Dawson	.15	.11	.06
358	*Jeff Brantley*(FC)	.10	.08	.04
359	Mike Bielecki	.08	.06	.03
360	Ken Oberkfell	.06	.05	.02
361	Kurt Stillwell	.07	.05	.03
362	Brian Holman	.09	.07	.04
363	Kevin Seitzer	.12	.09	.05
364	Alvin Davis	.15	.11	.06
365	Tom Gordon	.35	.25	.14
366	Bobby Bonilla	.10	.08	.04
367	Carlton Fisk	.10	.08	.04
368	*Steve Carter*(FC)	.15	.11	.06
369	Joel Skinner	.06	.05	.02
370	John Cangelosi	.06	.05	.02
371	Cecil Espy	.08	.06	.03
372	*Gary Wayne*(FC)	.15	.11	.06
373	Jim Rice	.08	.06	.03
374	*Mike Dyer*(FC)	.15	.11	.06
375	Joe Carter	.12	.09	.05
376	Dwight Smith	.20	.15	.08
377	*John Wetteland*(FC)	.20	.15	.08
378	Ernie Riles	.06	.05	.02
379	Otis Nixon	.06	.05	.02
380	Vance Law	.06	.05	.02
381	Dave Bergman	.06	.05	.02
382	Frank White	.07	.05	.03
383	Scott Bradley	.06	.05	.02
384	Israel Sanchez	.06	.05	.02
385	Gary Pettis	.06	.05	.02
386	Donn Pall(FC)	.06	.05	.02
387	John Smiley	.10	.08	.04
388	Tom Candiotti	.07	.05	.03
389	Junior Ortiz	.06	.05	.02
390	Steve Lyons	.06	.05	.02
391	Brian Harper	.06	.05	.02
392	Fred Manrique	.06	.05	.02
393	Lee Smith	.08	.06	.03
394	Jeff Kunkel	.06	.05	.02
395	Claudell Washington	.08	.06	.03

		MT	NR MT	EX
396	John Tudor	.07	.05	.03
397	Terry Kennedy	.07	.05	.03
398	Lloyd McClendon	.09	.07	.04
399	Craig Lefferts	.06	.05	.02
400	Checklist 301-400	.06	.05	.02
401	Keith Moreland	.06	.05	.02
402	Rich Gedman	.07	.05	.03
403	Jeff Robinson	.07	.05	.03
404	Randy Ready	.06	.05	.02
405	Rick Cerone	.06	.05	.02
406	Jeff Blauser	.07	.05	.03
407	Larry Andersen	.06	.05	.02
408	Joe Boever	.08	.06	.03
409	Felix Fermin	.06	.05	.02
410	Glenn Wilson	.06	.05	.02
411	Rex Hudler	.06	.05	.02
412	Mark Grant	.06	.05	.02
413	Dennis Martinez	.08	.06	.03
414	Darrin Jackson	.06	.05	.02
415	Mike Aldrete	.06	.05	.02
416	Roger McDowell	.09	.07	.04
417	Jeff Reardon	.10	.08	.04
418	Darren Daulton	.06	.05	.02
419	Tim Laudner	.08	.06	.03
420	Don Carman	.07	.05	.03
421	Lloyd Moseby	.09	.07	.04
422	Doug Drabek	.10	.08	.04
423	Lenny Harris	.09	.07	.04
424	Jose Lind	.07	.05	.03
425	*Dave Johnson*(FC)	.20	.15	.08
426	Jerry Browne	.09	.07	.04
427	*Eric Yelding*(FC)	.12	.09	.05
428	Brad Komminsk(FC)	.06	.05	.02
429	Jody Davis	.06	.05	.02
430	Mariano Duncan(FC)	.09	.07	.04
431	Mark Davis	.12	.09	.05
432	Nelson Santovenia	.10	.08	.04
433	Bruce Hurst	.10	.08	.04
434	*Jeff Huson*(FC)	.25	.20	.10
435	Chris James	.09	.07	.04
436	*Mark Guthrie*(FC)	.15	.11	.06
437	Charlie Hayes(FC)	.10	.08	.04
438	Shane Rawley	.08	.06	.03
439	Dickie Thon	.06	.05	.02
440	Juan Berenguer	.06	.05	.02
441	Kevin Romine	.06	.05	.02
442	Bill Landrum	.09	.07	.04
443	Todd Frohwirth	.07	.05	.03
444	Craig Worthington	.10	.08	.04
445	Fernando Valenzuela	.09	.07	.04
446	*Joey Belle*(FC)	1.50	1.25	.60
447	*Ed Whited*(FC)	.15	.11	.06
448	Dave Smith	.09	.07	.04
449	Dave Clark	.07	.05	.03
450	Juan Agosto	.06	.05	.02
451	Dave Valle	.06	.05	.02
452	Kent Hrbek	.15	.11	.06
453	Von Hayes	.10	.08	.04
454	Gary Gaetti	.15	.11	.06
455	Greg Briley	.20	.15	.08
456	Glenn Braggs	.08	.06	.03
457	Kirt Manwaring	.10	.08	.04
458	Mel Hall	.07	.05	.03
459	Brook Jacoby	.08	.06	.03
460	Pat Sheridan	.06	.05	.02
461	Rob Murphy	.06	.05	.02
462	Jimmy Key	.10	.08	.04
463	Nick Esasky	.10	.08	.04
464	Rob Ducey	.09	.07	.04
465	Carlos Quintana	.09	.07	.04
466	*Larry Walker*(FC)	.40	.30	.15
467	Todd Worrell	.10	.08	.04
468	Kevin Gross	.09	.07	.04
469	Terry Pendleton	.09	.07	.04
470	Dave Martinez	.07	.05	.02
471	Gene Larkin	.06	.05	.02
472	Len Dykstra	.09	.07	.04
473	Barry Lyons	.06	.05	.02
474	Terry Mulholland(FC)	.10	.08	.04
475	*Chip Hale*(FC)	.15	.11	.06
476	Jesse Barfield	.08	.06	.03
477	Dan Plesac	.09	.07	.04
478a	Scott Garrelts (Photo actually Bill Bathe)	3.00	2.25	1.25
478b	Scott Garrelts (Correct photo)	.10	.08	.04
479	Dave Righetti	.10	.08	.04
480	Gus Polidor(FC)	.06	.05	.02
481	Mookie Wilson	.09	.07	.04
482	Luis Rivera	.06	.05	.02
483	Mike Flanagan	.07	.05	.03
484	Dennis "Oil Can" Boyd	.07	.05	.03

		MT	NR MT	EX
485	John Cerutti	.07	.05	.03
486	John Costello	.07	.05	.03
487	Pascual Perez	.07	.05	.03
488	Tommy Herr	.09	.07	.04
489	Tom Foley	.06	.05	.02
490	Curt Ford	.06	.05	.02
491	Steve Lake	.06	.05	.02
492	Tim Teufel	.06	.05	.02
493	Randy Bush	.06	.05	.02
494	Mike Jackson	.06	.05	.02
495	Steve Jeltz	.06	.05	.02
496	Paul Gibson	.08	.06	.03
497	Steve Balboni	.06	.05	.02
498	Bud Black	.06	.05	.02
499	Dale Sveum	.06	.05	.02
500	Checklist 401-500	.06	.05	.02
501	Timmy Jones	.06	.05	.02
502	Mark Portugal	.06	.05	.02
503	Ivan Calderon	.07	.05	.03
504	Rick Rhoden	.06	.05	.02
505	Willie McGee	.09	.07	.04
506	Kirk McCaskill	.08	.06	.03
507	Dave LaPoint	.07	.05	.03
508	Jay Howell	.10	.08	.04
509	Johnny Ray	.08	.06	.03
510	Dave Anderson	.06	.05	.02
511	Chuck Crim	.06	.05	.02
512	Joe Hesketh	.06	.05	.02
513	Dennis Eckersley	.10	.08	.04
514	Greg Brock	.08	.06	.03
515	Tim Burke	.08	.06	.03
516	Frank Tanana	.07	.05	.03
517	Jay Bell	.07	.05	.03
518	Guillermo Hernandez	.07	.05	.03
519	Randy Kramer(FC)	.08	.06	.03
520	Charles Hudson	.06	.05	.02
521	Jim Corsi(FC)	.08	.06	.03
522	Steve Rosenberg	.08	.06	.03
523	Cris Carpenter	.10	.08	.04
524	*Matt Winters*(FC)	.12	.09	.05
525	Melido Perez	.08	.06	.03
526	Chris Gwynn	.08	.06	.03
527	Bert Blyleven	.09	.07	.04
528	Chuck Cary	.07	.05	.03
529	Daryl Boston	.06	.05	.02
530	Dale Mohorcic	.06	.05	.02
531	Geronimo Berroa(FC)	.09	.07	.04
532	Edgar Martinez	.09	.07	.04
533	Dale Murphy	.15	.11	.06
534	Jay Buhner	.09	.07	.04
535	John Smoltz	.15	.11	.06
536	Andy Van Slyke	.15	.11	.06
537	Mike Henneman	.09	.07	.04
538	Miguel Garcia(FC)	.07	.05	.03
539	Frank Williams	.06	.05	.02
540	R.J. Reynolds	.06	.05	.02
541	Shawn Hillegas	.06	.05	.02
542	Walt Weiss	.10	.08	.04
543	*Greg Hibbard*(FC)	.15	.11	.06
544	Nolan Ryan	1.00	.70	.40
545	*Todd Zeile*	.80	.60	.30
546	Hensley Meulens	.20	.15	.08
547	Tim Belcher	.10	.08	.04
548	Mike Witt	.08	.06	.03
549	Greg Cadaret	.06	.05	.02
550	Franklin Stubbs	.06	.05	.02
551	*Tony Castillo*(FC)	.12	.09	.05
552	Jeff Robinson	.08	.06	.03
553	*Steve Olin*(FC)	.12	.09	.05
554	Alan Trammell	.10	.08	.04
555	Wade Boggs	.50	.40	.20
556	Will Clark	.60	.45	.25
557	Jeff King(FC)	.10	.08	.04
558	Mike Fitzgerald	.06	.05	.02
559	Ken Howell	.06	.05	.02
560	Bob Kipper	.06	.05	.02
561	Scott Bankhead	.09	.07	.04
562a	*Jeff Innis* (Photo actually David West)(FC)	3.00	2.25	1.25
562b	*Jeff Innis* (Corrected)(FC)	.20	.15	.08
563	Randy Johnson	.10	.08	.04
564	*Wally Whithurst*	.10	.08	.04
565	*Gene Harris*(FC)	.10	.08	.04
566	Norm Charlton	.09	.07	.04
567	Robin Yount	.40	.30	.15
568	*Joe Oliver*(FC)	.35	.25	.14
569	Mark Parent	.07	.05	.03
570	John Farrell	.07	.05	.03
571	Tom Glavine	.10	.08	.04
572	Rod Nichols(FC)	.06	.05	.02
573	Jack Morris	.09	.07	.04

		MT	NR MT	EX
574	Greg Swindell	.12	.09	.05
575	Steve Searcy(FC)	.09	.07	.04
576	Ricky Jordan	.20	.15	.08
577	Matt Williams	.35	.25	.14
578	Mike LaValliere	.07	.05	.03
579	Bryn Smith	.08	.06	.03
580	Bruce Ruffin	.06	.05	.02
581	Randy Myers	.08	.06	.03
582	*Rick Wrona*(FC)	.15	.11	.06
583	Juan Samuel	.09	.07	.04
584	Les Lancaster	.07	.05	.03
585	Jeff Musselman	.07	.05	.03
586	Rob Dibble	.09	.07	.04
587	Eric Show	.07	.05	.03
588	Jesse Orosco	.06	.05	.02
589	Herm Winningham	.06	.05	.02
590	Andy Allanson	.06	.05	.02
591	Dion James	.06	.05	.02
592	Carmelo Martinez	.08	.06	.03
593	Luis Quinones(FC)	.08	.06	.03
594	Dennis Rasmussen	.08	.06	.03
595	Rich Yett	.06	.05	.02
596	Bob Walk	.08	.06	.03
597	Andy McGaffigan	.07	.05	.03
598	Billy Hatcher	.07	.05	.03
599	Bob Knepper	.06	.05	.02
600	Checklist 501-600	.06	.05	.02
601	Joey Cora(FC)	.10	.08	.04
602	*Steve Finley*	.20	.15	.08
603	Kal Daniels	.10	.08	.04
604	Gregg Olson	.30	.25	.12
605	Dave Steib	.09	.07	.04
606	*Kenny Rogers*(FC)	.15	.11	.06
607	Zane Smith	.06	.05	.02
608	*Bob Geren*(FC)	.15	.11	.06
609	Chad Kreuter	.10	.08	.04
610	Mike Smithson	.06	.05	.02
611	*Jeff Wetherby*(FC)	.15	.11	.06
612	*Gary Mielke*(FC)	.15	.11	.06
613	Pete Smith	.08	.06	.03
614	*Jack Daugherty*(FC)	.15	.11	.06
615	Lance McCullers	.08	.06	.03
616	Don Robinson	.06	.05	.02
617	Jose Guzman	.06	.05	.02
618	Steve Bedrosian	.08	.06	.03
619	Jamie Moyer	.06	.05	.02
620	Atlee Hammaker	.06	.05	.02
621	*Rick Luecken*(FC)	.15	.11	.06
622	Greg W. Harris	.09	.07	.04
623	Pete Harnisch	.10	.08	.04
624	Jerald Clark	.10	.08	.04
625	Jack McDowell	.07	.05	.03
626	Frank Viola	.12	.09	.05
627	Ted Higuera	.09	.07	.04
628	*Marty Pevey*(FC)	.15	.11	.06
629	Bill Wegman	.06	.05	.02
630	Eric Plunk	.06	.05	.02
631	Drew Hall	.06	.05	.02
632	Doug Jones	.08	.06	.03
633	Geno Petralli	.06	.05	.02
634	Jose Alvarez	.06	.05	.02
635	Bob Milacki(FC)	.10	.08	.04
636	Bobby Witt	.07	.05	.03
637	Trevor Wilson	.08	.06	.03
638	Jeff Russell	.08	.06	.03
639	Mike Krukow	.07	.05	.03
640	Rick Leach	.06	.05	.02
641	Dave Schmidt	.06	.05	.02
642	Terry Leach	.06	.05	.02
643	Calvin Schiraldi	.06	.05	.02
644	Bob Melvin	.06	.05	.02
645	Jim Abbott	.40	.30	.15
646	*Jaime Navarro*(FC)	.30	.25	.12
647	Mark Langston	.10	.08	.04
648	Juan Nieves	.08	.06	.03
649	Damaso Garcia	.06	.05	.02
650	Charlie O'Brien	.06	.05	.02
651	Eric King	.06	.05	.02
652	Mike Boddicker	.08	.06	.03
653	Duan Ward	.07	.05	.03
654	Bob Stanley	.06	.05	.02
655	Sandy Alomar, Jr.	.30	.25	.12
656	Danny Tartabull	.10	.08	.04
657	Randy McCament	.15	.11	.06
658	Charlie Leibrandt	.07	.05	.03
659	Dan Quisenberry	.07	.05	.03
660	Paul Assenmacher	.06	.05	.02
661	Walt Terrell	.07	.05	.03
662	Tim Leary	.07	.05	.03
663	Randy Milligan	.08	.06	.03
664	Bo Diaz	.06	.05	.02

		MT	NR MT	EX
665	Mark Lemke	.07	.05	.03
666	Jose Gonzalez	.08	.06	.03
667	Chuck Finley	.07	.05	.03
668	John Kruk	.08	.06	.03
669	Dick Schofield	.07	.05	.03
670	Tim Crews	.06	.05	.02
671	John Dopson	.09	.07	.04
672	*John Orton*(FC)	.15	.11	.06
673	Eric Hetzel(FC)	.10	.08	.04
674	Lance Parrish	.08	.06	.03
675	Ramon Martinez	.50	.40	.20
676	Mark Gubicza	.10	.08	.04
677	Greg Litton	.20	.15	.08
678	Greg Mathews	.07	.05	.03
679	Dave Dravecky	.07	.05	.03
680	Steve Farr	.07	.05	.03
681	Mike Devereaux	.09	.07	.04
682	Ken Griffey, Sr.	.08	.06	.03
683a	*Mickey Weston* (Jamie)(FC)	4.00	3.00	1.50
683b	*Mickey Weston* (corrected)(FC)	.30	.25	.12
684	Jack Armstrong	.07	.05	.03
685	Steve Buechele	.07	.05	.03
686	Bryan Harvey	.07	.05	.03
687	Lance Blankenship	.09	.07	.04
688	Dante Bichette	.09	.07	.04
689	Todd Burns	.09	.07	.04
690	Dan Petry	.06	.05	.02
691	*Kent Anderson*(FC)	.15	.11	.06
692	Todd Stottlemyre	.08	.06	.03
693	Wally Joyner	.15	.11	.06
694	Mike Rochford(FC)	.10	.08	.04
695	Floyd Bannister	.07	.05	.03
696	Rick Reuschel	.09	.07	.04
697	Jose DeLeon	.09	.07	.04
698	Jeff Montgomery	.08	.06	.03
699	Jeff Montgomery	.08	.06	.03
700a	Checklist 601-700 (Jamie Weston)	4.00	3.00	1.50
700b	Checklist 601-700 (Mickey Weston)	.10	.08	.04
701	Jim Gott	.10	.08	.04
702	"Rookie Threats" (Delino DeShields, Larry Walker, Marquis Grissom)	.60	.45	.25
703	Alejandro Pena	.10	.08	.04
704	Willie Randolph	.12	.09	.05
705	Tim Leary	.10	.08	.04
706	Chuck McElroy(FC)	.20	.15	.08
707	Gerald Perry	.10	.08	.04
708	Tom Brunansky	.12	.09	.05
709	John Franco	.15	.11	.06
710	Mark Davis	.10	.08	.04
711	Dave Justice(FC)	7.00	5.25	2.75
712	Storm Davis	.10	.08	.04
713	Scott Ruskin(FC)	.20	.15	.08
714	Glenn Braggs	.10	.08	.04
715	Kevin Bearse(FC)	.20	.15	.08
716	Jose Nunez(FC)	.15	.11	.06
717	Tim Layana(FC)	.20	.15	.08
718	Greg Myers(FC)	.12	.09	.05
719	Pete O'Brien	.10	.08	.04
720	John Candelaria	.10	.08	.04
721	Craig Grebeck(FC)	.25	.20	.10
722	Shawn Boskie(FC)	.30	.25	.12
723	Jim Leyritz(FC)	.20	.15	.08
724	Bill Sampen(FC)	.30	.25	.12
725	Scott Radinsky(FC)	.35	.25	.14
726	Todd Hundley(FC)	.30	.25	.12
727	Scott Hemond(FC)	.20	.15	.08
728	Lenny Webster(FC)	.25	.20	.10
729	Jeff Reardon	.12	.09	.05
730	Mitch Webster	.10	.08	.04
731	Brian Bohanon(FC)	.25	.20	.10
732	Rick Parker(FC)	.20	.15	.08
733	Terry Shumpert(FC)	.25	.20	.10
734a	6th No-Hitter (Nolan Ryan) (with 300 win stripe)	2.00	1.50	.80
734b	6th No-Hitter (Nolan Ryan) (without stripe)	13.00	9.75	5.25
735	John Burkett(FC)	.40	.30	.15
736	Derrick May(FC)	.80	.60	.30
737	Carlos Baerga(FC)	.80	.60	.30
738	Greg Smith(FC)	.15	.11	.06
739	Joe Kraemer(FC)	.15	.11	.06
740	Scott Sanderson	.10	.08	.04
741	Hector Villanueva(FC)	.30	.25	.12
742	Mike Fetters(FC)	.25	.20	.10
743	Mark Gardner(FC)	.30	.25	.12
744	Matt Nokes	.10	.08	.04
745	Dave Winfield	.20	.15	.08
746	Delino DeShields(FC)	1.00	.70	.40
747	Dann Howitt(FC)	.20	.15	.08

		MT	NR MT	EX
748	Tony Pena	.12	.09	.05
749	Oil Can Boyd	.12	.09	.05
750	Mike Benjamin(FC)	.25	.20	.10
751	Alex Cole(FC)	.80	.60	.30
752	Eric Gunderson(FC)	.30	.25	.12
753	Howard Farmer(FC)	.25	.20	.10
754	Joe Carter	.15	.11	.06
755	Ray Lankford(FC)	2.00	1.50	.80
756	Sandy Alomar,Jr.	.40	.30	.15
757	Alex Sanchez(FC)	.15	.11	.06
758	Nick Esasky	.10	.08	.04
759	Stan Belinda(FC)	.20	.15	.08
760	Jim Presley	.10	.08	.04
761	Gary DiSarcina(FC)	.20	.15	.08
762	Wayne Edwards(FC)	.20	.15	.08
763	Pat Combs(FC)	.20	.15	.08
764	Mickey Pina(FC)	.20	.15	.08
765	Wilson Alvarez(FC)	.50	.40	.20
766	Dave Parker	.15	.11	.06
767	Mike Blowers(FC)	.20	.15	.08
768	Tony Phillips	.10	.08	.04
769	Pascual Perez	.10	.08	.04
770	Gary Pettis	.10	.08	.04
771	Fred Lynn	.10	.08	.04
772	Mel Rojas(FC)	.20	.15	.08
773	David Segui(FC)	.30	.25	.12
774	Gary Carter	.15	.11	.06
775	Rafael Valdez(FC)	.15	.11	.06
776	Glenallen Hill(FC)	.15	.11	.06
777	Keith Hernandez	.12	.09	.05
778	Billy Hatcher	.12	.09	.05
779	Marty Clary(FC)	.10	.08	.04
780	Candy Maldonado	.12	.09	.05
781	Mike Marshall	.10	.08	.04
782	Billy Jo Robidoux(FC)	.10	.08	.04
783	Mark Langston	.12	.09	.05
784	Paul Sorrento(FC)	.25	.20	.10
785	Dave Hollins(FC)	.40	.30	.15
786	Cecil Fielder	1.00	.70	.40
787	Matt Young	.10	.08	.04
788	Jeff Huson	.15	.11	.06
789	Lloyd Moseby	.12	.09	.05
790	Ron Kittle	.12	.09	.05
791	Hubie Brooks	.12	.09	.05
792	Craig Lefferts	.10	.08	.04
793	Kevin Bass	.10	.08	.04
794	Bryn Smith	.10	.08	.04
795	Juan Samuel	.12	.09	.05
796	Sam Horn(FC)	.15	.11	.06
797	Randy Myers	.12	.09	.05
798	Chris James	.10	.08	.04
799	Bill Gullickson	.10	.08	.04
800	Checklist 701-800	.10	.08	.04

A player's name in *italic* indicates a rookie card. An (FC) indicates a player's first card for that particular card company.

1991 Upper Deck

115 rookies are included among the first 700 cards in the 1991 Upper Deck set. A 100-card high # series was once again planned for release in July or August. The 1991 Upper Deck cards feature high quality white stock and color photos on both the front and backs of the cards. A nine-card "Baseball Heroes" bonus set honoring Nolan Ryan, is among the many insert specials in the 1991 Upper Deck set. Others include a card of Chicago Bulls superstar Michael Jordan. Along with the Ryan bonus cards, 2,500 limited-edition cards personally autographed and numbered by Ryan will be randomly inserted. Upper Deck cards are packaged in tamper-proof foil packs. Each pack contains 15 cards and a 3-D team logo hologram sticker. The 1991 hologram stickers are full size.

NOTE: A card number in parentheses ( ) indicates the set is unnumbered.

	MT	NR MT	EX
Complete Set: 1-700	40.00	30.00	15.00
Common Player: 1-700	.05	.04	.02
Complete Set: 1-800	50.00	37.00	20.00
Common Player: 701-800	.10	.08	.04

		MT	NR MT	EX
1	Star Rookie Checklist	.05	.04	.02
2	Star Rookie (*Phil Plantier*)(FC)	2.00	1.50	.80
3	Star Rookie (*D.J. Dozier*)(FC)	.40	.30	.15
4	Star Rookie (Dave Hansen)(FC)	.25	.20	.10
5	Star Rookie (Maurice Vaughn)(FC)	1.50	1.25	.60
6	Star Rookie (*Leo Gomez*)(FC)	.60	.45	.25
7	Star Rookie (*Scott Aldred*)(FC)	.25	.20	.10
8	Star Rookie (*Scott Chiamparino*)(FC)	.30	.25	.12
9	Star Rookie (*Lance Dickson*)(FC)	.30	.25	.12
10	Star Rookie (*Sean Berry*)(FC)	.20	.15	.08
11	Star Rookie (Bernie Williams)(FC)	.70	.50	.30
12	Star Rookie (*Brian Barnes*)(FC)	.30	.25	.12
13	Star Rookie (*Narciso Elvira*)(FC)	.20	.15	.08
14	Star Rookie (*Mike Gardiner*)(FC)	.30	.25	.12
15	Star Rookie (*Greg Colbrunn*)(FC)	.20	.15	.08
16	Star Rookie (*Bernard Gilkey*)(FC)	.50	.40	.20
17	Star Rookie (Mark Lewis)(FC)	1.25	.90	.50
18	Star Rookie (*Mickey Morandini*)(FC)	.15	.11	.06
19	Star Rookie (Charles Nagy)(FC)	.30	.25	.12
20	Star Rookie (*Geronimo Pena*)(FC)	.25	.20	.10
21	Star Rookie (*Henry Rodriguez*)(FC)	.50	.40	.20
22	Star Rookie (Scott Cooper)(FC)	.20	.15	.08
23	Star Rookie (*Andujar Cedeno*)(FC)	1.00	.70	.40
24	Star Rookie (*Eric Karros*)(FC)	.60	.45	.25
25	Star Rookie (*Steve Decker*)(FC)	1.00	.70	.40
26	Star Rookie (*Kevin Belcher*)(FC)	.20	.15	.08
27	Star Rookie (*Jeff Conine*)(FC)	.40	.30	.15
28	Oakland Athletics Checklist	.10	.08	.04
29	Chicago White Sox Checklist	.08	.06	.03
30	Texas Rangers Checklist	.08	.06	.03
31	California Angels Checklist	.08	.06	.03
32	Seattle Mariners Checklist	.10	.08	.04
33	Kansas City Royals Checklist	.10	.08	.04
34	Minnesota Twins Checklist	.08	.06	.03
35	Scott Leius(FC)	.10	.08	.04
36	Neal Heaton	.06	.05	.02
37	*Terry Lee*(FC)	.20	.15	.08
38	Gary Redus	.05	.04	.02
39	Barry Jones	.06	.05	.02
40	Chuck Knoblauch(FC)	.80	.60	.30
41	Larry Andersen	.05	.04	.02
43	Darryl Hamilton	.06	.05	.02
44	Toronto Blue Jays Checklist	.08	.06	.03
45	Detroit Tigers Checklist	.10	.08	.04
46	Cleveland Indians Checklist	.08	.06	.03
47	Baltimore Orioles Checklist	.08	.06	.03
48	Milwaukee Brewers Checklist	.08	.06	.03
49	New York Yankees Checklist	.08	.06	.03
50	Top Prospect Checklist	.05	.04	.02
51	Top Prospect (Kyle Abbott)(FC)	.25	.20	.10
52	Top Prospect (Jeff Juden)(FC)	.25	.20	.10
53	Top Prospect (*Todd Van Poppel*)(FC)	3.00	2.25	1.25
54	Top Prospect (*Steve Karsay*)(FC)	.40	.30	.15

		MT	NR MT	EX
55	Top Prospect *(Chipper Jones)*(FC)	.50	.40	.20
56	Top Prospect *(Chris Johnson)*(FC)	.25	.20	.10
57	Top Prospect *(John Ericks)*(FC)	.25	.20	.10
58	Top Prospect *(Gary Scott)*(FC)	.50	.40	.20
59	Top Prospect (Kiki Jones)(FC)	.50	.40	.20
60	Top Prospect *(Wilfredo Cordero)*(FC)	.40	.30	.15
61	Top Prospect *(Royce Clayton)*(FC)	1.00	.70	.40
62	Top Prospect *(Tim Costo)*(FC)	.70	.50	.30
63	Top Prospect (Roger Salkeld)(FC)	.35	.25	.14
64	Top Prospect *(Brook Fordyce)*(FC)	.25	.20	.10
65	Top Prospect *(Mike Mussina)*(FC)	.60	.45	.25
66	Top Prospect *(Dave Staton)*(FC)	.40	.30	.15
67	Top Prospect *(Mike Lieberthal)*(FC)	.30	.25	.12
68	Top Prospect *(Kurt Miller)*(FC)	.30	.25	.12
69	Top Prospect *(Dan Peltier)*(FC)	.25	.20	.10
70	Top Prospect (Greg Blosser)(FC)	.40	.30	.15
71	Top Prospect *(Reggie Sanders)*(FC)	.70	.50	.30
72	Top Prospect (Brent Mayne)(FC)	.15	.11	.06
73	Top Prospect *(Rico Brogna)*(FC)	.35	.25	.14
74	Top Prospect *(Willie Banks)*(FC)	.40	.30	.15
75	Top Prospect *(Len Brutcher)*(FC)	.25	.20	.10
76	Top Prospect *(Pat Kelly)*(FC)	1.25	.90	.50
77	Cincinnati Reds Checklist	.08	.06	.03
78	Los Angeles Dodgers Checklist	.08	.06	.03
79	San Francisco Giants Checklist	.08	.06	.03
80	San Diego Padres Checklist	.08	.06	.03
81	Houston Astros Checklist	.08	.06	.03
82	Atlanta Braves Checklist	.10	.08	.04
83	"Fielder's Feat"	.20	.15	.08
84	*Orlando Merced*(FC)	1.00	.70	.40
85	Domingo Ramos	.05	.04	.02
86	Tom Bolton	.05	.04	.02
87	*Andres Santana*(FC)	.20	.15	.08
88	John Dopson	.05	.04	.02
89	Kenny Williams	.05	.04	.02
90	Marty Barrett	.06	.05	.02
91	Tom Pagnozzi	.06	.05	.02
92	Carmelo Martinez	.06	.05	.02
93	"Save Master"	.10	.08	.04
94	Pittsburgh Pirates Checklist	.10	.08	.04
95	New York Mets Checklist	.10	.08	.04
96	Montreal Expos Checklist	.08	.06	.03
97	Philadelphia Phillies Checklist	.08	.06	.03
98	St. Louis Cardinals Checklist	.08	.06	.03
99	Chicago Cubs Checklist	.10	.08	.04
100	Checklist 1-100	.05	.04	.02
101	Kevin Elster	.06	.05	.02
102	Tom Brookens	.05	.04	.02
103	Mackey Sasser	.08	.06	.03
104	Felix Fermin	.05	.04	.02
105	Kevin McReynolds	.12	.09	.05
106	Dave Steib	.12	.09	.05
107	Jeffrey Leonard	.06	.05	.02
108	Dave Henderson	.08	.06	.03
109	Sid Bream	.06	.05	.02
110	Henry Cotto	.05	.04	.02
111	Shawon Dunston	.12	.09	.05
112	Mariano Duncan	.08	.06	.03
113	Joe Girardi	.08	.06	.03
114	Billy Hatcher	.08	.06	.03
115	Greg Maddux	.12	.09	.05
116	Jerry Browne	.08	.06	.03
117	Juan Samuel	.08	.06	.03
118	Steve Olin	.06	.05	.02
119	Alfredo Griffin	.06	.05	.02
120	Mitch Webster	.06	.05	.02
121	Joel Skinner	.05	.04	.02
122	Frank Viola	.15	.11	.06
123	Cory Snyder	.10	.08	.04
124	Howard Johnson	.12	.09	.05
125	*Carlos Baerga*	.30	.25	.12
126	Tony Fernandez	.12	.09	.05
127	Dave Stewart	.15	.11	.06
128	Jay Buhner	.08	.06	.03
129	Mike LaValliere	.06	.05	.02
130	Scott Bradley	.05	.04	.02
131	Tony Phillips	.06	.05	.02
132	Ryne Sandberg	.20	.15	.08
133	Paul O'Neill	.08	.06	.03
134	Mark Grace	.15	.11	.06
135	Chris Sabo	.12	.09	.05
136	Ramon Martinez	.20	.15	.08
137	Brook Jacoby	.08	.06	.03
138	Candy Maldonado	.08	.06	.03
139	Mike Scioscia	.08	.06	.03
140	Chris James	.08	.06	.03
141	Craig Worthington	.08	.06	.03
142	Manny Lee	.06	.05	.02
143	Tim Raines	.15	.11	.06
144	Sandy Alomar,Jr.	.15	.11	.06
145	John Olerud	.40	.30	.15
146	*Ozzie Canseco*	.15	.11	.06
147	Pat Borders	.06	.05	.02
148	Harold Reynolds	.10	.08	.04
149	Tom Henke	.08	.06	.03
150	R.J. Reynolds	.05	.04	.02
151	Mike Gallego	.05	.04	.02
152	Bobby Bonilla	.20	.15	.08
153	Terry Steinbach	.06	.05	.02
154	Barry Bonds	.20	.15	.08
155	Jose Canseco	.50	.40	.20
156	Gregg Jefferies	.15	.11	.06
157	Matt Williams	.20	.15	.08
158	Craig Biggio	.08	.06	.03
159	Daryl Boston	.05	.04	.02
160	Ricky Jordan	.08	.06	.03
161	Stan Belinda	.20	.15	.08
162	Ozzie Smith	.10	.08	.04
163	Tom Brunansky	.08	.06	.03
164	Todd Zeile	.30	.25	.12
165	Mike Greenwell	.15	.11	.06
166	Kal Daniels	.10	.08	.04
167	Kent Hrbek	.12	.09	.05
168	Franklin Stubbs	.06	.05	.02
169	Dick Schofield	.05	.04	.02
170	Junior Ortiz	.05	.04	.02
171	*Hector Villanueva*	.20	.15	.08
172	Dennis Eckersley	.15	.11	.06
173	Mitch Williams	.08	.06	.03
174	Mark McGwire	.35	.25	.14
175	Fernando Valenzuela	.10	.08	.04
176	Gary Carter	.10	.08	.04
177	Dave Magadan	.10	.08	.04
178	Robby Thompson	.08	.06	.03
179	Bob Ojeda	.05	.04	.02
180	Ken Caminiti	.06	.05	.02
181	Don Slaught	.05	.04	.02
182	Luis Rivera	.05	.04	.02
183	Jay Bell	.06	.05	.02
184	Jody Reed	.08	.06	.03
185	Wally Backman	.06	.05	.02
186	Dave Martinez	.06	.05	.02
187	Luis Polonia	.05	.04	.02
188	Shane Mack	.06	.05	.02
189	Spike Owen	.06	.05	.02
190	Scott Bailes	.05	.04	.02
191	John Russell	.05	.04	.02
192	Walt Weiss	.08	.06	.03
193	Jose Oquendo	.06	.05	.02
194	Carney Lansford	.08	.06	.03
195	Jeff Huson	.08	.06	.03
196	Keith Miller	.06	.05	.02
197	Eric Yelding	.10	.08	.04
198	Ron Darling	.06	.05	.02
199	John Kruk	.06	.05	.02
200	Checklist 101-200	.05	.04	.02
201	John Shelby	.05	.04	.02
202	Bob Geren	.06	.05	.02
203	Lance McCullers	.05	.04	.02
204	Alvaro Espinoza	.06	.05	.02
205	Mark Salas	.05	.04	.02
206	Mike Pagliarulo	.06	.05	.02
207	Jose Uribe	.06	.05	.02
208	Jim Deshaies	.06	.05	.02
209	Ron Karkovice	.05	.04	.02
210	Rafael Ramirez	.06	.05	.02
211	Donnie Hill	.05	.04	.02
212	Brian Harper	.08	.06	.03
213	Jack Howell	.05	.04	.02
214	Wes Gardner	.05	.04	.02
215	Tim Burke	.08	.06	.03
216	Doug Jones	.08	.06	.03
217	Hubie Brooks	.10	.08	.04
218	Tom Candiotti	.06	.05	.02
219	Gerald Perry	.06	.05	.02
220	Jose DeLeon	.06	.05	.02
221	Wally Whitehurst	.08	.06	.03
222	*Alan Mills*(FC)	.15	.11	.06
223	Alan Trammell	.12	.09	.05
224	Dwight Gooden	.25	.20	.10
225	*Travis Fryman*(FC)	1.25	.90	.50
226	Joe Carter	.10	.08	.04
227	Julio Franco	.10	.08	.04
228	Craig Lefferts	.06	.05	.02
229	Gary Pettis	.06	.05	.02
230	Dennis Rasmussen	.06	.05	.02
231	Brian Downing	.06	.05	.02
232	Carlos Quintana	.10	.08	.04

		MT	NR MT	EX
233	Gary Gaetti	.12	.09	.05
234	Mark Langston	.15	.11	.06
235	Tim Wallach	.10	.08	.04
236	Greg Swindell	.10	.08	.04
237	Eddie Murray	.15	.11	.06
238	Jeff Manto(FC)	.20	.15	.08
239	Lenny Harris	.08	.06	.03
240	Jesse Orosco	.05	.04	.02
241	Scott Lusader	.05	.04	.02
242	Sid Fernandez	.08	.06	.03
243	*Jim Leyritz*	.25	.20	.10
244	Cecil Fielder	.20	.15	.08
245	Darryl Strawberry	.25	.20	.10
246	Frank Thomas(FC)	3.00	2.25	1.25
247	Kevin Mitchell	.20	.15	.08
248	Lance Johnson	.06	.05	.02
249	Rick Rueschel	.08	.06	.03
250	Mark Portugal	.05	.04	.02
251	Derek Lilliquist	.06	.05	.02
252	Brian Holman	.08	.06	.03
253	Rafael Valdez	.08	.06	.03
254	B.J. Surhoff	.06	.05	.02
255	Tony Gwynn	.15	.11	.06
256	Andy Van Slyke	.12	.09	.05
257	Todd Stottlemyre	.08	.06	.03
258	Jose Lind	.06	.05	.02
259	Greg Myers	.06	.05	.02
260	Jeff Ballard	.06	.05	.02
261	Bobby Thigpen	.10	.08	.04
262	*Jimmy Kremers*(FC)	.15	.11	.06
263	Robin Ventura	.30	.25	.12
264	John Smoltz	.10	.08	.04
265	Sammy Sosa	.20	.15	.08
266	Gary Sheffield	.15	.11	.06
267	Lenny Dykstra	.10	.08	.04
268	Bill Spiers	.06	.05	.02
269	Charlie Hayes	.08	.06	.03
270	Brett Butler	.08	.06	.03
271	Bip Roberts	.08	.06	.03
272	Rob Deer	.06	.05	.02
273	Fred Lynn	.08	.06	.03
274	Dave Parker	.15	.11	.06
275	Andy Benes	.10	.08	.04
276	Glenallen Hill	.08	.06	.03
277	*Steve Howard*(FC)	.12	.09	.05
278	Doug Drabek	.10	.08	.04
279	Joe Oliver	.08	.06	.03
280	Todd Benzinger	.06	.05	.02
281	Eric King	.06	.05	.02
282	Jim Presley	.06	.05	.02
283	Ken Patterson(FC)	.06	.05	.02
284	Jack Daugherty	.08	.06	.03
285	Ivan Calderon	.10	.08	.04
286	*Edgar Diaz*(FC)	.10	.08	.04
287	Kevin Bass	.08	.06	.03
288	Don Carman	.06	.05	.02
289	Greg Brock	.06	.05	.02
290	John Franco	.10	.08	.04
291	Joey Cora	.06	.05	.02
292	Bill Wegman	.06	.05	.02
293	Eric Show	.06	.05	.02
294	Scott Bankhead	.08	.06	.03
295	Garry Templeton	.06	.05	.02
296	Mickey Tettleton	.06	.05	.02
297	Luis Sojo(FC)	.15	.11	.06
298	Jose Rijo	.08	.06	.03
299	Dave Johnson	.06	.05	.02
300	Checklist 201-300	.05	.04	.02
301	Mark Grant	.05	.04	.02
302	Pete Harnisch	.08	.06	.03
303	Greg Olson(FC)	.10	.08	.04
304	*Anthony Telford*(FC)	.15	.11	.06
305	Lonnie Smith	.06	.05	.02
306	*Chris Hoiles*(FC)	.25	.20	.10
307	Bryn Smith	.06	.05	.02
308	Mike Devereaux	.06	.05	.02
309	Milt Thompson	.06	.05	.02
310	Bob Melvin	.05	.04	.02
311	Luis Salazar	.05	.04	.02
312	Ed Whitson	.06	.05	.02
313	Charlie Hough	.06	.05	.02
314	Dave Clark	.05	.04	.02
315	*Eric Gunderson*	.15	.11	.06
316	Dan Petry	.05	.04	.02
317	Dante Bichette	.08	.06	.03
318	Mike Heath	.05	.04	.02
319	Damon Berryhill	.06	.05	.02
320	Walt Terrell	.05	.04	.02
321	Scott Fletcher	.05	.04	.02
322	Dan Plesac	.08	.06	.03
323	Jack McDowell	.08	.06	.03

		MT	NR MT	EX
324	Paul Molitor	.12	.09	.05
325	Ozzie Guillen	.10	.08	.04
326	Gregg Olson	.10	.08	.04
327	Pedro Guererro	.10	.08	.04
328	Bob Milacki	.06	.05	.02
329	John Tudor	.08	.06	.03
330	Steve Finley	.08	.06	.03
331	Jack Clark	.10	.08	.04
332	Jerome Walton	.15	.11	.06
333	Andy Hawkins	.06	.05	.02
334	Derrick May	.20	.15	.08
335	Roberto Alomar	.10	.08	.04
336	Jack Morris	.08	.06	.03
337	Dave Winfield	.15	.11	.06
338	Steve Searcy	.08	.06	.03
339	Chili Davis	.08	.06	.03
340	Larry Sheets	.06	.05	.02
341	Ted Higuera	.08	.06	.03
342	*David Segui*	.30	.25	.12
343	Greg Cadaret	.05	.04	.02
344	Robin Yount	.15	.11	.06
345	Nolan Ryan	.30	.25	.12
346	*Ray Lankford*	.60	.45	.25
347	Cal Ripken, Jr.	.15	.11	.06
348	Lee Smith	.08	.06	.03
349	Brady Anderson	.05	.04	.02
350	Frank DiPino	.05	.04	.02
351	Hal Morris	.30	.25	.12
352	Deion Sanders	.10	.08	.04
353	Barry Larkin	.10	.08	.04
354	Don Mattingly	.35	.25	.14
355	Eric Davis	.20	.15	.08
356	Jose Offerman	.30	.25	.12
357	*Mel Rojas*	.12	.09	.05
358	Rudy Seanez(FC)	.10	.08	.04
359	Oil Can Boyd	.06	.05	.02
360	Nelson Liriano	.05	.04	.02
361	Ron Gant	.15	.11	.06
362	*Howard Farmer*	.15	.11	.06
363	David Justice	1.00	.70	.40
364	Delino DeShields	.30	.25	.12
365	Steve Avery	.25	.20	.10
366	David Cone	.12	.09	.05
367	lou Whitaker	.10	.08	.04
368	Von Hayes	.10	.08	.04
369	Frank Tanana	.06	.05	.02
370	Tim Teufel	.05	.04	.02
371	Randy Myers	.10	.08	.04
372	Roberto Kelly	.10	.08	.04
373	Jack Armstrong	.08	.06	.03
374	Kelly Gruber	.10	.08	.04
375	Kevin Maas	.50	.40	.20
376	Randy Johnson	.10	.08	.04
377	David West	.06	.05	.02
378	*Brent Knackert*(FC)	.12	.09	.05
379	Rick Honeycutt	.05	.04	.02
380	Kevin Gross	.08	.06	.03
381	Tom Foley	.05	.04	.02
382	Jeff Blauser	.06	.05	.02
383	*Scott Ruskin*	.15	.11	.06
384	Andres Thomas	.05	.04	.02
385	Dennis Martinez	.08	.06	.03
386	Mike Henneman	.08	.06	.03
387	Felix Jose	.15	.11	.06
388	Alejandro Pena	.05	.04	.02
389	Chet Lemon	.06	.05	.02
390	*Craig Wilson*(FC)	.20	.15	.08
391	Chuck Crim	.05	.04	.02
392	Mel Hall	.06	.05	.02
393	Mark Knudson	.05	.04	.02
394	Norm Charlton	.08	.06	.03
395	Mike Felder	.05	.04	.02
396	*Tim Layana*	.15	.11	.06
397	Steve Frey(FC)	.06	.05	.02
398	Bill Doran	.08	.06	.03
399	Dion James	.05	.04	.02
400	Checklist 301-400	.05	.04	.02
401	Ron Hassey	.05	.04	.02
402	Don Robinson	.06	.05	.02
403	Gene Nelson	.05	.04	.02
404	Terry Kennedy	.05	.04	.02
405	Todd Burns	.05	.04	.02
406	Roger McDowell	.08	.06	.03
407	Bob Kipper	.05	.04	.02
408	Darren Daulton	.08	.06	.03
409	Chuck Cary	.06	.05	.02
410	Bruce Ruffin	.06	.05	.02
411	Juan Berenguer	.05	.04	.02
412	Gary Ward	.05	.04	.02
413	Al Newman	.05	.04	.02
414	Danny Jackson	.08	.06	.02

		MT	NR MT	EX
415	Greg Gagne	.06	.05	.02
416	Tom Herr	.06	.05	.02
417	Jeff Parrett	.06	.05	.02
418	Jeff Reardon	.08	.06	.03
419	Mark Lemke	.06	.05	.02
420	Charlie O'Brien	.05	.04	.02
421	Willie Randolph	.08	.06	.03
422	Steve Bedrosian	.08	.06	.03
423	Mike Moore	.08	.06	.03
424	Jeff Brantley	.08	.06	.03
425	Bob Welch	.10	.08	.04
426	Terry Mulholland	.08	.06	.03
427	*Willie Blair*(FC)	.15	.11	.06
428	Darrin Fletcher(FC)	.10	.08	.04
429	Mike Witt	.06	.05	.02
430	Joe Boever	.05	.04	.02
431	Tom Gordon	.12	.09	.05
432	*Pedro Munoz*(FC)	.50	.40	.20
433	Kevin Seitzer	.10	.08	.04
434	Kevin Tapani	.15	.11	.06
435	Bret Saberhagen	.12	.09	.05
436	Ellis Burks	.20	.15	.08
437	Chuck Finley	.10	.08	.04
438	Mike Boddicker	.08	.06	.03
439	Francisco Cabrera	.08	.06	.03
440	*Todd Hundley*	.25	.20	.10
441	Kelly Downs	.06	.05	.02
442	*Dann Howitt*(FC)	.15	.11	.06
443	Scott Garrelts	.08	.06	.03
444	Rickey Henderson	.40	.30	.15
445	Will Clark	.40	.30	.15
446	Ben McDonald	.50	.40	.20
447	Dale Murphy	.12	.09	.05
448	Dave Righetti	.10	.08	.04
449	Dickie Thon	.05	.04	.02
450	Ted Power	.05	.04	.02
451	Scott Coolbaugh	.08	.06	.03
452	Dwight Smith	.08	.06	.03
453	Pete Incaviglia	.08	.06	.03
454	Andre Dawson	.15	.11	.06
455	Ruben Sierra	.20	.15	.08
456	Andres Galarraga	.10	.08	.04
457	Alvin Davis	.10	.08	.04
458	Tony Castillo	.06	.05	.02
459	Pete O'Brien	.06	.05	.02
460	Charlie Leibrandt	.06	.05	.02
461	Vince Coleman	.10	.08	.04
462	Steve Sax	.10	.08	.04
463	*Omar Oliveras*(FC)	.15	.11	.06
464	*Oscar Azocar*(FC)	.20	.15	.08
465	Joe Magrane	.08	.06	.03
466	*Karl Rhodes*(FC)	.30	.25	.12
467	Benito Santiago	.10	.08	.04
468	*Joe Klink*(FC)	.10	.08	.04
469	Sil Campusano	.05	.04	.02
470	Mark Parent	.05	.04	.02
471	*Shawn Boskie*	.20	.15	.08
472	Kevin Brown	.10	.08	.04
473	Rick Sutcliffe	.08	.06	.03
474	Rafael Palmeiro	.12	.09	.05
475	Mike Harkey	.10	.08	.04
476	Jaime Navarro	.15	.11	.06
477	Marquis Grissom	.20	.15	.08
478	Marty Clary	.05	.04	.02
479	Greg Briley	.10	.08	.04
480	Tom Glavine	.08	.06	.03
481	Lee Guetterman	.05	.04	.02
482	Rex Hudler	.06	.05	.02
483	Dave LaPoint	.06	.05	.02
484	Terry Pendleton	.08	.06	.03
485	Jesse Barfield	.08	.06	.03
486	Jose DeJesus	.08	.06	.03
487	*Paul Abbott*(FC)	.15	.11	.06
488	Ken Howell	.06	.05	.02
489	Greg W. Harris	.06	.05	.02
490	Roy Smith	.05	.04	.02
491	Paul Assenmacher	.05	.04	.02
492	Geno Petralli	.05	.04	.02
493	Steve Wilson	.08	.06	.03
494	Kevin Reimer(FC)	.08	.06	.03
495	Bill Long	.05	.04	.02
496	Mike Jackson	.06	.05	.02
497	Oddibe McDowell	.06	.05	.02
498	Bill Swift	.06	.05	.02
499	Jeff Treadway	.06	.05	.02
500	Checklist 401-500	.05	.04	.02
501	Gene Larkin	.06	.05	.02
502	Bob Boone	.08	.06	.03
503	Allan Anderson	.06	.05	.02
504	Luis Aquino	.06	.05	.02
505	Mark Guthrie	.06	.05	.02
506	Joe Orsulak	.06	.05	.02
507	*Dana Kiecker*(FC)	.15	.11	.06
508	Dave Gallagher	.05	.04	.02
509	Greg W. Harris	.06	.05	.02
510	Mark Williamson	.05	.04	.02
511	Casey Candaele	.05	.04	.02
512	Mookie Wilson	.06	.05	.02
513	Dave Smith	.08	.06	.03
514	*Chuck Carr*(FC)	.15	.11	.06
515	Glenn Wilson	.06	.05	.02
516	Mike Fitzgerald	.05	.04	.02
517	Devon White	.08	.06	.03
518	*Dave Hollins*	.25	.20	.10
519	Mark Eichhorn	.05	.04	.02
520	Otis Nixon	.05	.04	.02
521	*Terry Shumpert*	.20	.15	.08
522	*Scott Erickson*(FC)	4.00	3.00	1.50
523	Danny Tartabull	.10	.08	.04
524	Orel Hershiser	.15	.11	.06
525	George Brett	.15	.11	.06
526	Greg Vaughn	.20	.15	.08
527	*Tim Naehring*(FC)	.40	.30	.15
528	Curt Schilling(FC)	.06	.05	.02
529	Chris Bosio	.06	.05	.02
530	Sam Horn	.08	.06	.03
531	Mike Scott	.10	.08	.04
532	George Bell	.15	.11	.06
533	Eric Anthony	.20	.15	.08
534	*Julio Valera*(FC)	.15	.11	.06
535	Glenn Davis	.15	.11	.06
536	Larry Walker	.15	.11	.06
537	Pat Combs	.15	.11	.06
538	*Chris Nabholz*(FC)	.20	.15	.08
539	Kirk McCaskill	.08	.06	.03
540	Randy Ready	.05	.04	.02
541	Mark Gubicza	.10	.08	.04
542	Rick Aguilera	.08	.06	.03
543	*Brian McRae*(FC)	1.00	.70	.40
544	Kirby Puckett	.20	.15	.08
545	Bo Jackson	.50	.40	.20
546	Wade Boggs	.25	.20	.10
547	Tim McIntosh(FC)	.20	.15	.08
548	Randy Milligan	.08	.06	.03
549	Dwight Evans	.08	.06	.03
550	Billy Ripken	.05	.04	.02
551	Erik Hanson	.15	.11	.06
552	Lance Parrish	.10	.08	.04
553	Tino Martinez	.20	.15	.08
554	Jim Abbott	.15	.11	.06
555	Ken Griffey,Jr.	1.50	1.25	.60
556	Milt Cuyler(FC)	.30	.25	.12
557	*Mark Leonard*(FC)	.25	.20	.10
558	Jay Howell	.08	.06	.03
559	Lloyd Moseby	.08	.06	.03
560	Chris Gwynn	.06	.05	.02
561	*Mark Whiten*(FC)	.70	.50	.30
562	Harold Baines	.10	.08	.04
563	Junior Felix	.15	.11	.06
564	*Darren Lewis*(FC)	.50	.40	.20
565	Fred McGriff	.15	.11	.06
566	Kevin Appier	.15	.11	.06
567	*Luis Gonzalez*(FC)	1.00	.70	.40
568	Frank White	.08	.06	.03
569	Juan Agosto	.05	.04	.02
570	Mike Macfarlane	.06	.05	.02
571	Bert Blyleven	.10	.08	.04
572	Ken Griffey,Sr.	.10	.08	.04
573	Lee Stevens(FC)	.20	.15	.08
574	Edgar Martinez	.08	.06	.03
575	Wally Joyner	.10	.08	.04
576	Tim Belcher	.08	.06	.03
577	John Burkett	.10	.08	.04
578	Mike Morgan	.06	.05	.02
579	Paul Gibson	.05	.04	.02
580	Jose Vizcaino	.10	.08	.04
581	Duane Ward	.06	.05	.02
582	Scott Sanderson	.06	.05	.02
583	David Wells	.06	.05	.02
584	Willie McGee	.10	.08	.04
585	John Cerutti	.05	.04	.02
586	Danny Darwin	.08	.06	.03
587	Kurt Stillwell	.08	.06	.03
588	Rich Gedman	.05	.04	.02
589	Mark Davis	.08	.06	.03
590	Bill Gullickson	.06	.05	.02
591	Matt Young	.06	.05	.02
592	Bryan Harvey	.08	.06	.03
593	Omar Vizquel	.06	.05	.02
594	*Scott Lewis*(FC)	.20	.15	.08
595	Dave Valle	.06	.05	.02
596	Tim Crews	.05	.04	.02

		MT	NR MT	EX
597	Mike Bielecki	.06	.05	.02
598	Mike Sharperson	.06	.05	.02
599	Dave Bergman	.05	.04	.02
600	Checklist 501-600	.05	.04	.02
601	Steve Lyons	.06	.05	.02
602	Bruce Hurst	.08	.06	.03
603	Donn Pall	.05	.04	.02
604	*Jim Vatcher*(FC)	.15	.11	.06
605	Dan Pasqua	.06	.05	.02
606	Kenny Rogers	.08	.06	.03
607	*Jeff Schulz*(FC)	.15	.11	.06
608	Brad Arnsberg(FC)	.10	.08	.04
609	Willie Wilson	.08	.06	.03
610	Jamie Moyer	.06	.05	.02
611	Ron Oester	.05	.04	.02
612	Dennis Cook	.08	.06	.03
613	Rick Mahler	.05	.04	.02
614	Bill Landrum	.06	.05	.02
615	Scott Scudder	.15	.11	.06
616	*Tom Edens*(FC)	.08	.06	.03
617	"1917 Revisited"	.25	.20	.10
618	Jim Gantner	.06	.05	.02
619	Darrel Akerfelds(FC)	.06	.05	.02
620	Ron Robinson	.06	.05	.02
621	*Scott Radinsky*	.20	.15	.08
622	Pete Smith	.06	.05	.02
623	Melido Perez	.08	.06	.03
624	Jerald Clark	.06	.05	.02
625	Carlos Martinez	.08	.06	.03
626	*Wes Chamberlain*(FC)	1.00	.70	.40
627	Bobby Witt	.08	.06	.03
628	Ken Dayley	.06	.05	.02
629	*John Barfield*(FC)	.10	.08	.04
630	Bob Tewksbury	.06	.05	.02
631	Glenn Braggs	.06	.05	.02
632	*Jim Neidlinger*(FC)	.20	.15	.08
633	Tom Browning	.08	.06	.03
634	Kirk Gibson	.12	.09	.05
635	Rob Dibble	.12	.09	.05
636	"Stolen Base Leaders"	.30	.25	.12
637	Jeff Montgomery	.08	.06	.03
638	Mike Schooler	.08	.06	.03
639	Storm Davis	.06	.05	.02
640	*Rich Rodriguez*(FC)	.15	.11	.06
641	Phil Bradley	.08	.06	.03
642	Kent Mercker	.15	.11	.06
643	Carlton Fisk	.12	.09	.05
644	*Mike Bell*(FC)	.15	.11	.06
645	*Alex Fernandez*(FC)	.60	.45	.25
646	Juan Gonzalez	.30	.25	.12
647	Ken Hill	.06	.05	.02
648	Jeff Russell	.08	.06	.03
649	*Chuck Malone*(FC)	.15	.11	.06
650	Steve Buechele	.06	.05	.02
651	Mike Benjamin	.15	.11	.06
652	Tony Pena	.08	.06	.03
653	Trevor Wilson	.08	.06	.03
654	Alex Cole	.30	.25	.12
655	Roger Clemens	.25	.20	.10
656	"The Bashing Years"	.25	.20	.10
657	*Joe Grahe*(FC)	.20	.15	.08
658	Jim Eisenreich	.06	.05	.02
659	Dan Gladden	.06	.05	.02
660	Steve Farr	.06	.05	.02
661	*Bill Sampen*	.20	.15	.08
662	*Dave Rohde*(FC)	.15	.11	.06
663	Mark Gardner	.20	.15	.08
664	*Mike Simms*(FC)	.25	.20	.10
665	Moises Alou(FC)	.15	.11	.06
666	Mickey Hatcher	.06	.05	.02
667	Jimmy Key	.08	.06	.03
668	John Wetteland	.10	.08	.04
669	John Smiley	.06	.05	.02
670	Jim Acker	.05	.04	.02
671	Pascual Perez	.06	.05	.02
672	*Reggie Harris*(FC)	.30	.25	.12
673	Matt Nokes	.08	.06	.03
674	*Rafael Novoa*(FC)	.15	.11	.06
675	Hensley Meulens	.10	.08	.04
676	Jeff M. Robinson	.06	.05	.02
677	"Ground Breaking"	.25	.20	.10
678	Johnny Ray	.06	.05	.02
679	Greg Hibbard	.10	.08	.04
680	Paul Sorrento	.20	.15	.08
681	Mike Marshall	.06	.05	.02
682	Jim Clancy	.05	.04	.02
683	Rob Murphy	.05	.04	.02
684	Dave Schmidt	.05	.04	.02
685	*Jeff Gray*(FC)	.15	.11	.06
686	Mike Hartley(FC)	.20	.15	.08
687	Jeff King	.08	.06	.03

		MT	NR MT	EX
688	Stan Javier	.06	.05	.02
689	Bob Walk	.06	.05	.02
690	Jim Gott	.06	.05	.02
691	Mike LaCoss	.05	.04	.02
692	John Farrell	.06	.05	.02
693	Tim Leary	.06	.05	.02
694	*Mike Walker*(FC)	.20	.15	.08
695	Eric Plunk	.05	.04	.02
696	Mike Fetters(FC)	.15	.11	.06
697	Wayne Edwards	.10	.08	.04
698	Tim Drummond(FC)	.15	.11	.06
699	Willie Fraser	.05	.04	.02
700	Checklist 601-700	.05	.04	.02
701	Mike Heath	.10	.08	.04
702	"Rookie Threats"	.60	.45	.25
703	Jose Mesa	.10	.08	.04
704	Dave Smith	.10	.08	.04
705	Danny Darwin	.10	.08	.04
706	Rafael Belliard	.10	.08	.04
707	Rob Murphy	.10	.08	.04
708	Terry Pendleton	.15	.11	.06
709	Mike Pagliarulo	.10	.08	.04
710	Sid Bream	.12	.09	.05
711	Junior Felix	.12	.09	.05
712	Dante Bichette	.10	.08	.04
713	Kevin Gross	.10	.08	.04
714	Luis Sojo	.12	.09	.05
715	Bob Ojeda	.10	.08	.04
716	Julio Machado	.12	.09	.05
717	Steve Farr	.10	.08	.04
718	Franklin Stubbs	.10	.08	.04
719	Mike Boddicker	.12	.09	.05
720	Willie Randolph	.12	.09	.05
721	Willie McGee	.15	.11	.06
722	Chili Davis	.15	.11	.06
723	Danny Jackson	.12	.09	.05
724	Cory Snyder	.10	.08	.04
725	"MVP Lineup"	.25	.20	.10
726	Rob Deer	.10	.08	.04
727	Rich DeLucia(FC)	.15	.11	.06
728	Mike Perez(FC)	.15	.11	.06
729	Mickey Tettleton	.12	.09	.05
730	Mike Blowers	.10	.08	.04
731	Gary Gaetti	.12	.09	.05
732	Brett Butler	.12	.09	.05
733	Dave Parker	.15	.11	.06
734	Eddie Zosky(FC)	.20	.15	.08
735	Jack Clark	.12	.09	.05
736	Jack Morris	.12	.09	.05
737	Kirk Gibson	.12	.09	.05
738	Steve Bedrosian	.10	.08	.04
739	Candy Maldonado	.10	.08	.04
740	Matt Young	.10	.08	.04
741	Rich Garces(FC)	.20	.15	.08
742	George Bell	.15	.11	.06
743	Deion Sanders	.15	.11	.06
744	Bo Jackson	1.50	1.25	.60
745	Luis Mercedes(FC)	.40	.30	.15
746	Reggie Jefferson(FC)	.80	.60	.30
747	Pete Incaviglia	.10	.08	.04
748	Chris Hammond(FC)	.20	.15	.08
749	Mike Stanton	.12	.09	.05
750	Scott Sanderson	.10	.08	.04
751	Paul Faries(FC)	.20	.15	.08
752	Al Osuna(FC)	.15	.11	.06
753	Steve Chitren(FC)	.15	.11	.06
754	Tony Fernandez	.15	.11	.06
755	Jeff Bagwell(FC)	5.00	3.75	2.00
756	Kirk Dressendorfer(FC)	.50	.40	.20
757	Glenn Davis	.15	.11	.06
758	Gary Carter	.12	.09	.05
759	Zane Smith	.10	.08	.04
760	Vance Law	.10	.08	.04
761	Denis Boucher(FC)	.20	.15	.08
762	Turner Ward(FC)	.20	.15	.08
763	Roberto Alomar	.15	.11	.06
764	Albert Belle	.25	.20	.10
765	Joe Carter	.15	.11	.06
766	Pete Schourek(FC)	.15	.11	.06
767	Heathcliff Slocumb(FC)	.15	.11	.06
768	Vince Coleman	.15	.11	.06
769	Mitch Williams	.12	.09	.05
770	Brian Downing	.10	.08	.04
771	Dana Allison(FC)	.15	.11	.06
772	Pete Harnisch	.12	.09	.05
773	Tim Raines	.15	.11	.06
774	Darryl Kile(FC)	.25	.20	.10
775	Fred McGriff	.15	.11	.06
776	Dwight Evans	.12	.09	.05
777	Joe Slusarski(FC)	.20	.15	.08
778	Dave Righetti	.12	.09	.05

		MT	NR MT	EX
779	Jeff Hamilton	.10	.08	.04
780	Ernest Riles	.10	.08	.04
781	Ken Dayley	.10	.08	.04
782	Eric King	.10	.08	.04
783	Devon White	.12	.09	.05
784	Beau Allred	.10	.08	.04
785	Mike Timlin(FC)	.25	.20	.10
786	Ivan Calderon	.15	.11	.06
787	Hubie Brooks	.12	.09	.05
788	Juan Agosto	.10	.08	.04
789	Barry Jones	.10	.08	.04
790	Wally Backman	.10	.08	.04
791	Jim Presley	.10	.08	.04
792	Charlie Hough	.10	.08	.04
793	Larry Andersen	.10	.08	.04
794	Steve Finley	.12	.09	.05
795	Shawn Abner	.10	.08	.04
796	Jeff M. Robinson	.10	.08	.04
797	Joe Bitker(FC)	.10	.08	.04
798	Eric Show	.10	.08	.04
799	Bud Black	.10	.08	.04
800	Checklist 701-800	.10	.08	.04
----	Michael Jordan (Special Insert)	10.00	7.50	4.00

1991 Upper Deck Final Edition

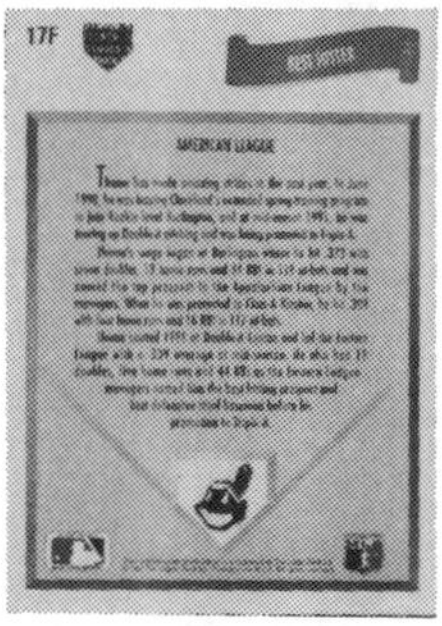

Upper Deck surprised the hobby with the release of this 100-card boxed set. The cards are numbered with an "F" designation. A special diamond skills subset features several top prospects. An all-star subset is also included in this set. The cards are styled like the regular 1991 Upper Deck issue. Special team hologram cards are also included with the set.

	MT	NR MT	EX
Complete Set:	25.00	20.00	10.00
Common Player:	.20	.15	.08

		MT	NR MT	EX
1	Diamond Skills Checklist (Klesko Sanders)	.80	.60	.30
2	Pedro Martinez(FC)	2.00	1.50	.80
3	Lance Dickson	.30	.25	.12
4	Royce Clayton	.50	.40	.20
5	Scott Bryant(FC)	.35	.25	.14
6	Dan Wilson(FC)	.40	.30	.15
7	Dmitri Young(FC)	1.25	.90	.50
8	Ryan Klesko(FC)	2.50	2.00	1.00
9	Tom Goodwin(FC)	.35	.25	.14
10	Rondell White(FC)	1.00	.70	.40
11	Reggie Sanders	.60	.45	.25
12	Todd Van Poppel	1.00	.70	.40
13	Arthur Rhodes(FC)	.50	.40	.20
14	Eddie Zosky	.20	.15	.08
15	Gerald Williams(FC)	.80	.60	.30
16	Robert Eenhoorn(FC)	.30	.25	.12
17	Jim Thome(FC)	1.00	.70	.40
18	Marc Newfield(FC)	2.00	1.50	.80
19	Kerwin Moore(FC)	.50	.40	.20
20	Jeff McNeely(FC)	.60	.45	.25
21	Frankie Rodriguez(FC)	2.50	2.00	1.00
22	Andy Mota(FC)	.30	.25	.12
23	Chris Haney(FC)	.30	.25	.12
24	Kenny Lofton(FC)	.80	.60	.30
25	Dave Nilsson(FC)	.70	.50	.30
26	Derek Bell(FC)	.70	.50	.30
27	Frank Castillo(FC)	.50	.40	.20
28	Candy Maldonado	.20	.15	.08
29	Chuck McElroy	.20	.15	.08
30	Chito Martinez(FC)	1.25	.90	.50
31	Steve Howe	.20	.15	.08
32	Freddie Benavides(FC)	.30	.25	.12
33	Scott Kamieniecki(FC)	.35	.25	.14
34	Denny Neagle(FC)	.70	.50	.30
35	Mike Humphreys(FC)	.35	.25	.14
36	Mike Remlinger(FC)	.25	.20	.10
37	Scott Coolbaugh	.20	.15	.08
38	Darren Lewis	.35	.25	.14
39	Thomas Howard(FC)	.20	.15	.08
40	John Candelaria	.20	.15	.08
41	Todd Benzinger	.20	.15	.08
42	Wilson Alvarez	.30	.25	.12
43	Patrick Lennon(FC)	.50	.40	.20
44	Rusty Meacham(FC)	.35	.25	.14
45	Ryan Bowen(FC)	.40	.30	.15
46	Rick Wilkins(FC)	.50	.40	.20
47	Ed Sprague(FC)	.30	.25	.14
48	Bob Scanlan(FC)	.20	.15	.08
49	Tom Candiotti	.20	.15	.08
50	Dennis Martinez (Perfecto)	.20	.15	.08
51	Oil Can Boyd	.20	.15	.08
52	Glenallen Hill	.30	.25	.12
53	Scott Livingstone(FC)	.50	.40	.20
54	Brian Hunter(FC)	1.50	1.25	.60
55	Ivan Rodriguez(FC)	4.00	3.00	1.50
56	Keith Mitchell(FC)	.80	.60	.30
57	Roger McDowell	.20	.15	.08
58	Otis Nixon	.20	.15	.08
59	Juan Bell	.20	.15	.08
60	Bill Krueger	.20	.15	.08
61	Chris Donnels(FC)	.50	.40	.20
62	Tommy Greene	.25	.20	.10
63	Doug Simons(FC)	.25	.20	.10
64	Andy Ashby(FC)	.25	.20	.10
65	Anthony Young(FC)	.60	.45	.25
66	Kevin Morton(FC)	.40	.30	.15
67	Bret Barberie(FC)	.50	.40	.20
68	Scott Servais(FC)	.25	.20	.10
69	Ron Darling	.20	.15	.08
70	Vicente Palacios	.20	.15	.08
71	Tim Burke	.20	.15	.08
72	Gerald Alexander(FC)	.20	.15	.08
73	Reggie Jefferson	.50	.40	.20
74	Dean Palmer	.60	.45	.25
75	Mark Whiten	.30	.25	.12
76	Randy Tomlin(FC)	.50	.40	.20
77	Mark Wohlers(FC)	.80	.60	.30
78	Brook Jacoby	.20	.15	.08
79	All-Star Checklist (Griffey/Sandberg)(FC)	1.00	.70	.40
80	Jack Morris (AS)	.30	.25	.12
81	Sandy Alomar, Jr. (AS)	.25	.20	.10
82	Cecil Fielder (AS)	.30	.25	.12
83	Roberto Alomar (AS)	.30	.25	.12
84	Wade Boggs (AS)	.30	.25	.12
85	Cal Ripken, Jr. (AS)	.50	.40	.20
86	Rickey Henderson (AS)	.40	.30	.15
87	Ken Griffey, Jr. (AS)	1.25	.90	.50
88	Dave Henderson (AS)	.25	.20	.10
89	Danny Tartabull (AS)	.25	.20	.10
90	Tom Glavine (AS)	.30	.25	.12
91	Benito Santiago (AS)	.25	.20	.10
92	Will Clark (AS)	.50	.40	.20
93	Ryne Sandberg (AS)	.50	.40	.20
94	Chris Sabo (AS)	.25	.20	.10
95	Ozzie Smith (AS)	.30	.25	.14
96	Ivan Calderon (AS)	.25	.20	.10
97	Tony Gwynn (AS)	.30	.25	.12
98	Andre Dawson (AS)	.30	.25	.12
99	Bobby Bonilla (AS)	.30	.25	.12
100	Checklist	.20	.15	.08

1991 Upper Deck Silver Sluggers

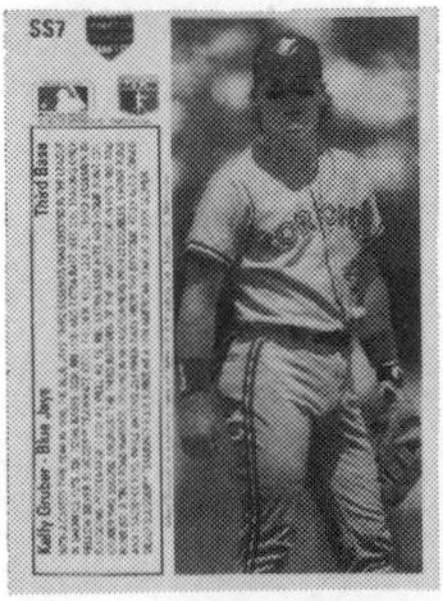

Each year the "Silver Slugger" award is presented to the top slugger at each position in the American and National Leagues. Upper Deck produced special cards in honor of the players who received this award for the 1990 season. The cards were randomly inserted in jumbo packs of Upper Deck cards. The cards feature a "SS" designation along with the card number. The cards are designed like the regular issue Upper Deck cards from 1991, but feature a Silver Slugger bat along the left border of the card.

		MT	NR MT	EX
Complete Set:		40.00	30.00	15.00
Common Player:		1.00	.70	.40
1	Julio Franco	1.50	1.25	.60
2	Alan Trammell	1.50	1.25	.60
3	Rickey Henderson	4.00	3.00	1.50
4	Jose Canseco	5.00	3.75	2.00
5	Barry Bonds	3.00	2.25	1.25
6	Eddie Murray	1.50	1.25	.60
7	Kelly Gruber	1.25	.90	.50
8	Ryne Sandberg	4.00	3.00	1.50
9	Darryl Strawberry	4.00	3.00	1.50
10	Ellis Burks	1.25	.90	.50
11	Lance Parrish	1.25	.90	.50
12	Cecil Fielder	4.00	3.00	1.50
13	Matt Williams	1.50	1.25	.60
14	Dave Parker	1.25	.90	.50
15	Bobby Bonilla	2.50	2.00	1.00
16	Don Robinson	1.00	.70	.40
17	Benito Santiago	1.25	.90	.50
18	Barry Larkin	2.00	1.50	.80

1991 Upper Deck Heroes of Baseball

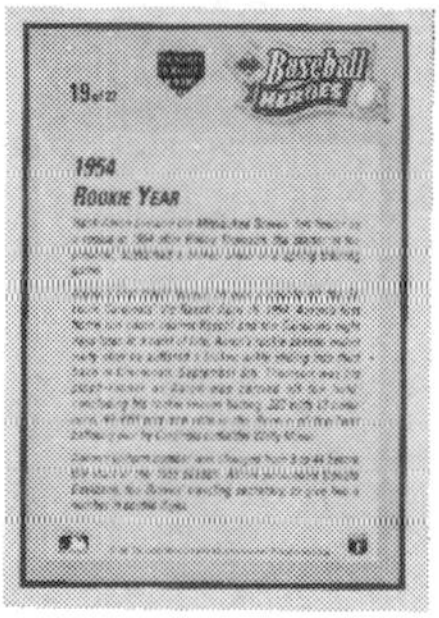

This set actually began in 1990 with the release of a 9-card Reggie Jackson subset in Upper Deck High number packs. It continued in 1991 with the release of a Nolan Ryan subset in first series packs and a Hank Aaron subset found in high number packs. The cards honor the players and their accomplishments at different points of their careers. Each player signed and numbered 2,500 cards which were randomly inserted into packs. The complete set price does not reflect the signed cards. Prices for each player reflects the standard price for a card in his subset. The header card explains the Baseball Heroes series.

		MT	NR MT	EX
Complete Set:		30.00	22.00	12.50
1	Reggie Jackson (Cards 1-9)	1.00	.70	.40
10	Nolan Ryan (Cards 10-18)	1.50	1.25	.60
19	Hank Aaron (Cards 19-27)	1.25	.90	.50
----	Reggie Jackson (Autographed & Numbered)	400.00	300.00	150.00
----	Nolan Ryan (Autographed & Numbered)	500.00	375.00	200.00
----	Hank Aaron (Hologram)	9.00	6.75	3.50
----	Hank Aaron (Autographed & Numbered)	400.00	300.00	150.00
----	Header Cards	.50	.40	.20

1992 Upper Deck

Upper Deck introduced a new look in 1992. The baseline style was no longer used. The 1992 cards feature full-color action photos on white stock, with the player's name and the Upper Deck logo along the top border. The team name is inserted in the bottom right corner of the photo.. Once again a 100-card high number series was set for release in July or August. 2,500 Ted Williams autographed Baseball Heroes cards were randomly inserted into Upper Deck packs. Several subsets are also featured in the 1992 issue including Star Rookies and Top Prospects. At press time, Upper Deck was considering changes in its 1992 card set. This explains any discrepancies in the price list from what was actually released from Upper Deck.

		MT	NR MT	EX
Complete Set:		30.00	22.00	12.50
Common Player:		.05	.04	.02
1	Star Rookie Checklist	.06	.05	.02
2	Star Rookie (Royce Clayton)	.20	.15	.08
3	Star Rookie (*Brian Jordan*)(FC)	.30	.25	.12
4	Star Rookie (*Dave Fleming*)(FC)	.25	.20	.10
5	Star Rookie (*Jim Thome*)	.40	.30	.15
6	Star Rookie (Jeff Juden)	.20	.15	.08
7	Star Rookie (*Roberto Hernandez*)(FC)	.20	.15	.08
8	Star Rookie (Kyle Abbott)(FC)	.10	.08	.04
9	Star Rookie (*Chris George*)(FC)	.20	.15	.08
10	Star Rookie (*Rob Maurer*)(FC)	.30	.25	.12
11	Star Rookie (Donald Harris)(FC)	.20	.15	.08
12	Star Rookie (*Mark Wohlers*)	.20	.15	.08
13	Star Rookie (*Patrick Lennon*)	.20	.15	.08
14	Star Rookie (Willie Banks)	.15	.11	.06
15	Star Rookie (Roger Salkeld)	.25	.20	.10
16	Star Rookie (Wilfredo Cordero)	.20	.15	.08
17	Star Rookie (*Arthur Rhodes*)	.20	.15	.08
18	Star Rookie (*Pedro Martinez*)	.80	.60	.30
19	Star Rookie (*Andy Ashby*)	.10	.08	.04
20	Star Rookie (Tom Goodwin)	.15	.11	.06
21	Star Rookie (*Braulio Castillo*)(FC)	.20	.15	.08
22	Star Rookie (Todd Van Poppel)	.60	.45	.25
23	Star Rookie (*Brian Williams*)(FC)	.30	.25	.12
24	Star Rookie (*Ryan Klesko*)	2.00	1.50	.80
25	Star Rookie (*Kenny Lofton*)	.25	.20	.10
26	Star Rookie (Derek Bell)	.35	.25	.14
27	Star Rookie (Reggie Sanders)	.15	.11	.06
28	"Winfield's 400th"	.10	.08	.04
29	Atlanta Checklist	.05	.04	.02
30	Cincinnati Checklist	.05	.04	.02
31	Houston Checklist	.05	.04	.02
32	Los Angeles Checklist	.05	.04	.02
33	San Diego Checklist	.05	.04	.02
34	San Francisco Checklist	.05	.04	.02
35	Chicago Checklist	.05	.04	.02
36	Montreal Checklist	.05	.04	.02
37	New York Checklist	.05	.04	.02
38	Philadelphia Checklist	.05	.04	.02
39	Pittsburgh Checklist	.05	.04	.02
40	St. Louis Checklist	.05	.04	.02
41	"Playoff Perfection"	.10	.08	.04
42	*Jeremy Hernandez*(FC)	.20	.15	.08
43	*Doug Henry*(FC)	.20	.15	.08
44	*Chris Donnels*	.25	.20	.10
45	*Mo Sanford*(FC)	.20	.15	.08

		MT	NR MT	EX
46	*Scott Kamieniecki*	.15	.11	.06
47	Mark Lemke	.06	.05	.02
48	Steve Farr	.05	.04	.02
49	Francisco Oliveras	.05	.04	.02
50	*Ced Landrum*(FC)	.10	.08	.04
51	Top Prospect Checklist	.06	.05	.02
52	Top Prospect *(Eduardo Perez)*(FC)	.35	.25	.14
53	Top Prospect *(Tom Nevers)*(FC)	.20	.15	.08
54	Top Prospect *(David Zancanaro)*(FC)	.20	.15	.08
55	Top Prospect *(Shawn Green)*(FC)	.20	.15	.08
56	Top Prospect *(Mike Kelly)*(FC)	.35	.25	.14
57	Top Prospect *(Dave Nilsson)*	.35	.25	.14
58	Top Prospect *(Dmitri Young)*	.70	.50	.30
59	Top Prospect *(Ryan Hawblitzel)*(FC)	.30	.25	.12
60	Top Prospect *(Raul Mondesi)*(FC)	.30	.25	.12
61	Top Prospect (Rondell White)(FC)	.35	.25	.14
62	Top Prospect (Steve Hosey)(FC)	.20	.15	.08
63	Top Prospect *(Manny Ramirez)*(FC)	.25	.20	.10
64	Top Prospect (Marc Newfield)	.30	.25	.12
65	Top Prospect (Jeromy Burnitz)(FC)	.40	.30	.15
66	Top Prospect *(Mark Smith)*(FC)	.30	.25	.12
67	Top Prospect *(Joey Hamilton)*(FC)	.25	.20	.10
68	Top Prospect *(Tyler Green)*(FC)	.35	.25	.14
69	Top Prospect *(John Farrell)*(FC)	.30	.25	.12
70	Top Prospect *(Kurt Miller)*(FC)	.20	.15	.08
71	Top Prospect *(Frankie Rodriguez)*	1.75	1.25	.70
72	Top Prospect (Dan Wilson)(FC)	.35	.25	.14
73	Top Prospect *(Joe Vitiello)*(FC)	.35	.25	.14
74	Top Prospect (Rico Brogna)(FC)	.10	.08	.04
75	Top Prospect *(David McCarty)*(FC)	.50	.40	.20
76	Top Prospect *(Bob Wickman)*(FC)	.30	.25	.12
77	Top Prospect *(Brien Taylor)*(FC)	2.50	2.00	1.00
78	"Stay In School"	.10	.08	.04
79	Bloodlines (Ramon & Pedro Martinez)	.40	.30	.15
80	Bloodlines (Kevin & Keith Mitchell)	.10	.08	.04
81	Bloodlines (Sandy Jr. & Roberto Alomar)	.10	.08	.04
82	Bloodlines (Cal Jr. & Billy Ripken)	.15	.11	.06
83	Bloodlines (Tony & Chris Gwynn)	.10	.08	.04
84	Bloodlines (Dwight Gooden & Gary Sheffield)	.10	.08	.04
85	Bloodlines (Ken Sr., Ken Jr. & Craig Griffey)	.80	.60	.30
86	California Checklist	.05	.04	.02
87	Chicago Checklist	.05	.04	.02
88	Kansas City Checklist	.05	.04	.02
89	Minnesota Checklist	.05	.04	.02
90	Oakland Checklist	.05	.04	.02
91	Seattle Checklist	.05	.04	.02
92	Texas Checklist	.05	.04	.02
93	Baltimore Checklist	.05	.04	.02
94	Boston Checklist	.05	.04	.02
95	Cleveland Checklist	.05	.04	.02
96	Detroit Checklist	.05	.04	.02
97	Milwaukee Checklist	.05	.04	.02
98	New York Checklist	.05	.04	.02
99	Toronto Checklist	.05	.04	.02
100	Checklist 1-100	.05	.04	.02
101	Joe Oliver	.05	.04	.02
102	Hector Villanueva	.06	.05	.02
103	Ed Whitson	.05	.04	.02
104	Danny Jackson	.05	.04	.02
105	Chris Hammond	.06	.05	.02
106	Ricky Jordan	.06	.05	.02
107	Kevin Bass	.05	.04	.02
108	Darrin Fletcher	.05	.04	.02
109	Junior Ortiz	.05	.04	.02
110	Tom Bolton	.05	.04	.02
111	Jeff King	.06	.05	.02
112	Dave Magadan	.08	.06	.03
113	Mike LaValliere	.06	.05	.02
114	Hubie Brooks	.06	.05	.02
115	Jay Bell	.06	.05	.02
116	David Wells	.05	.04	.02
117	Jim Leyritz	.05	.04	.02
118	Manuel Lee	.05	.04	.02
119	Alvaro Espinoza	.05	.04	.02
120	B.J. Surhoff	.06	.05	.02
121	Hal Morris	.20	.15	.08
122	Shawon Dunston	.08	.06	.03
123	Chris Sabo	.10	.08	.04
124	Andre Dawson	.15	.11	.06
125	Eric Davis	.15	.11	.06
126	Chili Davis	.08	.06	.03
127	Dale Murphy	.10	.08	.04
128	Kirk McCaskill	.06	.05	.02
129	Terry Mulholland	.06	.05	.02
130	Rick Aguilera	.08	.06	.03
131	Vince Coleman	.10	.08	.04
132	Andy Van Slyke	.12	.09	.05
133	Gregg Jefferies	.15	.11	.06
134	Barry Bonds	.20	.15	.08
135	Dwight Gooden	.15	.11	.06
136	Dave Stieb	.08	.06	.03
137	Albert Belle	.25	.20	.10
138	Teddy Higuera	.08	.06	.03
139	Jesse Barfield	.08	.06	.03
140	Pat Borders	.06	.05	.02
141	Bip Roberts	.06	.05	.02
142	Rob Dibble	.10	.08	.04
143	Mark Grace	.15	.11	.06
144	Barry Larkin	.15	.11	.06
145	Ryne Sandberg	.25	.20	.10
146	Scott Erickson	.25	.20	.10
147	Luis Polonia	.06	.05	.02
148	John Burkett	.06	.05	.02
149	Luis Sojo	.06	.05	.02
150	Dickie Thon	.05	.04	.02
151	Walt Weiss	.06	.05	.02
152	Mike Scioscia	.06	.05	.02
153	Mark McGwire	.15	.11	.06
154	Matt Williams	.15	.11	.06
155	Rickey Henderson	.25	.20	.10
156	Sandy Alomar, Jr.	.10	.08	.04
157	Brian McRae	.25	.20	.10
158	Harold Baines	.08	.06	.03
159	Kevin Appier	.06	.05	.02
160	Felix Fermin	.05	.04	.02
161	Leo Gomez	.15	.11	.06
162	Craig Biggio	.10	.08	.04
163	Ben McDonald	.20	.15	.08
164	Randy Johnson	.08	.06	.03
165	Cal Ripken, Jr.	.25	.20	.10
166	Frank Thomas	.80	.60	.30
167	Delino DeShields	.08	.06	.03
168	Greg Gagne	.05	.04	.02
169	Ron Karkovice	.05	.04	.02
170	Charlie Leibrandt	.05	.04	.02
171	Dave Righetti	.08	.06	.03
172	Dave Henderson	.10	.08	.04
173	Steve Decker	.15	.11	.06
174	Darryl Strawberry	.15	.11	.06
175	Will Clark	.25	.20	.10
176	Ruben Sierra	.15	.11	.06
177	Ozzie Smith	.15	.11	.06
178	Charles Nagy	.08	.06	.03
179	Gary Pettis	.05	.04	.02
180	Kirk Gibson	.08	.06	.03
181	Randy Milligan	.06	.05	.02
182	Dave Valle	.05	.04	.02
183	Chris Hoiles	.10	.08	.04
184	Tony Phillips	.05	.04	.02
185	Brady Anderson	.05	.04	.02
186	Scott Fletcher	.05	.04	.02
187	Gene Larkin	.05	.04	.02
188	Lance Johnson	.05	.04	.02
189	Greg Olson	.05	.04	.02
190	Melido Perez	.05	.04	.02
191	Lenny Harris	.05	.04	.02
192	Terry Kennedy	.05	.04	.02
193	Mike Gallego	.05	.04	.02
194	Willie McGee	.08	.06	.03
195	Juan Samuel	.06	.05	.02
196	Jeff Huson	.05	.04	.02
197	Alex Cole	.06	.05	.02
198	Ron Robinson	.06	.05	.02
199	Joel Skinner	.06	.05	.02
200	Checklist 101-200	.06	.05	.02
201	Kevin Reimer	.06	.05	.02
202	Stan Belinda	.05	.04	.02
203	Pat Tabler	.05	.04	.02
204	Jose Guzman	.05	.04	.02
205	Jose Lind	.05	.04	.02
206	Spike Owen	.05	.04	.02
207	Joe Orsulak	.05	.04	.02
208	Charlie Hayes	.05	.04	.02
209	Mike Devereaux	.06	.05	.02
210	Mike Fitzgerald	.05	.04	.02
211	Willie Randolph	.05	.04	.02
212	Rod Nichols	.05	.04	.02
213	Mike Boddicker	.05	.04	.02
214	Bill Spiers	.05	.04	.02
215	Steve Olin	.05	.04	.02
216	*David Howard*(FC)	.20	.15	.08
217	Gary Varsho	.05	.04	.02
218	Mike Harkey	.06	.05	.02
219	Luis Aquino	.05	.04	.02

		MT	NR MT	EX
220	Chuck McElroy	.05	.04	.02
221	Doug Drabek	.08	.06	.03
222	Dave Winfield	.15	.11	.06
223	Rafael Palmeiro	.12	.09	.05
224	Joe Carter	.12	.09	.05
225	Bobby Bonilla	.12	.09	.05
226	Ivan Calderon	.10	.08	.04
227	Gregg Olson	.10	.08	.04
228	Tim Wallach	.08	.06	.03
229	Terry Pendleton	.10	.08	.04
230	Gilberto Reyes(FC)	.08	.06	.03
231	Carlos Baerga	.10	.08	.04
232	Greg Vaughn	.10	.08	.04
233	Bret Saberhagen	.10	.08	.04
234	Gary Sheffield	.10	.08	.04
235	Mark Lewis	.15	.11	.06
236	George Bell	.10	.08	.04
237	Danny Tartabull	.10	.08	.04
238	Willie Wilson	.06	.05	.02
239	Doug Dascenzo	.05	.04	.02
240	Bill Pecota	.05	.04	.02
241	Julio Franco	.12	.09	.05
242	Ed Sprague	.10	.08	.04
243	Juan Gonzalez	.35	.25	.14
244	Chuck Finley	.10	.08	.04
245	*Ivan Rodriguez*	1.50	1.25	.60
246	Lenny Dykstra	.10	.08	.04
247	Deion Sanders	.15	.11	.06
248	Dwight Evans	.08	.06	.03
249	Larry Walker	.10	.08	.04
250	Billy Ripken	.05	.04	.02
251	Mickey Tettleton	.06	.05	.02
252	Tony Pena	.06	.05	.02
253	Benito Santiago	.08	.06	.03
254	Kirby Puckett	.20	.15	.08
255	Cecil Fielder	.20	.15	.08
256	Howard Johnson	.12	.09	.05
257	Andujar Cedeno	.20	.15	.08
258	Jose Rijo	.08	.06	.03
259	Al Osuna	.05	.04	.02
260	Todd Hundley	.15	.11	.06
261	Orel Hershiser	.08	.06	.03
262	Ray Lankford	.15	.11	.06
263	Robin Ventura	.15	.11	.06
264	Felix Jose	.10	.08	.04
265	Eddie Murray	.15	.11	.06
266	Kevin Mitchell	.15	.11	.06
267	Gary Carter	.10	.08	.04
268	Mike Benjamin	.05	.04	.02
269	Dick Schofield	.05	.04	.02
270	Jose Uribe	.05	.04	.02
271	Pete Incaviglia	.06	.05	.02
272	Tony Fernandez	.08	.06	.03
273	Alan Trammell	.10	.08	.04
274	Tony Gwynn	.15	.11	.06
275	Mike Greenwell	.10	.08	.04
276	*Jeff Bagwell*	1.00	.70	.40
277	Frank Viola	.10	.08	.04
278	Randy Myers	.06	.05	.02
279	Ken Caminiti	.06	.05	.02
280	Bill Doran	.06	.05	.02
281	Dan Pasqua	.05	.04	.02
282	Alfredo Griffin	.05	.04	.02
283	Jose Oquendo	.05	.04	.02
284	Kal Daniels	.08	.06	.03
285	Bobby Thigpen	.08	.06	.03
286	Robby Thompson	.05	.04	.02
287	Mark Eichhorn	.05	.04	.02
288	Mike Felder	.05	.04	.02
289	Dave Gallagher	.05	.04	.02
290	Dave Anderson	.05	.04	.02
291	Mel Hall	.06	.05	.02
292	Jerald Clark	.06	.05	.02
293	Al Newman	.05	.04	.02
294	Rob Deer	.05	.04	.02
295	Matt Nokes	.06	.05	.02
296	Jack Armstrong	.06	.05	.02
297	Jim Deshaies	.05	.04	.02
298	Jeff Innis	.05	.04	.02
299	Jeff Reed	.05	.04	.02
300	Checklist 201-300	.05	.04	.02
301	Lonnie Smith	.05	.04	.02
302	Jimmy Key	.06	.05	.02
303	Junior Felix	.08	.06	.03
304	Mike Heath	.05	.04	.02
305	Mark Langston	.10	.08	.04
306	Greg W. Harris	.06	.05	.02
307	Brett Butler	.08	.06	.03
308	Luis Rivera	.05	.04	.02
309	Bruce Ruffin	.05	.04	.02
310	Paul Faries	.08	.06	.03

		MT	NR MT	EX
311	Terry Leach	.05	.04	.02
312	*Scott Brosius*(FC)	.15	.11	.06
313	Scott Leius	.15	.11	.06
314	Harold Reynolds	.08	.06	.03
315	Jack Morris	.10	.08	.04
316	David Segui	.10	.08	.04
317	Bill Gullickson	.06	.05	.02
318	Todd Frohwirth	.05	.04	.02
319	*Mark Leiter*(FC)	.10	.08	.04
320	Jeff M. Robinson	.05	.04	.02
321	Gary Gaetti	.08	.06	.03
322	John Smotlz	.10	.08	.04
323	Andy Benes	.10	.08	.04
324	Kelly Gruber	.08	.06	.03
325	Jim Abbott	.10	.08	.04
326	John Kruk	.06	.05	.02
327	Kevin Seitzer	.06	.05	.02
328	Darrin Jackson	.05	.04	.02
329	Kurt Stillwell	.05	.04	.02
330	Mike Maddux	.05	.04	.02
331	Dennis Eckersley	.10	.08	.04
332	Dan Gladden	.05	.04	.02
333	Jose Canseco	.25	.20	.10
334	Kent Hrbek	.06	.05	.02
335	Ken Griffey, Sr.	.06	.05	.02
336	Greg Swindell	.08	.06	.03
337	Trevor Wilson	.06	.05	.02
338	Sam Horn	.05	.04	.02
339	Mike Henneman	.06	.05	.02
340	Jerry Browne	.05	.04	.02
341	Glenn Braggs	.05	.04	.02
342	Tom Glavine	.10	.08	.04
343	Wally Joyner	.10	.08	.04
344	Fred McGriff	.10	.08	.04
345	Ron Gant	.15	.11	.06
346	Ramon Martinez	.15	.11	.06
347	Wes Chamberlain	.20	.15	.08
348	Terry Shumpert	.05	.04	.02
349	Tim Teufel	.05	.04	.02
350	Wally Backman	.05	.04	.02
351	Joe Girardi	.05	.04	.02
352	Devon White	.08	.06	.03
353	Greg Maddux	.08	.06	.03
354	*Ryan Bowen*	.15	.11	.06
355	Roberto Alomar	.10	.08	.04
356	Don Mattingly	.25	.20	.10
357	Pedro Guerrero	.10	.08	.04
358	Steve Sax	.10	.08	.04
359	Joey Cora	.05	.04	.02
360	Jim Gantner	.05	.04	.02
361	Brian Barnes	.10	.08	.04
362	Kevin McReynolds	.10	.08	.04
363	*Bret Barberie*(FC)	.15	.11	.06
364	David Cone	.08	.06	.03
365	Dennis Martinez	.08	.06	.03
366	*Brian Hunter*	.60	.45	.25
367	Edgar Martinez	.08	.06	.03
368	Steve Finley	.08	.06	.03
369	Greg Briley	.05	.04	.02
370	Jeff Blauser	.05	.04	.02
371	Todd Stottlemyre	.06	.05	.02
372	Luis Gonzalez	.20	.15	.08
373	*Rick Wilkins*	.20	.15	.08
374	*Darryl Kile*	.15	.11	.06
375	John Olerud	.15	.11	.06
376	Lee Smith	.08	.06	.03
377	Kevin Maas	.20	.15	.08
378	Dante Bichette	.06	.05	.02
379	Tom Pagnozzi	.06	.05	.02
380	Mike Flanagan	.05	.04	.02
381	Charlie O'Brien	.05	.04	.02
382	Dave Martinez	.05	.04	.02
383	Keith Miller	.05	.04	.02
384	Scott Ruskin	.05	.04	.02
385	Kevin Elster	.05	.04	.02
386	Alvin Davis	.08	.06	.03
387	Casey Candaele	.05	.04	.02
388	Pete O'Brien	.05	.04	.02
389	Jeff Treadway	.05	.04	.02
390	Scott Bradley	.05	.04	.02
391	Mookie Wilson	.05	.04	.02
392	Jimmy Jones	.05	.04	.02
393	Candy Maldonado	.05	.04	.02
394	Eric Yelding	.05	.04	.02
395	Tom Henke	.06	.05	.02
396	Franklin Stubbs	.05	.04	.02
397	Milt Thompson	.05	.04	.02
398	Mark Carreon	.05	.04	.02
399	Randy Velarde	.05	.04	.02
400	Checklist 301-400	.05	.04	.02
401	Omar Vizquel	.05	.04	.02

		MT	NR MT	EX
402	Joe Boever	.05	.04	.02
403	Bill Krueger	.05	.04	.02
404	Jody Reed	.06	.05	.02
405	Mike Schooler	.06	.05	.02
406	Jason Grimsley	.06	.05	.02
407	Greg Myers	.05	.04	.02
408	Randy Ready	.05	.04	.02
409	*Mike Timlin*	.15	.11	.06
410	Mitch Williams	.08	.06	.03
411	Garry Templeton	.06	.05	.02
412	Greg Cadaret	.05	.04	.02
413	Donnie Hill	.05	.04	.02
414	Wally Whitehurst	.05	.04	.02
415	Scott Sanderson	.06	.05	.02
416	Thomas Howard	.06	.05	.02
417	Neal Heaton	.05	.04	.02
418	Charlie Hough	.06	.05	.02
419	Jack Howell	.05	.04	.02
420	Greg Hibbard	.06	.05	.02
421	Carlos Quintana	.06	.05	.02
422	*Kim Batiste*(FC)	.10	.08	.04
423	Paul Molitor	.10	.08	.04
424	Ken Griffey, Jr.	.80	.60	.30
425	Phil Plantier	.35	.25	.14
426	*Denny Neagle*(FC)	.20	.15	.08
427	Von Hayes	.06	.05	.02
428	Shane Mack	.08	.06	.03
429	Darren Daulton	.06	.05	.02
430	Dwayne Henry	.05	.04	.02
431	Lance Parrish	.06	.05	.02
432	*Mike Humphreys*(FC)	.10	.08	.04
433	Tim Burke	.05	.04	.02
434	Bryan Harvey	.06	.05	.02
435	Pat Kelly	.15	.11	.06
436	Ozzie Guillen	.08	.06	.03
437	Bruce Hurst	.06	.03	.02
438	Sammy Sosa	.08	.06	.03
439	Dennis Rasmussen	.05	.04	.02
440	Ken Patterson	.05	.04	.02
441	Jay Buhner	.08	.06	.03
442	Pat Combs	.06	.05	.02
443	Wade Boggs	.15	.11	.06
444	George Brett	.15	.11	.06
445	Mo Vaughn	.35	.25	.12
446	Chuck Knoblauch	.20	.15	.08
447	Tom Candiotti	.06	.05	.02
448	Mark Portugal	.05	.04	.02
449	Mickey Morandini	.10	.08	.04
450	Duane Ward	.05	.04	.02
451	Otis Nixon	.05	.04	.02
452	Bob Welch	.08	.06	.03
453	*Rusty Meacham*(FC)	.10	.08	.04
454	*Keith Mitchell*	.20	.15	.08
455	Marquis Grissom	.10	.08	.04
456	Robin Yount	.20	.15	.08
457	*Harvey Pulliam*(FC)	.20	.15	.08
458	Jose DeLeon	.05	.04	.02
459	Mark Gubicza	.06	.05	.02
460	Darryl Hamilton	.06	.05	.02
461	Tom Browning	.08	.06	.03
462	Monty Fariss	.10	.08	.04
463	Jerome Walton	.10	.08	.04
464	Paul O'Neill	.08	.06	.03
465	Dean Palmer	.20	.15	.08
466	Travis Fryman	.20	.15	.08
467	John Smiley	.06	.05	.02
468	Lloyd Moseby	.05	.04	.02
469	*John Wehner*(FC)	.25	.20	.10
470	Skeeter Barnes(FC)	.06	.05	.02
471	Steve Chitren	.06	.05	.02
472	Kent Mercker	.06	.05	.02
473	Terry Steinbach	.06	.05	.02
474	Andres Galarraga	.08	.06	.03
475	Steve Avery	.20	.15	.08
476	Tom Gordon	.10	.08	.04
477	Cal Eldred(FC)	.20	.15	.08
478	Omar Olivares(FC)	.08	.06	.03
479	Julio Machado	.05	.04	.02
480	Bob Milacki	.05	.04	.02
481	Les Lancaster	.05	.04	.02
482	John Candelaria	.05	.04	.02
483	Brian Downing	.05	.04	.02
484	Roger McDowell	.05	.04	.02
485	Scott Scudder	.05	.04	.02
486	Zane Smith	.06	.05	.02
487	John Cerutti	.05	.04	.02
488	Steve Buechele	.06	.05	.02
489	Paul Gibson	.05	.04	.02
490	Curtis Wilkerson	.05	.04	.02
491	Marvin Freeman	.05	.04	.02
492	Tom Foley	.05	.04	.02

		MT	NR MT	EX
493	Juan Berenguer	.05	.04	.02
494	Ernest Riles	.05	.04	.02
495	Sid Bream	.06	.05	.02
496	Chuck Crim	.05	.04	.02
497	Mike Macfarlane	.05	.04	.02
498	Dale Sveum	.05	.04	.02
499	Storm Davis	.05	.04	.02
500	Checklist 401-500	.05	.04	.02
501	Jeff Reardon	.08	.06	.03
502	Shawn Abner	.05	.04	.02
503	Tony Fossas	.05	.04	.02
504	Cory Snyder	.05	.04	.02
505	Matt Young	.05	.04	.02
506	Allan Anderson	.05	.04	.02
507	Mark Lee	.05	.04	.02
508	Gene Nelson	.05	.04	.02
509	Mike Pagliarulo	.05	.04	.02
510	Rafael Belliard	.05	.04	.02
511	Jay Howell	.06	.05	.02
512	Bob Tewksbury	.05	.04	.02
513	Mike Morgan	.05	.04	.02
514	John Franco	.06	.05	.02
515	Kevin Gross	.05	.04	.02
516	Lou Whitaker	.08	.06	.03
517	Orlando Merced	.20	.15	.08
518	Todd Benzinger	.05	.04	.02
519	Gary Redus	.05	.04	.02
520	Walt Terrell	.05	.04	.02
521	Jack Clark	.08	.06	.03
522	Dave Parker	.10	.08	.04
523	Tim Naehring	.15	.11	.06
524	Mark Whiten	.15	.11	.06
525	Ellis Burks	.10	.08	.04
526	*Frank Castillo*	.20	.15	.08
527	Brian Harper	.06	.05	.02
528	Brook Jacoby	.06	.05	.02
529	Rick Sutcliffe	.06	.05	.02
530	Joe Klink	.05	.04	.02
531	Terry Bross	.05	.04	.02
532	Jose Offerman	.15	.11	.06
533	Todd Zeile	.15	.11	.06
534	Eric Karros	.25	.20	.10
535	*Anthony Young*	.40	.30	.15
536	Milt Cuyler	.10	.08	.04
537	Randy Tomlin	.08	.06	.03
538	*Scott Livingstone*	.20	.15	.08
539	Jim Eisenreich	.05	.04	.02
540	Don Slaught	.05	.04	.02
541	Scott Cooper(FC)	.20	.15	.08
542	Joe Grahe	.06	.05	.02
543	Tom Brunansky	.06	.05	.02
544	Eddie Zosky	.10	.08	.04
545	Roger Clemens	.15	.11	.06
546	David Justice	.30	.25	.12
547	Dave Stewart	.10	.08	.04
548	David West	.05	.04	.02
549	Dave Smith	.06	.05	.02
550	Dan Plesac	.06	.05	.02
551	Alex Fernandez	.20	.15	.08
552	Bernard Gilkey	.10	.08	.04
553	Jack McDowell	.10	.08	.04
554	Tino Martinez	.10	.08	.04
555	Bo Jackson	.50	.40	.20
556	Bernie Williams	.25	.20	.10
557	Mark Gardner	.06	.05	.02
558	Glenallen Hill	.08	.06	.03
559	Oil Can Boyd	.05	.04	.02
560	Chris James	.05	.04	.02
561	*Scott Servais*	.15	.11	.06
562	*Rey Sanchez*(FC)	.15	.11	.06
563	*Paul McClellan*(FC)	.15	.11	.06
564	*Andy Mota*	.15	.11	.06
565	Darren Lewis	.15	.11	.06
566	*Jose Melendez*(FC)	.15	.11	.06
567	Tommy Greene	.08	.06	.03
568	Rich Rodriguez	.06	.05	.02
569	*Heathcliff Slocumb*	.10	.08	.04
570	Joe Hesketh	.05	.04	.02
571	Carlton Fisk	.15	.11	.06
572	Erik Hanson	.10	.08	.04
573	Wilson Alvarez	.10	.08	.04
574	*Rheal Cormier*(FC)	.20	.15	.08
575	Tim Raines	.10	.08	.04
576	Bobby Witt	.06	.05	.02
577	Roberto Kelly	.10	.08	.04
578	Kevin Brown	.06	.05	.02
579	Chris Nabholz	.06	.05	.02
580	Jesse Orosco	.05	.04	.02
581	Jeff Brantley	.06	.05	.02
582	Rafael Ramirez	.05	.04	.02
583	Kelly Downs	.05	.04	.02

		MT	NR MT	EX
584	Mike Simms	.10	.08	.04
585	*Mike Remlinger*	.10	.08	.04
586	Dave Hollins	.08	.06	.03
587	Larry Andersen	.05	.04	.02
588	Mike Gardiner	.08	.06	.03
589	Craig Lefferts	.05	.04	.02
590	Paul Assenmacher	.05	.04	.02
591	Bryn Smith	.05	.04	.02
592	Donn Pall	.05	.04	.02
593	Mike Jackson	.05	.04	.02
594	Scott Radinsky	.05	.04	.02
595	Brian Holman	.06	.05	.02
596	Geronimo Pena	.08	.06	.03
597	Mike Jeffcoat	.05	.04	.02
598	Carlos Martinez	.05	.04	.02
599	Geno Petralli	.05	.04	.02
600	Checklist 501-600	.05	.04	.02
601	Jerry Don Gleaton	.05	.04	.02
602	Adam Peterson	.05	.04	.02
603	Craig Grebeck	.05	.04	.02
604	Mark Guthrie	.05	.04	.02
605	Frank Tanana	.05	.04	.02
606	Hensley Meulens	.08	.06	.03
607	Mark Davis	.05	.04	.02
608	Eric Plunk	.05	.04	.02
609	Mark Williamson	.05	.04	.02
610	Lee Guetterman	.05	.04	.02
611	Bobby Rose	.05	.04	.02
612	Bill Wegman	.06	.05	.02
613	Mike Hartley	.05	.04	.02
614	*Chris Beasley*(FC)	.10	.08	.04
615	Chris Bosio	.05	.04	.02
616	Henry Cotto	.05	.04	.02
617	*Chico Walker*(FC)	.10	.08	.04
618	Russ Swan	.05	.04	.02
619	Bob Walk	.05	.04	.02
620	Billy Swift	.05	.04	.02
621	*Warren Newson*	.15	.11	.06
622	Steve Bedrosian	.05	.04	.02
623	*Ricky Bones*(FC)	.15	.11	.06
624	Kevin Tapani	.10	.08	.04
625	*Juan Guzman*(FC)	.60	.45	.25
626	*Jeff Johnson*(FC)	.15	.11	.06
627	Jeff Montgomery	.06	.05	.02
628	Ken Hill	.06	.05	.02
629	Gary Thurman	.05	.04	.02
630	Steve Howe	.06	.05	.02
631	Jose DeJesus	.06	.05	.02
632	Bert Blyleven	.06	.05	.02
633	Jaime Navarro	.06	.05	.02
634	Lee Stevens	.08	.06	.03
635	Pete Harnisch	.08	.06	.03
636	Bill Landrum	.05	.04	.02
637	Rich DeLucia	.06	.05	.02
638	Luis Salazar	.05	.04	.02
639	Rob Murphy	.05	.04	.02
640	Diamond Skills Checklist	.05	.04	.02
641	Roger Clemens (DS)	.25	.20	.10
642	Jim Abbott (DS)	.15	.11	.06
643	Travis Fryman (DS)	.25	.20	.10
644	Jesse Barfield (DS)	.10	.08	.04
645	Cal Ripken, Jr. (DS)	.25	.20	.10
646	Wade Boggs (DS)	.20	.15	.08
647	Cecil Fielder (DS)	.20	.15	.08
648	Rickey Henderson (DS)	.25	.20	.10
649	Jose Canseco (DS)	.25	.20	.10
650	Ken Griffey, Jr. (DS)	.50	.40	.20
651	Kenny Rogers	.05	.04	.02
652	*Luis Mercedes*(FC)	.35	.25	.14
653	Mike Stanton	.06	.05	.02
654	Glenn Davis	.10	.08	.04
655	Nolan Ryan	.30	.25	.12
656	Reggie Jefferson	.20	.15	.08
657	*Javier Ortiz*(FC)	.15	.11	.06
658	Greg A. Harris	.05	.04	.02
659	Mariano Duncan	.06	.05	.02
660	Jeff Shaw	.05	.04	.02
661	Mike Moore	.06	.05	.02
662	*Chris Haney*	.20	.15	.08
663	*Joe Slusarski*	.20	.15	.08
664	*Wayne Housie*(FC)	.20	.15	.08
665	Carlos Garcia(FC)	.08	.06	.03
666	Bob Ojeda	.05	.04	.02
667	*Bryan Hickerson*(FC)	.20	.15	.08
668	Tim Belcher	.06	.05	.02
669	Ron Darling	.06	.05	.02
670	Rex Hudler	.05	.04	.02
671	Sid Fernandez	.08	.06	.03
672	*Chito Martinez*	.50	.40	.20
673	*Pete Schourek*	.15	.11	.06
674	*Armando Renoso*(FC)	.15	.11	.06
675	Mike Mussina	.25	.20	.10
676	Kevin Morton(FC)	.15	.11	.06
677	Norm Charlton	.06	.05	.02
678	Danny Darwin	.05	.04	.02
679	Eric King	.05	.04	.02
680	Ted Power	.05	.04	.02
681	Barry Jones	.05	.04	.02
682	Carney Lansford	.08	.06	.03
683	Mel Rojas	.06	.05	.02
684	Rick Honeycutt	.05	.04	.02
685	*Jeff Fassero*(FC)	.15	.11	.06
686	Cris Carpenter	.06	.05	.02
687	Tim Crews	.05	.04	.02
688	Scott Terry	.05	.04	.02
689	Chris Gwynn	.05	.04	.02
690	Gerald Perry	.05	.04	.02
691	John Barfield	.05	.04	.02
692	Bob Melvin	.05	.04	.02
693	Juan Agosto	.05	.04	.02
694	Alejandro Pena	.06	.05	.02
695	Jeff Russell	.06	.05	.02
696	Carmelo Martinez	.05	.04	.02
697	Bud Black	.05	.04	.02
698	Dave Otto	.05	.04	.02
699	Billy Hatcher	.05	.04	.02
700	Checklist 601-700	.05	.04	.02

V

1989 Very Fine Pirates

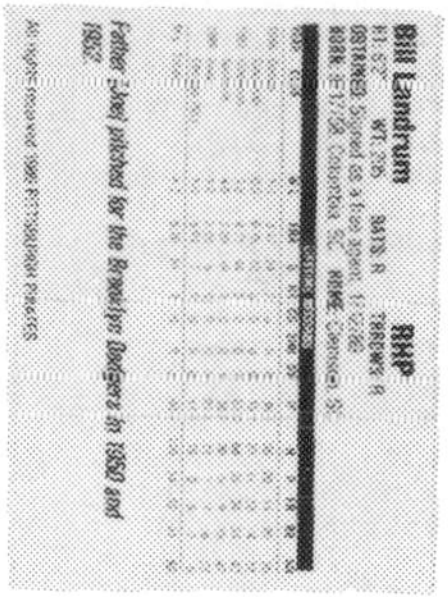

This 30-card set Pittsburgh Pirates team set was sponsored by Veryfine fruit juices, and was issued in the form of two uncut, perforated panels, each containing 15 standard-size cards. A third panel featured color action photographs. The panels were distributed in a stadium promotion to fans attending the April 23 Pirates game at Three Rivers Stadium. The cards display the Pirates traditional black and gold color scheme, and include the player's names and uniform number along the bottom. The "Veryfine" logo appears in the lower right corner. The backs include player data and complete stats.

		MT	NR MT	EX
Complete 3-Panel Set:		20.00	15.00	8.00
Complete Singles Card Set:		12.00	9.00	4.75
Common Player:		.20	.15	.08
0	Junior Ortiz	.20	.15	.08
2	Gary Redus	.30	.25	.12
3	Jay Bell	.30	.25	.12
5	Sid Bream	.30	.25	.12
6	Rafael Belliard	.25	.20	.10
10	Jim Leyland	.30	.25	.12
11	Glenn Wilson	.30	.25	.12
12	Mike La Valliere	.30	.25	.12
13	Jose Lind	.40	.30	.15
14	Ken Oberkfell	.25	.20	.10
15	Doug Drabek	.70	.50	.30
16	Bob Kipper	.20	.15	.08

		MT	NR MT	EX
17	Bob Walk	.25	.20	.10
18	Andy Van Slyke	1.00	.70	.40
23	R.J. Reynolds	.30	.25	.12
24	Barry Bonds	1.50	1.25	.60
25	Bobby Bonilla	1.50	1.25	.60
26	Neal Heaton	.30	.25	.12
30	Benny Distefano	.30	.25	.12
35	Jim Gott	.35	.25	.14
41	Mike Dunne	.30	.25	.12
43	Bill Landrum	.40	.30	.15
44	John Cangelosi	.25	.20	.10
49	Jeff Robinson	.35	.25	.12
52	Dorn Taylor	.30	.25	.12
54	Brian Fisher	.25	.20	.10
57	John Smiley	.50	.40	.20
---	Ray Miller, Tommy Sandt (31-37)	.20	.15	.08
---	Bruce Kimm (32-36)	.20	.15	.08
---	Gene Lamont (32-36)	.20	.15	.08
---	Milt May (39-45)	.20	.15	.08
---	Rich Donnelly (39-45)	.20	.15	.08

W

1950 W576
Callahan Hall Of Fame

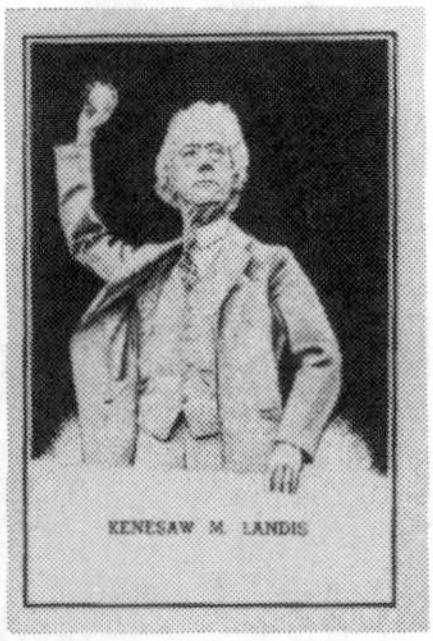

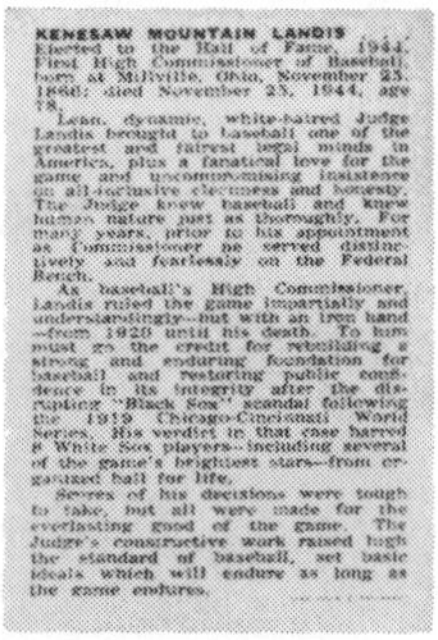

KENESAW MOUNTAIN LANDIS
Elected to the Hall of Fame, 1944. First High Commissioner of Baseball; born at Millville, Ohio, November 20, 1866; died November 25, 1944, age 78.

Lean, dynamic, white-haired Judge Landis brought to baseball one of the greatest and fairest legal minds in America, plus a fanatical love for the game and uncompromising insistence on all-inclusive cleanness and honesty. The Judge knew baseball and knew human nature just as thoroughly. For many years, prior to his appointment as Commissioner he served distinctively and fearlessly on the Federal Bench.

As baseball's High Commissioner, Landis ruled the game impartially and understandingly—but with an iron hand—from 1920 until his death. To him must go the credit for rebuilding a strong and enduring foundation for baseball and restoring public confidence in its integrity after the disrupting "Black Sox" scandal following the 1919 Chicago-Cincinnati World Series. His verdict in that case barred 8 White Sox players—including several of the game's brightest stars—from organized ball for life.

Scores of his decisions were tough to take, but all were made for the everlasting good of the game. The Judge's constructive work raised high the standard of baseball, set basic ideals which will endure as long as the game endures.

These cards, which feature drawings of Hall of Famers, were produced from 1950 through 1956 and sold by the Baseball Hall of Fame in Cooperstown. The cards measure 1-3/4" by 2-1/2" and include a detailed player biography on the back. When introduced in 1950 the set included all members of the Hall of Fame up to that time, and then new cards were added each year as more players were elected. Therefore, cards of players appearing in all previous editions are lesser in value than those players who appeared in just one or two years. When the set was discontinued in 1956 it consisted of 82 cards, which is now considered a complete set. The cards are not numbered and are listed here alphabetically.

		NR MT	EX	VG
Complete Set:		600.00	300.00	180.00
Common Player:		3.00	1.50	.90
(1)	Grover Alexander	6.00	3.00	1.75
(2)	"Cap" Anson	6.00	3.00	1.75
(3)	J. Franklin "Home Run" Baker	7.00	3.50	2.00
(4)	Edward G. Barrow	7.00	3.50	2.00
(5a)	Charles "Chief" Bender (different biography)	7.00	3.50	2.00
(5b)	Charles "Chief" Bender (different biography)	7.00	3.50	2.00
(6)	Roger Bresnahan	3.00	1.50	.90
(7)	Dan Brouthers	3.00	1.50	.90
(8)	Mordecai Brown	3.00	1.50	.90
(9)	Morgan G. Bulkeley	3.00	1.50	.90
(10)	Jesse Burkett	3.00	1.50	.90
(11)	Alexander Cartwright	3.00	1.50	.90
(12)	Henry Chadwick	3.00	1.50	.90
(13)	Frank Chance	3.00	1.50	.90
(14)	Albert B. Chandler	30.00	15.00	9.00
(15)	Jack Chesbro	3.00	1.50	.90
(16)	Fred Clarke	3.00	1.50	.90
(17)	Ty Cobb	50.00	25.00	15.00
(18a)	Mickey Cochran (name incorrect)	50.00	25.00	15.00
(18b)	Mickey Cochrane (name correct)	6.00	3.00	1.75
(19a)	Eddie Collins (different biography)	6.00	3.00	1.75
(19b)	Eddie Collins (different biography)	6.00	3.00	1.75
(20)	Jimmie Collins	3.00	1.50	.90
(21)	Charles A. Comiskey	3.00	1.50	.90
(22)	Tom Connolly	7.00	3.50	2.00
(23)	"Candy" Cummings	3.00	1.50	.90
(24)	Dizzy Dean	30.00	15.00	9.00
(25)	Ed Delahanty	3.00	1.50	.90
(26a)	Bill Dickey (different biography)	30.00	15.00	9.00
(26b)	Bill Dickey (different biography)	30.00	15.00	9.00
(27)	Joe DiMaggio	100.00	50.00	30.00
(28)	Hugh Duffy	3.00	1.50	.90
(29)	Johnny Evers	3.00	1.50	.90
(30)	Buck Ewing	3.00	1.50	.90
(31)	Jimmie Foxx	7.00	3.50	2.00
(32)	Frank Frisch	3.00	1.50	.90
(33)	Lou Gehrig	50.00	25.00	15.00
(34)	Charles Gehringer	3.00	1.50	.90
(35)	Clark Griffith	3.00	1.50	.90
(36)	Lefty Grove	6.00	3.00	1.75
(37)	Leo "Gabby" Hartnett	7.00	3.50	2.00
(38)	Harry Heilmann	3.00	1.50	.90
(39)	Rogers Hornsby	7.00	3.50	2.00
(40)	Carl Hubbell	6.00	3.00	1.75
(41)	Hughey Jennings	3.00	1.50	.90
(42)	Ban Johnson	3.00	1.50	.90
(43)	Walter Johnson	7.00	3.50	2.00
(44)	Willie Keeler	3.00	1.50	.90
(45)	Mike Kelly	3.00	1.50	.90
(46)	Bill Klem	7.00	3.50	2.00
(47)	Napoleon Lajoie	3.00	1.50	.90
(48)	Kenesaw M. Landis	3.00	1.50	.90
(49)	Ted Lyons	7.00	3.50	2.00
(50)	Connie Mack	7.00	3.50	2.00
(51)	Walter Maranville	7.00	3.50	2.00
(52)	Christy Mathewson	7.00	3.50	2.00
(53)	Tommy McCarthy	3.00	1.50	.90
(54)	Joe McGinnity	3.00	1.50	.90
(55)	John McGraw	6.00	3.00	1.75
(56)	Charles Nichols	3.00	1.50	.90
(57)	Jim O'Rourke	3.00	1.50	.90
(58)	Mel Ott	6.00	3.00	1.75
(59)	Herb Pennock	3.00	1.50	.90
(60)	Eddie Plank	3.00	1.50	.90
(61)	Charles Radbourne	3.00	1.50	.90
(62)	Wilbert Robinson	3.00	1.50	.90
(63)	Babe Ruth	100.00	50.00	30.00
(64)	Ray "Cracker" Schalk	7.00	3.50	2.00
(65)	Al Simmons	7.00	3.50	2.00
(66a)	George Sisler (different biography)	3.00	1.50	.90
(66b)	George Sisler (different biography)	3.00	1.50	.90
(67)	A. G. Spalding	3.00	1.50	.90
(68)	Tris Speaker	3.00	1.50	.90
(69)	Bill Terry	7.00	3.50	2.00
(70)	Joe Tinker	3.00	1.50	.90
(71)	"Pie" Traynor	3.00	1.50	.90
(72)	Clarence A. "Dizzy" Vance	7.00	3.50	2.00
(73)	Rube Waddell	3.00	1.50	.90
(74)	Hans Wagner	30.00	15.00	9.00
(75)	Bobby Wallace	7.00	3.50	2.00
(76)	Ed Walsh	3.00	1.50	.90
(77)	Paul Waner	6.00	3.00	1.75
(78)	George Wright	3.00	1.50	.90
(79)	Harry Wright	7.00	3.50	2.00
(80)	Cy Young	7.00	3.50	2.00
---a)	Museum Exterior View (different biography)	7.00	3.50	2.00
---b)	Museum Exterior View (different biography)	7.00	3.50	2.00
---a)	Museum Interior View (different biography)	7.00	3.50	2.00
---b)	Museum Interior View (different biography)	7.00	3.50	2.00

NOTE: A card number in parentheses ( ) indicates the set is unnumbered.

1985 Wendy's Tigers

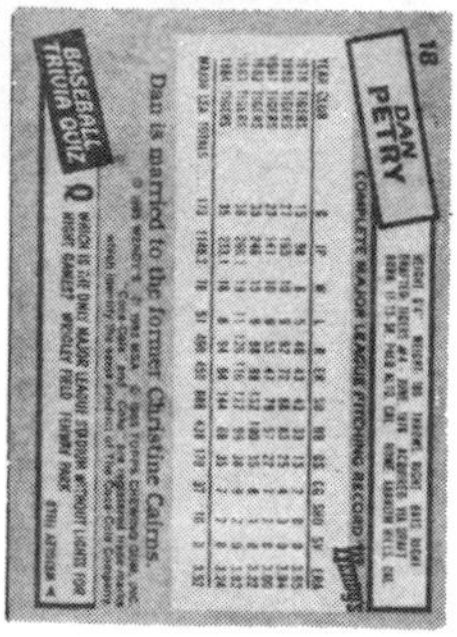

This 22-card set of cards measuring 2-1/2" by 3-1/2", which carry both Wendy's Hamburgers and Coca-Cola logos was produced by Topps. The cards feature a color photo with the player's team, name and position underneath the picture and the Wendy's logo in the lower left and Coke logo in the upper right. Backs are identical to 1985 Topps cards except they have different card numbers and are done in a red and black color scheme. Cards were distributed three to a pack along with a "Header" checklist in a cellophane package at selected Wendy's outlets in Michigan only.

		MT	NR MT	EX
Complete Set:		8.00	6.00	3.25
Common Player:		.15	.11	.06
1	Sparky Anderson	.30	.25	.12
2	Doug Bair	.15	.11	.06
3	Juan Berenguer	.15	.11	.06
4	Dave Bergman	.15	.11	.06
5	Tom Brookens	.15	.11	.06
6	Marty Castillo	.15	.11	.06
7	Darrell Evans	.40	.30	.15
8	Barbaro Garbey	.15	.11	.06
9	Kirk Gibson	.60	.45	.25
10	Johnny Grubb	.15	.11	.06
11	Willie Hernandez	.25	.20	.10
12	Larry Herndon	.15	.11	.06
13	Rusty Kuntz	.15	.11	.06
14	Chet Lemon	.25	.20	.10
15	Aurelio Lopez	.15	.11	.06
16	Jack Morris	1.00	.70	.40
17	Lance Parrish	.80	.60	.30
18	Dan Petry	.25	.20	.10
19	Bill Scherrer	.15	.11	.06
20	Alan Trammell	1.00	.70	.40
21	Lou Whitaker	.80	.60	.30
22	Milt Wilcox	.15	.11	.06

1954 Wilson Franks

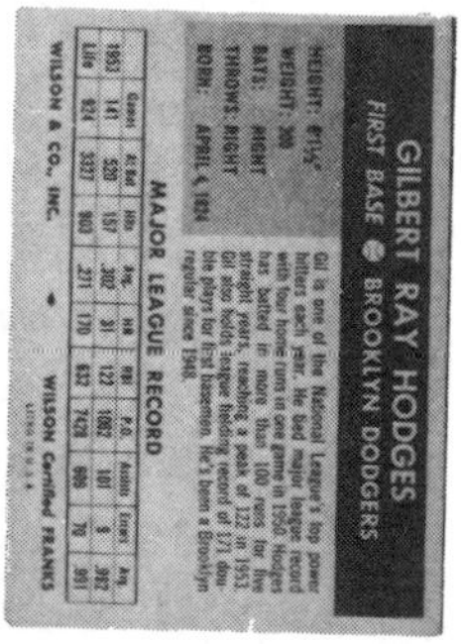

The 2-5/8" by 3-3/4" cards are among the most popular and difficult to find baseball card sets issued with hot dogs during the 1950s. The cards feature color-added photos on the front where the player's name, team and position appear at the top. The front also has a facsimile autograph and a color picture of a package of Wilson's frankfurters. The card backs feature personal information, a short career summary and 1953 and career statistics. The 20-card set includes players from a number of teams and was distributed nationally in the frankfurter packages. The problem with such distribution is that the cards are very tough to find without grease stains from the hot dogs.

		NR MT	EX	VG
Complete Set:		6500.00	3250.00	1950.
Common Player:		175.00	87.00	52.00
(1)	Roy Campanella	750.00	375.00	225.00
(2)	Del Ennis	175.00	87.00	52.00
(3)	Carl Erskine	300.00	150.00	90.00
(4)	Ferris Fain	175.00	87.00	52.00
(5)	Bob Feller	600.00	300.00	180.00
(6)	Nelson Fox	300.00	150.00	90.00
(7)	Johnny Groth	175.00	87.00	52.00
(8)	Stan Hack	175.00	87.00	52.00
(9)	Gil Hodges	500.00	250.00	150.00
(10)	Ray Jablonski	175.00	87.00	52.00
(11)	Harvey Kuenn	300.00	150.00	90.00
(12)	Roy McMillan	175.00	87.00	52.00
(13)	Andy Pafko	175.00	87.00	52.00
(14)	Paul Richards	175.00	87.00	52.00
(15)	Hank Sauer	175.00	87.00	52.00
(16)	Red Schoendienst	300.00	150.00	90.00
(17)	Enos Slaughter	450.00	225.00	135.00
(18)	Vern Stephens	175.00	87.00	52.00
(19)	Sammy White	175.00	87.00	52.00
(20)	Ted Williams	3000.00	1500.00	900.00

1988 Woolworth

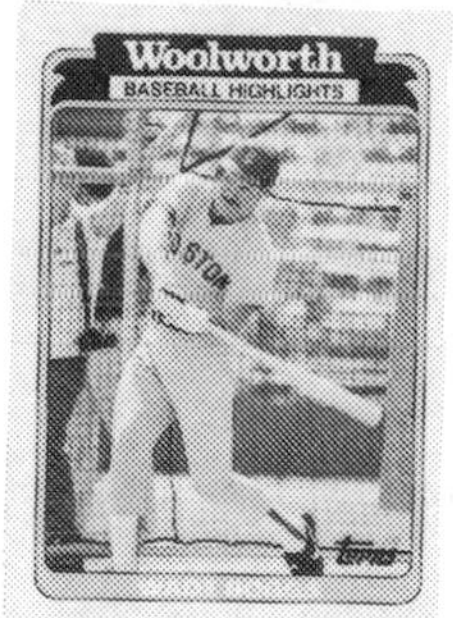

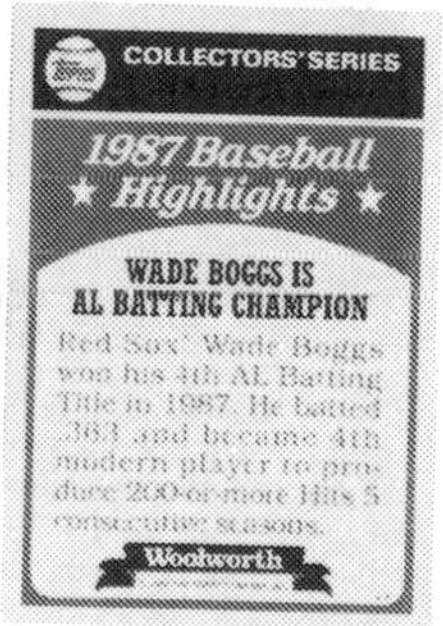

This 33-card boxed set was produced by Topps for exclusive distribution at Woolworth stores. The set includes 18 individual player cards and 15 World Series game action photo cards. World Series cards include two for each game of the Series, plus a card of 1987 Series MVP Frank Viola. Card front carry a Woolworth's Baseball Highlights heading on a red and yellow banner above the blue-bordered super glossy player photo. A white-lettered caption beneath the photo consists of either the player's name or a World Series game notation. Card backs are red, white and blue and contain the Topps logo, card number and "Collector's Series" label above a "1987 Baseball Highlights" logo and a brief description of the photo on the front.

		MT	NR MT	EX
Complete Set:		4.00	3.00	1.50
Common Player:		.09	.07	.04
1	Don Baylor	.12	.09	.05
2	Vince Coleman	.15	.11	.06
3	Darrell Evans	.12	.09	.05
4	Don Mattingly	.90	.70	.35
5	Eddie Murray	.30	.25	.12
6	Nolan Ryan	.30	.25	.12

		MT	NR MT	EX
7	Mike Schmidt	.35	.25	.14
8	Andre Dawson	.20	.15	.08
9	George Bell	.25	.20	.10
10	Steve Bedrosian	.12	.09	.05
11	Roger Clemens	.50	.40	.20
12	Tony Gwynn	.35	.25	.14
13	Wade Boggs	.40	.30	.15
14	Benny Santiago	.35	.25	.14
15	Mark McGwire	.40	.30	.15
16	Dave Righetti	.15	.11	.06
17	Jeffrey Leonard	.09	.07	.04
18	Gary Gaetti	.12	.09	.05
19	World Series Game #1 (Frank Viola)	.12	.09	.05
20	World Series Game #1 (Dan Gladden)	.09	.07	.04
21	World Series Game #2 (Bert Blyleven)	.12	.09	.05
22	World Series Game #2 (Gary Gaetti)	.12	.09	.05
23	World Series Game #3 (John Tudor)	.12	.09	.05
24	World Series Game #3 (Todd Worrell)	.12	.09	.05
25	World Series Game #4 (Tom Lawless)	.09	.07	.04
26	World Series Game #4 (Willie McGee)	.12	.09	.05
27	World Series Game #5 (Danny Cox)	.09	.07	.04
28	World Series Game #5 (Curt Ford)	.09	.07	.04
29	World Series Game #6 (Don Baylor)	.12	.09	.05
30	World Series Game #6 (Kent Hrbek)	.15	.11	.06
31	World Series Game #7 (Kirby Puckett)	.25	.20	.10
32	World Series Game #7 (Greg Gagne)	.09	.07	.04
33	World Series MVP (Frank Viola)	.12	.09	.05

1989 Woolworth

This 33-card set was produced by Topps for the Woolworth store chain and was sold in a special box with a checklist on the back. The glossy-coated cards commemorate the most memorable moments in baseball from the the 1988 season, and include the logo "Woolworth's Baseball Highlights" along the top. The player photos are framed in red, yellow and white and feature the player's name beneath the photo. The backs include a description of the various highlights. Orel Hershiser is pictured on four of the cards, and Jose Canseco appears on two.

		MT	NR MT	EX
Complete Set:		5.00	3.75	2.00
Common Player:		.09	.07	.04
1	Jose Canseco	.70	.50	.30
2	Kirk Gibson	.15	.11	.06
3	Frank Viola	.15	.11	.06
4	Orel Hershiser	.15	.11	.06
5	Walt Weiss	.20	.15	.11
6	Chris Sabo	.20	.15	.11
7	George Bell	.15	.11	.06
8	Wade Boggs	.50	.40	.20
9	Tom Browning	.12	.09	.05
10	Gary Carter	.12	.09	.05
11	Andre Dawson	.15	.11	.06
12	John Franco	.09	.07	.04
13	Randy Johnson	.15	.11	.06
14	Doug Jones	.09	.07	.04
15	Kevin McReynolds	.20	.15	.11
16	Gene Nelson	.09	.07	.04
17	Jeff Reardon	.09	.07	.04
18	Pat Tabler	.09	.07	.04
19	Tim Belcher	.25	.20	.10
20	Dennis Eckersley	.15	.11	.06
21	Orel Hershiser	.20	.15	.08
22	Gregg Jefferies	.50	.40	.20
23	Jose Canseco	.70	.50	.30
24	Kirk Gibson	.20	.15	.08
25	Orel Hershiser	.20	.15	.08
26	Mike Marshall	.09	.07	.04
27	Mark McGwire	.50	.40	.20
28	Rick Honeycutt	.09	.07	.04
29	Tim Belcher	.20	.15	.08
30	Jay Howell	.12	.09	.05
31	Mickey Hatcher	.09	.07	.04
32	Mike Davis	.09	.07	.04
33	Orel Hershiser	.15	.11	.06

1990 Woolworth

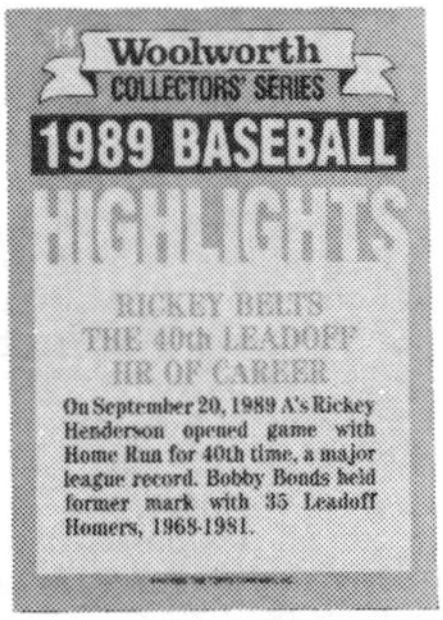

This 33-card set highlights the great baseball moments of 1989. The cards are styled like past Woolworth sets. The set features award winners and regular and post-season highlights.

		MT	NR MT	EX
Complete Set:		3.00	2.25	1.25
Common Player:		.06	.05	.02
1	Robin Yount	.20	.15	.08
2	Kevin Mitchell	.15	.11	.06
3	Bret Saberhagen	.10	.08	.04
4	Mark Davis	.06	.05	.02
5	Gregg Olson	.10	.08	.04
6	Jerome Walton	.10	.08	.04
7	Bert Blyleven	.06	.05	.02
8	Wade Boggs	.25	.20	.10
9	George Brett	.20	.15	.08
10	Vince Coleman	.10	.08	.04
11	Andre Dawson	.20	.15	.08
12	Dwight Evans	.10	.08	.04
13	Carlton Fisk	.20	.15	.08
14	Rickey Henderson	.40	.30	.15
15	Dale Murphy	.20	.15	.08
16	Eddie Murray	.20	.15	.08
17	Jeff Reardon	.08	.06	.03
18	Rick Reuschel	.06	.05	.02
19	Cal Ripken, Jr.	.25	.20	.10
20	Nolan Ryan	.40	.30	.15
21	Ryne Sandberg	.25	.20	.10
22	Robin Yount	.20	.15	.08
23	Rickey Henderson	.40	.30	.15
24	Will Clark	.40	.30	.15
25	Dave Stewart	.10	.08	.04
26	Walt Weiss	.08	.06	.03
27	Mike Moore	.06	.05	.02
28	Terry Steinbach	.08	.06	.03
29	Dave Henderson	.08	.06	.03
30	Matt Williams	.20	.15	.08

		MT	NR MT	EX
31	Rickey Henderson	.40	.30	.15
32	Kevin Mitchell	.15	.11	.06
33	Dave Stewart	.10	.08	.04

Z

1982 Zellers Expos

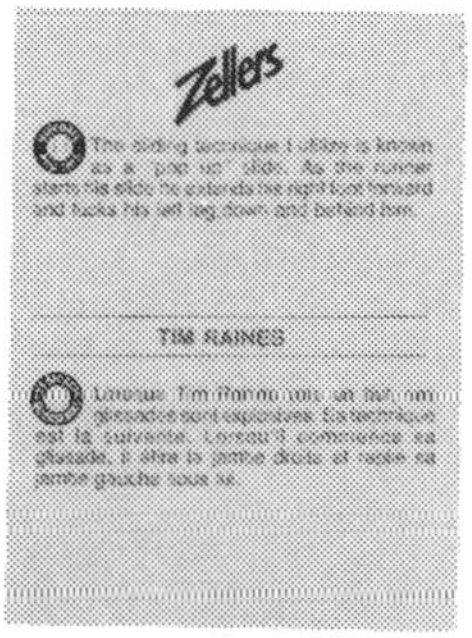

Produced and distributed by the Zellers department stores in Canada, this 60-card set was produced in the form of 20 three-card panels. The cards feature a photo of the player surrounded by rings and a yellow background. A red "Zellers" is above the photo and on either side of it are the words "Baseball Pro Tips" in English on the left and in French on the right. The player's name and the title of the playing tip are under the photo. Backs have the playing tip in both languages. Single cards measure 2-1/2" by 3-1/2" while the whole panel is 7-1/2" by 3-1/2". Although a number of stars are depicted, this set is not terribly popular as collectors do not generally like the playing tips idea. Total panels are worth more than separated cards.

		MT	NR MT	EX
	Complete Set:	12.00	9.00	4.75
	Common Player:	.40	.30	.15
1	Gary Carter (Catching Position)	1.00	.70	.40
2	Steve Rogers (Pitching Stance)	.50	.40	.20
3	Tim Raines (Sliding)	1.00	.70	.40
4	Andre Dawson (Batting Stance)	1.00	.70	.40
5	Terry Francona (Contact Hitting)	.40	.30	.15
6	Gary Carter (Fielding Pop Fouls)	1.00	.70	.40
7	Warren Cromartie (Fielding at First Base)	.40	.30	.15
8	Chris Speier (Fielding at Shortstop)	.40	.30	.15
9	Billy DeMars (Signals)	.40	.30	.15
10	Andre Dawson (Batting Stroke)	1.00	.70	.40
11	Terry Francona (Outfield Throws)	.40	.30	.15
12	Woodie Fryman (Holding the Runner-Left Handed)	.40	.30	.15
13	Gary Carter (Fielding Low Balls)	1.00	.70	.40
14	Andre Dawson (Playing Centerfield)	1.00	.70	.40
15	Bill Gullickson (The Slurve)	.50	.40	.20
16	Gary Carter (Catching Stance)	1.00	.70	.40
17	Scott Sanderson (Fielding as a Pitcher)	.40	.30	.15
18	Warren Cromartie (Handling Bad Throws)	.40	.30	.15
19	Gary Carter (Hitting Stride)	1.00	.70	.40
20	Ray Burris (Holding the Runner-Right Handed)	.40	.30	.15

Remember: All values quoted in this guide reflect the retail price of a card — the price a collector can expect to pay when buying a card from a dealer. The wholesale price — that which a collector can expect to receive from a dealer when selling a card — will be significantly lower, depending on desirability and condition of the particular card or cards.

Card Grading Guide

The following grading guide was originally formulated by *Baseball Cards* magazine and *Sports Collectors Digest* in 1981, and has been continually refined since that time to keep pace with actual market conditions. The staff of Krause Publications is eager to work toward the development of a standardized system of card grading that will be consistent with the realities of the hobby marketplace.

Mint (MT): A perfect card. Well-centered, with equal borders. Four sharp, square corners. No creases, edge dents, surface scratches, paper flaws, loss of luster, yellowing or fading, regardless of age. No imperfectly printed card — out of register, badly cut or ink flawed — or card stained by contact with gum, wax or other substances can be considered Mint, even if new out of the pack.

Near Mint (NM): A nearly perfect card. At first glance, a Near Mint card appears perfect. Upon closer examination, however, a minor flaw will be discovered. On well-centered cards, three of the four corners must be perfectly sharp. A slightly off-center card would also fit this grade, if otherwise perfect.

Excellent (EX): Corners are still fairly sharp with only moderate wear. Borders may be off-center. No creases. Minor gum, wax or product stains, front or back. Surfaces may show some loss of luster.

Very Good (VG): Shows obvious handling. Corners rounded and/or perhaps showing minor creases. Other minor creases may be visible. Surfaces may exhibit loss of luster, but all printing is intact. May show considerable gum, wax or other packaging stains. No major creases, tape marks or extraneous markings or writing. Card exhibits honest wear, but no damage.

Good (G): A well-worn card with no intentional damage or abuse. May have major or multiple creases. Corners rounded well into borders.

In addition to these widely-used grading terms, collectors will often encounter intermediate grades such as VG-EX (Very Good to Excellent), EX-MT (Excellent to Mint) or NM-MT (Near Mint to Mint). Persons who describe a card with such grades are usually trying to convey that the card has all the characteristics of the lower grade, with enough of those of the higher grade to merit mention. Such cards are usually priced at a point midway between the two grades.

1958 Bell Brand Dodgers

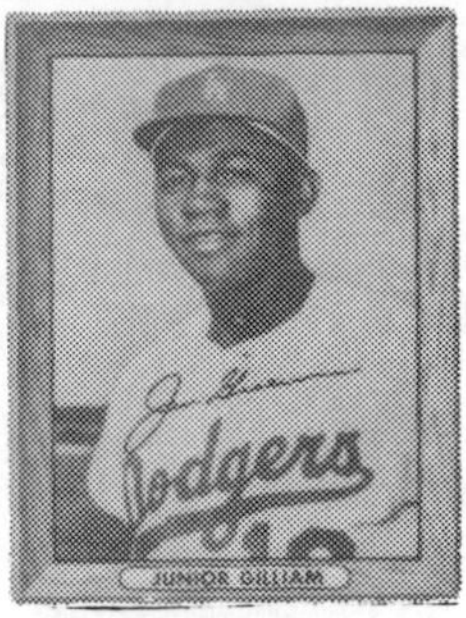

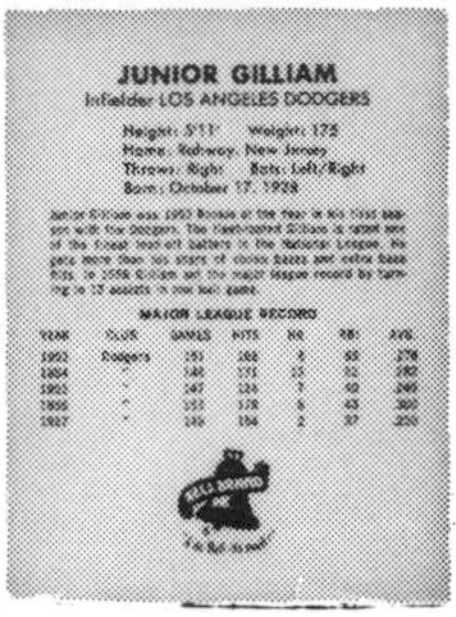

Celebrating the Dodgers first year in Los Angeles, Bell Brand inserted 10 different unnumbered cards in bags of potato chips and corn chips. The 3" by 4" cards have a sepia-colored photo inside a ¼" green woodgrain border. The backs have stats, biographies and a Bell Brand logo. Roy Campanella is in the set, despite a career-ending car wreck that prevented him from ever playing in Los Angeles.

		NR MT	EX	VG
Complete Set:		1000.00	500.00	300.00
Common Player:		35.00	17.50	10.50
1	Roy Campanella	125.00	56.00	35.00
2	Gino Cimoli	100.00	50.00	30.00
6	Sandy Koufax	125.00	56.00	35.00
7	Johnny Podres	100.00	50.00	30.00
9	Duke Snider	250.00	125.00	75.00

1960 Bell Brand Dodgers

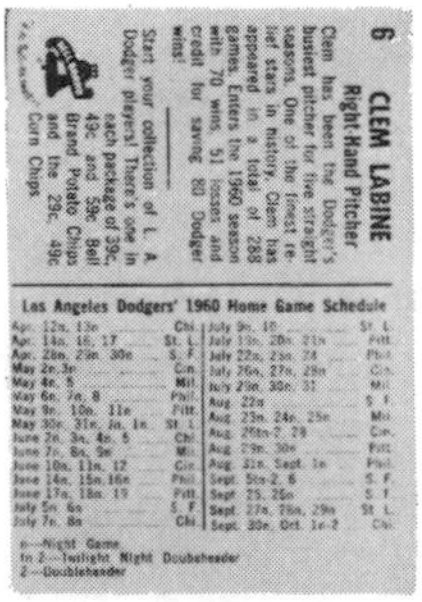

Bell Brand's 1960 cards, 2½" by 3½", feature beautiful, colored photos. The backs have a short player biography, the team's 1960 home schedule, and the Bell Brand logo. Twenty numbered cards were inserted in various size bags of potato chips and corn chips. Although sealed in cellophane, the cards were still subject to grease stains. Cards # 6, 12 and 18 are the scarcest in the set.

		NR MT	EX	VG
Complete Set:		800.00	400.00	250.00
Common Player:		15.00	7.50	4.50
2	Duke Snider	70.00	35.00	21.00
6	Clem Labine	90.00	45.00	27.00
9	Sandy Koufax	110.00	55.00	33.00
12	John Klippstein	90.00	45.00	27.00
18	Walter Alston	150.00	75.00	38.00

1961 Bell Brand Dodgers

The 1961 set is identical in format to 1960, but printed on thinner stock. Cards can be distinguished from the 1960 set by the 1961 schedule on the backs. The 2-7/16" by 3½" cards are numbered by the player's uniform number. Twenty different cards were inserted into various size potato chip and corn chip packages, each card being sealed in a cellophane wrapper.

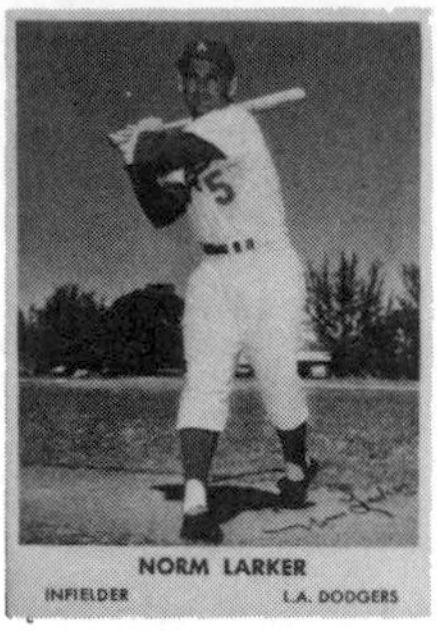

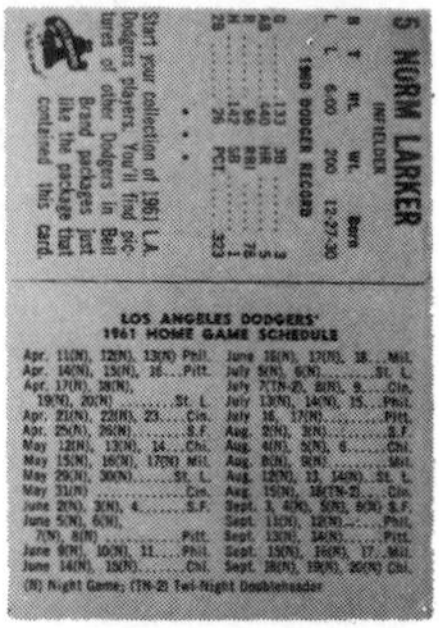

		NR MT	EX	VG
Complete Set:		400.00	200.00	125.00
Common Player:		12.00	6.00	3.50
4	Duke Snider	50.00	30.00	15.00
14	Gil Hodges	25.00	12.50	7.50
24	Walter Alston	25.00	12.50	7.50
30	Maury Wills	25.00	12.50	7.50
32	Sandy Koufax	100.00	50.00	30.00

1962 Bell Brand Dodgers

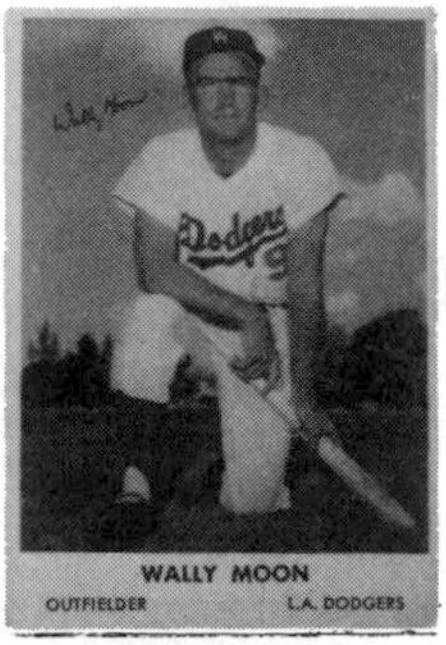

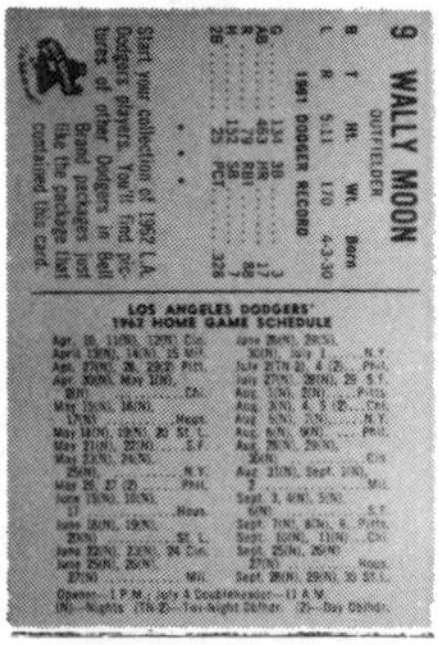

The 1962 set is identical in style to the previous two years but cards can be distinguished by the 1962 Dodgers schedule on the back. The set has 20 cards, each 2-7/16" by 3½" and numbered by the player's uniform number. Printed on glossy stock, the 1962 set was less susceptible to grease stains.

		NR MT	EX	VG
Complerte Set:		400.00	200.00	125.00
Common Player:		12.00	6.00	3.50
4	Duke Snider	50.00	30.00	15.00
24	Walter Alston	25.00	12.50	7.50
30	Maury Wills	25.00	12.50	7.50
32	Sandy Koufax	100.00	50.00	30.00
53	Don Drysdale	35.00	17.50	10.50

1987 French/Bray Orioles

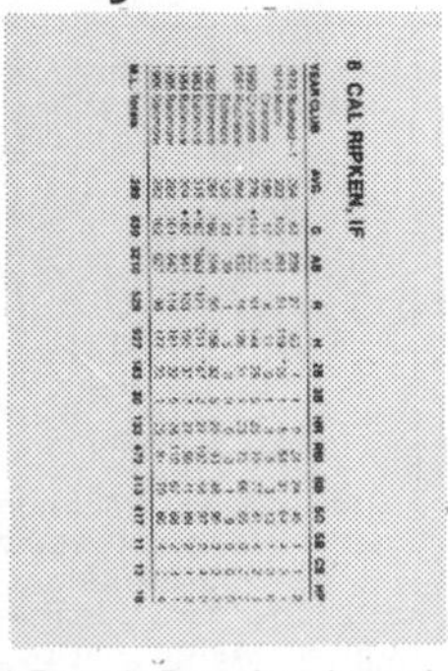

The Baltimore Orioles and French Bray Inc. issued this set which was distributed to fans at an Orioles

home game. Thirty perforated, detachable cards were printed within a three-panel fold-out piece measuring 9½'' by 11¼''. The fronts have the French/Bray logo and colored player photos surrounded by an orange border. The backs have only the player's name, uniform number, position and professional record.

		MT	NR MT	EX
Complete Set:		10.00	7.50	4.00
Common Player:		.15	.11	.06
3	Bill Ripken	.30	.25	.12
8	Cal Ripken	1.75	1.25	.70
20	Frank Robinson	.60	.45	.25
33	Eddie Murray	1.50	1.25	.60
38	Ken Gerhart	.25	.20	.10

1988 French/Bray Orioles

French-Bray sponsored a full-color brochure given to fans at an in-stadium promotion. A blue and orange front cover features inset photos of the Orioles in action in a flimstrip motif, the Orioles logo and 1988 slogan, "You Gotta Be There," above a baseball glove and ball. The 3-panel foldout, approximately 9½'' by 11¼'', includes a team photo on the inside cover, with two perforated pages of individual cards featuring players, coaches and the manager. Individual cards, 2¼'' by 3⅛'', have close-ups framed in white with an orange accent line. The player name and sponsor logo are also included. The black-and-white backs, numbered by player uniform, provide career stats. Additional copies of the brochure were available from the Orioles Baseball Store after the giveaway.

		MT	NR MT	EX
Complete Set:		8.00	6.00	3.25
Common Player:		.15	.11	.06
7	Bill Ripken	.20	.15	.08
8	Cal Ripken	1.75	1.25	.70
17	Pete Stanicek	.20	.15	.08
20	Frank Robinson	.60	.45	.25
33	Eddie Murray	1.50	1.25	.60

1989 French/Bray Orioles

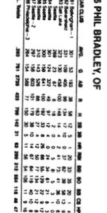

This 32-card Baltimore Orioles set, sponsored by French-Bray and the Wilcox Walter Furlong Paper Co., was distributed as an in-stadium promotion. The cards, 2¼'' by 3'', feature a colored player photo with number, name and position. The black-and-white backs include brief player data and complete major and minor league stats.

		MT	NR MT	EX
Complete Set:		8.00	6.00	3.25
Common Player:		.15	.11	.06
3	Bill Ripken	.20	.15	.08
8	Cal Ripken Jr.	1.75	1.25	.70
10	Steve Finley	.80	.60	.30
20	Frank Robinson	.60	.45	.25
30	Gregg Olson	1.50	1.25	.60
42	Pete Harnisch	.35	.25	.14

1983 Gardner's Brewers

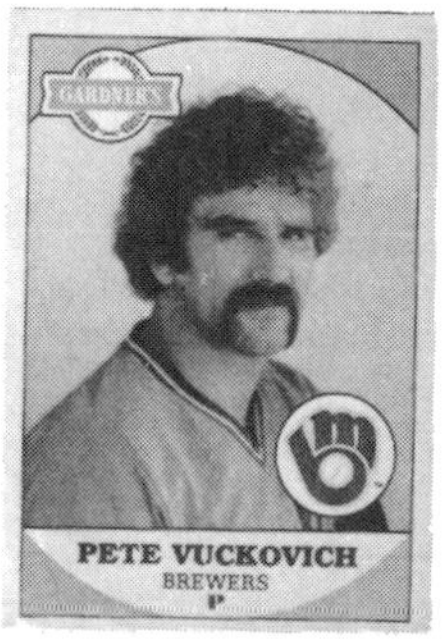

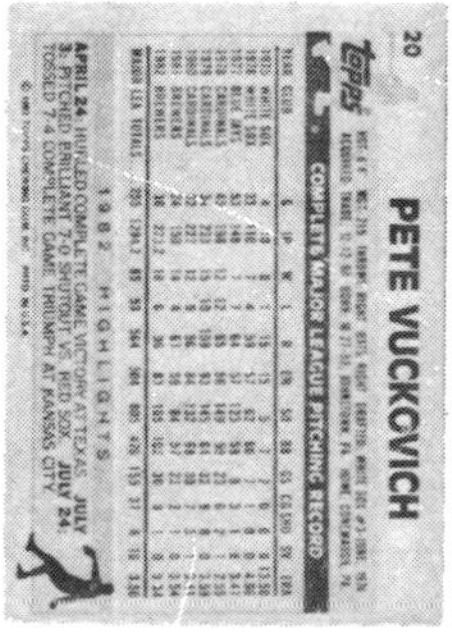

In 1983 Topps produced for Gardner's Bakery of Madison, Wis., this 22-card set featuring the American League champion Milwaukee Brewers. The cards, 2½'' by 3½'', have colorful fronts with the player's name, team, and position, and the Brewers and Gardner's logos. The backs are identical to the regular Topps issue but are numbered 1-22. The cards, inserted in specially-marked packages of Gardner's bread products, were susceptible to grease stains.

		MT	NR MT	EX
Complete Set:		30.00	22.00	12.50
Common Player:		.50	.40	.20
5	Cecil Cooper	1.25	.90	.50
7	Rollie Fingers	5.00	3.75	2.00
11	Paul Molitor	4.00	3.00	1.50
16	Ted Simmons	.90	.70	.35
18	Don Sutton	2.00	1.50	.80
22	Robin Yount	10.00	7.50	4.00

1984 Gardner's Brewers

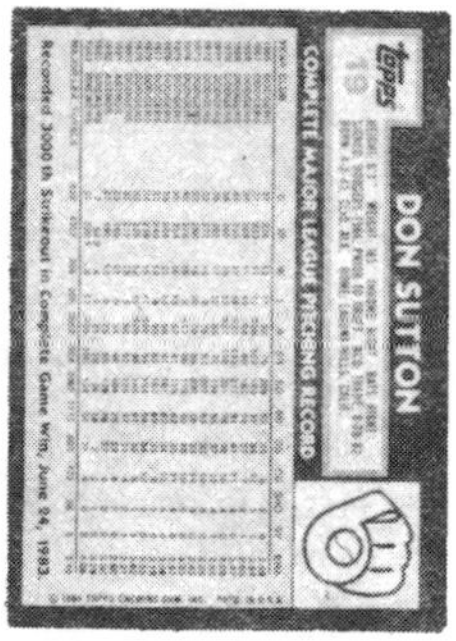

Gardner's Bakery inserted cards of the Milwaukee Brewers in its bread products. The 22-card set, entitled "1984 Series II", have multi-colored fronts with the Brewers and Gardner's logos. The backs are identical to the regular 1984 Topps issue except for the 1-22 numbering system. The Topps-produced cards, 2½'' by 3½'', are sometimes found with grease stains, resulting from contact with the bread.

		MT	NR MT	EX
Complete Set:		15.00	11.00	6.00
Common Player:		.50	.40	.20
5	Cecil Cooper	1.00	.70	.40
6	Rollie Fingers	2.00	1.50	.80
7	Jim Gantner	.70	.50	.30
13	Paul Molitor	2.00	1.50	.80
19	Don Sutton	1.25	.90	.50
22	Robin Yount	5.00	3.75	2.00

1985 Gardner's Brewers

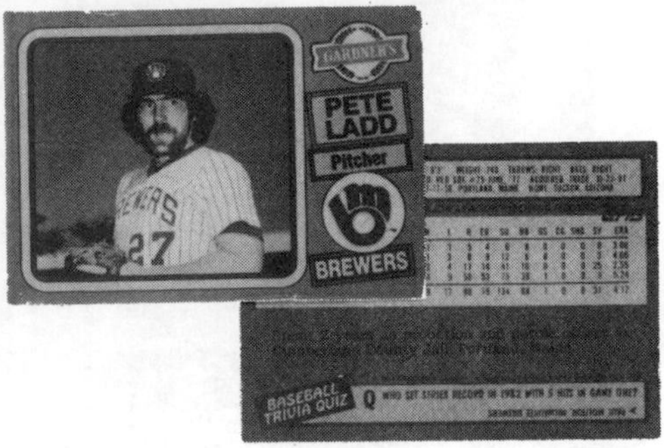

Gardner's Bakery issued this 22-card set featuring the Milwaukee Brewers. The set, produced by Topps, uses a horizontal format. The fronts have color photos inside blue, red and yellow frames. The player's name and position are in orange boxes and are accompanied by the Brewers and Gardner's logos. The backs, identical in design to the regular 1985 Topps set, are blue, not green, and are numbered 1-22. The cards, inserted in specially-marked bread products, often have grease stains.

		MT	NR MT	EX
Complete Set:		12.00	9.00	4.75
Common Player:		.35	.25	.14
5	Cecil Cooper	.90	.70	.35
6	Rollie Fingers	1.75	1.25	.70
13	Paul Molitor	2.00	1.50	.80
19	Ted Simmons	.70	.50	.30
22	Robin Yount	4.00	3.00	1.50

1989 Gardner's Brewers

Returning after a three-year hiatus, Gardner's Bread of Madison, Wis., issued a 15-card Milwaukee Brewers set. The blue and white-bordered cards, standard size, feature posed portrait photos. All Brewer logos are airbrushed from the players' caps. The Gardner's logo appears on the front, along with the player's name. The set, produced by Mike Schechter Associates, was issued in loaves of bread or packages of buns, one card per package.

		MT	NR MT	EX
Complete Set:		5.00	3.75	2.00
Common Player:		.10	.08	.04
1	Paul Molitor	1.00	.70	.40
2	Robin Yount	1.75	1.25	.70
3	Jim Gantner	.25	.20	.10
5	B.J. Surhoff	.25	.20	.10
7	Ted Higuera	.25	.20	.10
8	Dan Plesac	.25	.20	.10

1981 Granny Goose Potato Chips A's

The 1981 Granny Goose 15-card set of Oakland A's was issued one card per pack in bags of potato

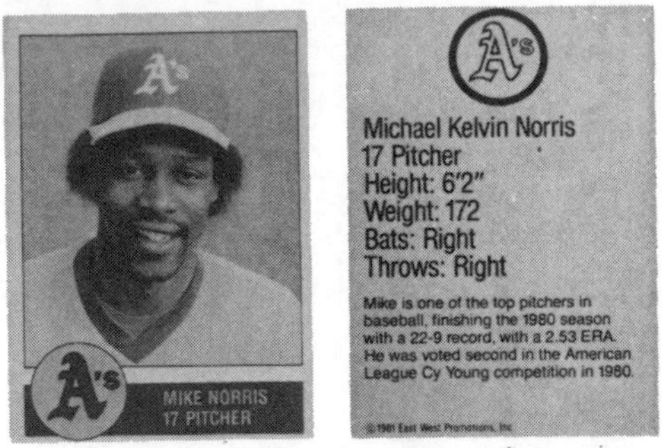

chips and are sometimes found with grease stains. The cards, 2½'' by 3½'', have colored fronts. The print is the team's green and yellow colors. The backs have the A's logo and a player biography. The Revering card, withdrawn from the set shortly after he was traded, is scarcer than the rest. The cards are numbered by the players' uniform numbers.

		MT	NR MT	EX
Complete Set:		100.00	75.00	40.00
Common Player:		2.00	1.50	.80
1	Billy Martin	10.00	7.50	4.00
13	Dave Revering	45.00	34.00	18.00
20	Tony Armas	4.00	3.00	1.50
35	Rickey Henderson	40.00	30.00	15.00

1982 Granny Goose Potato Chips A's

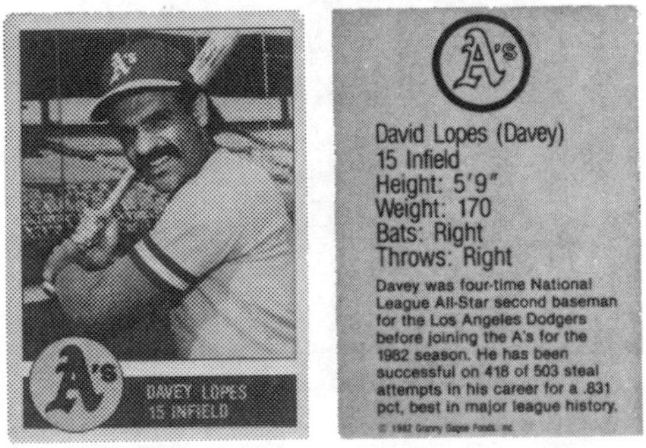

These 15 Oakland A's cards, 2½'' by 3½'', were distributed in two ways — in bags of potato chips and at Fan Appreciation Day at Oakland-Alameda Coliseum. The cards, identical in design to the 1981 set, can be distinguished from it by the date on the copyright on the bottom of the card back. The cards are numbered by the players' uniform numbers.

		MT	NR MT	EX
Complete Set:		20.00	15.00	7.50
Common Player:		.40	.30	.15
1	Billy Martin	3.00	2.25	1.25
15	Davey Lopes	.80	.60	.30
20	Tony Armas	.80	.60	.30
35	Rickey Henderson	12.00	9.00	4.75

1983 Granny Goose Potato Chip A's

This Oakland A's set of 15 was issued with or without a detachable coupon found at the bottom of each card. Issued in bags of potato chips were the coupon card, containing a scratch-off section offering prizes. The cards without the coupon section were given to fans at an A's home game. Cards with the detachable coupon command a 50 percent premium over the coupon-less variety. The cards are numbered by the players' uniform numbers.

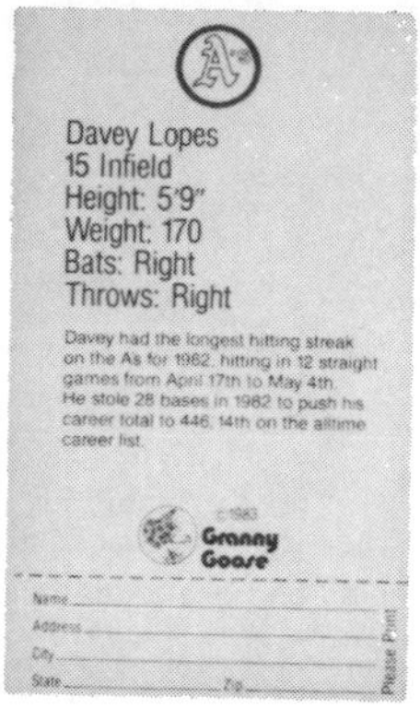

		MT	NR MT	EX
Complete Set:		12.00	9.00	4.75
Common Player:		.40	.30	.15
4	Carney Lansford	1.00	.70	.40
15	Davey Lopes	.80	.60	.30
16	Mike Davis	.80	.60	.30
35	Rickey Henderson	10.00	7.50	4.00

1953 Hunter Wieners St. Louis Cardinals

From the great era of the regionally-issued hot dog cards in the mid-1950s, the 1953 Hunter Wieners St. Louis Cardinals set of 26 is among the rarest today. Originally issued in two-card panels, the cards are most often found as 2¼'' by 3¼'' singles, if they are found. The cards have a light blue facsimile autograph printed over the stat box. They are blank-backed.

		NR MT	EX	VG
Complete SetL		3000.00	1500.00	800.00
Common Player:		60.00	30.00	18.00
(16)	Stanley Musial	600.00	300.00	175.00
(21)	Albert Schoendienst	110.00	55.00	33.00
(23)	Enos Slaughter	150.00	75.00	45.00
(25)	Edward Stanky	70.00	35.00	21.00

1954 Hunter Wieners St. Louis Cardinals

A nearly impossible set to complete today by virtue of the method of its issue, the 1954 Hunter hot dog set essentially features what would traditionally be the front and back of a normal baseball card on two different cards. The ''front'' has a color photo of one of 30 St. Louis Cardinals and a box challenging the collector to name him and quote his stats. The ''back'' features cartoon Cardinals in action and the answers. However, because both parts were printed on a single panel, and because most of the back (non-picture) panels were thrown away years ago, it is an

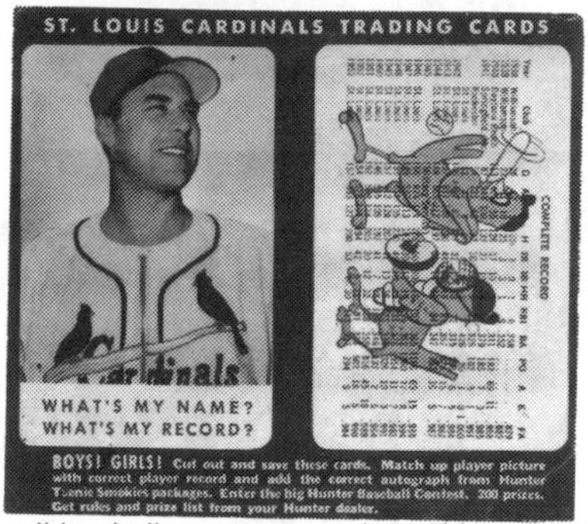

impossible challenge to complete this set today. There is no back printing on the 2¼'' by 3½'' cards.

		NR MT	EX	VG
Complete Set:		4000.00	2000.00	1200.00
Common Player:		60.00	30.00	18.00
(14)	Stan Musial	600.00	300.00	180.00
(24)	Red Schoendienst	110.00	55.00	33.00
(25)	Dick Schofield	100.00	50.00	30.00
(26)	Eddie Stanky	110.00	55.00	33.00
(27)	Enos Slaughter	150.00	75.00	45.00

1955 Hunter Wieners St. Louis Cardinals

The 1955 St. Louis Cardinals set was included in packages of Hunter hot dogs and features another format change. For 1955, the cards were printed in a tall, narrow 2'' by 4¾'' format, two to a panel. The fronts have a posed action photo and a portrait photo, and a facsimile autograph and brief biographical data. There is no back printing; the cards were part of the wrapping for packages of hot dogs.

		NR MT	EX	VG
Complete Set:		4000.00	2000.00	1200.
Common Player:		75.00	37.00	22.00
(2)	Kenton Lloyd Boyer	225.00	112.00	67.00
(7)	Harvey Haddix	125.00	62.00	37.00
(15)	Stanley Frank Musial	1000.00	500.00	300.00
(23)	Albert Fred Schoendienst	200.00	100.00	60.00
(26)	Edward R. Stanky	125.00	62.00	37.00
(28)	William Charles Virdon	175.00	87.00	52.00

1983 Minnesota Twins Team Issue

This Minnesota Twins' 36-card set was sold at concession stands and through the mail. The colored, borderless cards, 2½'' by 3½'', have the player's uniform number on a white Twins jersey. The backs have complete career statistics.

		MT	NR MT	EX
Complete Set:		9.00	6.75	3.50
Common Player:		.10	.08	.04
5	Gary Joseph Gaetti	.50	.40	.20
9	Kent Alan Hrbek	.75	.60	.30
11	Frank John Viola Jr.	.50	.40	.20

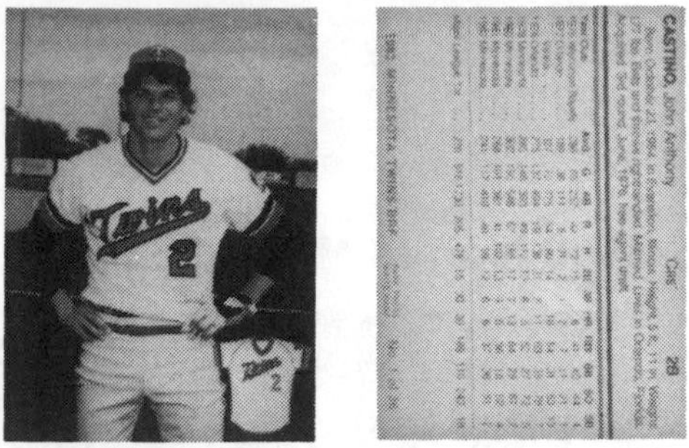

17	Thomas Andrew Brunansky	.50	.40	.20
33	The Lumber Company (Tom Brunansky, Gary Gaetti, Kent Hrbek, Gary Ward)	.35	.25	.14

1984 Minnesota Twins Team Issue

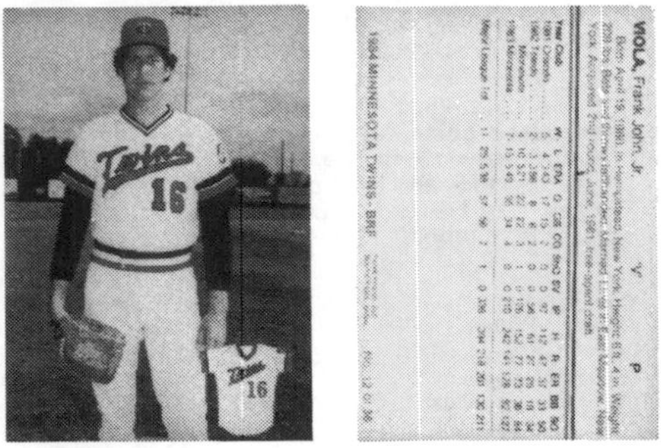

This team-issued Minnesota Twins set has 36 colored, borderless cards, each 2½" by 3½". The player's uniform number is on a white Twins jersey on the front. The backs, printed in red and blue on white stock, include career stats. The set includes several special cards, including one of Harmon Killebrew.

		MT	NR MT	EX
Complete Set:		6.00	4.50	2.50
Common Player:		.08	.06	.03
5	Gary Joseph Gaetti	.35	.25	.14
10	Kent Alan Hrbek	.50	.40	.20
12	Frank John Viola Jr.	.35	.25	.14
18	Thomas Andrew Brunansky	.35	.25	.14
33	Harmon Killebrew	.50	.40	.20

1985 Minnesota Twins Team Issue

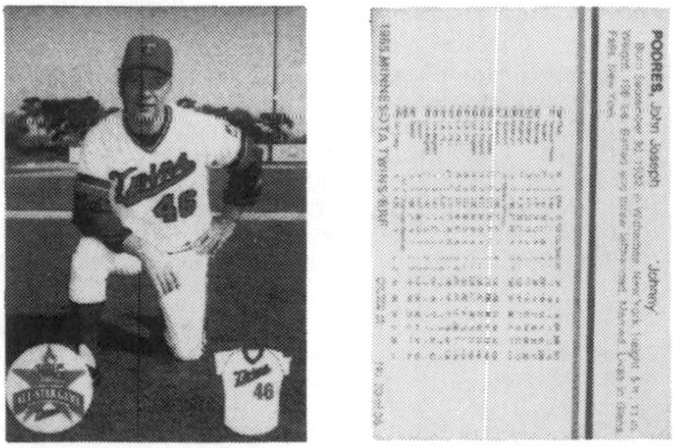

This 36-card, team-issued set also features colored, borderless cards. The player's uniform number is on a white Twins jersey on the front, as is the 1985 All-Star Game logo, which also appears on a special card in the set. The card back lists all Twins who have been selected for previous All-Star games. The set was sold at ballpark concession stands and through the mail.

		MT	NR MT	EX
Complete Set:		8.00	6.00	3.25
Common Player:		.08	.06	.03
5	Gary Joseph Gaetti	.35	.25	.14
10	Kent Alan Hrbek	.50	.40	.20
12	Frank John Viola Jr.	.35	.25	.14
19	Thomas Andrew Brunansky	.35	.25	.14
24	Kirby Puckett	1.50	1.25	.60

1986 Minnesota Twins Team Issue

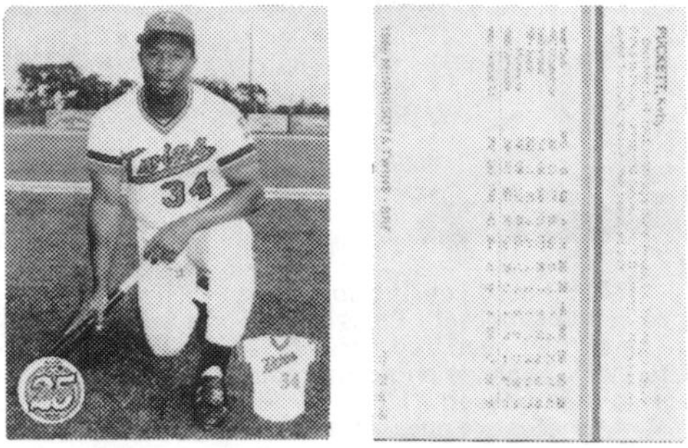

This team-issued set of 36 2-9/16" by 3½" colored cards features the Twins 25th anniversary logo and a jersey with the player's uniform number. All cards, except an action shot of Bert Blyleven, are posed photos, with a facsimile autograph. The set also includes a checklist and a team photo.

		MT	NR MT	EX
Complete Set:		6.00	4.50	2.50
Common Player:		.08	.06	.03
5	Gary Joseph Gaetti	.50	.40	.20
9	Kent Alan Hrbek	.60	.45	.25
11	Frank John Viola Jr.	.50	.40	.20
17	Thomas Andrew Brunansky	.35	.25	.14
24	Kirby Puckett	1.00	.70	.40

1987 Minnesota Twins Team Issue

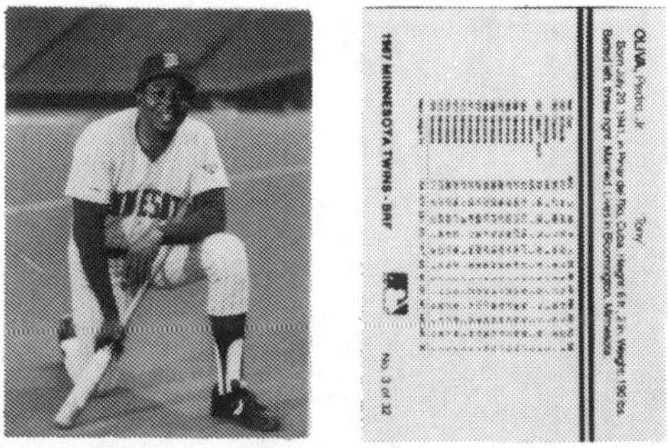

This Minnesota Twins 32-card set of 2½" by 3½" colored cards was sold at the ballpark and through a souvenir catalog. Card fronts are borderless, containing only the player photo. The backs, printed in blue and red on white card stock, have the player's personal data and career record. The Twins also produced a postcard set similar in design to the standard-size card set, but with different photos.

	MT	NR MT	EX
Complete Set:	6.00	4.50	2.50
Common Player:	.08	.06	.03

		MT	NR MT	EX
5	Gary Joseph Gaetti	.50	.40	.20
9	Kent Alan Hrbek	.60	.45	.25
11	Frank John Viola Jr.	.50	.40	.20
15	Thomas Andrew Brunansky	.35	.25	.14
21	Kirby Puckett	1.00	.70	.40

1988 Minnesota Twins Team Issue

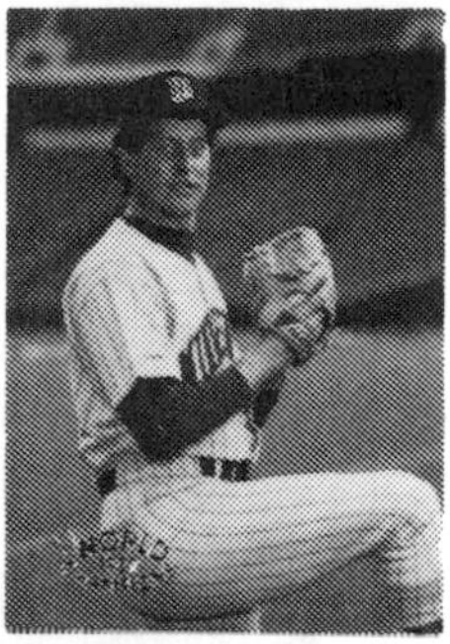
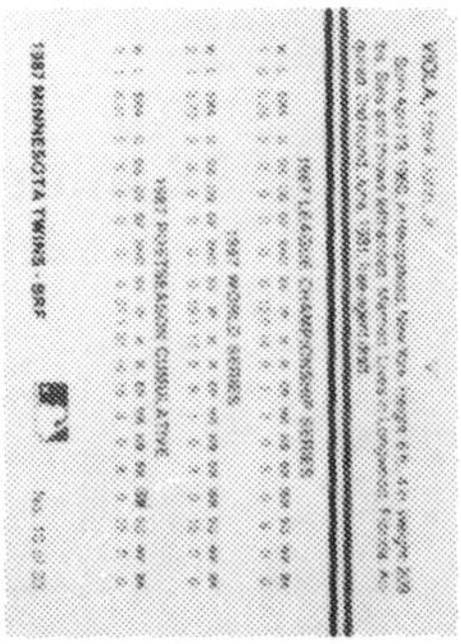

This 33-card set (including checklist) commemorates the Minnesota Twins 1987 World Series victory. The slightly oversized cards (2⅝" by 3-7/16") feature deluxe player photos printed on heavy stock with a gold-embossed "1987 World Champions" logo. Many photos are duplicates of the regular season set, but several new photos, including a group team shot, are included. Numbered card backs are red, white and blue and contain a player name, personal info and stats. A limited edition of 5,000 sets were printed but only a few hundred were sold before the cards were taken off the market due to Major League Baseball licensing restrictions.

		MT	NR MT	EX
Complete Set:		150.00	110.00	60.00
Common Player:		1.25	.90	.50
5	Gary Joseph Gaetti	12.00	9.00	4.75
8	Kent Alan Hrbek	12.00	9.00	4.75
10	Frank John Viola Jr.	15.00	11.00	6.00
15	Thomas Andrew Brunansky	8.00	6.00	3.25
19	Rik Aalbert Blyleven	8.00	6.00	3.25
23	Kirby Puckett	25.00	20.00	10.00

1959 Morrell Meats Dodgers

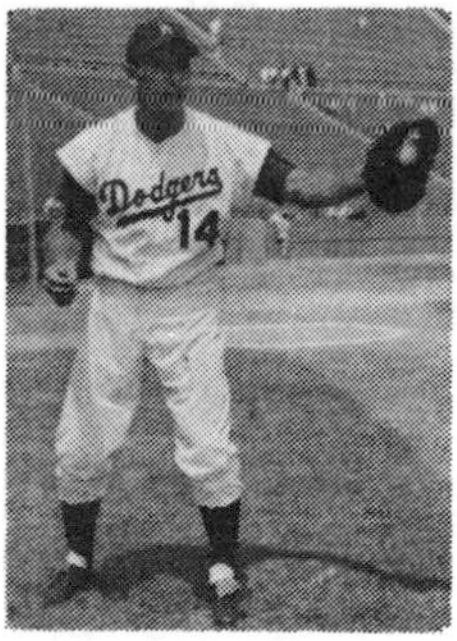
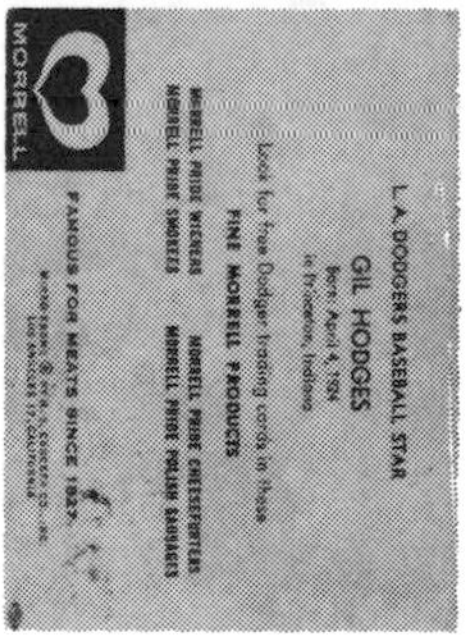

This popular Los Angeles Dodgers set was the first of three by the Southern California meat company. The 12 cards, 2½" by 3½", are unnumbered and feature fullframe, unbordered color photos. Backs have a company ad and list only the player's name, birthdate and birthplace. Two interesting errors exist; the Clem Labine and Norm Larker cards show photos of Stan Williams and Joe Pignatano, respectively. Dodger greats Sandy Koufax and Duke Snider are key cards.

		NR MT	EX	VG
Complete Set:		1200.00	600.00	350.00
Common Player:		50.00	25.00	15.00
(1)	Don Drysdale	110.00	55.00	33.00
(4)	Gil Hodges	110.00	55.00	33.00
(5)	Sandy Koufax	225.00	112.00	70.00
(11)	Duke Snider	225.00	112.00	70.00

1960 Morrell Meats Dodgers

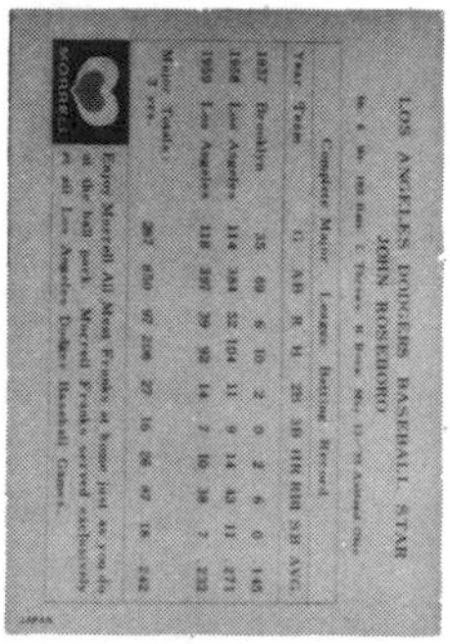

These 12 unnumbered cards, 2½" by 3½", feature unbordered color card fronts. Five of the players included are new to the Morrell's sets. Backs list player statistics and brief personal data. Cards for Gil Hodges, Carl Furlllo and Duke Snider are apparently scarcer than others in the set.

		NR MT	EX	VG
Complete Set:		800.00	400.00	250.00
Common Player:		15.00	7.50	4.50
(4)	Carl Furillo	100.00	50.00	30.00
(5)	Gil Hodges	125.00	62.00	37.00
(6)	Sandy Koufax	125.00	62.00	37.00
(12)	Duke Snider	225.00	112.00	70.00

1961 Morrell Meats Dodgers

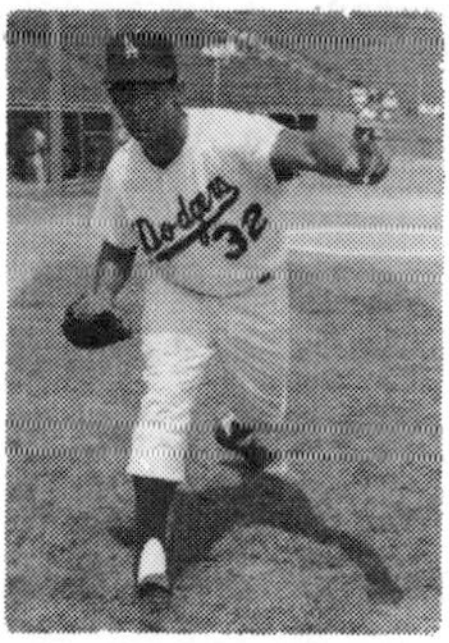
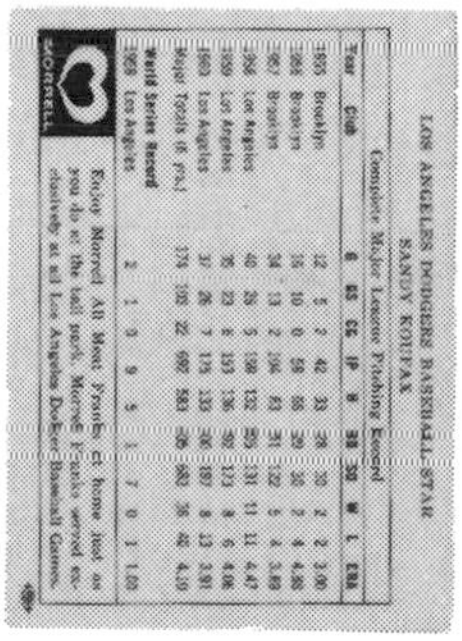

The 1961 Morrell set shrunk to six cards with a format almost identical to the 1960 cards. Fronts are colored, with unbordered photos. Backs have player-statistics. The unnumbered cards are a slightly smaller 2¼" by 3¼". Comparing statistical information helps distinguish the cards from the 1960 set. Key cards are of Don Drysdale and Sandy Koufax, the only two players to appear in three Morrell Meats sets.

		NR MT	EX	VG
Complete Set:		200.00	100.00	60.00
Common Player:		15.00	7.50	4.50
(1)	Tommy Davis	20.00	10.00	6.00
(2)	Don Drysdale	40.00	20.00	12.00
(3)	Frank Howard	20.00	10.00	6.00
(4)	Sandy Koufax	80.00	40.00	24.00
(5)	Norm Larker	15.00	7.50	4.50
(6)	Maury Wills	25.00	12.50	7.50

Mother's Cookies

1983 Giants

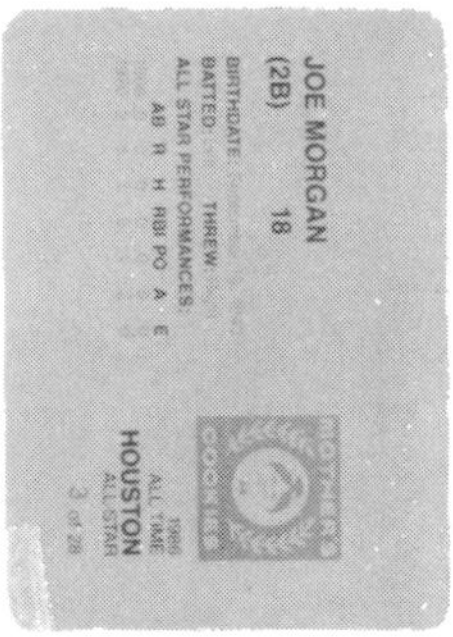

1986 Astros

After putting out Pacific Coast League sets in 1952 and 1953, Mother's Cookies began producing unbordered, rounded-corner, full-color sets again in 1983, starting with a 20-card San Francisco Giants set. Since then the company has produced 28-card sets annually through 1991. Teams featured on the 2½'' by 3½'' cards have included the Giants, Oakland A's, Houston Astros, Seattle Mariners, San Diego Padres, Texas Rangers and Los Angeles Dodgers.

The team sets were distributed during promotions at each representative teams' stadiums, along with redeemable coupons for additional cards. Most included a checklist featured on the back of a stadium photo, coaches or team logo card. The card backs are unnumbered and contain biographical information, the Mother's Cookies logo, and space for the players' autographs.

Three team sets feature All-Star team selections — the 1984 Giants, which uses drawings of former Giants All-Stars; the 1986 Astros set, which features paintings of past Astros All-Stars; and the 1987 A's set, which has photographs of every A's player to have been selected to the All-Star Game since 1968.

Several four-card sets, included inside packages of Mother's Cookies, have also been produced for players Jose Canseco, Will Clark, Ken Griffey Jr., Mark McGwire, Matt Williams, Nolan Ryan, and three Oakland A's Rookie of the Year award winners — Canseco, McGwire and Walt Weiss.

Included for each set is the year of issue, name of the set, number of cards, key cards and their Mint prices, and the value of the complete set in Mint condition.

Year	Set	Stars — Value	Set MT	Common MT
1983	Giants (20)	J. Clark $2.50; C. Davis, F. Robinson, D. Evans $1.50	$18	.50
1984	A's (28)	R. Henderson $3; J. Morgan $1.50; C. Lansford	$15	.50
1984	Astros (28)	N. Ryan $2.50; M. Scott $1.25; B. Doran $1	$15	.50
1984	Giants (28)	W. Mays $2.50; W. McCovey, J. Marichal, G. Perry $2; J. Clark $1.25; O. Cepeda $1	$15	.50
1984	Mariners (28)	A. Davis $1.75; M. Langston $1.50; P. Bradley $1.50	$15	.50
1984	Padres (28)	T. Gwynn $3.50; K. McReynolds $2.25; S. Garvey $2	$18	.50
1985	A's (28)	D. Sutton $1; C. Lansford 70¢; M. Tettleton 50¢	$12	.40
1985	Astros (28)	N. Ryan $3; M. Scott $1; J. Cruz, B. Doran 60¢	$13	.40
1985	Giants (28)	C. Brown, R. Deer $1; C. Davis, D. Gladden, V. Blue 60¢	$12	.40
1985	Mariners (28)	J. Presley $1.50; A. Davis $1.25; M. Langston, P. Bradley $1; H. Reynolds, I. Calderon 80¢	$13	.40
1985	Padres (28)	T. Gwynn $3; S. Garvey $1.75; K. McReynolds $1.50	$12	.40
1986	A's (28)	J. Canseco $18; J. Rijo 60¢; C. Lansford 50¢; M. Tettleton 30¢	$25	.30
1986	Astros (28)	N. Ryan $1.50; J. Morgan $1; J. Cruz 60¢; C. Cedeno 50¢	$10	.30
1986	Giants (28)	W. Clark $10; R. Thompson 80¢; C. Davis 60¢	$18	.30
1986	Mariners (28)	D. Tartabull $1.75; A. Davis $1; M. Langston 80¢	$12	.30
1987	A's (28)	J. Canseco $3; R. Jackson, Canseco/Jackson, R. Henderson $2; J. Hunter $1; R. Fingers 70¢	$18	.30
1987	Astros (28)	N. Ryan $3; M. Scott, G. Davis $1; J. Deshaies 50¢	$12	.30
1987	Dodgers (28)	F. Valenzuela, O. Hershiser $1; P. Guerrero 80¢	$12	.30
1987	Giants (28)	W. Clark $4.50; M. Williams $1.75; R. Thompson 40¢	$12	.30
1987	Mariners (28)	A. Davis 80¢; M. Langston 70¢; H. Reynolds 60¢	$9	.30
1987	Rangers (28)	R. Sierra $1.75; P. Incaviglia $1; B. Witt 60¢	$10	.30
1987	Mark McGwire	all four cards are $4 each	$20	$4.00
1988	A's (28)	J. Canseco, M. McGwire, Canseco/McGwire $3; W. Weiss $1.50; D. Parker 70¢; D. Eckersley 40¢	$16	.30
1988	Astros (28)	N. Ryan $2; M. Scott, G. Davis 90¢; G. Young 70¢	$10	.30

Mother's Cookies

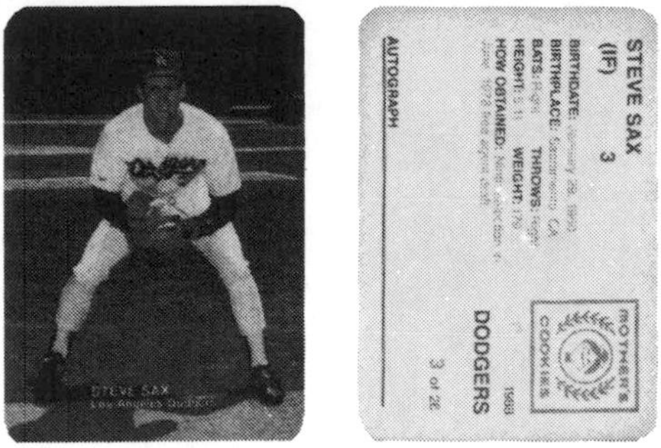

1988 Dodgers

1989 A's

1988 Dodgers (28)	K. Gibson, O. Hershiser, F. Valenzuela $1; P. Guerrero 80¢	$12	.30
1988 Giants (28)	W. Clark $3.50; K. Mitchell $1.50; R. Reuschel 50¢	$12	.30
1988 Mariners (28)	A. Davis 70¢; M. Langston 60¢; H. Reynolds 40¢	$10	.30
1988 Rangers (28)	R. Sierra 90¢; P. Incaviglia 70¢; B. Witt 50¢	$10	.30
1988 Will Clark (4)	all four cards are $4 each	$20	$4.00
1988 Mark McGwire	all four cards are $3 each	$15	$3.00
1989 A's (28)	J. Canseco $3; M. McGwire $2.75; Weiss/McGwire/Canseco 70¢; T. Steinbach 60¢	$12	.30
1989 A's Rookies of the year (4)	Canseco $3.50; McGwire, Weiss/Canseco/McGwire $3; Weiss $2	$10	$2.00
1989 Astros (28)	C. Biggio $1; M. Scott, G. Davis 90¢; K. Caminiti 60¢	$10	.30
1989 Dodgers (28)	O. Hershiser 80¢; K. Gibson 70¢; E. Murray, F. Valenzuela 60¢	$8	.30
1989 Giants (28)	W. Clark $1.25; K. Mitchell $1; M. Williams 70¢; B. Butler 40¢	$12	.30
1989 Mariners (28)	K. Griffey Jr. $5; M. Langston, J. Leonard, H. Reynolds 70¢; A. Davis 50¢; E. Martinez, E. Hanson 40¢	$10	.30
1989 Rangers (28)	N. Ryan $1.50; R. Sierra 90¢; J. Franco, R. Palmeiro 70¢;	$9	.30
1989 Jose Canseco (4)	all four cards are $3 each	$15	$3.00
1989 Will Clark (4)	all four cards are $2 each	$10	$2.00
1989 Ken Griffey Jr.	all four cards are $3.50 each	$16	$3.50
1989 Mark McGwire	all four cards are $3 each	$15	$3.00
1990 Jose Canseco (4)	all four cards are $4 each	$20	$4.00
1990 Will Clark (4)	all four cards are $3.50 each	$16	$3.50
1990 Mark McGwire	all four cards are $3.50 each	$16	$3.50
1990 Nolan Ryan (4)	all four cards are $4 each	$20	$4.00
1990 Matt Williams (4)	all four cards are $3.50 each	$16	$3.50
1990 Astros (28)	G.Davis 80¢; C. Biggio 50¢; E. Anthony 40¢	$8	.25
1990 A's (28)	R. Henderson, J. Canseco $1.75; McGwire 80¢	$10	.30
1990 Dodgers (28)	R. Martinez $1; O. Hershiser 70¢; K. Daniels 50¢	$8.00	.30
1990 Giants (28)	W. Clark $1.75; M. Williams, K. Mitchell $1	$9	.30
1990 Rangers (28)	N. Ryan $2; R. Sierra $1; Palmeiro 80¢	$10.00	.30
1991 Nolan Ryan (4)	all four cards are $3.50 each	$15	$3.50
1991 Ken Griffey Jr.	all four cards are $5 each	$20	$5

1989 Mariners

1990 Nolan Ryan

Police/Fire Safety

1979 Giants

Half of the 29 cards were distributed at the park; the others were given out by police agencies around San Francisco. Fronts have facsimile autographs.

		NR MT	EX	VG
Complete Set:		20.00	10.00	6.00
Common Player:		.40	.20	.12
14	Vida Blue	.80	.40	.25
18	Bill Madlock	1.25	.60	.40
22	Jack Clark	2.50	1.25	.70
41	Darrell Evans	1.25	.60	.40
44	Willie McCovey	3.00	1.50	.90

1980 Dodgers

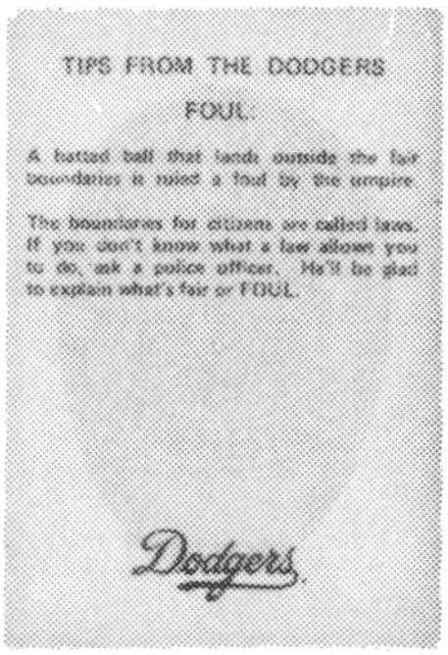

This 30-card set includes an unnumbered team photo. A Los Angeles Police Department logo is on the back; a facsimile autograph is on the front.

		NR MT	EX	VG
Complete Set:		10.00	5.00	3.00
Common Player:		.30	.15	.09
6	Steve Garvey	1.50	.70	.45
20	Don Sutton	.80	.40	.25
28	Pedro Guerrero	1.00	.50	.30
35	Bob Welch	.50	.25	.15
43	Rick Sutcliffe	.60	.30	.20

1980 Giants

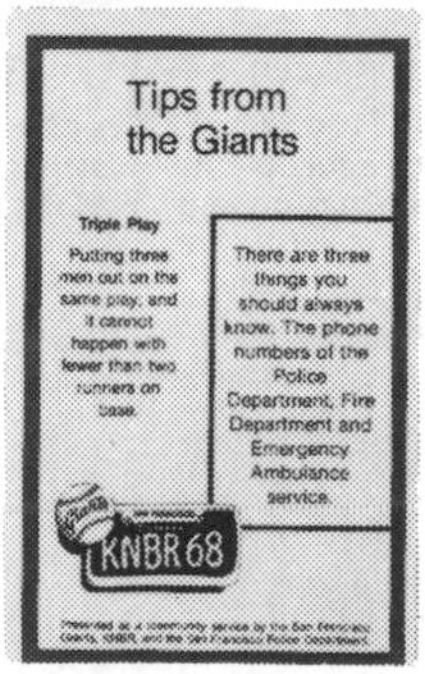

The 31 cards, numbered by player uniform numbers, have a similar design and distribution as the 1979 set. The fronts have facsimile autographs.

		NR MT	EX	VG
Complete Set:		12.00	9.00	4.75
Common Player:		.30	.15	.09
14	Vida Blue	.80	.40	.25
22	Jack Clark	2.25	1.25	.70
39	Bob Knepper	.50	.25	.15
41	Darrell Evans	.90	.45	.25
44	Willie McCovey	2.50	1.25	.70

1981 Braves

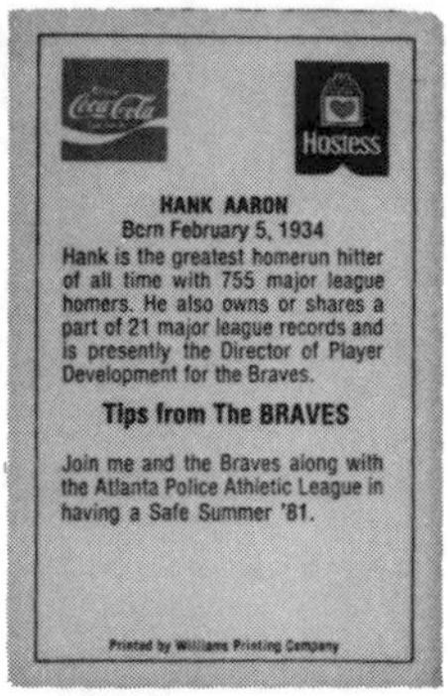

There were reportedly 30,000 sets printed of the first Braves police set. Terry Harper (#19) appears to be scarcer than the other 27 cards.

		NR MT	EX	VG
Complete Set:		12.00	9.00	4.75
Common Player:		.30	.25	.12
3	Dale Murphy	2.50	2.00	1.00
5	Bob Horner	.70	.50	.30
35	Phil Niekro	1.50	1.25	.60
46	Gaylord Perry	1.50	1.25	.60
--	Hank Aaron	2.50	2.00	1.00

1981 Dodgers

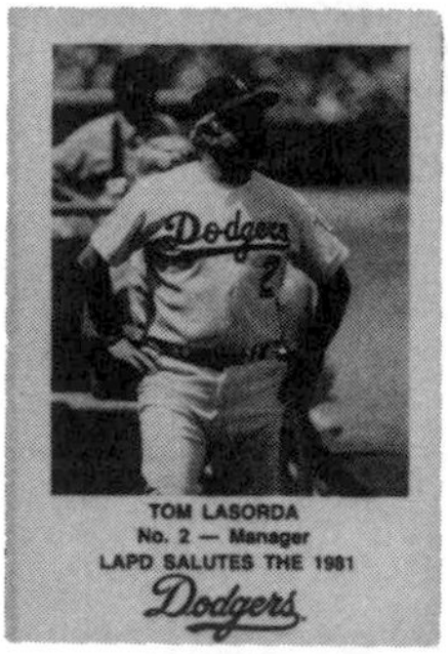

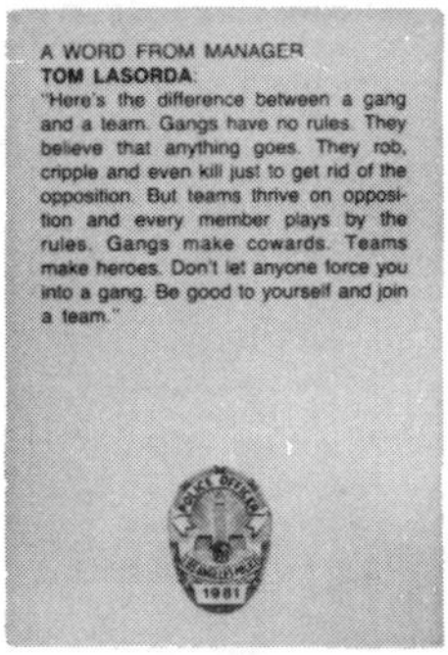

The 1981 Dodgers set has 32 cards. Dave Stewart and Ken Landreaux cards may have been added after the initial printing; they're more difficult to find.

		NR MT	EX	VG
Complete Set:		12.00	9.00	4.75
Common Player:		.20	.15	.08
6	Steve Garvey	1.25	.90	.50
28	Pete Guerrero	.70	.50	.30
34	Fernando Valenzuela	2.00	1.50	.80
44a	Mickey Hatcher	.25	.20	.10
44b	Ken Landreaux	.70	.50	.30
48	Dave Stewart	3.00	2.25	1.25

1981 Mariners

The Seattle Mariners' first police set has 16 cards. The cards, numbered on the lower left of the card back, measure 2⅝'' by 4⅛''.

		MT	NR MT	EX
Complete Set:		5.00	3.75	2.00
Common Player:		.25	.20	.10
1	Jeff Burroughs	.35	.25	.14
2	Floyd Bannister	.40	.30	.15
13	Richie Zisk	.35	.25	.14
14	Maury Wills	.50	.40	.20
16	Shane Rawley	.40	.30	.15

1981 Royals

This set, issued by the Ft. Myers, Fla., police department near the Royals' spring training site, features 10 Royals. Fronts have facsimile autographs.

		MT	NR MT	EX
Complete Set:		35.00	26.00	14.00
Common Player:		1.50	1.25	.60
(2)	George Brett	20.00	15.00	8.00
(6)	Hal McRae	2.25	1.75	.90
(9)	Frank White	3.50	2.75	1.50
(10)	Willie Wilson	4.00	3.00	1.50

1982 Braves

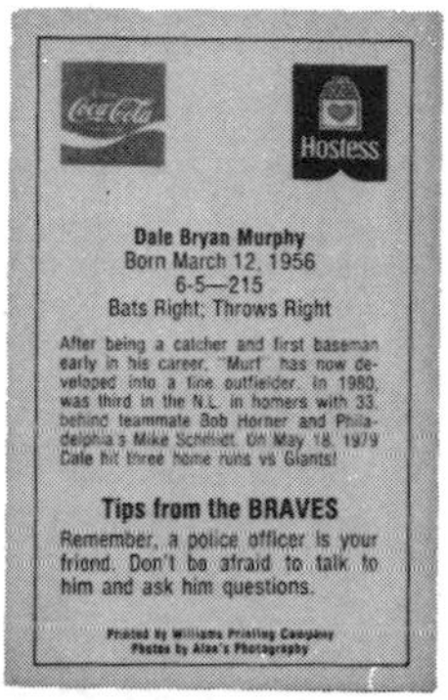

These 30 cards mark the 1982 team's record-breaking 13-game winning streak at the season's beginning. Reportedly only 8,000 sets were printed.

		MT	NR MT	EX
Complete Set:		20.00	15.00	8.00
Common Player:		.30	.25	.12
3	Dale Murphy	4.00	3.00	1.50
5	Bob Horner	1.25	.90	.50
8	Bob Watson	2.00	1.50	.80
22	Brett Butler	.70	.50	.30
32	Steve Bedrosian	1.00	.70	.40
35	Phil Niekro	2.00	1.50	.80
45	Bob Gibson	1.50	1.25	.60

1982 Brewers

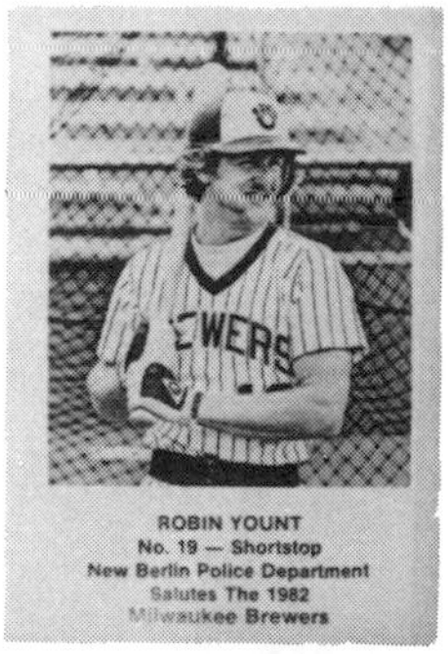

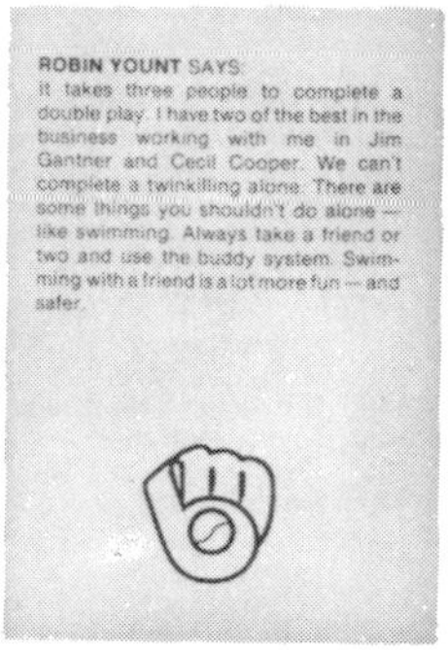

The first Brewers police set has 30 cards. Credit lines on the fronts note which Wisconsin law enforcement agency distributed them.

		MT	NR MT	EX
Complete Set:		15.00	11.00	6.00
Common Player:		.30	.25	12
4	Paul Molitor	1.00	.70	.40
15	Cecil Cooper	.50	.40	.20
19	Robin Yount	3.00	2.25	1.25
23	Ted Simmons	.50	.40	.20
26	Kevin Bass	.60	.45	.25
34	Rollie Fingers	.70	.50	.30

1982 Dodgers

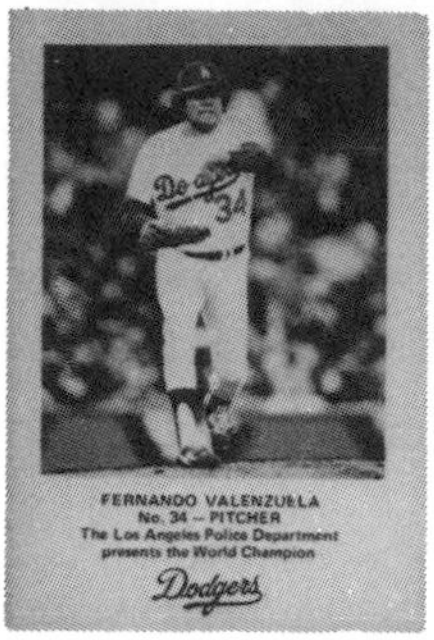

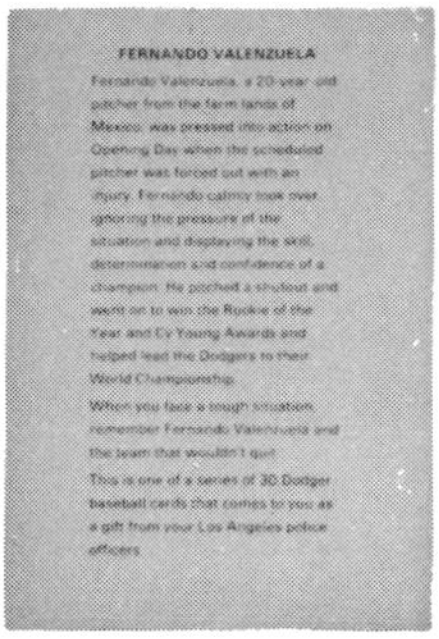

This set of 30 notes L.A.'s 1981 World Championship, with unnumbered cards for the divisional, league and World Series titles, and World Series trophy.

		MT	NR MT	EX
Complete Set:		7.00	5.25	2.75
Common Player:		.15	.11	.06
6	Steve Garvey	1.00	.70	.40
26	Alejandro Pena	.60	.45	.25
28	Pedro Guerrero	.80	.60	.30
34	Fernando Valenzuela	1.00	.70	.40
35	Bob Welch	.35	.25	.14
48	Dave Stewart	.30	.25	.12
52	Steve Sax	.90	.70	.35

1983 Braves

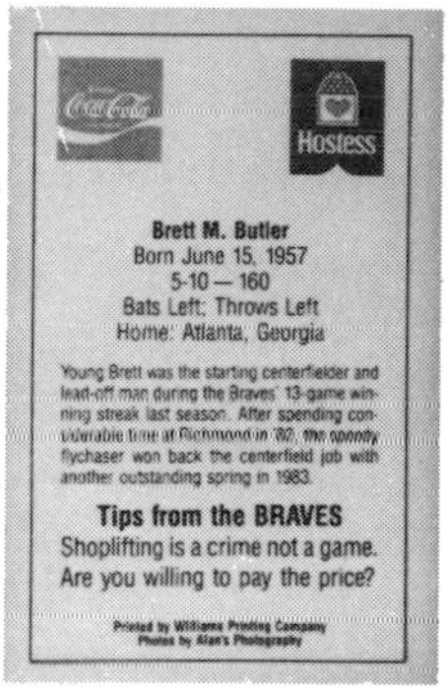

This set of 30 notes the team's 1982 National League Western Division title on the fronts. There were reportedly 8,000 sets printed.

		MT	NR MT	EX
Complete Set:		15.00	11.00	6.00
Common Player:		.30	.25	.12
3	Dale Murphy	3.50	2.75	1.50
5	Bob Horner	1.00	.70	.40
22	Brett Butler	.40	.30	.15
35	Phil Niekro	1.50	1.25	.60
45	Bob Gibson	1.25	.90	.50

1983 Brewers

Several law enforcement agency issuer variations exist for this Brewers 30-card set. Those distributed by smaller agencies are scarcer, with premium prices.

		MT	NR MT	EX
Complete Set:		10.00	7.50	4.00
Common Player:		.20	.15	.08
4	Paul Molitor	1.00	.70	.40
19	Robin Yount	2.00	1.50	.80
21	Don Sutton	.80	.60	.30
34	Rollie Fingers	.90	.70	.35

1983 Dodgers

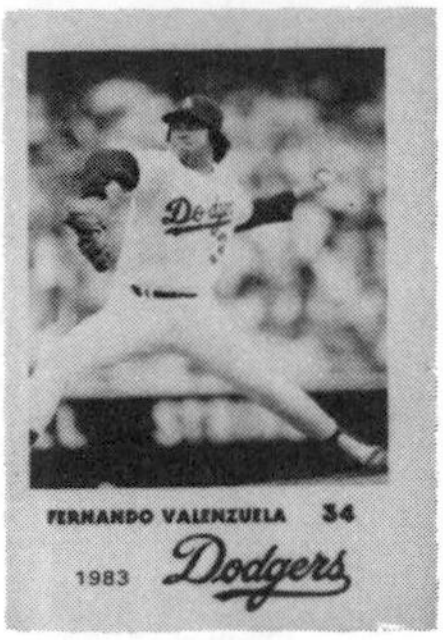

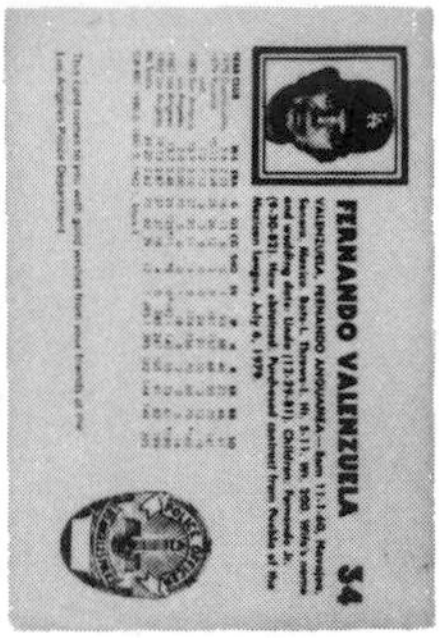

The 1983 backs differ from prior sets; a horizontal format and small portrait photos are used. Stats are fairly complete, but safety tips are not included.

		MT	NR MT	EX
Complete Set:		7.00	5.25	2.75
Common Player:		.15	.11	.06
3	Steve Sax	.60	.45	.25
28	Pedro Guerrero	.60	.45	.25
34	Fernando Valenzuela	.70	.50	.30
35	Bob Welch	.30	.25	.12
48	Dave Stewart	.25	.20	.10

1983 Royals

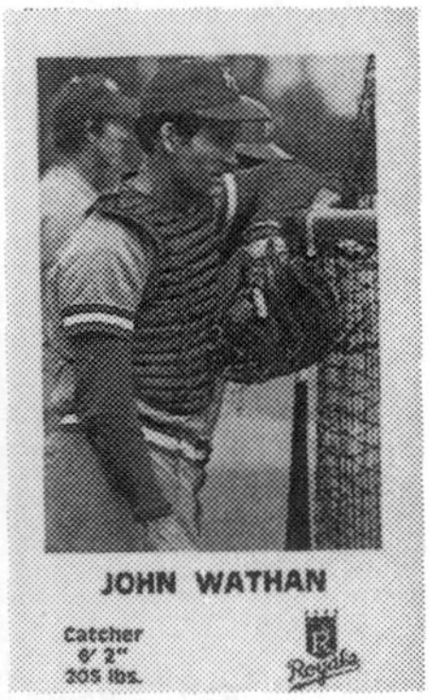

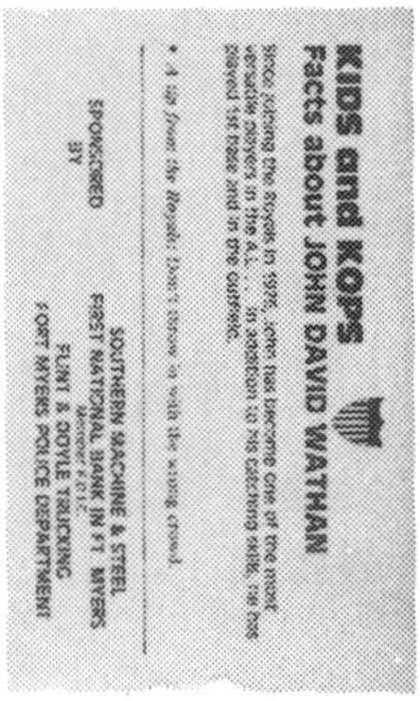

After skipping the 1982 season, the Ft. Myers polce department again issued 10 cards in 1983, with facsimilie autographs on the fronts.

		MT	NM	EX
Complete Set:		30.00	23.00	12.00
Common Player:		1.00	.70	.40
(2)	George Brett	18.00	13.50	7.25
(6)	Dan Quisenberry	3.00	2.75	1.25
(9)	Frank White	3.50	2.75	1.50
(10)	Willie Wilson	3.75	2.75	1.50

1984 Blue Jays

This 35-card set was issued by various Ontario area fire departments. The cards were distributed five at a time at two-week intervals in the summer of 1984.

		MT	NR MT	EX
Complete Set:		10.00	7.50	4.00
Common Player:		.20	.15	.08
1	Tony Fernandez	1.00	.70	.40
11	George Bell	1.50	1.25	.60
17	Kelly Gruber	.25	.20	.10
27	Jimmy Key	1.00	.70	.40
29	Jesse Barfield	.80	.60	.30

1984 Braves

A logo and date debut on the fronts. Pascual Perez and Rafael Ramirez cards are in Spanish. Cards were distributed two per week by Atlanta police officers, with reportedly 8,000 sets printed.

		MT	NR MT	EX
Complete Set:		12.00	9.00	4.75
Common Player:		.25	.20	.10
3	Dale Murphy	3.50	2.75	1.50
5	Bob Horner	1.00	.70	.40
28	Gerald Perry	1.50	1.25	.60
45	Bob Gibson	1.25	.90	.50

1984 Brewers

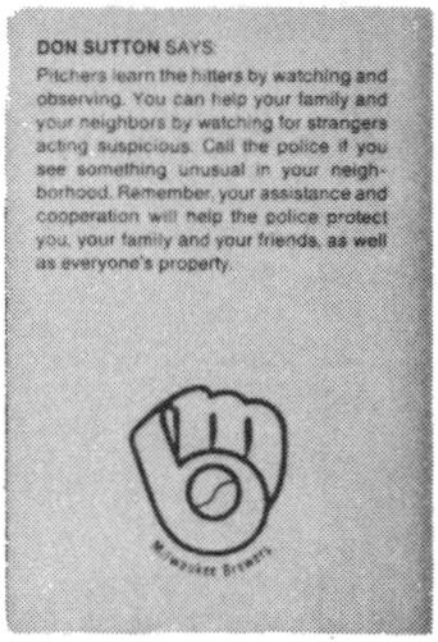

More than 50 Wisconsin police agencies distributed this 30-card set, as noted on the fronts. Cards issued by smaller departments may be worth premium prices.

		MT	NR MT	EX
Complete Set:		8.00	6.00	3.25
Common Player:		.15	.11	.06
4	Paul Molitor	.80	.60	.30
14	Dion James	.50	.40	.20
19	Robin Yount	1.50	1.25	.60
20	Don Sutton	.50	.40	.20
34	Rollie Fingers	.60	.45	.25

1984 Dodgers

Fronts differ from previous years; they have more posed photos, bolder names and a different team logo. Card backs again feature small portrait photos.

		MT	NR MT	EX
Complete Set:		8.00	6.00	3.25
Common Player:		.15	.11	.06
3	Steve Sax	.60	.45	.25
28	Pedro Guerrero	.70	.50	.30
34	Fernando Valenzuela	.70	.50	.30
55	Orel Hershiser	2.00	1.50	.80

1985 Blue Jays

For the second consecutive year, the Blue Jays issued a 35-card set, distributed throughout the Province of Ontario, Canada.

		MT	NR MT	EX
Complete Set:		8.00	6.00	3.25
Common Player:		.20	.15	.08
1	Tony Fernandez	.70	.50	.30
11	George Bell	1.25	.90	.50
22	Jimmy Key	.50	.40	.20
29	Jesse Barfield	.80	.60	.30
37	Dave Stieb	.50	.40	.20

1985 Braves

This fifth annual set includes 30 cards. Cards, similiar in size to previous efforts, differ from prior years; the year designation and team logo traded places.

		MT	NR MT	EX
Complete Set:		12.00	9.00	4.75
Common Player:		.25	.20	.10
3	Dale Murphy	3.25	2.50	1.25
11	Bob Horner	1.00	.70	.40
28	Gerald Perry	1.00	.70	.40
34	Zane Smith	.60	.45	.25
40	Bruce Sutter	.70	.50	.30

1985 Brewers

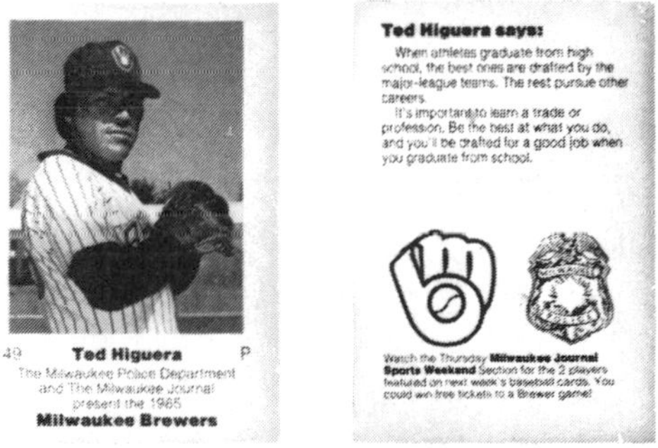

The cards were 1/16th narrower than before. The team and player names on the fronts are also much bolder. Nearly 60 agencies distributed the sets.

		MT	NR MT	EX
Complete Set:		8.00	6.00	3.25
Common Player:		.15	.11	.06
4	Paul Molitor	.70	.50	.30
19	Robin Yount	1.50	1.25	.60
34	Rollie Fingers	.60	.45	.25
49	Ted Higuera	1.25	.90	.50

NOTE: A card number in parentheses ( ) indicates the set is unnumbered.

1985 Phillies

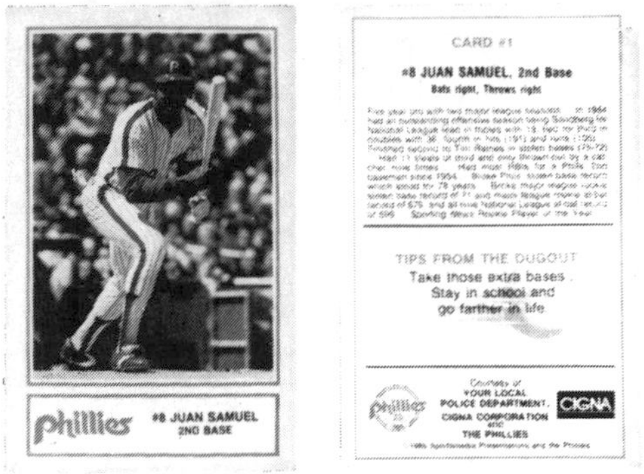

This 16-card set, sponsored by the Phillies and Cigna Corp., was distributed by several Philadelphia area police departments. The backs are numbered.

		MT	NR MT	EX
Complete Set:		8.00	6.00	3.25
Common Player:		.15	.11	.06
1	Juan Samuel	.50	.40	.20
2	Von Hayes	.35	.25	.14
4	Mike Schmidt	2.00	1.50	.80
12	Steve Carlton	1.50	1.00	.60

1986 Astros

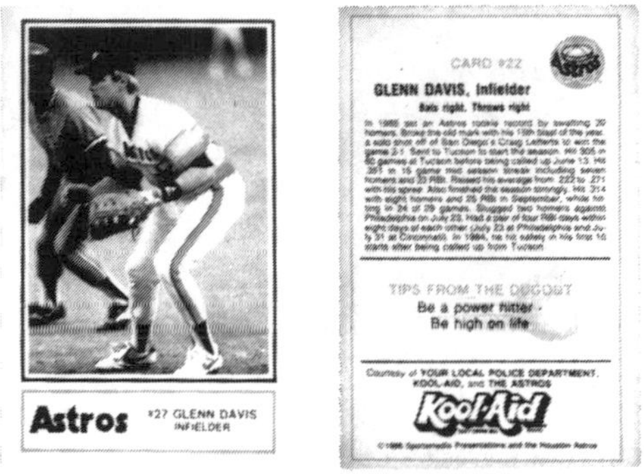

This 26-card set was distributed at an Astros' game; 15,000 sets of the first 12 cards were given away. The rest were distributed by the Houston police.

		MT	NR MT	EX
Complete Set:		8.00	6.00	3.25
Common Player:		.20	.15	.08
2	Nolan Ryan	2.00	1.50	.80
3	Mike Scott	.60	.45	.25
5	Bill Doran	.40	.30	.15
22	Glenn Davis	1.00	.70	.40
23	Billy Hatcher	.40	.30	.15
24	Jim Deshaies	.40	.30	.15

1986 Blue Jays

These sets of 36 cards, sponsored by Bubble Yum and the *Toronto Star*, were given out by many local fire stations in Ontario, Canada.

		MT	NR MT	EX
Complete Set:		10.00	7.50	4.00
Common Player:		.20	.15	.08
1	Tony Fernandez	.70	.50	.30
11	George Bell	1.25	.90	.50
17	Kelly Gruber	1.00	.70	.40
23	Cecil Fielder	1.00	.70	.40
29	Jesse Barfield	.80	.60	.30

1986 Braves

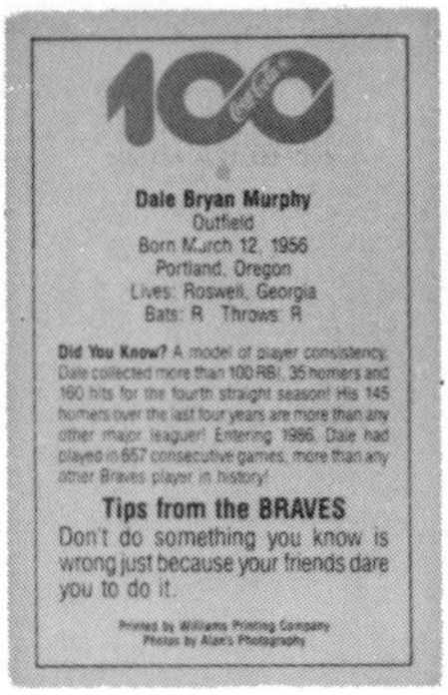

The Police Athletic League of Atlanta issued this 30-card set, available from police officers in Atlanta. The backs have the 100th anniversary Coca-Cola logo.

		MT	NR MT	EX
Complete Set:		11.00	8.25	4.50
Common Player:		.25	.20	.10
3	Dale Murphy	2.75	2.00	1.00
11	Bob Horner	.80	.60	.30
23	Ted Simmons	.50	.40	.20
40	Bruce Sutter	.60	.45	.25

1986 Brewers

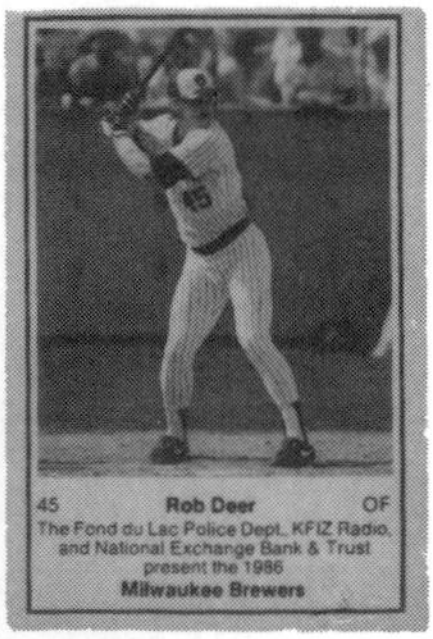

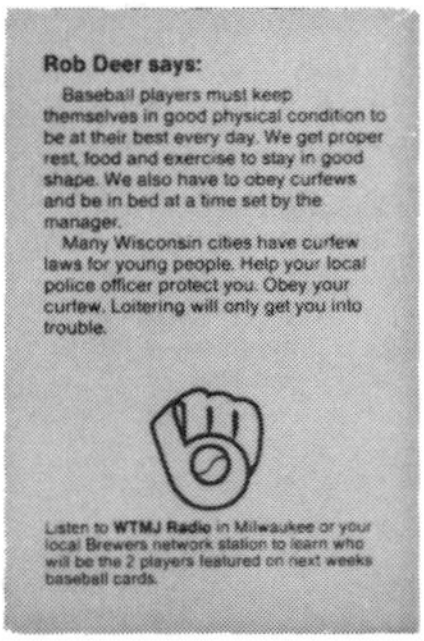

This 30-card set was again distributed in Wisconsin by numerous police departments; sets from smaller departments are considered scarcer.

		MT	NR MT	EX
Complete Set:		7.00	5.25	2.75
Common Player:		.15	.11	.06
4	Paul Molitor	.70	.50	.30
19	Robin Yount	1.00	.70	.40
20	Juan Nieves	.40	.30	.15
37	Dan Plesac	.60	.45	.25
45	Rob Deer	.40	.30	.15
49	Ted Higuera	.50	.40	.20

1986 Dodgers

After skipping the 1985 season, the Dodgers again issued a police set. The 30-card sets were given away May 18 during Baseball Card Day at Dodger Stadium.

		MT	NR MT	EX
Complete Set:		7.00	5.25	2.75
Common Player:		.15	.11	.06
3	Steve Sax	.50	.30	.15
28	Pedro Guerrero	.60	.45	.25
34	Fernando Valenzuela	.60	.45	.25
35	Bob Welch	.30	.25	.12
55	Orel Hershiser	1.00	.70	.40

1986 Phillies

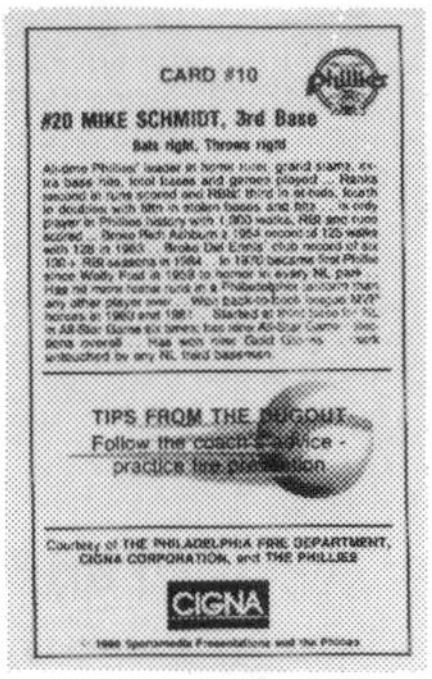

For the second straight year the Phillies issued a 16-card safety set, but this one was issued by the Philadelphia Fire Department, not the police.

		MT	NR MT	EX
Complete Set:		8.00	6.00	3.25
Common Player:		.15	.11	.06
1	Juan Samuel	.50	.40	.20
2	Don Carman	.35	.25	.14
3	Von Hayes	.30	.25	.12
10	Mike Schmidt	1.50	1.25	.60
11	Steve Bedrosian	.35	.25	.14

1987 Astros

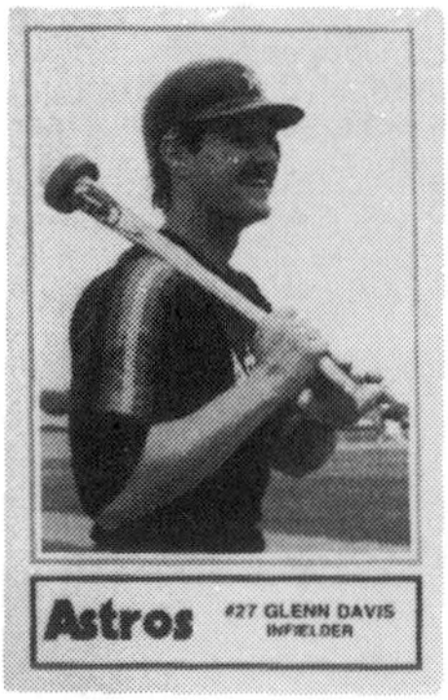

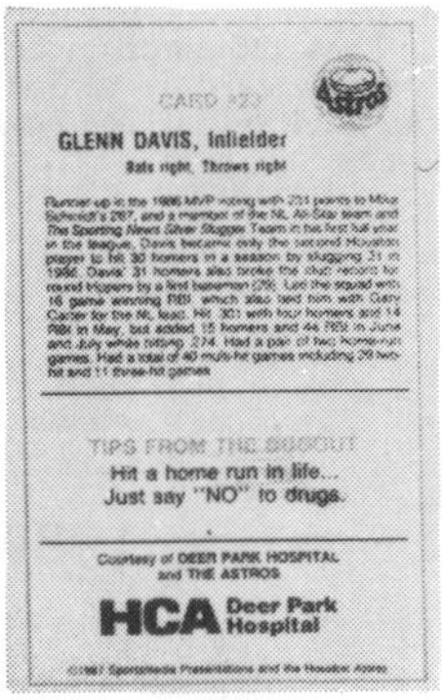

Card #s 1-12 of 26 were given to youngsters 14 and under at the Astrodome for a July 14 game. The rest of the distribution was handled by Deer Park Hospital.

		MT	NR MT	EX
Complete Set:		8.00	6.00	3.25
Common Player:		.20	.15	.08
5	Bill Doran	.40	.30	.15
6	Billy Hatcher	.40	.30	.15
11	Mike Scott	.60	.45	.25
16	Nolan Ryan	2.00	1.50	.80
23	Glenn Davis	1.00	.70	.40

1987 Blue Jays

For the fourth consecutive year the team issued a 36-card set, printed on thin stock. Sponsors included local fire departments and governing agencies.

		MT	NR MT	EX
Complete Set:		12.00	9.00	4.75
Common Player:		.15	.11	.06
1	Tony Fernandez	.50	.40	.20
11	George Bell	1.00	.70	.40
17	Kelly Gruber	.60	.45	.25
19	Fred McGriff	2.00	1.50	.80
23	Cecil Fielder	1.00	.70	.40
29	Jesse Barfield	.60	.45	.25

1987 Brewers

Several state police departments participated in distribution; the Milwaukee version as given to youngsters May 9 during Baseball Card Day at County Stadium. Chris Bosio occurs with uniform #26 or 29; the card was corrected to #29 in a later printing.

		MT	NR MT	EX
Complete Set:		6.00	4.50	2.50
Common Player:		.15	.11	.06
4	Paul Molitor	.60	.45	.25
5	B.J. Surhoff	.60	.45	.25
19	Robin Yount	1.00	.70	.40
26a	Glenn Braggs	.60	.45	.25
26b	Chris Bosio	1.00	.70	.40

1987 Dodgers

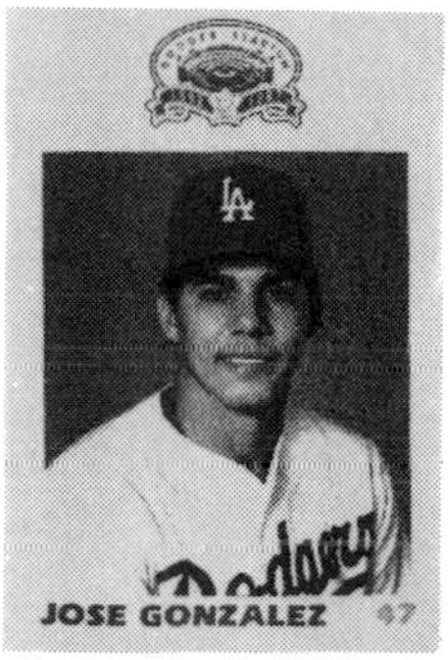

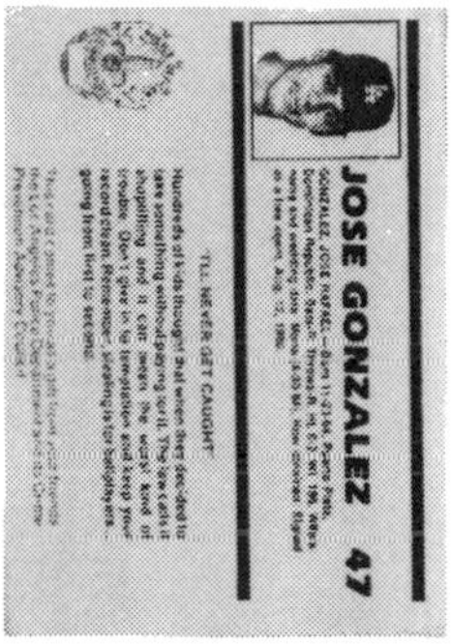

These 30 cards, including a Dodger Stadium anniversary card, were distributed at Dodger Stadium April 24 and by Los Angeles police officers, two per week.

		MT	NR MT	EX
Complete Set:		6.00	4.50	2.50
Common Player:		.15	.11	.06
3	Steve Sax	.50	.40	.20
5	Mike Marshall	.40	.30	.15
28	Pedro Guerrero	.60	.45	.25
34	Fernando Valenzuela	.60	.45	.25
55	Orel Hershiser	1.00	.70	.40

1988 Astros

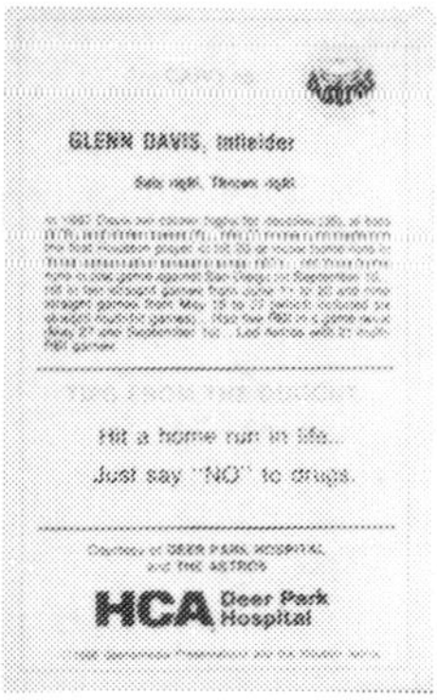

This 26-card set, distributed to fans 14 and under at a ballpark giveaway, is numbered and sponsored by the Deer Park Hospital and Sportsmedia Promotions.

		MT	NR MT	EX
Complete Set:		8.00	6.00	3.25
Common Player:		.20	.15	.08
6	Kevin Bass	.40	.30	.15
8	Glenn Davis	1.00	.70	.40
10	Bill Doran	.40	.30	.15
20	Nolan Ryan	2.00	1.50	.80
21	Mike Scott	.60	.45	.25
24	Gerald Young	.60	.45	.25

1988 Blue Jays

This 36-card set, numbered according to player uniform numbers, was distributed free as a part of a community service project.

		MT	NR MT	EX
Complete Set:		8.00	6.00	3.25
Common Player:		.15	.11	.06
1	Tony Fernandez	.60	.45	.25
11	George Bell	1.00	.70	.40
16	Todd Stottlemyre	.60	.45	.25
17	Kelly Gruber	.60	.45	.25
19	Fred McGriff	1.00	.70	.40
23	Cecil Fielder	1.00	.70	.40
29	Jesse Barfield	.60	.45	.25

1988 Brewers

This seventh annual set, 30 cards, uses the 1987 design. Two group photos — team coaches and the team — are unnumbered and printed horizontally.

		MT	NR MT	EX
Complete Set:		6.00	4.50	2.50
Common Player:		.15	.11	.06
4	Paul Molitor	.60	.45	.25
19	Robin Yount	1.00	.70	.40
23	Joey Meyer	.35	.25	.14
37	Dan Plesac	.40	.30	.15
49	Ted Higuera	.40	.30	.15

1988 Dodgers

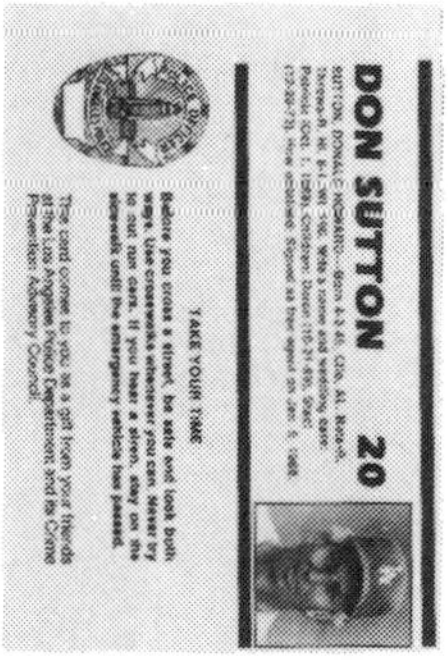

The Los Angeles police department sponsored this 30-card set, with three double-photo cards featuring posed closeups and two card numbers (players #'s).

		MT	NR MT	EX
Complete Set:		6.00	4.50	2.50
Common Player:		.15	.11	.06
3	Steve Sax	.50	.40	.20
23	Kirk Gibson	.60	.45	.25
28	Pedro Guerrero	.50	.40	.20
34	Fernando Valenzuela	.60	.45	.25
55	Orel Hershiser	.80	.60	.30

1988 Tigers

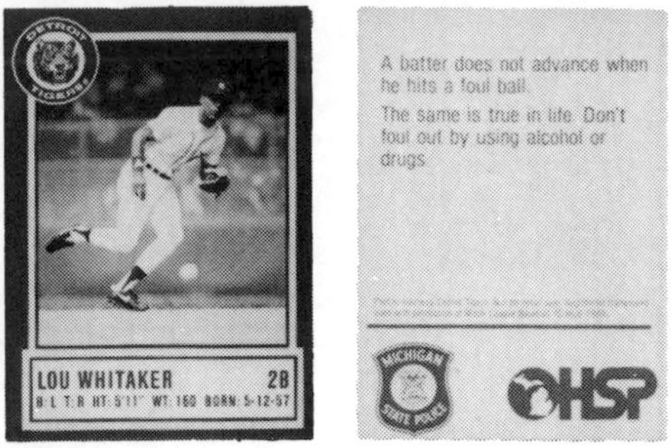

This unnumbered set, sponsored by the Michigan State Police, has 13 players and Sparky Anderson. The cards are 2½" by 3½".

		MT	NR MT	EX
Complete Set:		35.00	25.00	14.00
Common Player:		.50	.40	.20
(8)	Jack Morris	.80	.60	.30
(9)	Matt Nokes	.80	.60	.30
(13)	Alan Trammell	1.00	.70	.40
(14)	Lou Whitaker	.80	.60	.30

NOTE: A card number in parentheses ( ) indicates the set is unnumbered.

1989 Blue Jays

This safety set has 34 cards. The fronts have an "On the Move" logo and the players' uniform numbers in the upper left.

		MT	NR MT	EX
Complete Set:		6.00	4.50	2.50
Common Player:		.15	.11	.06
1	Tony Fernandez	.50	.40	.20
11	George Bell	.90	.70	.35
17	Kelly Gruber	.50	.40	.20
19	Fred McGriff	1.00	.70	.40
29	Jesse Barfield	.40	.30	.15
30	Todd Stottlemyre	.40	.30	.15
37	Dave Stieb	.40	.30	.15

1989 Brewers

Officers from more than 90 Wisconsin law enforcement agencies distributed this 30-card set in the summer. Complete sets were also a stadium giveaway.

		MT	NR MT	EX
Complete Set:		7.00	5.25	2.75
Common Player:		.15	.11	.06
1	Gary Sheffield	1.00	.70	.40
4	Paul Molitor	.60	.45	.25
6	Bill Spiers	.80	.60	.30
19	Robin Yount	1.00	.70	.40
37	Dan Plesac	.35	.25	.14
49	Teddy Higuera	.40	.30	.15

1989 Dodgers

The Dodgers and the Los Angeles Police Department sponsored this 30-card set.The Dodgers logo, 1989, and player uniform numbers are on the fronts.

		MT	NR MT	EX
Complete Set:		6.00	4.50	2.50
Common Player:		.15	.11	.06
23	Kirk Gibson	.40	.30	.15
33	Eddie Murray	.60	.45	.25
34	Fernando Valenzuela	.40	.30	.15
48	Ramon Martinez	2.00	1.50	.80
55	Orel Hershiser	.80	.60	.30

1989 Tigers

This unnumbered set, issued by the Michigan State Police Department, has 14 cards. Biographical information is on the fronts.

		MT	NR MT	EX
Complete Set:		9.00	6.75	3.50
Common Player:		.25	.20	.10
4	Mike Henneman	.50	.40	.20
8	Jack Morris	.50	.40	.20
13	Alan Trammell	.90	.70	.35
14	Lou Whitaker	.60	.45	.25

1990 Blue Jays

This 35-card set's fronts have a special Blue Jays fan club logo in the upper left corner. Cards are numbered according to player uniform numbers.

		MT	NR MT	EX
Complete Set:		8.00	6.00	3.25
Common Player:		.15	.11	.06
9	John Olreud	1.50	1.25	.60
11	George Bell	.60	.45	.25
17	Kelly Gruber	.50	.40	.20
19	Fred McGriff	.70	.50	.30
24	Glenallen Hill	.50	.40	.20
47	Junior Felix	.70	.50	.30

1990 Dodgers

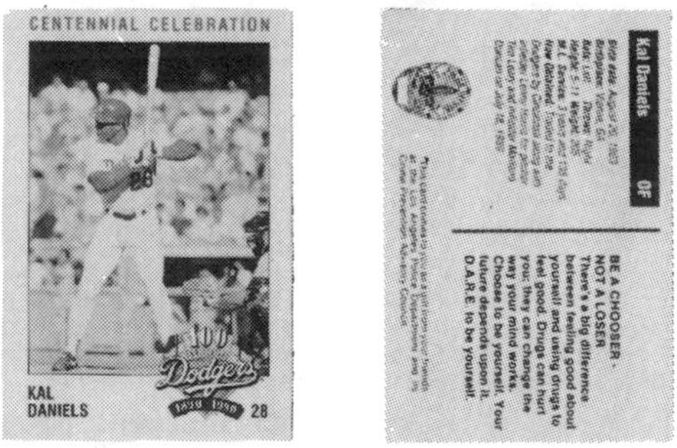

This set honors the centennial celebration of the Los Angeles Dodgers. A special 100th anniversary logo is on the fronts. The cards are 2¾" by 4¼".

		MT	NR MT	EX
Complete Set:		6.00	4.50	2.50
Common Player:		.15	.11	.06
21	Hubie Brooks	.40	.30	.15
28	Kal Daniels	.40	.30	.15
33	Eddie Murray	.60	.45	.25
48	Ramon Martinez	1.00	.70	.40
55	Orel Hershiser	.60	.45	.25

A player's name in *italic* type indicates a rookie card. An (FC) indicates a player's first card for that particular card company.

1984 Smokey Bear Dodgers

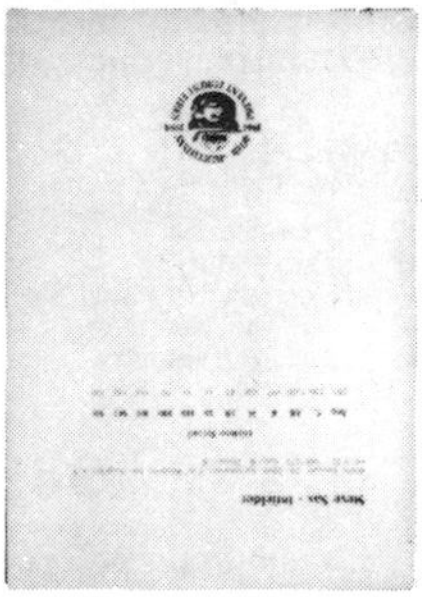

This Los Angeles Dodgers set of three players, on 5" by 7" cards, and a Smokey Bear card, were distributed at a Dodgers home game. Players are pictured in a forest scene on the colored fronts. Unnumbered backs have biographies and lifetime stats.

		MT	NR MT	EX
Complete Set:		12.00	9.00	4.75
Common Player:		2.50	2.00	1.00
(1)	Ken Landreaux	2.50	2.00	1.00
(2)	Tom Niedenfuer	2.50	2.00	1.00
(3)	Steve Sax	6.00	4.50	2.50
(4)	Smokey Bear	.50	.40	.20

1984 Smokey Bear Angels

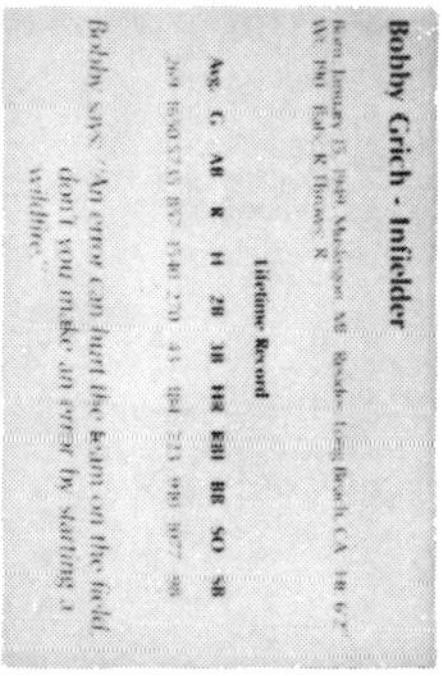

This 32-card set, distributed at an Angels game, has cards measuring 2½" by 3½". Colored fronts list the player name, team logo and a Forestry Service logo commemorating Smokey Bear's 40th birthday. The black-and-white backs have fire prevention tips.

		MT	NR MT	EX
Complete Set:		8.00	6.00	3.25
Common Player:		.20	.15	.08
(5)	Rod Carew	1.00	.70	.40
(11)	Reggie Jackson	1.25	.90	.50
(13)	Tommy John	.60	.45	.25
(17)	Fred Lynn	.60	.45	.25
(29)	Mike Witt	.50	.40	.20

1984 Smokey Bear Jackson Mets In Majors

This set, issued in conjunction with the Mississippi Forestry Commission, features big leaguers who played for the Mets' Double A farm club. Each of the 15 3" by 4" cards has a black-and-white portrait photo, player name, position and major league team shown in blue, and a Smokey Bear logo. Backs have player information and career highlights.

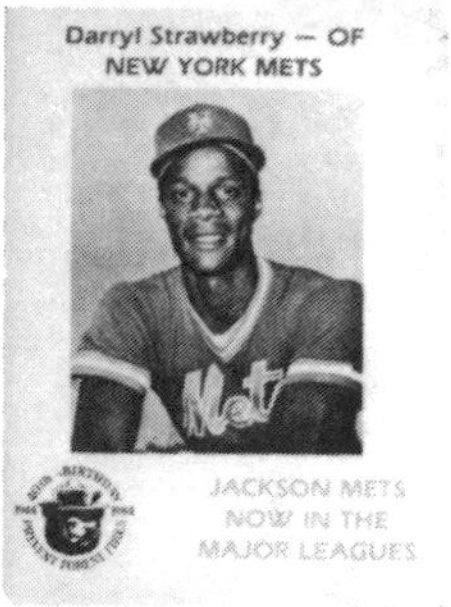

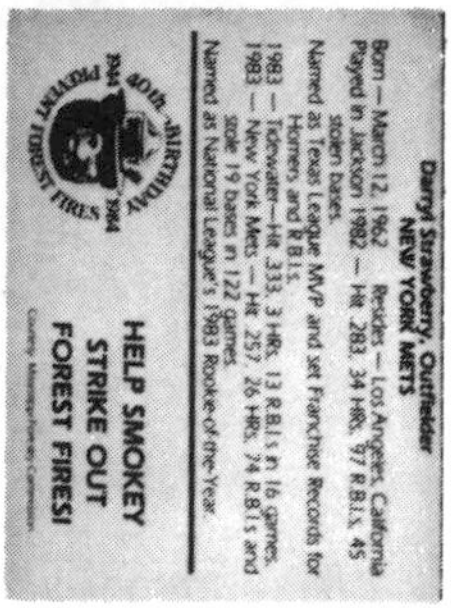

		MT	NR MT	EX
Complete Set:		60.00	45.00	25.00
Common Player:		1.00	.70	.40
(3)	Hubie Brooks	3.00	2.25	1.25
(10)	Jeff Reardon	3.00	2.25	1.25
(12)	Darryl Strawberry	20.00	15.00	8.00
(13)	Mookie Wilson	4.00	3.00	1.50

1984 Smokey Bear Padres

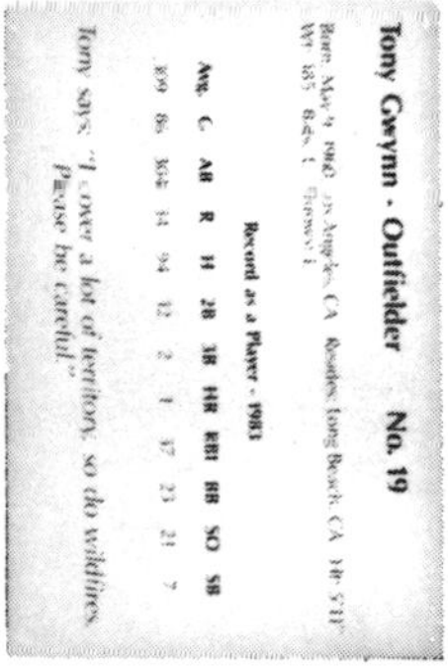

This 28-card set, distributed at a Padres home game, has Padres players, coaches, broadcasters and the Famous Chicken in posed colored photos with Smokey Bear. Forestry Department and team logos are also on the fronts. The backs have brief player information and a fire prevention tip.

		MT	NR MT	EX
Complete Set:		10.00	7.50	4.00
Common Player:		.25	.20	.10
6	Steve Garvey	1.25	.90	.50
18	Kevin McReynolds	1.25	.90	.50
19	Tony Gwynn	1.50	1.25	.60
30	Eric Show	.50	.40	.20

1985 Smokey Bear Angels

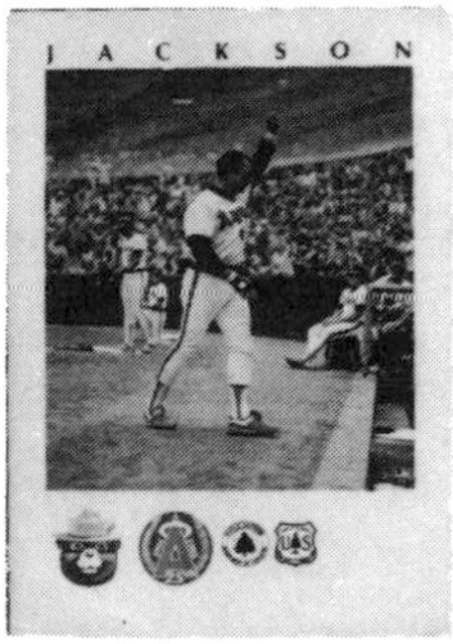

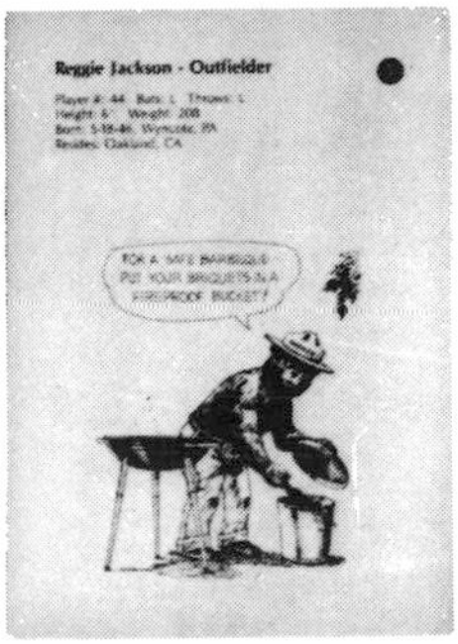

The California Forestry Service and the California Angels distributed this full-color, oversized (4¼" by 6"), 24-card set to fans attending an Angels home game. Fronts have player photos and last names. Bottoms have Smokey Bear, Angels, and the State Forestry Service and the U.S. Forestry Service logos. Black-and-white backs have personal data, limited playing stats and a wildfire safety tip.

		MT	NR MT	EX
Complete Set:		7.00	5.25	2.75
Common Player:		.20	.15	.08
1	Mike Witt	.50	.40	.20
2	Reggie Jackson	1.25	.90	.50
5	Rod Carew	1.00	.70	.40
23	Tommy John	.60	.45	.22

1986 Smokey Bear Angels

The California Angels, with the Forestry Service, issued this 24-card set, distributed at an Angels home game. The 4¼" by 6" cards have full-color fronts with the players'pictures in oval frames. The backs have stats and a drawing and slogan for fire prevention.

		MT	NR MT	EX
Complete Set:		8.00	6.00	3.25
Common Player:		.20	.15	.08
1	Mike Witt	.50	.40	.20
2	Reggie Jackson	1.25	.90	.50
4	Don Sutton	.60	.45	.25
5	Kirk McCaskill	.50	.40	.20
22	Wally Joyner	2.50	2.00	1.00

1987 Smokey Bear

The U.S. Forestry Service and Major League Baseball joined to promote National Smokey Bear Day. Two perforated colored sheets of cards, one each for the American and National Leagues, were produced by the Forestry Service. The 18" by 24" sheet of American Leaguers has 16 cards; the National League 20" by 18" sheet has 15. Each card is 4" by 6" and contains a fire prevention tip on the back. An average number of 25,000 sets was sent to all teams.

		MT	NR MT	EX
Complete Set:		8.00	6.00	3.25
Common Player:		.20	.15	.08
1A	Jose Canseco	1.50	1.25	.60
2Na	Dale Murphy (shirttail out)	5.00	3.75	2.00
2Nb	Dale Murphy (shirttail in)	.80	.60	.30
3Na	Jody Davis (standing)	3.50	2.75	1.50
8A	Kirby Puckett	.70	.50	.30
10N	Steve Garvey	.60	.45	.25

1987 Smokey Bear A's

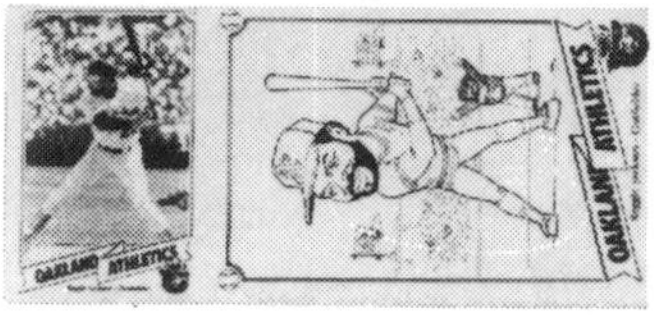

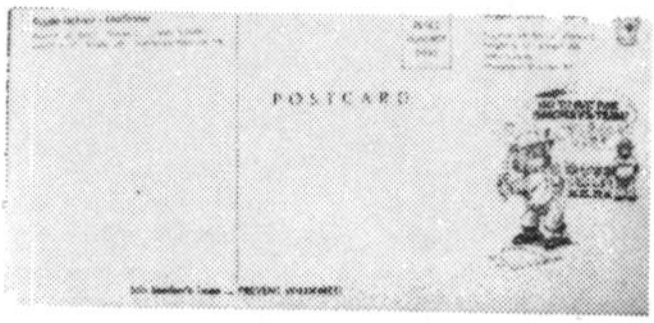

The 1987 Smokey Bear A's set of 12 is bound in a book titled "Smokey Bear's Fire Prevention Color-Grams." The Color-Gram cards, distributed at an A's game, feature two cards in one. A near-standard size (2½" by 3¾") black-and-white card is attached to a large perforated (3¾" by 6") card, also black-and-white, with a postcard back. It features a caricature photo of the player and is intended to be colored and then mailed. The backs have personal and statistical information and a Smokey Bear cartoon message.

		MT	NR MT	EX
Complete Book:		6.00	4.50	2.50
Complete Singles Set:		3.00	2.25	1.25
Common Single Player:		.15	.11	.06
(2)	Jose Canseco	1.50	1.25	.60
(7)	Reggie Jackson	.80	.60	.30
(8)	Carney Lansford	.30	.25	.12
(11)	Dave Stewart	.40	.30	.15

1987 Smokey Bear Angels

This 24-card set, produced by the U.S. Forestry Service, was distributed to approximately 25,000 fans at an Angels game. The full-color, 4" by 6" cards have a unique design — baseballs and bats framing the photos. Only the players' last names are on the fronts. The backs have the players' names, positions, stats, a Smokey Bear cartoon and a fire prevention tip.

	MT	NR MT	EX
Complete Set:	8.00	6.00	3.25
Common Player:	.20	.15	.08

		MT	NR MT	EX
2	Don Sutton	.60	.45	.25
3	Mike Witt	.50	.40	.20
12	Wally Joyner	2.00	1.50	.80
23	Devon White	1.25	.90	.50

1987 Smokey Bear Cardinals

This 25-card set, distributed to approximately 25,000 fans at a Cardinals home game, was produced by the U.S. Forestry Service. The cards, 4" by 6", feature colored photos set inside oval frames. Only the player's last name is on the front. The back has the player's name, position, personal data and a Smokey Bear cartoon with a fire prevention message.

		MT	NR MT	EX
Complete Set:		8.00	6.00	3.25
Common Player:		.20	.15	.08
2	Todd Worrell	.50	.40	.20
13	Jack Clark	.80	.60	.30
16	Terry Pendleton	.40	.30	.15
17	Ozzie Smith	.80	.60	.30
22	Willie McGee	.70	.50	.30
24	Vince Coleman	.80	.60	.30

1987 Smokey Bear Dodgers

This 40-card set features "25 Years of Dodger All-Stars." The 2½" by 3¾" cards, distributed at a Dodgers game, have colored photos set in the shape of Dodger Stadium, with silver borders. The backs have the players' All-Star game records and a fire prevention message. Many photos were from team-issued picture packs previously sold by the team.

		MT	NR MT	EX
Complete Set:		10.00	7.50	4.00
Common Player:		.20	.15	.08
(7)	Don Drysdale	.80	.60	.30
(8)	Steve Garvey	.80	.60	.30
(12)	Orel Hershiser	.60	.45	.25
(16)	Sandy Koufax	1.25	.90	.50
(35)	Don Sutton	.60	.45	.25
(36)	Fernando Valenzuela	.70	.50	.30

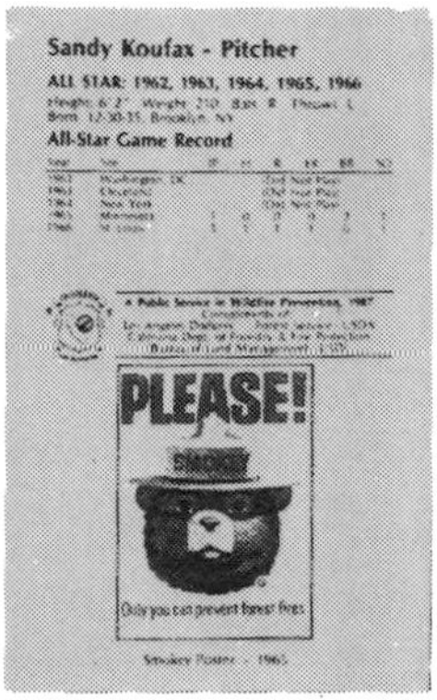

1987 Smokey Bear Rangers

This 32-card set, sponsored by the Texas Rangers, U.S. Forest Service and Texas Forest Service, was distributed to fans at promotions at Arlington Stadium. The cards, 4¼" by 6", have colored photos on the fronts. The backs have brief player personal information, a card number and a Smokey Bear message. The team withdrew cards of Mike Mason and Tom Paciorek from the set; they are quite scarce.

		MT	NR MT	EX
Complete Set:		70.00	52.00	27.00
Common Player:		.30	.25	.12
4	Mike Mason	25.00	20.00	10.00
6	Bobby Witt	.80	.60	.30
14	Tom Paciorek	25.00	20.00	10.00
15	Pete Incaviglia	1.00	.70	.40
17	Ruben Sierra	1.50	1.25	.60

1988 Smokey Bear Angels

This set has 25 borderless, color cards (2½" by 3½") that are highlighted by a thin white inset outline on the fronts. The player name, team logo and a Smokey Bear picture logo are in the lower right corner. The black-and-white backs have personal information and a large cartoon-style fire prevention logo. Cards, including a team logo checklist card, were part of the U.S. Forest Service fire prevention campaign and were distributed during three stadium giveaway days.

		MT	NR MT	EX
Complete Set:		10.00	7.50	4.00
Common Player:		.30	.25	.12
4	Mike Witt	.50	.40	.20
13	Devon White	.80	.60	.30
17	Wally Joyner	1.50	1.25	.60

1988 Smokey Bear Cardinals

This set of 25 oversized (3" by 5") cards features colored action photos on the entire card fronts. A thin white line frames the photos. The player's name, and team and Smokey Bear logos are also included. The black-and-white backs have player information and a Smokey Bear fire prevention cartoon. The sets, distributed to young St. Louis fans, were a Forest Service

fire prevention campaign, co-sponsored by the National Association of State Foresters.

		MT	NR MT	EX
Complete Set:		10.00	7.50	4.00
Common Player:		.20	.15	.08
6	Joe Magrane	.50	.40	.20
10	Todd Worrell	.50	.40	.20
18	Ozzie Smith	.80	.60	.30
19	Vince Coleman	.80	.60	.30
21	Willie McGee	.70	.50	.30
25	Tom Brunansky	.50	.40	.20

1988 Smokey Bear Dodgers

Record-breaking Dodgers from the past three decades are featured in this 32-card perforated sheet given to fans attending a Dodgers game. Individual cards, 2½'' by 4'', are printed on a light blue background. The black-and-white card backs have the player's name, a summary of the his record-breaking performance and a reproduction of one of several Smokey Bear fire prevention posters printed during the 1950s through 1980s. The sheets were sponsored by the Piedmont brand of the Liggert & Meyers Tobacco Co., the Forest Service, California Department of Forestry and the Bureau of Land Management.

		MT	NR MT	EX
Complete Set:		10.00	7.50	4.00
Common Player:		.20	.15	.08
4	Sandy Koufax	1.25	.90	.50
6	Record Pitchers (Sandy Koufax, Jerry Reuss, Bill Singer)	.70	.50	.30
11	Don Drysdale	.80	.60	.30
17	Steve Garvey	.80	.60	.30
24	Fernando Valenzuela	.70	.50	.30
30	Don Sutton	.60	.45	.25

1988 Smokey Bear Padres

This 33-card oversized (3'' by 5'') set, produced by the U.S. Forest Service as a fire prevention campaign, has colored photos, framed by a thin white line,

on the fronts, and the players' numbers, positions and a Smokey Bear logo. The black-and-white card backs, printed in a horizontal postcard format, have player information and a Smokey Bear cartoon. The set was available for sale at the Padres Gift Shop. Cards of Candy Sierra and Larry Bowa were not released by the team; they are quite rare. The complete set price does not include these rare cards.

		MT	NR MT	EX
Complete Set:		12.00	9.00	4.75
Common Player:		.30	.25	.12
(2)	Roberto Alomar	1.25	.90	.50
(5)	Larry Bowa	10.00	7.50	4.00
(11)	Tony Gwynn	1.50	1.25	.60
(15)	John Kruk	.80	.60	.30
(26)	Benito Santiago	.80	.60	.30
(28)	Candy Sierra	10.00	7.50	4.00

1988 Smokey Bear Rangers

This 21-card oversized (3½'' by 5'') set, distributed to Rangers' fans at Smokey Bear Game Day, has colored action photos framed in an oval blue and red border on a white background. A nameplate above the photo identifies the player. Wildfire prevention, Rangers and Smokey Bear logos are also shown. The black-and-white backs have player information, U.S. and Texas Forest Service logos, and fire prevention tips.

		MT	NR MT	EX
Complete Set:		9.00	6.75	3.50
Common Player:		.30	.25	.12
4	Pete Incaviglia	.70	.50	.30
7	Bobby Witt	.60	.45	.25
9	Ruben Sierra	1.00	.70	.40
13	Charlie Hough	.50	.40	.20
19	Mitch Williams	.40	.30	.15

1988 Smokey Bear Royals

This 28-card set, featuring color player caricatures by K.K. Goodale, was produced for an in-stadium promotion. The 3'' by 5'' cards depict players, the manager and coaches in action poses against a white background. A Royals logo and Smokey Bear logo also

appear. The black-and-white backs have brief player data and a Smokey cartoon.

	MT	NR MT	EX
Complete Set:	12.00	9.00	4.75
Common Player:	.20	.15	.08
4 Danny Tartabull	.70	.50	.30
5 Bo Jackson	1.50	1.25	.60
16 Bret Saberhagen	.70	.50	.30
20 George Brett	1.25	.90	.50
21 Kevin Seitzer	.80	.60	.30

1988 Smokey Bear Twins

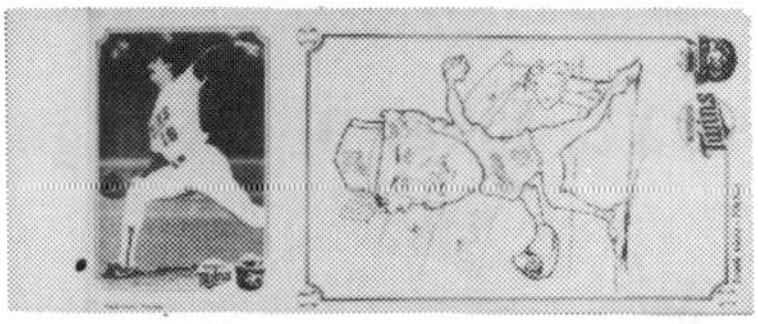

This 8¼" by 3¾" booklet contains 12 postcards called Color-Grams, featuring caricatures (suitable for coloring) of star Twins. Postcards are attached along a perforated edge to a baseball card-size stub with a black-and-white photo of the featured player. The postcard backs have the player names and personal information. The card stubs have the same information and a fire prevention tip. Twins Color-Grams, produced as a public service by the U.S. Forest Service and Department of Agriculture, were distributed to fans at a Twins home game.

	MT	NR MT	EX
Complete Set:	12.00	9.00	4.75
Common Player:	.70	.50	.30
(1) Bert Blyleven	1.00	.70	.40
(3) Gary Gaetti	1.50	1.25	.60
(6) Kent Hrbek	1.75	1.30	.70
(10) Kirby Puckett	2.00	1.50	.80
(11) Jeff Reardon	1.00	.70	.40
(12) Frank Viola	1.75	1.30	.70

1989 Smokey Bear Angels All-Stars

The U.S. Forest Service and Angels issued this 20-card set of "Angels All-Stars." The standard-size cards, printed on a silver background, with player

photos bordered in red, have a banner across home-plate which says "Angels All-Stars," and the player's name and position. A Smokey Bear and Angels 1989 All-Star Game logo are also included. Backs highlight the players' careers with the Angels and include an illustrated fire prevention tip.

	MT	NR MT	EX
Complete Set:	6.00	4.50	2.50
Common Player	.20	.15	.08
7 Nolan Ryan	1.00	.70	.40
8 Frank Robinson	.80	.60	.30
10 Rod Carew	.50	.40	.20
15 Reggie Jackson	.70	.50	.30
18 Wally Joyner	.60	.45	.25

1989 Smokey Bear Cardinals

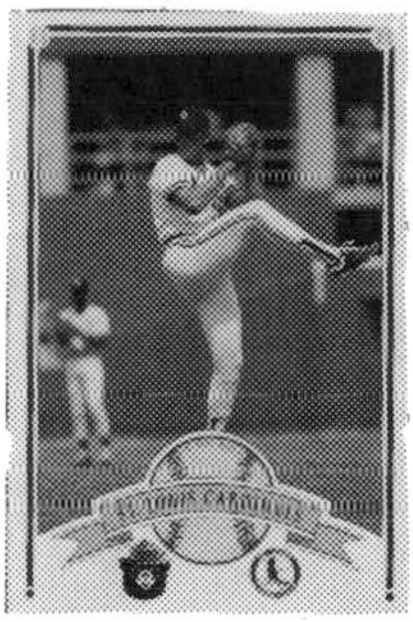

This 23-card set, featuring action player photos, was issued by the U.S. Forest Service to promote fire safety. The 4" by 6" card fronts have the players' names, team logo and small picture of Smokey Bear.

	MT	NR MT	EX
Complete Set:	10.00	7.50	4.00
Common Player:	.20	.15	.08
(3) Vince Coleman	.80	.60	.30
(9) Ken Hill	.80	.60	.30
(10) Pedro Guerrero	.80	.60	.30
(14) Willie McGee	.50	.40	.20
(21) Ozzie Smith	.80	.60	.30

1990 Smokey Bear Angels

This 20-card set, sponsored by the U.S. Forestry Service, was distributed at an Angels game. The cards have colored action photos surrounded by metallic-looking silver borders. The Angels and Smokey Bear logos are on the fronts. Backs have player data and a cartoon Smokey Bear fire prevention message.

	MT	NR MT	EX
Complete Set:	5.00	3.75	2.00
Common Player:	.20	.15	.08
1 Jim Abbott	.50	.40	.20
2 Bert Blyleven	.40	.30	.15
3 Chili Davis	.30	.25	12
5 Chuck Finley	.30	.25	.12
9 Wally Joyner	.40	.30	.15
10 Mark Langston	.30	.25	.12

1953 Stahl-Meyer Franks

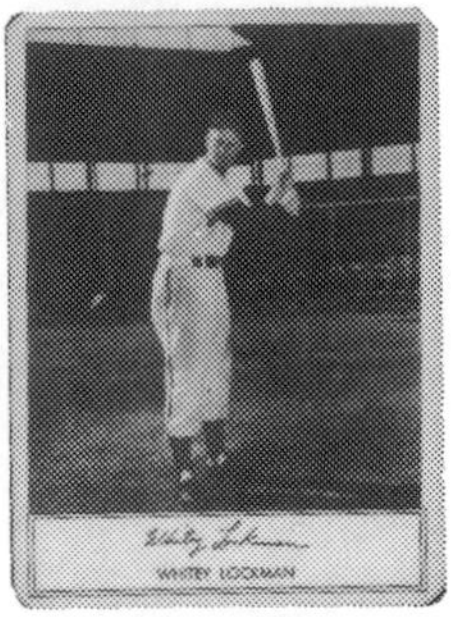

These nine cards, issued in packages of hot dogs by a New York area meat company, feature three players from each of the New York teams of the day - Dodgers Giants and Yankees. Cards in the set measure 3-1/4" by 4-1/2". The card fronts in this unnumbered set feature color photos with player name and facsimile autograph. The backs list both biographical and statistical information on half the card and a ticket offer promotion on the other half. The card corners are cut diagonally, although some cards (apparently cut from sheets) with square corners have been seen. Cards are white-bordered.

		NR MT	EX	VG
Complete Set:		4500.00	2250.00	1350.
Common Player:		125.00	62.00	37.00
(1)	Hank Bauer	150.00	75.00	45.00
(2)	Roy Campanella	550.00	275.00	165.00
(3)	Gil Hodges	300.00	150.00	90.00
(4)	Monte Irvin	200.00	100.00	60.00
(5)	Whitey Lockman	125.00	62.00	37.00
(6)	Mickey Mantle	2000.00	1000.00	600.00
(7)	Phil Rizzuto	300.00	150.00	90.00
(8)	Duke Snider	550.00	275.00	165.00
(9)	Bobby Thompson	150.00	75.00	45.00

1954 Stahl-Meyer Franks

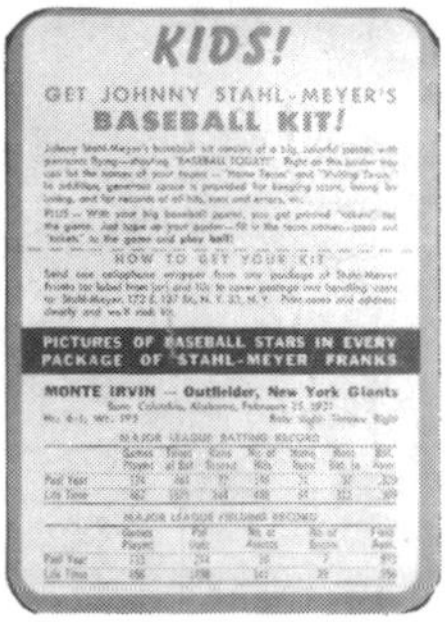

The 1954 set of Stahl-Meyer Franks was increased to 12 cards which retained the 3-1/4" by 4-1/2" size. The most prominent addition to the '54 set was New York Giants slugger Willie Mays. The card fronts are identical in format to the previous year's set. However, the backs are different as they are designed on a vertical format. The backs also contain an advertisement for a "Johnny Stahl-Meyer Baseball Kit." The cards in the set are unnumbered.

		NR MT	EX	VG
Complete Set:		6250.00	3125.00	1875.
Common Player:		125.00	62.00	37.00
(1)	Hank Bauer	150.00	75.00	45.00
(2)	Carl Erskine	150.00	75.00	45.00
(3)	Gil Hodges	300.00	150.00	90.00
(4)	Monte Irvin	225.00	112.00	67.00
(5)	Whitey Lockman	125.00	62.00	37.00
(6)	Gil McDougald	150.00	75.00	45.00
(7)	Mickey Mantle	2500.00	1250.00	750.00
(8)	Willie Mays	1250.00	625.00	375.00
(9)	Don Mueller	125.00	62.00	37.00
(10)	Don Newcombe	150.00	75.00	45.00
(11)	Phil Rizzuto	300.00	150.00	90.00
(12)	Duke Snider	575.00	287.00	172.00

1955 Stahl-Meyer Franks

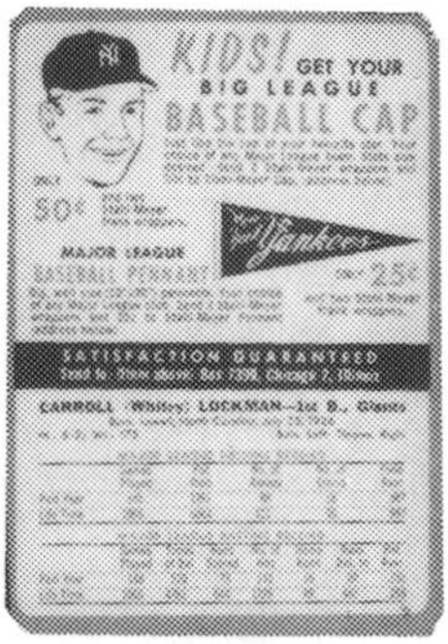

Eleven of the 12 players in the 1955 set are the same as those featured in 1954. The exception is the New York Giants Dusty Rhodes, who replaced Willie Mays on the 3-1/4" by 4-1/2" cards. The card fronts are again full-color photos bordered in yellow with diagonal corners, and four players from each of the three New York teams are featured. The backs offer a new promotion, with a drawing of Mickey Mantle and advertisements selling pennants and caps. Player statistics are still included on the vertical card backs. The cards in the set are unnumbered.

		NR MT	EX	VG
Complete Set:		5000.00	2500.00	1500.
Common Player:		125.00	62.00	37.00
(1)	Hank Bauer	150.00	75.00	45.00
(2)	Carl Erskine	150.00	75.00	45.00
(3)	Gil Hodges	300.00	150.00	90.00
(4)	Monte Irvin	200.00	100.00	60.00
(5)	Whitey Lockman	125.00	62.00	37.00
(6)	Mickey Mantle	2500.00	1250.00	750.00
(7)	Gil McDougald	150.00	75.00	45.00
(8)	Don Mueller	125.00	62.00	37.00
(9)	Don Newcombe	150.00	75.00	45.00
(10)	Jim Rhodes	125.00	62.00	37.00
(11)	Phil Rizzuto	300.00	150.00	90.00
(12)	Duke Snider	575.00	287.00	172.00

1983 Stuart Expos

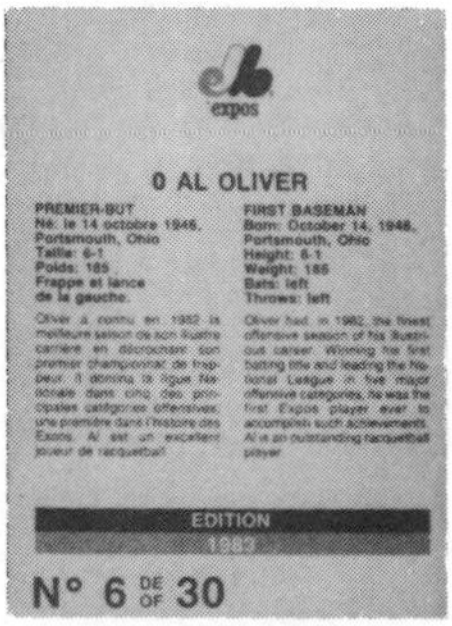

This set of Montreal Expos players and coaches was issued by a Montreal area baking company for

inclusion in packages of snack cakes. The 30 cards feature full-color player photos, with the player name, number and team logo also on the card fronts. The backs list brief player biographies in both English and French. Twenty-five players are pictured on the 2-1/2" by 3-1/2" cards.

		MT	NR MT	EX
Complete Set:		13.00	9.75	5.25
Common Player:		.25	.20	.10
1	Bill Virdon	.25	.20	.10
2	Woodie Fryman	.25	.20	.10
3	Vern Rapp	.25	.20	.10
4	Andre Dawson	2.00	1.50	.80
5	Jeff Reardon	.70	.50	.30
6	Al Oliver	.50	.40	.20
7	Doug Flynn	.25	.20	.10
8	Gary Carter	1.00	.70	.40
9	Tim Raines	1.50	1.25	.60
10	Steve Rogers	.30	.25	.12
11	Billy DeMars	.25	.20	.10
12	Tim Wallach	1.00	.70	.40
13	Galen Cisco	.25	.20	.10
14	Terry Francona	.25	.20	.10
15	Bill Gullickson	.25	.20	.10
16	Ray Burris	.25	.20	.10
17	Scott Sanderson	.35	.25	.14
18	Warren Cromartie	.25	.20	.10
19	Jerry White	.25	.20	.10
20	Bobby Ramos	.25	.20	.10
21	Jim Wolhford	.25	.20	.10
22	Dan Schatzeder	.25	.20	.10
23	Charlie Lea	.25	.20	.10
24	Bryan Little	.25	.20	.10
25	Mel Wright	.25	.20	.10
26	Tim Blackwell	.25	.20	.10
27	Chris Speier	.25	.20	.10
28	Randy Lerch	.25	.20	.10
29	Bryn Smith	.35	.25	.14
30	Brad Mills	.25	.20	.10

1984 Stuart Expos

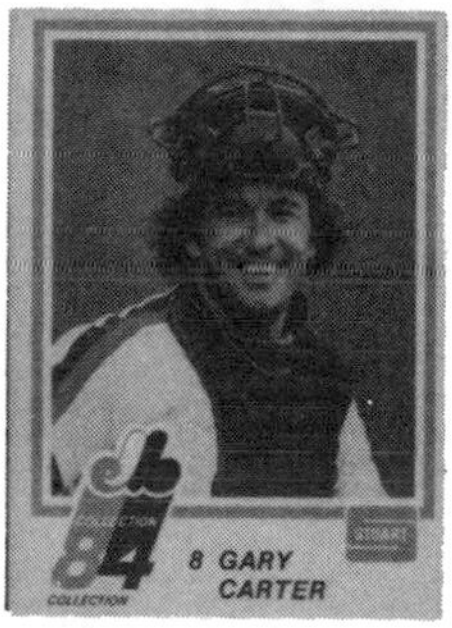

For the second year in a row, Stuart Cakes issued a full-color card set of the Montreal Expos. The 2-1/2" by 3-1/2" cards again list the player name and number along with the team and company logos on the card fronts. The backs are bilingual with biographical information in both English and French. The 40-card set was issued in two series. Card numbers 21-40, issued late in the summer, are more difficult to find than the first 20 cards. The 40 cards include players, the manager, coaches and team mascot.

		MT	NR MT	EX
Complete Set:		40.00	30.00	15.00
Common Player: 1-20		.25	.20	.10
Common Player: 21-40		.50	.40	.20
1	Youppi! (mascot)	.25	.20	.10
2	Bill Virdon	.25	.20	.10
3	Billy DeMars	.25	.20	.10
4	Galen Cisco	.25	.20	.10
5	Russ Nixon	.25	.20	.10
6	Felipe Alou	.25	.20	.10
7	Dan Schatzeder	.25	.20	.10
8	Charlie Lea	.25	.20	.10
9	Bobby Ramos	.25	.20	.10
10	Bob James	.25	.20	.10
11	Andre Dawson	2.00	1.50	.80
12	Gary Lucas	.25	.20	.10
13	Jeff Reardon	.50	.40	.20
14	Tim Wallach	1.00	.70	.40
15	Gary Carter	2.00	1.50	.80
16	Bill Gullickson	.25	.20	.10
17	Pete Rose	4.00	3.00	1.50
18	Terry Francona	.25	.20	.10
19	Steve Rogers	.30	.25	.12
20	Tim Raines	1.50	1.25	.60
21	Bryn Smith	.50	.40	.20
22	Greg Harris	.50	.40	.20
23	David Palmer	.50	.40	.20
24	Jim Wohlford	.50	.40	.20
25	Miguel Dilone	.50	.40	.20
26	Mike Stenhouse	.50	.40	.20
27	Chris Speier	.50	.40	.20
28	Derrel Thomas	.50	.40	.20
29	Doug Flynn	.50	.40	.20
30	Bryan Little	.50	.40	.20
31	Argenis Salazar	.50	.40	.20
32	Mike Fuentes	.50	.40	.20
33	Joe Kerrigan	.50	.40	.20
34	Andy McGaffigan	.45	.35	.20
35	Fred Breining	.50	.40	.20
36	Expos 1983 All-Stars (Gary Carter, Andre Dawson, Tim Raines, Steve Rogers)	1.50	1.25	.60
37	Co-Players Of The Year (Andre Dawson, Tim Raines)	1.50	1.25	.60
38	Expos' Coaching Staff (Felipe Alou, Galen Cisco, Billy DeMars, Joe Kerrigan, Russ Nixon, Bill Virdon)	.50	.40	.20
39	Team Photo	.50	.40	.20
40	Checklist	.50	.40	.20

1987 Stuart

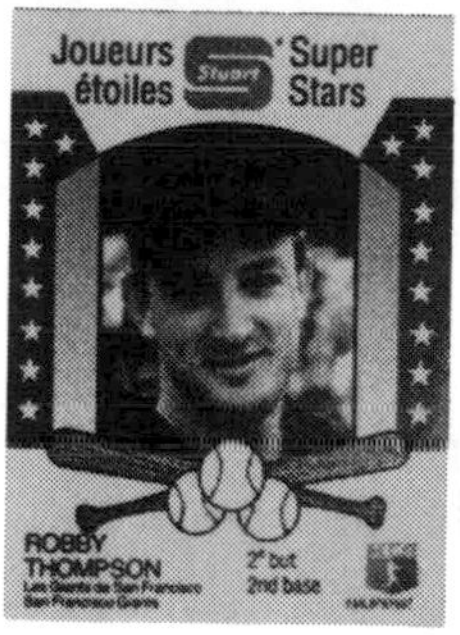

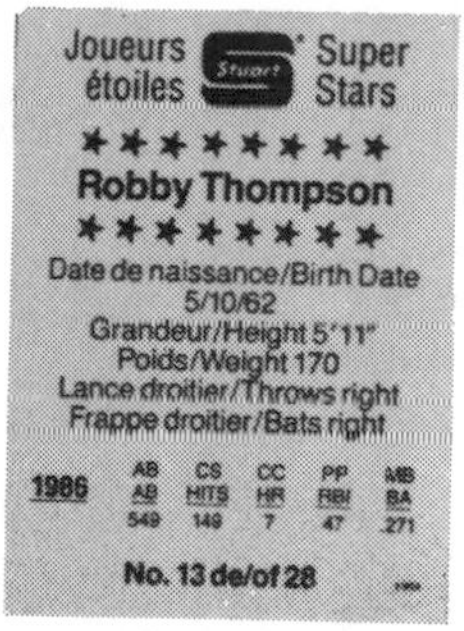

Twenty-eight four-part folding panels make up the 1987 Stuart Super Stars set, which was issued only in Canada. Three player cards and a sweepstakes entry form card comprise each panel. All 26 major league teams are included with the Montreal Expos and Toronto Blue Jays being represented twice. The cards, which are full color and measure 2-1/2" by 3-1/2", are written in both English and French. The card backs contain the player's previous year's statistics. All team insignias have been airbrushed away.

		MT	NR MT	EX
Complete Panel Set:		50.00	37.00	20.00
Complete Singles Set:		25.00	18.50	10.00
Common Panel:		.80	.60	.30
Common Single Player:		.10	.08	.04
	Panel (New York Mets)	4.00	3.00	1.50
1a	Gary Carter	.50	.40	.20
1b	Keith Hernandez	.40	.30	.15
1c	Darryl Strawberry	.60	.45	.25
	Panel (Atlanta Braves)	2.25	1.75	.90
2a	Bruce Benedict	.10	.08	.04
2b	Ken Griffey	.15	.11	.06
2c	Dale Murphy	.60	.45	.25
	Panel (Chicago Cubs)	1.50	1.25	.60
3a	Jody Davis	.15	.11	.06
3b	Andre Dawson	.30	.25	.12

3c	Leon Durham	.15	.11	.06
	Panel (Cincinnati Reds)	2.50	2.00	1.00
4a	Buddy Bell	.15	.11	.06
4b	Eric Davis	.60	.45	.25
4c	Dave Parker	.25	.20	.10
	Panel (Houston Astros)	2.25	1.75	.90
5a	Glenn Davis	.25	.20	.10
5b	Nolan Ryan	.70	.50	.30
5c	Mike Scott	.25	.20	.10
	Panel (Los Angeles Dodgers)	2.25	1.75	.90
6a	Pedro Guerrero	.25	.20	.10
6b	Mike Marshall	.20	.15	.08
6c	Fernando Valenzuela	.40	.30	.15
	Panel (Montreal Expos)	1.75	1.25	.70
7a	Tim Raines	.40	.30	.15
7b	Tim Wallach	.20	.15	.08
7c	Mitch Webster	.10	.08	.04
	Panel (Montreal Expos)	.80	.60	.30
8a	Hubie Brooks	.15	.11	.06
8b	Bryn Smith	.10	.08	.04
8c	Floyd Youmans	.10	.08	.04
	Panel (Philadelphia Phillies)	2.25	1.75	.90
9a	Shane Rawley	.10	.08	.04
9b	Juan Samuel	.20	.15	.08
9c	Mike Schmidt	.80	.60	.30
	Panel (Pittsburgh Pirates)	.80	.60	.30
10a	Jim Morrison	.10	.08	.04
10b	Johnny Ray	.15	.11	.06
10c	R.J. Reynolds	.10	.08	.04
	Panel (St. Louis Cardinals)	2.00	1.50	.80
11a	Jack Clark	.25	.20	.10
11b	Vince Coleman	.30	.25	.12
11c	Ozzie Smith	.25	.20	.10
	Panel (San Diego Padres)	3.00	2.25	1.25
12a	Steve Garvey	.50	.40	.20
12b	Tony Gwynn	.50	.40	.20
12c	John Kruk	.20	.15	.08
	Panel (San Francisco Giants)	.80	.60	.30
13a	Chili Davis	.10	.08	.04
13b	Jeffrey Leonard	.10	.08	.04
13c	Robbie Thompson	.10	.08	.04
	Panel (Baltimore Orioles)	3.00	2.25	1.25
14a	Fred Lynn	.25	.20	.10
14b	Eddie Murray	.50	.40	.20
14c	Cal Ripken	.50	.40	.20
	Panel (Boston Red Sox)	4.00	3.00	1.50
15a	Don Baylor	.15	.11	.06
15b	Wade Boggs	.80	.60	.30
15c	Roger Clemens	.60	.45	.25
	Panel	2.50	2.00	1.00
16a	Doug DeCinces	.10	.08	.04
16b	Wally Joyner	.80	.60	.30
16c	Mike Witt	.10	.08	.04
	Panel (Chicago White Sox)	1.50	1.25	.60
17a	Harold Baines	.20	.15	.08
17b	Carlton Fisk	.25	.20	.10
17c	Ozzie Guillen	.15	.11	.06
	Panel (Cleveland Indians)	1.00	.70	.40
18a	Joe Carter	.20	.15	.08
18b	Julio Franco	.15	.11	.06
18c	Pat Tabler	.10	.08	.04
	Panel (Detroit Tigers)	2.50	2.00	1.00
19a	Kirk Gibson	.40	.30	.15
19b	Jack Morris	.25	.20	.10
19c	Alan Trammell	.40	.30	.15
	Panel (Kansas City Royals)	2.50	2.00	1.00
20a	George Brett	.60	.45	.25
20b	Bret Saberhagen	.30	.25	.12
20c	Willie Wilson	.15	.11	.06
	Panel (Milwaukee Brewers)	2.00	1.50	.80
21a	Cecil Cooper	.15	.11	.06
21b	Paul Molitor	.20	.15	.08
21c	Robin Yount	.40	.30	.15
	Panel (Minnesota Twins)	2.50	2.00	1.00
22a	Tom Brunansky	.20	.15	.08
22b	Kent Hrbek	.30	.25	.12
22c	Kirby Puckett	.50	.40	.20
	Panel (New York Yankees)	5.00	3.75	2.00
23a	Rickey Henderson	.50	.40	.20
23b	Don Mattingly	1.00	.70	.40
23c	Dave Winfield	.50	.40	.20
	Panel (Oakland A's)	2.75	2.00	1.00
24a	Jose Canseco	.90	.70	.35
24b	Alfredo Griffin	.10	.08	.04
24c	Carney Lansford	.10	.08	.04
	Panel 25 (Seattle Mariners)	1.50	1.25	.60
25a	Phil Bradley	.15	.11	.06
25b	Alvin Davis	.20	.15	.08
25c	Mark Langston	.20	.15	.08
	Panel (Texas Rangers)	1.50	1.25	.60
26a	Pete Incaviglia	.30	.25	.12
26b	Pete O'Brien	.10	.08	.04
26c	Larry Parrish	.10	.08	.04
	Panel (Toronto Blue Jays)	2.25	1.75	.90
27a	Jesse Barfield	.20	.15	.08
27b	George Bell	.40	.30	.15
27c	Tony Fernandez	.20	.15	.08
	Panel (Toronto Blue Jays)	.80	.60	.30
28a	Lloyd Moseby	.10	.08	.04
28b	Dave Stieb	.15	.11	.06
28c	Ernie Whitt	.10	.08	.04

1962 Sugardale Weiners

The Sugardale Meats set of black and white cards measure 5-1/8" by 3-3/4". The 22-card set includes 18 Cleveland Indians and four Pittsburgh Pirates players. The Indians cards are numbered from 1-19 with card number 6 not issued. The Pirates cards are lettered from A to D. The card fronts contain a relatively small player photo, with biographical information and Sugardale logo. The backs are printed in red and offer playing tips and another company logo. Card number 10 (Bob Nieman) is considerably more scarce than other cards in the set.

		NR MT	EX	VG
Complete Set:		2250.00	1125.00	675.00
Common Player:		40.00	20.00	12.00
A	Dick Groat	70.00	35.00	21.00
B	Roberto Clemente	750.00	375.00	225.00
C	Don Hoak	55.00	27.00	16.50
D	Dick Stuart	55.00	27.00	16.50
1	Barry Latman	40.00	20.00	12.00
2	Gary Bell	45.00	22.00	13.50
3	Dick Donovan	40.00	20.00	12.00
4	Frank Funk	40.00	20.00	12.00
5	Jim Perry	60.00	30.00	18.00
6	Not issued			
7	Johnny Romano	40.00	20.00	12.00
8	Ty Cline	40.00	20.00	12.00
9	Tito Francona	45.00	22.00	13.50
10	Bob Nieman	300.00	150.00	90.00
11	Willie Kirkland	40.00	20.00	12.00
12	Woodie Held	45.00	22.00	13.50
13	Jerry Kindall	40.00	20.00	12.00
14	Bubba Phillips	40.00	20.00	12.00
15	Mel Harder	45.00	22.00	13.50
16	Salty Parker	40.00	20.00	12.00
17	Ray Katt	40.00	20.00	12.00
18	Mel McGaha	40.00	20.00	12.00
19	Pedro Ramos	40.00	20.00	12.00

1963 Sugardale Weiners

Sugardale Meats again featured Cleveland and Pittsburgh players in its 1963 set, which grew to 31 cards. The black and white cards again measure 5-1/8" by 3-3/4", and consist of 28 Indians and five Pirates players. Card formats are virtually identical to the 1962 cards, with the only real difference being the information included in the player biographies. The cards are numbered 1-38, with numbers 6, 21, 22 and 29-32 not issued. Cards for Bob Skinner (#35) and Jim Perry (#5) are scarce as these two players were traded during the season and their cards withdrawn from distribution. The red card backs again offer playing tips.

		NR MT	EX	VG
Complete Set:		2250.00	1125.00	675.00
A	Don Cardwell	40.00	20.00	12.00
B	Robert R. Skinner	200.00	100.00	60.00
C	Donald B. Schwall	40.00	20.00	12.00
D	Jim Pagliaroni	40.00	20.00	12.00
E	Dick Schofield	45.00	22.00	13.50
1	Barry Latman	40.00	20.00	12.00
2	Gary Bell	45.00	22.00	13.50
3	Dick Donovan	40.00	20.00	12.00
4	Joe Adcock	60.00	30.00	18.00
5	Jim Perry	175.00	87.00	52.00
6	Not issued			
7	Johnny Romano	40.00	20.00	12.00
8	Mike De La Hoz	40.00	20.00	12.00
9	Tito Francona	45.00	22.00	13.50
10	Gene Green	40.00	20.00	12.00
11	Willie Kirkland	40.00	20.00	12.00
12	Woodie Held	45.00	22.00	13.50
13	Jerry Kindall	40.00	20.00	12.00
14	Max Alvis	45.00	22.00	13.50
15	Mel Harder	45.00	22.00	13.50
16	George Strickland	40.00	20.00	12.00
17	Elmer Valo	40.00	20.00	12.00
18	Birdie Tebbetts	45.00	22.00	13.50
19	Pedro Ramos	40.00	20.00	12.00
20	Al Luplow	40.00	20.00	12.00
21	Not issued			
22	Not issued			
23	Jim Grant	45.00	22.00	13.50
24	Victor Davalillo	45.00	22.00	13.50
25	Jerry Walker	40.00	20.00	12.00
26	Sam McDowell	60.00	30.00	18.00
27	Fred Whitfield	40.00	20.00	12.00
28	Jack Kralick	40.00	20.00	12.00
29	Not issued			
30	Not issued			
31	Not issued			
32	Not issued			
33	Bob Allen	40.00	20.00	12.00

1986 Texas Gold Ice Cream Reds

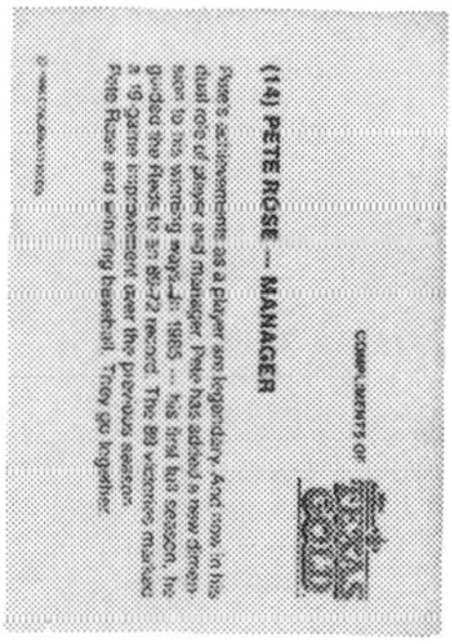

One of the last regional baseball card sets produced during the 1986 season was a 28-card team set sponsored by a Cincinnati-area ice cream company and given to fans attending a September 19th game. Photos on the 2-1/2" by 3-1/2" cards are game-action shots, and include three different cards of playing manager Pete Rose. The set is also notable for the inclusion of first cards of some of the Reds' young stars.

		MT	NR MT	EX
Complete Set:		30.00	22.00	12.00
Common Player:		.25	.20	.10
6	Bo Diaz	.35	.25	.14
9	Max Venable	.25	.20	.10
11	Kurt Stillwell	.80	.60	.30
12	Nick Esasky	.60	.45	.25
13	Dave Concepcion	.50	.40	.20
14a	Pete Rose (commemorative)	2.00	1.50	.80
14b	Pete Rose (infield)	2.00	1.50	.80
14c	Pete Rose (manager)	2.00	1.50	.80
16	Ron Oester	.25	.20	.10
20	Eddie Milner	.25	.20	.10
22	Sal Butera	.25	.20	.10
24	Tony Perez	.70	.50	.30
25	Buddy Bell	.35	.25	.14
28	Kal Daniels	1.50	1.25	.60
29	Tracy Jones	.80	.60	.30
31	John Franco	.80	.60	.30
32	Tom Browning	.60	.45	.25
33	Ron Robinson	.35	.25	.14
34	Bill Gullickson	.25	.20	.10
36	Mario Soto	.35	.25	.14
39	Dave Parker	1.00	.70	.40
40	John Denny	.25	.20	.10
44	Eric Davis	3.00	2.25	1.25
45	Chris Welsh	.25	.20	.10
48	Ted Power	.25	.20	.10
49	Joe Price	.25	.20	.10
----	Coaches Card (Scott Breeden, Billy DeMars, Tommy Helms, Bruce Kimm, Jim Lett, George Scherger)	.25	.20	.10
----	Logo/Coupon Card	.10	.08	.04

1983 Thorn Apple Valley Cubs

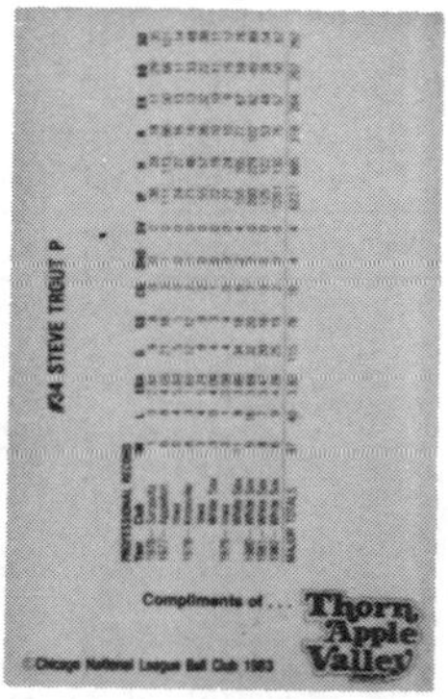

This set of 27 cards was issued in conjuction with a "Baseball Card Day" promotion at Wrigley Field in 1983. Thorn Apple Valley was the meat company which produced the hot dogs sold at the ballpark. The cards feature borderless color photos with the player's name, uniform number (also the card's number in the checklist) and an abbreviation for their position. Card backs feature annual statistics. Of the 27 cards, which measure 2-1/4" by 3-1/2", 25 feature players, one is a team card, and one features the manager and coaches.

		MT	NR MT	EX
Complete Set:		15.00	11.00	6.00
Common Player:		.20	.15	.08
1	Larry Bowa	.40	.30	.15
6	Keith Moreland	.40	.30	.15
7	Jody Davis	.40	.30	.15
10	Leon Durham	.40	.30	.15
11	Ron Cey	.40	.30	.15
16	Steve Lake	.20	.15	.08
20	Thad Bosley	.20	.15	.08
21	Jay Johnstone	.25	.20	.10
22	Bill Buckner	.40	.30	.15
23	Ryne Sandberg	4.00	3.00	1.50
24	Jerry Morales	.20	.15	.08
25	Gary Woods	.20	.15	.08
27	Mel Hall	.30	.25	.12
29	Tom Veryzer	.20	.15	.08
30	Chuck Rainey	.20	.15	.08
31	Fergie Jenkins	1.00	.70	.40
32	Craig Lefferts	.30	.25	.12
33	Joe Carter	3.00	2.25	1.25
34	Steve Trout	.25	.20	.10
36	Mike Proly	.20	.15	.08
39	Bill Campbell	.20	.15	.08
41	Warren Brusstar	.20	.15	.08
44	Dick Ruthven	.20	.15	.08
46	Lee Smith	.80	.60	.30
48	Dickie Noles	.20	.15	.08
----	Coaching Staff (Ruben Amaro, Billy Connors, Duffy Dyer, Lee Elia, Fred Koenig, John Vukovich)	.20	.15	.08
----	Team Photo	.20	.15	.08

Common Hobby Terms & Definitions

A

Airbrushing — An artist's technique used on baseball cards in which logos on uniforms or hats are altered or eliminated.

All-Star card (AS) — A card which denotes a player's selection to the previous year's All-Star Team.

Autographed card — Card which was personally autographed by the player depicted. Cards with facsimile signatures that are printed on many cards as part of the design, are not considered autographed cards.

Autograph guest — A current or former ball player or other celebrity who attends a card convention for the purpose of signing autographs for fans. Usually a fee is charged for the autograph, ranging from a few dollars to more than $30 for HOF players.

B

Baseball's Best — A set made by Donruss in 1988 and 1989. Also the name of a boxed set made by Fleer in 1987 and 1988, and the name of the set of insert cards made by *Baseball Cards* magazine in 1989 and 1990.

Bazooka cards — Cards issued with boxes of Bazooka Bubblegum (1959-1971, 1988-1990).

Big cards — Name for Topps' large, glossy-finish card issues produced in 1988-present. Cards reminiscent of Topps' cards from the 1950s.

Blank backs — A card that has a blank card back. Most collectors feel these cards are merely damaged, with a lower value than correctly-printed specimens, though some collectors will pay premiums on superstars or rookies.

Blanket — An early 20th-century collectible consisting of a square piece of felt or other fabric depicting a baseball player. Most popular are the 5" by 5" B-18 "blankets" from 1914, so-called because they were sometimes sewn together to form a blanket.

Blister pack — A blister pack is a method of card packaging in which cards are packaged in hard plastic on a cardboard backing, with three to four pockets of cards. Donruss (1987-present).

Borders — The portion of a card which surrounds the picture. They are usually white, but are sometimes other colors. Border condition is very important to the card's grade and value.

Bowman (B) — Sportscard manufacturer (1948-1955) bought out by Topps in 1956. Topps issued baseball sets under the Bowman name (1989-present).

Boxed sets — These are sets produced by one of the major card companies, usually in conjunction with a business, such as K-Mart or Walgreens. Boxed sets usually contain fewer than 60 cards, most of which are star players.

Box panel cards — Bonus cards which are featured on a panel of wax boxes of the major card companies. The idea was originated by Donruss in 1985. Complete sets range from four to 16 cards, and feature star players.

Brick — A "brick" of cards is any group of cards with similar characteristics, such as a 100-card brick of 1975 Topps cards. Bricks usually contain common cards.

Buy price — The price a dealer will to pay for cards or memorabilia.

Burger King cards (BK) — Cards issued in conjunction with Burger King (1977-1987).

C

Cabinet card — A large card from the 19th or early 20th centuries, usually issued on heavy cardboard.

Card lot — A "lot" of cards is the same card, such as a 1988 Topps Don Mattingly card, sold in a lot or "grouping" of five, 25, 50, 100 or whatever number of cards. A collector purchasing a "lot" of cards, gets the cards at a discounted price, as opposed to buying a single card. Example: a single Mattingly card costs $1, but 100 Mattingly cards cost $75 or 75-cents apiece.

Case — A sealed case containing wax boxes or other product units which card companies sell at wholesale to dealers or retail stores. For instance, a 1991 Topps "wax case" is made up of 20 "wax boxes."

Cello pack — A package of about 30 cards wrapped in a printed cellophane wrapper that allows you to see the top and bottom cards. There are usually 24 cello packs to a cello box, and 16 cello boxes to a cello case. Cello packs retail between for around $1. Issued by Topps, Fleer and Donruss.

Checklist (CL) — A list of every card in a particular set, usually with space allowing the collector to check whether or not he has the card. A checklist can appear on a card(s), in a book or elsewhere.

Classic cards — Baseball cards made by Game Time, Ltd., to go with its "Classic Baseball" trivia game (1987-present).

Coin — Can refer to an actual coin struck to commemorate an achievement made by a team or player; also, a collectible made soley from or with a combination of plastic, paper or metal, issued as a set, such as the 1988 Topps Coin set.

Collation — The act of putting cards in order, by hand or machine, usually numerically.

Collector issue — A set of cards produced primarily to be sold to collectors and not issued as a premium to be given away or sold with a commercial product.

Common card — A card which carries no premium value in a set. "Common" is a blunt way of saying the player depicted is not a star.

Convention — Also known as a "baseball card show" or "trading card show." A gathering of anywhere from one to 600 or more card dealers at a single location (convention center, hotel, school auditoriums or gymnasiums) for the purpose of buying, selling or trading cards.

Counterfeit cards — Cards made to look like original cards, and distributed with the intention of fooling a buyer. High demand cards are the most likely to be counterfeited.

D

Dealer — A person who buys, sells and trades baseball cards and other memorabilia for profit. A dealer may be full-time, part-time, own a shop, operate a mail-order business from his home, deal at baseball card shows on weekends, or any combination of the above.

Die-cut card — A baseball card in which the player's outline has been partially separated from the background, enabling the card to be folded into a "stand-up" figure. Die-cut cards that have never been folded are worth more to collectors.

Disc — Circular-shaped card.

Donruss (D) — Baseball card manufacturer (1981-present).

Donruss Rookies (DR) — 56-card post-season set issued by Donruss which includes rookie players (1986-present). Sold exclusively through hobby dealers in separate box.

Double print (DP) — A card printed twice on the same sheet, making it twice as common as other cards on the sheet. Topps double-printed cards in virtually every set from 1952 to 1981. This was done to accomodate the year's set size on standard company printing sheets.

Drakes — Ohio-based bakery which made baseball cards in the 1950s, and again from 1981-1988.

E

Error — An error is usually found on card backs in the statistical or personal information, and sometimes on the card front (such as a reversed negative). If an error is not corrected, the error adds nothing to the value of the card. If the error is corrected, it is called a "variation" card.

Exhibit card — Postcard-size cards picturing baseball players and other celebrities and sold in penny-arcade machines. Exhibit cards were produced from the 1920s to the 1960s.

F

Factory set (F or FAC.) — A complete set collated (packaged) by the card producing company. Issued by all companies.

First card (FC) — Price guide designation which refers to the first appearance of a player in the major card sets.

Fleer (F) — Baseball card manufacturer (1959-1963, 1981-present).

Fleer Glossy Tin (FG) — Limited edition set produced by Fleer, which features the year's regular issue set in a high gloss finish and sold in a tin box (1987-present). Fleer Update sets also done in glossy style.

Fleer Update (FU) — 132-card post-season set from Fleer which includes players traded to other teams during the season, and rookies (1984-present). Sold exclusively through hobby dealers in its own separate box.

Food issue — A set of baseball cards or related memorabilia which was issued in conjunction with a food product, such as Post cereal or Hostess snack cakes.

G

Gallery of Champions — Trade name for a set of metallic reproductions of Topps cards made and sold by Topps from 1986-1988. The metals used were bronze, aluminum, pewter and silver.

Goudey — Baseball card manufacturer (1933-1936, 1938, 1941).

Grades — The physical state or condition of a card.

H

Hand collated set (H or HC) — A complete set put together by hand using cards from wax, cello, rack or vending boxes.

High-numbers — A term used to describe the final series in a particular set of cards. "High numbers" were generally produced in smaller quantities than other series and are, therefore, scarcer and more valuable.

Hall of Famer (HOFer) - A card picturing a member of the Baseball Hall of Fame, in Cooperstown, N.Y. Hall of Famer cards almost always command a premium over other cards.

Hartland statues — Wisconsin plastics company which produced, among other things, statues of baseball players in the late 1950s and early 1960s. Company reproduced the set in 1989 as Hartland's 25th Anniversary Commemorative Edition. Original statues very collectible.

I

In Action card (IA) — A card featuring a star player, designated with the words "In Action" on the card front. Most notably from the 1972 and 1982 Topps sets.

Inserts — A collectible included inside a regular pack of baseball cards to boost sales. Inserts have included posters, coins, stamps, tatoos, special cards, etc.

J

Jell-O cards — Cards sold as premiums with Jell-O packages (1962-1963).

K

Kellog's cards — Simulated three-dimensional cards given away in cereal boxes or via a mail-in offer (1970-1983).

Key cards — The most important (valuable) cards in a set, such as the Mickey Mantle card, a "key" card in the 1952 Topps set.

L

Last card — The final regular card issued for a player, such as Hank Aaron's "last" card was in the 1976 Topps set. No particular extra value is added for last cards.

Leaf-Donruss — Baseball cards produced by Donruss specifically for the Canadian market (1985-1988). Leaf issued its own set in 1990.

Legitimate issue — A card set issued as a premium with a commerical product to increase sales; not a "collector issue."

Letter of authenticity — A letter stating that a certain piece of memorabilia, like a uniform, is authentic.

Lithograph — A high-quality art print made in limited quantities.

M

MVP — Most Valuable Player award.

Mail-bid auction — An auction where bids are sent through the mail, with the highest bidder winning the merchandise.

Major set — A large, nationally-distributed set produced by a major card maker like Topps, Fleer, Donruss, Score, Sportflics or Upper Deck.

Megalot — A megalot describes a group of cards, usually 1,000 or more of the same player, purchased for investment or speculation.

Memorabilia — Refers to items other than cards, such as uniforms, bats, autographed baseballs, magazines, scorecards, pins, statues and the like.

Minis — Cards which resemble the regular issue cards in every way, except they are smaller in size. Most noteable are the 1975 Topps Minis.

Minor league cards — A card depicting a player from the minor leagues. Minor league sets are a fast-growing segment of the hobby.

Mother's cards — An Oakland, (Calif.)-based cookie company which produces popular high quality glossy finish regional sets (1982-present).

Multi-player card — A card picturing more than one player.

N

Non-sport card — A trading card or bubblegum card picturing a subject other than sports. Non-sports cards have depicted movie stars, television shows, moments in history and other subjects.

O

Obverse — The front of the card displaying the picture.

O-Pee-Chee (OPC) — Canadian card producing company (1965-present). O-Pee-Chee is Topps' official Canadian licensee, and O-Pee-Chee cards are almost identical to Topps' issues of the same year.

P

Panel — A strip of two or more uncut cards. Some card sets are issued in "panels."

Phone auction — An auction where bids for baseball cards or other memorabilia are taken over the phone, with the highest bidder getting the merchandise.

Plastic sheet — A polyethelyne or polyvinyl sheet designed to store baseball cards, the most common being the nine-pocket sheet (which fits today's standard-sized cards). The sheets have pre-punched holes on the left side which allows them to be placed in a three-ring binder.

Play Ball — Name of baseball cards produced by Gum, Inc., (1939-1941).

Police/Fire/Safety sets — Card sets sponsored by public law enforcement or fire fighting agencies and a major or minor league team. Card backs usually contain anti-drug messages, fire prevention tips or other safety messages.

Post cards — Cards sold as premiums on boxes of Post cereal (1960-1963, 1990).

Pre-rookie card — Name given to a major league player's minor league cards.

Price guide — A periodical or book which contains checklists of cards, sets and other memorabilia and their values in varying conditions.

Price on request (POR) — A dealer will advertise a card P.O.R. if he believes the card will fluctuate in price from the time he places his ad until the time the ad is seen by the public.

Promotional cards — Cards produced by the card companies which serve as a marketing tool for their upcoming cards. Promotional or "promo" cards are often sent to dealers to entice them to order cards. Promo cards have limited distribution and can be very expensive.

Proof card — A card produced by the card companies prior to printing their sets, which is "proofed" for errors, and checked for card design, photography, colors, statisical accuracy and so on. Proof cards are not distributed and a few of the older proof cards on the hobby market can be quite expensive.

PPD — Postage Paid.

R

Rack pack — A three-sectioned card package with about 14-16 cards per section. There are usually 24 rack packs to a rack box, and six rack boxes to a rack case. Topps, Fleer, Donruss, Score.

Rare — Difficult to obtain and limited in number. See "Scarce."

Rated Rookie (RR) — Donruss subset featuring young players the company feels are the top rookie players from a particular year (1984-present).

Record Breaker card (RB) — A special Topps card found in a regular issue set which commemorates a record-breaking performance by a player from the previous season.

Regional set — A card set distributed in one geographical area. Regional sets often depict players from one team.

Regular issue set — See "Major set."

Reprint cards — Cards reprinted to closely match original cards, made with the intention of allowing collectors to buy them as substitutes for cards they could not ever afford. Reprints are usually labled — but not always — "reprint."

Reverse — The back of a card.

Rookie card (R or RC) — The first appearance of a player in one of the major sets (Topps, Fleer, etc.), excluding update and traded sets. It may or may not be issued during the player's actual rookie season.

S

SASE — Self-Addressed Stamped Envelope.

Score (S or SC) — Brand name of sports cards (1988-present). Major League Marketing is the manufacturer.

Score Traded (ScTr) - 110-card post-season set issued by Score to include players traded during the season, as well as rookie players. Sold exclusively by hobby dealers in its own separate box.

Second-year card — The second card of a player issued in the major sets. Usually, a second-year card is the most expensive card of a player, next to the rookie card.

Sell price — The price a dealer sells a card.

Series — A group of cards that is part of a set, and was issued at one time. The term usually applied to Topps sets from 1952-1973, when sets were issued in various "series." Cards of different series are valued at different prices since some series are scarcer than others.

Set — A complete run of cards, including one number of each card issued by a particular manufacturer in a particular year; for example, a 1985 Fleer "set."

Set case — Companies sell their factory sets in sealed cases containing 8 to 16 sets per case, depending on the company. Issued by all major companies.

Skip-numbered — A set of cards not numbered in exact sequence. Some manufacturers have issued "skip-numbered" sets to trick collectors into buying more cards, looking for card numbers that didn't exist. Other sets became skip-numbered when one or more players were dropped from the set at the last minute and were not replaced with another.

Sleeve — A specially-designed, plastic wrapper used to house and protect individual baseball cards.

Special card — A card in a set that depicts something other than a single player; for example a checklist card, All-Star card, team card or leaders card.

Sportflics — Brand name of baseball cards (1986-present). Major League Marketing is the manufacturer.

SCD — *Sports Collectors Digest.*

Standard size card — A card which measures 2½" wide by 3½" tall. In 1957, Topps baseball cards were produced in the 2½" by 3½" size, which set the standard for modern baseball cards.

Star card — Card featuring a star player, but not one of "superstar" caliber. The term "minor star" may also be used to differentiate between levels of skill and popularity. In terms of value, "star" cards fall between "commons" and "superstars."

Starter lot — A group of cards from the same set, usually more than 100, which serves as a starting point for a hobbyist to begin putting a set together. Starter lots usually contain common players. Also known as a "starter set."

Starting Lineup — A line of plastic sports statues produced by Kenner (1988-present). Also, the name for a computer-based baseball game from Parker Brothers.

Sticker — An adhesive-backed baseball card. Stickers can be card-size or smaller. Topps, Fleer and Panini have issued major baseball sticker sets over the past years. Stickers are not overly popular with older collectors, though younger collectors seem to enjoy them.

Subset — A set of cards with the same theme within a larger set. Examples: Donruss Diamond Kings are a "subset" of the Donruss set; or Topps All-Star cards are a subset of the Topps set.

Super card — A designation referring to the physical size of a card. Generally, any card postcard-size or larger is referred to as a "super."

Superstar card — A card picturing a true "superstar," a player of Hall of Fame caliber, like Mike Schmidt.

Stock — Refers to the type of paper or cardboard used on a baseball card.

Swap Meet — Term used to describe early baseball card shows where most of the cards were traded between hobbyists.

T

Team card — Card which depicts an entire team.

Team set — A set which includes all cards relating to a certain team from a particular year, by a particular manufacturer.

Team issued set — A set produced to be sold or given away by a baseball team.

Test issue — A set of cards test-marketed on a small scale in a limited geographic areas of the country. Topps test-marketed a variety of items from the 1950s-1980s.

Tobacco cards — Cards issued in the late 19th and early 20th centuries as premiums with cigarettes or other tobacco products.

Topps (T) — Sports card company (1951-present).

Topps Tiffany (TTF) — Limited edition set produced by Topps, featuring the year's regular complete set in a high gloss finish (1984-present). Topps Traded sets also done in this style.

Topps Traded (TT or TTR) — 132-card post-season set which includes players traded to other teams during the year, as well as rookie players (1981-present). Sold mainly through hobby dealers.

Traded set — An auxiliary set of cards issued toward the end of the season to reflect trades made after the printing of the regular set. Also called "Update" sets, they may also include rookies not included in the regular set.

U

Uncut sheet — A full sheet of baseball cards that has never been cut into individual cards.

Upper Deck (UD) — Sportscard company (1989-present).

Upper Deck High Numbers (UDH) — 100-card set featuring players traded during the season, as well as rookie players. This set was sold through hobby dealers and in Upper Deck foil packs, similar to the way cards before 1974 were released.

V

Variation — A variation is the result of a card company correcting a previous mistake on a card, resulting in two or more variations of the same card. Some variations have increased in value, if they were produced in lesser quantities.

Vending box — Vending boxes contain 500 cards per box. There are 24 vending boxes per vending case, for a total of 12,000 cards. Topps.

W

Want list — A collector's or dealer's list of items he is wishing to buy. Often, a collector will send a dealer a "want" list, and the dealer will try to locate the items on the list.

1992 ALPHABETICAL ROOKIE CARD CHECKLIST

A

Manny Alexander ....
1992 Topps #551
Ruben Amaro ....
1992 Fleer #52
Ruben Amaro ....
1992 Topps #269
Greg Anthony ....
1992 Topps #336
Alex Arias ....
1992 Topps #551
Andy Ashby ....
1992 Donruss #11
Andy Ashby ....
1992 Fleer #521
Andy Ashby ....
1992 Score #396
Andy Ashby ....
1992 Topps #497
Andy Ashby ....
1992 Upper Deck #19
Brad Asmus ....
1992 Topps #58

B

Jeff Bagwell ....
1992 Donruss #358
Jeff Bagwell ....
1992 Fleer #425
Jeff Bagwell ....
1992 Topps #520
Jeff Bagwell ....
1992 Upper Deck #276
Bret Barberie ....
1992 Fleer #472
Bret Barberie ....
1992 Score #419
Bret Barberie ....
1992 Topps #224
Bret Barberie ....
1992 Upper Deck #363
Kim Batiste ....
1992 Fleer #522
Kim Batiste ....
1992 Topps #514
Kim Batiste ....
1992 Upper Deck #422
Chris Beasley ....
1992 Fleer #54
Chris Beasley ....
1992 Upper Deck #614
Rod Beck ....
1992 Fleer #627
Esteban Beltre ....
1992 Fleer #75
Freddie Benavides ....
1992 Fleer #399
Cesar Bernhardt ....
1992 Topps #179
Brian Bohanon ....
1992 Topps #149
Frank Bolick ....
1992 Topps #473
Ricky Bones ....
1992 Fleer #600
Ricky Bones ....
1992 Topps #711
Ricky Bones ....
1992 Upper Deck #623
Ryan Bowen ....
1992 Topps #254
Ryan Bowen ....
1992 Upper Deck #354
Cliff Brantley ....
1992 Fleer #662
Cliff Brantley ....
1992 Topps #544
Jarvis Brown ....
1992 Fleer #669
Scott Brosius ....
1992 Fleer #671
Scott Brosius ....
1992 Upper Deck #312
Jacob Brumfield ....
1992 Topps #591

C

Jim Campanis ....
1992 Topps #58
Vinny Castilla ....
1992 Fleer #666
Braulio Castillo ....
1992 Topps #353
Braulio Castillo ....
1992 Upper Deck #21
Frank Castillo ....
1992 Fleer #378
Frank Castillo ....
1992 Score #399
Frank Castillo ....
1992 Topps #196
Frank Castillo ....
1992 Upper Deck #526
Mike Christopher ....
1992 Fleer #654

Alan Cockrell ....
1992 Topps #591
Rheal Comier ....
1992 Topps #346
Rheal Cormier ....
1992 Upper Deck #574
Chris Cron ....
1992 Fleer #656

D

Mike Dalton ....
1992 Fleer #131
Chris Donnels ....
1992 Score #212
Chris Donnels ....
1992 Topps #376
Chris Donnels ....
1992 Upper Deck #44
Brian Drahman ....
1992 Fleer #77
Brian Drahman ....
1992 Topps #231
Kirk Dressendorfer ....
1992 Topps #716

E

Shawn Estes ....
1992 Topps #624

F

John Farrell ....
1992 Upper Deck #69
Jeff Fassero ....
1992 Fleer #477
Jeff Fassero ....
1992 Topps #423
Jeff Fassero ....
1992 Upper Deck #685
Dave Fleming ....
1992 Topps #192
Dave Fleming ....
1992 Upper Deck #4

G

Dan Gakeler ....
1992 Fleer #135
Dan Gakeler ....
1992 Topps #621
Ramon Garcia ....
1992 Topps #176
Jeff Gardner ....
1992 Fleer #675
Brent Gates ....
1992 Topps # 216
Chris George ....
1992 Upper Deck #9
Benji Gil ....
1992 Topps #534
Shawn Green ....
1992 Topps #276
Shawn Green ....
1992 Upper Deck #55
Tyler Green ....
1992 Topps #764
Tyler Green ....
1992 Upper Deck #68
Kip Gross ....
1992 Fleer # 407
Kip Gross ....
1992 Topps #372
Juan Guzman ....
1992 Fleer #330
Juan Guzman ....
1992 Score #424
Juan Guzman ....
1992 Topps #662
Juan Guzman ....
1992 Upper Deck #625

H

Dave Haas ....
1992 Topps #665
Chris Haney ....
1992 Donruss #291
Chris Haney ....
1992 Fleer #483
Chris Haney ....
1992 Topps #626
Chris Haney ....
1992 Upper Deck #662
Scott Hatteberg ....
1992 Topps #734
Ryan Hawblitzel ....
1992 Upper Deck #59
Doug Henry ....
1992 Score #421
Doug Henry ....
1992 Topps #776
Doug Henry ....
1992 Upper Deck #43
Gil Heredia ....
1992 Fleer #665
Cesar Hernandez ....
1992 Topps #618
Jeremy Hernandez ....
1992 Topps #211
Jeremy Hernandez ....
1992 Upper Deck #42
Jose Hernandez ....
1992 Fleer #307
Jose Hernandez ....
1992 Topps #237
Roberto Hernandez ....
1992 Donruss #19
roberto Hernandez ....
1992 Fleer #677
Roberto Hernandez ....
1992 Topps # 667
Roberto Hernandez ....
1992 Upper Deck #7
Bryan Hickerson ....
1992 Fleer #638

Bryan Hickerson ....
1992 Topps #8
Bryan Hickerson ....
1992 Upper Deck # 667
Tyrone Hill ....
1992 Topps #444
Wayne Housie ....
1992 Topps #639
Wayne Housie ....
1992 Upper Deck #664
David Howard ....
1992 Fleer #160
David Howard ....
1992 Topps #641
David Howard ....
1992 Upper Deck #216
Mike Humphreys ....
1992 Fleer #231
Mike Humphreys ....
1992 Upper Deck #432
Brian Hunter ....
1992 Donruss #163
Brian Hunter ....
1992 Fleer #359
Brian Hunter ....
1992 Score #417
Brian Hunter ....
1992 Topps #611
Brian Hunter ....
1992 Upper Deck #366

J

John Jaha ....
1992 Topps #126
Jeff Johnson ....
1992 Donruss #275
Jeff Johnson ....
1992 Topps #449
Jeff Johnson ....
1992 Upper Deck #626
Joel Johnston ....
1992 Fleer #673
Chris Jones ....
1992 Fleer #410
Chris Jones ....
1992 Topps #332
Brian Jordan ....
1992 Upper Deck #3

K

Scott Kamieniecki ....
1992 Donruss #195
Scott Kamieniecki ....
1992 Fleer #232
Scott Kamieniecki ....
1992 Score #415
Scott Kamieniecki ....
1992 Topps #102
Scott Kamieniecki ....
1992 Upper Deck #46
Mike Kelly ....
1992 Upper Deck #56
Darryl Kile ....
1992 Donruss #309
Darryl Kile ....
1992 Fleer #439
Darryl Kile ....
1992 Upper Deck #374
Wayne Kirby ....
1992 Fleer #670
Ryan Klesko ....
1992 Donruss #13
Ryan Klesko ....
1992 Topps #126
Ryan Klesko ....
1992 Upper Deck #24

L

Ced Landrum ....
1992 Fleer #385
Ced Landrum ....
1992 Score #418
Ced Landrum ....
1992 Topps #81
Ced Landrum ....
1992 Upper Deck #50
Patrick Lennon ....
1992 Donruss #17
Patrick Lennon ....
1992 Upper Deck #13
Jim Lewis ....
1992 Fleer #612
Mike Linskey ....
1992 Fleer #663
Scott Livingstone ....
1992 Score #414
Scott Livingstone ....
1992 Topps #685
Scott Livingstone ....
1992 Upper Deck #538
Shawn Livsey ....
1992 Topps #124
Kenny Lofton ....
1992 Donruss #5
Kenny Lofton ....
1992 Fleer #655
Kenny Lofton ....
1992 Topps #69
Kenny Lofton ....
1992 Upper Deck #25

M

Rob MacDonald ....
1992 Score #405
Mike Magnante ....
1992 Topps #597
Chito Martinez ....
1992 Fleer #13
Chito Martinez ....
1992 Score #400

Chito Martinez ....
1992 Topps #479
Chito Martinez ....
1992 Upper Deck #672
Terry Mathews ....
1992 Fleer #310
Rob Mauer ....
1992 Fleer #659
Rob Mauer ....
1992 Upper Deck #10
David McCarty ....
1992 Upper Deck #75
Tom McKinnon ....
1992 Topps #96
Jeff McNeely ....
1992 Topps #618
Rusty Meacham ....
1992 Score #395
Rusty Meacham ....
1992 Upper Deck #453
Jose Melendez ....
1992 Fleer #615
Jose Melendez ....
1992 Score #397
Jose Melendez ....
1992 Topps #518
Jose Melendez ....
1992 Upper Deck #652
Luis Mercedes ....
1992 Donruss #6
Luis Mercedes ....
1992 Fleer #16
Luis Mercedes ....
1992 Topps #603
Luis Mercedes ....
1992 Upper Deck #652
Sam Militello ....
1992 Topps #676
Trever Miller ....
1992 Topps #684
Geno Minutelli ....
1992 Score #408
Keith Mitchell ....
1992 Fleer #364
Keith Mitchell ....
1992 Topps #542
Keith Mitchell ....
1992 Upper Deck #454
Armando Moreno ....
1992 Topps #179
Andy Mota ....
1992 Fleer #441
Andy Mota ....
1992 Topps #214
Andy Mota ....
1992 Upper Deck #564

N

Denny Neagle ....
1992 Fleer #213
Denny Neagle ....
1992 Topps #592
Denny Neagle ....
1992 Upper Deck #426
Warren Newson ....
1992 Fleer #91
Warren Newson ....
1992 Score #398
Warren Newson ....
1992 Topps #355
Warren Newson ....
1992 Upper Deck #621
Dave Nilsson ....
1992 Donruss #4
Dave Nilsson ....
1992 Topps #355
Dave Nilsson ....
1992 Upper Deck #57

O

Jim Olander ....
1992 Topps #7

P

Craig Paquette ....
1992 Topps #473
Rudy Pemberton ....
1992 Topps #656
Eduardo Perez ....
1992 Upper Deck #52
Doug Piatt ....
1992 Score #422
Doug Piatt ....
1992 Topps #526
Jason Pruitt ....
1992 Topps #426
Harvey Pulliam ....
1992 Fleer #166
Harvey Pulliam ....
1992 Topps #687
Harvey Pulliam ....
1992 Upper Deck #457

R

Manny Ramirez ....
1992 Topps #156
Manny Ramirez ....
1992 Upper Deck #63
John Ramos ....
1992 Donruss #15
John Ramos ....
1992 Fleer #242
Joe Redfield ....
1992 Fleer #563
Joe Redfield ....
1992 Score #412
Mike Remlinger ....
1992 Donruss #336
Mike Remlinger ....
1992 Fleer #646
Mike Remlinger ....
1992 Score #410

Mike Remlinger ....
1992 Upper Deck #585
Armando Reynoso ....
1992 Fleer #367
Armando Reynoso ....
1992 Topps #631
Armando Reynoso ....
1992 Upper Deck #674
Arthur Rhodes ....
1992 Fleer #367
Arthur Rhodes ....
1992 Topps #771
Arthur Rhodes ....
1992 Upper Deck #17
Pat Rice ....
1992 Fleer #658
Pat Rice ....
1992 Score #423
Carlos Rodriguez ....
1992 Score #411
Frankie Rodriguez ....
1992 Upper Deck #71
Ivan Rodriguez ....
1992 Donruss #289
Ivan Rodriguez ....
1992 Fleer #316
Ivan Rodriguez ....
1992 Topps #78
Ivan Rodriguez ....
1992 Upper Deck # 245
Wayne Rosenthal ....
1992 Fleer #318
Wayne Rosenthal ....
1992 topps #584
Mike Rossiter ....
1992 Topps #474
Rico Rossy ....
1992 Fleer #676
Scott Ruffcorn ....
1992 Topps # #36
Paul Russo ....
1992 Topps #473

S

Rey Sanchez ....
1992 Upper Deck #562
Pete Schourek ....
1992 Fleer #516
Pete Schourek ....
1992 Score #332
Pete Schourek ....
1992 Topps #287
Pete Schourek ....
1992 Upper Deck #673
Jose Segura ....
1992 Score #278
Aaron Sele ....
1992 Topps #504
Frank Seminara ....
1992 Donruss #10
Scott Servais ....
1992 Fleer #444
Scott Servais ....
1992 Topps #437
Scott Servais ....
1992 Upper Deck #561
Craig Shipley ....
1992 Fleer #621
Craig Shipley ....
1992 Topps #308
Doug Simons ....
1992 topps #82
Heathcliff Slocumb ....
1992 Donruss #334
Heathcliff Slocumb ....
1992 Fleer #390
Heahtcliff Slocumb ....
1992 Score #213
Heathcliff Slocumb ....
1992 Topps #576
Heathcliff Slocumb ....
1992 Upper Deck #569
Joe Slusarski ....
1992 Fleer #266
Joe Slusarski ....
1992 Topps #651
Joe Slusarski ....
1992 Upper Deck #663
Mark Smith ....
1992 Upper Deck #66
Tim Spehr ....
1992 Fleer #674
Tim Spehr ....
1992 Score #416
Tim Spehr ....
1992 Topps #342
Ed Sprague ....
1992 Donruss #187
Ed Sprague ....
1992 Fleer #340
Ed Sprague ....
1992 Topps #516
Scott Stahoviak ....
1992 Topps #66

T

Eddie Taubensee ....
1992 Donruss #18
Eddie Taubensee ....
1992 Topps #427
Brien Taylor ....
1992 Topps #245
Brien Taylor ....
1992 Upper Deck #77
Wade Taylor ....
1992 Fleer #245
Wade Taylor ....
1992 Topps #562
Jim Thome ....
1992 Fleer #125

Jim Thome ....
1992 Topps #768
Jim Thome ....
1992 Upper Deck #5
Mike Timlin ....
1992 Donruss #301
Mike Timlin ....
1992 Fleer #343
Mike Timlin ....
1992 Topps #108
Mike Timlin ....
1992 Upper Deck #409
Lee Tinsley ....
1992 Topps #656
Jose Tolentino ....
1992 Topps #541

V

Jon Vander Wal ....
1992 Topps #343
Joe Vitiello ....
1992 Upper Deck #73

W

Chico Walker ....
1992 Fleer #395
Chico Walker ....
1992 Topps #439
Chico Walker ....
1992 Upper Deck #617
Kevin Ward ....
1992 Fleer #623
Jeff Ware ....
1992 Topps #414
Allen Watson ....
1992 Topps #654
John Wehner ....
1992 Fleer # 573
John Wehner ....
1992 Topps #282
John Wehner ....
1992 Upper Deck #469
Turk Wendell ....
1992 Topps #676
Steve Whitaker ....
1992 Topps #369
Bob Wickman ....
1992 Upper Deck #76
Rick Wilkins ....
1992 Donruss #249
Rick Wilkins ....
1992 Fleer #397
Rick Wilkins ....
1992 Topps #348
Rick Wilkins ....
1992 Upper Deck #373
Gerald Williams ....
1992 Topps #656
Mark Wohlers ....
1992 Donruss #1
Mark Wohlers ....
1992 Fleer #374
Mark Wohlers ....
1992 Topps #703
Mark Wohlers ....
1992 Upper Deck #12
Ted Wood ....
1992 Fleer #678
Ted Wood ....
1992 Topps #358

Y

Anthony Young ....
1992 Fleer #520
Anthony Young ....
1992 Topps #148
Anthony Young ....
1992 Upper Deck #535

Z

Bob Zupcic ....
1992 Topps #377

Notes

Notes

Notes

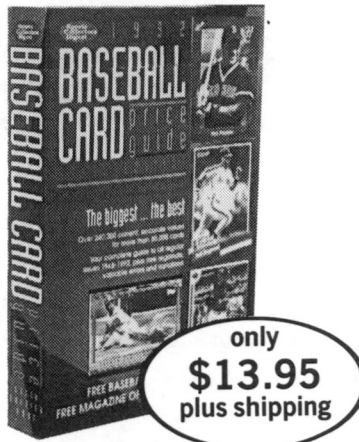

California Numismatic Investments

Krause Publications 5 Year Customer Service Award

Founding Member SCA

525 West Manchester Blvd.
Inglewood, CA 90301
Phone (213) 674-3330 • FAX (213) 330-3766

WE'RE BUYING THE FOLLOWING AUTOGRAPHS:

- **Deceased single signed baseballs - photos**
- **Documents and player contracts**
- **Autograph bats**
- **Game used bats**
- **Babe Ruth and Lou Gehrig autographs**
- **New York Yankees and Brooklyn Dodger team balls**
- **Championship baseballs**
- **Baseball flannel jerseys**
- **Cancelled Checks**
- **Championship sport rings**

All transactions confidential.
We will travel anywhere
for meaningful collections.
We can pay by Federal Express or bank wire.
Immediate payment is made
on all transactions.

oranges: carrot & orange soup 148
oysters: tomato & smoked shellfish soup 168

paprika
- bauernsuppe 180
- fish soup with semolina & dill dumplings 49
- goulash soup 78
- lamb & lemon soup 89
- lentil soup with ham 83
- sauerkraut & sausage soup 38
- tomato & white bean soup 16

parsley
- bacon & potato soup 26
- carrot & mussel soup 98
- chicken & corn soup 216
- chicken soup with leeks & rice 46
- chicken soup with matzo balls 43
- clam & pasta soup 52
- cream of clam soup 92
- cream of tomato soup 65
- cullen skink 191
- fish soup with semolina & dill dumplings 49
- garlic soup 122
- green vegetable soup 20
- harira 197
- lamb & eggplant soup 86
- lamb & vegetable broth 84
- lentil soup with ham 83
- Manhattan clam chowder 215
- mixed vegetable soup with lamb meatballs 32
- mushroom & ginger soup 71
- mussel soup 171
- mussel soup (Irish) 192
- tomato & white bean soup 16
- vegetable soup with semolina dumplings 113

parsnips
- carrot & parsnip soup 60
- curried vegetable soup 114
- tomato & parsnip soup 66

pasta
- chicken soup with matzo balls 43
- clam & pasta soup 52
- Mexican tomato & vermicelli soup 116
- minestrone 182
- quick sea scallop soup with pasta 55
- summer tomato soup 14

pearl barley
- barley, lentil & onion soup 19
- lamb & vegetable broth 84

pears: leek, potato & pear soup 154

peas
- chicken & almond soup 44
- green vegetable soup 20
- lamb & vegetable broth 84
- minestrone 182
- mixed vegetable soup with lamb meatballs 32
- pea soup 144
- quick sea scallop soup with pasta 55

plantain chips 218

pork
- Jamaican pepper pot 218
- Manhattan clam chowder 215
- pork rib soup with pickled mustard greens 126
- pork soup with bulgur wheat 28
- salt pork & lentil soup 31
- split pea and sausage soup 37
- wonton soup 200

potatoes
- apple & fennel soup 156
- apple soup 159
- bacon & potato soup 26
- bauernsuppe 180
- broccoli & Roquefort soup 107
- caldo verde 186
- carrot & cilantro soup 62
- cullen skink 191
- fish soup with semolina & dill dumplings 49
- goulash soup 78
- lamb & eggplant soup 86
- leek, potato & pear soup 154
- lentil soup with ham 83
- Manhattan clam chowder 215
- mixed vegetable soup with lamb meatballs 32
- ribollita 25
- salt pork & lentil soup 31
- vichyssoise 153

prosciutto: quick sea scallop soup with pasta 55

pumpkin
- bacon & pumpkin soup 80
- squash & lentil soup 22

ribollita 25

rice
- avgolemono 194
- chicken soup with ginger & coconut milk 212
- chicken soup with leeks & rice 46
- harira 197
- mixed vegetable soup with lamb meatballs 32

rutabaga
- lamb & vegetable broth 84
- mixed vegetable soup with lamb meatballs 32

saffron
- bouillabaisse 179
- chicken & corn soup 216
- fabada 185
- garlic soup 122
- leek, potato & pear soup 154

sauerkraut & sausage soup 38

sausages
- fabada 185
- sauerkraut & sausage soup 38
- split pea and sausage soup 37

scallions
- asparagus soup (chilled) 147
- beef noodle soup 34
- cauliflower & coconut soup 74
- chicken noodle soup 128
- chicken soup with ginger & coconut milk 212
- crab soup 206
- cucumber & mint soup 141
- cucumber & shrimp soup 166
- fish & corn soup 96
- hot & sour soup 125
- Jamaican pepper pot 218
- quick sea scallop soup with pasta 55
- spicy cucumber soup 108
- summer tomato soup 14
- tom yam goong 210
- wonton soup 200

scallops: quick sea scallop soup with pasta 55

seaweed
- seaweed soup with miso 204
- shiitake mushroom soup with egg 119

semolina
- fish soup with semolina & dill dumplings 49
- vegetable soup with semolina dumplings 113

sesame paste: quick-and-easy chickpea soup with sesame paste 162

shallots
- al fresco avocado soup 136
- avocado soup 104
- carrot & orange soup 148
- carrot & parsnip soup 60
- crab & noodle soup 131
- mushroom & ginger soup 71
- tomato & smoked shellfish soup 168

sherry
- beef noodle soup 34
- black bean soup 221
- egg flower soup 120
- fish & corn soup 96
- jellied vegetable consommé 165
- red bell pepper soup 72
- wonton soup 200

shrimp
- cucumber & shrimp soup 166
- laksa 209
- shrimp bisque 132
- three delicacy soup 203
- tom yam goong 210
- wonton soup 200

snow peas: vegetable broth 110

sour cream
- curried vegetable soup 114
- mushroom & ginger soup 71
- pea soup 144
- sauerkraut & sausage soup 38

spinach
- beef noodle soup 34
- green vegetable soup 20
- Jamaican pepper pot 218
- vegetable broth 110

split peas
- London particular 188
- split pea and sausage soup 37

squash & lentil soup 22
squid: laksa 209

stock 7–10
- basic recipe 10
- brown stock 9
- clarifying 9, 165
- light stock 8
- seasoning 9
- vegetable stock 7–10

sweet potatoes
- curried vegetable soup 114
- fish & sweet potato soup 50
- Jamaican pepper pot 218

three delicacy soup 203
tofu: hot & sour soup 125
tom yam goong 210

tomatoes
- borscht 174
- bouillabaisse 179
- chicken soup with matzo balls 43
- clam & pasta soup 52
- cream of tomato soup 65
- fish soup with semolina & dill dumplings 49
- harira 197
- jellied vegetable consommé 165
- lentil soup with ham 83
- Manhattan clam chowder 215
- Mexican tomato & vermicelli soup 116
- minestrone 182
- mixed vegetable soup with lamb meatballs 32
- ribollita 25
- roasted red bell pepper soup with garlic croutons 160
- shrimp bisque 132
- summer tomato soup 14
- tomato & parsnip soup 66
- tomato & smoked shellfish soup 168
- tomato & white bean soup 16

turnips
- lamb & vegetable broth 84
- vegetable soup with semolina dumplings 113

vichyssoise 153

watercress: green vegetable soup 20

wines & spirits
- Cajun crab & corn chowder 95
- carrot & mussel soup 98
- chicken noodle soup 128
- clam & pasta soup 52
- crab & noodle soup 131
- cream of clam soup 92
- fish & sweet potato soup 50
- French onion soup 176
- Manhattan clam chowder 215
- minestrone 182
- mushroom soup 68
- mussel soup 171
- pork soup with bulgur wheat 28
- quick sea scallop soup with pasta 55
- roasted red bell pepper soup with garlic croutons 160
- shrimp bisque 132
- *see also* cider; sherry

wonton soup 200

yogurt
- apple & fennel soup 156
- curried cucumber soup 142
- fava bean soup 138

pea soup 144

zucchini: ribollita 25

eshkaneh 198
jellied vegetable consommé 165
lamb & lemon soup 89
Mediterranean fish soup with garlic mayonnaise 56
shiitake mushroom soup with egg 119
eshkaneh 198

fabada 185
fava bean soup 138
fennel
apple & fennel soup 156
bouillabaisse 179
fish & seafood
bouillabaisse 179
cullen skink 191
fish & corn soup 96
fish & sweet potato soup 50
fish soup with semolina & dill dumplings 49
Mediterranean fish soup with garlic mayonnaise 56
see also clams; crabmeat; mussels; scallops; shrimp
French onion soup 176

garlic
apple & fennel soup 156
bacon & potato soup 26
bauernsuppe 180
beef noodle soup 34
black bean soup 221
borscht 174
bouillabaisse 179
Cajun crab & corn chowder 95
caldo verde 186
carrot & mussel soup 98
cauliflower & coconut soup 74
chicken soup with ginger & coconut milk 212
clam & pasta soup 52
crab soup 206
cream of clam soup 92
curried vegetable soup 114
fabada 185
French onion soup 176
garlic croutons 160
garlic soup 122
goulash soup 78
hot & sour soup 125
lentil soup with ham 83
Mediterranean fish soup with garlic mayonnaise 56
Mexican tomato & vermicelli soup 116
minestrone 182
pea soup 144
pork rib soup with pickled mustard greens 126
pork soup with bulgur wheat 28
quick-and-easy chickpea soup with sesame paste 162
ribollita 25
roasted red bell pepper soup with garlic croutons 160
salt pork & lentil soup 31
seaweed soup with miso 204
squash & lentil soup 22
summer tomato soup 14
tomato & parsnip soup 66
tomato & white bean soup 16
ginger
barley, lentil & onion soup 19
beef noodle soup 34
cauliflower & coconut soup 74
chicken & almond soup 44
chicken soup with ginger & coconut milk 212
egg flower soup 120
fish & corn soup 96
mushroom & ginger soup 71
seaweed soup with miso 204
squash & lentil soup 22
wonton soup 200
green beans
minestrone 182
vegetable broth 110

ham
fabada 185
lentil soup with ham 83
three delicacy soup 203
harira 197

Jamaican pepper pot 218
Jerusalem artichoke soup 77

kaffir lime leaves
chicken soup with ginger & coconut milk 212
hot & sour soup 125
tom yam goong 210
kidney beans: fabada 185

laksa 209
lamb
harira 197
lamb & eggplant soup 86
lamb & lemon soup 89
lamb & vegetable broth 84
mixed vegetable soup with lamb meatballs 32
langoustines: bouillabaisse 179
leeks
apple soup 159
asparagus soup 102
bouillabaisse 179
chicken & almond soup 44
chicken & lentil soup 40
chicken soup with leeks & rice 46
green vegetable soup 20
jellied vegetable consommé 165
lamb & vegetable broth 84
leek, potato & pear soup 154
mussel soup (Irish) 192
ribollita 25
split pea and sausage soup 37
vichyssoise 153
lemongrass
cauliflower & coconut soup 74
chicken soup with ginger & coconut milk 212
hot & sour soup 125
spicy cucumber soup 108
tom yam goong 210
lemons
al fresco avocado soup 136
apple & fennel soup 156
apple soup 159
avgolemono 194
avocado soup 104
barley, lentil & onion soup 19
beet & egg soup 150
black bean soup 221
eshkaneh 198
fava bean soup 138
lamb & lemon soup 89
Mediterranean fish soup with garlic mayonnaise 56
mixed vegetable soup with lamb meatballs 32
pork soup with bulgur wheat 28
quick-and-easy chickpea soup with sesame paste 162
squash & lentil soup 22
lentils
barley, lentil & onion soup 19
chicken & lentil soup 40
harira 197
lentil soup with ham 83
salt pork & lentil soup 31
squash & lentil soup 22
lettuce: green vegetable soup 20
lima beans: fabada 185
limes
avocado soup 104
cauliflower & coconut soup 74
curried vegetable soup 114
hot & sour soup 125
spicy cucumber soup 108
tom yam goong 210
London particular 188

Manhattan clam chowder 215
minestrone 182
mint
cucumber & mint soup 141
green vegetable soup 20
lamb & lemon soup 89
pea soup 144
quick-and-easy chickpea soup with sesame paste 162
miso paste: seaweed soup with miso 204

mushrooms
beef noodle soup 34
chicken & lentil soup 40
chicken soup with ginger & coconut milk 212
crab soup 206
jellied vegetable consommé 165
mushroom & ginger soup 71
mushroom soup 68
shiitake mushroom soup with egg 119
vegetable broth 110
mussels
bouillabaisse 179
carrot & mussel soup 98
mussel soup 171
mussel soup (Irish) 192
tomato & smoked shellfish soup 168
mustard greens: pork rib soup with pickled mustard greens 126

noodles
beef noodle soup 34
chicken & corn soup 216
chicken noodle soup 128
crab & noodle soup 131
laksa 209
pork rib soup with pickled mustard greens 126

okra: Jamaican pepper pot 218
onions
apple & fennel soup 156
bacon & potato soup 26
bacon & pumpkin soup 80
barley, lentil & onion soup 19
bauernsuppe 180
black bean soup 221
borscht 174
bouillabaisse 179
broccoli & Roquefort soup 107
Cajun crab & corn chowder 95
caldo verde 186
carrot & cilantro soup 62
chicken & corn soup 216
chicken & lentil soup 40
chicken soup with matzo balls 43
clam & pasta soup 52
cream of clam soup 92
cream of tomato soup 65
cullen skink 191
curried cucumber soup 142
curried vegetable soup 114
eshkaneh 198
fabada 185
fish & sweet potato soup 50
French onion soup 176
goulash soup 78
harira 197
jellied vegetable consommé 165
Jerusalem artichoke soup 77
lamb & eggplant soup 86
lamb & lemon soup 89
lamb & vegetable broth 84
lentil soup with ham 83
London particular 188
Mexican tomato & vermicelli soup 116
minestrone 182
mixed vegetable soup with lamb meatballs 32
mushroom soup 68
mussel soup (Irish) 192
pea soup 144
pork soup with bulgur wheat 28
red bell pepper soup 72
ribollita 25
roasted red bell pepper soup with garlic croutons 160
salt pork & lentil soup 31
seaweed soup with miso 204
shrimp bisque 132
split pea and sausage soup 37
squash & lentil soup 22
tomato & parsnip soup 66
tomato & white bean soup 16
vichyssoise 153
see also scallions; shallots

John the Baptist	Matthew 3	778
	Matthew 14:1–12	788
Jonah	Jonah 1—4	746
Jonathan	1 Samuel 20	232
Joseph	Genesis 39—50	31
Joseph	Matthew 1:18–25	777
Joshua	Numbers 13—14	115
	Joshua 1—6	170
Judas Iscariot	Matthew 26:14–25, 47–54	800
Laban	Genesis 29:16–30	22
Lazarus	John 11:1–44	860
Lot	Genesis 19:1–29	12
	2 Peter 2:7	974
Lydia	Acts 16:11–15	885
Mark	Acts 15:37–39	885
Mary	Luke 1:26—2:52	821
Mary and Martha	Luke 10:38–42	834
Mary Magdalene	John 20:1–18	869
Matthew	Mark 2:13–14	805
Miriam	Exodus 2:1–10	42
	Numbers 12:1–15	114
Moses	Exodus 2—4	42
	Exodus 12	50
Naomi	Ruth 1—4	213
Nebuchadnezzar	2 Kings 25:1–17	317
	Daniel 2:14–47	712
Nehemiah	Nehemiah 3:1—4:23	389
	Nehemiah 9:38—10:1	396
Nicodemus	John 3:1–21	851
Noah	Genesis 6:9—9:17	4
Paul (Saul)	Acts 9:1–19	879
	Acts 21—27	890
Peter	Matthew 14:22–33	789
	Acts 3:1–10	872
Philip	Acts 8:4–7, 26–40	877
Pontius Pilate	Matthew 27:11–26	802
Potiphar	Genesis: 39:1–20	31
Priscilla and Aquila	Acts 18:1–4	887
Rachel	Genesis 29—31	22
Rahab	Joshua 2	170
Rebekah	Genesis 24—27	60
Ruth	Ruth 1—4	213
Samson	Judges 13—16	204
Samuel	1 Samuel 1—3	216
Sarah	Genesis 12—23	8
Saul	1 Samuel 15	216
Shadrach, Meshach and Abednego	Daniel 3:1–30	713
Simeon	Luke 2:25–32	823
Solomon	1 Kings 2:1—3:28	266
	1 Kings 4:20–34	269
	1 Kings 10	276
Stephen	Acts 6:5—7:60	875
Tabitha	Acts 9:36–43	879
Thomas	John 20:24–29	870
Timothy	Acts 16:1	885
	Acts 17:14–15	886
Xerxes	Esther 3:12—7:10	403
Zacchaeus	Luke 19:1–10	842

Old Testament

Genesis

The Beginning

1 In the beginning, God created the heavens
and the earth. [2]The earth didn't have any
shape. And it was empty. Darkness was over
the surface of the ocean. At that time, the
ocean covered the earth. The Spirit of God
was hovering over the waters.

[3]God said, "Let there be light." And there was
light. [4]God saw that the light was good. He
separated the light from the darkness. [5]God
called the light "day." He called the darkness
"night." There was evening, and there was
morning. It was day one.
[6]God said, "Let there be a huge space between the
waters. Let it separate water from water."
[7]And that's exactly what happened. God
made the huge space between the waters. He
separated the water that was under the space
from the water that was above it. [8]God called
the huge space "sky." There was evening, and
there was morning. It was day two.
[9]God said, "Let the water under the sky be gathered into one place. Let dry ground appear."
And that's exactly what happened. [10]God
called the dry ground "land." He called the
waters that were gathered together "oceans."
And God saw that it was good.

[11]Then God said, "Let the land produce
plants. Let them bear their own seeds. And let
there be trees on the land that bear fruit with
seeds in it. Let each kind of plant or tree have
its own kind of seeds." And that's exactly
what happened.

[12]The land produced plants. Each kind of
plant had its own kind of seeds. The land produced trees that bore fruit with seeds in it.
Each kind of tree had its own kind of seeds.

God saw that it was good. [13]And there was
evening, and there was morning. It was day
three.
[14]God said, "Let there be lights in the huge space
of the sky. Let them separate the day from the
night. Let them serve as signs to mark off the
seasons and the days and the years. [15]Let them
serve as lights in the huge space of the sky to
give light on the earth." And that's exactly
what happened.

[16]God made two great lights. He made the
larger light to rule over the day. He made the
smaller light to rule over the night. He also
made the stars.

[17]God put the lights in the huge space of the
sky to give light on the earth. [18]He put them
there to rule over the day and the night. He put
them there to separate light from darkness.

God saw that it was good. [19]And there was
evening, and there was morning. It was day
four.
[20]God said, "Let the waters be filled with living
things. Let birds fly above the earth across the
huge space of the sky." [21]So God created the
great creatures of the ocean. He created every
living and moving thing that fills the waters. He
created all kinds of them. He created every kind
of bird that flies. And God saw that it was good.

[22]God blessed them. He said, "Have little
ones and increase your numbers. Fill the
water in the oceans. Let there be more and
more birds on the earth."

[23]There was evening, and there was morning. It was day five.
[24]God said, "Let the land produce all kinds of living creatures. Let there be livestock, and creatures that move along the ground, and wild
animals. Let there be all kinds of them." And
that's exactly what happened.

[25]God made all kinds of wild animals. He
made all kinds of livestock. He made all kinds
of creatures that move along the ground. And
God saw that it was good.

[26]Then God said, "Let us make man in our
likeness. Let them rule over the fish in the
waters and the birds of the air. Let them rule
over the livestock and over the whole earth.
Let them rule over all of the creatures that
move along the ground."

[27]So God created man in his own likeness.
He created him in the likeness of God.
He created them as male and female.

[28]God blessed them. He said to them, "Have children and increase your numbers. Fill the earth
and bring it under your control. Rule over the
fish in the waters and the birds of the air. Rule
over every living creature that moves on the
ground."

[29]Then God said, "I am giving you every
plant on the face of the whole earth that bears
its own seeds. I am giving you every tree that
has fruit with seeds in it. All of them will be
given to you for food.

[30]"I am giving every green plant to all of
the land animals and the birds of the air for
food. I am also giving the plants to all of the
creatures that move on the ground. I am giving them to every living thing that breathes."
And that's exactly what happened.

[31]God saw everything he had made. And it
was very good. There was evening, and there
was morning. It was day six.

2 So the heavens and the earth and everything in them were completed.

2By the seventh day God had finished the work he had been doing. So on the seventh day he rested from all of his work. 3God blessed the seventh day and made it holy. He rested on it. After he had created everything, he rested from all of the work he had done.

Adam and Eve

4Here is the story of the heavens and the earth when they were created.

The LORD God made the earth and the heavens. 5At that time, bushes had not appeared on the earth. Plants had not come up in the fields. The LORD God had not sent rain on the earth. And there wasn't any man to work the ground. 6But streams came up from the earth. They watered the whole surface of the ground.

7Then the LORD God formed a man. He made him out of the dust of the ground. He breathed the breath of life into him. And the man became a living person.

8The LORD God had planted a garden in the east. It was in Eden. There he put the man he had formed. 9The LORD God made all kinds of trees grow out of the ground. Their fruit was pleasing to look at and good to eat.

The tree that gives life forever was in the middle of the garden. The tree that gives the ability to tell the difference between good and evil was also there.

10A river watered the garden. It flowed from Eden. From there it separated into four other rivers.

11The name of the first river is the Pishon. It winds through the whole land of Havilah. Gold is found there. 12The gold of that land is good. Onyx and sweet-smelling resin are also found there.

13The name of the second river is the Gihon. It winds through the whole land of Cush. 14The name of the third river is the Tigris. It runs along the east side of Asshur. And the fourth river is the Euphrates.

15The LORD God put the man in the Garden of Eden. He put him there to work its ground and to take care of it.

16The LORD God gave the man a command. He said, "You can eat the fruit of any tree that is in the garden. 17But you must not eat the fruit of the tree of the knowledge of good and evil. If you do, you can be sure that you will die."

18The LORD God said, "It is not good for the man to be alone. I will make a helper who is just right for him."

19The LORD God had formed all of the wild animals. He had also formed all of the birds of the air. He had made all of them out of the ground. He brought them to the man to see what names he would give them. And the name the man gave each living creature became its name.

20So the man gave names to all of the livestock. He gave names to all of the birds of the air. And he gave names to all of the wild animals.

But Adam didn't find a helper that was right for him. 21So the LORD God caused him to fall into a deep sleep. While the man was sleeping, the LORD God took out one of his ribs. He closed up the opening that was in his side.

22Then the LORD God made a woman. He made her from the rib he had taken out of the man. And he brought her to him.

23The man said,

"Her bones have come from my bones.
  Her body has come from my body.
She will be named 'woman,'
  because she was taken out of a man."

24That's why a man will leave his father and mother and be joined to his wife. The two of them will become one.

25The man and his wife were both naked. They didn't feel any shame.

Adam and Eve Fall Into Sin

3 The serpent was more clever than any of the wild animals the LORD God had made. The serpent said to the woman, "Did God really say, 'You must not eat the fruit of any tree that is in the garden'?"

2The woman said to the serpent, "We can eat the fruit of the trees that are in the garden. 3But God did say, 'You must not eat the fruit of the tree that is in the middle of the garden. Do not even touch it. If you do, you will die.'"

4"You can be sure that you won't die," the serpent said to the woman. 5"God knows that when you eat the fruit of that tree, you will know things you have never known before. You will be able to tell the difference between good and evil. You will be like God."

6The woman saw that the fruit of the tree was good to eat. It was also pleasing to look at. And it would make a person wise. So she took some of the fruit and ate it. She also gave some to her husband, who was with her. And he ate it.

7Then both of them knew things they had never known before. They realized they were naked. So they sewed fig leaves together and made clothes for themselves.

8Then the man and his wife heard the LORD God walking in the garden. It was the coolest time of the day. They hid from the LORD God among the trees of the garden.

9But the LORD God called out to the man. "Where are you?" he asked.

10"I heard you in the garden," the man answered. "I was afraid. I was naked, so I hid."

11The LORD God said, "Who told you that you were naked? Have you eaten the fruit of the tree I commanded you not to eat?"

[12]The man said, "It was the woman you put here with me. She gave me some fruit from the tree. And I ate it."

[13]Then the LORD God said to the woman, "What have you done?"

The woman said, "The serpent tricked me. That's why I ate the fruit."

[14]So the LORD God spoke to the serpent. He said, "Because you have done this,

"I am putting a curse on you.
You are cursed more than all of the livestock
and all of the wild animals.
You will crawl on the ground.
You will eat dust
all of the days of your life.
15 I will put hatred
between you and the woman.
Your children and her children will be
enemies.
Her son will crush your head.
And you will crush his heel."

[16]The LORD God said to the woman,

"I will greatly increase your pain when you
give birth.
You will be in pain when you have children.
You will long for your husband.
And he will rule over you."

[17]The LORD God said to Adam, "You listened to your wife. You ate the fruit of the tree that I commanded you about. I said, 'You must not eat its fruit.'

"So I am putting a curse on the ground because
of what you did.
All the days of your life you will have to
work hard
to get food from the ground.
18 You will eat the plants of the field,
even though the ground produces thorns
and thistles.
19 You will have to work hard and sweat a lot
to produce the food you eat.
You were made out of the ground.
And you will return to it.
You are dust.
So you will return to it."

[20]Adam named his wife Eve. She would become the mother of every living person.

[21]The LORD God made clothes out of animal skins for Adam and his wife to wear. [22]The LORD God said, "The man has become like one of us. He can now tell the difference between good and evil. He must not be allowed to reach out his hand and pick fruit from the tree of life and eat it. If he does, he will live forever."

[23]So the LORD God drove the man out of the Garden of Eden to work the ground he had been made out of. [24]The LORD God drove him out and then placed cherubim on the east side of the Garden of Eden. He also placed a flaming sword there. It flashed back and forth. The cherubim and the sword guarded the way to the tree of life.

Cain and Abel

4 Adam made love to his wife Eve. She became pregnant and gave birth to Cain. She said, "With the LORD's help I have had a baby boy."
[2]Later she gave birth to his brother Abel.

Abel took care of sheep. Cain worked the ground. [3]After some time, Cain gathered some of the things he had grown. He brought them as an offering to the LORD.

[4]But Abel brought the fattest parts of some of the lambs from his flock. They were the male animals that were born first to their mothers.

The LORD was pleased with Abel and his offering. [5]But he wasn't pleased with Cain and his offering. So Cain became very angry. His face was sad.

[6]Then the LORD said to Cain, "Why are you angry? Why are you looking so sad? [7]Do what is right. Then you will be accepted. If you don't do what is right, sin is waiting at your door to grab you. It longs to have you. But you must rule over it."

[8]Cain said to his brother Abel, "Let's go out to the field." So they went out. There Cain attacked his brother Abel and killed him.

[9]Then the LORD said to Cain, "Where is your brother Abel?"

"I don't know," he replied. "Am I supposed to look after my brother?"

[10]The LORD said, "What have you done? Listen! Your brother's blood is crying out to me from the ground.

[11]"So I am putting a curse on you. I am driving you away from the ground. It has opened its mouth to receive your brother's blood from your hand.
[12]When you work the ground, it will not produce its crops for you anymore. You will be a restless person who wanders around on the earth."

[13]Cain said to the LORD, "You are punishing me more than I can take. [14]Today you are driving me away from the land. I will be hidden from you. I'll be a restless person who wanders around on the earth. Anyone who finds me will kill me."

[15]But the LORD said to him, "No. Anyone who kills you will be paid back seven times." The LORD put a mark on Cain. Then anyone who found him wouldn't kill him.

[16]So Cain went away from the LORD. He lived in the land of Nod. It was east of Eden.

[17]Cain made love to his wife. She became pregnant and gave birth to Enoch. At that time Cain was building a city. He named it after his son Enoch.

[18]Enoch had a son named Irad. Irad was the father of Mehujael. Mehujael was the father of Methushael. And Methushael was the father of Lamech.

[19]Lamech married two women. One was named Adah, and the other was named Zillah. [20]Adah

gave birth to Jabal. He was the father of those who live in tents and raise livestock. [21]His brother's name was Jubal. He was the father of everyone who plays the harp and flute.

[22]Zillah also had a son. His name was Tubal-Cain. He made all kinds of tools out of bronze and iron. Tubal-Cain's sister was Naamah.

[23]Lamech said to his wives,

"Adah and Zillah, listen to me.
You wives of Lamech, hear my words.
I have killed a man because he wounded me.
I have killed a young man because he hurt me.
24 Anyone who would have killed Cain would have been paid back seven times.
But anyone who hurts me will be paid back 77 times."

[25]Adam made love to his wife again. She gave birth to a son and named him Seth. She said, "God has given me another child. The child will take the place of Abel, because Cain killed him."

[26]Seth also had a son. He named him Enosh.

At that time people began to worship the LORD.

The Family Line of Adam

5 Here is the written story of Adam's family line.

When God created man, he made him in his own likeness. [2]He created them as male and female. He blessed them. And he called them "man" when they were created.

[3]When Adam was 130 years old, he had a son in his own likeness. He named him Seth. [4]Adam lived 800 years after Seth was born. He also had other sons and daughters. [5]Adam lived a total of 930 years. Then he died.

[6]Seth lived 105 years. Then he became the father of Enosh. [7]Seth lived 807 years after Enosh was born. He also had other sons and daughters. [8]Seth lived a total of 912 years. Then he died.

[9]Enosh lived 90 years. Then he became the father of Kenan. [10]Enosh lived 815 years after Kenan was born. He also had other sons and daughters. [11]Enosh lived a total of 905 years. Then he died.

[12]Kenan lived 70 years. Then he became the father of Mahalalel. [13]Kenan lived 840 years after Mahalalel was born. He also had other sons and daughters. [14]Kenan lived a total of 910 years. Then he died.

[15]Mahalalel lived 65 years. Then he became the father of Jared. [16]Mahalalel lived 830 years after Jared was born. He also had other sons and daughters. [17]Mahalalel lived a total of 895 years. Then he died.

[18]Jared lived 162 years. Then he became the father of Enoch. [19]Jared lived 800 years after Enoch was born. He also had other sons and daughters. [20]Jared lived a total of 962 years. Then he died.

[21]Enoch lived 65 years. Then he became the father of Methuselah. [22]Enoch walked with God 300 years after Methuselah was born. He also had other sons and daughters. [23]Enoch lived a total of 365 years.

[24]Enoch walked with God. Then he couldn't be found, because God took him from this life.

[25]Methuselah lived 187 years. Then he became the father of Lamech. [26]Methuselah lived 782 years after Lamech was born. He also had other sons and daughters. [27]Methuselah lived a total of 969 years. Then he died.

[28]Lamech lived 182 years. Then he had a son. [29]He named him Noah. Lamech said, "He will comfort us when we are working. He'll comfort us when our hands work so hard they hurt. We have to work hard. That's because the LORD has put a curse on the ground."

[30]Lamech lived 595 years after Noah was born. He also had other sons and daughters. [31]Lamech lived a total of 777 years. Then he died.

[32]After Noah was 500 years old, he became the father of Shem, Ham and Japheth.

The Flood

6 Men began to increase their numbers on the earth, and daughters were born to them. [2]The sons of God saw that the daughters of men were beautiful. So they married any of them they chose.

[3]Then the LORD said, "My Spirit will not struggle with man forever. He will die. He will have only 120 years to live until I judge him."

[4]The Nephilim were on the earth in those days. That was when the sons of God went to the daughters of men and had children by them. The Nephilim were the heroes of long ago. They were famous men. Nephilim were also on the earth later on.

[5]The LORD saw how bad the sins of man had become on the earth. All of the thoughts in his heart were always directed only toward what was evil. [6]The LORD was very sad that he had made man on the earth. His heart was filled with pain. [7]So the LORD said, "I created man on the earth. But I will wipe them out. I will destroy people and animals alike. I will also destroy the creatures that move along the ground and the birds of the air. I am very sad that I have made man."

[8]But the LORD was pleased with Noah.

[9]Here is the story of Noah.

Noah was a godly man. He was without blame among the people of his time. He walked with God. [10]Noah had three sons. Their names were Shem, Ham and Japheth.

[11]The earth was very sinful in God's eyes. It was full of mean and harmful acts. [12]God saw how sinful the earth had become. All of the people on earth were leading very sinful lives.

[13]So God said to Noah, "I am going to put an end to all people. They have filled the earth with

their harmful acts. You can be sure that I am going
to destroy both them and the earth.
14“So make yourself an ark out of cypress
wood. Make rooms in it. Cover it with tar inside
and out. 15Here is how I want you to build it. The
ark has to be 450 feet long. It has to be 75 feet
wide and 45 feet high. 16Make a roof for it. Leave
the sides of the ark open a foot and a half from the
top. Put a door in one side of the ark. Make lower,
middle and upper decks.
17“I am going to bring a flood on the earth. It
will destroy all life under the sky. It will destroy
every living creature that breathes. Everything on
earth will die.
18“But I will make my covenant with you. You
will enter the ark. Your sons and your wife and
your sons' wives will enter it with you.
19“Bring two of every living thing into the ark.
Bring male and female of them into it. They will
be kept alive with you. 20Two of every kind of bird
will come to you. Two of every kind of animal will
come to you. And two of every kind of creature
that moves along the ground will come to you. All
of them will be kept alive with you.
21“Take every kind of food that you will need.
Store it away. It will be food for you and for them.”
22Noah did everything exactly as God commanded him.

7 Then the LORD said to Noah, “Go into the ark
with your whole family. I know that you are a
godly man among the people of today.
2“Take seven of every kind of ‘clean’ animal
with you. Take male and female of them. Take two
of every kind of animal that is not ‘clean.’ Take
male and female of them. 3Also take seven of
every kind of bird. Take male and female of them.
That will keep every kind alive. Then they can
spread out again over the whole earth.
4“Seven days from now I will send rain on the
earth. It will rain for 40 days and 40 nights. I will
destroy from the face of the earth every living
thing I have made.”
5Noah did everything the LORD commanded
him to do.
6Noah was 600 years old when the flood came
on the earth. 7He and his sons entered the ark. His
wife and his sons' wives went with them. They
entered the ark to escape the waters of the flood.
8Pairs of “clean” animals and pairs of animals
that were not “clean” came to Noah. So did pairs
of birds and pairs of all of the creatures that move
along the ground. 9Male and female of all of them
came to Noah and entered the ark.
Everything happened exactly as God had commanded Noah. 10After seven days the flood came
on the earth.
11Noah was 600 years old. It was the 17th day of
the second month of the year. On that day all of
the springs at the bottom of the oceans burst open.
God opened the windows of the skies. 12Rain fell
on the earth for 40 days and 40 nights.
13On that same day Noah entered the ark
together with Shem, Ham and Japheth. Noah's
wife and the wives of his three sons also entered it.
14They had every kind of wild animal with
them. They had every kind of livestock. They had
every kind of creature that moves along the
ground. And they had every kind of bird that flies.
15Pairs of all living creatures that breathe came to
Noah and entered the ark. 16The animals going in
were male and female of every living thing.
Everything happened exactly as God had commanded Noah. Then the LORD shut him in.
17For 40 days the flood kept coming on the
earth. As the waters rose higher, they lifted the ark
high above the earth. 18The waters rose higher and
higher on the earth. And the ark floated on the
water.
19The waters rose on the earth until all of the
high mountains under the entire sky were covered.
20The waters continued to rise until they covered
the mountains by more than 20 feet.
21Every living thing that moved on the earth
died. The birds, the livestock and the wild animals
died. All of the creatures that fill the earth also
died. And so did every human being. 22Everything
on dry land that had the breath of life in it died.
23Every living thing on the earth was wiped out.
People and animals were destroyed. The creatures
that move along the ground and the birds of the air
were wiped out.
Everything was destroyed from the earth. Only
Noah and those who were with him in the ark were
left.
24The waters flooded the earth for 150 days.

8 But God showed concern for Noah. He also
showed concern for all of the wild animals
and livestock that were with Noah in the ark.
So God sent a wind over the earth. And the
waters began to go down. 2The springs at the bottom of the oceans had been closed. The windows
of the skies had been closed. And the rain had
stopped falling from the sky.
3The water continued to go down from the
earth. At the end of the 150 days the water had
gone down. 4On the 17th day of the seventh
month, the ark came to rest on the mountains of
Ararat. 5The waters continued to go down until the
tenth month. On the first day of the month, the tops
of the mountains could be seen.
6After 40 days Noah opened the window he had
made in the ark. 7He sent a raven out. It kept flying back and forth until the water had dried up
from the earth.
8Then Noah sent a dove out. He wanted to see
if the water had gone down from the surface of the
ground. 9But the dove couldn't find any place to
put its feet down. There was still water over the
whole surface of the earth. So the dove returned to
Noah in the ark. Noah reached out his hand and
took the dove in. He brought it back to himself in
the ark.

10 He waited seven more days. Then he sent the
dove out from the ark again. 11 In the evening the
dove returned to him. There in its beak was a
freshly picked olive leaf! So Noah knew that the
water on the earth had gone down.
12 He waited seven more days. Then he sent the
dove out again. But that time it didn't return to him.
13 It was the first day of the first month of
Noah's 601st year. The water had dried up from
the earth. Then Noah removed the covering from
the ark. He saw that the surface of the ground was
dry. 14 By the 27th day of the second month the
earth was completely dry.
15 Then God said to Noah, 16 "Come out of the
ark. Bring your wife and your sons and their wives
with you.
17 "Bring out every kind of living thing that is
with you. Bring the birds, the animals, and all of
the creatures that move along the ground. Then
they can multiply on the earth. They can have little ones and increase their numbers."
18 So Noah came out of the ark. His sons and his
wife and his sons' wives were with him. 19 All of the
animals came out of the ark. The creatures that
move along the ground also came out. So did all of
the birds. Everything that moves on the earth came
out of the ark. One kind after another came out.
20 Then Noah built an altar to honor the LORD.
He took some of all of the "clean" animals and
birds. He sacrificed burnt offerings to the LORD on
the altar.
21 Their smell was pleasant to the LORD. He said
to himself, "I will never put a curse on the ground
again because of man. I will not do it even though
his heart is always directed toward what is evil.
His thoughts are evil from the time he is young. I
will never destroy all living things again, as I have
just done.

22 "As long as the earth lasts,
there will always be a time to plant
and a time to gather the crops.
As long as the earth lasts,
there will always be cold and heat.
There will always be summer and winter,
day and night."

God Makes a Covenant With Noah

9 Then God gave his blessing to Noah and his
sons. He said to them, "Have children and
increase your numbers. Fill the earth.
2 "All of the land animals will be afraid of you.
All of the birds of the air will fear you. Every creature that moves along the ground will fear you.
Every fish in the oceans will also be afraid of you.
Every living thing is put under your control.
3 "Everything that lives and moves will be food
for you. I have already given you the green plants
for food. Now I am giving you everything.
4 "But you must not eat meat that still has blood
in it. 5 You can be sure that I will hold someone
accountable if you are murdered. I will even hold
animals accountable if they kill you. I will also
hold anyone accountable who murders another
person.

6 "Anyone who murders man
will be killed by man.
That is because I have made man
in my own likeness.

7 "Have children and increase your numbers.
Multiply on the earth and increase your numbers
on it."
8 Then God spoke to Noah and to his sons who
were with him. He said, 9 "I am now making my
covenant with you and with all of your children
who will be born after you. 10 I am making it also
with every living thing that was with you in the
ark. I am making my covenant with the birds, the
livestock and all of the wild animals. I am making
it with all of the creatures that came out of the ark
with you. I am making it with every living thing
on earth.
11 "Here is my covenant that I am making with
you. The waters of a flood will never destroy all
life again. A flood will never destroy the earth
again."
12 God continued, "My covenant is between me
and you and every living thing with you. It is a
covenant for all time to come.
"Here is the sign of the covenant I am making.
13 I have put my rainbow in the clouds. It will be
the sign of the covenant between me and the earth.
14 Sometimes when I bring clouds over the earth, a
rainbow will appear in them. 15 Then I will remember my covenant between me and you and every
kind of living thing. The waters will never become
a flood to destroy all life again.
16 "When the rainbow appears in the clouds, I
will see it. I will remember that my covenant will
last forever. It is a covenant between me and every
kind of living thing on earth."
17 So God said to Noah, "The rainbow is the sign
of my covenant. I have made my covenant
between me and all life on earth."

The Sons of Noah

18 The sons of Noah who came out of the ark
were Shem, Ham and Japheth. Ham was the father
of Canaan. 19 The people who were scattered over
the earth came from Noah's three sons.
20 Noah was a man who worked the ground. He
decided to plant a vineyard. 21 He drank some of its
wine. It made him drunk. Then he lay down inside
his tent without any clothes on. 22 Ham saw his
father's naked body. Ham was the father of Canaan. Ham went outside and told his two brothers.
23 But Shem and Japheth took a piece of clothing. They laid it across their shoulders. Then they
walked backward into the tent. They covered their
father's body. They turned their faces away. They
didn't want to see their father's naked body.

[24]Then Noah woke up from his sleep that was
caused by the wine. He found out what his
youngest son had done to him. [25]He said,

"May a curse be put on Canaan.
He will be the lowest of slaves to his
brothers."

[26]Noah also said,

"May the LORD, the God of Shem, be blessed.
May Canaan be the slave of Shem.
[27] May God add land to Japheth's territory.
May Japheth live in the tents of Shem.
And may Canaan be their slave."

[28]After the flood Noah lived 350 years. [29]Noah
lived a total of 950 years. Then he died.

A List of Nations

10 Here is the story of Shem, Ham and Japheth. They were Noah's sons. After the
flood, they too had sons.

The Sons of Japheth

[2] The sons of Japheth were
Gomer, Magog, Madai, Javan, Tubal,
Meshech and Tiras.
[3] The sons of Gomer were
Ashkenaz, Riphath and Togarmah.
[4] The sons of Javan were
Elishah, Tarshish, the Kittim and the
Rodanites. [5]The people who lived by the
sea came from all of them. Their tribes
and nations spread out into their own
territories. Each tribe and nation had its
own language.

The Sons of Ham

[6] The sons of Ham were
Cush, Egypt, Put and Canaan.
[7] The sons of Cush were
Seba, Havilah, Sabtah, Raamah and
Sabteca.
The sons of Raamah were
Sheba and Dedan.

[8]Cush was the father of Nimrod. Nimrod grew
up to be a mighty hero on the earth. [9]He was a
mighty hunter in the LORD's eyes. That's why people sometimes compare others with Nimrod. They
say, "They are like Nimrod, who is a mighty
hunter in the LORD's eyes."

[10]At first Nimrod's kingdom was made up of
Babylon, Erech, Akkad and Calneh. Those cities
were in the land of Babylonia.

[11]From that land he went to Assyria. There he
built Nineveh, Rehoboth Ir and Calah. [12]He also
built Resen. It is between Nineveh and Calah. Nineveh is the great city.

[13] Egypt was the father of
the Ludites, Anamites, Lehabites and
Naphtuhites. [14]He was also the father of
the Pathrusites, Casluhites and Caphtorites. The Philistines came from the Casluhites.
[15] Canaan was the father of
Sidon. Sidon was his oldest son. Canaan
was also the father of the Hittites, [16]Jeb-
usites, Amorites and Girgashites. [17]And
he was the father of the Hivites, Arkites,
Sinites, [18]Arvadites, Zemarites and Hamathites.

Later the Canaanite tribes scattered. [19]The borders
of Canaan went from Sidon toward Gerar all the way
to Gaza. Then they went toward Sodom, Gomorrah,
Admah and Zeboiim all the way to Lasha.

[20]Those are the sons of Ham. They are listed by
their tribes and languages in their territories and
nations.

The Sons of Shem

[21]Sons were also born to Shem. Shem was Japheth's younger brother. All of the sons of Eber
came from Shem.

[22] The sons of Shem were
Elam, Asshur, Arphaxad, Lud and Aram.
[23] The sons of Aram were
Uz, Hul, Gether and Meshech.
[24] Arphaxad was the father of Shelah.
Shelah was the father of Eber.
[25] Eber was the father of two sons.
One was named Peleg. That's because
the earth was divided up in his time. His
brother was named Joktan.
[26] Joktan was the father of
Almodad, Sheleph, Hazarmaveth and
Jerah. [27]He was also the father of Hadoram, Uzal, Diklah, [28]Obal, Abimael,
Sheba, [29]Ophir, Havilah and Jobab. All
of them were sons of Joktan.

[30]The area where they lived stretched from Mesha
toward Sephar. It was in the eastern hill country.

[31]Those are the sons of Shem. They are listed
by their tribes and languages in their territories and
nations.

[32]Those are the tribes of Noah's sons. They are
listed by their family lines within their nations.
From them the nations spread out over the earth
after the flood.

The Tower of Babel

11 The whole world had only one language.
All people spoke it. [2]They moved to the
east and found a broad valley in Babylonia. There
they settled down.

[3]They said to each other, "Come. Let's make
bricks and bake them well." They used bricks
instead of stones. They used tar to hold the bricks
together.

[4]Then they said, "Come. Let's build a city for
ourselves. Let's build a tower that reaches to the

sky. We'll make a name for ourselves. Then we won't be scattered over the face of the whole earth."

[5]But the LORD came down to see the city and the tower the people were building. [6]The LORD said, "They are one people. And all of them speak the same language. That is why they can do this. Now they will be able to do anything they plan to. [7]Come. Let us go down and mix up their language. Then they will not understand each other."

[8]So the LORD scattered them from there over the whole earth. And they stopped building the city. [9]The LORD mixed up the language of the whole world there. That's why the city was named Babel. From there the LORD scattered them over the face of the whole earth.

The Family Line of Shem

[10]Here is the story of Shem.

It was two years after the flood. When Shem was 100 years old, he became the father of Arphaxad. [11]After Arphaxad was born, Shem lived 500 years. And he had other sons and daughters.

[12]When Arphaxad had lived 35 years, he became the father of Shelah. [13]After Shelah was born, Arphaxad lived 403 years. And he had other sons and daughters.

[14]When Shelah had lived 30 years, he became the father of Eber. [15]After Eber was born, Shelah lived 403 years. And he had other sons and daughters.

[16]When Eber had lived 34 years, he became the father of Peleg. [17]After Peleg was born, Eber lived 430 years. And he had other sons and daughters.

[18]When Peleg had lived 30 years, he became the father of Reu. [19]After Reu was born, Peleg lived 209 years. And he had other sons and daughters.

[20]When Reu had lived 32 years, he became the father of Serug. [21]After Serug was born, Reu lived 207 years. And he had other sons and daughters.

[22]When Serug had lived 30 years, he became the father of Nahor. [23]After Nahor was born, Serug lived 200 years. And he had other sons and daughters.

[24]When Nahor had lived 29 years, he became the father of Terah. [25]After Terah was born, Nahor lived 119 years. And he had other sons and daughters.

[26]Terah lived for 70 years. Then he became the father of Abram, Nahor and Haran.

[27]Here is the story of Terah.

Terah became the father of Abram, Nahor and Haran. And Haran became the father of Lot. [28]Haran died in Ur in Babylonia. That was the land where he had been born. Haran died while his father Terah was still alive.

[29]Abram and Nahor both got married. The name of Abram's wife was Sarai. The name of Nahor's wife was Milcah. She was the daughter of Haran. Haran was the father of Milcah and Iscah. [30]But Sarai wasn't able to have children.

[31]Terah started out from Ur in Babylonia. He took his son Abram with him. He also took his grandson Lot. Lot was the son of Haran. And Terah took his daughter-in-law Sarai. She was the wife of his son Abram.

All of them left together to go to Canaan. But when they came to Haran, they settled down.

[32]Terah lived for 205 years. He died in Haran.

God Chooses Abram

12 The LORD had said to Abram, "Leave your country and your people. Leave your father's family. Go to the land I will show you.

[2]"I will make you into a great nation.
  I will bless you.
I will make your name great.
  You will be a blessing to others.
[3]I will bless those who bless you.
  I will put a curse on anyone who calls down a curse on you.
All nations on earth
  will be blessed because of you."

[4]So Abram left, just as the LORD had told him. Lot went with him. Abram was 75 years old when he left Haran.

[5]He took his wife Sarai and his nephew Lot. They took all of the things they had gotten in Haran. They also took the workers they had gotten there.

They set out for the land of Canaan. And they arrived there.

[6]Abram traveled through the land. He went as far as the large tree of Moreh at Shechem. At that time the people of Canaan were living in the land.

[7]The LORD appeared to Abram at Shechem. He said, "I will give this land to your children after you." So Abram built an altar there to honor the LORD, who had appeared to him.

[8]From there, Abram went on toward the hills east of Bethel. He set up his tent there. Bethel was to the west, and Ai was to the east.

Abram built an altar there and worshiped the LORD. [9]Then Abram left and continued toward the Negev Desert.

Abram Goes to Egypt

[10]At that time there wasn't enough food in the land. So Abram went down to Egypt to live there for a while.

[11]As he was about to enter Egypt, he spoke to his wife Sarai. He said, "I know what a beautiful woman you are. [12]The people of Egypt will see you. They will say, 'This is his wife.' And they will kill me. But they will let you live. [13]Say you are my sister. Then I'll be treated well because of you. My life will be spared because of you."

[14]Abram arrived in Egypt. The people of Egypt saw that Sarai was a very beautiful woman. [15]When Pharaoh's officials saw her, they bragged to Pharaoh about her. Sarai was taken into his palace.

[16]Pharaoh treated Abram well because of her. So Abram gained more sheep and cattle. He also got more male and female donkeys. And he gained more male and female servants and some camels.

[17]But the LORD sent terrible sicknesses on Pharaoh and everyone in his palace. He did it because of Abram's wife Sarai.

[18]So Pharaoh sent for Abram. "What have you done to me?" he said. "Why didn't you tell me she was your wife? [19]Why did you say, 'She's my sister'? That's why I took her to be my wife. Now then, here's your wife. Take her and go!"

[20]Then Pharaoh gave orders about Abram to his men. They sent him on his way. He left with his wife and everything he had.

Abram and Lot Separate

13 Abram went up from Egypt to the Negev Desert. He took his wife and everything he had. Lot went with him. [2]Abram had become very rich. He had a lot of livestock and silver and gold.

[3]From the Negev Desert, he went from place to place until he came to Bethel. He came to a place between Bethel and Ai. That's where his tent had been earlier. [4]He had also built an altar there. He worshiped the LORD there.

[5]Lot was moving around with Abram. Lot also had flocks and herds and tents.

[6]But the land didn't have enough food for both of them. They had large herds and many servants. So they weren't able to stay together. [7]The people who took care of Abram's herds and those who took care of Lot's herds began to argue.

The Canaanites and Perizzites were also living in the land at that time.

[8]So Abram said to Lot, "Let's not argue with each other. The people who take care of your herds and those who take care of mine shouldn't argue with one another. After all, we're part of the same family.

[9]"Isn't the whole land in front of you? Let's separate. If you go to the left, I'll go to the right. If you go to the right, I'll go to the left."

[10]Lot looked up. He saw that the whole Jordan River valley had plenty of water. It was like the garden of the LORD. It was like the land of Egypt near Zoar. That was before the LORD destroyed Sodom and Gomorrah.

[11]So Lot chose the whole Jordan River valley for himself. Then he started out toward the east.

The two men separated. [12]Abram lived in the land of Canaan. Lot lived among the cities of the Jordan River valley. He set up his tents near Sodom.

[13]The men of Sodom were evil. They were sinning greatly against the LORD.

[14]The LORD spoke to Abram after Lot had left him. He said, "Look up from where you are. Look north and south. Look east and west. [15]I will give you all of the land that you see. I will give it to you and your children after you forever.

[16]"I will make your children like the dust of the earth. Can dust be counted? If it can, then your children can be counted. [17]Go. Walk through the land. See how long and wide it is. I am giving it to you."

[18]So Abram moved his tents. He went to live near the large trees of Mamre at Hebron. There he built an altar to honor the LORD.

Abram Saves Lot

14 At that time Amraphel was the king of Babylonia. Arioch was the king of Ellasar. Kedorlaomer was the king of Elam. And Tidal was the king of Goiim.

[2]They went to war against five kings. The kings were Bera king of Sodom, Birsha king of Gomorrah, Shinab king of Admah, Shemeber king of Zeboiim, and the king of Bela. Bela was also called Zoar.

[3]Those five kings all gathered their armies together in the Valley of Siddim. It was the valley of the Dead Sea. [4]For 12 years they had been under the rule of Kedorlaomer. But in the 13th year they opposed him.

[5]In the 14th year, Kedorlaomer and the kings who helped him went to war. They won the battle against the Rephaites in Ashteroth Karnaim. They also won the battle against the Zuzites in Ham and the Emites in Shaveh Kiriathaim. [6]They did the same thing to the Horites in the hill country of Seir. They marched all the way to El Paran near the desert.

[7]Then they turned back. They went to En Mishpat. En Mishpat was also called Kadesh. They took over the whole territory of the Amalekites. They also won the battle against the Amorites who were living in Hazazon Tamar.

[8]Then the king of Sodom and the king of Gomorrah marched out. The kings of Admah, Zeboiim and Bela went with them. Bela was also called Zoar.

They lined up their armies for battle in the Valley of Siddim. [9]They got ready to fight against Kedorlaomer king of Elam, Tidal king of Goiim, Amraphel king of Babylonia, and Arioch king of Ellasar. There were four kings against five.

[10]The Valley of Siddim was full of tar pits. The kings of Sodom and Gomorrah ran away from the battle. Some of their men fell into the pits. The rest escaped to the hills.

[11]The four kings took all of the things that belonged to Sodom and Gomorrah. They also took all of their food. Then they went away.

[12]They carried away Lot, Abram's nephew, and the things he owned. Lot was living in Sodom at that time.

[13]One man escaped. He came and reported everything to Abram. Abram was a Hebrew. He was living near the large trees of Mamre the Amorite. Mamre was a brother of Eshcol and Aner. All of them helped Abram.

[14]Abram heard that Lot had been captured. So he called out his 318 trained men. All of them were sons of his servants. They chased the enemy as far

as Dan. 15During the night Abram separated his
men into groups. They attacked the enemy and
drove them away. They chased them north of Damascus as far as Hobah.
16Abram took back all of the things the kings
had taken. He brought back his nephew Lot and
the things Lot owned. He also brought back the
women and the other people.
17After Abram won the battle over Kedorlaomer
and the kings who helped him, he returned. The
king of Sodom came out to meet him in the Valley
of Shaveh. The Valley of Shaveh was also called
the King's Valley.
18Melchizedek was the king of Jerusalem. He
brought out bread and wine. He was the priest of
God Most High. 19He gave a blessing to Abram.
He said,

"May God Most High bless Abram.
May the Creator of heaven and earth bless
him.
20Give praise to God Most High.
He gave your enemies into your hand."

Then Abram gave Melchizedek a tenth of everything.
21The king of Sodom said to Abram, "Give me
the people. Keep everything else for yourself."
22But Abram said to the king of Sodom, "I have
raised my hand to the LORD. He is God Most High.
He is the Creator of heaven and earth. I have taken
an oath. 23I have said that I won't accept anything
that belongs to you. I won't take even a thread or
the strap of a sandal. You will never be able to say,
'I made Abram rich.'
24"I'll accept only what my men have eaten and
what belongs to Aner, Eshcol and Mamre. Those
three men went with me. Let them have their share."

God Makes a Covenant With Abram

15 Some time later, Abram had a vision. The
LORD said to him,

"Abram, do not be afraid.
I am like a shield to you.
I am your very great reward."

2But Abram said, "LORD and King, what can
you give me? I still don't have any children. My
servant Eliezer comes from Damascus. When I
die, he will get everything I own." 3Abram continued, "You haven't given me any children. So a
servant in my house will get everything I own."
4Then a message came to Abram from the
LORD. He said, "This man will not get what
belongs to you. A son will come from your own
body. He will get everything you own."
5The LORD took Abram outside and said, "Look
up at the sky. Count the stars, if you can." Then he
said to him, "That is how many children you will
have."
6Abram believed the LORD. The LORD accepted
Abram because he believed. So his faith made him
right with the LORD.
7He also said to Abram, "I am the LORD. I
brought you out of Ur in Babylonia. I wanted to
give you this land to take as your very own."
8But Abram said, "LORD and King, how can I
know I will take this land as my own?"
9So the LORD said to him, "Bring me a young
cow. Also bring a goat and a ram. All of them must
be three years old. Bring a dove and a young
pigeon along with them."
10Abram brought all of them to the LORD.
Abram cut them in two. He placed the halves
opposite each other. But he didn't cut the birds in
half. 11Then large birds came down to eat the dead
bodies of the animals and birds. But Abram chased
the large birds away.
12As the sun was going down, Abram fell into a
deep sleep. A thick and terrible darkness covered
him.
13Then the LORD said to him, "You can be sure
of what I am about to tell you. Your children who
live after you will be strangers in a country that
does not belong to them. They will become slaves.
They will be treated badly for 400 years. 14But I
will punish the nation that makes them slaves.
After that, they will leave with all kinds of valuable things.
15"But you will die in peace. You will join the
members of your family who have already died.
You will be buried when you are very old.
16"Your children's grandchildren will come
back here. That is because the sin of the Amorites
has not yet reached the point where I must judge
them."
17The sun set and darkness fell. Then a burning
torch and a fire pot filled with smoke appeared.
They passed between the pieces of the animals.
18On that day the LORD made a covenant with
Abram. He said, "I am giving this land to your
children after you. It reaches from the river of
Egypt to the great river Euphrates. 19It includes the
land of the Kenites, Kenizzites, Kadmonites, 20Hit-
tites, Perizzites and Rephaites. 21The Amorites, Canaanites, Girgashites and Jebusites also live there."

Hagar and Ishmael

16 Abram's wife Sarai had never had any children by him. But she had a female servant
from Egypt named Hagar. 2So she said to Abram,
"The LORD has kept me from having children. Go
and make love to my servant. Maybe I can have a
family through her."
Abram agreed to what Sarai had said. 3After he
had been living in Canaan for ten years, his wife
Sarai gave him her servant Hagar to be his wife.
4He made love to Hagar. And she became
pregnant.
When Hagar knew she was pregnant, she began
to look down on the woman who owned her.
5Then Sarai said to Abram, "It's your fault that
I'm suffering like this. I put my servant in your
arms. Now that she knows she's pregnant, she

looks down on me. May the LORD judge between you and me. May he decide which of us is right."

6"Your servant belongs to you," Abram said. "Do with her what you think is best." Then Sarai treated Hagar badly. So Hagar ran away from her.

7The angel of the LORD found Hagar near a spring of water in the desert. The spring was beside the road to Shur. 8He said, "Hagar, you are the servant of Sarai. Where have you come from? Where are you going?"

"I'm running away from my owner Sarai," she answered.

9Then the angel of the LORD told her, "Go back to the woman who owns you. Obey her." 10The angel continued, "I will greatly increase the number of your children after you. You will have more of them than anyone can count."

11The angel of the LORD also said to her,

"You are now pregnant.
You will have a son.
You will name him Ishmael.
That is because the LORD has heard about your suffering.
12He will be like a wild donkey.
He will use his power against everyone.
And everyone will be against him.
He will not be friendly
toward any of his relatives."

13She gave a name to the LORD who spoke to her. She called him "You are the God who sees me." That's because she said, "I have now seen the One who sees me."

14That's why the well was named Beer Lahai Roi. It's still there, between Kadesh and Bered.

15So Hagar had a son by Abram. And Abram gave the name Ishmael to the son she had by him. 16Abram was 86 years old when Hagar had Ishmael by him.

The Covenant of Circumcision

17 When Abram was 99 years old, the LORD appeared to him. He said, "I am the Mighty God. Walk with me and live without any blame. 2I will now put into practice my covenant between me and you. I will greatly increase your numbers."

3Abram fell with his face to the ground. God said to him, 4"As for me, this is my covenant with you. You will be the father of many nations.

5"You will not be called Abram anymore. Your name will be Abraham, because I have made you a father of many nations. 6I will give you many children. Nations will come from you. And kings will come from you.

7"I will make my covenant with you. It will last forever. It will be between me and you and your children after you for all time to come. I will be your God. And I will be the God of all of your family after you.

8"You are now living in Canaan as an outsider. But I will give you the whole land of Canaan. You will own it forever. So will your children after you. And I will be their God."

9Then God said to Abraham, "As for you, you must keep my covenant. You and your children after you for all time to come must keep it.

10"Here is my covenant that you and your children after you must keep. Every male among you must be circumcised. 11You must be circumcised. That will be the sign of the covenant between me and you. 12It must be done for all time to come.

"Every male among you who is eight days old must be circumcised. That includes those who are born in your house. It also includes those who are bought with money from a stranger. Even those who are not your own children must be included. 13Any male who is born in your house or bought with your money must be circumcised.

"My covenant will last forever. Your body will have the mark of my covenant on it.

14"Any male who has not been circumcised will be cut off from his people. He has broken my covenant."

15God also said to Abraham, "As for Sarai your wife, do not call her Sarai anymore. Her name will be Sarah. 16I will give her my blessing. You can be sure that I will give you a son by her. I will bless her so that she will be the mother of nations. Kings of nations will come from her."

17Abraham fell with his face to the ground. He laughed and said to himself, "Will a son be born to a man who is 100 years old? Will Sarah have a child at the age of 90?"

18Abraham said to God, "I wish Ishmael could receive your blessing!"

19Then God said, "I will bless Ishmael. But your wife Sarah will have a son by you. And you will name him Isaac. I will establish my covenant with him. It will be a covenant that lasts forever. It will be for Isaac and for his family after him.

20"As for Ishmael, I have heard you. You can be sure that I will bless him. I will give him children. I will greatly increase his numbers. He will be the father of 12 rulers. And I will make him into a great nation.

21"But I will establish my covenant with Isaac. By this time next year, Sarah will have a son by you."

22When he had finished speaking with Abraham, God left him.

23On that very day Abraham circumcised his son Ishmael. He also circumcised every male who was born in his house or bought with his money. He did exactly as God had told him. 24Abraham was 99 years old when he was circumcised. 25His son Ishmael was 13.

26Abraham and his son Ishmael were both circumcised on that same day. 27And every male in Abraham's house was circumcised along with him. That included those who were born in his house or bought from a stranger.

Three Men Visit Abraham

18 The LORD appeared to Abraham near the large trees of Mamre. Abraham was sitting at the entrance to his tent. It was the hottest time of the day.

[2]Abraham looked up and saw three men standing nearby. He quickly left the entrance to his tent to meet them. He bowed low to the ground.

[3]He said, "My lord, if you are pleased with me, don't pass me by. [4]Let a little water be brought. All of you can wash your feet and rest under this tree.

[5]"Let me get you something to eat to give you strength. Then you can go on your way. I want to do this for you now that you have come to me."

"All right," they answered. "Go ahead and do it."

[6]So Abraham hurried into the tent to Sarah. "Quick!" he said. "Get about half a bushel of fine flour. Mix it and bake some bread."

[7]Then he ran to the herd. He picked out a choice, tender calf. He gave it to a servant, who hurried to prepare it. [8]Then he brought some butter and milk and the calf that had been prepared. He served them to the three men.

While they ate, he stood near them under a tree.

[9]"Where is your wife Sarah?" they asked him.

"Over there, in the tent," he said.

[10]Then the LORD said, "You can be sure that I will return to you about this time next year. Your wife Sarah will have a son."

Sarah was listening at the entrance to the tent behind him. [11]Abraham and Sarah were already very old. Sarah was too old to have a baby. [12]So she laughed to herself. She thought, "I'm worn out, and my husband is old. Can I really know the joy of having a baby?"

[13]Then the LORD said to Abraham, "Why did Sarah laugh? Why did she say, 'Will I really have a baby, now that I am old?' [14]Is anything too hard for me? I will return to you at the appointed time next year. Sarah will have a son."

[15]Sarah was afraid. So she lied and said, "I didn't laugh."

But the LORD said, "Yes, you did."

Abraham Makes an Appeal for Sodom

[16]The men got up to leave. They looked down toward Sodom. Abraham walked along with them to see them on their way.

[17]Then the LORD said, "Should I hide from Abraham what I am about to do? [18]He will certainly become a great and powerful nation. All nations on earth will be blessed because of him.

[19]"I have chosen him. He must direct his children. He must see that the members of his family after him live the way I want them to. So he must direct them to do what is right and fair. Then I, the LORD, will do for Abraham what I have promised him."

[20]The LORD said, "The cries against Sodom and Gomorrah are very great. Their sin is so bad [21]that I will go down and see for myself. I want to see if what they have done is as bad as the cries that have reached me. If it is not, then I will know."

[22]The men turned away. They went toward Sodom. But Abraham remained standing in front of the LORD.

[23]Then Abraham came up to him. He said, "Will you sweep away godly people along with those who are evil? [24]What if there are 50 godly people in the city? Will you really sweep it away? Won't you spare the place because of the 50 godly people in it?

[25]"You would never kill godly people along with those who are evil, would you? You wouldn't treat godly and evil people alike. You would never do anything like that! Won't the Judge of the whole earth do what is right?"

[26]The LORD said, "If I find 50 godly people in the city of Sodom, I will save it. I will spare the whole place because of them."

[27]Then Abraham spoke up again. He said, "I have been very bold to speak to the Lord. After all, I'm only dust and ashes. [28]What if the number of godly people is five less than 50? Will you destroy the whole city because of five people?"

"If I find 45 there," he said, "I will not destroy it."

[29]Once again Abraham spoke to him. He asked, "What if only 40 are found there?"

He said, "If there are 40, I will not do it."

[30]Then Abraham said, "Lord, don't let your anger burn against me. Let me speak. What if only 30 can be found there?"

He answered, "If there are 30, I will not do it."

[31]Abraham said, "I have been very bold to speak to the Lord. What if only 20 are found there?"

He said, "If there are 20, I will not destroy it."

[32]Then he said, "Lord, don't let your anger burn against me. Let me speak just one more time. What if only ten are found there?"

He answered, "If there are ten, I will not destroy it."

[33]When the LORD had finished speaking with Abraham, he left. And Abraham returned home.

The LORD Destroys Sodom and Gomorrah

19 The two angels arrived at Sodom in the evening. Lot was sitting near the gate of the city.

When Lot saw them, he got up to meet them. He bowed down with his face to the ground. [2]"My lords," he said, "please come to my house. You can wash your feet and spend the night here. Then you can go on your way early in the morning."

"No," they answered. "We'll spend the night in the street."

[3]But Lot wouldn't give up. So they went with him and entered his house. He prepared a meal for them. He baked bread without using yeast. And they ate.

4Before Lot and his guests had gone to bed, all of the men came from every part of the city of Sodom. Young and old men alike surrounded the house. 5They called out to Lot. They said, "Where are the men who came to you tonight? Bring them out to us. We want to have sex with them."

6Lot went outside to meet them. He shut the door behind him. 7He said, "No, my friends. Don't do such an evil thing. 8Look, I have two daughters. No man has ever made love to them. I'll bring them out to you now. Then do to them what you want to. But don't do anything to these men. I've brought them inside so they can be safe."

9"Get out of our way!" the men of Sodom replied. They said, "This fellow came here as an outsider. Now he wants to act like a judge! We'll treat you worse than them." They kept trying to force Lot to open the door. Then they moved forward to break it down.

10But the men inside reached out and pulled Lot back into the house. They shut the door. 11Then they made the men who were at the door of the house blind. They blinded young and old men alike. So the men couldn't find the door.

12The two men said to Lot, "Do you have anyone else here? Do you have sons-in-law, sons or daughters? Does anyone else in the city belong to you? Get them out of here. 13We are going to destroy this place. There has been a great cry to the LORD against the people of this city. So he has sent us to destroy it."

14Then Lot went out and spoke to his sons-in-law. They had promised to get married to his daughters. He said, "Hurry up! Get out of this place! The LORD is about to destroy the city!" But his sons-in-law thought he was joking.

15The sun was coming up. So the angels tried to get Lot to leave. They said, "Hurry up! Take your wife and your two daughters who are here. Get out! If you don't, you will be swept away when the city is punished."

16Lot didn't move right away. So the men grabbed him by the hand. They also took hold of the hands of his wife and two daughters. They led all of them safely out of the city. The LORD had mercy on them.

17As soon as the angels had brought them out, one of them spoke. He said, "Run for your lives! Don't look back! Don't stop anywhere in the valley! Run to the mountains! If you don't, you will be swept away!"

18But Lot said to them, "No, my lords! Please! 19You have done me a big favor. You have been very kind to me by sparing my life. But I can't run to the mountains. This horrible thing that's going to happen will catch up with me. And then I'll die.

20"Look, here's a town near enough to run to. It's small. Let me run to it. It's very small, isn't it? Then my life will be spared."

21The LORD said to Lot, "All right. I will also give you what you are asking for. I will not destroy the town you are talking about. 22But run there quickly. I can't do anything until you reach it."

The town was named Zoar. Zoar means "small."

23By the time Lot reached Zoar, the sun had risen over the land. 24Then the LORD sent down burning sulfur. It came down like rain on Sodom and Gomorrah. It came from the LORD out of the sky. 25He destroyed those cities and the whole valley. All of the people who were living in the cities were wiped out. So were the plants in the land.

26But Lot's wife looked back. When she did, she became a pillar made out of salt.

27Early the next morning Abraham got up. He returned to the place where he had stood in front of the LORD. 28He looked down toward Sodom and Gomorrah and the whole valley. He saw thick smoke rising from the land. It looked like smoke from a furnace.

29So when God destroyed the cities of the valley, he showed concern for Abraham. He brought Lot out safely when he destroyed the cities where Lot had lived.

Lot and His Daughters

30Lot and his two daughters left Zoar. They went to settle down in the mountains. Lot was afraid to stay in Zoar. So he and his daughters lived in a cave.

31One day the older daughter spoke to the younger one. She said, "Our father is old. There aren't any other men around here to make love to, as people all over the earth do. 32So let's get our father to drink wine. Then we can make love to him. We can use our father to continue our family line."

33That night they got their father to drink wine. Then the older daughter went in and made love to him. He didn't know when she lay down or when she got up.

34The next day the older daughter spoke to the younger one again. She said, "Last night I made love to my father. Let's get him to drink wine again tonight. Then you go in and make love to him. In that way, we can use our father to continue our family line."

35So they got their father to drink wine that night also. Then the younger daughter went and made love to him. Again he didn't know when she lay down or when she got up.

36So both of Lot's daughters became pregnant by their father. 37The older daughter had a son. She named him Moab. He's the father of the Moabites of today. 38The younger daughter also had a son. She named him Ben-Ammi. He's the father of the Ammonites of today.

Abraham and Abimelech

20 Abraham moved away from there into the Negev Desert. He lived between Kadesh and Shur. For a while he stayed in Gerar.

2There Abraham said about his wife Sarah,
"She's my sister." Then Abimelech sent for Sarah
and took her. He was the king of Gerar.
3God came to Abimelech in a dream one night.
He said to him, "You are as good as dead because of
the woman you have taken. She is already married."
4But Abimelech hadn't gone near her. So he
said, "Lord, will you destroy a nation that hasn't
done anything wrong? 5Didn't Abraham say to me,
'She's my sister'? And didn't she also say, 'He's
my brother'? I had no idea I was doing anything
wrong. I'm not guilty."
6Then God spoke to him in the dream. He said,
"Yes, I know you had no idea you were doing anything wrong. So I have kept you from sinning
against me. That is why I did not let you touch her.
7"Now return the man's wife to him. He is a
prophet. He will pray for you, and you will live.
But what if you do not return her? Then you can be
sure that you and all of your people will die."
8Early the next morning Abimelech sent for all
of his officials. He told them everything that had
happened. They were really afraid.
9Then Abimelech called Abraham in. He said,
"What have you done to us? Have I done something wrong to you? Why have you brought so
much guilt on me and my kingdom? You have
done things to me that shouldn't be done."
10Abimelech also asked Abraham, "Why did
you do this?"
11Abraham replied, "I thought, 'There isn't any
respect for God in this place at all. They will kill
me because of my wife.' 12Besides, she really is my
sister. She's the daughter of my father, but not the
daughter of my mother. And she became my wife.
13"God had me wander away from my father's
house. So I said to her, 'Here is how you can show
your love to me. Everywhere we go, say about me,
"He's my brother."'"
14Then Abimelech gave Abraham sheep and
cattle and male and female slaves. He also
returned his wife Sarah to him. 15Abimelech said,
"Here is my land. Live anywhere you want to."
16He said to Sarah, "I'm giving your brother 25
pounds of silver. It will take care of the problem
we caused you. And all those who are with you
will know that you aren't guilty of doing anything
wrong."
17Then Abraham prayed to God. And God
healed Abimelech. He also healed his wife and his
female slaves so they could have children again.
18The LORD had kept the women in Abimelech's
house from having children. He had done it
because of Abraham's wife Sarah.

Isaac Is Born

21 The LORD was gracious to Sarah, just as he
had said he would be. He did for Sarah what
he had promised to do. 2Sarah became pregnant.
She had a son by Abraham when he was old. He
was born at the exact time God had promised him.
3Abraham gave the name Isaac to the son Sarah had by him. 4When his son Isaac was eight days
old, Abraham circumcised him. He did it exactly
as God had commanded him. 5Abraham was 100
years old when his son Isaac was born to him.
6Sarah said, "God has given laughter to me.
Everyone who hears about this will laugh with me."
7She continued, "Who would have said to Abraham that Sarah would nurse children? But I've had
a son by him when he is old."

Abraham Sends Hagar and Ishmael Away

8Isaac grew. The time came for his mother to
stop nursing him. On that day Abraham had a big
dinner prepared.
9But Sarah saw Ishmael making fun of Isaac.
Ishmael was the son Hagar had by Abraham. Hagar was Sarah's servant from Egypt.
10Sarah said to Abraham, "Get rid of that slave
woman. Get rid of her son. The slave woman's son
will never have a share of the family's property
with my son Isaac."
11What Sarah said upset Abraham very much.
After all, Ishmael was his son.
12But God said to him, "Do not be so upset
about the boy and your servant Hagar. Listen to
what Sarah tells you, because your family line will
continue through Isaac. 13I will make the son of
your servant into a nation also. I will do it because
he is your child."
14Early the next morning Abraham got some
food and a bottle of water. The bottle was made
out of animal skin. He gave the food and water to
Hagar. He placed them on her shoulders. Then he
sent her away with the boy. She went on her way
and wandered in the desert of Beersheba.
15When the water in the bottle was gone, she put
the boy under a bush. 16Then she went off and sat
down nearby. She was about as far away as a person can shoot an arrow. She thought, "I can't stand
to watch the boy die." As she sat nearby, she began
to sob.
17God heard the boy crying. Then the angel of
God called out to Hagar from heaven. He said to
her, "What is the matter, Hagar? Do not be afraid.
God has heard the boy crying as he lies there. 18Lift
the boy up. Take him by the hand. I will make him
into a great nation."
19Then God opened Hagar's eyes. She saw a
well of water. So she went and filled the bottle
with water. And she gave the boy a drink.
20God was with the boy as he grew up. He lived
in the desert and learned to shoot with a bow.
21While he was living in the Desert of Paran, his
mother got him a wife from Egypt.

The Peace Treaty at Beersheba

22At that time Abimelech and Phicol spoke to
Abraham. Phicol was the commander of Abimelech's army. They said, "God is with you in every-

thing you do. 23Now make a promise to me here while God is watching. Take an oath that you will treat me fairly. Promise that you will treat my children and their children the same way.

"I've been kind to you. Now you be kind to me. And be kind to the country where you are living as an outsider."

24Abraham said, "I promise with an oath that I'll do it."

25Then Abraham objected to Abimelech about what Abimelech's servants had done. They had taken over a well of water.

26But Abimelech said, "I don't know who has done this. You didn't tell me. Today is the first time I heard about it."

27So Abraham gave Abimelech sheep and cattle. The two men made a peace treaty. 28Then Abraham took out seven female lambs from his flock.

29Abimelech asked Abraham, "What's the meaning of these seven female lambs? Why have you taken them out and put them by themselves?"

30Abraham replied, "Accept the seven lambs from me. They will be a witness that I dug this well."

31That place was named Beersheba. That's because there the two men made a promise with an oath.

32After the peace treaty had been made at Beersheba, Abimelech went back to the land of the Philistines. His army commander Phicol went with him.

33Abraham planted a tamarisk tree in Beersheba. There he worshiped the LORD, the God who lives forever. 34Abraham stayed in the land of the Philistines for a long time.

God Puts Abraham to the Test

22 Some time later God put Abraham to the test. He said to him, "Abraham!"

"Here I am," Abraham replied.

2Then God said, "Take your son, your only son. He is the one you love. Take Isaac. Go to Moriah. Give him to me there as a burnt offering. Sacrifice him on one of the mountains I will tell you about."

3Early the next morning Abraham got up. He put a saddle on his donkey. He took two of his servants and his son Isaac with him. He cut enough wood for the burnt offering. Then he started out for the place God had told him about.

4On the third day Abraham looked up. He saw the place a long way off. 5He said to his servants, "Stay here with the donkey. The boy and I will go over there and worship. Then we'll come back to you."

6Abraham put the wood for the burnt offering on his son Isaac. He himself carried the fire and the knife. The two of them walked on together.

7Then Isaac spoke up. He said to his father Abraham, "Father?"

"Yes, my son?" Abraham replied.

"The fire and wood are here," Isaac said. "But where is the lamb for the burnt offering?"

8Abraham answered, "God himself will provide the lamb for the burnt offering, my son." The two of them walked on together.

9They reached the place God had told Abraham about. There Abraham built an altar. He arranged the wood on it. He tied up his son Isaac. He placed him on the altar, on top of the wood. 10Then he reached out his hand. He took the knife to kill his son.

11But the angel of the LORD called out to him from heaven. He said, "Abraham! Abraham!"

"Here I am," Abraham replied.

12"Do not lay a hand on the boy," he said. "Do not do anything to him. Now I know that you have respect for God. You have not held back from me your son, your only son."

13Abraham looked up. There in a bush he saw a ram. It was caught by its horns. He went over and took the ram. He sacrificed it as a burnt offering instead of his son.

14So Abraham named that place The LORD Will Provide. To this day people say, "It will be provided on the mountain of the LORD."

15The angel of the LORD called out to Abraham from heaven a second time. 16He said, "I am taking an oath in my own name. I will bless you because of what you have done," announces the LORD. "You have not held back your son, your only son.

17"So I will certainly bless you. I will make your children after you as many as the stars in the sky. I will make them as many as the grains of sand on the seashore. Your children will take over the cities of their enemies. 18All nations on earth will be blessed because of your children. All of that will happen because you have obeyed me."

19Then Abraham returned to his servants. They started out together for Beersheba. And Abraham stayed in Beersheba.

Nahor's Sons

20Some time later Abraham was told, "Milcah has become a mother. She has had sons by your brother Nahor. 21Uz was born first. Then came his brother Buz. Next came Kemuel, the father of Aram. 22The other sons are Kesed, Hazo, Pildash, Jidlaph and Bethuel." 23Bethuel became the father of Rebekah. Milcah had the eight sons by Abraham's brother Nahor. 24Nahor had a concubine named Reumah. She also had sons. They were Tebah, Gaham, Tahash and Maacah.

Sarah Dies

23 Sarah lived to be 127 years old. 2She died at Kiriath Arba. Kiriath Arba is also called Hebron. It's in the land of Canaan.

Sarah's death filled Abraham with sorrow. He went to the place where her body was lying. There he sobbed over her.

3Then Abraham got up from beside his dead wife. He spoke to the Hittites. He said, 4"I'm an outsider. I'm a stranger among you. Sell me some property here as a place for a family tomb. Then I can bury my wife's body."

5 The Hittites replied to Abraham, 6 "Sir, listen to
us. You are a mighty prince among us. Bury your
dead wife in the best of our tombs. None of us will
refuse to sell you his tomb for burying her."
7 Then Abraham bowed down in front of the Hittites, the people of the land. 8 He said to them, "If
you are willing to let me bury my dead wife, then
listen to me. Speak to Zohar's son Ephron for me.
9 Ask him to sell me the cave of Machpelah. It
belongs to him and is at the end of his field. Ask
him to sell it to me for the full price. I want it as a
place to bury my dead wife among you."
10 Ephron the Hittite was sitting there among his
people. He replied to Abraham. All of the Hittites
who had come to the gate of his city heard him.
11 "No, sir," Ephron said. "Listen to me. I will sell
you the field. I'll also sell you the cave that's in
the field. I will sell it to you in front of my people.
Bury your wife."
12 Again Abraham bowed down in front of the
people of the land. 13 He spoke to Ephron so they
could hear him. He said, "Please listen to me. I'll
pay the price of the field. Accept it from me. Then
I can bury my dead wife there."
14 Ephron answered Abraham, 15 "Sir, listen to
me. The land is worth ten pounds of silver. But
what is that between you and me? Bury your wife."
16 Abraham agreed to Ephron's offer. He
weighed out for him the price he had named. The
Hittites there had heard it. The price was ten pounds
of silver. Abraham measured it by the weights that
were used by those who bought and sold.
17 So Ephron sold his field in Machpelah near
Mamre to Abraham. He bought the field and the
cave that was in it. He also bought all of the trees
that were inside the borders of the field. Everything was sold 18 to Abraham as his property. He
bought it in front of all of the Hittites who had
come to the gate of the city.
19 Then Abraham buried the body of his wife
Sarah. He buried her in the cave in the field of
Machpelah near Mamre in the land of Canaan.
Mamre is at Hebron. 20 So the field and the cave
that was in it were sold to Abraham by the Hittites.
The property became a place for his family tomb.

Abraham's Servant Finds a Wife for Isaac

24 By that time Abraham was very old. The
LORD had blessed him in every way. 2 The
best servant in his house was in charge of everything he had.

Abraham said to him, "Put your hand under my
thigh. 3 The LORD is the God of heaven and the God
of earth. I want you to make a promise with an
oath in his name.

"I'm living among the people of Canaan. But I
want you to promise me that you won't get a wife
for my son from their daughters. 4 Instead, promise
me that you will go to my country and to my own
relatives. Get a wife for my son Isaac from there."
5 The servant asked him, "What if the woman
doesn't want to come back with me to this land?
Then should I take your son back to the country
you came from?"
6 "Make sure you don't take my son back there,"
Abraham said. 7 "The LORD, the God of heaven,
took me away from my father's family. He brought
me out of my own land. And he made me a
promise with an oath. He said, 'I will give this land
to your family after you.' The LORD will send his
angel ahead of you. So you will be able to get a
wife for my son from there.
8 "The woman may not want to come back with
you. If she doesn't, you will be free from your
oath. But don't take my son back there."
9 So the servant put his hand under Abraham's
thigh. He promised with an oath to do what his
master wanted.
10 The servant took ten of his master's camels
and left. He took with him all kinds of good things
from his master. He started out for Aram Naharaim. He made his way to the town of Nahor.
11 He stopped near the well outside the town.
There he made the camels get down on their knees.
It was almost evening. It was the time when
women go out to get water.
12 Then he prayed, "LORD, you are the God of
my master Abraham. Give me success today. Be
kind to my master Abraham. 13 I'm standing beside
this spring. The daughters of the people who live
in the town are coming out here to get water.
14 "I will speak to a young woman. I'll say,
'Please lower your jar so I can have a drink.' Suppose she says, 'Have a drink of water. And I'll get
some for your camels too.' Then let her be the one
you have chosen for your servant Isaac. That's
how I'll know you have been kind to my master."
15 Before he had finished praying, Rebekah came
out. She had a jar on her shoulder. She was the
daughter of Bethuel, the son of Milcah. Milcah was
the wife of Abraham's brother Nahor. 16 The young
woman was very beautiful. She was a virgin. No
man had made love to her. She went down to the
spring. She filled her jar and came up again.
17 The servant hurried to meet her. He said,
"Please give me a little water from your jar."
18 "Have a drink, sir," she said. She quickly lowered the jar to her hands. And she gave him a drink.
19 After she had given him a drink, she said, "I'll
get water for your camels too. I'll keep doing it
until they finish drinking." 20 So she quickly emptied her jar into the stone tub. Then she ran back
to the well to get more water. She got enough for
all of his camels.
21 The man didn't say a word. He watched her
closely. He wanted to learn whether the LORD had
given him success on the journey he had made.
22 The camels finished drinking. Then the man
took out a gold nose ring. It weighed a fifth of an
ounce. He also took out two gold bracelets. They
weighed four ounces.

23 Then he asked, “Whose daughter are you? And please tell me something else. Is there room in your father’s house for us? Can we spend the night there?”

24 She answered, “I’m the daughter of Bethuel. He’s the son Milcah had by Nahor.” 25 She continued, “We have plenty of straw and feed for your camels. We also have room for you to spend the night.”

26 Then the man bowed down and worshiped the LORD. 27 He said, “I praise the LORD, the God of my master Abraham. He hasn’t stopped being kind and faithful to my master. The LORD has led me on this journey. He has brought me to the house of my master’s relatives.”

28 The young woman ran home. She told her mother’s family what had happened.

29 Rebekah had a brother named Laban. He hurried out to the spring to meet the man. 30 Laban had seen the nose ring. He had seen the bracelets on his sister’s arms. And he had heard Rebekah tell what the man had said to her. So he went out to the man. He found him standing by the camels near the spring. 31 “The LORD has given you his blessing,” he said. “So come. Why are you standing out here? I’ve prepared my house for you. I also have a place for the camels.”

32 So the man went to the house. The camels were unloaded. Straw and feed were brought for the camels. And water was brought for him and his men to wash their feet.

33 Then food was placed in front of him. But he said, “I won’t eat until I’ve told you what I have to say.”

“Then tell us,” Laban said.

34 So he said, “I am Abraham’s servant. 35 The LORD has blessed my master greatly. He has become wealthy. The LORD has given him sheep and cattle. He has given him silver and gold. He has also given him male and female servants, and camels and donkeys.

36 “My master’s wife Sarah had a son by him when she was old. He has given that son everything he owns. 37 My master made me take an oath. He said, ‘I’m living in the land of the people of Canaan. But promise me that you won’t get a wife for my son from their daughters. 38 Instead, go to my father’s family and to my own relatives. Get a wife for my son there.’

39 “Then I asked my master, ‘What if the woman won’t come back with me?’

40 “He replied, ‘I have walked with the LORD. He will send his angel with you. He will give you success on your journey. So you will be able to get a wife for my son. You will get her from my own relatives and from my father’s family.

41 “‘When you go to my relatives, suppose they refuse to give her to you. Then you will be free from your oath.’

42 “Today I came to the spring. I said, ‘LORD, you are the God of my master Abraham. Please give me success on this journey I’ve made.

43 “‘I’m standing beside this spring. A young woman will come out to get water. I will speak to her. I’ll say, “Please let me drink a little water from your jar.” 44 Suppose she says, “Have a drink of water. And I’ll get some for your camels too.” Then let her be the one the LORD has chosen for my master’s son.’

45 “Before I finished praying in my heart, Rebekah came out. She had a jar on her shoulder. She went down to the spring and got water. I said to her, ‘Please give me a drink.’

46 “She quickly lowered her jar from her shoulder. She said, ‘Have a drink. And I’ll get water for your camels too.’ So I drank. She also got water for the camels.

47 “I asked her, ‘Whose daughter are you?’

“She said, ‘The daughter of Bethuel. He’s the son Milcah had by Nahor.’

“Then I put the ring in her nose. I put the bracelets on her arms. 48 And I bowed down and worshiped the LORD. I praised the LORD, the God of my master Abraham. He had led me on the right road. He had led me to get for my master’s son the granddaughter of my master’s brother.

49 “Now will you be kind and faithful to my master? If you will, tell me. And if you won’t, tell me. Then I’ll know which way to turn.”

50 Laban and Bethuel answered, “The LORD has done all of this. We can’t say anything to you one way or the other. 51 Here is Rebekah. Take her and go. Let her become the wife of your master’s son, just as the LORD has said.”

52 Abraham’s servant heard what they said. So he bowed down to the LORD with his face to the ground. 53 He brought out gold and silver jewelry. He brought out articles of clothing. He gave all of it to Rebekah. He also gave expensive gifts to her brother and her mother.

54 Then Abraham’s servant and the men who were with him ate and drank. They spent the night there.

They got up the next morning. Abraham’s servant said, “Send me back to my master.”

55 But her brother and her mother replied, “Let the young woman stay with us ten days or so. Then you can go.”

56 But he said to them, “Don’t make me wait. The LORD has given me success on my journey. Send me on my way so I can go to my master.”

57 Then they said, “Let’s get Rebekah. We’ll ask her about it.” 58 So they sent for her. They asked her, “Will you go with this man?”

“Yes,” she said.

59 So they sent their sister Rebekah on her way with Abraham’s servant and his men. They also sent Rebekah’s attendant with her. 60 And they gave Rebekah their blessing. They said to her,

“Dear sister, may your family grow
by thousands and thousands.
May your children after you take over
the cities of their enemies.”

61 Then Rebekah and her female servants got ready. They got on their camels to go with the man. So the servant took Rebekah and left.

62 By that time Isaac had come from Beer Lahai Roi. He was living in the Negev Desert. 63 One evening he went out to the field. He wanted to spend some time thinking. When he looked up, he saw camels approaching.

64 Rebekah also looked up and saw Isaac. She got down from her camel. 65 She asked the servant, "Who is that man in the field coming to meet us?"

"He's my master," the servant answered. So she took her veil and covered her face.

66 Then the servant told Isaac everything he had done.

67 Isaac brought Rebekah into the tent that had belonged to his mother Sarah. And he married Rebekah. She became his wife, and he loved her. So Isaac was comforted after his mother died.

Abraham Dies

25 Abraham married another woman. Her name was Keturah. 2 She had Zimran, Jokshan, Medan, Midian, Ishbak and Shuah by Abraham. 3 Jokshan was the father of Sheba and Dedan. The children of Dedan were the Asshurites, the Letushites and the Leummites. 4 The sons of Midian were Ephah, Epher, Hanoch, Abida and Eldaah. All of them came from Keturah.

5 Abraham left everything he owned to Isaac. 6 But while he was still living, he gave gifts to the sons of his concubines. Then he sent them away from his son Isaac. He sent them to the land of the east.

7 Abraham lived a total of 175 years. 8 He took his last breath and died when he was very old. He had lived a very long time. Then he joined the members of his family who had already died.

9 Abraham's sons Isaac and Ishmael buried his body. They put it in the cave of Machpelah near Mamre. It was in the field of Ephron, the son of Zohar the Hittite. 10 Abraham had bought it from the Hittites. He was buried there with his wife Sarah.

11 After Abraham died, God blessed his son Isaac. At that time Isaac lived near Beer Lahai Roi.

The Sons of Ishmael

12 Here is the story of Abraham's son Ishmael. Hagar had Ishmael by Abraham. She was Sarah's servant from Egypt.

13 Here are the names of the sons of Ishmael. They are listed in the order they were born. Nebaioth was Ishmael's oldest son. Then came Kedar, Adbeel, Mibsam, 14 Mishma, Dumah, Massa, 15 Hadad, Tema, Jetur, Naphish and Kedemah. 16 All of them were Ishmael's sons. They were rulers of 12 tribes. They all lived in their own settlements and camps.

17 Ishmael lived a total of 137 years. Then he took his last breath and died. He joined the members of his family who had already died. 18 His children settled in the area between Havilah and Shur. It was near the eastern border of Egypt, as you go toward Asshur.

Ishmael's children weren't friendly toward any of the tribes that were related to them.

Jacob and Esau

19 Here is the story of Abraham's son Isaac.

Abraham was the father of Isaac. 20 Isaac was 40 years old when he married Rebekah. She was the daughter of Bethuel the Aramean from Paddan Aram. She was also the sister of Laban the Aramean.

21 Rebekah couldn't have children. So Isaac prayed to the LORD for her. And the LORD answered his prayer. His wife Rebekah became pregnant.

22 The babies struggled with each other inside her. She said, "Why is this happening to me?" So she went to ask the LORD what she should do.

23 The LORD said to her,

"Two nations are in your body.
Two tribes that are now inside you will be separated.
One nation will be stronger than the other.
The older son will serve the younger one."

24 The time came for Rebekah to have her babies. There were twin boys in her body. 25 The first one to come out was red. His whole body was covered with hair. So they named him Esau.

26 Then his brother came out. His hand was holding onto Esau's heel. So he was named Jacob. Isaac was 60 years old when Rebekah had them.

27 The boys grew up. Esau became a skillful hunter. He was a man who liked the open country. But Jacob was a quiet man. He stayed at home among the tents. 28 Isaac liked the meat of wild animals. So Esau was his favorite son. But Rebekah's favorite was Jacob.

29 One day Jacob was cooking some stew. Esau came in from the open country. He was very hungry. 30 He said to Jacob, "Quick! Let me have some of that red stew! I'm very hungry!" That's why he was also named Edom.

31 Jacob replied, "First sell me the rights that belong to you as the oldest son in the family."

32 "Look, I'm dying of hunger," Esau said. "What good are those rights to me?"

33 But Jacob said, "First promise me with an oath that you are selling me your rights." So Esau promised to do it. He sold Jacob all of the rights that belonged to him as the oldest son.

34 Jacob gave Esau some bread and some lentil stew. Esau ate and drank. Then he got up and left.

So Esau didn't care anything at all about the rights that belonged to him as the oldest son.

Isaac and Abimelech

26 There was very little food in the land. The same thing had been true earlier, in Abraham's time. Isaac went to Abimelech in Gerar. Abimelech was the king of the Philistines.

[2]The LORD appeared to Isaac. He said, "Do not go down to Egypt. Live in the land where I tell you to live. [3]Stay here for a while. I will be with you and give you my blessing. I will give all of these lands to you and your children after you. And I will keep the promise I made with an oath to your father Abraham. [4]I will make your children after you as many as the stars in the sky. And I will give them all these lands. All nations on earth will be blessed because of your children.

[5]"I will do all of those things because Abraham obeyed me. He did what I required. He kept my commands, my rules and my laws." [6]So Isaac stayed in Gerar.

[7]The men of that place asked him about his wife. He said, "She's my sister." He was afraid to say, "She's my wife." He thought, "The men of this place might kill me because of Rebekah. She's a beautiful woman."

[8]Isaac had been there a long time. One day Abimelech, the king of the Philistines, looked down from a window. He saw Isaac hugging and kissing his wife Rebekah.

[9]So Abimelech sent for Isaac. He said, "She's really your wife, isn't she? Why did you say, 'She's my sister'?"

Isaac answered him, "I thought I might lose my life because of her."

[10]Then Abimelech said, "What have you done to us? What if one of the men had sex with your wife? Then you would have made us guilty."

[11]So Abimelech gave orders to all of the people. He said, "You can be sure that anyone who harms this man or his wife will be put to death."

[12]Isaac planted crops in that land. That same year he gathered 100 times more than he planted. That was because the LORD blessed him.

[13]Isaac became rich. His wealth continued to grow until he became very rich. [14]He had many flocks and herds and servants.

Isaac had so much that the Philistines became jealous of him. [15]So they stopped up all of the wells the servants of his father Abraham had dug. They filled them with dirt.

[16]Then Abimelech said to Isaac, "Move away from us. You have become too powerful for us."

[17]So Isaac moved away from there. He camped in the Valley of Gerar and settled there. [18]Isaac opened up the wells again. They had been dug in the time of his father Abraham. The Philistines had stopped them up after Abraham died. Isaac gave the wells the same names his father had given them.

[19]Isaac's servants dug for wells in the valley. There they discovered a well of fresh water. [20]But the people of Gerar who took care of their herds argued with the people who took care of Isaac's herds. "The water is ours!" the people of Gerar said. So Isaac named the well Esek. That's because they argued with him.

[21]Then Isaac's servants dug another well. They argued about that one too. So he named it Sitnah.

[22]He moved on from there and dug another well. But no one argued about that one. So he named it Rehoboth. He said, "Now the LORD has given us room. Now we will do well in the land."

[23]From there Isaac went up to Beersheba. [24]That night the LORD appeared to him. He said, "I am the God of your father Abraham. Do not be afraid. I am with you. I will bless you. I will increase the number of your children because of my servant Abraham."

[25]Isaac built an altar there and worshiped the LORD. There he set up his tent. And there his servants dug a well.

[26]During that time, Abimelech had come to him from Gerar. Ahuzzath had come with him. So had Phicol, Abimelech's army commander. Ahuzzath was Abimelech's personal adviser.

[27]Isaac asked them, "Why have you come to me? You were angry with me and sent me away."

[28]They answered, "We saw clearly that the LORD was with you. So we said, 'We should make an agreement by taking an oath.' The agreement should be between us and you. We want to make a peace treaty with you. [29]Promise that you won't harm us. We didn't harm you. We always treated you well. We sent you away in peace. Now the LORD has blessed you."

[30]Then Isaac had a big dinner prepared for them. They ate and drank. [31]Early the next morning the men made an agreement with an oath. Then Isaac sent the men of Gerar on their way. And they left in peace.

[32]That day Isaac's servants came to him. They told him about the well they had dug. They said, "We've found water!" [33]So he named it Shibah. To this day the name of the town has been Beersheba.

[34]When Esau was 40 years old, he got married to Judith. She was the daughter of Beeri the Hittite. He also married Basemath. She was the daughter of Elon the Hittite. [35]Isaac and Rebekah became very upset because Esau had married Hittite women.

Isaac Gives Jacob His Blessing

27 Isaac had become old. His eyes were so weak he couldn't see anymore. One day he called for his older son Esau. He said to him, "My son."

"Here I am," he answered.

[2]Isaac said, "I'm an old man now. And I don't know when I'll die. [3]Now then, get your weapons. Get your bow and arrows. Go out to the open country. Hunt some wild animals for me. [4]Prepare for me the kind of tasty food I like. Bring it to me to eat. Then I'll give you my blessing before I die."

[5]Rebekah was listening when Isaac spoke to his son Esau. Esau left for the open country. He went to hunt for a wild animal and bring it back.

[6]Then Rebekah said to her son Jacob, "Look, I heard your father speaking to your brother Esau. [7]He said, 'Bring me a wild animal. Prepare some

tasty food for me to eat. Then I'll give you my
blessing before I die. The LORD will be my
witness.'"
8Rebekah continued, "My son, listen carefully.
Do what I tell you. 9Go out to the flock. Bring me
two of the finest young goats. I will prepare tasty
food for your father. I'll make it just the way he
likes it. 10I want you to take it to your father to eat.
Then he'll give you his blessing before he dies."
11Jacob said to his mother Rebekah, "My
brother Esau's body is covered with hair. But my
skin is smooth. 12What if my father touches me?
He would know I was trying to trick him. That
would bring a curse down on me instead of a
blessing."
13His mother said to him, "My son, let the curse
fall on me. Just do what I say. Go and get the goats
for me."
14So he went and got the goats. He brought
them to his mother. And she prepared some tasty
food. She made it just the way his father liked it.
15The clothes of her older son Esau were in her
house. She took the best of them and put them on
her younger son Jacob. 16She covered his hands
with the skins of the goats. She also covered the
smooth part of his neck with them.
17Then she handed to her son Jacob the tasty
food and the bread she had made.
18He went to his father and said, "My father."
"Yes, my son," Isaac answered. "Who is it?"
19Jacob said to his father, "I'm your oldest son
Esau. I've done as you told me. Please sit up. Eat
some of my wild meat. Then give me your
blessing."
20Isaac asked his son, "How did you find it so
quickly, my son?"
"The LORD your God gave me success," he
replied.
21Then Isaac said to Jacob, "Come near so I can
touch you, my son. I want to know whether you
really are my son Esau."
22Jacob went close to his father. Isaac touched
him and said, "The voice is the voice of Jacob. But
the hands are the hands of Esau."
23Isaac didn't recognize him. His hands were
covered with hair like those of his brother Esau.
So Isaac blessed him. 24"Are you really my son
Esau?" he asked.
"I am," Jacob replied.
25Isaac said, "My son, bring me some of your
wild meat to eat. Then I'll give you my blessing."
Jacob brought it to him. So Isaac ate. Jacob also
brought some wine. And Isaac drank. 26Then Jacob's father Isaac said to him, "Come here, my
son. Kiss me."
27So Jacob went to him and kissed him. When
Isaac smelled the clothes, he gave Jacob his blessing. He said,

"It really is the smell of my son.
It's like the smell of a field
that the LORD has blessed.
28May God give you dew from heaven.
May he give you the richness of the earth.
May he give you plenty of grain and fresh
wine.
29May nations serve you.
May they bow down to you.
Rule over your brothers.
May the sons of your mother bow down
to you.
May those who call down curses on you
be cursed.
And may those who bless you be blessed."

30When Isaac finished blessing him, Jacob left
his father. Just then his brother Esau came in from
hunting. 31He too prepared some tasty food. He
brought it to his father. Then Esau said to him,
"My father, sit up. Eat some of my wild meat.
Then give me your blessing."
32His father Isaac asked him, "Who are you?"
"I'm your son," he answered. "I'm your oldest
son. I'm Esau."
33Isaac was shaking all over. He said, "Then
who was it that hunted a wild animal and brought
it to me? I ate it just before you came. I gave him
my blessing. And he will certainly be blessed!"
34Esau heard his father's words. Then he began
crying loudly and bitterly. He said to his father,
"Bless me! Bless me too, my father!"
35But Isaac said, "Your brother came and
tricked me. He took your blessing."
36Esau said, "Isn't Jacob just the right name for
him? He has cheated me two times. First, he took
my rights as the oldest son. And now he's taken
my blessing!" Then Esau asked, "Haven't you
saved any blessing for me?"
37Isaac answered Esau, "I've made him ruler
over you. I've made all of his relatives serve him.
And I've provided him with grain and fresh wine.
So what can I possibly do for you, my son?"
38Esau said to his father, "Do you have only one
blessing, my father? Bless me too, my father!"
Then Esau sobbed loudly.
39His father Isaac answered him,

"You will live far away from the richness of
the earth.
You will live far away from the dew of
heaven above.
40You will live by the sword.
And you will serve your brother.
But you will grow restless.
Then you will throw off the heavy load
he put on your shoulders."

Jacob Runs Away to Laban

41Esau was angry with Jacob. He was angry
because of the blessing his father had given to Jacob. He said to himself, "My father will soon die.
The days of sorrow over him are near. Then I'll
kill my brother Jacob."
42Rebekah was told what her older son Esau had
said. So she sent for her younger son Jacob. She

said to him, “Your brother Esau is comforting himself with the thought of killing you.
43“Now then, my son, do what I say. Go at once
to my brother Laban in Haran. 44Stay with him
until your brother’s anger calms down. 45Stay until
your brother isn’t angry with you anymore. When
he forgets what you did to him, I’ll let you know.
Then you can come back from there. Why should
I lose both of you in one day?”
46Then Rebekah spoke to Isaac. She said, “I’m
sick of living because of Esau’s Hittite wives. Suppose Jacob also marries a Hittite woman. If he
does, my life won’t be worth living.”

28 So Isaac called for Jacob and blessed him.
He commanded him, “Don’t get married to
a woman from Canaan. 2Go at once to Paddan Aram.
Go to the house of your mother’s father Bethuel.
Find a wife for yourself there. Take her from among
the daughters of your mother’s brother Laban.
3“May the Mighty God bless you. May he give
you children. May he increase your numbers until
you become a community of nations. 4May he give
you and your children after you the blessing he
gave to Abraham. Then you can take over the land
where you now live as an outsider. It’s the land
God gave to Abraham.”
5Isaac sent Jacob on his way. Jacob went to Paddan Aram. He went to Laban, the son of Bethuel
the Aramean. Laban was the brother of Rebekah.
And Rebekah was the mother of Jacob and Esau.
6Esau found out that Isaac had blessed Jacob
and had sent him to Paddan Aram. Isaac wanted
him to get a wife from there. Esau heard that when
Isaac blessed Jacob, he commanded him, “Don’t
get married to a woman from Canaan.” 7Esau also
learned that Jacob had obeyed his father and
mother and had gone to Paddan Aram.
8Then Esau realized how much his father Isaac
disliked the women of Canaan. 9So he went to Ishmael and married Mahalath. She was the sister of
Nebaioth and the daughter of Abraham’s son Ishmael. Esau added her to the wives he already had.

Jacob Has a Dream at Bethel

10Jacob left Beersheba and started out for Haran. 11He reached a certain place and stopped for
the night. The sun had already set. He took one of
the stones there and placed it under his head. Then
he lay down to sleep.
12In a dream he saw a stairway standing on the
earth. Its top reached to heaven. The angels of God
were going up and coming down on it.
13The LORD stood above the stairway. He said,
“I am the LORD. I am the God of your grandfather
Abraham and the God of Isaac. I will give you and
your children after you the land on which you are
lying. 14They will be like the dust of the earth that
can’t be counted. They will spread out to the west
and to the east. They will spread out to the north
and to the south. All nations on earth will be
blessed because of you and your children after you.
15“I am with you. I will watch over you everywhere you go. And I will bring you back to this
land. I will not leave you until I have done what I
have promised you.”
16Jacob woke up from his sleep. Then he
thought, “The LORD is certainly in this place. And
I didn’t even know it.”
17Jacob was afraid. He said, “How holy this
place is! This must be the house of God. This is
the gate of heaven.”
18Early the next morning Jacob took the stone
he had placed under his head. He set it up as a pillar. And he poured oil on top of it. 19He named that
place Bethel. But the city used to be called Luz.
20Then Jacob made a promise. He said, “May
God be with me. May he watch over me on this
journey I’m taking. May he give me food to eat
and clothes to wear. 21May he do as he has
promised so that I can return safely to my father’s
home. Then you, LORD, will be my God. 22This
stone I’ve set up as a pillar will be God’s house.
And I’ll give you a tenth of everything you
give me.”

Jacob Arrives in Paddan Aram

29 Then Jacob continued on his journey. He
came to the land where the eastern tribes
lived.
2There he saw a well in the field. Three flocks
of sheep were lying near it. The flocks were given
water from the well. The stone over the opening
of the well was large. 3All of the flocks would
gather there. The shepherds would roll the stone
away from the well’s opening. They would give
water to the sheep. Then they would put the stone
back in its place over the opening of the well.
4Jacob asked the shepherds, “My friends, where
are you from?”
“We’re from Haran,” they replied.
5He said to them, “Do you know Nahor’s grandson Laban?”
“Yes, we know him,” they answered.
6Then Jacob asked them, “How is he?”
“He’s fine,” they said. “Here comes his daughter Rachel with the sheep now.”
7“Look,” he said, “the sun is still high in the sky.
It’s not time for the flocks to be brought together.
Give water to the sheep and take them back to the
grasslands.”
8“We can’t,” they replied. “We have to wait
until all of the flocks are brought together. The
stone has to be rolled away from the opening of
the well. Then we’ll give water to the sheep.”
9He was still talking with them when Rachel
came with her father’s sheep. It was her job to take
care of the flock. 10Rachel was the daughter of Laban. He was the brother of Jacob’s mother.

When Jacob saw Rachel with Laban’s sheep, he
went over to the well. He rolled the stone away
from the opening. He gave water to his uncle’s
sheep.

11Jacob kissed Rachel. Then he began to sob
loudly. 12He had told Rachel he was a relative of
her father. He had also said he was Rebekah's son.
Rachel ran and told her father what Jacob had said.
13As soon as Laban heard the news about his
sister's son Jacob, he hurried to meet him. Laban
hugged Jacob and kissed him. Then he brought
him to his home. There Jacob told him everything.
14Then Laban said to him, "You are my own flesh
and blood."

Jacob Gets Married to Leah and Rachel

Jacob stayed with Laban for a whole month.
15Then Laban said to him, "You are one of my relatives. But is that any reason for you to work for
me for nothing? Tell me what your pay should be."
16Laban had two daughters. The name of the
older one was Leah. And the name of the younger
one was Rachel. 17Leah had weak eyes. But Rachel was beautiful. She had a nice figure.

18Jacob was in love with Rachel. He said to Laban, "I'll work for you for seven years to get your
younger daughter Rachel."

19Laban said, "It's better for me to give her to
you than to some other man. Stay here with me."
20So Jacob worked for seven years to get Rachel. But they seemed like only a few days to him
because he loved her so much.
21Then Jacob said to Laban, "Give me my wife.
I've completed my time. I want to make love to her."
22So Laban brought all of the people of the place
together and had a big dinner prepared. 23But when
evening came, he gave his daughter Leah to Jacob.
And Jacob made love to her. 24Laban gave his
female servant Zilpah to his daughter as her servant.
25When Jacob woke up the next morning, there
was Leah next to him! So he said to Laban, "What
have you done to me? I worked for you to get Rachel, didn't I? Why did you trick me?"
26Laban replied, "It isn't our practice here to
give the younger daughter to be married before the
older one. 27Complete this daughter's wedding
week. Then we'll give you the younger one also.
But you will have to work for another seven
years."
28So Jacob did it. He completed the week with
Leah. Then Laban gave him his daughter Rachel
to be his wife. 29Laban gave his female servant Bilhah to his daughter Rachel as her servant. 30Jacob
made love to Rachel also. He loved Rachel more
than he loved Leah. And he worked for Laban for
another seven years.

Jacob Becomes the Father of Many Children

31The LORD saw that Jacob didn't love Leah as
much as he loved Rachel. So he let Leah have children. But Rachel wasn't able to have children.
32Leah became pregnant. She had a son. She named
him Reuben. She said, "The LORD has seen me suffer. Certainly my husband will love me now."
33She became pregnant again. She had a son.
Then she said, "The LORD heard that Jacob doesn't
love me very much. That's why the LORD gave me
this one too." So she named him Simeon.
34She became pregnant again. She had a son.
Then she said, "Now at last my husband will want
me. I have had three sons by him." So the boy was
named Levi.
35She became pregnant again. She had a son.
Then she said, "This time I'll praise the LORD." So
she named him Judah. Then she stopped having
children.

30 Rachel saw that she couldn't have any
children by Jacob. So she became jealous
of her sister. She said to Jacob, "Give me children,
or I'll die!"
2Jacob became angry with her. He said, "Do
you think I'm God? He's the one who has kept you
from having children."
3Then she said, "Here's my servant Bilhah.
Make love to her so that she can have children for
me. Then I too can have a family through her."
4So she gave him her servant Bilhah as a wife. Jacob made love to her. 5And Bilhah became pregnant.
She had a son by him. 6Then Rachel said, "God has
stood up for my rights. He has listened to my prayer
and given me a son." So she named him Dan.
7Rachel's servant Bilhah became pregnant
again. She had a second son by Jacob. 8Then Rachel said, "I've had a great struggle with my sister.
Now I've won." So she named him Naphtali.
9Leah saw that she had stopped having children.
So she gave her servant Zilpah to Jacob as a wife.
10Leah's servant Zilpah had a son by Jacob. 11Then
Leah said, "What good fortune!" So she named
him Gad.
12Leah's servant Zilpah had a second son by Jacob. 13Then Leah said, "I'm so happy! The women
will call me happy." So she named him Asher.
14While the wheat harvest was being gathered,
Reuben went out into the fields. He found some
mandrake plants. He brought them to his mother
Leah. Rachel said to Leah, "Please give me some
of your son's mandrakes."
15But Leah said to her, "Isn't it enough that you
took my husband away? Are you going to take my
son's mandrakes too?"
Rachel said, "All right. Jacob can make love to
you tonight if you give me your son's mandrakes."
16Jacob came in from the fields that evening.
Leah went out to meet him. "You have to sleep
with me tonight," she said. "I've bought you with
my son's mandrakes." So he made love to her that
night.
17God listened to Leah. She became pregnant and
had a fifth son by Jacob. 18Then Leah said, "God
has rewarded me because I gave my female servant
to my husband." So she named the boy Issachar.
19Leah became pregnant again. She had a sixth
son by Jacob. 20Then Leah said, "God has given
me a priceless gift. This time my husband will treat

me with honor. I've had six sons by him." So she named the boy Zebulun.

21Some time later she had a daughter. She named her Dinah.

22Then God listened to Rachel. He showed concern for her. He made it possible for her to have children. 23She became pregnant. She had a son. She said, "God has taken my shame away." 24She continued, "May the LORD give me another son." So she named him Joseph.

Jacob's Flocks Increase Their Numbers

25After Rachel had Joseph, Jacob spoke to Laban. He said, "Send me on my way. I want to go back to my own home and country. 26Give me my wives and children. I worked for you to get them. So I'll be on my way. You know how much work I've done for you."

27But Laban said to him, "If you are pleased with me, stay here. I've discovered that the LORD has blessed me because of you." 28He continued, "Name your pay. I'll give it to you."

29Jacob said to him, "You know how hard I've worked for you. You know that your livestock has done better under my care. 30You had only a little before I came. But that little has become a lot. The LORD has blessed you everywhere I've been. But when can I do something for my own family?"

31"What should I give you?" Laban asked.

"Don't give me anything," Jacob replied. "Just do one thing for me. Then I'll go on taking care of your flocks and watching over them.

32"Let me go through all of your flocks today. Let me remove every sheep that has speckles or spots on it. Let me remove every dark-colored lamb. Let me remove every goat that has spots or speckles on it. They will be my pay.

33"My honesty will give witness about me in days to come. It will give witness every time you check on what you have paid me. Suppose I have a goat that doesn't have speckles or spots. Or suppose I have a lamb that isn't dark-colored. Then it will be considered stolen."

34"I agree," said Laban. "Let's do what you have said."

35That same day Laban removed all of the male goats that had stripes or spots. He removed all of the female goats that had speckles or spots. They were the ones that had white on them. He also removed all of the dark-colored lambs. He had his sons take care of them.

36Then he put a journey of three days between himself and Jacob. But Jacob continued to take care of the rest of Laban's flocks.

37Jacob took branches that were freshly cut from poplar, almond and plane trees. He made white stripes on them by peeling off the bark. He uncovered the white wood inside the branches.

38Then he placed the peeled branches in all of the stone tubs where the animals drank water. He placed them so they would be right in front of the flocks when they came to drink. The flocks were ready to mate when they came to drink. 39So they mated in front of the branches. And they had little ones that were striped or speckled or spotted. 40Jacob put the little ones of the flock to one side by themselves. But he made the older ones face the striped and dark-colored animals that belonged to Laban. In that way, he made separate flocks for himself. He didn't put them with Laban's animals.

41Every time the stronger females were ready to mate, Jacob would place the branches in the stone tubs. He would place them in front of the animals so they would mate near the branches.

42But if the animals were weak, he wouldn't place the branches there. So the weak animals went to Laban. And the strong ones went to Jacob.

43In this way, Jacob became very rich. He became the owner of large flocks. He also had many male and female servants. And he had many camels and donkeys.

Jacob Runs Away From Laban

31 Jacob heard what Laban's sons were saying. "Jacob has taken everything our father owned," they said. "He has gained all of this wealth from what belonged to our father."

2Jacob noticed that Laban's feelings toward him had changed.

3Then the LORD spoke to Jacob. He said, "Go back to your father's land and to your relatives. I will be with you."

4So Jacob sent word to Rachel and Leah. He told them to come out to the fields where his flocks were.

5He said to them, "I see that your father's feelings toward me have changed. But the God of my father has been with me. 6You know that I've worked for your father with all of my strength.

7"But your father has cheated me. He has changed my pay ten times. In spite of everything that's happened, God hasn't let him harm me. 8Sometimes Laban would say, 'The speckled ones will be your pay.' Then all the flocks had little ones with speckles. At other times he would say, 'The striped ones will be your pay.' Then all the flocks had little ones with stripes. 9So God has taken away your father's livestock and given it to me.

10"Once during the mating season I had a dream. In my dream I looked up and saw male goats mating with the flock. The goats had stripes, speckles or spots.

11"The angel of God said to me in the dream, 'Jacob.' I answered, 'Here I am.' 12He said, 'Look up. See the male goats mating with the flock. All of them have stripes, speckles or spots. That is because I have seen everything that Laban has been doing to you.

13" 'I am the God of Bethel. That is where you poured oil on a pillar. There you made a promise to me. Now leave this land. Go back to your own land.' "

[14]Rachel and Leah replied, "Do we still have any share in our father's property? [15]Doesn't our father think of us as strangers? First he sold us. Now he has used up what he was paid for us. [16]All of the wealth God took away from our father really belongs to us and our children. So do what God has told you to do."

[17]Then Jacob put his children and wives on camels. [18]He drove all of his livestock ahead of him. He also took with him everything he had gotten in Paddan Aram. He left to go to his father Isaac in the land of Canaan.

[19]Laban had gone to clip the wool from his sheep. While he was gone, Rachel stole the statues of family gods that belonged to her father. [20]And that's not all. Jacob tricked Laban the Aramean. He didn't tell him he was running away.

[21]So Jacob ran off with everything he had. He crossed the Euphrates River. And he headed for the hill country of Gilead.

Laban Chases Jacob

[22]On the third day Laban was told that Jacob had run away. [23]He took his relatives with him and went after Jacob. Seven days later he caught up with him in the hill country of Gilead.

[24]Then God came to Laban the Aramean in a dream at night. He said to him, "Be careful. Do not say anything to Jacob, whether it is good or bad."

[25]Jacob had set up his tent in the hill country of Gilead. That's where Laban caught up with him. Laban and his relatives camped there too.

[26]Laban said to Jacob, "What have you done? You have tricked me. You have taken my daughters away like prisoners of war. [27]Why did you run away in secret and trick me? Why didn't you tell me? Then I could have sent you away happily. We could have sung to the music of tambourines and harps. [28]You didn't even let me kiss my grandchildren and my daughters good-by. You have done a foolish thing.

[29]"I have the power to harm you. But last night the God of your father spoke to me. He said, 'Be careful. Do not say anything to Jacob, whether it is good or bad.'

[30]"Now you have run away. You longed to go back to your father's home. But why did you have to steal my gods?"

[31]Jacob answered Laban, "I was afraid. I thought you would take your daughters away from me by force.

[32]"But if you find anyone who has your gods, he will not remain alive. While our relatives are watching, look for yourself. See if there's anything of yours here with me. If you find anything belonging to you, take it." But Jacob didn't know that Rachel had stolen the gods.

[33]So Laban went into Jacob's tent and Leah's tent. He went into the tent of their two female servants. But he didn't find anything.

After he came out of Leah's tent, he entered Rachel's tent. [34]Rachel was the one who had taken his family gods. She had put them inside her camel's saddle. She was sitting on them. Laban searched the whole tent. But he didn't find anything.

[35]Rachel said to her father, "I'm sorry, sir. I can't get up for you right now. But don't be angry with me. I'm having my monthly period." So he searched everywhere but couldn't find his family gods.

[36]Jacob was very angry with Laban. "What have I done wrong?" he asked. "What sin have I committed to make you hunt me down like this? [37]You have searched through all of my things. What have you found that belongs to your family? Put it here in front of your relatives and mine. Let them decide between the two of us.

[38]"I've been with you for 20 years now. The little ones of your sheep and goats were not dead when they were born. I haven't eaten rams from your flocks. [39]I didn't bring you animals that were torn apart by wild beasts. I made up for the loss myself. Also, you made me pay for anything that was stolen by day or night.

[40]"And what was my life like? The heat burned me in the daytime. And it was so cold at night that I froze. I couldn't sleep. [41]That's what it was like for the 20 years I was living with you.

"I worked for 14 years to get your two daughters. I worked for six years to get my share of your flocks. You changed my pay ten times.

[42]"But the God of my father was with me. He is the God of Abraham and the God Isaac worshiped. If he hadn't been with me, you would certainly have sent me away without anything to show for all of my work. But God has seen my hard times. He has seen all of the work my hands have done. So last night he warned you."

[43]Laban answered Jacob, "The women are my daughters. The children are my children. The flocks are my flocks. Everything you see is mine. But what can I do today about these daughters of mine? What can I do about the children they've had?

[44]"Come now. Let's make a covenant, you and I. Let it be a witness between us."

[45]So Jacob took a stone. He set it up as a pillar. [46]He said to his relatives, "Get some stones." So they took stones and put them in a pile. And they ate there by it.

[47]Laban named the pile of stones Jegar Sahadutha. Jacob named it Galeed.

[48]Laban said, "This pile of stones is a witness between you and me today." That's why it was named Galeed. [49]It was also called Mizpah. That's because Laban said, "May the LORD keep watch between you and me when we are away from each other. [50]Don't treat my daughters badly. Don't get married to any women besides my daughters. There isn't anyone here to see what we're doing. But remember that God is a witness between you and me."

[51]Laban also said to Jacob, "Here is this pile of stones. And here is this pillar. I've set them up between you and me. [52]This pile is a witness. And

this pillar is a witness. They give witness that I won't go past this pile to harm you. And they give witness that you won't go past this pile and pillar to harm me.

53"The God of Abraham and Nahor is also the God of their father. May their God decide which of us is right."

So Jacob took an oath in the name of the God his father Isaac worshiped. 54He offered a sacrifice there in the hill country. And he invited his relatives to a meal. After they had eaten, they spent the night there.

55Early the next morning Laban kissed his grandchildren and his daughters. He gave them his blessing. Then he left and returned home.

Jacob Gets Ready to Meet Esau

32 Jacob also went on his way. The angels of God met him. 2Jacob saw them. He said, "This is the army of God!" So he named that place Mahanaim.

3Jacob sent messengers ahead of him to his brother Esau. Esau lived in the land of Seir. It was also called the country of Edom.

4Jacob told the messengers what to do. He said, "Here's what you must tell my master Esau. 'Your servant Jacob says, "I've been staying with Laban. I've remained there until now. 5I have cattle and donkeys and sheep and goats. I also have male and female servants. Now I'm sending this message to you. I hope I can please you." ' "

6The messengers came back to Jacob. They said, "We went to your brother Esau. He's coming now to meet you. He has 400 men with him."

7Jacob was very worried and afraid. So he separated the people who were with him into two groups. He also separated the flocks and herds and camels. 8He thought, "Esau may come and attack one group. If he does, the group that's left can escape."

9Then Jacob prayed, "You are the God of my grandfather Abraham. You are the God of my father Isaac.

"LORD, you are the one who said to me, 'Go back to your country and your relatives. Then I will give you success.' 10You have been very kind and faithful to me. But I'm not worthy of any of this. When I crossed this Jordan River, all I had was my walking stick. But now I've become two groups.

11"Please save me from the hand of my brother Esau. I'm afraid he'll come and attack me and the mothers with their children. 12But you have said, 'I will certainly give you success. I will make your children as many as the grains of sand on the seashore. People will not be able to count them.' "

13Jacob spent the night there. He chose a gift for his brother Esau from what he had with him. 14He chose 200 female goats and 20 male goats. He chose 200 female sheep and 20 male sheep. 15He chose 30 female camels with their little ones. He chose 40 cows and ten bulls. And he chose 20 female donkeys and ten male donkeys. 16He put each herd by itself.

Then he put his servants in charge of them. He said to his servants, "Go on ahead of me. Keep some space between the herds."

17Jacob spoke to his servant who was leading the way. He said, "My brother Esau will meet you. He'll ask, 'Who is your master? Where are you going? And who owns all of these animals in front of you?'

18"Then say to Esau, 'They belong to your servant Jacob. They are a gift to you from him. And he is coming behind us.' "

19He also spoke to the second and third servants. He told them and all of the others who followed the herds what to do. He said, "Say the same thing to Esau when you meet him. 20Make sure you say, 'Your servant Jacob is coming behind us.' " Jacob was thinking, "I'll make peace with him with these gifts I'm sending on ahead. When I see him later, maybe he'll welcome me."

21So Jacob's gifts went on ahead of him. But he himself spent the night in the camp.

Jacob Struggles With God

22That night Jacob got up. He took his two wives, his two female servants and his 11 sons and sent them across the Jabbok River. 23After they had crossed the stream, he sent over everything he owned.

24So Jacob was left alone. A man struggled with him until morning. 25The man saw that he couldn't win. So he touched the inside of Jacob's hip. As Jacob struggled with the man, Jacob's hip was twisted. 26Then the man said, "Let me go. It is morning."

But Jacob replied, "I won't let you go unless you bless me."

27The man asked him, "What is your name?"

"Jacob," he answered.

28Then the man said, "Your name will not be Jacob anymore. Instead, it will be Israel. You have struggled with God and with men. And you have won."

29Jacob said, "Please tell me your name."

But he replied, "Why do you want to know my name?" Then he blessed Jacob there.

30So Jacob named the place Peniel. He said, "I saw God face to face. But I'm still alive!"

31The sun rose above Jacob as he passed by Peniel. He was limping because of his hip. 32That's why the people of Israel don't eat the meat attached to the inside of the hip. They don't eat it to this very day. It's because the inside of Jacob's hip was touched.

Jacob Meets Esau

33 Jacob looked up. And there was Esau, coming with his 400 men! So Jacob separated the children. He put them with Leah, Rachel

and the two female servants. 2He put the servants and their children in front. He put Leah and her children next. And he put Rachel and Joseph last. 3He himself went on ahead. As he came near his brother, he bowed down to the ground seven times.

4But Esau ran to meet Jacob. He hugged him and threw his arms around his neck. He kissed him, and they cried. 5Then Esau looked up and saw the women and children. "Who are these people with you?" he asked.

Jacob answered, "They are the children God has so kindly given to me."

6Then the female servants and their children came near and bowed down. 7Next, Leah and her children came and bowed down. Last of all came Joseph and Rachel. They bowed down too.

8Esau asked, "Why did you send all of those herds I saw?"

"I hoped I could do something to please you," Jacob replied.

9But Esau said, "I already have plenty, my brother. Keep what you have for yourself."

10"No, please!" said Jacob. "If I've pleased you, accept this gift from me. Seeing your face is like seeing the face of God. You have welcomed me so kindly. 11Please accept the present that was brought to you. God has been gracious to me. I have everything I need." Jacob wouldn't give in. So Esau accepted it.

12Then Esau said, "Let's be on our way. I'll go with you."

13But Jacob said to him, "You know that the children are young. You also know that I have to take care of the cows and female sheep that are nursing their little ones. If the animals are driven hard for just one day, all of them will die.

14"So you go on ahead of me. I'll move along only as fast as the herds and the children can go. I'll go slowly until I come to you in Seir."

15Esau said, "Then let me leave some of my men with you."

"Why do that?" Jacob asked. "I just hope I've pleased you."

16So that day Esau started on his way back to Seir. 17But Jacob went to Succoth. There he built a place for himself. He also made shelters for his livestock. That's why the place is named Succoth.

18After Jacob came from Paddan Aram, he arrived safely at the city of Shechem in Canaan. He camped where he could see the city. 19For 100 pieces of silver he bought a piece of land. He got it from the sons of Hamor. Hamor was the father of Shechem. Jacob set up his tent on that piece of land. 20He also set up an altar there. He named it El Elohe Israel.

Simeon and Levi Kill the Men of Shechem

34 Dinah was the daughter Leah had by Jacob. Dinah went out to visit the women of the land. 2Hamor the Hivite was the ruler of that area. When his son Shechem saw Dinah, he took her and raped her. 3Then his heart longed for Jacob's daughter Dinah. He fell in love with her and spoke tenderly to her.

4Shechem said to his father Hamor, "Get me that woman. I want her to be my wife."

5Jacob heard that his daughter Dinah had been made "unclean." His sons were in the fields with his livestock. So he kept quiet about it until they came home.

6Then Shechem's father Hamor went out to talk with Jacob. 7Jacob's sons had come in from the fields. They came as soon as they heard what had happened. They were filled with sadness and anger.

Shechem had done a very terrible thing. He had forced Jacob's daughter to have sex with him. He had done something that should never be done in Israel.

8But Hamor said to them, "My son Shechem wants your daughter. Please give her to him to be his wife.

9"Let your people and ours get married to each other. Give us your daughters as our wives. You can have our daughters as your wives. 10You can settle among us. Here is the land. Live in it. Trade in it. Buy property in it."

11Then Shechem spoke to Dinah's father and brothers. He said, "I want to please you. I'll give you anything you ask. 12Make the price for the bride as high as you want to. I'll pay anything you ask me. Just give me the woman. I want to get married to her."

13Their sister Dinah had been made "unclean." So Jacob's sons lied to Shechem and his father Hamor. 14They said to them, "We can't do it. We can't give our sister to a man who isn't circumcised. That would bring shame on us. 15We'll agree, but only on one condition. You will have to become like us. You will have to circumcise all of your males.

16"Then we'll give you our daughters as your wives. And we'll take your daughters as our wives. We'll settle among you and become one people with you. 17But if you won't agree to it, then we'll take our sister and go."

18Their offer seemed good to Hamor and his son Shechem. 19The young man was the most honored of all of the men in his father's family. He didn't lose any time in doing what they said, because he was delighted with Jacob's daughter.

20Hamor and his son Shechem went to the city gate. They spoke to the other men in town. 21"These men are friendly toward us," they said. "Let them live in our land. Let them trade in it. The land has plenty of room for them. We can get married to their daughters. And they can marry ours.

22"But they will agree to live with us as one people only on one condition. All of our males must be circumcised, just as they are.

23"Won't their livestock and their property belong to us? Won't all of their animals become ours? So let's say yes to them. Then they'll settle among us."

24All of the men who went out through the city gate agreed with Hamor and his son Shechem. So every male in the city was circumcised.

25Three days later, all of them were still in pain. Then Simeon and Levi took their swords. They were Jacob's sons and Dinah's brothers. They attacked the city when the people didn't expect it. They killed every male. 26They also killed Hamor and his son Shechem with their swords. Then they took Dinah from Shechem's house and left.

27Jacob's other sons found the dead bodies. They robbed the city where their sister had been made "unclean." 28They took the flocks and herds and donkeys. They took everything that was in the city and out in the fields. 29They carried everything away. And they took all of the women and children. They took away everything that was in the houses.

30Then Jacob said to Simeon and Levi, "You have brought trouble on me. Now I'm like a very bad smell to the Canaanites and Perizzites who live in this land. There aren't many of us. They may join together against me and attack me. Then I and my family will be destroyed."

31But they replied, "Should he have treated our sister like a prostitute?"

Jacob Returns to Bethel

35 Then God said to Jacob, "Go up to Bethel and settle there. Build an altar there to honor me. That's where I appeared to you when you were running away from your brother Esau."

2So Jacob spoke to his family and to everyone who was with him. He said, "Get rid of the strange gods you have with you. Make yourselves pure, and change your clothes. 3Come, let's go up to Bethel. There I'll build an altar to honor God. He answered me when I was in trouble. He's been with me everywhere I've gone."

4So they gave Jacob all of the strange gods they had. They also gave him their earrings. Jacob buried them under the oak tree at Shechem.

5Then Jacob and everyone who was with him started out. The terror of God fell on the towns all around them. So no one chased them.

6Jacob and all of the people who were with him came to Luz. Luz is also called Bethel. It's in the land of Canaan. 7Jacob built an altar at Luz. He named the place El Bethel. There God made himself known to Jacob when he was running away from his brother.

8Rebekah's attendant Deborah died. They buried her body under the oak tree below Bethel. So it was called Allon Bacuth.

9After Jacob returned from Paddan Aram, God appeared to him again. And God blessed him. 10God said to him, "Your name is Jacob. But you will not be called Jacob anymore. Your name will be Israel." So he named him Israel.

11God said to him, "I am the Mighty God. Have children and increase your numbers. A nation and a community of nations will come from you. Kings will come from your body. 12I am giving you the land I gave to Abraham and Isaac. I will also give it to your children after you."

13Then God left him at the place where he had talked with him.

14Jacob set up a stone pillar at the place where God had talked with him. He poured out a drink offering on it. He also poured oil on it. 15Jacob named the place Bethel. That's where God had talked with him.

Rachel and Isaac Die

16They moved on from Bethel. Ephrath wasn't very far away when Rachel began to have a baby. She was having a very hard time of it.

17The woman who helped her saw that she was having problems. So she said to her, "Don't be afraid. You have another son."

18But Rachel was dying. As she took her last breath, she named her son Ben-Oni. But his father named him Benjamin.

19So Rachel died. Her body was buried beside the road to Ephrath. Ephrath was also called Bethlehem. 20Jacob set up a pillar over her tomb. The pillar marks the place of Rachel's tomb to this very day.

21Israel moved on again. He set up his tent beyond Migdal Eder.

22While Israel was living in that area, Reuben went in and made love to Bilhah. She was the concubine of Reuben's father. And Israel heard about it.

Here are the 12 sons Jacob had.

23 Leah was the mother of
    Reuben, Jacob's oldest son.
  Her other sons were
    Simeon, Levi, Judah, Issachar and Zebulun.
24 The sons of Rachel were
    Joseph and Benjamin.
25 The sons of Rachel's female servant Bilhah were
    Dan and Naphtali.
26 The sons of Leah's female servant Zilpah were
    Gad and Asher.

Those were Jacob's sons. They were born in Paddan Aram.

27Jacob came home to his father Isaac in Mamre. Mamre is near Kiriath Arba, where Abraham and Isaac had stayed. The place is also called Hebron.

28Isaac lived 180 years. 29Then he took his last breath and died. He was very old when he joined the members of his family who had already died. His sons Esau and Jacob buried his body.

The Family Line of Esau

36 Here is the story of Esau. Esau was also
called Edom.

2 Esau got his wives from among the
women of Canaan. He married Adah, the
daughter of Elon the Hittite. He also married
Oholibamah, the daughter of Anah and the
granddaughter of Zibeon the Hivite. 3 And he
married Basemath, the daughter of Ishmael
and the sister of Nebaioth.

4 Adah had Eliphaz by Esau. Basemath
had Reuel. 5 Oholibamah had Jeush, Jalam
and Korah. All of them were Esau's sons.
They were born in Canaan.

6 Esau moved to a land far away from his
brother Jacob. He took with him his wives,
his sons and daughters, and all of the people
who lived with him. He also took his livestock and all of his other animals. He took
everything he had gotten in Canaan.

7 Jacob and Esau owned so much that they
couldn't remain together. There wasn't enough
land for both of them. They had too much livestock. 8 So Esau settled in the hill country of
Seir. Esau was also called Edom.

9 Here is the story of Esau. He's the father of the
people of Edom. They live in the hill country of Seir.

10 Here are the names of Esau's sons.
They are Eliphaz, the son of Esau's wife
Adah, and Reuel, the son of Esau's wife
Basemath.
11 The sons of Eliphaz were
Teman, Omar, Zepho, Gatam and Kenaz.
12 Esau's son Eliphaz also had a concubine
named Timna. She had Amalek by Eliphaz. They were grandsons of Esau's
wife Adah.
13 The sons of Reuel were
Nahath, Zerah, Shammah and Mizzah.
They were grandsons of Esau's wife
Basemath.
14 Esau's wife Oholibamah was the daughter
of Anah and the granddaughter of Zibeon. She had Jeush, Jalam and Korah by
Esau.

15 Here are the chiefs who were among Esau's
sons.

Eliphaz was Esau's oldest son. The sons of
Eliphaz were
Chiefs Teman, Omar, Zepho, Kenaz,
16 Korah, Gatam and Amalek. They were
the chiefs in Edom who were sons of Eliphaz. They were Adah's grandsons.
17 The sons of Esau's son Reuel were
Chiefs Nahath, Zerah, Shammah and
Mizzah. They were the chiefs in Edom
who were sons of Reuel. They were
grandsons of Esau's wife Basemath.
18 The sons of Esau's wife Oholibamah were
Chiefs Jeush, Jalam and Korah. They
were the chiefs who were sons of Esau's
wife Oholibamah. She was Anah's
daughter.

19 That was the family line of Esau. And those
were the chiefs. Esau was also called Edom.

20 Seir the Horite had sons living in the same
area.
They were Lotan, Shobal, Zibeon, Anah,
21 Dishon, Ezer and Dishan. The sons of
Seir in Edom were Horite chiefs.
22 The sons of Lotan were
Hori and Homam. Timna was Lotan's
sister.
23 The sons of Shobal were
Alvan, Manahath, Ebal, Shepho and
Onam.
24 The sons of Zibeon were
Aiah and Anah. He was the Anah who
discovered the hot springs of water in
the desert. He found them while he was
taking care of the donkeys that belonged
to his father Zibeon.
25 The children of Anah were
Dishon and Oholibamah. Oholibamah
was the daughter of Anah.
26 The sons of Dishon were
Hemdan, Eshban, Ithran and Keran.
27 The sons of Ezer were
Bilhan, Zaavan and Akan.
28 The sons of Dishan were
Uz and Aran.
29 The Horite chiefs were
Lotan, Shobal, Zibeon, Anah, 30 Dishon,
Ezer and Dishan. They were the Horite
chiefs in the land of Seir. They are listed
tribe by tribe.

The Rulers of Edom

31 Before Israel had a king, there were kings who
ruled in Edom.

32 Bela became the king of Edom. Bela was
the son of Beor. Bela's city was called
Dinhabah.
33 When Bela died, Jobab became the next
king. Jobab was the son of Zerah from
Bozrah.
34 When Jobab died, Husham became the
next king. Husham was from the land of
the Temanites.
35 When Husham died, Hadad became the
next king. Hadad was the son of Bedad.
Hadad had won the battle over Midian
in the country of Moab. Hadad's city
was called Avith.
36 When Hadad died, Samlah became the next
king. Samlah was from Masrekah.
37 When Samlah died, Shaul became the next
king. Shaul was from Rehoboth on the
river.

38 When Shaul died, Baal-Hanan became the
next king. Baal-Hanan was the son of
Acbor.
39 When Baal-Hanan died, Hadad became the
next king. Hadad's city was called Pau.
His wife's name was Mehetabel. She
was the daughter of Matred. Matred was
the daughter of Me-Zahab.

40 Here are the chiefs who were in the family line
of Esau. They are listed by name as chiefs in charge
of their tribes and territories. They are
Timna, Alvah, Jetheth, 41 Oholibamah,
Elah, Pinon, 42 Kenaz, Teman, Mibzar,
43 Magdiel and Iram. They were the
chiefs of Edom. They ruled over their
settlements in the land where they lived.

That's the end of the story of Esau. He was the
father of the people of Edom.

Joseph Has Two Dreams

37 Jacob lived in the land of Canaan. It's the
land where his father had stayed.

2 Here is the story of Jacob.

Joseph was a young man. He was 17 years old.
He was taking care of the flocks with some of his
brothers. They were the sons of Bilhah and the sons
of Zilpah, his father's wives. Joseph brought their
father a bad report about them.
3 Israel loved Joseph more than any of his other
sons. Joseph had been born to him when he was
old. Israel made him a beautiful robe.
4 Joseph's brothers saw that their father loved
him more than any of them. So they hated Joseph.
They couldn't even speak one kind word to him.
5 Joseph had a dream. When he told it to his
brothers, they hated him even more. 6 He said to
them, "Listen to the dream I had. 7 We were tying
up bundles of grain out in the field. Suddenly my
bundle rose and stood up straight. Your bundles
gathered around my bundle and bowed down to it."
8 His brothers said to him, "Do you plan to be
king over us? Will you really rule over us?" So they
hated him even more because of his dream. They
didn't like what he had said.
9 Then Joseph had another dream. He told it to
his brothers. "Listen," he said. "I had another
dream. This time the sun and moon and 11 stars
were bowing down to me."
10 He told his father as well as his brothers. Then
his father objected. He said, "What about this
dream you had? Will your mother and I and your
brothers really do that? Will we really come and
bow down to the ground in front of you?"
11 His brothers were jealous of him. But his father
kept the matter in mind.

Joseph Is Sold by His Brothers

12 Joseph's brothers had gone to take care of
their father's flocks near Shechem. 13 Israel said to
Joseph, "As you know, your brothers are taking
care of the flocks near Shechem. Come. I'm going
to send you to them."
"All right," Joseph replied.
14 So Israel said to him, "Go to your brothers.
See how they are doing. Also see how the flocks
are doing. Then come back and tell me." So he
sent him away from the Hebron Valley.
Joseph arrived at Shechem. 15 A man found him
wandering around in the fields. He asked Joseph,
"What are you looking for?"
16 He replied, "I'm looking for my brothers. Can
you tell me where they are taking care of their
flocks?"
17 "They've moved on from here," the man
answered. "I heard them say, 'Let's go to Dothan.'"
So Joseph went to look for his brothers. He
found them near Dothan. 18 But they saw him a
long way off. Before he reached them, they made
plans to kill him.
19 "Here comes that dreamer!" they said to one
another. 20 "Come. Let's kill him. Let's throw him
into one of these empty wells. Let's say that a wild
animal ate him up. Then we'll see whether his
dreams will come true."
21 Reuben heard them. He tried to save Joseph
from them. "Let's not take his life," he said.
22 "Let's not spill any blood. Throw him into this
empty well here in the desert. But don't harm him
yourselves."
Reuben said that to save Joseph from them. He
was hoping he could take him back to his father.
23 When Joseph came to his brothers, he was
wearing his beautiful robe. They took it away from
him. 24 And they threw him into the well. The well
was empty. There wasn't any water in it.
25 Then they sat down to eat their meal. As they
did, they saw some Ishmaelite traders coming
from Gilead. Their camels were loaded with
spices, lotion and myrrh. They were on their way
to take them down to Egypt.
26 Judah said to his brothers, "What will we gain
if we kill our brother and try to cover up what
we've done? 27 Come. Let's sell him to these
traders. Let's not harm him ourselves. After all,
he's our brother. He's our own flesh and blood."
Judah's brothers agreed with him.
28 The traders from Midian came by. Joseph's
brothers pulled him up out of the well. They sold
him to the Ishmaelite traders for eight ounces of
silver. Then the traders took him to Egypt.
29 Later, Reuben came back to the empty well.
He saw that Joseph wasn't there. He was so upset
that he tore his clothes. 30 He went back to his
brothers and said, "The boy isn't there! Now what
should I do?"
31 Then they got Joseph's beautiful robe. They
killed a goat and dipped the robe in the blood.
32 They took it back to their father. They said, "We

found this. Take a look at it. See if it's your son's robe."

33Jacob recognized it. He said, "It's my son's robe! A wild animal has eaten him up. Joseph must have been torn to pieces."

34Jacob tore his clothes. He put on black clothes. Then he sobbed over his son for many days.

35All of Jacob's other sons and daughters came to comfort him. But they weren't able to. He said, "I'll be full of sorrow when I go down into the grave to be with my son." So Joseph's father sobbed over him.

36But the traders from Midian sold Joseph to Potiphar in Egypt. Potiphar was one of Pharaoh's officials. He was the captain of the palace guard.

Judah and Tamar

38 At that time, Judah left his brothers. He went down to stay with a man named Hirah. Hirah was from the town of Adullam.

2There Judah met the daughter of a man from Canaan. His name was Shua. Judah married her and made love to her. 3She became pregnant. She had a son. They named him Er. 4She became pregnant again and had another son. She named him Onan. 5She had still another son. She named him Shelah. He was born at Kezib.

6Judah got a wife for his oldest son Er. Her name was Tamar. 7But Judah's oldest son Er was evil in the LORD's eyes. So the LORD put him to death.

8Then Judah said to Onan, "Make love to your brother's wife. After all, you are her brother-in-law. So carry out your duty to her. Produce children for your brother."

9But Onan knew that the children wouldn't belong to him. So every time he made love to his brother's wife, he spilled his semen on the ground. He did it so he wouldn't produce children for his brother.

10What he did was evil in the LORD's eyes. So the LORD put him to death also.

11Then Judah spoke to his daughter-in-law Tamar. He said, "Live as a widow in your father's home. Wait there until my son Shelah grows up."

Judah was thinking, "Shelah might die too, just like his brothers." So Tamar went to live in her father's home.

12After a long time Judah's wife died. She was the daughter of Shua. When Judah got over his sadness, he went up to Timnah. His friend Hirah from Adullam went with him. Men were clipping the wool from Judah's sheep at Timnah.

13Tamar was told, "Your father-in-law is on his way to Timnah to clip the wool from his sheep." 14So she took off her widow's clothes. She covered her face with a veil so people wouldn't know who she was. Then she sat down at the entrance to Enaim. Enaim is on the road to Timnah. Tamar knew that Shelah had grown up. But she hadn't been given to him as his wife.

15Judah saw her. He thought she was a prostitute because she had covered her face with a veil. 16He didn't realize that she was his daughter-in-law. He went over to her by the side of the road. He said, "Come. Let me make love to you."

"What will you give me to make love to you?" she asked.

17"I'll send you a young goat from my flock," he said.

"Will you give me something that belongs to you?" she asked. "I'll keep it until you send the goat."

18He said, "What should I give you?"

"Give me your seal and its string," she answered. "And give me your walking stick."

So he gave them to her. Then he had sex with her. And she became pregnant by him. 19After she left, she took off her veil. She put on her widow's clothes again.

20Judah sent his friend Hirah with the young goat he had promised. He wanted to get back what he had given to the woman.

But his friend Hirah couldn't find her. 21He asked the men who lived at Enaim, "Where's the temple prostitute? She used to sit beside the road here."

"There hasn't been any temple prostitute here," they said.

22So Hirah went back to Judah. He said, "I couldn't find her. Besides, the men who lived there didn't know anything about her. They said, 'There hasn't been any temple prostitute here.'"

23Then Judah said, "Let her keep what she has. I don't want people making fun of us. After all, I did send her this young goat. We can't help it if you couldn't find her."

24About three months later people brought word to Judah. They said, "Your daughter-in-law Tamar is guilty of being a prostitute. Now she's pregnant."

Judah said, "Bring her out! Have her burned to death!"

25As Tamar was being brought out, she sent a message to her father-in-law. She said, "I am pregnant by the man who owns these." She continued, "Do you recognize this seal and string and walking stick? Do you know who they belong to?"

26Judah recognized them. He said, "She's a better person than I am. I should have given her to my son Shelah, but I didn't." Judah never had sex with Tamar again.

27The time came for Tamar to have her baby. There were twin boys inside her.

28As the babies were being born, one of them stuck out his hand. So the woman who was helping Tamar took a bright red thread. The woman tied it on the baby's wrist. She said, "This one came out first."

29But he pulled his hand back, and his brother came out first instead. She said, "Just look at how you have broken out!" So he was called Perez.

30Then his brother, who had the red thread on his wrist, came out. So he was named Zerah.

Joseph and Potiphar's Wife

39 Joseph had been taken down to Egypt. An Egyptian named Potiphar had bought him from the Ishmaelite traders who had taken him there. Potiphar was one of Pharaoh's officials. He was the captain of the palace guard.

2The LORD was with Joseph. He gave him great success. Joseph lived in Potiphar's house.

3Joseph's master saw that the LORD was with him. He saw that the LORD gave Joseph success in everything he did. 4So Potiphar was pleased with Joseph. He made him his attendant. He put Joseph in charge of his house. He told Joseph to take good care of everything he owned.

5From that time on, the LORD blessed Potiphar's family and servants because of Joseph. He blessed everything Potiphar had in his house and field.

6So Potiphar told Joseph to take good care of everything he owned. With Joseph in charge, he didn't have to worry about anything except the food he ate.

Joseph was strong and handsome. 7After a while, his master's wife noticed Joseph. She said to him, "Make love to me!"

8But he said no. "My master has put me in charge," he told her. "Now he doesn't have to worry about anything in the house. He trusts me to take care of everything he owns.

9"No one in this house is in a higher position than I am. My master hasn't held anything back from me, except you. You are his wife. So how could I do an evil thing like that? How could I sin against God?"

10She spoke to Joseph day after day. But he told her he wouldn't make love to her. He didn't even want to be with her.

11One day Joseph went into the house to take care of his duties. None of the family servants was inside.

12Potiphar's wife grabbed hold of him by his coat. "Make love to me!" she said. But he left his coat in her hand. And he ran out of the house.

13She saw that he had left his coat in her hand and had run out of the house. 14So she called her servants. "Look," she said to them, "this Hebrew slave has been brought here to make fun of us! He came in here to force me to have sex with him. But I screamed for help. 15He heard my scream. So he left his coat beside me and ran out of the house."

16She kept Joseph's coat with her until Potiphar came home. 17Then she told him her story. She said, "That Hebrew slave you brought us came to me to rape me. 18But I screamed for help. So he left his coat beside me and ran out of the house."

19Potiphar's wife told him, "That's how your slave treated me." When Joseph's master heard her story, he became very angry. 20So he put Joseph in prison. It was the place where the king's prisoners were kept.

While Joseph was there in the prison, 21the LORD was with him. He was kind to him.

So the man who was running the prison was pleased with Joseph. 22He put Joseph in charge of all of the prisoners. He made him accountable for everything that was done there. 23The man who ran the prison didn't pay attention to anything that was in Joseph's care.

The LORD was with Joseph. He gave Joseph success in everything he did.

The Wine Taster and the Baker

40 Some time later, the Egyptian king's baker and wine taster did something their master didn't like.

2So Pharaoh became angry with his two officials, the chief wine taster and the chief baker. 3He put them in prison in the house of the captain of the palace guard. It was the same prison where Joseph was kept.

4The captain put Joseph in charge of those men. So Joseph took care of them.

Some time passed while they were in prison. 5Then each of the two men had a dream. The men were the Egyptian king's baker and wine taster. They were being held in prison. Both of them had dreams the same night. Each of their dreams had its own meaning.

6Joseph came to them the next morning. He saw that they were sad. 7They were Pharaoh's officials, and they were in prison with Joseph in his master's house. So he asked them, "Why do you look so sad today?"

8"We both had dreams," they answered. "But no one can tell us what they mean."

Then Joseph said to them, "Only God knows what dreams mean. Tell me your dreams."

9So the chief wine taster told Joseph his dream. He said to him, "In my dream I saw a vine in front of me. 10There were three branches on the vine. As soon as it budded, it flowered. And bunches of ripe grapes grew on it.

11"Pharaoh's cup was in my hand. I took the grapes. I squeezed them into Pharaoh's cup. Then I put the cup in his hand."

12"Here's what your dream means," Joseph said to him. "The three branches are three days. 13In three days Pharaoh will let you out of prison. He'll give your position back to you. And you will put Pharaoh's cup in his hand. That's what you used to do when you were his wine taster.

14"But when everything is going well with you, remember me. Do me a favor. Speak to Pharaoh about me. Get me out of this prison. 15I was taken away from the land of the Hebrews by force. Even here I haven't done anything to be put in prison for."

16The chief baker saw that Joseph had given a positive meaning to the wine taster's dream. So he said to Joseph, "I had a dream too. There we[re] three baskets of bread on my head. 17All kinds [of] baked goods for Pharaoh were in the top ba[sket]. But the birds were eating them out of the b[asket] that was on my head."

18“Here’s what your dream means,” Joseph said. “The three baskets are three days. 19In three days Pharaoh will cut your head off. Then he will stick a pole through your body and set the pole up. The birds will eat up your body.”

20The third day was Pharaoh’s birthday. He had a big dinner prepared for all of his officials. He brought the chief wine taster and the chief baker out of prison. He did it in front of his officials. 21He gave the chief wine taster’s position back to him. Once again the wine taster put the cup into Pharaoh’s hand.

22But Pharaoh had a pole stuck through the chief baker’s body. Then he had the pole set up.

Everything happened exactly as Joseph had told them when he explained their dreams.

23But the chief wine taster didn’t remember Joseph. In fact, he forgot all about him.

Pharaoh Has Two Dreams

41 When two full years had passed, Pharaoh had a dream. In his dream, he was standing by the Nile River. 2Seven cows came up out of the river. They looked healthy and fat. They were eating some of the tall grass that was growing along the river.

3After them, seven other cows came up out of the Nile. They looked ugly and skinny. They were standing beside the other cows on the riverbank.

4The ugly, skinny cows ate up the seven cows that looked healthy and fat. Then Pharaoh woke up.

5He fell asleep again and had a second dream. In that dream, seven heads of grain were growing on one stem. They were healthy and good.

6After them, seven other heads of grain came up. They were thin and dried up by the east wind.

7The thin heads of grain swallowed up the seven healthy, full heads. Then Pharaoh woke up. It had been a dream.

8In the morning he was worried. So he sent for all of the magicians and wise men of Egypt. Pharaoh told them his dreams. But no one could tell him what they meant.

9Then the chief wine taster spoke up. He said to Pharaoh, “Now I remember that I’ve done something wrong. 10Pharaoh was once angry with his servants. He put me and the chief baker in prison. We were in the house of the captain of the palace guard. 11Each of us had a dream the same night. Each dream had its own meaning.

12“A young Hebrew servant was there with us. He was a servant of the captain of the guard. We ...d him our dreams. And he explained them to us. ...d each of us the meaning of our dreams. ...urned out exactly as he said they would. ...ck my position. The other man had ...gh his body.”

... for Joseph. He was quickly ...on. Joseph shaved himself ...es. Then he came to Pharaoh.

15Pharaoh said to Joseph, “I had a dream. No one can tell me what it means. But I’ve heard that when you hear a dream you can explain it.”

16“I can’t do it,” Joseph replied to Pharaoh. “But God will give Pharaoh the answer he wants.”

17Then Pharaoh told Joseph what he had dreamed. He said, “I was standing on the bank of the Nile River. 18Seven cows came up out of the river. They were fat and good-looking. They were eating the tall grass that was growing along the river.

19“After them, seven other cows came up. They were bony and very ugly and thin. I had never seen such ugly cows in the whole land of Egypt.

20“The thin, ugly cows ate up the seven fat cows that came up first. 21But even after the thin cows ate up the fat ones, no one could tell that they had eaten them. They looked just as ugly as before. Then I woke up.

22“In my dreams I also saw seven heads of grain. They were full and good. They were all growing on one stem.

23“After them, seven other heads of grain came up. They were weak and thin and dried up by the east wind.

24“The thin heads of grain swallowed up the seven good heads. I told my dreams to the magicians. But none of them could explain them to me.”

25Then Joseph said to Pharaoh, “Both of Pharaoh’s dreams have the same meaning. God has shown Pharaoh what he is about to do. 26The seven good cows are seven years. And the seven good heads of grain are seven years. Both dreams mean the same thing.

27“The seven thin, ugly cows that came up later are seven years. So are the seven worthless heads of grain that were dried up by the east wind. They are seven years when there won’t be enough food.

28“It’s exactly as I said to Pharaoh. God has shown Pharaoh what he’s about to do. 29Seven years with plenty of food are coming to the whole land of Egypt.

30“But seven years when there won’t be enough food will follow them. Then everyone will forget about all of the food Egypt had. Terrible hunger will destroy the land. 31There won’t be anything left to remind people of the years when there was plenty of food in the land. That’s how bad the hunger that follows will be.

32“God gave the dream to Pharaoh in two forms. That’s because the matter has been firmly decided by God. And it’s because God will do it soon.

33“So Pharaoh should look for a wise and understanding man. He should put him in charge of the land of Egypt.

34“Pharaoh should appoint officials to be in charge of the land. They should take a fifth of the harvest in Egypt during the seven years when there’s plenty of food. 35They should collect all of the extra food of the good years that are coming. Pharaoh should give them authority to store up the grain. They should keep it in the cities for food.

36“The grain should be stored up for the country to use later. It will be needed during the seven
years when there isn’t enough food in Egypt. Then
the country won’t be destroyed just because it
doesn’t have enough food.”
37The plan seemed good to Pharaoh and all of
his officials. 38So Pharaoh said to them, “The spirit
of God is in this man. We can’t find anyone else
like him, can we?”
39Then Pharaoh said to Joseph, “God has made
all of this known to you. No one is as wise and
understanding as you are. 40You will be in charge
of my palace. All of my people must obey your
orders. I will be greater than you only because I’m
the one who sits on the throne.”

Joseph Is Put in Charge of Egypt

41So Pharaoh said to Joseph, “I’m putting you
in charge of the whole land of Egypt.”
42Then Pharaoh took his ring off his finger. It
was the ring he used to stamp all of the official
papers. He put it on Joseph’s finger. He dressed
him in robes that were made out of fine linen. He
put a gold chain around his neck.
43He also had him ride in a chariot. Joseph was
now next in command after Pharaoh. People went
in front of him and shouted, “Get down on your
knees!”

By doing all of those things, Pharaoh put Joseph in charge of the whole land of Egypt.
44Then Pharaoh said to Joseph, “I am Pharaoh.
But without your word, no one will do anything in
the whole land of Egypt.”
45Pharaoh gave Joseph the name Zaphenath-
Paneah. He gave him a wife. She was Asenath, the
daughter of Potiphera. Potiphera was the priest
of On.

Joseph traveled all over the land of Egypt.
46Joseph was 30 years old when he began serving Pharaoh, the king of Egypt. He left Pharaoh’s
palace and traveled all over Egypt.
47During the seven years when there was plenty
of food, the land produced more than the people
needed.
48Joseph collected all of the extra food produced
in those seven years in Egypt. He stored it in the
cities. In each city he stored up the food that was
grown in the fields around it. 49Joseph stored up
huge amounts of grain. It was like the sand of the
sea. There was so much grain it couldn’t be measured. So Joseph stopped keeping records of it.
50Before the years when there wasn’t enough
food, two sons were born to Joseph. He had them
by Asenath, the daughter of Potiphera. Potiphera
was the priest of On.
51Joseph named his first son Manasseh. That’s
because he said, “God has made me forget all of
my trouble and my father’s whole family.”
52He named the second son Ephraim. That’s
because he said, “God has given me children in the
land where I’ve suffered so much.”
53The seven years when there was plenty of food
in Egypt came to an end. 54Then the seven years
when there wasn’t enough food began. It happened
exactly as Joseph had said it would. There wasn’t
enough food in any of the other lands. But in the
whole land of Egypt there was food.
55When all of the people of Egypt began to get
hungry, they cried out to Pharaoh for food. He told
all of the Egyptians, “Go to Joseph. Do what he
tells you.”
56There wasn’t enough food anywhere in the
country. So Joseph opened the storerooms. He sold
grain to the Egyptians because people were very
hungry all over Egypt.
57People from all of the other countries came to
Egypt. They came to buy grain from Joseph.
That’s because people were very hungry all over
the world.

Joseph’s Brothers Go Down to Egypt

42 Jacob found out that there was grain in
Egypt. So he said to his sons, “Why do you
just keep looking at each other?” 2He continued,
“I’ve heard there’s grain in Egypt. Go down there.
Buy some for us. Then we’ll live and not die.”
3So ten of Joseph’s brothers went down to
Egypt to buy grain there. 4But Jacob didn’t send
Joseph’s brother Benjamin with them. He was
afraid Benjamin might be harmed.
5Israel’s sons were among the people who went
to buy grain. There wasn’t enough food in the land
of Canaan.
6Joseph was the governor of the land. He was
the one who sold grain to all of its people. When
Joseph’s brothers arrived, they bowed down to him
with their faces to the ground.
7As soon as Joseph saw his brothers, he recognized them. But he pretended to be a stranger. He
spoke to them in a mean way. “Where do you
come from?” he asked.

“From the land of Canaan,” they replied.
“We’ve come to buy food.”
8Joseph recognized his brothers, but they didn’t
recognize him. 9Then Joseph remembered his
dreams about them. So he said to them, “You are
spies! You have come to see the places where our
land isn’t guarded very well.”
10“No, sir,” they answered. “We’ve come to buy
food. 11All of us are the sons of one man. We’re
honest men. We aren’t spies.”
12“No!” he said to them. “You have come to see
the places where our land isn’t guarded very well.”
13But they replied, “We were 12 brothers. All of
us were the sons of one man. He lives in the land
of Canaan. Our youngest brother is now with our
father. And one brother is gone.”
14Joseph said to them, “I still say you are spies!
15So I’m going to put you to the test. You can be
sure that Pharaoh lives. And you can be just as sure
that you won’t leave this place unless your youngest brother comes here. I promise with an oath that

you won't leave here. 16 Send one of you back to get your brother. The rest of you will be kept in prison.

"I'll put your words to the test. Then we'll find out whether you are telling the truth. You can be sure that Pharaoh lives. And you can be just as sure that if you aren't telling the truth, we'll know that you are spies!"

17 So Joseph kept all of them under guard for three days.

18 On the third day, Joseph spoke to them again. He said, "Do what I say. Then you will live, because I have respect for God. 19 If you are honest men, let one of your brothers stay here in prison. The rest of you may go and take grain back to your hungry families.

20 "But you must bring your youngest brother to me. That will prove that your words are true. Then you won't die." So they did what he said.

21 They said to one another, "God is certainly punishing us because of our brother. We saw how troubled he was when he begged us to let him live. But we wouldn't listen. That's why all of this trouble has come to us."

22 Reuben replied, "Didn't I tell you not to sin against the boy? But you wouldn't listen! Now we're being held accountable for killing him."

23 They didn't realize that Joseph could understand what they were saying. He was using someone else to explain their words to him in the Egyptian language.

24 Joseph turned away from them and began to sob. Then he turned around and spoke to them again. He had Simeon taken and tied up right there in front of them.

25 Joseph gave orders to have their bags filled with grain. He had each man's money put back into his sack. He also made sure they were given food for their journey.

26 Then the brothers loaded their grain on their donkeys and left.

27 When night came, they stopped. One of them opened his sack to get feed for his donkey. He saw his money in the top of his sack. 28 "My money has been given back," he said to his brothers. "Here it is in my sack."

They had a sinking feeling in their hearts. They began to tremble. They turned to each other and said, "What has God done to us?"

29 They came to their father Jacob in the land of Canaan. They told him everything that had happened to them.

They said, 30 "The man who is the governor of the land spoke to us in a mean way. He treated us as if we were spying on the land. 31 But we said to him, 'We're honest men. We aren't spies. 32 We were 12 brothers. All of us were the sons of one father. But now one brother is gone. And our youngest brother is with our father in Canaan.'

33 "Then the man who is the governor of the land spoke to us. He said, 'Here's how I will know whether you are honest men. Leave one of your brothers here with me. Take food for your hungry families and go.

34 " 'But bring your youngest brother to me. Then I'll know that you are honest men and not spies. I'll give your brother back to you. And you will be free to trade in the land.' "

35 They began emptying their sacks. There in each man's sack was his bag of money! When they and their father saw the money bags, they were afraid.

36 Their father Jacob said to them, "You have taken my children away from me. Joseph is gone. Simeon is gone. Now you want to take Benjamin. Everything is going against me!"

37 Then Reuben spoke to his father. He said, "You can put both of my sons to death if I don't bring Benjamin back to you. Place him in my care. I'll bring him back."

38 But Jacob said, "My son will not go down there with you. His brother is dead. He's the only one left here with me. Suppose he's harmed on the journey you are taking. Then I would die as a sad old man. I would go down into the grave full of sorrow."

Joseph's Brothers Go Down to Egypt Again

43 There still wasn't enough food anywhere in the land. 2 After a while Jacob's family had eaten all of the grain the brothers had brought from Egypt.

So their father said to them, "Go back. Buy us a little more food."

3 But Judah said to him, "The man gave us a strong warning. He said, 'You won't see my face again unless your brother comes with you.' 4 So send our brother along with us. Then we'll go down and buy food for you.

5 "If you won't send him, we won't go down. The man said to us, 'You won't see my face again unless your brother comes with you.' "

6 Israel asked, "Why did you bring this trouble to me? Why did you tell the man you had another brother?"

7 They replied, "The man questioned us closely about ourselves and our family. 'Is your father still living?' he asked us. 'Do you have another brother?'

"We just answered his questions. How could we possibly know he would say, 'Bring your brother down here'?"

8 Judah spoke to Israel his father. "Send the boy along with me," he said. "We'll go at once. Then we and you and our children will live and not die.

9 "I myself promise to keep him safe. You can hold me accountable for him. I'll bring him back to you. I'll set him right here in front of you. If I don't, you can put the blame on me for the rest of my life.

10 "As it is, we've already waited too long. We could have gone to Egypt and back twice by now."

11 Then their father Israel spoke to them. He said, "If that's the way it has to be, then do what I

tell you. Put some of the best things from our land in your bags. Take them down to the man as a gift. Take some lotion and a little honey. Take some spices and myrrh. Take some pistachio nuts and almonds. [12]Take twice the amount of money with you. You have to give back the money that was put in your sacks. Maybe it was a mistake.

[13]"Also take your brother. Go back to the man at once. [14]May the Mighty God cause him to show you mercy. May the man let your other brother and Benjamin come back with you. And if I lose my sons, I lose them."

[15]So the men took the gifts. They took twice the amount of money. They also took Benjamin. They hurried down to Egypt and went to Joseph.

[16]When Joseph saw Benjamin with them, he spoke to the manager of his house. "Take these men to my house," he said. "Kill an animal and prepare dinner. I want them to eat with me at noon."

[17]The manager did what Joseph told him to do. He took the men to Joseph's house.

[18]They were afraid when they were taken to Joseph's house. They thought, "We were brought here because of the money that was put back in our sacks the first time. He wants to attack us and overpower us. Then he can hold us as slaves and take our donkeys."

[19]So they went up to Joseph's manager. They spoke to him at the entrance to the house. [20]"Please, sir," they said. "We came down here the first time to buy food. [21]We opened our sacks at the place where we stopped for the night. Each of us found in our sacks the money we had paid. So we've brought it back with us. [22]We've also brought more money with us to buy food. We don't know who put our money in our sacks."

[23]"It's all right," the manager said. "Don't be afraid. Your God, the God of your father, has given you riches in your sacks. I received your money." Then he brought Simeon out to them.

[24]The manager took the men into Joseph's house. He gave them water to wash their feet. He provided feed for their donkeys. [25]They prepared their gifts for Joseph. He was planning to arrive at noon. They had heard that they were going to eat there.

[26]When Joseph came home, they gave him the gifts they had brought into the house. They bowed down to the ground in front of him.

[27]He asked them how they were. Then he said, "How is your old father you told me about? Is he still living?"

[28]They replied, "Your servant our father is still alive and well." And they bowed low to show him honor.

[29]Joseph looked around. Then he saw his brother Benjamin, his own mother's son. He asked, "Is this your youngest brother? Is he the one you told me about?" He continued, "May God be gracious to you, my son."

[30]It moved him deeply to see his brother. So Joseph hurried out and looked for a place to cry. He went into his own room and cried there.

[31]Then he washed his face and came out. He calmed down and said, "Serve the food."

[32]They served Joseph by himself. They served the brothers by themselves. They also served the Egyptians who ate with him by themselves. Because of their beliefs, Egyptians couldn't eat with Hebrews.

[33]The brothers had been given places in front of Joseph. They had been seated in the order of their ages, from the oldest to the youngest. That made them look at each other in great surprise.

[34]While they were eating, some food was brought to them from Joseph's table. Benjamin was given five times as much as anyone else. So all of Joseph's brothers ate and drank a lot with him.

A Silver Cup in a Sack

44 Joseph told the manager of his house what to do. "Fill the men's sacks with as much food as they can carry," he said. "Put each man's money in his sack.

[2]"Then put my silver cup in the youngest one's sack. Put it there along with the money he paid for his grain." So the manager did what Joseph told him to do.

[3]When morning came, the men were sent on their way with their donkeys.

[4]They hadn't gone very far from the city when Joseph spoke to his manager. "Go after those men at once," he said. "Catch up with them. Say to them, 'My master was good to you. Why have you paid him back by doing evil? [5]Isn't this the cup my master drinks from? Doesn't he also use it to figure things out? You have done an evil thing.'"

[6]When the manager caught up with them, he told them what Joseph had said.

[7]But they said to him, "Why do you say these things? We would never do anything like that! [8]We even brought back to you from Canaan the money we found in our sacks. So why would we steal silver or gold from your master's house?

[9]"If you find out that any of us has the cup, he will die. And the rest of us will become your slaves."

[10]"All right, then," he said. "As you wish. The one who is found to have the cup will become my slave. But the rest of you will be free from blame."

[11]Each of them quickly put his sack down on the ground and opened it.

[12]Then the manager started to search. He began with the oldest and ended with the youngest. The cup was found in Benjamin's sack.

[13]When that happened, they were so upset they tore their clothes. Then all of them loaded their donkeys and went back to the city.

[14]Joseph was still in the house when Judah and his brothers came in. They threw themselves down on the ground in front of him.

15 Joseph said to them, “What have you done? Don’t you know that a man like me has ways to figure things out?”

16 “What can we say to you?” Judah replied. “What can we say? How can we prove we haven’t done anything wrong? God has shown you that we are guilty. We are now your slaves. All of us are, including the one who was found to have the cup.”

17 But Joseph said, “I would never do anything like that! Only the man who was found to have the cup will become my slave. The rest of you may go back to your father in peace.”

18 Then Judah went up to him. He said, “Please, sir. Let me speak a word to you. Don’t be angry with me, even though you are equal to Pharaoh himself. 19 You asked us, ‘Do you have a father or a brother?’ 20 We answered, ‘We have an old father. A young son was born to him when he was old. His brother is dead. He’s the only one of his mother’s sons left. And his father loves him.’

21 “Then you said to us, ‘Bring him down to me. I want to see him for myself.’

22 “We said to you, ‘The boy can’t leave his father. If he does, his father will die.’

23 “But you told us, ‘Your youngest brother must come down here with you. If he doesn’t, you won’t see my face again.’ 24 So we went back to my father. We told him what you had said.

25 “Then our father said, ‘Go back. Buy a little more food.’

26 “But we said, ‘We can’t go down. We’ll only go if our youngest brother goes there with us. We can’t even see the man’s face unless our youngest brother goes with us.’

27 “Your servant my father said to us, ‘You know that my wife had two sons by me. 28 One of them went away from me. And I said, “He must have been torn to pieces.” I haven’t seen him since. 29 What if you take this one from me too and he is harmed? Then you would cause me to die as a sad old man. I would go down into the grave full of pain and suffering.’

30 “So now, what will happen if the boy isn’t with us when I go back to my father? His life is closely tied up with the boy’s life. 31 When he sees that the boy isn’t with us, he’ll die as a sad old man. Because of us, he’ll go down into the grave full of sorrow.

32 “I promised my father I would keep the boy safe. I said, ‘Father, I’ll bring him back to you. If I don’t, you can put the blame on me for the rest of my life.’

33 “Now then, please let me stay here. Let me be your slave in place of the boy. Let the boy return with his brothers. 34 How can I go back to my father if the boy isn’t with me? Don’t let me see the pain and suffering that would come to my father.”

Joseph Tells His Brothers Who He Is

45 Joseph couldn’t control himself anymore in front of all of his attendants. He cried out, “Have everyone leave me!”

So there wasn’t anyone with Joseph when he told his brothers who he was. 2 He sobbed so loudly that the Egyptians heard him. Everyone in Pharaoh’s house heard about it.

3 Joseph said to his brothers, “I am Joseph! Is my father still alive?”

But his brothers weren’t able to answer him. They were too afraid of him.

4 Joseph said to his brothers, “Come close to me.” So they did.

Then he said, “I am your brother Joseph. I’m the one you sold into Egypt. 5 But don’t be upset. And don’t be angry with yourselves because you sold me here. God sent me ahead of you to save many lives.

6 “For two years now, there hasn’t been enough food in the land. And for the next five years, people won’t be plowing or gathering crops. 7 But God sent me ahead of you to keep some of you alive on earth. He sent me here to save your lives by an act of mighty power.

8 “So then, it wasn’t you who sent me here. It was God. He made me like a father to Pharaoh. He made me master of Pharaoh’s whole house. He made me ruler of the whole land of Egypt.

9 “Now hurry back to my father. Say to him, ‘Your son Joseph says, “God has made me master of the whole land of Egypt. Come down to me. Don’t waste any time. 10 You will live in the area of Goshen. You, your children and grandchildren, your flocks and herds, and everything you have will be near me. 11 There I will provide everything you need.

“‘“Five years without enough food are still coming. If you don’t come down here, you and your family and everyone who belongs to you will lose everything.”’

12 “Brothers, you can see for yourselves that it’s really I, Joseph, speaking to you. My brother Benjamin can see it too.

13 “Tell my father about all of the honor that has been given to me in Egypt. Tell him about everything you have seen. And bring my father down here quickly.”

14 Then Joseph threw his arms around his brother Benjamin and sobbed. Benjamin also hugged him and sobbed. 15 Joseph kissed all of his brothers and sobbed over them. After that, his brothers talked with him.

16 The news reached Pharaoh’s palace that Joseph’s brothers had come. Pharaoh and all of his officials were pleased.

17 Pharaoh said to Joseph, “Here’s what I want you to tell your brothers. Say to them, ‘Load your animals. Return to the land of Canaan. 18 Bring your father and your families back to me. I’ll give you the best land in Egypt. You can enjoy all of the good things in the land.’

19 “And here’s something else I want you to tell them. Say to them, ‘Take some carts from Egypt. Your children and your wives can use them. Get your father and come back. 20 Don’t worry about

the things you have back there. The best of everything in Egypt will belong to you.'"
21 So the sons of Israel did it. Joseph gave them
carts, as Pharaoh had commanded. He also gave
them supplies for their journey. 22 He gave new
clothes to each of them.
But he gave more than seven pounds of silver to
Benjamin. He also gave him five sets of clothes.
23 He sent his father ten donkeys loaded with the
best things from Egypt. He also sent ten female
donkeys loaded with grain and bread and other
supplies for his journey.
24 Then Joseph sent his brothers away. As they
were leaving he said to them, "Don't argue on the
way!"
25 So they went up out of Egypt. They came to
their father Jacob in the land of Canaan. 26 They
told him, "Joseph is still alive! In fact, he is ruler
of the whole land of Egypt."
Jacob was shocked. He didn't believe them.
27 So they told him everything Joseph had said to
them.
Jacob saw the carts Joseph had sent to carry him
back. That gave new life to their father Jacob. 28 Israel said, "I believe it now! My son Joseph is still
alive. I'll go and see him before I die."

Jacob Goes Down to Egypt

46 So Israel started out with everything that
belonged to him. When he reached Beer-
sheba, he offered sacrifices to the God of his father
Isaac.
2 God spoke to Israel in a vision at night. "Jacob! Jacob!" he said.
"Here I am," Jacob replied.
3 "I am God. I am the God of your father," he
said. "Do not be afraid to go down to Egypt. There
I will make you into a great nation. 4 I will go down
to Egypt with you. You can be sure that I will bring
you back again. And when you die, Joseph will
close your eyes with his own hand."
5 Then Jacob left Beersheba. Israel's sons put
their father Jacob and their families in the carts
that Pharaoh had sent to carry them.
6 So Jacob and his whole family went to Egypt.
They took their livestock with them. And they took
everything they had gotten in Canaan. 7 Jacob took
his sons and grandsons with him to Egypt. He also
took his daughters and granddaughters. He took all
of his children and grandchildren with him.

8 Here are the names of Israel's children and
grandchildren who went to Egypt. Jacob and all of
his children and grandchildren are included.

Reuben was Jacob's oldest son.

9 The sons of Reuben were
Hanoch, Pallu, Hezron and Carmi.
10 The sons of Simeon were
Jemuel, Jamin, Ohad, Jakin, Zohar and
Shaul. Shaul was the son of a woman
from Canaan.
11 The sons of Levi were
Gershon, Kohath and Merari.
12 The sons of Judah were
Er, Onan, Shelah, Perez and Zerah. But
Er and Onan had died in the land of
Canaan. The sons of Perez were Hez-
ron and Hamul.
13 The sons of Issachar were
Tola, Puah, Jashub and Shimron.
14 The sons of Zebulun were
Sered, Elon and Jahleel.

15 Those were the sons and grandsons who were
born to Jacob and Leah in Paddan Aram. Leah also
had a daughter by Jacob. Her name was Dinah.
The total number of people in the family line of
Jacob and Leah was 33.

16 The sons of Gad were
Zephon, Haggi, Shuni, Ezbon, Eri, Arodi and Areli.
17 The sons of Asher were
Imnah, Ishvah, Ishvi and Beriah. Their
sister was Serah. The sons of Beriah
were Heber and Malkiel.

18 Those were the children and grandchildren
who were born to Jacob and Zilpah. Laban had
given Zilpah to his daughter Leah. The total number of people in the family line of Jacob and Zilpah was 16.

19 The sons of Jacob's wife Rachel were
Joseph and Benjamin. 20 In Egypt, Asenath
had Manasseh and Ephraim by Joseph.
Asenath was the daughter of Potiph-
era. Potiphera was the priest of On.
21 The sons of Benjamin were
Bela, Beker, Ashbel, Gera, Naaman, Ehi,
Rosh, Muppim, Huppim and Ard.

22 Those were the sons and grandsons who were
born to Jacob and Rachel. The total number of people in the family line of Jacob and Rachel was 14.

23 The son of Dan was
Hushim.
24 The sons of Naphtali were
Jahziel, Guni, Jezer and Shillem.

25 Those were the sons and grandsons who were
born to Jacob and Bilhah. Laban had given Bilhah
to his daughter Rachel. The total number of people
in the family line of Jacob and Bilhah was seven.

26 The total number of those who went to Egypt
with Jacob was 66. That number includes only his
own children and grandchildren. It doesn't include
his sons' wives or his grandsons' wives.
27 The total number of the members of Jacob's
family who went to Egypt was 70. That includes the
two sons who had been born to Joseph in Egypt.

28 Jacob sent Judah ahead of him to Joseph. He
sent him to get directions to Goshen. And so they
arrived in the area of Goshen.

29Then Joseph had his servants get his chariot
ready. He went to Goshen to meet his father Israel. As soon as he came to his father, Joseph threw
his arms around him. Then Joseph sobbed for a
long time.
30Israel said to Joseph, "I have seen for myself
that you are still alive. Now I'm ready to die."
31Then Joseph spoke to his brothers and to the
rest of his father's family. He said, "I will go up
and speak to Pharaoh. I'll say to him, 'My brothers and the rest of my father's family have come to
me. They were living in the land of Canaan. 32The
men are shepherds. They take care of livestock.
They've brought along their flocks and herds and
everything they own.'
33"Pharaoh will send for you. He'll ask, 'What do
you do for a living?' 34You should answer, 'We've
taken care of livestock from the time we were boys.
We've done just as our fathers did.' It's the practice
of the people of Egypt not to mix with shepherds.

"So Pharaoh will let you settle in the area of
Goshen."

47 Joseph went to Pharaoh. He told him, "My
father and brothers have come from the
land of Canaan. They've brought along their
flocks and herds and everything they own. They
are now in Goshen."
2Joseph had chosen five of his brothers to meet
with Pharaoh.
3Pharaoh asked the brothers, "What do you do
for a living?"

"We're shepherds," they replied to Pharaoh.
"And that's what our fathers were." 4They also
said to him, "We've come to live in Egypt for a
while. There isn't enough food anywhere in Canaan. There isn't any grass for our flocks. So
please let us settle in Goshen."
5Pharaoh said to Joseph, "Your father and your
brothers have come to you. 6The land of Egypt is
open to you. Settle your father and brothers in the
best part of the land. Let them live in Goshen. Do
any of them have special skills? If they do, put
them in charge of my own livestock."
7Then Joseph brought his father Jacob in. He
brought him in to meet Pharaoh. Jacob gave Pharaoh his blessing. 8Then Pharaoh asked him, "How
old are you?"
9Jacob said to Pharaoh, "The years of my journey through life are 130. My years have been few
and hard. They aren't as many as the years of my
fathers before me."
10Jacob gave Pharaoh his blessing. Then he left
him.
11So Joseph settled his father and his brothers in
Egypt. He gave them property in the best part of
the land, just as Pharaoh had directed him to do.
That part was known as the territory of Rameses.
12Joseph also provided food for his father and
brothers. He provided for them and the rest of his
father's family. He gave them enough for all of
their children.

Joseph Saves Many Lives

13But there wasn't any food in the whole area.
In fact, there wasn't enough food anywhere. Both
Egypt and Canaan lost their strength because there
wasn't enough food to go around.
14Joseph collected all of the money that was in
Egypt and Canaan. People paid it to him for the
grain they were buying. And Joseph brought it to
Pharaoh's palace.
15When the money of the people of Egypt and
Canaan was gone, all of the Egyptians came to Joseph. They said, "Give us food. Why should we die
right in front of your eyes? Our money is all gone."
16"Then bring your livestock," said Joseph.
"You say your money is gone. So I'll trade you
food for your livestock."
17They brought their livestock to Joseph. He
traded them food for their animals. They gave him
their horses, sheep, goats, cattle and donkeys. He
brought the people through that year by trading
them food for all of their livestock.
18When that year was over, they came to him
the next year. They said, "We can't hide the truth
from you. Our money is gone. Our livestock
belongs to you. We don't have anything left to give
you except our bodies and our land.
19"Why should we die right in front of your
eyes? Why should our land be destroyed as well?
Trade us food for ourselves and our land. Then we
and our land will belong to Pharaoh. Give us some
seeds so we can live and not die. We don't want
the land to become a desert."
20So Joseph bought all of the land in Egypt for
Pharaoh. All of the people of Egypt sold their
fields. They did that because there wasn't enough
food anywhere. In that way, the land became Pharaoh's. 21Joseph made the people slaves from one
end of Egypt to the other.
22But he didn't buy the land that belonged to the
priests. They received a regular share of food from
Pharaoh. They had enough food from what Pharaoh gave them. That's why they didn't have to sell
their land.
23Joseph said to the people, "I've bought you
and your land today for Pharaoh. So here are some
seeds for you to plant in the ground. 24But when
the crop comes in, give a fifth of it to Pharaoh.
Keep the other four-fifths for yourselves. They
will be seeds for the fields. And they will be food
for yourselves, your children, and the other people who live with you."
25"You have saved our lives," they said. "If you
are pleased with us, we will be slaves to Pharaoh."
26So Joseph made a law about land in Egypt. It's
still the law today. A fifth of the produce belongs
to Pharaoh. Only the land belonging to the priests
didn't become Pharaoh's.
27The people of Israel settled in Egypt in the
area of Goshen. They received property there.
They had children and greatly increased their
numbers.

28 Jacob lived 17 years in Egypt. He lived a total of 147 years.

29 The time came near for Israel to die. So he sent for his son Joseph. He said to him, "If you are pleased with me, put your hand under my thigh. Promise me that you will be kind and faithful to me. Don't bury me in Egypt. 30 When I join the members of my family who have already died, carry me out of Egypt. Bury me where they are buried."

"I'll do exactly as you say," Joseph said.

31 "Promise me with an oath that you will do it," Jacob said. So Joseph promised him. And Israel worshiped God as he leaned on the top of his wooden staff.

Ephraim and Manasseh

48 Some time later Joseph was told, "Your father is sick." So he took his two sons Manasseh and Ephraim along with him. 2 Jacob was told, "Your son Joseph has come to you." So Israel became stronger and sat up in bed.

3 Jacob said to Joseph, "The Mighty God appeared to me at Luz in the land of Canaan. He blessed me there. 4 He said to me, 'I am going to give you children. I will increase your numbers. I will make you a community of nations. And I will give this land to your children after you. It will belong to them forever.'

5 "Now then, two sons were born to you in Egypt. It happened before I came to you here. They will be counted as my own sons. Ephraim and Manasseh will belong to me, in the same way that Reuben and Simeon belong to me.

6 "Any children who are born to you after them will belong to you. Any territory they receive will come from the land that is given to Ephraim and Manasseh.

7 "As I was returning from Paddan, Rachel died. It made me very sad. She died in the land of Canaan while we were still on the way. We weren't very far away from Ephrath. So I buried her body there beside the road to Ephrath." Ephrath was also called Bethlehem.

8 Israel saw Joseph's sons. He asked, "Who are they?"

9 "They are the sons God has given me here," Joseph said to his father.

Then Israel said, "Bring them to me. I want to give them my blessing."

10 Israel's eyes were weak because he was old. He couldn't see very well. So Joseph brought his sons close to him. His father kissed them and hugged them.

11 Israel said to Joseph, "I never thought I'd see your face again. But now God has let me see your children too."

12 Then Joseph took his sons away from Israel's knees. He bowed down with his face to the ground.

13 Joseph placed Ephraim on his right, toward Israel's left hand. He placed Manasseh on his left, toward Israel's right hand. Then he brought them close to Jacob.

14 But Israel reached out his right hand and put it on Ephraim's head. He did it even though Ephraim was the younger son. He crossed his arms and put his left hand on Manasseh's head. He did it even though Manasseh was the older son.

15 Then Israel gave Joseph his blessing. He said,

"May God bless these boys.
He is the God of my grandfather Abraham and my father Isaac.
They walked with him.
He is the God who has been my shepherd all of my life to this very day.
16 He is the Angel who has saved me from all harm.
May he bless these boys.
May they be called by my name.
May they also be called by the names of my grandfather Abraham and my father Isaac.
And may they greatly increase their numbers on the earth."

17 Joseph saw his father putting his right hand on Ephraim's head. And Joseph didn't like it. So he took hold of his father's hand to move it over to Manasseh's head. 18 Joseph said to him, "No, my father. Here's my older son. Put your right hand on his head."

19 But his father wouldn't do it. He said, "I know, my son. I know. He too will become a nation. He too will become great. But his younger brother will be greater than he is. His children after him will become a group of nations."

20 On that day, Jacob gave them his blessing. He said,

"In the land of Israel, people will bless others in your names.
They will say, 'May God make you like Ephraim and Manasseh.'"

So he put Ephraim ahead of Manasseh.

21 Then Israel said to Joseph, "I'm about to die. But God will be with all of you. He'll take you back to the land of your fathers. 22 But you, Joseph, are over your brothers. So I'm giving you the range of hills I took from the Amorites. I took it with my sword and bow."

Jacob Gives Blessings to His Sons

49 Then Jacob sent for his sons. He said, "Gather around me so I can tell you what will happen to you in days to come.

2 "Sons of Jacob, come together and listen.
Listen to your father Israel.

3 "Reuben, you are my oldest son.
You were my first child. You were the first sign of my strength.

You were first in honor. You were first in
power.
4 But you are as unsteady as water. So you won't
be first anymore.
You had sex with your father's concubine in
his bed.
You lay on his couch and made it 'unclean.'

5 "Simeon and Levi are brothers.
Their swords have killed a lot of people.
6 I won't share in their plans.
I won't have anything to do with them.
They became angry and killed people.
They cut the legs of oxen just for the fun
of it.
7 May the LORD put a curse on them
because of their terrible anger.
I will scatter them in Jacob's land.
I will spread them around in Israel.

8 "Judah, your brothers will praise you.
Your enemies will be brought under your
control.
Your father's sons will bow down to you.
9 Judah, you are like a lion's cub.
You return from hunting, my son.
Like a lion, you lie down and sleep.
You are like a mother lion. Who dares to
wake you up?
10 The right to rule will not leave Judah.
The ruler's rod will not be taken from
between his feet.
It will be his until the king it belongs to comes.
It will be his until the nations obey him.
11 He will tie his donkey to a vine.
He will tie his colt to the very best branch.
He will wash his clothes in wine.
He will wash his robes in the red juice of
grapes.
12 His eyes will be darker than wine.
His teeth will be whiter than milk.

13 "Zebulun will live by the seashore.
He will become a safe harbor for ships.
His border will go out toward Sidon.

14 "Issachar is like a donkey
lying down between two saddlebags.
15 He sees how good his resting place is.
He sees that his land is pleasant.
So he'll carry a heavy load on his back.
He will obey when he's forced to work.

16 "Dan will do what is fair for his people.
He will do it as one of the tribes of Israel.
17 Dan will be a serpent by the side of the road.
He will be a poisonous snake along the path.
It bites the horse's heels
so that the rider falls off backward.

18 "LORD, I look to you to save me.

19 "Gad will be attacked by a group of robbers.
But he'll attack them as they run away.

20 "Asher's food will be rich and sweet.
He will provide food that even a king would
enjoy.

21 "Naphtali is a female deer that is set free
and gives birth to beautiful fawns.

22 "Joseph is a vine that grows a lot of fruit.
It grows close by a spring.
Its branches climb over a wall.
23 Mean people shot arrows at him.
They shot at him because they
were angry.
24 But his bow remained steady.
His strong arms moved freely.
The hand of the Mighty One of Jacob was
with him.
The Shepherd, the Rock of Israel, stood
by him.
25 Your father's God helps you.
The Mighty One blesses you.
He gives you blessings from the highest
heavens.
He gives you blessings from the deepest
oceans.
He blesses you with children and with a
mother's milk.
26 Your father's blessings are great.
They are greater than the blessings from the
age-old mountains.
They are greater than the gifts from the
ancient hills.
Let all of those blessings rest on the head of
Joseph.
Let them rest on the head of the one who is
prince among his brothers.

27 "Benjamin is a hungry wolf.
In the morning he eats what he has killed.
In the evening he shares what he has
stolen."

28 All of those are the 12 tribes of Israel. That's what their father said to them when he blessed them. He gave each one the blessing that was just right for him.

Jacob Dies

29 Then Jacob gave directions to his sons. He said, "I'm about to join the members of my family who have already died. Bury me with them in the cave in the field of Ephron the Hittite.

30 "The cave is in the field of Machpelah near Mamre in Canaan. Abraham had bought it as a place where he could bury his wife's body. He had bought the cave from Ephron the Hittite, along with the field.

31 "The bodies of Abraham and his wife Sarah were buried there. So were the bodies of Isaac and his wife Rebekah. I also buried Leah's body there.
32 Abraham bought the field and the cave from the Hittites."

33When Jacob had finished telling his sons what
to do, he pulled his feet up into his bed. Then he
took his last breath and joined the members of his
family who had already died.

50 Joseph threw himself on his father's body.
He sobbed over him and kissed him.
2Then Joseph talked to the doctors who served
him. He told them to prepare the body of his father
Israel to be buried. So the doctors prepared it.
3They took 40 days to do it. They needed that
much time to prepare a body in the right way. The
Egyptians sobbed over Jacob for 70 days.
4After the days of sorrow had passed, Joseph
went to Pharaoh's officials. He said to them, "If
you are pleased with me, speak to Pharaoh for me.
Tell him, 5'My father made me take an oath and
make a promise to him. He said, "I'm about to die.
Bury me in the tomb I dug for myself in the land
of Canaan." So let me go up and bury my father.
Then I'll come back.'"
6Pharaoh said, "Go up and bury your father. Do
what he made you promise to do."
7So Joseph went up to bury his father. All of
Pharaoh's officials went with him. They were the
important people of his court and all of the leaders
of Egypt.
8All of Joseph's family also went. His brothers
and all of the rest of his father's family went too.
Only their children and their flocks and herds were
left in Goshen.
9Chariots and horsemen also went up with him.
It was a very large group.
10They came to the threshing floor of Atad. It
was near the Jordan River. There they sobbed
loudly and bitterly. Joseph set apart seven days of
sadness to honor his father's memory.
11The people of Canaan who were living there
saw how sad all of them were at the threshing floor
of Atad. They said, "The Egyptians are having a
very special service for the dead." That's why that
place near the Jordan River is called Abel of the
Egyptians.
12So Jacob's sons did exactly as he had commanded them. 13They carried his body to the land
of Canaan. They buried it in the cave in the field of
Machpelah near Mamre. Abraham had bought the
cave as a place where he could bury his wife's
body. He had bought it from Ephron the Hittite,
along with the field.
14After Joseph buried his father, he went back
to Egypt. His brothers and all of the others who
had gone to help him bury his father went back
with him.

Joseph Sets His Brothers Free From Their Fears

15Now that their father was dead, Joseph's
brothers were worried. They said, "Remember all
of the bad things we did to Joseph? What if he
decides to hold those things against us? What if he
pays us back for them?"
16So they sent a message to Joseph. They said,
"Your father gave us directions before he died.
17He said, 'Here's what you must say to Joseph.
Tell him, "I'm asking you to forgive your brothers. Forgive the terrible things they did to you.
Forgive them for treating you so badly."' Now
then, please forgive our sins. We serve the God of
your father."
When their message came to Joseph, he sobbed.
18Then his brothers came and threw themselves
down in front of him. "We are your slaves," they
said.
19But Joseph said to them, "Don't be afraid. Do
you think I'm God? 20You planned to harm me. But
God planned it for good. He planned to do what is
now being done. He wanted to save many lives.
21"So then, don't be afraid. I'll provide for you
and your children." He set them free from their
fears. And he spoke in a kind way to them.

Joseph Dies

22Joseph stayed in Egypt, along with all of his
father's family. He lived 110 years. 23He lived long
enough to see Ephraim's children and grandchildren. When the children of Makir were born, they
were placed on Joseph's knees and counted as his
own children. Makir was the son of Manasseh.
24Joseph said to his brothers, "I'm about to die.
But I'm sure that God will come to help you. He'll
take you up out of this land. He'll bring you to the
land he promised with an oath to give to Abraham,
Isaac and Jacob."
25Joseph made the sons of Israel take an oath
and make a promise to him. He said, "I'm sure that
God will come to help you. Then you must carry
my bones up from this place."
26So Joseph died at the age of 110. They prepared his body to be buried. Then he was placed
in a casket in Egypt.

Exodus

The People of Israel Are Slaves in Egypt

1 Here are the names of Israel's children who went to Egypt with Jacob. Each one went with his family.

2Jacob's sons were Reuben, Simeon, Levi, Judah, 3Issachar, Zebulun, Benjamin, 4Dan, Naphtali, Gad and Asher. 5The total number of Jacob's children and grandchildren was 70. Joseph was already in Egypt.

6Joseph and all of his brothers died. So did all of their children.

7The people of Israel had many children. They greatly increased their numbers. There were so many of them that they filled the land.

8Then a new king came to power in Egypt. He didn't know anything about Joseph.

9"Look," he said to his people. "The Israelites are far too many for us. 10Come. We must deal with them carefully. If we don't, they will increase their numbers even more. Then if war breaks out, they'll join our enemies. They'll fight against us and leave the country."

11So the Egyptians put slave drivers over the people of Israel. The slave drivers beat them down and made them work hard. The Israelites built the cities of Pithom and Rameses so Pharaoh could store things there.

12But the more the slave drivers beat them down, the more the Israelites increased their numbers and spread out. So the Egyptians became afraid of them. 13They made them work hard. They didn't show them any pity. 14They made them suffer with hard labor. They forced them to work with bricks and mud. And they made them do all kinds of work in the fields. The Egyptians didn't show them any pity at all. They made them work very hard.

15There were two Hebrew women named Shiphrah and Puah. They helped other women who were having babies. The king of Egypt spoke to them. He said, 16"You are the ones who help the other Hebrew women. Watch them when they get into a sitting position to have their babies. Kill the boys. Let the girls live."

17But Shiphrah and Puah had respect for God. They didn't do what the king of Egypt had told them to do. They let the boys live.

18Then the king of Egypt sent for the women. He asked them, "Why have you done this? Why have you let the boys live?"

19The women answered Pharaoh, "Hebrew women are not like the women of Egypt. They are strong. They have their babies before we get there."

20So God was kind to Shiphrah and Puah. And the people of Israel increased their numbers more and more. 21Shiphrah and Puah had respect for God. So he gave them families of their own.

22Then Pharaoh gave an order to all of his people. He said, "You must throw every baby boy into the Nile River. But let every baby girl live."

Moses Is Born

2 A man and a woman from the tribe of Levi got married. 2She became pregnant and had a son by him. She saw that her baby was a fine child. So she hid him for three months.

3After that, she couldn't hide him any longer. So she got a basket that was made out of the stems of tall grass. She coated it with tar. Then she placed the child in it. She put the basket in the tall grass that grew along the bank of the Nile River. 4The child's sister wasn't very far away. She wanted to see what would happen to him.

5Pharaoh's daughter went down to the Nile River to take a bath. Her attendants were walking along the bank of the river. She saw the basket in the tall grass. So she sent her female slave to get it. 6When she opened it, she saw the baby. He was crying. She felt sorry for him. "This is one of the Hebrew babies," she said.

7Then his sister spoke to Pharaoh's daughter. She asked, "Do you want me to go and get one of the Hebrew women? She could nurse the baby for you."

8"Yes. Go," she answered. So the girl went and got the baby's mother.

9Pharaoh's daughter said to her, "Take this baby. Nurse him for me. I'll pay you." So the woman took the baby and nursed him.

10When the child grew older, she took him to Pharaoh's daughter. And he became her son. She named him Moses. She said, "I pulled him out of the water."

Moses Escapes to Midian

11Moses grew up. One day, he went out to where his own people were. He watched them while they were hard at work. He saw an Egyptian hitting a Hebrew man. The man was one of Moses' own people. 12Moses looked around and didn't see anyone. So he killed the Egyptian. Then he hid his body in the sand.

13The next day Moses went out again. He saw two Hebrew men fighting. He asked the one who had started the fight a question. He said, "Why are you hitting another Hebrew man?"

14The man said, "Who made you ruler and judge over us? Are you thinking about killing me as you killed the Egyptian?"

Then Moses became afraid. He thought, "People must have heard about what I did."

15When Pharaoh heard about what had happened, he tried to kill Moses. But Moses escaped from Pharaoh and went to live in Midian. There he sat down by a well.

16A priest of Midian had seven daughters. They came to fill the stone tubs with water. They wanted to give water to their father's flock. 17Some shepherds came along and drove the women away. But Moses got up and helped them. Then he gave water to their flock.

18The young women returned to their father Reuel. He asked them, "Why have you returned so early today?"

19They answered, "An Egyptian saved us from the shepherds. He even got water for us and gave it to the flock."

20"Where is he?" he asked his daughters. "Why did you leave him? Invite him to have something to eat."

21Moses agreed to stay with the man. And the man gave his daughter Zipporah to Moses to be his wife. 22Zipporah had a son by him. Moses named him Gershom. Moses said, "I'm an outsider in a strange land."

23After a long time, the king of Egypt died. The people of Israel groaned because they were slaves. They also cried out to God. Their cry for help went up to him. 24God heard their groans. He remembered his covenant with Abraham, Isaac and Jacob. 25So God looked on the Israelites with favor. He was concerned about them.

The LORD Sends Moses to Save His People

3 Moses was taking care of the flock of his father-in-law Jethro. Jethro was the priest of Midian. Moses led the flock to the western side of the desert. He came to Horeb. It was the mountain of God.

2There the angel of the LORD appeared to him from inside a burning bush. Moses saw that the bush was on fire. But it didn't burn up. 3So Moses thought, "I'll go over and see this strange sight. Why doesn't the bush burn up?"

4The LORD saw that Moses had gone over to look. So God spoke to him from inside the bush. He called out, "Moses! Moses!"

"Here I am," Moses said.

5"Do not come any closer," God said. "Take off your sandals. The place you are standing on is holy ground." 6He continued, "I am the God of your father. I am the God of Abraham. I am the God of Isaac. And I am the God of Jacob."

When Moses heard that, he turned his face away. He was afraid to look at God.

7The LORD said, "I have seen my people suffer in Egypt. I have heard them cry out because of their slave drivers. I am concerned about their suffering.

8"So I have come down to save them from the Egyptians. I will bring them up out of that land. I will bring them into a good land. It has a lot of room. It is a land that has plenty of milk and honey. It is the home of the Canaanites, Hittites, Amorites, Perizzites, Hivites and Jebusites.

9"And now Israel's cry for help has reached me. I have seen the way the Egyptians are beating them down. 10So now, go. I am sending you to Pharaoh. I want you to bring the Israelites out of Egypt. They are my people."

11But Moses spoke to God. "Who am I that I should go to Pharaoh?" he said. "Who am I that I should bring the Israelites out of Egypt?"

12God said, "I will be with you. I will give you a miraculous sign. It will prove that I have sent you. When you have brought the people out of Egypt, all of you will worship me on this mountain."

13Moses said to God, "Suppose I go to the people of Israel. Suppose I say to them, 'The God of your fathers has sent me to you.' Suppose they ask me, 'What is his name?' Then what should I tell them?"

14God said to Moses, "I AM WHO I AM. Here is what you must say to the Israelites. Tell them, 'I AM has sent me to you.'"

15God also said to Moses, "Say to the Israelites, 'The LORD is the God of your fathers. He has sent me to you. He is the God of Abraham. He is the God of Isaac. And he is the God of Jacob.' My name will always be The LORD. Remember me by that name for all time to come.

16"Go. Gather the elders of Israel together. Say to them, 'The LORD, the God of your fathers, appeared to me. He is the God of Abraham, Isaac and Jacob.

"'He said, "I have watched over you. I have seen what the Egyptians have done to you. 17I have promised to bring you up out of Egypt where you are suffering. I will bring you into the land of the Canaanites, Hittites, Amorites, Perizzites, Hivites and Jebusites. It is a land that has plenty of milk and honey."'

18"The elders of Israel will listen to you. Then you and the elders must go to the king of Egypt. You must say to him, 'The LORD has met with us. He is the God of the Hebrews. Let us take a journey that lasts about three days. We want to go into the desert to offer sacrifices to the LORD our God.'

19"But I know that the king of Egypt will not let you and your people go. Only a mighty hand could make him do that. 20So I will reach my hand out. I will strike the Egyptians with all kinds of miracles. After that, he will let you go.

21"I will cause the Egyptians to treat you in a kind way. Then when you leave, you will not go out with your hands empty. 22Every woman should ask her neighbor and any woman living in her house for articles made out of silver and gold. Ask them for clothes too. Put them on your children. In that way, you will take the wealth of Egypt along with you."

Miraculous Signs for Moses to Do

4 Moses answered, "What if the elders of Israel won't believe me? What if they won't listen to me? Suppose they say, 'The LORD didn't appear to you.' Then what should I do?"

2The LORD said to him, "What do you have in your hand?"

"A wooden staff," he said.

3The LORD said, "Throw it on the ground."

So Moses threw it on the ground. It turned into a snake. He ran away from it. 4Then the LORD said to Moses, "Reach your hand out. Take the snake by the tail." So he reached out and grabbed hold of the snake. It turned back into a staff in his hand.

5The LORD said, "When they see this miraculous sign, they will believe that I appeared to you. I am the God of their fathers. I am the God of Abraham. I am the God of Isaac. And I am the God of Jacob."

6Then the LORD said, "Put your hand inside your coat." So Moses put his hand inside his coat. When he took it out, it was as white as snow. It was covered with a skin disease.

7"Now put it back into your coat," the LORD said. So Moses put his hand back into his coat. When he took it out, the skin was healthy again. His hand was like the rest of his skin.

8Then the LORD said, "Suppose they do not believe you or pay attention to the first miracle. Then maybe they will believe the second one.

9"But suppose they do not believe either miracle. Suppose they will not listen to you. Then get some water from the Nile River. Pour it on the dry ground. The water you take from the river will turn to blood on the ground."

10Moses spoke to the LORD. He said, "Lord, I've never been a good speaker. And I haven't gotten any better since you spoke to me. I don't speak very well at all."

11The LORD said to him, "Who makes a man able to talk? Who makes him unable to hear or speak? Who makes him able to see? Who makes him blind? It is I, the LORD. 12Now go. I will help you speak. I will teach you what to say."

13But Moses said, "Lord, please send someone else to do it."

14Then the LORD's anger burned against Moses. He said, "What about your brother, Aaron the Levite? I know he can speak well. He is already on his way to meet you. He will be glad to see you. 15Speak to him. Put your words in his mouth. Tell him what to say. I will help both of you speak. I will teach you what to do. 16He will speak to the people for you. He will be like your mouth. And you will be like God to him.

17"But take this wooden staff in your hand. You will be able to do miraculous signs with it."

Moses Returns to Egypt

18Then Moses went back to his father-in-law Jethro. He said to him, "Let me go back to my own people in Egypt. I want to see if any of them are still alive."

Jethro said, "Go. I hope everything goes well with you."

19The LORD had said to Moses in Midian, "Go back to Egypt. All of the men who wanted to kill you are dead."

20So Moses got his wife and sons. He put them on a donkey. Together they started back to Egypt. And he took the wooden staff in his hand. It was the staff God would use in a powerful way.

21The LORD spoke to Moses. He said, "When you return to Egypt, do all of the miracles I have given you the power to do. Do them in the sight of Pharaoh. But I will make his heart stubborn. He will not let the people go.

22"Then say to Pharaoh, 'The LORD says, "Israel is like an oldest son to me. 23I told you, 'Let my son go. Then he will be able to worship me.' But you refused to let him go. So I will kill your oldest son."'"

24On the way to Egypt, Moses stopped for the night. There the LORD met him and was about to kill him.

25But Zipporah got a knife that was made out of hard stone. She circumcised her son with it. Then she touched Moses' feet with the skin she had cut off. "You are a husband who has forced me to spill my son's blood," she said. 26So the LORD didn't kill Moses. When she said "husband who has forced me to spill my son's blood," she was talking about circumcision.

27The LORD said to Aaron, "Go into the desert to see Moses." So he greeted Moses at the mountain of God and kissed him.

28Then Moses told Aaron everything the LORD had sent him to say. He also told him about all of the miraculous signs he had commanded him to do.

29Moses and Aaron gathered all of the elders of Israel together. 30Aaron told them everything the LORD had said to Moses. He also did the miracles in the sight of the people.

31And they believed. They heard that the LORD was concerned about them. He had seen their suffering. So they bowed down and worshiped him.

Pharaoh Makes the Israelites Work Even Harder

5 Later on, Moses and Aaron went to Pharaoh. They said, "The LORD is the God of Israel. He says, 'Let my people go. Then they will be able to hold a feast in my honor in the desert.'"

2Pharaoh said, "Who is the LORD? Why should I obey him? Why should I let Israel go? I don't even know the LORD. And I won't let Israel go."

3Then Moses and Aaron said, "The God of the Hebrews has met with us. Now let us take a journey that lasts about three days. We want to go into the desert to offer sacrifices to the LORD our God. If we don't, he might strike us with plagues. Or he might let us be killed with swords."

4But the king of Egypt said, "Moses and Aaron, why are you taking the people away from their work? Get back to work!" 5Pharaoh continued,

"There are large numbers of your people in the land. But you are stopping them from working."

6That same day Pharaoh gave orders to the slave drivers and the others who were in charge of the people. 7He said, "Don't give the people any more straw to make bricks. Let them go and get their own straw. 8But require them to make the same number of bricks as before. Don't lower the number they have to make. They don't want to work. That's why they are crying out, 'Let us go. We want to offer sacrifices to our God.' 9Make them work harder. Then they will be too busy to pay attention to lies."

10The slave drivers and the others who were in charge left. They said to the people, "Pharaoh says, 'I won't give you any more straw. 11Go and get your own straw anywhere you can find it. But you still have to make the same number of bricks.'"

12So the people scattered all over Egypt. They went to gather any pieces of straw that were left in the fields.

13The slave drivers kept making the people work hard. They said, "Finish the work you are required to do each day. Make the same number of bricks you made when you had straw." 14They whipped the Israelites who were in charge of the people. Those Israelites had been appointed by Pharaoh's slave drivers. The slave drivers asked, "Why didn't you make the same number of bricks yesterday or today, just as before?"

15Then the Israelites who were in charge of the people made their appeal to Pharaoh. They asked, "Why have you treated us like this? 16You didn't give us any straw. But you told us, 'Make bricks!' We are being whipped. But it's the fault of your own people."

17Pharaoh said, "You just don't want to work! That's why you keep saying, 'Let us go. We want to offer sacrifices to the LORD.' 18Now get to work. We won't give you any straw. But you still have to make the same number of bricks."

19The Israelites who were in charge of the people realized they were in trouble. They knew it when they were told, "Don't lower the number of bricks you are required to make each day."

20When they left Pharaoh, they found Moses and Aaron waiting to meet them. 21They said to Moses and Aaron, "We want the LORD to look at what you have done! We want him to judge you for it! We are like a very bad smell to Pharaoh and his officials. You have given them an excuse to kill us with their swords."

The LORD Promises to Save the Israelites

22Moses returned to the LORD. He said to him, "Lord, why have you brought trouble on these people? Is this why you sent me? 23I went to Pharaoh to speak to him in your name. Ever since then, he has brought nothing but trouble on these people. And you haven't saved your people at all."

6 Then the LORD spoke to Moses. He said, "Now you will see what I will do to Pharaoh. Because of my powerful hand, he will let the people of Israel go. Because of my mighty hand, he will drive them out of his country."

2God continued, "I am the LORD. 3I appeared to Abraham, Isaac and Jacob as the Mighty God. But I did not show them the full meaning of my name, The LORD.

4"I also made my covenant with them. I promised to give them the land of Canaan. That is where they lived as outsiders. 5Also, I have heard the groans of the Israelites. The Egyptians are keeping them as slaves. But I have remembered my covenant.

6"So tell the people of Israel, 'I am the LORD. I will throw off the heavy load the Egyptians have put on your shoulders. I will set you free from being slaves to them. I will reach out my arm and save you with mighty acts when I judge Egypt.

7"'I will take you to be my own people. I will be your God. You will know that I am the LORD your God when I throw off the load the Egyptians have put on your shoulders.

8"'I will bring you to the land I promised with an oath to give to Abraham, Isaac and Jacob. I lifted up my hand and promised it to them. The land will belong to you. I am the LORD.'"

9Moses reported those things to the Israelites. But they didn't listen to him. That's because they had lost all hope and had to work very hard.

10Then the LORD said to Moses, 11"Go. Tell Pharaoh, the king of Egypt, to let the people of Israel leave his country."

12But Moses spoke to the LORD. "The people won't listen to me," he said. "So why would Pharaoh listen to me? After all, I don't speak very well."

The Family Line of Moses and Aaron

13The LORD had spoken to Moses and Aaron. He had talked with them about the Israelites and about Pharaoh, the king of Egypt. He had commanded Moses and Aaron to bring the people of Israel out of Egypt.

14Here were the leaders of the family groups of Reuben, Simeon and Levi.

Reuben was the oldest son of Israel. His sons were Hanoch, Pallu, Hezron and Carmi. Those were the family groups of Reuben.

15The sons of Simeon were Jemuel, Jamin, Ohad, Jakin, Zohar and Shaul. Shaul was the son of a woman from Canaan. Those were the family groups of Simeon.

16Here were the names of the sons of Levi that were recorded in their family history. They were Gershon, Kohath and Merari. Levi lived for 137 years.

17The sons of Gershon, by their family groups, were Libni and Shimei.

18The sons of Kohath were Amram, Izhar, Hebron and Uzziel. Kohath lived for 133 years.

19The sons of Merari were Mahli and Mushi.

Those were the family groups of Levi that were recorded in their family history.

20Amram got married to his father's sister Jochebed. Aaron and Moses were born in Amram's family line. Amram lived for 137 years.

21The sons of Izhar were Korah, Nepheg and Zicri.

22The sons of Uzziel were Mishael, Elzaphan and Sithri.

23Aaron married Elisheba. She was the daughter of Amminadab and the sister of Nahshon. She had Nadab, Abihu, Eleazar and Ithamar by Aaron.

24The sons of Korah were Assir, Elkanah and Abiasaph. Those were the family groups of Korah.

25Eleazar, the son of Aaron, married one of the daughters of Putiel. She had Phinehas by Eleazar.

Those were the leaders of the families of Levi that were recorded by their groups.

26The LORD had spoken to that same Aaron and Moses. He had told them, "Bring the Israelites out of Egypt like an army on the march." 27They spoke to Pharaoh, the king of Egypt, about bringing the people of Israel out of Egypt. They were that same Moses and Aaron.

Aaron Speaks for Moses

28The LORD had spoken to Moses in Egypt. 29He had told him, "I am the LORD. Tell Pharaoh, the king of Egypt, everything I tell you."

30But Moses said to the LORD, "I don't speak very well. So why would Pharaoh listen to me?"

7 Then the LORD said to Moses, "I have made you like God to Pharaoh. And your brother Aaron will be like a prophet to you. 2You must say everything I command you to say. Then your brother Aaron must tell Pharaoh to let the people of Israel leave his country.

3"But I will make Pharaoh's heart stubborn. I will multiply my miraculous signs and wonders in Egypt. 4In spite of that, he will not listen to you. So I will use my powerful hand against Egypt. When I judge them with mighty acts, I will bring my people Israel out like an army on the march.

5"Then the Egyptians will know that I am the LORD. I will reach out my powerful hand against Egypt. I will bring the people of Israel out of it."

6Moses and Aaron did exactly as the LORD had commanded them. 7Moses was 80 years old and Aaron was 83 when they spoke to Pharaoh.

Aaron's Wooden Staff Becomes a Snake

8The LORD spoke to Moses and Aaron. 9He said, "Pharaoh will say to you, 'Do a miracle.' When he does, speak to Aaron. Tell him, 'Take your wooden staff and throw it down in front of Pharaoh.' It will turn into a snake."

10So Moses and Aaron went to Pharaoh. They did exactly as the LORD had commanded them. Aaron threw his staff down in front of Pharaoh and his officials. It turned into a snake.

11Then Pharaoh sent for wise men and those who do evil magic. By doing their magic tricks, the Egyptian magicians did the same things Aaron had done. 12Each one threw his staff down. Each staff turned into a snake. But Aaron's staff swallowed theirs up.

13In spite of that, Pharaoh's heart became stubborn. He wouldn't listen to them, just as the LORD had said.

The Nile River Turns Into Blood

14Then the LORD said to Moses, "Pharaoh's heart is very stubborn. He refuses to let the people go. 15In the morning Pharaoh will go down to the water. Go and wait on the bank of the Nile River to meet him. Take in your hand the wooden staff that turned into a snake.

16"Say to Pharaoh, 'The LORD, the God of the Hebrews, has sent me to you. He says, "Let my people go. Then they will be able to worship me in the desert. But up to now you have not listened."

17"'The LORD says, "Here is how you will know that I am the LORD. I will strike the water of the Nile River with the staff that is in my hand. The river will turn into blood. 18The fish in the river will die. The river will stink. The Egyptians will not be able to drink its water."'"

19The LORD said to Moses, "Tell Aaron, 'Get your staff. Reach your hand out over the waters of Egypt. The streams, waterways, ponds and all of the lakes will turn into blood. There will be blood everywhere in Egypt. It will even be in the wooden buckets and stone jars.'"

20Moses and Aaron did exactly as the LORD had commanded them. Aaron held out his staff in front of Pharaoh and his officials. He struck the water of the Nile River. And all of the water turned into blood.

21The fish in the Nile died. The river smelled so bad the Egyptians couldn't drink its water. There was blood everywhere in Egypt.

22But the Egyptian magicians did the same things by doing their magic tricks. So Pharaoh's heart became stubborn. He wouldn't listen to Moses and Aaron, just as the LORD had said. 23Even that miracle didn't change Pharaoh's mind. In fact, he turned around and went into his palace.

24All of the Egyptians dug holes near the Nile River to get drinking water. They couldn't drink water from the river.

The Plague of Frogs

25Seven days passed after the LORD struck the Nile River.

8 1Then the LORD said to Moses, "Go to Pharaoh. Tell him, 'The LORD says,

"Let my people go. Then they will be able to worship me.

[2]" ' "If you refuse to let them go, I will plague your whole country with frogs. [3]The Nile River will be full of frogs. They will come up into your palace. You will have frogs in your bedroom and on your bed. They will be in the homes of your officials and your people. They will be in your ovens and in your bread pans. [4]The frogs will be on you, your people and all of your officials." ' "

[5]Then the LORD spoke to Moses. He said, "Tell Aaron, 'Reach your hand out. Hold your staff over the streams, waterways and ponds. Make frogs come up on the land of Egypt.' "

[6]So Aaron reached his hand out over the waters of Egypt. The frogs came up and covered the land. [7]But the magicians did the same things by doing their magic tricks. They also made frogs come up on the land of Egypt.

[8]Pharaoh sent for Moses and Aaron. He said to them, "Pray to the LORD to take the frogs away from me and my people. Then I'll let your people go to offer sacrifices to the LORD."

[9]Moses said to Pharaoh, "You can have the honor of setting the time for me to pray. I will pray for you, your officials and your people. I'll pray that the frogs will leave you and your homes. The only frogs left will be the ones in the Nile River."

[10]"Tomorrow," Pharaoh said.

Moses replied, "It will happen just as you say. Then you will know that there is no one like the LORD our God. [11]The frogs will leave you and your houses. They will leave your officials and your people. They will remain only in the Nile River."

[12]Moses and Aaron left Pharaoh. Then Moses cried out to the LORD about the frogs he had brought on Pharaoh. [13]And the LORD did what Moses asked. The frogs died in the houses, courtyards and fields. [14]The Egyptians piled them up. The land smelled very bad because of them.

[15]But when Pharaoh saw that the frogs were dead, his heart became stubborn. He wouldn't listen to Moses and Aaron, just as the LORD had said.

The Plague of Gnats

[16]Then the LORD spoke to Moses. He said, "Tell Aaron, 'Reach your wooden staff out. Strike the dust on the ground with it.' Then all over the land of Egypt the dust will turn into gnats."

[17]So they did it. Aaron reached out the staff that was in his hand. He struck the dust on the ground with it. The dust all over the land of Egypt turned into gnats. They landed on people and animals alike.

[18]The magicians tried to produce gnats by doing their magic tricks. But they couldn't. The gnats stayed on people and animals alike.

[19]The magicians said to Pharaoh, "God's powerful finger has done this." But Pharaoh's heart was stubborn. He wouldn't listen, just as the LORD had said.

The Plague of Flies

[20]Then the LORD spoke to Moses. He said, "Get up early in the morning. Talk to Pharaoh as he goes down to the river. Say to him, 'The LORD says, "Let my people go. Then they will be able to worship me. [21]If you do not let my people go, I will send large numbers of flies. I will send them on you and your officials. I will send them on your people and into your homes. The houses of the Egyptians will be full of flies. Even the area where they live will be full of flies.

[22]" ' "But on that day I will treat the area of Goshen differently from yours. That is where my people live. There will not be large numbers of flies in Goshen. Then you will know that I, the LORD, am in this land. [23]I will treat my people differently from yours. The miraculous sign will take place tomorrow." ' "

[24]So the LORD did it. Huge numbers of flies poured into Pharaoh's palace. They came into the homes of his officials. All over Egypt the flies destroyed the land.

[25]Then Pharaoh sent for Moses and Aaron. He said to them, "Go. Offer sacrifices to your God here in the land."

[26]But Moses said, "That wouldn't be right. The sacrifices we offer to the LORD our God wouldn't be accepted by the Egyptians because of their beliefs. Suppose we offered sacrifices they couldn't accept. Then they would throw stones at us and try to kill us. [27]We have to take a journey that lasts about three days. We want to go into the desert to offer sacrifices to the LORD our God, exactly as he commands us."

[28]Pharaoh said, "I will let you and your people go to offer sacrifices. You can offer them to the LORD your God in the desert. But you must not go very far. And pray for me."

[29]Moses replied, "As soon as I leave you, I will pray to the LORD. Tomorrow the flies will leave you. They will also leave your officials and your people. Just be sure you don't try to trick us again. Let the people go to offer sacrifices to the LORD."

[30]Then Moses left Pharaoh and prayed to the LORD. [31]And the LORD did what Moses asked. The flies left Pharaoh, his officials and his people. Not one fly remained. [32]But Pharaoh's heart became stubborn that time also. He wouldn't let the people go.

The Plague on Livestock

9 Then the LORD spoke to Moses. He said, "Go to Pharaoh. Tell him, 'The LORD, the God of the Hebrews, says, "Let my people go. Then they will be able to worship me. [2]Do not refuse to let them go. Do not keep holding them back.

[3]" ' "If you refuse, my powerful hand will bring a terrible plague on you. I will strike your livestock in the fields. I will strike your horses, donkeys, camels, cattle, sheep and goats. [4]But I will treat Israel's livestock differently from yours. No animal that belongs to the people of Israel will die." ' "

5The LORD set a time for the plague. He said, "Tomorrow I will send it on the land." 6So the next day the LORD sent it. All of the livestock of the Egyptians died. But not one animal that belonged to the Israelites died.

7Pharaoh sent people to find out what had happened. They discovered that not even one animal that belonged to the Israelites had died. But his heart was still very stubborn. He wouldn't let the people go.

The Plague of Boils

8Then the LORD spoke to Moses and Aaron. He said, "Take handfuls of ashes from a furnace. Have Moses toss them into the air in front of Pharaoh. 9The ashes will turn into fine dust all over the whole land of Egypt. Then boils will break out on people and animals all over the land. Their bodies will be covered with them."

10So Moses and Aaron took ashes from a furnace and stood in front of Pharaoh. Moses tossed them into the air. Then boils broke out on people and animals alike. 11The bodies of all of the Egyptians were covered with boils. The magicians couldn't stand in front of Moses because of the boils that were all over them.

12But the LORD made Pharaoh's heart stubborn. Pharaoh wouldn't listen to Moses and Aaron, just as the LORD had said to Moses.

The Plague of Hail

13Then the LORD spoke to Moses. He said, "Get up early in the morning. Go to Pharaoh and say to him, 'The LORD, the God of the Hebrews, says, "Let my people go. Then they will be able to worship me.

14" ' "If you do not let them go, I will send the full force of my plagues against you this time. They will strike your officials and your people. Then you will know that there is no one like me in the whole earth.

15" ' "By now I could have reached out my hand. I could have struck you and your people with a plague that would have wiped you off the earth. 16But I had a special reason for making you king. I decided to show you my power. I wanted my name to become known everywhere on earth.

17" ' "But you are still against my people. You will not let them go. 18So at this time tomorrow I will send the worst hailstorm ever to fall on Egypt in its entire history.

19" ' "Give an order now to bring your livestock inside to a safe place. Bring in everything that is outside. The hail will fall on all of the people and animals that are left outside. They will die." ' "

20The officials of Pharaoh who had respect for what the LORD had said obeyed him. They hurried to bring their slaves and their livestock inside.

21But others didn't pay attention to what the LORD had said. They left their slaves and livestock outside.

22Then the LORD spoke to Moses. He said, "Reach your hand out toward the sky. Then hail will fall all over Egypt. It will beat down on people and animals alike. It will strike everything that is growing in the fields of Egypt."

23Moses reached his wooden staff out toward the sky. Then the LORD sent thunder and hail. Lightning flashed down to the ground. The LORD rained hail on the land of Egypt. 24Hail fell and lightning flashed back and forth. It was the worst storm in Egypt's entire history.

25All over Egypt hail struck everything in the fields. It fell on people and animals alike. It beat down everything that was growing in the fields. It tore all of the leaves off the trees.

26The only place it didn't hail was in the area of Goshen. That's where the people of Israel were.

27Then Pharaoh sent for Moses and Aaron. "This time I've sinned," he said to them. "The LORD has done what is right. I and my people have done what is wrong. 28Pray to the LORD, because we've had enough thunder and hail. I'll let you and your people go. You don't have to stay here any longer."

29Moses replied, "When I've left the city, I'll lift up my hands and pray to the LORD. The thunder will stop. There won't be any more hail. Then you will know that the earth belongs to the LORD. 30But I know that you and your officials still don't have any respect for the LORD God."

31The barley was ripe. The flax was blooming. So they were both destroyed. 32But the wheat and spelt weren't destroyed. That's because they ripen later.

33Then Moses left Pharaoh and went out of the city. He lifted up his hands and prayed to the LORD. The thunder and hail stopped. The rain didn't pour down on the land any longer.

34Pharaoh saw that the rain, hail and thunder had stopped. So he sinned again. He and his officials made their hearts stubborn. 35So Pharaoh's heart was stubborn. He wouldn't let the people of Israel go, just as the LORD had said through Moses.

The Plague of Locusts

10 Then the LORD said to Moses, "Go to Pharaoh. I have made his heart stubborn. I have also made the hearts of his officials stubborn so I can do my miraculous signs among them. 2Then you will be able to tell your children and grandchildren how hard I was on the Egyptians. You can tell them I did great miracles among the people of Egypt. And all of you will know that I am the LORD."

3So Moses and Aaron went to Pharaoh. They said to him, "The LORD, the God of the Hebrews, says, 'How long will you refuse to obey me? Let my people go. Then they will be able to worship me.

4" 'If you refuse to let them go, I will bring locusts into your country tomorrow. 5They will

Creation

God saw everything he had made. And it was very good.

—Genesis 1:31

Noah

God showed concern for Noah. He also showed concern for all of the wild animals and livestock that were with Noah in the ark.
—Genesis 8:1

cover the ground so that it can't be seen. They will
eat what little you have left after the hail. That
includes every tree that is growing in your fields.
6They will fill your houses. They will be in the
homes of all of your officials and your people.
Your parents and your people before them have
never seen anything like it as long as they have
lived here.'" Then Moses turned around and left
Pharaoh.

7Pharaoh's officials said to him, "How long will
this man be a trap for us? Let the people go. Then
they'll be able to worship the LORD their God.
After everything that's happened, don't you realize that Egypt is destroyed?"

8Moses and Aaron were brought back to Pharaoh. "Go. Worship the LORD your God," he said.
"But just who will be going?"

9Moses answered, "We'll go with our young
people and old people. We'll go with our sons and
daughters. We'll take our flocks and herds. We are
supposed to hold a feast in the LORD's honor."

10Pharaoh said, "The LORD will really be with
all of you if I ever let you go, along with your
women and children! Clearly you are planning to
do something bad. 11No! I'll only allow the men to
go. Then all of you can worship the LORD. After
all, that's what you have been asking for."

Then Pharaoh drove Moses and Aaron out of
his sight.

12The LORD said to Moses, "Reach out your
hand over Egypt. Locusts will cover the land. They
will eat up everything that is growing in the fields.
They will eat up everything that was left by the
hail."

13So Moses reached his wooden staff out over
Egypt. Then the LORD made an east wind blow
across the land. It blew all that day and all that
night. By morning the wind had brought the
locusts. 14They came into every part of Egypt.
They settled down in every area of the country in
large numbers. There had never been a plague of
locusts like it before. And there will never be one
like it again.

15The locusts covered the ground until it was
black. They ate up everything that was left after
the hail. They ate up everything that was growing
in the fields. They ate up the fruit on the trees.
There was nothing green left on any tree or plant
in the whole land of Egypt.

16Pharaoh quickly sent for Moses and Aaron.
He said, "I have sinned against the LORD your
God. I've also sinned against you. 17Now forgive
my sin one more time. Pray to the LORD your God
to take this deadly plague away from me."

18After Moses left Pharaoh, he prayed to the
LORD. 19The LORD changed the wind to a very
strong west wind. The wind picked up the locusts.
It blew them into the Red Sea. Not even one locust
was left anywhere in Egypt.

20But the LORD made Pharaoh's heart stubborn.
And Pharaoh wouldn't let the people of Israel go.

The Plague of Darkness

21The LORD spoke to Moses. He said, "Reach
out your hand toward the sky. Darkness will
spread over Egypt. It will be so dark that people
can feel it."

22So Moses reached out his hand toward the
sky. Then complete darkness covered Egypt for
three days. 23No one could see anyone else or go
anywhere for three days. But all of the people of
Israel had light where they lived.

24Then Pharaoh sent for Moses. He said to him,
"Go. Worship the LORD. Even your women and
children can go with you. Just leave your flocks
and herds behind."

25But Moses said, "You must allow us to take
animals to offer as sacrifices and burnt offerings to
the LORD our God. 26Our livestock must also go
with us. We have to use some of them to worship
the LORD our God. We can't leave even one animal
behind. Until we get there, we won't know what
we are supposed to use to worship the LORD."

27But the LORD made Pharaoh's heart stubborn.
So he wouldn't let the people go.

28Pharaoh said to Moses, "Get out of my sight!
Make sure you don't come to see me again! If you
do, you will die."

29"I'll do just as you say," Moses replied. "I will
never come to see you again."

The LORD Announces the Tenth Plague

11 The LORD had spoken to Moses. He had
said, "I will bring one more plague on
Pharaoh and on Egypt. After that, he will let you
and your people go. When he does, he will drive
you completely away. 2Tell the men and women
alike to ask their neighbors for articles made out
of silver and gold."

3The LORD caused the Egyptians to treat the Israelites in a kind way. Pharaoh's officials and the
people had great respect for Moses.

4Moses said, "The LORD says, 'About midnight
I will go through every part of Egypt. 5Every oldest son in Egypt will die. The oldest son of Pharaoh, who sits on the throne, will die. The oldest
son of the female slave, who works at her hand
mill, will die. All of the male animals that were
born first to their mothers among the cattle will
also die. 6There will be loud crying all over Egypt.
It will be worse than it's ever been before. And
nothing like it will ever be heard again.

7"'But among the people of Israel not even one
dog will bark at any man or animal.' Then you will
know that the LORD treats Egypt differently
from us.

8"All of your officials will come and bow down
to me. They will say, 'Go, you and all of the people who follow you!' After that, I will leave."

Moses burned with anger when he left Pharaoh.

9The LORD had spoken to Moses. He had said,
"Pharaoh will refuse to listen to you. So I will multiply my miracles in Egypt."

[10]Moses and Aaron did all of those miracles in the sight of Pharaoh. But the LORD made Pharaoh's heart stubborn. He wouldn't let the people of Israel go out of his country.

The First Passover Sacrifice

12 The LORD spoke to Moses and Aaron in Egypt. [2]He said, "From now on, this month will be your first month. Each of your years will begin with it.

[3]"Speak to the whole community of Israel. Tell them that on the tenth day of this month each man must get a lamb from his flock. A lamb should be chosen for each family and home.

[4]"Suppose there are not enough people in your family to eat a whole lamb. Then you must share some of it with your nearest neighbor. You must add up the total number of people there are. You must decide how much lamb is needed for each person.

[5]"The animals you choose must be males that are a year old. They must not have any flaws. You may choose either sheep or goats. [6]Take care of them until the 14th day of the month. Then the whole community of Israel must kill them when the sun goes down. [7]Take some of the blood. Put it on the sides and tops of the doorframes of the houses where you eat the lambs.

[8]"That same night eat the meat cooked over the fire. Also eat bitter plants. And eat bread that is made without yeast. [9]Do not eat the meat raw or boiled in water. Instead, cook it over the fire. Cook the head, legs and inside parts. [10]Do not leave any of it until morning. If some is left over until morning, burn it.

[11]"Eat the meat while your coat is tucked into your belt. Put your sandals on your feet. Take your walking stick in your hand. Eat the food quickly. It is the LORD's Passover.

[12]"That same night I will pass through Egypt. I will strike down every oldest son. I will also kill all of the male animals that were born first to their mothers. And I will judge all of the gods of Egypt. I am the LORD.

[13]"The blood on your houses will be a sign for you. When I see the blood, I will pass over you. No deadly plague will touch you when I strike Egypt.

[14]"Always remember this day. For all time to come, you and your children after you must celebrate this day as a feast in honor of the LORD. It is a law that will last forever.

[15]"Eat bread made without yeast for seven days. On the first day remove the yeast from your homes. For the next seven days, anyone who eats anything that has yeast in it must be cut off from Israel.

[16]"On the first and seventh days, come together for a special service. Do not work at all on those days. All you are allowed to do is prepare food for everyone to eat.

[17]"Celebrate the Feast of Unleavened Bread. I brought you out of Egypt on this very day like an army on the march. It is a law that will last for all time to come. [18]In the first month eat bread that is made without yeast. Eat it from the evening of the 14th day until the evening of the 21st day.

[19]"For seven days do not let any yeast be found in your homes. Anyone who eats anything that has yeast in it must be cut off from the community of Israel. That applies to outsiders and Israelites alike. [20]Do not eat anything that is made with yeast. No matter where you live, eat bread that is made without yeast."

[21]Then Moses sent for all of the elders of Israel. He said to them, "Go at once. Choose the animals for your families. Each family must kill a Passover lamb. [22]Get a branch of a hyssop plant. Dip it into the blood in the bowl. Put some of the blood on the top and on both sides of the doorframe. None of you can go out the door of your house until morning.

[23]"The LORD will go through the land to strike the Egyptians down. He'll see the blood on the top and sides of the doorframe. He will pass over that house. He won't let the destroying angel enter your homes to kill you.

[24]"Obey all of these directions. It's a law for you and your children after you for all time to come. [25]The LORD will give you the land, just as he promised. When you enter it, keep this holy day.

[26]"Your children will ask you, 'What does this holy day mean to you?' [27]Tell them, 'It's the Passover sacrifice in honor of the LORD. He passed over the houses of the people of Israel in Egypt. He spared our homes when he struck the Egyptians down.' "

Then the people of Israel bowed down and worshiped. [28]They did just what the LORD commanded Moses and Aaron.

[29]At midnight the LORD struck down every oldest son in Egypt. He killed the oldest son of Pharaoh, who sat on the throne. He killed all of the oldest sons of prisoners, who were in prison. He also killed all of the male animals that were born first to their mothers among the livestock.

[30]Pharaoh and all of his officials got up during the night. So did all of the Egyptians. There was loud crying in Egypt because someone had died in every home.

The People of Israel Leave Egypt

[31]During the night, Pharaoh sent for Moses and Aaron. He said to them, "Get out of here! You and the Israelites, leave my people! Go. Worship the LORD, just as you have asked. [32]Go. Take your flocks and herds, just as you have said. And also give me your blessing."

[33]The Egyptians begged the people of Israel to hurry up and leave the country. "If you don't," they said, "we'll all die!"

[34]So the people took their dough before the yeast was added to it. They carried it on their

shoulders in bread pans that were wrapped in clothes.

35They did just as Moses had directed them. They asked the Egyptians for articles that were made out of silver and gold. They also asked them for clothes. 36The LORD had caused the Egyptians to treat the people of Israel in a kind way. So they gave them what they asked for. The people of Israel took many expensive things that belonged to the Egyptians.

37The Israelites traveled from Rameses to Succoth. There were about 600,000 men who were old enough to go into battle. The women and children went with them. 38So did many other people. The Israelites also took large flocks and herds with them.

39They brought dough from Egypt. With it they baked bread without yeast. The dough didn't have any yeast in it. That's because the people had been driven out of Egypt before they had time to prepare their food.

40The people of Israel lived in Egypt for 430 years. 41At the end of the 430 years, to the very day, all of the LORD's people marched out of Egypt like an army.

42The LORD kept watch that night to bring them out of Egypt. So on that same night every year all of the Israelites must keep watch. They must do it to honor the LORD for all time to come.

Rules for the Passover

43The LORD spoke to Moses and Aaron. He said, "Here are the rules for the Passover.

"No one from another country is allowed to eat the Passover meal. 44Any slave you have bought is allowed to eat it after you have circumcised him. 45But a hired worker or someone who lives with you for a while is not allowed to eat it.

46"It must be eaten inside a house. Do not take any of the meat outside. Do not break any of the bones. 47The whole community of Israel must celebrate the Passover.

48"Suppose an outsider who is living among you wants to celebrate the LORD's Passover. Then all of the males in that home must be circumcised. After that, the person can take part, just like an Israelite. Only males who are circumcised can eat it.

49"The same law applies to Israelites and to outsiders who are living among you."

50All of the people of Israel did just what the LORD had commanded Moses and Aaron. 51On that very day the LORD brought the Israelites out of Egypt like an army on the march.

Setting Apart the Oldest Sons

13 The LORD said to Moses, 2"Set apart for me the first boy born in every family. The oldest son of every Israelite mother belongs to me. Every male animal that is born first to its mother also belongs to me."

3Then Moses said to the people, "Remember this day. It's the day you came out of Egypt. That's the land where you were slaves. The LORD used his mighty hand to bring you out of Egypt. Don't eat anything that has yeast in it. 4You are leaving today. It's the month of Abib.

5"The LORD will bring you into the land of the Canaanites, Hittites, Amorites, Hivites and Jebusites. He took an oath and promised your people of long ago that he would give that land to you. It's a land that has plenty of milk and honey. When you get there, keep this holy day in this month.

6"For seven days eat bread that is made without yeast. On the seventh day hold a feast in the LORD's honor. 7Eat bread that is made without yeast during those seven days. Nothing that has yeast in it should be found among you. No yeast should be seen anywhere inside your borders.

8"On that day talk to your son. Tell him, 'I'm doing this because of what the LORD did for me when I came out of Egypt.'

9"When you celebrate this day, it will be like a mark on your hand. It will be like a reminder on your forehead. The law of the LORD must be on your lips. The LORD used his mighty hand to bring you out of Egypt. 10Obey this law at the appointed time year after year.

11"The LORD will bring you into the land of Canaan. He will give it to you, just as he promised he would. He even took an oath when he made the promise to you and your people of long ago.

12"After you arrive there, give to the LORD the oldest son of every mother. Every male animal that is born first to its mother among your livestock belongs to the LORD. 13By sacrificing a lamb, buy back every male donkey that is born first to its mother. But if you don't buy the donkey back, break its neck. Buy back every oldest son.

14"In days to come, your son will ask you, 'What does this mean?'

"When he does, say to him, 'The LORD used his mighty hand to bring us out of Egypt. That's the land where we were slaves. 15Pharaoh was stubborn. He refused to let us go. So the LORD killed every oldest son in Egypt. He also killed every male animal that was born first to its mother. That's why I sacrifice to the LORD every male animal that was born first. And that's why I buy back each oldest son for him.'

16"This day will be like a mark on your hand. It will be like a sign on your forehead. It will remind you that the LORD used his mighty hand to bring us out of Egypt."

Israel Goes Through the Red Sea

17Pharaoh let the people go. The shortest road from Goshen to Canaan went through the Philistine country. But God didn't lead them that way. God said, "If they have to go into battle, they might change their minds. They might return to Egypt."

18 So God led the people toward the Red Sea by taking them on a road through the desert. The Israelites were prepared for battle when they went up out of Egypt.

19 Moses took the bones of Joseph along with him. Joseph had made the sons of Israel take an oath and make a promise. He had said, "I'm sure that God will come to help you. When he does, you must carry my bones up from this place with you." *(Genesis 50:25)*

20 The people left Succoth. They camped at Etham on the edge of the desert.

21 By day the LORD went ahead of them in a pillar of cloud. It guided them on their way. At night he led them with a pillar of fire. It gave them light. So they could travel by day or at night. 22 The pillar of cloud didn't leave its place in front of the people during the day. And the pillar of fire didn't leave its place at night.

14 Then the LORD spoke to Moses. 2 He said, "Tell the people of Israel to turn back. Have them camp near Pi Hahiroth between Migdol and the Red Sea. They must camp by the sea, right across from Baal Zephon. 3 Pharaoh will think, 'The people of Israel are wandering around the land. They don't know which way to go. The desert is all around them.'

4 "I will make Pharaoh's heart stubborn. He will chase them. But I will gain glory for myself because of what will happen to Pharaoh and his whole army. And the Egyptians will know that I am the LORD." So the Israelites camped by the Red Sea.

5 The king of Egypt was told that the people had gotten away. Then Pharaoh and his officials changed their minds about them. They said, "What have we done? We've let the people of Israel go! We've lost our slaves and all of the work they used to do for us!"

6 So he had his chariot made ready. He took his army with him. 7 He took 600 of the best chariots in Egypt. He also took along all of the other chariots. Officers were in charge of all of them.

8 The LORD made the heart of Pharaoh, the king of Egypt, stubborn. So he chased the Israelites, who were marching out boldly. 9 The Egyptians went after the Israelites. All of Pharaoh's horses and chariots and horsemen and troops went after them. They caught up with them as they camped by the sea. The Israelites were near Pi Hahiroth, across from Baal Zephon.

10 As Pharaoh approached, the people of Israel looked up. There were the Egyptians marching after them! The Israelites were terrified. They cried out to the LORD.

11 They said to Moses, "Why did you bring us to the desert to die? Weren't there any graves in Egypt? What have you done to us by bringing us out of Egypt? 12 We told you in Egypt, 'Leave us alone. Let us serve the Egyptians.' It would have been better for us to serve the Egyptians than to die here in the desert!"

13 Moses answered the people. He said, "Don't be afraid. Stand firm. You will see how the LORD will save you today. Do you see those Egyptians? You will never see them again. 14 The LORD will fight for you. Just be still."

15 Then the LORD spoke to Moses. He said, "Why are you crying out to me? Tell the people of Israel to move on. 16 Hold your wooden staff out. Reach your hand out over the Red Sea to part the water. Then the people can go through the sea on dry ground.

17 "I will make the hearts of the Egyptians stubborn. They will go in after the Israelites. I will gain glory for myself because of what will happen to Pharaoh, his whole army, his chariots and his horsemen.

18 "The Egyptians will know that I am the LORD. I will gain glory because of what will happen to all of them."

19 The angel of God had been traveling in front of Israel's army. Now he moved back and went behind them. The pillar of cloud also moved away from in front of them. Now it stood behind them. 20 It came between the armies of Egypt and Israel. All through the night the cloud brought darkness to one side and light to the other. Neither army went near the other all night long.

21 Then Moses reached his hand out over the Red Sea. All that night the LORD pushed the sea back with a strong east wind. He turned the sea into dry land. The waters were parted. 22 The people of Israel went through the sea on dry ground. There was a wall of water on their right side and on their left.

23 The Egyptians chased them. All of Pharaoh's horses and chariots and horsemen followed them into the sea.

24 Near the end of the night the LORD looked down from the pillar of fire and cloud. He saw the Egyptian army and threw it into a panic. 25 He kept their chariot wheels from turning freely. That made the chariots hard to drive.

The Egyptians said, "Let's get away from the Israelites! The LORD is fighting for Israel against Egypt."

26 Then the LORD spoke to Moses. He said, "Reach your hand out over the sea. The waters will flow back over the Egyptians and their chariots and horsemen." 27 So Moses reached his hand out over the sea. At sunrise the sea went back to its place. The Egyptians tried to run away from the sea. But the LORD swept them into it. 28 The water flowed back and covered the chariots and horsemen. It covered the entire army of Pharaoh that had followed the people of Israel into the sea. Not one of the Egyptians was left.

29 But the Israelites went through the sea on dry ground. There was a wall of water on their right side and on their left. 30 That day the LORD saved Israel from the power of Egypt. Israel saw the Egyptians lying dead on the shore. 31 The Israelites saw the great power the LORD showed against the

Egyptians. So they had respect for the LORD. They put their trust in him and in his servant Moses.

The Song of Moses and Miriam

15 Here is the song that Moses and the people of Israel sang to the LORD. They said,

"I will sing to the LORD.
He is greatly honored.
He has thrown Pharaoh's horses and their riders
into the Red Sea.
2 The LORD gives me strength. I sing about him.
He has saved me.
He is my God. I will praise him.
He is my father's God. I will honor him.
3 The LORD goes into battle.
The LORD is his name.
4 He has thrown Pharaoh's chariots and army
into the Red Sea.
Pharaoh's best officers
drowned in the sea.
5 The deep waters covered them.
They sank to the bottom like a stone.

6 "LORD, your right hand
was majestic and powerful.
LORD, your right hand
destroyed your enemies.
7 Because of your great majesty,
you threw down those who opposed you.
Your burning anger blazed out.
It burned them up like straw.
8 The powerful blast from your nose
piled up the waters.
The rushing waters stood firm like a wall.
The deep waters stood up in the middle of the sea.

9 "Your enemies bragged,
'We will chase Israel. We will catch them.
We'll divide up what we take from them.
We'll eat them alive.
We'll pull our swords out.
Our powerful hands will destroy them.'
10 But you blew with your breath.
The Red Sea covered your enemies.
They sank like lead
in the mighty waters.

11 "LORD, who among the gods is like you?
Who is like you?
You are majestic and holy.
Your glory fills me with wonder.
You do wonderful miracles.
12 You reached out your right hand.
The earth swallowed up the Egyptians.

13 "Because your love is faithful,
you will lead the people you have set free.
Because you are so strong,
you will guide them to the holy place where you live.
14 The nations will hear about it and tremble.
Pain and suffering will take hold of the Philistines.
15 The chiefs of Edom will be terrified.
The leaders of Moab will tremble with fear.
The people of Canaan will melt away.
16 Fear and terror will fall on them.
Your powerful arm
will make them as still as a stone.
Then your people will pass by, LORD.
Then the people you created will pass by.
17 You will bring them in.
You will plant them on the mountain you gave them.
LORD, you have made that place your home.
Lord, your hands have made your holy place secure.
18 "The LORD will rule
for ever and ever."

19 Pharaoh's horses, chariots and horsemen went into the Red Sea. The LORD brought the waters of the sea back over them. But the people of Israel walked through the sea on dry ground.

20 Aaron's sister Miriam was a prophet. She took a tambourine in her hand. All the women followed her. They played tambourines and danced.
21 Miriam sang to them,

"Sing to the LORD.
He is greatly honored.
He has thrown Pharaoh's horses and their riders
into the Red Sea."

At the Waters of Marah and Elim

22 Then Moses led Israel away from the Red Sea. They went into the Desert of Shur. For three days they traveled in the desert. They didn't find any water there.
23 When they came to Marah, they couldn't drink its water. It was bitter. That's why the place is named Marah.
24 The people told Moses they weren't happy with him. They said, "What are we supposed to drink?"

25 Then Moses cried out to the LORD. The LORD showed him a stick. Moses threw it into the water. The water became sweet.

There the LORD made a rule and a law for the people. And there he put them to the test.
26 He said, "I am the LORD your God. Listen carefully to my voice. Do what is right in my eyes. Pay attention to my commands. Obey all of my rules. If you do, I will not send on you any of the sicknesses I sent on the Egyptians. I am the LORD who heals you."

27 The people came to Elim. It had 12 springs and 70 palm trees. They camped there near the water.

The LORD Gives Israel Food Every Day

16 The whole community of Israel started out from Elim. They came to the Desert of Sin. It was between Elim and Sinai. They arrived there on the 15th day of the second month after they had come out of Egypt.

2In the desert the whole community told Moses and Aaron they weren't happy with them. 3The Israelites said to them, "We wish the LORD had put us to death in Egypt. There we sat around pots of meat. We ate all of the food we wanted. But you have brought us out into this desert. You must want this entire community to die of hunger."

4Then the LORD spoke to Moses. He said, "I will rain down bread from heaven for you. The people must go out each day. Have them gather enough bread for that day. Here is how I will put them to the test. I will see if they will follow my directions.

5"On the sixth day they must prepare what they bring in. On that day they must gather twice as much as on the other days."

6So Moses and Aaron spoke to all of the people of Israel. They said, "In the evening you will know that the LORD brought you out of Egypt. 7And in the morning you will see the glory of the LORD. He has heard you say you aren't happy with him. Who are we? Why are you telling us you aren't happy with us?"

8Moses also said, "You will know that the LORD has heard you speak against him. He will give you meat to eat in the evening. He'll give you all of the bread you want in the morning. But who are we? You aren't speaking against us. You are speaking against the LORD."

9Then Moses told Aaron, "Talk to the whole community of Israel. Say to them, 'Come to the LORD. He has heard you speak against him.'"

10While Aaron was talking to the whole community of Israel, they looked toward the desert. There was the glory of the LORD appearing in the cloud!

11The LORD said to Moses, 12"I have heard the people of Israel talking about how unhappy they are. Tell them, 'When the sun goes down, you will eat meat. In the morning you will be filled with bread. Then you will know that I am the LORD your God.'"

13That evening quail came and covered the camp. In the morning the ground around the camp was covered with dew. 14When the dew was gone, thin flakes appeared on the desert floor. They looked like frost on the ground. 15The people of Israel saw the flakes. They asked each other, "What's that?" They didn't know what it was.

Moses said to them, "It's the bread the LORD has given you to eat. 16Here is what the LORD has commanded. He has said, 'Each one of you should gather as much as you need. Take two quarts for each person who lives in your tent.'"

17The people of Israel did as they were told. Some gathered a lot, and some gathered a little. 18When they measured it out, those who gathered a lot didn't have too much. And those who gathered a little had enough. All of them gathered only what they needed.

19Then Moses said to them, "Don't keep any of it until morning."

20Some of them didn't pay any attention to Moses. They kept part of it until morning. But it was full of maggots and began to stink. So Moses became angry with them.

21Each morning all of them gathered as much as they needed. But by the hottest time of the day, the thin flakes had melted away.

22On the sixth day, the people gathered twice as much. It amounted to four quarts for each person. The leaders of the community came and reported that to Moses. 23He said to them, "Here is what the LORD commanded. He said, 'Tomorrow will be a day of rest. It will be a holy Sabbath day. It will be set apart for the LORD. So bake what you want to bake. Boil what you want to boil. Save what is left. Keep it until morning.'"

24So they saved it until morning, just as Moses commanded. It didn't stink or get maggots in it.

25"Eat it today," Moses said. "Today is a Sabbath day in the LORD's honor. You won't find any flakes on the ground today. 26Gather them for six days. But on the seventh day there won't be any. It's the Sabbath."

27In spite of what Moses said, some of the people went out on the seventh day to gather the flakes. But they didn't find any.

28Then the LORD spoke to Moses. He said, "How long will all of you refuse to obey my commands and my teachings? 29Keep in mind that I have given you the Sabbath day. That is why on the sixth day I give you bread for two days. All of you must stay where you are on the seventh day. No one can go out." 30So the people rested on the seventh day.

31The people of Israel called the bread manna. It was white like coriander seeds. It tasted like wafers that were made with honey.

32Moses said, "Here is what the LORD has commanded. He has said, 'Get two quarts of manna. Keep it for all time to come. Then those who live after you will see the bread I gave you to eat in the desert. I gave it to you when I brought you out of Egypt.'"

33So Moses said to Aaron, "Get a jar. Put two quarts of manna in it. Then place it in front of the LORD. Keep it there for all time to come."

34Aaron did exactly as the LORD had commanded Moses. He put the manna in front of the tablets of the covenant. He put it there so it would be kept for all time to come.

35The people of Israel ate manna for 40 years. They ate it until they came to a land that was settled. They ate it until they reached the border of Canaan.

36The jar had an omer of manna in it. An omer was two quarts.

The LORD Gives Israel Water Out of the Rock

17 The whole community of Israel started out from the Desert of Sin. They traveled from place to place, just as the LORD commanded.

They camped at Rephidim. But there wasn't any water for the people to drink. [2]So they argued with Moses. They said, "Give us water to drink."

Moses replied, "Why are you arguing with me? Why are you putting the LORD to the test?"

[3]But the people were thirsty for water there. So they told Moses they weren't happy with him. They said, "Why did you bring us up out of Egypt? Did you want us, our children and our livestock to die of thirst?"

[4]Then Moses cried out to the LORD. He said, "What am I going to do with these people? They are almost ready to kill me by throwing stones at me."

[5]The LORD answered Moses. He said, "Walk on ahead of the people. Take some of the elders of Israel along with you. Take in your hand the wooden staff you used when you struck the Nile River. Go. [6]I will stand there in front of you by the rock at Mount Horeb. Hit the rock. Then water will come out of it for the people to drink." So Moses hit the rock in the sight of the elders of Israel.

[7]Moses called the place Massah and Meribah. That's because the people of Israel argued with him there. They also put the LORD to the test. They asked, "Is the LORD among us or not?"

Joshua Wins the Battle Over the Amalekites

[8]The Amalekites came and attacked the Israelites at Rephidim. [9]Moses said to Joshua, "Choose some of our men. Then go out and fight against the Amalekites. Tomorrow I will stand on top of the hill. I'll stand there with the staff of God in my hands."

[10]So Joshua fought against the Amalekites, just as Moses had ordered.

Moses, Aaron and Hur went to the top of the hill. [11]As long as Moses held his hands up, the Israelites were winning. But every time he lowered his hands, the Amalekites began to win.

[12]When Moses' arms got tired, Aaron and Hur got a stone and put it under him. Then he sat on it. Aaron and Hur held his hands up. Aaron was on one side, and Hur was on the other. Moses' hands remained steady until sunset.

[13]So Joshua destroyed the Amalekite army with swords.

[14]Then the LORD said to Moses, "That is something to be remembered. So write it on a scroll. Make sure Joshua knows you have done it. I will completely erase the memory of the Amalekites from the earth."

[15]Then Moses built an altar. He called it The LORD Is My Banner. [16]He said, "I raised my hands toward the throne of the LORD. The LORD will fight against the Amalekites for all time to come."

Jethro Visits Moses

18 Moses' father-in-law Jethro was the priest of Midian. He heard about everything God had done for Moses and for his people Israel. He heard how the LORD had brought Israel out of Egypt.

[2]Moses had sent his wife Zipporah to his father-in-law. So Jethro welcomed her [3]and her two sons. One son was named Gershom. That's because Moses had said, "I'm an outsider in a strange land." [4]The other was named Eliezer. That's because Moses had said, "My father's God helped me. He saved me from Pharaoh's sword."

[5]Moses' father-in-law Jethro came to Moses in the desert. Moses' sons and wife came with Jethro. Moses was camped near the mountain of God. [6]Jethro had sent a message to him. It said, "I, your father-in-law Jethro, am coming to you. I'm bringing your wife and her two sons."

[7]So Moses went out to meet his father-in-law. Moses bowed down and kissed him. They greeted each other. Then they went into the tent.

[8]Moses told his father-in-law about everything the LORD had done to Pharaoh and the Egyptians because of how much he loved Israel. He told him about all of their hard times along the way. He told him about how the LORD had saved them.

[9]Jethro was delighted to hear about all of the good things the LORD had done for Israel. He heard about how God had saved them from the power of Egypt. [10]He said, "I praise the LORD. He saved you and your people from the power of Pharaoh and Egypt. [11]Now I know that the LORD is greater than all other gods. See what he did to those who looked down on Israel."

[12]Then Moses' father-in-law Jethro brought a burnt offering and other sacrifices to God. Aaron came with all of the elders of Israel. They ate with Moses' father-in-law in the sight of God.

[13]The next day Moses took his seat to serve the people as their judge. They stood around him from morning until evening. [14]His father-in-law saw everything Moses was doing for the people. So he said, "Aren't you trying to do too much for the people? You are the only judge. And all of these people are standing around you from morning until evening."

[15]Moses answered him. He said, "The people come to me to find out what God wants them to do. [16]Anytime they don't agree, they come to me. I decide between them. I tell them about God's rules and laws."

[17]Moses' father-in-law replied, "What you are doing isn't good. [18]You will just get worn out. And so will these people who come to you. There's too much work for you. You can't possibly handle it by yourself.

[19]"Listen to me. I'll give you some advice, and may God be with you. You must speak to God for the people. Take their problems to him. [20]Teach them the rules and laws. Show them how to live and what to do.

[21]"But choose men of ability from all of the people. They must have respect for God. You must be able to trust them. They must not try to get

money by cheating others. Appoint them as officials over thousands, hundreds, fifties and tens. 22Let them serve the people as judges. But have them bring every hard case to you. They can decide the easy ones themselves. That will make your load lighter. They will share it with you.

23"If this is what God wants and if you do it, then you will be able to carry the load. And all of these people will go home satisfied."

24Moses listened to his father-in-law. He did everything Jethro said. 25He chose men of ability from the whole community of Israel. He made them leaders of the people. They became officials over thousands, hundreds, fifties and tens. 26They judged the people at all times. They brought the hard cases to Moses. But they decided the easy ones themselves.

27Moses sent his father-in-law on his way. So Jethro returned to his own country.

Israel Comes to Mount Sinai

19 Exactly three months after the people of Israel left Egypt, they came to the Desert of Sinai. 2After they started out from Rephidim, they entered the Desert of Sinai. They camped there in the desert in front of the mountain.

3Then Moses went up to God. The LORD called out to him from the mountain. He said, "Here is what I want you to say to my people, who came from Jacob's family. Tell the Israelites, 4'You have seen for yourselves what I did to Egypt. You saw how I carried you on the wings of eagles and brought you to myself.

5"'Now obey me completely. Keep my covenant. If you do, then out of all of the nations you will be my special treasure. The whole earth is mine. 6But you will be a kingdom of priests to serve me. You will be my holy nation.' That is what you must tell the Israelites."

7So Moses went back. He sent for the elders of the people. He explained to them everything the LORD had commanded him to say. 8All of the people answered together. They said, "We will do everything the LORD has said."

So Moses brought their answer back to the LORD.

9The LORD spoke to Moses. He said, "I am going to come to you in a thick cloud. The people will hear me speaking with you. They will always put their trust in you." Then Moses told the LORD what the people had said.

10The LORD said to Moses, "Go to the people. Today and tomorrow set them apart for me. Have them wash their clothes. 11Have the people ready by the third day. On that day I will come down on Mount Sinai. Everyone will see it.

12"Put limits for the people around the mountain. Tell them, 'Be careful that you do not go up the mountain. Do not even touch the foot of it. You can be sure that all who touch the mountain will be put to death. 13Do not lay a hand on any of them. Kill them with stones or shoot them with arrows. Whether they are people or animals, do not let them live.' They may go up to the mountain only when the ram's horn gives out a long blast."

14Moses went down the mountain to the people. After he set them apart for the LORD, they washed their clothes. 15Then he spoke to the people. He said, "Get ready for the third day. Don't make love."

16On the morning of the third day there was thunder and lightning. A thick cloud covered the mountain. A trumpet gave out a very loud blast. Everyone in the camp trembled with fear.

17Then Moses led the people out of the camp to meet with God. They stood at the foot of the mountain.

18Smoke covered Mount Sinai, because the LORD came down on it in fire. The smoke rose up from it like smoke from a furnace. The whole mountain trembled and shook. 19The sound of the trumpet got louder and louder. Then Moses spoke. And the voice of God answered him.

20The LORD came down to the top of Mount Sinai. He told Moses to come to the top of the mountain. So Moses went up.

21The LORD said to him, "Go down and warn the people. They must not force their way through to see me. If they do, many of them will die. 22The priests approach me when they serve me. But even they must set themselves apart for me. If they do not, my anger will break out against them."

23Moses said to the LORD, "The people can't come up Mount Sinai. You yourself warned us. You said, 'Put limits around the mountain. Set it apart as holy.'"

24The LORD replied, "Go down. Bring Aaron up with you. But the priests and the people must not force their way through. They must not come up to me. If they do, my anger will break out against them."

25So Moses went down to the people and told them.

God Gives His People the Ten Commandments

20 Here are all of the words God spoke. He said,

2"I am the LORD your God. I brought you out of Egypt. That is the land where you were slaves.

3"Do not put any other gods in place of me.

4"Do not make statues of gods that look like anything in the sky or on the earth or in the waters. 5Do not bow down to them or worship them. I, the LORD your God, am a jealous God. I punish the children for the sin of their parents. I punish the grandchildren and great-grandchildren of those who hate me. 6But for all time to come I show love

to all those who love me and keep my
commandments.
7 "Do not misuse the name of the LORD your
God. The LORD will find guilty anyone
who misuses his name.
8 "Remember to keep the Sabbath day holy.
9 Do all of your work in six days. 10 But
the seventh day is a Sabbath in honor
of the LORD your God. Do not do any
work on that day. The same command
applies to your sons and daughters,
your male and female servants, and
your animals. It also applies to any
outsiders who live in your cities. 11 In
six days I made the heavens and the
earth. I made the oceans and everything in them. But I rested on the seventh day. So I blessed the Sabbath day
and made it holy.
12 "Honor your father and mother. Then you
will live a long time in the land the
LORD your God is giving you.
13 "Do not commit murder.
14 "Do not commit adultery.
15 "Do not steal.
16 "Do not give false witness against your
neighbor.
17 "Do not long for anything that belongs to
your neighbor. Do not long for your
neighbor's house, wife, male or female
servant, ox or donkey."

18 The people saw the thunder and lightning.
They heard the trumpet. They saw the mountain
covered with smoke. They trembled with fear and
stayed a long way off.

19 They said to Moses, "Speak to us yourself.
Then we'll listen. But don't let God speak to us. If
he does, we'll die."

20 Moses said to the people, "Don't be afraid.
God has come to put you to the test. He wants you
to have respect for him. That will keep you from
sinning."

21 Moses approached the thick darkness where
God was. But the people remained a long way off.

Worshiping the LORD

22 Then the LORD said to Moses, "Here is what
you must tell the people of Israel. Say to them,
'You have seen for yourselves what I said to you
from heaven. 23 Do not put any other gods in place
of me. Do not make silver or gold statues of them
for yourselves.

24 " 'Make an altar out of dirt for me. Sacrifice
your burnt offerings and friendship offerings on it.
Sacrifice your sheep, goats and cattle on it. I will
come to you and bless you everywhere I cause my
name to be honored.

25 " 'If you make an altar out of stones in honor
of me, do not build it with blocks of stone. You
will make it "unclean" if you use a tool on it.

26 " 'Do not walk up steps to my altar. If you do,
someone might see your naked body under your
robes.'

21 "Here are the laws you must explain to the
people of Israel.

Set Your Hebrew Servants Free

2 "Suppose you buy a Hebrew servant. He must
serve you for six years. But in the seventh year,
you must set him free. He does not have to pay
anything.

3 "If he does not have a wife when he comes, he
must go free alone. But if he has a wife when he
comes, she must go with him. 4 Suppose his master
gives him a wife. And suppose she has sons or
daughters by him. Then only the man will go free.
The woman and her children will belong to her
master.

5 "But suppose the servant says, 'I love my master and my wife and children. I don't want to go
free.' 6 Then his master must take him to the judges.
He must be taken to the door or doorpost of his
master's house. His master must poke a hole
through his ear lobe into the doorpost. Then he will
become his servant for life.

7 "Suppose a man sells his daughter as a servant.
Then she can't go free as male servants do.

8 "But what if the master who has chosen her
does not like her? Then he must let the man buy
her back. He has no right to sell her to strangers.
He has broken his promise to her.

9 "What if he chooses her to get married to his
son? Then he must grant her the rights of a
daughter.

10 "What if he marries another woman? He must
still give the first one her food and clothes and
make love to her. 11 If he does not provide her with
those three things, she can go free. She does not
have to pay anything.

Laws About Harming Others

12 "You can be sure that if anyone hits and kills
someone else, he will be put to death. 13 Suppose
he did not do it on purpose. Suppose I let it happen. Then he can escape to a place I will choose.
14 But suppose he kills someone on purpose. Then
take him away from my altar and put him to death.

15 "If anyone attacks his father or mother, he will
be put to death.

16 "If anyone kidnaps and sells another person,
he will be put to death. If he still has the person
with him when he is caught, he will be put to death.

17 "If anyone calls down a curse on his father or
mother, he will be put to death.

18 "Suppose two men get into a fight and argue
with each other. One hits the other with a stone or
his fist. He does not die but has to stay in bed.
19 And later he gets up and walks around outside
with his walking stick. Then the man who hit him
will not be held accountable. But he must pay the

one who was hurt for the time he spent in bed. He must be sure that the person is completely healed.

20“Suppose a man beats his male or female slave to death with a club. Then he must be punished. 21But he will not be punished if the slave gets up after a day or two. After all, the slave is his property.

22“Suppose some men are fighting and one of them hits a pregnant woman. And suppose she has her baby early but is not badly hurt. Then the man who hurt her must pay a fine. He must pay what the woman’s husband asks for and the court allows.

23“But if someone is badly hurt, a life must be taken for a life. 24An eye must be put out for an eye. A tooth must be knocked out for a tooth. A hand must be cut off for a hand and a foot for a foot. 25A burn must be given for a burn, a wound for a wound, and a bruise for a bruise.

26“Suppose a man hits his male or female servant in the eye and destroys it. Then he must let the servant go free to pay for the eye.

27“Suppose he knocks out the tooth of a male or female servant. Then he must let the servant go free to pay for the tooth.

28“Suppose a bull kills a man or woman with its horns. Then you must kill the bull by throwing stones at it. Its meat must not be eaten. The owner of the bull will not be held accountable.

29“But suppose the bull has had the habit of attacking people. And suppose the owner has been warned but has not kept it fenced in. Then if it kills a man or woman, you must kill it with stones. The owner must also be put to death.

30“But suppose payment is required of him instead. Then he can save his life by paying what is required.

31“The same law applies if the bull wounds a son or daughter with its horns.

32“Suppose the bull wounds a male or female slave. Then the owner must pay the slave’s master 12 ounces of silver. You must kill the bull with stones.

33“Suppose a man uncovers a pit or digs one and does not cover it. And suppose an ox or donkey falls into it. 34Then the owner of the pit must pay the animal’s owner for the loss. The dead animal will belong to the owner of the pit.

35“Suppose a man’s bull wounds a neighbor’s bull and it dies. Then they must sell the live one. And they must share the money and the dead animal equally.

36“But suppose people knew that the bull had the habit of attacking. And suppose the owner did not keep it fenced in. Then he must give another animal to pay for the dead animal. The dead animal will belong to him.

Laws About Keeping Property Safe

22 “Suppose a man steals an ox or a sheep. And suppose he kills it or sells it. Then he must pay back five head of cattle for the ox. Or he must pay back four sheep or goats for the sheep.

2“Suppose you catch a thief breaking into your house. And suppose you hit the thief and kill him. Then you are not guilty of murder. 3But suppose it happens after the sun has come up. Then you are guilty of murder.

“A thief must pay for what he has stolen. But suppose he does not have anything. Then he must be sold to pay for what he has stolen.

4“What if the stolen ox, donkey or sheep is found alive with him? Then the thief must pay back twice as much as he stole.

5“Suppose a man lets his livestock eat grass in someone else’s field or vineyard. Then he must pay that person back from the best crops of his own field or vineyard.

6“Suppose a fire breaks out and spreads into bushes. It burns grain that has been cut and stacked. Or it burns grain that is still growing. Or it burns the whole field. Then the one who started the fire must pay for the loss.

7“Suppose a man gives his neighbor silver or other things to keep safe. And suppose they are stolen from the neighbor’s house. If the thief is caught, he must pay back twice as much as he stole.

8“But suppose the thief is not found. Then the neighbor must go to the judges. They will decide whether the neighbor has stolen the other person’s property.

9“Suppose you have an ox, donkey, sheep or clothing that does not belong to you. Or you have other property that was lost by someone else. And suppose someone says, ‘That belongs to me.’ Then both people must bring their case to the judges. The one the judges decide is guilty must pay back twice as much to the other person.

10“Suppose a man asks his neighbor to take care of a donkey, ox, sheep or any other animal. And suppose the animal dies or gets hurt. Or suppose it is stolen while no one is looking. 11Then the problem will be settled by taking an oath and promising the LORD to tell the truth.

“Suppose the neighbor takes an oath and says, ‘I didn’t steal your property.’ Then the owner must accept what the neighbor says. No payment is required.

12“But suppose the animal really was stolen. Then the neighbor must pay the owner back.

13“Or suppose it was torn to pieces by a wild animal. Then the neighbor must bring in what is left as proof. No payment is required.

14“Suppose a man borrows an animal from his neighbor. And it gets hurt or dies while the owner is not there. Then the man must pay for it.

15“But suppose the owner is with the animal. Then the man will not have to pay. If he hired the animal, the money he paid to hire it covers the loss.

Laws About Social Problems

16“Suppose a man meets a virgin who is not engaged. And he talks her into having sex with

him. Then he must pay her father the price for a
bride. And he must get married to her.
17“But suppose her father absolutely refuses to
give her to him. Then he must still pay the price
for getting married to a virgin.
18“Do not let a woman who does evil magic stay
alive. Put her to death.
19“Anyone who has sex with an animal must be
put to death.
20“Anyone who sacrifices to any god other than
me must be destroyed.
21“Do not treat outsiders badly. Do not beat
them down. Remember, you were outsiders in
Egypt.
22“Do not take advantage of widows. Do not
take advantage of children whose fathers have
died.
23“If you do, they might cry out to me. Then I
will certainly hear them. 24And I will get angry. I
will kill you with a sword. Your wives will become
widows. Your children's fathers will die.
25“Suppose you lend money to one of my people among you who is in need. Then do not be like
those who lend money and charge interest. Do not
charge any interest.
26“Suppose your neighbor owes you money and
gives you a coat as a promise to pay it back. Then
return it to him by sunset. 27That coat is the only
thing he owns to wear or sleep in. When he cries out
to me, I will listen, because I am loving and kind.
28“Do not speak evil things against me. Do not
call down a curse on the ruler of your people.
29“Do not hold back your grain offerings or
wine offerings.
“You must give me the oldest of your sons. 30Do
the same with your cattle and sheep. Let them stay
with their mothers for seven days. But give them
to me on the eighth day.
31“I want you to be my holy people. So do not
eat the meat of any animal that has been torn by
wild animals. Throw it to the dogs.

Laws About Mercy and Fairness

23 “Do not spread reports that are false. Do
not help an evil person by telling lies in
court.
2“Do not follow the crowd when they do what
is wrong. When you are a witness in court, do not
turn what is right into wrong. Do not go along with
the crowd. 3Do not show favor to a poor person in
court.
4“Suppose you come across your enemy's ox or
donkey wandering away. Then be sure to take it
back to him.
5“Suppose you see that the donkey of someone
who hates you has fallen down under its load.
Then do not leave it there. Be sure you help him
with it.
6“Be fair to your poor people in their court
cases. 7Do not have anything to do with a charge
that is false. Do not put to death those who are not
guilty of doing anything wrong. I will not let those
who are guilty go free.
8“Do not take money from people who want
special favors. It makes you blind to the truth. It
twists the words of godly people.
9“Do not beat an outsider down. You yourselves
know how it feels to be outsiders. Remember, you
were outsiders in Egypt.

Laws About Sabbaths

10“For six years plant your fields and gather
your crops. 11But during the seventh year do not
plow your land or use it. Then the poor people who
are among you can get food from it. The wild animals can eat what is left over. Do the same thing
with your vineyards and your groves of olive trees.
12“Do all of your work in six days. But do not
do any work on the seventh day. Then your oxen
and donkeys can rest. The slaves who are born in
your house can be renewed. And so can the
outsiders.
13“Be careful to do everything I have said to
you. Do not use the names of other gods. Do not
even let them be heard on your lips.

Laws About Celebrating the Main Feasts

14“Three times a year you must celebrate a feast
in my honor.
15“Celebrate the Feast of Unleavened Bread.
Eat bread that is made without yeast for seven
days, just as I commanded you. Do it at the
appointed time in the month of Abib. You came
out of Egypt in that month.
“You must not come to worship me with your
hands empty.
16“Celebrate the Feast of Weeks. Bring the first
share of your crops from your field.
“Celebrate the Feast of Booths. Hold it in the
fall when you gather in your crops from the field.
17“Three times a year all of your men must
come to worship me. I am your LORD and King.
18“Do not include anything that is made with
yeast when you offer me the blood of a sacrifice.
“Suppose the fat from sacrifices is left over
from my feasts. Then do not keep it until morning.
19“Bring the best of the first share of your crops
to my house. I am the LORD your God.
“Do not cook a young goat in its mother's milk.

God's Angel Will Prepare the Way

20“I am sending an angel ahead of you. He will
guard you along the way. He will bring you to the
place I have prepared. 21Pay attention to him. Listen to what he says. Do not refuse to obey him. He
will not forgive you if you turn against him. My
very Name is in him. 22Listen carefully to what he
says. Do everything I say. Then I will be an enemy
to your enemies. I will fight against those who
fight against you.
23“My angel will go ahead of you. He will
bring you into the land of the Amorites, Hittites,

Perizzites, Canaanites, Hivites and Jebusites. I will wipe them out.

24“Do not do what they do. Do not bow down to their gods or worship them. You must destroy the statues of their gods. You must break their sacred stones to pieces.

25“I am the LORD your God. Worship me. Then I will bless your food and water. I will take away sickness from among you. 26In your land no woman will give birth to a dead baby. Every woman will be able to have children. I will give you a long life.

27“I will send my terror ahead of you. I will throw every nation you meet into a panic. I will make all of your enemies turn their backs and run away. 28I will send hornets ahead of you. They will drive the Hivites, Canaanites and Hittites out of your way.

29“But I will not drive them out in just one year. If I did, the land would be deserted. There would be too many wild animals for you. 30I will drive them out ahead of you little by little. I will do it until your numbers have increased enough for you to take control of the land.

31“I will make your borders secure from the Red Sea to the Mediterranean Sea. They will go from the desert to the Euphrates River.

“I will hand over to you the people who live in the land. You will drive them out to make room for you. 32Do not make a covenant with them or with their gods. 33Do not let them live in your land. If you do, they will cause you to sin against me. If you worship their gods, that will certainly be a trap for you.”

The Blood of the Covenant

24 The LORD said to Moses, “You and Aaron, Nadab and Abihu, and 70 of the elders of Israel must come up to me. Do not come close when you worship. 2Only Moses can come close to me. The others must not come near. And the people may not go up with him.”

3Moses went and told the people all of the LORD’s words and laws. They answered with one voice. They said, “We will do everything the LORD has told us to do.” 4Then Moses wrote down everything the LORD had said.

Moses got up early the next morning. He built an altar at the foot of the mountain. He set up 12 stone pillars. They stood for the 12 tribes of Israel. 5Then he sent young Israelite men to offer burnt offerings. They also sacrificed young bulls as friendship offerings to the LORD. 6Moses took half of the blood and put it in bowls. He sprinkled the other half on the altar.

7Then he took the Scroll of the Covenant and read it to the people.

They answered, “We will do everything the LORD has told us to do. We will obey him.”

8Then Moses took the blood and sprinkled it on the people. He said, “This is the blood that puts the covenant into effect. The LORD has made this covenant with you in keeping with all of these words.”

9Moses and Aaron, Nadab and Abihu, and the 70 elders of Israel went up. 10They saw the God of Israel. Under his feet was something like a street made out of sapphire. It was as clear as the sky itself. 11But God didn’t raise his hand against those leaders of the people of Israel. They saw God. And they ate and drank.

12The LORD said to Moses, “Come up to me on the mountain. Stay here. I will give you the stone tablets. They contain the law and commands I have written to teach the people.”

13Then Moses and Joshua, his helper, started out. Moses went up on the mountain of God. 14He said to the elders, “Wait for us here until we come back to you. Aaron and Hur are with you. Anyone who has a problem can go to them.”

15Moses went up on the mountain. Then the cloud covered it. 16The glory of the LORD settled on Mount Sinai. The cloud covered the mountain for six days.

On the seventh day the LORD called out to Moses from inside the cloud. 17The people of Israel saw the glory of the LORD. It looked like a fire burning on top of the mountain. 18Moses entered the cloud as he went on up the mountain. He stayed on the mountain for 40 days and 40 nights.

Offerings for the Holy Tent

25 The LORD said to Moses, 2“Tell the people of Israel to bring me an offering. You must receive the offering for me from all whose hearts move them to give.

3“Here are the offerings you must receive from them.

“gold, silver and bronze
4blue, purple and bright red yarn and fine linen
goat hair
5ram skins that are dyed red
the hides of sea cows
acacia wood
6olive oil for the lights
spices for the anointing oil and for the sweet-smelling incense
7onyx stones and other jewels for the linen apron and chest cloth

8“Have them make a sacred tent for me. I will live among them. 9Make the holy tent and everything that belongs to it. Make them exactly like the pattern I will show you.

The Ark of the Covenant

10“Have them make a chest out of acacia wood. Make it three feet nine inches long and two feet three inches wide and high. 11Cover it inside and outside with pure gold. Put a strip of gold around it.

12 “Make four gold rings for it. Join them to its four bottom corners. Put two rings on one side and two rings on the other.

13 “Then make poles out of acacia wood. Cover them with gold. 14 Put the poles through the rings on the sides of the chest to carry it. 15 The poles must remain in the rings of the chest. Do not remove them. 16 I will give you the tablets of the covenant. When I do, put them into the chest.

17 “Make its cover out of pure gold. The cover is the place where sin will be paid for. Make it three feet nine inches long and two feet three inches wide.

18 “Make two cherubim out of hammered gold at the ends of the cover. 19 Put one cherub on each end of it. Make the cherubim as part of the cover itself. 20 The cherubim must have their wings spread up over the cover. The cherubim must face each other and look toward the cover.

21 “Place the cover on top of the chest. I will give you the tablets of the covenant. Put them into the chest.

22 “The chest is the ark where the tablets of the covenant are kept. I will meet with you above the cover between the two cherubim that are over the ark. There I will give you all of my commands for the people of Israel.

The Table for the Holy Bread

23 “Make a table out of acacia wood. Make it three feet long, one foot six inches wide and two feet three inches high. 24 Cover it with pure gold. Put a strip of gold around it. 25 Also make a rim around it that is three inches wide. Put a strip of gold around the rim.

26 “Make four gold rings for the table. Join them to the four corners, where the four legs are. 27 The rings must be close to the rim. They must hold the poles that will be used to carry the table.

28 “Make the poles out of acacia wood. Cover them with gold. Use them to carry the table.

29 “Make its plates and dishes out of pure gold. Also make its pitchers and bowls out of pure gold. Use the pitchers and bowls to pour out drink offerings.

30 “Put the holy bread on the table. It must be near my holy throne on the ark of the covenant at all times.

The Gold Lampstand

31 “Make a lampstand out of pure gold. Hammer out its base and stem. Its buds, blooms and cups must branch out from it.

32 “Six branches must come out from the sides of the lampstand. Make three on one side and three on the other. 33 On one branch make three cups that are shaped like almond flowers with buds and blooms. Then put three on the next branch. Do the same with all six branches that come out from the lampstand.

34 “On the lampstand there must be four cups that are shaped like almond flowers with buds and blooms. 35 One bud must be under the first pair of branches that come out from the lampstand. Put a second bud under the second pair. And put a third bud under the third pair. Make a total of six branches. 36 The buds and branches must come out from the lampstand.

“The whole lampstand must be one piece that is hammered out of pure gold.

37 “Then make its seven lamps. Set them up on it so that they light the space in front of it. 38 The trays and wick cutters must be made out of pure gold. 39 Use 75 pounds of pure gold to make the lampstand and everything that is used with it.

40 “Be sure to make everything just like the pattern I showed you on the mountain.

The Holy Tent

26 “Make ten curtains out of finely twisted linen for the holy tent. Make them with blue, purple and bright red yarn. Have a skilled worker sew cherubim into the pattern. 2 Make all of the curtains the same size. They must be 42 feet long and six feet wide.

3 “Join five of the curtains together. Do the same thing with the other five. 4 Make loops out of blue strips of cloth along the edge of the end curtain in one set. Do the same thing with the end curtain in the other set. 5 Make 50 loops on the end curtain of the one set. Do the same thing on the end curtain of the other set. Put the loops across from each other. 6 Make 50 gold hooks. Use them to join the curtains together so that the holy tent is all one piece.

7 “Make a total of 11 curtains out of goat hair to put over the holy tent. 8 Make all 11 curtains the same size. They must be 45 feet long and six feet wide.

9 “Join five of the curtains together into one set. Do the same thing with the other six. Fold the sixth curtain in half at the front of the tent. 10 Make 50 loops along the edge of the end curtain in the one set. Do the same thing with the other set. 11 Then make 50 bronze hooks. Put them in the loops to join the tent together all in one piece.

12 “Let the extra half curtain hang down at the rear of the holy tent. 13 The tent curtains will be one foot six inches longer on both sides. What is left over will hang over the sides of the holy tent and cover it.

14 “Make a covering for the tent. Make it out of ram skins that are dyed red. Put a covering of the hides of sea cows over that.

15 “Make frames out of acacia wood for the holy tent. 16 Make each frame 15 feet long and two feet three inches wide. 17 Add two small wooden pins to each frame. Make the pins stick out so that they are even with each other. Make all of the frames for the holy tent in the same way.

18 “Make 20 frames for the south side of the holy tent. 19 And make 40 silver bases to go under them. Make two bases for each frame. Put one under each pin that sticks out.

[20]"For the north side of the holy tent make 20 frames [21]and 40 silver bases. Put two bases under each frame.

[22]"Make six frames for the west end of the holy tent. [23]Make two frames for the corners at the far end. [24]At those two corners the frames must be double from top to bottom. They must be fitted into a single ring. Make both of them the same. [25]There will be eight frames and 16 silver bases. There will be two bases under each frame.

[26]"Also make crossbars out of acacia wood. Make five for the frames on one side of the holy tent. [27]Make five for the frames on the other side. And make five for the frames on the west, at the far end of the holy tent. [28]The center crossbar must reach from end to end at the middle of the frames.

[29]"Cover the frames with gold. Make gold rings to hold the crossbars. Also cover the crossbars with gold.

[30]"Set up the holy tent in keeping with the plan I showed you on the mountain.

[31]"Make a curtain out of blue, purple and bright red yarn and finely twisted linen. Have a skilled worker sew cherubim into the pattern. [32]Hang the curtain with gold hooks on four posts that are made out of acacia wood. Cover the posts with gold. Stand them on four silver bases. [33]Hang the curtain from the hooks.

"Place the ark of the covenant behind the curtain. The curtain will separate the Holy Room from the Most Holy Room. [34]Put the cover on the ark of the covenant in the Most Holy Room. The cover will be the place where sin is paid for.

[35]"Place the table outside the curtain on the north side of the holy tent. And put the lampstand across from it on the south side.

[36]"For the entrance to the tent make a curtain out of blue, purple and bright red yarn and finely twisted linen. Have a person who sews skillfully make it. [37]Make gold hooks for the curtain. Make five posts out of acacia wood. Cover them with gold. And make five bronze bases for them.

The Altar for Burnt Offerings

27 "Build an altar out of acacia wood. It must be four feet six inches high and seven feet six inches square. [2]Make a horn stick out from each of its upper four corners. Cover the altar with bronze.

[3]"Make all of its tools out of bronze. Make its pots to remove the ashes. Make its shovels, sprinkling bowls, meat forks, and pans for carrying ashes.

[4]"Make a bronze grate for the altar. Make a bronze ring for each of the four corners of the grate. [5]Put the grate halfway up the altar on the inside.

[6]"Make poles out of acacia wood for the altar. Cover them with bronze. [7]Put the poles through the rings. They will be on two sides of the altar for carrying it.

[8]"Make the altar out of boards. Make it hollow. You must make it just as I showed you on the mountain.

The Courtyard

[9]"Make a courtyard for the holy tent. The south side must be 150 feet long. It must have curtains that are made out of finely twisted linen. [10]The curtains must be hung on 20 posts and 20 bronze bases. The posts must have silver hooks and bands on them.

[11]"The north side must also be 150 feet long. It must have curtains with 20 posts and 20 bronze bases. The posts must have silver hooks and bands on them.

[12]"The west end of the courtyard must be 75 feet wide. It must have curtains with ten posts and ten bases.

[13]"The east end of the courtyard, toward the sunrise, must also be 75 feet wide. [14]On one side of the entrance you must put curtains that are 22 feet six inches long. Hang them on three posts. Each post must have a base. [15]On the other side you must also put curtains that are 22 feet six inches long. Hang them on three posts. Each post must have a base.

[16]"For the entrance to the courtyard, provide a curtain that is 30 feet long. Make it out of blue, purple and bright red yarn and finely twisted linen. Have someone who sews skillfully make it. Hang it on four posts. Each post must have a base.

[17]"All of the posts that are around the courtyard must have silver bands and hooks. They must also have bronze bases. [18]The courtyard must be 150 feet long and 75 feet wide. It must have curtains that are made out of finely twisted linen. They must be seven feet six inches high. The posts must have bronze bases.

[19]"Make all of the other articles used for any purpose in the holy tent out of bronze. That includes all of the tent stakes for the tent and the courtyard.

Oil for the Lampstand

[20]"Command the people of Israel to bring you clear oil that is made from pressed olives. Use it to keep the lamps burning and giving light.

[21]"Aaron and his sons must keep the lamps burning in the Tent of Meeting. The lamps will be outside the curtain that is in front of the tablets of the covenant. The lamps must be kept burning in my sight from evening until morning. That is a law for the people of Israel that will last for all time to come.

Clothes for the Priests

28 "Have your brother Aaron brought to you from among the people of Israel. His sons Nadab, Abihu, Eleazar and Ithamar must also be brought. They will serve me as priests.

2“Make sacred clothes for your brother Aaron. When he is wearing them, people will honor him. They will have respect for him.

3“Speak to all of the skilled workers. I have given them the skill to do this kind of work. Tell them to make clothes for Aaron. He will wear them when he is set apart to serve me as priest. 4They must make a chest cloth, a linen apron, an outer robe, an inner robe, a turban and a belt. They must make sacred clothes for your brother Aaron and his sons. Then they will serve me as priests. 5Have them use fine gold wire, and blue, purple and bright red yarn, and fine linen.

The Linen Apron

6“Make the linen apron out of fine gold wire, and out of blue, purple and bright red yarn, and out of finely twisted linen. Have a skilled worker make it. 7It must have two shoulder straps joined to two of its corners.

8“Its skillfully made waistband must be like it. The waistband must be part of the apron itself. Make the waistband out of fine gold wire, and out of blue, purple and bright red yarn, and out of finely twisted linen.

9“Get two onyx stones. Carve the names of the sons of Israel on them. 10Arrange them in the order of their birth. Carve six names on one stone and six on the other. 11Carve the names of the sons of Israel on the two stones the way a jewel cutter carves a seal.

“Then put the stones in fancy gold settings. 12Connect them to the shoulder straps of the linen apron. The stones will stand for the sons of Israel. Aaron must carry the names on his shoulders as a reminder while he is serving me. 13Make fancy gold settings. 14Make two braided chains out of pure gold. Make them like ropes. Join the chains to the settings.

The Chest Cloth

15“Make a chest cloth that will be used for making decisions. Have a skilled worker make it. Make it like the linen apron. Use fine gold wire, and blue, purple and bright red yarn, and finely twisted linen. 16Make it nine inches square. Fold it in half.

17“Put four rows of valuable jewels on it. Put a ruby, a topaz and a beryl in the first row. 18Put a turquoise, a sapphire and an emerald in the second row. 19Put a jacinth, an agate and an amethyst in the third row. 20And put a chrysolite, an onyx and a jasper in the fourth row. Put them in fancy gold settings.

21“Use a total of 12 stones. Use one for each of the names of the sons of Israel. Each stone must be carved like a seal with the name of one of the 12 tribes.

22“Make braided chains out of pure gold for the chest cloth. Make them like ropes. 23Make two gold rings for the chest cloth. Connect them to two corners of it. 24Join the two gold chains to the rings at the corners of the chest cloth. 25Join the other ends of the chains to the two settings. Join them to the shoulder straps on the front of the linen apron.

26“Make two gold rings. Connect them to the other two corners of the chest cloth. Put them on the inside edge next to the apron. 27Make two more gold rings. Connect them to the bottom of the shoulder straps on the front of the apron. Put them close to the seam. Put them right above the waistband of the apron. 28The rings of the chest cloth must be tied to the rings of the apron. Tie them to the waistband with blue cord. Then the chest cloth will not swing out from the linen apron.

29“When Aaron enters the Holy Room, he will carry the names of the sons of Israel over his heart. Their names will be on the chest cloth of decision. They will be a continuing reminder while he is serving me.

30“Also put the Urim and Thummim into the chest cloth. Then they will be over Aaron’s heart when he comes to serve me. In that way, Aaron will always have what he needs to make decisions for the people of Israel. He will carry the Urim and Thummim over his heart while he is serving me.

More Clothes for the Priests

31“Make the outer robe of the linen apron completely from blue cloth. 32In the center of the robe, make an opening for the head of the priest. Make an edge like a collar around the opening. Then it will not tear.

33“Make pomegranates out of blue, purple and bright red yarn. Sew them around the hem of the robe. Sew gold bells between them. 34Sew a gold bell between every two pomegranates all around the hem of the robe.

35“Aaron must wear the robe when he serves. The bells will jingle when he enters the Holy Room while he is serving me. And they will jingle when he goes out. Then he will not die.

36“Make a plate out of pure gold. Carve words on it as if it were a seal. Carve the words SET APART FOR THE LORD. 37Tie the plate to the front of the turban with a blue cord.

38“Aaron must wear it on his forehead all the time. He will be held accountable for all of the sacred gifts the Israelites set apart. Then I will accept the gifts.

39“Make the inner robe out of fine linen. And make the turban out of fine linen. Have the belt made by a person who sews skillfully.

40“Make inner robes, belts and headbands for Aaron’s sons. When they are wearing them, people will honor them. They will also have respect for them.

41“Put all of the clothes on your brother Aaron and his sons. Then pour olive oil on them and prepare them to serve me. Set them apart to serve me as priests.

42“Make linen underwear that reaches from the waist to the thigh. 43Aaron and the priests who are in his family line must wear it when they enter the Tent of Meeting. They must wear it when they approach the altar to serve in the Holy Room. Then they will not be found guilty and die.

“For all time to come, that will be a law for Aaron and the priests who are in his family line.

Directions for Setting the Priests Apart

29 “Here is what you must do to set Aaron and his sons apart to serve me as priests.

“Get a young bull and two rams. They must not have any flaws. 2Get fine wheat flour that does not have yeast in it. Use the flour to make bread, flat cakes that are mixed with olive oil, and wafers that are spread with oil. 3Put everything in a basket. Offer them along with the bull and the two rams.

4“Then bring Aaron and his sons to the entrance to the Tent of Meeting. Wash them with water.

5“Take the inner robe, the outer robe of the linen apron, the apron itself and the chest cloth. Dress Aaron in them. Take the skillfully made waistband and tie the apron on him with it. 6Put the turban on his head. Connect the sacred crown to the turban. 7Take the anointing oil and pour it on his head.

8“Bring his sons and dress them in their inner robes. 9Put headbands on them. Tie belts on Aaron and his sons. The work of the priests belongs to them. This is my law that will last for all time to come.

“And that is how you must prepare Aaron and his sons to serve me.

10“Bring the bull to the front of the Tent of Meeting. Have Aaron and his sons place their hands on its head. 11Kill it in my sight at the entrance to the Tent of Meeting.

12“Dip your finger into some of the bull’s blood. Put it on the horns that stick out from the upper four corners of the altar. Pour the rest of it out at the base of the altar.

13“Then take all of the fat around the inside parts. Take the covering of the liver. Take both kidneys with the fat on them. And burn all of it on the altar.

14“But burn the bull’s meat, hide and guts outside the camp. It is a sin offering.

15“Get one of the rams. Have Aaron and his sons place their hands on its head. 16Kill it. Take the blood and sprinkle it against every side of the altar.

17“Cut the ram into pieces. Wash the inside parts and the legs. Put them with the head and the other pieces. 18Then burn the whole ram on the altar. It is a burnt offering to me. It has a pleasant smell. It is an offering that is made to me with fire.

19“Get the other ram. Have Aaron and his sons place their hands on its head. 20Kill it. Put some of its blood on the right ear lobes of Aaron and his sons. Put some on the thumbs of their right hands. Also put some on the big toes of their right feet. Then sprinkle blood against every side of the altar.

21“Get some of the blood from the altar. Also get some of the anointing oil. Sprinkle both of them on Aaron and his clothes and his sons and their clothes. Then he and his sons and their clothes will be set apart to serve me.

22“Here is what you must take from the second ram. Take the fat, the fat tail, the fat around the inside parts, the covering of the liver, both kidneys with the fat on them, and the right thigh. It is the ram you must use when you prepare the priests to serve me. 23Get a loaf, a flat cake that is made with oil, and a wafer. Take them from the basket of bread that was made without yeast. It is the one that is in front of me.

24“Put everything in the hands of Aaron and his sons. Tell them to lift it up and wave it in front of me as a wave offering. 25Then take it from their hands. Burn it on the altar along with the burnt offering. It gives a smell that is pleasant to me. It is an offering that is made to me with fire.

26“Get the breast of the ram that is used when you prepare Aaron to serve me. Wave it in front of me as a wave offering. It will be your share of the meat.

27“Here are the parts of the second ram that belong to Aaron and his sons. You must set apart the breast that was waved and the thigh that was offered. 28It will always be the regular share from the people of Israel for Aaron and his sons. The people must give it to me from their friendship offerings.

29“Aaron’s sacred clothes will belong to his sons who will come after him. Then they can wear them when you anoint them and prepare them to serve me. 30The son who comes after him as priest must wear them seven days. He will come and serve in the Holy Room in the Tent of Meeting.

31“Get the ram that is sacrificed when you prepare Aaron and his sons to serve me. Cook the meat in a sacred place.

32“Aaron and his sons must eat the ram’s meat. And they must eat the bread that is in the basket. They must eat all of it at the entrance to the Tent of Meeting. 33Those are the offerings to pay for their sins. They must eat them. The offerings must be made when Aaron and his sons are set apart and prepared to serve me. No one else can eat them. They are sacred.

34“And if any parts of the ram or bread that are sacrificed when you prepare Aaron and his sons to serve me are left until morning, burn them up. They must not be eaten. They are sacred.

35“Do everything I have commanded you to do for Aaron and his sons. Take seven days when you prepare them to serve me. 36Sacrifice a bull each day. It is a sin offering to pay for their sins.

“Make the altar pure. Pour olive oil on it to set it apart. 37Take seven days to make the altar pure. Set it apart. Then the altar will be a very holy place. Anything that touches it will be holy.

38“Every day offer on the altar two lambs that are a year old. 39Offer one in the morning. Offer the other one when the sun goes down. 40Along with the first lamb, offer eight cups of fine flour. Mix it with a quart of oil that is made from pressed olives. Along with that, offer a quart of wine as a drink offering.

41"Sacrifice the other lamb when the sun goes down. Sacrifice it along with the same grain offering and its drink offering as you do in the morning. It has a pleasant smell. It is an offering that is made to me with fire.

42"For all time to come, the burnt offering must be sacrificed regularly. Sacrifice it at the entrance to the Tent of Meeting in my sight. There I will meet you and speak to you. 43There I will also meet with the people of Israel. My glory will make the place holy.

44"So I will set the Tent of Meeting and the altar apart. And I will set Aaron and his sons apart to serve me as priests.

45"Then I will live among the people of Israel. And I will be their God. 46They will know that I am the LORD their God. They will know that I brought them out of Egypt so I could live among them. I am the LORD their God.

The Altar for Burning Incense

30 "Make an altar for burning incense. Make it out of acacia wood. 2It must be one foot six inches square and three feet high. Make a horn stick out from each of its upper four corners. 3Cover the top, sides and horns with pure gold. Put a strip of gold around it.

4"Make two gold rings for the altar below the strip. Put the rings across from each other. They will hold the poles that are used to carry it. 5Make the poles out of acacia wood. Cover them with gold.

6"Put the altar in front of the curtain that hangs in front of the ark where the tablets of the covenant are kept. The ark will have a cover. It will be the place where sin is paid for. There I will meet with you.

7"Aaron must burn sweet-smelling incense on the altar. He must do it every morning when he takes care of the lamps. 8He must burn incense again when he lights the lamps at sunset. Incense must be burned regularly to me. Do it for all time to come.

9"Do not burn any other incense on the altar. Do not use the altar for burnt offerings or grain offerings. Do not pour drink offerings on it.

10"Once a year Aaron must put the blood of a sin offering on its horns to make it pure. He must do it on the day Israel's sin is paid for. Do it for all time to come. The altar is a very holy place to me."

Money to Pay for the People's Lives

11Then the LORD spoke to Moses. He said, 12"When you make a list of the people of Israel and count them, they must pay me for their lives at the time they are counted. Then a plague will not come on them when you count them.

13"Each one who is counted must pay a fifth of an ounce of silver. It must be weighed out in keeping with the standard weights that are used in the sacred tent. The payment is an offering to me. 14Each one who is counted must be 20 years old or more. He must give an offering to me.

15"When you make the offering, rich people must not give more than a fifth of an ounce of silver. And poor people must not give less. The offering you give to me will pay for your lives.

16"Receive the money from the people of Israel. Use it for any purpose in the Tent of Meeting. It will remind the people that they are paying me for their lives."

The Large Bowl for Washing

17Then the LORD spoke to Moses. He said, 18"Make a large bronze bowl for washing. Make a bronze stand to put it on. Place the bowl between the Tent of Meeting and the altar. Put water in it.

19"Aaron and his sons must wash their hands and feet with water from it. 20When they enter the Tent of Meeting, they must wash with water so that they will not die. They will come to the altar to serve me. They will bring an offering that is made to me with fire. 21When they do, they must wash their hands and feet so that they will not die. For all time to come, that will be a law for Aaron and the priests who are in his family line."

Anointing Oil

22Then the LORD spoke to Moses. 23He said, "Get some fine spices. Get 12 pounds eight ounces of liquid myrrh. Get six pounds four ounces of sweet-smelling cinnamon and the same amount of sweet-smelling cane. 24Also get 12 pounds eight ounces of cassia. All of the spices must be weighed out in keeping with the standard weights that are used in the sacred tent. Get four quarts of olive oil.

25"Have a person who makes perfume mix everything into a sacred anointing oil. It will smell sweet.

26"Then anoint the Tent of Meeting and the ark where the tablets of the covenant are kept. 27Anoint the table for the holy bread and all of its articles. Anoint the lampstand and the things that are used with it. Anoint the altar for burning incense. 28Anoint the altar for burnt offerings and all of its tools. And anoint the large bowl together with its stand. 29You must set them apart so that they will be very holy. Anything that touches them will be holy.

30"Anoint Aaron and his sons. Set them apart so that they can serve me as priests.

31"Say to the people of Israel, 'This will be my sacred anointing oil for all time to come. 32Do not pour it on the bodies of any other men. Do not make any other oil in the same way. It is sacred. So you must think of it as sacred. 33Anyone who makes perfume in the same way and puts it on someone who is not a priest must be cut off from his people.' "

Incense

34Then the LORD spoke to Moses. He said, "Get
some sweet-smelling spices. Get some gum resin,
onycha and galbanum. Also get some pure frank-
incense. Make sure everything is in equal
amounts.
35"Have a person who makes perfume mix it all
up into a sweet-smelling incense. It must have salt
in it. It will be pure and sacred. 36Grind some of it
into powder. Place it in front of the tablets of the
covenant in the Tent of Meeting. There I will meet
with you. The incense will be very holy to you.
37"Do not make any incense for yourselves in
the same way. Think of it as holy to me. 38Anyone
who makes incense in the same way to enjoy its
sweet smell must be cut off from his people."

Bezalel and Oholiab

31 Then the LORD spoke to Moses. 2He said,
"I have chosen Bezalel, the son of Uri. Uri
is the son of Hur. Bezalel is from the tribe of Judah. 3I have filled him with the Spirit of God. I
have filled him with skill, ability and knowledge in
all kinds of crafts. 4He can make beautiful patterns
in gold, silver and bronze. 5He can cut and set
stones. He can work with wood. In fact, he can
work in all kinds of crafts.
6"I have also appointed Oholiab, the son of
Ahisamach, to help him. Oholiab is from the tribe
of Dan.
"I have given ability to all of the skilled workers. They can make everything I have commanded
you to make. Here is the complete list.

7"the Tent of Meeting
the ark where the tablets of the covenant are kept
the cover for the ark
8the table for the holy bread and its articles
the pure gold lampstand and everything that is used with it
the altar for burning incense
9the altar for burnt offerings and all of its tools
the large bowl with its stand
10the sacred clothes for Aaron the priest
the clothes for his sons when they serve as priests
11the anointing oil
the sweet-smelling incense for the Holy Room

"The skilled workers must make them just as I
commanded you."

The Sabbath Day

12Then the LORD spoke to Moses. 13He said,
"Tell the people of Israel, 'You must always keep
my Sabbath days. That will be the sign of the
covenant I have made between me and you for all
time to come. Then you will know that I am the
LORD. I make you holy.
14" 'Keep the Sabbath day. It is holy to you.
Those who misuse it must be put to death. Those
who do any work on that day must be cut off from
their people. 15Do your work in six days. But the
seventh day is a Sabbath. You must rest on it. It is
set apart for me. Those who work on the Sabbath
day must be put to death.
16" 'The people of Israel must keep the Sabbath.
They must celebrate it for all time to come. It will
be a covenant that lasts forever. 17It will be the sign
of the covenant I have made between me and the
people of Israel forever.
" 'I made the heavens and the earth in six days.
But on the seventh day I did not work. I rested.' "
18The LORD finished speaking to Moses on
Mount Sinai. Then he gave him the two tablets of
the covenant. They were made out of stone. The
words on them were written by the finger of God.

Israel Worships a Golden Calf

32 The people saw that Moses took a long
time to come down from the mountain. So
they gathered around Aaron. They said to him,
"Come. Make us a god that will lead us. This fellow Moses brought us up out of Egypt. But we
don't know what has happened to him."
2Aaron answered them, "Take the gold earrings
off your wives, your sons and your daughters.
Bring the earrings to me."
3So all of the people took off their earrings.
They brought them to Aaron. 4He took what they
gave him and made it into a metal statue of a god.
It looked like a calf. He shaped it with a tool.
Then the people said, "Israel, here is your god
who brought you up out of Egypt."
5When Aaron saw it, he built an altar in front of
the calf. He said, "Tomorrow will be a feast day in
the LORD's honor."
6So the next day the people got up early. They
sacrificed burnt offerings and brought friendship
offerings. They sat down to eat and drink. Then
they got up to dance wildly in front of their god.
7The LORD spoke to Moses. He said, "Go down.
Your people you brought up out of Egypt have
become very sinful. 8They have quickly turned
away from what I commanded them. They have
made themselves a statue of a god that looks like
a calf. They have bowed down and sacrificed to it.
And they have said, 'Israel, here is your god who
brought you up out of Egypt.'
9"I have seen those people," the LORD said to
Moses. "They are stubborn. 10Now leave me alone.
My anger will burn against them. I will destroy
them. Then I will make you into a great nation."
11But Moses asked the LORD his God to show
favor to the people. "LORD," he said, "why should
your anger burn against your people? You used your
great power and mighty hand to bring them out of
Egypt. 12Why should the Egyptians say, 'He brought
them out to hurt them. He wanted to kill them in the
mountains. He wanted to wipe them off the face of

the earth'? Turn away from your burning anger. Please take pity on your people. Don't destroy them!

13"Remember your servants Abraham, Isaac and Israel. You made a promise. You took an oath in your name. You said, 'I will make your children after you as many as the stars in the sky. I will give them all of this land I promised them. It will belong to them forever.'"

14Then the LORD took pity on his people. He didn't destroy them as he had said he would.

15Moses turned and went down the mountain. He had the two tablets of the covenant in his hands. Words were written on both sides of the tablets, front and back. 16The tablets were the work of God. The words had been written by God. They had been carved on the tablets.

17Joshua heard the noise of the people shouting. So he said to Moses, "It sounds like war in the camp."

18Moses replied,

"It's not the sound of winning.
It's not the sound of losing.
It's the sound of singing that I hear."

19As Moses approached the camp, he saw the calf. He also saw the people dancing. So he burned with anger. He threw the tablets out of his hands. They broke into pieces at the foot of the mountain.

20He took the calf the people had made. He burned it in the fire. Then he ground it into powder. He scattered it on the water. And he made the people of Israel drink it.

21He said to Aaron, "What did these people do to you? How did they make you lead them into such terrible sin?"

22"Please don't be angry," Aaron answered. "You know how these people like to do what is evil. 23They said to me, 'Make us a god that will lead us. This fellow Moses brought us up out of Egypt. But we don't know what has happened to him.'

24"So I told them, 'Anyone who has any gold jewelry, take it off.' They gave me the gold. I threw it into the fire. And out came this calf!"

25Moses saw that the people were running wild. Aaron had let them get out of control. The people had become a joke to their enemies.

26Moses stood at the entrance to the camp. He said, "Anyone who is on the LORD's side, come to me." All of the Levites joined him.

27Then he spoke to them. He said, "The LORD, the God of Israel, says, 'Each man must put on his sword. Then he must go back and forth through the camp from one end to the other. Each man must kill his brother, friend and neighbor.'" 28The Levites did as Moses commanded. About 3,000 of the people died that day. 29Then Moses said to the Levites, "You have been set apart for the LORD today. You stood against your own sons and brothers. And he has blessed you this day."

30The next day Moses said to the people, "You have committed a terrible sin. But now I will go up to the LORD. Maybe if I pray to him, he will forgive your sin."

31So Moses went back to the LORD. He said, "These people have committed a terrible sin. They have made a god out of gold for themselves. 32Now please forgive their sin. But if you won't, then erase my name from the scroll you have written."

33The LORD replied to Moses, "I will erase from my scroll only the names of those who have sinned against me. 34Now go. Lead the people to the place I spoke about. My angel will go ahead of you. But when the time comes for me to punish, I will punish them for their sin."

35The LORD struck the people with a plague. That's because of what they did with the calf Aaron had made.

33 Then the LORD spoke to Moses. He said, "Leave this place. You and the people you brought up out of Egypt must leave it. Go up to the land I promised with an oath to give to Abraham, Isaac and Jacob. I said to them, 'I will give it to your children after you.' 2I will send an angel ahead of you. I will drive out the Canaanites, Amorites, Hittites, Perizzites, Hivites and Jebusites.

3"Go up to the land that has plenty of milk and honey. But I will not go with you. You are stubborn. I might destroy you on the way."

4When the people heard those painful words, they became sad and began to sob. No one put on any jewelry.

5The LORD had said to Moses, "Tell the people of Israel, 'You are stubborn. If I went with you even for a moment, I might destroy you. Now take off your jewelry. Then I will decide what to do with you.'" 6So the people took off their jewelry at Mount Horeb.

The Tent of Meeting

7Moses used to take a tent and set it up far outside the camp. He called it the "tent of meeting." Anyone who wanted to ask the LORD a question would go to the tent of meeting that was outside the camp. 8When Moses would go out to the tent, all of the people would get up and stand at the entrances to their tents. They would watch Moses until he entered the tent.

9As Moses would go into the tent, the pillar of cloud would come down. It would stay at the entrance while the LORD spoke with Moses. 10The people would see the pillar of cloud standing at the entrance to the tent. Then all of them would stand and worship at the entrances to their tents.

11The LORD would speak to Moses face to face. It was like a man speaking to his friend. Then Moses would return to the camp.

But Joshua, his young helper, didn't leave the tent. Joshua was the son of Nun.

The LORD Shows Moses His Glory

12Moses said to the LORD, "You have been telling me, 'Lead these people.' But you haven't let me know whom you will send with me. You have said, 'I know your name. I know all about you. And I am pleased with you.' 13If you are pleased with me, teach me more about yourself. Then I can know you. And I can continue to please you. Remember that this nation is your people."

14The LORD replied, "I will go with you. And I will give you rest."

15Then Moses said to him, "If you don't go with us, don't send us up from here. 16How will anyone know that you are pleased with me and your people? You must go with us. How else will we be different from all of the other people on the face of the earth?"

17The LORD said to Moses, "I will do exactly what you have asked. I am pleased with you. And I know your name. I know all about you."

18Then Moses said, "Now show me your glory."

19The LORD said, "I will make all of my goodness pass in front of you. And I will announce my name, The LORD, in front of you. I will have mercy on whom I have mercy. And I will show love to those I love. 20But you can't see my face," he said. "No one can see me and stay alive."

21The LORD continued, "There is a place near me where you can stand on a rock. 22When my glory passes by, I will put you in an opening in the rock. I will cover you with my hand until I have passed by. 23Then I will remove my hand. You will see my back. But my face must not be seen."

The New Stone Tablets

34 The LORD said to Moses, "Cut out two stone tablets that are just like the first ones. I will write on them the words that were on the first tablets, which you broke.

2"Be ready in the morning. Then come up on Mount Sinai. Meet with me there on top of the mountain. 3No one must come with you. No one must be seen anywhere on the mountain. Not even the flocks and herds must be allowed to eat grass in front of the mountain."

4So Moses carved out two stone tablets that were just like the first ones. Early in the morning he went up Mount Sinai. He carried the two tablets in his hands. He did as the LORD had commanded him to do.

5Then the LORD came down in the cloud. He stood there with Moses and announced his name, The LORD.

6As he passed in front of Moses, he called out. He said, "I am the LORD, the LORD. I am a God who is tender and kind. I am gracious. I am slow to get angry. I am faithful and full of love. 7I continue to show my love to thousands of people. I forgive those who do evil. I forgive those who refuse to obey. And I forgive those who sin. But I do not let guilty people go without punishing them. I punish the children, grandchildren and great-grandchildren for the sin of their parents."

8Moses bowed down to the ground at once and worshiped. 9"Lord," he said, "if you are pleased with me, then go with us. Even though these people are stubborn, forgive the evil things we have done. Forgive our sin. And accept us as your people."

10Then the LORD said, "I am making a covenant with you. I will do wonderful things in front of all of your people. I will do miracles that have never been done before in any nation in the whole world. The people you live among will see the things that I, the LORD, will do for you. And they will see how wonderful those things really are.

11"Obey what I command you today. I will drive out the Amorites, Canaanites, Hittites, Perizzites, Hivites and Jebusites to make room for you.

12"Be careful. Do not make a peace treaty with those who live in the land where you are going. They will be a trap to you. 13Tear down their altars. Smash their sacred stones. Cut down the poles they use to worship the goddess Asherah. 14Do not worship any other god. I am a jealous God. In fact, my name is Jealous.

15"Be careful not to make a peace treaty with those who live in the land. They commit sin by offering sacrifices to their gods. They will invite you to eat their sacrifices. 16You will choose some of their daughters as wives for your sons. And those daughters will commit sin by worshiping their gods. Then they will lead your sons to do the same thing.

17"Do not make statues of gods.

18"Celebrate the Feast of Unleavened Bread. For seven days eat bread that is made without yeast, just as I commanded you. Do it at the appointed time in the month of Abib. You came out of Egypt in that month.

19"Every male animal that is born first to its mother belongs to me. That includes your livestock. It includes herds and flocks alike. 20Sacrifice a lamb to buy back every male donkey that is born first to its mother. But if you do not buy the donkey back, break its neck. Buy back every oldest son.

"You must not come to worship me with your hands empty.

21"Do your work in six days. But you must rest on the seventh day. Even when you are plowing your land or gathering your crops, you must rest on the seventh day.

22"Celebrate the Feast of Weeks. Bring the first share of your wheat crop.

"Celebrate the Feast of Booths. Hold it in the fall.

23"Three times a year all of your men must come to worship me. I am your LORD and King, the God of Israel. 24I will drive out nations ahead of you. I will increase your territory. Go up three times a year to worship me. While you are doing that, I will keep others from wanting to take any of your land for themselves. I am the LORD your God.

25"Do not include anything that is made with yeast when you offer me the blood of a sacrifice. You must not keep any of the meat from the sacrifice of the Passover Feast until morning.

26“Bring the best of the first share of your crops
to my house. I am the LORD your God.
“Do not cook a young goat in its mother’s milk.”
27Then the LORD said to Moses, “Write down
the words I have spoken. I have made a covenant
with you and with Israel in keeping with those
words.”
28Moses was there with the LORD for 40 days and
40 nights. He didn’t eat any food or drink any water.
The LORD wrote on the tablets the words of the
covenant. Those words are the Ten Commandments.

The Face of Moses Shines

29Moses came down from Mount Sinai. He had
the two tablets of the covenant in his hands. His
face was shining because he had spoken with the
LORD. But he didn’t realize it. 30Aaron and all of
the people of Israel saw Moses. His face was shining. So they were afraid to come near him.
31But Moses called out to them. So Aaron and all
of the leaders of the community came to him. And
Moses spoke to them. 32After that, all of the people
came near him. And he gave them all of the commands the LORD had given him on Mount Sinai.
33Moses finished speaking to them. Then he put
a veil over his face. 34But when he would go to
speak with the LORD, he would remove the veil.
He would keep it off until he came out. Then he
would tell the people what the LORD had commanded. 35They would see that his face was shining. So Moses would put the veil back over his
face. He would keep it on until he went in again to
speak with the LORD.

Rules for the Sabbath Day

35 Moses gathered the whole community of
Israel together. He said to them, “Here are
the things the LORD has commanded you to do.
2You must do your work in six days. But the seventh day will be your holy day. It will be a Sabbath in the LORD’s honor. You must rest on it.
Anyone who does any work on it must be put to
death. 3Do not even light a fire in any of your
homes on the Sabbath day.”

Supplies for the Holy Tent

4Moses spoke to the whole community of Israel. He said, “Here is what the LORD has commanded. 5Take an offering for the LORD from what
you have. Those who want to can bring an offering to the LORD. Here is what they can bring.

“gold, silver and bronze
6 blue, purple and bright red yarn and fine linen
goat hair
7 ram skins that are dyed red
the hides of sea cows
acacia wood
8 olive oil for the lights
spices for the anointing oil and for the sweet-smelling incense
9 onyx stones and other jewels for the linen apron and the chest cloth

10“All of the skilled workers among you must
come. They must make everything the LORD has
commanded 11for the holy tent and its covering.
Here is what they must make.

“hooks
frames
crossbars
posts
bases
12 the ark of the covenant
the poles and cover for the ark
the curtain that screens the ark
13 the table for the holy bread
the poles and all of the articles for the table
the holy bread
14 the lampstand for light and everything that is used with it
the lamps and the olive oil that gives light
15 the altar for burning incense
the poles for the altar
the anointing oil
the sweet-smelling incense
the curtain for the entrance to the holy tent
16 the altar for burnt offerings with its bronze grate
its poles and all of its tools
the large bronze bowl with its stand
17 the curtains of the courtyard with their posts and bases
the curtain for the entrance to the courtyard
18 the ropes and tent stakes for the holy tent and for the courtyard
19 the sacred clothes for Aaron the priest
the clothes for his sons when they serve as priests”

20Then the whole community of Israel left Moses. 21Everyone who wanted to give offerings to
the LORD brought them to him. The offerings were
for the work on the Tent of Meeting, for the sacred
clothes, and for any other purpose there.
22Every man and woman who wanted to give
came. They brought gold jewelry of all kinds.
They brought pins, earrings, rings and other jewelry. All of them gave their gold as a wave offering to the LORD.
23People brought what they had. They brought
blue, purple or bright red yarn or fine linen. They
brought goat hair, ram skins that were dyed red, or
the hides of sea cows. 24Some brought silver or
bronze as an offering to the LORD. Others brought
acacia wood for any part of the work.
25All of the skilled women spun yarn with their
hands. They brought blue, purple or bright red
yarn or fine linen. 26All of the skilled women who
wanted to spin the goat hair did so.
27The leaders brought onyx stones and other
jewels for the linen apron and the chest cloth.
28They also brought spices and olive oil. They

brought them for the light, for the anointing oil, and for the sweet-smelling incense.

29All of the men and women of Israel who wanted to bring offerings to the LORD brought them to him. The offerings were for all of the work the LORD had commanded Moses to tell them to do.

Bezalel and Oholiab

30Then Moses spoke to the people of Israel. He said, "The LORD has chosen Bezalel, the son of Uri. Uri is the son of Hur. Bezalel is from the tribe of Judah. 31The LORD has filled him with the Spirit of God. He has filled him with skill, ability and knowledge in all kinds of crafts. 32He can make beautiful patterns in gold, silver and bronze. 33He can cut and set stones. He can work with wood. In fact, he can work in all kinds of arts and crafts.

34"And the LORD has given both him and Oholiab the ability to teach others. Oholiab, the son of Ahisamach, is from the tribe of Dan.

35"The LORD has filled them with skill to do all kinds of work. They carve things and make patterns. They sew skillfully with blue, purple and bright red yarn and on fine linen. They use thread to make beautiful cloth. They have the skill to

36 work in all kinds of crafts. 1Bezalel and Oholiab must do the work just as the LORD has commanded. So must every skilled worker to whom the LORD has given skill and ability. They must know how to do all of the work for every purpose connected with the sacred tent. And that includes setting it up."

2Then Moses sent for Bezalel and Oholiab. He sent for every skilled worker to whom the LORD had given ability and who wanted to come and do the work.

3They received from Moses all of the offerings the people of Israel had brought. They had brought the offerings for all of the work for every purpose connected with the holy tent. That included setting it up. The people kept bringing the offerings they chose to give. They brought them morning after morning.

4So all of the skilled workers who were working on the holy tent stopped what they were doing. 5They said to Moses, "The people are bringing more than enough for doing the work the LORD commanded us to do."

6Then Moses gave an order. A message was sent through the whole camp. It said, "No man or woman should make anything else and offer it for the holy tent." And so the people were kept from bringing more offerings. 7There was already more than enough to do all of the work.

The Holy Tent

8All of the skilled workers made the holy tent. They made ten curtains out of finely twisted linen. They made them with blue, purple and bright red yarn. A skilled worker sewed cherubim into the pattern. 9All of the curtains were the same size. They were 42 feet long and six feet wide.

10The workers joined five of the curtains together. They did the same thing with the other five. 11Then they made loops out of blue strips of cloth along the edge of the end curtain in one set. They did the same thing with the end curtain in the other set. 12They also made 50 loops on the end curtain of the one set. They did the same thing on the end curtain of the other set. They put the loops across from each other. 13Then they made 50 gold hooks. They used them to join curtains together so that the holy tent was all one piece.

14The workers made a total of 11 curtains out of goat hair to put over the holy tent. 15All 11 curtains were the same size. They were 45 feet long and six feet wide.

16The workers joined five of the curtains together into one set. They did the same thing with the other six. 17Then they made 50 loops along the edge of the end curtain in the one set. They did the same thing with the other set. 18They made 50 bronze hooks. They used them to join the tent together all in one piece. 19They made a covering for the tent. They made it out of ram skins that were dyed red. They put a covering of the hides of sea cows over that.

20The workers made frames out of acacia wood for the holy tent. 21Each frame was 15 feet long and two feet three inches wide. 22The workers added two small wooden pins to each frame. The pins stuck out so that they were even with each other. The workers made all of the frames of the holy tent in the same way.

23They made 20 frames for the south side of the holy tent. 24And they made 40 silver bases to go under them. They made two bases for each frame. They put one under each pin that stuck out.

25For the north side of the holy tent they made 20 frames 26and 40 silver bases. They put two bases under each frame.

27The workers made six frames for the west end of the holy tent. 28They made two frames for the corners of the holy tent at the far end. 29At those two corners the frames were double from top to bottom. They were fitted into a single ring. The workers made both of them the same. 30So there were eight frames and 16 silver bases. There were two bases under each frame.

31The workers also made crossbars out of acacia wood. They made five for the frames on one side of the holy tent. 32They made five for the frames on the other side. And they made five for the frames on the west, at the far end of the holy tent. 33The center crossbar reached from end to end at the middle of the frames.

34They covered the frames with gold. They made gold rings to hold the crossbars. They also covered the crossbars with gold.

35They made the curtain out of blue, purple and bright red yarn and finely twisted linen. A skilled worker sewed cherubim into the pattern. 36The workers made four posts out of acacia wood for the curtain. They covered the posts with gold. They made gold hooks and four silver bases for the posts.

37For the entrance to the tent the workers made a curtain out of blue, purple and bright red yarn and finely twisted linen. A person who sewed skillfully made it. 38The workers made five posts with hooks for the curtains. They covered the tops of the posts and their bands with gold. And they made five bronze bases for them.

The Ark of the Covenant

37 Bezalel made the ark of the covenant out of acacia wood. It was three feet nine inches long and two feet three inches wide and high. 2He covered it inside and outside with pure gold. He put a strip of gold around it.

3He made four gold rings for it. He joined them to its four bottom corners. He put two rings on one side and two rings on the other.

4Then he made poles out of acacia wood. He covered them with gold. 5He put the poles through the rings on the sides of the ark to carry it.

6He made its cover out of pure gold. It was three feet nine inches long and two feet three inches wide. The cover is the place where sin is paid for.

7He made two cherubim out of hammered gold at the ends of the cover. 8He put one cherub on each end of it. 9He made the cherubim as part of the cover itself. The cherubim's wings spread up over the cover. The cherubim faced each other and looked toward the cover.

The Table for the Holy Bread

10The workers made the table out of acacia wood. It was three feet long, one foot six inches wide and two feet three inches high. 11They covered it with pure gold. They put a strip of gold around it. 12They also made a rim three inches wide around it. They put a strip of gold around the rim.

13They made four gold rings for the table. They joined them to the four corners, where the four legs were. 14The rings were close to the rim. They held the poles that were used to carry the table.

15The workers made the poles out of acacia wood. They covered them with gold.

16They made plates, dishes and bowls out of pure gold for the table. They also made pure gold pitchers to pour out drink offerings.

The Gold Lampstand

17The workers made the lampstand out of pure gold. They hammered out its base and stem. Its buds, blooms and cups branched out from it.

18Six branches came out from the sides of the lampstand. There were three on one side and three on the other. 19On one branch there were three cups that were shaped like almond flowers with buds and blooms. There were three on the next branch. There were three on all six branches that came out from the lampstand.

20On the lampstand there were four cups that were shaped like almond flowers with buds and blooms. 21One bud was under the first pair of branches that came out from the lampstand. A second bud was under the second pair. And a third bud was under the third pair. There was a total of six branches. 22The buds and branches came out from the lampstand.

The whole lampstand was one piece that was hammered out of pure gold.

23The workers made its seven lamps out of pure gold. They also made its trays and wick cutters out of pure gold. 24They used 75 pounds of pure gold to make the lampstand and everything that was used with it.

The Altar for Burning Incense

25The workers made an altar for burning incense. They made it out of acacia wood. It was one foot six inches square and three feet high. A horn stuck out from each of its upper four corners. 26The workers covered the top, sides and horns with pure gold. They put a strip of gold around it.

27They made two gold rings below the strip. They put the rings across from each other. The rings held the poles that were used to carry it. 28The workers made the poles out of acacia wood. They covered them with gold.

29They also made the sacred anointing oil and the pure, sweet-smelling incense. A person who makes perfume made them.

The Altar for Burnt Offerings

38 The workers made the altar for burnt offerings out of acacia wood. It was four feet six inches high and seven feet six inches square. 2They made a horn stick out from each of its four upper corners. They covered the altar with bronze.

3They made all of its tools out of bronze. They made its pots, shovels, sprinkling bowls, meat forks, and pans for carrying ashes.

4They made a bronze grate for the altar. They put the grate halfway up the altar on the inside. 5They made a bronze ring for each of the four corners of the grate.

6They made poles out of acacia wood. They covered them with bronze. 7They put the poles through the rings. The poles were on two sides of the altar for carrying it.

The workers made the altar out of boards. They made it hollow.

The Large Bowl for Washing

8The workers made the large bronze bowl and its bronze stand. They made them out of the bronze mirrors that belonged to the women who served at the entrance to the Tent of Meeting.

The Courtyard

9Next, the workers made the courtyard. The south side was 150 feet long. It had curtains that were made out of finely twisted linen. [10]The curtains had 20 posts and 20 bronze bases. The posts had silver hooks and bands on them.

[11]The north side was also 150 feet long. Its curtains had 20 posts and 20 bronze bases. The posts had silver hooks and bands on them.

[12]The west end was 75 feet wide. It had curtains with ten posts and ten bases. The posts had silver hooks and bands on them.

[13]The east end, toward the sunrise, was also 75 feet wide. [14]Curtains that were 22 feet six inches long were on one side of the entrance. They were hung on three posts. Each post had a base. [15]Curtains that were 22 feet six inches long were also on the other side of the entrance to the courtyard. They were hung on three posts. Each post had a base.

[16]All of the curtains that were around the courtyard were made out of finely twisted linen. [17]The bases for the posts were made out of bronze. The hooks and bands that were on the posts were made out of silver. Their tops were covered with silver. So all of the posts of the courtyard had silver bands.

[18]The curtain for the entrance to the courtyard was made out of blue, purple and bright red yarn and finely twisted linen. A person who sewed skillfully made it. It was 30 feet long. Like the curtains of the courtyard, it was seven feet six inches high. [19]It had four posts and four bronze bases. Their hooks and bands were made out of silver. Their tops were covered with silver.

[20]All of the tent stakes of the holy tent were made out of bronze. So were all of the stakes of the courtyard that was around it.

The Amounts of the Metals Used

[21]Here are the amounts of the metals that were used for the holy tent, where the tablets of the covenant were kept. Moses commanded the Levites to record the amounts. The Levites did the work under the direction of Ithamar. Ithamar was the son of the priest Aaron.

[22]Bezalel, the son of Uri, made everything the LORD had commanded Moses. Uri was the son of Hur. Bezalel was from the tribe of Judah. [23]Oholiab, the son of Ahisamach, helped Bezalel. Oholiab was from the tribe of Dan. He could carve things and make patterns. And he could sew skillfully with blue, purple and bright red yarn and on fine linen.

[24]The total weight of the gold from the wave offering was more than a ton. It was weighed out in keeping with the standard weights that are used in the sacred tent. The gold was used for all of the work that was done in connection with the sacred tent.

[25]The silver that was received from the men in the community who were listed and counted weighed four tons. It was weighed out in keeping with the weights used in the sacred tent. [26]It amounted to a fifth of an ounce for each person. It was weighed out in keeping with the weights used in the sacred tent. The silver was received from the men who had been listed and counted. All of them were 20 years old or more. Their total number was 603,550.

[27]The four tons of silver were used to make the bases for the holy tent and for the curtain. The 100 bases were made from the four tons. Each base used more than 75 pounds of silver. [28]The workers used 45 pounds to make the hooks for the posts, to cover the tops of the posts, and to make their bands.

[29]The bronze from the wave offering weighed two and a half tons. [30]The workers used some of it to make the bases for the entrance to the Tent of Meeting. They used some for the bronze altar for burnt offerings and its bronze grate and all of its tools. [31]They used some for the bases for the courtyard that was around the holy tent. They used some for the bases for the courtyard entrance. And they used the rest to make all of the tent stakes for the holy tent and the courtyard that was around it.

The Clothes for the Priests

39 The workers made clothes from the blue, purple and bright red yarn. The clothes were worn by those who served in the holy tent. The workers also made sacred clothes for Aaron. They made them just as the LORD had commanded Moses.

The Linen Apron

[2]The workers made the linen apron out of fine gold wire, and out of blue, purple and bright red yarn, and out of finely twisted linen. [3]They hammered out thin sheets of gold. They cut it into fine wire. They sewed it into the blue, purple and bright red yarn and fine linen. A skilled worker made it. [4]The workers made shoulder straps for the apron. The straps were joined to two of its corners.

[5]Its skillfully made waistband was made like it. The waistband was part of the apron itself. It was made out of fine gold wire, and out of blue, purple and bright red yarn, and out of finely twisted linen. The workers made it just as the LORD had commanded Moses.

[6]They put the onyx stones in fancy gold settings. They carved the names of the sons of Israel on them. They did it the way a person carves a seal. [7]Then they connected them to the shoulder straps of the linen apron. The stones stood for the sons of Israel and were a reminder for them. The workers did those things just as the LORD had commanded Moses.

The Chest Cloth

[8]Skilled workers made the chest cloth. They made it like the linen apron. They used fine gold wire, and blue, purple and bright red yarn, and finely twisted linen. [9]The chest cloth was nine inches square. It was folded in half.

10They put four rows of valuable jewels on it. A ruby, a topaz and a beryl were in the first row. 11A turquoise, a sapphire and an emerald were in the second row. 12A jacinth, an agate and an amethyst were in the third row. 13And a chrysolite, an onyx and a jasper were in the fourth row. The workers put them in fancy gold settings.

14They used a total of 12 stones. There was one stone for each of the names of the sons of Israel. Each stone was carved like a seal with the name of one of the 12 tribes.

15The workers made braided chains out of pure gold for the chest cloth. They made them like ropes. 16They made two fancy gold settings and two gold rings. They connected them to two corners of the chest cloth. 17They joined the two gold chains to the rings at the corners of the chest cloth. 18They joined the other ends of the chains to the two settings. They joined them to the shoulder straps on the front of the linen apron.

19The workers made two gold rings. They connected them to the other two corners of the chest cloth. They put them on the inside edge next to the apron. 20They made two more gold rings. They connected them to the bottom of the shoulder straps on the front of the apron. They put them close to the seam right above the waistband of the apron. 21They tied the rings of the chest cloth to the rings of the apron with blue cord. That connected it to the waistband. Then the chest cloth would not swing out from the linen apron. The workers did those things just as the LORD had commanded Moses.

More Clothes for the Priests

22The workers made the outer robe of the linen apron completely from blue cloth. The cloth was made by a skillful person. 23The workers made an opening like a collar in the center of the robe. They made an edge around the opening. Then it couldn't tear.

24They made pomegranates out of blue, purple and bright red yarn and finely twisted linen. They sewed them around the hem of the robe.

25They made bells out of pure gold. They sewed them around the hem between the pomegranates. 26They sewed a bell between every two pomegranates all around the hem of the robe. Aaron had to wear the robe when he served as priest. That's what the LORD commanded Moses.

27The workers made inner robes out of fine linen for Aaron and his sons. The linen cloth was made by a skillful person. 28The workers also made the turban out of fine linen. And they made the headbands and the underwear out of finely twisted linen. 29The belt was made out of finely twisted linen and blue, purple and bright red yarn. A person who sewed skillfully made it. The workers did those things just as the LORD had commanded Moses.

30They made the plate out of pure gold. It was a sacred crown. They carved words on it as if it were a seal. They carved the words SET APART FOR THE LORD. 31Then they tied the plate to the turban with a blue cord. They did those things just as the LORD had commanded Moses.

The Holy Tent is Completed

32So all of the work on the holy tent, the Tent of Meeting, was completed. The people of Israel did everything just as the LORD had commanded Moses.

33Then they brought the holy tent to Moses along with everything that belonged to it. Here are the things they brought.

hooks
frames
crossbars
posts
bases
34 the covering of ram skins that were dyed red
the covering of the hides of sea cows
the curtain that screens the ark
35 the ark where the tablets of the covenant are kept
the poles and cover for the ark
36 the table for the holy bread with all of its articles
the holy bread
37 the pure gold lampstand with its row of lamps and everything that is used with it
the olive oil that gives light
38 the gold altar for burning incense
the anointing oil
the sweet-smelling incense
the curtain for the entrance to the tent
39 the bronze altar for burnt offerings with its bronze grate
its poles and all of its tools
the large bowl with its stand
40 the curtains of the courtyard with their posts and bases
the curtain for the entrance to the courtyard
the ropes and tent stakes for the courtyard
41 the sacred clothes for the priest Aaron
the clothes for his sons when they serve as priests

42The people of Israel had done all of the work just as the LORD had commanded Moses. 43Moses looked over the work carefully. He saw that the workers had done it just as the LORD had commanded. So Moses gave them his blessing.

Moses Sets Up the Holy Tent

40 Then the LORD said to Moses, 2"Set up the holy tent, the Tent of Meeting. Set it up on the first day of the first month.

3"Place in it the ark where the tablets of the covenant are kept. Screen the ark with the curtain. 4Bring in the table for the holy bread. Arrange the loaves of bread on it. Then bring in the lampstand. Set up its lamps. 5Place the gold altar for burning incense in front of the ark where the tablets of the

covenant are kept. Put up the curtain at the entrance to the holy tent.
6"Place the altar for burnt offerings in front of
the entrance to the holy tent, the Tent of Meeting.
7Place the large bowl between the Tent of Meeting
and the altar. Put water in the bowl.
8"Set up the courtyard around the holy tent. Put
the curtain at the entrance to the courtyard.
9"Get the anointing oil. Anoint the holy tent and
everything that is in it. Set apart the holy tent and
everything that belongs to it. Then it will be holy.
10Anoint the altar for burnt offerings and all of its
tools. Set the altar apart. Then it will be a very holy
place. 11Anoint the large bowl and its stand. Set
them apart.
12"Bring Aaron and his sons to the entrance to
the Tent of Meeting. Wash them with water.
13Dress Aaron in the sacred clothes. Anoint him
and set him apart. Then he will be able to serve me
as priest.
14"Bring his sons and dress them in their inner
robes. 15Anoint them just as you anointed their
father. Then they will be able to serve me as
priests. They will be anointed to do the work of
priests. That work will last for all time to come."
16Moses did everything just as the LORD had
commanded him.
17So the holy tent was set up. It was the first day
of the first month in the second year. 18Moses set
up the holy tent. He put the bases in place. He put
the frames in them. He put in the crossbars. He set
up the posts. 19He spread the holy tent over the
frames. Then he put the coverings over the tent.
Moses did it as the LORD had commanded him.
20He got the tablets of the covenant. He placed
them in the ark. He put the poles through its rings.
And he put the cover on it. The cover was the
place where sin is paid for. 21Moses brought the
ark into the holy tent. He hung the curtain to screen
the ark where the tablets of the covenant are kept.
Moses did it as the LORD had commanded him.
22He placed the table for the holy bread in the
Tent of Meeting. It was on the north side of the
holy tent outside the curtain. 23He arranged the
loaves of bread on it in the sight of the LORD. Moses did it as the LORD had commanded him.
24He placed the lampstand in the Tent of Meeting. It stood across from the table on the south side
of the holy tent. 25He set up the lamps in the sight
of the LORD. Moses did it as the LORD had commanded him.
26He placed the gold altar for burning incense
in the Tent of Meeting. He placed it in front of the
curtain. 27He burned sweet-smelling incense on it.
Moses did it as the LORD had commanded him.
28Then he put up the curtain at the entrance to
the holy tent.
29He set the altar for burnt offerings near the
entrance to the holy tent, the Tent of Meeting. He
sacrificed burnt offerings and grain offerings on it.
Moses did it as the LORD had commanded him.
30He placed the large bowl between the Tent of
Meeting and the altar. He put water in the bowl for
washing. 31Moses and Aaron and his sons used it to
wash their hands and feet. 32They washed when they
entered the Tent of Meeting or approached the altar.
They did it as the LORD had commanded Moses.
33Then Moses set up the courtyard around the
holy tent and altar. He put up the curtain at the
entrance to the courtyard. And so Moses completed the work.

The Glory of the LORD

34Then the cloud covered the Tent of Meeting.
The glory of the LORD filled the holy tent. 35Moses
couldn't enter the Tent of Meeting because the
cloud had settled on it. The glory of the LORD
filled the holy tent.
36The people of Israel continued their travels.
When the cloud lifted from above the holy tent,
they started out. 37But if the cloud didn't lift, they
did not start out. They stayed until the day it lifted.
38So the cloud of the LORD was above the holy
tent during the day. Fire was in the cloud at night.
The whole community of Israel could see the
cloud during all of their travels.

Leviticus

Rules for Burnt Offerings

1 The LORD called out to Moses. He spoke to him from the Tent of Meeting. He said, 2“Speak to the people of Israel. Tell them, ‘Suppose any one of you brings an offering to the LORD. You must bring an animal from your herd or flock.

3“ ‘If a man brings a burnt offering from the herd, he must offer a male animal. It must not have any flaws. He must bring it to the entrance to the Tent of Meeting. Then the LORD will accept it.

4“ ‘The man must place his hand on the head of the burnt offering. Then the LORD will accept it in place of him. It will pay for his sin. 5The young bull must be killed there in the sight of the LORD.

“ ‘Then the priests who are in Aaron’s family line must bring its blood to the altar. They must sprinkle it against every side of the altar. The altar stands at the entrance to the Tent of Meeting.

6“ ‘The skin must be removed from the animal that is brought for the burnt offering. Then the animal must be cut into pieces.

7“ ‘The priests who are in Aaron’s family line must build a fire on the altar. They must place wood on the fire. 8Then they must place the pieces of the animal on the burning wood on the altar. The pieces include the head and the fat.

9“ ‘The inside parts of the animal must be washed with water. The legs must also be washed. The priest must burn all of it on the altar.

“ ‘It is a burnt offering. It is an offering that is made with fire. It gives a smell that is pleasant to the LORD.

10“ ‘If the offering is a burnt offering from the flock, it must be a male animal. It can be a sheep or a goat. It must not have any flaws.

11“ ‘It must be killed at the north side of the altar in the sight of the LORD. The priests who are in Aaron’s family line must sprinkle its blood against every side of the altar.

12“ ‘The animal must be cut into pieces. The priest must place them on the burning wood on the altar. The pieces include the head and the fat.

13“ ‘The inside parts must be washed with water. The legs must also be washed. The priest must bring all of it to the altar. He must burn it there.

“ ‘It is a burnt offering. It is an offering that is made with fire. It gives a smell that is pleasant to the LORD.

14“ ‘If the offering to the LORD is a burnt offering of birds, it must be a dove or a young pigeon.

15“ ‘The priest must bring it to the altar. He must twist its head off. Then he must burn the rest of the bird on the altar. Its blood must be emptied out on the side of the altar.

16“ ‘The priest must remove the small bag inside the bird’s throat. He must also remove what is in the bag. Then he must throw all of it to the east side of the altar. That is where the ashes are. 17He must take hold of the wings of the bird and tear it open. But he must not tear it in two. Then the priest will burn it on the wood that is on the fire on the altar.

“ ‘It is a burnt offering. It is an offering that is made with fire. It gives a smell that is pleasant to the LORD.

Rules for Grain Offerings

2 “ ‘Suppose someone brings a grain offering to the LORD. Then his offering must be made out of fine flour. He must pour olive oil on it. He must also put incense on it.

2“ ‘He must take it to the priests who are in Aaron’s family line. A priest must take a handful of the fine flour and oil. He must mix it with all of the incense. Then he must burn that part on the altar. It will be a reminder that all good things come from the LORD. It is an offering that is made with fire. It gives a smell that is pleasant to the LORD.

3“ ‘The rest of the grain offering belongs to Aaron and to the priests who are in his family line. It is a very holy part of the offerings that are made to the LORD with fire.

4“ ‘If you bring a grain offering that is baked in an oven, make it out of fine flour. It can be flat cakes that are made without yeast. Mix them with olive oil. Or it can be wafers that are made without yeast. Spread oil on them. 5If your grain offering is grilled on a metal plate, make it out of fine flour. Mix it with oil. Make it without yeast. 6Break it into pieces. Pour oil on it. It is a grain offering. 7If your grain offering is cooked in a pan, make it out of fine flour and oil.

8“ ‘Bring to the LORD your grain offering that is made out of all of those things. Give it to the priest. He must take it to the altar. 9He must take out the part of the grain offering that reminds you that all good things come from the LORD. He must burn it on the altar. It is an offering that is made with fire. It gives a smell that is pleasant to the LORD.

10“ ‘The rest of the grain offering belongs to Aaron and the priests who are in his family line. It is a very holy part of the offerings that are made to the LORD with fire.

11“ ‘Every grain offering you bring to the LORD must be made without yeast. You must not burn any yeast or honey in an offering that is made to the LORD with fire.

12“ ‘You can bring them to the LORD as an offering of the first share of the food you gather or produce. But they must not be offered on the altar as a pleasant smell.

13“‘Put salt on all of your grain offerings. Salt
stands for the lasting covenant between you and
your God. So do not leave it out of your grain
offerings. Add it to all of your offerings.
14“‘Suppose you bring to the LORD a grain
offering of the first share of your food. Then offer
crushed heads of your first grain that have been
cooked in fire. 15Put olive oil and incense on it. It
is a grain offering.
16“‘The priest must burn part of the crushed
grain and the oil. It will remind you that all good
things come from the LORD. The priest must burn
it together with all of the incense. It is an offering
that is made to the LORD with fire.

Rules for Friendship Offerings

3 “‘Suppose someone brings a friendship offering. If he offers an animal from the herd, it
can be either male or female. It must not have any
flaws. He must offer it in the sight of the LORD.
2“‘The man must place his hand on the animal's
head. It must be killed at the entrance to the Tent
of Meeting. Then the priests who are in Aaron's
family line must sprinkle the blood against every
side of the altar.
3“‘Part of the friendship offering must be given
to the LORD as an offering that is made with fire.
It must include all of the fat that covers the inside
parts or is connected to them. 4It must include both
kidneys with the fat on them next to the lower back
muscles. It must also include the covering of the
liver. All of it must be removed together with the
kidneys.
5“‘Then the priests who are in Aaron's family
line must burn it on the altar. They must burn it on
top of the burnt offering on the burning wood.
“‘It is an offering that is made with fire. It gives
a smell that is pleasant to the LORD.
6“‘If a man brings an animal from the flock as
a friendship offering to the LORD, it can be either
male or female. It must not have any flaws. 7If he
brings a lamb, he must offer it in the sight of the
LORD. 8The man must place his hand on the lamb's
head. It must be killed there in front of the Tent of
Meeting. Then the priests who are in Aaron's family line must sprinkle its blood against every side
of the altar. 9Part of the offering must be brought as
a sacrifice that is made to the LORD with fire. It
must include the lamb's fat and the entire fat tail
cut off close to the backbone. It must include all
of the fat that covers the inside parts or is connected to them. 10It must include both kidneys with
the fat on them next to the lower back muscles. It
must also include the covering of the liver. All of
it must be removed together with the kidneys.
11“‘Then the priest must burn it on the altar as
food. It is an offering that is made to the LORD with
fire.
12“‘If a man brings a goat, he must offer it in the
sight of the LORD. 13The man must place his hand
on its head. It must be killed there in front of the
Tent of Meeting. Then the priests who are in Aaron's family line must sprinkle its blood against
every side of the altar.
14“‘Part of the offering must be brought as an
offering that is made to the LORD with fire. It must
include all of the fat that covers the inside parts or
is connected to them. 15It must include both kidneys with the fat on them next to the lower back
muscles. It must also include the covering of the
liver. All of it must be removed together with the
kidneys.
16“‘Then the priest must burn it on the altar as
food. It is an offering that is made with fire. It has
a pleasant smell. All of the fat belongs to the LORD.
17“‘You must not eat any fat or any blood. That
is a law that will last for all time to come. It applies
no matter where you live.’”

Rules for Sin Offerings

4 The LORD spoke to Moses. He said, 2“Speak
to the people of Israel. Tell them, ‘Suppose
someone sins without meaning to. And that person
does something the LORD commands us not to do.
3“‘Suppose it is the anointed priest who sins.
And suppose he brings guilt on the people. Then
he must bring a young bull to the LORD. It must
not have any flaws. He must bring it as a sin offering for the sin he has committed. 4He must bring
the bull to the entrance to the Tent of Meeting in
the sight of the LORD. He must place his hand on
its head. He must kill it there in the sight of the
LORD.
5“‘Then the priest must take some of the bull's
blood. He must carry it into the Tent of Meeting.
6He must dip his finger into the blood. He must
sprinkle some of it seven times in the sight of the
LORD. He must do it in front of the curtain of the
Most Holy Room.
7“‘Then the priest must put some of the blood
on the horns that stick out from the upper four corners of the altar for burning incense. The incense
has a sweet smell. The altar stands in front of the
LORD in the Tent of Meeting. The priest must pour
out the rest of the bull's blood at the bottom of the
altar for burnt offerings. That altar stands at the
entrance to the tent.
8“‘He must remove all of the fat from the bull
for the sin offering. It includes the fat that covers
the inside parts or is connected to them. 9It
includes both kidneys with the fat on them next to
the lower back muscles. It also includes the covering of the liver. He must remove all of it together
with the kidneys. 10He must remove it in the same
way the fat is removed from an ox that is sacrificed
as a friendship offering. Then the priest must burn
all of it on the altar for burnt offerings.
11“‘But the bull's hide must be taken away. So
must all of its meat. So must its head and legs. And
so must its inside parts and guts. 12In other words,
all of the rest of the bull must be taken away. The

priest must take it outside the camp. He must take
it to a place that is "clean." He must take it to the
place where the ashes are thrown. There he must
burn it in a wood fire on a pile of ashes.

13" 'Or suppose the whole community of Israel
sins without meaning to. They do something the
LORD commands us not to do. Even if they are not
aware of what they have done, they are guilty.

14" 'But suppose they become aware of the sin
they have committed. Then they must bring a
young bull as a sin offering. They must offer it in
front of the Tent of Meeting. 15The elders of the
community must place their hands on the bull's
head in the sight of the LORD. The bull must be
killed in the sight of the LORD.

16" 'Then the anointed priest must take some of
the bull's blood into the Tent of Meeting. 17He
must dip his finger into the blood. He must sprinkle it seven times in the sight of the LORD. He must
do it in front of the curtain. 18He must put some of
the blood on the horns that stick out from the upper
four corners of the altar. The altar stands in front of
the LORD in the Tent of Meeting. The priest must
pour out the rest of the blood at the bottom of the
altar for burnt offerings. That altar stands at the
entrance to the tent.

19" 'He must remove all of the fat from the bull.
He must burn it on the altar. 20He must do the same
thing with that bull as he did with the bull for the
sin offering. When he does, he will pay for the sin
of the people. And they will be forgiven.

21" 'Then he must take the bull outside the camp.
He must burn it just as he burned the first bull. It
is the sin offering for the whole community.

22" 'Or suppose a leader sins without meaning
to. If he disobeys any of the commands of the
LORD his God, he is guilty.

23" 'But suppose he is made aware of the sin he
has committed. Then he must bring an offering. It
must be a male goat. It must not have any flaws.
24He must place his hand on the goat's head. He
must kill it. He must do it at the place where the
animals for burnt offerings are killed in the sight of
the LORD. His offering is a sin offering.

25" 'Then the priest must dip his finger into some
of the blood of the sin offering. He must put it on
the horns that stick out from the upper four corners
of the altar for burnt offerings. He must pour out
the rest of the blood at the bottom of the altar.

26" 'He must burn all of the fat on the altar. He
must burn it in the same way he burned the fat of
the friendship offering. When he does, he will pay
for the sin of the leader. And the leader will be forgiven.

27" 'Or suppose someone in the community sins
without meaning to. If he disobeys any of the
LORD's commands, he is guilty.

28" 'But suppose he is made aware of the sin he
has committed. Then he must bring an offering for
the sin he has committed. It must be a female goat.
It must not have any flaws. 29He must place his
hand on the head of the animal for the sin offering. It must be killed at the place where the animals for burnt offerings are killed.

30" 'Then the priest must dip his finger into
some of the blood. He must put it on the horns that
stick out from the upper four corners of the altar
for burnt offerings. He must pour out the rest of
the blood at the bottom of the altar.

31" 'He must remove all of the fat in the same
way the fat is removed from the friendship offering. He must burn it on the altar. It gives a smell
that is pleasant to the LORD. When the priest burns
the offering, he will pay for the sin of that person.
And he will be forgiven.

32" 'Suppose he brings a lamb as his sin offering. Then he must bring a female animal. It must
not have any flaws. 33He must place his hand on
its head. He must kill it as a sin offering. He must
do it at the place where the animals for burnt offerings are killed.

34" 'Then the priest must dip his finger into some
of the blood of the sin offering. He must put it on
the horns that stick out from the upper four corners
of the altar for burnt offerings. He must pour out
the rest of the blood at the bottom of the altar.

35" 'He must remove all of the fat in the same
way the fat is removed from the lamb for the
friendship offering. He must burn it on the altar on
top of the offerings that are made to the LORD with
fire. When he does, he will pay for the sin that person has committed. And he will be forgiven.

5 " 'Suppose a person has been called as a witness to something he has seen or learned
about. Then if he does not tell what he knows, he
has sinned. And he will be held accountable for it.

2" 'Or suppose a person touches something that
is not "clean." It could be the dead bodies of wild
animals or of livestock. Or it could be the dead
bodies of creatures that move along the ground.
Even though he is not aware that he touched them,
he has become "unclean." And he is guilty.

3" 'Or suppose he touches something "unclean"
that comes from a human being. It could be anything that would make him "unclean." Suppose he
is not aware that he touched it. When he finds out
about it, he will be guilty.

4" 'Or suppose a person takes an oath and makes
a promise to do something without thinking it
through. It does not matter what he promised. It
does not matter whether he took the oath without
thinking about it carefully. And suppose he is not
aware that he did not think it through. When he
finds out about it, he will be guilty.

5" 'When someone is guilty in any of those
ways, he must admit he has sinned. 6He must bring
a sin offering to pay for the sin he has committed.
He must bring to the LORD a female lamb or goat
from the flock. The priest will sacrifice the animal.
That will pay for the person's sin.

[7]"'Suppose he can't afford a lamb. Then he must get two doves or two young pigeons. He must bring them to the LORD to pay for his sin. One of them is for a sin offering. The other is for a burnt offering.

[8]"'He must bring them to the priest. The priest will offer the one for the sin offering first. He must twist its head. But he must not twist it off completely.

[9]"'Then he must sprinkle some of the blood of the sin offering against the side of the altar. He must empty out the rest of the blood at the bottom of the altar. It is a sin offering.

[10]"'Then the priest will offer the other bird as a burnt offering. He must do it in the way the law requires. That will pay for the sin the person has committed. And he will be forgiven.

[11]"'But suppose he can't afford two doves or two young pigeons. Then he must bring eight cups of fine flour as an offering for his sin. It is a sin offering. He must not put olive oil or incense on it. That is because it is a sin offering.

[12]"'He must bring it to the priest. The priest must take a handful of it. He must burn that part on the altar. It will be a reminder that all good things come from the LORD. The priest must burn it on top of the offerings that are made to the LORD with fire. It is a sin offering.

[13]"'In that way the priest will pay for any of the sins the person has committed. And he will be forgiven. The rest of the offering will belong to the priest. It is the same as in the case of the grain offering.'"

Rules for Guilt Offerings

[14]The LORD spoke to Moses. He said, [15]"Suppose a person sins by breaking the law. And he does it without meaning to. He sins against me or my priests by refusing to give them one of the holy things that are set apart for them.

"Then he must bring me a ram from the flock. It must not have any flaws. It must be worth the required amount of silver. It must be weighed out in keeping with the standard weights that are used in the sacred tent. It is a guilt offering. It will pay for his sin.

[16]"He must also pay for the holy thing he refused to give. He must add a fifth of its value to it. He must give all of it to the priest. The priest will pay for the person's sin with the ram. It is a guilt offering. And he will be forgiven.

[17]"Suppose a person sins by doing something I command him not to do. Even though he does not know it, he is guilty. He will be held accountable for it.

[18]"He must bring to the priest a ram from the flock as a guilt offering. It must not have any flaws. And it must be worth the required amount of money.

"The priest will sacrifice the animal. That will pay for what the person has done wrong without meaning to. And he will be forgiven. [19]It is a guilt offering. He has been guilty of doing wrong against me."

6 The LORD spoke to Moses. He said, [2]"Suppose a person sins by not being faithful to me. He does it by tricking his neighbors. He tricks them in connection with something they have placed in his care. He steals from them. Or he cheats them. [3]Or he finds something they have lost and then tells a lie about it. Or he goes to court. He takes an oath and tells a lie when he witnesses about it. Or he commits any other sin like those sins.

[4]"When he sins in any of those ways, he becomes guilty. He must return what he stole. He must give back what he took by cheating his neighbors. He must return what they placed in his care. He must return the lost property he found. [5]He must return anything he told a lie about when he witnessed in court. He must pay back everything in full. He must add a fifth of its value to it. He must give all of it to the owner on the day he brings his guilt offering.

[6]"He must bring his guilt offering to the priest to pay for his sin. It is an offering to me. He must bring a ram from the flock. It must not have any flaws. It must be worth the required amount of money.

[7]"The priest will sacrifice the ram to pay for the person's sin. He will do it in my sight. And the person will be forgiven for any of the things he did that made him guilty."

More Rules for Burnt Offerings

[8]The LORD spoke to Moses. He said, [9]"Give Aaron and the priests who are in his family line a command. Tell them, 'Here are some more rules for burnt offerings. The burnt offering must remain on the altar through the whole night. The fire on the altar must be kept burning until morning.

[10]"'The priest must put on his linen clothes. He must put on linen underwear next to his body. He must remove the ashes of the burnt offering that the fire has burned up on the altar. He must place them beside the altar. [11]Then he must take his clothes off and put others on. He must carry the ashes outside the camp to a place that is "clean."

[12]"'The fire on the altar must be kept burning. It must not go out. Every morning the priest must add more wood to the fire. He must place the burnt offering on the fire. He must burn the fat of the friendship offerings on it. [13]The fire must be kept burning on the altar all the time. It must not go out.

More Rules for Grain Offerings

[14]"'Here are some more rules for grain offerings. The priests who are in Aaron's family line must bring the grain offering to the LORD in front of the altar.

[15]"'The priest must take a handful of fine flour and olive oil. He must add to it all of the incense that is on the grain offering. He must burn that part

on the altar. It will remind him that all good things come from the LORD. It gives a smell that is pleasant to the LORD.

16"'Aaron and the priests who are in his family line will eat the rest of it. But they must eat it without yeast in a holy place. They must eat it in the courtyard of the Tent of Meeting. 17It must not be baked with yeast. The LORD has given it to the priests as their share of the offerings that are made to him with fire. It is very holy, just like the sin offering and the guilt offering.

18"'Any priests who are in Aaron's family line can eat it. It is their regular share of the offerings that are made to the LORD with fire. It is their share for all time to come. Anyone who touches those offerings will become holy.'"

19The LORD spoke to Moses. He said, 20"On the day each high priest who is in Aaron's family line is anointed, he must bring an offering to me. He must bring eight cups of fine flour as a regular grain offering. He must bring half of it in the morning. He must bring the other half in the evening. 21Mix it with olive oil. Grill it on a metal plate. Break it in pieces. Bring it as a grain offering. It gives a smell that is pleasant to me.

22"The son of Aaron who will become the next high priest after him will prepare the grain offering. It is my regular share. It must be completely burned up. 23Every grain offering a high priest offers must be completely burned up. It must not be eaten."

More Rules for Sin Offerings

24The LORD spoke to Moses. He said, 25"Speak to Aaron and the priests who are in his family line. Tell them, 'Here are some more rules for sin offerings. You must kill the animal for the sin offering in the sight of the LORD. Kill it in the place where the burnt offering is killed. It is very holy. 26The priest who offers it will eat it. He must eat it in a holy place. He must eat it in the courtyard of the Tent of Meeting.

27"'Anyone who touches any of its meat will become holy. Suppose some of the blood is spilled on someone's clothes. Then you must wash them in a holy place. 28Break the clay pot the meat is cooked in. But suppose you cook it in a bronze pot. Then you must scrub the pot and rinse it with water.

29"'Any male in a priest's family can eat the meat. It is very holy.

30"'But suppose some of the blood of a sin offering is brought into the Tent of Meeting. And that blood is brought into the Holy Room to pay for sin. Then that sin offering must not be eaten. It must be burned.

More Rules for Guilt Offerings

7 "'Here are some more rules for guilt offerings. The guilt offering is very holy. 2You must kill the animal for the guilt offering in the same place where you kill the animal for the burnt offering. Sprinkle its blood against every side of the altar.

3"'Offer all of its fat. It must include the fat tail and the fat that covers the inside parts. 4It must include both kidneys with the fat on them next to the lower back muscles. It must also include the covering of the liver. Remove all of it together with the kidneys. 5The priest must burn all of it on the altar. It is an offering that is made to the LORD with fire. It is a guilt offering.

6"'Any male in a priest's family can eat it. But he must eat it in a holy place. It is very holy.

7"'The same law applies to the sin offering and the guilt offering. Both of them belong to the priest who offers them to pay for sin. 8The priest who offers a burnt offering for anyone can keep its hide for himself.

9"'Every grain offering that is baked in an oven belongs to the priest who offers it. So does every grain offering that is cooked in a pan or grilled on a metal plate. 10Every grain offering belongs equally to all of the priests who are in Aaron's family line. That is true whether it is mixed with olive oil or it is dry.

More Rules for Friendship Offerings

11"'Here are some more rules for friendship offerings a person may bring to the LORD.

12"'Suppose he offers a friendship offering to show he is thankful. Then together with the thank offering he must offer flat cakes of bread. He must make them without yeast. He must mix them with olive oil. Or he must offer wafers that are made without yeast. He must spread oil on them. Or he must offer flat cakes that are made out of fine flour. He must add oil to it. He must work the flour and mix it well.

13"'He must bring another friendship offering along with his thank offering. It should be flat cakes of bread that are made with yeast. 14He must bring one of each kind of bread as an offering. One kind is made with yeast. The other is not. Both of them are a gift to the LORD. They belong to the priest who sprinkles the blood of the friendship offerings.

15"'The person must eat the meat from his thank offering on the day he offers it. He must not leave any of it until morning.

16"'But suppose he brings a friendship offering to keep a promise he has made. Or suppose he brings an offering he chooses to give. Then he must eat the sacrifice on the day he offers it. But if anything is left over, he may eat it the next day.

17"'He must burn up any meat from the sacrifice that is left over until the third day. 18Suppose he eats any meat from the friendship offering on the third day. Then the LORD will not accept the offering. He will not accept it as a gift from that person. It is not pure. If the person eats any of it, he will be held accountable for it.

19“‘He must not eat meat that touches anything that is “unclean.” He must burn it up. Anyone who is “clean” may eat any other meat.

20“‘But suppose a person is not “clean” and eats any meat from the friendship offering that belongs to the LORD. Then that person will be cut off from his people.

21“‘Suppose a person touches something that is not “clean.” It does not matter whether it comes from a human being who is not “clean.” It does not matter whether it comes from an animal that is not “clean.” It does not matter whether it comes from something that is hated and is not “clean.” And suppose the person eats any of the meat from the friendship offering that belongs to the LORD. Then that person will be cut off from his people.’”

Israel Must Not Eat Fat or Blood

22The LORD spoke to Moses. He said, 23“Speak to the people of Israel. Tell them, ‘Do not eat any of the fat of cattle, sheep or goats. 24Do not eat the fat of any animal that is found dead. Do not eat the fat of an animal that wild animals have torn apart. But you can use the fat for any other purpose.

25“‘Suppose an animal has been sacrificed as an offering that is made to the LORD with fire. No one may eat its fat. If he does, he will be cut off from his people.

26“‘No matter where you live, do not eat the blood of any bird or animal. 27If anyone does, he will be cut off from his people.’”

The Share That Belongs to the Priests

28The LORD spoke to Moses. He said, 29“Speak to the people of Israel. Tell them, ‘Suppose a person brings a friendship offering to the LORD. Then he must bring part of it as his special gift to the LORD. 30He must bring it with his own hands. It is an offering that is made to the LORD with fire. He must bring the fat together with the breast. He must lift the breast up and wave it in front of the LORD as a wave offering. 31The priest will burn the fat on the altar.

“‘But the breast belongs to Aaron and the priests who are in his family line. 32Give the right thigh from your friendship offerings to the priest as a gift. 33The priest who offers the blood and fat from the friendship offering must be given the right thigh. It is his share.

34“‘I, the LORD, have taken the breast that is waved and the thigh that is given. I have taken them from the friendship offerings of the people of Israel. And I have given them to the priest Aaron and the priests who are in his family line. The offerings are their regular share from the people of Israel.’”

35That is the part of the offerings that are made to the LORD with fire and given to Aaron and the priests who are in his family line. It was given to Aaron and his sons on the day they were set apart to serve the LORD as priests. 36On the day they were anointed, the LORD commanded the people of Israel to give that part to them. For all time to come, it will be the regular share of Aaron and the priests who are in his family line.

37Those are the rules for burnt offerings, grain offerings, sin offerings, guilt offerings and friendship offerings. They are also the rules for the offerings that are given when priests are being prepared to serve the LORD. 38They are the rules the LORD gave Moses on Mount Sinai. He gave them on the day he commanded the people of Israel to bring their offerings to the LORD. That took place in the Sinai Desert.

Preparing the Priests to Serve the LORD

8 The LORD spoke to Moses. He said, 2“Bring Aaron and his sons to the entrance to the Tent of Meeting. Bring their clothes and the anointing oil. Bring the bull for the sin offering. Also bring two rams. And bring the basket with the bread that is made without yeast. 3Then gather the whole community at the entrance to the Tent of Meeting.”

4Moses did just as the LORD had commanded him. All of the people gathered together at the entrance to the Tent of Meeting.

5Moses said to the people, “Here is what the LORD has commanded us to do.”

6Then Moses brought Aaron and his sons to the people. He washed Aaron and his sons with water. 7He put the inner robe on Aaron. He tied the belt around him. He dressed him in the outer robe. He put the linen apron on him. He took the skillfully made waistband and tied the apron on him with it. He wanted to make sure it was securely tied to him.

8Moses placed the chest cloth on Aaron. He put the Urim and Thummim in the chest cloth. 9Then he placed the turban on Aaron's head. On the front of the turban he put the gold plate. It was a sacred crown. Moses did everything just as the LORD had commanded him.

10Then Moses took the anointing oil and poured it on the holy tent. He also poured it on everything that was in it. That's how he set those things apart for the LORD. 11He sprinkled some of the oil on the altar seven times. He poured oil on the altar and all of its tools. He poured it on the large bowl and its stand. He did it to set them apart.

12He poured some of the anointing oil on Aaron's head. He anointed him to set him apart to serve the LORD. 13Then Moses brought Aaron's sons to the people. He put the inner robes on them. He tied belts around them. He put headbands on them. He did everything just as the LORD had commanded him.

14Then he brought the bull for the sin offering. Aaron and his sons placed their hands on its head. 15Moses killed the bull. He dipped his finger into some of the blood. He put it on all of the horns that stick out from the upper four corners of the altar. He did it to make the altar pure. He poured out the rest of the blood at the bottom of the altar. So he set it apart to make it pure.

16Moses also removed all of the fat that was around the inside parts of the bull. He removed the covering of the liver. He took both kidneys and their fat. Then he burned all of it on the altar.

17But he burned the rest of the bull outside the camp. He burned up its hide, its meat and its guts. He did it just as the LORD had commanded him.

18Then Moses brought the ram for the burnt offering. Aaron and his sons placed their hands on its head. 19Moses killed the ram. He sprinkled the blood against every side of the altar.

20He cut the ram into pieces. He burned the head, the other pieces and the fat. 21He washed the inside parts and the legs with water. He burned the whole ram on the altar as a burnt offering. It had a pleasant smell. It was an offering that was made to the LORD with fire. Moses did everything just as the LORD had commanded him.

22Then he brought the other ram. It was sacrificed to prepare the priests for serving the LORD. Aaron and his sons placed their hands on its head.

23Moses killed the ram. He put some of its blood on Aaron's right ear lobe. He put some on the thumb of Aaron's right hand. He also put some on the big toe of Aaron's right foot. 24Then Moses brought Aaron's sons to the people. He put some of the blood on their right ear lobes. He put some on the thumbs of their right hands. He also put some on the big toes of their right feet. Then he sprinkled the rest of the blood against every side of the altar.

25He removed the fat, the fat tail and all of the fat around the inside parts. He removed the covering of the liver. He removed both kidneys and their fat. And he removed the right thigh. 26Then he took a flat cake of bread from the basket of bread that was made without yeast. The basket was in front of the LORD. Moses took a cake of bread that was made with olive oil. He also took a wafer. He put all of it on the fat parts of the ram and on its right thigh.

27He put everything in the hands of Aaron and his sons. He told them to lift it up and wave it in front of the LORD as a wave offering.

28Then Moses took it from their hands. He burned it on the altar on top of the burnt offering. It was the offering that was sacrificed to prepare the priests for serving the LORD. It had a pleasant smell. It was an offering that was made to the LORD with fire.

29Moses also lifted the ram's breast up and waved it in front of the LORD as a wave offering. The breast was Moses' share of the ram that was sacrificed to prepare the priests for serving the LORD. Moses did everything just as the LORD had commanded him.

30Then Moses took some of the anointing oil. He also took some of the blood from the altar. He sprinkled some of the oil and blood on Aaron and his clothes. He also sprinkled some on Aaron's sons and their clothes. That's how he set apart Aaron and his clothes. And that's how he set apart Aaron's sons and their clothes.

31Then Moses spoke to Aaron and his sons. He said, "Cook the meat at the entrance to the Tent of Meeting. Eat it there along with the bread from the basket of the offerings that are brought to prepare the priests for serving the LORD. Do it just as I commanded you. I said, 'Aaron and his sons must eat it.' 32Then burn up the rest of the meat and the bread.

33"Don't leave the entrance to the Tent of Meeting for seven days. Don't leave until the days that are required to prepare you for serving the LORD have been completed. Stay here for the full seven days. 34The LORD commanded what has been done here today. It was done to pay for your sin. 35Stay at the entrance to the Tent of Meeting for seven days. Stay here day and night. Do what the LORD requires. Then you won't die. That's the command the LORD gave me."

36So Aaron and his sons did everything just as the LORD had commanded through Moses.

The Priests Offer Sacrifices

9 On the eighth day Moses sent for Aaron, his sons and the elders of Israel. 2He said to Aaron, "Bring a bull calf for your sin offering. Bring a ram for your burnt offering. They must not have any flaws. Offer them to the LORD.

3"Then speak to the people of Israel. Tell them, 'Bring a male goat for a sin offering. Bring a calf and a lamb for a burnt offering. Both of them must be a year old. They must not have any flaws. 4Bring an ox and a ram for a friendship offering. Sacrifice all of them to the LORD. Also bring a grain offering. Mix it with olive oil. Today the LORD will appear to you.'"

5The people got the things Moses commanded them to get. They took them to the front of the Tent of Meeting. The whole community came up close to the tent. They stood there in front of the LORD.

6Then Moses said, "You have done what the LORD has commanded. So the glory of the LORD will appear to you."

7Moses said to Aaron, "Come to the altar. Sacrifice your sin offering and your burnt offering. Pay for your sin and the sin of the people. Sacrifice the people's offering. Pay for their sin. Do just as the LORD has commanded."

8So Aaron came to the altar. He killed the calf as a sin offering for himself. 9His sons brought its blood to him. He dipped his finger into the blood. He put some on the horns that stick out from the upper four corners of the altar. He poured out the rest at the bottom of the altar.

10He burned the fat and the kidneys on the altar. He also burned the covering of the liver. All of those parts were from the sin offering. Aaron did just as the LORD had commanded Moses. [11]He burned up the meat and the hide outside the camp.

[12]Then he killed the animal for the burnt offering. His sons handed him its blood. He sprinkled it against every side of the altar. [13]They handed him the burnt offering piece by piece. It included the animal's head. Aaron burned everything on the altar. [14]He washed the inside parts and the legs. He burned them on top of the burnt offering on the altar.

[15]Then Aaron brought the people's offering. He took the goat for their sin offering and killed it. He offered it for a sin offering. He did just as he had done with his own sin offering.

[16]He brought the animal for the burnt offering. He offered it in the way the law requires. [17]He also brought the grain offering. He took a handful of it and burned it on the altar. It was in addition to that morning's burnt offering.

[18]Aaron killed the ox and the ram as the friendship offering for the people. His sons handed him the blood. He sprinkled it against every side of the altar.

[19]His sons also brought the fat parts of the ox and the ram. They included the fat tail and the layer of fat. They also included the kidneys and the covering of the liver. [20]Aaron's sons placed everything on the breasts of the animals.

Aaron burned the fat on the altar. [21]He lifted up the breasts and the right thigh and waved them in front of the LORD as a wave offering. He did it just as Moses had commanded.

[22]Then Aaron lifted up his hands toward the people. He gave them a blessing. He had already sacrificed the sin offering, the burnt offering and the friendship offering. So he stepped down from the altar.

[23]Moses and Aaron went into the Tent of Meeting. When they came out, they gave the people a blessing. The glory of the LORD appeared to all of the people. [24]The LORD sent fire on the altar. It burned up the burnt offering and the fat parts that were on it. All of the people saw it. Then they shouted for joy. They fell with their faces to the ground.

The Lord Kills Nadab and Abihu

10 Nadab and Abihu were two of Aaron's sons. They got their shallow cups for burning incense. They put fire in them. They added incense to it. They made an offering to the LORD by using fire that wasn't allowed. They did it against his command. [2]So the LORD sent fire on them. It burned them up. They died in front of the LORD.

[3]Then Moses spoke to Aaron. He said, "That's what the LORD was talking about when he said,

"'Among those who approach me
I will show that I am holy.
In the sight of all of the people
I will be honored.'"

So Aaron remained silent.

[4]Moses sent for Mishael and Elzaphan. They were sons of Aaron's uncle Uzziel. Moses said to them, "Come here. Carry the bodies of your cousins outside the camp. Take them away from in front of the Holy Room." [5]So they came and carried them outside the camp. It was just as Moses had ordered. The bodies of Nadab and Abihu still had their inner robes on them.

[6]Moses spoke to Aaron and to Eleazar and Ithamar. They were Aaron's sons. Moses said, "Don't let your hair hang loose. Don't tear your clothes. If you do, you will die. And the LORD will be angry with the whole community.

"But all of the people of Israel are allowed to show they are sad. They are your relatives. They can sob over those the LORD has destroyed with fire.

[7]"Don't leave the entrance to the Tent of Meeting. If you do, you will die. That's because the LORD's anointing oil has made you holy." So they did what Moses told them to do.

[8]Then the LORD spoke to Aaron. He said, [9]"You and your sons must not drink any kind of wine when you go into the Tent of Meeting. If you do, you will die. That is a law that will last for all time to come.

[10]"You must be able to tell the difference between what is holy and what is not. You must be able to tell the difference between what is 'clean' and what is not. [11]You must teach the people of Israel all of the rules I have given them through Moses."

[12]Moses spoke to Aaron and to Eleazar and Ithamar. They were Aaron's two remaining sons. Moses said, "Take the grain offering that is left over from the offerings that are made to the LORD with fire. It is very holy. Make bread without yeast from it. Eat it beside the altar. [13]Eat it in a holy place. It's your share and your sons' share of the offerings that are made to the LORD with fire. Those rules are in keeping with the command the LORD gave me.

[14]"But you and your sons and your daughters can eat the breast that was waved. You can also eat the thigh that was offered. Eat them in a place that is 'clean.' They have been given to you and your children. They are your share of the friendship offerings the people of Israel bring.

[15]"The thigh that was offered must be brought together with the fat parts of the offerings that are made with fire. The breast that was waved must be brought in the same way. All of it must be lifted up and waved in front of the LORD as a wave offering. It will be the regular share for you and your children. That's what the LORD has commanded."

[16]Moses asked about the goat that was brought as the sin offering. He found out that it had been burned up. So he became angry with Eleazar and Ithamar. They were Aaron's two remaining sons.

Moses asked them, [17]"Why didn't you eat the sin offering in a place that is near the Holy Room? The offering is very holy. It was given to you to take the people's guilt away. It paid for their sin in the sight of the LORD. [18]The blood of the offering

wasn't taken into the Holy Room. So you should
have eaten the goat in a place that is near the Holy
Room. That's what I commanded."
19 Aaron replied to Moses, "Today the people
sacrificed their sin offering to the LORD. They also
sacrificed their burnt offerings to him. But a terrible thing has happened to me. Two of my sons
have died. Would the LORD have been pleased if I
had eaten the sin offering today?" 20 When Moses
heard that, he was satisfied.

Food That Is "Clean" and Food That Is Not

11 The LORD spoke to Moses and Aaron. He
said to them, 2 "Speak to the people of Israel. Tell them, 'Many animals live on land. Here are
the only ones you can eat. 3 You can eat any animal
that has hoofs that are separated completely in
two. But it must also chew the cud.
4 " 'Some animals only chew the cud. Some only
have hoofs that are separated in two. You must not
eat those animals.
" 'Camels chew the cud. But their hoofs are not
separated in two. So they are not "clean" for you.
5 " 'Rock badgers chew the cud. But their hoofs
are not separated in two. So they are not "clean"
for you.
6 " 'Rabbits chew the cud. But their hoofs are not
separated in two. So they are not "clean" for you.
7 " 'Pigs have hoofs that are separated completely in two. But they do not chew the cud. So
they are not "clean" for you.
8 " 'You must not eat the meat of those animals.
You must not even touch their dead bodies. They
are not "clean" for you.
9 " 'Many creatures live in the water of the
oceans and streams. You can eat all of those that
have fins and scales.
10 " 'But be sure to avoid all of the creatures in
the oceans or streams that do not have fins and
scales. That includes all of those that move
together in groups and all of those that do not. 11 Be
sure to avoid them. Do not eat their meat. Do not
even touch their dead bodies. 12 Be sure to avoid
everything that lives in the water that does not
have fins and scales.
13 " 'Here are the birds you must be sure to avoid.
Do not eat them. Be sure to avoid them.
" 'They include eagles, vultures and black vultures. 14 They include red kites and all kinds of
black kites. 15 They include all kinds of ravens.
16 They include horned owls, screech owls, gulls
and all kinds of hawks.
17 " 'They include little owls, cormorants and
great owls. 18 They include white owls, desert owls
and ospreys. 19 They also include storks, hoopoes,
bats and all kinds of herons.
20 " 'Be sure to avoid every flying insect that
walks on all fours. 21 But you can eat some creatures that have wings and walk on all fours. Their
legs have joints so they can hop on the ground.
22 " 'Here are the insects you can eat. You can eat
all kinds of locusts, katydids, crickets and
grasshoppers. 23 But be sure to avoid every other
creature that has wings and four legs.
24 " 'You will make yourselves "unclean" if you
eat those things. If you touch their dead bodies,
you will be "unclean" until evening. 25 If a person
picks up one of their dead bodies, he must wash
his clothes. He will be "unclean" until evening.
26 " 'Suppose an animal has hoofs that are not
separated completely in two. Or suppose an animal does not chew the cud. Then those animals are
not "clean" for you. If you touch the dead body of
any of them, you will not be "clean."
27 " 'Many animals walk on all fours. But those
that walk on their paws are not "clean" for you.
Anyone who touches their dead bodies will be
"unclean" until evening. 28 If he picks up their dead
bodies, he must wash his clothes. He will be
"unclean" until evening. They are not "clean" for
him.
29 " 'Many animals move around on the ground.
Here are the ones that are not "clean" for you. They
include weasels, rats and all kinds of large lizards.
30 They also include geckos, monitor lizards, wall
lizards, skinks and chameleons. 31 Those are the animals that move around on the ground that are not
"clean" for you. If you touch their dead bodies, you
will be "unclean" until evening.
32 " 'Suppose one of them dies and falls on something. Then that article will not be "clean." It does
not matter what it is used for. It does not matter
whether it is made out of wood, cloth, hide or
black cloth. Put it in water. It will be "unclean"
until evening. After that, it will be "clean."
33 " 'Suppose one of those animals falls into a
clay pot. Then everything that is in the pot will be
"unclean." You must break the pot. 34 Any food that
could be eaten but has water on it that came from
that pot is not "clean." And any liquid that could
be drunk from it is not "clean."
35 " 'Anything that the dead body of one of those
animals falls on becomes "unclean." If it is an
oven or cooking pot, break it. It is "unclean." And
you must consider it "unclean."
36 " 'But a spring or a well for collecting water
remains "clean." That is true even if the dead body
of one of those animals falls into it. But anyone
who touches the dead body is not "clean."
37 " 'If the dead body falls on any seeds that have
not been planted yet, the seeds remain "clean."
38 But suppose water has already been put on the
seeds. And suppose the dead body falls on them.
Then they are not "clean" for you.
39 " 'Suppose an animal you are allowed to eat
dies. If anyone touches its dead body, he will be
"unclean" until evening. 40 If he eats part of the
dead body, he must wash his clothes. He will be
"unclean" until evening. If he picks up the dead
body, he must wash his clothes. He will be
"unclean" until evening.

41“‘Be sure to avoid every creature that moves around on the ground. Do not eat it. 42Do not eat any of those creatures. It does not matter whether they move on their bellies. It does not matter whether they walk on all fours or on many feet. Be sure to avoid them. 43Do not make yourselves “unclean” by eating any of those animals. Do not make yourselves “unclean” because of them. Do not let them make you “unclean.”

44“‘I am the LORD your God. Set yourselves apart. Be holy, because I am holy. Do not make yourselves “unclean” by eating any creatures that move around on the ground. 45I am the LORD. I brought you up out of Egypt to be your God. So be holy, because I am holy.

46“‘Those are the rules about animals and birds. Those are the rules about every living thing that moves in the water. And those are the rules about every creature that moves around on the ground. 47You must be able to tell the difference between what is “clean” and what is not. You must also be able to tell the difference between the living creatures that can be eaten and those that can’t.’”

Becoming “Clean” After Having a Baby

12 The LORD spoke to Moses. He said, 2“Speak to the people of Israel. Tell them, ‘Suppose a woman becomes pregnant and has a baby boy. Then she will be “unclean” for seven days. It is the same as when she is “unclean” during her monthly period. 3On the eighth day the boy must be circumcised.

4“‘After that, the woman must wait for 33 days to be made pure from her bleeding. She must not touch anything that is sacred until the 33 days are over. During that time she must not go to the sacred tent.

5“‘But suppose she has a baby girl. Then she will be “unclean” for two weeks. It is the same as during her period. After the two weeks, she must wait for 66 days to be made pure from her bleeding.

6“‘After she has waited the required number of days to be made pure, she must bring two offerings. She must take them to the priest at the entrance to the Tent of Meeting. She must bring a lamb that is a year old for a burnt offering. She must also bring a young pigeon or a dove for a sin offering. 7The priest must offer them to the LORD. They will pay for her sin. Then she will be “clean” from her bleeding.

“‘Those are the rules for a woman who has a baby boy or girl.

8“‘But suppose she can’t afford a lamb. Then she must bring two doves or two young pigeons. One is for a burnt offering. The other is for a sin offering. The priest will sacrifice those offerings. That will pay for her sin. And she will be “clean.”’”

Rules About Skin Diseases

13 The LORD spoke to Moses and Aaron. He told them to say to the people, 2“Suppose someone’s skin has a swelling or a rash or a bright spot. And suppose it could become a skin disease. Then he must be brought to the priest Aaron. Or he must be brought to a priest who is in Aaron’s family line.

3“The priest must look carefully at the sore on the person’s skin. He must see whether the hair in the sore has turned white. He must also see whether the sore seems to be under the skin. If the sore is white and is under the skin, it is a skin disease. When the priest looks that person over carefully, he must announce that the person is ‘unclean.’

4“Suppose the spot on the skin is white but does not seem to be under the skin. And suppose the hair in the spot has not turned white. Then the priest must make the person stay away from everyone else for seven days. 5On the seventh day the priest must look carefully at the sore again. Suppose it has not changed and has not spread in the skin. Then the priest must make the person stay away from everyone else for another seven days. 6On the seventh day the priest must look carefully at the sore again. If it has faded and has not spread, he must announce that the person is ‘clean.’ It is only a rash. He must wash his clothes. He will be ‘clean.’

7“But suppose the rash spreads in the skin after he has shown himself to the priest a second time. Then he must appear in front of the priest again. 8The priest must look carefully at the sore. If the rash has spread, he must announce that the person is ‘unclean.’ He has a skin disease.

9“When anyone has a skin disease, he must be brought to the priest. 10The priest must look him over carefully. Suppose there is a white swelling in the skin. Suppose it has turned the hair white. And suppose there are open sores in the swelling. 11Then the person has a skin disease that will never go away. The priest must announce that he is ‘unclean.’ The priest must not make the person stay away from everyone else. He is already ‘unclean.’

12“Suppose the disease breaks out all over his skin. And suppose it covers him from head to foot, as far as the priest can tell. 13Then the priest must look him over carefully. If the disease has covered his whole body, the priest must announce that he is ‘clean.’ All of his skin has turned white. So he is ‘clean.’

14“But when open sores appear on his skin, he will not be ‘clean.’ 15When the priest sees the open sores, he must announce that he is ‘unclean.’ The open sores are not ‘clean.’ He has a skin disease.

16“But if the open sores change and turn white, he must go to the priest. 17The priest must look him over carefully. If the sores have turned white, the priest must announce that the person is ‘clean.’ Then he will be ‘clean.’

18“Suppose someone has a boil on his skin and it heals. 19And suppose a white swelling or shiny pink spot appears where the boil was. Then he must show himself to the priest.

[20]"The priest must look at the boil carefully. Suppose it seems to be under the skin. And suppose the hair in it has turned white. Then the priest must announce that the person is 'unclean.' A skin disease has broken out where the boil was.

[21]"But suppose that when the priest looks at the boil carefully, there is no white hair in it. The boil is not under the skin. And it has faded. Then the priest must make the person stay away from everyone else for seven days. [22]If the boil is spreading in the skin, the priest must announce that the person is 'unclean.' He has a skin disease.

[23]"But suppose the spot has not changed. And suppose it has not spread. Then it is only a scar from the boil. And the priest must announce that the person is 'clean.'

[24]"Suppose someone has a burn on his skin. And suppose a white or shiny pink spot shows up in the open sores of the burn. [25]Then the priest must look at the spot carefully. Suppose the hair in it has turned white. And suppose the spot seems to be under the skin. Then the person has a skin disease. It has broken out where he was burned. The priest must announce that the person is 'unclean.' He has a skin disease.

[26]"But suppose the priest looks at the spot carefully. Suppose there is no white hair in it. Suppose the spot is not under the skin. And suppose it has faded. Then the priest must make the person stay away from everyone else for seven days. [27]On the seventh day the priest must look him over carefully. If the spot is spreading in the skin, the priest must announce that the person is 'unclean.' He has a skin disease.

[28]"But suppose the spot has not changed. It has not spread in the skin. And it has faded. Then the burn has caused it to swell. The priest must announce that the person is 'clean.' It is only a scar from the burn.

[29]"Suppose a man or woman has a sore on the head or chin. [30]Then the priest must look at the sore carefully. Suppose it seems to be under the skin. And suppose the hair in the sore is yellow and thin. Then the priest must announce that the person is 'unclean.' The sore is an itch. It is a skin disease on the head or chin.

[31]"But suppose the priest looks carefully at that kind of sore. It does not seem to be under the skin. And there is no black hair in it. Then the priest must make the person stay away from everyone else for seven days.

[32]"On the seventh day the priest must look at the sore carefully. Suppose the itch has not spread in the skin. It does not have any yellow hair in it. And it does not seem to be under the skin. [33]Then the person must shave his head. But he must not shave the area where the disease is. And the priest must make him stay away from everyone else for another seven days.

[34]"On the seventh day the priest must look at the itch carefully. Suppose it has not spread in the skin. And suppose it does not seem to be under the skin. Then the priest must announce that the person is 'clean.' He must wash his clothes. He will be 'clean.'

[35]"But suppose the itch spreads in the skin after the priest announces that the person is 'clean.' [36]Then the priest must look him over carefully. Suppose the itch has spread. Then the priest does not have to look for yellow hair. The person is not 'clean.'

[37]"But suppose the itch has been stopped and black hair has grown in it, as far as the priest can tell. Then the itch is healed. The person is 'clean.' The priest must announce that he is 'clean.'

[38]"Suppose a man or woman has white spots on the skin. [39]Then the priest must look at them carefully. Suppose he sees that the spots are dull white. Then a harmless rash has broken out on the skin. That person is 'clean.'

[40]"Suppose a man loses all of the hair on his head. Then he is 'clean.' [41]Suppose he loses only the hair on the front of his head. Then he is 'clean.'

[42]"But suppose he has a shiny pink sore on his head where his hair was. Then he has a skin disease. It is breaking out on his whole head or on the front of his head.

[43]"The priest must look him over carefully. Suppose the swollen sore on his head or on the front of it is pink and shiny. And suppose it looks like a skin disease. [44]Then he has a skin disease. He is not 'clean.' The priest must announce that the man is 'unclean.' That is because he has a sore on his head.

[45]"Suppose someone has a skin disease that makes him 'unclean.' Then he must wear torn clothes. He must let his hair hang loose. He must cover the lower part of his face. He must cry out, 'Unclean! Unclean!' [46]As long as he has the disease, he remains 'unclean.' He must live alone. He must live outside the camp.

Rules About Mold

[47]"Suppose some clothes have mold on them. The clothes could be made out of wool or linen. [48]Or there could be cloth that is woven or knitted out of linen or wool. There could be pieces of leather. Or there could be articles that are made out of leather. [49]And suppose the mold that is on the clothes or on the woven or knitted cloth looks green or red. Or suppose the green or red mold is on the pieces of leather or the leather articles. Then it is mold that spreads. It must be shown to the priest.

[50]"The priest must look at it carefully. He must keep the article with the mold on it away from everything else for seven days. [51]On the seventh day he must look at it carefully. Suppose the mold has spread in the clothes or in the woven or knitted cloth. Or suppose it has spread on the pieces of leather or on the leather articles. Then it is mold that destroys. The article is not 'clean.'

52"The priest must burn up everything that has the mold in it. He must burn up the clothes or the woven or knitted cloth that is made out of wool or linen. He must burn up the leather articles. The mold destroys. So everything must be burned up.

53"But suppose the priest looks at the article carefully. The mold has not spread in the clothes. And it has not spread in the woven or knitted cloth or in the leather articles. 54Then he will order someone to wash the article that has the mold on it. After that, the priest must keep the articles away from everything else for another seven days.

55"After the article that has the mold on it has been washed, the priest must look at it carefully. Suppose the way the mold looks has not changed. Then even though the mold has not spread, it is not 'clean.' Burn it up. It does not matter which side of the article the mold is on.

56"But suppose the priest looks at it carefully. And suppose the mold has faded after the article has been washed. Then the priest must tear out the part that has mold on it. He must tear it out of the clothes or leather. He must tear it out of the woven or knitted cloth.

57"But suppose it shows up again in the clothes. Or suppose it shows up again in the woven or knitted cloth or in the leather articles. Then it is spreading. Everything that has the mold on it must be burned up.

58"The clothes that have been washed and do not have any more mold on them must be washed again. So must the woven or knitted cloth or the leather articles. Then they will be 'clean.'"

59Those are the rules about what to do with anything that has mold on it. They apply to clothes that are made out of wool or linen. They apply to woven and knitted cloth and to leather articles. They give a priest directions about when to announce whether something is "clean" or not.

Making People "Clean" From Skin Diseases

14 The LORD spoke to Moses. He told him to say to the people, 2"Here are the rules for making someone 'clean' if he has had a skin disease. They apply when he is brought to the priest.

3"The priest must go outside the camp. He must look the person over carefully. Suppose he has been healed of his skin disease. 4Then the priest will order someone to bring him two live 'clean' birds. He will also order someone to bring him some cedar wood, bright red yarn and branches of a hyssop plant. All of those things will be used to make the person 'clean.'

5"The priest will order someone to kill one of the birds. It must be killed over fresh water in a clay pot. 6Then the priest must take the live bird. He must dip it into the blood of the bird that was killed over the fresh water. He must dip it into the blood together with the cedar wood, the bright red yarn and the hyssop plant.

7"The priest will sprinkle the blood on the person who had the skin disease. That will make him 'clean.' The priest must sprinkle him seven times. Then the priest must announce that he is 'clean.' After that, the priest must let the live bird go free in the open fields.

8"The person must also wash his clothes to be made 'clean.' He must shave off all of his hair. He must take a bath. Then he will be 'clean.' After that, he may come into the camp. But he must stay outside his tent for seven days.

9"On the seventh day he must shave off all of his hair. He must shave his head. He must shave off his beard. He must also shave off his eyebrows and the rest of his hair. He must wash his clothes. He must take a bath. Then he will be 'clean.'

10"On the eighth day he must bring two male lambs and one female lamb as an offering. The female must be a year old. The lambs must not have any flaws. He must also bring 24 cups of fine flour as a grain offering. He must mix it with olive oil. He must also bring five ounces of oil. 11The priest who announces that the person is 'clean' must bring him and his offerings to me. He must do it at the entrance to the Tent of Meeting.

12"Then the priest must take one of the male lambs. He must offer it as a guilt offering. He must offer it along with five ounces of oil. He must lift all of it up and wave it in front of me as a wave offering.

13"He must kill the lamb in the holy place where sin offerings and burnt offerings are killed. The guilt offering belongs to the priest, just as the sin offering does. The guilt offering is very holy.

14"The priest must take some of the blood from the guilt offering and put it on the person's right ear lobe. He must put some on the thumb of his right hand. He must also put some on the big toe of his right foot.

15"Then the priest must take some of the oil and pour it into his own left hand. 16He must dip his right forefinger into the oil that is in his hand. He must use his finger to sprinkle some of the oil in front of me seven times.

17"The priest must put some of the oil that is in his hand on the same places he put the blood of the guilt offering. He must put some on the person's right ear lobe. He must put some on the thumb of his right hand. He must put some on the big toe of his right foot. 18He must put on his head the rest of the oil that is in his hand. It will pay for the person's sin in my sight.

19"Then the priest must sacrifice the sin offering. It will pay for the person's sin. He will be made 'clean' after being 'unclean.' After that, the priest will kill the burnt offering. 20He will offer it on the altar. He will offer it together with the grain offering. It will pay for the person's sin. Then he will be 'clean.'

21"But suppose he is poor. Suppose he can't afford all of those offerings. Then he must bring one male lamb as a guilt offering. It must be lifted up and waved in front of me to pay for his sin. He must also bring eight cups of fine flour along with the lamb. He must mix the flour with olive oil. It is a grain offering. He must offer it along with five ounces of oil. 22He must also bring two doves or two young pigeons that he can afford. One is for a sin offering. The other is for a burnt offering.

23"On the eighth day he must bring them to the priest so he can be made 'clean.' He must bring them to the entrance to the Tent of Meeting. He must do it in my sight.

24"The priest must take the lamb for the guilt offering. He must take it together with the five ounces of oil. He must lift all of it up and wave it in front of me as a wave offering. 25He must kill the lamb for the guilt offering. He must take some of its blood and put it on the person's right ear lobe. He must put some on the thumb of his right hand. He must also put some on the big toe of his right foot.

26"The priest must pour some of the oil into his own left hand. 27He must dip his right forefinger into the oil that is in his hand. He must use his finger to sprinkle some of it seven times in front of me.

28"He must put some of the oil that is in his hand on the same places he put the blood of the guilt offering. He must put some on the person's right ear lobe. He must put some on the thumb of his right hand. He must also put some on the big toe of his right foot. 29He must put on his head the rest of the oil that is in his hand. It will pay for the person's sin in my sight.

30"The priest will sacrifice the doves or the young pigeons that the person can afford. 31One is for a sin offering. The other is for a burnt offering. The priest must offer them together with the grain offering. In that way he will pay for the person's sin in my sight. He will do it to make him 'clean.'"

32Those are the rules for anyone who has a skin disease. They are for people who can't afford the regular offerings that are required to make them "clean."

Making Things "Clean" From Mold

33The LORD spoke to Moses and Aaron. He told them to say to the people, 34"You will enter the land of Canaan. I am giving it to you as your own. When you enter it, suppose I put mold in one of your houses. And suppose the mold spreads. 35Then the owner of that house must go and speak to the priest. He must say, 'I've seen something that looks like mold in my house.'

36"The priest must order everything to be taken out of the house. It must be done before he goes in to look carefully at the mold. If it is not done, the priest must announce that everything in the house is 'unclean.'

"After the house is empty the priest must go in and check it. 37He must look carefully at the mold that is on the walls. Suppose it looks as if it has green or red dents in it. And suppose the dents look as if they are behind the surface of the wall. 38Then the priest must go out the door. He must close the house up for seven days.

39"On the seventh day the priest will return to check the house. Suppose the mold that is on the walls has spread. 40Then he must order someone to tear out the stones that have mold on them. He must have them thrown into an 'unclean' place outside the town. 41He must have all of the inside walls of the house scraped. Everything that is scraped off must be dumped into an 'unclean' place outside the town.

42"Then other stones must be put in the place of the stones that had mold on them. The inside walls of the house must be coated with new clay.

43"Suppose the stones have been torn out. The house has been scraped. And the walls have been coated with new clay. But the mold appears again.

44"Then the priest must go and look things over carefully. Suppose the mold has spread in the house. Then it is the kind of mold that destroys things. The house is not 'clean.'

45"It must be torn down. The stones, the wood and all of the clay coating must be torn out. All of it must be taken out of the town to an 'unclean' place.

46"Suppose someone goes into the house while it is closed up. Then he will be 'unclean' until evening. 47If he sleeps or eats in the house, he must wash his clothes.

48"But suppose the priest comes to look things over carefully. And suppose the mold has not spread after the walls had been coated with new clay. Then he will announce that the house is 'clean.' The mold is gone.

49"To make the house pure, the priest must get two birds. He must also get some cedar wood, bright red yarn and branches of a hyssop plant. 50He must kill one of the birds over fresh water in a clay pot.

51"Then he must take the cedar wood, the hyssop plant, the bright red yarn and the live bird. He must dip all of them into the blood of the dead bird. He must also dip them into the fresh water. He must sprinkle the house seven times.

52"The priest will use the blood and the water to make the house pure. He will use the live bird to make it pure. He will also use the cedar wood, the hyssop plant and the bright red yarn to make it pure.

53"Then he must let the live bird go free in the open fields outside the town. In that way he will make the house pure. It will be 'clean.'"

54Those are the rules for skin diseases. They apply to itches. 55They apply to mold in clothes or in houses. 56They also apply to swellings, rashes or bright red spots on the skin. 57Use those rules to decide whether something is "clean" or not.

Those are the rules for skin diseases and for mold.

Rules About Liquid Body Wastes

15 The LORD spoke to Moses and Aaron. He said, 2“Speak to the people of Israel. Tell them, ‘Suppose liquid waste is flowing out of a man’s body. That liquid is not “clean.” 3It does not matter whether it continues to flow out of his body or is blocked. It will make him “unclean.” Here is how his liquid body waste will make him “unclean.”

4“ ‘Any bed the man who has the flow of liquid body waste lies on will not be “clean.” Anything he sits on will not be “clean.”

5“ ‘If any of you touches the man’s bed, you must wash your clothes. You must take a bath. You will be “unclean” until evening. 6Suppose you sit on anything the man sat on. Then you must wash your clothes. You must take a bath. You will be “unclean” until evening.

7“ ‘Suppose you touch the man who has the flow of liquid body waste. Then you must wash your clothes. You must take a bath. You will be “unclean” until evening.

8“ ‘Suppose you are “clean.” And suppose the man who has the flow of liquid waste spits on you. Then you must wash your clothes. You must take a bath. You will be “unclean” until evening.

9“ ‘Everything the man sits on when he is riding will be “unclean.” 10Suppose you touch any of the things that were under him. Then you will be “unclean” until evening. Even if you pick up those things, you must wash your clothes. You must take a bath. You will be “unclean” until evening.

11“ ‘Suppose the man who has the liquid flow touches you. And suppose he does it without rinsing his hands with water. Then you must wash your clothes. You must take a bath. You will be “unclean” until evening.

12“ ‘Suppose the man touches a clay pot. Then that pot must be broken. Any wooden article he touches must be rinsed with water.

13“ ‘Suppose the man has been healed from his liquid flow. Then he must wait seven days. He must wash his clothes. He must take a bath in fresh water. After that, he will be “clean.”

14“ ‘On the eighth day he must get two doves or two young pigeons. He must come to the LORD at the entrance to the Tent of Meeting. There he must give the birds to the priest. 15The priest must sacrifice them. One is for a sin offering. The other is for a burnt offering. In that way the priest will pay for the man’s sin in the sight of the LORD. He will do it because the man had a liquid flow.

16“ ‘Suppose semen flows from a man’s body. Then he must wash his whole body with water. He will be “unclean” until evening.

17“ ‘Suppose clothes or leather have semen on them. Then they must be washed with water. They will be “unclean” until evening.

18“ ‘Suppose a man makes love to a woman. And suppose semen flows from his body and touches both of them. Then they must take a bath. They will be “unclean” until evening.

19“ ‘Suppose a woman is having her regular period. Then for seven days she will not be pure. Anyone who touches her will be “unclean” until evening.

20“ ‘Anything she lies on during her period will be “unclean.” Anything she sits on will be “unclean.”

21“ ‘If anyone touches her bed, he must wash his clothes. He must take a bath. He will be “unclean” until evening. 22If anyone touches anything she sits on, he must wash his clothes. He must take a bath. He will be “unclean” until evening.

23“ ‘It does not matter whether it was her bed or anything she was sitting on. If anyone touches it, he will be “unclean” until evening.

24“ ‘Suppose a man makes love to that woman. And suppose blood from her monthly period touches him. Then he will be “unclean” for seven days. Any bed he lies on will be “unclean.”

25“ ‘Suppose blood flows from a woman’s body for many days. And it happens at a time other than her monthly period. Or blood keeps flowing after her period is over. Then she will be “unclean” as long as the blood continues to flow. She will be “unclean,” just as she is during the days of her period.

26“ ‘Any bed she lies on while her blood continues to flow will be “unclean.” It is the same as it is when she is having her period. Anything she sits on will be “unclean.” It is the same as it is when she is having her period.

27“ ‘If anyone touches those things, he will not be “clean.” He must wash his clothes. He must take a bath. He will be “unclean” until evening.

28“ ‘Suppose the woman has been healed from her flow of blood. Then she must wait seven days. After that, she will be “clean.” 29On the eighth day she must get two doves or two young pigeons. She must bring them to the priest at the entrance to the Tent of Meeting.

30“ ‘The priest must sacrifice them. One is for a sin offering. The other is for a burnt offering. In that way he will pay for her sin in the sight of the LORD. He will do it because her flow of blood made her “unclean.”

31“ ‘You must keep the people of Israel away from things that make them “unclean.” Then they will not die for being “unclean.” And they will not die for making the place where the LORD lives “unclean.” It is in the middle of the camp.’ ”

32Those are the rules for a man who has liquid waste flowing out of his body. They apply to a man who is made “unclean” by semen that flows from his body. 33They apply to a woman who is having her monthly period. They apply to a man or woman who has a liquid flow. And they apply to a man who makes love to a woman who is not “clean.”

The Day When Sin Is Paid For

16 The LORD spoke to Moses after two of Aaron's sons had died. They were the sons who died when they came near the LORD. 2The LORD said to Moses, "Speak to your brother Aaron. Tell him not to come into the Most Holy Room just anytime he wants to. Tell him not to come behind the curtain that is in front of the cover of the ark. The cover is the place where sin is paid for. If he comes behind the curtain, he will die. That is because I appear in the cloud over the cover.

3"Aaron must not enter the area of the sacred tent without bringing a sacrifice. He must bring a young bull for a sin offering. He must also bring a ram for a burnt offering.

4"He must put on the sacred inner robe that is made out of linen. He must wear linen underwear next to his body. He must tie the linen belt around him. And he must put on the linen turban. Those are sacred clothes. So he must take a bath before he puts them on.

5"The community of Israel must give him two male goats and a ram. The goats are for a sin offering. The ram is for a burnt offering.

6"Aaron must offer the bull for his own sin offering. It will pay for his own sin and the sin of his whole family.

7"Then he must take the two goats and bring them to me at the entrance to the Tent of Meeting.
8He must cast lots for the two goats. One lot is for me. The other is for the goat that carries the people's sins away. 9Aaron must bring the goat that is chosen for me by lot. He must sacrifice it for a sin offering.

10"But the goat that is chosen by the other lot must remain alive. First it must be brought in to me to pay for the people's sin. Then it must be sent into the desert as a goat that carries the people's sins away.

11"Aaron must bring the bull for his own sin offering. It will pay for his own sin and the sin of his whole family. He must kill the bull for his own sin offering.

12"He must take a shallow cup full of burning coals from the altar in my sight. He must get two handfuls of incense that is completely ground up. The incense must smell sweet. He must take the cup and the incense behind the curtain. 13He must put the incense on the fire in my sight. The smoke from the incense will hide the cover of the ark where the tablets of the covenant are kept. The cover is the place where sin is paid for. Aaron must burn the incense so that he will not die.

14"He must dip his finger in the bull's blood. He must sprinkle it on the front of the cover of the ark. He must sprinkle some in front of the cover. He must do it seven times.

15"Then Aaron must kill the goat for the sin offering for the people. He must take its blood behind the curtain. There he must do the same thing with it as he did with the bull's blood. He must sprinkle it on the cover of the ark. He must also sprinkle some in front of it.

16"That is how he will make the Most Holy Room pure. He must do it because the people of Israel are not 'clean.' They have not obeyed me. They have also committed other sins. Aaron must do the same for the Tent of Meeting because it stands in the middle of the camp. And the camp is not 'clean.'

17"No one can be in the Tent of Meeting when Aaron goes into the Most Holy Room to pay for the people's sin. No one can enter the tent until Aaron comes out. He will not come out until he has paid for his own sin and the sin of his whole family. He will not come out until he has also paid for the sin of the whole community of Israel.

18"Then he will come out to the altar for burnt offerings. It is in front of the tent where the ark of the LORD is. He will make the altar pure and clean. He will take some of the bull's blood and some of the goat's blood. Then he will put the blood on all of the horns that stick out from the upper four corners of the altar. 19He will sprinkle some of the blood on it with his finger seven times. He will do it to make the altar pure. He will do it to set it apart from the people of Israel. They are not 'clean.'

20"Aaron will finish making the Most Holy Room pure and clean. He will finish making the Tent of Meeting and the altar pure.

"Then he will bring the live goat out. 21He must place both of his hands on its head. While he does that, he must tell me about all of the sins the people of Israel have committed. He must tell me about all of their evil acts and the times they did not obey me. In that way he puts their sins on the goat's head.

"Then he will send the goat away into the desert. The goat will be led away by a man who was appointed to do it. 22The goat will carry all of their sins on itself to a place where there are no people. And the man will set the goat free in the desert.

23"Then Aaron must go into the Tent of Meeting. He must take off the linen clothes he put on before he entered the Most Holy Room. He must leave them there. 24He must take a bath in a holy place. And he must put on his regular clothes.

"Then he will come out and sacrifice the burnt offering for himself. He will also sacrifice the burnt offering for the people. That will pay for his own sin and the people's sin. 25He will also burn the fat of the sin offering on the altar.

26"The man who sets free the goat that carries the people's sins away must wash his clothes. He must take a bath. After that, he can come back into the camp.

27"The bull and the goat for the sin offerings must be taken outside the camp. Their blood was brought into the Most Holy Room. It paid for sin. The hides, meat and guts must be burned up.

28“The man who burns them must wash his clothes. He must take a bath. After that, he can come back into the camp.

29“Here is a law for you that will last for all time to come. On the tenth day of the seventh month you must not eat anything. You must not do any work. It does not matter whether you are Israelites or outsiders.

30“On that day your sin will be paid for. You will be made pure and clean. You will be clean from all of your sins in my sight. 31That day is a sabbath for you. You must rest on it. You must not eat anything on that day. That is a law that will last for all time to come.

32“The high priest must pay for sin. He must make everything pure and clean. He has been anointed and prepared to become the next high priest after his father. He must put on the sacred clothes that are made out of linen. 33He must make the Most Holy Room, the Tent of Meeting and the altar pure. And he must pay for the sin of the priests and all of the people in the whole community.

34“Here is a law for you that will last for all time to come. Once a year you must pay for all of the sin of the people of Israel.”

So it was done, just as the LORD commanded Moses.

Do Not Eat Meat That Has Blood in It

17 The LORD spoke to Moses. He said, 2“Speak to Aaron and his sons. Speak to all of the people of Israel. Tell them, ‘Here is what the LORD has commanded. He has said, 3“Suppose someone sacrifices an ox, a lamb or a goat. He sacrifices it in the camp or outside of it. 4He does it instead of bringing the animal to the entrance to the Tent of Meeting. He sacrifices it instead of giving it as an offering to me in front of my holy tent. Then he will be thought of as guilty of spilling blood. Because he has done that, he must be cut off from his people.

5“ ‘ “The people of Israel are now making sacrifices in the open fields. But they must bring their sacrifices to the priest. They must bring them to me at the entrance to the Tent of Meeting. There they must sacrifice them as friendship offerings. 6The priest must sprinkle the blood against my altar. It is the altar at the entrance to the Tent of Meeting. He must burn the fat. It will give a pleasant smell to me.

7“ ‘ “Israel must stop offering any of their sacrifices to statues of gods that look like goats. When they offer sacrifices to those statues, they are not faithful to me. That is a law for them that will last for all time to come.” ’

8“Tell them, ‘Suppose someone offers a burnt offering or sacrifice. It does not matter whether he is an Israelite or an outsider. 9And suppose he does not bring it to the entrance to the Tent of Meeting to sacrifice it to me. Then he must be cut off from his people.

10“ ‘Suppose someone eats meat that still has blood in it. It does not matter whether he is an Israelite or an outsider. I will turn against him if he eats it. I will cut him off from his people.

11“ ‘The life of each creature is in its blood. So I have given you the blood of animals to pay for your sin on the altar. Blood is life. That is why blood pays for your sin.

12“ ‘So I say to the people of Israel, “You must not eat meat that still has blood in it. And an outsider who lives among you must not eat it either.”

13“ ‘Suppose any of you hunts any animal or bird that can be eaten. It does not matter whether you are an Israelite or an outsider. You must let the blood flow out of the animal or bird. You must cover the blood with dirt.

14“ ‘That is because every creature’s life is its blood. And that is why I have said to the people of Israel, “You must not eat any creature’s meat that still has blood in it. Every creature’s life is its blood. Anyone who eats that kind of meat must be cut off.”

15“ ‘Suppose someone eats anything that is found dead or is torn apart by wild animals. It does not matter whether he is an Israelite or an outsider. He must wash his clothes. He must take a bath. He will be “unclean” until evening. After that, he will be “clean.”

16“ ‘But suppose he does not wash his clothes. And suppose he does not take a bath. Then he will be held accountable for what he has done.’ ”

Do Not Commit Sexual Sins

18 The LORD spoke to Moses. He said, 2“Speak to the people of Israel. Tell them, ‘I am the LORD your God. 3You must not do what the people of Egypt do. You used to live there. And you must not do what the people of Canaan do. I am bringing you into their land. Do not follow their practices.

4“ ‘You must obey my laws. You must be careful to follow my rules. I am the LORD your God. 5Keep my rules and laws. The one who obeys them will live by them. I am the LORD.

6“ ‘Do not have sex with any of your close relatives. I am the LORD.

7“ ‘Do not bring shame on your father by having sex with your mother. Do not have sex with her. She is your mother.

8“ ‘Do not have sex with any other wife of your father. That would bring shame on your father.

9“ ‘Do not have sex with your sister. It does not matter whether she is your father’s daughter or your mother’s daughter. It does not matter whether she was born in the same home as you were or somewhere else.

10“ ‘Do not have sex with your son’s daughter or your daughter’s daughter. That would bring shame on you.

11“ ‘Do not have sex with the daughter of your father’s wife. She was born to your father. She is your sister.

12"'Do not have sex with your father's sister.
She is a close relative on your father's side.
13"'Do not have sex with your mother's sister.
She is a close relative on your mother's side.
14"'Do not bring shame on your father's brother
by having sex with his wife. She is your aunt.
15"'Do not have sex with your daughter-in-law.
She is your son's wife. Do not have sex with her.
16"'Do not have sex with your brother's wife.
That would bring shame on your brother.
17"'Do not have sex with both a woman and her
daughter. Do not have sex with either her son's
daughter or her daughter's daughter. They are
close relatives on her side. Having sex with them
is an evil thing.
18"'Do not take your wife's sister as another
wife and have sex with her. Do not do it while your
wife is still living.
19"'Do not make love to a woman during her
monthly period. She is not "clean" at that time.
20"'Do not have sex with your neighbor's wife.
That would make you "unclean."
21"'Do not hand over any of your children to be
sacrificed to the god Molech. That would be treating my name as if it were not holy. I am the LORD
your God.
22"'Do not have sex with a man as you would
have sex with a woman. I hate that.
23"'Do not have sex with an animal. Do not
make yourself "unclean" by doing that. A woman
must not offer herself to an animal to have sex
with it. That is a twisted use of sex.
24"'Do not make yourselves "unclean" in any of
those ways. That is how other nations became
"unclean." So I am going to drive those nations out
of the land to make room for you. 25Even their land
was not "clean." So I punished it because of its sin.
The land itself threw out the people who lived
there.
26"'But you must keep my rules and my laws.
You must not do any of the things I hate. It does
not matter whether you are Israelites or outsiders.
27"'All of those things were done by the people
who lived in the land before you. That is how the
land became "unclean." 28If you make the land
"unclean," it will throw you out. It will get rid of
you just as it got rid of the nations that were there
before you.
29"'Suppose you do any of the things I hate.
Then you must be cut off from your people.
30"'Do exactly what I require. When you arrive
in Canaan, do not follow any of the practices of its
people. I hate the things they do. Do not make
yourselves "unclean" by doing them. I am the
LORD your God.'"

Other Laws

19 The LORD spoke to Moses. He said,
2"Speak to the whole community of Israel.
Tell them, 'Be holy, because I am holy. I am the
LORD your God.
3"'All of you must have respect for your mother
and father. You must always keep my Sabbath
days. I am the LORD your God.
4"'Do not turn away from me to worship statues of gods. Do not make gods out of metal for
yourselves. I am the LORD your God.
5"'Suppose you sacrifice a friendship offering
to me. Then do it in the right way. And I will
accept it from you. 6You must eat it on the same
day you sacrifice it or on the next day. Anything
that is left over until the third day must be
burned up.
7"'If you eat any of it on the third day, it is not
pure. I will not accept it. 8If you eat it, you will be
held accountable. You have misused what is holy
to me. You will be cut off from your people.
9"'Suppose you are harvesting your crops. Then
do not harvest all the way to the edges of your
field. And do not pick up the grain you missed.
10Do not go over your vineyard a second time. Do
not pick up the grapes that have fallen to the
ground. Leave them for poor people and outsiders.
I am the LORD your God.
11"'Do not steal.
"'Do not tell lies.
"'Do not cheat one another.
12"'Do not take an oath and give false witness in
my name. That would be treating it as if it were
not holy. I am the LORD your God.
13"'Do not cheat your neighbor. Do not rob him.
"'Do not hold back the pay of a hired worker
until morning.
14"'Do not call a curse down on deaf people. Do
not put anything in front of blind people that will
make them trip. Instead, have respect for me. I am
the LORD your God.
15"'Do not make something that is wrong
appear to be right. Treat poor people and rich people in the same way. Do not favor one person over
another. Instead, judge everyone fairly.
16"'Do not go around spreading lies among your
people.
"'Do not do anything that puts your neighbor's
life in danger. I am the LORD.
17"'Do not hate your brother in your heart. Correct your neighbor boldly when he does something
wrong. Then you will not share his guilt.
18"'Do not try to get even. Do not hold anything
against one of your people. Instead, love your
neighbor as you love yourself. I am the LORD.
19"'Obey my rules.
"'Do not let different kinds of animals mate
with each other.
"'Do not mix two kinds of seeds and then plant
them in your field.
"'Do not wear clothes that are made out of two
kinds of cloth.
20"'Suppose a man has sex with a female slave.
But she and another man have promised to get
married to each other. And her freedom has not yet
been paid for or given to her. Then she and the

man who had sex with her must be punished. But
they must not be put to death, because she had not
been set free.
21" 'The man must bring a ram to the entrance
to the Tent of Meeting. It is for a guilt offering to
me. 22The priest must take the ram for the guilt
offering. He must sacrifice it to pay for the man's
sin in my sight. Then his sin will be forgiven.
23" 'When you enter the land, suppose you plant
a fruit tree. Then do not eat its fruit for the first
three years. The fruit is not "clean." 24In the fourth
year all of the fruit will be holy. Offer it as a way
of showing praise to me. 25But in the fifth year you
can eat the fruit. Then you will gather more and
more fruit. I am the LORD your God.
26" 'Do not eat any meat that still has blood in it.
" 'Do not practice any kind of evil magic at all.
27" 'Do not cut the hair on the sides of your
head. Do not clip off the edges of your beard.
28" 'Do not make cuts on your bodies when
someone dies. Do not put marks on your skin. I am
the LORD.
29" 'Do not dishonor your daughter's body by
making a prostitute out of her. If you do, the people of Israel will start using prostitutes. The land
will be filled with evil.
30" 'You must always keep my Sabbath days.
Have respect for my sacred tent. I am the LORD.
31" 'Do not look for advice from people who get
messages from those who have died. Do not go to
people who talk to the spirits of the dead. If you
do, they will make you "unclean." I am the LORD
your God.
32" 'Stand up in order to show your respect for
old people. Also have respect for me. I am the
LORD your God.
33" 'Suppose an outsider lives with you in your
land. Then do not treat him badly. 34Treat him as if
he were one of your own people. Love him as you
love yourself. Remember that all of you were outsiders in Egypt. I am the LORD your God.
35" 'Be honest when you measure lengths,
weights or amounts. 36Use honest scales and honest weights. Use honest dry measures. And use
honest liquid measures. I am the LORD your God.
I brought you out of Egypt.
37" 'Obey all of my rules and laws. Follow them.
I am the LORD.' "

Israel Will Be Punished for Their Sins

20 The LORD spoke to Moses. He said, 2"Say
to the people of Israel, 'Suppose a person
sacrifices one of his children to the god Molech. It
does not matter whether that person is an Israelite
or an outsider who lives in Israel. He must be put
to death. The people of the community must kill
him by throwing stones at him. 3I will turn against
that man. I will cut him off from his people. That
is because he sacrificed his child to Molech. He
has made my sacred tent "unclean." He has treated
my name as if it were not holy.
4" 'Suppose the people of the community close
their eyes to the fact that the man sacrificed his
child to Molech. And suppose they fail to put him
to death. 5Then I will turn against that man and his
family. I will cut him off from his people. I will
also cut off all those who follow him by joining
themselves to Molech. They are not faithful to me.
6" 'Suppose someone looks for advice from people who get messages from those who have died.
Or he goes to people who talk to the spirits of the
dead. And he follows their advice. Then he has not
been faithful to me. So I will turn against him. I
will cut him off from his people.
7" 'Set yourselves apart for me. Be holy, because
I am the LORD your God. 8Obey my rules. Follow
them. I am the LORD. I make you holy.
9" 'If anyone calls down a curse on his father or
mother, he will be put to death. He has cursed his
father or mother. Anything that happens to him
will be his own fault.
10" 'Suppose a man commits adultery with his
neighbor's wife. Then the man and the woman
must be put to death.
11" 'Suppose a man has sex with his father's
wife. Then he has brought shame on his father.
The man and the woman must be put to death.
Anything that happens to them will be their own
fault.
12" 'Suppose a man has sex with his daughter-
in-law. Then they must be put to death. They have
used sex in a twisted way. Anything that happens
to them will be their own fault.
13" 'Suppose a man has sex with another man as
he would have sex with a woman. I hate what they
have done. They must be put to death. Anything
that happens to them will be their own fault.
14" 'Suppose a man gets married to both a
woman and her mother. That is evil. All of them
must be burned to death. Then there will not be
any evil among you.
15" 'Suppose a man has sex with an animal.
Then he must be put to death. You must also kill
the animal.
16" 'Suppose a woman has sex with an animal.
Then kill the woman and the animal. They must
be put to death. Anything that happens to them will
be their own fault.
17" 'Suppose a man gets married to his sister and
has sex with her. That is a shameful thing to do. It
does not matter whether she is the daughter of his
father or of his mother. They must be cut off right
in front of their own people. That man has brought
shame on his sister. He will be held accountable
for what he has done.
18" 'Suppose a man makes love to a woman during her monthly period. He has uncovered the
place where her bleeding was coming from. And
she has let him do it. So they must be cut off from
their people.
19" 'Do not have sex with the sister of either
your mother or your father. That would bring

shame on a close relative. Both of you would be held accountable for what you have done.

20"'Suppose a man has sex with his aunt. Then he has brought shame on his uncle. Both of them will be held accountable for what they have done. They will die without having any children.

21"'Suppose a man gets married to his brother's wife. That is something that should never be done. He has brought shame on his brother. Neither of them will have any children.

22"'Obey all of my rules and laws. Follow them. Then the land where I am bringing you to live will not throw you out. 23To make room for you, I am going to drive out the nations that are in the land. You must not follow the practices of those nations. I hated those nations because they did all of those things.

24"'But I said to you, "You will take over their land as your own. I will give it to you. It will belong to you. It is a land that has plenty of milk and honey." I am the LORD your God. I have set you apart from the other nations.

25"'So you must be able to tell the difference between animals that are "clean" and those that are not. You must know which birds are "clean" and which are not. Do not make yourselves "unclean" by eating any animal or bird that is not "clean." Do not make yourselves "unclean" by eating anything that moves along the ground. I have set all of them apart. They are "unclean" for you.

26"'You must be holy. You must be set apart to me. I am the LORD. I am holy. I have set you apart from the other nations to be my own people.

27"'Suppose a man or woman gets messages from those who have died. Or suppose a man or woman talks to the spirits of the dead. Then you must put that man or woman to death. You must kill them by throwing stones at them. Anything that happens to them will be their own fault.'"

Rules for Priests

21 The LORD said to Moses, "Speak to the priests, the sons of Aaron. Tell them, 'A priest must not make himself "unclean" by going near the dead body of any of his people. 2But he can go near the body of a close relative. It could be his mother, father, son, daughter or brother. 3He can also go near a sister who is not married. She would have depended on him because she did not have a husband. The priest can make himself "unclean" by going near her body. 4But he must not make himself "unclean" by going near the bodies of people who were only related to him by marriage. Going near them would make him "unclean."

5"'Priests must not shave any part of their heads. They must not shave off the edges of their beards. They must not make cuts on their bodies when someone dies.

6"'Priests must be holy. They must be set apart for me. I am their God. They must not treat my name as if it were not holy. They must be holy because they bring offerings that are made to me with fire. That is my food.

7"'They must not get married to women who are "unclean" because they are prostitutes. They must not marry women who are divorced from their husbands. That is because priests are holy. They are set apart for me. I am their God. 8Consider them as holy, because they offer up food to me. Consider them as holy, because I am holy. I am the LORD. I make you holy.

9"'Suppose a priest's daughter makes herself "unclean" by becoming a prostitute. Then she brings shame on her father. She must be burned to death.

10"'The high priest is the one among his brothers whose head has been anointed with olive oil. He has been appointed to wear the priest's clothes.

"'When someone dies, the high priest must not let his hair hang loose. He must not tear his clothes to show how sad he is. 11He must not enter a place where there is a dead body. He must not make himself "unclean," even if his father or mother dies. 12He must not leave my sacred tent to take part in burying a body. That would bring shame on the tent. My anointing oil has set the high priest apart. I am the LORD.

13"'The woman the high priest gets married to must be a virgin. 14He must not marry a widow or a woman who is divorced. He must not marry a woman who is "unclean" because she is a prostitute. He must only get married to a virgin. She must come from his own people. 15If he marries a virgin, he makes the children he has by her "clean." I am the LORD. I make him holy.'"

16The LORD spoke to Moses. He said, 17"Speak to Aaron. Tell him, 'For all time to come, no man in your family line who has any flaws can come near to offer food to me.

18"'No man who has any flaws can come near. No man who is blind or disabled can come. No man whose body is scarred or twisted can come. 19No man whose foot or hand is disabled can come. 20No man whose back is bent can come. No man who is too short can come. No man who has anything wrong with his eyes can come. No man who has boils or running sores can come. No man whose sex glands are crushed can come.

21"'No man in the family line of the priest Aaron who has any flaws can come near me. He can't come to bring the offerings that are made to me with fire. If he has any flaws, he must not come near to offer food to me. 22He can eat the holy food. He can also eat my very holy food. 23But because he has a flaw, he must not go near the curtain or approach the altar. If he does, he will make my sacred tent "unclean." I am the LORD. I make everything holy.'"

24So Moses told all of those things to Aaron and his sons. He also told them to all of the people of Israel.

22

The LORD spoke to Moses. He said, 2“Here is what I want you to tell Aaron and his sons. Tell them to treat the sacred offerings with respect. They are the offerings the people of Israel set apart to honor me. So Aaron and his sons must never treat my name as if it were not holy. I am the LORD.

3“Say to them, ‘Suppose a man in your family line is “unclean.” And suppose he comes near the sacred offerings. They are the offerings the people of Israel set apart to honor me. That man must be cut off from serving me as a priest. That applies for all time to come. I am the LORD.

4“ ‘Suppose a man in Aaron’s family line has a skin disease. Or suppose liquid waste is flowing out of his body. Then he can’t eat the sacred offerings until he is made pure and clean.

“ ‘Suppose he touches something that has been made “unclean” by coming near a dead body. Or suppose he touches someone who has semen flowing from his body. Then he will not be “clean.” 5Or suppose he touches any crawling thing that makes him “unclean.” Or suppose he touches any person who makes him “unclean.” It does not matter what he touches that is “unclean.” It will make him “unclean.”

6“ ‘The one who touches anything of that kind will be “unclean” until evening. He must not eat any of the sacred offerings unless he has taken a bath. 7When the sun goes down, he will be “clean.” After that, he can eat the sacred offerings. They are his food.

8“ ‘He must not eat anything that is found dead or torn apart by wild animals. If he does, it will make him “unclean.” I am the LORD.

9“ ‘The priests must do what I require. But suppose they make fun of what I require. Then they will become guilty and die. I am the LORD. I make them holy.

10“ ‘Only a member of a priest’s family can eat the sacred offering. The guest of a priest can’t eat it. A priest’s hired worker can’t eat it either.

11“ ‘But suppose a priest buys a slave with money. Or suppose a slave is born in his house. Then that slave can eat the sacred food.

12“ ‘Suppose a priest’s daughter gets married to someone who is not a priest. Then she can’t eat any of the food that is brought as a sacred gift. 13But suppose the priest’s daughter becomes a widow or is divorced. She does not have any children. And she returns to live in her father’s house, where she lived when she was young. Then she can eat her father’s food. But a person who does not belong to a priest’s family can’t eat any of it.

14“ ‘Suppose someone eats a sacred offering by mistake. Then he must pay back the priest for the offering. He must also add a fifth of its value to it.

15“ ‘The priests must not allow the sacred offerings to become “unclean.” They are the offerings the people of Israel bring to me. 16The priests must not allow the offerings to become “unclean” by letting the people eat them. If they do, they will bring guilt on the people. They will have to pay for what they have done. I am the LORD. I make them holy.’ ”

Sacrifices the LORD Does Not Accept

17The LORD spoke to Moses. He said, 18“Speak to Aaron and his sons. Speak to all of the people of Israel. Tell them, ‘Suppose any of you brings a gift for a burnt offering to the LORD. It does not matter whether you are an Israelite or an outsider who lives in Israel. It does not matter whether you bring the offering to keep a promise or because you choose to give it. 19You must bring a male animal that does not have any flaws if you want the LORD to accept it from you. It does not matter whether it is from your cattle, sheep or goats. 20Do not bring an animal that has any flaws. If you do, the LORD will not accept it from you.

21“ ‘Suppose any of you brings an animal for a friendship offering to the LORD. Then it must not have any flaws at all. If it does, the LORD will not accept it. It does not matter whether the animal is from your herd or flock. It does not matter whether you bring it to keep a promise or because you choose to give it. 22Do not offer a blind animal to the LORD. Do not bring an animal that is hurt or wounded. And do not offer one that has warts or boils or running sores. Do not place any of them on the altar as an offering that is made to the LORD with fire.

23“ ‘But suppose you bring an offering you choose to give. Then you can bring an ox or a sheep whose body is twisted or too small. But the LORD will not accept it if you offer it to keep a promise.

24“ ‘You must not offer the LORD a male animal whose sex glands have been hurt. The glands also must not be crushed, torn or cut. You must not offer that kind of animal in your own land. 25And you must not accept that kind of animal from someone who comes from another land. You must not offer it as food for your God. He will not accept it from you. Its body is twisted and has flaws.’ ”

26The LORD spoke to Moses. He said, 27“When a calf, lamb or goat is born, it must remain with its mother for seven days. From the eighth day on, I will accept it as an offering that is made to me with fire. 28Do not kill a cow and its calf on the same day. Do not kill a female sheep and its lamb on the same day.

29“Sacrifice a thank offering to me in the right way. Then I will accept it from you. 30You must eat it that same day. Do not leave any of it until morning. I am the LORD.

31“Obey my commands. Follow them. I am the LORD. 32Do not treat my name as if it were not holy. The people of Israel must recognize me as the holy God. I am the LORD. I make you holy. 33I brought you out of Egypt to be your God. I am the LORD.”

23 The LORD spoke to Moses. He said, 2“Speak to the people of Israel. Tell them, ‘Here are my appointed feast days. They are the appointed feast days of the LORD. Tell the people that they must come together for these sacred feasts.

The Sabbath Day

3“ ‘There are six days when you can work. But the seventh day is a Sabbath. You must rest on it. Come together on that sacred day. You must not do any work on it. No matter where you live, it is a Sabbath day in my honor.

Passover and Unleavened Bread

4“ ‘Here are my appointed feasts. Tell the people that they must come together for these sacred feasts at their appointed times. 5My Passover begins when the sun goes down on the 14th day of the first month.

6“ ‘My Feast of Unleavened Bread begins on the 15th day of that month. For seven days you must eat bread that is made without yeast. 7On the first day you must come together for a special service. Do not do any regular work on that day. 8On each of the seven days bring an offering that is made to me with fire. On the seventh day come together for a special service. Do not do any regular work on that day.’ ”

The First Share of Israel’s Crops Belongs to the LORD

9The LORD spoke to Moses. He said, 10“Speak to the people of Israel. Tell them, ‘When you enter the land I am going to give you, bring an offering to me. Gather your crops. Bring the first bundle of grain to the priest. 11He must lift the grain up and wave it in front of me. Then I will accept it from you. The priest must wave it on the day after the Sabbath.

12“ ‘On the day he waves the grain for you, you must sacrifice a burnt offering to me. It must be a lamb that does not have any flaws. It must be a year old. 13You must bring it together with its grain offering. The grain offering must be 16 cups of fine flour. Mix it with olive oil. It is an offering that is made to me with fire. It has a pleasant smell. You must offer a drink offering along with the burnt offering. It must be a quart of wine.

14“ ‘You must not eat any bread until the very day you bring your offering to me. You must not eat any grain that has been cooked or any of your first grain until that time. That is a law that will last for all time to come. It applies no matter where you live.

The Feast of Weeks

15“ ‘The day you brought the grain for the wave offering was the day after the Sabbath. Count off seven full weeks from that day. 16Count off 50 days up to the day after the seventh Sabbath. On that day bring me an offering of your first grain. 17Bring two loaves of bread that are made with 16 cups of fine flour. They must be baked with yeast. Bring them to me as a wave offering from the first share of your crops. That applies no matter where you live.

18“ ‘Together with the bread, bring seven male lambs. Each lamb must be a year old. It must not have any flaws. Also bring one young bull and two rams. They will be a burnt offering to me. They will be offered together with their grain offerings and drink offerings. They are an offering that is made with fire. They give a pleasant smell to me.

19“ ‘Then sacrifice one male goat for a sin offering. Also sacrifice two lambs for a friendship offering. Each of the lambs must be a year old. 20The priest must lift the two lambs up and wave them in front of me as a wave offering. He must offer them together with the bread that is made out of the first share of your crops. They are a sacred offering to me. They will be given to the priest.

21“ ‘On that same day tell the people that they must come together for a special service. They must not do any regular work. That is a law that will last for all time to come. It applies no matter where you live.

22“ ‘Suppose you are gathering your crops. Then do not harvest all the way to the edges of your field. And do not pick up the grain you missed. Leave some for poor people and outsiders. I am the LORD your God.’ ”

The Feast of Trumpets

23The LORD spoke to Moses. He said, 24“Say to the people of Israel, ‘On the first day of the seventh month you must have a day of rest. It must be a special service that is announced with trumpet blasts. 25Do not do any regular work on that day. Instead, bring an offering that is made to me with fire.’ ”

The Day When Sin Is Paid For

26The LORD spoke to Moses. He said, 27“The tenth day of the seventh month is the day when sin is paid for. Come together for a special service. Do not eat any food. Bring an offering that is made to me with fire. 28Do not do any work on that day. It is the day when sin is paid for. On that day your sin will be paid for in my sight. I am the LORD your God.

29“Suppose you do eat food on that day. Then you will be cut off from your people. 30I will destroy anyone among your people who does any work on that day. 31You must not do any work at all. That is a law that will last for all time to come. It applies no matter where you live.

32“That day is a sabbath for you. You must rest on it. You must not eat anything on that day. You must keep your sabbath from the evening of the ninth day of the month until the following evening.”

The Feast of Booths

33The LORD spoke to Moses. He said, 34"Say to the people of Israel, 'On the 15th day of the seventh month my Feast of Booths begins. It lasts for seven days.

35" 'On the first day you must come together for a special service. Do not do any regular work on that day. 36On each of the seven days bring an offering that is made to me with fire. On the eighth day come together for a special service. Bring an offering that is made to me with fire. That special service is the closing service. Do not do any regular work on that day.

37" 'Those are my appointed feasts. Tell the people that they must come together for those sacred feasts. During those times, the people must bring offerings that are made to me with fire. They are burnt offerings and grain offerings. They are sacrifices and drink offerings. Each offering must be brought at its required time.

38" 'The feasts are in addition to my Sabbath days. The offerings are in addition to your gifts and anything you have promised. They are also in addition to all of the offerings you choose to give me.

39" 'Begin with the 15th day of the seventh month. That is after you have gathered your crops. On that day celebrate my Feast of Booths for seven days. The first day is a day of rest. The eighth day is also a day of rest. 40On the first day you must get the best fruit from the trees. You must also get palm leaves, leafy branches and poplar branches. You must be filled with joy in my sight for seven days. I am the LORD your God.

41" 'Celebrate my Feast of Booths for seven days each year. That is a law that will last for all time to come. Celebrate the feast in the seventh month. 42Live in booths for seven days. All of the people of Israel must live in booths. 43Then your children after you will know that I made the people of Israel live in booths. I made them do it after I brought them out of Egypt. I am the LORD your God.' "

44So Moses announced to the people of Israel the appointed feasts of the LORD.

Olive Oil, Bread and Incense

24 The LORD spoke to Moses. He said, 2"Command the people of Israel to bring you clear oil that is made from pressed olives. Use it to keep the lamps burning and giving light all the time.

3"Aaron must take care of the lamps in my sight from evening until morning all the time. That is a law that will last for all time to come. The lamps are outside the curtain that is in front of the tablets of the covenant in the Tent of Meeting. 4The lamps are on the pure gold lampstand in front of me. They must be taken care of all the time.

5"Get fine flour and bake 12 loaves of bread. Use 16 cups of flour for each loaf. 6Place them in two rows. Put six loaves in each row on the table that is made out of pure gold. The table stands in front of me.

7"Along each row put some pure incense. It will remind you that all good things come from me. Burn the incense in place of the bread. The incense is an offering that is made to me with fire.

8"The bread must be set out in front of me regularly. Do it every Sabbath day. It will be Israel's duty to provide it for all time to come.

9"The bread belongs to Aaron and his sons. They must eat it in a holy place. It is a very holy part of their regular share of the offerings that are made to me with fire."

A Person Who Speaks Evil Is Put to Death

10There was a man who had an Israelite mother. His father was born in Egypt. The man went out among the people of Israel. A fight broke out in the camp between him and an Israelite. 11The son of the Israelite woman spoke evil things against the LORD by using a curse. So the people brought him to Moses. The name of the man's mother was Shelomith. She was the daughter of Dibri. Dibri was from the tribe of Dan. 12The people kept her son under guard until they could find out what the LORD wanted them to do.

13Then the LORD spoke to Moses. He said, 14"Get the man who spoke evil things against me. Take him outside the camp. All those who heard him say those things must place their hands on his head. Then the whole community must kill him by throwing stones at him.

15"Say to the people of Israel, 'If anyone calls down a curse on me, he will be held accountable. 16If anyone speaks evil things against my Name, he must be put to death. The whole community must kill him by throwing stones at him. It does not matter whether he is an outsider or an Israelite. When he speaks evil things against my Name, he must be put to death.

17" 'If anyone kills another human being, he must be put to death. 18If anyone kills someone's animal, he must pay its owner. A life must be taken for a life.

19" 'Suppose someone hurts his neighbor. Then what he has done must be done to him. 20A bone must be broken for a bone. An eye must be put out for an eye. A tooth must be knocked out for a tooth. He must be hurt in the same way he hurt someone else.

21" 'If anyone kills an animal, he must pay its owner. But if he kills a human being, he must be put to death. 22The same law applies whether he is an outsider or an Israelite. I am the LORD your God.' "

23Then Moses spoke to the people of Israel. They got the man who had spoken evil things against the LORD. They took him outside the camp. There they killed him by throwing stones at him. The people of Israel did just as the LORD had commanded Moses.

The Sabbath Year

25 The LORD spoke to Moses on Mount Sinai.
He said, 2“Speak to the people of Israel.
Tell them, ‘You will enter the land I am going to
give you. When you do, you must honor me every
seventh year by not farming the land that year.
3“ ‘For six years plant your fields. Trim the
branches in your vineyards and gather your crops.
4“ ‘But the seventh year must be a sabbath for
the land. The land must rest during it. It is a sabbath year in my honor. Do not plant your fields.
Do not trim the branches in your vineyards. 5Do
not gather what grows without being planted. And
do not gather the grapes from the vines you have
not taken care of. The land must have a year of
rest.
6“ ‘Anything the land produces during the sabbath year will be food for you. It will be for you
and your male and female servants. Your hired
workers will eat it. So will people who live with
you for a while. 7And so will your livestock and
the wild animals that are in your land. Anything
the land produces can be eaten.

The Year of Jubilee

8“ ‘Count off seven sabbaths of years. Count off
seven times seven years. The seven sabbaths of
years add up to a total of 49 years. 9The tenth day
of the seventh month is the day when sin is paid
for. On that day blow the trumpet all through your
land.
10“ ‘Set the 50th year apart. Announce freedom
all over the land to everyone who lives there. The
50th year will be a Year of Jubilee for you. Each of
you must return to your own family property. And
each of you must return to your own tribe.
11“ ‘The 50th year will be a Year of Jubilee for
you. Do not plant anything. Do not gather what
grows without being planted. And do not gather
the grapes from the vines you have not taken care
of. 12It is a Year of Jubilee. It will be holy for you.
Eat only what the fields produce.
13“ ‘In the Year of Jubilee all of you must return
to your own property.
14“ ‘Suppose you sell land to one of your own
people. Or you buy land from him. Then do not
take advantage of each other. 15The price you pay
must be based on the number of years since the last
Year of Jubilee. And the price you charge must be
based on the number of years left for gathering
crops before the next Year of Jubilee.
16“ ‘When there are many years left, you must
raise the price. When there are only a few years
left, you must lower the price. That is because
what the man is really selling you is the number of
crops the land will produce. 17Do not take advantage of each other. Instead, have respect for me. I
am the LORD your God.
18“ ‘Follow my rules. Be careful to obey my
laws. Then you will live safely in the land. 19The
land will produce its fruit. You will eat as much as
you want. And you will live there in safety.
20“ ‘Suppose you say, “In the seventh year we
will not plant anything or gather our crops. So
what will we eat?” 21I will send you a great blessing in the sixth year. The land will produce enough
for three years. 22While you plant during the eighth
year, you will eat food from the old crop. You will
continue to eat food from it until the crops from
the ninth year are gathered.
23“ ‘The land must not be sold without a way of
getting it back. That is because it belongs to me.
You are only outsiders who rent my land. 24You
must make sure that you can buy the land back.
That applies to all of the land that belongs to you.
25“ ‘Suppose one of your own people becomes
poor. And suppose he has to sell some of his land.
Then his nearest relative must come and buy back
what he has sold.
26“ ‘But suppose he does not have anyone to buy
it back for him. And suppose things go well for
him and he earns enough money to buy it back
himself. 27Then he must decide how much the
crops have become worth since the time he sold
the land. He must take that amount off the price
the land was sold for. He must give the man who
is selling it back to him the money that is left. Then
he can go back to his own property.
28“ ‘But suppose he has not earned enough
money to pay the man back. Then the buyer he
sold the land to will keep it until the Year of
Jubilee. At that time it will be returned to him.
Then he can go back to his property.
29“ ‘Suppose a man sells a house in a city that
has a wall around it. Then for a full year after he
sells it he has the right to buy it back.
30“ ‘But suppose he does not buy it back before
the full year has passed. Then the house in the
walled city will continue to belong to the buyer
and his children after him. It will not be returned
to the seller in the Year of Jubilee.
31“ ‘But houses in villages that do not have walls
around them must be treated like property outside
walled cities. Those houses can be bought back at
any time. And they must be returned in the Year of
Jubilee.
32“ ‘The Levites always have the right to buy
back their houses in the towns that belong to them.
33So their property among the people of Israel can
be bought back. That applies to a house that is sold
in any of their towns. Any house that is sold must
be returned to its original owner in the Year of
Jubilee. That is because the houses of the Levites
will always belong to them.
34“ ‘But the grasslands around their towns must
never be sold. They will belong to them for all
time to come.
35“ ‘Suppose one of your own people becomes
poor. And suppose he can’t take care of himself.
Then help him just as you would help an outsider
or someone who is living among you for a while.

In that way, the man who is poor can continue to
live among you.
36"'Do not charge him interest of any kind.
Instead, have respect for me. Then the man who
has become poor can continue to live among you.
37If you lend him money, you must not charge him
interest. And you must not sell him food for more
than it cost you.
38"'I am the LORD your God. I brought you out
of Egypt. I did it to give you the land of Canaan. I
wanted to be your God.
39"'Suppose one of your own people becomes
poor. And suppose he sells himself to you. Then
do not make him work as a slave. 40You must treat
him like a hired worker. Or you must treat him like
someone who is living among you for a while.
"'He must work for you until the Year of
Jubilee. 41Then he and his children must be set free.
He will go back to his own tribe. He will go back
to the property his people have always owned.
42"'The people of Israel are my servants. I
brought them out of Egypt. So they must not be
sold as slaves. 43Show them pity when you rule
over them. Have respect for me.
44"'You must get your male and female slaves
from the nations that are around you. You can buy
slaves from them. 45You can buy as slaves some of
the people who are living among you for a while.
You can also buy members of their families who
were born among you. They will become your
property. 46You can leave them to your children as
their share of your property. You can make them
slaves for life. But when you rule over your own
people, you must be kind to them.
47"'Suppose an outsider or someone who is living among you for a while becomes rich. Then
suppose one of your own people becomes poor. He
sells himself to the outsider who is living among
you. Or he sells himself to a member of the outsider's family. 48Then he keeps the right to buy
himself back after he has sold himself. One of his
relatives can buy him back. 49An uncle or a cousin
can buy himself back after he has sold himself. In
fact, any relative in his tribe can do it. Or suppose
things go well for him. Then he can buy himself
back.
50"'He and his buyer must count the number of
years from the time of the sale up to the Year of
Jubilee. The price for his freedom must be based
on the amount that is paid to a hired man for that
number of years.
51"'Suppose there are many years until the Year
of Jubilee. Then for his freedom he must pay a
larger share of the price that was paid for him.
52But suppose there are only a few years left until
the Year of Jubilee. Then he must count the number of years that are left. The payment for his freedom must be based on that number.
53"'He must be treated as if he had been hired
from year to year. You must make sure that his
owner is kind to him when he rules over him.
54"'Suppose he is not bought back in any of
those ways. Then he and his children must still be
set free in the Year of Jubilee. 55That is because the
people of Israel belong to me. They are my servants. I brought them out of Egypt. I am the LORD
their God.

Rewards for Obeying the LORD

26 "'Do not make statues of gods for yourselves. Do not set up a likeness of a god or
a sacred stone for yourselves. Do not place a
carved stone in your land and bow down in front
of it. I am the LORD your God.
2"'You must always keep my Sabbath days.
Have respect for my sacred tent. I am the LORD.
3"'Follow my rules. Be careful to obey my
commands. 4Then I will send you rain at the right
time. The ground will produce its crops. The trees
of the field will bear their fruit. 5You will continue
to thresh your grain until you gather your grapes.
You will continue to gather your grapes until you
plant your crops. You will have all you want to eat.
And you will live in safety in your land.
6"'I will give you peace in the land. You will
sleep, and no one will make you afraid. I will
remove wild animals from the land. There will not
be any war in your country. 7You will hunt down
your enemies. You will kill them with your
swords. 8Five of you will chase 100. And 100 of
you will chase 10,000. You will kill your enemies
with your swords.
9"'I will look with favor on you. I will give you
many children and increase your numbers. And I
will keep my covenant with you. 10You will still be
eating last year's crops when you have to move
them out to make room for new crops.
11"'I will live among you. I will not turn away
from you. 12I will walk among you. I will be your
God. And you will be my people. 13I am the LORD
your God. I brought you out of Egypt. I did not
want you to be slaves in Egypt anymore. I threw
off your heavy load. I helped you walk with your
heads held high.

Punishment for Not Obeying the LORD

14"'But suppose you will not listen to me. You
will not carry out all of my commands. 15You will
say no to my rules and turn away from my laws.
And you will break my covenant by failing to carry
out all of my commands. 16Then here is what I will
do to you. All at once I will bring terror on you. I
will send sicknesses that will make you weak. I will
send fever that will destroy your sight. It will
slowly take your life away. When you plant seeds,
it will not do you any good. Instead, your enemies
will eat what you have planted. 17I will turn against
you. Then your enemies will win the battle over
you. Those who hate you will rule over you. You
will run away even when no one is chasing you.
18"'After all of that, suppose you still will not
listen to me. Then I will punish you for your sins

seven times. 19I will break down your stubborn pride. I will make the sky above you like iron, and it will not rain. I will make the ground under you like bronze, and you will not be able to farm it. 20You will work with all of your strength, but it will not do you any good. That is because your soil will not produce any crops. The trees of the land will not bear any fruit.

21" 'Suppose you continue to be my enemy. And suppose you still refuse to listen to me. Then I will multiply your troubles many times because of your sins. 22I will send wild animals against you. They will kill your children. They will destroy your cattle. There will be so few of you left that your roads will be deserted.

23" 'After all of those things, suppose you still do not accept my warnings. And suppose you continue to be my enemy. 24Then I myself will be your enemy. I will make you suffer for your sins again and again. 25I will send war against you to punish you for breaking my covenant. When you go back into your cities, I will send a plague among you. You will be handed over to your enemies. 26I will cut off your supply of bread. Ten women will need only one oven to bake your bread. They will weigh out the bread piece by piece. Even when you eat all of it, it will not be enough to satisfy you.

27" 'After all of that, suppose you still do not listen to me. And suppose you continue to be my enemy. 28Then I will be angry with you. I will be your enemy. I myself will again punish you for your sins over and over. 29You will eat the dead bodies of your sons. You will also eat the dead bodies of your daughters.

30" 'I will destroy the high places where you worship other gods. I will pull down your incense altars. I will pile up your dead bodies on the lifeless statues of your gods. And I will turn away from you. 31I will completely destroy your cities. I will destroy your places of worship. The pleasant smell of your offerings will not give me any delight.

32" 'I will destroy your land so completely that your enemies who live there will be shocked. 33I will scatter you among the nations. I will pull out my sword and hunt you down. Your land and your cities will be completely destroyed.

34" 'Then the deserted land will enjoy its sabbath years. It will rest. It will not be farmed. It will enjoy its sabbaths. But you will become prisoners in the country of your enemies. 35The land will rest the whole time it is deserted. It was not able to rest during the sabbaths you lived in it.

36" 'Some of you will be left in the lands of your enemies. I will fill your hearts with fear. The sound of a leaf that is blown by the wind will scare you away. You will run as if you were escaping from swords. You will fall down, even though no one is chasing you. 37You will trip over one another as if you were running away from the battle. You will run away, even though no one is chasing you. You will not be able to stand and fight against your enemies.

38" 'While you are still scattered among the nations, you will die. The lands of your enemies will destroy you. 39You who are left in those lands will become weaker and weaker. You will die because of your sins and the sins of your parents.

40" 'But suppose you admit that you and your parents have sinned. You admit the evil and dishonest things you have done against me. And you admit you have become my enemy. 41What you did made me become your enemy. I let your enemies take you into their land. But suppose you stop being stubborn. You stop being proud. And you pay for your sin. 42Then I will remember my covenant with Jacob. I will remember my covenant with Isaac. I will remember my covenant with Abraham. I will remember what I said to them about the land.

43" 'You will leave the land. It will enjoy its sabbaths while it lies deserted because you are not there. You will pay for your sins because you said no to my laws. You turned away from my rules.

44" 'But even after all of that, I will not say no to you or turn away from you. I will not destroy you completely in the land of your enemies. I will not break my covenant with you. I am the LORD your God. 45Because of you, I will remember the covenant I made with the people of Israel who lived before you. I brought them out of Egypt to be their God. The nations saw me do it. I am the LORD.' "

46Those are the orders, the laws and the rules of the covenant the LORD made on Mount Sinai. He made it between himself and the people of Israel through Moses.

Keep Your Promises to the LORD

27 The LORD spoke to Moses. He said, 2"Speak to the people of Israel. Tell them, 'Suppose someone makes a special promise to set a person apart to serve me. Here is how much it will cost to set that person free from the promise to serve.

3" 'The cost for a male between the ages of 20 and 60 is 20 ounces of silver. It must be weighed out in keeping with the standard weights that are used in the sacred tent. 4The cost for a female of the same age is 12 ounces of silver.

5" 'The cost for a male between the ages of five and 20 is eight ounces of silver. The cost for a female of the same age is four ounces of silver.

6" 'The cost for a male between the ages of one month and five years is two ounces of silver. The cost for a female of the same age is one and a fourth ounces of silver.

7" 'The cost for a male who is 60 years old or more is six ounces of silver. The cost for a female of the same age is four ounces of silver.

8" 'But suppose the one who makes the special promise is too poor to pay the required amount. Then he must bring to the priest the person who will be set free. The priest will decide the right

value for that person. It will be based on how
much the one who makes the promise can afford.
9“ ‘Suppose what he promised is an animal that
I will accept as an offering. Then the animal that is
given to me becomes holy. 10The one who makes
the promise must not trade it. He must not trade a
good animal for a bad one. And he must not trade
a bad animal for a good one. Suppose he chooses
one animal instead of another. Then both animals
become holy.
11“ ‘Suppose the animal he promised is not
“clean.” Suppose I will not accept it as an offering. Then the animal must be brought to the priest.
12He will decide whether it is good or bad. Its value
will be what he decides it will be. 13Suppose the
owner wants to buy the animal back. Then he must
add a fifth to its cost.
14“ ‘Suppose a man sets his house apart as something that is holy to me. Then the priest will decide
whether it is good or bad. Its value will remain
what he decides it will be. 15Suppose the man sets
his house apart. And suppose later he wants to buy
it back. Then he must add a fifth to its value. The
house will belong to him again.
16“ ‘Suppose a man sets apart a piece of his family’s land to me. Then its value must be decided
based on the number of seeds that are required to
grow a full crop on it. That value will be 20 ounces
of silver for every six bushels of barley seeds.
17“ ‘Suppose he sets his field apart during the
Year of Jubilee. Then the value that has been
decided will not be changed. 18But suppose he sets
his field apart after the Year of Jubilee. Then the
priest will decide its value based on the number of
years that are left until the next Year of Jubilee.
The value that was decided will be reduced.
19“ ‘Suppose the man who sets his field apart
wants to buy it back. Then he must add a fifth to its
value. The field will belong to him again. 20But
suppose he does not buy the field back. Instead,
suppose he sells it to someone else. Then he can
never buy it back.
21“ ‘When the field is set free in the Year of
Jubilee, it will become holy. It will be like a field
that is set apart to me. It will become the property
of the priests.
22“ ‘Suppose a man sets apart to me a field he
has bought. And suppose it is not part of his family’s land. 23Then the priest will decide its value
based on the number of years that are left until the
Year of Jubilee. The man must pay that value on
the day it is decided. The money is holy. It is set
apart for me.
24“ ‘In the Year of Jubilee the field will go back
to the person the man bought it from. That person
is the one who had owned the land before.
25“ ‘Every amount of money must be weighed
out in keeping with the standard weights that are
used in the sacred tent.
26“ ‘But no one can set apart the first male animal that is born to its mother. That animal already
belongs to me. It does not matter whether it is an
ox or a sheep. It belongs to me.
27“ ‘Suppose it is an animal that is not “clean.”
Then the owner may buy it back at the value that
has been decided. And he must add a fifth to its
value. But suppose he does not buy it back. Then
it must be sold at the value that has been decided.
28“ ‘But nothing a man owns and sets apart to
me can be sold or bought back. It does not matter
whether it is a person or an animal or a family’s
land. Everything that is set apart to me is very holy
to me.
29“ ‘No one who is set apart in a special way to
be destroyed can be bought back. He must be put
to death.
30“ ‘A tenth of everything the land produces
belongs to me. That includes grain from the soil
and fruit from the trees. It is holy. It is set apart for
me. 31Suppose a man buys back some of his tenth.
Then he must add a fifth of the cost to it.
32“ ‘The whole tenth of his herds and flocks will
be holy. They will be set apart for me. That
includes every tenth animal that its shepherd
marks with his wooden staff. 33The owner must not
pick out the good animals from the bad. He must
not choose one animal instead of another. But if he
does, both animals become holy. They can’t be
bought back.’ ”

34The LORD gave Moses all of those commands
on Mount Sinai for the people of Israel.

Numbers

The Men of Israel Are Counted

1 The LORD spoke to Moses in the Tent of Meeting. It happened in the Desert of Sinai. The
LORD spoke to him on the first day of the second
month. It was the second year after the people of
Israel came out of Egypt.
The LORD said, 2“Count all of the men of Israel. Make a list of them by their tribes and families.
List every man by name. List them one by one.
3Count all of the men who are able to serve in the
army. They must be 20 years old or more. I want
you and Aaron to make a list of them company by
company. 4One man from each tribe must help
you. Those who help must be the heads of their
families.

5“Here are the names of the men who must help
you.

> “From the tribe of Reuben will come Elizur, the son of Shedeur.
> 6From the tribe of Simeon will come Shelumiel, the son of Zurishaddai.
> 7From the tribe of Judah will come Nahshon, the son of Amminadab.
> 8From the tribe of Issachar will come Nethanel, the son of Zuar.
> 9From the tribe of Zebulun will come Eliab, the son of Helon.
> 10From the tribe of Ephraim will come Elishama, the son of Ammihud.
> From the tribe of Manasseh will come Gamaliel, the son of Pedahzur.
> Ephraim and Manasseh were Joseph’s two sons.
> 11From the tribe of Benjamin will come Abidan, the son of Gideoni.
> 12From the tribe of Dan will come Ahiezer, the son of Ammishaddai.
> 13From the tribe of Asher will come Pagiel, the son of Ocran.
> 14From the tribe of Gad will come Eliasaph, the son of Deuel.
> 15From the tribe of Naphtali will come Ahira, the son of Enan.”

16Those were the men who were appointed from
the community. They were the leaders of the tribes
of their people. They were the heads of the major
families in Israel.
17Moses and Aaron went and got the men whose
names had been given to them. 18Then Moses and
Aaron gathered all of the men of Israel together. It
was the first day of the second month. The men
announced the tribe and family they belonged to.
Those who were 20 years old or more were listed
by name. They were listed one by one.
19Everything was done just as the LORD had
commanded Moses. So Moses counted them in the
Desert of Sinai.

20Here is the number of men from the tribe of Reuben, Israel’s oldest son.

> All of the men who were able to serve in the army were counted. They were 20 years old or more. They were listed by name. They were listed one by one. They were listed in keeping with the records of their tribes and families.
> 21The number from the tribe of Reuben was 46,500.

22Here is the number of men from the tribe of Simeon.

> All of the men who were able to serve in the army were counted. They were 20 years old or more. They were listed by name. They were listed one by one. They were listed in keeping with the records of their tribes and families.
> 23The number from the tribe of Simeon was 59,300.

24Here is the number of men from the tribe of Gad.

> All of the men who were able to serve in the army were counted. They were 20 years old or more. They were listed by name. They were listed in keeping with the records of their tribes and families.
> 25The number from the tribe of Gad was 45,650.

26Here is the number of men from the tribe of Judah.

> All of the men who were able to serve in the army were counted. They were 20 years old or more. They were listed by name. They were listed in keeping with the records of their tribes and families.
> 27The number from the tribe of Judah was 74,600.

28Here is the number of men from the tribe of Issachar.

> All of the men who were able to serve in the army were counted. They were 20 years old or more. They were listed by name. They were listed in keeping with the records of their tribes and families.
> 29The number from the tribe of Issachar was 54,400.

30Here is the number of men from the tribe of Zebulun.

> All of the men who were able to serve in the army were counted. They were 20 years old or more. They were listed by

name. They were listed in keeping with the records of their tribes and families.
[31]The number from the tribe of Zebulun was 57,400.

[32]Here is the number of men from the tribe of Ephraim, the son of Joseph.

All of the men who were able to serve in the army were counted. They were 20 years old or more. They were listed by name. They were listed in keeping with the records of their tribes and families.
[33]The number from the tribe of Ephraim was 40,500.

[34]Here is the number of men from the tribe of Manasseh, the son of Joseph.

All of the men who were able to serve in the army were counted. They were 20 years old or more. They were listed by name. They were listed in keeping with the records of their tribes and families.
[35]The number from the tribe of Manasseh was 32,200.

[36]Here is the number of men from the tribe of Benjamin.

All of the men who were able to serve in the army were counted. They were 20 years old or more. They were listed by name. They were listed in keeping with the records of their tribes and families.
[37]The number from the tribe of Benjamin was 35,400.

[38]Here is the number of men from the tribe of Dan.

All of the men who were able to serve in the army were counted. They were 20 years old or more. They were listed by name. They were listed in keeping with the records of their tribes and families.
[39]The number from the tribe of Dan was 62,700.

[40]Here is the number of men from the tribe of Asher.

All of the men who were able to serve in the army were counted. They were 20 years old or more. They were listed by name. They were listed in keeping with the records of their tribes and families.
[41]The number from the tribe of Asher was 41,500.

[42]Here is the number of men from the tribe of Naphtali.

All of the men who were able to serve in the army were counted. They were 20 years old or more. They were listed by name. They were listed in keeping with the records of their tribes and families.
[43]The number from the tribe of Naphtali was 53,400.

[44]Those were the men Moses and Aaron counted. The 12 leaders of Israel helped them. There was one leader from each tribe. [45]The men who were counted were able to serve in Israel's army. All of them were 20 years old or more. They were counted family by family. [46]The total number was 603,550.

[47]But the families of the tribe of Levi were not counted along with the others. [48]The LORD had spoken to Moses. He had said, [49]"You must not count the men from the tribe of Levi. Do not include them when you list the other men of Israel.

[50]"Instead, put the Levites in charge of the holy tent. That is where the tablets of the covenant are kept. The Levites will be in charge of everything that belongs to the holy tent. They must carry the tent and everything that belongs to it. They must take care of it. They must set up camp around it.

[51]"When the holy tent must be moved, the Levites must take it down. And when the tent must be set up, the Levites must do it. Anyone else who goes near it will be put to death.

[52]"The people of Israel must set up their tents by companies. All of them must be in their own camps under their own flags.

[53]"But the Levites must set up their tents around the holy tent where the tablets of the covenant are kept. Then my anger will not fall on the community of Israel. The Levites will be held accountable for taking care of the tent."

[54]The people of Israel did everything just as the LORD had commanded Moses.

The Tribes Camp Around the Tent of Meeting

2 The LORD spoke to Moses and Aaron. He said, [2]"The people of Israel must camp around the Tent of Meeting. But they must not camp too close to it. All of them must camp under their flags and under the banners of their families."

[3]The companies of the camp of Judah must be on the east side. They must set up camp toward the sunrise. They must camp under their flag. The leader of the tribe of Judah is Nahshon, the son of Amminadab. [4]There are 74,600 men in his company.

[5]The tribe of Issachar will camp next to them. The leader of the tribe of Issachar is Nethanel, the son of Zuar. [6]There are 54,400 men in his company.

[7]The tribe of Zebulun will be next. The leader of the tribe of Zebulun is Eliab, the son of Helon. [8]There are 57,400 men in his company.

[9]So a total of 186,400 men will be set apart for the camp of Judah. They will be arranged company by company. They will start out first.

[10]The companies of the camp of Reuben will be on the south side. They will be under their flag. The leader of the tribe of Reuben is Elizur, the son of Shedeur. [11]There are 46,500 men in his company.

12The tribe of Simeon will camp next to them. The leader of the tribe of Simeon is Shelumiel, the son of Zurishaddai. 13There are 59,300 men in his company.

14The tribe of Gad will be next. The leader of the tribe of Gad is Eliasaph, the son of Deuel. 15There are 45,650 men in his company.

16So a total of 151,450 men will be set apart for the camp of Reuben. They will be arranged company by company. They will start out second.

17Then the camp of the Levites will start out. The Tent of Meeting will go with them. They will march in the middle of the other camps. They will start out in the same order as they do when they set up camp. Each one will be in his own place under his flag.

18The companies of the camp of Ephraim will be on the west side. They will be under their flag. The leader of the tribe of Ephraim is Elishama, the son of Ammihud. 19There are 40,500 men in his company.

20The tribe of Manasseh will be next to them. The leader of the tribe of Manasseh is Gamaliel, the son of Pedahzur. 21There are 32,200 men in his company.

22The tribe of Benjamin will be next. The leader of the tribe of Benjamin is Abidan, the son of Gideoni. 23There are 35,400 men in his company.

24So a total of 108,100 men will be set apart for the camp of Ephraim. They will be arranged company by company. They will start out third.

25The companies of the camp of Dan will be on the north side. They will be under their flag. The leader of the tribe of Dan is Ahiezer, the son of Ammishaddai. 26There are 62,700 men in his company.

27The tribe of Asher will camp next to them. The leader of the tribe of Asher is Pagiel, the son of Ocran. 28There are 41,500 men in his company.

29The tribe of Naphtali will be next. The leader of the tribe of Naphtali is Ahira, the son of Enan. 30There are 53,400 men in his company.

31So a total of 157,600 men will be set apart for the camp of Dan. They will start out last. They will march under their flags.

32Those are the men of Israel. They were counted in keeping with their families. The total number of all of the men who were in the camps is 603,550, company by company. 33But the Levites weren't counted along with the other men of Israel. That's what the LORD had commanded Moses.

34So the people of Israel did everything the LORD had commanded Moses. That's the way they set up camp under their flags. And that's the way they started out. Each man marched out with his own tribe and family.

The Levites

3 Here is the story of the family of Aaron and Moses. It belongs to the time when the LORD talked with Moses on Mount Sinai.

2Aaron's oldest son was Nadab. His other sons were Abihu, Eleazar and Ithamar. 3Those were the names of Aaron's sons. They were the anointed priests. They were prepared to serve the LORD as priests. 4But Nadab and Abihu made an offering to the LORD by using fire that wasn't allowed. So they fell dead in front of him. That happened in the Desert of Sinai. They didn't have any sons. Only Eleazar and Ithamar served as priests while their father Aaron was living.

5The LORD spoke to Moses. He said, 6"Bring the men of the tribe of Levi to the priest Aaron. They will help him. 7They must work at the Tent of Meeting for Aaron and for the whole community. They must do what needs to be done at the holy tent. 8They must take care of everything that is connected with the Tent of Meeting. When they do, they are acting for all of the people of Israel. 9Give the Levites to Aaron and his sons. They are the men of Israel who must be given completely to him.

10"Appoint Aaron and his sons to serve as priests. Anyone else who approaches the sacred tent must be put to death."

11The LORD also said to Moses, 12"I have taken the Levites from among the people of Israel. I have taken them in place of the oldest son who is born to each woman in Israel. The Levites belong to me. 13That is because every male that is born first to a mother is mine. In Egypt I struck down all of the males that were born first. I did it when I set apart for myself every male that is born first to a mother in Israel. That is true for men and animals alike. They belong to me. I am the LORD."

14The LORD spoke to Moses in the Desert of Sinai. He said, 15"Count the Levites by their family groups. Count every male who is a month old or more." 16So Moses counted them. He did just as the word of the LORD had commanded him.

17 The sons of Levi were
Gershon, Kohath and Merari.
18 The major families from Gershon were
Libni and Shimei.
19 The major families from Kohath were
Amram, Izhar, Hebron and Uzziel.
20 The major families from Merari were
Mahli and Mushi.
Those were the major families of the Levites.

21The families of Libni and Shimei belonged to the family of Gershon. 22All of the males who were a month old or more were counted. There were 7,500 of them. 23The families of Gershon had to camp on the west side. They had to camp behind the holy tent. 24The leader of the families of Gershon was Eliasaph, the son of Lael.

25Here are the duties of the families of Gershon at the Tent of Meeting. They were held accountable for taking care of the holy tent and its coverings. They took care of the curtain at the entrance to the Tent of Meeting. 26They took care of the curtains of the courtyard. They took care of the curtain at the entrance to the courtyard. The courtyard was all around the holy tent and altar. They also took care of the ropes. In fact, they had to take care of everything that was connected with the use of all of those things.

27The families of Amram, Izhar, Hebron and Uzziel belonged to the family of Kohath. 28All of the males who were a month old or more were counted. There were 8,600 of them. The families of Kohath were held accountable for taking care of the sacred tent. 29They had to camp on the south side of the holy tent. 30The leader of the families of Kohath was Elizaphan, the son of Uzziel.

31They were held accountable for taking care of the ark of the covenant. They took care of the table for the holy bread. They took care of the lampstand and the two altars. They took care of the articles that were used for serving in the sacred tent. They also took care of the inner curtain. In fact, they had to take care of everything that was connected with the use of all of those things.

32The chief leader of the Levites was Eleazar. He was the son of the priest Aaron. Eleazar was appointed over those who were held accountable for taking care of the sacred tent.

33The families of Mahli and Mushi belonged to the family of Merari. 34All of the males who were a month old or more were counted. There were 6,200 of them. 35The leader of the families of Merari was Zuriel, the son of Abihail. They had to camp on the north side of the holy tent.

36They were appointed to take care of the frames of the tent. They took care of its crossbars, posts and bases. They took care of all of its supplies. In fact, they had to take care of everything that was connected with the use of all of those things. 37They also took care of the posts of the courtyard that was around the holy tent. And they took care of the bases, tent stakes and ropes.

38Moses, Aaron and Aaron's sons had to camp to the east of the holy tent. They had to camp toward the sunrise in front of the Tent of Meeting. They were held accountable for taking care of the sacred tent. They had to do it for the people of Israel. Anyone else who approached the tent would be put to death.

39The total number of the Levites was 22,000. They were counted family by family. Every male who was a month old or more was counted. Moses and Aaron counted them, just as the LORD had commanded.

40The LORD said to Moses, "Count the males among the people of Israel who were the oldest sons born in their families. Count all those who are a month old or more. Make a list of their names. 41Take the Levites for me in their place. And take the livestock of the Levites in place of all of the male animals in Israel that were born first to their mothers. I am the LORD."

42So Moses counted all of the oldest sons in Israel. He did just as the LORD had commanded him. 43There were 22,273 of those sons who were a month old or more. They were listed by name.

44The LORD also said to Moses, 45"Take the Levites in place of all the males who were born first in Israel. Also take the livestock of the Levites in place of the livestock of Israel. The Levites belong to me. I am the LORD.

46"But there are 273 more males who were born first in Israel than there are male Levites. 47Collect two ounces of silver for each of them. Weigh it out in keeping with the standard weights that are used in the sacred tent. 48Give the silver to Aaron and his sons. It will buy the freedom of the additional sons in Israel."

49So Moses collected the silver from the additional sons in Israel to buy their freedom. The Levites took the place of all of the others. 50Moses collected 35 pounds of silver. It was weighed out in keeping with the weights that are used in the sacred tent. Moses collected it from the oldest sons in Israel. 51He gave the silver to Aaron and his sons. He did just as the LORD had commanded him.

The Kohath Families

4 The LORD spoke to Moses and Aaron. He said, 2"Count the Kohath families of the Levites. Make a list of them family by family. 3Count all of the men who are from 30 to 50 years old. Those are the men who must come and serve at the Tent of Meeting.

4"Here is the work the men of Kohath must do at the Tent of Meeting. They must take care of the things that are very holy.

5"When the camp is ready to move, Aaron and his sons must go into the tent. They must take down the curtain that screens the ark where the tablets of the covenant are kept. They must cover the ark with the curtain. 6Then they must cover that with the hides of sea cows. They must spread a solid blue cloth over the hides. And they must put the poles in place.

7"They must spread a blue cloth over the table for the holy bread. They must put the plates, dishes and bowls on the cloth. They must also put the jars for drink offerings on it. The bread that is always kept there must remain on it. 8They must spread a bright red cloth over everything. Then they must cover that with the hides of sea cows. And they must put the poles of the table in place.

9“They must get a blue cloth. With it they must cover the lampstand that gives light. They must also cover its lamps, trays and wick cutters. And they must cover all of its jars. The jars are for the olive oil that is used in the lampstand. 10Then Aaron and his sons must wrap the lampstand and all of the things that are used with it. They must cover it with the hides of sea cows. And they must put it on a frame to carry it.

11“They must spread a blue cloth over the gold altar for burning incense. They must cover that with the hides of sea cows. And they must put the poles of the altar in place.

12“They must get all of the articles that are used for serving in the sacred tent. They must wrap them in a blue cloth. They must cover that with the hides of sea cows. Then they must put the articles on a frame to carry them.

13“They must remove the ashes from the bronze altar for burnt offerings. They must spread a purple cloth over it. 14Then they must place all of the tools on it. The tools are used for serving at the altar. They include the pans for carrying ashes. They also include the meat forks, shovels and sprinkling bowls. Aaron and his sons must cover the altar with the hides of sea cows. And they must put its poles in place.

15“Aaron and his sons must cover all of the holy articles that belong to the holy tent. Then the men of Kohath must get ready to carry everything. They must do it when the camp is ready to move. But they must not touch the holy things. If they do, they will die. The men of Kohath must carry everything that is in the Tent of Meeting.

16“The priest Eleazar will be in charge of the olive oil for the light. He is the son of Aaron. Eleazar will be in charge of the sweet-smelling incense. He will be in charge of the regular grain offering and the anointing oil. He will be in charge of the entire holy tent. He will also be in charge of everything that is in it. That includes all of the articles that belong to the tent.”

17The LORD spoke to Moses and Aaron. He said, 18“Make sure that the Kohath families are not cut off from the Levites. 19I want them to live and not die when they come near the very holy things. So here is what you must do for them. Aaron and his sons must go into the sacred tent and tell each man what to do. They must tell each man what to carry. 20But the men of Kohath must not go in and look at the holy things. They must not look at them even for a moment. If they do, they will die.”

The Gershon Families

21The LORD said to Moses, 22“Count the Gershon families. Make a list of them family by family. 23Count all of the men who are from 30 to 50 years old. Those are the men who must come and serve at the Tent of Meeting.

24“Here is how the Gershon families must serve. They must carry things. 25They must carry the curtains of the holy Tent of Meeting. They must carry its covering and the outside covering of the hides of sea cows. They must carry the curtains that cover the entrance to the Tent of Meeting. 26They must carry the curtains of the courtyard. The courtyard is all around the holy tent and altar. They must carry the curtain for the entrance. They must carry the ropes. They must also carry all of the supplies that are used for any purpose in the tent. The men of Gershon must do everything that needs to be done with those things.

27“All of their work must be done under the direction of Aaron and his sons. That includes carrying and everything else they do. Aaron and his sons must tell them what to carry. And that will be their work. 28It is what the Gershon families must do at the Tent of Meeting. They must work under the direction of the priest Ithamar. He is the son of Aaron.

The Merari Families

29“Count the Merari families. Count them family by family. 30Count all of the men who are from 30 to 50 years old. Those are the men who must come and serve at the Tent of Meeting.

31“Here is the work they must do at the Tent of Meeting. They must carry the frames of the holy tent. They must carry its crossbars, posts and bases. 32They must also carry the posts of the courtyard. The courtyard is all around the holy tent. And they must carry the bases for the posts as well as their tent stakes and ropes. They must also carry all of the supplies and everything that is connected with their use. Tell each man exactly what to carry. 33That is the work the Merari families must do at the Tent of Meeting. They must work under the direction of the priest Ithamar. He is the son of Aaron.”

Counting the Families of the Levites

34Moses, Aaron and the leaders of the community counted the men of Kohath. They counted them family by family. 35They counted all of the men who were from 30 to 50 years old. Those were the men who came and served at the Tent of Meeting. 36There were 2,750 men. They were counted family by family. 37That was the total of all of the men in the Kohath families who served at the Tent of Meeting. Moses and Aaron counted them. They did just as the LORD had commanded through Moses.

38The men of Gershon were counted family by family. 39All of the men who were from 30 to 50 years old were counted. They were the men who came and served at the Tent of Meeting. 40There were 2,630 men. They were counted family by family. 41That was the total of the men in the Gershon families who served at the Tent of Meeting.

Moses and Aaron counted them. They did just as
the LORD had commanded.
42The men of Merari were counted family by
family. 43All of the men who were from 30 to 50
years old were counted. They were the men who
came and served at the Tent of Meeting. 44There
were 3,200 men. They were counted family by
family. 45That was the total of the men in the Merari families. Moses and Aaron counted them.
They did just as the LORD had commanded
through Moses.
46So Moses and Aaron counted all of the Levites. The leaders of Israel helped them. They
counted the Levites family by family. 47All of the
men who were from 30 to 50 years old were
counted. They were the men who came and served
at the Tent of Meeting. They were also supposed to
carry it. 48The total number of men was 8,580.
49Everything was done as the LORD had commanded through Moses. Each man was given his
work. And each one was told what to carry.

So they were counted, just as the LORD had
commanded Moses.

Making the Camp Pure

5 The LORD spoke to Moses. He said, 2"Tell the
Israelites that certain people must be sent
away from the camp. Command them to send
away anyone who has a skin disease. They must
send away all those who have a liquid waste coming from their bodies. And they must send away
those who are not 'clean' because they have
touched a dead body. 3That applies to men and
women alike. Send them out of the camp. They
must not make their camp 'unclean.' That is where
I live among them."
4So the people of Israel did what the LORD commanded. They sent those who were not "clean" out
of the camp. They did just as the LORD had
directed Moses.

Sins Against Others Must Be Paid For

5The LORD said to Moses, 6"Speak to the people
of Israel. Say to them, 'Suppose a man or woman
does something wrong to someone else. Then that
person is not being faithful to the LORD. People
like that are guilty.
7" 'They must admit they have committed a sin.
They must pay in full for what they did wrong.
And they must add a fifth to it. Then they must
give all of it to the person they have sinned against.
8" 'But suppose the person has died. And suppose there is not a close relative who can be paid
for the sin that was committed. Then what is paid
belongs to the LORD. It must be given to the priest.
A ram must be given along with it. The ram must
be sacrificed to the LORD to pay for the sin.
9" 'All of the sacred gifts the people of Israel
bring to a priest will belong to him. 10Sacred gifts
belong to the man who gives them. But what he
gives to a priest will belong to the priest.' "

The Test for a Wife Who Is Not Faithful

11Then the LORD spoke to Moses again. He said,
12"Speak to the people of Israel. Say to them,
'Suppose a man's wife goes down the wrong path.
And suppose she is not faithful to him. 13She has
sex with another man. And suppose what she has
done is hidden from her husband. No one knows
she is not "clean." So there is no witness against
her. And she has not been caught in the act.
14" 'Suppose her husband becomes jealous. He
does not trust his wife, and she is really not
"clean." Or suppose he does not trust her even
though she is "clean." 15Then he must take his wife
to the priest.
" 'He must also bring an offering. It must be
eight cups of barley flour. The offering is for his
wife. He must not pour olive oil on it. And he must
not put incense on it. It is a grain offering for being
jealous. It calls attention to a person's guilt.
16" 'The priest must have her stand in front of
the LORD. 17He must pour some holy water into a
clay jar. He must get some dust from the floor of
the holy tent. And he must put it into the water.
18The priest must have the woman stand in front of
the LORD. Then he must untie her hair. He must
place in her hands the offering that calls attention
to a person's guilt. It is the grain offering for being
jealous. The priest must keep the bitter water with
him. It is the water that brings a curse.
19" 'Then the priest must have the woman take
an oath. He must say to her, "Suppose no other
man has had sex with you. And suppose you
haven't gone down the wrong path. You have kept
yourself pure while you are married to your husband. Then may the bitter water that brings a curse
not harm you. 20But suppose you have gone down
the wrong path while you are married to your husband. You have made yourself 'unclean.' You have
had sex with a man who isn't your husband."
21" 'At that point the priest must put the woman
under the curse of the oath. He must say, "May the
LORD cause your people to call a curse down on
you. May he cause them to speak against you. May
they do it when the LORD makes your body unable
to have children. 22May this water that brings a
curse enter your body. May it make your body
unable to have children."
" 'Then the woman must say, "Amen. Let it
happen."
23" 'The priest must write the curses on a scroll.
He must wash them off in the bitter water. 24It is
the water he will have the woman drink. It is bitter water that brings a curse. It will enter her body.
And it will cause her to suffer bitterly.
25" 'The priest must take from her hands the
grain offering for being jealous. He must lift it up
and wave it in front of the LORD. He must bring it
to the altar. 26Then the priest must take a handful of
the grain offering. It is the offering that calls attention to a person's guilt. He must burn it on the

altar. After that, he must have the woman drink the water.

27"'Suppose she has made herself "unclean." She has not been faithful to her husband. And she has drunk the water that brings a curse. Then it will go into her body. It will cause her to suffer bitterly. It will make her body unable to have children. Her people will call a curse down on her.

28"'But suppose the woman has not made herself "unclean." And suppose she is free from anything that is not "clean." Then she will be free of guilt. And she will be able to have children.

29"'That is the law about being jealous. It applies to a woman who has gone down the wrong path. She has made herself "unclean" while she is married to her husband. 30And it applies to a man who becomes jealous. He has doubts about his wife. The priest must have her stand in front of the LORD. He must apply the entire law to her. 31The husband will not be guilty of doing anything wrong. But the woman will be punished for her sin.'"

Becoming a Nazirite

6 The LORD said to Moses, 2"Speak to the people of Israel. Say to them, 'Suppose a man or woman wants to make a special promise. They want to set themselves apart to the LORD for a certain period of time. They want to be Nazirites.

3"'Then they must not drink any kind of wine. They must not drink vinegar that is made out of wine of any kind. They must not drink grape juice. They must not eat grapes or raisins. 4As long as they are Nazirites, they must not eat anything grapevines produce. They must not even eat the seeds or skins of grapes.

5"'They must not use razors on their heads. They must not cut their hair during the whole time they have set themselves apart to the LORD. They must be holy until that time is over. They must let the hair on their heads grow long. 6And they must not go near a dead body during that whole time.

7"'But what if their father or mother dies? Or what if their brother or sister dies? Then they must not make themselves "unclean" because of them. The hair on their heads shows they are set apart for God. 8During the whole time they are set apart they are holy to the LORD.

9"'Suppose someone dies suddenly in front of them. That makes the hair they have set apart to the LORD "unclean." So they must shave their heads on the day they will be made "clean." That is the seventh day.

10"'Then on the eighth day they must bring two doves. Or they can bring two young pigeons. They must bring them to the priest. He will be at the entrance to the Tent of Meeting. 11The priest must offer one of the birds as a sin offering. And he must offer the other as a burnt offering. The sacrifices will pay for the sin of the Nazirite man or woman. They sinned by being near a dead body. That same day they must set their heads apart as holy.

12"'They must set themselves apart to the LORD again. They must do it for the same period of time they had agreed to at first. And they must bring a male lamb that is a year old as a guilt offering. The days before that day do not count. That is because they became "unclean" during the time they were set apart.

13"'The time when the Nazirites are set apart will come to an end. Here is the law that applies to them at that time. They must be brought to the entrance to the Tent of Meeting.

14"'There they must sacrifice their offerings to the LORD. They must bring a male lamb that is a year old. It must not have any flaws. It is for a burnt offering. Then they must bring a female lamb that is a year old. It must not have any flaws. It is for a sin offering. And they must bring a ram that does not have any flaws. It is for a friendship offering.

15"'They must sacrifice the offerings together with their grain offerings and drink offerings. And they must also bring a basket of bread that is made without yeast. The offering must include flat cakes that are made out of fine flour mixed with olive oil. And it must include wafers that are spread with oil.

16"'The priest must bring all of those things to the LORD. He must sacrifice the sin offering and the burnt offering. 17He must bring the basket of bread that is made without yeast. And he must sacrifice the ram. It will be a friendship offering to the LORD. The priest must bring it together with its grain offering and drink offering.

18"'Then the Nazirites must shave off the hair they had set apart to the Lord. They must do it at the entrance to the Tent of Meeting. And they must put the hair in the fire that burns the sacrifice of the friendship offering.

19"'After the Nazirites have shaved off their hair, the priest must take a boiled shoulder of the ram. He must remove a cake and a wafer from the basket. They must be made without yeast. And he must place the shoulder and the bread in the hands of the Nazirites.

20"'Then he must lift up the shoulder and bread and wave them in front of the LORD. They are a wave offering. They are holy. They belong to the priest. The breast that was waved belongs to him. The thigh that was offered belongs to him too. After the offering is waved, the Nazirites can drink wine.

21"'That is the law of the Nazirites. They promise to sacrifice offerings to the LORD. They do it when they set themselves apart. And they should bring anything else they can afford. They must carry out the promises they have made. They must do it in keeping with the law of the Nazirites.'"

How the Priests Bless the People

22The LORD spoke to Moses. He said, 23"Tell Aaron and his sons, 'Here is how I want you to bless the people of Israel. Say to them,

24“ ‘ “May the LORD bless you
and take good care of you.
25May the LORD smile on you
and be gracious to you.
26May the LORD look on you with favor
and give you his peace.” ’

27“In that way they will put the blessing of my
name on the people of Israel. And I will bless
them.”

Israel’s Leaders Bring Offerings for the Holy Tent

7 Moses finished setting up the holy tent. Then
he anointed it with olive oil. He set it apart to
the LORD. He did the same thing with everything
that belonged to it. He also anointed the altar. And
he set apart to the LORD the altar and all of its tools.
2Then the leaders of Israel brought their offerings. The leaders were the heads of the families.
They were the leaders of the tribes. They were in
charge of the men who had been counted. 3They
brought gifts to the LORD. They brought six covered carts and 12 oxen. Each leader gave an ox.
And every two leaders gave a cart. They put their
gifts in front of the holy tent.
4The LORD spoke to Moses. He said, 5“Accept
the gifts from the leaders. I want their gifts to be
used in the work at the Tent of Meeting. Give them
to the Levites. They need them to do their work.”
6So Moses gave the carts and the oxen to the
Levites. 7He gave two carts and four oxen to the
men from the family of Gershon. They needed
them to do their work. 8He gave four carts and
eight oxen to the men from the family of Merari.
They needed them to do their work. All of those
men were under the direction of the priest Ithamar,
the son of Aaron.
9But Moses didn’t give any carts or oxen to the
men from the family of Kohath. They had to carry
the holy things on their shoulders. They were
accountable for the holy things.
10When the altar was anointed, the leaders
brought their offerings. They placed them in front
of the altar. They brought their offerings to set the
altar apart. 11The LORD had spoken to Moses. He
had said, “Each day one leader must bring his
offering. He must bring it to set the altar apart.”

12On the first day Nahshon, the son of Amminadab, brought his offering. Nahshon was from the
tribe of Judah.

13He brought one silver plate and one silver sprinkling bowl. The plate weighed three
pounds four ounces. The sprinkling bowl
weighed one pound 12 ounces. They were
weighed in keeping with the standard weights
that are used in the sacred tent. Each plate
and bowl was filled with fine flour that was
mixed with olive oil. It was a grain offering.
14He brought one gold dish. It weighed four
ounces. It was filled with incense.

15Nahshon brought one young bull, one
ram, and one male lamb that was a year old.
They would be sacrificed as a burnt offering.
16He brought one male goat to be sacrificed
as a sin offering. 17He brought two oxen, five
rams and five male goats. He also brought
five male lambs that were a year old. All of
them would be sacrificed as a friendship
offering.

That was everything that Nahshon, the
son of Amminadab, brought as his offering.

18On the second day Nethanel, the son of Zuar,
brought his offering. Nethanel was the leader of
the tribe of Issachar.

19He brought one silver plate and one silver sprinkling bowl. The silver plate
weighed three pounds four ounces. The
sprinkling bowl weighed one pound 12
ounces. Both were weighed in keeping with
the standard weights that are used in the
sacred tent. Each plate and bowl was filled
with fine flour that was mixed with olive oil.
It was a grain offering. 20He brought one
gold dish. It weighed four ounces. It was
filled with incense.

21Nethanel brought one young bull, one
ram, and one male lamb that was a year old.
They would be sacrificed as a burnt offering.
22He brought one male goat to be sacrificed
as a sin offering. 23He brought two oxen, five
rams and five male goats. He also brought
five male lambs that were a year old. All of
them would be sacrificed as a friendship
offering.

That was everything that Nethanel, the
son of Zuar, brought as his offering.

24On the third day Eliab, the son of Helon, brought
his offering. Eliab was the leader of the people of
Zebulun.

25He brought one silver plate and one silver sprinkling bowl. The plate weighed three
pounds four ounces. The sprinkling bowl
weighed one pound 12 ounces. They were
weighed in keeping with the standard
weights that are used in the sacred tent. Each
plate and bowl was filled with fine flour that
was mixed with olive oil. It was a grain
offering. 26He brought one gold dish. It
weighed four ounces. It was filled with
incense.

27Eliab brought one young bull, one ram,
and one male lamb that was a year old. They
would be sacrificed as a burnt offering. 28He
brought one male goat to be sacrificed as a
sin offering. 29He brought two oxen, five rams
and five male goats. He also brought five
male lambs that were a year old. All of them
would be sacrificed as a friendship offering.

That was everything that Eliab, the son of
Helon, brought as his offering.

30On the fourth day Elizur, the son of Shedeur,
brought his offering. Elizur was the leader of the
people of Reuben.

31He brought one silver plate and one silver sprinkling bowl. The plate weighed three
pounds four ounces. The sprinkling bowl
weighed one pound 12 ounces. They were
weighed in keeping with the standard
weights that are used in the sacred tent. Each
plate and bowl was filled with fine flour that
was mixed with olive oil. It was a grain
offering. 32He brought one gold dish. It
weighed four ounces. It was filled with
incense.

33Elizur brought one young bull, one ram,
and one male lamb that was a year old. They
would be sacrificed as a burnt offering. 34He
brought one male goat to be sacrificed as a
sin offering. 35He brought two oxen, five
rams and five male goats. He also brought
five male lambs that were a year old. All of
them would be sacrificed as a friendship
offering.

That was everything that Elizur, the son of Shedeur, brought as his offering.

36On the fifth day Shelumiel, the son of Zurishaddai, brought his offering. Shelumiel was the leader
of the people of Simeon.

37He brought one silver plate and one silver sprinkling bowl. The plate weighed three
pounds four ounces. The sprinkling bowl
weighed one pound 12 ounces. They were
weighed in keeping with the standard
weights that are used in the sacred tent. Each
plate and bowl were filled with fine flour
that was mixed with olive oil. It was a grain
offering. 38He brought one gold dish. It
weighed four ounces. It was filled with
incense.

39Shelumiel brought one young bull, one
ram, and one male lamb that was a year old.
They would be sacrificed as a burnt offering.
40He brought one male goat to be sacrificed
as a sin offering. 41He brought two oxen, five
rams and five male goats. He also brought
five male lambs that were a year old. All of
them would be sacrificed as a friendship
offering.

That was everything that Shelumiel, the son of Zurishaddai, brought as his offering.

42On the sixth day Eliasaph, the son of Deuel,
brought his offering. Eliasaph was the leader of the
people of Gad.

43He brought one silver plate and one silver sprinkling bowl. The plate weighed three
pounds four ounces. The sprinkling bowl
weighed one pound 12 ounces. They were
weighed in keeping with the standard
weights that are used in the sacred tent. Each
plate and bowl was filled with fine flour that
was mixed with olive oil. It was a grain
offering. 44He brought one gold dish. It
weighed four ounces. It was filled with
incense.

45Eliasaph brought one young bull, one
ram, and one male lamb that was a year old.
They would be sacrificed as a burnt offering.
46He brought one male goat to be sacrificed
as a sin offering. 47He brought two oxen, five
rams and five male goats. He also brought
five male lambs that were a year old. All of
them would be sacrificed as a friendship
offering.

That was everything that Eliasaph, the son of Deuel, brought as his offering.

48On the seventh day Elishama, the son of Ammihud, brought his offering. Elishama was the leader
of the people of Ephraim.

49He brought one silver plate and one silver sprinkling bowl. The plate weighed three
pounds four ounces. The sprinkling bowl
weighed one pound 12 ounces. They were
weighed in keeping with the standard
weights that are used in the sacred tent. Each
plate and bowl was filled with fine flour that
was mixed with olive oil. It was a grain
offering. 50He brought one gold dish. It
weighed four ounces. It was filled with
incense.

51Elishama brought one young bull, one
ram, and one male lamb that was a year old.
They would be sacrificed as a burnt offering.
52He brought one male goat to be sacrificed
as a sin offering. 53He brought two oxen, five
rams and five male goats. He also brought
five male lambs that were a year old. All of
them would be sacrificed as a friendship
offering.

That was everything that Elishama, the son of Ammihud, brought as his offering.

54On the eighth day Gamaliel, the son of Pedahzur,
brought his offering. Gamaliel was the leader of
the people of Manasseh.

55He brought one silver plate and one silver sprinkling bowl. The plate weighed three
pounds four ounces. The sprinkling bowl
weighed one pound 12 ounces. They were
weighed in keeping with the standard
weights that are used in the sacred tent. Each
plate and bowl was filled with fine flour that
was mixed with olive oil. It was a grain
offering. 56He also brought one gold dish. It
weighed four ounces. It was filled with
incense.

57Gamaliel brought one young bull, one
ram, and one male lamb that was a year old.
They would be sacrificed as a burnt offering.
58He brought one male goat to be sacrificed
as a sin offering. 59He brought two oxen, five
rams and five male goats. He also brought

five male lambs that were a year old. All of them would be sacrificed as a friendship offering.

That was everything that Gamaliel, the son of Pedahzur, brought as his offering.

60On the ninth day Abidan, the son of Gideoni, brought his offering. Abidan was the leader of the people of Benjamin.

61He brought one silver plate and one silver sprinkling bowl. The plate weighed three pounds four ounces. The sprinkling bowl weighed one pound 12 ounces. They were weighed in keeping with the standard weights that are used in the sacred tent. Each plate and bowl was filled with fine flour that was mixed with olive oil. It was a grain offering.
62He brought one gold dish. It weighed four ounces. It was filled with incense.

63Abidan brought one young bull, one ram, and one male lamb that was a year old. They would be sacrificed as a burnt offering.
64He brought one male goat to be sacrificed
as a sin offering. 65He brought two oxen, five rams and five male goats. He also brought five male lambs that were a year old. All of them would be sacrificed as a friendship offering.

That was everything that Abidan, the son of Gideoni, brought as his offering.

66On the tenth day Ahiezer, the son of Ammishaddai, brought his offering. Ahiezer was the leader of the people of Dan.

67He brought one silver plate and one silver sprinkling bowl. The plate weighed three pounds four ounces. The sprinkling bowl weighed one pound 12 ounces. They were weighed in keeping with the standard weights that are used in the sacred tent. Each plate and bowl was filled with fine flour that was mixed with olive oil. It was a grain
offering. 68He brought one gold dish. It weighed four ounces. It was filled with incense.

69Ahiezer brought one young bull, one ram, and one male lamb that was a year old. They would be sacrificed as a burnt offering.
70He brought one male goat to be sacrificed
as a sin offering. 71He brought two oxen, five rams and five male goats. He also brought five male lambs that were a year old. All of them would be sacrificed as a friendship offering.

That was everything that Ahiezer, the son of Ammishaddai, brought as his offering.

72On the eleventh day Pagiel, the son of Ocran, brought his offering. Pagiel was the leader of the people of Asher.

73He brought one silver plate and one silver sprinkling bowl. The plate weighed three pounds four ounces. The sprinkling bowl weighed one pound 12 ounces. They were weighed in keeping with the standard weights that are used in the sacred tent. Each plate and bowl was filled with fine flour that was mixed with olive oil. It was a grain
offering. 74He brought one gold dish. It weighed four ounces. It was filled with incense.

75Pagiel brought one young bull, one ram, and one male lamb that was a year old. They
would be sacrificed as a burnt offering. 76He
brought one male goat to be sacrificed as a
sin offering. 77He brought two oxen, five rams and five male goats. He also brought five male lambs that were a year old. All of them would be sacrificed as a friendship offering.

That was everything that Pagiel, the son of Ocran, brought as his offering.

78On the twelfth day Ahira, the son of Enan, brought his offering. Ahira was the leader of the people of Naphtali.

79He brought one silver plate and one silver sprinkling bowl. The plate weighed three pounds four ounces. The sprinkling bowl weighed one pound 12 ounces. They were weighed in keeping with the standard weights that are used in the sacred tent. Each plate and bowl was filled with fine flour that was mixed with olive oil. It was a grain
offering. 80He brought one gold dish. It weighed four ounces. It was filled with incense.

81Ahira brought one young bull, one ram, and one male lamb that was a year old. They
would be sacrificed as a burnt offering. 82He
brought one male goat to be sacrificed as a
sin offering. 83He brought two oxen, five rams and five male goats. He also brought five male lambs that were a year old. All of them would be sacrificed as a friendship offering.

That was everything that Ahira, the son of Enan, brought as his offering.

84Those were the offerings the leaders of the people of Israel brought. They gave them to set the altar apart when it was anointed with olive oil. They gave 12 silver plates, 12 silver sprinkling
bowls and 12 gold dishes. 85Each silver plate
weighed three pounds four ounces. Each sprinkling bowl weighed one pound 12 ounces. The total weight of the silver dishes was 60 pounds. Everything was weighed in keeping with the standard weights that are used in the sacred tent.

86Each of the 12 gold dishes weighed four ounces. They were filled with incense. They were weighed in keeping with the weights used in the sacred tent. The total weight of the gold dishes was three pounds.

[87]The leaders brought 12 young bulls, 12 rams and 12 male lambs that were a year old. That was the total number of animals they gave for the burnt offering. They gave them together with the grain offering. They brought 12 male goats for the sin offering.

[88]The leaders brought 24 oxen, 60 rams, 60 male goats and 60 male lambs that were a year old. That was the total number of animals that were sacrificed as the friendship offering.

Those were the offerings they brought to set the altar apart. The leaders brought them after the altar was anointed with oil.

[89]Moses entered the Tent of Meeting. He wanted to speak with the LORD. There Moses heard the LORD talking to him. The LORD's voice was speaking to him from between the two cherubim. The cherubim were over the place where sin is paid for. It was the cover on the ark where the tablets of the covenant were kept. The LORD spoke with Moses there.

Aaron Sets Up the Lamps

8 The LORD said to Moses, [2]"Speak to Aaron. Say to him, 'Set up the seven lamps. They will give light to the area that is in front of the lampstand.'"

[3]So Aaron did it. He set up the lamps so that they faced forward on the lampstand. He did just as the LORD had commanded Moses. [4]The lampstand was made out of hammered gold. From its base to its blooms it was made out of hammered gold. The lampstand was made exactly like the pattern the LORD had shown Moses.

Moses Sets the Levites Apart

[5]The LORD spoke to Moses. He said, [6]"Take the Levites from among the other men of Israel. Make them 'clean' in the usual way. [7]Here is how to make them pure. Sprinkle the special water on them. Then have them shave their whole bodies. Also have them wash their clothes. That is how they will make themselves pure.

[8]"Have them get a young bull along with its grain offering. The offering must be made out of fine flour mixed with olive oil. Then you must get a second young bull. You must sacrifice it as a sin offering.

[9]"Bring the Levites to the front of the Tent of Meeting. Gather the whole community of Israel together. [10]You must bring the Levites to me. The men of Israel must place their hands on them. [11]Aaron must bring the Levites to me. They are a wave offering from the people of Israel. That is how they will be set apart to do my work.

[12]"I want the Levites to place their hands on the heads of the bulls. Then they must sacrifice one bull as a sin offering to me. And they must sacrifice the other as a burnt offering. The blood of the bulls will pay for the sin of the Levites.

[13]"Have the Levites stand in front of Aaron and his sons. Then give them as a wave offering to me. [14]That is how I want you to set the Levites apart from the other men of Israel. The Levites will belong to me.

[15]"Make the Levites pure. Give them to me as a wave offering. Then they must come to do their work at the Tent of Meeting. [16]They are the men of Israel who will be given to me completely. I have taken them to be my own. I have taken them in place of every son who is born first in his family in Israel.

[17]"Every male that is born first in Israel belongs to me. That is true whether it is a man or an animal. I struck down all of the males that were born first to a mother in Egypt. Then I set apart for myself all of the males that were born first in Israel. [18]And I have taken the Levites in place of all of the sons who are born first in Israel.

[19]"I have given the Levites as gifts to Aaron and his sons. I have taken them from all of the men of Israel. I have appointed them to do the work at the Tent of Meeting. They will do it in place of the men of Israel.

"That is how they will keep the men of Israel from being guilty when they go near the sacred tent. Then no plague will strike the people of Israel when they go near the tent."

[20]So Moses and Aaron and the whole community of Israel did with the Levites just as the LORD had commanded Moses. [21]The Levites made themselves pure. They washed their clothes. Then Aaron gave them to the LORD as a wave offering. That's how he paid for their sin to make them pure. [22]After that, the Levites came to do their work at the Tent of Meeting. They worked under the direction of Aaron and his sons. And so Moses and Aaron and the whole community of Israel did with the Levites just as the LORD had commanded Moses.

[23]The LORD spoke to Moses. He said, [24]"Here is what the Levites must do. Men who are 25 years old or more must come and take part in the work at the Tent of Meeting.

[25]"But when they reach the age of 50, they must not work any longer. They must stop doing their regular work. [26]They can help their brothers with their duties at the Tent of Meeting. But they themselves should not do the work. That is how you must direct the Levites to do their work."

Israel Celebrates the Passover Feast

9 The LORD spoke to Moses in the Desert of Sinai. It was the first month of the second year after the people came out of Egypt. He said, [2]"Tell the people of Israel to celebrate the Passover Feast. Have them do it at the appointed time. [3]Celebrate it when the sun goes down on the 14th day of this month. Obey all of its rules and laws."

[4]So Moses told the people of Israel to celebrate the Passover Feast. [5]They did it in the Desert of Sinai. They celebrated it when the sun went down on

the 14th day of the first month. The people of Israel did everything just as the LORD had commanded Moses.
6But some of them couldn't celebrate the Passover Feast on that day. That's because they weren't
"clean." They had gone near a dead body. So they
came to Moses and Aaron that same day. 7They
said to Moses, "We went near a dead body. So we
aren't 'clean.' But why should we be kept from
bringing the LORD's offering at the appointed
time? Why shouldn't we bring it along with the
other people of Israel?"
8Moses answered them, "Wait until I find out
what the LORD wants you to do."
9Then the LORD spoke to Moses. He said, 10"Tell
the people of Israel, 'Suppose any of you or your
children are not "clean" because you have gone
near a dead body. Or suppose you are away on a
journey. You can still celebrate the LORD's Passover.
11" 'I want you to celebrate it on the 14th day of
the second month. You have to do it when the sun
goes down. You have to eat the lamb together with
bread that is made without yeast. Eat it with bitter
plants. 12Do not leave any of it until morning. Do
not break any of its bones. When you celebrate the
Passover Feast, follow all of the rules.
13" 'But suppose a man is "clean." He is not on a
journey. And he fails to celebrate the Passover
Feast. Then he must be cut off from the community
of Israel. He did not bring the LORD's offering at
the appointed time. He will be punished for his sin.
14" 'What if there is an outsider living among
you? And what if he wants to celebrate the LORD's
Passover? Then he must obey its rules and laws.
You must have the same laws for outsiders as you
do for the people of Israel.' "

The Cloud Covers the Holy Tent

15The holy tent was set up. It was the tent where
the tablets of the covenant were kept. On the day
it was set up, the cloud covered it. From evening
until morning the cloud that was above the tent
looked like fire. 16That's what continued to happen. The cloud covered the tent. At night the cloud
looked like fire.
17When the cloud lifted from its place above the
tent, the people of Israel started out. Where the
cloud settled, the people of Israel camped. 18When
the LORD gave the command, the people of Israel
started out. And when he gave the command, they
camped. As long as the cloud stayed above the
holy tent, they remained in camp.
19Sometimes the cloud remained above the tent
for a long time. Then the people of Israel obeyed
the LORD's order. They didn't start out. 20Some-
times the cloud was above the tent for only a few
days. When the LORD would give the command,
they would camp. Then when he would give the
command, they would start out.
21Sometimes the cloud stayed only from
evening until morning. When it lifted in the morning, they started out. It didn't matter whether it was
day or night. When the cloud lifted, the people
started out. 22It didn't matter whether the cloud
stayed above the holy tent for two days or a month
or a year. The people of Israel would remain in
camp. They wouldn't start out. But when the cloud
lifted, they would start out.
23When the LORD gave the command, they
camped. And when he gave the command, they
started out. They obeyed the LORD's order. They
obeyed him, just as he had commanded them
through Moses.

The Silver Trumpets

10 The LORD spoke to Moses. He said,
2"Make two trumpets out of hammered silver. Blow them when you want the community to
gather together. And blow them when you want the
camps to start out. 3When both trumpets are
blown, the whole community must gather in front
of you. They must come to the entrance to the Tent
of Meeting. 4Suppose only one trumpet is blown.
Then the leaders must gather in front of you. They
are the heads of the tribes of Israel. 5When a trumpet blast is blown, the tribes that are camped on
the east side must start out. 6When the second blast
is blown, the camps on the south side must start
out. The blast will tell them when to start. 7Blow
the trumpets to gather the people together. But do
not use the same kind of blast.
8"The sons of Aaron, the priests, must blow the
trumpets. That is a law for you and your children
after you for all time to come. 9Suppose you go
into battle in your own land. And suppose it is
against an enemy who is beating you down. Then
blow a blast on the trumpets. If you do, I will
remember you. I will save you from your enemies.
I am the LORD your God. 10You must also blow the
trumpets when you are happy. Blow them at your
appointed feasts. Blow them at your New Moon
Feasts. Blow them when you sacrifice your burnt
offerings. Blow them when you sacrifice your
friendship offerings. They will remind me of you.
I am the LORD your God."

The People of Israel Leave the Sinai Desert

11It was the 20th day of the second month of the
second year. On that day the cloud began to move.
It went up from above the holy tent where the
tablets of the covenant were kept.
12Then the people of Israel started out from the
Desert of Sinai. They traveled from place to place.
They kept going until the cloud came to rest in the
Desert of Paran. 13The first time they started out,
the LORD commanded Moses to tell them to do it.
And they did it.
14The companies of the camp of Judah went
first. They went out under their flag. Nahshon was
their commander. He was the son of Amminadab.
15Nethanel was over the company of the tribe of

Abraham

"I will make your name great. You will be a blessing to others."
—Genesis 12:2

Moses

Then the LORD spoke to Moses. "Hold your wooden staff out.
Reach your hand out over the Red Sea to part the water.
Then the people can go through the sea on dry ground."
—Exodus 14:15–16

Issachar. Nethanel was the son of Zuar. 16 Eliab was
over the company of the tribe of Zebulun. Eliab
was the son of Helon.
17 The holy tent was taken down. The men of
Gershon and Merari started out. They carried the
tent.
18 The companies of the camp of Reuben went
next. They went out under their flag. Elizur was
their commander. He was the son of Shedeur.
19 Shelumiel was over the company of the tribe of
Simeon. Shelumiel was the son of Zurishaddai.
20 Eliasaph was over the company of the tribe of
Gad. Eliasaph was the son of Deuel.
21 The men of Kohath started out. They carried
the holy things. The holy tent had to be set up
before they arrived.
22 The companies of the camp of Ephraim went
next. They went out under their flag. Elishama was
their commander. He was the son of Ammihud.
23 Gamaliel was over the company of the tribe of
Manasseh. Gamaliel was the son of Pedahzur.
24 Abidan was over the company of the tribe of
Benjamin. Abidan was the son of Gideoni.
25 Finally, the companies of the camp of Dan
started out. They marched out under their flag.
They followed behind all of the other companies
and guarded them. Ahiezer was their commander.
He was the son of Ammishaddai. 26 Pagiel was over
the company of the tribe of Asher. Pagiel was the
son of Ocran. 27 Ahira was over the company of the
tribe of Naphtali. Ahira was the son of Enan.
28 As the companies of Israel started out, that
was the order they marched in.
29 Moses spoke to Hobab, the son of Reuel. Reuel was Moses' father-in-law. Reuel was from Midian. Moses said to Hobab, "We're starting out for
the place the LORD promised to us. He said to us,
'I will give it to you.' So come with us. We'll treat
you well. The LORD has promised to give good
things to Israel."
30 Hobab answered, "No. I can't go. I'm going
back to my own land. I'm returning to my own
people."
31 But Moses said, "Please don't leave us. You
know where we should camp in the desert. You
can be our guide. 32 So come with us. The LORD
will give us good things. We'll share them with
you."
33 So they started out from the mountain of the
LORD. They traveled for three days. The ark of the
covenant of the LORD went in front of them during those three days. It went ahead of them to find
a place for them to rest. 34 They started out from the
camp by day. And the cloud of the LORD was
above them.
35 When the ark started out, Moses said,

"LORD, rise up!
Let your enemies be scattered.
Let them run away from you."

36 When the ark came to rest, Moses said,

"LORD, return.
Return to the many thousands of people
in Israel."

The LORD Sends Fire Among the People

11 The people weren't happy about the hard
times they were having. The LORD heard
what they were saying. It made him burn with
anger. Then the LORD sent fire on them. It blazed
out among the people. It burned up some of the
outer edges of the camp.
2 The people cried out to Moses. Then he prayed
to the LORD. And the fire died down.
3 So that place was named Taberah. That's because fire from the LORD had blazed out among
them there.

The LORD Sends Meat for the People

4 Some people who were with them began to
long for other food. Again the people of Israel
began to cry out. They said, "We wish we had
meat to eat. 5 We remember the fish we ate in
Egypt. It didn't cost us anything. We also remember the cucumbers, melons, leeks, onions and gar
lic. 6 But now we've lost all interest in eating. We
never see anything but this manna!"
7 The manna was like coriander seeds. It looked
like sap from a tree. 8 The people went around gathering it. Then they ground it in a small mill they
held in their hands. Or they crushed it in a stone
bowl. They cooked it in a pot. Or they made cakes
out of it. It tasted like something made with olive
oil. 9 When the dew came down on the camp at
night, the manna also came down.
10 Moses heard people from every family crying.
They were sobbing at the entrances to their tents.
The LORD burned with hot anger. So Moses
became troubled. 11 He asked the LORD, "Why have
you brought this trouble on me? Why aren't you
pleased with me? Why have you loaded me down
with the troubles of all of these people?
12 "Am I like a mother to them? Are they my
children? Why do you tell me to carry them in my
arms? Do I have to carry them the way a nurse carries a baby? Do I have to carry them to the land
you promised? You took an oath and promised the
land to their people of long ago.
13 "Where can I get meat for all of these people?
They keep crying out to me. They say, 'Give us
meat to eat!' 14 I can't carry all of these people by
myself. The load is too heavy for me.
15 "Is this how you are going to treat me? If you
are pleased with me, just put me to death right
now. Don't let me live if I have to see myself
destroyed anyway."
16 The LORD said to Moses, "Bring me 70 of Israel's elders. Bring men that you know are leaders
and officials among the people. Have them come
to the Tent of Meeting. I want them to stand there
with you. 17 I will come down. I will speak wit'
you there. I will take some of my Spirit that i-

you. And I will put the Spirit on them. They will
help you carry the people's load. Then you will not
have to carry it alone.
18"Tell the people, 'Set yourselves apart for
tomorrow. At that time you will eat meat. The LORD
heard you when you cried out. You said, "We wish
we had meat to eat. We were better off in Egypt."
"'Now the LORD will give you meat. And you
will eat it. 19You will not eat it for just one or two
days. You will not eat it for just five, ten or 20
days. 20Instead, you will eat it for a whole month.
You will eat it until it comes out of your nose. You
will eat it until you hate it.
"'The LORD is among you. But you have turned
your back on him. You have cried out while he was
listening. You have said, "Why did we ever leave
Egypt?"'"
21But Moses said, "Here I am among 600,000
men on the march. And you say, 'I will give them
meat to eat for a whole month'! 22Would they have
enough if flocks and herds were killed for them?
Would they have enough even if all of the fish in
the ocean were caught for them?"
23The LORD answered Moses, "Am I not strong
enough? Now you will see whether what I say will
come true for you."
24So Moses went out. He told the people what
the LORD had said. He gathered 70 of their elders
together. He had them stand around the Tent of
Meeting.
25Then the LORD came down in the cloud. He
spoke with Moses. He took some of his Spirit that
was on Moses. And he put the Spirit on the 70
elders. When the Spirit came on them, they prophesied. But they didn't do it again.
26Two men had remained in the camp. Their
names were Eldad and Medad. They were listed
among the elders. But they didn't go out to the
Tent of Meeting. In spite of that, the Spirit came
on them too. So they prophesied in the camp.
27A young man ran up to Moses. He said, "Eldad and Medad are prophesying in the camp."
28Joshua spoke up. He was the son of Nun.
Joshua had been Moses' helper from the time he
was young. He said, "Moses! Please stop them!"
29But Moses replied, "Are you jealous for me?
I wish that all of the LORD's people were prophets.
And I wish that the LORD would put his Spirit on
them." 30Then Moses and the elders of Israel
returned to the camp.
31The LORD sent out a wind. It drove quail in
from the Red Sea. It brought them down all around
the camp. They were about three feet above the
ground. They could be seen in every direction as
far as a person could walk in a day.
32The people went out all day and gathered
quail. They gathered them all night and all the next
day. No one gathered less than 60 bushels. Then
they spread the quail out all around the camp.
33But while the meat was still in their mouths,
the LORD acted. Before the people could swallow
it, his anger burned against them. He struck them
with a terrible plague.
34So the place was named Kibroth Hattaavah.
That's where the bodies of the people who had
longed for other food were buried.
35From Kibroth Hattaavah the people traveled
to Hazeroth. And they stayed there.

Miriam and Aaron Speak Against Moses

12 Miriam and Aaron began to say bad things
about Moses. That's because Moses had
married a woman from Cush. 2"Has the LORD spoken only through Moses?" they asked. "Hasn't he
also spoken through us?" The LORD heard what
they said.
3Moses wasn't very proud at all. In fact, he had
less pride than anyone else on the face of the earth.
4The LORD spoke to Moses, Aaron and Miriam.
He said, "All three of you, come out to the Tent of
Meeting." So they did. 5Then the LORD came down
in a pillar of cloud. He stood at the entrance to the
tent. And he told Aaron and Miriam to come to
him. Both of them stepped forward.
6Then the LORD said, "Listen to my words.

"Suppose one of my prophets is among you.
I make myself known to him in visions.
I speak to him in dreams.
7 But that is not true of my servant Moses.
He is faithful in everything he does in
my house.
8 With Moses I speak face to face.
I speak with him clearly. I do not speak
in riddles.
I let him see something of what I look like.
So why were you not afraid
to speak against my servant Moses?"

9The anger of the LORD burned against them.
And he left them.
10When the cloud went up from above the tent,
there stood Miriam. She had a disease that made
her skin as white as snow.
Aaron turned toward her. He saw that she had a
skin disease. 11So he said to Moses, "We have
committed a very foolish sin. Please don't hold it
against us. 12Don't let Miriam be like a baby that
was born dead. Don't let her look like a dead baby
whose body is half eaten away."
13So Moses cried out to the LORD. He said,
"God, please heal her!"
14The LORD answered Moses. He said, "Suppose her father had spit in her face. Then she
would have been put to shame for seven days. So
keep her outside the camp for seven days. After
that, you can bring her back."
15So Miriam was kept outside the camp for
seven days. The people didn't move on until she
was brought back.
16After that, the people left Hazeroth. They
camped in the Desert of Paran.

Some Men Check Out the Land of Canaan

13 The LORD spoke to Moses. He said, 2"Send
some men to check out the land of Canaan.
I am giving it to the people of Israel. Send one
leader from each of Israel's tribes."
3So Moses sent them out from the Desert of Paran. He sent them as the LORD had commanded.
All of them were leaders of the people of Israel.
4Here are their names.

There was Shammua from the tribe of Reuben. Shammua was the son of Zaccur.
5 There was Shaphat from the tribe of Simeon. Shaphat was the son of Hori.
6 There was Caleb from the tribe of Judah.
Caleb was the son of Jephunneh.
7 There was Igal from the tribe of Issachar.
Igal was the son of Joseph.
8 There was Hoshea from the tribe of Ephraim. Hoshea was the son of Nun.
9 There was Palti from the tribe of Benjamin. Palti was the son of Raphu.
10 There was Gaddiel from the tribe of Zebulun. Gaddiel was the son of Sodi.
11 There was Gaddi from the tribe of Manasseh. Gaddi was the son of Susi. Manasseh was a tribe of Joseph.
12 There was Ammiel from the tribe of Dan.
Ammiel was the son of Gemalli.
13 There was Sethur from the tribe of Asher.
Sethur was the son of Michael.
14 There was Nahbi from the tribe of Naphtali. Nahbi was the son of Vophsi.
15 There was Geuel from the tribe of Gad.
Geuel was the son of Maki.

16Those are the men Moses sent to check out the
land. He gave the name Joshua to Hoshea, the son
of Nun.
17Moses sent them to check out Canaan. He
said, "Go up through the Negev Desert. Go on into
the central hill country. 18See what the land is like.
See whether the people who live there are strong
or weak. See whether they are few or many.
19"What kind of land do they live in? Is it good
or bad? What kind of towns do they live in? Do
the towns have high walls around them or not?
20How is the soil? Is it rich land or poor land? Are
there trees on it or not? Do your best to bring back
some of the fruit of the land." It was the season for
the first ripe grapes.
21So the men went up and checked out the land.
They went from the Desert of Zin as far as Rehob.
It was in the direction of Lebo Hamath. 22They
went up through the Negev Desert and came to
Hebron. That's where Ahiman, Sheshai and Talmai lived. They belonged to the family line of
Anak. Hebron had been built seven years before
Zoan. Zoan was a city in Egypt.
23The men came to the Valley of Eshcol. There
they cut off a branch that had a single bunch of
grapes on it. Two of them carried it on a pole
between them. They carried some pomegranates
and figs along with it. 24That place was called the
Valley of Eshcol. That's because the men of Israel cut off a bunch of grapes there.
25At the end of 40 days, the men returned from
checking out the land.

The Men Report on What They Found

26The men came back to Moses, Aaron and the
whole community of Israel. The people were at
Kadesh in the Desert of Paran. There the men
reported to Moses and Aaron and all of the people.
They showed them the fruit of the land.
27They gave Moses their report. They said, "We
went into the land you sent us to. It really does
have plenty of milk and honey! Here's some fruit
from the land.
28"But the people who live there are powerful.
Their cities have high walls around them and are
very large. We even saw members of the family
line of Anak there. 29The Amalekites live in the
Negev Desert. The Hittites, Jebusites and Amorites
live in the central hill country. The Canaanites live
near the Mediterranean Sea. They also live along
the Jordan River."
30Then Caleb interrupted the men who were
speaking to Moses. He said, "We should go up and
take the land. We can certainly do it."
31But the men who had gone up with him spoke.
They said, "We can't attack those people. They are
stronger than we are." 32The men spread a bad
report about the land among the people of Israel.
They said, "The land we checked out destroys
those who live in it. All of the people we saw there
are very big and tall. 33We saw the Nephilim there.
We seemed like grasshoppers in our own eyes.
And that's also how we seemed to them." The children of Anak came from the Nephilim.

The People Refuse to Obey the LORD

14 That night all of the people in the community raised their voices. They sobbed out
loud.
2The people of Israel spoke against Moses and
Aaron. The whole community said to them, "We
wish we had died in Egypt or even in this desert.
3Why is the LORD bringing us to this land? We're
going to be killed with swords. Our enemies will
capture our wives and children. Wouldn't it be better for us to go back to Egypt?"
4They said to one another, "We should choose
another leader. We should go back to Egypt."
5Then Moses and Aaron fell with their faces to
the ground. They did it in front of the whole community of Israel that was gathered there.
6Joshua, the son of Nun, tore his clothes. So did
Caleb, the son of Jephunneh. Joshua and Caleb
were two of the men who had checked out the
land. 7They spoke to the whole community of Israel. They said, "We passed through the land and

checked it out. It's very good. 8 If the LORD is pleased with us, he'll lead us into that land. It's a land that has plenty of milk and honey. He'll give it to us.

9 "But don't refuse to obey him. And don't be afraid of the people of the land. We will swallow them up. The LORD is with us. So nothing can save them. Don't be afraid of them."

10 But all of the people talked about killing Joshua and Caleb by throwing stones at them.

Then the glory of the LORD appeared at the Tent of Meeting. All of the people of Israel saw it. 11 The LORD spoke to Moses. He said, "How long will these people make fun of me? How long will they refuse to believe in me? They refuse even though I have done many miraculous signs among them. 12 So I will strike them down with a plague. I will destroy them. But I will make you into a greater and stronger nation than they are."

13 Moses said to the LORD, "Then the Egyptians will hear about it. You used your power to bring these people up from among them.

14 "And the Egyptians will tell the people who live in Canaan about it. LORD, they have already heard a lot about you. They've heard that you are with these people. They've heard that you have been seen face to face. They've been told that your cloud stays over them. They've heard that you go in front of them in a pillar of cloud by day. They've been told that you go in front of them in a pillar of fire at night.

15 "Suppose you put these people to death all at one time. Then the nations who have heard those things about you will talk. They'll say, 16 'The LORD took an oath. He promised to give these people the land of Canaan. But he wasn't able to bring them into it. So he killed them in the desert.'

17 "Now, Lord, show your strength. You have said, 18 'I am the LORD. I am slow to get angry. I am full of love. I forgive those who sin. I forgive those who refuse to obey. But I do not let guilty people go without punishing them. I punish the children, grandchildren and great-grandchildren for the sin of their parents.'

19 "LORD, your love is great. So forgive the sin of these people. Forgive them just as you have done from the time they left Egypt until now."

20 The LORD replied, "I have forgiven them, just as you asked. 21 You can be sure that I live. You can be sure that my glory fills the whole earth.

22 "And you can be just as sure that these men will not see the land I promised to give them. They have seen my glory. They have seen the miraculous signs I did in Egypt. And they have seen what I did in the desert. But they did not obey me. And they have put me to the test ten times. 23 So not even one of them will ever see the land I promised with an oath to give to their people of long ago. No one who has made fun of me will ever see it.

24 "But my servant Caleb has a different spirit. He follows me with his whole heart. So I will bring him into the land he went to. And his children after him will receive land there.

25 "The Amalekites and Canaanites are living in the valleys. So turn back tomorrow. Start out toward the desert. Go along the way that leads to the Red Sea."

26 The LORD spoke to Moses and Aaron. He said, 27 "How long will this evil community speak against me? I have heard these Israelites talk about how unhappy they are. 28 So tell them, 'Here is what I, the LORD, am announcing. You can be sure that I live. And you can be just as sure that I will do to you the very things that I heard you say.

29 " 'You will die in this desert. Every one of you who is 20 years old or more will die. Every one of you who was counted in the list of the people will die. Every one of you who has spoken out against me will be wiped out. 30 I lifted up my hand and promised with an oath to make this land your home. But now not all of you will enter the land. Caleb, the son of Jephunneh, will enter it. So will Joshua, the son of Nun. They are the only ones who will enter the land.

31 " 'You have said that your enemies would capture your children. But I will bring your children in to enjoy the land you have turned your backs on. 32 As for you, you will die in the desert. 33 Your children will be shepherds here for 40 years. They will suffer because you were not faithful. They will suffer until the last of your bodies lies here in the desert. 34 For 40 years you will suffer for your sins. That is one year for each of the 40 days you checked out the land. You will know what it is like to have me against you.'

35 "I, the LORD, have spoken. You can be sure that I will do those things to this whole evil community. They have joined together against me. They will meet their end in this desert. They will die here."

36 So the LORD struck down the men Moses had sent to check out the land. They had returned and had spread a bad report about the land. And that had made the whole community speak out against Moses. 37 Those men were to blame for spreading the bad report. So the LORD struck them down. They died of a plague.

38 Only two of the men who went to check out the land remained alive. One of them was Joshua, the son of Nun. The other was Caleb, the son of Jephunneh.

39 Moses reported to all of the people of Israel what the LORD had said. And they became very sad. 40 Early the next morning they went up toward the high hill country. "We have sinned," they said. "We will go up to the place the LORD promised to give us."

41 But Moses said, "Why aren't you obeying the LORD's command? You won't succeed. 42 So don't go up. The LORD isn't with you. Your enemies will win the battle over you. 43 The Amalekites and Canaanites will meet you on the field of battle. You

have turned away from the LORD. So he won't be with you. And you will be killed with swords."

44But they wouldn't listen. They still went up toward the high hill country. They went up even though Moses didn't move from the camp. They went even though the ark of the LORD's covenant didn't move from the camp.

45Then the Amalekites and Canaanites who lived in that hill country came down. They attacked the people of Israel. They won the battle over them. They chased them all the way to Hormah.

Other Offerings

15 The LORD said to Moses, 2"Speak to the people of Israel. Say to them, 'You are going to enter the land I am giving you as a home. 3When you do, you will give offerings that are made to the LORD with fire. The animals must come from your herd or flock. The offerings will give a smell that is pleasant to the LORD. They can be either burnt offerings or sacrifices. They can be either for special promises or for feast offerings. Or they can be for offerings you choose to give.

4" 'With each of the offerings, the one who brings it must give the LORD a grain offering. It must be eight cups of fine flour. It must be mixed with a quart of olive oil. 5Also prepare a quart of wine as a drink offering. You must give it with each lamb that you bring for the burnt offering or the sacrifice.

6" 'With a ram prepare a grain offering. It must be 16 cups of fine flour. It must be mixed with two and a half pints of olive oil. 7You must bring two and a half pints of wine as a drink offering. Offer everything as a smell that is pleasant to the LORD.

8" 'Suppose you prepare a young bull as a burnt offering or sacrifice. You prepare it to keep a special promise to the LORD. Or you prepare it to give as a friendship offering. 9Then bring a grain offering with the bull. The grain offering must be 24 cups of fine flour. It must be mixed with two quarts of olive oil. 10Also bring two quarts of wine as a drink offering. It will be an offering that is made with fire. It will give a smell that is pleasant to the LORD.

11" 'Each bull or ram must be prepared in the same way. Each lamb or young goat must also be prepared in that way. 12Do it for each animal. Do it for as many animals as you prepare.

13" 'Everyone in Israel must do those things in that way. He must do them when he brings an offering that is made with fire. Offerings like that give a smell that is pleasant to the LORD.

14" 'Everyone must always do what the law requires. It does not matter whether he is an outsider or someone else who is living among you. He must do exactly as you do when he brings an offering that is made with fire. Offerings like that give a smell that is pleasant to the LORD.

15" 'The community must have the same rules for you and for the outsider who is living among you. That law will last for all time to come. In the sight of the LORD, the law applies to you and the outsider alike. 16The same laws and rules will apply to you and to the outsider who is living among you.' "

17The LORD said to Moses, 18"Speak to the people of Israel. Say to them, 'You are going to enter the land I am taking you to. 19You will eat its food. When you do, bring part of it as an offering to the LORD. 20Bring a loaf that is made from the first flour you grind. Give it as an offering from the threshing floor. 21You must bring the offering to the LORD. You must give it from the first grain you grind. You must do it for all time to come.

Offerings for Sins That Aren't Committed on Purpose

22" 'Suppose you fail to keep any of the commands the LORD gave Moses. And suppose you do it without meaning to. 23That applies to any of the commands the LORD told Moses to give you. And they are in effect from the day the LORD gave them and for all time to come. 24Suppose the community sins without meaning to. And suppose they do not know they have sinned. Then the whole community must offer a young bull. They must offer it for a burnt offering. It will give a smell that is pleasant to the LORD. Along with it, they must offer its required grain offering and drink offering. They must also offer a male goat for a sin offering.

25" 'With it the priest will pay for the sin of the whole community of Israel. Then they will be forgiven. They did not mean to commit that sin. And they have brought to the LORD an offering that is made with fire for the wrong thing they did. They have brought a sin offering with it.

26" 'The LORD will forgive the whole community of Israel and the outsiders living among them. All of the people had a part in the sin, even though they did not mean to do it.

27" 'But suppose just one person sins without meaning to. Then he must bring a female goat for a sin offering. It must be a year old. 28With it the priest will pay for the person's sin in the sight of the LORD. He will do it for the one who did wrong by sinning without meaning to. When the sin is paid for, that person will be forgiven.

29" 'The same law applies to everyone who sins without meaning to. It does not matter whether he is an Israelite or an outsider.

30" 'But suppose someone sins on purpose. It does not matter whether he is an Israelite or an outsider. He speaks evil things against the LORD. He must be cut off from his people. 31He has made fun of what the LORD has said. He has broken the LORD's commands. He must certainly be cut off. He is still guilty.' "

A Man Breaks the Sabbath Day

32The people of Israel were in the desert. One Sabbath day, people saw a man gathering wood.

33They brought him to Moses and Aaron and the
whole community. 34They kept him under guard.
It wasn't clear what should be done to him.
35Then the LORD said to Moses, "The man must
die. The whole community must kill him by
throwing stones at him. They must do it outside
the camp."
36So the people took the man outside the camp.
There they killed him by throwing stones at him.
They did just as the LORD had commanded Moses.

Tassels on Clothes

37The LORD said to Moses, 38"Speak to the people of Israel. Say to them, 'You must make tassels
on the corners of your clothes. A blue cord must be
on each tassel. You must do it for all time to come.
39You will have the tassels to look at. They will
remind you to obey all of the LORD's commands.
Then you will be faithful to him. You will not go
after what your own hearts and eyes long for.
40" 'You will remember to obey all of my commands. And you will be set apart for your God. 41I
am the LORD your God. I brought you out of Egypt
to be your God. I am the LORD your God.' "

Korah, Dathan and Abiram

16 Korah was the son of Izhar, the son of Kohath. Kohath was the son of Levi. Korah
and certain men from the tribe of Reuben turned
against Moses. The men from Reuben were Dathan, Abiram and On. Dathan and Abiram were the
sons of Eliab. On was the son of Peleth. 2All of
those men rose up against Moses. And 250 men of
Israel joined them. All of them were known as
leaders in the community. They had been
appointed as members of the ruling body.
3They came as a group to oppose Moses and Aaron. They said to Moses and Aaron, "You have gone
too far! The whole community is holy. Every one
in it is holy. And the LORD is with them. So why do
you put yourselves above the LORD's people?"
4When Moses heard what they said, he fell with
his face to the ground. 5Then he spoke to Korah
and all of his followers. He said, "In the morning
the LORD will show who belongs to him. He will
show who is holy. He'll bring that person near
him. He'll bring the man he chooses near him.
6"Korah, here's what you and all of your followers must do. Get some shallow cups for burning incense. 7Tomorrow put fire and incense in
them. Offer it to the LORD. The man the LORD
chooses will be the one who is holy. You Levites
have gone too far!"
8Moses also said to Korah, "Listen, you Levites! 9The God of Israel has separated you from
the rest of the community of Israel. He has brought
you near him to work at the LORD's holy tent. He
has given you to the people so that you can serve
them. Isn't all of that enough for you? 10He has
already brought you and all of the other Levites
near him. But now you want to be priests too.
11You and all of your followers have joined
together against the LORD. Why are you telling
Aaron you aren't happy with him?"
12Then Moses sent for Dathan and Abiram, the
sons of Eliab. But they said, "We won't come!
13You have brought us up out of a land that has
plenty of milk and honey. You have brought us
here to kill us in this desert. Isn't that enough?
Now do you also want to act as if you were ruling
over us?
14"Besides, you haven't brought us into a land
that has plenty of milk and honey. You haven't
given us fields and vineyards of our own. Are you
going to poke out the eyes of these men? No! We
won't come!"
15Then Moses became very angry. He said to
the LORD, "Don't accept their offering. I haven't
taken even a donkey from them. In fact, I haven't
done anything wrong to any of them."
16Moses said to Korah, "You and all of your followers must stand in front of the LORD tomorrow.
You must appear there along with Aaron. 17Each
man must get his shallow cup. He must put incense
in it. There will be a total of 250 incense cups.
Each man must bring his cup to the LORD. You and
Aaron must also bring your cups."
18So each man got his cup. He put fire and
incense in it. All of the men came with Moses and
Aaron. They stood at the entrance to the Tent of
Meeting. 19Korah gathered all of his followers
together at the entrance to the tent. They opposed
Moses and Aaron.
Then the glory of the LORD appeared to the
whole community. 20The LORD spoke to Moses
and Aaron. He said, 21"Separate yourselves from
these people. Then I can put an end to all of them
at once."
22But Moses and Aaron fell with their faces to
the ground. They cried out, "God, you are the God
who creates the spirits of all people. Will you be
angry with the whole community when only one
man sins?"
23Then the LORD spoke to Moses. He said,
24"Tell the community, 'Move away from the tents
of Korah, Dathan and Abiram.' "
25Moses got up. He went to Dathan and Abiram.
The elders of Israel followed him. 26Moses warned
the community. He said, "Move away from the
tents of those evil men! Don't touch anything that
belongs to them. If you do, the LORD will sweep
you away because of all of their sins."
27So they moved away from the tents of Korah,
Dathan and Abiram. Dathan and Abiram had
already come out. They were standing at the
entrances to their tents. Their wives, children and
little ones were standing there with them.
28Then Moses said, "What is about to happen
wasn't my idea. The LORD has sent me to do
everything I'm doing. Here is how you will know
I'm telling you the truth. 29Those men won't die a
natural death. Something will happen to them that

doesn't usually happen to people. If what I'm telling you isn't true, then you will know that the LORD hasn't sent me.

30"But the LORD will make something totally new happen. The ground will open its mouth and swallow them up. It will swallow up everything that belongs to them. They will go down into the grave alive. When that happens, you will know that those men have made fun of the LORD."

31As soon as Moses finished speaking all of those words, what he had said came true. The ground under them broke open. 32It opened its mouth. It swallowed up those men. In fact, it swallowed up everyone who lived in their houses. It swallowed all of Korah's men. And it swallowed up everything they owned. 33They went down into the grave alive. Everything they owned went down with them. The ground closed over them. They died. And so they disappeared from the community.

34All of the people of Israel who were around them heard their cries. They ran away from them. They shouted, "The ground is going to swallow us up too!"

35Then the LORD sent down fire. It burned up the 250 men who were offering the incense.

36The LORD spoke to Moses. He said, 37"Speak to the priest Eleazar. He is the son of Aaron. Remind him that the shallow cups are holy. He must take them out of the fire. He must scatter the burning coals away from there. 38The men who sinned used those cups. And it cost them their lives. Hammer the cups into bronze sheets that will cover the altar. The cups were offered to the LORD. They have become holy. Let them serve as a warning to the people of Israel."

39So the priest Eleazar collected the bronze incense cups. They had been brought by the men who had been burned up. He had them hammered out to cover the altar. 40He did just as the LORD had directed Moses to tell him to do. The covering would be a reminder to the people of Israel. It would remind them that no one except a son of Aaron should come and burn incense to the LORD. If people other than priests did that, they would become like Korah and his followers.

41The next day the whole community of Israel told Moses and Aaron they weren't happy with them. "You have killed the LORD's people," they said.

42The community gathered together to oppose Moses and Aaron. The people walked toward the Tent of Meeting. Suddenly the cloud covered it. The glory of the LORD appeared. 43Then Moses and Aaron went to the front of the Tent of Meeting. 44The LORD spoke to Moses. He said, 45"Get away from these people. Then I can put an end to all of them at once." And Moses and Aaron fell with their faces to the ground.

46Moses said to Aaron, "Take your incense cup. Put incense in it. And put fire from the altar in it. Then hurry to the people and pay for their sin. The LORD has sent his anger. The plague has started."

47So Aaron did as Moses said. He ran in among the people. The plague had already started among them. But Aaron offered the incense and paid for their sin. 48He stood between those who were alive and those who were dead. And the plague stopped. 49But 14,700 people died from the plague. That doesn't include those who had died because of what Korah did. 50Then Aaron returned to Moses at the entrance to the Tent of Meeting. The plague had stopped.

Aaron's Wooden Staff Produces Buds

17 The LORD spoke to Moses. He said, 2"Speak to the people of Israel. Get 12 wooden staffs from them. Get one from the leader of each of Israel's tribes. Write the name of each man on his staff. 3Write Aaron's name on the staff of Levi. There must be one staff for the head of each of Israel's tribes.

4"Put the staffs in the Tent of Meeting. Place them in front of the ark where the tablets of the covenant are kept. That is where I meet with you. 5The staff that belongs to the man I choose will begin to grow new shoots. The people of Israel are never happy with what you do. I will put an end to what they are saying."

6So Moses spoke to the people of Israel. Their leaders gave him 12 wooden staffs. They gave one for the leader of each of Israel's tribes. Aaron's staff was among them. 7Moses put the staffs in front of the LORD in the tent where the tablets of the covenant were kept.

8The next day Moses entered the tent. He looked at Aaron's staff. It stood for the tribe of Levi. Moses saw that it had not only begun to grow new shoots. It had also produced buds and flowers and almonds.

9Then Moses brought out all of the staffs from in front of the LORD. He brought them to all of the people of Israel. They looked at them. And each man took his own staff.

10The LORD said to Moses, "Put Aaron's staff back in front of the ark where the tablets of the covenant are kept. The staff will be kept there as a warning to those who refuse to obey. They are never happy with what I do. Aaron's staff will put an end to what they are saying. Then they will not die." 11Moses did just as the LORD commanded him.

12The people of Israel said to Moses, "We'll die! We are lost! All of us are lost! 13Anyone who even comes near the LORD's holy tent will die. Are all of us going to die?"

Duties of Priests and Levites

18 The LORD spoke to Aaron. He said, "You, your sons and your father's family are in charge of the sacred tent. You will be held accountable for sins that are committed against it. And you

and your sons will be held accountable for sins that are committed against the office of priest.

2“Bring the Levites from your tribe to join you. They will help you when you and your sons serve at the tent where the tablets of the covenant are kept. 3They will work for you. They must do everything that needs to be done at the tent. But they must not go near anything that belongs to the sacred tent. And they must not go near the altar. If they do, they and you will die. 4They will help you take care of the Tent of Meeting. They will join you in all of the work at the tent. No one else can come near you there.

5“You will be held accountable for taking care of the sacred tent and the altar. Then my anger will not fall on the people of Israel again. 6I myself have chosen the Levites. I have chosen them from among the people of Israel. They are a gift to you. I have set them apart to do the work at the Tent of Meeting.

7“But only you and your sons can serve as priests. Only you and your sons can work with everything at the altar and inside the curtain. I am letting you serve as priests. It is a gift from me. Anyone else who comes near the sacred tent must be put to death.”

Offerings for Priests and Levites

8Then the LORD spoke to Aaron. He said, “I have put you in charge of the offerings that are brought to me. The people of Israel will give me holy offerings. I will give all of their offerings to you and your sons. They are the part that belongs to you. They are your regular share.

9“You will have a part of the very holy offerings. It is the part that is not burned in the fire. That part belongs to you and your sons. You will have a part of all of the gifts the people bring me as very holy offerings. It does not matter whether they are grain offerings or sin offerings or guilt offerings. 10Eat your part as something that is very holy. Every male will eat it. You must consider it holy.

11“Part of the gifts the people of Israel bring as wave offerings will be set to one side. That part will also belong to you. I will give it to you and your sons and daughters. It is your regular share. Everyone in your home who is ‘clean’ can eat it.

12“I will give you all of the finest olive oil and grain the people give me. And I will give you all of the finest fresh wine they give me. They give all of those things as the first share of their harvest. 13All of the first shares of the harvest they bring me will belong to you. Everyone in your home who is ‘clean’ can eat it.

14“Everything in Israel that is set apart to me belongs to you. 15Offer to me every male that is born first to its mother. It belongs to you. That is true for men and animals alike. But you must buy back every oldest son. Suppose certain animals are not ‘clean.’ Then you must buy back every male that is born first to its mother. 16When they are a month old, you must buy them back. You must pay the price to buy them back. The price is set at two ounces of silver. It must be weighed out in keeping with the standard weights that are used in the sacred tent.

17“But you must not buy back any male calf that is born first. And you must not buy back any male sheep or goat that is born first. They are holy. Sprinkle their blood on the altar. And burn their fat as an offering that is made with fire. It gives a smell that is pleasant to me.

18“The meat will belong to you. It is just like the breast and the right thigh of the wave offering. Those parts belong to you. 19Part of the holy offerings the people of Israel bring to me will be set to one side. No matter what it is, I will give it to you and your sons and daughters. It is your regular share. It is a covenant of salt from me. The salt means that the covenant will last for all time to come for you and your children.”

20The LORD spoke to Aaron. He said, “You will not receive any part of the land I am giving to Israel. You will not have any share among them. I am your share. I am what you will receive among the people of Israel.

21“The people of Israel will give me a tenth of everything they produce. And I will give it to the Levites. They serve at the Tent of Meeting. I will give them the tenth for the work they do there. 22From now on the people of Israel must not go near the Tent of Meeting. If they do, they will be punished for their sin. They will die.

23“The Levites will do the work at the Tent of Meeting. They will be held accountable for sins that are committed against it. That is a law that will last for all time to come. The Levites will not receive any share among the people of Israel. 24Instead, I will give the Levites the tenth as their share. It is the tenth that the people of Israel bring me as an offering. That is why I said the Levites would not have any share of land among the people of Israel.”

25The LORD said to Moses, 26“Speak to the Levites. Say to them, ‘You will receive the tenth from the people of Israel. I will give it to you as your share. When I do, you must give a tenth of that tenth as an offering to the LORD. 27Your offering will be considered as if you gave grain from a threshing floor. It will be considered as juice from a winepress.

28“‘In that way, you also will bring an offering to the LORD. You will bring it from the tenth you receive from the people of Israel. You must give the LORD’s part to the priest Aaron. You must bring it from the tenth you receive. 29You must bring to the LORD a part of everything that is given to you. It must be the best and holiest part.’

30“Say to the Levites, ‘You must bring the best part. Then it will be considered as if you gave grain from a threshing floor. It will be considered as juice from a winepress. 31You and your families can eat the rest of it anywhere. It is your pay for your work at the Tent of Meeting. 32 Bring the best part of what you receive. Then you will not be guilty of holding anything back. You will not make the holy offerings of the people of Israel "unclean." You will not die.'"

The Special Water That Makes People "Clean"

19 The LORD spoke to Moses and Aaron. He said, 2 "Here is what the law I have commanded requires. Tell the people of Israel to bring you a young red cow. It must not have any flaws at all. It must never have pulled a load.

3 "Give it to the priest Eleazar. It must be taken outside the camp and killed in front of him. 4 Then the priest Eleazar must put some of its blood on his finger. He must sprinkle the blood toward the front of the Tent of Meeting. He must do it seven times.

5 "While he watches, the young cow must be burned. Its hide, meat, blood and guts must be burned. 6 The priest must get some cedar wood, branches of a hyssop plant, and bright red wool. He must throw them on the young cow as it burns.

7 "After that, the priest must wash his clothes. He must also take a bath. Then he can come into the camp. But he will be 'unclean' until evening.

8 "The man who burns the young cow must wash his clothes. He must also take a bath. He too will be 'unclean' until evening.

9 "A man who is 'clean' will gather up the ashes of the young cow. He must put them in a place that is 'clean.' The place must be outside the camp. The ashes will be kept by the community of Israel. They will be added to the special water. The water will be used to make people pure from their sin.

10 "The man who gathers up the ashes of the young cow must wash his clothes. He too will be 'unclean' until evening. That law is for the people of Israel. It is also for the outsiders who are living among them. The law will last for all time to come.

11 "Anyone who touches a dead person's body will be 'unclean' for seven days. 12 He must make himself pure and clean with the special water. He must do it on the third day. He must also do it on the seventh day. Then he will be 'clean.'

"But suppose he does not make himself pure and clean on the third and seventh days. Then he will not be 'clean.' 13 Anyone who touches a dead person's body and does not make himself pure and clean makes my holy tent 'unclean.' He must be cut off from Israel. The special water has not been sprinkled on him. So he is 'unclean.' And he remains 'unclean.'

14 "Here is the law that applies when a person dies in a tent. Anyone who enters the tent will be 'unclean' for seven days. Anyone who is in the tent will also be 'unclean' for seven days. 15 And anything in it that is open and has no lid will be 'unclean.'

16 "Suppose someone is out in the country. And suppose he touches someone who has been killed with a sword. Or he touches someone who has died a natural death. Or he touches a human bone or a grave. Then anyone who touches any of those things will be 'unclean' for seven days.

17 "Here is what I want you to do for someone who is not 'clean.' Put some ashes from the burned young cow into a jar. Pour fresh water on the ashes. 18 Then a man who is 'clean' must dip branches of a hyssop plant in the water. He must sprinkle the tent with it. Everything that belongs to the tent must be sprinkled with it. The people who were in the tent must also be sprinkled. Anyone who has touched a human bone or a grave must be sprinkled. So must anyone who has touched someone who has been killed. So must anyone who has touched someone who has died a natural death.

19 "The man who is 'clean' must sprinkle the person who is not. That must be done on the third and seventh days. On the seventh day the person who is not 'clean' must be made pure and clean. The one who is being made 'clean' must wash his clothes. He must take a bath. Then that evening he will be 'clean.'

20 "But what if a person who is 'unclean' does not make himself pure and clean? Then he must be cut off from the community. He has made my holy tent 'unclean.' The special water has not been sprinkled on him. He is not 'clean.' 21 That law will apply to all of those people for all time to come.

"The man who sprinkles the special water must also wash his clothes. Anyone who touches the water will be 'unclean' until evening. 22 Anything that an 'unclean' person touches becomes 'unclean.' And anyone who touches it becomes 'unclean' until evening."

The LORD Gives Israel Water Out of the Rock

20 In the first month the whole community of Israel arrived at the Desert of Zin. They stayed at Kadesh. Miriam died there. Her body was also buried there.

2 The people didn't have any water. So they gathered together to oppose Moses and Aaron. 3 They argued with Moses. They said, "We wish we had died when our people fell dead in front of the LORD.

4 "Why did you bring the LORD's people into this desert? We and our livestock will die here. 5 Why did you bring us up out of Egypt? Why did you bring us to this terrible place? It doesn't have any grain or figs. It doesn't have any grapes or pomegranates. There isn't even any water for us to drink!"

6 Moses and Aaron left the people. They went to the entrance to the Tent of Meeting. There they fell with their faces to the ground.

Then the glory of the LORD appeared to them. 7 The LORD spoke to Moses. He said, 8 "Get your

wooden staff. You and your brother Aaron gather
the people together. Then speak to that rock while
everyone is watching. It will pour out its water.
You will bring water out of the rock for the community. Then they and their livestock can drink it."
9So Moses took the wooden staff from the tent.
He did just as the LORD had commanded him. 10He
and Aaron gathered the people together in front of
the rock. Moses said to them, "Listen, you who
refuse to obey! Do we have to bring water out of
this rock for you?"
11Then Moses raised his arm. He hit the rock
twice with his staff. Water poured out. And the
people and their livestock drank it.
12But the LORD spoke to Moses and Aaron. He
said, "You did not trust in me enough to honor me.
You did not honor me as the holy God in front of
the people of Israel. So you will not bring this
community into the land I am giving them."
13Those were the waters of Meribah. That's
where the people of Israel argued with the LORD.
And that's where he showed them he is holy.

Edom Doesn't Let Israel Pass Through Its Territory

14Moses sent messengers from Kadesh to the
king of Edom. The messengers said,

"The nation of Israel is your brother. They
say, 'You know about all of the hard times
we've had. 15Long ago our people went
down into Egypt. We lived there for many
years. The Egyptians treated us and our people badly. 16But we cried out to the LORD. He
heard our cry. He sent an angel and brought
us out of Egypt.

"'Now here we are at the town of Kadesh.
It's on the edge of your territory. 17Please let
us pass through your country. We won't go
through any field or vineyard. We won't
drink water from any well. We'll travel along
the king's highway. We won't turn to the
right or the left. We'll just go straight
through your territory.'"

18But the people of Edom answered,

"You can't pass through here. If you try
to, we'll march out against you. We'll attack
you with our swords."

19The people of Israel replied,

"We'll go along the main road. We and our
livestock won't drink any of your water. If we
do, we'll pay for it. We only want to walk
through your country. That's all we ask."

20Again the people of Edom answered,

"You can't pass through here."

Then the people of Edom came out against
them. They came with a large and powerful army.
21Edom refused to let Israel go through their territory. So Israel turned away from them.

Aaron Dies

22The whole community of Israel started out
from Kadesh. They arrived at Mount Hor. 23It was
near the border of Edom. There the LORD spoke to
Moses and Aaron. He said, 24"Aaron will join the
members of his family who have already died. He
will not enter the land I am giving to the people of
Israel. Both of you refused to obey my command.
You did it at the waters of Meribah.
25"So get Aaron and his son Eleazar. Take them
up Mount Hor. 26Take Aaron's official robes off
him. Put them on his son Eleazar. Aaron will die
on Mount Hor. He will join the members of his
family who have already died."
27Moses did just as the LORD had commanded.
The three men went up Mount Hor while the
whole community was watching. 28Moses took
Aaron's official robes off him. He put them on
Aaron's son Eleazar. And Aaron died there on top
of the mountain. Then Moses and Eleazar came
down from the mountain.
29The whole community found out that Aaron
had died. So the entire nation of Israel sobbed over
him for 30 days.

Israel Destroys Arad

21 The Canaanite king of the city of Arad
lived in the Negev Desert. He heard that
Israel was coming along the road to Atharim. So
he attacked the people of Israel. He captured some
of them.
2Then Israel made a promise to the LORD. They
said, "Hand these people over to us. If you do, we
will set their cities apart to you in a special way to
be destroyed."
3The LORD gave Israel what they asked for. He
handed the Canaanites over to them. Israel completely destroyed them. They also destroyed their
towns. So that place was named Hormah.

Moses Makes a Bronze Snake

4The people of Israel traveled from Mount Hor
along the way to the Red Sea. They wanted to go
around Edom. But they grew tired on the way. 5So
they spoke against God. They also spoke against
Moses. They said to them, "Why have you brought
us up out of Egypt? Do you want us to die here in
the desert? We don't have any bread! We don't
have any water! And we hate this awful food!"
6Then the LORD sent poisonous snakes among the
people of Israel. The snakes bit them. Many of the
people died. 7The others came to Moses. They said,
"We sinned when we spoke against the LORD and
against you. Pray that the LORD will take the snakes
away from us." So Moses prayed for the people.
8The LORD said to Moses, "Make a snake. Put it
up on a pole. Then anyone who is bitten can look
at it and remain alive." 9So Moses made a bronze

snake. He put it up on a pole. Then anyone who
was bitten by a snake and looked at the bronze
snake remained alive.

The People Continue On to Moab

10 The people of Israel moved on. They camped
at Oboth. 11 Then they started out from Oboth.
They camped in Iye Abarim. It's in the desert on
the eastern border of Moab. 12 From there they
moved on. They camped in the Zered Valley.
13 They started out from there and camped by the
Arnon River. It's in the desert that spreads out into
the territory of the Amorites. The Arnon is the border of Moab. It's between Moab and the Amorites.
14 Here is what the Book of the Wars of the LORD
says about it. It says,

"Sing about Waheb in Suphah and the valleys.
  Sing about the Arnon 15 and the slopes of
    the valleys.
They lead to the place called Ar.
  They lie along the border of Moab."

16 From there the people of Israel continued on
to Beer. That was the well where the LORD spoke
to Moses. He said, "Gather the people together. I
will give them water to drink."
17 Then Israel sang a song. They said,

"Spring up, you well!
  Sing about it.
18 Sing about the well the princes dug.
  Sing about the well the nobles of the
    people dug.
  All of their rulers were holding their rods
    and staffs."

Then the people of Israel went from the desert
to Mattanah. 19 They went from Mattanah to Nahaliel. They went from Nahaliel to Bamoth. 20 And
they went from Bamoth to a valley in Moab. It's
the valley where the highest slopes of Pisgah look
out over a dry and empty land.

Israel Wins the Battle Over Sihon and Og

21 The people of Israel sent messengers to speak
to Sihon. He was the king of the Amorites. The
messengers said to him,

22 "Let us pass through your country. We
won't go off the road into any field or vineyard. We won't drink water from any well.
We'll travel along the king's highway. We'll
just go straight through your territory."

23 But Sihon wouldn't let Israel pass through his
territory. He gathered his whole army together.
Then he marched out into the desert against Israel.
When he reached Jahaz, he fought against Israel.
24 But Israel put him to death with their swords.
They took over his land. They took everything
from the Arnon River to the Jabbok River. But
they didn't take over any of the land of the Ammonites. That's because the Ammonites had built
strong forts along their border. 25 The people of Israel captured all of the cities of the Amorites. Then
they settled down in them. They captured the city
of Heshbon. They also captured all of the settlements that were around it.
26 Sihon, the king of the Amorites, ruled in
Heshbon. He had fought against an earlier king of
Moab. Sihon had taken from him all of his land all
the way to the Arnon River.
27 That's why the poets say,

"Come to Heshbon. Let it be built again.
  Let Sihon's city be made as good as new.
28 "Fire went out from Heshbon.
  A blaze went out from the city of Sihon.
It burned up Ar in Moab.
  It burned up the citizens who lived on
    Arnon's hills.
29 Moab, how terrible it is for you!
  People of Chemosh, you are destroyed!
Chemosh has deserted his sons and daughters.
  His sons have run away from the battle.
His daughters have become prisoners.
  He has handed all of them over to Sihon,
  the king of the Amorites.

30 "But we have taken them over.
  Heshbon is destroyed all the way to Dibon.
We have destroyed them as far as Nophah.
  Nophah goes all the way to Medeba."

31 So Israel settled in the land of the Amorites.
32 Moses sent spies to the city of Jazer. The people of Israel captured the settlements that were
around it. They drove out the Amorites who were
there. 33 Then they turned and went up along the
road toward Bashan. Og was the king of Bashan.
He and his whole army marched out. They went to
fight against Israel at Edrei.
34 The LORD said to Moses, "Do not be afraid of
Og. I have handed him over to you. I have given
you his whole army. I have also given you his land.
Do to him what you did to Sihon, the king of the
Amorites. He ruled in Heshbon."
35 So the people of Israel struck Og down. They
struck his sons down. And they wiped out his
whole army. They didn't leave anyone alive. They
took over his land for themselves.

Balak Sends For Balaam

22 Then the people of Israel traveled to the
flatlands of Moab. They camped along the
Jordan River across from Jericho.
2 Balak saw everything that Israel had done to
the Amorites. Balak was the son of Zippor. 3 The
people of Moab were terrified because there were
so many Israelites. In fact, Moab was filled with
panic because of the people of Israel.
4 The Moabites spoke to the elders of Midian.
They said, "This huge mob is going to lick up
everything around us. They'll lick it up as an ox
licks up all of the grass in the fields."

Balak, the son of Zippor, was the king of Moab at that time. 5He sent messengers to get Balaam. Balaam was the son of Beor. Balaam was at the city of Pethor near the Euphrates River. Pethor was in the land where Balaam had been born. Balak told the messengers to say to Balaam,

> "A nation has come out of Egypt. They are covering the face of the land. They've settled down next to me. 6So come and put a curse on those people. They are too powerful for me. Maybe I'll be able to win the battle over them. Maybe I'll be able to drive them out of the country. I know that those you bless will be blessed. And I know that those you put a curse on will be cursed."

7The elders of Moab and Midian left. They took with them the money they knew Balaam would ask for. They wanted him to use magic and figure things out for them. They came to where Balaam was. And they told him what Balak had said.

8"Spend the night here," Balaam said to them. "I'll bring you back the answer the LORD gives me." So the princes of Moab stayed with him.

9God came to Balaam. He asked, "Who are these men who are with you?"

10Balaam said to God, "Balak king of Moab, the son of Zippor, sent me a message. 11He said, 'A nation has come out of Egypt. They are covering the whole surface of the land. So come. Put a curse on them for me. Maybe I'll be able to fight them. Maybe I'll be able to drive them away.'"

12But God said to Balaam, "Do not go with them. You must not put a curse on those people. I have blessed them."

13The next morning Balaam got up. He said to Balak's princes, "Go back to your own country. The LORD won't let me go with you."

14So the princes of Moab returned to Balak. They said, "Balaam wouldn't come with us."

15Then Balak sent other princes. They were more important than the first ones. And there were more of them. 16They came to Balaam. They said,

> "Balak, the son of Zippor, says, 'Don't let anything keep you from coming to me. 17I'll make you very rich. I'll do anything you say. Come. Put a curse on those people for me.'"

18But Balaam gave them his answer. He said, "Balak could give me his palace filled with silver and gold. Even then, I still couldn't do anything at all that goes beyond what the LORD my God commands. 19Stay here tonight, just as the others did. I'll find out what else the LORD will tell me."

20That night God came to Balaam. He said, "These men have come to get you. So go with them. But do only what I tell you to do."

Balaam's Donkey

21Balaam got up in the morning. He put a saddle on his donkey. Then he went with the princes of Moab.

22But God was very angry when Balaam went. So the angel of the LORD stood in the road to oppose him. Balaam was riding on his donkey. His two servants were with him. 23The donkey saw the angel of the LORD standing in the road. The angel was holding a sword. He was ready for battle. So the donkey left the road and went into a field. Balaam hit the donkey. He wanted to get it back on the road.

24Then the angel of the LORD stood in a narrow path. The path went between two vineyards. There were walls on both sides. 25The donkey saw the angel of the LORD. So it moved close to the wall. It crushed Balaam's foot against the wall. He hit the donkey again.

26Then the angel of the LORD moved on ahead. He stood in a narrow place. There was no room to turn, either right or left. 27The donkey saw the angel of the LORD. So it lay down under Balaam. That made him angry. He hit the donkey with his walking stick.

28Then the LORD opened the donkey's mouth. It said to Balaam, "What have I done to you? Why did you hit me those three times?"

29Balaam answered the donkey. He said, "You have made me look foolish! I wish I had a sword in my hand. If I did, I'd kill you right now."

30The donkey said to Balaam, "I'm your own donkey. I'm the one you have always ridden. Haven't you been riding me to this very day? Have I ever made you look foolish before?"

"No," he said.

31Then the LORD opened Balaam's eyes. He saw the angel of the LORD standing in the road. He saw that the angel was holding a sword. The angel was ready for battle. So Balaam bowed down. He fell with his face to the ground.

32The angel of the LORD spoke to him. He asked him, "Why have you hit your donkey three times? I have come here to oppose you. What you are doing is foolish. 33The donkey saw me. It turned away from me three times. Suppose it had not turned away. Then I would certainly have killed you by now. But I would have spared the donkey."

34Balaam spoke to the angel of the LORD. He said, "I have sinned. I didn't realize you were standing in the road to oppose me. Tell me whether you are pleased with me. If you aren't, I'll go back."

35The angel of the LORD spoke to Balaam. He said, "Go with the men. But say only what I tell you to say." So Balaam went with the princes of Balak.

36Balak heard that Balaam was coming. So he went out to meet him. They met at a Moabite town near the Arnon River. The town was on the border of Balak's territory. 37Balak spoke to Balaam. He said, "Didn't I send messengers to you? I wanted you to come quickly. So why didn't you come? I can make you very rich."

38“Well, I’ve come to you now,” Balaam
replied. “But I can’t say just anything. I can only
speak the words God puts in my mouth.”
39Then Balaam went with Balak to Kiriath Hu-
zoth. 40Balak sacrificed cattle and sheep. He gave
some to Balaam. He also gave some to the princes
who were with him.
41The next morning Balak took Balaam up to
Bamoth Baal. From there he saw part of the people of Israel.

Balaam’s First Message From God

23 Balaam said to Balak, “Build me seven
altars here. Prepare seven bulls and seven
rams for me to sacrifice.” 2Balak did just as Balaam said. The two of them offered a bull and a
ram on each altar.
3Then Balaam said to Balak, “Stay here beside
your offering. I’ll go and try to find out what the
LORD wants me to do. Maybe he’ll come and meet
with me. Then I’ll tell you what he says to me.” So
Balaam went off to a bare hilltop.
4God met with him there. Balaam said, “I’ve
prepared seven altars. On each altar I’ve offered a
bull and a ram.”
5The LORD put a message in Balaam’s mouth.
The LORD said, “Go back to Balak. Give him my
message.”
6So Balaam went back to him. He found Balak
standing beside his offering. All of the princes of
Moab were with him.
7Then Balaam spoke the message he had
received from God. He said,

“Balak brought me from the land of Aram.
The king of Moab sent for me from the
mountains in the east.
‘Come,’ he said. ‘Put a curse on Jacob’s people
for me.
Come. Speak against Israel.’
8 But how can I put a curse on
people God hasn’t cursed?
How can I speak against
people the LORD hasn’t spoken against?
9 I see them from the rocky peaks.
I view them from the hills.
I see a group of people who live by
themselves.
They don’t consider themselves to be one
of the nations.
10 Jacob’s people are like the dust of the earth.
Can dust be counted?
Who can count even a fourth of the people
of Israel?
Let me die as godly people die.
Let my death be like theirs!”

11Balak said to Balaam, “What have you done
to me? I brought you here to put a curse on my
enemies! But all you have done is give them a
blessing!”
12He answered, “I have to speak only the words
the LORD puts in my mouth.”

Balaam’s Second Message From God

13Then Balak said to Balaam, “Come with me
to another place. You can see the people of Israel
from there. You will see only some of them. You
won’t see all of them. From there, put a curse on
them for me.”
14So Balak took Balaam to the field of Zophim.
It was on the highest slopes of Pisgah. There he
built seven altars. He offered a bull and a ram on
each altar.
15Balaam said to Balak, “Stay here beside your
offering. I’ll meet with the LORD over there.”
16The LORD met with Balaam. He put a message
in Balaam’s mouth. The LORD said, “Go back to
Balak. Give him my message.”
17So he went to him. He found him standing
beside his offering. The princes of Moab were with
him. Balak asked him, “What did the LORD say?”
18Then Balaam spoke the message he had
received from God. He said,

“Balak, rise up and listen.
Son of Zippor, hear me.
19 God isn’t a mere man. He can’t lie.
He isn’t a human being. He doesn’t change
his mind.
He speaks, and then he acts.
He makes a promise, and then he keeps it.
20 He has commanded me to bless Israel.
He has given them his blessing. And I can’t
change it.

21 “I don’t see any trouble coming on the people
of Jacob.
I don’t see any suffering in Israel.
The LORD their God is with them.
The shout of the King is among them.
22 God brought them out of Egypt.
They are as strong as a wild ox.
23 There isn’t any magic that can hurt the people
of Jacob.
No one can use magic words to harm Israel.
Here is what will be said about the people
of Jacob.
Here is what will be said about Israel.
People will say, ‘See what God has done!’
24 The people of Israel are going to wake up like
a female lion.
They are going to get up like a male lion.
They are like a lion that won’t rest
until it eats what it has caught.
They are like a lion that won’t rest
until it drinks the blood of what it has
killed.”

25Then Balak said to Balaam, “Don’t put a curse
on them at all! And don’t give them a blessing at
all!”
26Balaam answered, “Didn’t I tell you that I
have to do only what the LORD says?”

Balaam's Third Message From God

27 Then Balak said to Balaam, "Come. Let me
take you to another place. Perhaps God will be
pleased to let you put a curse on them for me from
there." 28 Balak took Balaam to the top of Mount
Peor. It looks out over a dry and empty land.
29 Balaam said, "Build me seven altars here. Prepare seven bulls and seven rams for me to sacrifice." 30 Balak did just as Balaam said. He offered
a bull and a ram on each altar.

24 Balaam saw that the LORD was pleased to
give his blessing to Israel. So he didn't try
to use evil magic as he had done at other times.
Instead, he turned and looked toward the desert.
2 He looked out and saw Israel. They had set up
their camps tribe by tribe. The Spirit of God came
on him.

3 Balaam spoke the message he had received
from God. He said,

"Here is the message God gave Balaam, the
son of Beor.
It's the message God gave to the one who
sees clearly.
4 It's the message God gave to the one who hears
the words of God.
He sees a vision from the Mighty One.
He falls down flat with his face toward
the ground.
His eyes have been opened by the LORD.

5 "People of Jacob, your tents are very beautiful.
Israel, the places where you live are very
beautiful.

6 "They spread out like valleys.
They are like gardens beside a river.
They are like aloes the LORD has planted.
They are like cedar trees beside a stream.
7 Their water buckets will run over.
Their seeds will have plenty of water.

"Their king will be greater than King Agag.
Their kingdom will be honored.

8 "God brought them out of Egypt.
They are as strong as a wild ox.
They eat up nations that are at war with them.
They break their bones in pieces.
They wound them with their arrows.
9 Like a male lion they lie down and sleep.
They are like a female lion.
Who dares to wake them up?

May those who bless you be blessed!
May those who call down a curse on you
be cursed!"

10 Then Balak's anger burned against Balaam. He
slapped his hands together. He said to Balaam, "I
sent for you to put a curse on my enemies. But you
have given them a blessing three times. 11 Get out of
here right away! Go home! I said I'd make you very
rich. But the LORD has kept you from getting rich."

12 Balaam answered Balak, "Here is what I told
the messengers you sent me. 13 I said, 'Balak could
give me his palace filled with silver and gold.
Even if I wanted to, I still couldn't do anything at
all that goes beyond what the LORD commands. I
have to say only what the LORD tells me to say.'

14 "Now I'm going back to my people. But
come. Let me warn you about what these people
will do to your people in days to come."

Balaam's Fourth Message From God

15 Then Balaam spoke the message he had
received from God. He said,

"Here is the message God gave Balaam, the
son of Beor.
It's the message God gave to the one who
sees clearly.
16 It's the message God gave to the one who hears
the words of God.
The Most High God has given him
knowledge.
He sees a vision from the Mighty One.
He falls down flat with his face toward
the ground.
His eyes have been opened by the LORD.

17 "I see him, but I don't see him now.
I view him, but he isn't near.
A star will come from among the people
of Jacob.
A king will rise up out of Israel.
He'll crush the foreheads of the people
of Moab.
He'll crush the skulls of all of the sons
of Sheth.
18 He'll win the battle over Edom.
He'll win the battle over his enemy Seir.
But Israel will grow strong.
19 A ruler will come from among the people
of Jacob.
He'll destroy those from the city who are
still alive."

Balaam's Fifth Message From God

20 Then Balaam saw the people of Amalek. He
spoke the message he had received from God. He
said,

"Amalek was the first nation to attack Israel.
But they will finally be destroyed."

Balaam's Sixth Message From God

21 Then he saw the Kenites. He spoke the message he had received from God. He said,

"The place where you live is safe.
Your nest is on a high cliff.
22 But you Kenites will be destroyed.
Assyria will take you as prisoners."

Balaam's Seventh Message From God

23 Then he spoke the message he had received
from God. He said,

"Who can live when God does this?
24 Ships will come from the shores of Kittim.
They will bring Assyria and Eber under
their control.
But they themselves will also be destroyed."

25Then Balaam got up and returned home. And Balak went on his way.

Moab Leads Israel Down the Wrong Path

25 Israel was staying in Shittim. The men of Israel began to commit sexual sins with the women of Moab. 2The women invited the men to feasts and sacrifices in honor of their gods. The people ate and bowed down in front of the statues of those gods.

3So Israel joined in worshiping the god Baal that was worshiped at Peor. The LORD's anger burned against Israel.

4The LORD said to Moses, "Take all of the leaders of these people. Kill them. Put their dead bodies out in the open. I want to see you do it in the middle of the day. Then my anger will not burn against Israel."

5So Moses spoke to Israel's judges. He said, "Some of your men have joined in worshiping the god Baal that is worshiped at Peor. Each of you must kill the men in your tribe who have done that."

6Then a man of Israel brought a woman of Midian to his family. He did it right in front of the eyes of Moses and the whole community of Israel. They were sobbing at the entrance to the Tent of Meeting.

7Phinehas was a priest. He was the son of Eleazar, the son of Aaron. When Phinehas saw what had happened, he left the people. He took a spear in his hand. 8He followed the man into a tent. Phinehas stuck the spear through both the man and the woman.

Then the LORD stopped the plague against the people of Israel. 9But the plague had already killed 24,000 of them.

10The LORD spoke to Moses. He said, 11"Phinehas is a priest. He is the son of Eleazar, the son of Aaron. Phinehas has turned my anger away from the people of Israel. I am committed to making sure I am honored among them. And he is as committed as I am. Even though I was angry with them, I did not put an end to them.

12"So tell Phinehas I am making my covenant with him. It promises to give him peace. 13He and his sons after him will have a covenant to be priests forever. That is because he was committed to making sure that I, his God, was honored. In that way he paid for the sin of the people of Israel."

14The name of the man of Israel who was killed was Zimri. He was the son of Salu. Zimri was killed along with the woman of Midian. Salu was a family leader in the tribe of Simeon. 15The name of the woman of Midian who was killed was Cozbi. She was the daughter of Zur. Zur was the chief of a family in Midian.

16The LORD spoke to Moses. He said, 17"Treat the people of Midian just as you would treat enemies. Kill them. 18After all, they treated you like enemies. They tricked you into worshiping the god Baal that is worshiped at Peor. They also tricked you because of what Cozbi did. She was the woman who was killed when the plague that was connected with Peor came. Cozbi was the daughter of a leader of Midian."

The Men of Israel Are Counted a Second Time

26 After the plague the LORD spoke to Moses and the priest Eleazar. Eleazar was the son of Aaron. The LORD said, 2"Count all of the men of Israel. Make a list of them by their families. Count all of the men who are able to serve in Israel's army. They must be 20 years old or more."

3At that time the people of Israel were on the flatlands of Moab. They were by the Jordan River across from Jericho. Moses and the priest Eleazar spoke with them. They said, 4"Count all of the men who are 20 years old or more. Do it just as the LORD commanded Moses."

Here are the men of Israel who came out of Egypt.

5Reuben was Israel's oldest son. Here are the names of his sons.

The Hanochite family came from Hanoch.
The Palluite family came from Pallu.
6 The Hezronite family came from Hezron.
The Carmite family came from Carmi.

7Those were the families of Reuben. The number of men was 43,730.

8Eliab was the son of Pallu. 9Eliab's sons were Nemuel, Dathan and Abiram. Dathan and Abiram were the same community officials who refused to obey Moses and Aaron. They were among the followers of Korah who refused to obey the LORD. 10The ground opened its mouth. It swallowed them up along with Korah. The followers of Korah died when fire burned up 250 men. Their deaths were a warning to the rest of Israel. 11But the family line of Korah didn't die out completely.

12Here are the names of Simeon's sons. They are listed by their families.

The Nemuelite family came from Nemuel.
The Jaminite family came from Jamin.
The Jakinite family came from Jakin.
13 The Zerahite family came from Zerah.
The Shaulite family came from Shaul.

14Those were the families of Simeon. The number of the men was 22,200.

15Here are the names of Gad's sons. They are listed by their families.

The Zephonite family came from Zephon.
The Haggite family came from Haggi.
The Shunite family came from Shuni.

16 The Oznite family came from Ozni.
The Erite family came from Eri.
17 The Arodite family came from Arodi.
The Arelite family came from Areli.
18 Those were the families of Gad. The number of the men was 40,500.

19 Er and Onan were sons of Judah. But they died in Canaan.
20 Here are the names of Judah's sons. They are listed by their families.
The Shelanite family came from Shelah.
The Perezite family came from Perez.
The Zerahite family came from Zerah.
21 Here are the names of the sons of Perez.
The Hezronite family came from Hezron.
The Hamulite family came from Hamul.
22 Those were the families of Judah. The number of the men was 76,500.

23 Here are the names of Issachar's sons. They are listed by their families.
The Tolaite family came from Tola.
The Puite family came from Puah.
24 The Jashubite family came from Jashub.
The Shimronite family came from Shimron.
25 Those were the families of Issachar. The number of the men was 64,300.

26 Here are the names of Zebulun's sons. They are listed by their families.
The Seredite family came from Sered.
The Elonite family came from Elon.
The Jahleelite family came from Jahleel.
27 Those were the families of Zebulun. The number of the men was 60,500.

28 Here are the names of Joseph's sons. They are listed by their families. The families came from Manasseh and Ephraim, the sons of Joseph.

29 Here are the names of Manasseh's sons.
The Makirite family came from Makir.
Makir was the father of Gilead.
The Gileadite family came from Gilead.
30 Here are the names of Gilead's sons.
The Iezerite family came from Iezer.
The Helekite family came from Helek.
31 The Asrielite family came from Asriel.
The Shechemite family came from Shechem.
32 The Shemidaite family came from Shemida.
The Hepherite family came from Hepher.
33 Zelophehad was the son of Hepher. Zelophehad didn't have any sons. All he had was daughters. Their names were Mahlah, Noah, Hoglah, Milcah and Tirzah.
34 Those were the families of Manasseh. The number of the men was 52,700.

35 Here are the names of Ephraim's sons. They are listed by their families.
The Shuthelahite family came from Shuthelah.
The Bekerite family came from Beker.
The Tahanite family came from Tahan.
36 The sons of Shuthelah were the Eranite family.
They came from Eran.
37 Those were the families of Ephraim. The number of the men was 32,500.

Those were the sons of Joseph. They are listed by their families.

38 Here are the names of Benjamin's sons. They are listed by their families.
The Belaite family came from Bela.
The Ashbelite family came from Ashbel.
The Ahiramite family came from Ahiram.
39 The Shuphamite family came from Shupham.
The Huphamite family came from Hupham.
40 Bela's sons came from Ard and Naaman.
The Ardite family came from Ard.
The Naamite family came from Naaman.
41 Those were the families of Benjamin. The number of the men was 45,600.

42 Here is the name of Dan's son. He is listed by his family.
The Shuhamite family came from Shuham.
That was the family of Dan. 43 All of the men in Dan's family were Shuhamites. The number of the men was 64,400.

44 Here are the names of Asher's sons. They are listed by their families.
The Imnite family came from Imnah.
The Ishvite family came from Ishvi.
The Beriite family came from Beriah.
45 Here are the names of the families that came from Beriah's sons.
The Heberite family came from Heber.
The Malkielite family came from Malkiel.
46 Asher also had a daughter named Serah.
47 Those were the families of Asher. The number of the men was 53,400.

48 Here are the names of Naphtali's sons. They are listed by their families.
The Jahzeelite family came from Jahzeel.
The Gunite family came from Guni.
49 The Jezerite family came from Jezer.
The Shillemite family came from Shillem.
50 Those were the families of Naphtali. The number of the men was 45,400.

51 The total number of the men of Israel was 601,730.

52 The LORD spoke to Moses. He said, 53 "I will give the land to them. The amount of land each family receives will be based on the number of its men. 54 Give a larger share to a larger family. Give

a smaller share to a smaller family. Each family will receive its share based on the number of men who are listed in it.

55"Be sure that you use lots when you give out the land. What each family receives will be based on the number of men listed in its tribe. 56Use lots when you give out each share. Use lots for the larger and smaller families alike."

57Here are the names of the Levites. They are listed by their families.

The Gershonite family came from Gershon.
The Kohathite family came from Kohath.
The Merarite family came from Merari.

58Here are the names of the other Levite families. They are
the Libnite family,
the Hebronite family,
the Mahlite family,
the Mushite family,
the Korahite family.

Amram came from the Kohathite family.

59The name of Amram's wife was Jochebed. She was from the family line of Levi. She was born to the Levites in Egypt. Aaron, Moses and their sister Miriam were born in the family line of Amram and Jochebed.

60Aaron was the father of Nadab and Abihu. He was also the father of Eleazar and Ithamar. 61But Nadab and Abihu made an offering to the LORD by using fire that wasn't allowed. So they died.

62The number of male Levites who were a month old or more was 23,000. They weren't listed along with the other men of Israel. That's because they didn't receive a share among them.

63Those are the men who were counted by Moses and the priest Eleazar. At that time the people of Israel were on the flatlands of Moab. They were by the Jordan River across from Jericho.

64The men of Israel had been counted before in the Sinai Desert by Moses and the priest Aaron. But not one of them was among the men who were counted this time. 65The LORD had told the people of Israel at Kadesh Barnea that they would certainly die in the desert. Not one of them was left alive except Caleb, the son of Jephunneh, and Joshua, the son of Nun.

Zelophehad's Daughters

27 The daughters of Zelophehad belonged to the family groups of Manasseh. Zelophehad was the son of Hepher. Hepher was the son of Gilead. Gilead was the son of Makir. Makir was the son of Manasseh. And Manasseh was the son of Joseph. The names of Zelophehad's daughters were Mahlah, Noah, Hoglah, Milcah and Tirzah. They approached 2the entrance to the Tent of Meeting. There they stood in front of Moses and the priest Eleazar. The leaders and the whole community were there too.

Zelophehad's daughters said, 3"Our father died in the Sinai Desert. But he wasn't one of the men who followed Korah. He wasn't one of those who joined together against the LORD. Our father died because of his own sin. He didn't leave any sons.

4"Why should our father's name disappear from his family just because he didn't have a son? Give us property among our father's relatives."

5So Moses brought their case to the LORD. 6The LORD spoke to him. He said, 7"What Zelophehad's daughters are saying is right. You must certainly give them property. Give them a share among their father's relatives. Turn their father's property over to them.

8"Say to the people of Israel, 'Suppose a man dies who doesn't have a son. Then turn his property over to his daughter. 9Suppose the man doesn't have a daughter. Then give his property to his brothers. 10Suppose the man doesn't have any brothers. Then give his property to his father's brothers. 11Suppose his father doesn't have any brothers. Then give his property to the nearest male relative in his family group. It will belong to him. That is what the law will require of the people of Israel. It is just as the LORD commanded me.'"

Joshua Becomes Israel's New Leader

12Then the LORD spoke to Moses. He said, "Go up this mountain in the Abarim range. See the land I have given the people of Israel. 13After you have seen it, you too will join the members of your family who have already died. You will die, just as your brother Aaron did.

14"The community refused to obey me at the waters of Meribah Kadesh. At that time, you and Aaron did not obey my command. You did not honor me in front of them as the holy God." Meribah Kadesh is in the Desert of Zin.

15Moses spoke to the LORD. He said, 16"LORD, you are the God who creates the spirits of all people. Please appoint a man to lead this community. 17Put him in charge of them. Tell him to take care of them. Then your people won't be like sheep that don't have a shepherd."

18So the LORD said to Moses, "Joshua, the son of Nun, has the ability to be a wise leader. Get him and place your hand on him. 19Have him stand in front of the priest Eleazar and the whole community. Put him in charge while everyone is watching. 20Give him some of your authority. Then the whole community of Israel will obey him.

21"Joshua will stand in front of the priest Eleazar. Eleazar will help him make decisions. Eleazar will get help from me by using the Urim. Joshua and the whole community of Israel must not make any move at all unless I command them to."

22Moses did just as the LORD commanded him. He got Joshua and had him stand in front of the priest Eleazar and the whole community. 23Then Moses placed his hands on Joshua. And he put him in charge of the people. He did just as the LORD had directed through Moses.

Offerings That Israel Must Bring Each Day

28 The LORD spoke to Moses. He said, 2“Here is a command I want you to give the people of Israel. Tell them, ‘Be sure to bring to the LORD the food for the offerings that are made to him with fire. Do it at the appointed time. It will give a smell that is pleasant to him.’

3“Tell them, ‘Here is the offering you must bring to the LORD. It should be made with fire. Bring him two lambs that are a year old. They must not have any flaws. Bring them as a regular burnt offering each day.

4“ ‘Prepare one lamb in the morning. Prepare the other when the sun goes down. 5Bring a grain offering along with them. It must have eight cups of fine flour. Mix it with a quart of oil that is made from pressed olives. 6It is the regular burnt offering. The LORD established it at Mount Sinai. It has a pleasant smell. It is an offering that is made to him with fire. 7Along with that, offer a quart of wine as a drink offering. It must be given along with each lamb. Pour out the drink offering to the LORD at the sacred tent.

8“ ‘Prepare the second lamb when the sun goes down. Sacrifice it along with the same kind of grain offering and drink offering that you prepare in the morning. It is an offering that is made with fire. It gives a smell that is pleasant to the LORD.

Offerings That Israel Must Bring on the Sabbath Day

9“ ‘On the Sabbath day, bring an offering of two lambs. They must be a year old. They must not have any flaws. Offer them along with their drink offering. Offer them along with a grain offering of 16 cups of fine flour. Mix it with olive oil. 10It is the burnt offering for every Sabbath day. It is in addition to the regular burnt offering and its drink offering.

Offerings That Israel Must Bring Every Month

11“ ‘On the first day of every month, bring to the LORD a burnt offering. Bring two young bulls and one ram. Also bring seven male lambs that are a year old. They must not have any flaws.

12“ ‘Bring a grain offering along with each bull. It must have 24 cups of fine flour. Mix it with olive oil. Bring a grain offering along with the ram. It must have 16 cups of fine flour. Mix it with oil. 13Bring a grain offering along with each lamb. It must have eight cups of fine flour. Mix it with oil. It is for a burnt offering. It has a pleasant smell. It is an offering that is made to the LORD with fire.

14“ ‘Bring a drink offering along with each bull. It must have two quarts of wine. Offer two and a half pints along with the ram. And offer one quart along with each lamb.

“ ‘It is the burnt offering for each month. It must be made on the day of each New Moon Feast during the year.

15“ ‘One male goat must be brought to the LORD as a sin offering. It is in addition to the regular burnt offering and its drink offering.

The Passover Feast

16“ ‘The LORD’s Passover Feast must be held on the 14th day of the first month. 17On the 15th day of the month there must be a feast. For seven days eat bread that is made without yeast. 18On the first day come together for a special service. Do not do any regular work.

19“ ‘Bring to the LORD an offering that is made with fire. Bring a burnt offering of two young bulls and one ram. Also bring seven male lambs that are a year old. They must not have any flaws.

20“ ‘Prepare a grain offering along with each bull. The offering must have 24 cups of fine flour. Mix it with olive oil. Offer 16 cups along with the ram. 21Offer eight cups along with each of the seven lambs.

22“ ‘Include a male goat as a sin offering. It will pay for your sin.

23“Prepare everything in addition to the regular morning burnt offering. 24Prepare the food in that way for the offering that is made with fire. Do it every day for seven days. The offering will give a smell that is pleasant to the LORD. You must prepare the offering in addition to the regular burnt offering and its drink offering.

25“ ‘On the seventh day come together for a special service. Do not do any regular work.

The Feast of Weeks

26“ ‘On the day you gather the first share of your crops, bring to the LORD an offering of your first grain. Do it during the Feast of Weeks. Come together for a special service. Do not do any regular work.

27“ ‘Bring a burnt offering of two young bulls and one ram. Also bring seven male lambs that are a year old. The offering will give a smell that is pleasant to the LORD.

28“ ‘Bring a grain offering along with each bull. It must have 24 cups of fine flour. Mix it with olive oil. Offer 16 cups along with the ram. 29Offer eight cups along with each of the seven lambs.

30“ ‘Include a male goat to pay for your sin.

31“ ‘Prepare everything along with the drink offerings. Do it in addition to the regular burnt offering and its grain offering. Be sure the animals do not have any flaws.

The Feast of Trumpets

29 “ ‘On the first day of the seventh month, come together for a special service. Do not do any regular work. Blow the trumpets on that day.

[2]"'Prepare a burnt offering. It will give a smell that is pleasant to the LORD. Prepare one young bull and one ram. Also prepare seven male lambs that are a year old. They must not have any flaws.
[3]"'Prepare a grain offering along with the bull. It must have 24 cups of fine flour. Mix it with olive oil. Offer 16 cups along with the ram. [4]Offer eight cups along with each of the seven lambs.
[5]"'Include a male goat as a sin offering. It will pay for your sin.
[6]"'Each month and each day you must bring burnt offerings. Bring them along with their grain offerings and drink offerings as they are required.

"'The offerings for the Feast of Trumpets are in addition to them. They are offerings that are made to the LORD with fire. They have a pleasant smell.

The Day When Sin Is Paid For

[7]"'On the tenth day of the seventh month, come together for a special service. You must not eat anything on that day. You must not do any work on it.
[8]"'Bring a burnt offering. It will give a smell that is pleasant to the LORD. Bring one young bull and one ram. Also bring seven male lambs that are a year old. They must not have any flaws.
[9]"'Prepare a grain offering along with the bull. It must have 24 cups of fine flour. Mix it with olive oil. Offer 16 cups along with the ram. [10]Offer eight cups along with each of the seven lambs.
[11]"'Include a male goat as a sin offering. It is in addition to the offering that pays for sin. It is in addition to the regular burnt offering along with its grain offering. It is also in addition to their drink offerings.

The Feast of Booths

[12]"'On the 15th day of the seventh month, come together for a special service. Do not do any regular work. Celebrate the Feast of Booths in honor of the LORD for seven days.
[13]"'Bring an offering that is made with fire. It will give a smell that is pleasant to the LORD. Bring a burnt offering of 13 young bulls and two rams. Also bring 14 male lambs that are a year old. They must not have any flaws.
[14]"'Prepare a grain offering along with each of the 13 bulls. It must have 24 cups of fine flour. Mix it with olive oil. Offer 16 cups along with each of the two rams. [15]Offer eight cups along with each of the 14 lambs.
[16]"'Include a male goat as a sin offering. It is in addition to the regular burnt offering. It is also in addition to its grain offering and drink offering.
[17]"'On the second day prepare 12 young bulls and two rams. Also prepare 14 male lambs that are a year old. They must not have any flaws.
[18]"'Prepare their grain offerings and drink offerings. Prepare them along with the bulls, rams and lambs. Prepare them in keeping with the required number.
[19]"'Include a male goat as a sin offering. It is in addition to the regular burnt offering along with its grain offering. It is also in addition to their drink offerings.
[20]"'On the third day prepare 11 bulls and two rams. Also prepare 14 male lambs that are a year old. They must not have any flaws.
[21]"'Prepare their grain offerings and drink offerings. Prepare them along with the bulls, rams and lambs. Prepare them in keeping with the required number.
[22]"'Include a male goat as a sin offering. It is in addition to the regular burnt offering. It is also in addition to its grain offering and drink offering.
[23]"'On the fourth day prepare ten bulls and two rams. Also prepare 14 male lambs that are a year old. They must not have any flaws.
[24]"'Prepare their grain offerings and drink offerings. Prepare them along with the bulls, rams and lambs. Prepare them in keeping with the required number.
[25]"'Include a male goat as a sin offering. It is in addition to the regular burnt offering. It is also in addition to its grain offering and drink offering.
[26]"'On the fifth day prepare nine bulls and two rams. Also prepare 14 male lambs that are a year old. They must not have any flaws.
[27]"'Prepare their grain offerings and drink offerings. Prepare them along with the bulls, rams and lambs. Prepare them in keeping with the required number.
[28]"'Include a male goat as a sin offering. It is in addition to the regular burnt offering. It is also in addition to its grain offering and drink offering.
[29]"'On the sixth day prepare eight bulls and two rams. Also prepare 14 male lambs that are a year old. They must not have any flaws.
[30]"'Prepare their grain offerings and drink offerings. Prepare them along with the bulls, rams and lambs. Prepare them in keeping with the required number.
[31]"'Include a male goat as a sin offering. It is in addition to the regular burnt offering. It is also in addition to its grain offering and drink offering.
[32]"'On the seventh day prepare seven bulls and two rams. Also prepare 14 male lambs that are a year old. They must not have any flaws.
[33]"'Prepare their grain offerings and drink offerings. Prepare them along with the bulls, rams and lambs. Prepare them in keeping with the required number.
[34]"'Include a male goat as a sin offering. It is in addition to the regular burnt offering. It is also in addition to its grain offering and drink offering.
[35]"'On the eighth day come together for a sacred service. Do not do any regular work.
[36]"'Bring an offering that is made with fire. It will give a smell that is pleasant to the LORD. Bring a burnt offering of one bull and one ram. Also bring seven male lambs that are a year old. They must not have any flaws.

37“‘Prepare their grain offerings and drink offerings. Prepare them along with the bull, the ram and the lambs. Prepare them in keeping with the required number.

38“‘Include a male goat as a sin offering. It is in addition to the regular burnt offering. It is also in addition to the grain offering and drink offering.

39“‘Here are the offerings you must prepare for the LORD at your appointed feasts. They are burnt offerings, grain offerings, drink offerings and friendship offerings. They are in addition to the offerings you bring to keep a special promise you make to the LORD. They are also in addition to the offerings you choose to give.’”

40Moses told the people of Israel everything the LORD had commanded him.

Oaths and Special Promises

30 Moses spoke to the heads of the tribes of Israel. He said, “Here is what the LORD commands. 2Suppose a man makes a special promise to the LORD. Or suppose he takes an oath and agrees to do something. Then he must keep his promise. He must do everything he said he would do.

3“Suppose a young woman is still living in her father’s house. She makes a special promise to the LORD. Or she takes an oath and agrees to do something.

4“Suppose her father hears about her promise or oath. And he doesn’t say anything to her about it. Then she must keep her promise. She must do what she agreed to do.

5“But suppose her father doesn’t allow her to keep her promises when he hears about them. Then she doesn’t have to do what she promised or agreed to do. The LORD will set her free. He’ll do it because her father hasn’t allowed her to keep her promises.

6“Suppose she gets married after she makes a special promise. Or she gets married after agreeing to do something without thinking it through. 7Suppose her husband hears about what she did. And he doesn’t say anything to her about it. Then she must keep her promise. She must do what she agreed to do.

8“But suppose her husband doesn’t allow her to keep her promises when he hears about them. Then she doesn’t have to do what she promised. She doesn’t have to do what she agreed to do without thinking it through. The LORD will set her free.

9“Suppose a widow makes a special promise. Or suppose she takes an oath and agrees to do something. Then she must keep her promise. She must do what she agreed to do. The same rules apply to a woman who has been divorced.

10“Suppose a woman who is living with her husband makes a special promise. Or she takes an oath and agrees to do something. 11Suppose her husband hears about what she did. He doesn’t say anything to her about it. And he doesn’t try to stop her from keeping her promises. Then she must keep her promise. She must do what she agreed to do.

12“But suppose her husband doesn’t allow her to keep her promises when he hears about them. Then she doesn’t have to do what she promised. She doesn’t have to do what she agreed to do. Her husband has kept her from doing what she said she would do. The LORD will set her free.

13“Her husband can let her keep any special promise she makes. Or he can refuse to let her keep it.

“Suppose she takes an oath and agrees not to eat anything. Then her husband can let her keep her promise. Or he can refuse to let her keep it.

14“But suppose day after day her husband doesn’t say anything to her about what she did. Then he lets her keep all of her promises. He lets her do everything she agreed to do. That’s because he didn’t say anything to her when he heard about what she had done.

15“But suppose some time after he hears about her promises he doesn’t let her keep them. Then she will be guilty. But he will be held accountable for it.”

16Those are the rules the LORD gave Moses about a man and his wife. And those are the rules the LORD gave about a father and his young daughter who is still living in his house.

The LORD Punishes the People of Midian

31 The LORD spoke to Moses. He said, 2“Pay the people of Midian back for what they did to the Israelites. After that, you will join the members of your family who have already died.”

3So Moses said to the people, “Prepare some of your men for battle. They must go to war against Midian. They will carry out the LORD’s plan to punish Midian. 4Send 1,000 men from each of the tribes of Israel into battle.” 5So Moses prepared 12,000 men for battle. There were 1,000 from each tribe. They came from the families of Israel.

6Moses sent them into battle. He sent 1,000 from each tribe. The priest Phinehas went along with them. Phinehas was the son of Eleazar. Phinehas took some articles from the sacred tent with him. He also took the trumpets. The trumpet blasts would tell the people what to do and when to do it.

7They fought against Midian, just as the LORD had commanded Moses. They killed every man. 8Evi, Rekem, Zur, Hur and Reba were among the men they killed. Those men were the five kings of Midian. The people of Israel also killed Balaam, the son of Beor, with a sword.

9They captured the women and children of Midian. They took for themselves all of the herds, flocks and goods.

10They burned up all of the towns where the people of Midian had settled. They also burned up all of their camps.

11They carried off everything they had taken. That included the people and the animals. 12They brought back to Israel’s camp the prisoners and everything else they had taken. They took them to Moses and to the priest Eleazar. They brought them to the whole community. Israel was camped on the flatlands of Moab. They were by the Jordan River across from Jericho.

[13]Moses and the priest Eleazar went to meet them outside the camp. So did all of the leaders of the community. [14]Moses was angry with the officers of the army who had returned from the battle. Some of them were the commanders of thousands of men. Others were the commanders of hundreds.

[15]"Have you let all of the women remain alive?" Moses asked them. [16]"The women followed Balaam's advice. They caused the people of Israel to turn away from the LORD. The people worshiped the god Baal that was worshiped at Peor. So a plague struck them. [17]Kill all of the boys. And kill every woman who has made love to a man. [18]But save for yourselves every woman who has never made love to a man.

[19]"All of you who have killed anyone must stay outside the camp for seven days. And all of you who have touched anyone who was killed must do the same thing. On the third and seventh days you must make yourselves pure. You must also make your prisoners pure. [20]Make all of your clothes pure and clean. Everything that is made out of leather, goat hair or wood must be made pure."

[21]Then the priest Eleazar spoke to the soldiers who had gone into battle. He said, "Here is what the law the LORD gave Moses requires. [22]All of your gold, silver, bronze, iron, tin and lead [23]must be put through fire. So must everything else that doesn't burn up. Then those things will be 'clean.' But they must also be made pure with the special water. In fact, everything that won't burn up must be put through that water. [24]On the seventh day wash your clothes. And you will be 'clean.' Then you can come into the camp."

The People Divide Up What They Had Taken

[25]The LORD spoke to Moses. He said, [26]"Here is what you and the priest Eleazar and the family heads of the community must do. You must count all of the people and animals you took. [27]Divide up some of what you took with the soldiers who fought in the battle. Divide up the rest with the others in the community.

[28]"Set apart a gift for me. Take something from the soldiers who fought in the battle. Set apart one out of every 500 people, cattle, donkeys, sheep and goats. [29]Take my gift from the soldiers' half. Give it to the priest Eleazar. It is my share.

[30]"Also take something from the half that belongs to the people of Israel. Choose one out of every 50 people, cattle, donkeys, sheep, goats or other animals. Give them to the Levites. They are accountable for taking care of my holy tent."

[31]So Moses and the priest Eleazar did just as the LORD had commanded Moses.

[32]What the soldiers took included 675,000 sheep. [33]There were also 72,000 cattle [34]and 61,000 donkeys. [35]And there were 32,000 women who had never made love to a man.

[36]Here is the half that belonged to those who had fought in the battle.

There were 337,500 sheep. [37]From among them, the LORD's gift was 675.
[38]There were 36,000 cattle. From among them, the LORD's gift was 72.
[39]There were 30,500 donkeys. From among them, the LORD's gift was 61.
[40]There were 16,000 women. From among them, the LORD's gift was 32.

[41]Moses gave the gift to the priest Eleazar. It was the LORD's share. Moses did just as the LORD had commanded him.

[42]The other half belonged to the people of Israel. Moses set it apart from what belonged to the fighting men. [43]The community's half was 337,500 sheep, [44]36,000 cattle, [45]30,500 donkeys [46]and 16,000 women. [47]Moses chose one out of every 50 people and animals. He gave them to the Levites. They were accountable for taking care of the LORD's holy tent. Moses did just as the LORD had commanded him.

[48]Then the army officers went to Moses. Some of them were the commanders of thousands of men. Others were the commanders of hundreds. [49]All of them said to Moses, "We have counted the soldiers under our command. Not a single one is missing.

[50]"So we've brought an offering to the LORD. We've brought the gold articles each of us took in the battle. We've also brought armbands, bracelets, rings, earrings and necklaces. We've brought them to pay for our sin in the sight of the LORD."

[51]Moses and the priest Eleazar accepted the beautiful gold articles from the army officers. [52]The gold that was received from the commanders of thousands and commanders of hundreds weighed 420 pounds. Moses and Eleazar offered all of it as a gift to the LORD. [53]Each soldier had taken things from the battle for himself. [54]Moses and the priest Eleazar accepted the gold from all of the commanders. They brought it into the Tent of Meeting. It reminded the LORD of the people of Israel.

The Tribes on the East Side of the Jordan River

32 The tribes of Reuben and Gad had very large herds and flocks. They looked at the lands of Jazer and Gilead. They saw that those lands were just right for livestock.

[2]So they came to Moses and the priest Eleazar. They also came to the leaders of the community. They said, [3]"We have seen the cities of Ataroth, Dibon, Jazer, Nimrah and Heshbon. We've seen Elealeh, Sebam, Nebo and Beon. [4]All of them are

in the land the LORD has brought under Israel's
control. This land is just right for livestock. And
we have livestock.
5"We hope you are pleased with us," they continued. "If you are, please give us this land. Then
it will belong to us. But don't make us go across
the Jordan River."
6Moses spoke to the people of Gad and Reuben.
He said, "Should the rest of us go to war while you
stay here? 7The LORD has given the land of Canaan
to the people of Israel. So why would you want to
keep them from going over into it?
8"That's what your fathers did. I sent them from
Kadesh Barnea to check out the land. 9They went
up to the Valley of Eshcol and looked at the land.
Then they talked the people of Israel out of entering the land the LORD had given them.
10"The LORD's anger was stirred up that day. So
he took an oath and made a promise. He said,
11'Not one of the men who is 20 years old or more
who came up out of Egypt will see the land. They
have not followed me with their whole heart. I
took an oath and promised to give the land to
Abraham, Isaac and Jacob.
12" 'But not one of these men will see it except
Caleb and Joshua. Caleb is the son of Jephunneh,
the Kenizzite. And Joshua is the son of Nun. They
will see the land. They followed me with their
whole heart.'
13"The LORD's anger burned against Israel. He
made them wander around in the desert for 40
years. They wandered until all of the people who
had done evil in his sight had died.
14"Now here you are, you bunch of sinners! You
have taken the place of your fathers. And you are
making the LORD even more angry with Israel.
15What if you turn away from following him? Then
he'll leave all of these people in the desert again.
And it will be your fault when they are destroyed."
16Then they came up to Moses. They said, "We
would like to build pens here for our livestock. We
would also like to build cities for our women and
children.
17"But we're ready to prepare ourselves for battle. We're even ready to go ahead of the people of
Israel. We'll go with them until we've brought
them to their place. While we're gone, our women
and children will live in cities that have high walls
around them. That will keep them safe from the
people who are living in this land.
18"We won't return to our homes until all of the
people of Israel have received their share of the
land.
19"We won't receive any share with them on the
west side of the Jordan River. We've already
received our share here on the east side."
20Then Moses said to them, "Do what you have
promised to do. Prepare yourselves to fight for the
LORD. 21Prepare yourselves and go across the Jordan River. Fight for the LORD until he has driven
out his enemies in front of him.
22"When the land is under the LORD's control,
you can come back here. Your duty to the LORD
and Israel will be over. Then the LORD will give
you this land as your own.
23"But what if you fail to do your duty? Then
you will be sinning against the LORD. And you can
be sure that your sin will be discovered. It will be
brought out into the open.
24"So build up cities for your women and children. Make sheep pens for your flocks. But do
what you have promised to do."
25The people of Gad and Reuben spoke to Moses. They said, "We will do just as you command.
26Our children and wives will remain here in the
cities of Gilead. So will our flocks and herds. 27But
we will prepare ourselves for battle. We'll go
across the Jordan River and fight for the LORD. We
will do just as you have said."
28Then Moses gave orders about them to the
priest Eleazar. He gave the same orders to Joshua,
the son of Nun. He also spoke to the family heads
of the tribes of Israel.
29He said, "The men of Gad and Reuben must
prepare themselves for battle. They must go across
the Jordan River with you. They must help you
fight for the LORD. They must stay with you until
the land has been brought under your control. If
they do, give them the land of Gilead as their own.
30"But what if they don't get ready for battle?
What if they don't go across the Jordan with you?
Then they must accept a share with you in Canaan."
31The people of Gad and Reuben gave their
answer. They said, "We will do what the LORD has
said. 32We'll get ready for battle. We'll go across
the Jordan into Canaan. We'll fight for the LORD
there. But the property we receive will be on this
side of the Jordan River."
33Then Moses gave their land to them. He gave
it to the tribes of Gad and Reuben and half of the
tribe of Manasseh. Manasseh was Joseph's son.
One part of that land had belonged to the kingdom
of Sihon, the king of the Amorites. The other part
had belonged to the kingdom of Og, the king of
Bashan. Moses gave that whole land to those two
and a half tribes. It included its cities and the territory around them.
34The people of Gad built up the cities of Dibon,
Ataroth and Aroer. 35They built up Atroth Sho-
phan, Jazer, Jogbehah, 36Beth Nimrah and Beth
Haran. They built a high wall around each of those
cities. They also built sheep pens for their flocks.
37The people of Reuben built up Heshbon, Elealeh and Kiriathaim. 38They also built up Nebo,
Baal Meon and Sibmah. They gave new names to
the cities they had built up.
39The people of Makir, the son of Manasseh,
went to the land of Gilead. They captured it. They
drove out the Amorites who were living there. 40So
Moses gave Gilead to the people of Makir, the son
of Manasseh. And they settled there. 41Jair was a
man in the family line of Manasseh. Jair captured

Gilead's settlements. He called them Havvoth Jair. 42Nobah captured Kenath and the settlements that were around it. He named it after himself.

The Places Where Israel Stopped During Their Journey

33 Here are the places where the people of Israel stopped during their journey. When they came out of Egypt, they marched in companies like an army. Moses and Aaron led them. 2The LORD commanded Moses to record their journey. Here are the places where they stopped.

3The people of Israel started out from Rameses. It was the 15th day of the first month. It was the day after the Passover Feast. They marched out boldly in plain sight of all of the Egyptians. 4The Egyptians were burying all of their oldest sons. The LORD had struck them down. He had done it when he punished their gods.

5The people of Israel left Rameses and camped at Succoth.

6They left Succoth and camped at Etham. Etham was on the edge of the desert.

7They left Etham and turned back to Pi Hahiroth. It was east of Baal Zephon. They camped near Migdol.

8They left Pi Hahiroth. Then they passed through the Red Sea into the desert. They traveled for three days in the Desert of Etham. Then they camped at Marah.

9They left Marah and went to Elim. Twelve springs and 70 palm trees were there. So they camped at Elim.

10They left Elim and camped by the Red Sea.

11They left the Red Sea and camped in the Desert of Sin.

12They left the Desert of Sin and camped at Dophkah.

13They left Dophkah and camped at Alush.

14They left Alush and camped at Rephidim. But there was no water there for the people to drink.

15They left Rephidim and camped in the Desert of Sinai.

16They left the Desert of Sinai and camped at Kibroth Hattaavah.

17They left Kibroth Hattaavah and camped at Hazeroth.

18They left Hazeroth and camped at Rithmah.

19They left Rithmah and camped at Rimmon Perez.

20They left Rimmon Perez and camped at Libnah.

21They left Libnah and camped at Rissah.

22They left Rissah and camped at Kehelathah.

23They left Kehelathah and camped at Mount Shepher.

24They left Mount Shepher and camped at Haradah.

25They left Haradah and camped at Makheloth.

26They left Makheloth and camped at Tahath.

27They left Tahath and camped at Terah.

28They left Terah and camped at Mithcah.

29They left Mithcah and camped at Hashmonah.

30They left Hashmonah and camped at Moseroth.

31They left Moseroth and camped at Bene Jaakan.

32They left Bene Jaakan and camped at Hor Haggidgad.

33They left Hor Haggidgad and camped at Jotbathah.

34They left Jotbathah and camped at Abronah.

35They left Abronah and camped at Ezion Geber.

36They left Ezion Geber and camped at Kadesh. Kadesh was in the Desert of Zin.

37They left Kadesh and camped at Mount Hor. It was on the border of Edom.

38The priest Aaron went up Mount Hor when the LORD commanded him to. That's where he died. It happened on the first day of the fifth month. It was the 40th year after the people of Israel came out of Egypt. 39Aaron was 123 years old when he died on Mount Hor.

40The Canaanite king of Arad lived in the Negev Desert in Canaan. He heard that the people of Israel were coming.

41They left Mount Hor and camped at Zalmonah.

42They left Zalmonah and camped at Punon.

43They left Punon and camped at Oboth.

44They left Oboth and camped at Iye Abarim. It was on the border of Moab.

45They left Iyim and camped at Dibon Gad.

46They left Dibon Gad and camped at Almon Diblathaim.

47They left Almon Diblathaim and camped in the mountain range of Abarim near Nebo.

48They left the mountain range of Abarim and camped on the flatlands of Moab. They were by the Jordan River across from Jericho. 49They camped there along the Jordan River from Beth Jeshimoth to Abel Shittim.

50On the flatlands of Moab the LORD spoke to Moses. He spoke to him by the Jordan River across from Jericho. The LORD said, 51"Speak to the people of Israel. Tell them, 'Go across the Jordan River into Canaan. 52Drive out all those who are living in the land. The statues of their gods are made out of stone and metal. Destroy all of those statues. And destroy all of the high places where they are worshiped.

53 " 'Take the land as your own. Settle down in it. I have given it to you. 54 Use lots when you give out the land. Do it based on the number of men who are in each tribe and family. Give a larger share to a larger group. And give a smaller group a smaller share. The share they receive by using lots will belong to them. Give out the shares based on the number of men in Israel's tribes.

55 " 'But suppose you do not drive out the people who are living in the land. Then those you allow to remain there will become like needles in your eyes. They will become like thorns in your sides. They will give you trouble in the land where you will live. 56 Then I will do to you what I plan to do to them.' "

Israel Arrives at the Borders of Canaan

34 The LORD spoke to Moses. He said, 2 "Give the people of Israel a command. Tell them, 'You are going to enter Canaan. The land will be given to you as your own. Here are the borders it will have.

3 " 'Your southern border will include some of the Desert of Zin. It will be along the border of Edom. On the east, your southern border will start from the end of the Dead Sea. 4 It will cross south of Scorpion Pass. It will continue on to Zin. From there it will go south of Kadesh Barnea. Then it will go to Hazar Addar and over to Azmon. 5 There it will turn and join the Wadi of Egypt. It will come to an end at the Mediterranean Sea.

6 " 'Your western border will be the coast of the Mediterranean Sea. That will be your border on the west.

7 " 'For your northern border, run a line from the Mediterranean Sea to Mount Hor. 8 Continue it from Mount Hor to Lebo Hamath. Then the border will go to Zedad. 9 It will continue to Ziphron. It will come to an end at Hazar Enan. That will be your border on the north.

10 " 'For your eastern border, run a line from Hazar Enan to Shepham. 11 The border will go down from Shepham to Riblah. Riblah is on the east side of Ain. From there the border will continue along the slopes east of the Sea of Galilee. 12 Then the border will go down along the Jordan River. It will come to an end at the Dead Sea.

" 'That will be your land. And those will be its borders on every side.' "

13 Moses gave the people of Israel a command. He said, "Use lots when you give out the land. Each tribe will have its own share. The LORD has ordered it to be given to the nine and a half tribes. 14 "The families of the tribes of Reuben and Gad have already received their shares. The families of half of the tribe of Manasseh have also received their share. 15 Those two and a half tribes have received their shares east of the Jordan River. It flows near Jericho. Their land is toward the sunrise."

16 The LORD spoke to Moses. He said, 17 "Here are the names of the men who will give out the shares of the land to your people. They are the priest Eleazar and Joshua, the son of Nun. 18 Also appoint one leader from each tribe to help give out the land. 19 Here are their names.

"Caleb, the son of Jephunneh,
 is from the tribe of Judah.
20 Shemuel, the son of Ammihud,
 is from the tribe of Simeon.
21 Elidad, the son of Kislon,
 is from the tribe of Benjamin.
22 Bukki, the son of Jogli,
 is the leader from the tribe of Dan.
23 Hanniel, the son of Ephod,
 is the leader from the tribe of Manasseh.
 Manasseh was the son of Joseph.
24 Kemuel, the son of Shiphtan,
 is the leader from the tribe of Ephraim.
 Ephraim was the son of Joseph.
25 Elizaphan, the son of Parnach,
 is the leader from the tribe of Zebulun.
26 Paltiel, the son of Azzan,
 is the leader from the tribe of Issachar.
27 Ahihud, the son of Shelomi,
 is the leader from the tribe of Asher.
28 Pedahel, the son of Ammihud,
 is the leader from the tribe of Naphtali."

29 Those are the men the LORD commanded to give out the shares of the land. They were commanded to give them to Israel in the land of Canaan.

The Levites Receive Their Towns

35 On the flatlands of Moab, the LORD spoke to Moses. It was by the Jordan River across from Jericho. The LORD said, 2 "Command the people of Israel to give the Levites towns to live in. The towns must come from the shares of land the people will have as their own. Also give the Levites the grasslands that are around the towns. 3 Then the Levites will have towns to live in. They will also have grasslands that are for their cattle, flocks and all of their other livestock.

4 "The grasslands that are around each town you give them will go out to 1,500 feet from the town wall. 5 Outside each town, the east side will measure 3,000 feet. The south side will measure 3,000 feet. The west side will measure 3,000 feet. And the north side will measure 3,000 feet. The town must be in the center. The Levites will have the area around it as grasslands.

Cities to Go to for Safety

6 "Six of the towns you give the Levites will be cities to go to for safety. A person who has killed someone can run to one of them. Also give the Levites 42 other towns. 7 You must give the Levites a

total of 48 towns. Also give them the grasslands
that are around the towns.
8"The towns you give the Levites must come
from the land the people of Israel have as their
own. So the number you give from each tribe will
depend on the size of that tribe's share. Take many
towns from a tribe that has many. But take only a
few towns from a tribe that has only a few."
9Then the LORD spoke to Moses. He said,
10"Speak to the people of Israel. Tell them, 'You
will soon go across the Jordan River. You will
enter Canaan. 11When you do, choose the cities to
go to for safety. People who have killed someone
by accident can run to one of those cities. 12They
will be places of safety for them. People will be
safe there from those who want to kill them. Then
those who are charged with murder will not die
before their case has been brought to the community court.
13" 'Six towns will be the cities you can go to for
safety. 14Three will be east of the Jordan River. The
other three will be in Canaan.
15" 'Those six towns will be places where the
people of Israel can go for safety. Outsiders and
any other people living in Israel can also go to
them for safety. So anyone who has killed another
person by accident can run there.
16" 'Suppose a person uses an iron object to hit
and kill someone. Then he is a murderer. He must
be put to death. 17Or suppose a person is holding a
stone that could kill. And he uses it to hit and kill
someone. Then he is a murderer. He must be put to
death. 18Or suppose a person is holding a wooden
object that could kill. And he uses it to hit and kill
someone. Then he is a murderer. He must be put to
death.
19" 'The dead person's nearest male relative
should kill the murderer. When he meets him, he
should kill him.
20" 'What if a person makes evil plans against
someone else? And what if that person pushes him
so that he dies? Or what if that person throws
something at him so that he dies? 21Or what if that
person hits the other person with a fist so that the
other dies? Then the person who does any of those
things must be put to death. He is a murderer.
" 'The dead person's nearest male relative
should kill the murderer. When he meets him, he
should kill him.
22" 'But what if a person suddenly pushes someone else without being angry? Or what if that person throws something at him without meaning to?
23Or what if that person does not see him and drops
a stone on him that kills him? He was not the dead
person's enemy. He did not mean to harm him.
24" 'Then the court must decide between the person who did the act and the nearest male relative
of the one who was killed. Here are the rules the
court must follow.
25" 'The court must provide a safe place for the
person who is charged with murder. It must keep
him safe from those who want to kill him. The
court must send him back to the city he ran to for
safety. He must stay there until the high priest dies.
The priest is the one who has been anointed with
the holy oil.
26" 'But suppose the one who has been charged
with murder goes outside that city. 27And suppose
the dead person's nearest male relative finds that
one outside the city. Then the relative can kill the
one who has been charged. The relative will not be
guilty of murder.
28" 'The one who has been charged must stay in
that city until the high priest dies. Only then can
the one who has been charged return home.
29" 'That is what the law requires of you for all
time to come. It will apply to you no matter where
you live.
30" 'Suppose a person kills someone. That person must be put to death as a murderer. But do it
only when there are witnesses who can tell what
happened. Do not put anyone to death if only one
witness tells what happened.
31" 'Do not accept payment for a murderer's life.
He should die. He must certainly be put to death.
32" 'Do not accept payment for anyone who has
run to a city for safety. Do not let him buy his freedom to return home. He must not go back and live
on his own land before the high priest dies.
33" 'Do not pollute the land where you are. Murder pollutes the land. Only one thing can pay to
remove the pollution in the land where murder has
been committed. The blood of the one who spilled
another's blood must be spilled. 34So do not make
the land where you live "unclean." I live there too.
I live among the people of Israel. I am the LORD.' "

The Property Zelophehad's Daughters Will Receive

36 The heads of the families of Gilead came
to Moses. Gilead was the son of Makir.
The family heads were from the tribe of Manasseh. So they were in the family line of Joseph.
They spoke to Moses in front of the leaders of the
families of Israel.
2They said, "The LORD commanded you to give
shares of the land to the people of Israel. He told
you to use lots when you do it. At that time the
LORD ordered you to give our brother Zelophehad's share to his daughters.
3"Suppose they get married to men who are
from other tribes in Israel. Then their share will be
taken away from our family's land. It will be
added to the land of the tribe they marry into. So
a part of the share that was given to us will be
taken away. 4The Year of Jubilee for the people of
Israel will come. Then their share will be added to
the land of the tribe they marry into. Their land
will be taken away from the share that was given
to our tribe."
5Then the LORD gave a command to Moses. He
told Moses to give an order to the people of Israel.

Moses said, "What the tribe in the family line of Joseph is saying is right.

6"Here is what the LORD commands for Zelophehad's daughters. They can get married to anyone they want to. But they have to get married to someone in their own family's tribe.

7"Property in Israel must not pass from one tribe to another. Everyone in Israel must keep his family's share of his tribe's land.

8"Suppose a daughter in any tribe of Israel receives land from her parents. Then she must get married to someone in her father's family and tribe. In that way, every family's share will remain in its family line in Israel.

9"Property can't pass from one tribe to another. Each tribe of Israel must keep the land it receives."

10So Zelophehad's daughters did just as the LORD commanded Moses. 11The names of the daughters were Mahlah, Tirzah, Hoglah, Milcah and Noah. All of them got married to their cousins on their father's side. 12They married men who were in the family line of Manasseh, the son of Joseph. So the land they received remained in their father's family and tribe.

13Those are the commands and rules the LORD gave through Moses. He gave them to the people of Israel on the flatlands of Moab. They were by the Jordan River across from Jericho.

Deuteronomy

The LORD Commands Israel to Leave Mount Horeb

1 These are the words Moses spoke to all of the people of Israel. At that time, they were in the desert east of the Jordan River. It's in the Arabah Valley across from Suph. They were between Paran and Tophel, Laban, Hazeroth and Dizahab. [2]It takes 11 days to go from Mount Horeb to Kadesh Barnea if you travel on the Mount Seir road.

[3]It was now the 40th year since the people of Israel had left Egypt. On the first day of the 11th month, Moses spoke to them. He told them everything the LORD had commanded him to tell them. [4]They had already won the battle over Sihon. Sihon was the king of the Amorites. He had ruled in Heshbon. Israel had also won the battle over Og at Edrei. Og was the king of Bashan. He had ruled in Ashtaroth.

[5]The people were east of the Jordan River in the territory of Moab. There Moses began to explain the law. Here is what he said.

[6]The LORD our God spoke to us at Mount Horeb. He said, "You have stayed long enough at this mountain. [7]Take your tents down. Go into the hill country of the Amorites. Go to all of the people who are their neighbors. Go to the people who live in the Arabah Valley. Travel to the mountains and the western hills. Go to the people in the Negev Desert and along the coast. Travel to the land of Canaan and to Lebanon. Go as far as the great Euphrates River.

[8]"I have given you all of that land. Go in and take it as your own. I took an oath. I promised I would give the land to your fathers. I promised it to Abraham, Isaac and Jacob. I also said I would give it to their children after them."

Some Officials Help Moses

[9]At that time I spoke to you. I said, "You are too heavy a load for me to carry alone. [10]The LORD your God has increased your numbers. Today you are as many as the stars in the sky. [11]The LORD is the God of your people. May he increase your numbers a thousand times. May he bless you, just as he promised he would. [12]But I can't handle your problems and troubles all by myself. I can't settle your arguments.

[13]"So choose some wise men from each of your tribes. They must understand how to give good advice. The people must have respect for them. I will appoint those men to have authority over you."

[14]You answered me, "Your suggestion is good."

[15]So I took the leading men of your tribes who were wise and respected. I appointed them to have authority over you. I made them commanders of thousands, hundreds, fifties and tens. I appointed them to be officials over the tribes.

[16]Here is what I commanded your judges at that time. I said, "Listen to your people's cases when they argue with one another. Judge them fairly. It doesn't matter whether the case is between fellow Israelites or between an Israelite and an outsider. [17]When you judge them, treat everyone the same. Listen to those who are important and those who are not. Don't be afraid of any man. God is the highest judge. Bring me any case that is too hard for you. I'll listen to it." [18]At that time I told you everything you should do.

Twelve Men Check Out the Land of Canaan

[19]The LORD our God commanded us to start out from Mount Horeb. So we did. We went toward the hill country of the Amorites. We traveled all through the huge and terrible desert you saw. Finally, we reached Kadesh Barnea.

[20]Then I said to you, "You have reached the hill country of the Amorites. The LORD our God is giving it to us. [21]The LORD your God has given you the land. Go up and take it. Do what the LORD says. He's the God of your people. Don't be afraid. Don't lose hope."

[22]Then all of you came to me. You said, "Let's send some men ahead of us. They can check out the land for us and bring back a report. They can suggest to us which way to go. They can tell us about the towns we'll come to."

[23]That seemed like a good idea to me. So I chose 12 of you. I picked one man from each tribe. [24]They left and went up into the hill country. There they came to the Valley of Eshcol. They checked it out. [25]They got some of the fruit of that land. They brought it down to us and gave us their report. They said, "The LORD our God is giving us a good land."

Israel Refuses to Obey the LORD

[26]But you wouldn't go up. You refused to obey the command of the LORD your God. [27]You spoke against him in your tents. You said, "The LORD hates us. That's why he brought us out of Egypt to hand us over to the Amorites. He wanted to destroy us. [28]Where can we go? The men who checked out the land have made us lose hope. They say, 'The people are stronger and taller than we are. The cities are large. They have walls that reach up to the sky. We even saw the Anakites there.'"

[29]Then I said to you, "Don't be terrified. Don't be afraid of them. [30]The LORD your God will go ahead of you. He will fight for you. With your own eyes you saw how he fought for you in Egypt.

31"You also saw how the LORD your God
brought you through the desert. He carried you
everywhere you went, just as a father carries his
son. And now you have arrived here."
32In spite of that, you didn't trust in the LORD
your God. 33He went ahead of you on your journey. He was in the fire at night and in the cloud
during the day. He found places for you to camp.
He showed you the way you should go.
34The LORD heard what you said. So he became
angry. He took an oath and made a promise. He
said, 35"I promised to give this good land to your
people long ago. But not one of you evil men who
are alive today will see it.
36"Only Caleb will see the land. He is the son
of Jephunneh. I will give him and his children after
him the land he walked on. He followed me with
his whole heart."
37Because of you, the LORD became angry with
me also. He said, "You will not enter the land
either. 38But Joshua, the son of Nun, is your helper.
Joshua will enter the land. Help him to be brave.
Give him hope. He will lead Israel to take the land
as their own.
39"You said your little ones would be taken prisoner. But they will enter the land. They do not
know right from wrong yet. But I will give them
the land. They will take it as their own. 40As for
you, turn around. Start out toward the desert. Go
along the road that leads to the Red Sea."
41Then you replied, "We have sinned against the
LORD. We will go up and fight. We'll do just as the
LORD our God has commanded us." So all of you
got your swords and put them on. You thought it
would be easy to go up into the hill country.
42But the LORD spoke to me. He said, "Tell
them, 'Do not go up and fight. I will not be with
you. Your enemies will win the battle over you.'"
43So I told you what the LORD said. But you
wouldn't listen. You refused to obey his command.
You were so filled with pride that you marched up
into the hill country. 44The Amorites who lived in
those hills came out and attacked you. Like large
numbers of bees they chased you. They beat you
down from Seir all the way to Hormah.
45You came back and sobbed in front of the LORD.
But he didn't pay any attention to your sobs. He
wouldn't listen to you. 46So you stayed in Kadesh
for many years. You spent a long time in that area.

Israel Wanders in the Desert

2 We turned back and started out toward the
desert. We went along the road that leads to
the Red Sea. That's how the LORD had directed
me. For a long time we made our way around the
hill country of Seir.
2Then the LORD spoke to me. He said, 3"You
have made your way around this hill country long
enough. So now turn north.
4"Here are the orders I want you to give the people. Tell them, 'You are about to pass through the
territory of your relatives. They are from the family line of Esau. They live in Seir. They will be
afraid of you. But be very careful. 5Do not make
them angry. If you do, they will go to war against
you. I will not give you any of their land. You will
not have even enough to put your foot on. I have
given Esau the hill country of Seir as his own. 6Pay
them with silver for the food you eat and the water
you drink.'"
7The LORD your God has blessed you in everything your hands have done. He watched over you
when you traveled through that huge desert. For
these 40 years the LORD your God has been with
you. So you have had everything you need.
8We went on past our relatives. They are from
the family line of Esau. They live in Seir. We
turned away from the Arabah Valley road. It comes
up from Elath and Ezion Geber. We traveled along
the desert road of Moab.
9Then the LORD said to me, "Do not attack the
Moabites. Do not even make them angry. If you
do, they will go to war against you. I will not give
you any part of their land. I have given Moab to
the people in the family line of Lot. I have given
it to them as their own."
10The Emites used to live there. They were
strong people. There were large numbers of them.
They were as tall as the Anakites. 11Like the Anakites, they too were thought of as Rephaites. But
the Moabites called them Emites.
12The Horites used to live in Seir. But the people of Esau drove them out. They destroyed the
Horites to make room for themselves. Then they
settled in their territory. They did just as Israel has
done in the land the LORD gave them as their own.
13The LORD said, "Now get up. Go across the
Zered Valley." So we went across it.
14Between the time we left Kadesh Barnea and
the time we went across the Zered Valley, 38 years
passed. By then, all of the fighting men who had
been in our camp from the beginning had died.
The LORD had warned them with an oath that it
would happen. 15He used his power against them
until he had gotten rid of all of them. Not one was
left in the camp.
16Finally, the last of the fighting men among the
people died.
17Then the LORD spoke to me. He said, 18"Today
you must pass near the border of Moab. Moab is
also called Ar.
19"When you come to the Ammonites, do not
attack them. Do not make them angry. If you do,
they will go to war against you. I will not give you
any of their land as your own. I have given it to the
people in the family line of Lot. I have given it to
them as their own."
20That land was also thought of as a land of the
Rephaites. They used to live there. But the Ammonites called them Zamzummites. 21The Rephaites were strong people. There were large numbers
of them. They were as tall as the Anakites. The

LORD destroyed the Rephaites to make room for the
Ammonites. So the Ammonites drove them out.
Then they settled in the territory of the Rephaites.
22The LORD had done the same thing for the
people of Esau. They lived in Seir. He destroyed
the Horites to make room for them. They drove the
Horites out. So the people of Esau have lived in
Seir in the territory of the Horites to this very day.
23The Avvites lived in villages as far away as
Gaza. But people came from Crete. They destroyed the Avvites. Then they settled in the territory of the Avvites.

Israel Wins the Battle Over Sihon

24The LORD said, "Start out and go across the
valley of the Arnon River. I have handed Sihon
over to you. He is the Amorite king of Heshbon. I
have also given you his country. Begin to take it
as your own. Go to war against him.
25"This very day I will bring fear and terror on
all of the nations because of you. They will hear
about you. They will tremble with fear. Pain and
suffering will take hold of them because of you."
26I sent messengers from the Desert of Kedemoth. I told them to go to Sihon, the king of Heshbon. They offered him peace. They said, 27"Let us
pass through your country. We'll stay on the main
road. We won't turn off it to one side or the other.
28We'll pay you the right amount of silver for food
to eat and water to drink. Just let us walk through
your country. 29The people of Esau, who live in
Seir, allowed us to do that. The people of Moab,
who live in Ar, also allowed us to do it. So let us
walk through until we go across the Jordan River.
Then we'll be able to go into the land the LORD our
God is giving us."
30But Sihon, the king of Heshbon, refused to let
us walk through. The LORD your God had made
his heart and spirit stubborn. The LORD wanted to
hand him over to you. And that's exactly what he
has done.
31The LORD said to me, "I have begun to hand
Sihon and his country over to you. So begin the
battle to take his land as your own."
32Sihon and his whole army came out to fight
against us at Jahaz. 33But the LORD our God
handed him over to us. We struck him down
together with his sons and his whole army. 34At
that time we took all of his towns. We completely
destroyed them. We killed all of the men, women
and children. We didn't leave any of them alive.
35But we took for ourselves the livestock and
everything else from the towns we had captured.
36Not a single town was too strong for us. That
includes all of the towns from Aroer on the rim of
the Arnon River valley all the way to Gilead. It
also includes the town in the valley. The LORD our
God gave us all of them.
37And you obeyed the LORD's command. You
didn't go near any part of the land of the Ammonites. That includes the land along the Jabbok River.
It also includes the land around the towns that are
in the hills.

Israel Wins the Battle Over Og

3 Next, we turned and went up along the road
toward Bashan. Og, the king of Bashan,
marched out with his whole army. They fought
against us at Edrei.
2The LORD said to me, "Do not be afraid of Og.
I have handed him over to you. I have also handed
over his whole army and his land. Do to him what
you did to Sihon. Sihon was the Amorite king who
ruled in Heshbon."
3So the LORD our God also handed Og, the king
of Bashan, and his whole army over to us. We
struck them down. We didn't leave any of them
alive. 4At that time we took all of his cities. There
were 60 of them. We took the whole area of Argob. That was Og's kingdom in Bashan.
5All of those cities had high walls around them.
The city gates were made secure with heavy metal
bars. There were also large numbers of villages
that didn't have walls. 6We completely destroyed
them. We did to them just as we had done to Sihon, the king of Heshbon. We destroyed all of their
cities. We destroyed the men, women and children.
7But we kept for ourselves the livestock and everything else we took from their cities.
8So at that time we took the territory east of the
Jordan River. We captured it from those two Amorite kings. The territory goes all the way from the
Arnon River valley to Mount Hermon. 9Hermon is
called Sirion by the people of Sidon. The Amorites
call it Senir.
10We captured all of the towns on the high flatlands. We took the whole land of Gilead. And we
captured the whole land of Bashan as far away as
Salecah and Edrei. Those were towns that
belonged to Og's kingdom in Bashan.
11Og, the king of Bashan, was the only Rephaite
left. His bed was made out of iron. It was more
than 13 feet long and six feet wide. It is still in the
Ammonite city of Rabbah.

Moses Divides Up the Land

12I divided up the land we took over at that time.
I gave the tribes of Reuben and Gad the territory
north of Aroer by the Arnon River valley. It
includes half of the hill country of Gilead together
with its towns.
13I gave the rest of Gilead to half of the tribe of
Manasseh. I also gave them the whole land of Bashan, the kingdom of Og. The whole area of Argob in Bashan used to be known as a land of the
Rephaites.
14Jair took the whole area of Argob. He was
from the family line of Manasseh. Argob goes all
the way to the border of the people of Geshur and
Maacah. It was named after Jair. So Bashan is
called Havvoth Jair to this very day. 15I gave Gilead to Makir.

[16]But I gave to the tribes of Reuben and Gad the territory that reaches from Gilead down to the Arnon River valley. It reaches all the way to the Jabbok River. The Jabbok is the northern border of Ammon. The middle of the Arnon River valley is its southern border.

[17]The western border of Reuben and Gad is the Jordan River in the Arabah Valley. It reaches from the Sea of Galilee to the Dead Sea. It runs below the slopes of Pisgah.

[18]Here is the command I gave at that time to the tribes of Reuben and Gad and half of the tribe of Manasseh. I said, "The LORD your God has given you this land as your very own. But all of your strong men must be prepared for battle. They must cross over ahead of the rest of your fellow Israelites.

[19]"But your wives and children can stay in the towns I've given you. You can keep your livestock there too. I know you have a lot of livestock. [20]Let your families and livestock stay in those towns until the LORD gives peace and rest to the other tribes, just as he has given you peace and rest. And let them stay until the other tribes have taken over the land the LORD your God is giving them. That land is across the Jordan River. After that, each of you may go back to the land I've given you as your very own."

The LORD Will Not Allow Moses to Cross the Jordan River

[21]At that time I gave Joshua a command. I said, "Your own eyes have seen everything the LORD your God has done to Sihon and Og. He will do the same thing to all of the kingdoms in the land where you are going. [22]Don't be afraid of them. The LORD your God himself will fight for you."

[23]At that time I made my appeal to the LORD. I said, [24]"LORD and King, you have begun to show me how great you are. You have shown me how strong your hand is. You do great works and mighty acts. There isn't any god in heaven or on earth that can do what you do. [25]Let me go across the Jordan River. Let me see the good land that is beyond it. I want to see that fine hill country and Lebanon."

[26]But the LORD was angry with me because of what you did. He wouldn't listen to me. "That is enough!" the LORD said. "Do not speak to me anymore about this matter. [27]Go up to the highest slopes of Pisgah. Look west and north and south and east. Look at the land with your own eyes. But you are not going to go across that Jordan River.

[28]"So appoint Joshua as the new leader. Help him to be brave. Give him hope and strength. He will take these people across the Jordan. You will see the land. But he will lead them into it to take it as their own." [29]So we stayed in the valley near Beth Peor.

Obey the LORD

4 Israel, listen to the rules and laws I'm going to teach you. Follow them. Then you will live. You will go in and take over the land. The LORD was the God of your people long ago. He's giving you the land. [2]Don't add to what I'm commanding you. Don't subtract from it either. Instead, obey the commands of the LORD your God that I'm giving you.

[3]Your own eyes saw what the LORD your God did at Baal Peor. He destroyed every one of your people who followed the Baal that was worshiped at Peor. [4]But all of you who remained true to the LORD your God are still alive today.

[5]I have taught you rules and laws, just as the LORD my God commanded me. Follow them in the land you are entering to take as your very own. [6]Be careful to keep them. That will show the nations how wise and understanding you are. They will hear about all of those rules. They'll say, "That great nation certainly has wise and understanding people."

[7]The LORD our God is near us every time we pray to him. What other nation is great enough to have its gods that close to them? [8]I'm giving you the laws of the LORD today. What other nation is great enough to have rules and laws that are as fair as these?

[9]Don't be careless. Instead, be very careful. Don't forget the things your eyes have seen. As long as you live, don't let them slip from your mind. Teach them to your children and their children after them. [10]Remember the day you stood at Mount Horeb. The LORD your God was there. He said to me, "Bring the people to me to hear my words. I want them to learn to have respect for me as long as they live in the land. I want them to teach my words to their children."

[11]You came near and stood at the foot of the mountain. It blazed with fire that reached as high as the very heavens. There were black clouds and deep darkness.

[12]Then the LORD spoke to you out of the fire. You heard the sound of his words. But you didn't see any shape or form. You only heard a voice. [13]He announced his covenant to you. That covenant is the Ten Commandments. He commanded you to follow them. Then he wrote them down on two stone tablets.

[14]At that time the LORD directed me to teach you his rules and laws. You must follow them in the land you are crossing the Jordan River to take as your own.

Don't Make or Worship Statues of Gods

[15]The LORD spoke to you at Mount Horeb out of the fire. But you didn't see any shape or form that day. So be very careful.

[16]Make sure you don't commit a horrible sin. Don't make for yourselves a statue of a god. Don't make a god that looks like a man or woman or anything else. [17]Don't make one that looks like any animal on earth or any bird that flies in the sky. [18]Don't make a statue that looks like any creature that moves along the ground or any fish that swims in the water.

19When you look up at the heavens, you will see
the sun and moon. And you will see huge numbers
of stars. Don't let anyone tempt you to bow down
to the sun, moon or stars. Don't worship things the
LORD your God has provided for all of the nations
on earth.

20Egypt was like a furnace that melts iron down
and makes it pure. But the LORD took you and
brought you out of Egypt. He wanted you to be his
very own people. And that's exactly what you are.

21The LORD was angry with me because of what
you did. He took an oath that he would never let
me go across the Jordan River. He promised that I
would never enter that good land. It's the land the
LORD your God is giving you as your own. 22I'll
die here in this land. I won't go across the Jordan.
But you are about to cross over it. And you are
about to take that good land as your own.

23Be careful. Don't forget the covenant the
LORD your God made with you. Don't make for
yourselves a statue of any god at all. He has told
you not to. So don't do it.

24The LORD your God is like a fire that burns
everything up. He's a jealous God.

25You will have children and grandchildren.
And you will live in the land a long time.

But don't commit a horrible sin. Don't make a
statue of a god. If you do, that will be an evil thing
in the sight of the LORD your God. You will make
him angry. 26I'm calling out to heaven and earth to
be witnesses against you this very day. If you do
those things, you will quickly die in the land you
are going across the Jordan River to take over. You
won't live there very long. You will certainly be
destroyed. 27The LORD will drive you out of your
land. He will scatter you among the nations. Only
a few of you will remain alive there. 28There you
will worship gods that men have made out of
wood and stone. Those gods can't see, hear, eat or
smell.

29Perhaps while you are there, you will look to
the LORD your God. You will find him if you look
for him with all your heart and with all your soul.

30All of the things I've told you about might
happen to you. And you will be in trouble. But
later you will return to the LORD your God. You
will obey him. 31The LORD your God is tender and
loving. He won't leave you or destroy you. He
won't forget the covenant he made with your people long ago. He took an oath when he made it.

The LORD Is God

32Ask now about the days of long ago. Learn
what happened long before your time. Ask about
what has happened since the time God created
man on the earth. Ask from one end of the world
to the other. Has anything as great as this ever happened? Has anything like it ever been heard of?
33You heard the voice of God speaking out of fire.
And you lived! Has that happened to any other
people?

34Has any god ever tried to take one nation out
of another to be his own? Has any god done it by
putting his people to the test? Has any god done it
with miraculous signs and wonders or with a war?
Has any god reached out his mighty hand and
powerful arm? Or has any god shown his people
his great and wonderful acts?

The LORD your God did all of those things for
you in Egypt. With your very own eyes you saw
him do them.

35The LORD showed you those things so that
you might know he is God. There is no other God
except him. 36From heaven he made you hear his
voice. He wanted to teach you. On earth he
showed you his great fire. You heard his words
coming out of the fire.

37He loved your people long ago. He chose their
children after them. So he brought you out of Egypt.
He used his great strength to do it. 38He drove out
nations to make room for you. They were greater
and stronger than you are. He will bring you into
their land. He wants to give it to you as your very
own. The whole land is as good as yours right now.

39The LORD is God in heaven above and on the
earth below. Today you must agree with that and
take it to heart. There is no other God.

40I'm giving you his rules and commands today.
Obey them. Then things will go well with you and
your children after you. You will live a long time
in the land. The LORD your God is giving you the
land for all time to come.

Cities to Go to for Safety

41I set apart three cities east of the Jordan River.
42Anyone who killed a person he didn't hate and
without meaning to do it could run to one of those
cities. He could go there and stay alive.

43Here are the names of the cities. Bezer was for
the people of Reuben. It was in the high flatlands
in the desert. Ramoth was for the people of Gad. It
was in Gilead. Golan was for the people of Manasseh. It was in Bashan.

Moses Gives the Law to Israel

44Here is the law I gave the people of Israel.
45Here are its terms, rules and laws. I gave them to
the people when they came out of Egypt.

46They were now east of the Jordan River in the
valley near Beth Peor. They were in the land of Sihon, the king of the Amorites. He ruled in Heshbon. But the people of Israel and I won the battle
over him after we came out of Egypt. 47We captured his land and made it our own. We also took
the land of Og, the king of Bashan. Sihon and Og
were the two Amorite kings east of the Jordan
River.

48Their land reached from Aroer on the rim of
the Arnon River valley to Mount Hermon. 49It
included the whole Arabah Valley east of the Jordan. It included land all the way to the Dead Sea
below the slopes of Pisgah.

The Ten Commandments

5 I sent for all of the people of Israel. Here is
what I said to them.

Israel, listen to me. Here are the rules and laws
I'm announcing to you today. Learn them well. Be
sure to follow them.
2 The LORD our God made a covenant with us at
Mount Horeb. 3 He didn't make it only with our
parents. He also made it with us. In fact, he made
it with all of us who are alive here today. 4 The
LORD spoke to you face to face. His voice came
out of the fire on the mountain.
5 At that time I stood between the LORD and you.
I announced to you the LORD's message. I did it
because you were afraid of the fire. You didn't go
up the mountain.
The LORD said,

6 "I am the LORD your God. I brought
you out of Egypt. That is the land
where you were slaves.
7 "Do not put any other gods in place of me.
8 "Do not make statues of gods that look like
anything in the sky or on the earth or in
the waters. 9 Do not bow down to them
or worship them. I am the LORD your
God. I am a jealous God. I punish the
children for the sin of their parents. I
judge the grandchildren and great-
grandchildren of those who hate me.
10 But for all time to come I show love
to all those who love me and keep my
commandments.
11 "Do not misuse the name of the LORD your
God. The LORD will find guilty anyone
who misuses his name.
12 "Observe the Sabbath day. Keep it holy,
just as the LORD your God commanded
you. 13 Do all of your work in six days.
14 But the seventh day is a Sabbath in
honor of the LORD your God. Do not
do any work on that day. The same
command applies to your sons and
daughters, your male and female servants, your oxen, your donkeys and
your other animals. It also applies to
any outsiders who live in your cities. I
want your male and female servants to
rest, just as you do. 15 Remember that
you were slaves in Egypt. The LORD
your God reached out his mighty hand
and powerful arm and brought you out
of there. So he has commanded you to
observe the Sabbath day.
16 "Honor your father and mother, just as the
LORD your God commanded you.
Then you will live a long time in the
land he is giving you. And things will
go well with you there.
17 "Do not commit murder.
18 "Do not commit adultery.
19 "Do not steal.
20 "Do not give false witness against your
neighbor.
21 "Do not long for your neighbor's wife. Do
not long to have anything that belongs
to your neighbor. Do not long to have
your neighbor's house or land, male or
female servant, ox or donkey."

22 Those are the commandments the LORD
announced in a loud voice to your whole community. He gave them to you there on the mountain.
He spoke out of the fire, cloud and deep darkness.
He didn't add anything else. Then he wrote the
commandments on two stone tablets. And he gave
them to me.
23 The mountain was blazing with fire. You
heard the voice coming out of the darkness. So
your elders and all of the leaders of your tribes
came to me.
24 You said, "The LORD our God has shown us
his glory and majesty. We have heard his voice
coming out of the fire. Today we have seen that a
man can still stay alive even if God speaks with
him. 25 But why should we die? This great fire will
burn us up. We'll die if we hear the voice of the
LORD our God again.
26 "We have heard the voice of the living God.
We've heard him speaking out of the fire. Has any
other human being ever heard him speak like that
and stayed alive? 27 Go near and listen to everything the LORD our God says. Then tell us what he
tells you. We will listen and obey."
28 The LORD heard you when you spoke to me.
He said to me, "I have heard what these people
said to you. Everything they said was good. 29 But
I wish they would always have respect for me in
their hearts. I wish they would always obey all of
my commands. Then things would go well with
them and their children forever.
30 "Go and tell them to return to their tents. 31 But
you stay here with me. Then I will give you all of
my commands, rules and laws. You must teach the
people to follow them in the land I am giving them
as their very own."
32 So be careful to do what the LORD your God
has commanded you. Don't turn away from his
commands to the right or the left. 33 Live exactly as
the LORD your God has commanded you to live.
Then you will enjoy life in the land you will soon
own. Things will go well with you there. You will
live there for a long time.

Love the LORD Your God

6 The LORD your God has directed me to teach
you his commands, rules and laws. Obey
them in the land you will take over when you go
across the Jordan River. 2 Then you, your children
and their children after them will have respect for
the LORD your God as long as you live. Keep all

of his rules and commands I'm giving you. If you do, you will enjoy long life.

3Israel, listen to me. Make sure you obey me. Then things will go well with you. Your numbers will increase greatly in a land that has plenty of milk and honey. That's what the LORD, the God of your parents, promised you.

4Israel, listen to me. The LORD is our God. The LORD is the one and only God. 5Love the LORD your God with all your heart and with all your soul. Love him with all your strength.

6The commandments I give you today must be in your hearts. 7Make sure your children learn them. Talk about them when you are at home. Talk about them when you walk along the road. Speak about them when you go to bed. And speak about them when you get up. 8Write them down and tie them on your hands as a reminder. Also tie them on your foreheads. 9Write them on the doorframes of your houses. Also write them on your gates.

10The LORD your God will bring you into the land of Canaan. He took an oath. He promised he would give the land to your fathers. He promised it to Abraham, Isaac and Jacob.

The land has large, wealthy cities you didn't build. 11It has houses that are filled with all kinds of good things you didn't provide. It has wells you didn't dig. And it has vineyards and groves of olive trees you didn't plant. You will have plenty to eat.

12But be careful that you don't forget the LORD. Remember that he brought you out of Egypt. That's the land where you were slaves.

13Worship the LORD your God. He is the only one you should serve. When you make promises, take your oaths in his name. 14Don't follow other gods. Don't worship the gods of the nations that are around you.

15The LORD your God is among you. He is a jealous God. If you worship other gods, his anger will burn against you. And he will destroy you from the face of the land. 16Don't put the LORD your God to the test as you did at Massah.

17Be sure to obey the LORD's commands. Follow the terms and rules he has given you. 18Do what is right and good in the LORD's eyes. Then things will go well with you. You will go in and take over the land. It's the good land the LORD promised with an oath to your people long ago. 19You will drive out all of your enemies to make room for you. That's what the LORD said would happen.

20Later on, your son might ask you, "What is the meaning of the terms, rules and laws the LORD our God has commanded you to obey?"

21If he does, tell him, "We were Pharaoh's slaves in Egypt. But the LORD used his mighty hand to bring us out of Egypt. 22With our own eyes we saw the LORD send miraculous signs and wonders. They were great and terrible. He sent them on Egypt and Pharaoh and everyone in his house.

23"But the LORD brought us out of Egypt. He planned to bring us into the land of Canaan and give it to us. It's the land he promised with an oath to our people long ago.

24"The LORD our God commanded us to obey all of his rules. He commanded us to have respect for him. If we do, we will always succeed and be kept alive. That's what is happening today. 25We must make sure we obey the whole law in the sight of the LORD our God. That's what he has commanded us to do. If we obey his law, we'll be doing what he requires of us."

The LORD Will Drive Many Nations Out

7 The LORD your God will bring you into the land. You are going to enter it and take it as your own. He'll drive many nations out to make room for you. He'll drive out the Hittites, Girgashites, Amorites, Canaanites, Perizzites, Hivites and Jebusites. Those seven nations are larger and stronger than you are.

2The LORD your God will hand them over to you. You will win the battle over them. You must completely destroy them. Don't make a peace treaty with them. Don't show them any mercy. 3Don't get married to any of them. Don't give your daughters to their sons. And don't take their daughters for your sons. 4If you do, those people will turn your children away from following the LORD. Then your children will serve other gods. The LORD's anger will burn against you. It will quickly destroy you.

5So here is what you must do to those people. Break down their altars. Smash their sacred stones. Cut down the poles they use to worship the goddess Asherah. Burn the statues of their gods in the fire.

6You are a holy nation. The LORD your God has set you apart for himself. He has chosen you to be his special treasure. He chose you out of all of the nations on the face of the earth to be his people.

7The LORD chose you because he loved you very much. He didn't choose you because you had more people than other nations. In fact, you had the smallest number of all.

8The LORD chose you because he loved you. He wanted to keep the promise he had made with an oath to your people long ago. That's why he brought you out of Egypt with a mighty hand. He bought you back from the land where you were slaves. He set you free from the power of Pharaoh, the king of Egypt.

9So I want you to realize that the LORD your God is God. He is the faithful God. He keeps his covenant for all time to come. He keeps it with those who love him and obey his commands. He shows them his love. 10But he will pay back those who hate him. He'll destroy them. He'll quickly pay back those who hate him. 11So be careful to follow the commands, rules and laws I'm giving you today.

12Pay attention to the laws of the LORD your God. Be careful to obey them. Then he will keep his covenant of love with you. That's what he promised with an oath to your people long ago.

13The LORD will love you and bless you. He'll increase your numbers. He'll give you many children. He'll bless the crops of your land. He'll give you plenty of grain, olive oil and fresh wine. He'll bless your herds with many calves. He'll give your flocks many lambs. He'll do all of those things for you in the land of Canaan. It's the land he promised your people long ago that he would give you. 14He will bless you more than any other nation. All of your men and women will have children. All of your livestock will have little ones.

15The LORD will keep you from getting sick. He won't send on you any of the horrible sicknesses you saw all around you in Egypt. But he'll send them on everyone who hates you.

16You must destroy all of the nations the LORD your God hands over to you. Don't feel sorry for them. Don't serve their gods. If you do, they will be a trap for you.

17You might say to yourselves, "These nations are stronger than we are. How can we drive them out?" 18But don't be afraid of them.

Be sure to remember what the LORD your God did to Pharaoh and all of the Egyptians. 19With your own eyes you saw what the LORD did to them. You saw his miraculous signs and wonders. He reached out his mighty hand and powerful arm. The LORD your God used all of those things to bring you out. He will do the same things to all of the nations you are now afraid of.

20The LORD your God will also send hornets among them. Some of the people who are left alive will hide from you. But even they will die. 21So don't be terrified by them. The LORD your God is with you. He is a great and wonderful God.

22The LORD your God will drive out those nations to make room for you. But he will do it little by little. You won't be allowed to get rid of them all at once. If you did, wild animals would multiply all around you.

23But the LORD your God will hand those nations over to you. He will throw them into a panic until they are destroyed. 24He will hand their kings over to you. You will wipe out their names from the earth. No one will be able to stand up against you. You will destroy them.

25Burn the statues of their gods in the fire. Don't long for the silver and gold that is on those statues. Don't take it for yourselves. If you do, it will be a trap for you. The LORD your God hates it. 26Don't bring anything he hates into your house. If you do, you will be completely destroyed along with it. So hate it with all your heart. It is set apart to be destroyed.

Remember What the LORD Has Done

8 Make sure you follow every command I'm giving you today. Then you will live. You will increase your numbers. You will enter the land and take it as your own. It's the land the LORD promised with an oath to your people long ago.

2Remember how the LORD your God led you all the way. He guided you in the desert for these 40 years. He wanted to take your pride away. He wanted to put you to the test and know what was in your hearts. He wanted to see whether you would obey his commands.

3He took your pride away. He let you go hungry. Then he gave you manna to eat. You and your parents had never even known anything about manna before. He tested you to teach you that man doesn't live only on bread. He also lives on every word that comes from the mouth of the LORD. 4Your clothes didn't wear out during these 40 years. Your feet didn't swell.

5Here is what I want you to know in your hearts. The LORD your God trains you, just as parents train their children.

6Obey the commands of the LORD your God. Live as he wants you to live. Have respect for him.

7The LORD your God is bringing you into a good land. It has streams and pools of water. Springs flow in its valleys and hills. 8It has wheat, barley, vines, fig trees, pomegranates, olive oil and honey. 9There is plenty of food in that land. You will have everything you need. Its rocks have iron in them. And you can dig copper out of its hills.

10When you have eaten and are satisfied, praise the LORD your God. Praise him for the good land he has given you. 11Make sure you don't forget the LORD your God. Don't fail to obey his commands, laws and rules. I'm giving them to you today.

12But suppose you don't obey his commands. And suppose you have plenty to eat. You build fine houses and settle down in them. 13Your herds and flocks increase their numbers. You also get more and more silver and gold. And everything you have multiplies. 14Then your hearts will become proud. And you will forget the LORD your God.

The LORD brought you out of Egypt. That's the land where you were slaves. 15He led you through that huge and terrible desert. It was a dry land. It didn't have any water. It had poisonous snakes and scorpions. The LORD gave you water out of solid rock. 16He gave you manna to eat in the desert. Your parents had never even known anything about manna before.

The LORD took your pride away. He put you to the test. He did it so that things would go well with you in the end. 17You might say to yourselves, "Our power and our strong hands have made us rich."

18But remember the LORD your God. He gives you the ability to produce wealth. That shows he stands by the terms of his covenant. He promised it with an oath to your people long ago. And he's still faithful to his covenant today.

19Don't forget the LORD your God. Don't follow other gods. Don't worship them and bow down to them. I give witness against you today that if you do, you will certainly be destroyed. 20You will be destroyed just like the nations the LORD your God is destroying to make room for you. That's what will happen if you don't obey him.

Why the LORD Gave Canaan to Israel

9 Israel, listen to me. You are now about to go across the Jordan. You will take over the land of the nations that live there.

Those nations are greater and stronger than you are. Their large cities have walls that reach up to the sky. 2The people who live there are Anakites. They are strong and tall. You know all about them. You have heard people say, "Who can stand up against the Anakites?"

3But today you can be sure the LORD your God will go over there ahead of you. He is like a fire that will burn them up. He'll destroy them. He'll bring them under your control. You will drive them out. You will put an end to them quickly, just as the LORD has promised you.

4The LORD your God will drive them out to make room for you. When he does, don't say to yourselves, "The LORD has done it because we are godly. That's why he brought us here to take over this land." That isn't true. The LORD is going to drive out those nations to make room for you because they are very evil.

5You are not going in to take over their land because you have done what is right or honest. It's because those nations are so evil. That's why the LORD your God will drive them out ahead of you. He will do what he said he would do. He took an oath and made a promise to your fathers. He made it to Abraham, Isaac and Jacob.

6The LORD your God is giving you this good land to take as your own. But you must understand that it isn't because you are a godly nation. In fact, you are stubborn.

Israel Worshiped the Golden Calf

7Here is something you must remember. Never forget it. You made the LORD your God angry in the desert. You refused to obey him from the day you left Egypt until you arrived here.

8At Mount Horeb you made the LORD angry enough to destroy you. 9I went up the mountain. I went there to receive the tablets of the covenant. They were made out of stone. It was the covenant the LORD had made with you. I stayed on the mountain for 40 days and 40 nights. I didn't eat any food or drink any water.

10The LORD gave me two stone tablets. The words on them were written by the finger of God. All of the commandments the LORD gave you were written on the tablets. He announced them to you out of the fire on the mountain. He wrote them on the day you gathered together there.

11The 40 days and 40 nights came to an end. Then the LORD gave me the two stone tablets. They were the tablets of the covenant. 12The LORD told me, "Go down from here right away. The people you brought out of Egypt have become very sinful. They have quickly turned away from what I commanded them. They have made a metal statue of a god for themselves."

13The LORD said to me, "I have seen these people. They are so stubborn! 14Do not try to stop me. I am going to destroy them. I will wipe them out from the earth. Then I will make you into a great nation. Your people will be stronger than they were. There will be more of you than there were of them."

15So I turned and went down the mountain. It was blazing with fire. I was carrying the two tablets of the covenant.

16When I looked, I saw that you had sinned against the LORD your God. You had made for yourselves a metal statue of a god. It looked like a calf. You had quickly turned away from the path the LORD had commanded you to follow.

17So I threw the two tablets out of my hands. You watched them break into pieces.

18Then once again I fell down flat in front of the LORD with my face toward the ground. I lay there for 40 days and 40 nights. I didn't eat any food or drink any water. You had committed a terrible sin. You had done an evil thing in the LORD's sight. You had made him angry.

19I was afraid of the LORD's burning anger. He was so angry with you he wanted to destroy you. But the LORD listened to me again. 20And he was so angry with Aaron he wanted to destroy him too. But at that time I prayed for Aaron.

21I also got that sinful calf you had made. I burned it in the fire. I crushed it and ground it into fine powder. Then I threw the powder into a stream that was flowing down the mountain.

22You also made the LORD angry at Taberah, Massah and Kibroth Hattaavah.

23The LORD sent you out from Kadesh Barnea. He said, "Go up and take over the land I have given you." But you refused to do what the LORD your God had commanded you to do. You didn't trust him or obey him. 24You have been refusing to obey the LORD as long as I've known you.

25I lay down in front of the LORD with my face toward the ground for 40 days and 40 nights. I did it because the LORD had said he would destroy you.

26I prayed to him. "LORD and King," I said, "don't destroy your people. They belong to you. You set them free by your great power. You used your mighty hand to bring them out of Egypt. 27Remember your servants Abraham, Isaac and Jacob. Forgive the people of Israel for being so stubborn. Don't judge them for the evil and sinful things they've done.

28"If you do, the Egyptians will say, 'The LORD wasn't able to take them into the land he had promised to give them. He hated them. So he brought them out of Egypt to put them to death in the desert.' 29But they are your people. They belong to you. You used your great power to bring them out of Egypt. You reached out your mighty arm and saved them."

The New Stone Tablets

10 At that time the LORD spoke to me. He said, "Carve out two stone tablets, just like the first ones. Then come up to me on the mountain. Also make a wooden chest. [2]I will write on the tablets the words that were on the first tablets, which you broke. Then you must put the tablets in the chest."

[3]So I made the ark out of acacia wood. I carved out two stone tablets that were just like the first ones. I went up the mountain. I carried the two tablets in my hands.

[4]The LORD wrote on the tablets what he had written before. It was the Ten Commandments. He had announced them to you out of the fire on the mountain. It was on the day you had gathered together there. So the LORD gave the tablets to me.

[5]Then I came back down the mountain. I put the tablets in the ark I had made, just as the LORD had commanded me. And that's where they are now.

[6]Remember how the people of Israel traveled from the wells of Bene Jaakan to Moserah. That's where Aaron died. And his body was buried there. His son Eleazar became the next priest after him. [7]From Moserah the people traveled to Gudgodah. Then they went on to Jotbathah. That land has streams of water.

[8]At that time the LORD set the tribe of Levi apart. He appointed them to carry the ark of the covenant of the LORD. He wanted them to serve him. He told them to bless the people in his name. And they still do it today. [9]That's why the Levites don't have any part of the land the LORD gave the other tribes in Israel. They don't have any share among them. The LORD himself is their share. That's what the LORD your God told them.

[10]I had stayed on the mountain for 40 days and nights, just as I did the first time. The LORD listened to me that time also. He didn't want to destroy you.

[11]"Go," the LORD said to me. "Lead the people on their way. Then they can enter the land and take it over. I have taken an oath. I promised I would give the land to their fathers. I promised it to Abraham, Isaac and Jacob."

Have Respect for the LORD

[12]And now, Israel, what is the LORD your God asking you to do? Have respect for him. Live exactly as he wants you to live. Love him. Serve him with all your heart and with all your soul. [13]Obey the LORD's commands and rules. I'm giving them to you today for your own good.

[14]The heavens belong to the LORD your God. Even the highest heavens belong to him. He owns the earth and everything in it.

[15]But the LORD loved your people very much long ago. You are their children. And he chose you above all of the other nations. His love and his promise remain with you to this very day. [16]So don't let your hearts be stubborn anymore. Obey the LORD.

[17]The LORD your God is the greatest God of all. He is the greatest Lord of all. He is the great God. He is mighty and wonderful. He treats everyone the same. He doesn't accept any money from those who want special favors. [18]He stands up for widows and for children whose fathers have died. He loves outsiders. He gives them food and clothes. [19]So you also must love outsiders. Remember that you yourselves were outsiders in Egypt.

[20]Have respect for the LORD your God. Serve him. Remain true to him. When you make promises, take your oaths in his name. [21]He is the one you should praise. He's your God. With your own eyes you saw the great and wonderful miracles he did for you.

[22]Long ago, your people went down into Egypt. The total number of them was 70. And now the LORD your God has made you as many as the stars in the sky.

Love and Obey the LORD

11 Love the LORD your God. Do what he requires. Always obey his rules, laws and commands.

[2]Remember today that your children weren't the ones the LORD your God taught and trained. They didn't see his majesty. They weren't in Egypt when he reached out his mighty hand and powerful arm. [3]They didn't see the miraculous signs and the other things he did in Egypt. They didn't see what he did to Pharaoh, the king of Egypt, and to his whole country. [4]They weren't there when he destroyed the army of Egypt and its horses and chariots. The LORD swept the waters of the Red Sea over the Egyptians while they were chasing you. He wiped them out forever.

[5]Your children didn't see what he did for you in the desert before you arrived here. [6]They didn't see what he did to Dathan and Abiram, who were the sons of Eliab. Eliab was from the tribe of Reuben. The earth opened its mouth right in the middle of the Israelite camp. It swallowed up Dathan and Abiram. It swallowed them up together with their families, tents and every living thing that belonged to them.

[7]But with your own eyes you saw all of the great things the LORD has done.

[8]So obey all of the commands I'm giving you today. Then you will be strong enough to go in and take over the land. You will go across the Jordan River and take it as your own.

[9]You will live in the land for a long time. It's the land the LORD promised to give to Abraham, Isaac and Jacob and their children after them. He took an oath when he made that promise. It's a land that has plenty of milk and honey. [10]You will enter it and take it over.

It isn't like the land of Egypt. That's where you came from. You planted your seeds there. You had to water them, just as you have to water a vegetable garden.

11But you will soon go across the Jordan River. The land you are going to take over has mountains and valleys in it. It drinks rain from heaven. 12It's a land the LORD your God takes care of. His eyes always look on it with favor. He watches over it from the beginning of the year to its end.

13So be faithful. Obey the commands the LORD your God is giving you today. Love him. Serve him with all your heart and with all your soul.

14Then the LORD will send rain on your land at the right time. He'll send rain in the fall and in the spring. You will be able to gather your grain. You will also be able to make olive oil and fresh wine. 15He'll provide grass in the fields for your cattle. You will have plenty to eat.

16But be careful. Don't let anyone tempt you to do something wrong. Don't turn away and worship other gods. Don't bow down to them. 17If you do, the LORD's anger will burn against you. He'll close up the sky. It won't rain. The ground won't produce its crops. Soon you will die. You won't live to enjoy the good land the LORD is giving you.

18So keep my words in your hearts and minds. Write them down and tie them on your hands as a reminder. Also tie them on your foreheads. 19Teach them to your children. Talk about them when you are at home. Talk about them when you walk along the road. Speak about them when you go to bed. And speak about them when you get up. 20Write them on the doorframes of your houses. Also write them on your gates.

21Then you and your children will live for a long time in the land. The LORD took an oath and promised to give the land to Abraham, Isaac and Jacob. Your family line will continue as long as the heavens remain above the earth.

22So be careful. Obey all of the commands I'm giving you to follow. Love the LORD your God. Live exactly as he wants you to live. Remain true to him. 23Then the LORD will drive out all of the nations to make room for you. They are larger and stronger than you are. But you will take their land.

24Every place you walk on will belong to you. Your territory will go all the way from the desert to Lebanon. It will go from the Euphrates River to the Mediterranean Sea.

25No man will be able to stand up against you. The LORD your God will throw the whole land into a panic because of you. He'll do it everywhere you go, just as he promised you.

26Listen to me. I'm setting a blessing and a curse in front of you today. 27I'm giving you the commands of the LORD your God today. You will be blessed if you obey them. 28But you will be cursed if you don't obey them. So don't turn away from the path I'm now commanding you to take. Don't worship other gods. You haven't known anything about them before.

29The LORD your God will bring you into the land to take it over. When he does, you must announce the blessings from Mount Gerizim. You must announce the curses from Mount Ebal. 30As you know, those mountains are across the Jordan River. They are beyond the road that runs along the west side of the Jordan. They are near the large trees of Moreh. The mountains are in the territory of the Canaanites, who live in the Arabah Valley near Gilgal.

31You are about to go across the Jordan River. You will enter the land and take it over. The LORD your God is giving it to you. You will take it over and live there. 32When you do, make sure you obey all of the rules and laws I'm giving you today.

Worship Only Where the LORD Wants You To

12 Here are the rules and laws you must obey. Be careful to follow them in the land the LORD has given you to take as your own. He's the God of your people who lived long ago. Obey these rules and laws as long as you live in the land.

2You will soon drive the nations out of it. Completely destroy all of the places where they worship their gods. Destroy them on the high mountains, on the hills, and under every green tree. 3Break down their altars. Smash their sacred stones. Burn up the poles they use to worship the goddess Asherah. Cut down the statues of their gods. Wipe out the names of their gods from those places.

4You must not worship the LORD your God the way those nations worship their gods. 5Instead, go to the special place he will choose from among all of your tribes. He will put his Name there. That's where you must go.

6Take your burnt offerings and sacrifices to that place. Bring your special gifts and a tenth of everything you produce. Take with you what you have promised to give. Bring any other offerings you choose to give. And bring the male animals among your livestock that were born first to their mothers.

7You and your families will eat at the place the LORD your God will choose. He will be with you there. You will find joy in everything you have done. That's because he has blessed you.

8You must not do as we're doing here today. All of us are doing only what we think is right. 9That's because you haven't yet reached the place the LORD is giving you. Your God will give you peace and rest there.

10But first you will go across the Jordan River. You will settle in the land he's giving you. It will belong to you as your share. He will give you peace and rest from all of your enemies around you. You will live in safety.

11The LORD your God will choose a special place. He will put his Name there. That's where you must bring everything I command you to bring. That includes your burnt offerings and sacrifices. It includes your special gifts and a tenth of everything you produce. It also includes all of the things of value that you promised to give to the LORD.

12 Be filled with joy there in the sight of the LORD your God. Your children should also be joyful. So should your male and female servants. And so should the Levites from your towns. The Levites won't receive any part of the land as their share.

13 Be careful not to sacrifice your burnt offerings anywhere you want to. 14 Offer them only at the place the LORD will choose in one of your tribes. There obey everything I command you.

15 But you can kill your animals in any of your towns. You can eat as much of the meat as you want to. You can eat it as if it were antelope or deer meat. That's in keeping with the blessing the LORD your God is giving you. Those who are "clean" and those who are not can eat it.

16 But you must not eat meat that still has blood in it. Pour the blood out on the ground like water.

17 Here are the things you must not eat in your own towns. You must not eat the tenth part of your grain, olive oil and fresh wine. It belongs to the LORD. You must not eat the male animals among your livestock that were born first to their mothers. Don't eat anything you have promised to give. Don't eat any offerings you have chosen to give. And you must not eat any of your special gifts.

18 Instead, you must eat all of those things in the sight of the LORD your God. Do it at the place he will choose. You, your children, your male and female servants and the Levites from your towns can eat them.

Be filled with joy in the sight of the LORD your God. Be joyful in everything you do.

19 Don't forget to take care of the Levites as long as you live in your land.

20 The LORD your God will increase your territory, just as he has promised you. When he does, you might get hungry for meat. You might say, "I'd really like some meat." Then you can eat as much of it as you want to.

21 The LORD your God will choose a special place. He will put his Name there. But suppose it's too far away for you to go to it. Then you can kill animals from the herds and flocks the LORD has given you. Do it just as I have commanded you. In your own towns you can eat as much of the meat as you want to. 22 Eat it as you would eat antelope or deer meat. Those who are "clean" and those who are not can eat it.

23 But be sure you don't eat meat that still has blood in it. The blood is the animal's life. So you must not eat the life along with the meat. 24 You must not eat the blood. Pour it out on the ground like water. 25 Don't eat it. Then things will go well with you and your children after you. You will be doing what is right in the eyes of the LORD.

26 But go to the place the LORD will choose. Take with you the things you have set apart for him. Bring what you have promised to give him. 27 Sacrifice your burnt offerings on the altar of the LORD your God. Offer the meat and the blood there. The blood of your sacrifices must be poured out beside his altar. But you can eat the meat.

28 Make sure you obey all of the rules I'm giving you. Then things will always go well with you and your children after you. That's because you will be doing what is good and right in the eyes of the LORD your God.

29 You are about to attack the land and take it over as your own. When you do, the LORD your God will cut off the nations who live there. He will do it to make room for you. You will drive them out. You will settle in their land. 30 They will be destroyed to make room for you. But when they are, be careful.

Don't be trapped. Don't ask questions about their gods. Don't say, "How do these nations serve their gods? We'll do it in the same way." 31 You must not worship the LORD your God the way they worship their gods. When they worship, they do all kinds of evil things the LORD hates. They even burn up their children in the fire as sacrifices to their gods.

32 Be sure you do everything I'm commanding you to do. Don't add anything to my commands. And don't take anything away from them.

Don't Worship Other Gods

13 Suppose a prophet appears among you. Or someone comes who uses dreams to tell what's going to happen. He tells you that a miraculous sign or wonder is going to take place. 2 The sign or wonder he has spoken about might really take place. And he might say, "Let's follow other gods. Let's worship them." But you haven't known anything about those gods before. 3 So you must not listen to what that prophet or dreamer has said.

The LORD your God is putting you to the test. He wants to know whether you love him with all your heart and with all your soul. 4 You must follow him. You must have respect for him. Keep his commands. Obey him. Serve him. Remain true to him.

5 That prophet or dreamer must be put to death. He told you not to obey the LORD your God. The LORD brought you out of Egypt. He set you free from the land where you were slaves. He commanded you to live the way he wants you to. But that prophet or dreamer has tried to make you turn away from it. Get rid of that evil person.

6 Suppose your very own brother or sister secretly tempts you to do something wrong. Or your child or the wife you love tempts you. Or your closest friend does it. Suppose one of them says, "Let's go and worship other gods." But you and your people long ago hadn't known anything about those gods before. 7 They are the gods of the

nations that are around you. Those nations might
be near or far away. In fact, they might reach from
one end of the land to the other. 8Don't give in to
those who are tempting you. Don't listen to them.
Don't feel sorry for them. Don't spare them or
save them.

9You must certainly put them to death. You
must be the first to throw stones at them. Then all
of the people must do the same thing. 10Put them to
death by throwing stones at them. They tried to
turn you away from the LORD your God. He
brought you out of Egypt. That's the land where
you were slaves.

11After you kill those who tempted you, all of
the people of Israel will hear about it. And they
will be too scared to do an evil thing like that
again.

12The LORD your God is giving you towns to
live in. But suppose you hear something bad about
one of those towns. 13You hear that evil men have
appeared among you. They've tried to get the people of their town to do something wrong. They've
said, "Let's go and worship other gods." But you
haven't known anything about those gods before.
14So you must question people. You must check
the matter out carefully.

If it's true, an evil thing has really happened
among you. It's something the LORD hates. 15Then
you must certainly kill with your swords everyone
who lives in that town. Destroy it completely.
Wipe out its people and livestock. 16Gather all of
the goods of that town into the middle of the main
street. Burn the town completely. Burn up everything in it.

It's a whole burnt offering to the LORD your
God. The town must remain a pile of stones forever. It must never be built again.

17Don't keep anything that should be destroyed.
Then the LORD will turn away from his burning
anger. He will show you mercy. He'll have deep
concern for you. He'll increase your numbers.
That's what he promised your people long ago. He
took an oath when he made the promise.

18The LORD your God will do those things if
you obey him. I'm giving you his commands
today. And you must obey all of them. You must
do what is right in his eyes.

Food That Is "Clean" and Food That Is Not

14 You are the children of the LORD your God.
Don't cut yourselves to honor the dead.
Don't shave the front of your heads to honor them.

2You are a holy nation. The LORD your God has
set you apart for himself. He has chosen you to be
his special treasure. He chose you out of all of the
nations on the face of the earth.

3Don't eat anything the LORD hates. 4Here are
the only animals you can eat. You can eat oxen,
sheep, goats, 5deer, gazelles, roe deer, wild goats,
ibexes, antelope and mountain sheep.

6You can eat any animal that has hoofs that are
separated completely in two. But it must also chew
the cud. 7Some animals only chew the cud. Others
only have hoofs that are completely separated in
two. The camel, rabbit and rock badger chew the
cud, but they don't have hoofs that are completely
separated. So you can't eat them. They are not
"clean" for you.

8Pigs aren't "clean" for you either. They have
hoofs that are completely separated, but they don't
chew the cud. So don't eat their meat. And don't
touch their dead bodies.

9Many creatures live in water. You can eat all of
the ones that have fins and scales. 10But don't eat
anything that doesn't have fins and scales. It isn't
"clean" for you.

11You can eat any "clean" bird. 12But there are
many birds you can't eat. They include eagles, vultures, and black vultures. 13They include red kites,
black kites and all kinds of falcons. 14They include
all kinds of ravens. 15They include horned owls,
screech owls, gulls and all kinds of hawks. 16They
include little owls, great owls, white owls 17and
desert owls. They include ospreys and cormorants.
18They include storks and all kinds of herons. They
also include hoopoes and bats.

19All insects that fly together in groups are
"unclean" for you. So don't eat them. 20But you
can eat any creature that has wings and is "clean."

21If you find something that's already dead,
don't eat it. You can give it to an outsider who is
living in any of your towns. He can eat it. Or you
can sell it to someone who is from another country. But you are a holy nation. The LORD your God
has set you apart for himself.

Don't cook a young goat in its mother's milk.

Give a Tenth of What You Produce

22Be sure to set apart a tenth of everything your
fields produce each year. 23Here are the things you
should eat in the sight of the LORD your God. You
should eat a tenth part of your grain, olive oil and
fresh wine. You should also eat the male animals
among your livestock that were born first to their
mothers. Eat all of those things at the special place
the LORD your God will choose. He will put his
Name there. You will learn to have respect for him
always.

24But suppose the place the LORD will choose for
his Name is too far away from you. And suppose
your God has blessed you. And your tenth part is too
heavy for you to carry. 25Then sell it for silver. Take
the silver with you. Go to the place the LORD your
God will choose. 26Use the silver to buy anything
you like. It can be cattle or sheep. It can be any kind
of wine. In fact, it can be anything else you wish.
Then you and your family can eat there in the sight
of the LORD your God. You can be filled with joy.

27Don't forget to take care of the Levites who
will live in your towns. They won't receive any
part of the land as their share.

[28]At the end of every three years, bring a tenth of everything you produce that year. Store it in your towns. [29]Then the Levites can come and eat. That's because they won't receive any part of the land as their share. The outsiders and widows who live in your towns can come. So can the children whose fathers have died. Everyone can have plenty to eat. Then the LORD your God will bless you in everything you do.

The Year for Forgiving People What They Owe

15 At the end of every seven years you must forgive people what they owe you. [2]Have you made a loan to one of your own people? Then forgive what is owed to you. You can't require that person to pay you back. The LORD's time to forgive what is owed has been announced. [3]You can require someone from another nation to pay you back. But you must forgive your own people what they owe you.

[4]There shouldn't be any poor people among you. The LORD will greatly bless you in the land he is giving you. You will take it over as your own. [5]The LORD your God will bless you if you obey him completely. Be careful to follow all of the commands I'm giving you today.

[6]The LORD your God will bless you, just as he has promised. You will lend money to many nations. But you won't have to borrow from any of them. You will rule over many nations. But none of them will rule over you.

[7]Suppose there are poor people among you. And suppose they live in one of the towns in the land the LORD your God is giving you. Then don't be mean to them. They are poor. So don't hold back money from them. [8]Instead, open your hands and lend them what they need. Do it freely. [9]Be careful not to have an evil thought in your mind. Don't say to yourself, "The seventh year will soon be here. It's the year for forgiving people what they owe." If you think like that, you might treat your needy people badly. You might not give them anything. Then they might make their appeal to the LORD against you. And he will find you guilty of sin.

[10]So give freely to those who are needy. Open your hearts to them. Then the LORD your God will bless you in all of your work. He will bless you in everything you do. [11]There will always be poor people in the land. So I'm commanding you to give freely to those who are poor and needy in your land. Open your hands to them.

Set Your Hebrew Servants Free

[12]Suppose Hebrew men or women sell themselves to you. If they do, they will serve you for six years. Then in the seventh year you must let them go free.

[13]But when you set them free, don't send them away without anything to show for all of their work. [14]Freely give them some animals from your flock. Also give them some of your grain and wine. The LORD your God has blessed you richly. Give to them as he has given to you.

[15]Remember that you were slaves in Egypt. The LORD your God set you free. That's why I'm giving you this command today.

[16]But suppose your servant says to you, "I don't want to leave you." He loves you and your family. And you are taking good care of him. [17]Then take him to the door of your house. Poke a hole through his ear lobe into the doorpost. And he will become your servant for life. Do the same with your female servant.

[18]Don't think you are being cheated when you set your servants free. After all, they have served you for six years. The service of each of them has been worth twice as much as the service of a hired worker. And the LORD your God will bless you in everything you do.

Male Animals That Are Born First to Their Mothers

[19]Set apart to the LORD your God every male animal among your livestock that was born first to its mother. Don't put that kind of ox to work. Don't clip the wool from that kind of sheep. [20]Each year you and your family must eat them. Do it in the sight of the LORD your God at the place he will choose.

[21]Suppose an animal has something wrong with it. It might not be able to see or walk. Or it might have a bad flaw. Then you must not sacrifice it to the LORD your God. [22]You must eat it in your own towns. Those who are "clean" and those who are not can eat it. Eat it as if it were antelope or deer meat. [23]But you must not eat meat that still has blood in it. Pour the blood out on the ground like water.

The Passover Feast

16 Celebrate the Passover Feast of the LORD your God in the month of Abib. In that month he brought you out of Egypt at night.

[2]Sacrifice an animal from your flock or herd. It is the Passover sacrifice in honor of the LORD your God. Sacrifice it at the special place the LORD will choose. He will put his Name there.

[3]Don't eat the animal along with bread that is made with yeast. Instead, for seven days eat bread that is made without yeast. It's the bread that reminds you of how much you suffered. Remember that you left Egypt in a hurry. Remember it all the days of your life. Don't forget the day you left Egypt. [4]Don't keep any yeast anywhere in your land for seven days.

Don't let any of the meat you sacrifice on the evening of the first day be left over until the next morning.

[5]You must not sacrifice the Passover animal in any town the LORD your God is giving you. [6]Sacrifice it only in the special place he will choose for his Name. Sacrifice it there in the evening when the

sun goes down. Do it on the same day every year. Be sure it's the day you left Egypt. 7Cook it and eat it. Do it at the place the LORD your God will choose. Then in the morning return to your tents.

8For six days eat bread that is made without yeast. On the seventh day come together for a service in honor of the LORD your God. Don't do any work.

The Feast of Weeks

9Count off seven weeks from the time you begin to cut your grain in the field. 10Then celebrate the Feast of Weeks in honor of the LORD your God. Give anything you choose to give as an offering. Do it in keeping with the blessings the LORD has given you.

11Be filled with joy in the sight of the LORD your God. Be joyful at the special place he will choose for his Name. You, your children, and your male and female servants should be joyful. So should the Levites who are living in your towns. So should the outsiders and widows who are living among you. And so should the children whose fathers have died. 12Remember that you were slaves in Egypt. Be careful to obey the rules I'm giving you.

The Feast of Booths

13Gather the grain from your threshing floors. Take the fresh wine from your winepresses. Then celebrate the Feast of Booths for seven days. 14Be filled with joy at your Feast. You, your children, and your male and female servants should be joyful. So should the Levites, the outsiders, and the widows who are living in your towns. And so should the children whose fathers have died.

15For seven days celebrate the Feast in honor of the LORD your God. Do it at the place he will choose. The LORD will bless you when you gather all of your crops. He'll bless you in everything you do. And you will be full of joy.

16All of your men must appear in front of the LORD your God at the holy tent. They must go to the place he will choose. They must do it three times a year. They must go there to celebrate the Feast of Unleavened Bread, the Feast of Weeks and the Feast of Booths.

No man should appear in front of the LORD without bringing something with him. 17Each of you must bring a gift. Do it in keeping with the way the LORD your God has blessed you.

Appoint Judges and Officials

18Appoint judges and officials for each of your tribes. Do it in every town the LORD your God is giving you. They must judge the people fairly. 19Do what is right. Treat everyone the same. Don't take money from people who want special favors. It makes those who are wise close their eyes to the truth. It twists the words of those who do what is right. 20Follow only what is right. If you do, you will live. You will take over the land the LORD your God is giving you.

Don't Worship Other Gods

21Don't set up a wooden pole that is used to worship the goddess Asherah. Don't set it up beside the altar you build to worship the LORD your God. 22Don't set up a sacred stone to honor another god. The LORD your God hates Asherah poles and sacred stones.

17 Suppose an ox or sheep has anything at all wrong with it. Then don't sacrifice it to the LORD your God. He hates it.

2Someone who is living among you might do what is evil in the sight of the LORD your God. It might happen in one of the towns the LORD is giving you. That person is breaking the LORD's covenant. 3The person might have worshiped or bowed down to other gods. That person might have bowed down to the sun or moon or stars in the sky. I have commanded you not to do those things. 4When you hear that people have done something like that, check the matter out carefully. If it's true, an evil thing has been done in Israel. It's something the LORD hates.

5So take the person who has done that evil thing to your city gate. Put that person to death with stones. 6The witness of two or three people is required to put someone to death. No one can be put to death because of what only one witness says. It needs the witness of two or three people. 7The witnesses must throw the first stones. Then the rest of the people must also throw stones. Get rid of that evil person.

Law Courts

8People will bring their cases to your courts. But some cases will be too hard for you to judge. They might be about murders, attacks or other crimes. Then take those hard cases to the place the LORD your God will choose. 9Go to a priest, who is a Levite. And go to the judge who is in office at that time. Ask them for their decision. They will give it to you.

10They'll hand down their decisions at the place the LORD will choose. You must do what they decide. Be careful to do everything they direct you to do. 11Act in keeping with the laws they teach you. Accept the decisions they give you. Don't turn away from what they tell you. Don't turn to the right or the left.

12Someone might make fun of the judge. Or he might make fun of the priest who serves the LORD your God at the place he will choose. If the man does that, he must be put to death. Remove that evil person from Israel. 13All of the people of Israel will hear about it. And they will be afraid to make fun of a judge or priest again.

Appoint the King the LORD Chooses

14You will enter the land the LORD your God is giving you. You will take it as your own. You will settle down in it. When you do, you will say, "Let's appoint a king over us, just like all of the nations around us." [15]When that happens, make sure you appoint over you the king the LORD your God chooses. He must be from among your own people. Don't appoint over you someone from another country. Don't choose anyone who isn't from one of the tribes of Israel.

[16]The king must not get large numbers of horses for himself. He must not make the people return to Egypt to get more horses. The LORD has told you, "You must not go back there again."

[17]The king must not have a lot of wives. If he does, he will be led down the wrong path. He must not store up large amounts of silver and gold.

[18]When he sits on the throne of his kingdom, he must make himself a copy of the law I'm teaching you. He must write it on a scroll. He must copy it from the scroll of a priest, who is a Levite.

[19]The king must keep the scroll close to him at all times. He must read it all the days of his life. Then he can learn to have respect for the LORD his God. He can carefully follow all of the words of that law and those rules. [20]He won't think of himself as being better than his people are. He won't turn away from the law. He won't turn to the right or the left. Then he and his sons after him will rule over his kingdom in Israel for a long time.

Offerings for Priests and Levites

18 The priests, who are Levites, won't receive any part of the land of Israel. That also applies to the whole tribe of Levi. They will eat the offerings that are made to the LORD with fire. That will be their share. [2]They won't have any part of the land the LORD gave the other tribes in Israel. The LORD himself is their share, just as he promised them.

[3]Anyone who sacrifices a bull or a sheep owes a share of it to the priests. Their share is the shoulder, jaws and inside parts. [4]You must give the priests the first share of the harvest of your grain, olive oil and fresh wine. You must also give them the first wool you clip from your sheep. [5]The LORD your God has chosen the Levites and their sons after them to serve him in his name always. He hasn't chosen priests from any of your other tribes.

[6]Sometimes a Levite will move from the town in Israel where he's living. And he will come to the place the LORD will choose. He'll do it because he really wants to. [7]Then he can serve in the name of the LORD his God. He'll be like all of the other Levites who serve the LORD there. [8]He must have an equal share of the good things they have. That applies even if he has already received money by selling things his family owned.

Practices the LORD Hates

[9]You will enter the land the LORD your God is giving you. When you do, don't copy the practices of the nations that are there. The LORD hates those practices.

[10]Here are things you must not do. Don't sacrifice your children in the fire to other gods. Don't practice any kind of evil magic at all. Don't use magic to try to explain the meaning of warnings in the sky or of any other signs. Don't take part in worshiping evil powers. [11]Don't put a spell on anyone. Don't get messages from those who have died. Don't talk to the spirits of the dead. Don't get advice from the dead.

[12]The LORD your God hates it when anyone does those things. The nations that are in the land he's giving you practice the things he hates. So he will drive out those nations to make room for you. [13]You must be without blame in the sight of the LORD your God.

The Prophet of the LORD

[14]You will take over the nations that are in the land the LORD is giving you. They listen to those who practice all kinds of evil magic. But you belong to the LORD your God. He says you must not do those things.

[15]The LORD your God will raise up for you a prophet like me. He will be one of your own people. You must listen to him. [16]At Mount Horeb you asked the LORD your God for a prophet. You asked him on the day you gathered together. You said, "We don't want to hear the voice of the LORD our God. We don't want to see this great fire anymore. If we do, we'll die."

[17]The LORD said to me, "What they are saying is good. [18]I will raise up for them a prophet like you. He will be one of their own people. I will put my words in his mouth. He will tell them everything I command him to say.

[19]"The prophet will speak in my name. But someone might not listen to what I say through the prophet. Then that person will be accountable to me.

[20]"But suppose a prophet dares to speak in my name something I have not commanded him to say. Or he speaks in the name of other gods. Then that prophet must be put to death."

[21]You will say to yourselves, "How can we know when a message hasn't been spoken by the LORD?" [22]Sometimes a prophet will announce something in the name of the LORD. And it won't take place or come true. Then that's a message the LORD hasn't told him to speak. That prophet has dared to speak on his own authority. So don't be afraid of him or what he says.

Cities to Go to for Safety

19 The LORD your God will destroy the nations whose land he is giving you. You will drive them out. And you will settle down in their towns and houses.

[2]When you do, set apart for yourselves three cities in the land. It's the land the LORD your God is giving you to take as your own. [3]Build roads to

those cities and separate the land into three parts. Then anyone who kills another person can run to one of the cities for safety. They are in the land the Lord your God is giving you as your own.

[4]Here is the rule about a person who kills someone. That person can run to one of those cities for safety. The rule applies to all those who kill a neighbor they didn't hate and didn't mean to kill.

[5]For example, suppose a man goes into a forest with his neighbor to cut wood. When he swings his ax to chop down a tree, the head of the ax flies off. And it hits his neighbor and kills him. Then that man can run to one of those cities and save his life.

[6]If he doesn't go to one of those cities, the dead man's nearest male relative might become very angry. He might chase the man. If the city is too far away, he might catch him and kill him. But he isn't worthy of death, because he didn't hate his neighbor. [7]That's why I command you to set apart for yourselves three cities.

[8]The Lord your God will increase the size of your territory. He took an oath and promised your fathers he would do it. He will give you the whole land he promised them. [9]But he'll do it only if you are careful to obey all of the laws I'm commanding you today. I'm commanding you to love the Lord your God. I want you to live always as he wants you to live.

When he gives you additional land, you must set apart three more cities. [10]Do it so the blood of those who aren't guilty of murder won't be spilled in your land. It's the land the Lord your God is giving you as your own.

[11]But suppose a man hates his neighbor. So he hides and waits for him. Then he attacks him and kills him. And he runs to one of those cities for safety. [12]If he does, the elders of his own town must send for him. He must be brought back from the city and handed over to the dead man's nearest male relative. The relative will kill him.

[13]Don't feel sorry for him. He has killed someone who hadn't done anything wrong. Crimes like that must be punished in Israel. Then things will go well with you.

[14]Don't move your neighbor's boundary stone. It was set up by people who lived there before you. It marks the border of a field in the land you will receive as your own. The Lord your God is giving you that land. You will take it over.

Witnesses

[15]Suppose someone is charged with committing a crime of any kind. Then one witness won't be enough to prove he is guilty. Every matter must be proved by the words of two or three witnesses.

[16]Suppose a witness who tells lies goes to court and brings charges against someone. The witness says that person committed a crime. [17]Then the two people in the case must stand in front of the Lord. They must stand in front of the priests and the judges who are in office at that time. [18]The judges must check out the matter carefully. And suppose the witness is proved to be lying. Then he has given false witness against another Israelite.

[19]So do to the lying witness what he tried to do to the other person. Get rid of that evil person. [20]The rest of the people will hear about it. And they will be afraid. They won't allow such an evil thing to be done among them again.

[21]Don't feel sorry for that evil person. A life must be taken for a life. An eye must be put out for an eye. A tooth must be knocked out for a tooth. A hand must be cut off for a hand and a foot for a foot.

Going to War

20 When you go to war against your enemies, you might see that they have horses and chariots. They might even have an army that is stronger than yours. But don't be afraid of them. The Lord your God will be with you. After all, he brought you up out of Egypt.

[2]Just before you go into battle, the priest will come forward. He'll speak to the army. [3]He'll say, "Men of Israel, listen to me. Today you are going into battle against your enemies. Don't be scared. Don't be afraid. Don't panic. Don't be terrified by them. [4]The Lord your God is going with you. He'll fight for you. He'll help you win the battle over your enemies."

[5]The officers will speak to the army. They will say, "Has anyone built a new house and not started to live in it? Let him go home. If he doesn't, he might die in battle. Then someone else will live in his house. [6]Has anyone planted a vineyard and not started to enjoy it? Let him go home. If he doesn't, he might die in battle. Then someone else will enjoy his vineyard. [7]Has anyone promised to get married to a woman but hasn't done it yet? Let him go home. If he doesn't, he might die in battle. Then someone else will marry her." [8]The officers will continue, "Is any man afraid? Is anyone scared? Let him go home. Then the other men won't lose hope too."

[9]The officers will finish speaking to the army. When they do, they'll appoint commanders over it.

[10]Suppose you march up to attack a city. Before you attack it, offer peace to its people. [11]Suppose they accept your offer and open their gates. Then force all of the people in the city to be your slaves. They will have to work for you.

[12]But suppose they refuse your offer of peace and prepare for battle. Then surround that city. Get ready to attack it. [13]The Lord your God will hand it over to you. When he does, kill all of the men with your swords.

[14]But you can take the women and children for yourselves. You can also take the livestock and everything else in the city. What you have captured from your enemies you can use for yourselves. The Lord your God has given it to you.

[15]That's how you must treat all of the cities that are far away from you. Those cities don't belong to the nations that are nearby.

16 But what about the cities the LORD your God is giving you as your own? Kill everything in those cities that breathes. 17 Completely destroy them. Wipe out the Hittites, Amorites, Canaanites, Perizzites, Hivites and Jebusites. That's what the LORD your God commanded you to do.

18 If you don't destroy them, they'll teach you to follow all of the things the LORD hates. He hates the way they worship their gods. If you do those things, you will sin against the LORD your God.

19 Suppose you surround a city and get ready to attack it. And suppose you fight against it for a long time in order to capture it. Then don't chop its trees down and destroy them. You can eat their fruit. So don't cut them down. The trees of the field aren't people. So why should you attack them?

20 But you can cut down trees that you know aren't fruit trees. You can build war machines out of their wood. You can use them until you capture the city you are fighting against.

What to Do When You Don't Know Who Killed Someone

21 Suppose you find someone who has been killed. The body is lying in a field in the land the LORD your God is giving you to take as your own. But no one knows who the killer was. 2 Then your elders and judges will go out and measure how far it is from the body to the nearby towns.

3 The elders from the town that is nearest to the body will get a young cow. It must never have been used for work. It must never have pulled a load. 4 The elders must lead it down into a valley. The valley must not have been farmed. There must be a stream flowing through it. There in the valley the elders must break the cow's neck.

5 The priests, who are sons of Levi, will step forward. The LORD your God has chosen them to serve him. He wants them to bless the people in his name. He wants them to decide all cases that have to do with people arguing and attacking others.

6 Then all of the elders from the town that is nearest to the body will wash their hands. They will wash them over the young cow whose neck they broke in the valley. 7 They'll say to the LORD, "We didn't kill that person. We didn't see it happen. 8 Accept this payment for the sin of your people Israel. LORD, you have set your people free. Don't hold them guilty for spilling the blood of someone who hasn't done anything wrong." That will pay for the death of that person.

9 So you will get rid of the guilt of killing someone who didn't do anything wrong. That's because you have done what is right in the LORD's eyes.

Getting Married to a Woman Who Is Your Prisoner

10 Suppose you go to war against your enemies. And the LORD your God hands them over to you and you take them as prisoners. 11 Then you notice a beautiful woman among them. If you like her, you can get married to her.

12 Bring her home. Have her shave her head. Have her cut her nails. 13 Have her throw away the clothes she was wearing when she was captured. Let her live in your house and sob over her parents for a full month. Then you can go to her and be her husband. And she will be your wife.

14 But suppose you aren't pleased with her. Then let her go where she wants to. You must not sell her. You must not treat her as a slave. You have already brought shame on her.

The Rights of the Oldest Son

15 Suppose a man has two wives. He loves one but not the other. And both of them have sons by him. But the oldest son is the son of the wife the man doesn't love. 16 Someday he'll leave his property to his sons. When he does, he must not give the rights of the oldest son to the son of the wife he loves. He must give those rights to his oldest son. He must do it even though his oldest son is the son of the wife he doesn't love.

17 He must recognize the full rights of the oldest son, even though that son is the son of the wife he doesn't love. He must give that son a double share of everything he has. That son is the first sign of his father's strength. So the rights of the oldest son belong to him.

A Stubborn Son

18 Suppose someone has a very stubborn son. He doesn't obey his father and mother. And he won't listen to them when they try to correct him. 19 Then his parents will take hold of him and bring him to the elders at the gate of his town. 20 They will say to the elders, "This son of ours is very stubborn. He won't obey us. He wastes his money. He's always getting drunk."

21 Then all of the people in his town will put him to death by throwing stones at him. Get rid of that evil person. All of the people of Israel will hear about it. And they will be afraid to disobey their parents.

Several Other Laws

22 Suppose a man is put to death for a crime that is worthy of death. And a pole is stuck through his body and set up where people can see it. 23 Then you must not leave the body on the pole all night. Make sure you bury it that same day.

Everyone who is hung on a pole is under God's curse. You must not make the land "unclean." The LORD your God is giving it to you as your own.

22 Suppose you see your neighbor's ox or sheep wandering away. Then don't act as if you didn't see it. Instead, make sure you take it back to him.

2 Your neighbor might not live near you. Or you might not know who he is. Then take the animal

home with you. Keep it until he comes looking for it. Then give it back.

[3]Do the same thing if you find his donkey, coat or anything he loses. Don't act as if you didn't see it.

[4]Suppose you see your neighbor's donkey or ox that has fallen down on the road. Then don't act as if you didn't see it. Help him get it up on its feet again.

[5]A woman must not wear men's clothes. And a man must not wear women's clothes. The LORD your God hates it when anyone does that.

[6]Suppose you happen to find a bird's nest beside the road. It might be in a tree or on the ground. And suppose the mother bird is sitting on her little birds or on the eggs. Then don't take the mother along with the little ones. [7]You can take the little ones. But make sure you let the mother go. Then things will go well with you. You will live for a long time.

[8]If you build a new house, put a low wall around the edge of your roof. Then you won't be held accountable if someone falls off your roof and dies.

[9]Don't plant two kinds of seeds in your vineyard. If you do, the crops you grow there will be polluted. Your grapes will also be polluted.

[10]Don't let an ox and a donkey pull the same plow together.

[11]Don't wear clothes made of wool and linen that are woven together.

[12]Make tassels on the four corners of the coat you wear.

Breaking Marriage Laws

[13]Suppose a man gets married to a woman and makes love to her. But then he doesn't like her. [14]So he tells lies about her and says she's a bad woman. He says, "I got married to this woman. But when I made love to her, I discovered she wasn't a virgin." [15]Then the woman's parents must bring proof that she was a virgin. They must give the proof to the elders at the gate of the town.

[16]The woman's father will speak to the elders. He'll say, "I gave my daughter to this man to be his wife. But he doesn't like her. [17]So now he has told lies about her. He has said, 'I discovered that your daughter wasn't a virgin.' But here's the proof that my daughter was a virgin." Then her parents will show the elders of the town the cloth that has her blood on it.

[18]The elders will punish the man. [19]They'll make him weigh out two and a half pounds of silver. They'll give it to the woman's father. That's because the man has said an Israelite virgin is a bad woman. She will continue to be his wife. He must not divorce her as long as he lives.

[20]But suppose the charge is true. And there isn't any proof that the woman was a virgin. [21]Then she must be brought to the door of her father's house. There the people of her town will put her to death by throwing stones at her. She has done a very terrible thing in Israel. She has had sex before she got married. Get rid of that evil person.

[22]Suppose a man is seen having sex with another man's wife. Then the man and the woman must both die. Get rid of those evil people.

[23]Suppose a man happens to see a virgin in a town. And she has promised to get married to another man. But the man who happens to see her has sex with her. [24]Then you must take both of them to the gate of that town. You must put them to death by throwing stones at them. You must kill the woman because she was in a town and didn't scream for help. And you must kill the man because he had sex with another man's wife. Get rid of those evil people.

[25]But suppose a man happens to see a woman out in the country. And she has promised to marry another man. But the man who happens to see her rapes her. Then only the man who has done that will die. [26]Don't do anything to the woman. She hasn't committed a sin that is worthy of death. That case is like the case of someone who attacks and murders his neighbor. [27]The man found the woman out in the country. And she screamed. But there wasn't anyone around who could save her.

[28]Suppose a man happens to see a virgin who hasn't promised to marry another man. And the man who happens to see her rapes her. But someone discovers them. [29]Then the man must weigh out 20 ounces of silver. He must give it to the woman's father. The man must marry the woman, because he raped her. And he can never divorce her as long as he lives.

[30]A man must not get married to his stepmother. He must not bring shame on his father by having sex with her.

Who Can Worship With the LORD's People?

23 No man whose sex organs have been crushed or cut can join in worship with the LORD's people.

[2]No one who was born to a woman who wasn't married can join in worship with the LORD's people. That also applies to the person's children for all time to come.

[3]The people of Ammon and Moab can't join in worship with the LORD's people. That also applies to their children after them for all time to come. [4]The Ammonites and Moabites didn't come to meet you with food and water on your way out of Egypt. They even hired Balaam from Pethor in Aram Naharaim to call down a curse on you. Balaam was the son of Beor. [5]The LORD your God wouldn't listen to Balaam. Instead, he turned the curse into a blessing for you. He did it because he loves you. [6]So don't make a peace treaty with the Ammonites and Moabites as long as you live.

[7]Don't hate the people of Edom. They are your relatives. Don't hate the people of Egypt. After all,

you lived as outsiders in their country. 8The great-grandchildren of the Edomites and Egyptians can join in worship with the LORD's people.

Keep the Camp of the Soldiers Pure and Clean

9There will be times when you are at war with your enemies. And your soldiers will be in camp. Then keep away from anything that isn't pure and clean.

10Suppose semen flows from the body of one of your soldiers during the night. Then that will make him "unclean." He must go outside the camp and stay there. 11But as evening approaches, he must wash himself. When the sun goes down, he can return to the camp.

12Choose a place outside the camp where you can go to the toilet. 13Keep a shovel among your tools. When you go to the toilet, dig a hole. Then cover up your waste.

14The LORD your God walks around in your camp. He's there to keep you safe. He's also there to hand your enemies over to you. So your camp must be holy. Then he won't see anything among you that is shameful. He won't turn away from you.

Several Other Laws

15If a slave comes to you for safety, don't hand him over to his master. 16Let him live among you anywhere he wants to. Let him live in any town he chooses. Don't crush him.

17A man or woman in Israel must not become a temple prostitute. 18The LORD your God hates the money that men and women get for being prostitutes. So don't take that money into the house of the LORD to pay what you promised to give.

19Don't charge your own people any interest. Don't charge them when they borrow money, food or anything else. 20You can charge interest to people from another country. But don't charge your own people. Then the LORD your God will bless you in everything you do. He will bless you in the land you are entering to take as your own.

21Don't put off giving to the LORD your God everything you promise him. He will certainly require it from you. And you will be guilty of committing a sin. 22But if you don't make a promise, you won't be guilty. 23Make sure you do what you promised to do. With your own mouth you made the promise to the LORD your God. No one forced you to do it.

24When you enter your neighbor's vineyard, you can eat all of the grapes you want. But don't put any of them in your basket. 25When you enter your neighbor's field, you can pick heads of grain. But don't cut down his standing grain.

24 Suppose a man gets married to a woman. But later he decides he doesn't like her. He finds something shameful about her. So he gives her a letter of divorce and sends her away from his house. 2Then after she leaves his house she becomes another man's wife. 3But her second husband doesn't like her either. So he gives her a letter of divorce and sends her away from his house. Or perhaps he dies. 4Then her first husband isn't allowed to marry her again. The LORD would hate that. When her first husband divorced her, she became "unclean." Don't bring sin on the land the LORD your God is giving you as your own.

5Suppose a man has just gotten married. Then don't send him into battle. Don't give him any other duty either. He's free to stay home for one year. He needs time to make his new wife happy.

6Someone might borrow money from you and give you two millstones to keep until you are paid back. Don't keep them. Don't even keep the upper one. That person depends on the millstones to make a living.

7Suppose a man is caught kidnapping another Israelite. And he sells or treats that person as a slave. Then the kidnapper must die. Get rid of that evil person.

8What about skin diseases? Be very careful to do exactly what the priests, who are Levites, tell you to do. You must be careful to follow the commands I've given them. 9Remember what the LORD your God did to Miriam on your way out of Egypt.

10Suppose your neighbor borrows something from you. And he offers you something to keep until you get paid back. Then don't go into his house to get it. 11Stay outside. Let the man bring it out to you.

12He might be poor. You might be given his coat to keep until you get paid back. Don't go to sleep while you still have it. 13Return it before the sun goes down. He needs it to sleep in and will thank you for returning it. The LORD your God will see it and know that you have done the right thing.

14Don't take advantage of any hired worker who is poor and needy. That applies to your own people. It also applies to outsiders who are living in one of your towns. 15Give them their pay every day. They are poor and are counting on it. If you don't pay them, they might cry out to the LORD against you. Then you will be guilty of committing a sin.

16Parents must not be put to death because of what their children do. And children must not be put to death because of what their parents do. People must die because of their own sins.

17Do what is right and fair for outsiders and for children whose fathers have died. Suppose a widow borrows something from you. And she offers to give you her coat until she pays you back. Don't take it.

18Remember that you were slaves in Egypt. Remember that the LORD your God set you free from there. That's why I'm commanding you to do those things.

19When you are gathering crops in your field, you might leave some grain behind by mistake. Don't go back to get it. Leave it for outsiders and widows. Leave it for children whose fathers have died. Then the LORD your God will bless you in everything you do.

20When you knock olives off your trees, don't go back over the branches a second time. Leave what remains for outsiders and widows. Leave it for children whose fathers have died. 21When you pick grapes in your vineyard, don't go back over the vines a second time. Leave what remains for outsiders and widows. Leave it for children whose fathers have died.

22Remember that you were slaves in Egypt. That's why I'm commanding you to do those things.

25 Suppose two men don't agree about something. Then they must take their case to court. The judges will decide the case. They will let the one who isn't guilty go free. And they will punish the one who is guilty.

2The guilty one might have done something that's worthy of a beating. Then the judge will make him lie down and be beaten with a whip right there in court. The number of strokes should fit the crime. 3But the judge must not give the guilty man more than 40 strokes. If more than that are used, you will look down on your Israelite neighbor.

4Don't stop an ox from eating while you use it to separate grain from straw.

5Suppose two brothers are living near each other. And one of them dies without having a son. Then his widow must not get married to anyone outside the family. Her husband's brother should marry her. That's what a brother-in-law is supposed to do. 6Her first baby boy will be named after her first husband. Then the dead man's name will not be wiped out in Israel.

7But suppose the man doesn't want to get married to his brother's wife. Then she will go to the elders at the gate of the town. She will say, "My husband's brother refuses to keep his brother's name alive in Israel. He won't do for me what a brother-in-law is supposed to do."

8Then the elders in his town will send for him. They will talk to him. But he still might say, "I don't want to marry her." 9Then his brother's widow will go up to him in front of the elders. She'll pull one of his sandals off his foot. She'll spit in his face. And she'll say, "That's what we do to a man who won't build up his brother's family line." 10That man's family line will be known in Israel as The Family of the Man Whose Sandal Was Pulled Off.

11Suppose two men are fighting. And the wife of one of them comes to save her husband from his attacker. So she reaches out and grabs hold of his sex organs. 12Then you must cut off her hand. Don't feel sorry for her.

13Don't have two different scales. You must not have one that weighs things heavier than they really are and another that weighs them lighter than they are. 14And don't have two different sets of measures. You must not have one set that measures things larger than they really are and another that measures them smaller than they are. 15You must use weights and measures that are honest and exact. Then you will live a long time in the land the LORD your God is giving you. 16He hates anyone who cheats.

17Remember what the Amalekites did to you on your way out of Egypt. 18You were tired and worn out. They met you on your journey. They attacked everyone who was lagging behind. They didn't have any respect for God. 19The LORD your God will give you peace and rest from all of the enemies who are around you. He'll do it in the land he's giving you to take over as your very own. Then you will wipe out the memory of the Amalekites from the earth. Don't forget to do it!

Give the LORD His Share

26 You will enter the land the LORD your God is giving you as your own. You will take it over. You will settle down in it. 2When you do, get some of the first share of everything your soil produces. Put it in a basket. It's from the land the LORD your God is giving you. Take your gifts and go to the special place he will choose. He will put his Name there.

3Speak to the priest who is in office at that time. Tell him, "I announce today to the LORD your God that I have come to this land. It's the land he promised with an oath to our fathers to give us." 4The priest will take the basket from you. He'll set it down in front of the altar of the LORD your God.

5Then you will speak while the LORD is listening. You will say, "My father Jacob was a wanderer from the land of Aram. He went down into Egypt with a few people. He lived there and became the father of a great nation. It had huge numbers of people.

6"But the people of Egypt treated us badly. They made us suffer. They made us work very hard. 7Then we cried out to the LORD. He is the God of our people who lived long ago. He heard our voice. He saw how much we were suffering. The Egyptians were crushing us. They were making us work very hard.

8"So the LORD reached out his mighty hand and powerful arm and brought us out of Egypt. He did great and wonderful things. He did miraculous signs and wonders. 9He brought us to this place. He gave us this land. It's a land that has plenty of milk and honey.

10"Now, LORD, I'm bringing you the first share of crops from the soil. After all, you have given them to me." Place the basket in front of the LORD your God. Bow down to him.

11You and the Levites and the outsiders among you will be full of joy. You will enjoy all of the good things the LORD your God has given to you and your family.

12 You will set apart a tenth of everything you
produce in the third year. That's the year for giving the tenth to people who have special needs.
You will give it to the Levites, outsiders and widows. You will also give it to children whose fathers
have died. Then all of them will have plenty to eat
in your towns.
13 Speak to the LORD your God. Say to him, "I
have taken your sacred share from my house. I
have given it to the Levites, outsiders and widows.
I have also given it to children whose fathers have
died. I've done everything you commanded me to
do. I haven't turned away from your commands. I
haven't forgotten any of them. 14 I haven't eaten
any part of your sacred share while I was sobbing
over someone who had died. I haven't taken any of
it from my house while I was 'unclean.' And I
haven't offered any of it to the dead. LORD my
God, I've obeyed you. I've done everything you
commanded me to do.
15 "Look down from the holy place where you
live in heaven. Bless your people Israel. Bless the
land you have given us. It's the land you promised
with an oath to give to our fathers. It's a land that
has plenty of milk and honey."

Follow the LORD's Commands

16 This very day the LORD your God commands
you to follow all of those rules and laws. Be careful to obey them with all your heart and with all
your soul.
17 Today you have announced that the LORD is
your God. You have said you would live exactly
as he wants you to live. You have agreed to keep
his rules, commands and laws. And you have said
you would obey him.
18 Today the LORD has announced that you are his
people. He has said that you are his special treasure.
He promised that you would be. He has told you to
keep all of his commands. 19 He has announced that
he will make you famous. He'll give you more
praise and honor than all of the other nations he has
made. And he has said that you will be a holy
nation. The LORD your God has set you apart for
himself. That's exactly what he promised to do.

The Altar on Mount Ebal

27 The elders of Israel and I gave commands
to the people. We said, "Obey all of the
commands we're giving you today.
2 "You will go across the Jordan River. You will
enter the land the LORD your God is giving you.
When you do, set up some large stones. Put a coat
of plaster on them. 3 Write all of the words of this
law on them. Do it when you have crossed over
into the land the LORD your God is giving you. It's
a land that has plenty of milk and honey. The LORD
is the God of your fathers. He promised you that
you would enter the land. 4 After you have gone
across the Jordan, set up those stones on Mount
Ebal. Put a coat of plaster on them. We're commanding you today to do that.
5 "Build an altar there to honor the LORD your
God. Make it out of stones. Don't use any iron tool
on them. 6 Use stones you find in the fields to build
his altar. Then offer burnt offerings on it to the
LORD your God. 7 Sacrifice friendship offerings
there. Eat them and be filled with joy in the sight
of the LORD your God.
8 "You must write all of the words of this law on
the stones you have set up. Write the words very
clearly."

Curses for Not Obeying the LORD

9 Then the priests, who are Levites, and I spoke
to all of the people of Israel. We said, "Israel, be
quiet! Listen! You have now become the people of
the LORD your God. 10 Obey him. Follow his commands and rules that we're giving you today."
11 Here are the commands I gave the people that
very day.
12 You will go across the Jordan River. When
you do, I want six tribes to stand on Mount Gerizim to bless the people. Those tribes are Simeon,
Levi, Judah, Issachar, Joseph and Benjamin. 13 I
want the other six tribes to stand on Mount Ebal
to announce some curses. Those tribes are Reuben,
Gad, Asher, Zebulun, Dan and Naphtali.
14 The Levites will speak to all of the people of
Israel in a loud voice. They will say,

15 "May any man who makes a wooden or metal
statue of a god and sets it up in secret be under the
LORD's curse. That statue is made by a skilled
worker. And the LORD hates it."
Then all of the people will say, "Amen!"
16 "May anyone who brings shame on his father
or mother be under the LORD's curse."
Then all of the people will say, "Amen!"
17 "May anyone who moves his neighbor's
boundary stone be under the LORD's curse."
Then all of the people will say, "Amen!"
18 "May anyone who leads blind people down
the wrong road be under the LORD's curse."
Then all of the people will say, "Amen!"
19 "May anyone who isn't fair in the way he
treats outsiders, widows, and children whose
fathers have died be under the LORD's curse."
Then all of the people will say, "Amen!"
20 "May any man who has sex with his stepmother be under the LORD's curse. That man
brings shame on his father by doing that."
Then all of the people will say, "Amen!"
21 "May anyone who has sex with animals be
under the LORD's curse."
Then all of the people will say, "Amen!"
22 "May any man who has sex with his sister be
under the LORD's curse. It doesn't matter whether
she is his full sister or his half sister."
Then all of the people will say, "Amen!"
23 "May any man who has sex with his mother-
in-law be under the LORD's curse."
Then all of the people will say, "Amen!"

24"May anyone who kills his neighbor secretly be under the LORD's curse."

Then all of the people will say, "Amen!"

25"May anyone who accepts money to kill someone who isn't guilty of doing anything wrong be under the LORD's curse."

Then all of the people will say, "Amen!"

26"May anyone who doesn't honor the words of this law by obeying them be under the LORD's curse."

Then all of the people will say, "Amen!"

Blessings for Obeying the LORD

28 Make sure you obey the LORD your God completely. Be careful to follow all of his commands. I'm giving them to you today. If you do those things, the LORD will honor you more than all of the other nations on earth. 2If you obey the LORD your God, here are the blessings that will come to you and remain with you.

3You will be blessed in the cities. You will be blessed out in the country.

4Your children will be blessed. Your crops will be blessed. The young animals among your livestock will be blessed. That includes your calves and lambs.

5Your baskets and bread pans will be blessed.

6You will be blessed no matter where you go.

7Enemies will rise up against you. But the LORD will help you win the battle over them. They will come at you from one direction. But they'll run away from you in seven directions.

8The LORD your God will bless your barns with plenty of grain and other food. He will bless everything you do. He'll bless you in the land he's giving you.

9The LORD your God will make you his holy people. He will set you apart for himself. He took an oath and promised to do that. He promised to do it if you would keep his commands and live exactly as he wants you to live. 10All of the nations on earth will see that you belong to the LORD. And they will be afraid of you.

11The LORD will give you more than you need. You will have many children. Your livestock will have many little ones. Your crops will do very well. All of that will happen in the land he promised with an oath to your fathers to give you.

12The LORD will open up the heavens. That's where he stores his riches. He will send rain on your land at just the right time. He'll bless everything you do. You will lend money to many nations. But you won't have to borrow from any of them. 13The LORD your God will make you leaders, not followers.

Pay attention to his commands that I'm giving you today. Be careful to follow them. Then you will always be on top. You will never be on the bottom.

14Don't turn away from any of the commands I'm giving you today. Don't turn to the right or the left. Don't follow other gods. Don't worship them.

More Curses for Not Obeying the LORD

15But suppose you don't obey the LORD your God. And you aren't careful to follow all of his commands and rules I'm giving you today. Then he will send curses on you. They'll catch up with you. Here are those curses.

16You will be cursed in the cities. You will be cursed out in the country.

17Your baskets and bread pans will be cursed.

18Your children will be cursed. Your crops will be cursed. Your calves and lambs will be cursed.

19You will be cursed no matter where you go.

20The LORD will send curses on you. You won't know what's going on. In everything you do, he will be angry with you. You will be destroyed suddenly and completely. That will happen because you did an evil thing when you deserted the LORD.

21He will send all kinds of sicknesses on you. He'll send them until he has destroyed you. He'll remove you from the land you are entering to take as your own. 22The LORD will make you sick and very weak. He will strike you with fever and swelling. He'll send burning heat. There won't be any rain. The hot winds will completely dry up your crops. All of those things will happen until you die.

23The sky above you will be like bronze. The ground beneath you will be like iron. 24The LORD will turn the rain of your country into dust and powder. It will come down from the skies until you are destroyed.

25The LORD will help your enemies win the battle over you. You will come at them from one direction. But you will run away from them in seven directions. You will look so bad that all of the kingdoms on earth will be completely shocked when they see you. 26Birds and wild animals will eat up your dead bodies. There won't be anyone left to scare them away.

27The LORD will send boils on you, just like the ones he sent on the Egyptians. You will have growths in your bodies and boils on your skin. You will itch all over. No one will be able to heal you.

28The LORD will make you lose your mind. He will make you blind. You won't know what's going on. 29Even at noon you will have to feel your way around like a blind person in the dark. You won't have success in anything you do. Day after day you will be robbed and beaten down. No one will be able to save you.

30You and a woman will promise to get married to each other. But another man will take her and rape her. You will build a house. But you won't live in it. You will plant a vineyard. But you won't eat a single grape from it. 31Your ox will be killed right in front of your eyes. But you won't eat any of it. Your donkey will be taken away from you by force. And you will never get it back. Your sheep will be given to your enemies. No one will be able to save them.

32Your children will be given to another nation. Day after day you will watch for them to come back. But you will only wear out your eyes. You won't be able to help your children.

33A nation you don't know anything about will eat what you work to produce on your land. You will be completely beaten down as long as you live. 34The things you see will make you lose your mind. 35The LORD will send painful boils on your knees and legs. No one will be able to heal them. They will cover you from head to toe.

36The LORD will drive you out of the land. And he will drive out the king you place over you. All of you will go to a nation you and your people long ago didn't know anything about. There you will worship other gods. They will be made out of wood and stone. 37You will look very bad to all of the nations where the LORD sends you. They will be completely shocked when they see you. They will laugh at you and make fun of you.

38You will plant many seeds in your field. But you will gather very little food. Locusts will eat it up. 39You will plant vineyards and take care of them. But you won't drink the wine. You won't gather the grapes. Worms will eat them up. 40You will have olive trees through your whole country. But you won't use the oil. The olives will drop off the trees. 41You will have children. But you won't be able to keep them. They'll be taken away as prisoners. 42Large numbers of locusts will eat up the leaves on all of your trees. They will also eat up the crops on your land.

43Outsiders who live among you will become your leaders. They will rise higher and higher. But you will sink lower and lower. 44They will lend money to you. But you won't be able to lend money to them. They will be the leaders. But you will be the followers.

45The LORD your God will send all of those curses on you. They will follow you everywhere. They'll catch up with you. You will be under the LORD's curse until you are destroyed. That's because you didn't obey him. You didn't keep the commands and rules he gave you. 46Those curses will remain as miraculous signs and wonders against you and your children after you forever.

47You didn't serve the LORD your God with joy and gladness when times were good. 48So he will send enemies against you. You will have to serve them. You will be hungry and thirsty. You will be naked and poor. The LORD will put the iron chains of slavery around your necks until he has destroyed you.

49The LORD will bring a nation against you from far away. It will come from the ends of the earth. It will dive down on you like an eagle. You won't understand that nation's language. 50Its people will look mean. They won't have any respect for old people. They won't show any kindness to young people.

51They will eat up the young animals among your livestock. They'll eat up the crops on your land. They'll destroy you. They won't leave you any grain, olive oil or fresh wine. They won't leave you any calves or lambs. They'll destroy you. 52They'll surround all of the cities through your whole land. They'll get ready to attack them. They'll do those things until the high, strong walls you trust in fall down. That's what will happen to the cities in the land the LORD your God is giving you.

53Your enemies will surround you and get ready to attack you. They will make you suffer greatly. So you will eat your own children. You will eat the dead bodies of the sons and daughters the LORD your God has given you.

54There may be a gentle and caring man among you. But he will treat his own brother badly. He'll be just as mean to the wife he loves and to any of his children who are still alive. 55He won't give to a single one of them any part of the dead bodies of his children that he's eating. It will be all he has left to eat. That's how much your enemies will make you suffer when they surround all of your cities to attack them.

56There may be a gentle and caring woman among you. She wouldn't even touch the ground with her feet without first putting her sandals on. But she will not share anything with the husband she loves. She won't share with her own children either. 57She will eat what comes out of her body after she has a baby. Then she'll even eat her baby. She won't share it with anyone in her family. She'll plan to eat it in secret. There won't be anything else for her to eat because the city she lives in will be surrounded. That's an example of how much your enemies will make you suffer when they are getting ready to attack your cities.

58Be careful to follow all of the words of this law. They are written in this scroll. Have respect for the glorious and wonderful name of the LORD your God. If you don't, 59he will send terrible plagues on you and your children after you. He'll send horrible and lasting troubles. He'll make you very sick for a long time. 60He'll bring on you all of the sicknesses you were afraid of getting when you were in Egypt. You won't be able to get rid of them. 61The LORD will also bring on you all of the other kinds of sickness and trouble I haven't written down in this Scroll of the Law. You will be destroyed.

62At one time you were as many as the stars in the sky. But there will only be a few of you left. That's because you didn't obey the LORD your God. 63It pleased the LORD to give you success and to increase your numbers. But it will please him just as much to wipe you out and destroy you. You will be removed from the land you are entering to take as your own.

[64]Then the LORD will scatter you among all of the nations. He'll spread you around from one end of the earth to the other. There you will worship statues of gods that are made out of wood and stone. You and your people long ago hadn't known anything about those gods.

[65]Among those nations you won't find any peace. There won't be any place where you can settle down and rest your feet. There the LORD will give you minds that are filled with worry. He'll give you eyes that are worn out from sobbing. Your hearts won't have any hope.

[66]Your lives will always be in danger. You will be filled with fear night and day. You will never be sure you are safe. [67]In the morning you will say, "We wish it were evening!" In the evening you will say, "We wish it were morning!" Your hearts will be filled with fear. The things you see will terrify you.

[68]The LORD will send you back to Egypt in ships. He'll send you on a journey I said you should never have to make again. You will offer to sell yourselves to your enemies as slaves in Egypt. But no one will buy you.

Follow the Terms of the Covenant

29 These are the terms of the covenant the LORD commanded me to make with the people of Israel in Moab. The terms were added to the covenant he had made with them at Mount Horeb.

[2]I sent for all of the Israelites. Here is what I said to them.

With your own eyes you have seen everything the LORD did in Egypt to Pharaoh. You have seen what he did to all of Pharaoh's officials and to his whole land. [3]With your own eyes you saw how the LORD really made them suffer. You saw his miraculous signs and great wonders.

[4]But to this very day the LORD hasn't given you a mind that understands. He hasn't given you eyes that see. He hasn't given you ears that hear.

[5]He led you through the desert for 40 years. During that time your clothes didn't wear out. The sandals on your feet didn't wear out either. [6]You didn't eat any bread. You didn't drink any kind of wine. The LORD did all of those things because he wanted you to know that he is the LORD your God.

[7]When we got here, Sihon and Og came out to fight against us. Sihon was the king of Heshbon. And Og was the king of Bashan. But we won the battle over them. [8]We took their land. We gave it to the tribes of Reuben and Gad and half of the tribe of Manasseh as their share.

[9]Be careful to obey the terms of this covenant. Then you will have success in everything you do.

[10]Today all of you are standing here in the sight of the LORD your God. Your leaders and chief men are here. Your elders and officials are here. So are all of the other men of Israel. [11]Your children and wives are here with you too. So are the outsiders who are living in your camps. They chop your wood and carry your water.

[12]All of you are standing here in order to enter into a covenant with the LORD your God. He is making the covenant with you today. He's sealing it with an oath. [13]Today he wants to show you that you are his people and that he is your God. That's what he promised with an oath to your fathers. He promised it to Abraham, Isaac and Jacob.

[14]I'm making this covenant. I'm sealing it with an oath. I'm not making it only with you [15]who are standing here with us today in the sight of the LORD our God. I'm also making it with those who aren't here today.

[16]You yourselves know how we lived in Egypt. You also know how we passed through other countries on the way here. [17]You saw the statues of their gods that were made out of wood, stone, silver and gold. The LORD hates those statues.

[18]Make sure there isn't a man or woman among your families or tribes who turns away from the LORD our God. No one must worship the gods of those nations. Make sure that kind of worship doesn't spread like bitter poison through your whole community.

[19]Some people who worship those gods will hear the oath that seals the covenant I'm making. They think they can escape trouble by saying to themselves, "We'll be safe, even though we're stubborn and go our own way." But trouble will come on them everywhere in the land.

[20]The LORD will never be willing to forgive those people. His burning anger will blaze out against them. All of the curses I've written down in this scroll will fall on them. And the LORD will wipe out their names from the earth. [21]He will find those people in all of the tribes of Israel and give them nothing but trouble. That will be in keeping with all of the curses of the covenant. They are written down in this Scroll of the Law.

[22]Even your children's children will see the troubles that have fallen on the land. They'll see the sicknesses the LORD has brought on it. People who come from countries far away will also see those things.

[23]The whole land will be burned up. Nothing but salt and sulfur will be left. Nothing will be planted there. Nothing will grow there. In fact, nothing will even start to grow there. The land will be like Sodom, Gomorrah, Admah and Zeboiim after they were destroyed. The LORD wiped out those cities because he was very angry.

[24]All of the nations will ask, "Why has the LORD done this to the land? What could have made him so very angry?"

[25]And they will hear the answer, "It's because the people who are living there have broken the covenant of the LORD. He's the God of their parents. He made that covenant with them when

he brought them out of Egypt. 26They went off and
worshiped other gods. They bowed down to them.
They hadn't known anything about those gods
before. The LORD hadn't given those gods to them.
27"So the LORD's anger burned against the land.
He brought on it all of the curses that are written
down in this scroll. 28The LORD's anger blazed out
against his people. So he pulled them up out of
their land. He threw them into another land. And
that's where they are now."
29The LORD our God keeps certain things hidden. But he makes other things known to us and
our children forever. He does it so we can obey all
of the words of this law.

The LORD Will Bless His People

30 I have told you about all of those blessings
and curses. The LORD will bring them on
you. Then you will think carefully about them
everywhere the LORD your God scatters you
among the nations. 2You and your children will
return to the LORD your God. You will obey him
with all your heart and with all your soul. That will
be in keeping with everything I'm commanding
you today.
3When all of that happens, the LORD your God
will bless you with great success again. He will be
very kind to you. He'll bring you back from all of
the nations where he scattered you. 4Suppose you
have been forced to go away to the farthest land
on earth. The LORD your God will bring you back
even from there.
5He will bring you to the land that belonged to
your people long ago. You will take it over. He'll
make you better off than your people were. He'll
increase your numbers more than he increased
theirs. 6The LORD your God will keep your hearts
from being stubborn. He'll do the same thing for
your children and their children. Then you will
love him with all your heart and with all your soul.
And you will live.
7The LORD your God will put all of those curses
on your enemies. They hated you and hunted you
down.
8You will obey the LORD again. You will follow
all of his commands that I'm giving you today.
9Then the LORD your God will give you great success in everything you do. You will have many
children. Your livestock will have many little ones.
Your crops will do very well. The LORD will take
delight in you again. He'll give you success. That's
what he did for your people long ago.
10But you must obey the LORD your God. You
must keep his commands and rules. They are written in this Scroll of the Law. You must turn to the
LORD your God with all your heart and with all
your soul.

Choose Life

11What I'm commanding you today is not too
hard for you. It isn't beyond your reach. 12It isn't
up in heaven. So you don't have to ask, "Who will
go up into heaven to get it? Who will announce it
to us so we can obey it?" 13And it isn't beyond the
ocean. So you don't have to ask, "Who will go
across the ocean to get it? Who will announce it to
us so we can obey it?"
14No, the message isn't far away at all. In fact,
it's really near you. It's in your mouth and in your
heart so that you can obey it.
15Today I'm giving you a choice. You can have
life and success. Or you can have death and harm.
16I'm commanding you today to love the LORD your
God. I'm commanding you to live exactly as he
wants you to live. You must obey his commands,
rules and laws. Then you will live. Your numbers
will increase. The LORD your God will bless you in
the land you are entering to take as your own.
17Don't let your hearts turn away from the
LORD. Instead, obey him. Don't let yourselves be
drawn away to other gods. And don't bow down
to them and worship them. 18If you do, I announce
to you this very day that you will certainly be
destroyed. You are about to go across the Jordan
River and take over the land. But you won't live
there very long.
19I'm calling for heaven and earth to give witness against you this very day. I'm offering you the
choice of life or death. You can choose either blessings or curses. But I want you to choose life. Then
you and your children will live. 20And you will love
the LORD your God. You will obey him. You will
remain true to him. The LORD is your very life. He
will give you many years in the land. He took an
oath. He promised to give that land to your fathers.
He promised it to Abraham, Isaac and Jacob.

Joshua Becomes the New Leader

31 Here are the words I spoke to all of the
people of Israel. 2I said, "I am now 120
years old. I'm not able to lead you anymore. The
LORD has said to me, 'You will not go across the
Jordan River.'
3"The LORD your God himself will go across
ahead of you. He'll destroy the nations that are
there in order to make room for you. You will take
over their land. Joshua will also go across ahead
of you, just as the LORD said he would.
4"The LORD will do to those nations what he did
to Sihon and Og. He destroyed those Amorite
kings along with their land. 5The LORD will hand
those nations over to you. Then you must do to
them everything I've commanded you to do.
6"Be strong and brave. Don't be afraid of them.
Don't be terrified because of them. The LORD your
God will go with you. He will never leave you.
He'll never desert you."
7Then I sent for Joshua. I spoke to him in front
of all of the people of Israel. I said, "Be strong and
brave. You must go with these people. They are
going into the land the LORD promised with an
oath to give to their fathers. You must divide it up

among them. They will each receive their share.
8The LORD himself will go ahead of you. He will
be with you. He will never leave you. He'll never
desert you. So don't be afraid. Don't lose hope."

The Law Must Be Read

9I wrote down that law. I gave it to the priests,
who are sons of Levi. They carried the ark of the
covenant of the LORD. I also gave the law to all of
the elders of Israel.
10Then I commanded them, "You must read this
law at the end of every seven years. Do it in the
year when you forgive people what they owe.
Read it during the Feast of Booths. 11That's when
all of the people of Israel come to appear in front
of the LORD your God at the holy tent. It will be at
the place he will choose. You must read this law
to them.
12"Gather the people together. Gather the men,
women and children. Also bring together the outsiders who are living in your towns. Then they can
listen and learn to have respect for the LORD your
God. And they'll be careful to obey all of the
words of this law. 13Their children must hear it
read too. They don't know this law yet. They too
must learn to have respect for the LORD your God.
They must respect him as long as you live in the
land. You are about to go across the Jordan River
and take that land as your very own."

Israel Will Refuse to Obey the LORD

14The LORD spoke to me. He said, "The day
when you will die is near. Have Joshua go to the
Tent of Meeting. Join him there. That is where I
will appoint him as the new leader." So Joshua and
I went to the Tent of Meeting.
15Then the LORD appeared at the tent in a pillar
of cloud. It stood over the entrance to the tent.
16The LORD spoke to me. He said, "You are going
to join the members of your family who have
already died. The people will not be faithful to me.
They will soon join themselves to the strange gods
that are worshiped in the land they are entering.
The people will desert me. They will break the
covenant I made with them.
17"On that day I will become angry with them.
I will desert them. I will turn my face away from
them. And they will be destroyed. Many horrible
troubles and hard times will come on them. On
that day they will say, 'Trouble has come on us.
Our God isn't with us!'
18"I will certainly turn away from them on that
day. I will do it because they did a very evil thing
when they turned to other gods.
19"I want you to write down a song for yourselves. Teach it to the people of Israel. Have them
sing it. It will be my witness against them.
20"I will bring them into a land that has plenty
of milk and honey. I promised the land to their
fathers. I took an oath when I promised it. In that
land they will eat until they have had enough.
They will get fat. When they do, they will turn to
other gods and worship them. They will turn their
backs on me. They will break my covenant.
21"Many horrible troubles and hard times will
come on them. Then the song I am giving you will
be a witness against them. That is because the song
will not be forgotten by their children and their
children's children. I know what they are likely to
do. I know it even before I bring them into the land
I promised them with an oath."
22So that day I wrote the song down. And I
taught it to the people of Israel.
23The LORD gave a command to Joshua, the son
of Nun. He said, "Be strong and brave. You will
bring the Israelites into the land I promised them
with an oath. I myself will be with you."
24I finished writing the words of that law in a
scroll. I wrote them down from beginning to end.
25Then I gave a command to the Levites who
carried the ark of the covenant of the LORD. I said,
26"Take this Scroll of the Law. Place it beside the
ark of the covenant of the LORD your God. It will
remain there as a witness against you. 27I know
how you refuse to obey the LORD. I know how
stubborn you are. You have refused to obey him
while I've been living among you. So you will certainly refuse to obey him after I'm dead!
28Gather together all of the elders of your tribes
and all of your officials. Bring them to me. Then I
can speak these words to them. I can call for
heaven and earth to give witness against them. 29I
know that after I'm dead you will certainly
become very sinful. You will turn away from the
path I've commanded you to take. In days to
come, trouble will fall on you. That's because you
will do what is evil in the sight of the LORD. You
will make him very angry because of the statues
of gods your hands have made."

The Song of Moses

30I spoke the words of this song from beginning
to end. The whole community of Israel heard
them. Here is what I said.

32 Heavens, listen to me. Then I will speak.
Earth, hear the words of my mouth.
2 Let my teaching fall like rain.
Let my words come down like dew.
Let them be like raindrops on new grass.
Let them be like rain on tender plants.

3 I will make known the name of the LORD.
Praise God! How great he is!
4 He is the Rock. His works are perfect.
All of his ways are right.
He is faithful. He doesn't do anything wrong.
He is honest and fair.

5 Israel, you have sinned against him very much.
It's too bad for you that you aren't his
children anymore.
You have become a twisted and evil nation.

[6] Is that how you thank the LORD?
You aren't wise. You are foolish.
Remember, he's your Father. He's your Creator.
He made you. He formed you.
[7] Remember the days of old.
Think about what the LORD did through those many years.
Ask your father. He will tell you.
Ask your elders. They'll explain it to you.
[8] The Most High God gave the nations their lands.
He divided up the human race.
He set up borders for the nations.
He did it based on the number of the sons of Israel.
[9] The LORD's people are his share.
Jacob is the nation he has received.
[10] The LORD found Israel in a desert land.
He found them in an empty and windy wasteland.
He took care of them and kept them safe.
He guarded them as he would guard his own eyes.
[11] He was like an eagle that stirs up its nest.
It hovers over its little ones.
It spreads out its wings to catch them.
It carries them on its feathers.
[12] The LORD was the only one who led Israel.
No other god was with them.
[13] The LORD made them ride on the highest places in the land.
He fed them what grew in the fields.
He gave them the sweetest honey.
He fed them olive oil from a rocky hillside.
[14] He gave them butter and milk from the herds and flocks.
He fed them the fattest lambs and goats.
He gave them the best of Bashan's rams.
He fed them the finest wheat.
They drank the bubbling red juice of grapes.
[15] When Israel grew fat, they became stubborn.
When they were filled with food, they became fat and heavy.
They left the God who made them.
They turned away from the Rock who saved them.
[16] They made him jealous by serving strange gods.
They made him angry by worshiping statues of gods.
He hated those gods.
[17] The people sacrificed to demons, not to God.
The demons were gods they hadn't known anything about.
Those gods were new to them.
Their people long ago didn't worship them.
[18] But then they deserted the Rock. He was their Father.
They forgot the God who created them.

[19] When the LORD saw that, he turned away from them.
His sons and daughters made him angry.
[20] "I will turn my face away from them," he said.
"I will see what will happen to them in the end.
They are sinful people.
They are unfaithful children.
[21] They made me jealous by serving what is not even a god.
They made me angry by worshiping worthless statues of gods.
I will use people who are not a nation to make them jealous.
I will use a nation that has no understanding to make them angry.
[22] My anger has started a fire.
It burns down to the kingdom of the dead.
It will eat up the earth and its crops.
It will set the base of the mountains on fire.

[23] "I will pile troubles on my people.
I will shoot all of my arrows at them.
[24] I will send them hunger. It will make them weak.
I will send terrible sickness. I will send deadly plagues.
I will send wild animals that will tear them apart.
Snakes that glide through the dust will bite them.
[25] In the streets their children will be killed with swords.
Their homes will be filled with terror.
Young men and women will die.
Babies and old people will die.
[26] I said I would scatter them.
I said I would wipe them from human memory.
[27] But I was afraid their enemies would make fun of that.
I was afraid their attackers would not understand.
I was sure they would say, 'We're the ones who've beaten them!
The LORD isn't the one who did it.'"
[28] Israel is a nation that doesn't have any sense.
They can't understand anything.
[29] I wish they were wise. Then they would understand what's coming.
They'd realize what would happen to them in the end.
[30] How could one person chase a thousand?
How could two make ten thousand run away?
It couldn't happen unless their Rock had deserted them.
It couldn't take place unless the LORD had given them up.
[31] Their rock is not like our Rock.
Even our enemies know that.

32 Their vine comes from the vines of Sodom.
It comes from the vineyards of Gomorrah.
Their grapes are filled with poison.
Their bunches of grapes taste bitter.
33 Their wine is like the poison of snakes.
It's like the deadly poison of cobras.

34 The LORD says, "I have kept all of those terrible things stored away.
I have kept them sealed up in my strongbox.
35 I punish people. I will pay them back.
The time will come when their feet will slip.
Their day of trouble is near.
Very soon they will be destroyed."

36 The LORD will judge his people.
He'll show tender love to those who serve him.
He will know when their strength is gone.
He'll see that no one at all is left.
37 He'll say, "Where are their gods now?
Where is the rock they went to for safety?
38 Where are the gods who ate the fat of their sacrifices?
Where are the gods who drank the wine of their drink offerings?
Let them rise up to help you!
Let them keep you safe!

39 "Look! I am the One!
There is no other God except me.
I put some people to death. I bring others to life.
I have wounded, and I will heal.
No one can save you from my powerful hand.
40 I raise my hand to heaven. Here is the oath I take.
You can be sure that I live forever.
41 And you can be just as sure
that I will sharpen my flashing sword.
My hand will hold it when I judge.
I will get even with my enemies.
I will pay back those who hate me.
42 I will make my arrows drip with blood.
My sword will destroy people.
It will kill some. It will even kill prisoners.
It will cut off the heads of enemy leaders."

43 You nations, be full of joy. Be joyful together with God's people.
The LORD will get even with his enemies.
He will pay them back for killing those who serve him.
He will wipe away the sin of his land and people.

44 I spoke all of the words of that song to the
people. Joshua, the son of Nun, was with me. 45 I
finished speaking all of those words to all of the
people of Israel.

46 Then I said to the people, "Think carefully
about all of the words I have announced to you
today. I want you to command your children to be
careful to obey all of the words of this law. 47 They
aren't just useless words for you. They are your
very life. If you obey them, you will live in the
land for a long time. It's the land you are going
across the Jordan River to take as your own."

Moses Will Die on Mount Nebo

48 On that same day the LORD spoke to me. He
said, 49 "Go up into the Abarim Mountains. Go to
Mount Nebo in Moab. It is across from Jericho.
From there look out over Canaan. It is the land I
am giving the people of Israel to take as their own.

50 "You will die there on the mountain you have
climbed. You will join the members of your family who have already died. In the same way, your
brother Aaron died on Mount Hor. He joined the
members of his family who had already died.

51 "You and Aaron disobeyed me in front of the
Israelites. It happened at the waters of Meribah
Kadesh in the Desert of Zin. You did not honor me
among the Israelites as the holy God. 52 So you will
see the land. But you will see it only from far
away. You will not enter the land I am giving to
the people of Israel."

Moses Blesses the Tribes

33 Here is the blessing that Moses, the man of God, gave to the people of Israel before he
died. 2 He said,

"The LORD came from Mount Sinai.
Like the rising sun, he shone on his people from Mount Seir.
He shone on them from Mount Paran.
He came with large numbers of angels.
He came from his mountain slopes in the south.
3 LORD, I'm sure you love your people.
All of the Israelites are in your hands.
At your feet all of them bow down.
And you teach them.
4 They learn the law I gave them.
It belongs to the community of the people of Jacob.
5 The LORD was king over Israel
when the leaders of the people came together.
The tribes of Israel were also there."

6 Here's what Moses said about Reuben.

"Let Reuben live. Don't let him die.
But let his people be few."

7 Here's what Moses said about Judah.

"LORD, listen to Judah cry out.
Bring him to his people.
By his own power he stands up for himself.
LORD, help him fight against his enemies!"

8 Here's what Moses said about Levi.

"Your Thummim and Urim belong to the man
you favored.
You put him to the test at Massah.
You argued with him at the waters
of Meribah.
9 Levi didn't show special favor to anyone.
He did not spare his father and mother.
He didn't excuse his relatives or his
children.
But he watched over your word.
He guarded your covenant.
10 He teaches your rules to the people of Jacob.
He teaches your law to Israel.
He offers incense to you.
He sacrifices whole burnt offerings on
your altar.
11 LORD, bless all of his skills.
Be pleased with everything he does.
Destroy those who rise up against him.
Strike down his enemies until they can't
get up."

12 Here's what Moses said about Benjamin.

"Let the one the LORD loves rest safely in him.
The LORD guards him all day long.
The one the LORD loves rests in his arms."

13 Here's what Moses said about Joseph.

"May the LORD bless Joseph's land.
May he bless it with dew from the highest
heavens.
May he bless it with water from the deepest
oceans.
14 May he bless it with the best crops the sun
can produce.
May he bless it with the finest crops the
moon can give.
15 May he bless it with the best products of the
age-old mountains.
May he bless it with the many crops of
the ancient hills.
16 May he bless it with the best gifts that fill
the earth.
May he bless it with the favor of the One
who spoke out of the burning bush.
Let all of those blessings rest on the head
of Joseph.
Let them rest on the head of the one who is
prince among his brothers.
17 His glory is like the glory of a bull that was
born first to its mother.
His horns are like the horns of a wild ox.
He will destroy the nations with them.
He'll wipe out the nations that are very
far away.
The ten thousands of men in Ephraim's army
are like the bull and the ox.
So are the thousands in the army of
Manasseh."

18 Here's what Moses said about Zebulun and Issachar.

"Zebulun, be filled with joy when you go out.
Issachar, be joyful in your tents.
19 You will call for all of the other Israelites to go
to the mountain.
There you will offer proper sacrifices.
You will enjoy the many good things your
ships bring you.
You will enjoy treasures that are hidden in
the sand."

20 Here's what Moses said about Gad.

"May the One who gives Gad more land
be praised!
Gad lives there like a lion
that tears off arms and heads.
21 He chose the best land for his livestock.
The leader's share was kept for him.
The leaders of the people came together.
Then Gad carried out the LORD's holy plan.
He carried out the LORD's decisions
for Israel."

22 Here's what Moses said about Dan.

"Dan is like a lion's cub
that charges out of the land of Bashan."

23 Here's what Moses said about Naphtali.

"The LORD greatly favors Naphtali.
The LORD fills him with his blessing.
Naphtali's land will reach south to the Sea
of Galilee."

24 Here's what Moses said about Asher.

"Asher is the most blessed of sons.
Let his brothers show favor to him.
Let him wash his feet with olive oil.
25 The bars of his gates will be made out of iron
and bronze.
His strength will last as long as he lives.
26 "There is no one like the God of Israel.
He rides in the heavens to help you.
He rides on the clouds in his glory.
27 God lives forever! You can run to him
for safety.
His powerful arms are always there to
carry you.
He will drive out your enemies to make room
for you.
He'll say to you, 'Destroy them!'
28 So Israel will live alone in safety.
Jacob's spring of water is safe
in a land that has grain and fresh wine.
There the heavens drop their dew.
29 Israel, how blessed you are!
Who is like you?
The LORD has saved you.
He keeps you safe. He helps you.
He's like a glorious sword to you.
Your enemies will bow down to you in fear.
You will bring them under your control."

Moses Dies

34 Moses climbed Mount Nebo. He went up from the flatlands of Moab to the highest slopes of Pisgah. It's across from Jericho.

At Pisgah the LORD showed him the whole land from Gilead all the way to Dan. 2Moses saw the whole land of Naphtali. He saw the territory of Ephraim and Manasseh. The LORD showed him the whole land of Judah all the way to the Mediterranean Sea. 3Moses saw the Negev Desert. He saw the whole area from the Valley of Jericho all the way to Zoar. Jericho was also known as The City of Palm Trees.

4Then the LORD spoke to Moses. He said, "This is the land I promised with an oath to Abraham, Isaac and Jacob. I told them, 'I will give this land to your children and their children.' Moses, I have let you see it with your own eyes. But you will not go across the Jordan River to enter it."

5Moses, the servant of the LORD, died there in Moab, just as the LORD had said. 6The LORD buried the body of Moses in Moab. His grave is in the valley across from Beth Peor. But to this day no one knows where it is. 7Moses was 120 years old when he died. But his eyes were not weak. He was still very strong.

8The people of Israel sobbed over Moses on the flatlands of Moab for 30 days. They did it until their time for sobbing and crying was over.

9Joshua, the son of Nun, was filled with wisdom. That's because Moses had placed his hands on him. So the Israelites listened to Joshua. They did what the LORD had commanded Moses.

10Since then, Israel has never had a prophet like Moses. The LORD knew him face to face. 11Moses did many miraculous signs and wonders. The LORD had sent him to do them in Egypt. Moses did them against Pharaoh, against all of his officials and against his whole land. 12No one has ever had the mighty power Moses had. No one has ever done the wonderful acts he did in the sight of all of the people of Israel.

Joshua

The LORD Gives Commands to Joshua

1 Moses, the servant of the LORD, died. After that, the LORD spoke to Joshua, the son of Nun. Joshua was Moses' helper. The LORD said to Joshua, 2"My servant Moses is dead. Now then, I want you and all of these people to get ready to go across the Jordan River. I want all of you to go into the land I am about to give to the people of Israel.

3"I will give all of you every place you walk on, just as I promised Moses. 4Your territory will reach from the Negev Desert all the way to Lebanon. The great Euphrates River will be to the east. The Mediterranean Sea will be to the west. Your territory will include all of the Hittite country.

5"Joshua, no one will be able to stand up against you as long as you live. I will be with you, just as I was with Moses. I will never leave you. I will never desert you.

6"Be strong and brave. You will lead these people, and they will take the land as their very own. It is the land I promised with an oath to give their people long ago.

7"Be strong and very brave. Make sure you obey the whole law my servant Moses gave you. Do not turn away from it to the right or the left. Then you will have success everywhere you go. 8Never stop reading this Scroll of the Law. Day and night you must think about what it says. Make sure you do everything that is written in it. Then things will go well with you. And you will have great success.

9"Here is what I am commanding you to do. Be strong and brave. Do not be terrified. Do not lose hope. I am the LORD your God. I will be with you everywhere you go."

Joshua Gives Commands to the People

10So Joshua gave orders to the officers of the people. He said, 11"Go through the camp. Tell the people, 'Get your supplies ready. Three days from now you will go across the Jordan River right here. You will go in and take over the land. The LORD your God is giving it to you as your very own.'"

12Joshua also spoke to the tribes of Reuben and Gad and half of the tribe of Manasseh. He said to them, 13"Remember what Moses, the servant of the LORD, commanded you. He said, 'The LORD your God is giving you this land. It's a place where you can settle down and live in peace and rest.'

14"Your wives, children and livestock can stay here east of the Jordan River. Moses gave you this land. But all of your fighting men must get ready for battle. They must go across ahead of the other tribes. You must help them 15until the LORD gives them rest. In the same way, he has already given you rest. You must help them until they also have taken over their land. It's the land the LORD your God is giving them. After that, you can come back here. Then you can live in your own land. It's the land that Moses, the servant of the LORD, gave you east of the Jordan River. It's toward the sunrise."

16Then the tribes of Reuben and Gad and half of the tribe of Manasseh answered Joshua. They said, "We'll do what you have commanded us to do. We'll go where you send us. 17We obeyed Moses completely. And we'll obey you just as completely. But may the LORD your God be with you, just as he was with Moses.

18"Suppose people question your authority. And suppose they refuse to obey anything you command them to do. Then they will be put to death. Just be strong and brave!"

Rahab Helps the Spies

2 Joshua, the son of Nun, sent two spies from Shittim. He sent them in secret. He said to them, "Go. Look the land over. Most of all, check out Jericho."

So they went to Jericho. They stayed at the house of a prostitute. Her name was Rahab.

2The king of Jericho was told, "Look! Some of the people of Israel have come here tonight. They've come to check out the land."

3So the king sent a message to Rahab. It said, "Bring out the men who came into your house. They've come to check out the whole land."

4But the woman had hidden the two men. She said, "It's true that the men came here. But I didn't know where they had come from. 5They left at sunset, when it was time to close the city gate. I don't know which way they went. Go after them quickly. You might catch up with them."

6But in fact she had taken them up on the roof. There she had hidden them under some flax she had piled up.

7The king's men left to hunt down the spies. They took the road that leads to where the Jordan River can be crossed. As soon as they had gone out of the city, the gate was shut.

8Rahab went up on the roof before the spies settled down for the night. 9She said to them, "I know that the LORD has given this land to you. We are very much afraid of you. Everyone who lives in this country is weak with fear because of you.

10"We've heard how the LORD dried up the Red Sea for you when you came out of Egypt. We've heard what you did to Sihon and Og, the two Amorite kings. They ruled east of the Jordan River. You completely destroyed them.

11"When we heard about it, our hearts melted away in fear. Because of you, we aren't brave any-

more. The LORD your God is the God who rules
over heaven above and earth below.
12"Now then, please take an oath. Promise me
in the name of the LORD that you will be kind to
my family. I've been kind to you. Promise me
13that you will spare the lives of my father and
mother. Spare my brothers and sisters. Also spare
everyone in their families. Promise that you won't
put any of us to death."
14So the men made a promise to her. "We'll give
up our lives to save yours," they said. "But don't
tell anyone what we're doing. Then we'll be kind
and faithful to you when the LORD gives us the
land."
15The house Rahab lived in was part of the city
wall. So she let the spies down by a rope through
the window. 16She had said to them, "Go up into the
hills. The men who are chasing you won't be able
to find you. Hide yourselves there for three days
until they return. Then you can go on your way."
17The men said to her, "You made us take an
oath and make a promise. But we won't keep it
18unless you do what we say. When we enter the
land, you must tie this bright red rope in the window. Tie it in the window you let us down through.
"Bring your father and mother into your house.
Also bring your brothers and everyone else in your
family into your house. 19None of you must go out
into the street. If you do, anything that happens to
you will be your own fault. Don't hold us
accountable.
"But if anyone hurts someone who is inside the
house with you, it will be our fault. And you can
hold us accountable.
20"Don't tell anyone what we're doing. If you
do, we won't have to keep the promise you asked
us to make."
21"I agree," Rahab replied. "I'll do as you say."
So she sent them away, and they left. Then she tied
the bright red rope in the window.
22When the spies left, they went up into the
hills. They stayed there for three days. By that time
the men who were chasing them had searched all
along the road. They couldn't find them. So they
returned.
23Then the two spies started back. They went
down out of the hills. They went across the Jordan
River. They came to Joshua, the son of Nun. They
told him everything that had happened to them.
24They said, "We're sure the LORD has given the
whole land over to us. All of the people there are
weak with fear because of us."

Israel Goes Across the Jordan River

3 Early one morning Joshua and all of the people of Israel started out from Shittim. They
went down to the Jordan River. They camped there
before they went across it.
2After three days the officers went all through
the camp. 3They gave orders to the people. They
said, "Watch for the ark of the covenant of the
LORD your God. The priests, who are Levites, will
be carrying it. When you see it, you must move out
from where you are and follow it. 4Then you will
know which way to go. You have never gone this
way before. But don't go near the ark. Stay about
1,000 yards away from it."
5Joshua spoke to the people. He said, "Set yourselves apart to the LORD. Tomorrow he'll do amazing things among you."
6Joshua said to the priests, "Go and get the ark
of the covenant. Walk on ahead of the people." So
they went and got it. Then they walked on ahead of
them.
7The LORD said to Joshua, "Today I will begin
to honor you in the eyes of all of the people of Israel. Then they will know that I am with you, just
as I was with Moses. 8Speak to the priests who
carry the ark of the covenant. Tell them, 'When
you reach the edge of the Jordan River, go into the
water and stand there.'"
9Joshua spoke to the people of Israel. He said,
"Come here. Listen to what the LORD your God is
saying. 10You will soon know that the living God
is among you. You can be sure that he'll drive out
the people who are now living in the land. He'll
do it to make room for you. He'll drive out the Canaanites, Hittites, Hivites, Perizzites, Girgashites,
Amorites and Jebusites.
11"The ark will go into the Jordan River ahead
of you. It's the ark of the covenant of the Lord of
the whole earth.
12"Choose 12 men from the tribes of Israel.
Choose one from each tribe.
13"The priests will carry the ark of the LORD.
He's the Lord of the whole earth. As soon as the
priests step into the Jordan, it will stop flowing.
The water that's coming down the river will pile
up in one place. That's how you will know that the
living God is among you."
14So the people took their tents down. They prepared to go across the Jordan River. The priests
who were carrying the ark of the covenant went
ahead of them.
15The water of the Jordan was going over its
banks. It always does that at the time the crops are
being gathered. The priests came to the river. Their
feet touched the water's edge. 16Right away the
water that was coming down the river stopped
flowing. It piled up far away at a town called
Adam near Zarethan. The water that was flowing
down to the Dead Sea was completely cut off. So
the people went across the Jordan River opposite
Jericho.
17The priests carried the ark of the covenant of
the LORD. They stood firm on dry ground in the
middle of the river. They stayed there until the
whole nation of Israel had gone across on dry
ground.
4 After the whole nation had gone across the
Jordan River, the LORD spoke to Joshua. He
said, 2"Choose 12 men from among the people.

Choose one from each tribe. [3]Tell them to get 12 stones from the middle of the river. They must pick them up from right where the priests stood. They must carry the stones over with all of you. And they must put them down at the place where you will stay tonight."

[4]So Joshua called together the 12 men he had appointed from among the people of Israel. There was one man from each tribe. [5]He said to them, "Go back to the middle of the Jordan River. Go to where the ark of the LORD your God is. Each one of you must pick up a stone. You must carry it on your shoulder. There will be as many stones as there are tribes in Israel.

[6]"The stones will serve as a reminder to you. In days to come, your children will ask you, 'What do these stones mean?' [7]Tell them that the LORD cut off the flow of water in the Jordan River. Tell them its water stopped flowing when the ark of the covenant of the LORD went across. The stones will always remind the Israelites of what happened there."

[8]So the people of Israel did as Joshua commanded them. They took 12 stones from the middle of the Jordan River. There was one stone for each of the tribes of Israel. It was just as the LORD had told Joshua. The people carried the stones with them to their camp. There they put them down.

[9]Joshua piled up the 12 stones that had been in the middle of the river. They had been right where the priests who carried the ark of the covenant had stood. And they are still there to this very day.

[10]The priests who carried the ark remained standing in the middle of the Jordan River. They stayed there until the people had done everything the LORD had commanded Joshua. It was just as Moses had directed Joshua. All of the people went across quickly. [11]As soon as they did, the ark of the LORD and the priests also went across to the other side. The people were watching them.

[12]Among the people who went across the river were men from the tribes of Reuben and Gad and half of the tribe of Manasseh. The men were armed. They went across ahead of the rest of the people of Israel. It was just as Moses had directed them. [13]There were about 40,000 of them. All of them were ready for battle. They went across in front of the ark of the LORD. They went to the flatlands around Jericho. They were prepared to go to war.

[14]That day the LORD honored Joshua in the eyes of all of the people of Israel. They had respect for Joshua as long as he lived. They respected him just as much as they had respected Moses.

[15]Then the LORD spoke to Joshua. He said, [16]"Command the priests to come up out of the Jordan River. They are carrying the ark where the tablets of the covenant are kept."

[17]So Joshua gave a command to the priests. He said, "Come up out of the Jordan River."

[18]Then the priests came up out of the river. They were carrying the ark of the covenant of the LORD. As soon as they stepped out on dry ground, the water of the Jordan began to flow again. It went over its banks, just as it had done before.

[19]On the tenth day of the first month the people went up out of the Jordan River. They camped at Gilgal on the eastern border of Jericho.

[20]Joshua set up the 12 stones at Gilgal. They were the ones the people had taken out of the Jordan.

[21]Then he spoke to the people of Israel. He said, "In days to come, your children after you will ask their parents, 'What do these stones mean?' [22]Their parents must tell them, 'Israel went across the Jordan River on dry ground.' [23]The LORD your God dried up the Jordan for you until you had gone across it. He did to the Jordan River the same thing he had done to the Red Sea. He dried up the Red Sea ahead of us until we had gone across it. [24]He did it so that all of the nations on earth would know that he is powerful. He did it so that you would always have respect for the LORD your God."

Joshua Circumcises the Men of Israel

5 All of the Amorite and Canaanite kings heard how the LORD had dried up the Jordan River. They heard how he had dried it up for the people of Israel until they had gone across it. The Amorite kings lived west of the Jordan. The kings of Canaan lived along the Mediterranean Sea.

When all of those kings heard what the LORD had done, their hearts melted away in fear. They weren't brave enough to face the people of Israel anymore.

[2]At that time the LORD spoke to Joshua. He said, "Make knives out of hard stone. Circumcise the men of Israel."

[3]So Joshua made knives out of hard stone. Then he circumcised the men of Israel at Gibeath Haaraloth.

[4]Here is why Joshua circumcised them. All of the men who came out of Egypt had died. They died while they were going through the Sinai Desert after they had left Egypt. They were the men who were old enough to serve in the army. [5]All of the men who came out had been circumcised. But all of the men who were born in the desert during the journey from Egypt hadn't been circumcised.

[6]The people of Israel had moved around in the desert for 40 years. By the end of that time all of the men who were old enough to serve in the army when they left Egypt had died. That's because they hadn't obeyed the LORD. The LORD had taken an oath. He had told them they wouldn't see the land. It's the land he had promised with an oath to their people to give us. It's a land that has plenty of milk and honey.

[7]Because they hadn't obeyed him, he raised up their sons to take their place. They were the ones Joshua circumcised. They hadn't been circumcised

yet. That's because no one had circumcised them during the journey. 8So Joshua circumcised all of those men. The whole nation remained in the camp until the men were healed.

9Then the LORD spoke to Joshua. He said, "Today I have taken away from you the shame of being laughed at by Egypt." That's why the place where the men were circumcised has been called Gilgal to this very day.

10The people of Israel celebrated the Passover Feast. They observed it on the evening of the 14th day of the month. They did it while they were camped at Gilgal on the flatlands around Jericho. 11The day after the Passover, they ate some of the food that was grown in the land. On that very day they ate grain that had been cooked. They also ate bread that was made without yeast. 12The manna stopped coming down the day after they ate the food that was grown in the land. The people of Israel didn't have manna anymore. Instead, that year they ate food that was grown in Canaan.

Israel Captures Jericho

13When Joshua was near Jericho, he looked up and saw a man standing in front of him. The man was holding a sword. He was ready for battle. Joshua went up to him. He asked, "Are you on our side? Or are you on the side of our enemies?"

14"I am not on either side," he replied. "I have come as the commander of the LORD's army." Then Joshua fell with his face to the ground. He asked the man, "What message does my Lord have for me?"

15The commander of the LORD's army replied, "Take off your sandals. The place you are standing on is holy ground." So Joshua took them off.

6 The gates of Jericho were shut tight and guarded closely because of the people of Israel. No one went out. No one came in.

2Then the LORD spoke to Joshua. He said, "I have handed Jericho over to you. I have also handed its king and its fighting men over to you.

3"March around the city once with all of your fighting men. In fact, do it for six days. 4Have seven priests get trumpets that are made out of rams' horns. They must carry them in front of the ark. On the seventh day, march around the city seven times. Have the priests blow the trumpets as you march.

5"You will hear them blow a long blast on the trumpets. When you do, have all of the men give a loud shout. The wall of the city will fall down. Then the whole army will go up to the city. Every man will go straight in."

6So Joshua, the son of Nun, called for the priests. He said to them, "Go and get the ark of the covenant of the LORD. I want seven of you to carry trumpets in front of it." 7He gave an order to the men. He said, "Move out! March around the city. Some of the fighting men must march in front of the ark of the LORD."

8When Joshua had spoken to the men, the seven priests went forward. They were carrying the seven trumpets as they marched in front of the ark of the LORD. They were blowing the trumpets. The ark of the LORD's covenant was carried behind the priests. 9Some of the fighting men marched ahead of the priests who were blowing the trumpets. The others followed behind the ark and guarded all of them. That whole time the priests were blowing the trumpets.

10But Joshua had given an order to the fighting men. He had said, "Don't give a war cry. Don't raise your voices. Don't say a word until the day I tell you to shout. Then shout!"

11So he had the ark of the LORD carried around the city once. Then the men returned to camp. They spent the night there.

12Joshua got up early the next morning. The priests went and got the ark of the LORD. 13The seven priests who were carrying the seven trumpets started out. They marched in front of the ark of the LORD. They blew the trumpets. Some of the fighting men marched ahead of them. The others followed behind the ark and guarded all of them. The priests kept blowing the trumpets.

14On the second day they marched around the city once. Then the men returned to camp. They did all of those things for six days.

15On the seventh day, they got up at sunrise. They marched around the city, just as they had done before. But on that day they went around it seven times.

16On the seventh time around, the priests blew a long blast on the trumpets.

Then Joshua gave a command to the men. He said, "Shout! The LORD has given you the city! 17The city and everything that is in it must be set apart to the LORD in a special way to be destroyed. But the prostitute Rahab and all those who are with her in her house must be spared. That's because she hid the spies we sent.

18"But keep away from the things that have been set apart to the LORD. If you take any of them, you will be destroyed. And you will bring trouble on the camp of Israel. You will cause it to be destroyed. 19All of the silver and gold is holy. It is set apart to the LORD. So are all of the articles that are made out of bronze and iron. All of those things must be added to the treasures that are kept in the LORD's house."

20The priests blew the trumpets. As soon as the fighting men heard the sound, they gave a loud shout. Then the wall fell down. Every man charged straight in. So they took the city. 21They set it apart to the LORD in a special way to be destroyed. They destroyed every living thing in it with their swords. They killed men and women. They wiped out young people and old people. They destroyed cattle, sheep and donkeys.

22Then Joshua spoke to the two men who had gone in to check out the land. He said, "Go into the

prostitute's house. Bring her out. Also bring out
everyone who is with her. That's what you promised
her you would do when you took an oath."
23So the young men who had checked out the
land went into Rahab's house. They brought her
out along with her parents and brothers. They
brought out everyone else who was there with her.
They put them in a place that was outside the camp
of Israel.
24Then they burned the whole city and everything that was in it. But they added the silver and
gold to the treasures that were kept in the LORD's
house. They also put there the articles that were
made out of bronze and iron.
25But Joshua spared the prostitute Rahab. He
spared her family. He also spared everyone else
who was in the house with her. He did it because
she hid the spies he had sent to Jericho. Rahab
lives among the people of Israel to this very day.
26At that time Joshua took an oath and called
down a curse. He said, "May the man who tries to
rebuild this city of Jericho be under the LORD's
curse.

"If he lays its foundations,
  it will cost the life of his oldest son.
If he sets up its gates,
  it will cost the life of his youngest son."

27So the LORD was with Joshua. And Joshua
became famous everywhere in the land.

Achan Sins Against the LORD

7 But the people of Israel weren't faithful to the
LORD. They didn't do what they were told to
do with the things that had been set apart to him in
a special way to be destroyed.
Achan had taken some of those things. So the
LORD's anger burned against Israel. Achan was the
son of Carmi. Carmi was the son of Zimri. And
Zimri was the son of Zerah. They were from the
tribe of Judah.
2Joshua sent men from Jericho to Ai. Ai is near
Beth Aven east of Bethel. Joshua told the men,
"Go up and check out the area around Ai." So the
men went up and checked it out.
3Then they returned to Joshua. They said, "The
whole army doesn't have to go up and attack Ai.
Send only two or three thousand men. They can
take the city. Don't make the whole army go up
there. Ai only has a few men."
4So only about 3,000 men went up. But the men
of Ai drove them away. 5They chased the men of
Israel from the city gate all the way to Shebarim.
They killed about 36 of them on the way down.
So the hearts of the people of Israel melted
away in fear.
6Joshua and the elders of Israel became sad.
Joshua tore his clothes. He fell in front of the ark of
the LORD with his face to the ground. He remained
there until evening. The elders did the same thing.
They also sprinkled dust on their heads.
7Joshua said, "LORD and King, why did you
ever bring these people across the Jordan River?
Did you want to hand us over to the Amorites? Did
you want them to destroy us? I wish we had been
content to stay on the other side of the Jordan!
8"Lord, our enemies have driven us away. What
can I say? 9The people of Canaan will hear about
it. So will everyone else in the country. They will
surround us. They'll wipe our name from the face
of the earth. Then what will you do when people
don't honor your great name anymore?"
10The LORD said to Joshua, "Get up! What are
you doing down there on your face?
11"Israel has sinned. I made a covenant with
them. I commanded them to keep it. But they have
broken it. They have taken some of the things that
had been set apart to me in a special way to be
destroyed. They have stolen. They have lied. They
have taken the things they stole and have put them
with their own things.
12"That is why the men of Israel can't stand up
against their enemies. They turn their backs and
run. It is because I have decided to let them be
destroyed. You must destroy the things you took
that had been set apart to me. If you do not, I will
not be with you anymore.
13"Go. Set the people apart. Tell them, 'Make
yourselves pure. Get ready for tomorrow. Here is
what the LORD, the God of Israel, wants you to do.
He says, "People of Israel, you have kept some of
the things that had been set apart to me in a special
way to be destroyed. You can't stand up against
your enemies until you get rid of those things."
14"'In the morning, come forward tribe by tribe.
The tribe the LORD chooses will come forward
group by group. The group the LORD chooses will
come forward family by family. And the men in
the family the LORD chooses will come forward
one by one.
15"'Anyone who is caught with the things that
had been set apart to the LORD will be destroyed by
fire. Everything that belongs to that person will also
be destroyed. He has broken the LORD's covenant.
He has done a very terrible thing in Israel!'"
16Early the next morning Joshua had Israel
come forward by tribes. The tribe of Judah was
picked. 17The groups of Judah came forward. Joshua picked the group of Zerah. He had the group of
Zerah come forward by families. The family of
Zimri was picked. 18He had their men come forward one by one. Achan was picked. Achan was
the son of Carmi. Carmi was the son of Zimri. And
Zimri was the son of Zerah. Zerah was from the
tribe of Judah.
19Joshua spoke to Achan. He said, "My son, the
LORD is the God of Israel. So give him glory by
telling the truth! Give him praise by admitting you
have sinned! Tell me what you have done. Don't
hide it from me."
20Achan replied, "It's true! I've sinned against
the LORD, the God of Israel. Here is what I've done.

21I saw a beautiful robe from Babylonia among the
things we had taken. I saw five pounds of silver.
And I saw a gold bar that weighed 20 ounces. I
wanted them, so I took them. I hid them in the
ground inside my tent. The silver is on the bottom."
22So Joshua sent some messengers. They ran to
Achan's tent. And there was everything, hidden in
his tent! The silver was on the bottom. 23They
brought the things out of the tent. They took them
to Joshua and all of the people of Israel. And they
spread them out in the sight of the LORD.
24Then Joshua and all of the people grabbed
hold of Achan, the son of Zerah. They took the silver, the robe and the gold bar. They took Achan's
sons and daughters. They took his cattle, donkeys
and sheep. They also took his tent and everything
he had. They took all of it to the Valley of Achor.
25Joshua said to Achan, "Why have you brought
this trouble on us? The LORD will bring trouble on
you today."
Then all of the people killed Achan by throwing
stones at him. They also killed the rest of his family with stones. They burned all of them up. 26They
placed a large pile of rocks on top of Achan's body.
The place has been called the Valley of Achor ever
since. That pile is still there to this very day.
After the people killed Achan, the LORD turned
his burning anger away from them.

Israel Destroys Ai

8 Then the LORD spoke to Joshua. He said, "Do
not be afraid. Do not lose hope. Go up and
attack Ai. Take the whole army with you. I have
handed the king of Ai over to you. I have given
you his people, his city and his land.
2"Remember what you did to Jericho and its
king. You will do the same thing to Ai and its king.
But this time you can keep for yourselves the livestock and everything else you take from them.
Have some of your fighting men hide behind the
city and take them by surprise."
3So Joshua and the whole army moved out to
attack Ai. He chose 30,000 of his best fighting
men. He sent them out at night. 4He gave them
orders. He said, "Listen carefully to what I'm saying. You must hide behind the city. Don't go very
far away from it. All of you must be ready to
attack it.
5"I and all of the men who are with me will go
up to the city. The men of Ai will come out to fight
against us, just as they did before. Then we'll run
away from them. 6They'll chase us until we've
drawn them away from the city. They'll say, 'They
are running away from us, just as they did before.'
"When we run away from them, 7come out of
your hiding place. Take over the city. The LORD
your God will hand it over to you. 8When you have
taken it, set it on fire. Do what the LORD has commanded. Make sure you obey my orders."
9Then Joshua sent them away. They went to the
place where they had planned to hide. They hid in
a place west of Ai. It was between Bethel and Ai.
But Joshua spent that night with his men.
10Early the next morning Joshua brought his
men together. He and the leaders of Israel marched
in front of them to Ai. 11The whole army that was
with him marched up to the city. They stopped in
front of it. They set up camp north of Ai. There
was a valley between them and the city.
12Joshua had chosen about 5,000 soldiers. He
had ordered them to hide in a place west of Ai. It
was between Bethel and Ai.
13The men took up their battle positions. All of
the men who were in the camp that was north of
the city took up their positions. So did those who
were supposed to hide west of the city. That night
Joshua went into the valley.
14The king of Ai saw what the army of Israel
was doing. So he and all of his men hurried out of
the city early in the morning. They marched out to
meet Israel in battle. They went to a place that
looked out over the Arabah Valley. The king didn't
know that some of Israel's fighting men were hiding behind the city.
15Joshua and all of his men let the men of Ai
drive them back. The men of Israel ran away
toward the desert.
16All of the men of Ai were called out to chase
them. They chased Joshua. So they were drawn
away from the city. 17Not even one man remained
in Ai or Bethel. All of them went out to chase Israel. When they did, they left the city wide open.
18Then the LORD spoke to Joshua. He said,
"Point the javelin that is in your hand at Ai. I will
hand the city over to you." So Joshua pointed his
javelin at Ai.
19As soon as he did, the men who were hiding
behind the city got up quickly. They came out of
their hiding places and rushed forward. They
entered the city and captured it. They quickly set
it on fire.
20The men of Ai looked back. They saw smoke
rising up from the city into the sky. But they
couldn't escape in any direction.
The men of Israel had been running away
toward the desert. But now they turned around to
face those who were chasing them. 21Joshua and
all of his men saw that the men who had been hiding behind the city had captured it. They also saw
the smoke that was going up from it. So they
turned around and attacked the men of Ai. 22The
men who had set Ai on fire came out of the city.
They also fought against the men of Ai.
So the men of Ai were caught in the middle.
The army of Israel was on both sides of them. Israel struck them down. They didn't let anyone
remain alive or get away. 23But they took the king
of Ai alive. They brought him to Joshua.
24Israel finished killing all of the men of Ai.
They destroyed them in the fields and in the desert
where they had chased them. They struck every
one of them down with their swords. Then all of

the men of Israel returned to Ai. And they killed those who were left in it.

25 The total number of men and women they killed that day was 12,000. They put to death all of the people of Ai.

26 Joshua kept the javelin that was in his hand pointed at Ai. He didn't lower his hand until he and his men had totally destroyed everyone who lived there.

27 But this time Israel kept for themselves the livestock and everything else they had taken from the city. The LORD had directed Joshua to let them do it.

28 So Joshua burned Ai down. He tore it down so it could never be built again. It has been deserted to this very day.

29 Joshua killed the king of Ai. He stuck a pole through the body. Then he set it up where people could see it. He left it there until evening. At sunset, Joshua ordered his men to remove the body from the pole. He told them to throw the body down at the entrance of the city gate. They put a large pile of rocks over the body. That pile is still there to this very day.

Joshua Reads the Scroll of the Law to the People

30 Joshua built an altar to honor the LORD, the God of Israel. He built it on Mount Ebal. 31 Moses, the servant of the LORD, had commanded the people of Israel to do that. Joshua built the altar in keeping with what is written in the Scroll of the Law of Moses. He built an altar out of stones that iron tools had never touched. Then the people offered on the altar burnt offerings to the LORD. They also sacrificed friendship offerings on it.

32 Joshua copied the written law of Moses on stones. He did it while all of the people of Israel were watching. 33 They were standing on both sides of the ark of the covenant of the LORD. All of the people of Israel, including outsiders and citizens, were there. Israel's elders, officials and judges were also there. All of them faced the priests, who were Levites. They were carrying the ark. Half of the people stood in front of Mount Gerizim. The other half stood in front of Mount Ebal. Moses, the servant of the LORD, had earlier told them to do it. It was when he had given directions to bless the people of Israel.

34 Then Joshua read all of the words of the law out loud. He read the blessings and the curses. He read them in keeping with what is written in the Scroll of the Law. 35 Joshua read every word Moses had commanded. He read them to the whole community of Israel. That included the women and children. It also included the outsiders who were living among them.

The People of Gibeon Trick Israel

9 All of the kings who ruled west of the Jordan River heard about the battles Israel had won. That included the kings who ruled in the central hill country and the western hills. It also included those who ruled along the entire coast of the Mediterranean Sea all the way to Lebanon. They were the kings of the Hittites, Amorites, Canaanites, Perizzites, Hivites and Jebusites. 2 They brought their armies together to fight against Joshua and Israel.

3 The people of Gibeon heard about what Joshua had done to Jericho and Ai. 4 So they decided to trick the people of Israel. They packed supplies as if they were going on a long trip. They loaded their donkeys with old sacks and old wineskins. The wineskins were cracked but had been mended. 5 The men put worn-out sandals on their feet. The sandals had been patched. The men also wore old clothes. All of the bread they took along was dry and moldy.

6 They went to Joshua in the camp at Gilgal. They spoke to him and the men of Israel. They said, "We've come from a country that's far away. Make a peace treaty with us."

7 The men of Israel spoke to the Hivites. They said, "But suppose you live close to us. If you do, we can't make a peace treaty with you."

8 "We'll serve you," they said to Joshua.

But Joshua asked, "Who are you? Where do you come from?"

9 They answered, "We've come from a country that's very far away. We've come because the LORD your God is famous. We've heard reports about him. We've heard about everything he did in Egypt.

10 "We've heard about everything he did to Sihon and Og. They were the two kings of the Amorites. They ruled east of the Jordan River. Sihon was the king of Heshbon. Og was the king of Bashan. He ruled in Ashtaroth.

11 "Our elders and all of the people who are living in our country spoke to us. They said, 'Take supplies for your trip. Go and meet the people of Israel. Say to them, "We'll serve you. Make a peace treaty with us."'

12 "Look at our bread. It was warm when we packed it. We packed it at home on the day we left to come and see you. But look at how dry and moldy it is now. 13 When we filled these wineskins, they were new. But look at how cracked they are now. And our clothes and sandals are worn out because we've traveled so far."

14 The men of Israel looked over the supplies those men had brought. But they didn't ask the LORD what they should do.

15 Joshua made a peace treaty with the men who had come. He agreed to let them live. The leaders of the community took an oath to show that they agreed with the treaty.

16 The people of Israel made a peace treaty with the people of Gibeon. But three days later they heard that the people of Gibeon lived close to them. 17 So the people of Israel started out to go to the cities of those men. On the third day they came to Gibeon, Kephirah, Beeroth and Kiriath Jearim.

Joshua

On the seventh time around, the priests blew a long blast on the trumpets. Then Joshua said, "Shout! The LORD has given you the city!"
—Joshua 6:16

Samuel

The LORD said, "Samuel! Samuel!"
Then Samuel replied, "Speak. I'm listening."
—1 Samuel 3:10

[18]But they didn't attack those cities. That's because the leaders of the community had taken an oath and made a peace treaty with them. They had taken the oath in the name of the LORD, the God of Israel.

The whole community told the leaders they weren't happy with them.

[19]But all of the leaders answered, "We've made a peace treaty with them. We've taken an oath in the name of the LORD, the God of Israel. So we can't touch them now.

[20]"But here is what we'll do to them. We'll let them live. Then the LORD's anger won't fall on us because we didn't keep the oath we took." [21]They continued, "Let them live. But let them cut wood and carry water for the whole community." So the leaders kept their promise to them.

[22]Joshua sent for the people of Gibeon. He said, "Why did you trick us? You said, 'We live far away from you.' But in fact you live close to us. [23]So now you are under a curse. You will always serve us. You will always cut wood and carry water for the house of my God."

[24]They answered Joshua, "We were clearly told what the LORD your God had commanded his servant Moses to do. He commanded him to give you the whole land. He also ordered him to wipe out all of its people to make room for you. So we were afraid you would kill us. That's why we tricked you. [25]We are now in your hands. Do to us what you think is good and right."

[26]So Joshua saved the people of Gibeon. He didn't let the people of Israel kill them. [27]That day he made them cut wood and carry water. They had to serve the community of Israel. They also had to serve at the altar of the LORD at the place where he would choose to put it. And they still serve the people of Israel to this very day.

The Sun Stands Still

10 Adoni-Zedek was the king of Jerusalem. He heard that Joshua had taken Ai. He found out that the city had been set apart to the LORD in a special way to be destroyed. He heard that Joshua had done to Ai and its king the same thing he had done to Jericho and its king.

Adoni-Zedek heard that the people of Gibeon had made a peace treaty with Israel. He also found out that they were living among the people of Israel. [2]The things he heard alarmed him and his people very much. That's because Gibeon was an important city. It was like one of the royal cities. It was larger than Ai. All of its men were good soldiers.

[3]So Adoni-Zedek, the king of Jerusalem, made an appeal to Hoham, the king of Hebron. He appealed to Piram, the king of Jarmuth. He appealed to Japhia, the king of Lachish. He also made an appeal to Debir, the king of Eglon. [4]"Come up and help me attack Gibeon," he said. "Its people have made peace with Joshua and the people of Israel."

[5]The kings of Jerusalem, Hebron, Jarmuth, Lachish and Eglon gathered their armies together. Those five Amorite kings moved all of their troops into position to fight against Gibeon. Then they attacked it.

[6]Joshua was in the camp at Gilgal. The people of Gibeon sent a message to him there. It said, "Don't desert us. We serve you. Come up to us quickly! Save us! Help us! All of the Amorite kings from the central hill country have gathered their armies together to fight against us."

[7]So Joshua marched up from Gilgal with his whole army. The army included all of his best fighting men.

[8]The LORD said to Joshua, "Do not be afraid of them. I have handed them over to you. Not one of them will be able to fight against you and win."

[9]Joshua marched all night from Gilgal. He took the Amorite armies by surprise. [10]The LORD threw them into a panic as Israel marched toward them. Then Israel won a great battle over them at Gibeon. They chased them along the road that goes up to Beth Horon. They struck them down all the way to Azekah and Makkedah.

[11]The Amorites ran away as Israel marched toward them. They ran down the road from Beth Horon to Azekah. As they ran, the LORD threw large hailstones down on them from the sky. The hailstones killed more of them than the swords of the men of Israel did.

[12]So the LORD gave the Amorites over to Israel. On that day Joshua spoke to the LORD while the people of Israel were listening. He said,

"Sun, stand still over Gibeon.
Moon, stand still over the Valley
of Aijalon."
13 So the sun stood still.
The moon stopped.
They didn't move again until the nation
won the battle over its enemies.

You can read about it in the Book of Jashar.

The sun stopped in the middle of the sky. It didn't go down for about a full day. [14]There has never been a day like it before or since. It was a day when the LORD listened to a mere man. You can be sure that the LORD was fighting for Israel!

[15]Joshua and his whole army returned to the camp at Gilgal.

Joshua Kills the Five Amorite Kings

[16]The five Amorite kings had run away. They had hidden in the cave at Makkedah.

[17]Joshua was told that the five kings had been found. He was also told that they were hiding in the cave at Makkedah. [18]He said, "Roll some large rocks up to the opening of the cave. Put some men there to guard it. [19]But keep on going! Chase your enemies. Attack them from behind. Don't let them get back to their cities. The LORD your God has handed them over to you."

[20]So Joshua and the men of Israel completely destroyed them. They killed almost every one of them. But a few escaped. They went back to their cities that had high walls around them.

[21]Then Israel's whole army returned safely to Joshua. He was in the camp at Makkedah. No one in the land dared to say anything against the people of Israel.

[22]Joshua said, "Open up the cave. Bring those five kings out to me." [23]So Joshua's men brought the five kings out of the cave. They were the kings of Jerusalem, Hebron, Jarmuth, Lachish and Eglon.

[24]The men brought them to Joshua. Then he sent for all of the men of Israel. He spoke to the army commanders who had come with him. He said, "Come here. Put your feet on the necks of these kings." So they came forward and placed their feet on the necks of the kings.

[25]Joshua said to them, "Don't be afraid. Don't lose hope. Be strong and brave. This is what the LORD will do to all of the enemies you are going to fight."

[26]Joshua struck the five kings down and killed them. He stuck a pole through each of their bodies. Then he set the poles up where people could see the bodies. He left them there until evening.

[27]At sunset Joshua ordered his men to take the bodies down. So they took them down and threw them into the cave where the kings had been hiding. They placed large rocks at the opening of the cave. And the rocks are still there to this very day.

[28]That day Joshua took Makkedah. He killed its people and their king with the sword. He totally destroyed everyone in it. He didn't leave anyone alive. He did to the king of Makkedah the same thing he had done to the king of Jericho.

The Campaign Against the Cities in the South

[29]Joshua moved on from Makkedah to Libnah. Israel's whole army went with him. They attacked Libnah. [30]The LORD also handed that city and its king over to Israel. Joshua destroyed the city. He and his men killed everyone in it with their swords. He didn't leave anyone alive there. He did to its king the same thing he had done to the king of Jericho.

[31]Joshua moved on from Libnah to Lachish. Israel's whole army went with him. The men took up their battle positions. Then Joshua attacked Lachish. [32]The LORD handed it over to Israel. Joshua took the city on the second day of the battle. He destroyed the city. He and his men killed everyone in it with their swords. He had done the same thing to Libnah.

[33]While all of that was happening, Horam had come up to help Lachish. He was the king of Gezer. But Joshua won the battle over him and his army. No one was left alive.

[34]Joshua moved on from Lachish to Eglon. Israel's whole army went with him. They took up their battle positions. Then they attacked Eglon. [35]They captured it that same day. They totally destroyed everyone in it with their swords. They had done the same thing to Lachish.

[36]Joshua went up from Eglon to Hebron. Israel's whole army went with him. Then they attacked Hebron. [37]They took the city. They destroyed it and its villages. They killed all of its people and their king with their swords. They didn't leave anyone alive. They totally destroyed the city and everyone in it. They had done the same thing at Eglon.

[38]Joshua turned back and attacked Debir. Israel's whole army went with him. [39]They took the city, its king and its villages. They totally destroyed everyone in Debir with their swords. They didn't leave anyone alive. They did to Debir and its king the same thing they had done to Libnah and its king. They had also done the same thing to Hebron.

[40]So Joshua brought the whole area under his control. That included the central hill country and the Negev Desert. It included the western hills and the mountain slopes. It also included all of the kings in that whole area. Joshua didn't leave anyone alive. He totally destroyed everyone who breathed. He did just as the LORD, the God of Israel, had commanded.

[41]Joshua brought everyone from Kadesh Barnea to Gaza under his control. He also brought everyone from the whole area of Goshen to Gibeon under his control. [42]He won the battle over all of those kings and their lands. He did it in one campaign. That's because the LORD, the God of Israel, fought for Israel.

[43]Then Joshua returned to the camp at Gilgal. Israel's whole army went with him.

The Campaign Against the Cities in the North

11 Jabin was the king of Hazor. He heard about the battles Israel had won. So he sent a message to Jobab. Jobab was the king of Madon. Jabin sent the same message to the kings of Shimron and Acshaph. [2]He also sent it to a lot of other kings. Some ruled in the mountains in the north. Some ruled in the Arabah Valley south of Kinnereth. Others ruled in the western hills. Still others ruled in Naphoth Dor in the west. [3]Jabin sent the same message to the people of east Canaan and west Canaan. He sent it to the Amorites, Hittites, Perizzites and Jebusites. They lived in the central hill country. He also sent it to the Hivites who lived below Mount Hermon in the area of Mizpah.

[4]Those kings marched out with all of their troops. They had a large number of horses and chariots. It was a huge army. The fighting men were as many as the grains of sand on the seashore. [5]All of those kings gathered their armies together to fight against Israel. They set up camp together at the Waters of Merom.

6The LORD spoke to Joshua. He said, "Do not
be afraid of them. By this time tomorrow I will
hand all of them over to Israel. All of them will be
killed. You must cut the legs of their horses. You
must burn up their chariots."
7So Joshua and his whole army attacked them
suddenly. They fought against them at the Waters
of Merom. 8The LORD handed them over to Israel.
Israel won the battle over them. They hunted them
down all the way to Greater Sidon. They chased
them to Misrephoth Maim. They chased them to
the Valley of Mizpah in the east. Not one of them
was left alive.
9Joshua did to them what the LORD had directed
him to do. He cut the legs of their horses. He
burned up their chariots.
10At that time Joshua turned back. He captured
Hazor. He killed its king with his sword. Hazor
was the most important city in all of those kingdoms. 11The army of Israel killed everyone in Hazor with their swords. Its people had been set apart
to the LORD in a special way to be destroyed. Israel's army didn't spare anything that breathed. Then
Joshua burned up the city.
12Joshua took all of those royal cities and their
kings. He and his men killed everyone in those
cities with their swords. He totally destroyed them.
He did just as Moses, the servant of the LORD, had
commanded. 13Many cities were built on top of
earlier cities that had been destroyed. Israel didn't
burn up any of those except Hazor. Joshua burned
it up.
14The army of Israel kept for themselves the
livestock and everything else they took from those
cities. But they killed all of the people with their
swords. They completely destroyed them. They
didn't spare anyone who breathed.
15The LORD had commanded his servant Moses
to do all of those things. Moses had passed that
command on to Joshua. And Joshua carried it out.
He did everything the LORD had commanded
Moses.
16So Joshua took the whole land. He took the
central hill country and the whole Negev Desert.
He took the whole area of Goshen. He took the
western hills. He took the Arabah Valley. He took
the mountains of Israel and the hills around them.
17He took the area that begins at Mount Halak,
which rises toward Seir. The area ends at Baal Gad
in the Valley of Lebanon below Mount Hermon.
Joshua captured the kings who ruled over that
whole land. He struck them down and killed them.
18He fought battles against all of those kings for a
long time.
19Only the Hivites who lived in Gibeon made a
peace treaty with the people of Israel. No other city
made a treaty with them. So Israel captured all of
those cities in battle. 20The LORD himself made the
hearts of their people stubborn. He made them go
to war against Israel so he could totally destroy
them. He wanted to wipe them out. He didn't show
them any mercy. The LORD had commanded Moses to destroy the people of Canaan.
21At that time Joshua went and destroyed the
Anakites. They lived all through the hill country
of Judah and Israel. They lived in Hebron, Debir
and Anab. Joshua totally destroyed the Anakites
and their towns. 22There weren't any Anakites left
alive in Israel's territory. But a few were left alive
in Gaza, Gath and Ashdod.
23So Joshua took the whole land, just as the
LORD had directed Moses. Joshua gave the land to
Israel as their very own. He divided it up and gave
each tribe its share.
Then the land had peace and rest.

Israel Wins the Battle Over the Kings in the Land

12 The people of Israel took over the territory
east of the Jordan River. The land they took
reached from the Arnon River valley to Mount
Hermon. It included the whole east side of the Arabah Valley. Israel won the battle over the kings of
that whole territory. Here are the lands Israel took
from the kings they won the battle over.

2They took the land of Sihon. He was the king of
the Amorites.
He ruled in Heshbon. The land he ruled over
begins at Aroer. Aroer is on the rim of the Arnon River valley. He ruled from the middle
of the valley to the Jabbok River. The Jabbok
is the border of Ammon. Sihon's territory
included half of Gilead. 3He also ruled over
the east side of the Arabah Valley. That land
begins at the Sea of Galilee. It goes to the
Dead Sea and over to Beth Jeshimoth. Then
it goes south, below the slopes of Pisgah.

4Israel also took the territory of Og. He was the
king of Bashan.
He was one of the last of the Rephaites. He
ruled in Ashtaroth and Edrei. 5He ruled over
Mount Hermon, Salecah and the whole land
of Bashan. He ruled all the way to the border of Geshur and Maacah. He ruled over
half of Gilead. His land reached the border
of Sihon. Sihon was the king of Heshbon.

6Moses was the servant of the LORD. Moses and
the people of Israel won the battle over those two
kings. He gave their land to the tribes of Reuben
and Gad and half of the tribe of Manasseh. He
gave it to them as their share.
7Joshua and the people of Israel won the battle
over the kings who ruled west of the Jordan River.
The lands of the kings reached from Baal Gad in
the Valley of Lebanon to Mount Halak, which rises
toward Seir.
Joshua gave their lands to the tribes of Israel as
their very own. He divided them up and gave each
tribe its share. 8Those lands included the central
hill country, the western hills and the Arabah

Valley. They also included the mountain slopes,
the Desert of Judah and the Negev Desert. Those
lands belonged to the Hittites, Amorites, Canaanites, Perizzites, Hivites and Jebusites. Here are the
kings Israel won the battle over.

9 the king of Jericho — one
the king of Ai, which is near Bethel — one
10 the king of Jerusalem — one
the king of Hebron — one
11 the king of Jarmuth — one
the king of Lachish — one
12 the king of Eglon — one
the king of Gezer — one
13 the king of Debir — one
the king of Geder — one
14 the king of Hormah — one
the king of Arad — one
15 the king of Libnah — one
the king of Adullam — one
16 the king of Makkedah — one
the king of Bethel — one
17 the king of Tappuah — one
the king of Hepher — one
18 the king of Aphek — one
the king of Lasharon — one
19 the king of Madon — one
the king of Hazor — one
20 the king of Shimron Meron — one
the king of Acshaph — one
21 the king of Taanach — one
the king of Megiddo — one
22 the king of Kedesh — one
the king of Jokneam in Carmel — one
23 the king of Dor in Naphoth Dor — one
the king of Goyim in Gilgal — one
24 the king of Tirzah — one

The total number of kings was 31.

The Land That Remained to Be Taken Over

13 Joshua was now very old. The LORD said
to him, "You are very old. And there are
still very large areas of land that have not been
taken over yet.

2 "Here is the land that remains to be taken
over. It includes all of the areas of Philistia
and Geshur. 3 Those areas begin at the Shihor
River in the eastern part of Egypt. They go
to the territory of Ekron in the north. All of
that land is considered as belonging to the
people of Canaan. The land that remains to
be taken over includes the territory of the
five rulers of Philistia. They rule over Gaza,
Ashdod, Ashkelon, Gath and Ekron. The Avvites 4 live south of them. The rest of the land
of Canaan that remains to be taken over
reaches from Arah all the way to Aphek.
Arah belongs to the people of Sidon. The
land that remains to be taken over includes
the area where the Amorites live. 5 It includes
the area where the people of Byblos live. It
also includes all of Lebanon to the east. It
reaches from Baal Gad below Mount Hermon to Lebo Hamath.

6 "I myself will drive out all of the people who
live in the mountain areas. Those areas reach from
Lebanon to Misrephoth Maim. They include the
area where all of the people of Sidon live. I myself
will drive those people out to make room for the
people of Israel.

"Make sure you set that land apart for Israel.
Give it to them as their share, just as I have
directed you. 7 Divide it up among the nine tribes
and half of the tribe of Manasseh. Give each tribe
its share."

Moses Had Given the Eastern Tribes Their Land

8 The other half of Manasseh's tribe had already
received the share of land Moses had given them.
Their share was east of the Jordan River. The tribes
of Reuben and Gad had already received their
share too. Moses, the servant of the LORD, had
given it to them.

9 That land starts at Aroer on the rim of the
Arnon River valley. It includes the town in
the middle of the valley. It includes the high
flatlands of Medeba all the way to Dibon. 10 It
also includes all of the towns of Sihon, the
king of the Amorites. He had ruled in Heshbon. That area reaches to the border of Ammon. 11 It also includes Gilead. It includes the
territory of Geshur and Maacah. It includes
Mount Hermon and the whole land of Bashan all the way to Salecah.

12 So it includes the entire kingdom of Og
in Bashan. Og had ruled in Ashtaroth and
Edrei. He was one of the last of the Rephaites. Moses had won the battle over Sihon
and Og. He had taken over their land.

13 But the people of Israel didn't drive out
the people of Geshur and Maacah. So they
continue to live among the people of Israel
to this very day.

14 Moses hadn't given any share of the land to
the tribe of Levi. That's because the offerings that
are made with fire are their share. Those offerings
are made to the LORD, the God of Israel. Moses
gave the Levites what he had promised them.

15 Here is what Moses had given to the tribe of Reuben, family group by family group.

16 Their territory starts at Aroer on the rim of
the Arnon River valley. It includes the town
in the middle of the valley. It includes all of
the high flatlands that are near Medeba. 17 It
includes Heshbon and all of its towns on
those flatlands. Those towns include Dibon,

Bamoth Baal, Beth Baal Meon, [18]Jahaz, Kedemoth and Mephaath. [19]They include Kiriathaim, Sibmah and Zereth Shahar on the hill in the valley. [20]They also include Beth Peor, Beth Jeshimoth and the slopes of Pisgah. [21]All of those towns are on the high flatlands.

The territory includes the whole kingdom of Sihon, the king of the Amorites. He had ruled in Heshbon. Moses had won the battle over him and over the chiefs of Midian. Those chiefs were Evi, Rekem, Zur, Hur and Reba. They were princes who helped Sihon fight against Israel. They lived in that country. [22]The people of Israel killed many of them in battle. They also killed Balaam with a sword. He was the son of Beor. Balaam used magic to find out what was going to happen.

[23]The border of the tribe of Reuben was the bank of the Jordan River. All of those towns and their villages were given to the tribe of Reuben as their very own. Each family group received its share.

[24]Here is what Moses had given to the tribe of Gad, family group by family group.

[25]Their territory includes Jazer and all of the towns of Gilead. It includes half of the country of Ammon all the way to Aroer, which was near Rabbah. [26]Their territory reaches from Heshbon to Ramath Mizpah and Betonim. It reaches from Mahanaim to the territory of Debir. [27]In the valley their land includes Beth Haram, Beth Nimrah, Succoth and Zaphon. It also includes the rest of the kingdom of Sihon. He was the king of Heshbon. His kingdom included the east side of the Jordan River. It reached up to the south end of the Sea of Galilee. [28]All of those towns and their villages were given to the tribe of Gad as their very own. Each family group received its share.

[29]Here is what Moses had given to half of the tribe of Manasseh, family group by family group. It's what Moses had given to half of Manasseh's family line.

[30]Their territory starts at Mahanaim. It includes the whole land of Bashan. That was the entire kingdom of Og, the king of Bashan. Manasseh's territory includes all of the 60 towns of Jair in Bashan. [31]It includes half of the land of Gilead. It also includes Ashtaroth and Edrei. They were the royal cities of Og in Bashan. That land was given to half of the family line of Makir. He was the son of Manasseh. Each family group received its share.

[32]Those were the shares of land Moses had given the eastern tribes when he was in the flatlands of Moab. The flatlands are across the Jordan River east of Jericho. [33]But Moses hadn't given any share to the tribe of Levi. The LORD, the God of Israel, is their share. Moses gave the Levites what he had promised them.

The Western Tribes Are Given Their Land

14 The rest of the tribes of Israel received their shares of land in Canaan. The priest Eleazar and Joshua, the son of Nun, decided what each of the tribes should receive. The leaders of the tribes helped them make those decisions.

[2]The shares of nine tribes and half of the tribe of Manasseh were decided by using lots. That's what the LORD had commanded through Moses.

[3]Moses had given two tribes and the other half of the tribe of Manasseh their shares east of the Jordan River. But Moses had not given the Levites a share among the other tribes. [4]Manasseh and Ephraim were the sons of Joseph. They had become two tribes. The Levites didn't receive any share of the land. They only received towns to live in and grasslands for their flocks and herds.

[5]So the people of Israel divided up the land, just as the LORD had commanded Moses.

Joshua Gives Hebron to Caleb

[6]The men of Judah approached Joshua at Gilgal. Caleb, the son of Jephunneh the Kenizzite, spoke to Joshua. He said, "You know what the LORD said to Moses, the man of God. He spoke to him at Kadesh Barnea about you and me. [7]Moses, the servant of the LORD, sent me from Kadesh Barnea to check out the land. I was 40 years old at that time. I brought back an honest report to him. I told him exactly what I had seen. [8]Several other men of Israel went up with me. What they reported made the hearts of the people melt away in fear. But I followed the LORD my God with my whole heart.

[9]"So on that day Moses took an oath and made a promise to me. He said, 'The land your feet have walked on will be your share. It will be the share of your children forever. That's because you have followed the LORD my God with your whole heart.' *(Deuteronomy 1:36)*

[10]"The LORD has done just as he promised. He made the promise while Israel was wandering around in the desert. That was 45 years ago. He has kept me alive all of this time. So here I am today, 85 years old! [11]I'm still as strong today as I was the day Moses sent me out. I'm just as able to go out to battle now as I was then.

[12]"So give me this hill country. The LORD promised it to me that day. At that time you yourself heard that the Anakites were living there. You also heard that their cities were large and had high walls. But I'll drive them out, just as the LORD said I would. He will help me do it."

[13]Then Joshua blessed Caleb, the son of Jephunneh. He gave him Hebron as his share.

14So ever since that time Hebron has belonged to Caleb, the son of Jephunneh the Kenizzite. That's because he followed the LORD, the God of Israel, with his whole heart.

15Hebron used to be called Kiriath Arba. It was named after Arba. He was the greatest man among the Anakites.

So the land had peace and rest.

Land Is Given to Judah

15 Land was given to the tribe of Judah, family group by family group. It reached down to the territory of Edom. It went as far south as the Desert of Zin.

2Judah's border on the south started from
the bay at the south end of the Dead Sea. 3It
went across to the south of Scorpion Pass. It
continued on to Zin. It went over to the south
of Kadesh Barnea. Then it ran past Hezron
up to Addar. It curved around to Karka. 4It
then went along to Azmon. There it joined
the Wadi of Egypt and ended at the Mediterranean Sea. That was the southern border of Judah.

5The border on the east was the Dead Sea. It went north all the way to where the Jordan River enters the sea.

The border on the north started at the bay
of the Dead Sea. That's where the Jordan
River enters the sea. 6From there it went up
to Beth Hoglah. It continued north of Beth
Arabah to the Stone of Bohan, the son of
Reuben. 7Then it went from the Valley of
Achor up to Debir. It turned north to Gilgal.
Gilgal faces the Pass of Adummim south of
the valley. The border continued along to the
springs of En Shemesh. It came to an end at
En Rogel. 8Then it ran up the Valley of Ben
Hinnom. It went along the south slope of Jerusalem. From there it climbed to the top of
the hill that is west of the Hinnom Valley.
The hill is also at the north end of the Valley
of Rephaim. 9From the top of the hill the border headed toward the springs of Nephtoah.
It went to the towns near Mount Ephron. It
went down toward Kiriath Jearim. 10Then it
curved west from Kiriath Jearim to Mount
Seir. It ran along the north slope of Mount
Kesalon. It continued down to Beth Shemesh
and crossed over to Timnah. 11It went to the
north slope of Ekron. Then it turned toward
Shikkeron. It passed along to Mount Baalah
and reached Jabneel. The border came to an
end at the Mediterranean Sea.

12The border on the west was the coastline of the Mediterranean Sea.

Those were the borders of the family groups of the tribe of Judah.

13Joshua gave a part of Judah's share of land to
Caleb, the son of Jephunneh. That was in keeping
with the LORD's command to Joshua. The share
Caleb received was the city of Hebron. It was also
called Kiriath Arba. Anak came from the family
line of Arba. 14Caleb drove three Anakites out of
Hebron. Their names were Sheshai, Ahiman and
Talmai. They were from the family line of Anak.

15From Hebron, Caleb marched out against the
people who were living in Debir. It used to be
called Kiriath Sepher. 16Caleb said, "I will give my
daughter Acsah to be married. I'll give her to the
man who attacks and captures Kiriath Sepher."

17Othniel captured it. So Caleb gave his daughter Acsah to him to be his wife. Othniel was the son of Kenaz. He was Caleb's brother.

18One day Acsah came to Othniel. She begged him to ask her father for a field. When she got off her donkey, Caleb spoke to her. He asked, "What can I do for you?"

19She replied, "Do me a special favor. You have given me some land in the Negev Desert. Give me springs of water also." So Caleb gave her the upper and lower springs.

20Here is the share of land that was given to the tribe of Judah, family group by family group.

21The towns farthest south that were given to Judah were in the Negev Desert. They were near the border of Edom. Here is a list of those towns.

Kabzeel, Eder, Jagur, 22Kinah, Dimonah,
Adadah, 23Kedesh, Hazor, Ithnan, 24Ziph, Telem, Bealoth, 25Hazor Hadattah, Hazor,
26Amam, Shema, Moladah, 27Hazar Gaddah,
Heshmon, Beth Pelet, 28Hazar Shual, Beersheba, Biziothiah, 29Baalah, Iim, Ezem, 30Eltolad, Kesil, Hormah, 31Ziklag, Madmannah,
Sansannah, 32Lebaoth, Shilhim, Ain and
Rimmon. The total number of towns was 29.
Some of them had villages near them.

33Towns were also given to Judah in the western hills. Here is a list of those towns.

Eshtaol, Zorah, Ashnah, 34Zanoah, En
Gannim, Tappuah, Enam, 35Jarmuth, Adullam, Socoh, Azekah, 36Shaaraim, Adithaim
and Gederah. Gederah is also called Gederothaim. The total number of towns was 14.
Some of them had villages near them.

37Here's another list of towns that were given to Judah in the western hills.

Zenan, Hadashah, Migdal Gad, 38Dilean,
Mizpah, Joktheel, 39Lachish, Bozkath, Eglon, 40Cabbon, Lahmas, Kitlish, 41Gederoth,
Beth Dagon, Naamah and Makkedah. The total number of towns was 16. Some of them had villages near them.

42Here's another list of towns that were given to Judah in the western hills.

Libnah, Ether, Ashan, 43Iphtah, Ashnah,
Nezib, 44Keilah, Aczib and Mareshah. The total number of towns was nine. Some of them had villages near them.

[45]Judah was also given Ekron and the settlements and villages that were around it.
[46]West of Ekron, Judah was given all of the
settlements and villages that were near Ashdod. [47]Judah was given Ashdod and the settlements and villages that were around it.
And Judah was given Gaza and its settlements and villages. Judah's territory went all
the way to the Wadi of Egypt and the coast of
the Mediterranean Sea.

[48]Towns were also given to Judah in the central hill
country. Here is a list of those towns.
Shamir, Jattir, Socoh, [49]Dannah, Debir,
[50]Anab, Eshtemoh, Anim, [51]Goshen, Holon
and Giloh. The total number of towns was
11. Some of them had villages near them.
[52]Here's another list of towns that were given to
Judah in the central hill country.
Arab, Dumah, Eshan, [53]Janim, Beth Tap-
puah, Aphekah, [54]Humtah, Hebron and Zior.
The total number of towns was nine. Some
of them had villages near them.
[55]Here's another list of towns that were given to
Judah in the central hill country.
Maon, Carmel, Ziph, Juttah, [56]Jezreel,
Jokdeam, Zanoah, [57]Kain, Gibeah and Timnah. The total number of towns was ten.
Some of them had villages near them.
[58]Here's another list of towns that were given to
Judah in the central hill country.
Halhul, Beth Zur, Gedor, [59]Maarath, Beth
Anoth and Eltekon. The total number of
towns was six. Some of them had villages
near them.
[60]Here's another list of towns that were given to
Judah in the central hill country.
Kiriath Jearim and Rabbah. The total
number of towns was two. They had villages
near them.

[61]Towns were also given to Judah in the desert.
Here is a list of those towns.
Beth Arabah, Middin, Secacah, [62]Nib-
shan, the City of Salt and En Gedi. The total
number of towns was six. Some of them had
villages near them.

[63]Judah couldn't drive out the Jebusites who
were living in Jerusalem. So they live there with
the people of Judah to this very day.

Land Is Given to Ephraim and Manasseh

16 The land that was given to the two
tribes in the family line of Joseph
began at the Jordan River near Jericho. Their
border started east of the springs of Jericho.
It went up from there through the desert into
the hill country of Bethel. [2]Bethel is also
called Luz. From Bethel it crossed over to
Ataroth. That's where the Arkites live. [3]Then
it went west down to the territory of the
Japhletites. It went all the way to the area of
Lower Beth Horon. It went on to Gezer. It
came to an end at the Mediterranean Sea.
[4]The tribes of Manasseh and Ephraim were from
the family line of Joseph. So they received that
land as their share.

[5]Here is the territory that was given to the tribe of
Ephraim, family group by family group.
The border of their share of land started
at Ataroth Addar in the east. It went to Upper
Beth Horon. [6]It continued toward the
Mediterranean Sea. From Micmethath on the
north, it curved toward the east. It went to
Taanath Shiloh. It passed by Taanath Shiloh
to Janoah on the east. [7]Then it went down
from Janoah to Ataroth and Naarah. It
touched Jericho and came to an end at the
Jordan River. [8]From Tappuah the border
went west to the Kanah Valley. It came to an
end at the Mediterranean Sea. That was the
land that was given to the tribe of Ephraim.
Each family group received its share.
[9]The tribe of Ephraim was also given
other towns and villages that were set apart
for them. Those towns and villages were in
the share of land that was given to the tribe
of Manasseh.
[10]The people of Ephraim didn't drive out the people of Canaan who were living in Gezer. The people of Canaan live among the people of Ephraim to
this very day. But they are forced to work hard for
the people of Ephraim.

17 Land was given to the tribe of Manasseh. It
was given to Makir. Manasseh was Joseph's
oldest son. Makir was Manasseh's oldest son. The
people of Gilead came from the family line of Makir. The people of Gilead had received the lands of
Gilead and Bashan. That's because the people of
Makir were great soldiers. [2]So land was given to the
rest of the people of Manasseh. It was given to the
family groups of Abiezer, Helek, Asriel, Shechem,
Hepher and Shemida. They were the other men in
the family line of Manasseh, the son of Joseph.
Those were their names by their family groups.
[3]Makir was the son of Manasseh. Gilead was
the son of Makir. Hepher was the son of Gilead.
And Zelophehad was the son of Hepher. Zelophehad didn't have any sons. He only had daughters.
Their names were Mahlah, Noah, Hoglah, Milcah
and Tirzah.
[4]The daughters of Zelophehad went to the priest
Eleazar and to Joshua, the son of Nun. They also
went to the other leaders. They said, "The LORD
commanded Moses to give us our share of land
among our male relatives." So Joshua gave them
land along with their male relatives. That was in
keeping with what the LORD had commanded.
[5]Manasseh's share was made up of ten pieces
of land. That land was in addition to Gilead and

Bashan east of the Jordan River. 6So the five granddaughters of Hepher in the family line of Manasseh received land, just as the other five sons of Manasseh did. The land of Gilead belonged to the rest of the family line of Manasseh.

7The territory of Manasseh reached from Asher to Micmethath. Micmethath was east of Shechem. The border ran south from Micmethath. The people who were living at En Tappuah were inside the border. 8Manasseh had the land around Tappuah. But the town of Tappuah itself was on the border of Manasseh's land. It belonged to the people of Ephraim. 9The border continued south to the Kanah Valley. Some of the towns that belonged to Ephraim were located among the towns of Manasseh. But the border of Manasseh was the north side of the valley. The border came to an end at the Mediterranean Sea.

10The land on the south belonged to Ephraim. The land on the north belonged to Manasseh. The territory of Manasseh reached the Mediterranean Sea. The tribe of Asher was the border on the north. The tribe of Issachar was the border on the east.

11Inside the land that was given to Issachar and Asher, the towns of Beth Shan and Ibleam belonged to Manasseh. The towns of Dor, Endor, Taanach and Megiddo and their people also belonged to Manasseh. Manasseh was given all of those towns and the settlements that were around them. The third town in the list was also called Naphoth Dor.

12But the people of Manasseh weren't able to take over those towns. That's because the people of Canaan had made up their minds to live in that area. 13The people of Israel grew stronger. Then they forced the people of Canaan to work hard for them. But they didn't drive them out completely.

14The people in the family line of Joseph spoke to Joshua. They said, "Why have you given us only one share of the land to have as our own? There are large numbers of us. The LORD has blessed us greatly."

15"That's true," Joshua said. "There are large numbers of you. And the hill country of Ephraim is too small for you. So go up into the forest. Clear out some land for yourselves in the territory of the Perizzites and Rephaites."

16The people in Joseph's family line replied. They said, "The hill country isn't big enough for us. And all of the people of Canaan who live in the flatlands use chariots that have iron parts. They include the people of Beth Shan and its settlements. They also include the people who live in the Valley of Jezreel."

17Joshua spoke again to the people in Joseph's family line. He said to the people of Ephraim and Manasseh, "There are large numbers of you. And you are very powerful. You will have more than one piece of land. 18You will also have the central hill country. It's covered with trees. Cut them down and clear the land. That whole land from one end to the other will belong to you. The people of Canaan use chariots that have iron parts. And those people are strong. But you can drive them out."

The Rest of the Land Is Divided Up

18 The whole community of Israel gathered together at Shiloh. They set up the Tent of Meeting there. The country was brought under their control. 2But there were still seven tribes in Israel who had not yet received their shares of land.

3So Joshua spoke to the people of Israel. He said, "The LORD, the God of your people, has given you this land. How long will you wait before you begin to take it over? 4Appoint three men from each tribe. I'll send them to map out the land. Then they'll write a report about its features. The report will point out the share of land each tribe will receive. Then the men will return to me.

5"You must divide the land up into seven shares. Judah must remain in its territory in the south. The people in Joseph's family line must remain in their territory in the north. 6Write reports about the features of those seven shares of land. Bring them here to me. Then I'll cast lots for you in the sight of the LORD our God.

7"But the Levites don't get any share of your land. That's because their share is to serve the LORD as priests.

"The tribes of Gad and Reuben and half of the tribe of Manasseh have already received their shares. They are on the east side of the Jordan River. Moses, the servant of the LORD, gave their shares to them."

8The men started out on their way to map out the land. Joshua directed them, "Go and map out the land. Write a report about its features. Then return to me. I'll cast lots for you here at Shiloh in the sight of the LORD."

9So the men left and went through the land. They wrote a report about its features on a scroll. It showed how they divided up the land into seven shares. It listed the towns that were in each share. The men returned to Joshua in the camp at Shiloh.

10Then Joshua cast lots for them in Shiloh in the sight of the LORD. There he gave out a share of land to each of the remaining tribes in Israel.

Land Is Given to Benjamin

11The first lot that was drawn out was for the tribe of Benjamin, family group by family group. The territory they were given was located between the tribes of the people of Judah and the people of Joseph. Here are the borders of Benjamin's territory.

12On the north side their border started at the Jordan River. It went past the north slope of Jericho. Then it headed west into the central hill country. It came to an end at the

Desert of Beth Aven. [13]From there it crossed to the south slope of Bethel. Then it went down to Ataroth Addar on the hill south of Lower Beth Horon.

[14]From the hill that faces Beth Horon on the south the border turned south along the west side of the hill. It came to an end at Kiriath Jearim. That town belongs to the people of Judah. That was the border on the west.

[15]The border on the south side started at the west edge of Kiriath Jearim. It came to an end at the springs of Nephtoah. [16]It went down to the foot of the hill that faces the Valley of Ben Hinnom. The hill is north of the Valley of Rephaim. The border continued down the Hinnom Valley. It went along the south slope of Jerusalem, where the people of Jebus live. It continued on to En Rogel. [17]Then it curved north. It went to En Shemesh. It continued on to Geliloth. Geliloth faces the Pass of Adummim. The border ran down to the Stone of Bohan, the son of Reuben. [18]It continued to the north slope of Beth Arabah. It went on down into the Arabah Valley. [19]From there it went to the north slope of Beth Hoglah. It came to an end at the north bay of the Dead Sea. That's where the Jordan River flows into the Dead Sea. That was the border on the south.

[20]The Jordan River formed the border on the east side.

Those were the borders that marked out on all sides the land the family groups of Benjamin received as their share.

[21]Here is a list of towns that were given to the tribe of Benjamin, family group by family group.

Jericho, Beth Hoglah, Emek Keziz, [22]Beth Arabah, Zemaraim, Bethel, [23]Avvim, Parah, Ophrah, [24]Kephar Ammoni, Ophni and Geba. The total number of towns and their villages was 12.

[25]Here is another list of towns that were given to Benjamin.

Gibeon, Ramah, Beeroth, [26]Mizpah, Kephirah, Mozah, [27]Rekem, Irpeel, Taralah, [28]Zelah, Haeleph, Jerusalem, Gibeah and Kiriath. The total number of towns and their villages was 14.

That was the share of land the family groups of Benjamin received.

Land Is Given to Simeon

19 The second lot that was drawn out was for the tribe of Simeon, family group by family group. The share of land they were given was in the territory of Judah. [2]Here is what Simeon's share included.

Beersheba, Moladah, [3]Hazar Shual, Balah, Ezem, [4]Eltolad, Bethul, Hormah, [5]Ziklag, Beth Marcaboth, Hazar Susah, [6]Beth Lebaoth and Sharuhen. The total number of towns was 13. Some of them had villages near them.

[7]Here's another list of towns that were given to Simeon.

Ain, Rimmon, Ether and Ashan. The total number of towns was four. Some of them had villages near them. [8]The towns and all of the villages that were around them reached all the way to Ramah in the Negev Desert.

That was the share of land the tribe of Simeon received, family group by family group. [9]Simeon's share of land was taken from Judah's share. That's because Judah had more land than they needed. So the people of Simeon received their share of land inside the territory of Judah.

Land Is Given to Zebulun

[10]The third lot that was drawn out was for the tribe of Zebulun, family group by family group. Here are the borders of Zebulun's territory.

The border of their share of land went as far as Sarid. [11]It ran west to Maralah and touched Dabbesheth. It reached to the valley near Jokneam. [12]It turned east from Sarid toward the sunrise. It went to the territory of Kisloth Tabor. It went on to Daberath and up to Japhia. [13]Then it continued east to Gath Hepher and Eth Kazin. It came to an end at Rimmon and turned toward Neah. [14]There the border went around on the north to Hannathon. It came to an end at the Valley of Iphtah El. [15]Zebulun's territory included Kattath, Nahalal, Shimron, Idalah and Bethlehem. The total number of towns was 12. Some of them had villages near them.

[16]Those towns and their villages were Zebulun's share, family group by family group.

Land Is Given to Issachar

[17]The fourth lot that was drawn out was for the tribe of Issachar, family group by family group. [18]Here is what Issachar's share included.

Jezreel, Kesulloth, Shunem, [19]Hapharaim, Shion, Anaharath, [20]Rabbith, Kishion, Ebez, [21]Remeth, En Gannim, En Haddah and Beth Pazzez. [22]The border touched Tabor, Shahazumah and Beth Shemesh. It came to an end at the Jordan River. The total number of towns was 16. Some of them had villages near them.

[23]Those towns and their villages were the share the tribe of Issachar received, family group by family group.

Land Is Given to Asher

[24]The fifth lot that was drawn out was for the tribe of Asher, family group by family group. [25]Here is what Asher's share included.

Helkath, Hali, Beten, Acshaph, [26]Allammelech, Amad and Mishal. On the west the

border touched Carmel and Shihor Libnath.
27Then it turned east toward Beth Dagon. It
touched Zebulun and the Valley of Iphtah El.
It went north to Beth Emek and Neiel. It
went past Cabul on the left. 28It went to Abdon, Rehob, Hammon and Kanah. It reached
all the way to Greater Sidon. 29The border
then turned back toward Ramah. It went to
Tyre, a city that had high walls around it. It
turned toward Hosah. It came to an end at the
Mediterranean Sea in the area of Aczib,
30Ummah, Aphek and Rehob. The total number of towns was 22. Some of them had villages near them.
31Those towns and their villages were the share the
tribe of Asher received, family group by family
group.

Land Is Given to Naphtali

32The sixth lot that was drawn out was for Naphtali, family group by family group.
33Their border started at Heleph and the
large tree in Zaanannim. It went past Adami
Nekeb and Jabneel. It went to Lakkum and
came to an end at the Jordan River. 34The
border ran west through Aznoth Tabor. It
came to an end at Hukkok. It touched Zebulun on the south. It touched Asher on the
west. It touched the Jordan on the east.
35The cities that had high walls around
them were Ziddim, Zer, Hammath, Rakkath,
Kinnereth, 36Adamah, Ramah, Hazor, 37Ke-
desh, Edrei, En Hazor, 38Iron, Migdal El, Ho-
rem, Beth Anath and Beth Shemesh. The
total number of towns was 19. Some of them
had villages near them.
39Those towns and their villages were the share the
tribe of Naphtali received, family group by family
group.

Land Is Given to Dan

40The seventh lot that was drawn out was for the
tribe of Dan, family group by family group. 41Here
is what Dan's share of land included.
Zorah, Eshtaol, Ir Shemesh, 42Shaalabbin,
Aijalon, Ithlah, 43Elon, Timnah, Ekron, 44Elte-
keh, Gibbethon, Baalath, 45Jehud, Bene Berak,
Gath Rimmon, 46Me Jarkon and Rakkon.
Dan's share included the area that faces Joppa.
47The people of Dan had trouble taking over
their territory. So they went up and attacked Leshem. They took it. They killed its people with
their swords. Then they moved into Leshem and
settled down there. They named it Dan. That's
because they traced their family line back to him.
48All of those towns and their villages were the
share the tribe of Dan received, family group by
family group.

Land Is Given to Joshua

49The people of Israel finished dividing up the
shares of land the tribes received. Then they gave
a share to Joshua, the son of Nun. 50They did what
the LORD had commanded them to do. They gave
Joshua the town he asked for. It was Timnath Serah in the hill country of Ephraim. He built up the
town and settled down there.
51All of those territories were given out by using
lots at Shiloh. The lots were drawn out by the
priest Eleazar and by Joshua, the son of Nun. The
leaders of the tribes of Israel helped them. The lots
were drawn out in front of the LORD at the entrance
to the Tent of Meeting. So the work of dividing up
the land was finished.

Cities to Go to for Safety

20 Then the LORD spoke to Joshua. He said,
2"Tell the people of Israel to choose the
cities to go to for safety, just as I directed you
through Moses. 3Anyone who kills a person by accident can run there for safety. So can anyone who
kills a person without meaning to. The one who is
charged with murder will be kept safe from the
nearest male relative of the person who was killed.
4"Suppose the one who is charged runs for
safety to one of those cities. Then he must stand in
the entrance of the city gate. He must state his case
in front of the elders of that city. They must let him
come into their city. They must give him a place
to live there.
5"Suppose the nearest male relative of the person who was killed comes after him. Then the
elders must not hand him over to that relative.
That's because he didn't mean to kill his neighbor.
He didn't make evil plans to do it.
6"He must stay in that city until his case has
been brought to the community court. He must stay
there until the high priest who is serving at that
time dies. Then he can go back to his own home.
He can return to the town he ran away from."
7So the people of Israel set apart Kedesh in Galilee. It's in the hill country of Naphtali. They set
apart Shechem. It's in the hill country of Ephraim.
They set apart Kiriath Arba. It's in the hill country
of Judah. Kiriath Arba is also called Hebron.
8On the east side of the Jordan River near Jericho
they chose Bezer. It's in the desert on the high flatlands. It's in the territory of the tribe of Reuben.
They chose Ramoth in Gilead. It's in the territory of
the tribe of Gad. They chose Golan in the land of
Bashan. It's in the territory of the tribe of Manasseh.
9Suppose you kill someone by accident. Or
another Israelite does it. Or an outsider who lives
among you does it. Then any of you can run for
safety to one of those cities that have been chosen.
There you won't be killed by the nearest male relative of the person who was killed. First your case
must be brought to the community court.

Towns Are Given to the Levites

21 The leaders of the Levite family groups
approached the priest Eleazar and Joshua,
the son of Nun. They also approached the leaders

of the family groups of Israel's other tribes. 2They went to all of them at Shiloh in Canaan. They said to them, "Give us towns to live in. Also give us grasslands for our livestock. That's what the LORD commanded through Moses."

3So the people of Israel gave the Levites towns and grasslands out of their own shares of land. They did what the LORD had commanded. Here are the towns the Levites were given.

4The first lot that was drawn out was for the people of Kohath, family group by family group. Some of the Levites came from the family line of the priest Aaron. They were given 13 towns from the tribes of Judah, Simeon and Benjamin. 5The rest of Kohath's family groups were given ten towns from the family groups of the tribes of Ephraim and Dan and half of the tribe of Manasseh.

6The family groups of Gershon were given 13 towns from the family groups of the tribes of Issachar, Asher and Naphtali and half of the tribe of Manasseh. That part of Manasseh was in the land of Bashan.

7The family groups of Merari received 12 towns from the tribes of Reuben, Gad and Zebulun. Each family group received its share.

8So the people of Israel gave those towns and their grasslands to the Levites. They did what the LORD had commanded through Moses.

9They gave some towns from the territories of the tribes of Judah and Simeon 10to the members of the family line of Aaron. The towns were given to the family groups of Kohath. They were Levites. The first lot that was drawn out was for them. Here are the towns the family groups of Kohath were given.

11The people of Israel gave them Kiriath Arba and the grasslands that were around it. Kiriath Arba is also called Hebron. It's in the hill country of Judah. Anak came from the family line of Arba. 12But Israel had already given away the fields and villages around the city. They had given them to Caleb as his share. Caleb was the son of Jephunneh.

13So they gave Hebron to the members of the family line of the priest Aaron. Hebron was a city where anyone who was charged with murder could go for safety. They also gave them Libnah, 14Jattir, Eshtemoa, 15Holon, Debir, 16Ain, Juttah and Beth Shemesh. They gave those towns and their grasslands to the family groups of Kohath. The total number of towns from the tribes of Judah and Simeon was nine.

17The people of Israel gave some towns from the tribe of Benjamin to the family groups of Kohath. The towns were Gibeon, Geba, 18Anathoth and Almon. The total number of those towns and their grasslands was four.

19So the total number of towns and their grasslands that were given to the priests in the family line of Aaron was 13.

20There were other family groups of Kohath among the Levites. They were given towns from the tribe of Ephraim. Here are the towns those other family groups of Kohath were given.

21In the hill country of Ephraim they were given Shechem. It was a city where anyone who was charged with murder could go for safety. They were also given Gezer, 22Kibzaim and Beth Horon. The total number of those towns and their grasslands was four.

23From the tribe of Dan they received Eltekeh, Gibbethon, 24Aijalon and Gath Rimmon. The total number of those towns and their grasslands was four.

25From half of the tribe of Manasseh they received Taanach and Gath Rimmon. The total number of those towns and their grasslands was two.

26So all of those ten towns and their grasslands were given to the other family groups of Kohath.

27Here are the towns the family groups of Gershon among the Levites were given.

From half of the tribe of Manasseh they received Golan in the land of Bashan. Golan was a city where anyone who was charged with murder could go for safety. They also received Be Eshtarah. The total number of those towns and their grasslands was two.

28From the tribe of Issachar
they received Kishion, Daberath, 29Jarmuth and En Gannim. The total number of those towns and their grasslands was four.

30From the tribe of Asher
they received Mishal, Abdon, 31Helkath and Rehob. The total number of those towns and their grasslands was four.

32From the tribe of Naphtali
they received Kedesh in Galilee. Kedesh was a city where anyone who was charged with murder could go for safety. They also received Hammoth Dor and Kartan. The total number of those towns and their grasslands was three.

33So the total number of towns and their grasslands that were given to the family groups of Gershon was 13.

34The rest of the Levites were from the family groups of Merari. Here are the towns they were given.

From the tribe of Zebulun
they received Jokneam, Kartah, 35Dimnah and Nahalal. The total number of those towns and their grasslands was four.

36From the tribe of Reuben
they received Bezer, Jahaz, 37Kedemoth and Mephaath. The total number of those towns and their grasslands was four.

38From the tribe of Gad
they received Ramoth in Gilead. Ramoth was a city where anyone who was charged

with murder could go for safety. They also
received Mahanaim, 39Heshbon and Jazer.
The total number of those towns and their
grasslands was four.
40So the total number of towns that were given to
the family groups of Merari was 12. That con-
cludes the list of towns the rest of the Levites
received.

41The total number of Levite towns and their
grasslands in the territory that was given to Israel
was 48. 42Each of those towns had grasslands
around it. That was true of all of them.

43So the LORD gave Israel all of the land he had
promised with an oath to give to Abraham, Isaac
and Jacob. And Israel took it over. Then they settled down there. 44The LORD gave them peace and
rest on every side. That's what he had promised
their fathers he would do. Not one of their enemies
was able to fight against Israel and win. The LORD
handed all of their enemies over to them.

45The LORD kept all of the good promises he
had made to the people of Israel. Every one of
them came true.

The Eastern Tribes Return Home

22 Joshua sent for the tribes of Reuben and
Gad and half of the tribe of Manasseh. 2He
said to them, "You have done everything that Moses, the servant of the LORD, commanded. You
have also obeyed everything I commanded. 3For a
long time now you haven't deserted the other Israelites. Instead, you have done what the LORD your
God sent you to do. You have obeyed him to this
very day.

4"Now the LORD your God has given the other
tribes peace and rest. That's what he promised to
do. So return to your homes. They are in the land
that Moses, the servant of the LORD, gave you. It's
on the east side of the Jordan River.

5"Be very careful to obey the law that Moses,
the servant of the LORD, gave you. He commanded you to love the LORD your God. He told
you to live exactly as the LORD wants you to. He
told you to obey the LORD's commands. He told
you to remain true to the LORD. And he told you
to serve the LORD with all your heart and with all
your soul."

6Joshua gave the eastern tribes his blessing.
Then he sent them home. So they went.

7Moses had given land in Bashan to half of the
tribe of Manasseh. Joshua had given land to the
other half of the tribe along with the other tribes
on the west side of the Jordan River.

When Joshua sent them home, he blessed them.
8He said, "Return to your homes. Take your great
wealth with you. Return with your large herds of
livestock. Take your silver, gold, bronze and iron
with you. Return with all of your clothes. Divide
up the things you have taken from your enemies.
Share them with your people."

9So the tribes of Reuben and Gad and half of the
tribe of Manasseh went home. They left the other
people of Israel at Shiloh in Canaan. They returned
to Gilead. That was their own land. They had gotten it in keeping with the LORD's command
through Moses.

10The tribes of Reuben and Gad and half of the
tribe of Manasseh came to Geliloth. It was near the
Jordan River in the land of Canaan. They built a
large altar there by the Jordan.

11The rest of the people of Israel heard that they
had built the altar. They heard that they had built
it on the border of Canaan at Geliloth. It was near
the Jordan River on the west side.

12So the whole community of Israel gathered
together at Shiloh. They decided to go to war
against the eastern tribes.

13The people of Israel sent the priest Phinehas
to the land of Gilead. Phinehas was the son of Eleazar. They sent him to the tribes of Reuben and
Gad and half of the tribe of Manasseh.

14They sent ten of their leaders with him. There
was one for each of the tribes of Israel. Each man
was the leader of a family group among the larger
family groups of Israel.

15They went to the tribes of Reuben and Gad
and half of the tribe of Manasseh in the land of
Gilead. They said to them, 16"We're speaking for
the LORD's whole community. How could you disobey the God of Israel like this? How could you
turn away from the LORD? How could you disobey
him by building an altar for yourselves?

17"Don't you remember how we sinned at Peor?
The LORD struck us with a plague because of what
we did. Up to this very day we're still suffering
because of that sin. 18Are you turning away from
the LORD now?

"Suppose you disobey the LORD today. If you
do, he'll be angry with the whole community of
Israel tomorrow.

19"If your own land isn't 'clean,' come over to
the LORD's land. It's where his holy tent stands.
Share our land with us. But don't disobey the
LORD. Don't turn against us by building an altar
for yourselves. Don't build any altar other than the
altar of the LORD our God.

20"Remember Achan, the son of Zerah. Achan
wasn't faithful to the LORD. He took the things that
had been set apart to the LORD in a special way to
be destroyed. Didn't the LORD's anger come on the
whole community of Israel? And Achan wasn't the
only one who died because of his sin."

21Then the tribes of Reuben and Gad and half
of the tribe of Manasseh replied. They answered
the leaders of the family groups of Israel. 22They
said, "The Mighty One, God, the LORD! The
Mighty One, God, the LORD! He knows! And we
want Israel to know! Have we opposed the LORD?
Have we refused to obey him? If we have, don't
spare us today.

23“Have we built our own altar so we can turn
away from the LORD? Have we built it to offer
burnt offerings and grain offerings on it? Have we
built it to sacrifice friendship offerings on it? If we
have, may the LORD himself hold us accountable.
24“No! We built it because we were afraid.
Someday your children might speak to our children. We were afraid they might say, ‘What do you
have to do with the LORD? What do you have to do
with the God of Israel? 25The LORD has made the
Jordan River a border between us and you. You
people of Reuben! You people of Gad! You don’t
have anything to do with the LORD.’ If your children say that, they might cause our children to stop
worshiping the LORD.
26“That’s why we said to ourselves, ‘Let’s get
ready and build an altar. But let’s not build it to
offer burnt offerings or sacrifices on it.’
27“So just the opposite is true. The altar will be
a witness between us and you. It will be a witness
between our children and yours after us. It will
also be a witness that we will worship the LORD at
his sacred tent. We’ll worship him there with our
burnt offerings, sacrifices and friendship offerings.
Then in days to come your children won’t be able
to say to ours, ‘You don’t have anything to do with
the LORD.’
28“So we said to ourselves, ‘Suppose they say
that to us sometime. Or suppose they say it to our
children after us. Then we’ll answer, “Look at this
altar. It’s exactly like the LORD’s altar. Our people
built it. They didn’t build it to offer burnt offerings
and sacrifices on it. Instead, they built it to be a
witness between us and you.” ’
29“We would never refuse to obey the LORD. We
would never turn away from him now. We
wouldn’t build an altar to offer burnt offerings,
grain offerings and sacrifices on it. We wouldn’t
use any altar other than the altar of the LORD our
God. That altar stands in front of his holy tent.”
30The priest Phinehas heard what the tribes of
Reuben, Gad and Manasseh had to say. The leaders of the family groups of the community of Israel heard it too. All of them were pleased with what
they heard.
31The priest Phinehas spoke to the tribes of Reuben, Gad and Manasseh. Phinehas was the son of
Eleazar. He said, “Today we know that the LORD is
with us. That’s because you have been faithful to
him in this matter. Now you have saved the people
of Israel from the LORD’s anger against them.”
32Then the priest Phinehas, the son of Eleazar,
returned to Canaan. So did the leaders. All of them
went back from their meeting with the tribes of
Reuben and Gad in Gilead. They brought a report
back to the people of Israel. 33The people were
glad to hear the report. They praised God. They
didn’t talk anymore about going to war against the
eastern tribes. And they didn’t talk anymore about
destroying the country where the tribes of Reuben
and Gad lived.
34The tribes of Reuben and Gad gave the altar a
name. They called it A Witness Between Us That
the LORD Is God.

Joshua Says Good-by to the Leaders

23 A long time had passed. The LORD had
given Israel peace and rest from all of
their enemies who were around them. By that
time Joshua was very old. 2So he sent for all of
the elders, leaders, judges and officials of Israel.
He said to them, “I’m very old. 3You yourselves
have seen everything the LORD your God has
done. You have seen what he’s done to all of those
nations because of you. The LORD your God
fought for you.
4“Remember how I’ve given you all of the land of
the nations that remain here. I’ve given each of your
tribes a share of it. It’s the land of the nations I won
the battle over. It’s between the Jordan River and the
Mediterranean Sea in the west. 5The LORD your God
himself will drive those nations out of your way. He
will push them out to make room for you. You will
take over their land, just as the LORD your God
promised you.
6“Be very strong. Be careful to obey everything
that is written in the Scroll of the Law of Moses.
Don’t turn away from it to the right or the left.
7“Don’t have anything to do with the nations
that remain among you. Don’t use the names of
their gods for any reason at all. Don’t take oaths
and make promises in their names. You must not
serve them. You must not bow down to them. 8You
must remain true to the LORD your God, just as
you have done until now.
9“The LORD has driven out great and powerful
nations to make room for you. To this very day no
one has been able to fight against you and win.
10One of you can chase a thousand away. That’s
because the LORD your God fights for you, just as
he promised he would. 11So be very careful to love
the LORD your God.
12“But suppose you turn away from him. You
mix with the people who are left alive in the
nations that remain among you. Later, you and
they get married to each other. And you do other
kinds of things with them. 13Then you can be sure
of what the LORD your God will do. He won’t
drive out those nations to make room for you anymore. Instead, they will become traps and snares
for you. They will be like whips on your backs.
They will be like thorns in your eyes. All of that
will continue until you are destroyed. It will continue until you are removed from this good land.
It’s the land the LORD your God has given you.
14“Now I’m about to die, just as everyone else
on earth does. The LORD your God has kept all of
the good promises he gave you. Every one of them
has come true. Not one has failed to come true.
And you know that with all your heart and soul.
15“Every good promise of the LORD your God
has come true. So you know that the LORD will

bring on you all of the evil things he has warned
you about. He'll do it until he has destroyed you.
He'll do it until he has removed you from this
good land. It's the land he has given you.
16"Suppose you break the covenant the LORD
your God made with you. He commanded you to
obey it. But suppose you go and serve other gods.
And you bow down to them. Then the LORD's
anger will burn against you. You will quickly be
destroyed. You will be removed from the good
land he has given you."

Joshua Tells Israel to Serve the LORD

24 Joshua gathered all of Israel's tribes
together at Shechem. He sent for the
elders, leaders, judges and officials of Israel. They
came and stood there in the sight of God.
2Joshua spoke to all of the people. He said, "The
LORD is the God of Israel. He says, 'Long ago your
people lived east of the Euphrates River. They
worshiped other gods there. Your people included
Terah. He was the father of Abraham and Nahor.
3" 'I took your father Abraham from the land
that is east of the Euphrates. I led him all through
Canaan. I gave him many children and grandchildren. I gave him Isaac. 4To Isaac I gave Jacob and
Esau. I gave the hill country of Seir to Esau. But
Jacob and his children went down to Egypt.
5" 'Then I sent Moses and Aaron. I made the
people of Egypt suffer because of the plagues I
sent on them. But I brought you out of Egypt.
6" 'When I brought your parents out, they came
to the Red Sea. The people of Egypt chased them
with chariots and with men on horses. They chased
them all the way to the sea. 7But your people cried
out to me for help. So I put darkness between you
and the people of Egypt. I swept them into the sea.
It completely covered them. Your own eyes saw
what I did to them. After that, you lived in the
desert for a long time.
8" 'I brought you to the land of the Amorites.
They lived east of the Jordan River. They fought
against you. But I handed them over to you. I
destroyed them to make room for you. Then you
took over their land.
9" 'Balak, the son of Zippor, prepared to fight
against Israel. Balak was king of Moab. He sent
for Balaam. He wanted him to put a curse on you.
Balaam was the son of Beor. 10But I would not listen to Balaam's curses. So he blessed you again
and again. And I saved you from his power.
11" 'Then you went across the Jordan River. You
came to Jericho. Its people fought against you. So
did the Amorites, Perizzites, Canaanites, Hittites,
Girgashites, Hivites and Jebusites. But I handed
them over to you.
12" 'I sent hornets ahead of you. They drove
your enemies out to make room for you. That
included the two Amorite kings. You did not do
that with your own swords and bows. 13So I gave
you a land you had never farmed. I gave you cities
you had not built. You are now living in them. And
you are eating the fruit of vineyards and olive trees
you did not plant.'
14"So have respect for the LORD. Serve him. Be
completely faithful to him. Throw away the gods
your people worshiped east of the Euphrates River
and in Egypt. Serve the LORD.
15"But suppose you don't want to serve him.
Then choose for yourselves right now whom you
will serve. You can choose the gods your people
served east of the Euphrates River. Or you can
choose the gods the Amorites serve. After all, you
are living in their land. But as for me and my family, we will serve the LORD."
16Then the people answered Joshua. They said,
"We would never desert the LORD! We would
never serve other gods! 17The LORD our God himself brought us and our parents up out of Egypt.
He brought us out of that land where we were
slaves. With our own eyes, we saw those great and
miraculous signs he did. He kept us safe on our
entire journey. He kept us safe as we traveled
through all of the nations. 18He drove them out to
make room for us. That included the Amorites.
They also lived in the land. We too will serve the
LORD. That's because he is our God."
19Joshua spoke to the people. He said, "You
aren't able to serve the LORD. He is a holy God.
He is a jealous God. He won't forgive you when
you disobey him. He won't forgive you when you
sin against him.
20"Suppose you desert the LORD. Suppose you
serve the gods that people in other lands serve. If
you do, he will turn against you. He will bring
trouble on you. He will destroy you, even though
he has been good to you."
21But the people spoke to Joshua. They said,
"No! We will serve the LORD."
22Then Joshua said, "You are witnesses against
yourselves. You have said that you have chosen to
serve the LORD."
"Yes. We are witnesses," they replied.
23"Now then," said Joshua, "throw away the
gods that are among you. People from other lands
serve those gods. Give yourselves completely to
the LORD, the God of Israel."
24Then the people spoke to Joshua. They said,
"We will serve the LORD our God. We will obey
him."
25On that day Joshua made a covenant for the
people. There at Shechem he wrote down rules and
laws for them. 26He recorded those things in the
Scroll of the Law of God. Then he got a large
stone. He set it up in Shechem under the oak tree.
It was near the place that had been set apart for the
LORD.
27"Look!" he said to all of the people. "This
stone will be a witness against us. It has heard all
of the words the LORD has spoken to us. Suppose
you aren't true to your God. Then the stone will be
a witness against you."

Joshua Dies

28Joshua sent the people away. He sent all of them to their own shares of land.

29Then Joshua, the servant of the LORD, died. He was the son of Nun. He was 110 years old when he died. 30His people buried his body at Timnath Serah on his own property. It's north of Mount Gaash in the hill country of Ephraim.

31Israel served the LORD as long as Joshua lived. They also served him as long as the elders lived. Those were the elders who lived longer than Joshua did. They had seen for themselves everything the LORD had done for Israel.

32The people of Israel had brought Joseph's bones up from Egypt. They buried his bones at Shechem in the piece of land Jacob had bought. He had bought it from the sons of Hamor. He had paid 100 pieces of silver for it. Hamor was the father of Shechem. That piece of land became the share that belonged to Joseph's children after him.

33Aaron's son Eleazar died. His body was buried at Gibeah in the hill country of Ephraim. Gibeah had been given to Eleazar's son Phinehas.

Judges

Israel Fights Against the Canaanites Who Are Still Left

1 Joshua died. After that, the people of Israel
spoke to the LORD. They asked him, "Who
will go up first and fight for us against the people
of Canaan?"
2 The LORD answered, "The tribe of Judah will
go. I have handed the land over to them."
3 Then the men of Judah spoke to their fellow Israelites, the men of Simeon. They said, "Come up
with us. Come into the territory Joshua gave us.
Help us fight against the people of Canaan. Then
we'll go with you into your territory." So the men
of Simeon went with them.
4 When the men of Judah attacked, the LORD
helped them. He handed the Canaanites and Perizzites over to them. They struck down 10,000 men
at Bezek.
5 Judah found Adoni-Bezek there. They fought
against him. They struck down the Canaanites and
Perizzites. 6 But Adoni-Bezek ran away. Judah
chased him and caught him. Then they cut off his
thumbs and big toes.
7 Adoni-Bezek said, "I cut off the thumbs and
big toes of 70 kings. I made them pick up scraps
under my table. Now God has paid me back for
what I did to them." The men of Judah brought
Adoni-Bezek to Jerusalem. That's where he died.
8 The men of Judah attacked Jerusalem and took
it. They set the city on fire. They killed its people
with their swords.
9 After that, the men of Judah went down to fight
against the people of Canaan who were living in
the central hill country. They also fought against
those who were living in the Negev Desert and the
western hills.
10 Then the men of Judah marched out against
the Canaanites who were living in Hebron. The
men of Judah won the battle over Sheshai, Ahiman
and Talmai. Hebron used to be called Kiriath Arba.
11 From Hebron they marched out against the
people who were living in Debir. It used to be
called Kiriath Sepher.
12 Caleb said, "I will give my daughter Acsah to
be married. I'll give her to the man who attacks
and captures Kiriath Sepher."
13 Othniel captured it. So Caleb gave his daughter Acsah to him to be his wife. Othniel was the
son of Kenaz. He was Caleb's younger brother.
14 One day Acsah came to Othniel. She begged
him to ask her father for a field. When she got off
her donkey, Caleb spoke to her. He said, "What
can I do for you?"
15 She replied, "Do me a special favor. You have
given me some land in the Negev Desert. Give me
springs of water also." So Caleb gave her the
upper and lower springs.
16 Moses' father-in-law was a Kenite. His family
went up from Jericho. They went up with the people of Judah to the Desert of Judah. They went
there to live among its people. Those people were
living in the Negev Desert near Arad. Jericho was
also known as The City of Palm Trees.
17 The men of Judah went with their fellow Israelites, the men of Simeon. They attacked the people of Canaan who were living in Zephath. They
set the city apart to the LORD in a special way to be
destroyed. That's why the city was called Hormah.
18 The men of Judah took Gaza, Ashkelon and
Ekron. They also took the territory that was around
each of those cities.
19 The LORD was with the men of Judah. They
took over the central hill country. But they weren't
able to drive the people out of the flatlands. That's
because those people used chariots that had some
iron parts.
20 Moses had promised to give Hebron to Caleb.
So Hebron was given to Caleb. He drove the three
sons of Anak out of it.
21 But the people of Benjamin failed to drive out
the Jebusites who were living in Jerusalem. So
they live there with the people of Benjamin to this
very day.
22 The men of Joseph attacked Bethel. The LORD
was with them. 23 They sent men to Bethel to check
it out. It used to be called Luz.
24 Those who were sent saw a man coming out
of the city. They said to him, "Show us how to get
into the city. If you do, we'll see that you are
treated well." 25 So he showed them how to get in.
The men of Joseph killed the people in the city
with their swords. But they spared the man from
Bethel. They also spared his whole family. 26 Then
he went to the land of the Hittites. He built a city
there. He called it Luz. That's still its name to this
very day.
27 But the tribe of Manasseh didn't drive out the
people of Beth Shan. They didn't drive out the
people of Taanach, Dor, Ibleam and Megiddo. And
they didn't drive out the people of the settlements
that are around those cities either. That's because
the people of Canaan had made up their minds to
continue living in that land.
28 Later, Israel became stronger. Then they
forced the people of Canaan to work hard for
them. But Israel never drove them out completely.
29 The tribe of Ephraim didn't drive out the Canaanites who were living in Gezer. So they continued to live there among them.
30 The tribe of Zebulun didn't drive out the Canaanites who were living in Kitron and Nahalol.

So they remained among them. But Zebulun
forced the Canaanites to work hard for them.
31The tribe of Asher didn't drive out the people
who were living in Acco and Sidon. They didn't
drive out the people of Ahlab, Aczib, Helbah,
Aphek and Rehob. 32So the people of Asher lived
among the Canaanites who were in the land.
33The tribe of Naphtali didn't drive out the people who were living in Beth Shemesh and Beth
Anath. So the people of Naphtali lived among the
Canaanites who were in the land. The people of
Beth Shemesh and Beth Anath were forced to
work hard for them.
34The Amorites made the people of Dan stay in
the central hill country. They didn't let them come
down into the flatlands. 35The Amorites made up
their minds to stay in Mount Heres. They also
stayed in Aijalon and Shaalbim.
But the power of the tribes of Joseph grew. Then
the Amorites were forced to work hard for them.
36The border of the Amorites started at Scorpion
Pass. It went to Sela and even past it.

The Angel of the Lord Warns Israel

2 The angel of the Lord went up from Gilgal to
Bokim. There he spoke to the people of Israel. "I brought you up out of Egypt," he said. "I led
you into this land. It is the land I promised with an
oath to give to Abraham, Isaac and Jacob. I said, 'I
will never break the covenant I made with you. 2So
you must not make a covenant with the people of
this land. Instead, you must tear down their altars.'
"But you have disobeyed me. Why did you do
it? 3I have something to tell you. I will not drive
those people out to make room for you. They will
be like thorns in your sides. Their gods will be a
trap to you."
4The angel of the Lord spoke those things to all
of the people of Israel. Then the people began to
sob out loud. 5So that place was called Bokim. The
people offered sacrifices to the Lord there.

The People Turn Away From the Lord

6Joshua sent the people of Israel away. Then
they went to take over the land. All of them went
to their own shares of land.
7The people served the Lord as long as Joshua
lived. They also served him as long as the elders
lived. Those were the elders who lived longer than
Joshua did. They had seen all of the great things
the Lord had done for Israel.
8Joshua, the servant of the Lord, died. He was
the son of Nun. He was 110 years old when he
died. 9His people buried his body on his own property at Timnath Heres. It's north of Mount Gaash
in the hill country of Ephraim.
10All of the people of Joshua's time joined the
members of their families who had already died.
Then those who were born after them grew up.
They didn't know the Lord. They didn't know
what he had done for Israel.
11The people of Israel did what was evil in the
sight of the Lord. They served the gods that were
named after Baal. 12They deserted the Lord, the
God of their people. He had brought them out of
Egypt. But now the people of Israel followed other
gods and worshiped them. They served the gods
of the nations that were around them. They made
the Lord angry 13because they deserted him. They
served Baal. They also served the goddesses that
were named after Ashtoreth.
14The Lord became angry with Israel. So he
handed them over to robbers. The robbers stole
everything from them. He gave them over to their
enemies who were all around them. Israel wasn't
able to fight against them anymore and win.
15When Israel went out to fight, the Lord's power
was against them. He let their enemies win the battle over them. The Lord had warned them with an
oath that it would happen. And now they were suffering terribly.
16Then the Lord gave them leaders. The leaders
saved them from the power of those robbers. 17But
the people wouldn't listen to their leaders. They
weren't faithful to the Lord. They joined themselves to other gods and worshiped them. They
didn't obey the Lord's commands as their people
before them had done. They quickly turned away
from the path their people had taken.
18When the Lord gave them a leader, he was
with that leader. He saved the people from the
power of their enemies. He did it as long as the
leader lived. He was very sorry for the people.
They groaned because of what their enemies did
to them. The enemies beat them down. They
treated them badly.
19But when the leader died, the people returned
to their evil ways. The things they did were even
more sinful than the things their people before
them had done. They followed other gods. They
served them. They worshiped them. They refused
to give up their evil practices. They wouldn't
change their stubborn ways.
20So the Lord's anger burned against the people
of Israel. He said, "This nation has broken my
covenant. I made it with their people of long ago.
But this nation has not listened to me. 21Joshua left
some nations in the land when he died. I will not
drive those nations out to make room for you anymore. 22I will use them to put Israel to the test. I
will see whether Israel will live the way I want
them to. I will see whether they will follow my
path, just as their people did long ago."
23The Lord had let those nations remain in the
land. He didn't drive them out right away. He
didn't hand them over to Joshua.

3 The Lord left some nations in the land. He left
them there in order to put the people of Israel
to the test. He did it for all those who hadn't lived
through any of the wars in Canaan. 2He wanted to
teach the men in Israel who had never been in battle before. He wanted them to learn how to fight.

3So he left the five rulers of the Philistines. He left
the people of Canaan and the people of Sidon. He
left the Hivites who were living in the Lebanon
mountains. They lived in the area that was between
Mount Baal Hermon and Lebo Hamath.
4The LORD left those nations where they were
in order to put Israel to the test. He wanted to see
whether they would obey his commands. He had
given those commands through Moses to their
people of long ago.
5So the people of Israel lived among the Canaanites, Hittites, Amorites, Perizzites, Hivites and
Jebusites. 6They got married to the daughters of
those people. They gave their own daughters to the
sons of those people. And they served the gods of
those people.

Othniel

7The people of Israel did what was evil in the
sight of the LORD. They forgot the LORD their God.
They served the gods that were named after Baal.
They also served the goddesses that were named
after Asherah.
8So the LORD's anger burned against Israel. He
gave them over to the power of Cushan-Rishathaim. He was the king of Aram Naharaim. For eight
years Israel was under his rule.
9They cried out to the LORD. Then he gave them
a man to save them. His name was Othniel, the son
of Kenaz. He was Caleb's younger brother. 10The
Spirit of the LORD came on Othniel. So he became
Israel's leader. He went to war. The LORD handed
Cushan-Rishathaim, the king of Aram, over to
him. Othniel overpowered him.
11So the land was at peace for 40 years. Then
Othniel, the son of Kenaz, died.

Ehud

12Once again the people of Israel did what was
evil in the sight of the LORD. Because they did that,
the LORD gave Eglon power over Israel. Eglon was
the king of Moab. 13He got the Ammonites and
Amalekites to join him. All of them came and
attacked Israel. They took over Jericho. Jericho
was also known as The City of Palm Trees. 14For
18 years the people of Israel were under the rule
of Eglon, the king of Moab.
15Again the people of Israel cried out to the
LORD. Then he gave them a man to save them. His
name was Ehud, the son of Gera. Ehud was left-
handed. He was from the tribe of Benjamin.

The people of Israel sent Ehud to Eglon, the
king of Moab. They sent him to give the king what
he required them to bring him. 16Ehud had made a
sword that had two edges. It was about a foot and
a half long. He tied it to his right leg under his
clothes. 17Eglon, the king of Moab, was a very fat
man. Ehud gave him the gift he had brought.
18After that, he sent away those who had carried it.
19At the place where some statues of gods stood
near Gilgal, Ehud turned back. He said, "King Eglon, I have a secret message for you."

The king said, "I want everyone to be quiet."
And all of his attendants left him.
20Then Ehud approached him. King Eglon was
sitting alone in the upstairs room of his summer
palace. Ehud said, "I have a message from God for
you." So the king got up from his seat.
21Then Ehud reached out his left hand. He
pulled out the sword that was tied to his right leg.
He stuck it into the king's stomach. 22Even the
handle sank in after the blade. The blade came
right out the king's back. Ehud didn't pull the
sword out. And the fat closed over it.
23Ehud went out to the porch. He shut the doors
of the upstairs room behind him. Then he locked
them.
24After he had gone, the servants came. They
found the doors of the upstairs room locked. They
said, "Eglon must be going to the toilet in the
inside room of the house."
25They waited for a long time. They waited so
long they became worried. But the king still didn't
open the doors of the room. So they took a key and
unlocked them. There they saw their king. He had
fallen to the floor. He was dead.
26While Eglon's servants had been waiting,
Ehud had gotten away. He passed by the statues of
gods and escaped to Seirah. 27There in the hill
country of Ephraim he blew a trumpet. Then he led
the people of Israel down from the hills.
28"Follow me," Ehud ordered. "The LORD has
handed your enemy Moab over to you."

So they followed him down. They took over the
only places where people could go across the Jordan River to get to Moab. They didn't let anyone
go across. 29At that time they struck down about
10,000 men of Moab. All of those men were strong
and powerful. But not even one escaped. 30That
day Moab was brought under the rule of Israel.

So the land was at peace for 80 years.

Shamgar

31After Ehud, Shamgar became the next leader.
He was the son of Anath. He struck down 600
Philistines with a large, pointed stick that was used
to drive oxen. He saved Israel too.

Deborah

4 After Ehud died, the people of Israel once
again did what was evil in the sight of the
LORD.
2So the LORD gave them over to the power of
Jabin. He was a king in Canaan. He ruled in Hazor.
The commander of his army was Sisera. Sisera
lived in Harosheth Haggoyim. 3Jabin used 900
chariots that had some iron parts. He treated the
people of Israel very badly for 20 years. So they
cried out to the LORD for help.
4Deborah was a prophet. She was the wife of
Lappidoth. She was leading Israel at that time.
5Under The Palm Tree of Deborah she served the
people as their judge. That place was between Ra-

mah and Bethel in the hill country of Ephraim. The
people of Israel came to her there. They came to
have her decide cases for them. She settled matters between them.
6 Deborah sent for Barak. He was the son of
Abinoam. Barak was from Kedesh in the land of
Naphtali. Deborah said to Barak, "The LORD, the
God of Israel, is giving you a command. He says,
'Go! Take 10,000 men from the tribes of Naphtali and Zebulun with you. Then lead the way to
Mount Tabor. 7 I will draw Sisera into a trap. He is
the commander of Jabin's army. I will bring him,
his chariots and his troops to the Kishon River.
There I will hand him over to you.' "
8 Barak said to her, "If you go with me, I'll go.
But if you don't go with me, I won't go."
9 "All right," Deborah said. "I'll go with you.
But because of the way you are doing this, you
won't receive any honor. The LORD will hand Sisera over to a woman."
So Deborah went to Kedesh with Barak.
10 There he sent for Zebulun and Naphtali. And
10,000 men followed him. Deborah also went with
him.
11 Heber, the Kenite, had left the other Kenites.
They came from the family line of Hobab. He was
the brother-in-law of Moses. Heber set up his tent
by the large tree in Zaanannim near Kedesh.
12 Sisera was told that Barak, the son of Abinoam, had gone up to Mount Tabor. 13 So Sisera gathered together his 900 chariots that had some iron
parts. He also gathered all of his men together. He
brought them from Harosheth Haggoyim to the
Kishon River.
14 Then Deborah said to Barak, "Go! Today the
LORD will hand Sisera over to you. Hasn't the
LORD gone ahead of you?" So Barak went down
Mount Tabor. His 10,000 men followed him.
15 As Barak's men marched out, the LORD drove
Sisera away from the field of battle. He scattered
all of Sisera's chariots. Barak's men struck down
Sisera's army with their swords. Sisera left his
chariot behind. He ran away on foot.
16 But Barak chased Sisera's chariots and army.
He chased them all the way to Harosheth Haggoyim. All of Sisera's men were killed with
swords. Not even one was left.
17 But Sisera ran away on foot. He ran to the tent
of Jael. She was the wife of Heber, the Kenite. Sisera ran there because Heber's family was friendly
toward Jabin, the king of Hazor.
18 Jael went out to meet Sisera. "Come in, sir,"
she said. "Come right in. Don't be afraid." So he
entered her tent. Then she covered him up.
19 "I'm thirsty," he said. "Please give me some
water." So Jael opened a bottle of milk. The bottle
was made out of animal skin. She gave him a drink
of milk. Then she covered him up again.
20 "Stand in the doorway of the tent," he told her.
"Someone might come by and ask you, 'Is anyone
here?' If that happens, say 'No.' "
21 But Heber's wife Jael picked up a tent stake
and a hammer. She went quietly over to Sisera. He
was lying there, fast asleep. He was very tired. She
drove the stake through his head right into the
ground. So he died.
22 Barak came by because he was chasing Sisera. Jael went out to meet him. "Come right in,"
she said. "I'll show you the man you are looking
for." So he went in with her. Sisera was lying there
with the stake through his head. He was dead.
23 On that day God brought Jabin under Israel's
control. He was a king in Canaan. 24 Israel's power
grew stronger and stronger against Jabin, a king in
Canaan. They became so strong that they destroyed him.

The Song of Deborah

5 On that day Deborah and Barak sang a song.
Barak was the son of Abinoam. Here is what
Deborah and Barak sang.

2 "The princes in Israel lead the way.
The people follow them just because they
want to.
Praise the LORD!

3 "Kings, hear this! Rulers, listen!
I will sing to the LORD. I will sing.
I will make music to the LORD. He is the
God of Israel.

4 "LORD, you went out from Mount Seir.
You marched out from the land of Edom.
The earth shook. The heavens poured.
The clouds poured down their water.
5 The mountains shook because of the LORD.
He was at Mount Sinai.
They shook because of the LORD. He is the
God of Israel.

6 "The roads were deserted. So travelers used
the winding paths.
That happened in the days of Shamgar,
the son of Anath.
It happened in the days of Jael.
7 Life in the villages of Israel stopped.
It stopped until I, Deborah, came.
I came as a mother in Israel.
8 The people chose new gods.
Then war came to the city gates.
But no shields or spears were seen anywhere.
There weren't any among 40,000 men
in Israel.
9 My heart is with the princes in Israel.
It's with the people who follow them just
because they want to.
Praise the LORD!

10 "Some of you ride on white donkeys.
Some of you sit on your saddle blankets.
Some of you walk along the road.
Think about 11 the voices of the singers at the
watering places.

They sing about the right things the
LORD does.
They sing about the right things his warriors
in Israel do.

"The people of the LORD
went down to the city gates.
12 'Wake up, Deborah! Wake up!' they said.
'Wake up! Wake up! Begin to sing!
Barak, get up!
Son of Abinoam, capture your prisoners!'

13 "Then the people who were left came down to
the nobles.
The people of the LORD
came to me against the powerful enemy.
14 Some came from the part of Ephraim where
some Amalekites lived.
Benjamin was with the people who
followed Ephraim.
Captains came down from Makir.
Those who rule like commanders came
down from Zebulun.
15 The princes of Issachar were with Deborah.
The men of Issachar were with Barak.
They rushed behind him into the valley.
In the territories of Reuben,
men looked deeply into their hearts.
16 Why did they stay among the campfires?
Why did they stay to hear shepherds
whistling for the flocks?
In the territories of Reuben,
men looked deeply into their hearts.
17 Gilead stayed east of the Jordan River.
Why did Dan stay near the ships?
The men of Asher remained on the coast of
the Mediterranean Sea.
They stayed in their safe harbors.
18 The people of Zebulun put their very lives
in danger.
So did Naphtali on the hills in the open
country.

19 "Kings came and fought.
The kings of Canaan fought
at Taanach by the streams of Megiddo.
But they didn't carry any silver away.
They didn't take anything at all.
20 From the heavens the stars fought.
From the sky they fought against Sisera.
21 The Kishon River swept them away.
The Kishon is a very old river.
My spirit, march on! Be strong!
22 The hoofs of the horses pounded like thunder.
The powerful horses of our enemies
galloped away.
23 'Let Meroz be cursed,' said the angel
of the LORD.
'Let bitter curses fall on its people.
They did not come to help the LORD.
They did not come to help him against our
powerful enemies.'

24 "May Jael be the most blessed woman of all.
May the wife of the Kenite Heber
be blessed.
May she be the most blessed woman of all
those who live in tents.
25 Sisera asked for water. She gave him milk.
In a bowl that was fit for nobles she brought
him buttermilk.
26 Her hand reached out for a tent stake.
Her right hand reached for a hammer.
She hit Sisera. She crushed his head.
She drove the stake right through his head.
27 He sank down. He fell at her feet.
He was lying there.
At her feet he sank down. He fell.
He fell where he sank down.
That's where he died.

28 "Sisera's mother looked out through
the window.
From behind the wooden screen she
cried out.
'Why is his chariot taking so long to get here?'
she said.
'Why can't I hear the noise of his chariots
yet?'
29 Her wisest ladies answer her.
And here's what she keeps saying to herself.
30 She says, 'They must be finding riches to
bring back.
They must be dividing them up.
Each man is getting a woman or two.
They are giving colorful clothes
to Sisera.
The clothes are very beautiful.
He will bring some for me to wear.
The men must be finding many things
to bring home.'

31 "LORD, may all of your enemies be destroyed.
But may those who love you be like the
morning sun.
May they be like the sun when it shines the
brightest."

So the land was at peace for 40 years.

Gideon

6 Once again the people of Israel did what was evil in the sight of the LORD. So for seven years he handed them over to the people of Midian.

2 The Midianites treated the people of Israel very badly. That's why they made hiding places for themselves. They hid in holes in the mountains. They also hid in caves and in other safe places.

3 Each year the people planted their crops. When they did, the Midianites came into the country and attacked it. So did the Amalekites and other tribes
from the east. 4 They camped on the land. They destroyed the crops all the way to Gaza. They didn't spare any living thing for Israel. They didn't spare sheep or cattle or donkeys.

5 The Midianites came up with their livestock and tents. They came like huge numbers of locusts. It was impossible to count all of those men and their camels. They came into the land to destroy it.

6 Midian made the people of Israel very poor. So they cried out to the LORD for help.

7 They cried out to the LORD because of what Midian had done. 8 So he sent a prophet to them. The prophet said, "The LORD is the God of Israel. He says, 'I brought you up out of Egypt. That is the land where you were slaves. 9 I saved you from the power of Egypt. I saved you from all those who were beating you down. I drove the people of Canaan out to make room for you. I gave you their land.

10 " 'I said to you, "I am the LORD your God. You are now living in the land of the Amorites. Do not worship their gods." But you have not listened to me.' "

11 The angel of the LORD came. He sat down under an oak tree in Ophrah. The tree belonged to Joash. He was from the family line of Abiezer.

Gideon was threshing wheat in a winepress at Ophrah. He was the son of Joash. Gideon was threshing in a winepress to hide the wheat from the Midianites.

12 The angel of the LORD appeared to Gideon. He said, "Mighty warrior, the LORD is with you."

13 "But sir," Gideon replied, "you say the LORD is with us. Then why has all of this happened to us? Where are all of the wonderful things he has done? Our parents told us about them. They said, 'Didn't the LORD bring us up out of Egypt?' But now the LORD has deserted us. He has handed us over to Midian."

14 The LORD turned to Gideon. He said to him, "You are strong. Go and save Israel from the power of Midian. I am sending you."

15 "But Lord," Gideon asked, "how can I possibly save Israel? My family group is the weakest in the tribe of Manasseh. And I'm the least important member of my family."

16 The LORD answered, "I will be with you. So you will strike down the men of Midian all at one time."

17 Gideon replied, "If you are pleased with me, give me a special sign. Then I'll know that it's really you talking to me. 18 Please don't go away until I come back. I'll bring my offering and set it down in front of you."

The LORD said, "I will wait until you return."

19 Gideon went and prepared a young goat. From more than half a bushel of flour he made bread without using yeast. He put the meat in a basket. In a pot he put soup that was made from the meat. Then he brought all of it and offered it to the LORD under the oak tree.

20 The angel of God spoke to Gideon. He said, "Take the meat and the bread. Place them on this rock. Then pour out the soup." So Gideon did it.

21 The angel of the LORD had a wooden staff in his hand. With the tip of his staff he touched the meat and the bread. Fire blazed out of the rock. It burned up the meat and the bread. Then the angel of the LORD disappeared.

22 Gideon realized it was the angel of the LORD. He cried out, "LORD and King, I have seen the angel of the LORD face to face!"

23 But the LORD said to him, "May peace be with you! Do not be afraid. You are not going to die."

24 So Gideon built an altar to honor the LORD there. He called it The LORD Is Peace. It still stands in Ophrah to this very day. Ophrah is in the territory that belongs to the family line of Abiezer.

25 That same night the LORD spoke to Gideon. He said, "Get the second bull from your father's herd. Get the one that is seven years old. Tear down the altar your father built in honor of Baal. Cut down the pole that is beside it. The pole is used to worship the goddess Asherah.

26 "Then build the right kind of altar. Build it in honor of the LORD your God. Build it on top of this hill. Then use the wood from the Asherah pole you cut down. Sacrifice the second bull as a burnt offering."

27 So Gideon went and got ten of his servants. He did just as the LORD had told him. But he was afraid of his family. He was also afraid of the men in the town. So he did everything at night instead of during the day.

28 In the morning the men in the town got up. They saw that Baal's altar had been torn down. The Asherah pole that was beside it had been cut down. And the second bull had been sacrificed on the new altar that had been built.

29 They asked each other, "Who did this?"

They looked into the matter carefully. Someone told them, "Gideon, the son of Joash, did it."

30 The men in the town spoke to Joash. They ordered him, "Bring your son out here. He must die. He has torn down Baal's altar. He has cut down the Asherah pole that was beside it."

31 But Joash replied to the angry crowd that was around him. He said, "Are you going to stand up for Baal? Are you trying to save him? Those who stand up for him will be put to death by morning! Is Baal really a god? If he is, he can stand up for himself when someone tears down his altar."

32 That's why Gideon was called Jerub-Baal that day. He said, "Let Baal take his stand against him." Gideon had torn down Baal's altar.

33 All of the Midianites and Amalekites gathered their armies together. Other tribes from the east joined them. All of them went across the Jordan River. They camped in the Valley of Jezreel.

34 Then the Spirit of the LORD came on Gideon. So Gideon blew the trumpet to send for the men of Abiezer. He told them to follow him. 35 He sent messengers all through Manasseh. He called for the men of Manasseh to fight. He also sent messengers to the men of Asher, Zebulun and Naphtali. So all of those men went up to join the others.

36 Gideon said to God, "You promised you would use me to save Israel. 37 Please do something

for me. I'll put a piece of wool on the threshing floor. Suppose dew is only on the wool tomorrow morning. And suppose the ground all around it is dry. Then I will know that you will use me to save Israel. I'll know that your promise will come true."

38And that's what happened. Gideon got up early the next day. He squeezed the dew out of the wool. The water filled a bowl.

39Then Gideon said to God, "Don't let your anger burn against me. Let me ask you for just one more thing. Let me use the wool for one more test. This time make the wool dry. And cover the ground with dew."

40So that night God did it. Only the wool was dry. The ground all around it was covered with dew.

Gideon Wins the Battle Over the Midianites

7 Early in the morning Jerub-Baal and all of his men camped at the spring of Harod. Jerub-Baal was another name for Gideon. The camp of Midian was north of Gideon's camp. It was in the valley near the hill of Moreh.

2The LORD spoke to Gideon. He said, "I want to hand Midian over to you. But you have too many men for me to do that. I do not want Israel to brag that their own strength has saved them. 3So here is what I want you to announce to your men. Tell them, 'Those who tremble with fear can turn back. They can leave Mount Gilead.'" So 22,000 men left. But 10,000 remained.

4The LORD spoke to Gideon again. He said, "There are still too many men. So take them down to the water. I will sort them out for you there. If I say, 'This one will go with you,' he will go. But if I say, 'That one will not go with you,' he will not go."

5So Gideon took the men down to the water. There the LORD spoke to him. He said, "Some men will drink the way dogs do. They will lap up the water with their tongues. Separate them from those who get down on their knees to drink."

6Three hundred men lapped up the water. They brought it up to their mouths with their hands. All of the rest got down on their knees to drink.

7The LORD spoke to Gideon. He said, "With the help of the 300 men who lapped up the water I will save you. I will hand the Midianites over to you. Let all of the other men go home."

8So Gideon sent the rest of the men of Israel to their tents. But he kept the 300 men. They took over the supplies and trumpets the others had left.

The Midianites had set up their camp in the valley below where Gideon was.

9During that night the LORD spoke to Gideon. He said, "Get up. Go down against the camp. I am going to hand it over to you. 10But what if you are afraid to attack? Then go down to the camp with your servant Purah. 11Listen to what they are saying. After that, you will not be afraid to attack the camp."

So Gideon and his servant Purah went down to the edge of the camp. 12The Midianites had settled in the valley. So had the Amalekites and all of the other tribes from the east. There were so many of them that they looked like huge numbers of locusts. Like the grains of sand on the seashore, their camels couldn't be counted.

13Gideon arrived just as a man was telling a friend about his dream. "I had a dream," he was saying. "A round loaf of barley bread came rolling into the camp of Midian. It hit a tent with great force. The tent turned over and fell down flat."

14His friend replied, "That can only be the sword of Gideon, the son of Joash. Gideon is from Israel. God has handed the Midianites over to him. He has given him the whole camp."

15Gideon heard the man explain what the dream meant. Then Gideon worshiped God. He returned to the camp of Israel. He called out, "Get up! The LORD has handed the Midianites over to you."

16Gideon separated the 300 men into three companies. He put a trumpet and an empty jar into the hands of each man. And he put a torch inside each jar.

17"Watch me," he told them. "Do what I do. I'll go to the edge of the enemy camp. Then do exactly as I do. 18I and everyone who is with me will blow our trumpets. Then blow your trumpets from your positions all around the camp. And shout the battle cry, 'For the LORD and for Gideon!'"

19Gideon and the 100 men who were with him reached the edge of the enemy camp. It was about ten o'clock at night. It was just after the guard had been changed. Gideon and his men blew their trumpets. They broke the jars that were in their hands.

20The three companies blew their trumpets. They smashed their jars. They held their torches in their left hands. They held in their right hands the trumpets they were going to blow. Then they shouted the battle cry, "A sword for the LORD and for Gideon!"

21Each man stayed in his position around the camp. But all of the Midianites ran away in fear. They were crying out as they ran.

22When the 300 trumpets were blown, the LORD caused all of the men in the enemy camp to start fighting each other. They attacked each other with their swords. The army ran away to Beth Shittah toward Zererah. They ran all the way to the border of Abel Meholah near Tabbath.

23The men of Israel from the tribes of Naphtali, Asher and all of Manasseh were called out. They chased the Midianites.

24Gideon sent messengers through the entire hill country of Ephraim. They said, "Come on down against the Midianites. Take control of the waters of the Jordan River before they get there. Do it all the way to Beth Barah."

So all of the men of Ephraim were called out. They took control of the waters of the Jordan all the way to Beth Barah.

25They also captured Oreb and Zeeb. Those men were two of the Midianite leaders. The men of Ephraim killed Oreb at the rock of Oreb. They killed Zeeb at the winepress of Zeeb. They chased the Midianites. And they brought the heads of Oreb and Zeeb to Gideon. He was by the Jordan River.

Gideon Destroys Midian's Whole Army

8 The men of Ephraim spoke to Gideon. They asked, "Why have you treated us like this? Why didn't you ask us to help you when you went out to fight against Midian?" They spoke very sharply against Gideon.

2But he answered them, "What I've done isn't anything compared to what you have done. After Ephraim's grapes have been gathered, isn't what is left over better than all of the grapes that have been gathered from Abiezer's vines? 3God handed Oreb and Zeeb over to you. They were Midianite leaders. So what was I able to do compared to what you did?"

After Gideon had said that, they didn't feel angry with him anymore.

4Gideon and his 300 men were very tired. But they kept on chasing their enemies. They came to the Jordan River and went across it. 5Gideon spoke to the men of Succoth. He said, "Give my troops some bread. They are worn out. And I'm still chasing Zebah and Zalmunna. They are the kings of Midian."

6But the officials of Succoth objected. They said, "Have you already killed Zebah and Zalmunna? Have you cut their hands off and brought them back to prove it? If you haven't, why should we give bread to your troops?"

7Gideon replied, "The LORD will hand Zebah and Zalmunna over to me. When he does, I'll tear your skin with thorns from desert bushes."

8From there Gideon went up to Peniel. He asked its men for the same thing. But they answered as the men of Succoth had. 9So he said to the men of Peniel, "I'll be back after I've won the battle. Then I'll tear down this tower."

10Zebah and Zalmunna were in Karkor. They had an army of about 15,000 men. That's all that was left of the armies of the tribes from the east. About 120,000 men who carried swords had died in battle.

11Gideon went up the trail the people of the desert had made. It ran east of Nobah and Jogbehah. He attacked the army by surprise. 12Zebah and Zalmunna ran away. They were the two kings of Midian. Gideon chased them and captured them. He destroyed their whole army.

13Then Gideon, the son of Joash, returned from the battle. He came back through the Pass of Heres.

14He caught a young man from Succoth. He asked him about the elders of the town. The young man wrote down for him the names of Succoth's 77 officials.

15Then Gideon came and spoke to the men of Succoth. He said, "Here are Zebah and Zalmunna. You made fun of me because of them. You said, 'Have you already killed Zebah and Zalmunna? Have you cut their hands off and brought them back to prove it? If you haven't, why should we give bread to your tired men?'"

16Gideon went and got the elders of the town. Then he taught the men of Succoth a lesson. He tore their skin with thorns from desert bushes. 17He also pulled down the tower at Peniel. He killed the men in the town.

18Then he spoke to Zebah and Zalmunna. He asked, "What were the men like that you killed at Tabor?"

"Men like you," they answered. "Each one walked as if he were a prince."

19Gideon replied, "Those were my brothers. They were the sons of my own mother. You can be sure that the LORD lives. And you can be just as sure that if you had spared their lives, I wouldn't kill you."

20Then Gideon turned to his oldest son Jether. He said, "Kill them!" But Jether didn't pull out his sword. He was only a boy. So he was afraid.

21Zebah and Zalmunna said, "Come on. Do it yourself. 'The older the man, the stronger he is.'"

So Gideon stepped forward and killed them. Then he took the moon-shaped necklaces off the necks of their camels.

Gideon Refuses to Be Israel's Ruler

22The people of Israel spoke to Gideon. They said, "Rule over us. We want you, your son and your grandson to be our rulers. You have saved us from the power of Midian."

23But Gideon told them, "I will not rule over you. My son won't rule over you either. The LORD will rule over you."

24He continued, "I do ask one thing. I want each of you to give me an earring. I'm talking about the earrings you took from your enemies." It was the practice of the people in the family line of Ishmael to wear gold earrings.

25The people of Israel said, "We'll be glad to give them to you." So they spread out a piece of clothing. Each man threw a ring on it from what he had taken. 26The weight of the gold rings Gideon asked for was 43 pounds. That didn't include the moon-shaped necklaces the kings of Midian had worn. It didn't include their other necklaces or their purple clothes. And it didn't include the gold chains that had been on the necks of their camels.

27Gideon made an object out of all of the gold. It looked like the linen apron the high priest of Israel wore. He placed it in Ophrah. That was his hometown. All of the people of Israel worshiped it there. They weren't faithful to the LORD. So the gold object became a trap to Gideon and his family.

Gideon Dies

28Israel brought Midian under their control.
Midian wasn't able to attack Israel anymore. So
the land was at peace for 40 years. The peace
lasted as long as Gideon was living.
29Jerub-Baal, the son of Joash, went back home
to live. Jerub-Baal was another name for Gideon.
30He had 70 sons of his own. That's because he had
a lot of wives. 31And he had a concubine who lived
in Shechem. She also had a son by him. Gideon
named that son Abimelech.
32Gideon, the son of Joash, died when he was
very old. His body was buried in the tomb of his
father Joash in Ophrah. Ophrah was in the territory that belonged to the family line of Abiezer.
33As soon as Gideon had died, the people of Israel joined themselves to the gods that were named
after Baal. Israel wasn't faithful to the LORD. They
worshiped Baal-Berith as their god. 34They forgot
what the LORD their God had done for them. He
had saved them from the power of their enemies
who were all around them.
35Jerub-Baal had done many good things for the
people of Israel. But they weren't kind to his family. Jerub-Baal was another name for Gideon.

Abimelech Becomes King of Shechem

9 Abimelech was the son of Jerub-Baal. He went
to his mother's brothers in Shechem. He spoke
to them and to all of the members of his mother's
family group. He said, 2"Speak to all of the citizens
of Shechem. Tell them, 'You can have all 70 of Jerub-Baal's sons rule over you. Or you can have just
one man rule over you. Which would you rather
have?' Remember, I'm your own flesh and blood."
3The brothers told all of that to the citizens of
Shechem. Then the people decided to follow
Abimelech. They said, "He's related to us."
4They gave him 28 ounces of silver. They had
taken it from the temple of the god Baal-Berith.
Abimelech used it to hire some men. They were
wild. They weren't good for anything. They
became his followers.
5Abimelech went to his father's home in Ophrah. There on a big rock he murdered his 70 brothers. All of them were the sons of Jerub-Baal. But
Jotham escaped by hiding. He was Jerub-Baal's
youngest son.
6All of the citizens of Shechem and Beth Millo
came together. They gathered at the stone pillar
that was beside the large tree in Shechem. They
wanted to crown Abimelech as their king.
7Jotham was told about it. So he climbed up on
top of Mount Gerizim. He shouted down to them,
"Citizens of Shechem! Listen to me! Then God
will listen to you. 8One day the trees went out to
anoint a king for themselves. They said to an olive
tree, 'Be our king.'
9"But the olive tree answered, 'Should I give up
my olive oil? It's used to honor gods and people
alike. Should I give that up just to rule over the
trees?'
10"Next, the trees spoke to a fig tree. They said,
'Come and be our king.'
11"But the fig tree replied, 'Should I give up my
fruit? It's so good and sweet. Should I give that up
just to rule over the trees?'
12"Then the trees spoke to a vine. They said,
'Come and be our king.'
13"But the vine answered, 'Should I give up my
wine? It cheers up gods and people alike. Should
I give that up just to rule over the trees?'
14"Finally, all of the trees spoke to a bush that
had thorns. They said, 'Come and be our king.'
15"The bush spoke to the trees. It said, 'Do you
really want to anoint me as king over you? If you
do, come and rest in my shade. But if you don't, I
will destroy you! Fire will come out of me and
burn up the cedar trees of Lebanon!'
16"Did you act in an honest way when you made
Abimelech your king? Did you really do the right
thing? Have you been fair to Jerub-Baal and his
family? Have you given him the honor he's worthy of?
17"Remember that my father fought for you. He
put his life in danger for you. He saved you from
the power of Midian. 18But today you have turned
against my father's family. You have murdered his
70 sons on a big rock. Abimelech is only the son
of my father's female slave. But you have made
him king over the citizens of Shechem. You have
done that because he's related to you.
19"Have you citizens of Shechem and Beth
Millo acted in an honest way toward Jerub-Baal?
Have you done the right thing to his family today?
If you have, may you be happy with Abimelech!
And may he be happy with you! 20But if you
haven't, let fire come out from Abimelech and
burn you up! And let fire come out from you and
burn Abimelech up!"
21Then Jotham ran away. He escaped to Beer.
He lived there because he was afraid of his brother
Abimelech.
22Abimelech ruled over Israel for three years.
23Then God sent an evil spirit to cause trouble
between Abimelech and the citizens of Shechem.
They turned against Abimelech. They decided not
to follow him anymore.
24God made that happen because of what Abimelech had done to Jerub-Baal's 70 sons. He had
spilled their blood. God wanted to pay back their
brother Abimelech for doing that. He also wanted
to pay back the citizens of Shechem. They had
helped Abimelech murder his brothers.
25The citizens of Shechem opposed Abimelech.
So they hid some men on top of the hills. They
wanted them to attack and rob everyone who
passed by. Abimelech was told about it.
26Gaal and his relatives moved into Shechem.
He was the son of Ebed. The citizens of Shechem
put their trust in Gaal.

27The people of Shechem went out into the fields. They gathered the grapes. They pressed the juice out of them by stomping on them. Then they held a feast in the temple of their god. While they were eating and drinking, they called down curses on Abimelech.

28Then Gaal, the son of Ebed, spoke up. "Who is Abimelech?" he said. "And who is Shechem? Why should we be under Abimelech's rule? Isn't he Jerub-Baal's son? Isn't Zebul his helper? It would be better to serve the men of Hamor. He was the father of Shechem. So why should we serve Abimelech? 29I wish these people were under my command. Then I would get rid of him. I would say to him, 'Call out your whole army!'"

30Zebul was the governor of Shechem. He heard about what Gaal, the son of Ebed, had said. So he burned with anger.

31Zebul sent messengers to Abimelech secretly. They said, "Gaal, the son of Ebed, has come to Shechem. His relatives have come with him. They are stirring up the city against you. 32So come with your men during the night. Hide in the fields and wait. 33In the morning at sunrise, attack the city. Gaal and his men will come out against you. Then do what you can."

34So Abimelech and all of his troops started out at night. They went into their hiding places near Shechem. Abimelech had separated them into four companies.

35Gaal, the son of Ebed, had already gone out. He was standing at the entrance of the city gate. He had arrived there just as Abimelech and his troops came out of their hiding places.

36Gaal saw them. He said to Zebul, "Look! People are coming down from the tops of the mountains!"

Zebul replied, "You are wrong. Those aren't people. They are just the shadows of the mountains."

37But Gaal spoke up again. He said, "Look! People are coming down from the center of the land. Another company is coming from the direction of the fortune tellers' tree."

38Then Zebul said to Gaal, "Where is your big talk now? You said, 'Who is Abimelech? Why should we be under his rule?' Aren't these the people you looked down on? Go out and fight against them!"

39So Gaal led the citizens out of Shechem. They fought against Abimelech. 40He chased Gaal from the field of battle. Many men were wounded as they ran away. Abimelech chased them all the way to the entrance of the city gate. 41He stayed in Arumah. Zebul drove Gaal and his relatives out of Shechem.

42The next day the people of Shechem went out to work in the fields. Abimelech was told about it. 43So he gathered his men together. He separated them into three companies. Then he hid them in the fields and told them to wait. When he saw the people coming out of the city, he got up to attack them. 44Abimelech and the men who were with him ran forward. They placed themselves at the entrance of the city gate. Then the other two companies rushed over to the people who were in the fields. There they struck them down. 45Abimelech kept up his attack against the city all day long. He didn't stop until he had captured it. Then he killed its people. He destroyed the city. He scattered salt on it to make sure that nothing would be able to grow there.

46The citizens who were in the tower of Shechem heard about what was happening. So they went to the safest place in the temple of the god El-Berith.

47Abimelech heard that they had gathered together there. 48He and all of his men went up Mount Zalmon. He got an ax and cut off some branches. He carried them on his shoulders. He ordered the men who were with him to do the same thing. "Quick!" he said. "Do what you have seen me do!"

49So all of the men cut branches and followed Abimelech. They piled them against the place where the people had gone for safety. Then they set the place on fire with the people inside. There were about 1,000 men and women in the tower of Shechem. All of them died.

50Next, Abimelech went to Thebez. He surrounded it. Then he attacked it and captured it.

51But inside the city there was a strong tower. All of the people in the city ran to it for safety. All of the men and women went into it. They locked themselves in. They climbed up on the roof of the tower. 52Abimelech went to the tower and attacked it. He approached the entrance to the tower to set it on fire. 53But a woman dropped a large millstone on him. It broke his head open.

54He quickly called out to the man who was carrying his armor. He said, "Pull out your sword and kill me. Then people can't say, 'A woman killed him.'" So his servant stuck his sword through him. And Abimelech died. 55When the people of Israel saw he was dead, they went home.

56That's how God paid Abimelech back for the evil thing he had done to his father. He had murdered his 70 brothers. 57God also made the men of Shechem pay for all of the evil things they had done. The curse of Jotham came down on them. He was the son of Jerub-Baal.

Tola

10 Tola rose up to save Israel. That happened after the time of Abimelech. Tola was from the tribe of Issachar. He was the son of Puah, who was the son of Dodo. Tola lived in Shamir. It's in the hill country of Ephraim. 2Tola led Israel for 23 years. After he died, his body was buried in Shamir.

Jair

3Jair became the leader after Tola. Jair was from the land of Gilead. He led Israel for 22 years. 4He had 30 sons. They rode on 30 donkeys. They controlled 30 towns in Gilead. Those towns are called Havvoth Jair to this very day. 5After Jair died, his body was buried in Kamon.

Jephthah

6Once again the people of Israel did what was evil in the sight of the LORD. They served the gods that were named after Baal. They served the goddesses that were named after Ashtoreth. They worshiped the gods of Aram and Sidon. They served the gods of Moab and Ammon. They also worshiped the gods of the Philistines. The people of Israel deserted the LORD. They didn't serve him anymore.

7So the LORD's anger burned against them. He handed them over to the Philistines and the Ammonites. 8That year they broke Israel's power completely. They treated the people of Israel badly for 18 years. Those people lived east of the Jordan River. They lived in Gilead. That was the land of the Amorites.

9The Ammonites also went across the Jordan. They crossed over to fight against Judah, Benjamin and the people of Ephraim. Israel was suffering terribly.

10Then the people of Israel cried out to the LORD. They said, "We have sinned against you. We have deserted our God. We have served the gods that are named after Baal."

11The LORD replied, "The Egyptians and Amorites beat you down. So did the Ammonites and Philistines. 12And so did the Amalekites and the people of Sidon and Maon. Each time you cried out to me for help. And I saved you from their power.

13"But you have deserted me. You have served other gods. So I will not save you anymore. 14Go and cry out to the gods you have chosen. Let them save you when you get into trouble!"

15But the people of Israel replied to the LORD. They said, "We have sinned. Do to us what you think is best. But please save us now." 16Then they got rid of the strange gods that were among them. They served the LORD. And he couldn't stand to see Israel suffer anymore.

17The Ammonites were called together to fight. They camped in the land of Gilead. Then the men of Israel gathered together. They camped at the city of Mizpah.

18The leaders of Gilead spoke to each other. They said, "Who will lead the attack against the Ammonites? That man will be the ruler of all of the people who live in Gilead."

11 Jephthah was a mighty warrior. He was from the land of Gilead. His father's name was Gilead. Jephthah's mother was a prostitute.

2Gilead's wife also had sons by him. When they had grown up, they drove Jephthah away. "You aren't going to get any share of our family's property," they said. "You are the son of another woman."

3So Jephthah ran away from his brothers. He settled in the land of Tob. A group of men who weren't good for anything gathered around him there. And they followed him.

4Some time later, the Ammonites went to war against Israel. 5So the elders of Gilead went to get Jephthah from the land of Tob. 6"Come with us," they said. "Be our commander. Then we can fight against the Ammonites."

7Jephthah said to them, "Didn't you hate me? Didn't you drive me away from my father's house? Why are you coming to me only when you are in trouble?"

8The elders of Gilead replied to him. "You are right," they said. "That's why we're turning to you now. Come with us and fight against the Ammonites. Then you will be our leader. You will rule over everyone who lives in Gilead."

9Jephthah said, "Suppose you take me back to fight against the Ammonites. And suppose the LORD gives them over to me. Then will I really be your leader?"

10The elders of Gilead replied, "The LORD is our witness. We'll certainly do as you say." 11So Jephthah went with the elders of Gilead. And the people made him their leader and commander. He went to Mizpah. There he repeated to the LORD everything he had said.

12Then Jephthah sent messengers to the king of Ammon. They asked, "What do you have against us? Why have you attacked our country?"

13The king of Ammon answered Jephthah's messengers. He said, "Israel came up out of Egypt. At that time they took my land away. They took all of the land that was between the Arnon River and the Jabbok River. It reached all the way to the Jordan River. Now give it back. Then there will be peace."

14Jephthah sent messengers back to the king of Ammon. 15They said,

> "Here is what Jephthah says to you. Israel didn't take the land of Moab. They didn't take the land of Ammon. 16When Israel came up out of Egypt, they went through the desert to the Red Sea. From there they went on to Kadesh.
>
> 17"Then Israel sent messengers to the king of Edom. They said, 'Please let us go through your country.' But the king of Edom wouldn't listen to them.
>
> "They sent the same message to the king of Moab. But he refused too. So Israel stayed at Kadesh.
>
> 18"Next, they traveled through the desert. They traveled along the borders of the lands of Edom and Moab. They passed along the east side of the country of Moab. They camped on the other side of the Arnon River. They didn't enter the territory of Moab. The Arnon River was Moab's border.

19“Then Israel sent messengers to Sihon. He was the king of the Amorites. He ruled in Heshbon. They said to him, ‘Let us pass through your country to our own land.’

20“But Sihon didn’t trust Israel to pass through his territory. Instead, he gathered all of his men together. They camped at Jahaz. And they fought against Israel.

21“Then the LORD, the God of Israel, handed Sihon and all of his men over to Israel. Israel won the battle over them. Amorites were living in the country at that time. And Israel took over all of their land. 22They captured all of the land that was between the Arnon River and the Jabbok River. It reached from the desert all the way to the Jordan River.

23“The LORD, the God of Israel, has driven the Amorites out to make room for his people. So what right do you have to take it over? 24You will take what your god Chemosh gives you, won’t you? In the same way, we will take over what the LORD our God has given us. 25Are you better than Balak, the son of Zippor? Balak was the king of Moab. Did he ever argue with Israel? Did he ever fight against them?

26“For 300 years Israel has been living in Heshbon and Aroer. They have been living in the settlements that are around those cities. They have also been living in all of the towns that are along the Arnon River. Why didn’t you take those places back during that time?

27“I haven’t done anything wrong to you. But you are doing something wrong to me. You have gone to war against me. The LORD is the Judge. So let him decide our case today. Let him settle matters between the people of Israel and the people of Ammon.”

28But the king of Ammon didn’t pay any attention to the message Jephthah sent him.

29Then the Spirit of the LORD came on Jephthah. He went across the territories of Gilead and Manasseh. He passed through Mizpah in the land of Gilead. From there he attacked the people of Ammon.

30Jephthah made a promise to the LORD. He said, “Hand the Ammonites over to me. 31If you do, here’s what I’ll do when I come back from winning the battle. Anything that comes out the door of my house to meet me will belong to you. I will sacrifice it as a burnt offering.”

32Then Jephthah went over to fight against the Ammonites. The LORD handed them over to him. 33Jephthah destroyed 20 towns between Aroer and the area of Minnith. He destroyed them all the way to Abel Keramim. So Israel brought Ammon under their control.

34Jephthah returned to his home in Mizpah. And guess who came out to meet him. It was his daughter! She was dancing to the music of tambourines. She was his only child. He didn’t have any other sons or daughters.

35When Jephthah saw her, he was so upset that he tore his clothes. He cried out, “My daughter! You have filled me with trouble and sorrow. I’ve made a promise to the LORD. And I can’t break it.”

36“My father,” she replied, “you have given your word to the LORD. So do to me just what you promised to do. The Ammonites were your enemies. And the LORD has paid them back for what they did to you.

37“But please do one thing for me,” she continued. “Give me two months to wander around in the hills. Let me sob there with my friends. I want to do that because I’ll never get married.”

38“You can go,” he said. He let her go for two months. She and her friends went into the hills. They were filled with sadness because she would never get married.

39After the two months were over, she returned to her father. He did to her just what he had promised to do. And she was a virgin.

So that became a practice in Israel. 40Each year the young women of Israel go away for four days. They do it in honor of the daughter of Jephthah. He was from the land of Gilead.

Jephthah Wins the Battle Over Ephraim

12 The men of Ephraim called out their troops. The troops went across the Jordan River to Zaphon. When they arrived, they said to Jephthah, “You went to fight against the Ammonites. Why didn’t you ask us to go with you? We’re going to burn down your house over your head.”

2Jephthah answered, “I and my people were taking part in a great struggle. We were at war with the Ammonites. I asked you for help. But you didn’t come to save me from their power. 3I saw that you wouldn’t help. So I put my own life in danger. I went across the Jordan to fight against the Ammonites. The LORD helped me win the battle over them. So why have you come up today to fight against me?”

4Then Jephthah called the men of Gilead together. They fought against Ephraim. The men of Gilead struck them down. The people of Ephraim had said, “You people of Gilead are nothing but deserters from Ephraim and Manasseh.”

5The men of Gilead captured the places where people go across the Jordan River to get to Ephraim. Some men of Ephraim weren’t killed in the battle. When they arrived at the river, they would say, “Let us go across.”

Then the men of Gilead would ask each one, “Are you from Ephraim?” Suppose he replied, “No.” 6Then they would say, “All right. Say ‘Shibboleth.’ ” If he said “Sibboleth,” the way he said the word would give him away. He couldn’t say it correctly. So they would grab hold of him. Then they would kill him at one of the places where

people go across the Jordan. At that time, 42,000
men of Ephraim were killed.
7Jephthah led Israel for six years. Then he died.
His body was buried in a town in Gilead. Jephthah
was from the land of Gilead.

Ibzan, Elon and Abdon

8After Jephthah, Ibzan from Bethlehem led Israel. 9He had 30 sons and 30 daughters. He gave
his daughters to be married to men who were outside his family group. He brought in 30 young
women to be married to his sons. Those women
also came from outside his family group. Ibzan led
Israel for seven years. 10Then he died. His body
was buried in Bethlehem.
11After Ibzan, Elon led Israel. He was from the
tribe of Zebulun. Elon led Israel for ten years.
12Then he died. His body was buried in Aijalon. It
was in the land of Zebulun.
13After Elon, Abdon led Israel. Abdon was the
son of Hillel. Abdon was from Pirathon. 14He had
40 sons and 30 grandsons. They rode on 70 donkeys. He led Israel for eight years. 15Then he died.
His body was buried at Pirathon in Ephraim. Pirathon was in the hill country of the Amalekites.
Abdon was the son of Hillel.

Samson Is Born

13 Once again the people of Israel did what
was evil in the sight of the LORD. So the
LORD handed them over to the Philistines for 40
years.
2A certain man from Zorah was named Manoah.
He was from the tribe of Dan. Manoah had a wife
who wasn't able to have children.
3The angel of the LORD appeared to Manoah's
wife. He said, "You are not able to have children.
But you are going to become pregnant. You will
have a baby boy. 4Make sure you do not drink any
kind of wine. Also make sure you do not eat anything that is 'unclean.'
5"You will become pregnant. You will have a
son. He must not use a razor on his head. He must
not cut his hair. That is because the boy will be a
Nazirite. He will be set apart to God from the day
he is born. He will begin to save Israel from the
power of the Philistines."
6Then the woman went to her husband. She told
him, "A man of God came to me. He looked like
an angel of God. His appearance was so amazing
that it filled me with great wonder. I didn't ask him
where he came from. And he didn't tell me his
name.
7"But he said to me, 'You will become pregnant. You will have a son. So do not drink any kind
of wine. Do not eat anything that is "unclean."
That is because the boy will be a Nazirite. He will
belong to God in a special way from the day he is
born until the day he dies.'"
8Then Manoah prayed to the LORD. He said,
"Lord, I beg you to let the man of God you sent to
us come again. He told us we would have a son.
We want the man of God to teach us how to bring
up the boy."
9God heard Manoah. And the angel of God
came again to the woman. He came while she was
out in the field. But her husband Manoah wasn't
with her. 10The woman hurried to her husband. She
told him, "He's here! The man who appeared to
me the other day is here!"
11Manoah got up and followed his wife. When
he came to the man, he spoke to him. He said,
"Are you the one who talked to my wife?"
"I am," he replied.
12So Manoah asked him, "What will happen
when your words come true? What rules should
we follow for the boy's life and work?"
13The angel of the LORD answered him. He said,
"Your wife must do everything I have told her to
do. 14She must not eat anything that comes from
grapevines. She must not drink any kind of wine.
She must not eat anything that is 'unclean.' She
must do everything I have commanded her to do."
15Manoah spoke to the angel of the LORD. He
said, "We would like you to stay and eat. We want
to prepare a young goat for you."
16The angel of the LORD replied, "Even if I stay,
I will not eat any of your food. But if you still want
to prepare a burnt offering, you must offer it to the
LORD." Manoah didn't realize it was the angel of
the LORD.
17Then Manoah asked the angel of the LORD a
question. "What is your name?" he said. "We want
to honor you when your word comes true."
18The angel replied, "Why are you asking me
what my name is? You would not be able to understand it."
19Manoah got a young goat. He brought it
together with the grain offering. He sacrificed it
on a rock to the LORD.
Then the LORD did an amazing thing. It happened while Manoah and his wife were watching.
20A flame blazed up from the altar toward heaven.
The angel of the LORD rose up in the flame. When
Manoah and his wife saw it, they fell with their
faces to the ground.
21The angel of the LORD didn't show himself
again to Manoah and his wife. Then Manoah realized it was the angel of the LORD.
22"We're going to die!" he said to his wife.
"We've seen God!"
23But his wife answered, "The LORD doesn't
want to kill us. If he did, he wouldn't have
accepted a burnt offering and a grain offering
from us. He wouldn't have shown us all of those
things. He wouldn't have told us we're going to
have a son."
24Later, the woman had a baby boy. She named
him Samson. As he grew up, the LORD blessed
him. 25The Spirit of the LORD began to work in his
life. It happened while he was in Mahaneh Dan.
It's between Zorah and Eshtaol.

Samson Gets Married

14 Samson went down to Timnah. There he saw a young Philistine woman. 2When he returned, he spoke to his father and mother. He said, "I've seen a Philistine woman in Timnah. Get her for me. I want her to be my wife."

3His father and mother replied, "Can't we find a wife for you among your relatives? Isn't there one among any of our people? Do you have to go to the Philistines to get a wife? They aren't God's people. They haven't even been circumcised."

But Samson said to his father, "Get her for me. She's the right one for me."

4Samson's parents didn't know that the LORD wanted things to happen that way. He was working out his plans against the Philistines. That's because the Philistines were ruling over Israel at that time.

5Samson went down to Timnah. His father and mother went with him. They approached the vineyards of Timnah. Suddenly a young lion came roaring toward Samson.

6Then the Spirit of the LORD came on Samson with power. He tore the lion apart with his bare hands. He did it as easily as he might have torn a young goat apart. But he didn't tell his father or mother what he had done.

7Then he went down and talked with the woman. He liked her.

8Some time later, he was going back to get married to her. But he turned off the road to look at the lion's dead body. Large numbers of bees and some honey were in it. 9He dug the honey out with his hands. He ate it as he walked along. Then he joined his parents again. He gave them some honey. They ate it too. But he didn't tell them he had taken it from the lion's dead body.

10Samson's father went down to see the woman. Samson had a big dinner prepared there. He was following the practice of men when they got married. 11When the people saw Samson, they gave him 30 companions.

12"Let me tell you a riddle," Samson said to the companions. "The dinner will last for seven days. Give me the answer to the riddle before the dinner ends. If you do, I'll give you 30 linen shirts. I'll also give you 30 sets of clothes. 13But suppose you can't give me the answer. Then you must give me 30 linen shirts. You must also give me 30 sets of clothes."

"Tell us your riddle," they said. "Let's hear it."

14Samson replied,

"Out of the eater came something to eat.
 Out of the strong came something sweet."

For three days they couldn't give him the answer.

15On the fourth day they spoke to Samson's wife. "Get your husband to explain the riddle for us," they said. "If you don't, we'll burn you to death. We'll burn up everyone in your family. Did you invite us here to rob us?"

16Then Samson's wife threw herself on him. She sobbed, "You hate me! You don't really love me. You have given my people a riddle. But you haven't told me the answer."

"I haven't even explained it to my father or mother," he replied. "So why should I explain it to you?"

17She cried during the whole seven days the dinner was going on. So on the seventh day he finally told her the answer to the riddle. That's because she kept on asking him to tell her. Then she explained the riddle to her people.

18Before sunset on the seventh day the men of the town spoke to Samson. They said,

"What is sweeter than honey?
 What is stronger than a lion?"

Samson said to them,

"You have plowed with my young cow.
 If you hadn't, you wouldn't have known the
 answer to my riddle."

19Then the Spirit of the LORD came on Samson with power. He went down to Ashkelon. He struck down 30 of their men. He took everything they had with them. And he gave their clothes to those who had explained the riddle. Samson was burning with anger as he went up to his father's house.

20Samson's wife was given to someone else. She was given to a friend of Samson. The friend had helped him at his wedding.

Samson Gets Even With the Philistines

15 Later on, Samson went to visit his wife. He took a young goat with him. He went at the time the wheat was being gathered. He said, "I'm going to my wife's room." But her father wouldn't let him go in.

2Her father said, "I was sure you really hated her. So I gave her to your friend. Isn't her younger sister more beautiful? Take her instead."

3Samson said to them, "This time I have a right to get even with the Philistines. I'm going to hurt them badly."

4So he went out and caught 300 foxes. He tied them in pairs by their tails. Then he tied a torch to each pair of tails. 5He lit the torches. He let the foxes loose in the fields of grain that belonged to the Philistines. He burned up the grain that had been cut and stacked. He burned up the grain that was still growing. He also burned up the vineyards and olive trees.

6The Philistines asked, "Who did this?" They were told, "Samson did. He's the son-in-law of the man from Timnah. Samson did it because his wife was given to his friend."

So the Philistines went up and burned the woman and her father to death.

7Samson said to them, "Is that how you act? Then I won't stop until I pay you back." 8He struck them down with heavy blows. He killed many of them. Then he went down and stayed in a cave. It was in the rock of Etam.

9The Philistines went up and camped in Judah. They spread out near Lehi. 10The men of Judah asked, "Why have you come to fight against us?"

"We've come to take Samson as our prisoner," they answered. "We want to do to him what he did to us."

11Then 3,000 men from Judah went to get Samson. They went down to the cave that was in the rock of Etam. They said to Samson, "Don't you realize the Philistines are ruling over us? What have you done to us?"

Samson answered, "I only did to them what they did to me."

12The men of Judah said to him, "We've come to tie you up. We're going to hand you over to the Philistines."

Samson said, "Take an oath and promise me you won't kill me yourselves."

13"We agree," they answered. "We'll only tie you up and hand you over to them. We won't kill you." So they tied him up with two new ropes. They led him up from the rock.

14Samson approached Lehi. The Philistines came toward him shouting. Then the Spirit of the LORD came on Samson with power. The ropes on his arms became like burned thread. They dropped off his hands. 15He found a fresh jawbone of a donkey. He grabbed hold of it and struck down 1,000 men.

16Then Samson said,

"By using a donkey's jawbone
 I've made them look like donkeys.
By using a donkey's jawbone
 I've struck down 1,000 men."

17Samson finished speaking. Then he threw the jawbone away. That's why the place was called Ramath Lehi.

18Samson was very thirsty. So he cried out to the LORD. He said, "You have helped me win this great battle. Do I have to die of thirst now? Must I fall into the power of people who haven't even been circumcised? They aren't your people."

19Then God opened up the hollow place in Lehi. Water came out of it. When Samson drank the water, his strength returned. He felt as good as new. So the spring was called En Hakkore. It's still there in Lehi.

20Samson led Israel for 20 years. In those days the Philistines were in the land.

Samson and Delilah

16 One day Samson went to Gaza. There he saw a prostitute. He went in to spend the night with her.

2The people of Gaza were told, "Samson is here!" So they surrounded the place. They hid and waited for him at the city gate all night long. They didn't make any move against him during the night. They said, "Let's wait until the sun comes up. Then we'll kill him."

3But Samson stayed there only until the middle of the night. Then he got up. He took hold of the doors of the city gate. He also took hold of the two doorposts. He tore them loose, together with their metal bar. He picked them up and put them on his shoulders. Then he carried them to the top of the hill that faces Hebron.

4Some time later, Samson fell in love again. The woman lived in the Valley of Sorek. Her name was Delilah.

5The rulers of the Philistines went to her. They said, "See if you can get him to tell you the secret of why he's so strong. Find out how we can overpower him. Then we can tie him up. We can bring him under our control. Each of us will give you 28 pounds of silver."

6So Delilah spoke to Samson. She said, "Tell me the secret of why you are so strong. Tell me how you can be tied up and controlled."

7Samson answered her, "Let someone tie me up with seven new leather straps. They must be straps that aren't completely dry. Then I'll become as weak as any other man."

8So the Philistine rulers brought seven new leather straps to her. They weren't completely dry. Delilah tied Samson up with them.

9Men were hiding in the room. She called out to him. She said, "Samson! The Philistines are attacking you!" But he snapped the leather straps easily. They were like pieces of string that had come too close to a flame. So the secret of why he was so strong wasn't discovered.

10Delilah spoke to Samson again. "You have made me look foolish," she said. "You told me a lie. Come on. Tell me how you can be tied up."

11Samson said, "Let someone tie me tightly with new ropes. They must be ropes that have never been used. Then I'll become as weak as any other man."

12So Delilah got some new ropes. She tied him up with them. Men were hiding in the room. She called out to him. She said, "Samson! The Philistines are attacking you!" But he snapped the ropes off his arms. They fell off just as if they were threads.

13Delilah spoke to Samson again. "Until now, you have been making me look foolish," she said. "You have been telling me lies. This time really tell me how you can be tied up."

He replied, "Weave the seven braids of my hair into the cloth on a loom. Then pin my hair to the loom. If you do, I'll become as weak as any other man."

So while Samson was sleeping, Delilah took hold of the seven braids of his hair. She wove them into the cloth on a loom. 14Then she pinned his hair to the loom.

Again she called out to him. She said, "Samson! The Philistines are attacking you!" He woke up from his sleep. He pulled up the pin and the loom, together with the cloth.

15Then she said to him, "How can you say, 'I love you'? You won't even share your secret with me. This is the third time you have made me look foolish. And you still haven't told me the secret of why you are so strong."

16She continued to pester him day after day. She nagged him until he was sick and tired of it.

17So he told her everything. "I've never used a razor on my head," he said. "I've never cut my hair. That's because I've been a Nazirite since the day I was born. A Nazirite is set apart to God. If you shave my head, I won't be strong anymore. I'll become as weak as any other man."

18Delilah realized he had told her everything. So she sent a message to the Philistine rulers. She said, "Come back one more time. He has told me everything." So the rulers returned. They brought the silver with them.

19Delilah got Samson to go to sleep on her lap. Then she called for a man to shave off the seven braids of his hair. That's how she began to bring him under her control. And he wasn't strong anymore.

20She called out, "Samson! The Philistines are attacking you!"

He woke up from his sleep. He thought, "I'll go out just as I did before. I'll shake myself free." But he didn't know that the LORD had left him.

21Then the Philistines grabbed hold of him. They poked his eyes out. They took him down to Gaza. They put bronze chains around him. Then they made him grind grain in the prison. 22His head had been shaved. But the hair on it began to grow again.

Samson Dies

23The rulers of the Philistines gathered together. They were going to offer a great sacrifice to their god Dagon. They were going to celebrate. They said, "Our god has handed our enemy Samson over to us."

24When the people saw Samson, they praised their god. They said,

"Our god has handed our enemy over to us.
 Our enemy has destroyed our land.
 He has killed large numbers of our people."

25After they had drunk a lot of wine, they shouted, "Bring Samson out. Let him put on a show for us." So they called Samson out of the prison. He put on a show for them.

They had him stand near the temple pillars. 26Then he spoke to the servant who was holding his hand. He said, "Put me where I can feel the pillars. I'm talking about the ones that hold the temple up. I want to lean against them."

27The temple was crowded with men and women. All of the Philistine rulers were there. About 3,000 men and women were on the roof. They were watching Samson put on a show.

28Then he prayed to the LORD. He said, "LORD and King, show me that you still have concern for me. God, please make me strong just one more time. Let me pay the Philistines back for what they did to my two eyes. Let me do it with only one blow."

29Then Samson reached toward the two pillars that were in the middle of the temple. They held the temple up. He put his right hand on one of them. He put his left hand on the other. He leaned hard against them.

30Samson said, "Let me die together with the Philistines!" Then he pushed with all his might. The temple came down on the rulers. It fell on all of the people who were in it. So Samson killed many more Philistines when he died than he did while he lived.

31Then his brothers went down to get him. So did his father's whole family. All of them brought Samson's body back home. They buried his body in the tomb of his father Manoah. It's between Zorah and Eshtaol. Samson had led Israel for 20 years.

Micah Makes Some Statues of Gods

17 A man named Micah lived in the hill country of Ephraim. 2He said to his mother, "Someone took 28 pounds of silver from you. I heard you call down a curse because of it. I have the silver with me. I'm the one who took it."

Then his mother said, "My son, may the LORD bless you!"

3He gave the 28 pounds of silver back to his mother. She said to him, "I'm taking an oath and setting my silver apart to the LORD. My son, I want you to use part of it for a statue of a god that is made out of wood or stone and covered with silver. Use the rest of it to have another statue made out of silver. That's why I'll give the silver back to you."

4He gave the silver back to his mother. She gave five pounds of it to a skilled worker who made things out of silver. He used the silver for the two statues. They were put in Micah's house.

5That same Micah had a small temple. He made a sacred linen apron and some statues of gods. He prepared one of his sons to serve as his priest.

6In those days Israel didn't have a king. The people did anything they thought was right.

7A young Levite had been living in land that belonged to the tribe of Judah. He was from Bethlehem in Judah. 8He left that town to look for some other place to stay. On his way he came to Micah's house. It was in the hill country of Ephraim.

9Micah asked him, "Where are you from?"

"I'm a Levite," he said. "I'm from Bethlehem in Judah. I'm looking for a place to stay."

10Then Micah said to him, "Live with me. Be my father and priest. I'll give you four ounces of silver a year. I'll also give you clothes and food."

11So the Levite agreed to live with him. The young man was just like a son to Micah.

12 Then Micah prepared the Levite to serve as
his priest. He lived in Micah's house. 13 Micah said,
"Now I know that the LORD will be good to me.
This Levite has become my priest."

The People of Dan Settle Down in Laish

18 In those days Israel didn't have a king.
And in those days the tribe of Dan was
looking for a place where they could settle down.
They hadn't been able to take over their own share
of land among the tribes of Israel.

2 So the people of Dan sent out five warriors
from Zorah and Eshtaol. They told them to look
the land over and check it out. Those men did it
for all of their family groups. The people of Dan
told the men, "Go. Check out the land."

So they entered the hill country of Ephraim.
They went to the house of Micah. That's where
they spent the night.

3 When they came near Micah's house, they recognized a voice. It was the voice of the young Levite. So they turned off the road and stopped there.
They asked him, "Who brought you here? What
are you doing in this place? Why are you here?"

4 The Levite told them what Micah had done for
him. He said, "He has hired me. I'm his priest."

5 Then they said to him, "Please ask God for
advice. Try to find out whether we'll have success
on our journey."

6 The priest answered them, "Go in peace. The
LORD is pleased with your journey."

7 So the five men left. They came to Laish.
There they saw that the people felt secure. They
were living in safety. Like the people in Sidon,
they weren't expecting anything bad to happen to
them. Their land had everything they needed.
Things were going very well for them. They lived
a long way from the people of Sidon. And they
didn't think they would ever need help from anyone else.

8 The men returned to Zorah and Eshtaol. Their
people asked them, "What did you find out?"

9 They answered, "Come on! Let's attack them!
We've seen that the land is very good. Aren't you
going to do something? Don't wait any longer. Go
there and take it over. 10 When you get there, you
will find people who aren't expecting anything bad
to happen to them. Their land has plenty of room.
God has handed it over to you. It's a land that has
everything you will ever need."

11 So 600 men from the tribe of Dan started out
from Zorah and Eshtaol. They were prepared for
battle. 12 On their way they set up camp. Their
camp was near Kiriath Jearim in Judah. That's
why the place is called Mahaneh Dan to this very
day. It's west of Kiriath Jearim. 13 From there they
went to the hill country of Ephraim. They came to
Micah's house.

14 Then the five men who had looked over the
land of Laish spoke to the other members of their
tribe. They said, "Don't you know that one of
these houses has a sacred linen apron in it? Some
statues of family gods are there. It also has two
statues of other gods in it. One of them is made out
of wood or stone. The other is made out of silver.
Now you know what to do."

15 So they turned off the road and stopped there.
They went to the house of the young Levite. He
was at Micah's place. They greeted the young
man. 16 The 600 men from Dan stood at the
entrance of the gate. They were prepared for battle.

17 The five men who had looked over the land
went inside. They took the two statues. They also
took the family gods and the linen apron.

During that time, the priest stood at the entrance
of the gate. The 600 men stood there with him.
They were prepared for battle.

18 When those men went into Micah's house and
took all of those things, the priest spoke to them.
He asked, "What are you doing?"

19 They answered him, "Be quiet! Don't say a
word. Come with us. Be our father and priest. You
can serve a whole tribe and family group in Israel
as our priest. Isn't that better than serving just one
man's family?"

20 The priest was glad. He took the linen apron
and the family gods. He also took the statue of a
god that was made out of wood or stone. Then he
left with the people.

21 They put their little children and their livestock in front of them. They also put everything
else they owned in front of them. And they turned
and went on their way.

22 The men who lived near Micah were called
together. Then they left and caught up with the
people of Dan. That's because Dan's people hadn't
gone very far from Micah's house. 23 Those who
lived near Micah shouted at them. The people of
Dan turned around and spoke to Micah. "What's
the matter with you?" they asked. "Why did you
call your men out to fight against us?"

24 He replied, "You took away the gods I made.
And you took my priest away. What do I have left?
So how can you ask, 'What's the matter with
you?'"

25 The people of Dan answered, "Don't argue
with us. Some men get angry quickly. They might
attack you. Then you and your family will lose
your lives."

26 So the people of Dan went on their way. Micah saw that they were too strong for him. So he
turned around and went back home.

27 The people of Dan took what Micah had
made. They also took his priest. They continued
on their way to Laish. They went there to fight
against peaceful people who weren't expecting to
be attacked. They struck them down with their
swords. They burned their city down. 28 No one
could save them. They lived a long way from Sidon. And they didn't think they would ever need
help from anyone else. Their city was located in a
valley near Beth Rehob.

The people of Dan rebuilt the city. Then they settled down there. 29They named it Dan. That's because they traced their family line back to Dan. He was a son of Israel. The city used to be called Laish.

30There the people of Dan set up the statues of gods for themselves. Jonathan and his sons were priests for the tribe of Dan. Jonathan was the son of Gershom, the son of Moses. Jonathan and his sons were priests until the time when the land was captured. 31They continued to use the statues Micah had made. They used them during the whole time the house of God was in Shiloh.

A Levite and His Concubine

19 In those days Israel didn't have a king. There was a Levite who lived deep in the hill country of Ephraim. He got a concubine from Bethlehem in Judah. 2But she wasn't faithful to him. She left him. She went back to her father's house in Bethlehem in Judah. She stayed there for four months.

3Then her husband went to see her. He tried to talk her into coming back with him. He had his servant and two donkeys with him. She took her husband into her father's house. When her father saw him, he gladly welcomed him.

4His father-in-law, the woman's father, begged him to stay. So he remained with him for three days. He ate, drank and slept there.

5On the fourth day they got up early. The Levite prepared to leave. But the woman's father spoke to his son-in-law. He said, "Have something to eat. It will give you strength. Then you can go on your way."

6So the two of them sat down. They ate and drank together. After that, the woman's father said, "Please stay tonight. Enjoy yourself."

7The man got up to go. But his father-in-law talked him into staying. So he stayed there that night.

8On the morning of the fifth day, he got up to go. But the woman's father said, "Have something to eat. It will give you strength. Wait until this afternoon!" So the two of them ate together.

9Then the man got up to leave. His concubine and his servant got up when he did. But his father-in-law, the woman's father, spoke to him again. "Look," he said. "It's almost evening. The day is nearly over. So spend another night here. Please stay. Enjoy yourself. Early tomorrow morning you can get up and go back home."

10But the man didn't want to stay another night. So he left. He went toward Jebus. He had his two donkeys and his concubine with him. The donkeys had saddles on them. Jebus is also called Jerusalem.

11By the time the travelers came near Jebus, the day was almost over. So the servant said to his master, "Come. Let's stop at this Jebusite city. Let's spend the night here."

12His master replied, "No. We won't go into a city where strangers live. The people there aren't from Israel. We'll continue on to Gibeah." 13He added, "Come. Let's try to reach Gibeah or Ramah. We can spend the night in one of those places."

14So they continued on. As they came near Gibeah in Benjamin, the sun went down. 15They stopped there to spend the night. They went to the city's main street and sat down. But no one took them home for the night.

16That evening an old man came into the city. He had been working in the fields. He was from the hill country of Ephraim. But he was living in Gibeah. The people who lived there were from the tribe of Benjamin. 17The old man saw the traveler in the main street. He asked, "Where are you going? Where did you come from?"

18The Levite answered, "We've come from Bethlehem in Judah. We're on our way to Ephraim. I live deep in the hill country there. I've been to Bethlehem. Now I'm going to the house of the LORD. But no one has taken me home for the night. 19We have straw and feed for our donkeys. We have food and wine for ourselves. We have enough for me, my female servant and the young man who is with us. We don't need anything."

20"You are welcome at my house," the old man said. "I'd be happy to supply anything you might need. But don't spend the night in the street."

21So the old man took him into his house and fed his donkeys. After the travelers had washed their feet, they had something to eat and drink.

22They were inside enjoying themselves. But some of the evil men who lived in the city surrounded the house. They pounded on the door. They shouted to the old man who owned the house. They said, "Bring out the man who came to your house. We want to have sex with him."

23The owner of the house went outside. He said to them, "No, my friends. Don't do such an evil thing. This man is my guest. So don't do this terrible thing.

24"Look, here is my virgin daughter. And here's the Levite's concubine. I'll bring them out to you now. You can have them. Do to them what you want to. But don't do such a terrible thing to this man."

25The men wouldn't listen to him. So the Levite sent his concubine out to them. They forced her to have sex with them. They raped her all night long. As the night was ending, they let her go.

26At sunrise she went back to the house where her master was staying. She fell down at the door. She stayed there until daylight.

27Later that morning her master got up. He opened the door of the house. He stepped out to continue on his way. But his concubine was lying there. She had fallen at the doorway of the house. Her hands were reaching out toward the door. 28He said to her, "Get up. Let's go." But there wasn't any answer. Then he put her dead body on his donkey. And he started out for home.

29When he reached home, he got a knife. He cut up his concubine. He cut her into 12 pieces. He sent them into all of the territories of Israel.

30Everyone who saw it said, "Nothing like this has ever been seen or done before. Nothing like this has happened since the day the people of Israel came up out of Egypt. Think about it! Consider it! Tell us what to do!"

The Tribe of Benjamin Is Attacked by the Other Tribes

20 Then all of the people of Israel came out. They came from the whole land between Dan and Beersheba. They also came from the land of Gilead. All of them gathered together in the sight of the LORD at Mizpah. 2The leaders of all of the tribes of Israel came. They took their places among the people of God who were gathered together. There were 400,000 fighting men who were carrying swords. 3The tribe of Benjamin heard that the people of Israel had gone up to Mizpah. The people of Israel said, "Tell us how that awful thing happened."

4So the Levite spoke. He was the husband of the woman who had been murdered. He said, "I and my concubine went to Gibeah in Benjamin. We spent the night there. 5During the night the men of Gibeah came after me. They surrounded the house. They were planning to kill me. They raped my concubine, and she died.

6"I took my concubine and cut her into pieces. I sent one piece to each part of Israel's territory. I did it because they had done a very terrible thing in Israel. 7All of you men of Israel, speak up now. Give your decision."

8All of the men got up together. They said, "None of us will go home. Not one of us will return to his house. 9Here is what we'll do to Gibeah. We'll use lots to tell us how to attack the city. 10We'll take ten men out of every 100 from all of the tribes of Israel. We'll take 100 from every 1,000. We'll take 1,000 from every 10,000. The men we take will get supplies for the army. Then the army will go to Gibeah in Benjamin. They'll give Gibeah exactly what they should get because of the evil thing they did in Israel."

11So all of the men of Israel came together to fight against the city.

12The tribes of Israel sent men through the whole tribe of Benjamin. They said, "What about this awful crime that was committed among you? 13Hand over those evil men of Gibeah. We'll put them to death. In that way we'll get rid of those evil people."

But the people of Benjamin wouldn't listen to the other people of Israel. 14They came together at Gibeah from their towns. They came to fight against the other people of Israel.

15Right away the people of Benjamin gathered together 26,000 men from their towns. They were carrying swords. The men were added to the 700 who had been chosen from those who were living in Gibeah. 16Among all of those men there were 700 who were left-handed. Each of them could sling a stone at a hair and not miss.

17Israel gathered 400,000 men together. They were carrying swords. All of them were fighting men. That number didn't include the tribe of Benjamin.

18The people of Israel went up to Bethel. There they spoke to God. They asked him, "Who will go up first and fight for us against the people of Benjamin?"

The LORD answered, "The tribe of Judah will go first."

19The next morning the people of Israel got up. They set up camp near Gibeah. 20The men of Israel went out to fight against the men of Benjamin. They took up their battle positions against them at Gibeah. 21The men of Benjamin came out of Gibeah. They killed 22,000 men of Israel on the field of battle that day. 22But the men of Israel cheered each other on. They again took up their positions in the places where they had been the first day.

23The men of Israel went and sobbed in the sight of the LORD until evening. They spoke to the LORD. They asked, "Should we go up again to fight against the men of Benjamin? They are our fellow Israelites."

The LORD answered, "Go up and fight against them."

24The men of Israel came near the men of Benjamin on the second day. 25The men of Benjamin came out from Gibeah to oppose them. That time they killed 18,000 more men of Israel. All of the men who died had been carrying swords.

26Then all of the people of Israel went up to Bethel. They sat there and sobbed in the sight of the LORD. They didn't eat anything that day until evening. Then they brought burnt offerings and friendship offerings to the LORD.

27Again the people of Israel spoke to the LORD. In those days the ark of the covenant of God was there. 28Phinehas was serving as priest at the ark. He was the son of Eleazar. Eleazar was the son of Aaron. The people of Israel asked, "Should we go up again to fight against the men of Benjamin? They are our fellow Israelites."

The LORD answered, "Go. Tomorrow I will hand them over to you."

29Then Israel hid some men and had them wait all around Gibeah. 30They went up to fight against the men of Benjamin on the third day. They took up their positions against Gibeah, just as they had done before.

31The men of Benjamin came out to fight against them. They were drawn away from the city. They began to wound and kill the men of Israel just as they had done before. About 30 men fell in battle. They fell in the open fields and on the roads. One of the roads led to Bethel. The other led to Gibeah.

32The men of Benjamin said, "We're winning
the battle over them, just as we did before."
But the men of Israel said, "Let's pull back.
Let's draw them away from the city to the roads."
33All of the men of Israel moved away from
their places. They took up new battle positions at
Baal Tamar. The men who had been hiding
charged out. They came from west of Gibeah.
34Then 10,000 of Israel's finest men attacked
Gibeah. The men of Benjamin didn't realize they
were about to be destroyed. The fighting was very
heavy.
35The LORD helped Israel win the battle over
Benjamin. On that day the men of Israel struck
down 25,100 men of Benjamin. All of the men
who died had been carrying swords. 36Then the
men of Benjamin saw that they had lost the battle.
The men of Israel had moved away from their
positions in front of Benjamin. They had depended
on the men they had hidden near Gibeah. 37Sud-
denly the men who had been hiding rushed into
Gibeah. They spread out. Then they killed everyone in the city with their swords.
38The men of Israel had made a plan with those
who had been hiding. They had told them to send
up a large cloud of smoke from the city. 39Then the
men of Israel would turn around and attack.
The men of Benjamin had begun to wound and
kill the men of Israel. They had struck down about
30 of them. They had said, "We're winning the
battle over them, just as we did the first time."
40But a column of smoke began to go up from
the city. The men of Benjamin turned around.
They saw the smoke of the whole city going up
into the sky.
41Then the men of Israel turned around and
attacked them.
The men of Benjamin were terrified. They realized they were going to be destroyed. 42So they ran
away from the men of Israel. They ran toward the
desert. But they couldn't escape the battle. Other
men of Israel came out of the towns. There they
struck the men of Benjamin down. 43They surrounded them. They chased them and easily caught
up with them. That happened east of Gibeah.
44So 18,000 men of Benjamin fell in battle. All
of them were brave fighters.
45Some men of Benjamin turned back. They ran
toward the desert to the rock of Rimmon. As they
did, the men of Israel struck down 5,000 of them
along the roads. They kept chasing the men of
Benjamin all the way to Gidom. Along the way
they struck down 2,000 more.
46On that day 25,000 men of Benjamin fell in
battle. They had been carrying swords. All of them
were brave fighters. 47But 600 men turned back.
They ran into the desert to the rock of Rimmon.
They stayed there for four months.
48The men of Israel went back to Benjamin.
They killed the people in all of the towns with their
swords. They even killed the animals. So they
killed everything they found. They set on fire all of
the towns they came to.

The Men of Benjamin Receive Wives

21 The men of Israel had taken an oath and
made a promise at Mizpah. They had said,
"Not one of us will give his daughter to be married to a man from Benjamin."
2The people went to Bethel. They sat there until
evening in the sight of God. They sobbed loudly
and bitterly. 3"LORD, you are the God of Israel,"
they cried. "Why has this happened to Israel? Why
is one tribe missing from Israel today?"
4Early the next day the people built an altar.
They brought burnt offerings and friendship
offerings.
5Then the people of Israel asked, "Has anyone
failed to come here in the sight of the LORD? Is
anyone missing from all of the tribes of Israel?"
The people had made a promise with an oath.
They had said that anyone who failed to come to
Mizpah in the sight of the LORD should certainly
be put to death.
6The people of Israel were very sad because of
what had happened to the tribe of Benjamin. After
all, they were their fellow Israelites. "Today one
tribe has been cut off from Israel," they said.
7"How can we provide wives for the men who are
left? We've made a promise with an oath in the
sight of the LORD. We've promised not to give any
of our daughters to be married to them."
8Then they asked, "Has any tribe of Israel failed
to come here to Mizpah in the sight of the LORD?"
They discovered that no one from Jabesh Gilead had come. No one from there had gathered
together with the others in the camp. 9They
counted the people. They found that none of the
people of Jabesh Gilead had come to Mizpah.
10So the community sent 12,000 fighting men
to Jabesh Gilead. They directed them to take their
swords and kill those who were living there. That
included the women and children.
11"Here is what you must do," they said. "Kill
every male. Also kill every woman who is not a
virgin."
12They found 400 young women in Jabesh Gilead who had never made love to a man. So they
took them to the camp at Shiloh in Canaan.
13Then the whole community sent an offer of
peace to the men of Benjamin. The men were at
the rock of Rimmon. 14So the men of Benjamin
returned at that time. They were given the women
of Jabesh Gilead who had been spared. But there
weren't enough women for all of them.
15The people were very sad because of what had
happened to the tribe of Benjamin. The LORD had
left a gap in the tribes of Israel. They weren't complete without Benjamin.
16The elders of the community spoke up. They
said, "All of the women of Benjamin have been
wiped out. So how will we find wives for the men
who are left? 17The men of Benjamin who are still

alive need to have children," they said. "If they don't, a tribe of Israel will be wiped out.

18"But we can't give them our daughters to be their wives. We Israelites have taken an oath and made a promise. We've said, 'May anyone who gives a wife to a man from Benjamin be under the LORD's curse.'

19"Look, a feast is celebrated every year in Shiloh in honor of the LORD. Shiloh is north of Bethel. It's east of the road that goes from Bethel to Shechem. It's south of Lebonah."

20So they told the men of Benjamin what to do.
They said, "Go. Hide in the vineyards 21and watch.
The young women of Shiloh will come out. They'll join in the dancing. When they do, run out of the vineyards. Each of you grab hold of a young woman from Shiloh to be your wife. Then go to the land of Benjamin.

22"Their fathers or brothers might not be happy with what we're doing. If they aren't, we'll say to them, 'Do us a favor. Help the men of Benjamin. We didn't get wives for them during the battle. You aren't guilty of doing anything wrong. After all, you didn't give your daughters to them. They were stolen from you.'"

23So that's what the men of Benjamin did. While the young women were dancing, each man caught one. He carried her away to be his wife. Then the men returned to their own share of land. They built the towns again. They settled down in them.

24At that time the men of Israel also left. They went home to their tribes and family groups. Each one went to his own share of land.

25In those days Israel didn't have a king. The people did anything they thought was right.

Ruth

Ruth Goes to Bethlehem With Naomi

1 There was a time when Israel didn't have kings to rule over them. But they had leaders to help them. This is a story about some things that happened during that time.

There wasn't enough food in the land of Judah. So a man went to live in the country of Moab for a while. He was from Bethlehem in Judah. His wife and two sons went with him.

[2]The man's name was Elimelech. His wife's name was Naomi. The names of his two sons were Mahlon and Kilion. They were Ephrathites from Bethlehem in Judah. They went to Moab and lived there.

[3]Naomi's husband Elimelech died. So she was left with her two sons. [4]They got married to women from Moab. One was named Orpah. The other was named Ruth. Naomi's family lived in Moab for about ten years. [5]Then Mahlon and Kilion also died. So Naomi was left without her two sons and her husband.

[6]While Naomi was in Moab, she heard that the LORD had helped his people. He had begun to provide food for them again. So Naomi and her daughters-in-law prepared to go from Moab back to her home. [7]She left the place where she had been living. Her two daughters-in-law went with her. They started out on the road that would take them back to the land of Judah.

[8]Naomi spoke to her two daughters-in-law. "Both of you go back," she said. "Each of you go to your own mother's home. You were kind to your husbands, who have died. You have also been kind to me. So may the LORD be just as kind to you. [9]May he help each of you find a secure place in the home of another husband. May he give you peace and rest."

Then she kissed them good-by. They broke down and sobbed loudly. [10]They said to her, "We'll go back to your people with you."

[11]But Naomi said, "Go home, my daughters. Why would you want to come with me? AmI going to have any more sons who could become your husbands?

[12]"Go home, my daughters. I'm too old to have another husband. Suppose I thought there was still some hope for me. Suppose I got married to a man tonight. And later I had sons by him. [13]Would you wait until they grew up? Would you stay single until you could get married to them? No, my daughters. My life is more bitter than yours. The LORD's powerful hand has been against me!"

[14]When they heard that, they broke down and sobbed again. Then Orpah kissed her mother-in-law good-by. But Ruth held on to her.

[15]"Look," said Naomi. "Your sister-in-law is going back to her people and her gods. Go back with her."

[16]But Ruth replied, "Don't try to make me leave you and go back. Where you go I'll go. Where you stay I'll stay. Your people will be my people. Your God will be my God. [17]Where you die I'll die. And there my body will be buried. I won't let anything except death separate you from me. If I do, may the LORD punish me greatly."

[18]Naomi realized that Ruth had made up her mind to go with her. So she stopped trying to make her go back.

[19]The two women continued on their way. At last they arrived in Bethlehem. The whole town was stirred up because of them. The women asked, "Can this possibly be Naomi?"

[20]"Don't call me Naomi," she told them. "Call me Mara. The Mighty One has made my life very bitter. [21]I was full when I went away. But the LORD has brought me back empty. So why are you calling me Naomi? The LORD has made me suffer. The Mighty One has brought trouble on me."

[22]So Naomi returned from Moab. Ruth, her daughter-in-law from Moab, came with her. They arrived in Bethlehem just when people were beginning to harvest the barley.

Ruth Meets Boaz

2 Naomi had a relative on her husband's side of the family. Her husband's name was Elimelech. The relative's name was Boaz. He was a very important man.

[2]Ruth, who was from Moab, spoke to Naomi. She said, "Let me go out to the fields. I'll pick up the grain that has been left. I'll do it behind anyone who is pleased with me."

Naomi said to her, "My daughter, go ahead."

[3]So Ruth went out and began to pick up grain. She worked in the fields behind those who were cutting and gathering the grain. As it turned out, she was working in a field that belonged to Boaz. He was from the family of Elimelech.

[4]Just then Boaz arrived from Bethlehem. He greeted those who were cutting and gathering the grain. He said, "May the LORD be with you!"

"And may the LORD bless you!" they replied.

[5]Boaz spoke to the man who was in charge of his workers. He asked, "Who is that young woman?"

[6]The man replied, "She's from Moab. She came back from there with Naomi. [7]She said, 'Please let me walk behind the workers. Let me pick up the grain that is left.' Then she went into the field. She has kept on working there from morning until now. She took only one short rest in the shade."

8So Boaz said to Ruth, "Dear woman, listen to
me. Don't pick up grain in any other field. Don't
go anywhere else. Stay here with my female servants. 9Keep your eye on the field where the men
are cutting grain. Walk behind the women who are
gathering it. Pick up the grain that is left. I've told
the men not to touch you. When you are thirsty, go
and get a drink. Take water from the jars the men
have filled."
10When Ruth heard that, she bowed down with
her face to the ground. She asked, "Why are you
being so kind to me? In fact, why are you even
noticing me? I'm from another country."
11Boaz replied, "I've been told all about you.
I've heard about everything you have done for
your mother-in-law since your husband died. I
know that you left your father and mother. I know
that you left your country. You came to live with
people you didn't know before.
12"May the LORD reward you for what you have
done. May the God of Israel bless you richly. You
have come to him to find safety under his care."
13"Sir, I hope you will continue to be kind to
me," Ruth said. "You have comforted me. You
have spoken kindly to me. And I'm not even as
important as one of your female servants!"
14When it was time to eat, Boaz spoke to Ruth
again. "Come over here," he said. "Have some
bread. Dip it in the wine vinegar."

She sat down with the workers. Then Boaz
offered her some grain that had been cooked. She
ate all she wanted. She even had some left over.
15Ruth got up to pick up more grain. Then Boaz
gave orders to his men. He said, "Suppose she
takes some stalks from what the women have tied
up. If she does, don't make her look bad. 16Instead,
pull some stalks out for her. Leave them for her to
pick up. Don't tell her she shouldn't do it."
17So Ruth picked up grain in the field until
evening. Then she separated the barley from the
straw. It amounted to more than half a bushel.
18She carried it back to town. Her mother-in-law
saw how much she had gathered. Ruth also
brought out the food that was left over from the
lunch Boaz had given her. She gave it to Naomi.
19Her mother-in-law asked her, "Where did you
pick up grain today? Where did you work? May
the man who noticed you be blessed!"

Then Ruth told her about the man whose field
she had worked in. "The name of the man I
worked with today is Boaz," she said.
20"May the LORD bless him!" Naomi said to her
daughter-in-law. "The LORD is still being kind to
those who are living and those who are dead."

She continued, "That man is a close relative of
ours. He's one of our family protectors."
21Then Ruth, who was from Moab, said, "He told
me more. He even said, 'Stay with my workers until
they have finished bringing in all of my grain.'"
22Naomi replied to her daughter-in-law Ruth.
She said, "That will be good for you, my daughter.
Go with his female servants. You might be harmed
if you go to someone else's field."
23So Ruth stayed close to the female servants of
Boaz as she picked up grain. She worked until the
time when all of the barley and wheat had been
harvested. And she lived with her mother-in-law.

Ruth Goes to Boaz at the Threshing Floor

3 One day Ruth's mother-in-law Naomi spoke
to her. She said, "My daughter, shouldn't I try
to find a secure place for you? Shouldn't you have
peace and rest? Shouldn't I find a home where
things will go well with you? 2You have been with
the female servants of Boaz. He's a relative of
ours. Tonight he'll be separating the straw from his
barley on the threshing floor.
3"So wash yourself. Put on some perfume. And
put on your best clothes. Then go down to the
threshing floor. But don't let Boaz know you are
there. Wait until he has finished eating and drinking. 4Notice where he lies down. Then go over and
uncover his feet. Lie down there. He'll tell you
what to do."
5"I'll do everything you say," Ruth answered.
6So she went down to the threshing floor. She did
everything her mother-in-law had told her to do.
7When Boaz had finished eating and drinking,
he was in a good mood. He went over to lie down
at the far end of the grain pile. Then Ruth
approached quietly. She uncovered his feet and lay
down there.
8In the middle of the night, something surprised
Boaz and woke him up. He turned and found a
woman lying there at his feet.
9"Who are you?" he asked.

"I'm Ruth," she said. "You are my family protector. So take good care of me by making me your
wife."
10"Dear woman, may the LORD bless you," he
replied. "You are showing even more kindness
now than you did earlier. You didn't run after the
younger men, whether they were rich or poor.
11Dear woman, don't be afraid. I'll do for you
everything you ask. All of the people of my town
know that you are a noble woman.
12"It's true that I'm a relative of yours. But
there's a family protector who is more closely
related to you than I am. 13So stay here for the
night. In the morning if he wants to help you,
good. Let him help you. But if he doesn't want to,
then I'll do it. You can be sure that the LORD lives.
And you can be just as sure that I'll help you. Lie
down here until morning."
14So she stayed at his feet until morning. But
she got up before anyone could be recognized.
Boaz thought, "No one must know that a woman
came to the threshing floor."
15He said to Ruth, "Bring me the coat you have
around you. Hold it out." So she did. He poured
more than fifty pounds of barley into it and helped
her pick it up. Then he went back to town.

16Ruth came to her mother-in-law. Naomi asked, "How did it go, my daughter?"

Then Ruth told her everything Boaz had done for her. 17She said, "He gave me all of this barley. He said, 'Don't go back to your mother-in-law with your hands empty.'"

18Naomi said, "My daughter, sit down until you find out what happens. The man won't rest until he settles the whole matter today."

Boaz Gets Married to Ruth

4 Boaz went up to the town gate and sat down there. The family protector he had talked about came by. Then Boaz said, "Come over here, my friend. Sit down." So the man went over and sat down.

2Boaz brought ten of the elders of the town together. He said, "Sit down here." So they did.

3Then he spoke to the family protector. He said, "Naomi has come back from Moab. She's selling the piece of land that belonged to our relative Elimelech. 4I thought I should bring the matter to your attention. I suggest that you buy the land while those who are sitting here and the elders of my people are looking on as witnesses.

"If you are willing to buy it back, do it. But if you aren't, tell me. Then I'll know. No one has the right to buy it back except you. And I'm next in line."

"I'll buy it," he said.

5Then Boaz said, "When you buy the land from Naomi and Ruth, who is from Moab, you must get married to Ruth. She's the dead man's widow. So you must take her as your wife. His name must stay with his property."

6When the family protector heard that, he said, "Then I can't buy the land. If I did, I might put my own property in danger. So you buy it. I can't do it."

7In earlier times in Israel, there was a certain practice. It was used when family land was bought back and changed owners. The practice made the sale final. One person would take his sandal off and give it to the other. That was how people in Israel showed that a business matter had been settled.

8So the family protector said to Boaz, "Buy it yourself." And he took his sandal off.

9Then Boaz spoke to the elders and all of the people. He said, "Today you are witnesses. You have seen that I have bought land from Naomi. I have bought all of the property that had belonged to Elimelech, Kilion and Mahlon.

10"I've also taken Ruth, who is from Moab, to become my wife. She is Mahlon's widow. I've decided to get married to her so the dead man's name will stay with his property. Now his name won't disappear from his family line. It won't disappear from the town records. Today you are witnesses!"

11Then the elders and all who were at the gate spoke. They said, "We are witnesses. The woman is coming into your home. May the LORD make her to be like Rachel and Leah. Together they built up the nation of Israel. May you be an important person in Ephrathah. May you be famous in Bethlehem. 12The LORD will give you children through this young woman. May your family be like the family of Perez. He was the son Tamar had by Judah."

The Family Line of David

13So Boaz got married to Ruth. She became his wife. Then he made love to her. The LORD blessed her so that she became pregnant. And she had a son.

14The women said to Naomi, "We praise the LORD. Today he has provided a family protector for you. May this child become famous all over Israel! 15He will make your life new again. He'll take care of you when you are old. He's the son of your very own daughter-in-law. She loves you. She is better to you than seven sons."

16Then Naomi put the child on her lap and took care of him. 17The women who were living there said, "Naomi has a son." They named him Obed. He was the father of Jesse. Jesse was the father of David.

18Here is the family line of Perez.

Perez was the father of Hezron.
19 Hezron was the father of Ram.
Ram was the father of Amminadab.
20 Amminadab was the father of Nahshon.
Nahshon was the father of Salmon.
21 Salmon was the father of Boaz.
Boaz was the father of Obed.
22 Obed was the father of Jesse.
And Jesse was the father of David.

1 Samuel

Samuel Is Born

1 A certain man from Ramathaim in the hill
country of Ephraim was named Elkanah. He
was the son of Jeroham. Jeroham was the son of
Elihu. Elihu was the son of Tohu. Tohu was the son
of Zuph. Elkanah belonged to the family line of
Zuph. Elkanah lived in the territory of Ephraim.
[2]Elkanah had two wives. One was named Hannah. The other was named Peninnah. Peninnah had
children, but Hannah didn't.
[3]Year after year Elkanah went up from his town
to Shiloh. He went there to worship and sacrifice
to the LORD who rules over all. Hophni and Phinehas served as priests of the LORD at Shiloh. They
were the two sons of Eli.
[4]Every time the day came for Elkanah to offer
a sacrifice, he would give a share of the meat to
his wife Peninnah. He would also give a share to
each of her sons and daughters. [5]But he would give
two shares of meat to Hannah. That's because he
loved her. He also gave her two shares because the
LORD had kept her from having children.
[6]Peninnah teased Hannah to make her angry.
She did it because the LORD had kept Hannah from
having children. [7]Peninnah teased Hannah year
after year. Every time Hannah would go up to the
house of the LORD, Elkanah's other wife would
tease her. She would keep doing it until Hannah
cried and wouldn't eat.
[8]Her husband Elkanah would speak to her. He
would say, "Hannah, why are you crying? Why
don't you eat? Why are you so angry and unhappy?
Don't I mean more to you than ten sons?"
[9]One time when they had finished eating and
drinking in Shiloh, Hannah stood up. The priest
Eli was sitting on a chair by the doorpost of the
LORD's house. [10]Hannah was very bitter. She
sobbed and sobbed. She prayed to the LORD. [11]She
made a promise to him. She said, "LORD, you rule
over all. Please see how I'm suffering! Show concern for me! Don't forget about me! Please give
me a son! If you do, I'll give him back to you.
Then he will serve you all the days of his life. He'll
never use a razor on his head. He'll never cut his
hair."
[12]As Hannah kept on praying to the LORD, Eli
watched her lips. [13]She was praying in her heart.
Her lips were moving. But she wasn't making a
sound.
Eli thought Hannah was drunk. [14]He said to her,
"How long will you keep on getting drunk? Get
rid of your wine."
[15]"That's not true, sir," Hannah replied. "I'm a
woman who is deeply troubled. I haven't been
drinking wine or beer. I was telling the LORD all of
my troubles. [16]Don't think of me as an evil woman.
I've been praying here because I'm very sad. My
pain is so great."
[17]Eli answered, "Go in peace. May the God of
Israel give you what you have asked him for."
[18]She said, "May you be pleased with me."
Then she left and had something to eat. Her face
wasn't sad anymore.
[19]Early the next morning Elkanah and his family got up. They worshiped the LORD. Then they
went back to their home in Ramah.
Elkanah made love to his wife Hannah. And the
LORD showed concern for her. [20]After some time,
Hannah became pregnant. She had a baby boy. She
said, "I asked the LORD for him." So she named
him Samuel.

Hannah Gives Samuel to the LORD

[21]Elkanah went up to Shiloh to offer the yearly
sacrifice to the LORD. He also went there to keep
a promise he had made. His whole family went
with him.
[22]But Hannah didn't go. She said to her husband, "When the boy doesn't need me to nurse
him anymore, I'll take him to the LORD's house.
I'll give him to the LORD there. He'll stay there for
the rest of his life."
[23]Her husband Elkanah told her, "Do what you
think is best. Stay here at home until Samuel
doesn't need you to nurse him anymore. May the
LORD make his promise to you come true."
So Hannah stayed home. She nursed her son
until he didn't need her milk anymore.
[24]When the boy didn't need her to nurse him
anymore, she took him with her to Shiloh. She
took him there even though he was still very
young. She brought him to the LORD's house. She
brought along a bull that was three years old. She
brought more than half a bushel of flour. She also
brought a bottle of wine. The bottle was made out
of animal skin.
[25]After the bull was killed, Elkanah and Hannah
brought the boy to Eli. [26]Hannah said to Eli, "Sir,
I'm the woman who stood here beside you praying
to the LORD. And that's just as sure as you are alive.
[27]I prayed for this child. The LORD has given me
what I asked him for. [28]So now I'm giving him to
the LORD. As long as he lives he'll be given to the
LORD." And all of them worshiped the LORD there.

Hannah Gives Thanks to the LORD

2 Then Hannah prayed. She said,

"The LORD has filled my heart with joy.
He has made me strong.
I can laugh at my enemies.
I'm so glad he saved me.

2“There isn't anyone holy like the LORD.
    There isn't anyone except him.
    There isn't any Rock like our God.

3“Don't keep talking so proudly.
    Don't let your mouth say such proud things.
The LORD is a God who knows everything.
    He judges everything people do.

4“The bows of great heroes are broken.
    But those who trip and fall are made strong.
5Those who used to be full have to work
        for food.
    But those who used to be hungry aren't
        hungry anymore.
The woman who couldn't have children has
        seven of them now.
    But the woman who has had many children
        is sad now because hers have died.

6“The LORD causes people to die. He also gives
        people life.
    He brings people down to the grave. He also
        brings people up.
7The LORD makes people poor. He also makes
        people rich.
    He brings people down. He also lifts
        people up.
8He raises poor people up from the trash pile.
    He lifts needy people out of the ashes.
He lets them sit with princes.
    He gives them places of honor.
“The foundations of the earth belong to
        the LORD.
    On them he has set the world.
9He guards the paths of those who are faithful
        to him.
    But evil people will lie silent in their
        dark graves.

“People don't win just because they are strong.
10 Those who oppose the LORD will be totally
        destroyed.
He will thunder against them from heaven.
    He will judge the earth from one end to
        the other.

“He will give power to his king.
    He will give honor to his anointed one.”

11Then Elkanah went home to Ramah. But the
boy Samuel served the LORD under the direction
of the priest Eli.

Eli's Evil Sons

12Eli's sons were evil men. They didn't know
the LORD. 13When anyone came to offer a sacrifice,
here is what the priests would do. While the meat
was being boiled, the servant of the priest would
come with a large fork in his hand. 14He would
stick it into the pan or pot or small or large kettle.
Then the priest would take for himself everything
the fork brought up. That's how Eli's sons treated
all of the people of Israel who came to Shiloh.

15Even before the fat was burned, the servant of
the priest would come over. He would speak to the
man who was offering the sacrifice. He would say,
“Give the priest some meat to cook. He won't
accept boiled meat from you. All he'll accept is
raw meat.”

16Sometimes the man would say to him, “Let
the fat be burned up first. Then take what you
want.”

But the servant would answer, “No. Hand it over right now. If you don't, I'll take it away from you by force.”

17That sin of Eli's sons was very great in the
LORD's sight. That's because they were making fun
of his offering.

18But the boy Samuel served the LORD. He wore
a sacred linen apron. 19Each year his mother made
him a little robe. She took it to him when she went
up to Shiloh with her husband. She did it when her
husband went to offer the yearly sacrifice.

20Eli would bless Elkanah and his wife. He
would say, “May the LORD give you children by
this woman. May they take the place of the boy
she prayed for and gave to him.” Then they would
go home.

21The LORD was gracious to Hannah. She became pregnant. Over a period of years she had three
more sons and two daughters. During that whole
time the boy Samuel grew up serving the LORD.

22Eli was very old. He kept hearing about everything his sons were doing to all of the people of Israel. He also heard how they were having sex with
the women who served at the entrance to the Tent
of Meeting.

23So Eli said to his sons, “Why are you doing
those things? All of the people are telling me about
the evil things you are doing. 24No, my sons. The
report I hear isn't good. And it's spreading among
the LORD's people. 25If a man sins against someone else, God can help that sinner. But if a man
sins against the LORD, who can help him?”

In spite of what their father Eli said, his sons didn't pay any attention to his warning. That's because the LORD had already decided to put them to death.

26The boy Samuel continued to grow stronger.
He also became more and more pleasing to the
LORD and to people.

A Man of God Prophesies Against Eli's Family

27A man of God came to Eli. He told him, “The
LORD says, 'I made myself clearly known to your
relatives who lived long ago. I did it when they
were in Egypt under Pharaoh. 28I chose your father
Aaron to be my priest. I chose him out of all of the
tribes of Israel. I told him to go up to my altar. I
told him to burn incense. I chose him to wear a
linen apron when he served me. I also gave his
family all of the offerings that are made with fire
by the people of Israel.

29“‘Why do all of you laugh at my sacrifices
and offerings? I require them to be brought to the
house where I live. Why do you honor your sons
more than me? Why do you fatten yourselves on
the best parts of every offering that is made by my
people Israel?’

30“The LORD is the God of Israel. He announced,
‘I promised that your family and the family of Aaron would serve me as priests forever.’

“But now the LORD announces, ‘I will not let
that happen! I will honor those who honor me. But
I will turn away from those who look down on me.
31The time is coming when I will cut your life
short. I will also cut short the lives of those in your
family. No man in your family line will grow old.

32“‘You will see nothing but trouble in the house
where I live. Good things will still happen to Israel. But no man in your family line will ever grow
old. 33A member of your family will serve me at my
altar. But what he does will bring tears to your eyes.
Your heart will be sad. And the rest of the men in
your family line will die while they are still young.

34“‘Something is going to happen to your two
sons Hophni and Phinehas. When it does, it will
show you that what I am saying is true. They will
both die on the same day.

35“‘I will raise up for myself a faithful priest.
He will do what my heart and mind want him to
do. I will make his family line very secure. They
will always serve as priests to my anointed king.
36Everyone who is left in your family line will
come and bow down to him. They will beg him for
a piece of silver and a crust of bread. They will say,
“Please give me a place to serve among the priests.
Then I can have food to eat.”’”

The LORD Calls Out to Samuel

3 The boy Samuel served the LORD under the
direction of Eli. In those days the LORD didn’t
give many messages to his people. He didn’t give
them many visions.

2One night Eli was lying down in his usual
place. His eyes were becoming so weak he
couldn’t see very well. 3Samuel was lying down in
the LORD’s house. That’s where the ark of God was
kept. The lamp of God was still burning. 4The
LORD called out to Samuel.

Samuel answered, “Here I am.” 5He ran over to
Eli. He said, “Here I am. You called out to me.”

But Eli said, “I didn’t call you. Go back and lie
down.” So he went and lay down.

6Again the LORD called out, “Samuel!” Samuel
got up and went to Eli. He said, “Here I am. You
called out to me.”

“My son,” Eli said, “I didn’t call you. Go back
and lie down.”

7Samuel didn’t know the LORD yet. That’s
because the LORD still hadn’t given him a message.

8The LORD called out to Samuel for the third
time. Samuel got up and went to Eli. He said,
“Here I am. You called out to me.”

Then Eli realized that the LORD was calling the
boy. 9So Eli told Samuel, “Go and lie down. If
someone calls out to you again, say, ‘Speak, LORD.
I’m listening.’” So Samuel went and lay down in
his place.

10The LORD came and stood there. He called
out, just as he had done the other times. He said,
“Samuel! Samuel!”

Then Samuel replied, “Speak. I’m listening.”

11The LORD said to Samuel, “Pay attention! I am
about to do something terrible in Israel. It will
make the ears of everyone who hears about it ring.

12“At that time I will do everything to Eli and
his family that I said I would. I will finish what I
have started. 13I told Eli I would punish his family
forever. He knew his sons were sinning. He knew
they were making fun of me. In spite of that, he
failed to stop them.

14“So I took an oath and made a promise to the
family of Eli. I said, ‘The sins of Eli’s family will
never be paid for by bringing sacrifices or
offerings.’”

15Samuel lay down until morning. Then he
opened the doors of the LORD’s house. He was afraid
to tell Eli about the vision he had received. 16But Eli
called out to him. He said, “Samuel, my son.”

Samuel answered, “Here I am.”

17“What did the LORD say to you?” Eli asked.
“Don’t hide from me anything he told you. If you
do, may God punish you greatly.”

18So Samuel told him everything. He didn’t hide
anything from him.

Then Eli said, “He is the LORD. Let him do what
he thinks is best.”

19As Samuel grew up, the LORD was with him.
He made everything Samuel said come true. 20So
all of the people of Israel recognized that Samuel
really was a prophet of the LORD. Everyone from
Dan all the way to Beersheba knew it.

21The LORD continued to appear at Shiloh.
There he made himself known to Samuel through
the messages he gave him.

4 And Samuel gave those messages to all of the
people of Israel.

The Philistines Capture the Ark

The people of Israel went out to fight against
the Philistines. The Israelites camped at Ebenezer.
The Philistines camped at Aphek. 2The Philistines
brought their forces together to fight against Israel. As the fighting spread, the men of Israel lost the
battle to the Philistines. The Philistines killed
about 4,000 of them on the field of battle.

3The rest of the Israelite soldiers returned to
camp. Then the elders asked them, “Why did the
LORD let the Philistines win the battle over us
today? Let’s bring the ark of the LORD’s covenant
from Shiloh. Let’s take it with us. It will save us
from the power of our enemies.”

4So the people sent men to Shiloh. They
brought back the ark of the covenant of the LORD.

He sits there on his throne between the cherubim. He is the One who rules over all. Eli's two sons Hophni and Phinehas were with the ark of the covenant of God in Shiloh.

5The ark of the LORD's covenant was brought into the camp. Then all of the people of Israel shouted so loudly that the ground shook.

6The Philistines heard the noise. They asked, "What's all that shouting about in the Hebrew camp?"

Then the Philistines found out that the ark of the LORD had come into the camp. 7So they were afraid. "A god has come into their camp," they said. "We're in trouble! Nothing like this has ever happened before. 8How terrible it will be for us! Who will save us from the power of those mighty gods? They struck down the people of Egypt in the desert. They sent all kinds of plagues on them.

9"Philistines, be strong! Fight like men! If you don't, you will come under the control of the Hebrews. You will become their slaves, just as they have been your slaves. Fight like men!"

10So the Philistines fought. The people of Israel lost the battle. Every man ran back to his tent. A large number of them were killed. Israel lost 30,000 soldiers who were on foot.

11The ark of God was captured. And Eli's two sons Hophni and Phinehas died.

Eli Dies

12That same day a man from the tribe of Benjamin ran from the front lines of the battle. He went to Shiloh. His clothes were torn. He had dust on his head. 13When he arrived, there was Eli sitting on his chair. He was by the side of the road. He was watching because his heart was really concerned about the ark of God. The man entered the town and told everyone what had happened. Then the whole town cried out.

14Eli heard the people crying out. He asked, "What's the meaning of all of this noise?"

The man hurried over to Eli. 15Eli was 98 years old. His eyes were so bad he couldn't see. 16The man told Eli, "I've just come from the front lines of the battle. I ran away from there this very day."

Eli asked, "What happened, son?"

17The man who brought the news replied, "Israel ran away from the Philistines. Large numbers of men in the army were wounded or killed. Your two sons Hophni and Phinehas are also dead. And the ark of God has been captured."

18When the man spoke about the ark of God, Eli fell backward off his chair. He had been sitting by the side of the gate. When he fell, he broke his neck and died. He was old and fat. He had led Israel for 40 years.

19The wife of Phinehas was pregnant. She was Eli's daughter-in-law. It was near the time for her baby to be born. She heard the news that the ark of God had been captured. She heard that her father-in-law and her husband were dead. So she went into labor and had her baby. Her pain was so great that her life was slipping away.

20As she was dying, the women who were helping her spoke up. They said, "Don't be afraid. You have had a son." But she didn't reply. She didn't pay any attention.

21She named the boy Ichabod. She said, "The God of glory has left Israel." She said it because the ark of God had been captured. She also said it because her father-in-law and her husband had died. 22She said, "The God of glory has left Israel." She said it because the ark of God had been captured.

The Ark Is Taken to Ashdod and Ekron

5 The Philistines had captured the ark of God. They took it from Ebenezer to Ashdod. 2They carried the ark into the temple of their god Dagon. They set it down beside the statue of Dagon.

3The people of Ashdod got up early the next day. They saw the statue of Dagon. There it was, lying on the ground! It had fallen on its face in front of the ark of the LORD. So they picked the statue of Dagon up. They put it back in its place.

4But the following morning when they got up, they saw the statue of Dagon. There it was, lying on the ground again! It had fallen on its face in front of the ark of the LORD. Its head and hands had been broken off. Only the body of the statue was left. Its head and hands were lying in the doorway of the temple. 5That's why to this very day no one steps on the bottom part of the doorway of Dagon's temple at Ashdod. Not even the priests of Dagon step there.

6The LORD's powerful hand punished the people of Ashdod and the settlements that were near it. He destroyed them. He made them suffer with growths in their bodies.

7The people of Ashdod saw what was happening. They said, "The ark of the god of Israel must not stay here with us. His powerful hand is punishing us and our god Dagon."

8So they called all of the rulers of the Philistines together. They asked them, "What should we do with the ark of the god of Israel?"

The rulers answered, "Have the ark moved to Gath." So they moved it.

9But after the people of Ashdod had moved the ark, the LORD's hand punished Gath. That threw its people into a great panic. The LORD made them break out with growths in their bodies. It happened to young people and old people alike. 10So the ark of God was sent to Ekron.

As the ark was entering Ekron, the people of the city cried out. They shouted, "They've brought the ark of the god of Israel to us. They want to kill us and our people."

11So they called all of the rulers of the Philistines together. They said, "Send the ark of the god of Israel away. Let it go back to its own place. If you don't, it will kill us and our people." The death of so many people had filled the city with panic. God's powerful hand was punishing the city. 12Those who didn't die suffered with growths in their bodies. The people of Ekron cried out to heaven for help.

The Philistines Return the Ark to Israel

6 The ark of the LORD had been in Philistine territory for seven months. 2The Philistines called for the priests and for those who practice evil magic. They wanted their advice. They said to them, "What should we do with the ark of the LORD? Tell us how we should send it back to its place."

3They answered, "If you return the ark of the god of Israel, don't send it away empty. Be sure you send a guilt offering to their god along with it. Then you will be healed. You will find out why his hand hasn't stopped punishing you."

4The Philistines asked, "What guilt offering should we send to him?"

Their advisers replied, "There are five Philistine rulers. So send five gold models of the growths that are in your bodies. Also send five gold models of rats. Do it because the same plague has struck you and your rulers alike. 5Make models of the growths and of the rats that are destroying the country. Pay honor to Israel's god. Perhaps his hand will stop punishing you. Maybe it will stop punishing your gods and your land.

6"Why are you stubborn, as Pharaoh and the people of Egypt were? God was very hard on them. Only then did they send the people of Israel out. Only then did they let them go on their way.

7"Now then, get a new cart ready. Get two cows that have just had calves. Be sure the cows have never pulled a cart before. Tie the cart to them. But take their calves away and put them in a pen.

8"Then put the ark of the LORD on the cart. Put the gold models in a chest beside the ark. Send them back to the LORD as a guilt offering. Send the cart on its way.

9"But keep an eye on the cart. See if it goes up toward Beth Shemesh to its own territory. If it does, then it's the LORD who has brought this horrible trouble on us. But if it doesn't, then we'll know it wasn't his hand that struck us. We'll know it happened to us by chance."

10So that's what they did. They took the two cows and tied the cart to them. They put the calves in a pen. 11They placed the ark of the LORD on the cart. They put the chest there along with it. The chest held the gold models of the rats and of the growths.

12Then the cows went straight up toward Beth Shemesh. They stayed on the road. They were mooing all the way. They didn't turn to the right or the left. The Philistine rulers followed them all the way to the border of Beth Shemesh.

13The people of Beth Shemesh were working in the valley. They were gathering their wheat crop. They looked up and saw the ark. When they saw it, they were filled with joy.

14The cart came to the field of Joshua of Beth Shemesh. It stopped there beside a large rock. The people chopped up the wood the cart was made out of. They sacrificed the cows as a burnt offering to the LORD.

15Some Levites had taken the ark of the LORD off the cart. They had also taken off the chest that held the gold models. They placed them on the large rock. On that day the people of Beth Shemesh offered burnt offerings to the LORD. They also made sacrifices to him.

16The five Philistine rulers saw everything that happened. On that same day they returned to Ekron.

17The Philistines sent gold models of growths as a guilt offering to the LORD. There was one each for Ashdod, Gaza, Ashkelon, Gath and Ekron. 18They also sent five gold models of rats. There was one for each of the Philistine towns that belonged to the five rulers. Each of those towns had high walls around it. The towns also had country villages around them.

The Levites set the ark of the LORD on a large rock. To this very day the rock gives witness to what happened there. It's in the field of Joshua of Beth Shemesh.

19But some of the people of Beth Shemesh looked into the ark of the LORD. So he struck them down. He put 70 of them to death. The rest of the people were filled with sorrow. That's because the LORD had killed so many of them.

20The people of Beth Shemesh said, "The LORD is a holy God. Who can stand in front of him? Where can the ark go up to from here?"

21Then messengers were sent to the people of Kiriath Jearim. They said, "The Philistines have returned the ark of the LORD. Come down and take
7 it up to your place." 1So the men of Kiriath Jearim came and got the ark of the LORD. They took it up to Abinadab's house on the hill. They set his son Eleazar apart to guard the ark.

Samuel Brings the Philistines Under Israel's Control

2The ark remained at Kiriath Jearim for a long time. It was there for a full 20 years. All of the people of Israel were filled with sorrow. They looked to the LORD for help.

3Samuel spoke to the whole community of Israel. He said, "Do you really want to return to the LORD with all your hearts? If you do, get rid of your strange gods. Get rid of your statues of goddesses that are named after Ashtoreth. Commit yourselves to the LORD. Serve him only. Then he will save you from the powerful hand of the Philistines."

4So the people of Israel put away their statues of gods that were named after Baal. They put away their statues of goddesses named after Ashtoreth. They served the LORD only.

5Then Samuel said, "Gather all of the people of
Israel together at Mizpah. I will pray to the LORD
for you."
6When the people had come together at Mizpah,
they went to the well and got water. They poured
it out in the sight of the LORD. On that day they
didn't eat any food. They admitted they had
sinned. They said, "We've sinned against the
LORD." Samuel was the leader of Israel at Mizpah.
7The Philistines heard that Israel had gathered
together at Mizpah. So the Philistine rulers came
up to attack them.
When the people of Israel heard about it, they
were afraid. 8They said to Samuel, "Don't stop
crying out to the LORD our God to help us. Keep
praying that he'll save us from the powerful hand
of the Philistines."
9Then Samuel got a very young lamb. He sacrificed it as a whole burnt offering to the LORD. He
cried out to the LORD to help Israel. And the LORD
answered his prayer.
10The Philistines came near to attack Israel. At
that time Samuel was sacrificing the burnt offering.
But that day the LORD thundered loudly against the
Philistines. He threw them into such a panic that
the Israelites were able to chase them away. 11The
men of Israel rushed out of Mizpah. They chased
the Philistines all the way to a point below Beth
Car. They killed them all along the way.
12Then Samuel got a big stone. He set it up
between Mizpah and Shen. He named it Ebenezer.
He said, "The LORD has helped us every step of the
way."
13So Samuel brought the Philistines under Israel's control. The Philistines didn't attack their territory again.
The LORD used his powerful hand against the
Philistines as long as Samuel lived. 14The Philistines had captured many towns between Ekron and
Gath. But they had to give all of them back. Israel took back the territories near those towns from
the powerful hand of the Philistines.
During that time Israel and the Amorites were
friendly toward each other.
15Samuel continued to lead Israel all the days of
his life. 16From year to year he traveled from Bethel to Gilgal to Mizpah. He served Israel as judge in
all of those places. 17But he always went back to
Ramah. That's where his home was. He served Israel as judge there too. And he built an altar there
to honor the LORD.

Israel Asks Samuel for a King

8 When Samuel became old, he appointed his
sons to serve as judges for Israel. 2The name of
his oldest son was Joel. The name of his second son
was Abijah. They served as judges at Beersheba.
3But his sons didn't live as he did. They were only
interested in making money. They accepted money
from people who wanted special favors. They made
things that were wrong appear to be right.
4So all of the elders of Israel gathered together.
They came to Samuel at Ramah. 5They said to
him, "You are old. Your sons don't live as you do.
So appoint a king to lead us. We want a king just
like the kings all of the other nations have."
6Samuel wasn't pleased when they said, "Give
us a king to lead us." So he prayed to the LORD.
7The LORD told him, "Listen to everything the
people are saying to you. You are not the one they
have turned their backs on. I am the one they do
not want as their king. 8They are doing just as they
have always done. They have deserted me and
served other gods. They have done that from the
time I brought them up out of Egypt until this very
day. Now they are deserting you too.
9"Let them have what they want. But give them
a strong warning. Let them know what the king
who rules over them will do."
10Samuel told the people who were asking him
for a king everything the LORD had said. 11Samuel
told them, "Here's what the king who rules over
you will do. He will take your sons. He'll make
them serve with his chariots and horses. They will
run in front of his chariots. 12He'll choose some of
your sons to be commanders of thousands of men.
Some will be commanders of fifties. Others will
have to plow his fields and gather his crops. Still
others will have to make weapons of war and parts
for his chariots.
13"He'll also take your daughters. Some will
have to make perfume. Others will be forced to
cook and bake.
14"He will take away your best fields and vineyards and olive groves. He'll give them to his attendants. 15He will take a tenth of your grain and a
tenth of your grapes. He'll give it to his officials
and attendants. 16He will also take your male and
female servants. He'll take your best cattle and
donkeys. He'll use all of them any way he wants to.
17"He will take a tenth of your sheep and goats.
You yourselves will become his slaves.
18"When that time comes, you will cry out for
help because of the king you have chosen. But the
LORD won't answer you at that time."
19In spite of what Samuel said, the people
refused to listen to him. "No!" they said. "We want
a king to rule over us. 20Then we'll be like all of
the other nations. We'll have a king to lead us.
He'll go out at the head of our armies and fight our
battles."
21Samuel heard everything the people said. He
told the LORD about it. 22The LORD answered, "Listen to them. Give them a king."
Then Samuel said to the men of Israel, "Each
of you go back to your own town."

Samuel Anoints Saul to Be Israel's Leader

9 There was a man named Kish from the tribe
of Benjamin. Kish was a very important person. He was the son of Abiel, the son of Zeror. Zeror was the son of Becorath, the son of Aphiah

from the tribe of Benjamin. 2Kish had a son named Saul. Saul was a handsome young man. There wasn't anyone like him among the people of Israel. He was a head taller than any of them.

3The donkeys that belonged to Saul's father Kish were lost. So Kish spoke to his son Saul. He said, "Go and look for the donkeys. Take one of the servants with you."

4Saul and his servant went through the hill country of Ephraim. They also went through the area around Shalisha. But they didn't find the donkeys. So they went on into the area of Shaalim. But the donkeys weren't there either. Then Saul went through the territory of Benjamin. But they still didn't find the donkeys.

5When Saul and the servant who was with him reached the area of Zuph, Saul spoke to him. He said, "Come on. Let's go back. If we don't, my father will stop thinking about the donkeys and start worrying about us."

6But the servant replied, "There's a man of God here in Ramah. People have a lot of respect for him. Everything he says comes true. So let's go and see him now. Perhaps he'll tell us which way to go."

7Saul said to his servant, "If we go to see the man, what can we give him? There isn't any food in our sacks. We don't have a gift for the man of God. So what can we give him?"

8The servant answered Saul again. "Look," he said. "I've got a tenth of an ounce of silver. I'll give it to the man of God. Then maybe he'll tell us which way to go."

9In Israel, prophets used to be called seers. So if a man wanted to ask God for advice, he would say, "Come on. Let's go to the seer."

10Saul said to his servant, "That's a good idea. Come on. Let's go and ask the seer." So they started out for the town where the man of God lived.

11They were going up the hill toward the town. Along the way they met some young women who were coming out to get water from the well. Saul and his servant asked them, "Is the seer here?"

12"Yes, he is," they answered. "In fact, he's just up ahead of you. So hurry along. He has just come to our town today. The people are going to offer a sacrifice at the high place where they worship. 13As soon as you enter the town, you will find him. He'll be there until he goes up to the high place to eat. The people won't start eating until he gets there. He must bless the sacrifice first. After that, those who are invited will eat. So go on up. You should find him there just about now."

14They went up to the town. As they were entering it, they saw Samuel. He was coming toward them. He was on his way up to the high place.

15The LORD had spoken to Samuel the day before Saul came. He had said, 16"About this time tomorrow I will send you a man. He is from the land of Benjamin. Anoint him to be the leader of my people Israel. He will save them from the powerful hand of the Philistines. I have seen how much my people are suffering. Their cry for help has reached me."

17When Samuel saw a man coming toward him, the LORD spoke to Samuel again. He said, "He is the man I told you about. His name is Saul. He will govern my people."

18Saul approached Samuel at the gate of the town. He asked Samuel, "Can you please show me the house where the seer is staying?"

19"I'm the seer," Samuel replied. "Go on up to the high place ahead of me. I want you and your servant to eat with me today. Tomorrow morning I'll tell you what's on your mind. Then I'll let you go. 20Don't worry about the donkeys you lost three days ago. They've already been found. But who are all of the people of Israel longing for? You and your father's whole family!"

21Saul answered, "But I'm from the tribe of Benjamin. It's the smallest tribe in Israel. And my family group is the least important in the whole tribe of Benjamin. So why are you saying that to me?"

22Then Samuel brought Saul and his servant into the room where they would be eating. He seated them at the head table. About 30 people had been invited. 23Samuel said to the cook, "Bring the piece of meat I gave you. It's the one I told you to put to one side."

24So the cook went and got a choice piece of thigh. He set it in front of Saul. Samuel said, "Here is what has been kept for you. Eat it. It was put to one side for you for this special occasion. We've saved it for you ever since I invited the guests." And Saul ate with Samuel that day.

25They came down from the high place to the town. After that, Samuel talked with Saul on the roof of Samuel's house.

26The next day they got up at about the time the sun was rising. Samuel called out to Saul on the roof. He said, "Get ready. Then I'll send you on your way." So Saul got ready. And he and Samuel went outside together.

27As they were on their way down to the edge of town, Samuel spoke to Saul. He said, "Tell the servant to go ahead of us." So the servant went on ahead. Then Samuel continued, "Stay here awhile. I'll give you a message from God."

10 Then Samuel took a bottle of olive oil. He poured it on Saul's head and kissed him. He said, "The LORD has anointed you to be the leader of his people. 2When you leave me today, you will meet two men. They will be near Rachel's tomb at Zelzah on the border of Benjamin. They'll say to you, 'The donkeys you have been looking for have been found. Now your father has stopped thinking about them. Instead, he's worried about you. He's asking, "What can I do to find my son?"'

3"You will go on from Zelzah until you come to the large tree at Tabor. Three men will meet you

there. They'll be on their way up to Bethel to worship God. One of them will be carrying three
young goats. Another will be carrying three loaves
of bread. A third will be carrying a bottle of wine.
It will be a bottle that is made out of animal skin.
4The men will greet you. They'll offer you two
loaves of bread. You will accept the loaves from
them.

5"After that, you will go to Gibeah of God.
Some Philistine soldiers are stationed there. As
you approach the town, you will meet a group of
prophets. They'll be coming down from the high
place where they worship. People will be playing
lyres, tambourines, flutes and harps at the head of
the group. The prophets will be prophesying. 6The
Spirit of the LORD will come on you with power.
Then you will prophesy along with them. You will
become a different person.

7"All of those things will happen. Then do what
you want to do. God is with you.

8"Go down ahead of me to Gilgal. You can be
sure that I'll come down to you there. I'll come
and sacrifice burnt offerings and friendship offerings. But you must wait there for seven days until
I come to you. Then I'll tell you what to do."

Saul Is Made King of Israel

9As Saul turned to leave Samuel, God changed
Saul's heart. All of those things happened that day.
10When Saul and his servant arrived at Gibeah, a
group of prophets met Saul. Then the Spirit of God
came on him with power. He prophesied along
with them. 11Those who had known Saul before
saw him prophesying with the prophets. They
asked one another, "What has happened to the son
of Kish? Is Saul also one of the prophets?"

12A man who lived in Gibeah answered, "Yes,
he is. In fact, he's their leader." That's why people
say, "Is Saul also one of the prophets?"

13After Saul stopped prophesying, he went to
the high place to worship.

14Later, Saul's uncle spoke to him and his servant. He asked, "Where have you been?"

"Looking for the donkeys," he said. "But we
couldn't find them. So we went to Samuel."

15Saul's uncle said, "Tell me what Samuel said
to you."

16Saul replied, "He told us the donkeys had
been found." But Saul didn't tell his uncle that
Samuel had said he would become king.

17Samuel sent a message to the people of Israel. He told them to meet with the LORD at Mizpah.
18He said to them, "The LORD is the God of Israel.
He says, 'Israel, I brought you up out of Egypt. I
saved you from their powerful hand. I also saved
you from the powerful hand of all of the kingdoms
that had beaten you down.'

19"But now you have turned your backs on your
God. He saves you out of all of your trouble and
suffering. In spite of that, you have said, 'We
refuse to listen. Place a king over us.'

"So now gather together to meet with the LORD.
Do it tribe by tribe and family group by family
group."

20Then Samuel had each tribe of Israel come
forward. The tribe of Benjamin was chosen. 21Next
he had the tribe of Benjamin come forward, family group by family group. Matri's group was chosen. Finally Saul, the son of Kish, was chosen. But
when people looked for him, they realized he
wasn't there. 22They needed more help from the
LORD. So they asked him, "Has the man come here
yet?"

The LORD said, "Yes. He has hidden himself
among the supplies."

23So they ran over there and brought him out.
When he stood up, the people saw that he was a
head taller than any of them.

24Samuel spoke to all of the people. He said,
"Look at the man the LORD has chosen! There isn't
anyone like him among all of the people."

Then the people shouted, "May the king live a
long time!"

25Samuel explained to the people what the king
who ruled over them should do. He wrote it down
on a scroll. He placed it in front of the LORD in the
holy tent. Then he sent the people away. He sent
each of them to their own homes.

26Saul also went to his home in Gibeah. Some
brave men whose hearts God had touched went
with Saul.

27But some evil people who wanted to stir up
trouble said, "How can this fellow save us?" They
looked down on him. They didn't bring him any
gifts. But Saul kept quiet about it.

Saul Saves the City of Jabesh Gilead

11 Nahash was the king of Ammon. He and
his army went up to Jabesh Gilead. They
surrounded it and got ready to attack it. All of the
men of Jabesh spoke to Nahash. They said, "Make
a peace treaty with us. Then we'll be under your
control."

2Nahash, the king of Ammon, replied, "I will
make a peace treaty with you. But I'll do it only
on one condition. You must let me put out the right
eye of every one of you. I want to bring shame on
the whole nation of Israel."

3The elders of Jabesh said to him, "Give us
seven days to report back to you. We'll send messengers all through Israel. If no one comes to save
us, we'll hand ourselves over to you."

4The messengers came to Gibeah of Saul. They
reported to the people the terms Nahash had
required. Then all of the people sobbed out loud.

5Just then Saul was coming in from the fields.
He was walking behind his oxen. He asked,
"What's wrong with the people? Why are they
sobbing?" He was told what the men of Jabesh had
said.

6When Saul heard their words, the Spirit of God
came on him with power. He burned with anger.

7 He got a pair of oxen and cut them into pieces. He
sent the pieces by messengers all through Israel.
They announced, "You must follow Saul and Samuel. If you don't, this is what will happen to your
oxen."
The terror of the LORD fell on the people. So all
of them came together with one purpose in mind.
8 Saul brought his army together at Bezek. There
were 300,000 men from Israel and 30,000 from
Judah.
9 The messengers who had come were told, "Go
back and report to the men of Jabesh Gilead. Tell
them, 'By the hottest time of the day tomorrow,
you will be saved.'"
The messengers went and reported it to the men
of Jabesh. It made those men very happy. 10 They
said to the people of Ammon, "Tomorrow we'll
hand ourselves over to you. Then you can do to us
what seems best to you."
11 The next day Saul separated his men into three
groups. While it was still dark, they broke into the
camp of the Ammonite army. They kept killing the
men of Ammon until the hottest time of the day.
Those who got away alive were scattered. There
weren't two of them left together anywhere.

The People Agree to Have Saul as King

12 The people said to Samuel, "Who asked, 'Is
Saul going to rule over us?' Bring those people to
us. We'll put them to death."
13 But Saul said, "We won't put anyone to death
today! After all, this is the day the LORD has saved
Israel."
14 Then Samuel said to the people, "Come on.
Let's go to Gilgal. There we'll agree to have Saul
as our king."
15 So all of the people went to Gilgal. There,
with the LORD as witness, they agreed to have Saul
as their king. There they sacrificed friendship
offerings to the LORD. And there Saul and all of the
people of Israel celebrated with great joy.

Samuel Tells Israel to Serve the LORD

12 Samuel spoke to all of the people of Israel.
He said, "I've done everything you asked
me to do. I've placed a king over you. 2 Now you
have a king as your leader. But I'm old. My hair is
gray. My sons are here with you. I've been your
leader from the time I was young until this very day.
3 "Here I stand. Bring charges against me if you
can. The LORD is a witness. And so is his anointed
king. Whose ox have I taken? Whose donkey have
I taken? Have I cheated anyone? Have I beaten
anyone down? Have I accepted money from anyone who wanted special favors? If I've done any of
those things, I'll make it right."
4 "You haven't cheated us," they replied. "You
haven't beaten us down. You haven't taken anything from anyone."
5 Samuel said to them, "The LORD is a witness
against you this very day. And so is his anointed
king. They are witnesses that I haven't taken anything from any of you."
"The LORD is a witness," they said.
6 Then Samuel said to the people, "The LORD
appointed Moses and Aaron. He brought up out of
Egypt your people who lived long ago. 7 Now then,
stand here. I'm going to remind you of all of the
good things the LORD has done for you and your
people. He is a witness.
8 "After Jacob's family entered Egypt, they cried
out to the LORD for help. The LORD sent Moses and
Aaron. They brought your people out of Egypt.
They settled them in this land.
9 "But the people forgot the LORD their God. So
he gave them over to the powerful hand of Sisera.
Sisera was the commander of the army of Hazor.
The LORD also gave the people of Israel over to the
powerful hand of the Philistines and the king of
Moab. All of those nations fought against Israel.
10 "So the people cried out to the LORD. They
said, 'We have sinned. We've deserted the LORD.
We've served the gods that are named after Baal.
We've served the goddesses that are named after
Ashtoreth. But save us now from the powerful
hands of our enemies. Then we will serve you.'
11 "The LORD sent Gideon, Barak, Jephthah and
me. He saved you from the hands of your enemies,
who were all around you. So you lived in safety.
12 "But then you saw that Nahash, the king of
Ammon, was about to attack you. So you said to
me, 'No! We want a king to rule over us.' You said
it even though the LORD your God was your king.
13 Now here is the king you have chosen. He's the
one you asked for. The LORD has placed a king
over you.
14 "But you must have respect for the LORD. You
must serve him and obey him. You must not say
no to his commands. Both you and the king who
rules over you must follow the LORD your God. If
you do, that's good. 15 But you must not disobey
him. You must not say no to his commands. If you
do, his powerful hand will punish you. That's what
happened to your people who lived before you.
16 "So stand still. Watch the great thing the LORD
is about to do right here in front of you! 17 It's time
to gather in the wheat, isn't it? I'll call out to the
LORD to send thunder and rain. Then you will realize what an evil thing you did in the sight of the
LORD. You shouldn't have asked for a king."
18 Samuel called out to the LORD. That same day
the LORD sent thunder and rain. So all of the people had great respect for the LORD and for Samuel.
19 They said to Samuel, "Pray to the LORD your
God for us. Pray that we won't die because we
asked for a king. That was an evil thing to do. We
added it to all of our other sins."
20 "Don't be afraid," Samuel replied. "It's true that
you have done all of those evil things. But don't turn
away from the LORD. Serve him with all your heart.
21 "Don't turn away and worship statues of gods.
They are useless. They can't do you any good.

They can't save you either. They are completely
useless.
22"But the LORD will be true to his great name.
He won't turn his back on his people. That's because
he was pleased to make you his own people.
23"I would never sin against the LORD by failing to pray for you. I'll teach you to live in a way
that is good and right.
24"But be sure to have respect for the LORD.
Serve him faithfully. Do it with all your heart.
Think about the great things he has done for you.
25But don't be stubborn. Don't continue to do what
is evil. If you do, both you and your king will be
swept away."

Saul Refuses to Obey the LORD's Command

13 Saul was 30 years old when he became
king. He ruled over Israel for 42 years.
2He chose 3,000 of Israel's men. Two thousand
of them were with him at Micmash and in the hill
country of Bethel. One thousand were with Jonathan at Gibeah in the land of Benjamin. Saul sent
the rest back to their homes.
3Some Philistine soldiers were stationed at
Geba. Jonathan attacked them. The other Philistines heard about it.
Saul announced, "Let the Hebrew people hear
about what has happened!" He had trumpets
blown all through the land. 4So all of the people of
Israel heard the news. They were told, "Saul has
attacked the Philistine army camp at Geba. He has
made Israel smell very bad to the Philistines." The
people of Israel were called out to join Saul at
Gilgal.
5The Philistines gathered together to fight
against Israel. They had 3,000 chariots and 6,000
chariot drivers. Their soldiers were as many as the
grains of sand on the seashore. They went up and
camped at Micmash. It was east of Beth Aven.
6The men of Israel saw that their army was in
deep trouble. So they hid in caves and bushes.
They hid among the rocks. They hid in pits and
empty wells. 7Some of them even went across the
Jordan River. They went to the lands of Gad and
Gilead.
Saul remained at Gilgal. All of the troops who
were with him were shaking with fear. 8He waited
seven days, just as Samuel had told him to. But
Samuel didn't come to Gilgal. And Saul's men
began to scatter. 9So he said, "Bring me the burnt
offering and the friendship offerings." Then he
offered up the burnt offering.
10Just as Saul finished offering the sacrifice,
Samuel arrived. Saul went out to greet him.
11"What have you done?" asked Samuel.
Saul replied, "I saw that the men were scattering. I saw that the Philistines were gathering
together at Micmash. You didn't come when you
said you would. 12So I thought, 'Now the Philistines will come down to attack me at Gilgal. And
I haven't asked the LORD to show us his favor.' So
I felt I had to sacrifice the burnt offering."
13"You did a foolish thing," Samuel said. "You
haven't obeyed the command the LORD your God
gave you. If you had, he would have made your
kingdom secure over Israel for all time to come.
14But now your kingdom won't last. The LORD has
already looked for a man who is dear to his heart.
He has appointed him leader of his people. That's
because you haven't obeyed the LORD's
command."
15Then Samuel left Gilgal and went up to Gibeah
in the land of Benjamin. Saul counted the men who
stayed with him. The total number was about 600.

Israel Doesn't Have Swords or Spears

16Saul and his son Jonathan were staying in
Gibeah in the land of Benjamin. What was left of
the army was there with them. At the same time,
the Philistines camped at Micmash.
17Three groups of soldiers went out from the
Philistine camp to attack Israel. One group turned
and went toward Ophrah in the area of Shual.
18Another went toward Beth Horon. The third went
toward the border that looked out over the Valley
of Zeboim. That valley faces the desert.
19There weren't any blacksmiths in the whole
land of Israel. That's because the Philistines had
said, "The Hebrews might hire them to make
swords or spears!"
20So all of the people of Israel had to go down
to the Philistines. They had to go to them to get
their plows, hoes, axes and sickles sharpened. 21It
cost a fourth of an ounce of silver to sharpen a
plow or a hoe. It cost an eighth of an ounce to
sharpen a pitchfork or an axe. That's also what it
cost to put new tips on large sticks that were used
to drive oxen.
22So not one of Saul's or Jonathan's soldiers had
a sword or spear in his hand when he went out to
battle. Only Saul and his son Jonathan had those
weapons.

Jonathan Attacks the Philistines

23A group of Philistine soldiers had gone out to
14 the pass at Micmash. 1One day Jonathan,
the son of Saul, spoke to the young man
who was carrying his armor. "Come on," he said.
"Let's go over to the Philistine army camp on the
other side of the pass." But he didn't tell his father
about it.
2Saul was staying just outside Gibeah. He was
under a pomegranate tree in Migron. He had about
600 men with him. 3Ahijah was one of them. He
was wearing a sacred linen apron. He was a son of
Ichabod's brother Ahitub. Ahitub was the son of
Eli's son Phinehas. Eli had been the LORD's priest
in Shiloh. No one was aware that Jonathan had left.
4Jonathan planned to go across the pass to reach
the Philistine camp. But there was a cliff on each
side of the pass. One cliff was called Bozez. The

other was called Seneh. 5One cliff stood on the
north side of the pass toward Micmash. The other
stood on the south side toward Geba.
6Jonathan spoke to the young man who was carrying his armor. He said, "Come on. Let's go over
to the camp of those fellows who aren't circumcised. Perhaps the LORD will help us. If he does, it
won't matter how many or how few of us there
are. That won't keep the LORD from saving us."
7"Go ahead," the young man said. "Do everything you have in mind. I'm with you all the way."
8Jonathan said, "Come on, then. We'll go across
the pass toward the Philistines and let them see us.
9Suppose they say to us, 'Wait there until we come
to you.' Then we'll stay where we are. We won't
go up to them. 10But suppose they say, 'Come up
to us.' Then we'll climb up. That will show us that
the LORD has handed them over to us."
11So Jonathan and the young man let the soldiers in the Philistine camp see them. "Look!" said
the Philistines. "Some of the Hebrews are crawling
out of the holes they were hiding in."
12The men in the Philistine camp shouted to
Jonathan and the young man who was carrying his
armor. They said, "Come on up here. We'll teach
you a thing or two."
So Jonathan said to the young man, "Climb up
after me. The LORD has handed them over to Israel."
13Using his hands and feet, Jonathan climbed
up. The young man was right behind him. Jonathan struck the Philistines down. The young man
followed him and killed those who were still alive.
14In that first attack, Jonathan and the young man
killed about 20 men. They did it in an area of about
half an acre.

Israel Chases the Philistines Away

15Then panic struck the whole Philistine army.
It struck those who were in the camp and the field.
It struck those who were at the edge of the camp.
It also struck those who were in the groups that
had been sent out to attack Israel. The ground
shook. It was a panic that God had sent.
16Saul's lookouts at Gibeah in the land of Benjamin saw what was happening. They saw the
Philistine army melting away in all directions.
17Then Saul spoke to the men who were with
him. He said, "Bring the troops together. See who
has left our camp." When they did, they discovered that Jonathan and the young man who was
carrying his armor weren't there.
18Saul said to the priest Ahijah, "Bring the ark
of God." At that time it was with the people of
Israel.
19While Saul was talking to the priest, the noise
in the Philistine camp increased more and more.
So Saul said to him, "Stop what you are doing."
20Then Saul and all of his men gathered
together. They went to the battle. They saw that the
Philistines were in total disorder. They were striking each other with their swords.
21At an earlier time some of the Hebrews had
been on the side of the Philistines. They had gone
up with them to their camp. But now they changed
sides. They joined the people of Israel who were
with Saul and Jonathan.
22Some of the people had hidden in the hill
country of Ephraim. They heard that the Philistines were running away. They quickly joined the
battle and chased after them.
23So the LORD saved Israel that day. And the
fighting continued on past Beth Aven.

Jonathan Eats Honey

24The men of Israel became very hungry that
day. That's because Saul had put the army under
an oath. He had said, "None of you must eat any
food before evening comes. You must not eat until
I've paid my enemies back for what they did. If
you do, may you be under a curse!" So none of the
troops ate any food at all.
25The whole army entered the woods. There
was honey on the ground. 26When they went into
the woods, they saw the honey dripping out of a
honeycomb. No one put any of the honey in his
mouth. That's because they were afraid of the oath.
27But Jonathan hadn't heard that his father had
put the army under an oath. Jonathan had a long
stick in his hand. He reached out and dipped the
end of it into the honeycomb. He put some honey
in his mouth. It gave him new life.
28Then one of the soldiers told him, "Your
father put the army under a strong oath. He said,
'None of you must eat any food today. If you do,
may you be under a curse!' That's why the men are
weak and ready to faint."
29Jonathan said, "My father has made trouble for
the country. See how I gained new life after I tasted
a little of this honey. 30Our soldiers took food from
their enemies today. Suppose they had eaten some
of it. How much better off they would have been!
Even more Philistines would have been killed."
31That day the men of Israel struck the Philistines down. They killed them from Micmash to Aijalon. By that time they were tired and worn out.
32They grabbed what they had taken from their
enemies. They killed some of the sheep, cattle and
calves right there on the ground. They ate the meat
while the blood was still in it.
33Then someone said to Saul, "Look! The men
are sinning against the LORD. They're eating meat
that still has blood in it."
Saul said to them, "You have broken your
promise. Roll a large stone over here at once."
34He continued, "Go out among the men. Tell
them, 'Each of you bring me your cattle and sheep.
Kill them here and eat them. Don't sin against the
LORD by eating meat that still has blood in it.'"
So that night everyone brought the ox he had
taken and killed it there.
35Then Saul built an altar to honor the LORD. It
was the first time he had done that.

36Saul said, "Let's go down after the Philistines tonight. Let's not leave even one of them alive. Let's take everything they have before it gets light."

"Do what you think is best," they replied.

But the priest said, "Let's ask God for advice first."

37So Saul asked God, "Should I go down after the Philistines? Will you hand them over to Israel?" But God didn't answer him that day.

38Saul said to the leaders of the army, "Come here. Let's find out what sin has been committed today. 39You can be sure that the LORD who saves Israel lives. And you can be just as sure that the sinner must die. He must die even if he's my son Jonathan." But no one said anything.

40Then Saul spoke to all of Israel's men. He said, "You stand over there. I and my son Jonathan will stand over here."

"Do what you think is best," the men replied.

41Then Saul prayed to the LORD, the God of Israel. He said, "Give me an answer." Jonathan and Saul were chosen by using lots. The other men were cleared of blame.

42Saul said, "Cast the lot to find out whether I or my son Jonathan is to blame." And Jonathan was chosen.

43Then Saul said to Jonathan, "Tell me what you have done."

So Jonathan told him, "I only used the end of my stick to get a little honey and taste it. And now do I have to die?"

44Saul said, "Jonathan, I must certainly put you to death. If I don't, may God punish me greatly."

45But the men said to Saul, "Should Jonathan be put to death? Never! He has saved Israel in a wonderful way. He did it today with God's help. You can be sure that the LORD lives. And you can be just as sure that not even one hair on Jonathan's head will fall to the ground." So the men saved Jonathan. He wasn't put to death.

46Then Saul stopped chasing the Philistines. They went back to their own land.

47After Saul's kingdom was set firmly in place in Israel, he fought against their enemies who were all around them. He went to war against Moab, Ammon and Edom. He fought against the kings of Zobah and the Philistines. No matter where he went, he punished his enemies. 48He fought bravely. He won the battle over the Amalekites. He saved Israel from the power of those who had carried off what belonged to Israel.

Saul's Family

49Saul's sons were Jonathan, Ishvi and Malki-Shua. His older daughter was named Merab. His younger daughter was named Michal. 50Saul's wife was named Ahinoam. She was the daughter of Ahimaaz.

The commander of Saul's army was named Abner. He was the son of Ner. Ner was Saul's uncle. 51Saul's father Kish and Abner's father Ner were sons of Abiel.

52As long as Saul was king, he had to fight hard against the Philistines. So every time Saul saw a strong or brave man, he took him into his army.

The LORD Is Sorry He Has Made Saul King

15 Samuel said to Saul, "The LORD sent me to anoint you as king over his people Israel. So listen now to a message from him. 2The LORD who rules over all says, 'I will punish the Amalekites because of what they did to Israel. As the people of Israel came up from Egypt, the Amalekites attacked them.

3"'Now go. Attack the Amalekites. Set everything apart that belongs to them. Set it apart to me in a special way to be destroyed. Do not spare the Amalekites. Put the men and women to death. Put the children and babies to death. Also kill the cattle, sheep, camels and donkeys.'"

4So Saul brought his men together at Telaim. The total number was 200,000 soldiers on foot from Israel and 10,000 men from Judah. 5He went to the city of Amalek. He had some of his men hide and wait in the valley.

6Then Saul said to the Kenites, "You were kind to all of the people of Israel when they came up out of Egypt. Get away from the Amalekites. Then I won't have to destroy you along with them." So the Kenites moved away from the Amalekites.

7Saul attacked the Amalekites. He struck them down all the way from Havilah to Shur. Shur was near the eastern border of Egypt. 8He took Agag, the king of the Amalekites, alive. He and his men totally destroyed all of Agag's people with swords.

9But Saul and the army spared Agag. They spared the best of the sheep and cattle. They spared the fat calves and lambs. They spared everything that was valuable. They weren't willing to completely destroy any of those things. But they totally destroyed everything that was worthless and weak.

10Then the LORD gave Samuel a message. He said, 11"I am very sorry I have made Saul king. He has turned away from me. He has not done what I directed him to do."

When Samuel heard that, he was troubled. He cried out to the LORD during that whole night.

12Early the next morning Samuel got up. He went to see Saul. But Samuel was told, "Saul went to Carmel. There he set up a monument in his own honor. Now he has gone on down to Gilgal."

13When Samuel got there, Saul said, "May the LORD bless you. I've done what he directed me to do."

14But Samuel said, "Then why do I hear the baaing of sheep? Why do I hear the mooing of cattle?"

15Saul answered, "The soldiers brought them from the Amalekites. They spared the best of the sheep and cattle. They did it to sacrifice them to

the LORD your God. But we totally destroyed
everything else."
16"Stop!" Samuel said to Saul. "Let me tell you
what the LORD said to me last night."
"Tell me," Saul replied.
17Samuel said, "There was a time when you
didn't think you were important. But you became
the leader of the tribes of Israel. The LORD
anointed you to be king over Israel. 18He sent you
to do something for him. He said, 'Go and set the
Amalekites apart. Set those sinful people apart to
me in a special way to be destroyed. Fight against
them until you have wiped them out.'
19"Why didn't you obey the LORD? Why did
you grab what you had taken from your enemies?
Why did you do what is evil in the sight of the
LORD?"
20"But I did obey the LORD," Saul said. "I went
to do what he sent me to do. I totally destroyed the
Amalekites. I brought back Agag, their king.
21"The soldiers took sheep and cattle from what
had been taken from our enemies. They took the
best of what had been set apart to God. They
wanted to sacrifice them to the LORD your God at
Gilgal."
22But Samuel replied,

"What pleases the LORD more?
Burnt offerings and sacrifices, or obeying him?
It is better to obey than to offer a sacrifice.
It is better to do what he says than to offer the fat of rams.
23Refusing to obey him is as sinful as using evil magic.
Being proud is as evil as worshiping statues of gods.
You have refused to do what the LORD told you to do.
So he has refused to have you as king."

24Then Saul said to Samuel, "I have sinned. I've
broken the LORD's command. I haven't done what
you directed me to do. I was afraid of the people.
So I did what they said I should do. 25Now I beg
you, forgive my sin. Come back into town with me
so I can worship the LORD."
26But Samuel said to him, "I won't go back with
you. You have refused to do what the LORD told
you to do. So he has refused to have you as king
over Israel!"
27Samuel turned to leave. But Saul grabbed hold
of the hem of his robe, and it tore.
28Samuel said to Saul, "The LORD has torn the
kingdom of Israel away from you today. He has
given it to one of your neighbors. He has given it
to someone who is better than you. 29The One who
is the Glory of Israel does not lie. He doesn't
change his mind. That's because he isn't a mere
man. If he were, he might change his mind."
30Saul replied, "I have sinned. But please honor
me in front of the elders of my people and in front
of Israel. Come back with me so I can worship the
LORD your God."
31So Samuel went back with Saul. And Saul
worshiped the LORD.
32Then Samuel said, "Bring me Agag, the king
of the Amalekites."
Agag wasn't afraid when he came to Samuel.
He thought, "The time for me to be put to death
must have passed by now."
33But Samuel said,

"Your sword has killed the children of other women.
So the child of your mother will be killed."

Samuel put Agag to death at Gilgal in the sight of
the LORD.
34Then Samuel left to go to Ramah. But Saul
went up to his home in Gibeah of Saul. 35Until the
day Samuel died, he didn't go to see Saul again.
Samuel was filled with sorrow because of Saul.
And the LORD was very sorry he had made Saul
king over Israel.

Samuel Anoints David to Be Israel's King

16 The LORD said to Samuel, "How long will
you be filled with sorrow because of Saul?
I have refused to have him as king over Israel. Fill
your animal horn with olive oil and go on your
way. I am sending you to Jesse in Bethlehem. I
have chosen one of his sons to be king."
2But Samuel said, "How can I go? Saul will
hear about it. Then he'll kill me."
The LORD said, "Take a young cow with you.
Tell the elders of Bethlehem, 'I've come to offer a
sacrifice to the LORD.' 3Invite Jesse to the sacrifice.
Then I will show you what to do. You must anoint
for me the one I point out to you."
4Samuel did what the LORD said. He arrived at
Bethlehem. The elders of the town met him. They
were trembling with fear. They asked, "Have you
come in peace?"
5Samuel replied, "Yes, I've come in peace. I've
come to offer a sacrifice to the LORD. Set yourselves apart to him and come to the sacrifice
with me."
Then he set Jesse and his sons apart to the
LORD. He invited them to the sacrifice.
6When they arrived, Samuel saw Eliab. He
thought, "This has to be the one the LORD wants
me to anoint for him."
7But the LORD said to Samuel, "Do not consider
how handsome or tall he is. I have not chosen him.
I do not look at the things people look at. Man
looks at how someone appears on the outside. But
I look at what is in the heart."
8Then Jesse called for Abinadab. He had him
walk in front of Samuel. But Samuel said, "The
LORD hasn't chosen him either."
9Then Jesse had Shammah walk by. But Samuel said, "The LORD hasn't chosen him either."

[10]Jesse had seven of his sons walk in front of Samuel. But Samuel said to him, "The LORD hasn't chosen any of them." [11]So he asked Jesse, "Are these the only sons you have?"

"No," Jesse answered. "My youngest son is taking care of the sheep."

Samuel said, "Send for him. We won't sit down to eat until he arrives."

[12]So Jesse sent for his son and had him brought in. His skin was tanned. He had a fine appearance and handsome features.

Then the LORD said, "Get up and anoint him. He is the one."

[13]So Samuel got the animal horn that was filled with olive oil. He anointed David in front of his brothers. From that day on, the Spirit of the LORD came on David with power. Samuel went back to Ramah.

David Serves Saul

[14]The Spirit of the LORD had left Saul. And an evil spirit that was sent by the LORD terrified him.

[15]Saul's attendants said to him, "An evil spirit that was sent by God is terrifying you. [16]Give us an order to look for someone who can play the harp. He will play it when the evil spirit that was sent by God comes on you. Then you will feel better."

[17]So Saul said to his attendants, "Find someone who plays the harp well. Bring him to me."

[18]One of the servants said, "I've seen someone who knows how to play the harp. He is a son of Jesse from Bethlehem. He's a brave man. He would make a good soldier. He's a good speaker. He's very handsome. And the LORD is with him."

[19]Then Saul sent messengers to Jesse. He said, "Send me your son David, the one who takes care of your sheep."

[20]So Jesse got some bread and a bottle of wine. The bottle was made out of animal skin. He also got a young goat. He loaded everything on the back of a donkey. He sent all of it to Saul with his son David.

[21]David went to Saul and began to serve him. Saul liked him very much. David became one of the men who carried Saul's armor.

[22]Saul sent a message to Jesse. It said, "Let David stay here. I want him to serve me. I'm pleased with him."

[23]When the evil spirit that was sent by God would come on Saul, David would get his harp and play it. That would help Saul. He would feel better, and the evil spirit would leave him.

David Kills Goliath

17 The Philistines gathered their army together for war. They came to Socoh in Judah. They set up camp at Ephes Dammim. It was between Socoh and Azekah. [2]Saul and the army of Israel gathered together. They camped in the Valley of Elah. They lined up their men to fight against the Philistines. [3]The Philistine army was camped on one hill. Israel's army was on another. The valley was between them.

[4]A mighty hero named Goliath came out of the Philistine camp. He was from Gath. He was more than nine feet tall. [5]He had a bronze helmet on his head. He wore a coat of bronze armor. It weighed 125 pounds. [6]On his legs he wore bronze guards. He carried a bronze javelin on his back. [7]His spear was as big as a weaver's rod. Its iron point weighed 15 pounds. The man who carried his shield walked along in front of him.

[8]Goliath stood and shouted to the soldiers of Israel. He said, "Why do you come out and line up for battle? I'm a Philistine. You are servants of Saul. Choose one of your men. Have him come down and face me. [9]If he's able to fight and kill me, we'll become your slaves. But if I win and kill him, you will become our slaves and serve us." [10]Goliath continued, "This very day I dare the soldiers of Israel to send a man down to fight against me."

[11]Saul and the whole army of Israel heard what the Philistine said. They were terrified.

[12]David was the son of an Ephrathite. His name was Jesse. He was from Bethlehem in Judah. Jesse had eight sons. When Saul was king, Jesse was already very old. [13]Jesse's three oldest sons had followed Saul into battle. The oldest son was Eliab. The second was Abinadab. The third was Shammah. [14]David was the youngest. The three oldest sons followed Saul. [15]But David went back and forth from Saul's camp to Bethlehem. He went to Bethlehem to take care of his father's sheep.

[16]Every morning and evening Goliath came forward and stood there. He did it for 40 days.

[17]Jesse said to his son David, "Get at least half a bushel of grain that has been cooked. Also get ten loaves of bread. Take all of it to your brothers. Hurry to their camp. [18]Take along these ten chunks of cheese to the commander of their company. Find out how your brothers are doing. Bring me back some word about them. [19]They are with Saul and all of the men of Israel. They are in the Valley of Elah. They are fighting against the Philistines."

[20]Early in the morning David left his father's flock in the care of a shepherd. David loaded up the food and started out, just as Jesse had directed.

David reached the camp as the army was going out to its battle positions. The soldiers were shouting the war cry. [21]Israel and the Philistines were lining up their armies for battle. The armies were facing each other.

[22]David left what he had brought with the man who took care of the supplies. He ran to the battle lines and greeted his brothers. [23]As David was talking with them, Goliath stepped forward from his line. Goliath was a mighty Philistine hero from Gath. He again dared someone to fight him, and David heard it.

[24]When Israel's army saw Goliath, all of them ran away from him. That's because they were filled with fear.

25The men of Israel had been saying, “Just look
at how this man keeps stepping forward! Again
and again he dares Israel to fight him. The king
will make the man who kills him very wealthy. He
will also give him his daughter to be his wife. He
won’t require anyone in his family to pay any
taxes in Israel.”

26David spoke to the men who were standing
near him. He asked them, “What will be done for
the man who kills this Philistine? Goliath is bringing shame on Israel. What will be done for the one
who removes it? This Philistine isn’t even circumcised. He dares the armies of the living God
to fight him. Who does he think he is?”

27The men told David what Israel’s soldiers had
been saying. The men told him what would be
done for the man who killed Goliath.

28David’s oldest brother Eliab heard him speaking with the men. So he burned with anger at him.
He asked him, “Why have you come down here?
Who did you leave those few sheep in the desert
with? I know how proud you are. I know how evil
your heart is. The only reason you came down here
was to watch the battle.”

29“What have I done now?” said David. “Can’t
I even speak?”

30Then he turned away to speak to some other
men. He asked them the same question he had
asked before. And they gave him the same answer.

31Someone heard what David said and reported
it to Saul. So Saul sent for him.

32David said to Saul, “Don’t let anyone lose
hope because of that Philistine. I’ll go out and fight
him.”

33Saul replied, “You aren’t able to go out there
and fight that Philistine. You are too young. He’s
been a fighting man ever since he was a boy.”

34But David said to Saul, “I’ve been taking care
of my father’s sheep. Sometimes a lion or a bear
would come and carry off a sheep from the flock.
35Then I would go after it and hit it. I would save
the sheep it was carrying in its mouth. If it turned
around to attack me, I would grab hold of its hair.
I would strike it down and kill it. 36In fact, I’ve
killed both a lion and a bear. I’ll do the same thing
to this Philistine. He isn’t even circumcised. He
has dared the armies of the living God to fight him.

37“The LORD saved me from the paw of the lion.
He saved me from the paw of the bear. And he’ll
save me from the powerful hand of this Philistine
too.”

Saul said to David, “Go. And may the LORD be
with you.”

38Then Saul dressed David in his own military
clothes. He put a coat of armor on him. He put a
bronze helmet on his head. 39David put on Saul’s
sword over his clothes. He walked around for a
while in all of that armor because he wasn’t used
to it.

“I can’t go out there in all of this armor,” he said
to Saul. “I’m not used to it.” So he took it off.

40Then David picked up his wooden staff. He
went down to a stream and chose five smooth
stones. He put them in the pocket of his shepherd’s
bag. Then he took his sling in his hand and approached Goliath.

41At that same time, the Philistine kept coming
closer to David. The man who was carrying Goliath’s shield walked along in front of him.

42Goliath looked David over. He saw how young
he was. He also saw how tanned and handsome he
was. And he hated him. 43He said to David, “Why
are you coming at me with sticks? Do you think
I’m only a dog?” The Philistine called down curses
on David in the name of his god. 44“Come over
here,” he said. “I’ll feed your body to the birds of
the air! I’ll feed it to the wild animals!”

45David said to Goliath, “You are coming to
fight against me with a sword, a spear and a
javelin. But I’m coming against you in the name
of the LORD who rules over all. He is the God of
the armies of Israel. He’s the one you have dared
to fight against.

46“This very day the LORD will hand you over
to me. I’ll strike you down. I’ll cut your head off.
This very day I’ll feed the bodies of the Philistine
army to the birds of the air. I’ll feed them to the
wild animals. Then the whole world will know
there is a God in Israel.

47“The LORD doesn’t save by using a sword or
a spear. And everyone who is here will know it.
The battle belongs to the LORD. He will hand all
of you over to us.”

48As the Philistine moved closer to attack him,
David ran quickly to the battle line to meet him.
49He reached into his bag. He took out a stone. He
put it in his sling. He slung it at Goliath. The stone
hit him on the forehead and sank into it. He fell to
the ground on his face.

50So David won the fight against Goliath with
a sling and a stone. He struck the Philistine down
and killed him. He did it without even using a
sword.

51David ran and stood over him. He took hold
of Goliath’s sword and pulled it out. After he killed
him, he cut off his head with the sword.

The Philistines saw that their hero was dead. So
they turned around and ran away.

52Then the men of Israel and Judah shouted and
rushed forward. They chased the Philistines to the
entrance of Gath. They chased them to the gates
of Ekron. The dead bodies of the Philistines were
scattered all along the road to Gath and Ekron.
That’s the road that leads to Shaaraim.

53Israel’s army returned from chasing the Philistines. They had taken everything from the Philistine camp.

54David picked up Goliath’s head. He brought
it to Jerusalem. He put Goliath’s weapons in his
own tent.

55Saul had been watching David as he went out
to meet the Philistine. He spoke to Abner, the com-

mander of the army. He said to him, "Abner, whose son is that young man?"

Abner replied, "King Saul, I don't know. And that's just as sure as you are alive."

56 The king said, "Find out whose son that young man is."

57 After David killed Goliath, he returned to the camp. Then Abner brought him to Saul. David was still carrying Goliath's head.

58 "Young man, whose son are you?" Saul asked him.

David said, "I'm the son of Jesse from Bethlehem."

Saul Becomes Jealous of David

18 David finished talking with Saul. After that, Jonathan and David became close friends. Jonathan loved David just as he loved himself.

2 From that time on, Saul kept David with him. He didn't let him return to his father's home.

3 Jonathan made a covenant with David because he loved him just as he loved himself. 4 Jonathan took off the robe he was wearing and gave it to David. He also gave him his military clothes. He even gave him his sword, his bow and his belt.

5 David did everything Saul sent him to do. He did it so well that Saul gave him a high rank in the army. That pleased Saul's whole army, including his officers.

6 After David had killed Goliath, the men of Israel returned home. The women came out of all of the towns of Israel to meet King Saul. They danced and sang joyful songs. They played lutes and tambourines. 7 As they danced, they sang,

"Saul has killed thousands of men.
David has killed tens of thousands."

8 That song made Saul very angry. It really upset him. He said to himself, "They are saying David has killed tens of thousands of men. But they are saying I've killed only thousands. The only thing left for him to get is the kingdom itself." 9 From that time on, Saul became very jealous of David. So he watched him closely.

10 The next day an evil spirit that was sent by God came on Saul with power. Saul began to prophesy in his house. At that same time David began to play the harp, just as he usually did. Saul was holding a spear. 11 He threw it at David. As he did, he said to himself, "I'll pin David to the wall." But David got away from him twice.

12 The LORD had left Saul and was with David. So Saul was afraid of David. 13 He sent David away. He put him in command of 1,000 men. David led the troops in battle. 14 In everything he did, he was very successful. That's because the LORD was with him.

15 When Saul saw how successful David was, he became afraid of him. 16 But all of the troops of Israel and Judah loved David. That's because he led them in battle.

17 Saul said to David, "Here is my older daughter Merab. I'll give her to you to be your wife. Just serve me bravely and fight the LORD's battles."

Saul said to himself, "I won't have to lift my hand to strike him down. The Philistines will do that!"

18 But David said to Saul, "Who am I? Is anyone in my whole family that important in Israel? Am I worthy to become the king's son-in-law?"

19 The time came for Saul to give his daughter Merab to David. Instead, Saul gave her to Adriel from Meholah to be his wife.

20 Saul's daughter Michal was in love with David. When they told Saul about it, he was pleased. 21 "I'll give her to him to be his wife," he said to himself. "Then maybe she'll trap him. And maybe the powerful hand of the Philistines will strike him down." So Saul said to David, "Now you have a second chance to become my son-in-law."

22 Then Saul gave an order to his attendants. He said, "Speak to David in private. Tell him, 'The king is pleased with you. All of his attendants like you. So become his son-in-law.'"

23 Saul's attendants spoke those very words to David. But David said, "Do you think it's a small thing to become the king's son-in-law? I'm only a poor man. I'm not very well known."

24 Saul's attendants told him what David had said. 25 Saul said, "Tell David, 'Here's the price the king wants for the bride. He wants you to kill 100 Philistines. Then bring back the skins you cut off when you circumcise them. That's how Saul will get even with his enemies.'" Saul hoped that the powerful hand of the Philistines would strike David down.

26 Saul's attendants also told David those things. Then David was pleased to become the king's son-in-law. So before the day that was set for the wedding, 27 David and his men went out and killed 200 Philistines. They circumcised them. Then David brought all of the skins and gave them to the king. By doing that, he could become the king's son-in-law. So Saul gave David his daughter Michal to be his wife.

28 Saul realized that the LORD was with David. He also realized that his daughter Michal loved David. 29 So Saul became even more afraid of him. He remained David's enemy as long as he was king.

30 The Philistine commanders kept on going out to battle. Every time they did, David had more success against them than the rest of Saul's officers. So his name became well known.

Michal Helps David Get Away

19 Saul told his son Jonathan and all of the attendants to kill David. But Jonathan liked David very much. 2 So Jonathan warned him, "My father Saul is looking for a chance to kill you. Be very careful tomorrow morning. Find a place to hide and stay there. 3 My father and I will come and

stand in the field where you are hiding. I'll speak to
him about you. Then I'll tell you what I find out."
4Jonathan told his father Saul some good things
about David. He said to him, "Please don't do anything to harm David. He hasn't done anything to
harm you. And what he's done has helped you a
lot. 5He put his own life in danger when he killed
Goliath. The LORD used him to win a great battle
for the whole nation of Israel. When you saw it,
you were glad. So why would you do anything to
harm a man like David? He isn't guilty of doing
anything to harm you. Why would you want to kill
him without any reason?"
6Saul paid attention to Jonathan. He took an
oath and made a promise. He said, "You can be
sure that the LORD lives. And you can be just as
sure that David will not be put to death."
7So Jonathan sent for David and told him everything he and Saul had said. Then he brought David
to Saul. David served Saul as he had done before.
8Once more war broke out. So David went out
and fought against the Philistines. He struck them
down with so much force that they ran away from
him.
9But an evil spirit that was sent by the LORD
came on Saul. It happened as he was sitting in his
house and holding his spear. While David was
playing the harp, 10Saul tried to pin him to the wall
with his spear. But David got away from him just
as Saul drove the spear into the wall. That night
David escaped.
11Saul sent some men to watch David's house.
He told them to kill David the next morning.
But David's wife Michal warned him. She said,
"You must run for your life tonight. If you don't,
tomorrow you will be killed." 12So Michal helped
David escape through a window. He ran and got
away.
13Then Michal got a statue of a god. She laid it
on David's bed. She covered it with clothes. And
she put some goat hair at the place where David's
head would have been.
14Saul sent the men to capture David. But Michal told them, "He's sick."
15Then Saul sent the men back to see David. He
told them, "Bring him up here to me in his bed.
Then I'll kill him."
16But when the men entered, they found nothing but the statue in the bed. Some goat hair was
at the place where David's head would have been.
17Saul said to Michal, "Why did you trick me
like this? Why did you help my enemy escape?"
Michal told him, "He said to me, 'Help me get
away. If you don't, I'll kill you.'"
18After David had run away and escaped, he
went to Samuel at Ramah. He told him everything
Saul had done to him. Then David and Samuel
went to Naioth and stayed there.
19Saul was told, "David is in Naioth at Ramah."
20So Saul sent some men to capture him. When
they got there, they saw a group of prophets who
were prophesying. Samuel was standing there as
their leader. Then the Spirit of God came on Saul's
men. So they also began to prophesy. 21Saul was
told about it. So he sent some more men. They
began to prophesy too. Saul sent some men a third
time. And they also began to prophesy.
22Finally, Saul decided to go to Ramah himself.
He went to the large well at Secu. He asked some
people, "Where are Samuel and David?"
"Over in Naioth at Ramah," they said.
23So Saul went to Naioth at Ramah. But the
Spirit of God even came on him. He walked along
and prophesied until he came to Naioth. 24There he
took off his royal robes. Then he prophesied in
front of Samuel. He lay there without his robes on
all that day and night. That's why people say, "Is
Saul also one of the prophets?"

Jonathan Helps David Get Away

20 David was in Naioth at Ramah. He ran
away from there to where Jonathan was.
He asked him, "What have I done? What crime
have I committed? I haven't done anything to
harm your father. So why is he trying to kill me?"
2"That will never happen!" Jonathan replied.
"You aren't going to die! My father doesn't do
anything at all without telling me. So why would
he hide that from me? He isn't going to kill you!"
3But David took an oath. Then he said, "Your
father knows very well that you are pleased with
me. He has said to himself, 'I don't want Jonathan
to know I'm planning to kill David. If he finds out,
he'll be very sad.' But I'm very close to being
killed. And that's just as sure as the LORD and you
are alive."
4Jonathan said to David, "I'll do anything you
want me to do for you."
5So David said, "Tomorrow is the time for the
New Moon Feast. I'm supposed to eat with the
king. But let me go and hide in the field. I'll stay
there until the evening of the day after tomorrow.
6Your father might miss me. If he does, then tell
him, 'David begged me to let him hurry home to
Bethlehem. A yearly sacrifice is being offered
there for his whole family group.' 7Your father
might say, 'That's all right.' If he does, it will mean
I'm safe. But he might become very angry. If he
does, you can be sure he's made up his mind to
harm me.
8"Please be kind to me. You have made a
covenant with me in the sight of the LORD. If I'm
guilty, kill me yourself! Don't hand me over to
your father!"
9"I would never do that!" Jonathan said. "Suppose I had even the smallest clue that my father
had made up his mind to harm you. Then I would
tell you."
10David asked, "Who will tell me if your father
answers you in a mean way?"
11"Come on," Jonathan said. "Let's go out to the
field." So they went there together.

12 Then Jonathan spoke to David. He said, "I promise you that I'll find out what my father is planning to do. I'll find out by this time the day after tomorrow. The LORD, the God of Israel, is my witness. Suppose my father feels kind toward you. Then I'll send you a message and let you know. 13 But suppose he wants to harm you. And I don't let you know about it. I don't help you get away safely. Then may the LORD punish me greatly. May he be with you, just as he has been with my father.

14 "But always be kind to me, just as the LORD is. Be kind to me as long as I live. Then I won't be killed. 15 And never stop being kind to my family. Don't stop even when the LORD has cut off every one of your enemies from the face of the earth."

16 So Jonathan made a covenant with David and his family. He said, "May the LORD make David's enemies accountable for what they've done." 17 Jonathan had David take an oath again because he loved him. In fact, Jonathan loved David just as he loved himself.

18 Then Jonathan said to David, "Tomorrow is the time for the New Moon Feast. You will be missed, because your seat at the table will be empty. 19 Go to the place where you hid when all of this trouble began. Go there the day after tomorrow, when evening is approaching. There's a stone out there called Ezel. 20 Wait by it.

"I'll shoot three arrows to one side of the stone. I'll pretend I'm practicing my shooting. 21 Then I'll send a boy out there. I'll tell him, 'Go and find the arrows.' Suppose I say to him, 'The arrows are on this side of you. Bring them here.' Then come. That will mean you are safe. You won't be in any danger. And that's just as sure as the LORD is alive. 22 But suppose I tell the boy, 'The arrows are far beyond you.' Then go. That will mean the LORD is sending you away.

23 "And remember what we talked about. Remember that the LORD is a witness between you and me forever."

24 So David hid in the field. When the time for the New Moon Feast came, the king sat down to eat. 25 He sat in his usual place by the wall. Jonathan sat across from him. Abner sat next to Saul. But David's place was empty.

26 Saul didn't say anything that day. He said to himself, "Something must have happened to David to make him 'unclean.' That must be why he isn't here."

27 But the next day, David's place was empty again. It was the second day of the month.

Finally, Saul spoke to his son Jonathan. He said, "Why hasn't the son of Jesse come to the meal? He hasn't been here yesterday or today."

28 Jonathan replied, "David begged me to let him go to Bethlehem. 29 He said, 'Let me go. Our family is offering a sacrifice in the town. My brother has ordered me to be there. Are you pleased with me? If you are, let me go and see my brothers.' That's why he hasn't come to eat at your table."

30 Saul burned with anger against Jonathan. He said to him, "You are an evil son. You have refused to obey me. I know that you are on the side of Jesse's son. You should be ashamed of that. And your mother should be ashamed of having a son like you. 31 You will never be king as long as Jesse's son lives on this earth. And you will never have a kingdom either. So send for the son of Jesse. Bring him to me. He must die!"

32 "Why do you want to put him to death?" Jonathan asked his father. "What has he done?"

33 But Saul threw his spear at Jonathan to kill him. Then Jonathan knew that his father wanted to kill David.

34 So Jonathan got up from the table. He was burning with anger. On that second day of the month, he refused to eat. He was very sad that his father was treating David so badly.

35 The next morning Jonathan went out to the field to meet David. He took a young boy with him. 36 He said to the boy, "Run and find the arrows I shoot." As the boy ran, Jonathan shot an arrow far beyond him. 37 The boy came to the place where Jonathan's arrow had fallen.

Then Jonathan shouted to him, "The arrow went far beyond you, didn't it?" 38 He continued, "Hurry up! Run fast! Don't stop!"

The boy picked up the arrow and returned to his master. 39 The boy didn't know what was going on. Only Jonathan and David knew. 40 Jonathan gave his weapons to the boy. He told him, "Go back to town. Take the weapons with you."

41 After the boy had gone, David got up from the south side of the stone. He bowed down in front of Jonathan with his face to the ground. He did it three times. Then they kissed each other and cried. But David cried more than Jonathan did.

42 Jonathan said to David, "Go in peace. In the name of the LORD we have taken an oath. We've promised to be friends. We've said, 'The LORD is a witness between you and me. He's a witness between your children and my children forever.'"

Then David left, and Jonathan went back to the town.

Ahimelech Helps David

21 David went to the priest Ahimelech at Nob. Ahimelech trembled with fear when he met him. He asked David, "Why are you alone? Why isn't anyone with you?"

2 David answered the priest Ahimelech, "The king gave me a special job to do. He said to me, 'I don't want anyone to know what I'm sending you to do. So don't say anything about it.' I've told my men to meet me at a certain place. 3 Do you have anything for us to eat? Give me five loaves of bread, or anything else you can find."

4 But the priest answered David, "I don't have any bread that isn't holy. I only have some holy bread here. But it's for men who haven't made love to women recently."

5David replied, "Well, we haven't made love to
women recently. That's the way it is every time I
lead my men out to battle. We keep ourselves holy
even when we do jobs that aren't holy. And that's
even more true today."
6So the priest gave him the holy bread. It was
the only bread he had. It had been removed from
the table that was in front of the LORD. On the
same day, hot bread had been put in its place.
7One of Saul's servants was there that day. He
had been made to stay at the holy tent for a while.
He was Doeg from Edom. He was Saul's chief
shepherd.
8David asked Ahimelech, "Don't you have a
spear or sword here? I haven't brought my sword
or any other weapon. That's because the king's
business had to be done right away."
9The priest replied, "The sword of Goliath, the
Philistine, is here. You killed him in the Valley of
Elah. His sword is wrapped in a cloth. It's behind
the sacred linen apron. If you want it, take it. It's
the only sword here."
David said, "There isn't any sword like it. Give
it to me."

David Meets a Philistine King

10That day David ran away from Saul. He went
to Achish, the king of Gath. 11But the servants of
Achish spoke to him. They said, "Isn't this David,
the king of the land? Isn't he the one the Israelites
sing about when they dance? They sing,

"'Saul has killed thousands of men.
David has killed tens of thousands.'"

12David paid close attention to what the servants
were saying. He became very much afraid of what
Achish, the king of Gath, might do. 13So he pretended to be out of his mind when he was with
them. As long as he was in Gath, he acted like
someone who was crazy. He made marks on the
doors of the city gate. He let spit run down his
beard.
14Achish said to his servants, "Just look at the
man! He's out of his mind! Why are you bringing
him to me? 15Don't I have enough crazy people
around me already? So why do you have to bring
this fellow here? Just look at how he's carrying on
in front of me! Why do you have to bring this man
into my house?"

David Goes to Adullam and Mizpah

22 David left Gath and escaped to the cave of
Adullam. His brothers and the other members of his family heard about it. So they went
down to join him there. 2Everyone who was in
trouble or owed money or was unhappy gathered
around him. He became their leader. About 400
men were with him.
3From there David went to Mizpah in Moab. He
spoke to the king of Moab. He said, "Please let my
father and mother come and stay with you. Let
them stay until I learn what God will do for me."
4So David left his parents with the king of Moab.
They stayed with him as long as David was in his
usual place of safety.
5But the prophet Gad spoke to David. He said,
"Don't stay in your usual place of safety. Go into
the land of Judah." So David left and went to the
forest of Hereth.

Saul Kills the Priests of Nob

6Saul heard that the place where David and his
men were hiding had been discovered. Saul was
sitting under a tamarisk tree on the hill at Gibeah.
He was holding his spear. All of his officials were
standing around him.
7Saul said to them, "Men of Benjamin, listen to
me! Do you think Jesse's son will give all of you
fields and vineyards? Do you think he'll make
some of you commanders of thousands of men?
Do you think he'll make the rest of you commanders of hundreds? 8Is that why all of you have
joined together against me? No one tells me when
my son makes a covenant with Jesse's son. None
of you is concerned about me. No one tells me that
my son has stirred up Jesse's son to hide and wait
to attack me. But that's exactly what's happening
now."
9Doeg was standing with Saul's officials. He
was from Edom. He said, "I saw Jesse's son David
come to Ahimelech at Nob. Ahimelech is the son
of Ahitub. 10Ahimelech asked the LORD a question
for David. He also gave him food and the sword
of Goliath, the Philistine."
11Then the king sent for the priest Ahimelech,
the son of Ahitub. He sent for all of the men in his
family. They were the priests at Nob. All of them
came to the king.
12Saul said, "Son of Ahitub, listen to me."
"Yes, master," he answered.
13Saul said to him, "Why have you and Jesse's
son joined together against me? Why did you give
him bread and a sword? Why did you ask God a
question for him? Now he has turned against me.
He is hiding and waiting to attack me right now."
14Ahimelech answered the king, "David is true
to you. In fact, he's more true to you than anyone
else who serves you. He's your own son-in-law.
He's the captain of your own personal guards. He's
highly respected by everyone in your palace. 15Was
that day the first time I asked God a question for
him? Of course not!
"Please don't bring charges against me. Please
don't bring charges against anyone in my family.
I don't know anything at all about this whole
matter."
16But the king said, "Ahimelech, you will certainly be put to death. You and your whole family
will be put to death."
17Then the king gave an order to the guards who
were at his side. He said, "Go and kill the priests
of the LORD. They are on David's side too. They

knew he was running away from me. And they didn't even tell me."

But the king's officials wouldn't raise a hand to strike down the priests of the LORD.

18 Then the king ordered Doeg, "You go and strike the priests down."

So Doeg, the Edomite, went and struck them down. That day he killed 85 men who wore linen aprons. 19 He also killed the people of Nob with his sword. Nob was a town where priests lived. Doeg killed its men and women. He killed its children and babies. He also destroyed its cattle, donkeys and sheep.

20 But Abiathar, a son of Ahimelech, escaped. Ahimelech was the son of Ahitub. Abiathar ran away and joined David. 21 He told David that Saul had killed the priests of the LORD.

22 Then David said to Abiathar, "One day I was at Nob. I saw Doeg, the Edomite, there. I knew he would be sure to tell Saul. Your whole family has been killed. And I'm accountable for it. 23 So stay with me. Don't be afraid. The man who wants to kill you wants to kill me too. You will be safe with me."

David Saves the People of Keilah

23 David was told, "The Philistines are fighting against the town of Keilah. They are stealing grain from the threshing floors." 2 So he asked the LORD for advice. He said, "Should I go and attack those Philistines?"

The LORD answered him, "Go and attack them. Save Keilah."

3 But David's men said to him, "We're afraid here in Judah. Suppose we go to Keilah and fight against the Philistine army. Then we'll be even more afraid."

4 Once again David asked the LORD what he should do.

The LORD answered him, "Go down to Keilah. I am going to hand the Philistines over to you."

5 So David and his men went to Keilah. They fought against the Philistines and carried off their livestock. David wounded and killed large numbers of Philistines. And he saved the people of Keilah.

6 Abiathar, the son of Ahimelech, had brought the linen apron down with him from Nob. He did it when he ran away to David at Keilah.

Saul Chases David

7 Saul was told that David had gone to Keilah. He said, "God has handed him over to me. David has trapped himself by entering a town that has gates and heavy metal bars." 8 So Saul brought together all of his soldiers to go to battle. He ordered them to go down to Keilah. He told them to surround David and his men. He told them to get ready to attack them.

9 David learned that Saul was planning to attack him. So he said to the priest Abiathar, "Bring the linen apron." 10 Then David said, "LORD, you are the God of Israel. I know for sure that Saul plans to come to Keilah. He plans to destroy the town because of me. 11 Will the citizens of Keilah hand me over to him? Will Saul come down here, as I've heard he would? LORD, you are the God of Israel. Please answer me."

The LORD said, "He will come down."

12 Again David asked, "Will the citizens of Keilah hand me and my men over to Saul?"

And the LORD said, "They will."

13 So David and his men left Keilah. The total number of them was about 600. They kept moving from place to place. Saul was told that David had escaped from Keilah. So he didn't go there.

14 Sometimes David stayed in places of safety in the desert. At other times he stayed in the hills of the Desert of Ziph. Day after day Saul looked for him. But God didn't hand David over to him.

15 David was at Horesh in the Desert of Ziph. There he learned that Saul had come out to kill him.

16 Saul's son Jonathan went to David at Horesh. He told David that God would make him strong. 17 "Don't be afraid," he said. "My father Saul won't lay a hand on you. You will be king over Israel. And I will be next in command. Even my father Saul knows this."

18 The two of them made a covenant in the sight of the LORD. Then Jonathan went home. But David remained at Horesh.

19 The people of Ziph went up to Saul at Gibeah. They said, "David is hiding among us. He's hiding in places of safety at Horesh. Horesh is south of Jeshimon on the hill of Hakilah. 20 King Saul, come down when it pleases you to come. It will be our duty to hand David over to you."

21 Saul replied, "May the LORD bless you because you were concerned about me. 22 Make sure you are right. Go and check things out again. Find out where David usually goes. Find out who has seen him there. People tell me he's very tricky. 23 Find out about all of the hiding places he uses. Come back to me with all of the facts. I'll go with you. Suppose he's in the area. Then I'll track him down among all of the family groups of Judah."

24 So they started out. They went to Ziph ahead of Saul. David and his men were in the Desert of Maon. Maon is south of Jeshimon in the Arabah Valley. 25 Saul and his men started out to look for David. David was told about it. So he went down to a rock in the Desert of Maon to hide. Saul heard he was there. So he went into the Desert of Maon to chase David.

26 Saul was going along one side of the mountain. David and his men were on the other side. They were hurrying to get away from Saul. Saul and his army were closing in on David and his men. They were about to capture them. 27 Just then a messenger came to Saul. He said, "Come quickly! The Philistines are attacking the land."

[28]So Saul stopped chasing David. He went to
fight against the Philistines. That's why they call
that place Sela Hammahlekoth.
[29]David left that place. He went and lived in
places of safety near En Gedi.

David Spares Saul's Life

24 Saul returned from chasing the Philistines.
Then he was told, "David is in the Desert
of En Gedi." [2]So Saul took 3,000 of the best soldiers from the whole nation of Israel. He started
out to look for David and his men. He planned to
look near the Rocky Cliffs of the Wild Goats.
[3]He came to some sheep pens along the way. A
cave was there. Saul went in to go to the toilet. David and his men were far back in the cave.
[4]David's men said, "This is the day the LORD
told you about. He said to you, 'I will hand your
enemy over to you. Then you can deal with him as
you want to.' "

So David came up close to Saul without being
seen. He cut off a corner of Saul's robe.
[5]Later, David felt sorry that he had cut off a corner of Saul's robe. [6]He said to his men, "May the
LORD keep me from doing a thing like that to my
master again. He is the LORD's anointed king. So
I promise that I will never lift my hand to strike
him down. The LORD has anointed him."
[7]David said that to warn his men. He didn't
allow them to attack Saul. So Saul left the cave
and went on his way.
[8]Then David went out of the cave. He called out
to Saul, "King Saul! My master!" When Saul
looked behind him, David bowed down. He lay
down flat with his face toward the ground.
[9]He said to Saul, "Why do you listen when men
say, 'David is trying to harm you'? [10]This very day
you have seen with your own eyes how the LORD
handed you over to me in the cave. Some of my
men begged me to kill you. But I spared you. I
said, 'I will never lift my hand to strike my master
down. He is the LORD's anointed king.'
[11]"Look, my father! Look at this piece of your
robe in my hand! I cut off the corner of your robe.
But I didn't kill you. I want you to know and
understand that I'm not guilty of doing anything
wrong. I haven't turned against you. I haven't
done anything to harm you. But you are hunting
me down. You want to kill me.
[12]"May the LORD judge between you and me.
And may the LORD pay you back because of the
wrong things you have done to me. But I won't lay
a hand on you. [13]People say, 'Evil acts come from
those who do evil.' So I won't lay a hand on you.
[14]"King Saul, who are you trying to catch? Who
do you think you are chasing? I'm nothing but a
dead dog or a flea! [15]May the LORD be our judge.
May he decide between us. May he consider my
case and stand up for me. May he show that I'm
not guilty of doing anything wrong. May he save
me from your powerful hand."
[16]When David finished speaking, Saul asked him
a question. He said, "My son David, is that your
voice?" And Saul sobbed out loud. [17]"You are a better person than I am," he said. "You have treated
me well. But I've treated you badly. [18]You have just
now told me about the good things you did to me.
The LORD handed me over to you. But you didn't
kill me. [19]Suppose a man finds his enemy. He
doesn't let him get away without harming him. May
the LORD reward you with many good things. May
he do it because of the way you treated me today. [20]I
know for sure that you will be king. I know that the
kingdom of Israel will be made secure under your
control. [21]Now take an oath in the name of the
LORD. Promise me that you won't cut off my children from my family. Also promise me that you
won't wipe out my name from my family line."
[22]So David took an oath and made that promise
to Saul. Then Saul returned home. But David and
his men went up to his usual place of safety.

David Gets Married to Abigail

25 Samuel died. The whole nation of Israel
gathered together. They were filled with
sorrow because he was dead. They buried his body
at his home in Ramah.

Then David went down into the Desert of
Maon. [2]A certain man in Maon was very wealthy.
He owned property there at Carmel. He had 1,000
goats and 3,000 sheep. He was clipping the wool
off the sheep in Carmel. [3]His name was Nabal. His
wife's name was Abigail. She was a wise and
beautiful woman. But her husband was rude and
mean in the way he treated others. He was from
the family of Caleb.
[4]David was staying in the Desert of Maon.
While he was there, he heard that Nabal was clipping the wool off his sheep. [5]So he sent for ten
young men. He said to them, "Go up to Nabal at
Carmel. Greet him for me. [6]Say to him, 'May you
live a long time! May everything go well with you
and your family! And may things go well with
everything that belongs to you!
[7]" 'I hear that you are clipping the wool off your
sheep. When your shepherds were with us, we
treated them well. The whole time they were at
Carmel nothing that belonged to them was stolen.
[8]Ask your own servants. They'll tell you. We've
come to you now at a happy time of the year.
Please show favor to my young men. Please give
me and my men anything you can find for us.' "
[9]When David's men arrived, they gave Nabal
the message from David. Then they waited.
[10]Nabal answered David's servants, "Who is
this David? Who is this son of Jesse? Many servants are running away from their masters these
days. [11]Why should I give away my bread and
water? Why should I give away the meat I've prepared for those who clip the wool off my sheep?
Why should I give food to men who come from
who knows where?"

12 So David's men turned around and went back. When they arrived, they reported to David every word Nabal had spoken. 13 David said to his men, "Put on your swords!" So they put their swords on. David put his on too. About 400 men went up with David. Two hundred men stayed behind with the supplies.

14 One of the servants warned Nabal's wife Abigail. He said, "David sent some messengers from the desert to give his greetings to our master. But Nabal shouted at them and made fun of them.

15 "David's men had been very good to us. They treated us well. The whole time we were near them out in the fields, nothing was stolen. 16 We were taking care of our sheep near them. During that time, they were like a wall around us night and day. They kept us safe.

17 "Now think it over. See what you can do. Horrible trouble will soon come to our master and his whole family. He's such an evil man that no one can even talk to him."

18 Abigail didn't waste any time. She got 200 loaves of bread and two bottles of wine. The bottles were made out of animal skins. She got five sheep that were ready to be cooked. She got a bushel of grain that had been cooked. She got 100 raisin cakes. And she got 200 cakes of pressed figs. She loaded all of it on the backs of donkeys. 19 Then she told her servants, "Go on ahead. I'll follow you." But she didn't tell her husband Nabal about it.

20 Abigail rode her donkey into a mountain valley. There she saw David and his men. They were coming down toward her. 21 David had just said, "Everything we've done hasn't been worth a thing! I watched over that fellow's property in the desert. I made sure none of it was stolen. But he has paid me back evil for good. 22 I won't leave even one of his men alive until morning. If I do, may God punish me greatly!"

23 When Abigail saw David, she quickly got off her donkey. She bowed down in front of David with her face toward the ground. 24 She fell at his feet. She said, "Please let me speak to you, sir. Listen to what I'm saying. Let me take the blame myself. 25 Don't pay any attention to that evil man Nabal. His name means Foolish Person. And that's exactly what he is. He's always doing foolish things. I'm sorry I didn't get a chance to see the men you sent.

26 "Sir, the LORD has kept you from killing Nabal and his men. He has kept you from using your own hands to get even. May what's about to happen to Nabal happen to all of your enemies. May it also happen to everyone who wants to harm you. And may it happen just as surely as the LORD and you are alive.

27 "I've brought a gift for you. Give it to the men who follow you. 28 Please forgive me for what I've done wrong.

"The LORD will certainly give you and your family line a kingdom that will last. That's because you fight the LORD's battles. Don't do anything wrong as long as you live.

29 "Someone may chase you and try to kill you. But the LORD your God will keep your life safe like a treasure that is hidden in a bag. And he'll destroy your enemies. Their lives will be thrown away, just as a stone is thrown from a sling.

30 "The LORD will do for you every good thing he promised to do. He'll appoint you leader over Israel. 31 When that happens, you won't have this heavy load on your mind. You won't have to worry about how you killed people without any reason. You won't have to worry about how you got even. The LORD will give you success. When that happens, please remember me."

32 David said to Abigail, "Give praise to the LORD. He is the God of Israel. He has sent you today to find me. 33 May the LORD bless you for what you have done. You have shown a lot of good sense. You have kept me from killing Nabal and his men this very day. You have kept me from using my own hands to get even.

34 "It's a good thing you came quickly to meet me. If you hadn't come, not one of Nabal's men would have been left alive by sunrise. And that's just as sure as the LORD, the God of Israel, is alive. He has kept me from harming you."

35 Then David accepted from her what she had brought him. He said, "Go home in peace. I've heard your words. I'll do what you have asked."

36 Abigail went back to Nabal. He was having a dinner party in the house. It was the kind of dinner a king would have. He had been drinking too much wine. He was very drunk. So she didn't tell him anything at all until sunrise.

37 The next morning Nabal wasn't drunk anymore. Then his wife told him everything. When she did, his heart grew weak. He became like a stone. 38 About ten days later, the LORD struck Nabal down. And he died.

39 David heard that Nabal was dead. So he said, "Give praise to the LORD. Nabal made fun of me. But the LORD stood up for me. He has kept me from doing something wrong. He has paid Nabal back for the wrong things he did."

Then David sent a message to Abigail. He asked her to become his wife. 40 His servants went to Carmel. They said to Abigail, "David has sent us to you. He wants you to come back with us and become his wife."

41 Abigail bowed down with her face toward the ground. She said, "Here I am. I'm ready to serve him. I'm ready to wash the feet of his servants."

42 Abigail quickly got on a donkey and went with David's messengers. Her five female servants went with her. She became David's wife.

43 David had also gotten married to Ahinoam from Jezreel. Both of them became his wives.

44 But Saul had given his daughter Michal, David's first wife, to Paltiel. Paltiel was from Gallim. He was the son of Laish.

David Spares Saul's Life Again

26 Some people from Ziph went to Saul at Gibeah. They said, "David is hiding on the hill of Hakilah. It faces Jeshimon."

2So Saul went down to the Desert of Ziph. He took 3,000 of the best soldiers in Israel with him. They went to the desert to look for David. 3Saul set up his camp beside the road. It was on the hill of Hakilah facing Jeshimon.

But David stayed in the desert. He saw that Saul had followed him there. 4So he sent out scouts. From them he learned that Saul had arrived.

5Then David started out. He went to the place where Saul had camped. He saw where Saul and Abner were lying down. Saul was lying inside the camp. The army was camped all around him. Abner was commander of the army. He was the son of Ner.

6Then David spoke to Ahimelech, the Hittite. He also spoke to Joab's brother Abishai, the son of Zeruiah. He asked them, "Who will go down with me into the camp to Saul?"

"I'll go with you," said Abishai.

7So that night David and Abishai went into the camp. They found Saul lying asleep inside the camp. His spear was stuck in the ground near his head. Abner and the soldiers were lying asleep around him.

8Abishai said to David, "Today God has handed your enemy over to you. So let me pin him to the ground. I can do it with one jab of my spear. I won't even have to strike him twice."

9But David said to Abishai, "Don't destroy him! No one can lay a hand on the LORD's anointed king and not be guilty. 10You can be sure that the LORD lives," he said. "And you can be just as sure that the LORD himself will strike Saul down. Perhaps he'll die a natural death. Or perhaps he'll go into battle and be killed. 11May the LORD keep me from laying a hand on his anointed king. Now get the spear and water jug that are near his head. Then let's leave."

12So David took the spear and water jug that were near Saul's head. Then he and Abishai left. No one saw them. No one knew about what they had done. In fact, no one even woke up. Everyone was sleeping. That's because the LORD had put them into a deep sleep.

13David went across to the other side of the valley. He stood on top of a hill far away from Saul's camp. There was a wide space between them. 14He called out to the army and to Abner, the son of Ner. He said, "Abner! Aren't you going to answer me?"

Abner replied, "Who is calling out to the king?"

15David said, "You are a great soldier, aren't you? There isn't anyone else like you in Israel. So why didn't you guard the king? He's your master, isn't he? Someone came into the camp to destroy him. 16You didn't guard him. And that isn't good. You can be sure that the LORD lives. And you can be just as sure that you and your men are worthy of death. That's because you didn't guard your master. He's the LORD's anointed king. Look around you. Where are the king's spear and water jug that were near his head?"

17Saul recognized David's voice. He said, "My son David, is that your voice?"

David replied, "Yes it is, King Saul, my master." 18He continued, "Why are you chasing me? What evil thing have I done? What am I guilty of?

19"King Saul, please listen to what I'm saying. Was it the LORD who made you angry with me? If it was, may he accept my offering. Was it people who made you angry at me? If it was, may the LORD send down a curse on them. They have now driven me from my share of the LORD's land. By doing that, they might as well have said, 'Go and serve other gods.'

20"Don't spill my blood on the ground far away from where the LORD lives. King Saul, you have come out to look for nothing but a flea. It's as if you were hunting a partridge in the mountains."

21Then Saul said, "I have sinned. My son David, come back. Today you thought my life was very special. So I won't try to harm you again. I've really acted like a foolish person. I've made a huge mistake."

22"Here's your spear," David answered. "Send one of your young men over to get it.

23"The LORD rewards everyone for doing what is right and being faithful. He handed you over to me today. But I wouldn't lay a hand on you. You are the LORD's anointed king. 24Today I thought your life had great value. In the same way, may the LORD think of my life as having great value. May he save me from all trouble."

25Then Saul said to David, "My son David, may the LORD bless you. You will do great things. You will also have great success."

So David went on his way. And Saul returned home.

David Lives in Philistine Territory

27 David thought, "Some day the powerful hand of Saul will destroy me. So the best thing I can do is escape. I'll go to the land of the Philistines. Then Saul will stop looking for me everywhere in Israel. His hand won't be able to reach me."

2So David and his 600 men left Israel. They went to Achish, the king of Gath. He was the son of Maoch. 3David and his men settled down in Gath near Achish. Each of David's men had his family with him. David had his two wives with him. They were Ahinoam from Jezreel and Abigail from Carmel. Abigail was Nabal's widow.

4Saul was told that David had run away to Gath. So he didn't look for David anymore.

5David said to Achish, "If you are pleased with me, give me a place in one of your country towns. I can live there. I don't really need to live near you in the royal city."

6 So on that day Achish gave David the town of
Ziklag. It has belonged to the kings of Judah ever
since that time. 7 David lived in Philistine territory
for a year and four months.
8 Sometimes David and his men would go up
and attack the Geshurites. At other times they
would attack the Girzites or the Amalekites. All of
those people had lived in the land that reached all
the way to Shur and Egypt. They had been there
for a long time.
9 When David would attack an area, he wouldn't
leave a man or woman alive. But he would take
their sheep, cattle, donkeys, camels and clothes.
Then he would return to Achish.
10 Achish would ask, "Who did you attack
today?" David would answer, "The people who
live in the Negev Desert of Judah." Or he would
answer, "The people in the Negev Desert of Jerahmeel." Or he would answer, "The people in the
Negev Desert of the Kenites."
11 David wouldn't leave a man or woman alive
to be brought back to Gath. He thought, "They
might tell on us. They might tell Achish who we
really attacked." That's what David did as long as
he lived in Philistine territory.
12 Achish trusted David. He thought, "David has
made himself smell very bad to his people, the Israelites. So he'll serve me forever."

Saul Disobeys the Lord at Endor

28 While David was living in Ziklag, the Philistines gathered their army together. They
planned to fight against Israel.
Achish said to David, "I want you to understand
that you and your men must march out with me
and my army."
2 David said, "I understand. You will see for
yourself what I can do."
Achish replied, "All right. I'll make you my
own personal guard for life."
3 Samuel had died. The whole nation of Israel
was filled with sorrow because he was dead. They
had buried his body in his own town of Ramah.
Saul had gotten rid of people who get messages
from those who have died. He had also gotten rid
of people who talk to the spirits of the dead. He
had thrown all of them out of the land.
4 The Philistines gathered together and set up
camp at Shunem. At the same time, Saul gathered
all of the fighting men of Israel together. They set
up camp at Gilboa.
5 When Saul saw the Philistine army, he was
afraid. Terror filled his heart. 6 He asked the Lord
for advice. But the Lord didn't answer him
through dreams or prophets. He didn't answer him
when Saul had the priest use the Urim.
7 Saul spoke to his attendants. He said, "Find me
a woman who gets messages from those who have
died. Then I can go and ask her some questions."
"There's a woman like that in Endor," they said.
8 Saul put on different clothes so people
wouldn't know who he was. At night he and two of
his men went to see the woman. "I want you to talk
to a spirit for me," he said. "Bring up the spirit of
the dead person I choose."
9 But the woman said to him, "By now you must
know what Saul has done. He has cut off everyone
who gets messages from those who have died. He
has also cut off everyone who talks to the spirits
of the dead. He has thrown all of them out of the
land. Why are you trying to trap me? Why do you
want to have me put to death?"
10 Saul took an oath in the name of the Lord. He
promised the woman, "You can be sure that the
Lord lives. And you can be just as sure that you
won't be punished for helping me."
11 Then the woman asked, "Whose spirit should
I bring up for you?"
"Bring Samuel up," he said.
12 When the woman saw Samuel, she let out a
loud scream. She said to Saul, "Why have you
tricked me? You are King Saul!"
13 He said to her, "Don't be afraid. Tell me what
you see."
The woman said, "I see a spirit. He's coming up
out of the ground."
14 "What does he look like?" Saul asked.
"An old man wearing a robe is coming up," she
said.
Then Saul knew it was Samuel. He bowed
down. He lay down flat with his face toward the
ground.
15 Samuel said to Saul, "Why have you troubled
me by bringing me up from the dead?"
"I'm having big problems," Saul said. "The
Philistines are fighting against me. God has turned
away from me. He doesn't answer me anymore.
He doesn't speak to me through prophets or
dreams. So I've called on you to tell me what
to do."
16 Samuel said, "The Lord has turned away
from you. He has become your enemy. So why are
you asking me what you should do? 17 The Lord
has spoken through me and has done what he said
he would do. He has torn the kingdom out of your
hands. He has given it to one of your neighbors.
He has given it to David. 18 You didn't obey the
Lord. You didn't carry out his burning anger
against the Amalekites. So he's punishing you
today.
19 "He will hand both Israel and you over to the
Philistines. Tomorrow you and your sons will be
down here with me. The Lord will also hand Israel's army over to the Philistines."
20 Immediately Saul fell flat on the ground. What
Samuel had said filled Saul with fear. His strength
was gone. He hadn't eaten anything all that day
and night.
21 The woman went over to Saul because she
saw that he was very upset. She said, "Look, I've
obeyed you. I put my own life in danger by doing

what you told me to do. 22So please listen to me. Let me give you some food. Eat it. Then you will have the strength to go on your way."

23But he refused. He said, "I don't want anything to eat."

Then his men joined the woman in begging him to eat. Finally, he paid attention to them. He got up from the ground and sat on a couch.

24The woman had a fat calf at her house. She killed it at once. She got some flour. She mixed it and baked some bread that didn't have any yeast in it. 25Then she set the food in front of Saul and his men. They ate it. That same night they got up and left.

Achish Sends David Back to Ziklag

29 The Philistines gathered their whole army together at Aphek. Israel's army camped by the spring of water at Jezreel. 2The Philistine rulers marched out in companies of hundreds and thousands. David and his men were marching with Achish behind the others.

3The commanders of the Philistines asked, "Why are these Hebrews here?"

Achish replied, "That's David, isn't it? Wasn't he an officer of Saul, the king of Israel? He has already been with me for more than a year. I haven't found any fault in him. That's been true from the day he left Saul until now."

4But the Philistine commanders were angry with Achish. They said, "Send David back. Let him return to the town you gave him. He must not go with us into battle. If he does, he'll turn against us during the fighting. In fact, he might even cut off the heads of our own men. What better way could he choose to win back his master's favor? 5Isn't David the one the Israelites sang about when they danced? They sang,

"'Saul has killed thousands of men.
David has killed tens of thousands.'"

6So Achish called David over to him. He said, "You have been faithful to me. And that's just as sure as the LORD is alive. I would be pleased to have you serve with me in the army. I haven't found any fault in you. That's been true from the day you came to me until now. But the Philistine rulers aren't pleased to have you come along. 7So go back home in peace. Don't do anything that wouldn't please the Philistine rulers."

8"But what have I done?" asked David. "What have you found against me from the day I came to you until now? Why can't I go and fight against your enemies? After all, you are my king and master."

9Achish answered, "You have been as pleasing to me as an angel of God. But the Philistine commanders have said, 'We don't want David to go up with us into battle.' 10So get up early in the morning. Take with you the men who used to serve Saul. Leave as soon as the sun begins to come up."

11So David and his men got up early in the morning. They went back to the land of the Philistines. And the Philistines went up to Jezreel.

David Destroys the Amalekites

30 On the third day David and his men arrived in Ziklag. The Amalekites had attacked the people of the Negev Desert. They had also attacked Ziklag and burned it. 2They had captured the women and everyone else who was in Ziklag. They had taken as prisoners young people and old people alike. But they didn't kill any of them. Instead, they carried them off as they went on their way.

3David and his men came to Ziklag. They saw that it had been destroyed by fire. They found out that their wives and sons and daughters had been captured. 4So David and his men began to sob out loud. They sobbed until they couldn't sob anymore. 5David's two wives had been captured. Their names were Ahinoam from Jezreel and Abigail from Carmel. Abigail was Nabal's widow.

6David was greatly troubled. His men were even talking about killing him by throwing stones at him. All of them were very bitter because their sons and daughters had been taken away. But David was made strong by the LORD his God.

7Then David spoke to the priest Abiathar, the son of Ahimelech. He said, "Bring me the linen apron." Abiathar brought it to him. 8David asked the LORD for advice. He said, "Should I chase after the men who attacked Ziklag? If I do, will I catch up with them?"

"Chase after them," the LORD answered. "You will certainly catch up with them. You will succeed in saving those who were captured."

9David and his 600 men came to the Besor Valley. Some of them stayed behind there. 10That's because 200 of them were too tired to go across the valley. But David and the other 400 continued the chase.

11David's men found an Egyptian in a field. They brought him to David. They gave him water to drink and food to eat. 12They gave him part of a cake of pressed figs. They also gave him two raisin cakes. After he ate them, he felt as good as new. That's because he hadn't eaten any food for three days and three nights. He hadn't drunk any water during that time either.

13David asked him, "Who do you belong to? Where do you come from?"

The man said, "I'm from Egypt. I'm the slave of an Amalekite. My master deserted me when I became ill three days ago. 14We attacked the people in the Negev Desert of the Kerethites. We attacked the territory that belongs to Judah. We attacked the people in the Negev Desert of Caleb. And we burned Ziklag."

15David asked him, "Can you lead me down to the men who attacked Ziklag?"

He answered, "Take an oath in the name of God. Promise me that you won't kill me. Promise

Elijah

Suddenly a chariot and horses appeared.
Then Elijah went up to heaven in a strong wind.
—2 Kings 2:11

David

The LORD is my shepherd. He gives me everything I need.
—Psalm 23:1

that you won't hand me over to my master. Then
I'll take you down to them."
16He led David down to where the men were.
They were scattered all over the countryside. They
were eating and drinking and dancing wildly.
That's because they had taken a large amount of
goods from those they had attacked. They had
taken it from the land of the Philistines and from
the people of Judah.
17David fought against them from sunset until
the evening of the next day. None of them escaped
except 400 young men. They rode off on camels
and got away.
18David got everything back that the Amalekites had taken. That included his two wives.
19Nothing was missing. Not one young person or
old person or boy or girl was missing. None of the
goods or anything else the Amalekites had taken
was missing. David brought everything back. 20He
brought back all of the flocks and herds. His men
drove them on ahead of the other livestock. They
said, "Here's what David has captured."
21Then David came to the 200 men who had
been too tired to follow him. They had been left
behind in the Besor Valley. They came out to welcome David and the people who were with him.
As David and his men approached, he greeted
them. 22But some of the men who had gone out
with David were evil. They wanted to stir up trouble. They said, "The 200 men didn't go out into
battle with us. So we won't share with them the
goods we brought back. But each man can take his
wife and children and go home."
23David replied, "No, my friends. You must not
hold back their share of what the LORD has given
us. He has kept us safe. He has handed over to us
the men who attacked Ziklag. 24So no one will pay
any attention to what you are saying. Each man
who stayed with the supplies will receive the same
share as each man who went down to the battle.
Everyone's share will be the same." 25David made
that a law and a rule for Israel. It has been followed
from that day until now.
26David arrived in Ziklag. He sent some of the
goods to the elders of Judah. They were his
friends. He said, "Here's a present for you. It's
part of the things we took from the LORD's
enemies."
27He sent some goods to the elders who were in
Bethel, Ramoth Negev and Jattir. 28He sent some
to those who were in Aroer, Siphmoth, Eshtemoa
29and Racal. He sent some to those who were in
the towns of the Jerahmeelites and Kenites. 30He
sent some to those who were in Hormah, Bor
Ashan, Athach 31and Hebron. He also sent some to
those who were in all of the other places where he
and his men had wandered around.

Saul Takes His Own Life

31 The Philistines fought against Israel. The
men of Israel ran away from them. But
many Israelites were killed on Mount Gilboa.
2The Philistines kept chasing Saul and his sons.
They killed his sons Jonathan, Abinadab and Malki-Shua. 3The fighting was heavy around Saul.
Men who were armed with bows and arrows
caught up with him. They shot their arrows at him
and wounded him badly.
4Saul spoke to the man who was carrying his
armor. He said, "Pull out your sword. Stick it
through me. If you don't, those fellows who aren't
circumcised will come. They'll stick their swords
through me and hurt me badly."
But the man was terrified. He wouldn't do it. So
Saul took his own sword and fell on it. 5The man
saw that Saul was dead. So he fell on his own
sword and died with him.
6Saul and his three sons died together that same
day. The man who carried his armor also died with
them that day. So did all of Saul's men.
7The Israelites who lived along the valley saw
that their army had run away. So did those who
lived across the Jordan River. They saw that Saul
and his sons were dead. So they left their towns
and ran away. Then the Philistines came and settled down in them.
8The day after the Philistines had won the battle, they came to take what they wanted from the
dead bodies. They found Saul and his three sons
dead on Mount Gilboa. 9So they cut off Saul's
head. They took his armor from his body. Then
they sent messengers through the whole land of
the Philistines. They announced the news in the
temple where they had set up statues of their gods.
They also announced it among their people.
10They put Saul's armor in the temple where
they had set up statues of goddesses that were
named after Ashtoreth. They hung his body up on
the wall of Beth Shan.
11The people of Jabesh Gilead heard about what
the Philistines had done to Saul. 12So all of their
brave men traveled through the night to Beth Shan.
They took down the bodies of Saul and his sons
from the wall of Beth Shan. They brought them to
Jabesh. There they burned them.
13Then they got the bones of Saul and his sons
and buried them under a tamarisk tree at Jabesh.
They didn't eat anything for seven days.

2 Samuel

David Hears That Saul Has Died

1 After Saul died, David returned to Ziklag. He
had won the battle over the Amalekites. He
stayed in Ziklag for two days.
2 On the third day a man arrived from Saul's
camp. His clothes were torn. He had dust on his
head. When he came to David, he fell to the
ground to show him respect.
3 "Where have you come from?" David asked him.
He answered, "I've escaped from Israel's camp."
4 "What happened?" David asked. "Tell me."
He said, "Israel's men ran away from the battle. Many of them were killed. Saul and his son
Jonathan are dead."
5 David spoke to the young man who brought
him the report. He asked him, "How do you know
that Saul and his son Jonathan are dead?"
6 "I just happened to be there on Mount Gilboa,"
the young man said. "Saul was there too. He was
leaning on his spear. The enemy chariots and chariot drivers had almost caught up with him. 7 Then
he turned around and saw me. He called out to me.
I said, 'What do you want me to do?'
8 "He asked me, 'Who are you?'
"'An Amalekite,' I answered.
9 "Then he said to me, 'Stand over me and kill
me! I'm close to death, but I'm still alive.'
10 "So I stood over him and killed him. I did it
because I knew that after he had lost the battle he
would be killed anyway. So I took the crown that
was on his head. I also took his armband. I've
brought them here to you. You are my master."
11 Then David took hold of his clothes and tore
them. All of his men did the same thing. 12 All of
them were filled with sadness. They sobbed over
the whole nation of Israel. They didn't eat anything
until evening. That's because Saul and Jonathan
and the LORD's army had been killed with swords.
13 David spoke to the young man who had brought
him the report. He asked, "Where are you from?"
"I'm the son of an outsider, an Amalekite," he
answered.
14 David asked him, "Why weren't you afraid to
lift your hand to kill the LORD's anointed king?"
15 Then David called for one of his men. He said,
"Go! Strike him down!" So he struck the man
down, and the man died. 16 That's because David
had said to him, "Anything that happens to you
will be your own fault. What your own mouth has
spoken is a witness against you. You said, 'I killed
the LORD's anointed king.'"

David's Song of Sadness About Saul and Jonathan

17 David sang a song of sadness about Saul and
his son Jonathan. 18 He ordered that it be taught to
the people of Judah. It is called The Song of the
Bow. It is written down in the Book of Jashar.
David sang,

19 "Israel, your glorious leaders lie dead on
your hills.
Your mighty men have fallen.

20 "Don't announce it in Gath.
Don't tell it in the streets of Ashkelon.
If you do, the daughters of the Philistines
will be glad.
The daughters of men who haven't been
circumcised will be joyful.

21 "Mountains of Gilboa,
may no dew or rain fall on you.
May your fields not produce any offerings
of grain.
The shield of the mighty king lies polluted
there.
The shield of Saul lies there. It isn't rubbed
with oil anymore.
22 The bow of Jonathan didn't turn back.
The sword of Saul didn't return without
being satisfied.
They spilled the blood of their enemies.
They killed mighty men.
23 "In life Saul and Jonathan were loved and
gracious.
In death they were not parted.
They were faster than eagles.
They were stronger than lions.

24 "Daughters of Israel, sob over Saul.
He dressed you in the finest clothes.
He decorated your clothes with ornaments
of gold.

25 "Your mighty men have fallen in battle.
Jonathan lies dead on your hills.
26 My brother Jonathan, I'm filled with sadness
because of you.
You were very special to me.
Your love for me was wonderful.
It was more wonderful than the love
of women.

27 "Israel's mighty men have fallen.
Their weapons of war are broken."

David Is Anointed to Be King Over Judah

2 After Saul and Jonathan died, David asked the
LORD for advice. "Should I go up to one of the
towns of Judah?" he asked.
The LORD said, "Go up."
David asked, "Where should I go?"
"To Hebron," the LORD answered.

2So David went up there with his two wives. Their names were Ahinoam from Jezreel and Abigail from Carmel. Abigail was Nabal's widow. 3David also took his men and their families with him. They settled down in Hebron and its towns.

4Then the men of Judah came to Hebron. There they anointed David to be king over the people of Judah.

David was told that the men of Jabesh Gilead had buried Saul's body. 5So he sent messengers to them to speak for him.

The messengers said, "You were kind to bury the body of your master Saul. May the LORD bless you for that. 6And may he now be kind and faithful to you. David will treat you well for being kind to Saul's body. 7Now then, be strong and brave. Your master Saul is dead. And the people of Judah have anointed David to be king over them."

The Armies of David and Saul Fight Each Other

8Abner, the son of Ner, was commander of Saul's army. He had brought Saul's son Ish-Bosheth to Mahanaim. 9There he made him king over Gilead, Ashuri and Jezreel. He also made him king over Ephraim, Benjamin and other areas of Israel.

10Ish-Bosheth was 40 years old when he became king over Israel. He ruled for two years. But the people of Judah followed David. 11David was king in Hebron over the people of Judah for seven and a half years.

12Abner, the son of Ner, left Mahanaim and went to Gibeon. The men of Ish-Bosheth, the son of Saul, went with him. 13Joab, the son of Zeruiah, and David's men also went out. All of them met at the pool in Gibeon. One group sat down on one side of the pool. The other group sat on the other side.

14Then Abner said to Joab, "Let's have some of the young men get up and fight. Let's tell them to fight hand to hand in front of us."

"All right. Let them do it," Joab said.

15So the young men stood up and were counted off. There were 12 on the side of Benjamin and Saul's son Ish-Bosheth. And there were 12 on David's side. 16Each man grabbed one of his enemies by the head. Each one stuck his dagger into the other man's side. And all of them fell down together and died. So that place in Gibeon was named Helkath Hazzurim.

17The fighting that day was very heavy. Abner and the men of Israel lost the battle to David's men.

18The three sons of Zeruiah were there. Their names were Joab, Abishai and Asahel. Asahel was as quick on his feet as a wild antelope. 19He chased Abner. He didn't turn to the right or the left as he chased him. 20Abner looked behind him. He asked, "Asahel, is that you?"

"It is," he answered.

21Then Abner said to him, "Turn to the right or the left. Fight one of the young men. Take his weapons away from him." But Asahel wouldn't stop chasing him.

22Again Abner warned Asahel, "Stop chasing me! If you don't, I'll strike you down. Then how could I look your brother Joab in the face?"

23But Asahel refused to give up the chase. So Abner drove the dull end of his spear into Asahel's stomach. The spear came out of his back. He fell and died right there on the spot. Every man stopped when he came to the place where Asahel had fallen and died.

24But Joab and Abishai chased Abner. As the sun was going down, they came to the hill of Ammah. It was near Giah on the way to the dry and empty land close to Gibeon. 25The men of Benjamin gathered in a group around Abner. They took their stand on top of a hill.

26Abner called out to Joab, "Do you want our swords to keep on killing us off? Don't you know that all of this fighting will end in bitter feelings? How long will it be before you order your men to stop chasing their fellow Israelites?"

27Joab answered, "It's a good thing you spoke up. If you hadn't, the men would have kept on chasing their fellow Israelites until morning. And that's just as sure as God is alive."

28So Joab blew a trumpet. All of the men stopped. They didn't chase Israel anymore. They didn't fight anymore either.

29All that night Abner and his men marched through the Arabah Valley. They went across the Jordan River. They kept on going through the whole Bithron. Finally, they came to Mahanaim.

30Then Joab returned from chasing Abner. He gathered all of his men together. Besides Asahel, only 19 of David's men were missing. 31But David's men had killed 360 men from Benjamin who were with Abner. 32They got Asahel's body and buried it in his father's tomb at Bethlehem. Then Joab and his men marched all night. They arrived at Hebron at sunrise.

3 The war between Saul's royal house and David's royal house lasted a long time. David grew stronger and stronger. But the royal house of Saul grew weaker and weaker.

2 Sons were born to David in Hebron.

His first son was Amnon. Amnon's mother was Ahinoam from Jezreel.

3 His second son was Kileab. Kileab's mother was Abigail. She was Nabal's widow from Carmel.

The third son was Absalom. His mother was Maacah. She was the daughter of Talmai, the king of Geshur.

4 The fourth son was Adonijah. His mother was Haggith.

The fifth son was Shephatiah. His mother was Abital.

5 The sixth son was Ithream. His mother was David's wife Eglah.

Those sons were born to David in Hebron.

Abner Goes Over to David's Side

6 The fighting continued between David's royal house and Saul's royal house. Abner gained more and more power in the royal house of Saul.

7 While Saul was still alive, he had a concubine named Rizpah. She was the daughter of Aiah. Ish-Bosheth said to Abner, "Why did you have sex with my father's concubine?"

8 Abner burned with anger because of what Ish-Bosheth said. He answered, "Do you think I'm only a dog's head? Am I on Judah's side? To this very day I've been true to the royal house of your father Saul. I've been true to his family and friends. I haven't handed you over to David. But now you claim that I've sinned with this woman!

9 "I will do for David what the LORD promised him with an oath. If I don't, may God punish me greatly. 10 I'll take the kingdom away from Saul's royal house. I'll set up the throne of David's kingdom over Israel and Judah. He will rule from Dan all the way to Beersheba."

11 Ish-Bosheth didn't dare to say another word to Abner. He was much too afraid of him.

12 Then Abner sent messengers to David to speak for him. They said, "Who will rule over this land? Make a covenant with me. Then I'll help you bring all of the people of Israel over to your side."

13 "Good," said David. "I will make a covenant with you. But there's one thing I want you to do. Bring Saul's daughter Michal to me. Don't come to see me unless she's with you."

14 Then David sent messengers to Saul's son Ish-Bosheth. He ordered them to say, "Give me my wife Michal. She was promised to me. I paid for her with the skins I cut off when I circumcised 100 Philistines."

15 So Ish-Bosheth gave the order. He sent men who took Michal away from her husband Paltiel. Paltiel was the son of Laish. 16 But her husband followed her to Bahurim. He was crying all the way. Then Abner said to him, "Go back home!" So he did.

17 Abner talked with the elders of Israel. He said, "For some time you have wanted to make David your king. 18 Now do it! The LORD made a promise to David. He said, 'I will save my people Israel from the powerful hand of the Philistines. I will also save them from all of their enemies. I will save them through my servant David.' "

19 Abner also spoke to the people of Benjamin in person. Then he went to Hebron to tell David everything. He told him what Israel and all of the people of Benjamin wanted to do. 20 Abner had 20 men with him. They came to David at Hebron. So David prepared a big dinner for Abner and his men.

21 Then Abner said to David, "Let me go right now. I'll gather together all of the people of Israel for you. After all, you are now my king and master. The people can make a covenant with you. Then you can rule over everyone you want to." So David sent Abner away. And he went in peace.

Joab Murders Abner

22 Just then David's men and Joab came back from attacking their enemies. They brought with them the large amount of goods they had taken. But Abner wasn't with David in Hebron anymore. That's because David had sent him away, and he had gone in peace.

23 Joab and all of the soldiers who were with him arrived. Then he was told that Abner, the son of Ner, had come to see the king. He was told that the king had sent Abner away. He was also told that Abner had gone in peace.

24 So Joab went to the king. He said, "What have you done? Abner came to you. Why did you let him get away? Now he's gone! 25 You know what Abner, the son of Ner, is like. He came to trick you. He wanted to watch your every move. He came to find out everything you are doing."

26 Then Joab left David. He sent messengers to get Abner. They brought Abner back from the well of Sirah. But David didn't know about it.

27 When Abner returned to Hebron, Joab took him to one side. He brought him to the entrance of the city gate. Joab acted as if he wanted to speak to him in private. But he really wanted to get even with him. That's because Abner had spilled the blood of Joab's brother Asahel. So Joab stabbed him in the stomach. And Abner died.

28 Later on, David heard about it. He said, "I and the people of my kingdom aren't guilty of spilling the blood of Abner, the son of Ner. We are free of blame forever in the sight of the LORD.

29 "May Joab and his whole family line be held accountable for spilling Abner's blood! May someone in Joab's family always have an open sore or skin disease. May someone in his family always have to use a crutch to walk. May someone in his family be killed with a sword. And may someone in his family never have enough food to eat."

30 Joab and his brother Abishai murdered Abner. They did it because he had killed their brother Asahel in the battle at Gibeon.

31 David spoke to Joab and all of the people who were with him. He said, "Tear your clothes. Put on black clothes. Sob when you walk in front of Abner's body." King David himself walked behind it.

32 Abner's body was buried in Hebron. The king sobbed out loud at Abner's tomb. So did the rest of the people.

33 King David sang a song of sadness over Abner. He said,

"Should Abner have died as sinful people do?
34 His hands were not tied.
His feet were not chained.
He died as if he had been killed by
evil people."

All of the people sobbed over Abner again.

35 Then all of them came and begged David to eat something. They wanted him to eat while it

was still day. But David took an oath. He said, "I
won't taste bread or anything else before the sun
goes down. If I do, may God punish me greatly!"
[36]All of the people heard it and were pleased. In
fact, everything the king did pleased them. [37]So on
that day all of the people of Judah and Israel
understood. They knew that the king didn't have
anything to do with the murder of Abner, the son
of Ner.
[38]The king spoke to his men. He said, "Don't
you realize that a great commander has died in Israel today? [39]I'm the anointed king. But today I'm
weak. These sons of Zeruiah are too powerful for
me. May the LORD pay back the one who killed
Abner! May he pay him back for the evil thing he
has done!"

Ish-Bosheth Is Murdered

4 Ish-Bosheth, the son of Saul, heard that Abner had died in Hebron. Then he wasn't so
brave anymore. And all of the people of Israel
became alarmed.
[2]Two men in Ish-Bosheth's army led small
companies that attacked their enemies. The names
of the men were Baanah and Recab. They were
sons of Rimmon from the town of Beeroth. Rimmon was from the tribe of Benjamin. Beeroth is
considered to be part of Benjamin. [3]That's because
the people who used to live in Beeroth had run
away to Gittaim. They have lived there as outsiders to this very day.
[4]Jonathan, the son of Saul, had a son named
Mephibosheth. Both of Mephibosheth's feet were
hurt. He was five years old when the news that
Saul and Jonathan had died came from Jezreel. His
nurse picked him up and ran. But as she hurried to
get away, he fell down. That's how his feet were
hurt.
[5]Recab and Baanah started out for the house of
Ish-Bosheth. They were the sons of Rimmon from
Beeroth. They arrived there during the hottest time
of the day. Ish-Bosheth was taking his early afternoon nap. [6]Recab and his brother Baanah went
into the inside part of the house. They acted as if
they were going to get some wheat. Instead, they
stabbed Ish-Bosheth in the stomach. Then they
slipped away.
[7]They had gone into the house while Ish-Bosheth was lying on his bed in his bedroom. They
stabbed him and killed him. Then they cut off his
head and took it with them. They traveled all night
through the Arabah Valley. [8]They brought the head
of Ish-Bosheth to King David at Hebron. They
said to him, "Here's the head of Ish-Bosheth, the
son of Saul. Saul was your enemy. He often tried
to kill you. Today the LORD has paid Saul and his
family back. He has let you get even with them.
You are our king and master."
[9]David gave an answer to Recab and his brother
Baanah. They were the sons of Rimmon of Beeroth. David said, "The LORD has saved me from all
of my troubles. [10]A man once told me, 'Saul is
dead.' He thought he was bringing me good news.
But I grabbed hold of him. I had him put to death
in Ziklag. That's the reward I gave him for his
news! And that's just as sure as the LORD is alive.
[11]"Now you evil men have killed a man in his
own house. He hadn't done anything wrong. You
killed him while he was lying on his own bed. You
spilled his blood. So shouldn't I spill your blood?
Shouldn't I wipe you off the face of the earth?"
[12]Then David gave an order to his men. They
killed Recab and Baanah. They cut off their hands
and feet. They hung their bodies by the pool in Hebron. But they buried the head of Ish-Bosheth in
Abner's tomb at Hebron.

David Becomes King Over Israel

5 All of the tribes of Israel came to see David
at Hebron. They said, "We are your own flesh
and blood. [2]In the past, Saul was our king. But you
led the men of Israel on their military campaigns.
And the LORD said to you, 'You will be the shepherd over my people Israel. You will become their
ruler.' "
[3]All of the elders of Israel came to see King David at Hebron. There the king made a covenant
with them in the sight of the LORD. They anointed
David as king over Israel.
[4]David was 30 years old when he became king.
He ruled for 40 years. [5]In Hebron he ruled over Judah for seven and a half years. In Jerusalem he
ruled over all of Israel and Judah for 33 years.

David Captures Jerusalem

[6]The king and his men marched to Jerusalem.
They went to attack the Jebusites who lived there.
The Jebusites said to David, "You won't get in
here. Even blind people and those who are disabled can keep you from coming in." They
thought, "David can't get in here."
[7]But David captured the fort of Zion. It became
known as the City of David.
[8]On that day David said, "Anyone who wins the
battle over the Jebusites will have to crawl through
the water tunnel to get into the city. That's the only
way he can reach those 'disabled and blind' enemies of mine." That's why people say, "Those who
are 'blind and disabled' won't enter David's
palace."
[9]David moved into the fort. He called it the City
of David. He built up the area around the fort. He
filled in the low places. He started at the bottom
and worked his way up. [10]David became more and
more powerful. That's because the LORD God who
rules over all was with him.
[11]Hiram was king of Tyre. He sent messengers
to David. He sent cedar logs along with them. He
also sent skilled workers. They worked with wood
and stone. They built a palace for David.
[12]David knew that the LORD had made his position as king secure. He knew that he had made him

king over the whole nation of Israel. He knew that the LORD had greatly honored his kingdom. The LORD had done it because the Israelites were his people.

[13]After David left Hebron, he got more concubines and wives in Jerusalem. More sons and daughters were born to him there. [14]Here is a list of the children who were born to him in Jerusalem. Their names were Shammua, Shobab, Nathan, Solomon, [15]Ibhar, Elishua, Nepheg, Japhia, [16]Elishama, Eliada and Eliphelet.

David Wins the Battle Over the Philistines

[17]The Philistines heard that David had been anointed king over Israel. So their whole army went to look for him. But David heard about it. He went down to his usual place of safety. [18]The Philistines had come and spread out in the Valley of Rephaim.

[19]So David asked the LORD for advice. He said, "Should I go and attack the Philistines? Will you hand them over to me?"

The LORD answered him, "Go. You can be sure that I will hand the Philistines over to you."

[20]So David went to Baal Perazim. There he won the battle over the Philistines. He said, "The LORD has broken through against my enemies when I've attacked them, just as water breaks through a dam." That's why the place was called Baal Perazim. [21]The Philistines left the statues of their gods there. So David and his men carried the statues off.

[22]Once more the Philistines came up. They spread out in the Valley of Rephaim.

[23]So David asked the LORD for advice. The LORD answered, "Do not go straight up. Instead, circle around behind them. Attack them in front of the balsam trees. [24]Listen for the sound of marching in the tops of the trees. Then move quickly. The sound will mean that I have gone out in front of you. I will strike down the Philistine army."

[25]So David did just as the LORD had commanded him. He struck down the Philistines. He struck them down from Gibeon all the way to Gezer.

David Brings the Ark to Jerusalem

6 Again David brought together the best soldiers in Israel. The total number was 30,000. [2]He and all of his men started out from Baalah in Judah. They wanted to bring the ark of God up to Jerusalem from there. The ark is named after the LORD. He is the LORD who rules over all. He sits on his throne between the cherubim that are on the ark.

[3]The ark of God was placed on a new cart. Then it was brought from Abinadab's house, which was on a hill. Uzzah and Ahio were guiding the cart. They were the sons of Abinadab. [4]The ark of God was on the cart. Ahio was walking in front of it.

[5]David was celebrating with all his might in the sight of the LORD. So was the whole community of Israel. All of them were singing songs. They were also playing harps, lyres, tambourines, rattles and cymbals.

[6]They came to the threshing floor of Nacon. The oxen nearly fell there. So Uzzah reached out and took hold of the ark of God.

[7]Then the LORD's anger burned against Uzzah. That's because what Uzzah did showed that he didn't have any respect for the LORD. So God struck him down. He died there beside the ark of God.

[8]David was angry because the LORD's burning anger had broken out against Uzzah. That's why the place is still called Perez Uzzah to this very day.

[9]David was afraid of the LORD that day. He asked, "How can the ark of the LORD ever be brought to me?" [10]He didn't want to take the ark of the LORD to be with him in the City of David. Instead, he took it to the house of Obed-Edom. Obed-Edom was from Gath. [11]The ark of the LORD remained in Obed-Edom's house for three months. And the LORD blessed him and his whole family.

[12]King David was told, "The LORD has blessed the family of Obed-Edom. He has also blessed everything that belongs to him. That's because the ark of God is in Obed-Edom's house."

So David went down there and brought up the ark. With great joy he brought it up from the house of Obed-Edom. He took it to the City of David. [13]Those who were carrying the ark of the LORD took six steps forward. Then David sacrificed a bull and a fat calf. [14]David was wearing a sacred linen apron. He danced in the sight of the LORD with all his might. [15]He did it while he was bringing up the ark of the LORD. The whole community of Israel helped him bring it up. They shouted. They blew trumpets.

[16]The ark of the LORD was brought into the City of David. Saul's daughter Michal was watching from a window. She saw King David leaping and dancing in the sight of the LORD. That made her hate him in her heart.

[17]The ark of the LORD was brought into Jerusalem. It was put in its place in the tent David had set up for it. David sacrificed burnt offerings and friendship offerings to the LORD.

[18]After he finished sacrificing those offerings, he blessed the people in the name of the LORD who rules over all. [19]He gave to each Israelite man and woman a loaf of bread. He also gave each one a date cake and a raisin cake. Then all of the people went home.

[20]David returned home to bless his family. Saul's daughter Michal came out to meet him. She said, "You are the king of Israel. You have really brought honor to yourself today, haven't you? You have taken off your royal robe right in front of the female slaves of your officials. You acted like someone who is very foolish!"

[21]David said to Michal, "I did it to honor the LORD. He chose me instead of your father or anyone else in Saul's family. He appointed me ruler over his people Israel. I will celebrate in honor of the LORD. [22]And that's not all. I will bring even less

honor to myself. I will bring even more shame on myself. But those female slaves you spoke about will honor me."

23Saul's daughter Michal didn't have any children as long as she lived.

God Makes a Promise to David

7 The king settled down in his palace. The LORD had given him peace and rest from all of his enemies who were around him.

2Then the king spoke to the prophet Nathan. He said, "Here I am, living in a palace that has beautiful cedar walls. But the ark of God remains in a tent."

3Nathan replied to the king, "Go ahead and do what you want to. The LORD is with you."

4That night the word of the LORD came to Nathan. The LORD said,

5"Go and speak to my servant David. Tell him, 'The LORD says, "Are you the one to build me a house to live in? 6I have not lived in a house from the day I brought the people of Israel up out of Egypt until now. I have been moving from place to place. I have been living in a tent. 7I have moved from place to place with all of the people of Israel. I commanded their rulers to be shepherds over them. I never asked any of those rulers, 'Why haven't you built me a house that has beautiful cedar walls?'"'

8"So tell my servant David, 'The LORD who rules over all says, "I took you away from the grasslands. That's where you were taking care of your father's sheep and goats. I made you ruler over my people Israel. 9I have been with you everywhere you have gone. I cut off all of your enemies when you were attacking them.

"'"Now I will make you famous. Your name will be just as respected as the names of the most important people on earth. 10I will provide a place where my people Israel can live. I will plant them in the land. Then they will have a home of their own. They will not be bothered anymore. Evil people will no longer crush them, as they did at first. 11That is what your enemies have done ever since I appointed leaders over my people Israel. But I will give you peace and rest from all of them.

"'"I tell you that I myself will set up a royal house for you. 12Some day your life will come to an end. You will join the members of your family who have already died. Then I will make one of your own sons the next king after you. And I will make his kingdom secure. 13He is the one who will build a house where I will put my Name.

"'"I will set up the throne of his kingdom. It will last forever. 14I will be his father. And he will be my son. When he does what is wrong, I will use other men to beat him with rods and whips. 15I took my love away from Saul. I removed him from being king. You were there when I did it. But I will never take my love away from your son.

16"'"Your royal house and your kingdom will last forever in my sight. Your throne will last forever."'"

17Nathan reported to David all of the words that the LORD had spoken to him.

David Prays to the LORD

18Then King David went into the holy tent. He sat down in front of the LORD. He said,

"LORD and King, who am I? My family isn't important. So why have you brought me this far? 19I would have thought that you had already done more than enough for me. But now, LORD and King, you have also spoken about what is going to happen to my royal house in days to come. LORD and King, is this your usual way of dealing with people?

20"What more can I say to you? LORD and King, you know all about me. 21You have done a wonderful thing. You have made it known to me. You have done it because that's what you said you would do. It's exactly what you wanted to do for me.

22"LORD and King, how great you are! There isn't anyone like you. There isn't any God but you. We have heard about it with our own ears.

23"Who is like your people Israel? God, we are the one nation on earth you have saved. You have set us free for yourself. Your name has become famous. You have done great and wonderful things. You have driven out nations and their gods to make room for your people. You saved us when you set us free from Egypt. 24You made Israel your very own people forever. LORD, you have become our God.

25"And now, LORD God, keep forever the promise you have made to me and my royal house. Do exactly as you promised. 26Then your name will be honored forever. People will say, 'The LORD rules over all. He is God over Israel.' My royal house will be made secure in your sight.

27"LORD who rules over all, you are the God of Israel. Here's what you have shown me. You told me, 'I will build you a royal house.' So I can boldly offer this prayer to you. 28LORD and King, you are God! Your words can be trusted. You have promised many good things to me.

29"Now please bless my royal house. Then it will continue forever in your sight. LORD and King, you have spoken. Because you have given my royal house your blessing, it will be blessed forever."

David Wins Many Battles

8 While David was king of Israel, he won many battles over the Philistines. He brought them under his control. He took Metheg Ammah away from them.

2David also won the battle over the people of Moab. He made them lie down on the ground. Then he measured them off with a piece of rope. He put two-thirds of them to death. He let the other third remain alive. So the Moabites were brought under David's rule. They gave him the gifts he required them to bring him.

3David fought against Hadadezer, the son of Rehob. Hadadezer was king of Zobah. He had gone to take back control of the land along the Euphrates River. 4David captured 1,000 of Hadadezer's chariots, 7,000 chariot riders and 20,000 soldiers on foot. He cut the legs of all but 100 of the chariot horses.

5The Arameans of Damascus came to help Hadadezer, the king of Zobah. But David struck down 22,000 of them. 6He stationed some soldiers in the Aramean kingdom of Damascus. The people of Aram were brought under his rule. They gave him the gifts he required them to bring him. The LORD helped David win his battles everywhere he went.

7David took the gold shields that belonged to the officers of Hadadezer. He brought the shields to Jerusalem. 8He took a huge amount of bronze from Tebah and Berothai. Those towns belonged to Hadadezer.

9Tou was king of Hamath. He heard that David had won the battle over the entire army of Hadadezer. 10So Tou sent his son Joram to King David. Joram greeted David. He praised him because he had won the battle over Hadadezer. Hadadezer had been at war with Tou. So Joram brought with him articles that were made out of silver, gold and bronze.

11King David set those articles apart for the LORD. He had done the same thing with the silver and gold he had taken from the other nations he had brought under his control. 12Those nations were Edom, Moab, Ammon, Philistia and Amalek. He also set apart for the LORD what he had taken from Hadadezer, the son of Rehob. Hadadezer was king of Zobah.

13David returned after he had struck down 18,000 men of Edom in the Valley of Salt. He became famous for doing it.

14He stationed some soldiers all through Edom. The whole nation of Edom was brought under his rule. The LORD helped David win his battles everywhere he went.

David's Officials

15David ruled over the whole nation of Israel. He did what was fair and right for all of his people. 16Joab, the son of Zeruiah, was commander over the army. Jehoshaphat, the son of Ahilud, kept the records. 17Zadok, the son of Ahitub, was a priest. Ahimelech, the son of Abiathar, was also a priest. Seraiah was the secretary. 18Benaiah, the son of Jehoiada, was commander over the Kerethites and Pelethites. And David's sons were royal advisers.

David Is Kind to Mephibosheth

9 David asked, "Is anyone left from the royal house of Saul? If there is, I want to be kind to him because of Jonathan."

2Ziba was a servant in Saul's family. David sent for him to come and see him. The king said to him, "Are you Ziba?"

"I'm ready to serve you," he replied.

3The king asked, "Isn't anyone left from the royal house of Saul? God has been very kind to me. I would like to be kind to someone in the same way."

Ziba answered the king, "A son of Jonathan is still living. Both of his feet were hurt."

4"Where is he?" the king asked.

Ziba answered, "He's in the town of Lo Debar. He's staying at the house of Makir, the son of Ammiel."

5So King David had Mephibosheth brought from Makir's house in Lo Debar.

6Mephibosheth came to David. He was the son of Jonathan, the son of Saul. Mephibosheth bowed down to David to show him respect.

David said, "Mephibosheth!"

"I'm ready to serve you," he replied.

7"Don't be afraid," David told him. "You can be sure that I will be kind to you because of your father Jonathan. I'll give back to you all of the land that belonged to your grandfather Saul. And I'll always provide what you need."

8Mephibosheth bowed down to David. He said, "Who am I? Why should you pay attention to me? I'm nothing but a dead dog."

9Then the king sent for Saul's servant Ziba. He said to him, "I'm giving your master's grandson everything that belonged to Saul and his family. 10You and your sons and your servants must farm the land for him. You must bring in the crops. Then he'll be taken care of. I'll always provide what he needs." Ziba had 15 sons and 20 servants.

11Then Ziba said to the king, "I'll do anything you command me to do. You are my king and master." So David provided what Mephibosheth needed. He treated him like one of the king's sons.

12Mephibosheth had a young son named Mica. All of the members of Ziba's family became servants of Mephibosheth. 13Mephibosheth lived in Jerusalem. The king always provided what he needed. Both of his feet were hurt.

David Goes to War Against the People of Ammon

10 The king of Ammon died. His son Hanun became the next king after him. 2David thought, "I'm going to be kind to Hanun. His father Nahash was kind to me." So David sent

messengers to Hanun. He wanted them to tell Hanun how sad he was that Hanun's father had died.

David's messengers went to the land of Ammon. 3The Ammonite nobles spoke to their master Hanun. They said, "David has sent messengers to tell you he is sad. They say he wants to honor your father. But the real reason they've come is to look the city over. They want to destroy it."

4So Hanun grabbed hold of David's men. He shaved off half of each man's beard. He cut their clothes off just below the waist and left them half naked. Then he sent them away.

5David was told about it. So he sent messengers to his men because they were filled with shame. King David said to them, "Stay at Jericho until your beards grow out again. Then come back here."

6The Ammonites realized that what they had done had made David very angry with them. So they hired 20,000 Aramean soldiers who were on foot. The soldiers came from Beth Rehob and Zobah. The Ammonites also hired the king of Maacah and 1,000 men. And they hired 12,000 men from Tob.

7David heard about it. So he sent Joab out with the entire army of Israel's fighting men.

8The Ammonites marched out. They took up their battle positions at the entrance of their city gate. The Arameans of Zobah and Rehob gathered their troops together in the open country. So did the men of Tob and Maacah.

9Joab saw that there were lines of soldiers in front of him and behind him. So he chose some of the best troops in Israel. He sent them to march out against the Arameans.

10He put the rest of the men under the command of his brother Abishai. Joab sent them to march out against the Ammonites. 11He said, "Suppose the Arameans are too strong for me. Then you must come and help me. But suppose the Ammonites are too strong for you. Then I'll come and help you.

12"Be strong. Let's be brave as we fight for our people and the cities of our God. The LORD will do what he thinks is best."

13Then Joab and the troops who were with him marched out to attack the Arameans. They ran away from him. 14The Ammonites saw that the Arameans were running away. So they ran away from Abishai. They went inside the city. After Joab had fought against the Ammonites, he went back to Jerusalem.

15The Arameans saw that they had been driven away by Israel. So they brought their troops together. 16Hadadezer had some Arameans brought from east of the Euphrates River. They went to Helam under the command of Shobach. He was the commander of Hadadezer's army.

17David was told about it. So he gathered the whole army of Israel together. They went across the Jordan River to Helam. The Arameans lined up their soldiers to go to war against David. They began to fight against him. 18But then they ran away from Israel. David killed 700 of their chariot riders. He killed 40,000 of their soldiers who were on foot. He also struck down Shobach, the commander of their army. Shobach died there.

19All of the kings who were under the rule of Hadadezer saw that Israel had won the battle over them. So they made a peace treaty with the Israelites. They were brought under Israel's rule.

After that, the Arameans were afraid to help the Ammonites anymore.

David and Bathsheba

11 It was spring. It was the time when kings go off to war. So David sent Joab out with the king's special troops and the whole army of Israel. They destroyed the Ammonites. They went to the city of Rabbah. They surrounded it and got ready to attack it. But David remained in Jerusalem.

2One evening David got up from his bed. He walked around on the roof of his palace. From the roof he saw a woman taking a bath. She was very beautiful.

3David sent a messenger to find out who she was. The messenger returned and said, "She is Bathsheba. She's the daughter of Eliam. She's the wife of Uriah. He's a Hittite."

4Then David sent messengers to get her. She came to him. And he had sex with her. Then she went back home. All of that took place after she had already made herself "clean" from her monthly period.

5Later, Bathsheba found out she was pregnant. She sent a message to David. It said, "I'm pregnant."

6So David sent a message to Joab. It said, "Send me Uriah, the Hittite." Joab sent him to David.

7Uriah came to David. David asked him how Joab and the soldiers were doing. He also asked him how the war was going.

8David said to Uriah, "Go home and enjoy some time with your wife." So Uriah left the palace. Then the king sent him a gift.

9But Uriah didn't go home. Instead, he slept at the entrance to the palace. He stayed there with all of his master's servants.

10David was told, "Uriah didn't go home." So he sent for Uriah. He said to him, "You have been away for a long time. Why didn't you go home?"

11Uriah said to David, "The ark and the army of Israel and Judah are out there in tents. My master Joab and your special troops are camped in the open fields. How could I go to my house to eat and drink? How could I go there and make love to my wife? I could never do a thing like that. And that's just as sure as you are alive!"

12Then David said to him, "Stay here one more day. Tomorrow I'll send you back to the battle." So Uriah remained in Jerusalem that day and the next.

13David invited Uriah to eat and drink with him. David got him drunk. But Uriah still didn't go home. In the evening he went out and slept on his mat. He stayed there among his master's servants.

14The next morning David wrote a letter to Joab. He sent it along with Uriah. 15In it he wrote, "Put Uriah on the front lines. That's where the fighting is the heaviest. Then pull your men back from him. When you do, the Ammonites will strike him down and kill him."

16So Joab attacked the city. He put Uriah at a place where he knew the strongest enemy fighters were. 17The troops came out of the city. They fought against Joab. Some of the men in David's army were killed. Uriah, the Hittite, also died.

18Joab sent David a full report of the battle. 19He told the messenger, "Tell the king everything that happened in the battle. When you are finished, 20his anger might explode. He might ask you, 'Why did you go so close to the city to fight against it? Didn't you know that the enemy soldiers would shoot arrows down from the wall? 21Don't you remember how Abimelech, the son of Jerub-Besheth, was killed? A woman dropped a large millstone on him from the wall. That's how he died in Thebez. So why did you go so close to the wall?' If the king asks you that, tell him, 'Your servant Uriah, the Hittite, is also dead.'"

22The messenger started out for Jerusalem. When he arrived there, he told David everything Joab had sent him to say. 23The messenger said to David, "The men who were in the city were more powerful than we were. They came out to fight against us in the open. But we drove them back to the entrance of the city gate. 24Then those who were armed with bows shot arrows at us from the wall. Some of your special troops were killed. Your servant Uriah, the Hittite, is also dead."

25David told the messenger, "Tell Joab, 'Don't get upset over what happened. Swords kill one person as well as another. So keep on attacking the city. Destroy it.' Tell that to Joab. It will cheer him up."

26Uriah's wife heard that her husband was dead. She sobbed over him. 27When her time of sadness was over, David had her brought to his house. She became his wife. And she had a son by him. But the LORD wasn't pleased with what David had done.

David's Son Dies

12 The LORD sent the prophet Nathan to David. When Nathan came to him, he said, "Two men lived in the same town. One was rich. The other was poor. 2The rich man had a very large number of sheep and cattle. 3But all the poor man had was one little female lamb. He had bought it. He raised it. It grew up with him and his children. It shared his food. It drank from his cup. It even slept in his arms. It was just like a daughter to him.

4"One day a traveler came to the rich man. The rich man wanted to prepare a meal for him. But he didn't want to kill one of his own sheep or cattle. Instead, he took the little female lamb that belonged to the poor man. Then he cooked it for the traveler who had come to him."

5David burned with anger against the rich man. He said to Nathan, "The man who did that is worthy of death. And that's just as sure as the LORD is alive. 6The man must pay back four times as much as that lamb was worth. How could he do such a thing? And he wasn't even sorry he had done it."

7Then Nathan said to David, "You are the man! The LORD, the God of Israel, says, 'I anointed you king over Israel. I saved you from Saul's powerful hand. 8I gave you everything that belonged to your master Saul. I even put his wives into your arms. I made you king over the people of Israel and Judah. And if all of that had not been enough for you, I would have given you even more.

9"'Why did you turn your back on what I told you to do? You did what is evil in my sight. You made sure that Uriah, the Hittite, would be killed in battle. You took his wife to be your own. You let the men of Ammon kill him with their swords.

10"'So time after time members of your own royal house will be killed with swords. That's because you turned your back on me. You took the wife of Uriah, the Hittite, to be your own.'

11"The LORD also says, 'I am going to bring trouble on you. It will come from your own family. I will take your wives away. Your own eyes will see it. I will give your wives to a man who is close to you. He will have sex with them in the middle of the day. 12You committed your sins in secret. But I will make sure that the sin the man commits with your wives will take place in the middle of the day. Everyone in Israel will see it.'"

13Then David said to Nathan, "I have sinned against the LORD."

Nathan replied, "The LORD has taken away your sin. You aren't going to die. 14But you have dared to make fun of the LORD. So the son who has been born to you will die."

15Nathan went home. Then the LORD made the child that had been born to Uriah's wife by David very sick.

16David begged God to heal the child. David didn't eat anything. He spent his nights lying on the ground. 17His most trusted servants stood beside him. They wanted him to get up from the ground. But he refused to do it. And he wouldn't eat any food with them.

18On the seventh day the child died. David's servants were afraid to tell him the child was dead. They thought, "While the child was still alive, we spoke to David. But he wouldn't listen to us. So how can we tell him the child is dead? He might do something terrible to himself."

19David saw that his servants were whispering to each other. Then he realized the child was dead. "Has the child died?" he asked.

"Yes," they replied. "He's dead."

20Then David got up from the ground. After he washed himself, he put on lotions. He changed his clothes. He went into the house of the LORD and worshiped him. Then he went to his own house. He asked for some food. They served it to him. And he ate it.

21His servants asked him, "Why are you acting like this? While the child was still alive, you wouldn't eat anything. You cried a lot. But now that the child is dead, you get up and eat!"

22He answered, "While the child was still alive, I didn't eat anything. And I cried a lot. I thought, 'Who knows? The LORD might show favor to me. He might let the child live.' 23But now he's dead. So why should I go without eating? Can I bring him back to life again? Someday I'll go to him. But he won't return to me."

24Then David comforted his wife Bathsheba. He went to her and made love to her. Some time later she had a son. He was given the name Solomon. The LORD loved him. 25So the LORD sent a message through the prophet Nathan. It said, "Name the boy Jedidiah."

David Captures the City of Rabbah

26During that time, Joab fought against Rabbah. It was the royal city of the Ammonites. It had high walls around it. Joab was about to capture it. 27He sent messengers to David. He told them to say, "I have fought against Rabbah. I've taken control of its water supply. 28So bring the rest of the troops together. Surround the city and get ready to attack it. Then capture it. If you don't, I'll capture it myself. Then it will be named after me."

29So David brought the whole army together and went to Rabbah. He attacked it and captured it. 30He took the gold crown off the head of the king of Ammon. The crown weighed 75 pounds. It had jewels in it. It was placed on David's head. He took a huge amount of goods from the city. 31He brought out the people who were there. He made them work with saws and iron picks and axes. He forced them to make bricks. He did that to all of the towns in Ammon. Then he and his entire army returned to Jerusalem.

Amnon Rapes Tamar

13 Some time later, David's son Amnon fell in love with Tamar. She was the beautiful sister of Absalom. He was another one of David's sons.

2Amnon's sister Tamar was a virgin. It seemed impossible for him to do what he wanted to do with her. But he wanted her so much it almost made him sick.

3Amnon had a friend named Jonadab. He was the son of David's brother Shimeah. Jonadab was a very clever man. 4He asked Amnon, "You are the king's son, aren't you? So why do you look so worn out every morning? Won't you tell me?"

Amnon answered, "I'm in love with Tamar. She's the sister of my brother Absalom."

5"Go to bed," Jonadab said. "Pretend to be sick. Your father will come to see you. When he does, tell him, 'I would like my sister Tamar to come and give me something to eat. Let her prepare the food right here in front of me where I can watch her. Then she can feed it to me.'"

6So Amnon went to bed. He pretended to be sick. The king came to see him. Amnon said to him, "I would like my sister Tamar to come here. I want to watch her make some special bread. Then she can feed it to me."

7David sent a message to Tamar at the palace. It said, "Go to your brother Amnon's house. Prepare some food for him."

8So Tamar went to the house of her brother Amnon. He was lying in bed. She got some dough and mixed it. She shaped the bread right there in front of him. And she baked it. 9Then she took the bread out of the pan and served it to him. But he refused to eat it.

"Send everyone out of here," Amnon said. So everyone left him.

10Then he said to Tamar, "Bring the food here into my bedroom. Please feed it to me."

So Tamar picked up the bread she had prepared. She brought it to her brother Amnon in his bedroom. 11She took it to him so he could eat it.

But he grabbed hold of her. He said, "My sister, come and have sex with me."

12"Don't do this, my brother!" she said to him. "Don't force me to have sex with you. An evil thing like that should never be done in Israel! Don't do it! 13What about me? How could I ever get rid of my shame? And what about you? You would be as foolish as any evil person in Israel. Please speak to the king. He won't keep me from getting married to you."

14But Amnon refused to listen to her. He was stronger than she was. So he raped her.

15Then Amnon was filled with deep hatred for Tamar. In fact, he hated her now more than he had loved her before. He said to her, "Get up! Get out!"

16"No!" she said to him. "Don't send me away. That would be worse than what you have already done to me."

But he refused to listen to her. 17He sent for his personal servant. He said, "Get this woman out of here. Lock the door behind her."

18So his servant threw her out. Then he locked the door behind her.

Tamar was wearing a beautiful robe. It was the kind of robe the virgin daughters of the king wore. 19She put ashes on her head. She tore the beautiful robe she was wearing. She put her hands on her head and went away. She was sobbing out loud as she went.

20When her brother Absalom saw her, he spoke to her. He said, "Has Amnon, that brother of yours, forced you to have sex with him? My sister, don't let it upset you. Don't let it bother you. He's your brother."

After that, Tamar lived in her brother Absalom's house. She was very lonely.

21King David heard about everything that had
happened. So he became very angry.
22Absalom never said a word of any kind to
Amnon. He hated Amnon because he had brought
shame on his sister Tamar.

Absalom Kills Amnon

23Two years later, Absalom invited all of the
king's sons to come to Baal Hazor. It was near the
border of Ephraim. The workers who clipped the
wool off Absalom's sheep were there.
24Absalom went to the king. He said, "I've had
my workers come to clip the wool. Will you and
your officials please join me?"
25"No, my son," the king replied. "All of us
shouldn't go. It would be too much trouble for
you." Although Absalom begged him, the king still
refused to go. But he gave Absalom his blessing.
26Then Absalom said, "If you won't come,
please let my brother Amnon come with us."
The king asked him, "Why should he go with
you?" 27But Absalom begged him. So the king sent
Amnon with him. He also sent the rest of his sons.
28Absalom ordered his men, "Listen! When
Amnon has had too much wine to drink, I'll say to
you, 'Strike Amnon down.' When I do, kill him.
Don't be afraid. I've given you an order, haven't I?
Be strong and brave."
29So Absalom's men killed Amnon, just as Absalom had ordered. Then all of the king's sons got
on their mules and rode away.
30While they were on their way, a report came to
David. It said, "Absalom has struck down all of
your sons. Not one of them is left alive."
31The king stood up and tore his clothes. Then
he lay down on the ground. All of his servants
stood near him. They had also torn their clothes.
32Jonadab, the son of David's brother Shimeah,
spoke up. He said, "You shouldn't think that all of
the princes have been killed. The only one who is
dead is Amnon. Absalom had planned to kill him
ever since the day Amnon raped his sister Tamar.
33You are my king and master. You shouldn't be concerned about this report. It's not true that all of your
sons are dead. The only one who is dead is Amnon."
34While all of that was taking place, Absalom
ran away.
The man on guard duty at Jerusalem looked up.
He saw many people coming on the road west of
him. They were coming down the side of the hill.
He went and spoke to the king. He said, "I see men
coming down the road from Horonaim. They are
coming down the side of the hill."
35Jonadab said to the king, "See, your sons are
coming. It has happened just as I said it would."
36As he finished speaking, the king's sons came
in. They were sobbing out loud. The king and all
of his servants were also sobbing very bitterly.
37When Absalom ran away, he went to Talmai,
the son of Ammihud. Talmai was king of Geshur.
King David sobbed over his son every day.
38So Absalom ran away and went to Geshur. He
stayed there for three years.
39After some time the king got over his sorrow
because of Amnon's death. Then he longed to go
to Absalom.

Absalom Returns to Jerusalem

14 Joab, the son of Zeruiah, knew that the
king longed to see Absalom. 2So Joab sent
someone to Tekoa to have a wise woman brought
back from there. Joab said to her, "Pretend you are
filled with sadness. Put on black clothes. Don't use
any makeup. Act like a woman who has spent
many days sobbing over someone who has died.
3Then go to the king. Give him the message I'm
about to give you." And Joab told her what to say.
4The woman from Tekoa went to the king. She
bowed down with her face toward the ground. She
did it to show him respect. She said, "King David,
please help me!"
5The king asked her, "What's bothering you?"
She said, "I'm a widow. My husband is dead. 6I
had two sons. They got into a fight with each other
in the field. No one was there to separate them.
One of my sons struck the other one down and
killed him.
7"Now my whole family group has risen up
against me. They say, 'Hand over the one who
struck his brother down. Then we can put him to
death for killing his brother. That will also get rid
of the one who will receive the family property.'
They want to kill the only living son I have left,
just as someone would put out a burning coal. That
would leave my husband without any son on the
face of the earth to carry on his name."
8The king said to the woman, "Go home. I'll
give an order to make sure you are taken care of."
9But the woman from Tekoa said to him, "You
are my king and master. No matter what you do, I
and my family will take the blame for it. You and
your royal family won't be guilty of doing anything wrong."
10The king replied, "If people give you any trouble, bring them to me. They won't bother you
again."
11She said, "Please pray to the LORD your God.
Pray that he will keep our nearest male relative
from killing my other son. Then my son won't be
destroyed."
"You can be sure that the LORD lives," the king
said. "And you can be just as sure that not one hair
of your son's head will fall to the ground."
12Then the woman said, "King David, please let
me say something else to you."
"Go ahead," he replied.
13The woman said, "You are the king. So why
have you done something that brings so much harm
on God's people? When you do that, you hand
down a sentence against yourself. You won't let the
son you drove away come back. 14All of us must
die. We are like water that is spilled on the ground.

It can’t be put back into the jar. But God doesn’t
take life away. Instead, he finds a way to bring back
anyone who was driven away from him.
15“King David, I’ve come here to say this to you
now. I’ve done it because people have made me
afraid. I thought, ‘I’ll go and speak to the king.
Perhaps he’ll do what I’m asking. 16Perhaps he’ll
agree to save me from the man who is trying to cut
off me and my son from the property God
gave us.’
17“So now I’m saying, ‘May what you have told
me bring me peace and rest. You are like an angel
of God. You know what is good and what is evil.
May the LORD your God be with you.’ ”
18Then the king said to the woman, “I’m going
to ask you a question. I want you to tell me the
truth.”
“Please ask me anything you want to,” the
woman said.
19The king asked, “Joab told you to say all of
this, didn’t he?”
The woman answered, “What you have told me
is exactly right. And that’s just as sure as you are
alive. It’s true that Joab directed me to do this. He
told me everything he wanted me to say. 20He did
it to change the way things now are. You are as
wise as an angel of God. You know everything that
happens in the land.”
21Later the king said to Joab, “All right. I’ll do
what you want. Go. Bring the young man Absalom back.”
22Joab bowed down with his face toward the
ground. He did it to honor the king. And he asked
God to bless the king. He said, “You are my king
and master. Today I know that you are pleased
with me. You have given me what I asked for.”
23Then Joab went to Geshur. He brought Absalom back to Jerusalem. 24But the king said, “He
must go to his own house. I don’t want him to
come and see me.”
So Absalom went to his own house. He didn’t
go to see the king.
25In the whole land of Israel there wasn’t any
man as handsome as Absalom was. That’s why
everyone praised him. From the top of his head to
the bottom of his feet he didn’t have any flaws.
26He used to cut his hair when it became too heavy
for him. Then he would weigh it. It weighed five
pounds in keeping with the standard weights that
were used in the palace.
27Three sons and a daughter were born to Absalom. The daughter’s name was Tamar. She became
a beautiful woman.
28Absalom lived in Jerusalem for two years
without going to see the king.
29Then Absalom sent for Joab. He wanted to
send him to the king. But Joab refused to come to
Absalom. So Absalom sent for him a second time.
But Joab still refused to come.
30Then Absalom said to his servants, “Joab’s
field is next to mine. He has barley growing there.
Go and set it on fire.” So Absalom’s servants set
the field on fire.
31Joab finally went to Absalom’s house. He said
to Absalom, “Why did your servants set my field
on fire?”
32Absalom said to Joab, “I sent a message to
you. It said, ‘Come here. I want to send you to the
king. I want you to ask him for me, “Why did you
bring me back from Geshur? I would be better off
if I were still there!” ’ Now then, I want to go and
see the king. If I’m guilty of doing anything
wrong, let him put me to death.”
33So Joab went to the king and told him that.
Then the king sent for Absalom. He came in and
bowed down to the king with his face toward the
ground. And the king kissed Absalom.

Absalom Makes Secret Plans Against David

15 Some time later, Absalom got a chariot and
horses for himself. He also got 50 men to
run in front of him. 2He would get up early. He
would stand by the side of the road that led to the
city gate. Sometimes a person would come with a
case for the king to decide.
Then Absalom would call out to him, “What
town are you from?”
He would answer, “I’m from one of the tribes of
Israel.”
3Absalom would say, “Look, your claims are
based on the law. So you have every right to make
them. But the king doesn’t have anyone here who
can listen to your case.” 4Absalom would continue,
“I wish I were appointed judge in the land! Then
anyone who has a case or a claim could come to
me. I would make sure he is treated fairly.”
5Sometimes people would approach Absalom
and bow down to him. Then he would reach out
his hand. He would take hold of them and kiss
them.
6Absalom did that to all of the people of Israel
who came to the king with their cases or claims.
That’s why the hearts of the people were turned
toward him.
7After Absalom had lived in Jerusalem for four
years, he went and spoke to the king. He said, “Let
me go to Hebron. I want to keep a promise I made
to the LORD. 8When I was living at Geshur in
Aram, I made a promise. I said, ‘If the LORD takes
me back to Jerusalem, I’ll go to Hebron and worship him there.’ ”
9The king said to him, “Go in peace.” So he
went to Hebron.
10Then Absalom sent messengers secretly to all
of the tribes of Israel. They said, “Listen for the
sound of trumpets. As soon as you hear them, say,
‘Absalom has become king in Hebron.’ ”
11Absalom had taken 200 men from Jerusalem
with him to Hebron. He had invited them to be
his guests. They went without having any idea
what was going to happen. 12While Absalom was

offering sacrifices, he sent for Ahithophel. Ahithophel was David's adviser. He came to Absalom from Giloh, his hometown. The number of people who followed Absalom kept growing. So he became more and more able to carry out his plans against David.

David Runs Away From Absalom

13A messenger came and spoke to David. He told him, "The hearts of the people are turned toward Absalom."

14Then David spoke to all of his officials who were with him in Jerusalem. He said, "Come on! We have to leave right away! If we don't, none of us will escape from Absalom. He'll move quickly to catch up with us. He'll destroy us. His men will kill everyone in the city with their swords."

15The king's officials answered him, "You are our king and master. We're ready to do anything you want."

16The king started out. Everyone in his whole family went with him. But he left ten concubines behind to take care of the palace. 17So the king and all those who were with him left. They stopped at a place that wasn't very far away.

18All of David's officials marched past him. All of the Kerethites and Pelethites marched along with them. And all of the 600 men who had come with him from Gath marched in front of him.

19The king spoke to Ittai. He was from Gath. The king said to him, "Why do you want to come along with us? Go back. Stay with King Absalom. You are a stranger. You left your own country. 20You came to join me only a short time ago. So why should I make you wander around with us now? I don't even know where I'm going. So go on back. Take with you the others who are from your country. And may the LORD be kind and faithful to you."

21But Ittai replied to the king, "You are my king and master. I want to be where you are. It doesn't matter whether I live or die. And that's just as sure as the LORD and you are alive."

22David said to Ittai, "Go ahead then. Keep marching with my men."

So Ittai, the Gittite, kept marching. All of his men and their families marched with him.

23All of the people in the countryside sobbed out loud as David and all of his followers passed by. The king went across the Kidron Valley. He and all of the people who were with him moved on toward the desert.

24Zadok also went with them. Some of the Levites went with him. They were carrying the ark of the covenant of God. They set the ark down. Abiathar offered sacrifices until all of the people had left the city.

25Then the king said to Zadok, "Take the ark of God back into the city. If the LORD is pleased with me, he'll bring me back. He'll let me see the ark again. He'll also let me see Jerusalem again. That's the place where he lives. 26But suppose he says, 'I am not pleased with you.' Then I accept that. Let him do to me what he thinks is best."

27The king spoke again to the priest Zadok. He said, "You are a prophet, aren't you? Go back to the city in peace. Take your son Ahimaaz with you. Also take Abiathar and his son Jonathan with you. 28I'll wait at the place in the desert where we can go across the Jordan River. I'll wait there until you send word to let me know what's happening."

29So Zadok and Abiathar took the ark of God back to Jerusalem. They stayed there.

30But David went on up the Mount of Olives. He was sobbing as he went. His head was covered, and he was barefoot. All of the people who were with him covered their heads too. And they were sobbing as they went up.

31David had been told, "Ahithophel is one of those who are making secret plans with Absalom against you." So David prayed, "LORD, make Ahithophel's advice look foolish."

32David arrived at the top of the Mount of Olives. That's where people used to worship God. Hushai, the Arkite, was there to meet him. His robe was torn. There was dust on his head.

33David said to him, "If you go with me, you will be too much trouble for me. 34So return to the city. Say to Absalom, 'King Absalom, I'll be your servant. In the past, I was your father's servant. But now I'll be your servant.' If you do that, you can help me by making sure Ahithophel's advice fails. 35The priests Zadok and Abiathar will be there with you. Tell them everything you hear in the king's palace. 36They have their sons Ahimaaz and Jonathan there with them. Send them to tell me everything you hear."

37So David's friend Hushai went to Jerusalem. He arrived just as Absalom was entering the city.

Ziba Lies to David

16 David went just beyond the top of the Mount of Olives. Ziba was waiting there to meet him. He was Mephibosheth's manager. He had several donkeys with saddles on them. They were carrying 200 loaves of bread and 100 raisin cakes. They were also carrying 100 fig cakes and a bottle of wine. The bottle was made out of animal skin.

2The king asked Ziba, "Why have you brought all of these things?"

Ziba answered, "The donkeys are for the king's family to ride on. The bread and fruit are for the people to eat. The wine will make those who get tired in the desert feel like new again."

3Then the king asked, "Where is your master's grandson Mephibosheth?"

Ziba said to him, "He's staying in Jerusalem. He thinks, 'Today the people of Israel will give me back my grandfather Saul's kingdom.'"

4Then the king said to Ziba, "Everything that belonged to Mephibosheth belongs to you now."

"You are my king and master," Ziba said. "I
make myself low in front of you. I bow down to
you. May you be pleased with me."

Shimei Calls Down Curses on David

5King David approached Bahurim. As he did, a
man came out toward him. The man was from the
same family group that Saul was from. His name
was Shimei. He was the son of Gera. As he came
out of the town, he called down curses on David.
6He threw stones at David and all of his officials.
He did it even though all of the troops and the special guard were there. They were to the right and
left of David.
7As Shimei called down curses, he said, "Get
out! Get out, you murderer! You are a worthless
and evil man! 8You spilled the blood of a lot of
people in Saul's family. You took over his kingdom. Now the LORD is paying you back. He has
handed the kingdom over to your son Absalom.
You have been destroyed because you are a
murderer!"
9Then Abishai, the son of Zeruiah, spoke to the
king. He said, "King David, why should we let this
dead dog call down curses on you? Let me go over
there. I'll cut off his head."
10But the king said, "You and Joab are sons of
Zeruiah. What do you and I have in common?
Maybe the LORD said to him, 'Call down curses on
David.' If he did, who can ask him, 'Why are you
doing this?'"
11Then David spoke to Abishai and all of his
officials. He said, "My very own son Absalom is
trying to kill me. How much more should this man
from Benjamin want to kill me! Leave him alone.
Let him call down curses. The LORD has told him
to do it. 12Maybe the LORD will see how much I'm
suffering. Maybe he'll reward me with good things
in place of the curses that are being called down
on me today."
13So David and his men kept going along the
road. At the same time, Shimei was going along
the hillside across from him. He was calling down
curses as he went. He was throwing stones at David. He was showering him with dirt.
14The king and all of the people who were with
him came to the place they had planned to go to.
They were very tired. So David rested there.

Hushai and Ahithophel Give Advice to Absalom

15During that time, Absalom and all of the men
of Israel came to Jerusalem. Ahithophel was with
him.
16Then Hushai, the Arkite, went to Absalom. He
said to him, "May the king live a long time! May
the king live a long time!" Hushai was David's
friend.
17Absalom asked Hushai, "Is this the way you
show love to your friend? Why didn't you go with
him?"
18Hushai said to Absalom, "Why should I? You
are the one the LORD has chosen. These people and
all of the men of Israel have also chosen you. I
want to be on your side. I want to stay with you.
19After all, who else should I serve? Shouldn't I
serve the king's son? I will serve you, just as I
served your father."
20Absalom said to Ahithophel, "Give us your
advice. What should we do?"
21Ahithophel answered, "Your father left some
concubines behind to take care of the palace. Go
and have sex with them. Then all of the people of
Israel will hear about it. They will hear that you
have made yourself smell very bad to your father.
Everyone who is with you will become braver."
22So they set up a tent for Absalom on the roof
of the palace. He went in and had sex with his
father's concubines. Everyone in Israel saw it.
23In those days the advice Ahithophel gave was
as good as advice from someone who asks God for
guidance. That's what David and Absalom thought
about all of Ahithopel's advice.
17 One day Ahithophel said to Absalom,
"Here's what I suggest. Choose 12,000
men. Start out tonight and go after David. 2Attack
him while he's tired and weak. Fill him with terror.
Then all of the people who are with him will run
away. Don't strike down anyone except the king.
3Bring all of the other people back. After the man
you want to kill is dead, everyone else will return
to you. And none of the people will be harmed."
4Ahithophel's plan seemed good to Absalom. It
also seemed good to all of the elders of Israel.
5But Absalom said, "Send for Hushai, the Arkite. Then we can find out what he suggests."
6Hushai came to him. Absalom said, "Ahithophel has given us his advice. Should we do what he
says? If we shouldn't, tell us what you would do."
7Hushai replied to Absalom, "The advice Ahithophel has given you isn't good this time. 8You
know your father and his men. They are fighters.
They are as strong as a wild bear whose cubs have
been stolen from her. Besides, your father really
knows how to fight. He won't spend the night with
his troops. 9In fact, he's probably hiding in a cave
or some other place right now.
"Suppose he attacks your troops first. When
people hear about it, they'll say, 'Many of the
troops who followed Absalom have been killed.'
10Then the hearts of your soldiers will melt away
in fear. Even those who are as brave as a lion will
be terrified. That's because everyone in Israel
knows that your father is a fighter. They know that
those who are with him are brave.
11"So here's what I suggest. Bring together all
of the men of Israel from the town of Dan all the
way to Beersheba. They are as many as the grains
of sand on the seashore. You yourself should lead
them into battle.
12"Then we'll attack David no matter where we
find him. As dew completely covers the ground,

we'll completely overpower his entire army. We won't leave him or any of his men alive. 13He might try to get away by going into a city. If he does, all of us will bring ropes to that city. We'll drag the whole city down into the valley. No one will be able to find even a piece of that city."

14Absalom and all of the men of Israel agreed. They said, "The advice of Hushai, the Arkite, is better than the advice of Ahithophel." The LORD had decided that Ahithophel's good advice would fail. The LORD wanted to bring horrible trouble on Absalom.

15Hushai spoke to the priests Zadok and Abiathar. He said, "Ahithophel has given advice to Absalom and the elders of Israel. He suggested that they should do one thing. But I suggested something else.

16"Send a message right away. Tell David, 'Don't spend the night at the place in the desert where people can go across the Jordan River. Make sure you go on across. If you don't, you and all of the people who are with you will be swallowed up.'"

17Jonathan and Ahimaaz were staying at En Rogel just outside Jerusalem. They knew they would be in danger if anyone saw them entering the city. A female servant was supposed to go and tell them what had happened. Then they were supposed to go and tell King David. 18But a young man saw Jonathan and Ahimaaz and told Absalom about it. So the two men left quickly. They went to the house of a man in Bahurim. He had a well in his courtyard. They climbed down into it. 19The man's wife got a covering and spread it out over the opening of the well. Then she scattered grain on the covering. So no one knew that the men were hiding in the well.

20Absalom's men came to the house. They asked the woman, "Where are Ahimaaz and Jonathan?"

She answered, "They went across the brook." When the men looked around, they didn't find anyone. So they returned to Jerusalem.

21After the men had gone, Jonathan and Ahimaaz climbed out of the well. They went to tell King David what they had found out. They said to him, "Go across the river right away. Ahithophel has told Absalom how to come after you and strike you down."

22So David and all of the people who were with him started out. They went across the Jordan River. By sunrise, everyone had crossed over.

23Ahithophel saw that his advice wasn't being followed. So he put a saddle on his donkey. He started out for his house in his hometown. When he got there, he put everything in order. He made out his will. Then he killed himself. So he died, and his body was buried in his father's tomb.

24David went to Mahanaim. Absalom went across the Jordan River with all of the men of Israel.

25Absalom had made Amasa commander of the army in place of Joab. Amasa was the son of a man named Jether. Jether belonged to the family line of Ishmael. He had gotten married to Abigail. She was the daughter of Nahash and the sister of Zeruiah. Zeruiah was the mother of Joab. 26Absalom and the people of Israel camped in the land of Gilead.

27David came to Mahanaim. Shobi, the son of Nahash, met him there. Shobi was from Rabbah in the land of Ammon. Makir, the son of Ammiel from Lo Debar, met him there too. So did Barzillai from Rogelim in the land of Gilead. 28They brought beds, bowls and clay pots. They brought wheat, barley, flour, and grain that had been cooked. They brought beans and lentils. 29They brought honey, butter, sheep and cheese that was made from cows' milk. They brought all of that food for David and his people to eat. They said, "These people have become hungry. They've become tired and thirsty in the desert."

Absalom Dies

18 David brought together the men who were with him. He appointed commanders of thousands over some of them. He appointed commanders of hundreds over the others.

2Then David sent the troops out in three companies. One company was under the command of Joab. Another was under Joab's brother Abishai, the son of Zeruiah. The last was under Ittai, the Gittite. The king told the troops, "You can be sure that I myself will march out with you."

3But the men said, "You must not march out. If we are forced to run away, our enemies won't care about us. Even if half of us die, they won't care. But you are worth 10,000 of us. So it would be better for you to stay here in the city. Then you can send us help if we need it."

4The king said, "I'll do what you think is best."

So the king stood beside the city gate. The whole army marched out in companies of hundreds and companies of thousands.

5The king gave an order to Joab, Abishai and Ittai. He commanded them, "Be gentle with the young man Absalom. Do it for me." All of the troops heard the king give the commanders that order about Absalom.

6David's army marched into the field to fight against Israel. The battle took place in the forest of Ephraim. 7There David's men won the battle over Israel's army. A huge number of men were wounded or killed that day. The total number was 20,000. 8The fighting spread out over the whole countryside. But more men were killed in the forest that day than out in the open.

9Absalom happened to come across some of David's men. He was riding his mule. The mule went under the thick branches of a large oak tree. Absalom's head got caught in the tree. He was left hanging in the air. The mule he was riding kept on going.

10One of David's men saw what had happened. He told Joab, "I just saw Absalom hanging in an oak tree."

11Joab said to the man, "What! You saw him? Why didn't you strike him down right there? Then I would have had to give you four ounces of silver and a soldier's belt."

12But the man replied, "I wouldn't lift my hand to harm the king's son. I wouldn't do it even for 25 pounds of silver. We heard the king's command to you and Abishai and Ittai. He said, 'Be careful not to hurt the young man Absalom. Do it for me.' 13Suppose I had put my life in danger by killing him. The king would have found out about it. Nothing is hidden from him. And you wouldn't have stood up for me."

14Joab said, "I'm not going to waste any more time on you." So he got three javelins. Then he went over and drove them into Absalom's heart. He did it while Absalom was still hanging there alive in the oak tree.

15Ten of the men who were carrying Joab's armor surrounded Absalom. They struck him down and killed him.

16Then Joab blew his trumpet. He ordered his troops to stop chasing Israel's army. 17Joab's men threw Absalom's body into a big pit in the forest. They covered his body with a large pile of rocks. While all of that was going on, all of the Israelites ran back to their homes.

18Earlier in his life Absalom had set up a pillar in the King's Valley. He had put it up as a monument to himself. He thought, "I don't have a son to carry on the memory of my name." So he named the pillar after himself. It is still called Absalom's Monument to this very day.

David Sobs Over Absalom

19Ahimaaz said to Joab, "Let me run and take the news to the king. Let me tell him that the LORD has saved him from the power of his enemies." Ahimaaz was the son of Zadok.

20"I don't want you to take the news to the king today," Joab told him. "You can do it some other time. But you must not do it today, because the king's son is dead."

21Then Joab said to a man from Cush, "Go. Tell the king what you have seen." The man bowed down in front of Joab. Then he ran off.

22Ahimaaz, the son of Zadok, spoke again to Joab. He said, "I don't care what happens to me. Please let me run behind the man from Cush."

But Joab replied, "My son, why do you want to go? You don't have any news that will bring you a reward."

23He said, "I don't care what happens. I want to run."

So Joab said, "Run!" Then Ahimaaz ran across the flatlands of the Jordan River. As he ran, he passed the man from Cush.

24David was sitting in the area between the inner and outer gates of the city. The man on guard duty went up to the roof over the entrance of the gate by the wall. As he looked out, he saw someone running alone. 25He called out to the king and reported it.

The king said, "If the runner is alone, he must be bringing good news." The man came closer and closer.

26Then the man on guard duty saw another man running. He called out to the man who was guarding the gate. He said, "Look! There's another man running alone!"

The king said, "He must be bringing good news too."

27The man on guard duty said, "I can see that the first one runs like Ahimaaz, the son of Zadok."

"He's a good man," the king said. "He's bringing good news."

28Then Ahimaaz called out to the king, "Everything's all right!" He bowed down in front of the king with his face toward the ground. He said, "You are my king and master. Give praise to the LORD your God! He has handed over to you the men who lifted their hands to kill you."

29The king asked, "Is the young man Absalom safe?"

Ahimaaz answered, "I saw total disorder. I saw it just as Joab was about to send the king's servant and me to you. But I don't know what it was all about."

30The king said, "Stand over there and wait." So he stepped over to one side and stood there.

31Then the man from Cush arrived. He said, "You are my king and master. I'm bringing you some good news. The LORD has saved you today from all those who were trying to kill you."

32The king asked the man from Cush, "Is the young man Absalom safe?"

The man replied, "King David, may your enemies be like that young man. May all those who rise up to harm you be like him."

33The king was very upset. He went up to the room over the entrance of the gate and sobbed. As he went, he said, "My son Absalom! My son, my son Absalom! I wish I had died instead of you. Absalom! My son, my son!"

19 Someone told Joab, "The king is sobbing over Absalom. He's filled with sadness because his son has died."

2The army had won a great battle that day. But their joy turned into sadness. That's because someone had told the troops, "The king is filled with sorrow because his son is dead." 3The men came quietly into the city that day. They were like fighting men who are ashamed because they've run away from a battle.

4The king covered his face. He sobbed out loud, "My son Absalom! Absalom, my son, my son!"

5Then Joab went into the king's house. He said to him, "Today you have made all of your men feel ashamed. They have just saved your life. They have saved the lives of your sons and daughters. And they have saved the lives of your wives and concubines.

6“You love those who hate you. You hate those who love you. The commanders and their troops don’t mean anything to you. You made that very clear today. I can see that you would be pleased if Absalom were alive today and all of us were dead.

7“Now go out there and cheer up your men. If you don’t, you won’t have any of them left with you by sunset. That will be worse for you than all of the troubles you have ever had in your whole life. That’s what I promise you with an oath in the LORD’s name.”

8So the king got up and took his seat in the entrance of the city gate. His men were told, “The king is sitting in the entrance of the gate.” Then all of them came and stood in front of him.

David Returns to Jerusalem

While all of that was going on, the Israelites had run back to their homes. 9People from all of the tribes of Israel began to argue with one another. They were saying, “The king saved us from the power of our enemies. He saved us from the power of the Philistines. But now he has left the country because of Absalom. 10We anointed Absalom to rule over us. But he has died in battle. So why aren’t any of you talking about bringing the king back?”

11King David sent a message to the priests Zadok and Abiathar. It said, “Speak to the elders of Judah. Tell them I said, ‘News has reached me where I’m staying. People all over Israel are talking about bringing me back to my palace. Why should you be the last to do something about it? 12You are my relatives. You are my own flesh and blood. So why should you be the last to bring me back?’

13“Say to Amasa, ‘Aren’t you my own flesh and blood? From now on you will be the commander of my army in place of Joab. If that isn’t true, may God punish me greatly.’”

14So the hearts of all of the men of Judah were turned toward David. All of them had the same purpose in mind. They sent a message to the king. It said, “We want you to come back. We want all of your men to come back too.” 15Then the king returned. He went as far as the Jordan River.

The men of Judah had come to Gilgal to welcome the king back. They had come to bring him across the Jordan. 16Shimei, the son of Gera, was among them. Shimei was from Bahurim in the territory of Benjamin. He hurried down to welcome King David back. 17There were 1,000 people from Benjamin with him. Ziba, the manager of Saul’s house, was with him too. And so were Ziba’s 15 sons and 20 servants. All of them rushed down to the Jordan River. That’s where the king was. 18They went across at the place where people usually cross it. Then they brought the king’s family back over with them. They were ready to do anything he wanted them to do.

Shimei, the son of Gera, had also gone across the Jordan. When he did, he fell down flat with his face toward the ground in front of the king. 19He said to him, “You are my king and master. Please don’t hold me guilty. Please forgive me for the wrong things I did on the day you left Jerusalem. Please forget all about them. 20I know I’ve sinned. But today I’ve come down here to welcome you. I’m the first member of Joseph’s whole family to do it.”

21Then Abishai, the son of Zeruiah, said, “Shouldn’t Shimei be put to death for what he did? He called down curses on you. And you are the LORD’s anointed king.”

22But David replied, “You and Joab are sons of Zeruiah. What do you and I have in common? Abishai, you have now become my enemy! Should anyone be put to death in Israel today? Don’t I know that today I am king over Israel again?”

23So the king took an oath and made a promise to Shimei. He said to him, “You aren’t going to be put to death.”

24Mephibosheth was Saul’s grandson. He had also gone down to welcome the king back. He had not taken care of his feet. He hadn’t trimmed his mustache or washed his clothes. He hadn’t done any of those things from the day the king left Jerusalem until the day he returned safely. 25He came from Jerusalem to welcome the king. The king asked him, “Mephibosheth, why didn’t you go with me?”

26He said, “You are my king and master. I’m disabled. So I thought, ‘I’ll have a saddle put on my donkey. I’ll ride on it. Then I can go with the king.’ But my servant Ziba turned against me. 27He has told you lies about me. King David, you are like an angel of God. So do what pleases you. 28You should have put all of the members of my grandfather’s family to death, including me. Instead, you always provided what I needed. So what right do I have to make any more appeals to you?”

29The king said to him, “You don’t have to say anything else. I order you and Ziba to divide up Saul’s fields between you.”

30Mephibosheth said to the king, “I’m happy that you have arrived home safely. So just let Ziba have everything.”

31Barzillai had also come down to go across the Jordan River with the king. He wanted to send the king on his way from there. Barzillai was from Rogelim in the land of Gilead. 32He was a very old man. He was 80 years old. He had given the king everything he needed while the king was staying in Mahanaim. That’s because Barzillai was very wealthy.

33The king said to Barzillai, “Come across the river with me. Stay with me in Jerusalem. I’ll take good care of you.”

34But Barzillai said to the king, “I won’t live for many more years. So why should I go up to Jerusalem with you? 35I’m already 80 years old. I can hardly tell the difference between what is good and what isn’t. I can hardly taste what I eat and drink. I can’t even hear the voices of male and female singers anymore. So why should I add my problems to yours?

36“I’ll go across the Jordan River with you for a little way. Why should you reward me by taking care of me? 37Let me go back home. Then I can die in my own town. I can be buried there in the tomb of my father and mother. But let Kimham take my place. Let him go across the river with you. Do for him what pleases you.”

38The king said, “Kimham will go across with me. I’ll do for him what pleases you. And I’ll do for you anything you want me to do.”

39So all of the people went across the Jordan River. Then the king crossed over. The king kissed Barzillai and gave him his blessing. And Barzillai went back home.

40After the king had gone across the river, he went to Gilgal. Kimham had gone across with him. All of the troops of Judah and half of the troops of Israel had taken the king across.

41Soon all of the men of Israel were coming to the king. They were saying to him, “Why did the men of Judah take you away from us? They are our relatives. What right did they have to bring you and your family across the Jordan River? What right did they have to bring all of your men over with you?”

42All of the men of Judah answered the men of Israel. They said, “We did that because the king is our close relative. So why should you be angry about what happened? Have we eaten any of the king’s food? Have we taken anything for ourselves?”

43Then the men of Israel answered the men of Judah. They said, “We have ten of the 12 tribes in the kingdom. So we have a stronger claim on David than you have. Why then are you acting as if you hate us? Weren’t we the first ones to talk about bringing back our king?”

But the men of Judah answered in an even meaner way than the men of Israel.

Sheba Tells Israel Not to Follow David

20 An evil man who always stirred up trouble happened to be in Gilgal. His name was Sheba, the son of Bicri. Sheba was from the tribe of Benjamin. He blew his trumpet. Then he shouted,

“We don’t have any share in David’s kingdom!
Jesse’s son is not our king!
Men of Israel, every one of you go back home!”

2So all of the men of Israel deserted David. They followed Sheba, the son of Bicri. But the men of Judah stayed with their king. They remained with him from the Jordan River all the way to Jerusalem.

3David returned to his palace in Jerusalem. He had left ten concubines there to take care of the palace. He put them in a house and kept them under guard. He gave them what they needed. But he didn’t make love to them. They were kept under guard until the day they died. They lived as if they were widows.

4The king said to Amasa, “Send for the men of Judah. Tell them to come to me within three days. And be here yourself.” 5So Amasa went to get the men of Judah. But he took longer than the time the king had set for him.

6David said to Abishai, “Sheba, the son of Bicri, will do more harm to us than Absalom ever did. Take my men and go after him. If you don’t, he’ll find cities that have high walls around them. He’ll go into one of them and escape from us.”

7So Joab’s men marched out with the Kerethites and Pelethites. They went out with all of the mighty soldiers. All of them were under Abishai’s command. They marched out from Jerusalem and went after Sheba, the son of Bicri.

8They arrived at the great rock in Gibeon. Amasa went there to welcome them. Joab was wearing his military clothes. Over them at his waist he strapped on a belt that held a dagger. As he stepped forward, the dagger fell out.

9Joab said to Amasa, “How are you, my friend?” Then Joab reached out his right hand. He took hold of Amasa’s beard to kiss him.

10Amasa didn’t pay any attention to the dagger that was in Joab’s left hand. Joab stuck it into his stomach. His insides spilled out on the ground. Joab didn’t have to stab him again. Amasa was already dead. Then Joab and his brother Abishai went after Sheba, the son of Bicri.

11One of Joab’s men stood beside Amasa’s body. He said to the other men, “Are you pleased with Joab? Are you on David’s side? Then follow Joab!”

12Amasa’s body lay covered with his blood in the middle of the road. The man saw that all of the troops stopped there. He realized that everyone was stopping to look at Amasa’s body. So he dragged it from the road into a field. Then he threw some clothes on top of it. 13After that happened, all of the men continued on with Joab. They went after Sheba, the son of Bicri.

14Sheba passed through all of the territory of the tribes of Israel. He arrived at the city of Abel Beth Maacah. He had gone through the entire area of the Berites. They had gathered together and followed him.

15Joab and all of his troops came to Abel Beth Maacah. They surrounded it because Sheba was there. They built a ramp up to the city. It stood against the outer wall. They pounded the wall with huge logs to bring it down.

16While that was going on, a wise woman called out from the city. She shouted, “Listen! Listen! Tell Joab to come here. I want to speak to him.”

17 So Joab went toward her. She asked, "Are you Joab?"

"I am," he answered.

She said, "Listen to what I have to say."

"I'm listening," he said.

18 She continued, "Long ago people used to say, 'Get your answer at Abel.' And that would settle the matter. 19 We are the most peaceful and faithful people in Israel. You are trying to destroy a city that is like a mother in Israel. Why do you want to swallow up what belongs to the LORD?"

20 "I would never do anything like that!" Joab said. "I would never swallow up or destroy what belongs to the LORD! 21 That isn't what I have in mind at all. There's a man named Sheba, the son of Bicri, in your city. He's from the hill country of Ephraim. He's trying to kill King David. Hand that man over to me. Then I'll pull my men back from your city."

The woman said to Joab, "We'll throw his head down to you from the wall."

22 Then the woman gave her wise advice to all of the people in the city. They cut off the head of Sheba, the son of Bicri. They threw it down to Joab. So he blew his trumpet. Then his men pulled back from the city. Each of them returned to his home. And Joab went back to the king in Jerusalem.

23 Joab was commander over Israel's entire army. Benaiah, the son of Jehoiada, was commander over the Kerethites and Pelethites. 24 Adoniram was in charge of those who were forced to work hard. Jehoshaphat, the son of Ahilud, kept the records. 25 Sheva was the secretary. Zadok and Abiathar were priests. 26 Ira, the Jairite, was David's priest.

David Makes Things Right for the People of Gibeon

21 For three years in a row there wasn't enough food in the land. That was while David was king. So David asked the LORD why he wasn't showing his favor to his people. The LORD said, "It is because Saul and his family committed murder. He put the people of Gibeon to death."

2 The people of Gibeon weren't a part of Israel. Instead, they were some of the Amorites who were still left alive. The people of Israel had promised with an oath to spare them. But Saul had tried to put an end to them. That's because he wanted to make Israel and Judah strong.

So now King David sent for the people of Gibeon and spoke to them. 3 He asked them, "What would you like me to do for you? How can I make up for the wrong things that were done to you? I want you to be able to pray that the LORD will once again bless his land."

4 The people of Gibeon answered him. They said, "No amount of silver or gold can make up for what Saul and his family did to us. And we can't put anyone in Israel to death."

"What do you want me to do for you?" David asked.

5 They answered the king, "Saul nearly destroyed us. He made plans to wipe us out. We don't have anywhere to live in Israel. 6 So let seven of the males in his family line be given to us. We'll kill them. We'll put their dead bodies out in the open in the sight of the LORD. We'll do it at Gibeah of Saul. Saul was the LORD's chosen king."

So King David said, "I'll give seven males to you."

7 The king spared Mephibosheth. He was the son of Jonathan and the grandson of Saul. David had taken an oath in the sight of the LORD. He had promised to be kind to Jonathan and the family line of his father Saul.

8 But the king chose Armoni and another Mephibosheth. They were the two sons of Aiah's daughter Rizpah. Saul was their father. The king also chose the five sons of Saul's daughter Merab. Adriel, the son of Barzillai, was their father. Adriel was from Meholah.

9 King David handed them over to the people of Gibeon. They killed them. They put their dead bodies out in the open on a hill in the sight of the LORD. All seven of them died together. They were put to death during the first days of the harvest. It happened just when people were beginning to harvest the barley.

10 Aiah's daughter Rizpah got some black cloth. She spread it out for herself on a rock. She stayed there from the beginning of the harvest until it rained. The rain poured down from the sky on the dead bodies of the seven males. She didn't let the birds of the air touch them by day. She didn't let the wild animals touch them at night.

11 Someone told David what Rizpah had done. She was Aiah's daughter and Saul's concubine.

12 David got the bones of Saul and his son Jonathan. He got them from the citizens of Jabesh Gilead. They had taken them in secret from the main street in Beth Shan. That's where the Philistines had hung their bodies up on the city wall. They had done it after they struck Saul down on Mount Gilboa.

13 David brought the bones of Saul and his son Jonathan from Jabesh Gilead. The bones of the seven males who had been killed and put out in the open were also gathered up.

14 The bones of Saul and his son Jonathan were buried in the tomb of Saul's father Kish. The tomb was at Zela in the territory of Benjamin. Everything the king commanded was done. After that, God answered prayer and blessed the land.

Israel Goes to War Against the Philistines

15 Once again there was a battle between the Philistines and Israel. David went down with his men to fight against the Philistines. He became very tired.

16 Ishbi-Benob belonged to the family line of Rapha. The tip of his bronze spear weighed seven and a half pounds. He was also armed with a new sword. He said he would kill David.

[17]But Abishai, the son of Zeruiah, came to save David. He struck the Philistine down and killed him.

Then David's men took an oath and made a promise. They said to David, "We never want you to go out with us to battle again. You are the lamp of Israel's kingdom. We want that lamp to keep on burning brightly."

[18]There was another battle against the Philistines. It took place at Gob. At that time Sibbecai killed Saph. Sibbecai was a Hushathite. Saph was from the family line of Rapha.

[19]In another battle against the Philistines at Gob, Elhanan killed Goliath's brother. Elhanan was the son of Jaare-Oregim from Bethlehem. Goliath was from the city of Gath. His spear was as big as a weaver's rod.

[20]There was still another battle. It took place at
Gath. A huge man lived there. He had six fingers
on each hand and six toes on each foot. So the total
number of his toes and fingers was 24. He was also
from the family of Rapha. [21]He made fun of Israel. So Jonathan killed him. Jonathan was the son of
David's brother Shimeah.

[22]Those four Philistine men lived in Gath. They were from the family line of Rapha. David and his men killed them.

David Sings Praises to the LORD

22 David sang the words of this song to the
LORD. He sang them when the LORD saved
him from the powerful hand of all of his enemies
and of Saul. [2]He said,

"The LORD is my rock and my fort. He is the
One who saves me.
[3] My God is my rock. I go to him for safety.
He is like a shield to me. He's the power
that saves me.
He's my place of safety. I go to him for help.
He's my Savior.
He saves me from those who want to
hurt me.
[4] I call out to the LORD. He is worthy of praise.
He saves me from my enemies.

[5] "The waves of death were all around me.
A destroying flood swept over me.
[6] The ropes of the grave were tight around me.
Death set its trap in front of me.
[7] When I was in trouble I called out to the LORD.
I called out to my God.
From his temple he heard my voice.
My cry for help reached his ears.

[8] "The earth trembled and shook.
The pillars of the heavens rocked back
and forth.
They trembled because the LORD was angry.
[9] Smoke came out of his nose.
Flames of fire came out of his mouth.
Burning coals blazed out of it.
[10] He opened the heavens and came down.
Dark clouds were under his feet.
[11] He got on the cherubim and flew.
The wings of the wind lifted him up.
[12] He covered himself with darkness.
The dark rain clouds of the sky were like a
tent around him.
[13] From the brightness that was all around him
flashes of lightning blazed out.
[14] The LORD thundered from heaven.
The voice of the Most High God was heard.
[15] He shot his arrows and scattered our enemies.
He sent flashes of lightning and chased the
enemies away.
[16] The bottom of the sea could be seen.
The foundations of the earth were uncovered.
It happened when the LORD's anger blazed out.
It came like a blast of breath from his nose.

[17] "He reached down from heaven. He took hold
of me.
He lifted me out of deep waters.
[18] He saved me from my powerful enemies.
He set me free from those who were too
strong for me.
[19] They stood up to me when I was in trouble.
But the LORD helped me.
[20] He brought me out into a wide and safe place.
He saved me because he was pleased
with me.

[21] "The LORD has been good to me because I do
what is right.
He has rewarded me because I lead a
pure life.
[22] I have lived the way the LORD wanted me to.
I haven't done evil by turning away from
my God.
[23] I keep all of his laws in mind.
I haven't turned away from his commands.
[24] He knows that I am without blame.
He knows I've kept myself from sinning.
[25] The LORD has rewarded me for doing what
is right.
He has rewarded me because I haven't done
anything wrong.

[26] "LORD, to those who are faithful you show that
you are faithful.
To those who are without blame you show
that you are without blame.
[27] To those who are pure you show that you
are pure.
But to those whose paths are crooked you
show that you are clever.
[28] You save those who aren't proud.
But you watch the proud to bring them
down.
[29] LORD, you are my lamp.
You bring light into my darkness.
[30] With your help I can attack a troop of soldiers.
With the help of my God I can climb over
a wall.

31 "God's way is perfect.
The word of the LORD doesn't have any flaws.
He is like a shield
to all who go to him for safety.
32 Who is God except the LORD?
Who is the Rock except our God?
33 God gives me strength for the battle.
He makes my way perfect.
34 He makes my feet like the feet of a deer.
He helps me stand on the highest places.
35 He trains my hands to fight every battle.
My arms can bend a bow of bronze.
36 LORD, you are like a shield that keeps me safe.
You help me win the battle.
You bend down to make me great.
37 You give me a wide path to walk in
so that I don't twist my ankles.

38 "I chased my enemies and crushed them.
I didn't turn back until they were destroyed.
39 I crushed them completely so that they couldn't get up.
They fell under my feet.
40 LORD, you gave me strength to fight the battle.
You made my enemies bow down at my feet.
41 You made them turn their backs and run away.
So I destroyed my enemies.
42 They cried out for help. But there was no one to save them.
They called out to you. But you didn't answer them.
43 I beat them as fine as the dust of the earth.
I pounded them and walked on them like mud in the streets.

44 "You saved me when my own people attacked me.
You have kept me as the ruler over nations.
People I didn't know serve me now.
45 People from other lands bow down to me in fear.
As soon as they hear me, they obey me.
46 All of them give up hope.
They come trembling out of their hiding places.

47 "The LORD lives! Give praise to my Rock!
Give honor to God, the Rock! He is my Savior!
48 He is the God who pays my enemies back.
He brings the nations under my control.
49 He sets me free from my enemies.
You have honored me more than them.
You have saved me from men who want to hurt me.
50 LORD, I will praise you among the nations.
I will sing praises to you.
51 You help me win great battles.
You show your faithful love to your anointed king.
You show it to me and my family forever."

David's Last Words

23 Here are David's last words. He said,

"I am David, the son of Jesse. God has given me a message.
The Most High God has greatly honored me.
The God of Jacob anointed me as king.
I am Israel's singer of songs.
2 "The Spirit of the LORD spoke through me.
I spoke his word with my tongue.
3 The God of Israel spoke.
The Rock of Israel said to me,
'A king must rule over people in a way that is right.
He must have respect for me when he rules.
4 Then he will be like the light of morning at sunrise
when there aren't any clouds.
He will be like the bright sun after rain
that makes the grass grow on the earth.'

5 "Isn't my royal family right with God?
Hasn't he made a covenant with me that will last forever?
Every part of it was well prepared and made secure.
Won't he save me completely?
Won't he give me everything I long for?
6 But evil people are like thorns that are thrown away.
You can't pick them up with your hands.
7 Even if you touch them,
you must use an iron tool or a spear.
Thorns are burned up right where they are."

David's Mighty Men

8 Here are the names of David's mighty men.
Josheb-Basshebeth was chief of the Three. He
was a Tahkemonite. He used his spear against 800
men. He killed all of them at one time.
9 Next to him was Eleazar. He was one of the
three mighty men. He was the son of Dodai, the
Ahohite. Eleazar was with David at Pas Dammim.
That's where Israel's army made fun of the Philistines who were gathered there for battle. Then the
men of Israel pulled back.
10 But Eleazar stayed right where he was. He
struck the Philistines down until his hand grew
tired. But he still held on to his sword. The LORD
helped him win a great battle that day. The troops
returned to Eleazar. They came back to him only to
take what they wanted from the dead bodies.
11 Next to him was Shammah, the son of Agee.
Shammah was a Hararite. The Philistines gathered
together at a place where there was a field full of
lentils. Israel's troops ran away from them.
12 But Shammah took his stand in the middle of
the field. He didn't let the Philistines capture it. He
struck them down. The LORD helped him win a
great battle.

13David was at the cave of Adullam. During
harvest time, three of the 30 chief men came down
to him there. A group of Philistines was camped in
the Valley of Rephaim. 14At that time David was
in his usual place of safety. Some Philistine troops
were stationed at Bethlehem.

15David longed for water. He said, "I wish
someone would get me a drink of water from the
well that is near the gate of Bethlehem."

16So the three mighty men fought their way past
the Philistine guards. They got some water from
the well that was near the gate of Bethlehem. They
took the water back to David.

But David refused to drink it. Instead, he
poured it out as a drink offering to the LORD.
17"LORD, I would never drink that water!" David
said. "It stands for the blood of these men. They
put their lives in danger by going to Bethlehem to
get it." So David wouldn't drink it.

Those were some of the brave things the three
mighty men did.

18Abishai was chief over the Three. He was the
brother of Joab, the son of Zeruiah. He used his
spear against 300 men. He killed all of them. So
he became as famous as the Three were. 19In fact,
he was even more honored than the Three. He
became their commander. But he wasn't included
among them.

20Benaiah was a great hero from Kabzeel. He
was the son of Jehoiada. Benaiah did many brave
things. He struck down two of Moab's best fighting men. He also went down into a pit on a snowy
day. He killed a lion there.

21And he struck down a huge Egyptian. The Egyptian was holding a spear. Benaiah went out to fight
against him with a club. He grabbed the spear out of
the Egyptian's hand. Then he killed him with it.

22Those were some of the brave things Benaiah,
the son of Jehoiada, did. He too was as famous as
the three mighty men were. 23He was honored
more than any of the Thirty. But he wasn't
included among the Three. David put him in
charge of his own personal guards.

24 Here is a list of David's men who were among the Thirty.

Asahel, the brother of Joab
Elhanan, the son of Dodo, from Bethlehem
25 Shammah, the Harodite
Elika, the Harodite
26 Helez, the Paltite
Ira, the son of Ikkesh, from Tekoa
27 Abiezer from Anathoth
Mebunnai, the Hushathite
28 Zalmon, the Ahohite
Maharai from Netophah
29 Heled, the son of Baanah, from Netophah
Ithai, the son of Ribai, from Gibeah in Benjamin
30 Benaiah from Pirathon
Hiddai from the valleys of Gaash
31 Abi-Albon, the Arbathite
Azmaveth, the Barhumite
32 Eliahba, the Shaalbonite
the sons of Jashen
Jonathan, 33the son of Shammah, the Hararite
Ahiam, the son of Sharar, the Hararite
34 Eliphelet, the son of Ahasbai, the Maacathite
Eliam, the son of Ahithophel, from Giloh
35 Hezro from Carmel
Paarai, the Arbite
36 Igal, the son of Nathan, from Zobah
the son of Hagri
37 Zelek from Ammon
Naharai from Beeroth, who carried the armor of Joab, the son of Zeruiah
38 Ira, the Ithrite
Gareb, the Ithrite
39 Uriah, the Hittite

The total number of men was 37.

David Counts His Fighting Men

24 The LORD's anger burned against Israel.
He stirred up David against them. He said,
"Go! Count the men of Israel and Judah."

2So the king spoke to Joab and the army commanders who were with him. He said, "Go all
through the territories of the tribes of Israel. Go
from Dan all the way to Beersheba. Count the
fighting men. Then I'll know how many there are."

3Joab replied to the king. He said, "King David,
you are my master. May the LORD your God multiply the troops 100 times. And may you live to see
it. But why would you want me to count the fighting men?"

4In spite of what Joab said, the king's word had
more authority than the word of Joab and the army
commanders did. So they left the king and went
out to count the fighting men of Israel.

5They went across the Jordan River. They
camped south of the town in the middle of the Arnon River valley near Aroer. Then they went
through Gad and continued on to Jazer. 6They
went to Gilead and the area of Tahtim Hodshi.
They continued to Dan Jaan and on around toward
Sidon. 7Then they went toward the fort of Tyre.
They went to all of the towns of the Hivites and
Canaanites. Finally, they went on to Beersheba. It
was in the Negev Desert of Judah.

8They finished going through the entire land.
Then they came back to Jerusalem. They had been
gone for nine months and 20 days.

9Joab reported to the king how many fighting
men he had counted. In Israel there were 800,000
men who were able to handle a sword. In Judah
there were 500,000.

10David felt sorry that he had counted the fighting men. So he said to the LORD, "I committed a
great sin when I counted Judah and Israel's men.
LORD, I beg you to take away my guilt. I've done
a very foolish thing."

11Before David got up the next morning, a message from the LORD came to the prophet Gad. He was David's seer. The message said, 12"Go and tell David, 'The LORD says, "I could punish you in three different ways. Choose one of them for me to use against you."'"

13So Gad went to David. He said to him, "Take your choice. Do you want three years when there won't be enough food in your land? Or do you want three months when you will run away from your enemies while they chase you? Or do you want three days when there will be a plague in your land? Think it over. Then take your pick. Tell me how to answer the One who sent me."

14David said to Gad, "I'm suffering terribly. Let us fall into the hands of the LORD. His mercy is great. But don't let me fall into the hands of men."

15So the LORD sent a plague on Israel. It lasted from that morning until he decided to end it. From Dan all the way to Beersheba 70,000 people died.

16The angel reached his hand out to destroy Jerusalem. But the LORD was very sad because of the plague. So he spoke to the angel who was making the people suffer. He said, "That is enough! Do not kill any more people." The angel of the LORD was at Araunah's threshing floor. Araunah was from the city of Jebus.

17David saw the angel who was striking the people down. David said to the LORD, "I'm the one who has sinned. I'm the one who has done what is wrong. These people are like sheep. What have they done? Let your powerful hand punish me and my family."

David Builds an Altar

18On that day Gad went to David. Gad said to him, "Go up to the threshing floor of Araunah, the Jebusite. Build an altar there to honor the LORD."

19So David went up and did it. He did what the LORD had commanded through Gad.

20Araunah looked and saw the king and his officials coming toward him. So he went out to welcome them. He bowed down to the king with his face toward the ground.

21Araunah said, "King David, you are my master. Why have you come to see me?"

"To buy your threshing floor," David answered. "I want to build an altar there to honor the LORD. When I do, the plague on the people will be stopped."

22Araunah said to David, "Take anything that pleases you. Offer it up. Here are oxen for the burnt offering. Here are threshing sleds. And here are wooden collars from the necks of the oxen. Use all of the wood to burn the offering. 23King David, I'll give all of it to you." Araunah continued, "And may the LORD your God accept you."

24But the king replied to Araunah, "No. I want to pay you for it. I won't sacrifice to the LORD my God burnt offerings that haven't cost me anything."

So David bought the threshing floor and the oxen. He paid 20 ounces of silver for them. 25David built an altar there to honor the LORD. He sacrificed burnt offerings and friendship offerings.

Then the LORD answered prayer and blessed the land. The plague on Israel was stopped.

1 Kings

Adonijah Makes Himself King

1 King David was now very old. He couldn't keep warm even when blankets were spread over him. 2So his servants spoke to him. They said, "You are our king and master. Please let us try to find a young virgin to help you. She can take care of you. She can lie down beside you. Then you can keep warm."

3So David's servants looked all over Israel for a beautiful young woman. They found Abishag. She was from the town of Shunem. They brought her to the king. 4The woman was very beautiful. She took care of the king and served him. But the king didn't have sex with her.

5Adonijah was the son of David and his wife Haggith. He came forward and announced, "I'm going to be the next king." So he got chariots and horses ready. He also got 50 men to run in front of him.

6His father had never tried to stop him from doing what he wanted to. His father had never asked him, "Why are you acting the way you do?"

Adonijah was also very handsome. Now that Absalom was dead, Adonijah was David's oldest son.

7Adonijah talked things over with Joab, the son of Zeruiah. He also talked with the priest Abiathar. They agreed to help him.

8But the priest Zadok and Benaiah, the son of Jehoiada, didn't join Adonijah. The prophet Nathan didn't join him. Shimei and Rei didn't join him. And neither did David's special guard.

9Adonijah sacrificed sheep, cattle and fat calves. He sacrificed them at the Stone of Zoheleth near En Rogel. He invited all of his brothers, the king's sons, and all of the men of Judah who were royal officials.

10But he didn't invite Benaiah or the prophet Nathan. He didn't invite the special guard or his brother Solomon either.

11Nathan spoke to Solomon's mother Bathsheba. He asked, "Haven't you heard? Adonijah, the son of Haggith, has made himself king. And King David doesn't even know about it.

12"So let me tell you what to do to save your life. It will also save the life of your son Solomon. 13Go in and see King David. Say to him, 'You are my king and master. You took an oath. You promised me, "You can be sure that your son Solomon will be king after me. He will sit on my throne." If that's really true, why has Adonijah become king?'

14"While you are still talking to the king, I'll come in. I'll tell him that what you have said is true."

15So Bathsheba went to see the old king in his room. Abishag, the Shunammite, was taking care of him there. 16Bathsheba bowed low. She got down on her knees in front of the king.

"What do you want?" the king asked.

17She said to him, "My master, you took an oath in the name of the LORD your God. You promised me, 'Your son Solomon will be king after me. He will sit on my throne.'

18"But now Adonijah has made himself king. And you don't even know about it. 19He has sacrificed large numbers of cattle, fat calves and sheep. He has invited all of the king's sons. He has also invited the priest Abiathar and Joab, the commander of the army. But he hasn't invited your son Solomon.

20"You are my king and master. All of the people of Israel are watching to see what you will do. They want to find out from you who will sit on the throne after you. 21If you don't do something, I and my son Solomon will be treated like people who have committed crimes. That will happen as soon as you join the members of your family who have already died."

22While she was still speaking with the king, the prophet Nathan arrived. 23The king was told, "The prophet Nathan is here." So Nathan went to the king. He bowed down with his face toward the ground.

24Nathan said, "You are my king and master. Have you announced that Adonijah will be king after you? Have you said he will sit on your throne? 25Today he has gone down outside the city. He has sacrificed large numbers of cattle, fat calves and sheep. He has invited all of the king's sons. He has also invited the commanders of the army and the priest Abiathar. Even now they are eating and drinking with him. They are saying, 'May King Adonijah live a long time!'

26"But he didn't invite me. He didn't invite the priest Zadok or Benaiah, the son of Jehoiada. He didn't invite your son Solomon either.

27"King David, have you allowed all of that to happen? Did you do it without letting us know about it? Why didn't you tell us who is going to sit on your throne after you?"

David Makes Solomon King

28King David said, "Tell Bathsheba to come in." So she came and stood in front of the king.

29Then the king took an oath and made a promise. He said, "The LORD has saved me from all of my troubles. You can be sure that he lives. 30And you can be just as sure that I will do today what I promised in the name of the LORD. He is the God of Israel. I promised you that your son Solomon would be king after me. He will sit on my throne in my place."

31Then Bathsheba bowed low with her face
toward the ground. She got down on her knees in
front of the king. She said, "King David, you are
my master. May you live forever!"
32King David said, "Tell the priest Zadok and
the prophet Nathan to come in. Also tell Benaiah,
the son of Jehoiada, to come." So they came to the
king.
33He said to them, "Take my officials with you.
Put my son Solomon on my own mule. Take him
down to the Gihon spring. 34Have the priest Zadok
and the prophet Nathan anoint him as king over Israel there. Blow a trumpet. Shout, 'May King Solomon live a long time!' 35Then come back up to
the city with him. Have him sit on my throne. He
will rule in my place. I've appointed him ruler
over Israel and Judah."
36Benaiah, the son of Jehoiada, answered the
king. "Amen!" he said. "May the LORD your God
make it come true. 37You are my king and master.
The LORD has been with you. May he also be with
Solomon. King David, may the LORD make Solomon's kingdom even greater than yours!"
38So the priest Zadok and the prophet Nathan
left the palace. Benaiah, the son of Jehoiada, went
with them. So did the Kerethites and Pelethites.
They put Solomon on King David's mule. And
they brought him down to the Gihon spring.
39The priest Zadok had gotten an animal horn
that was filled with olive oil. He had taken it from
the sacred tent. He anointed Solomon with the oil.
The trumpet was blown. All of the people shouted,
"May King Solomon live a long time!"
40Then they went up toward the city. Solomon
was leading the way. The people were playing
flutes. They were filled with great joy. The ground
shook because of all of the noise.
41Adonijah and all of his guests heard it. They
were just finishing their meal. Joab heard the
sound of the trumpet. So he asked, "What does all
of that noise in the city mean?"
42While Joab was still speaking, Jonathan
arrived. Jonathan was the son of the priest Abiathar. Adonijah said, "Come in. I have respect for
you. You must be bringing good news."
43"No! I'm not!" Jonathan answered. "Our master King David has made Solomon king. 44David
sent the priest Zadok and the prophet Nathan along
with Solomon. He also sent Benaiah, the son of Jehoiada, with him. He sent the Kerethites and Pelethites with him too. They put him on the king's
mule. 45They took him down to the Gihon spring.
There the priest Zadok and the prophet Nathan
anointed him as king. Now they've gone back up
to the city. They were cheering all the way. The
city is filled with the sound of it. That's the noise
you hear.
46"And that's not all. Solomon has taken his seat
on the royal throne. 47The royal officials came to
give their blessing to our master King David. They
said, 'May your God make Solomon's name more
famous than yours! May he make Solomon's kingdom greater than yours!'
"While King David was sitting on his bed, he
bowed in worship. 48He said, 'I praise the LORD.
He is the God of Israel. He has let me live to see
my son sitting on my throne today as the next
king.'"
49When all of Adonijah's guests heard that, they
were terrified. So they got up and scattered.
50Adonijah was afraid of what Solomon might
do to him. So he went and grabbed hold of the
horns that stuck out from the upper corners of the
altar for burnt offerings.
51Then Solomon was told, "King Solomon, Adonijah is afraid of you. He's holding onto the horns
of the altar. He says, 'I want King Solomon to take
an oath today. I want him to promise that he won't
kill me with his sword.'"
52Solomon replied, "Let him show that he's a
man people can respect. Then not even one hair on
his head will fall to the ground. But if I find out
he's done something evil, he will die."
53King Solomon got some men to bring Adonijah down from the altar. He came and bowed down
to King Solomon. Solomon said, "Go on home."

David Gives Orders to Solomon

2 The time came near for David to die. So he
gave orders to his son Solomon. He said,
2"I'm about to die, just as everyone else on
earth does. So be strong. Show how brave you are.
3Do everything the LORD your God requires. Live
the way he wants you to. Obey his orders and commands. Keep his laws and rules. Do everything
that is written in the Law of Moses. Then you will
have success in everything you do. You will succeed everywhere you go.
4"The LORD will keep the promise he made to
me. He said, 'Your sons must be careful about how
they live. They must be faithful to me with all their
heart and soul. Then you will always have a man
sitting on the throne of Israel.'
5"You yourself know what Joab, the son of Zeruiah, did to me. You know that he killed Abner, the
son of Ner, and Amasa, the son of Jether. They
were the two commanders of Israel's armies. He
killed them in a time of peace. It wasn't a time of
war. Joab spilled the blood of Abner and Amasa. It
stained the belt that was around his waist. It also
stained the sandals on his feet. 6You are wise. So I
leave him in your hands. Just don't let him live to
become an old man. Don't let him die peacefully.
7"But be kind to the sons of Barzillai from Gilead. Provide what they need. They were faithful
to me when I had to run away from your brother
Absalom.
8"Don't forget Shimei, the son of Gera. He's
still around. He's from Bahurim in the territory of
Benjamin. He called down bitter curses on me. He
did it on the day I went to Mahanaim. Later, he
came down to welcome me at the Jordan River. At

that time I took an oath in the name of the LORD. I promised Shimei, 'I won't put you to death with my sword.' 9But now I want you to think of him as guilty. You are wise. You will know what to do to him. Don't let him live to become an old man. Put him to death."

10David joined the members of his family who had already died. His body was buried in the City of David. 11He had ruled over Israel for 40 years. He ruled for seven years in Hebron. Then he ruled for 33 years in Jerusalem.

12So Solomon sat on the throne of his father David. His position as king was made secure.

Solomon's Kingdom Is Made Secure

13Adonijah was the son of David's wife Haggith. He went to Bathsheba. She was Solomon's mother. She asked Adonijah, "Have you come in peace?"

He answered, "Yes. I've come in peace." 14He continued, "I want to ask you something."

"Go ahead," she replied.

15He said, "As you know, the kingdom belonged to me. The whole nation of Israel thought of me as their king. But now things have changed. The kingdom belongs to my brother. The LORD has given it to him. 16But I have a favor to ask of you. Don't say no to me."

"Go ahead," she said.

17So he continued, "Please ask King Solomon for a favor. He won't say no to you. Ask him to give me Abishag from Shunem to be my wife."

18"All right," Bathsheba replied. "I'll speak to the king for you."

19So Bathsheba went to King Solomon. She went to him to speak for Adonijah. The king stood up to greet her. He bowed down to her. Then he sat down on his throne. He had a throne brought for his mother. She sat down at his right side.

20"I have one small favor to ask of you," she said. "Don't say no to me."

The king replied, "Mother, go ahead and ask. I won't say no to you."

21She said, "Let your brother Adonijah get married to Abishag, the Shunammite."

22King Solomon answered his mother, "Why are you asking for Abishag, the Shunammite, for Adonijah? You might as well ask me to give him the whole kingdom! After all, he's my older brother. And he doesn't want the kingdom only for himself. He also wants it for the priest Abiathar and for Joab, the son of Zeruiah."

23Then King Solomon took an oath and made a promise in the name of the LORD. He said, "Adonijah will pay with his life because of what he has asked for. If he doesn't, may God punish me greatly. 24The LORD has made my position as king secure. I'm sitting on the throne of my father David. The LORD has built a royal house for me, just as he promised. You can be sure that the LORD lives. And you can be just as sure that Adonijah will be put to death today."

25So King Solomon gave the order to Benaiah, the son of Jehoiada. Benaiah struck Adonijah down. And Adonijah died.

26The king spoke to the priest Abiathar. He said, "Go back to your fields in Anathoth. You should really be put to death. But I won't have it done now. That's because you carried the ark of the LORD and King. You did it for my father David. You shared all of his hard times."

27So Solomon wouldn't let Abiathar serve as a priest of the LORD anymore. That's how the message the LORD had spoken at Shiloh came true. He had spoken it about the family of Eli.

28News of what Solomon had done reached Joab. Joab had never made evil plans along with Absalom. But he had joined Adonijah. So he ran to the tent of the LORD. He took hold of the horns that stuck out from the upper corners of the altar for burnt offerings.

29King Solomon was told that Joab had run to the tent. He was also told that Joab was by the altar.

Then Solomon gave the order to Benaiah, the son of Jehoiada. He told him, "Go! Strike him down!"

30So Benaiah entered the tent of the LORD. He said to Joab, "The king says, 'Come on out!'"

But Joab answered, "No. I'd rather die here."

Benaiah told the king what Joab had said to him.

31Then the king commanded Benaiah, "Do what he says. Strike him down. Bury his body. Then I and my family won't be held accountable for the blood Joab spilled. He killed people who weren't guilty of doing anything wrong. 32The LORD will pay him back for the blood he spilled. Joab attacked two men. He killed them with his sword. And my father David didn't even know anything about it.

"Joab killed Abner, the son of Ner. Abner was the commander of Israel's army. Joab also killed Amasa, the son of Jether. Amasa was the commander of Judah's army. Abner and Amasa were better men than Joab is. They were more honest than he is. 33May Joab and his children after him be held forever accountable for spilling the blood of Abner and Amasa.

"But may David and his children after him enjoy the LORD's peace and rest forever. May the LORD also give his peace to David's royal house and kingdom forever."

34So Benaiah, the son of Jehoiada, went up to the LORD's tent. There he struck Joab down. And he killed him. Joab's body was buried on his own land in the desert.

35The king put Benaiah in charge of the army. Benaiah took Joab's place. The king also put the priest Zadok in Abiathar's place.

36Then the king sent for Shimei. He said to him, "Build yourself a house in Jerusalem. Live there. Don't go anywhere else. 37You must not leave the city and go across the Kidron Valley. If you do, you can be sure you will die. And it will be your own fault."

[38]Shimei replied to the king, "You are my king and master. What you say is good. I'll do it." Shimei stayed in Jerusalem for a long time.

[39]Three years after Solomon had talked with Shimei, two of Shimei's slaves ran off. They went to Achish, the king of Gath. He was the son of Maacah. Shimei was told, "Your slaves are in Gath." [40]When Shimei heard that, he put a saddle on his donkey. Then he went to Achish at Gath to look for his slaves. Shimei found them and brought them back from Gath.

[41]Solomon was told that Shimei had left Jerusalem. He was told he had gone to Gath and had returned.

[42]So the king sent for Shimei. He said to him, "Didn't I make you take an oath in the name of the LORD? Didn't I warn you? I said, 'You must not leave the city and go somewhere else. If you do, you can be sure you will die.' At that time you said to me, 'What you say is good. I'll obey your command.' [43]So why didn't you keep your oath to the LORD? Why didn't you obey the command I gave you?"

[44]The king continued, "You know all of the wrong things you did to my father David. In your heart you know them. Now the LORD will pay you back for what you did. [45]But I will be blessed. The LORD will make David's kingdom secure forever."

[46]Then the king gave the order to Benaiah, the son of Jehoiada. Benaiah left the palace and struck Shimei down. And he killed him.

So the kingdom was now made secure in Solomon's hands.

Solomon Asks God for Wisdom

3 Solomon and Pharaoh, the king of Egypt, agreed to help each other. So Solomon got married to Pharaoh's daughter. He brought her to the City of David. She stayed there until he finished building his palace, the LORD's temple, and the wall that was around Jerusalem.

[2]But the people continued to offer sacrifices at the high places where they worshiped. That's because a temple hadn't been built yet where the LORD would put his Name.

[3]Solomon showed his love for the LORD. He did it by obeying the laws his father David had taught him. But Solomon offered sacrifices at the high places. He also burned incense there.

[4]King Solomon went to the city of Gibeon to offer sacrifices. That's where the most important high place was. He offered 1,000 burnt offerings on the altar that was there.

[5]The LORD appeared to Solomon at Gibeon. He spoke to him in a dream during the night. God said, "Ask for anything you want me to give you."

[6]Solomon answered, "You have been very kind to my father David, your servant. That's because he was faithful to you. He did what was right. His heart was honest. And you have continued to be very kind to him. You have given him a son to sit on his throne this very day.

[7]"LORD my God, you have now made me king. You have put me in the place of my father David. But I'm only a little child. I don't know how to carry out my duties. [8]I'm here among the people you have chosen. They are a great nation. They are more than anyone can count. [9]So give me a heart that understands. Then I can rule over your people. I can tell the difference between what is right and what is wrong. Who can possibly rule over this great nation of yours?"

[10]The Lord was pleased that Solomon had asked for that. [11]So God said to him, "You have not asked to live for a long time. You have not asked to be wealthy. You have not even asked to have your enemies killed. Instead, you have asked for understanding. You want to do what is right and fair when you judge people. Because that is what you have asked for, [12]I will give it to you. I will give you a wise and understanding heart. So here is what will be true of you. There has never been anyone like you. And there never will be.

[13]"And that is not all. I will give you what you have not asked for. I will give you riches and honor. As long as you live, no other king will be as great as you are. [14]Live the way I want you to. Obey my laws and commands, just as your father David did. Then I will let you live for a long time."

[15]Solomon woke up. He realized he had been dreaming.

He returned to Jerusalem. He stood in front of the ark of the LORD's covenant. He sacrificed burnt offerings and friendship offerings. Then he gave a big dinner for all of his officials.

Solomon Judges Wisely

[16]Two prostitutes came to the king. They stood in front of him. [17]One of them said, "My master, this woman and I live in the same house. I had a baby while she was there with me. [18]Three days after my child was born, this woman also had a baby. We were alone. There wasn't anyone in the house but the two of us.

[19]"During the night this woman's baby died. It happened because she was lying on top of him. [20]So she got up in the middle of the night. She took my son from my side while I was asleep. She put him by her breast. Then she put her dead son by my breast. [21]The next morning, I got up to nurse my son. But he was dead! I looked at him closely in the morning light. And I saw that it wasn't my baby."

[22]The other woman said, "No! The living baby is my son. The dead one belongs to you."

But the first woman said, "No! The dead baby is yours. The living one belongs to me." So they argued in front of the king.

[23]The king said, "One of you says, 'My son is alive. Your son is dead.' The other one says, 'No! Your son is dead. Mine is alive.'"

24He continued, "Bring me a sword." So a sword was brought to him. 25Then he gave an order. He said, "Cut the living child in two. Give half to one woman and half to the other."

26The woman whose son was alive was filled with deep concern for her son. She said to the king, "My master, please give her the living baby! Don't kill him!"

But the other woman said, "Neither one of us will have him. Cut him in two!"

27Then the king made his decision. He said, "Give the living baby to the first woman. Don't kill him. She's his mother."

28All of the people of Israel heard about the decision the king had given. That gave them great respect for him. They saw that God had given him wisdom. They knew that Solomon would do what was right and fair when he judged people.

Solomon's Officials and Governors

4 So King Solomon ruled over the whole nation of Israel. 2Here are the names of his chief officials.

Azariah was the priest. He was the son of Zadok.
3 Elihoreph and Ahijah were secretaries. They were the sons of Shisha.
Jehoshaphat kept the records. He was the son of Ahilud.
4 Benaiah was the commander in chief. He was the son of Jehoiada.
Zadok and Abiathar were priests.
5 Azariah was in charge of the local officials. He was the son of Nathan.
Zabud was a priest. He was the king's personal adviser. He was the son of Nathan.
6 Ahishar was in charge of the palace.
Adoniram was in charge of those who were forced to work for the king. He was the son of Abda.

7Solomon also had 12 local governors over the whole land of Israel. They provided supplies for the king and the royal family. Each governor had to provide supplies for one month out of each year. 8Here are their names and areas.

Ben-Hur's area was the hill country of Ephraim.
9 Ben-Deker's area was Makaz, Shaalbim, Beth Shemesh and Elon Bethhanan.
10 Ben-Hesed's area was Arubboth. Socoh and the whole land of Hepher were included in his area.
11 Ben-Abinadab's area was Naphoth Dor. He got married to Solomon's daughter Taphath.
12 Baana's area was Taanach, Megiddo and the whole territory of Beth Shan. Beth Shan was next to Zarethan below Jezreel. Baana's area reached from Beth Shan all the way to Abel Meholah. It also went across to Jokmeam. Baana was the son of Ahilud.
13 Ben-Geber's area was Ramoth Gilead. The settlements of Jair, the son of Manasseh, were included in his area in Gilead. The area of Argob in Bashan was also included. That area had 60 large cities that had high walls around them. The city gates were made secure with heavy bronze bars.
14 Ahinadab's area was Mahanaim. He was the son of Iddo.
15 Ahimaaz's area was Naphtali. He had gotten married to Basemath. She was Solomon's daughter.
16 Baana's area was Asher and Aloth. He was the son of Hushai.
17 Jehoshaphat's area was Issachar. He was the son of Paruah.
18 Shimei's area was Benjamin. He was the son of Ela.
19 Geber's area was Gilead. He was the only governor over the area. He was the son of Uri. Gilead had been the country of Sihon and Og. Sihon had been king of the Amorites. Og had been king of Bashan.

Solomon's Daily Supplies

20There were many people in Judah and Israel. In fact, they were as many as the grains of sand on the seashore. They ate, drank and were happy.

21Solomon ruled over all of the kingdoms from the Euphrates River to the land of the Philistines. He ruled as far as the border of Egypt. All of those countries brought the gifts he required them to bring him. And Solomon ruled over those countries for his whole life.

22Here are the supplies Solomon required every day.

185 bushels of fine flour
375 bushels of meal
23 ten head of cattle that had been fed by hand
20 head of cattle that had been fed on grasslands
100 sheep and goats
deer, antelopes and roebucks
the finest birds

24Solomon ruled over all of the kingdoms that were west of the Euphrates River. He ruled from Tiphsah all the way to Gaza. And he had peace and rest on every side.

25While Solomon was king, Judah and Israel lived in safety. They were secure from Dan all the way to Beersheba. Each man had his own vine and fig tree.

26Solomon had 4,000 spaces where he kept his chariot horses. He had a total of 12,000 horses.

27The local officials provided supplies for King Solomon. They provided them for all who ate at the king's table. Each official provided supplies for one month every year. The officials made sure the king had everything he needed. 28They also brought barley and straw for the chariot horses and the other horses. Each of them brought the amounts that were required of them. They brought them to the proper places.

God Makes Solomon Very Wise

29God made Solomon very wise. His understanding couldn't even be measured. It was like the sand on the seashore. People can't measure that either.

30Solomon's wisdom was greater than the wisdom of all of the people of the east. It was greater than all of the wisdom of Egypt. 31Solomon was wiser than any other man. He was wiser than Ethan, the Ezrahite. He was wiser than Heman, Calcol and Darda. They were the sons of Mahol. Solomon became famous in all of the nations that were around him.

32He spoke 3,000 proverbs. He wrote 1,005 songs. 33He explained all about plants. He knew everything about them, from the cedar trees in Lebanon to the hyssop plants that grow out of walls. He taught about animals and birds. He also taught about reptiles and fish.

34The kings of all of the world's nations heard about how wise Solomon was. So they sent their people to listen to him.

Solomon Asks Hiram to Help Build the Temple

5 Hiram was the king of Tyre. He heard that Solomon had been anointed as king. He heard that Solomon had become the next king after his father David. Hiram had always been David's friend. So Hiram sent his messengers to Solomon.

2Then Solomon sent a message back to Hiram. It said,

> 3"As you know, my father David had to fight many battles. His enemies attacked him from every side. So he couldn't build a temple where the LORD his God would put his Name. That wouldn't be possible until the LORD had put his enemies under his control.
>
> 4"But now the LORD my God has given me peace and rest on every side. We don't have any enemies. And we don't have any other major problems either. 5So I'm planning to build a temple. I want to build it for the Name of the LORD my God. That's what he told my father David he wanted me to do. He said, 'I will put your son on the throne in your place. He will build a temple. I will put my Name there.'
>
> 6"So give your men orders to cut down cedar trees in Lebanon for me. My men will work with yours. I'll pay you for your men's work. I'll pay any amount you decide on. As you know, we don't have anyone who is as skilled in cutting down trees as the men of Sidon are."

7When Hiram heard Solomon's message, he was very pleased. He said, "May the LORD be praised today. He has given David a wise son to rule over that great nation."

8So Hiram sent a message to Solomon. It said,

> "I have received the message you sent me. I'll do everything you want me to. I'll provide the cedar and pine logs. 9My men will bring them from Lebanon down to the Mediterranean Sea. I'll make them into rafts. I'll float them to the place you want me to. When the rafts arrive, I'll separate the logs from each other. Then you can take them away.
>
> "And here's what I want in return. Provide food for all of the people in my palace."

10So Hiram supplied Solomon with all of the cedar and pine logs he wanted.

11Solomon gave Hiram 125,000 bushels of wheat as food for the people in his palace. He also gave him 115,000 gallons of oil that was made from pressed olives. He did that for Hiram year after year.

12The LORD made Solomon wise, just as he had promised him. There was peace between Hiram and Solomon. The two of them made a peace treaty.

13King Solomon forced men from all over Israel to work hard for him. There were 30,000 of them. 14He sent them off to Lebanon in groups of 10,000 each month. They spent one month in Lebanon. Then they spent two months at home. Adoniram was in charge of the people who were forced to work. 15Solomon had 70,000 people who carried things. He had 80,000 who cut stones in the hills. 16He had 3,300 men who were in charge of the project. They also directed the workers.

17The people did what the king commanded. They removed large blocks of fine stone from a rock pit. They used them to provide a foundation for the temple. 18The skilled workers of Solomon and Hiram cut and prepared the logs and stones. They would later be used in building the temple. The people of Byblos helped the workers.

Solomon Builds the Temple

6 Solomon began to build the temple of the LORD. It was 480 years after the people of Israel had come out of Egypt. It was in the fourth year of Solomon's rule over Israel. He started in the second month. That was the month of Ziv.

2The temple King Solomon built for the LORD was 90 feet long. It was 30 feet wide. And it was 45 feet high. 3The temple had a porch in front of the main hall. The porch was as wide as the temple itself. It was 30 feet wide. It came out 15 feet from the front of the temple. 4Solomon made narrow windows high up in the temple walls.

5He built side rooms around the temple. They were built against the walls of the main hall and the Most Holy Room. 6On the first floor the side rooms were seven and a half feet wide. On the second floor they were nine feet wide. And on the third floor they were ten and a half feet wide. Solomon made the walls of the temple thinner as they went up floor by floor. The result was ledges along the walls. So the floor beams of the side rooms rested on the ledges. The beams didn't go into the temple walls.

7All of the stones that were used for building the temple were shaped where they were cut. So hammers, chisels and other iron tools couldn't be heard where the temple was being built.

8The entrance to the first floor was on the south side of the temple. A stairway led up to the second floor. From there it went on up to the third floor.

9So Solomon built the temple and finished it. He made its roof out of beams and cedar boards. 10He built side rooms all along the temple. Each room was seven and a half feet high. They were joined to the temple by cedar beams.

11A message came to Solomon from the LORD. The LORD said, 12"You are now building this temple. Follow my orders. Keep my rules. Obey all of my commands. Then I will make the promise I gave your father David come true. I will do it through you. 13I will live among my people Israel. I will not desert them."

14So Solomon built the temple and finished it. 15He put cedar boards on its inside walls. He covered them from floor to ceiling. He covered the temple floor with pine boards. 16He put up a wall 30 feet from the back of the temple. He made it with cedar boards from floor to ceiling. That formed a room inside the temple. It was the Most Holy Room. 17The main hall in front of the room was 60 feet long. 18The inside of the temple was covered with cedar wood. Gourds and open flowers were carved on the wood. Everything was cedar. There wasn't any stone showing anywhere.

19Solomon prepared the Most Holy Room inside the temple. That's where the ark of the covenant of the LORD would be placed. 20The Most Holy Room was 30 feet long. It was 30 feet wide. And it was 30 feet high. Solomon covered the inside of it with pure gold. He prepared the cedar altar for burning incense. He covered it with gold. 21Solomon covered the inside of the main hall with pure gold. He placed gold chains across the front of the Most Holy Room. That room was covered with gold. 22So Solomon covered the inside of the whole temple with gold. He also covered the altar for burning incense with gold. It was right in front of the Most Holy Room.

23For the Most Holy Room Solomon made a pair of cherubim. He made them out of olive wood. Each cherub was 15 feet high. 24One wing of the first cherub was seven and a half feet long. The other wing was also seven and a half feet long. So the wings measured 15 feet from tip to tip. 25The second cherub's wings also measured 15 feet from tip to tip. The two cherubim had the same size and shape. 26Each cherub was 15 feet high.

27Solomon placed the cherubim inside the Most Holy Room in the temple. Their wings were spread out. The wing tip of one cherub touched one wall. The wing tip of the other touched the other wall. The tips of their wings touched each other in the middle of the room. 28Solomon covered the cherubim with gold.

29On the walls that were all around the temple he carved cherubim, palm trees and open flowers. He carved them on the walls of the Most Holy Room and the main hall. 30He also covered the floors of those two rooms with gold.

31For the entrance to the Most Holy Room he made two doors out of olive wood. Each doorpost had five sides. 32On the two olive wood doors he carved cherubim, palm trees and open flowers. He covered the cherubim and palm trees with hammered gold.

33In the same way he made olive wood doorposts for the entrance to the main hall. Each doorpost had four sides. 34He also made two pine doors. Each door had two parts. They turned in bases that were shaped like cups. 35He carved cherubim, palm trees and open flowers on the doors. He covered the doors with gold. He hammered the gold evenly over the carvings.

36He used blocks of stone to build a wall around the inside courtyard. The first three layers of the wall were made out of stone. The top layer was made out of beautiful cedar wood.

37The foundation of the LORD's temple was laid in Solomon's fourth year. It was in the month of Ziv. 38The temple was finished in his 11th year. It was in the month of Bul. That was the eighth month. Everything was finished just as the plans required. Solomon had spent seven years building the temple.

Solomon Builds His Palace

7 But it took Solomon 13 years to finish constructing his palace and the other buildings that were related to it.

2He built the Palace of the Forest of Lebanon. It was 150 feet long. It was 75 feet wide. And it was 45 feet high. It had four rows of cedar columns. They held up beautiful cedar beams. 3Above the beams was a roof that was made out of cedar boards. It rested on the columns. There were three rows of beams with 15 in each row. The total number of beams was 45. 4The windows of the palace were placed high up in the walls. They were in groups of three. And they faced each other. 5All of the doorways had frames that were shaped like rectangles. They were in front. They were in groups of three. And they faced each other.

6Solomon made a covered area. It was 75 feet long. And it was 45 feet wide. Its roof was held up by columns. In front of it was a porch. In front of that were pillars and a roof that went out beyond them.

[7]Solomon built the throne hall. It was called the Hall of Justice. That's where he would serve as judge. He covered the hall with cedar boards from floor to ceiling.

[8]The palace where he would live was set farther back. Its plan was something like the plan for the hall. Solomon had gotten married to Pharaoh's daughter. He made a palace for her. It was like the hall.

[9]All of those buildings were made out of blocks of very fine stone. They were cut to the right size. They were shaped with a saw on the back and front sides. Those stones were used for the outside of each building and for the large courtyard. They were also used from the foundations up to the roofs. [10]Large blocks of very fine stone were used for the foundations. Some were 15 feet long. Others were 12 feet long. [11]The walls that were above them were made out of very fine stones. The stones were cut to the right size. On top of them was a layer of cedar beams.

[12]The large courtyard had a wall around it. The first three layers of the wall were made out of blocks of stone. The top layer was made out of beautiful cedar wood. The same thing was done with the inside courtyard of the LORD's temple and its porch.

More Facts About the Temple

[13]King Solomon sent messengers to Tyre. He wanted them to bring Huram back with them. [14]Huram's mother was a widow. She was from the tribe of Naphtali. Huram's father was from Tyre. He was skilled in working with bronze. Huram also was very skilled. He had done all kinds of work with bronze. He came to King Solomon and did all of the work he was asked to do.

[15]Huram made two bronze pillars. Each of them was 27 feet high. And each was 18 feet around. [16]Each pillar had a decorated top that was made out of bronze. Each top was seven and a half feet high.

[17]Chains that were linked together hung down from the tops of the pillars. There were seven chains for each top. [18]Huram made two rows of pomegranates. They circled the chains. The pomegranates decorated the tops of the pillars. Huram did the same thing for each pillar. [19]The tops on the pillars of the porch were shaped like lilies. The lilies were 6 feet high. [20]On the tops of both pillars were 200 pomegranates. They were in rows all around the tops. They were above the part that was shaped like a bowl. And they were next to the chains.

[21]Huram set the pillars up at the temple porch. The pillar on the south he named Jakin. The one on the north he named Boaz. [22]The tops of the pillars were shaped like lilies. So the work on the pillars was finished.

[23]Huram made a huge metal bowl for washing. Its shape was round. It measured 15 feet from rim to rim. It was seven and a half feet high. And it was 45 feet around. [24]Below the rim there was a circle of gourds around the bowl. In every 18 inches around the bowl there were ten gourds. The gourds were arranged in two rows. They were made as part of the bowl itself.

[25]The huge bowl stood on 12 bulls. Three of them faced north. Three faced west. Three faced south. And three faced east. The bowl rested on top of them. Their rear ends were toward the center. [26]The bowl was three inches thick. Its rim was like the rim of a cup. The rim was shaped like the bloom of a lily. The bowl held 11,500 gallons of water.

[27]Huram also made ten stands out of bronze. They could be moved around. Each stand was six feet long. It was six feet wide. And it was four and a half feet high. [28]Here is how the stands were made. They had sides that were joined to posts. [29]On the sides between the posts were lions, bulls and cherubim. They were also on all of the posts. Above and below the lions and bulls were wreaths that were made out of hammered metal.

[30]Each stand had four bronze wheels with bronze axles. Each one had a bowl that rested on four supports. They had wreaths on each side.

[31]There was a round opening on the inside of each stand. The opening had a frame that was 18 inches deep. The sides were 27 inches high from the top of the opening to the bottom of the base. There was carving around the opening. The sides of the stands were square, not round.

[32]The four wheels were under the sides. The axles of the wheels were connected to the stand. Each wheel was 27 inches across. [33]The wheels were made like chariot wheels. All of the axles, rims, spokes and hubs were made out of metal.

[34]Each stand had four handles on it. There was one on each corner. They came out from the stand. [35]At the top of the stand there was a round band. It was nine inches deep. The sides and supports were connected to the top of the stand.

[36]Huram carved cherubim, lions and palm trees on the sides of the stands. He also carved them on the surfaces of the supports. His carving covered every open space. He had also carved wreaths all around.

[37]That's how he made the ten stands. All of them were made in the same molds. And they had the same size and shape.

[38]Then Huram made ten bronze bowls. Each one held 230 gallons. The bowls measured six feet across. There was one bowl for each of the ten stands. [39]He placed five of the stands on the south side of the temple. He placed the other five on the north side. He put the huge bowl on the south side. It was at the southeast corner of the temple. [40]He also made the bowls, shovels and sprinkling bowls.

So Huram finished all of the work he had started for King Solomon. Here's what he made for the LORD's temple.

41 He made the two pillars.
He made the two tops for the pillars. The tops were shaped like bowls.
He made the two sets of chains that were linked together. They decorated the two bowl-shaped tops of the pillars.
42 He made the 400 pomegranates for the two sets of chains. There were two rows of pomegranates for each chain. They decorated the bowl-shaped tops of the pillars.
43 He made the ten stands with their ten bowls.
44 He made the huge bowl. He made the 12 bulls that were under it.
45 He made the pots, shovels and sprinkling bowls.

Huram made all of those objects for King Solomon for the LORD's temple. He made them out of
bronze. Then he shined them up. 46The king had
made them in clay molds. It was done on the flatlands of the Jordan River between Succoth and
Zarethan.

47Solomon didn't weigh any of those things.
There were too many of them to weigh. No one
even tried to weigh the bronze they were made
out of.

48Solomon also made all of the articles that
were in the LORD's temple.

He made the golden altar.
He made the golden table for the holy bread.
49 He made the pure gold lampstands. There were five on the right and five on the left. They were in front of the Most Holy Room.
He made the gold flowers. He made the gold lamps and tongs.
50 He made the bowls, wick cutters, sprinkling bowls, dishes, and shallow cups for burning incense. All of them were made out of pure gold.
He made the gold bases for the doors of the inside room. That's the Most Holy Room. He also made gold bases for the doors of the main hall of the temple.

51King Solomon finished all of the work for the
LORD's temple. Then he brought in the things his
father David had set apart for the LORD. They
included the silver and gold and all of the articles
for the LORD's temple. Solomon placed them with
the other treasures that were there.

Solomon Brings the Ark to the Temple

8 Then King Solomon sent for the elders of Israel. He told them to come to him in Jerusalem. They included all of the leaders of the tribes.
They also included the chiefs of the families of Israel. Solomon wanted them to bring up the ark of
the LORD's covenant from Zion. Zion was the City
of David. 2All of the men of Israel came together
to where King Solomon was. It was at the time of
the Feast of Booths. The feast was held in the
month of Ethanim. That's the seventh month.

3All of the elders of Israel arrived. Then the
priests picked up the ark and carried it. 4They
brought up the ark of the LORD. They also brought
up the Tent of Meeting and all of the sacred articles
that were in the tent. The priests and Levites carried everything up.

5The entire community of Israel had gathered
around King Solomon. All of them were in front
of the ark. They sacrificed huge numbers of sheep
and cattle. There were so many that they couldn't
be recorded. In fact, they couldn't even be
counted.

6The priests brought the ark of the LORD's
covenant to its place in the Most Holy Room of
the temple. They put it under the wings of the
cherubim. 7The cherubim's wings were spread out
over the place where the ark was. They covered
the ark. They also covered the poles that were used
to carry it. 8The poles were so long that their ends
could be seen from the Holy Room in front of the
Most Holy Room. But they couldn't be seen from
outside the Holy Room. They are still there to this
very day.

9There wasn't anything in the ark except the
two stone tablets. Moses had placed them in it at
Mount Horeb. That's where the LORD had made a
covenant with the Israelites. He made it after they
came out of Egypt.

10The priests left the Holy Room. Then the
cloud filled the temple of the LORD. 11The priests
couldn't do their work because of it. That's
because the glory of the LORD filled his temple.

12Then Solomon said, "LORD, you have said you
would live in a dark cloud. 13As you can see, I've
built a beautiful temple for you. You can live in it
forever."

14The whole community of Israel was standing
there. The king turned around and gave them his
blessing. 15Then he said,

"I praise the LORD. He is the God of Israel. With his own mouth he made a promise to
my father David. With his own powerful
hand he made it come true. He said, 16'I
brought my people Israel out of Egypt. Ever
since I did that, I have not chosen a city in
any tribe of Israel where a temple could be
built for my Name. But I have chosen David
to rule over my people Israel.'

17"With all his heart my father David
wanted to build a temple. He wanted to do it
so the LORD could put his Name there. The
LORD is the God of Israel.

18"But the LORD spoke to my father David. He said, 'With all your heart you wanted
to build a temple for my Name. It is good

that you wanted to do that. 19But you will not build the temple. Instead, your son will build the temple for my Name. He is your own flesh and blood.'

20"The LORD has kept the promise he made. I've become the next king after my father David. Now I'm sitting on the throne of Israel. That's exactly what the LORD promised would happen. I've built the temple where the LORD will put his Name. He is the God of Israel. 21I've provided a place for the ark there. The tablets of the LORD's covenant are inside it. He made that covenant with our people of long ago. He made it when he brought them out of Egypt."

Solomon Prays to Set the Temple Apart to the LORD

22Then Solomon stood in front of the LORD's altar. He stood in front of the whole community of Israel. He spread out his hands toward heaven. 23He said,

"LORD, you are the God of Israel. There is no God like you in heaven above or on earth below. You keep the covenant you made with us. You show us your love. You do that when we follow you with all our hearts. 24You have kept your promise to my father David. He was your servant. With your mouth you made a promise. With your powerful hand you have made it come true. And today we can see it.

25"LORD, you are the God of Israel. Keep the promises you made to my father David. Do it for him. He was your servant. You said to him, 'You will always have a man to sit on the throne of Israel in my sight. That will be true only if your sons are careful in everything they do. They must live in my sight the way you have lived.' 26God of Israel, let your promise to my father David come true.

27"But will you really live on earth? After all, the heavens can't hold you. In fact, even the highest heavens can't hold you. So this temple I've built certainly can't hold you!

28"But please pay attention to my prayer. LORD my God, show me your favor as I make my appeal to you. Listen to my cry for help. Hear the prayer I'm praying to you today. 29Let your eyes look toward this temple night and day. You said, 'I will put my Name there.' So please listen to the prayer I'm praying toward this place.

30"Hear me when I ask you to show us your favor. Listen to your people Israel when they pray toward this place. Listen to us from heaven. It's the place where you live. When you hear us, forgive us.

31"Suppose a man does something wrong to his neighbor. And he is required to take an oath and make a promise. He must come and do it in front of your altar in this temple. 32When he does, listen to him from heaven. Take action. Judge between those people. Punish the one who is guilty. Do to him what he has done to his neighbor. Tell everyone that the one who hasn't done anything wrong is free from blame. That will prove he isn't guilty.

33"Suppose your people Israel have lost the battle against their enemies. And suppose they've sinned against you. But they turn back to you and praise your name. They pray to you in this temple. And they ask you to show them your favor. 34Then listen to them from heaven. Forgive the sin of your people Israel. Bring them back to the land you gave to their people who lived long ago.

35"Suppose your people have sinned against you. And because of that, the sky is closed up and there isn't any rain. But your people pray toward this place. They praise you by admitting they've sinned. And they turn away from their sin because you have made them suffer. 36Then listen to them from heaven. Forgive the sin of your people Israel. Teach them the right way to live. Send rain on the land you gave them as their share.

37"Suppose there isn't enough food in the land. And a plague strikes the land. The hot winds completely dry up our crops. Or locusts or grasshoppers come and eat them up. Or an enemy surrounds one of our cities and gets ready to attack it. Or trouble or sickness comes. 38But suppose one of your people prays to you. He asks you to show him your favor. He is aware of how much his own heart is suffering. And he spreads out his hands toward this temple to pray. 39Then listen to him from heaven. It's the place where you live. Forgive him. Take action. Deal with him in keeping with everything he does. You know his heart. In fact, you are the only one who knows every human heart. 40Your people will have respect for you. They will respect you as long as they are in the land you gave our people long ago.

41"Suppose there are strangers who don't belong to your people Israel. And they have come from a land far away. They've come because they've heard about your name. 42When they get here, they will find out even more about your great name. They'll hear about how you reached out your mighty hand and powerful arm. So they'll come and pray toward this temple.

43"Then listen to them from heaven. It's the place where you live. Do what those strangers ask you to do. Then all of the nations on earth will know you. They will have respect for you. They'll respect you just as your own people Israel do. They'll know that your Name is in this house I've built.

44"Suppose your people go to war against their enemies. It doesn't matter where you send them. And suppose they pray to you toward the city you have chosen. They pray toward the temple I've built for your Name. 45Then listen to them from heaven. Listen to their prayer. Listen to them when they ask you to show them your favor. Stand up for them.

46"Suppose your people sin against you. After all, there isn't anyone who doesn't sin. And suppose you get angry with them. You hand them over to their enemies. They take them as prisoners to their own land. It doesn't matter whether it's near or far away. 47"But suppose your people change their ways in the land where they are held as prisoners. They turn away from their sins. They beg you to help them in the land of those who won the battle over them. They say, 'We have sinned. We've done what is wrong. We've done what is evil.' 48And they turn back to you with all their heart and soul. Suppose it happens in the land of their enemies who took them away as prisoners. There they pray to you toward the land you gave their people long ago. They pray toward the city you have chosen. And they pray toward the temple I've built for your Name.

49"Then listen to them from heaven. It's the place where you live. Listen to their prayer. Listen to them when they ask you to show them your favor. Stand up for them.

50"Your people have sinned against you. Please forgive them. Forgive them for all of the wrong things they've done against you. And make those who won the battle over them show mercy to them. 51After all, they are your people. They belong to you. You brought them out of Egypt. You brought them out of that furnace that melts iron down and makes it pure.

52"Let your eyes be open to me when I ask you to show us your favor. Let them be open to your people Israel when they ask you to show them your favor. Pay attention to them every time they cry out to you.

53"After all, you chose them out of all of the nations in the world. You made them your very own people. You did it just as you had announced through your servant Moses. That's when you brought our people out of Egypt. You are our LORD and King."

54Solomon finished all of those prayers. He finished asking the LORD to show his favor to his people. Then he got up from in front of the LORD's altar. He had been down on his knees with his hands spread out toward heaven. 55He stood in front of the whole community of Israel. He blessed them with a loud voice. He said,

56"I praise the LORD. He has given peace and rest to his people Israel. That's exactly what he promised to do. He gave his people good promises through his servant Moses. Every single word of those promises has come true.

57"May the LORD our God be with us, just as he was with our people who lived long ago. May he never leave us. May he never desert us. 58May he turn our hearts to him. Then we will live the way he wants us to. We'll obey the commands, rules and directions he gave our people.

59"I've prayed these words to the LORD our God. May he keep them close to him day and night. May he stand up for me. May he also stand up for his people Israel. May he give us what we need every day. 60Then all of the nations on earth will know that the LORD is God. They'll know that there isn't any other god.

61"But you must commit your lives completely to the LORD our God. You must live by his rules. You must obey his commands. You must always do as you are doing now."

Solomon Sets the Temple Apart to the LORD

62Then the king and the whole community of Israel offered sacrifices to the LORD. 63Solomon sacrificed friendship offerings to the LORD. He sacrificed 22,000 head of cattle. He also sacrificed 120,000 sheep and goats. So the king and the whole community set the temple of the LORD apart to him.

64On that same day the king set the middle area of the courtyard apart to the LORD. It was in front of the LORD's temple. There Solomon sacrificed burnt offerings and grain offerings. He also sacrificed the fat of the friendship offerings there. He did it there because the bronze altar in front of the LORD was too small. It wasn't big enough to hold all of the burnt offerings, the grain offerings and the fat of the friendship offerings.

65At that time Solomon celebrated the Feast of Booths. The whole community of Israel was with him. It was a huge crowd. People came from as far away as Lebo Hamath and the Wadi of Egypt. For seven days they celebrated in front of the LORD our God. The feast continued for seven more days. That made a total of 14 days.

66On the following day Solomon sent the people away. They asked the LORD to bless the king. Then they went home. The people were glad. Their hearts were full of joy. That's because the LORD had done so many good things for his servant David and his people Israel.

The LORD Appears to Solomon

9 Solomon finished building the LORD's temple and the royal palace. He had accomplished everything he had planned to do. 2The LORD appeared to him a second time. He had already appeared to him at Gibeon. 3The LORD said to him,

> "I have heard you pray to me. I have heard you ask me to show you my favor. You have built this temple. I have set it apart for myself. My Name will be there forever. My eyes and my heart will always be there.
>
> 4"But you must walk with me, just as your father David did. Your heart must be honest. It must be without blame. Do everything I command you to do. Obey my rules and laws. 5Then I will set up your royal throne over Israel forever. I promised your father David I would do that. I said to him, 'You will always have a man on the throne of Israel.'
>
> 6"But suppose all of you turn away from me. Or your sons turn away from me. You refuse to obey the commands and rules I have given you. And you go off to serve other gods and worship them. 7Then I will cut Israel off from the land. It is the land I gave them. I will turn my back on this temple. I will do it even though I have set it apart for my Name to be there. Then Israel will be hated by all of the nations. They will laugh and joke about Israel.
>
> 8"This temple is now grand and beautiful. But the time is coming when all those who pass by it will be shocked. They will make fun of it. And they will say, 'Why has the LORD done a thing like this to this land and temple?'
>
> 9"People will answer, 'Because they have deserted the LORD their God. He brought their people out of Egypt. But they have been holding on to other gods. They've been worshiping them. They've been serving them. That's why the LORD has brought all of this horrible trouble on them.'"

Other Things Solomon Did

10Solomon built the LORD's temple and the royal palace. It took him 20 years to construct those two buildings.

11King Solomon gave 20 towns in Galilee to Hiram. That's because Hiram had provided him with all of the cedar and pine logs he wanted. He had also provided him with all of the gold he wanted. Hiram was king of Tyre.

12Hiram went from Tyre to see the towns Solomon had given him. But he wasn't pleased with them. 13"My friend," he asked, "what have you given me? What kind of towns are these?" So he called them the Land of Cabul. And that's what they are still called to this very day. 14Hiram had sent four and a half tons of gold to Solomon.

15King Solomon forced people to work hard for him. Here is a record of what they did. They built the LORD's temple and Solomon's palace. They filled in the low places. They rebuilt the wall of Jerusalem. They built up Hazor, Megiddo and Gezer.

16Pharaoh, the king of Egypt, had attacked Gezer and captured it. He had set it on fire. He had killed the Canaanites who lived there. Then he had given Gezer as a wedding gift to his daughter. She was Solomon's wife.

17Solomon rebuilt Gezer. He built up Lower Beth Horon 18and Baalath. He built up Tadmor in the desert. All of those towns were in his land. 19He built up all of the cities where he could store things. He also built up the towns for his chariots and horses. He built anything he wanted to build in Jerusalem, Lebanon and all of the territory he ruled over.

20There were still many people left in the land who weren't Israelites. They included Amorites, Hittites, Perizzites, Hivites and Jebusites. 21They were children of the people who had lived in the land before the Israelites came. Those people had been set apart to the LORD in a special way to be destroyed. But the Israelites hadn't been able to kill all of them. Solomon had forced them to work very hard as his slaves. And they still work for Israel to this very day.

22But Solomon didn't force any of the men of Israel to work as his slaves. Instead, some were his fighting men. Others were his government officials, his officers and his captains. Others were commanders of his chariots and chariot drivers. 23Still others were the chief officials who were in charge of his projects. There were 550 officials in charge of those who did the work.

24Pharaoh's daughter moved from the City of David up to the palace Solomon had built for her. After that, he filled in the low places near the palace.

25Three times a year Solomon sacrificed burnt offerings and friendship offerings. He sacrificed them on the altar he had built to honor the LORD. Along with the offerings, he burned incense to the LORD. So he carried out his duties for the temple.

26King Solomon also built ships at Ezion Geber. It's near Elath in Edom. It's on the shore of the Red Sea.

27Hiram sent his men to serve on the ships together with Solomon's men. Hiram's sailors knew the sea. 28All of them sailed to Ophir. They brought back 16 tons of gold. They gave it to King Solomon.

The Queen of Sheba Visits Solomon

10 The queen of Sheba heard about how famous Solomon was. She also heard about how he served and worshiped the LORD. So she came to test him with hard questions.

2She arrived in Jerusalem with a very large group of attendants. Her camels were carrying spices, huge amounts of gold, and valuable jewels. She came to Solomon and asked him about everything she wanted to know.

3Solomon answered all of her questions. There wasn't anything that was too hard for the king to explain to her.

4So the queen of Sheba saw how very wise Solomon was. She saw the palace he had built. 5She saw the food that was on his table. She saw his officials sitting there. She saw the robes of the servants who waited on everyone. She saw his wine tasters. And she saw the burnt offerings Solomon sacrificed at the LORD's temple. She could hardly believe everything she had seen.

6She said to the king, "Back in my own country I heard a report about you. I heard about how much you had accomplished. I also heard about how wise you are. Everything I heard is true. 7But I didn't believe those things. So I came to see for myself. And now I believe it! You are twice as wise and wealthy as people say you are. The report I heard doesn't even begin to tell the whole story about you.

8"How happy your men must be! How happy your officials must be! They always get to serve you and hear the wise things you say.

9"May the LORD your God be praised. He must take great delight in you. He placed you on the throne of Israel. The LORD will love Israel for all time to come. That's why he has made you king. He knows that you will do what is fair and right."

10She gave the king four and a half tons of gold. She also gave him huge amounts of spices and valuable jewels. No one would ever bring to King Solomon as many spices as the queen of Sheba gave him.

11Hiram's ships brought gold from Ophir. From there they also brought huge amounts of almugwood and valuable jewels. 12The king used the almugwood to make supports for the LORD's temple and the royal palace. He also used it to make harps and lyres for those who played the music. That much almugwood has never been brought into Judah or seen there since that day.

13King Solomon gave the queen of Sheba everything she wanted and asked for. That was in addition to what he had given her out of his royal riches. Then she left. She returned to her own country with her attendants.

Solomon in All of His Glory

14Each year Solomon received 25 tons of gold. 15That didn't include the money that was brought in by business and trade. It also didn't include the money from all of the kings of Arabia and the governors of Israel.

16King Solomon made 200 large shields out of hammered gold. Each one weighed seven and a half pounds. 17He also made 300 small shields out of hammered gold. Each one weighed almost four pounds. The king put all of the shields in the Palace of the Forest of Lebanon.

18Then he made a large throne. It was decorated with ivory. It was covered with fine gold. 19The throne had six steps. Its back had a rounded top. The throne had armrests on both sides of the seat. A statue of a lion stood on each side of the throne. 20Twelve lions stood on the six steps. There was one at each end of each step. Nothing like that throne had ever been made for any other kingdom.

21All of King Solomon's cups were made out of gold. All of the articles that were used in the Palace of the Forest of Lebanon were made out of pure gold. Nothing was made out of silver. When Solomon was king, silver wasn't considered to be worth very much.

22He had many ships that carried goods to be traded. His ships went to sea along with Hiram's ships. Once every three years the ships returned. They brought gold, silver, ivory, apes and baboons.

23King Solomon was richer than all of the other kings on earth. He was also wiser than they were. 24People from the whole world wanted to meet Solomon in person. They wanted to see for themselves how wise God had made him. 25Year after year, everyone who came to him brought a gift. They brought articles that were made out of silver and gold. They brought robes, weapons and spices. They also brought horses and mules.

26Solomon had 1,400 chariots and 12,000 horses. He kept some of his horses and chariots in the chariot cities. He kept the others with him in Jerusalem.

27The king made silver as common in Jerusalem as stones. He made cedar wood as common there as sycamore-fig trees in the western hills.

28Solomon got horses from Egypt and from Kue. The royal traders bought them from Kue. 29They weighed out 15 pounds of silver for a chariot from Egypt. And they weighed out almost four pounds of silver for a horse. They also sold horses and chariots to all of the kings of the Hittites and the kings of the Arameans.

Solomon's Wives Turn Him Away From the LORD

11 King Solomon loved many women besides Pharaoh's daughter. They were from other lands. They were Moabites, Ammonites, Edomites, Sidonians and Hittites.

2The LORD had warned Israel about women from other nations. He had said, "You must not get married to them. If you do, you can be sure they will turn your hearts toward their gods." But Solomon continued to love them anyway. He wouldn't give them up. 3He had 700 wives who came from royal families. And he had 300 concubines. His wives led him down the wrong path.

4As Solomon grew older, his wives turned his heart toward other gods. He didn't follow the LORD his God with all his heart. So he wasn't like his father David. 5Solomon worshiped Ashtoreth. Ashtoreth was the goddess of the people of Sidon.

He also worshiped Molech. Molech was the god
of the people of Ammon. The LORD hated that god.
[6]Solomon did what was evil in the sight of the
LORD. He didn't follow the LORD completely. He
didn't do what his father David had done.
[7]There is a hill east of Jerusalem. Solomon built
a high place for worshiping Chemosh there. He
built a high place for worshiping Molech there too.
Chemosh was the god of Moab. Molech was the
god of Ammon. The LORD hated both of those
gods.
[8]Solomon also built high places so that all of his
wives from other nations could worship their gods.
Those women burned incense and offered sacrifices to their gods.
[9]The LORD became angry with Solomon. That's
because his heart had turned away from the LORD.
He is the God of Israel. He had appeared to Solomon twice. [10]He had commanded Solomon not to
follow other gods. But Solomon didn't obey him.
[11]So the LORD said to Solomon, "You have chosen not to keep my covenant. You have decided
not to obey my rules. I commanded you to do what
I told you. But you did not do it. So you can be
absolutely sure I will tear the kingdom away from
you. I will give it to one of your officials.
[12]"But I will not do that while you are still living. Because of your father David I will wait. I will
tear the kingdom out of your son's hand. [13]But I
will not tear the whole kingdom away from him. I
will give him one of the tribes because of my servant David. I will also do it because of Jerusalem.
That is the city I have chosen."

The LORD Brings Enemies Against Solomon

[14]Then the LORD brought an enemy against Solomon. The enemy's name was Hadad. He was
from Edom. In fact, he belonged to the royal family of Edom.
[15]David had fought against Edom. Joab had been
the commander of the army. He had gone up to
bury the dead bodies of the Israelites who had been
killed in battle. At that time he had struck down all
of the men in Edom. [16]In fact, Joab and all of the
men of Israel stayed there for six months. During
that time they destroyed all of the men in Edom.
[17]But when Hadad was only a boy, he ran away
to Egypt. Some officials from Edom went with
him. They had served Hadad's father. [18]They
started out from Midian and went to Paran. They
took some men from Paran with them. Then they
went to Egypt. They went to Pharaoh, the king of
Egypt. He gave Hadad a house and some land. He
also supplied him with food.
[19]Pharaoh was very pleased with Hadad. Pharaoh's wife was Queen Tahpenes. He gave Hadad
her sister to be his wife. [20]The sister of Tahpenes
had a son by Hadad. The baby was named Genubath. Tahpenes brought him up in the royal palace.
Genubath lived there with Pharaoh's own children.
[21]Hadad heard that David had joined the members of his family who had already died. He also
heard that Joab, the commander of the army, was
dead. Hadad heard those things while he was in
Egypt. He said to Pharaoh, "Let me go. I want to
return to my own country."
[22]"Why do you want to go back to your own
country?" Pharaoh asked. "Don't you have everything you need right here?"
"Yes," Hadad replied. "But I want you to let me
go anyway!"
[23]God brought another enemy against Solomon.
The enemy's name was Rezon. He was the son of
Eliada. Rezon had run away from his master Hadadezer, the king of Zobah. [24]He gathered some
men together to follow him. He became the leader
of a group of men who had refused to follow David. It happened when David destroyed the troops
of Zobah. Then the group that was against David
went to Damascus. They settled down there and
took control of it. [25]Rezon was Israel's enemy as
long as Solomon was living. Rezon added to the
trouble Hadad had caused. So Rezon ruled in
Aram. He was Israel's enemy.

Jeroboam Refuses to Follow Solomon

[26]Jeroboam refused to follow King Solomon.
He was one of Solomon's officials. He was from
Zeredah in the territory of Ephraim. His father was
Nebat. His mother was a widow named Zeruah.
[27]Here is the story of how Jeroboam refused to
follow the king. Solomon had filled in the low
places near the palace. He had also repaired the
wall of the city of his father David. [28]Jeroboam
was a very important young man. Solomon saw
how well he did his work. So he put him in charge
of all of the workers in northern Israel.
[29]About that time Jeroboam was going out of
Jerusalem. The prophet Ahijah met him on the
road. Ahijah was from Shiloh. He was wearing a
new coat. The two of them were all alone out in
the country.
[30]Ahijah grabbed hold of the new coat he had
on. He tore it up into 12 pieces. [31]Then he said to
Jeroboam, "Take ten pieces for yourself. The
LORD is the God of Israel. He says, 'I am going to
tear the kingdom out of Solomon's hand. I will
give you ten of its tribes. [32]Solomon will have one
of its tribes. I will let him keep it because of my
servant David and because of Jerusalem. I have
chosen that city out of all of the cities in the tribes
of Israel.
[33]"'I will do those things because the tribes
have deserted me. They have worshiped Ashtoreth, the goddess of the people of Sidon. They
have worshiped Chemosh, the god of the people
of Moab. And they have worshiped Molech, the
god of the people of Ammon. They have not lived
the way I wanted them to. They have not done
what is right in my eyes. They have not obeyed my
rules and laws as Solomon's father David did.

34"'But I will not take the whole kingdom out of Solomon's hand. I have made him ruler all the days of his life. I have done it because of my servant David. I chose him. He obeyed my commands and rules.

35"'I will take the kingdom out of his son's hands. And I will give you ten of the tribes.

36"'I will give one of the tribes to David's son. Then my servant David will always have a son on his throne in Jerusalem. The lamp of David's kingdom will always burn brightly in my sight. Jerusalem is the city I chose for my Name.

37"'But I will make you king over Israel. You will rule over everything your heart longs for. So you will be the king of Israel. 38Do everything I command you to do. Live the way I want you to. Do what is right in my eyes. Obey my rules and commands. That is what my servant David did. If you do those things, I will be with you. I will build you a kingdom. It will last as long as the one I built for David. I will give Israel to you.

39"'I will punish David's family because of what Solomon has done. But I will not punish them forever.'"

40Solomon tried to kill Jeroboam. But Jeroboam ran away to Egypt. He went to Shishak, the king of Egypt. He stayed there until Solomon died.

Solomon Dies

41The other events of Solomon's rule are written down. Everything he did and the wisdom he showed are written down. They are written in the official records of Solomon.

42Solomon ruled in Jerusalem over the whole nation of Israel for 40 years. 43Then he joined the members of his family who had already died. His body was buried in the city of his father David. Solomon's son Rehoboam became the next king after him.

Israel Refuses to Follow Rehoboam

12 Rehoboam went to Shechem. All of the people of Israel had gone there to make him king. 2Jeroboam heard about it. He was the son of Nebat. Jeroboam was still in Egypt at that time. He had gone there for safety. He wanted to get away from King Solomon. But now he returned from Egypt.

3So the people sent for Jeroboam. He and the whole community of Israel went to Rehoboam. They said to him, 4"Your father put a heavy load on our shoulders. But now make our hard work easier. Make the heavy load on us lighter. Then we'll serve you."

5Rehoboam answered, "Go away for three days. Then come back to me." So the people went away.

6King Rehoboam asked the elders for advice. They had served his father Solomon while he was still living. Rehoboam asked them, "What advice can you give me? How should I answer these people?"

7They replied, "Serve them today. Give them what they are asking for. Then they'll always serve you."

8But Rehoboam didn't accept the advice the elders gave him. Instead, he asked for advice from the young men who had grown up with him and were now serving him. 9He asked them, "What's your advice? How should I answer these people? They say to me, 'Make the load your father put on our shoulders lighter.'"

10The young men who had grown up with him gave their answer. They replied, "These people say to you, 'Your father put a heavy load on our shoulders. Make it lighter.' Tell them, 'My little finger is stronger than my father's legs. 11My father put a heavy load on your shoulders. But I'll make it even heavier. My father beat you with whips. But I'll beat you with bigger whips.'"

12Three days later Jeroboam and all of the people returned to Rehoboam. That's because the king had said, "Come back to me in three days."

13The king answered the people in a mean way. He didn't accept the advice the elders had given him. 14Instead, he followed the advice of the young men. He said, "My father put a heavy load on your shoulders. But I'll make it even heavier. My father beat you with whips. But I'll beat you with bigger whips."

15So the king didn't listen to the people. That's because the LORD had planned it that way. What he had said through Ahijah came true. Ahijah had spoken the LORD's message to Jeroboam, the son of Nebat. Ahijah was from Shiloh.

16All of the people of Israel saw that the king refused to listen to them. So they answered the king. They said,

"We don't have any share in David's royal family.
We don't have any share in Jesse's son.
People of Israel, let's go back to our homes.
David's royal family, take care of your own kingdom!"

So the people of Israel went home.

17But Rehoboam still ruled over the Israelites who were living in the towns of Judah.

18Adoniram was in charge of those who were forced to work hard for King Rehoboam. The king sent him out among all of the Israelites. But they killed him by throwing stones at him. King Rehoboam was able to get away in his chariot. He escaped to Jerusalem. 19Israel has refused to follow the royal family of David to this very day.

20All of the people of Israel heard that Jeroboam had returned. They sent for him. They wanted him to meet with the whole community. Then they made him king over the entire nation of Israel. Only the tribe of Judah remained true to David's royal family.

21Rehoboam arrived in Jerusalem. He brought together 180,000 fighting men from the royal house of Judah and the tribe of Benjamin. He had decided to make war against the royal house of Israel. Solomon's son Rehoboam wanted his fighting men to get the kingdom of Israel back for him.

22But a message from God came to Shemaiah. He was a man of God. God said to him, 23"Speak to Solomon's son Rehoboam, the king of Judah. Speak to the royal house of Judah and Benjamin. Also speak to the rest of the people. Tell all of them, 24'The LORD says, "Do not go up to fight against the Israelites. They are your relatives. I want every one of you to go back home. Things have happened exactly the way I planned them."'" So the fighting men obeyed the LORD's message. They went home again, just as he had ordered.

Jeroboam Sets Up Golden Calves at Bethel and Dan

25Jeroboam built up the walls of Shechem. It was in the hill country of Ephraim. Jeroboam made Shechem his home. From there he went out and built up Peniel.

26Jeroboam thought, "My kingdom still isn't secure. It could very easily go back to the royal family of David. 27Suppose the people of Israel go up to Jerusalem to offer sacrifices at the LORD's temple. If they do, they will again decide to follow Rehoboam as their master. Then they'll kill me. They'll return to King Rehoboam. He is king of Judah."

28So King Jeroboam asked for advice. Then he made two golden statues that looked like calves. He said to the people, "It's too hard for you to go up to Jerusalem. Israel, here are your gods who brought you up out of Egypt." 29He set up one statue in Bethel. He set up the other one in Dan.

30What Jeroboam did was sinful. And it caused Israel to sin. The people even went all the way to Dan to worship the statue that was there.

31Jeroboam built temples for worshiping gods on high places. He appointed all kinds of people as priests. They didn't even have to be Levites. 32He established a feast. It was on the 15th day of the eighth month. He wanted to make it like the Feast of Booths that was held in Judah.

Jeroboam built an altar at Bethel. He offered sacrifices on it. He sacrificed to the calves he had made. He also put priests in Bethel. He did it at the high places he had made. 33He offered sacrifices on the altar he had built at Bethel. It was on the 15th day of the eighth month. That's the month he had chosen for it. So he established the feast for the people of Israel. And he went up to the altar to sacrifice offerings.

A Man of God Goes to Bethel

13 A man of God went from Judah to Bethel. He had received a message from the LORD. He arrived in Bethel just as Jeroboam was standing by the altar to offer a sacrifice. 2The man cried out. He shouted a message from the LORD against the altar. He said, "Altar! Altar! The LORD says, 'A son named Josiah will be born into the royal family of David. Altar, listen to me! Josiah will sacrifice the priests of the high places on you. They will be the children of the priests who are offering sacrifices here now. So human bones will be burned on you.'"

3That same day the man of God spoke about a miraculous sign. He said, "Here is the sign the LORD has announced. This altar will be broken to pieces. The ashes on it will be spilled out."

4The man of God announced that message against the altar at Bethel. When King Jeroboam heard it, he reached out his hand from the altar. He said, "Grab him!" But as he reached out his hand toward the man, it dried up. He couldn't even pull it back.

5Also, the altar broke into pieces. Its ashes spilled out. That happened in keeping with the miraculous sign the man of God had announced. He had received a message from the LORD.

6King Jeroboam spoke to the man of God. He said, "Pray to the LORD your God for me. Pray that my hand will be as good as new again."

So the man of God prayed to the LORD for the king. And the king's hand became as good as new. It was just as healthy as it had been before.

7The king said to the man of God, "Come home with me. Have something to eat. I'll give you a gift."

8But the man of God replied to the king. He said, "What if you were to give me half of what you own? Even then I wouldn't go with you. I wouldn't eat bread or drink water here. 9The LORD gave me a command. He said, 'Do not eat bread or drink water there. Do not return the same way you came.'" 10So he took another road. He didn't go back on the same road he had taken when he came to Bethel.

11An old prophet was living in Bethel. His sons came and spoke to him. They told him everything the man of God had done there that day. They also told their father what the man had said to the king. 12Their father asked them, "Which way did he go?"

His sons showed him the road the man of God from Judah had taken.

13So he said to his sons, "Put a saddle on the donkey for me."

When they had done it, he got on the donkey. 14He traveled on the same road the man of God had taken. He found the man sitting under an oak tree. He asked him, "Are you the man of God who came from Judah?"

"I am," he replied.

15So the prophet said to him, "Come home with me. I'll give you something to eat."

16The man of God said, "I can't go back to Bethel with you. I can't eat bread or drink water with you there. 17I've received a message from the LORD. He told me, 'Do not eat bread or drink water there. Do not return the same way you came.'"

18The old prophet answered, "I'm also a
prophet, just like you. An angel gave me a message from the LORD. The message said, 'Bring the
man of God back with you to your house. Then he
can eat bread and drink water with you.'" But the
old prophet was telling him a lie.
19The man of God returned with him. He ate
and drank in his house.
20They were sitting at the table. The LORD gave
a message to the old prophet who had brought the
man of God back. 21He cried out to the man who
had come from Judah. He told him, "The LORD
says, 'You have not done what I told you to do.
You have not obeyed the command I gave you. I
am the LORD your God. 22You came back here and
ate bread and drank water. You did it in the place
where I told you not to. So your body will not be
buried in your family tomb.'"
23The man of God finished eating and drinking.
Then the old prophet who had brought him back
put a saddle on the man's donkey for him. 24And
the man went on his way. A lion attacked him on
the road and killed him. His body was left lying on
the road. The donkey and the lion were standing
beside it.
25Some people passed by. They saw the body
lying on the road. They saw the lion standing
beside the body. Then they went and reported it in
the city where the old prophet lived.
26The prophet who had brought the man back
from his journey heard about what had happened.
He said, "It's the man of God. He didn't do what
the LORD told him to do. So the LORD has given
him over to the lion. The lion has attacked him and
killed him. Everything has happened just as the
LORD's message had warned him it would."
27The old prophet said to his sons, "Put a saddle
on the donkey for me." So they did. 28Then he
went out. He found the body of the man of God
lying on the road. The donkey and the lion were
standing beside it. The lion hadn't eaten the body.
It hadn't attacked the donkey either.
29So the prophet picked up the man's body. He
put it on the donkey. He brought it back to his own
city. He wanted to sob over him and bury him.
30Then he placed the body in his own tomb. People sobbed over him. They said, "My friend! My
dear friend!"
31After the old prophet had buried the body of
the man of God, he spoke to his sons. He said,
"When I die, bury my body in the grave where the
man of God is buried. Put my bones next to his
bones. 32I want you to do that because he
announced a message from the LORD. He spoke
against the altar in Bethel. He also spoke against
all of the temples that were on the high places.
They are in the towns of Samaria. What the man of
God said will certainly come true."
33Even after all of that happened, Jeroboam still
didn't change his evil ways. Once more he
appointed priests for the high places. He made
priests out of all kinds of people. In fact, he let
anyone become a priest who wanted to. He set
them apart to serve at the high places. 34All of that
was the great sin the royal family of Jeroboam
committed. It led to their fall from power. Because
of it, they were destroyed from the face of the
earth.

Ahijah Prophesies Against Jeroboam

14 At that time Abijah became sick. He was
the son of Jeroboam. 2Jeroboam said to his
wife, "Go. Put on some different clothes. Then no
one will recognize you as my wife. Go to Shiloh.
That's where the prophet Ahijah is. He told me I
would be king over the people of Israel. 3Take ten
loaves of bread with you. Take some cakes and a
jar of honey. Go to him. He'll tell you what will
happen to our son."
4So Jeroboam's wife did what he said. She went
to Ahijah's house in Shiloh.
Ahijah couldn't see. He was blind because he
was so old. 5But the LORD had told Ahijah, "Jeroboam's wife is coming. Her son is sick. She'll ask
you about him. Give her the answer I give you.
When she arrives, she'll pretend to be someone
else."
6Ahijah heard the sound of her footsteps at the
door. He said, "Come in. I know that you are Jeroboam's wife. Why are you pretending to be
someone else? I have some bad news for you.
7"Go. Tell Jeroboam that the LORD has a message for him. The LORD is the God of Israel. He
says, 'I chose you from among the people. I made
you the leader of my people Israel. 8I tore the kingdom away from the royal house of David. I gave it
to you. But you have not been like my servant David. He obeyed my commands. He followed me
with all his heart. He did only what was right in
my eyes. 9You have done more evil things than all
those who lived before you. You have made other
gods for yourself. You have made statues of gods
out of metal. You have made me very angry. You
have turned your back on me.
10"'Because of that, I am going to bring horrible
trouble on your royal house. I will cut off from you
every male in Israel. It does not matter whether
they are slaves or free. I will burn up your royal
house, just as someone burns up trash. I will burn
it until it is all gone. 11Some of the people who
belong to you will die in the city. Dogs will eat
them up. Others will die in the country. The birds
of the air will eat them. I have spoken!'
12"Now go back home. When you enter your
city, your son will die. 13All of the people of Israel will sob over him. Then his body will be buried.
He is the only one who belongs to Jeroboam who
will be buried. That is because he is the only one
in Jeroboam's royal house in whom I have found
anything good. I am the LORD, the God of Israel.
14"I will choose for myself a king over Israel.
He will cut off the family of Jeroboam. This very

day your son will die. Can that really be true? Yes. Even now, that is what I am telling you.

15“I will strike Israel down. Israel will be like tall grass swaying in the water. I will pull Israel up from this good land by the roots. I gave it to their people who lived long ago. I will scatter Israel to the east side of the Euphrates River. That is because they made me very angry. They made poles that were used to worship the goddess Asherah.

16“I will give Israel up because of the sins Jeroboam has committed. He has also caused Israel to commit those same sins.”

17Then Jeroboam’s wife got up and left. She went to the city of Tirzah. As soon as she stepped through the doorway of the house, her son died. 18His body was buried. All of the people of Israel sobbed over him. That’s what the LORD had said would happen. He had said it through his servant, the prophet Ahijah.

19The other events of Jeroboam’s rule are written down. His wars and how he ruled are written down. They are written in the official records of the kings of Israel. 20Jeroboam ruled for 22 years. Then he joined the members of his family who had already died. Jeroboam’s son Nadab became the next king after him.

Rehoboam, the King of Judah

21Rehoboam was king in Judah. He was the son of Solomon. Rehoboam was 41 years old when he became king. He ruled for 17 years in Jerusalem. It was the city the LORD had chosen out of all of the cities in the tribes of Israel. He wanted to put his Name there. Rehoboam’s mother was Naamah from Ammon.

22The people of Judah did what was evil in the sight of the LORD. The sins they had committed stirred up his jealous anger. They did more to make him angry than their people who lived before them had done.

23Judah also set up for themselves high places for worship. They set up sacred stones. They set up poles that were used to worship the goddess Asherah. They did it on every high hill and under every green tree.

24There were even male prostitutes at the temples in the land. The people took part in all of the practices of other nations. The LORD hated those practices. He had driven those nations out to make room for the people of Israel.

25Shishak attacked Jerusalem. It was in the fifth year that Rehoboam was king. Shishak was king of Egypt. 26He carried away the treasures of the LORD’s temple. He also carried the treasures of the royal palace away. He took everything. That included all of the gold shields Solomon had made.

27So King Rehoboam made bronze shields to take their place. He gave them to the commanders of the guards who were on duty at the entrance to the royal palace. 28Every time the king went to the LORD’s temple, the guards carried the shields. Later, they took them back to the room where they were kept.

29The other events of Rehoboam’s rule are written down. Everything he did is written down. All of those things are written in the official records of the kings of Judah. 30Rehoboam and Jeroboam were always at war with each other. 31Rehoboam joined the members of his family who had already died. His body was buried in his family tomb in the City of David. His mother was Naamah from Ammon. His son Abijah became the next king after him.

Abijah Becomes King of Judah

15 Abijah became king of Judah. It was in the 18th year of Jeroboam’s rule over Israel. Jeroboam was the son of Nebat. 2Abijah ruled in Jerusalem for three years. His mother’s name was Maacah. She was Abishalom’s daughter.

3Abijah committed all of the sins his father had committed before him. Abijah didn’t follow the LORD his God with all his heart. He didn’t do what King David had done.

4But the LORD still kept the lamp of Abijah’s kingdom burning brightly in Jerusalem. He did it by giving him a son to be the next king after him. He also did it by making Jerusalem strong. The LORD did those things because of David. 5David had done what was right in the eyes of the LORD. He had kept all of the LORD’s commands. He had obeyed them all the days of his life. But he hadn’t obeyed the LORD in the case of Uriah, the Hittite.

6There was war between Jeroboam and Abijah’s father Rehoboam. The war continued all through Abijah’s life. 7The other events of Abijah’s rule are written down. Everything he did is written down. All of those things are written in the official records of the kings of Judah. There was war between Abijah and Jeroboam.

8Abijah joined the members of his family who had already died. His body was buried in the City of David. His son Asa became the next king after him.

Asa Becomes King of Judah

9Asa became king of Judah. It was in the 20th year that Jeroboam was king of Israel. 10Asa ruled in Jerusalem for 41 years. His grandmother’s name was Maacah. She was Abishalom’s daughter.

11Asa did what was right in the eyes of the LORD. That’s what King David had done.

12Asa threw out of the land the male prostitutes who were at the temples. He got rid of all of the statues of gods his people before him had made. 13He even removed his grandmother Maacah from her position as queen mother. That’s because she had made a pole that was used to worship the goddess Asherah. The LORD hated it. So Asa cut it down. He burned it in the Kidron Valley.

14Asa didn’t remove the high places from Israel. But he committed his whole life completely to

the LORD. 15He and his father had set apart silver,
gold and other articles to the LORD. He brought
them into the LORD's temple.
16There was war between Asa and Baasha, the
king of Israel. It lasted the whole time they were
kings. 17Baasha was king of Israel. He marched out
against Judah. He built up the walls of Ramah. He
did it to keep people from leaving or entering the
territory of Asa, the king of Judah.
18Asa took all of the silver and gold that was left
among the treasures of the LORD's temple and his
own palace. He put his officials in charge of it. He
sent the officials to Ben-Hadad. Ben-Hadad was
king of Aram. He was ruling in Damascus. He was
the son of Tabrimmon and the grandson of Hezion.
19"Let's make a peace treaty between us," Asa
said. "My father and your father had made a peace
treaty between them. Now I'm sending you a gift
of silver and gold. So break your treaty with Baasha, the king of Israel. Then he'll go back home."
20Ben-Hadad agreed with King Asa. He sent his
army commanders against the towns of Israel. He
attacked Ijon, Dan, Abel Beth Maacah and the
whole area of Kinnereth in addition to Naphtali.
21Baasha heard about it. So he stopped building
up Ramah. He went back home to Tirzah.
22Then King Asa gave an order to all of the men
of Judah. Everyone was required to help. They carried away from Ramah the stones and wood Baasha had been using there. King Asa used them to
build up Geba in the territory of Benjamin. He also
used them to build up Mizpah.
23All of the other events of Asa's rule are written down. Everything he accomplished is written
down. Everything he did and the cities he built are
written down. They are written in the official
records of the kings of Judah. But when Asa
became old, his feet began to give him trouble.
24He joined the members of his family who had
already died. His body was buried in his family
tomb. It was in the city of King David. Asa's son
Jehoshaphat became the next king after him.

Nadab Becomes King of Israel

25Nadab became king of Israel. It was in the second year that Asa was king of Judah. Nadab ruled
over Israel for two years. He was the son of Jeroboam. 26Nadab did what was evil in the sight of the
LORD. He lived the way his father had lived. He
sinned as his father had sinned. Jeroboam had also
caused Israel to commit the same sins.
27Baasha was from the tribe of Issachar. He was
the son of Ahijah. Baasha made plans against Nadab and struck him down at Gibbethon. It was a
Philistine town. Baasha struck him down while
Nadab and all of the men of Israel were getting
ready to attack Gibbethon. 28He killed Nadab in
the third year that Asa was king of Judah. Baasha
became the next king after Nadab.
29As soon as Baasha became king, he killed Jeroboam's whole family. He didn't leave any of
them alive. He destroyed every one of them. He
did what the LORD had said would happen. The
LORD had spoken that message through his servant
Ahijah from Shiloh.
30The LORD judged Jeroboam's family because
of the sins Jeroboam had committed. He had also
caused Israel to commit those same sins. He had
made the LORD very angry. The LORD is the God of
Israel.
31The other events of Nadab's rule are written
down. Everything he did is written down. All of
those things are written in the official records of
the kings of Israel.
32There was war between Asa and Baasha, the
king of Israel. It lasted the whole time they were
kings.

Baasha Becomes King of Israel

33Baasha became king of Israel in Tirzah. It was
in the third year that Asa was king of Judah. Baasha ruled for 24 years. He was the son of Ahijah.
34Baasha did what was evil in the sight of the
LORD. He lived the way Jeroboam had lived. He
sinned as Jeroboam had sinned. Jeroboam had also
caused Israel to commit the same sins.
16 The LORD's message against Baasha came
to Jehu. Jehu was the son of Hanani. The
LORD said, 2"I lifted you up from the dust. I made
you leader of my people Israel. But you lived the
way Jeroboam had lived. You also caused my people Israel to sin. And their sins made me very
angry.
3"So I am about to destroy you and your royal
house. I will make your house like the royal house
of Jeroboam, the son of Nebat. 4Some of the people who belong to you will die in the city. Dogs
will eat them up. Others will die in the country.
The birds of the air will eat them."
5The other events of Baasha's rule are written
down. What he did and what he accomplished are
written down. All of those things are written in the
official records of the kings of Israel. 6Baasha
joined the members of his family who had already
died. His body was buried in Tirzah. His son Elah
became the next king after him.
7The LORD's message came through the prophet
Jehu, the son of Hanani. It was against Baasha and
his royal house. Baasha had done all kinds of evil
things in the sight of the LORD. What he did had
made the LORD very angry. So Baasha had become
as sinful as the royal house of Jeroboam had been.
He had also destroyed it.

Elah Becomes King of Israel

8Elah became king of Israel. It was in the 26th
year that Asa was king of Judah. Elah ruled in Tirzah for two years. He was the son of Baasha.
9Zimri was one of Elah's officials. He commanded half of Elah's chariot drivers. He made
plans against Elah. Elah was in Tirzah at the time.
He was getting drunk in the home of Arza. Arza

was in charge of the palace at Tirzah. 10Zimri came in. He struck Elah down and killed him. It was in the 27th year of Asa, the king of Judah. Zimri became the next king after Elah.

11As soon as Zimri was seated on the throne as king, he killed off Baasha's whole family. He didn't even spare one male. It didn't matter whether it was a relative or a friend. 12So Zimri destroyed the whole family of Baasha. That's what the LORD had said would happen. He had spoken against Baasha through the prophet Jehu.

13Baasha and his son Elah had committed all kinds of sin. They had also caused Israel to commit the same sins. So Israel made the LORD very angry. They did it by worshiping worthless statues of gods. The LORD is the God of Israel.

14The other events of Elah's rule are written down. Everything he did is written down. All of those things are written in the official records of the kings of Israel.

Zimri Becomes King of Israel

15Zimri ruled in Tirzah for seven days. It was in the 27th year that Asa was king of Judah. The army of Israel had set up camp near Gibbethon. It was a Philistine town.

16The people of Israel who were in the camp heard that Zimri had made plans against King Elah. They also heard that Zimri had murdered him. So they announced that Omri was king over Israel. He was the commander of the army. They made him king that very day in the camp.

17Then Omri and all of his men pulled back from Gibbethon. They marched to Tirzah and surrounded it. They attacked it and captured it.

18Zimri saw that they had taken over the city. So he went into the safest place in the royal palace. He set the palace on fire all around him. He died there 19because of the sins he had committed. He had done what was evil in the sight of the LORD. He had lived the way Jeroboam had lived. He had sinned as Jeroboam had sinned. Jeroboam had also caused Israel to commit the same sins.

20The other events of Zimri's rule are written down. The way he turned against King Elah and killed him is written down. All of those things are written in the official records of the kings of Israel.

Omri Becomes King of Israel

21The people of Israel divided up into two groups. Half of them wanted Tibni to be king. He was the son of Ginath. The other half wanted Omri. 22But Omri's followers were stronger than those of Tibni, the son of Ginath. So Tibni died. And Omri began to rule.

23Omri became king of Israel. It was in the 31st year that Asa was king of Judah. Omri ruled for 12 years. He ruled in Tirzah for six of those years. 24He bought the hill of Samaria from Shemer. He weighed out 150 pounds of silver for it. Then he built a city on the hill. He called it Samaria. He named it after Shemer. Shemer had owned the hill before him.

25But Omri did what was evil in the sight of the LORD. He sinned more than all of the kings who had ruled before him. 26He lived the way Jeroboam, the son of Nebat, had lived. He sinned as Jeroboam had sinned. Jeroboam had also caused Israel to commit the same sins. Israel made the LORD very angry. They did it by worshiping worthless statues of gods. The LORD is the God of Israel.

27The other events of Omri's rule are written down. Everything he did and the things he accomplished are written down. All of those things are written in the official records of the kings of Israel. 28Omri joined the members of his family who had already died. His body was buried in Samaria. His son Ahab became the next king after him.

Ahab Becomes King of Israel

29Ahab became king of Israel. It was in the 38th year that Asa was king of Judah. Ahab ruled over Israel in Samaria for 22 years. He was the son of Omri. 30Ahab, the son of Omri, did what was evil in the sight of the LORD. He did more evil things than any of the kings who had ruled before him. 31He thought it was only a small thing to commit the sins Jeroboam, the son of Nebat, had committed.

Ahab also got married to Jezebel. She was Ethbaal's daughter. Ethbaal was king of the people of Sidon. Ahab began to serve the god Baal and worship him. 32He set up an altar to honor Baal. He set it up in the temple of Baal that he built in Samaria. 33Ahab also made a pole that was used to worship the goddess Asherah.

He made the LORD very angry. He did more to make him angry than all of the kings of Israel had done before him. The LORD is the God of Israel.

34In Ahab's time, Hiel from Bethel rebuilt Jericho. When he laid its foundations, it cost him the life of his oldest son Abiram. When he set up its gates, it cost him the life of his youngest son Segub. That's what the LORD had said would happen. He had spoken it through Joshua, the son of Nun.

Elijah Is Fed by Ravens

17 Elijah was from Tishbe in the land of Gilead. He said to Ahab, "I serve the LORD. He is the God of Israel. You can be sure that he lives. And you can be just as sure that there won't be any dew or rain on the whole land. There won't be any during the next few years. It won't come until I say so."

2Then a message from the LORD came to Elijah. It said, 3"Leave this place. Go east and hide in the Kerith Valley. It is east of the Jordan River. 4You will drink water from the brook. I have ordered some ravens to feed you there."

5So Elijah did what the LORD had told him to do. He went to the Kerith Valley. It was east of the

Jordan River. He stayed there. 6The ravens brought
him bread and meat in the morning. They also
brought him bread and meat in the evening. He
drank water from the brook.

Elijah Visits a Widow at Zarephath

7Some time later the brook dried up. It hadn't
rained in the land for quite a while. 8A message
came to Elijah from the LORD. He said, 9"Go right
away to Zarephath in the territory of Sidon. Stay
there. I have commanded a widow in that place to
supply you with food."
10So Elijah went to Zarephath. He came to the
town gate. A widow was there gathering sticks. He
called out to her. He asked, "Would you bring me
a little water in a jar? I need a drink."
11She went to get the water.
Then he called out to her, "Please bring me a
piece of bread too."
12"I don't have any bread," she replied. "And
that's just as sure as the LORD your God is alive.
All I have is a small amount of flour in a jar and
a little olive oil in a jug. I'm gathering a few
sticks to take home. I'll make one last meal for
myself and my son. We'll eat it. After that, we'll
die."
13Elijah said to her, "Don't be afraid. Go home.
Do what you have said. But first make a little
bread for me. Make it out of what you have. Bring
it to me. Then make some for yourself and your
son.
14"The LORD is the God of Israel. He says, 'The
jar of flour will not be used up. The jug will always
have oil in it. You will have flour and oil until the
day the LORD sends rain on the land.'"
15She went away and did what Elijah had told
her to do. So Elijah had food every day. There was
also food for the woman and her family. 16The jar
of flour wasn't used up. The jug always had oil in
it. That's what the LORD had said would happen.
He had spoken that message through Elijah.
17Some time later the son of the woman who
owned the house became sick. He got worse and
worse. Finally he stopped breathing.
18The woman said to Elijah, "You are a man of
God. What do you have against me? Did you come
to bring my sin out into the open? Did you come
to kill my son?"
19"Give me your son," Elijah replied. He took
him from her arms. He carried him to the upstairs
room where he was staying. He put him down on
his bed.
20Then Elijah cried out to the LORD. He said,
"LORD my God, I'm staying with this widow. Have
you brought pain and sorrow to her? Have you
caused her son to die?"
21Then he lay down on the boy three times. He
cried out to the LORD. He said, "LORD my God,
give this boy's life back to him!"
22The LORD answered Elijah's prayer. He gave
the boy's life back to him. So the boy lived. 23Eli-
jah picked up the boy. He carried him down from
the upstairs room into the house. He gave him to
his mother. He said, "Look! Your son is alive!"
24Then the woman said to Elijah, "Now I know
that you are a man of God. I know that the message you have brought from the LORD is true."

Elijah Gives Obadiah a Message for Ahab

18 It was now three years since it had rained.
A message came to Elijah from the LORD.
He said, "Go. Speak to Ahab. Then I will send rain
on the land."
2So Elijah went to speak to Ahab.
There wasn't enough food in Samaria. The people there were very hungry. 3Ahab had sent for
Obadiah. He was in charge of Ahab's palace. Obadiah had great respect for the LORD.
4Ahab's wife Jezebel had been killing off the
LORD's prophets. So Obadiah had hidden 100
prophets in two caves. He had put 50 in each cave.
He had supplied them with food and water.
5Ahab had said to Obadiah, "Go through the
land. Go to all of the springs of water and to the
valleys. Maybe we can find some grass there. It
will keep the horses and mules alive. Then we
won't have to kill any of our animals." 6So they
decided where each of them would look. Ahab
went in one direction. Obadiah went in another.
7As Obadiah was walking along, Elijah met
him. Obadiah recognized him. He bowed down to
the ground. He said, "My master Elijah! Is it really
you?"
8"Yes," he replied. "Go and tell your master
Ahab, 'Elijah is here.'"
9"What have I done wrong?" asked Obadiah.
"Why are you handing me over to Ahab to be put
to death?
10"My master has sent people to look for you
everywhere. There isn't a nation or kingdom
where he hasn't sent someone to look for you.
Suppose a nation or kingdom would claim you
weren't there. Then Ahab would make them take
an oath and say they couldn't find you. And that's
just as sure as the LORD your God is alive.
11"But now you are telling me to go to my master. You want me to say, 'Elijah is here.' 12But the
Spirit of the LORD might carry you away when I
leave you. Then I won't know where you are. If I
go and tell Ahab and he doesn't find you, he'll
kill me.
"But I've worshiped the LORD ever since I was
young. 13My master, haven't you heard what I did?
Jezebel was killing the LORD's prophets. But I hid
100 of them in two caves. I put 50 in each cave. I
supplied them with food and water. 14And now you
are telling me to go to my master Ahab. You want
me to say to him, 'Elijah is here.' He'll kill me!"
15Elijah said, "I serve the LORD who rules over
all. You can be sure that he lives. And you can be
just as sure that I will speak to Ahab today."

The LORD Answers Elijah's Prayer on Mount Carmel

[16]Obadiah went back to Ahab. He told Ahab that Elijah wanted to see him. So Ahab went to where Elijah was. [17]When he saw Elijah, he said to him, "Is that you? You are always stirring up trouble in Israel."

[18]"I haven't made trouble for Israel," Elijah replied. "But you and your father's family have. You have turned away from the LORD's commands. You have followed the gods that are named after Baal.

[19]"Now send for people from all over Israel. Tell them to meet me on Mount Carmel. And bring the 450 prophets of the god Baal. Also bring the 400 prophets of the goddess Asherah. All of them eat at Jezebel's table."

[20]So Ahab sent that message all through Israel. He gathered the prophets together on Mount Carmel.

[21]Elijah went there and stood in front of the people. He said, "How long will it take you to make up your minds? If the LORD is the one and only God, follow him. But if Baal is the one and only God, follow him."

The people didn't say anything.

[22]Then Elijah said to them, "I'm the only one of the LORD's prophets left. But Baal has 450 prophets. [23]Get two bulls for us. Let Baal's prophets choose one for themselves. Let them cut it into pieces. Then let them put it on the wood. But don't let them set fire to it. I'll prepare the other bull. I'll put it on the wood. But I won't set fire to it. [24]Then you pray to your god. And I'll pray to the LORD. The god who answers by sending fire down is the one and only God."

Then all of the people said, "What you are saying is good."

[25]Elijah spoke to the prophets of Baal. He said, "Choose one of the bulls. There are many of you. So prepare your bull first. Pray to your god. But don't light the fire."

[26]So they prepared the bull they had been given.

They prayed to Baal from morning until noon. "Baal! Answer us!" they shouted. But there wasn't any reply. No one answered. Then they danced around the altar they had made.

[27]At noon Elijah began to tease them. "Shout louder!" he said. "I'm sure Baal is a god! Perhaps he has too much to think about. Or maybe he has gone to the toilet. Or perhaps he's away on a trip. Maybe he's sleeping. You might have to wake him up."

[28]So they shouted louder. They cut themselves with swords and spears until their blood flowed. That's what they usually did when things really looked hopeless. [29]It was now past noon. The prophets of Baal continued to prophesy with all their might. They did it until the time came to offer the evening sacrifice. But there wasn't any reply. No one answered. No one paid any attention.

[30]Then Elijah said to all of the people, "Come here to me." So they went to him. He rebuilt the altar of the LORD. It had been destroyed. [31]Elijah got 12 stones. There was one for each tribe in the family line of Jacob. The LORD's message had come to Jacob. It had said, "Your name will be Israel." [32]Elijah used the stones to build an altar in honor of the LORD. He dug a ditch around it. The ditch was large enough to hold 13 quarts of seeds. [33]He arranged the wood for the fire. He cut the bull into pieces. He placed the pieces on the wood.

Then he said to some of the people, "Fill four large jars with water. Pour it on the offering and the wood." So they did.

[34]"Do it again," he said. So they did it again.

"Do it a third time," he ordered. And they did it the third time. [35]The water ran down around the altar. It even filled the ditch.

[36]When it was time to offer the evening sacrifice, the prophet Elijah stepped forward. He prayed, "LORD, you are the God of Abraham, Isaac and Israel. Today let everyone know that you are God in Israel. Let them know I'm your servant. Let them know I've done all of these things because you commanded me to. [37]Answer me. LORD, answer me. Then these people will know that you are the one and only God. They'll know that you are turning their hearts back to you again."

[38]The fire of the LORD came down. It burned up the sacrifice. It burned up the wood and the stones and the soil. It even licked up the water in the ditch.

[39]All of the people saw it. Then they fell down flat with their faces toward the ground. They cried out, "The LORD is the one and only God! The LORD is the one and only God!"

[40]Then Elijah commanded them, "Grab hold of the prophets of Baal. Don't let a single one of them get away!"

So they grabbed them. Elijah had them brought down to the Kishon Valley. There he had them put to death.

[41]Elijah said to Ahab, "Go. Eat and drink. I can hear the sound of a heavy rain."

[42]So Ahab went off to eat and drink.

But Elijah climbed to the top of Mount Carmel. He bent down toward the ground. Then he put his face between his knees.

[43]"Go and look toward the sea," he told his servant. So he went up and looked.

"I don't see anything there," he said.

Seven times Elijah said, "Go back."

[44]The seventh time the servant said, "I see a cloud. It's as small as a man's hand. It's coming up over the sea."

Elijah said, "Go to Ahab. Tell him, 'Tie your chariot to your horse. Go down to Jezreel before the rain stops you.'"

[45]Black clouds filled the sky. The wind came up, and a heavy rain began to fall. Ahab rode off to Jezreel.

[46]The power of the LORD came on Elijah. He tucked his coat into his belt. And he ran ahead of Ahab all the way to Jezreel.

Elijah Runs Away to Mount Horeb

19 Ahab told Jezebel everything Elijah had done. He told her how Elijah had killed all of the prophets with his sword.

2So Jezebel sent a message to Elijah. She said, "You can be sure that I will kill you, just as I killed the other prophets. I'll do it by this time tomorrow. If I don't, may the gods punish me greatly."

3Elijah was afraid. So he ran for his life. He came to Beersheba in Judah. He left his servant there.

4Then he traveled for one day into the desert. He came to a small tree. He sat down under it. He prayed that he would die. "LORD, I've had enough," he said. "Take my life. I'm no better than my people of long ago." 5Then he lay down under the tree. And he fell asleep.

Suddenly an angel touched him. The angel said, "Get up and eat." 6Elijah looked around. Near his head he saw a flat cake of bread. It had been baked over hot coals. A jar of water was also there. So Elijah ate and drank. Then he lay down again.

7The angel of the LORD came to him a second time. He touched him and said, "Get up and eat. Your journey will be long and hard."

8So he got up. He ate and drank. The food gave him new strength. He traveled for 40 days and 40 nights. He kept going until he arrived at Horeb. It was the mountain of God. 9There he went into a cave and spent the night.

The LORD Appears to Elijah

A message came to Elijah from the LORD. He said, "Elijah, what are you doing here?"

10He replied, "LORD God who rules over all, I've been very committed to you. The people of Israel have turned their backs on your covenant. They have torn down your altars. They've put your prophets to death with their swords. I'm the only one left. And they are trying to kill me."

11The LORD said, "Go out. Stand on the mountain in front of me. I am going to pass by."

As the LORD approached, a very powerful wind tore the mountains apart. It broke up the rocks. But the LORD wasn't in the wind.

After the wind there was an earthquake. But the LORD wasn't in the earthquake.

12After the earthquake a fire came. But the LORD wasn't in the fire.

And after the fire there was only a gentle whisper. 13When Elijah heard it, he pulled his coat over his face. He went out and stood at the entrance to the cave.

Then a voice said to him, "Elijah, what are you doing here?"

14He replied, "LORD God who rules over all, I've been very committed to you. The people of Israel have turned their backs on your covenant. They have torn down your altars. They've put your prophets to death with their swords. I'm the only one left. And they are trying to kill me."

15The LORD said to him, "Go back the way you came. Go to the Desert of Damascus. When you get there, anoint Hazael as king over Aram. 16Also anoint Jehu as king over Israel. He is the son of Nimshi. And anoint Elisha from Abel Meholah as the next prophet after you. He is the son of Shaphat. 17Jehu will put to death anyone who escapes Hazael's sword. And Elisha will put to death anyone who escapes Jehu's sword.

18"But I will keep 7,000 people in Israel for myself. They have not bowed down to Baal. And they have not kissed him."

The LORD Chooses Elisha

19Elijah left Mount Horeb. He saw Elisha, the son of Shaphat. Elisha was plowing in a field. He was driving the last of 12 pairs of oxen. Elijah went up to him. He threw his coat around him. 20Then Elisha left his oxen. He ran after Elijah. "Let me kiss my father and mother good-by," he said. "Then I'll come with you."

"Go back," Elijah replied. "What have I done to you?"

21So Elisha left him and went back. He got his two oxen and killed them. He burned the plow to cook the meat. He gave it to the people, and they ate it. Then he started to follow Elijah. He became Elijah's assistant.

Ben-Hadad Attacks Samaria

20 Ben-Hadad brought his whole army together. He was king of Aram. He went up to Samaria. He took 32 kings and their horses and chariots with him. All of them surrounded Samaria and attacked it.

2Ben-Hadad sent messengers into the city. They spoke to Ahab, the king of Israel. They told him, "Ben-Hadad says, 3'Your silver and gold belong to me. The best of your wives and children also belong to me.'"

4The king of Israel replied, "What you say is true. You are my king and master. I belong to you. And everything I have belongs to you."

5The messengers came again. They told Ahab, "Ben-Hadad says, 'I commanded you to give me your silver and gold. I also commanded you to give me your wives and children. 6But now I'm going to send my officials to you. They will come about this time tomorrow. They'll search your palace. They'll search the houses of your officials. They'll take everything you value. And they'll carry all of it away.'"

7The king of Israel sent for all of the elders of the land. He said to them, "This man is really looking for trouble! He sent for my wives and children. He sent for my silver and gold. And I agreed to give them to him."

8All of the elders and people answered, "Don't listen to him. Don't agree to give him what he wants."

9So Ahab replied to Ben-Hadad's messengers. He said, "Tell my king and master, 'I will do

everything you commanded me to do the first
time. But this time, I can't do what you want me
to do.'"

They took Ahab's answer back to Ben-Hadad.

10Then Ben-Hadad sent another message to
Ahab. It said, "There won't be enough dust left in
Samaria to give each of my followers even a hand-
ful. If there is, may the gods punish me greatly."

11The king of Israel replied. He said, "Tell him,
'Someone who puts his armor on shouldn't brag
like someone who takes it off.'"

12Ben-Hadad and the kings were in their tents
drinking. That's when he heard the message. He
ordered his men, "Get ready to attack." So they
prepared to attack the city.

Ahab Wins the Battle Over Ben-Hadad

13During that time a prophet came to Ahab, the
king of Israel. He announced, "The LORD says, 'Do
you see this huge army? I will hand it over to you
today. Then you will know that I am the LORD.'"

14"But who will do it?" Ahab asked.

The prophet answered, "The LORD says, 'The
young officers who are under the area commanders will do it.'"

"And who will start the battle?" he asked.

The prophet answered, "You will."

15So Ahab sent for the young officers who were
under the area commanders. The total number of
officers was 232. Ahab gathered together the rest
of the men of Israel. The total number of them was
7,000. 16They started out at noon. At that time Ben-
Hadad and the 32 kings who were helping him
were in their tents. They were getting drunk. 17The
young officers who were under Ahab's area commanders marched out first.

Ben-Hadad had sent out scouts. They came
back and reported, "Men are marching against us
from Samaria."

18Ben-Hadad said, "They might be coming to
make peace. If they are, take them alive. Or they
might be coming to make war. If they are, take
them alive."

19The young officers marched out of the city.
The army was right behind them. 20Each man
struck down the one who was fighting against him.
When that happened, the army of Aram ran away.
The men of Israel chased them. But Ben-Hadad,
the king of Aram, escaped on a horse. Some of his
horsemen escaped with him.

21The king of Israel attacked them. He overpowered the horses and chariots. Large numbers
of the men of Aram were wounded or killed.

22After that, the prophet came to the king of Is-
rael again. He said, "Make your position stronger.
Do what needs to be done. Next spring the king of
Aram will attack you again."

23During that time, the officials of the king of
Aram gave him advice. They said, "The gods of
Israel are gods of the hills. That's why they were
too strong for us. But suppose we fight them on
the flatlands. Then we'll certainly be stronger than
they are.

24"Here's what you should do. Don't let any of
the kings continue as military leaders. Have other
officers take their places. 25You must also put
another army together. It should be just like the
one you lost. It should have the same number of
horses and chariots. Then we'll be able to fight
against Israel on the flatlands. And we'll certainly
be stronger than they are."

Ben-Hadad agreed with their advice. He did
what they suggested.

26The next spring Ben-Hadad brought together
the men of Aram. They went up to the city of
Aphek to fight against Israel.

27The men of Israel were also brought together.
They were given supplies. They marched out to
fight against their enemies. Israel's army camped
across from Aram's army. The men of Israel
looked like two small flocks of goats that had
become separated from the others. But the men of
Aram covered the countryside.

28The man of God came up to the king of Israel again. He told him, "The LORD says, 'The men
of Aram think I am a god of the hills. They do not
think I am a god of the valleys. So I will hand their
huge army over to you. Then you will know that I
am the LORD.'"

29For seven days the two armies camped across
from each other. On the seventh day the battle
began. The men of Israel wounded or killed
100,000 Aramean soldiers on foot. That happened
in a single day. 30The rest of the men of Aram
escaped to the city of Aphek. Its wall fell down on
27,000 of them. Ben-Hadad ran to the city. He hid
in a secret room.

31His officials said to him, "Look, we've heard
that the kings of Israel's royal house often show
mercy. So let's go to the king of Israel. Let's wear
black clothes. Let's tie ropes around our heads.
Perhaps Ahab will spare your life."

32So they wore black clothes. They tied ropes
around their heads. Then they went to the king of
Israel. They told him, "Your servant Ben-Hadad
says, 'Please let me live.'"

The king answered, "Is he still alive? He used to
be my friend."

33The men thought that was good news. So they
quickly used the word Ahab had used. "Yes! Your
friend Ben-Hadad!" they said.

"Go and get him," the king said.

Ben-Hadad came out of the secret room. Then
Ahab had him get into his chariot.

34"I'll return the cities my father took from your
father," Ben-Hadad offered. "You can set up your
own market areas in Damascus. That's what my
father did in Samaria."

Ahab said, "If we sign a peace treaty, I'll set
you free."

So he made a treaty with him. Then Ahab let
him go.

A Prophet Brings Charges Against Ahab

35 There was a group that was called the company of the prophets. A message from the LORD
came to one of their members. He said to his companion, "Strike me down with your weapon." But
the man wouldn't do it.
36 The prophet said, "You haven't obeyed the
LORD. So as soon as you leave me, a lion will kill
you."
The companion went away. And a lion found
him and killed him.
37 The prophet found another man. He said,
"Please strike me down."
So the man struck him down and wounded him.
38 Then the prophet went and stood by the road.
He waited for the king to come by. He pulled his
headband down over his eyes so no one would recognize him.
39 The king passed by. Then the prophet called
out to him. He said, "I went into the middle of the
battle. Someone came to me with a prisoner. He
said, 'Guard this man. Don't let him get away. If
he does, you will pay for his life with yours. Or
you can pay 75 pounds of silver.' 40 While I was
busy here and there, the man disappeared."
"That's your sentence," the king of Israel told
him. "You have said so yourself."
41 Then the prophet quickly removed the headband from his eyes. The king of Israel recognized
him as one of the prophets. 42 He told the king,
"The LORD says, 'You have set a man free. But I
had said he should be set apart to the LORD in a
special way to be destroyed. So you must pay for
his life with yours. You must pay for his people's
lives with the lives of your people.'"
43 The king of Israel was angry. He was in a bad
mood. He went back to his palace in Samaria.

Ahab Takes Over Naboth's Vineyard

21 Some time later King Ahab wanted a certain vineyard. It belonged to Naboth from
Jezreel. The vineyard was in Jezreel. It was close
to the palace of Ahab, the king of Samaria.
2 Ahab said to Naboth, "Let me have your vineyard. It's close to my palace. I want to use it for a
vegetable garden. I'll trade you a better vineyard
for it. Or, if you prefer, I'll pay you what it's
worth."
3 But Naboth replied, "May the LORD keep me
from giving you the land my family handed down
to me."
4 So Ahab went home. He was angry. He was in
a bad mood because of what Naboth from Jezreel
had said. He had told him, "I won't give you the
land my family handed down to me."
So Ahab lay on his bed. He was in a very bad
mood. He wouldn't even eat anything.
5 His wife Jezebel came in. She asked him,
"Why are you in such a bad mood? Why won't
you eat anything?"
6 He answered her, "Because I spoke to Naboth
from Jezreel. I said, 'Sell me your vineyard. Or, if
you prefer, I'll give you another vineyard in its
place.' But he said, 'I won't sell you my
vineyard.'"
7 His wife Jezebel said, "Is this how the king of
Israel acts? Get up! Eat something! Cheer up. I'll
get you the vineyard of Naboth from Jezreel."
8 So she wrote some letters in Ahab's name. She
stamped them with his seal. Then she sent them to
the elders and nobles who lived in the city where
Naboth lived. 9 In those letters she wrote,

> "Announce a day when people are sup-
> posed to go without eating. Have Naboth sit
> in an important place among the people.
> 10 But put two worthless and evil men in seats
> across from him. Have them witness to the
> fact that he has called down curses on God
> and the king. Then take him out of the city.
> Kill him by throwing stones at him."

11 So the elders and nobles who lived in that city
did what Jezebel wanted. They did everything she
directed in the letters she had written to them.
12 They announced a day of fasting. They had Naboth sit in an important place among the people.
13 Then two worthless and evil men came and sat
across from him. They brought charges against
Naboth in front of the people. The two men said,
"Naboth has called down curses on God and the
king." So they took him outside the city. They
killed him by throwing stones at him.
14 Then they sent a message to Jezebel. They
said, "Naboth is dead. We killed him by throwing
stones at him."
15 Jezebel heard that Naboth had been killed. As
soon as she heard it, she said to Ahab, "Get up.
Take over the vineyard of Naboth from Jezreel. It's
the one he wouldn't sell to you. He isn't alive anymore. He's dead."
16 Ahab heard that Naboth was dead. So he got
up. He went down to take over Naboth's vineyard.
17 Then a message from the LORD came to Elijah, who was from Tishbe. It said, 18 "Go down to
see Ahab, the king of Israel. He rules in Samaria.
You will find him in Naboth's vineyard. He has
gone there to take it over. 19 Tell him, 'The LORD
says, "Haven't you murdered a man? Haven't you
taken over his property?"' Then tell him, 'The
LORD says, "Dogs licked up Naboth's blood. In
that same place dogs will lick up your blood. Yes,
I said your blood!"'"
20 Ahab said to Elijah, "My enemy! You have
found me!"
"I have found you," he answered. "That's
because you gave yourself over to do evil things.
You did what was evil in the sight of the LORD.
21 So the LORD says, 'I am going to bring horrible
trouble on you. I will destroy your children after
you. I will cut off every male in Israel who is
related to you. It does not matter whether they are

slaves or free. 22I will make your royal house like
the house of Jeroboam, the son of Nebat. I will
make it like the house of Baasha, the son of Ahijah. You have made me very angry. You have
caused Israel to commit sin.'
23"The LORD also says, 'Dogs will eat up Jezebel near the wall of Jezreel.'
24"Some of the people who belong to Ahab will
die in the city. Dogs will eat them up. Others will
die in the country. The birds of the air will eat them."
25There was never anyone like Ahab. He gave
himself over to do what was evil in the sight of the
LORD. His wife Jezebel talked him into it. 26He
acted in the most evil way. He worshiped statues
of gods. He was like the Amorites. The LORD
drove them out to make room for Israel.
27When Ahab heard what Elijah had said, he
tore his clothes. He put on black clothes. He went
without eating. He even slept in his clothes. He
went around looking sad.
28Then a message from the LORD came to Elijah, who was from Tishbe. It said, 29"Have you
seen how Ahab has made himself low in my sight?
Because he has done that, I will not bring trouble
on him while he lives. But I will bring it on his
royal house when his son is king."

Micaiah Prophesies Against Ahab

22 For three years there wasn't any war
between Aram and Israel. 2In the third year
Jehoshaphat went down to see Ahab, the king of
Israel. Jehoshaphat was king of Judah.
3The king of Israel had spoken to his officials.
He had said, "Don't you know that Ramoth Gilead belongs to us? And we aren't even doing anything to take it back from the king of Aram."
4So Ahab asked Jehoshaphat, "Will you go with
me to fight against Ramoth Gilead?"
Jehoshaphat replied to the king of Israel, "Yes.
I'll go with you. My men will go with you. My
horses will also go with you." 5Jehoshaphat continued, "First ask the LORD for advice."
6So the king of Israel brought about 400 prophets
together. He asked them, "Should I go to war
against Ramoth Gilead? Or should I stay here?"
"Go," they answered. "The Lord will hand it
over to you."
7But Jehoshaphat asked, "Isn't there a prophet
of the LORD here? If there is, ask him what we
should do."
8The king of Israel answered Jehoshaphat. He
said, "There is still one other man we can go to.
We can ask the LORD for advice through him. But
I hate him. He never prophesies anything good
about me. He only prophesies bad things. His
name is Micaiah. He's the son of Imlah."
"You shouldn't say bad things about him," Jehoshaphat replied.
9So the king of Israel called for one of his officials. He told him, "Bring Micaiah, the son of Imlah, at once."
10The king of Israel and Jehoshaphat, the king
of Judah, were wearing their royal robes. They
were sitting on their thrones at the threshing floor.
It was near the entrance of the gate of Samaria. All
of the prophets were prophesying in front of them.
11Zedekiah was the son of Kenaanah. Zedekiah
had made horns out of iron. They looked like animal horns. He announced, "The LORD says, 'With
these horns you will drive back the men of Aram
until they are destroyed.'"
12All of the other prophets were prophesying the
same thing. "Attack Ramoth Gilead," they said.
"Win the battle over it. The LORD will hand it over
to you."
13A messenger went to get Micaiah. He said to
him, "Look. The other prophets agree. All of them
are saying the king will have success. So agree
with them. Say the same thing they do."
14But Micaiah said, "You can be sure that the
LORD lives. And you can be just as sure that I can
only tell the king what the LORD tells me to say."
15When Micaiah arrived, the king spoke to him.
He asked, "Should we go to war against Ramoth
Gilead? Or should I stay here?"
"Attack," he answered. "You will win. The
LORD will hand Ramoth Gilead over to you."
16The king said to him, "I've made you promise
to tell the truth many times before. So don't tell
me anything but the truth in the name of the
LORD."
17Then Micaiah answered, "I saw all of the people of Israel scattered on the hills. They were like
sheep that didn't have a shepherd. The LORD said,
'These people do not have a master. Let each of
them go home in peace.'"
18The king of Israel spoke to Jehoshaphat. He
said, "Didn't I tell you he never prophesies anything good about me? He only prophesies bad
things."
19Micaiah continued, "Listen to the LORD's
message. I saw the LORD sitting on his throne.
Some of the angels of heaven were standing at his
right side. The others were standing at his left side.
So all of them were standing around him. 20The
LORD said, 'Who will try to get Ahab to attack Ramoth Gilead? I want him to die there.'
"One angel suggested one thing. Another suggested something else. 21Finally, a spirit came forward and stood in front of the LORD. The spirit
said, 'I'll try to get Ahab to do it.'
22"'How?' the LORD asked.
"The spirit said, 'I'll go out and put lies in the
mouths of all of his prophets.'
"'You will have success in getting Ahab to
attack Ramoth Gilead,' said the LORD. 'Go and
do it.'
23"So the LORD has put lies in the mouths of all
of your prophets. He has said that great harm will
come to you."
24Then Zedekiah, the son of Kenaanah, went up
and slapped Micaiah in the face. "So you think the

spirit that was sent by the LORD went away from me to speak to you, do you?" he asked. "Which way did he go?"

25 Micaiah replied, "You will find out on the day you go to hide in an inside room to save your life."

26 Then the king of Israel gave an order. He said, "Take Micaiah away. Send him back to Amon. Amon is the ruler of the city of Samaria. And send him back to Joash. Joash is a member of the royal court. 27 Tell him, 'The king says, "Put this fellow in prison. Don't give him anything but bread and water until I return safely." ' "

28 Micaiah announced, "Do you really think you will return safely? If you do, the LORD hasn't spoken through me." He continued, "All of you people, remember what I've said!"

Ahab Is Killed at Ramoth Gilead

29 So the king of Israel went up to Ramoth Gilead. Jehoshaphat, the king of Judah, went there too.

30 The king of Israel spoke to Jehoshaphat. He said, "I'll go into battle wearing different clothes. Then people won't recognize me. But you wear your royal robes."

So the king of Israel put on different clothes. Then he went into battle.

31 The king of Aram had given an order to his 32 chariot commanders. He had said, "Fight only against the king of Israel. Don't fight against anyone else."

32 The chariot commanders saw Jehoshaphat. They thought, "That has to be the king of Israel." So they turned to attack him. But Jehoshaphat cried out. 33 Then the commanders saw he wasn't the king of Israel after all. So they stopped chasing him.

34 But someone shot an arrow without taking aim. The arrow hit the king of Israel between the parts of his armor. The king told his chariot driver, "Turn the chariot around. Get me out of this battle. I've been wounded." 35 All day long the battle continued. The king kept himself standing up by leaning against the inside of his chariot. He kept his face toward the men of Aram. The blood from his wound ran down onto the floor of the chariot. That evening he died.

36 As the sun was setting, a cry spread through the army. "Every man must go to his own town!" they said. "Everyone must go to his own land!"

37 So the king died. He was brought to Samaria. They buried his body there. 38 They washed the chariot at a pool in Samaria. It was where the prostitutes took baths. The dogs licked up Ahab's blood. It happened exactly as the LORD had said it would.

39 The other events of Ahab's rule are written down. Everything he did is written down. That includes the palace he built and decorated with ivory. It also includes the cities he built up and put high walls around. All of those things are written in the official records of the kings of Israel. 40 Ahab joined the members of his family who had already died. His son Ahaziah became the next king after him.

Jehoshaphat's Rule Comes to an End

41 Jehoshaphat began to rule over Judah. It was in the fourth year that Ahab was king of Israel. Jehoshaphat was the son of Asa. 42 Jehoshaphat was 35 years old when he became king. He ruled in Jerusalem for 25 years. His mother's name was Azubah. She was the daughter of Shilhi.

43 Jehoshaphat followed all of the ways of his father Asa. He didn't wander away from them. He did what was right in the eyes of the LORD. But the high places weren't removed. The people continued to offer sacrifices and burn incense at them.

44 Jehoshaphat was also at peace with the king of Israel.

45 The other events of Jehoshaphat's rule are written down. The brave things he did in battle and everything else he accomplished are written down. All of those things are written in the official records of the kings of Judah.

46 Jehoshaphat got rid of the rest of the male prostitutes who were at the temples. They had remained in the land even after the rule of his father Asa.

47 At that time Edom didn't have a king. An appointed official was in charge.

48 Jehoshaphat built many ships that he used to carry goods to be traded. The ships were supposed to go to Ophir for gold. But they never had a chance to sail. They were wrecked at Ezion Geber. 49 At that time Ahaziah, the son of Ahab, spoke to Jehoshaphat. He said, "Let my men sail with yours." But Jehoshaphat refused.

50 Jehoshaphat joined the members of his family who had already died. His body was buried in the family tomb in the city of King David. His son Jehoram became the next king after him.

Ahaziah Becomes King of Israel

51 Ahaziah became king of Israel in Samaria. It was in the 17th year that Jehoshaphat was king of Judah. Ahaziah ruled over Israel for two years. He was the son of Ahab.

52 Ahaziah did what was evil in the sight of the LORD. He lived the way his father and mother had lived. He lived the way Jeroboam, the son of Nebat, had lived. Jeroboam had caused Israel to commit sin. 53 Ahaziah served and worshiped the god Baal. He made the LORD, the God of Israel, very angry. That's exactly what his father had done.

2 Kings

The LORD Judges Ahaziah

1 After Ahab died, Moab refused to remain under Israel's control.

2Ahaziah had fallen through the window of his upstairs room in Samaria. He had hurt himself. So he sent messengers to ask the god Baal-Zebub for advice. Baal-Zebub was the god of the city of Ekron. Ahaziah said to the messengers, "Go and ask Baal-Zebub whether I will get well again."

3But the angel of the LORD spoke to Elijah, who was from Tishbe. He said, "Go up to see the messengers of Ahaziah, the king of Samaria. Tell them, 'You are on your way to ask Baal-Zebub for advice. He is the god of Ekron. Are you going to that god because you think there is no God in Israel?' 4The LORD says to Ahaziah, 'You will never leave the bed you are lying on. You can be sure that you will die!'" So Elijah went to see the messengers.

5They returned to the king. He asked them, "Why have you come back?"

6"A man met us on our way there," they replied. "He said to us, 'Go back to the king who sent you. Tell him, "The LORD says, 'You are sending messengers to ask Baal-Zebub for advice. He is the god of Ekron. Are you going to that god because you think there is no God in Israel? You will never leave the bed you are lying on. You can be sure that you will die!'"'"

7The king asked them, "What kind of man came to see you? Who told you those things?"

8They replied, "He was wearing clothes that were made out of hair. He had a leather belt around his waist."

The king said, "That was Elijah from Tishbe."

9Then Ahaziah sent a captain to Elijah. The captain had his company of 50 men with him. Elijah was sitting on top of a hill. The captain went up to him. He said to Elijah, "Man of God, the king says, 'Come down!'"

10Elijah answered the captain, "If I'm really a man of God, may fire come down from heaven! May it burn you and your 50 men up!"

Then fire came down from heaven. It burned up the captain and his men.

11After that happened, the king sent another captain to Elijah. The captain had his 50 men with him. He said to Elijah, "Man of God, the king says, 'Come down at once!'"

12Elijah replied, "If I'm really a man of God, may fire come down from heaven! May it burn you and your 50 men up!"

Then the fire of God came down from heaven. It burned up the captain and his 50 men.

13So the king sent a third captain with his 50 men. The captain went up to Elijah. He fell on his knees in front of him. "Man of God," he begged, "please have respect for my life! Please have respect for the lives of these 50 men! 14Fire has come down from heaven. It has burned up the first two captains and all of their men. But please have respect for my life!"

15The angel of the LORD spoke to Elijah. He said, "Go down with him. Don't be afraid of him."

So Elijah got up. He went down with the captain to the king.

16Elijah told the king, "The LORD says, 'You have sent messengers to ask Baal-Zebub for advice. He is the god of Ekron. Did you go to that god for advice because you think there is no God in Israel? You will never leave the bed you are lying on. You can be sure that you will die!'"

17So Ahaziah died. It happened just as the LORD had said it would. He had spoken that message through Elijah.

Ahaziah didn't have any sons. So Joram, his younger brother, became the next king after him. It was the second year of Jehoram, the king of Judah. Jehoram was the son of Jehoshaphat.

18All of the other events of Ahaziah's rule are written down. The things he did are written down. All of those things are written in the official records of the kings of Israel.

Elijah Is Taken Up to Heaven

2 Elijah and Elisha were on their way from Gilgal. The LORD was going to use a strong wind to take Elijah up to heaven. 2Elijah said to Elisha, "Stay here. The LORD has sent me to Bethel."

But Elisha said, "I won't leave you. And that's just as sure as the LORD and you are alive." So they went down to Bethel.

3There was a company of prophets at Bethel. They came out to where Elisha was. They asked him, "Do you know what the LORD is going to do? He's going to take your master away from you today."

"Yes, I know," Elisha replied. "But don't talk about it."

4Then Elijah said to him, "Stay here, Elisha. The LORD has sent me to Jericho."

Elisha replied, "I won't leave you. And that's just as sure as the LORD and you are alive." So they went to Jericho.

5There was a company of prophets at Jericho. They went up to where Elisha was. They asked him, "Do you know what the LORD is going to do? He's going to take your master away from you today."

"Yes, I know," Elisha replied. "But don't talk about it."

6Then Elijah said to him, "Stay here. The LORD has sent me to the Jordan River."

Elisha replied, "I won't leave you. And that's just as sure as the LORD and you are alive." So the two of them walked on.

7Fifty men from the company of the prophets followed them. The men stopped and stood not far away from them. They faced the place where Elijah and Elisha had stopped at the Jordan River. 8Elijah rolled his coat up. Then he struck the water with it. The water parted to the right and to the left. The two of them went across the river on dry ground.

9After they had gone across, Elijah spoke to Elisha. He said, "Tell me. What can I do for you before I'm taken away from you?"

"Please give me a double share of your spirit," Elisha replied.

10"You have asked me for something I can't give you," Elijah said. "Only the LORD can give it. But suppose you see me when I'm taken away from you. Then you will receive what you have asked for. If you don't see me, you won't receive it."

11They kept walking along and talking together. Suddenly a chariot and horses appeared. Fire was all around them. The chariot and horses came between the two men. Then Elijah went up to heaven in a strong wind.

12Elisha saw it. He cried out to Elijah, "My father! You are like a father to me! You are the true chariots and horsemen of Israel!"

Elisha didn't see Elijah anymore. Then Elisha took hold of his own clothes and tore them apart.

13He picked up the coat that had fallen from Elijah. He went back and stood on the bank of the Jordan River. 14Then he struck the water with Elijah's coat. "Where is the power of the LORD?" he asked. "Where is the power of the God of Elijah?" When Elisha struck the water, it parted to the right and to the left. He went across the river.

15The company of the prophets from Jericho were watching. They said, "The spirit of Elijah has been given to Elisha." They went over to him. They bowed down to him with their faces toward the ground. 16"Look," they said. "We have 50 able men. Let them go and look for your master. Perhaps the Spirit of the LORD has lifted him up. Maybe he has put him down on a mountain or in a valley."

"No," Elisha replied. "Don't send them."

17But they kept asking until he felt he couldn't say no. So he said, "Send them." And they sent 50 men. They looked for Elijah for three days. But they didn't find him.

18So they returned to Elisha. He was staying in Jericho. Elisha said to them, "Didn't I tell you not to go?"

Elisha Makes Jericho's Water Pure

19The men of Jericho spoke to Elisha. "Look," they said. "This town has a good location. You can see that for yourself. But the spring of water here is bad. So the land doesn't produce anything."

20"Bring me a new bowl," Elisha said. "Put some salt in it." So they brought it to him.

21Then he went out to the spring. He threw the salt into it. He told them, "The LORD says, 'I have made this water pure. It will never cause death again. It will never keep the land from producing crops again.'" 22The water has stayed pure to this very day. That's what Elisha had said would happen.

Some Young Fellows Make Fun of Elisha

23Elisha left Jericho and went up to Bethel. He was walking along the road. Some young fellows came out of the town. They made fun of him. "Go on up! You don't even have any hair on your head!" they said. "Go on up! You don't even have any hair on your head!"

24He turned around and looked at them. And he called down a curse on them. He did it in the name of the LORD. Then two bears came out of the woods. They attacked 42 of the young fellows.

25Elisha went on to Mount Carmel. From there he returned to Samaria.

Moab's King Refuses to Obey Israel's King

3 Joram became king of Israel in Samaria. It was in the 18th year that Jehoshaphat was king of Judah. Joram ruled for 12 years. He was the son of Ahab.

2Joram did what was evil in the sight of the LORD. But he wasn't as bad as his father and mother had been. His father had made a sacred stone that was used to worship the god Baal. Joram got rid of it. 3But he kept on committing the sins of Jeroboam, the son of Nebat. Jeroboam had also caused Israel to commit those same sins. Joram didn't turn away from them.

4Mesha raised sheep. He was king of Moab. He had to supply the king of Israel with 100,000 lambs a year. He also had to supply him with the wool of 100,000 rams a year.

5Ahab died. Moab's king refused to obey the next king of Israel. 6So at that time King Joram started out from Samaria. He gathered all of Israel's troops together.

7He also sent a message to Jehoshaphat, the king of Judah. It said, "The king of Moab is refusing to obey me. Will you go with me to fight against Moab?"

"Yes. I'll go with you," he replied. "My men will go with you. My horses will also go with you."

8"What road should we take to attack Moab?" Joram asked.

"The one that goes through the Desert of Edom," Jehoshaphat answered.

9So the king of Israel started out. The king of Judah and the king of Edom went with him. Their armies marched around the southern end of the Dead Sea. After seven days they ran out of water.

There wasn't any water for the men or their animals.

10“What should we do now?” exclaimed the king of Israel. “The LORD has called us three kings together. Did he do it only to hand us over to Moab?”

11But Jehoshaphat asked, “Isn't there a prophet of the LORD here? Can't we ask the LORD for advice through him?”

An officer of the king of Israel spoke up. He answered, “Elisha is here. He's the son of Shaphat. Elisha used to serve Elijah.”

12Jehoshaphat said, “The LORD speaks through him.” So the king of Israel went down to see Elisha. Jehoshaphat and the king of Edom also went there.

13Elisha spoke to the king of Israel. He said, “What do you and I have in common? Go to your father's prophets. Go to your mother's prophets.”

“No,” the king of Israel answered. “The LORD called us three kings together. He did it to hand us over to Moab.”

14Elisha said, “I serve the LORD who rules over all. You can be sure that he lives. And you can be just as sure that I have respect for Jehoshaphat, the king of Judah. If I didn't, I wouldn't look at you or even notice you. 15But now bring me someone who plays the harp.”

While that person was playing the harp, the LORD's powerful hand came on Elisha. 16Elisha announced, “The LORD says, ‘Dig a lot of ditches in this valley.’ 17Do it because the LORD says, ‘You will not see wind or rain. But this valley will be filled with water. Then you, your cattle and your other animals will have water to drink.’

18“That's an easy thing for the LORD to do. He will also hand Moab over to you. 19You will destroy every city that has high walls around it. You will destroy every major town. You will cut down every good tree. You will stop up all of the springs of water. And you will cover every good field with stones.”

20The next day, the time came to offer the morning sacrifice. And then it happened! Water was flowing from the direction of Edom! In fact, the land was filled with water!

21Now all of the people of Moab had heard that the kings had come to fight against them. So Moab sent for all of its fighting men. It didn't matter whether they were young or old. They sent for everyone who could carry a weapon. All of them were stationed at the border.

22They got up early in the morning. The sun was already shining on the water. Across the way, the water looked red to the men of Moab. It looked like blood. 23“That's blood!” they said. “Those kings must have fought and killed each other. Let's go, Moab! Let's take everything that has any value.”

24So the men of Moab went to the camp of Israel. Just as they arrived there, the men of Israel got ready to fight. They fought against the men of Moab until they ran away. The men of Israel marched into the land and attacked it. They killed the people of Moab. 25They destroyed the towns. Each man threw a large stone on every good field. They did that until the fields were covered. They stopped up all of the springs of water. And they cut down every good tree. The only town that was left with any stones in place was Kir Hareseth. But men who were armed with slings surrounded it. Then they attacked it.

26The king of Moab saw that the battle had gone against him. So he took with him 700 men who had swords. They tried to break through the battle lines to the king of Edom. But they couldn't do it.

27Then the king of Moab got his oldest son. He was the son who would become the next king after him. He offered his son as a sacrifice on the city wall. That shocked and terrified the men of Israel. So they pulled back. And they returned to their own land.

Elisha Provides Olive Oil for a Widow

4 The wife of a man from the company of the prophets cried out to Elisha. She said, “My husband is dead. You know how much respect he had for the LORD. But he owed money to someone. And now that person is coming to take my two boys away. They will become his slaves.”

2Elisha replied to her, “How can I help you? Tell me. What do you have in your house?”

“I don't have anything there at all,” she said. “All I have is a little olive oil.”

3Elisha said, “Go around to all of your neighbors. Ask them for empty jars. Get as many as you can. 4Then go inside your house. Shut the door behind you and your sons. Pour oil into all of the jars. As each jar is filled, put it over to one side.”

5The woman left him. After that, she shut the door behind her and her sons. They brought the jars to her. And she kept pouring. 6When all of the jars were full, she spoke to one of her sons. She said, “Bring me another jar.”

But he replied, “There aren't any more left.” Then the oil stopped flowing.

7She went and told the man of God about it. He said, “Go and sell the oil. Pay what you owe. You and your sons can live on what is left.”

The Son of a Woman From Shunem Is Brought Back to Life

8One day Elisha went to the town of Shunem. A rich woman lived there. She begged him to stay and have a meal. So every time he came by, he stopped there to eat.

9The woman said to her husband, “That man often comes by here. I know that he is a holy man of God. 10Let's make a small room for him on the roof. We'll put a bed and a table in it. We'll also put a chair and a lamp in it. Then he can stay there when he comes to visit us.”

11One day Elisha came. He went up to his room. He lay down there. 12He said to his servant Gehazi, "Go and get the Shunammite woman." So he did. She stood in front of Elisha.

13He said to Gehazi, "Tell her, 'You have gone to a lot of trouble for us. Now what can we do for you? Can we speak to the king for you? Or can we speak to the commander of the army for you?' "

She replied, "I live among my own people. I have everything I need here."

14After she left, Elisha asked Gehazi, "What can we do for her?"

Gehazi said, "Well, she doesn't have a son. And her husband is old."

15Then Elisha said, "Bring her here again." So he did. She stood in the doorway. 16"You will hold a son in your arms," Elisha said. "It will be about this time next year."

"No, my master!" she objected. "You are a man of God. So don't lie to me!"

17But the woman became pregnant. She had a baby boy. It happened the next year about that same time. That's exactly what Elisha had told her would happen.

18The child grew. One day he went out to get his father. His father was with those who were gathering the crops.

19The boy said to his father, "My head hurts! It really hurts!"

His father told a servant, "Carry him to his mother." 20The servant lifted the boy up. He carried him to his mother.

The boy sat on her lap until noon. Then he died. 21She went up to the room on the roof. There she laid him on the bed of the man of God. Then she shut the door and went out.

22She sent for her husband. She said, "Please send me one of the servants and a donkey. Then I can go quickly to the man of God and return."

23"Why do you want to go to him today?" he asked. "It isn't the time for the New Moon Feast. It isn't the Sabbath day."

"Don't let that bother you," she said.

24She put a saddle on her donkey. She said to her servant, "Let's go. Don't slow down for me unless I tell you to." 25So she started out. She came to Mount Carmel. That's where the man of God was.

When she was still a long way off, he saw her coming. He said to his servant Gehazi, "Look! There's the woman from Shunem! 26Run out there to meet her. Ask her, 'Are you all right? Is your husband all right? Is your child all right?' "

"Everything is all right," she said.

27She came to the man of God at the mountain. Then she took hold of his feet. Gehazi came over to push her away. But the man of God said, "Leave her alone! She is suffering terribly. But the LORD hasn't told me the reason for it. He has hidden it from me."

28"My master, did I ask you for a son?" she said. "Didn't I tell you, 'Don't get my hopes up'?"

29Elisha said to Gehazi, "Tuck your coat into your belt. Take my wooden staff and run to Shunem. Don't say hello to anyone you see. If anyone says hello to you, don't answer. Lay my staff on the boy's face."

30But the child's mother said, "I won't leave you. And that's just as sure as the LORD and you are alive." So Elisha got up and followed her.

31Gehazi went on ahead. He laid Elisha's wooden staff on the boy's face. But there wasn't any sound. The boy didn't move at all.

So Gehazi went back to Elisha. He told him, "The boy hasn't awakened."

32Elisha arrived at the house. The boy was dead. He was lying on Elisha's bed.

33Elisha went into the room. He shut the door. He was alone with the boy. He prayed to the LORD. 34Then he got on the bed. He lay down on the boy. His mouth touched the boy's mouth. His eyes touched the boy's eyes. And his hands touched the boy's hands. As Elisha lay on the boy, the boy's body grew warm.

35Elisha turned away. He walked back and forth in the room. Then he got on the bed again. He lay down on the boy once more. The boy sneezed seven times. After that, he opened his eyes.

36Elisha sent for Gehazi. He said to him, "Go and get the Shunammite woman." So he did. When she came, Elisha said, "Take your son." 37She came in. She fell at Elisha's feet. She bowed down with her face toward the ground. Then she took her son and went out.

Deadly Food in a Pot

38Elisha returned to Gilgal. There wasn't enough food to eat in that area. The company of the prophets was meeting with Elisha. So he said to his servant, "Put the large pot over the fire. Cook some stew for these men."

39One of them went out into the fields to gather herbs. He found a wild vine. He gathered up some of its gourds. He brought them back with him in his coat. Then he cut them up into the pot of stew. But no one knew what they were.

40The stew was poured out for the men. They began to eat it. But then they cried out, "Man of God, the food in that pot will kill us!" They couldn't eat it.

41Elisha said, "Get some flour." He put it in the pot. He said, "Serve it to the men to eat." Then there wasn't anything in the pot that could harm them.

Elisha Feeds 100 People

42A man came from Baal Shalishah. He brought the man of God 20 loaves of barley bread. They had been baked from the first grain that had ripened. He also brought some heads of new grain. "Give this food to the people to eat," Elisha said.

43"How can I put this in front of 100 men?" his servant asked.

But Elisha answered, "Give it to the people to
eat. Do it because the LORD says, 'They will eat
and have some left over.'"
44Then the servant put the food in front of them.
They ate it and had some left over. It happened just
as the LORD had said it would.

Naaman Is Healed of a Skin Disease

5 Naaman was commander of the army of the
king of Aram. He was a very important man
in the eyes of his master. And he was highly
respected. That's because the LORD had helped
him win the battle over Aram's enemies. He was a
brave soldier. But he had a skin disease.
2Companies of soldiers from Aram had
marched out. They had captured a young girl from
Israel. She became a servant of Naaman's wife.
3She spoke to the woman she was serving. She
said, "I wish my master would go and see the
prophet who is in Samaria. He would heal my
master of his skin disease."
4Naaman went to see his own master. He told
him what the girl from Israel had said.
5"I think you should go," the king of Aram
replied. "I'll give you a letter to take to the king of
Israel."
So Naaman left. He took 750 pounds of silver
with him. He also took 150 pounds of gold. And
he took ten sets of clothes. 6He carried the letter to
the king of Israel. It said, "I'm sending my servant
Naaman to you with this letter. I want you to heal
him of his skin disease."
7The king of Israel read the letter. As soon as he
did, he tore his royal robes. He said, "AmI God?
Can I kill people and bring them back to life? Why
does this fellow send someone to me to be healed
of his skin disease? He must be trying to pick a
fight with me!"
8Elisha, the man of God, heard that the king of
Israel had torn his robes. So he sent the king a message. It said, "Why have you torn your robes? Tell
the man to come to me. Then he will know there is
a prophet in Israel."
9So Naaman went to see Elisha. He took his
horses and chariots with him. He stopped at the
door of Elisha's house.
10Elisha sent a messenger out to him. The messenger said, "Go. Wash yourself in the Jordan
River seven times. Then your skin will be healed.
You will be pure and clean again."
11But Naaman went away angry. He said, "I was
sure he would come out to me. I thought he would
stand there and pray to the LORD his God. I thought
he would wave his hand over my skin. Then I
would be healed. 12And what about the Abana and
Pharpar rivers of Damascus? Aren't they better
than any of the rivers of Israel? Couldn't I wash in
them and be made pure and clean?" So he turned
and went away. He was burning with anger.
13Naaman's servants went over to him. They
said, "You are like a father to us. What if the
prophet Elisha had told you to do some great
thing? Wouldn't you have done it? But he only
said, 'Wash yourself. Then you will be pure and
clean.' You should be even more willing to do
that!"
14So Naaman went down to the Jordan River.
He dipped himself in it seven times. He did exactly
what the man of God had told him to do. Then his
skin was made pure again. It became clean like the
skin of a young boy.
15Naaman and all of his attendants went back to
the man of God. Naaman stood in front of Elisha.
He said, "Now I know that there is no God anywhere in the whole world except in Israel. Please
accept a gift from me."
16The prophet answered, "I serve the LORD. You
can be sure that he lives. And you can be just as
sure that I won't accept a gift from you." Even
though Naaman begged him to take it, Elisha
wouldn't.
17"I can see that you won't accept a gift from
me," said Naaman. "But please let me have some
soil from your land. Give me as much as a pair of
mules can carry. Here's why I want it. I won't ever
bring burnt offerings and sacrifices to any other
god again. I'll bring them only to the LORD. I'll
worship him on his own soil.
18"But there is one thing I hope the LORD will
forgive me for. From time to time my master will
enter the temple to bow down to his god Rimmon.
When he does, he'll lean on my arm. Then I'll
have to bow down there also. I hope the LORD will
forgive me for that."
19"Go in peace," Elisha said.
Naaman started out on his way.
20Gehazi was the servant of Elisha, the man of
God. Gehazi said to himself, "My master was too
easy on Naaman from Aram. He should have
accepted the gift he brought. I'm going to run after
Naaman. I'm going to get something from him.
And that's just as sure as the LORD is alive."
21Gehazi hurried after Naaman. Naaman saw
him running toward him. So he got down from the
chariot to greet him. "Is everything all right?" he
asked.
22"Everything is all right," Gehazi answered.
"My master sent me to say, 'Two young men from
the company of the prophets have just come to me.
They've come from the hill country of Ephraim.
Please give them 75 pounds of silver and two sets
of clothes.'"
23"I wish you would take twice as much silver,"
said Naaman. He begged Gehazi to accept it. Then
Naaman tied up 150 pounds of silver in two bags.
He also gave Gehazi two sets of clothes. He gave
all of it to two of his own servants. They carried it
ahead of Gehazi.
24Gehazi came to the hill where Elisha lived.
Then the servants handed the things over to Gehazi. He put them away in Elisha's house. He sent
the men away, and they left. 25Then he went back

inside the house. He stood in front of his master Elisha.

"Gehazi, where have you been?" Elisha asked.

"I didn't go anywhere," Gehazi answered.

26But Elisha said to him, "Didn't my spirit go with you? I know that the man got down from his chariot to greet you. Is this the time for you to accept money or clothes? Is it the time to take olive groves, vineyards, flocks or herds? Is it the time to accept male and female servants? 27You and your children after you will have Naaman's skin disease forever."

Then Gehazi left Elisha. And he had Naaman's skin disease. His skin was as white as snow.

An Ax Blade Floats

6 The company of the prophets spoke to Elisha. They said, "Look. The place where we meet with you is too small for us. 2We would like to go to the Jordan River. Each of us can get some wood there. We want to build a place there for us to live in."

Elisha said, "Go."

3Then one of them said, "Won't you please come with us?"

"I will," Elisha replied. 4And he went with them.

They went to the Jordan. There they began to cut down trees. 5One of them was cutting a tree down. The iron blade of his ax fell into the water. "Master!" he cried out. "This ax was borrowed!"

6The man of God asked, "Where did the blade fall?" He showed him the place. Then Elisha cut a stick and threw it there. That made the iron blade float. 7"Take it out of the water," he said. So the man reached out and took it.

Elisha Makes the Soldiers of Aram Blind

8The king of Aram was at war with Israel. He talked things over with his officers. Then he said, "I'm going to set up my camp in a certain place."

9The man of God sent a message to the king of Israel. It said, "Try to stay away from that place. Aram's army is going to be down there." 10The king of Israel checked on the place the man of God had told him about. Time after time Elisha warned the king. So the king was on guard in those places.

11All of that made the king of Aram very angry. He sent for his officers. He said to them, "Tell me. Which of us is on the side of the king of Israel?"

12"You are my king and master," said one of his officers. "None of us is on Israel's side. But Elisha is a prophet in Israel. He tells the king of Israel the very words you speak in your own bedroom."

13"Go and find out where he is," the king ordered. "Then I can send my men and capture him." The report came back. It said, "He's in Dothan."

14Then the king sent horses and chariots and a strong army there. They went at night and surrounded the city.

15The servant of the man of God got up the next morning. He went out early. He saw that an army with horses and chariots had surrounded the city. "My master!" the servant said. "What can we do?"

16"Don't be afraid," the prophet answered. "Those who are with us are more than those who are with them."

17Elisha prayed, "LORD, open my servant's eyes so he can see." Then the LORD opened his eyes. He looked up and saw the hills. He saw that Elisha was surrounded by horses and chariots. Fire was all around them.

18Aram's army came down toward Elisha. Then he prayed to the LORD. He said, "Make these soldiers blind." So the LORD made them blind, just as Elisha had prayed.

19Elisha told them, "This isn't the right road. This isn't the right city. Follow me. I'll lead you to the man you are looking for." He led them to Samaria.

20They entered the city. Then Elisha said, "LORD, open the eyes of these men. Help them see again." Then the LORD opened their eyes. They looked around. And there they were, inside Samaria!

21The king of Israel saw them. So he asked Elisha, "Should I kill them? I need your advice. You are like a father to me. Should I kill them?"

22"Don't kill them," he answered. "Would you kill men you have captured with your own sword or bow? Put some food and water in front of them. Then they can eat and drink. They can go back to their master."

23So he prepared a big dinner for them. After they had finished eating and drinking, he sent them away. They returned to their master. So the companies of soldiers from Aram stopped attacking Israel's territory.

Aram's Army Attacks Samaria

24Some time later, Ben-Hadad gathered his entire army together. Ben-Hadad was the king of Aram. His army marched up and surrounded Samaria. Then they attacked it.

25There wasn't enough food anywhere in the city. It was surrounded for so long that people had to weigh out two pounds of silver for a donkey's head. They had to weigh out two ounces of silver for half a pint of seed pods.

26One day the king of Israel was walking on top of the wall. A woman cried out to him, "You are my king and master. Please help me!"

27The king replied, "If the LORD doesn't help you, where can I get help for you? From the threshing floor? From the winepress?" 28He continued, "What's wrong?"

She answered, "A woman said to me, 'Give up your son. Then we can eat him today. Tomorrow we'll eat my son.' 29So we cooked my son. Then we ate him. The next day I said to her, 'Give up your son. Then we can eat him.' But she had hidden him."

30When the king heard the woman's words, he tore his royal robes. As he walked along the wall, the people looked up at him. They saw that he was wearing black clothes under his robes. 31He said, "I'll cut the head of Shaphat's son Elisha off his shoulders today. If I don't, may God punish me greatly!"

32Elisha was sitting in his house. The elders were sitting there with him. The king went to see Elisha. He sent a messenger on ahead of him. Before the messenger arrived, Elisha spoke to the elders. He said, "That murderer is sending someone here to cut my head off. Can't you see that? When the messenger comes, close the door. Hold it shut against him. Can't you hear his master's footsteps right behind him?"

33Elisha was still talking to the elders when the messenger came down to him. The king also arrived. He said, "The LORD has sent this horrible trouble on us. Why should I wait any longer for him to help us?"

7 Elisha said, "Listen to a message from the LORD. He says, 'About this time tomorrow, you will be able to buy seven quarts of flour for less than half of an ounce of silver. You will also be able to buy 13 quarts of barley for the same price. That's all you will have to pay for those things at the gate of Samaria.'"

2The king was leaning on an officer's arm. The officer spoke to the man of God. He said, "Suppose the LORD opens the windows of the skies. Suppose he pours food down on us. Even if he does, could what you are saying really happen?"

"You will see it with your own eyes," answered Elisha. "But you won't eat any of it!"

The Attack on Samaria Ends

3There were four men who had a skin disease. They were at the entrance of the gate of Samaria. They said to one another, "Why should we stay here until we die? 4Suppose we say, 'We'll go into the city.' There isn't any food there, and we'll die. But if we stay here, we'll die anyway. So let's go over to Aram's army camp. Let's give ourselves up. If they spare us, we'll live. If they kill us, we'll die."

5At sunset they got up. They went to Aram's army camp. They arrived at the edge of it. But no one was there. 6The Lord had caused the soldiers of Aram to hear a noise. It sounded like chariots and horses and a huge army. So the soldiers spoke to one another. They said, "Listen! The king of Israel has hired the Hittite and Egyptian kings. He has paid them to attack us!" 7So they had gotten up and had run away at sunset. They had left their tents and horses and donkeys behind. They had left the camp as it was. And they had run for their lives.

8The men who had a skin disease arrived at the edge of the camp. They entered one of the tents. They ate and drank. Then they carried away silver, gold and clothes. They went off and hid them. They returned and entered another tent. They took some things from it and hid them also.

9But then they said to one another, "What we're doing isn't right. This is a day of good news. And we're keeping it to ourselves. If we wait until sunrise, we'll be punished. Let's go at once. Let's report this to the royal palace."

10So they went. They called out to the people who were guarding the city gates. They told them, "We went into Aram's army camp. No one was there. We didn't hear anyone. The horses and donkeys were still tied up. The tents were left just as they were."

11The people who guarded the gates shouted the news. It was reported inside the palace.

12The king of Israel got up in the night. He spoke to his officers. He said, "I'll tell you what the men of Aram have done to us. They know we are very hungry. So they have left the camp to hide in the countryside. They are thinking, 'We are sure they'll come out. Then we'll take them alive. And we'll get into the city.'"

13One of the king's officers spoke up. He said, "A few horses are still left in the city. Have some men get five of them. They won't be any worse off than all of the other Israelites who are left here. In fact, all of us will soon be dead. So let's send the men to find out what happened."

14The men chose two chariots and their horses. The king sent them out to look for Aram's army. He commanded the drivers, "Go and find out what has happened."

15They followed the trail of Aram's soldiers all the way to the Jordan River. They found clothes and supplies all along the road. The soldiers had thrown them down when they ran away. So the men returned. They reported to the king what they had seen.

16Then the people went out of the city. They took everything of value from Aram's army camp. So seven quarts of flour sold for less than half of an ounce of silver. And 13 quarts of barley sold for the same price. That's exactly what the LORD had said would happen.

17The king had put an officer in charge of the city gate. He was the officer on whose arm the king leaned. On their way out of the city, the people knocked the officer down. In the entrance of the gate they walked all over him. And he died. That's exactly what the man of God had said would happen. He had said it when the king came down to his house.

18What the man of God had told the king came true. He had said, "About this time tomorrow, you will be able to buy seven quarts of flour for less than half of an ounce of silver. You will also be able to buy 13 quarts of barley for the same price. That's all you will have to pay for those things at the gate of Samaria."

19The officer had spoken to the man of God. He had said, "Suppose the LORD opens the windows of the skies. Suppose he pours food down on us. Even if he does, could what you are saying really happen?" The man of God had replied, "You will see it with your own eyes. But you won't eat any of it!"

20And that's exactly what happened to the officer. On their way out of the city, the people knocked him down. In the entrance of the gate they walked all over him. And he died.

The Woman from Shunem Gets Her Land Back

8 Elisha had brought a woman's son back to life. He had said to her, "Go away with your family. Stay for a while anywhere you can. The LORD has decided that there won't be enough food in the land. That will be true for seven years."

2The woman did just as the man of God told her to. She and her family went away. They stayed in the land of the Philistines for seven years.

3The seven years passed. Then she came back from the land of the Philistines. She went to the king of Israel. She wanted to beg him to get her house and land back.

4The king was talking to Gehazi. Gehazi was the servant of the man of God. The king had said, "Tell me about all of the great things Elisha has done." 5Gehazi was telling the king how Elisha had brought a dead boy back to life. Just then the woman came to beg the king to get her house and land back. She was the woman whose son Elisha had brought back to life.

Gehazi said, "King Joram, this is the woman I've been telling you about. And this is her son. He's the one Elisha brought back to life." 6The king asked the woman about her house and land. And she told him.

Then he appointed an official to look into her case. The king told him, "Give her back everything that belonged to her. That includes all of the money that was earned from her land. It was earned from the day she left the country until now."

Hazael Murders Ben-Hadad

7Elisha went to Damascus. Ben-Hadad was sick. He was king of Aram. The king was told, "The man of God has come all the way up here."

8Then the king said to Hazael, "Take a gift with you. Go and see the man of God. Ask him for the LORD's advice. Ask him whether I will get well again."

9Hazael went to see Elisha. He took 40 camels with him as a gift. The camels were loaded with all of the finest goods of Damascus. Hazael went into Elisha's house and stood in front of him. He said, "Ben-Hadad has sent me. He is the king of Aram. He asks, 'Will I get well again?'"

10Elisha answered, "Go and speak to him. Tell him, 'Yes. You will get well again.' But the LORD has shown me that he will in fact die."

11Elisha stared at him without looking away. He did it until Hazael felt ashamed. Then the man of God began to sob.

12"Why are you sobbing?" asked Hazael.

"Because I know how much harm you will do to the people of Israel," he answered. "You will set fire to their cities that have high walls around them. You will kill their young men with your sword. You will smash their little children on the ground. You will rip open their pregnant women."

13Hazael said, "How could I possibly do a thing like that? I'm nothing but a dog. I don't have that kind of power."

"You will become king of Aram," Elisha answered. "That's what the LORD has shown me."

14Then Hazael left Elisha. He returned to his master. Ben-Hadad asked, "What did Elisha say to you?"

Hazael replied, "He told me you would get well again."

15But the next day Hazael got a thick cloth. He soaked it in water. He spread it over the king's face. He held it there until the king died. Then Hazael became the next king after him.

Jehoram Becomes King of Judah

16Jehoram began to rule as king over Judah. It was in the fifth year that Joram was king of Israel. Joram was the son of Ahab. Jehoram was the son of Jehoshaphat. 17Jehoram was 32 years old when he became king. He ruled in Jerusalem for eight years.

18He followed the ways of the kings of Israel, just as the royal family of Ahab had done. In fact, he got married to a daughter of Ahab. Jehoram did what was evil in the sight of the LORD.

19But the LORD didn't want to destroy Judah. That's because the LORD had made a covenant with his servant David. He had promised to keep the lamp of David's kingdom burning brightly for him and his children after him forever.

20When Jehoram was king over Judah, Edom refused to remain under Judah's control. They set up their own king. 21So Jehoram went to Zair. He took all of his chariots with him. The men of Edom surrounded him and his chariot commanders. He got up at night and fought his way out. But his army ran back home.

22To this very day Edom has refused to remain under Judah's control. At that same time, Libnah also refused to remain under the control of Judah.

23The other events of Jehoram's rule are written down. Everything he did is written down. All of those things are written in the official records of the kings of Judah.

24Jehoram joined the members of his family who had already died. His body was buried in the family tomb in the City of David. His son Ahaziah became the next king after him.

Ahaziah Becomes King of Judah

25Ahaziah began to rule as king over Judah. It was in the 12th year that Joram was king of Israel. Joram was the son of Ahab. Ahaziah was the son of Jehoram. 26Ahaziah was 22 years old when he became king. He ruled in Jerusalem for one year. His mother's name was Athaliah. She was a granddaughter of Omri. Omri had been the king of Israel.

27Ahaziah followed the ways of the royal family of Ahab. Ahaziah did what was evil in the sight of the LORD, just as the family of Ahab had done. That's because he had married into Ahab's family.

28Ahaziah joined forces with Joram. They went to war against Hazael at Ramoth Gilead. Joram was the son of Ahab. Hazael was king of Aram. The soldiers of Aram wounded King Joram. 29So he returned to Jezreel to give his wounds time to heal. The soldiers of Aram had wounded him at Ramoth in his battle against Hazael, the king of Aram.

Ahaziah, the son of Jehoram, went down to Jezreel. He went there to see Joram. That's because Joram had been wounded. Ahaziah was king of Judah. Joram was the son of Ahab.

Jehu Is Anointed as King of Israel

9 The prophet Elisha sent for a man from the company of the prophets. Elisha said to him, "Tuck your coat into your belt. Take this bottle of olive oil with you. Go to Ramoth Gilead.

2"When you get there, look for Jehu. He's the son of Jehoshaphat, the son of Nimshi. Go to him. Get him away from his companions. Take him into an inside room. 3Then get the bottle. Pour the oil on his head. Announce to him, 'The LORD says, "I anoint you as king over Israel."' After that, open the door and run away. Do it quickly!"

4So the young prophet went to Ramoth Gilead. 5When he arrived, he found the army officers sitting together. "Commander, I have a message for you," he said.

"For which one of us?" asked Jehu.

"For you, commander," he replied.

6Jehu got up and went into the house. Then the prophet poured the oil on Jehu's head. He announced, "The LORD is the God of Israel. He says, 'I am anointing you as king over my people Israel. 7You must destroy the royal house of your master Ahab. I will pay them back for spilling the blood of my servants the prophets. I will also pay them back for the blood of all of my servants that Jezebel spilled. 8The whole house of Ahab will die out. I will cut off every male in Israel who is related to Ahab. It does not matter whether they are slaves or free.

9"'I will make Ahab's royal house like the house of Jeroboam, the son of Nebat. I will make it like the house of Baasha, the son of Ahijah. 10Dogs will eat up Jezebel on a piece of land at Jezreel. No one will bury her.'" Then the prophet opened the door and ran away.

11Jehu went out to where the other officers were. One of them asked him, "Is everything all right? Why did that crazy man come to you?"

"You know the man. You know the kinds of things he says," Jehu replied.

12"That's not true!" they said. "Tell us."

Jehu said, "Here is what he told me. He announced, 'The LORD says, "I am anointing you as king over Israel."'"

13The officers quickly grabbed their coats. They spread them out under Jehu on the bare steps of the house. Then they blew a trumpet. They shouted, "Jehu is king!"

Jehu Kills Joram and Ahaziah

14Jehu was the son of Jehoshaphat, the son of Nimshi. Jehu made plans against Joram. During that time Joram and Israel's whole army had been guarding Ramoth Gilead. They had been guarding it against Hazael, the king of Aram.

15But King Joram had returned to Jezreel. He had gone there to give his wounds time to heal. The soldiers of Aram had wounded him in his battle against Hazael, the king of Aram.

Jehu said to his men, "Are you really on my side? If you are, don't let anyone sneak out of the city. Don't let them go and tell the news in Jezreel." 16Then Jehu got into his chariot. He rode off to Jezreel. Joram was resting there. And Ahaziah, the king of Judah, had gone down to see him.

17A lookout was standing on the roof of the tower in Jezreel. He saw Jehu's troops approaching. So he called out, "I see some troops coming."

"Get a horseman," Joram ordered. "Send him to ride out to them. Have him ask, 'Are you coming in peace?'"

18The horseman rode out to where Jehu was. He said, "The king asks, 'Are you coming in peace?'"

"What do you know about peace?" Jehu answered. "Get in line behind me."

The lookout reported, "The messenger has reached them. But he isn't coming back."

19So the king sent out a second horseman. When he came to them, he told them, "The king asks, 'Are you coming in peace?'"

Jehu replied, "What do you know about peace? Get in line behind me."

20The lookout reported, "The second messenger has reached them. But he isn't coming back either. The one driving the chariot drives like Jehu, the son of Nimshi. He's driving like a crazy man."

21"Get my chariot ready," King Joram ordered. When it was ready, he rode out. Ahaziah, the king of Judah, rode out with him. Each of them was in his own chariot. They both went to meet Jehu. They met him at the piece of land that had belonged to Naboth from Jezreel.

22When Joram saw Jehu he asked, "Have you come here in peace, Jehu?"

"Your mother Jezebel worships statues of gods," Jehu replied. "She also worships evil powers. The evil things she does have spread everywhere. As long as all of that goes on, how can there be peace?"

23Joram turned around and tried to get away. He called out to Ahaziah. He said, "It's treason, Ahaziah!"

24Then Jehu shot an arrow at Joram. It hit him between the shoulders. It went through his heart. He sank down slowly in his chariot.

25Jehu spoke to Bidkar, his chariot officer. He said, "Pick him up. Throw him on the field that belonged to Naboth from Jezreel. Remember how you and I were riding together in chariots behind Joram's father Ahab? It was when the LORD made a prophecy about him. He announced, 26'Yesterday I saw the blood of Naboth and the blood of his sons. You can be sure that I will make you pay for it on this piece of land.' So pick him up. Throw him on that piece of land. That's what the LORD said would happen."

27Ahaziah, the king of Judah, saw what had happened. So he tried to get away. He went up the road toward Beth Haggan.

Jehu chased him. He shouted, "Kill him too!" Jehu's men wounded Ahaziah in his chariot. It happened on the way up to Gur near Ibleam. But he escaped to Megiddo. And that's where he died.

28Ahaziah's servants took him to Jerusalem in his chariot. They buried his body in his family tomb in the City of David. 29Ahaziah had become king of Judah. It was in the 11th year of Joram, the son of Ahab.

Jehu Kills Jezebel

30Jehu went to Jezreel. Jezebel heard about it. So she put makeup on her eyes and fixed her hair. She looked out of a window. 31Jehu entered the gate below. Then Jezebel said, "You are just like Zimri. You murdered your master. Have you come here in peace?"

32He looked up at the window. "Who is on my side?" he called out. "Who?" Two or three officials looked down at him. 33"Throw her down!" Jehu said. So they threw her down. Some of her blood splashed on the wall. Some of it splashed on Jehu's chariot horses as they ran over her.

34Jehu went inside. He ate and drank. "The LORD put a curse on that woman," he said. "Take proper care of her body. Bury it. After all, she was a king's daughter."

35So they went out to bury her body. But all they found was her skull, feet and hands.

36They went back and reported it to Jehu. He told them, "That's what the LORD said would happen. He announced it through his servant Elijah, who was from Tishbe. He said, 'On a piece of land at Jezreel, dogs will eat up Jezebel's body. 37Her body will be left to rot on that piece of land. So no one will be able to say, "Here's where Jezebel is buried." ' "

Jehu Wipes Out Ahab's Royal House

10 Ahab's royal family in the city of Samaria had a total of 70 sons. Jehu wrote some letters to the officials of the city. He also sent them to the elders there. And he sent them to those who took care of Ahab's children. He said, 2"Your master's sons are with you. You also have chariots and horses and weapons. And you are living in a city that has high walls around it. As soon as you read this letter, here's what I want you to do. 3Choose the best and most respected son of your master. Place him on his father Joram's throne. Then fight for your master's royal house."

4The leaders of Samaria were terrified. They said, "King Joram and King Ahaziah couldn't stand up against Jehu. So how can we?"

5The city governor and the person who was in charge of the palace sent a message to Jehu. The message was also from the elders and those who took care of Ahab's children. It said, "We will serve you. We'll do anything you say. We won't appoint anyone to be king. Do what you think is best."

6Then Jehu wrote them a second letter. It said, "You say you are on my side. You say you will obey me. If you really mean it, bring me the heads of your master's sons. Meet me in Jezreel by this time tomorrow."

There were 70 royal princes. They were with the most important men of the city. Those men were in charge of raising them. 7When Jehu's letter arrived, the men went and got the princes. They killed all 70 of them. They put their heads in baskets. Then they sent them to Jehu in Jezreel.

8When the messenger arrived, he spoke to Jehu. He told him, "The heads of the princes have been brought here."

Then Jehu ordered his men, "Put them in two piles. Stack them up at the entrance of the city gate until morning."

9The next morning Jehu went out. He stood in front of all of the people. He said, "You aren't guilty of doing anything wrong. I'm the one who made plans against my master Joram. I killed him. But who killed all of these? 10I want you to know that the LORD has spoken against Ahab's royal house. Not a word of what he has said will fail. The LORD has done exactly what he promised through his servant Elijah."

11So Jehu killed everyone from Ahab's family who was in Jezreel. He also killed all of Ahab's chief men. And he killed Ahab's close friends and his priests. He didn't leave anyone in Ahab's family alive.

12Then Jehu started out for Samaria. At Beth Eked of the Shepherds, 13he saw some people. They were relatives of Ahaziah, the king of Judah. Jehu asked them, "Who are you?"

They said, "We are Ahaziah's relatives. We've come down to visit the families of the king and of his mother."

14"Take them alive!" Jehu ordered. So his men took them alive. Then they killed them by the well of Beth Eked. They killed a total of 42 men. Jehu didn't leave anyone alive.

15After Jehu left there, he came upon Jehonadab. He was the son of Recab. Jehonadab was on his way to see Jehu. Jehu greeted him. He asked, "Are you my friend? You know I'm your friend."

"I am," Jehonadab answered.

"If that's true," said Jehu, "hold out your hand." So he did. Then Jehu helped him up into the chariot. 16Jehu said, "Come along with me. See how committed I am to serve the LORD." He had him ride along in his chariot.

17Jehu came to Samaria. He killed everyone who was left there from Ahab's family. And so he wiped out Ahab's royal house. That's what the LORD had said would happen. He had spoken that message to Elijah.

Jehu Kills Those Who Serve Baal

18Then Jehu brought all of the people together. He said to them, "Ahab served the god Baal a little. I will serve him a lot. 19Send for all of Baal's prophets. Also send for all of his priests and the others who serve him. Make sure that not a single one is missing. I'm going to hold a great sacrifice to honor Baal. Anyone who doesn't come will be killed." But Jehu was lying to them. He was planning to destroy those who served Baal.

20Jehu said, "Call everyone together to honor Baal." So they did. 21Then he sent a message all through Israel. All of those who served Baal came. Not a single one of them stayed away. They crowded into Baal's temple. It was full from one end to the other.

22Jehu spoke to the one who took care of the sacred robes. He told him, "Bring robes for everyone who serves Baal." So he brought the robes out for them.

23Then Jehu went into Baal's temple. Jehonadab, the son of Recab, went with him. Jehu spoke to those who served Baal. He said, "Look around. Make sure that no one who serves the LORD is here with you. Make sure only those who serve Baal are here." 24So they went in to offer sacrifices and burnt offerings.

Jehu had stationed 80 men outside. He warned them, "I'm placing some men in your hands. Don't let a single one of them escape. If you do, you will pay for his life with yours."

25Jehu finished sacrificing the burnt offering. As soon as he did, he gave an order to the guards and officers. He commanded them, "Go inside and kill everyone. Don't let a single one of them escape."

So they cut them down with their swords. The guards and officers threw the bodies outside. Then they entered the most sacred area inside Baal's temple.

26They brought the sacred stone of Baal outside. They burned it up. 27So they destroyed Baal's sacred stone. They also tore down Baal's temple. People have used it as a public toilet to this very day.

28So Jehu destroyed the worship of the god Baal in Israel. 29But he didn't turn away from the sins of Jeroboam, the son of Nebat. Jeroboam had caused Israel to commit those same sins. Jehu worshiped the golden calves at Bethel and Dan.

30The LORD said to Jehu, "You have done well. You have accomplished what is right in my eyes. You have done to Ahab's royal house everything I wanted you to do. So your sons after you will sit on the throne of Israel. They will rule until the time of your children's grandchildren."

31But Jehu wasn't careful to obey the law of the LORD. He didn't obey the God of Israel with all his heart. He didn't turn away from the sins of Jeroboam. Jeroboam had caused Israel to commit those same sins.

32In those days the LORD began to make the kingdom of Israel smaller. Hazael gained control over many parts of Israel. He gained control over all of their territory 33east of the Jordan River. It included the whole land of Gilead from Aroer by the Arnon River valley all the way to Bashan. That was the territory of Gad, Reuben and Manasseh.

34The other events of Jehu's rule are written down. Everything he did and accomplished is written down. All of those things are written in the official records of the kings of Israel.

35Jehu joined the members of his family who had already died. His body was buried in Samaria. His son Jehoahaz became the next king after him. 36Jehu had ruled over Israel in Samaria for 28 years.

Athaliah and Joash

11 Athaliah was Ahaziah's mother. She saw that her son was dead. So she began to wipe out the whole royal house of Judah.

2But Jehosheba went and got Joash, the son of Ahaziah. She was the daughter of King Jehoram and the sister of Ahaziah. She stole Joash away from among the royal princes. All of them were about to be murdered. She put Joash and his nurse in a bedroom. That's how she hid him from Athaliah. And that's why Athaliah didn't kill him. 3The child remained hidden with his nurse at the LORD's temple for six years. Athaliah ruled over the land during that time.

4In the seventh year the priest Jehoiada sent for the commanders of companies of 100 men. They were the commanders over the Carites and guards. He had them brought to him at the temple of the LORD. He made a covenant with them. He made them take an oath at the temple. Then he showed them the king's son.

5He gave them a command. He said, "Here's what you must do. There are five companies of you. Some of you are in the three companies that are going on duty on the Sabbath day. A third of you must guard the royal palace. 6A third of you must guard the Sur Gate. And a third of you must guard the gate that is behind the guard. All of you must take turns guarding the temple.

7"The rest of you are in the other two companies. Normally you are not on duty on the Sabbath.

But you also must guard the temple for the king. 8Station yourselves around the king. Each man must have his weapon in his hand. Anyone else who approaches your companies must be put to death. Stay close to the king no matter where he goes."

9The commanders of the companies did just as the priest Jehoiada ordered. Each commander got his men and came to Jehoiada. Some of the men were going on duty on the Sabbath day. Others were going off duty.

10Then Jehoiada gave weapons to the commanders. He gave them spears and shields. The weapons had belonged to King David. They had been in the LORD's temple.

11The guards stationed themselves around the new king. Each man had his weapon in his hand. They were near the altar and the temple. They stood from the south side of the temple to its north side. Their line formed half of a circle.

12Jehoiada brought Ahaziah's son out. He put the crown on him. He gave him a copy of the covenant. And he announced that Joash was king. Jehoiada and his sons anointed him. The people clapped their hands. Then they shouted, "May the king live a long time!"

13Athaliah heard the noise the guards and the people were making. So she went to the people at the LORD's temple. 14She looked. And there was the king! He was standing next to the pillar. That was the usual practice. The officers and trumpet players were standing beside the king. All of the people of the land were filled with joy. They were blowing trumpets.

Then Athaliah tore her royal robes. She called out, "Treason! It's treason!"

15The priest Jehoiada gave an order to the commanders of the companies. They were in charge of the troops. He said to them, "Bring her away from the temple between the line of guards. Use your swords to kill anyone who follows her." The priest had said, "She must not be put to death at the LORD's temple."

16So they grabbed hold of her as she reached the place where the horses enter the palace grounds. There she was put to death.

17Then Jehoiada made a covenant between the LORD and the king and people. He had the king and people promise that they would be the LORD's people. Jehoiada also made a covenant between the king and the people.

18All of the people of the land went to Baal's temple. They tore it down. They smashed to pieces the altars and the statues of gods. They killed Mattan in front of the altars. He was the priest of Baal.

Then the priest Jehoiada stationed guards at the temple of the LORD. 19He took with him the commanders of companies of 100 men. They were the commanders over the Carites and guards. He also took with him all of the people of the land. All of them brought the new king down from the LORD's temple. They went into the palace. They entered it by going through the gate of the guards. Then the king sat down on the royal throne.

20All of the people of the land were filled with joy. And the city was quiet. That's because Athaliah had been killed with a sword at the palace.

21Joash was seven years old when he became king.

Joash Repairs the Temple

12 Joash became king of Judah. It was in the seventh year of Jehu's rule. Joash ruled in Jerusalem for 40 years. His mother's name was Zibiah. She was from Beersheba.

2Joash did what was right in the eyes of the LORD. He lived that way as long as the priest Jehoiada was teaching him.

3But the high places weren't removed. The people continued to offer sacrifices and burn incense there.

4Joash spoke to the priests. He said, "Collect all of the money the people bring as sacred offerings to the LORD's temple. That includes the money that is collected when the men who are able to serve in the army are counted. It includes the money that is received from people who make a special promise to the LORD. It also includes the money people bring to the temple just because they want to.

5"Let each priest receive the money from one of the people who are in charge of the temple's treasures. Let all of that money be used to repair the temple where it needs it."

6It was now the 23rd year of King Joash. And the priests still hadn't repaired the temple. 7So the king sent for the priest Jehoiada and the other priests. He asked them, "Why aren't you repairing the temple where it needs it? Don't take any more money from the people who are in charge of the treasures. Instead, hand it over so the temple can be repaired."

8The priests agreed that they wouldn't collect any more money from the people. They also agreed that they wouldn't repair the temple themselves.

9The priest Jehoiada got a chest. He drilled a hole in its lid. He placed the chest beside the altar for burnt offerings. The chest was on the right side as people enter the LORD's temple. Some priests guarded the entrance. They put into the chest all of the money the people brought to the temple.

10From time to time there was a large amount of money in the chest. When that happened, the royal secretary and the high priest came. They counted the money the people had brought to the temple. Then they put it into bags.

11After they added it all up, they used it to repair the temple. They gave it to the men who had been put in charge of the work. Those men used it to pay the workers. They paid the builders and those who worked with wood. 12They paid those who cut stones and those who laid them. They bought lumber and blocks of stone. So they used the money to repair the LORD's temple. They also paid all of the other costs to make the temple like new again.

13The money the people brought to the LORD's temple wasn't used to make silver bowls. It wasn't used for wick cutters, sprinkling bowls or trumpets. And it wasn't used for any other articles made out of gold or silver. 14Instead, it was paid to the workers. They used it to repair the temple. 15The royal secretary and the high priest didn't require a report from those who were in charge of the work. That's because they were completely honest. They always paid the workers. 16Money was received from those who brought guilt offerings and sin offerings. But it wasn't taken to the LORD's temple. It belonged to the priests.

17About that time Hazael, the king of Aram, went up and attacked Gath. Then he captured it. After that, he turned back to attack Jerusalem.

18But Joash, the king of Judah, didn't want to go to war. So he got all of the sacred objects. They had been set apart to the LORD by the kings who had ruled over Judah before him. They were Jehoshaphat, Jehoram and Ahaziah. Joash got the gifts he himself had set apart. He got all of the gold that was among the temple treasures. He also got all of the gold from the royal palace. He sent all of those things to Hazael, the king of Aram. Then Hazael pulled his army back from Jerusalem.

19The other events of the rule of Joash are written down. Everything he did is written down. All of those things are written in the official records of the kings of Judah.

20The officials of Joash made evil plans against him. They killed him at Beth Millo. It happened on the road that goes down to Silla. 21The officials who murdered him were Jozabad and Jehozabad. Jozabad was the son of Shimeath. Jehozabad was the son of Shomer.

After Joash died, his body was buried in the family tomb in the City of David. His son Amaziah became the next king after him.

Jehoahaz Becomes King of Israel

13 Jehoahaz became king of Israel in Samaria. It was in the 23rd year of Joash, the king of Judah. Jehoahaz ruled for 17 years. Joash was the son of Ahaziah. Jehoahaz was the son of Jehu.

2Jehoahaz did what was evil in the sight of the LORD. He committed the sins Jeroboam, the son of Nebat, had committed. Jeroboam had caused Israel to commit those same sins. Jehoahaz didn't turn away from them.

3So the LORD's anger burned against Israel. For a long time he kept them under the power of Hazael, the king of Aram. He also kept them under the power of his son Ben-Hadad.

4Then Jehoahaz asked the LORD to show him his favor. The LORD listened to him. The LORD saw how badly the king of Aram was treating Israel. 5The LORD provided someone to save Israel. And they escaped from the power of Aram. So the people of Israel lived in their own homes, just as they had before.

6But the people didn't turn away from the sins of the royal house of Jeroboam. He had caused Israel to commit those same sins. The people continued to commit them. And the pole that was used to worship the goddess Asherah remained standing in Samaria.

7The army of Jehoahaz had almost nothing left. All it had was 50 horsemen, 10 chariots and 10,000 soldiers on foot. The king of Aram had destroyed the rest of them. He had made them like dust at threshing time.

8The other events of the rule of Jehoahaz are written down. Everything he did and accomplished is written down. All of those things are written in the official records of the kings of Israel.

9Jehoahaz joined the members of his family who had already died. His body was buried in Samaria. His son Jehoash became the next king after him.

Jehoash Becomes King of Israel

10Jehoash became king of Israel in Samaria. It was in the 37th year that Joash was king of Judah. Jehoash ruled for 16 years. He was the son of Jehoahaz.

11Jehoash did what was evil in the sight of the LORD. He didn't turn away from any of the sins of Jeroboam, the son of Nebat. Jeroboam had caused Israel to commit those same sins. And Jehoash continued to commit them.

12The other events of the rule of Jehoash are written down. Everything he did and accomplished is written down. That includes his war against Amaziah, the king of Judah. All of those things are written in the official records of the kings of Israel.

13Jehoash joined the members of his family who had already died. His body was buried in the royal tombs in Samaria. Jeroboam became the next king on Israel's throne after him.

14Elisha was suffering from a sickness. Later he would die from it. Jehoash, the king of Israel, went down to see him. He sobbed over him. "My father!" he cried. "You are like a father to me! You are the true chariots and horsemen of Israel!"

15Elisha said to Jehoash, "Get a bow and some arrows." So he did.

16"Hold the bow in your hands," Elisha said to the king of Israel. So Jehoash took hold of the bow. Then Elisha put his hands on the king's hands.

17"Open the east window," Elisha said. So he did. "Shoot!" Elisha said. So he shot.

"That's the LORD's arrow!" Elisha announced. "It means you will win the battle over Aram! You will completely destroy the men of Aram at Aphek."

18He continued, "Get some arrows." So the king did. Elisha told him, "Strike the ground." He struck it three times. Then he stopped.

19The man of God was angry with him. He said,
"You should have struck the ground five or six
times. Then you would have won the war over
Aram. You would have completely destroyed
them. But now you will win only three battles over
them."
20Elisha died. And his body was buried.
Some robbers from Moab used to enter the
country of Israel every spring. 21One day some
people of Israel were burying a man's body. Suddenly they saw a group of robbers. So they threw
the man's body into Elisha's tomb. The body
touched Elisha's bones. When it did, the man came
back to life again. He stood up on his feet.
22Hazael, the king of Aram, treated Israel badly.
He did it the whole time Jehoahaz was king.
23But the LORD showed his favor to Israel. He
was tender and kind to them. He showed concern
for them. He did all of those things because of the
covenant he had made with Abraham, Isaac and
Jacob. To this very day he hasn't been willing to
destroy them. And he hasn't driven them out of his
land.
24Hazael, the king of Aram, died. His son Ben-
Hadad became the next king after him. 25Then Jehoash took some towns back from Ben-Hadad, the
son of Hazael. Ben-Hadad had captured them in
battle from Jehoahaz, the father of Jehoash. Jehoash won three battles over Ben-Hadad. So Jehoash
took back the Israelite towns.

Amaziah Becomes King of Judah

14 Amaziah began to rule as king over Judah.
It was in the second year that Jehoash was
king of Israel. He was the son of Jehoahaz. Amaziah was the son of Joash. 2Amaziah was 25 years
old when he became king. He ruled in Jerusalem
for 29 years. His mother's name was Jehoaddin.
She was from Jerusalem.
3Amaziah did what was right in the eyes of the
LORD. But he didn't do what King David had done.
He always followed the example of his father Joash. 4The high places weren't removed. The people continued to offer sacrifices and burn incense
there.
5The kingdom was firmly under his control. So
he put to death the officials who had murdered his
father, the king.
6But he didn't put their children to death. He
obeyed what is written in the Scroll of the Law of
Moses. There the LORD commanded, "Parents
must not be put to death because of what their children do. And children must not be put to death
because of what their parents do. People must die
because of their own sins." *(Deuteronomy 24:16)*
7Amaziah won the battle over 10,000 men of
Edom. It happened in the Valley of Salt. During the
battle he captured the town of Sela. He called it Joktheel. That's the name it still has to this very day.
8Then Amaziah sent messengers to Jehoash, the
king of Israel. He was the son of Jehoahaz, the son
of Jehu. The message said, "Come on. Meet me
face to face in battle."
9But Jehoash, the king of Israel, answered Amaziah, the king of Judah. He said, "A thorn bush in
Lebanon sent a message to a cedar tree there. It
said, 'Give your daughter to be married to my
son.' Then a wild animal in Lebanon came along.
It walked all over the thorn bush. 10It's true that
you have won the battle over Edom. So you are
proud. Enjoy your success while you can. But stay
home and enjoy it! Why ask for trouble? Why
bring yourself crashing down? Why bring Judah
down with you?"
11But Amaziah wouldn't listen. So Jehoash, the
king of Israel, attacked. He and Amaziah, the king
of Judah, faced each other in battle. The battle took
place at Beth Shemesh in Judah.
12Israel drove Judah away. Every man ran
home. 13Jehoash king of Israel captured Amaziah
king of Judah at Beth Shemesh. Amaziah was the
son of Joash. Joash was the son of Ahaziah. Jehoash went to Jerusalem. He broke down part of its
wall. It's the part that went from the Ephraim Gate
to the Corner Gate. That part of the wall was 600
feet long.
14Jehoash took all of the gold, silver and articles
that were in the LORD's temple. He also took all of
those same kinds of things that were among the
treasures of the royal palace. And he took the prisoners. Then he returned to Samaria.
15The other events of the rule of Jehoash are written down. Everything he did and accomplished is
written down. That includes his war against Amaziah, the king of Judah. All of those things are written
in the official records of the kings of Israel.
16Jehoash joined the members of his family who
had already died. His body was buried in Samaria
in the royal tombs of Israel. His son Jeroboam
became the next king after him.
17Amaziah king of Judah lived for 15 years after
Jehoash king of Israel died. Amaziah was the son
of Joash. Jehoash was the son of Jehoahaz. 18The
other events of Amaziah's rule are written down.
They are written in the official records of the kings
of Judah.
19Some people made evil plans against Amaziah in Jerusalem. So he ran away to Lachish. But
they sent men to Lachish after him. There they
killed him. 20His body was brought back on a
horse. Then he was buried in the family tomb in
Jerusalem, the City of David.
21All of the people of Judah made Uzziah king.
He was 16 years old. They made him king in place
of his father Amaziah. 22Uzziah rebuilt Elath. He
brought it under Judah's control again. He did it
after Amaziah joined the members of his family
who had already died.

Jeroboam II Becomes King of Israel

23Jeroboam became king of Israel in Samaria. It
was in the 15th year that Amaziah was king of Ju-

dah. Jeroboam ruled for 41 years. Amaziah was the son of Joash. Jeroboam was the son of Jehoash.

24 Jeroboam did what was evil in the sight of the LORD. He didn't turn away from any of the sins the earlier Jeroboam, the son of Nebat, had committed. That Jeroboam had caused Israel to commit those same sins.

25 Jeroboam, the son of Jehoash, made the borders of Israel the same as they were before. They reached from Lebo Hamath all the way to the Dead Sea. That's what the LORD, the God of Israel, had said would happen. He had spoken that message through his servant Jonah. The prophet Jonah was the son of Amittai. Jonah was from Gath Hepher.

26 The LORD had seen how much everyone in Israel was suffering. It didn't matter whether they were slaves or free. They didn't have anyone to help them. 27 The LORD hadn't said he would wipe out Israel's name from the earth. So he saved them by using the powerful hand of Jeroboam, the son of Jehoash.

28 The other events of the rule of Jeroboam are written down. Everything he did is written down. What he and his army accomplished is written down. That includes how he brought Damascus and Hamath back under Israel's control. Damascus and Hamath had belonged to the territory of Yaudi. All of those things are written in the official records of the kings of Israel.

29 Jeroboam joined the members of his family who had already died. His body was buried in the royal tombs of Israel. His son Zechariah became the next king after him.

Uzziah Becomes King of Judah

15 Uzziah began to rule as king over Judah. It was in the 27th year that Jeroboam was king of Israel. Uzziah was the son of Amaziah. 2 Uzziah was 16 years old when he became king. He ruled in Jerusalem for 52 years. His mother's name was Jecoliah. She was from Jerusalem.

3 Uzziah did what was right in the eyes of the LORD, just as his father Amaziah had done.

4 But the high places weren't removed. The people continued to offer sacrifices and burn incense there.

5 The LORD caused King Uzziah to suffer from a skin disease until the day he died. He lived in a separate house. His son Jotham was in charge of the palace. Jotham ruled over the people of the land.

6 The other events of the rule of Uzziah are written down. Everything he did is written down. All of those things are written in the official records of the kings of Judah.

7 Uzziah joined the members of his family who had already died. His body was buried near them in the City of David. His son Jotham became the next king after him.

Zechariah Becomes King of Israel

8 Zechariah became king of Israel in Samaria. It was in the 38th year that Uzziah was king of Judah. Zechariah ruled for six months. He was the son of Jeroboam, the son of Jehoash.

9 Zechariah did what was evil in the sight of the LORD. He did what the kings of Israel before him had done. He didn't turn away from the sins Jeroboam, the son of Nebat, had committed. Jeroboam had caused Israel to commit those same sins.

10 Shallum made evil plans against Zechariah. He attacked Zechariah in front of the people and killed him. Then he became the next king after him. Shallum was the son of Jabesh.

11 The other events of the rule of Zechariah are written down. They are written in the official records of the kings of Israel. 12 That's what the LORD had said would happen. He had spoken that message to Jehu. It had said, "Your sons after you will sit on the throne of Israel. They will rule until the time of your children's grandchildren." *(2 Kings 10:30)*

Shallum Becomes King of Israel

13 Shallum became king of Israel. It was in the 39th year that Uzziah was king of Judah. Shallum ruled in Samaria for one month. He was the son of Jabesh.

14 Menahem went from Tirzah up to Samaria. There he attacked Shallum, the son of Jabesh. He killed him and became the next king after him. Menahem was the son of Gadi.

15 The other events of Shallum's rule are written down. The evil things he planned are written down. All of those things are written in the official records of the kings of Israel.

16 At that time Menahem started out from Tirzah and attacked Tiphsah. He attacked everyone in the city and the area around it. That's because they refused to open their gates for him. He destroyed Tiphsah. He ripped open all of their pregnant women.

Menahem Becomes King of Israel

17 Menahem became king of Israel. It was in the 39th year that Uzziah was king of Judah. Menahem ruled in Samaria for ten years. He was the son of Gadi.

18 Menahem did what was evil in the sight of the LORD. During his entire rule he didn't turn away from the sins Jeroboam, the son of Nebat, had committed. Jeroboam had caused Israel to commit those same sins.

19 Then Tiglath-Pileser marched into the land of Israel. He was king of Assyria. Menahem gave him 37 tons of silver to get his help. He wanted to make his control over the kingdom stronger. 20 Menahem forced Israel to give him that money. Every wealthy person had to give him 20 ounces of silver. All of it went to the king of Assyria. So

he pulled his troops back. He didn't stay in the land anymore.

21The other events of the rule of Menahem are written down. Everything he did is written down. All of those things are written in the official records of the kings of Israel.

22Menahem joined the members of his family who had already died. His son Pekahiah became the next king after him.

Pekahiah Becomes King of Israel

23Pekahiah became king of Israel in Samaria. It was in the 50th year that Uzziah was king of Judah. Pekahiah ruled for two years. He was the son of Menahem.

24Pekahiah did what was evil in the sight of the LORD. He didn't turn away from the sins Jeroboam, the son of Nebat, had committed. Jeroboam had caused Israel to commit those same sins.

25One of Pekahiah's chief officers was Pekah. He was the son of Remaliah. Pekah made evil plans against Pekahiah. He took 50 men of Gilead with him and killed Pekahiah. He also killed Argob and Arieh. He killed all of them in the safest place in the royal palace at Samaria. So Pekah killed Pekahiah. He became the next king after him.

26The other events of the rule of Pekahiah are written down. Everything he did is written down. All of those things are written in the official records of the kings of Israel.

Pekah Becomes King of Israel

27Pekah became king of Israel in Samaria. It was in the 52nd year that Uzziah was king of Judah. Pekah ruled for 20 years. He was the son of Remaliah.

28Pekah did what was evil in the sight of the LORD. He didn't turn away from the sins Jeroboam, the son of Nebat, had committed. Jeroboam had caused Israel to commit those same sins.

29During the rule of Pekah, the king of Israel, Tiglath-Pileser marched into the land again. He was king of Assyria. He took the towns of Ijon, Abel Beth Maacah, Janoah, Kedesh and Hazor. He also took the lands of Gilead and Galilee. That included the whole territory of Naphtali. He took the people away from their own land. He sent them off to Assyria.

30Then Hoshea made evil plans against Pekah, the son of Remaliah. Hoshea was the son of Elah. Hoshea attacked Pekah and killed him. Then Hoshea became the next king after him. It was in the 20th year of the rule of Jotham, the son of Uzziah.

31The other events of the rule of Pekah are written down. Everything he did is written down. All of those things are written in the official records of the kings of Israel.

Jotham Becomes King of Judah

32Jotham began to rule as king over Judah. It was in the second year that Pekah was king of Israel. He was the son of Remaliah. Jotham was the son of Uzziah. 33Jotham was 25 years old when he became king. He ruled in Jerusalem for 16 years. His mother's name was Jerusha. She was the daughter of Zadok.

34Jotham did what was right in the eyes of the LORD, just as his father Uzziah had done.

35But the high places weren't removed. The people continued to offer sacrifices and burn incense there. Jotham rebuilt the Upper Gate of the LORD's temple.

36The other events of the rule of Jotham are written down. Everything he did is written down. All of those things are written in the official records of the kings of Judah.

37In those days the LORD began to send Rezin and Pekah against Judah. Rezin was king of Aram. Pekah was the son of Remaliah.

38Jotham joined the members of his family who had already died. His body was buried in the family tomb in the city of King David. His son Ahaz became the next king after him.

Ahaz Becomes King of Judah

16 Ahaz began to rule as king over Judah. It was in the 17th year of the rule of Pekah, the son of Remaliah. Ahaz was the son of Jotham. 2Ahaz was 20 years old when he became king. He ruled in Jerusalem for 16 years.

Ahaz didn't do what was right in the eyes of the LORD his God. He didn't do what King David had done. 3He followed the ways of the kings of Israel. He even sacrificed his son in the fire to another god. He followed the practices of the nations. The LORD hated those practices. He had driven out those nations to make room for the people of Israel. 4Ahaz offered sacrifices and burned incense at the high places. He also did it on the tops of hills and under every green tree.

5Rezin and Pekah marched up to Jerusalem and surrounded it. Rezin was king of Aram. Pekah, the son of Remaliah, was king of Israel. They attacked Ahaz. But they couldn't overpower him. 6At that time Rezin, the king of Aram, got back Elath for Aram. He drove out the people of Judah. Then the people of Edom moved into Elath. And they still live there to this very day.

7Ahaz sent messengers to Tiglath-Pileser. He was king of Assyria. The message of Ahaz said, "I am your servant. You are my master. Come up and save me from the powerful hands of the kings of Aram and Israel. They are attacking me."

8Ahaz took the silver and gold that were in the LORD's temple. He also took the silver and gold that were among the treasures in the royal palace. He sent all of it as a gift to the king of Assyria.

9So the king of Assyria did what Ahaz asked him to do. He attacked the city of Damascus and captured it. He sent its people away to Kir. And he put Rezin to death.

10Then King Ahaz went to Damascus. He went there to see Tiglath-Pileser, the king of Assyria.

Ahaz saw an altar in Damascus. He sent a drawing of it to the priest Uriah. He also sent him plans
for building it.
11So the priest Uriah built an altar. He followed
all of the plans King Ahaz had sent from Damascus. He finished it before Ahaz returned.
12The king came back from Damascus. When
he saw the altar, he approached it. Then he offered
sacrifices on it. 13He offered up his burnt offering
and grain offering. He poured out his drink offering. And he sprinkled blood from his friendship
offerings on the altar.
14The bronze altar for burnt offerings stood in
front of the LORD. It was between the new altar and
the LORD's temple. Ahaz took it away from the
front of the temple. He put it on the north side of
the new altar.
15Then King Ahaz gave orders to the priest
Uriah. He said, "Offer sacrifices on the large new
altar. Offer the morning burnt offering and the
evening grain offering. Offer my burnt offering
and my grain offering. Offer the burnt offering of
all of the people of the land. Offer their grain offering and their drink offering. Sprinkle on the altar
all of the blood from the burnt offerings and sacrifices. But I will use the bronze altar to look for
advice and direction."
16The priest Uriah did just as King Ahaz had
ordered.
17Ahaz took away the sides of the bronze
stands. He removed the bowls from the stands. He
removed the huge bowl from the bronze bulls it
stood on. He placed the bowl on a stone base. 18He
took away the covered area that had been used on
the Sabbath day. It had been built at the LORD's
temple. He removed the royal entrance that was
outside the temple. Ahaz did all of that to honor
the king of Assyria.
19The other events of the rule of Ahaz are written down. Everything he did is written down. All
of those things are written in the official records
of the kings of Judah.
20Ahaz joined the members of his family who
had already died. His body was buried in the family tomb in the City of David. His son Hezekiah
became the next king after him.

Hoshea Becomes the Last King of Israel

17 Hoshea became king of Israel in Samaria.
It was in the 12th year that Ahaz was king
of Judah. Hoshea ruled for nine years. He was the
son of Elah.
2Hoshea did what was evil in the sight of the
LORD. But he wasn't as evil as the kings of Israel
who ruled before him.
3Shalmaneser came up to attack Hoshea. Shalmaneser was king of Assyria. He had been Hoshea's master. He had forced Hoshea to bring him
gifts. 4But the king of Assyria found out that Hoshea had turned against him. Hoshea had sent messengers to So, the king of Egypt. Hoshea didn't
send gifts to the king of Assyria anymore. He had
been sending them every year. So Shalmaneser
grabbed hold of him and put him in prison.
5The king of Assyria marched into the whole
land of Israel. He marched to Samaria and surrounded it for three years. From time to time he
attacked it. 6Finally, the king of Assyria captured
Samaria. It was in the ninth year of Hoshea. The
king of Assyria took the people of Israel away
from their own land. He sent them off to Assyria.
He settled some of them in Halah. He settled others in Gozan on the Habor River. And he settled
still others in the towns of the Medes.

Israel Is Forced to Go Away to Assyria

7All of that took place because the people of Israel had committed sins against the LORD their
God. He had brought them up out of Egypt. He
had brought them out from under the power of
Pharaoh, the king of Egypt. But they worshiped
other gods.
8The LORD had driven out other nations to make
room for them. But they followed the evil practices
of those nations. They also followed the practices
that the kings of Israel had started. 9The people of
Israel did things against the LORD their God in
secret. What they did wasn't right. They built high
places for worship in all of their towns. They built
them at lookout towers. They also built them at
cities that had high walls around them. 10They set
up sacred stones. And they set up poles that were
used to worship the goddess Asherah. They did that
on every high hill and under every green tree.
11The LORD had driven out nations to make
room for Israel. But the people of Israel burned
incense at every high place, just as those nations
had done. The Israelites did evil things that made
the LORD very angry. 12They worshiped statues of
gods. They did it even though the LORD had said,
"Do not do that."
13The LORD warned Israel and Judah through all
of his prophets and seers. He said, "Turn from
your evil ways. Keep my commands and rules.
Obey every part of my Law. I commanded your
people who lived long ago to obey it. And I gave
it to you through my servants the prophets."
14But the people wouldn't listen. They were as
stubborn as their people of long ago had been.
Those people didn't trust in the LORD their God.
15They refused to obey his rules. They broke the
covenant he had made with them. They didn't pay
any attention to the warnings he had given them.
They worshiped worthless statues of gods. Then
they themselves became worthless. They followed
the example of the nations that were around them.
They did it even though the LORD had ordered
them not to. He had said, "Do not do as they do."
They did the very things the LORD had told them
not to do.
16They turned away from all of the commands
of the LORD their God. They made two statues of

gods for themselves. The statues were shaped like calves. They made a pole that was used to worship the goddess Asherah. They bowed down to all of the stars. And they worshiped the god Baal.

17They sacrificed their sons and daughters in the fire. They practiced all kinds of evil magic. They gave themselves over to do what was evil in the sight of the LORD. All of those things made him very angry.

18So the LORD was filled with anger against Israel. He removed them from his land. Only the tribe of Judah was left. 19And even Judah didn't obey the commands of the LORD their God. They followed the practices Israel had started.

20So the LORD turned his back on all of the people of Israel. He made them suffer. He handed them over to people who stole everything they had. And finally he threw them out of his land.

21He tore Israel away from the royal house of David. The people of Israel made Jeroboam, the son of Nebat, their king. Jeroboam tried to get Israel to stop following the LORD. He caused them to commit a terrible sin. 22The people of Israel were stubborn. They continued to commit all of the sins Jeroboam had committed. They didn't turn away from them.

23So the LORD removed them from his land. That's what he had warned them he would do. He had given that warning through all of his servants the prophets. So the people of Israel were taken away from their country. They were forced to go to Assyria. And that's where they still are.

Assyria Brings Other People to Samaria

24The king of Assyria brought people from Babylon. He also brought them from Cuthah, Avva, Hamath and Sepharvaim. He settled all of them in the towns of Samaria. They took the place of the people of Israel. They took over Samaria and lived in its towns.

25When they first lived there, they didn't worship the LORD. So he sent lions among them. And the lions killed some of the people.

26A report was given to the king of Assyria. He was told, "You forced people to leave their own homes. You settled them in the towns of Samaria. But they don't know what the god of that country requires. So he has sent lions among them. And the lions are killing the people off. That's because the people don't know what that god requires."

27Then the king of Assyria gave an order. He said, "Get one of the priests you captured from Samaria. Send him back to live there. Have him teach the people what the god of that land requires."

28So one of the priests went back to live in Bethel. He was one of those who had been forced to leave Samaria. He taught the people there how to worship the LORD.

29In spite of that, the people from each nation made statues of their own gods. They made them in all of the towns where they had settled. They set up those statues in small temples. The people of Samaria had built the temples at the high places. 30The people from Babylon made statues of the god Succoth Benoth. Those from Cuthah made statues of Nergal. Those from Hamath made statues of Ashima. 31The Avvites made statues of Nibhaz and Tartak. The Sepharvites sacrificed their children in the fire to Adrammelech and Anammelech. They were the gods of Sepharvaim.

32So the people of Samaria worshiped the LORD. But they also appointed all kinds of their own people to serve them as priests. The priests served in the small temples at the high places. 33The people worshiped the LORD. But they also served their own gods. They followed the evil practices of the nations from which they had been brought.

34They are still stubborn. They continue in their old practices to this very day. And now they don't even worship the LORD. They don't follow his directions and rules. They don't obey his laws and commands. The LORD had given all of those laws to the family of Jacob. He gave the name Israel to Jacob.

35The LORD made a covenant with the people of Israel. At that time he commanded them, "Do not worship any other gods. Do not bow down to them. Do not serve them or sacrifice to them. 36I am the one you must worship. I brought you up out of Egypt by my great power. I saved you by reaching out my mighty arm. You must bow down to me. You must offer sacrifices to me. 37You must always be careful to follow my directions and rules. You must obey the laws and commands I wrote for you. Do not worship other gods.

38"Do not forget the covenant I made with you. And remember, you must not worship other gods. 39Instead, worship me. I will save you from the powerful hand of all of your enemies. I am the LORD your God."

40But the people wouldn't listen. Instead, they were stubborn. They continued in their old practices. 41They worshiped the LORD. But at the same time, they served the statues of their gods. And to this very day their children and grandchildren continue to do what their people before them did.

Hezekiah Becomes King of Judah

18 Hezekiah began to rule as king over Judah. It was in the third year that Hoshea was king of Israel. He was the son of Elah. Hezekiah was the son of Ahaz. 2Hezekiah was 25 years old when he became king. He ruled in Jerusalem for 29 years. His mother's name was Abijah. She was the daughter of Zechariah.

3Hezekiah did what was right in the eyes of the LORD, just as King David had done. 4Hezekiah removed the high places. He smashed the sacred stones. He cut down the poles that were used to worship the goddess Asherah. He broke into pieces the bronze snake Moses had made. Up to that time

the people of Israel had been burning incense to it.
They called it Nehushtan.
5Hezekiah trusted in the LORD, the God of Israel. There was no one like him among all of the
kings of Judah. There was no king like him either
before him or after him. 6Hezekiah remained true
to the LORD. He didn't stop following him. He
obeyed the commands the LORD had given Moses.
7The LORD was with Hezekiah. He was successful in everything he did. He refused to remain
under the control of the king of Assyria. He didn't
serve him. 8He won the war against the Philistines.
He won battles at their lookout towers. He won
battles at their cities that had high walls around
them. He won battles against the Philistines all the
way to Gaza and its territory.
9Shalmaneser marched to Samaria and surrounded it. It was in the fourth year of King Hezekiah. That was the seventh year of Hoshea, the
king of Israel. He was the son of Elah. Shalmaneser was king of Assyria.
10At the end of three years the army of Assyria
took Samaria. So it was captured in the sixth year
of Hezekiah. That was the ninth year of Hoshea,
the king of Israel. 11The king of Assyria took the
people of Israel away from their own land. He sent
them off to Assyria. He settled some of them in
Halah. He settled others in Gozan on the Habor
River. And he settled still others in the towns of
the Medes.
12Those things happened because the Israelites
hadn't obeyed the LORD their God. They had broken the covenant he had made with them. They
had refused to do everything Moses, the servant of
the LORD, had commanded. They hadn't paid any
attention to those commands. They hadn't obeyed
them.
13Sennacherib attacked and captured all of the
cities of Judah that had high walls around them. It
was in the 14th year of the rule of Hezekiah. Sennacherib was king of Assyria.
14Hezekiah, the king of Judah, sent a message
to the king of Assyria at Lachish. It said, "I have
done what is wrong. Pull your troops back from
me. Then I'll pay you anything you ask me to."

The king of Assyria forced Hezekiah, the king
of Judah, to give him 11 tons of silver. Hezekiah
also had to give him a ton of gold. 15So Hezekiah
gave him all of the silver that was in the LORD's
temple. He also gave him all of the silver that was
among the treasures in the royal palace.
16Hezekiah, the king of Judah, had covered the
doors and doorposts of the LORD's temple with
gold. But now he had to strip it off. He had to give
it to the king of Assyria.

Sennacherib Warns Jerusalem

17The king of Assyria sent his highest commander from Lachish to King Hezekiah at Jerusalem. He also sent his chief officer and his field
commander along with a large army. All of them
came up to Jerusalem. They stopped at the channel
that brings water from the Upper Pool. It was on
the road to the Washerman's Field. 18They called
for King Hezekiah. Eliakim, Shebna and Joah
went out to them. Eliakim, the son of Hilkiah, was
in charge of the palace. Shebna was the secretary.
Joah, the son of Asaph, kept the records.
19The field commander said to them, "Give
Hezekiah this message. Tell him,

"'Sennacherib is the great king of Assyria. He says, "Why are you putting your faith
in what your king says? 20You say you have
a military plan. You say you have a strong
army. But your words don't mean anything.
Who are you depending on? Why don't you
want to stay under my control?
21"'"You are depending on Egypt. Why
are you doing that? Egypt is nothing but a
broken papyrus stem. Try leaning on it. It
will only cut your hand. Pharaoh, the king of
Egypt, is just like that to everyone who
depends on him.
22"'"Suppose you say to me, 'We are
depending on the LORD our God.' Didn't
Hezekiah remove your god's high places and
altars? Didn't Hezekiah say to the people of
Judah and Jerusalem, 'You must worship at
the altar in Jerusalem'?
23"'"Come on. Make a deal with my master, the king of Assyria. I'll give you 2,000
horses. But only if you can put riders on
them! 24You are depending on Egypt for
chariots and horsemen. You can't drive away
even the least important officer among my
master's officials.
25"'"Besides, do you think I've come
without receiving a message from the LORD?
Have I come to attack and destroy this place
without a message from him? The LORD
himself told me to march out against your
country. He told me to destroy it."'"

26Then Shebna, Joah and Eliakim, the son of
Hilkiah, spoke to the field commander. They said,
"Please speak to us in the Aramaic language. We
understand it. Don't speak to us in Hebrew. If you
do, the people who are on the wall will be able to
understand you."
27But the commander replied, "My master sent
me to say these things. Are these words only for
your master and you to hear? Aren't they also for
the men who are sitting on the wall? They are
going to suffer just like you. They'll have to eat
their own waste. They'll have to drink their own
urine."

28Then the commander stood up and spoke in
the Hebrew language. He called out, "Pay attention to what the great king of Assyria is telling you.
29He says, 'Don't let Hezekiah trick you. He can't
save you from my powerful hand. 30Don't let Hezekiah talk you into trusting in the LORD. Don't

believe him when he says, “You can be sure that the LORD will save us. This city will not be handed over to the king of Assyria.”’

31“Don’t listen to Hezekiah. The king of Assyria says, ‘Make a peace treaty with me. Come over to my side. Then every one of you will eat fruit from your own vine and fig tree. Every one of you will drink water from your own well. 32You will do that until I come back. Then I’ll take you to a land that is just like yours. It’s a land that has a lot of grain and fresh wine. It has plenty of bread and vineyards. It has olive trees and honey. So choose life! Don’t choose death!’

“Don’t pay any attention to Hezekiah. He’s telling you a lie when he says, ‘The LORD will save us.’

33“Has the god of any nation ever saved his land from the powerful hand of the king of Assyria? 34Where are the gods of Hamath and Arpad? Where are the gods of Sepharvaim, Hena and Ivvah? Have they saved Samaria from my power?

35“Which one of all of the gods of those countries has been able to save his land from me? So how can the LORD save Jerusalem from my power?”

36But the people remained silent. They didn’t say anything. That’s because King Hezekiah had commanded, “Don’t answer him.”

37Then Eliakim, the son of Hilkiah, went to Hezekiah. Eliakim was in charge of the palace. The secretary Shebna went with him. So did Joah, the son of Asaph. Joah kept the records. All of them went to Hezekiah with their clothes torn. They told him what the field commander had said.

Isaiah Prophesies That Jerusalem Will Be Saved

19 When King Hezekiah heard what the field commander had said, he tore his clothes. He put on black clothes. Then he went into the LORD’s temple.

2Hezekiah sent Eliakim, who was in charge of the palace, to the prophet Isaiah, the son of Amoz. He also sent the leading priests and the secretary Shebna to him. All of them were wearing black clothes.

3They told Isaiah, “Hezekiah says, ‘Today we’re in great trouble. The LORD is warning us. He’s bringing shame on us. Sometimes babies come to the moment when they should be born. But their mothers aren’t strong enough to allow them to be born. Today we are like those mothers. We aren’t strong enough to save ourselves.

4“‘Perhaps the LORD your God will hear everything the field commander has said. His master, the king of Assyria, has sent him to make fun of the living God. Maybe the LORD your God will punish him for what he has heard him say. So pray for the remaining people who are still alive here.’”

5King Hezekiah’s officials came to Isaiah. 6Then Isaiah said to them, “Tell your master, ‘The LORD says, “Do not be afraid of what you have heard. The officers who are under the king of Assyria have spoken evil things against me. 7Listen! I will send him news from his own country. It will upset him so much that he will return home. There I will have him cut down with a sword.”’”

8The field commander heard that the king of Assyria had left Lachish. So the commander pulled his troops back from Jerusalem. He went to join the king. He found out that the king was fighting against Libnah.

9During that time Sennacherib received a report. He was told that Tirhakah was marching out to fight against him. Tirhakah was the king of Egypt. He was from the land of Cush.

Sennacherib sent messengers again to Hezekiah with a letter. It said, 10“Tell Hezekiah, the king of Judah, ‘Don’t let the god you depend on trick you. He says, “Jerusalem will not be handed over to the king of Assyria.” But don’t believe him.

11“‘I’m sure you have heard about what the kings of Assyria have done to all of the other countries. They have destroyed them completely. So do you think you will be saved? 12The kings who ruled before me destroyed many nations. Did the gods of those nations save them? Did the gods of Gozan, Haran or Rezeph save them? What about the gods of the people of Eden who were in Tel Assar? 13Where is the king of Hamath? Where is the king of Arpad? Where is the king of the city of Sepharvaim? Where are the kings of Hena or Ivvah?’”

Hezekiah Prays to the LORD

14When Hezekiah received the letter from the messengers, he read it. Then he went up to the LORD’s temple. There he spread the letter out in front of the LORD.

15Hezekiah prayed to the LORD. He said, “LORD, you are the God of Israel. You sit on your throne between the cherubim. You alone are God over all of the kingdoms on earth. You have made heaven and earth. 16Listen, LORD. Hear us. Open your eyes, LORD. Look at the trouble we’re in. Listen to what Sennacherib is saying. You are the living God. And he dares to make fun of you!

17“LORD, it’s true that the kings of Assyria have completely destroyed many nations and their lands. 18They have thrown the statues of the gods of those nations into the fire. And they have destroyed them. That’s because they weren’t really gods at all. They were nothing but statues that were made out of wood and stone. They were made by the hands of men.

19“LORD our God, save us from the powerful hand of Sennacherib. Then all of the kingdoms on earth will know that you alone are God.”

Isaiah Prophesies That Sennacherib Will Fall From Power

20Isaiah sent a message to Hezekiah. Isaiah was the son of Amoz. Isaiah said, “The LORD is the

God of Israel. He says, 'I have heard your prayer about Sennacherib, the king of Assyria.'
21"Here is the message the LORD has spoken against him. The LORD says,

"'You will not win the battle over Zion.
Its people hate you and make fun of you.
The people of Jerusalem lift up their heads proudly
as you run away.
22 Who have you laughed at?
Who have you spoken evil things against?
Who have you raised your voice against?
Who have you looked at so proudly?
You have done it against me.
I am the Holy One of Israel!
23 Through your messengers
you have laughed at me again and again.
And you have said,
"I have many chariots.
With them I have climbed to the tops of the mountains.
I've climbed the highest mountains in Lebanon.
I've cut down its tallest cedar trees.
I've cut down the best of its pine trees.
I've reached its farthest parts.
I've reached its finest forests.
24 I've dug wells in strange lands.
I've drunk the water from them.
I've walked through all of Egypt's streams.
I've dried up every one of them."

25"'But I, the LORD, say, "Haven't you heard what I have done?
Long ago I arranged for you to do all of that.
In days of old I planned it.
Now I have made it happen.
You have turned cities with high walls into piles of stone.
26 Their people do not have any power left.
They are troubled and put to shame.
They are like plants in the field.
They are like new green plants.
They are like grass that grows on a roof.
It dries up before it is completely grown.

27"'"But I know where you live.
I know when you come and go.
I know how very angry you are with me.
28 You roar against me and brag.
And I have heard your bragging.
So I will put my hook in your nose.
I will put my bit in your mouth.
And I will make you go home
by the same way you came."'"

29The LORD said, "Hezekiah, here is a miraculous sign for you.

"This year you will eat what grows by itself.
In the second year you will eat what grows from that.
But in the third year you will plant your crops and gather them in.
You will plant your grapevines and eat their fruit.
30 The people of Judah who are still alive will be like plants.
Once more they will put down roots and produce fruit.
31 Out of Jerusalem will come those who remain.
Out of Mount Zion will come those who are still left alive.

"My great love will make sure that happens.
I rule over all.

32"Here is a message from me about the king of Assyria. It says,

"'He will not enter this city.
He will not even shoot an arrow at it.
He will not come near it with a shield.
He will not build a ramp in order to climb over its walls.
33 By the same way he came he will go home.
He will not enter this city,'
announces the LORD.
34"'I will guard this city and save it.
I will do it for myself. And I will do it for my servant David.'"

35That night the angel of the LORD went into the camp of the Assyrians. He put to death 185,000 soldiers there. The people of Jerusalem got up the next morning. They looked out and saw all of the dead bodies. 36So Sennacherib, the king of Assyria, took the army tents down. Then he left. He returned to Nineveh and stayed there.

37One day Sennacherib was worshiping in the temple of his god Nisroch. His sons Adrammelech and Sharezer cut him down with their swords. Then they escaped to the land of Ararat. Esarhaddon became the next king after his father Sennacherib.

Hezekiah Becomes Sick

20 In those days Hezekiah became very sick. He knew he was about to die.

The prophet Isaiah, the son of Amoz, went to him. Isaiah told Hezekiah, "The LORD says, 'Put everything in order. Make out your will. You are going to die soon. You will not get well again.'"

2Hezekiah turned his face toward the wall. He prayed to the LORD. He said, 3"LORD, please remember how faithful I've been to you. I've lived the way you wanted me to. I've served you with all my heart. I've done what is good in your sight." And Hezekiah cried bitterly.

4Isaiah was leaving the middle courtyard. Before he had left it, a message came to him from the LORD. He said, 5"Go back and speak to Hezekiah. He is the leader of my people. Tell him, 'The LORD, the God of King David, says, "I have heard your prayer. I have seen your tears. And I will heal

you. On the third day from now you will go up to
my temple. 6I will add 15 years to your life. And I
will save you and this city from the powerful hand
of the king of Assyria. I will guard this city. I will
do it for myself. And I will do it for my servant
David."'"

7Then Isaiah said, "Press some figs together.
Spread them on a piece of cloth." So that's what
they did. Then they applied it to Hezekiah's boil.
And he got well again.

8Hezekiah had said to Isaiah, "You say the
LORD will heal me. You say that I'll go up to his
temple on the third day from now. What will the
miraculous sign be to prove he'll really do that?"

9Isaiah answered, "The LORD will do what he
has promised. Here is his sign to you. Do you want
the shadow the sun makes to go forward ten steps?
Or do you want it to go back ten steps?"

10"It's easy for the shadow to go forward ten
steps," said Hezekiah. "So have it go back ten
steps."

11Then the prophet Isaiah called out to the
LORD. And the LORD made the shadow go back ten
steps. It went back the ten steps it had gone down
on the stairway Ahaz had made.

Messengers Come From Babylon to Hezekiah

12At that time Merodach-Baladan, the king of
Babylonia, sent Hezekiah letters and a gift. He had
heard that Hezekiah had been sick. Merodach-Baladan was the son of Baladan.

13Hezekiah received the messengers. He showed
them everything that was in his storerooms. He
showed them the silver and gold. He showed them
the spices and the fine olive oil. He showed
them where he kept his weapons. And he
showed them all of his treasures. In fact, he showed
them everything that was in his palace and in his
whole kingdom.

14Then Isaiah the prophet went to King Hezekiah. He asked him, "What did those men say?
Where did they come from?"

"They came from a land far away," Hezekiah
said. "They came from Babylon."

15The prophet asked, "What did they see in your
palace?"

"They saw everything in my palace," Hezekiah
said. "I showed them all of my treasures."

16Then Isaiah said to Hezekiah, "Listen to the
LORD's message. He says, 17'You can be sure the
time will come when everything in your palace
will be carried off to Babylon. Everything the
kings before you have stored up until this day will
be taken away. There will not be anything left,'
says the LORD. 18'Some of the members of your
family line will be taken away. They will be your
own flesh and blood. They will include the children who will be born into your family line in
years to come. And they will serve the king of
Babylonia in his palace.'"

19"The message the LORD has spoken through
you is good," Hezekiah replied. He thought,
"There will be peace and safety while I'm still
living."

20The other events of the rule of Hezekiah are
written down. Everything he accomplished is written down. That includes how he made the pool and
the tunnel. He used them to bring water into Jerusalem. All of those things are written in the official records of the kings of Judah.

21Hezekiah joined the members of his family
who had already died. His son Manasseh became
the next king after him.

Manasseh Becomes King of Judah

21 Manasseh was 12 years old when he
became king. He ruled in Jerusalem for 55
years. His mother's name was Hephzibah.

2Manasseh did what was evil in the sight of the
LORD. He followed the practices of the nations. The
LORD hated those practices. He had driven those
nations out to make room for the people of Israel.

3Manasseh rebuilt the high places. His father
Hezekiah had destroyed them. Manasseh also set
up altars to the god Baal. He made a pole that was
used to worship the goddess Asherah. Ahab, the
king of Israel, had done those same things. Manasseh even bowed down to all of the stars. And he
worshiped them.

4He built altars in the LORD's temple. The LORD
had said about his temple, "I will put my Name
there in Jerusalem." 5In both courtyards of the
LORD's temple Manasseh built altars to honor all
of the stars.

6He sacrificed his own son in the fire to another
god. He practiced all kinds of evil magic. He got
messages from those who had died. He talked to
the spirits of the dead. He did many things that
were evil in the sight of the LORD. He made him
very angry.

7Manasseh had carved a pole for worshiping
Asherah. He put it in the temple. The LORD had
spoken to David and his son Solomon about the
temple. He had said, "My Name will be in this
temple and in Jerusalem forever. Out of all of the
cities in the tribes of Israel I have chosen Jerusalem. 8I gave this land to your people who lived
long ago. I will not make the Israelites wander
away from it again. But they must be careful to do
everything I commanded them. They must obey
the whole Law that my servant Moses gave them."

9But the people didn't pay any attention. Manasseh led them down the wrong path. They did
more evil things than the nations the LORD had
destroyed to make room for the people of Israel.

10The LORD spoke through his servants the
prophets. He said, 11"Manasseh, the king of Judah,
has committed terrible sins. I hate them. Manasseh
has done more evil things than the Amorites who
were in the land before him. And he has led Judah
to commit sin by worshiping his statues of gods.

12"I am the God of Israel. I tell you, 'I am going to bring trouble on Jerusalem and Judah. It will be so horrible that the ears of everyone who hears about it will ring. 13I will measure out punishment against Jerusalem, just as I did against Samaria. I used a plumb line against the royal family of Ahab to prove that they did not measure up to my standards. I will use the same plumb line against Jerusalem. I will wipe out Jerusalem, just as someone wipes a dish. I will wipe it and turn it upside down. 14I will desert those who remain among my people. I will hand them over to their enemies. All of their enemies will rob them.

15" 'That is because my people have done what is evil in my sight. They have made me very angry. They have done that from the day their own people came out of Egypt until this very day.' "

16Manasseh also spilled the blood of many people who weren't guilty of doing anything wrong. He spilled so much blood that he filled Jerusalem with it from one end of the city to the other. And he caused Judah to commit sin. So they also did what was evil in the sight of the LORD.

17The other events of the rule of Manasseh are written down. Everything he did is written down. That includes the sin he committed. All of those things are written in the official records of the kings of Judah.

18Manasseh joined the members of his family who had already died. His body was buried in his palace garden. It was called the garden of Uzza. Manasseh's son Amon became the next king after him.

Amon Becomes King of Judah

19Amon was 22 years old when he became king. He ruled in Jerusalem for two years. His mother's name was Meshullemeth. She was the daughter of Haruz. She was from Jotbah.

20Amon did what was evil in the sight of the LORD, just as his father Manasseh had done. 21He lived the way his father had lived. He worshiped the statues of the gods his father had worshiped. He bowed down to them. 22He deserted the LORD, the God of his people. He didn't live the way the LORD wanted him to.

23Amon's officials made plans against him. They murdered the king in his palace. 24Then the people of the land killed all those who had made plans against King Amon. They made his son Josiah king in his place.

25The other events of the rule of Amon are written down. Everything he did is written down. All of those things are written in the official records of the kings of Judah. 26Amon's body was buried in his grave in the garden of Uzza. His son Josiah became the next king after him.

Hilkiah Finds the Scroll of the Law

22 Josiah was eight years old when he became king. He ruled in Jerusalem for 31 years. His mother's name was Jedidah. She was the daughter of Adaiah. She was from Bozkath.

2Josiah did what was right in the eyes of the LORD. He lived the way King David had lived. He didn't turn away from it to the right or the left.

3King Josiah sent his secretary Shaphan to the LORD's temple. It was in the 18th year of Josiah's rule. Shaphan was the son of Azaliah. Azaliah was the son of Meshullam. Josiah said, 4"Go up to the high priest Hilkiah. Have him add up the money that has been brought into the LORD's temple. Those who guard the doors have collected it from the people.

5"Have them put all of the money in the care of the men who have been put in charge of the work on the LORD's temple. Have them pay the workers who repair it. 6Have them pay the builders and those who work with wood. Have them pay those who lay the stones. Also have them buy lumber and blocks of stone to repair the temple.

7"But they don't have to report how they use the money that is given to them. That's because they are completely honest."

8The high priest Hilkiah spoke to the secretary Shaphan. He said, "I've found the Scroll of the Law in the LORD's temple." He gave it to Shaphan, who read it.

9Then Shaphan went to King Josiah. He told him, "Your officials have paid out the money that was in the LORD's temple. They've put it in the care of the workers and directors there." 10Shaphan continued, "The priest Hilkiah has given me a scroll." Shaphan read some of it to the king.

11The king heard the words of the Scroll of the Law. When he did, he tore his royal robes. 12He gave orders to the priest Hilkiah, Ahikam, Acbor, the secretary Shaphan and Asaiah. Ahikam was the son of Shaphan. Acbor was the son of Micaiah. And Asaiah was the king's attendant.

Josiah commanded them, 13"Go. Ask the LORD for advice. Ask him about what is written in this scroll that has been found. Do it for me. Also do it for the people and the whole nation of Judah. The LORD's anger is burning against us. That's because our people before us didn't obey the words of this scroll. They didn't do everything that is written there about us."

14The priest Hilkiah went to speak to the prophet Huldah. So did Ahikam, Acbor, Shaphan and Asaiah. Huldah was the wife of Shallum. Shallum was the son of Tikvah. Tikvah was the son of Harhas. Shallum took care of the sacred robes. Huldah lived in the New Quarter of Jerusalem.

15She said to them, "The LORD is the God of Israel. He says, 'Tell the man who sent you to me, 16"The LORD says, 'I am going to bring horrible trouble on this place and its people. Everything that is written in the scroll the king of Judah has read will take place.

17" ' " 'That is because the people have deserted me. They have burned incense to other gods. They have made me very angry because of the statues of gods their hands have made. So my anger will burn against this place. The fire of my anger will not be put out.'"'

18"The king of Judah sent you to ask the LORD for advice. Tell him, 'The LORD is the God of Israel. He has a message for you about the things you heard. He says, 19"Your heart was tender. You made yourself low in my sight. You heard what I spoke against this place and its people. I said they would be under a curse. I told them they would be destroyed. You tore your royal robes and sobbed. And I have heard you," announces the LORD.

20""You will join the members of your family who have already died. Your body will be buried in peace. Your eyes will not see all of the trouble I am going to bring on this place."'"

Huldah's answer was taken back to the king.

Josiah Promises to Follow the Covenant

23 Then the king called together all of the elders of Judah and Jerusalem. 2He went up to the LORD's temple. The people of Judah and Jerusalem went with him. So did the priests and prophets. All of them went, from the least important of them to the most important.

The king had all of the words of the Scroll of the Covenant read to them. The scroll had been found in the LORD's temple.

3The king stood next to his pillar. He agreed to the terms of the covenant in front of the LORD. He promised to follow him and obey his commands, directions and rules. He promised to obey them with all his heart and with all his soul. So he agreed to the terms of the covenant that were written down in that scroll. Then all of the people committed themselves to the covenant.

4Certain articles that were in the LORD's temple had been made to honor the god Baal and the goddess Asherah and all of the stars in the sky. The king ordered the high priest Hilkiah to remove those articles. He ordered the priests who were under him and the men who guarded the doors to help Hilkiah. Josiah burned the articles outside Jerusalem. He burned them in the fields in the Kidron Valley. And he took the ashes to Bethel.

5He got rid of the priests who served other gods. The kings of Judah had appointed them to burn incense. They burned the incense on the high places of the towns of Judah. And they burned it on the high places around Jerusalem. They burned incense to honor Baal and the sun and moon. They burned it to honor all of the stars.

6Josiah removed the Asherah pole from the LORD's temple. It had been used to worship Asherah. He took it to the Kidron Valley outside Jerusalem. There he burned it. He ground it into powder. And he scattered it over the graves of the ordinary people.

7He also tore down the rooms where the male temple prostitutes stayed. Those rooms were in the LORD's temple. The women had made cloth for Asherah in them.

8Josiah brought all of the priests from the towns of Judah and destroyed the high places. He destroyed them from Geba all the way to Beersheba. The priests had burned incense on them. Josiah broke down the high places at the gates. That included the high place at the entrance of the Gate of Joshua. It was on the left side of one of Jerusalem's gates. Joshua was the city governor.

9The priests of the high places didn't serve at the LORD's altar in Jerusalem. In spite of that, they ate with the other priests. All of them ate bread that was made without yeast.

10Josiah destroyed the high places at Topheth in the Valley of Ben Hinnom. He didn't want anyone to use them to sacrifice his son or daughter in the fire to the god Molech.

11He removed the statues of horses from the entrance to the LORD's temple. The kings of Judah had set them apart to honor the sun. The statues were in the courtyard. They were near the room of an official named Nathan-Melech. Josiah burned the chariots that had been set apart to honor the sun.

12He pulled down the altars the kings of Judah had set up. They had put them on the palace roof near the upstairs room of Ahaz. Josiah also pulled down the altars Manasseh had built. They were in the two courtyards of the LORD's temple. Josiah removed the altars from there. He smashed them to pieces. Then he threw the broken pieces into the Kidron Valley.

13The king also destroyed the high places that were east of Jerusalem. They were at the southern end of the Mount of Olives. They were the ones Solomon, the king of Israel, had built. He had built a high place for worshiping Ashtoreth. She was the evil goddess of the people of Sidon. Solomon had also built one for worshiping Chemosh. He was the evil god of Moab. And Solomon had built one for worshiping Molech. He was the god of the people of Ammon. The LORD hated that god.

14Josiah smashed the sacred stones. He cut down the poles that were used to worship the goddess Asherah. Then he covered all of those places with human bones.

15There was an altar at Bethel. It was at the high place that had been made by Jeroboam, the son of Nebat. Jeroboam had caused Israel to commit sin. Even that altar and high place were destroyed by Josiah. He burned the high place. He ground it into powder. He also burned the Asherah pole.

16Then Josiah looked around. He saw the tombs that were on the side of the hill. He had the bones removed from them. And he burned them on the altar to make it "unclean." That's what the LORD had said would happen. He had spoken that message through a man of God. The man had announced those things long before they took place.

17 The king asked, "What's that stone on the
grave over there?"
The men of the city said, "It marks the tomb
where the body of a man of God is buried. He came
from Judah. He spoke against the altar at Bethel.
He announced the very things you have done to it."
18 "Leave it alone," Josiah said. "Don't let anyone touch his bones."
So they spared his bones. They also spared the
bones of the prophet who had come from the
northern kingdom of Israel.
19 Josiah did in the rest of the northern kingdom
the same things he had done at Bethel. He
removed all of the small temples at the high
places. He made them "unclean." The kings of Israel had built them in the towns of the northern
kingdom. The people in those towns had made the
LORD very angry.
20 Josiah killed all of the priests of those high
places on the altars. He burned human bones on
the altars. Then he went back to Jerusalem.
21 The king gave an order to all of the people. He
said, "Celebrate the Passover Feast to honor the
LORD your God. Do what is written in this Scroll
of the Covenant."
22 A Passover Feast like that one had not been
held for a long time. There hadn't been any like it
since the days of the judges who led Israel. And
there hadn't been any like it during the whole time
the kings of Israel and Judah were ruling.
23 King Josiah celebrated the Passover in Jerusalem to honor the LORD. It was in the 18th year
of his rule.
24 And that's not all. Josiah got rid of those who
got messages from people who had died. He got
rid of those who talked to the spirits of the dead.
He got rid of the statues of family gods and the
statues of other gods. He got rid of everything else
the LORD hates that was in Judah and Jerusalem.
He did it to carry out what the law required. That
law was written in the scroll the priest Hilkiah had
found in the LORD's temple.
25 There was no king like Josiah either before him
or after him. None of them turned to the LORD as he
did. He followed the LORD with all his heart and all
his soul. He followed him with all his strength. He
did everything the Law of Moses required.
26 In spite of that, the LORD didn't turn away
from his burning anger. It blazed out against Judah. That's because of everything Manasseh had
done to make him very angry.
27 So the LORD said, "I will remove Judah from
my land. I will do to them what I did to Israel. I
will turn my back on Jerusalem. It is the city I
chose. I will also turn my back on this temple. I
spoke about it. I said, 'I will put my Name here.'"
(1 Kings 8:29)
28 The other events of the rule of Josiah are written down. Everything he did is written down. All
of those things are written in the official records
of the kings of Judah.
29 Pharaoh Neco was king of Egypt. He marched
up to the Euphrates River. He went there to help
the king of Assyria. It happened while Josiah was
king. Josiah marched out to meet Neco in battle.
When Neco saw him at Megiddo, he killed him.
30 Josiah's servants brought his body in a chariot
from Megiddo to Jerusalem. They buried his body
in his own tomb. Then the people of the land went
and got Jehoahaz. They anointed him as king in
place of his father Josiah.

Jehoahaz Becomes King of Judah

31 Jehoahaz was 23 years old when he became
king. He ruled in Jerusalem for three months. His
mother's name was Hamutal. She was the daughter of Jeremiah. She was from Libnah.
32 Jehoahaz did what was evil in the sight of the
LORD. He did just as the kings who had ruled
before him had done. 33 Pharaoh Neco put him in
chains at Riblah in the land of Hamath. That kept
him from ruling in Jerusalem. Neco made the people of Judah pay him a tax of almost four tons of
silver and 75 pounds of gold.
34 Pharaoh Neco made Eliakim king in place of
his father Josiah. He changed Eliakim's name to
Jehoiakim. But he took Jehoahaz with him to
Egypt. And that's where Jehoahaz died.
35 Jehoiakim paid Pharaoh Neco the silver and
gold he required. To get the money, Jehoiakim
taxed the land. He forced the people to give him
the silver and gold. He made each one pay him
what he required.

Jehoiakim Becomes King of Judah

36 Jehoiakim was 25 years old when he became
king. He ruled in Jerusalem for 11 years. His
mother's name was Zebidah. She was the daughter of Pedaiah. She was from Rumah.
37 Jehoiakim did what was evil in the sight of the
LORD. He did just as the kings who had ruled
before him had done.
24 During Jehoiakim's rule, Nebuchadnezzar
marched into the land and attacked it. He
was king of Babylonia. He became Jehoiakim's
master for three years. But then Jehoiakim decided
he didn't want to remain under Nebuchadnezzar's
control.
2 The LORD sent robbers against Jehoiakim from
Babylonia, Aram, Moab and Ammon. He sent
them to destroy Judah. That's what the LORD had
said would happen. He had spoken that message
through his servants the prophets.
3 Those things happened to Judah in keeping
with what the LORD had commanded. He brought
enemies against his people in order to remove
them from his land. He removed them because of
all of the sins Manasseh had committed. 4 He had
spilled the blood of many people who weren't
guilty of doing anything wrong. In fact, he spilled
so much of their blood that he filled Jerusalem
with it. So the LORD refused to forgive him.

5The other events of the rule of Jehoiakim are
written down. Everything he did is written down.
All of those things are written in the official
records of the kings of Judah.
6Jehoiakim joined the members of his family
who had already died. His son Jehoiachin became
the next king after him.
7The king of Egypt didn't march out from his
own country again. That's because the king of
Babylonia had taken so much of his territory. That
territory reached from the Wadi of Egypt all the
way to the Euphrates River.

Jehoiachin Becomes King of Judah

8Jehoiachin was 18 years old when he became
king. He ruled in Jerusalem for three months. His
mother's name was Nehushta. She was the daughter of Elnathan. She was from Jerusalem.
9Jehoiachin did what was evil in the sight of the
LORD. He did just as his father Jehoiakim had
done.
10At that time the officers of Nebuchadnezzar,
the king of Babylonia, marched to Jerusalem. They
surrounded it and got ready to attack it. 11Nebu-
chadnezzar himself came up to the city. He arrived
while his officers were attacking it.
12Jehoiachin, the king of Judah, handed himself
over to him. Jehoiachin's mother did the same
thing. And so did all of his attendants, nobles and
officials.
The king of Babylonia took Jehoiachin away as
his prisoner. It was in the eighth year of Nebuchadnezzar's rule.
13He removed all of the treasures from the
LORD's temple. He also removed all of the treasures from the royal palace. He took away all of
the gold articles that Solomon, the king of Israel,
had made for the temple. That's what the LORD had
announced would happen.
14Nebuchadnezzar took all of the people of Jerusalem to Babylonia as prisoners. That included
all of the officers and fighting men. It also
included all of the skilled workers. The total number of prisoners was 10,000. Only the poorest people were left in the land.
15Nebuchadnezzar took Jehoiachin to Babylon
as his prisoner. He also took the king's mother
from Jerusalem to Babylon. And he took Jehoiachin's wives, his officials and the most important
men in the land.
16The king also forced the whole army of 7,000
soldiers to go away to Babylonia. Those men were
strong and able to go to war. And the king forced
1,000 skilled workers to go to Babylonia.
17Nebuchadnezzar made Jehoiachin's uncle
Mattaniah king in his place. And he changed Mattaniah's name to Zedekiah.

Zedekiah Becomes King of Judah

18Zedekiah was 21 years old when he became
king. He ruled in Jerusalem for 11 years. His
mother's name was Hamutal. She was the daughter of Jeremiah. She was from Libnah.
19Zedekiah did what was evil in the sight of the
LORD. He did just as Jehoiakim had done. 20The
enemies of Jerusalem and Judah attacked them
because the LORD was angry. In the end he threw
them out of his land.

Nebuchadnezzar Destroys Jerusalem

Zedekiah also refused to remain under the control of Nebuchadnezzar.
25 Nebuchadnezzar was king of Babylonia.
He marched out against Jerusalem. All of
his armies went with him. It was in the ninth year
of the rule of Zedekiah. It was on the tenth day of
the tenth month. Nebuchadnezzar set up camp outside the city. He brought in war machines all
around it. 2It was surrounded until the 11th year of
King Zedekiah's rule.
3By the ninth day of the fourth month, there
wasn't any food left in the city. So the people
didn't have anything to eat.
4Then the Babylonians broke through the city
wall. Judah's whole army ran away at night. They
went out through the gate between the two walls
that were near the king's garden. They escaped
even though the Babylonians surrounded the city.
Judah's army ran toward the Arabah Valley.
5But the armies of Babylonia chased King Zedekiah. They caught up with him in the flatlands
near Jericho. All of his soldiers were separated
from him. They had scattered in every direction.
6The king was captured. He was taken to the
king of Babylonia at Riblah. That's where Nebuchadnezzar decided how he would be punished.
7His men killed the sons of Zedekiah. They forced
him to watch it with his own eyes. Then they
poked out his eyes. They put him in bronze chains.
And they took him to Babylon.
8Nebuzaradan was an official of the king of
Babylonia. In fact, he was commander of the royal
guard. He came to Jerusalem. It was in the 19th
year that Nebuchadnezzar was king of Babylonia.
It was on the seventh day of the fifth month.
9Nebuzaradan set the LORD's temple on fire. He
also set fire to the royal palace and all of the
houses in Jerusalem. He burned down every
important building. 10The armies of Babylonia
broke down the walls around Jerusalem. That's
what the commander told them to do.
11Some people still remained in the city. But the
commander Nebuzaradan took them away as prisoners. He also took the rest of the people of the
land. That included those who had joined the king
of Babylonia.
12But the commander left some of the poorest
people of the land behind. He told them to work in
the vineyards and fields.
13The armies of Babylonia destroyed the LORD's
temple. They broke the bronze pillars into pieces.
They broke up the bronze stands that could be

moved around. And they broke up the huge bronze
bowl. Then they carried the bronze away to Babylon. 14 They also took away the pots, shovels, wick
cutters and dishes. They took away all of the bronze
articles that were used for any purpose in the temple. 15 The commander of the royal guard took away
the shallow cups for burning incense. He took away
the sprinkling bowls. So he took away everything
that was made out of pure gold or silver.

16 The bronze was more than anyone could
weigh. It included the bronze from the two pillars.
It also included the bronze from the huge bowl and
the stands. Solomon had made all of those things
for the LORD's temple. 17 Each pillar was 27 feet
high. The bronze top of one pillar was four and a
half feet high. It was decorated with a set of bronze
chains and pomegranates all around it. The other
pillar was just like it. It also had a set of chains.

18 The commander of the guard took some prisoners. They included the chief priest Seraiah and
the priest Zephaniah who was under him. They
also included the three men who guarded the temple doors.

19 Some people were still left in the city. The
commander took as a prisoner the officer who was
in charge of the fighting men. He took the five
men who gave advice to the king. He also took the
secretary who was the chief officer in charge of
getting the people of the land to serve in the army.
And he took 60 of the secretary's men who were
still in the city.

20 The commander Nebuzaradan took all of
them away. He brought them to the king of Babylonia at Riblah. 21 There the king had them put to
death. Riblah was in the land of Hamath.

So the people of Judah were taken as prisoners.
They were taken far away from their own land.

22 Nebuchadnezzar, the king of Babylonia,
appointed Gedaliah to be over the people he had
left behind in Judah. Gedaliah was the son of Ahikam. Ahikam was the son of Shaphan.

23 All of Judah's army officers and their men
heard about what had happened. They heard that
the king had appointed Gedaliah as governor. So
they came to Gedaliah at Mizpah. Ishmael, the
son of Nethaniah, came. So did Johanan, the son
of Kareah. Seraiah, the son of Tanhumeth, also
came. And so did Jaazaniah, the son of the Maacathite. All of their men came too. Seraiah was
from Netophah.

24 Gedaliah took an oath to give hope to all of
those men. He spoke in a kind way to them. He
said, "Don't be afraid of the officials from Babylonia. Settle down in the land of Judah. Serve the
king of Babylonia. Then things will go well with
you."

25 But in the seventh month Ishmael, the son of
Nethaniah, came with ten men. He killed Gedaliah. He also killed the people of Judah and Babylonia who were with Gedaliah at Mizpah. Nethaniah
was the son of Elishama. Ishmael was a member of
the royal family.

26 After he had killed Gedaliah, all of the people
ran away to Egypt. Everyone from the least important of them to the most important ran away. The
army officers went with them. All of them went to
Egypt because they were afraid of the Babylonians.

Jehoiachin Is Set Free

27 Evil-Merodach set Jehoiachin, the king of Judah, free from prison. It was in the 37th year after
Jehoiachin had been taken away to Babylon. It was
also the year Evil-Merodach became king of Babylonia. It was on the 27th day of the 12th month.
28 Evil-Merodach spoke kindly to Jehoiachin. He
gave him a place of honor. Other kings were with
Jehoiachin in Babylon. But his place was more
important than theirs.

29 So Jehoiachin put his prison clothes away. For
the rest of Jehoiachin's life the king provided what
he needed. 30 The king did that for Jehoiachin day
by day as long as he lived.

1 Chronicles

A List of Names From Adam to Abraham

A List of Names From Adam to the Sons of Noah

1 Adam, Seth, Enosh, 2 Kenan, Mahalalel, Jared,
3 Enoch, Methuselah, Lamech, Noah.

4 The sons of Noah were
Shem, Ham and Japheth.

The Sons of Japheth

5 The sons of Japheth were
Gomer, Magog, Madai, Javan, Tubal, Meshech and Tiras.
6 The sons of Gomer were
Ashkenaz, Riphath and Togarmah.
7 The sons of Javan were
Elishah, Tarshish, the Kittim and the Rodanites.

The Sons of Ham

8 The sons of Ham were
Cush, Egypt, Put and Canaan.
9 The sons of Cush were
Seba, Havilah, Sabta, Raamah and Sabteca.
The sons of Raamah were
Sheba and Dedan.
10 Cush was the father of
Nimrod. Nimrod grew up to be a mighty hero on the earth.
11 Egypt was the father of
the Ludites, Anamites, Lehabites and
Naphtuhites. 12 He was also the father of
the Pathrusites, Casluhites and Caphtorites. The Philistines came from the Casluhites.
13 Canaan was the father of Sidon. Sidon was his oldest son.
Canaan was also the father of the Hittites, 14 Jebusites, Amorites and Girga-
shites. 15 And he was the father of the
Hivites, Arkites, Sinites, 16 Arvadites,
Zemarites and Hamathites.

The Sons of Shem

17 The sons of Shem were
Elam, Asshur, Arphaxad, Lud and Aram.
The sons of Aram were
Uz, Hul, Gether and Meshech.
18 Arphaxad was the father of Shelah.
Shelah was the father of Eber.
19 Eber was the father of two sons.
One was named Peleg. The earth was divided up in his time. His brother was named Joktan.
20 Joktan was the father of
Almodad, Sheleph, Hazarmaveth and
Jerah. 21 He was also the father of Hado-
ram, Uzal, Diklah, 22 Obal, Abimael,
Sheba, 23 Ophir, Havilah and Jobab. All of them were sons of Joktan.

A List of Names From Shem to Abraham

24 Shem, Arphaxad, Shelah,
25 Eber, Peleg, Reu,
26 Serug, Nahor, Terah,
27 Abram. Abram was also called Abraham.

The Family Line of Abraham

28 The sons of Abraham were
Isaac and Ishmael.

The Family Line of Hagar

29 Here are the members of the family line of Hagar.
Nebaioth was Ishmael's oldest son. Then came Kedar, Adbeel, Mibsam,
30 Mishma, Dumah, Massa, Hadad,
Tema, 31 Jetur, Naphish and Kedemah.
All of them were Ishmael's sons.

The Family Line of Keturah

32 Here are the sons that were born to Abraham's concubine Keturah.
They were Zimran, Jokshan, Medan, Midian, Ishbak and Shuah.
The sons of Jokshan were
Sheba and Dedan.
33 The sons of Midian were
Ephah, Epher, Hanoch, Abida and Eldaah.
All of them came from Keturah.

The Family Line of Sarah

34 Abraham was the father of Isaac.
The sons of Isaac were
Esau and Israel.

The Family Line of Esau

35 The sons of Esau were
Eliphaz, Reuel, Jeush, Jalam and Korah.
36 The sons of Eliphaz were
Teman, Omar, Zepho, Gatam and Kenaz.
Timna had Amalek by Eliphaz.
37 The sons of Reuel were
Nahath, Zerah, Shammah and Mizzah.

The People of Seir in Edom

38 The sons of Seir were
Lotan, Shobal, Zibeon, Anah, Dishon, Ezer and Dishan.
39 The sons of Lotan were
Hori and Homam. Timna was Lotan's sister.

40 The sons of Shobal were
Alvan, Manahath, Ebal, Shepho and
Onam.
The sons of Zibeon were
Aiah and Anah.
41 The son of Anah was
Dishon.
The sons of Dishon were
Hemdan, Eshban, Ithran and Keran.
42 The sons of Ezer were
Bilhan, Zaavan and Akan.
The sons of Dishan were
Uz and Aran.

The Rulers of Edom

43 Before Israel had a king, there were kings
who ruled in Edom.
Bela was the son of Beor. Bela's city
was called Dinhabah.
44 When Bela died, Jobab became the next
king. Jobab was the son of Zerah from
Bozrah.
45 When Jobab died, Husham became the
next king. Husham was from the land of
the people of Teman.
46 When Husham died, Hadad became the
next king. Hadad was the son of Bedad.
Hadad had won the battle over Midian
in the country of Moab. Hadad's city
was called Avith.
47 When Hadad died, Samlah became the
next king. Samlah was from Masrekah.
48 When Samlah died, Shaul became the next
king. Shaul was from Rehoboth on the
river.
49 When Shaul died, Baal-Hanan became the
next king. Baal-Hanan was the son of
Acbor.
50 When Baal-Hanan died, Hadad became the
next king. Hadad's city was called Pau.
His wife's name was Mehetabel. She was
the daughter of Matred. Matred was the
daughter of Me-Zahab. 51 Hadad also died.

The chiefs of Edom were
Timna, Alvah, Jetheth, 52 Oholibamah,
Elah, Pinon, 53 Kenaz, Teman, Mibzar,
54 Magdiel and Iram. They were the
chiefs of Edom.

The Sons of Israel

2 Here are the names of the sons of Israel.

Reuben, Simeon, Levi, Judah, Issachar,
Zebulun, 2 Dan, Joseph, Benjamin,
Naphtali, Gad, Asher.

The Family Line of Judah

The Family Line From Judah's Sons to Hezron's Sons

3 The sons of Judah were
Er, Onan and Shelah. A woman from Canaan had those three sons by him. She
was the daughter of Shua. Er was Judah's
oldest son. He was evil in the LORD's
eyes. So the LORD put him to death. 4 Tamar was Judah's daughter-in-law. She
had Perez and Zerah by him. The total
number of Judah's sons was five.

5 The sons of Perez were
Hezron and Hamul.
6 The sons of Zerah were
Zimri, Ethan, Heman, Calcol and Darda. The total number of Zerah's sons
was five.
7 The son of Carmi was Achar.
He brought trouble on Israel. He took
some of the things that had been set
apart to the LORD in a special way to be
destroyed. When he did that, he disobeyed the LORD's command.
8 The son of Ethan was
Azariah.
9 Hezron was the father of
Jerahmeel, Ram and Caleb.

The Family Line of Ram

10 Ram was the father of
Amminadab. Amminadab was the
father of Nahshon. Nahshon was the
leader of the people of Judah. 11 Nahshon was the father of Salmon. Salmon
was the father of Boaz. 12 Boaz was the
father of Obed. And Obed was the
father of Jesse.
13 Jesse's first son was
Eliab. His second son was Abinadab.
The third was Shimea. 14 The fourth was
Nethanel. The fifth was Raddai. 15 The
sixth was Ozem. And the seventh was
David. 16 Their sisters were Zeruiah and
Abigail. Zeruiah's three sons were
Abishai, Joab and Asahel. 17 Abigail was
the mother of Amasa. Amasa's father
was Jether. Jether belonged to the family line of Ishmael.

The Family Line of Caleb

18 Caleb was the son of Hezron. Caleb's wife
Azubah had children by him. Jerioth
also had children by him. Azubah's sons
were Jesher, Shobab and Ardon. 19 When
Azubah died, Caleb got married to Ephrath. She had Hur by him. 20 Hur was the
father of Uri. And Uri was the father of
Bezalel.
21 Later, Hezron made love to the daughter of
Makir. He had gotten married to her
when he was 60 years old. She had Segub by him. Makir was the father of
Gilead. 22 Segub was the father of Jair.

Jair controlled 23 towns in Gilead. 23But
Geshur and Aram captured Havvoth
Jair. They also captured Kenath and the
settlements that were around it. The
total number of towns that were captured was 60. Hezron, Segub and Jair
belonged to the family line of Makir.
Makir was the father of Gilead.

24 Hezron died in Caleb Ephrathah. Abijah
was Hezron's wife. She had Ashhur by
him. Ashhur was born after Hezron
died. Ashhur was the father of Tekoa.

The Family Line of Jerahmeel

25 Here are the sons of Jerahmeel. He was the
oldest son of Hezron. Ram was Jerahmeel's oldest son. Then came Bunah,
Oren, Ozem and Ahijah. 26Jerahmeel
had another wife. Her name was Atarah.
She was the mother of Onam.

27 Here are the sons of Ram. He was the oldest son of Jerahmeel. The sons of Ram
were
Maaz, Jamin and Eker.

28 The sons of Onam were
Shammai and Jada.
The sons of Shammai were
Nadab and Abishur.

29 Abishur's wife was named Abihail. She
had Ahban and Molid by him.

30 The sons of Nadab were
Seled and Appaim. Seled died without
having any children.

31 The son of Appaim was
Ishi. Ishi was the father of Sheshan.
Sheshan was the father of Ahlai.

32 The sons of Jada were
Jether and Jonathan. Jada was Shammai's brother. Jether died without having any children.

33 The sons of Jonathan were
Peleth and Zaza.
They belonged to the family line of Jerahmeel.

34 Sheshan didn't have any sons. All he had
was daughters.
He had a servant from Egypt named Jarha. 35Sheshan gave his daughter to be
married to his servant Jarha. She had
Attai by Jarha.

36 Attai was the father of Nathan.
Nathan was the father of Zabad.
37 Zabad was the father of Ephlal.
Ephlal was the father of Obed.
38 Obed was the father of Jehu.
Jehu was the father of Azariah.
39 Azariah was the father of Helez.
Helez was the father of Eleasah.
40 Eleasah was the father of Sismai.
Sismai was the father of Shallum.
41 Shallum was the father of Jekamiah.
And Jekamiah was the father of Elishama.

The Family Groups of Caleb

42 Caleb was the brother of Jerahmeel.
Caleb's oldest son was Mesha. Mesha
was the father of Ziph. Caleb had
another son named Mareshah. Mareshah was the father of Hebron.

43 The sons of Hebron were
Korah, Tappuah, Rekem and Shema.
44Shema was the father of Raham. Raham was the father of Jorkeam. Rekem
was the father of Shammai. 45The son of
Shammai was Maon. Maon was the
father of Beth Zur.

46 Caleb had a concubine named Ephah. She
was the mother of Haran, Moza and Gazez. Haran was the father of Gazez.

47 The sons of Jahdai were
Regem, Jotham, Geshan, Pelet, Ephah
and Shaaph.

48 Caleb had a concubine named Maacah.
She was the mother of Sheber and Tirhanah. 49She was also the mother of
Shaaph and Sheva. Shaaph was the
father of Madmannah. Sheva was the
father of Macbenah and Gibea. Caleb's
daughter was Acsah. 50All of them
belonged to the family line of Caleb.

Hur was the oldest son of Ephrathah.
Hur was the brother of Shobal. Shobal
was the father of Kiriath Jearim. 51Hur
was the father of Salma. Salma was the
father of Bethlehem. Hur was also the
father of Hareph. Hareph was the father
of Beth Gader.

52 Here is the family line of Shobal, the father
of Kiriath Jearim. It included
Haroeh and half of the people of Manahath. 53It also included the family
groups of Kiriath Jearim. They were the
Ithrites, Puthites, Shumathites and
Mishraites. The people of Zorah and
Eshtaol belonged to those family
groups.

54 Here is the family line of Salma. It
included
Bethlehem, the people of Netophah, Atroth Beth Joab, half of the people of
Manahath, and the Zorites. 55It also
included the family groups of secretaries
who lived at Jabez. They were the Tirathites, Shimeathites and Sucathites. They
were the Kenites who belonged to the
family line of Hammath. Hammath was
the father of the family line of Recab.

The Sons of David

3 Here are the sons of David who were born to
him in Hebron.

His first son was Amnon. Amnon's mother was Ahinoam from Jezreel.
The second son was Daniel. His mother was Abigail from Carmel.
2 The third son was Absalom. His mother was Maacah. She was the daughter of Talmai, the king of Geshur.
The fourth son was Adonijah. His mother was Haggith.
3 The fifth son was Shephatiah. His mother was Abital.
The sixth son was Ithream. David's wife Eglah had Ithream by him.
4 Those six sons were born to David in Hebron. He ruled there for seven and a half years.

After that, he ruled in Jerusalem for 33 years.
5 Children were born to him there.
They included Shammua, Shobab, Nathan and Solomon. The mother of those four sons was Bathsheba. She was the daughter of Ammiel. 6 David's children also included Ibhar, Elishua, Eliphelet, 7 Nogah, Nepheg, Japhia, 8 Elishama, Eliada and Eliphelet. There were nine of them. 9 David was the father of all of those sons. His concubines also had sons by him. David's sons had a sister named Tamar.

The Kings of Judah

10 Solomon's son was Rehoboam.
Abijah was the son of Rehoboam.
Asa was the son of Abijah.
Jehoshaphat was the son of Asa.
11 Jehoram was the son of Jehoshaphat.
Ahaziah was the son of Jehoram.
Joash was the son of Ahaziah.
12 Amaziah was the son of Joash.
Azariah was the son of Amaziah.
Jotham was the son of Azariah.
13 Ahaz was the son of Jotham.
Hezekiah was the son of Ahaz.
Manasseh was the son of Hezekiah.
14 Amon was the son of Manasseh.
Josiah was the son of Amon.
15 Josiah's first son was Johanan.
Jehoiakim was his second son.
Zedekiah was the third son.
Shallum was the fourth son.
16 The next king after Jehoiakim was his son Jehoiachin.
After that, Josiah's son Zedekiah became king.

The Royal Family Line After Jehoiachin

17 Here are the members of the family line of Jehoiachin. He was taken as a prisoner to Babylon.
His sons were Shealtiel, 18 Malkiram, Pedaiah, Shenazzar, Jekamiah, Hoshama and Nedabiah.
19 The sons of Pedaiah were
Zerubbabel and Shimei.
The sons of Zerubbabel were
Meshullam and Hananiah.
Shelomith was their sister.
20 There were also five other sons.
They were Hashubah, Ohel, Berekiah, Hasadiah and Jushab-Hesed.
21 The family line of Hananiah included
Pelatiah and Jeshaiah. It also included the sons of Rephaiah, Arnan, Obadiah and Shecaniah.
22 The family line of Shecaniah included
Shemaiah and his sons.
They were Hattush, Igal, Bariah, Neariah and Shaphat. The total number of men was six.
23 The sons of Neariah were
Elioenai, Hizkiah and Azrikam. The total number of sons was three.
24 The sons of Elioenai were
Hodaviah, Eliashib, Pelaiah, Akkub, Johanan, Delaiah and Anani. The total number of sons was seven.

Other Family Groups of Judah

4 The family line of Judah included
Perez, Hezron, Carmi, Hur and Shobal.
2 Reaiah was the son of Shobal and the father of Jahath. Jahath was the father of Ahumai and Lahad. Those were the family groups of the people of Zorah.
3 The sons of Etam were
Jezreel, Ishma and Idbash. Their sister was named Hazzelelponi. 4 Penuel was the father of Gedor. Ezer was the father of Hushah.
Those people belonged to the family line of Hur. He was the oldest son of Ephrathah and the father of Bethlehem.
5 Ashhur was the father of Tekoa. Ashhur had two wives. Their names were Helah and Naarah.
6 Naarah had Ahuzzam, Hepher, Temeni and Haahashtari by Ashhur. They belonged to the family line of Naarah.
7 The sons of Helah were
Zereth, Zohar, Ethnan 8 and Koz. Koz was the father of Anub and Hazzobebah. He was also the father of the family groups of Aharhel. Aharhel was the son of Harum.

9 Jabez was more respected than his brothers. His mother had named him Jabez. She had said, "I was in a lot of pain when he was born."
10 Jabez cried out to the God of Israel. He said, "I wish you would bless me. I wish you would give me more territory. Let your powerful hand be with me. Keep me from harm. Then I won't have any pain." God gave him what he asked for.

[11]Kelub was the brother of Shuhah and the
father of Mehir. Mehir was the father of
Eshton. [12]Eshton was the father of Beth
Rapha, Paseah and Tehinnah. Tehinnah
was the father of Ir Nahash. Those were
the men of Recah.

[13]The sons of Kenaz were
Othniel and Seraiah.
The sons of Othniel were
Hathath and Meonothai. [14]Meonothai
was the father of Ophrah.
Seraiah was the father of Joab. Joab was
the father of GeHarashim. GeHarashim
was called by that name because all of
its people were skilled workers.
[15]The sons of Caleb were
Iru, Elah and Naam. Caleb was the son
of Jephunneh.
The son of Elah was
Kenaz.
[16]The sons of Jehallelel were
Ziph, Ziphah, Tiria and Asarel.
[17]The sons of Ezrah were
Jether, Mered, Epher and Jalon. One of
Mered's wives had Miriam, Shammai
and Ishbah by him. Ishbah was the
father of Eshtemoa. [18]Those were the
children of Pharaoh's daughter Bithiah.
Mered had gotten married to her. His
wife from Judah had Jered, Heber and
Jekuthiel by him. Jered was the father
of Gedor. Heber was the father of Soco.
Jekuthiel was the father of Zanoah.
[19]Hodiah's wife was the sister of Naham.
Her sons were
the father of Keilah the Garmite and
Eshtemoa the Maacathite.
[20]The sons of Shimon were
Amnon, Rinnah, Ben-Hanan and Tilon.
The family line of Ishi included
Zoheth and Ben-Zoheth.
[21]Shelah was the son of Judah.
The sons of Shelah were Er and Laadah.
Er was the father of Lecah. Laadah was
the father of Mareshah. He was also the
father of the family groups of the linen
workers who lived in Beth Ashbea.
[22]Other sons of Shelah were Jokim, Joash, Saraph and the men of Cozeba.
Moab and Jashubi Lehem were ruled by
sons of Shelah. The records of all of
those matters are very old. [23]Some of
Shelah's sons were potters who lived in
Netaim and Gederah. They stayed there
and worked for the king.

The Family Line of Simeon

[24]The family line of Simeon included
Nemuel, Jamin, Jarib, Zerah and Shaul.
[25]Shallum was Shaul's son. Mibsam was
Shallum's son. Mishma was Mibsam's
son.
[26]The family line of Mishma included Hammuel. Hammuel was Mishma's son.
Zaccur was Hammuel's son. Shimei
was Zaccur's son.
[27]Shimei had 16 sons and six daughters. But his
brothers didn't have many children. So their whole
family group didn't have as many people as Judah
had. [28]Shimei's family group lived in Beersheba,
Moladah, Hazar Shual, [29]Bilhah, Ezem, Tolad,
[30]Bethuel, Hormah, Ziklag, [31]Beth Marcaboth, Hazar Susim, Beth Biri and Shaaraim. Those were
their towns until David became king. [32]Five of the
villages that were around those towns were Etam,
Ain, Rimmon, Token and Ashan. [33]The territory of
all of the villages that were around those towns
reached all the way to Baalath. Those were their
settlements. The tribe of Simeon kept its own family history.

[34]Simeon's family line included Meshobab,
Jamlech and Joshah. Joshah was the son of
Amaziah. [35]Simeon's family line also
included Joel and Jehu. Jehu was the son of
Joshibiah. Joshibiah was the son of Seraiah.
Seraiah was the son of Asiel. [36]And the fam-
ily line included Elioenai, Jaakobah, Jesho-
haiah, Asaiah, Adiel, Jesimiel, Benaiah [37]and
Ziza. Ziza was the son of Shiphi. Shiphi was
the son of Allon. Allon was the son of Jeda-
iah. Jedaiah was the son of Shimri. And
Shimri was the son of Shemaiah.

[38]The men whose names are listed above were
leaders of their family groups. Their families
greatly increased their numbers.
[39]They spread out all the way to the edge of Ge
dor east of the valley. They looked for grasslands
for their flocks. [40]They found grasslands that were
rich and good. The land had plenty of room. It was
peaceful and quiet. Some of the people of Ham
had lived there before.
[41]The men whose names are listed lived at the
time when Hezekiah was king of Judah. They
came and attacked the Hamites in their homes.
They also attacked the Meunites who were there.
And they completely destroyed them. What happened to them is clear even to this very day. The
men of Simeon settled down where the Meunites
had lived. They had enough grasslands for their
flocks.
[42]Five hundred of those men came into the hill
country of Seir and attacked it. They were led by
Pelatiah, Neariah, Rephaiah and Uzziel. Those
four men were the sons of Ishi. [43]They killed the
rest of the Amalekites who had escaped. And they
still live there to this very day.

The Family Line of Reuben

5 Here is a list of the sons of Reuben. First, here
are a few things about him. Reuben was the
oldest son of Israel. But he had sex with his
father's concubine. He made his father's bed

"unclean." That's why his rights as the oldest son
were given to the sons of Joseph, the son of Israel. So Reuben isn't listed in the family history as
the one who had the rights of the oldest son. 2Ju-
dah was the leader among his brothers. A ruler
came from his family line. But the rights of the
oldest son belonged to Joseph. 3Reuben was the
oldest son of Israel. Reuben's sons were
Hanoch, Pallu, Hezron and Carmi.
4The family line of Joel includes
his son Shemaiah. Gog was the son of
Shemaiah.
Shimei was the son of Gog. 5Micah was
the son of Shimei.
Reaiah was the son of Micah. Baal was
the son of Reaiah.
6And Beerah was the son of Baal. Beerah was a leader of the people of Reuben. Tiglath-Pileser took Beerah as a
prisoner to another country. Tiglath-
Pileser was the king of Assyria.
7Here are the relatives of the family groups
of Reuben. They are listed in their family history.
They include Chief Jeiel, Zechariah
8and Bela. Bela was the son of Azaz.
Azaz was the son of Shema. Shema was
the son of Joel. All of them settled in the
area from Aroer to Nebo and Baal
Meon. 9To the east they settled in the
land up to the edge of the desert. That
desert reaches all the way to the Euphrates River. They settled there because
their livestock had increased their numbers in Gilead.
10While Saul was king, the people of
Reuben went to war against the Hagrites. They won the battle over them.
Then they settled down in their houses.
They settled through the entire area east
of Gilead.

The Family Line of Gad

11The people of Gad lived next to the people
of Reuben in Bashan. They spread out
all the way to Salecah.
12Joel was their chief. Shapham was next.
Then came Janai and Shaphat in Bashan.
13Here are their relatives family by family.
They included
Michael, Meshullam, Sheba, Jorai, Ja-
can, Zia and Eber. The total number of
them was seven.
14Those were the sons of Abihail. Abihail
was the son of Huri. Huri was the son of
Jaroah. Jaroah was the son of Gilead.
Gilead was the son of Michael. Michael was the son of Jeshishai. Jeshishai
was the son of Jahdo. And Jahdo was
the son of Buz.
15Ahi was the leader of some of the families of Gad. Ahi was the son of Abdiel.
Abdiel was the son of Guni.
16The people of Gad lived in the land of Gilead. They lived in the villages of Bashan.
They also lived on all of the grasslands
of Sharon as far as they reached.
17All of those names were written down in the
family history. They were written during the time
when Jotham was king of Judah and Jeroboam was
king of Israel.

18The tribes of Reuben and Gad and half of the
tribe of Manasseh had 44,760 men who were able
to serve in the army. They were able to handle a
shield and sword. They were also able to use a bow.
They were trained for battle. 19They went to war
against the Hagrites, Jetur, Naphish and Nodab.
20God helped his people fight against the Hagrites and all who were helping them. He handed all
of those enemies over to his people. That's because
they cried out to him during the battle. He answered
their prayers, because they trusted in him.
21They captured the livestock of the Hagrites.
They captured 50,000 camels, 250,000 sheep and
2,000 donkeys. They also took 100,000 people as
prisoners. 22Many others were killed, because God
won the battle over them. His people lived in the
land until they themselves were taken as prisoners
to other countries.

The Family Line of Half of the Tribe of Manasseh

23The people in half of the tribe of Manasseh
greatly increased their numbers. They settled in the
land from Bashan to Baal Hermon. Baal Hermon
is also called Senir. Another name for it is Mount
Hermon.
24Here are the leaders of their families. They
included Epher, Ishi, Eliel, Azriel, Jeremiah, Hodaviah and Jahdiel. They were brave fighting men.
They were famous. They were the leaders of their
families. 25But they weren't faithful to the God of
their people. They joined themselves to the gods
of the nations of the land and worshiped them.
God had destroyed those nations to make room for
his people.
26So the God of Israel stirred up the spirit of Pul.
He was king of Assyria. He was also called Tiglath-Pileser. He took the tribes of Reuben and Gad
and half of the tribe of Manasseh to other countries as his prisoners. He took them to Halah,
Habor, Hara and the river of Gozan. And that's
where they still are to this very day.

The Family Line of Levi

6 The sons of Levi were
Gershon, Kohath and Merari.
2The sons of Kohath were
Amram, Izhar, Hebron and Uzziel.
3Aaron, Moses and Miriam
were born in the family line of Amram.

The sons of Aaron were
Nadab, Abihu, Eleazar and Ithamar.
4 Eleazar was the father of Phinehas.
Phinehas was the father of Abishua.
5 Abishua was the father of Bukki.
Bukki was the father of Uzzi.
6 Uzzi was the father of Zerahiah.
Zerahiah was the father of Meraioth.
7 Meraioth was the father of Amariah.
Amariah was the father of Ahitub.
8 Ahitub was the father of Zadok.
Zadok was the father of Ahimaaz.
9 Ahimaaz was the father of Azariah.
Azariah was the father of Johanan.
10 Johanan was the father of Azariah. Azariah served as priest in the temple Solomon built in Jerusalem.
11 Azariah was the father of Amariah.
Amariah was the father of Ahitub.
12 Ahitub was the father of Zadok.
Zadok was the father of Shallum.
13 Shallum was the father of Hilkiah.
Hilkiah was the father of Azariah.
14 Azariah was the father of Seraiah.
And Seraiah was the father of Jehozadak.
15 Jehozadak was taken away from his own land. The LORD took the people of Judah and Jerusalem to Babylonia. He used Nebuchadnezzar to take them there as prisoners.

16 The sons of Levi were
Gershon, Kohath and Merari.
17 The names of the sons of Gershon were
Libni and Shimei.
18 The sons of Kohath were
Amram, Izhar, Hebron and Uzziel.
19 The sons of Merari were
Mahli and Mushi.
Here are the members of the family groups of the Levites. They are listed under the names of their fathers.
20 Gershon was the father of Libni.
Jahath was Libni's son.
Zimmah was Jahath's son.
21 Joah was Zimmah's son.
Iddo was Joah's son.
Zerah was Iddo's son.
And Jeatherai was Zerah's son.
22 The family line of Kohath included his son Amminadab.
Korah was Amminadab's son.
Assir was Korah's son.
23 Elkanah was Assir's son.
Ebiasaph was Elkanah's son.
Assir was Ebiasaph's son.
24 Tahath was Assir's son.
Uriel was Tahath's son.
Uzziah was Uriel's son.
And Shaul was Uzziah's son.
25 The family line of Elkanah included his son Amasai.
Amasai was the father of Ahimoth.
26 Elkanah was Ahimoth's son.
Zophai was Elkanah's son.
Nahath was Zophai's son.
27 Eliab was Nahath's son.
Jeroham was Eliab's son.
Elkanah was Jeroham's son.
And Samuel was Elkanah's son.
28 The sons of Samuel were
his first son Joel
and his second son Abijah.
29 The family line of Merari included his son Mahli.
Libni was Mahli's son.
Shimei was Libni's son.
Uzzah was Shimei's son.
30 Shimea was Uzzah's son.
Haggiah was Shimea's son.
And Asaiah was Haggiah's son.

The Levites Who Were in Charge of the Music

31 Here are the Levites David put in charge of
the music in the house of the LORD. He did it after
the ark was placed there. 32 The men used their
music to serve in front of the holy tent, the Tent of
Meeting. They served there until Solomon built
the temple of the LORD in Jerusalem. They did
their work based on the rules they had been given.
33 Here are the men who served. The list also
includes their sons.
The family line of Kohath included
Heman. He led the music.
He was the son of Joel.
Joel was the son of Samuel.
34 Samuel was the son of Elkanah.
Elkanah was the son of Jeroham.
Jeroham was the son of Eliel.
Eliel was the son of Toah.
35 Toah was the son of Zuph.
Zuph was the son of Elkanah.
Elkanah was the son of Mahath.
Mahath was the son of Amasai.
36 Amasai was the son of Elkanah.
Elkanah was the son of Joel.
Joel was the son of Azariah.
Azariah was the son of Zephaniah.
37 Zephaniah was the son of Tahath.
Tahath was the son of Assir.
Assir was the son of Ebiasaph.
Ebiasaph was the son of Korah.
38 Korah was the son of Izhar.
Izhar was the son of Kohath.
Kohath was the son of Levi.
And Levi was the son of Israel.
39 Heman had a relative named Asaph. Asaph served as Heman's helper at his right side.
Asaph was the son of Berekiah.
Berekiah was the son of Shimea.

[40]Shimea was the son of Michael.
Michael was the son of Baaseiah.
Baaseiah was the son of Malkijah.
[41]Malkijah was the son of Ethni.
Ethni was the son of Zerah.
Zerah was the son of Adaiah.
[42]Adaiah was the son of Ethan.
Ethan was the son of Zimmah.
Zimmah was the son of Shimei.
[43]Shimei was the son of Jahath.
Jahath was the son of Gershon.
And Gershon was the son of Levi.
[44]Here are the Levites in the family line of Merari who served as Heman's helpers at his left side. They were relatives of the Kohathites.
Ethan was the son of Kishi.
Kishi was the son of Abdi.
Abdi was the son of Malluch.
[45]Malluch was the son of Hashabiah.
Hashabiah was the son of Amaziah.
Amaziah was the son of Hilkiah.
[46]Hilkiah was the son of Amzi.
Amzi was the son of Bani.
Bani was the son of Shemer.
[47]Shemer was the son of Mahli.
Mahli was the son of Mushi.
Mushi was the son of Merari.
And Merari was the son of Levi.

[48]The rest of the Levites were appointed to do all of the other work at the holy tent. It was the house of God.

[49]Aaron and his sons after him brought the offerings. They sacrificed them on the altar of burnt offering. They also burned incense on the altar of incense. That was part of what they did in the Most Holy Room. That's how they paid for the sin of Israel. They did everything just as Moses, the servant of God, had commanded.

[50]Here are the members of the family line of Aaron.
Eleazar was Aaron's son.
Phinehas was Eleazar's son.
Abishua was Phinehas's son.
[51]Bukki was Abishua's son.
Uzzi was Bukki's son.
Zerahiah was Uzzi's son.
[52]Meraioth was Zerahiah's son.
Amariah was Meraioth's son.
Ahitub was Amariah's son.
[53]Zadok was Ahitub's son.
And Ahimaaz was Zadok's son.

[54]Here were the places where they settled. They were given to them as their territory. Some were given to the children of Aaron who were from the family group of Kohath. They were given out by using lots. The first lot was for Kohath.

[55]The Kohathites were given Hebron in Judah. They also received the grasslands that were around Hebron. [56]But the fields and villages that were around the city were given to Caleb, the son of Jephunneh.

[57]So the people in the family line of Aaron received Hebron. It was a city where people could go for safety. Aaron's family line received Libnah, Jattir, Eshtemoa, [58]Hilen and Debir. [59]They also received Ashan, Juttah and Beth Shemesh. They were given all of those towns together with their grasslands. [60]From the tribe of Benjamin they received Gibeon, Geba, Alemeth and Anathoth. They received those towns together with their grasslands.

All of those towns were handed out to the family groups of Kohath. The total number of towns was 13.

[61]The rest of the members of the family line of Kohath were given ten towns. The towns were from the family groups of half of the tribe of Manasseh.

[62]The members of the family line of Gershon were given 13 towns. They received them family group by family group. Most of the towns were from the tribes of Issachar, Asher and Naphtali. The rest were from the other half of the tribe of Manasseh. It's in Bashan.

[63]The members of the family line of Merari were given 12 towns. They received them family group by family group. The towns were from the tribes of Reuben, Gad and Zebulun.

[64]So the people of Israel gave the Levites all of those towns and their grasslands. [65]They gave other towns to them from the tribes of Judah, Simeon and Benjamin.

[66]Some of the family groups of Kohath were given towns from the tribe of Ephraim as their territory.

[67]In the hill country of Ephraim they received Shechem. Shechem was a city where people could go for safety. The Kohathites also received Gezer, [68]Jokmeam, Beth Horon, [69]Aijalon and Gath Rimmon. They were given all of those towns together with their grasslands.

[70]From half of the tribe of Manasseh the people of Israel gave the towns of Aner and Bileam. They gave them to the rest of the family groups of Kohath. They gave them together with their grasslands.

[71]Here is what the members of the family line of Gershon were given.
They received Golan in Bashan and also Ashtaroth. They received them together with their grasslands.
They received them from half of the tribe of Manasseh.
[72]From the tribe of Issachar
they received Kedesh, Daberath, [73]Ramoth and Anem. They received them together with their grasslands.

74 From the tribe of Asher
they received Mashal, Abdon, 75Hukok and Rehob. They received them together with their grasslands.
76 From the tribe of Naphtali
they received Kedesh in Galilee. They also received Hammon and Kiriathaim. They were given all of those towns together with their grasslands.
77 The members of the family line of Merari make up the rest of the Levites. Here is what they were given.
From the tribe of Zebulun
they received Jokneam, Kartah, Rimmono and Tabor. They received them together with their grasslands.
78 The tribe of Reuben was across the Jordan River east of Jericho. From that tribe the Merarites
received Bezer in the desert, Jahzah, 79Kedemoth and Mephaath. They received them together with their grasslands.
80 From the tribe of Gad
they received Ramoth in Gilead. They also received Mahanaim, 81Heshbon and Jazer. They received all of those towns together with their grasslands.

The Family Line of Issachar

7 The sons of Issachar were
Tola, Puah, Jashub and Shimron. The total number of sons was four.
2 The sons of Tola were
Uzzi, Rephaiah, Jeriel, Jahmai, Ibsam and Samuel. They were the leaders of their families. The total number of fighting men who were listed in the history of the family line of Tola was 22,600. That was when David was king.
3 The son of Uzzi was
Izrahiah.
The sons of Izrahiah were
Michael, Obadiah, Joel and Isshiah. All five of them were chiefs. 4Based on their family history, 36,000 of their men were ready for battle. That's because they had many wives and children.
5 The total number of fighting men who belonged to all of the family groups of Issachar was 87,000. The men were listed in their family history.

The Family Line of Benjamin

6 The three sons of Benjamin were
Bela, Beker and Jediael.
7 The sons of Bela were
Ezbon, Uzzi, Uzziel, Jerimoth and Iri. They were the leaders of their families. The total number of sons was five. Their family history listed 22,034 fighting men.
8 The sons of Beker were
Zemirah, Joash, Eliezer, Elioenai, Omri, Jeremoth, Abijah, Anathoth and Alemeth. All of them were the sons of Beker. 9Their family history listed the leaders of their families. It also listed 20,200 fighting men.
10 The son of Jediael was
Bilhan.
The sons of Bilhan were
Jeush, Benjamin, Ehud, Kenaanah, Zethan, Tarshish and Ahishahar. 11All of those sons of Jediael were the leaders of their families. There were 17,200 fighting men who were ready to go to war.
12 The Shuppites and Huppites belonged to the family line of Ir. The Hushites belonged to the family line of Aher.

The Family Line of Naphtali

13 The sons of Naphtali were
Jahziel, Guni, Jezer and Shillem. They belonged to the family line of Bilhah.

The Family Line of Manasseh

14 Here is the family line of Manasseh.
He had a concubine who was from the land of Aram. She had Asriel and Makir by him. Makir was the father of Gilead. 15Makir got married to a woman from among the Huppites and Shuppites. He had a sister named Maacah.
Another member of Manasseh's family line was Zelophehad. All he had was daughters.
16Makir's wife Maacah had a son by him. She named the boy Peresh. He had a brother named Sheresh. The sons of Sheresh were Ulam and Rakem.
17 The son of Ulam was
Bedan.
Those were the members of the family line of Makir, the son of Manasseh. Gilead was the son of Makir. 18Gilead's sister was Hammoleketh. She was the mother of Ishhod, Abiezer and Mahlah.
19 The sons of Shemida were
Ahian, Shechem, Likhi and Aniam.

The Family Line of Ephraim

20 Here are the members of the family line of Ephraim.
Shuthelah was Ephraim's son.
Bered was Shuthelah's son.
Tahath was Bered's son.
Eleadah was Tahath's son.
Tahath was Eleadah's son.
21 Zabad was Tahath's son.
And Shuthelah was Zabad's son.

Men from Gath killed Ezer and Ele-
ad when they went down to steal their
livestock. 22Their father Ephraim
sobbed over them for many days. His
relatives came to comfort him. 23Then
he made love to his wife. She became
pregnant and had a baby boy. Ephraim
named him Beriah. That's because
something bad had happened in his
family. 24His daughter was Sheerah. She
built Lower and Upper Beth Horon. She
also built Uzzen Sheerah.

25 Rephah was Beriah's son.
Resheph was Rephah's son.
Telah was Resheph's son.
Tahan was Telah's son.
26 Ladan was Tahan's son.
Ammihud was Ladan's son.
Elishama was Ammihud's son.
27 Nun was Elishama's son.
And Joshua was the son of Nun.

28The lands and settlements of the members of
Ephraim's line included Bethel and the villages
that were around it. Naaran was on the east. Gezer
and its villages were on the west. The lands and
settlements included Shechem. They also included
the villages that were around Shechem all the way
to Ayyah and its villages. 29Along the borders of
Manasseh were Beth Shan, Taanach, Megiddo and
Dor, together with their villages. The members of
the family line of Joseph lived in those towns. Joseph was the son of Israel.

The Family Line of Asher

30 The sons of Asher were
Imnah, Ishvah, Ishvi and Beriah. They had a sister named Serah.

31 The sons of Beriah were
Heber and Malkiel. Malkiel was the father of Birzaith.

32 Heber was the father of Japhlet, Shomer, Hotham and their sister Shua.

33 The sons of Japhlet were
Pasach, Bimhal and Ashvath. They were Japhlet's sons.

34 The sons of Shomer were
Ahi, Rohgah, Hubbah and Aram.

35 The sons of Shomer's brother Helem were
Zophah, Imna, Shelesh and Amal.

36 The sons of Zophah were
Suah, Harnepher, Shual, Beri, Imrah,
37Bezer, Hod, Shamma, Shilshah, Ithran
and Beera.

38 The sons of Jether were
Jephunneh, Pispah and Ara.

39 The sons of Ulla were
Arah, Hanniel and Rizia.

40All of them were members of the family line
of Asher. They were the leaders of their families.
They were fine men. They were brave fighting
men. They were outstanding leaders. The total
number of men who were ready for battle was
26,000. They were listed in their family history.

The Family History of Saul

8 Benjamin was the father of Bela. Bela was his first son.
Ashbel was his second son. Aharah was the third.
2 Nohah was the fourth. And Rapha was the fifth.

3 The sons of Bela were
Addar, Gera, Abihud, 4Abishua, Naa-
man, Ahoah, 5Gera, Shephuphan and
Huram.

6 Here are the members of the family line of
Ehud. They were the leaders of the families who were living in Geba. Later,
they were taken away from their own
land. They were forced to go to Manahath.
7 The sons of Ehud were Naaman, Ahijah
and Gera. Gera took them away from
their land. He was the father of Uzza
and Ahihud.

8 Sons were born to Shaharaim in Moab.
That happened after he had divorced his
wives Hushim and Baara. 9His wife Ho-
desh had sons by him. Their names
were Jobab, Zibia, Mesha, Malcam,
10Jeuz, Sakia and Mirmah. His sons
were the leaders of their families. 11His
wife Hushim had Abitub and Elpaal by
him.

12 The sons of Elpaal were
Eber, Misham and Shemed. Shemed
built Ono and Lod and the villages that
were around it. 13Beriah and Shema
were also sons of Elpaal. They were the
leaders of the families who were living
in Aijalon. Beriah and Shema drove out
the people who were living in Gath.

14 Ahio, Shashak, Jeremoth, 15Zebadiah,
Arad, Eder, 16Michael, Ishpah and Joha
were the sons of Beriah.

17 Zebadiah, Meshullam, Hizki, Heber, 18Ish-
merai, Izliah and Jobab were other sons
of Elpaal.

19 Jakim, Zicri, Zabdi, 20Elienai, Zillethai,
Eliel, 21Adaiah, Beraiah and Shimrath
were the sons of Shimei.

22 Ishpan, Eber, Eliel, 23Abdon, Zicri, Hanan,
24Hananiah, Elam, Anthothijah, 25Iphde-
iah and Penuel were the sons of Shashak.

26 Shamsherai, Shehariah, Athaliah, 27Jaare-
shiah, Elijah and Zicri were the sons of
Jeroham.

28All of those men were the leaders of their families. They were listed as chiefs in their family history. They lived in Jerusalem.

29 Jeiel lived in the city of Gibeon. He was the father of Gibeon.
Jeiel had a wife named Maacah. 30His oldest son was Abdon. His other sons were Zur, Kish, Baal, Ner, Nadab, 31Gedor, Ahio, Zeker 32and Mikloth. Mikloth was the father of Shimeah. Mikloth and Shimeah also lived in Jerusalem. They lived near their relatives.
33 Ner was the father of Kish. Kish was the father of Saul. Saul was the father of Jonathan, Malki-Shua, Abinadab and Esh-Baal.
34 The son of Jonathan was
Merib-Baal. Merib-Baal was the father of Micah.
35 The sons of Micah were
Pithon, Melech, Tarea and Ahaz.
36 Ahaz was the father of Jehoaddah. Jehoaddah was the father of Alemeth, Azmaveth and Zimri. Zimri was the father of Moza. 37Moza was the father of Binea. Raphah was Binea's son. Eleasah was Raphah's son. And Azel was Eleasah's son.
38 Azel had six sons. Their names were
Azrikam, Bokeru, Ishmael, Sheariah, Obadiah and Hanan. All of them were the sons of Azel.
39 Here are the sons of Azel's brother Eshek. Ulam was his first son. Jeush was the second. Eliphelet was the third. 40The sons of Ulam were brave fighting men. They could handle a bow. They had many sons and grandsons. The total number of sons and grandsons was 150.
All of those men belonged to the family line of Benjamin.

9 The whole community of Israel was listed in their family histories. They were written down in the records of the kings of Israel.

The People Who Lived in Jerusalem

The people of Judah were taken away from their own land. They were taken as prisoners to Babylonia. That's because they weren't faithful to the LORD. 2The first ones who came back from there were some Israelites, priests, Levites and temple servants. They settled down again in their own towns on their own property.

3Some of them lived in Jerusalem. They included people from Judah, Benjamin, Ephraim and Manasseh.

4 They included Uthai. He was the son of Ammihud. Ammihud was the son of Omri. Omri was the son of Imri. Imri was the son of Bani. Bani belonged to the family line of Perez. Perez was the son of Judah.
5 The family line of Shelah included his oldest son Asaiah. It also included the sons of Asaiah.
6 The family line of Zerah included Jeuel.
The total number of the people of Judah was 690.
7 The family line of Benjamin included Sallu. He was the son of Meshullam. Meshullam was the son of Hodaviah. Hodaviah was the son of Hassenuah.
8 Ibneiah was the son of Jeroham. Elah was the son of Uzzi. Uzzi was the son of Micri. Meshullam was the son of Shephatiah. Shephatiah was the son of Reuel. Reuel was the son of Ibnijah.
9 The total number of the people of Benjamin was 956. They were listed in their family history. All of those men were the leaders of their families.
10 The family line of the priests included Jedaiah, Jehoiarib and Jakin.
11 It also included Azariah. He was the son of Hilkiah. Hilkiah was the son of Meshullam. Meshullam was the son of Zadok. Zadok was the son of Meraioth. Meraioth was the son of Ahitub. Azariah was the official who was in charge of the house of God.
12 Adaiah was the son of Jeroham. Jeroham was the son of Pashhur. Pashhur was the son of Malkijah. Maasai was the son of Adiel. Adiel was the son of Jahzerah. Jahzerah was the son of Meshullam. Meshullam was the son of Meshillemith. Meshillemith was the son of Immer.
13 The total number of priests was 1,760. They were the leaders of their families. They were able men. It was their duty to serve in the house of God.
14 The family line of the Levites included Shemaiah. He was the son of Hasshub. Hasshub was the son of Azrikam. Azrikam was the son of Hashabiah. Shemaiah belonged to the family line of Merari. 15The family line of the Levites also included Bakbakkar, Heresh, Galal and Mattaniah. Mattaniah was the son of Mica. Mica was the son of Zicri. Zicri was the son of Asaph. 16Obadiah was the son of Shemaiah. Shemaiah was the son of Galal. Galal was the son of Jeduthun. Berekiah was the son of Asa. Asa was the son of Elkanah. He lived in the villages of the people of Netophah.
17 The men who guarded the gates were Shallum, Akkub, Talmon, Ahiman and other Levites. Shallum was their chief. 18He was stationed at the King's Gate on the east side of the temple. That duty has continued to this very day. Those guards belonged to the camp of the Levites.
19 Shallum was the son of Kore. Kore was the son of Ebiasaph. Ebiasaph was the son of Korah. Shallum and the other

Levites in his family belonged to the
family line of Korah. They had the duty
of guarding the entrances to the temple.
Their fathers had also had the duty of
guarding the entrance to the house of
the LORD. 20Long ago Phinehas, the son
of Eleazar, was in charge of those who
guarded the gate. And the LORD was
with him.
21 Zechariah guarded the entrance to the
Tent of Meeting. He was the son of Meshelemiah.
22The total number of the men who were chosen to guard the entrances was 212. They were
listed in their family history in their villages. David and the prophet Samuel had appointed them to
their positions. They appointed them because they
trusted them.
23Those Levites and their children after them
were in charge of guarding the gates of the house
of the LORD. The house of the LORD was also
called the temple. 24The men who guarded the
gates were on the four sides of the temple. They
were on the east, west, north and south sides.
25From time to time, their relatives in their villages
had to come to the temple. They had to share their
duties for a week at a time.
26The four main men who guarded the gates
were Levites. They were trusted with the duty of
taking care of the storerooms and the other rooms
in the house of God. 27They spent the night in their
positions around the house of God. That's because
they had to guard it. They were in charge of the
key that opened the temple each morning.
28Some Levites were in charge of the articles that
were used when they served at the temple. They
counted the articles when they were brought in.
They also counted them when they were taken out.
29Other Levites were appointed to take care of
all of the other articles that belonged to the temple. They also took care of the flour, wine, olive
oil, incense and spices. 30Some of the priests took
care of mixing the spices.
31There was a Levite named Mattithiah. He was
the oldest son of Shallum. Shallum belonged to the
family line of Korah. Mattithiah was trusted with
the duty of baking the offering bread. 32The bread
was placed on the table every Sabbath day. Some
Levites in the family line of Kohath were in charge
of preparing the bread.
33Those who led the music lived in rooms in the
temple. They were the leaders of their Levite families. Their only duty was to lead the music. They
had to do that work day and night.
34All of them were the leaders of their Levite
families. They were listed as chiefs in their family
history. They lived in Jerusalem.

The Family History of Saul

35 Jeiel lived in the city of Gibeon. He was
the father of Gibeon.
Jeiel had a wife named Maacah. 36His
oldest son was Abdon. His other sons
were Zur, Kish, Baal, Ner, Nadab, 37Ge-
dor, Ahio, Zechariah and Mikloth.
38Mikloth was the father of Shimeam.
Mikloth and Shimeam lived in Jerusalem. They lived near their relatives.
39 Ner was the father of Kish. Kish was the
father of Saul. Saul was the father of
Jonathan, Malki-Shua, Abinadab and
Esh-Baal.
40 The son of Jonathan was
Merib-Baal. Merib-Baal was the father
of Micah.
41 The sons of Micah were
Pithon, Melech, Tahrea and Ahaz.
42 Ahaz was the father of Jadah. Jadah was
the father of Alemeth, Azmaveth and
Zimri. Zimri was the father of Moza.
43Moza was the father of Binea. Rephaiah was Binea's son. Eleasah was Rephaiah's son. And Azel was Eleasah's
son.
44 Azel had six sons. Their names were
Azrikam, Bokeru, Ishmael, Sheariah,
Obadiah and Hanan. They were the sons
of Azel.

Saul Takes His Own Life

10 The Philistines fought against Israel. The
men of Israel ran away from them. But
many Israelites were killed on Mount Gilboa.
2The Philistines kept chasing Saul and his sons.
They killed his sons Jonathan, Abinadab and Malki-Shua. 3The fighting was heavy around Saul.
Men who were armed with bows and arrows
caught up with him. They shot their arrows at him
and wounded him badly.
4Saul spoke to the man who was carrying his
armor. He said, "Pull out your sword. Stick it
through me. If you don't, those men who aren't
circumcised will come and hurt me badly."
But the man was terrified. He wouldn't do it. So
Saul took his own sword and fell on it. 5The man
saw that Saul was dead. So he fell on his own
sword and died. 6Saul and his three sons died. All
of them died together.
7All of the Israelites who lived in the valley saw
that their army had run away. They saw that Saul
and his sons were dead. So they left their towns
and ran away. Then the Philistines came and settled down in them.
8The day after the Philistines had won the battle, they came to take what they wanted from the
dead bodies. They found Saul and his sons dead
on Mount Gilboa. 9So they took what they wanted
from Saul's body. They took his head and his
armor. Then they sent messengers through the
whole land of the Philistines. They announced the
news to the statues of their gods. They also
announced it among their people. 10They put

Saul's armor in the temple of their gods. They hung his head up in the temple of their god Dagon.

11 The people of Jabesh Gilead heard about everything the Philistines had done to Saul. 12 So all of their brave men went and got the bodies of Saul and his sons. They brought them to Jabesh. Then they buried the bones of Saul and his sons under the great tree that was there. They didn't eat anything for seven days.

13 Saul died because he wasn't faithful to the LORD. He didn't obey the word of the LORD. He even asked for advice from a person who gets messages from those who have died. 14 He didn't ask the LORD for advice. So the LORD put him to death. He turned the kingdom over to David. David was the son of Jesse.

David Becomes King Over Israel

11 The whole community of Israel came together to see David at Hebron. They said, "We are your own flesh and blood. 2 In the past, Saul was our king. But you led the men of Israel in battle. The LORD your God said to you, 'You will be the shepherd over my people Israel. You will become their ruler.' "

3 All of the elders of Israel came to see King David at Hebron. There he made a covenant with them in the sight of the LORD. They anointed David as king over Israel. It happened just as the LORD had promised through Samuel.

David Captures Jerusalem

4 David and all of the men of Israel marched to Jerusalem. Jerusalem was also called Jebus.

The Jebusites who lived there 5 spoke to David. They said, "You won't get in here."

But David captured the fort of Zion. It became known as the City of David.

6 David had said, "Anyone who leads the attack against the Jebusites will become the commander of Israel's army." Joab went up first. So he became the commander of the army. He was the son of Zeruiah.

7 David moved into the fort. So it was called the City of David. 8 He built up the city around the fort. He filled in the low places. He built a wall around it. During that time, Joab built up the rest of the city. 9 David became more and more powerful. That's because the LORD who rules over all was with him.

David's Mighty Men

10 The chiefs of David's mighty men and the whole community of Israel helped David greatly. They helped him become king over the entire land. That's exactly what the LORD had promised him. 11 Here is a list of David's mighty men.

Jashobeam was chief of the officers. He was a Hacmonite. He used his spear against 300 men. He killed all of them at one time.

12 Next to him was Eleazar. He was one of the three mighty men. He was the son of Dodai, the Ahohite. 13 Jashobeam was with David at Pas Dammim. The Philistines had gathered there for battle. Israel's troops ran away from the Philistines. At the place where that happened, there was a field that was full of barley. 14 The three mighty men took their stand in the middle of the field. They didn't let the Philistines capture it. They struck them down. The LORD helped them win a great battle.

15 David was near the rock at the cave of Adullam. Three of the 30 chiefs came down to him there. A group of Philistines was camped in the Valley of Rephaim. 16 At that time David was in his usual place of safety. Some Philistine troops were stationed at Bethlehem.

17 David longed for water. He said, "I wish someone would get me a drink of water from the well that is near the gate of Bethlehem!"

18 So the Three fought their way past the Philistine guards. They got some water from the well that was near the gate of Bethlehem. They took the water back to David.

But David refused to drink it. Instead, he poured it out as a drink offering to the LORD. 19 "I would never drink that water!" David said. "It would be like drinking the blood of these men. They put their lives in danger by going to Bethlehem." The men had put their lives in danger by bringing the water back. So David wouldn't drink it.

Those were some of the brave things the three mighty men did.

20 Abishai was chief over the Three. He was the brother of Joab. He used his spear against 300 men. He killed all of them. So he became as famous as the Three were. 21 He was honored twice as much as the Three. He became their commander. But he wasn't included among them.

22 Benaiah was a great hero from Kabzeel. He was the son of Jehoiada. Benaiah did many brave things. He struck down two of Moab's best fighting men. He also went down into a pit on a snowy day. He killed a lion there.

23 And Benaiah struck down an Egyptian who was seven and a half feet tall. The Egyptian was holding a spear as big as a weaver's rod. Benaiah went out to fight against him with a club. He grabbed the spear out of the Egyptian's hand. Then he killed him with it.

24 Those were some of the brave things Benaiah, the son of Jehoiada, did. He too was as famous as the three mighty men were. 25 He was honored more than any of the Thirty. But he wasn't included among the Three. And David put him in charge of his own personal guards.

26 Here is a list of David's mighty men.
Asahel, the brother of Joab
Elhanan, the son of Dodo, from Bethlehem
27 Shammoth, the Harorite
Helez, the Pelonite

28 Ira, the son of Ikkesh, from Tekoa
Abiezer from Anathoth
29 Sibbecai, the Hushathite
Ilai, the Ahohite
30 Maharai from Netophah
Heled, the son of Baanah, from Netophah
31 Ithai, the son of Ribai, from Gibeah in Benjamin
Benaiah from Pirathon
32 Hurai from the valleys of Gaash
Abiel, the Arbathite
33 Azmaveth, the Baharumite
Eliahba, the Shaalbonite
34 the sons of Hashem, the Gizonite
Jonathan, the son of Shagee, the Hararite
35 Ahiam, the son of Sacar, the Hararite
Eliphal, the son of Ur
36 Hepher, the Mekerathite
Ahijah, the Pelonite
37 Hezro from Carmel
Naarai, the son of Ezbai
38 Joel, the brother of Nathan
Mibhar, the son of Hagri
39 Zelek from Ammon
Naharai, from Beeroth, who carried the armor of Joab, the son of Zeruiah
40 Ira, the Ithrite
Gareb, the Ithrite
41 Uriah, the Hittite
Zabad, the son of Ahlai
42 Adina, the son of Shiza, the Reubenite, who was chief of the Reubenites and the 30 men with him
43 Hanan, the son of Maacah
Joshaphat, the Mithnite
44 Uzzia, the Ashterathite
Shama and Jeiel, the sons of Hotham from Aroer
45 Jediael, the son of Shimri
his brother Joha, the Tizite
46 Eliel, the Mahavite
Jeribai and Joshaviah, the sons of Elnaam
Ithmah from Moab
47 Eliel
Obed
Jaasiel, the Mezobaite

Fighting Men Join David

12 Some fighting men came to David at Ziklag. They were among those who helped
him in battle. David had been forced to hide from
Saul, the son of Kish. 2The men were armed with
bows. They were able to shoot arrows or throw
stones from a sling with either hand. They were
relatives of Saul from the tribe of Benjamin. Here
is a list of them.

3Their chief Ahiezer and Joash, the sons of Shemaah the Gibeathite
Jeziel and Pelet, the sons of Azmaveth
Beracah
Jehu from Anathoth
4 Ishmaiah, the Gibeonite, who was a mighty man among the Thirty and a leader of the Thirty
Jeremiah
Jahaziel
Johanan
Jozabad from Gederah
5 Eluzai
Jerimoth
Bealiah
Shemariah
Shephatiah, the Haruphite
6 the Korahites Elkanah, Isshiah, Azarel, Joezer and Jashobeam
7 Joelah and Zebadiah, the sons of Jeroham from Gedor

8Some men of Gad went over to David's side at his usual place of safety in the desert. They were brave fighting men. They were ready for battle. They were able to use shields and spears. Their faces were like the faces of lions. They could run as fast as antelopes in the mountains.

9 Ezer was their chief.
Obadiah was next in command. Eliab was third.
10 Mishmannah was fourth. Jeremiah was fifth.
11 Attai was sixth. Eliel was seventh.
12 Johanan was eighth. Elzabad was ninth.
13 Jeremiah was tenth. And Macbannai was eleventh.

14All of those men of Gad were army commanders. The least important of them was equal to 100 men. The most important was equal to 1,000.
15They went across the Jordan River when it was flowing over its banks. That happened in the first month of spring. They chased away everyone who lived in the valleys. They chased them away from the east and west sides of the river.

16Some men from the territories of Benjamin and Judah also came to David at his usual place of safety.
17David went out to meet them. He said to them, "Have you come to me in peace? Have you come to help me? If you have, I'm ready to have you join me. But suppose you have come to hand me over to my enemies when I haven't even harmed anyone. Then may the God of our people see it and judge you."
18The Spirit of God came on Amasai. He was chief of the Thirty. He said,

"David, we belong to you!
Son of Jesse, we're on your side!
May you have great success.
May those who help you also have success.
Your God will help you."

So David welcomed them. He made them leaders in his army.

[19]Some men of Manasseh went over to David's side when he marched out with the Philistines to fight against Saul.

But David and his men didn't help the Philistines. That's because after all of the Philistine rulers had discussed the matter, they sent him away. They said, "Suppose he deserts to his master Saul. Then our heads will be cut off!"

[20]So David went to Ziklag. Here are the men of Manasseh who went over to his side. They were Adnah, Jozabad, Jediael, Michael, Jozabad, Elihu and Zillethai. They were leaders of companies of 1,000 men in Manasseh. [21]They helped David fight against enemy armies. All of the men of Manasseh were brave fighting men. They were commanders in David's army.

[22]Day after day men came to help him. Soon he had a large army. It was like the army of God.

Other Fighting Men Join David at Hebron

[23]Large numbers of men came to David at Hebron. They were prepared for battle. They came to hand Saul's kingdom over to him, just as the LORD had said. Here are the numbers of the men who came.

[24]The men from Judah carried shields and spears. They were prepared for battle. The total number of them was 6,800.

[25]The fighting men from Simeon were ready for battle. The total number of them was 7,100.

[26]The total number of men from Levi was 4,600. [27]They included Jehoiada. He was the leader of the family of Aaron. He came with 3,700 men. [28]They also included Zadok. He was a brave young fighter. He came with 22 officers from his family.

[29]The men from Benjamin were Saul's relatives. Most of them had remained faithful to Saul's family until that time. The total number of them was 3,000.

[30]The men from Ephraim were brave fighting men. They were famous in their own family groups. The total number of them was 20,800.

[31]The men from half of the tribe of Manasseh had been chosen by name to come and make David king. The total number of them was 18,000.

[32]The men from Issachar understood what was going on at that time. They knew what Israel should do. The total number of their chiefs was 200. They came with all of their relatives who were under their command.

[33]The men from Zebulun knew how to fight well. That's because they had done it many times before. They were prepared for battle. They had every kind of weapon. They came to help David with their whole heart. The total number of them was 50,000.

[34]The total number of officers from Naphtali was 1,000. They came with 37,000 men who carried shields and spears.

[35]The men from Dan were ready for battle. The total number of them was 28,600.

[36]The men from Asher knew how to fight well. That's because they had done it many times before. They were prepared for battle. The total number of them was 40,000.

[37]The men from the tribes of Reuben and Gad and half of the tribe of Manasseh were armed with every kind of weapon. The men came from the east side of the Jordan River. The total number of them was 120,000.

[38]All of those fighting men offered to serve in the army. Before they came to Hebron, they had agreed completely to make David king over all of the people of Israel. All of the rest of the people also agreed to make David king.

[39]The men spent three days there with David. They ate and drank what their families had given them. [40]Their neighbors also brought food. They brought it on donkeys, camels, mules and oxen. They came from as far away as the territories of Issachar, Zebulun and Naphtali. There was plenty of flour, fig cakes, raisin cakes, wine, olive oil, cattle and sheep. The people of Israel brought all of those things because they were so happy.

David Wants to Bring the Ark Back

13 David talked with each of his officers. He wanted to get their advice. Some of them were commanders of thousands of men. Others were commanders of hundreds.

[2]David spoke to the whole community of Israel. He said, "Let's send word to the rest of our people no matter how far away they live. They live in all of the territories of Israel. Let's also send word to the priests and Levites who are with them in their towns and grasslands. Let's invite everyone to come and join us. Let's do it if it seems good to you and if that's what the LORD our God wants. [3]Let's bring the ark of our God back here to us. We didn't use it to ask God for advice during the whole time Saul was king."

[4]So that's what the whole community agreed to do. It seemed right to them.

[5]David gathered all of the people together. They came from the area between the Shihor River in Egypt and Lebo Hamath. They came to bring the ark of God from Kiriath Jearim to Jerusalem. [6]David went to Baalah of Judah. The whole community of Israel went with him. Baalah is also called Kiriath Jearim. All of the people went there to get the ark of God the LORD. He sits on his throne between the cherubim. The ark is named after the LORD.

7The ark of God was placed on a new cart. Then it was moved from Abinadab's house. Uzzah and Ahio were guiding it.

8David was celebrating with all his might in the sight of God. So was the whole community of Israel. All of them were singing songs. They were also playing harps, lyres, tambourines, cymbals and trumpets.

9They came to the threshing floor of Kidon. The oxen nearly fell there. So Uzzah reached out his hand to hold the ark steady.

10Then the LORD's anger burned against Uzzah. He struck him down because he had put his hand on the ark. So Uzzah died there in front of God.

11David was angry because the LORD's burning anger had broken out against Uzzah. That's why the place is still called Perez Uzzah to this very day.

12David was afraid of God that day. He asked, "How can I ever bring the ark of God back here to me?"

13So he didn't take the ark to be with him in the City of David. Instead, he took it to the house of Obed-Edom. Obed-Edom was from Gath. 14The ark of God remained with the family of Obed-Edom. It stayed in his house for three months. And the LORD blessed his family. He also blessed everything that belonged to him.

David's Palace and Family

14 Hiram was king of Tyre. He sent messengers to David. He sent cedar logs along with them. He also sent skilled workers to build a palace for David. They worked with stone and wood.

2David knew that the LORD had made his position as king secure. He knew that he had made him king over the whole nation of Israel. He knew that the LORD had greatly honored his kingdom. The LORD had done it because the Israelites were his people.

3In Jerusalem David got married to more women. He also became the father of more sons and daughters. 4Here is a list of the children who were born to him in Jerusalem. Their names were Shammua, Shobab, Nathan, Solomon, 5Ibhar, Elishua, Elpelet, 6Nogah, Nepheg, Japhia, 7Elishama, Beeliada and Eliphelet.

David Wins the Battle Over the Philistines

8The Philistines heard that David had been anointed king over the entire nation of Israel. So their whole army went to look for him. But David heard about it. He went out to where they were. 9The Philistines had come and attacked the people in the Valley of Rephaim.

10So David asked God for advice. He said, "Should I go and attack the Philistines? Will you hand them over to me?"

The LORD answered him, "Go. I will hand them over to you."

11So David and his men went up to Baal Perazim. There David won the battle over the Philistines. He said, "God has broken through against my enemies, just as water breaks through a dam." That's why the place was called Baal Perazim.

12The Philistines had left the statues of their gods there. So David gave orders to burn them up.

13Once more the Philistines attacked the people in the valley. 14So David asked God for advice again.

God answered him, "Do not go straight up. Instead, circle around them. Attack them in front of the balsam trees. 15Listen for the sound of marching in the tops of the trees. Then move out to fight. The sound will mean that I have gone out in front of you. I will strike down the Philistine army."

16So David did just as God had commanded him. He and his men struck down the Philistine army. They struck them down from Gibeon all the way to Gezer.

17So David became famous in every land. The LORD made all of the nations afraid of him.

David Brings the Ark to Jerusalem

15 David constructed buildings for himself in the City of David. Then he prepared a place for the ark of God. He set up a tent for it. 2He said, "Only Levites can carry the ark of God. That's because the LORD chose them to carry his ark. He chose them to serve him forever in front of the place where his throne is."

3David gathered the whole community of Israel together in Jerusalem. He wanted to bring the ark of the LORD up to the place he had prepared for it. 4He called together the members of the family line of Aaron. He also called the Levites together.

Here are the men who came from the families of the Levites.

5From the families of Kohath
came the leader Uriel and 120 relatives.
6From the families of Merari
came the leader Asaiah and 220 relatives.
7From the families of Gershon
came the leader Joel and 130 relatives.
8From the families of Elizaphan
came the leader Shemaiah and 200 relatives.
9From the families of Hebron
came the leader Eliel and 80 relatives.
10From the families of Uzziel
came the leader Amminadab and 112 relatives.

11David sent for the priests Zadok and Abiathar. He also sent for Uriel, Asaiah, Joel, Shemaiah, Eliel and Amminadab. They were Levites. 12He said to them, "You are the leaders of the families of Levi. You and the other Levites must set yourselves apart to serve the LORD and his people. You must bring up the ark of the LORD. He is the God

of Israel. Put the ark in the place I've prepared
for it.
13 "Remember when the anger of the LORD our
God broke out against us? It was because you Levites didn't bring the ark up the first time. We
didn't ask the LORD how to do it in the way the law
requires."
14 So the priests and Levites set themselves
apart. Then they brought up the ark of the LORD.
He is the God of Israel. 15 This time the Levites
used the poles to carry the ark of God on their
shoulders. That's what Moses had commanded in
keeping with the word of the LORD.
16 David told the Levite leaders to appoint their
relatives as singers. He wanted them to sing joyful
songs. He also wanted them to play lyres, harps
and cymbals along with their singing.
17 So the Levites appointed Heman, the son of
Joel. From his relatives they chose Asaph, the son of
Berekiah. Other relatives were from the family of
Merari. From them they chose Ethan, the son of Ku-
shaiah. 18 Along with them they chose their relatives
who were next in line. Their names were Zechariah,
Jaaziel, Shemiramoth, Jehiel, Unni, Eliab, Benaiah,
Maaseiah, Mattithiah, Eliphelehu, Mikneiah, Obed-
Edom and Jeiel. They guarded the gates.
19 Heman, Asaph and Ethan played the bronze
cymbals. 20 Zechariah, Aziel, Shemiramoth, Jehiel,
Unni, Eliab, Maaseiah and Benaiah played the
high notes on the lyres. 21 Mattithiah, Eliphelehu,
Mikneiah, Obed-Edom, Jeiel and Azaziah played
the low notes on the harps.
22 Kenaniah was the leader of the Levites. He was
in charge of the singing because he was good at it.
23 Berekiah and Elkanah guarded the ark. 24 Some
of the priests blew trumpets in front of the ark of
God. Their names were Shebaniah, Joshaphat, Nethanel, Amasai, Zechariah, Benaiah and Eliezer.
Obed-Edom and Jehiah also helped guard the ark.
25 David and the elders of Israel went to bring up
the ark of the covenant of the LORD. So did the
commanders of companies of 1,000 men. With
great joy they brought the ark up from the house of
Obed-Edom.
26 God had helped the Levites who were carrying the ark of the covenant of the LORD. So seven
bulls and seven rams were sacrificed.
27 David was wearing a robe that was made out
of fine linen. So were all of the Levites who were
carrying the ark. And so were the singers and the
choir director Kenaniah. David was also wearing
a sacred linen apron.
28 So the whole community of Israel brought up
the ark of the covenant of the LORD. They shouted.
They blew rams' horns and trumpets. They played
cymbals, lyres and harps.
29 The ark of the covenant of the LORD was
brought into the City of David. Saul's daughter
Michal was watching from a window. She saw
King David dancing and celebrating. That made
her hate him in her heart.

16 The ark of God was brought into Jerusalem. It was put in the tent David had set up
for it. The priests brought burnt offerings and
friendship offerings to God.
2 After David finished sacrificing those offerings, he blessed the people in the name of the
LORD. 3 He gave to each Israelite man and woman
a loaf of bread. He also gave each one a date cake
and a raisin cake.
4 He appointed some of the Levites to serve in
front of the ark of the LORD. David wanted them to
pray, give thanks and praise the LORD. He is the
God of Israel. 5 Asaph was the leader of those Levites. Zechariah was next. Then came Jeiel, Shemiramoth, Jehiel, Mattithiah, Eliab, Benaiah,
Obed-Edom and Jeiel. They played the lyres and
harps. Asaph played the cymbals. 6 The priests Benaiah and Jahaziel blew the trumpets. They blew
them at regular times in front of the ark of the
covenant of God.

David's Psalm of Thanks to the LORD

7 That day was the first time David gave Asaph
and his helpers this psalm of thanks to the LORD.

8 Give thanks to the LORD. Worship him.
Tell the nations what he has done.
9 Sing to him. Sing praise to him.
Tell about all of the wonderful things he
has done.
10 Praise him, because his name is holy.
Let the hearts of those who trust in the LORD
be glad.
11 Look to the LORD and to his strength.
Always look to him.
12 Remember the wonderful things he has done.
Remember his miracles and how he judged
our enemies.
13 Remember what he has done, you children of
his servant Israel.
Remember it, you people of Jacob. You are
God's chosen ones.

14 He is the LORD our God.
He judges the whole earth.
15 He will keep his covenant forever.
He will keep his promise for all time
to come.
16 He will keep the covenant he made with
Abraham.
He will keep the oath he took when he made
his promise to Isaac.
17 He made it stand as a law for Jacob.
He made it stand as a covenant for Israel.
It will last forever.
18 He said, "I will give you the land of Canaan.
It will belong to you."

19 At first there weren't very many of
God's people.
There were only a few. And they were
strangers in the land.

20 They wandered from nation to nation.
They wandered from one kingdom
to another.
21 But God didn't allow anyone to beat them
down.
To keep them safe, he gave a command
to kings.
22 He said to them, "Do not touch my
anointed ones.
Do not harm my prophets."

23 All you people of the earth, sing to the LORD.
Day after day tell about how he saves us.
24 Tell the nations about his glory.
Tell all people about the wonderful things he
has done.
25 The LORD is great. He is really worthy of
praise.
People should have respect for him as the
greatest God of all.
26 All of the gods of the nations are like their
statues.
They can't do anything.
But the LORD made the heavens.
27 Glory and majesty are all around him.
Strength and joy can be seen in the place
where he lives.
28 Praise the LORD, all you nations.
Praise the LORD for his glory and strength.
29 Praise the LORD for the glory that belongs
to him.
Bring an offering and come to him.
Worship the LORD because of his beauty and
holiness.
30 All you people of the earth, tremble when you
are with him.
The world is firmly set in place. It can't be
moved.
31 Let the heavens be filled with joy. Let the earth
be glad.
Let them say among the nations, "The LORD
rules!"
32 Let the ocean and everything in it roar.
Let the fields and everything in them
be glad.
33 Then the trees in the forest will sing with joy.
They will sing to the LORD.
He will judge the people of the world.

34 Give thanks to the LORD, because he is good.
His faithful love continues forever.
35 Cry out, "Save us, God our Savior.
Save us. Bring us back from among the
nations.
Then we will give thanks to you, because your
name is holy.
We will celebrate by praising you."
36 Give praise to the LORD, the God of Israel,
for ever and ever.

Then all of the people said, "Amen!" They also said, "Praise the LORD."

37 David left Asaph and his helpers to serve in front of the ark of the covenant of the LORD. They served there at regular times. They did it as they were required to do each day.
38 David also left Obed-Edom and his 68 helpers to serve with them. Obed-Edom and Hosah guarded the gates. Obed-Edom was the son of Jeduthun.

39 David left the priest Zadok and some other priests in front of the holy tent of the LORD. It was at the high place in Gibeon.
40 David left them there to sacrifice burnt offerings to the LORD on the altar every morning and evening. They did it in keeping with everything that is written in the Law of the LORD. That's the Law he had given to Israel.

41 Heman and Jeduthun were with the priests. So were the rest of those who had been chosen by name and appointed to serve. They had been chosen to give thanks to the LORD, "because his faithful love continues forever."
42 It was the duty of Heman and Jeduthun to blow the trumpets. They also had the duty of playing the cymbals and other instruments for the sacred songs. The sons of Jeduthun were stationed at one of the gates.

43 All of the people left. Everyone went home. And David returned home to bless his family.

God Makes a Promise to David

17 David settled down in his palace. Then he spoke to the prophet Nathan. He said, "Here I am, living in a palace that has beautiful cedar walls. But the ark of the covenant of the LORD is under a tent."

2 Nathan replied to David, "Do what you want to. God is with you."

3 That night a message came to Nathan from God. He said,

4 "Go and speak to my servant David. Tell him, 'The LORD says, "You are not the one who will build me a house to live in.
5 I have not lived in a house from the day I brought Israel up out of Egypt until now. I have moved my tent from one place to another. I have moved my home from one place to another.
6 I have moved from place to place with all of the people of Israel. I commanded their leaders to be shepherds over them. I never asked any of those leaders, 'Why haven't you built me a house that has beautiful cedar walls?'"'

7 "So tell my servant David, 'The LORD who rules over all says, "I took you away from the grasslands. That is where you were taking care of your father's sheep and goats. I made you ruler over my people Israel.
8 I have been with you everywhere you have gone. I cut off all of your enemies when you were attacking them. Now I will make you famous. Your name will be just as respected as the names of the most important people on earth.

9“ ‘ ‘I will provide a place where my people Israel can live. I will plant them in the
land. Then they will have a home of their
own. They will not be bothered anymore.
Sinful people will no longer crush them, as
they did at first. 10That is what your enemies
have done ever since I appointed leaders
over my people Israel. But I will bring all of
them under your control.

“ ‘ ‘I tell you that I will build a royal house
for your family. 11Some day your life will
come to an end. You will join the members
of your family who have already died. Then
I will give you one of your own sons to
become the next king after you. I will make
his kingdom secure.

12“ ‘ ‘He is the one who will build me a
house. I will set up his throne. It will last forever. 13I will be his father. And he will be my
son. I took my love away from the man who
ruled before you. But I will never take my
love away from your son. 14I will place him
over my house and my kingdom forever. His
throne will last forever.’ ’ ”

15Nathan reported to David all of the words that
the LORD had spoken to him.

David Prays to the LORD

16Then King David went into the holy tent. He
sat down in front of the LORD. He said,

“LORD God, who am I? My family isn’t
important. So why have you brought me this
far? 17I would have thought that you had
already done more than enough for me. But
now, God, you have spoken about what is
going to happen to my royal house in days
to come. LORD God, you have treated me as
if I were the most honored man of all.

18“What more can I say to you for honoring me? You know all about me. 19LORD, you
have done a wonderful thing. You have given
me many great promises. All of them are for
my good. They are exactly what you wanted
to give me.

20“LORD, there isn’t anyone like you.
There isn’t any God but you. We have heard
about it with our own ears.

21“Who is like your people Israel? God,
we are the one nation on earth you have
saved. You have set us free for yourself. Your
name has become famous. You have done
great and wonderful things. You have driven
nations out to make room for your people.
You saved us when you set us free from
Egypt. No other god has done any of those
things for its people. 22You made Israel your
very own people forever. LORD, you have
become our God.

23“And now, LORD, let the promise you
have made to me and my royal house stand
forever. Do exactly as you promised. 24When
your promise comes true, your name will be
honored forever. People will say, ‘The LORD
rules over all. He is the God over Israel. He
is Israel’s God.’ My royal house will be
made secure in your sight.

25“My God, you have shown me that you
will build me a royal house. So I can pray to
you boldly. 26LORD, you are God! You have
promised many good things to me. 27You
have been pleased to bless my royal house.
Now it will continue forever in your sight.
LORD, you have blessed it. And it will be
blessed forever.”

David Wins Many Battles

18 While David was king of Israel, he won
many battles over the Philistines. He
brought them under his control. He took Gath
away from the Philistines. He also captured the
villages that were around Gath.

2David also won the battle over the people of
Moab. They were brought under his rule. They
gave him the gifts he required them to bring him.

3David fought against Hadadezer all the way to
Hamath. Hadadezer was king of Zobah. He had
gone to take complete control of the land along the
Euphrates River. 4David captured 1,000 of Hadadezer’s chariots, 7,000 chariot riders and 20,000
soldiers on foot. He cut the legs of all but 100 of
the chariot horses.

5The Arameans of Damascus came to help Hadadezer, the king of Zobah. But David struck down
22,000 of them. 6He stationed some soldiers in the
Aramean kingdom of Damascus. The people of
Aram were brought under his rule. They gave him
the gifts he required them to bring him. The LORD
helped David win his battles everywhere he went.

7David took the gold shields that were carried
by the officers of Hadadezer. He brought the
shields to Jerusalem. 8He took a huge amount of
bronze from Tebah and Cun. Those towns
belonged to Hadadezer. Later, Solomon used the
bronze to make the huge bronze bowl for washing.
He also used it to make the pillars and many other
bronze articles for the temple.

9Tou was king of Hamath. He heard that David
had won the battle over the entire army of Hadadezer, the king of Zobah. 10So Tou sent his son Hadoram to King David. Hadoram greeted David. He
praised him because he had won the battle over
Hadadezer. Hadadezer had been at war with Tou.
So Hadoram brought David all kinds of articles
that were made out of gold, silver and bronze.

11King David set those articles apart for the
LORD. He had done the same thing with the silver
and gold he had taken from other nations. The
nations were Edom, Moab, Ammon, Philistia and
Amalek.

12Abishai struck down 18,000 men of Edom in
the Valley of Salt. Abishai was the son of Zeruiah.

[13]He stationed some soldiers in Edom. The whole nation of Edom was brought under his rule. The LORD helped David win his battles everywhere he went.

David's Officials

[14]David ruled over the whole nation of Israel. He did what was fair and right for all of his people. [15]Joab, the son of Zeruiah, was commander over the army. Jehoshaphat, the son of Ahilud, kept the records. [16]Zadok, the son of Ahitub, was a priest. Ahimelech, the son of Abiathar, was also a priest. Shavsha was the secretary. [17]Benaiah, the son of Jehoiada, was commander over the Kerethites and Pelethites. And King David's sons were the chief officials who served at his side.

David Goes to War Against the People of Ammon

19 Nahash was king of Ammon. After he died, his son became the next king after him. [2]David thought, "I'm going to be kind to Hanun. His father Nahash was kind to me." So David sent messengers to Hanun. He wanted them to tell Hanun how sad he was that Hanun's father had died.

David's messengers went to the land of Ammon. They told Hanun how sad David was.

[3]The Ammonite nobles spoke to Hanun. They said, "David has sent messengers to tell you he is sad. They say he wants to honor your father. But the real reason they've come is to look the land over. They want to destroy it."

[4]So Hanun grabbed hold of David's men. He shaved them. He cut their clothes off just below the waist and left them half naked. Then he sent them away.

[5]Someone came and told David what had happened to his men. So David sent messengers to them because they were filled with shame. King David said to them, "Stay at Jericho until your beards grow out again. Then come back here."

[6]The Ammonites realized that what they had done had made David very angry with them. So Hanun and the Ammonites got 37 tons of silver. They used it to hire chariots and chariot riders from Aram Naharaim, Aram Maacah and Zobah. [7]They hired 32,000 chariots and riders. They also hired the king of Maacah and his troops. All of them came out and camped near Medeba. At the same time the Ammonites brought their troops together from their towns. Then they marched out to fight.

[8]David heard about it. So he sent Joab out with the entire army of Israel's fighting men. [9]The Ammonites marched out. They took up their battle positions at the entrance to their city. The kings who came to help them gathered their troops together in the open country.

[10]Joab saw that there were lines of soldiers in front of him and behind him. So he chose some of the best troops in Israel. He sent them to march out against the Arameans. [11]He put the rest of the men under the command of his brother Abishai. They were sent to march out against the Ammonites.

[12]Joab said, "Suppose the Arameans are too strong for me. Then you must come and help me. But suppose the Ammonites are too strong for you. Then I'll come and help you. [13]Be strong. Let's be brave as we fight for our people and the cities of our God. The LORD will do what he thinks is best."

[14]Then Joab and the troops who were with him marched out to attack the Arameans. They ran away from him. [15]The Ammonites saw that the Arameans were running away. So they also ran away from Joab's brother Abishai. They went inside the city. Then Joab went back to Jerusalem.

[16]The Arameans saw that they had been driven away by Israel. So they sent messengers to get some Arameans from east of the Euphrates River. The Arameans were under the command of Shophach. He was the commander of Hadadezer's army.

[17]David was told about it. So he gathered the whole army of Israel together. They went across the Jordan River. David marched out against the Arameans. He lined up his soldiers opposite them. He lined them up to meet the Arameans in battle.

The Arameans began to fight against him. [18]But then they ran away from Israel. David killed 7,000 of their chariot riders. He killed 40,000 of their soldiers who were on foot. He also killed Shophach, the commander of their army.

[19]The people who were under the rule of Hadadezer saw that Israel had won the battle over them. So they made a peace treaty with David. They were brought under his rule.

After that, the Arameans wouldn't help the Ammonites anymore.

Joab Captures the City of Rabbah

20 In the spring, Joab led Israel's army out. It was the time when kings go off to war. Joab destroyed the land of Ammon. He went to the city of Rabbah. He surrounded it and got ready to attack it. But David remained in Jerusalem. Later, Joab attacked Rabbah and completely destroyed it.

[2]David took the gold crown off the head of the king of Ammon. The crown weighed 75 pounds. It had jewels in it. It was placed on David's head. He took a huge amount of goods from the city. [3]He brought out the people who were there. He made them work with saws and iron picks and axes. David did that to all of the towns in Ammon. Then he and his entire army returned to Jerusalem.

Israel Goes to War Against the Philistines

[4]War broke out at Gezer against the Philistines. At that time Sibbecai killed Sippai. So the Philistines were brought under Israel's control. Sibbecai was a Hushathite. Sippai was from the family line of Rapha.

5 In another battle against the Philistines, Elhanan killed Lahmi. Elhanan was the son of Jair.
Lahmi was the brother of Goliath. Goliath was
from the city of Gath. Lahmi's spear was as big as
a weaver's rod.
6 There was still another battle. It took place at
Gath. A huge man lived there. He had six fingers
on each hand and six toes on each foot. So the total
number of his toes and fingers was 24. He was also
from the family line of Rapha. 7 He made fun of Israel. So Jonathan killed him. Jonathan was the son
of David's brother Shimea.
8 Those Philistine men lived in Gath. They were
from the family line of Rapha. David and his men
killed them.

David Counts His Fighting Men

21 Satan rose up against Israel. He stirred up
David to count the men of Israel. 2 So David spoke to Joab and the commanders of the
troops. He said, "Go! Count the men of Israel from
Beersheba all the way to Dan. Report back to me.
Then I'll know how many there are."
3 Joab replied, "May the LORD multiply his
troops 100 times. King David, you are my master.
Aren't all of the men under your control? Why
would you want me to count them? Do you want
to make Israel guilty?"
4 In spite of what Joab said, the king's word had
more authority than Joab's word did. So Joab left
and went all through Israel. Then he came back to
Jerusalem. 5 Joab reported to David how many
fighting men he had counted. In the whole land of
Israel there were 1,100,000 men who could use a
sword well. That included 470,000 men in Judah.
6 But Joab didn't include the tribes of Levi and
Benjamin in the total number. The king's command was sickening to Joab. 7 It was also evil in
the sight of God. So he punished Israel.
8 Then David said to God, "I committed a great
sin when I counted Israel's men. I beg you to take
away my guilt. I've done a very foolish thing."
9 The LORD spoke to David's prophet Gad. He
said, 10 "Go and tell David, 'The LORD says, "I
could punish you in three different ways. Choose
one of them for me to use against you." ' "
11 So Gad went to David. He said to him, "The
LORD says, 'Take your choice. 12 You can have
three years when there will not be enough food in
the land. You can have three months when your
enemies will sweep you away. They will catch up
with you. They will cut you down with their
swords. Or you can have three days when my
sword will punish you. That means there would be
three days of plague in the land. My angel would
strike people down in every part of Israel.'
"So take your pick. Tell me how to answer the
One who sent me."
13 David said to Gad, "I'm suffering terribly. Let
me fall into the hands of the LORD. His mercy is very
great. But don't let me fall into the hands of men."
14 So the LORD sent a plague on Israel. And
70,000 Israelites died. 15 God sent an angel to
destroy Jerusalem. But as the angel was doing it,
the LORD saw it. He was very sad because of the
plague. So he spoke to the angel who was destroying the people. He said, "That is enough! Do not
kill any more people!"
The angel of the LORD was standing at Araunah's threshing floor. Araunah was from the city
of Jebus.
16 David looked up. He saw the angel of the
LORD standing between heaven and earth. The
angel was holding out a sword over Jerusalem. David and the elders fell with their faces to the
ground. They were wearing black clothes.
17 David said to God, "I ordered the fighting
men to be counted. I'm the one who has sinned.
I'm the one who has done what is wrong. These
people are like sheep. What have they done? LORD
my God, let your powerful hand punish me and
my family. But don't let this plague continue to
strike your people."

David Builds an Altar

18 Then the angel of the LORD ordered Gad to tell
David to go up to the threshing floor of Araunah,
the Jebusite. He wanted David to build an altar
there to honor the LORD.
19 So David went up and did it. He obeyed the
message that Gad had spoken in the LORD's name.
20 Araunah was threshing wheat. He turned and
saw the angel. His four children were with him.
They hid themselves. 21 David approached the
threshing floor. Araunah looked up and saw him.
So Araunah left the threshing floor. He bowed
down to David with his face toward the ground.
22 David said to him, "Let me have the property
your threshing floor is on. I want to build an altar
there to honor the LORD. When I do, the plague on
the people will be stopped. Sell the threshing floor
to me for the full price."
23 Araunah said to David, "Take it! King David,
you are my master. Do what you please. I'll even
provide the oxen for the burnt offerings. Use
boards from the threshing sleds for the wood. Use
the wheat for the grain offering. I'll give all of it to
you."
24 But King David replied to Araunah, "No! I
want to pay the full price. I won't take what
belongs to you and give it to the LORD. I won't sacrifice a burnt offering that hasn't cost me
anything."
25 So David paid Araunah 15 pounds of gold for
the property. 26 David built an altar there to honor
the LORD. He sacrificed burnt offerings and friendship offerings. He called out to the LORD. The
LORD answered him by sending fire from heaven
on the altar for burnt offerings.
27 Then the LORD spoke to the angel. And the
angel put his sword away. 28 When the angel did that,
David was still at the threshing floor of Araunah,

the Jebusite. David saw that the LORD had answered
him. So he offered sacrifices there.
29At that time, the LORD's holy tent was at the
high place in Gibeon. The altar for burnt offerings
was there too. Moses had made the holy tent in the
desert. 30David couldn't go to the tent to pray to
God. That's because he was afraid of the sword of
the angel of the LORD.
22 David announced, "The house of the LORD
God will be built here. Israel's altar for
burnt offerings will also be here."

David Makes Plans for Building the Temple

2David gave orders to bring together the outsiders who were living in Israel. He appointed
some of them to cut stones. He wanted them to
prepare blocks of stone for building the house of
God.
3David provided a large amount of iron to make
nails. They were for the doors of the gates and for
the fittings. He provided more bronze than anyone
could weigh. 4He also provided more cedar logs
than anyone could count. The people of Sidon and
Tyre brought large numbers of logs to David.
5David said, "My son Solomon is young. He's
never done anything like this before. The house
that will be built for the LORD should be very
grand and wonderful. It should be famous and
beautiful in the eyes of all of the nations. I'll get
things ready for it." So David got many things
ready before he died.
6Then he sent for his son Solomon. He told him
to build a house for the LORD, the God of Israel.
7David said to Solomon, "My son, with all my
heart I wanted to build a house for the LORD my
God. That's where his Name will be. 8But a message from the LORD came to me. It said, 'You have
spilled the blood of many people. You have fought
many wars. You are not the one who will build a
house for my Name. That is because I have seen
you spill the blood of many people on the earth.
9" 'But you are going to have a son. He will be
a man of peace. And I will give him peace and rest
from all of his enemies on every side. His name
will be Solomon. I will give Israel peace and quiet
while he is king. 10He will build a house for my
Name. He will be my son. And I will be his father.
I will make his kingdom secure over Israel. It will
last forever.'
11"My son, may the LORD be with you. May you
have success. May you build the house of the
LORD your God, just as he said you would. 12May
the LORD give you good sense. May he give you
understanding when he makes you king over Israel. Then you will keep the law of the LORD your
God.
13"Be careful to obey the rules and laws the
LORD gave Moses for Israel. Then you will have
success. Be strong and brave. Don't be afraid.
Don't lose hope.
14"I've tried very hard to provide for the LORD's
temple. I've provided 3,750 tons of gold and
37,500 tons of silver. I've provided more bronze
and iron than anyone can weigh. I've also given
plenty of wood and stone. You can add to it.
15"You have a lot of workers. You have people
who can cut stones and people who can lay the
stones. You have people who can work with wood.
You also have people who are skilled in every
other kind of work. 16Some of them can work with
gold and silver. Others can work with bronze and
iron. There are more workers than anyone can
count. So begin the work. May the LORD be with
you."
17Then David ordered all of Israel's leaders to
help his son Solomon. 18He said to them, "The
LORD your God is with you. He's given you peace
and rest on every side. He's handed the people
who are living in the land over to me. The land has
been brought under the control of the LORD and his
people.
19"So look to the LORD your God with all your
heart and soul. Start building the temple of the
LORD God. Then bring the ark of the covenant of
the LORD into it. Also bring in the sacred articles
that belong to God. The temple will be built for the
Name of the LORD."

The Family Line of Levi

23 David had become very old. So he made
his son Solomon king over Israel.
2He gathered together all of the leaders of Israel. He also gathered the priests and the Levites
together. 3The Levites who were 30 years old or
more were counted. The total number of men was
38,000.
4David said, "From them, 24,000 will direct the
work of the LORD's temple. And 6,000 will be officials and judges. 5Another 4,000 will guard the
gates. And 4,000 will praise the LORD with the
instruments of music I've provided for that
purpose."
6David separated the Levites into groups. He
did it based on the sons of Levi. The sons were
Gershon, Kohath and Merari.

The Family of Gershon

7Ladan and Shimei belonged to the family of Gershon.
8The sons of Ladan were
Jehiel, Zetham and Joel. Jehiel was the
oldest son. The total number of sons
was three.
9The sons of Shimei were
Shelomoth, Haziel and Haran. The total
number of sons was three. They were
the leaders of the families of Ladan.
10The sons of Shimei were
Jahath, Ziza, Jeush and Beriah. The
total number of the sons of Shimei was
four.

11 Jahath was the first son. Ziza was the second son. But Jeush and Beriah didn't have many sons. So they were counted as one family. They had only one task.

The Family of Kohath

12 The sons of Kohath were
Amram, Izhar, Hebron and Uzziel. The total number of sons was four.
13 Aaron and Moses belonged to Amram's family line.
Aaron and his family line were set apart forever as the LORD's priests.
They had the duty of setting the most holy things apart to the LORD. They offered sacrifices to the LORD. They served him. They gave blessings in his
name forever. 14The sons of Moses, the
man of God, were counted as part of the tribe of Levi.
15 The sons of Moses were
Gershom and Eliezer.
16 Shubael was the oldest son in the family line of Gershom.
17 Rehabiah was the oldest son in the family line of Eliezer.
Eliezer didn't have any other sons. But Rehabiah had a great many sons.
18 Shelomith was the oldest son of Izhar.
19 Jeriah was the first son of Hebron.
Amariah was his second son. Jahaziel was the third. Jekameam was the fourth.
20 Micah was the first son of Uzziel. Isshiah was his second son.

The Family of Merari

21 The sons of Merari were
Mahli and Mushi.
The sons of Mahli were
Eleazar and Kish.
22 Eleazar died without having any sons. All he had was daughters. They got married to their cousins. The cousins were the sons of Kish.
23 The sons of Mushi were
Mahli, Eder and Jerimoth. The total number of sons was three.

24Those were the family lines of Levi. They
were recorded under the names of the family leaders. Each worker who was 20 years old or more
was counted. They served in the LORD's temple.
25David had said, "The LORD is the God of Israel. He has given peace and rest to his people. He
has come to Jerusalem to live there forever. 26So
the Levites don't need to carry the holy tent anymore. They don't need to carry any of its articles
anymore. Those were the articles that were used
to serve there."
27The Levites who were 20 years old or more
were counted. That was in keeping with David's
final directions.
28The Levites had the duty of helping the members of Aaron's family line. They helped them
serve in the LORD's temple. They were in charge
of the courtyards and the side rooms. They made
all of the sacred things pure and clean.
They also had other duties at the house of God.
29They were in charge of setting the holy bread out
on the table. They prepared the flour for the grain
offerings. They made the wafers without using any
yeast. They did the baking and the mixing. They
measured the amount and size of everything.
30They stood every morning to thank and praise
the LORD. They did the same thing every evening.
31They also did it every time burnt offerings were
brought to the LORD. Those offerings were brought
every Sabbath day. They were also brought at
every New Moon Feast and during the appointed
yearly feasts.
The Levites served in front of the LORD at regular times. The proper number of Levites was always used when they served. They served in the way the law required of them.
32So the Levites carried out their duties for the
Tent of Meeting and for the Holy Room. They
worked under their relatives who were in the family line of Aaron. They helped them serve at the
LORD's temple.

The Groups of Priests

24 Here are the groups of priests the sons of Aaron were separated into.
The sons of Aaron were Nadab, Abihu, Eleazar
and Ithamar. 2But Nadab and Abihu died before
their father did. They didn't have any sons. So Eleazar and Ithamar served as the priests.
3With the help of Zadok and Ahimelech, David
separated the priests into groups. Each group
served in its appointed order and time. Zadok
belonged to the family line of Eleazar. Ahimelech
belonged to the family line of Ithamar. 4More leaders were found among Eleazar's family line than
among Ithamar's. So the priests were separated
into their groups based on that fact. There were 16
family leaders from Eleazar's line. There were
eight family leaders from Ithamar's line.
5The priests were separated into their groups by
using lots. That was the fair way to do it. The
priests were officials of the temple and officials of
God. They came from the family lines of Eleazar
and Ithamar.
6Shemaiah was a Levite. He was the son of Nethanel. He was the writer who recorded the names
of the priests. He wrote them down in front of the
king and the officials. The officials included the
priest Zadok and Ahimelech. Ahimelech was the
son of Abiathar. They also included the leaders of
the families of the priests and the Levites. One
family was chosen by lot from Eleazar. Then one
was chosen from Ithamar.

7 The 1st lot that was drawn out was for Jehoiarib.
The 2nd was for Jedaiah.
8 The 3rd was for Harim.
The 4th was for Seorim.
9 The 5th was for Malkijah.
The 6th was for Mijamin.
10 The 7th was for Hakkoz.
The 8th was for Abijah.
11 The 9th was for Jeshua.
The 10th was for Shecaniah.
12 The 11th was for Eliashib.
The 12th was for Jakim.
13 The 13th was for Huppah.
The 14th was for Jeshebeab.
14 The 15th was for Bilgah.
The 16th was for Immer.
15 The 17th was for Hezir.
The 18th was for Happizzez.
16 The 19th was for Pethahiah.
The 20th was for Jehezkel.
17 The 21st was for Jakin.
The 22nd was for Gamul.
18 The 23rd was for Delaiah.
The 24th was for Maaziah.

19 That was their appointed order for serving when they entered the LORD's temple. That order was based on the rules Aaron had given them long ago. Everything was done exactly as the LORD had commanded Aaron. The LORD is the God of Israel.

The Rest of the Levites

20 Here are the other members of the family line of Levi.

From the sons of Amram came Shubael.
From the sons of Shubael came Jehdeiah.
21 From the sons of Rehabiah came Isshiah.
Isshiah was the oldest.
22 From the people of Izhar came Shelomoth.
From the sons of Shelomoth came Jahath.
23 Jeriah was the first son of Hebron. Amariah was his second son. Jahaziel was the third. Jekameam was the fourth.
24 The son of Uzziel was Micah.
From the sons of Micah came Shamir.
25 The brother of Micah was Isshiah.
From the sons of Isshiah came Zechariah.
26 The sons of Merari were Mahli and Mushi.
The son of Jaaziah was Beno.
27 The sons of Merari
from Jaaziah were Beno, Shoham, Zaccur and Ibri.
28 From Mahli came Eleazar. Eleazar didn't have any sons.
29 From Kish came
Jerahmeel. Jerahmeel was the son of Kish.
30 The sons of Mushi were Mahli, Eder and Jerimoth.

Those were the Levites, family by family.
31 They cast lots, just as their relatives, the sons of Aaron, had done. They did it in front of King David, Zadok and Ahimelech. They did it in front of the family leaders of the priests. They also did it in front of the family leaders of the Levites. The families of the oldest brother were treated in the same way as the families of the youngest.

The Singers

25 David and the commanders of the army set apart some of the sons of Asaph, Heman and Jeduthun. They set them apart to serve the LORD by prophesying while harps, lyres and cymbals were being played. Here is the list of the men who served in that way.

2 From the sons of Asaph came
Zaccur, Joseph, Nethaniah and Asarelah. The sons of Asaph were under the direction of Asaph. He prophesied under the king's direction.
3 From the sons of Jeduthun came
Gedaliah, Zeri, Jeshaiah, Shimei, Hashabiah and Mattithiah. The total number was six. They were under the direction of their father Jeduthun. He prophesied while playing the harp. He used it to thank and praise the LORD.
4 From the sons of Heman came
Bukkiah, Mattaniah, Uzziel, Shubael, Jerimoth, Hananiah, Hanani, Eliathah, Giddalti, Romamti-Ezer, Joshbekashah, Mallothi, Hothir and Mahazioth.
5 All of them were sons of the king's prophet Heman. They were given to Heman to bring him honor. That's what God had promised. God gave him 14 sons and three daughters.

6 All of them were under the direction of their fathers. They played music for the LORD's temple. They served at the house of God by playing cymbals, lyres and harps. Asaph, Jeduthun and Heman were under the king's direction.

7 All of them were trained and skilled in playing music for the LORD. Their total number was 288. That included their relatives.
8 Young and old alike cast lots for their duties. That was true for students as well as teachers.

9 The 1st lot that was drawn out was for Asaph. It was for Joseph
and his sons and relatives. The total number was 12.
The 2nd lot was for Gedaliah
and his relatives and sons. The total number was 12.
10 The 3rd was for Zaccur
and his sons and relatives. The total number was 12.
11 The 4th was for Izri
and his sons and relatives. The total number was 12.
12 The 5th was for Nethaniah
and his sons and relatives. The total number was 12.

13 The 6th was for Bukkiah
and his sons and relatives. The total number was 12.
14 The 7th was for Jesarelah
and his sons and relatives. The total number was 12.
15 The 8th was for Jeshaiah
and his sons and relatives. The total number was 12.
16 The 9th was for Mattaniah
and his sons and relatives. The total number was 12.
17 The 10th was for Shimei
and his sons and relatives. The total number was 12.
18 The 11th was for Azarel
and his sons and relatives. The total number was 12.
19 The 12th was for Hashabiah
and his sons and relatives. The total number was 12.
20 The 13th was for Shubael
and his sons and relatives. The total number was 12.
21 The 14th was for Mattithiah
and his sons and relatives. The total number was 12.
22 The 15th was for Jerimoth
and his sons and relatives. The total number was 12.
23 The 16th was for Hananiah
and his sons and relatives. The total number was 12.
24 The 17th was for Joshbekashah
and his sons and relatives. The total number was 12.
25 The 18th was for Hanani
and his sons and relatives. The total number was 12.
26 The 19th was for Mallothi
and his sons and relatives. The total number was 12.
27 The 20th was for Eliathah
and his sons and relatives. The total number was 12.
28 The 21st was for Hothir
and his sons and relatives. The total number was 12.
29 The 22nd was for Giddalti
and his sons and relatives. The total number was 12.
30 The 23rd was for Mahazioth
and his sons and relatives. The total number was 12.
31 The 24th was for Romamti-Ezer
and his sons and relatives. The total number was 12.

The Men Who Guarded the Gates

26 Here are the groups of men who guarded the gates.

From the family of Korah came Meshelemiah, the son of Kore. Kore was one of the sons of Asaph.
2 Meshelemiah had sons.
Zechariah was his first son.
Jediael was his second son.
Zebadiah was the third.
Jathniel was the fourth.
3 Elam was the fifth.
Jehohanan was the sixth.
And Eliehoenai was the seventh.
4 Obed-Edom also had sons.
Shemaiah was his first son.
Jehozabad was his second son.
Joah was the third.
Sacar was the fourth.
Nethanel was the fifth.
5 Ammiel was the sixth.
Issachar was the seventh.
And Peullethai was the eighth.
God had blessed Obed-Edom.

6 His son Shemaiah also had sons. They were leaders in their family. That's because they were men of great ability.
7 The sons of Shemaiah were Othni, Rephael, Obed and Elzabad. Elzabad's brothers Elihu and Semakiah were also able men.
8 All of them belonged to the family line of Obed-Edom. They and their sons and relatives were men of ability. They were strong enough to do their work. The total number of men in the family line of Obed-Edom was 62.
9 Meshelemiah's sons and relatives were able men. Their total number was 18.
10 Hosah belonged to the family line of Merari. Hosah's first son was Shimri. But Shimri wasn't the oldest son. His father had made him the first.
11 Hilkiah was Hosah's second son. Tabaliah was the third. Zechariah was the fourth. The total number of Hosah's sons and relatives was 13.

12 Those groups of men guarded the gates. They worked under their chief men. They served at the LORD's temple, just as their relatives had served.
13 Lots were cast for each gate, family by family. Young and old alike were chosen.

14 The lot that was drawn out for the East Gate was for Shelemiah. Then lots were cast for his son Zechariah. He gave wise advice. The lot that was drawn out for the North Gate was for him.
15 The lot for the South Gate was for Obed-Edom. The lot for the storeroom was for his sons.
16 Lots were drawn out for the West Gate and the Shalleketh Gate on the upper road. Those lots were for Shuppim and Hosah.

One guard stood next to another.
17 There were six Levites a day on the east. There were four a day on the north. There were four a day on the south.

And there were two at a time at the storeroom.
18 Two Levite guards were at the courtyard to the
west. And four were at the road.
19 Those were the groups of the men who
guarded the gates. They belonged to the family
lines of Korah and Merari.

Other Officials

20 The Levite relatives of the men who guarded
the gates were in charge of the treasures in the
house of God. They were also in charge of other
treasures that had been set apart for God.
21 Ladan was from the family line of Gershon.
Some leaders of families belonged to Ladan's family line. One of them was Jehieli. 22 The sons of Jehieli were Zetham and his brother Joel. They were
in charge of the treasures in the LORD's temple.
23 Here are the officials who were from the family lines of Amram, Izhar, Hebron and Uzziel.

24 Shubael was from the family line of Moses' son Gershom. Shubael was the officer in charge of the treasures. 25 His
relatives through Eliezer included his
son Rehabiah. Jeshaiah was Rehabiah's
son. Joram was Jeshaiah's son. Zicri
was Joram's son. And Shelomith was
Zicri's son.

26 Shelomith and his relatives were in
charge of all of the treasures that had
been set apart for God. King David had
set those treasures apart. Some family
leaders had also set them apart. They
were the commanders of thousands of
men and commanders of hundreds. The
treasures had also been set apart by
other army commanders.

27 Some of the goods that had been taken
in battle were set apart to repair the
LORD's temple. 28 The prophet Samuel
had set apart some things for God. Saul,
the son of Kish, had set apart other
things. So had Abner, the son of Ner.
And so had Joab, the son of Zeruiah.
All of those things and all of the others
that had been set apart were taken care
of by Shelomith and his relatives.

29 From the family line of Izhar came Kenaniah and his sons. They were given duties
that were away from the temple. They
were officials and judges over Israel.

30 From the family line of Hebron came
Hashabiah and his relatives. They were
able men. The total number was 1,700.
It was their duty to serve the king in Israel west of the Jordan River. It was also
their duty to do all of the LORD's work
there.

31 Jeriah was the chief of the family line of
Hebron. That's based on their family
history. In the 40th year of David's rule,
a search was made in the records. That's
how men of ability were found in the
family line of Hebron at Jazer in Gilead. 32 Jeriah had 2,700 relatives. They
were able men. They were family leaders. King David had put them in charge
of the tribes of Reuben and Gad and
half of the tribe of Manasseh. They
were in charge of matters having to do
with God and the king.

The Companies in the King's Army

27 Here is the list of the Israelites who served
in the king's army. They included leaders
of families. They included commanders of thousands of men and commanders of hundreds. They
also included other officers. All of them served the
king in everything concerning the army companies
that were on duty month by month all through the
year. The total number of men in each company
was 24,000.

2 Jashobeam was in charge of the first company
for the first month. He was the son of Zabdiel. The total number of men in Jashobeam's
company was 24,000. 3 He belonged to the
family line of Perez. He was chief of all of the
army officers for the first month.

4 Dodai was in charge of the second company for
the second month. He belonged to the family
line of Ahoah. Mikloth was the leader of Dodai's company. The total number of men in
Dodai's company was 24,000.

5 The third army commander for the third month
was the priest Benaiah, the son of Jehoiada.
Benaiah was the chief. The total number of
men in Benaiah's company was 24,000. 6 That
same Benaiah was a mighty man among the
Thirty. In fact, he was leader over the Thirty.
His son Ammizabad was in charge of his
company.

7 The fourth commander for the fourth month was
Joab's brother Asahel. Asahel's son Zebadiah
was the next commander after him. The total
number of men in Asahel's company was
24,000.

8 The fifth commander for the fifth month was
Shamhuth. He was an Izrahite. The total number of men in Shamhuth's company was
24,000.

9 The sixth commander for the sixth month was
Ira. He was the son of Ikkesh from Tekoa. The
total number of men in Ira's company was
24,000.

10 The seventh commander for the seventh month
was Helez. He was a Pelonite from Ephraim.
The total number of men in Helez's company
was 24,000.

11 The eighth commander for the eighth month was
Sibbecai. He was a Hushathite from Zerah.
The total number of men in Sibbecai's com-
pany was 24,000.

[12]The ninth commander for the ninth month was Abiezer. He was from Anathoth in Benjamin. The total number of men in Abiezer's company was 24,000.
[13]The tenth commander for the tenth month was Maharai. He was a Netophathite from Zerah. The total number of men in Maharai's company was 24,000.
[14]The 11th commander for the 11th month was Benaiah. He was from Pirathon in Ephraim. The total number of men in Benaiah's company was 24,000.
[15]The 12th commander for the 12th month was Heldai. He was a Netophathite from the family line of Othniel. The total number of men in Heldai's company was 24,000.

The Officers Over the Tribes

[16]Here are the officers over the tribes of Israel.

Over the tribe of Reuben was Eliezer, the son of Zicri.
Over Simeon was Shephatiah, the son of Maacah.
[17]Over Levi was Hashabiah, the son of Kemuel.
Over Aaron was Zadok.
[18]Over Judah was Elihu. He was David's brother.
Over Issachar was Omri, the son of Michael.
[19]Over Zebulun was Ishmaiah, the son of Obadiah.
Over Naphtali was Jerimoth, the son of Azriel.
[20]Over Ephraim was Hoshea, the son of Azaziah.
Over half of the tribe of Manasseh was Joel, the son of Pedaiah.
[21]Over the half of the tribe of Manasseh in Gilead was Iddo, the son of Zechariah.
Over Benjamin was Jaasiel, the son of Abner.
[22]Over Dan was Azarel, the son of Jeroham.

Those were the officers over the tribes of Israel.

[23]David didn't count the men who were 20 years
old or less. That's because the LORD had promised
to make the people of Israel as many as the stars in
the sky. [24]Joab, the son of Zeruiah, began to count
the men. But he didn't finish. The LORD was angry
with Israel because David had begun to count the
men. So the number wasn't written down in the
official records of King David.

Other Officials of the King

[25]Azmaveth was in charge of the royal storerooms. He was the son of Adiel.

Jonathan was in charge of the storerooms in the fields, towns, villages and lookout towers. He was the son of Uzziah.

[26]Ezri was in charge of the workers who farmed the land. He was the son of Kelub.

[27]Shimei was in charge of the vineyards. He was from Ramah.

Zabdi was in charge of the grapes from the vineyards. He was also in charge of storing the wine. He was a Shiphmite.

[28]Baal-Hanan was in charge of the olive trees and sycamore-fig trees in the western hills. He was from Geder.

Joash was in charge of storing the olive oil.

[29]Shitrai was in charge of the herds that ate grass in Sharon. He was from Sharon.

Shaphat was in charge of the herds in the valleys. He was the son of Adlai.

[30]Obil was in charge of the camels. He was from the family line of Ishmael.

Jehdeiah was in charge of the donkeys. He was from Meronoth.

[31]Jaziz was in charge of the flocks. He was a Hagrite.

All of those men were the officials in charge of King David's property.

[32]Jonathan was David's uncle. He gave good
advice. He was a man of understanding. He was
also a secretary. Jehiel took care of the king's sons.
He was the son of Hacmoni.
[33]Ahithophel was the king's adviser.
Hushai was the king's friend. He was an Arkite.
[34]Jehoiada and Abiathar became the next advisers
after Ahithophel. Jehoiada was the son of Benaiah.
Joab was the commander of the royal army.

David Talks About His Plans for the Temple

28 David asked all of the officials of Israel to
come together at Jerusalem. He sent for the
officers who were over the tribes. He sent for the
commanders of the companies who served the
king. He sent for the commanders of thousands of
men and commanders of hundreds. He sent for the
officials who were in charge of all of the royal
property and livestock. They belonged to the king
and his sons. He sent for the palace officials and
the mighty men. He also sent for all of the brave
fighting men.
[2]King David stood up. He said, "All of you, listen to me. With all my heart I wanted to build a
house for the LORD. I wanted it to be a place of
peace and rest for the ark of the covenant of the
LORD. The ark is the stool for our God's feet. I
made plans to build the LORD's house. [3]But God
said to me, 'You are not the one who will build a
house for my Name. That is because you are a
fighting man. You have spilled people's blood.'
[4]"But the LORD chose me. He is the God of Israel. He chose me from my whole family to be
king over Israel forever. He chose Judah to lead
the tribes. From the families of Judah he chose my
family. From my father's sons he chose me. He
was pleased to make me king over the whole
nation of Israel.

5“The LORD has given me many sons. From all of them he has chosen my son Solomon. He wants Solomon to sit on the throne of the LORD’s kingdom. He wants him to rule over Israel. 6He said to me, ‘Your son Solomon is the one who will build my house and my courtyards. I have chosen him to be my son. And I will be his father. 7I will make his kingdom secure. It will last forever. That will happen if he does not turn away from my commands and laws. He must continue to obey them, just as he is doing now.’

8“So I’m giving you a command in the sight of all of the people of Israel. The LORD’s community is watching. And our God is listening. I command you to be careful to follow all of the commands of the LORD your God. Then you will own this good land. You will pass it on to your children after you as their share forever.

9“My son Solomon, always remember the God of your father. Serve him with all your heart. Do it with a mind that wants to obey him. The LORD looks deep down inside every heart. He understands the real reasons for everything you think. If you look to him, you will find him. But if you desert him, he will turn his back on you forever. 10Think about it. The LORD has chosen you to build a temple as a holy place where he can live. So be strong. Get to work.”

11Then David gave his son Solomon the plans for the porch of the temple. He gave him the plans for its buildings and its storerooms. He gave him the plans for its upper parts and its inside rooms. He gave him the plans for the place where sin is paid for and forgiven. 12He gave him the plans for everything the Spirit of the LORD had put in his mind. There were plans for the courtyards of the LORD’s temple. There were plans for all of the rooms that were around it. There were plans for the places where the treasure of God’s temple would be kept. There were plans for the places where the things that were set apart for God would be kept.

13David told Solomon how to separate the priests and Levites into groups. He gave him directions for all of the work they should do when they served in the LORD’s temple.

He also showed him how all of the articles should be used at the temple. 14Different articles were used for different purposes.

David told Solomon how much gold should be used for each gold article. He also told him how much silver should be used for each silver article. 15He told him how much gold should be used to make each gold lampstand and its lamps. He told him how much silver should be used to make each silver lampstand and its lamps. The amount depended on how each lampstand would be used.

16David told Solomon how much gold should be used to make each table for holy bread. He told him how much silver should be used to make the silver tables. 17He told him how much pure gold should be used to make the forks, sprinkling bowls and pitchers. He told him how much gold should be used to make each gold dish. He told him how much silver should be used to make each silver dish.

18And he told him how much pure gold should be used to make the altar for burning incense. David also gave Solomon the plan for the chariot of the gold cherubim. They spread their wings over the ark of the covenant of the LORD.

19David said, “I have written everything down. The LORD’s powerful hand helped me. He helped me understand every part of the plan.”

20David also said to his son Solomon, “Be strong and brave. Get to work. Don’t be afraid. Don’t lose hope. The LORD God is my God. He is with you. He won’t fail you. He won’t desert you until all of the work for serving in the LORD’s temple is finished. 21The groups of the priests and Levites are ready to do all of the work on God’s temple. Every worker who is willing and skilled can help you do all of the work. The officials and all of the people will obey every command you give them.”

Gifts Are Brought for the Temple

29 Then King David spoke to the whole community. He said, “God has chosen my son Solomon. But Solomon is young. He’s never done anything like this before. The task is huge. This grand and wonderful temple won’t be built for human beings. It will be built for the LORD God.

2“With all of my riches I’ve done everything I could for the temple of my God. I’ve provided gold for the gold work and silver for the silver work. I’ve provided bronze for the bronze work and iron for the iron work. I’ve given wood for the things that will be made out of wood. I’ve given onyx and turquoise for the settings. I’ve given stones of different colors and all kinds of fine stone and marble. I’ve provided everything in huge amounts.

3“With all my heart I want the temple of my God to be built. So I’m giving my personal treasures of gold and silver for it. I’m adding them to everything else I’ve provided for the holy temple. 4I’m giving 110 tons of gold and 260 tons of pure silver. Cover the walls of the buildings with it. 5Use it for the gold work and the silver work. Use it for everything the skilled workers will do. How many of you are willing to set yourselves apart to the LORD today?”

6Many people were willing to give. They included the leaders of families and the officers of the tribes of Israel. They included the commanders of thousands of men and commanders of hundreds. They also included the officials who were in charge of the king’s work. 7All of them gave to the work on God’s temple. They gave more than 190 tons of gold and 375 tons of silver. They also gave 675 tons of bronze and 3,750 tons of iron.

[8]Anyone who had valuable jewels added them to the treasure for the LORD's temple. Jehiel was in charge of the temple treasure. He was from the family line of Gershon.

[9]The people were happy when they saw what their leaders had been willing to give. The leaders had given freely. With their whole heart they had given everything to the LORD. King David was filled with joy.

David Praises the LORD

[10]David praised the LORD in front of the whole community. He said,

"LORD, we give you praise.
You are the God of our father Israel.
We give you praise for ever and ever.
11 LORD, you are great and powerful.
Glory, majesty and beauty belong to you.
Everything in heaven and on earth belongs to you.
LORD, the kingdom belongs to you.
You are honored as the One who rules over all.
12 Wealth and honor come from you.
You are the ruler of all things.
In your hands are strength and power.
You can give honor and strength to everyone.
13 Our God, we give you thanks.
We praise your glorious name.

[14]"But who am I? And who are my people? Without your help we wouldn't be able to give this much. Everything comes from you. We've given back to you only what comes from you. [15]We are outsiders and strangers in your sight. So were all of our people who lived long ago. Our days on this earth are like a shadow. We don't have any hope.

[16]"LORD our God, we've given more than enough. We've provided it to build you a temple where you will put your holy Name. But all of it comes from you. All of it belongs to you. [17]My God, I know that you put our hearts to the test. And you are pleased when we are honest. I've given all of these things just because I wanted to. When I did it, I was completely honest with you. And I've been happy to see that your people who are here have also been willing to give to you.

[18]"LORD, you are the God of our fathers Abraham, Isaac and Israel. Keep this longing in the hearts of your people forever. Keep their hearts true to you. [19]Help my son Solomon serve you with all his heart. Then he will keep your commands and rules. He will do what you require. He'll do everything to build the grand and wonderful temple I've provided for."

[20]Then David spoke to the whole community. He said, "Praise the LORD your God." So all of them praised the LORD. He's the God of their people who lived long ago. The whole community bowed low. They fell down flat with their faces toward the ground. They did it in front of the LORD and the king.

Solomon Becomes the Next King

[21]The next day they offered sacrifices to the LORD. They brought burnt offerings to him. They sacrificed 1,000 bulls, 1,000 rams and 1,000 male lambs. They also brought the required drink offerings. And they offered many other sacrifices for the whole community of Israel. [22]They ate and drank with great joy that day. They did it in the sight of the LORD.

Then they announced a second time that Solomon was king. He was the son of David. They anointed Solomon to be ruler in the sight of the LORD. They also anointed Zadok to be priest.

[23]So Solomon sat on the throne of the LORD. He ruled as king in place of his father David. Things went well with him. All of the people of Israel obeyed him. [24]All of the officers and mighty men promised to be completely faithful to King Solomon. So did all of King David's sons.

[25]The LORD greatly honored Solomon in the sight of all of the people. He gave him royal majesty. Solomon was given more glory than any king over Israel had ever had.

David Dies

[26]David was king over the whole nation of Israel. He was the son of Jesse. [27]He ruled over Israel for 40 years. He ruled for seven years in Hebron and for 33 years in Jerusalem. [28]He died when he was very old. He had enjoyed a long life. He had enjoyed wealth and honor. His son Solomon became the next king after him.

[29]The events of King David's rule from beginning to end are written down. They are written in the records of the prophets Samuel, Nathan and Gad. [30]The records tell all about David's rule and power. They tell about what happened concerning him and Israel and the kingdoms of all of the other lands.

2 Chronicles

Solomon Asks God for Wisdom

1 Solomon was the son of David. Solomon made his position secure over his kingdom. The LORD his God was with him. He made Solomon very great.

2Solomon spoke to the whole community of Israel. He spoke to the commanders of thousands of men and commanders of hundreds. He spoke to the judges and all of the leaders in Israel. He spoke to the leaders of Israel's families. 3Solomon and the whole community went to the high place at Gibeon. That's because God's Tent of Meeting was there. The LORD's servant Moses had made the tent in the desert.

4David had brought the ark of God up from Kiriath Jearim. He had brought it to the place he had prepared for it. He had set up a tent for it in Jerusalem.

5But the bronze altar that Bezalel had made was in Gibeon. Bezalel was the son of Uri. Uri was the son of Hur. The altar was in front of the LORD's holy tent. So Solomon and the whole community asked the LORD for advice there.

6Solomon went up to the bronze altar in front of the LORD at the Tent of Meeting. Solomon sacrificed 1,000 burnt offerings on the altar.

7That night God appeared to Solomon. He said to him, "Ask for anything you want me to give you."

8Solomon answered God, "You were very kind to my father David. Now you have made me king in his place. 9LORD God, let the promise you gave to my father David come true. You have made me king. My people are like the dust of the earth. They can't be counted. 10Give me wisdom and knowledge. Then I'll be able to lead these people. Without your help, who would be able to rule this great nation of yours?"

11God said to Solomon, "I am glad that those are the things you really want. You have not asked for wealth, riches or honor. You have not even asked to have your enemies killed. You have not asked to live for a long time. Instead, you have asked for wisdom and knowledge. You want to be able to rule my people wisely. I have made you king over them.

12"So wisdom and knowledge will be given to you. I will also give you wealth, riches and honor. You will have more than any king before you ever had. And no king after you will have as much."

13Then Solomon left the high place at Gibeon. He went from the Tent of Meeting there to Jerusalem. And he ruled over Israel.

14Solomon had 1,400 chariots and 12,000 horses. He kept some of them in the chariot cities. He kept others with him in Jerusalem.

15The king made silver and gold as common in Jerusalem as stones. He made cedar wood as common there as sycamore-fig trees in the western hills.

16Solomon got horses from Egypt and Kue. The king's buyers purchased them from Kue. 17They could get a chariot from Egypt for 15 pounds of silver. They could get a horse for less than four pounds of silver. They sold horses and chariots to all of the Hittite and Aramean kings.

Solomon Asks Hiram to Help Build the Temple

2 Solomon gave orders to build a temple. That's where the LORD would put his Name. Solomon also gave orders to build a royal palace for himself. 2He chose 70,000 men to carry things. He chose 80,000 to cut stones in the hills. He put 3,600 men in charge of them.

3Solomon sent a message to Hiram. Hiram was king of Tyre. The message said,

> "Send me cedar logs, just as you did for my father David. You sent him cedar to build a palace to live in. 4Now I'm about to build a temple. The Name of the LORD my God will be there. I'll set the temple apart for him.
>
> "Sweet-smelling incense will be burned in front of him there. The holy bread will be set out at regular times. Burnt offerings will be sacrificed there every morning and evening. They will be sacrificed every Sabbath day. They will be sacrificed at every New Moon Feast. And they will be sacrificed at every yearly appointed feast of the LORD our God. That's a law for Israel that will last for all time to come.
>
> 5"The temple I'm going to build will be beautiful. That's because our God is greater than all other gods. 6So who is able to build a temple for him? After all, the heavens can't hold him. In fact, not even the highest heavens can hold him. So who am I to build a temple for him? It will only be a place to burn sacrifices to him.
>
> 7"Send me someone who is skilled at working with gold, silver, bronze and iron. He must also be able to work with purple, blue and bright red yarn. He must be skilled in the art of carving. Send him to work in Judah and Jerusalem with my skilled workers. My father David provided them to help me.
>
> 8"Also send me cedar, pine and algum logs from Lebanon. I know that your men are skilled in cutting wood there. My men will work with yours. 9They'll provide me with plenty of lumber. That's because the

temple I'm building must be large and beautiful.

10"I'll pay your servants. They will cut the wood. I'll pay them 125,000 bushels of wheat that has been ground up. I'll pay them 125,000 bushels of barley. I'll also pay them 115,000 gallons of wine and 115,000 gallons of olive oil."

11King Hiram of Tyre replied to Solomon. He wrote a letter to him. It said,

"The LORD loves his people. That's why he has made you their king."

12Hiram continued,

"I praise the LORD. He is the God of Israel. He made heaven and earth. He has given King David a wise son. You have good sense. You understand what is right. You will build a temple for the LORD. You will also build a palace for yourself.

13"I'm sending Huram-Abi to you. He is very skillful. 14His mother was from Dan. His father was from Tyre. He is trained to work with gold, silver, bronze and iron. He knows how to work with stone and wood. He can also work with purple, blue and bright red yarn and fine linen. He's skilled in all kinds of carving. He can follow any pattern you give him. He'll work with your skilled workers. He'll also work with those of your father David. David was my master.

15"Now please send us what you promised. Send us the wheat, barley, olive oil and wine. 16And we'll cut all of the logs from Lebanon you need. We'll make rafts out of them. We'll float them by sea down to Joppa. Then you can take them up to Jerusalem."

17Solomon counted all of the outsiders who were living in Israel. He did it after his father David had counted them. There were 153,600 of them. 18He chose 70,000 to carry things. He chose 80,000 to cut stones in the hills. He put 3,600 men in charge of the people to keep them working.

Solomon Builds the Temple

3 Then Solomon began to build the temple of the LORD. He built it on Mount Moriah in Jerusalem. That's where the LORD had appeared to Solomon's father David. He had appeared at the threshing floor of Araunah. Araunah was from Jebus. David had provided the threshing floor. 2Solomon began building the temple on the second day of the second month. It was in the fourth year of his rule.

3Solomon laid the foundation for God's temple. It was 90 feet long and 30 feet wide. Solomon's men followed the standard measure that was used at that time. 4The porch in front of the temple was 30 feet across and 30 feet high.

Solomon covered the inside of the temple with pure gold. 5He covered the inside of the main hall with pine boards. Then he covered the boards with fine gold. He decorated the hall with palm tree patterns and chain patterns. 6He decorated the temple with valuable jewels. The gold he used came from Parvaim. 7He covered the ceiling beams, doorframes, walls and doors of the temple with gold. He carved cherubim on the walls.

8He built the Most Holy Room. It was as long as the temple was wide. It was 30 feet long and 30 feet wide. He covered the inside of the Most Holy Room with 23 tons of fine gold. 9He also covered the upper parts with gold. The gold on the nails weighed 20 ounces.

10For the Most Holy Room, Solomon made a pair of carved cherubim. He covered them with gold. 11The total length of the cherubim's wings from tip to tip was 30 feet. One wing of the first cherub was seven and a half feet long. Its tip touched the temple wall. The other wing was also seven and a half feet long. Its tip touched the wing tip of the other cherub.

12In the same way one wing of the second cherub was seven and a half feet long. Its tip touched the other temple wall. The other wing was also seven and a half feet long. Its tip touched the wing tip of the first cherub. 13So the total length of the wings of the two cherubim was 30 feet from tip to tip. The cherubim stood facing the main hall.

14Solomon made the curtain out of blue, purple and bright red yarn and fine linen. A skilled worker sewed cherubim into its pattern.

15In front of the temple, Solomon made two pillars. Each pillar was 26 feet tall. Each had a decorated top that was seven and a half feet high. 16Solomon made chains that were linked together. He put them on top of the pillars. He also made 100 pomegranates. He fastened them to the chains.

17Solomon set the pillars up in front of the temple. One was on the south. The other was on the north. He named the one on the south Jakin. The one on the north he named Boaz.

More Facts About the Temple

4 Solomon made a bronze altar that was 30 feet long, 30 feet wide and 15 feet high. 2He made a huge metal bowl for washing. Its shape was round. It measured 15 feet from rim to rim. It was seven and a half feet high. And it was 45 feet around. 3Below the rim there was a circle of bull figures around the bowl. In every 18 inches around the bowl there were ten bulls. The bulls were arranged in two rows. They were made as part of the bowl itself.

4The bowl stood on 12 bulls. Three of them faced north. Three faced west. Three faced south. And three faced east. The bowl rested on top of them. Their rear ends were toward the center. 5The bowl was three inches thick. Its rim was like the rim of a cup. The rim was shaped like the bloom of a lily. The bowl held 17,500 gallons of water.

6 Solomon made ten smaller bowls for washing.
He placed five of them on the south side of the huge
bowl. He placed the other five on the north side.
The things that were used for the burnt offerings were rinsed in the smaller bowls. But the
priests used the huge bowl for washing.
7 Solomon made ten gold lampstands. He followed the pattern the LORD had given him. He
placed the lampstands in the temple. He put five
of them on the south side. He put the other five on
the north side.
8 He made ten tables. He placed them in the temple. He put five of them on the south side. He put
the other five on the north side. He also made 100
gold sprinkling bowls.
9 He made the courtyard of the priests. He also
made the large courtyard. He made doors for it. He
covered the doors with bronze.
10 He placed the huge bowl on the south side of
the courtyard. He put it at the southeast corner.
11 He also made the pots, shovels and sprinkling
bowls.
So Huram finished the work he had started for
King Solomon. Here's what he made for God's
temple.

12 He made the two pillars.
He made the two tops for the pillars. The
tops were shaped like bowls.
He made the two sets of chains that were
linked together. They decorated the two
bowl-shaped tops of the pillars.
13 He made the 400 pomegranates for the two
sets of chains. There were two rows of
pomegranates for each chain. They decorated the bowl-shaped tops of the
pillars.
14 He made the stands and their bowls.
15 He made the huge bowl. He made the 12
bulls that were under it.
16 He made the pots, shovels and meat forks.
He also made all of the articles that
were connected with them.

Huram-Abi made all of those objects for King
Solomon for the LORD's temple. He made them out
of bronze. Then he shined them up. 17 The king had
them made in clay molds. It was done on the flatlands of the Jordan River between Succoth and
Zarethan.
18 Solomon made huge numbers of those articles. There were too many of them to weigh. No
one even tried to weigh the bronze they were made
out of.
19 Solomon also made all of the articles that
were in God's temple.

He made the golden altar.
He made the tables for the holy bread.
20 He made the pure gold lampstands and
their lamps. The lamps burned in front
of the Most Holy Room, just as the law
required.
21 He made the gold flowers. He made the
gold lamps and tongs. They were made
out of solid gold.
22 He made the wick cutters, sprinkling
bowls, dishes, and shallow cups for
burning incense. All of them were made
out of pure gold. He made the gold
doors of the temple. They were the
inner doors to the Most Holy Room and
the doors of the main hall.

5 Solomon finished all of the work for the
LORD's temple. Then he brought in the things
his father David had set apart for the LORD. They
included the silver and gold and all of the articles
for God's temple. Solomon placed them with the
other treasures that were there.

Solomon Brings the Ark to the Temple

2 Then Solomon sent for the elders of Israel. He
told them to come to Jerusalem. They included all
of the leaders of the tribes. They also included the
chiefs of the families of Israel. Solomon wanted
them to bring up the ark of the LORD's covenant
from Zion. Zion was the City of David. 3 All of the
men of Israel came together to where the king was.
It was at the time of the Feast of Booths. The feast
was held in the seventh month.
4 All of the elders of Israel arrived. Then the Levites picked up the ark and carried it. 5 They
brought up the ark. They also brought up the Tent
of Meeting and all of the sacred articles that were
in the tent. The priests, who were Levites, carried
everything up.
6 The entire community of Israel had gathered
around King Solomon. All of them were in front of
the ark. They sacrificed huge numbers of sheep and
cattle. There were so many that they couldn't be
recorded. In fact, they couldn't even be counted.
7 The priests brought the ark of the LORD's
covenant to its place in the Most Holy Room of
the temple. They put it under the wings of the
cherubim.
8 The cherubim's wings were spread out over the
place where the ark was. They covered the ark.
They also covered the poles that were used to carry
it. 9 The poles reached out from the ark. They were
so long that their ends could be seen from in front
of the Most Holy Room. But they couldn't be seen
from outside the Holy Room. They are still there
to this very day.
10 There wasn't anything in the ark except the
two tablets. Moses had placed them in it at Mount
Horeb. That's where the LORD had made a
covenant with the Israelites. He made it after they
came out of Egypt.
11 The priests left the Holy Room. All of the
priests who were there had set themselves apart to
the LORD. It didn't matter what group they were in.
12 All of the Levites who played music stood
near the east side of the altar. They included

Asaph, Heman, Jeduthun and their sons and relatives. They were dressed in fine linen. They were playing cymbals, harps and lyres. They were joined by 120 priests who were blowing trumpets.

13The trumpet players and singers made music together as if they were only one voice. They praised the LORD. They gave thanks to him. Some of them played their trumpets, cymbals and other instruments. The others raised their voices to praise the LORD. They sang,

"He is good.
His faithful love continues forever."

Then a cloud filled the temple of the LORD. 14The priests couldn't do their work because of it. The glory of the LORD filled God's temple.

6 Then Solomon said, "LORD, you have said you would live in a dark cloud. 2I've built a beautiful temple for you. You can live in it forever."

3The whole community of Israel was standing there. The king turned around and gave them his blessing. 4Then he said,

"I praise the LORD. He is the God of Israel. With his mouth he made a promise to my father David. With his powerful hands he made it come true. He said, 5'I brought my people out of Egypt. Ever since I did that, I have not chosen a city in any tribe of Israel where a temple could be built for my Name. I have not chosen anyone to be the leader over my people Israel. 6But now I have chosen Jerusalem. I will put my Name there. And I have chosen David to rule over my people Israel.'

7"With all his heart my father David wanted to build a temple. He wanted to do it so the Name of the LORD could be there. The LORD is the God of Israel.

8"But the LORD spoke to my father David. He said, 'With all your heart you wanted to build a temple for my Name. It is good that you wanted to do that. 9But you will not build the temple. Instead, your son will build the temple for my Name. He is your own flesh and blood.'

10"The LORD has kept the promise he made. I've become the next king after my father David. Now I'm sitting on the throne of Israel. That's exactly what the LORD promised would happen. I've built the temple for the Name of the LORD. He is the God of Israel. 11I've placed the ark there. The tablets of the LORD's covenant are inside it. He made that covenant with the people of Israel."

Solomon Prays to Set the Temple Apart to the LORD

12Then Solomon stood in front of the LORD's altar. He stood in front of the whole community of Israel. He spread out his hands to pray. 13He had made a bronze stage. It was seven and a half feet long and seven and a half feet wide. It was four and a half feet high. He had placed it in the center of the outer courtyard. He stood on the stage. Then he got down on his knees in front of the whole community of Israel. He spread out his hands toward heaven. 14He said,

"LORD, you are the God of Israel. There is no God like you in heaven or on earth. You keep the covenant you made with us. You show us your love. You do that when we follow you with all our hearts. 15You have kept your promise to my father David. He was your servant. With your mouth you made a promise. With your powerful hand you have made it come true. And today we can see it.

16"LORD, you are the God of Israel. Keep the promises you made to my father David. Do it for him. He was your servant. You said to him, 'You will always have a son to sit on the throne of Israel in my sight. That will be true only if your sons are careful in everything they do. They must live the way my law tells them to. That is the way you have lived.' 17LORD, you are the God of Israel. So let your promise to your servant David come true.

18"But will you really live on earth with human beings? After all, the heavens can't hold you. In fact, even the highest heavens can't hold you. So this temple I've built certainly can't hold you!

19"But please pay attention to my prayer. LORD my God, show me your favor as I make my appeal to you. Listen to my cry for help. Hear the prayer I'm praying to you. 20Let your eyes look toward this temple day and night. You said you would put your Name here. Listen to the prayer I'm praying toward this place.

21"Hear me when I ask you to show us your favor. Listen to your people Israel when they pray toward this place. Listen to us from heaven. It's the place where you live. When you hear us, forgive us.

22"Suppose a man does something wrong to his neighbor. And he is required to take an oath and make a promise. He must come and do it in front of your altar in this temple. 23When he does, listen to him from heaven. Take action. Judge between the man and his neighbor. Pay back the one who is guilty. Do to him what he has done to the other person. Tell everyone that the person who hasn't done anything wrong is free of blame. That will prove he isn't guilty.

24"Suppose your people Israel have lost the battle against their enemies. And suppose they've sinned against you. But they turn

back to you and praise your name. They pray
to you in this temple. And they ask you to
show them your favor. 25Then listen to them
from heaven. Forgive the sin of your people
Israel. Bring them back to the land you gave
to them and their people who lived long ago.
26"Suppose your people have sinned
against you. And because of that, the sky is
closed up and there isn't any rain. But your
people pray toward this place. They praise
you by admitting they've sinned. And they
turn away from their sin because you have
made them suffer. 27Then listen to them from
heaven. Forgive the sin of your people Israel. Teach them the right way to live. Send
rain on the land you gave them as their share.
28"Suppose there isn't enough food in the
land. And a plague strikes the land. The hot
winds completely dry up our crops. Or
locusts or grasshoppers come and eat them
up. Or enemies surround one of our cities
and get ready to attack it. Or trouble or sickness comes. 29But suppose one of your people prays to you. He asks you to show him
your favor. He is aware of how much he is
suffering. And he spreads out his hands
toward this temple to pray. 30Then listen to
him from heaven. It's the place where you
live. Forgive him. Deal with him in keeping
with everything he does. You know his heart.
In fact, you are the only one who knows
every human heart.
31"Your people will have respect for you.
They will live the way you want them to.
They'll live that way as long as they are in
the land you gave our people long ago.
32"Suppose a stranger who doesn't belong
to your people Israel has come from a land
far away. He has come because he's heard
about your great name. He has heard that
you reached out your mighty hand and powerful arm. So he comes and prays toward this
temple. 33Then listen to him from heaven.
It's the place where you live. Do what that
stranger asks you to do.

"Then all of the nations on earth will
know you. They will have respect for you.
They'll respect you just as your own people
Israel do. They'll know that your Name is in
this house I've built.
34"Suppose your people go to war against
their enemies. It doesn't matter where you
send them. And suppose they pray to you
toward this city you have chosen. They pray
toward the temple I've built for your Name.
35Then listen to them from heaven. Listen to
their prayer. Listen to them when they ask you
to show them your favor. Stand up for them.
36"Suppose they sin against you. After all,
there isn't anyone who doesn't sin. And suppose you get angry with them. You hand
them over to their enemies. They take them
as prisoners to another land. It doesn't matter whether it's near or far away. 37But suppose your people change their ways in the
land where they are held as prisoners. They
turn away from their sins. They beg you to
help them in the land where they are prisoners. They say, 'We have sinned. We've done
what is wrong. We've done what is evil.'
38And they turn back to you with all their
heart and soul. Suppose it happens in the
land where they were taken as prisoners.
There they pray toward the land you gave
their people long ago. They pray toward the
city you have chosen. And they pray toward
the temple I've built for your Name. 39Then
listen to them from heaven. It's the place
where you live. Listen to their prayer. Listen
to them when they ask you to show them
your favor. Stand up for them. Your people
have sinned against you. Please forgive
them.
40"My God, let your eyes see us. Let your
ears pay attention to the prayers that are
offered in this place.

41 "LORD God, rise up and come to your
resting place.
Come in together with the ark.
It's the sign of your power.
LORD God, may your priests put on
salvation as if it were their
clothes.
May your faithful people be glad
because you are so good.
42 LORD God, don't turn your back on
your anointed king.
Remember the great love you
promised to your servant
David."

Solomon Sets the Temple Apart to the LORD

7 Solomon finished praying. Then fire came
down from heaven. It burned up the burnt
offering and the sacrifices. The glory of the LORD
filled the temple. 2The priests couldn't enter the
temple of the LORD. His glory filled it.
3All of the people of Israel saw the fire coming
down. They saw the glory of the LORD above the
temple. So they got down on their knees in the
courtyard with their faces toward the ground. They
worshiped the LORD. They gave thanks to him.
They said,

"He is good.
His faithful love continues forever."

4Then the king and all of the people offered sacrifices to the LORD. 5King Solomon sacrificed
22,000 head of cattle and 120,000 sheep and goats.
So the king and all of the people set the temple of
God apart.

[6]The priests and Levites took their positions. The Levites played the LORD's musical instruments. King David had made them for praising the LORD. They were used when he gave thanks to the LORD. He said, "His faithful love continues forever."

Across from where the Levites were, the priests blew their trumpets. All of the people of Israel were standing.

[7]Solomon set the middle area of the courtyard apart to the LORD. It was in front of the LORD's temple. There Solomon sacrificed burnt offerings. He also sacrificed the fat of the friendship offerings there. He did it there because the bronze altar he had made couldn't hold all of the burnt offerings, the grain offerings and the fat parts.

[8]At that time Solomon celebrated the Feast of Booths for seven days. The whole community of Israel was with him. It was a huge crowd. People came from as far away as Lebo Hamath and the Wadi of Egypt. [9]On the eighth day they held a service. For seven days they had celebrated by setting the altar apart to honor God. The feast continued for seven more days.

[10]Then Solomon sent the people home. It was the 23rd day of the seventh month. The people were glad. Their hearts were full of joy. That's because the LORD had done good things for David and Solomon and his people Israel.

The LORD Appears to Solomon

[11]Solomon finished the LORD's temple and the royal palace. He had done everything he had planned to do in the LORD's temple and his own palace.

[12]The LORD appeared to him at night. He said,

"I have heard your prayer. I have chosen this place for myself. It is a temple where sacrifices will be offered.

[13]"Suppose I close up the sky and there isn't any rain. Suppose I command locusts to eat up the crops. And I send a plague among my people. [14]But they make themselves low in my sight. They pray and look to me. And they turn from their evil ways. Then I will listen to them from heaven. I will forgive their sin. And I will heal their land. After all, they are my people.

[15]"Now my eyes will see them. My ears will pay attention to the prayers they offer in this place. [16]I have chosen this temple. I have set it apart for myself. My Name will be there forever. My eyes and my heart will always be there.

[17]"But you must walk with me, just as your father David did. Do everything I command you to do. Obey my rules and laws. [18]Then I will set up your royal throne. I made a covenant with your father David to do that. I said to him, 'You will always have a son to rule over Israel.'

[19]"But suppose all of you turn away from me. You refuse to obey the rules and commands I have given you. And you go off to serve other gods and worship them. [20]Then I will remove Israel from my land. It is the land I gave them. I will turn my back on this temple. I will do it even though I have set it apart for my Name to be there. I will make all of the nations hate it. They will laugh and joke about it.

[21]"This temple is now so grand and beautiful. But the time is coming when all those who pass by it will be shocked. They will say, 'Why has the LORD done a thing like this to this land and temple?'

[22]"People will answer, 'Because they have deserted the LORD. He is the God of their people who lived long ago. He brought them out of Egypt. But they have been holding on to other gods. They've been worshiping them. They've been serving them. That's why he has brought all of this horrible trouble on them.'"

Other Things Solomon Did

8 Solomon built the LORD's temple and his own palace. It took him 20 years to build them. After that, [2]Solomon rebuilt the villages Hiram had given him. He settled Israelites in them.

[3]Then Solomon went to Hamath Zobah. He captured it. [4]He also built up Tadmor in the desert. He built up all of the cities in Hamath where he could store things. [5]He rebuilt Lower Beth Horon and Upper Beth Horon. He put up high walls around them. He made their city gates secure with heavy metal bars. [6]He rebuilt Baalath and all of the cities where he could store things. He also rebuilt all of the cities for his chariots and horses.

Solomon built anything he wanted to build in Jerusalem, Lebanon and all of the territory he ruled over.

[7]There were still many people left in the land who weren't Israelites. They included Hittites, Amorites, Perizzites, Hivites and Jebusites. [8]They were children of the people who had lived in the land before the Israelites came. The people of Israel hadn't destroyed them. Solomon had forced them to work very hard as his slaves. And they still work for Israel to this very day.

[9]But Solomon didn't force the men of Israel to work as his slaves. Instead, some were his fighting men. Others were commanders of his captains, chariots and chariot drivers. [10]Still others were King Solomon's chief officials. There were 250 officials in charge of the other men.

[11]Solomon brought Pharaoh's daughter up from the City of David to the palace he had built for her. He said, "My wife must not live in the palace of David, who was the king of Israel. It's one of the places the ark of the LORD has entered. That makes it holy."

[12]Solomon had built the LORD's altar. It stood in front of the temple porch. On that altar Solomon sacrificed burnt offerings to the LORD. [13]Each day he sacrificed what the Law of Moses required. He

sacrificed the required offerings every Sabbath day. He also sacrificed them at each New Moon Feast and during the three yearly feasts. Those three were the Feast of Unleavened Bread, the Feast of Weeks and the Feast of Booths.

[14]Solomon followed the orders his father David had given him. He appointed the groups of priests for their duties. He appointed the Levites to lead the people in praising the LORD. They also helped the priests do their required tasks each day. Solomon appointed the groups of men who guarded all of the gates. That's what David, the man of God, had ordered. [15]King David's commands were followed completely. They applied to the priests and Levites. They also applied to the temple treasure.

[16]All of Solomon's work was carried out. It started the day the foundation of the LORD's temple was laid. It ended when the LORD's temple was finished.

[17]Solomon went to Ezion Geber and Elath on the coast of Edom. [18]Hiram sent him ships that his own officers commanded. They were men who knew the sea. Together with Solomon's men they sailed to Ophir. They brought back 17 tons of gold. They gave it to King Solomon.

The Queen of Sheba Visits Solomon

9 The queen of Sheba heard about how famous Solomon was. So she came to Jerusalem to test him with hard questions. She arrived with a very large group of attendants. Her camels were carrying spices, huge amounts of gold, and valuable jewels. She came to Solomon and asked him about everything she wanted to know.

[2]He answered all of her questions. There wasn't anything that was too hard for him to explain to her.

[3]So the queen of Sheba saw how wise Solomon was. She saw the palace he had built. [4]She saw the food that was on his table. She saw his officials sitting there. She saw the robes of the servants who waited on everyone. She saw the robes the wine tasters were wearing. And she saw the burnt offerings Solomon sacrificed at the LORD's temple. She could hardly believe everything she had seen.

[5]She said to the king, "Back in my own country I heard a report about you. I heard about how much you had accomplished. I also heard about how wise you are. Everything I heard is true. [6]But I didn't believe what people were saying. So I came to see for myself. And now I believe it! You are twice as wise as people say you are. The report I heard doesn't even begin to tell the whole story about you.

[7]"How happy your men must be! How happy your officials must be! They always get to serve you and hear the wise things you say.

[8]"May the LORD your God be praised. He must take great delight in you. He placed you on his throne as king. He put you there to rule for him. Your God loves Israel very much. He longs to take good care of them forever. That's why he has made you king over them. He knows that you will do what is fair and right."

[9]She gave the king four and a half tons of gold. She also gave him huge amounts of spices and valuable jewels. There had never been as many spices as the queen of Sheba gave to King Solomon.

[10]The servants of Hiram and those of Solomon brought gold from Ophir. They also brought algumwood and valuable jewels. [11]The king used the algumwood to make steps for the LORD's temple and the royal palace. He also used it to make harps and lyres for those who played the music. No one had ever seen that much algumwood in Judah before.

[12]King Solomon gave the queen of Sheba everything she wanted and asked for. In fact, he gave her more than she had brought to him. Then she left. She returned to her own country with her attendants.

Solomon in All of His Glory

[13]Each year Solomon received 25 tons of gold. [14]That didn't include the money that was brought in by business and trade. All of the kings of Arabia also brought gold and silver to Solomon. So did the governors of Israel.

[15]King Solomon made 200 large shields out of hammered gold. Each one weighed seven and a half pounds. [16]He also made 300 small shields out of hammered gold. Each one weighed almost four pounds. The king put all of the shields in the Palace of the Forest of Lebanon.

[17]Then he made a large throne. It was decorated with ivory. It was covered with pure gold. [18]The throne had six steps. A gold stool for the king's feet was connected to it. The throne had armrests on both sides of the seat. A statue of a lion stood on each side of the throne. [19]Twelve lions stood on the six steps. There was one at each end of each step. Nothing like that throne had ever been made for any other kingdom.

[20]All of King Solomon's cups were made out of gold. All of the articles that were used in the Palace of the Forest of Lebanon were made out of pure gold. Nothing was made out of silver. When Solomon was king, silver wasn't considered to be worth very much.

[21]He had many ships that carried goods to be traded. The crews of those ships were made up of Hiram's men. Once every three years the ships returned. They brought gold, silver, ivory, apes and baboons.

[22]King Solomon was richer than all of the other kings on earth. He was also wiser than they were.

[23]All of these kings wanted to meet Solomon in person. They wanted to see for themselves how wise God had made him. [24]Year after year, everyone who came to him brought a gift. They brought articles that were made out of silver and gold. They brought robes, weapons and spices. They also brought horses and mules.

[25]Solomon had 4,000 spaces where he kept his
horses and chariots. He had 12,000 horses. He kept
some of his horses and chariots in the chariot
cities. He kept the others with him in Jerusalem.
[26]Solomon ruled over all of the kings from the
Euphrates River to the land of the Philistines. He
ruled all the way to the border of Egypt.
[27]The king made silver as common in Jerusalem
as stones. He made cedar wood as common there
as sycamore-fig trees in the western hills.
[28]Solomon got horses from Egypt. He also got
them from many other countries.

Solomon Dies

[29]The other events of Solomon's rule from
beginning to end are written down. They are written in the records of the prophet Nathan. They are
written in the prophecy of Ahijah. He was from
Shiloh. They are also written in the records of the
visions of the prophet Iddo about Jeroboam. Jeroboam was the son of Nebat.
[30]Solomon ruled in Jerusalem over the whole
nation of Israel for 40 years. [31]Then he joined the
members of his family who had already died. His
body was buried in the city of his father David.
Solomon's son Rehoboam became the next king
after him.

Israel Refuses to Follow Rehoboam

10 Rehoboam went to Shechem. All of the
people of Israel had gone there to make
him king.
[2]Jeroboam heard about it. He was the son of Nebat. Jeroboam was in Egypt at that time. He had
gone there for safety. He wanted to get away from
King Solomon. But now he returned from Egypt.
[3]So the people sent for Jeroboam. He and all of
the people went to Rehoboam. They said to him,
[4]"Your father put a heavy load on our shoulders.
But now make our hard work easier. Make the
heavy load on us lighter. Then we'll serve you."
[5]Rehoboam answered, "Come back to me in
three days." So the people went away.
[6]Then King Rehoboam asked the elders for
advice. They had served his father Solomon while
he was still living. Rehoboam asked them, "What
advice can you give me? How should I answer
these people?"
[7]They replied, "Be kind to them. Please them.
Give them what they are asking for. Then they'll
always serve you."
[8]But Rehoboam didn't accept the advice the
elders gave him. He asked for advice from the
young men who had grown up with him and were
now serving him. [9]He asked them, "What's your
advice? How should I answer these people? They
said to me, 'Make the load your father put on our
shoulders lighter.'"
[10]The young men who had grown up with him
gave their answer. They replied, "The people have
said to you, 'Your father put a heavy load on our
shoulders. Make it lighter.' Tell them, 'My little
finger is stronger than my father's legs. [11]My
father put a heavy load on your shoulders. But I'll
make it even heavier. My father beat you with
whips. But I'll beat you with bigger whips.'"
[12]Three days later Jeroboam and all of the people returned to Rehoboam. That's because the king
had said, "Come back to me in three days."
[13]The king answered them in a mean way. He
didn't accept the advice of the elders. [14]Instead, he
followed the advice of the young men. He said,
"My father put a heavy load on your shoulders.
But I'll make it even heavier. My father beat you
with whips. But I'll beat you with bigger whips."
[15]So the king didn't listen to the people. That's
because God had planned it that way. What the
LORD had said through Ahijah came true. Ahijah
had spoken the LORD's message to Jeroboam, the
son of Nebat. Ahijah was from Shiloh.
[16]All of the people of Israel saw that the king
refused to listen to them. So they answered the
king. They said,

"We don't have any share in David's royal
family.
We don't have any share in Jesse's son.
People of Israel, let's go back to our homes.
David's royal family, take care of your own
kingdom!"

So all of the people of Israel went home.
[17]But Rehoboam still ruled over the Israelites
who were living in the towns of Judah.
[18]Adoniram was in charge of those who were
forced to work hard for King Rehoboam. The king
sent him out among the Israelites. But they killed
him by throwing stones at him. Rehoboam was
able to get away in his chariot. He escaped to Jerusalem. [19]Israel has refused to follow the royal
family of David to this very day.

11 Rehoboam arrived in Jerusalem. He brought
together 180,000 fighting men from the
tribes of Judah and Benjamin. He had decided to
make war against Israel. He wanted his fighting
men to get the kingdom of Israel back for him.
[2]But a message came to Shemaiah from the
LORD. He was a man of God. The LORD said to
him, [3]"Speak to Solomon's son Rehoboam, the
king of Judah. Speak to all of the people of Israel
in Judah and Benjamin. Tell them, [4]'The LORD
says, "Do not go up to fight against your relatives.
I want every one of you to go back home. Things
have happened exactly the way I planned them."'"
So the fighting men obeyed the LORD's message. They turned back. They didn't march out
against Jeroboam.

Rehoboam Builds Up Judah's Towns

[5]Rehoboam lived in Jerusalem. He made Judah
more secure by building up their towns. [6]He built
up Bethlehem, Etam, Tekoa, [7]Beth Zur, Soco and
Adullam. [8]He also built up Gath, Mareshah, Ziph,

9Adoraim, Lachish, Azekah, 10Zorah, Aijalon and
Hebron. All of them were cities in Judah and Benjamin that had high walls around them.

11Rehoboam made those cities even more
secure. He put commanders in them. He gave them
plenty of food, olive oil and wine. 12He put shields
and spears in all of those cities. He made them
very strong. So he ruled over Judah and Benjamin.

13The priests and Levites were on Rehoboam's
side. They came from their territories all over Israel. 14The Levites even left their grasslands and
other property behind. They came to Judah and Jerusalem. That's because Jeroboam and his sons
had refused to accept them as priests of the LORD.
15Jeroboam appointed his own priests to serve at
the high places. He had made statues of gods that
looked like goats and calves. His priests served
those gods.

16Some people from every tribe in Israel followed the Levites to Jerusalem. With all their
hearts they wanted to worship the LORD. He is the
God of Israel. They came to Jerusalem to offer sacrifices to him. He was the God of their people of
long ago.

17All those who came to Jerusalem made the
kingdom of Judah strong. They helped Solomon's
son Rehoboam for three years. During that time
they lived the way David and Solomon had lived.

Rehoboam's Family

18Rehoboam got married to Mahalath. She was
the daughter of David's son Jerimoth. Her mother
was Abihail. Abihail was the daughter of Jesse's
son Eliab. 19Mahalath had sons by Rehoboam.
Their names were Jeush, Shemariah and Zaham.

20Then Rehoboam married Maacah. She was
the daughter of Absalom. She had sons by Rehoboam. Their names were Abijah, Attai, Ziza and
Shelomith. 21Rehoboam loved Absalom's daughter Maacah. In fact, he loved her more than any of
his other wives and concubines. He had a total of
18 wives and 60 concubines. And he had a total of
28 sons and 60 daughters.

22Rehoboam appointed Maacah's son Abijah to
be the chief prince among his brothers. He did it
to make him king. 23He acted wisely. He scattered
some of his sons through all of the territories of
Judah and Benjamin. He put them in all of the
cities that had high walls around them. He gave
them plenty of food and everything else they
needed. He also gave them many wives.

Shishak Attacks Jerusalem

12 Rehoboam had made his position as king
secure. He had become very strong. Then
he turned away from the law of the LORD. So did
all of the people of Judah.

2They hadn't been faithful to the LORD. So Shishak attacked Jerusalem. It was in the fifth year
that Rehoboam was king. Shishak was king of
Egypt. 3He came with 1,200 chariots and 60,000
horsemen. Troops of Libyans, Sukkites and Cushites came with him from Egypt. There were so
many of them they couldn't be counted. 4Shishak
captured the cities of Judah that had high walls
around them. He came all the way to Jerusalem.

5Then the prophet Shemaiah came to Rehoboam and the leaders of Judah. They had gathered
together in Jerusalem. They were afraid of Shishak.
Shemaiah said to them, "The LORD says, 'You have
left me. So now I am leaving you to Shishak.'"

6The king and the leaders of Israel made themselves low in the LORD's sight. They said, "The
LORD does what is right and fair."

7The LORD saw they had made themselves low.
So he gave a message to Shemaiah. It said, "They
have made themselves low in my sight. So I will
not destroy them. Instead, I will soon save them. I
will not pour out my burning anger on Jerusalem
through Shishak. 8But its people will be brought
under his control. Then they will learn the difference between serving me and serving the kings of
other lands."

9Shishak, the king of Egypt, attacked Jerusalem.
He carried away the treasures of the LORD's temple. He also carried the treasures of the royal
palace away. He took everything. That included
the gold shields Solomon had made.

10So King Rehoboam made bronze shields to
take their place. He gave them to the commanders
of the guards who were on duty at the entrance to
the royal palace. 11Every time the king went to the
LORD's temple, the guards went with him. They
carried the shields. Later, they took them back to
the room where they were kept.

12Rehoboam had made himself low in the
LORD's sight. So the LORD turned his anger away
from him. Rehoboam wasn't totally destroyed. In
fact, some good things happened in Judah.

13King Rehoboam had made his position secure
in Jerusalem. He continued as king. He was 41
years old when he became king. He ruled for 17
years in Jerusalem. It was the city the LORD had
chosen out of all of the cities in the tribes of Israel. He wanted to put his Name there. The name of
Rehoboam's mother was Naamah from Ammon.

14Rehoboam did what was evil. That's because
he hadn't worshiped the LORD with all his heart.

15The events of Rehoboam's rule from beginning to end are written down. They are written in
the records of the prophets Shemaiah and Iddo.
The records deal with family histories. Rehoboam
and Jeroboam were always at war with each other.

16Rehoboam joined the members of his family
who had already died. His body was buried in the
City of David. His son Abijah became the next
king after him.

Abijah Becomes King of Judah

13 Abijah became king of Judah. It was in the
18th year of Jeroboam's rule over Israel.
2Abijah ruled in Jerusalem for three years. His

mother's name was Maacah. She was a daughter of Uriel. Uriel was from Gibeah.

There was war between Abijah and Jeroboam. 3Abijah went into battle with an army of 400,000 able fighting men. Jeroboam lined up his soldiers against them. He had 800,000 able troops.

4Abijah stood on Mount Zemaraim. It's in the hill country of Ephraim. Abijah said, "Jeroboam and all you men of Israel, listen to me! 5The LORD is the God of Israel. Don't you know that he has placed David and his sons after him on Israel's throne forever? The LORD made a covenant of salt with David. The salt means the covenant will last for all time to come.

6"Jeroboam, the son of Nebat, was an official of David's son Solomon. But he refused to obey his master. 7Some worthless and evil men gathered around him. They opposed Solomon's son Rehoboam. At that time Rehoboam was young. He couldn't make up his mind. He wasn't strong enough to stand up against those men.

8"Now you plan to stand up against the kingdom of the LORD. His kingdom is in the hands of men in David's family line. It's true that you have a huge army. You have the golden calves that Jeroboam made to be your gods.

9"But you drove out the priests of the LORD, the sons of Aaron. You also drove out the Levites. You appointed your own priests. That's what the people of other nations do. Anyone can come and set himself apart. All he has to do is sacrifice a young bull and seven rams. Then he becomes a priest of gods that aren't really gods at all!

10"But the LORD is our God. We haven't deserted him. The priests who serve the LORD belong to the family line of Aaron. The Levites help them. 11Every morning and evening the priests bring burnt offerings and sweet-smelling incense to the LORD. They set out the holy bread on the table. That table is 'clean.' They light the lamps on the gold lampstand every evening.

"We always do what the LORD our God requires in his law. But you have deserted him. 12God is with us. He's our leader. His priests will blow their trumpets. They will sound the battle cry against you. Men of Israel, don't fight against the LORD. He's the God of your people who lived long ago. You can't possibly succeed."

13Jeroboam had sent some troops behind Judah's battle lines. He told them to hide and wait there. He and his men stayed in front of Judah's lines.

14Judah turned and saw that they were being attacked from the front and from the back. Then they cried out to the LORD. The priests blew their trumpets. 15The men of Judah shouted the battle cry. When they did, God drove Jeroboam and all of Israel's men away from Abijah and Judah.

16The men of Israel ran away from them. God handed Israel over to Judah. 17Abijah and his men wounded and killed large numbers of them. In fact, 500,000 of Israel's able men lay dead or wounded.

18So at that time the men of Israel were brought under Judah's control. The men of Judah won the battle over them. That's because they trusted in the LORD. He's the God of their people.

19Abijah chased Jeroboam. He took from him the towns of Bethel, Jeshanah and Ephron. He also took the villages that were around them. 20Jeroboam didn't get his power back during the time of Abijah. In fact, the LORD struck him down. And he died.

21But Abijah grew stronger. He got married to 14 wives. He had 22 sons and 16 daughters.

22The other events of Abijah's rule are written down. The things he did and said are written in the notes of the prophet Iddo.

14 Abijah joined the members of his family who had already died. His body was buried in the City of David. His son Asa became the next king after him. While Asa was king, the country had peace and rest for ten years.

Asa Becomes King of Judah

2Asa did what was good and right in the eyes of the LORD his God. 3He removed the altars where strange gods were worshiped. He took away the high places. He smashed the sacred stones. He cut down the poles that were used to worship the goddess Asherah. 4He commanded Judah to worship the LORD, the God of their people. He commanded them to obey the LORD's laws and commands.

5He removed the high places and incense altars from every town in Judah. The kingdom had peace and rest under him. 6He built up the cities of Judah that had high walls around them. The land was at peace. No one was at war with Asa during those years. That's because the LORD gave him peace and rest.

7"Let's build up our towns," Asa said to the people of Judah. "Let's put walls around them. Let's provide them with towers. Let's make them secure with gates that have heavy metal bars. The land still belongs to us. That's because we've trusted in the LORD our God. We trusted in him, and he has given us peace and rest on every side." So they built. And things went well for them.

8Asa had an army of 300,000 men from Judah. They carried spears and large shields. There were 280,000 men from Benjamin. They were armed with bows and small shields. All of those men were brave soldiers.

9Zerah marched out against them. He was from Cush. He had a huge army. He also had 300 chariots. They came all the way to Mareshah.

10Asa went out to meet Zerah in battle. They took up their positions in the Valley of Zephathah. It's near Mareshah.

11Then Asa called out to the LORD his God. He said, "LORD, there isn't anyone like you. You help the weak against the strong. LORD our God, help us. We trust in you. In your name we have come out to fight against this huge army. LORD, you are our God. Don't let mere men win the battle over you."

12The LORD struck down the men of Cush for Asa and Judah. The Cushites ran away. 13Asa and his army chased them all the way to Gerar. A large number of Cushites fell down wounded or dead. So they couldn't fight back. The LORD and his army crushed them. The men of Judah carried off a large amount of goods.

14They attacked all of the villages around Gerar. The LORD had made the people in those villages afraid of him. The men of Judah took everything from all of the villages. 15They also attacked the camps of those who took care of the herds. They carried off large numbers of sheep, goats and camels. Then they returned to Jerusalem.

Asa Makes Judah a Better Nation

15 The Spirit of God came on Azariah. He was the son of Oded. 2Azariah went out to meet Asa. He said to him, "Asa and all you people of Judah and Benjamin, listen to me. The LORD is with you when you are with him. If you really look for him, you will find him. But if you desert him, he will desert you.

3"For a long time Israel didn't worship the true God. They didn't have a priest who taught them. So they didn't know God's law. 4But when they were in trouble, they turned to the LORD, the God of Israel. When they did, they found him.

5"In those days it wasn't safe to travel around. The people who lived in all of the areas of the land were having a lot of trouble. 6One nation was crushing another. One city was crushing another. That's because God was causing them to suffer terribly.

7"But be strong. Don't give up. God will reward you for your work."

8Asa heard that prophecy. He paid attention to the words of the prophet Azariah, the son of Oded. So Asa became bolder than ever. He removed the statues of gods from the whole land of Judah and Benjamin. He also removed them from the towns he had captured in the hills of Ephraim. He did it because he hated those gods. He repaired the altar of the LORD. It was in front of the porch of the LORD's temple.

9Then he gathered all of the people of Judah and Benjamin together. He also gathered together the people from Ephraim, Manasseh and Simeon who had settled among them. Large numbers of people had come over to him from Israel. They came because they saw that the LORD his God was with him.

10They gathered in Jerusalem. It was the third month of the 15th year of Asa's rule. 11At that time they sacrificed to the LORD 700 head of cattle and 7,000 sheep and goats. The animals were among the things they had taken after the battle.

12They made a covenant to look to the LORD, the God of their people. They looked to him with all their heart and soul. 13All those who wouldn't look to the LORD, the God of Israel, would be killed. It wouldn't matter how important they were. It wouldn't matter whether they were men or women. 14They took an oath and made a promise to the LORD. They praised him out loud. They shouted. They blew trumpets and horns.

15All of the people of Judah were happy about the promise they had made. They turned to God with all their heart. When they did, they found him. So the LORD gave them peace and rest on every side.

16King Asa also removed his grandmother Maacah from her position as queen mother. That's because she had made a pole that was used to worship the goddess Asherah. The LORD hated it. So Asa cut it down. He broke it up. He burned it in the Kidron Valley.

17Asa didn't remove the high places from Israel. But he committed his whole life completely to the LORD. 18He and his father had set apart silver, gold and other articles to the LORD. He brought them into God's temple.

19There weren't any more wars until the 35th year of Asa's rule.

The Last Years of Asa's Rule

16 Baasha was king of Israel. He marched out against Judah. It was in the 36th year of Asa's rule over Judah. Baasha built up the walls of Ramah. He did it to keep people from leaving or entering the territory of Asa, the king of Judah.

2Asa took the silver and gold from among the treasures of the LORD's temple and his own palace. He sent it to Ben-Hadad. Ben-Hadad was king of Aram. He was ruling in Damascus. 3"Let's make a peace treaty between us," Asa said. "My father and your father had made a peace treaty between them. Now I'm sending you silver and gold. So break your treaty with Baasha, the king of Israel. Then he'll go back home."

4Ben-Hadad agreed with King Asa. He sent his army commanders against the towns of Israel. They attacked Ijon, Dan, Abel Maim and all of the cities in Naphtali where Baasha stored things.

5Baasha heard about it. So he stopped building up Ramah. He stopped working there. 6Then King Asa brought all of the men of Judah to Ramah. They carried away the stones and wood Baasha had been using. Asa used them to build up Geba and Mizpah.

7At that time the prophet Hanani came to Asa, the king of Judah. He said to him, "You trusted the king of Aram. You didn't trust in the LORD your God. So the army of the king of Aram has escaped from you. 8The people of Cush and Libya had a strong army. They had large numbers of chariots and horsemen. But you trusted in the LORD. So he handed them over to you. 9The LORD looks out over the whole earth. He gives strength to those who commit their lives completely to him. You have done a foolish thing. From now on you will be at war."

[10]Asa was angry with the prophet because of what he had said. In fact, he was so angry he put him in prison. At the same time, Asa treated some of his own people very badly.

[11]The events of Asa's rule from beginning to end are written down. They are written in the records of the kings of Judah and Israel.

[12]In the 39th year of Asa's rule his feet began to hurt. The pain was terrible. But even though he was suffering, he didn't look to the LORD for help. All he did was go to the doctors.

[13]In the 41st year of Asa's rule he joined the members of his family who had already died. [14]His body was buried in a tomb. He had cut it out for himself in the City of David. His body was laid on a wooden frame. It was covered with spices and different mixes of perfume. A huge fire was made in his honor.

Jehoshaphat Becomes King of Judah

17 Jehoshaphat was the son of Asa. Jehoshaphat became the next king after him. He made his kingdom strong in case Israel would attack him. [2]He placed troops in all of the cities of Judah that had high walls around them. He stationed some soldiers in Judah. He also put some in the towns of Ephraim that his father Asa had captured.

[3]The LORD was with Jehoshaphat. That's because in his early years he lived the way King David had lived. He didn't ask for advice from the gods that were named after Baal. [4]Instead, he looked to the God of his father. He followed the LORD's commands instead of the practices of Israel.

[5]The LORD made the kingdom secure under Jehoshaphat's control. All of the people of Judah brought gifts to Jehoshaphat. So he had great wealth and honor. [6]His heart was committed to living the way the LORD wanted him to. He removed the high places from Judah. He also removed the poles that were used to worship the goddess Asherah.

[7]In the third year of his rule, he sent his officials to teach in the towns of Judah. The officials were Ben-Hail, Obadiah, Zechariah, Nethanel and Micaiah. [8]Some Levites were with them. Their names were Shemaiah, Nethaniah, Zebadiah, Asahel, Shemiramoth, Jehonathan, Adonijah, Tobijah and Tob-Adonijah. The priests Elishama and Jehoram were also with them. [9]They taught people all through Judah. They took the Scroll of the Law of the LORD with them. They went around to all of the towns of Judah. And they taught the people.

[10]All of the kingdoms of the lands around Judah became afraid of the LORD. So they didn't go to war against Jehoshaphat. [11]Some Philistines brought to Jehoshaphat the gifts and silver he required of them. The Arabs brought him their flocks. They brought him 7,700 rams and 7,700 goats.

[12]Jehoshaphat became more and more powerful. He built forts in Judah. He also built cities in Judah where he could store things. [13]He had large supplies in the towns of Judah. In Jerusalem he kept men who knew how to fight well. [14]Here is a list of them, family by family.

From Judah there were commanders of companies of 1,000.
One of them was Adnah. He commanded 300,000 fighting men.
[15] Another was Jehohanan. He commanded 280,000.
[16] Another was Amasiah, the son of Zicri. Amasiah commanded 200,000. He had offered to serve the LORD.
[17] From Benjamin there were also commanders.
One of them was Eliada. He was a brave soldier. He commanded 200,000 men. They were armed with bows and shields.
[18] Another was Jehozabad. He commanded 180,000 men. They were prepared for battle.

[19]Those were the men who served the king. He stationed some other men in the cities all through Judah. The cities had high walls around them.

Micaiah Prophesies Against Ahab

18 Jehoshaphat had great wealth and honor. He joined forces with Ahab by getting married to Ahab's daughter. [2]Some years later he went down to visit Ahab in Samaria. Ahab killed a lot of sheep and cattle for him and the people who were with him. Ahab tried to get Jehoshaphat to attack Ramoth Gilead. [3]Ahab was the king of Israel. He spoke to Jehoshaphat, the king of Judah. He asked, "Will you go with me to fight against Ramoth Gilead?"

Jehoshaphat replied, "Yes. I'll go with you. My men will also go with you. We'll join you in the war." [4]He continued, "First ask the LORD for advice."

[5]So the king of Israel brought 400 prophets together. He asked them, "Should we go to war against Ramoth Gilead? Or should I stay here?"

"Go," they answered. "God will hand it over to you."

[6]But Jehoshaphat asked, "Isn't there a prophet of the LORD here? If there is, ask him what we should do."

[7]The king of Israel answered Jehoshaphat. He said, "There is still one other man we can go to. We can ask the LORD for advice through him. But I hate him. He never prophesies anything good about me. He only prophesies bad things. His name is Micaiah. He's the son of Imlah."

"You shouldn't say bad things about him," Jehoshaphat replied.

[8]So the king of Israel called for one of his officials. He told him, "Bring Micaiah, the son of Imlah, at once."

9 The king of Israel and Jehoshaphat, the king of Judah, were wearing their royal robes. They were sitting on their thrones at the threshing floor. It was near the entrance of the gate of Samaria. All of the prophets were prophesying in front of them.

10 Zedekiah was the son of Kenaanah. Zedekiah had made horns out of iron. They looked like animal horns. He announced, "The LORD says, 'With these horns you will drive back the men of Aram until they are destroyed.'"

11 All of the other prophets were prophesying the same thing. "Attack Ramoth Gilead," they said. "Win the battle over it. The LORD will hand it over to you."

12 A messenger went to get Micaiah. He said to him, "Look. The other prophets agree. All of them are saying the king will have success. So agree with them. Say the same thing they do."

13 But Micaiah said, "You can be sure that the LORD lives. And you can be just as sure that I can only tell the king what my God says."

14 When Micaiah arrived, the king spoke to him. He asked, "Should we go to war against Ramoth Gilead? Or should I stay here?"

"Attack," he answered. "You will win. The people of Ramoth Gilead will be handed over to you."

15 The king said to him, "I've made you promise to tell the truth many times before. So don't tell me anything but the truth in the name of the LORD."

16 Then Micaiah answered, "I saw all of the people of Israel scattered on the hills. They were like sheep that didn't have a shepherd. The LORD said, 'These people do not have a master. Let each of them go home in peace.'"

17 The king of Israel spoke to Jehoshaphat. He said, "Didn't I tell you he never prophesies anything good about me? He only prophesies bad things."

18 Micaiah continued, "Listen to the LORD's message. I saw the LORD sitting on his throne. Some of the angels of heaven were standing at his right side. The others were standing at his left side. 19 The LORD said, 'Who will try to get Ahab, the king of Israel, to attack Ramoth Gilead? I want him to die there.'

"One angel suggested one thing. Another suggested something else. 20 Finally, a spirit came forward and stood in front of the LORD. The spirit said, 'I'll try to get Ahab to do it.'

"'How?' the LORD asked.

21 "The spirit said, 'I'll go and put lies in the mouths of all of his prophets.'

"'You will have success in getting Ahab to attack Ramoth Gilead,' said the LORD. 'Go and do it.'

22 "So the LORD has put lies in the mouths of your prophets. He has said that great harm will come to you."

23 Then Zedekiah, the son of Kenaanah, went up and slapped Micaiah in the face. "So you think the spirit that was sent by the LORD went away from me to speak to you, do you?" he asked. "Which way did he go?"

24 Micaiah replied, "You will find out on the day you go to hide in an inside room to save your life."

25 Then the king of Israel gave an order. He said, "Take Micaiah away. Send him back to Amon. Amon is the ruler of the city of Samaria. And send him back to Joash. Joash is a member of the royal court. 26 Tell them, 'The king says, "Put this fellow in prison. Don't give him anything but bread and water until I return safely."'"

27 Micaiah announced, "Do you really think you will return safely? If you do, the LORD hasn't spoken through me." He continued, "All of you people, remember what I've said!"

Ahab Is Killed at Ramoth Gilead

28 So the king of Israel went up to Ramoth Gilead. Jehoshaphat, the king of Judah, went there too.

29 The king of Israel spoke to Jehoshaphat. He said, "I'll go into battle wearing different clothes. Then people won't recognize me. But you wear your royal robes." So the king of Israel put on different clothes. Then he went into battle.

30 The king of Aram had given an order to his chariot commanders. He had said, "Fight only against the king of Israel. Don't fight against anyone else."

31 The chariot commanders saw Jehoshaphat. They thought, "That's the king of Israel." So they turned to attack him. But Jehoshaphat cried out. And the LORD helped him. God drew the commanders away from him. 32 They saw he wasn't the king of Israel after all. So they stopped chasing him.

33 But someone shot an arrow without taking aim. The arrow hit the king of Israel between the parts of his armor. The king told the chariot driver, "Turn the chariot around. Get me out of this battle. I've been wounded."

34 All day long the battle continued. The king of Israel kept himself standing up by leaning against the inside of his chariot. He kept his face toward the men of Aram until evening. At sunset he died.

19 Jehoshaphat, the king of Judah, returned safely to his palace in Jerusalem. 2 The prophet Jehu went out to meet him. He was the son of Hanani. Jehu said to the king, "You shouldn't help evil people. You shouldn't love those who hate the LORD. The LORD is angry with you. 3 But there's some good in you. You have gotten rid of all of the poles in the land that are used to worship the goddess Asherah. And you have worshiped God with all your heart."

Jehoshaphat Appoints Judges

4 Jehoshaphat lived in Jerusalem. He went out again among the people. He went from Beersheba to the hill country of Ephraim. He turned the people back to the LORD, the God of Israel.

5Jehoshaphat appointed judges in the land. He
put them in all of the cities of Judah that had high
walls around them. 6He told the judges, "Think
carefully about what you do. After all, you aren't
judging for mere men. You are judging for the
LORD. He's with you every time you make a decision. 7Have respect for the LORD. Judge carefully.
He is always right. He treats everyone the same.
He doesn't want his judges to take money from
people who want special favors."
8In Jerusalem, Jehoshaphat chose some Levites
and priests. He also chose some leaders of Israelite families. He appointed all of them to apply the
law of the LORD fairly. He wanted them to decide
cases. He wanted them to settle matters between
people. All of those judges lived in Jerusalem.
9Here are the orders Jehoshaphat gave them. He
said, "Have respect for the LORD. Serve him faithfully. Do it with all your heart. 10Cases will come
to you from your fellow judges who live in the
other cities. The cases might be about murder or
other matters that the law, commands, directions
and rules deal with. Warn the judges not to sin
against the LORD. If you don't warn them, he will
be angry with you and your fellow judges. Do
what I say. Then you won't sin.
11"The chief priest Amariah will be over you in
any matter that concerns the LORD. Zebadiah is the
leader of the tribe of Judah. He is the son of Ishmael. Zebadiah will be over you in any matter that
concerns the king. The Levites will serve as your
officials. Be brave. And may the LORD be with
those of you who do well."

Jehoshaphat Wins the Battle Over Moab and Ammon

20 After that, the Moabites, Ammonites and
some Meunites went to war against Jehoshaphat.
2Some people came and told him, "A huge army
is coming from Edom to fight against you. They
have come across the Dead Sea. They are already
in Hazazon Tamar." Hazazon Tamar is also called
En Gedi.
3Jehoshaphat was alarmed. So he decided to ask
the LORD for advice. He told all of the people of
Judah to go without eating. 4The people came
together to ask the LORD for help. In fact, they
came from every town in Judah to pray to him.
5Then Jehoshaphat stood up among the people
of Judah and Jerusalem. He was in front of the new
courtyard at the LORD's temple. 6He said,

"LORD, you are the God of our people.
You are the God who is in heaven. You rule
over all of the kingdoms of the nations. Your
hands are strong and powerful. No one can
fight against you and win.
7"Our God, you drove out the people who
lived in this land. You drove them out to
make room for your people Israel. You gave
this land forever to those who belong to the
family line of your friend Abraham.
8"They have lived in this land. They've
built a temple here for your Name. They
have said, 9'Suppose trouble comes on us. It
doesn't matter whether it's a punishing
sword, plague or hunger. We'll serve you.
We'll stand in front of this temple where
your Name is. We'll cry out to you when
we're in trouble. Then you will hear us. You
will save us.'
10"But here are men from Ammon, Moab
and Mount Seir. You wouldn't allow Israel
to march in and attack their territory when
the Israelites came from Egypt. So Israel
turned away from them. They didn't destroy
them. 11See how they are paying us back.
They are coming to drive us out. They want
to take over the land you gave us as our
share.
12"Our God, won't you please judge
them? We don't have the power to face this
huge army that's attacking us. We don't
know what to do. But we're looking to you
to help us."

13All of the men of Judah stood there in front of
the LORD. Their wives, children and little ones
were with them.
14Then the Spirit of the LORD came on Jahaziel.
He was standing among the people of Israel. He
was the son of Zechariah. Zechariah was the son of
Benaiah. Benaiah was the son of Jeiel. Jeiel was
the son of Mattaniah. Jahaziel was a Levite. He
was from the family line of Asaph.
15Jahaziel said, "King Jehoshaphat, listen! All
you who live in Judah and Jerusalem, listen! The
LORD says to you, 'Do not be afraid. Do not lose
hope because of this huge army. The battle is not
yours. It is mine.
16" 'Tomorrow march down against them. They
will be climbing up by the Pass of Ziz. You will
find them at the end of the valley in the Desert of
Jeruel. 17You will not have to fight this battle. Take
your positions. Stand firm. You will see how I will
save you. Judah and Jerusalem, do not be afraid.
Do not lose hope. Go out and face them tomorrow.
I will be with you.' "
18Jehoshaphat bowed down with his face
toward the ground. All of the people of Judah and
Jerusalem also bowed down. They worshiped the
LORD.
19Then some Levites from the families of Kohath and Korah stood up. They praised the LORD,
the God of Israel. They praised him with very loud
voices.
20Early in the morning all of the people left for
the Desert of Tekoa. As they started out, Jehoshaphat stood up. He said, "Judah, listen to me! People of Jerusalem, listen to me! Have faith in the
LORD your God. He'll take good care of you. Have
faith in his prophets. Then you will have success."

21 Jehoshaphat asked the people for advice. Then he appointed men to sing to the LORD. He wanted them to praise him because of his glory and holiness. They marched out in front of the army. They said,

"Give thanks to the LORD.
His faithful love continues forever."

22 They began to sing and praise him. Then the LORD hid some men and told them to wait. He wanted them to attack the people of Ammon, Moab and Mount Seir. They had gone into Judah and attacked it. But they lost the battle. 23 The men of Ammon and Moab rose up against the men from Mount Seir. They destroyed them. They put an end to them. When they finished killing the men from Seir, they destroyed each other.

24 The men of Judah came to the place that looks out over the desert. They turned to look down at the huge army. But all they saw was dead bodies lying there on the ground. No one had escaped.

25 So Jehoshaphat and his men went down there to carry off anything of value. Among the dead bodies they found a lot of supplies, clothes and articles of value. There was more than they could take away. There was so much it took three days to collect all of it.

26 On the fourth day they gathered together in the Valley of Beracah. There they praised the LORD. That's why it's called the Valley of Beracah to this very day.

27 Then all of the men of Judah and Jerusalem returned to Jerusalem. They were filled with joy. Jehoshaphat led them. The LORD had made them happy because all of their enemies were dead. 28 They entered Jerusalem and went to the LORD's temple. They were playing harps, lutes and trumpets.

29 All of the kingdoms of the surrounding countries began to have respect for God. They had heard how the LORD had fought against Israel's enemies.

30 The kingdom of Jehoshaphat was at peace. His God had given him peace and rest on every side.

Jehoshaphat's Rule Comes to an End

31 So Jehoshaphat ruled over Judah. He was 35 years old when he became Judah's king. He ruled in Jerusalem for 25 years. His mother's name was Azubah. She was the daughter of Shilhi.

32 Jehoshaphat followed the ways of his father Asa. He didn't wander away from them. He did what was right in the eyes of the LORD.

33 But the high places weren't removed. The people still hadn't worshiped the God of Israel with all their hearts.

34 The other events of Jehoshaphat's rule from beginning to end are written down. They are written in the official records of Jehu, the son of Hanani. They are written in the records of the kings of Israel.

35 Jehoshaphat king of Judah and Ahaziah king of Israel agreed to be friends. Ahaziah was guilty of doing what was evil. 36 Jehoshaphat agreed with him to build a lot of ships. They were built at Ezion Geber. They carried goods that were traded for other goods.

37 Eliezer was the son of Dodavahu from Mareshah. Eliezer prophesied against Jehoshaphat. He said, "You have joined forces with Ahaziah. So the LORD will destroy what you have made." The ships were wrecked. They were never able to sail or trade goods.

21 Jehoshaphat joined the members of his family who had already died. His body was buried in the family tomb in the City of David. His son Jehoram became the next king after him.

2 Jehoram's brothers, the sons of Jehoshaphat, were Azariah, Jehiel, Zechariah, Azariahu, Michael and Shephatiah. All of them were sons of Jehoshaphat, the king of Israel. 3 Their father had given them many gifts. He had given them silver, gold and articles of value. He had also given them cities in Judah that had high walls around them. But he had made Jehoram king. That's because Jehoram was his oldest son.

Jehoram Becomes King of Judah

4 Jehoram made his position secure over his father's kingdom. Then he killed all of his brothers with his sword. He also killed some of the princes of Israel.

5 Jehoram was 32 years old when he became king. He ruled in Jerusalem for eight years. 6 He followed the ways of the kings of Israel, just as the royal family of Ahab had done. In fact, he got married to a daughter of Ahab. Jehoram did what was evil in the sight of the LORD.

7 But the LORD didn't want to destroy the royal family of David. That's because the LORD had made a covenant with him. He had promised to keep the lamp of David's kingdom burning brightly for him and his children after him forever.

8 When Jehoram was king over Judah, Edom refused to remain under Judah's control. They set up their own king. 9 So Jehoram went to Edom. He took his officers and all of his chariots with him. The men of Edom surrounded him and his chariot commanders. But he got up at night and fought his way out. 10 To this very day Edom has refused to remain under Judah's control.

At that same time, Libnah also refused to remain under the control of Judah. That's because Jehoram had deserted the LORD, the God of his people. 11 He had also built high places on the hills of Judah. He had caused the people of Jerusalem to worship other gods. They weren't faithful to the LORD. Jehoram had led Judah down the wrong path.

12 Jehoram received a letter from the prophet Elijah. It said,

"The LORD is the God of your father David. The LORD says, 'You have not followed the ways of your own father Jehoshaphat or of Asa, the king of Judah. [13]Instead, you have followed the ways of the kings of Israel. You have led Judah and the people of Jerusalem to worship other gods, just as the royal family of Ahab did. Also, you have murdered your own brothers. They were members of your own family. They were better men than you are.

[14]" 'So now I am about to strike your people down with a heavy blow. I will strike down your sons, your wives and everything that belongs to you. [15]And you yourself will be very sick for a long time. The sickness will finally cause your insides to come out.' "

[16]The LORD stirred up the anger of the Philistines against Jehoram. He also stirred up the anger of the Arabs. They lived near the people of Cush. [17]The Philistines and Arabs attacked Judah. They went in and carried off all of the goods they found in the king's palace. They also took his sons and wives. The only son he had left was Ahaziah. He was the youngest son.

[18]After all of that, the LORD made Jehoram very sick. He couldn't be healed. [19]After he had been sick for two years, the sickness caused his insides to come out. He died in great pain. His people didn't make a fire in his honor, as they had done for the kings who ruled before him.

[20]Jehoram was 32 years old when he became king. He ruled in Jerusalem for eight years. No one was sorry when he passed away. His body was buried in the City of David. But it wasn't placed in the tombs of the kings.

Ahaziah Becomes King of Judah

22 The people of Jerusalem made Ahaziah king in place of Jehoram. Ahaziah was Jehoram's youngest son. Robbers had come with the Arabs into Jehoram's camp. The robbers had killed all of his older sons. So Ahaziah, the king of Judah, began to rule. He was the son of Jehoram.

[2]Ahaziah was 22 years old when he became king. He ruled in Jerusalem for one year. His mother's name was Athaliah. She was a granddaughter of Omri.

[3]Ahaziah also followed the ways of the royal family of Ahab. That's because Ahaziah's mother gave him bad advice. She told him to do what was wrong. [4]So he did what was evil in the sight of the LORD, just as the family of Ahab had done.

After Ahaziah's father died, the members of Ahab's family became his advisers. That's what destroyed him. [5]He also followed their advice when he joined forces with Joram, the king of Israel. They went to war against Hazael at Ramoth Gilead. Joram was the son of Ahab. Hazael was king of Aram. The soldiers of Aram wounded Joram. [6]So he returned to Jezreel to give his wounds time to heal. His enemies had wounded him at Ramoth in his battle against Hazael, the king of Aram.

Ahaziah, the son of Jehoram, went down to Jezreel. He went there to see Joram. That's because Joram had been wounded. Ahaziah was king of Judah. Joram was the son of Ahab.

[7]Through Ahaziah's visit to Joram, God caused Ahaziah to fall from power. When Ahaziah arrived, he rode out with Joram to meet Jehu, the son of Nimshi. The LORD had anointed Jehu to destroy the royal family of Ahab. [8]So Jehu punished Ahab's family, just as the LORD had told him to. While he was doing it, he found the princes of Judah and the sons of Ahaziah's relatives. They had been serving Ahaziah. So Jehu killed them. [9]Then he went to look for Ahaziah. Jehu's men captured him while he was hiding in Samaria. Ahaziah was brought to Jehu and put to death. People buried his body, because they said, "He was a grandson of Jehoshaphat, who followed the LORD with all his heart."

So no one in the royal family of Ahaziah was powerful enough to keep the kingdom.

Athaliah and Joash

[10]Athaliah was Ahaziah's mother. She saw that her son was dead. So she began to wipe out the whole royal house of Judah.

[11]But Jehosheba went and got Joash, the son of Ahaziah. She was the daughter of King Jehoram. She stole Joash away from among the royal princes. All of them were about to be murdered. She put Joash and his nurse in a bedroom. Jehosheba, the daughter of King Jehoram, was the wife of the priest Jehoiada. She was also Ahaziah's sister.

So Jehosheba hid the child from Athaliah. That's why Athaliah couldn't kill him. [12]The child remained hidden with the priest and his wife at God's temple for six years. Athaliah ruled over the land during that time.

23 When Joash was seven years old, Jehoiada showed how strong he was. He made a covenant with the commanders of companies of 100 men. The commanders were Azariah son of Jeroham, Ishmael son of Jehohanan, Azariah son of Obed, Maaseiah son of Adaiah, and Elishaphat son of Zicri. [2]They went all through Judah. They gathered together the Levites and the leaders of Israelite families from all of the towns. They came to Jerusalem. [3]The whole community made a covenant with the new king at God's temple.

Jehoiada said to them, "Ahaziah's son will rule over Judah. That's what the LORD promised concerning the family line of David. [4]Here's what I want you to do. A third of you priests and Levites who are going on duty on the Sabbath day must guard the doors. [5]A third of you must guard the royal palace. And a third of you must guard the

Foundation Gate. All of the other men must guard the courtyards of the LORD's temple.

6"Don't let anyone enter the temple except the priests and Levites who are on duty. They can enter because they are set apart to the LORD. But all of the other men must guard the places where the LORD has sent them.

7"The Levites must station themselves around the new king. Each man must have his weapons in his hand. Anyone else who enters the temple must be put to death. Stay close to the king no matter where he goes."

8The Levites did just as the priest Jehoiada ordered. So did all of the men of Judah. Each commander got his men. Some of the men were going on duty on the Sabbath day. Others were going off duty. Jehoiada didn't let any of the groups go. 9Then he gave weapons to the commanders of the companies. He gave them spears, large shields and small shields. The weapons had belonged to King David. They had been in God's temple.

10Jehoiada stationed all of the men around the new king. Each man had his weapon in his hand. They were standing near the altar and the temple. They stood from the south side of the temple to its north side. Their line formed half of a circle.

11Jehoiada and his sons brought Ahaziah's son out. They put the crown on him. They gave him a copy of the covenant. And they announced that he was king. They anointed him. Then they shouted, "May the king live a long time!"

12Athaliah heard the noise of the people running and cheering the new king. So she went to them at the LORD's temple.

13She looked. And there was the king! He was standing next to his pillar at the entrance. The officers and trumpet players were standing beside the king. All of the people of the land were filled with joy. They were blowing trumpets. Singers with their musical instruments were leading the songs of praise.

Then Athaliah tore her royal robes. She shouted, "Treason! It's treason!"

14The priest Jehoiada sent out the commanders of the companies of 100 men. They were in charge of the troops. He said to them, "Bring her away from the temple between the line of guards. Use your swords to kill anyone who follows her." The priest had said, "Don't put her to death at the LORD's temple."

15So they grabbed hold of her as she reached the entrance of the Horse Gate on the palace grounds. There they put her to death.

16Then Jehoiada made a covenant. He promised that he, the people and the king would be the LORD's people.

17All of the people went to Baal's temple. They tore it down. They smashed the altars and the statues of gods. They killed Mattan in front of the altars. He was the priest of Baal.

18Then Jehoiada put the priests, who were Levites, in charge of the LORD's temple. David had given them their duties in the temple. He had appointed them to sacrifice burnt offerings to the LORD. He wanted them to do it in keeping with what was written in the Law of Moses. David wanted them to sing and be full of joy.

19Jehoiada stationed guards at the gates of the LORD's temple. No one who was "unclean" in any way could enter.

20Jehoiada took with him the commanders of hundreds, the nobles, the rulers of the people, and all of the people of the land. He brought the new king down from the LORD's temple. They went into the palace through the Upper Gate. Then they seated the king on the royal throne.

21All of the people of the land were filled with joy. And the city was quiet. That's because Athaliah had been killed with a sword.

Joash Repairs the Temple

24 Joash was seven years old when he became king. He ruled in Jerusalem for 40 years. His mother's name was Zibiah. She was from Beersheba.

2Joash did what was right in the eyes of the LORD. He lived that way as long as the priest Jehoiada was alive. 3Jehoiada chose two wives for Joash. They had sons and daughters by Joash.

4Some time later Joash decided to make the LORD's temple look like new again. 5He called together the priests and Levites. He said to them, "Go to the towns of Judah. Collect the money that the nation of Israel owes every year. Use it to repair the temple of your God. Do it now." But the Levites didn't do it right away.

6So the king sent for the chief priest Jehoiada. He said to him, "Why haven't you required the Levites to bring in the tax from Judah and Jerusalem? It was set up by the LORD's servant Moses and the whole community of Israel. It was used for the tent where the tablets of the covenant were kept."

7The children of that evil woman Athaliah had broken into God's temple. They had used even its sacred objects for the gods that were named after Baal.

8King Joash commanded that a wooden chest be made. It was placed outside near the gate of the LORD's temple. 9Then a message went out in Judah and Jerusalem. It said that the people should bring the tax to the LORD. God's servant Moses had required Israel to pay that tax when they were in the desert.

10All of the officials and people gladly brought their money. They dropped it into the chest until it was full.

11The chest was brought in by the Levites to the king's officials. Every time the officials saw there was a large amount of money in the chest, it was emptied out. The royal secretary and the officer of the chief priest came and emptied it. Then they carried it back to its place. They did it regularly. They collected a great amount of money.

12The king and Jehoiada gave it to the men who were doing the work on the LORD's temple. They hired people who could lay the stones and people who could work with wood. They also hired people who could work with iron and bronze. They hired all of them to repair the temple.

13The men who were in charge of the work did their best. The repairs went very well under them. They rebuilt God's temple. They did it in keeping with its original plans. They made it stronger.

14So they finished the work. Then they brought the rest of the money to the king and Jehoiada. It was used to pay for the articles that were made for the LORD's temple. The articles were used for serving at the temple. They were also used for the burnt offerings. The articles included dishes and other objects that were made out of gold and silver. As long as Jehoiada lived, burnt offerings were sacrificed continually at the LORD's temple.

15Jehoiada had become very old. He died at the age of 130. 16His body was buried with the kings in the City of David. That's because he had done so many good things in Israel for God and his temple.

The Evil Things Joash Did

17After Jehoiada died, the officials of Judah came to King Joash. They bowed down to him. He listened to them. 18They turned their backs on the temple of the LORD, the God of their people. They worshiped poles that were made to honor the goddess Asherah. They also worshiped statues of other gods.

Because Judah and Jerusalem were guilty of sin, God became angry with them. 19The LORD sent prophets to the people to bring them back to him. The prophets gave witness against the people. But they wouldn't listen.

20Then the Spirit of God came on the priest Zechariah. He was the son of Jehoiada. Zechariah stood in front of the people. He told them, "God says, 'Why do you refuse to obey my commands? You will not have success. You have deserted me. So I have deserted you.'"

21But the people made evil plans against Zechariah. The king ordered them to kill Zechariah by throwing stones at him. They did it in the courtyard of the LORD's temple. 22King Joash didn't remember how kind Zechariah's father Jehoiada had been to him. So he killed Jehoiada's son.

As Zechariah was dying he said, "May the LORD see this. May he hold you accountable."

23In the spring, the army of Aram marched into Judah and Jerusalem against Joash. They killed all of the leaders of the people. They took a large amount of goods from Judah. They sent it to their king in Damascus. 24The army of Aram had come with only a few men. But the LORD allowed them to win the battle over a much larger army. Judah had deserted the LORD, the God of their people. That's why the LORD punished Joash.

25The army of Aram pulled back. They left Joash badly wounded. His officials planned to do evil things to him. That's because he murdered the son of the priest Jehoiada. They killed Joash in his bed. So he died. His body was buried in the City of David. But it wasn't placed in the tombs of the kings.

26Those who made the plans against Joash were Zabad and Jehozabad. Zabad was the son of Shimeath. She was from Ammon. Jehozabad was the son of Shimrith. She was from Moab.

27The story of the sons of Joash is written in the notes on the records of the kings. The many prophecies about him are written there too. So is the record of how he made God's temple look like new again. His son Amaziah became the next king after him.

Amaziah Becomes King of Judah

25 Amaziah was 25 years old when he became king. He ruled in Jerusalem for 29 years. His mother's name was Jehoaddin. She was from Jerusalem.

2Amaziah did what was right in the eyes of the LORD. But he didn't do it with all his heart. 3The kingdom was firmly under his control. So he put to death the officials who had murdered his father, the king.

4But he didn't put their children to death. He obeyed what is written in the Law, the Scroll of Moses. There the LORD commanded, "Parents must not be put to death because of what their children do. And children must not be put to death because of what their parents do. People must die because of their own sins." *(Deuteronomy 24:16)*

5Amaziah called the people of Judah together. He arranged them by families under commanders of thousands and commanders of hundreds. He did it for all of the people of Judah and Benjamin. Then he brought together the men who were 20 years old or more. He found out there were 300,000 men who were able to serve in the army. They could handle spears and shields. 6He also hired 100,000 fighting men from Israel. He had to pay them almost four tons of silver.

7But a man of God came to him. He said, "King Amaziah, these troops from Israel must not march out with you. The LORD is not with Israel. He isn't with any of the people of Ephraim. 8Go and fight bravely in battle if you want to. But God will destroy you right in front of your enemies. God has the power to help you or destroy you."

9Amaziah asked the man of God, "But what about all of that silver I paid for these Israelite troops?"

The man of God replied, "The LORD can give you much more than that."

10So Amaziah let the troops go who had come to him from Ephraim. He sent them home. They were very angry with Judah. In fact, they were burning with anger when they went home.

[11]Then Amaziah showed how strong he was. He led his army to the Valley of Salt. There he killed 10,000 men of Seir. [12]The army of Judah also captured 10,000 men alive. They took them to the top of a cliff. Then they threw them down. All of them were smashed to pieces.

[13]The troops Amaziah had sent back attacked some towns in Judah. He hadn't allowed the troops to take part in the war. They attacked towns from Samaria to Beth Horon. They killed 3,000 people. They carried off huge amounts of goods.

[14]Amaziah returned from killing the men of Edom. He brought back the statues of the gods of Seir. He set them up as his own gods. He bowed down to them. He burned sacrifices to them.

[15]The LORD's anger burned against Amaziah. He sent a prophet to him. The prophet said, "Why do you ask the gods of those people for advice? They couldn't even save their own people from your power!"

[16]While the prophet was still speaking, the king spoke to him. He said, "Did I ask you for advice? Stop! If you don't, you will be struck down."

So the prophet stopped. But then he said, "I know that God has decided to destroy you. That's because you have worshiped other gods. You haven't listened to my advice."

[17]Amaziah, the king of Judah, spoke to his advisers. Then he sent a message to Jehoash, the king of Israel. Jehoash was the son of Jehoahaz. Jehoahaz was the son of Jehu. Amaziah dared Jehoash, "Come on. Meet me face to face in battle."

[18]But Jehoash, the king of Israel, answered Amaziah, the king of Judah. He said, "A thorn bush in Lebanon sent a message to a cedar tree there. It said, 'Give your daughter to be married to my son.' Then a wild animal in Lebanon came along. It walked all over the thorn bush. [19]You brag that you have won the battle over Edom. You are very proud. But stay home! Why ask for trouble? Why bring yourself crashing down? Why bring Judah down with you?"

[20]But Amaziah wouldn't listen. That's because God had planned to hand Judah over to Jehoash. After all, they had asked the gods of Edom for advice.

[21]So Jehoash, the king of Israel, attacked. He and Amaziah, the king of Judah, faced each other in battle. The battle took place at Beth Shemesh in Judah. [22]Israel drove Judah away. Every man ran home.

[23]Jehoash king of Israel captured Amaziah king of Judah at Beth Shemesh. Amaziah was the son of Joash. Joash was the son of Ahaziah. Jehoash brought Amaziah to Jerusalem. He broke down part of its wall. It's the part that went from the Ephraim Gate to the Corner Gate. That part of the wall was 600 feet long.

[24]Jehoash took all of the gold and silver. He took all of the articles he found in God's temple. Obed-Edom had been in charge of them. Jehoash also took the palace treasures and the prisoners. Then he returned to Samaria.

[25]Amaziah king of Judah lived for 15 years after Jehoash king of Israel died. Amaziah was the son of Joash. Jehoash was the son of Jehoahaz.

[26]The other events of Amaziah's rule from beginning to end are written down. They are written in the records of the kings of Judah and Israel.

[27]Amaziah turned away from following the LORD. From that time on, some people made evil plans against him in Jerusalem. So he ran away to Lachish. But they sent men to Lachish after him. There they killed him. [28]His body was brought back on a horse. Then he was buried in the family tomb in Jerusalem, the City of Judah.

Uzziah Becomes King of Judah

26 All of the people of Judah made Uzziah king. He was 16 years old. They made him king in place of his father Amaziah.

[2]Uzziah rebuilt Elath. He brought it under Judah's control again. He did it after Amaziah joined the members of his family who had already died.

[3]Uzziah was 16 years old when he became king. He ruled in Jerusalem for 52 years. His mother's name was Jecoliah. She was from Jerusalem.

[4]Uzziah did what was right in the eyes of the LORD, just as his father Amaziah had done. [5]He looked to God during the days of Zechariah. Zechariah taught him to have respect for God. As long as Uzziah looked to the LORD, God gave him success.

[6]Uzziah went to war against the Philistines. He broke down the walls of Gath, Jabneh and Ashdod. Then he rebuilt some towns that were near Ashdod. He also rebuilt some other towns where Philistines lived. [7]God helped him fight against the Philistines. He also helped him fight against the Meunites and against the Arabs who lived in Gur Baal. [8]The Ammonites brought to Uzziah the gifts he required of them. He became famous all the way to the border of Egypt. That's because he had become very powerful.

[9]Uzziah built towers in Jerusalem. They were at the Corner Gate, the Valley Gate and the angle of the wall. He made the towers very strong. [10]He also built towers in the desert.

He dug many wells, because he had a lot of livestock. The livestock were in the western hills and on the flatlands. Uzziah had people working in his fields and vineyards in the hills and in the rich lands. That's because he loved the soil.

[11]Uzziah's army was well trained. It was ready to march out by companies in keeping with their numbers. Jeiel and Maaseiah brought them together. Jeiel was the secretary. Maaseiah was the officer. They were under the direction of Hananiah. He was one of the royal officials. [12]The total number of family leaders who were over the fighting men was 2,600. [13]An army of 307,500 men was under their command. The men were trained for war. They

were a powerful force. They helped the king against
his enemies. [14]Uzziah provided the entire army with
shields, spears, helmets, coats of armor, bows, and
stones for their slings. [15]In Jerusalem he made
machines that were based on patterns that skilled
men had drawn up. The machines were used on the
towers and on the corners of walls. They could
shoot arrows. They could also throw large stones.

Uzziah became famous everywhere. God
greatly helped him until he became powerful.

[16]But after Uzziah became powerful, his pride
brought him down. He wasn't faithful to the LORD
his God. He entered the LORD's temple to burn
incense on the altar for burning incense.

[17]The priest Azariah followed him in. So did 80
other brave priests of the LORD. [18]They stood up to
Uzziah. They said, "Uzziah, it isn't right for you
to burn incense to the LORD. Only the priests are
supposed to do that. They are members of the family line of Aaron. They have been set apart to burn
incense. So get out of here. Leave the temple. You
haven't been faithful. The LORD God won't honor
you."

[19]Uzziah was holding a shallow cup. He was
ready to burn incense. He became angry. He
shouted at the priests in the LORD's temple. He did
it near the altar for burning incense.

While he was shouting, a skin disease suddenly
broke out on his forehead. [20]The chief priest Azariah looked at him. So did all of the other priests.
They saw that Uzziah had a skin disease on his
forehead. So they hurried him out of the temple.
Actually, he himself really wanted to leave. He
knew that the LORD was making him suffer.

[21]King Uzziah had the skin disease until the day
he died. He lived in a separate house because he
had the disease. And he wasn't allowed to enter the
LORD's temple.

Uzziah's son Jotham was in charge of the
palace. Jotham ruled over the people of the land.

[22]The other events of Uzziah's rule from beginning to end were written down by the prophet Isaiah. Isaiah was the son of Amoz.

[23]Uzziah joined the members of his family who
had already died. His body was buried near theirs
in a royal burial ground. People said, "He had a
skin disease." His son Jotham became the next
king after him.

Jotham Becomes King of Judah

27 Jotham was 25 years old when he became
king. He ruled in Jerusalem for 16 years.
His mother's name was Jerusha. She was the
daughter of Zadok.

[2]Jotham did what was right in the eyes of the
LORD, just as his father Uzziah had done. But Jotham didn't enter the LORD's temple as Uzziah had
done. In spite of that, the people continued to do
very sinful things.

[3]Jotham rebuilt the Upper Gate of the LORD's
temple. He did a lot of work on the wall at the hill
of Ophel. [4]He built towns in the hills of Judah. He
also built forts and towers in areas that had a lot of
trees in them.

[5]Jotham went to war against the king of Ammon. He won the battle over the people of Ammon. That year they paid Jotham almost four tons
of silver. They paid him 62,000 bushels of wheat
and 62,000 bushels of barley. They also brought
him the same amount in the second and third
years.

[6]Jotham became powerful. That's because he
had worshiped the LORD his God with all his heart.

[7]The other events of Jotham's rule are written
down. That includes all of his wars and the other
things he did. All of those things are written in the
records of the kings of Israel and Judah. [8]Jotham
was 25 years old when he became king. He ruled
in Jerusalem for 16 years.

[9]Jotham joined the members of his family who
had already died. His body was buried in the City
of David. His son Ahaz became the next king after
him.

Ahaz Becomes King of Judah

28 Ahaz was 20 years old when he became
king. He ruled in Jerusalem for 16 years.

He didn't do what was right in the eyes of the
LORD. He didn't do what King David had done.
[2]He followed the ways of the kings of Israel. He
also made metal statues of gods that were named
after Baal. [3]He burned sacrifices in the Valley of
Ben Hinnom. He sacrificed his children in the fire
to other gods. He followed the practices of the
nations. The LORD hated those practices. He had
driven out those nations to make room for the people of Israel. [4]Ahaz offered sacrifices and burned
incense at the high places. He also did it on the
tops of hills and under every green tree.

[5]So the LORD his God handed him over to the
king of Aram. The men of Aram won the battle
over him. They took many of his people as prisoners. They brought them to Damascus.

God also handed Ahaz over to Pekah. His army
wounded or killed many of the troops of Ahaz. Pekah was king of Israel. [6]In one day Pekah killed
120,000 soldiers in Judah. That's because Judah
had deserted the LORD, the God of their people.
Pekah was the son of Remaliah.

[7]Zicri was a fighting man from Ephraim. He
killed Maaseiah, Azrikam and Elkanah. Maaseiah
was the king's son. Azrikam was the officer who
was in charge of the palace. And Elkanah was next
in command after the king. [8]The men of Israel captured 200,000 wives, sons and daughters from their
relatives in Judah. They also took a large amount
of goods. They carried all of it back to Samaria.

[9]But a prophet of the LORD was there. His name
was Oded. When the army returned to Samaria, he
went out to meet them. He said to them, "The
LORD is the God of your people. He burned with
anger against Judah. So he handed them over to

you. But you have killed them. Your anger reached all the way to heaven.

10“Now you are planning to make the men and women of Judah and Jerusalem your slaves. But aren’t you also guilty of sins against the LORD your God? 11Listen to me! You have taken your relatives from Judah as prisoners. The LORD’s anger is burning against you. So send your relatives back.”

12Then some of the leaders in Ephraim stood up to those who were returning from the war. The leaders were Azariah, Berekiah, Jehizkiah and Amasa. Azariah was the son of Jehohanan. Berekiah was the son of Meshillemoth. Jehizkiah was the son of Shallum. And Amasa was the son of Hadlai. 13“Don’t bring those prisoners here,” they said. “If you do, we’ll be guilty in the sight of the LORD. Do you really want to add to our sin and guilt? We’re already very guilty. The LORD’s anger is burning against Israel.”

14So the soldiers gave up the prisoners and the goods they had taken. They did it in front of the officials and the whole community. 15Azariah, Berekiah, Jehizkiah and Amasa received the prisoners. From the goods that had been taken they gave clothes to all those who were naked. They gave them clothes, sandals, food, drink and healing lotion. They put all of the weak people on donkeys. They took them back to their relatives at Jericho. Then they returned to Samaria. Jericho was also known as the City of Palm Trees.

16At that time King Ahaz sent men to the king of Assyria to get help. 17The men of Edom had come again and attacked Judah. They had carried prisoners away. 18At the same time the Philistines had attacked towns in the western hills and in the Negev Desert of Judah. They had captured Beth Shemesh, Aijalon and Gederoth. They had also captured Soco, Timnah and Gimzo and the villages that were around them. They had settled down in all of them.

19The LORD had brought Judah down because of Ahaz, their king. Ahaz had stirred up the people of Judah to do evil things. He hadn’t been faithful to the LORD at all.

20Tiglath-Pileser came to Ahaz. But he gave Ahaz trouble instead of help. Tiglath-Pileser was king of Assyria. 21Ahaz took some things from the LORD’s temple. He also took some from the royal palace and from the princes. He gave all of them to the king of Assyria. But that didn’t help him.

22When King Ahaz was in trouble, he became even more unfaithful to the LORD. 23He offered sacrifices to the gods of Damascus. They had won the battle over him. He thought, “The gods of the kings of Aram have helped them. So I’ll sacrifice to them. Then they’ll help me.” But they brought him down. In fact, they brought the whole nation of Israel down.

24Ahaz gathered together everything that belonged to God’s temple. He took all of it away. He shut the doors of the LORD’s temple. He set up altars at every street corner in Jerusalem. 25In every town in Judah he built high places. Sacrifices were burned there to other gods. That made the LORD, the God of his people, very angry.

26The other events of the rule of Ahaz and all of his evil practices from beginning to end are written down. They are written in the records of the kings of Judah and Israel.

27Ahaz joined the members of his family who had already died. His body was buried in the city of Jerusalem. But it wasn’t placed in the tombs of the kings of Israel. His son Hezekiah became the next king after him.

Hezekiah Purifies the Temple

29 Hezekiah was 25 years old when he became king. He ruled in Jerusalem for 29 years. His mother’s name was Abijah. She was the daughter of Zechariah.

2Hezekiah did what was right in the eyes of the LORD, just as King David had done.

3In the first month of Hezekiah’s first year as king, he opened the doors of the LORD’s temple. He repaired them. 4He brought the priests and Levites in. He gathered them together in the open area on the east side of the temple.

5He said, “Levites, listen to me! Set yourselves apart to the LORD. Set apart the temple of the LORD. He’s the God of your people. Remove anything that is ‘unclean’ from the temple. 6Our people weren’t faithful. They did what was evil in the sight of the LORD our God. They deserted him. They turned their faces away from the place where he lives. They turned their backs on him. 7They also shut the doors of the temple porch. They put the lamps out. They didn’t burn incense at the temple. They didn’t sacrifice burnt offerings to the God of Israel there.

8“So the LORD has become angry with Judah and Jerusalem. He has made them look so bad that everyone is shocked when they see them. They laugh at them. You can see it with your own eyes. 9That’s why our people have been killed with swords. That’s why our sons and daughters and wives have become prisoners.

10“So I’m planning to make a covenant with the LORD, the God of Israel. Then he’ll turn his burning anger away from us.

11“My sons, don’t fail to obey the LORD. He has chosen you to stand in front of him and work for him. He wants you to serve him and burn incense to him.”

12Here are the Levites who went to work.

Mahath and Joel were from the family line of Kohath.
Mahath was the son of Amasai. Joel was the son of Azariah.
Kish and Azariah were from the family line of Merari.
Kish was the son of Abdi. Azariah was the son of Jehallelel.

Jonah

The L*ORD* *gave the fish a command.*
And it spit Jonah up onto dry land.
—Jonah 2:10

Baby Jesus

She gave birth to her first baby. It was a boy. She wrapped him in large strips of cloth. Then she placed him in a manger.

—Luke 2:7

Joah and Eden were from the family line of Gershon.
Joah was the son of Zimmah. Eden was the son of Joah.
13 Shimri and Jeiel were from
the family line of Elizaphan.
Zechariah and Mattaniah were from
the family line of Asaph.
14 Jehiel and Shimei were from
the family line of Heman.
Shemaiah and Uzziel were from
the family line of Jeduthun.

15 All of those Levites gathered the other Levites together. They set themselves apart to the LORD. Then they went in to purify the LORD's temple. That's what the king had ordered them to do. They did what the LORD told them to. 16 The priests went into the LORD's temple to make it pure. They brought out to the temple courtyard everything that was "unclean." They had found "unclean" things in the LORD's temple. The Levites took them and carried them out to the Kidron Valley.

17 On the first day of the first month they began to set everything in the temple apart to the LORD. By the eighth day of the month they reached the LORD's porch. For eight more days they set the LORD's temple itself apart to him. They finished on the 16th day of the first month.

18 Then they went to King Hezekiah. They reported, "We've purified the whole temple of the LORD. That includes the altar for burnt offerings and all of its tools. It also includes the table for the holy bread and all of its articles. 19 We've prepared all of the articles King Ahaz had removed. We've set them apart to the LORD. Ahaz had removed them while he was king. He wasn't faithful to the LORD. The articles are now in front of the LORD's altar."

20 Early the next morning King Hezekiah gathered the city officials together. They went up to the LORD's temple. 21 They brought seven bulls, seven rams, seven male lambs and seven male goats with them. They sacrificed the animals as a sin offering for the kingdom, for the temple and for Judah. The king commanded the priests to offer them on the LORD's altar. The priests were from the family line of Aaron.

22 They killed the bulls. Then they sprinkled the blood on the altar. Next they killed the rams and sprinkled the blood on the altar. Then they killed the lambs and sprinkled the blood on the altar.

23 The goats for the sin offering were brought to the king and the whole community. They placed their hands on them. 24 Then the priests killed the goats. They put the blood on the altar as a sin offering. It paid for the sin of the whole nation of Israel. The king had ordered the burnt offering and the sin offering for the whole nation.

25 He stationed the Levites in the LORD's temple. They had cymbals, harps and lyres. They did everything in the way King David, his prophet Gad, and the prophet Nathan had required. The LORD had given commands about all of those things through his prophets. 26 So the Levites stood ready with David's musical instruments. And the priests had their trumpets ready.

27 Hezekiah gave the order to sacrifice the burnt offering on the altar. The offering began. Singing to the LORD also began. The singing was accompanied by the trumpets and by the instruments of David. He had been king of Israel. 28 The whole community bowed down. They worshiped the LORD. At the same time the singers sang. The priests blew their trumpets. All of that continued until the burnt offering had been sacrificed.

29 So the offerings were finished. King Hezekiah got down on his knees. He worshiped the LORD. So did everyone who was with him.

30 The king and his officials ordered the Levites to praise the LORD. They used the words of David and the prophet Asaph. They sang praises with joy. They bowed their heads and worshiped the LORD.

31 Then Hezekiah said, "You have set yourselves apart to the LORD. Come and bring sacrifices and thank offerings to his temple."

So the whole community brought sacrifices and thank offerings. Everyone who wanted to brought burnt offerings.

32 The whole community brought 70 bulls, 100 rams and 200 male lambs. They brought all of them as burnt offerings to the LORD. 33 The total number of animals that were set apart as sacrifices to the LORD was 600 bulls and 3,000 sheep and goats.

34 But there weren't enough priests to skin all of the burnt offerings. So their brother Levites helped them. They worked until the task was finished. By that time other priests had been set apart to the LORD. The Levites had been more careful than the priests when they set themselves apart. 35 There were large numbers of burnt offerings, along with the drink offerings and the fat from the friendship offerings. They were offered along with the burnt offerings.

So the service of the LORD's temple was started up again. 36 Hezekiah and all of the people were filled with joy. That's because everything had been done so quickly. God had provided for his people in a wonderful way.

Hezekiah Celebrates the Passover Feast

30 Hezekiah sent a message to all of the people of Israel and Judah. He also wrote letters to the tribes of Ephraim and Manasseh. He invited everyone to come to the LORD's temple in Jerusalem. He wanted them to celebrate the Passover Feast in honor of the LORD. He is the God of Israel.

2 The king, his officials and the whole community in Jerusalem decided to celebrate the Passover in the second month. 3 They hadn't been able to celebrate it at the regular time. That's because

there weren't enough priests who had set themselves apart to the LORD. Also, the people hadn't gathered together in Jerusalem.

[4]The plan seemed good to the king and the whole community. [5]They decided to send a message all through Israel. It was sent out from Beersheba all the way to Dan. The message invited the people to come to Jerusalem. It invited them to celebrate the Passover in honor of the LORD, the God of Israel.

The Passover hadn't been celebrated by large numbers of people for a long time. It hadn't been done in keeping with what was written in the law.

[6]Messengers went all through Israel and Judah. They carried letters from the king and his officials. The king had ordered them to do that. The letters said,

> "People of Israel, return to the LORD. He is the God of Abraham, Isaac and Israel. Return to him. Then he will return to you who are left in the land. You have escaped from the power of the kings of Assyria.
>
> [7]"Don't be like the rest of your people and relatives. They weren't faithful to the LORD, the God of their people. That's why he punished them. He made them look so bad that everyone was shocked when they saw them. You can see it for yourselves.
>
> [8]"Don't be stubborn. Don't be as your people were. Obey the LORD. Come to the temple. He has set it apart to himself forever. Serve the LORD your God. Then he'll turn his burning anger away from you.
>
> [9]"Suppose you return to the LORD. Then those who captured your relatives and children will be kind to them. In fact, your relatives and children will come back to this land. The LORD your God is kind and tender. He won't turn away from you if you return to him."

[10]The messengers went from town to town in Ephraim and Manasseh. They went all the way to Zebulun. But the people made fun of them. They laughed at them. [11]In spite of that, some men from Asher, Manasseh and Zebulun made themselves low in the LORD's sight. They went to Jerusalem.

[12]God's powerful hand helped the people of Judah. He helped them agree with one another. So they did what the king and his officials had ordered. They did what the LORD told them to do.

[13]A very large crowd of people gathered together in Jerusalem. They went there to celebrate the Feast of Unleavened Bread. It took place in the second month. [14]They removed the altars in Jerusalem. They cleared away the altars for burning incense. They threw all of the altars into the Kidron Valley.

[15]They killed the Passover lamb on the 14th day of the second month. The priests and Levites were filled with shame. They set themselves apart to the LORD. They brought burnt offerings to his temple. [16]Then they went to their regular positions. They did it just as the Law of Moses, the man of God, required. The Levites gave the blood of the animals to the priests. The priests sprinkled it on the altar.

[17]Many people in the crowd hadn't set themselves apart to the LORD. They weren't "clean." They couldn't set their lambs apart to him. So the Levites had to kill the Passover lambs for all of them.

[18]Many people came from Ephraim, Manasseh, Issachar and Zebulun. Most of them hadn't made themselves pure and clean. But they still ate the Passover meal. That was against what was written in the law. But Hezekiah prayed for them. He said, "The LORD is good. May he forgive everyone [19]who wants to worship God with all his heart. God is the LORD, the God of their people. May God forgive them even if they aren't 'clean' in keeping with the rules of the temple."

[20]The LORD answered Hezekiah's prayer. He healed the people.

[21]The people of Israel who were in Jerusalem celebrated the Feast of Unleavened Bread. They celebrated for seven days with great joy.

The Levites and priests sang to the LORD every day. Their singing was accompanied by musical instruments. The instruments were used to praise the LORD.

[22]Hezekiah spoke words that gave hope to all of the Levites. They understood how to serve the LORD well. For the seven days of the Feast they ate the share that was given to them. They also sacrificed friendship offerings. They praised the LORD, the God of their people.

[23]Then the whole community agreed to celebrate the Feast for seven more days. So for another seven days they celebrated with joy.

[24]Hezekiah, the king of Judah, provided 1,000 bulls and 7,000 sheep and goats for the community. The officials provided 1,000 bulls and 10,000 sheep and goats for them. A large number of priests set themselves apart to the LORD.

[25]The entire community of Judah was filled with joy. So were the priests and Levites. And so were all of the people who had gathered together from Israel. That included the outsiders who had come from Israel. It also included those who lived in Judah.

[26]There was great joy in Jerusalem. There hadn't been anything like it in Israel since the days of Solomon, the son of David. Solomon had been king of Israel.

[27]The priests and Levites gave their blessing to the people. God heard them. Their prayer reached all the way to heaven. It's the holy place where he lives.

31 The Feast came to an end. The people of Israel who were in Jerusalem went out to the towns of Judah. They smashed the sacred

stones. They cut down the poles that were used to worship the goddess Asherah. They destroyed the high places and the altars. They did those things all through Judah and Benjamin. They also did them in Ephraim and Manasseh. They destroyed all of the objects that were used to worship other gods. Then the people returned to their own towns and property.

The People Bring Gifts to the LORD

2Hezekiah put the priests and Levites in groups based on their duties. The priests sacrificed burnt offerings and friendship offerings. The Levites served the LORD by giving thanks and singing praises at the gates of his house.

3The king gave some of his own possessions to the temple. He gave them for the morning and evening burnt offerings. He gave them for the burnt offerings for every Sabbath day. He gave them for the burnt offerings for every New Moon feast. And he gave them for the burnt offerings for every yearly appointed feast. He did it in keeping with what is written in the Law of the LORD.

4Hezekiah gave an order to the people who were living in Jerusalem. He commanded them to give to the priests and Levites the share they owed them. Then the priests and Levites could give their full attention to the Law of the LORD.

5The order went out. Right away the people of Israel began to give freely. They gave the first share of the harvest of their grain, fresh wine, olive oil and honey. They also gave the first share of everything else their fields produced. They brought a large amount. It was a tenth of everything.

6The people of Israel and Judah who lived in the towns of Judah brought a tenth of their herds and flocks. They also brought a tenth of the holy things they had set apart to the LORD their God. They put them in piles. 7They began doing it in the third month. They finished in the seventh month. 8Hezekiah and his officials came and saw the piles. When they did, they praised the LORD. And they blessed his people Israel.

9Hezekiah asked the priests and Levites about the piles. 10The chief priest Azariah answered him. He said, "The people have been bringing their gifts to the LORD's temple. Ever since they began to bring them, we've had enough to eat. We have even had plenty to spare. That's because the LORD has blessed his people. So we have a large amount left over." Azariah was from the family line of Zadok.

11Hezekiah gave orders to prepare storerooms in the LORD's temple. And it was done. 12The people were faithful. They brought in their offerings, a tenth of everything they produced, and the gifts they had set apart to the LORD. The Levite Conaniah was in charge of those things. His brother Shimei was next in command after him. 13Conaniah and his brother Shimei had directors who worked under them. Their names were Jehiel, Azaziah, Nahath, Asahel, Jerimoth, Jozabad, Eliel, Ismakiah, Mahath and Benaiah. King Hezekiah and Azariah had appointed them. Azariah was the official who was in charge of God's temple.

14The Levite Kore guarded the East Gate. He was in charge of the offerings people chose to give to God. He handed out the offerings that were made to the LORD. He also handed out the gifts that had been set apart to the LORD. Kore was the son of Imnah. 15Eden, Miniamin, Jeshua, Shemaiah, Amariah and Shecaniah helped Kore. They were faithful in helping him in the towns of the priests. They handed out gifts to their brother priests, group by group. They gave the gifts to young men and old men alike.

16In addition to that, they handed out gifts to the males who were three years old or more. The names of those males were listed in their family history. All of them would enter the LORD's temple. They would carry out their duties each day. Each group did all of the different things it was supposed to do.

17Kore and his Levite companions also handed out gifts to the priests. The priests were listed by their families in their family history. Those Levites also handed out gifts to the Levites who were 20 years old or more. Each group did all of the different things it was supposed to do.

18Those groups included all of the little ones, the wives, and the sons and daughters of the whole community. All of them were listed in their family history. They were faithful in setting themselves apart to serve the LORD.

19Some of the priests, who were from the family line of Aaron, lived in other towns or on farms around their towns. Men were chosen by name to hand out shares to those priests. They gave a share to every male among them. They also gave a share to everyone whose name was written down in the family history of the Levites.

20That's what Hezekiah did all through Judah. He did what was good and right. He was faithful to the LORD his God. 21He looked to his God. He worked for him with all his heart. That's the way he worked in everything he did to serve God's temple. He obeyed the law. He followed the LORD's commands. So he had success.

Sennacherib's Army Surrounds Jerusalem

32 Hezekiah had been completely faithful to the LORD. But in spite of that, Sennacherib came and marched into Judah. He was the king of Assyria. He surrounded the cities that had high walls around them. He got ready to attack them. He thought he could win the battle over them. He thought he could take them for himself.

2Hezekiah saw that Sennacherib had come to Jerusalem to make war against it. 3So he asked his officials and military leaders for advice. He asked them about blocking off the water from the springs

that were outside the city. They gave him the
advice he asked for.
4A large group of men gathered together. They
blocked all of the springs. They also blocked the
stream that flowed through the land. "Why should
the kings of Assyria come and find plenty of
water?" they asked.
5Then Hezekiah worked hard repairing all of
the broken parts of the wall. He built towers on it.
He built another wall outside that one. He built up
the areas that had been filled in around the City of
David. He also made large numbers of weapons
and shields.
6He appointed military officers over the people.
He gathered the officers together in front of him in
the open area at the city gate. He gave them words
of hope. He said, 7"Be strong. Be brave. Don't be
afraid. Don't lose hope. The king of Assyria has a
huge army with him. But there's a greater power
with us than there is with him. 8The only thing he
has is human strength. But the LORD our God is
with us. He will help us. He'll fight our battles."
The people had great faith in what Hezekiah,
the king of Judah, said.
9Later Sennacherib, the king of Assyria, and all
of his forces surrounded Lachish. They got ready
to attack it. At that time, he sent his officers to Jerusalem. They went there with a message for Hezekiah, the king of Judah. The message was also for
all of the people of Judah who were there. The
message said,

10"Sennacherib, the king of Assyria, says,
'Why are you putting your faith in what your
king says? Why do you remain in Jerusalem
when you are surrounded?
11"'Hezekiah says, "The LORD our God
will save us from the powerful hand of the
king of Assyria." But he isn't telling you the
truth. If you listen to him, you will die of
hunger and thirst.
12"'Didn't Hezekiah himself remove your
god's high places and altars? Didn't Hezekiah say to the people of Judah and Jerusalem,
"You must worship at one altar. You must
burn sacrifices on it"?
13"'Don't you know what I and the kings
who ruled before me have done? Don't you
know what we've done to all of the peoples
of the other lands? Were the gods of those
nations ever able to save their lands from my
power? 14The kings who ruled before me
destroyed many nations. Which one of the
gods of those nations has been able to save
his people from me? So how can your god
save you from my power?
15"'Don't let Hezekiah trick you. He's
telling you lies. Don't believe him. No god
of any nation or kingdom has been able to
save his people from my power. No god has
been able to save his people from the power
of the kings who ruled before me. So your
god won't save you from my power either!'"

16Sennacherib's officers spoke even more things
against the LORD God and his servant Hezekiah.
17The king also wrote letters against the LORD. His
letters made fun of the God of Israel. They said,
"The peoples of other lands have their gods. But
those gods didn't save their people from my powerful hand. So the god of Hezekiah won't save his
people from my powerful hand either."
18Then the officers called out in the Hebrew language to the people of Jerusalem who were on the
wall. They were trying to scare them and make
them afraid. That's because they wanted to capture
the city. 19They were comparing the God of Jerusalem to the gods of the other nations of the world.
But those gods were only statues. They had been
made by the hands of men.
20King Hezekiah cried out in prayer to God in
heaven. He prayed about the problem Jerusalem
was facing. So did the prophet Isaiah. He was the
son of Amoz.
21The LORD sent an angel. The angel wiped out
all of the enemy's fighting men, leaders and officers. He put an end to them right there in the camp
of the Assyrian king.
So Sennacherib went back to his own land in
shame. He went into the temple of his god. There
some of his own sons cut him down with their
swords.
22So the LORD saved Hezekiah and the people
of Jerusalem. He saved them from the power of
Sennacherib, the king of Assyria. He also saved
them from all of their other enemies. He took care
of them on every side.
23Many people brought offerings to Jerusalem
for the LORD. They brought expensive gifts for
Hezekiah, the king of Judah. From then on, all of
the nations thought highly of him.

Hezekiah's Pride, Success and Death

24In those days Hezekiah became sick. He knew
he was about to die. So he prayed to the LORD. And
the LORD answered him. He gave him a miraculous sign.
25But Hezekiah's heart was proud. He didn't
give thanks for the many kind things the LORD had
done for him. So the LORD became angry with him.
He also became angry with Judah and Jerusalem.
26Then Hezekiah had a change of heart. He was
sorry he had been proud. The people of Jerusalem
were also sorry they had sinned. So the LORD
wasn't angry with them as long as Hezekiah was
king.
27Hezekiah was very rich. He received great
honor. He made storerooms for his silver and gold.
He also made them for his jewels, spices, shields
and all kinds of expensive things. 28He made buildings to store the harvest of grain, fresh wine and
olive oil. He made barns for all kinds of cattle. He

made sheep pens for his flocks. 29 He built villages.
He gained large numbers of flocks and herds. God
had made him very rich.
30 Hezekiah blocked up the upper opening of the
Gihon spring. He directed the water to flow down
to the west side of the City of David. He had success in everything he did.
31 The rulers of Babylon sent messengers to him.
They asked him about the miraculous sign that had
taken place in the land. Then God left him to put
him to the test. He wanted to know everything that
was in his heart.
32 Hezekiah did many things that showed he was
faithful to the LORD. Those things and the other
events of his rule are written down. They are written in the record of the vision of the prophet Isaiah,
the son of Amoz. That record is part of the records
of the kings of Judah and Israel.
33 Hezekiah joined the members of his family
who had already died. His body was buried on the
hill where the tombs of David's family are. The
whole nation of Judah honored him when he died.
So did the people of Jerusalem. Hezekiah's son
Manasseh became the next king after him.

Manasseh Becomes King of Judah

33 Manasseh was 12 years old when he
became king. He ruled in Jerusalem for 55
years.
2 Manasseh did what was evil in the sight of the
LORD. He followed the practices of the nations.
The LORD hated those practices. He had driven
those nations out to make room for the people of
Israel.
3 Manasseh rebuilt the high places. His father
Hezekiah had destroyed them. Manasseh also set
up altars to the gods that were named after Baal.
He made poles that were used to worship the goddess Asherah. He even bowed down to all of the
stars. And he worshiped them.
4 He built altars in the LORD's temple. The LORD
had said about his temple, "My Name will remain
in Jerusalem forever." 5 In both courtyards of the
LORD's temple Manasseh built altars to honor all
of the stars.
6 He sacrificed his children in the fire to other
gods. He did it in the Valley of Ben Hinnom. He
practiced all kinds of evil magic. He took part in
worshiping evil powers. He got messages from
those who had died. He talked to the spirits of the
dead. He did many things that were evil in the
sight of the LORD. He made him very angry.
7 Manasseh had carved a statue of a god. He put
it in God's temple. God had spoken to David and
his son Solomon about the temple. He had said,
"My Name will be in this temple and in Jerusalem
forever. Out of all of the cities in the tribes of Israel I have chosen Jerusalem. 8 I gave this land to
your people who lived long ago. I will not make
the Israelites leave it again. But they must be careful to do everything I commanded them. They
must follow all of the laws, directions, and rules I
gave them through Moses."
9 But Manasseh led Judah and the people of Jerusalem down the wrong path. They did more evil
things than the nations the LORD had destroyed to
make room for the people of Israel.
10 The LORD spoke to Manasseh and his people.
But they didn't pay any attention to him. 11 So the
LORD brought the army commanders of the king
of Assyria against them. They took Manasseh as a
prisoner. They put a hook in his nose. They put
him in bronze chains. And they took him to Babylon.
12 When Manasseh was in trouble, he asked the
LORD his God to show favor to him. He made himself very low in the sight of the God of his people.
13 Manasseh prayed to him. When he did, the LORD
felt sorry for him. He answered his prayer. He
brought him back to Jerusalem and his kingdom.
Then Manasseh knew that the LORD is God.
14 After that, Manasseh rebuilt the outer wall of
the City of David. It was west of the Gihon spring
in the valley. It reached all the way to the entrance
of the Fish Gate. It went around the entire hill of
Ophel. Manasseh also made the wall much higher.
He stationed military commanders in all of the
cities in Judah that had high walls around them.
15 Manasseh got rid of the strange gods. He
removed the statue of one of those gods from the
LORD's temple. He also removed all of the altars
he had built on the temple hill and in Jerusalem.
He threw them out of the city. 16 Then he made the
LORD's altar look like new again. He sacrificed
friendship offerings and thank offerings on it. He
told the people of Judah to serve the LORD, the
God of Israel. 17 The people continued to offer sacrifices at the high places. But they offered them
only to the LORD their God.
18 The other events of Manasseh's rule are written down in the official records of the kings of Israel. They include his prayer to his God. They also
include the words the prophets spoke to him in the
name of the LORD, the God of Israel. 19 Everything
about Manasseh is written in the records of the
prophets. That includes his prayer and the fact that
God felt sorry for him. It includes everything he
did before he made himself low in the LORD's
sight. It includes all of his sins and the fact that he
wasn't faithful to the LORD. It includes the loca-
tions where he built high places. It includes the
places where he set up poles that were used to worship the goddess Asherah. And it includes the
places where he set up statues of other gods.
20 Manasseh joined the members of his family
who had already died. His body was buried in his
palace. His son Amon became the next king after
him.

Amon Becomes King of Judah

21 Amon was 22 years old when he became king.
He ruled in Jerusalem for two years.

22Amon did what was evil in the sight of the LORD, just as his father Manasseh had done. Amon worshiped and offered sacrifices to all of the statues of gods that Manasseh had made. 23He didn't make himself low in the LORD's sight as his father Manasseh had done. So Amon became even more guilty.

24Amon's officials made plans against him. They murdered him in his palace. 25Then the people of the land killed all those who had made plans against King Amon. They made his son Josiah king in his place.

Josiah Makes Judah a Better Nation

34 Josiah was eight years old when he became king. He ruled in Jerusalem for 31 years.

2He did what was right in the eyes of the LORD. He lived the way King David had lived. He didn't turn away from it to the right or the left.

3While he was still young, he began to worship the God of King David. It was the eighth year of Josiah's rule.

In his 12th year he began to get rid of the high places in Judah and Jerusalem. He removed the poles that were used to worship the goddess Asherah. He also removed the wooden and metal statues of gods. 4He ordered the altars of the gods that were named after Baal to be torn down. He cut to pieces the altars for burning incense that were above them. He smashed the Asherah poles. He also smashed the wooden and metal statues of gods. He broke all of them to pieces. He scattered the pieces over the graves of those who had offered sacrifices to those gods. 5He burned the bones of the priests on their altars. That's the way he made Judah and Jerusalem pure and clean.

6He went to the towns of Manasseh, Ephraim and Simeon. He went all the way to Naphtali. He also went to the destroyed places around all of those towns. 7Everywhere he went he tore down the altars and the Asherah poles. He crushed the statues of gods to powder. He cut to pieces all of the altars for burning incense. He destroyed all of those things everywhere in Israel. Then he went back to Jerusalem.

8In the 18th year of Josiah's rule, he decided to make the land and temple pure and clean. So he sent Shaphan, Maaseiah and Joah to repair the temple of the LORD his God. Shaphan was the son of Azaliah. Maaseiah was ruler of the city. And Joah, the son of Joahaz, kept the records.

9They went to the high priest Hilkiah. They gave him the money that had been brought into God's temple. The Levites who guarded the doors had collected it. They had received some of the money from the people of Manasseh, Ephraim and the others who remained in Israel. They had received the rest of it from the people of Judah and Benjamin and those who lived in Jerusalem.

10They put all of the money in the care of the men who had been appointed to direct the work on the LORD's temple. Those men paid the workers who repaired the temple and made it look like new again. 11They also gave money to the builders and those who worked with wood. The workers used it to buy lumber and blocks of stone. The lumber was used for the supports and beams for the buildings. The kings of Judah had let the buildings fall down.

12The men were faithful in doing the work. Jahath and Obadiah directed them. They were Levites from the family line of Merari. Zechariah and Meshullam also directed them. They were from the family line of Kohath. The Levites were skilled in playing musical instruments. 13They were in charge of the laborers. They directed all of the workers from job to job. Some of the Levites were secretaries and writers. Others guarded the doors.

Hilkiah Finds the Scroll of the Law

14The money that had been taken into the LORD's temple was being brought out. At that time the priest Hilkiah found the Scroll of the Law of the LORD. It had been given through Moses. 15Hilkiah spoke to the secretary Shaphan. He said, "I've found the Scroll of the Law in the LORD's temple." He gave it to Shaphan.

16Then Shaphan took the scroll to King Josiah. He told him, "Your officials are doing everything they've been asked to do. 17They have paid out the money that was in the LORD's temple. They've put it in the care of the directors and workers." 18Shaphan continued, "The priest Hilkiah has given me a scroll." Shaphan read some of it to the king.

19The king heard the words of the Law. When he did, he tore his royal robes. 20He gave orders to Hilkiah, Ahikam, Abdon, the secretary Shaphan and Asaiah. Ahikam was the son of Shaphan. Abdon was the son of Micah. And Asaiah was the king's attendant. Josiah commanded them, 21"Go. Ask the LORD for advice. Ask him about what is written in this scroll that has been found. Do it for me. Also do it for those who remain in Israel and Judah. The LORD has poured out his burning anger on us. That's because our people before us didn't obey what the LORD had said. They didn't do everything that is written in this scroll."

22Hilkiah and those the king had sent with him went to speak to the prophet Huldah. She was the wife of Shallum. Shallum was the son of Tokhath. Tokhath was the son of Hasrah. Shallum took care of the sacred robes. Huldah lived in the New Quarter of Jerusalem.

23She said to them, "The LORD is the God of Israel. He says, 'Tell the man who sent you to me, 24"The LORD says, 'I am going to bring horrible trouble on this place and its people. All of the curses that are written down in the scroll that has been read to the king of Judah will take place. 25That is because the people have deserted me. They have burned incense to other gods. They have made me very angry because of everything their hands have made. So I will pour out my burning anger on this place. The fire of my anger will not be put out.'"'

26"The king of Judah sent you to ask for advice. Tell him, 'The LORD is the God of Israel. He has a message for you about the things you heard. 27He says, "Your heart was tender. You made yourself low in my sight. You heard what I spoke against this place and its people. So you made yourself low. You tore your royal robes and sobbed. And I have heard you," announces the LORD.

28"'"You will join the members of your family who have already died. Your body will be buried in peace. Your eyes will not see all of the trouble I am going to bring on this place and those who live here."'"

Huldah's answer was taken back to the king.

29Then the king called together all of the elders of Judah and Jerusalem. 30He went up to the LORD's temple. The people of Judah and Jerusalem went with him. So did the priests and Levites. All of them went, from the least important of them to the most important. The king had all of the words of the Scroll of the Covenant read to them. The scroll had been found in the LORD's temple.

31The king stood next to his pillar. He agreed to the terms of the covenant in front of the LORD. He promised to follow him and obey his commands, directions and rules. He promised to obey them with all his heart and with all his soul. So he promised to obey the terms of the covenant that were written down in that scroll.

32Then he had everyone in Jerusalem and in Benjamin commit themselves to the covenant. The people of Jerusalem did it in keeping with the covenant of the God of Israel.

33Josiah removed all of the statues of gods from the whole territory that belonged to the people of Israel. The LORD hated those statues. Josiah had everyone in Israel serve the LORD their God. As long as he lived, they didn't fail to follow the LORD, the God of their people.

Josiah Celebrates the Passover Feast

35 Josiah celebrated the Passover Feast in Jerusalem in honor of the LORD. The Passover lamb was killed on the 14th day of the first month. 2Josiah appointed the priests to their duties. He cheered them up as they served the LORD at his temple.

3The Levites taught all of the people of Israel. The Levites had been set apart to the LORD. Josiah said to them, "Put the sacred ark of the covenant in the temple Solomon built. He was the son of David and king of Israel. The ark must not be carried around on your shoulders. Serve the LORD your God. Serve his people Israel. 4Prepare yourselves by families in your groups. Do it based on the directions that were written by David, the king of Israel, and by his son Solomon.

5"Stand at the temple. Stand there with a group of Levites for each group of families among your people. 6Kill the Passover lambs. Set yourselves apart to the LORD. Prepare the lambs for your people. Do what the LORD commanded through Moses."

7Josiah provided animals for the Passover offerings. He gave them for all of the people who were there. He gave a total of 30,000 sheep and goats and 3,000 head of cattle. He gave all of them from his own possessions.

8His officials also gave freely. They gave to the people and the priests and Levites. Hilkiah, Zechariah and Jehiel were in charge of God's temple. They gave the priests 2,600 Passover lambs and 300 head of cattle. 9Conaniah and his brothers Shemaiah and Nethanel also gave offerings. So did Hashabiah, Jeiel and Jozabad. All of them were the leaders of the Levites. They gave 5,000 Passover lambs and 500 head of cattle for the Levites.

10The Passover service was arranged. The priests stood in their places. The Levites were in their groups. That's what the king had ordered.

11The Passover lambs were killed. The priests sprinkled the blood that had been handed to them. The Levites skinned the animals.

12They set the burnt offerings to one side. Those offerings were for the smaller family groups of the people to offer to the LORD. That's what was written in the Scroll of Moses. The Levites did the same thing with the cattle.

13They cooked the Passover animals over the fire, just as the law required. They boiled the holy offerings in pots, large kettles and pans. They served the offerings quickly to all of the people.

14After that, they got things ready for themselves and the priests. That's because the priests, who were from the family line of Aaron, were busy until dark. They were sacrificing the burnt offerings and the fat parts. The Levites got things ready for themselves and for the priests, who belonged to Aaron's family line.

15Those who played music were from the family line of Asaph. They were in the places that had been set up by David, Asaph, Heman and Jeduthun. Jeduthun had been the king's prophet. The guards at each gate didn't have to leave their places. That's because their brother Levites got things ready for them.

16So at that time the entire service in honor of the LORD was carried out. The Passover Feast was celebrated. The burnt offerings were sacrificed on the LORD's altar. That's what King Josiah had ordered.

17The people of Israel who were there celebrated the Passover at that time. They observed the Feast of Unleavened Bread for seven days. 18The Passover hadn't been observed like that in Israel since the days of the prophet Samuel. None of the kings of Israel had ever celebrated a Passover like Josiah's. He celebrated it with the priests and Levites. All of the people of Judah and Israel were there along with the people of Jerusalem. 19That Passover Feast was celebrated in the 18th year of Josiah's rule.

Josiah Dies

[20]Josiah had put the temple in order. After all of that, Neco went up to fight at Carchemish. He was king of Egypt. Carchemish was on the Euphrates River. Josiah marched out to meet Neco in battle.

[21]But Neco sent messengers to him. They said, "King Josiah, there isn't any trouble between you and me. I'm not attacking you at this time. I'm at war with another country. God told me to hurry. He's with me. So stop opposing him. If you don't, he'll destroy you."

[22]But Josiah wouldn't turn away from Neco. He wore different clothes so people wouldn't recognize him. He wanted to go to war against Neco. He wouldn't listen to what God had commanded Neco to say. Instead, he went out to fight him on the flatlands of Megiddo.

[23]Men who had bows shot arrows at King Josiah. After he was hit, he told his officers, "Take me away. I'm badly wounded." [24]So they took him out of his chariot. They put him in his other chariot. They brought him to Jerusalem. There he died. His body was buried in the tombs of his family. All of the people of Judah and Jerusalem sobbed over him.

[25]Jeremiah wrote songs of sadness about Josiah. To this very day all of the male and female singers remember Josiah by singing those songs. That became a practice in Israel. The songs are written down in the Book of the Songs of Sadness.

[26]Josiah did many things that showed he was faithful to the LORD. Those things and the other events of Josiah's rule were in keeping with what is written in the Law of the LORD. [27]All of the events from beginning to end are written down. They are written in the records of the kings of Israel and Judah.

36 [1]The people of the land went and got Jehoahaz. He was the son of Josiah. The people made Jehoahaz king in Jerusalem in place of his father.

Jehoahaz Becomes King of Judah

[2]Jehoahaz was 23 years old when he became king. He ruled in Jerusalem for three months. [3]The king of Egypt removed him from his throne in Jerusalem. The king of Egypt made the people of Judah pay him a tax of almost four tons of silver and 75 pounds of gold.

[4]Neco, the king of Egypt, made Eliakim king over Judah and Jerusalem. Eliakim was a brother of Jehoahaz. Neco changed Eliakim's name to Jehoiakim. But he took Eliakim's brother Jehoahaz with him to Egypt.

Jehoiakim Becomes King of Judah

[5]Jehoiakim was 25 years old when he became king. He ruled in Jerusalem for 11 years. He did what was evil in the sight of the LORD his God.

[6]Nebuchadnezzar attacked him. Nebuchadnezzar was king of Babylonia. He put Jehoiakim in bronze chains. And he took him to Babylon. [7]Nebuchadnezzar also took articles from the LORD's temple. He took them to Babylon. He put them in his own temple there.

[8]The other events of Jehoiakim's rule are written in the records of the kings of Israel and Judah. He did things the LORD hated. Those things and everything that happened to him are also written in those records. His son Jehoiachin became the next king after him.

Jehoiachin Becomes King of Judah

[9]Jehoiachin was 18 years old when he became king. He ruled in Jerusalem for three months and ten days. He did what was evil in the sight of the LORD.

[10]In the spring, King Nebuchadnezzar sent for him. He brought him to Babylon. He also brought articles of value from the LORD's temple. He made Zedekiah king over Judah and Jerusalem. Zedekiah was Jehoiachin's uncle.

Zedekiah Becomes King of Judah

[11]Zedekiah was 21 years old when he became king. He ruled in Jerusalem for 11 years.

[12]He did what was evil in the sight of the LORD his God. He didn't pay any attention to the message the LORD spoke through the prophet Jeremiah.

[13]Zedekiah also refused to remain under the control of King Nebuchadnezzar. The king had made him take an oath in God's name. But his heart became very stubborn. He wouldn't turn to the LORD, the God of Israel.

[14]And that's not all. The people and the leaders of the priests became more and more unfaithful. They followed all of the practices of the nations. The LORD hated those practices. The people and leaders made the LORD's temple "unclean." The LORD had set the temple in Jerusalem apart in a special way for himself.

Nebuchadnezzar Destroys Jerusalem

[15]The LORD, the God of Israel, sent word to his people through his messengers. He sent it to them again and again. He took pity on his people. He also took pity on the temple where he lived.

[16]But God's people made fun of his messengers. They hated his words. They laughed at his prophets. Finally the LORD's burning anger was stirred up against his people. Nothing could save them.

[17]The LORD brought the king of Babylonia against them. The Babylonian army killed their young people with their swords at the temple. They didn't spare young men or women. They didn't spare the old people either. God handed all of them over to Nebuchadnezzar.

[18]Nebuchadnezzar carried off to Babylon all of the articles from God's temple. Some of the articles were large. Others were small. He carried off the treasures of the temple. He also carried off the

treasures that belonged to the king and his officials.
[19]The Babylonians set God's temple on fire.
They broke down the wall of Jerusalem. They
burned all of the palaces. They destroyed everything of value there.
[20]Nebuchadnezzar took the rest of the people to
Babylon as prisoners. They had escaped from
being killed with swords. They served him and his
sons. That lasted until the kingdom of Persia
became stronger than Babylonia.
[21]The land of Israel enjoyed its sabbath years. It
rested. That deserted land wasn't farmed for a full
70 years. What the LORD had spoken through Jeremiah came true.
[22]It was the first year of the rule of Cyrus. He
was king of Persia. The LORD stirred him up to
send a message all through his kingdom. It happened so that what the LORD had spoken through
Jeremiah would come true. The message was written down. It said,

[23]Cyrus, the king of Persia, says,
"'The LORD is the God of heaven. He has
given me all of the kingdoms on earth. He
has appointed me to build a temple for him at
Jerusalem in Judah. Any one of his people
among you can go up to Jerusalem. And may
the LORD your God be with you.'"

Ezra

Cyrus Helps the Jews Build the LORD's Temple

1 It was the first year of the rule of Cyrus. He was king of Persia. The LORD stirred him up to send a message all through his kingdom. It happened so that what the LORD had spoken through Jeremiah would come true. The message was written down. It said,

2 "Cyrus, the king of Persia, says,

> "'The LORD is the God of heaven. He has given me all of the kingdoms on earth. He has appointed me to build a temple for him at Jerusalem in Judah.
>
> 3 "'Any one of his people among you can go up to Jerusalem. And may your God be with you. You can build the LORD's temple. He is the God of Israel. He is the God who is in Jerusalem.
>
> 4 "'The people who are still left alive in every place must bring him gifts. They must provide him with silver and gold. They must bring goods and livestock. They should also bring any offerings they choose to. All of those gifts will be for God's temple in Jerusalem.'"

5 Then everyone God had stirred up got ready to go. They wanted to go up to Jerusalem and build the LORD's temple there. They included the family leaders of Judah and Benjamin. They also included the priests and Levites.

6 All of their neighbors helped them. They gave them silver and gold articles. They gave them goods and livestock. And they gave them gifts of great value. All of those things were added to the other offerings the people chose to give.

7 King Cyrus also brought out the articles that
belonged to the LORD's temple. Nebuchadnezzar
had carried them off from Jerusalem. He had put
them in the temple of his own god. 8 Cyrus, the
king of Persia, told Mithredath to bring them out.
Mithredath was in charge of the temple treasures.
He counted the articles. Then he gave them to
Sheshbazzar, the prince of Judah.

9 Here is a list of the articles.

> There were 30 gold dishes.
> There were 1,000 silver dishes.
> There were 29 silver pans.
> 10 There were 30 gold bowls.
> There were 410 matching silver bowls.
> There were 1,000 other articles.

11 The total number of gold and silver articles was 5,400. Sheshbazzar took all of them with him to Jerusalem. He brought them along when the Jews who had been forced to leave Judah came back from Babylon.

A List of People Who Returned to Judah

2 Nebuchadnezzar had taken many Jews away
from the land of Judah. He had forced them
to go to Babylonia as prisoners. Now they returned
to Jerusalem and Judah. All of them went back to
their own towns. Nebuchadnezzar was king of
Babylonia. 2 The leaders of the Jews included Zerubbabel, Jeshua, Nehemiah, Seraiah and Reela-
iah. They also included Mordecai, Bilshan,
Mispar, Bigvai, Rehum and Baanah.

Here is a list of the men of Israel who returned home.

3 There were 2,172 from the family line of Parosh.
4 There were 372 from Shephatiah.
5 There were 775 from Arah.
6 There were 2,812 from Pahath-Moab through the family line of Jeshua and Joab.
7 There were 1,254 from Elam.
8 There were 945 from Zattu.
9 There were 760 from Zaccai.
10 There were 642 from Bani.
11 There were 623 from Bebai.
12 There were 1,222 from Azgad.
13 There were 666 from Adonikam.
14 There were 2,056 from Bigvai.
15 There were 454 from Adin.
16 There were 98 from Ater through the family line of Hezekiah.
17 There were 323 from Bezai.
18 There were 112 from Jorah.
19 There were 223 from Hashum.
20 There were 95 from Gibbar.

21 There were 123 from the men of Bethlehem.
22 There were 56 from Netophah.
23 There were 128 from Anathoth.
24 There were 42 from Azmaveth.
25 There were 743 from Kiriath Jearim, Kephirah and Beeroth.
26 There were 621 from Ramah and Geba.
27 There were 122 from Micmash.
28 There were 223 from Bethel and Ai.
29 There were 52 from Nebo.
30 There were 156 from Magbish.
31 There were 1,254 from the other Elam.
32 There were 320 from Harim.
33 There were 725 from Lod, Hadid and Ono.
34 There were 345 from Jericho.
35 There were 3,630 from Senaah.

36 Here is a list of the priests.

There were 973 from the family line of Jedaiah through the line of Jeshua.

37 There were 1,052 from Immer.
38 There were 1,247 from Pashhur.
39 There were 1,017 from Harim.

40 Here is a list of the Levites.

There were 74 from the family lines of Jeshua and Kadmiel through the line of Hodaviah.

41 Here is a list of the singers.

There were 128 from the family line of Asaph.

42 Here is a list of the men who guarded the temple gates.

There were 139 from the family lines of
Shallum, Ater, Talmon,
Akkub, Hatita and Shobai.

43 Here is a list of the members of the family lines of the temple servants.

Ziha, Hasupha, Tabbaoth,
44 Keros, Siaha, Padon,
45 Lebanah, Hagabah, Akkub,
46 Hagab, Shalmai, Hanan,
47 Giddel, Gahar, Reaiah,
48 Rezin, Nekoda, Gazzam,
49 Uzza, Paseah, Besai,
50 Asnah, Meunim, Nephussim,
51 Bakbuk, Hakupha, Harhur,
52 Bazluth, Mehida, Harsha,
53 Barkos, Sisera, Temah,
54 Neziah, Hatipha

55 Here is a list of the members of the family lines of the servants of Solomon.

Sotai, Hassophereth, Peruda,
56 Jaala, Darkon, Giddel,
57 Shephatiah, Hattil,
Pokereth-Hazzebaim, Ami

58 The total number of the members of the family lines of the temple servants and the servants of Solomon was 392.

59 Many people came up to Judah from the towns of Tel Melah, Tel Harsha, Kerub, Addon and Immer. But they weren't able to prove that their families belonged to the people of Israel.

60 There were 652 of them from the family lines of
Delaiah, Tobiah and Nekoda.

61 Here is a list of the members of the family lines of the priests.

They were Hobaiah, Hakkoz and Barzillai. Barzillai had married a daughter of Barzillai from Gilead. So he was also called Barzillai.

62 The priests looked for their family records. But they couldn't find them. So they weren't able to serve as priests. They weren't "clean."

63 The governor gave them an order. He told them not to eat any of the most sacred food. They had to wait until there was a priest who could use the Urim and Thummim to find out what the LORD wanted them to do.

64 The total number of the entire group that returned was 42,360. 65 That didn't include their 7,337 male and female slaves. There were also 200 male and female singers. 66 And there were 736 horses, 245 mules, 67 435 camels and 6,720 donkeys.

68 All of the people arrived at the LORD's temple in Jerusalem. Then some of the leaders of the families brought offerings they chose to give. They would be used for rebuilding the house of God. It would stand in the same place it had been before. 69 The people gave money for the work. It was based on how much they had. They gave 1,100 pounds of gold. They also gave three tons of silver. And they gave 100 sets of clothes for the priests. All of that was added to the temple treasure.

70 The priests and Levites settled in their own towns. So did the singers, the men who guarded the gates, and the temple servants. The rest of the people of Israel also settled in their own towns.

The People Rebuild the Altar

3 The people of Israel had settled down in their towns. In the seventh month all of them gathered together in Jerusalem.

2 Then Jeshua began to build the altar for burnt offerings to honor the God of Israel. Jeshua was the son of Jehozadak. The other priests helped Jeshua. So did Zerubbabel and his men. They built the altar in keeping with what is written in the Law of Moses. Moses was a man of God. Zerubbabel was the son of Shealtiel.

3 The people who built the altar were afraid of the nations that were around them. But they built it anyway. They set it up where it had stood before. They sacrificed burnt offerings on it to the LORD. They offered the morning and evening sacrifices on it.

4 Then they celebrated the Feast of Booths. They did it in keeping with what is written in the Law. They sacrificed the number of burnt offerings that were required for each day.

5 After they celebrated the Feast of Booths, they sacrificed the regular burnt offerings. They offered the New Moon sacrifices. They also offered the sacrifices for all of the appointed sacred feasts of the LORD. And they sacrificed the offerings the people chose to give him. 6 On the first day of the seventh month they began to offer burnt offerings to the LORD. They did it even though the foundation of the LORD's temple hadn't been finished yet.

The People Begin to Rebuild the Temple

7The people gave money to those who worked
with stone and those who worked with wood. They
gave food and drink and olive oil to the people of
Sidon and Tyre. Then those people brought cedar
logs down from Lebanon to the Mediterranean
Sea. They floated them down to Joppa. Cyrus, the
king of Persia, authorized them to do it.

8It was the second month of the second year
after they had arrived at the house of God in Jerusalem. Zerubbabel, the son of Shealtiel, began the
work. Jeshua, the son of Jehozadak, helped him.
So did everyone else. That included the priests and
Levites. It also included the rest of those who had
returned to Jerusalem. They had been prisoners in
Babylonia. Levites who were 20 years old or more
were appointed to be in charge of building the
LORD's house.

9Those who joined together to direct the work
included Jeshua and his sons and brothers. They
also included Kadmiel and his sons. And they
included the sons of Henadad and all of their sons
and brothers. All of those men were Levites. Kadmiel and his sons were members of the family line
of Hodaviah.

10The builders laid the foundation of the LORD's
temple. Then the priests came. They were wearing
their special clothes. They brought their trumpets
with them. The Levites who belonged to the family line of Asaph also came. They brought their
cymbals with them. The priests and Levites took
their places to praise the LORD. They did everything just as King David had required them to.
11They sang to the LORD. They praised him. They
gave thanks to him. They said,

"The LORD is good.
His faithful love to Israel continues
forever."

All of the people gave a loud shout. They praised
the LORD. They were glad because the foundation
of the LORD's temple had been laid.

12But many of the older priests and Levites and
family leaders sobbed out loud. They had seen the
first temple. So when they saw the foundation of
the second temple being laid, they sobbed. Others
shouted with joy.

13No one could tell the difference between the
shouts of joy and the sounds of sobbing. That's
because the people made so much noise. The
sound was heard far away.

Enemies Oppose the Rebuilding of the Temple

4 The enemies of Judah and Benjamin heard
about what the people who had returned from
Babylonia were doing. They heard that they were
building a temple to honor the LORD. He is the
God of Israel. 2The enemies came to Zerubbabel.
The family leaders of Israel were with him. The
enemies said, "We want to help you build. We're
just like you. We worship your God. We offer sacrifices to him. We've been doing that ever since
the time of Esarhaddon. He was king of Assyria.
He brought our people here."

3Zerubbabel and Jeshua answered them. So did
the rest of the family leaders of Israel. They said,
"You can't help us build a temple to honor our God.
You aren't part of us. We'll build it ourselves. We'll
do it to honor the LORD. He is the God of Israel. Cyrus, the king of Persia, commanded us to build it."

4Then the nations that were around Judah tried
to make its people lose hope. They wanted to make
them afraid to go on building. 5So they hired advisers to work against them. They wanted their plans
to fail. They did it during the whole time Cyrus
was king of Persia. They kept doing it until Darius became king.

Later Enemies Also Oppose the Jews

6The enemies of the Jews brought charges
against the people of Judah and Jerusalem. It happened when Xerxes began to rule over Persia.

7Then Artaxerxes became king of Persia. During his rule, Bishlam, Mithredath, Tabeel and their
friends wrote a letter to him. It was written in the
Aramaic language. And it used the Aramaic
alphabet.

8Rehum and Shimshai also wrote a letter to
King Artaxerxes. Rehum was the commanding
officer. Shimshai was the secretary. Their letter
was against the people of Jerusalem. It said,

9We, Rehum and Shimshai, are writing this
letter. Rehum is the commanding officer.
Shimshai is the secretary. Our friends join us
in writing. They include the judges and officials who are in charge of the people from
Tripolis, Persia, Erech and Babylon. They
are also over the Elamites from Susa. 10And
they are over those who were forced to leave
their countries. The great King Ashurbani-
pal, who is worthy of honor, forced them to
leave. He settled them in the city of Samaria. He also settled them in other places west
of the Euphrates River.

11Here is a copy of the letter that was sent to Artaxerxes.

We are sending this letter to you, King Artaxerxes.

It is from your servants who live west of the
Euphrates River.

12We want you to know that the Jews who
left you and came up to us have gone to Jerusalem. They are rebuilding that evil city. It
has caused trouble for a long time. The Jews
are making its walls like new again. They are
repairing the foundations.

13Here is something else we want you to
know. Suppose this city is rebuilt. And suppose its walls are made like new again. Then

no more taxes, gifts or fees will be collected.
And there will be less money for you.
14We owe a lot to you. We don't want to
see dishonor brought on you. So we're sending this letter to tell you what is going on.
15Then you can have a search made in the
official records. Have someone check the
records of the kings who ruled before you.
If you do, you will find out that Jerusalem
is an evil city. It causes trouble for kings and
countries. For a long time the city has
refused to let anyone rule over it. That's why
it was destroyed. 16We want you to know that
this city shouldn't be rebuilt. Its walls
shouldn't be made like new again. If that
happens, you won't have anything left west
of the Euphrates River.

17The king replied,

I am writing this letter to Rehum, the commanding officer. I am also writing it to Shimshai, the secretary. And I am writing it to your friends who are living in Samaria and in other places west of the Euphrates River.

I give you my greetings.

18The letter you sent us has been read to
me. It has been explained to me in my language. 19I gave an order. I had a search made.
We found out that Jerusalem has a long history of turning against the kings of the countries that have ruled over it. It has refused to
remain under their control. It is always stirring up trouble. 20Jerusalem has had powerful
kings. Some of them ruled over everything
west of the Euphrates. Taxes, gifts and fees
were paid to them.
21So give an order to those men. Make
them stop their work. Then the city won't be
rebuilt until I give the order. 22Pay careful
attention to this matter. Why should we let
this danger grow? That would not be in our
best interests.

23The copy of the letter of King Artaxerxes was
read to Rehum and the secretary Shimshai. It was
also read to their friends. Right away they went to
the Jews in Jerusalem. They forced them to stop
their work.

24And so the work on the house of God in Jerusalem came to an end. Nothing more was done on
it until the second year that Darius was king of
Persia.

Tattenai Sends a Letter to King Darius

5 The prophets Haggai and Zechariah prophesied to the Jews in Judah and Jerusalem. They
spoke to them in the name of the God of Israel. He
had spoken to those prophets. Zechariah belonged
to the family line of Iddo.

2Zerubbabel, the son of Shealtiel, began to
work. So did Jeshua, the son of Jehozadak. They
began to rebuild the house of God in Jerusalem.
The prophets of God were right there with them.
They were helping them.
3At that time Tattenai was governor of the land
west of the Euphrates River. He and Shethar-Bozenai and their friends went to the Jews. They asked
them, "Who authorized you to rebuild this temple?
Who told you that you could make this building like
new again?" 4They also asked, "What are the names
of the men who are putting up this building?"
5But the God of the Jews was watching over
their elders. So they didn't have to stop their work.
First a report would have to be sent to Darius.
Then they would have to receive his answer in
writing.
6Here is a copy of the letter that was sent to
King Darius. It was from Tattenai, the governor of
the land west of the Euphrates. Shethar-Bozenai
joined him in writing it. So did their friends. They
were officials of that land. 7The report they sent to
the king said,

We are sending this letter to you, King Darius.

We give you our most friendly greetings.

8We want you to know that we went to the
land of Judah. We went to the temple of the
great God. The people are building it with
large stones. They are putting wooden beams
in the walls. The people are working hard.
The work is moving ahead very quickly
under the direction of the people.
9We asked the elders some questions. We
said to them, "Who authorized you to rebuild
this temple? Who told you that you could
make this building like new again?" 10We
also asked them their names. We wanted to
write down the names of their leaders for
your information.
11Here is the answer they gave us. They
said,

"We serve the God of heaven and earth.
We are rebuilding the temple that was built
many years ago. The great King Solomon
built it and finished it. 12But our people made
the God of heaven angry. So he handed them
over to Nebuchadnezzar from Chaldea. He
was king of Babylonia. He destroyed this
temple. He forced the Jews to leave their
own country. He took them away to Babylonia.
13"But King Cyrus gave an order to
rebuild this house of God. He gave it in the
first year he was king of Babylonia. 14He
even removed some gold and silver articles
from the temple of Babylon. Nebuchadnezzar had brought them there from the house
of God in Jerusalem. He had taken them to
the temple in Babylon.

"Then King Cyrus brought them out. He gave them to a man named Sheshbazzar. Cyrus had appointed him as governor. 15He told him, 'Take these articles with you. Go and put them in the temple in Jerusalem. Rebuild the house of God in the same place where it stood before.'

16"So Sheshbazzar made the trip to Jerusalem. He laid the foundations of the house of God there. From that day until now the people have been working on it. But they haven't finished it yet."

17If it pleases you, King Darius, let a search be made in the official records of the kings of Babylonia. Find out whether King Cyrus really did give an order to rebuild this house of God in Jerusalem. Then tell us what you decide to do.

King Darius Sends a Reply to Tattenai

6 King Darius gave an order. He had a search made in the official records that were stored among the treasures at Babylon. 2A scroll was found in a safe storeroom at Ecbatana in the land of Media. Here is what was written on it.

This is my official reply to your letter.

3In the first year that Cyrus was king, he gave an order. It concerned God's temple in Jerusalem. It said,

Rebuild the temple. Then the Jews can offer sacrifices there. Lay its foundations. The temple must be 90 feet high and 90 feet wide. 4Its walls must have three layers of large stones. They must also have a layer of beautiful wood. Use money from the royal treasures to pay for everything.

5The gold and silver articles from the house of God must be returned. Nebuchadnezzar had taken them from the first temple in Jerusalem. And he had brought them to Babylon. Now they must be returned to their places in the temple at Jerusalem. They must be put in the house of God there.

6Tattenai, you are governor of the land west of the Euphrates River. I want you to stay away from the temple in Jerusalem. Shethar-Bozenai and the other officials of that area must also stay away from it. 7Don't try to stop the work on God's temple. Let the governor of the Jews and their elders rebuild the house of their God. Let them build it in the same place where it stood before.

8Here is what I want you to do for the elders of the Jews. Here is how you must help the men who build the house of their God.

Pay all of their expenses from the royal treasures. Use the money you collect from the people who live west of the Euphrates. Don't let the work on the temple stop. 9Don't fail to give the priests in Jerusalem what they ask for each day. Give them what they need. Give them young bulls, rams and male lambs. The priests can use them to sacrifice burnt offerings to the God of heaven. Also give them wheat, salt, wine and olive oil. 10Give them those things so they can offer sacrifices that please the God of heaven. And I want them to pray that things will go well for me and my sons.

11Don't change this order. If a man tries to change it, he must be put to death. A pole must be pulled from his house. The pole must be stuck through his body. Then it must be set up where people can see it. Because the man tried to change my royal order, his house must be broken to pieces. 12God has chosen to put his Name in the temple at Jerusalem. May he wipe out any king or nation that lifts a hand to change this order. May he also wipe out anyone who tries to destroy the temple in Jerusalem.

That's what I have ordered. I am King Darius. Make sure you carry out my order.

The Temple Is Completed and Set Apart to God

13The governor Tattenai carried out the order King Darius had sent. So did Shethar-Bozenai and their friends.

14The elders of the Jews continued to build the temple. They enjoyed great success because of the preaching of the prophets Haggai and Zechariah. Zechariah belonged to the family line of Iddo.

The people finished building the temple. That's what the God of Israel had commanded them to do. Cyrus and Darius had given orders allowing them to do it. Later, Artaxerxes supplied many things that were needed in the temple. Those three men were kings of Persia.

15So the temple was completed on the third day of the month of Adar. It was in the sixth year that Darius was king.

16When the house of God was set apart, the people of Israel celebrated with joy. The priests and Levites joined them. So did the rest of those who had returned from Babylonia. 17When the house of God was set apart to him, the people sacrificed 100 bulls. They also sacrificed 200 rams and 400 male lambs. As a sin offering for the whole nation of Israel, the people sacrificed 12 male goats. One goat was sacrificed for each tribe in Israel.

18The priests were appointed to their companies. And the Levites were appointed to their groups. All of them served God at Jerusalem. They served him in keeping with what is written in the Scroll of Moses.

The People Celebrate the Passover Feast

19Those who had returned from Babylonia celebrated the Passover Feast. It was on the 14th day of the first month. [20]The priests and Levites had made themselves pure and clean. The Levites killed the Passover lamb for everyone who had returned from Babylonia. They also did it for themselves and their relatives, the priests.

[21]So the people of Israel who had returned ate the Passover lamb. They ate it together with all those who had separated themselves from the practices of their neighbors who weren't Jews. Those practices were "unclean." The people worshiped the LORD. He is the God of Israel.

[22]For seven days they celebrated the Feast of Unleavened Bread with joy. That's because the LORD had filled them with joy. They were glad because he had changed the mind of the king of Persia. So the king had helped them with the work on the house of the God of Israel.

Ezra Comes to Jerusalem

7 After all of those things had happened, Ezra came up to Jerusalem from Babylonia. It was during the rule of Artaxerxes. He was king of Persia. Ezra was the son of Seraiah. Seraiah was the son of Azariah. Azariah was the son of Hilkiah. [2]Hilkiah was the son of Shallum. Shallum was the son of Zadok. Zadok was the son of Ahitub. [3]Ahitub was the son of Amariah. Amariah was the son of Azariah. Azariah was the son of Meraioth. [4]Meraioth was the son of Zerahiah. Zerahiah was the son of Uzzi. Uzzi was the son of Bukki. [5]Bukki was the son of Abishua. Abishua was the son of Phinehas. Phinehas was the son of Eleazar. And Eleazar was the son of the chief priest Aaron.

[6]So Ezra came up from Babylonia. He was a teacher. He knew the Law of Moses very well. The LORD had given Israel that law. He is the God of Israel. The king had given Ezra everything he asked for. That's because the powerful hand of the LORD his God helped him.

[7]Some of the people of Israel came up to Jerusalem too. They included priests, Levites and singers. They also included the temple servants and those who guarded the temple gates. It was in the seventh year that Artaxerxes was king.

[8]Ezra arrived in Jerusalem in the fifth month of the seventh year of the king's rule. [9]Ezra had begun his journey from Babylonia on the first day of the first month. He arrived in Jerusalem on the first day of the fifth month. That's because the gracious hand of his God helped him.

[10]Ezra had committed himself to study and obey the Law of the LORD. He also wanted to teach the LORD's rules and laws in Israel.

King Artaxerxes Gives Ezra a Letter

[11]Ezra was a priest and teacher. He was an educated man. He knew the LORD's commands and rules for Israel very well. Here is a copy of a letter King Artaxerxes had given to Ezra. It said,

> [12]I, Artaxerxes, am writing this letter. I am the greatest king of all.
>
> I have given it to the priest Ezra. He is a teacher of the Law of the God of heaven.
>
> I give you my greetings.
>
> [13]Ezra, there are people from Israel in my kingdom. I am giving an order that any of them who want to go to Jerusalem with you can go. The order also allows priests and Levites to go with you.
>
> [14]I and my seven advisers are sending you to see how things are going in Judah and Jerusalem. Find out whether the people there are obeying the Law of your God. You have a copy of that law with you.
>
> [15]I and my advisers have freely given some silver and gold to the God of Israel. He lives in Jerusalem. Take the silver and gold with you. [16]Also take any other silver and gold you can get from the land of Babylonia. And take the offerings the people and priests choose to give for the temple of their God in Jerusalem. [17]Make sure you use the money to buy bulls, rams and male lambs. Also buy their grain offerings and drink offerings. Then sacrifice them on the altar of the temple of your God in Jerusalem.
>
> [18]You and the other Jews can do what you think is best with the rest of the silver and gold. Do what your God wants you to do. [19]Give to the God of Jerusalem all of the articles you are accountable for. Use them for worshiping your God in his temple. [20]You might need to supply some other things for the temple of your God. If you do, take them from among the royal treasures.
>
> [21]I, King Artaxerxes, also give this order. It applies to all those who are in charge of the treasures west of the Euphrates River. Make sure you provide anything the priest Ezra might ask you to give. He is a teacher of the Law of the God of heaven. [22]Give Ezra up to three and three-fourths tons of silver. Give him up to 600 bushels of wheat. Give him up to 600 gallons of wine. Also give him up to 600 gallons of olive oil. And give him as much salt as he needs.
>
> [23]Work hard for the temple of the God of heaven. Do everything he has required. I don't want him to be angry with my kingdom and the kingdom of my sons.
>
> [24]I want you to know that you don't have any authority to collect taxes, gifts or fees from these people. You can't collect them from the priests, Levites, singers or those who guard the temple gates. And you can't collect them from the temple servants or other workers at the house of God in Jerusalem.
>
> [25]Ezra, appoint judges and other court officials. When you do it, use the wisdom your God gives you. Those you appoint should do what is right and fair when they

judge people. They should do it for everyone who lives west of the Euphrates. They should do it for everyone who knows the laws of your God. And I want you to teach the people who don't know those laws.

26Anyone who doesn't obey the law of your God must be punished. The same thing applies to anyone who doesn't obey my law. The people must be punished in keeping with the laws they have broken. Some of them must be put to death. Others must be forced to leave the places where they live. Others must have their property taken away from them. Still others must be put in prison.

Ezra Praises the LORD

27People of Israel, give praise to the LORD. He is the God of our people who lived long ago. He has put it in the king's heart to bring honor to the LORD's temple in Jerusalem. The king has honored the LORD in his letter. 28The LORD has shown his good favor to me. He has caused the king and his advisers to show me their favor. In fact, all of the king's powerful officials have shown favor to me. The strong hand of the LORD my God helped me. That gave me new strength. So I gathered together leaders from Israel to go up to Jerusalem with me.

The Family Leaders Who Returned to Jerusalem With Ezra

8 Many family leaders came up to Jerusalem with me from Babylonia. So did others who were listed with them. It was during the time when Artaxerxes was king. Here is a list of those who came.

2Gershom came from the family line of Phinehas.

Daniel came from the family line of Ithamar.

Hattush came from the family line of David. 3Hattush also belonged to the family of Shecaniah.

Zechariah came from the family line of Parosh. The total number of men who were listed with him was 150.

4Eliehoenai came from the family line of Pahath-Moab. Eliehoenai was the son of Zerahiah. The total number of men with him was 200.

5Shecaniah came from the family line of Zattu. Shecaniah was the son of Jahaziel. The total number of men with him was 300.

6Ebed came from the family line of Adin. Ebed was the son of Jonathan. The total number of men with him was 50.

7Jeshaiah came from the family line of Elam. Jeshaiah was the son of Athaliah. The total number of men with him was 70.

8Zebadiah came from the family line of Shephatiah. Zebadiah was the son of Michael. The total number of men with him was 80.

9Obadiah came from the family line of Joab. Obadiah was the son of Jehiel. The total number of men with him was 218.

10Shelomith came from the family line of Bani. Shelomith was the son of Josiphiah. The total number of men with him was 160.

11Zechariah came from the family line of Bebai. Zechariah was the son of Bebai. The total number of men with him was 28.

12Johanan came from the family line of Azgad. Johanan was the son of Hakkatan. The total number of men with him was 110.

13Eliphelet, Jeuel and Shemaiah came from the family line of Adonikam. Some members of their family had gone up to Jerusalem before them. The total number of men with them was 60.

14Uthai and Zaccur came from the family line of Bigvai. The total number of men with them was 70.

Ezra Leads Many Jews Back to Jerusalem

15I gathered the people together at the waterway that flows toward Ahava. We camped there for three days. I looked for Levites among the people and priests. But I didn't find any. 16So I sent for Eliezer, Ariel, Shemaiah, Elnathan and Jarib. I also sent for Elnathan, Nathan, Zechariah and Meshullam. All of them were leaders. And I sent for Joiarib and Elnathan. They were very well educated.

17I sent all of those men to Iddo. He was the leader in Casiphia. He and his relatives were temple servants there. I told my men what to say to them. I wanted Iddo and his relatives to bring some attendants to us for the house of our God.

18The gracious hand of our God helped us. So they brought us Sherebiah. He was a man of ability. He came from the family line of Mahli. Mahli was the son of Levi. Levi was a son of Israel. They also brought us Sherebiah's sons and brothers. The total number of men was 18. 19And they brought Hashabiah and his brothers and nephews. They brought them together with Jeshaiah. He came from the family line of Merari. The total number of men was 20. 20They also brought 220 of the temple servants. That was a special group David and his officials had established. They were supposed to help the Levites. All of them were listed by name.

21I announced a fast by the waterway that flows toward Ahava. I told the people not to eat any food. In that way, we made ourselves low in the sight of God. We prayed that he would give us and our children a safe journey. We asked him to keep safe everything we owned.

22I was ashamed to ask King Artaxerxes for soldiers and horsemen. They could have kept us safe from enemies on the road. But we had told the king that our God would keep us safe. We had said, "The gracious hand of our God helps everyone who looks to him. But he becomes very angry with anyone who deserts him."

23So we didn't eat anything. We prayed to our God about all of those matters. And he answered our prayers.

24Then I set 12 of the leading priests apart. I also set apart Sherebiah, Hashabiah and ten of their relatives.

25I weighed out to them the offering of silver and gold and other articles. They had been given for the house of our God. The king, his advisers and officials, and all of the people of Israel who were there had given them. 26I weighed out 25 tons of silver to those men. I weighed out almost four tons of silver articles. I weighed out almost four tons of gold. 27I weighed out 20 gold bowls. They weighed 19 pounds. I also weighed out two fine articles. The bronze they were made out of was highly polished. They were as priceless as gold.

28I said to those men, "You are set apart to the LORD. So are these articles. The silver and gold were offered to the LORD by those who chose to give them. He is the God of your people. 29Guard all of those things carefully until you weigh them out. Weigh them in the special rooms of the LORD's temple in Jerusalem. Do it in front of the leading priests and the Levites. Make sure the family leaders of Israel are watching."

30Then the priests and Levites received the silver and gold and sacred articles. All of them had been weighed out. They were going to take them to the house of our God in Jerusalem.

31On the 12th day of the first month we started out. We left the waterway that flows toward Ahava. And we headed for Jerusalem. The powerful hand of our God helped us. He kept us safe from enemies and robbers along the way. 32So we arrived in Jerusalem. There we rested for three days.

33On the fourth day we weighed out the silver and gold. We also weighed out the sacred articles. We weighed everything in the house of our God. We handed all of it over to the priest Meremoth. He was the son of Uriah. Eleazar, Jozabad and Noadiah were with him. Eleazar was the son of Phinehas. Jozabad was the son of Jeshua. Noadiah was the son of Binnui. Jozabad and Noadiah were Levites. 34Everything was listed by number and weight. And the total weight was recorded at that time.

35Then the people sacrificed burnt offerings to the God of Israel. They had returned from Babylonia. They offered 12 bulls for the whole nation of Israel. They offered 96 rams and 77 male lambs. All of that was a burnt offering to the LORD. They sacrificed 12 male goats as a sin offering.

36They also handed over the king's orders. They gave them to the royal officials and governors who ruled over the land west of the Euphrates River. Then those men helped the people. They also did many things for the house of God.

Ezra Prays for the People

9 After all of those things had been done, the leaders came to me. They said, "The people of Israel have committed sins. Even the priests and Levites have sinned. They haven't kept themselves separate from the nations that are around them. The LORD hates the practices of those nations. He hates what the Canaanites, Hittites, Perizzites and Jebusites do. He also hates what the Ammonites, Moabites, Egyptians and Amorites do.

2"The men of Israel have gotten married to the daughters of some of those people. They've also taken some of those women for their sons to marry. So they've mixed our holy nation with the nations around us. By getting married to women who don't worship the LORD, we leaders and officials have led the way in breaking our covenant with him. We haven't been faithful to him."

3When I heard that, I tore my inner robe and my coat. I pulled hair from my head and beard. I was so shocked I sat down. 4Then everyone who trembled with fear because of what the God of Israel had said gathered around me. They came because the people who had returned from Babylonia had not been faithful. So I sat there in shock until the time of the evening sacrifice.

5Then I got up. I had been very sad for quite a while. My inner robe and my coat were torn. I fell down on my knees. I spread my hands out to the LORD my God. 6I prayed,

> "You are my God. I'm filled with shame and dishonor. I can hardly look to you and pray. That's because our sins are piled up above our heads. Our guilt reaches all the way to the heavens. 7We are filled with it. It has been like that ever since the days of our people who lived long ago.
>
> "Kings of other countries have killed many of us and our kings and priests with their swords. They've forced others to leave their own land. They've taken them away as prisoners. They've robbed others. They've made still others feel ashamed and dishonored.
>
> "All of those things have happened to us because we've committed so many sins. And that's how things still are to this very day.
>
> 8"But you are the LORD our God. Now you have shown us your favor for a short time. You have allowed a few of us to remain here. Your temple has given us new hope. So you have made things easier for us. You have

given us a little rest from our slavery. [9]We are still slaves. But you are our God. You haven't deserted us. You haven't left us in our slavery. You have been kind to us. The kings of Persia have seen it. You have given us new life to repair your temple and rebuild it. You have given us a place of safety in Judah and Jerusalem.

[10]"You are our God. What can we say after the way you have blessed us? We said no to what you commanded us to do.

[11]"You gave us your commands through your servants the prophets. You said, 'You are entering the land to take it as your own. The sinful practices of its people have polluted it. They have filled it with their unclean acts from one end to the other. The LORD hates all of their practices. [12]So don't let your daughters get married to their sons. And don't let their daughters marry your sons. Don't make a peace treaty with them at any time. Then you will be strong. You will eat the good things the land produces. And you will leave all of it to your children as their share. They and their children after them will enjoy it forever.'

[13]"Our evil acts and our terrible sins have brought about the things that have happened to us. You are our God. Because we sinned so much, you should have punished us even more than you have. But you have left many of your people alive. [14]Suppose we don't obey your commands again. And suppose we continue to get married to people who commit sins that you hate. If we do, you will be so angry with us that you will destroy us. You won't leave us even a few people. You won't leave anyone alive.

[15]"LORD, you are the God of Israel. You are holy. You always do what is right. Today you have left many of your people alive. Here we are with all of our guilt. You see the guilt of our sin. Because we have sinned, not one of us can stand in front of you."

The People Admit They Have Sinned

10 Ezra was praying and admitting to God that his people had sinned. He was sobbing and throwing himself down in front of the house of God. Then a large crowd gathered around him. Men, women and children were there. They too sobbed bitterly.

[2]Shecaniah spoke to Ezra. Shecaniah was the son of Jehiel. He belonged to the family line of Elam. Shecaniah said, "We haven't been faithful to our God. We've gotten married to women from the nations that are around us. In spite of that, there is still hope for Israel. [3]So let's make a covenant in the sight of our God. Let's promise to send away all of those women and their children. That's what you have advised us to do. Those who respect our God's commands have given us the same advice. We want to do what the Law says.

[4]"Get up, Ezra. This matter is in your hands. Do what you need to. We will be behind you all the way. Be brave and do it."

[5]So Ezra got up. He made the leading priests and Levites and all of the people of Israel take an oath. He made them promise they would do what Shecaniah had suggested. And they took the oath.

[6]Then Ezra left the house of God. He went to Jehohanan's room. Jehohanan was the son of Eliashib. While Ezra was there, he didn't eat any food. He didn't drink any water. That's because he was filled with sadness. He sobbed because the people weren't faithful to the LORD's commands. Those people were the ones who had returned from Babylonia.

[7]Then an announcement was sent all through Judah and Jerusalem. All those who had returned were told to gather together in Jerusalem. [8]They were supposed to come there before three days had passed. If they didn't, they would lose all of their property. They would also be removed from the community of those who had returned. That's what the officials and elders had decided.

[9]Before the three days were over, all of the men of Judah and Benjamin had gathered together in Jerusalem. It was the 20th day of the ninth month. They were sitting in the open area in front of the house of God. They were very upset by what they knew would happen. And they were upset because it was raining.

[10]Then the priest Ezra stood up. He said, "You haven't been faithful to the LORD. You have gotten married to women from other lands. So you have added to Israel's guilt. [11]Admit to the LORD that you have sinned. Tell the God of your people what you have done. Then do what he wants you to do. Separate yourselves from the nations that are around you. Send away your wives from other lands."

[12]The whole community answered with a loud voice. They said, "You are right! We must do as you say. [13]But there are a lot of people here. And it's the rainy season. So we can't stand outside. Besides, this matter can't be taken care of in just a day or two. That's because we have sinned terribly by what we've done.

[14]"Our officials can act for the whole community. Have everyone in our towns who has married a woman from another land come at a certain time. Tell them to come together with the elders and judges of each town. Then our God will turn his burning anger away from us concerning this whole matter."

[15]Only a few men opposed that. They included Jonathan and Jahzeiah. Meshullam and the Levite Shabbethai joined them. Jonathan was the son of Asahel. Jahzeiah was the son of Tikvah.

[16]So those who had returned did what had been suggested. The priest Ezra chose some family

leaders. There was one from each family group. All of them were chosen by name. They sat down to check out each case. They started on the first day of the tenth month. [17]By the first day of the first month they were finished. They had handled all of the cases of the men who had gotten married to women from other lands.

A List of Those Who Had Married Women From Other Lands

18 Among the family lines of the priests, here are the men who had married women from other lands.

Maaseiah, Eliezer, Jarib and Gedaliah
came from the family line of Jeshua and his brothers. Jeshua was the son of Jehozadak. [19]All of them made a firm promise to send their wives away. Each of those men brought a ram from his flock as a guilt offering.

20 Hanani and Zebadiah
came from the family line of Immer.

21 Maaseiah and Elijah
came from the family line of Harim. So did Shemaiah, Jehiel and Uzziah.

22 Elioenai, Maaseiah and Ishmael
came from the family line of Pashhur. So did Nethanel, Jozabad and Elasah.

23 Among the Levites, here are the men who had married women from other lands.

There were Jozabad, Shimei and Kelaiah. There were also Pethahiah, Judah and Eliezer. Kelaiah's other name was Kelita.

24 Eliashib came from the singers.
Shallum, Telem and Uri
came from the men who guarded the temple gates.

25 Among the other Israelites, here are the men who had married women from other lands.

Ramiah, Izziah, Malkijah and Mijamin
came from the family line of Parosh. So did Eleazar, Malkijah and Benaiah.

26 Mattaniah, Zechariah and Jehiel
came from the family line of Elam. So did Abdi, Jeremoth and Elijah.

27 Elioenai, Eliashib and Mattaniah
came from the family line of Zattu. So did Jeremoth, Zabad and Aziza.

28 Jehohanan, Hananiah, Zabbai and Athlai
came from the family line of Bebai.

29 Meshullam, Malluch and Adaiah
came from the family line of Bani. So did Jashub, Sheal and Jeremoth.

30 Adna, Kelal, Benaiah and Maaseiah
came from the family line of Pahath-Moab. So did Mattaniah, Bezalel, Binnui and Manasseh.

31 Eliezer, Ishijah, Malkijah, Shemaiah and Shimeon
came from the family line of Harim.
[32]So did Benjamin, Malluch and Shemariah.

33 Mattenai, Mattattah, Zabad and Eliphelet
came from the family line of Hashum. So did Jeremai, Manasseh and Shimei.

34 Maadai, Amram and Uel
came from the family line of Bani. [35]So
did Benaiah, Bedeiah, Keluhi, [36]Vaniah,
Meremoth, Eliashib, [37]Mattaniah, Mattenai and Jaasu.

38 Shimei came from the family line of Binnui. [39]So did Shelemiah, Nathan, Adaiah, [40]Macnadebai, Shashai, Sharai,
[41]Azarel, Shelemiah, Shemariah, [42]Shallum, Amariah and Joseph.

43 Jeiel, Mattithiah, Zabad and Zebina
came from the family line of Nebo. So did Jaddai, Joel and Benaiah.

[44]All of those men had married women from other lands. Some of them had even had children by those wives.

Nehemiah

Nehemiah Prays to the LORD

1 These are the words of Nehemiah. He was the son of Hacaliah.

I was in the safest place in Susa. I was there in the 20th year that Artaxerxes was king. It was in the month of Kislev. 2At that time Hanani came from Judah with some other men. He was one of my brothers. I asked him and the other men about the Jews who were left alive in Judah. They had returned from Babylonia. I also asked him about Jerusalem.

3He and the men who were with him said to me, "Some of the people who returned are still alive. They are back in the land of Judah. But they are having a hard time. People are making fun of them. The wall of Jerusalem is broken down. Its gates have been burned with fire."

4When I heard about those things, I sat down and sobbed. For several days I was very sad. I didn't eat any food. And I prayed to the God of heaven. 5I said,

"LORD, you are the God of heaven. You are a great and wonderful God. You keep the covenant you made with those who love you and obey your commands. You show them your love.

6"Please pay careful attention to my prayer. See how your people are suffering. Please listen to me. I'm praying to you day and night. I'm praying for the people of Israel. We Israelites have committed sins against you. All of us admit it. I and my family have also sinned against you. 7We've done some very evil things. We haven't obeyed the commands, rules and laws you gave your servant Moses.

8"Remember what you told him. You said, 'If you people are not faithful, I will scatter you among the nations. 9But if you return to me, I will bring you back. If you obey my commands, I will gather you together again. I will bring you back from the farthest places on earth. I will bring you to the special place where I have chosen to put my Name.'

10"LORD, they are your people. They serve you. You used your great strength and mighty hand to set them free from Egypt. 11Lord, please pay careful attention to my prayer. Listen to the prayers of all of us. We take delight in bringing honor to your name. Give me success today. Help King Artaxerxes show me his favor."

I was the king's wine taster.

Artaxerxes Sends Nehemiah to Jerusalem

2 Wine was brought in for King Artaxerxes. It was the month of Nisan in the 20th year of his rule. I got the wine and gave it to him. I hadn't been sad in front of him before. But now I was. 2So the king asked me, "Why are you looking so sad? You aren't sick. You must be feeling sad deep down inside."

I was really afraid. 3But I said to the king, "May you live forever! Why shouldn't I look sad? The city where my people of long ago are buried has been destroyed. And fire has burned up its gates."

4The king said to me, "What do you want?"

I prayed to the God of heaven. 5Then I answered the king, "Are you pleased with me, King Artaxerxes? If it pleases you, send me to Judah. Let me go to the city of Jerusalem. That's where my people are buried. I want to rebuild it."

6The queen was sitting beside the king. He turned and asked me, "How long will your journey take? When will you get back?" It pleased the king to send me. So I chose a certain time.

7I also said to him, "If it pleases you, may I take some letters with me? I want to give them to the governors of the land west of the Euphrates River. Then they'll help me travel safely through their territory until I arrive in Judah.

8"May I also have a letter to Asaph? He takes care of your forest. I want him to give me some logs so I can make beams out of them. I want to use them for the gates of the fort that is by the temple. Some of the logs will be used in the city wall. And I'll need some for the house I'm going to live in." The gracious hand of my God helped me. So the king gave me what I asked for.

9Then I went to the governors of the land west of the Euphrates. I gave them the king's letters. He had also sent army officers and horsemen along with me.

10Sanballat and Tobiah heard about what was happening. They were very upset that someone had come to work for the good of Israel's people. Sanballat was a Horonite. Tobiah was an official from Ammon.

Nehemiah Checks Out the Walls of Jerusalem

11I went to Jerusalem. I stayed there for three days. 12Then at night I took a few men with me to check out the walls. I hadn't told anyone what my God wanted me to do for Jerusalem. There weren't any donkeys with me except the one I was riding on.

13That night I went out through the Valley Gate. I went toward the Jackal Well and the Dung Gate.

I checked out the walls of Jerusalem. They had been broken down. I also checked the city gates. Fire had burned them up. 14I moved on toward the Fountain Gate and the King's Pool. But there wasn't enough room for my donkey to get through. 15It was still night. I went up the Kidron Valley. I kept checking the wall. Finally, I turned back. I went back in through the Valley Gate.

16The officials didn't know where I had gone. They didn't know what I had done either. That's because I hadn't said anything to anyone yet. I hadn't told the priests or nobles or officials. And I hadn't spoken to any others who would be rebuilding the wall.

17I said to them, "You can see the trouble we're in. Jerusalem has been destroyed. Fire has burned up its gates. Come on. Let's rebuild the wall of Jerusalem. Then people won't make fun of us anymore." 18I also told them how the gracious hand of my God was helping me. And I told them what the king had said to me.

They replied, "Let's start rebuilding." So they began that good work.

19But Sanballat, the Horonite, heard about it. So did Tobiah, the official from Ammon. Geshem, the Arab, heard about it too. All of them laughed at us. They made fun of us. "What do you think you are doing?" they asked. "Are you turning against the king?"

20I answered, "The God of heaven will give us success. We serve him. So we'll start rebuilding the walls. But you don't have any share in Jerusalem. You don't have any claim to it. You don't have any right to worship here."

A List of the People Who Repaired the Wall

3 The high priest Eliashib and the other priests went to work. They rebuilt the Sheep Gate. They set it apart to God. They put its doors in place. They continued to rebuild the wall up to the Tower of the Hundred. They set the tower apart to God. Then they continued to rebuild the wall all the way to the Tower of Hananel. 2Some men from Jericho rebuilt the next part of the wall. And Zaccur rebuilt the next part. He was the son of Imri.

3The sons of Hassenaah rebuilt the Fish Gate. They laid its beams. They put its doors and metal bolts and bars in place. 4Meremoth repaired the next part of the wall. He was the son of Uriah. Uriah was the son of Hakkoz. Next to Meremoth, Meshullam made some repairs. He was the son of Berekiah. Berekiah was the son of Meshezabel. Next to Meshullam, Zadok also made some repairs. He was the son of Baana. 5Some men from Tekoa repaired the next part of the wall. But their nobles refused to do any work at all. They didn't pay any attention to the people who were in charge of the work.

6Joiada and Meshullam repaired the Jeshanah Gate. Joiada was the son of Paseah. Meshullam was the son of Besodeiah. Joiada and Meshullam laid the beams of the gate. They put its doors and metal bolts and bars in place. 7Next to them, some men from Gibeon and Mizpah made repairs. They included Melatiah from Gibeon and Jadon from Meronoth. Those places were under the authority of the governor of the land west of the Euphrates River.

8Uzziel repaired the next part of the wall. He made his living by working with gold. He was the son of Harhaiah. Hananiah made repairs on the next part. He made his living by making perfume. So the wall of Jerusalem was made like new again all the way to the Broad Wall. 9Rephaiah repaired the next part. He was the son of Hur. Rephaiah ruled over half of the territory where Jerusalem was located.

10Jedaiah repaired the part of the wall that was across from his house. He was the son of Harumaph. Hattush made repairs next to Jedaiah. Hattush was the son of Hashabneiah. 11Malkijah and Hasshub repaired another part of the wall. They also repaired the Tower of the Ovens. Malkijah was the son of Harim. Hasshub was the son of Pahath-Moab.

12Shallum repaired the next part. His daughters helped him. He was the son of Hallohesh. Shallum ruled over the other half of the territory where Jerusalem was located.

13Hanun repaired the Valley Gate. Some people who lived in Zanoah helped him. They rebuilt it. They put its doors and metal bolts and bars in place. They also repaired 500 yards of the wall. They repaired it all the way to the Dung Gate.

14Malkijah repaired the Dung Gate. He was the son of Recab. Malkijah ruled over the territory where Beth Hakkerem was located. He rebuilt the gate. He put its doors and metal bolts and bars in place.

15Shallun repaired the Fountain Gate. He was the son of Col-Hozeh. Shallun ruled over the territory where Mizpah was located. He rebuilt the gate. He put a roof over it. And he put the doors and metal bolts and bars of the gate in place. He also repaired the wall by the Pool of Siloam. It was near the King's Garden. Shallun repaired the wall as far as the steps that go down from the City of David.

16Next to Shallun, Nehemiah made some repairs. He was the son of Azbuk. Nehemiah ruled over half of the territory where Beth Zur was located. He repaired the wall up to the part that was across from the tombs of David. He repaired it all the way to the man-made pool and the House of Heroes.

17Next to Nehemiah, some Levites made repairs. They worked under the direction of Rehum. He was the son of Bani. Next to Rehum, Hashabiah made repairs for his territory. He ruled over half of the territory where Keilah was located. 18Next to him, other people from that territory made some repairs. They worked under the direction of Binnui. He was the son of Henadad. Binnui ruled over the other half of the territory where Keilah was located.

19Next to him, Ezer repaired another part of the wall. He was the son of Jeshua. Ezer ruled over the territory where Mizpah was located. He repaired the part that was across from the place that went up to the storeroom where the weapons were kept. He repaired the wall up to the angle.

20Next to him, Baruch worked hard to repair another part of the wall. He was the son of Zabbai. He repaired the part from the angle to the entrance to Eliashib's house. Eliashib was high priest. 21Next to Baruch, Meremoth repaired another part. He was the son of Uriah. Uriah was the son of Hakkoz. Meremoth repaired the part from the entrance to Eliashib's house to the end of the house.

22Next to Meremoth, some priests from the surrounding area made repairs. 23Next to them, Benjamin and Hasshub repaired the part of the wall that was in front of their house. Next to them, Azariah repaired the part that was beside his house. He was the son of Maaseiah. Maaseiah was the son of Ananiah.

24Next to Azariah, Binnui made repairs on another part. Binnui was the son of Henadad. Binnui repaired the wall from Azariah's house to the angle and the corner. 25Palal worked across from the angle. He was the son of Uzai. Palal also worked across from the tower that was part of the upper palace. It was near the courtyard of the guard. Next to him, Pedaiah made some repairs. He was the son of Parosh.

26The temple servants who lived on the hill of Ophel helped him. They repaired the wall up to the part that was across from the Water Gate. It was toward the east and the palace tower. 27Next to the temple servants, the men from Tekoa repaired another part. They made repairs from the large palace tower to the wall of Ophel.

28The priests made repairs above the Horse Gate. Each priest repaired the part of the wall that was in front of his own house. 29Next to them, Zadok made repairs across from his house. He was the son of Immer. Next to Zadok, Shemaiah made some repairs. He was the son of Shecaniah. Shemaiah guarded the East Gate.

30Next to him, Hananiah and Hanun repaired another part of the wall. Hananiah was the son of Shelemiah. Hanun was the sixth son of Zalaph. Next to Hananiah and Hanun, Meshullam made some repairs. He was the son of Berekiah. Meshullam repaired the part that was across from where he lived.

31Next to him, Malkijah made some repairs. He made his living by working with gold. He repaired the wall up to the house of the temple servants and the traders. It was across from the Inspection Gate. He also repaired the wall as far as the room that was above the corner. 32The traders and those who made their living by working with gold made some repairs. They repaired the wall from the room above the corner to the Sheep Gate.

Nehemiah's Enemies Oppose Him

4 Sanballat heard that we were rebuilding the wall. So he burned with anger. He became very upset. He made fun of the Jews. 2He spoke to his friends and the army of Samaria. He said, "What are those Jews trying to do? Can they make their city wall like new again? Will they offer sacrifices? Can they finish everything in a single day? The stones from their city wall and buildings are piled up like trash. And everything has been badly burned. Can they use those stones to rebuild everything again?"

3Tobiah from Ammon was at Sanballat's side. He said, "What are they building? They're putting up a stone wall. But suppose a fox climbs on top of it. Even that will break it down!"

4I prayed to God. I said, "Our God, please listen to our prayer. Some people hate us. They're making fun of us. So let others make fun of them. Let them be carried off like stolen goods. Let them be taken to another country as prisoners. 5Don't hide your eyes from their guilt. Don't forgive their sins. They have made fun of the builders."

6So we rebuilt the wall. We repaired it until all of it was half as high as we wanted it to be. The people worked with all their heart.

7But Sanballat and Tobiah heard that Jerusalem's walls continued to be repaired. The Arabs and some people from Ammon heard the same thing. Some men from Ashdod heard about it too. They heard that the gaps in the wall were being filled in. So they burned with anger. 8All of them made evil plans to come and fight against Jerusalem. They wanted to stir up trouble against it.

9But we prayed to our God. We put guards on duty day and night to watch out for danger.

10During that time, the people in Judah spoke up. They said, "The workers are getting weaker and weaker all the time. Broken stones are piled up everywhere. They are in our way. So we can't rebuild the wall."

11And our enemies said, "We will be right there among them. We'll kill them. We'll put an end to their work. We'll do it before they even know it or see us."

12Then the Jews who lived near our enemies came to us. They told us ten times, "No matter where you are, they'll attack us."

13So I stationed some people behind the lowest parts of the wall. That's where our enemies could easily attack us. I stationed the people family by family. They had their swords, spears and bows with them.

14I looked things over. Then I stood up and spoke to the nobles, the officials and the rest of the people. I said, "Don't be afraid of your enemies. Remember the Lord. He is great and powerful. So fight for your brothers and sisters. Fight for your sons and daughters. Fight for your wives and homes."

15Our enemies heard that we knew what they were trying to do. They heard that God had blocked their evil plans. So all of us returned to the wall. Each of us did our own work.

16From that day on, half of my men did the work. The other half were given spears, shields, bows and armor. The officers stationed themselves behind all of the people of Judah. 17The people continued to build the wall. Those who carried supplies did their work with one hand. They held a weapon in the other hand. 18Each of the builders wore his sword at his side as he worked. But the man who blew the trumpet stayed with me.

19Then I spoke to the nobles, the officials and the rest of the people. I said, "This is a big job. It covers a lot of territory. We're separated too far from one another along the wall. 20When you hear the sound of the trumpet, join us at that location. Our God will fight for us!"

21So we continued the work. Half of the men held spears. We worked from the first light of sunrise until the stars came out at night. 22At that time I also spoke to the people. I told them, "Have every man and his helper stay inside Jerusalem at night. Then they can guard us at night. And they can work during the day."

23My relatives and I didn't take our clothes off. My men and the guards didn't take theirs off either. Each man kept his weapon with him, even when he went to get water.

Nehemiah Helps Some Poor People

5 Some men and their wives cried out against their Jewish brothers and sisters. 2Some of them were saying, "We and our sons and daughters have increased our numbers. Now there are many of us. We have to get some grain so we can eat and stay alive."

3Others were saying, "We're being forced to sell our fields, vineyards and homes. We have to do it to buy grain. There isn't enough food for everyone."

4Still others were saying, "We've had to borrow money. We needed it to pay the king's tax on our fields and vineyards. 5We belong to the same family lines as the rest of our people. Our sons and daughters are as good as theirs. But we've had to sell them off as slaves. Some of our daughters have already been made slaves. But we can't do anything about it. That's because our fields and vineyards now belong to others."

6I heard them when they cried out. And I burned with anger when I heard what they were saying. 7I thought it over for a while. Then I brought charges against the nobles and officials. I told them, "You are forcing your own people to pay too much interest!"

So I called together a large group of people to handle the matter. 8I said, "Our Jewish brothers and sisters were sold to other nations. We've done everything we could to buy them back and bring them home. But look at what you are doing! You are actually selling your own people! Now we'll have to buy them back too!"

The people kept quiet. They couldn't think of anything to say.

9So I continued, "What you are doing isn't right. Shouldn't you show respect for our God? Shouldn't you live in a way that will keep our enemies from making fun of us?

10"I'm lending the people money and grain. So are my relatives and my men. But you must stop charging too much interest!

11"Give the people's fields back to them. Give them back their vineyards, olive groves and houses. Do it right away. You have charged them too much. Give everything back to them. Give them back the one percent on the money, grain, fresh wine and olive oil you have charged them."

12"We'll give it back," they said. "And we won't require anything more from them. We'll do exactly as you say."

Then I sent for the priests. I made the nobles and officials take an oath to do what they had promised. 13I also shook out my pockets and emptied them. I said, "Some of you might decide not to keep the promise you have made. If that happens, may God shake you out of your house! May he empty you of everything you own! May you be left with nothing at all!"

The whole community said, "Amen." They praised the LORD. And the leaders did what they had promised to do.

14And that's not all. I was appointed as governor of Judah in the 20th year that Artaxerxes was king of Persia. I remained in that position until his 32nd year. During those 12 years, I and my relatives didn't eat the food that was provided for my table.

15But there had been governors before me. They had put a heavy load on the people. They had taken a pound of silver from each of them. They had also taken food and wine from them. Their officials had acted like high and mighty rulers over them.

But I have great respect for God. So I didn't act like that. 16Instead, I spent all of my time working on this wall. All of my men were gathered there to work on it too. We didn't receive any land for ourselves.

17Many people ate at my table. They included 150 Jews and officials. They also included leaders who came to us from the nations that were around us. 18Each day one ox, six of the best sheep and some birds were prepared for me. Every ten days plenty of wine of all kinds was brought in as well. In spite of all that, I never asked for the food that was provided for my table. That's because the people were already paying too many taxes.

19You are my God. Please remember me. Show me your favor. Keep in mind everything I've done for these people.

Nehemiah's Enemies Continue to Oppose Him

6 Sanballat, Tobiah and Geshem, the Arab, heard about what I had done. So did the rest of our enemies. All of them heard I had rebuilt the wall. In fact, they heard there weren't any gaps left in it. But up to that time I hadn't put up the gates at the main entrances to the city.

2Sanballat and Geshem sent me a message. They said, "Come. Let's talk with one another. Let's meet in one of the villages on the flatlands of Ono."

But they were planning to harm me. 3So I sent messengers to them with my answer. I replied, "I'm working on a huge project. So I can't get away. Why should the work stop while I leave it? Why should I go down and talk with you?"

4They sent me the same message four times. And I gave them the same answer each time.

5Sanballat sent his helper to me a fifth time. He brought the same message. He was carrying a letter that wasn't sealed. 6It said,

> "A report is going around among the nations. Geshem says it's true. We hear that you and the other Jews are planning to turn against the Persian rulers. And that's why you are building the wall.
>
> "It's also reported that you are about to become their king. 7People say that you have even appointed prophets to make an announcement about you. In Jerusalem they are going to say, 'Judah has a king!' That report will get back to the king of Persia. So come. Let's talk things over."

8I sent a reply to Sanballat. I said, "What you are saying isn't really happening. You are just making it up."

9All of them were trying to frighten us. They thought, "Their hands will get too weak to do the work. So it won't be completed."

But I prayed to God. I said, "Make my hands stronger."

10One day I went to Shemaiah's house. He was the son of Delaiah. Delaiah was the son of Mehetabel. Shemaiah had shut himself up in his home. He said, "Let's go to God's house. Let's meet inside the temple. Let's close the temple doors. Some people want to kill you. They will come at night."

11But I said, "Should a man like me run away? Should someone like me go into the temple just to save his life? No! I won't go!"

12I realized that God hadn't sent Shemaiah. Tobiah and Sanballat had hired him. That's why he had prophesied lies about me. 13They had hired him to scare me. They wanted me to commit a sin by doing what he said. That would give me a bad name in the community. People would find fault with me and my work.

14You are my God. Remember what Tobiah and Sanballat have done. Also remember the prophet Noadiah. She and the rest of the prophets have been trying to scare me.

The City Wall Is Completed

15So the city wall was completed on the 25th day of the month of Elul. It was finished in 52 days. 16All of our enemies heard about it. All of the nations that were around us became afraid. They weren't sure of themselves anymore. They realized that our God had helped us finish the work.

17In those days the nobles of Judah sent many letters to Tobiah. And replies from Tobiah came back to them. 18Many people in Judah had taken an oath that they would be faithful to him. That's because he was Shecaniah's son-in-law. Shecaniah was the son of Arah. Tobiah's son Jehohanan had married Meshullam's daughter. Meshullam was the son of Berekiah. 19Tobiah's friends kept reporting to me the good things he did. They also kept telling him what I said. And Tobiah himself sent letters to scare me.

7 The wall had been rebuilt. I had put up the gates at the main entrances to the city. Those who guarded the gates were appointed to their positions. So were the singers and Levites. 2I put my brother Hanani in charge of Jerusalem. Hananiah helped him. Hananiah was commander of the fort that was by the temple. Hanani was an honest man. He had more respect for God than most people do.

3I said to Hanani and Hananiah, "Don't open the gates of Jerusalem until the hottest time of the day. Tell the men who guard the gates to shut them before they go off duty. Make sure they lock them up tight. Also appoint as guards some people who live in Jerusalem. Station some of them at their appointed places. Station others near their own homes."

A List of People Who Returned to Judah

4Jerusalem was large. It had a lot of room. But only a few people lived there. The houses hadn't been rebuilt yet. 5So my God stirred me up to gather the people together. He also told me to gather the nobles and officials together with them. He wanted me to list them by families. I found the family history of those who had been the first to return. Here is what I found written in it.

> 6Nebuchadnezzar had taken many Jews away from the land of Judah. He had forced them to go to Babylonia as prisoners. Now they returned to Jerusalem and Judah. All of them went back to their own towns. Nebu-

chadnezzar was king of Babylonia. 7The leaders of the Jews included Zerubbabel, Jeshua,
Nehemiah, Azariah, Raamiah and Nahamani.
They also included Mordecai, Bilshan, Mis-
pereth, Bigvai, Nehum and Baanah.

Here is a list of the men of Israel who returned home.

8 There were 2,172 from the family line of Parosh.
9 There were 372 from Shephatiah.
10 There were 652 from Arah.
11 There were 2,818 from Pahath-Moab through the family line of Jeshua and Joab.
12 There were 1,254 from Elam.
13 There were 845 from Zattu.
14 There were 760 from Zaccai.
15 There were 648 from Binnui.
16 There were 628 from Bebai.
17 There were 2,322 from Azgad.
18 There were 667 from Adonikam.
19 There were 2,067 from Bigvai.
20 There were 655 from Adin.
21 There were 98 from Ater through the family line of Hezekiah.
22 There were 328 from Hashum.
23 There were 324 from Bezai.
24 There were 112 from Hariph.
25 There were 95 from Gibeon.

26 There were 188 from the men of Bethlehem and Netophah.
27 There were 128 from Anathoth.
28 There were 42 from Beth Azmaveth.
29 There were 743 from Kiriath Jearim, Kephirah and Beeroth.
30 There were 621 from Ramah and Geba.
31 There were 122 from Micmash.
32 There were 123 from Bethel and Ai.
33 There were 52 from Nebo.
34 There were 1,254 from the other Elam.
35 There were 320 from Harim.
36 There were 345 from Jericho.
37 There were 721 from Lod, Hadid and Ono.
38 There were 3,930 from Senaah.

39 Here is a list of the priests.

There were 973 from the family line of Jedaiah through the line of Jeshua.
40 There were 1,052 from Immer.
41 There were 1,247 from Pashhur.
42 There were 1,017 from Harim.

43 The Levites belonged to
the family line of Jeshua through Kadmiel through the line of Hodaviah. The total number of men was 74.

44 The singers belonged to
the family line of Asaph. The total number of men was 148.

45 The men who guarded the temple gates belonged to
the family lines of Shallum, Ater, Talmon, Akkub, Hatita and Shobai. The total number of men was 138.

46Here is a list of the members of the family lines of the temple servants.

Ziha, Hasupha, Tabbaoth,
47 Keros, Sia, Padon,
48 Lebana, Hagaba, Shalmai,
49 Hanan, Giddel, Gahar,
50 Reaiah, Rezin, Nekoda,
51 Gazzam, Uzza, Paseah,
52 Besai, Meunim, Nephussim,
53 Bakbuk, Hakupha, Harhur,
54 Bazluth, Mehida, Harsha,
55 Barkos, Sisera, Temah,
56 Neziah, Hatipha

57Here is a list of the members of the family lines of the servants of Solomon.

Sotai, Sophereth, Perida,
58 Jaala, Darkon, Giddel,
59 Shephatiah, Hattil,
Pokereth-Hazzebaim, Amon

60 The total number of the members of the family lines of the temple servants and the servants of Solomon was 392.

61Many people came up to Judah from the
towns of Tel Melah, Tel Harsha, Kerub, Addon and Immer. But they weren't able to
prove that their families belonged to the people of Israel.

62 There were 642 of them from the family lines of
Delaiah, Tobiah and Nekoda.

63Here is a list of the members of the family lines of the priests.

They were
Hobaiah, Hakkoz and Barzillai. Barzillai had married a daughter of Barzillai from Gilead. So he was also called Barzillai.

64The priests looked for their family
records. But they couldn't find them. So they
weren't able to serve as priests. They weren't
"clean."

65The governor gave them an order. He
told them not to eat any of the most sacred
food. They had to wait until there was a
priest who could use the Urim and Thummim to get decisions from the LORD.

66The total number of the entire group that
returned was 42,360. 67That didn't include their
7,337 male and female slaves. There were also
245 male and female singers. 68And there were
736 horses, 245 mules, 69435 camels and 6,720
donkeys.

[70]Some of the family leaders helped pay for the work. The governor gave 19 pounds of gold to be added to the temple treasure. He also gave 50 bowls and 530 sets of clothes for the priests. [71]Some of the family leaders gave 375 pounds of gold for the work. They also gave one and a third tons of silver. All of that was added to the temple treasure. [72]The rest of the people gave a total of 375 pounds of gold and one and a fourth tons of silver. They also gave 67 sets of clothes for the priests.

[73]The priests and Levites settled down in their own towns. So did the singers, the temple servants and the men who guarded the gates. The rest of the people of Israel also settled in their own towns.

Ezra Reads the Law to the People

8 The people of Israel had settled down in their towns. In the seventh month, [1]all of them gathered together. They went to the open area in front of the Water Gate. They told Ezra to bring out the Scroll of the Law of Moses. The LORD had given Israel that law so they would obey him. Ezra was a teacher of the law.

[2]The priest Ezra brought the Law out to the whole community. It was the first day of the seventh month. The group was made up of men and women and everyone who was old enough to understand what Ezra was going to read.

[3]He read the Law to them from sunrise until noon. He did it as he faced the open area in front of the Water Gate. He read it to the men, women and others who could understand. And all of the people paid careful attention as Ezra was reading the Scroll of the Law.

[4]Ezra, the teacher, stood on a high wooden stage. It had been built for the occasion. Mattithiah, Shema and Anaiah stood at his right side. So did Uriah, Hilkiah and Maaseiah. Pedaiah, Mishael and Malkijah stood at his left side. So did Hashum, Hashbaddanah, Zechariah and Meshullam.

[5]Ezra opened the scroll. All of the people could see him. That's because he was standing above them. As he opened the scroll, the people stood up. [6]Ezra praised the LORD. He is the great God. All of the people lifted up their hands. They said, "Amen! Amen!" Then they bowed down. They turned their faces toward the ground. And they worshiped the LORD.

[7]The Levites taught the Law to the people. They remained standing while the Levites taught them. The Levites who were there included Jeshua, Bani, Sherebiah, Jamin, Akkub, Shabbethai and Hodiah. They also included Maaseiah, Kelita, Azariah, Jozabad, Hanan and Pelaiah. [8]All of those Levites read parts of the Scroll of the Law of God to the people. They made it clear to them. They told them what it meant. So the people were able to understand what was being read.

[9]Then Nehemiah and Ezra spoke up. So did the Levites who were teaching the people. All of those men said to the people, "This day is set apart to honor the LORD your God. So don't sob. Don't be sad." All of the people had been sobbing as they listened to the words of the Law. Nehemiah was governor. Ezra was a priest and a teacher of the law.

[10]Nehemiah said, "Go and enjoy some good food and sweet drinks. Send some of it to those who don't have any. This day is set apart to honor our Lord. So don't be sad. The joy of the LORD makes you strong."

[11]The Levites calmed all of the people down. They said, "Be quiet. This is a sacred day. So don't be sad."

[12]Then all of the people went away to eat and drink. They shared their food with others. They celebrated with great joy. Now they understood the words they had heard. That's because everything had been explained to them.

[13]All of the family leaders gathered around Ezra, the teacher. So did the priests and Levites. All of them paid attention to the words of the Law. It was the second day of the month.

[14]The LORD had given the Law through Moses. He wanted the people of Israel to obey it. It is written there that they were supposed to live in booths during the Feast of Booths. That Feast was celebrated in the seventh month. [15]They were also supposed to spread the message all through their towns and in Jerusalem. They were supposed to announce, "Go out into the central hill country. Bring back some branches from olive and wild olive trees. Also bring some from myrtle, palm and shade trees. Use the branches to make booths."

[16]So the people went out and brought some branches back. They built themselves booths on their own roofs. They made them in their courtyards. They put them up in the courtyards of the house of God. They built them in the open area in front of the Water Gate. And they built them in the open area in front of the Gate of Ephraim.

[17]All those who had returned from Babylonia made booths. They lived in them during the Feast of Booths. They hadn't celebrated the Feast with so much joy for a long time. In fact, they had never celebrated it like that from the days of Joshua, the son of Nun, until that very day. So their joy was very great.

[18]Day after day, Ezra read parts of the Scroll of the Law of God to them. He read it out loud from the first day to the last. They celebrated the Feast of Booths for seven days. On the eighth day they gathered together. They followed the required rules for celebrating the Feast.

The People of Israel Pray to the LORD

9 It was the 24th day of the seventh month. The people of Israel gathered together again. They didn't eat any food. They wore black clothes. They put dust on their heads. [2]The people of Israel separated themselves from everyone else. They stood

and admitted they had sinned. They also admitted
that their people before them had done evil things.
[3]They stood where they were. They listened
while the Levites read parts of the Scroll of the
Law of the LORD their God. They listened for a
fourth of the day. They spent another fourth of the
day admitting their sins. They also worshiped the
LORD their God.
[4]The Levites stood on the stairs. They included
Jeshua, Bani, Kadmiel and Shebaniah. They also
included Bunni, Sherebiah, Bani and Kenani. With
loud voices they called out to the LORD their God.
[5]Then some Levites spoke up. They included Jeshua, Kadmiel, Bani and Hashabneiah. They also
included Sherebiah, Hodiah, Shebaniah and Pethahiah. They said to the people, "Stand up. Praise
the LORD your God. He lives for ever and ever!"

So the people said, "LORD, may your glorious name be praised. May it be lifted high
above every other name that is blessed and
praised. [6]You are the one and only LORD.
You made the heavens. You made even the
highest heavens. You created all of the stars
in the sky. You created the earth and everything that is on it. And you made the oceans
and everything that is in them. You give life
to everything. Every living being in heaven
worships you.
[7]"You are the LORD God. You chose
Abram. You brought him out of Ur in Babylonia. You named him Abraham. [8]You knew
that his heart was faithful to you. And you
made a covenant with him. You promised to
give to his children after him a land of their
own. It was the land of the Canaanites, Hittites and Amorites. The Perizzites, Jebusites
and Girgashites also lived there. You have
kept your promise. That's because you
always do what is right and fair.
[9]"You saw how our people suffered long
ago in Egypt. You heard them cry out to you
at the Red Sea. [10]You did miraculous signs
and wonders against Pharaoh. You sent
plagues on all of his officials. In fact, you sent
them on all of the people of Egypt. You knew
how they treated our people. They looked
down on them. But you made a name for
yourself. That name remains to this very day.
[11]"You parted the Red Sea for the people
of Israel. They passed through it on dry
ground. But you threw into the sea those
who chased them. They sank down like a
stone into the mighty waters. [12]By day you
led them with a pillar of cloud. At night you
led them with a pillar of fire. It gave them
light to show them the way you wanted them
to go.
[13]"You came down on Mount Sinai. From
heaven you spoke to our people. You gave
them rules and laws. Those laws are right
and fair. You gave them orders and commands that are good. [14]You taught them
about your holy Sabbath day. You gave them
commands, orders and laws. You did it
through your servant Moses.
[15]"When the people were hungry, you
gave them bread from heaven. When they
were thirsty, you brought them water out of
a rock.
"You told them to go into the land of Canaan. You told them to take it as their own. It
was the land you had promised to give them.
You had even raised your hand and taken an
oath to do it.
[16]"But our people before us became proud
and stubborn. They didn't obey your commands. [17]They refused to listen to you. They
forgot the miracles you had done among
them. So they became stubborn. When they
refused to obey you, they appointed a leader
for themselves. They wanted to go back to
being slaves in Egypt. But you are a God
who forgives. You are gracious. You are tender and kind. You are slow to get angry. You
are full of love. So you didn't desert them.
[18]"They made for themselves a metal
statue of a god that looked like a calf. They
said, 'Here is your god. He brought you up
out of Egypt.' And they did evil things that
dishonored you. But you still didn't desert
them.
[19]"Because you loved them so much, you
didn't leave them in the desert. During the
day the pillar of cloud didn't stop guiding
them on their path. At night the pillar of fire
didn't stop shining on the way you wanted
them to go. [20]You gave them your good
Spirit to teach them. You didn't hold back
your manna from their mouths. And you
gave them water when they were thirsty.
[21]For 40 years you took good care of them in
the desert. They had everything they needed.
Their clothes didn't wear out. And their feet
didn't swell up.
[22]"You gave them kingdoms and nations.
You even gave them lands far away. They
took over the country of Sihon. He was king
of Heshbon. They also took over the country
of Og. He was king of Bashan. [23]You gave
them as many children as there are stars in
the sky. You told their parents to enter the
land. You told them to take it over. And you
brought their children into it. [24]Their children
went into the land. They took it as their own.
You brought the people of Canaan under Israel's control. The Canaanites lived in the
land. But you handed them over to Israel.
You also handed their kings and the other
nations in the land over to Israel. You
allowed Israel to deal with them just as they
wanted to.

25"Your people captured cities that had high walls around them. They also took over the rich land in Canaan. They took houses that were filled with all kinds of good things. They took over wells that had already been dug. They took many vineyards, olive groves and fruit trees. They ate until they were very full and satisfied. They were filled with joy because you were so good to them.

26"But they didn't obey you. Instead, they turned against you. They turned their backs on your law. They killed your prophets. The prophets had warned them to turn back to you. But they did very evil things that dishonored you.

27"So you handed them over to their enemies, who beat them down. Then they cried out to you. From heaven you heard them. You loved them very much. So you sent leaders to help them. The leaders saved them from the powerful hand of their enemies.

28"But as soon as the people were enjoying peace and rest again, they did what was evil in your sight. Then you handed them over to their enemies. So their enemies ruled over them. When they cried out to you again, you heard them from heaven. You loved them very much. So you saved them time after time.

29"You warned them to obey your law again. But they became proud. They didn't obey your commands. They sinned against your rules. Anyone who obeys them will live by them. But the people didn't care about that. They turned their backs on you. They became very stubborn. They refused to listen to you.

30"For many years you put up with them. By your Spirit you warned them through your prophets. In spite of that, they didn't pay any attention. So you handed them over to the nations that were around them.
31But you loved them very much. So you didn't put an end to them. You didn't desert them. That's because you are a gracious God. You are tender and kind.

32"Our God, you are great, mighty and wonderful. You keep the covenant you made with us. You show us your love. So don't let all of our suffering seem like a small thing in your sight. We've suffered greatly. So have our kings and leaders. So have our priests and prophets. Our people who lived long ago also suffered. And all of your people are suffering right now. In fact, we've been suffering from the time of the kings of Assyria until today.

33"In spite of everything that has happened to us, you have been fair. You have been faithful in what you have done. But we did what was wrong.
34Our kings and leaders didn't follow your law. Our priests and our people before us didn't follow it either. They didn't pay any attention to your commands. They didn't listen to the warnings you gave them.
35They didn't serve you. They didn't turn from their evil ways. They didn't obey you even when they had a kingdom. You were very good to them. And they enjoyed it. You gave them a rich land. It had plenty of room in it. But they still didn't serve you.

36"Now look at us. We are slaves today. We're slaves in the land you gave our people long ago. You gave it to them so they could eat its fruit and the other good things it produces.
37But we have sinned against you. So its great harvest goes to the kings of Persia. You have placed them over us. They rule over our bodies and cattle just as they please. And we are suffering terribly.

The People Agree to Obey God's Law

38"So we are making a firm agreement. We're writing it down. Our leaders are stamping it with their seals. And so are our Levites and priests."

10 Here are the names of those who stamped the agreement with their seals.

The governor Nehemiah, the son of Hacaliah
Zedekiah, 2Seraiah, Azariah, Jeremiah,
3Pashhur, Amariah, Malkijah,
4Hattush, Shebaniah, Malluch,
5Harim, Meremoth, Obadiah,
6Daniel, Ginnethon, Baruch,
7Meshullam, Abijah, Mijamin,
8Maaziah, Bilgai, Shemaiah

They were the priests.

9Here are the names of the Levites.

Jeshua, the son of Azaniah
Binnui, one of the sons of Henadad
Kadmiel

10Here are the names of those who helped them.

Shebaniah, Hodiah, Kelita, Pelaiah, Hanan,
11Mica, Rehob, Hashabiah,
12Zaccur, Sherebiah, Shebaniah,
13Hodiah, Bani, Beninu

14Here are the names of the leaders of the people.

Parosh, Pahath-Moab, Elam, Zattu, Bani,
15Bunni, Azgad, Bebai,
16Adonijah, Bigvai, Adin,
17Ater, Hezekiah, Azzur,
18Hodiah, Hashum, Bezai,
19Hariph, Anathoth, Nebai,
20Magpiash, Meshullam, Hezir,
21Meshezabel, Zadok, Jaddua,
22Pelatiah, Hanan, Anaiah,
23Hoshea, Hananiah, Hasshub,

24 Hallohesh, Pilha, Shobek,
25 Rehum, Hashabnah, Maaseiah,
26 Ahiah, Hanan, Anan,
27 Malluch, Harim, Baanah

28 The rest of the people gathered together. They included the priests, the Levites and the men who guarded the gates. They included the singers and temple servants. They also included all those who separated themselves from the surrounding nations to obey the Law of God. All of those men brought their wives with them. And they brought all of their sons and daughters who were old enough to understand what was being agreed to. 29 All of the men joined the nobles of their people. They made a firm agreement. They put themselves under a curse and took an oath. They promised to follow the Law of God. It had been given through Moses, the servant of God. They promised to obey carefully all of the commands, rules and laws of the LORD our Lord.

30 The priests, Levites and people said, "We promise not to give our daughters to be married to men from the nations that are around us. And we promise not to let their daughters get married to our sons.

31 "The people around us will bring goods and grain to sell on the Sabbath day. But we won't buy anything from them on the Sabbath. In fact, we won't buy anything from them on any holy day. Every seventh year we won't farm the land. And we'll forgive people what they owe us.

32 "We will be accountable for carrying out the commands for serving in the house of our God. Each of us will give an eighth of an ounce of silver every year. 33 It will pay for the holy bread that is placed on the table in the temple. It will pay for the regular grain offerings and burnt offerings. It will pay for the offerings on the Sabbath days. It will pay for the offerings at the New Moon Feasts and appointed feasts. It will pay for the holy offerings. It will be used for sin offerings to pay for the sin of Israel. It will also pay for everything else that needs to be done at the house of our God.

34 "We are the priests, Levites and people. We have cast lots to decide when each of our families should bring a gift of wood to the house of our God. They will bring it at certain appointed times every year. The wood will be burned on the altar of the LORD our God. That's what the Law requires.

35 "We will also be accountable for bringing the first share of our crops each year. And we'll bring the first share of every fruit tree. We'll bring them to the LORD's house.

36 "Each of us will bring our oldest son to the priests who serve there. We'll also bring the male animals that were born first to their mothers among our cattle, herds and flocks. We'll bring them to the house of our God. That's what the Law requires.

37 "We will also bring the first part of the meal we grind. We'll bring the first of our grain offerings. We'll bring the first share of fruit from all of our trees. And we'll bring the first share of our olive oil and fresh wine. We'll give all of those things to the priests. They'll put them in the storerooms of the house of our God.

"And we'll give a tenth of our crops to the Levites. They collect the tenth shares. They do it in all of the towns where we work. 38 A priest from Aaron's family line must go with the Levites when they receive the tenth shares. And the Levites must bring a tenth of those shares up to the house of our God. They must put it in the rooms where the treasures are stored.

39 "The people of Israel, including the Levites, must bring their gifts. They must bring grain, olive oil and fresh wine. They must put them in the storerooms where the articles for the temple are kept. That's where the priests stay when they are serving at the temple. The singers and the men who guard the gates also stay there.

"We won't forget to take care of the house of our God."

People Are Chosen to Live in Jerusalem

11 The leaders of the people settled down in Jerusalem. The rest of the people cast lots. They did it to choose one person out of every ten. That person was brought to live in the holy city of Jerusalem. The other nine had to stay in their own towns. 2 The people praised all those who agreed to live in Jerusalem.

3 Here are the leaders from different parts of the country who settled down in Jerusalem. Some Israelites, priests and Levites lived in the towns of Judah. So did some temple servants and some members of the family lines of Solomon's servants. All of them lived on their own property in the towns of Judah. 4 At the same time, other people from the tribes of Judah and Benjamin lived in Jerusalem.

Here are the leaders from the family line of Judah.

> There was Athaiah. He was the son of Uzziah. Uzziah was the son of Zechariah. Zechariah was the son of Amariah. Amariah was the son of Shephatiah. Shephatiah was the son of Mahalalel. Mahalalel belonged to the family line of Perez. 5 There was also Maaseiah. He was the son of Baruch. Baruch was the son of Col-Hozeh. Col-Hozeh was the son of Hazaiah. Hazaiah was the son of Adaiah. Adaiah was the son of Joiarib. Joiarib was the son of Zechariah. Zechariah belonged to the family line

of Shelah. [6]Many able men who belonged to the family line of Perez lived in Jerusalem. The total number of them was 468.

[7]Here are the leaders from the family line of Benjamin.

There was Sallu. He was the son of Meshullam. Meshullam was the son of Joed. Joed was the son of Pedaiah. Pedaiah was the son of Kolaiah. Kolaiah was the son of Maaseiah. Maaseiah was the son of Ithiel. Ithiel was the son of Jeshaiah. [8]There were also Gabbai and Sallai. They were Sallu's followers. The total number of men was 928. [9]Joel was their chief officer. He was the son of Zicri. A man named Judah was in charge of the New Quarter of Jerusalem. He was the son of Hassenuah.

[10]Here are the leaders from among the priests.

There were Jedaiah, Jakin and the son of Joiarib. [11]There was also Seraiah. He was the son of Hilkiah. Hilkiah was the son of Meshullam. Meshullam was the son of Zadok. Zadok was the son of Meraioth. Meraioth was the son of Ahitub. Ahitub was a ruler in God's house. [12]There were also those who helped them. They carried out the work for the temple. The total number of men was 822.

There was also Adaiah. He was the son of Jeroham. Jeroham was the son of Pelaliah. Pelaliah was the son of Amzi. Amzi was the son of Zechariah. Zechariah was the son of Pashhur. Pashhur was the son of Malkijah. [13]There were also those who helped Adaiah. They were family leaders. The total number of men was 242.

There was also Amashsai. He was the son of Azarel. Azarel was the son of Ahzai. Ahzai was the son of Meshillemoth. Meshillemoth was the son of Immer. [14]There were also those who helped Amashsai. They were able men. The total number of them was 128. Their chief officer was Zabdiel. He was the son of Haggedolim.

[15]Here are the leaders from among the Levites.

There was Shemaiah. He was the son of Hasshub. Hasshub was the son of Azrikam. Azrikam was the son of Hashabiah. Hashabiah was the son of Bunni. [16]There were also Shabbethai and Jozabad. They were two of the leaders of the Levites. They were in charge of the work that was done outside God's house.

[17]There was also Mattaniah. He led in prayer and in giving thanks. He was the son of Mica. Mica was the son of Zabdi. Zabdi was the son of Asaph. There was also Bakbukiah. He was second among those who helped Mattaniah. And there was Abda. He was the son of Shammua. Shammua was the son of Galal. Galal was the son of Jeduthun. [18]The total number of Levites in the holy city was 284.

[19]Here are the leaders from among the men who guarded the gates.

There were Akkub, Talmon and those who helped them. They stood guard at the gates. The total number of men was 172.

[20]The rest of the Israelites were in all of the towns of Judah. The priests and Levites were with them. All of them lived on their own family property.

[21]The temple servants lived on the hill of Ophel. Ziha and Gishpa were in charge of them.

[22]Uzzi was the chief officer of the Levites in Jerusalem. He was the son of Bani. Bani was the son of Hashabiah. Hashabiah was the son of Mattaniah. Mattaniah was the son of Mica. Uzzi was one of the members of Asaph's family line. They were singers. They were in charge of the worship services at God's house. [23]The singers received their orders from the Persian king. He told them what they should do every day.

[24]Pethahiah worked for the king in all matters that were connected with the people. He was the son of Meshezabel. Meshezabel belonged to the family line of Zerah. Zerah was the son of Judah.

[25]Many of the people of Judah lived in villages that had fields around them. Some of them lived in Kiriath Arba and the settlements that were around it. Others lived in Dibon and its settlements. Others lived in Jekabzeel and its villages. [26]Others lived in Jeshua, Moladah and Beth Pelet.

[27]Others lived in Hazar Shual and in Beersheba and its settlements. [28]Others lived in Ziklag and in Meconah and its settlements. [29]Others lived in En Rimmon and Zorah. Others lived in Jarmuth, [30]Zanoah and Adullam and their villages. Others lived in Lachish and its fields. Still others lived in Azekah and its settlements. So the people of Judah were living all the way from Beersheba to the Valley of Hinnom.

[31]Some of the members of the family line of Benjamin who were from Geba lived in Micmash. Others lived in Aija and in Bethel and its settlements. [32]Others lived in Anathoth, Nob and Ananiah. [33]Others lived in Hazor, Ramah and Gittaim. [34]Others lived in Hadid, Zeboim and Neballat. [35]Others lived in Lod and Ono. Still others lived in the Valley of Skilled Workers.

[36]Some of the groups of the Levites from Judah settled in the territory of Benjamin.

The Priests and Levites Who Returned to Judah

12 Some priests and Levites returned to Judah with Zerubbabel and Jeshua. Zerubbabel was the son of Shealtiel. Here are the names of those priests and Levites.

Seraiah, Jeremiah, Ezra,
2 Amariah, Malluch, Hattush,
3 Shecaniah, Rehum, Meremoth,
4 Iddo, Ginnethon, Abijah,
5 Mijamin, Moadiah, Bilgah,
6 Shemaiah, Joiarib, Jedaiah,
7 Sallu, Amok, Hilkiah, Jedaiah

All of them were the leaders of the priests and those
who helped them. They lived in the days of Jeshua.
8 The Levites were Jeshua, Binnui, Kadmiel,
Sherebiah and Judah. There were also Mattaniah
and those who helped him. They were in charge of
the songs for giving thanks. 9 Bakbukiah and Unni
helped them. They stood and sang across from
them during the services.
10 Jeshua was the father of Joiakim. Joiakim was
the father of Eliashib. Eliashib was the father of
Joiada. 11 Joiada was the father of Jonathan. And
Jonathan was the father of Jaddua.
12 Here are the names of the family leaders of the
priests. They were the leaders in the days of Joiakim.

Meraiah was from Seraiah's family.
Hananiah was from Jeremiah's family.
13 Meshullam was from Ezra's family.
Jehohanan was from Amariah's family.
14 Jonathan was from Malluch's family.
Joseph was from Shecaniah's family.
15 Adna was from Harim's family.
Helkai was from Meremoth's family.
16 Zechariah was from Iddo's family.
Meshullam was from Ginnethon's family.
17 Zicri was from Abijah's family.
Piltai was from Miniamin's and Moadiah's family.
18 Shammua was from Bilgah's family.
Jehonathan was from Shemaiah's family.
19 Mattenai was from Joiarib's family.
Uzzi was from Jedaiah's family.
20 Kallai was from Sallu's family.
Eber was from Amok's family.
21 Hashabiah was from Hilkiah's family.
And Nethanel was from Jedaiah's family.

22 The names of the family leaders of the Levites
in the days of Eliashib, Joiada, Johanan and Jaddua
were written down. So were the names of the family leaders of the priests. That happened while Darius ruled over Persia. 23 The names of the leaders
in Levi's family line up to the time of Johanan
were written down. They were written in the official records. Johanan was the son of Eliashib.
24 The leaders of the Levites were Hashabiah, Sherebiah and Jeshua. Jeshua was the son of Kadmiel.

Those who helped them stood across from them to sing praises and give thanks. One group would sing back to the other. That's what David, the man of God, had ordered.

25 Mattaniah, Bakbukiah, Obadiah, Meshullam,
Talmon and Akkub stood at the gates of the temple. They guarded the storerooms at the gates.
26 They served in the days of Joiakim. He was the
son of Jeshua. Jeshua was the son of Jehozadak.
They also served in the days of Nehemiah and
Ezra. Nehemiah was governor. Ezra was a priest
and a teacher of the law.

The Wall of Jerusalem Is Set Apart to God

27 The wall of Jerusalem was set apart to God.
For that occasion, the Levites were gathered
together from where they lived. They were
brought to Jerusalem to celebrate that happy occasion. They celebrated the fact that the wall was
being set apart to God. They did it by singing and
giving their thanks to him. They celebrated by
playing music on cymbals, harps and lyres.
28 The singers were also brought together. Some
of them came in from the area around Jerusalem.
Others came from the villages where the people of
Netophah lived. 29 Others came from Beth Gilgal.
Still others came from the area of Geba and Azmaveth. The singers had built villages for themselves around Jerusalem.
30 The priests and Levites made themselves
pure. Then they made the people, the gates and the
wall pure and clean.
31 I, Nehemiah, had the leaders of Judah go up
on top of the wall. I also appointed two large
choirs to sing and give thanks. I told one of them
to walk south on top of the wall. That was toward
the Dung Gate. 32 Hoshaiah and half of the leaders
of Judah followed them. 33 Azariah, Ezra, Meshullam, 34 Judah, Benjamin, Shemaiah and Jeremiah
also followed them.
35 Some priests who had trumpets followed
them. So did Zechariah. He was the son of Jonathan. Jonathan was the son of Shemaiah. Shemaiah was the son of Mattaniah. Mattaniah was the
son of Micaiah. Micaiah was the son of Zaccur.
Zaccur was the son of Asaph. 36 Those who helped
Zechariah also marched along. They were Shemaiah, Azarel, Milalai, Gilalai, Maai, Nethanel, Judah and Hanani. They brought instruments of
music with them. That's what David, the man of
God, had ordered. Ezra led the group that was
marching south. He was a teacher of the law.
37 At the Fountain Gate they continued straight
up the steps of the City of David that went up to the
wall. Then the group passed above David's house.
They continued on to the Water Gate on the east.
38 The second choir went north. I followed them
on top of the wall. Half of the people went with
me. They went past the Tower of the Ovens. They
went to the Broad Wall. 39 They marched over the
Gate of Ephraim. They went over the Jeshanah
Gate and the Fish Gate. They went past the Tower
of Hananel and the Tower of the Hundred. They
continued on to the Sheep Gate. At the Gate of the
Guard they stopped.
40 Then the two choirs that sang and gave thanks
took their places in God's house. So did I. So did
half of the officials. 41 And so did the priests. They

were Eliakim, Maaseiah, Miniamin, Micaiah, Elioenai, Zechariah and Hananiah. They had their trumpets with them. 42Maaseiah, Shemaiah, Eleazar, Uzzi, Jehohanan, Malkijah, Elam and Ezer were also there. The choirs sang under the direction of Jezrahiah.

43On that day large numbers of sacrifices were offered. The people were glad because God had given them great joy. The women and children were also very happy. The joyful sound in Jerusalem could be heard far away.

44At that time some men were put in charge of the storerooms. That's where all of the gifts the people brought were placed. They included the first shares of their crops. They also included a tenth of everything the Law required. From the fields that were around the towns the people had to bring the shares of their crops that were required by the Law. They gave them to the priests and Levites. That's because the people of Judah were pleased with the priests and Levites who were serving God.

45The priests and Levites did everything their God wanted them to do. They made things pure and clean. The singers and those who guarded the temple gates also served God. Everything was done just as David and his son Solomon had commanded. 46A long time ago there had been directors for the singers. There had also been directors for the songs for giving thanks and praise to God. It was in the time of David and Asaph.

47So now in the days of Zerubbabel and Nehemiah, all of the people of Israel brought their gifts. They gave the singers and those who guarded the gates what they were supposed to give them every day. They also set apart the shares for the other Levites. And the Levites set apart the shares for the priests in the family line of Aaron.

Nehemiah Warns the People

13 On that same day the Scroll of Moses was read out loud. All of the people heard it. It was written there that no one from Ammon or Moab should ever be allowed to become a member of the community of God. 2That's because they hadn't given the people of Israel food and water. Instead, they had hired Balaam to call a curse down on them. But our God turned the curse into a blessing.

3When that law was read, the people of Judah obeyed it. They put out of Israel everyone who was from another nation.

4The priest Eliashib had been put in charge of the storerooms in the house of our God. He had worked closely with Tobiah. 5He had also provided a large room for Tobiah. It had been used to store the grain offerings. The incense and temple articles had been put there. And a tenth of the grain, olive oil and fresh wine had been kept there. That's what the Law required for the Levites. That's also what it required for the singers and those who guarded the temple gates. The gifts for the priests had been kept there too.

6But I wasn't in Jerusalem while all of that was going on. I had returned to the Persian King Artaxerxes, the king of Babylonia. I went to him in the 32nd year of his rule. Some time later I asked him to let me return to Jerusalem.

7When I got back, I learned about the evil thing Eliashib had done. He had provided a room for Tobiah. It was in the courtyards of God's house. 8So I was very unhappy. I threw all of Tobiah's things out of the room.

9I gave orders to make the rooms pure and clean again. Then I put the supplies from God's house back into them. That included the grain offerings and the incense.

10I also learned that the shares the Levites were supposed to receive hadn't been given to them. So all of the Levites and singers had to leave their regular temple duties. They had to go back and farm their own fields.

11I gave a warning to the officials. I asked them, "Why aren't you taking care of God's house?" Then I brought them together. I stationed them in their proper places. I put them back to work.

12All of the people of Judah brought a tenth of the grain, olive oil and fresh wine. They took it to the storerooms.

13I put some men in charge of the storerooms. They were Shelemiah, Zadok and Pedaiah. Shelemiah was a priest. Zadok was a teacher of the law. And Pedaiah was a Levite. I made Hanan their assistant. He was the son of Zaccur. Zaccur was the son of Mattaniah. I knew that those men could be trusted. They were put in charge of handing out the supplies to their people.

14You are my God. Remember me because of what I've done. I've worked faithfully for your temple and its services. So please don't forget the good things I've done.

15In those days I saw some men of Judah stomping on grapes in winepresses. They were doing it on the Sabbath day. Others were bringing in grain. They were loading it on donkeys. Still others were loading up wine, grapes, figs and other kinds of things. They were bringing all of it into Jerusalem on the Sabbath. So I warned them not to sell food on that day. 16People from Tyre who lived in Jerusalem were bringing in fish. In fact, they were bringing in all kinds of goods. They were selling them in Jerusalem on the Sabbath. The people of Judah were buying them.

17I gave a warning to the nobles of Judah. I said, "Why are you doing such an evil thing? You are misusing the Sabbath day! 18Your people before you did the very same things. That's why our God has brought all of this trouble on us. That's why he's making this city suffer so much. Now you are stirring up even more of his anger against Israel. You are misusing the Sabbath day."

19Evening shadows fell on the gates of Jerusalem before the Sabbath started. So I ordered the
gates to be shut. They had to remain closed until
the Sabbath was over. I stationed some of my own
men at the gates. I told them not to let anything be
brought in on the Sabbath day.
20Once or twice some traders and sellers spent the
night outside Jerusalem. They were hoping to sell
all kinds of goods. 21But I gave them a warning. I
said, "Why are you spending the night by the wall?
If you do this again, I'll arrest you." So from that
time on they didn't come on the Sabbath anymore.
22I commanded the Levites to make themselves
pure. Then I told them to go and guard the gates. I
wanted the Sabbath day to be kept holy.

You are my God. Remember me because of the good things I've done. Be kind to me in keeping with your great love.

23In those days I also saw that some men of Judah had gotten married to women from Ashdod.
Others had married women from Ammon or
Moab. 24Half of their children spoke the language
of Ashdod. Or they spoke the language of one of
the other nations. They didn't even know how to
speak the language of Judah.
25So I gave them a warning. I called curses
down on them. I beat some of them up. I pulled
their hair out. I made them take an oath in God's
name. I said, "You must promise not to give your
daughters to be married to their sons. You must
promise not to let their daughters marry your sons.
And you must not marry their daughters either.
26"That's how Solomon, the king of Israel,
sinned. He married women from other nations.
There wasn't a king like him anywhere. His God
loved him. In fact, God made him king over the
whole nation of Israel. But even he was led into
sin by women from other lands. 27Now I hear that
you too are doing all of the same terrible and evil
things. You aren't being faithful to our God. You
are marrying women from other lands."
28One of the sons of Joiada was the son-in-law
of Sanballat. Joiada was the high priest. He was
the son of Eliashib. I drove Joiada's son away
from me. Sanballat was a Horonite.

29You are my God. Remember what those
priests have done. They have polluted their own
work. They have also polluted the covenant that
God made with the priests and Levites long ago.

30So I made the priests and Levites pure. I made
them pure from every practice that had come from
other countries and had polluted them. I gave them
their duties. Each one had his own job to do. 31I
also made plans for gifts of wood to be brought at
certain appointed times. And I made plans for the
first share of the crops to be brought.

You are my God. Please remember me. Show me your favor.

Esther

Vashti Is Removed From Her Position as Queen

1 King Xerxes ruled over the 127 territories in his kingdom. They reached from India all the way to Cush. Here is what happened during the time Xerxes ruled over the whole Persian kingdom. 2He was ruling from his royal throne in the safest place in Susa.

3In the third year of his rule King Xerxes gave a big dinner. It was for all of his nobles and officials. The military leaders of Persia and Media were there. So were the princes and the nobles of the territories he ruled over. 4Every day for 180 days he showed his guests the great wealth of his kingdom. He also showed them how glorious his kingdom was.

5When those days were over, the king gave another big dinner. It lasted for seven days. It was held in the garden of the king's courtyard. It was for all of the people who lived in the safest place in Susa. Everyone from the least important person to the most important was invited.

6The garden was decorated with white and blue linen banners. They hung from ropes that were made out of white linen and purple cloth. The ropes were connected to silver rings on marble pillars. There were gold and silver couches in the garden. They were placed on a floor that was made out of small stones. The floor had purple crystal, marble, mother-of-pearl and other stones of great value.

7Royal wine was served in gold cups. Each cup was different from all of the others. There was plenty of wine. The king always provided as much as his guests wanted. 8He commanded that they should be allowed to drink as much or as little as they wished. He directed all of his servants to give them what they asked for.

9Queen Vashti also gave a big dinner. Only women were invited. It was held in the royal palace of King Xerxes.

10On the seventh day Xerxes was in a good mood because he had drunk a lot of wine. So he gave a command to the seven officials who served him. They were Mehuman, Biztha, Harbona, Bigtha, Abagtha, Zethar and Carcas. 11He told them to bring Queen Vashti to him. He wanted her to come wearing her royal crown. He wanted to show off her beauty to the people and nobles. She was lovely to look at.

12The attendants told Queen Vashti what the king had ordered her to do. But she refused to come. So the king became very angry. In fact, he burned with anger.

13It was the king's practice to ask advice from those who knew a lot about matters of law and fairness. So he spoke with the wise men who were supposed to understand what was going on at that time. 14They were the men who were closest to the king. They were Carshena, Shethar, Admatha, Tarshish, Meres, Marsena and Memucan. They were the seven nobles of Persia and Media. They were the king's special advisers. In fact, they were the most important men in the kingdom.

15"You know the law," the king said. "What should I do to Queen Vashti? She hasn't obeyed my command. The officials told her what I ordered her to do, didn't they?"

16Then Memucan gave a reply to the king and the nobles. He said, "Queen Vashti has done what is wrong. But she didn't do it only against you, King Xerxes. She did it also against all of the nobles. And she did it against the people in all of the territories you rule over.

17"All of the women will hear about what the queen has done. Then they will look down on their husbands. They'll say, 'King Xerxes commanded Queen Vashti to be brought to him. But she wouldn't come.' 18Starting today, the leading women in Persia and Media who have heard about the queen's actions will act in the same way. They'll disobey all of your nobles, just as she disobeyed you. They won't have any respect for their husbands. They won't honor them.

19"So if it pleases you, send out a royal order. Let it be written down in the laws of Persia and Media. They can never be changed. Let the royal order say that Vashti can never see you again. Also let her position as queen be given to someone who is better than she is.

20"And let your order be announced all through your entire kingdom. Then all of the other women will have respect for their husbands from the least important of them to the most important."

21The king and his nobles were pleased with that advice. So he did what Memucan had suggested. 22He sent messages out to every territory in the kingdom. He sent them to each territory in its own writing. He sent them to every nation in its own language. The messages announced in each nation's language that every man should rule over his own family.

Esther Becomes Queen of Persia

2 Later, the anger of King Xerxes calmed down. Then he remembered Vashti and what she had done. He also remembered the royal order he had sent out concerning her.

2At that time the king's personal attendants made a suggestion. They said, "King Xerxes, let a search be made for some beautiful young virgins for you. 3Appoint some officials in every territory

in your kingdom. Have them bring all of those
beautiful virgins into the safest place in Susa. Put
them in the special place where the virgins stay.
Then put Hegai in charge of them. He's the eunuch
who serves you. He's in charge of the virgins. Let
beauty care be given to the new group of virgins.
4 Then let the one who pleases you the most
become queen in Vashti's place."
The king liked that advice. So he followed it.
5 There was a Jew living in the safest place in
Susa. He was from the tribe of Benjamin. His
name was Mordecai. He was the son of Jair. Jair
was the son of Shimei. Shimei was the son of
Kish. 6 Nebuchadnezzar had forced Mordecai to
leave Jerusalem. He was among the prisoners who
were carried off along with Jehoiachin. Jehoiachin
had been king of Judah. Nebuchadnezzar was king
of Babylonia.
7 Mordecai had a cousin named Hadassah. He
had brought her up in his own home. She didn't
have a father or mother. Hadassah was also called
Esther. She was very beautiful. Mordecai had
adopted her as his own daughter. He had done it
when her father and mother died.
8 After the king's order and law were announced, many virgins were brought to the safest
place in Susa. Hegai was put in charge of them.
Esther was also taken to the king's palace. She was
put under the control of Hegai. He was in charge
of the place where the virgins stayed.
9 Esther pleased him. He showed her his favor.
Right away he provided her with her beauty care
and special food. He appointed seven female attendants to help her. They were chosen from the
king's palace. He moved her and her attendants
into the best part of the place where the virgins
stayed.
10 Esther hadn't told anyone who her people
were. She hadn't talked about her family. That's
because Mordecai had told her not to.
11 Mordecai tried to find out how Esther was getting along. He wanted to know what was happening to her. So he walked back and forth near the
courtyard by the place where the virgins stayed.
He did it every day.
12 Each virgin had to complete 12 months of
beauty care. They used oil of myrrh for six
months. And they used perfume and make-up for
the other six months. A virgin's turn to go in to
King Xerxes could come only after a full 12
months had passed.
13 And here is how she would go to the king. She
would be given anything she wanted from the
place where the virgins stayed. She could take it
with her to the king's palace. 14 In the evening she
would go there. In the morning she would leave.
Then she would go to the special place where the
king's concubines stayed. She would be put under
the control of Shaashgaz. He was the king's
eunuch who was in charge of the concubines. She
would never return to the king unless he was
pleased with her. He had to send for her by name
before she could go to him again.
15 Mordecai had adopted Esther. She had been
the daughter of his uncle Abihail. Her turn came
to go in to the king. She only asked for what Hegai suggested. He was the king's eunuch who was in
charge of the place where the virgins stayed.
Everyone who saw Esther was pleased with her.
16 She was taken to King Xerxes in the royal house.
It was now the tenth month. That was the month
of Tebeth. It was the seventh year of the rule of
Xerxes.
17 The king liked Esther more than he liked any
of the other women. She pleased him more than
any of the other virgins. So he put a royal crown on
her head. He made her queen in Vashti's place.
18 Then the king gave a big dinner. It was in
honor of Esther. All of his nobles and officials
were invited. He announced a holiday all through
the territories he ruled over. He freely gave many
gifts in keeping with his royal wealth.

Mordecai Uncovers a Plan to Kill the King

19 The virgins were gathered together a second
time. At that time Mordecai was sitting at the
palace gate. 20 Esther had kept her family history a
secret. She hadn't told anyone who her people
were. Mordecai had told her not to. She continued
to follow his directions. That's what she had
always done when he was bringing her up.
21 Bigthana and Teresh were two of the king's
officers. They guarded the door of the royal palace.
They became angry with King Xerxes. So they
decided to kill him. They made their evil plans
while Mordecai was sitting at the palace gate.
22 So he found out about it. And he told Queen
Esther. Then she reported it to the king. She told
him that Mordecai had uncovered the plans against
him. 23 Some people checked Esther's report. And
they found out it was true. So the two officials
were put to death. Then poles were stuck through
them. They were set up where people could see
them. All of that was written in the official records.
It was written down while the king was watching.

Haman Plans to Destroy the Jews

3 After those events, King Xerxes honored Haman. Haman was the son of Hammedatha. He
was from the family line of Agag. The king gave
Haman a higher position than he had before. He
gave him a seat of honor. It was higher than the
positions any of the other nobles had. 2 All of the
royal officials at the palace gate got down on their
knees. They gave honor to Haman. That's because
the king had commanded them to do it.
But Mordecai refused to get down on his knees.
He wouldn't give Haman any honor at all.
3 The royal officials at the palace gate asked
Mordecai a question. They said, "Why don't you
obey the king's command?" 4 Day after day they

spoke to him. But he still refused to obey. So they
told Haman about it. They wanted to see whether
he would let Mordecai get away with what he was
doing. Mordecai had told them he was a Jew.
[5]Haman noticed that Mordecai wouldn't get
down on his knees. He wouldn't give Haman any
honor. So Haman burned with anger. [6]But he had
found out who Mordecai's people were. So he
decided not to kill just Mordecai. He also looked
for a way to destroy all of Mordecai's people. They
were Jews. He wanted to kill all of them everywhere in the kingdom of Xerxes.
[7]The lot was cast in front of Haman. That was
done to choose a day and a month. It was the 12th
year that Xerxes was king. It was in the first
month. That was the month of Nisan. The lot chose
the 12th month. That was the month of Adar. The
lot was also called *pur*.
[8]Then Haman said to King Xerxes, "Certain
people are scattered among the nations. They live
in all of the territories in your kingdom. Their
practices are different from the practices of all
other people. They don't obey your laws. It really
isn't good for you to put up with them.
[9]"If it pleases you, give the order to destroy
them. I'll even add 375 tons of silver to the royal
treasures. You can use it to pay the men who take
care of the matter."
[10]So the king took his ring off his finger. The
ring had his royal seal on it. He gave the ring to
Haman. Haman was the son of Hammedatha, the
Agagite. He was the enemy of the Jews.
[11]"Keep the money," the king said to Haman.
"Do what you want to with those people."
[12]The king sent for the royal secretaries. It was
the 13th day of the first month. The secretaries
wrote down all of Haman's orders. They wrote
them down in the writing of each territory in the
kingdom. They also wrote them in the language of
each nation. The orders were sent to the royal officials. They were also sent to the governors of the
territories. And they went out to the nobles of the
nations. The orders were written in the name of
King Xerxes himself. And they were stamped with
his own royal seal. [13]They were carried by messengers. They were sent to all of the king's
territories.

The orders commanded people to destroy, kill
and wipe out all of the Jews. That included young
people and old people alike. It included women
and little children. All of the Jews were supposed
to be killed on a single day. That day was the 13th
day of the 12th month. It was the month of Adar.
The orders also commanded people to take the
goods that belonged to the Jews.
[14]A copy of the order had to be sent out as law.
It had to be sent to every territory in the kingdom.
It had to be announced to the people of every
nation. Then they would be ready for that day.
[15]The king commanded the messengers to go
out. So they did. The order was sent out from the
safest place in Susa. Then the king and Haman sat
down to drink wine. But the people in the city
were bewildered.

Mordecai Talks Esther Into Helping the Jews

4 Mordecai found out about everything that had
been done. So he tore his clothes. He put on
black clothes. He sat down in ashes. Then he went
out into the city. He sobbed out loud. He cried bitter tears. [2]But he only went as far as the palace
gate. That's because no one who was dressed in
black clothes was allowed to go through it.
[3]All of the Jews were very sad. They didn't eat
anything. They sobbed and cried. Many of them
put on black clothes. They were lying down in
ashes. They did all of those things in every territory where the king's order and law had been sent.
[4]Esther's eunuchs and female attendants came
to her. They told her about Mordecai. So she
became very troubled. She wanted him to take his
black clothes off. So she sent him other clothes to
wear. But he wouldn't accept them. [5]Then Esther
sent for Hathach. He was one of the king's
eunuchs. He had been appointed to take care of
her. She ordered him to find out what was troubling Mordecai. She wanted to know why he was
so upset.
[6]So Hathach went out to see Mordecai. He was
in the open area in front of the palace gate. [7]Mor-
decai told him everything that had happened to
him. He told him about the exact amount of money
Haman had promised to add to the royal treasures.
He said Haman wanted it to be used to pay some
men to destroy the Jews.
[8]Mordecai also gave Hathach a copy of the
order. It commanded people to wipe out the Jews.
The order had been sent from Susa.

Mordecai told Hathach to show the order to Esther. He wanted him to explain it to her. He told
him to try and get her to go to the king. He wanted
her to beg for mercy. He wanted her to make an
appeal to the king for her people.
[9]Hathach went back. He reported to Esther what
Mordecai had said. [10]Then Esther directed him to
give an answer to Mordecai. She told him to say,
[11]"There is a certain law that everyone knows
about. All of the king's officials know about it. The
people in the royal territories know about it. It
applies to any man or woman who approaches the
king in the inner courtyard without being sent for.
It says they must be put to death. But there is a
way out. Suppose the king reaches out his gold rod
toward them. Then their lives will be spared. But
30 days have gone by since the king sent for me."
[12]Esther's words were reported to Mordecai.
[13]Then he sent back an answer. He said, "You live
in the king's palace. But don't think that just
because you are there you will be the only Jew
who will escape. [14]What if you don't say anything
at this time? Then help for the Jews will come

from another place. But you and your family will die. Who knows? It's possible that you became queen for a time just like this."

15Then Esther sent a reply to Mordecai. She said, 16"Go. Gather together all of the Jews who are in Susa. And fast for my benefit. Don't eat or drink anything for three days. Don't do it night or day. I and my attendants will fast just as you do. Then I'll go to the king. I'll do it even though it's against the law. And if I have to die, I'll die."

17So Mordecai went away. He carried out all of Esther's directions.

Esther Invites the King and Haman to a Big Dinner

5 On the third day Esther put her royal robes on. She stood in the inner courtyard of the palace. It was in front of the king's hall.

The king was sitting on his royal throne in the hall. He was facing the entrance. 2He saw Queen Esther standing in the courtyard. He was pleased with her. So he reached out toward her the gold rod that was in his hand. Then Esther approached him. She touched the tip of the rod.

3The king asked, "What is it, Queen Esther? What do you want? I'll give it to you. I'll even give you up to half of my kingdom."

4Esther replied, "King Xerxes, if it pleases you, come to a big dinner today. I've prepared it for you. Please have Haman come with you."

5"Bring Haman at once," the king said to his servants. "Then we'll do what Esther asks."

So the king and Haman went to the big dinner Esther had prepared. 6As they were drinking wine, the king asked Esther the same question again. He said, "What do you want? I'll give it to you. What do you want me to do for you? I'll even give you up to half of my kingdom."

7Esther replied, "Here is what I want. Here is my appeal to you. 8I hope you will show me your favor. I hope you will be pleased to give me what I want. And I hope you will be pleased to listen to my appeal. If you are, I'd like you and Haman to come tomorrow to the big dinner I'll prepare for you. Then I'll answer your question."

Haman Brags About Being Invited to Esther's Dinner

9That day Haman was happy. So he left the palace in a good mood. But then he saw Mordecai at the palace gate. He noticed that Mordecai didn't stand up when he walked by. In fact, Mordecai didn't have any respect for him at all. So he burned with anger against him. 10But Haman was able to control himself. He went on home.

Haman called his friends and his wife Zeresh together. 11He bragged to them about how rich he was. He talked about how many sons he had. He spoke about all of the ways the king had honored him. He bragged about how the king had given him a higher position than any of the other nobles and officials had. 12"And that's not all!" Haman added. "I'm the only person Queen Esther invited to come with the king to the big dinner she gave. Now she has invited me along with the king tomorrow.

13"But even all of that doesn't satisfy me. I won't be satisfied as long as I see that Jew Mordecai sitting at the palace gate."

14Haman's wife Zeresh and all of his friends spoke up. They said to him, "Get a pole. In the morning, ask the king to have Mordecai put to death. Have the pole stuck through his body. Set it up at a place where it will be 75 feet above the ground. Everyone will be able to see it there. Then go to the dinner with the king. Have a good time."

Haman was delighted with that suggestion. So he got the pole ready.

The King Honors Mordecai

6 That night the king couldn't sleep. So he ordered the official records of his rule to be brought in. He ordered someone to read them to him. 2It was written there that Mordecai had uncovered the plans of Bigthana and Teresh against the king. They had been two of the king's officers who guarded the door of the royal palace. They had decided to kill King Xerxes.

3"What great honor has Mordecai received for doing that?" the king asked.

"Nothing has been done for him," his attendants answered.

4The king asked, "Who is in the courtyard?"

Haman had just entered the outer courtyard of the palace. He had come to speak to the king about putting Mordecai to death. He wanted to talk about putting Mordecai's body up on the pole he had gotten ready for him.

5The king's attendants said to him, "Haman is standing in the courtyard."

"Bring him in," the king ordered.

6Haman entered. Then the king asked him, "What should be done for the man I want to honor?"

Haman said to himself, "Is there anyone the king would rather honor than me?" 7So he answered the king. He said, "Here is what you should do for the man you want to honor. 8Have your servants get a royal robe you have worn. Have them bring a horse you have ridden on. Have a royal crest placed on its head. 9Then give the robe and horse to one of your most noble princes. Let the robe be put on the man you want to honor. Let him be led on the horse through the city streets. Let people announce in front of him, 'This is what is done for the man the king wants to honor!'"

10"Go right away," the king commanded Haman. "Get the robe. Bring the horse. Do exactly what you have suggested. Do it for the Jew Mordecai. He's sitting out there at the palace gate. Make sure you do everything you have suggested."

[11]So Haman got the robe and the horse. He put the robe on Mordecai. And he led him on horseback through the city streets. He walked along in front of him and announced, "This is what is done for the man the king wants to honor!"

[12]After that, Mordecai returned to the palace gate. But Haman rushed home. He covered his head because he was very sad. [13]He told his wife Zeresh everything that had happened to him. He also told all of his friends.

His advisers and his wife Zeresh spoke to him. They said, "Your fall from power started with Mordecai. He's a Jew. So now you can't stand up against him. You are going to be destroyed!" [14]They were still talking with him when the king's officials arrived. They hurried Haman away to the big dinner Esther had prepared.

Haman Is Put to Death

7 So the king and Haman went to dine with Queen Esther. [2]They were drinking wine on the second day. The king again asked, "What do you want, Queen Esther? I'll give it to you. What do you want me to do for you? I'll even give you up to half of my kingdom."

[3]Then Queen Esther answered, "King Xerxes, I hope you will show me your favor. I hope you will be pleased to let me live. That's what I want. Please spare my people. That's my appeal to you. [4]"My people and I have been sold to be destroyed. We've been sold to be killed and wiped out. Suppose we had only been sold as male and female slaves. Then I wouldn't have said anything. That kind of suffering wouldn't be a good enough reason to bother you."

[5]King Xerxes asked Queen Esther, "Who is the man who has dared to do such a thing? And where is he?"

[6]Esther said, "The man hates us! He's our enemy! He's this evil Haman!"

Then Haman was terrified in front of the king and queen.

[7]The king got up. He was burning with anger. He left his wine and went out into the palace garden.

But Haman realized that the king had already decided what he was going to do to him. So he stayed behind to beg Queen Esther for his life.

[8]The king returned from the palace garden to the dinner hall. Just then he saw Haman falling on the couch where Esther was lying.

The king shouted, "Will he even rape the queen? Is he going to rape her while she's right here with me in the palace?"

As soon as the king finished speaking, his men covered Haman's face.

[9]Then Harbona said, "There's a pole standing near Haman's house. He has gotten it ready for Mordecai. Mordecai is the one who spoke up to help you. Haman had planned to have him put to death. He was going to have the pole stuck through his body. Then he was going to set it up at a place where it would be 75 feet above the ground." Harbona was one of the officials who attended the king.

The king said to his men, "Put Haman to death! Stick the pole through his body! Set it up where everyone can see it!" [10]So they did. And they used the pole Haman had gotten ready for Mordecai. Then the king's anger calmed down.

The King Allows the Jews to Fight for Their Lives

8 That same day King Xerxes gave Queen Esther everything Haman had owned. Haman had been the enemy of the Jews.

Esther had told the king that Mordecai was her cousin. So Mordecai came to see the king. [2]The king took his ring off. It had his royal seal on it. He had taken it back from Haman. Now he gave it to Mordecai. And Esther put Mordecai in charge of everything Haman had owned.

[3]Esther made another appeal to the king. She fell at his feet and sobbed. She begged him to put an end to the evil plan of Haman, the Agagite. He had decided to kill the Jews.

[4]The king reached out his gold rod toward Esther. She got up and stood in front of him.

[5]"King Xerxes, I hope you will show me your favor," she said. "I hope you will think that what I'm asking is the right thing to do. I hope you are pleased with me. If you are, and if it pleases you, let an order be written. Let it take the place of the messages Haman wrote. Haman was the son of Hammedatha, the Agagite. He planned to kill the Jews. He wrote orders to destroy us in all of your territories. [6]I couldn't stand by and see the horrible trouble that would fall on my people! I couldn't stand to see my family destroyed!"

[7]King Xerxes gave a reply to Queen Esther and the Jew Mordecai. He said, "Haman attacked the Jews. So I've given Esther everything he owned. My men have stuck a pole through his dead body. And they've set it up where everyone can see it.

[8]"Now write another order in my name. Do it for the benefit of the Jews. Do what seems best to you. Stamp the order with my royal seal. Nothing that is written in my name and stamped with my seal can ever be changed."

[9]Right away the king sent for the royal secretaries. It was the 23rd day of the third month. That was the month of Sivan. They wrote down all of Mordecai's orders to the Jews. They also wrote them to the royal officials, the governors and the nobles of the 127 territories in his kingdom. The territories reached from India all the way to Cush. The orders were written down in the writing of each territory. They were written in the language of each nation. They were also written to the Jews in their own writing and language.

[10]Mordecai wrote the orders in the name of King Xerxes. He stamped them with the king's

royal seal. He sent them by messengers on horseback. They rode fast horses that were raised just for the king.

11The Jews in every city could now gather together and fight for their lives. The king's order gave them that right. But what if soldiers from any nation or territory attacked them? What if they attacked their women and children? Then the Jews could destroy, kill and wipe out those soldiers. They could also take the goods that belonged to their enemies. 12A day was appointed for the Jews to do that in all of the king's territories. It was the 13th day of the 12th month. That was the month of Adar.

13A copy of the order was sent out as law in every territory. It was announced to the people of every nation. So the Jews would be ready on that day. They could pay their enemies back.

14The messengers rode on the royal horses. They raced along. That's what the king commanded them to do. The order was also sent out in the safest place in Susa.

15Mordecai left the king and went on his way. Mordecai was wearing royal clothes. They were blue and white. He was also wearing a large gold crown. And he was wearing a purple coat. It was made out of fine linen. The city of Susa celebrated with great joy.

16The Jews were filled with joy and happiness. They were very glad because now they were being honored. 17They celebrated and enjoyed good food. They were glad and full of joy. That was true everywhere the king's order went out. It was true in every territory and every city. Many people from other nations announced that they had become Jews. That's because they were so afraid of the Jews.

The Jews Win the Battle Over Their Enemies

9 The king's order had to be carried out on the 13th day of the 12th month. That was the month of Adar. On that day the enemies of the Jews had hoped to win the battle over them. But now everything had changed. The Jews had gained the advantage over those who hated them.

2The Jews gathered together in their cities. They gathered in all of the territories King Xerxes ruled over. They came together to attack those who were trying to destroy them. No one could stand up against them. The people from all of the other nations were afraid of them.

3All of the nobles in the territories helped the Jews. So did the royal officials, the governors and the king's officers. That's because they were so afraid of Mordecai. 4He was well known in the palace. His fame spread all through the territories. So he became more and more important.

5The Jews struck down all of their enemies with swords. They killed them and destroyed them. They did what they pleased to those who hated them. 6The Jews killed 500 men. They destroyed them in the safest place in Susa.

7They also killed Parshandatha, Dalphon, Aspatha, 8Poratha, Adalia, Aridatha, 9Parmashta, Arisai, Aridai and Vaizatha. 10They were the ten sons of Haman. He was the son of Hammedatha. Haman had been the enemy of the Jews. They didn't take anything that belonged to their enemies.

11A report was brought to the king that same day. He was told how many men had been killed in the safest place in Susa. 12He said to Queen Esther, "The Jews have killed 500 men. They destroyed them in the safest place in Susa. They also killed the ten sons of Haman there. What have they done in the rest of my territories? Now what do you want? I'll give it to you. What do you want me to do for you? I'll do that too."

13"If it pleases you," Esther answered, "let the Jews in Susa carry out today's order tomorrow also. Stick poles through the dead bodies of Haman's ten sons. Set them up where everyone can see them."

14So the king commanded that it be done. An order was sent out in Susa. And the king's men did to the bodies of Haman's sons everything they were told to do. 15The Jews in Susa came together on the 14th day of the month of Adar. They put 300 men to death in Susa. But they didn't take anything that belonged to those men.

16During that time, the rest of the Jews also gathered together. They lived in the king's territories. They came together to fight for their lives. They didn't want their enemies to bother them anymore. They wanted to get some peace and rest. So they killed 75,000 of their enemies. But they didn't take anything that belonged to them. 17It happened on the 13th of Adar. On the 14th day they rested. They made it a day to celebrate with great joy. And they enjoyed good food.

Purim Is Celebrated

18But the Jews in Susa had gathered together on the 13th and 14th. Then on the 15th they rested. They made it a day to celebrate with great joy. And they enjoyed good food.

19That's why Jews who live out in the villages celebrate on the 14th of Adar. They celebrate that day with great joy. And they enjoy good food. They also give presents to each other on that day.

20Mordecai wrote down those events. He sent letters to all of the Jews all through the territories of King Xerxes. It didn't matter whether the Jews lived nearby or far away. 21Mordecai told them to celebrate the 14th and 15th days of the month of Adar. He wanted them to do it every year.

22Mordecai told the Jews to celebrate the time when they got rest from their enemies. That was the month when their sadness was turned into joy. It was when their sobbing turned into a day for celebrating. He wrote the letters to celebrate those days as times of joy. He wanted the people to enjoy good food. He told them to give presents of food to one another. He also wanted them to give gifts to those who were poor.

23So the Jews agreed to continue the celebrating they had started. They kept doing what Mordecai had written to them.

24Haman was the son of Hammedatha, the Agagite. He had been the enemy of all of the Jews. He had planned to destroy them. He had cast the lot to destroy them completely. The lot was also called *pur*.
25But the king had found out about Haman's evil plan. So the king had sent out written orders. He had ordered that the evil plan Haman had made against the Jews should come back on his own head. He had also commanded that Haman and his sons should be put to death. Poles should be stuck through their dead bodies. Then they should be set up where everyone could see them.

26The days the Jews were celebrating were called Purim. Purim comes from the word *pur*. *Pur* means "lot." Now the Jews celebrate those two days every year. They do it because of everything that was written in Mordecai's letter. They also do it because of what they had seen and what had happened to them.

27So they established it as a regular practice. They decided they would always observe those two days of the year. They would celebrate in the required way. And they would celebrate at the appointed time. They and their children after them and everyone who joined them would always observe those days.
28The days should be remembered and celebrated. They should be remembered by every family for all time to come. They should be celebrated in every territory and in every city. The Jews should never stop celebrating the days of Purim. Their children after them should always remember those days.

29So Queen Esther, the daughter of Abihail, wrote a second letter. She wrote it together with the Jew Mordecai. They wanted to give their full authority to this second letter about Purim.
30Mordecai sent letters to all of the Jews in the 127 territories of the kingdom of Xerxes. The letters had messages of kindness and hope in them.

31The letters established the days of Purim at their appointed times. They spoke about what the Jew Mordecai and Queen Esther had ordered the people to do. Everything should be done in keeping with the directions the Jews had set up for themselves and their children after them. The directions applied to their times of fasting and sadness.
32Esther's order established the rules about Purim. It was written down in the records.

The Greatness of Mordecai

10 King Xerxes required people all through his kingdom to bring him gifts. He required gifts from its farthest shores.
2All of his powerful and mighty acts are written down. That includes the whole story of how important Mordecai was. The king had given him a position of great honor. All of those things are written in the official records of the kings of Media and Persia.

3The Jew Mordecai's position was second only to the position of King Xerxes. Mordecai was the most important Jew. All of the other Jews had the highest respect for him. That's because he worked for the good of his people. And he spoke up for the benefit of all of the Jews.

Job

The Story Begins

1 There was a man who lived in the land of Uz. His name was Job. He was honest. He did what was right. He had respect for God and avoided evil.

2Job had seven sons and three daughters. 3He owned 7,000 sheep and 3,000 camels. He owned 500 pairs of oxen and 500 donkeys. He also had a large number of servants. He was the most important man among all of the people in the east.

4His sons used to take turns giving big dinners in their homes. They would invite their three sisters to eat and drink with them.

5When the time for enjoying good food was over, Job would have his children made pure and clean. He would sacrifice a burnt offering for each of them. He would do it early in the morning. He would think, "Perhaps my children have sinned. Maybe they have spoken evil things against God in their hearts."

That's what Job always did for his children when he felt they had sinned.

Job Is Put to the Test

6One day angels came to the LORD. Satan also came with them. 7The LORD said to Satan, "Where have you come from?"

Satan answered, "From traveling all around the earth. I've been going from one end of it to the other."

8Then the LORD said to Satan, "Have you thought about my servant Job? There isn't anyone on earth like him. He is honest. He does what is right. He has respect for me and avoids evil."

9"You always give Job everything he needs," Satan replied. "That's why he has respect for you. 10Haven't you guarded him and his family? Haven't you taken care of everything he has? You have blessed everything he does. His flocks and herds are spread all through the land.

11"But reach out your hand and strike down everything he has. Then I'm sure he will speak evil things against you. In fact, he'll do it right in front of you."

12The LORD said to Satan, "All right. I am handing everything he has over to you. But do not touch the man himself."

Then Satan left the LORD and went on his way.

13One day Job's sons and daughters were at their oldest brother's house. They were enjoying good food and drinking wine.

14During that time a messenger came to Job. He said, "The oxen were plowing. The donkeys were eating grass near them. 15Then the Sabeans attacked us and carried the animals off. They killed some of the servants with their swords. I'm the only one who has escaped to tell you!"

16While he was still speaking, a second messenger came. He said, "God sent lightning from the sky. It struck the sheep and killed them. It burned up some of the servants. I'm the only one who has escaped to tell you!"

17While he was still speaking, a third messenger came. He said, "The Chaldeans separated themselves into three groups. They attacked your camels and carried them off. They killed the rest of the servants with their swords. I'm the only one who has escaped to tell you!"

18While he was still speaking, a fourth messenger came. He said, "Your sons and daughters were at their oldest brother's house. They were enjoying good food and drinking wine. 19Suddenly a strong wind blew in from the desert. It struck the four corners of the house. The house fell down on your children. Now all of them are dead. I'm the only one who has escaped to tell you!"

20After Job heard all of those reports, he got up and tore his robe. He shaved his head. Then he fell to the ground and worshiped the LORD. 21He said,

"I was born naked.
　And I'll leave here naked.
You have given, and you have taken away.
　May your name be praised."

22In spite of everything, Job didn't sin by blaming God for doing anything wrong.

Job Is Put to the Test Again

2 On another day angels came to the LORD. Satan also came to him along with them. 2The LORD said to Satan, "Where have you come from?"

Satan answered, "From traveling all around the earth. I've been going from one end of it to the other."

3Then the LORD said to Satan, "Have you thought about my servant Job? There isn't anyone on earth like him. He is honest. He does what is right. He has respect for me and avoids evil. You tried to turn me against him. You wanted me to destroy him without any reason. But he still continues to be faithful."

4Satan replied, "A man will give everything he has to save himself. So Job is willing to give up the lives of his family to save his own life.

5"But reach out your hand and strike his flesh and bones. Then I'm sure he will speak evil things against you. In fact, he'll do it right in front of you."

6The LORD said to Satan, "All right. I am handing him over to you. But you must spare his life."

7Then Satan left the LORD and went on his way. He sent painful sores on Job. They covered him from the bottom of his feet to the top of his head. 8He got part of a broken pot. He used it to scrape his skin. He did it while he was sitting in ashes.

9His wife said to him, "Are you still continuing to be faithful to the LORD? Speak evil things against him and die!"

10Job replied, "You are talking like a foolish woman. We accept good things from God. So we should also accept trouble when he sends it."

In spite of everything, Job didn't say anything that was sinful.

Job's Three Friends Come to Comfort Him

11Job had three friends named Eliphaz the Temanite, Bildad the Shuhite, and Zophar the Naamathite. They heard about all of the troubles that had come to Job. So they started out from their homes. They had agreed to meet together. They wanted to go and show their concern for Job. They wanted to comfort him.

12When they got closer to where he lived, they could see him. But they could hardly recognize him. They began to sob out loud. They tore their robes and sprinkled dust on their heads.

13Then they sat down on the ground with him for seven days and seven nights. No one said a word to him. That's because they saw how much he was suffering.

Job Wishes He Had Never Been Born

3 After a while, Job opened his mouth to speak. He called down a curse on the day he had been born. 2He said,

3"May the day I was born be wiped out.
May the night be wiped away when people said, 'A boy is born!'
4May that day turn into darkness.
May God in heaven not care about it.
May no light shine on it.
5May darkness and deep shadow take it back.
May a cloud settle over it.
May blackness cover up its light.
6May deep darkness take over the night I was born.
May it not be included among the days of the year.
May it never appear in any of the months.
7May no children ever have been born on that night.
May no shout of joy be heard in it.
8May people call down a curse on that day.
May those who are ready to wake up the sea monster Leviathan curse that day.
9May its morning stars become dark.
May it lose all hope of ever seeing daylight.
May it not see the first light of the morning sun.
10It didn't keep my mother from letting me be born.
It didn't keep my eyes from seeing trouble.

11"Why didn't I die when I was born?
Why didn't I die as I came out of my mother's body?
12Why was I placed on her knees?
Why did her breasts give me milk?
13If all of that hadn't happened,
I would be lying down in peace.
I'd be asleep and at rest in the grave.
14I'd be with the earth's kings and advisers.
They had built for themselves places that are now destroyed.
15I'd be with rulers who used to have gold.
They had filled their houses with silver.
16Why wasn't I buried like a baby who was born dead?
Why wasn't I buried like a child who never saw the light of day?
17In the grave, sinful people don't cause trouble anymore.
And there those who are tired find rest.
18Prisoners also enjoy peace there.
They don't hear a slave driver shouting at them anymore.
19The least important and most important people are there.
And there the slaves are set free from their owners.

20"Why is the light that leads to life given to those who suffer?
Why is it given to those whose spirits are bitter?
21Why is life given to those who long for death that doesn't come?
Why is it given to those who would rather search for death
than for hidden treasure?
22Why is life given to those who are actually happy and glad
when they reach the grave?
23Why is life given to a man like me?
God hasn't told me what will happen to me.
He has surrounded me with nothing but trouble.
24I sigh instead of eating food.
Groans pour out of me like water.
25What I was afraid of has come on me.
What I worried about has happened to me.
26I don't have any peace and quiet.
I can't find any rest. All I have is trouble."

The First Speech of Eliphaz

4 Then Eliphaz the Temanite replied,

2"Job, suppose someone tries to talk to you.
Will that make you uneasy?
I can't keep from speaking up.
3Look, you taught many people.
You made weak hands strong.

[4] Your words helped those who had fallen down.
You made shaky knees strong.
[5] Now trouble comes to you. And you are unhappy about it.
It strikes you down. And you are afraid.
[6] Shouldn't you worship God and trust in him?
Shouldn't your honest life give you hope?

[7] "Here's something to think about.
Have blameless people ever been wiped out?
Have honest people ever been completely destroyed?
[8] Here's what I've observed.
People gather a crop from what they plant.
If they plant evil and trouble, that's what they will harvest.
[9] The breath of God destroys them.
The blast of his anger wipes them out.
[10] Powerful lions might roar and growl.
But their teeth are broken.
[11] Lions die because they don't have any food.
Then their cubs are scattered.

[12] "A message came to me in secret.
It was as quiet as a whisper.
[13] I had a scary dream one night.
I was sound asleep.
[14] Fear and trembling grabbed hold of me.
That made every bone in my body shake.
[15] A spirit glided past my face.
The hair on my body stood on end.
[16] Then the spirit stopped.
But I couldn't tell what it was.
Something stood there in front of me.
I heard a soft voice.
[17] It said, 'Can a human being be more right than God?
Can a mere man be more pure than the One who made him?
[18] God doesn't trust those who serve him.
He even brings charges against his angels.
[19] So he'll certainly find fault with human beings.
After all, they are made out of dust.
They can be crushed more easily than a moth.
[20] Between sunrise and sunset they are broken to pieces.
Nobody even notices. They disappear forever.
[21] Like a tent that falls down, they get weak.
They die because they didn't follow God's wisdom.' "

5 Eliphaz continued,

"Call out if you want to, Job.
But who will answer you?
Which one of the holy angels will you turn to?
[2] Anger kills foolish people.
Jealousy destroys those who are childish.
[3] I saw that foolish people were having success.
But suddenly a curse came down on their houses.
[4] Their children aren't safe at all.
They lose their case in court.
No one speaks up for them.
[5] Hungry people eat up the crops of those who are foolish.
They even take the food that grows among thorns.
Thirsty people long for the wealth of the foolish.
[6] Hard times don't just grow out of the soil.
Trouble doesn't jump out of the ground.
[7] People are born to have trouble.
And that's just as sure as sparks fly up.

[8] "If I were you, I'd make my appeal to God.
I'd bring my case to be judged by him.
[9] He does wonderful things that can't be understood.
He does miracles that can't even be counted.
[10] He sends rain on the earth.
He sends water on the countryside.
[11] He lifts up those who are lowly in spirit.
He lifts up those who are sad.
He keeps them safe.
[12] He stops those who are tricky from doing what they plan to do.
The work of their hands doesn't succeed.
[13] Some people think they are so wise.
But God catches them in their own tricks.
He sweeps away the evil plans of sinful people.
[14] Darkness covers them in the daytime.
At noon they feel their way around as if it were night.
[15] God saves needy people from the cutting words of their enemies.
He saves them from their powerful hands.
[16] So those who are poor have hope.
And God shuts the mouths of people who don't treat others fairly.

[17] "Blessed is the person God corrects.
So don't hate the Mighty One's training.
[18] He wounds. But he also bandages up those he wounds.
He harms. But his hands also heal those he harms.
[19] From six troubles he will save you.
Even if you are in trouble seven times, no harm will come to you.
[20] When there isn't enough food, God will keep you from dying.
When you go into battle, he won't let a sword strike you down.
[21] He will keep you safe from words that can hurt you.
You won't need to be afraid
when everything is being destroyed.

22 You will laugh when things are being destroyed.
You will enjoy life even when there isn't enough food.
You won't be afraid of wild animals.
23 You will make a covenant with the stones in the fields.
They won't keep your crops from growing.
Even wild animals will be at peace with you.
24 You will know that the tent you live in is secure.
You will check out your property.
You will see that nothing is missing.
25 You can be sure you will have a lot of children.
They will be as many as the blades of grass on the earth.
26 You will go down to the grave
while you are still very strong.
You will be like a crop that is gathered at the right time.
27 "We have carefully studied all of those things.
And they are true.
So pay attention to them.
Apply them to yourself."

Job's Reply

6 Job replied,
2 "I wish my great pain could be weighed!
I wish all of my suffering could be weighed on scales!
3 I'm sure they would weigh more than the grains of sand on the seashore.
No wonder I've been so quick to speak!
4 The Mighty One has shot me with his arrows.
I have to drink their poison.
God's terrors are aimed at me.
5 Does a wild donkey cry out when it has enough grass?
Does an ox call out when it has plenty of food?
6 Is food that doesn't have any taste eaten without salt?
Is there any flavor in the white of an egg?
7 I refuse to touch that kind of food.
It makes me sick.
8 "I wish I could have what I'm asking for!
I wish God would give me what I'm hoping for!
9 I wish he would crush me!
I wish his powerful hand would cut off my life!
10 Then I'd still have one thing to comfort me.
It would be that I haven't said no to the Holy One's commands.
That would give me joy in spite of my pain that never ends.
11 "I'm so weak that I no longer have any hope.
Things have gotten so bad that I can't wait for help anymore.
12 Am I as strong as stone?
Is my body made out of bronze?
13 I don't have the power to help myself.
All hope of success has been taken away from me.
14 "A man's friends should love him when his hope is gone.
They should be faithful to him
even if he stops showing respect for the Mighty One.
15 But my friends aren't faithful to me.
They are like streams that only flow for part of the year.
They are like rivers that flow over their banks
16 when the ice begins to break up.
The streams rise when the snow starts to melt.
17 But they stop flowing when the dry season comes.
They disappear from their stream beds when the weather warms up.
18 Groups of traders turn away from their usual paths.
They go up into the dry and empty land.
And they die there.
19 Traders from Tema look for water.
Traveling merchants from Sheba also hope to find it.
20 They become troubled because they had expected to find some.
But when they arrive at the stream beds,
they don't find any water at all.
21 And now, my friends, you haven't helped me either.
You see the horrible condition I'm in.
And that makes you afraid.
22 I've never said, 'Give me something to help me.
Use your wealth to set me free.
23 Save me from the powerful hand of my enemy.
Set me free from the power of mean people.'
24 "Teach me. Then I'll be quiet.
Show me what I've done wrong.
25 Honest words are so painful!
But your reasoning doesn't prove anything.
26 Are you trying to correct what I'm saying?
You are treating the words of this hopeless man
like nothing but wind.
27 You would even cast lots for those whose fathers have died.
You would even trade away your closest friend.
28 "But now please look at me.
Would I tell you a lie right here in front of you?
29 Stop what you are saying. Don't be so unfair.
Think it over again.
You are trying to take my honesty away from me.

30 Has my mouth spoken anything that is evil?
Do my lips say things that are hateful?"

7 Job continued,

"Doesn't every man have to work hard on this earth?
Aren't his days like the days of a hired worker?
2 I've been like a slave
who longs for the evening shadows to come.
I've been like a hired worker
who can hardly wait to get paid.
3 I've been given several months that were useless to me.
My nights have been filled with suffering.
4 When I lie down I think,
'How long will it be before I can get up?'
The night drags on.
I toss and turn until sunrise.
5 My body is covered with worms and sores.
My skin is broken. It has boils all over it.

6 "My days pass by faster than a weaver can work.
They come to an end. I don't have any hope.
7 God, remember that my life is only a breath.
I'll never be happy again.
8 The eyes that see me now won't see me anymore.
You will look for me. But I'll be gone.
9 When a cloud disappears, it's gone forever.
And anyone who goes down to the grave never returns.
10 He never comes home again.
Even his own family doesn't remember him.

11 "So I won't keep quiet.
When I'm suffering greatly, I'll speak out.
When my spirit is bitter, I'll tell you how unhappy I am.
12 AmI the ocean? Am I the sea monster?
If I'm not, why do you guard me so closely?
13 Sometimes I think my bed will comfort me.
I think my couch will keep me from being unhappy.
14 But even then you send me dreams that frighten me.
You send me visions that terrify me.
15 So I would rather choke to death.
That would be better than living in this body of mine.
16 I hate my life. I don't want to live forever.
Leave me alone. My days don't mean anything to me.

17 "What are human beings that you think so much of them?
What are they that you pay so much attention to them?
18 You check up on them every morning.
You put them to the test every moment.
19 Won't you ever look away from me?
Won't you leave me alone even for one second?
20 If I've really sinned, tell me what I've done to you.
Why do you watch people so closely?
Why do you shoot your arrows at me?
Have I become a problem to you?
21 Why don't you forgive the wrong things I've done?
Why don't you forgive me for my sins?
I'll soon lie down in the dust of my grave.
You will search for me. But I'll be gone."

The First Speech of Bildad

8 Then Bildad the Shuhite replied,

2 "Job, how long will you talk like that?
Your words don't have any meaning.
3 Does God ever treat people unfairly?
Does the Mighty One make what is wrong
appear to be right?
4 Your children sinned against him.
So he punished them for their sin.
5 But look to God.
Make your appeal to the Mighty One.
6 Be pure and honest.
And he will rise up and help you now.
He'll return you to the place where you belong.
7 In the past, things went well with you.
But in days to come, things will get even better.

8 "Find out what your people who lived long ago taught.
Discover what those who lived before them learned.
9 After all, we were born only yesterday.
So we don't know anything.
Our days on this earth are like a shadow that disappears.
10 Won't your people of long ago teach you and tell you?
Won't the things they said help you understand?
11 Can grass grow tall where there isn't any swamp?
Can plants grow well where there isn't any water?
12 While they are still growing and haven't been cut,
they dry up faster than grass does.
13 The same thing happens to everyone who forgets God.
The hope of ungodly people dies out.
14 What they trust in is very weak.
What they depend on is like a spider's web.
15 A person leans on it, but it falls apart.
He holds on to it, but it gives way.

16 He is like a plant in the sunshine
that receives plenty of water.
It spreads its new growth all over
the garden.
17 It wraps its roots around a pile of rocks.
It tries to find places to grow among
the stones.
18 But when a plant is pulled up from its spot,
that place says, 'I never saw you.'
19 The life of that plant is sure to dry up.
But from the same soil other plants
will grow.

20 "I'm sure God doesn't turn his back on anyone
who is honest.
And he doesn't help those who do what
is evil.
21 He will fill your mouth with laughter.
Shouts of joy will come from your lips.
22 Your enemies will put on shame as if it were
clothes.
The tents of sinful people will be gone."

Job's Reply

9 Job replied,

2 "I'm sure that what you have said is true.
But how can human beings be right
with God?
3 They might wish to argue with him.
But they couldn't answer him
even once in a thousand times.
4 His wisdom is deep. His power is great.
No one opposes him and comes away
unharmed.
5 He moves mountains, and they don't even
know it.
When he is angry, he turns them upside
down.
6 He shakes the earth loose from its place.
He makes its pillars tremble.
7 When he tells the sun not to shine, it doesn't.
He turns off the light of the stars.
8 He's the only one who can spread the
heavens out.
He alone can walk on the waves of
the ocean.
9 He made the Big Dipper and Orion.
He created the Pleiades and the southern
stars.
10 He does wonderful things that can't be
understood.
He does miracles that can't even be counted.
11 When he passes by me, I can't see him.
When he goes past me, I can't recognize
him.
12 If he takes something, who can stop him?
Who would dare to ask him, 'What are you
doing?'
13 God doesn't hold back his anger.
Even the helpers of the sea monster Rahab
bowed in fear at his feet.

14 "So how can I disagree with God?
How can I possibly argue with him?
15 Even if I hadn't done anything wrong,
I couldn't answer him.
I could only beg my Judge to have mercy
on me.
16 Suppose I called out to him and he answered.
I don't believe he'd listen to me.
17 He would send a storm to crush me.
He'd increase my wounds without any
reason.
18 He wouldn't let me catch my breath.
He'd make my life very bitter.
19 If it's a matter of strength, he is mighty!
And if it's a matter of being fair,
who would dare to bring charges
against him?
20 Even if I hadn't sinned, what I said would
prove me guilty.
Even if I were honest, my words would
show that I'm wrong.

21 "Even though I'm honest,
I'm not concerned about myself.
I hate my own life.
22 It all amounts to the same thing. That's why
I say,
'God destroys honest people and sinful
people alike.'
23 Suppose a plague brings sudden death.
Then he laughs when those who haven't
sinned lose hope.
24 Suppose a nation falls into the power of
sinful people.
Then God makes its judges blind to
the truth.
If he isn't the one doing it, who is?

25 "God, my days race by like a runner.
They fly away without seeing any joy.
26 They speed along like papyrus boats.
They are like eagles swooping down on
their food.
27 Suppose I say, 'I'll forget about all of my
problems.
I'll change my frown into a smile.'
28 Then I'd still be afraid I'd go on suffering.
That's because I know you would say
I had done something wrong.
29 In fact, you have already said I'm guilty.
So why should I struggle without any
reason?
30 Suppose I clean myself with soap.
Suppose I wash my hands with cleanser.
31 Even then you would throw me into a
muddy pit.
And even my clothes would hate me.

32 "God isn't a man like me. I can't answer him.
We can't take each other to court.
33 I wish someone would settle matters
between us.

I wish someone would force us to work
things out.
34 I wish someone would keep God from
punishing me.
Then his terror wouldn't frighten me
anymore.
35 I would speak up without being afraid of him.
But as things stand now, I can't do that.

10 "I'm sick of living.
So I'll talk openly about my problems.
I'll speak out because my spirit is bitter.
2 I'll say to God, 'Don't find me guilty.
Instead, tell me what charges
you are bringing against me.
3 Does it make you happy when you crush me?
Does it please you to turn your back on
what you have made?
While you do those things,
you smile on the plans of sinful people!
4 You don't have human eyes.
You don't see as people see.
5 Your days aren't like the days of a human
being.
Your years aren't like the years of a
mere man.
6 So you search for my mistakes.
You look for my sin.
7 You already know I'm not guilty.
No one can save me from your powerful
hand.

8 "'Your hands shaped me and made me.
So are you going to destroy me now?
9 Remember, you molded me like clay.
So are you going to turn me back into dust?
10 Didn't you pour me out like milk?
Didn't you form me like cheese?
11 Didn't you put skin and flesh on me?
Didn't you sew me together with bones and
muscles?
12 You gave me life. You were kind to me.
You took good care of me. You watched
over me.

13 "'But here's what you hid in your heart.
Here's what you had on your mind.
14 If I sinned, you would be watching me.
You wouldn't let me go without
punishing me.
15 If I were guilty, how terrible that would be
for me!
Even if I haven't sinned,
I can't be proud of what I've done.
That's because I'm so full of shame.
I'm drowning in my suffering.
16 If I become proud, you hunt me down like
a lion.
You show your mighty power against me.
17 You bring new witnesses against me.
You become more and more angry with me.
You use your power against me again
and again.

18 "'Why did you bring me out of my
mother's body?
I wish I had died before anyone saw me.
19 I wish I'd never been born!
I wish I'd been carried straight from my
mother's body to the grave!
20 Aren't my few days almost over?
Leave me so I can have a moment of joy.
21 Turn away before I go to the place I can't
return from.
It's the land of darkness and deep shadow.
22 It's the land of darkest night
and deep shadow and disorder.
There even the light is like darkness.'"

The First Speech of Zophar

11 Then Zophar the Naamathite replied,

2 "Don't all of your words require an answer?
I'm sure that what you are saying can't
be right.
3 Your useless talk won't keep us quiet.
Someone has to correct you when you make
fun of truth.
4 You say to God, 'My beliefs are perfect.
I'm pure in your sight.'
5 I wish God would speak.
I wish he'd answer you.
6 I wish he'd show you the secrets of wisdom.
After all, true wisdom has two sides.
Here's what I want you to know.
God has forgotten some of your sins.

7 "Do you know how deep the mysteries of
God are?
Can you discover the limits of the Mighty
One's knowledge?
8 They are higher than the heavens.
What can you do?
They are deeper than the deepest grave.
What can you know?
9 They are longer than the earth.
They are wider than the ocean.

10 "Suppose God comes along and puts you
in prison.
Suppose he takes you to court.
Then who can oppose him?
11 He certainly knows when people tell lies.
When he sees evil, he pays careful attention
to it.
12 A wild donkey's colt can't be born a human
being.
And a man who doesn't have any sense
can't become wise.

13 "So commit yourself to God completely.
Reach out your hands to him for help.
14 Get rid of all of the sin you have.
Don't let anything that is evil stay in
your tent.
15 Then you can face others without feeling any
shame.
You can stand firm without being afraid.

[16] You can be sure you will forget your troubles.
They will be like water that has flowed on by.
[17] Life will be brighter than the sun at noon.
And darkness will become like morning.
[18] You will be secure, because there is hope.
You will look around you and find a safe place to rest.
[19] You will lie down, and no one will make you afraid.
Many people will want you to show them your favor.
[20] But sinful people won't find what they are looking for.
They won't be able to escape.
All they can hope for is to die."

Job's Reply

12 Job replied,

[2] "You people think you know everything, don't you?
You are sure that wisdom will die with you!
[3] But I have a brain, just like you.
I'm as clever as you are.
In fact, everyone knows as much as you do.

[4] "My friends laugh at me all the time,
even though I called out to God and he answered.
My friends laugh at me,
even though I'm honest and right.
[5] People who have an easy life look down on those who have problems.
They think trouble comes only to those whose feet are slipping.
[6] Why doesn't anyone bother the tents of robbers?
Why do those who make God angry remain secure?
They carry the statues of their gods in their hands!

[7] "But ask the animals what God does.
They will teach you.
Or ask the birds of the air.
They will tell you.
[8] Or speak to the earth. It will teach you.
Or let the fish of the ocean educate you.
[9] Are there any of those creatures that don't know
what the powerful hand of the LORD has done?
[10] He holds the life of every creature in his hand.
He controls the breath of every human being.
[11] Our tongues tell us what tastes good and what doesn't.
And our ears tell us what's true and what isn't.
[12] Old people are wise.
Those who live a long time have understanding.

[13] "Wisdom and power belong to God.
Advice and understanding also belong to him.
[14] What he tears down can't be rebuilt.
Any man he puts in prison can't be set free.
[15] If he holds back the water, everything dries up.
If he lets the water loose, it floods the land.
[16] Strength and success belong to him.
Those who tell lies and those who believe them also belong to him.
[17] He removes the wisdom of advisers and leads them away.
He makes judges look foolish.
[18] He sets people free from the chains that kings put on them.
Then he dresses the kings in the clothes of slaves.
[19] He removes the authority of priests and leads them away.
He removes from their positions
those who have been in control for a long time.
[20] He shuts the mouths of trusted advisers.
He takes away the understanding of elders.
[21] He looks down on proud leaders.
He takes away the strength of those who are mighty.
[22] He tells people the secrets of darkness.
He brings evil plans out into the light.
[23] He makes nations great, and then he destroys them.
He makes nations grow, and then he scatters them.
[24] He takes away the understanding of the leaders of the earth.
He makes them wander in a desert where no one lives.
[25] Without any light, they feel their way along in darkness.
God makes them unsteady like those who get drunk.

13 "My eyes have seen everything God has done.
My ears have heard it and understood it.
[2] What you know, I also know.
I'm as clever as you are.
[3] In fact, I long to speak to the Mighty One.
I want to argue my case with God.
[4] But you spread lies about me and take away my good name.
If you are trying to heal me,
you aren't very good doctors!
[5] I wish you would keep your mouths shut!
Then people would think you were wise.
[6] Listen to my case.
Listen as I make my appeal.
[7] Will you say evil things in order to help God?
Will you tell lies for him?
[8] Do you want to be on God's side?
Will you argue his case for him?

9 Would it turn out well if he looked you over carefully?
Could you fool him as you fool others?
10 He would certainly correct you
if you took his side in secret.
11 Wouldn't his glory terrify you?
Wouldn't the fear of him fall on you?
12 Your sayings are as useless as ashes.
The answers you give are as weak as clay.

13 "So be quiet and let me speak.
Then I won't care what happens to me.
14 Why do I put myself in danger?
Why do I take my life in my hands?
15 Even if God kills me, I'll still put my hope in him.
I'll argue my case in front of him.
16 No matter how things turn out,
I'm sure I'll still be saved.
After all, no ungodly person
would dare to come into his court.
17 Listen carefully to what I'm saying.
Pay close attention to my words.
18 I've prepared my case.
And I know I'll be proved right.
19 Can others bring charges against me?
If they can, I'll keep quiet and die.

20 "God, I won't hide from you.
Here are the only two things I want.
21 Keep your powerful hand far away from me.
And stop making me so afraid.
22 Then send for me, and I'll answer.
Or let me speak, and you reply.
23 How many things have I done wrong?
How many sins have I committed?
Show me my crime. Show me my sin.
24 Why do you turn your face away from me?
Why do you think of me as your enemy?
25 I'm already like a leaf that is blown by the wind.
Are you going to terrify me even more?
I'm already like dry straw.
Are you going to keep on chasing me?
26 You write down bitter things against me.
You make me suffer for the sins
I committed when I was young.
27 You put my feet in chains.
You watch every step I take.
You do it by putting marks on the bottom of my feet.

28 "People waste away like something that is rotten.
They are like clothes that are eaten by moths.

14 They have only a few days to live.
Their lives are full of trouble.
2 They grow like flowers, and then they dry up.
They are like shadows that quickly disappear.
3 "God, why do you keep looking at someone like me?
Are you planning to take me to court?
4 Who can bring what is pure from something that isn't pure?
No one!
5 You decide how long anyone will live.
You have established the number of his months.
You have set a limit to the number of his days.
6 So look away from him. Leave him alone.
Let him put in his time like a hired worker.

7 "At least there is hope for a tree.
If it's cut down, it will begin to grow again.
New branches will appear on it.
8 Its roots may grow old in the ground.
Its stump may die in the soil.
9 But when it smells water, it will begin to grow.
It will send out new growth like a plant.
10 No man is like that. When he dies, he is buried in a grave.
He takes his last breath. Then he is gone.
11 Water disappears from lakes.
Riverbeds become empty and dry.
12 In the same way, a man lies down and never gets up.
He won't wake up or rise from his sleep
until the heavens are gone.

13 "I wish you would hide me in a grave!
I wish you would cover me up until your anger passes by!
I wish you would set the time for me to spend in the grave
and then bring me back up!
14 If a man dies, will he live again?
All the days of my hard work
I will wait for the time when you give me new life.
15 You will call out to me, and I will answer you.
Your hands created me. So you will long for me.
16 Then you will count every step I take.
But you won't keep track of my sin.
17 The wrong things I've done will be sealed up in a bag.
You will wipe out my sins by forgiving them.

18 "A mountain wears away and crumbles.
A rock is moved from its place.
19 Water wears stones away.
Storms wash soil away.
In the same way, you destroy our hope.
20 You overpower us completely, and then we're gone.
You change the way we look and send us to our graves.
21 If our children are honored, we don't even know it.
If they are dishonored, we don't even see it.

22 All we feel is the pain of our own bodies.
We are full of sadness only for ourselves."

The Second Speech of Eliphaz

15 Then Eliphaz the Temanite replied,

2 "Job, if you were wise,
would you answer us with a lot of meaningless talk?
Would you fill your stomach with the hot east wind?
3 Would you argue with useless words?
Would you give worthless speeches?
4 But you even cause others to lose their respect for God.
You make it hard for them to be faithful to him.
5 Your sin makes you say evil things.
You talk like people who twist the truth.
6 Your own mouth judges you, not mine.
Your own lips witness against you.

7 "Are you the first man who was ever born?
Were you created before the hills?
8 Do you listen in when God speaks with his angels?
Do you think you are the only wise person?
9 What do you know that we don't know?
What understanding do you have that we don't have?
10 People who are old and gray are on our side.
And they are even older than your parents!
11 Aren't God's words of comfort enough for you?
He speaks them to you gently.
12 Why have you let your wild ideas carry you away?
Why do your eyes flash with anger?
13 Why do you get so angry with God?
Why do words like those pour out of your mouth?

14 "Can human beings really be pure?
Can mere men really be right with God?
15 God doesn't trust his holy angels.
Even the heavens aren't pure in his sight.
16 So he'll certainly find fault with human beings.
After all, they are evil and sinful.
They drink up evil as if it were water.

17 "Listen to me. I'll explain things to you.
Let me tell you what I've seen.
18 I'll tell you what those who are wise have said.
They don't hide anything they've received
from their people of long ago.
19 The land was given only to those people.
Their wisdom didn't come from outsiders.
And here's what those who are wise have said.
20 Sinful people always suffer pain.
Mean people suffer all their lives.
21 Terrifying sounds fill their ears.
When everything seems to be going well,
robbers attack them.
22 They lose all hope of escaping the darkness of death.
They will certainly be killed with swords.
23 They wander around. They are like food for vultures.
They know that the day they will die is near.
24 Suffering and pain terrify them.
Their troubles overpower them,
like a king ready to attack his enemies.
25 They shake their fists at God.
They brag about themselves and oppose the Mighty One.
26 They boldly charge against him
with their thick, strong shields.

27 "Their faces are very fat.
Their stomachs hang out.
28 They'll live in towns that have been destroyed.
They'll live in houses where no one else lives.
The houses will crumble to pieces.
29 They won't be rich anymore. Their wealth won't last.
Their property will no longer spread out over the land.
30 They won't escape the darkness of death.
A flame will dry up everything they have.
The breath of God will blow them away.
31 Don't let them fool themselves
by trusting in what is worthless.
They won't get anything out of it.
32 Even before they die, they'll be paid back in full.
No matter what they do, it won't succeed.
33 They'll be like vines
that are stripped of their unripe grapes.
They'll be like olive trees
that drop their flowers.
34 People who are ungodly won't have any children.
Fire will burn up the tents of people who accept money
from those who want special favors.
35 Instead of having children,
ungodly people create suffering.
All they produce is evil.
They are full of lies."

Job's Reply

16 Job replied,

2 "I've heard many of those things before.
You are terrible at comforting me!
3 Your speeches go on forever.
Won't they ever end?
What's wrong with you?
Why do you keep on arguing?
4 If you and I changed places,
I could say the same things you are saying.

I could make fine speeches against you.
I could shake my head at you.
5 But what I might say would give you hope.
My words of comfort would help you.

6 "If I speak, it doesn't help me.
And if I keep quiet, my pain doesn't go away.
7 God has worn me out completely.
He has destroyed my whole family.
8 People can see the condition he has put me in.
My thin body stands as a witness against me.
9 God is angry with me.
He attacks me and tears me up.
He grinds his teeth at me.
He stares at me as if he were my enemy.
10 People make fun of me.
They slap my face and laugh at me.
All of them join together against me.
11 God has turned me over to sinful people.
He has handed me over to them.
12 Everything was going well with me.
But he broke me into pieces like a clay pot.
He grabbed me by the neck and crushed me.
He has taken aim at me.
13 He shoots his arrows at me from all sides.
Without pity, he stabs me in the kidneys.
He spills my insides on the ground.
14 He smashes through me as if I were a wall.
He rushes at me like a fighting man.

15 "I've sewed black cloth over my skin.
All I can do is sit here in the dust.
16 My face is red from crying.
I have deep circles under my eyes.
17 But I haven't harmed anyone.
My prayers to God are pure.

18 "Earth, please don't cover up my blood!
May God always hear my cry for help!
19 Even now my witness is in heaven.
The one who speaks up for me is there.
20 My go-between is my friend
as I pour out my tears to God.
21 He makes his appeal to God to help me
as a man begs someone to help his friend.

22 "Only a few years will pass by.
Then I'll go on a journey I won't return from.

17 1 My strength is almost gone.
I won't live much longer.
A grave is waiting for me.
2 People who make fun of me are all around me.
I'm forced to watch as they attack me with their words.

3 "God, please pay the price to have me set free.
Who else would put up money for me?
4 You have closed the minds of those who are trying to comfort me.
They don't understand that I haven't done anything wrong.
So don't let them win the argument.
5 Suppose a man tells lies about his friends to get a reward.
Then his own children will suffer for it.

6 "God has made everyone laugh at me.
People spit in my face.
7 My eyes have grown weak because I'm so sad.
My body is so thin it hardly casts a shadow.
8 Those who claim to be honest
are shocked when they see me.
Those who think they haven't sinned
are stirred up against me.
They think I'm ungodly.
9 But godly people will keep doing what is right.
Those who have clean hands will grow stronger.

10 "Come on, all of you! Try again!
I can't find a wise person among you.
11 My life is almost over. My plans are destroyed.
And so are the longings of my heart.
12 People like you turn night into day.
Even though it's dark you say,
'Light is nearby.'
13 Suppose the only home I can hope for is a grave.
And suppose I make my bed in the darkness of death.
14 Suppose I say to the grave,
'You are like a father to me.'
And suppose I say to its worms,
'You are like a mother or sister to me.'
15 Then what hope do I have?
Who can give me any hope?
16 Will hope go down to the gates of death with me?
Will we go down together into the dust of the grave?"

The Second Speech of Bildad

18 Then Bildad the Shuhite replied,

2 "Job, when will you stop these speeches of yours?
Be reasonable! Then we can talk.
3 Why do you look at us as if we were cattle?
Why do you think of us as being stupid?
4 Your anger is tearing you to pieces.
Does the earth have to be deserted just to prove you are right?
Must all of the rocks be moved from their places?

5 "The lamps of sinful people are blown out.
Their flames will never burn again.
6 The lights in their tents become dark.
The lamps beside those who are evil go out.
7 They walk more slowly than they used to.
Their own evil plans make them fall.
8 Their feet take them into a net.
They wander right into it.

9 A trap grabs hold of their heels.
It refuses to let them go.
10 A trap lies in their path.
A rope to catch them is hidden on the ground.
11 Terrors alarm them on every side.
They follow them every step of the way.
12 Trouble would like to eat them up.
Danger waits for them when they fall.
13 It eats away parts of their skin.
Death itself feeds on their arms and legs.
14 They are torn away from the safety of their tents.
They are marched off to the one who rules over death.
15 Fire races through their tents.
Burning sulfur is scattered over their homes.
16 Their roots dry up under them.
Their branches dry up above them.
17 No one on earth remembers them.
Their names are forgotten in the land.
18 They are driven from light into darkness.
They are thrown out of the world.
19 Their family dies out among their people.
No one is left where they used to live.
20 What has happened to them shocks the people in the west.
It terrifies the people in the east.
21 Now you know what the homes of sinners are like.
Those who don't know God live in places like that."

Job's Reply

19 Job replied,

2 "How long will you people make me suffer?
How long will you crush me with your words?
3 You have already made fun of me many times.
You have attacked me without feeling any shame.
4 Suppose it's true that I've gone down the wrong path.
Then it's my concern, not yours.
5 Suppose you want to place yourselves above me.
Suppose you want to use my shame to prove I'm wrong.
6 Then I want you to know that God hasn't treated me right.
In fact, he has captured me in his net.

7 "I cry out, 'Someone harmed me!'
But I don't get any reply.
I call out for help.
But I'm not treated fairly.
8 God has blocked my way, and I can't get through.
He has made my paths so dark I can't see where I'm going.
9 He has taken my wealth away from me.
He has stripped me of my honor.
10 He tears me down on every side until I'm gone.
He pulls up the roots of my hope as if I were a tree.
11 His anger burns against me.
He thinks I'm one of his enemies.
12 His troops march toward me in force.
They come at me from every direction.
They camp around my tent.

13 "God has caused my brothers to desert me.
The people I used to know are now strangers to me.
14 My family has gone away.
My friends have forgotten me.
15 My guests and my female servants think of me as a stranger.
They look at me as if I were an outsider.
16 I send for my servant, but he doesn't answer.
He doesn't come, even though I beg him to.
17 My wife can't stand the way my breath smells.
My own relatives won't have anything to do with me.
18 Even little children laugh at me.
When I appear, they make fun of me.
19 All of my close friends hate me.
Those I love have turned against me.
20 I'm nothing but skin and bones.
I've only escaped by the skin of my teeth.

21 "Have pity on me, my friends! Please have pity!
God has struck me down with his powerful hand.
22 Why do you chase after me as he does?
Aren't you satisfied with what you have done to me already?

23 "I wish my words were written down!
I wish they were written on a scroll!
24 I wish they were cut into lead with an iron tool!
I wish they were carved in rock forever!
25 I know that my Redeemer lives.
In the end he will stand on the earth.
26 After my skin has been destroyed,
in my body I'll still see God.
27 I myself will see him with my own eyes.
I'll see him, and he won't be a stranger to me.
How my heart longs for that day!

28 "You might say, 'Let's keep bothering Job.
After all, he's the cause of all of his suffering.'
29 But you should be afraid when God comes to judge you.
He'll be angry. He'll punish you with his sword.
Then you will know that he is the Judge."

The Second Speech of Zophar

20 Then Zophar the Naamathite replied,

2 "My troubled thoughts force me to answer you.
That's because I'm very upset.
3 What you have just said makes fun of me.
So I really have to reply to you.

4 "I'm sure you must know how things have always been.
They've been that way
ever since man was placed on this earth.
5 Those who are evil are happy for only a short time.
The joy of ungodly people lasts only for a moment.
6 Their pride might reach all the way up to the heavens.
Their heads might touch the clouds.
7 But they will disappear forever,
like the waste from their own bodies.
Anyone who has seen them will say,
'Where did they go?'
8 Like a dream they will fly away.
They will never be seen again.
They will be driven away like visions in the night.
9 The eyes that saw them won't see them anymore.
Even their own families won't remember them.
10 Their children must pay back what they took from poor people.
Their own hands must give back the wealth they stole.
11 They might feel young and very strong.
But they will soon lie down in the dust of their graves.

12 "Anything that is evil tastes sweet to them.
They keep it under their tongues for a while.
13 They can't stand to let it go.
So they hold it in their mouths.
14 But their food will turn sour in their stomachs.
It will become like the poison of a serpent inside them.
15 They will spit out the rich food they swallowed.
God will make their stomachs throw it up.
16 They will suck the poison of a serpent.
The fangs of an adder will kill them.
17 They won't enjoy streams that flow with honey.
They won't enjoy rivers that flow with cream.
18 What they worked for they must give back before they can eat it.
They won't enjoy what they have earned.
19 They've crushed poor people and left them with nothing.
They've taken over houses they didn't even build.

20 "No matter how much they have,
they always long for more.
But their treasure can't save them.
21 There isn't anything left for them to eat up.
Their success won't last.
22 While they are enjoying the good life,
trouble will catch up with them.
Terrible suffering will come on them.
23 When they've filled their stomachs,
God will pour out his burning anger on them.
He'll strike them down with blow after blow.
24 They might run away from iron weapons.
But arrows that have bronze tips will wound them.
25 They will pull the arrows out of their backs.
They will remove the shining tips from their livers.
They will be filled with terror.
26 Total darkness hides and waits for their treasures.
God will send a fire that will destroy them.
It will burn up everything that's left in their tents.
27 Heaven will show their guilt to everyone.
The earth will be a witness against them.
28 A flood will carry their houses away.
Rushing water will wash them away
on the day when God judges.
29 Now you know what God will do to sinful people.
Now you know what he has planned for them."

Job's Reply

21 Job replied,

2 "Listen carefully to what I'm saying.
Let that be the comfort you people give me.
3 Put up with me while I speak.
After I've spoken, you can make fun of me!

4 "I'm not arguing with mere human beings.
So why shouldn't I be angry and uneasy?
5 Look at me and be amazed.
Put your hand over your mouth and stop talking!
6 When I think about these things, I'm terrified.
My whole body trembles.
7 Why do sinful people keep on living?
The older they grow, the richer they get.
8 They see their children grow up around them.
They watch their family increase in number.
9 Their homes are safe.
They don't have to be afraid.
God isn't punishing them.
10 Every time their bulls mate, their cows become pregnant.
And the calves don't die before they are born.

[11] Sinful people send their children out like a
flock of lambs.
Their little ones dance around.
[12] They sing to the music of tambourines
and harps.
They have a good time while flutes are
being played.
[13] Those who are evil spend their years living
well.
They go down to their graves in peace.
[14] But they say to God, 'Leave us alone!
We don't want to know how you want us
to live.
[15] Who is the Mighty One? Why should we
serve him?
What would we get if we prayed to him?'
[16] But they aren't in control of their own success.
So I don't pay any attention to the advice
they give.

[17] "How often are their lamps blown out?
How often does trouble come on them?
How often does God punish them when
he's angry?
[18] How often are they like dried-up seed
coverings blowing in the wind?
How often are they like straw swept away
by a storm?
[19] People say, 'God punishes a man's children for
his sins.'
But let him punish the man himself.
Then he'll learn a lesson from it.
[20] Let his own eyes see how he is destroyed.
Let him drink the wine of the Mighty One's
anger.
[21] What does he care about the family he leaves
behind?
What does he care about them
when his life comes to an end?

[22] "Can anyone teach God anything?
After all, he judges even the angels in
heaven.
[23] Some people die while they are still very
strong.
They are completely secure. They have an
easy life.
[24] They are well fed.
Their bodies are healthy.
[25] Others die while their spirits are bitter.
They've never enjoyed anything good.
[26] Side by side they lie in the dust of death.
The worms in their graves cover all of them.

[27] "I know exactly what you people are thinking.
I know you are planning to do bad things
to me.
[28] You are saying to yourselves,
'Where is the great man's house now?
Where are the tents where his evil family
lived?'
[29] Haven't you ever asked questions of those
who travel?
Haven't you paid any attention to their
stories?
[30] They'll tell you that sinful people
are spared from the day of trouble.
They'll say that those people
are saved from the day when God will
judge.
[31] Who speaks against them for the way they act?
Who pays them back for what they've
done?
[32] Their bodies will be carried to their graves.
Guards will watch over their tombs.
[33] The soil in the valley will be pleasant
to those who have died.
Many people will walk along behind their
bodies.
Many others will walk in front of them.

[34] "So how can you comfort me with your
speeches?
They don't make any sense at all.
Your answers are nothing but lies!"

The Third Speech of Eliphaz

22 Then Eliphaz the Temanite replied,

[2] "Can any man be of benefit to God?
Can even a wise man be of any help to him?
[3] Job, what pleasure would it give the Mighty
One if you were right?
What would he get if you were completely
honest?

[4] "You say you have respect for him.
Is that why he corrects you?
Is that why he brings charges against you?
[5] Haven't you done many evil things?
Don't you sin again and again?
[6] You took clothes away from your relatives
just because they owed you some money.
You left them naked for no reason at all.
[7] You didn't give any water to people who
were tired.
You held food back from those who were
hungry.
[8] You did it even though you were honored and
powerful.
You owned land and lived on it.
[9] But you sent widows away without anything.
You mistreated children whose fathers
had died.
[10] That's why traps have been set all around you.
That's why sudden danger terrifies you.
[11] That's why it's so dark you can't even see.
That's why a flood covers you up.

[12] "Isn't God in the highest parts of heaven?
See how high the highest stars are!
[13] But you still say, 'What does God know?
Can he see through the darkest clouds to
judge us?
[14] He goes around in the highest heavens.
Thick clouds keep him from seeing us.'

[15] Will you stay on the old path
that sinful people have walked on?
[16] They were carried off even before they died.
Their foundations were washed away by a flood.
[17] They said to God, 'Leave us alone!
What can you do to us, you Mighty One?'
[18] But he was the one who filled their houses with good things.
So I don't pay any attention to the advice they give.

[19] "Those who do what is right are joyful
when they see sinners destroyed.
Those who haven't done anything wrong make fun of them.
[20] They say, 'Our enemies are completely destroyed.
Fire has burned up their wealth.'

[21] "Job, obey God and be at peace with him.
Then he will help you succeed.
[22] Do what he teaches you to do.
Keep his words in your heart.
[23] If you return to the Mighty One,
you will have what you had before.
But first you must remove
everything that is evil far from your tent.
[24] You must throw your gold nuggets away.
You must toss your gold from Ophir into a valley.
[25] Then the Mighty One himself will be your gold.
He'll be like the finest silver to you.
[26] You will find delight in the Mighty One.
You will honor God and trust in him.
[27] You will pray to him, and he will hear you.
You will keep the promises you made to him.
[28] What you decide to do will be done.
Light will shine on the path you take.
[29] When people are brought low you will say,
'Lift them up!'
Then God will help them.
[30] He'll even save those who are guilty.
He'll save them because your hands are clean."

Job's Reply

23 Job replied,

[2] "Even today my problems are more than I can handle.
In spite of my groans, God's hand is heavy on me.
[3] I wish I knew where I could find him!
I wish I could go to the place where he lives!
[4] I would state my case to him.
I'd give him all of my arguments.
[5] I'd find out what his answers would be.
I'd think about what he would say.
[6] Would he oppose me with his great power?
No. He wouldn't bring charges against me.
[7] I'm an honest person. I could state my case to him.
Then my Judge would tell me once and for all that I'm not guilty.

[8] "But if I go to the east, God isn't there.
If I go to the west, I don't find him.
[9] When he's working in the north, I don't see him there.
When he turns to the south, I don't see him there either.
[10] But he knows every step I take.
When he has put me to the test,
I'll come out as pure as gold.
[11] My feet have closely followed his steps.
I've stayed on his path without turning away.
[12] I haven't disobeyed his commands.
I've treasured his words more than my daily bread.

[13] "But he's the only God. Who can oppose him?
He does anything he wants to do.
[14] He carries out his plans against me.
And he still has many other plans just like them.
[15] That's why I'm so terrified.
When I think about all of this, I'm afraid of him.
[16] God has made my heart weak.
The Mighty One has filled me with terror.
[17] But even the darkness of death won't make me silent.
When the darkness of the grave covers my face, I won't be quiet.

24 "Why doesn't the Mighty One set a time for judging sinful people?
Why do those who know him have to keep waiting for that day?
[2] People move their neighbor's boundary stones.
They steal their neighbor's flocks.
[3] They take away the donkeys
that belong to children whose fathers have died.
They take a widow's ox until she has paid what she owes.
[4] They push those who are needy out of their way.
They force all of the poor people in the land to go into hiding.
[5] The poor are like wild donkeys in the desert.
They have to go around looking for food.
The dry and empty land provides the only food for their children.
[6] The poor go to the fields and get a little grain.
They gather up what is left in the vineyards of sinners.
[7] The poor don't have any clothes. So they spend the night naked.

They don't have anything to cover
themselves in the cold.
8 They are soaked by mountain rains.
They hug the rocks because they don't have
anything to keep them warm.
9 Children whose fathers have died
are torn away from their mothers.
A poor person's baby is taken away to pay
back what is owed.
10 The poor don't have any clothes. They go
around naked.
They carry bundles of grain, but they still
go hungry.
11 They work very hard as they crush olives.
They stomp on grapes in winepresses,
but they are still thirsty.
12 The groans of those who are dying are heard
from the city.
Those who are wounded cry out for help.
But God doesn't charge anyone with doing
what is wrong.

13 "Some people hate it when daylight comes.
In the daytime they never walk outside.
14 When daylight is gone, murderers get up.
They kill poor people and those who are
in need.
In the night they sneak around like robbers.
15 Those who commit adultery wait until the sun
goes down.
They think, 'No one will see us.'
They keep their faces hidden.
16 In the dark, people break into houses.
But by day they shut themselves in.
They don't want anything to do with
the light.
17 The deepest darkness is like morning to them.
The terrors of darkness are their friends.

18 "But sinners are like bubbles on the surface
of water.
Their share of the land is under God's curse.
So no one goes to their vineyards.
19 Melted snow disappears when the air is hot
and dry.
And sinners disappear when they go down
into their graves.
20 Even their mothers forget them.
The worms in their graves eat them up.
No one remembers sinful people anymore.
They are cut down like trees.
21 They mistreat women who aren't able to have
children.
They aren't kind to widows.
22 But God is powerful.
He even drags away people who are strong.
When he rises up against them,
they can never be sure they are safe.
23 God might let them rest and feel secure.
But his eyes see how they live.
24 For a little while they are honored.
Then they are gone.
They are brought low.
And they die like everyone else.
They are cut off like heads of grain.

25 "Who can prove that what I'm saying
is wrong?
Who can prove that my words aren't true?"

The Third Speech of Bildad

25 Then Bildad the Shuhite replied,

2 "God is King. He should be feared.
He establishes peace in the highest parts
of heaven.
3 Can anyone count his troops?
Is there anyone his light doesn't shine on?
4 How can human beings be right with God?
How can mere people really be pure?
5 Even the moon isn't bright
and the stars aren't pure in God's eyes.
6 So how about human beings? They are like
maggots.
How about mere people? They are like
worms."

Job's Reply

26 Job replied,

2 "Bildad, you haven't helped people who aren't
strong!
You haven't saved people who are weak!
3 You haven't offered advice to those who
aren't wise!
In fact, you haven't understood anything
at all!
4 Who helped you say those things?
Whose spirit was speaking through you?

5 "The spirits of the dead are suffering greatly.
So are those that are under the waters.
And so are all those that live in them.
6 Death is naked in the sight of God.
The Grave lies open in front of him.
7 He spreads out the northern skies over empty
space.
He hangs the earth over nothing.
8 He wraps up water in his clouds.
They are heavy, but they don't burst.
9 He covers the face of the full moon.
He spreads his clouds over it.
10 He marks out the place where the sky meets
the sea.
He marks out the boundary between light
and darkness.
11 The pillars of the heavens shake.
They are terrified when his anger blazes out.
12 With his power he stirred up the oceans.
In his wisdom he cut the sea monster Rahab
to pieces.
13 His breath made the skies bright and clear.
His hand wounded the serpent that glides
through the sea.

[14]Those are only on the edges of what he does.
They are only the soft whispers that we hear from him.
So who can understand how very powerful he is?"

27 Job continued to speak. He said,

[2]"God hasn't treated me fairly.
The Mighty One has made my spirit bitter.
You can be sure that God lives.
And here's something else you can be sure of.
[3]As long as I have life
and God gives me breath,
[4]my mouth won't say evil things.
My lips won't tell lies.
[5]I'll never admit you people are right.
Until I die, I'll say I'm telling the truth.
[6]I'll continue to say I'm right.
I'll never let go of that.
I won't blame myself as long as I live.

[7]"May my enemies suffer like sinful people!
May my attackers be punished like those who aren't fair!
[8]What hope do ungodly people have when their lives are cut off?
What hope do they have when God takes away their lives?
[9]God won't listen to their cry
when trouble comes on them.
[10]They won't take delight in the Mighty One.
They'll never call out to God.

[11]"I'll teach all of you about God's power.
I won't hide the things the Mighty One does.
[12]You have seen those things yourselves.
So why do you continue your useless talk?

[13]"Here's what God does to sinful people.
Here's what those who are mean receive from the Mighty One.
[14]All of their children will be killed with swords.
They'll never have enough to eat.
[15]A plague will kill those who are left alive.
The widows of sinful men
won't even sob over their own children.
[16]Sinners might store up silver like dust
and clothes like piles of clay.
[17]But people who do what is right will wear those clothes.
People who haven't done anything wrong
will divide up that silver.
[18]The house an evil person builds is like a moth's cocoon.
It's like a hut that's made by someone on guard duty.
[19]Sinful people lie down wealthy, but their wealth is taken away.
When they open their eyes, everything is gone.
[20]Terrors sweep over them like a flood.
A storm takes them away during the night.
[21]The east wind carries them off, and they are gone.
It sweeps them out of their houses.
[22]It blows against them without mercy.
They try to escape from its power.
[23]It claps its hands and makes fun of them.
It hisses them out of their houses.

28 "There are mines where silver is found.
There are places where gold is purified.
[2]Iron is taken out of the earth.
Copper is melted down from ore.
[3]A miner lights up the darkness.
He searches for ore in the deepest pits.
He looks for it in the blackest darkness.
[4]Far from where people live he cuts a tunnel.
He does it in places where others don't go.
Far away from people he swings back and forth on ropes.
[5]Food grows on the surface of the earth.
But far below, the earth is changed as if by fire.
[6]Sapphires are taken from its rocks.
Its dust contains nuggets of gold.
[7]No bird knows the miner's hidden path.
No falcon's eye has seen it.
[8]Proud animals don't walk on it.
Lions don't prowl there.
[9]The miner attacks the hardest rock.
His strong hands uncover the base of the mountains.
[10]He tunnels through the rock.
His eyes see all of its treasures.
[11]He searches the places where the rivers begin.
He brings hidden things out into the light.

[12]"And where can wisdom be found?
Where does understanding live?
[13]No one knows how much it's worth.
It can't be found anywhere in the world.
[14]The ocean says, 'It's not in me.'
The sea says, 'It's not here either.'
[15]It can't be bought with the finest gold.
Its price can't be weighed out in silver.
[16]It can't be bought with gold from Ophir.
It can't be bought with priceless onyx or sapphires.
[17]Gold or crystal can't compare with it.
It can't be bought with jewels made of gold.
[18]Don't bother to talk about coral and jasper.
Wisdom is worth far more than rubies.
[19]A topaz from Cush can't compare with it.
It can't be bought with the purest gold.

[20]"So where does wisdom come from?
Where does understanding live?
[21]It's hidden from the eyes of every living thing.
Even the birds of the air can't find it.
[22]Death and the Grave say,
'Only reports about it have reached our ears.'

23 But God understands the way to it.
He's the only one who knows where it lives.
24 He sees from one end of the earth to the other.
He views everything in the world.
25 He made the mighty wind.
He measured out the waters.
26 He gave orders for the rain to fall.
He made paths for the thunderstorms.
27 Then he looked at wisdom and set its price.
He established it and put it to the test.
28 He said to human beings,
'Have respect for me. That will prove you are wise.
Avoid evil. That will show you have understanding.' "

29 Job continued to speak. He said,

2 "How I long for the good old days!
That's when God watched over me.
3 The light of his lamp shone on me.
I walked through darkness by his light.
4 Those were the best days of my life.
That's when God's friendship blessed my house.
5 The Mighty One was still with me.
My children were all around me.
6 The path in front of me was like sweet cream.
It was as if the rock poured out olive oil for me.

7 "In those days I went to the city gate.
I took my seat as a member of the council.
8 Young people who saw me stepped to one side.
Old people stood up as I approached.
9 The leaders stopped speaking.
They covered their mouths with their hands.
10 The voices of the nobles became quiet.
Their tongues stuck to the roofs of their mouths.
11 Everyone who heard me said good things about me.
Those who saw me honored me.
12 That's because I saved poor people who cried out for help.
I saved helpless children whose fathers had died.
13 Those who were dying gave me their blessing.
I made the hearts of widows sing.
14 I put on a godly life as if it were my clothes.
Fairness was my robe and my turban.
15 I was like eyes for those who were blind.
I was like feet for those who couldn't walk.
16 I was like a father to needy people.
I stood up for strangers in court.
17 Sinners are like animals that have powerful teeth.
But I took from their mouths the people they had caught.

18 "I thought, 'I'll die in my own house.
The days of my life will be as many as the grains of sand.
19 My roots will reach down to the water.
The dew will lie all night on my branches.
20 I will remain healthy and strong.
My bow will stay as good as new in my hand.'

21 "People wanted to hear what I had to say.
They waited silently for the advice I gave them.
22 After I had spoken, they didn't speak anymore.
My words fell gently on their ears.
23 They waited for me just as they would wait for showers.
They drank my words just as they would drink the spring rain.
24 When I smiled at them, they could hardly believe it.
The light of my face lifted their spirits.
25 I chose the way they should go. I sat as their chief.
I lived as a king lives among his troops.
I was like someone who comforts those who are sad.

30 "But now those who are younger than I am make fun of me.
I wouldn't put even their parents with my sheep dogs!
2 Their strong hands couldn't give me any help.
That's because their strength was gone.
3 They were weak because they were needy and hungry.
They wandered through dry and empty deserts at night.
4 Among the bushes they gathered salty plants.
They ate the roots of desert trees.
5 They were driven away from society.
They were shouted at as if they were robbers.
6 They were forced to live in dry stream beds.
They had to stay among rocks
and in holes in the ground.
7 Like donkeys they cried out among the bushes.
There they crowded together and hid.
8 They were so foolish that no one respected them.
They were driven out of the land.

9 "Now their children laugh at me.
They make fun of me with their songs.
10 They hate me. They stay away from me.
They even dare to spit in my face.
11 God has made my body weak.
It's like a tent that has fallen down.
So those children do what they want to in front of me.
12 Many people attack me on my right side.
They lay traps for my feet.
They come at me from every direction.
13 They tear up the road I walk on.
They succeed in destroying me.
They do it without any help.

14 They attack me like troops smashing through
a wall.
Among the destroyed buildings they come
rolling in.
15 Terrors sweep over me.
My honor is driven away as if by the wind.
My safety vanishes like a cloud.

16 "Now my life is slipping away.
Days of suffering grab hold of me.
17 At night my bones hurt.
My gnawing pains never stop.
18 God's great power becomes like clothes
to me.
He chokes me like the neck of my shirt.
19 He throws me down into the mud.
I'm nothing but dust and ashes.

20 "God, I cry out to you. But you don't
answer me.
I stand up. But all you do is look at me.
21 You do mean things to me.
Your mighty hand attacks me.
22 You pick me up and blow me away with
the wind.
You toss me around in the storm.
23 I know that you will bring me down to death.
That's what you have appointed for
everyone.

24 "No one would crush people
when they cry out for help in their trouble.
25 Haven't I sobbed over those who are in
trouble?
Haven't I felt sorry for poor people?
26 I hoped good things would happen, but
something evil came.
I looked for light, but all I saw was
darkness.
27 My insides are always churning.
Nothing but days of suffering are ahead
of me.
28 My skin has become dark, but the sun didn't
do it.
I stand up in the community and cry out
for help.
29 I've become a brother to wild dogs.
Owls are my companions.
30 My skin grows black and peels.
My body burns with fever.
31 My harp is tuned to sadness.
My flute makes a sound like sobbing.

31 "I made an agreement with my eyes.
I promised not to look at another woman
with sexual longing.
2 What do human beings receive from God
above?
What do they get from the Mighty One
in heaven?
3 Sinful people are destroyed.
Trouble comes to those who do what
is wrong.
4 Doesn't God see how I live?
Doesn't he count every step I take?

5 "I haven't told any lies.
My feet haven't hurried to cheat others.
6 So let God weigh me in honest scales.
Then he'll know I haven't done anything
wrong.
7 Suppose my steps have turned away from the
right path.
Suppose my heart has longed for what my
eyes have seen.
Or suppose my hands have become
'unclean.'
8 Then may others eat what I've planted.
May my crops be pulled up by the roots.

9 "Suppose my heart has been tempted by a
woman.
Or suppose I've prowled around my
neighbor's door.
10 Then may my wife grind another man's grain.
May other men have sex with her.
11 Wanting another woman would have been a
shameful thing.
It would have been a sin that should be
judged.
12 It's like a fire that burns down to the grave.
It would have caused my crops to be pulled
up by the roots.

13 "Suppose I haven't treated my male and female
servants fairly
when they've brought charges against me.
14 Then what will I do when God opposes me?
What answer will I give him
when he asks me to explain myself?
15 Didn't he who made me make my servants
also?
Didn't the same God form us inside our
mothers?

16 "I haven't said no to what poor people have
wanted.
I haven't let widows lose their hope.
17 I haven't kept my bread to myself.
I've shared it with children whose fathers
had died.
18 From the time I was young, I've helped those
widows.
I've raised those children as a father
would.
19 Suppose I've seen people dying
because they didn't have any clothes.
I've seen needy people
who had nothing to wear.
20 And they didn't give me their blessing
when I warmed them with wool from
my sheep.
21 Suppose I've raised my hand
against children whose fathers have died.
And I did it because I knew
I had power in the courts.

Then let my arm fall from my shoulder.
Let it be broken off at the joint.
23 I was afraid God would destroy me.
His glory terrifies me.
So I'd never do things like that.

24 "Suppose I've put my trust in gold.
I've said to pure gold, 'You make me feel secure.'
25 And I'm happy because I'm so wealthy.
I'm glad because my hands have earned so much.
26 Suppose I've worshiped the sun in all of its glory.
I've bowed down to the moon in all of its beauty.
27 My heart has been secretly tempted.
My hand has thrown kisses to the sun and moon.
28 Then those things would have been sins that should be judged.
And I wouldn't have been faithful to God in heaven.

29 "I wasn't happy when hard times came to my enemies.
I didn't enjoy seeing the trouble they had.
30 I didn't allow my mouth to sin
by calling down curses on them.
31 The workers in my house always said,
'Job always gives plenty of food to everyone.'
32 No stranger ever had to spend the night in the street.
My door was always open to travelers.
33 I didn't hide my sin as others do.
I didn't hide my guilt in my heart.
34 I was never afraid of the crowd.
I never worried that my relatives might hate me.
I didn't have to keep quiet or stay inside.

35 "I wish someone would listen to me!
I'm signing my name to everything I've said.
I hope the Mighty One will give me his answer.
I hope the one who brings charges against me will write them down.
36 I'll wear them on my shoulder.
I'll put them on my head like a crown.
37 I'll give that person a report of every step I take.
I'll approach him like a prince.

38 "Suppose my land cries out against me.
And all of its soil is wet with tears.
39 Suppose I've used up its crops without paying for them.
Or I've broken the spirit of its renters.
40 Then let thorns grow instead of wheat.
Let weeds come up instead of barley."

The words of Job end here.

The Speech of Elihu

32 So the three men stopped answering Job, because he thought he was right.
2 But Elihu the Buzite burned with anger against
Job. That's because Job said he himself was right
instead of God. Elihu was the son of Barakel. He
was from the family of Ram.
3 Elihu's anger also burned against Job's three
friends. They hadn't found any way to prove that
Job was wrong. But they still said he was guilty.
4 Elihu had waited before he spoke to Job. That's
because the others were older than he was. 5 But he
saw that the three men didn't have anything more
to say. So he burned with anger.
6 Elihu the Buzite, the son of Barakel, said,

"I'm young, and you are old.
So I was afraid to tell you what I know.
7 I thought, 'Those who are older should speak first.
Those who have lived for many years should teach people how to be wise.'
8 But the spirit in people gives them understanding.
The breath of the Mighty One gives them wisdom.
9 Older people aren't the only ones who are wise.
They aren't the only ones who understand what is right.

10 "So I'm saying you should listen to me.
I'll tell you what I know.
11 I waited while you men spoke.
I listened to your reasoning.
While you were searching for words,
12 I paid careful attention to you.
But not one of you has proved that Job is wrong.
None of you has answered his arguments.
13 Don't claim, 'We have enough wisdom to answer Job.'
Let God, not a mere man, prove that he's wrong.
14 Job hasn't directed his words against me.
I won't answer him with your arguments.

15 "Job, those men are afraid.
They don't have anything else to say.
They've run out of words.
16 Do I have to keep on waiting, now that they are silent?
They are just standing there with nothing to say.
17 I too have something to say.
I too will tell what I know.
18 I'm full of words.
My spirit inside me forces me to speak.
19 Inside I'm like wine that is bottled up.
I'm like new wineskins ready to burst.
20 I must speak so I can feel better.
I must open my mouth and reply.

21 I'll treat everyone the same.
I won't praise anyone without meaning it.
22 If I weren't honest when I praised people,
my Maker would soon take me from this life.

33 "Job, listen now to my words.
Pay attention to everything I say.
2 I'm about to open my mouth.
My words are on the tip of my tongue.
3 What I say comes from an honest heart.
My lips speak only what I know is true.
4 The Spirit of God has made me.
The breath of the Mighty One gives me life.
5 So answer me if you can.
Prepare yourself to face me.
6 In God's sight I'm just like you.
I too have been made out of clay.
7 You don't have to be afraid of me.
My hand won't be too heavy on you.

8 "But I heard what you said.
And here are the exact words I heard.
9 You said, 'I'm pure. I haven't sinned in the ways you have charged.
I'm clean. I'm not guilty of doing anything wrong.
10 But God has found fault with me.
He thinks I'm his enemy.
11 He puts my feet in chains.
He watches every step I take.'

12 "But I'm telling you that you aren't right when you talk like that.
After all, God is greater than a mere man.
13 Why do you claim that God
never answers any of our questions?
14 He speaks in one way and then another.
We might not even realize it.
15 He might speak in a dream or in a vision at night.
That's when people are sound asleep in their beds.
16 He might speak in their ears.
His warnings might terrify them.
17 He warns men in order to turn them away from sinning.
He wants to keep them from being proud.
18 He wants to stop them from going down into the grave.
He doesn't want them to be killed with swords.
19 Someone might be punished by suffering in bed.
The pain in his bones might never go away.
20 He might feel so bad he can't eat anything.
He might even hate the finest food.
21 His body might waste away to nothing.
His bones might have been hidden.
But now they stick out.
22 He might approach the very edge of the grave.
The messengers of death might come for him.

23 "But suppose there is an angel who will speak up for him.
The angel is very special. He's one out of a thousand.
He will tell that person what is right for him.
24 He'll be gracious to him. He'll say to God,
'Spare him from going down into the grave.
I know a way that can set him free.'
25 Then his body is made like new again.
He becomes as strong and healthy as when he was young.
26 He prays to God and finds favor with him.
He sees God's face and shouts with joy.
God makes him right with himself again.
27 Then the person comes to others and says,
'I sinned. I made what was wrong appear to be right.
But I wasn't punished as I should have been.
28 God set me free. He kept me from going down into the grave.
So I'll live to enjoy the light that leads to life.'

29 "God does all of those things to people.
In fact, he does them again and again.
30 He wants to stop people from going down into the grave.
Then the light that leads to life will shine on them.

31 "Pay attention, Job! Listen to me!
Be quiet so I can speak.
32 If you have anything to say, answer me.
Speak up. I want to help you be cleared of all charges.
33 But if you don't have anything to say, listen to me.
Be quiet so I can teach you how to be wise."

34 Elihu continued,

2 "Hear what I'm saying, you wise men.
Listen to me, you who have learned so much.
3 Our tongues tell us what tastes good and what doesn't.
And our ears tell us what's true and what isn't.
4 So let's choose for ourselves what is right.
Let's learn together what is good.

5 "Job says, 'I'm not guilty of doing anything wrong.
But God doesn't treat me fairly.
6 Even though I'm right,
he thinks I'm a liar.
Even though I'm not guilty,
his arrows give me wounds that can't be healed.'
7 Is there any other man like Job?
He laughs at God and makes fun of him.
8 He's a companion of those who do evil.
He spends his time with sinful people.

He asks, 'What good is it
to try to please God?'

10 "So listen to me, you men who have
understanding.
God would never do what is evil.
The Mighty One would never do what
is wrong.
11 He pays a man back for what he's done.
He gives him exactly what he should get.
12 It isn't possible for God to do wrong.
The Mighty One would never treat people
unfairly.
13 Who appointed him to rule over the earth?
Who put him in charge of the
whole world?
14 If he really wanted to,
he could hold back his spirit and breath.
15 Then everyone would die together.
They would return to the dust.

16 "Job, if you have understanding, listen to me.
Pay attention to what I'm saying.
17 Can someone who hates to be fair govern?
Will you bring charges against the holy and
mighty One?
18 He says to kings, 'You are worthless.'
He says to nobles, 'You are evil.'
19 He doesn't favor princes.
He treats rich people and poor people
the same.
His hands created all of them.
20 They die suddenly in the middle of the night.
God strikes them down, and they
pass away.
Those who are mighty are removed, but not
by human hands.

21 "His eyes see how people live.
He watches every step they take.
22 There isn't a dark place or deep shadow
where those who do what is evil can hide.
23 God doesn't need to bring charges against men.
He knows they are guilty.
So he doesn't need to have them appear in
his court to be judged.
24 He destroys the mighty without asking them
questions in court.
Then he sets others up in their places.
25 He knows what they do.
So he crushes them during the night.
26 He punishes them for the sins they commit.
He does it where everyone can see them.
27 That's because they turned away from
following him.
They didn't have respect for anything
he does.
28 They caused poor people to cry out to him.
He heard the cries of those who were
in need.
29 But if he remains silent, who can judge him?
If he turns his face away, who can see him?
He rules over people and nations alike.
30 He keeps those who are ungodly from
ruling.
He keeps them from laying traps for others.

31 "Someone might say to God,
'I'm guilty of sinning,
but I won't do it anymore.
32 Show me my sins that I'm not aware of.
If I've done what is wrong,
I won't do it again.'
33 But you refuse to turn away from your sins.
So God won't treat you the way you want to
be treated.
You must decide, Job. I can't do it for you.
So tell me what you know.

34 "You men who have understanding have
spoken.
You wise men who hear me have said
to me,
35 'Job doesn't know what he's talking about.
The things he has said don't make any
sense.'
36 I wish Job would be put to the hardest test!
He answered like someone who is evil.
37 To his sin he adds even more sin.
He claps his hands and makes fun of us.
He multiplies his words against God."

35

Elihu continued,

2 "Job, do you think it's fair for you to say,
'God will clear me of all charges'?
3 You ask him, 'What good is it for me not
to sin?
What do I get by not sinning?'

4 "I'd like to reply to you
and to your friends who are with you.
5 Look up at the heavens.
Observe the clouds that are high above you.
6 If you sin, what does that mean to God?
If you sin many times, what does that do
to him?
7 If you do what is right, how does that
help him?
What does he get from you?
8 The evil things you do only hurt someone like
yourself.
The right things you do only help other
human beings.

9 "People cry out when they are beaten down.
They beg to be set free from the power of
those who are over them.
10 But no one says, 'Where is the God who
made me?
He gives us songs even during the night.
11 He teaches more to us than to wild animals.
He makes us wiser than the birds of the air.'
12 He doesn't answer sinful people when they cry
out to him.
That's because they are so proud.

[13] In fact, God doesn't listen to their empty cries.
The Mighty One doesn't pay any attention to them.
[14] So he certainly won't listen to you.
When you say you don't see him, he won't hear you.
He won't listen when you state your case to him.
He won't pay attention even if you wait for him.
[15] When you say his anger never punishes sin, he won't hear you.
He won't listen when you say he doesn't pay any attention to evil.
[16] So you say things that don't mean anything.
You use a lot of words,
but you don't know what you are talking about."

36 Elihu continued,

[2] "Put up with me a little longer.
I'll show you I can speak up for God even more.
[3] I get my knowledge from far away.
I'll announce that the One who made me is fair.
[4] You can be sure that my words are true.
One who has perfect knowledge is talking to you.

[5] "God is mighty, but he doesn't hate people.
He's mighty, and he knows exactly what he's going to do.
[6] He doesn't keep alive those who are evil.
Instead, he gives suffering people their rights.
[7] He watches over those who do what is right.
He puts them on thrones as if they were kings.
He honors them forever.
[8] But some people are held by chains.
They are tied up with painful ropes.
[9] God tells them what they've done.
He tells them they've become proud and sinned against him.
[10] He makes them listen when he corrects them.
He commands them to turn away
from the evil things they've done.
[11] If they obey him and serve him,
they'll enjoy a long and happy life.
Things will go well with them.
[12] But if they don't listen to him,
they'll be killed with swords.
They'll die because they didn't want to know anything about him.

[13] "Those whose hearts are ungodly are always angry.
Even when God puts them in chains,
they don't cry out for help.
[14] They die while they are still young.
They die among the male prostitutes at the temples.
[15] But God saves suffering people while they are suffering.
He speaks to them while they are hurting.

[16] "Job, he wants to take you out of the jaws of trouble.
He wants to bring you to a wide and safe place.
He'd like to seat you at a table that is loaded with the best food.
[17] But now you are loaded down
with the punishment sinners will receive.
You have been judged fairly.
[18] Be careful that no one tempts you with riches.
Don't take money from people who want special favors,
no matter how much it is.
[19] Can your wealth keep you out of trouble?
Can all of your mighty efforts keep you going?
[20] Don't long for the night to come
so you can drag people away from their homes.
[21] Be careful not to do what is evil.
You seem to like evil better than suffering!

[22] "God is honored because he is so powerful.
He has no equal as a teacher.
[23] Who has told him what he can do?
Who has said to him, 'You have done what is wrong'?
[24] Remember to thank him for what he's done.
People have praised him with their songs.
[25] Every human being has seen his work.
People can see it from far away.
[26] How great God is! We'll never completely understand him.
We'll never find out how long he has lived.

[27] "He makes mist rise from the water.
Then it falls as rain into the streams.
[28] The clouds pour down their moisture.
Rain showers fall on people everywhere.
[29] Who can understand how God spreads out the clouds?
Who can explain how he thunders from his home in heaven?
[30] See how he scatters his lightning around him!
He lights up the deepest parts of the ocean.
[31] The rain he sends makes things grow for the nations.
He provides them with plenty of food.
[32] He holds lightning bolts in his hands.
He commands them to strike their marks.
[33] His thunder announces that a storm is coming.
Even the cattle let us know it's approaching.

37 "When I hear the thunder, my heart pounds.
It beats faster inside me.
[2] Listen! Listen to the roar of his voice!
Listen to the thunder that comes from him!

3 He sends his lightning across the sky.
It reaches from one end of the earth to the other.
4 Next comes the sound of his roaring thunder.
He thunders with his majestic voice.
When his voice fills the air,
he doesn't hold anything back.
5 God's voice thunders in wonderful ways.
We'll never understand the great things he does.
6 He says to the snow, 'Fall on the earth.'
He tells the rain, 'Pour down your mighty waters.'
7 He stops everyone from working.
He wants them to see his work.
8 The animals go inside.
They remain in their dens.
9 The storm comes out of its storeroom in the heavens.
The cold comes from the driving winds.
10 The breath of God produces ice.
The shallow water freezes over.
11 He loads the clouds with moisture.
He scatters his lightning through them.
12 He directs the clouds to circle
above the surface of the whole earth.
They do everything he commands them to do.
13 He tells the clouds to punish people.
Or he brings them to water his earth and show his love.

14 "Job, listen to me.
Stop and think about the wonderful things God does.
15 Do you know how he controls the clouds?
Do you understand how he makes his lightning flash?
16 Do you know how the clouds stay up in the sky?
Do you understand the wonders of the One who has perfect knowledge?
17 Even your clothes are too hot for you
when the land lies quiet under the south wind.
18 Can you help God spread out the skies?
They are as hard as a mirror
that's made out of bronze.

19 "Job, tell us what we should say to God.
We can't prepare our case
because our minds are dark.
20 Should he be told that I want to speak?
Would any man ask to be destroyed by him?
21 No one can look at the sun.
It's too bright after the wind has swept the skies clean.
22 Out of the north, God comes in his shining glory.
He comes in all of his wonderful majesty.
23 We can't reach up to the Mighty One.
He is lifted high because of his power.
Everything he does is fair and right.
So he doesn't crush people.
24 That's why they have respect for him.
He cares about all those who are wise."

The First Speech of the LORD

38 The LORD spoke to Job out of a storm. He said,

2 "Who do you think you are to disagree with my plans?
You do not know what you are talking about.
3 Get ready to stand up for yourself.
I will ask you some questions.
Then I want you to answer me.

4 "Where were you when I laid the earth's foundation?
Tell me, if you know.
5 Who measured it? I am sure you know!
Who stretched a measuring line across it?
6 What was it built on?
Who laid its most important stone?
7 When it happened, the morning stars sang together.
All of the angels shouted with joy.

8 "Who created the ocean?
Who caused it to be born?
9 I put clouds over it as if they were its clothes.
I wrapped it in thick darkness.
10 I set limits for it.
I put its doors and metal bars in place.
11 I said, 'You can come this far.
But you can't come any farther.
Here is where your proud waves have to stop.'

12 "Job, have you ever commanded the morning to come?
Have you ever shown the sun where to rise?
13 The daylight takes the earth by its edges
as if it were a blanket.
Then it shakes sinful people out of it.
14 The earth takes shape like clay under a seal.
Its features stand out
like the different parts of your clothes.
15 Sinners would rather have darkness than light.
When the light comes, their power is broken.

16 "Have you traveled to the springs at the bottom of the ocean?
Have you walked in its deepest parts?
17 Have the gates of death been shown to you?
Have you seen the gates of darkness?
18 Do you understand how big the earth is?
Tell me, if you know all of those things.

19 "Where does light come from?
And where does darkness live?
20 Can you take them to their places?
Do you know the paths to their houses?

21 I am sure you know! After all, you were
already born!
You have lived so many years!

22 "Have you entered the places where the snow
is kept?
Have you seen the storerooms for the hail?
23 I store up snow and hail for times of trouble.
I keep them for days of war and battle.
24 Where does lightning come from?
Where do the east winds that blow across
the earth live?
25 Who tells the rain where it should fall?
Who makes paths for the thunderstorms?
26 They bring water to places where no one lives.
They water deserts that do not have anyone
in them.
27 They satisfy the needs of dry and empty lands.
They make grass start growing there.
28 Does the rain have a father?
Who is the father of the drops of dew?
29 Does the ice have a mother?
Who is the mother of the frost from the
heavens?
30 The waters become as hard as stone.
The surface of the ocean freezes over.

31 "Can you tie up the beautiful Pleiades?
Can you untie the ropes that hold Orion
together?
32 Can you bring out all of the stars in their
seasons?
Can you lead out the Big Dipper and the
Little Dipper?
33 Do you know the laws that govern the heavens?
Can you rule over the earth the way I do?

34 "Can you give orders to the clouds?
Can you make them pour rain down on you?
35 Do you send the lightning bolts on their way?
Do they report to you, 'Here we are'?
36 Who put wisdom in people's hearts?
Who gave understanding to their minds?
37 Who is wise enough to count the clouds?
Who can tip over the water jars of the
heavens?
38 I tip them over when the ground becomes hard.
I do it when the dirt sticks together.

39 "Do you hunt for food for mother lions?
Do you satisfy the hunger of their cubs?
40 Some of them lie low in their dens.
Others lie waiting in the bushes.
41 Who provides food for ravens
when their babies cry out to me?
They wander around because they do not
have anything to eat.

39 "Job, do you know when mountain goats
have their babies?
Do you watch when female deer give birth?
2 Do you count the months until the animals
have their babies?
Do you know the time when they give birth?
3 They bend their back legs and have their
babies.
Then their labor pains stop.
4 Their little ones grow strong and healthy in
the wild.
They leave and do not come home again.

5 "Who let the wild donkeys go free?
Who untied their ropes?
6 I gave them the dry and empty land as their
home.
I gave them salt flats to live in.
7 They laugh at all of the noise in town.
They do not hear the shouts of the donkey
drivers.
8 They wander over the hills to look for grass.
They search for anything green to eat.

9 "Job, will wild oxen agree to serve you?
Will they stay by your feed box at night?
10 Can you keep them in straight rows with
harnesses?
Will they plow the valleys behind you?
11 Will you depend on them for their great
strength?
Will you let them do your heavy work?
12 Can you trust them to bring in your grain?
Will they take it to your threshing floor?

13 "The wings of ostriches flap with joy.
But they can't compare with the wings and
feathers of storks.
14 Ostriches lay their eggs on the ground.
They let them get warm in the sand.
15 They do not know that something might step
on them.
A wild animal might walk all over them.
16 Ostriches are mean to their little ones.
They treat them as if they did not belong
to them.
They do not care that their work was
useless.
17 I did not provide ostriches with wisdom.
I did not give them good sense.
18 But when they spread their feathers to run,
they laugh at a horse and its rider.

19 "Job, do you give horses their strength?
Do you put flowing manes on their necks?
20 Do you make them jump like locusts?
They terrify others with their proud
snorting.
21 They paw the ground wildly.
They are filled with joy.
They charge at their enemies.
22 They laugh at fear. They are not afraid of
anything.
They do not run away from swords.
23 Many arrows rattle at their sides.
Flashing spears and javelins are also there.
24 They are so stirred up that they eat up the
ground.
They can't stand still when trumpets
are blown.

25 When they hear the trumpets they snort, 'Aha!'
They catch the smells of battle far away.
They hear the shouts of commanders and the battle cries.

26 "Job, are you wise enough to teach hawks where to fly?
They spread their wings and fly toward the south.
27 Do you command eagles to fly so high?
They build their nests as high as they can.
28 They live on cliffs and stay there at night.
High up on the rocks they think they are safe.
29 From there they look for their food.
They can see it from far away.
30 Their little ones like to eat blood.
Eagles gather where they see dead bodies."

40 The LORD continued,

2 "I am the Mighty One.
Will the man who argues with me correct me?
Let him who brings charges against me answer me!"

Job's Reply

3 Job replied to the LORD,

4 "I'm not worthy. How can I reply to you?
I'm putting my hand over my mouth. I'll stop talking.
5 I spoke once. But I really don't have any answer.
I spoke twice. But I won't say anything else."

The Second Speech of the LORD

6 Then the LORD spoke to Job out of the storm. He said,

7 "Get ready to stand up for yourself.
I will ask you some more questions.
Then I want you to answer me.

8 "Would you dare to claim that I am not being fair?
Would you judge me in order to make yourself seem right?
9 Is your arm as powerful as mine is?
Can your voice thunder as mine does?
10 Then put on glory and beauty as if they were your clothes.
Also put honor and majesty on.
11 Let loose your great anger.
Look at those who are proud and bring them low.
12 Look at proud people and bring them down.
Crush those who are evil right where they are.
13 Bury their bodies in the dust together.
Cover their faces in the grave.
14 Then I myself will admit to you
that your own right hand can save you.

15 "Look at the behemoth. It is a huge animal.
I made both of you.
It eats grass like an ox.
16 Look at the strength it has in its hips!
What power it has in the muscles of its stomach!
17 Its tail sways back and forth like a cedar tree.
The tendons of its thighs are close together.
18 Its bones are like tubes made out of bronze.
Its legs are like rods made out of iron.
19 It ranks first among my works.
I made it. I can approach it with my sword.
20 The hills produce food for it.
All of the other wild animals play near it.
21 It lies under lotus plants.
It hides in tall grass in the swamps.
22 The lotus plants hide it in their shade.
Poplar trees near streams surround it.
23 It is not afraid when the river roars.
It is secure even when the Jordan River rushes against its mouth.
24 Can anyone capture it by its eyes?
Can anyone trap it and poke a hole through its nose?

41 "Job, can you pull the leviathan out of the sea with a fish hook?
Can you tie down its tongue with a rope?
2 Can you put a rope through its nose?
Can you stick a hook through its jaw?
3 Will it keep begging you for mercy?
Will it speak gently to you?
4 Will it make an agreement with you?
Can you make it your slave for life?
5 Can you make a pet out of it like a bird?
Can you put it on a leash for your young women?
6 Will traders offer you something for it?
Will they divide it up among the merchants?
7 Can you fill its body with harpoons?
Can you throw fishing spears into its head?
8 If you touch it, it will fight you.
Then you will remember never to touch it again!
9 No one can possibly control the leviathan.
Just looking at it will terrify you.
10 No one dares to wake it up.
So who can possibly stand up to me?
11 Who has a claim against me that I must pay?
Everything on earth belongs to me.

12 "Now I will speak about the leviathan's legs.
I will talk about its strength and its graceful body.
13 Who can strip off its outer coat?
Who would try to put a bridle on it?
14 Who dares to open its jaws?
Its mouth is filled with terrifying teeth.
15 Its back has rows of shields
that are close together.

16 Each one is so close to the next one
that not even air can pass between them.
17 They are joined tightly to one another.
They stick together and can't be forced apart.
18 The leviathan's snorting throws out flashes
of light.
Its eyes shine like the first light of day.
19 Fire seems to spray out of its mouth.
Sparks of fire shoot out.
20 Smoke pours out of its nose.
It is like smoke from a boiling pot over
burning grass.
21 Its breath sets coals on fire.
Flames fly out of its mouth.
22 Its neck is very strong.
People run to get out of its way.
23 Its rolls of fat are close together.
They are firm and can't be moved.
24 Its chest is as hard as rock.
It is as hard as a lower millstone.
25 When the leviathan rises up,
even mighty people are terrified.
They run away when it moves around
wildly.
26 A sword that strikes it has no effect.
Neither does a spear or dart or javelin.
27 It treats iron as if it were straw.
It crushes bronze as if it were rotten wood.
28 Arrows do not make it run away.
Stones that are thrown from slings are like
straw hitting it.
29 A club seems like a piece of straw to it.
It laughs when it hears a javelin rattling.
30 Its undersides are like broken pieces of pottery.
It leaves a trail in the mud like a threshing
sled.
31 It makes the ocean churn like a boiling pot.
It stirs up the sea like perfume someone
is making.
32 It leaves a shiny trail behind it.
You would think the ocean had white hair.
33 Nothing on earth is equal to the leviathan.
That creature is not afraid of anything.
34 It looks down on proud people.
It rules over all those who are proud."

Job's Reply

42 Job replied to the LORD,

2 "I know that you can do anything.
No one can keep you from doing what you
plan to do.
3 You asked me, 'Who do you think you are to
disagree with my plans?
You do not know what you are talking
about.'
I spoke about things I didn't completely
understand.
I talked about things that were too
wonderful for me to know.

4 "You said, 'Listen now, and I will speak.
I will ask you some questions.
Then I want you to answer me.'
5 My ears had heard about you.
But now my own eyes have seen you.
6 So I hate myself.
I'm really sorry for what I said about you.
That's why I'm sitting in dust and ashes."

The Story Ends

7 After the LORD finished speaking to Job, he
spoke to Eliphaz the Temanite. He said, "I am
angry with you and your two friends. You have not
said what is true about me, as my servant Jobhas.
8 "So now get seven bulls and seven rams. Go to
my servant Job. Then sacrifice a burnt offering for
yourselves. My servant Jobwill pray for you. And
I will accept his prayer. I will not punish you for
saying the foolish things you said. You have not
said what is true about me, as my servant Jobhas."
9 So Eliphaz the Temanite, Bildad the Shuhite,
and Zophar the Naamathite did what the LORD told
them to do. And the LORD accepted Job's prayer.
10 After Job had prayed for his friends, the LORD
made him successful again. He gave him twice as
much as he had before. 11 All of his brothers and
sisters and everyone who had known him before
came to see him. They ate with him in his house.
They showed their concern for him. They comforted him because of all of the troubles the LORD
had brought on him. Each one gave him a piece of
silver and a gold ring.
12 The LORD blessed the last part of Job's life
even more than the first part. He gave Job 14,000
sheep and 6,000 camels. He gave him 1,000 pairs
of oxen and 1,000 donkeys.
13 Job also had seven sons and three daughters.
14 He named the first daughter Jemimah. He named
the second Keziah. And he named the third Ker-
en-Happuch. 15 Job's daughters were more beautiful than any other women in the whole land. Their
father gave them a share of property along with
their brothers.
16 After all of that happened, Job lived for 140
years. He saw his children, his grandchildren and
his great-grandchildren. 17 And so he died. He had
lived for a very long time.

Psalms

BOOK I

Psalms 1–41

Psalm 1

1 Blessed is the one who obeys the law of
the LORD.
He doesn't follow the advice of evil people.
He doesn't make a habit of doing what
sinners do.
He doesn't join those who make fun of the
LORD and his law.
2 Instead, he takes delight in the law of
the LORD.
He thinks about his law day and night.
3 He is like a tree that is planted near a stream
of water.
It always bears its fruit at the right time.
Its leaves don't dry up.
Everything godly people do turns out well.

4 Sinful people are not like that at all.
They are like straw
that the wind blows away.
5 When the LORD judges them, their life will
come to an end.
Sinners won't have any place among those
who are godly.

6 The LORD watches over the lives of those who
are godly.
But the lives of sinful people will lead to
their death.

Psalm 2

1 Why do the nations plan evil together?
Why do they make useless plans?
2 The kings of the earth take their stand against
the LORD.
The rulers of the earth gather together
against his anointed king.
3 "Let us break free from their chains," they say.
"Let us throw off their ropes."

4 The One who sits on his throne in heaven
laughs.
The Lord makes fun of those rulers and
their plans.
5 When he is angry, he warns them.
When his anger blazes out, he terrifies them.
6 He says to them,
"I have placed my king on my holy
mountain of Zion."

7 I will announce what the LORD has promised.

He said to me, "You are my son.
Today I have become your father.
8 Ask me, and I will give the nations to you.
All nations on earth will belong to you.
9 You will rule them with an iron rod.
You will break them to pieces like
clay pots."

10 Kings, be wise!
Rulers of the earth, be warned!
11 Serve the LORD and have respect for him.
Serve him with joy and trembling.
12 Obey the son completely, or he will be angry.
Your way of life will lead to your death.
His anger can blaze out at any moment.
Blessed are all those who go to him
for safety.

Psalm 3

A psalm of David when he ran away
from his son Absalom.

1 LORD, I have so many enemies!
So many people are rising up against me!
2 Many are saying about me,
"God will not save him." *Selah*

3 LORD, you are like a shield that keeps me safe.
You honor me. You help me win the battle.
4 I call out to the LORD.
He answers me from his holy hill. *Selah*

5 I lie down and sleep.
I wake up again, because the LORD takes
care of me.
6 I won't be afraid of the tens of thousands
who are lined up against me on every side.

7 LORD, rise up!
My God, save me!
Strike all my enemies in the face.
Break the teeth of sinful people.

8 LORD, you are the one who saves.
May your blessing be on your people. *Selah*

Psalm 4

For the director of music. A psalm of David
to be played on stringed instruments.

1 My faithful God,
answer me when I call out to you.
Give me rest from my trouble.
Show me your favor. Hear my prayer.

2 How long will you people turn my glory into
shame?
How long will you love what will certainly
fail you?
How long will you pray to statues of gods?
Selah

3 Remember that the LORD has set his faithful
people apart for himself.
The LORD will hear me when I call out
to him.
4 When you are angry, do not sin.
When you are in bed,
look deep down inside you and be silent.
Selah
5 Offer sacrifices to the LORD in the right way.
Trust in him.
6 Many are asking, "Who can show us
anything good?"
LORD, let us see your face smiling on us
with favor.
7 You have filled my heart with great joy.
It is greater than the joy of people who
have lots of grain and fresh wine.
8 I will lie down and sleep in peace.
LORD, you alone keep me safe.

Psalm 5

For the director of music. A psalm of David
to be played on flutes.

1 LORD, listen to my words.
Pay attention when I sigh.
2 My King and my God,
listen to me when I cry for help.
I pray to you.
3 LORD, in the morning you hear my voice.
In the morning I pray to you.
I wait for you in hope.
4 God, you aren't happy with anything that
is evil.
Those who do what is wrong can't live
where you are.
5 Those who are proud can't stand in front
of you.
You hate everyone who does what is evil.
6 You destroy those who tell lies.
LORD, you hate murderers and those who
cheat others.
7 Because of your great love
I will come into your house.
With deep respect I will bow down
toward your holy temple.
8 LORD, I have many enemies.
Lead me in your right path.
Make your way smooth and straight for me.
9 Not a word from their mouths can be trusted.
Their hearts are filled with plans to destroy
others.
Their throats are like open graves.
With their tongues they tell lies.
10 God, show that they are guilty.
Let their evil plans bring them down.
Send them away because of their many sins.
They have refused to obey you.
11 But let all those who go to you for safety
be glad.
Let them always sing with joy.
Spread your cover over them and keep
them safe.
Then those who love you will be glad
because of you.
12 LORD, you bless those who do what is right.
Like a shield, your loving care keeps
them safe.

Psalm 6

For the director of music. For *sheminith*.
A psalm of David to be played
on stringed instruments.

1 LORD, don't correct me when you are angry.
Don't punish me when you are burning
with anger.
2 LORD, have mercy on me. I'm so weak.
LORD, heal me. My body is full of pain.
3 My soul is very troubled.
LORD, how long will it be until you save me?
4 LORD, turn to me and help me.
Save me. Your love never fails.
5 People can't remember you when they
are dead.
How can they praise you when they are in
the grave?
6 My groaning has worn me out.
All night long my tears flood my bed.
My bed is wet because of my crying.
7 I'm so sad I can't see very well.
My eyesight gets worse because of all of
my enemies.
8 Get away from me, all of you who do evil.
The LORD has heard my sobbing.
9 The LORD has heard my cry for his favor.
The LORD accepts my prayer.
10 All of my enemies will be troubled and put
to shame.
They will turn back in dishonor. It will
happen suddenly.

Psalm 7

A *shiggaion* of David. He sang it to the LORD
about Cush, who was from the tribe of Benjamin.

1 LORD my God, I go to you for safety.
Help me. Save me from all those who are
chasing me.
2 If you don't, they will tear me apart as if they
were lions.
They will rip me to pieces so that no one
can save me.
3 LORD my God, suppose I have done something
wrong.
Suppose I am guilty.

4 I have done evil to my friend.
Or I have robbed my enemy without any reason.
5 If I have done any of those things, let my enemy chase me and catch me.
Let him walk all over me.
Let him bury me in the dust. *Selah*

6 LORD, rise up in your anger.
Rise up against the great anger of my enemies.
My God, wake up. Command that the right thing be done.
7 Let all the people of the earth gather around you.
Rule over them from your throne in heaven.
8 LORD, judge all people.
LORD, judge me. But remember that I have done what is right.
Most High God, remember that I am honest.
9 God, you always do what is right.
You look deep down inside the hearts and minds of people.
Bring to an end the terrible things sinful people do.
Make godly people safe.

10 The Most High God is like a shield that keeps me safe.
He saves those whose hearts are honest.
11 God judges fairly.
He shows his anger every day.
12 If evil people don't change their ways,
God will sharpen his sword.
He will get his bow ready to use.
13 He has prepared his deadly weapons.
He has made his flaming arrows ready.

14 Anyone who is full of evil
plans trouble and ends up telling lies.
15 Anyone who digs a hole and shovels it out
falls into the pit he has made.
16 The trouble he causes comes back on him.
The terrible things he does come down on his own head.

17 I will give thanks to the LORD because he does what is right.
I will sing praise to the LORD Most High.

Psalm 8

For the director of music. For *gittith*.
A psalm of David.

1 LORD, our Lord,
how majestic is your name in the whole earth!

You have made your glory
higher than the heavens.
2 You have made sure that children
and infants praise you.
You have done it because of your enemies.
You have done it to put a stop to their talk.
3 I think about the heavens.
I think about what your fingers have created.
I think about the moon and stars
that you have set in place.
4 What is a human being that you think about him?
What is a son of man that you take care of him?
5 You made him a little lower than the heavenly beings.
You placed on him a crown of glory and honor.

6 You made human beings the rulers over all that your hands have created.
You put everything under their control.
7 They rule over all flocks and herds
and over the wild animals.
8 They rule over the birds of the air
and over the fish in the ocean.
They rule over everything that swims in the oceans.

9 LORD, our Lord,
how majestic is your name in the whole earth!

Psalm 9

For the director of music. A psalm of David
to the tune of "The Death of the Son."

1 LORD, I will praise you with all my heart.
I will tell about all of the miracles you have done.
2 I will be glad and full of joy because of you.
Most High God, I will sing praise to you.

3 My enemies turn back.
They fall down and die right in front of you.
4 You have proved that I haven't done anything wrong.
You have sat on your throne and judged fairly.
5 You have punished the nations. You have destroyed evil people.
You have erased their names from your book for ever and ever.
6 The enemy has been destroyed forever.
You have leveled their cities to the ground.
Even the memory of them is gone.

7 The LORD rules forever.
He has set up his throne so that he can judge people.
8 He will judge the world in keeping with what is right.
He will rule over all of its people fairly.
9 The LORD is a place of safety for those who have been beaten down.
He keeps them safe in times of trouble.

10 LORD, those who know you will trust in you.
You have never deserted those who look
to you.
11 Sing praises to the LORD. He rules from his
throne in Zion.
Tell among the nations what he has done.
12 The One who pays back murderers remembers.
He doesn't forget the cries of those who
are hurting.

13 LORD, see how badly my enemies treat me!
Show me your favor. Don't let me go down
to the gates of death.
14 Then I can give praise to you
at the gates of the city of Zion.
There I will be full of joy
because you have saved me.
15 The nations have fallen into the pit they
have dug.
Their feet are caught in the net they have
hidden.
16 The LORD is known to be fair.
Evil people are trapped by what they
have done. *Higgaion. Selah*
17 Sinful people go down to the grave.
So do all the nations that forget God.
18 But those who are in need will always be
remembered.
The hope of those who are hurting will
never die.

19 LORD, rise up. Don't let people win the battle.
Let the nations come to you and be judged.
20 LORD, strike them with terror.
Let the nations know they are only human.
Selah

Psalm 10

1 LORD, why are you so far away?
Why do you hide yourself in times of
trouble?
2 An evil person is proud and hunts down those
who are weak.
He catches weak people by making
clever plans.
3 He brags about what his heart longs for.
He speaks well of those who always
want more.
He attacks the LORD with his words.
4 Because he is proud, that evil person doesn't
turn to the LORD.
There is no room for God in any of his
thoughts.
5 Everything always goes well for him.
So he is proud.
He doesn't want to have anything to do with
God's laws.
He makes fun of all of his enemies.
6 He says to himself, "I will always be secure.
I will always be happy. I'll never have any
trouble."
7 His mouth is full of curses and lies and
warnings.
With his tongue he speaks evil and makes
trouble.
8 Sinful people hide and wait near the villages.
From their hiding places they murder
those who aren't guilty of doing
anything wrong.
They watch in secret for those they want
to attack.
9 They hide and wait like a lion in the bushes.
From their hiding places they wait to catch
those who are helpless.
They catch them and drag them off in
their nets.
10 Those they have attacked are beaten up. They
fall to the ground.
They fall because their attackers are too
strong for them.
11 Sinful people say to themselves, "God doesn't
pay any attention.
He covers his face. He never sees us."

12 LORD, rise up! God, show your power!
Don't forget those who are helpless.
13 Why do sinful people attack you with their
words?
Why do they say to themselves,
"He won't hold us accountable"?
14 God, you see trouble and sadness.
You take note of it. You do something
about it.
So those who are attacked place themselves in
your care.
You help children whose fathers have died.
15 Take away the power of bad and sinful people.
Hold them accountable for the evil things
they do.
Uncover all the evil they have done.

16 The LORD is King for ever and ever.
The nations will disappear from his land.
17 LORD, you hear the longings of those who
are hurting.
You cheer them up and give them hope.
You listen to their cries.
18 You stand up for those whose fathers have died
and for those who have been beaten down.
You do it so that no one made of dust
may terrify others anymore.

Psalm 11

For the director of music. A psalm of David.

1 I run to the LORD for safety.
So how can you say to me,
"Fly away like a bird to your mountain.
2 Look! Evil people are bending their bows.
They are placing their arrows against
the strings.
They are planning to shoot from the shadows
at those who have honest hearts.

[3] When law and order are being destroyed,
what can godly people do?"
[4] The LORD is in his holy temple.
The LORD is on his throne in heaven.
He watches all people.
His eyes study them.
[5] The LORD watches over those who do what is right.
But he hates sinful people and those who love to hurt others.
[6] He will pour out flaming coals and burning sulfur
on those who do what is wrong.
A hot and dry wind will destroy them.

[7] The LORD always does what is right.
So he loves it when people do what is fair.
Those who are honest will enjoy his blessing.

Psalm 12

For the director of music. For *sheminith.* A psalm of David.

[1] Help, LORD! Those who do what is right are gone.
Those who are faithful have disappeared from the earth.
[2] Everyone tells lies to his neighbors.
With his lips he praises others, but he doesn't really mean it.

[3] May the LORD cut off all lips that don't mean what they say.
May he cut out every tongue that brags.
[4] They say, "We will win the battle with our tongues.
Our lips belong to us. No one else is in charge of us."

[5] The LORD says, "The weak are beaten down.
Those who are in need groan.
So I will stand up to help them.
I will keep them safe from those who tell lies about them."
[6] The words of the LORD are perfect.
They are like silver made pure in a clay furnace.
They are like silver made pure seven times over.

[7] LORD, you will keep us safe.
You will always keep sinners from hurting us.
[8] Proud and sinful people walk around openly
when the evil they do is praised by others.

Psalm 13

For the director of music. A psalm of David.

[1] LORD, how long must I wait? Will you forget me forever?
How long will you turn your face away from me?
[2] How long must I struggle with my thoughts?
How long must my heart be sad day after day?
How long will my enemies keep winning the battle over me?

[3] LORD my God, look at me and answer me.
Give me new life, or I will die.
[4] Then my enemies will say, "We have beaten him."
They will be filled with joy when I die.

[5] But I trust in your faithful love.
My heart is filled with joy because you will save me.
[6] I will sing to the LORD.
He has been so good to me.

Psalm 14

For the director of music. A psalm of David.

[1] Foolish people say in their hearts,
"There is no God."
They do all kinds of horrible and evil things.
No one does anything good.

[2] The LORD looks down from heaven
on all people.
He wants to see if there are any who understand.
He wants to see if there are any who trust in God.
[3] All of them have turned away.
They have all become evil.
No one does anything good,
no one at all.

[4] Won't those who do evil ever learn?
They eat up my people as if they were eating bread.
They don't call out to the LORD for help.
[5] Just look at them! They are filled with terror
because God is among those who do right.
[6] You who do evil make it hard for poor people to do what they plan to do.
But the LORD is their place of safety.

[7] How I pray that the One who saves Israel will come out of Zion!
Then the LORD will bless his people with great success again.
So let the people of Jacob be filled with joy!
Let Israel be glad!

Psalm 15

A psalm of David.

[1] LORD, who can live in your sacred tent?
Who can stay on your holy hill?

[2] Anyone who lives without blame
and does what is right.

He speaks the truth from his heart.
3 He doesn't tell lies about others.
He doesn't do wrong to his neighbors.
He doesn't say anything bad about them.
4 He hates sinful people.
He honors those who have respect for the LORD.
He keeps his promises
even when it hurts.
5 He lends his money without charging too much interest.
He doesn't accept money to harm those who aren't guilty.

Anyone who lives like that
will always be secure.

Psalm 16

A *miktam* of David.

1 God, keep me safe.
I go to you for safety.
2 I said to the LORD, "You are my Lord.
Without you, I don't have anything that is good."
3 God's people who live in our land are glorious.
I take great delight in them.
4 Those who run after other gods
will have nothing but trouble.
I will not pour out offerings of blood to those gods.
My lips will not speak their names.

5 LORD, everything you have given me is good.
You have made my life secure.
6 I am very pleased with what you have given me.
I am very happy with what I've received from you.

7 I will praise the LORD. He gives me good advice.
Even at night my heart teaches me.
8 I know that the LORD is always with me.
He is at my right hand.
I will always be secure.

9 So my heart is glad. Joy is on my tongue.
My body also will be secure.
10 You will not leave me in the grave.
You will not let your faithful one rot away.
11 You always show me the path that leads to life.
You will fill me with joy when I am with you.
You will give me endless pleasures at your right hand.

Psalm 17

A prayer of David.

1 LORD, hear me when I ask you to treat me fairly.
Listen to my cry for help.
Hear my prayer.
It doesn't come from lips that tell lies.
2 When you hand down your sentence, may it be in my favor.
May your eyes see what is right.

3 Look deep down into my heart.
Study me carefully at night.
Put me to the test.
You won't find anything wrong.
I have made up my mind
that my mouth won't say sinful things.
4 I don't do the things other people do.
By obeying your word
I have kept myself from acting
like those who try to hurt others.
5 My steps have stayed on your paths.
My feet have not slipped.

6 God, I call out to you because you will answer me.
Listen to me. Hear my prayer.
7 Show the wonder of your great love.
By using your powerful right hand,
you save those who go to you for safety from their enemies.
8 Take good care of me, just as you would take care of your own eyes.
Hide me in the shadow of your wings.
9 Save me from the sinful people who attack me.
Save me from my deadly enemies who are all around me.

10 They make their hearts hard and stubborn.
Their mouths speak with pride.
11 They have tracked me down. They are all around me.
Their eyes watch for a chance to throw me to the ground.
12 They are like a hungry lion, waiting to attack.
They are like a powerful lion, hiding in the bushes.

13 LORD, rise up. Oppose them and bring them down.
With your sword, save me from those evil people.
14 LORD, by your power save me from people like that.
They belong to this world. They get their reward in this life.

You satisfy the hunger of those you love.
Their children have plenty.
And those children store up wealth for their children.
15 Because I do what is right, I will enjoy your blessing.
When I wake up, I will be satisfied because I will see you.

Psalm 18

For the director of music. A psalm of David, the servant of the LORD. He sang the words of this song to the LORD. He sang them when the LORD saved him from the powerful hand of all of his enemies and of Saul. He said,

1 I love you, LORD.
You give me strength.
2 The LORD is my rock and my fort. He is the One who saves me.
My God is my rock. I go to him for safety.
He is like a shield to me. He's the power that saves me. He's my place of safety.
3 I call out to the LORD. He is worthy of praise.
He saves me from my enemies.

4 The ropes of death were almost wrapped around me.
A destroying flood swept over me.
5 The ropes of the grave were tight around me.
Death set its trap in front of me.
6 When I was in trouble, I called out to the LORD.
I cried to my God for help.
From his temple he heard my voice.
My cry for help reached his ears.

7 The earth trembled and shook.
The base of the mountains rocked back and forth.
It trembled because the LORD was angry.
8 Smoke came out of his nose.
Flames of fire came out of his mouth.
Burning coals blazed out of it.
9 He opened the heavens and came down.
Dark clouds were under his feet.
10 He got on the cherubim and flew.
The wings of the wind lifted him up.
11 He covered himself with darkness.
The dark rain clouds of the sky were like a tent around him.
12 Clouds came out of the brightness that was all around him.
They came with hailstones and flashes of lightning.
13 The LORD thundered from heaven.
The voice of the Most High God was heard.
14 He shot his arrows and scattered our enemies.
He sent great flashes of lightning and chased the enemies away.
15 The bottom of the sea could be seen.
The foundations of the earth were uncovered.
LORD, it happened when your anger blazed out.
It came like a blast of breath from your nose.

16 He reached down from heaven. He took hold of me.
He lifted me out of deep waters.
17 He saved me from my powerful enemies.
He set me free from those who were too strong for me.
18 They stood up to me when I was in trouble.
But the LORD helped me.
19 He brought me out into a wide and safe place.
He saved me because he was pleased with me.

20 The LORD has been good to me because I do what is right.
He has rewarded me because I lead a pure life.
21 I have lived the way the LORD wanted me to.
I haven't done evil by turning away from my God.
22 I keep all of his laws in mind.
I haven't turned away from his commands.
23 He knows that I am without blame.
He knows I've kept myself from sinning.
24 The LORD has rewarded me for doing what is right.
He has rewarded me because I haven't done anything wrong.

25 LORD, to those who are faithful you show that you are faithful.
To those who are without blame you show that you are without blame.
26 To those who are pure you show that you are pure.
But to those whose paths are crooked you show that you are clever.
27 You save those who aren't proud.
But you bring down those whose eyes are proud.
28 LORD, you keep the lamp of my life burning brightly.
You are my God. You bring light into my darkness.
29 With your help I can attack a troop of soldiers.
With the help of my God I can climb over a wall.

30 God's way is perfect.
The word of the LORD doesn't have any flaws.
He is like a shield
to all who go to him for safety.
31 Who is God except the LORD?
Who is the Rock except our God?
32 God gives me strength for the battle.
He makes my way perfect.
33 He makes my feet like the feet of a deer.
He helps me stand on the highest places.
34 He trains my hands to fight every battle.
My arms can bend a bow of bronze.
35 LORD, you are like a shield that keeps me safe.
You help me win the battle.
Your strong right hand keeps me going.
You bend down to make me great.
36 You give me a wide path to walk on
so that I don't twist my ankles.

37 I chased my enemies and caught them.
I didn't turn back until they were destroyed.
38 I crushed them so that they couldn't get up.
They fell under my feet.
39 LORD, you gave me strength to fight the battle.
You made my enemies bow down at
my feet.
40 You made them turn their backs and run away.
So I destroyed my enemies.
41 They cried out for help. But there was no one
to save them.
They called out to you. But you didn't
answer them.
42 I beat them as fine as dust blown by the wind.
I poured them out like mud in the streets.

43 You saved me when my own people
attacked me.
You made me the ruler over nations.
People I didn't know serve me now.
44 As soon as they hear me, they obey me.
People from other lands bow down to me
in fear.
45 All of them give up hope.
They come trembling out of their hiding
places.

46 The LORD lives! Give praise to my Rock!
Give honor to God my Savior!
47 He is the God who pays my enemies back.
He brings the nations under my control.
48 He saves me from my enemies.
You have honored me more than them.
You have saved me from men who want to
hurt me.
49 LORD, I will praise you among the nations.
I will sing praises to you.
50 The LORD helps his king win great battles.
He shows his faithful love to his anointed
king.
He shows it to me and my family forever.

Psalm 19

For the director of music. A psalm of David.

1 The heavens tell about the glory of God.
The skies show that his hands created them.
2 Day after day they speak about it.
Night after night they make it known.
3 But they don't speak or use words.
No sound is heard from them.
4 At the same time, their voice goes out into the
whole earth.
Their words go out from one end of the
world to the other.

God has set up a tent in the heavens for the sun.
5 The sun is like a groom coming out of
the room where he spent his
wedding night.
The sun is like a great runner who takes
delight in running a race.
6 It rises at one end of the heavens.
Then it moves across to the other end.
Nothing can hide from its heat.

7 The law of the LORD is perfect.
It gives us new strength.
The laws of the LORD can be trusted.
They make childish people wise.
8 The rules of the LORD are right.
They give joy to our hearts.
The commands of the LORD shine brightly.
They give light to our minds.
9 The law that brings respect for the LORD
is pure.
It lasts forever.
The directions the LORD gives are true.
All of them are completely right.
10 They are more priceless than gold.
They have greater value than huge amounts
of pure gold.
They are sweeter than honey
that is taken from the honeycomb.
11 I am warned by them.
When I obey them, I am greatly rewarded.

12 Can I know my mistakes?
Forgive my hidden faults.
13 Keep me also from the sins I want to commit.
May they not be my master.
Then I will be without blame.
I will not be guilty of any great sin against
your law.

14 LORD, may the words of my mouth and the
thoughts of my heart
be pleasing in your eyes.
You are my Rock and my Redeemer.

Psalm 20

For the director of music. A psalm of David.

1 May the LORD answer you when you are
in trouble.
May the God of Jacob keep you safe.
2 May he send you help from the sacred tent.
May he give you aid from Zion.
3 May he remember all of your sacrifices.
May he accept your burnt offerings. *Selah*
4 May he give you what your heart longs for.
May he make all of your plans succeed.
5 We will shout with joy when you win
the battle.
We will lift up our flags in the name of
our God.
May the LORD give you everything you
ask for.

6 Now I know that the LORD saves his anointed
king.
He answers him from his holy heaven.
The power of God's right hand saves
the king.

7 Some trust in chariots. Some trust in horses.
But we trust in the LORD our God.
8 They are brought to their knees and fall down.
But we get up and stand firm.

9 LORD, save the king!
Answer us when we call out to you!

Psalm 21

For the director of music. A psalm of David.

1 LORD, the king is filled with joy because you are strong.
How great is his joy because you help him win his battles!
2 You have given him what his heart longed for.
You haven't kept back from him what his lips asked for. *Selah*
3 You welcomed him with rich blessings.
You placed a crown of pure gold on his head.
4 He asked you for life, and you gave it to him.
You promised him days that would never end.
5 His glory is great because you helped him win his battles.
You have honored him with glory and majesty.
6 You have given him blessings that will last forever.
You have made him glad and joyful because you are with him.

7 The king trusts in the LORD.
The faithful love of the Most High God will keep the king secure.

8 You, the king, will capture all of your enemies.
Your right hand will take hold of them.
9 When you appear,
you will be like a flaming furnace to them.
The LORD will swallow them up in his anger.
His fire will burn them up.
10 You will wipe their children from the face of the earth.
You will remove them from the human race.
11 Your enemies make evil plans against you.
They think up evil things to do. But they can't succeed.
12 You will make them turn their backs and run away
when you aim your arrows at them.

13 LORD, may you be honored because you are strong.
We will sing and praise your might.

Psalm 22

For the director of music. A psalm of David
to the tune of "The Doe of the Morning."

1 My God, my God, why have you deserted me?
Why do you seem to be so far away when I need you to save me?
Why do you seem to be so far away that you can't hear my groans?
2 My God, I cry out in the daytime. But you don't answer.
I cry out at night. I can't keep quiet.
3 But you rule from your throne as the Holy One.
You are the God Israel praises.
4 Our people of long ago put their trust in you.
They trusted in you, and you saved them.
5 They cried out to you and were saved.
They trusted in you, and you didn't let them down.

6 People treat me like a worm and not a man.
They hate me and look down on me.
7 All those who see me laugh at me.
They shout at me and make fun of me.
They shake their heads at me.
8 They say, "He trusts in the LORD.
Let the LORD help him.
If the LORD is pleased with him,
let him save him."

9 But you brought me out of my mother's body.
You made me trust in you
even when I was at my mother's breast.
10 From the time I was born, you took good care of me.
Ever since I came out of my mother's body, you have been my God.
11 Don't be far away from me.
Trouble is near,
and there is no one to help me.

12 Many enemies are all around me.
They are like strong bulls from the land of Bashan.
13 They are like roaring lions that tear to pieces what they kill.
They open their mouths wide to attack me.
14 My strength is like water that is poured out on the ground.
I feel as if my bones aren't connected.
My heart has turned to wax.
It has melted away inside me.
15 My strength is dried up like a piece of broken pottery.
My tongue sticks to the roof of my mouth.
You bring me down to the edge of the grave.
16 A group of sinful people has closed in on me.
They are all around me like a pack of dogs.
They have pierced my hands and my feet.
17 I can see all of my bones right through my skin.
People stare at me. They laugh when I suffer.
18 They divide up my clothes among them.
They cast lots for what I am wearing.

19 LORD, don't be so far away.
You give me strength. Come quickly to help me.
20 Save me from the sword.
Save the only life I have. Save me from the power of those dogs.
21 Save me from the mouths of those lions.
Save me from the horns of those wild oxen.
22 I will announce your name to my brothers and sisters.
I will praise you among those who worship you.
23 You who have respect for the LORD, praise him!
All you people of Jacob, honor him!
All you people of Israel, worship him!
24 He has not forgotten the one who is hurting.
He has not turned away from his suffering.
He has not turned his face away from him.
He has listened to his cry for help.

25 Because of what you have done,
I will praise you in the whole community of those who worship you.
In front of those who respect you,
I will keep my promises.
26 Those who are poor will eat and be satisfied.
Those who look to the LORD will praise him.
May their hearts be filled with new hope!
27 People from one end of the earth to the other
will remember and turn to the LORD.
The people of all the nations
will bow down before him.
28 The LORD is King.
He rules over the nations.
29 All the rich people of the earth will worship God and take part in his feasts.
All those who go down to the edge of the grave will fall on their knees in front of him.
I'm talking about those who can hardly keep themselves alive.
30 Those who are not yet born will serve him.
Those who are born later will be told about the Lord.
31 And they will tell people who have not yet been born
that he has done what is right.

Psalm 23

A psalm of David.

1 The LORD is my shepherd. He gives me everything I need.
2 He lets me lie down in fields of green grass.
He leads me beside quiet waters.
3 He gives me new strength.
He guides me in the right paths
for the honor of his name.
4 Even though I walk
through the darkest valley,
I will not be afraid.
You are with me.
Your shepherd's rod and staff
comfort me.

5 You prepare a feast for me
right in front of my enemies.
You pour oil on my head.
My cup runs over.
6 I am sure that your goodness and love will follow me
all the days of my life.
And I will live in the house of the LORD
forever.

Psalm 24

A psalm of David.

1 The earth belongs to the LORD. And so does everything in it.
The world belongs to him. And so do all those who live in it.
2 He set it firmly on the oceans.
He made it secure on the waters.

3 Who can go up to the temple on the hill of the LORD?
Who can stand in his holy place?
4 Anyone who has clean hands and a pure heart.
He does not worship the statue of a god.
He doesn't use the name of that god when he makes a promise.
5 People like that will receive the LORD's blessing.
When God their Savior hands down his sentence, it will be in their favor.
6 The people who look to God are like that.
God of Jacob, they look to you. *Selah*

7 Open wide, you gates.
Open up, you age-old doors.
Then the King of glory will come in.
8 Who is the King of glory?
The LORD, who is strong and mighty.
The LORD, who is mighty in battle.
9 Open wide, you gates.
Open wide, you age-old doors.
Then the King of glory will come in.
10 Who is he, this King of glory?
The LORD who rules over all.
He is the King of glory. *Selah*

Psalm 25

A psalm of David.

1 LORD, I worship you.
2 My God, I trust in you.
Don't let me be put to shame.
Don't let my enemies win the battle over me.
3 Those who put their hope in you
will never be put to shame.

But those who can't be trusted
will be put to shame. They have no excuse.
4 LORD, show me your ways.
Teach me how to follow you.
5 Guide me in your truth. Teach me.
You are God my Savior.
I put my hope in you all day long.
6 LORD, remember your great mercy and love.
You have shown them to your people for a long time.
7 Don't remember the sins I committed when I was young.
Don't remember how often I refused to obey you.
Remember me because you love me.
LORD, you are good.
8 The LORD is honest and good.
He teaches sinners to walk in his ways.
9 He shows those who aren't proud how to do what is right.
He teaches them his ways.
10 All of the LORD's ways are loving and faithful
for those who obey what his covenant commands.
11 LORD, be true to your name.
Forgive my sin, even though it is great.
12 Who is the man who has respect for the LORD?
God will teach him the way he has chosen for him.
13 Things will always go well for him.
His children will be given the land.
14 The LORD shares his plans with those who have respect for him.
He makes his covenant known to them.
15 My eyes always look to the LORD.
He alone can set my feet free from the trap.
16 Turn to me and show me your favor.
I am lonely and hurting.
17 The troubles of my heart have increased.
Set me free from my great pain.
18 Look at how I'm hurting! See how much I suffer!
Take away all of my sins.
19 Look at how many enemies I have!
See how terrible their hatred is for me!
20 Guard my life. Save me.
Don't let me be put to shame.
I go to you for safety.
21 May my honest and good life keep me safe.
I have put my hope in you.

22 God, set Israel free
from all of their troubles!

Psalm 26

A psalm of David.

1 LORD, when you hand down your sentence, let it be in my favor.
I have lived without blame.
I have trusted in the LORD.
I have never doubted him.
2 LORD, test me. Try me out.
Look deep down into my heart and mind.
3 Your love is always with me.
I have always lived by your truth.
4 I don't spend time with people who tell lies.
I don't keep company with pretenders.
5 I hate to be with a group of sinful people.
I refuse to spend time with those who are evil.
6 I wash my hands to show that I'm not guilty.
LORD, I come near your altar.
7 I shout my praise to you.
I tell about all the wonderful things you have done.
8 LORD, I love the house where you live.
I love the place where your glory is.
9 Don't destroy me together with sinners.
Don't take my life away along with murderers.
10 Their hands are always planning to do evil.
Their right hands are full of money that bought them off.
11 But I live without blame.
Set me free and show me your favor.
12 My feet stand on level ground.
In the whole community I will praise the LORD.

Psalm 27

A psalm of David.

1 The LORD gives me light and saves me.
Why should I fear anyone?
The LORD is my place of safety.
Why should I be afraid?
2 My enemies are evil.
They will trip and fall
when they attack me
and try to eat me alive.
3 Even if an army attacks me,
my heart will not be afraid.
Even if war breaks out against me,
I will still trust in God.

4 I'm asking the LORD for only one thing.
Here is what I want.
I want to live in the house of the LORD
all the days of my life.
I want to look at the beauty of the LORD.
I want to worship him in his temple.
5 When I'm in trouble,
he will keep me safe in his house.
He will hide me in the safety of his holy tent.
He will put me on a rock that is very high.
6 Then I will win the battle
over my enemies who are all around me.
At his holy tent I will offer my sacrifice with shouts of joy.
I will sing and make music to the LORD.

7 LORD, hear my voice when I call out to you.
Show me your favor and answer me.
8 My heart says, "Look to him!"
LORD, I will look to you.
9 Don't turn your face away from me.
Don't turn me away because you are angry.
You have helped me.
God my Savior, don't say no to me.
Don't desert me.
10 My father and mother may desert me,
but the LORD will accept me.
11 LORD, teach me your ways.
Lead me along a straight path.
There are many people who beat me down.
12 My enemies want to harm me. So don't turn
me over to them.
Witnesses who tell lies are rising up
against me.
They are trying to destroy me.

13 Here is something I am still sure of.
I will see the LORD's goodness
while I'm still alive.
14 Wait for the LORD.
Be strong and don't lose hope.
Wait for the LORD.

Psalm 28

A psalm of David.

1 LORD, my Rock, I call out to you.
Pay attention to me.
If you remain silent, I will die.
I will be like those who have gone down
into the grave.
2 Hear my cry for your favor
when I call out to you for help.
Hear me when I lift up my hands in prayer
toward your Most Holy Room.

3 Don't drag me away with sinners.
Don't drag me away with those who do evil.
They speak in a friendly way to their
neighbors.
But their hearts are full of hatred.
4 Pay them back for their evil actions.
Pay them back for what their hands
have done.
Give them exactly what they should get.
5 They don't care about the LORD's mighty acts.
They don't care about what his hands
have done.
So he will tear them down.
He will never build them up again.
6 Give praise to the LORD.
He has heard my cry for his favor.
7 The LORD gives me strength. He is like a shield
that keeps me safe.
My heart trusts in him, and he helps me.
My heart jumps for joy.
I will sing and give thanks to him.

8 The LORD gives strength to his people.
He guards and saves his anointed king.
9 Save your people. Bless those who belong
to you.
Be their shepherd. Take care of them
forever.

Psalm 29

A psalm of David.

1 Praise the LORD, you mighty angels.
Praise the LORD for his glory and strength.
2 Praise the LORD for the glory that belongs
to him.
Worship the LORD because of his beauty and
holiness.

3 The voice of the LORD is heard over the waters.
The God of glory thunders.
The LORD thunders over the mighty waters.
4 The voice of the LORD is powerful.
The voice of the LORD is majestic.
5 The voice of the LORD breaks the cedar trees.
The LORD breaks the cedars of Lebanon
into pieces.
6 He makes the mountains of Lebanon skip like
a calf.
He makes Mount Hermon jump like a
young wild ox.
7 The voice of the LORD strikes
with flashes of lightning.
8 The voice of the LORD shakes the desert.
The LORD shakes the Desert of Kadesh.
9 The voice of the LORD twists the oak trees.
It strips the forests bare.
And in his temple everyone cries out,
"Glory!"

10 The LORD on his throne rules over the flood.
The LORD rules from his throne as King
forever.
11 The LORD gives strength to his people.
The LORD blesses his people with peace.

Psalm 30

A psalm of David. A song for committing the completed temple to God.

1 LORD, I will give you honor.
You brought me out of deep trouble.
You didn't give my enemies the joy of
seeing me die.
2 LORD my God, I called out to you for help.
And you healed me.
3 LORD, you brought me up from the edge of
the grave.
You kept me from going down into the pit.

4 Sing to the LORD, you who are faithful to him.
Praise him, because his name is holy.
5 His anger lasts for only a moment.
But his favor lasts for a person's whole life.

Sobbing can remain through the night.
But joy comes in the morning.

6 When I felt safe, I said,
"I will always be secure."
7 LORD, when you showed me your favor,
you made my mountain stand firm.
But when you turned your face away
from me,
I was terrified.

8 LORD, I called out to you.
I cried to you for your favor.
9 I said, "What good will come if I die?
What good will come if I go down into
the grave?
Can the dust of my dead body praise you?
Can it tell how faithful you are?
10 LORD, hear me. Show me your favor.
LORD, help me."
11 You turned my loud crying into dancing.
You removed my black clothes and
dressed me with joy.
12 So my heart will sing to you. I can't
keep silent.
LORD, my God, I will give you thanks
forever.

Psalm 31

For the director of music.
A psalm of David.

1 LORD, I have gone to you for safety.
Don't let me ever be put to shame.
Save me, because you do what is right.
2 Pay attention to me.
Come quickly to help me.
Be the rock I go to for safety.
Be the strong fort that saves me.
3 You are my rock and my fort.
Lead me and guide me for the honor of
your name.
4 Free me from the trap that is set for me.
You are my place of safety.
5 Into your hands I commit my very life.
LORD, set me free. You are my
faithful God.

6 I hate those who worship worthless statues
of gods.
I trust in the LORD.
7 I will be glad and full of joy because you
love me.
You saw that I was hurting.
You took note of my great pain.
8 You have not handed me over to the enemy.
You have put me in a wide and safe place.

9 LORD, show me your favor. I'm in deep
trouble.
I'm so sad I can hardly see.
My whole body grows weak with sadness.
10 Pain has taken over my life.
My years are spent in groaning.
I have no strength because I'm hurting
so much.
My body is getting weaker and weaker.
11 My neighbors make fun of me
because I have so many enemies.
My friends are afraid of me.
Those who see me on the street run away
from me.
12 They have forgotten me. I might as well
be dead.
I have become like broken pottery.
13 I hear the lies many people tell about me.
There is terror all around me.
Many have joined together against me.
They plan to kill me.

14 But I trust in you, LORD.
I say, "You are my God."
15 My whole life is in your hands.
Save me from my enemies.
Save me from those who are chasing me.
16 Let your face smile on me with favor.
Save me because your love is faithful.
17 LORD, I have cried out to you.
Don't let me be put to shame.
But let sinners be put to shame.
Let them lie silent in the grave.
18 Their lips tell lies. Let them be silenced.
They speak with pride against those
who do right.
They make fun of them.

19 How great your goodness is!
You have stored it up for those who have
respect for you.
While other people watch, you give it to
those who run to you for safety.
20 They are safe because you are with them.
You hide them from the evil plans of
their enemies.
In your house you keep them safe
from those who bring charges against them.

21 Give praise to the LORD.
He showed me his wonderful love
when my enemies attacked the city
I was in.
22 I was afraid and said,
"I've been cut off from you!"
But you heard my cry for your favor.
You heard me when I called out to you
for help.

23 Love the LORD, all of you who are faithful
to him!
The LORD watches over the faithful.
But he completely pays back those who
are proud.
24 Be strong, all of you who put your hope
in the LORD.
Never give up.

Psalm 32

A *maskil* of David.

1 Blessed is the one whose lawless acts are forgiven.
His sins have been taken away.
2 Blessed is the man whose sin the LORD never counts against him.
He doesn't want to cheat anyone.

3 When I kept silent about my sin,
my body became weak
because I groaned all day long.
4 Day and night
your heavy hand punished me.
I became weaker and weaker
as I do in the heat of summer. *Selah*
5 Then I admitted my sin to you.
I didn't cover up the wrong I had done.
I said, "I will admit my lawless acts to the LORD."
And you forgave the guilt of my sin. *Selah*

6 Let everyone who is godly pray to you
while they can still look to you.
When troubles come like a flood,
they certainly won't reach those who are godly.
7 You are my hiding place.
You will keep me safe from trouble.
You will surround me with songs sung by those who praise you
because you save your people. *Selah*

8 I will guide you and teach you the way you should go.
I will give you good advice and watch over you.
9 Don't be like the horse or the mule.
They can't understand anything.
They have to be controlled by bits and bridles.
If they aren't, they won't come to you.
10 Sinful people have all kinds of trouble.
But the LORD's faithful love
is all around those who trust in him.

11 Be glad because of what the LORD has done for you.
Be joyful, you who do what is right!
Sing, all of you whose hearts are honest!

Psalm 33

1 You who are godly, sing with joy to the LORD.
It is right for honest people to praise him.
2 Praise the LORD with the harp.
Make music to him on the lyre that has ten strings.
3 Sing a new song to him.
Play with skill, and shout with joy.

4 What the LORD says is right and true.
He is faithful in everything he does.
5 The LORD loves what is right and fair.
The earth is full of his faithful love.

6 The heavens were made when the LORD commanded it to happen.
All of the stars were created by the breath of his mouth.
7 He gathers the waters of the sea together.
He puts the oceans in their places.
8 Let the whole earth have respect for the LORD.
Let all of the people in the world honor him.
9 He spoke, and the world came into being.
He commanded, and it stood firm.
10 The LORD blocks the sinful plans of the nations.
He keeps them from doing what they want to do.
11 But the plans of the LORD stand firm forever.
What he wants to do will last for all time.

12 Blessed is the nation whose God is the LORD.
Blessed are the people he chose to be his own.
13 From heaven the LORD looks down
and sees everyone.
14 From his throne he watches
all those who live on the earth.
15 He creates the hearts of all people.
He is aware of everything they do.
16 A king isn't saved just because his army is big.
A soldier doesn't escape just because he is very strong.
17 People can't trust a horse to save them either.
Though it is very strong, it can't save them.
18 But the LORD looks with favor on those who respect him.
He watches over those who put their hope in his faithful love.
19 He watches over them to save them from death.
He wants to keep them alive when there is no food in the land.

20 We wait in hope for the LORD.
He helps us. He is like a shield that keeps us safe.
21 Our hearts are full of joy because of him.
We trust in him, because he is holy.
22 LORD, may your faithful love rest on us.
We put our hope in you.

Psalm 34

A psalm of David when he was in front of Abimelech and pretended to be out of his mind. Abimelech drove him away, and he left.

1 I will thank the LORD at all times.
My lips will always praise him.
2 I will honor the LORD.
Let those who are hurting hear and be joyful.
3 Join me in giving glory to the LORD.
Let us honor him together.

4 I looked to the LORD, and he answered me.
He saved me from everything I was afraid of.
5 Those who look to him beam with joy.
They are never put to shame.
6 This poor man called out, and the LORD heard him.
He saved him out of all of his troubles.
7 The angel of the LORD stands guard
around those who have respect for him.
And he saves them.

8 Taste and see that the LORD is good.
Blessed is the man who goes to him for safety.
9 You people of God, have respect for the LORD.
Those who respect him have everything they need.
10 The lions may grow weak and hungry.
But those who look to the LORD have every good thing they need.

11 My children, come. Listen to me.
I will teach you to have respect for the LORD.
12 Do you love life
and want to see many good days?
13 Then keep your tongues from speaking evil.
Keep your lips from telling lies.
14 Turn away from evil, and do good.
Look for peace, and go after it.

15 The LORD looks with favor on those who are godly.
His ears are open to their cry.
16 The LORD doesn't look with favor on those who do evil.
He removes all memory of them from the earth.
17 Godly people cry out, and the LORD hears them.
He saves them from all of their troubles.
18 The LORD is close to those whose hearts have been broken.
He saves those whose spirits have been crushed.

19 Anyone who does what is right may have many troubles.
But the LORD saves him from all of them.
20 The LORD watches over all of his bones.
Not one of them will be broken.

21 Sinners will be killed by their own evil.
The enemies of godly people will be judged.
22 The LORD sets those who serve him free.
No one who goes to him for safety will be judged.

Psalm 35

A psalm of David.

1 LORD, stand up against those who stand up against me.
Fight against those who fight against me.
2 Pick up your large shields and your small shields.
Rise up and help me.
3 Get your spear and javelin ready to fight
against those who are chasing me.
Say to me, "I will save you."

4 Let those who are trying to kill me
be brought down in dishonor.
Let those who plan to destroy me
be turned back in terror.
5 Let them be like straw blowing in the wind,
while the angel of the LORD drives them away.
6 Let their path be dark and slippery,
while the angel of the LORD chases them.
7 They set a trap for me without any reason.
Without any reason they dug a pit to catch me.
8 So let them be destroyed without warning.
Let the trap they set for me catch them.
Let them fall into the pit and be destroyed.
9 Then I will be full of joy because of what the LORD has done.
I will be glad because he has saved me.
10 My whole being will cry out,
"Who is like you, LORD?
You save poor people from those who are too strong for them.
You save poor and needy people from those who rob them."

11 Mean people come forward to give witness against me.
They ask me things I don't know anything about.
12 They pay me back with evil, even though I was good to them.
They leave me without hope.
13 But when they were sick, I put on black clothes.
I made myself low by going without food.
My prayers for them weren't always answered.
14 So I went around crying
as if I were crying over my friend or relative.
I bowed my head in sadness
as if I were sobbing over my mother.
15 But when I tripped and fell, they were all very happy.
Attackers gathered against me when I didn't even know it.
They kept on telling lies about me.
16 They were like ungodly people. They made fun of me.
They ground their teeth at me in hate.
17 Lord, how much longer will you just look on?
Save me from their deadly attacks.
Save the only life I have.
Save me from those lions.
18 I will give you thanks in the whole community.
Among all of your people I will praise you.

19 Don't let those who are my enemies without any reason
laugh at me and make fun of me.
Don't let those who hate me without any reason
wink at me with an evil purpose.
20 They don't speak words of peace.
They make up false charges
against those who live quietly in the land.
21 They open their mouths wide at me. They make fun of me.
They say, "With our own eyes we have seen what you did."

22 LORD, you have seen this. Don't be silent.
Lord, don't be far away from me.
23 Wake up! Rise up to help me!
My God and Lord, stand up for me.
24 LORD my God, when you hand down your sentence, let it be in my favor.
You always do what is right.
Don't let my enemies have the joy of seeing me fall.
25 Don't let them think, "That's exactly what we wanted!"
Don't let them say, "We have swallowed him up."

26 Let all those who laugh at me because I'm in trouble
be ashamed and bewildered.
Let all who think they are better than I am
put on shame and dishonor as if they were clothes.
27 Let those who are happy when my name is cleared
shout with joy and gladness.
Let them always say, "May the LORD be honored.
He is pleased when everything goes well with the one who serves him."
28 You always do what is right. My tongue will speak about it
and praise you all day long.

Psalm 36

For the director of music. A psalm of David, the servant of the LORD.

1 Here are the words God has given me to say
about the evil ways of anyone who sins.
He doesn't have any respect for God.
2 He praises himself so much
that he can't see his sin or hate it.
3 His mouth speaks words that are evil and false.
He has stopped being wise. He has stopped doing good.
4 Even as he lies in bed he makes evil plans.
He commits himself to a sinful way of life.
He never says no to what is wrong.

5 LORD, your love is as high as the heavens.
Your faithful love reaches up to the skies.
6 You are as holy as the mountains are high.
You are as honest as the oceans are deep.
LORD, you keep people and animals safe.
7 How priceless your faithful love is!
Important and ordinary people alike
find safety in the shadow of your wings.
8 They eat well because there is more than enough in your house.
You let them drink from your river that flows with good things.
9 You have the fountain of life.
We are filled with light because you give us light.

10 Keep on loving those who know you.
Keep on doing right to those whose hearts are honest.
11 Don't let the feet of those who are proud step on me.
Don't let the hands of those who are evil drive me away.
12 See how those who do evil have fallen!
They are thrown down. They aren't able to get up.

Psalm 37

A psalm of David.

1 Don't be upset because of sinful people.
Don't be jealous of those who do wrong.
2 Like grass, they will soon dry up.
Like green plants, they will soon die.

3 Trust in the LORD and do good.
Then you will live in the land and enjoy its food.
4 Find your delight in the LORD.
Then he will give you everything your heart really wants.

5 Commit your life to the LORD.
Here is what he will do if you trust in him.
6 He will make your godly ways shine like the dawn.
He will make your honest life shine like the sun at noon.

7 Be still. Be patient. Wait for the LORD to act.
Don't be upset when other people succeed.
Don't be upset when they carry out their evil plans.

8 Keep from being angry. Turn away from anger.
Don't be upset. That only leads to evil.
9 Sinful people will be cut off from the land.
But it will be given to those who put their hope in the LORD.

10 In a little while, there won't be any more sinners.
Even if you look for them, you won't be able to find them.
11 But those who are free of pride will be given the land.
They will enjoy great peace.

12 Sinful people make plans to harm those who
do what is right.
They grind their teeth at them.
13 But the Lord laughs at those who do evil.
He knows the day is coming when he will
judge them.

14 Sinners pull out their swords.
They bend their bows.
They want to kill poor and needy people.
They plan to murder those who lead
honest lives.
15 But they will be killed with their own swords.
Their own bows will be broken.

16 Those who do what is right may have
very little.
But it's better than the wealth of many
sinners.
17 The power of those who are evil will
be broken.
But the LORD takes good care of those
who do what is right.
18 Every day the LORD watches over those who
are without blame.
What he has given them will last forever.
19 When trouble comes to them, they will have
what they need.
When there is little food in the land, they
will still have plenty.

20 But sinful people will die.
The LORD's enemies will be like flowers in
the field.
They will disappear like smoke.

21 Sinful people borrow and don't pay back.
But those who are godly give freely
to others.
22 The LORD will give the land to those he blesses.
But he will cut off those he puts a curse on.

23 If the LORD is pleased with the way a
man lives,
he makes his steps secure.
24 Even if the man trips, he won't fall.
The LORD's hand takes good care of him.

25 I once was young, and now I'm old.
But I've never seen godly people deserted.
I've never seen their children begging for
bread.
26 The godly are always giving and lending
freely.
Their children will be blessed.

27 Turn away from evil and do good.
Then you will live in the land forever.
28 The LORD loves those who are honest.
He will not desert those who are faithful
to him.

They will be kept safe forever.
But the children of sinners will be cut off
from the land.

29 Those who do what is right will be given
the land.
They will live in it forever.

30 The mouths of those who do what is right
speak words of wisdom.
They say what is honest.
31 God's law is in their hearts.
Their feet do not slip.

32 Those who are evil hide and wait for godly
people.
They are trying to kill them.
33 But the LORD will not leave the godly in
their power.
He will not let them be found guilty when
they are brought into court.

34 Wait for the LORD to act.
Live as he wants you to.
He will honor you by giving you the land.
When sinners are cut off from it, you will
see it.

35 I saw a mean and sinful person.
He was doing well, like a green tree in its
own soil.
36 But he soon passed away and was gone.
Even though I looked for him, I couldn't
find him.

37 Think about those who are without blame.
Look at those who are honest.
A man who loves peace will have a
tomorrow.
38 But all sinners will be destroyed.
Those who are evil won't have a tomorrow.
They will be cut off from the land.

39 The LORD saves those who do what is right.
He is their place of safety when trouble
comes.
40 The LORD helps them and saves them.
He saves them from sinful people
because they go to him for safety.

Psalm 38

A psalm of David. A prayer.

1 LORD, don't correct me when you are angry.
Don't punish me when you are burning
with anger.
2 You have wounded me with your arrows.
You have struck me with your hand.
3 Because of your anger, my whole body is sick.
Because of my sin, I'm not healthy.
4 My guilt has become too much for me.
It is a load too heavy to carry.

5 My wounds are ugly. They stink.
I've been foolish. I have sinned.
6 I am bent over. I've been brought very low.
All day long I go around sobbing.
7 My back is filled with burning pain.
My whole body is sick.

8 I am weak. I feel as if I've been broken
in pieces.
I groan because of the great pain in
my heart.
9 Lord, everything I really want is clearly
known to you.
You always hear me when I sigh.
10 My heart pounds. My strength is gone.
My eyes can hardly see.
11 My friends and companions avoid me because
of my wounds.
My neighbors stay far away from me.
12 Those who are trying to kill me set their traps.
Those who want to harm me talk about
destroying me.
All day long they plan ways to trick me.

13 I'm like a deaf person. I can't hear.
I'm like someone who can't speak, who
can't say a word.
14 I'm like a man who doesn't hear.
I'm like someone whose mouth can't make
any reply.
15 LORD, I wait for you to help me.
LORD my God, I know you will answer.
16 I said, "Don't let my enemies have the joy of
seeing me fall.
Don't let them brag when my foot slips."

17 I am about to fall.
My pain never leaves me.
18 I admit that I have done wrong.
I am troubled by my sin.
19 I have many powerful enemies. They are
strong and healthy.
They hate me without any reason.
20 They pay me back with evil, even though I was
good to them.
They tell lies about me because I try to do
what is good.

21 LORD, don't desert me.
My God, don't be far away from me.
22 Lord my Savior,
come quickly to help me.

Psalm 39

For the director of music. For Jeduthun.
A psalm of David.

1 I said, "I will be careful about how I live.
I will not sin by what I say.
I will keep my mouth closed
when sinful people are near me."
2 I was silent and kept quiet.
I didn't even say anything good.
But the pain inside me grew worse.
3 My heart was deeply troubled.
As I thought about what was happening
to me,
I became even more troubled.
Then I spoke out.

4 I said, "LORD, show me when my life will end.
Show me how many days I have left.
Tell me how short my life will be.
5 You have given me only a few days to live.
My whole life doesn't seem like anything
to you.
No man's life lasts any longer than a breath.
Selah
6 People are only shadows as they go here
and there.
They rush around, but it doesn't mean
anything.
They pile up wealth, but they don't know
who will get it.

7 "Lord, what can I look forward to now?
You are the only hope I have.
8 Save me from all the wrong things I've done.
Don't let foolish people make fun of me.
9 I keep silent. I don't open my mouth.
You are the one who has caused all of this
to happen.
10 Please stop beating me.
I'm about to die from the blows of your hand.
11 You correct and punish people for their sin.
Just as a moth eats cloth, you destroy their
wealth.
No one's life lasts any longer than a breath.
Selah

12 "LORD, hear my prayer.
Listen to my cry for help.
Pay attention to my sobbing.
I'm like a guest in your home.
I'm only a visitor, like all of my family
who lived before me.
13 Leave me alone.
Let me be full of joy again before I die."

Psalm 40

For the director of music. A psalm of David.

1 I was patient while I waited for the LORD.
He turned to me and heard my cry for help.
2 I was sliding down into the pit of death, and
he pulled me out.
He brought me up out of the mud and dirt.
He set my feet on a rock.
He gave me a firm place to stand on.
3 He gave me a new song to sing.
It is a hymn of praise to our God.
Many people will see what he has done and
will worship him.
They will put their trust in the LORD.

4 Blessed is the man
who trusts in the LORD.
He doesn't look to proud people for help.
He doesn't turn away to worship statues
of gods.
5 LORD my God,
no one can compare with you.

You have done many miracles.
And you plan to do many more for us.
There are too many of them
for me to talk about.

6 You didn't want sacrifices and offerings.
You weren't pleased with burnt offerings
and sin offerings.
You gave me ears to hear you and obey you.
7 Then I said, "Here I am.
It is written about me in the scroll.
8 My God, I have come to do what you want.
Your law is in my heart."

9 I have told the whole community of those who
worship you
that what you do is right.
LORD, you know
that I haven't kept quiet.
10 I haven't kept to myself that what you did for
me was right.
I have spoken about how faithful you were
when you saved me.
I haven't hidden your love and truth
from the whole community.

11 LORD, don't hold back your mercy from me.
May your love and truth always keep
me safe.
12 There are more troubles all around me than I
can count.
My sins have caught up with me, and I can't
see any longer.
My sins are more than the hairs of my head.
I have lost all hope.

13 LORD, please save me.
LORD, come quickly to help me.
14 Let all those who are trying to kill me be
put to shame.
Let them not be honored.
Let all those who want to destroy me
be turned back in shame.
15 Some people make fun of me.
Let them be shocked when their plans fail.
16 But let all those who look to you
be joyful and glad because of what you
have done.
Let those who love you because you save them
always say,
"May the LORD be honored!"

17 But I am poor and needy.
May the Lord be concerned about me.
You are the One who helps me and saves me.
My God, please don't wait any longer.

Psalm 41

For the director of music. A psalm of David.

1 Blessed is the one who cares about
weak people.
When he is in trouble, the LORD saves him.
2 The LORD will guard him and keep him alive.
He will bless him in the land.
He won't hand him over to the wishes of
his enemies.
3 The LORD will take care of him when he is
lying sick in bed.
He will make him well again.

4 I said, "LORD, show me your favor.
Heal me. I have sinned against you."
5 My enemies are saying bad things about me.
They say, "When will he die and be
forgotten?"
6 When anyone comes to see me,
he says things he doesn't mean.
At the same time, he thinks up lies to tell
against me.
Then he goes out and spreads those lies
around.

7 All of my enemies whisper to each other
about me.
They want something terrible to happen
to me.
8 They say, "He is sick and will die very soon.
He will never get up from his bed again."
9 Even my close friend, whom I trusted, has
deserted me.
I even shared my bread with him.

10 But LORD, show me your favor.
Make me well, so I can pay them back.
11 Then I will know that you are pleased with me,
because my enemies haven't won the battle
over me.
12 You will take good care of me because I've
been honest.
You will let me be with you forever.

13 Give praise to the LORD, the God of Israel,
for ever and ever.
Amen and Amen.

BOOK II

Psalms 42–72

Psalm 42

For the director of music.
A *maskil* of the Sons of Korah.

1 A deer longs for streams of water.
God, I long for you in the same way.
2 I am thirsty for God. I am thirsty for the
living God.
When can I go and meet with him?
3 My tears have been my food
day and night.
All day long people say to me,
"Where is your God?"
4 When I remember what has happened,
I tell God all of my troubles.

I remember how I used to walk along with the
crowd of worshipers.
I led them to the house of God.
We shouted with joy and gave thanks
as we went to the holy feast.

5 My spirit, why are you so sad?
Why are you so upset deep down inside me?
Put your hope in God.
Once again I will have reason to praise him.
He is my Savior and 6 my God.

My spirit is very sad deep down inside me.
So I will remember you here where the Jordan River begins.
I will remember you here on the Hermon
mountains
and on Mount Mizar.
7 You have sent wave upon wave of trouble
over me.
It roars down on me like a waterfall.
All of your waves and breakers have rolled
over me.

8 During the day the LORD sends his love to me.
During the night I sing about him.
I say a prayer to the God who gives me life.

9 I say to God my Rock,
"Why have you forgotten me?
Why must I go around in sorrow?
Why am I beaten down by my enemies?"
10 My body suffers deadly pain
as my enemies make fun of me.
All day long they say to me,
"Where is your God?"

11 My spirit, why are you so sad?
Why are you so upset deep down inside me?
Put your hope in God.
Once again I will have reason to praise him.
He is my Savior and my God.

Psalm 43

1 God, when you hand down your decision, let it
be in my favor.
Stand up for me against an ungodly nation.
Save me from those lying and sinful people.
2 You are God, my place of safety.
Why have you turned your back on me?
Why must I go around in sorrow?
Why am I beaten down by my enemies?
3 Send out your light and your truth.
Let them guide me.
Let them bring me back to your holy mountain,
to the place where you live.
4 Then I will go to the altar of God.
I will go to God. He is my joy and my
delight.
God, you are my God.
I will praise you by playing the harp.

5 My spirit, why are you so sad?
Why are you so upset deep down inside me?
Put your hope in God.
Once again I will have reason to praise him.
He is my Savior and my God.

Psalm 44

For the director of music.
A *maskil* of the Sons of Korah.

1 God, we have heard what you did.
Those who came before us have told us
what you did in their days,
in days long ago.
2 With your powerful hand you drove out
the nations.
You settled our people in the land.
You crushed the people who were there.
And you made our people do well.
3 They didn't win the land with their swords.
They didn't gain success with their
powerful arms.
Your powerful right hand and your mighty arm
gave them success.
You looked on them with favor. You
loved them.

4 You are my King and my God.
You give success to the people of Jacob.
5 With your help we push our enemies back.
By your power we walk all over them.
6 I don't trust in my bow.
My sword doesn't bring me success.
7 But you give us success over our enemies.
You put them to shame.
8 All day long we talk about how great God is.
We will praise your name forever. *Selah*

9 But now you have turned your back on us and
made us low.
You don't march out with our armies
anymore.
10 You made us turn and run from our enemies.
They have taken what belongs to us.
11 You handed us over to be eaten up like sheep.
You have scattered us among the nations.
12 You sold your people for very little.
You didn't gain anything when you sold them.

13 You have made us something that our
neighbors laugh at.
Those who live around us make fun of us
and tease us.
14 The nations make jokes about us.
They shake their heads at us.
15 All day long I am reminded of my shame.
My face is covered with it
16 because of those who laugh at me and attack
me with their words.
They want to get even with me.

17 All of this happened to us,
even though we had not forgotten you.
We had been true to the covenant you made
with us.

[18]Our hearts had not turned away from you.
Our feet had not wandered from your path.
[19]But you crushed us and left us to the wild dogs.
You covered us over with deep darkness.

[20]We didn't forget our God.
We didn't spread out our hands in prayer to a strange god.
[21]If we had, God would have discovered it.
He knows the secrets of our hearts.
[22]But because of you, we face death all day long.
We are considered as sheep to be killed.

[23]Lord, wake up! Why are you sleeping?
Get up! Don't say no to us forever.
[24]Why do you turn your face away from us?
Why do you forget our pain and troubles?

[25]We are brought down to the dust.
Our bodies lie flat on the ground.
[26]Rise up and help us.
Save us because of your faithful love.

Psalm 45

For the director of music.
A *maskil* of the Sons of Korah.
A wedding song to the tune of "Lilies."

[1]My heart is full of beautiful words
as I say my poem for the king.
My tongue is like the pen of a skillful writer.

[2]You are the most excellent of men.
Your lips have been given the ability to speak gracious words.
God has blessed you forever.
[3]Mighty one, put your sword at your side.
Put on glory and majesty as if they were your clothes.
[4]In your majesty ride out with power
in honor of what is true and right.
Do it in honor of all those who are not proud.
Let your right hand do wonderful things.
[5]Shoot your sharp arrows into the hearts of your enemies.
Let the nations come under your control.
[6]Your throne is the very throne of God.
Your kingdom will last for ever and ever.
You will rule by treating everyone fairly.
[7]You love what is right and hate what is evil.
So your God has placed you above your companions.
He has filled you with joy by pouring the sacred oil on your head.
[8]Myrrh and aloes and cassia make all of your robes smell good.
In palaces decorated with ivory
the music played on stringed instruments makes you glad.
[9]Daughters of kings are among the women you honor.
At your right hand is the royal bride dressed in gold from Ophir.

[10]Royal bride, listen. Think about this and pay attention to it.
Forget about your people and the home you came from.
[11]The king is charmed by your beauty.
Honor him. He is now your master.
[12]The people of Tyre will come with gifts.
Wealthy people will try to gain your favor.

[13]The princess comes into the palace in all her glory.
Her gown has gold threads running through it.
[14]Dressed in beautiful clothes, she is led to the king.
Her virgin companions follow her
and are brought to him.
[15]They are led in with joy and gladness.
They enter the palace of the king.

[16]Your sons will rule just as your father and grandfather did.
You will make them princes through the whole land.
[17]I will make sure that people will always remember you.
The nations will praise you for ever and ever.

Psalm 46

For the director of music.
A song of the Sons of Korah. For *alamoth*.

[1]God is our place of safety. He gives us strength.
He is always there to help us in times of trouble.
[2]The earth may fall apart.
The mountains may fall into the middle of the sea.
But we will not be afraid.
[3]The waters of the sea may roar and foam.
The mountains may shake when the waters rise.
But we will not be afraid. *Selah*

[4]God's blessings are like a river. They fill the city of God with joy.
That city is the holy place where the Most High God lives.
[5]Because God is there, the city will not fall.
God will help it at the beginning of the day.
[6]Nations are in disorder. Kingdoms fall.
God speaks, and the people of the earth melt in fear.

[7]The LORD who rules over all is with us.
The God of Jacob is like a fort to us. *Selah*

[8]Come and see what the LORD has done.
See the places he has destroyed on the earth.
[9]He makes wars stop from one end of the earth to the other.

He breaks every bow. He snaps every spear.
He burns every shield with fire.
10 He says, "Be still, and know that I am God.
I will be honored among the nations.
I will be honored in the earth."

11 The LORD who rules over all is with us.
The God of Jacob is like a fort to us. *Selah*

Psalm 47

For the director of music.
A psalm of the Sons of Korah.

1 Clap your hands, all you nations.
Shout to God with cries of joy.
2 How wonderful is the LORD Most High!
He is the great King over the whole earth.
3 He brought nations under our control.
He made them fall under us.
4 He chose our land for us.
The people of Jacob are proud of their land,
and God loves them. *Selah*

5 God went up to his throne while his people
were shouting with joy.
The LORD went up while trumpets were
playing.
6 Sing praises to God. Sing praises.
Sing praises to our King. Sing praises.

7 God is the King of the whole earth.
Sing a psalm of praise to him.
8 God rules over the nations.
He is seated on his holy throne.
9 The nobles of the nations come together.
They are now part of the people of the God
of Abraham.
The kings of the earth belong to God.
He is greatly honored.

Psalm 48

A song. A psalm of the Sons of Korah.

1 The LORD is great. He is really worthy of praise.
Praise him in the city of our God, his holy
mountain.
2 Mount Zion is high and beautiful.
It brings joy to everyone on earth.
Mount Zion is like the highest parts of
Mount Zaphon.
It is the city of the Great King.
3 God is there to keep it safe.
He has shown himself to be like a fort
to the city.

4 Many kings joined forces.
They entered Israel together.
5 But when they saw Mount Zion, they were
amazed.
They ran away in terror.
6 Trembling took hold of them.
They felt pain like a woman giving birth
to a baby.
7 LORD, you destroyed them like ships
of Tarshish
that were torn apart by an east wind.
8 What we heard we have also seen.
We have seen it
in the city of the LORD who rules over all.
We have seen it in the city of our God.
We have heard and seen that God makes
her secure forever. *Selah*

9 God, inside your temple
we think about your faithful love.
10 God, your fame reaches from one end of the
earth to the other.
In the same way, people praise you from one
end of the earth to the other.
You use your power to do what is right.
11 Mount Zion is filled with joy.
The villages of Judah are glad.
That's because you judge fairly.

12 Walk around Zion. Go all around it.
Count its towers.
13 Think carefully about its outer walls.
Just look at how safe it is!
Then you can tell its people that God keeps
them safe.
14 This God is our God for ever and ever.
He will be our guide to the very end.

Psalm 49

For the director of music.
A psalm of the Sons of Korah.

1 Hear this, all you nations.
Listen, all you who live in this world.
2 Listen, ordinary and important people alike.
Listen, those of you who are rich or poor.
3 My mouth will speak wise words.
What I say from my heart will give
understanding.
4 I will pay attention to a proverb.
I will explain my riddle as I play the harp.

5 Why should I be afraid when trouble comes?
Why should I fear when sinners are all
around me?
They are the kind of people who want to
take advantage of me.
6 They trust in their wealth.
They brag about how rich they are.
7 No man can pay for the life of anyone else.
No one can give God what that
would cost.
8 The price for a life is very high.
No payment is ever enough.
9 No one can pay enough to live forever
and not rot in the grave.

10 Everyone can see that even wise people die.
Foolish and dumb people also pass away.
All of them leave their wealth to others.

[11] Their graves will remain their houses forever.
Their graves will be their homes for all time to come.
Naming lands after themselves won't help either.
[12] Even though people may be very rich, they don't live on and on.
They are like the animals. They die.
[13] That's what happens to those who trust in themselves.
It also happens to their followers, who agree with what they say. *Selah*
[14] Like sheep they will end up in the grave.
Death will swallow them up.
When honest people come to power, a new day will dawn.
The bodies of sinners will waste away in the grave.
They will end up far away from their princely houses.
[15] But God will save me from the grave.
He will certainly take me to himself. *Selah*
[16] Don't be upset when someone becomes rich.
Don't be troubled when he becomes more and more wealthy.
[17] He won't take anything with him when he dies.
His riches won't go down to the grave with him.
[18] While he lived, he believed he was blessed.
People praised him when things were going well for him.
[19] But he will die, like his people of long ago.
He will never again see the light that leads to life.
[20] People who have riches but don't understand are like the animals. They die.

Psalm 50

A psalm of Asaph.

[1] The Mighty One, God, the LORD, speaks.
He calls out to the earth
from the sunrise in the east
to the sunset in the west.
[2] From Zion, perfect and beautiful,
God's glory shines out.
[3] Our God comes, and he won't be silent.
A burning fire goes ahead of him.
A terrible storm is all around him.
[4] He calls out to heaven and earth to be his witnesses.
Then he judges his people.
[5] He says, "Gather my holy people around me.
They made a covenant with me by offering a sacrifice."
[6] The heavens announce that what God decides is right.
He himself is the Judge. *Selah*
[7] God says, "Listen, my people, and I will speak.
Listen, Israel, and I will give witness against you.
I am God, your God.
[8] I don't find fault with you because of your sacrifices.
I don't find fault with the burnt offerings you always bring me.
[9] I don't need a bull from your barn.
I don't need goats from your pens.
[10] Every animal in the forest already belongs to me.
And so do the cattle on a thousand hills.
[11] I own every bird in the mountains.
The creatures of the field belong to me.
[12] If I were hungry, I wouldn't tell you.
The world belongs to me. And so does everything in it.
[13] Do I eat the meat of bulls?
Do I drink the blood of goats?
[14] Bring me thank offerings, because I am your God.
Carry out the promises you made to me, because I am the Most High God.
[15] Call out to me when trouble comes.
I will save you. And you will honor me."

[16] But here is what God says to sinful people.

"What right do you have to speak the words of my laws?
How dare you speak the words of my covenant!
[17] You hate my teaching.
You turn your back on what I say.
[18] When you see a thief, you join him.
You make friends with those who commit adultery.
[19] You use your mouth to speak evil.
You use your tongue to spread lies.
[20] You always speak against your brother.
You always tell lies about your own mother's son.
[21] You have done those things, and I kept silent.
So you thought I was just like you.
But now I'm going to correct you.
I will bring charges against you.

[22] "You who forget God, think about this.
If you don't, I will tear you to pieces.
No one will be able to save you.
[23] Anyone who sacrifices thank offerings to me honors me.
He makes it possible for me to show him that I am the God who saves."

Psalm 51

For the director of music. A psalm of David when the prophet Nathan came to him after David had committed adultery with Bathsheba.

[1] God, show me your favor
in keeping with your faithful love.

Because your love is so tender and kind,
wipe out my lawless acts.
2 Wash away all of the evil things I've done.
Make me pure from my sin.

3 I know the lawless acts I've committed.
I can't forget my sin.
4 You are the one I've really sinned against.
I've done what is evil in your sight.
So you are right when you sentence me.
You are fair when you judge me.
5 I know I've been a sinner ever since I
was born.
I've been a sinner ever since my mother
became pregnant with me.
6 I know that you want truth to be in my heart.
You teach me wisdom deep down
inside me.

7 Make me pure by sprinkling me with hyssop
plant. Then I will be clean.
Wash me. Then I will be whiter than snow.
8 Let me hear you say, "Your sins are forgiven."
That will bring me joy and gladness.
Let the body you have broken be glad.
9 Take away all of my sins.
Wipe away all of the evil things I've done.

10 God, create a pure heart in me.
Give me a new spirit that is faithful to you.
11 Don't send me away from you.
Don't take your Holy Spirit away from me.
12 Give me back the joy that comes from being
saved by you.
Give me a spirit that obeys you. That will
keep me going.

13 Then I will teach your ways to those who
commit lawless acts.
And sinners will turn back to you.
14 You are the God who saves me.
I have committed murder.
Take away my guilt.
Then my tongue will sing about how right
you are
no matter what you do.
15 Lord, open my lips so that I can speak.
Then my mouth will praise you.
16 You don't take delight in sacrifice.
If you did, I would bring it.
You don't take pleasure in burnt
offerings.
17 The greatest sacrifice you want is a
broken spirit.
God, you will gladly accept a heart
that is broken because of sadness over sin.

18 May you be pleased to give Zion success.
Build up the walls of Jerusalem.
19 Then holy sacrifices will be offered in the
right way.
Whole burnt offerings will bring delight
to you.
And bulls will be offered on your altar.

Psalm 52

For the director of music. A *maskil* of David when Doeg, who was from Edom, had gone to Saul. Doeg had told Saul, "David has gone to the house of Ahimelech."

1 You think you are such a big, strong man!
Why do you brag about the evil things
you've done?
You are a dishonor to God all the time.
2 You plan ways to destroy others.
Your tongue is like a blade that has a
sharp edge.
You are always telling lies.
3 You love evil instead of good.
You would rather lie than tell
the truth. *Selah*
4 You love to harm others with your
words, you liar!

5 So God will destroy you forever.
He will grab hold of you and throw you
out of your tent.
He will remove you from this life. *Selah*
6 Those who do what is right will see it and
learn a lesson from it.
They will laugh at you and say,
7 "Just look at this fellow!
He didn't depend on God for his safety.
He put his trust in all his wealth.
He grew strong by destroying others!"

8 But I am like a healthy olive tree.
My roots are deep in the house of God.
I trust in your faithful love
for ever and ever.
9 I will praise you forever for what you
have done.
I will put my hope in you because you
are good.
I will praise you when I'm with your
faithful people.

Psalm 53

For the director of music. For *mahalath*. A *maskil* of David.

1 Foolish people say in their hearts,
"There is no God."
They do all kinds of horrible and evil things.
No one does anything good.

2 God looks down from heaven
on all people.
He wants to see if there are any who
understand.
He wants to see if there are any who trust
in God.
3 All of them have turned away.
They have all become evil.
No one does anything good,
no one at all.

4 Won't those who do evil ever learn?
They eat up my people as if they were eating bread.
They don't call out to God for help.
5 Just look at them! They are filled with terror
even when there is nothing to be afraid of!
People of Israel, God will scatter the bones of those who attack you.
You will put them to shame, because God hates them.

6 How I pray that the One who saves Israel will come out of Zion!
God will bless his people with great success again.
So let the people of Jacob be filled with joy!
Let Israel be glad!

Psalm 54

For the director of music. To be played on stringed instruments. A *maskil* of David when the men from Ziph had gone to Saul. They had said, "Isn't David hiding among us?"

1 God, save me by your power.
Set me free by your might.
2 God, hear my prayer.
Listen to what I'm saying.

3 Strangers are attacking me.
Mean people are trying to kill me.
They don't care about God. *Selah*

4 But I know that God helps me.
The Lord is the one who keeps me going.

5 My enemies tell lies about me.
Do to them the evil things they planned against me.
God, be faithful and destroy them.

6 I will sacrifice an offering to you
just because I choose to.
LORD, I will praise your name
because it is good.
7 You have saved me from all of my troubles.
With my own eyes I have seen you win the battle over my enemies.

Psalm 55

For the director of music. A *maskil* of David to be played on stringed instruments.

1 God, listen to my prayer.
Pay attention to my cry for help.
2 Hear me and answer me.
My thoughts upset me. I'm very troubled.
3 I'm troubled by what my enemies say about me.
I'm upset because sinful people stare at me.
They cause me all kinds of suffering.
When they are angry, they attack me with their words.

4 I feel great pain deep down inside me.
The terrors of death are crushing me.
5 Fear and trembling have taken hold of me.
Panic has overpowered me.
6 I said, "I wish I had wings like a dove!
Then I would fly away and be at rest.
7 I would escape to a place far away.
I would stay out in the desert. *Selah*
8 I would hurry to my place of safety.
It would be far away from the winds and storms I'm facing."

9 Lord, destroy the plans of sinners. Keep them from understanding one another.
I see people destroying things and fighting in the city.
10 Day and night they prowl around on top of its walls.
The city is full of crime and trouble.
11 Forces that destroy are at work inside it.
Its streets are full of people who cheat others and take advantage of them.

12 If an enemy were making fun of me,
I could stand it.
If he were looking down on me,
I could hide from him.
13 But it's you, someone like myself.
It's my companion, my close friend.
14 We used to enjoy good friendship
as we walked with the crowds at the house of God.

15 Let death take my enemies by surprise.
Let them be buried alive,
because their hearts and homes are full of evil.

16 But I call out to God.
And the LORD saves me.
17 Evening, morning and noon
I groan and cry out.
And he hears my voice.
18 Even though many enemies are fighting against me,
he brings me safely back from the battle.
19 God sits on his throne forever.
He hears my prayers and makes my enemies suffer. *Selah*
They never change their ways.
They don't have any respect for God.

20 My companion attacks his friends.
He breaks his promise.
21 His talk is as smooth as butter.
But he has war in his heart.
His words flow like olive oil.
But they are like swords ready for battle.

22 Turn your worries over to the LORD.
He will keep you going.
He will never let godly people fall.

23 God, you will bring sinners
down to the grave.
Murderers and liars
won't live out even half of their lives.

But I trust in you.

Psalm 56

For the director of music. A *miktam* of David after the Philistines had captured him in Gath. To the tune of "A Dove on Distant Oak Trees."

1 God, show me your favor. Men are chasing me.
All day long they keep attacking me.
2 Those who tell lies about me chase me all
day long.
Many proud people are attacking me.

3 When I'm afraid,
I will trust in you.
4 I trust in God. I praise his word.
I trust in God. I will not be afraid.
What can people do to me?

5 All day long they twist my words.
They are always making plans to harm me.
6 They get together and hide.
They watch my steps.
They hope to kill me.

7 Make sure you don't let them escape.
God, bring down the nations in your anger.
8 Write down my poem of sadness.
List my tears on your scroll.
Aren't you making a record of them?

9 My enemies will turn back
when I call out to you for help.
Then I will know that God is on my side.
10 I trust in God. I praise his word.
I trust in the LORD. I praise his word.
11 I trust in God. I will not be afraid.
What can mere men do to me?

12 God, I have made promises to you.
I will bring my thank offerings to you.
13 You have saved me from death.
You have kept me from tripping
and falling.
Now I can live with you
in the light that leads to life.

Psalm 57

For the director of music. A *miktam* of David when he had run away from Saul into the cave. To the tune of "Do Not Destroy."

1 Show me your favor, God. Show me
your favor.
I go to you for safety.
I will find safety in the shadow of your wings.
There I will stay until the danger is gone.

2 I cry out to God Most High.
I cry out to God, and he carries out his plan
for me.
3 He answers from heaven and saves me.
He puts to shame those who chase me. *Selah*
He shows me his love and his truth.

4 Men who are like lions are all around me.
I am lying down among hungry animals.
Their teeth are like spears and arrows.
Their tongues are like sharp swords.

5 God, may you be honored above the heavens.
Let your glory be over the whole earth.

6 My enemies spread a net to catch me by
the feet.
I felt helpless.
They dug a pit in my path.
But they fell into it themselves. *Selah*

7 God, my heart feels secure.
My heart feels secure.
I will sing and make music to you.
8 My spirit, wake up!
Harp and lyre, wake up!
I want to sing and make music before the
sun rises.

9 Lord, I will praise you among the nations.
I will sing about you among the people of
the earth.
10 Great is your love. It reaches to the heavens.
Your truth reaches to the skies.

11 God, may you be honored above the heavens.
Let your glory be over the whole earth.

Psalm 58

For the director of music. A *miktam* of David to the tune of "Do Not Destroy."

1 Are you rulers really fair when you speak?
Do you judge people honestly?
2 No, in your hearts you plan to be unfair.
With your hands you do terrible things on
the earth.
3 Even from birth those who are evil go down
the wrong path.
From the day they are born they go the
wrong way and speak lies.
4 Their words are like the poison of a snake.
They are like the poison of a cobra that has
covered up its ears.
5 It won't listen to any tune of a snake charmer,
even if the charmer really plays well.

6 God, break the teeth in the mouths of those
sinners!
LORD, tear out the sharp teeth of those lions!
7 Let those people disappear like water that
flows away.
When they draw their bows, let their arrows
be dull.

8 Let them be like a slug that melts away as it moves along.
Let them be like a baby that is born dead and never sees the sun.

9 Evil people will be swept away quicker than a pot can feel the heat of thorns burning under it.
And it doesn't matter if the thorns are green or dry.

10 Godly people will be glad when those who have hurt them are paid back.
They will wash their feet in the blood of those who do evil.

11 Then people will say,
"The godly will get their reward.
There really is a God who judges the earth."

Psalm 59

For the director of music. A *miktam* of David when Saul had sent men to watch David's house in order to kill him. To the tune of "Do Not Destroy."

1 God, save me from my enemies.
Keep me safe from those who rise up against me.

2 Save me from those who do evil.
Save me from murderers.

3 See how they hide and wait for me!
LORD, angry people plan to harm me,
even though I haven't hurt them in any way or sinned against them.

4 I haven't done anything wrong to them. But they are ready to attack me.
Rise up and help me! Look at what I'm up against!

5 LORD God who rules over all, rise up. God of Israel,
punish all of the nations.
Don't show any mercy to those sinful people who have turned against me. *Selah*

6 My enemies are like a pack of barking dogs that come back to the city in the evening.
They prowl around the city.

7 Listen to what pours out of their mouths.
The words from their lips are like swords.
They think, "Who can hear us?"

8 But you laugh at them, LORD.
You make fun of all those nations.

9 You give me strength. I look to you.
God, you are like a fort to me. 10 You are my loving God.
God will march out in front of me.
He will let me look down on those who tell lies about me.

11 Lord, you are like a shield that keeps us safe.
Don't kill my enemies all at once.
If you do, my people will forget about it.
Use your power to make my enemies wander around.
Destroy them.

12 They have sinned with their mouths.
Their lips have spoken evil words.
They have called down a curse on me and lied.
Let them be caught in their pride.

13 Burn them up in your anger.
Burn them up until there isn't anything left of them.
Then everyone from one end of the earth to the other will know
that God rules over the people of Jacob. *Selah*

14 My enemies are like a pack of barking dogs that come back into the city in the evening.
They prowl around the city.

15 They wander around looking for food.
They groan if they don't find something that will satisfy them.

16 But I will sing about your strength.
In the morning I will sing about your love.
You are like a fort to me.
You keep me safe in times of trouble.

17 You give me strength. I sing praise to you.
God, you are like a fort to me. You are my loving God.

Psalm 60

For the director of music. For teaching. A *miktam* of David when he fought against Aram Naharaim and Aram Zobah. That was when Joab returned and struck down 12,000 people from Edom in the Valley of Salt. To the tune of "The Lily of the Covenant."

1 God, you have turned away from us. You have attacked us.
You have been angry. Now turn back to us!

2 You have shaken the land and torn it open.
Fix its cracks, because it is falling apart.

3 You have shown your people hard times.
You have made us drink the wine of your anger.
Now we can't even walk straight.

4 But you lead into battle those who have respect for you.
You give them a flag to wave against the enemy's weapons. *Selah*

5 Save us. Help us with your powerful right hand,
so that those you love may be saved.

6 God has spoken from his temple.
He has said, "I will win the battle.
Then I will divide up the land around Shechem.
I will divide up the Valley of Succoth.

7 Gilead belongs to me.
So does the land of Manasseh.

Ephraim is the strongest tribe.
It is like a helmet for my head.
Judah is the royal tribe.
It is like a ruler's staff.
8 Moab serves me like one who washes my feet.
I toss my sandal on Edom to show that I own it.
I shout to Philistia that I have won the battle."

9 Who will bring me to the city that has high walls around it?
Who will lead me to the land of Edom?
10 God, isn't it you, even though you have now turned away from us?
Isn't it you, even though you don't lead our armies into battle anymore?
11 Help us against our enemies.
The help people give doesn't amount to anything.
12 With your help we will win the battle.
You will walk all over our enemies.

Psalm 61

For the director of music. A psalm of David to be played on stringed instruments.

1 God, hear my cry for help.
Listen to my prayer.

2 From a place far away I call out to you.
I call out as my heart gets weaker.
Lead me to the safety of a rock that is high above me.
3 You have always kept me safe from my enemies.
You are like a strong tower to me.

4 I long to live in your holy tent forever.
There I find safety in the shadow of your wings. *Selah*
5 God, you have heard my promises.
You have given me what belongs to those who worship you.
6 Add many days to the king's life.
Let him live on and on for many years.
7 May he always enjoy your blessing as he rules.
Let your love and truth keep him safe.

8 Then I will always sing praise to you.
I will keep my promises day after day.

Psalm 62

For the director of music. For Jeduthun. A psalm of David.

1 I find my rest in God alone.
He is the One who saves me.
2 He alone is my rock. He is the One who saves me.
He is like a fort to me. I will always be secure.

3 How long will you enemies attack me?
Will all of you throw me down?
I'm like a leaning wall.
I'm like a fence that is about to fall.
4 You only want to pull me down
from my place of honor.
You take delight in telling lies.
You bless me with what you say.
But in your hearts you call down curses on me. *Selah*

5 I will find my rest in God alone.
He is the One who gives me hope.
6 He alone is my rock. He is the One who saves me.
He is like a fort to me. I will always be secure.
7 I depend on God to save me and to honor me.
He is my mighty rock. He is my place of safety.
8 Trust in him at all times, you people.
Tell him all of your troubles.
God is our place of safety. *Selah*

9 Ordinary people are only a breath.
Important people are not what they seem to be.
If they were weighed on a scale, they wouldn't amount to anything.
Together they are only a breath.
10 Don't trust in money you have taken from others.
Don't be proud of things you have stolen.
Even if your riches grow,
don't put your trust in them.

11 God, I have heard you say two things.
One is that you, God, are strong.
12 The other is that you, Lord, are loving.
I'm sure you will reward each person
in keeping with what he has done.

Psalm 63

A psalm of David when he was in the Desert of Judah.

1 God, you are my God.
I greatly long for you.
With all my heart I thirst for you
in this dry desert
where there isn't any water.

2 I have seen you in the sacred tent.
There I have seen your power and your glory.
3 Your love is better than life.
I will bring glory to you with my lips.
4 I will praise you as long as I live.
I will lift up my hands when I pray to you.
5 I will be as satisfied as if I had eaten the best food there is.
I will sing praise to you with my mouth.

[6] As I lie on my bed I remember you.
I think of you all night long.
[7] Because you have helped me,
I sing in the shadow of your wings.
[8] I hold on to you.
Your powerful right hand takes good care of me.

[9] Those who are trying to kill me will be destroyed.
They will go down into the grave.
[10] They will be killed with swords.
They will become food for wild dogs.

[11] But the king will be filled with joy because of what God has done.
All those who take an oath in God's name will praise him.
But the mouths of liars will be shut.

Psalm 64

For the director of music. A psalm of David.

[1] God, hear me as I tell you my problem.
Don't let my enemies kill me.
[2] Hide me from those who make evil plans against me.
Hide me from that crowd of people who are doing evil.
[3] They make their tongues like sharp swords.
They aim their words like deadly arrows.
[4] They shoot from their hiding places at people who aren't guilty of doing anything wrong.
They shoot quickly. They aren't afraid of being caught.

[5] They help each other make evil plans.
They talk about hiding their traps.
They say, "Who can see what we are doing?"
[6] They make plans to do what is evil.
They say, "We have thought up a perfect plan!"
The hearts and minds of people are so clever!

[7] But God will shoot my enemies with his arrows.
He will suddenly strike them down.
[8] He will turn their own words against them.
He will destroy them.
All those who see them will shake their heads and look down on them.

[9] Everyone will respect God.
They will tell about his works.
They will think about what he has done.
[10] Let godly people be full of joy because of what the LORD has done.
Let them go to him for safety.
Let all those whose hearts are honest praise him.

Psalm 65

For the director of music.
A psalm of David. A song.

[1] God, we look forward to praising you in Zion.
We will keep our promises to you.
[2] All people will come to you,
because you hear and answer prayer.
[3] When our sins became too much for us,
you forgave our lawless acts.
[4] Blessed are those you choose
and bring near to worship you.
You bring us into the courtyards of your holy temple.
There in your house we are filled with all kinds of good things.

[5] God our Savior, you answer us by doing wonderful things.
You save us by your power.
People all over the world and beyond the farthest oceans
put their hope in you.
[6] You formed the mountains by your power.
You showed how strong you are.
[7] You calmed the oceans and their roaring waves.
You calmed the angry words and actions of the nations.
[8] Those who live far away are amazed at the miracles you have done.
What you do makes people from one end of the earth to the other sing for joy.

[9] You take care of the land and water it.
You make it very rich.
You fill your streams with water.
You provide the people with grain.
That's how you prepare the land.
[10] You water its rows.
You smooth out its bumps.
You soften it with showers.
And you bless its crops.
[11] You bring the year to a close with huge crops.
You provide more than enough food.
[12] The grass grows thick even in the desert.
The hills are dressed with gladness.
[13] The meadows are covered with flocks and herds.
The valleys are dressed with grain.
They sing and shout with joy.

Psalm 66

For the director of music. A song. A psalm.

[1] Shout to God with joy, everyone on earth!
[2] Sing about the glory of his name!
Give him glorious praise!
[3] Say to God, "What wonderful things you do!
Your power is so great
that your enemies bow down to you in fear.

[4] Everyone on earth bows down to you.
They sing praise to you.
They sing praise to your name." *Selah*

[5] Come and see what God has done.
See what wonderful things he has done for his people!
[6] He turned the Red Sea into dry land.
The people of Israel passed through the waters on foot.
Come, let us be full of joy because of what he did.
[7] He rules by his power forever.
His eyes watch the nations.
Let no one who refuses to obey him rise up against him. *Selah*
[8] Praise our God, you nations.
Let the sound of the praise you give him be heard.
[9] He has kept us alive.
He has kept our feet from slipping.
[10] God, you have put us to the test.
You put us through fire to make us like silver.
[11] You put us in prison.
You placed heavy loads on our backs.
[12] You let people run over our heads.
We went through fire and water.
But you brought us to a place
where we have everything we need.

[13] I will come to your temple with burnt offerings.
I will keep my promises to you.
[14] I made them with my lips.
My mouth spoke them when I was in trouble.
[15] I will sacrifice fat animals to you as burnt offerings.
I will offer rams, bulls and goats to you. *Selah*

[16] Come and listen, all of you who have respect for God.
Let me tell you what he has done for me.
[17] I cried out to him with my mouth.
I praised him with my tongue.
[18] If I had enjoyed having sin in my heart,
the Lord would not have listened.
[19] But God has listened.
He has heard my prayer.
[20] Give praise to God.
He has accepted my prayer.
He has not held his love back from me.

Psalm 67

For the director of music. A psalm.
A song to be played on stringed instruments.

[1] God, show us your favor. Bless us.
May you smile on us with your favor. *Selah*
[2] Then your ways will be known on earth.
All nations will see that you have the power to save.

[3] God, may the nations praise you.
May all of the people on earth praise you.
[4] May the nations be glad and sing with joy.
You rule the people of the earth fairly.
You guide the nations of the earth. *Selah*
[5] God, may the nations praise you.
May all of the people on earth praise you.

[6] Then the land will produce its crops.
God, our God, will bless us.
[7] God will bless us.
People from one end of the earth to the other
will have respect for him.

Psalm 68

For the director of music.
A psalm of David. A song.

[1] May God rise up and scatter his enemies.
May they turn and run away from him.
[2] As wind blows smoke away,
so may God blow them away.
As fire melts wax,
so may he destroy sinful people.
[3] But may those who do what is right be glad
and filled with joy when they are with him.
May they be happy and joyful.

[4] Sing to God. Sing praise to his name.
Lift up a song to the One who rides on the clouds.
His name is the LORD.
Be glad when you are with him.
[5] God is in his holy temple.
He is a father to those whose fathers have died.
He takes care of women whose husbands have died.
[6] God gives lonely people a family.
He sets prisoners free, and they go out singing.
But those who refuse to obey him
live in a land that is baked by the sun.

[7] God, you led your people out.
You marched through a dry and empty land. *Selah*
[8] The ground shook
when you, the God of Sinai, appeared.
The heavens poured down rain
when you, the God of Israel, appeared.
[9] God, you gave us plenty of rain.
You renewed your worn-out land.
[10] God, your people settled in it.
From all of your riches, you provided for those who were poor.

[11] The Lord gave a message.
Many people made it widely known.

12 They said, "Kings and armies are running away.
In the camps, Israel's soldiers are dividing up
the things they have taken from their enemies.
13 Even while the soldiers sleep near the campfires,
God wins the battle for them.
He gives the enemy's silver and gold
to Israel, his dove."
14 The Mighty One has scattered the kings around the land.
It was like snow falling on Mount Zalmon.
15 The mountains of Bashan are majestic.
The mountains of Bashan are very rocky.
16 You rocky mountains are jealous of Mount Zion, aren't you?
That's where God chooses to rule.
That's where the LORD himself will live forever.
17 God has come with tens of thousands of his chariots.
He has come with thousands and thousands of them.
The Lord has come from Mount Sinai.
He has entered his holy place.
18 When he went up to his place on high,
he led a line of prisoners.
He received gifts from people,
even from those who refused to obey him.
The LORD God went up to live on Mount Zion.
19 Give praise to the Lord. Give praise to God our Savior.
He carries our heavy loads day after day. *Selah*
20 Our God is a God who saves.
He is the King and the LORD. He saves us from death.
21 God will certainly smash the heads of his enemies.
He will break the hairy heads of those who keep on sinning.
22 The Lord says, "I will bring your enemies from Bashan.
I will bring them up from the bottom of the sea.
23 Then your feet can wade in their blood.
The tongues of your dogs can lick up all the blood they want."
24 God, those who worship you come marching into view.
My God and King, those who follow you have entered the sacred tent.
25 The singers are walking in front.
Next come those who play the music.
Young women playing tambourines are with them.
26 The leaders sing, "Praise God among all those who worship him.
Praise the LORD in the community of Israel."
27 The little tribe of Benjamin leads the worshipers.
Next comes the great crowd of Judah's princes.
Then come the princes of Zebulun and the princes of Naphtali.
28 God, show us your power.
Show us your strength.
God, do as you have done before.
29 Do it from your temple at Jerusalem,
where kings will bring you gifts.
30 Give a strong warning to Egypt, that beast among the tall grass.
Warn the leaders of the nations, who are like bulls among the calves.
May they bow down before you with gifts of silver.
Scatter the nations who like to make war.
31 Messengers will come from Egypt.
The people of Cush will be quick to bring gifts to you.
32 Sing to God, you kingdoms of the earth.
Sing praise to the Lord. *Selah*
33 He rides in the age-old skies above.
He thunders with his mighty voice.
34 Tell how powerful God is.
He rules as king over Israel.
The skies show how powerful he is.
35 How wonderful is God in his holy place!
The God of Israel gives power and strength to his people.

Give praise to God!

Psalm 69

For the director of music.
A psalm of David to the tune of "Lilies."

1 God, save me.
My troubles are like a flood.
I'm up to my neck in them.
2 I'm sinking in deep mud.
I have no firm place to stand.
I am out in deep water.
The waves roll over me.
3 I'm worn out from calling for help.
My throat is very dry.
My eyes grow tired
looking for my God.
4 Those who hate me without any reason
are more than the hairs on my head.
Many people who don't have any reason to be my enemies
are trying to destroy me.
They force me to give back
what I didn't steal.

5 God, you know how foolish I've been.
My guilt is not hidden from you.

6 Lord, you are the LORD who rules over all.
May those who put their hope in you not be dishonored because of me.
You are the God of Israel.
May those who worship you not be put to shame because of me.
7 Because of you, people laugh at me.
My face is covered with shame.
8 I'm a stranger to my brothers.
I'm an outsider to my own mother's sons.
9 My great love for your house destroys me.
Those who make fun of you make fun of me also.
10 When I sob and go without eating,
they laugh at me.
11 When I put on black clothes to show how sad I am,
people make jokes about me.
12 Those who gather in public places make fun of me.
Those who get drunk make up songs about me.

13 But LORD, I pray to you.
May this be the time you show me your favor.
God, answer me because you love me so much.
Save me, as you always do.
14 Save me from the trouble I'm in.
It's like slippery mud. Don't let me sink in it.
Save me from those who hate me.
Save me from the deep water I'm in.
15 Don't let the floods cover me.
Don't let the deep water swallow me up.
Don't let the grave close its mouth over me.
16 LORD, answer me because your love is so good.
Turn to me because you are so kind.
17 Don't turn your face away from me.
Answer me quickly. I'm in trouble.
18 Come near and save me.
Set me free from my enemies.

19 You know how they make fun of me.
They dishonor me and put me to shame.
You know all about my enemies.
20 They have broken my heart by saying evil things about me.
It has left me helpless.
I looked for pity, but I didn't find any.
I looked for someone to comfort me, but I didn't find anyone.
21 They put bitter spices in my food.
They gave me vinegar when I was thirsty.

22 Let their feast be a trap and a snare.
Let my enemies get what's coming to them.
23 Let their eyes grow weak so they can't see.
Let their backs be bent forever.
24 Pour out your anger on them.
Let them feel its burning heat.
25 May their homes be deserted.
May no one live in their tents.
26 They attack those you have wounded.
They talk about the pain of those you have hurt.
27 Charge them with one crime after another.
Don't save them.
28 May their names be erased from the Book of Life.
Don't include them in the list of those who do right.

29 I'm in pain. I'm in deep trouble.
God, save me and keep me safe.

30 I will praise God's name by singing to him.
I will bring him glory by giving him thanks.
31 That will please the LORD more than offering him an ox.
It will please him more than offering him a bull with its horns and hoofs.
32 Poor people will see it and be glad.
The hearts of those who worship God will be strengthened.
33 The LORD hears those who are in need.
He doesn't forget his people in prison.
34 Let heaven and earth praise him.
Let the oceans and everything that moves in them praise him.
35 God will save Zion.
He will build the cities of Judah again.
Then people will live in them and own the land.
36 The children of those who serve God will receive it.
Those who love him will live there.

Psalm 70

For the director of music. A prayer of David.

1 God, hurry and save me.
LORD, come quickly and help me.
2 Let those who are trying to kill me be put to shame.
Let them not be honored.
Let all those who want to destroy me
be turned back in shame.
3 Some people make fun of me.
Let them be turned back when their plans fail.
4 But let all those who look to you
be joyful and glad because of what you have done.
Let those who love you because you save them always say,
"May God be honored!"

5 But I am poor and needy.
God, come quickly to me.
You are the One who helps me and saves me.
LORD, please don't wait any longer.

Psalm 71

1 LORD, I have gone to you for safety.
Let me never be put to shame.
2 You do what is right. Save me and help me.
Pay attention to me and save me.
3 Be my rock of safety
that I can always go to.
Give the command to save me.
You are my rock and my fort.
4 My God, save me from the power of sinners.
Save me from the hands of those who are mean and evil.

5 You are the King and the LORD. You have always been my hope.
I have trusted in you ever since I was young.
6 From the time I was born I have depended on you.
You brought me out of my mother's body.
I will praise you forever.
7 To many people I am an example of how much you care.
You are strong. You are my place of safety.
8 My mouth is filled with praise for you.
All day long I will talk about your glory.

9 Don't push me away when I'm old.
Don't desert me when my strength is gone.
10 My enemies speak against me.
Those who want to kill me get together and make evil plans.
11 They say, "God has deserted him.
Go after him and grab him.
No one will save him."
12 God, don't stay so far away from me.
My God, come quickly and help me.
13 May those who bring charges against me die in shame.
May those who want to harm me
be covered with shame and dishonor.

14 But I will always have hope.
I will praise you more and more.
15 I will say that what you have done is right.
All day long I will talk about how you have saved your people.
It is more than I can understand.
16 LORD and King, I will come and announce your mighty acts.
I will announce that you alone do what is right.
17 God, ever since I was young you have taught me about what you have done.
To this very day I tell about your wonderful acts.
18 God, don't leave me
even when I'm old and have gray hair.
Let me live to tell my children about your power.
Let me tell all of them about your mighty acts.
19 God, your saving acts reach to the skies.
You have done great things.
God, who is like you?
20 You have sent many bitter troubles my way.
But you will give me new life.
Even if I'm almost in the grave,
you will bring me back.
21 You will honor me more and more.
You will comfort me once again.

22 My God, I will use the harp to praise you
because you are always faithful.
Holy One of Israel,
I will use the lyre to sing praise to you.
23 My lips will shout with joy
when I sing praise to you.
You have saved me.
24 All day long my tongue will say
that you have done what is right.
Those who wanted to harm me have been put to shame.
They have not been honored.

Psalm 72

A psalm of Solomon.

1 God, give the king the ability to judge fairly.
He is your royal son. Help him to do what is right.
2 Then he will rule your people in the right way.
He will be fair to those among your people who are hurting.
3 The mountains and the hills will produce rich crops,
because the people will do what is right.
4 The king will stand up for those who are hurting.
He will save the children of those who are in need.
He will crush those who beat others down.

5 He will rule as long as the sun shines
and the moon gives its light.
He will rule for all time to come.
6 He will be like rain falling on the fields.
He will be like showers watering the earth.
7 Godly people will do well as long as he rules.
They will have more than they need as long as the moon lasts.

8 He will rule from ocean to ocean.
His kingdom will reach from the Euphrates River to the ends of the earth.
9 The desert tribes will bow down to him.
His enemies will lick the dust.
10 The kings of Tarshish and of places far away
will bring him gifts.
The kings of Sheba and Seba
will give him presents.
11 All kings will bow down to him.
All nations will serve him.

12 People who are in need will cry out, and he
will save them.
He will save those who are hurting.
They don't have anyone else who can
help them.
13 He will take pity on those who are weak and
in need.
He will save them from death.
14 He will save them from people who beat
others down.
He will save them from people who do
mean things to them.
Their lives are very special to him.

15 May he live a long time!
May gold from Sheba be given to him.
May people always pray for him.
May they ask the LORD to bless him all
day long.
16 Let there be plenty of grain everywhere in
the land.
May it sway in the wind on the tops of
the hills.
Let crops grow well, like those in Lebanon.
Let them grow like the grass of the field.
17 May the king's name be remembered forever.
May his fame last as long as the sun shines.

All nations will be blessed because of him.
They will call him blessed.

18 Give praise to the LORD God, the God of Israel.
Only he can do wonderful things.
19 Give praise to his glorious name forever.
May his glory fill the whole earth.
Amen and Amen.

20 The prayers of David, the son of Jesse,
end here.

BOOK III

Psalms 73–89

Psalm 73

A psalm of Asaph.

1 God is truly good to Israel.
He is good to those who have pure hearts.

2 But my feet had almost slipped.
I had almost tripped and fallen.
3 I saw that proud and sinful people were
doing well.
And I began to long for what they had.

4 They don't have any troubles.
Their bodies are healthy and strong.
5 They don't have the problems others have.
They don't suffer as other people do.
6 Their pride is like a necklace.
They put on meanness as if it were their
clothes.
7 Many sins come out of their hard and stubborn
hearts.
There is no limit to their proud and evil
thoughts.
8 They laugh at others and speak words
of hatred.
They are proud. They warn others about the
harm they can do to them.
9 They brag as if they owned heaven itself.
They talk as if they controlled the earth.
10 So people listen to them.
They lap up their words like water.
11 They say, "How can God know what we're
doing?
Does the Most High God really know
that much?"
12 Here is what sinful people are like.
They don't have a care in the world.
They keep getting richer and richer.

13 It seems as if I have kept my heart pure
without any reason.
It didn't do me any good to wash my hands
to show that I wasn't guilty of doing
anything wrong.
14 Day after day I've been in pain.
God has punished me every morning.
15 What if I had said, "I will speak as evil
people do"?
Then I wouldn't have been faithful to
God's children.
16 I tried to understand it all.
But it was more than I could handle.
17 It troubled me until I entered God's temple.
Then I understood what will happen to
bad people in the end.
18 God, I'm sure you will make them slip
and fall.
You will throw them down and
destroy them.
19 It will happen very suddenly.
A terrible death will take them away
completely.
20 A dream goes away when a person wakes up.
Lord, it will be like that when you rise up.
It will be as if those people were only
a dream.

21 At one time my heart was sad
and my spirit was bitter.
22 I didn't have any sense. I didn't know
anything.
I acted like a wild animal toward you.

23 But I am always with you.
You hold me by my right hand.
24 You give me wise advice to guide me.
And when I die, you will take me away
into the glory of heaven.
25 I don't have anyone in heaven but you.
I don't want anything on earth besides you.

26 My body and my heart may grow weak.
God, you give strength to my heart.
You are everything I will ever need.

27 Those who don't want anything to do with you will die.
You destroy all those who aren't faithful to you.
28 But I am close to you. And that's good.
LORD and King, I have made you my place of safety.
I will talk about everything you have done.

Psalm 74

A *maskil* of Asaph.

1 God, why have you turned your back on us for so long?
Why does your anger burn against us? We are your very own sheep.
2 Remember that you chose us to be your own people a long time ago.
Remember that you set us free from slavery to be your very own tribe.
Remember Mount Zion, where you lived.
3 Walk through this place that has been torn down beyond repair.
See how completely your enemies have destroyed the temple!

4 In the place where you used to meet with us, your enemies have shouted, "We've won the battle!"
They have set up their flags to show they have beaten us.
5 They acted like people cutting down a forest with axes.
6 They smashed all of the beautiful wooden walls
with their axes and hatchets.
7 They burned your temple to the ground.
They polluted the place where your Name is.
8 They had said in their hearts, "We will crush them completely!"
They burned every place where you were worshiped in the land.
9 You don't give us miraculous signs anymore.
There aren't any prophets left.
None of us knows how long that will last.

10 God, how long will your enemies make fun of you?
Will they attack you with their words forever?
11 Why don't you help us? Why do you hold back your powerful right hand?
Use your strong arms to destroy your enemies!

12 God, you have been my king for a long time.
The whole earth has seen you save us over and over again.
13 You parted the Red Sea by your power.
You broke the heads of that sea monster in Egypt.
14 You crushed the heads of the sea monster Leviathan.
You fed it to the creatures of the desert.
15 You opened up streams and springs.
You dried up rivers that flow all year long.
16 You rule over the day and the night.
You created the sun and the moon.
17 You decided where the borders of the earth would be.
You made both summer and winter.

18 LORD, remember how your enemies have made fun of you.
Remember how foolish people have attacked you with their words.
19 Don't hand Israel, your dove, over to those wild animals.
Don't forget your suffering people forever.
20 Honor the covenant you made with us.
Horrible things are happening in every dark corner of the land.
21 Don't let your suffering people be put to shame.
May those who are poor and needy praise you.

22 God, rise up. Stand up for your cause.
Remember how foolish people make fun of you all day long.
23 Pay close attention to the shouts of your enemies.
The trouble they cause never stops.

Psalm 75

For the director of music. A psalm of Asaph.
A song to the tune of "Do Not Destroy."

1 God, we give thanks to you.
We give thanks because your Name is near.
People talk about the wonderful things you have done.

2 You say, "I choose the appointed time to judge people.
And I judge them fairly.
3 When the earth and all of its people tremble,
I keep everything from falling to pieces. *Selah*
4 To the proud I say, 'Don't brag anymore.'
To sinners I say, 'Don't show off your power.
5 Don't show it off against me.
Don't speak with your noses in the air.' "

6 No one from east or west or north or south can act as judge.
7 God is the One who judges.
He says to one person, "You are guilty."
To another he says, "You are not guilty."

8 In the hand of the LORD is a cup.
It is full of wine mixed with spices.
It is the wine of his anger.
He pours it out. All of the evil people on earth
drink it down to the very last drop.
9 I will speak about this forever.
I will sing praise to the God of Jacob.
10 God will destroy the power of all sinful people.
But he will make godly people more
powerful.

Psalm 76

For the director of music.
A psalm of Asaph. A song to be played
on stringed instruments.

1 In the land of Judah, God is known.
His name is great in Israel.
2 His tent is in Jerusalem.
The place where he lives is on Mount Zion.
3 There he broke the deadly arrows of
his enemies.
He broke their shields and swords.
He broke their weapons of war. *Selah*

4 God, you shine like a very bright light.
You are more majestic than mountains full
of wild animals.
5 Brave soldiers have been robbed of everything
they had.
Now they lie there, sleeping in death.
Not one of them can even lift his hands.
6 God of Jacob, at your command
both horse and chariot lie still.
7 People should have respect for you alone.
Who can stand in front of you when you
are angry?
8 From heaven you handed down your sentence.
The land was afraid and became quiet.
9 God, that happened when you rose up to judge.
It happened when you came to save all
of your suffering people in the land.
Selah
10 Your anger against sinners brings you praise.
Those who live through your anger gather to
worship you.

11 Make promises to the LORD your God and
keep them.
Let all of the neighboring nations
bring gifts to the One who should be
respected.
12 He breaks the proud spirit of rulers.
The kings of the earth have respect for him.

Psalm 77

For the director of music.
For Jeduthun. A psalm of Asaph.

1 I cried out to God for help.
I cried out to God to hear me.
2 When I was in trouble, I looked to the Lord.
During the night I lifted up my hands
in prayer.
But I refused to be comforted.

3 God, I remembered you, and I groaned.
I thought about you, and I became weak.
Selah
4 You kept me from going to sleep.
I was so troubled I couldn't speak.
5 I thought about days gone by.
I thought about the years of long ago.
6 I remembered how I used to sing praise to you
in the night.
I thought about it, and here is what I
asked myself.
7 "Will the Lord turn away from us forever?
Won't he ever show us his kindness
again?
8 Has his faithful love disappeared forever?
Has his promise failed for all time?
9 Has God forgotten to show us his favor?
Has he held back his tender love because
he was angry?" *Selah*

10 Then I thought, "Here is what I will make my
appeal to.
For many years the Most High God showed
how powerful his right hand is."
11 LORD, I will remember what you did.
Yes, I will remember your miracles of
long ago.
12 I will spend time thinking about everything
you have done.
I will consider all of your mighty acts.

13 God, everything you do is holy.
What god is so great as our God?
14 You are the God who does miracles.
You show your power among
the nations.
15 With your mighty arm you set your
people free.
You set the children of Jacob and
Joseph free. *Selah*

16 God, the water of the Red Sea saw you.
It saw you and boiled up.
The deepest waters were stirred up.
17 The clouds poured down rain.
The skies rumbled with thunder.
Lightning flashed back and forth like
arrows.
18 Your thunder was heard in the windstorm.
Your lightning lit up the world.
The earth trembled and shook.
19 Your path led through the Red Sea.
You walked through the mighty waters.
But your footprints were not seen.

20 You led your people like a flock.
You led them by the hands of Moses
and Aaron.

Psalm 78

A *maskil* of Asaph.

1 My people, listen to my teaching.
Pay attention to what I say.
2 I will open my mouth and tell stories.
I will speak about things that were hidden.
They happened a long time ago.
3 We have heard about them and we know them.
Our people who lived before us have told us about them.
4 We won't hide them from our children.
We will tell them to those who live after us.
We will tell them about what the LORD has done that is worthy of praise.
We will talk about his power and the wonderful things he has done.
5 He gave laws to the people of Jacob.
He gave Israel their law.
He commanded our people who lived before us
to teach his laws to their children.
6 Then those born later would know his laws.
Even their children yet to come would know them.
And they in turn would tell their children.
7 Then they would put their trust in God.
They would not forget what he had done.
They would obey his commands.
8 They would not be like their people who lived before them.
Those people were stubborn. They refused to obey God.
Their hearts were not true to him.
Their spirits were not faithful to him.

9 The soldiers of Ephraim were armed with bows.
But they ran away on the day of battle.
10 They didn't keep the covenant God had made with them.
They refused to live by his law.
11 They forgot what he had done.
They didn't remember the wonders he had shown them.
12 He did miracles right in front of our people who lived long ago.
At that time they were living in the land of Egypt, in the area of Zoan.
13 God parted the Red Sea and led them through it.
He made the water stand up like a wall.
14 He guided them with the cloud during the day.
He led them with the light of a fire all night long.
15 He broke the rocks open in the desert.
He gave them as much water as there is in the oceans.
16 He brought streams out of a rocky cliff.
He made water flow down like rivers.

17 But they continued to sin against him.
In the desert they refused to obey the Most High God.
18 They were stubborn and put God to the test.
They ordered him to give them the food they longed for.
19 They spoke against God. They said,
"Can God put food on a table in the desert?
20 When he struck the rock, streams of water poured out.
Huge amounts of water flowed down.
But can he also give us food?
Can he supply meat for his people?"
21 When the LORD heard what they said, he was very angry.
His anger broke out like fire against the people of Jacob.
He became very angry with Israel.
22 That was because they didn't believe in God.
They didn't trust in his power to save them.
23 But he gave a command to the skies above.
He opened the doors of the heavens.
24 He rained down manna for the people to eat.
He gave them the grain of heaven.
25 Mere men ate the bread of angels.
He sent them all of the food they could eat.
26 He made the east wind blow from the heavens.
By his power he caused the south wind to blow.
27 He rained meat down on them like dust.
He sent them birds like sand on the seashore.
28 He made the birds come down inside their camp.
The birds fell all around their tents.
29 People ate until they had more than enough.
He gave them what they had longed for.
30 But even before they had finished eating, God acted.
He did it while the food was still in their mouths.
31 His anger rose up against them.
He put to death the strongest among them.
He struck down Israel's young men.

32 But even after all that, they kept on sinning.
Even after they had seen the miracles he did, they still didn't believe.
33 So he brought their days to an end like a puff of smoke.
He ended their years with terror.
34 Every time God killed some of them, the others would look to him.
They gladly turned back to him again.
35 They remembered that God was their Rock.
They remembered that God Most High had set them free.
36 But they didn't mean it when they praised him.
They lied to him when they spoke.
37 Their hearts were not true to him.
They weren't faithful to the covenant he had made with them.
38 But he was full of tender love.
He forgave their sins
and didn't destroy his people.

Time after time he held back his anger.
He didn't let all of his burning anger
blaze out.
39 He remembered that they were only human.
He remembered they were only a breath
of air
that drifts by and doesn't return.
40 How often they refused to obey him in
the desert!
How often they caused him sorrow in that
dry and empty land!
41 Again and again they put God to the test.
They made the Holy One of Israel sad
and angry.
42 They didn't remember his power.
They forgot the day he set them free
from those who had beaten them down.
43 They forgot how he had shown them his
miraculous signs in Egypt.
They forgot his miracles in the area
of Zoan.
44 He turned the rivers of Egypt into blood.
The people of Egypt couldn't drink water
from their streams.
45 He sent large numbers of flies that bit them.
He sent frogs that destroyed their land.
46 He gave their crops to the grasshoppers.
He gave their food to the locusts.
47 He destroyed their vines with hail.
He destroyed their fig trees with sleet.
48 He killed their cattle with hail.
Their livestock were struck by lightning.
49 He brought great trouble on Egypt by pouring
out his blazing anger.
In his hot anger he sent destroying angels
against them.
50 God prepared a path for his anger.
He didn't spare their lives.
He gave them over to the plague.
51 He killed the oldest son of each family
in Egypt.
He struck down the oldest son in every
house in the land of Ham.
52 But he brought his people out like a flock.
He led them like sheep through the desert.
53 He guided them safely, and they weren't afraid.
But the Red Sea swallowed up their
enemies.
54 He brought his people to the border of his
holy land.
He led them to the central hill country he
had taken by his power.
55 He drove the nations out to make room for
his people.
He gave to each family a piece of land to
pass on to their children.
He settled the tribes of Israel in their homes.

56 But they put God to the test.
They refused to obey the Most High God.
They didn't keep his laws.
57 Like their people who lived before them,
they turned away from him and were not
faithful.
They were like a bow that doesn't shoot straight.
They couldn't be trusted.
58 They made God angry by going to their
high places.
They made him jealous by worshiping the
statues of their gods.
59 When God saw what the people were doing,
he was very angry.
He turned away from them completely.
60 He deserted the holy tent at Shiloh.
He left the tent he had set up among
his people.
61 He allowed the ark to be captured.
Into the hands of his enemies he sent the ark
where his glory rested.
62 He let his people be killed with swords.
He was very angry with them.
63 Fire destroyed their young men.
Their young women had no one to get
married to.
64 Their priests were killed with swords.
Their widows weren't able to cry.

65 Then the Lord woke up as if he had been
sleeping.
He was like a man waking up from the deep
sleep caused by wine.
66 He drove his enemies back.
He put them to shame that will last forever.
67 He turned his back on the tents of the people
of Joseph.
He didn't choose to live in the tribe
of Ephraim.
68 Instead, he chose to live in the tribe of Judah.
He chose Mount Zion, which he loved.
69 There he built his holy place as secure as
the heavens.
He built it to last forever, like the earth.
70 He chose his servant David.
He took him from the sheep pens.
71 He brought him from tending sheep
to be the shepherd of his people Jacob.
He made him the shepherd of Israel, his
special people.
72 David cared for them with a faithful and
honest heart.
With skilled hands he led them.

Psalm 79

A psalm of Asaph.

1 God, an army from the nations has attacked
your land.
They have polluted your holy temple.
They have completely destroyed Jerusalem.
2 They have given the dead bodies of
your people
as food to the birds of the air.

They have given the bodies of your faithful people
to the animals of the earth.
3 They have poured out the blood of your people like water
all around Jerusalem.
No one is left to bury the dead.
4 We are something our neighbors joke about.
The nations around us laugh at us and make fun of us.

5 LORD, how long will you be angry with us?
Will it be forever?
How long will your jealousy burn like fire?
6 Pour out your burning anger on the nations
that don't pay any attention to you.
Pour it out on the kingdoms
that don't worship you.
7 They have swallowed up the people of Jacob.
They have destroyed Israel's homeland.
8 Don't hold against us the sins of our people who lived before us.
May you be quick to show us your tender love.
We are in great need.

9 God our Savior, help us.
Then glory will come to you.
Be true to your name.
Save us and forgive our sins.
10 Why should the nations say,
"Where is their God?"
Show the nations that you punish those who kill your people.
We want to see it happen.
11 Listen to the groans of the prisoners.
Use your powerful arm
to save the lives of those who have been sentenced to death.

12 Lord, our neighbors have laughed at you.
Pay them back seven times for what they have done.
13 We are your people. We are your very own sheep.
We will praise you forever.
For all time to come
we will keep on praising you.

Psalm 80

For the director of music. A psalm of Asaph to the tune of "The Lilies of the Covenant."

1 Shepherd of Israel, hear us.
You lead the people of Joseph like a flock.
You sit on your throne between the cherubim.
Show your glory
2 to the people of Ephraim, Benjamin and Manasseh.
Call your strength into action.
Come and save us.

3 God, make us new again.
Let your face smile on us with favor.
Then we will be saved.

4 LORD God who rules over all,
how long will your anger burn
against the prayers of your people?
5 You have given us tears as our food.
You have made us drink tears by the bowlful.
6 You have let our neighbors fight against us.
Our enemies laugh at us.

7 God who rules over all, make us new again.
Let your face smile on us with favor.
Then we will be saved.

8 You brought Israel out of Egypt.
Israel was like a vine.
After you drove the nations out of Canaan,
you planted the vine in their land.
9 You prepared the ground for it.
It took root and spread out over the whole land.
10 The mountains were covered with its shade.
The shade of its branches covered the mighty cedar trees.
11 Your vine sent its branches out all the way to the Mediterranean Sea.
They reached as far as the Euphrates River.

12 Why have you broken down the walls around your vine?
Now all who pass by it can pick its grapes.
13 Wild pigs from the forest destroy it.
The creatures of the field feed on it.
14 God who rules over all, return to us!
Look down from heaven and see us!
Watch over your vine.
15 Guard the root you have planted with your powerful right hand.
Take care of the branch you have raised up for yourself.

16 Your vine has been cut down. Fire has burned it up.
You have been angry with us, and we are dying.
17 May you honor the people at your right hand.
May you honor the nation you have raised up for yourself.
18 Then we won't turn away from you.
Give us new life. We will worship you.

19 LORD God who rules over all, make us new again.
Let your face smile on us with favor.
Then we will be saved.

Psalm 81

For the director of music. For *gittith*. A psalm of Asaph.

1 Sing joyfully to God! He gives us strength.
Give a loud shout to the God of Jacob!

2 Let the music begin. Play the tambourines.
Play sweet music on harps and lyres.

3 Blow the ram's horn on the day of the New Moon Feast.
Blow it again when the moon is full and the Feast of Booths begins.
4 This is an order given to Israel.
It is a law of the God of Jacob.
5 He gave it as a covenant law for the people of Joseph
when God went out to punish Egypt.
There we heard a language we didn't understand.

6 God said, "I removed the load from your shoulders.
I set your hands free from carrying heavy baskets.
7 You called out when you were in trouble, and I saved you.
I answered you out of a thundercloud.
I put you to the test at the waters of Meribah. *Selah*

8 "My people, listen and I will warn you.
Israel, I wish you would listen to me!
9 Don't have anything to do with the gods of other nations.
Don't bow down and worship strange gods.
10 I am the LORD your God.
I brought you up out of Egypt.
Open your mouth wide, and I will fill it with good things.

11 "But my people wouldn't listen to me.
Israel wouldn't obey me.
12 So I let them go their own stubborn way.
I let them follow their own sinful plans.

13 "I wish my people would listen to me!
I wish Israel would live as I want them to live!
14 Then I would quickly bring their enemies under control.
I would use my power against their attackers.
15 Those who hate me would bow down to me in fear.
They would be punished forever.
16 But you would be fed with the finest wheat.
I would satisfy you with the sweetest honey."

Psalm 82

A psalm of Asaph.

1 God takes his place at the head of a large gathering of rulers and judges.
He announces his decisions among them.

2 He says, "How long will you stand up for those who aren't fair to others?
How long will you show favor to sinful people? *Selah*
3 Stand up for those who are weak and for those whose fathers have died.
See to it that those who are poor and those who are beaten down are treated fairly.
4 Save the weak and those who are in need.
Save them from the power of sinful people.

5 "You rulers and judges don't know anything.
You don't understand anything.
You are in the dark about what is right.
Law and order have been destroyed all over the world.

6 "I said, 'Rulers and judges, you are "gods."
You are all children of the Most High God.'
7 But you will die, just like everyone else.
You will die like every other ruler."

8 God, rise up. Judge the earth.
All of the nations belong to you.

Psalm 83

A song. A psalm of Asaph.

1 God, don't keep silent.
God, don't keep quiet. Don't be still.
2 See how your enemies are getting ready for action.
See how they are rising up against you.
3 They make clever plans against your people.
They make evil plans against those you love.
4 "Come," they say. "Let's destroy that whole nation.
Then the name of Israel won't be remembered anymore."

5 All of them agree on the evil plans they have made.
They join forces against you.
6 Their forces include the people of Edom,
Ishmael, Moab and Hagar.
7 They also include the people of Byblos, Ammon, Amalek,
Philistia and Tyre.
8 Even Assyria has joined them
to give strength to the people of Moab and Ammon. *Selah*

9 Do to them what you did to the people of Midian.
Do to them what you did to Sisera and Jabin at the Kishon River.
10 Sisera and Jabin died near the town of Endor.
Their bodies were left to rot on the ground.
11 Do to the nobles of your enemies what you did to Oreb and Zeeb.
Do to all of their princes what you did to Zebah and Zalmunna.
12 They said, "Let's take over
the grasslands that belong to God."

13 My God, make them like straw that the wind blows away.
Make them like tumbleweed.

[14] Destroy them as fire burns up a forest.
Destroy them as a flame sets mountains on fire.
[15] Chase them with your mighty winds.
Terrify them with your storm.
[16] LORD, put them to shame
so that people will worship you.
[17] May they always be filled with terror and shame.
May they die in dishonor.
[18] Your name is the LORD. Let them know
that you alone are the Most High God
over the whole earth.

Psalm 84

For the director of music. For *gittith*.
A psalm of the Sons of Korah.

[1] LORD who rules over all,
how lovely is the place where you live!
[2] I long to be in the courtyards of the LORD's temple.
I deeply long to be there.
My whole being cries out
for the living God.
[3] LORD who rules over all,
even the sparrow has found a home near your altar.
My King and my God,
the swallow also has a nest there,
where she may have her young.
[4] Blessed are those who live in your house.
They are always praising you. *Selah*
[5] Blessed are those whose strength comes from you.
They have decided to travel to your temple.
[6] As they pass through the dry Valley of Baca,
they make it a place where water flows.
The rain in the fall covers it with pools.
[7] Those people get stronger as they go along,
until each of them appears in Zion, where God lives.
[8] LORD God who rules over all, hear my prayer.
God of the people of Jacob, listen to me. *Selah*
[9] God, look with favor on your anointed king.
You appointed him to be like a shield that keeps us safe.
[10] A single day in your courtyards is better
than a thousand anywhere else.
I would rather guard the door of the house of my God
than live in the tents of sinful people.
[11] The LORD God is like the sun that gives us light.
He is like a shield that keeps us safe.
The LORD blesses us with favor and honor.
He doesn't hold back anything good
from those whose lives are without blame.
[12] LORD who rules over all,
blessed is everyone who trusts in you.

Psalm 85

For the director of music.
A psalm of the Sons of Korah.

[1] LORD, you showed favor to your land.
You blessed the people of Jacob with great success again.
[2] You forgave the evil things your people did.
You took away all of their sins. *Selah*
[3] You stopped being angry with them.
You turned your burning anger away from them.
[4] God our Savior, make us new again.
Stop being unhappy with us.
[5] Will you be angry with us forever?
Will you be angry for all time to come?
[6] Won't you give us new life again?
Then we'll be joyful because of what you have done.
[7] LORD, show us your faithful love.
Save us.
[8] I will listen to what God the LORD will say.
He promises peace to his faithful people.
But they must not return to their foolish ways.
[9] I know he's ready to save those who have respect for him.
Then his glory can be seen in our land.
[10] God's truth and faithful love join together.
His peace and holiness kiss each other.
[11] His truth springs up from the earth.
His holiness looks down from heaven.
[12] The LORD will certainly give what is good.
Our land will produce its crops.
[13] God's holiness leads the way in front of him.
It prepares the way for his coming.

Psalm 86

A prayer of David.

[1] LORD, hear me and answer me.
I am poor and needy.
[2] Keep my life safe. I am faithful to you.
You are my God. Save me.
I trust in you.
[3] Lord, show me your favor.
I call out to you all day long.
[4] Bring joy to me.
Lord, I worship you.
[5] Lord, you are good. You are forgiving.
You are full of love for all who call out to you.
[6] LORD, hear my prayer.
Listen to my cry for your favor.
[7] When I'm in trouble, I will call out to you.
And you will answer me.

8 Lord, there's no one like you among the gods.
No one can do what you do.
9 Lord, all of the nations you have made
will come and worship you.
They will bring glory to you.
10 You are great. You do wonderful things.
You alone are God.
11 LORD, teach me how you want me to live.
Then I will follow your truth.
Give me a heart that doesn't want anything
more than to worship you.
12 Lord my God, I will praise you with all
my heart.
I will bring glory to you forever.
13 Great is your love for me.
You have kept me from going down into
the grave.

14 God, proud people are attacking me.
A gang of mean people is trying to kill me.
They don't care about you.
15 But Lord, you are a God who is tender and kind.
You are gracious.
You are slow to get angry.
You are faithful and full of love.
16 Turn to me and show me your favor.
Give me strength and save me.
17 Prove your goodness to me.
Then my enemies will see it and be put
to shame.
LORD, you have helped me and given me
comfort.

Psalm 87

A psalm of the Sons of Korah. A song.

1 The LORD has built his city
on the holy mountain.
2 He loves the city of Zion
more than all of the other places
where the people of Jacob live.
3 City of God,
the LORD says glorious things
about you. *Selah*
4 He says, "I will include Egypt and Babylon
in a list of those who recognize me as king.
I will also include Philistia and Tyre,
along with Cush.
I will say about them, 'They were born
in Zion.'"
5 Certainly it will be said about Zion,
"This nation and that nation were born
in her.
The Most High God himself will make
her secure."
6 Here is what the LORD will write in his list of
the nations.
"Each of them was born in Zion." *Selah*
7 As they make music they will sing,
"Zion, all of our blessings come from you."

Psalm 88

For the director of music.
For *mahalath leannoth*. A song.
A psalm of the Sons of Korah. A *maskil*
of Heman the Ezrahite.

1 LORD, you are the God who saves me.
Day and night I cry out to you.
2 Please hear my prayer.
Pay attention to my cry for help.

3 I have so many troubles
I'm about to die.
4 People think my life is over.
I'm like someone who doesn't have
any strength.
5 People treat me as if I were dead.
I'm like those who have been killed and
are now in the grave.
You don't even remember them anymore.
They are cut off from your care.

6 It seems as if you have put me deep down
in the grave,
that deep and dark place.
7 Your burning anger lies heavy on me.
All the waves of your anger have
crashed over me. *Selah*
8 You have taken my closest friends away
from me.
You have made me sickening to them.
I feel trapped. I can't escape.
9 I'm crying so much I can't see
very well.

LORD, I call out to you every day.
I lift up my hands to you in prayer.
10 Do you work miracles for those who
are dead?
Do dead people rise up and praise you?
Selah
11 Do those who are dead speak about your love?
Do those who are in the grave tell how
faithful you are?
12 Are your miracles known in that dark place?
Are your holy acts known in that land where
the dead are forgotten?

13 LORD, I cry out to you for help.
In the morning I pray to you.
14 LORD, why do you say no to me?
Why do you turn your face away from me?

15 I've been in pain ever since I was young.
I've been close to death.
You have made me suffer terrible things.
I have lost all hope.
16 Your burning anger has swept over me.
Your terrors have destroyed me.
17 All day long they surround me like a flood.
They have closed in all around me.
18 You have taken my companions and loved
ones away from me.
The darkness is my closest friend.

Psalm 89

A *maskil* of Ethan the Ezrahite.

1 LORD, I will sing about your great love
forever.
For all time to come, I will tell how
faithful you are.
2 I will tell everyone that your love stands
firm forever.
I will tell them that you are always faithful,
even in heaven itself.

3 You said, "Here is the covenant I have made
with my chosen one.
Here is the promise I have made to my
servant David.
4 'I will make your family line continue forever.
I will make your kingdom secure for all
time to come.' " *Selah*

5 LORD, the heavens praise you for your
miracles.
When your holy angels gather together,
they praise you for how faithful you are.
6 Who in the skies above can compare with
the LORD?
Who among the angels is like the LORD?
7 God is highly respected among his holy angels.
He's more wonderful than all those who are
around him.
8 LORD God who rules over all, who is like you?
LORD, you are mighty. You are faithful in
everything you do.

9 You rule over the stormy sea.
When its waves rise up, you calm them
down.
10 You crushed Egypt and killed her people.
With your powerful arm you scattered
your enemies.
11 The heavens belong to you. The earth is
yours also.
You made the world and everything that
is in it.
12 You created everything from north to south.
Mount Tabor and Mount Hermon sing to
you with joy.
13 Your arm is powerful.
Your hand is strong.
Your right hand is mighty.

14 Your kingdom is built on what is right and fair.
Your truth and faithful love lead the way in
front of you.
15 Blessed are those who have learned to shout
praise to you.
LORD, they live in the light of your favor.
16 All day long they are full of joy because of
who you are.
They praise you because you do what
is right.
17 You are their glory. You give them strength.
You favor them by honoring our king.
18 Our king is like a shield that keeps us safe.
He belongs to the LORD.
He belongs to the Holy One of Israel.

19 You once spoke to your faithful people in
a vision.
You said, "I have given strength to a soldier.
I have raised up a young man from among
the people.
20 I have found my servant David.
I have poured my sacred oil on his head.
21 My powerful hand will keep him going.
My mighty arm will give him strength.
22 No enemies will require him to bring gifts
to them.
No evil person will beat him down.
23 I will crush the king's enemies.
I will completely destroy them.
24 I will love him and be faithful to him.
Because of me his power will increase.
25 I will give him a great kingdom.
It will reach from the Mediterranean Sea to
the Euphrates River.
26 He will call out to me, 'You are my Father.
You are my God. You are my Rock
and Savior.'
27 I will also make him my oldest son.
Among all the kings of the earth, he will be
the most important one.
28 I will continue to love him forever.
I will never break my covenant with him.
29 I will make his family line continue forever.
His kingdom will last as long as the
heavens.

30 "What if his sons turn away from my laws
and do not follow them?
31 What if they disobey my orders
and fail to keep my commands?
32 Then I will punish them for their sins.
I will strike them with the rod.
I will whip them for their evil acts.
33 But I will not stop loving David.
I will always be faithful to him.
34 I will not break my covenant.
I will not go back on my word.
35 Once and for all, I have made a promise
with an oath.
It is based on my holiness.
And I will not lie to David.
36 His family line will continue forever.
His kingdom will last as long as the sun.
37 It will last forever like the moon,
that faithful witness in the sky." *Selah*

38 But you have turned your back on your
anointed king.
You have been very angry with him.
39 You have broken the covenant you made
with him.
You have thrown your servant's crown into
the dirt.

40 You have broken through the walls around
his city.
You have completely destroyed his
secure places.
41 All those who pass by have carried off what
belonged to him.
His neighbors make fun of him.
42 You have made his enemies strong.
You have made all of them happy.
43 You have made his sword useless.
You have not helped him in battle.
44 You have put an end to his glory.
You have knocked his throne to
the ground.
45 You have cut short the days of his life.
You have covered him with shame. *Selah*

46 LORD, how long will you hide yourself?
Will it be forever?
How long will your anger burn like fire?
47 Remember how short my life is.
You have created all people for such a
useless purpose!
48 What man can live and not die?
Who can escape the power of the grave?
Selah
49 Lord, where is the great love you used to have?
You faithfully promised it to David.
50 Lord, remember how my enemies have made
fun of me.
I've had to put up with mean words from
all of the nations.
51 LORD, your enemies have said mean things.
They have laughed at everything your
anointed king has done.

52 Give praise to the LORD forever!
Amen and Amen.

BOOK IV

Psalms 90–106

Psalm 90

A prayer of Moses, the man of God.

1 Lord, from the very beginning
you have been like a home to us.
2 Before you created the world and the
mountains were made,
from the beginning to the end you are God.

3 You turn human beings back to dust.
You say to them, "Return to dust."
4 To you a thousand years
are like a day that has just gone by.
They are like a few hours of the night.
5 You sweep people away, and they die.
They are like new grass that grows in
the morning.
6 In the morning it springs up new,
but by evening it's all dried up.

7 Your anger destroys us.
Your burning anger terrifies us.
8 You have put our sins right in front of you.
You have placed our secret sins where you
can see them clearly.
9 You have been angry with us all of our days.
We groan as we come to the end of our
lives.
10 We live to be about 70.
Or we may live to be 80, if we stay healthy.
But all that time is filled with trouble
and sorrow.
The years quickly pass, and we are gone.

11 Who knows how powerful your anger is?
It's as great as the respect we should have
for you.
12 Teach us to realize how short our lives are.
Then our hearts will become wise.

13 LORD, please stop punishing us!
How long will you keep it up?
Be kind to us.
14 Satisfy us with your faithful love every
morning.
Then we can sing with joy and be glad all
of our days.
15 Make us glad for as many days as you have
made us suffer.
Give us joy for as many years as we've
had trouble.
16 Show us your mighty acts.
Let our children see your glorious power.

17 May the Lord our God show us his favor.
Lord, make what we do succeed.
Please make what we do succeed.

Psalm 91

1 The person who rests in the shadow of the
Most High God
will be kept safe by the Mighty One.
2 I will say about the LORD,
"He is my place of safety.
He is like a fort to me.
He is my God. I trust in him."

3 He will certainly save you from hidden traps
and from deadly sickness.
4 He will cover you with his wings.
Under the feathers of his wings you will
find safety.
He is faithful. He will keep you safe like a
shield or a tower.
5 You won't have to be afraid of the terrors that
come during the night.
You won't have to fear the arrows that come
at you during the day.
6 You won't have to be afraid of the sickness that
attacks in the darkness.
You won't have to fear the plague that
destroys at noon.

7 A thousand may fall dead at your side.
Ten thousand may fall near your right hand.
But no harm will come to you.
8 You will see with your own eyes
how God punishes sinful people.
9 The LORD is the one who keeps you safe.
So let the Most High God be like a home to you.
10 Then no harm will come to you.
No terrible plague will come near your tent.
11 The LORD will command his angels
to take good care of you.
12 They will lift you up in their hands.
Then you won't trip over a stone.
13 You will walk all over lions and cobras.
You will crush mighty lions and poisonous snakes.
14 The LORD says, "I will save the one who loves me.
I will keep him safe, because he trusts in me.
15 He will call out to me, and I will answer him.
I will be with him in times of trouble.
I will save him and honor him.
16 I will give him a long and full life.
I will save him."

Psalm 92

A psalm. A song for the Sabbath day.

1 LORD, it is good to praise you.
Most High God, it is good to make music to honor you.
2 It is good to sing every morning about your love.
It is good to sing every night about how faithful you are.
3 I sing about it to the music of the lyre that has ten strings.
I sing about it to the music of the harp.
4 LORD, you make me glad by what you have done.
I sing with joy about the works of your hands.
5 LORD, how great are the things you do!
How wise your thoughts are!
6 Here is something a man who isn't wise doesn't know.
Here is what a foolish person doesn't understand.
7 Those who are evil spring up like grass.
Those who do wrong succeed.
But they will be destroyed forever.
8 But LORD, you are honored forever.
9 LORD, your enemies will certainly die.
All those who do evil will be scattered.
10 You have made me as strong as a wild ox.
You have poured the finest olive oil on me.
11 I've seen my evil enemies destroyed.
I've heard that they have lost the battle.
12 Those who do what is right will grow like a palm tree.
They will grow strong like a cedar tree in Lebanon.
13 Their roots will be firm in the house of the LORD.
They will grow strong and healthy in the courtyards of our God.
14 When they get old, they will still bear fruit.
Like young trees they will stay fresh and strong.
15 They will say to everyone, "The LORD is honest.
He is my Rock. There is no evil in him."

Psalm 93

1 The LORD rules.
He puts on majesty as if it were clothes.
The LORD puts on majesty and strength.
The world is firmly set in place.
It can't be moved.
2 LORD, you began to rule a long time ago.
You have always existed.
3 LORD, the seas have lifted up their voice.
They have lifted up their pounding waves.
4 But LORD, you are more powerful than the roar of the ocean.
You are stronger than the waves of the sea.
LORD, you are powerful in heaven.
5 Your laws do not change.
LORD, your temple will be holy
for all time to come.

Psalm 94

1 LORD, you are the God who punishes.
Since you are the one who punishes, come and show your anger.
2 Judge of the earth, rise up.
Pay back proud people for what they have done.
3 LORD, how long will those who are evil be glad?
How long will they be full of joy?
4 Proud words pour out of their mouths.
All those who do evil are always bragging.
5 LORD, they crush your people.
They beat down those who belong to you.
6 They kill outsiders. They kill widows.
They murder children whose fathers have died.
7 They say, "The LORD doesn't see what's happening.
The God of Jacob doesn't pay any attention to it."
8 You who aren't wise, pay attention.
You foolish people, when will you become wise?

9 Does he who made the ear not hear?
Does he who formed the eye not see?
10 Does he who corrects nations not punish?
Does he who teaches human beings not know anything?
11 The LORD knows what people think.
He knows that their thoughts don't amount to anything.

12 LORD, blessed is the man you correct.
Blessed is the person you teach from your law.
13 You give him rest from times of trouble,
until a pit is dug to trap sinners.
14 The LORD won't say no to his people.
He will never desert those who belong to him.
15 He will again judge people in keeping with what is right.
All those who have honest hearts will follow the right way.

16 Who will rise up for me against sinful people?
Who will stand up for me against those who do evil?
17 Suppose the LORD had not helped me.
Then I would soon have been lying quietly in the grave.
18 I said, "My foot is slipping."
But LORD, your love kept me from falling.
19 I was very worried.
But your comfort brought joy to my heart.
20 Can you have anything to do with rulers who aren't fair?
Can those who make laws that cause suffering be friends of yours?
21 They join together against those who do what is right.
They sentence to death those who aren't guilty of doing anything wrong.
22 But the LORD has become like a fort to me.
My God is my rock. I go to him for safety.
23 He will pay them back for their sins.
He will destroy them for their evil acts.
The LORD our God will destroy them.

Psalm 95

1 Come, let us sing with joy to the LORD.
Let us give a loud shout to the Rock who saves us.
2 Let us come to him and give him thanks.
Let us praise him with music and song.

3 The LORD is the great God.
He is the greatest King.
He rules over all of the gods.
4 He owns the deepest parts of the earth.
The mountain peaks belong to him.
5 The ocean is his, because he made it.
He formed the dry land with his hands.

6 Come, let us bow down and worship him.
Let us fall on our knees in front of the LORD our Maker.
7 He is our God.
We are the sheep belonging to his flock.
We are the people he takes good care of.

Listen to his voice today.
8 If you hear it, don't be stubborn as you were at Meribah.
Don't be stubborn as you were that day at Massah in the desert.
9 There your people of long ago really put me to the test.
They did it even though they had seen what I had done for them.
10 For 40 years I was angry with them.
I said, "Their hearts are always going down the wrong path.
They do not know how I want them to live."
11 So when I was angry, I took an oath.
I said, "They will never enjoy the rest I planned for them."

Psalm 96

1 Sing a new song to the LORD.
All you people of the earth, sing to the LORD.
2 Sing to the LORD. Praise him.
Day after day tell about how he saves us.
3 Tell the nations about his glory.
Tell all people about the wonderful things he has done.
4 The LORD is great. He is really worthy of praise.
People should have respect for him as the greatest God of all.
5 All of the gods of the nations are like their statues.
They can't do anything.
But the LORD made the heavens.
6 Glory and majesty are all around him.
Strength and glory can be seen in his temple.

7 Praise the LORD, all you nations.
Praise the LORD for his glory and strength.
8 Praise the LORD for the glory that belongs to him.
Bring an offering and come into the courtyards of his temple.
9 Worship the LORD because of his beauty and holiness.
All you people of the earth, tremble when you are with him.

10 Say to the nations, "The LORD rules."
The world is firmly set in place. It can't be moved.
The LORD will judge the people of the world fairly.
11 Let the heavens be full of joy. Let the earth be glad.
Let the ocean and everything in it roar.

12 Let the fields and everything in them
be glad.
Then all of the trees in the forest will sing
with joy.
13 They will sing to the LORD,
because he is coming to judge the earth.
He will judge the people of the world
in keeping with what is right and true.

Psalm 97

1 The LORD rules. Let the earth be glad.
Let countries that are far away be full of joy.

2 Clouds and thick darkness surround him.
His rule is built on what is right and fair.
3 The LORD sends fire ahead of him.
It burns up his enemies all around him.
4 His lightning lights up the world.
The earth sees it and trembles.
5 The mountains melt like wax when the LORD
is near.
He is the Lord of the whole earth.
6 The heavens announce that what he does
is right.
All people everywhere see his glory.

7 All who worship statues of gods or brag about
them are put to shame.
All you gods, worship the LORD!

8 Zion hears about it and is filled with joy.
LORD, the villages of Judah are glad
because of how you judge.
9 LORD, you are the Most High God.
You rule over the whole earth.
You are honored much more than all gods.

10 Let those who love the LORD hate evil.
He guards the lives of those who are faithful
to him.
He saves them from the power of sinful
people.
11 The light of his favor shines on those who do
what is right.
Joy comes to those whose hearts are honest.
12 You who are godly, be glad because of what
the LORD has done.
Praise him, because his name is holy.

Psalm 98

A psalm.

1 Sing a new song to the LORD.
He has done wonderful things.
By the power of his right hand and his
holy arm
he has saved his people.
2 The LORD has made known his power to save.
He has shown the nations that he does what
is right.
3 He has shown his faithful love
to the people of Israel.
People from one end of the earth to the other
have seen that our God has saved us.

4 Shout to the LORD with joy, everyone on earth.
Burst into joyful songs and make music.
5 Make music to the LORD with the harp.
Sing and make music with the harp.
6 Blow the trumpets. Give a blast on the
ram's horn.
Shout to the LORD with joy. He is the King.

7 Let the ocean and everything in it roar.
Let the world and all who live in it shout.
8 Let the rivers clap their hands.
Let the mountains sing together with joy.
9 Let them sing to the LORD,
because he is coming to judge the earth.
He will judge the nations of the world
in keeping with what is right and fair.

Psalm 99

1 The LORD rules.
Let the nations tremble.
He sits on his throne between the cherubim.
Let the earth shake.
2 Great is the LORD in Zion.
He is honored over all of the nations.
3 Let them praise his great and wonderful name.
He is holy.

4 The King is mighty. He loves what is fair.
He has set up the rules for fairness.
He has done what is right and fair
for the people of Jacob.
5 Honor the LORD our God.
Worship at his feet.
He is holy.

6 Moses and Aaron were two of his priests.
Samuel was one of those who worshiped
him.
They called out to the LORD.
And he answered them.
7 He spoke to them from the pillar of cloud.
They obeyed his laws and the orders he
gave them.

8 LORD our God, you answered them.
You showed Israel that you are a God who
forgives.
But when they did wrong, you punished
them.
9 Honor the LORD our God.
Worship at his holy mountain.
The LORD our God is holy.

Psalm 100

A psalm for giving thanks.

1 Shout to the LORD with joy, everyone on earth.
2 Worship the LORD with gladness.
Come to him with songs of joy.

3 I want you to realize that the LORD is God.
He made us, and we belong to him.
We are his people.
We are the sheep belonging to his flock.

4 Give thanks as you enter the gates of
his temple.
Give praise as you enter its courtyards.
Give thanks to him and praise his name.
5 The LORD is good. His faithful love continues
forever.
It will last for all time to come.

Psalm 101

A psalm of David.

1 I will sing about your love and fairness.
LORD, I will sing praise to you.
2 I will be careful to lead a life
that is without blame.
When will you come and help me?

I will lead a life
that is without blame in my house.
3 I won't look at anything that is evil.

I hate the acts of people who aren't faithful
to you.
I don't even want people like that
around me.
4 I will stay away from those whose hearts are
twisted.
I don't want to have anything to do
with evil.

5 I will get rid of anyone
who tells lies about his neighbor in secret.
I won't put up with anyone
whose eyes and heart are proud.
6 I will look with favor on the faithful people in
the land.
They will live with me.
Those whose lives are without blame will
serve me.

7 No one who lies and cheats
will live in my house.
No one who tells lies
will serve me.

8 Every morning I will get rid of
all the sinful people in the land.
I will remove from the city of the LORD
everyone who does what is evil.

Psalm 102

A prayer of a suffering man when he is weak
and pours out his problems to the LORD.

1 LORD, hear my prayer.
Listen to my cry for help.
2 Don't turn your face away from me
when I'm in trouble.
Pay attention to me.
When I call out for help, answer me quickly.

3 My days are disappearing like smoke.
My body burns like glowing coals.
4 My strength has dried up like grass.
I even forget to eat my food.
5 I groan out loud because of my suffering.
I'm nothing but skin and bones.
6 I'm like a desert owl.
I'm like an owl among destroyed buildings.
7 I can't sleep. I've become
like a bird alone on a roof.
8 All day long my enemies laugh at me.
Those who make fun of me use my name as
a curse.
9 I eat ashes as my food.
My tears fall into what I'm drinking.
10 You were very angry with me.
So you picked me up and threw me away.
11 The days of my life are like an evening
shadow.
I dry up like grass.

12 But LORD, you are seated on your throne
forever.
Your fame will continue for all time
to come.
13 You will rise up and show deep concern
for Zion.
The time has come for you to show favor
to it.
14 The stones of your destroyed city are priceless
to us.
Even its dust brings deep concern to us.
15 The nations will worship the LORD.
All of the kings on earth will respect his
glorious power.
16 The LORD will build Zion again.
He will appear in his glory.
17 He will answer the prayer of those who don't
have anything.
He won't say no to their cry for help.

18 Let this be written down for those born
after us.
Then people who are not yet born can praise
the LORD.
19 Here is what should be written.
"The LORD looked down from his temple in
heaven.
From heaven he viewed the earth.
20 He heard the groans of the prisoners.
He set free those who were sentenced
to death."
21 So people will talk about him in Zion.
They will praise him in Jerusalem.
22 Nations and kingdoms
will gather there to worship the LORD.

23 When I was still young, he took away my
strength.
He wasn't going to let me live much longer.

24 So I said, "My God, don't let me die in the
middle of my life.
You will live for all time to come.
25 In the beginning you made the earth secure.
You placed it on its foundations.
Your hands created the heavens.
26 They will pass away. But you will remain.
They will all wear out like a piece
of clothing.
You will make them like clothes
that are taken off and thrown away.
27 But you remain the same.
Your years will never end.
28 Our children will live with you.
Their sons and daughters will be safe in
your care."

Psalm 103

A psalm of David.

1 I will praise the LORD.
Deep down inside me, I will praise him.
I will praise him, because his name is holy.
2 I will praise the LORD.
I won't forget anything he does for me.
3 He forgives all my sins.
He heals all my sicknesses.
4 He saves my life from going down into
the grave.
His faithful and tender love makes me feel
like a king.
5 He satisfies me with the good things I long for.
Then I feel young and strong again, just like
an eagle.

6 The LORD does what is right and fair
for all who are beaten down.

7 He told Moses all about his plans.
He let the people of Israel see his
mighty acts.
8 The LORD is tender and kind. He is gracious.
He is slow to get angry. He is full of love.
9 He won't keep bringing charges against us.
He won't stay angry with us forever.
10 He doesn't punish us for our sins as much as
we should be punished.
He doesn't pay us back in keeping with the
evil things we've done.
11 His love for those who have respect for him
is as high as the heavens are above the earth.
12 He has removed our lawless acts from us
as far as the east is from the west.
13 A father is tender and kind to his children.
In the same way, the LORD is tender
and kind
to those who have respect for him.
14 He knows what we are made of.
He remembers that we are dust.
15 People's lives are like grass.
People grow like the flowers in the field.
16 When the wind blows on them, they are gone.
No one can tell that they had ever been
there.
17 But the LORD's love
for those who have respect for him
lasts for ever and ever.
Their children's children will know
that he always does what is right.
18 He always loves those who keep his covenant.
He always does what is right for those who
remember to obey his commands.

19 The LORD has set up his throne in heaven.
His kingdom rules over all.

20 Praise the LORD, you angels of his.
Praise him, you mighty ones
who carry out his orders and obey his word.
21 Praise the LORD, all you angels in heaven.
Praise him, all you who serve him and do
what he wants.
22 Let everything the LORD has made praise him
everywhere in his kingdom.

I will praise the LORD.

Psalm 104

1 I will praise the LORD.

LORD my God, you are very great.
You are dressed in glory and majesty.
2 You wrap yourself in light as if it were a robe.
You spread the heavens out like a tent.
3 You build your palace high in the heavens.
You make the clouds serve as your chariot.
You ride on the wings of the wind.
4 You make the winds serve as your messengers.
You make flashes of lightning serve you.

5 You placed the earth on its foundations.
It can never be moved.
6 You covered it with the oceans like a blanket.
The waters covered the mountains.
7 But you commanded the waters, and they
ran away.
At the sound of your thunder they rushed off.
8 They flowed down the mountains.
They went into the valleys.
They went to the place you appointed for
them.
9 You drew a line they can't cross.
They will never cover the earth again.

10 You make springs pour water into the valleys.
It flows between the mountains.
11 The springs give water to all of the wild
animals.
The wild donkeys satisfy their thirst.
12 The birds of the air build nests by the waters.
They sing among the branches.
13 You water the mountains from your palace
high in the clouds.
The earth is filled with the things you
have made.

14 You make grass grow for the cattle
and plants for people to take care of.
That's how they get food from the earth.
15 There is wine to make people glad.
There is olive oil to make them healthy.
And there is bread to make them strong.
16 The cedar trees of Lebanon belong to the LORD.
You planted them and gave them plenty of water.
17 There the birds make their nests.
The stork has its home in the pine trees.
18 The high mountains belong to the wild goats.
The cliffs are a safe place for the rock badgers.

19 The moon serves to mark off the seasons.
The sun knows when to go down.
20 You bring darkness, and it becomes night.
Then all the animals of the forest prowl around.
21 The lions roar while they hunt.
All of their food comes from God.
22 The sun rises, and they slip away.
They return to their dens and lie down.
23 Then a man gets up and goes to work.
He keeps working until evening.

24 LORD, you have made so many things!
How wise you were when you made all of them!
The earth is full of your creatures.
25 Look at the ocean, so big and wide!
It is filled with more creatures than people can count.
It is filled with living things, from the largest to the smallest.
26 Ships sail back and forth on it.
The leviathan, the sea monster you made, plays in it.

27 All of those creatures depend on you
to give them their food when they need it.
28 When you give it to them,
they eat it.
When you open your hand,
they are satisfied with good things.
29 When you turn your face away from them,
they are terrified.
When you take away their breath,
they die and turn back into dust.
30 When you send your Spirit,
you create them.
You give new life to the earth.

31 May the glory of the LORD continue forever.
May the LORD be happy with what he has made.
32 When he looks at the earth, it trembles.
When he touches the mountains, they pour out smoke.

33 I will sing to the LORD all my life.
I will sing praise to my God as long as I live.
34 May these thoughts of mine please him.
I find my joy in the LORD.
35 But may those who sin be gone from the earth.
May evil people disappear.

I will praise the LORD.

Praise the LORD.

Psalm 105

1 Give thanks to the LORD. Worship him.
Tell the nations what he has done.
2 Sing to him. Sing praise to him.
Tell about all of the wonderful things he has done.
3 Praise him, because his name is holy.
Let the hearts of those who trust in the LORD be glad.
4 Look to the LORD and to his strength.
Always look to him.
5 Remember the wonderful things he has done.
Remember his miracles and how he judged our enemies.
6 Remember what he has done, you children of his servant Abraham.
Remember it, you people of Jacob, God's chosen ones.
7 He is the LORD our God.
He judges the whole earth.

8 He will keep his covenant forever.
He will keep his promise for all time to come.
9 He will keep the covenant he made with Abraham.
He will keep the oath he took when he made his promise to Isaac.
10 He made it stand as a law for Jacob.
He made it stand as a covenant for Israel.
It will last forever.
11 He said, "I will give you the land of Canaan.
It will belong to you."

12 At first there weren't very many of God's people.
There were only a few. And they were strangers in the land.
13 They wandered from nation to nation.
They wandered from one kingdom to another.
14 But God didn't allow anyone to beat them down.
To keep them safe, he gave a command to kings.
15 He said to them, "Do not touch my anointed ones.
Do not harm my prophets."

16 He made the people in the land go hungry.
He destroyed all their food supplies.
17 He sent a man ahead of them into Egypt.
That man was Joseph. He had been sold as a slave.

18 The Egyptians put his feet in chains.
They put an iron collar around his neck.
19 He was in prison until what he said would happen came true.
The word of the LORD proved that he was right.
20 The king of Egypt sent for Joseph and let him out of prison.
The ruler of many nations set him free.
21 He put Joseph in charge of his palace.
He made him ruler over everything he owned.
22 Joseph was in charge of teaching the princes.
He taught the elders how to think and live wisely.
23 Then the rest of Jacob's family went to Egypt.
The people of Israel lived as outsiders in the land of Ham.
24 The LORD gave his people so many children that there were too many of them for their enemies.
25 He made the Egyptians hate his people.
The Egyptians made evil plans against them.
26 The LORD sent his servant Moses to the king of Egypt.
He sent Aaron, his chosen one, along with him.
27 The LORD gave them the power to do miraculous signs among the Egyptians.
They did his wonders in the land of Ham.
28 He sent darkness over the land.
He did it because the Egyptians had refused to obey his words.
29 He turned their rivers and streams into blood.
He caused the fish in them to die.
30 Their land was covered with frogs.
Frogs even went into the bedrooms of the rulers.
31 The LORD spoke, and large numbers of flies came.
Gnats filled the whole country.
32 He turned their rain into hail.
Lightning flashed all through their land.
33 He destroyed their vines and fig trees.
He broke down the trees in Egypt.
34 He spoke, and the locusts came.
There were so many of them they couldn't be counted.
35 They ate up every green thing in the land.
They ate up what the land produced.
36 Then he killed the oldest son of every family in Egypt.
He struck down the oldest of all of their sons.

37 He brought the people of Israel out of Egypt.
The Egyptians loaded them down with silver and gold.
From among the tribes of Israel no one got tired or fell down.
38 The Egyptians were glad when the people of Israel left.
They were terrified because of Israel.
39 The LORD spread out a cloud to cover his people.
He gave them a fire to light up the night.
40 They asked for meat, and he brought them quail.
He satisfied them with manna, the bread of heaven.
41 He broke open a rock, and streams of water poured out.
They flowed like a river in the desert.

42 He remembered the holy promise he had made to his servant Abraham.
43 His chosen people shouted for joy as he brought them out of Egypt.
44 He gave them the lands of other nations.
He let them take over what others had worked for.
45 He did it so they might obey his rules and follow his laws.

Praise the LORD.

Psalm 106

1 Praise the LORD.

Give thanks to the LORD, because he is good.
His faithful love continues forever.
2 Who can speak enough about the mighty acts of the LORD?
Who can praise him as much as he should be praised?
3 Blessed are those who always do what is fair.
Blessed are those who keep doing what is right.
4 LORD, remember me when you show favor to your people.
Help me when you save them.
5 Then I will enjoy the good things you give your chosen ones.
I will be joyful together with your people.
I will join them when they praise you.

6 We have sinned, just as our people of long ago did.
We too have done what is evil and wrong.
7 When our people were in Egypt,
they forgot about the LORD's miracles.
They didn't remember his many kind acts.
At the Red Sea they refused to obey him.
8 But he saved them for the honor of his name.
He did it to make his mighty power known.
9 He ordered the Red Sea to dry up, and it did.
He led his people through it as if it were a desert.
10 He saved them from the power of their enemies.
He set them free from their control.
11 The waters covered their enemies.
Not one of them escaped alive.

[12] Then his people believed his promises
and sang praise to him.

[13] But they soon forgot what he had done.
They didn't wait for his advice.
[14] In the desert they longed for food.
In that dry and empty land they put God to the test.
[15] So he gave them what they asked for.
But he also sent a sickness that killed many of them.

[16] In their camp some of them became jealous of Moses.
They were also jealous of Aaron. He had been set apart to serve the LORD.
[17] The ground opened up and swallowed Dathan.
It buried Abiram and his followers.
[18] Fire blazed among all of them.
Flames destroyed those evil people.

[19] At Mount Horeb they made a metal statue of a bull calf.
They worshiped that statue of a god.
[20] They traded their glorious God
for a statue of a bull that eats grass.
[21] They forgot the God who saved them.
They forgot the One who had done great things in Egypt.
[22] They forgot the miracles he did in the land of Ham.
They forgot the wonderful things he did by the Red Sea.
[23] So he said he would destroy them.
But Moses, his chosen one,
stood up for them.
He kept God's anger from destroying them.

[24] Later on, they refused to enter the pleasant land of Canaan.
They didn't believe God's promise.
[25] In their tents they told the LORD how unhappy they were.
They didn't obey him.
[26] So he lifted up his hand and promised with an oath
that he would make them die in the desert.
[27] He promised he would scatter their children's children among the nations.
He would make them die in other lands.

[28] They joined in worshiping the Baal that was worshiped at Peor.
They ate food that had been offered to gods that aren't even alive.
[29] Their evil ways made the LORD angry.
So a plague broke out among them.
[30] But Phinehas stood up and took action.
Then the plague stopped.
[31] What Phinehas did made him right with the LORD.
It will be remembered for all time to come.

[32] By the waters of Meribah the LORD's people made him angry.
Moses got in trouble because of them.
[33] They refused to obey the Spirit of God.
So Moses spoke without thinking.

[34] They didn't destroy the nations in Canaan
as the LORD had commanded them.
[35] Instead, they mixed with those nations
and adopted their ways.
[36] They worshiped statues of their gods.
That became a trap for them.
[37] They sacrificed their sons and daughters
as offerings to demons.
[38] They killed those who weren't guilty of doing anything wrong.
They killed their own sons and daughters.
They sacrificed them as offerings to statues of the gods of Canaan.
The land became "unclean" because of the blood of their children.
[39] The people polluted themselves by what they had done.
They weren't faithful to the LORD.

[40] So the LORD became angry with his people.
He turned away from his own children.
[41] He handed them over to the nations.
Their enemies ruled over them.
[42] They beat them down
and kept them under their power.
[43] Many times the LORD saved them.
But they refused to obey him.
So he destroyed them because of their sins.

[44] But he heard them when they cried out.
He paid special attention to their suffering.
[45] Because they were his people, he remembered his covenant.
Because of his great love, he felt sorry for them.
[46] He made all those who held them as prisoners
show concern for them.

[47] LORD our God, save us.
Bring us back from among the nations.
Then we will give thanks to you, because your name is holy.
We will celebrate by praising you.

[48] Give praise to the LORD, the God of Israel,
for ever and ever.
Let all of the people say, "Amen!"

Praise the LORD.

BOOK V

Psalms 107–150

Psalm 107

[1] Give thanks to the LORD, because he is good.
His faithful love continues forever.

[2] That's what those who have been set free by the LORD should say.
He set them free from the power of the enemy.
[3] He brought them back from other lands.
He brought them back from east and west, from north and south.

[4] Some of them wandered in deserts that were dry and empty.
They couldn't find their way to a city where they could settle down.
[5] They were hungry and thirsty.
Their lives were slipping away.
[6] Then they cried out to the LORD because of their problems.
And he saved them from their troubles.
[7] He led them straight
to a city where they could settle down.
[8] Let them give thanks to the LORD for his faithful love.
Let them give thanks for the miracles he does for his people.
[9] He gives those who are thirsty all of the water they want.
He gives those who are hungry all of the good food they can eat.

[10] Others lived in the deepest darkness.
They suffered as prisoners in iron chains.
[11] That's because they hadn't obeyed the words of God.
They had refused to follow the advice of the Most High God.
[12] So he made them do work that was hard and bitter.
They tripped and fell, and there was no one to help them.
[13] Then they cried out to the LORD because of their problems.
And he saved them from their troubles.
[14] He brought them out of the deepest darkness.
He broke their chains off.
[15] Let them give thanks to the LORD for his faithful love.
Let them give thanks for the miracles he does for his people.
[16] He breaks down gates that are made of bronze.
He cuts through bars that are made of iron.

[17] Others were foolish. They suffered because of their sins.
They suffered because they wouldn't obey the LORD.
[18] They refused to eat anything.
They came close to passing through the gates of death.
[19] Then they cried out to the LORD because of their problems.
And he saved them from their troubles.
[20] He gave his command and healed them.
He saved them from the grave.
[21] Let them give thanks to the LORD for his faithful love.
Let them give thanks for the miracles he does for his people.
[22] Let them sacrifice thank offerings.
Let them talk about what he has done as they sing with joy.

[23] Others sailed out on the ocean in ships.
They traded goods on the mighty waters.
[24] They saw the works of the LORD.
They saw the miracles he did on the ocean.
[25] He spoke and stirred up a storm.
It lifted the waves high.
[26] They rose up to the heavens. Then they went down deep into the ocean.
In that kind of danger the people's boldness melted away.
[27] They were unsteady like those who get drunk.
They didn't know what to do.
[28] Then they cried out to the LORD because of their problems.
And he brought them out of their troubles.
[29] He made the storm as quiet as a whisper.
The waves of the ocean calmed down.
[30] The people were glad when the ocean became calm.
Then he guided them to the harbor they were looking for.
[31] Let them give thanks to the LORD for his faithful love.
Let them give thanks for the miracles he does for his people.
[32] Let them honor him among his people who gather for worship.
Let them praise him in the meeting of the elders.

[33] He turned rivers into a desert.
He turned flowing springs into thirsty ground.
[34] He turned land that produced crops into a salty land where nothing could grow.
He did it because the people who lived there were evil.
[35] He turned the desert into pools of water.
He turned the dry and cracked ground into flowing springs.
[36] He brought hungry people there to live.
They built a city where they could settle down.
[37] They planted fields and vineyards
that produced large crops.
[38] He blessed the people, and they greatly increased their numbers.
He kept their herds from getting smaller.

[39] Then the number of God's people got smaller.
They were brought low by trouble, suffering and sorrow.
[40] The One who looks down on proud nobles made them wander in a desert where no one lives.

[41] But he lifted needy people out of their
suffering.
He made their families increase like flocks
of sheep.
[42] Honest people see it and are filled with joy.
But no one who is evil has anything to say.

[43] Let those who are wise pay attention to these
things.
Let them think about the LORD's great love.

Psalm 108

A song. A psalm of David.

[1] God, my heart feels secure.
I will sing and make music to you with all
my heart.
[2] Harp and lyre, wake up!
I want to sing and make music before the
sun rises.
[3] LORD, I will praise you among the nations.
I will sing about you among the people of
the earth.
[4] Great is your love. It is higher than the
heavens.
Your truth reaches to the skies.
[5] God, may you be honored above the heavens.
Let your glory be over the whole earth.

[6] Save us. Help us with your powerful
right hand,
so that those you love may be saved.
[7] God has spoken from his temple.
He has said, "I will win the battle.
Then I will divide up the land around
Shechem.
I will divide up the Valley of Succoth.
[8] Gilead belongs to me. So does the land
of Manasseh.
Ephraim is the strongest tribe. It is like
a helmet for my head.
Judah is the royal tribe. It is like a
ruler's staff.
[9] Moab serves me like one who washes
my feet.
I toss my sandal on Edom to show that
I own it.
I shout to Philistia that I have won
the battle."

[10] Who will bring me to the city that has high
walls around it?
Who will lead me to the land of Edom?
[11] God, isn't it you, even though you have now
turned away from us?
Isn't it you, even though you don't lead our
armies into battle anymore?
[12] Help us against our enemies.
The help people give doesn't amount to
anything.
[13] With your help we will win the battle.
You will walk all over our enemies.

Psalm 109

For the director of music.
A psalm of David.

[1] God, I praise you.
Don't remain silent.
[2] Sinful people who lie and cheat have spoken
against me.
They have used their tongues to tell lies
about me.
[3] They gather all around me with their words
of hatred.
They attack me without any reason.
[4] They bring charges against me,
even though I love them
and pray for them.
[5] They pay me back with evil for the good
things I do.
They pay back my love with hatred.

[6] Appoint an evil person to take my enemies
to court.
Let him stand at their right hand and bring
charges against them.
[7] When they are tried, let them be found guilty.
May even their prayers judge them.
[8] May their days be few.
Let others take their places as leaders.
[9] May their children's fathers die.
May their wives become widows.
[10] May their children be driven from their
destroyed homes.
May they wander around like beggars.
[11] May everything those people own be taken
away to pay for what they owe.
May strangers rob them of everything
they've worked for.
[12] May no one be kind to them
or take pity on the children they leave
behind.
[13] May their family line come to an end.
May their names be forgotten by those who
live after them.
[14] May the LORD remember the evil things their
fathers have done.
May he never erase the sins of their
mothers.
[15] May the LORD never forget their sins.
Then he won't let people remember those
sinners anymore.

[16] They never thought about doing
anything kind.
Instead, they drove those who were poor
and needy to their deaths.
They did the same thing to those whose
hearts were broken.
[17] They loved to call down curses on others.
May their curses come back on them.
They didn't find any pleasure in giving anyone
their blessing.
May no blessing ever come to them.

18 They called down curses on others as easily as
they put on clothes.
Cursing was as natural to them as getting a
drink of water
or putting olive oil on their bodies.
19 May their curses cover them like coats.
May their curses be wrapped around them
like a belt forever.
20 May that be the LORD's way of paying back
those who bring charges against me.
May it happen to those who say
evil things about me.

21 But LORD and King,
be true to your name. Treat me well.
Because your love is so good, save me.
22 I am poor and needy.
My heart is wounded deep down inside me.
23 I fade away like an evening shadow.
I'm like a locust that someone brushes off.
24 My knees are weak because I've gone
without food.
My body is very thin.
25 Those who bring charges against me laugh
at me.
When they see me, they shake their heads
at me.

26 LORD my God, help me.
Save me because you love me.
27 LORD, let my enemies know that you yourself
have saved me.
You have done it with your own hand.
28 They may call down a curse on me.
But you will give me your blessing.
When they attack me, they will be put
to shame.
But I will be filled with joy.
29 Those who bring charges against me will be
clothed with dishonor.
They will be wrapped in shame as if it
were a coat.

30 With my mouth I will continually praise
the LORD.
I will praise him when all of his people
gather for worship.
31 He stands ready to help those who need it.
He saves them from those who have
sentenced them to death.

Psalm 110

A psalm of David.

1 The LORD says to my Lord,
"Sit at my right hand
until I put your enemies
under your control."

2 The LORD will make your royal authority
spread out from Zion to other lands.
You will rule over your enemies who are all
around you.
3 Your troops will be willing to fight for you
on the day of battle.
You will be wrapped in holy majesty.
Just as the dew falls fresh early in the
morning,
you will always be young and strong.

4 The LORD has taken an oath and made a
promise.
He will not change his mind.
He has said, "You are a priest forever,
just like Melchizedek."

5 The Lord is at your right hand.
He will crush kings on the day when he
is angry.
6 He will judge the nations. He will pile up dead
bodies on the field of battle.
He will crush the rulers of the
whole earth.
7 He will drink from a brook along the way
and receive new strength.
And so he will win the battle.

Psalm 111

1 Praise the LORD.
I will praise the LORD with all my heart.
I will praise him where honest people gather
for worship.

2 The LORD has done great things.
All who take delight in what he has done
will spend time thinking about it.
3 What he does shows his glory and majesty.
He will always do what is right.
4 The LORD causes his miracles to be
remembered.
He is kind and tender.
5 He provides food for those who have respect
for him.
He remembers his covenant forever.
6 He has shown his people what his power
can do.
He has given them the lands of other
nations.
7 He is faithful and right in everything he does.
All his rules can be trusted.
8 They will stand firm for ever and ever.
They were given by the LORD.
He is faithful and honest.
9 He set his people free.
He made a covenant with them that will
last forever.
His name is holy and wonderful.
10 If you really want to become wise,
you must begin by having respect for
the LORD.
All those who follow his rules have good
understanding.
People should praise him forever.

Psalm 112

[1] Praise the LORD.

Blessed is the one who has respect for the LORD.
He finds great delight when he obeys God's commands.

[2] His children will be powerful in the land.
Because he is honest, his children will be blessed.
[3] His family will have wealth and riches.
He will always be blessed for doing what is right.
[4] Even in the darkness light shines on honest people.
It shines on those who are kind and tender and godly.
[5] Good things will come to those who are willing to lend freely.
Good things will come to those who are fair in everything they do.
[6] They will always be secure.
Those who do what is right will be remembered forever.
[7] They aren't afraid when bad news comes.
They stand firm because they trust in the LORD.
[8] Their hearts are secure. They aren't afraid.
In the end they will see their enemies destroyed.
[9] They have spread their gifts around to poor people.
Their good works continue forever.
They will be powerful and honored.

[10] Evil people will see it and be upset.
They will grind their teeth and become weaker and weaker.
What evil people long to do can't succeed.

Psalm 113

[1] Praise the LORD.

Praise him, you who serve the LORD.
Praise the name of the LORD.
[2] Let us praise the name of the LORD,
both now and forever.
[3] From the sunrise in the east to the sunset in the west,
may the name of the LORD be praised.

[4] The LORD is honored over all of the nations.
His glory reaches to the highest heavens.
[5] Who is like the LORD our God?
He sits on his throne in heaven.
[6] He bends down to look
at the heavens and the earth.

[7] He raises poor people up from the trash pile.
He lifts needy people out of the ashes.
[8] He lets them sit with princes.
He lets them sit with the princes of their own people.
[9] He gives children to the woman who doesn't have any children.
He makes her a happy mother in her own home.

Praise the LORD.

Psalm 114

[1] The people of Israel came out of Egypt.
The people of Jacob left a land where a different language was spoken.
[2] Then Judah became the holy place where God lived.
Israel became the land he ruled over.

[3] The Red Sea saw him and parted.
The Jordan River stopped flowing.
[4] The mountains leaped like rams.
The hills skipped like lambs.

[5] Red Sea, why did you part?
Jordan River, why did you stop flowing?
[6] Why did you mountains leap like rams?
Why did you hills skip like lambs?

[7] Earth, tremble with fear when the Lord comes.
Tremble when the God of Jacob is near.
[8] He turned the rock into a pool.
He turned the hard rock into springs of water.

Psalm 115

[1] LORD, may glory be given to you, not to us.
You are loving and faithful.

[2] Why do the nations ask,
"Where is their God?"
[3] Our God is in heaven.
He does anything he wants to do.
[4] But the statues of their gods are made out of silver and gold.
They are made by the hands of men.
[5] They have mouths, but they can't speak.
They have eyes, but they can't see.
[6] They have ears, but they can't hear.
They have noses, but they can't smell.
[7] They have hands, but they can't feel.
They have feet, but they can't walk.
They have throats, but they can't say anything.
[8] Those who make statues of gods will be like them.
So will all those who trust in them.

[9] People of Israel, trust in the LORD.
He helps you. He is like a shield that keeps you safe.
[10] Priests of Aaron, trust in the LORD.
He helps you. He is like a shield that keeps you safe.
[11] You who have respect for the LORD, trust in him.
He helps you. He is like a shield that keeps you safe.

12 The LORD remembers us and will bless us.
He will bless the people of Israel.
He will bless the priests of Aaron.
13 The LORD will bless those who have respect for him.
He will bless important and unimportant people alike.

14 May the LORD give you many children.
May he give them to you and to your children after you.
15 May the LORD bless you.
He is the Maker of heaven and earth.

16 The highest heavens belong to the LORD.
But he has given the earth to human beings.
17 Dead people don't praise the LORD.
Those who lie quietly in the grave don't praise him.
18 But we who are alive praise the LORD,
both now and forever.

Praise the LORD.

Psalm 116

1 I love the LORD, because he heard my voice.
He heard my cry for his favor.
2 Because he paid attention to me,
I will call out to him as long as I live.

3 The ropes of death were wrapped around me.
The horrors of the grave came over me.
I was overcome by trouble and sorrow.
4 Then I called out to the LORD.
I cried out, "LORD, save me!"

5 The LORD is holy and kind.
Our God is full of tender love.
6 The LORD takes care of those who are as helpless as children.
When I was in great need, he saved me.

7 I said to myself, "Be calm.
The LORD has been good to me."

8 LORD, you have saved me from death.
You have dried the tears from my eyes.
You have kept me from tripping and falling.
9 So now I can enjoy life here with you
while I'm still living.
10 I believed in you even when I said to myself,
"I'm in great pain."
11 When I was terrified, I said to myself,
"No one tells the truth."

12 The LORD has been so good to me!
How can I ever pay him back?
13 I will bring an offering of wine to the LORD
and thank him for saving me.
I will worship him.
14 In front of all of the LORD's people,
I will do what I promised him.
15 The LORD pays special attention
when his faithful people die.

16 LORD, I serve you.
I serve you just as my mother did.
You have set me free from the chains of my suffering.
17 LORD, I will sacrifice a thank offering to you.
I will worship you.
18 In front of all of the LORD's people,
I will do what I promised him.
19 I will keep my promise in the courtyards of the LORD's temple.
I will keep my promise in Jerusalem itself.

Praise the LORD.

Psalm 117

1 All you nations, praise the LORD.
All you people on earth, praise him.
2 Great is his love for us.
The LORD is faithful forever.

Praise the LORD.

Psalm 118

1 Give thanks to the LORD, because he is good.
His faithful love continues forever.
2 Let the people of Israel say,
"His faithful love continues forever."
3 Let the priests of Aaron say,
"His faithful love continues forever."
4 Let those who have respect for the LORD say,
"His faithful love continues forever."

5 When I was in great pain, I cried out to the LORD.
He answered me and set me free.
6 The LORD is with me. I will not be afraid.
What can mere men do to me?
7 The LORD is with me. He helps me.
I will win the battle over my enemies.

8 It is better to go to the LORD for safety
than to trust in mere men.
9 It is better to go to the LORD for safety
than to trust in human leaders.

10 The nations were all around me.
But by the LORD's power I destroyed them.
11 They were around me on every side.
But by the LORD's power I destroyed them.
12 They attacked me like large numbers of bees.
But they died out as quickly as burning thorns.
By the LORD's power I destroyed them.

13 I was pushed back. I was about to be killed.
But the LORD helped me.
14 The LORD gives me strength. I sing about him.
He has saved me.

15 Shouts of joy ring out in the tents of godly people.
They praise him for his help in battle.
They shout, "The LORD's powerful right hand has done mighty things!

16 The LORD's powerful right hand has won
the battle!
The LORD's powerful right hand has done
mighty things!"
17 I will not die. I will live.
I will talk about what the LORD has done.
18 The LORD has really punished me.
But he didn't let me die.

19 Open the gates of the temple for me.
I will enter and give thanks to the LORD.
20 This is the gate of the LORD.
Only those who do what is right can go
through it.
21 LORD, I will give thanks to you, because you
answered me.
You have saved me.

22 The stone the builders didn't accept
has become the most important stone of all.
23 The LORD has done it.
It is wonderful in our eyes.
24 The LORD has done it on this day.
Let us be joyful and glad in it.

25 LORD, save us.
LORD, give us success.
26 Blessed is the one who comes in the name of
the LORD.
From the temple of the LORD we bless you.
27 The LORD is God.
He has made the light of his favor shine
on us.
Take branches in your hands. Join in the march
on the day of the feast.
March up to the corners of the altar.

28 You are my God, and I will give thanks to you.
You are my God, and I will honor you.

29 Give thanks to the LORD, because he is good.
His faithful love continues forever.

Psalm 119

א Aleph

1 Blessed are those who live without blame.
They live in keeping with the law of
the LORD.
2 Blessed are those who obey his covenant laws.
They trust in him with all their hearts.
3 They don't do anything wrong.
They live as he wants them to live.
4 You have given me rules
that I must obey completely.
5 I hope I will always stand firm
in following your orders.
6 Then I won't be put to shame
when I think about all of your commands.
7 I will praise you with an honest heart
as I learn about how fair your decisions are.
8 I will obey your orders.
Please don't leave me all alone.

ב Beth

9 How can a young person keep his life pure?
By living in keeping with your word.
10 I trust in you with all my heart.
Don't let me wander away from your
commands.
11 I have hidden your word in my heart
so that I won't sin against you.
12 LORD, I give praise to you.
Teach me your orders.
13 With my lips I talk about
all of the decisions you have made.
14 Following your covenant laws gives me joy
just as great riches give joy to others.
15 I spend time thinking about your rules.
I consider how you want me to live.
16 I take delight in your orders.
I won't fail to obey your word.

ג Gimel

17 Be good to me, and I will live.
I will obey your word.
18 Open my eyes so that I can see
the wonderful truths in your law.
19 I'm a stranger on earth.
Don't hide your commands from me.
20 My heart is filled with longing
for your laws at all times.
21 You correct proud people. They are under
your curse.
They wander away from your commands.
22 I obey your covenant laws.
So don't let evil people laugh at me or
hate me.
23 Even if rulers sit together and tell lies about me,
I will spend time thinking about your orders.
24 Your covenant laws are my delight.
They give me wise advice.

ד Daleth

25 I lie in the dust. I'm about to die.
Keep me alive as you have promised.
26 I told you how I've lived, and you gave me
your answer.
Teach me your orders.
27 Help me understand what your rules can
teach me.
Then I'll spend time thinking about the
miracles you have done.
28 My sadness has worn me out.
Give me strength as you have promised.
29 Keep me from cheating and telling lies.
Be kind and teach me your law.
30 I have chosen to be faithful to you.
I put my trust in your laws.
31 LORD, I'm careful to obey your covenant laws.
Don't let me be put to shame.
32 I am quick to follow your commands,
because you have set my heart free.

ה He

33 LORD, teach me to follow your orders.
Then I will obey them to the very end.
34 Help me understand your law. Then I will follow it
and obey it with all my heart.
35 Teach me to live as you command,
because that makes me very happy.
36 Make me want to follow your covenant laws
instead of wanting to gain things only for myself.
37 Turn my eyes away from things that are worthless.
Keep me alive as you have promised.
38 Keep your promise to me.
Then other people will have respect for you.
39 Please don't let me be put to shame.
Your laws are good.
40 I really want to follow your rules.
Keep me alive, because you do what is right.

ו Waw

41 LORD, show me your faithful love.
Save me as you have promised.
42 Then I will answer those who make fun of me,
because I trust in your word.
43 Help me always to tell the truth about how faithful you are.
I have put my hope in your laws.
44 I will always obey your law,
for ever and ever.
45 I will lead a full and happy life,
because I've tried to obey your rules.
46 I will talk about your covenant laws to kings.
I will not be put to shame.
47 I take delight in obeying your commands
because I love them.
48 I praise your commands, and I love them.
I spend time thinking about your orders.

ז Zayin

49 Remember what you have said to me.
You have given me hope.
50 Even when I suffer, I am comforted
because you promised to keep me alive.
51 Proud people are always making fun of me.
But I don't turn away from your law.
52 LORD, I remember the laws you gave long ago.
I find comfort in them.
53 I am very angry
because evil people have turned away from your law.
54 No matter where I live,
I sing about your orders.
55 LORD, during the night I remember who you are.
That's why I keep your law.
56 I have really done my best
to obey your rules.

ח Heth

57 LORD, you are everything I need.
I have promised to obey your words.
58 I have looked to you with all my heart.
Be kind to me as you have promised.
59 I have thought about the way I live.
And I have decided to follow your covenant laws.
60 I won't waste any time.
I will be quick to obey your commands.
61 Evil people may tie me up with ropes.
But I won't forget to obey your law.
62 At midnight I get up to give you thanks
because your decisions are very fair.
63 I'm a friend to everyone who has respect for you.
I'm a friend to everyone who follows your rules.
64 LORD, the earth is filled with your love.
Teach me your orders.

ט Teth

65 LORD, be good to me
as you have promised.
66 Increase my knowledge and give me good sense,
because I believe in your commands.
67 Before I went through suffering, I went down the wrong path.
But now I obey your word.
68 You are good, and what you do is good.
Teach me your orders.
69 Proud people have spread lies about me and have taken away my good name.
But I follow your rules with all my heart.
70 Their hearts are hard and stubborn. They don't feel anything.
But I take delight in your law.
71 It was good for me to suffer.
That's what helped me to understand your orders.
72 The law you gave is worth more to me
than thousands of pieces of silver and gold.

י Yodh

73 You made me and formed me with your own hands.
Give me understanding so that I can learn your commands.
74 May those who have respect for you be filled with joy when they see me.
I have put my hope in your word.
75 LORD, I know that your laws are right.
You were faithful to your promise when you made me suffer.
76 May your faithful love comfort me
as you have promised me.
77 Show me your tender love so that I can live.
I take delight in your law.

78 Proud people have treated me badly without
any reason. May they be put to shame.
I will spend time thinking about your rules.
79 May those who have respect for you come
to me.
Then I can teach them your covenant laws.
80 May my heart be without blame as I follow
your orders.
Then I won't be put to shame.

כ Kaph

81 I deeply long for you to save me.
I have put my hope in your word.
82 My eyes grow tired looking for what you have
promised.
I say, "When will you comfort me?"
83 I'm as useless as a wineskin that smoke has
dried up.
But I don't forget to follow your orders.
84 How long do I have to wait?
When will you punish those who attack me?
85 Proud people do what is against your law.
They dig pits for me to fall into.
86 All of your commands can be trusted.
Help me, because people attack me without
any reason.
87 They almost wiped me off the face of the earth.
But I have not turned away from your rules.
88 Keep me alive, because you love me.
Then I will obey the covenant laws you
have given.

ל Lamedh

89 LORD, your word lasts forever.
It stands firm in the heavens.
90 You will be faithful for all time to come.
You made the earth, and it continues
to exist.
91 Your laws continue to this very day,
because all things serve you.
92 If I had not taken delight in your law,
I would have died because of my suffering.
93 I will never forget your rules.
You have kept me alive, because I
obey them.
94 Save me, because I belong to you.
I've tried to obey your rules.
95 Sinful people are waiting to destroy me.
But I will spend time thinking about your
covenant laws.
96 I've learned that everything has its limits.
But your commands are perfect. They are
always there when I need them.

מ Mem

97 LORD, I really love your law!
All day long I spend time thinking about it.
98 Your commands make me wiser than
my enemies,
because your commands are always in
my heart.
99 I know more than all of my teachers do,
because I spend time thinking about your
covenant laws.
100 I understand more than the elders do,
because I obey your rules.
101 I've kept my feet from every path that
sinners take
so that I might obey your word.
102 I haven't turned away from your laws,
because you yourself have taught me.
103 Your words are very sweet to my taste!
They are sweeter than honey to me.
104 I gain understanding from your rules.
So I hate every path that sinners take.

נ Nun

105 Your word is like a lamp that shows me
the way.
It is like a light that guides me.
106 I have taken an oath. I have promised
to follow your laws, because they are right.
107 I have suffered very much.
LORD, keep me alive as you have promised.
108 LORD, accept the praise I freely give you.
Teach me your laws.
109 I keep putting my life in danger.
But I won't forget to obey your law.
110 Evil people have set a trap for me.
But I haven't wandered away from
your rules.
111 Your covenant laws are your gift to me
forever.
They fill my heart with joy.
112 I have decided to obey your orders
to the very end.

ס Samekh

113 I hate people who can't make up their minds.
But I love your law.
114 You are my place of safety.
You are like a shield that keeps me safe.
I have put my hope in your word.
115 Get away from me, you who do evil!
Then I can do what my God commands
me to do.
116 Keep me going as you have promised. Then
I will live.
Don't let me lose all hope.
117 Take good care of me, and I will be saved.
I will always honor your orders.
118 You turn your back on all those who wander
away from your orders.
They lie and cheat, but it doesn't amount
to anything.
119 You throw away all of the sinners on earth as
if they were trash.
So I love your covenant laws.
120 My body trembles because I have respect
for you.
I have great respect for your laws.

ע Ayin

121 I have done what is right and fair.
So don't leave me to those who beat me down.
122 Make sure that everything goes well with me.
Don't let proud people beat me down.
123 My eyes grow tired as I look to you to save me.
Please save me as you have promised.
124 Be good to me, because you love me.
Teach me your orders.
125 I serve you. Help me to understand what is right.
Then I will understand your covenant laws.
126 LORD, it's time for you to act.
People are breaking your law.
127 I love your commands more than gold.
I love them more than pure gold.
128 I consider all of your rules to be right.
So I hate every path that sinners take.

פ Pe

129 Your covenant laws are wonderful.
So I obey them.
130 When your words are made clear, they bring light.
They bring understanding to childish people.
131 I open my mouth and pant like a dog,
because I long to know your commands.
132 Turn to me and show me your favor.
That's what you've always done for those who love you.
133 Teach me how to live as you have promised.
Don't let any sin be my master.
134 Set me free from men who beat me down.
Then I will obey your rules.
135 Let your face smile on me with favor.
Teach me your orders.
136 Streams of tears flow from my eyes,
because people don't obey your law.

צ Tsadhe

137 LORD, you do what is fair.
And your laws are right.
138 The laws you have made are fair.
They can be completely trusted.
139 My anger is wearing me out,
because my enemies don't pay any attention to your words.
140 Your promises have proved to be true.
I love them.
141 I'm not important. People look down on me.
But I don't forget to obey your rules.
142 You always do what is right.
And your law is true.
143 I've had my share of trouble and suffering.
But I take delight in your commands.
144 Your covenant laws are always right.
Help me to understand them. Then I will live.

ק Qoph

145 LORD, I call out to you with all my heart.
Answer me, and I will obey your orders.
146 I call out to you.
Save me, and I will keep your covenant laws.
147 I get up before the sun rises. I cry out for help.
I've put my hope in your word.
148 My eyes stay open all night long.
I spend my time thinking about your promises.
149 Listen to me, because you love me.
LORD, keep me alive as you have promised.
150 Those who think up evil plans are near.
They have wandered far away from your law.
151 But LORD, you are near.
All your commands are true.
152 Long ago I learned from your covenant laws
that you made them to last forever.

ר Resh

153 Look at how I'm suffering!
Save me, because I haven't forgotten to obey your law.
154 Stand up for me and set me free.
Keep me alive as you have promised.
155 Those who are evil are far from being saved.
They don't want to obey your orders.
156 LORD, you have deep concern for me.
Keep me alive as you have promised.
157 Many enemies attack me.
But I haven't turned away from your covenant laws.
158 I get very angry when I see people who aren't faithful to you.
They don't obey your word.
159 See how I love your rules!
LORD, keep me alive, because you love me.
160 All your words are true.
All your laws are right. They last forever.

ש Sin and Shin

161 Rulers attack me without any reason.
But my heart trembles because of your word.
162 I'm filled with joy because of your promise.
It's like finding a great fortune.
163 I hate lies with a deep hatred.
But I love your law.
164 Seven times a day I praise you
for your laws, because they are right.
165 Those who love your law enjoy great peace.
Nothing can make them trip and fall.
166 LORD, I wait for you to save me.
I follow your commands.
167 I obey your covenant laws,
because I love them greatly.
168 I obey your rules and your covenant laws,
because you know all about how I live.

©2005 Mission City Press

Boy Jesus

The child grew and became strong. He was very wise.
He was blessed by God's grace.
—Luke 2:40

Five Thousand Fed

All of them ate and were satisfied. The disciples picked up 12 baskets of leftover pieces.
—Matthew 14:20

ת Taw

[169] LORD, may you hear my cry.
Give me understanding, just as you said you would.
[170] May you hear my prayer.
Save me, just as you promised.
[171] May my lips pour out praise to you,
because you teach me your orders.
[172] May my tongue sing about your word,
because all of your commands are right.
[173] May your hand be ready to help me,
because I have chosen to obey your rules.
[174] LORD, I long for you to save me.
I take delight in your law.
[175] Let me live so that I can praise you.
May your laws keep me going.
[176] Like a lost sheep, I've gone down the wrong path.
Come and look for me,
because I haven't forgotten to obey your commands.

Psalm 120

A song for those who go up to Jerusalem to worship the LORD.

[1] I call out to the LORD when I'm in trouble,
and he answers me.
[2] LORD, save me from people whose lips tell lies.
Save me from people whose tongues don't tell the truth.

[3] What will the LORD do to you, you lying tongue?
And what more will he do?
[4] He will punish you with the sharp arrows of a soldier.
He will punish you with burning wood from a desert tree.

[5] How terrible it is for me to live in the tents of the people of Meshech!
How terrible to live in the tents of the people of Kedar!
[6] I have lived too long
among those who hate peace.
[7] I want peace.
But when I speak, they want war.

Psalm 121

A song for those who go up to Jerusalem to worship the LORD.

[1] I look up to the hills.
Where does my help come from?
[2] My help comes from the LORD.
He is the Maker of heaven and earth.

[3] He won't let your foot slip.
He who watches over you won't get tired.
[4] In fact, he who watches over Israel
won't get tired or go to sleep.

[5] The LORD watches over you.
The LORD is like a shade tree at your right hand.
[6] The sun won't harm you during the day.
The moon won't harm you during the night.

[7] The LORD will keep you from every kind of harm.
He will watch over your life.
[8] The LORD will watch over your life no matter where you go,
both now and forever.

Psalm 122

A song for those who go up to Jerusalem to worship the LORD. A psalm of David.

[1] I was very glad when they said to me,
"Let us go up to the house of the LORD."
[2] Jerusalem, our feet are standing
inside your gates.

[3] Jerusalem is built like a city
where everything is close together.
[4] The tribes of the LORD go there to praise his name.
They do it in keeping with the law he gave to Israel.
[5] The thrones of the family line of David are there.
That's where the people are judged.

[6] Pray for the peace of Jerusalem. Say,
"May those who love you be secure.
[7] May there be peace inside your walls.
May your people be kept safe."
[8] I'm concerned for my family and friends.
So I say to Jerusalem, "May you enjoy peace."
[9] I'm concerned about the house of the LORD our God.
So I pray that things will go well with Jerusalem.

Psalm 123

A song for those who go up to Jerusalem to worship the LORD.

[1] I look up and pray to you.
Your throne is in heaven.
[2] Slaves depend on their masters.
Maids depend on the women they work for.
In the same way, we depend on the LORD our God.
We wait for him to show us his favor.

[3] LORD, show us your favor. Show us your favor,
because people have made so much fun of us.
[4] We have had to put up with a lot from those who are proud.
They were always laughing at us.

Psalm 124

A song for those who go up
to Jerusalem to worship the LORD.
A psalm of David.

1 Here is what Israel should say.
Suppose the LORD had not been on our side.
2 Suppose the LORD had not been on our side
when our enemies attacked us.
3 Suppose he had not been on our side
when their anger blazed out against us.
Then they would have swallowed us alive.
4 They would have been like a flood that
drowned us.
They would have swept over us like a
rushing river.
5 They would have washed us away
like a swollen stream.

6 Give praise to the LORD.
He has not let our enemies chew us up.
7 We have escaped like a bird
from a hunter's trap.
The trap has been broken,
and we have escaped.
8 Our help comes from the LORD.
He is the Maker of heaven and earth.

Psalm 125

A song for those who go up to Jerusalem
to worship the LORD.

1 Those who trust in the LORD are like
Mount Zion.
They will always be secure. They will
last forever.
2 Like the mountains around Jerusalem,
the LORD is all around his people
both now and forever.

3 Evil people will not always rule
the land the LORD gave to those who
do right.
If they did, those who do right
might do what is evil.

4 LORD, do good to those who are good.
Do good to those whose hearts are honest.
5 But what about those who have taken paths
that are crooked?
The LORD will drive them out, along with
those who do what is evil.

May Israel enjoy peace.

Psalm 126

A song for those who go up to Jerusalem
to worship the LORD.

1 Our enemies took us away from Zion.
But when the LORD brought us home,
it seemed like a dream to us.
2 Our mouths were filled with laughter.
Our tongues sang with joy.
Then the people of other nations said,
"The LORD has done great things for them."
3 The LORD has done great things for us.
And we are filled with joy.

4 LORD, bless us with great success again,
as rain makes streams flow in the
Negev Desert.
5 Those who cry as they plant their crops
will sing with joy when they gather
them in.
6 Those who go out sobbing
as they carry seeds to plant
will come back singing with joy.
They will bring the new crop back
with them.

Psalm 127

A song for those who go up to Jerusalem
to worship the LORD. A psalm of Solomon.

1 If the LORD doesn't build a house,
the work of its builders is useless.
If the LORD doesn't watch over a city,
it's useless for those on guard duty to stand
watch over it.
2 It's useless for you to work from early morning
until late at night
just to get food to eat.
God provides for those he loves even while
they sleep.

3 Children are a gift from the LORD.
They are a reward from him.
4 Children who are born to people when they
are young
are like arrows in the hands of a soldier.
5 Blessed are those
who have many children.
They won't be put to shame
when they go up against their enemies
in court.

Psalm 128

A song for those who go up to Jerusalem
to worship the LORD.

1 Blessed are all those who have respect for
the LORD.
They live as he wants them to live.
2 Your work will give you what you need.
Blessings and good things will come to you.
3 As a vine bears a lot of fruit,
so your wife will have many children
by you.
They will sit around your table
like young olive trees.
4 Only a man who has respect for the LORD
will be blessed like that.

5 May the LORD bless you from Zion.
May you enjoy the good things that come to Jerusalem
all the days of your life.
6 May you live to see your grandchildren.

May Israel enjoy peace.

Psalm 129

A song for those who go up to Jerusalem to worship the LORD.

1 Here is what Israel should say.
Many times my enemies have beaten me down ever since I was a young nation.
2 Many times my enemies have beaten me down ever since I was a young nation,
but they haven't won the battle.
3 They have made deep wounds in my back.
It looks like a field a farmer has plowed.
4 The LORD does what is right.
Sinners had tied me up with ropes. But the LORD has set me free.
5 May all those who hate Zion
be driven back in shame.
6 May they be like grass that grows on the roof of a house.
It dries up before it can grow.
7 There isn't enough of it to fill a person's hand.
There isn't enough to tie up and carry away.
8 May no one who passes by say to those who hate Zion,
"May the blessing of the LORD be on you.
We bless you in the name of the LORD."

Psalm 130

A song for those who go up to Jerusalem to worship the LORD.

1 LORD, I cry out to you
because I'm suffering so deeply.
2 Lord, listen to me.
Pay attention to my cry for your favor.

3 LORD, suppose you kept a record of sins,
Lord, who then wouldn't be found guilty?
4 But you forgive.
So people have respect for you.

5 With all my heart I wait for the LORD to help me.
I put my hope in his word.
6 I wait for the Lord to help me.
I wait with more longing than those on guard duty wait for the morning.
I'll say it again.
I wait with more longing than those on guard duty wait for the morning.

7 Israel, put your hope in the LORD,
because the LORD's love never fails.
He sets his people completely free.
8 He himself will set Israel
free from all of their sins.

Psalm 131

A song for those who go up to Jerusalem to worship the LORD. A psalm of David.

1 LORD, my heart isn't proud.
My eyes aren't proud either.
I don't concern myself with important matters.
I don't concern myself with things that are too wonderful for me.
2 I have made myself calm and content
like a young child in its mother's arms.
Deep down inside me, I am as content as a young child.

3 Israel, put your hope in the LORD
both now and forever.

Psalm 132

A song for those who go up to Jerusalem to worship the LORD.

1 LORD, remember David
and all of the hard times he went through.

2 LORD, he took an oath.
Mighty One of Jacob, he made a promise to you.
3 He said, "I won't enter my house
or go to bed.
4 I won't let my eyes sleep.
I won't close my eyelids
5 until I find a place for the LORD.
I want to build a house for the Mighty One of Jacob."

6 Here are the words we heard in Ephrathah.
We heard them again in the fields of Kiriath Jearim.
7 "Let us go to the LORD's house.
Let us worship at his feet.
8 LORD, rise up and come to your resting place.
Come in together with the ark. It's the sign of your power.
9 May your priests put on godliness as if it were their clothes.
May your faithful people sing with joy."

10 In honor of your servant David,
don't turn your back on your anointed king.

11 The LORD took an oath and made a promise to David.
It is a firm promise that he will never break.
He said, "After you die,
I will place one of your own sons on your throne.
12 If your sons keep my covenant
and the laws I teach them,
then their sons will sit
on your throne for ever and ever."

13 The LORD has chosen Zion.
That's the place where he wants to live.

[14] He has said, "This will be my resting place for ever and ever.
Here I will sit on my throne, because that's what I want.
[15] I will greatly bless Zion with everything it needs.
I will give plenty of food to the poor people living there.
[16] I will put salvation on its priests as if it were their clothes.
God's faithful people will always sing with joy.

[17] "Here in Jerusalem I will raise up a mighty king from the family of David.
I will set up the lamp of David's kingdom for my anointed king.
Its flame will burn brightly forever.
[18] I will put shame on his enemies as if it were their clothes.
But the royal crown he wears will shine with glory."

Psalm 133

A song for those who go up to Jerusalem to worship the LORD. A psalm of David.

[1] How good and pleasant it is
when God's people live together in peace!
[2] It's like the special olive oil
that was poured on Aaron's head.
It ran down on his beard
and on the collar of his robe.
[3] It's as if the dew of Mount Hermon
were falling on Mount Zion.
There the LORD gives his blessing.
He gives life that never ends.

Psalm 134

A song for those who go up to Jerusalem to worship the LORD.

[1] All of you who serve the LORD, praise the LORD.
All of you who serve at night in the house of the LORD, praise him.
[2] Lift up your hands in the temple
and praise the LORD.

[3] May the LORD bless you from Zion.
He is the Maker of heaven and earth.

Psalm 135

[1] Praise the LORD.

Praise the name of the LORD.
You who serve the LORD, praise him.
[2] You who serve in the house of the LORD, praise him.
You who serve in the courtyards of the temple of our God, praise him.
[3] Praise the LORD, because he is good.
Sing praise to his name, because that is pleasant.
[4] The LORD has chosen the people of Jacob to be his own.
He has chosen Israel to be his special treasure.

[5] I know that the LORD is great.
I know that our Lord is greater than all gods.
[6] The LORD does anything he wants to do
in the heavens and on the earth.
He does it even in the deepest parts of the oceans.
[7] He makes clouds rise from one end of the earth to the other.
He sends lightning with the rain.
He brings the wind out of his storerooms.

[8] He killed the oldest son of each family in Egypt.
He struck down the oldest males that were born to people and animals.
[9] He did miraculous signs in Egypt.
He did wonders against Pharaoh and everyone who served him.
[10] He destroyed many nations.
He killed mighty kings.
[11] He killed Sihon, the king of the Amorites,
and Og, the king of Bashan.
He killed all of the kings of Canaan.
[12] He gave their land as a gift
to his people Israel.

[13] LORD, your name continues forever.
LORD, your fame will last for all time to come.
[14] When the LORD hands down his sentence, it will be in his people's favor.
He will show deep concern for those who serve him.

[15] The statues of the gods of the nations are made of silver and gold.
They are made by the hands of men.
[16] They have mouths, but they can't speak.
They have eyes, but they can't see.
[17] They have ears, but they can't hear.
They have mouths, but they can't breathe.
[18] Those who make statues of gods will be like them.
So will all those who trust in them.

[19] People of Israel, praise the LORD.
Priests of Aaron, praise the LORD.
[20] Tribe of Levi, praise the LORD.
You who have respect for the LORD, praise him.
[21] Give praise to the LORD in Zion.
Give praise to the One who lives in Jerusalem.

Praise the LORD.

Psalm 136

1 Give thanks to the LORD, because he
is good.
His faithful love continues forever.
2 Give thanks to the greatest God of all.
His faithful love continues forever.
3 Give thanks to the most powerful Lord of all.
His faithful love continues forever.

4 Give thanks to the only one who can do
great miracles.
His faithful love continues forever.
5 By his understanding he made the heavens.
His faithful love continues forever.
6 He spread out the earth on the waters.
His faithful love continues forever.
7 He made the great lights in the sky.
His faithful love continues forever.
8 He made the sun to rule over the day.
His faithful love continues forever.
9 He made the moon and stars to rule over
the night.
His faithful love continues forever.

10 Give thanks to the One who killed the oldest
son of each family in Egypt.
His faithful love continues forever.
11 He brought the people of Israel out of Egypt.
His faithful love continues forever.
12 He did it by reaching out his mighty hand and
powerful arm.
His faithful love continues forever.

13 Give thanks to the One who parted the
Red Sea.
His faithful love continues forever.
14 He brought Israel through the middle of it.
His faithful love continues forever.
15 But he swept Pharaoh and his army into
the Red Sea.
His faithful love continues forever.

16 Give thanks to the One who led his people
through the desert.
His faithful love continues forever.
17 He killed great kings.
His faithful love continues forever.
18 He struck down mighty kings.
His faithful love continues forever.
19 He killed Sihon, the king of the Amorites.
His faithful love continues forever.
20 He killed Og, the king of Bashan.
His faithful love continues forever.
21 He gave their land as a gift.
His faithful love continues forever.
22 He gave it as a gift to his servant Israel.
His faithful love continues forever.

23 Give thanks to the One who remembered us
when things were going badly for us.
His faithful love continues forever.
24 He set us free from our enemies.
His faithful love continues forever.
25 He gives food to every creature.
His faithful love continues forever.
26 Give thanks to the God of heaven.
His faithful love continues forever.

Psalm 137

1 We were sitting by the rivers of Babylon.
We cried when we remembered what had
happened to Zion.
2 On the nearby poplar trees
we hung up our harps.
3 Those who held us as prisoners asked us
to sing.
Those who enjoyed hurting us ordered us
to sing joyful songs.
They said, "Sing one of the songs of Zion
to us!"

4 How can we sing the songs of the LORD
while we are in another land?
5 Jerusalem, if I forget you,
may my right hand never be able to play the
harp again.
6 If I don't remember you,
may my tongue stick to the roof of my
mouth so I can't sing.
May it happen if I don't consider Jerusalem
to be my greatest joy.

7 LORD, remember what the people of Edom did
on the day Jerusalem fell.
"Tear it down!" they cried.
"Tear it down to the ground!"

8 People of Babylon, you are sentenced to
be destroyed.
Happy are those who pay you back
for what you have done to us.
9 Happy are those who grab your babies
and smash them against the rocks.

Psalm 138

A psalm of David.

1 LORD, I will praise you with all my heart.
In front of those who think they are gods
I will sing praise to you.
2 I will bow down facing your holy temple.
I will praise your name,
because you are loving and faithful.
You have honored your name and your word
more than anything else.
3 When I called out to you, you answered me.
You made me strong and brave.

4 LORD, may all of the kings on earth praise you
when they hear about what you have
promised.
5 LORD, may they sing about what you have
done,
because your glory is great.

[6]The LORD is in heaven. But he watches over
those who are free of pride.
He knows those who are proud and stays far
away from them.
[7]Trouble is all around me,
but you keep me alive.
You reach out your hand to put a stop to the
anger of my enemies.
With your powerful right hand you save me.
[8]LORD, you will do everything you have
planned for me.
LORD, your faithful love continues forever.
You have done so much for us. Don't
stop now.

Psalm 139

For the director of music. A psalm of David.

[1]LORD, you have seen what is in my heart.
You know all about me.
[2]You know when I sit down and when I get up.
You know what I'm thinking even though
you are far away.
[3]You know when I go out to work and when I
come back home.
You know exactly how I live.
[4]LORD, even before I speak a word,
you know all about it.

[5]You are all around me. You are behind me and
in front of me.
You hold me in your power.
[6]I'm amazed at how well you know me.
It's more than I can understand.
[7]How can I get away from your Spirit?
Where can I go to escape from you?
[8]If I go up to the heavens, you are there.
If I lie down in the deepest parts of the
earth, you are also there.
[9]Suppose I were to rise with the sun in the east
and then cross over to the west where it
sinks into the ocean.
[10]Your hand would always be there to guide me.
Your right hand would still be holding
me close.
[11]Suppose I were to say, "I'm sure the darkness
will hide me.
The light around me will become as dark
as night."
[12]Even that darkness would not be dark to you.
The night would shine like the day,
because darkness is like light to you.

[13]You created the deepest parts of my being.
You put me together inside my mother's
body.
[14]How you made me is amazing and wonderful.
I praise you for that.
What you have done is wonderful.
I know that very well.
[15]None of my bones was hidden from you
when you made me inside my mother's
body.
That place was as dark as the deepest parts
of the earth.
When you were putting me together there,
[16]your eyes saw my body even before it
was formed.
You planned how many days I would live.
You wrote down the number of them in
your book
before I had lived through even one of them.

[17]God, your thoughts about me are priceless.
No one can possibly add them all up.
[18]If I could count them,
they would be more than the grains of sand.
If I were to fall asleep counting and then
wake up,
you would still be there with me.
[19]God, I wish you would kill the people who
are evil!
I wish those murderers would get away
from me!
[20]They are your enemies. They misuse your name.
They misuse it for their own evil purposes.
[21]LORD, I really hate those who hate you!
I really hate those who rise up against you!
[22]I have nothing but hatred for them.
I consider them to be my enemies.

[23]God, see what is in my heart.
Know what is there.
Put me to the test.
Know what I'm thinking.
[24]See if there's anything in my life you
don't like.
Help me live in the way that is always right.

Psalm 140

For the director of music. A psalm of David.

[1]LORD, save me from sinful men.
Keep me safe from those who want to
hurt me.
[2]They make evil plans in their hearts.
They are always starting fights.
[3]Their tongues are as deadly as the tongue
of a serpent.
The words from their lips are like the
poison of a snake. *Selah*

[4]LORD, keep me out of the hands of sinful
people.
Keep me safe from men who want to
hurt me.
They plan to trip me up and make me fall.
[5]Proud people have hidden their traps to
catch me.
They have spread out their nets.
They have set traps for me along my path.
Selah

[6] LORD, I say to you, "You are my God."
LORD, hear my cry for your favor.
[7] LORD and King, you save me because you are strong.
You are like a shield that keeps me safe in the day of battle.
[8] LORD, don't give sinners what they want.
Don't let their plans succeed.
If you do, they will become proud. *Selah*
[9] Those who are all around me have caused me trouble
by what their lips have said.
Let that trouble fall on their own heads.
[10] Let burning coals fall on people like that.
May they be thrown into the fire.
May they be thrown into muddy pits and never get out.
[11] Don't let men who tell lies about me settle down in the land.
May trouble hunt down those who want to hurt me.
[12] I know that the LORD makes sure that poor people are treated fairly.
He stands up for those who are in need.
[13] I'm sure that those who do right will praise your name.
Those who are honest will live with you.

Psalm 141

A psalm of David.

[1] LORD, I call out to you. Come quickly to help me.
Listen to me when I call out to you.
[2] May my prayer come to you like the sweet smell of incense.
When I lift up my hands in prayer, may it be like the evening sacrifice.

[3] LORD, guard my mouth.
Keep watch over the door of my lips.
[4] Don't let my heart be drawn to what is evil.
Don't let me join men who do evil.
They don't do what is right.
Don't let me join them and eat their fancy food.
[5] If a person who does what is right were to strike me, it would be an act of kindness.
If that person were to correct me, it would be like pouring olive oil on my head.
I wouldn't say no to it.
But I always pray against the things that sinful people do.
[6] When their rulers are thrown down from the rocky cliffs,
those evil people will realize that my words were true.
[7] They will say, "As clumps of dirt are left from plowing up the ground,
so our bones will be scattered near an open grave."

[8] But LORD and King, I keep looking to you.
I go to you for safety. Don't let me die.
[9] Keep me from the traps of those who do evil.
Save me from the traps they have set for me.
[10] Let evil people fall into their own nets.
But let me go safely on my way.

Psalm 142

A prayer of David when he was in the cave.
A *maskil.*

[1] I call out to the LORD.
I pray to him for his favor.
[2] I pour out my problem to him.
I tell him about my trouble.

[3] When I grow weak,
you know what I'm going through.
In the path where I walk,
people have hidden a trap to catch me.
[4] Look around me, and you will see
that no one is concerned about me.
I have no place of safety.
No one cares whether I live or die.

[5] LORD, I cry out to you.
I say, "You are my place of safety.
You are everything I need in this life."
[6] Listen to my cry.
I am in great need.
Save me from those who are chasing me.
They are too strong for me.
[7] My troubles are like a prison.
Set me free so I can praise your name.

Then those who do what is right will gather around me
because you have been good to me.

Psalm 143

A psalm of David.

[1] LORD, hear my prayer.
Listen to my cry for your favor.
You are faithful and right.
Come and help me.
[2] Don't take me to court and judge me,
because in your eyes no living person does what is right.

[3] My enemies chase me.
They crush me down to the ground.
They make me live in darkness
like those who died long ago.
[4] So I grow weak.
Deep down inside me, I'm afraid.

[5] I remember what happened long ago.
I spend time thinking about all of your acts.
I consider what your hands have done.
[6] I spread out my hands to you in prayer.
I'm thirsty for you, just as dry ground is thirsty for rain. *Selah*

[7] LORD, answer me quickly.
I'm growing weak.
Don't turn your face away from me,
or I will be like those who go down into the grave.
[8] In the morning let me hear about your faithful love,
because I've put my trust in you.
Show me the way I should live,
because I pray to you.
[9] LORD, save me from my enemies,
because I go to you for safety.
[10] Teach me to do what you want,
because you are my God.
May your good Spirit
lead me on a level path.

[11] LORD, be true to your name. Keep me alive.
Because you do what is right, get me out of trouble.
[12] Because your love is faithful, put an end to my enemies.
Destroy all of them, because I serve you.

Psalm 144

A psalm of David.

[1] Give praise to the LORD. He is my rock.
He trains my hands for war.
He trains my fingers for battle.
[2] He is my loving God. He is like a fort to me.
He is my place of safety and the One who saves me.
He is like a shield that keeps me safe. I go to him for safety.
He brings nations under my control.

[3] LORD, what is a human being that you take care of him?
What is a son of man that you think about him?
[4] His life doesn't last any longer than a breath.
His days are like a shadow that quickly disappears.

[5] LORD, open up your heavens and come down.
Touch the mountains, and they will pour out smoke.
[6] Send flashes of lightning and scatter my enemies.
Shoot your arrows and chase them away.
[7] My enemies are like a mighty flood.
Reach down from heaven and save me.
Save me from strangers who attack me.
[8] They tell all kinds of lies with their mouths.
Even when they make a promise by raising their right hands, they don't mean it.

[9] God, I will sing a new song to you.
I will make music to you on a harp that has ten strings.
[10] You are the One who helps kings win battles.
You save your servant David from dying by the sword.

[11] Save me. Set me free
from strangers who attack me.
They tell all kinds of lies with their mouths.
Even when they make a promise by raising their right hands, they don't mean it.

[12] While our sons are young,
they will be like healthy plants.
Our daughters will be like pillars
that have been made to decorate a palace.
[13] Our storerooms will be filled
with every kind of food.
The sheep in our fields will increase
by thousands.
They will increase by tens of thousands.
[14] Our oxen will pull heavy loads.
None of our city walls will be broken down.
No one will be carried off as a prisoner.
No cries of pain will be heard in our streets.

[15] Blessed are the people about whom all of those things are true.
Blessed are the people whose God is the LORD.

Psalm 145

A psalm of praise. A psalm of David.

[1] I will honor you, my God the King.
I will praise your name for ever and ever.
[2] Every day I will praise you.
I will praise your name for ever and ever.

[3] LORD, you are great. You are really worthy of praise.
No one can completely understand how great you are.
[4] Parents will praise your works to their children.
They will tell about your mighty acts.
[5] They will speak about your glorious majesty.
I will spend time thinking about your miracles.
[6] They will speak about the powerful and wonderful things you do.
I will talk about the great things you have done.
[7] They will celebrate your great goodness.
They will sing with joy about your holy acts.

[8] The LORD is gracious. He is kind and tender.
He is slow to get angry. He is full of love.
[9] The LORD is good to all.
He shows deep concern for everything he has made.
[10] LORD, every living thing you have made will praise you.
Your faithful people will praise you.
[11] They will tell about your glorious kingdom.
They will speak about your power.
[12] Then all people will know about the mighty things you have done.
They will know about the glorious majesty of your kingdom.

13 Your kingdom is a kingdom that will last
forever.
Your rule will continue for all time to come.

The LORD is faithful and will keep all of
his promises.
He is loving toward everything he
has made.
14 The LORD takes good care of all those
who fall.
He lifts up all those who feel helpless.
15 Every living thing looks to you for food.
You give it to them exactly when they
need it.
16 You open your hand
and satisfy the needs of every living
creature.

17 The LORD is right in everything he does.
He is loving toward everything he has made.
18 The LORD is ready to help all those who call
out to him.
He helps those who really mean it when
they call out to him.
19 He satisfies the needs of those who have
respect for him.
He hears their cry and saves them.
20 The LORD watches over all those who
love him.
But he will destroy all sinful people.

21 I will praise the LORD with my mouth.
Let every creature praise his holy name
for ever and ever.

Psalm 146

1 Praise the LORD.

I will praise the LORD.
2 I will praise the LORD all my life.
I will sing praise to my God as long as
I live.

3 Don't put your trust in human leaders.
Don't trust in people. They can't save you.
4 When they die, they return to the ground.
On that very day their plans are bound
to fail.

5 Blessed are those who depend on the God of
Jacob for help.
Blessed are those who put their hope in the
LORD their God.
6 He is the Maker of heaven and earth and
the ocean.
He made everything in them.
The LORD remains faithful forever.
7 He stands up for those who are beaten down.
He gives food to hungry people.
The LORD sets prisoners free.
8 The LORD gives sight to those who are
blind.
The LORD lifts up those who feel helpless.
The LORD loves those who do what is right.
9 The LORD watches over the outsiders who live
in our land.
He takes good care of children whose
fathers have died.
He also takes good care of widows.
But he causes evil people to fail
in everything they do.

10 The LORD rules forever.
The God of Zion will rule for all time to come.

Praise the LORD.

Psalm 147

1 Praise the LORD.

How good it is to sing praises to our God!
How pleasant and right it is to praise him!

2 The LORD builds up Jerusalem.
He gathers the scattered people of Israel.
3 He heals those who have broken hearts.
He takes care of their wounds.

4 He decides how many stars there should be.
He gives each one of them a name.
5 Great is our Lord. His power is mighty.
There is no limit to his understanding.
6 The LORD gives strength to those who
aren't proud.
But he throws evil people down to
the ground.

7 Sing to the LORD and give thanks to him.
Make music to our God on the harp.
8 He covers the sky with clouds.
He supplies the earth with rain.
He makes grass grow on the hills.
9 He provides food for the cattle.
He provides for the young ravens when
they cry out.

10 He doesn't take pleasure in the strength
of horses.
He doesn't take delight in the strong legs
of men.
11 The LORD takes delight in those who have
respect for him.
They put their hope in his faithful love.

12 Jerusalem, praise the LORD.
Zion, praise your God.
13 He makes the bars of your gates stronger.
He blesses the people who live inside you.
14 He keeps your borders safe and secure.
He satisfies you with the finest wheat.

15 He sends his command to the earth.
His word arrives there quickly.
16 He spreads the snow like wool.
He scatters the frost like ashes.
17 He throws down his hail like small stones.
No one can stand his icy blast.
18 He gives his command, and the ice melts.
He stirs up his winds, and the waters flow.

19 He has made his word known to the people
of Jacob.
He has made his laws and rules known
to Israel.
20 He hasn't done that for any other nation.
They don't know his laws.

Praise the LORD.

Psalm 148

1 Praise the LORD.

Praise the LORD from the heavens.
Praise him in the heavens above.
2 Praise him, all his angels.
Praise him, all his angels in heaven.
3 Praise him, sun and moon.
Praise him, all you shining stars.
4 Praise him, you highest heavens.
Praise him, you waters above the skies.
5 Let all of them praise the name of the LORD,
because he gave a command and they
were created.
6 He set them in place for ever and ever.
He gave them laws they will always have
to obey.
7 Praise the LORD from the earth,
you great sea creatures and all of the deepest
parts of the ocean.
8 Praise him, lightning and hail, snow and clouds.
Praise him, you stormy winds that
obey him.
9 Praise him, all you mountains and hills.
Praise him, all you fruit trees and cedar trees.
10 Praise him, all you wild animals and cattle.
Praise him, you small creatures and
flying birds.
11 Praise him, you kings of the earth and
all nations.
Praise him, all you princes and rulers
on earth.
12 Praise him, young men and young women.
Praise him, old people and children.

13 Let them praise the name of the LORD.
His name alone is honored.
His glory is higher than the earth and
the heavens.
14 He has given his people a strong king.
All of his faithful people praise him for
that gift.
All of the people of Israel are close to
his heart.

Praise the LORD.

Psalm 149

1 Praise the LORD.

Sing a new song to the LORD.
Sing praise to him in the community of his
faithful people.

2 Let Israel be filled with joy because God is
their Maker.
Let the people of Zion be glad because he is
their King.
3 Let them praise his name with dancing.
Let them make music to him with harps and
tambourines.
4 The LORD takes delight in his people.
He saves those who aren't proud. He makes
them feel like kings.
5 Let his faithful people be filled with joy
because of that honor.
Let them sing with joy even when they are
lying in bed.

6 May they praise God with their mouths.
May they hold in their hands a sword that
has two edges.
7 Let them pay the nations back.
Let them punish the people of the earth.
8 Let them put the kings of those nations
in chains.
Let them put their nobles in iron chains.
9 Let them carry out God's sentence against
the nations.
That will bring glory to all of his faithful
people.

Praise the LORD.

Psalm 150

1 Praise the LORD.

Praise God in his holy temple.
Praise him in his mighty heavens.
2 Praise him for his powerful acts.
Praise him because he is greater than
anything else.
3 Praise him by blowing trumpets.
Praise him with harps and lyres.
4 Praise him with tambourines and dancing.
Praise him with stringed instruments and
flutes.
5 Praise him with clashing cymbals.
Praise him with clanging cymbals.

6 Let everything that has breath praise the LORD.

Praise the LORD.

Proverbs

Purpose

1 These are the proverbs of Solomon. He was the son of David and the king of Israel.

2 Proverbs teach you wisdom and train you.
They help you understand wise sayings.
3 They provide you with training and help you live wisely.
They lead to what is right and honest and fair.
4 They give understanding to childish people.
They give knowledge and good sense to those who are young.
5 Let wise people listen and add to what they have learned.
Let those who understand what is right get guidance.
6 What I'm teaching also helps you understand proverbs and stories.
It helps you understand the sayings and riddles of those who are wise.

Main Point

7 If you really want to gain knowledge, you must begin by having respect for the LORD.
But foolish people hate wisdom and training.

Think and Live Wisely

A Warning Against a Life of Crime

8 My son, listen to your father's advice.
Don't turn away from your mother's teaching.
9 What they teach you will be like a beautiful crown on your head.
It will be like a chain to decorate your neck.

10 My son, if sinners tempt you,
don't give in to them.
11 They might say, "Come along with us.
Let's hide and wait to spill someone's blood.
Let's catch some harmless people in our trap.
12 Let's swallow them alive, as the grave does.
Let's swallow them whole, like those who go down into the pit.
13 We'll get all kinds of valuable things.
We'll fill our houses with what we steal.
14 Come and join our gang.
We'll share everything we have."
15 My son, don't go along with them.
Don't even set your feet on their paths.
16 They are always in a hurry to sin.
They are quick to spill someone's blood.
17 How useless it is to spread a net
while all the birds are watching!
18 Those who hide and wait will spill their own blood.
They will be caught in their own trap.
19 That's what happens to everyone
who goes after money in the wrong way.
That kind of money takes away
the lives of those who get it.

A Warning Against Turning Away From Wisdom

20 Wisdom calls out in the street.
She raises her voice in public places.
21 At the noisy street corners she cries out.
Here is what she says near the gates of the city.

22 "How long will you childish people love your childish ways?
How long will you rude people enjoy making fun of God and others?
How long will you foolish people hate knowledge?
23 Suppose you had paid attention to my warning.
Then I would have poured out my heart to you.
I would have told you what I was thinking.
24 But you turned away from me when I called out to you.
None of you paid attention when I reached out my hand.
25 You turned away from all my advice.
You wouldn't accept my warning.
26 So I will laugh at you when you are in danger.
I will make fun of you when hard times come.
27 I will laugh when hard times hit you like a storm.
I will laugh when danger comes your way like a windstorm.
I will make fun of you when suffering and trouble come.

28 "Then you will call to me. But I won't answer.
You will look for me. But you won't find me.
29 You hated knowledge.
You didn't choose to have respect for the LORD.
30 You wouldn't accept my advice.
You turned your backs on my warnings.
31 So you will eat the fruit of the way you have lived.
You will choke on the fruit of what you have planned.

32 "Childish people go down the wrong path.
They will die.
Foolish people are satisfied with the way they live. They will be destroyed.
33 But those who listen to me will live in safety.
They will not worry. They won't be afraid of getting hurt."

Good Things Come From Wisdom

2 My son, accept my words.
Store up my commands inside you.
2 Let your ears listen to wisdom.
Apply your heart to understanding.
3 Call out for the ability to be wise.
Cry out for understanding.
4 Look for it as you would look for silver.
Search for it as you would search for hidden treasure.
5 Then you will understand how to have respect for the LORD.
You will find out how to know God.
6 The LORD gives wisdom.
Knowledge and understanding come from his mouth.
7 He stores up success for honest people.
He is like a shield to those who live without blame. He keeps them safe.
8 He guards the path of those who are honest.
He watches over the way of his faithful ones.

9 You will understand what is right and honest and fair.
You will understand the right way to live.
10 Your heart will become wise.
Your mind will delight in knowledge.
11 Good sense will keep you safe.
Understanding will guard you.

12 Wisdom will save you from the ways of evil men.
It will save you from men who twist their words.
13 Men like that leave the straight paths
to walk in dark ways.
14 They take delight in doing what is wrong.
They take joy in twisting everything around.
15 Their paths are crooked.
Their ways are not straight.

16 Wisdom will save you from a woman who commits adultery.
It will save you from a sinful wife and her tempting words.
17 She leaves the man she married when she was young.
She breaks the promise she made to her God.
18 Her house leads down to death.
Her paths lead to the spirits of the dead.
19 No one who goes to her comes back
or reaches the paths of life.

20 You will walk in the ways of good people.
You will follow the paths of those who do right.
21 Honest people will live in the land.
Those who are without blame will remain in it.
22 But sinners will be cut off from the land.
Those who aren't faithful will be torn away from it.

More Good Things Come From Wisdom

3 My son, do not forget my teaching.
Keep my commands in your heart.
2 They will help you live for many years.
They will bring you success.

3 Don't let love and truth ever leave you.
Tie them around your neck.
Write them on the tablet of your heart.
4 Then you will find favor and a good name
in the eyes of God and people.
5 Trust in the LORD with all your heart.
Do not depend on your own understanding.
6 In all your ways remember him.
Then he will make your paths smooth and straight.

7 Don't be wise in your own eyes.
Have respect for the LORD and avoid evil.
8 That will bring health to your body.
It will make your bones strong.
9 Honor the LORD with your wealth.
Give him the first share of all your crops.
10 Then your storerooms will be so full they can't hold everything.
Your huge jars will spill over with fresh wine.

11 My son, do not hate the LORD's training.
Do not object when he corrects you.
12 The LORD trains those he loves.
He is like a father who trains the son he is pleased with.

13 Blessed is the one who finds wisdom.
Blessed is the one who gains understanding.
14 Wisdom pays better than silver does.
She earns more than gold does.
15 She is worth more than rubies.
Nothing you want can compare with her.
16 Long life is in her right hand.
In her left hand are riches and honor.
17 Her ways are pleasant ways.
All her paths lead to peace.
18 She is a tree of life to those who hold her close.
Those who hold on to her will be blessed.

19 By wisdom the LORD laid the earth's foundations.
Through understanding he set the heavens in place.
20 By his knowledge the seas were separated,
and the clouds dropped their dew.

21 My son, hold on to good sense and the
understanding of what is right.
Don't let them out of your sight.
22 They will be life for you.
They will be like a gracious necklace
around your neck.
23 Then you will go on your way in safety.
You will not trip and fall.
24 When you lie down, you won't be afraid.
When you lie down, you will sleep soundly.
25 Don't be terrified by sudden trouble.
Don't be afraid when sinners are destroyed.
26 The LORD is the one you will trust in.
He will keep your feet from being caught
in a trap.

27 Don't hold back good from those who are
worthy of it.
Don't hold it back when you can help.
28 Suppose you have something to give.
Don't say to your neighbor,
"Come back later.
I'll give it to you tomorrow."
29 Don't plan to harm your neighbor.
He lives near you and trusts you.
30 Don't bring charges against a man without
any reason.
He has not harmed you.

31 Don't be jealous of a man who hurts others.
Don't choose any of his ways.
32 The LORD really hates sinful people.
But he makes honest people his closest
friends.

33 The LORD puts a curse on the houses of sinners.
But he blesses the homes of those who
do what is right.
34 He laughs at proud people who make fun
of others.
But he gives grace to those who are
not proud.
35 Wise people receive honor.
But the LORD puts foolish people to shame.

Wisdom Is Best

4 My children, listen to a father's teaching.
Pay attention and gain understanding.
2 I give you good advice.
So don't turn away from what I teach you.
3 I was once a young boy in my father's house.
I was my mother's only child.
4 My father taught me.
He said, "Hold on to my words with all
your heart.
Keep my commands. Then you will live.
5 Get wisdom. Get understanding.
Don't forget my words. Don't turn away
from them.
6 Stay close to wisdom, and she will keep
you safe.
Love her, and she will watch over you.
7 Wisdom is best. So get wisdom.
No matter what it costs, get understanding.
8 Value wisdom, and she will lift you up.
Hold her close, and she will honor you.
9 She will set a beautiful crown on your head.
She will give you a glorious crown."

10 My son, listen. Accept what I say.
Then you will live for many years.
11 I guide you in the way of wisdom.
I lead you along straight paths.
12 When you walk, nothing will slow you down.
When you run, you won't trip and fall.
13 Hold on to my teaching. Don't let it go.
Guard it well. It is your life.
14 Don't take the path of evil people.
Don't live the way sinners do.
15 Stay away from their path. Don't travel on it.
Turn away from it. Go on your way.
16 Sinners can't sleep until they do what is evil.
They can't rest until they make someone
fall.
17 They do evil just as easily as they eat food.
They hurt others as easily as they
drink wine.

18 The path of those who do what is right is like
the first gleam of dawn.
It shines brighter and brighter until the full
light of day.
19 But the way of those who do what is wrong is
like deep darkness.
They don't know what makes them trip
and fall.

20 My son, pay attention to what I say.
Listen closely to my words.
21 Don't let them out of your sight.
Keep them in your heart.
22 They are life to those who find them.
They are health to your whole body.
23 Above everything else, guard your heart.
It is where your life comes from.
24 Don't speak with twisted words.
Keep evil talk away from your lips.
25 Let your eyes look straight ahead.
Keep looking right in front of you.
26 Make level paths for your feet to walk on.
Only go on ways that are firm.
27 Don't turn to the right or left.
Keep your feet from the path of evil.

A Warning Against Committing Adultery

5 My son, pay attention to my wisdom.
Listen carefully to my wise sayings.
2 Then you will continue to have good sense.
Your lips will keep on speaking words of
knowledge.
3 A woman who commits adultery has lips that
drip honey.
What she says is smoother than oil.

4 But in the end she is like bitter poison.
She cuts like a sword that has two edges.
5 Her feet go down to death.
Her steps lead straight to the grave.
6 She doesn't give any thought to her way of life.
Her paths are crooked, but she doesn't realize it.

7 My sons, listen to me.
Don't turn away from what I say.
8 Stay on a path far away from that evil woman.
Don't even go near the door of her house.
9 If you do, you will give your best strength to others.
You will give the best years of your life to someone who is mean.
10 Strangers will use up all of your wealth.
Your hard work will make someone else rich.
11 At the end of your life you will groan.
Your skin and your body will be worn out.
12 You will say, "How I hated to take advice!
How my heart refused to be corrected!
13 I would not obey my teachers.
I wouldn't listen to those who taught me.
14 I was almost totally destroyed.
It happened right in front of the whole community."
15 Drink water from your own well.
Drink running water from your own spring.
16 Should your springs pour out into the streets?
Should your streams of water pour out in public places?
17 No! Let them belong to you alone.
Never share them with strangers.
18 May your fountain be blessed.
May the wife you married when you were young make you happy.
19 She is like a loving doe, a graceful deer.
May her breasts always satisfy you.
May you always be captured by her love.
20 My son, why be captured by a woman who commits adultery?
Why hug the wife of another man?

21 The LORD watches a man's ways.
He studies all of his paths.
22 A sinner is trapped by his own evil acts.
He is held tight by the ropes of his sins.
23 He will die because he refused to be corrected.
His sins will capture him because he was very foolish.

Warnings Against Foolish Acts

6 My son, don't put up money for what your neighbor owes.
Don't agree to pay up for someone else.
2 Don't be trapped by what you have said.
Don't be caught by the words of your mouth.
3 Instead, my son, do something to free yourself.
Don't fall into your neighbor's hands.
Don't be proud.
Hurry and make your appeal to your neighbor.
4 Don't let your eyes go to sleep.
Don't let your eyelids close.
5 As a deer frees itself from a hunter, free yourself.
As a bird frees itself from a trapper, free yourself.

6 You people who don't want to work, think about the ant!
Consider its ways and be wise!
7 It has no commander.
It has no leader or ruler.
8 But it stores up its food in summer.
It gathers its food at harvest time.

9 You lazy people, how long will you lie there?
When will you get up from your sleep?
10 You might sleep a little or take a little nap.
You might even fold your hands and rest.
11 Then you would be poor, as if someone had robbed you.
You would have little, as if someone had stolen from you.

12 A worthless and evil man
goes around saying twisted things with his mouth.
13 He winks with his eyes.
He makes signals with his feet.
He motions with his fingers.
14 His plans are evil. He has lies in his heart.
He is always stirring up fights.
15 Trouble will catch up with him in an instant.
He will suddenly be destroyed. Nothing can save him.

16 There are six things the LORD hates.
In fact, he hates seven things.
17 The LORD hates proud eyes,
a lying tongue,
and hands that kill those who aren't guilty.
18 He also hates hearts that make evil plans,
feet that are quick to do evil,
19 any witness who pours out lies,
and anyone who stirs up family fights.

A Warning Against Committing Adultery

20 My son, keep your father's commands.
Don't turn away from your mother's teaching.
21 Tie them to your heart forever.
Put them around your neck.
22 When you walk, they will guide you.
When you sleep, they will watch over you.
When you wake up, they will speak to you.

23 Your father's commands are like a lamp.
Your mother's teaching is like a light.
And the training that corrects you
leads to life.
24 It keeps you from a sinful woman.
It keeps you from the smooth tongue of a woman who commits adultery.
25 Don't hunger in your heart after her beauty.
Don't let her eyes capture you.
26 A prostitute leaves you with only a loaf of bread.
Another man's wife hunts your very life.
27 You can't shovel fire into your lap
without burning your clothes.
28 You can't walk on hot coals
without burning your feet.
29 It's the same for anyone who has sex with another man's wife.
Anyone who touches her will be punished.
30 People don't hate a thief who steals
to fill his empty stomach.
31 But when he is caught, he must pay seven times as much as he stole.
It may even cost him everything he has.
32 A man who commits adultery has no sense.
Anyone who does it destroys himself.
33 He will be beaten up and dishonored.
His shame will never be wiped away.
34 Jealousy stirs up a husband's anger.
He will show no mercy when he gets even.
35 He won't accept any payment.
He won't take any money, no matter how much he is offered.

A Warning Against a Woman Who Commits Adultery

7 My son, obey my words.
Store up my commands inside you.
2 Obey my commands and you will live.
Guard my teachings as you would your own eyes.
3 Tie them on your fingers.
Write them on the tablet of your heart.
4 Say to wisdom, "You are my sister."
Call understanding a member of your family.
5 They will keep you from a woman who commits adultery.
They will keep you from the smooth talk of a sinful wife.

6 I stood at the window of my house.
I looked out through it.
7 Among those who were childish
I saw a young man who had no sense.
8 He went down the street near that sinful woman's corner.
He walked toward her house.
9 The sun had gone down. Day was fading.
The darkness of night was falling.
10 A woman came out to meet him.
She was dressed like a prostitute and had a clever plan.
11 She was a loud and pushy woman.
She never stayed at home.
12 Sometimes in the streets, sometimes at other places,
at every corner she would wait.
13 She took hold of the young man and kissed him.
With a bold face she spoke to him.

14 She said, "At home I have meat left over from my offerings.
Today I offered what I had promised I would.
15 So I came out to meet you.
I looked for you. And I have found you!
16 I have covered my bed
with colored sheets from Egypt.
17 I've perfumed my bed with spices.
I used myrrh, aloes and cinnamon.
18 Come, let's drink our fill of love until morning.
Let's enjoy ourselves by having sex!
19 My husband isn't home.
He's gone on a long journey.
20 He took his bag full of money.
He won't be home for several days."

21 She led him down the wrong path with her clever words.
She charmed him with her smooth talk.
22 All at once he followed her.
He was like an ox going to be killed.
He was like a deer stepping into a trap
23 until an arrow struck its liver.
He was like a bird rushing into a trap.
Little did he know it would cost him his life!

24 My sons, listen to me.
Pay attention to what I say.
25 Don't let your hearts turn to her ways.
Don't step onto her paths.
26 She has brought down a lot of men.
She has killed a huge crowd.
27 Her house is a road to the grave.
It leads down to the place of the dead.

Wisdom Is Worth More Than Anything

8 Doesn't wisdom call out?
Doesn't understanding raise her voice?
2 On the high roads along the way,
she takes her place where the paths meet.
3 Beside the gates leading into the city,
she cries out at the entrances.
4 She says, "Men, I call out to you.
I raise my voice to all human beings.
5 You who are childish, get some good sense.
You who are foolish, gain understanding.
6 Listen! I have worthy things to say.
I open my lips to speak what is right.

7 My mouth speaks what is true.
My lips hate evil.
8 All the words of my mouth are honest.
None of them is twisted or sinful.
9 To those who have understanding, all my words are right.
To those who have knowledge, they are true.
10 Choose my teaching instead of silver.
Choose knowledge rather than fine gold.
11 Wisdom is worth more than rubies.
Nothing you want can compare with her.

12 "I, wisdom, live together with understanding.
I have knowledge and good sense.
13 To have respect for the LORD is to hate evil.
I hate pride and bragging.
I hate evil ways and twisted words.
14 I have good sense and give good advice.
I have understanding and power.
15 By me kings rule.
Leaders make laws that are fair.
16 By me princes govern.
By me all nobles rule on earth.
17 I love those who love me.
Those who look for me find me.
18 With me are riches and honor.
With me are lasting wealth and success.
19 My fruit is better than fine gold.
My gifts are better than the finest silver.
20 I walk in ways that are honest.
I take paths that are right.
21 I leave riches to those who love me.
I give them more than they have room for.

22 "The LORD created me as the first of his works,
before his acts of long ago.
23 I was formed at the very beginning.
I was formed before the world began.
24 Before there were any oceans, I was born.
There weren't any springs of water at that time.
25 Before the mountains were settled in place, I was born.
Before there were any hills, I was born.
26 It happened before the LORD made the earth and its fields.
It was before he made the dust of the world.
27 I was there when he set the heavens in place.
When he marked out the place where the sky meets the sea, I was there.
28 That was when he put the clouds above.
It was when he fixed the ocean springs in place.
29 It was when he set limits for the sea
so that the waters had to obey his command.
When he marked out the foundations of the earth, I was there.
30 I was the skilled worker at his side.
I was filled with delight day after day.
I was always happy to be with him.
31 His whole world filled me with joy.
I took delight in all human beings.

32 "My children, listen to me.
Blessed are those who keep my ways.
33 Listen to my teaching and be wise.
Don't turn away from it.
34 Blessed is the one who listens to me.
He watches every day at my doors.
He waits beside my doorway.
35 Those who find me find life.
They receive favor from the LORD.
36 But those who don't find me harm only themselves.
Everyone who hates me loves death."

Wisdom and Foolishness Call Out

9 Wisdom has built her house.
She has made its seven pillars.
2 She has prepared her meat and mixed her wine.
She has also set her table.
3 She has sent out her female servants.
She calls out from the highest point of the city.
4 She says, "Let all who are childish come in here!"
She speaks to those who have no sense.
5 "Come and eat my food.
Drink the wine I have mixed.
6 Leave your childish ways and you will live.
Walk in the way that leads to understanding.

7 "When you correct someone who makes fun of others, you might be laughed at.
When you warn a sinner, you might get hurt.
8 Don't warn those who make fun of others.
They will hate you.
Warn those who are wise. They will love you.
9 Teach a wise man. He will become even wiser.
Teach a person who does right. He will learn even more.

10 "If you really want to become wise, you must begin by having respect for the LORD.
To know the Holy One is to gain understanding.
11 Through me, you will live a long time.
Years will be added to your life.
12 If you are wise, your wisdom will reward you.
If you make fun of others, you alone will suffer."

13 The woman called Foolishness is loud.
She doesn't control herself. She doesn't know anything.
14 She sits at the door of her house.
She sits at the highest point of the city.
15 She calls out to those who pass by.
She calls out to those who go straight on their way.
16 She says, "Let all who are childish come in here!"
She speaks to those who have no sense.
17 She says, "Stolen water is sweet.
Food eaten in secret tastes good!"

18 But they don't know that dead people are there.
They don't know that her guests are in the deepest parts of the grave.

The Proverbs of Solomon

10 These are the proverbs of Solomon.

A wise son makes his father glad.
But a foolish son brings sorrow to his mother.

2 Riches that are gained by sinning aren't worth anything.
But doing what is right saves you from death.

3 The LORD gives those who do right the food they need.
But he lets those who do wrong go hungry.

4 Hands that don't want to work make you poor.
But hands that work hard bring wealth to you.

5 A child who gathers crops in summer is wise.
But a child who sleeps at harvest time brings shame.

6 Blessings are like crowns on the heads of those who do right.
But the trouble caused by what sinners say destroys them.

7 To remember those who do right is a blessing.
But the names of those who do wrong will rot.

8 A wise heart accepts commands.
But foolish chattering destroys you.

9 Anyone who lives without blame walks safely.
But anyone who takes a crooked path will get caught.

10 An evil wink gets you into trouble.
And foolish chattering destroys you.

11 The mouths of those who do right are a fountain of life.
But the trouble caused by what sinners say destroys them.

12 Hate stirs up fights.
But love erases all sins by forgiving them.

13 Wisdom is found on the lips of those who understand what is right.
But those who have no sense are punished.

14 Wise people store up knowledge.
But the mouths of foolish people destroy them.

15 The wealth of rich people is like a city that makes them feel safe.
But having nothing destroys those who are poor.

16 People who do what is right earn life.
But what sinners earn causes them to be punished.

17 Anyone who pays attention to his training is on his way to life.
But anyone who refuses to be corrected leads others down the wrong path.

18 Anyone who hides hatred has lying lips.
And anyone who spreads lies is foolish.

19 Those who talk a lot are likely to sin.
But those who control their tongues are wise.

20 The tongues of those who do right are like fine silver.
But the hearts of those who do wrong aren't worth very much.

21 The words of those who do right benefit many people.
But those who are foolish die because they have no sense.

22 The blessing of the LORD brings wealth.
Trouble doesn't come with it.

23 A foolish person finds pleasure in doing evil things.
But a man who has understanding takes delight in wisdom.

24 What sinners are afraid of will catch up with them.
But those who do right will get what they want.

25 When the storm is over, sinners are gone.
But those who do right stand firm forever.

26 Anyone who doesn't want to work hurts those who send him.
He is like vinegar on the teeth or smoke in the eyes.

27 Having respect for the LORD leads to a longer life.
But the years of evil people are cut short.

28 Those who do right can expect joy.
But the hopes of sinners are bound to fail.

29 The way of the LORD leads to a safe place for those who do right.
But it destroys those who do evil.

30 Those who do right will never be removed from the land.
But those who do wrong will not remain in it.

31 The mouths of those who do right produce wisdom.
But tongues that speak twisted words will be cut out.

32 Those who do right know the proper thing to say.
But those who do wrong speak only twisted words.

11 The LORD hates it when people use scales
to cheat others.
But he is delighted when people use honest
weights.

2 When pride comes, shame follows.
But wisdom comes to those who are
not proud.

3 Those who do what is right are guided by their
honest lives.
But those who aren't faithful are destroyed
by their trickery.

4 Wealth isn't worth anything when God
judges you.
But doing what is right saves you from
death.

5 The ways of honest people are made straight
because they do what is right.
But those who do what is wrong are brought
down by their own sins.

6 Godly people are saved by doing what is right.
But those who aren't faithful are trapped by
evil longings.

7 When an evil man dies, his hope dies with him.
Everything he expected to gain from his
power will be lost.

8 Those who do right are saved from trouble.
But trouble comes on those who do wrong.

9 With their words ungodly people destroy their
neighbors.
But those who do what is right escape
because of their knowledge.

10 When those who do right succeed, their city
is glad.
When those who do wrong die, people shout
for joy.

11 The blessing of honest people builds up a city.
But the words of sinners destroy it.

12 A person who has no sense makes fun of his
neighbor.
But a man who has understanding controls
his tongue.

13 Those who talk about others tell secrets.
But those who can be trusted keep things to
themselves.

14 Without the guidance of good leaders a nation
falls.
But many good advisers can save it.

15 Anyone who puts up money for what someone
else owes will certainly suffer.
But a person who doesn't agree to pay up
for someone else is safe.

16 A woman who has a kind heart gains respect.
But men who are not kind gain only wealth.

17 A kind man benefits himself.
But a mean person brings trouble on
himself.

18 Those who do what is wrong really earn
nothing.
But those who plant what is right will
certainly be rewarded.

19 Right living leads to life.
But anyone who runs after evil will die.

20 The LORD hates those whose hearts are twisted.
But he is pleased with those who live
without blame.

21 You can be sure that sinners will be punished.
And you can also be sure that godly people
will go free.

22 A beautiful woman who has no sense
is like a gold ring in a pig's nose.

23 What godly people long for ends only in what
is good.
But what sinners hope for ends only in
God's anger.

24 Some give freely but get even richer.
Others don't give what they should but get
even poorer.

25 Anyone who gives a lot will succeed.
Anyone who renews others will be renewed.

26 People call down curses on those who store up
grain for themselves.
But blessing makes those who are willing to
sell feel like kings.

27 Anyone who looks for what is good finds
favor.
But bad things happen to a person who
plans to do evil.

28 Those who trust in their riches will fall.
But those who do right will be as healthy as
a green leaf.

29 Those who bring trouble on their families will
receive nothing but wind.
And foolish people will serve wise people.

30 The fruit that godly people bear is like a tree
of life.
And those who lead others to do what is
right are wise.

31 Godly people get what they should get
on earth.
So ungodly people and sinners will certainly
get what they should get!

12 Anyone who loves to be trained loves
knowledge.
Anyone who hates to be corrected is stupid.

2 The LORD blesses anyone who does good.
But he judges any man who is tricky.

3 If a man does what is evil, he can't become strong and steady.
But if people do what is right, they can't be removed from the land.

4 A noble wife is her husband's crown.
But a wife who brings shame is like sickness in his bones.

5 The plans of godly people are right.
But the advice of sinners will lead you the wrong way.

6 The words of those who are evil hide and wait to spill people's blood.
But the speech of those who are honest saves them from traps like that.

7 Sinners are destroyed and taken away.
But the houses of godly people stand firm.

8 A man is praised for how wise he is.
But people hate those who have twisted minds.

9 Being nobody and having a servant
is better than pretending to be somebody and having no food.

10 Those who do what is right take good care of their animals.
But the kindest acts of those who do wrong are mean.

11 Anyone who farms his land will have plenty of food.
But a person who chases dreams has no sense.

12 Those who do what is wrong want to steal from others.
But those who do what is right bear good fruit because of their deep roots.

13 A sinner is trapped by his sinful talk.
But a godly person escapes trouble.

14 Many good things come from what a man says.
And the work of his hands rewards him.

15 The way of a foolish person seems right to him.
But a wise person listens to advice.

16 Foolish people are easily upset.
But wise people pay no attention to hurtful words.

17 An honest witness tells the truth.
But a dishonest witness tells lies.

18 Thoughtless words cut like a sword.
But the tongue of wise people brings healing.

19 Truthful words last forever.
But lies last for only a moment.

20 There are lies in the hearts of those who plan evil.
But there is joy for those who work to bring peace.

21 No harm comes to godly people.
But sinners have all the trouble they can handle.

22 The LORD hates those whose lips tell lies.
But he is pleased with people who tell the truth.

23 Wise people keep their knowledge to themselves.
But the hearts of foolish people shout foolish things.

24 Hands that work hard will rule.
But people who don't want to work will become slaves.

25 Worry makes a man's heart heavy.
But a kind word cheers him up.

26 Godly people are careful about the friends they choose.
But the way of sinners leads them down the wrong path.

27 Anyone who refuses to work doesn't even cook what he catches.
But a man who works hard values what he has.

28 There is life in doing what is right.
Along that path you will never die.

13 A wise child pays attention to what his father teaches him.
But anyone who makes fun of others doesn't listen to warnings.

2 The good things a man says benefit him.
But a liar loves to hurt others.

3 Anyone who guards what he says guards his life.
But anyone who speaks without thinking will be destroyed.

4 People who refuse to work want things and get nothing.
But the longings of people who work hard are completely satisfied.

5 Those who do right hate what is false.
But those who do wrong bring shame and dishonor.

6 Doing right guards those who are honest.
But evil destroys those who are sinful.

7 Some people pretend to be rich but have nothing.
Others pretend to be poor but have great wealth.

8 A man who is rich might have to pay to save his life.
But a poor person is not in danger of that.

9 The lights of godly people shine brightly.
But the lamps of sinners are blown out.

10 Pride only leads to arguing.
But those who take advice are wise.

11 Money that is gained in the wrong way
disappears.
But money that is gathered little by little
grows.

12 Hope that is put off makes one sick at heart.
But a longing that is met is like a tree of life.

13 Anyone who hates what he is taught will pay
for it later.
But a person who respects a command will
be rewarded.

14 The teaching of wise people is like a fountain
that gives life.
It turns those who listen to it away from the
jaws of death.

15 Good understanding wins favor.
But the way of liars doesn't last.

16 Wise people act in keeping with the knowledge
they have.
But foolish people show how foolish
they are.

17 An evil messenger gets into trouble.
But a messenger who is trusted brings
healing.

18 Those who turn away from their training
become poor and ashamed.
But those who accept warnings are honored.

19 A longing that is met is like something that
tastes sweet.
But foolish people hate to turn away
from evil.

20 Anyone who walks with wise people
grows wise.
But a companion of foolish people
suffers harm.

21 Hard times chase those who are sinful.
But success is the reward of those who
do right.

22 A good person leaves what he owns to his
children and grandchildren.
But a sinner's wealth is stored up for those
who do right.

23 The fields of poor people might produce a lot
of food.
But those who beat them down destroy
it all.

24 Those who don't correct their children hate
them.
But those who love them are careful to train
them.

25 Those who do right eat until they are full.
But the stomachs of those who do wrong
go hungry.

14 A wise woman builds her house.
But a foolish woman tears hers down
with her own hands.

2 An honest person has respect for the LORD.
But a person whose paths are crooked
hates him.

3 Foolish people are punished for what they say.
But the things wise people say keep them
safe.

4 Where there are no oxen, the feed box is
empty.
But a strong ox brings in a great harvest.

5 An honest witness does not lie.
But a dishonest witness pours out lies.

6 Those who make fun of others look for
wisdom and don't find it.
But knowledge comes easily to those who
understand what is right.

7 Stay away from a foolish man.
You won't find knowledge in what he says.

8 People are wise and understanding when they
think about the way they live.
But people are foolish when their foolish
ways trick them.

9 Foolish people laugh at making things right
when they sin.
But honest people try to do the right thing.

10 Each heart knows its own sadness.
And no one else can share its joy.

11 The houses of sinners will be destroyed.
But the tents of honest people will stand
firm.

12 There is a way that may seem right to a man.
But in the end it leads to death.

13 Even when you laugh, your heart can be
hurting.
And your joy can end in sadness.

14 Those who aren't faithful will be paid back
for what they've done.
And good men will receive rewards
for how they've lived.

15 A childish person believes anything.
But a wise person thinks about how he lives.

16 A wise person has respect for the LORD and
avoids evil.
But a foolish person gets mad and is
thoughtless.

17 Anyone who gets angry quickly does foolish
things.
And a man who is tricky is hated.

18 Childish people act in keeping with their foolish ways.
But knowledge makes wise people feel like kings.

19 Evil people will bow down in front of good people.
And those who do wrong will bow down at the gates of those who do right.

20 Poor people are avoided even by their neighbors.
But rich people have many friends.

21 Anyone who hates his neighbor commits sin.
But blessed is the person who is kind to those in need.

22 Those who plan evil go down the wrong path.
But those who plan good find love and truth.

23 All hard work pays off.
But if all you do is talk, you will be poor.

24 The wealth of wise people is their crown.
But the foolish ways of foolish people lead to what is foolish.

25 An honest witness saves lives.
But a dishonest witness tells lies.

26 Anyone who shows respect for the LORD has a strong tower.
It will be a safe place for his children.

27 Respect for the LORD is like a fountain that gives life.
It turns you away from the jaws of death.

28 A large population is a king's glory.
But a prince without followers is destroyed.

29 Anyone who is patient has great understanding.
But anyone who gets angry quickly shows how foolish he is.

30 A peaceful heart gives life to the body.
But jealousy rots the bones.

31 Anyone who crushes poor people makes fun of their Maker.
But anyone who is kind to those in need honors God.

32 When trouble comes, sinners are brought down.
But godly people have a safe place even when they die.

33 Wisdom rests in the hearts of those who understand what is right.
And even among foolish people she makes herself known.

34 Doing what is right lifts people up.
But sin brings shame to any nation.

35 A king is pleased with a wise servant.
But a servant who is full of shame invites the king's anger.

15 A gentle answer turns anger away.
But mean words stir up anger.

2 The tongues of wise people use knowledge well.
But the mouths of foolish people pour out foolish words.

3 The eyes of the LORD are everywhere.
They watch those who are evil and those who are good.

4 A tongue that brings healing is like a tree of life.
But a tongue that tells lies produces a broken spirit.

5 A foolish person turns his back on how his father has trained him.
But anyone who accepts being corrected shows understanding.

6 The houses of those who do what is right hold great wealth.
But those who do what is wrong earn only trouble.

7 The lips of wise people spread knowledge.
But that's not true of the hearts of foolish people.

8 The LORD hates the sacrifice of sinful people.
But the prayers of honest people please him.

9 The LORD hates how sinners live.
But he loves those who run after what is right.

10 Hard training is in store for anyone who leaves the right path.
A person who hates to be corrected will die.

11 Death and the Grave lie open in front of the LORD.
So the hearts of mere men certainly lie open to him!

12 Anyone who makes fun of others doesn't like to be corrected.
He won't ask wise people for advice.

13 A happy heart makes a face look cheerful.
But a sad heart produces a broken spirit.

14 A heart that understands what is right looks for knowledge.
But the mouths of foolish people feed on what is foolish.

15 All the days of those who are crushed are filled with pain and suffering.
But a cheerful heart enjoys a good time that never ends.

16 It is better to have respect for the LORD and have little
than to be rich and have trouble.

17 A meal of vegetables where there is love
is better than the finest meat where there is hatred.

18 A man who burns with anger stirs up fights.
But a person who is patient calms things down.
19 The way of people who don't want to work is blocked with thorns.
But the path of honest people is a wide road.
20 A wise son makes his father glad.
But a foolish son hates his mother.
21 A person who has no sense enjoys doing foolish things.
But a man who has understanding walks straight ahead.
22 Plans fail without good advice.
But they succeed when there are many advisers.
23 Joy is found in giving the right answer.
And how good is a word spoken at the right time!
24 The path of life leads up for those who are wise.
It keeps them from going down to the grave.
25 The LORD tears down the proud person's house.
But he keeps the widow's property safe.
26 The LORD hates the thoughts of sinful people.
But the thoughts of pure people are pleasing to him.
27 Anyone who always wants more brings trouble to his family.
But a person who refuses to be paid off will live.
28 The hearts of those who do right think about how they will answer.
But the mouths of those who do wrong pour out evil.
29 The LORD is far away from those who do wrong.
But he hears the prayers of those who do right.
30 A cheerful look brings joy to your heart.
And good news gives health to your body.
31 If you listen to a warning, you will live.
You will be at home among those who are wise.
32 Anyone who turns away from his training hates himself.
But anyone who accepts being corrected gains understanding.
33 Having respect for the LORD teaches you how to live wisely.
So don't be proud if you want to be honored.

16 People make plans in their hearts.
But the LORD controls what they say.
2 Everything a man does might seem right to him.
But the LORD knows what that man is thinking.
3 Commit to the LORD everything you do.
Then your plans will succeed.
4 The LORD works everything out for his own purposes.
Even those who do wrong were made for a day of trouble.
5 The LORD hates all those who have proud hearts.
You can be sure that they will be punished.
6 Through love and truth sin is paid for.
People avoid evil when they have respect for the LORD.
7 When the way you live pleases the LORD,
he makes even your enemies live at peace with you.
8 It is better to have a little and do right
than to have a lot and be unfair.
9 In your heart you plan your life.
But the LORD decides where your steps will take you.
10 A king might speak as if his words come from God.
But what he says should not turn right into wrong.
11 Honest scales and balances come from the LORD.
He made all of the weights in the bag.
12 A king hates it when his people do what is wrong.
A ruler is made secure when they do what is right.
13 Kings are pleased when what you say is honest.
They value people who speak the truth.
14 An angry king can order your death.
But a wise man will try to calm him down.
15 When a king's face is happy, it means life.
His favor is like rain in the spring.
16 It is much better to get wisdom than gold.
It is much better to choose understanding than silver.
17 The path of honest people takes them away from evil.
Those who guard their ways guard their lives.
18 If you are proud, you will be destroyed.
If you are proud, you will fall.

19 Suppose you are lowly in spirit and are with
those who are beaten down.
That's better than sharing stolen goods with
those who are proud.

20 If anyone pays attention to what he is taught,
he will succeed.
Blessed is the person who puts his trust in
the LORD.

21 Wise hearts are known for understanding what
is right.
Pleasant words make people want to learn
more.

22 Understanding is like a fountain of life to those
who have it.
But foolish people are punished for the
foolish things they do.

23 The hearts of wise people guide their mouths.
Their words make people want to learn
more.

24 Pleasant words are like honey.
They are sweet to the spirit and bring
healing to the body.

25 There is a way that may seem right to a man.
But in the end it leads to death.

26 The hunger of a worker makes him work.
His hunger drives him on.

27 A worthless man plans to do evil things.
His words are like a burning fire.

28 A twisted person stirs up fights.
Anyone who talks about others comes
between close friends.

29 A man who wants to hurt others tries to get
them to sin.
He leads them down a path that isn't good.

30 When he winks with his eyes, he is planning to
do wrong.
When his lips are tightly closed, he is up to
no good.

31 Gray hair is a glorious crown.
You get it by living the right way.

32 It is better to be patient than to fight.
It is better to control your temper than to
take a city.

33 Lots are cast into the lap to make decisions.
But everything they decide comes from
the LORD.

17 It is better to eat a dry crust of bread in
peace and quiet
than to eat a big dinner in a house that is full
of fighting.

2 A wise servant will rule over a shameful child.
He will be given part of the property as if he
were a family member.

3 Fire tests silver. Heat tests gold.
But the LORD tests our hearts.

4 An evil person listens to evil words.
A liar pays attention to words that are
harmful.

5 Anyone who laughs at those who are poor
makes fun of their Maker.
Anyone who is happy when others suffer
will be punished.

6 Grandchildren are like a crown to older people.
And children are proud of their parents.

7 It isn't proper for foolish people to brag.
And it certainly isn't proper for rulers to
tell lies!

8 Money buys favors for those who give it.
No matter where they turn, they succeed.

9 Those who erase a sin by forgiving it show love.
But those who talk about it come between
close friends.

10 A person who understands what is right learns
more from just a warning
than a foolish person learns from 100
strokes with a whip.

11 An evil person never wants to obey.
An official who shows no mercy will be
sent against him.

12 It is better to meet a bear whose cubs have
been stolen
than to meet a foolish person who is acting
foolishly.

13 Evil will never leave the house
of anyone who pays back evil for good.

14 Starting to argue is like making a crack in
a dam.
So drop the matter before a fight breaks out.

15 The LORD hates two things.
He hates it when the guilty are set free.
He also hates it when those who aren't
guilty are punished.

16 What good is money in the hands of a foolish
person?
He doesn't want to become wise.

17 A friend loves at all times.
He is there to help when trouble comes.

18 A man who has little sense agrees to pay what
other people owe.
It isn't wise to put up money for others.

19 The one who loves to argue loves to sin.
The one who builds a high gate is just
asking to be destroyed.

20 If your heart is twisted, you won't succeed.
If your tongue tells lies, you will get into
trouble.

[21] It is sad to have a foolish child.
The parents of a foolish person have no joy.

[22] A cheerful heart makes you healthy.
But a broken spirit dries you up.

[23] Anyone who does wrong accepts favors in secret.
Then he turns what is right into wrong.

[24] Anyone who understands what is right keeps wisdom in view.
But the eyes of a foolish person look everywhere else.

[25] A foolish child makes his father sad and his mother sorry.

[26] It isn't good to punish those who aren't guilty.
It isn't good to whip officials just because they are honest.

[27] Anyone who has knowledge controls his words.
A man who has understanding is not easily upset.

[28] We think even a foolish person is wise if he keeps silent.
We think he understands what is right if he controls his tongue.

18 A person who isn't friendly looks out only for himself.
He opposes all good sense.

[2] A foolish person doesn't want to understand.
He takes delight in saying only what he thinks.

[3] People hate it when evil comes.
And they refuse to honor those who bring shame.

[4] The words of a person's mouth are like deep water.
But the fountain of wisdom is like a flowing stream.

[5] It isn't good to favor those who do wrong.
And it isn't good to hold back what is fair from those who aren't guilty.

[6] What a foolish person says leads to arguing.
He is just asking for a beating.

[7] The words of a foolish person drag him down.
He is trapped by what he says.

[8] The words of anyone who talks about others are like tasty bites of food.
They go deep down inside you.

[9] Anyone who doesn't want to work is like someone who destroys.

[10] The name of the LORD is like a strong tower.
Godly people run to it and are safe.

[11] The wealth of rich people is like a city that makes them feel safe.
They think of it as a city with walls that can't be climbed.

[12] If a man's heart is proud, he will be destroyed.
So don't be proud if you want to be honored.

[13] To answer before listening is foolish and shameful.

[14] A man's cheerful heart gives him strength when he is sick.
You can't keep going if you have a broken spirit.

[15] Those whose hearts understand what is right get knowledge.
The ears of those who are wise listen for it.

[16] A gift opens the way for the one who gives it.
It helps him meet important people.

[17] The first one to tell his case seems right.
Then someone else comes forward and questions him.

[18] Casting lots will put a stop to arguing.
It will keep the strongest enemies apart.

[19] A broken friendship is harder to deal with than a city that has high walls around it.
And arguing is like the locked gates of a mighty city.

[20] A man can fill his stomach with what he says.
The words from his lips can satisfy him.

[21] Your tongue has the power of life and death.
Those who love to talk will eat the fruit of their words.

[22] The one who finds a wife finds what is good.
He receives favor from the LORD.

[23] Poor people beg for mercy.
But rich people answer in a mean way.

[24] Even a man who has many companions can be destroyed.
But there is a friend who sticks closer than a brother.

19 It is better to be poor and to live without blame
than to be foolish and to twist words around.

[2] It isn't good to get all stirred up without knowledge.
And it isn't good to be in a hurry and miss the way.

[3] A man's own foolish acts destroy his life.
But his heart is angry with the LORD.

[4] Wealth brings many friends.
But the friends of poor people leave them alone.

5 A dishonest witness will be punished.
And those who pour out lies will not go free.

6 Many try to win the favor of rulers.
And everyone is the friend of a man who gives gifts.

7 A poor person is avoided by his whole family.
His friends avoid him even more.
The poor person runs after them to beg.
But he can't find them.

8 Anyone who gets wisdom loves himself.
Anyone who values understanding succeeds.

9 A dishonest witness will be punished.
And those who pour out lies will die.

10 It isn't proper for a foolish person to live in great comfort.
And it is much worse when a slave rules over princes!

11 A man's wisdom makes him patient.
He will be honored if he forgives someone who sins against him.

12 A king's anger is like a lion's roar.
But his favor is like dew on the grass.

13 If a child is foolish, he destroys his father.
A nagging wife is like dripping that never stops.

14 You will receive houses and wealth from your parents.
But a wise wife is given by the LORD.

15 Anyone who doesn't want to work sleeps his life away.
And a person who refuses to work goes hungry.

16 Those who obey what they are taught guard their lives.
But those who don't care how they live will die.

17 Anyone who is kind to poor people lends to the LORD.
God will reward him for what he has done.

18 Train your child. Then there is hope.
Don't do anything to bring about his death.

19 Anyone who burns with anger must pay for it.
If you save him, you will have to do it again.

20 Listen to advice and accept what you are taught.
In the end you will be wise.

21 A man may have many plans in his heart.
But the LORD's purpose wins out in the end.

22 Every man longs for love that never fails.
It is better to be poor than to be a liar.

23 Having respect for the LORD leads to life.
Then you will be content and free from trouble.

24 A person who doesn't want to work leaves his hand in the dish.
He won't even bring it back up to his mouth!

25 If you whip a person who makes fun of others,
childish people will learn to be wise.
If you warn someone who already understands what is right,
he will gain even more knowledge.

26 A child who robs his father and drives out his mother
brings shame and dishonor.

27 My son, if you stop listening to what I teach you,
you will wander away from the words of knowledge.

28 A dishonest witness makes fun of what is right.
The mouths of those who do wrong gulp down evil.

29 Those who make fun of others will be judged.
Foolish people will be punished.

20 Wine causes you to make fun of others,
and beer causes you to start fights.
Anyone who is led down the wrong path by them is not wise.

2 A king's anger is like a lion's roar.
Anyone who makes him angry may lose his life.

3 Avoiding a fight brings honor to a man.
But every foolish person is quick to argue.

4 Anyone who refuses to work doesn't plow in the right season.
When he looks for a crop at harvest time, he doesn't find it.

5 The purposes of a man's heart are like deep water.
But a man who has understanding brings them out.

6 Many claim to have love that never fails.
But who can find a faithful man?

7 Anyone who does what is right lives without blame.
Blessed are his children after him.

8 A king sits on his throne to judge.
He gets rid of all evil when he sees it.

9 No one can say, "I have kept my heart pure.
I'm clean. I haven't sinned."

10 The LORD hates two things.
He hates weights that weigh things heavier or lighter than they really are.

He also hates measures that measure things
larger or smaller than they really are.

11 A child is known by his actions.
He is known by whether his conduct is pure
and right.

12 The LORD has made two things.
He has made ears that hear.
He has also made eyes that see.

13 Don't love sleep, or you will become poor.
Stay awake, and you will have more food
than you need.

14 "It's no good. It's no good!" says a buyer.
Then off he goes and brags about what
he bought.

15 There is gold. There are plenty of rubies.
But lips that speak knowledge are a
priceless jewel.

16 Take the coat of one who puts up money for
what a stranger owes.
Hold it until you get paid back if he does it
for a woman who commits adultery.

17 Food gained by cheating tastes sweet to a man.
But he will end up with a mouth full
of sand.

18 Make plans by asking for guidance.
If you go to war, get good advice.

19 A person who talks about others tells secrets.
So avoid anyone who talks too much.

20 If anyone calls down curses on his father
or mother,
his lamp will be blown out in total darkness.

21 Property you gain quickly at the beginning
will not be blessed in the end.

22 Don't say, "I'll get even with you for the
wrong you did to me!"
Wait for the LORD, and he will save you.

23 The LORD hates weights that weigh things
heavier or lighter than they really are.
Scales that are not honest don't please him.

24 The LORD directs a man's steps.
So how can anyone understand his
own way?

25 A man is trapped if he makes a hasty promise
to God
and only later thinks about what he said.

26 A wise king gets rid of evil people.
He runs the threshing wheel over them.

27 The lamp of the LORD searches a
man's heart.
It searches deep down inside him.

28 Love and truth keep a king safe.
Faithful love makes his throne secure.

29 Young men are proud of their strength.
Gray hair brings honor to old men.

30 Blows and wounds wash evil away.
And beatings make you pure deep down
inside.

21 The king's heart is in the hand of the
LORD.
He directs it like a stream of water
anywhere he pleases.

2 Everything a man does might seem right
to him.
But the LORD knows what he is thinking.

3 Do what is right and fair.
The LORD accepts that more than sacrifices.

4 Proud eyes and a proud heart are the lamp of
sinful people.
But those things are evil.

5 The plans of people who work hard succeed.
You can be sure that those in a hurry will
become poor.

6 A fortune made by people who tell lies
amounts to nothing and leads to death.

7 The harmful things that evil people do will
drag them away.
They refuse to do what is right.

8 The path of those who are guilty is crooked.
But the conduct of those who are not guilty
is honest.

9 It is better to live on a corner of a roof
than to share a house with a nagging wife.

10 A sinful person longs to do evil.
He doesn't show his neighbor any mercy.

11 When you punish someone who makes fun of
others, childish people get wise.
If you teach a person who is already wise,
he will get even more knowledge.

12 The Blameless One knows where
sinners live.
And he destroys them.

13 If you refuse to listen to the cries of
poor people,
you too will cry out and not be answered.

14 A secret gift calms anger down.
A hidden favor softens great anger.

15 When you do what is fair, you make godly
people glad.
But you terrify those who do what is evil.

16 A man who leaves the path of understanding
ends up with those who are dead.

17 Anyone who loves pleasure will become poor.
Anyone who loves wine and oil will never
be rich.

18 Those who do what is evil pay the price for
setting godly people free.
Those who aren't faithful pay the price for
honest people.

19 It is better to live in a desert
than to live with a nagging, angry wife.

20 The best food and olive oil are stored up in the
houses of wise people.
But a foolish man eats up everything he has.

21 Anyone who wants to be godly and loving
finds life, success and honor.

22 Those who are wise can attack a strong city.
They can pull down the place of safety its
people trust in.

23 Anyone who is careful about what he says
keeps himself out of trouble.

24 A proud person is called a "mocker."
He thinks much too highly of himself.

25 Some people will die while they are still
hungry.
That's because their hands refuse to work.
26 All day long they hunger for more.
But godly people give without holding back.

27 God hates sacrifices that are brought by
evil people.
He hates it even more when they bring them
for the wrong reason.

28 Witnesses who aren't honest will die.
And anyone who listens to them will be
destroyed forever.

29 A sinful man tries to look as if he were bold.
But an honest person thinks about how
he lives.

30 No wisdom, wise saying or plan
can succeed against the LORD.

31 You can prepare a horse for the day of battle.
But the power to win comes from the LORD.

22 You should want a good name more than
you want great riches.
To be highly respected is better than having
silver or gold.

2 The LORD made rich people and poor people.
That's what they have in common.

3 Wise people see danger and go to a safe place.
But childish people keep going and suffer
for it.

4 Have respect for the LORD and don't be proud.
That will bring you wealth and honor
and life.

5 Thorns and traps lie in the paths of evil people.
But those who guard themselves stay far
away from them.

6 Train a child in the way he should go.
When he is old, he will not turn away
from it.

7 Rich people rule over those who are poor.
Borrowers are slaves to lenders.

8 Anyone who plants evil gathers a harvest of
trouble.
His power to beat others down will be
destroyed.

9 Anyone who gives freely will be blessed.
That's because he shares his food with those
who are poor.

10 If you drive away those who make fun of
others, fighting also goes away.
Arguing and unkind words will stop.

11 Have a pure and loving heart, and speak
kindly.
Then you will be a friend of the king.

12 The eyes of the LORD keep watch over
knowledge.
But he does away with the words of those
who aren't faithful.

13 People who don't want to work say, "There's a
lion outside!"
Or they say, "I'll be murdered if I go out
into the streets!"

14 The mouth of a woman who commits adultery
is like a deep pit.
Any man the LORD is angry with will fall
into it.

15 A child is going to do foolish things.
But correcting him will drive his foolishness
far away from him.

16 One person may beat poor people down in
order to get rich.
Another person may give gifts to rich people.
Both of them will become poor.

Sayings of Those Who Are Wise

17 Pay attention and listen to the sayings of those
who are wise.
Apply your heart to the sayings I teach.
18 It is pleasing when you keep them in
your heart.
Have all of them ready on your lips.
19 You are the one I am teaching today.
I want you to trust in the LORD.
20 I have written 30 sayings for you.
They will give you knowledge and
good advice.
21 I am teaching you words that are completely
true.
Then you can give the right answers to the
one who sent you.

1.

22 Don't take advantage of poor people just
because they are poor.
Don't beat down those who are in need by
taking them to court.
23 The LORD will stand up for them in court.
He will take back the stolen goods from
those who have robbed them.

2.

24 Don't be a friend with anyone who burns
with anger.
Don't go around with a person who gets
angry easily.
25 You might learn his habits.
And then you will be trapped by them.

3.

26 Don't agree to pay for
what someone else owes.
27 Don't put up money for him.
If you don't have the money to pay,
your bed will be taken right out from
under you!

4.

28 Don't move old boundary stones
that your people set up long ago.

5.

29 Do you see a man who does good work?
He will serve kings.
He won't serve ordinary people.

6.

23 When you sit down to eat with a ruler,
look carefully at what's in front of you.
2 Put a knife to your throat
if you like to eat too much.
3 Don't long for his fancy food.
It can fool you.

7.

4 Don't wear yourself out to get rich.
Be wise enough to say no.
5 When you take even a quick look at riches,
they are gone.
They grow wings and fly away into the sky
like an eagle.

8.

6 Don't eat the food of anyone who won't
share it.
Don't long for his fancy food.
7 He is the kind of person
who is always thinking about how much
it costs.
"Eat and drink," he says to you.
But he doesn't mean it.
8 You will throw up what little you have eaten.
You will have wasted your words of praise.

9.

9 Don't speak to a foolish person.
He will laugh at your wise words.

10.

10 Don't move old boundary stones.
Don't try to take over the fields of children
whose fathers have died.
11 The One who guards them is strong.
He will stand up for them in court
against you.

11.

12 Apply your heart to what you are taught.
Listen carefully to words of knowledge.

12.

13 Don't hold back training from a child.
If you correct him, he won't die.
14 So correct him.
Then you will save him from death.

13.

15 My child, if your heart is wise,
my heart will be glad.
16 Deep down inside, I will be happy
when you say what is right.

14.

17 Do not long for what sinners have.
But always show great respect for the LORD.
18 There really is hope for you tomorrow.
So your hope will not be cut off.

15.

19 My child, listen and be wise.
Keep your heart on the right path.
20 Don't join those who drink too much wine.
Don't join those who stuff themselves
with meat.
21 Those who drink or eat too much will
become poor.
If they sleep too much, they'll have to
wear rags.

16.

22 Listen to your father, who gave you life.
Don't hate your mother when she is old.

23 Buy the truth. Don't sell it.
Get wisdom, training and understanding.
24 The father of a godly child is very happy.
Anyone who has a wise child is glad.
25 May your father and mother be glad.
May the woman who gave birth to you
be happy.

17.

26 My son, give me your heart.
Keep your eyes on the way I live.
27 A prostitute is like a deep pit.
A wife who commits adultery is like a
narrow well.
28 She hides and waits like a thief.
She causes many men to sin.

18.

29 Who has trouble? Who has sorrow?
Who argues? Who has problems?
Who has wounds for no reason? Who has
red eyes?
30 Those who spend too much time with wine.
Or those who like to taste wine that is mixed
with spices.
31 Don't look at wine when it is red.
Don't look at it when it bubbles in the cup.
And don't look at it when it goes down
smoothly.
32 In the end it bites like a snake.
It bites like a poisonous serpent.
33 Your eyes will see strange sights.
Your mind will imagine weird things.
34 You will feel like someone sleeping on
the ocean.
You will think you are lying among the
ropes in a boat.
35 "They hit me," you will say. "But I'm not hurt!
They beat me. But I don't feel it!
When will I wake up
so I can find another drink?"

19.

24 Do not want what evil men have.
Don't long to be with them.
2 In their hearts they plan to hurt others.
With their lips they talk about making trouble.

20.

3 By wisdom a house is built.
Through understanding it is made secure.
4 Through knowledge its rooms are filled
with priceless and beautiful things.

21.

5 A wise man has great power.
A man who has knowledge increases his
strength.
6 If you go to war, you need guidance.
If you want to win, you need many good
advisers.

22.

7 Wisdom is too high for anyone who is
foolish.
He has nothing to say when people meet at
the city gate to conduct business.

23.

8 Anyone who thinks up sinful things to do
will be known as one who plans evil.
9 Foolish plans are sinful.
People hate those who make fun of others.

24.

10 If you grow weak when trouble comes,
your strength is very small!

25.

11 Save those who are being led away to death.
Hold back those who are about to
be killed.
12 Don't say, "But we didn't know anything
about this."
The One who knows what you are thinking
sees it.
The One who guards your life knows it.
He will pay each person back for what he
has done.

26.

13 Eat honey, my child. It is good.
Honey from a honeycomb has a sweet taste.
14 I want you to know that wisdom is sweet
to you.
If you find it, there is hope for you
tomorrow.
So your hope will not be cut off.

27.

15 Don't hide and wait like a burglar at a godly
person's house.
Don't rob his home.
16 Even if godly people fall down seven times,
they always get up.
But those who are evil are brought down
by trouble.

28.

17 Don't be happy when your enemy falls.
When he trips, don't let your heart be glad.
18 The LORD will see it, but he won't be pleased.
He might turn his anger away from your
enemy.

29.

19 Don't be upset because of evil people.
Don't long for what sinners have.
20 Tomorrow evil people won't have any hope.
The lamps of sinners will be blown out.

30.

21 My son, have respect for the LORD and the king.
Don't join those who disobey them.
22 The LORD and the king will suddenly destroy them.
Who knows what trouble those two can bring?

More Sayings of Those Who Are Wise

23 Here are more sayings of those who are wise.

Taking sides in court is not good.
24 A curse will fall on those who say the guilty are not guilty.
Nations will call down curses on them.
People will speak against them.
25 But it will go well with those who sentence guilty people.
Rich blessings will come to them.

26 An honest answer
is like a kiss on the lips.

27 Finish your outdoor work.
Get your fields ready.
After that, build your house.

28 Don't give witness against your neighbor without any reason.
Don't use your lips to tell lies.
29 Don't say, "I'll do to him what he did to me.
I'll get even with that man for what he did."

30 I went past the field of someone who didn't want to work.
I went past the vineyard of a man who didn't have any sense.
31 Thorns had grown up everywhere.
The ground was covered with weeds.
The stone wall had fallen down.
32 I applied my heart to what I observed.
I learned a lesson from what I saw.
33 You might sleep a little or take a little nap.
You might even fold your hands and rest.
34 Then you would be poor, as if someone had robbed you.
You would have little, as if someone had stolen from you.

More Proverbs of Solomon

25 These are more proverbs of Solomon. They were copied down by the men of Hezekiah, the king of Judah.

2 When God hides a matter, he gets glory.
When kings figure out a matter, they get glory.

3 The heavens are high and the earth is deep.
In the same way, the minds of kings are hard to figure out.

4 Remove the scum from the silver.
Then the master worker can make something.
5 Remove sinful people from where the king is.
When he does what is right, his kingdom will be secure.

6 Don't brag in front of the king.
Don't claim a place among great people.
7 Let the king say to you, "Come up here."
That's better than for him to shame you in front of nobles.

What you have seen with your own eyes
8 don't bring too quickly to court.
What will you do in the end
if your neighbor puts you to shame?

9 If you talk about a matter with your neighbor,
don't tell others what was said.
10 If you do, someone might hear it and put you to shame.
Then no one will ever respect you again.

11 The right word at the right time
is like golden apples in silver jewelry.

12 A wise person's warning to a listening ear
is like a gold earring or jewelry made of fine gold.

13 A messenger trusted by those who send him
is like cool snow at harvest time.
He renews the spirit of his masters.

14 A man who brags about gifts he doesn't give
is like wind and clouds that don't produce rain.

15 If you are patient, you can win an official over to your side.
And gentle words can break a bone.

16 If you find honey, eat just enough.
If you eat too much of it, you will throw up.
17 Don't go to your neighbor's home very often.
If he sees too much of you, he will hate you.

18 A man who gives false witness against his neighbor
is like a club, a sword or a sharp arrow.

19 Trusting someone who is not faithful when trouble comes
is like a bad tooth or a disabled foot.

20 You may sing songs to a troubled heart.
But that's like taking a coat away on a cold day.
It's like pouring vinegar on baking soda.

21 If your enemy is hungry, give him food
to eat.
If he is thirsty, give him water to drink.
22 By doing those things, you will pile up burning
coals on his head.
And the LORD will reward you.

23 The north wind brings rain.
And a crafty tongue brings angry looks.

24 It is better to live on a corner of a roof
than to share a house with a nagging wife.

25 Hearing good news from a land far away
is like drinking cold water when you
are tired.

26 Sometimes a godly person gives in to those
who are evil.
Then he becomes like a muddy spring of
water or a polluted well.

27 It isn't good for you to eat too much honey.
And you shouldn't try to get others to
honor you.

28 A man who can't control himself
is like a city whose walls are broken down.

26 It isn't proper to honor a foolish person.
That's like having snow in summer or
rain at harvest time.

2 A curse given for no reason is like a wandering
bird or a flying sparrow.
It doesn't go anywhere.

3 A whip is for a horse. A harness is for
a donkey.
And a beating is for the backs of foolish
people.

4 Don't answer a foolish person in keeping with
his foolish acts.
If you do, you will be like him yourself.

5 Answer a foolish person in keeping with his
foolish acts.
If you do, he won't be wise in his own eyes.

6 Sending a message in the hand of a foolish
person
is like cutting off your feet or drinking
something harmful.

7 A proverb in the mouth of a foolish person
is like disabled legs that are useless.

8 Giving honor to a foolish person
is like tying a stone in a slingshot.

9 A proverb in the mouth of a foolish person
is like a thorn in the hand of someone who
is drunk.

10 Anyone who hires a foolish person or someone
who is passing by
is like a person who shoots arrows at just
anybody.

11 A foolish person who does the same foolish
things again
is like a dog that returns to where it has
thrown up.

12 Do you see a man who is wise in his own eyes?
There is more hope for a foolish person than
for him.

13 A person who doesn't want to work says,
"There's a lion in the road!
There's an angry lion wandering in the
streets!"

14 A person who doesn't want to work turns over
in bed
just like a door that swings back and forth.

15 A person who doesn't want to work leaves his
hand in the dish.
He acts as if he is too tired to bring it back
up to his mouth.

16 A person who doesn't want to work is wiser in
his own eyes
than seven people who give careful answers.

17 Don't get mixed up in someone else's fight as
you are passing by.
That's like picking a dog up by its ears.

18 Suppose a crazy person shoots
flaming arrows that can kill.
19 A man who lies to his neighbor
and says, "I was only joking!" is just like
that person.

20 If you don't have wood, your fire goes out.
If you don't talk about others, arguing
dies down.
21 Coal glows. Wood burns.
And a man who argues stirs up fights.
22 The words of anyone who talks about others
are like tasty bites of food.
They go deep down inside you.

23 Warm words that come from an evil heart
are like shiny paint on a clay pot.

24 Someone who wants to hurt you uses his words
to hide his hatred.
But his heart is full of lies that cover up his
evil plans.
25 What a person says can be charming. But don't
believe him.
Seven things that God hates can fill that
person's heart.
26 Hatred can be hidden by lies.
But what is evil will be shown to everyone.

27 If anyone digs a pit, he will fall into it.
If he rolls a big stone, it will roll back
on him.

28 A tongue that tells lies hates the people it hurts.
And words that seem to praise you destroy
you.

27 Don't brag about tomorrow.
You don't know what a day will bring.
2 Let another person praise you, and not your own mouth.
Let someone else praise you, and not your own lips.

3 Stones are heavy. Sand weighs a lot.
But letting a foolish person make you angry is a heavier load than both of them.

4 Anger is mean. Great anger overpowers you.
But who can face jealousy?
5 Being warned openly is better
than being loved in secret.

6 Wounds from a friend can be trusted.
But an enemy kisses you many times.
7 When you are full, you even hate honey.
When you are hungry, even what is bitter tastes sweet.

8 A man who wanders away from his home
is like a bird that wanders from its nest.

9 Perfume and incense bring joy to your heart.
And a friend is sweeter when he gives you honest advice.

10 Don't desert your friend or your father's friend.
And don't go to your family when trouble strikes you.
A neighbor nearby is better than a family member far away.

11 My child, be wise and bring joy to my heart.
Then I can answer anyone who makes fun of me.
12 Wise people see danger and go to a safe place.
But childish people keep on going and suffer for it.
13 Take the coat of one who puts up money for what a stranger owes.
Hold it until you get paid back if he does it for a woman who commits adultery.
14 Suppose you loudly bless your neighbor early in the morning.
Then you might as well be calling down a curse on him.

15 A nagging wife is like
dripping that never stops on a rainy day.
16 Stopping her is like trying to stop the wind.
It's like trying to grab oil with your hand.

17 As iron sharpens iron,
so one person sharpens another.

18 A person who takes good care of a fig tree will eat its fruit.
And a person who looks after his master will be honored.

19 When you look into water, you see a likeness of your face.
When you look into your heart, you see what you are really like.

20 Death and the Grave are never satisfied.
A man's eyes are never satisfied either.

21 Fire tests silver. Heat tests gold.
But a man is tested by the praise he receives.

22 You can grind a foolish person in a mill.
You can grind him as you would grind grain with a tool.
But you can't remove his foolishness from him.

23 Be sure you know how your flocks are doing.
Pay careful attention to your herds.
24 Riches don't last forever.
And a crown is not secure for all time to come.
25 The hay is removed, and new growth appears.
The grass from the hills is gathered in.
26 Then your lambs will provide you with clothes.
And the money from selling your goats will buy you a field.
27 You will have plenty of goats' milk.
It will feed you and your family.
It will also feed your female servants.

28 Sinners run away even when no one is chasing them.
But those who do what is right are as bold as lions.

2 A country has many rulers when its people don't obey.
But an understanding king knows how to keep order.

3 A ruler who beats poor people down
is like a pounding rain that leaves no crops.

4 Those who turn away from the law praise sinners.
But those who obey the law oppose them.

5 Sinful men don't understand what is fair.
But those who worship the LORD understand it completely.

6 It is better to be poor and live without blame
than to be rich and follow a crooked path.

7 A child who obeys the law understands what is right.
But a child who likes to eat too much brings shame on his father.

8 A person who increases his wealth by charging high interest
piles it up for someone who will be kind to poor people.

9 If you don't pay attention to the law,
even your prayers are hated.

10 Those who lead honest people down an
evil path
will fall into their own trap.
But those who are without blame
will receive good things.

11 Rich people may be wise in their own eyes.
But a poor person who understands what is
right knows what they are really like.

12 When godly people win, everyone is very
happy.
But when sinners take charge, everyone
hides.

13 Anyone who hides his sins doesn't succeed.
But anyone who admits his sins and gives
them up finds mercy.

14 Blessed is the one who always has respect for
the LORD.
But anyone who is stubborn will get
into trouble.

15 An evil person who rules over helpless people
is like a roaring lion or an angry bear.

16 A ruler who is mean to his people doesn't have
any sense.
But anyone who hates money gained in the
wrong way will enjoy a long life.

17 A man who is troubled because he is guilty of
murder
will be on the run until the day he dies.
No one should give him any help.

18 Anyone who lives without blame is kept safe.
But anyone whose path is crooked will
suddenly fall.

19 Anyone who farms his land will have plenty
of food.
But anyone who chases dreams will be
very poor.

20 A faithful man will be richly blessed.
But anyone who wants to get rich will be
punished.

21 Favoring one person over another is not good.
But some men will do wrong for a piece
of bread.

22 A man who won't share what he has wants to
get rich.
He doesn't know he is going to be poor.

23 It is better to warn a man than to pretend to
praise him.
In the end he will be more pleased with you.

24 Anyone who steals from his parents and says,
"It's not wrong,"
is just like a man who destroys.

25 A person who always wants more stirs
up fights.
But anyone who trusts in the LORD will
succeed.

26 Anyone who trusts in himself is foolish.
But a person who lives wisely is kept safe.

27 Those who give to poor people
will have everything they need.
But those who close their eyes to the poor
will be under many curses.

28 When those who are evil take charge, other
people hide.
But when those who are evil die, godly
people grow stronger.

29 A man who still won't obey after being
warned many times
will suddenly be destroyed. Nothing can
save him.

2 When those who do right grow stronger, the
people are glad.
But when those who do wrong become
rulers, the people groan.

3 A man who loves wisdom makes his
father glad.
But a man who spends time with prostitutes
wastes his father's wealth.

4 By doing what is fair, a king makes a country
secure.
But the one who wants to be paid off tears
it down.

5 A man who only pretends to praise his
neighbor
is spreading a net to catch him by the feet.

6 A sinful man is trapped by his own sin.
But a godly person can sing and be glad.

7 Those who do what is right want to treat poor
people fairly.
But those who do what is wrong don't care
about the poor.

8 Those who make fun of others stir up a city.
But wise people turn anger away.

9 Suppose a wise man goes to court with a
foolish person.
Then the foolish person gets mad and pokes
fun. And there is no peace.

10 Murderers hate honest people.
They try to kill those who do what is right.

11 A foolish person lets his anger run wild.
But a wise person keeps himself under
control.

12 If rulers listen to lies,
all their officials become evil.

13 The LORD gives sight to the eyes of poor people and those who beat others down.
That's what they both have in common.

14 If a king judges poor people fairly,
his throne will always be secure.

[15] If a child is corrected, he becomes wise.
But a child left to himself brings shame to his mother.

[16] When those who do wrong grow stronger, so does sin.
But those who do right will see them destroyed.

[17] If you train your children, they will give you peace.
They will bring delight to you.

[18] Where there is no message from God, the people don't control themselves.
But blessed are those who obey the law.

[19] A servant can't be corrected only by words.
Even if he understands, he won't obey.

[20] Have you seen a man who speaks without thinking?
There is more hope for foolish people than for him.

[21] If you spoil your servant while he is young,
he will bring you sorrow later on.

[22] An angry man stirs up fights.
And a person who burns with anger commits many sins.

[23] If a man is proud, he will be made low.
But if he isn't proud, he will be honored.

[24] Anyone who helps a thief is his own enemy.
When he is put under oath, he doesn't dare give witness.

[25] If you are afraid of people, it will trap you.
But if you trust in the LORD, he will keep you safe.

[26] Many people want to meet a ruler.
But only the LORD sees that people are treated fairly.

[27] Those who do what is right hate dishonest people.
Those who do what is wrong hate honest people.

The Sayings of Agur

30 These sayings are the words of Agur, son of Jakeh. He spoke them as if they came from God.

He spoke them to Ithiel
and to Ucal.

[2] He said, "I know less than anyone.
I don't understand as other men do.
[3] I haven't learned wisdom.
And I don't know the Holy One.
[4] Who has gone up to heaven and come down?
Who has gathered up the wind in the palms of his hands?
Who has wrapped up the waters in his coat?
Who has set all the boundaries of the earth in place?
What is his name? What is his son's name?
Tell me if you know!

[5] "Every word of God is perfect.
He is like a shield to those who trust in him.
He keeps them safe.
[6] Don't add to his words.
If you do, he will correct you.
He will prove that you are a liar.

[7] "LORD, I ask you for two things.
Don't refuse me before I die.
[8] Keep lies far away from me.
Don't make me either poor or rich,
but give me only the bread I need each day.
[9] If you don't, I might have too much.
Then I might say I don't know you.
I might say, 'Who is the LORD?'
Or I might become poor and steal.
Then I would bring shame to the name of my God.

[10] "Don't tell lies about a servant when you talk to his master.
If you do, he will call down curses on you.
And you will pay for it.

[11] "Some people call down curses on their fathers.
Others don't bless their mothers.
[12] Some are pure in their own eyes.
But their dirty sins haven't been washed away.
[13] Some have eyes that are very proud.
They look down on others.
[14] Some people have teeth like swords.
The teeth in their jaws are as sharp as knives.
They are ready to eat up the poor people of the earth.
They are ready to eat up those who are the most needy.

[15] "A bloodsucking worm has two daughters.
They cry out, 'Give! Give!'
"Three things are never satisfied.
Four things never say, 'Enough!'
[16] The first is the grave.
The second is a woman who can't have a baby.
The third is land. It never gets enough water.
And the fourth is fire. It never says, 'Enough!'

[17] "Some make fun of their fathers.
Others laugh about obeying their mothers.
The ravens of the valley will peck their eyes out.
Then the vultures will eat them.

[18] "Three things are too amazing for me.
There are four things I don't understand.

19 The first is the way of an eagle in the sky.
The second is the way of a snake on a rock.
The third is the way of a ship on the ocean.
And the fourth is the way of a man with a young woman.

20 "This is the way of a woman who commits adultery.
She eats. She wipes her mouth.
Then she says, 'I haven't done anything wrong.'

21 "Under three things the earth shakes.
Under four things it can't stand up.
22 The first is a servant who becomes a king.
The second is a foolish person who is full of food.
23 The third is a woman who is married but not loved by her husband.
And the fourth is a woman servant who takes the place of the woman she works for.

24 "Four things on earth are small.
But they are very wise.
25 The first are ants. They aren't very strong.
But they store up their food in the summer.
26 The second are rock badgers. They aren't very powerful.
But they make their home among the rocks.
27 The third are locusts. They don't have a king.
But they all march forward in ranks.
28 And the fourth are lizards. Your hand can catch them.
But you will find them in kings' palaces.

29 "Three things walk as if they were kings.
Four things move as kings do.
30 The first is a lion. It is mighty among the animals.
It doesn't back away from anything.
31 The second is a rooster that walks proudly.
The third is a billy goat.
And the fourth is a king who has his army around him.

32 "Have you been foolish?
Have you thought you were better than others?
Have you planned evil?
If you have, put your hand over your mouth and stop talking!
33 If you churn cream, you will produce butter.
If you twist a nose, you will produce blood.
And if you stir up anger, you will produce a fight."

The Sayings of King Lemuel

31 These are the sayings of King Lemuel. His mother taught them to him. She spoke them as if they came from God.

2 She said, "My son! My very own son!
The son I prayed for!
3 Don't waste your strength on women.
Don't waste it on those who destroy kings.
4 "Lemuel, it isn't good for kings to drink wine.
It isn't good for rulers to long for beer.
5 If they do, they might drink and forget what the law commands.
They might take away the rights of all those who are beaten down.
6 Give beer to those who are dying.
Give wine to those who are sad and troubled.
7 Let them drink and forget how poor they are.
Let them forget their suffering.

8 "Speak up for those who can't speak for themselves.
Speak up for the rights of all those who are poor.
9 Speak up and judge fairly.
Speak up for the rights of those who are poor and needy."

The Noble Wife

10 Who can find a noble wife?
She is worth far more than rubies.
11 Her husband trusts her completely.
She gives him all the important things he needs.
12 She brings him good, not harm,
all the days of her life.
13 She chooses wool and flax.
She loves to work with her hands.
14 She is like the ships of traders.
She brings her food from far away.
15 She gets up while it is still dark.
She provides food for her family.
She also gives some to her female servants.
16 She considers a field and buys it.
She uses some of the money she earns to plant a vineyard.
17 She gets ready to work hard.
Her arms are strong.
18 She sees that her trading earns a lot of money.
Her lamp doesn't go out at night.
19 With one hand she holds the wool.
With the other she spins the thread.
20 She opens her arms to those who are poor.
She reaches out her hands to those who are needy.
21 When it snows, she's not afraid for her family.
All of them are dressed in the finest clothes.
22 She makes her own bed coverings.
She is dressed in fine linen and purple clothes.
23 Her husband is respected at the city gate.
There he takes his seat among the elders of the land.
24 She makes linen clothes and sells them.
She supplies belts to the traders.

25 She puts on strength and honor as if they were
her clothes.
She can laugh at the days that are coming.
26 She speaks wisely.
She teaches faithfully.
27 She watches over family matters.
She is busy all the time.
28 Her children stand up and call her blessed.
Her husband also rises up, and he praises her.
29 He says, "Many women do noble
things.
But you are better than all the others."
30 Charm can fool you. Beauty fades.
But a woman who has respect for the LORD
should be praised.
31 Give her the reward she has earned.
Let everything she has done bring praise to
her at the city gate.

Ecclesiastes

Nothing Has Any Meaning

1 These are the words of the Teacher. He was the son of David. He was also king in Jerusalem.

2 "Meaningless! Everything is meaningless!"
says the Teacher.
"Everything is completely meaningless!
Nothing has any meaning."

3 What does a man get for all of his work?
Why does he work so hard on this earth?
4 People come and people go.
But the earth remains forever.
5 The sun rises. Then it sets.
And then it hurries back to where it rises.
6 The wind blows to the south.
Then it turns to the north.
Around and around it goes.
It always returns to where it started.
7 Every stream flows into the ocean.
But the ocean never gets full.
The streams return
to the place they came from.
8 All things are tiresome.
They are more tiresome than anyone can say.
But our eyes never see enough of anything.
Our ears never hear enough.
9 Everything that has ever been will come back again.
Everything that has ever been done will be done again.
Nothing is new on earth.
10 There isn't anything about which someone can say,
"Look! Here's something new."
It was already here long ago.
It was here before we were.
11 No one remembers the men of long ago.
Even those who haven't been born yet
won't be remembered
by those who will be born after them.

Wisdom Doesn't Have Any Meaning

12 I, the Teacher, was king over Israel in Jerusalem. 13 I spent all of my time studying. I used my
wisdom to check everything out. I looked into
everything that is done on earth. What a heavy
load God has put on men!
14 I've seen what is done on this earth. It doesn't
have any meaning. It's like chasing the wind.

15 People can't straighten things that are twisted.
They can't count things that don't even exist.

16 I said to myself, "Look, my wisdom has really
been growing. In fact, I'm now wiser than anyone
who ruled over Jerusalem in the past. I have a lot
of wisdom and knowledge."
17 Then I used my mind to understand what it
really means to be wise. And I wanted to know
what foolish pleasure is all about. But I found out
that that's also like chasing the wind.

18 A lot of human wisdom leads to a lot of sorrow.
More knowledge only brings more sadness.

Pleasure Doesn't Have Any Meaning

2 I said to myself, "Come on. I'll put pleasure to
the test. I want to find out what is good." But
that also proved to be meaningless.
2 "Laughter is foolish," I said. "And what can
pleasure do for me?" 3 I tried cheering myself up
by drinking wine. I even tried living in a foolish
way. But wisdom was still guiding my mind. I
wanted to see what was really important for men
to do on earth during the few days of their lives.
4 So I started some large projects. I built houses
for myself. I planted vineyards. 5 I made gardens
and parks. I planted all kinds of fruit trees in them.
6 I made lakes to water groves of healthy trees.
7 I bought male and female slaves. And I had
other slaves who were born in my house. I also
owned more herds and flocks than anyone in Jerusalem ever had before. 8 I stored up silver and
gold for myself. I gathered up the treasures of
kings and their kingdoms. I got some male and
female singers. I also got many women for myself.
Women delight the hearts of men.
9 I became far more important than anyone in Jerusalem had ever been before. And in spite of
everything, I didn't lose my wisdom.

10 I gave myself everything my eyes wanted.
There wasn't any pleasure that I refused to give myself.
I took delight in everything I did.
And that was what I got for all of my work.
11 But then I looked over everything my hands had done.
I saw what I had worked so hard to get.
And nothing had any meaning.
It was like chasing the wind.
Nothing was gained on this earth.

Wisdom and Foolish Pleasure Don't Have Any Meaning

12 I decided to think about wisdom.
I also thought about foolish pleasure.
What more can a new king do?
Can he do anything more than others have already done?
13 I saw that wisdom is better than foolishness,
just as light is better than darkness.

[14] The eyes of a wise man see things clearly.
A person who is foolish lives in darkness.
But I finally realized that death catches up
with both of them.

[15] Then I thought,

"What happens to a foolish person will catch
up with me too.
So what do I gain by being wise?"
I said to myself,
"That doesn't have any meaning either."
[16] Like a foolish person, a wise man won't be
remembered very long.
In days to come, both of them will be
forgotten.
Like a person who is foolish,
a wise man must die too!

Work Doesn't Have Any Meaning

[17] So I hated life. That's because the work that is done on this earth made me sad. None of it has any meaning. It's like chasing the wind.

[18] I hated everything I had worked for on earth. I'll have to leave all of it to someone who lives after me. [19] And who knows whether he will be wise or foolish? Either way, he'll take over everything on earth I've worked so hard for. That doesn't have any meaning either.

[20] So I began to lose hope because of all of my hard work on this earth. [21] A man might use wisdom, knowledge and skill to do his work. But then he has to leave everything he owns to someone who hasn't worked for it. That doesn't have any meaning either. In fact, it isn't fair.

[22] What does a man get for all of his hard work on earth? What does he get for all of his worries? [23] As long as he lives, his work is nothing but pain and sorrow. Even at night his mind can't rest. That doesn't have any meaning either.

[24] A man can't do anything better than eat and drink and be satisfied with his work. I'm finally seeing that those things also come from the hand of God. [25] Without his help, who can eat or find pleasure?

[26] God gives wisdom, knowledge and happiness to a man who pleases him. But to a sinner he gives the task of gathering and storing up wealth. Then the sinner must hand it over to the one who pleases God. That doesn't have any meaning either. It's like chasing the wind.

There Is a Time for Everything

3 There is a time for everything.
There's a time for everything that is done on
earth.

[2] There is a time to be born.
And there's a time to die.
There is a time to plant.
And there's a time to pull up what is
planted.
[3] There is a time to kill.
And there's a time to heal.
There is a time to tear down.
And there's a time to build up.
[4] There is a time to cry.
And there's a time to laugh.
There is a time to be sad.
And there's a time to dance.
[5] There is a time to scatter stones.
And there's a time to gather them.
There is a time to hug.
And there's a time not to hug.
[6] There is a time to search.
And there's a time to stop searching.
There is a time to keep.
And there's a time to throw away.
[7] There is a time to tear.
And there's a time to mend.
There is a time to be silent.
And there's a time to speak.
[8] There is a time to love.
And there's a time to hate.
There is a time for war.
And there's a tim.e for peace.

[9] What does the worker get for his hard work?
[10] I've seen the heavy load God has put on men.
[11] He has made everything beautiful in its time. He
has also given men a sense of what he's been
doing down through the ages. But they can't completely figure out what he's done from the beginning to the end.

[12] They should be happy and do good while they live. I know there's nothing better for them to do than that. [13] Everyone should eat and drink. People should be satisfied with all of their hard work. That is God's gift to them.

[14] I know that everything God does will last forever. Nothing can be added to it. And nothing can be taken from it. God does that so men will have respect for him.

[15] Everything that now exists has already been.
And what is coming has existed before.
God will judge those who treat others badly.

[16] Here's something else I saw on earth.

Where people should be treated right,
they are treated wrong.
Where people should be treated fairly,
they are treated unfairly.

[17] I said to myself,

"God will judge
godly and sinful people alike.
He has a time for every act.
He has a time for everything that is done."

[18] I also thought, "God puts human beings to the
test. Then they can see they are just like animals.
[19] What happens to animals happens to people too.
Death waits for people and animals alike. People

die, just as animals do. All of them have the same breath. People don't have any advantage over animals. Nothing has any meaning.

20"People and animals go to the same place. All of them come from dust. And all of them return to dust. 21Who can know whether the spirit of a man goes up? Who can tell whether the spirit of an animal goes down into the earth?"

22So man should enjoy his work. That's what God made him for. I saw that there's nothing better for him to do than that. After all, who can show him what will happen after he is gone?

Suffering, Hard Work and Friendship

4 I looked and saw how much people were suffering on this earth.

I saw the tears of those who are suffering.
They don't have anyone to comfort them.
Power is on the side of those who beat them down.
Those who are suffering don't have anyone to comfort them.
2 Then I announced that those
who have already died
are happier than those
who are still alive.
3 But someone who hasn't been born yet
is better off than the dead or the living.
That's because he hasn't seen the evil things
that are done on earth.

4I also saw that man works hard and accomplishes a lot. But he does it only because he wants what his neighbor has. That doesn't have any meaning either. It's like chasing the wind.

5 A foolish person folds his hands and doesn't work.
And that destroys him.
6 One handful with peace and quiet
is better than two handfuls with hard work.
Working too hard is like chasing the wind.

7Again I saw something on earth that didn't mean anything.

8 A man lived all by himself.
He didn't have any sons or brothers.
His hard work never ended.
But he wasn't happy with what he had.
"Who am I working so hard for?" he asked.
"Why don't I get the things I enjoy?"
That doesn't have any meaning either.
In fact, it's a very bad deal!

9 Two people are better than one.
They can help each other in everything they do.
10 Suppose someone falls down.
Then his friend can help him up.
But suppose the man who falls down doesn't have anyone to help him up.
Then feel sorry for him!
11 Or suppose two people lie down together.
Then they'll keep warm.
But how can one person keep warm alone?
12 One person could be overpowered.
But two people can stand up for themselves.
And a rope made out of three cords isn't easily broken.

Getting Ahead Doesn't Have Any Meaning

13A poor but wise young man is better off than an old but foolish king. That king doesn't pay attention to a warning anymore. 14The young man might have come from prison to become king. Or he might have been born poor within the kingdom but still became king. 15I saw that everyone was following the young man who had become the new king.

16At first, all of the people served him when he became king. But those who came later weren't pleased with the way he was ruling. That doesn't have any meaning either. It's like chasing the wind.

Have Respect for God

5 Be careful what you say when you go to God's house. Go there to listen. Don't be like foolish people when you offer your sacrifice. They do what is wrong and don't even know it.

2 Don't be too quick to speak.
Don't be in a hurry to say anything to God.
He is in heaven. You are on earth.
So use only a few words when you speak.
3 Dreams come to people when they worry a lot.
When foolish people talk, they use too many words.

4When you make a promise to God, don't wait too long to carry it out. He isn't pleased with foolish people. So do what you have promised. 5It is better to make no promise at all than to make a promise and not keep it.

6Don't let your mouth cause you to sin. Don't object to the temple messenger. Don't say, "My promise was a mistake." Why should God be angry with what you say? Why should he destroy what you have done? 7Dreaming too much and talking too much are meaningless. So have respect for God.

Riches Don't Have Any Meaning

8Suppose you see poor people being mistreated somewhere. And what is being done to them isn't right or fair. Don't be surprised by that. One official is watched by a higher one. Others who are even higher are watching both of them. 9All of them take what the land produces. And the king himself takes his share from the fields.

10 Anyone who loves money never has enough.
Anyone who loves wealth is never satisfied with what he gets.
That doesn't have any meaning either.

11 As more and more goods are made,
more and more people use them up.
So how can those goods benefit their owner?
All he can do is look at them
with longing.
12 The sleep of a worker is sweet.
It doesn't matter whether he eats a little or
a lot.
But the wealth of a rich man
keeps him awake at night.

13 I've seen something very evil on earth.

It's when wealth is stored up
and then brings harm to its owner.
14 It's also when wealth is lost
because of an unwise business deal.
Then there won't be anything left
for the owner's son.
15 A man is born naked.
He comes into the world with nothing.
And he goes out of it with nothing.
He doesn't get anything from his work
that he can take with him.

16 Here's something else that is very evil.

A man is born, and a man dies.
And what does he get for his work?
Nothing. It's like working for the wind.
17 All his life he eats in darkness.
His life is full of trouble, suffering
and anger.

18 I realized that it's good and proper for a man
to eat and drink. It's good for him to be satisfied
with his hard work on this earth. That's what he
should do during the few days of life God has
given him. That's what God made him for.
19 Sometimes God gives a man wealth and possessions. He makes it possible for him to enjoy
them. He helps him accept the life he has given
him. He helps him to be happy in his work. All of
those things are gifts from God. 20 A man like that
doesn't have to think about how his life is going.
That's because God fills his heart with joy.

6 I've seen another evil thing on this earth. And
it's a heavy load on men. 2 God gives a man
wealth, possessions and honor. He has everything
his heart longs for. But God doesn't let him enjoy
those things. Instead, strangers enjoy them. That
doesn't have any meaning. It's a very evil thing.
3 A man might have a hundred children. He
might live a long time. But suppose he can't enjoy
his wealth. And suppose he isn't buried in the
proper way. Then it doesn't matter how long he
lives.

I'm telling you that a baby that is born dead is
better off than he is. 4 That kind of birth doesn't
have any meaning. The baby dies in darkness and
leaves this world. And in darkness it is forgotten.
5 It didn't even see the sun. It didn't know anything
at all. But it has more rest than that man does. 6 And
that's true even if he lives for 2,000 years but
doesn't get to enjoy his wealth. All people die and
go to the grave, don't they?

7 Man eats up everything he works to get.
But he is never satisfied.
8 What advantage does a wise man have
over someone who is foolish?
What does a poor man gain
by knowing how to act toward others?
9 Being satisfied with what you have
is better than always wanting more.
That doesn't have any meaning either.
It's like chasing the wind.

10 God has already planned what now exists.
He has already decided what man is.
A man can't argue with the One
who is stronger than he is.
11 The more words people use,
the less meaning there is.
And that doesn't help anyone.

12 Who knows what's good for a man? He lives
for only a few meaningless days. He passes
through life like a shadow. Who can tell him what
will happen on earth after he is gone?

Good Advice About How to Live

7 A good name is better than fine perfume.
People can learn more from sobbing when
someone dies
than from being happy when someone is
born.
2 So it's better to go where people are sobbing
than to go where people are having a good
time.
Everyone will die someday.
Those who are still living
should really think about that.
3 Sadness is good for the heart.
That's why sorrow is better than laughter.
4 Those who are wise are found where there
is sorrow.
But foolish people are found where there
is pleasure.
5 Pay attention to a wise man's warning.
That's better than listening to the songs of
those who are foolish.
6 A foolish person's laughter
is like the crackling of thorns burning under
a pot.
That doesn't have any meaning either.
7 When a wise man takes wealth by force, he
becomes foolish.
It is sinful to take money from people who
want special favors.
8 The end of a matter is better than its beginning.
So it's better to be patient than proud.
9 Don't become angry quickly.
Anger lives in the hearts of foolish people.

[10]Don't say, "Why were things better in the good old days?"
It isn't wise to ask that kind of question.

[11]Wisdom is a good thing.
It's like getting a share of the family wealth.
It benefits those who live on this earth.
[12]Wisdom provides safety,
just as money provides safety.
But here's the advantage of wisdom.
It guards the lives of those who have it.

[13]Think about what God has done.

Who can make straight
what he has made crooked?
[14]When times are good, be happy.
But when times are bad, here's something to think about.
God has made bad times.
He has also made good times.
So a man can't find out anything
about what's ahead for him.

[15]In my meaningless life here's what I've seen.

I've seen a godly man dying
even though he is godly.
And I've seen a sinful man living a long time
even though he is sinful.
[16]Don't claim to be better than you are.
And don't claim to be wiser than you are.
Why destroy yourself?
[17]Don't be too sinful.
And don't be foolish.
Why die before your time comes?
[18]It's good to hold on to both of those things.
Don't let go of either one.
A man who has respect for God will avoid
going too far in either direction.

[19]Wisdom makes one wise man more powerful
than ten rulers in a city.

[20]There isn't anyone on earth
who does only what is right and never sins.

[21]Don't pay attention to everything people say.
If you do, you might hear your servant
calling down a curse on you.
[22]Many times you yourself have called down
curses on others.
Deep down inside, you know that's true.

[23]I used wisdom to put all of those things to the test. I said,

"I've made up my mind to be wise."
But it was more than I could accomplish.
[24]No matter what else wisdom may be,
it's far away and very deep.
Who can find it?
[25]So I tried to understand wisdom more completely.
I wanted to study it and figure it out.
I tried to find out everything I could about it.
I tried to understand why it's foolish to be evil.
I wanted to see why choosing foolishness is so unwise.

[26]A woman who hunts a man down
is more painful than death.
Her heart is like a trap.
Her hands are like chains.
A man who pleases God will try to get away from her.
But she will trap a sinner.

[27]"Look," says the Teacher. "Here's what I've discovered.

"I added one thing to another to find out
everything I could about wisdom.
[28]I searched and searched
but found very little.
I did find one honest man among a thousand.
But I didn't find one honest woman among a thousand.
[29]Here's the only other thing I found.
God made men honest.
But they've made many evil plans."

8 Who is like a wise man?
Who knows how to explain things?
Wisdom makes a man's face bright.
It softens the look on his face.

Obey the King

[2]I'm telling you to obey the king's command.
You took an oath to serve him. You made a
promise to God. [3]Don't be in a hurry to quit your
job in the palace. Don't stand up for something the
king doesn't like. He'll do anything he wants to.
[4]He has the final word. So who can ask him,
"What are you doing?"

[5]No one who obeys his command will be harmed.
Those who are wise will know the proper
time and way to approach him.
[6]There's a proper time and way for people to do everything.
That's true even though a man might be suffering greatly.

[7]No one knows what lies ahead.
So who can tell a person what's going to happen?
[8]He can't stop the wind from blowing.
And he doesn't have the power to decide
when he will die.
No one is let out of the army in times of war.
And evil won't let go of those who practice it.

[9]I understood all of those things. I used my
mind to study everything that's done on earth. A
man sometimes makes life hard for others. But he
ends up hurting himself.
[10]I also saw sinful people being buried. They
used to come and go from the place of worship.

And others praised them in the city where they
worshiped. That doesn't have any meaning either.
11Sometimes the sentence for a crime isn't carried out quickly. So people make plans to commit
even more crimes.
12An evil man may be guilty of a hundred
crimes and still live a long time. But I know that
things will go better with men who have great
respect for God. 13Sinful people don't respect God.
So things won't go well with them. Like a shadow,
they won't be around very long.
14Here's something else on this earth that
doesn't have any meaning. Sometimes godly men
get what sinful people should receive. And sinful
men get what godly people should receive. Here's
what I'm telling you. That doesn't have any meaning either.
15So I advise everyone to enjoy life. A man on
this earth can't do anything better than eat and
drink and be glad. Then he will enjoy his work.
He'll be happy all the days of the life God has
given him on earth.
16I used my mind to understand what it really
means to be wise. I wanted to observe the hard
work man does on earth. He doesn't close his eyes
and go to sleep day or night.
17I saw everything God has done. No one can
understand what happens on earth. Man might try
very hard to figure it out. But he still can't discover
what it all means. A wise man might claim he
knows. But he can't really understand it either.

Everyone Dies

9 I thought about all of those things. I realized
that those who are wise and do what is right
are under God's control. What they do is also
under his control.
But a man doesn't know whether God will
show favor to him. 2Everyone will die someday.
Death comes to godly and sinful people alike. It
comes to good and bad people alike. It comes to
"clean" and "unclean" people alike. Those who
offer sacrifices and those who don't offer them
also die.

A good person dies,
and so does a sinner.
Those who take oaths die.
So do those who are afraid to take them.

3Here's what is so bad about everything that
happens on this earth. Death catches up with all of
us. Also, the hearts of people are full of evil. They
live in foolish pleasure. After that, they join those
who have already died.
4Anyone who is living still has hope. Even a
live dog is better off than a dead lion!

5 People who are still alive know they'll die.
But those who have died don't know
anything.
They don't receive any more rewards.
And they are soon forgotten.
6 Their love, hate and jealousy disappear.
They will never share again
in anything that happens on earth.

7Go and enjoy your food. Be joyful as you drink
your wine. Now is the time God favors what you
do. 8Always wear white clothes to show you are
happy. Anoint your head with olive oil.
9You love your wife. So enjoy life with her. Do
it all the days of this meaningless life God has given
you on earth. That's what he made you for. That's
what you get for all of your hard work on earth.
10No matter what you do, work at it with all
your might. Remember, you are going to your
grave. And there isn't any work or planning or
knowledge or wisdom there.
11Here's something else I've seen on this earth.

Races aren't always won by those who
run fast.
Battles aren't always won by those who
are strong.
Wise people don't always have plenty of food.
Clever people aren't always wealthy.
Those who have learned a lot aren't always
favored.
God controls the timing of every event.
He also controls how things turn out.

12A man doesn't know when trouble will come
to him.

Fish are caught in nets.
Birds are taken in traps.
And people are trapped by hard times
that come when they don't expect them.

Being Wise Is Better Than Being Foolish

13Here's something else I saw on this earth. I
saw an example of wisdom that touched me
deeply. 14There was once a small city. Only a few
people lived there. A powerful king attacked it. He
brought in war machines all around it.
15A certain man lived in that city. He was poor
but wise. He used his wisdom to save the city. But
no one remembered that poor man. 16So I said,
"It's better to be wise than to be powerful." But
people looked down on the poor man's wisdom.
No one paid any attention to what he said.

17 People should listen to the quiet words
of those who are wise.
That's better than paying attention to the shouts
of a ruler of foolish people.
18 Wisdom is better than weapons of war.
But one sinner destroys a lot of good.

10 Dead flies give perfume a bad smell.
And a little foolishness can make a lot of
wisdom useless.
2 The hearts of wise people lead them on the
right path.
But the hearts of foolish people take them
down the wrong path.

3 A foolish person doesn't have any sense at all.
He shows everyone he is foolish.
He does it even when he is walking along the road.
4 Suppose a ruler gets very angry with you.
If he does, don't quit your job in the palace.
Stay calm. That will overcome the effects of your big mistakes.

5 Here's something evil I've seen on this earth.
And it's the kind of mistake that rulers make.
6 Foolish people are given many important jobs.
Rich people are given unimportant ones.
7 I've seen slaves on horseback.
I've also seen princes who were forced to walk as if they were slaves.

8 Anyone who digs a pit might fall into it.
Anyone who breaks through a wall might be bitten by a snake.
9 Anyone who removes stones from rock pits might get hurt.
Anyone who cuts logs might get wounded.

10 Suppose the blade of an ax is dull.
And its edge hasn't been sharpened.
Then more effort is needed to use it.
But skill will bring success.

11 Suppose a snake bites before it is charmed.
Then there isn't any benefit in being a snake charmer.

12 A man who is wise says gracious things.
But a foolish person is destroyed by what his own lips speak.
13 At first what he says is foolish.
In the end his words are very evil.
14 He talks too much.

No one knows what lies ahead for him.
Who can tell him what will happen after he is gone?

15 The work a foolish person does makes him tired.
He doesn't even know the way to town.

16 How terrible it is for a land whose king used to be a servant!
How terrible if its princes get drunk in the morning!
17 How blessed is the land whose king was born into the royal family!
How blessed if its princes eat and drink at the proper time!
How blessed if they eat and drink to become strong and not to get drunk!

18 When a man won't work, the roof falls down.
When his hands aren't busy, the house leaks.

19 People laugh at a dinner party.
And wine makes life happy.
People think money can buy everything.

20 Don't call down curses on the king.
Don't even think about doing it.
Don't call down curses on rich people.
Don't even do it in your bedroom.
A bird might fly away and carry your words.
It might report what you said.

Be Bold

11 Put your money into trade across the ocean.
After a while you will earn something from it.
2 Give shares of what you earn to a lot of people.
After all, you don't know what great trouble might come on the land.

3 Clouds that are full of water
pour rain down on the earth.
A tree might fall to the south or the north.
It will stay in the place where it falls.
4 Anyone who keeps on watching the wind won't plant seeds.
Anyone who keeps looking at the clouds won't gather crops.

5 You don't know the path the wind takes.
You don't know how a baby is made inside its mother.
So you can't understand how God works either.
He made everything.

6 In the morning plant your seeds.
In the evening keep your hands busy.
You don't know what will succeed.
It may be one or the other.
Or both might do equally well.

Remember the One Who Created You

7 Light is sweet.
People enjoy being out in the sun.
8 No matter how many years a man might live, let him enjoy all of them.
But let him remember the dark days.
There will be many of them.
Nothing that's going to happen will have any meaning.

9 Young man, be happy while you are still young.
Let your heart be joyful while you are still strong.
Do what your heart tells you to do.
Go after what your eyes look at.
But I want you to know
that God will judge you for everything you do.
10 So drive worry out of your heart.
Get rid of all of your troubles.
Being young and strong doesn't have any meaning.

12 Remember the One who created you.
Remember him while you are still young.

Think about him before your times of trouble
come.
The years will come when you will say,
"I don't find any pleasure in them."
2 That's when the sunlight will become dark.
The moon and the stars will also
grow dark.
And the clouds will return after it rains.
3 Remember your Creator before those who
guard the house tremble with old age.
That's when strong men will be bent over.
The women who grind grain will stop because
there are so few of them left.
Those who look through the windows won't
be able to see very well.
4 Remember your Creator before the front doors
are closed.
That's when the sound of grinding will
fade away.
Old men will rise up when they hear birds
singing.
But they will barely hear any of
their songs.
5 Remember your Creator before you become
afraid of places that are too high.
You will also be terrified because of danger
in the streets.
Remember your Creator before the almond
trees have buds on them.
That's when grasshoppers will drag
themselves along.
Old men will not want to make love
anymore.
Man will go to his dark home in the grave.
And those who sob over the dead will walk
around in the streets.

6 Remember your Creator before the silver cord
is cut.
That's when the golden bowl will be broken.
The wheel will be broken at the well.
The pitcher will be smashed at the spring.
7 Remember your Creator before you return to
the dust you came from.
That's when your spirit will go back to God
who gave it.

8 "Meaningless! Everything is meaningless!"
says the Teacher.
"Nothing has any meaning."

Have Respect for God

9 The Teacher was wise. He gave knowledge to
people. He put many proverbs to the test. He
thought about them carefully. Then he wrote them
down in order.
10 He did his best to find just the right
words. And what he wrote was honest and true.

11 The sayings of those who are wise move people to take action. Their collected sayings really nail
things down. They are given to us by one Shepherd.
12 My son, be careful not to pay attention to anything
that is added to them.

Books will never stop being written. Too much
studying makes people tired.

13 Everything has now been heard.
And here's the final thing I want to say.
Have respect for God and obey his
commandments.
That's what everyone should do.
14 God will judge everything people do.
That includes everything they try to hide.
He'll judge everything, whether it's good
or evil.

Song of Songs

1 This is the greatest song Solomon ever wrote.

A Shulammite woman says to King Solomon,

2 "I long for your lips to kiss me!
Your love makes me happier than wine does.
3 The lotion you have on pleases me.
Your name is like perfume that is poured out.
No wonder the young women love you!
4 Take me away with you. Let us hurry!
King Solomon, bring me into your palace."

The other women say,

"King Solomon, you fill us with joy. You make us happy.
We praise your love more than we praise wine."

The woman says to the king,

"It is right for them to love you!

5 "Women of Jerusalem,
my skin is dark but lovely.
It is dark like the tents in Kedar.
It's like the curtains of Solomon's tent.
6 Don't stare at me because I'm dark.
The sun has made my skin look like this.
My brothers burned with anger against me.
They made me take care of the vineyards.
I haven't even taken care of my own vineyard.

7 "King Solomon, I love you.
So tell me where you take care of your flock.
Tell me where you rest your sheep at noon.
Why should I have to act like a prostitute
near the flocks of your friends?"

The other women say,

8 "You are the most beautiful woman of all.
Don't you know where to find the king?
Follow the tracks the sheep make.
Take care of your young goats
near the tents of the shepherds."

King Solomon says to the Shulammite woman,

9 "You are my love.
You are like a mare that pulls one of Pharaoh's chariots.
10 Your earrings make your cheeks even more beautiful.
Your strings of jewels make your neck even more lovely."

The other women say to her,

11 "We will make gold earrings for you.
We'll decorate them with silver."

The woman says,

12 "The king was at his table.
My perfume gave off a sweet smell.
13 The one who loves me is like a small bag of myrrh
resting between my breasts.
14 He is like henna flowers
from the vineyards of En Gedi."

The king says,

15 "You are so beautiful, my love!
So beautiful!
Your eyes are like doves."

The woman says,

16 "You are so handsome, my love!
So charming!
The green field is our bed.
17 Cedar trees above us are the beams of our house.
Fir trees overhead are its rafters.

2 "I am like a rose on the coast of Sharon.
I'm like a lily in the valleys."

The king says,

2 "My love, among the young women
you are like a lily among thorns."

The woman says,

3 "My love, among the young men
you are like an apple tree among the trees of the forest.
I'm happy to sit in your shade.
Your fruit tastes so sweet to me.
4 You have taken me to the dinner hall.
Your banner of love is lifted high above me.
5 Give me some raisins to make me strong.
Give me some apples to make me feel like new again.
Our love has made me weak.
6 Your left arm is under my head.
Your right arm is around me.
7 Women of Jerusalem, take an oath and make me a promise.
Let the antelopes and the does serve as witnesses.
Don't stir up love.
Don't wake it up until it's ready.

8 "Listen! I hear my love!
Look! Here he comes!
He's leaping across the mountains.
He's coming over the hills.

9 The one who loves me is like an antelope or a young deer.
Look! There he stands behind our wall.
He's gazing through the window.
He's peering through the screen.
10 He said to me, 'Rise up, my love.
Come with me, my beautiful one.
11 Look! The winter is past.
The rains are over and gone.
12 Flowers are appearing on the earth.
The season for singing has come.
The cooing of doves
is heard in our land.
13 The fig trees are producing their early fruit.
The flowers on the vines are giving off their sweet smell.
Rise up and come, my love.
Come with me, my beautiful one.'"

The king says,

14 "You are like a dove in an opening in the rocks.
You are like a dove in a hiding place on a mountainside.
Show me your face.
Let me hear your voice.
Your voice is so sweet.
Your face is so lovely.
15 Catch the foxes for us.
Catch the little foxes.
They destroy our vineyards.
The vineyards are in bloom."

The woman says,

16 "My love belongs to me, and I belong to him.
Like an antelope, he eats among the lilies.
17 Until the day begins
and the shadows fade away,
turn to me, my love.
Be like an antelope
or like a young deer
on the rocky hills.

3 "All night long on my bed
I searched for the one my heart loves.
I looked for him but didn't find him.
2 I will get up. I'll go around in the city.
I'll look through all of its streets.
I'll search for the one my heart loves.
So I looked for him but didn't find him.
3 Those on guard duty found me
as they were walking around in the city.
'Have you seen the one my heart loves?'
I asked.
4 As soon as I had passed by them
I found the one my heart loves.
I threw my arms around him. I didn't let him go
until I had brought him to my mother's house.
I took him to my mother's room.
5 Women of Jerusalem, take an oath and make me a promise.
Let the antelopes and the does serve as witnesses.
Don't stir up love.
Don't wake it up until it's ready."

The other women say,

6 "Who is this man coming up from the desert
like a column of smoke?
He smells like myrrh and incense
made from all of the spices of the trader.
7 Look! There's Solomon's movable throne.
Sixty soldiers accompany it.
They have been chosen from the best warriors in Israel.
8 All of them are wearing swords.
They have fought many battles.
Each one has his sword at his side.
Each is prepared for the terrors of the night.
9 King Solomon made the movable throne for himself.
He made it out of wood from Lebanon.
10 He formed its posts out of silver.
He made its base out of gold.
Its seat was covered with purple cloth.
It was decorated inside with loving care
by the women of Jerusalem.
11 Women of Zion, come out.
Look at King Solomon wearing his crown.
His mother placed it on him.
She did it on his wedding day.
His heart was full of joy."

4 The king says to the Shulammite woman,

"You are so beautiful, my love!
So beautiful!
Your eyes behind your veil are like doves.
Your hair flows like a flock of black goats
coming down from Mount Gilead.
2 Your teeth are as clean as a flock of sheep.
Their wool has just been clipped.
They have just come up from being washed.
Each of your teeth has its twin.
Not one of them is alone.
3 Your lips are like a bright red ribbon.
Your mouth is so lovely.
Your cheeks behind your veil
are like the halves of a pomegranate.
4 Your neck is strong and beautiful like the tower of David.
That tower is built with beautiful stones.
A thousand shields are hanging on it.
All of them belong to mighty soldiers.
5 Your two breasts are lovely.
They are like two young antelopes
that eat among the lilies.
6 I will go to the mountain of myrrh.
I'll go to the hill of incense.
I'll stay there until the day begins
and the shadows fade away.

7 Every part of you is so beautiful, my love.
There is no flaw in you.

8 "Come with me from Lebanon, my bride.
Come with me from Lebanon.
Come down from the top of Mount Amana.
Come down from the top of Senir.
Come to me from the peak of Mount Hermon.
Leave the dens where the lions live.
Leave the places in the mountains where the leopards stay.
9 My bride, you have stolen my heart
with one glance of your eyes.
My sister, you have stolen my heart
with one jewel in your necklace.
10 My bride, your love is so delightful.
My sister, your love makes me happier than wine does.
Your perfume smells better than any spice.
11 Your lips are as sweet as a honeycomb, my bride.
Milk and honey are under your tongue.
Your clothes smell like the cedar trees in Lebanon.
12 My bride, you are like a garden that is locked up.
My sister, you are like a spring of water that has a fence around it.
You are like a fountain that is sealed up.
13 You are like trees whose branches are loaded
with pomegranates, fine fruits, henna and nard,
14 with saffron, cane and cinnamon.
You are like every kind of incense tree.
You have myrrh, aloes
and all of the finest spices.
15 You are like a fountain in a garden.
You are like a well of flowing water
streaming down from Lebanon."

The woman says,

16 "Wake up, north wind!
Come, south wind!
Blow on my garden.
Then its sweet smell will spread everywhere.
Let my love come into his garden.
Let him taste its fine fruits."

5 The king says,

"My bride, I have come into my garden.
My sister, I've gathered my myrrh and my spice.
I've eaten my honeycomb and my honey.
I've drunk my wine and my milk."

The other women say to the Shulammite woman and to Solomon,

"Friends, eat and drink.
Lovers, drink all you want."

The woman says,

2 "I slept, but my heart was awake.
Listen! The one who loves me is knocking.
He says, 'My sister, I love you.
Open up so I can come in.
You are my dove.
You are perfect in every way.
My head is soaked with dew.
The night air has made my hair wet.'

3 "But I've taken my robe off.
Must I put it on again?
I've washed my feet.
Must I get them dirty again?
4 My love put his hand through the opening.
My heart began to pound for him.
5 I got up to open the door for my love.
My hands dripped with myrrh.
It flowed from my fingers
onto the handles of the lock.
6 I opened the door for my love.
But he had left. He was gone.
My heart sank because he had left.
I looked for him but didn't find him.
I called out to him, but he didn't answer.
7 Those on guard duty found me
as they were walking around in the city.
They beat me. They hurt me.
Those on guard duty at the walls
took my coat away from me.
8 Women of Jerusalem, take an oath and make me a promise.
If you find the one who loves me,
tell him our love has made me weak."

The other women say,

9 "You are the most beautiful woman of all.
How is the one you love better than others?
How is he better than anyone else?
Why do you ask us to make you a promise?"

The woman says,

10 "The one who loves me is tanned and handsome.
He's the finest man among 10,000.
11 His head is like the purest gold.
His hair is wavy and as black as a raven.
12 His eyes are like doves
by streams of water.
They look as if they've been washed in milk.
They are set like jewels in his head.
13 His cheeks are like beds of spice
that give off perfume.
His lips are like lilies
that drip with myrrh.
14 His arms are like gold
that are set with chrysolite.
His body is like polished ivory
that is decorated with sapphires.

15 His legs are like pillars of marble
that are set on bases of pure gold.
He looks like the finest cedar tree
in the mountains of Lebanon.
16 His mouth is very sweet.
Everything about him is delightful.
That's what the one who loves me is like.
That's what my friend is like, women of Jerusalem."

6 The other women say,

"You are the most beautiful woman of all.
Where has the one who loves you gone?
Which way did he turn?
We'll help you look for him."

The woman says,

2 "My love has gone down to his garden.
He's gone to the beds of spices.
He's eating in the gardens.
He's gathering lilies.
3 I belong to my love, and he belongs to me.
He's eating among the lilies."

The king says,

4 "My love, you are as beautiful as the city of Tirzah.
You are as lovely as Jerusalem.
You are as majestic as troops carrying their banners.
5 Turn your eyes away from me.
They overpower me.
Your hair flows like a flock of black goats
coming down from Mount Gilead.
6 Your teeth are as clean as a flock of sheep
coming up from being washed.
Each of your teeth has its twin.
Not one of them is alone.
7 Your cheeks behind your veil
are like the halves of a pomegranate.
8 There might be 60 queens and 80 concubines.
There might be more virgins than anyone can count.
9 But you are my perfect dove.
There isn't anyone like you.
You are your mother's favorite daughter.
The young women see you and call you blessed.
The queens and concubines praise you."

The other women say,

10 "Who is this woman?
She is like the sunrise in all of its glory.
She is as beautiful as the moon.
She is as bright as the sun.
She is as majestic as troops carrying their banners."

The king says,

11 "I went down to a grove of nut trees.
I wanted to look at the new plants growing in the valley.
I wanted to find out whether the vines had budded.
I wanted to see if the pomegranate trees had bloomed.
12 Before I realized it,
I was among the royal chariots of my people."

The other women say,

13 "Come back to us.
Come back, Shulammite woman.
Come back to us.
Come back. Then we can look at you."

The woman says,

"Why do you want to look at me
as you would watch a dancer at Mahanaim?"

7 The king says to the Shulammite woman,

"You are like a prince's daughter.
Your feet in sandals are so beautiful.
Your graceful legs are like jewels.
The hands of a skilled worker must have shaped them.
2 Your navel is like a round bowl
that always has mixed wine in it.
Your waist is like a mound of wheat
that is surrounded by lilies.
3 Your two breasts are lovely.
They are like two young antelopes.
4 Your neck is smooth and beautiful like an ivory tower.
Your eyes are like the pools of Heshbon
by the gate of Bath Rabbim.
Your nose is like the towering mountains of Lebanon
that face the city of Damascus.
5 Your head is like a crown on you.
It is as beautiful as Mount Carmel.
Your hair is as smooth as purple silk.
I am captured by your flowing curls.
6 You are so beautiful! You please me so much!
You are so delightful, my love!
7 You are as graceful as a palm tree.
Your breasts are as sweet as the freshest fruit.
8 I said, 'I will climb the palm tree.
I'll take hold of its fruit.'
May your breasts be as sweet as the fruit on the vine.
May your breath smell like the tastiest apples.
9 May your lips be like the finest wine."

The woman says,

"May my wine go straight to you, my love.
May it flow gently over our lips as we sleep.

10 "I belong to you, my love.
And you long for me.

11 Come, my love. Let's go to the country.
Let's spend the night in the villages.
12 Let's go out to the vineyards early.
Let's go and see if the vines
have budded.
Let's find out whether their flowers have
opened.
Let's see if the pomegranate trees are
blooming.
I'll make love to you in the vineyards.
13 The mandrake flowers give off their strong
smell.
All of the best things are waiting
for us,
new and old alike.
I've stored them up for you, my love.

8 "I wish you were like a brother to me.
I wish my mother's breasts had nursed
you.
Then if I found you outside,
I could kiss you.
No one would look down on me.
2 I'd bring you to my mother's house.
She taught me everything I know.
I'd give you spiced wine to drink.
It's the juice of my pomegranates.
3 Your left arm is under my head.
Your right arm is around me.
4 Women of Jerusalem, take an oath and make
me a promise.
Don't stir up love.
Don't wake it up until it's ready."

The other women say,

5 "Who is this woman coming up from the
desert?
She's leaning on the one who loves her."

The woman says to the king,

"Under the apple tree I woke you up.
That's where your mother became pregnant
with you.
She went into labor, and you were
born there.
6 Hold me close to your heart like the seal
around your neck.
Keep me close to yourself like the ring on
your finger.
My love for you is so strong it won't let
you go.
Love is as powerful as death.
Love's jealousy is as strong as the grave.
Love is like a blazing fire.
It burns like a mighty flame.
7 No amount of water can put it out.
Rivers can't drown it.
Suppose someone offers
all of his wealth to buy love.
That won't even come close to being
enough."

The woman's brothers say,

8 "We have a little sister.
Her breasts are still small.
What should we do for our sister
when she gets engaged?
9 If she were a wall,
we'd build silver towers on her.
If she were a door,
we'd cover her with cedar boards."

The woman says to the king,

10 "I am a wall.
My breasts are like well-built towers.
So in your eyes I've become
like someone who makes you happy.
11 Solomon, you had a vineyard in Baal Hamon.
You rented your vineyard to others.
They had to pay 25 pounds
of silver for its fruit.
12 But I can give my own vineyard to anyone I
want to.
So I give my 25 pounds of silver to you,
Solomon.
Give 5 pounds to those who take care of
its fruit."

The king says,

13 "My love, you live in the gardens.
My friends listen for your voice.
But let me hear it now."

The woman says,

14 "Come away with me, my love.
Be like an antelope
or like a young deer
on mountains that are full of spices."

Isaiah

1 Here is the vision about Judah and Jerusalem that Isaiah had. It came to him when Uzziah, Jotham, Ahaz and Hezekiah were ruling. They were kings of Judah. Isaiah was the son of Amoz.

Israel Refuses to Obey the LORD

2 Listen to me, heavens! Pay attention to me,
earth!
The LORD has said,
"I raised children. I brought them up.
But they have refused to obey me.
3 The ox knows its master.
The donkey knows where its owner feeds it.
But Israel does not know me.
My people do not understand me."

4 They are a sinful nation.
They are loaded down with guilt.
They are people who do nothing but evil.
They are children who are always sinning.
They have deserted the LORD.
They have turned against the Holy One
of Israel.
They have turned their backs on him.

5 Israel, why do you want to be beaten all
the time?
Why do you always refuse to obey
the LORD?
Your head is covered with wounds.
Your whole heart is weak.
6 There isn't a healthy spot on your body
from the bottom of your feet to the top of
your head.
There are only wounds, cuts
and open sores.
They haven't been cleaned up or bandaged
or treated with olive oil.

7 Your country has been deserted.
Your cities have been burned down.
The food from your fields is being eaten up by
outsiders.
They are doing it right in front of you.
Your land has been completely destroyed.
It looks as if strangers have taken it over.
8 The city of Zion is left like a hut
where someone stands guard in a vineyard.
It is left like an empty cabin in a melon field.
It's like a city that is being attacked.
9 The LORD who rules over all
has let some people live through that time of
trouble.
If he hadn't, we would have become like
Sodom.
We would have been like Gomorrah.

10 Rulers of Sodom,
hear the LORD's message.
People of Gomorrah,
listen to the law of our God.
11 "Do you think I need any more of your
sacrifices?"
asks the LORD.
"I have more than enough of your burnt
offerings.
I have more than enough of rams
and the fat of your fattest animals.
I do not find any pleasure
in the blood of your bulls, lambs
and goats.
12 Who asked you to bring all of those animals
when you come to worship me?
Who asked you and your animals
to walk all over my courtyards?
13 Stop bringing offerings that do not mean
anything to me!
I hate your incense.
I can't stand your evil gatherings.
I can't stand the way you celebrate your
New Moon Feasts,
Sabbath days and special services.
14 I hate your New Moon Feasts
and your other appointed feasts.
They have become a heavy load to me.
I am tired of carrying it.
15 You might spread out your hands toward me
when you pray.
But I will not look at you.
You might even offer many prayers.
But I will not listen to them.
Your hands are covered with the blood of the
people you have murdered.
16 So wash your hands. Make yourselves
clean.
Get your evil actions out of my sight!
Stop doing what is wrong!
17 Learn to do what is right!
Treat people fairly.
Give hope to those who are beaten down.
Cheer them up.
Stand up in court for children whose fathers
have died.
And do the same thing for widows.

18 "Come. Let us talk some more about
this matter,"
says the LORD.
"Even though your sins are bright red,
they will be as white as snow.
Even though they are deep red,
they will be white like wool.
19 But you have to be willing to change and
obey me.
If you are, you will eat the best food that
grows on the land.

20 You must follow me. You must obey me.
If you do not, you will be killed with swords."
The LORD has spoken.

21 See how the faithful city of Jerusalem
has become like a prostitute!
Once it was full of people who treated others fairly.
Those who did what was right used to live in it.
But now murderers live there!
22 Jerusalem, your silver isn't pure anymore.
Your best wine has been made weak with water.
23 Your rulers refuse to obey the LORD.
They are companions of robbers.
All of them love to accept money from those who want special favors.
They are always looking for gifts from other people.
They don't stand up in court for children whose fathers have died.
They don't do it for widows either.
24 The Lord is the Mighty One of Israel.
The LORD who rules over all announces,
"Israel, you have become my enemies.
I will pay you back for what you have done.
Then you will not trouble me anymore.
25 I will turn my powerful hand against you.
I will make you completely clean.
I will remove everything that is not pure.
26 I will give judges to you like the ones you had long ago.
I will give you advisers like those you had at the beginning.
Then you will be called
The City That Does What Is Right.
You will also be called The Faithful City."

27 Zion will be saved when others are treated fairly.
Those who are sorry for their sins will be saved
when what is right is done.
28 But sinners and those who refuse to obey the LORD will be destroyed.
And those who desert the LORD will die.

29 Israel, you take delight in worshiping among the sacred oak trees.
You will be full of shame for doing that.
You have chosen to worship in the sacred gardens.
You will be dishonored for doing that.
30 You will be like an oak tree whose leaves are dying.
You will be like a garden that doesn't have any water.
31 Your strongest men will become like dry pieces of wood.
Their worship of other gods will be the spark that lights the fire.
Everything will be burned up.
No one will be there to put the fire out.

People From Many Nations Will Worship at Mount Zion

2 Here is a vision that Isaiah, the son of Amoz, had about Judah and Jerusalem.

2 In the last days
the mountain where the LORD's temple is located will be famous.
It will be the most important mountain of all.
It will stand out above the hills.
All of the nations will go to it.

3 People from many nations will go there. They will say,

"Come. Let us go up to the LORD's mountain.
Let's go to the house of Jacob's God.
He will teach us how we should live.
Then we will live the way he wants us to."
The law of the LORD will be taught at Zion.
His message will go out from Jerusalem.
4 He will judge between the nations.
He'll settle problems among many of them.
They will hammer their swords into plows.
They'll hammer their spears into pruning tools.
Nations will not go to war against one another.
They won't even train to fight anymore.

5 People of Jacob, come.
Let us live the way the LORD has taught us to.

The Day of the LORD Is Coming

6 LORD, you have deserted the people of Jacob.
They are your people.
The land is full of false beliefs from the east.
The people practice evil magic, just as the Philistines do.
They make ungodly people their friends.
7 Their land is full of silver and gold.
There is no end to their treasures.
Their land is full of horses.
There is no end to their chariots.
8 Their land is full of statues of gods.
They bow down to what their own hands have made.
They bow down to what their fingers have shaped.
9 So man will be brought low.
People will be put to shame.
Do not forgive them.

10 Go and hide in caves in the rocks, you people!
Hide in holes in the ground.
Hide from the terror of the LORD!
Hide when he comes in glory and majesty!

11 A man who brags will be brought low.
Men who are proud will be put to shame.
The LORD alone will be honored at that time.
12 The LORD who rules over all has set apart a day when he will judge.
He has set it apart for all those who are proud and think they are important.
He has set it apart for all those who brag about themselves.
All of them will be brought low.
13 The LORD has set that day apart for all of the cedar trees in Lebanon.
They are very tall.
He has set it apart for all of the oak trees in Bashan.
14 He has set it apart for all of the towering mountains.
He has set it apart for all of the high hills.
15 He has set it apart for every high tower and every strong wall.
16 He has set it apart for every trading ship and every beautiful boat.
17 A man who brags will be brought low.
Men who are proud will be put to shame.
The LORD alone will be honored at that time.
18 And the statues of gods will totally disappear.

19 People will run and hide in caves in the rocks.
They will go into holes in the ground.
They will run away from the terror of the LORD.
They will run when he comes in glory and majesty.
When he comes, he will shake the earth.
20 Men had made some statues of gods out of silver.
They had made others out of gold.
Then they worshiped them.
But when the LORD comes,
they will throw the statues away to the rodents and bats.
21 They will run and hide in caves in the rocks.
They will go into holes in the cliffs.
They will run away from the terror of the LORD.
They will run when he comes in glory and majesty.
When he comes, he will shake the earth.
22 Stop trusting man. He can't help you.
He only lives for a little while.
What good is he?

The LORD Will Judge Jerusalem and Judah

3 Here is what
the LORD who rules over all is about to do.
The Lord will take away from Jerusalem and Judah
supplies and help alike.
He will take away all of the supplies of food and water.
2 He'll take away heroes and soldiers.
He'll take away judges and prophets.
He'll take away fortune tellers and elders.
3 He'll take away captains of companies of 50 men.
He'll take away government leaders.
He'll take away advisers, skilled workers
and those who are clever at doing evil magic.

4 The LORD will make young boys rule over all of them.
Mere children will govern them.
5 People will crush one another.
They will fight against each other.
They will fight against their neighbors.
Young people will attack old people.
Ordinary people will attack those who are more important.

6 A man will grab hold of one of his brothers at his father's home. He will say,
"You have a coat. So you be our leader.
Take charge of all of these broken-down buildings!"
7 But at that time the brother will cry out,
"I can't help you.
I don't have any food or clothing in my house.
Don't make me the leader of these people."

8 Jerusalem is about to fall.
And so is Judah.
They say and do things against the LORD.
They dare to disobey him to his very face.
9 The look on their faces is a witness against them.
They show off their sin, just as the people of Sodom did.
They don't even try to hide it.
How terrible it will be for them!
They have brought trouble on themselves.

10 Tell those who do what is right that things will go well with them.
They will enjoy the results of the good things they've done.
11 But how terrible it will be for those who do what is evil!
Trouble is about to fall on them.
They will be paid back for the evil things they've done.

12 Those who are young crush my people.
Women rule over them.
My people, your leaders have taken you down the wrong path.
They have turned you away from the right path.

13 The LORD takes his place in court.
He stands up to judge the people.

[14] He judges the elders and leaders of his people.
He says to them,
"My people are like a vineyard.
You have destroyed them.
The things you have taken from poor
people are in your houses.
[15] What do you mean by crushing my
people?
Why are you grinding the faces of the
poor into the dirt?"
announces the Lord.
He is the LORD who rules over all.

[16] The LORD continues,
"The women in Zion are very proud.
They walk along with their noses in the air.
They tease men with their eyes.
They walk with quick, short steps.
Little chains jingle on their ankles.
[17] So I will put sores on the heads of Zion's
women.
And I will remove the hair from their
heads."

[18]At that time the Lord will take away the beautiful things they wear. He will take away their decorations, headbands and moon-shaped necklaces.
[19]He'll take away their earrings, bracelets and
veils. [20]He'll remove their headdresses, ankle
chains and belts. He'll take away their perfume
bottles and charms. [21]He'll remove the rings they
wear on their fingers and in their noses. [22]He'll
take away their fine robes and their capes and
coats. He'll take away their purses [23]and mirrors.
And he'll take away their linen clothes, turbans
and shawls.

[24] Instead of smelling sweet,
the women will smell bad.
Instead of wearing belts,
they will wear ropes.
Instead of having beautiful hair,
they won't have any hair at all.
Instead of wearing fine clothes,
they'll wear black clothes to show how sad
they are.
Instead of being beautiful,
they'll have the brands of slaves on their
bodies.
[25] Jerusalem, your men will be killed with
swords.
Your soldiers will die in battle.
[26] The city of Zion will be very sad.
Like a widow, she will lose everything.
She will sit on the ground and sob.

4 At that time seven women
will grab hold of one man.
They'll say to him, "We will eat our own food.
We'll provide our own clothes.
Just let us become your wives.
Take away our shame!"

The Branch of the LORD

[2]At that time Israel's king will be beautiful and
glorious. He will be called The Branch of the
LORD. The fruit of the land will be the pride and
glory of those who are still left alive in Israel.
[3]Those who are left in Zion will be called holy.
They will be recorded among those who are alive
in Jerusalem. [4]The Lord will wash away the sin of
the women in Zion. He will clean up the blood that
was spilled there. He will judge those who spilled
that blood. His burning anger will blaze out at
them.
[5]Then the LORD will create over Jerusalem a
cloud of smoke by day. He will also create a glow
of flaming fire at night. They will appear over all
of Mount Zion and those who gather together
there. The LORD's glory will be like a tent over
them. [6]It will cover them and give them shade
from the hot sun all day long. It will be a safe place
where they can hide from storms and rain.

The Song of the Vineyard

5 I will sing a song for the LORD.
He is the one I love.
It's a song about his vineyard Israel.
The one I love had a vineyard.
It was on a hillside that had rich soil.
[2] He dug up the soil and removed its stones.
He planted the very best vines in it.
He built a lookout tower there.
He also cut out a winepress for it.
Then he kept looking for a crop of good
grapes.
But the vineyard produced only bad fruit.
[3] So the LORD said, "People of Jerusalem
and Judah,
you be the judge between me and my
vineyard.
[4] What more could I have done for my vineyard?
I did everything I could.
I kept looking for a crop of good grapes.
So why did it produce only bad ones?
[5] Now I will tell you
what I am going to do to my vineyard.
I will take away its fence.
And it will be destroyed.
I will break down its wall.
And people will walk all over it.
[6] I will turn my vineyard into a dry and empty
desert.
It will not be pruned or taken care of.
Thorns and bushes will grow there.
I will command the clouds
not to rain on it."

[7] The vineyard of the LORD who rules over all
is the nation of Israel.
The people of Judah
are the garden he takes delight in.
He kept looking for them to do what is fair.
But all he saw was blood being spilled.

He kept looking for them to do what is right.
But all he heard were cries of suffering.

The LORD Judges His Vineyard

8 How terrible it will be for you who get too many houses!
How terrible for you who get too many fields!
Finally there won't be any space left in the land.
Then you will live all alone.

9 I heard the LORD who rules over all announce
a message. He said,

"You can be sure that the great houses will become empty.
The fine homes will be left with no one living in them.
10 A ten-acre vineyard will produce only six gallons of wine.
Six bushels of seeds will produce less than a bushel of grain."

11 How terrible it will be for those who get up early in the morning
to start drinking!
How terrible for those who stay up late at night
until they are drunk with wine!
12 They have harps and lyres at their big dinners.
They have tambourines, flutes and wine.
But they don't have any concern for the mighty acts of the LORD.
They don't have any respect for what his powerful hands have done.
13 So my people will be taken away as prisoners.
That's because they don't understand what the LORD has done.
Their government leaders will die of hunger.
The rest of the people won't have any water to drink.
14 So the grave is hungry to receive them.
Its mouth is open wide to swallow them up.
Their nobles and the rest of the people will go down into it.
They will go there together with all those who have wild parties.
15 So man will be brought low.
People will be put to shame.
Those who brag will be brought down.
16 But the LORD who rules over all will be honored
because he judges fairly.
The holy God will show that he is holy
by doing what is right.
17 Then sheep will graze as if they were in their own grasslands.
Lambs will eat grass among the destroyed buildings
where rich people used to live.

18 How terrible it will be for those who continue to sin
and lie about it!
How terrible for those who keep on doing what is evil
as if they were tied to it!
19 How terrible for those who say,
"Let God hurry up and do what he says he will.
We want to see it happen.
Let the Holy One of Israel carry out his plan soon.
We want to know what it is."

20 How terrible it will be for those who say
that what is evil is good!
How terrible for those who say
that what is good is evil!
How terrible for those who say
that darkness is light
and light is darkness!
How terrible for those who say
that what is bitter is sweet
and what is sweet is bitter!

21 How terrible it will be for those who think they are wise!
How terrible for those who think they are really clever!

22 How terrible it will be for those
who are heroes at drinking wine!
How terrible for those
who are heroes at mixing drinks!
23 How terrible for those
who take money to set guilty people free!
How terrible for those
who don't treat good people fairly!
24 Flames of fire burn up straw.
Dry grass sinks down into those flames.
Evil people will be like plants whose roots rot away.
They will be like flowers that are blown away like dust.
That's because they have said no to the law of the LORD who rules over all.
They have turned against the message of the Holy One of Israel.
25 So the LORD's anger burns against his people.
He raises his hand against them. He strikes them down.
The mountains shake.
The bodies of dead people lie in the streets like trash.

Even then, the LORD is still angry.
His hand is still raised against them.

26 He lifts up a banner to gather the nations that are far away.
He whistles for them to come
from the farthest places on earth.
Here they come.
They are moving very quickly.
27 None of them grows tired.
None of them falls down.
None of them sleeps or even takes a nap.

All of them are ready for battle.
Every belt is pulled tight.
Not a single sandal strap is broken.
28 The enemies' arrows are sharp.
All of their bows are ready.
The hoofs of their horses are as hard as rock.
Their chariot wheels turn like a twister.
29 The sound of their army is like the roar of lions.
It's like the roar of young lions.
They growl as they capture what they were chasing.
They carry it off.
No one can take it away from them.
30 At that time the enemy army will roar over Israel.
It will sound like the roaring of the ocean.
If someone looks at the land of Israel,
he will see darkness and trouble.
The clouds will make even the light become dark.

The Lord Appoints Isaiah to Speak for Him

6 In the year that King Uzziah died, I saw the
Lord. He was seated on his throne. His long
robe filled the temple. He was highly honored.
2 Above him were seraphs. Each of them had six
wings. With two wings they covered their faces.
With two wings they covered their feet. And with
two wings they were flying.
3 They were calling out
to one another. They were saying,

"Holy, holy, holy is the LORD who rules over all.
The whole earth is full of his glory."

4 The sound of their voices caused the stone doorframe to shake. The temple was filled with smoke.
5 "How terrible it is for me!" I cried out. "I'm
about to be destroyed! My mouth speaks sinful
words. And I live among people who speak sinful
words. Now I have seen the King with my own
eyes. He is the LORD who rules over all."
6 A seraph flew over to me. He was holding a hot
coal. He had used tongs to take it from the altar.
7 He touched my mouth with the coal. He said,
"This has touched your lips. Your guilt has been
taken away. Your sin has been paid for."
8 Then I heard the voice of the Lord. He said,
"Who will I send? Who will go for us?"
I said, "Here I am. Send me!"
9 So he said, "Go and speak to these people. Tell
them,

" 'You will hear but never understand.
You will see but never know what you are seeing.'
10 Make the hearts of these people stubborn.
Plug up their ears.
Close their eyes.
Otherwise they might see with their eyes.
They might hear with their ears.
They might understand with their hearts.
And they might turn to me and be healed."

11 Then I said, "Lord, how long will it be like
that?"
He answered,

"It will last until the cities of Israel are destroyed
and no one is living in them.
It will last until the houses are deserted.
The fields will be completely destroyed.
12 It will last until I have sent everyone far away.
The land will be totally deserted.
13 Even if a tenth of the people remain there,
the land will be completely destroyed again.
But when oak trees and terebinth trees
are cut down, stumps are left.
And my holy people will be like stumps
that begin to grow again."

The Miraculous Sign of Immanuel

7 Ahaz was king of Judah. Rezin was king of
Aram. And Pekah was king of Israel. Rezin
and Pekah marched up to fight against Jerusalem.
But they couldn't overpower it. Ahaz was the son
of Jotham and the grandson of Uzziah. Pekah was
the son of Remaliah.
2 The royal family of Ahaz was told, "The army
of Aram has joined forces with Ephraim's army."
So the hearts of Ahaz and his people trembled with
fear. They shook just as trees in the forest shake
when the wind blows through them.
3 The LORD said to me, "Go out and see Ahaz.
Take your son Shear-Jashub with you. Meet Ahaz
at the end of the channel that brings water from the
Upper Pool. It is on the road to the Washerman's
Field.
4 "Tell Ahaz, 'Be careful. Stay calm. Do not be
afraid. Do not lose hope because of the burning
anger of Rezin, Aram and the son of Remaliah.
After all, they are nothing but a couple of pieces of
smoking firewood.
5 Aram, Ephraim and Remaliah's
son have planned to destroy you. They said,
6 "Let's
march into Judah and attack it. Let's tear everything
down. Then we can share the land among ourselves.
And we can make Tabeel's son king over it."
7 " 'But I am the LORD and King. I say,

" ' "That will not happen.
It will not take place.
8 The capital of Aram is Damascus.
And the ruler of Damascus is only Rezin.
Do not worry about the people of Ephraim.
They will be too crushed to be considered a people.
That will happen before 65 years are over.
9 The capital of Ephraim is Samaria.
And the ruler of Samaria is only Remaliah's son.
If you do not stand firm in your faith,
you will not stand at all." ' "

10The LORD spoke to Ahaz through me again.
He said, 11"I am the LORD your God. Ask me to
give you a miraculous sign. It can be anything in
the deepest grave or in the highest heaven."
12But Ahaz said, "I won't ask. I won't put the
LORD to the test."
13Then I said, "Listen, you members of the royal
family of Ahaz! Isn't it enough for you to test the
patience of men? Are you also going to test the
patience of my God? 14The LORD himself will give
you a miraculous sign. The virgin is going to have
a baby. She will give birth to a son. And he will be
called Immanuel.
15"The time will come when he is old enough to
decide between what is wrong and what is right.
By that time he will have only butter and honey to
eat. 16But even before that happens, the lands of
the two kings you are afraid of will be completely
destroyed.
17"The LORD will also bring the king of Assyria against you. And he will bring him against your
people and the whole royal family. That will be a
time of trouble unlike any since the people of
Ephraim broke away from Judah."
18At that time the LORD will whistle for the
Egyptians. They will come like flies from the
streams of Egypt. He will also whistle for the Assyrians. They will come from their country like
bees. 19All of them will come and camp in the deep
valleys. They will camp in caves in the rocks. And
they'll camp near bushes and water holes.
20At that time the Lord will use the Assyrians to
punish you. Ahaz had hired them earlier from east
of the Euphrates River. Now their king will be like
a razor in the Lord's hand. He will shave the hair
from your head and legs. He will also shave off
your beards.
21At that time a man will only be able to keep
one young cow and two goats alive. 22But they will
give enough milk and butter to live on. Everyone
who is left alive in the land will have nothing but
butter and honey to eat.
23The land used to have vineyards with 1,000
vines worth 25 pounds of silver. But soon the
whole land will be covered with thorns and
bushes. 24Men will go there to hunt with bows and
arrows. That's because it will be covered with
bushes and thorns. 25All of the hills used to be
plowed with hoes. But you won't go there anymore. That's because you will be afraid of the
thorns and bushes. Cattle will be turned loose on
those hills. And sheep will run there.

The LORD Uses Assyria to Judge Judah

8 The LORD said to me, "Get a large scroll.
Write 'Maher-Shalal-Hash-Baz' on it with a
pen. 2I will send for Zechariah and the priest Uriah.
They can be trusted. They will be witnesses for
me. Zechariah is the son of Jeberekiah."
3Then I went and made love to my wife, who
was a prophet. She became pregnant and had a
baby boy. The LORD said to me, "Name him Maher-Shalal-Hash-Baz.
4"The king of Assyria will carry off the wealth
of Damascus. He will also carry away the goods
that were taken from Samaria. That will happen
before the boy knows how to say 'My father' or
'My mother.'"
5The LORD continued,

6"I am like the gently flowing stream of Siloam.
But the people of Judah have turned their
backs on me.
They are filled with joy because of the fall
of Rezin
and the son of Remaliah.
7So I am about to bring against these people
the king of Assyria and his whole army.
The Assyrians will be like the mighty
Euphrates River
when it is flooding.
They will run over everything in
their path.
8They will sweep on into Judah like a flood.
They will pass through Judah and reach all
the way to Jerusalem.
Immanuel, they will attack your land like
an eagle.
Their wings will spread out and cover it."
9Sound the battle cry, you nations!
But you will be torn apart.
Listen, all of you lands far away!
Prepare for battle! But you will be torn apart.
Prepare for battle! But you will be torn
apart.
10Make your battle plans! But you won't
succeed.
Give your orders! But they won't be
carried out.
That's because God is with us.

Have Respect for God

11The LORD put his powerful hand on me and
spoke to me. He warned me not to live the way
these people live. He said,

12"People of Judah, do not agree with those
who say
Isaiah is guilty of treason.
Do not fear what they fear.
Do not be afraid.
13I am the LORD who rules over all.
You must think about me as holy.
You must have respect for me.
You must fear me.
14Then I will be a holy place of safety for you.
But for many people in Israel and Judah I
will be
a stone that causes them to trip.
I will be a rock that makes them fall.
And for the people of Jerusalem I will be
a trap and a snare.

15 Many of them will trip.
They will fall and be broken.
They will be trapped and captured."
16 Keep safe what the LORD said to you through me.
Seal up among my followers what he taught you through me.
17 I will wait for the LORD.
He is turning his face away from Jacob's people.
I will put my trust in him.

18 Here I am. Here are the children the LORD has given me. We are signs and reminders to Israel from the LORD who rules over all. He lives on Mount Zion.

19 Some will tell you to ask for advice from people who get messages from those who have died. Others will tell you to ask for advice from people who talk to the spirits of the dead. But those people only whisper. Their words are barely heard. So shouldn't you ask for advice from your God? Why should you get advice from dead people to help those who are alive?

20 Follow what the LORD taught you and said to
you through me. People who don't speak in keeping with those words won't have any hope in the
morning.
21 They will suffer and be hungry. They'll wander through the land. When they are very hungry, they will become angry. They'll look up toward heaven. They'll call down curses on their
king and their God.
22 Then they will look at the earth. They'll see nothing but suffering and darkness. They'll see terrible sadness. They'll be driven into total darkness.

A Son Will Be Given to Us

9 But there won't be any more sadness for those who were suffering. In the past the LORD brought shame on the land of Zebulun. He also brought shame on the land of Naphtali. But in days to come he will honor Galilee, where people from other nations live. He will honor the land along the Mediterranean Sea. And he will honor the territory east of the Jordan River.

2 The people who are now living in darkness
will see a great light.
They are now living in a very dark land.
But a light will shine on them.
3 LORD, you will make our nation larger.
You will increase their joy.
They will show you how glad they are.
They will be as glad as people are at harvest time.
They will be as glad as soldiers are
when they share the things they've taken after a battle.
4 You set Israel free from Midian long ago.
In the same way, you will break
the heavy yoke that weighs Israel down.
You will break the wooden beams that are on their shoulders.
You will break the rods of those who strike them down.
5 Every fighting man's boot that is used in battle will be burned up.
So will every piece of clothes
that is covered with blood.
All of them will be thrown into the fire.
6 A child will be born to us.
A son will be given to us.
He will rule over us.
And he will be called
Wonderful Adviser and Mighty God.
He will also be called Father Who Lives Forever
and Prince Who Brings Peace.
7 The authority of his rule will continue to grow.
The peace he brings will never end.
He will rule on David's throne
and over his kingdom.
He will make the kingdom strong and secure.
His rule will be based on what is fair and right.
It will last forever.
The LORD's great love will make sure that happens.
He rules over all.

The LORD Is Angry With Israel

8 The Lord has sent a message against Jacob's people.
He will punish Israel.
9 All of the people will know about it.
Ephraim's people and those who live in Samaria will know about it.
Their hearts are very proud.
They say,
10 "The brick buildings have fallen down.
But we will rebuild them with blocks of stone.
The fig trees have been chopped down.
But we'll plant cedar trees in place of them."
11 In spite of that, the LORD has made Rezin's enemies stronger.
He has stirred up Assyria to fight against Israel.
12 Arameans from the east
have opened their mouths and swallowed Israel up.
So have Philistines from the west.

Even then, the LORD is still angry.
His hand is still raised against them.

13 But his people have not returned
to the One who struck them down.
They haven't turned for help
to the LORD who rules over all.

14 So he will cut off from Israel heads and tails alike.
In a single day he will cut off palm branches and tall grass alike.
The palm branches are the people who rule over others.
The tall grass is the people who bow down to them.
15 The elders and important leaders are the heads.
The prophets who teach lies are the tails.
16 Those who guide the people of Israel are leading them down the wrong path.
So those who follow them aren't on the right road.
17 The Lord will not be pleased with the young men.
He won't take pity on widows and on children whose fathers have died.
All of them are ungodly and evil.
They say sinful things with their mouths.

Even then, the LORD is still angry.
His hand is still raised against them.

18 What is evil burns like a fire.
It burns up bushes and thorns.
It sets the forest on fire.
It sends up a huge column of smoke.
19 The LORD rules over all.
When he gets angry, he will burn up the land.
The people will die.
Men will eat their brothers.
20 People will eat up everything they can find on their right.
But they'll still be hungry.
They will eat everything they can find on their left.
But they won't be satisfied.
So they will eat the dead bodies of their children.
21 That's what Manasseh's people will do to Ephraim.
And that's what Ephraim's people will do to Manasseh.
Together they will turn against Judah.

Even then, the LORD is still angry.
His hand is still raised against them.

10 How terrible it will be for you who make laws that aren't fair!
How terrible for you who write laws that make life hard for others!
2 You take away the rights of poor people.
You hold back what is fair from my people who are suffering.
You take for yourselves what belongs to widows.
You rob children whose fathers have died.
3 What will you do on the day when the LORD punishes you?
On that day trouble will come from far away.
Who will you run to for help?
Who will you trust your riches with?
4 All you can do is bow down in fear among the prisoners.
All you can do is fall among those who have died in battle.

Even then, the LORD is still angry.
His hand is still raised against them.

The LORD Will Judge Assyria

5 The LORD says, "How terrible it will be for the people of Assyria!
They are the war club that carries out my anger.
6 I will send them against the ungodly nation of Judah.
I will order them to fight against my own people.
They make me angry.
I will order them to take their goods and carry them away.
I will order them to walk on my people as if they were walking on mud.
7 But that is not what the king of Assyria plans.
It is not what he has in mind.
His purpose is to destroy many nations.
His purpose is to put an end to them.
8 'Aren't all of my commanders kings?' he says.
9 'I took over Calno just as I took Carchemish.
I took over Hamath just as I did Arpad.
I took Samaria just as I did Damascus.
10 My powerful hand grabbed hold of kingdoms whose people worship statues of gods.
They had more gods than Jerusalem and Samaria did.
11 I took over Samaria and its statues of gods.
In the same way, I will take Jerusalem and its gods.'"

12 The Lord will finish everything he has planned to do against Mount Zion and Jerusalem. Then he'll say, "Now I will punish the king of Assyria. I will punish him because his heart and his eyes are so proud.
13 "The king of Assyria says,

"'I have used my powerful hand to take over all of those nations.
I am very wise.
I have great understanding.
I have wiped out the borders between nations.
I've taken their treasures.
Like a great hero I've brought their kings under my control.

14 I've taken the wealth of the nations.
It was as easy as reaching into a bird's nest.
I've gathered the riches of all of those countries.
It was as easy as gathering eggs
that have been left in a nest.
Not a single baby bird flapped its wings.
Not one of them opened its mouth to chirp.'"

15 Does an ax claim to be more important
than the one who swings it?
Does a saw brag that it is better
than the one who uses it?
That would be like a stick
swinging someone who picks it up!
It would be like a war club
waving the one who carries it!
16 So the LORD who rules over all will send a sickness.
The Lord will send it on the king of Assyria's strong fighting men.
It will make them weaker and weaker.
The army he was so proud of will be completely destroyed.
It will be as if it had been burned up in a fire.
17 The LORD is the light of Israel.
He will become a fire.
Israel's Holy One will become a flame.
In a single day he will burn up all of Assyria's bushes.
He will destroy all of their thorns.
18 He will completely destroy the beauty
of their forests and rich farm lands.
The Assyrian army will be like a sick man
who becomes weaker and weaker.
19 It will be like the trees of their forests.
So few of them will be left standing
that even a child could count them.

Israel Will Return to the LORD

20 In days to come, some people will still be left alive in Israel.
They will be from Jacob's family line.
But they won't depend any longer on
the nation that struck them down.
Instead, they will truly depend on the LORD.
He is the Holy One of Israel.
21 The people of Jacob who are still alive
will return to the Mighty God.
22 Israel, your people might be as many as the grains of sand by the sea.
But only a few of them will return.
The LORD has handed down a death sentence.
He will destroy his people.
What he does is right.
23 The LORD who rules over all will carry out his sentence.
The Lord will destroy the whole land.

24 The LORD rules over all. The Lord says,

"My people who live in Zion,
do not be afraid of the Assyrian army.
They beat you with rods.
They lift up war clubs against you,
just as the Egyptians did.
25 Very soon I will not be angry with you anymore.
I will turn my anger against the Assyrians.
I will destroy them."

26 The LORD who rules over all will beat them with a whip.
He will strike them down as he struck Midian down at the rock of Oreb.
And he will reach his wooden staff out over the waters.
That's what he did in Egypt.
27 People of Zion, in days to come he will lift
the heavy load of the Assyrians from your shoulders.
He will remove their yokes from your necks.
They will be broken
because you have become so strong.

28 The Assyrian army has entered the town of Aiath.
They have passed through Migron.
They have stored up supplies at Micmash.
29 They have marched through the pass there.
They said,
"Let's camp for the night at Geba."
The people of Ramah tremble with fear.
Those who live in Gibeah of Saul run away.
30 Town of Gallim, cry out!
Laishah, listen!
Poor Anathoth!
31 The people of Madmenah are running away.
Those who live in Gebim are hiding.
32 Today the Assyrians have stopped at Nob.
They are shaking their fists
at Mount Zion in the city of Jerusalem.

33 The Assyrian soldiers are like trees in a forest.
The LORD who rules over all
will chop them down.
The Lord will cut off their branches
with his great power.
He will chop the tall trees down.
He will cut down even the highest ones.
34 The Mighty One will chop down the forest with his ax.
He will cut down the cedar trees in Lebanon.

A Branch Will Come From Jesse's Family Line

11 Jesse's family is like a tree that has been cut down.
A new little tree will grow from its stump.
From its roots a Branch will grow and produce fruit.

2 The Spirit of the LORD will rest on that Branch.
He will help him to be wise and understanding.
He will help him make wise plans and carry them out.
He will help him know the LORD and have respect for him.
3 The Branch will take delight
in respecting the LORD.

He will not judge things only by the way they look.
He won't make decisions based simply on what people say.
4 He will always do what is right
when he judges those who are in need.
He'll be completely fair
when he makes decisions about poor people.
When he commands that people be punished,
it will happen.
When he orders that evil people be put to death,
it will take place.
5 He will put godliness on as if it were his belt.
He'll wear faithfulness around his waist.

6 Wolves will live with lambs.
Leopards will lie down with goats.
Calves and lions will eat together.
And little children will lead them around.
7 Cows will eat with bears.
Their little ones will lie down together.
And lions will eat straw like oxen.
8 A baby will play near a hole where cobras live.
A young child will put his hand into a nest
where poisonous snakes live.
9 None of those animals will harm or destroy anything or anyone
on my holy mountain of Zion.
The oceans are full of water.
In the same way, the earth will be filled
with the knowledge of the LORD.

10 At that time the man who is called the Root
from Jesse's family line will be like a banner that
brings nations together. They will come to him.
And the place where he rules will be glorious.
11 At that time the Lord will reach out his hand
to gather his people a second time. He will bring
back those who are left alive. He'll bring them
back from Assyria, Lower Egypt, Upper Egypt and
Cush. He'll bring them from Elam, Babylonia and
Hamath. He will also bring them from the islands
of the Mediterranean Sea.

12 He will lift up a banner.
It will show the nations that he is gathering the people of Israel.
He'll bring back those who had been taken away as prisoners.
He'll gather together the scattered people of Judah.
He'll bring them back from all four directions.

13 Ephraim's people won't be jealous anymore.
Judah's attackers will be cut off.
Ephraim won't be jealous of Judah.
And Judah won't attack Ephraim.
14 Together they will rush down the slopes of Philistia to the west.
They'll take what belongs to the people of the east.
They'll take over Edom and Moab.
The people of Ammon will be under their control.
15 The LORD will dry up
the Red Sea in Egypt.
With his powerful hand he'll send a burning wind
to sweep over the Euphrates River.
He will break it up into many streams.
Then people will be able to go across it wearing sandals.
16 There was a road the people of Israel used
when they came up from Egypt.
In the same way, there will be a wide road coming out of Assyria.
It will be used by the LORD's people who are left alive there.

Two Songs of Praise

12 In days to come, the people of Israel will sing,

"LORD, we will praise you.
You were angry with us.
But now your anger has turned away from us.
And you have brought us comfort.
2 God, you are the one who saves us.
We will trust in you.
Then we won't be afraid.
LORD, you give us strength.
We sing about you.
LORD, you have saved us."
3 People of Israel, he will save you.
That will bring you joy like water that is brought up from wells.

4 In days to come, the people of Israel will sing,

"Give thanks to the LORD. Worship him.
Tell the nations what he has done.
Announce how honored he is.
5 Sing to the LORD. He has done glorious things.
Let it be known all over the world.
6 People of Zion, give a loud shout!
Sing with joy!
The Holy One of Israel is among you.
And he is great."

A Message About Babylonia

13 Here is the vision about Babylonia that Isaiah, the son of Amoz, saw.

2 Lift up a banner on the top of a bare hill.
Shout to the enemy soldiers.
Wave for them to enter the gates
that are used by the nobles of Babylon.

[3] The LORD has set those soldiers apart to fight
for him.
He has sent for them to carry out his anger
against Babylon.
They will be happy when he wins the battle
for them.

[4] Listen! I hear a noise in the mountains.
It sounds like a huge crowd.
Listen! I hear a loud noise among the
kingdoms.
It sounds like nations gathering together.
The LORD who rules over all is bringing
an army together for war.
[5] They come from lands far away.
They come from the farthest places on earth.
The LORD and those weapons of his anger
are coming to destroy the whole country of
Babylonia.

[6] Cry out! The day of the LORD is near.
The Mighty One is coming to destroy them.
[7] Their hands won't be able to help them.
Everyone's heart will melt away in fear.
[8] The people will be filled with terror.
Pain and suffering will grab hold of them.
They will groan with pain like a woman
having a baby.
They'll look at one another in terror.
Their faces will burn with shame.

[9] The day of the LORD is coming.
It will be a terrible day.
The LORD's burning anger will blaze out.
He will make the land dry and empty.
He'll destroy the sinners in it.
[10] All of the stars in the sky
will stop giving their light.
The sun will be darkened as soon as it rises.
The moon will not shine.
[11] The LORD will punish the world because it is
so evil.
He will punish evil people for their sins.
He'll put an end to the bragging of those who
are proud.
He'll bring down the pride of those who
don't show any pity.
[12] He'll make men harder to find than pure gold.
They will be harder to find than gold
from Ophir.
[13] He will make the heavens tremble.
He'll shake the earth out of its place.
The LORD who rules over all will show how
angry he is.
At that time his burning anger will
blaze out.

[14] Outsiders who live in Babylonia will scatter
like antelope that are chased by a hunter.
They are like sheep that don't have a
shepherd.
All of them will return to their own people.
They will run back to their own countries.
[15] Those who are captured will have spears stuck
through them.
Those who are caught will be killed with
swords.
[16] Their babies will be smashed to pieces
right in front of their eyes.
Their houses will be robbed.
Their wives will be raped.

[17] The LORD will stir up the Medes to attack the
Babylonians.
They aren't interested in getting silver.
They don't delight in gold.
[18] Instead, they will use their bows and arrows
to strike the young men down.
They won't even show any mercy to babies.
They won't take pity on children.
[19] The city of Babylon is the jewel of kingdoms.
It is the glory and pride of the Babylonians.
But God will destroy it
just as he did Sodom and Gomorrah.
[20] No one will ever live in Babylon again.
No one will live there for all time to come.
Arabs will never set up their tents there.
Shepherds will never rest their flocks there.
[21] But desert creatures will lie down there.
Wild dogs will fill its houses.
Owls will live there.
Wild goats will jump around in it.
[22] Hyenas will cry out in its forts.
Wild dogs will bark in its beautiful palaces.
The time for Babylon to be punished is near.
Its days are numbered.

14 The LORD will show tender love toward
Jacob's people.
Once again he will choose Israel.
He'll settle them in their own land.
Outsiders will join them.
They and the people of Jacob will become
one people.
[2] Nations will help Israel
return to their own land.
People from other nations will belong to Israel.
They will serve them as male and female
servants in the LORD's land.
The Israelites will make prisoners of those who
had held them as prisoners.
They will rule over those who had crushed
them.

[3] The LORD will put an end to Israel's suffering
and trouble. They won't be slaves anymore. [4] They
will make fun of the king of Babylonia. They will
say,

"See how the one who crushed others has
fallen!
See how his anger has come to an end!
[5] The LORD has taken away the authority of evil
people.
He has broken the power of rulers.

[6] When they became angry, they struck nations down.
Their blows never stopped.
In their anger they brought nations under their control.
They attacked them again and again.
[7] All of the lands now enjoy peace and rest.
They break out into singing.
[8] Even the pine trees are glad.
The cedar trees of Lebanon are happy too.
They say, 'Babylon, you have fallen.
Now no one comes and cuts us down.'

[9] "King of Babylonia, many people in the grave are really excited
about meeting you when you go down there.
The spirits of the dead get up to welcome you.
At one time all of them were leaders in the world.
They were kings over the nations.
They get up from their thrones.
[10] All of them call out to you.
They say,
'You have become weak, just as we are.
You have become like us.'
[11] Your grand show of power has been brought down to the grave.
The noise of your harps has come down here along with your power.
Maggots are spread out under you.
Worms cover you.

[12] "King of Babylonia, you thought you were the bright morning star.
But now you have fallen from heaven!
You once brought nations down.
But now you have been thrown down to the earth!
[13] You said in your heart,
'I will go up to heaven.
I'll raise my throne
above the stars of God.
I'll sit as king on the mountain where the gods meet.
I'll set up my throne on the highest slopes of the sacred mountain.
[14] I will rise above the tops of the clouds.
I'll make myself like the Most High God.'
[15] But now you have been brought down to the grave.
You have been thrown into the deepest part of the pit.

[16] "Those who see you stare at you.
They think about what has happened to you.
They say to themselves,
'Is this the man who shook the earth?
Is he the one who made kingdoms tremble with fear?
[17] Did he turn the world into a desert?
Did he destroy its cities?
Did he refuse to let his prisoners go home?'

[18] "All of the kings of the nations are buried with honor.
Each of them lies in his own tomb.
[19] But you have been thrown out of your tomb.
You are like a branch that is cut off and thrown away.
You are covered with the bodies
of those who have been killed with swords.
You have been tossed into a stony pit along with them.
You are like a dead body that people have walked on.
[20] You won't be buried like other kings.
That's because you have destroyed your land.
You have killed your people.

"The children of that evil man will be killed.
None of them will be left to carry on the family name.
[21] So prepare a place to kill his children.
Kill them because of the sins of the rulers who lived before them.
They must not rise to power.
They must not rule over the world.
They must not cover the earth with their cities."

[22] "I will rise up against them,"
announces the LORD who rules over all.
"I will destroy Babylon.
It will not be remembered anymore.
No one will be left alive there.
I will destroy its people and their children after them,"
announces the LORD.
[23] "I will turn it into a place where nothing but owls can live.
I will turn it into a swamp.
I will sweep through it like a broom and destroy everything,"
announces the LORD who rules over all.

A Message About Assyria

[24] The LORD who rules over all has taken an oath. He has said,

"You can be sure that what I have planned will happen.
What I have decided will take place.
[25] I will crush the Assyrians in my land.
On my mountains I will walk all over them.
The yokes they put on my people will be removed.
The heavy load they put on their shoulders will be taken away."

[26] That's how the LORD carries out his plan all over the world.
That's how he reaches out his powerful hand to punish all of the nations.
[27] The LORD who rules over all has planned it.
Who can stop him?

He has reached out his powerful hand.
Who can keep him from using it?

A Message About the Philistines

28 A message came to me from the LORD in the year King Ahaz died. The LORD said,

29 "The rod of Assyria has struck all of you Philistines.
But do not be glad that it is broken.
That rod is like a snake that will produce an even more poisonous snake.
It will produce a darting, poisonous serpent.
30 Even the poorest people in Israel will have plenty to eat.
Those who are in need will lie down in safety.
But I will destroy your families.
They will die of hunger.
I will kill any of them who are still left alive.

31 "Cities of Philistia, cry out for help! Scream in pain!
All of you Philistines, melt away in fear!
An army is coming from the north in a cloud of dust.
No one in its ranks is falling behind.
32 What answer should be given
to the messengers from that nation?
Tell them, 'The LORD has made Zion secure.
His suffering people will find safety there.'"

A Message About Moab

15 Here is a message the LORD gave me about Moab.

The city of Ar in Moab is destroyed.
It happened in a single night.
Kir in Moab is also destroyed.
It happened in a single night.
2 The people of Dibon go up to their temple to worship.
They go to their high places to sob.
The people of Moab cry over the cities of Nebo and Medeba.
All of their heads are shaved.
All of their beards have been cut off.
3 In the streets they wear black clothes.
On their roofs and in the market places
all of them are crying.
They fall down flat with their faces toward the ground.
And they sob.
4 The people of Heshbon and Elealeh cry out.
Their voices are heard all the way to Jahaz.
So the fighting men of Moab cry out.
Their hearts are weak.

5 My heart cries out over Moab.
Some who run away get as far as Zoar.
Others run all the way to Eglath Shelishiyah.
Others go up the road to Luhith.
They are sobbing as they go.
Still others travel the road to Horonaim.
They sing a song of sadness because their town is being destroyed.
6 The waters at Nimrim are dried up.
And so is the grass.
The plants have died.
Nothing green is left.
7 The people are trying to escape
through the Valley of the Poplar Trees.
They are carrying with them the wealth
they have collected and stored up.
8 Their loud cries echo along the border of Moab.
They reach as far as Eglaim.
Their songs of sadness reach all the way to Beer Elim.
9 The waters of the city of Dimon are full of blood.
But the LORD will bring even more trouble on Dimon.
He will bring lions against those who run away from Moab.
They will also attack those who remain in the land.

16 People of Moab, send lambs as a gift to the ruler of Judah.
Send them from Sela.
Send them across the desert.
Send them to Mount Zion in the city of Jerusalem.
2 The women of Moab are at the places
where people go across the Arnon River.
They are like birds that flap their wings
when they are pushed from their nest.

3 The Moabites say to the rulers of Judah,
"Give us advice. Make a decision.
Cover us with your shadow.
Make it like night even at noon.
Hide those of us who are running away.
Don't turn them over to their enemies.
4 Let those who have run away from Moab stay with you.
Keep them safe from those who are trying to destroy them."

Those who crush others will be destroyed.
The killing will stop.
The attackers will disappear from the earth.
5 A man from the royal house of David will sit on Judah's throne.
He will rule with faithful love.
When he judges he will do what is fair.
He will be quick to do what is right.
6 We have heard all about Moab's pride.
We have heard how very proud they are.
They think they are so much better than others.

They brag about themselves.
But all of their bragging is nothing but empty words.

7 So the people of Moab cry out.
All of them cry over their country.
Sing a song of sadness.
Sob over the men of Kir Hareseth.
8 The vineyards of Heshbon dry up.
So do the vines of Sibmah.
The rulers of the nations
have walked all over its finest vines.
Those vines once reached as far as Jazer.
They spread out toward the desert.
Their new growth went
all the way to the Dead Sea.
9 Jazer sobs over the vines of Sibmah.
And so do I.
Heshbon and Elealeh,
I soak you with my tears!
There isn't any ripe fruit for people to shout about.
There isn't any harvest to make them happy.
10 Joy and gladness are taken away from the orchards.
No one sings or shouts in the vineyards.
No one stomps on grapes at the winepresses.
That's because the LORD has put an end to the shouting.
11 My heart sobs over Moab like a song of sadness played on a harp.
Deep down inside me I sob over Kir Hareseth.
12 Moab's people go to their high place to pray.
But all they do is wear themselves out.
Their god Chemosh can't help them at all.

13 That's the message the LORD has already spoken about Moab. 14 But now he says, "In exactly three years, people will look down on Moab's glory. Now Moab has many people. But by that time only a few of them will be left alive. And even they will be weak."

Messages About Damascus and Israel

17 Here is a message the LORD gave me about Damascus. He said,

"Damascus will not be a city anymore.
Instead, all of its buildings will be knocked down.
2 The cities of Aroer will be deserted.
They will be left to the flocks that lie down there.
No one will make them afraid.
3 Ephraim's people will no longer have cities with high walls around them.
Royal power will disappear from Damascus.
Those who are left alive in Aram
will be like the glory of the people of Israel,"
announces the LORD who rules over all.

4 "In days to come, the glory of Jacob's people will fade.
Their strength will get weaker and weaker.
5 It will be as when a worker cuts and gathers grain
in the Valley of Rephaim.
He gathers up stalks with his arms.
Only a few heads of grain are left.
6 In the same way, only a few people will be left alive.
It will be as when workers knock olives off the trees.
Only two or three olives are left on the highest branches.
Four or five at most are left on the limbs that produce fruit,"
announces the LORD, the God of Israel.

7 In days to come, men will look to their Maker for help.
They will turn their eyes to the Holy One of Israel.
8 They won't trust in the altars
they made with their own hands.
They won't pay any attention to the poles they used
to worship the goddess Asherah.
And they won't depend on the incense altars
they made with their own fingers.

9 At that time the strong cities in Israel will be deserted. They will be as they were when the Israelites drove the Canaanites out of them. They will be like places that are taken over by bushes and weeds. The whole land will become dry and empty.

10 Israel, you have forgotten God, who saves you.
You have not remembered the Rock, who keeps you safe.
You might set out the finest plants.
You might plant vines from other lands.
11 The plants might start to grow on the day you set them out.
The vines might begin to bud on the morning you plant them.
But even if they do, there won't be any harvest.
Instead, there will be sickness and pain that won't go away.

12 How terrible it looks for us!
Many nations are marching against us.
The noise of their armies is like the sound of the ocean.
They are making a lot of noise.
It sounds like huge waves crashing on the shore.
13 It sounds like the roar of rushing waters.
But when the LORD speaks out against them, they run far away.
The wind blows them away like straw on the hills.
A strong wind drives them along like tumbleweeds.

14 In the evening, the nations terrify us.
But before morning comes, they are gone.
That's what happens to those who steal our goods.
That's what happens to those who take what belongs to us.

A Message About Cush

18 How terrible it will be for the land whose armies are like large numbers of flying insects!
That land is along the rivers of Cush.
2 Its people send messengers on the Nile River.
They travel over the water in papyrus boats.

Messengers, hurry back home!
Go back to your people,
who are tall and have smooth skin.
Everyone is afraid of them.
They are warriors.
Their language is different from ours.
Their land is divided up by rivers.

3 Pay attention, all you people of the world!
Listen, all you who live on earth!
Banners will be lifted up on the mountains.
And you will see them.
Trumpets will be blown.
And you will hear them.
4 The LORD says to me,
"I will look down from heaven, where I live.
I will be as quiet as summer heat in the sunshine.
I will be as quiet as a cloud of dew in the heat of harvest."
5 A farmer cuts off new growth with pruning knives.
He cuts down spreading branches and takes them away.
He does it before the grapes are harvested.
That's when the blooms are gone and the grapes are ripe.
In the same way, the LORD will cut off the nations
that are gathered against his people.
6 Their dead bodies will be left for the birds of the mountains to eat.
They will be left for the wild animals.
The birds will eat the dead bodies all summer long.
The wild animals will eat them all through the winter.

7 At that time gifts will be brought to the LORD who rules over all.

The people who are tall and have smooth skin will bring them.
Everyone is afraid of those people.
They are warriors. Their language is different from ours.
Their land is divided up by rivers.

They will bring their gifts to Mount Zion. That's where the LORD who rules over all has put his Name.

A Message About Egypt

19 Here is a message the LORD gave me about Egypt.

The LORD is coming to Egypt.
He's riding on a cloud that moves very fast.
The statues of the gods in Egypt tremble with fear because of him.
The hearts of the people there melt away inside them.

2 The LORD says, "I will stir up one Egyptian against another.
Relatives will fight against relatives.
Neighbors will fight against one another.
Cities will fight against cities.
Kingdoms will fight against one another.
3 The people of Egypt will lose hope.
I will keep them from doing what they plan to do.
They will ask their gods for advice.
They will turn to the spirits of dead people for help.
They will go to people who get messages from those who have died.
They will ask for advice from people who talk to the spirits of the dead.
4 I will hand the Egyptians over
to a mean and unkind master.
A powerful king will rule over them,"
announces the Lord.
He is the LORD who rules over all.

5 The waters of the Nile River will dry up.
The bottom of it will be cracked and dry.
6 Its waterways will stink.
And the streams of Egypt will get smaller and smaller
until they dry up.
The tall grass that grows along the river will dry up.
7 So will the plants along the banks of the Nile.
Even the planted fields along the Nile will dry up.
Everything that grows there will blow away and disappear.
8 The fishermen will moan.
All those who drop hooks into the Nile will sob.
Those who throw their nets on the water
will become very sad.
9 Those who make clothes out of flax will lose hope.
So will those who weave fine linen.
10 Those who work with cloth will be unhappy.
And all those who work for money will be sick at heart.

11 The officials of the city of Zoan are very
foolish.
Pharaoh's wise men give advice that doesn't
make any sense.
How can they dare to say to Pharaoh,
"We're among the wise men"?
How can they say to him,
"We're like the advisers to the kings of
long ago"?
12 Pharaoh, where are your wise men now?
Let them tell you
what the LORD who rules over all
has planned against Egypt.
13 The officials of Zoan have become foolish.
The leaders of Memphis have been lied to.
The most important leaders in Egypt
have led its people down the wrong path.
14 The LORD has given them
a spirit that makes them feel dizzy.
They make Egypt unsteady in everything
it does.
Egypt is like a person who drinks too much.
He throws up and then walks around in the
mess he's made.
15 No one in Egypt can do anything to help them.
Its elders and important leaders can't help
them.
Its prophets and priests can't do anything.
Those who rule over others can't help.
And those who bow down to them can't
help either.

16 In days to come, the people of Egypt will be as
terrified as women. The LORD who rules over all
will raise his hand against them. Then they will
tremble with fear. 17 The people of Judah will bring
terror to the Egyptians. Everyone in Egypt who
hears the name of Judah will be terrified. That's
because of what the LORD who rules over all is
planning to do to them.

18 At that time the people of five cities in Egypt
will use the Hebrew language when they worship
the LORD who rules over all. They will take an
oath. And they will promise to be faithful to him.
One of those cities is called The City of the Sun.

19 At that time there will be an altar to the LORD
in the middle of Egypt. There will be a monument
to him at its border. 20 They will remind people that
the LORD who rules over all is worshiped in Egypt.
The people there will cry out to the LORD because
of those who treat them badly. He will send someone to stand up for them and save them. And he
will set them free.

21 So the LORD will make himself known to the
people of Egypt. At that time they will recognize that
he is the LORD. They will worship him by bringing
sacrifices and grain offerings to him. They will make
promises to the LORD. And they will keep them.
22 The LORD will strike Egypt with a plague. But then
he will heal them. They will turn to the LORD. And
he will answer their prayers and heal them.

23 At that time there will be a wide road from
Egypt to Assyria. The people of Assyria will go to
Egypt. And the people of Egypt will go to Assyria. The people of Egypt and Assyria will worship
the LORD together.

24 At that time Egypt, Assyria and Israel will be
a blessing to the whole earth. 25 The LORD who
rules over all will bless those three nations. He will
say, "Let the Egyptians be blessed. They are my
people. Let the Assyrians be blessed. My hands
created them. And let the Israelites be blessed.
They are my very own people."

A Message About Egypt and Cush

20 Sargon sent his highest commander to the
city of Ashdod. He attacked it and captured
it. Sargon was king of Assyria. 2 Three years earlier
the LORD had spoken to me. He had said, "Take off
the black clothes you are wearing. And take your
sandals off." So I did. I went around barefoot. I
didn't have anything on but my underwear.

3 After Ashdod was captured, the LORD said,
"My servant Isaiah has gone around barefoot for
three years. He has not worn anything but his
underwear. He is a sign and reminder to Egypt and
Cush about what will happen to them.

4 "The king of Assyria will lead prisoners away
from Egypt and Cush. Young people and old people alike will be taken away. Like Isaiah, they will
be barefoot. They will not be wearing anything but
their underwear. And their backsides will be bare.
So the Egyptians will be put to shame.

5 "People trusted in Cush to help them. They
bragged about what Egypt could do for them. But
they will be afraid and put to shame. 6 At that time
the people who live on the coast of Philistia will
speak up. They will say, 'See what has happened
to those we depended on! We ran to them for help.
We wanted them to save us from the king of Assyria. Now how can we escape?' "

A Message About Babylonia

21 Here is a message the LORD gave me about
Babylonia. It is known as the Desert by the
Two Rivers.

An attack is coming through the desert.
It is coming from a land of terror.
It's sweeping along like a windstorm
blowing across the Negev Desert.

2 I have seen a vision about something terrible
that will happen.
People are turning against Babylon.
Robbers are taking its goods.
Elamites, attack the city! Medes, surround it!
The LORD will put an end to all of the
suffering Babylon has caused.

3 The vision fills my body with pain.
Pains take hold of me.
They are like the pains of a woman having
a baby.

I am shaken by what I hear.
I'm terrified by what I see.
4 My heart grows weak.
Fear makes me tremble.
I longed for evening to come.
But it brought me horror instead of rest.

5 In my vision the Babylonians set the tables.
They spread the rugs out.
They eat. They drink.
Get up, you officers!
Rub your shields with oil!

6 The Lord said to me,

"Go. Put a guard on duty on Jerusalem's walls.
Have him report what he sees.
7 Tell him to watch for chariots
that are pulled by teams of horses.
Tell him to watch for men riding on donkeys
or camels.
Make sure he stays awake.
Make sure he stays wide awake."

8 "My master!" the guard shouts back.

"Day after day I stand here on the lookout
tower.
Every night I stay here on duty.
9 Look! Here comes a man in a chariot!
It's being pulled by a team of horses.
He's calling out the news,
'Babylon has fallen! It has fallen!
All of the statues of its gods
lie broken in pieces on the ground!'"

10 My people, you have been crushed
like grain on a threshing floor.
But now I'm telling you the good news
I've heard.
It comes from the LORD who rules over all.
He is the God of Israel.

A Message About Edom

11 Here is a message the LORD gave me about Edom.

Someone is calling out to me from the land of
Seir. He says,
"Guard, when will the night be over?
Guard, how soon will it end?"
12 The guard answers,
"Morning is coming. But the night will
return.
If you want to ask again,
come back and ask."

A Message About Arabia

13 Here is a message the LORD gave me about Arabia.

He told me to give orders to traders from
Dedan.
They were camping in the bushes
of Arabia.
14 I told them to bring water for those who
are thirsty.
I also gave orders to those who live
in Tema.
I told them to bring food for those who are
running away.
15 They are running away from where the fighting
is heaviest.
That's where the swords are ready to strike.
That's where the bows are ready to shoot.

16 The Lord says to me, "In exactly one year, Kedar's grand show of power will come to an end.
17 Only a few of Kedar's soldiers who shoot arrows
will be left alive." The LORD has spoken. He is the
God of Israel.

A Message About Jerusalem

22 Here is a message the LORD gave me about the Valley of Vision.

People of Jerusalem, what's the matter
with you?
Why have all of you gone up on the roofs
of your houses?
2 Why is your town so full of noise?
Why is your city so full of the sound of
wild parties?
Those among you who died weren't killed
with swords.
They didn't die in battle.
3 All of your leaders have run away.
They've been captured without a single
arrow being shot.
All those who were caught were taken away
as prisoners.
They ran off while your enemies were still
far away.
4 So I said, "Leave me alone.
Let me sob bitter tears.
Don't try to comfort me.
My people have been destroyed."

5 The LORD who rules over all sent the noise of
battle against you.
The Lord brought disorder and terror
to the Valley of Vision.
The walls of the city were knocked down.
Cries for help were heard in the mountains.
6 Soldiers from Elam came armed with bows
and arrows.
They came with their chariots and horses.
Soldiers from Kir got their shields ready.
7 Your rich valleys filled up with chariots.
Horsemen took up their battle positions at
your city gates.
8 Judah wasn't a safe place to live in
anymore.
When all of that happened, you depended
on the weapons in the Palace of the Forest
of Lebanon.

9 You saw that the City of David
had many holes in its walls.
They needed to be repaired.
You stored up water
in the Lower Pool.
10 You picked out the weaker buildings in
Jerusalem.
You tore them down and used their stones
to strengthen the city walls against attack.
11 You built a pool between the two walls.
You used it to save the water
that was running down from the Old Pool.
But you didn't look to the One who made it
all possible.
You didn't pay any attention to the One
who planned everything long ago.

12 The LORD who rules over all
called out to you at that time.
The Lord told you to sob and cry.
He told you to tear your hair out.
And he told you to put black clothes on.
13 Instead, you are enjoying yourselves at wild
parties!
You are killing cattle and sheep.
You are eating their meat and drinking wine.
You are saying, "Let's eat and drink,
because tomorrow we'll die."

14 I heard the LORD who rules over all speaking.
"Your sin can never be paid for as long as you people live," says the Lord.

15 The LORD who rules over all speaks. The Lord says,

"Go. Speak to the head servant Shebna.
He is in charge of the palace. Tell him,
16 'What are you doing here outside the city?
Who allowed you to cut out a tomb for
yourself here?
Who said you could carve out your grave on
the hillside?
Who allowed you to cut out your resting
place in the rock?

17 "'Watch out, you mighty man!
The LORD is about to grab hold of you.
He is about to throw you away.
18 He will roll you up tightly like a ball.
He will throw you into a very large
country.
There you will die.
And there the chariots you are so proud of
will remain.
You bring shame on your master's family!
19 The LORD will remove you from your job.
You will be brought down from your high
position.

20 "'At that time he will send for his servant Eliakim. He is the son of Hilkiah.
21 The LORD will put
your robe on Eliakim. He will tie your belt around
him. He will hand your authority over to him. Eliakim will be like a father to the people of Jerusalem and Judah.

22 "'The LORD will give Eliakim the key of
authority in David's royal house. No one can shut
what he opens. And no one can open what he
shuts.
23 The LORD will set him firmly in place like
a peg that is driven into a wall. He will hold a position of honor in his family.
24 The good name of his
whole family will depend on him. They will be
like bowls and jars hanging on a peg.

25 "'But a new day is coming,'" announces the LORD who rules over all. "'At that time the peg that was driven into the wall will give way. It will break off and fall down. And the heavy load hanging on it will also fall.'" The LORD has spoken.

A Message About Tyre

23 Here is a message the LORD gave me about Tyre.

Men in the ships of Tarshish, cry out!
The city of Tyre is destroyed.
Its houses and harbor are gone.
That's the message you have received
from the island of Cyprus.

2 People on the island of Tyre, be silent.
Traders from the city of Sidon, be quiet.
Those who sail on the Mediterranean Sea
have made you rich.
3 Grain from Egypt
came across the mighty waters.
The harvest of the Nile River brought wealth
to Tyre.
It became the market place of the nations.

4 Sidon, be ashamed. Mighty Tyre out in the sea,
be ashamed.
The sea has spoken. It has said,
"It's as if I had never felt labor pains or had
children.
It's as if I had never brought up sons or
daughters.
It's as if the city of Tyre had never existed."
5 The Egyptians will hear about what has
happened to Tyre.
They'll be very sad and troubled.

6 People of the island of Tyre, cry out!
Go across the sea to Tarshish.
7 Just look at Tyre.
It's no longer the old, old city that was
known for its wild parties.
It no longer sends its people out
to settle in lands far away.
8 Tyre was a city that produced kings.
Its traders were princes.
They were honored all over the earth.
So who planned to destroy such a city?
9 The LORD who rules over all planned to do it.
He wanted to bring down all of its pride
and glory.

He wanted to put to shame those who were
honored all over the earth.

10 People of Tarshish, spread out over your land
like the waters of the Nile.
There isn't anything to hold you back
anymore.
11 The LORD has reached his powerful hand out
over the sea.
He has made its kingdoms tremble with fear.
He has given a command concerning
Phoenicia.
He has ordered that its forts be destroyed.
12 He said, "No more wild parties for you!
People of Sidon, you are now destroyed!

"Leave your city. Go across the sea to Cyprus.
Even there you will not find any rest."
13 Look at the land of the Babylonians.
No one lives there anymore.
The Assyrians have turned it
into a place for desert creatures.
They built their towers in order to attack it.
They took everything out of its forts.
They knocked all of its buildings down.

14 Men in the ships of Tarshish, cry out!
Mighty Tyre is destroyed!

15 A time is coming when people will forget
about Tyre for 70 years. That's the length of a
king's life. But at the end of those 70 years, Tyre
will be like the prostitute that people sing about.
They say,

16 "Forgotten prostitute, pick up a harp.
Walk through the city.
Play the harp well. Sing many songs.
Then you will be remembered."

17 At the end of the 70 years, the LORD will punish Tyre. He will let it return to its way of life as a
prostitute. It will earn its living with all of the
kingdoms on the face of the earth. 18 But the money
it earns will be set apart for the LORD. The money
won't be stored up or kept for Tyre. Instead, it will
go to those who live the way the LORD wants them
to. It will pay for plenty of food and fine clothes
for them.

The LORD Will Destroy the Earth

24 The LORD is going to completely destroy
everything on earth.
He will twist its surface.
He'll scatter those who live on it.
2 Priests and people alike will suffer.
So will masters and their servants.
And so will women and their female
servants.
Sellers and buyers alike will suffer.
So will those who borrow and those who
lend.
And so will those who owe money and
those who lend it.
3 The earth will be completely destroyed.
Everything of value will be taken out of it.
That's what the LORD has said.

4 The earth will dry up completely.
The world will dry up and waste away.
The most important people on earth will
fade away.
5 The earth is polluted by its people.
They haven't obeyed the laws of the LORD.
They haven't done what he told them to do.
They've broken the covenant that will last
forever.
6 So the LORD will send a curse on the earth.
Its people will pay for what they've done.
They will be burned up.
Very few of them will be left.
7 The vines and fresh wine will dry up
completely.
Those who used to have a good time
will groan.
8 The happy sounds of tambourines will be gone.
The noise of those who enjoy wild parties
will stop.
The joyful music of harps will become
silent.
9 People will no longer sing as they drink wine.
Beer will taste bitter to those who drink it.
10 Destroyed cities will lie empty.
People will lock themselves inside their
houses.
11 In the streets people will cry out for wine.
All joy will turn into sadness.
All happiness will be driven out of the earth.
12 All of the buildings will be knocked down.
Every city gate will be smashed to pieces.
13 That's how it will be on the earth.
And that's how it will be among the nations.
It will be as when workers knock all but a few
olives off the trees.
It will be like a vine that has only a few
grapes left after the harvest.

14 Those who are left alive will shout with joy.
People from the west will praise the LORD
because he is the King.
15 So give glory to him, you who live in the east.
Honor the name of the LORD, you who are
in the islands of the sea.
He is the God of Israel.
16 From one end of the earth to the other we hear
singing.
People are saying,
"Give glory to the One who always does
what is right."

But I said, "I feel very bad.
I'm getting weaker and weaker.
How terrible it is for me!
People turn against one another.
They can't be trusted.
So they turn against each other."

[17] People of the earth,
terror, a pit and a trap are waiting for you.
[18] Anyone who runs away from the terror
will fall into the pit.
Anyone who climbs out of the pit
will be caught in the trap.
The LORD will open the windows of the skies.
He will flood the land.
The foundations of the earth will shake.
[19] The earth will be broken up.
It will split open.
It will be shaken to pieces.
[20] The earth will be unsteady like someone who is drunk.
It will sway like a tent in the wind.
Its sin will weigh so heavily on it that it will fall.
It will never get up again.

[21] At that time the LORD will punish
the spiritual forces of evil in the heavens above.
He will also punish the kings on the earth below.
[22] They will be brought together
like prisoners in chains.
They'll be locked up in prison.
After many days the LORD will punish them.
[23] The LORD who rules over all will rule
on Mount Zion in Jerusalem.
The elders of the city will be there.
They will see his glory.
His rule will be so glorious that the sun and moon
will be too ashamed to shine.

A Song of Praise

25 LORD, you are my God.
I will honor you.
I will praise your name.
You have been perfectly faithful.
You have done wonderful things.
You had planned them long ago.
[2] You have turned cities into piles of trash.
You have pulled down the high walls that were around them.
You have destroyed our enemies' forts.
They will never be rebuilt.
[3] Powerful nations will honor you.
Even sinful people from their cities will have respect for you.
[4] Poor people have come to you for safety.
You have kept needy people safe when they were in trouble.
You have been a place to hide when storms came.
You have been a shade from the heat of the sun.
Evil people attack us.
They are like a storm beating against a wall.
[5] They are like the heat of the desert.
You stopped the noisy shouts of our enemies.
You kept them from winning the battle over us and singing about it.
You are like the shadow of a cloud that cools the earth.

[6] On Mount Zion the LORD who rules over all will prepare
a feast for all of the nations.
The best and richest foods
and the finest aged wines will be served.
[7] On that mountain the LORD will destroy
the veil of sadness that covers all of the nations.
He will destroy the gloom that is spread over everyone.
[8] He will swallow up death forever.
The LORD and King will wipe away the tears
from everyone's face.
He will remove the shame of his people
from the whole earth.
The LORD has spoken.

[9] At that time they will say,

"He is our God.
We trusted in him, and he saved us.
He is the LORD. We trusted in him.
Let us be filled with joy because he saved us."

[10] The LORD's powerful hand will keep Mount Zion safe.
But he will walk all over Moab.
Its people will be crushed,
just as straw is crushed in animal waste.
[11] They will try to swim their way out of it.
They will spread their hands out in it,
just as a swimmer spreads his hands out to swim.
But God will bring down Moab's pride.
None of their skill will help them.
[12] He will pull down their high, strong walls.
He will bring them down to the ground.
He'll bring them right down to the dust.

Another Song of Praise

26 At that time a song will be sung in the land of Judah. It will say,

"We have a strong city.
God's saving power surrounds it
like walls and towers.
[2] Open its gates
so that those who do what is right can enter.
They are the people who remain faithful to God.
[3] LORD, you will give perfect peace
to anyone who commits himself to be faithful to you.
That's because he trusts in you.

4 "Trust in the LORD forever.
The LORD is the Rock.
The LORD will keep us safe forever.
5 He brings down those who are proud.
He pulls down cities that have high walls.
They fall down flat on the ground.
He throws them down to the dust.
6 The feet of those who were crushed stomp on them.
Those who were helpless walk all over them."

7 LORD, you are honest and fair.
You guide those who do what is right.
You lead them on a straight path.
You make their way smooth.
8 LORD, we are living the way your laws command us to live.
We are waiting for you to act.
Our hearts long for you to be true to your name.
That's what you are known for.
9 My heart longs for you at night.
My spirit longs for you in the morning.
You will come and judge the earth.
Then the people of the world will learn to do what is right.
10 Grace is shown to sinful people.
But they still don't learn to do what is right.
They keep on doing evil even in a land where others are honest and fair.
They don't have any respect for the majesty of the LORD.
11 LORD, you have raised your hand high to punish them.
But they don't even see it.
Let them see how much you love your people.
Then they will be put to shame.
Let the fire you are saving for your enemies burn them up.

12 LORD, you give us peace.
You are the one who has done everything we've accomplished.
13 LORD, you are our God.
Other masters besides you have ruled over us.
But your name is the only one we honor.
14 Those other masters are now dead.
They will never live again.
Their spirits won't rise from the dead.
You punished them and destroyed them.
You wiped out all memory of them.
15 LORD, you have made our nation grow.
You have made it larger.
You have gained glory for yourself.
You have increased the size of our land.

16 LORD, when your people were suffering, they came to you.
When you punished them,
they could barely whisper a prayer.
17 LORD, you made us like a woman who is having a baby.
She groans and cries out in pain.
18 We were pregnant. We groaned with pain.
But nothing was born.
We didn't bring your saving power to the earth.
We didn't give life to the people of the world.

19 Israel, those among you who have died will live again.
Their bodies will rise from the dead.
You who lie in the grave,
wake up and shout with joy.
The dew of the morning gives life to the earth.
So the earth will give up its dead people.

20 My people, go into your houses.
Shut the doors behind you.
Hide yourselves for a little while.
Do it until the LORD's anger is over.
21 He is coming from the place where he lives.
He will punish the people of the earth for their sins.
The blood that has been spilled on the earth will be brought out into the open.
The ground will no longer hide those who have been killed.

Israel Will Be Saved

27 At that time
the LORD will punish Leviathan with his sword.
His great, powerful and deadly sword will punish
the serpent that glides through the sea.
He will kill that twisting sea monster.

2 At that time the LORD will sing about his fruitful vineyard. He will say,

3 "I am the LORD. I watch over my vineyard.
I water it all the time.
I guard it day and night.
I do it so no one can harm it.
4 I am not angry with my vineyard.
I wish thorns and bushes would come up in it.
Then I would march out against them in battle.
I would set all of them on fire.
5 So the enemies of my people had better come to me for safety.
They should make peace with me.
I will say it again.
They should make peace with me."

6 In days to come, Jacob's people will put down roots like a vine.
Israel will bud and bloom.
They will fill the whole world with fruit.

7 The LORD struck down those who struck Israel down.
But he hasn't punished Israel as much.

The LORD killed those who killed many of
his people.
But he hasn't punished his people as much.
8 The LORD will use war to punish Israel.
He will make them leave their land.
With a strong blast of his anger he will drive
them out.
It will be as if the east wind were blowing.
9 The people of Jacob will have to pay for
their sin.
That must happen in order for their sin to be
taken away.
They will make all of the altar stones like chalk.
They will crush them to pieces.
No poles that had been used to worship the
goddess Asherah will be left standing.
No incense altars will be left either.
10 Cities that have high walls around them will
become empty.
They will be deserted settlements.
They will be like a desert.
Calves will eat and lie down in them.
They will strip the branches of their
trees bare.
11 When their twigs are dry, they will be
broken off.
Then women will come and make fires
with them.
The people of Jacob don't understand
the LORD.
So the One who made them won't be
concerned about them.
Their Creator won't show them his favor.

12 At that time the LORD will separate Israel from
other people. He will gather the Israelites together.
He will gather them one by one from the Euphrates River all the way to the Wadi of Egypt. 13 At
that time a loud trumpet will be blown. Those who
were dying in Assyria will come and worship the
LORD. So will those who were taken away to
Egypt. All of them will worship the LORD on his
holy mountain in Jerusalem.

The LORD Will Judge Israel

28 How terrible it will be for the city of
Samaria!
It sits on a hill like a crown of flowers.
The leaders of Ephraim are drunk.
They take pride in their city.
It sits above a valley that has rich soil.
How terrible it will be for the glorious
beauty of that fading flower!
2 The Lord will bring the strong and powerful
king of Assyria against Samaria.
The Lord will throw that city down to the
ground with great force.
It will be like a hailstorm.
It will be like a wind that destroys
everything.
It will be like a driving rain and a flooding
storm.
3 That city is like a crown.
The leaders of Ephraim are drunk.
They take pride in their city.
But its enemies will walk all over it.
4 It sits on a hill above a rich valley.
It's like a crown of flowers whose glorious
beauty is fading away.
But it will become like a fig that is ripe before
harvest.
As soon as someone sees it,
he picks it and swallows it.

5 At that time the LORD who rules over all
will be like a glorious crown.
He will be like a beautiful wreath
for those of his people who will be
left alive.
6 He will help those
who are fair when they judge.
He will give strength to those
who turn back their enemies at the
city gate.

7 Israel's leaders are drunk from wine.
They can't walk straight.
They are drunk from beer.
They are unsteady on their feet.
Priests and prophets drink beer.
They can't walk straight.
They are mixed up from drinking too
much wine.
They drink too much beer.
They are unsteady on their feet.
The prophets see visions but don't really
understand them.
The priests aren't able to make good
decisions.
8 They throw up. All of the tables are covered
with the mess they've made.
There isn't one spot on the tables
that isn't smelly and dirty.

9 My people are making fun of me. They say,
"Who does he think he's trying to teach?
Who does he think he's explaining his
message to?
Is it to children who do not need their mother's
milk anymore?
Is it to those who have just been taken from
her breast?
10 Here is how he teaches.
Do this and do that.
Do that and do this.
Obey this rule and obey that rule.
Obey that rule and obey this rule.
Learn a little here and learn a little there."

11 All right then, these people won't listen to me.
So God will speak to them.
He will speak by using people who speak
unfamiliar languages.
He will speak by using the mouths of
strangers.

12 He said to his people,
"I am offering you a resting place.
Let those who are tired rest."
He continued, "I am offering you a place of peace and quiet."
But they wouldn't listen.
13 So then, here is what the LORD's message will become to them.
Do this and do that.
Do that and do this.
Obey this rule and obey that rule.
Obey that rule and obey this rule.
Learn a little here and learn a little there.
So when they try to go forward,
they'll fall back and be wounded.
They'll be trapped and captured.

14 Listen to the LORD's message,
you who make fun of the truth.
Listen, you who rule over these people in Jerusalem.
15 You brag, "We have entered into a covenant with death.
We have made an agreement with the grave.
When a terrible plague comes to punish us,
it can't touch us.
That's because we depend on lies to keep us safe.
We hide behind what isn't true."

16 So the LORD and King speaks. He says,

"Look! I am laying a stone in Zion.
It is a stone that has been tested.
It is the most important stone for a firm foundation.
The one who trusts in that stone will never be shaken.
17 I will use a measuring line to prove that you have not been fair.
I will use a plumb line to prove that you have not done what is right.
Hail will sweep away the lies you depend on to keep you safe.
Water will flood your hiding place.
18 Your covenant with death will be called off.
The agreement you made with the grave will not stand.
When the terrible plague comes to punish you,
you will be beaten down by it.
19 As often as it comes, it will carry you away.
Morning after morning, day and night,
it will come to punish you."

If you understand this message,
it will bring you absolute terror.
20 You will be like someone whose bed is too short to lie down on.
You will be like those whose blankets are too small to wrap themselves in.
21 The LORD will rise up to judge, just as he did at Mount Perazim.
He will get up to act, just as he did in the Valley of Gibeon.
He'll do his work, but it will be strange work.
He'll carry out his task, but it will be an unexpected one.
22 Now stop making fun of me.
If you don't, your chains will become heavier.
The LORD who rules over all has spoken to me.
The Lord has told me he has ordered that the whole land be destroyed.

23 Listen and hear my voice.
Pay attention to what I'm saying.
24 When a farmer plows in order to plant, does he plow without stopping?
Does he keep on breaking up the soil and making the field level?
25 When he's made the surface even, doesn't he plant caraway seeds?
Doesn't he scatter cummin?
Doesn't he plant wheat in its proper place?
Doesn't he plant barley where it belongs?
Doesn't he plant spelt along the edge of the field?
26 His God directs him.
He teaches him the right way to do his work.

27 Caraway seeds are beaten out with a rod.
They aren't separated out under a threshing sled.
Cummin seeds are beaten out with a stick.
The wheel of a cart isn't rolled over them.
28 Grain must be ground up to make bread.
A farmer separates it out.
But he doesn't go on doing it forever.
He drives the wheels of a threshing cart over it.
But he doesn't let the horses grind it to dust.
29 All of those insights come from the LORD who rules over all.
His advice is wonderful. His wisdom is glorious.

The LORD Will Judge Jerusalem

29 Jerusalem, how terrible it will be for you!
Ariel, you are the city where David settled.
The years will come and go.
Keep on celebrating your regular feasts.
2 The LORD says, "Ariel, I will surround you.
Jerusalem, I will get ready to attack you.
Your people will sob.
They will sing songs of sadness.
I will make you like the front of an altar
that is covered with blood.
3 I will be like an army that is camped against you on all sides.
I will surround you with towers in order to attack you.
I will build my ramps all around you and set up my ladders.

4 You will be brought down to the grave.
You will speak from deep down inside the ground.
Your words will be barely heard out of the dust.
Your voice will sound like the voice of a ghost
coming from under the ground.
Your words will sound like a whisper out of the dust."

5 Jerusalem, all of your enemies will become like fine dust.
Their terrifying armies will become like straw
that the wind blows away.
All of a sudden, in an instant,
6 the LORD who rules over all will come.
He will come with thunder, earthquakes and a lot of noise.
He'll bring windstorms and rainstorms with him.
He'll send a blazing fire that will burn everything up.

7 Armies from all of the nations will fight against Ariel.
They will attack it and its fort.
They'll surround it completely.
But suddenly those armies will disappear like a dream.
They will vanish like a vision in the night.
8 They will be like a hungry person who dreams he is eating.
But when he wakes up, he's still hungry.
They will be like a thirsty person who dreams he is drinking.
But when he wakes up, he is weak.
His thirst hasn't been satisfied.
In the same way, the armies from all of the nations
that fight against Mount Zion will disappear.

9 People of Jerusalem, be shocked and amazed.
Make yourselves blind so you can't see anything.
Get drunk, but not from wine.
Be unsteady on your feet, but not because of beer.
10 The LORD has made you fall into a deep sleep.
He has closed the eyes of your prophets.
He has covered the heads of your seers so they can't see.

11 For you, this whole vision is like words that
are sealed up in a scroll. Suppose you give it to
someone who can read. And suppose you say to
him, "Please read this for us." Then he'll answer,
"I can't. It's sealed up." 12 Or suppose you give the
scroll to someone who can't read. And suppose
you say, "Please read this for us." Then he'll
answer, "I don't know how to read."

13 The Lord says,

"These people worship me only with their words.
They honor me by what they say.
But their hearts are far away from me.
Their worship doesn't mean anything to me.
They teach nothing but human rules.
14 So once more I will shock these people
with many wonderful acts.
I will destroy the wisdom of those who think they are so wise.
I will do away with the cleverness of those who think they are so smart."
15 How terrible it will be for people who do everything they can
to hide their plans from the LORD!
They do their work in darkness.
They think, "Who sees us? Who will know?"
16 They turn everything upside down.
How silly they are to think that potters are like the clay they work with!
Can what is made say to the one who made it,
"You didn't make me"?
Can the pot say to the potter,
"You don't know anything"?

17 In a very short time, Lebanon will be turned into rich farm lands.
The rich farm lands will seem like a forest.
18 At that time those who can't hear will hear what is read from the scroll.
Those who are blind will come out of gloom and darkness.
They will be able to see.
19 Those who aren't proud will once again find their joy in the LORD.
And those who are in need will find their joy in the Holy One of Israel.
20 Those who don't show any pity will vanish.
Those who make fun of others will disappear.
All those who look for ways to do what is evil will be cut off.
21 Without any proof, they claim that a man is guilty.
In court they try to trap
the one who speaks up for others.
By using dishonest witnesses they keep those who aren't guilty
from being treated fairly.

22 Long ago the LORD saved Abraham from trouble. Now he says to Jacob's people,

"You will not be ashamed anymore.
Your faces will no longer grow pale with fear.
23 You will see your children living among you.
I myself will give you those children.
Then you will honor my name.
You will recognize how holy I am.
I am the Holy One of Jacob.

You will have great respect for me.
I am the God of Israel.
24 I will give understanding to you
who find yourselves going down the wrong path.
You who are always speaking against others
will accept what I teach you."

The LORD Will Judge His Stubborn People

30 "How terrible it will be for these
stubborn children of mine!"
announces the LORD.
"How terrible for those who carry out plans
that did not come from me!
Their agreement with Egypt did not come
from my Spirit.
So they pile up one sin on top of another.
2 They go down to Egypt
without asking me for advice.
They look to Pharaoh to help them.
They ask Egypt to keep them safe.
3 But looking to Pharaoh will only bring them
shame.
Asking Egypt for help will bring them
dishonor.
4 Their officials have gone to the city of Zoan.
Their messengers have arrived in Hanes.
5 But the people of Judah will be put to shame
because they are trusting in a nation that is
useless to them.
Egypt will not bring them any help or
advantage.
Instead, it will bring them shame and
dishonor."

6 Here is a message the LORD gave me about the
animals in the Negev Desert.

Judah's messengers carry their riches on the
backs of donkeys.
They carry their treasures on the humps
of camels.
They travel through a land of danger and
suffering.
It's a land that is filled with lions.
Poisonous snakes are also there.
The messengers travel to a nation
that can't do them any good.
7 They travel to Egypt, whose help is totally
useless.
That's why I call it Rahab the Do-Nothing.

8 The LORD said to me, "Go now.
Write on a tablet for the people of Judah
what I am about to say.
Also write it on a scroll.
In days to come
it will be a witness that lasts forever.
9 The people of Judah refuse to obey me.
They are children who tell lies.
They will not listen to what I want to teach
them.
10 They say to the seers,
'Don't see any more visions!'
They say to the prophets,
'Don't give us any more visions of what is
right!
Tell us pleasant things.
Prophesy things we want to hear even
if they aren't true.
11 Get out of our way!
Get off our path!
Keep the Holy One of Israel away
from us!'"

12 So the Holy One of Israel speaks. He says,

"You have turned your backs on what I have
said.
You have depended on telling people lies.
You have crushed others.
13 Those sins are like cracks in a high wall.
They get bigger and bigger.
Suddenly the wall breaks apart.
Then it quickly falls down.
14 It breaks into small pieces like a clay pot.
It breaks up completely.
Not one piece is left big enough
for taking coals from a fireplace.
Not one piece is left for dipping water out
of a well."

15 The LORD and King is the Holy One of Israel.
He says,

"You will find peace and rest
when you turn away from your sins and
depend on me.
You will receive the strength you need
when you stay calm and trust in me.
But you do not want to do what I tell you to.
16 You said, 'No. We'll escape on horses.'
So you will have to escape!
You said, 'We'll ride off on fast horses.'
So those who chase you will use faster
horses!
17 When one of them dares you to fight,
a thousand of you will run away.
When five of them dare you,
all of you will run away.
So few of you will be left that you will be
like a flagpole on top of a mountain.
You will be like only one banner on a hill."

18 But the LORD longs to show you his favor.
He wants to give you his tender love.
The LORD is a God who is always fair.
Blessed are all those who wait for him
to act!

19 People of Zion, who live in Jerusalem, you
won't sob anymore. When you cry out to the Lord
for help, he will show you his favor. As soon as he
hears you, he'll answer you. 20 He might treat you
like prisoners. You might eat the bread of trouble.
You might drink the water of suffering. But he will

be your Teacher. He won't hide himself anymore.
You will see him with your own eyes. 21You will
hear your Teacher's voice behind you. You will
hear it whether you turn to the right or the left. It
will say, "Here is the path I want you to take. So
walk on it."

22Then you will get rid of the silver statues of
your gods. You won't have anything to do with the
gold statues either. All of them are "unclean." So
you will throw them away like dirty rags. You will
say to them, "Get away from us!"

23The LORD will send rain on the seeds you
plant in the ground. The crops that grow will be
rich and plentiful. At that time your cattle will eat
grass in rolling meadows. 24The oxen and donkeys
that work the soil will eat the finest feed and
crushed grain. The farmers will use pitchforks and
shovels to separate it from the straw.

25At that time the towers of your enemies will
fall down. Their soldiers will die. Streams of water
will flow on every high mountain and hill.

26The moon will shine like the sun. And the sunlight will be seven times brighter than usual. It will
be like the light of seven full days. That will happen when the LORD bandages and heals the
wounds and bruises he has brought on his people.

27 The LORD will come from far away
in all of his power and glory.
He will show his burning anger.
Thick clouds of smoke will be all around
him.
His mouth will speak angry words.
The words from his tongue will be like a
destroying fire.
28 His breath will be like a rushing flood
that rises up to the neck.
He'll separate out the nations he is going to
destroy.
He'll place a bit in their jaws.
It will lead them down the road to death.
29 You will sing
as you do on the night you celebrate a
holy feast.
Your hearts will be filled with joy.
You will be as joyful as people playing
their flutes
as they go up to the mountain of the LORD.
He is the Rock of Israel.
30 The LORD will cause people to hear his
powerful voice.
He will make them see his arm coming
down to punish them.
It will come down with burning anger and
destroying fire.
It will come down with rain, thunderstorms
and hail.
31 The voice of the LORD will tear the Assyrians
apart.
He will strike them down with his mighty
rod.
32 He will strike them
with his rod to punish them.
Each time he does, his people will celebrate
with the music of harps and tambourines.
He will use his powerful arm
to strike the Assyrians down in battle.
33 In the Valley of Ben Hinnom, Topheth has been
prepared for a long time.
It has been made ready for the king
of Assyria.
Its fire pit has been made deep and wide.
It has plenty of wood for the fire.
The breath of the LORD
will be like a stream of burning sulfur.
It will set the wood on fire.

The LORD Will Judge Those Who Depend on Egypt

31 How terrible it will be for those who go
down to Egypt for help!
How terrible for those who depend on
horses!
They trust in how many chariots they have.
They trust in how strong their horsemen are.
But they don't look to the Holy One of Israel.
They don't ask the LORD for his help.
2 He too is wise. He can bring horrible
trouble.
He does what he says he'll do.
He'll rise up against everyone who does what
is evil.
He'll fight against those who help them.
3 The men of Egypt are only human.
They aren't God.
Their horses are only flesh and blood.
They aren't spirits.
The LORD will reach out his powerful hand
to punish everyone.
The Egyptians provide help.
But they will be tripped up.
The people of Judah receive the help.
But they will fall down.
All of them will be destroyed.

4The LORD says to me,

"A powerful lion stands over its food and
growls.
A lot of shepherds can be brought together
to drive it away.
But the lion is not frightened by their shouts.
It is not upset by the noise they make.
In the same way, I will come down from
heaven.
I will fight on Mount Zion and on its hills.
Nothing will drive me away.
I am the LORD who rules over all.
5 Like a bird hovering over its nest, I will guard
Jerusalem.
I will keep it safe.
I will pass over it and save it.
I am the LORD who rules over all."

[6]People of Israel, return to the LORD. He's the one you have so strongly opposed. [7]The time will come when every one of you will turn your backs on your gods of silver and gold. You sinned when you made them with your own hands.

[8]The LORD says, "The Assyrians will be killed
with swords.
But it will not be men who use them.
The swords that kill them will not be used
by human beings.
The Assyrians will run away from those
swords.
But their young men will be caught
and forced to work hard.
[9]Their hiding places will be destroyed
when terror strikes them.
When their commanders see their enemy's
battle flags,
they will be filled with panic,"
announces the LORD.
His fire blazes out from Mount Zion.
His furnace burns in Jerusalem.

The King Who Will Do What Is Right

32 A king will come who will do what
is right.
His officials will govern fairly.
[2]Each man will be like a place to get out of
the wind.
He will be like a place to hide from storms.
He'll be like streams of water flowing in
the desert.
He'll be like the shadow of a huge rock in a
dry and thirsty land.

[3]Then the eyes of those who see won't be
closed anymore.
The ears of those who hear will listen to
the truth.
[4]The minds of thoughtless people will know
and understand.
Tongues that stutter will speak clearly.
[5]Foolish people won't be considered noble
anymore.
Those who are worthless won't be highly
respected.
[6]A foolish person says foolish things.
His mind is full of evil thoughts.
He doesn't do what is right.
He tells lies about the LORD.
He doesn't give hungry people any food.
He doesn't let thirsty people have any water.
[7]The one who is worthless uses sinful methods.
He makes evil plans against poor people.
He destroys them with his lies.
He does it even when those people are right.
[8]But the man who is noble makes noble plans.
And by doing noble things he succeeds.

The Sinful Women in Jerusalem

[9]You women who are so contented,
pay attention to me.
You who feel so secure,
listen to what I have to say.
[10]You feel secure now.
But in a little over a year you will tremble
with fear.
The grape harvest will fail.
There won't be any fruit.
[11]So tremble, you contented women.
Tremble with fear, you who feel so secure.
Take your fine clothes off.
Put black clothes on.
[12]Beat your chests to show how sad you are.
The pleasant fields have been destroyed.
The fruitful vines have dried up.
[13]My people's land is overgrown with thorns
and bushes.
Sob over all of the houses that were once
filled with joy.
Cry over this city that used to be full of
wild parties.
[14]The royal palace will be left empty.
The noisy city will be deserted.
The fort and lookout tower will become
a dry and empty desert forever.
Donkeys will enjoy being there.
Flocks will eat there.
[15]That will continue until the Holy Spirit
is poured out on us from heaven.
Then the desert will be turned into rich farm
lands.
The rich farm lands will seem like a forest.
[16]In the desert and the rich farm lands
people will do what is right.
And they will treat one another fairly.
[17]Doing what is right will bring peace and rest.
When my people do that, they will stay
calm
and trust in the LORD forever.
[18]They will live in a peaceful land.
Their homes will be secure.
They will enjoy peace and quiet.
[19]Hail might strip the forests bare.
Cities might be completely destroyed.
[20]But how blessed you people will be!
You will plant your seeds by every stream.
You will let your cattle and donkeys
wander anywhere they want to.

The LORD Will Judge Assyria

33 How terrible it will be for you, you who
destroy others!
Assyria, you haven't been destroyed yet.
How terrible for you, you who turn against
others!
Others haven't turned against you yet.
When you stop destroying,
you will be destroyed.
When you stop turning against others,
others will turn against you.

[2]LORD, show us your favor.
We long for you to help us.

Make us strong every morning.
Save us when we're in trouble.
3 When the nations hear you thunder, they run away.
When you rise up against them, they scatter.
4 Nations, what you have taken in battle is destroyed.
It's as if young locusts had eaten it up.
Like large numbers of locusts,
people rush to get it.

5 The LORD is honored. He lives in heaven.
He will fill Zion's people with what is fair and right.
6 He will be the firm foundation for their entire lives.
He will give them all of the wisdom, knowledge and saving power they will ever need.
Respect for the LORD is the key to that treasure.

7 Look! Judah's brave men cry out loud in the streets.
The messengers who were sent to bring peace sob bitter tears.
8 The wide roads are deserted.
No one travels on them.
Our peace treaty with Assyria is broken.
Those who witnessed it are looked down on.
No one is respected.
9 The land is filled with sadness and wastes away.
Lebanon is full of shame and dries up.
The rich land of Sharon is like the Arabah Desert.
The trees of Bashan and Carmel drop their leaves.

10 "Now I will take action," says the LORD.
"Now I will be honored.
Now I will be respected.
11 Assyria, your plans and actions are like straw.
Your anger is a fire that will destroy you.
12 The nations will be burned to ashes.
They will be like bushes that are cut down and set on fire.

13 "You nations far away, listen to what I have done!
My people who are near, recognize how powerful I am!
14 The sinners in Zion are terrified.
They tremble with fear.
They say, 'Who of us can live through the LORD's destroying fire?
Who of us can live through the fire that burns forever?'
15 A person must do what is right.
He must be honest and tell the truth.
He must not get rich by cheating others.
His hands must not receive money from those who want special favors.
He must not let his ears listen to plans to commit murder.
He must close his eyes to even thinking about doing what is evil.
16 A person like that will be kept safe.
It will be as if he were living on high mountains.
It will be as if he were living in a mountain fort.
He will have all of the food he needs.
And he will never run out of water."

17 People of Judah, you will see the king in all of his glory and majesty.
You will view his kingdom spreading far and wide.
18 You will think about what used to terrify you.
You will say to yourself,
"Where is that chief officer of Assyria?
Where is the one who forced us to send gifts to his king?
Where is the officer in charge of the towers that were used when we were attacked?"
19 You won't see those proud people anymore.
They spoke a strange language.
None of us could understand it.

20 Just look at Zion! It's the city
where we celebrate our regular feasts.
Turn your eyes toward Jerusalem.
It will be a peaceful place to live in.
It will be like a tent that will never be moved.
Its stakes will never be pulled up.
None of its ropes will be broken.
21 There the LORD will be our Mighty One.
It will be like a place of wide rivers and streams.
No boat with oars will travel on them.
No mighty ship will sail on them.
22 That's because the LORD is our judge.
The LORD gives us our law.
The LORD is our king.
He will save us.

23 The ropes on your ship hang loose.
The mast isn't very secure.
The sail isn't spread out.
But the LORD will strike the Assyrians down.
Then a large amount of goods will be taken from them and divided up.
Even people who are disabled will carry off what was taken.
24 No one living in Zion will ever say again, "I'm sick."
And the sins of those who live there will be forgiven.

The LORD Will Judge the Nations

34 Nations, come near and listen to me!
Pay attention to what I'm about to say.
Let the earth and everything in it listen.

Let the world and everything that comes out
of it pay attention.
2 The LORD is angry with all of the nations.
His anger burns against all of their armies.
He will totally destroy them.
He will have them killed.
3 Those who are killed won't be buried.
Their dead bodies will be thrown on the
ground.
They will give off a very bad smell.
Their blood will cover the mountains.
4 All of the stars in the heavens will vanish.
The sky will be rolled up like a scroll.
All of the stars in the sky will fall like dried-up
leaves from a vine.
They will drop like wrinkled figs from a
fig tree.
5 The sword of the LORD will finish its deadly
work in the sky.
Then it will come down to strike Edom.
He will totally destroy that nation.
6 His sword will be red with blood.
It will be covered with fat.
The blood will flow like the blood
of lambs and goats being sacrificed.
The fat will be like the fat
taken from the kidneys of rams.
That's because the LORD will offer a sacrifice
in the city of Bozrah.
He will kill many people in Edom.
7 The people and their leaders will be killed
like wild oxen and young bulls.
Their land will be wet with their blood.
The dust will be covered with their fat.

8 That's because the LORD has set aside a day to
pay Edom back.
He has set aside a year to pay them back for
what they did to the city of Zion.
9 The streams of Edom will be turned into tar.
Its dust will be turned into blazing sulfur.
Its land will become burning tar.
10 The fire will keep burning night and day.
It can't be put out.
Its smoke will go up forever.
Edom will lie empty for all time to come.
No one will ever travel through it again.
11 The desert owl and screech owl will make it
their home.
The great owl and the raven will build their
nests there.
God will use his measuring line
to show how completely Edom will be
destroyed.
He will use his plumb line
to show how empty Edom will become.
12 Edom's nobles won't have anything left there
that can be called a kingdom.
All of its princes will vanish.
13 Thorns will cover its forts.
Bushes and weeds will cover its safest
places.
It will become a home for wild dogs.
It will become a place where owls live.
14 Desert creatures will meet with hyenas.
Wild goats will call out to each other.
Night creatures will also sleep there.
They will find places where they can rest.
15 Owls will make their nests and lay their eggs
there.
And they will hatch them.
They will take care of their little ones
under the shadow of their wings.
Male and female falcons will also gather
there.

16 Look in the scroll of the LORD. There you will
read that

none of those animals will be missing.
Male and female alike will be there.
The LORD himself has commanded it.
And his Spirit will gather them together.
17 The LORD will decide what part of the land
goes to each animal.
Then he will give each one its share.
It will belong to them forever.
And they will live there for all time to come.

The LORD Will Set His People Free

35 The desert and the dry ground will be glad.
The dry places will be full of joy.
Flowers will grow there.
Like the first crocus in the spring,
2 the desert will bloom with flowers.
It will be very glad and shout with joy.
The glorious beauty of Lebanon will be given
to it.
It will be as beautiful as the rich lands
of Carmel and Sharon.
Everyone will see the glory of the LORD.
They will see the beauty of our God.

3 Strengthen the hands of those who are weak.
Help those whose knees give way.
4 Say to those whose hearts are afraid,
"Be strong. Do not fear.
Your God will come.
He will pay your enemies back.
He will come to save you."

5 Then the eyes of those who are blind will be
opened.
The ears of those who can't hear will be
unplugged.
6 Those who can't walk will leap like a deer.
And those who can't speak will shout
with joy.
Water will pour out in dry places.
Streams will flow in the desert.
7 The burning sand will become a pool of water.
The thirsty ground will become bubbling
springs.
In the places where wild dogs once lay down,
tall grass and papyrus will grow.

8 A wide road will go through the land.
It will be called The Way of Holiness.
Only those who are pure and clean can travel
on it.
Only those who lead a holy life can use it.
Evil and foolish people can't walk on it.
9 No lions will use it.
No wild animals will be on it.
None of them will be there.
Only people who have been set free will walk
on it.
10 Those the LORD has saved will return to
their land.
They will sing as they enter the city of Zion.
Joy that lasts forever will be
like beautiful crowns on their heads.
They will be filled with gladness and joy.
Sorrow and sighing will be gone.

Sennacherib Warns Jerusalem

36 Sennacherib attacked and captured all of
the cities of Judah that had high walls
around them. It was in the 14th year of the rule of
Hezekiah. Sennacherib was king of Assyria. 2He
sent his field commander from Lachish to King
Hezekiah at Jerusalem. He sent him along with a
large army. The commander stopped at the channel
that brings water from the Upper Pool. It was on
the road to the Washerman's Field.
3Eliakim, Shebna and Joah went out to him. Eliakim, the son of Hilkiah, was in charge of the
palace. Shebna was the secretary. Joah, the son of
Asaph, kept the records.
4The field commander said to them, "Give Hezekiah this message. Tell him,

"'Sennacherib is the great king of Assyria. He says, "Why are you putting your faith
in what your king says? 5You say you have a
military plan. You say you have a strong
army. But your words don't mean anything.
Who are you depending on? Why don't you
want to stay under my control?
6"'"You are depending on Egypt. Why are
you doing that? Egypt is nothing but a broken papyrus stem. Try leaning on it. It will
only cut your hand. Pharaoh, the king of
Egypt, is just like that to everyone who
depends on him.
7"'"Suppose you say to me, 'We are
depending on the LORD our God.' Didn't
Hezekiah remove your god's high places and
altars? Didn't Hezekiah say to the people of
Judah and Jerusalem, 'You must worship at
the altar in Jerusalem'?
8"'"Come on. Make a deal with my master, the king of Assyria. I'll give you 2,000
horses. But only if you can put riders on
them! 9You are depending on Egypt for chariots and horsemen. You can't drive away
even the least important officer among my
master's officials.
10"'"Besides, do you think I've come
without being sent by the LORD? Have I
come to attack and destroy this land without
receiving a message from him? The LORD
himself told me to march out against your
country. He told me to destroy it."'"

11Then Eliakim, Shebna and Joah spoke to the
field commander. They said, "Please speak to us
in the Aramaic language. We understand it. Don't
speak to us in Hebrew. If you do, the people who
are on the wall will be able to understand you."
12But the commander replied, "My master sent
me to say these things. Are these words only for
your master and you to hear? Aren't they also for
the men who are sitting on the wall? They are going
to suffer just like you. They'll have to eat their own
waste. They'll have to drink their own urine."
13Then the commander stood up and spoke in
the Hebrew language. He called out, "Pay attention
to what the great king of Assyria is telling you. 14He
says, 'Don't let Hezekiah trick you. He can't save
you! 15Don't let Hezekiah talk you into trusting in
the LORD. Don't believe him when he says, "You
can be sure that the LORD will save us. This city
will not be handed over to the king of Assyria."'
16"Don't listen to Hezekiah. The king of Assyria says, 'Make a peace treaty with me. Come over
to my side. Then every one of you will eat fruit
from your own vine and fig tree. Every one of you
will drink water from your own well. 17You will
do that until I come back. Then I'll take you to a
land that is just like yours. It's a land that has a lot
of grain and fresh wine. It has plenty of bread and
vineyards.
18"'Don't let Hezekiah fool you. He's telling
you a lie when he says, "The LORD will save us."
Has the god of any nation ever saved his land from
the powerful hand of the king of Assyria? 19Where
are the gods of Hamath and Arpad? Where are the
gods of Sepharvaim? Have they saved Samaria
from my power? 20Which one of all of the gods of
those countries has been able to save his land from
me? So how can the LORD save Jerusalem from
my power?'"
21But the people remained silent. They didn't
say anything. That's because King Hezekiah had
commanded, "Don't answer him."
22Then Eliakim, the son of Hilkiah, went to
Hezekiah. Eliakim was in charge of the palace.
The secretary Shebna went with him. So did Joah,
the son of Asaph. Joah kept the records. All of
them went to Hezekiah with their clothes torn.
They told him what the field commander had said.

Isaiah Prophesies That Jerusalem Will Be Saved

37 When King Hezekiah heard what the field
commander had said, he tore his clothes.
He put on black clothes. Then he went into the
LORD's temple. 2Hezekiah sent Eliakim, who was

in charge of the palace, to me. He also sent the
leading priests and the secretary Shebna to me. All
of them were wearing black clothes.
3They told me, "Hezekiah says, 'Today we're
in great trouble. The LORD is warning us. He's
bringing shame on us. Sometimes babies come to
the moment when they should be born. But their
mothers aren't strong enough to allow them to be
born. Today we are like those mothers. We aren't
strong enough to save ourselves.
4" 'Perhaps the LORD your God will hear everything the field commander has said. His master,
the king of Assyria, has sent him to make fun of
the living God. Maybe the LORD your God will
punish him for what he has heard him say. So pray
for the remaining people who are still alive here.' "
5King Hezekiah's officials came to me. 6Then I
said to them, "Tell your master, 'The LORD says,
"Do not be afraid of what you have heard. The
officers who are under the king of Assyria have
spoken evil things against me. 7Listen! I will send
him news from his own country. It will upset him
so much that he will return home. There I will
have him cut down with a sword." ' "
8The field commander heard that the king of
Assyria had left Lachish. So the commander
pulled his troops back from Jerusalem. He went to
join the king. He found out that the king was fighting against Libnah.
9During that time Sennacherib received a
report. He was told that Tirhakah was marching
out to fight against him. Tirhakah was king of
Egypt. He was from the land of Cush.
When Sennacherib heard the report, he sent
messengers again to Hezekiah with a letter. It said,
10"Tell Hezekiah, the king of Judah, 'Don't let the
god you depend on trick you. He says, "Jerusalem
will not be handed over to the king of Assyria."
But don't believe him. 11I'm sure you have heard
about what the kings of Assyria have done to all
of the other countries. They have destroyed them
completely. So do you think you will be saved?
12" 'The kings who ruled before me destroyed
many nations. Did the gods of those nations save
them? Did the gods of Gozan, Haran or Rezeph
save them? What about the gods of the people of
Eden who were in Tel Assar? 13Where is the king
of Hamath? Where is the king of Arpad? Where is
the king of the city of Sepharvaim? Where are the
kings of Hena or Ivvah?' "

Hezekiah Prays to the LORD

14When Hezekiah received the letter from the
messengers, he read it. Then he went up to the
LORD's temple. There he spread the letter out in
front of the LORD.
15Hezekiah prayed to the LORD. He said,
16"LORD who rules over all, you are the God of Israel. You sit on your throne between the cherubim.
You alone are God over all of the kingdoms on
earth. You have made heaven and earth. 17Listen,
LORD. Hear us. Open your eyes, LORD. Look at the
trouble we're in. Listen to what Sennacherib is
saying. You are the living God. And he dares to
make fun of you!
18"LORD, it's true that the kings of Assyria have
completely destroyed many nations and their
lands. 19They have thrown the statues of the gods
of those nations into the fire. And they have
destroyed them. That's because they weren't really
gods at all. They were nothing but statues that
were made out of wood and stone. They were
made by human hands.
20"LORD our God, save us from the powerful
hand of Sennacherib. Then all of the kingdoms on
earth will know that you alone are God."

Sennacherib Falls From Power

21I sent a message to Hezekiah. I said, "The
LORD is the God of Israel. He says, 'You have
prayed to me about Sennacherib, the king of Assyria. 22So here is the message I have spoken
against him. I am telling him,

" ' "You will not win the battle over Zion.
Its people hate you and make fun of you.
The people of Jerusalem lift up their heads
proudly
as you run away.
23 Who have you laughed at?
Who have you spoken evil things against?
Who have you raised your voice against?
Who have you looked at so proudly?
You have done it against me.
I am the Holy One of Israel!
24 Through your messengers
you have laughed at me again and
again.
And you have said,
'I have many chariots.
With them I have climbed to the tops of
the mountains.
I've climbed the highest mountains in
Lebanon.
I've cut down its tallest cedar trees.
I've cut down the best of its pine trees.
I've reached its farthest mountains.
I've reached its finest forests.
25 I've dug wells in strange lands.
I've drunk the water from them.
I've walked through all of Egypt's streams.
I've dried up every one of them.'
26 " ' "But I, the LORD, say, 'Haven't you heard
what I have done?
Long ago I arranged for you to do all
of that.
In days of old I planned it.
Now I have made it happen.
You have turned cities with high walls
into piles of stone.
27 Their people do not have any power left.
They are troubled and put to shame.

They are like plants in the field.
They are like new green plants.
They are like grass that grows on a roof.
It dries up before it is completely grown.

28 "'"'But I know where you live.
I know when you come and go.
I know how very angry you are with me.
29 You roar against me and brag.
And I have heard your bragging.
So I will put my hook in your nose.
I will put my bit in your mouth.
And I will make you go home
by the same way you came.'"'"

30 The LORD said, "Hezekiah, here is a miraculous sign for you.

"This year you will eat what grows by itself.
Next year you will eat what grows from that.
But in the third year you will plant your crops and gather them in.
You will plant your grapevines and eat their fruit.
31 The people of Judah who are still alive will be like plants.
Once more they will put down roots and produce fruit.
32 Out of Jerusalem will come those who remain.
Out of Mount Zion will come those who are still left alive.
My great love will make sure that happens.
I rule over all.

33 "Here is a message from me about the king of Assyria. It says,

"'He will not enter this city.
He will not even shoot an arrow at it.
He will not come near it with a shield.
He will not build a ramp in order to climb over its walls.
34 By the way that he came he will go home.
He will not enter this city,'
announces the LORD.
35 "I will guard this city and save it.
I will do it for myself.
And I will do it for my servant David."

36 Then the angel of the LORD went into the
camp of the Assyrians. He put to death 185,000
soldiers there. The people of Jerusalem got up the
next morning. They looked out and saw all of the
dead bodies. 37 So Sennacherib, the king of Assyria, took the army tents down. Then he left. He
returned to Nineveh and stayed there.
38 One day Sennacherib was worshiping in the
temple of his god Nisroch. His sons Adrammelech
and Sharezer cut him down with their swords. Then
they escaped to the land of Ararat. Esarhaddon
became the next king after his father Sennacherib.

Hezekiah Praises the LORD for Healing Him

38 In those days Hezekiah became very sick.
He knew he was about to die. I went to see
him. I told him, "The LORD says, 'Put everything
in order. Make out your will. You are going to die
soon. You will not get well again.'"
2 Hezekiah turned his face toward the wall. He
prayed to the LORD. He said, 3 "LORD, please
remember how faithful I've been to you. I've lived
the way you wanted me to. I've served you with
all my heart. I've done what is good in your sight."
And Hezekiah cried bitterly.
4 A message came to me from the LORD. He
said, 5 "Go and speak to Hezekiah. Tell him, 'The
LORD, the God of King David, says, "I have heard
your prayer. I have seen your tears. I will add 15
years to your life. 6 And I will save you and this
city from the powerful hand of the king of Assyria. I will guard this city.
7 "'"Here is a miraculous sign from me. It will
show you that I will heal you, just as I promised I
would. 8 The shadow that was made by the sun has
gone down ten steps on the stairway of Ahaz. I will
make it go back up those ten steps."'" So the
shadow went back up the ten steps it had gone
down.

9 Here is a song of praise that was written by
Hezekiah, the king of Judah. He wrote it after he
was sick and had gotten well again.

10 I said, "I'm enjoying the best years of my life.
Must I now go through the gates of death?
Will the rest of my years be taken away from me?"
11 I said, "LORD, I'll never see you again
while I'm still alive.
I'll never see people anymore.
I'll never again be with those who live in this world.
12 My body is like a shepherd's tent.
It has been pulled down and carried off.
My life is like a piece of cloth that I've rolled up.
You have cut it off from the loom.
In a short period of time you have brought my life to an end.
13 I waited patiently until sunrise.
But like a lion you broke all of my bones.
In a short period of time you have brought my life to an end.
14 I cried softly like a weak little bird.
I groaned like a sad dove.
My eyes grew tired as I looked up toward heaven.
Lord, I'm in trouble. Please come and help me!
15 "But what can I say?
You have promised to heal me.
And you yourself have done it.

Once I was proud and bitter.
But now I will live the rest of my life free of pride.
16 Lord, people find the will to live because you keep your promises.
And my spirit also finds life in your promises.
You brought me back to health.
You let me live.
17 I'm sure it was for my benefit
that I suffered such great pain.
You love me. You kept me
from going down into the pit of death.
You have put all of my sins
behind your back.
18 People in the grave can't praise you.
Dead people can't sing praise to you.
Those who go down to the grave
can't hope for you to be faithful to them.
19 It is those who are alive who praise you.
And that's what I'm doing today.
Fathers tell their children
about how faithful you are.

20 "You will save me.
So we will sing and play music on stringed instruments.
We will sing all the days of our lives
in your temple."

21 When Hezekiah was sick, I had said, "Press
some figs together. Spread them on a piece of
cloth. Apply them to Hezekiah's boil. Then he'll
get well again."
22 At that time Hezekiah had asked me, "What
will the miraculous sign be to prove I'll go up to
the LORD's temple?" That's when the LORD had
made the shadow go back ten steps.

Messengers Come From Babylon to Hezekiah

39 At that time Merodach-Baladan, the king
of Babylonia, sent Hezekiah letters and a
gift. He had heard that Hezekiah had been sick but
had gotten well again. Merodach-Baladan was the
son of Baladan.
2 Hezekiah gladly received the messengers. He
showed them what was in his storerooms. He
showed them the silver and gold. He took them to
where the spices and the fine olive oil were kept.
He showed them where he kept all of his weapons.
And he showed them all of his treasures. In fact, he
showed them everything that was in his palace and
in his whole kingdom.
3 Then I went to King Hezekiah. I asked him,
"What did those men say? Where did they come
from?"

"They came from a land far away," Hezekiah said. "They came to me from Babylon."

4 I asked, "What did they see in your palace?"

"They saw everything in my palace," Hezekiah said. "I showed them all of my treasures."

5 Then I said to Hezekiah, "Listen to the message of the LORD who rules over all. He says,
6 'You can be sure the time will come when everything in your palace will be carried off to Babylon.
Everything the kings before you have stored up
until this day will be taken away. There will not be
anything left,' says the LORD.
7 "'Some of the members of your family line
will be taken away. They will be your own flesh
and blood. They will include the children who will
be born into your family line in years to come. And
they will serve the king of Babylonia in his
palace.'"
8 "The message the LORD has spoken through
you is good," Hezekiah replied. He thought,
"There will be peace and safety while I'm still
living."

God Comforts His People

40 "Comfort my people," says your God.
"Comfort them.
2 Speak tenderly to the people of Jerusalem.
Announce to them
that their hard service has been completed.
Tell them that their sin has been paid for.
Tell them I have punished them enough
for all of their sins."

3 A messenger is calling out,
"In the desert prepare
the way for the LORD.
Make a straight road through it
for our God.
4 Every valley will be filled in.
Every mountain and hill will be made level.
The rough ground will be smoothed out.
The rocky places will be made flat.
5 Then the glory of the LORD will appear.
And everyone will see it.
The LORD has spoken."

6 Another messenger says, "Cry out."
And I said, "What should I cry?"

"Cry out, 'All people are like grass.
They don't last any longer than flowers in the field.
7 The grass dries up. The flowers fall to the ground.
That happens when the LORD makes his wind blow on them.
So people are just like grass.
8 The grass dries up. The flowers fall to the ground.
But what our God says will stand forever.'"

9 Zion, you are bringing good news to your people.
Go up on a high mountain and announce it.
Jerusalem, you are bringing good news to them.
Shout the message loudly.

Shout it out loud. Don't be afraid.
Say to the towns of Judah,
"Your God is coming!"
10 The LORD and King is coming with power.
His powerful arm will rule for him.
He has set his people free.
He is bringing them back as his reward.
He has won the battle over their enemies.
11 He takes care of his flock like a shepherd.
He gathers the lambs in his arms.
He carries them close to his heart.
He gently leads those that have little ones.

12 Who has measured the oceans by using the palm of his hand?
Who has used the width of his hand to mark off the sky?
Who has measured out the dust of the earth in a basket?
Who has weighed the mountains on scales?
Who has weighed the hills in a balance?
13 Who can ever understand what is in the LORD's mind?
Who can ever give him advice?
14 Did the LORD have to ask anyone to help him understand?
Did he have to ask someone to teach him the right way?
Who taught him what he knows?
Who showed him how to understand?

15 The nations are only a drop in a bucket to him.
He considers them as nothing but dust on the scales.
He weighs the islands as if they were only fine dust.
16 Lebanon doesn't have enough trees to keep his altar fires burning.
It doesn't have enough animals to sacrifice as burnt offerings to him.
17 To him, all of the nations don't amount to anything.
He considers them to be worthless.
In fact, they are less than nothing in his sight.

18 So who will you compare God to?
Is there any other god like him?
19 Will you compare him to a statue of a god?
Any skilled worker can make a statue.
Then another worker covers it with gold
and makes silver chains for it.
20 But someone who is too poor to bring that kind of offering
will choose some wood that won't rot.
Then he looks for a skilled worker.
He pays the worker to make a statue of a god that won't fall over.

21 Don't you know who made everything?
Haven't you heard about him?
Hasn't it been told to you from the beginning?
Haven't you understood it ever since the earth was made?
22 God sits on his throne high above the earth.
Its people look like grasshoppers to him.
He spreads the heavens out like a cover.
He sets it up like a tent to live in.
23 He takes the power of princes away from them.
He reduces the rulers of this world to nothing.
24 They are planted.
They are scattered like seeds.
They put down roots in the ground.
But as soon as that happens, God blows on them and they dry up.
Then a windstorm sweeps them away like straw.

25 "So who will you compare me to?
Who is equal to me?" says the Holy One.
26 Look up toward the sky.
Who created everything you see?
The LORD causes the stars to come out at night one by one.
He gives each one of them a name.
His power and strength are great.
So none of the stars is missing.

27 Family of Jacob, why do you say,
"The LORD doesn't notice our condition"?
People of Israel, why do you say,
"Our God doesn't pay any attention to our rightful claims"?
28 Don't you know who made everything?
Haven't you heard about him?
The LORD is the God who lives forever.
He created everything on earth.
He won't become worn out or get tired.
No one will ever know how great his understanding is.
29 He gives strength to those who are tired.
He gives power to those who are weak.
30 Even young people become worn out and get tired.
Even the best of them trip and fall.
31 But those who trust in the LORD
will receive new strength.
They will fly as high as eagles.
They will run and not get tired.
They will walk and not grow weak.

The LORD Helps Israel

41 The LORD says, "People who live on the islands,
come and stand quietly in front of me.
Let the nations gain new strength
in order to state their case.
Let them come forward and speak.
Let us go to court and find out who is right.

2 "Who has stirred up a king from the east?
Who has helped him win his battles?
I hand nations over to him.
I bring kings under his control.

He turns them into dust with his sword.
With his bow he turns them into straw
blowing in the wind.
3 He hunts them down. Then he moves on
unharmed.
He travels so fast that his feet
don't seem to touch the ground.
4 Who has made that happen? Who has carried
it out?
Who has created all of the people who have
ever lived?
I, the LORD, have done it.
I was with the first of them.
And I will be with the last of them."

5 The people on the islands have seen that king
coming.
And it has made them afraid.
People tremble with fear from one end of
the earth to the other.
They come and gather together.
6 They help each other.
They say to one another, "Be strong!"
7 One skilled worker makes a statue of a god.
Another covers it with gold.
The first worker says to the second,
"You have done a good job."
Another worker smooths out the metal with a
hammer.
Still another gives the statue its final shape.
The third worker says to the last one,
"You have done a good job."
Then they nail the statue down so it won't
fall over.
8 The LORD says, "People of Israel, you are my
servants.
Family of Jacob, I have chosen you.
You are the children of my friend Abraham.
9 I gathered you from one end of the earth to the
other.
From the farthest places on earth I brought
you together.
I said, 'You are my servants.'
I have chosen you.
I have not turned my back on you.
10 So do not be afraid. I am with you.
Do not be terrified. I am your God.
I will make you strong and help you.
My powerful right hand will take good care
of you.
I always do what is right.

11 "All those who are angry with you will be put
to shame.
And they will be dishonored.
Those who oppose you will be destroyed.
And they will vanish.
12 You might search for your enemies.
But you will not find them.
Those who go to war against you
will completely disappear.
13 I am the LORD your God.
I take hold of your right hand.
I say to you, 'Do not be afraid.
I will help you.'
14 Family of Jacob, you are as weak as a worm.
But do not be afraid.
People of Israel, there are only a few of you.
But do not be afraid.
I myself will help you," announces the LORD.
He is the one who sets his people free.
He is the Holy One of Israel.
15 He says, "I will make you into a threshing sled.
It will be new and sharp.
It will have many teeth.
You will grind the mountains down and
crush them.
You will turn the hills into nothing but
straw.
16 You will toss them in the air.
A strong wind will catch them and blow
them away.
You will be glad because I will make that
happen.
You will praise me.
I am the Holy One of Israel.

17 "Those who are poor and needy search
for water.
But there isn't any.
Their tongues are dry because they are
thirsty.
But I will help them. I am the LORD.
I will not desert them.
I am Israel's God.
18 I will make streams flow on the bare hilltops.
I will make springs come up in the valleys.
I will turn the desert into pools of water.
I will turn the dry and cracked ground into
flowing springs.
19 I will make trees grow in the desert.
I will plant cedar and acacia trees there.
I will plant myrtle and olive trees there.
I will make pine trees grow in the dry and
empty desert.
I will plant fir and cypress trees there.
20 Then people will see and know
that my powerful hand has done it.
They will consider and understand
that I have created it.
I am the Holy One of Israel."

21 The LORD says to the nations and their gods,
"State your case."
Jacob's King says to them,
"Prove your case to me.
22 Show me your facts. Tell me and my people
what is going to happen.
Tell us what happened in the past.
Then we can check it out
and see if it is really true.
Or announce to us the things that will take
place.

23 Tell us what will happen in the days ahead.
Then we will know that you are gods.
Do something. It does not matter whether it is good or bad.
Then we will be terrified and filled with fear.
24 But you are less than nothing.
Your actions are completely worthless.
I hate it when people worship you.

25 "I have stirred up a king
who will come from the north.
He lives in the east.
He will bring honor to me.
He walks all over rulers as if they were mud.
He steps on them just as a potter stomps on clay.
26 Which one of you gods said those things
would happen before they did?
Who told us about them
so we could know them?
Who told us ahead of time?
Who told us so we could say,
'You are right'?
None of you told us about them.
None of you told us ahead of time.
In fact, no one heard you say anything at all.
27 I was the first to tell Zion.
I said, 'Look! The people of Israel are coming back!'
I sent a prophet to Jerusalem with the good news.
28 I look, but there is no one
among the gods that can give me advice.
None of them can answer
when I ask them the simplest question.
29 So they are not really gods at all.
What they do does not amount to anything.
They are as useless as wind.

The LORD's Chosen Servant

42 "Here is my servant. I take good care of him.
I have chosen him. I am very pleased with him.
I will put my Spirit on him.
He will make everything right among the nations.
2 He will not shout or cry out.
He will not raise his voice in the streets.
3 He will not break a bent twig.
He will not put out a dimly burning flame.
He will be faithful and make everything right.
4 He will not grow weak or lose hope.
He will not give up until he makes everything right on the earth.
The islands will put their hope in his law."

5 God created the heavens and spread them out.
The LORD made the earth and everything that grows on it.
He gives breath to its people.
He gives life to those who walk on it.
He says to his servant,
6 "I, the LORD, have chosen you to do what is right.
I will take hold of your hand.
I will keep you safe.
You will put my covenant with the people of Israel into effect.
And you will be a light for the other nations.
7 You will open eyes that can't see.
You will set prisoners free.
Those who sit in darkness will come out of their cells.

8 "I am the LORD. That is my name!
I will not let any other god share my glory.
I will not let statues of gods share my praise.
9 What I said would happen has taken place.
Now I announce new things to you.
Before they even begin to happen,
I announce them to you."

A Song of Praise to the LORD

10 Sing a new song to the LORD.
Sing praise to him from one end of the earth to the other.
Sing, you who sail out on the ocean.
Sing, all of you creatures in it.
Sing, you islands.
Sing, all of you who live there.
11 Let the desert and its towns raise their voices.
Let those who live in the settlements of Kedar be glad.
Let the people of Sela sing with joy.
Let them shout from the tops of the mountains.
12 Let them give glory to the LORD.
Let them praise him in the islands.
13 The LORD will march out like a mighty warrior.
He will stir up his anger like a soldier getting ready to fight.
He will shout the battle cry.
And he will win the battle over his enemies.

14 The LORD says, "For a long time I have kept silent.
I have been calm and quiet.
But now, like a woman having a baby,
I cry out. I am struggling to breathe.
15 I will completely destroy the mountains and hills.
I will dry up everything that grows there.
I will turn rivers into dry land.
I will dry up the pools.
16 Israel is blind.
So I will lead them along paths
they had not known before.
I will guide them on roads they are not familiar with.
I will turn the darkness into light as they travel.
I will make the rough places smooth.

Those are the things I will do.
I will not desert my people.
17 Some people trust in statues of gods.
They say to them, 'You are our gods.'
But they will be dishonored.
They will be put to shame.

Israel Can't See or Hear

18 "Israel, listen to me! You can hear,
but you do not understand.
Look to me! You can see,
but you do not know what you are seeing.
19 The people of Israel serve me. But who is more blind than they are?
Who is more deaf than the messengers I send?
Who is more blind than those who have committed themselves to be faithful to me?
Who is more blind than my servants?
20 Israel, you have seen many things.
But you have not paid any attention to me.
Your ears are open.
But you do not hear anything I say."
21 The LORD wanted his people to see
how great and glorious his law is.
He wanted to show them
that he always does what is right.
22 Enemies have carried off everything they own.
All of my people are trapped in pits
or hidden away in prisons.
They themselves have become like stolen goods.
No one can save them.
They have been carried off.
And there is no one who will say, "Send them back."

23 Family of Jacob, who among you will listen to what I'm saying?
People of Israel, which one of you will pay close attention in days to come?
24 Who allowed you to be carried off like stolen goods?
Who handed you over to robbers?
The LORD did it!
We have sinned against him.
Israel, you wouldn't follow his ways.
You didn't obey his law.
25 So he poured his burning anger out on you.
He had many of you killed off in battle.
You were surrounded by flames.
But you didn't realize what was happening.
Many of you were destroyed.
But you didn't learn anything from it.

The LORD Saves Israel

43 Family of Jacob, the LORD created you.
People of Israel, he formed you.
He says, "Do not be afraid.
I will set you free.
I will send for you by name.
You belong to me.
2 You will pass through deep waters.
But I will be with you.
You will pass through the rivers.
But their waters will not sweep over you.
You will walk through fire.
But you will not be burned.
The flames will not harm you.
3 I am the LORD your God.
I am the Holy One of Israel.
I am the one who saves you.
I will give up Egypt to set you free.
I will give up Cush and Seba for you.
4 You are priceless to me.
I love you and honor you.
So I will trade other people for you.
I will give up other nations to save your lives.
5 Do not be afraid. I am with you.
I will bring your people back from the east.
I will gather you from the west.
6 I will say to the north, 'Let them go!'
And I will say to the south, 'Do not hold them back.'
Bring my sons from far away.
Bring my daughters from the farthest places on earth.
7 Bring back everyone who belongs to me.
I created them to bring glory to me.
I formed them and made them."

8 Lead my people into court.
They have eyes but can't see.
Bring those who have ears but can't hear.
9 All of the nations are gathering together.
All of them are coming.
Which one of their gods said ahead of time
that the people of Israel would return?
Which of them told us anything at all about the past?
Let them bring in their witnesses to prove they were right.
Then others will hear them. And they will say,
"What they said is true."
10 "People of Israel, you are my witnesses," announces the LORD.
"I have chosen you to be my servants.
I wanted you to know me and believe in me.
I wanted you to understand that I am the one and only God.
Before me, there was no other god at all.
And there will not be any god after me.
11 I am the one and only LORD.
I am the only one who can save you.
12 I have made known what would happen.
I told you about it. And I saved you.
I did it. It was not some other god you worship.
You are my witnesses that I am God," announces the LORD.

13 "And that is not all! I have always been God,
and I always will be.
No one can save people from my powerful hand.
When I do something, who can undo it?"

The LORD Forgives Israel but Also Punishes Them

14 The LORD sets his people free.
He is the Holy One of Israel. He says,
"People of Israel, I will send an army to
Babylon to save you.
I will cause all of the Babylonians to
run away.
They will try to escape in the ships they
were so proud of.
15 I am your LORD and King.
I am your Holy One.
I created you."
16 Long ago the LORD opened
a way for his people to go through the
Red Sea.
He made a path through the mighty waters.
17 He caused Egypt to send out its chariots
and horses.
He sent its entire army to its death.
Its soldiers lay down there.
They never got up again.
They were destroyed.
They were blown out like a dimly burning
flame.
But the LORD says,
18 "Forget the things that happened in the past.
Do not keep on thinking about them.
19 I am about to do something new.
It is beginning to happen even now.
Don't you see it coming?
I am going to make a way for you to go
through the desert.
I will make streams of water in the dry and
empty land.
20 Even wild dogs and owls honor me.
That is because I provide water in the desert
for my people to drink.
I cause streams to flow in the dry and
empty land
for my chosen ones.
21 I do it for the people I made for myself.
I want them to sing praise to me.

22 "Family of Jacob, you have not prayed to me
as you should.
People of Israel, you have not even begun to
get tired while doing it.
23 You have not brought me sheep for burnt
offerings.
You have not honored me with your
sacrifices.
I have not loaded you down
by requiring grain offerings.
I have not made you tired
by requiring you to burn incense.
24 But you have not bought any sweet-smelling
cane for me.
You have not given me the fattest parts
of your animal sacrifices.
Instead, you have loaded me down with
your sins.
You have made me tired with the wrong
things you have done.

25 "I am the one who wipes out your lawless acts.
I do it because of who I am.
I will not remember your sins anymore.
26 But let us go to court together.
Remind me of what you have done.
State your case.
Prove to me that you are not guilty.
27 Your father Jacob sinned.
Your priests and prophets refused to
obey me.
28 So I will put the high officials of your temple
to shame.
I will let Jacob's family be totally destroyed.
And I will let people make fun of Israel.

The LORD Chooses Israel

44 "Family of Jacob, listen to me. You are
my servants.
People of Israel, I have chosen you.
2 I made you. I formed you when you were born
as a nation.
I will help you.
So listen to what I am saying.
Family of Jacob, do not be afraid. You are my
servants.
People of Israel, I have chosen you.
3 I will pour water out on the thirsty land.
I will make streams flow on the dry ground.
I will pour out my Spirit on your children.
I will pour out my blessing on their children
after them.
4 They will spring up like grass in a meadow.
They will grow like poplar trees near
flowing streams.
5 Some will say, 'We belong to the LORD.'
Others will call themselves by Jacob's
name.
Still others will write on their hands,
'We belong to the Lord.'
And they will be called by the name
of Israel.

Worship the LORD, Not Other Gods

6 "I am Israel's King. I set them free.
I am the LORD who rules over all.
So listen to what I am saying.
I am the First and the Last.
I am the one and only God.
7 Who is like me? Let him come forward and
speak boldly.
Let him tell me everything that has
happened
since I created my people long ago.

And let him tell me what has not happened yet.
Let him announce ahead of time what is going to take place.
8 Do not tremble with fear. Do not be afraid.
Didn't I announce everything that has happened?
Didn't I tell you about it long ago?
You are my witnesses. Is there any other God but me?
No! There is no other Rock. I do not know even one."
9 Those who make statues of gods don't amount to anything.
And the statues they think so much of are worthless.
Those who would speak up for them are blind.
They don't know anything.
So they will be put to shame.
10 People make statues of gods.
But those gods can't do them any good.
11 People like that will be put to shame.
Those who make statues of gods are mere men.
Let all of them come together and state their case.
They will be terrified and put to shame.
12 A blacksmith gets his tool.
He uses it to shape metal over the burning coals.
He uses his hammers to make a statue of a god.
He forms it with his powerful arm.
He gets hungry and loses his strength.
He doesn't drink any water.
He gets weaker and weaker.
13 A carpenter measures a piece of wood with a line.
He draws a pattern on it with a marker.
He cuts out a statue with sharp tools.
He marks it with compasses.
He shapes it into the form of a handsome man.
He does all of that so he can put it in a temple.
14 He cuts down a cedar tree.
Or perhaps he takes a cypress or an oak tree.
It might be a tree that grew in the forest.
Or it might be a pine tree he planted.
And the rain made it grow.
15 Man gets wood from trees for fuel.
He uses some of it to warm himself.
He starts a fire and bakes bread.
But he also uses some of it to make a god and worship it.
He makes a statue of a god and bows down to it.
16 He burns half of the wood in the fire.
He prepares a meal over it.
He cooks meat over it.
He eats until he is full.
He also warms himself. He says,
"Good! I'm getting warm.
The fire is nice and hot."
17 From the rest of the wood he makes a statue.
It becomes his god.
He bows down and worships it.
He prays to it. He says,
"Save me. You are my god."
18 People like that don't even know what they are doing.
Their eyes are shut so that they can't see the truth.
Their minds are closed so that they can't understand it.
19 No one even stops to think about this.
No one has any sense or understanding.
If anyone did, he would say,
"I used half of the wood for fuel.
I even baked bread over the fire.
I cooked meat. Then I ate it.
Should I now make a statue of a god out of the wood that's left over?
Should I bow down to a block of wood?
The LORD would hate that."
20 That's as foolish as eating ashes!
The mind of someone like that has led him down the wrong path.
He can't save himself.
He can't bring himself to say,
"This thing I'm holding in my right hand isn't really a god at all."
21 The LORD says, "Family of Jacob, remember those things.
People of Israel, you are my servants.
I have made you. You are my servants.
Israel, I will not forget you.
22 I will sweep your sins away as if they were a cloud.
I will blow them away as if they were the morning mist.
Return to me.
Then I will set you free."
23 Sing with joy, you heavens!
The LORD does wonderful things.
Shout out loud, you earth!
Burst into song, you mountains!
Sing, you forests and all of your trees!
The LORD sets the family of Jacob free.
He shows his glory in Israel.

People Will Live in Jerusalem Again

24 The LORD says,
"People of Israel, I set you free.
I formed you when you were born as a nation.

"I am the LORD. I have made everything.
I alone spread out the heavens.
I formed the earth by myself.

25 "Some prophets are not really prophets at all.
I show that their miraculous signs are fake.
I make those who practice evil magic look foolish.

I destroy the learning of those who think they
are wise.
Their knowledge does not make any sense
at all.
26 I make the words of my servants the prophets
come true.
I carry out what my messengers say will
happen.

"I say about Jerusalem,
'My people will live there again.'
I say about the towns of Judah,
'They will be rebuilt.'
I say about their broken-down buildings,
'I will make them like new again.'
27 I say to the deep waters,
'Dry up. Let your streams become dry.'
28 I say about Cyrus,
'He is my shepherd.
He will accomplish everything I want
him to.
He will say about Jerusalem,
"Let it be rebuilt."
And he will say about the temple,
"Let its foundations be laid."'

45 "Cyrus is my anointed king.
I take hold of his right hand.
I give him the power
to bring nations under his control.
I help him strip kings of their power
to go to war against him.
I break city gates open so he can go through
them.
I say to him,
2 'I will march out ahead of you.
I will make the mountains level.
I will break down bronze gates.
I will cut through their heavy iron bars.
3 I will give you treasures that are hidden away
in dark places.
I will give you riches that are stored up in
secret places.
Then you will know that I am the LORD.
I am the God of Israel.
I am sending for you by name.
4 Cyrus, I am sending for you by name.
I am doing it for the good of the family
of Jacob.
They are my servants.
I am doing it for Israel.
They are my chosen people.
You do not know anything about me.
But I am giving you a title of honor.
5 I am the LORD. There is no other LORD.
I am the one and only God.
You do not know anything about me.
But I will make you strong.
6 Then people will know there is no God but me.
Everyone from where the sun rises in the
east
to where it sets in the west will know it.
I am the LORD.
There is no other LORD.
7 I cause light to shine. I also create
darkness.
I bring good times. I also create
hard times.
I do all of those things. I am the LORD.
8 "'Rain down godliness, you heavens above.
Let the clouds shower it down.
Let the earth open wide to receive it.
Let freedom spring to life.
Let godliness grow along with it.
I have created all of those things.
I am the LORD.'"

9 How terrible it will be for anyone who argues
with his Maker!
He is like a broken piece of pottery lying on
the ground.
Does clay say to a potter,
"What are you making?"
Does a pot say,
"You don't have any skill"?
10 How terrible it will be for anyone who says to
his father,
"Why did you give me life?"
How terrible for anyone who says to his
mother,
"Why have you brought me into the world?"

11 The LORD is the Holy One of Israel.
He made them.
He says to them,
"Are you asking me about what will happen
to my children?
Are you telling me what I should do with
what my hands have made?
12 I made the earth.
I created man to live there.
My own hands spread out the heavens.
I put all of the stars in their places.
13 I will stir up Cyrus and help him win his
battles.
I will make all of his roads straight.
He will rebuild Jerusalem.
My people have been taken away from their
country.
But he will set them free.
I will not pay him to do it.
He will not receive a reward for it,"
says the LORD who rules over all.

14 The LORD says to the people of Jerusalem,

"You will get everything Egypt produces.
You will receive everything the people
of Cush
and the tall Sabeans get in trade.
All of it will belong to you.
And all of those people will walk behind you
as slaves.
They will be put in chains and come over
to you.

They will bow down to you.
They will admit,
'God is with you.
There is no other God.'"

15 You are a God who hides yourself.
You are the God of Israel. You save us.
16 All those who make statues of gods will be put to shame.
They will be dishonored.
They will be led away in shame together.
17 But the LORD will save Israel.
He will save them forever.
They will never be put to shame or dishonored.
That will be true for all time to come.

18 The LORD created the heavens.
He is God.
He formed the earth and made it.
He set it firmly in place.
He didn't create it to be empty.
Instead, he formed it for people to live on.
He says, "I am the LORD.
There is no other LORD.
19 I have not spoken in secret.
I have not spoken from a dark place.
I have not said to Jacob's people,
'It is useless to look for me.'
I am the LORD. I always speak the truth.
I always say what is right.

20 "Come together, you people of the nations
who escaped from Babylonia.
Gather together and come into court.
Only people who do not know anything
would carry around gods that are made out of wood.
They pray to gods that can't save them.
21 Tell me what will happen. State your case.
Talk it over together.
Who spoke long ago about what would happen?
Who said it a long time ago?
I did. I am the LORD.
I am the one and only God.
I always do what is right.
I am the one who saves.
There is no God but me.

22 "All of you who live anywhere on earth,
turn to me and be saved.
I am God. There is no other God.
23 I have made a promise with an oath in my own name.
I have spoken with complete honesty.
I will not take back a single word. I said,
'Everyone's knee will bow down to me.
Everyone's mouth will take an oath in my name.'
24 They will say, 'The LORD always does what is right.
Only he can make us strong.'"
All those who have been angry with the LORD
will come to him.
And they will be put to shame.
25 But the LORD will help all of the people of Israel.
He will make them right with himself.
And they will praise him.

There Is No Other God

46 The gods Bel and Nebo are brought down in shame.
The statues of them are being carried away on the backs of animals.
They used to be carried around by the people who worshiped them.
But now they've become a heavy load for tired animals.
2 Bel and Nebo are brought down in shame together.
They aren't able to save their own statues.
They themselves are carried off as prisoners.

3 The LORD says, "Family of Jacob, listen to me.
Pay attention, you people of Israel who are left alive.
I have taken good care of you since your life began.
I have carried you since you were born as a nation.
4 I will continue to carry you even when you are old.
I will take good care of you even when your hair is gray.
I have made you. And I will carry you.
I will take care of you. And I will save you.
I am the LORD.

5 "Who will you compare me to?
Who is equal to me?
What am I like?
Who can you compare me to?
6 Some people pour gold out of their bags.
They weigh out silver on the scales.
They hire someone who works with gold to make it into a god.
They bow down to it and worship it.
7 They lift it up on their shoulders and carry it.
They set it up in its place. And there it stands.
It can't move from that spot.
Someone might cry out to it.
But it does not answer him.
It can't save him from his troubles.
8 So remember that, you who refuse to obey me.
Keep it in your minds and hearts.

9 "Remember what happened in the past.
Think about what took place long ago.
I am God. There is no other God.
I am God. There is no one like me.

10 Before something even happens, I announce
how it will end.
In fact, from times long ago I announced
what was still to come.
I say, 'My plan will succeed.
I will do anything I want to do.'
11 I will send for a man from the east to carry out
my plan.
From a land far away, he will come like a
bird that eats dead bodies.
I will bring about what I have said.
I will do what I have planned.
12 Listen to me, you stubborn people.
Pay attention, you who refuse to do what
is right.
13 The time is almost here for me to make
everything right.
It is not far away.
The time for me to save you will not be
put off.
I will save the city of Zion.
I will bring honor to Israel.

Babylon Will Fall

47 "City of Babylon,
go down and sit in the dust.
Leave your throne and sit on the ground.
City of the Babylonians,
your life will not be comfortable
and easy anymore.
2 Get millstones and grind some flour like a
female slave.
Take your veil off.
Lift your skirts up. Make your legs bare.
Wade through the streams.
3 Everyone will see your naked body.
Everyone will see your shame.
I will pay you back for what you did.
I will not spare any of your people."

4 The one who sets us free is the Holy One
of Israel.
His name is The LORD Who Rules Over All.

5 The LORD says, "City of the Babylonians,
go into a dark prison and sit there quietly.
You will not be called
the queen of kingdoms anymore.
6 I was angry with my people.
I treated them as if they did not belong
to me.
I handed them over to you.
And you did not show them any pity.
You even placed heavy loads on their
old people.
7 You said, 'I will continue to be queen
forever!'
But you did not think about what you
were doing.
You did not consider how things might
turn out.

8 "So listen, you who love pleasure.
You think you are safe and secure.
You say to yourself,
'I am like a god.
No one is greater than I am.
I'll never be a widow.
And my children will never be taken away
from me.'
9 But both of those things will happen to you in
a moment.
They will take place on a single day.
You will lose your children.
And you will become a widow.
That is what will happen to you.
All of your evil magic
and powerful spells will not save you.
10 You have felt secure in your evil ways.
You have said, 'No one sees what I'm
doing.'
Your wisdom and knowledge lead you down
the wrong path.
You say to yourself,
'I am like a god. No one is greater than
I am.'
11 So horrible trouble will come on you.
You will not know how to use your evil
magic to make it go away.
Great trouble will fall on you.
No amount of money can keep it away.
Something terrible will happen to you all
at once.
You will not see it coming ahead of time.

12 "So keep on casting your magic spells.
Keep on practicing your evil magic.
You have been doing those things ever since
you were a child.
Perhaps they will help you.
Maybe they will scare your enemies away.
13 All of the advice you have received
has only worn you out!
Let those who study the heavens come
forward.
They claim to know what is going to happen
by watching the stars every month.
So let them save you from the trouble
that is coming on you.
14 They are just like straw.
Fire will burn them up.
They can't even save themselves
from the powerful flames.
They are not like coals that can warm
anyone.
They are not like a fire to sit by.
15 They can't do you any good.
You have done business with them ever
since you were a child.
You have always asked them for advice.
All of them are bewildered and continue in
their own ways.
None of them can save you."

Israel Is Stubborn

48 People of Jacob, listen to me.
You are called by the name of Israel.
You come from the family line of Judah.
You take oaths in the name of the LORD.
You pray to Israel's God.
But you aren't honest.
You don't mean what you say.
2 You call yourselves citizens of the holy city of Jerusalem.
You say you depend on Israel's God.
His name is The LORD Who Rules Over All.
He says,
3 "Long ago I told you ahead of time what would happen.
I announced it and made it known.
Then all of a sudden I acted.
And those things took place.
4 I knew how stubborn you were.
Your neck was as unbending as iron.
Your forehead was as hard as bronze.
5 So I told you those things long ago.
Before they happened I announced them to you.
I did it so you would not be able to say,
'My statues of gods did them.
My wooden and metal gods made them happen.'
6 You have heard me tell you those things.
Think about all of them.
Won't you admit they have taken place?

"From now on I will tell you about new things that will happen.
I have not made them known to you before.
7 Those things are taking place right now.
They did not happen long ago.
You have not heard of them before today.
So you can't say,
'Oh, yes. I already knew about them.'
8 You have not heard or understood what I said.
Your ears have been plugged up for a long time.
I knew very well that you would turn against me.
From the day you were born, you have refused to obey me.
9 For the honor of my own name I put off showing my anger.
I hold it back from you so people will continue to praise me.
I do not want to destroy you.
10 I have put you to the test in the furnace of suffering.
I have tried to make you pure.
But I did not use as much heat as it takes to make silver pure.
11 I tried to purify you for my own honor.
I did it for the honor of my name.
How can I let myself be dishonored?
I will not give up my glory to any other god.

Israel Is Set Free

12 "Family of Jacob, listen to me.
People of Israel, pay attention.
I have chosen you.
I am the First and the Last.
I am the LORD.
13 With my own hand I laid the foundations of the earth.
With my right hand I spread out the heavens.
When I send for them,
they come and stand ready to obey me.

14 "People of Israel, come together and listen to me.
What other god has said ahead of time that certain things would happen?
I have chosen Cyrus.
He will carry out my plans against Babylon.
He will use his powerful arm against the Babylonians.
15 I myself have spoken.
I have chosen him to carry out my purpose.
I will bring him to Babylon.
He will succeed in what I tell him to do.

16 "Come close and listen to me.

"From the first time I said Cyrus was coming,
I did not do it in secret.
When he comes, I will be there."

The LORD and King has filled me with his Spirit.
People of Israel, he has sent me to you.

17 The LORD is the Holy One of Israel.
He sets his people free. He says to them,
"I am the LORD your God.
I teach you what is best for you.
I direct you in the way you should go.
18 I wish you would pay attention to my commands.
If you did, peace would flow over you like a river.
Holiness would sweep over you like the waves of the ocean.
19 Your family would be like the sand.
Your children after you would be as many as the grains of sand by the sea.
It would be impossible to count them.
I would always accept the members of your family line.
They would never be cut off or destroyed."

20 People of Israel, leave Babylon!
Hurry up and get away from the Babylonians!
Here is what I want you to announce.
Make it known with shouts of joy.
Send the news out from one end of the earth to the other.
Say, "The LORD has set Jacob's people free.
They are his servants."

21 They didn't get thirsty when he led them
through the deserts.
He made water flow out of the rock
for them.
He broke the rock open,
and water came out of it.

22 "There is no peace for those who are evil,"
says the LORD.

The Servant of the LORD

49 People who live on the islands, listen
to me.
Pay attention, you nations far away.
Before I was born the LORD chose me to
serve him.
He appointed me by name.
2 He made my words like a sharp sword.
He hid me in the palm of his hand.
He made me into a sharpened arrow.
He took good care of me and kept me safe.
3 He said to me, "You are my true servant Israel.
I will show my glory through you."
4 But I said, "In spite of my hard work,
I feel as if I haven't accomplished anything.
I've used up all of my strength.
It seems as if everything I've done is
worthless.
But the LORD will give me what I should
receive.
My God will reward me."
5 The LORD formed me in my mother's body to
be his servant.
He wanted me to bring the family of Jacob
back to him.
He wanted me to gather the people of Israel
to himself.
The LORD will honor me.
My God will give me strength.

6 The LORD says to me,

"It is not enough for you as my servant
to bring the tribes of Jacob back to their
land.
It is not enough for you to bring back
the people of Israel I have kept alive.
I will also make you a light for other nations.
Then you will make it possible for the
whole world to be saved."

7 The LORD sets his people free.
He is the Holy One of Israel.
He speaks to his servant, who is looked down
on and hated by the nations.
He speaks to the servant of rulers. He says
to him,
"Kings will see you and rise up to honor you.
Princes will see you and bow down to show
you their respect.
I am the LORD. I am faithful.
I am the Holy One of Israel.
I have chosen you."

Israel Is Brought Back to Their Land

8 The LORD says to his servant,

"When it is time to show you my favor, I will
answer your prayers.
When it is time to save you, I will help you.
I will keep you safe.
You will put my covenant with the people of
Israel into effect.
Then their land will be made like new again.
Each tribe will be sent back to its territory
that was left empty.
9 I want you to say to the prisoners, 'Come out.'
Tell those who are in their dark cells, 'You
are free!'

"On their way home they will eat beside
the roads.
They will find plenty to eat on every
bare hill.
10 They will not get hungry or thirsty.
The heat from the desert sun will not beat
down on them.
The One who shows his tender love to them
will guide them.
Like a shepherd, he will lead them beside
springs of water.
11 I will make roads across the mountains.
I will build wide roads for my people.
12 They will come from far away.
Some of them will come from the north.
Others will come from the west.
Still others will come from Aswan in
the south."

13 Shout with joy, you heavens!
Be glad, you earth!
Burst into song, you mountains!
The LORD will comfort his people.
He will show his tender love to those who
are suffering.

14 But the city of Zion said, "The LORD has
deserted me.
The Lord has forgotten me."

15 The LORD answers, "Can a mother forget
the baby
who is nursing at her breast?
Can she stop showing her tender love
to the child who was born to her?
She might forget her child.
But I will not forget you.
16 I have written your name on the palms of
my hands.
Your walls are never out of my sight.
17 Your people will hurry back.
Those who destroyed you so completely
will leave you.
18 Look up. Look all around you.
All of your people are getting together
to come back to you.
You can be sure that I live,"
announces the LORD.

"And you can be just as sure that your people
will be like decorations you will wear.
Like a bride, you will wear them proudly.

19 "Zion, you were destroyed. Your land was
left empty.
It was turned into a dry and empty desert.
But now you will be too small to hold all of
your people.
And those who destroyed you will be
far away.
20 The children who were born during your time
of sorrow
will speak to you. They will say,
'This city is too small for us.
Give us more space to live in.'
21 Then you will say to yourself,
'Whose children are these?
I lost my children.
And I couldn't have any more.
My children were taken far away from me.
And no one wanted them.
Who brought these children up?
I was left all alone.
So where have these children come from?'"

22 The LORD and King continues,

"I will call out to the nations.
I will give a signal to them.
They will bring back your sons in their arms.
They will carry your daughters on their
shoulders.
23 Their kings will become like fathers to you.
Their queens will be like mothers who
nurse you.
They will bow down to you with their faces
toward the ground.
They will kiss the dust at your feet to show
you their respect.
Then you will know that I am the LORD.
Those who put their hope in me will not
be ashamed."

24 Can goods that were stolen by soldiers be
taken away from them?
Can prisoners be set free from the powerful
Babylonians?

25 "Yes, they can," the LORD answers.

"Prisoners will be taken away from soldiers.
Stolen goods will be taken back from the
powerful Babylonians.
Zion, I will fight against those who fight
against you.
And I will save your people.
26 I will make those who beat you down eat the
flesh of others.
They will drink blood and get drunk on it as
if it were wine.
Then everyone on earth will know
that I am the one who saves you.
I am the LORD. I set you free.
I am the Mighty One of Jacob."

The LORD's Servant Obeys Him

50 The LORD says to the people in Jerusalem,

"Do you think I divorced your people
before you?
Is that why I sent them away?
If it is, show me the letter of divorce.
I did not sell you into slavery to pay
someone I owe.
You were sold because you sinned
against me.
Your people were sent away because of
their lawless acts.
2 When I came to save you, why didn't anyone
welcome me?
When I called out to you, why didn't anyone
answer me?
Wasn't my arm powerful enough to set
you free?
Wasn't I strong enough to save you?
I dry up the sea with a single command.
I turn rivers into a desert.
Then fish rot because they do not have
any water.
They die because they are thirsty.
3 I make the sky turn dark.
It looks as if it is dressed in black clothes."

4 The LORD and King has taught me what
to say.
He has taught me how to help those who
are tired.
He wakes me up every morning.
He makes me want to listen like a good
student.
5 The LORD and King has unplugged my ears.
I've always obeyed him.
I haven't turned away from him.
6 I let my enemies beat me on my bare back.
I let them pull the hair out of my beard.
I didn't turn my face away
when they made fun of me and spit on me.
7 The LORD and King helps me.
He won't let me be dishonored.
So I've made up my mind to keep on
serving him.
I know he won't let me be put to shame.
8 He is near. He will prove I haven't done
anything wrong.
So who will bring charges against me?
Let's face each other in court!
Who can bring charges against me?
Let him come and face me!
9 The LORD and King helps me.
So who will judge me?
My enemies will be like clothes that moths
have eaten up.
They will disappear.

10 Does anyone among you have respect for
the LORD?
Does anyone obey the message of the
LORD's servant?
Let the person who walks in the dark
trust in the LORD.
Let the one who doesn't have any light to
guide him
depend on his God.
11 But all of you sinners who light fires
should go ahead and walk in their light.
You who carry flaming torches
should walk in their light.
Here's what I'm going to do to you.
I'll make you lie down in great pain.

Zion Will Be Saved

51 The LORD says, "Listen to me, you who
want to do what is right.
Pay attention, you who look to me.
Consider the rock you were cut out of.
Think about the rock pit you were dug from.
2 Consider Abraham. He is the father of
your people.
Think about Sarah. She is your mother.
When I chose Abraham, he did not have any
children.
But I blessed him and gave him many of
them.
3 You can be sure that I will comfort Zion's
people.
I will look with loving concern on all of
their destroyed buildings.
I will make their deserts like Eden.
I will make their dry and empty land like
my very own garden.
Joy and gladness will be there.
People will sing and give thanks to me.

4 "Listen to me, my people.
Pay attention, my nation.
My law will go out to the nations.
I make everything right.
That will be a guiding light for them.
5 The time for me to set you free is near.
I will soon save you.
My powerful arm will make everything
right among the nations.
The islands will put their hope in me.
They will wait for my powerful arm to act.
6 Look up toward the heavens.
Then look at the earth.
The heavens will vanish like smoke.
The earth will wear out like clothes.
Those who live there will die like flies.
But I will save you forever.
My saving power will never end.

7 "Listen to me, you who know what is right.
Pay attention, you who have my law in
your hearts.
Do not be afraid when mere people make
fun of you.
Do not be terrified when they laugh at you.
8 They will be like clothes that moths have
eaten up.
They will be like wool that worms have
chewed up.
But my saving power will last forever.
I will save you for all time to come."

9 Wake up! LORD, wake up! Dress your powerful
arm with strength
as if it were your clothes.
Wake up, just as you did in the past.
Wake up, as you did long ago.
Didn't you cut Rahab to pieces?
Didn't you stab that sea monster to death?
10 Didn't you dry up the Red Sea?
Didn't you dry up those deep waters?
You made a road on the bottom of that sea.
Then those who were set free went across.
11 Those the LORD has saved will return to
their land.
They will sing as they enter the city of Zion.
Joy that lasts forever will be like beautiful
crowns on their heads.
They will be filled with gladness and joy.
Sorrow and sighing will be gone.

12 The LORD says to his people,
"I comfort you because of who I am.
Why are you afraid of mere men?
They are only human beings.
They are like grass that dries up.
13 How can you forget me? I made you.
I spread out the heavens.
I laid the foundations of the earth.
Why are you terrified every day?
Is it because those who are angry with you
are crushing you?
Is it because they are trying to destroy you?
Their anger can't harm you anymore.
14 You prisoners who are so afraid will soon be
set free.
You will not die in your prison cells.
You will not go without food.
15 I am the LORD your God.
I stir up the ocean. I make its waves roar.
My name is The LORD Who Rules Over All.
16 I have put my words in your mouth.
I have kept you safe in the palm of
my hand.
I set the heavens in place.
I laid the foundations of the earth.
I say to Zion, 'You are my people.'"

The Cup of the LORD's Burning Anger

17 Wake up, Jerusalem!
Wake up! Get up!
The LORD has handed you the cup of his
burning anger.
And you have drunk from it.

That cup makes men unsteady on their feet.
And you have drunk from it to the very last drop.
18 None of the children who were born to you are left to guide you.
None of the children you brought up are left to lead you by the hand.
19 Nothing but trouble has come to you.
You have been wiped out and destroyed.
And you have suffered hunger and war.
No one feels sorry for you.
No one can comfort you.
20 Your children have fainted.
They lie helpless at every street corner.
They are like antelope that have been caught in a net.
They have felt the full force of the LORD's burning anger.
Jerusalem, your God had to warn them strongly.

21 So listen to me, you suffering people of Jerusalem.
You have been made drunk, but not by drinking wine.
22 Your LORD and King speaks.
He is your God.
He stands up for his people. He says,
"I have taken from you the cup of my burning anger.
It made you unsteady on your feet.
But you will never drink from that cup again.
23 Instead, I will give it to those who made you suffer.
They said to you,
'Fall down flat on the ground.
Then we can walk all over you.'
And that is exactly what you did.
You made your back like a street to be walked on."

52 Wake up! Zion, wake up!
Dress yourself with strength as if it were your clothes.
Holy city of Jerusalem,
put on your clothes of glory.
Those who haven't been circumcised will never enter you again.
Neither will those who are "unclean."
2 Get up, Jerusalem! Shake off your dust.
Take your place on your throne.
Captured people of Zion,
remove the chains from your neck.

3 The LORD says,

"When you were sold as slaves, no one paid anything for you.
Now no one will pay any money to set you free."

4 The LORD and King continues,

"Long ago my people went down to Egypt.
They lived there for a while.
Later, Assyria crushed them without any reason.

5 "Now look at what has happened to them," announces the LORD.

"Once again my people have been taken away.
And no one paid anything for them.
Those who rule over them brag about it,"
announces the LORD.
"All day long without stopping,
people speak evil things against my name.
6 So the day will come when my people will really know the meaning of my name.
They will know what kind of God I am.
They will know that I told them ahead of time they would return to their land.
They will know that it was I."

7 What a beautiful sight it is
to see messengers coming with good news!
How beautiful to see them coming down from the mountains
with a message about peace!
How wonderful it is when they bring the good news
that we are saved!
How wonderful when they say to Zion,
"Your God rules!"
8 Listen! Those on guard duty are shouting out the message.
With their own eyes
they see the LORD returning to Zion.
So they shout with joy.
9 Burst into songs of joy together,
you broken-down buildings in Jerusalem.
The LORD has comforted his people.
He has set Jerusalem free.
10 The LORD will use the power of his holy arm to save his people.
All of the nations will see him do it.
Everyone from one end of the earth to the other will see it.

11 You who carry the articles that belong to the LORD's temple, leave Babylon!
Leave it! Get out of there!
Don't touch anything that isn't pure and clean.
Come out of Babylon and be pure.
12 But this time you won't have to leave in a hurry.
You won't have to rush away.
The LORD will go ahead of you and lead you.
The God of Israel will follow behind you and guard you.

The Suffering and Glory of the LORD's Servant

13 The LORD says, "My servant will act wisely and accomplish his task.
He will be highly honored. He will be greatly respected.

14 Many people were shocked when they
saw him.
He was so scarred that he did not look like
a man at all.
His body was so twisted that he did not look
like a human being anymore.
15 But many nations will be surprised when they
see what he has done.
Kings will be so amazed that they will not
be able to say anything.
They will understand things they were never
told about.
They will know the meaning of things they
never heard about."

53 Who has believed what we've been
saying?
Who has seen the LORD's saving power?
2 His servant grew up like a tender young plant.
He grew like a root coming up out of dry
ground.
He didn't have any beauty or majesty that
made us notice him.
There wasn't anything special about the way
he looked that drew us to him.
3 Men looked down on him. They didn't accept
him.
He knew all about sorrow and suffering.
He was like someone people turn their faces
away from.
We looked down on him. We didn't have
any respect for him.

4 He suffered the things we should have
suffered.
He took on himself the pain that should
have been ours.
But we thought God was punishing him.
We thought God was wounding him and
making him suffer.
5 But the servant was pierced because we had
sinned.
He was crushed because we had done what
was evil.
He was punished to make us whole again.
His wounds have healed us.
6 All of us are like sheep. We have wandered
away from God.
All of us have turned to our own way.
And the LORD has placed on his servant
the sins of all of us.

7 He was beaten down and made to suffer.
But he didn't open his mouth.
He was led away like a sheep to be killed.
Lambs are silent while their wool is being
cut off.
In the same way, he didn't open his
mouth.
8 He was arrested and sentenced to death.
Then he was taken away.
He was cut off from this life.
He was punished for the sins of my people.
Who among those who were living at
that time
could have understood those things?
9 He was given a grave with those who
were evil.
But his body was buried in the tomb of a
rich man.
He was killed even though he hadn't harmed
anyone.
And he had never lied to anyone.

10 The LORD says, "It was my plan to crush him
and cause him to suffer.
I made his life a guilt offering to pay for sin.
But he will see all of his children after him.
In fact, he will continue to live.
My plan will be brought about through him.
11 After he suffers, he will see the light that leads
to life.
And he will be satisfied.
My godly servant will make many people
godly
because of what he will accomplish.
He will be punished for their sins.
12 So I will give him a place of honor among
those who are great.
He will be rewarded just like others who
win the battle.
That is because he was willing to give his life
as a sacrifice.
He was counted among those who had
committed crimes.
He took the sins of many people on himself.
And he gave his life for those who had done
what is wrong."

Jerusalem Will Be Glorious

54 "Jerusalem, sing!
You are now like a woman who never
had a child.
Burst into song! Shout with joy!
You who have never had labor pains,
you are now all alone.
But you will have more children than a
woman who still has a husband,"
says the LORD.
2 "Make a large area for your tent.
Spread out its curtains.
Go ahead and make your tent wider.
Make its ropes longer.
Drive the stakes down deeper.
3 You will spread out to the right and the left.
Your children after you will drive out the
nations that are now living in your land.
They will settle down in the deserted cities
of those nations.

4 "Do not be afraid. You will not be put to shame
anymore.
Do not be afraid of being dishonored.
People will no longer make fun of you.

You will forget the time when you suffered as
slaves in Egypt.
You will no longer remember the shame
of being a widow in Babylonia.
5 I made you. I am now your husband.
My name is The LORD Who Rules
Over All.
I am the Holy One of Israel.
I have set you free.
I am the God of the whole earth.
6 You were like a wife who was deserted.
And her heart was broken.
You were like a wife who married young.
And her husband sent her away.
But now I am calling you to come back,"
says your God.
7 "For a brief moment I left you.
But because I love you so much, I will
bring you back.
8 For a moment I turned my face away
from you.
I was very angry with you.
But I will show you my loving concern.
My faithful love will continue forever,"
says the LORD. He is the one who set
you free.

9 "During Noah's time I took an oath and made
a promise.
I said I would never cover the earth with
water again.
In the same way, I have promised not to be
angry with you.
I will never punish you again.
10 The mountains might shake.
The hills might be removed.
But my faithful love for you will never be
shaken.
And my covenant that promises peace to
you will never be broken,"
says the LORD. He shows you his loving
concern.

11 "Suffering city, you have been beaten
by storms.
You have not been comforted.
I will rebuild you with turquoise stones.
I will rebuild your foundations with
sapphires.
12 I will line the top of your city wall with rubies.
I will make your gates out of gleaming
jewels.
And I will make all of your walls out of
precious stones.
13 I will teach all of your children.
And they will enjoy great peace.
14 When you do what is right,
you will be made secure.
Your leaders will not be mean to you.
You will not have anything to be afraid of.
You will not be terrified anymore.
Terror will not come near you.
15 People might attack you. But I will not be the
cause of it.
Those who attack you will give themselves
up to you.

16 "I created blacksmiths.
They fan the coals into flames of fire.
They make weapons that are fit for their work.
I also created those who destroy others.
17 But no weapon that is used against you will
succeed.
People might bring charges against you.
But you will prove that they are wrong.
Those are the things I do for my servants.
I make everything right for them,"
announces the LORD.

The LORD Invites His People to Come to Him

55 "Come, all of you who are thirsty.
Come and drink the water I offer to you.
You who do not have any money, come.
Buy and eat the grain I give you.
Come and buy wine and milk.
You will not have to pay anything for it.
2 Why spend money on what is not food?
Why work for what does not satisfy you?
Listen carefully to me.
Then you will eat what is good.
You will enjoy the richest food there is.
3 Listen and come to me.
Pay attention to me.
Then you will live.
I will make a covenant with you that will last
forever.
I will give you my faithful love.
I promised it to David.
4 I made him a witness to the nations.
He became a leader and commander
over them.
5 You too will send for nations you do
not know.
Even though they do not know you,
they will hurry and come to you.
That is what I will do. I am the LORD
your God.
I am the Holy One of Israel.
I have honored you."

6 Turn to the LORD before it's too late.
Call out to him while he's still ready to
help you.
7 Let the one who is evil stop doing evil things.
And let him quit thinking evil thoughts.
Let him turn to the LORD.
The LORD will show him his tender love.
Let him turn to our God.
He is always ready to forgive.

8 "My thoughts are not like your thoughts.
And your ways are not like my ways,"
announces the LORD.

9 "The heavens are higher than the earth.
And my ways are higher than your ways.
My thoughts are higher than your thoughts.
10 The rain and the snow
come down from the sky.
They do not return to it
without watering the earth.
They make plants come up and grow.
The plants produce seeds for farmers.
They also produce food for people to eat.
11 The words I speak are like that.
They will not return to me without producing results.
They will accomplish what I want them to.
They will do exactly what I sent them to do.

12 "My people, you will leave Babylonia with joy.
You will be led out of it in peace.
The mountains and hills
will burst into song as you go.
And all of the trees in the fields
will clap their hands.
13 Pine trees will grow where there used to be bushes that had thorns on them.
And myrtle trees will grow where there used to be thorns.
That will bring me great fame.
It will be a lasting reminder of what I can do.
It will not be forgotten."

The LORD Will Save Those Who Come to Him

56 The LORD says,

"Do what is fair and right.
I will soon come and save you.
Soon everyone will know that what I do is right.
2 Blessed is the man who does what I want him to.
He is faithful in keeping the Sabbath day.
He does not misuse it.
He does not do what is evil on that day."

3 Suppose an outsider wants to follow the LORD.
Then he shouldn't say,
"The LORD won't accept me as one of his people."
And a eunuch shouldn't say,
"I'm like a dry tree
that doesn't bear any fruit."

4 The LORD says,

"Suppose some eunuchs keep my Sabbath days.
They choose to do what pleases me.
And they are faithful in keeping my covenant.
5 Then I will set up a monument in the area of my temple.
Their names will be written on it.
That will be better for them than having sons and daughters.
The names of the eunuchs will be remembered forever.
They will never be forgotten.

6 "Suppose outsiders want to follow me
and serve me.
They want to love me
and worship me.
They keep the Sabbath day and do not misuse it.
And they are faithful in keeping my covenant.
7 Then I will bring them to my holy mountain of Zion.
I will give them joy in my house.
They can pray there.
I will accept their burnt offerings and sacrifices on my altar.
My house will be called
a house where people from all nations can pray."
8 The LORD and King will gather
those who were taken away from their homes in Israel.
He announces, "I will gather them to myself.
And I will gather others to join them."

The LORD Judges Israel's Evil Leaders

9 Come, all of you enemy nations! Come like wild animals.
Come and destroy like animals in the forest.
10 Israel's prophets are blind.
They don't know the LORD.
All of them are like watchdogs that can't even bark.
They just lie around and dream.
They love to sleep.
11 They are like dogs that love to eat.
They never get enough.
They are like shepherds who don't have any understanding.
All of them do as they please.
They only look for what they can get for themselves.
12 "Come!" they shout. "Let's get some wine!
Let's drink all the beer we can!
Tomorrow we'll do the same thing.
And that will be even better than today."

57 Those who are right with God die.
And no one really cares about it.
Men who are faithful to the LORD are swept away by trouble.
And no one understands why that happens
to those who do what is right.

2 Those who lead honest lives
will enjoy peace and rest when they die.

3 The LORD says, "Come here,
you children of women who practice evil magic!
You are children of prostitutes and those who commit adultery.
4 Who are you making fun of?
Who are you laughing at?
Who are you sticking your tongue out at?
You are people who refuse to obey me.
You are just a bunch of liars!
5 You burn with sinful longing among the oak trees.
You worship your gods by having sex under every green tree.
You sacrifice your children in the valleys.
You also do it under the cliffs.
6 You have chosen some of the smooth stones in the valleys to be your gods.
You have joined yourselves to them.
You have even poured out drink offerings to them.
You have given grain offerings to them.
So why should I take pity on you?
7 You have made your bed to have sex on a very high hill.
You went up there to offer your sacrifices.
8 You have set up statues to remind you of your gods.
You have put them behind your doors and doorposts.
You deserted me. You invited other lovers into your bed.
You climbed into it and welcomed them.
You made a deal with them.
And you looked at their naked bodies.
9 You went to the god Molech with olive oil.
You took a lot of perfume along with you.
You sent your messengers to places far away.
You even sent them down to the place of the dead.
10 All of your efforts wore you out.
But you would not say, 'It's hopeless.'
You received new strength.
So you did not give up.

11 "Who are you so afraid of
that you have not been true to me?
You have not remembered me.
You do not even care about me.
I have not punished you for a long time.
That is why you are not afraid of me.
12 You have not done what is right or good.
I will let everyone know about it.
And that will not be of any benefit to you.
13 Go ahead and cry out for help to all of the statues of your gods.
See if they can save you!
The wind will carry them off.
Just a puff of air will blow them away.
But anyone who comes to me for safety
will receive the land.
He will possess my holy mountain of Zion."

The LORD Comforts Those Who Aren't Proud

14 A messenger says,

"Build up the road! Build it up! Get it ready!
Remove anything that would keep my people from coming back."
15 The One who is highly honored lives forever.
His name is holy. He says,
"I live in a high and holy place.
But I also live with anyone who turns away from his sins.
I live with anyone who is not proud.
I give new life to him.
I give it to anyone who turns away from his sins.
16 I will not find fault with my people forever.
I will not always be angry with them.
If I were, I would cause their spirits to grow weak.
The very breath of life would go out of the people I created.
17 I was very angry with them.
They always longed for more and more of everything.
So I punished them for that sin.
I turned my face away from them because I was angry.
But they kept on wanting their own way.
18 I have seen what they have done.
But I will heal them.
I will guide them.
And I will comfort them just as I did before.
19 Then the people of Israel who are sorry for their sins will praise me.
I will give perfect peace to those who are far away and those who are near.
And I will heal them," says the LORD.
20 But those who are evil are like the rolling sea.
It never rests.
Its waves toss up mud and sand.

21 "There is no peace for those who are evil," says my God.

What True Worship Is All About

58 The LORD told me,

"Shout out loud. Do not hold back.
Raise your voice like a trumpet.
Tell my people that they have refused to obey me.
Tell the family of Jacob how much they have sinned.
2 Day after day they worship me.
They seem ready and willing to know how I want them to live.

They act as if they were a nation that does
what is right.
They act as if they have not turned away
from my commands.
They claim to want me to give them fair
decisions.
They seem ready and willing to come near
and worship me.
3 'We have gone without food,' they say.
'Why haven't you noticed it?
We have made ourselves suffer.
Why haven't you paid any attention to us?'

"On the day when you fast, you do as you
please.
You take advantage of all of your workers.
4 When you fast, it ends in arguing and fighting.
You hit one another with your fists.
That is an evil thing to do.
The way you are now fasting
keeps your prayers from being heard in
heaven.
5 Do you think that is the way I want you to fast?
Is it only a time for a man to make himself
suffer?
Is it only for people to bow their heads like tall
grass that is bent by the wind?
Is it only for people to lie down on black
cloth and ashes?
Is that what you call a fast?
Do you think I can accept that?

6 "Here is the way I want you to fast.

"Set free those who are held by chains without
any reason.
Untie the ropes that hold people as slaves.
Set free those who are crushed.
Break every evil chain.
7 Share your food with hungry people.
Provide homeless people with a place
to stay.
Give naked people clothes to wear.
Provide for the needs of your own family.
8 Then the light of my blessing will shine on you
like the rising sun.
I will heal you quickly.
I will march out ahead of you.
And my glory will follow behind you and
guard you.
That is because I always do what is right.
9 You will call out to me for help.
And I will answer you.
You will cry out.
And I will say, 'Here I am.'

"Get rid of the chains you use to hold others
down.
Stop pointing your finger at others as if they
had done something wrong.
Stop saying harmful things about them.
10 Work hard to feed hungry people.
Satisfy the needs of those who are crushed.
Then my blessing will light up your darkness.
And the night of your suffering will become
as bright as the noonday sun.
11 I will always guide you.
I will satisfy your needs in a land that is
baked by the sun.
I will make you stronger.
You will be like a garden that has plenty of
water.
You will be like a spring whose water never
runs dry.
12 Your people will rebuild the cities that were
destroyed long ago.
And you will build again on the old
foundations.
You will be called The One Who Repairs
Broken Walls.
You will be called The One Who Makes
City Streets Like New Again.

13 "Do not work on the Sabbath day.
Do not do just anything you want to on my
holy day.
Make the Sabbath a day you can enjoy.
Honor my holy day.
Do not work on it.
Do not do just anything you want to.
Do not talk about things that are worthless.
14 Then you will find your joy in me.
I will give you control over the most
important places in the land.
And you will enjoy all of the good things
in the land I gave your father Jacob."
The LORD has spoken.

The LORD Sets His People Free

59 People of Israel, the LORD's arm is not
too weak to save you.
His ears aren't too deaf to hear your cry for
help.
2 But your sins have separated you from
your God.
They have caused him to turn his face away
from you.
So he won't listen to you.
3 Your hands and fingers are stained with blood.
You are guilty of committing murder.
Your mouth has told lies.
Your tongue says evil things.
4 People aren't fair when they present their
cases in court.
They aren't honest when they state
their case.
They depend on weak arguments. They
tell lies.
They plan to make trouble.
Then they carry it out.
5 The plans they make are like the eggs of
poisonous snakes.
Anyone who eats those eggs will die.
When one of them is broken, a snake comes
out.

[6]Those people weave their evil plans together
like a spider's web.
But the webs they make can't be used as
clothes.
They can't cover themselves with what
they make.
Their acts are evil.
They do things to harm others.
[7]They are always in a hurry to sin.
They run quickly to murder those who
aren't guilty.
Their thoughts are evil.
They leave a trail of suffering and pain.
[8]They don't know how to live at peace with
others.
What they do isn't fair.
They lead twisted lives.
No one who lives like that will enjoy peace
and rest.

[9]We aren't being treated fairly.
We haven't been set free yet.
The God who always does what is right
hasn't come to help us.
We look for light. But we see nothing but
darkness.
We look for brightness. But we walk in deep
shadows.
[10]Like blind people we feel our way along the
wall.
We are like those who can't see.
At noon we trip and fall as if the sun had
already set.
Compared to those who are healthy, we are
like dead people.
[11]All of us growl like hungry bears.
We cry like sad doves.
We want the LORD to do what is fair and
save us.
But he doesn't do it.
We long for him to set us free.
But the time for that seems far away.

[12]That's because we've done so many things he
considers wrong.
Our sins prove that we are guilty.
The wrong things we've done are always
troubling us.
We admit that we have sinned.
[13]We've refused to obey the LORD.
We've made evil plans against him.
We've turned our backs on our God.
We've stirred up trouble and refused to
follow him.
We've told lies that came from our own
minds.
[14]So people stop others from doing what is fair.
They keep them from doing what is right.
No one tells the truth in court anymore.
No one is honest there.
[15]In fact, truth can't be found anywhere.
Those who refuse to do evil are attacked.

The LORD sees that people aren't treating
others fairly.
That makes him unhappy.
[16]He sees that there is no one who helps his
people.
He is shocked that no one stands up
for them.
So he will use his own powerful arm to
save them.
He has the strength to do it because he
is holy.
[17]He will put the armor of holiness on his chest.
He'll put the helmet of salvation on his
head.
He'll pay people back for the wrong things
they do.
He'll wrap himself in anger as if it were
a coat.
[18]He will pay his enemies back for what they
have done.
He'll pour his anger out on them.
He'll punish those who attack him.
He'll give the people in the islands what
they have coming to them.
[19]People in the west will show respect for the
LORD's name.
People in the east will worship him because
of his glory.
The LORD will come like a rushing river that
was held back.
His breath will drive it along.

[20]"I set my people free. I will come to Mount
Zion.
I will come to those in Jacob's family who
turn away from their sins,"
announces the LORD.

[21]"Here is the covenant I will make with them,"
says the LORD. "My Spirit is on you. I have put my
words in your mouth. They will never leave your
mouth. And they will never leave the mouths of
your children or their children after them. That will
be true for all time to come," says the LORD.

Zion Will Be Glorious

60 "People of Jerusalem, get up.
Shine, because your light has come.
My glory will shine on you.
[2]Darkness covers the earth.
Thick darkness spreads over the nations.
But I will rise and shine on you.
My glory will appear over you.
[3]Nations will come to your light.
Kings will come to the brightness of your
new day.

[4]"Look up. Look all around you.
All of your people are getting together to
come back to you.
Your sons will come from far away.
Your daughters will be carried like little
children.

5 Then your face will glow with joy.
Your heart will beat fast because you are so happy.
Wealth from across the ocean will be brought to you.
The riches of the nations will come to you.
6 Herds of young camels will cover your land.
They will come from Midian and Ephah.
They will also come from Sheba.
They'll carry gold and incense.
And people will shout praises to me.
7 All of Kedar's flocks will be gathered to you.
The rams of Nebaioth will serve as your sacrifices.
I will accept them as offerings on my altar.
That is how I will bring honor to my glorious temple.

8 "Whose ships are these that sail along like clouds?
They fly like doves to their nests.
9 People from the islands are coming to me.
The ships of Tarshish are out in front.
They are bringing your children back from far away.
Your children are bringing their silver and gold with them.
They are coming to honor me.
I am the LORD your God.
I am the Holy One of Israel.
I have honored you.

10 "People from other lands will rebuild your walls.
Their kings will serve you.
When I was angry with you, I struck you.
But now I will show you my tender love.
11 Your gates will always stand open.
They will never be shut, day or night.
Then people can bring you the wealth of the nations.
Their kings will come along with them.
12 The nation or kingdom that will not serve you will be destroyed.
It will be completely wiped out.

13 "Lebanon's glorious trees will be brought to you.
Its pines, firs and cypress trees will be brought.
They will be used to make my temple beautiful.
And I will bring glory to the place where my throne is.
14 The children of those who crush you will come and bow down to you.
All those who hate you will kneel down at your feet.
Jerusalem, they will call you The City of the LORD.
They will name you Zion, the City of the Holy One of Israel.

15 "You have been deserted and hated.
No one even travels through you.
But I will make you into something to be proud of forever.
You will be a place of joy for all time to come.
16 You will get everything you need from kings and nations.
You will be like children who are nursing at their mother's breasts.
Then you will know that I am the one who saves you.
I am the LORD. I set you free.
I am the Mighty One of Jacob.
17 Instead of bronze I will bring you gold.
In place of iron I will give you silver.
Instead of wood I will bring you bronze.
In place of stones I will give you iron.
I will make peace govern you.
I will make godliness rule over you.
18 People will no longer harm one another in your land.
They will not wipe out or destroy anything inside your borders.
You will call your walls Salvation.
And you will name your gates Praise.
19 You will not need the light of the sun by day anymore.
The bright light of the moon will no longer have to shine on you.
I will be your light forever.
My glory will shine on you.
I am the LORD your God.
20 Your sun will never set again.
Your moon will never lose its light.
I will be your light forever.
Your days of sorrow will come to an end.
21 Then all of your people will do what is right.
The land will belong to them forever.
They will be like a young tree I have planted.
My hands have created them.
They will show how glorious I am.
22 The smallest family among you will become a tribe.
The smallest tribe will become a mighty nation.
I am the LORD.
When it is the right time, I will act quickly."

The LORD's Servant Accomplishes His Work

61 The Spirit of the LORD and King is on me.
The LORD has anointed me
to tell the good news to poor people.
He has sent me to comfort
those whose hearts have been broken.
He has sent me to announce freedom
for those who have been captured.
He wants me to set prisoners free
from their dark prisons.

[2] He has sent me to announce the year
when he will set his people free.
He wants me to announce the day
when he will pay his enemies back.
Our God has sent me to comfort all those who are sad.
[3] He wants me to help those in Zion who are filled with sorrow.
I will put beautiful crowns on their heads
in place of ashes.
I will anoint them with oil to give them gladness
instead of sorrow.
I will give them a spirit of praise
in place of a spirit of sadness.
They will be like oak trees that are strong and straight.
The LORD himself will plant them in the land.
That will show how glorious he is.

[4] They will rebuild the places that were destroyed long ago.
They will repair the buildings that have been broken down for many years.
They will make the destroyed cities like new again.
They have been broken down for a very long time.
[5] Outsiders will serve you by taking care of your flocks.
People from other lands will work in your fields and vineyards.
[6] You will be called priests of the LORD.
You will be named workers for our God.
You will enjoy the wealth of nations.
You will brag about getting their riches.

[7] Instead of being put to shame
my people will receive a double share of wealth.
Instead of being dishonored
they will be glad to be in their land.
They will receive a double share of riches there.
And they'll be filled with joy that will last forever.
[8] The LORD says, "I love those who do what is right.
I hate it when people steal and do other sinful things.
So I will be faithful to those who do what is right.
And I will bless them.
I will make a covenant with them
that will last forever.
[9] Their children after them will be famous among the nations.
Their families will be praised by people everywhere.
All those who see them will agree
that I have blessed them."

[10] The people of Jerusalem will say,
"We take great delight in the LORD.
We are joyful because we belong to our God.
He has dressed us with salvation as if it were our clothes.
He has put robes of godliness on us.
We are like a groom who is dressed up for his wedding.
We are like a bride who decorates herself with her jewels.
[11] The soil makes the young plant come up.
A garden causes seeds to grow.
In the same way, the LORD and King will make godliness grow.
And all of the nations will praise him."

The LORD Gives Zion a New Name

62 The LORD says, "For the good of Zion
I will not keep silent.
For Jerusalem's benefit I will not remain quiet.
I will not keep silent until its people's godliness
shines like the sunrise.
I will not remain quiet until they are saved
and shine like a blazing torch.
[2] Jerusalem, the nations will see
that I have made everything right for you.
All of their kings will see your glory.
You will be called by a new name.
I myself will give it to you.
[3] You will be like a glorious crown in my strong hand.
You will be like a royal crown in my powerful hand.
[4] People will not call you Deserted anymore.
They will no longer name your land Empty.
Instead, you will be called The One the LORD Delights In.
Your land will be named The Married One.
I will take delight in you.
And your land will be like a bride.
[5] As a young man gets married to a young woman,
your people will marry you.
As a groom is happy with his bride,
I will be full of joy over you."

[6] Jerusalem, I have stationed guards on your walls.
They must never be silent day or night.
You who call out to the LORD
must not give yourselves any rest.
[7] And don't give him any rest
until he makes Jerusalem secure.
Don't give him any peace
until people all over the earth praise that city.

[8] The LORD has taken an oath and made
a promise.
He has lifted up his right hand and
mighty arm.
He has promised, "I will never give your grain
to your enemies for food again.
Outsiders will never again drink the fresh wine
you have worked so hard for.
[9] Instead, those who gather the grain will eat it
themselves.
And they will praise me.
Those who gather grapes to make the wine will
enjoy it.
They will drink it in the courtyards of my
temple."

[10] Go out through your gates, people of
Jerusalem! Go out!
Prepare the way for the rest of your people
to return.
Build up the road! Build it up!
Remove the stones.
Raise a banner over the city
for the nations to see.

[11] The LORD has announced a message
from one end of the earth to the other.
He has said, "Tell the people of Zion,
'Look! Your Savior is coming!
He is bringing his people back as his reward.
He has won the battle over their enemies.'"
[12] They will be called The Holy People.
The LORD will set them free.
And Jerusalem will be named The City the
LORD Cares About.
It won't be deserted anymore.

God Will Save His People and Punish Their Enemies

63 Who is this man coming from the city of
Bozrah in Edom?
His clothes are stained bright red.
Who is he? He is dressed up in all of his glory.
He is marching toward us with great
strength.

The LORD answers, "It is I.
I have won the battle.
I am mighty.
I have saved my people."

[2] Why are your clothes red?
They look as if you have been stomping
on grapes in a winepress.

[3] The LORD answers, "I have been stomping on
the nations
as if they were grapes.
No one was there to help me.
I walked all over the nations because I was
angry.
That is why I stomped on them.
Their blood splashed all over my clothes.
So my clothes were stained bright red.
[4] I decided it was time to pay Israel's enemies
back.
The year for me to set my people free
had come.
[5] I looked around, but no one was there to
help me.
I was shocked that no one gave me any help.
So I used my own powerful arm to save
my people.
I had the strength to do it because I
was angry.
[6] I walked all over the nations because I was
angry with them.
I made them drink from the cup of my
burning anger.
I poured their blood out on the ground."

Isaiah Prays to the LORD

[7] I will talk about the kind things the LORD
has done.
I'll praise him for everything he's done
for us.
He has done many good things
for the nation of Israel.
That's because he loves us and is very kind
to us.
[8] In the past he said, "They are my people.
They will not turn against me."
So he saved them.
[9] When they suffered, he suffered with them.
He sent his angel to save them.
He set them free because he is loving and kind.
He lifted them up and carried them.
He did it again and again in days long ago.
[10] But they refused to obey him.
They made his Holy Spirit sad.
So he turned against them and became their
enemy.
He himself fought against them.

[11] Then his people remembered what he did
long ago.
They recalled the days of Moses and his
people.
They asked, "Where is the One who brought
Israel through the Red Sea?
Moses led them as the shepherd of his flock.
Where is the One who put
his Holy Spirit among them?
[12] He used his glorious and powerful arm
to help Moses.
He parted the waters of the sea in front
of them.
That mighty act made him famous forever.
[13] He led them through that deep sea.
Like a horse in open country,
they didn't trip and fall.
[14] Like cattle that are taken down to the flatlands,
they were given rest by the Spirit of the
LORD."
That's how he guided his people.
So he made a glorious name for himself.

15 LORD, look down from heaven.
Look down from your holy and glorious throne.
Where is your great love for us?
Where is your power?
Why don't you show us
your tender love and concern?
16 You are our Father.
Abraham might not accept us as his children.
Jacob might not recognize us as his family.
But you are our Father, LORD.
Your name is The One Who Always Sets Us Free.
17 LORD, why do you let us wander away from you?
Why do you let us become so stubborn
that we don't respect you?
Come back and help us.
We are the tribes that belong to you.
18 For a little while your holy people possessed the land.
But now our enemies have torn your temple down.
19 We are like people you never ruled over.
We are like those who don't belong to you.

64 I wish you would open up your heavens
and come down to us!
I wish the mountains would tremble
when you show your power!
2 Be like a fire that causes twigs to burn.
It also makes water boil.
So come down and make yourself known to your enemies.
Cause the nations to shake with fear
when they see your power!
3 Long ago you did some wonderful things we didn't expect.
You came down, and the mountains trembled
when you showed your power.
4 No one's ears have ever heard of a God like you.
No one's eyes have ever seen a God who is greater than you.
No God but you acts for the good
of those who trust in him.
5 You come to help those who enjoy doing what is right.
You help those who thank you for teaching them how to live.
But when we continued to disobey you,
you became angry with us.
So how can we be saved?
6 All of us have become like someone who is "unclean."
All of the good things we do are like polluted rags to you.
All of us are like leaves that have dried up.
Our sins sweep us away like the wind.
7 No one prays to you.
No one asks you for help.
You have turned your face away from us.
You have let us waste away
because we have sinned so much.

8 LORD, you are our Father.
We are the clay. You are the potter.
Your hands made all of us.
9 Don't be so angry with us, LORD.
Don't remember our sins anymore.
Please show us your favor.
All of us belong to you.
10 Your sacred cities have become a desert.
Even Zion is a desert.
Jerusalem is a dry and empty place.
11 Our people used to praise you in our holy and glorious temple.
But now it has been burned down.
Everything we treasured has been destroyed.
12 LORD, won't you help us even after everything that's happened?
Will you keep silent and punish us more than we can stand?

The LORD Answers Isaiah's Prayer

65 The LORD says, "I made myself known to those who were not asking for me.
I was found by those who were not trying to find me.
I spoke to a nation that did not pray to me.
'Here I am,' I said. 'Here I am.'
2 All day long I have held out my hands
to welcome a stubborn nation.
They lead sinful lives.
They go where their evil thoughts take them.
3 They are always making me very angry.
They do it right in front of me.
They offer sacrifices in the gardens of other gods.
They burn incense on altars that are made out of bricks.
4 They sit among the graves.
They spend their nights talking to the spirits of the dead.
They eat the meat of pigs.
Their cooking pots hold soup that has 'unclean' meat in it.
5 They say, 'Keep away! Don't come near us!
We are too sacred for you!'
Those people are like smoke in my nose.
They are like a fire that keeps burning all day.

6 "I will judge them. I have even written it down.
I will not keep silent.
Instead, I will pay them back for all of their sins.
7 I will punish them for their sins
and the sins of their people before them,"
says the LORD.

"They burned sacrifices on the mountains.
They disobeyed me by worshiping other gods on the hills.
So I will really punish them
for all of the sins they have committed."

8 The LORD says,

"Sometimes juice is still left in grapes that have been crushed.
So people say, 'Don't destroy them.
Some good juice is still left in them.'
That is what I will do for the good of those who serve me.
I will not destroy all of my people.
9 I will give children
to the families of Jacob and Judah.
They will possess my entire land.
My chosen people will be given all of it.
Those who serve me will live there.
10 Their flocks will eat in the rich grasslands of Sharon.
Their herds will rest in the Valley of Achor.
That is what I will do for my people who follow me.

11 "But some of you have deserted me.
You no longer worship on my holy mountain of Zion.
You spread a table for the god that is called Good Fortune.
You offer bowls of mixed wine to the god named Fate.
12 So I will make it your fate to be killed with swords.
Each of you will die a horrible death.
That is because I called out to you, but you did not answer me.
I spoke to you, but you did not listen.
You did what is evil in my sight.
You chose to do what does not please me."

13 So the LORD and King says,

"Those who serve me will have food to eat.
But you will be hungry.
My servants will have plenty to drink.
But you will be thirsty.
Those who serve me will be full of joy.
But you will be put to shame.
14 My servants will sing
with joy in their hearts.
But you will cry out
because of the great pain in your hearts.
You will cry because your spirits are sad.
15 My chosen ones will use your names
when they call down curses on others.
I am your LORD and King.
I will put you to death.
But I will give new names to those who serve me.
16 They will ask me to bless their land.
They will do it in my name.
I am the God of truth.
They will take oaths and make promises in their land.
They will do it in my name.
I am the God of truth.
The troubles of the past will be forgotten.
They will be hidden from my eyes.

The LORD Will Create New Heavens and a New Earth

17 "I will create new heavens and a new earth.
The things that have happened before will not be remembered.
They will not even enter your minds.
18 So be glad and full of joy forever
because of what I will create.
I will cause others to take delight in Jerusalem.
They will be filled with joy
when they see its people.
19 And I will be full of joy because of Jerusalem.
I will take delight in my people.
Sobbing and crying
will not be heard there anymore.

20 "Babies in Jerusalem will no longer
live only a few days.
Old people will not fail
to live for a very long time.
Those who live to the age of 100
will be thought of as still being young when they die.
Those who die before they are 100
will be considered as having been under God's curse.
21 My people will build houses and live in them.
They will plant vineyards and eat their fruit.
22 They will no longer build houses
only to have others live in them.
They will no longer plant crops
only to have others eat them.
My people will live to be as old as trees.
My chosen ones will enjoy for a long time
the things they have worked for.
23 Their work will not be worthless anymore.
They will not have children who are sure to face sudden terror.
Instead, I will bless them.
I will also bless their children after them.
24 Even before they call out to me, I will answer them.
While they are still speaking, I will hear them.
25 Wolves and lambs will eat together.
Lions will eat straw like oxen.
Serpents will not bite anyone.
They will eat nothing but dust.
None of those animals will harm or destroy
anything or anyone on my holy mountain of Zion,"
says the LORD.

The LORD Judges Some People and Blesses Others

66 The LORD says,
"Heaven is my throne.
The earth is under my control.
So how could you ever build a house for me?
Where would my resting place be?
2 Didn't my powerful hand make everything?
That is how all things were created,"
announces the LORD.

"The person I value is not proud.
He is sorry for the wrong things he
has done.
He has great respect for what I say.
3 But others are not like that.
They sacrifice bulls to me,
but at the same time they kill people.
They offer lambs to me,
but they also sacrifice dogs to other gods.
They bring grain offerings to me,
but they also offer pig's blood to other gods.
They burn incense to me,
but they also worship statues of gods.
They have chosen to go their own way.
They take delight in things I hate.
4 So I have also made a choice.
I will make them suffer greatly.
I will bring on them what they are afraid of.
When I called out to them, no one
answered me.
When I spoke to them, no one listened.
They did what is evil in my sight.
They chose to do what displeases me."

5 Listen to the word of the LORD.
Listen, you who tremble with fear when he
speaks. He says,
"Some of your own people hate you.
They turn their backs on you because you
are faithful to me.
They make fun of you and say,
'Let the LORD show his glory by saving you.
Then we can see how happy you are.'
But they will be put to shame.
6 Hear the loud sounds coming from the city!
Listen to the noise coming from the temple!
I am the one who is causing it.
I am paying my enemies back for
everything they have done.

7 "Zion is like a woman who has a baby
before she goes into labor.
She has a son
even before her labor pains begin.
8 Who has ever heard of anything like that?
Who has ever seen such a thing?
Can a country be born in a day?
Can a nation be created in a moment?
But as soon as Zion goes into labor,
her people increase their numbers.
9 Zion, would I bring you to the moment of birth
and not let it happen?" says the LORD.
"Would I close up a mother's body
when it is time for her baby to be born?"
says your God.
10 "Be glad along with Jerusalem, all you who
love her.
Be filled with joy because of her.
Take great delight in her,
all you who sob over her.
11 You will nurse at her comforting breasts.
And you will be satisfied.
You will drink until you are full.
And you will delight in her rich and
plentiful supply."

12 The LORD continues,

"I will cause peace to flow over her like a river.
I will make the wealth of nations sweep
over her like a flooding stream.
You will nurse and be carried in her arms.
You will play on her lap.
13 As a mother comforts her child,
I will comfort you.
You will find comfort in Jerusalem."

14 When you see that happen, your hearts will be
filled with joy.
Just as grass grows quickly, you will
succeed.
The LORD will show his power to those who
serve him.
But he will pour out his anger on his
enemies.
15 The LORD will judge them with fire.
His chariots are coming like a windstorm.
He will pour out his burning anger on his
enemies.
It will blaze out like flames of fire.
16 The LORD will bring everyone into court.
He will use fire and his sword to punish
those he finds guilty.
He will put many people to death.

17 "Some people set themselves apart and make
themselves pure. They do it so they can go into the
gardens to worship other gods. They do what the
worship leader tells them to do. They eat the meat
of pigs and rats. They also eat other things I hate.
All of those people will come to a horrible end,"
announces the LORD.

18 "They have done many evil things. And they
plan to do even more. So I will come and gather
the people of every nation and language. They will
see my glory when I act.

19 "I will do a miracle among them. I will send to
the nations some of those who are left alive. I will
send some of them to the people of Tarshish, Libya and Lydia, who are famous for using bows. I
will send others to Tubal and Greece. And I will
send still others to islands far away. The people
who live there have not heard about my fame.

They have not seen my glory. Those I send will tell the nations about my glory when I act.

[20]"And they will bring back all of the people of Israel from all of those nations. They will bring them to my holy mountain in Jerusalem. My people will ride on horses, mules and camels. They will come in chariots and wagons," says the LORD. "Those messengers will bring my people as an offering to me. They will bring them to my temple, just as the Israelites bring their grain offerings in bowls that are 'clean.' [21]And I will choose some of them to be priests and Levites," says the LORD.

[22]"I will make new heavens and a new earth. And they will last forever," announces the LORD. "In the same way, your name and your children after you will last. [23]Everyone will come and bow down to me. They will do it at every New Moon Feast and on every Sabbath day," says the LORD.

[24]"When they go out of Jerusalem, they will see the dead bodies of those who refused to obey me. The worms that eat the bodies will not die. The fire that burns them will not be put out. It will make everyone sick just to look at them."

Jeremiah

1 These are the words Jeremiah received from the LORD. He was the son of Hilkiah. Jeremiah was one of the priests at Anathoth. That's a town in the territory of Benjamin. 2A message came to Jeremiah from the LORD. It came in the 13th year that Josiah was king over Judah. Josiah was the son of Amon.

3The LORD's message also came to Jeremiah during the whole time Jehoiakim was king over Judah. Jehoiakim was the son of Josiah. The LORD continued to speak to Jeremiah until the fifth month of the 11th year that Zedekiah was king over Judah. That's when the people of Jerusalem were forced to leave their country. Zedekiah was the son of Josiah. Here is what Jeremiah said.

The LORD Chooses Jeremiah

4A message came to me from the LORD. He said,

5"Before I formed you in your mother's body
I chose you.
Before you were born I set you apart to
serve me.
I appointed you to be a prophet to the
nations."

6"You are my LORD and King," I said. "I don't know how to speak. I'm only a child."

7But the LORD said to me, "Do not say, 'I'm only a child.' You must go to everyone I send you to. You must say everything I command you to say. 8Do not be afraid of the people I send you to. I am with you. I will save you," announces the LORD.

9Then the LORD reached out his hand. He touched my mouth and spoke to me. He said, "I have put my words in your mouth. 10Today I am appointing you to speak to nations and kingdoms. I want you to pull them up by the roots and tear them down. I want you to destroy them and crush them. But I also want you to build them up and plant them."

11A message came to me from the LORD. He asked me, "What do you see, Jeremiah?"

"The branch of an almond tree," I replied.

12The LORD said to me, "You have seen correctly. I am watching to see that my word comes true."

13Another message came to me from the LORD. He asked me, "What do you see?"

"A pot that has boiling water in it," I answered. "It's leaning toward us from the north."

14The LORD said to me, "Something very bad will be poured out on everyone who lives in this land. It will come from the north. 15I am about to send for all of the armies in the northern kingdoms," announces the LORD.

"Their kings will come to Jerusalem.
They will set up their thrones at the very
gates of the city.
They will attack all of the walls that surround
the city.
They will go to war against all of the towns
of Judah.
16I will judge my people.
They have done many evil things.
They have deserted me.
They have burned incense to other gods.
They have worshiped the gods
their own hands have made.

17"So get ready! Stand up! Tell them everything I command you to. Do not let them terrify you. If you do, I will terrify you in front of them. 18Today I have made you like a city that has a high wall around it. I have made you like an iron pillar and a bronze wall. Now you can stand up against the whole land. You can stand against the kings and officials of Judah. You can stand against its priests and its people. 19They will fight against you. But they will not overcome you. I am with you. I will save you," announces the LORD.

Israel Deserts the LORD

2 A message came to me from the LORD. He said, 2"Go. Announce my message to the people in Jerusalem. I want everyone to hear it. Tell them,

"'I remember how faithful you were to me
when you were young.
You loved me as if you were my bride.
You followed me through the desert.
Nothing had been planted there.
3Your people were holy to me.
They were the first share of my harvest.
All those who destroyed them were held guilty.
And trouble came to their enemies,'"
announces the LORD.

4People of Jacob, hear the LORD's message.
Listen, all you tribes of Israel.

5The LORD says,

"What did your people find wrong with me?
Why did they wander so far away from me?
They worshiped worthless statues of gods.
Then they themselves became worthless.
6They did not ask, 'Where is the LORD?
He brought us up out of Egypt.
He led us through a dry and empty land.
He guided us through deserts and deep
valleys.
It was a land of darkness where there wasn't
any rain.
No one lived or traveled there.'

7 But I brought you into a land that has rich soil.
I gave you its fruit and its finest food.
In spite of that, you polluted my land.
You turned it into something I hate.
8 The priests did not ask,
'Where is the LORD?'
Those who taught my law did not know me.
The leaders refused to obey me.
The prophets prophesied in the name of Baal.
They worshiped worthless statues
of gods.

9 "So I am bringing charges against you again,"
announces the LORD.
"And I will bring charges against your
children's children.
10 Go over to the coasts of the western nations
and look.
Send people to the land of Kedar and have
them look closely.
See if there has ever been anything like this.
11 Has a nation ever changed its gods?
Actually, they are not even gods at all.
But my people have traded away their
glorious God.
They have traded me for worthless statues
of gods.
12 Sky above, be shocked over that.
Tremble with horror,"
announces the LORD.
13 "My people have sinned twice.
They have deserted me,
even though I am the spring of water that
gives life.
And they have dug their own wells.
But those wells are broken.
They can't hold any water.
14 Are you people of Israel servants?
You were not born as slaves, were you?
Then why have you been carried off like
stolen goods?
15 Lions have roared.
They have growled at you.
They have destroyed your land.
Your towns are burned and deserted.
16 The men of Memphis and Tahpanhes
have shaved your heads to dishonor you.
17 Haven't you brought that on yourselves?
I am the LORD your God, but you
deserted me.
You left me even while I was leading you.
18 Why do you go to Egypt
to drink water from the Shihor River?
Why do you go to Assyria
to drink from the Euphrates River?
19 You will be punished because you have sinned.
You will be corrected for turning away
from me.
I am the LORD your God.
If you desert me, bad things will happen
to you.
If you do not respect me, you will suffer
bitterly.
I want you to understand that,"
announces the LORD who rules over all.

20 "Long ago you broke off the yoke I put on you.
You tore off the ropes I tied you up with.
You said, 'I won't serve you!'
In fact, on every high hill
you lay down like a prostitute.
You worshiped other gods under every
green tree.
21 You were like a good vine when I planted you.
You were a healthy plant.
Then how did you turn against me?
How did you become a bad, wild vine?
22 You might wash yourself with baking soda.
You might use plenty of soap.
But I can still see the stains your guilt
covers you with,"
announces the LORD and King.
23 "You say, 'I am "clean."
I haven't followed the gods that are named
after Baal.'
How can you say that?
Remember how you acted in the valley.
Consider what you have done.
You are like a female camel running quickly
here and there.
24 You are like a wild donkey that lives in
the desert.
She smells the wind when she longs for
a mate.
Who can hold her back?
The males that run after her do not need to
wear themselves out.
At mating time they will easily find her.
25 Do not run after other gods
until your sandals are worn out and your
throat is dry.
But you said, 'It's no use!
I love those gods.
I must go after them.'

26 "A thief is dishonored when he is caught.
And you people of Israel are filled with
shame.
Your kings and officials are dishonored.
So are your priests and your prophets.
27 You say to a piece of wood, 'You are
my father.'
You say to a stone, 'You are my mother.'
You have turned your backs to me.
You refuse to look at me.
But when you are in trouble, you say,
'Come and save us!'
28 So where are the gods you made for
yourselves?
Let them come when you are in trouble!
Let them save you if they can!
Judah, you have as many gods
as you have towns.

29 "Why do you bring charges against me?
All of you have refused to obey me,"
announces the LORD.
30 "I punished your people. But it did not do them any good.
They did not pay attention when they were corrected.
You have killed your prophets with swords.
You have swallowed them up like a hungry lion.

31 "You who are now living, consider my message. I am saying,

"Have I been like a desert to Israel?
Have I been like a land of deep darkness?
Why do my people say, 'We are free to wander.
We won't come to you anymore'?
32 Does a young woman forget all about her jewelry?
Does a bride forget her wedding jewels?
But my people have forgotten me
more days than anyone can count.
33 You are very skilled at chasing after love!
Even the worst of women can learn from how you act.
34 The blood of those you have killed is on your clothes.
You have destroyed poor people who were not guilty.
You did not catch them in the act of breaking in.
In spite of all of that,
35 you say, 'I'm not guilty of doing anything wrong.
The LORD isn't angry with me.'
But I will judge you.
That is because you say, 'I haven't sinned.'
36 Why do you keep on
changing your ways so much?
Assyria did not help you.
And Egypt will not help you either.
37 So you will also leave Egypt
with your hands tied together above your heads.
I have turned my back on those you trust.
They will not help you.

3 "Suppose a man divorces his wife.
What if she then gets married to another man?
Should her first husband return to her again?
If he does, won't the land become
completely 'unclean'?
People of Israel, you have lived like a prostitute.
You have loved many other gods.
So do you think you can return to me now?"
announces the LORD.
2 "Look up at the bare hilltops.
Is there any place where you have not
committed adultery with other gods?
By the side of the road you sat waiting
for lovers.
You sat there like someone who wanders in the desert.
You have polluted the land.
You are like a sinful prostitute.
3 So I have held the showers back.
I have kept the spring rains from falling.
But you still have the bold face of a prostitute.
You refuse to blush with shame.
4 You have just now called out to me.
You said,
'My Father, you have been my friend
ever since I was young.
5 Will you always be angry with me?
Will your anger continue forever?'
That is how you talk.
But you do all of the evil things
you can."

Israel Is Not Faithful to the LORD

6 During the time Josiah was king, the LORD
spoke to me. He said, "Have you seen what the
people of Israel have done? They have not been
faithful to me. They have committed adultery with
other gods. They worshiped them on every high
hill and under every green tree.
7 "I thought that after they had done all of those
things, they would return to me. But they did not.
Their sister nation Judah saw it. And they were not
faithful to me either.
8 "I gave Israel their letter of divorce. I sent them
away because they were unfaithful to me so many
times. But I saw that their sister nation Judah did
not have any respect for me. They were not faithful to me either. They also went out and committed adultery with other gods.
9 "Israel was not faithful to me, but that did not
bother them at all. They made the land 'unclean.'
They worshiped gods that were made out of stone
and wood. 10 In spite of all that, their sister Judah
did not come back to me. They were not faithful
to me either. They did not return with all their
heart. They only pretended to," announces the
LORD.
11 The LORD said to me, "Israel and Judah have
not been faithful to me. But Israel was not as bad
as Judah was.
12 "Go. Announce this message to the people in
the north. Tell them,

" 'Israel, you have not been faithful,'
announces the LORD.
'Return to me. Then I will look on you with favor again.
My love is faithful,' announces the LORD.
'I will not be angry with you forever.
13 Admit that you are guilty of doing what is wrong.
You have refused to obey me. I am the
LORD your God.

You have committed adultery with other gods.
You worshiped them under every green tree.
And you have not obeyed me,'"
announces the LORD.

14"You people have not been faithful," the LORD. "Return to me. I am your husband. I will choose one of you from each town. I will choose two from each territory. And I will bring you to the city of Zion.

15"Then I will give you shepherds who are dear to my heart. Their knowledge and understanding will help them lead you. 16In those days your numbers will increase greatly in the land," announces the LORD.

"Then people will not talk about the ark of the covenant of the LORD anymore. It will never enter their minds. They will not remember it. The ark will not be missed. And another one will not be made.

17"At that time they will call Jerusalem The Throne of the LORD. All of the nations will gather together there. They will go there to honor me. They will no longer do what their stubborn and evil hearts want them to do.

18"In those days the people of Judah will join the people of Israel. Together they will come from a land in the north. They will come to the land I gave to your people long ago. I wanted them to have it as their very own.

19"I myself said,

"'I would gladly treat you like my children.
I would give you a pleasant land.
It is the most beautiful land any nation could have.'
I thought you would call me 'Father.'
I hoped you would always follow me.
20 But you people are like a woman who is not faithful to her husband.
Israel, you have not been faithful to me,"
announces the LORD.
21 A cry is heard on the bare hilltops.
The people of Israel are sobbing and praying.
That's because their lives are so twisted.
They've forgotten the LORD their God.

22 "You have not been faithful,"
says the LORD.
"Return to me. I will heal you.
Then you will not turn away from me anymore."

"Yes," the people say. "We will come to you.
You are the LORD our God.
23 The gods we worship on the hills
and mountains are useless.
You are the LORD our God.
You are the only one who can save us.
24 From our earliest years shameful gods have eaten up
everything our people worked for.
They have eaten up our flocks and herds.
They've destroyed our sons and daughters.
25 Let us lie down in our shame.
Let our dishonor cover us.
You are the LORD our God. But we have sinned against you.
We and our people before us have sinned.
We haven't obeyed you
from our earliest years until now."

4 "If you will return, Israel,
return to me,"
announces the LORD.
"Put the statues of your gods out of my sight.
I hate them.
Stop going down the wrong path.
2 Take all of your oaths in my name.
Say, 'You can be sure that the LORD is alive.'
Let all of your promises be truthful, fair and honest.
Then I will bless the nations.
And they will take delight in me."

3Here is what the LORD is telling the people of Judah and Jerusalem. He says,

"Your hearts are as hard as a field
that has not been plowed.
So change your ways and produce good crops.
Do not plant seeds among thorns.
4 People of Judah and Jerusalem, obey me.
Do not let your hearts be stubborn.
If you do, my anger will blaze out against you.
It will burn like fire because of the evil things you have done.
No one will be able to put it out.

Trouble Will Come From the North

5 "Announce my message in Judah.
Tell it in Jerusalem.
Say, 'Blow trumpets all through the land!'
Give a loud shout and say,
'Gather together!
Let's run to cities that have high walls around them!'
6 Warn everyone to go to Zion!
Run for safety! Do not wait!
I am bringing trouble from the north.
Everything will be totally destroyed."

7 Lions have come out of their den.
Those who destroy nations have begun to march out.
They have left their place
to destroy your land completely.
Your towns will be broken to pieces.
No one will live in them.
8 So put on black clothes.
Sob and cry over what has happened.
The LORD hasn't turned
his burning anger away from us.

9 "A dark day is coming," announces the LORD.
"The king and his officials will lose hope.
The priests will be shocked.
And the prophets will be terrified."

10 Then I said, "You are my LORD and King. You
have completely tricked the people of Judah and Jerusalem. You have told them, 'You will have peace
and rest.' But swords are pointed at our throats."
11 At that time the people of Judah and Jerusalem will be warned. They will be told, "A hot and
dry wind is coming, my people. It is blowing
toward you from the bare hilltops in the desert. But
it does not separate straw from grain. 12 It is much
too strong for that. The wind is coming from me.
I am making my decision against you."

13 Look! Our enemies are approaching like the clouds.
Their chariots are coming like a strong wind.
Their horses are faster than eagles.
How terrible it will be for us!
We'll be destroyed!
14 People of Jerusalem, wash your sins from your hearts and be saved.
How long will you hold on to your evil thoughts?
15 A voice is speaking all the way from the city of Dan.
From the hills of Ephraim it announces that trouble is coming.
16 "Tell the nations.
Warn Jerusalem.
Say, 'An army will attack you.
It is coming from a land far away.
It will shout a war cry
against the cities of Judah.
17 It will surround them like people who guard a field.
Judah has refused to obey me,'"
announces the LORD.
18 "The army will attack you
because of your conduct and actions.
That is how you will be punished.
It will be so bitter!
It will cut deep down into your hearts!"
19 I'm suffering! I'm really suffering!
I'm hurting badly.
My heart is suffering so much!
It's pounding inside me.
I can't keep silent.
I've heard the sound of trumpets.
I've heard the battle cry.
20 One trouble follows another.
The whole land is destroyed.
In an instant my tents are gone.
My home disappears in a moment.
21 How long must I look at our enemy's battle flag?
How long must I hear the sound of the trumpets?
22 The LORD says, "My people are foolish.
They do not know me.
They are children who do not have any sense.
They have no understanding at all.
They are skilled in doing what is evil.
They do not know how to do what is good."

23 I looked at the earth.
It didn't have any shape. And it was empty.
I looked at the sky.
Its light was gone.
24 I looked at the mountains.
They were shaking.
All of the hills were swaying.
25 I looked. And there weren't any people.
Every bird in the sky had flown away.
26 I looked. And the fruitful land had become a desert.
All of its towns were destroyed.
The LORD had done all of that because of his burning anger.

27 The LORD says,

"The whole land will be destroyed.
But I will not destroy it completely.
28 So the earth will be filled with sadness.
The sky above will grow dark.
I have spoken, and I will not take pity on them.
I have made my decision, and I will not change my mind."
29 People can hear the sound of horsemen.
Men who are armed with bows are coming.
The people in every town run away.
Some of them go into the bushes.
Others climb up among the rocks.
All of the towns are deserted.
No one is living in them.

30 What are you doing, you who are destroyed?
Why do you dress yourself in bright red clothes?
Why do you put on jewels of gold?
Why do you put makeup on your eyes?
You make yourself beautiful for no reason at all.
Your lovers hate you.
They are trying to kill you.

31 I hear a cry like the cry of a woman having a baby.
I hear a groan like someone having her first child.
It's the cry of the people of Zion struggling to breathe.
They reach out their hands and say,
"Help us! We're fainting!
Murderers are about to kill us!"

No One Is Honest

5 The LORD says, "Go up and down the streets of Jerusalem.
Look around.
Think about what you see.

Search through the market places.
See if you can find one honest person who tries to be truthful.
If you can, I will forgive this city.
2 They take all of their oaths in my name.
They say, 'You can be sure that the LORD is alive.'
But their oaths can't be trusted."
3 LORD, don't your eyes look for truth?
You struck your people down.
But they didn't feel any pain.
You crushed them.
But they refused to be corrected.
They made their faces harder than stone.
They refused to turn away from their sins.
4 I thought, "The people of Jerusalem are foolish.
They don't know how the LORD wants them to live.
They don't know what their God requires of them.
5 So I will go to the leaders.
I'll speak to them.
They should know how the LORD wants them to live.
They must know what their God requires of them."
But all of them had broken off the yoke the LORD had put on them.
They had torn off the ropes he had tied them up with.
6 So a lion from the forest will attack them.
A wolf from the desert will destroy them.
A leopard will hide and wait near their towns.
It will tear to pieces anyone who dares to go out.
Again and again they have refused to obey the LORD.
They have turned away from him many times.

7 The LORD says, "Jerusalem, why should I forgive you?
Your people have deserted me.
They have taken their oaths in the names of gods
that are not really gods at all.
I supplied everything they needed.
But they committed adultery.
Large crowds went to the houses of prostitutes.
8 Your people are like stallions that have plenty to eat.
Their sinful longings are out of control.
Each of them goes after another man's wife.
9 Shouldn't I punish them for that?"
announces the LORD.
"Shouldn't I pay back the nation
that does those things?
10 "Armies of Babylonia, go through their vineyards and destroy them.
But do not destroy them completely.
Strip off their branches.
Those people do not belong to me.
11 The people of Israel and Judah
have not been faithful to me at all,"
announces the LORD.
12 They have told lies about the LORD.
They said, "He won't do anything!
No harm will come to us.
We will never see war or be hungry.
13 The prophets are nothing but wind.
Their message doesn't come from the LORD.
So let what they say will happen be done to them."

14 The LORD God rules over all. He says to me,
"The people have spoken those words.
So my words will be like fire in your mouth.
I will make the people like wood.
And the fire will burn them up."

15 "People of Israel, listen to me,"
announces the LORD.
"I am bringing against you
a nation from far away.
It is an old nation. And it will last for a long time.
Its people speak a language you do not know.
You can't understand what they are saying.
16 The bags they carry their arrows in are like an open grave.
All of their soldiers are mighty.
17 They will eat up your crops and your food.
They will strike down your sons and daughters.
They will kill your sheep and cattle.
They will destroy your vines and fig trees.
You trust in your cities that have high walls around them.
But the people in them will be killed with swords.

18 "In spite of that, even in those days I will not destroy you completely," announces the LORD.
19 "'Jeremiah,' the people will ask, 'Why has the LORD our God done all of this to us?'

"Then you will tell them, 'You have deserted the LORD. You have served other gods in your own land. So now you will serve another nation in a land that is not your own.'

20 "Here is what I want you to announce
to the people of Jacob.
Tell it in Judah.
Tell them I say,
21 'Listen to this, you foolish people,
who do not have any sense.
You have eyes, but you do not see.
You have ears, but you do not hear.
22 Shouldn't you have respect for me?' announces the LORD.
'Shouldn't you tremble with fear in front of me?

I made the sand to hold the ocean back.
It will do that forever.
The ocean can't go past it.
The waves might roll, but they can't sweep over it.
They might roar, but they can't go across it.
23 But you people have stubborn hearts.
You refuse to obey me.
You have turned away from me.
You have gone down the wrong path.
24 You do not say to yourselves,
"Let us have respect for the LORD our God.
He sends rain in the fall and the spring.
He promises us that the harvest will come at the same time each year."
25 But the things you have done wrong
have robbed you of those gifts.
Your sins have kept those good things
far away from you.'

26 "Jeremiah, some of my people are evil.
They hide and wait just as people hide to catch birds.
They set traps for men.
27 A hunter uses tricks to fill his cage with birds.
And my people have filled their houses with a lot of goods.
They have become rich and powerful.
28 They have grown fat and heavy.
There is no limit to the evil things they do.
In court they do not state the case
of children whose fathers have died.
They do not stand up for poor people.
29 Shouldn't I punish them for that?"
announces the LORD.
"Shouldn't I pay back the
nation that does those things?

30 "Something horrible and shocking
has happened in the land.
31 The prophets prophesy lies.
The priests rule by their own authority.
And my people love it that way.
But what will they do in the end?"

Babylonia Will Attack Jerusalem

6 The LORD says, "People of Benjamin, run for safety!
Run away from Jerusalem!
Blow trumpets in Tekoa!
Warn everyone in Beth Hakkerem!
Horrible trouble is coming from the north.
The Babylonians will destroy everything with awful power.
2 I will destroy the city of Zion,
even though it is very beautiful.
3 Shepherds will come against it with their flocks.
They will set up their tents around it.
All of them will take care of their own sheep."

4 The Babylonians say, "Prepare for battle against Judah!
Get up! Let's attack them at noon!
But the daylight is fading.
The shadows of evening are getting longer.
5 So get up! Let's attack them at night!
Let's destroy their strongest forts!"

6 The LORD who rules over all speaks to the Babylonians. He says,

"Cut some trees down.
Use the wood to build ramps against Jerusalem's walls.
I must punish that city.
It is filled with people who treat others badly.
7 Wells keep giving fresh water.
And Jerusalem keeps on sinning.
Its people are always fighting and causing trouble.
When I look at them,
I see nothing but sickness and wounds.
8 Jerusalem, listen to my warning.
If you do not, I will turn away from you.
Your land will become a desert.
No one will be able to live there."

9 The LORD rules over all. He says to me,
"People gather the few grapes that are left on a vine.
So let Israel's enemies gather the few people who are left alive in the land.
Look carefully at the branches again.
Do it like someone who gathers the last few grapes."

10 Who can I speak to? Who can I warn?
Who will even listen to me?
Their ears are closed
so they can't hear.
The LORD's message displeases them.
They don't take any delight in it.
11 But the LORD's anger burns inside me.
I can no longer hold it in.

The LORD says to me, "Pour out my anger on the children in the street.
Pour it out on the young people who are gathered together.
Husband and wife alike will be caught in it.
So will those who are very old.
12 I will reach out my hand
against those who live in the land,"
announces the LORD.
"Then their houses will be turned over to others.
So will their fields and their wives.
13 Everyone wants to get richer and richer,
from the least important of them to the most important.
Prophets and priests alike
try to fool everyone they can.

14 They bandage the wounds of my people
as if they were not very deep.
'Peace, peace,' they say.
But there isn't any peace.
15 Are they ashamed of their hateful actions?
No. They do not feel any shame at all.
They do not even know how to blush.
So they will fall like others who have already fallen.
They will be brought down when I punish them,"
says the LORD.

16 The LORD tells the people of Judah,

"Stand where the roads cross, and look around.
Ask where the old paths are.
Ask for the good path, and walk on it.
Then your hearts will find rest in me.
But you said, 'We won't walk on it.'
17 I appointed prophets to warn you. I said,
'Listen to the sound of the trumpets!'
But you said, 'We won't listen.'
18 So pay attention, you nations.
Be witnesses for me.
Watch what will happen to my people.
19 Earth, pay attention.
I am going to bring trouble on them.
I will punish them because of the evil things they have done.
They have not listened to my words.
They have said no to my law.
20 What do I care about incense from the land of Sheba?
Why should I bother with sweet-smelling cane from a land far away?
I do not accept your burnt offerings.
Your sacrifices do not please me."

21 So the LORD says,

"I will bring an army against the people of Judah.
Parents and children alike will trip and fall.
Neighbors and friends will die."

22 The LORD says to Jerusalem,

"Look! An army is coming
from the land of the north.
I am stirring up a great nation.
Its army is coming from a land that is very far away.
23 Its soldiers are armed with bows and spears.
They are mean. They do not show any mercy at all.
They come riding in on their horses.
They sound like the roaring ocean.
They are lined up for battle.
They are marching out
to attack you, city of Zion."

24 We have heard reports about them.
And our hands can't help us.
We are suffering greatly.
It's like the pain of a woman having a baby.
25 Don't go out to the fields.
Don't walk on the roads.
Our enemies have swords.
And there is terror on every side.
26 Put on black clothes, my people.
Roll among the ashes.
Cry with bitter sobbing
just as you would cry for an only child.
The one who is going to destroy us
will come suddenly.

27 The LORD says to me, "I have made you like one who tests metals.
My people are the ore.
I want you to watch them
and test the way they live.
28 All of them are used to disobeying me.
They go around telling lies about others.
They are like bronze mixed with iron.
All of them do very sinful things.
29 The fire is made very hot
so the lead will burn away.
But it is impossible to make those people pure.
Those who are evil are not removed.
30 They are like silver that is thrown away.
That is because I have not accepted them."

Worshiping Other Gods Is Worthless

7 A message came to me from the LORD. He
said, 2 "Stand at the gate of my house.
Announce my message to the people there. Say,
"'Listen to the LORD's message, all of you people of Judah. You always come through these gates
to worship the LORD. 3 The God of Israel is speaking to you. He is the LORD who rules over all. He
says, "Change the way you live and act. Then I
will let you live in this place.
4 "'"Do not trust in lies. Do not say, 'This is the
temple of the LORD! This is the temple of the
LORD! This is the temple of the LORD!'
5 "'"You must really change the way you live
and act. Treat each other fairly. 6 Do not treat outsiders or widows badly in this place. Do not take
advantage of children whose fathers have died. Do
not kill those who are not guilty of doing anything
wrong. Do not worship other gods. That will only
bring harm to you.
7 "'"If you obey me, I will let you live in this
place. It is the land I gave your people who lived
long ago. It was promised to them for ever and ever.
8 "'"But look! You are trusting in worthless lies.
9 "'"You continue to steal and commit murder.
You commit adultery and tell lies. You burn
incense to Baal. You worship other gods you have
not known anything about before.
10 "'"Then you come and stand in front of me.
You keep coming to this house where I have put
my Name. You say, 'We are safe.' You think you
are safe when you do so many things I hate. 11 My

Name is in this house. But you have made it a den
for robbers! I have been watching you!" announces the LORD.
12"'"Go now to the town of Shiloh. Go to the
place where I first made a home for my Name. See
what I did to it because of the evil things my people Israel were doing.
13"'"I spoke to you again and again," announces
the LORD. "I warned you while you were doing all
of those things. But you did not listen. I called out
to you. But you did not answer. 14So what I did to
Shiloh I will now do to the house where my Name
is. It is the temple you trust in. It is the place I gave
to you and your people of long ago.
15"'"But I will throw you out of my land. That
is exactly what I did to the people of Ephraim. And
they are your relatives."'
16"Jeremiah, do not pray for those people. Do
not make any appeal or request for them. Do not
beg me. I will not listen to you.
17"Don't you see what they are doing? They are
worshiping other gods in the towns of Judah. They
are offering sacrifices to them in the streets of Jerusalem. 18The children go out and gather wood.
The fathers light the fire. The women mix the
dough. They make flat cakes of bread for the goddess who is called the Queen of Heaven. They
pour out drink offerings to other gods. That makes
me very angry.
19"But am I the one they are hurting?" announces the LORD. "Aren't they only harming
themselves? They should be ashamed of it."
20So the LORD and King says, "I will pour out
my burning anger on this place. It will strike people and animals alike. It will destroy the trees and
the crops in the fields. It will burn, and no one will
be able to put it out."
21The LORD who rules over all is the God of Israel. He says, "Go ahead! Add your burnt offerings to your other sacrifices. Eat the meat
yourselves! 22When I brought your people out of
Egypt, I spoke to them. But I did not just give them
commands about burnt offerings and sacrifices. 23I
also gave them another command. I said, 'Obey
me. Then I will be your God. And you will be my
people. Live the way I command you to live. Then
things will go well with you.'
24"But they did not listen. They refused to pay
any attention to me. Instead, they did what their
stubborn and evil hearts wanted them to do. They
went backward and not forward.
25"Again and again I sent my servants the
prophets to you. They came to you day after day.
They prophesied from the time your people left
Egypt until now.
26"But the people did not listen. They refused to
pay any attention to me. They were stubborn. They
did more evil things than their people who lived
before them.
27"Jeremiah, when you tell them all of that, they
will not listen to you. When you call out to them,
they will not answer.
28"So say to them, 'You are a nation that has not
obeyed the LORD your God. You did not pay attention when you were corrected. Truth has died out.
You do not tell the truth anymore.'"
29The LORD says to the people of Jerusalem,
"Cut off your hair. Throw it away. Sing a song of
sadness on the bare hilltops. I am very angry with
you. I have turned my back on you. I have deserted you.

The Valley of Death

30"The people of Judah have done what is evil
in my eyes," announces the LORD. "They have set
up statues of their gods. They have worshiped
them in the house where my Name is. They have
made my house 'unclean.' I hate those statues.
31The people have built the high places of Topheth
in the Valley of Ben Hinnom. There they worship
other gods. And there they sacrifice their children
in the fire. That is something I did not command.
It did not even enter my mind.
32"So watch out!" announces the LORD. "The
days are coming when people will not call it Topheth anymore. And they will not call it the Valley of Ben Hinnom either. Instead, they will call it
the Valley of Death. They will bury the dead bodies of some people in Topheth. But they will run
out of room. 33Then they will not be able to bury
the bodies of other people there. So the bodies will
become food for the birds of the air and the wild
animals. And no one will scare them away.
34"I will put an end to the sounds of joy and
gladness. The voices of brides and grooms will not
be heard anymore. There will not be any sounds
of joy in the towns of Judah and the streets of Jerusalem. The land will become a desert.
8 "At that time the tombs will be opened," announces the LORD. "The bones of the kings
and officials of Judah will be brought out. The
bones of the priests and prophets will be removed.
So will the bones of the people of Jerusalem.
2They will lie outside under the sun, moon and all
of the stars.

"All of those people had loved and served those
things. They had followed them and worshiped
them. They had asked them for advice. So the
bones of those people will not be gathered up or
buried again. Instead, they will be like trash lying
there on the ground.
3"Everyone who is left alive in this evil nation
will want to die rather than live. That is what they
will long for in the lands where I force them to
go," announces the LORD who rules over all.

The LORD Punishes His Sinful People

4"Jeremiah, tell them, 'The LORD says,

"'"When people fall down, don't they get up
again?
When someone turns away, doesn't he come
back?

5 Then why have the people of Jerusalem turned
away from me?
Why do they always turn away?
They keep on telling lies.
They refuse to come back to me.
6 I have listened carefully.
But they do not say what is right.
They refuse to turn away from their sins.
No one says, 'What have I done?'
All of them go their own way.
They are like horses charging into battle.
7 Storks know when to fly south.
So do doves, swifts and thrushes.
But my people do not know
what I require them to do.

8 "'"How can you people say, 'We are wise.
We have the law of the LORD'?
Actually, the teachers of the law have told lies
about it.
Their pens have not written what is true.
9 Those who think they are wise will be put
to shame.
They will become terrified. They will
be trapped.
They have not accepted my message.
So what kind of wisdom do they have?
10 I will give their wives to other men.
I will give their fields to new owners.
Everyone wants to get richer and richer,
from the least important of them to the
most important.
Prophets and priests alike
try to fool everyone they can.
11 They bandage the wounds of my people
as if they were not very deep.
'Peace, peace,' they say.
But there isn't any peace.
12 Are they ashamed of their hateful actions?
No. They do not feel any shame at all.
They do not even know how to blush.
So they will fall like others who have already
fallen.
They will be brought down when I punish
them,"
says the LORD.

13 "'"I will take away their harvest,"
announces the LORD.
"There will not be any grapes on the vines.
The trees will not bear any figs.
The leaves on the trees will dry up.
What I have given them
will be taken away from them."'"

14 Why are we sitting here?
Let's gather together!
Let's run to the cities that have high walls
around them!
Let's die there!
The LORD our God has sentenced us to death.
He has given us poisoned water to drink.
That's because we've sinned against him.
15 We hoped peace would come.
But nothing good has happened to us.
We hoped we would finally be healed.
But all we got was terror.
16 When our enemy's horses snort,
the noise is heard all the way from Dan.
When their stallions neigh,
the whole land trembles with fear.
They have come to destroy
the land and everything in it.
The city and everyone who lives there will
be destroyed.

17 "People of Judah, I will send poisonous snakes
among you.
No one will be able to charm them.
And they will bite you,"
announces the LORD.

18 LORD, my heart is weak inside me.
You comfort me when I'm sad.
19 Listen to the cries of my people
from a land far away.
They cry out, "Isn't the LORD in Zion?
Isn't its King there anymore?"

The LORD says, "Why have they made me
so angry
by worshiping their wooden gods?
Why have they made me angry
with their worthless statues
of gods from other lands?"

20 The people say, "The harvest is over.
The summer has ended.
And we still haven't been saved."

21 My people are crushed, so I am crushed.
I sob, and I am filled with horror.
22 Isn't there any healing lotion in Gilead?
Isn't there a doctor there?
Then why doesn't someone heal
the wounds of my people?

9 1 I wish my head were a spring of water!
I wish my eyes were a fountain of tears!
I would sob day and night
over my people who have been killed.
2 I wish I had somewhere to go in
the desert
where a traveler could stay!
Then I could leave my people.
I could get away from them.
All of them commit adultery by worshiping
other gods.
They aren't faithful to the LORD.

3 "They get ready to use
their tongues like bows,"
announces the LORD.
"Their mouths shoot out lies like arrows.
They tell lies to gain power in
the land.
They go from one sin to another.
They do not pay any attention to me.

4 Be on guard against your friends.
Do not trust the members of your own family.
Every one of them cheats.
Every friend tells lies.
5 One friend cheats another.
No one tells the truth.
They have taught their tongues how to lie.
They wear themselves out sinning.
6 Jeremiah, you live among people who tell lies.
When they lie, they refuse to pay any attention to me,"
announces the LORD.

7 So the LORD who rules over all says,

"I will put them through the fire to test them.
What else can I do?
My people are so sinful!
8 Their tongues are like deadly arrows.
They tell lies.
With their mouths all of them speak kindly to their neighbors.
But in their hearts they set traps for them.
9 Shouldn't I punish them for that?"
announces the LORD.
"Shouldn't I pay back the nation
that does those things?"

10 I will cry and sob over the fields in the hills.
I will sing a song of sadness about the desert grasslands.
They are dry and empty. No one travels through them.
The mooing of cattle isn't heard there.
The birds of the air have flown away.
All of the animals are gone.

11 The LORD says, "I will knock all of Jerusalem's buildings down.
I will make it a home for wild dogs.
The towns of Judah will be completely destroyed.
No one will be able to live in them."

12 Who is wise enough to understand those things? Who has been taught by the LORD? Who can explain them? Why has the land been destroyed so completely? Why has it become like a desert that no one can go across?

13 The LORD answered me, "Because my people have turned away from my law. I gave it to them. But they have not kept it. They have not obeyed me.
14 Instead, they have done what their stubborn hearts wanted them to do. They have worshiped the gods that are named after Baal. They have done what their people have taught them to do down through the years."

15 So now the LORD who rules over all speaks. He is the God of Israel. He says, "I will make these people eat bitter food. I will make them drink poisoned water.
16 I will scatter them among the nations. They and their people before them have not had anything to do with those nations before. I will chase these people with swords. I will hunt them down until I have destroyed them."

17 The LORD rules over all. He says,

"Here is something I want you to think about.
Send for the women who sob over the dead.
Send for the most skilled among them."

18 Let them come quickly
and sob over us.
Let them cry until tears flow from our eyes.
Let them sob until water pours out of our eyes.
19 People are heard sobbing in Zion.
They are saying, "We are destroyed!
We are filled with shame!
We must leave our land.
Our houses have been torn down."

20 Women, hear the LORD's message.
Listen to what he's saying.
Teach your daughters how to sob over the dead.
Teach one another a song of sadness.
21 Death has climbed in through our windows.
It has entered our forts.
It has removed the children from the streets.
It has taken the young people out of the market places.

22 Say, "The LORD announces,

" 'The dead bodies of men will be like trash lying in the open fields.
They will lie there like grain
that is cut down at harvest time.
No one will gather them up.' "

23 The LORD says,

"Do not let a wise man brag about how wise he is.
Do not let a strong man boast about how strong he is.
Do not let a rich person brag about how rich he is.
24 But here is what the one who brags should boast about.
He should brag that he has understanding and knows me.
I want him to know that I am the LORD.
No matter what I do on earth, I am always kind, fair and right.
And I take delight in that,"
announces the LORD.

25 "The days are coming when I will judge people," announces the LORD. "I will punish all those who are circumcised only in their bodies.
26 That includes the people of Egypt, Judah, Edom, Ammon and Moab. It also includes all those who live in the desert in places far away. None of the people in those nations is really circumcised. And not even the people of Israel are circumcised in their hearts."

The LORD Is the Only True God

10 People of Israel, listen to what the LORD is telling you. [2]He says,

"Do not follow the practices of other nations.
Do not be terrified by warnings in the sky.
Do not be afraid, even though the nations are terrified by them.
3 The practices of those nations are worthless.
People cut a tree out of the forest.
A skilled worker shapes the wood with a sharp tool.
4 Others decorate it with silver and gold.
They use a hammer to nail it to the floor.
They want to keep it from falling down.
5 The statues of their gods can't speak.
They are like scarecrows in a field of melons.
They have to be carried around
because they can't walk.
So do not worship them.
They can't do you any harm.
And they can't do you any good either."
6 LORD, no one is like you.
You are great.
You are mighty and powerful.
7 King of the nations,
everyone should have respect for you.
That's what people should give you.
Among all of the wise people in the nations
there is no one like you.
No one can compare with you in all of their kingdoms.
8 All of them are foolish. They don't have any sense.
They think they are taught by worthless wooden gods.
9 Hammered silver is brought from Tarshish.
Gold is brought from Uphaz.
People who are skilled in working with wood and gold make a statue.
Then they put blue and purple clothes on it.
The whole thing is made by skilled workers.
10 But you are the only true God.
You are the only living God.
You are the King who rules forever.
When you are angry, the earth trembles with fear.
The nations can't stand up under your anger.

11 The LORD says to the Jews who are living in Babylonia, "Tell the people of the nations, 'Your gods did not make the heavens and the earth. In fact, those gods will disappear from the earth. They will vanish from under the heavens.'"

12 But God used his power to make the earth.
His wisdom set the world in place.
His understanding spread the heavens out.
13 When he thunders, the waters in the heavens roar.
He makes clouds rise from one end of the earth to the other.
He sends lightning along with the rain.
He brings the wind out from his storerooms.

14 No one has any sense. No one knows anything at all.
Everyone who works with gold is put to shame by his wooden gods.
The metal gods he worships are fakes.
They can't even breathe.
15 They are worthless. People make fun of them.
When the LORD judges them, they will be destroyed.
16 The God of Jacob is not like them.
He gives his people everything they need.
He made everything that exists.
And that includes Israel.
It's the nation that belongs to him.
His name is The LORD Who Rules Over All.

The Land Will Be Destroyed

17 People of Jerusalem, your enemies have surrounded you.
They are attacking you.
So gather up what belongs to you.
Then leave the land.
18 The LORD says,
"I am about to throw out of this land
everyone who lives in it.
I will bring trouble on them.
They will be captured."

19 How terrible it will be for me!
I've been wounded!
And my wound can't be healed!
In spite of that, I said to myself,
"I'm sick. But I'll have to put up with it."
20 Jerusalem is like a tent that has been destroyed.
All of its ropes have snapped.
My people have gone away from me.
Now no one is left to set up my tent.
I have no one to set it up for me.
21 The leaders of my people are like shepherds who don't have any sense.
They don't ask the LORD for advice.
That's why they don't succeed.
And that's why their whole flock is scattered like sheep.
22 Listen! A message is coming!
I hear the sound of a great army
marching down from the north!
It will turn Judah's towns into a desert.
They will become a home for wild dogs.

Jeremiah Prays to the LORD

23 LORD, I know that a man doesn't control his own life.
He doesn't direct his own steps.

24 Correct me, LORD. But please be fair.
Don't correct me when you are angry.
If you do, nothing will be left of me.
25 Pour out your burning anger on the nations.
They don't pay any attention to you.
They refuse to worship you.
They have destroyed the people of Jacob.
They've wiped them out completely.
They've also destroyed the land they
lived in.

The LORD's People Have Broken His Covenant

11 A message came to me from the LORD. He
said, 2"Listen to the terms of the covenant
I made with my people long ago. Tell Judah the
terms still apply to them. Tell those who live in Jerusalem that they must obey them too.
3"I am the God of Israel. So let the people know
what I want them to do. Tell them I am saying,
'May the man who does not obey the terms of the
covenant be under my curse. 4I gave those terms
to your people long ago. That was when I brought
them out of Egypt. I saved them out of that furnace
that melts iron down and makes it pure.' I said,
'Obey me. Do everything I command you to do.
Then you will be my people. And I will be your
God.
5" 'I raised my hand and made an oath to your
people long ago. I promised them I would give
them a land that had plenty of milk and honey.' It
is the land you own today. I kept my promise."
I replied, "Amen, LORD."
6The LORD said to me, "Here is what I want you
to announce in the towns of Judah. Say it also in
the streets of Jerusalem. Tell the people, 'Listen to
the terms of my covenant. Obey them. 7Long ago
I brought your people up from Egypt. From that
time until today, I warned them again and again. I
said, "Obey me."
8" 'But they did not listen. They did not pay any
attention to me. Instead, they did what their stubborn and evil hearts wanted them to do. So I
brought down on them all of the curses of the
covenant. I commanded them to obey it. But they
refused.' "
9The LORD continued, "The people of Judah
have made some evil plans. So have those who
live in Jerusalem. 10All of them have returned to
the sins their people committed long ago. Those
people refused to listen to what I told them. And
now the people of Israel and Judah alike have worshiped other gods and served them. They have
broken the covenant I made with their people who
lived before them.
11"So I say, 'I will bring trouble on them. They
will not be able to escape it. They will cry out to
me. But I will not listen to them.
12" 'The people of Jerusalem and of the towns
of Judah will cry out to the gods they burn incense
to. But those gods will not help them at all when
trouble strikes them. 13Judah, you have as many
gods as you have towns. And in Jerusalem you
have set up as many altars as there are streets. You
are burning incense to that shameful god Baal.'
14"Jeremiah, do not pray for those people. Do
not make any appeal or request for them. They will
call out to me when they are in trouble. But I will
not listen to them.

15 "I love the people of Judah.
But they are working out their evil plans
along with many others.
So what are they doing in my temple?
Can meat that is offered to me keep me from
punishing you?
When you do evil things, you get a lot of
pleasure from them."
16 People of Judah, the LORD once called you a
healthy olive tree.
He thought its fruit was beautiful.
But now he will come with the roar of a
mighty storm.
He will set the tree on fire.
And its branches will be broken.

17The LORD who rules over all planted you. But
now he has ordered your enemies to destroy you.
The people of Israel and Judah have done what is
evil. They have made the LORD very angry by
burning incense to Baal.

Jeremiah's Enemies Make Evil Plans Against Him

18The LORD told me about the evil plans of my
enemies. That's how I knew about them. He
showed me what they were doing. 19I had been like
a gentle lamb that was led off to be killed. I didn't
realize they had made plans against me. They had
said,

"Let's destroy the tree and its fruit.
Let's cut him off while he's still living.
Then his name won't be remembered
anymore."
20 But LORD, you rule over all.
You always judge fairly.
You put people's hearts and minds to
the test.
So pay them back for what they've done.
I've committed my cause to you.

21The LORD says, "Jeremiah, here is what I am
telling you about the men of Anathoth. They want
to kill you. They are saying, 'Don't prophesy in
the LORD's name. If you do, we will kill you with
our own hands.' "
22So the LORD who rules over all says, "I will
punish them. Their young men will be killed with
swords. Their sons and daughters will die of
hunger. 23Only a few people will be left alive. I
will judge the men of Anathoth. I will destroy
them when the time to punish them comes."

Jeremiah Argues With the LORD

12 LORD, when I bring a matter to you,
you always do what is right.
But now I would like to speak with you
about whether you are being fair.
Why are sinful people successful?
Why do those who can't be trusted have an easy life?
2 You have planted them.
Their roots are deep in the ground.
They grow and produce fruit.
They honor you by what they say.
But their hearts are far away from you.
3 LORD, you know me and see me.
You test my thoughts about you.
Drag those people off like sheep to be killed!
Set them apart for the day of their death!
4 How long will the land be thirsty for water?
How long will the grass in every field be dry?
The people who live in the land are evil.
So the animals and birds have died.
And that's not all. The people are saying,
"The LORD won't see what happens to us."

The LORD Replies to Jeremiah

5 The LORD says, "Suppose you have run in a race with other men.
And suppose they have worn you out.
Then how would you be able to race against horses?
Suppose you feel safe only in open country.
Then how would you get along in the bushes near the Jordan River?
6 Even your own family has turned against you.
They have shouted loudly at you.
They might say nice things about you.
But do not trust them.

7 "I will turn my back on my people.
I will desert my land.
I love the people of Judah.
In spite of that, I will hand them over to their enemies.
8 My land has become to me
like a lion in the forest.
It roars at me.
So I hate it.
9 My own land has become like a spotted hawk.
And other hawks surround it and attack it.
Come, all of you wild animals!
Gather together!
Come together to eat up my land.
10 Many shepherds will destroy my vineyard.
They will walk all over it.
They will turn my pleasant vineyard
into a dry and empty land.
11 My vineyard will become a desert.
It will be dry and empty in my sight.
The whole land will be completely destroyed.
And no one even cares.
12 Many will come to destroy it.
They will gather on the bare hilltops in the desert.
I will use them as my sword to destroy my people.
They will kill them from one end of the land to the other.
No one will be safe.
13 People will plant wheat. But all they will gather is thorns.
They will wear themselves out. But they will not have anything to show for it.
My anger is burning against you.
So you will be ashamed of the crop you gather."

14 The LORD continues, "All of my evil neighbors have taken over the land I gave my people Israel. So I will pull them up by their roots from the
lands they live in. And I will pull up the roots of
the people of Judah from among them.
15 "But after I pull those nations up, I will show
my tender love to them again. I will bring all of
them back to their own lands. I will take all of
them back to their own countries.
16 "Suppose they learn to follow the practices of
my people. And they take an oath and make a
promise in my name. They say, 'You can be sure
that the LORD is alive.' They do it just as they once
taught my people to take oaths in Baal's name.
Then I will give them a place among my people.
17 "But what if one of those nations does not listen? Then you can be sure I will pull it up by the
roots and destroy it," announces the LORD.

A Linen Belt

13 The LORD said to me, "Go and buy a linen
belt. Put it around your waist. But do not
let it get wet."
2 So I bought a belt, just as the LORD had told me
to do. And I put it around my waist.
3 Then another message came to me from the
LORD. He said, 4 "Take off the belt you bought and
are wearing around your waist. Go to Perath. Hide
the belt there in a crack in the rocks."
5 So I went and hid it at Perath. I did just as the
LORD had told me to do.
6 Many days later the LORD spoke to me again.
He told me, "Go to Perath. Get the belt I told you
to hide there."
7 So I went to Perath. I dug up the belt. I took it
from the place where I had hidden it. But it had
rotted. It was completely useless.
8 Then another message came to me from the
LORD. He said, 9 "In the same way, I will destroy
Judah's pride. And I will destroy the great pride of
Jerusalem.
10 "Those people are evil. They refuse to listen
to what I say. They do what their stubborn hearts
want them to do. They chase after other gods.
They serve them and worship them. So they will

be like this belt. They will be completely useless.
11A belt is tied around a man's waist. In the same way, I tied all of the people of Israel and Judah to me," announces the LORD. "I wanted them to be my people. They should have brought me fame and praise and honor. But they have not listened to me.

Wineskins

12"Tell them, 'The LORD is the God of Israel. He says, "Every wineskin should be filled with wine."'

"The people might say to you, 'Don't we know that every wineskin should be filled with wine?'

13"If they do, tell them, 'The LORD says, "I am going to fill with wine everyone who lives in this land. I will make the kings who sit on David's throne drunk. And I will fill with wine the priests, the prophets and everyone who lives in Jerusalem.
14I will smash them against one another. I will punish parents and children alike," announces the LORD. "I will not feel sorry for them. I will not show them any kindness. My tender love for them will not keep me from destroying them."'"

Judah Will Be Taken Away From Their Land

15 People of Judah, listen to me.
Pay attention. Don't be proud.
The LORD has spoken.
16 Give glory to the LORD your God.
Honor him before he sends
darkness to cover the land.
Do it before you trip and fall
on the darkened hills.
You hope that light will come.
But he will turn it into thick darkness.
He will change it to deep shadows.
17 If you don't listen,
I will sob in secret.
Because you are so proud,
I will sob bitterly.
Tears will flow from my eyes.
The LORD's flock will be taken away as prisoners.
18 Speak to the king and his mother. Tell them,
"Come down from your thrones.
Your glorious crowns
are about to fall from your heads."
19 The gates of the cities in the Negev Desert will be shut tight.
There won't be anyone to open them.
You will be carried away as prisoners.
You will be taken away completely.

20 Jerusalem, look up!
Your enemies are coming from the north.
Where is the flock you were supposed to take care of?
Where are the sheep you were so proud of?
21 You have worked hard to make special friends.
But the LORD will let them rule over you.
Then what will you say?
Suffering will take hold of you.
It will be like the pain of a woman having a baby.
22 Suppose you ask yourself,
"Why has this happened to me?"
It's because you have committed so many sins.
That's the reason your skirt has been torn off.
That's why your body has been treated so badly.
23 Can people from Ethiopia change their skin?
Can leopards change their spots?
It's the same with you.
You have always done what is evil.
So how can you do what is good?

24 The LORD says, "I will scatter you like straw
that the desert wind blows away.
25 That is what will happen to you.
I have appointed it for you,"
announces the LORD.
"You have forgotten me.
You have trusted in other gods.
26 So I will pull your skirt up over your face.
Then people will see the shame of your naked body.
27 They will see that you have not been faithful to me.
You have committed adultery with other gods.
And you have acted like a prostitute
who does not have any shame.
I have seen what you did
on the hills and in the fields.
And I hate it.
How terrible it will be for you, Jerusalem!
How long will you choose to be 'unclean'?"

War and Hunger

14 A message came to me from the LORD. He told me there wouldn't be any rain in the land. He said,

2 "Judah is filled with sadness.
Its cities are wasting away.
The people sob over the land.
Crying is heard in Jerusalem.
3 The nobles send their servants to get water.
They go to the wells.
But they do not find any water.
They return with empty jars.
They are terrified. They do not have any hope.
They cover their heads.
4 The ground is dry and cracked.
There isn't any rain in the land.
The farmers are terrified.
They cover their heads.

5 Even the does in the fields
desert their newborn fawns.
There isn't any grass to eat.
6 Wild donkeys stand on the bare hilltops.
They long for water as wild dogs do.
Their eyesight fails
because they do not have any grass to eat."

7 Our sins are a witness against us.
LORD, do something for the honor of
your name.
We have completely turned away from you.
We've sinned against you.
8 You are Israel's only hope.
You save us when we're in trouble.
Why are you like a stranger to us?
Why are you like a traveler who stays for
only one night?
9 Why are you like a man who is taken by
surprise?
Why are you like a soldier who can't save
anyone?
LORD, you are among us.
And we are your people.
Please don't desert us!

10 The LORD has given me a message about these
people. He says,

"They really love to wander away from me.
Their feet go down the wrong path.
I do not accept these people.
I will remember the evil things they have
done.
I will punish them for their sins."

11 The LORD continued, "Do not pray that things
will go well with them. 12 Even if they go without
food, I will not listen to their cry for help. They
might sacrifice burnt offerings and grain offerings.
But I will not accept them. Instead, I will destroy
them with war, hunger and plague."

13 But I said, "LORD and King, the prophets keep
telling them something else. They say, 'You won't
have to suffer from war or hunger. Instead, the
LORD will give you peace and rest in this place.'"

14 Then the LORD said to me, "The prophets are
prophesying lies in my name. I have not sent them
or appointed them. I have not even spoken to
them. Everything they tell you about their visions
or secret knowledge is a lie. They pretend to bring
you messages from other gods. They try to get you
to believe their own mistaken ideas.

15 "So here is what I am saying about the
prophets who are prophesying in my name. I did
not send them. But they are saying, 'No war or
hunger will come to this land.' Those same
prophets will die because of war and hunger. 16 And
the people they are prophesying to will be thrown
out into the streets of Jerusalem. They will die
because of hunger and war. No one will bury their
bodies. No one will bury their wives or children. I
will pour trouble out on them. That is exactly what
they should get.

17 "Jeremiah, give them this message. Tell them,

"'Let tears flow from my eyes.
Let them pour out night and day.
Never let them stop.
The people of my own nation
have suffered a terrible wound.
They have been crushed.
18 Suppose I go into the country.
Then I see people who have been killed with
swords.
Or suppose I go into the city.
Then I see people who have died of hunger.
Prophet and priest alike have gone to a land
they hadn't had anything to do with
before.'"

19 LORD, have you turned your back on Judah
completely?
Do you hate the city of Zion?
Why have you made us suffer?
We can't be healed.
We hoped peace would come.
But nothing good has happened to us.
We hoped we would finally be healed.
But all we got was terror.
20 LORD, we admit we've done evil things.
We also admit that our people of long ago
were guilty.
It's true that we've sinned against you.
21 For the honor of your name, don't turn your
back on us.
Don't bring shame on your glorious throne
in the temple.
Remember the covenant you made with us.
Please don't break it.
22 Do any of the worthless gods of the nations
bring rain?
Do the skies send down showers all by
themselves?
No. LORD our God, you send the rain.
So we put our hope in you.
You are the one who does all of those
things.

15 Then the LORD said to me, "Suppose Moses and Samuel were standing in front of
me. Even then my heart would not feel sorry for
these people. Send them away from me! Let
them go!

2 "Suppose they ask you, 'Where should
we go?'

"Then tell them, 'The LORD says,

"'"Those I have appointed to die will die.
Those I have appointed to be killed with
swords
will be killed with swords.
Those I have appointed to die of hunger
will die of hunger.
Those I have appointed to be taken away as
prisoners
will be taken away."'

3"I will send four kinds of destroyers against them," announces the LORD. "Swords will kill them. Dogs will drag them away. Birds of the air will eat them up. And wild animals will destroy them.

4"I will make all of the kingdoms on earth hate them. That will happen because of what Manasseh did in Jerusalem. He was king of Judah and the son of Hezekiah.

5"Jerusalem, who will have pity on you?
Who will sob over you?
Who will stop to ask how you are doing?
6You have said no to me," announces the LORD.
"You keep on turning away from me.
So I will destroy you with my own hands.
I can't show you my tender love anymore.
7I will stand at the city gates of the land.
I will separate the straw from the grain.
I will destroy my people. I will bring great sorrow on them.
They have not changed their ways.
8I will increase the number of their widows.
They will be more than the grains of sand on the seashore.
At noon I will bring a destroyer
against the mothers of the young men among my people.
All at once I will bring down on them
great suffering and terror.
9Mothers who have many children will grow weak.
They will take their last breath.
The sun will set on them while it is still day.
They will be dishonored and put to shame.
All those who are left alive I will kill with swords.
I will have their enemies do it,"
announces the LORD.

10My mother, I wish I had never been born!
The whole land opposes me.
They fight against me.
I haven't made loans to anyone.
And I haven't borrowed anything.
But everyone still calls down curses on me.

11The LORD said,

"Jeremiah, I will keep you safe for a good purpose.
I will make your enemies ask you to pray for them.
They will make their appeal to you
when they are in great trouble.
12"People of Judah, the armies of Babylonia will come from the north.
They are as strong as iron and bronze.
Can anyone break their power?
13I will give away your wealth and your treasures.
Your enemies will carry off everything.
And they will not pay anything for it.
That will happen because you have sinned so much.
You have done it all through your country.
14I will make you slaves to your enemies.
You will serve them in a land
you have not had anything to do with before.
My anger will start a fire
that will burn you up."

15LORD, you understand how much I'm suffering.
Show concern for me. Take care of me.
Pay back those who are trying to harm me.
You are patient. Don't take my life away from me.
Think about how much shame I suffer because of you.
16When I received your words, I ate them.
They filled me with joy.
My heart took delight in them.
LORD God who rules over all,
I belong to you.
17I never sat around with those who go to wild parties.
I never had a good time with them.
I sat alone because you had put your powerful hand on me.
Your anger against sin was burning inside me.
18Why does my pain never end?
Why is my wound so deep?
Why can't I ever get well?
To me you are like a stream that runs dry.
You are like a spring that doesn't have any water.

19So the LORD says,

"Turn away from your sins. Then I will heal you.
And then you will be able to serve me.
Speak words that are worthy, not worthless.
Then you will be speaking for me.
Let these people turn to you.
But you must not turn to them.
20I will make you like a wall to them.
I will make you like a strong bronze wall.
The people will fight against you.
But they will not overcome you.
I am with you.
I will save you,"
announces the LORD.
21"I will save you from the hands of evil people.
I will set you free from those who treat you badly."

Times of Trouble Are Coming

16 A message came to me from the LORD. He said, 2"You must not get married. You must not have any sons or daughters in this land."

3 Here is the LORD's message about the children
who are born in this place. He says about them and
their parents, 4 "Some of them will die of deadly
sicknesses. No one will sob over them. Their bodies will not be buried. Instead, they will be like
trash lying there on the ground. Others will die
because of war and hunger. Their bodies will not
be buried. Instead, they will become food for the
birds of the air and the wild animals."

5 The LORD says, "Jeremiah, do not enter a
house where a meal is being served because someone has died. Do not go there to sob or to comfort
the family. I will not bless these people anymore.
I have taken my love and pity away from them,"
announces the LORD.

6 "Important and ordinary people alike will die
in this land. Their bodies will not be buried. No
one will sob over them. No one will cut himself or
shave his head because of them. 7 No one will offer
food or drink to comfort those who sob over the
dead. No one will do it even if someone's father
or mother has died.

8 "Do not enter a house where a big dinner party
is being held. Do not sit down there to eat and
drink. 9 I am the LORD who rules over all. I am the
God of Israel. I am telling you, 'In your days I will
judge your people. You will see it with your own
eyes. I will put an end to the sounds of joy and
gladness here in Jerusalem. The voices of brides
and grooms will not be heard anymore.'

10 "Tell these people all of those things. They
will ask you, 'Why has the LORD decided to send
so much trouble on us? We haven't done anything
wrong. We haven't committed any sins against the
LORD our God.'

11 "When they say that, tell them, 'I did it
because your people of long ago deserted me,'
announces the LORD. 'They followed other gods.
They served them and worshiped them. They
deserted me. They did not obey my law.

12 " 'But you have done more evil things than
they did. All of you are doing what your stubborn
and evil hearts want you to do. You are not obeying me.

13 " 'So I will throw you out of this land. I will
send you away to a land that you and your people
have not had anything to do with before. There
you will serve other gods day and night. And I will
not show you any favor.'

14 "But a new day is coming," announces the
LORD. "At that time people will no longer say,
'The LORD brought the people of Israel up out of
Egypt. And that's just as sure as he is alive.'

15 "Instead, they will say, 'The LORD brought the
people of Israel up out of the land of the north. He
gathered them out of all of the countries where he
had forced them to go. And that's just as sure as he
is alive.' I will bring them back to the land I gave
their people long ago.

16 "But now I will send for many fishermen,"
announces the LORD. "They will catch some of
these people. After that, I will send for many
hunters. They will hunt the others down on every
mountain and hill. They will bring them out of the
cracks in the rocks. 17 My eyes see everything these
people do. What they do is not hidden from me. I
always see their sin. 18 I will pay them back double
for their sin and the evil things they have done.
They have made my land 'unclean.' They have set
up lifeless statues of their evil gods. They have
filled my land with them. I hate those gods."

19 LORD, you give me strength.
You are like a fort to me.
When I'm in trouble,
I go to you for safety.
The nations will come to you
from one end of the earth to the other.
They will gather together and say,
"Our people of long ago didn't own anything
except statues of gods.
The statues were worthless.
They didn't do them any good.
20 Do men really make their own gods?
Yes. But they aren't really gods at all!"

21 The LORD says, "So I will teach them about
myself.
This time I will show them
how powerful and mighty I am.
Then they will know
that I am the LORD.

17

"Judah's sin is carved with an iron tool.
It is written with a sharp stone.
It is carved on the tablets of their hearts.
It is written on the horns that stick out
from the corners of their altars.
2 Even their children offer sacrifices
to other gods on those altars.
They use the poles that were made
to worship the goddess Asherah.
They worship strange gods beside the
green trees
and on the high hills.
3 I will give away my holy Mount Zion to the
Babylonians.
Your enemies will carry off your wealth
and all of your treasures.
I will give away your high places.
That will happen because you have sinned.
You have done it all through your country.
4 You will lose the land I gave you.
And it will be your own fault.
I will make you slaves to your enemies.
You will serve them in a land you have not
had anything to do with before.
You have set my anger on fire.
It will burn forever."

5 The LORD says,

"Those who trust in man are under my curse.
They depend on human strength.
Their hearts turn away from me.

Jesus and the Children

Jesus said, "Let the little children come to me. Don't keep them away. The kingdom of heaven belongs to people like them."
—Matthew 19:14

©2005 Mission City Press

Jesus Enters Jerusalem

Some of the people went ahead of him, and some followed.
They all shouted, "Hosanna to the Son of David!"
—Matthew 21:9

6 They will be like a bush in a dry and empty land.
They will not enjoy success when it comes.
They will live in dry places in the desert.
It is a land of salt where no one else lives.

7 "But I will bless any man who trusts in me.
I will show my favor to the one who depends on me.
8 He will be like a tree that is planted near water.
It sends out its roots beside a stream.
It is not afraid when heat comes.
Its leaves are always green.
It does not worry when there is no rain.
It always bears fruit."

9 A human heart is more dishonest than anything else.
It can't be healed.
Who can understand it?

10 The LORD says, "I look deep down inside human hearts.
I see what is in people's minds.
I reward a man in keeping with his conduct.
I bless him based on what he has done."

11 Some people get rich in the wrong way.
They are like a partridge that hatches eggs it didn't lay.
When their lives are half over, their riches will desert them.
In the end they will prove how foolish they have been.

12 Our temple is where the LORD's glorious throne is.
From the beginning it has been high and lifted up.
13 LORD, you are Israel's only hope.
Everyone who deserts you will be put to shame.
The names of those who turn away from you will be listed among the dead.
LORD, they have deserted you.
You are the spring of water that gives life.

14 LORD, heal me. Then I will be healed.
Save me from my enemies. Then I will be saved.
You are the one I praise.
15 They keep saying to me,
"What has happened to the message the LORD gave you?
Let it come true right now!"
16 I haven't run away from being the shepherd of your people.
You know I haven't wanted the day of Jerusalem's fall to come.
You are aware of every word that comes from my lips.
17 Don't be a terror to me.
When I'm in trouble, I go to you for safety.
18 Let those who attack me be put to shame.
But keep me from shame.
Let them be terrified.
But keep me from terror.
Bring the day of trouble on them.
Destroy them once and for all.

Keep the Sabbath Day Holy

19 The LORD said to me, "Go. Stand at the city
gate where the people gather together. That is
where the kings of Judah go in and out. Also go to
all of the other gates of Jerusalem. 20 Say, 'Listen
to the LORD's message, you kings of Judah and all
of you people of Judah and Jerusalem. You always
come through these gates.

21 "'The LORD says, "Make sure you do not
carry a load on the Sabbath day. Do not bring it
through the gates of Jerusalem. 22 Do not bring a
load out of your houses on the Sabbath. Do not do
any work on that day. Instead, keep the Sabbath
day holy. Do as I commanded your people long
ago. 23 But they did not listen. They did not pay any
attention to me. They were stubborn. They would
not listen or pay attention when I corrected them.

24 "'"Be careful to obey me," announces the
LORD. "Do not bring a load through the gates of
this city on the Sabbath. Instead, keep the Sabbath
day holy. Do not do any work on it.

25 "'"Then kings who sit on David's throne will
come through the gates of this city. They and their
officials will come riding in chariots and on
horses. The people of Judah and Jerusalem will
come along with them. And this city will always
have people living in it. 26 Some will come from the
towns of Judah. And some will come in from the
villages around Jerusalem. Others will come from
the territory of Benjamin. And others will come in
from the western hills. Still others will come from
the central hill country and the Negev Desert. All
of them will bring burnt offerings and sacrifices.
They will come bringing grain offerings, incense
and thank offerings. They will take all of those
offerings to my house.

27 "'"But what if you do not obey me? Suppose
you do not keep the Sabbath day holy. And suppose you carry a load through the gates of Jerusalem on the Sabbath. Then I will start a fire that
can't be put out. It will begin at the gates of Jerusalem. It will destroy its mighty towers."'"

The LORD Sends Jeremiah to the Potter's House

18 A message came to me from the LORD. He
said, 2 "Go down to the potter's house. I
will give you my message there."

3 So I went down to the potter's house. I saw
him working at his wheel. 4 His hands were shaping a pot out of clay. But he saw that something
was wrong with it. So he formed it into another
pot. He shaped it in the way that seemed best to
him.

5Then the LORD's message came to me. He said,
6"People of Israel, I can do with you just as this
potter does," announces the LORD. "The clay is in
the potter's hand. And you are in my hand, people
of Israel.

7"Suppose at any time I announce that a nation
or kingdom is going to be pulled up by the roots.
And I tell it that it will be torn down and destroyed.
8But suppose the nation I warned turns away from
its sins. Then I will not do what I said I would. I
will not bring trouble on it as I had planned.

9"Suppose at another time I announce that a
nation or kingdom is going to be built up and
planted. 10But it does what is evil in my sight. It
does not obey me. Then I will think again about
the good things I had wanted to do for it.

11"So speak to the people of Judah and Jerusalem. Tell them, 'The LORD says, "Look! I am making plans against you. I am going to bring trouble
on you. So each one of you must turn from your
evil ways. Change the way you live and act."'

12"But they will reply, 'It's no use. We will continue to do what we've already planned. All of us
will do what our stubborn and evil hearts want us
to do.'"

13So the LORD says,

"Ask the nations a question. Say to them,
'Who has ever heard anything like this?
The people of Israel have done
a very horrible thing.
14 Does the snow ever disappear
from Lebanon's rocky slopes?
Do its cool waters ever stop
flowing from places far away?
15 But my people have forgotten me.
They burn incense to worthless gods.
Their gods made them trip and fall
as they walked on the old paths.
They made them use side roads
instead of roads that were built up.
16 So their land will be completely destroyed.
People will make fun of it again and again.
All those who pass by it will be shocked.
They will shake their heads.
17 I will sweep over my people like a wind from
the east.
I will use the Babylonians to scatter them.
I will show them my back and not my face.
I will desert them when their day of trouble
comes.'"

18They said, "Come on. Let's make plans
against Jeremiah. We'll still have priests to teach
us the law. We'll always have wise people to give
us advice. We'll have prophets to bring us messages from the LORD. So come on. Let's speak out
against Jeremiah. We shouldn't pay any attention
to what he says."

19 LORD, please listen to me!
Hear what my enemies are saying about me!
20 Should the good things I've done be paid back
with evil?
But my enemies have dug a pit for me.
Remember that I stood in front of you
and spoke up for them.
I tried to turn your anger away from them.
21 So let their children die of hunger.
Let my enemies be killed in war.
Let their wives lose their children and
husbands.
Let their men be put to death.
Let their young men be killed in battle.
22 Bring their enemies against them without
warning.
Let cries be heard from their houses.
They have dug a pit to capture me.
They have hidden traps for my feet.
23 But LORD, you know
all about their plans to kill me.
Don't forgive their crimes.
Don't erase their sins from your sight.
Destroy my enemies.
Punish them when the time to show your
anger comes.

19 The LORD said to me, "Go and buy a clay
jar from a potter. Take along some of the
elders of the people. Also tell some of the priests
to go with you. 2Go out to the Valley of Ben Hinnom. Stand near the entrance of the gate where
broken pieces of pottery are thrown away.

"There announce the message I give you. 3Tell
the people, 'Listen to the LORD's message, you
kings of Judah and people of Jerusalem. The LORD
who rules over all is the God of Israel. He says,
"Listen! I am going to bring trouble on Jerusalem.
It will be so horrible that it will make the ears of
everyone who hears about it ring.

4"'"My people have deserted me. They have
made this city a place where other gods are worshiped. They have burned sacrifices to them here.
They and their people and the kings of Judah had
never had anything to do with those gods before.
My people have also filled this place with the
blood of those who are not guilty of anything.
5They have built the high places where they worship Baal. There they sacrifice their children in the
fire as offerings to Baal. That is something I did
not command or talk about. It did not even enter
my mind.

6"'"So watch out!" announces the LORD. "The
days are coming when people will not call this
place Topheth anymore. And they will not call it
the Valley of Ben Hinnom either. Instead, they will
call it the Valley of Death.

7"'"In this place I will make the plans of Judah
and Jerusalem as useless as a broken jar. I will use
their enemies to kill my people with swords. They
will die at the hands of those who want to take
their lives. I will give their dead bodies as food to
the birds of the air and the wild animals.

8“‘“I will destroy this city completely. People
will make fun of it. All those who pass by it will be
shocked. They will laugh at its people because of
all of their wounds. 9 I will make the people of this
city eat the dead bodies of their sons and daughters. And they will eat one another. They will do it
because things will be so bad during the attack.
The enemies who want to take their lives will
bring all of that trouble on them.”’

10“Jeremiah, break the jar while those who go
with you are watching. 11 Tell them, ‘The LORD
who rules over all says, “This potter’s jar is
smashed and can’t be repaired. And I will smash
this nation and this city. People will bury their
dead in Topheth. But they will run out of room.
12 Here is what I will do to Jerusalem and those
who live here,” announces the LORD. “I will make
this city like Topheth. 13 The houses in Jerusalem
will be made ‘unclean’ like Topheth. So will the
houses of the kings of Judah. All of those people
burned incense on their roofs to all of the stars.
They poured out drink offerings to other gods.”’”

14 Then I returned from Topheth. That’s where
the LORD had sent me to prophesy. I stood in the
courtyard of the LORD’s temple. I spoke to all of the
people. I said, 15“The LORD who rules over all is the
God of Israel. He says, ‘Listen! I am going to punish this city and the villages that are around it. I am
going to bring against them all of the trouble I have
announced. That is because my people were stubborn. They would not listen to what I said.’”

Jeremiah and Pashhur

20 The priest Pashhur was chief officer in the
LORD’s temple. He was the son of Immer.
Pashhur heard me prophesying that Jerusalem
would be destroyed. 2 So he had me beaten. Then
he put me in prison at the Upper Gate of Benjamin
at the LORD’s temple.

3 The next day Pashhur set me free. I said to him,
“The LORD’s name for you isn’t Pashhur. It’s Ma-
gor-Missabib. That name means Terror on Every
Side.

4“The LORD says to you, ‘I will make you a terror to yourself. You will also be a terror to all of
your friends. With your own eyes you will see
them die. Their enemies will kill them with
swords. I will hand all of the people of Judah over
to the king of Babylonia. He will carry them away
to Babylonia or kill them with swords.

5“‘I will hand all of the wealth of this city over
to Judah’s enemies. I will give them all of its products and everything of value. I will turn over to
them all of the treasures that belonged to the kings
of Judah. They will take those things and carry
them off to Babylon.

6“‘Pashhur, you and everyone who lives in your
house will also be forced to go there. You have
prophesied lies to all of your friends. So all of you
will die in Babylonia. And that’s where your bodies will be buried.’”

Jeremiah Argues With the LORD

7 LORD, you tricked me, and I was tricked.
You overpowered me and won.
People make fun of me all day long.
Everyone laughs at me.

8 Every time I speak, I cry out.
All you ever tell me to talk about
is fighting and trouble.
Your message has brought me nothing but
dishonor.
It has made me suffer shame all day long.
9 Sometimes I think, “I won’t talk about him
anymore.
I’ll never speak in his name again.”
But then your message burns in my heart.
It’s like a fire inside my very bones.
I’m tired of holding it in.
In fact, I can’t.
10 I hear many people whispering,
“There is terror on every side!
Report Jeremiah! Let’s report him to the
authorities!”
All of my friends
are waiting for me to slip.
They are saying, “Perhaps he will be tricked
into making a mistake.
Then we’ll win out over him.
We’ll get even with him.”

11 But you are with me like a mighty warrior.
So those who are trying to harm me will trip
and fall.
They won’t win out over me.
They will fail. They’ll be totally put
to shame.
Their dishonor will never be forgotten.

12 LORD, you rule over all.
You test those who do what is right.
You see what is in people’s hearts
and minds.
So pay them back for what they’ve done.
I’ve committed my cause to you.

13 Sing to the LORD, you people!
Give praise to him!
He saves the lives of those who are in need.
He saves them from the powerful hands
of sinful people.

14 May the day I was born be under a curse!
May the day I was born to my mother not
be blessed!
15 May the man who brought my father the news
be under a curse!
He’s the one who made my father very glad.
He said, “You have had a baby!
It’s a boy!”
16 May that man be like the towns
the LORD destroyed without pity.
May that man hear loud sobs in the morning.
May he hear a battle cry at noon.

[17]He should have killed me in my mother's body.
He should have made my mother my grave.
He should have let her body stay large
forever.
[18]Why did I ever come out of my mother's body?
I've seen nothing but trouble and sorrow.
My days will end in shame.

The LORD Refuses Zedekiah's Appeal

21 A message came to me from the LORD. It
came when King Zedekiah sent Pashhur to
me. Pashhur was the son of Malkijah. Zedekiah
sent the priest Zephaniah along with him. Zephaniah was the son of Maaseiah. They said to me,
[2]"Ask the LORD to help us. Nebuchadnezzar is
attacking us. He is king of Babylonia. In the past
the LORD did wonderful things for us. Maybe he'll
do them again. Then Nebuchadnezzar will pull his
armies back from us."

[3]But I answered them, "Tell Zedekiah and his
people, [4]'The LORD is the God of Israel. He says,
"The king of Babylonia and his armies are all
around this city. They are getting ready to attack
you. You have weapons of war in your hands to
fight against them. But I am about to turn your
weapons against you. And I will bring your enemies inside this city.

[5]" ' "I myself will fight against you. I will reach
out my powerful hand and mighty arm. I will come
against you with all of my burning anger. [6]I will
strike down those who live in this city. I will kill
people and animals alike. They will die of a terrible plague.

[7]" ' "After that, I will hand you over to your enemies who want to kill you," announces the LORD.
"I will hand over Zedekiah, the king of Judah. I
will hand over his officials and the people in this
city who live through the plague, war and hunger.
All of them will be turned over to Nebuchadnezzar, the king of Babylonia. He will kill them with
swords. He will not show them any kindness. He
will not feel sorry for them. In fact, he will not
have any concern for them at all." '

[8]"Tell the people, 'The LORD says, "I am offering you a choice. You can choose the way that leads
to life. Or you can choose the way that leads to
death. [9]Those who stay in this city will die of war,
hunger or plague. But those who go out and give
themselves up to the Babylonians who are attacking you will live. They will escape with their lives.

[10]" ' "I have decided to do this city harm and not
good," announces the LORD. "It will be handed
over to the king of Babylonia. And he will destroy
it with fire." '

[11]"Also speak to Judah's royal family. Tell
them, 'Listen to the LORD's message. [12]The LORD
says to you who belong to David's royal house,

" ' "Every morning do what is right and fair.
Save those who have been robbed.
Set them free from the people who have
treated them badly.
If you do not, my anger will blaze out
against you.
It will burn like fire because of the evil
things you have done.
No one will be able to put it out.
[13]Jerusalem, I am against you,"
announces the LORD.
"You live above this valley.
You are on a high, rocky flatland.
And you say, 'Who can come against us?
Who can enter our place of safety?'
[14]But I will punish you in keeping with what
you have done,"
announces the LORD.
"I will start a fire in your forests.
It will burn up everything around you." ' "

The LORD Judges Evil Kings

22 The LORD said to me, "Jeremiah, go down
to the palace of the king of Judah. Announce my message there. Tell him, [2]'King of Judah, listen to the LORD's message. You are sitting
on David's throne. You and your officials and
your people come through these gates. [3]The LORD
says, "Do what is fair and right. Save those who
have been robbed. Set them free from the people
who have treated them badly. Do not do anything
wrong to outsiders or widows in this place. Do not
harm children whose fathers have died. Do not
kill those who are not guilty of doing anything
wrong.

[4]" ' "Be careful to obey those commands. Then
kings who sit on David's throne will come through
the gates of this palace. They will come riding in
chariots and on horses. Their officials and their
people will come along with them.

[5]" ' "But suppose you do not obey those commands," announces the LORD. "Then I promise
you that this palace will be destroyed. I make that
promise by taking an oath in my own name." ' "

[6]The LORD speaks about the palace of the king
of Judah. He says,

"You are like the land of Gilead to me.
You are like the highest mountain
in Lebanon.
But I will make you like a desert.
You will become like towns that no one
lives in.
[7]I will send destroyers against you.
All of them will come with their weapons.
They will cut up your fine cedar beams.
They will throw them into the fire.

[8]"People from many nations will pass by this
city. They will ask one another, 'Why has the
LORD done such a thing to this great city?'

[9]"And the answer will be, 'Because its people
have turned away from the covenant the LORD
their God made with them. They have worshiped
other gods. And they have served them.' "

10 Don't sob over dead King Josiah.
Don't be sad because he's gone.
Instead, sob bitterly over King Jehoahaz.
He was forced to leave his country.
He will never return.
He'll never see his own land again.

11 Jehoahaz became king of Judah after his father
Josiah. But he has gone away from this place.
That's because the LORD says about him, "He will
never return. 12 He will die in Egypt. That is where
he was taken as a prisoner. He will not see this land
again."

13 The LORD says, "How terrible it will be for
King Jehoiakim!
He builds his palace
by mistreating his people.
He builds its upstairs rooms
with money that was gained by sinning.
He makes his own people work for nothing.
He does not pay them for what they do.
14 He says, 'I will build myself a great palace.
It will have large rooms upstairs.'
So he makes big windows in it.
He covers its walls with cedar boards.
He decorates it with red paint.

15 "Jehoiakim, does having more and more cedar
boards
make you a king?
Your father Josiah had enough to eat and drink.
He did what was right and fair.
So everything went well with him.
16 He stood up for those who were poor or needy.
So everything went well with him.
That is what it means to know me,"
announces the LORD.
17 "Jehoiakim, the only thing on your mind
is to get rich by cheating others.
You would even kill people who are not guilty
of doing anything wrong.
You would mistreat them.
You would take everything they own."

18 So the LORD speaks about King Jehoiakim, the
son of Josiah. He says,
"His people will not sob over him.
They will not say,
'My poor brother! My poor sister!'
They will not sob over him.
They will not say,
'My poor master! How sad that his glory
is gone!'
19 In fact, he will be buried like a donkey.
His body will be dragged away and thrown
outside the gates of Jerusalem."

20 The LORD says, "People of Jerusalem, go up to
Lebanon.
Cry out for help.
Let your voice be heard in the land of
Bashan.
Cry out from the mountains of Abarim.
All those who were going to help you are
crushed.
21 When you felt secure, I warned you.
But you said, 'I won't listen!'
You have acted like that ever since you
were young.
You have not obeyed me.
22 The wind will drive all of your shepherds
away.
All those who were going to help you will
be carried off as prisoners.
Then you will be dishonored and put to shame.
That will happen because you have been
so sinful.
23 Some of you live in Jerusalem in the Palace of
the Forest of Lebanon.
You are comfortable in your cedar
buildings.
But you will groan when pain comes on you.
It will be like the pain of a woman having
a baby.

24 "King Jehoiachin, you are the son of Jehoiakim," announces the LORD. "Suppose you were a
ring on my right hand. And suppose the ring even
had my royal seal on it. Then I would still pull you
off my finger. And that is just as sure as I am alive.
25 "I will hand you over to those who are trying
to kill you. I will turn you over to people you are
afraid of. I will give you to Nebuchadnezzar, the
king of Babylonia. I will hand you over to his
armies.
26 "I will throw you out into another country. I
will throw your mother out. Neither of you was
born in that country. But both of you will die there.
27 You will never come back to the land you long
to return to."

28 This man Jehoiachin is like a broken pot.
Everyone hates him. No one wants him.
Why will he and his children be thrown out of
this land?
Why will they be sent to a land
they didn't have anything to do with before?
29 Land, land, land,
listen to the LORD's message!
30 The LORD says,
"Let the record say that this man did not have
any children.
Let it report that he did not have any success
in life.
None of his children will have success either.
None of them will sit on David's throne.
None of them will ever rule over Judah.

The True and Rightful Branch

23 "How terrible it will be for the shepherds
who lead my people down the wrong
path!" announces the LORD. "They are destroying
and scattering the sheep that belong to my flock."

[2]So the LORD, the God of Israel, speaks to the
shepherds who take care of my people. He tells
them, "You have scattered my sheep. You have
driven them away. You have not taken good care
of them. So I will punish you for the evil things
you have done," announces the LORD.
[3]"I myself will gather together those who are left
alive in my flock. I will gather them out of all of the
countries where I have driven them. And I will bring
them back to their own land. There my sheep will
have many lambs. Their numbers will increase.
[4]"I will place shepherds over them who will
take good care of them. My sheep will not be
afraid or terrified anymore. And none of them will
be missing," announces the LORD.

[5]"A new day is coming," announces the LORD.
"At that time I will raise up from David's
royal line
a true and rightful Branch.
He will be a King who will rule wisely.
He will do what is fair and right in the land.
[6]In his days Judah will be saved.
Israel will live in safety.
And the Branch will be called
The LORD Who Makes Us Right With
Himself.

[7]"Other days are also coming," announces the
LORD. "At that time people will no longer say,
'The LORD brought the people of Israel up out of
Egypt. And that's just as sure as he is alive.'
[8]"Instead, they will say, 'The LORD brought the
people of Israel up out of the land of the north. He
gathered them out of all of the countries where he
had forced them to go. And that's just as sure as he
is alive.' Then they will live in their own land."

Prophets Who Tell Lies

[9]Here is my message about the prophets.

My heart is broken inside me.
All of my bones tremble with fear.
I am like a man who is drunk.
I am like someone who has had too
much wine.
That's what the LORD's holy words
have done to me.
[10]The land is full of people
who aren't faithful to the LORD.
Now the land is under his curse.
And that's why it is thirsty for water.
That's why the grasslands in the desert
are dry.
The prophets are leading sinful lives.
They don't use their power in the right way.

[11]"Prophets and priests alike are ungodly,"
announces the LORD.
"Even in my temple I find them sinning.
[12]So their path will become slippery.
They will be thrown out into darkness.
There they will fall.
I will bring trouble on them
when the time to punish them comes,"
announces the LORD.

[13]"Among the prophets of Samaria
I saw something I can't stand.
They were prophesying in the name of Baal.
They were leading my people Israel down
the wrong path.
[14]I have also seen something horrible among Jerusalem's prophets.
They are not faithful to me.
They are not living by the truth.
They strengthen the hands of those who
do evil.
So the people do not turn from their sinful
ways.
All of them are like the people of Sodom
to me.
They are just like the people of Gomorrah."

[15]So the LORD who rules over all speaks about
the prophets. He says,

"I will make them eat bitter food.
I will make them drink poisoned water.
The prophets of Jerusalem have spread
their ungodly ways all through the land."

[16]The LORD who rules over all says to the people of Judah,

"Do not listen to what the prophets are saying
to you.
They fill you with false hopes.
They talk about visions that come from their
own minds.
What they say does not come from my
mouth.
[17]They keep speaking to those who hate me.
They say,
'The LORD says you will have peace.'
They speak to all those who do
what their stubborn hearts want them to do.
They tell them, 'No harm will come to you.'
[18]But which of them has ever stood in my
courts?
Have they been there to see a vision or hear
my message?
Who has listened and heard my message
there?
[19]A storm will burst out
because of my burning anger.
A windstorm will sweep down
on the heads of sinful people.
[20]My anger will not turn back.
I will accomplish everything
I plan to do.
In days to come
you will understand it clearly.
[21]I did not send those prophets.
But they have run to tell you their message
anyway.

I did not speak to them.
But they have still prophesied.
22 Suppose they had stood in my courts.
Then they would have announced my
message to my people.
They would have turned my people from their
evil ways.
They would have turned them away from
their sins.
23 “Am I only a God who is nearby?”
announces the LORD.
“Am I not a God who is also far away?
24 Can anyone hide in secret places
so that I can’t see him?”
announces the LORD.
“Don’t I fill heaven and earth?”
announces the LORD.

25“I have heard what the prophets are saying.
They prophesy lies in my name. They say, ‘I had
a dream! The LORD has given me a dream!’ 26How
long will that continue in the hearts of those
prophets who tell lies? They try to get others to
believe their own mistaken ideas. 27They tell one
another their dreams. They think that will make
my people forget my name. In the same way, their
people of long ago forgot my name when they
worshiped Baal.

28“Let the prophet who has a dream tell his
dream. But let the one who has my message speak
it faithfully. Your prophets have given you straw
to eat instead of grain,” announces the LORD.

29“My message is like fire,” announces the
LORD. “It is like a hammer that breaks a rock in
pieces.

30“So I am against those prophets,” announces
the LORD. “I am against those who steal messages
from one another. They claim that the messages
come from me.

31“Yes,” announces the LORD. “I am against the
prophets who wag their own tongues but still say,
‘Here is what the LORD says.’ 32I am against
prophets who talk about dreams that did not come
from me,” announces the LORD. “They tell foolish
lies. Their lies lead my people down the wrong
path.

“But I did not send those prophets. I did not
appoint them. They do not help my people in the
least,” announces the LORD.

Prophets Who Give Messages That Are Not From the LORD

33“Jeremiah, those people might ask you a question. Or a prophet or priest might do it. They might
ask, ‘What message have you received from the
LORD?’

“Then tell them, ‘You ask, “What message?”
Here it is. “I will desert you,” announces the
LORD.’

34“A prophet or priest might make a claim. Or
someone else might do it. He might claim, ‘I have
received a message from the LORD.’ Then I will
punish him and his family.

35“Here is what each of you people keeps on
saying to your friend or relative. You ask, ‘What
is the LORD’s answer?’ Or you ask, ‘What has the
LORD spoken?’ 36But you must not talk about ‘a
message from the LORD’ again. That is because
your message becomes your own message. And so
you twist my words. I am the living God. I am the
LORD who rules over all. And I am your God.

37“Here is what you keep saying to a prophet.
You ask, ‘What is the LORD’s answer to you?’ Or
you ask, ‘What has the LORD spoken?’ 38You
claim, ‘I have received a message from the LORD.’
But I really say, ‘You used the words, “I have
received a message from the LORD.” But I told you
that you must not claim, “I have received a message from the LORD.”’

39“So you can be sure I will forget you. I will
throw you out of my sight. I will also destroy the
city I gave you and your people. 40I will bring
shame on you that will last forever. It will never
be forgotten.”

Judah Is Like Two Baskets of Figs

24 King Jehoiachin was forced to leave Jerusalem. He was the son of Jehoiakim. Jehoiachin was taken to Babylon by Nebuchadnezzar,
the king of Babylonia. The officials and all of the
skilled workers were forced to leave with him.

After they left, the LORD showed me two baskets of figs. They were in front of his temple. 2One
basket had very good figs in it. They were like figs
that ripen early. The other basket had figs that
weren’t good at all. In fact, they were so bad they
couldn’t even be eaten.

3Then the LORD asked me, “What do you see,
Jeremiah?”

“Figs,” I answered. “The good ones are very
good. But the others are so bad they can’t be eaten.”

4Then a message came to me from the LORD. He
said, 5“I am the LORD, the God of Israel. I say, ‘I
consider the people who were forced to leave Judah to be like those good figs. I sent them away
from this place. I forced them to go to Babylonia.
6My eyes will watch over them. I will be good to
them. And I will bring them back to this land. I will
build them up. I will not tear them down. I will
plant them. I will not pull them up by the roots.

7“ ‘I will change their hearts. Then they will
know that I am the LORD. They will be my people.
And I will be their God. They will return to me
with all their heart.

8“ ‘But there are also figs that are not very good.
In fact, they are so bad they can’t be eaten,’ says
the LORD. ‘Zedekiah, the king of Judah, is like
those bad figs. So are his officials and the people of
Jerusalem who are still left alive. I will punish them
whether they remain in this land or live in Egypt.

9“ ‘I will make all of the kingdoms on earth displeased with them. In fact, they will hate them a

great deal. They will laugh and joke about them.
They will call down curses on them. All of that
will happen no matter where I force them to go. 10I
will send war, hunger and plague against them.
They will be destroyed from the land I gave them
and their people of long ago.'"

Seventy Years in Babylonia

25 A message about all of the people of Judah
came to me from the LORD. It came in the
fourth year that Jehoiakim was king of Judah. It
was the first year that Nebuchadnezzar was king
of Babylonia. Jehoiakim was the son of Josiah.
2I, the LORD's prophet, spoke to all of the people of Judah and Jerusalem. I said, 3"For 23 years
the LORD's messages have been coming to me.
They began to come in the 13th year that Josiah
was king of Judah. He was the son of Amon. The
LORD's messages still come to me today. I've spoken to you people again and again. But you
haven't listened to me.
4"The LORD has sent all of his servants the
prophets to you. They've come to you again and
again. But you haven't listened. You haven't paid
any attention to them.
5"They said, 'Each of you must turn from your
evil ways and practices. Then you can stay in the
land forever. It's the land the LORD gave you and
your people long ago. 6Don't follow other gods.
Don't serve them or worship them. Don't make the
LORD angry with the gods your own hands have
made. Then he won't harm you.'
7"'But you did not listen to me,' announces the
LORD. 'You have made me very angry with the
gods your hands have made. And you have
brought harm on yourselves.'
8"The LORD who rules over all says, 'You have
not listened to my words. 9So I will send for all of
the nations in the north. And I will send for my servant Nebuchadnezzar, the king of Babylonia,'
announces the LORD.
"'I will bring all of them against this land and
against you who live here. They will march out
against all of the nations that are around this land.
I will set them apart in a special way to be
destroyed. People will be shocked because of
them. And they will make fun of them. Those
nations will be destroyed forever.
10"'I will put an end to the sounds of joy and
gladness. I will put an end to the voices of brides
and grooms. The sound of grinding millstones will
not be heard anymore. And lamps will not be lit
anymore. 11This whole country will become dry
and empty. And those nations will serve the king
of Babylonia for 70 years.
12"'But I will punish that king and his nation
because they are guilty. I will do it when the 70
years are over,' announces the LORD. 'I will make
that land a desert forever.
13"'I have spoken against that land. And I will
make all of those things happen to it. Everything
will happen that is written in this scroll. And I will
make everything Jeremiah prophesied against all
of the nations come true. 14The people of Babylonia will become slaves of many other nations and
great kings. I will pay them back for what their
hands have done.'"

The LORD Judges the Nations

15The LORD is the God of Israel. He said to me,
"Take this cup from my hand. It is filled with the
wine of my burning anger. Make all of the nations
to which I send you drink it. 16When they drink it,
they will not even be able to walk straight. It will
drive them out of their minds. I am going to send
war against them."
17So I took the cup from the LORD's hand. I
made all of the nations to which he sent me drink
from it. 18He sent me to Judah's kings and officials.
He told me to go to Jerusalem and the towns of Judah. He wanted me to tell them they would be
destroyed. Then people would be shocked because
of them. They would make fun of them. They
would call down curses on them. And that's how
things still are today.
19Here is a list of the other kings and nations he
sent me to.

Pharaoh, the king of Egypt
his attendants, his officials, all of his people
20 all of the people from other lands who lived there
all of the kings of Uz
the Philistine kings of Ashkelon, Gaza and Ekron
the Philistines who were still living in Ashdod
21 Edom, Moab, Ammon
22 all of the kings of Tyre and Sidon
the kings of the islands and other lands along the Mediterranean Sea
23 Dedan, Teman, Buz
all of the other places far away in the east
24 all of the kings of Arabia
all of the other kings of people who live in the desert
25 all of the kings of Zimri, Elam and Media
26 all of the kings in the north, near and far

So he sent me to all of the kingdoms on the face
of the earth, one after the other. After all of them
drink from the cup of the LORD's anger, the king
of Babylonia will drink from it too.
27The LORD says, "Tell them, 'The LORD who
rules over all is the God of Israel. He says, "Drink
from this cup. Get drunk and throw up. Fall down
and do not get up again. I am going to send war
against you."'
28"But they might refuse to take the cup from
your hand. They might not want to drink from it.
Then tell them, 'The LORD who rules over all says,
"You have to drink from it! 29I am beginning to
bring trouble on the city where I have put my

Name. You might think you will not be punished.
But you will certainly be punished. I am sending
war against everyone who lives on earth,”
announces the LORD who rules over all.’
30“Jeremiah, prophesy against them. Tell them,

“‘The LORD will roar from heaven like a lion.
His voice will sound like thunder
from his holy temple there.
He will roar loudly against his land.
He will shout like those who stomp on
grapes in winepresses.
He will shout against everyone who lives on
earth.
31 The noise of battle will be heard
from one end of the earth to the other.
That’s because the LORD will bring charges
against the nations.
He will judge every human being.
He will kill sinful people with his sword,’”
announces the LORD.

32The LORD who rules over all says,

“Look! Horrible trouble is spreading
from one nation to another.
A mighty storm is rising.
It is coming from a place
that is very far away.”
33At that time those the LORD kills will be lying
around everywhere. They will be found from one
end of the earth to the other. No one will sob over
them. Their dead bodies will not be gathered up or
buried. Instead, they will be like trash lying there
on the ground.

34 Sob and cry, you shepherds.
Roll in the dust, you leaders of the flock.
Your time to be killed has come.
You will fall and be broken to pieces like
fine clay pots.
35 The shepherds won’t have any place to run to.
The leaders of the flock won’t be able to
escape.
36 Listen to the cries of the shepherds.
Hear the sobs of the leaders of the flock.
The LORD is destroying their grasslands.
37 Their peaceful meadows will be completely
destroyed
because of the LORD’s burning anger.
38 Like a lion he will leave his den.
The land of those leaders will become
a desert.
That’s because the sword of the LORD brings
great harm.
His anger will burn against them.

Jeremiah’s Enemies Try to Have Him Killed

26 A message came to me from the LORD. It
was shortly after Jehoiakim became king
of Judah. He was the son of Josiah. 2The LORD
said, “Stand in the courtyard of my house. Speak
to the people of the towns in Judah. Speak to all
those who come to worship in my house. Tell them
everything I command you. Do not leave out a single word. 3Perhaps they will listen. Maybe they
will turn from their evil ways. Then I will not do
what I said I would. I will not bring trouble on
them. I had planned to punish them because of the
evil things they had done.
4“Tell them, ‘The LORD says, “Listen to me.
Obey my law that I gave you. 5And listen to the
words my servants the prophets are speaking. I
have sent them to you again and again. But you
have not listened to them. 6So I will make this
house like Shiloh. All of the nations on earth will
call down curses on this city.”’”
7I spoke those words in the LORD’s house. The
priests, the prophets and all of the people heard
me. 8I finished telling all of the people everything
the LORD had commanded me to say.

But as soon as I did, the priests, the prophets and
all of the people grabbed hold of me. They said,
“You must die! 9Why do you prophesy those things
in the LORD’s name? Why do you say that this house
will become like Shiloh? Why do you say that this
city will be empty and deserted?” And all of the
people crowded around me in the LORD’s house.
10The officials of Judah heard what had happened. So they went up from the royal palace to
the LORD’s house. There they took their places at
the entrance of the New Gate. 11Then the priests
and prophets spoke to the officials and all of the
people. They said, “This man should be sentenced
to death. He has prophesied against this city. You
have heard it with your own ears!”
12Then I spoke to all of the officials and people.
I said, “The LORD sent me to prophesy against this
house and this city. He told me to say everything
you have heard. 13So change the way you live and
act. Obey the LORD your God. Then he won’t do
what he said he would. He won’t bring on you the
trouble he said he would bring.
14“As for me, I’m in your hands. Do to me what
you think is good and right. 15But you can be sure
of one thing. If you put me to death, you will be
held accountable for spilling my blood. And I
haven’t even done anything wrong. You will bring
guilt on yourselves and this city and those who live
in it. The LORD has sent me to you. He wanted me
to say all of those things so you could hear them.
And that’s the truth.”
16Then the officials and all of the people spoke
to the priests and prophets. They said, “This man
shouldn’t be sentenced to death! He has spoken to
us in the name of the LORD our God.”
17Some of the elders of the land stepped forward. They spoke to the whole community that
was gathered there. They said, 18“Micah from Moresheth prophesied. It was during the time Hezekiah was king over Judah. Micah spoke to all of the
people of Judah. He told them, ‘The LORD who
rules over all says,

"'"Zion will be plowed up like a field.
Jerusalem will be turned into a pile of trash.
The temple hill will be covered with bushes
and weeds."' *(Micah 3:12)*

19"Did King Hezekiah or anyone else in Judah put
Micah to death? Hezekiah had respect for the
LORD. He asked the LORD to show him his favor.
And the LORD didn't judge Jerusalem as he said he
would. He didn't bring on it the trouble he said he
would bring. But we are about to bring horrible
trouble on ourselves!"

20Uriah was another man who prophesied in the
name of the LORD. He was from Kiriath Jearim.
He was the son of Shemaiah. Uriah prophesied
against this city and this land. He said the same
things I did.

21King Jehoiakim and all of his officers and
officials heard Uriah's words. So the king tried to
have him put to death.

But Uriah heard about it. He was afraid. And he
ran away to Egypt.

22So King Jehoiakim sent Elnathan to Egypt. He
also sent some other men along with him. Elnathan was the son of Acbor. 23Those men brought
Uriah out of Egypt. They took him to King Jehoiakim. Then the king had Uriah struck down with a
sword. He had Uriah's body thrown into one of the
graves of the ordinary people.

24In spite of that, Ahikam stood up for me. He
was the son of Shaphan. Because of Ahikam, I
wasn't handed over to the people to be put to death.

Judah Will Serve Nebuchadnezzar

27 A message came to me from the LORD. It
was shortly after Zedekiah became king of
Judah. He was the son of Josiah. 2The LORD said,
"Make a yoke out of ropes and wooden boards. Put
it on your neck.

3"Then write down a message for the kings of
Edom, Moab, Ammon, Tyre and Sidon. Give it to
their messengers who have come to Jerusalem.
They have come to see Zedekiah, the king of Judah. 4Give them a message for the kings who sent
them. It should say, 'The LORD who rules over all
is the God of Israel. He says, "Here is what I want
you to tell your masters. 5I reached out my great
and powerful arm. I made the earth. I made its people and animals. And I can give the earth to anyone I please.

6"'"Now I will hand all of your countries over
to my servant Nebuchadnezzar. He is king of Babylonia. I will put even the wild animals under his
control. 7All of the nations will serve him and his
son and grandson. After that, I will judge his land.
Then many nations and great kings will make him
serve them.

8"'"But suppose any nation or kingdom will not
serve Nebuchadnezzar, the king of Babylonia. And
suppose it refuses to put its neck under his yoke.
Then I will punish that nation with war, hunger
and plague," announces the LORD. "I will punish it
until his powerful hand destroys it.

9"'"So do not listen to your prophets. Do not
listen to those who claim to have secret knowledge. Do not listen to those who try to explain
your dreams. Do not listen to those who get messages from people who have died. Do not listen to
those who practice evil magic. All of them will tell
you, 'You won't serve the king of Babylonia.'

10"'"But they prophesy lies to you. If you listen
to them, you will be removed far away from your
lands. I will drive you away from them. And you
will die.

11"'"But suppose any nation will put its neck
under the yoke of the king of Babylonia. And suppose it serves him. Then I will let that nation
remain in its own land. I will let its people plow
the land and live there,"'" announces the LORD.

12I gave the same message to Zedekiah, the king
of Judah. I said, "Put your neck under the yoke of
the king of Babylonia. Obey him. Serve his people. Then you will live. 13Why should you and
your people die? Why should you die of war,
hunger and plague? That's what the LORD said
would happen to any nation that won't serve the
king of Babylonia.

14"Don't listen to the words of the prophets who
say to you, 'You won't serve the king of Babylonia.' They are prophesying lies to you. 15'I have not
sent them,' announces the LORD. 'They are prophesying lies in my name. So I will drive you away
from your land. And you will die. So will the
prophets who prophesy to you.'"

16Then I spoke to the priests and all of those
people. I said, "The LORD says, 'Do not listen to
the prophets who say, "Very soon the articles from
the LORD's house will be brought back from Babylon." They are prophesying lies to you. 17Do not
listen to them. Serve the king of Babylonia. Then
you will live. Why should this city be destroyed?

18"'If they are prophets and have received a
message from me, let them pray to me. I am the
LORD who rules over all. Those prophets should
pray that what is still in Jerusalem will remain
here. They should pray that the articles in my
house and the king's palace will not be taken to
Babylon.

19"'I am the LORD who rules over all. Do you
know what those articles are? They include the
two pillars in front of the temple. They include the
huge metal bowl. They include the bronze stands
that can be moved around. And they include the
other articles that are left in this city. 20Nebuchad-
nezzar, the king of Babylonia, did not take those
things away at first. That was when he took King
Jehoiachin from Jerusalem to Babylon. He also
took all of the nobles of Judah and Jerusalem along
with him. Jehoiachin is the son of Jehoiakim.

21"'I am the LORD who rules over all. I am the
God of Israel. Here is what will happen to the
things that are left in my house, the king's palace

and Jerusalem. 22They will be taken to Babylon.
They will remain there until the day I come for
them,' announces the LORD. 'Then I will bring
them back. I will return them to this place.'"

Hananiah Opposes Jeremiah

28 The prophet Hananiah spoke to me in the
LORD's house. It was shortly after Zedekiah became king of Judah. It was in the fifth month
of his fourth year. Hananiah was from Gibeon. He
was the son of Azzur. In front of the priests and all
of the people Hananiah said to me, 2"The LORD
who rules over all is the God of Israel. He says, 'I
will break the yoke of the king of Babylonia. 3Neb-
uchadnezzar, the king of Babylonia, removed all
of the articles that belong to my house. He took
them to Babylon. Before two years are over, I will
bring them back to this place.

4"'I will also bring King Jehoiachin back. He is
the son of Jehoiakim. And I will bring back all of
the others who were taken from Judah to Babylon,' announces the LORD. 'I will break the yoke
of the king of Babylonia.'"

5Then I, the prophet Jeremiah, replied to the
prophet Hananiah. I spoke to him in front of the
priests and all of the people. They were standing in
the LORD's house. 6I said, "Amen, Hananiah! May
the LORD do those things! May he make the words
you have prophesied come true. May he bring
back from Babylon the articles that belong to the
LORD's house. May he bring back to this place all
of the people who were taken away.

7"But listen to what I have to say. I want you and
all of the people to hear it. 8There have been
prophets long before you and I were ever born.
They have prophesied against many countries and
great kingdoms. They have spoken about war, trouble and plague. 9But what if a prophet says peace
will come? Only if it comes true will he be recognized as one who has been truly sent by the LORD."

10The prophet Hananiah took the yoke off my
neck. Then he broke it. 11In front of all of the people he said, "The LORD says, 'In the same way, I
will break the yoke of Nebuchadnezzar, the king
of Babylonia. Before two years are over, I will
remove it from the necks of all of the nations.'"
When I heard that, I went on my way.

12A message came to me from the LORD. It was
shortly after the prophet Hananiah had broken the
yoke off my neck. The message said, 13"Go. Tell
Hananiah, 'The LORD says, "You have broken a
wooden yoke. But in its place you will get an iron
yoke." 14The LORD who rules over all is the God
of Israel. He says, "I will put an iron yoke on the
necks of all of those nations. I will make them
serve Nebuchadnezzar, the king of Babylonia. So
they will serve him. I will even give him control
over the wild animals."'"

15Then I, the prophet Jeremiah, spoke to the
prophet Hananiah. I said, "Listen, Hananiah! The
LORD hasn't sent you. But you have tricked these
people. Now they trust in lies. 16So the LORD says,
'I am about to remove you from the face of the
earth. Before this year is over, you will die. You
have taught the people to turn against me.'"

17In the seventh month of that very year, the
prophet Hananiah died.

Jeremiah's Letter to the Jews in Babylonia

29 I, the prophet Jeremiah, sent a letter from
Jerusalem to Babylonia. It was for the Jewish elders who were still alive there. It was also for
the priests and prophets in Babylonia. And it was
for all of the other people Nebuchadnezzar had
taken from Jerusalem to Babylon. 2It was sent to
them after King Jehoiachin had been forced to
leave Jerusalem. His mother and the court officials
were taken with him. The leaders of Judah and Jerusalem and all of the skilled workers had also
been forced to go to Babylon.

3I gave the letter to Elasah and Gemariah. Zedekiah, the king of Judah, had sent them to King
Nebuchadnezzar in Babylon. Elasah was the son
of Shaphan. Gemariah was the son of Hilkiah.
Here is what the letter said.

4The LORD who rules over all is the God
of Israel. He speaks to all those he forced to
go from Jerusalem to Babylon. He says,
5"Build houses and settle down. Plant gardens and eat what they produce. 6Get married. Have sons and daughters. Find wives
for your sons. Give your daughters to be
married. Then they too can have sons and
daughters. Increase your numbers there. Do
not let the number of your people get
smaller.

7"Also work for the success of the city I
have sent you to. Pray to the LORD for that
city. If it succeeds, you too will enjoy
success."

8The LORD who rules over all is the God
of Israel. He says, "Do not let the prophets
trick you. Do not be fooled by those who
claim to have secret knowledge. Do not listen to people who try to explain their dreams
to you. 9All of them are prophesying lies to
you in my name. I have not sent them,"
announces the LORD.

10The LORD says, "You will be forced to
live in Babylonia for 70 years. After they are
over, I will come to you. My gracious
promise to you will come true. I will bring
you back home.

11"I know the plans I have for you,"
announces the LORD. "I want you to enjoy
success. I do not plan to harm you. I will
give you hope for the years to come. 12Then
you will call out to me. You will come and
pray to me. And I will listen to you. 13When
you look for me with all your heart, you will
find me.

14“I will be found by you,” announces the
LORD. “And I will bring you back from
where you were taken as prisoners. I will
gather you from all of the nations. I will
gather you from the places where I have
forced you to go,” announces the LORD. “I
will bring you back to the place from which
I sent you away.”
15You might say, “The LORD has given us
prophets in Babylonia.” 16But here is what
the LORD says about the king who now sits
on David’s throne. He also says it about all
of the people who remain in this city. And he
says it about all those who did not go with
you to Babylon. 17The LORD who rules over
all says, “I will send war, hunger and plague
against them. I will make them like bad figs.
They are so bad they can’t be eaten. 18I will
hunt them down with war, hunger and
plague. I will make all of the kingdoms on
earth displeased with them. They will call
down curses on them. All of the nations
where I drive them will be shocked at them.
They will make fun of them. And they will
bring shame on them.
19“That is because they have not listened
to my words,” announces the LORD. “I sent
messages to them again and again. I sent
them through my servants the prophets. And
you who were taken to Babylon have not listened either,” announces the LORD.
20So listen to the LORD’s message. Listen,
all of you whom he has sent away from Jerusalem to Babylon. 21The LORD who rules
over all is the God of Israel. He speaks about
Ahab and Zedekiah. They are prophesying
lies to you in my name. Ahab is the son of
Kolaiah. Zedekiah is the son of Maaseiah.
The LORD says about Ahab and Zedekiah, “I
will hand them over to Nebuchadnezzar, the
king of Babylonia. He will put them to death.
You will see it with your own eyes.
22“Because of what happens to them, people will use their names when they call down
curses on someone. All those who have been
taken from Judah to Babylon will use their
names in that way. They will say, ‘May the
LORD treat you like Zedekiah and Ahab. The
king of Babylonia burned them in the fire.’
23“That will happen because they have
done awful things in Israel. They have committed adultery with their neighbors’ wives.
They have spoken lies in my name. I did not
tell them to do that. I know what they have
done. And I am a witness to it,” announces
the LORD.

Shemaiah Opposes Jeremiah

24Tell Shemaiah, the Nehelamite, 25“The LORD
who rules over all is the God of Israel. He says,
‘You sent letters in your own name to all of the
people in Jerusalem. You also sent them to the
priest Zephaniah, the son of Maaseiah. And you
sent them to all of the other priests.
“ ‘You said to Zephaniah, 26“The LORD has
appointed you priest in place of Jehoiada. He has
put you in charge of the LORD’s house. You are
supposed to arrest any crazy person who claims to
be a prophet. You should put him in prison. You
should put iron bands around his neck.
27“ ‘ “So why haven’t you punished Jeremiah
from Anathoth? He claims to be a prophet among
you. 28He has sent a message to us in Babylon. It
says, ‘You will be there a long time. So build
houses and settle down. Plant gardens and eat what
they produce.’ ” ’ ”
29But the priest Zephaniah read the letter to me.
30Then a message came to me from the LORD. He
said, 31“Send a message to all of the people who
were taken away. Tell them, ‘The LORD speaks
about Shemaiah, the Nehelamite. He says, “Shemaiah has prophesied to you. But I did not send
him. He has made you believe a lie.
32“ ‘ “So I say, ‘I will certainly punish Shemaiah,
the Nehelamite. I will also punish his children after
him. He will not have any children left among
these people. I will do good things for my people.
But he will not see them,’ ” ’ ” announces the LORD.
“ ‘ “ ‘That is because he has taught people to turn
against me.’ ” ’ ”

Israel Will Return to the LORD

30 A message came to me from the LORD. He
said, 2“I am the LORD. I am the God of Israel. I say, ‘Write on a scroll all of the words I have
spoken to you. 3A new day is coming,’ ” announces
the LORD. “ ‘At that time I will bring my people Israel and Judah back from where they have been
taken as prisoners. I will bring them back to this
land. Long ago I gave it to their people to have as
their own,’ ” says the LORD.
4Here are the words the LORD spoke about Israel and Judah. He said, 5“I am the LORD. I say,

“ ‘Cries of fear are heard.
There is terror. There isn’t any peace.
6Ask and see.
Can a man give birth to children?
Then why do I see every strong man
with his hands on his stomach?
Each of them is acting like a woman having
a baby.
Every face is as pale as death.
7How awful that day will be!
No other day will be like it.
It will be a time of trouble for the people
of Jacob.
But they will be saved out of it.

8“ ‘At that time I will break the yoke off their
necks,’
announces the LORD who rules over all.

'I will tear off the ropes that hold them.
People from other lands will not make them slaves anymore.
9 Instead, they will serve me.
And they will serve David their king.
I will raise him up for them.
I am the LORD their God.

10 "'People of Jacob, do not be afraid.
You are my servant.
Israel, do not be terrified,'"
announces the LORD.
"'You can be sure that I will save you.
I will bring you out of a place far away.
I will bring your children back
from the land where they were taken.
Your people will have peace and security again.
And no one will make them afraid.
11 I am with you. I will save you,'"
announces the LORD.
"'I will completely destroy all of the nations
among which I scatter you.
But I will not completely destroy you.
I will correct you. But I will be fair.
I will punish you in a way that is fair and right.'"

12 The LORD says,

"Your wound can't be cured.
Your pain can't be healed.
13 No one will stand up for you.
There isn't any medicine for your sore.
There isn't any healing for you.
14 All those who were going to help you have forgotten you.
They do not care about you.
I have struck you as if I were your enemy.
I have punished you as if I were very mean.
That is because your guilt is so great.
You have sinned so much.
15 Why do you cry out about your wound?
Your pain can't be healed.
Your guilt is very great.
And you have committed many sins.
That is why I have done all of those things to you.

16 "But everyone who destroys you will be destroyed.
All of your enemies will be forced
to leave their countries.
Those who steal from you will be stolen from.
I will take the belongings
of those who take things from you.
17 But I will make you healthy again.
I will heal your wounds,"
announces the LORD.
"That is because you have been thrown out.
You are called Zion, the one no one cares about."

18 The LORD says,

"I will bless Jacob's people with great success again.
I will show tender love to Israel.
Jerusalem will be rebuilt where it was destroyed.
The palace will stand in its proper place.
19 From those places the songs of people giving thanks will be heard.
The sound of great joy will come from there.
I will increase the numbers of my people.
Their numbers will not become smaller.
I will bring them honor.
People will have respect for them.
20 Things will be as they used to be for Jacob's people.
I will make their community firm and secure.
I will punish everyone who treats them badly.
21 Their leader will be one of their own people.
Their ruler will rise up from among them.
I will bring him near.
And he will come close to me.
He will commit himself to serve me,"
announces the LORD.
22 "So you will be my people.
And I will be your God."

23 A storm will burst out
because of the LORD's burning anger.
A strong wind will sweep down
on the heads of evil people.
24 The LORD's burning anger won't turn back.
He will accomplish everything
his heart plans to do.
In days to come
you will understand that.

31

"At that time I will be the God of all of the tribes of Israel," announces the LORD. "And they will be my people."

2 The LORD says,

"Some of my people will live through
everything their enemies do to them.
They will find help in the desert.
I will come to give peace and rest to Israel."

3 The LORD appeared to us in the past. He said,

"I have loved you with a love that lasts forever.
I have kept on loving you with faithful love.
4 I will build you up again.
Nation of Israel, you will be rebuilt.
Once again you will use your tambourines to celebrate.
You will go out and dance with joy.
5 Once again you will plant vineyards
on the hills of Samaria.
Farmers will plant them.
They will enjoy their fruit.

[6]There will be a day when those on guard duty
will cry out.
They will stand on the hills of Ephraim.
And they will shout,
'Come! Let's go up to Zion.
Let's go up to where the LORD our God is.'"

[7]The LORD says,

"Sing with joy because the people of Jacob are
blessed.
Shout because the LORD has made them the
greatest nation.
Make your praises heard.
Say, 'LORD, save your people.
Save the people who are left alive in Israel.'
[8]I will bring them from the land of the north.
I will gather them from one end of the earth
to the other.
Even those who are blind and those who
can't walk
will be among them.
Pregnant women and women having their
babies
will be among them also.
A large number will return.
[9]Their eyes will be filled with tears as they
come.
They will pray as I bring them back.
I will lead them beside streams of water.
I will lead them on a level path
where they will not trip or fall.
I am Israel's father.
And Ephraim is my oldest son.

[10]"Listen to my message, you nations.
Announce it on shores far away.
Say, 'He who scattered Israel will gather them.
He will watch over his flock like a
shepherd.'
[11]I will set the people of Jacob free.
I will save them from those who are
stronger than they are.
[12]They will come and shout for joy on Mount
Zion.
They will be joyful because of everything I
give them.
I give them grain, olive oil and fresh wine.
I give them the young animals in their
flocks and herds.
Israel will be like a garden that has plenty of
water.
And they will not be sad anymore.
[13]Then young women will dance and be glad.
And so will the men, young and old alike.
I will turn their sobbing into gladness.
I will comfort them.
And I will give them joy instead of sorrow.
[14]I will satisfy the priests. I will give them more
than enough.
And my people will be filled with the good
things I give them,"
announces the LORD.

[15]The LORD says,

"A voice is heard in Ramah.
It is the sound of crying and deep sadness.
Rachel is crying over her children.
She refuses to be comforted,
because they are gone."

[16]The LORD says,

"Do not sob anymore.
Do not let tears fall from your eyes.
I will reward you for your work,"
announces the LORD.
"Your children will return from the land of
the enemy.
[17]So I am giving you hope for the years
to come,"
announces the LORD.
"Your children will return to their own land.

[18]"I have heard the groans of Ephraim's people.
They say,
'You corrected us like a calf you were
training.
And we have been trained.
Bring us back to you, and we will come back.
You are the LORD our God.
[19]After we wandered away from you,
we turned away from our sins.
After we learned our lesson,
we beat our chests in sorrow.
We were full of shame.
What we did when we were young brought
dishonor on us.'
[20]Aren't the people of Ephraim my dear
children?
Aren't they the children I take delight in?
I often speak against them.
But I still remember them.
So my heart longs for them.
I love them with a tender love,"
announces the LORD.

[21]The LORD says, "Put up road signs.
Set up stones to show the way.
Look carefully for the highway.
Look for the road you will take.
Return, people of Israel.
Return to your towns.
[22]How long will you wander,
you people who are not faithful to me?
I will create a new thing on earth.
A woman will guard a man."

[23]The LORD who rules over all is the God of Israel. He says, "I will bring them back from the
place where they were taken. The people in Judah
and its towns will say once again, 'Holy temple in
Jerusalem, may the LORD bless you. Sacred mountain, may he bless you.'
[24]"People will live together in Judah and all of
its towns. Farmers and shepherds will live there.
[25]I will give rest to those who are tired. I will satisfy those who are weak."

[26]When I heard that, I woke up and looked around. My sleep had been pleasant.

[27]The LORD announces, "The days are coming when I will plant the nation of Israel and Judah again. I will plant it with children and young animals.

[28]"I watched over Israel and Judah to pull them up by the roots. I tore them down. I crushed them. I destroyed them. I brought horrible trouble on them. But now I will watch over them to build them up and plant them," announces the LORD.

[29]"In those days people will no longer say,

'The fathers have eaten sour grapes.
But the children have a bitter taste in their mouths.'

[30]Instead, everyone will die for his own sin. The one who eats sour grapes will taste how bitter they are.

[31]"A new day is coming," announces the LORD.
"I will make a new covenant
with the people of Israel.
I will also make it with the people of Judah.
[32]It will not be like the covenant
I made with their people long ago.
That was when I took them by the hand.
I led them out of Egypt.
But they broke my covenant.
They did it even though I was like a husband to them,"
announces the LORD.
[33]"This is the covenant I will make with Israel
after that time," announces the LORD.
"I will put my law in their minds.
I will write it on their hearts.
I will be their God.
And they will be my people.
[34]A man will not need to teach his neighbor anymore.
And he will not need to teach his friend anymore.
He will not say, 'Know the LORD.'
Everyone will know me.
From the least important of them to the most important,
all of them will know me,"
announces the LORD.
"I will forgive their evil ways.
I will not remember their sins anymore."

[35]The LORD speaks.

He makes the sun
shine by day.
He orders the moon and stars
to shine at night.
He stirs up the ocean.
He makes its waves roar.
His name is The LORD Who Rules Over All.
[36]"Suppose my orders for creation disappear from my sight,"
announces the LORD.
"Only then will the people of Israel stop being a nation in my sight."

[37]The LORD says,

"Suppose the sky above could be measured.
Suppose the foundations of the earth below could be completely discovered.
Only then would I turn the people of Israel away.
Even though they have committed many sins,
I will still accept them,"
announces the LORD.

[38]"A new day is coming," announces the LORD. "At that time Jerusalem will be rebuilt for me. It will be rebuilt from the Tower of Hananel to the Corner Gate. [39]The measuring line will reach out from there. It will go straight to the hill of Gareb. Then it will turn and reach as far as Goah.

[40]"There is a valley where dead bodies and ashes are thrown. That whole valley will be holy to me. The side of the Kidron Valley east of the city will be holy to me. It will be holy all the way to the corner of the Horse Gate. The city will never again be pulled up by the roots. It will never be destroyed."

Jeremiah Buys a Field

32 A message came to me from the LORD. It came in the 10th year that Zedekiah was king of Judah. It was in the 18th year of the rule of Nebuchadnezzar. [2]The armies of the king of Babylonia were getting ready to attack Jerusalem. I, the prophet Jeremiah, was being held as a prisoner. I was kept in the courtyard of the guard. It was part of Judah's royal palace.

[3]Zedekiah, the king of Judah, had made me a prisoner there. He had said to me, "Why do you prophesy as you do? You say, 'The LORD says, "I am about to hand this city over to the king of Babylonia. He will capture it.

[4]"'"Zedekiah, the king of Judah, will not escape from the powerful hands of the armies of Babylonia. He will certainly be handed over to the king of Babylonia. Zedekiah will speak with him face to face. He will see him with his own eyes. [5]Nebuchadnezzar will take Zedekiah to Babylon. Zedekiah will remain there until I deal with him," announces the LORD. "Suppose you fight against the armies of Babylonia. If you do, you will not succeed."'"

[6]I said, "A message came to me from the LORD. He said, [7]'Hanamel is going to come to you. He is the son of your uncle Shallum. Hanamel will say, "Buy my field at Anathoth. You are my closest relative. So it's your right and duty to buy it."'

[8]"Then my cousin Hanamel came to me. I was in the courtyard of the guard. It happened just as the LORD had said it would. Hanamel said, 'Buy my field at Anathoth. It is in the territory of Benjamin.

It is your right to buy it and own it. So buy it for yourself.'

"I knew that this was the LORD's message. 9So I bought the field at Anathoth from my cousin Hanamel. I weighed out seven ounces of silver for him. 10I signed and sealed the deed of purchase. I had some people witness everything. And I weighed out the silver on the scales.

11"There were two copies of the deed. One was sealed and the other wasn't. The deed included the terms and conditions of the sale. 12I gave Baruch the copies of the deed. My cousin Hanamel saw me do it. The witnesses who had signed the deed were there too. So were all of the Jews who were sitting in the courtyard of the guard. Baruch was the son of Neriah. Neriah was the son of Mahseiah.

13"I gave Baruch directions in front of all of them. I said, 14'The LORD who rules over all is the God of Israel. He says, "Take this deed of purchase. Take the sealed and unsealed copies. Put them in a clay jar. Then they will last a long time." 15The LORD who rules over all is the God of Israel. He says, "Houses, fields and vineyards will again be bought in this land."'

16"I gave the deed of purchase to Baruch, the son of Neriah. Then I prayed to the LORD. I said,

> 17" 'LORD and King, you have reached out your great and powerful arm. You have made the heavens and the earth. Nothing is too hard for you.
>
> 18" 'You show your love to thousands of people. But you punish children for the sins of their fathers. Great and powerful God, your name is The LORD Who Rules Over All. 19Your purposes are great. Your acts are mighty. Your eyes see everything people do. You reward each one of them in keeping with his conduct. You do it based on what he has done.
>
> 20" 'You performed miraculous signs and wonders in Egypt. And you have continued to do them to this very day. You have done them in Israel and among all people. You are still known for doing them. 21You brought your people Israel out of Egypt. You did it with miraculous signs and wonders. You reached out your mighty hand and powerful arm. You did great and wonderful things.
>
> 22" 'You gave Israel this land. Long before that, you took an oath. You promised to give their people a land that had plenty of milk and honey. 23They came in and took it over. But they did not obey you. They didn't follow your law. They didn't do what you commanded them to do. So you brought all of this trouble on them.
>
> 24" 'See how ramps are built up against Jerusalem's walls to attack it. The city will be handed over to the armies of Babylonia. They are attacking it. It will fall because of war, hunger and plague. What you said would happen is now happening, as you can see. 25LORD and King, the city will be handed over to the armies of Babylonia. In spite of that, you tell me to buy a field. You say, "Pay for it with silver. And have the sale witnessed." ' "

26Then a message came to me from the LORD. He said, 27"I am the LORD. I am the God of all people. Is anything too hard for me?"

28So the LORD says, "I am about to hand this city over to the armies of Babylonia. I will give it to Nebuchadnezzar, the king of Babylonia. He will capture it. 29The armies of Babylonia are now attacking this city. They will come in and set it on fire. They will burn it down. They will burn up the houses where the people made me very angry. They burned incense on their roofs to the god Baal. And they poured out drink offerings to other gods.

30"The people of Israel and Judah have done nothing but evil in my sight. They have done it since the nation was young. In fact, they have done nothing but make me very angry. They have worshiped statues of gods their own hands have made," announces the LORD. 31"This city has always stirred up my burning anger. It has done it since the day it was built. Now I must remove it from my sight.

32"The people of Israel and Judah have made me very angry. They have done many evil things. They, their kings and officials have sinned. So have their priests and prophets. And the people of Judah and Jerusalem have also sinned. 33They turned their backs to me. They would not face me. I taught them again and again. But they would not listen or pay attention when they were corrected.

34"They set up statues of their gods. They did it in the house where I have put my Name. They made my house 'unclean.' I hate those statues.

35"The people built high places for Baal in the Valley of Ben Hinnom. That is where they sacrifice their children to Molech in the fire. That is something I did not command. It did not even enter my mind. They did something I hate. They made Judah sin."

36You people of Judah are saying about this city, "By war, hunger and plague it will be handed over to the king of Babylonia."

But the LORD, the God of Israel, says, 37"You can be sure that I will gather my people again. I will bring them from all of the lands where I send them when my burning anger blazes out against them. I will bring them back to this place. And I will let them live in safety.

38"They will be my people. And I will be their God. 39I will give them a single purpose in life. Then, they will always have respect for me. I will do it for their own good. And it will be for the good of their children after them.

40“I will make a covenant with them that will last forever. I promise that I will never stop doing good to them. I will cause them to respect me. Then they will never turn away from me again. 41I will take pleasure in doing good things for them. I will certainly plant them in this land. I will do those things with all my heart and soul.”

42The LORD says, “I have brought all of this horrible trouble on these people. But now I will give them all of the good things I have promised them.

43“Once more fields will be bought in this land. It is the land about which you now say, ‘It is a dry and empty desert. It doesn’t have any people or animals in it. It has been handed over to the armies of Babylonia.’ 44Fields will be bought with silver. Deeds will be signed, sealed and witnessed. That will be done in the territory of Benjamin. It will be done in the villages around Jerusalem and in the towns of Judah. It will also be done in the towns of the central hill country. And it will be done in the towns of the western hills and the Negev Desert. I will bless their people with great success again,” announces the LORD.

The LORD Keeps His Promises

33 I was still being held as a prisoner. I was kept in the courtyard of the guard. Then another message came to me from the LORD. He said, 2“I made the earth. I formed it. And I set it in place. The LORD is my name. 3Call out to me. I will answer you. I will tell you great things you do not know. You will not be able to understand them.”

4The LORD is the God of Israel. He speaks about the houses in Jerusalem. He talks about the royal palaces of Judah. The people had torn many of them down. They had used their stones to strengthen the city walls against attack. 5That was during their fight with the armies of Babylonia. The LORD says, “The houses will be filled with dead bodies. They will be the bodies of the men I will kill when my anger burns against them. I will hide my face from this city. That is because its people have committed so many sins.

6“But now I will bring health and healing to Jerusalem. I will heal my people. I will let them enjoy great peace and security. 7I will bring Judah and Israel back from the places where they have been taken. I will build up the nation again. It will be just as it was before.

8“I will wash from its people all of the sins they have committed against me. And I will forgive all of the sins they committed when they turned away from me.

9“Then this city will bring me fame, joy, praise and honor. All of the nations on earth will hear about the good things I do for this city. They will see the great success and peace I give it. Then they will be filled with wonder. And they will tremble with fear.”

10The LORD says, “You say about this place, ‘It’s a dry and empty desert. It doesn’t have any people or animals in it.’ The towns of Judah and the streets of Jerusalem are now deserted. So they do not have any people or animals living in them. But happy sounds will be heard there once more. 11They will be the sounds of joy and gladness. The voices of brides and grooms will fill the streets.

“And the voices of those who bring thank offerings to my house will be heard there. They will say,

‘Give thanks to the LORD who rules over all,
because he is good.
His faithful love continues forever.’

That is because I will bless this land with great success again. It will be as it was before,” says the LORD.

12The LORD who rules over all says, “This place is a desert. It does not have any people or animals in it. But there will again be grasslands near all of its towns. Shepherds will rest their flocks there. 13Flocks will again pass under the hands of shepherds as they count their sheep,” says the LORD. “That will be done in the towns of the central hill country. It will be done in the western hills and the Negev Desert. It will be done in the territory of Benjamin. And it will be done in the villages around Jerusalem and in the towns of Judah.

14“A new day is coming,” announces the LORD. “At that time my gracious promise to my people will come true. I made it to the people of Israel and the people of Judah.

15“In those days and at that time
I will make a true and rightful Branch grow
from David’s royal line.
He will do what is fair and right in the land.
16In those days Judah will be saved.
Jerusalem will live in safety.
And it will be called
The LORD Who Makes Us Right With
Himself.”

17The LORD says, “David will always have a son to sit on the throne of the nation of Israel.

18“The priests, who are Levites, will always have a man to serve me. He will sacrifice burnt offerings. He will burn grain offerings. And he will offer sacrifices.”

19A message came to me from the LORD. 20He said, “Could you ever break my covenant with the day? Could you ever break my covenant with the night? Could you ever stop day and night from coming at their appointed times? 21Only then could my covenant with my servant David be broken. Only then could my covenant with the Levites who serve me as priests be broken. Only then would David no longer have someone from his family line to rule on his throne.

22“Here is what I will do for my servant David. And here is what I will do for the Levites who serve me. I will make their children after them as many as the stars in the sky. And I will make them as many as the grains of sand on the seashore. It will be impossible to count them."

23A message came to me from the LORD. He said, 24"Haven't you noticed what these people are saying? They say, 'The LORD once chose the two kingdoms of Israel and Judah. But now he has turned his back on them.' So they hate my people. They do not think of them as a nation anymore.

25"I say, 'What if I had not made my covenant with day and night? What if I had not established the laws of heaven and earth? 26Only then would I turn my back on the children of Jacob and my servant David. Only then would I not choose one of David's sons to rule over the children of Abraham, Isaac and Jacob. But I will bless my people with great success again. I will love them with tender love.'"

Zedekiah Is Warned

34 Nebuchadnezzar, the king of Babylonia, and all of his armies were fighting against Jerusalem. They were also fighting against all of the towns that were around it. All of the kingdoms and nations Nebuchadnezzar ruled over were helping him.

At that time a message came to me from the LORD. He said, 2"I am the LORD, the God of Israel. Go to Zedekiah, the king of Judah. Tell him, 'The LORD says, "I am about to hand this city over to the king of Babylonia. He will burn it down. 3You will not escape from his powerful hand. You will certainly be captured. You will be handed over to him. You will see the king of Babylonia with your own eyes. He will speak with you face to face. And you will go to Babylon.

4""'But listen to my promise, Zedekiah. Listen, king of Judah. I say that you will not be killed with a sword. 5You will die in a peaceful way. People made fires to honor the kings who died before you. In the same way, they will make a fire in your honor. They will sob over you. They will say, 'My poor master!' I myself make this promise," announces the LORD.'"

6Then I, the prophet Jeremiah, told all of that to King Zedekiah in Jerusalem. 7At that time Nebuchadnezzar's armies were fighting against Jerusalem. They were also fighting against Lachish and Azekah. Those two cities were still holding out. They were the only cities left in Judah that had high walls around them.

The People Set Their Slaves Free

8A message came to me from the LORD. King Zedekiah had made a covenant with all of the people in Jerusalem. He had told them to set their Hebrew slaves free. 9All of them had to do it. That applied to male and female slaves alike. No one was allowed to hold another Jew as a slave.

10So all of the officials and people entered into that covenant. They agreed to set their male and female slaves free. They agreed not to hold them as slaves anymore. Instead, they set them free. 11But later they changed their minds. They took back the people they had set free. They made them slaves again.

12Then a message came to me from the LORD. 13The LORD is the God of Israel. He says, "I made a covenant with your people long ago. I brought them out of Egypt. That is the land where they were slaves. I said, 14'Every seventh year you must set your people free. You must set free all of the Hebrews who have sold themselves to you. Let them serve you for six years. Then you must let them go free.' *(Deuteronomy 15:12)* But your people did not listen to me. They did not pay any attention to me.

15"Recently you turned away from your sins. You did what is right in my eyes. Each of you set your Hebrew slaves free. You even made a covenant in front of me. You did it in the house where I have put my Name. 16But now you have turned around. You have treated my name as if it were not holy. Each of you has taken back your male and female slaves. You had set them free to go where they wished. But now you have forced them to become your slaves again."

17So the LORD says, "You have not obeyed me. You have not set your Hebrew slaves free. So now I will set you free," announces the LORD. "I will set you free to be destroyed by war, plague and hunger. I will make all of the kingdoms on earth displeased with you.

18"The men who have broken my covenant will be punished. They have not lived up to the terms of the covenant they made in front of me. When you made that covenant, you cut a calf in two. Then you walked between its pieces. Now I will cut you to pieces. 19That includes all of you who walked between the pieces of the calf. It includes the leaders of Judah and Jerusalem, the court officials and the priests. It also includes some of the people of the land.

20"So I will hand all of those people over to their enemies who are trying to kill them. Their dead bodies will become food for the birds of the air and the wild animals.

21"I will hand King Zedekiah and his officials over to their enemies. I will hand them over to those who want to kill them. I will give them over to the armies of the king of Babylonia. They have now pulled back from you. 22But I am going to give an order," announces the LORD. "I will bring them back to this city. They will fight against it. They will take it and burn it down. And I will completely destroy the towns of Judah. No one will be able to live there."

The Family of Recab

35 A message came to me from the LORD. It came during the time Jehoiakim was king over Judah. He was the son of Josiah. The message said, 2"Go to the members of the family line of Re-

cab. Invite them to come to one of the side rooms
in my house. Then give them wine to drink."
3So I went to get Jaazaniah. He was the son of
Jeremiah. Jeremiah was the son of Habazziniah. I
also went to get Jaazaniah's brothers and all of his
sons. That included all of the members of the family line of Recab. 4I brought them into the LORD's
house. I took them into the room of the sons of Hanan. He was the son of Igdaliah. He was also a
man of God. His room was next to the room of the
officials. Their room was above the room of Maaseiah. He was the son of Shallum. He also was one
of those who guarded the temple doors. 5Then I
got bowls full of wine and some cups. I set them
down in front of the men from the family line of
Recab. I said to them, "Drink some wine."
6But they replied, "We don't drink wine. That's
because Jonadab gave us a command. He was the
son of Recab. He was also one of our own people
from long ago. He commanded, 'You and your
children after you must never drink wine. 7Also
you must never build houses. You must never plant
crops or vineyards. You must never have any of
those things. Instead, you must always live in
tents. Then you will live a long time in the land
where you are wandering around.'
8"We have done everything Jonadab, the son of
Recab, commanded us to do. So we and our wives
and our children have never drunk wine. 9We have
never built houses to live in. We've never had
vineyards, fields or crops. 10We've always lived in
tents. We've completely obeyed everything Jonadab commanded our people of long ago.
11"But Nebuchadnezzar, the king of Babylonia,
marched into this land. Then we said, 'Come. We
must go to Jerusalem. There we can escape the
armies of Babylonia and Aram.' So we have
remained in Jerusalem."
12Then a message came to me from the LORD.
It said, 13"The LORD who rules over all is the God
of Israel. He says, 'Go. Speak to the people of Judah and Jerusalem. Tell them, "Won't you ever
learn a lesson? Won't you ever obey my words?"
announces the LORD.
14" ' "Jonadab, the son of Recab, ordered his
children not to drink wine. And they have kept his
command. To this very day they do not drink wine.
They obey the command Jonadab gave their people long ago. But I have spoken to you again and
again. In spite of that, you have not obeyed me.
15" ' "Again and again I sent all of my servants
the prophets to you. They said, 'Each of you must
turn from your evil ways. You must change the way
you act. Do not worship other gods. Do not serve
them. Then you will live in the land. I gave it to you
and your people long ago.' But you have not paid
any attention. You have not listened to me.
16" ' "The children of Jonadab, the son of Recab,
have obeyed the command Jonadab gave them
long ago. But the people of Judah have not
obeyed me." ' "
17So the LORD God who rules over all speaks.
The God of Israel says, "Listen! I am going to
bring horrible trouble on Judah. I will also bring it
on everyone who lives in Jerusalem. I will bring
on them every trouble I said I would. I spoke to
them. But they did not listen. I called out to them.
But they did not answer."
18Then I spoke to the members of the family
line of Recab. I said, "The LORD who rules over
all is the God of Israel. He says, 'You have obeyed
the command Jonadab gave your people long ago.
You have followed all of his directions. You have
done everything he ordered.' 19So the LORD who
rules over all speaks. The God of Israel says, 'Jonadab, the son of Recab, will always have a man
from his family to serve me.' "

Jehoiakim Burns Up Jeremiah's Scroll

36 A message came to me from the LORD. It
came in the fourth year that Jehoiakim was
king of Judah. He was the son of Josiah. The message said, 2"Get a scroll. Write on it all of the
words I have spoken to you. Write down what I
have said about Israel, Judah and all of the other
nations. Write what I have said to you from the
time of King Josiah until now. 3The people of Judah will hear about all of the trouble I plan to bring
on them. Maybe then all of them will turn from
their evil ways. If they do, I will forgive their sins
and the evil things they have done."
4So I sent for Baruch, the son of Neriah. I told
him to write down all of the words the LORD had
spoken to me. And Baruch wrote them on the scroll.
5Then I said to him, "I'm not allowed to go to
the LORD's temple. 6So you go there. Go on a day
when the people are fasting. Read to them from the
scroll. Read the words of the LORD you wrote
down as I gave them to you. Read them to all of
the people of Judah who come in from their towns.
7They will hear what the LORD will do to them
when his burning anger blazes out against them.
Then perhaps they will pray to him. And maybe all
of them will turn from their evil ways."
8Baruch, the son of Neriah, did everything I told
him to do. He went to the LORD's temple. There he
read the words of the LORD from the scroll. 9It was
in the fifth year that Jehoiakim, the son of Josiah,
was king of Judah. It was the ninth month of that
year. A time of fasting at the LORD's temple had
been ordered. All of the people in Jerusalem were
told to take part in it. So were those who had come
in from the towns of Judah.
10Baruch read to all of the people who were at
the LORD's temple. He read my words from the
scroll. He was in the room of the secretary Gemariah. It was located in the upper courtyard at the
entrance of the New Gate of the temple. Gemariah was the son of Shaphan.
11Micaiah was the son of Gemariah, the son of
Shaphan. Micaiah heard Baruch reading all of the
LORD's words that were written on the scroll.

12 Then he went down to the secretary's room in the royal palace. All of the officials were sitting there. They included the secretary Elishama and Delaiah, the son of Shemaiah. Elnathan, the son of Acbor, was also there. So was Gemariah, the son of Shaphan. Zedekiah, the son of Hananiah, was there too. And so were all of the other officials. 13 Micaiah told all of them what he had heard. He told them everything Baruch had read to the people from the scroll.

14 All of the officials sent Jehudi to speak to Baruch, the son of Neriah. Jehudi was the son of Nethaniah. Nethaniah was the son of Shelemiah. Shelemiah was the son of Cushi. Jehudi said to Baruch, "Come. Bring the scroll you have read to the people."

So Baruch went to them. He carried the scroll with him. 15 The officials said to him, "Please sit down. Read the scroll to us."

So Baruch read it to them. 16 They heard all of its words. Then they looked at each other in fear. They said to Baruch, "We must report all of these words to the king."

17 They said to Baruch, "Tell us. How did you happen to write all of these things? Did Jeremiah tell you to do it?"

18 "Yes," Baruch replied. "He told me to write down all of these words. So I wrote them in ink on the scroll."

19 Then the officials spoke to Baruch. They said, "You and Jeremiah must go and hide. Don't let anyone know where you are."

20 The officials put the scroll in the room of the secretary Elishama. Then they went to the king in the courtyard. They reported everything to him.

21 The king sent Jehudi to get the scroll. Jehudi brought it from the room of the secretary Elishama. He read it to the king. All of the officials were standing beside the king. So they heard it too. 22 It was the ninth month. The king was sitting in his winter apartment. A fire was burning in the fire pot in front of him. 23 Jehudi read three or four columns from the scroll. Then the king cut them off with a secretary's knife. He threw them into the fire pot. He did that until the entire scroll was burned up in the fire. 24 The king and some of his attendants heard all of those words. But they weren't afraid. They didn't tear their clothes.

25 Elnathan, Delaiah and Gemariah begged the king not to burn the scroll. But he wouldn't listen to them. 26 Instead, the king commanded three men to arrest the secretary Baruch and the prophet Jeremiah. But the LORD had hidden them. The three were Jerahmeel, Seraiah and Shelemiah. Jerahmeel was a member of the royal court. Seraiah was the son of Azriel. And Shelemiah was the son of Abdeel.

27 A message came to me from the LORD. It came after the king burned the scroll that had the words Baruch had written down. I had told him to write them. The message said, 28 "Get another scroll. Write on it all of the words that were on the first one. King Jehoiakim burned that one up.

29 "Also tell King Jehoiakim, 'The LORD says, "You burned that scroll. You said to Baruch, 'Why did you write that the king of Babylonia would certainly come? Why did you write that he would destroy this land? Why did you write that he would cut off people and animals alike from it?'"

30 "'So now the LORD has something to say about Jehoiakim, the king of Judah. He says, "No one from Jehoiakim's family line will sit on David's throne. Jehoiakim's body will be thrown out. It will lie outside in the heat by day and in the frost at night. 31 I will punish him and his children and his attendants. I will punish them for their sinful ways. I will bring on them all of the trouble I said I would. And I will bring it on the people of Jerusalem and Judah. They have not listened to me."'"

32 So I got another scroll. I gave it to the secretary Baruch, the son of Neriah. I told him what to write on it. He wrote down all of the words that were on the scroll King Jehoiakim had burned up in the fire. And he added many more words the LORD had given to me. They were similar to those that had already been written.

Jeremiah Is Put in Prison

37 Nebuchadnezzar, the king of Babylonia, appointed Zedekiah to be king of Judah. He was the son of Josiah. Zedekiah ruled in place of Jehoiachin, the son of Jehoiakim. 2 Zedekiah and his attendants didn't pay any attention to what the LORD had said through me. And the people of the land didn't pay any attention either.

3 But King Zedekiah sent Jehucal to me. He sent the priest Zephaniah along with him. Jehucal was the son of Shelemiah. Zephaniah was the son of Maaseiah. Jehucal and Zephaniah brought the king's message to me. It said, "Please pray to the LORD our God for us."

4 At that time I was free to come and go among the people. I had not yet been put in prison. 5 The armies of Babylonia were attacking Jerusalem. They received a report that Pharaoh's army had marched out of Egypt to help Zedekiah. So they pulled back from Jerusalem.

6 A message came to me from the LORD. 7 The LORD is the God of Israel. He says, "The king of Judah has sent you to ask me for advice. Tell him, 'Pharaoh's army has marched out to help you. But it will go back to its own land. It will return to Egypt. 8 Then the armies of Babylonia will come back here. They will attack this city. They will capture it. Then they will burn it down.'

9 "The LORD says, 'Do not fool yourselves. You think, "The Babylonians will leave us alone." But they will not! 10 Suppose you destroy all of the armies of Babylonia that are attacking you. Suppose only wounded men are left in their tents. Even then they will come out and burn this city down.'"

11The armies of Babylonia had pulled back from Jerusalem because of Pharaoh's army. 12So I started to leave the city. I was planning to go to the territory of Benjamin. I wanted to get my share of the property among the people there. 13I got as far as the Benjamin Gate. But the captain of the guard arrested me. He said, "You are going over to the side of the Babylonians!" The captain's name was Irijah, the son of Shelemiah. Shelemiah was the son of Hananiah.

14I said to Irijah, "That isn't true! I'm not going to the side of the Babylonians."

But Irijah wouldn't listen to me. Instead, he arrested me. He brought me to the officials. 15They were angry with me. So they had me beaten. Then they took me to the house of the secretary Jonathan. It had been made into a prison. That's where they put me.

16I was put into a prison cell that was below ground level. I remained there a long time. 17Then King Zedekiah sent for me. He had me brought to the palace. There he spoke to me in private. He asked, "Do you have a message from the LORD for me?"

"Yes," I replied. "You will be handed over to the king of Babylonia."

18Then I continued, "Why have you put me in prison? What crime have I committed against you? What have I done to your officials or these people? 19Where are your prophets who prophesied to you? They said, 'The king of Babylonia won't attack you. He won't march into this land.'

20"But now please listen, my king and master. Let me make my appeal to you. Please don't send me back to the house of the secretary Jonathan. If you do, I'll die there."

21Then King Zedekiah gave the order. His men put me in the courtyard of the guard. They gave me bread from the street of the bakers. They did it every day until all of the bread in the city was gone. So I remained in the courtyard of the guard.

Jeremiah Is Thrown Into an Empty Well

38 Shephatiah, Gedaliah, Jehucal and Pashhur heard what I was telling all of the people. Shephatiah was the son of Mattan. Gedaliah was the son of Pashhur. Jehucal was the son of Shelemiah. And Pashhur was the son of Malkijah. Those four men heard me say, 2"The LORD says, 'Those who stay in this city will die of war, hunger or plague. But those who go over to the side of the Babylonians will live. They will escape with their lives. They will remain alive.' 3The LORD also says, 'This city will certainly be handed over to the armies of the king of Babylonia. They will capture it.'"

4Then those officials said to the king, "That man should be put to death. What he says is making the soldiers who are left in this city lose hope. It's making all of the people lose hope too. He isn't interested in what is best for the people. In fact, he's trying to destroy them."

5"He's in your hands," King Zedekiah answered. "I can't do anything to oppose you."

6So they took me and put me into an empty well. It belonged to Malkijah. He was a member of the royal court. His well was in the courtyard of the guard. Zedekiah's men lowered me by ropes into the well. It didn't have any water in it. All it had was mud. And I sank down into the mud.

7Ebed-Melech was an official in the royal palace. He was from the land of Cush. He heard that I had been put into the well. The king was sitting by the Benjamin Gate at that time. 8Ebed-Melech went out of the palace. He said to the king, 9"My king and master, everything those men have done to the prophet Jeremiah is evil. They have thrown him into an empty well. Soon there won't be any more bread in the city. Then he'll starve to death."

10So the king gave an order to Ebed-Melech from Cush. He said, "Take 30 men from here with you. Lift the prophet Jeremiah out of the well before he dies."

11Then Ebed-Melech took the men with him. He went to a room under the place in the palace where the treasures were stored. He got some old rags and worn-out clothes from there. Then he let them down with ropes to me in the well.

12Ebed-Melech from Cush told me what to do. He said, "Put these old rags and worn-out clothes under your arms. They'll pad the ropes." So I did. 13Then the men pulled me up with the ropes. They lifted me out of the well. And I remained in the courtyard of the guard.

Zedekiah Questions Jeremiah Again

14Then King Zedekiah sent for me. He had me brought to the third entrance to the LORD's temple. "I want to ask you something," the king said to me. "Don't hide anything from me."

15I said to Zedekiah, "Suppose I give you an answer. You will kill me, won't you? Suppose I give you good advice. You won't listen to me, will you?"

16But King Zedekiah took an oath. He promised me secretly, "I won't kill you. And I won't hand you over to those who want to take your life. That's just as sure as the LORD is alive. He's the one who has given us breath."

17So I said to Zedekiah, "The LORD God who rules over all is the God of Israel. He says, 'Give yourself up to the officers of the king of Babylonia. Then your life will be spared. And this city will not be burned down. You and your family will remain alive.

18"'But what if you do not give yourself up to them? Then this city will be handed over to the Babylonians. They will burn it down. And you yourself will not escape from their powerful hands.'"

19King Zedekiah said to me, "I'm afraid of some of the Jews. They are the ones who have gone over to the side of the Babylonians. The Babylonians might hand me over to them. And those Jews will treat me badly."

[20]"They won't hand you over to them," I replied. "Obey the LORD. Do what I tell you to do. Then things will go well with you. Your life will be spared.

[21]"Don't refuse to give yourself up. The LORD has shown me what will happen if you do. [22]All of the women who are left in your palace will be brought out. They'll be given to the officials of the king of Babylonia. Those women will say to you,

"'Your trusted friends have tricked you.
They have gotten the best of you.
Your feet are sunk down in the mud.
Your friends have deserted you.'

[23]"All of your wives and children will be brought out to the Babylonians. You yourself won't escape from their powerful hands. You will be captured by the king of Babylonia. And this city will be burned down."

[24]Then Zedekiah said to me, "Don't let anyone know about the talk we've had. If you do, you might die. [25]Suppose the officials find out that I've talked with you. And suppose they come to you and say, 'Tell us what you said to the king. Tell us what the king said to you. Don't hide it from us. If you do, we'll kill you.' [26]Then tell them, 'I was begging the king not to send me back to Jonathan's house. I don't want to die there.'"

[27]All of the officials came to me. And they questioned me. I told them everything the king had ordered me to say. None of them had heard what I told the king. So they didn't say anything else to me.

[28]I remained in the courtyard of the guard. I stayed there until the day Jerusalem was captured.

Jerusalem Is Destroyed

39 Here is how Jerusalem was captured. [1]Nebuchadnezzar, the king of Babylonia, marched out against it. He came with all of his armies and attacked it. It was in the ninth year that Zedekiah was king of Judah. It was in the tenth month. [2]The city wall was broken through. It happened on the ninth day of the fourth month. It was in the 11th year of Zedekiah's rule.

[3]All of the officials of the king of Babylonia came. They took seats near the Middle Gate. Nergal-Sharezer from Samgar was there. Nebo-Sarsekim, a chief officer, was also there. So was Nergal-Sharezer, a high official. And all of the other officials of the king of Babylonia were there too.

[4]King Zedekiah and all of the soldiers saw them. Then they ran away. They left the city at night. They went by way of the king's garden. They went out through the gate between the two walls. And they headed toward the Arabah Valley.

[5]But the armies of Babylonia chased them. They caught up with Zedekiah in the flatlands near Jericho. They captured him there. And they took him to Nebuchadnezzar, the king of Babylonia. He was at Riblah in the land of Hamath. That's where Nebuchadnezzar decided how he would be punished. [6]The king of Babylonia killed the sons of Zedekiah at Riblah. He forced Zedekiah to watch it with his own eyes. He also killed all of the nobles of Judah. [7]Then he poked out Zedekiah's eyes. He put him in bronze chains. And he took him to Babylon.

[8]The Babylonians set the royal palace on fire. They also set fire to the houses of the people. And they broke down the walls of Jerusalem.

[9]Nebuzaradan was commander of the royal guard. Some people still remained in the city. But he took them away to Babylon as prisoners. He also took along those who had gone over to his side. And he took the rest of the people.

[10]Nebuzaradan, the commander of the guard, left some of the poor people of Judah behind. They didn't own anything. So at that time he gave them vineyards and fields.

[11]Nebuchadnezzar, the king of Babylonia, had given orders about me. He had given them to Nebuzaradan, the commander of the royal guard. Nebuchadnezzar had said, [12]"Take him. Look after him. Don't harm him. Do for him anything he asks."

[13]So that's what Nebuzaradan, the commander of the guard, did. Nebushazban and Nergal-Sharezer were with him. So were all of the other officers of the king of Babylonia. Nebushazban was a chief officer. Nergal-Sharezer was a high official. All of those men [14]sent for me. They had me taken out of the courtyard of the guard. They turned me over to Gedaliah. They told him to take me back to my home. So I remained among my own people. Gedaliah was the son of Ahikam, the son of Shaphan.

[15]A message came to me from the LORD. It came while I was being kept in the courtyard of the guard. He said, [16]"Go. Speak to Ebed-Melech from Cush. Tell him, 'The LORD who rules over all is the God of Israel. He says, "I am about to make the words I spoke against this city come true. I will not give success to it. Instead, I will bring horrible trouble on it. At that time my words will come true. You will see it with your own eyes.

[17]"'"But I will save you on that day," announces the LORD. "You will not be handed over to those you are afraid of. [18]I will save you. You will not be killed with a sword. Instead, you will escape with your life. That is because you trust in me," announces the LORD.'"

Jeremiah Is Set Free From His Chains

40 A message came to me from the LORD. It came after Nebuzaradan, the commander of the royal guard, had set me free at Ramah. I was being held by chains when he found me. I was among all of the prisoners from Jerusalem and Judah. We were being taken to Babylon.

2But the commander of the guard found me. He said to me, "The LORD your God ordered that this place be destroyed. 3And now he has brought it about. He has done exactly what he said he would do. All of these things have happened because you people sinned against the LORD. You didn't obey him. 4But today I'm setting you free from the chains that are on your wrists. Come with me to Babylon if you want to. I'll take good care of you there. But if you don't want to come, then don't. The whole country lies in front of you. Go anywhere you want to."

5But before I turned to go, Nebuzaradan continued, "Go back to Gedaliah, the son of Ahikam. The king of Babylonia has appointed Gedaliah to be over the towns of Judah. Go and live with him among your people. Or go anywhere else you want to." Ahikam was the son of Shaphan.

The commander gave me food and water. He also gave me a gift. Then he let me go. 6So I went to Mizpah to see Gedaliah, the son of Ahikam. I stayed with him. I lived among the people who were left behind in the land.

Gedaliah Is Murdered

7Some of Judah's army officers and their men were still in the open country. They heard that the king of Babylonia had appointed Gedaliah, the son of Ahikam, as governor over Judah. He had put him in charge of the men, women and children who were still there. They were the poorest people in the land. They hadn't been taken to Babylon. 8When the army officers and their men heard those things, they came to Gedaliah at Mizpah. Ishmael, the son of Nethaniah, came. So did Johanan and Jonathan, the sons of Kareah. Seraiah, the son of Tanhumeth, also came. The sons of Ephai from Netophah came too. And so did Jaazaniah, the son of the Maacathite. All of their men came with them.

9Gedaliah son of Ahikam, the son of Shaphan, took an oath to give hope to all of those men. He spoke in a kind way to them. He said, "Don't be afraid to serve the Babylonians. Settle down in the land of Judah. Serve the king of Babylonia. Then things will go well with you. 10I myself will stay at Mizpah. I'll speak for you to the officials of Babylonia who come to us. But you must harvest the wine, summer fruit and olive oil. Put them in your jars. Store them up. And live in the towns you have taken over."

11All of the Jews in Moab, Ammon and Edom heard what had happened. So did the Jews in all of the other countries. They heard that the king of Babylonia had left some people behind in Judah. They also heard that he had appointed Gedaliah, the son of Ahikam, as governor over them. Ahikam was the son of Shaphan.

12When they heard those things, all of them came back to the land of Judah. They went to Gedaliah at Mizpah. They came from all of the countries where they had been scattered. And they harvested a large amount of wine and summer fruit.

13Johanan and all of the other army officers who were still in the open country came to Gedaliah at Mizpah. Johanan was the son of Kareah. 14The officers said to Gedaliah, "Don't you know that Baalis, the king of Ammon, has sent someone to take your life? It's Ishmael, the son of Nethaniah." But Gedaliah, the son of Ahikam, didn't believe them.

15Then Johanan, the son of Kareah, spoke in private to Gedaliah in Mizpah. He said, "Let me go and kill Ishmael, the son of Nethaniah. No one will know about it. Why should he take your life? Why should he cause all of the Jews who are gathered around you to be scattered? Why should he cause the people who remain in Judah to die?"

16But Gedaliah, the son of Ahikam, spoke to Johanan, the son of Kareah. He said, "Don't do an awful thing like that! What you are saying about Ishmael isn't true."

41 In the seventh month Ishmael, the son of Nethaniah, came with ten men to Gedaliah, the son of Ahikam, at Mizpah. Nethaniah was the son of Elishama. Ishmael was a member of the royal family. He had been one of the king's officers. Ishmael and his ten men were eating together at Mizpah.

2They got up and struck down Gedaliah, the son of Ahikam, with their swords. They killed him even though the king of Babylonia had appointed him as governor over Judah. Ahikam was the son of Shaphan. 3Ishmael also killed all of the Jews who were with Gedaliah at Mizpah. And he killed the Babylonian soldiers who were there.

4On the next day, people still hadn't found out that Gedaliah had been murdered. 5On that day 80 men came from Shechem, Shiloh and Samaria. They had shaved off their beards. They had torn their clothes. And they had cut themselves. They brought grain offerings and incense with them. They took them to the LORD's house.

6Ishmael, the son of Nethaniah, went out from Mizpah to meet them. He was sobbing as he went. When he met them, he said, "Come to Gedaliah, the son of Ahikam."

7They went with him into the city. Then Ishmael, the son of Nethaniah, and the men who were with him killed them. And they threw them into an empty well.

8But ten of the men had spoken to Ishmael. They had said, "Don't kill us! We have some wheat and barley. We also have olive oil and honey. We've hidden all of it in a field." So he let them alone. He didn't kill them along with the others.

9But he had thrown all of the bodies of the men he had killed into the empty well. That included Gedaliah's body. The well was the one King Asa had made. He had made it when he strengthened Mizpah against attack by Baasha, the king of Israel.

Ishmael, the son of Nethaniah, filled it with the
bodies of those he had killed.
10 Ishmael made prisoners of all the rest of the
people who were in Mizpah. That included women
who were members of the royal court. It also
included all of the others who were left there. Nebuzaradan had appointed Gedaliah, the son of Ahikam, over them. Ishmael, the son of Nethaniah,
took them as prisoners. Then he started out to go
across the Jordan River to the land of Ammon.
Nebuzaradan was the commander of the royal
guard.
11 Johanan, the son of Kareah, and all of the
other army officers who were with him were told
what had happened. They heard about all of the
crimes Ishmael, the son of Nethaniah, had committed. 12 So they brought all of their men together.
Then they went to fight against Ishmael, the son
of Nethaniah. They caught up with him near the
large pool in Gibeon.
13 Ishmael had many people with him. They saw
Johanan, the son of Kareah. And they saw the
other army officers who were with him. So the
people who had been forced to go with Ishmael
were glad. 14 All those whom Ishmael had taken as
prisoners at Mizpah turned and went over to the
side of Johanan, the son of Kareah. 15 But Ishmael,
the son of Nethaniah, and eight of his men escaped
from Johanan. They ran away to the land of Ammon.

Some Jews Take Jeremiah to Egypt

16 Then Johanan, the son of Kareah, led away all
of the people from Mizpah who were still alive.
All of the other army officers who were with Johanan helped him do it. He had taken them away
from Ishmael, the son of Nethaniah. That happened after Ishmael had murdered Gedaliah, the
son of Ahikam. The people Johanan had taken
away included the soldiers, women, children and
court officials he had brought from Gibeon.
17 They went on their way. They stopped at Ge-
ruth Kimham near Bethlehem. They were going to
Egypt. 18 They wanted to get away from the Babylonians. They were afraid of them because Ishmael, the son of Nethaniah, had killed Gedaliah,
the son of Ahikam. The king of Babylonia had
appointed Gedaliah as governor over Judah.
42 Then all of the army officers approached
me. They included Johanan, the son of Kareah, and Jezaniah, the son of Hoshaiah. All of the
people from the least important of them to the
most important also came. 2 All of them said to me,
"Please listen to our appeal. Pray to the LORD your
God. Pray for all of us who are left here. Once
there were many of us. But as you can see, only a
few of us are left now. 3 So pray to the LORD your
God. Pray that he'll tell us where we should go.
Pray that he'll tell us what we should do."
4 "I've heard you," I replied. "I'll certainly pray
to the LORD your God. I'll do what you have asked
me to do. In fact, I'll tell you everything the LORD
says. I won't keep anything back from you."
5 Then they said to me, "We'll do everything the
LORD your God sends you to tell us to do. If we
don't, may he be a true and faithful witness against
us. 6 It doesn't matter whether what you say is in
our favor or not. We're asking you to pray to the
LORD our God. And we'll obey him. Things will
go well with us. That's because we will obey the
LORD our God."
7 Ten days later a message came to me from the
LORD. 8 So I sent for Johanan, the son of Kareah,
and all of the other army officers who were with
him. I also gathered together all of the people from
the least important of them to the most important.
9 I said to all of them, "The LORD is the God of
Israel. You asked me to present your appeal to him.
10 He told me, 'Stay in this land. Then I will build
you up. I will not tear you down. I will plant you.
I will not pull you up by the roots. I am very sad
that I had to bring all of this trouble on you.
11 "'Do not be afraid of the king of Babylonia.
You are afraid of him now. Do not be,' announces
the LORD. 'I am with you. I will keep you safe. I
will save you from his powerful hands. 12 I will
show you my loving concern. Then he will have
concern for you. And he will let you return to your
land.'
13 "But suppose you say, 'We won't stay in this
land.' If you do, you will be disobeying the LORD
your God. 14 And suppose you say, 'No! We'll go
and live in Egypt. There we won't have to face war
anymore. We won't hear the trumpets of war. And
we won't get hungry.'
15 "Then listen to what the LORD says to you
who are left in Judah. He is the LORD who rules
over all. He is the God of Israel. He says, 'Have
you already made up your minds to go to Egypt?
Are you going to settle down there?
16 "'Then the war you fear will catch up with
you there. The hunger you are afraid of will follow you into Egypt. And you will die there. 17 In
fact, that will happen to all those who go and settle in Egypt. All of them will die of war, hunger
and plague. Not one of them will live. None of
them will escape the trouble I will bring on them.'
18 "He is the LORD who rules over all. He is the
God of Israel. He says, 'My burning anger has
been poured out on those who used to live in Jerusalem. In the same way, it will be poured out on
you when you go to Egypt. People will call down
curses on you. They will be shocked at you. They
will say bad things about you. And they will bring
shame on you. You will never see this place again.'
19 "The LORD has spoken to you who are left in
Judah. He has said, 'Do not go to Egypt.' Here is
something you can be sure of. I am warning you
about it today. 20 You made a big mistake when you
asked me to pray to the LORD your God. You said,
'Pray to the LORD our God for us. Tell us everything he says. We'll do it.'

21“I have told you today what the LORD your God wants you to do. But you still haven’t obeyed him. You haven’t done anything he sent me to tell you to do. 22So here is something else you can be sure of. You will die of war, hunger and plague. You want to go and settle down in Egypt. But you will die there.”

43 I finished telling the people everything the LORD their God had said. I told them everything he had sent me to tell them. 2After that, Azariah, the son of Hoshaiah, and Johanan, the son of Kareah, spoke to me. And all of the proud men joined them. They said, “You are lying! The LORD our God hasn’t sent you to speak to us. He hasn’t told you to say, ‘You must not go to Egypt and settle down there.’ 3But Baruch, the son of Neriah, is turning you against us. He wants us to be handed over to the Babylonians. Then they can kill us. Or they can take us away to Babylon.”

4So Johanan, the son of Kareah, disobeyed the LORD’s command. So did all of the other army officers and all of the people. They didn’t stay in the land of Judah.

5Instead Johanan, the son of Kareah, and all of the other army officers led away all of the people who were left in Judah. Those people had returned to Judah from all of the nations where they had been scattered. 6Johanan and the other officers also led away many people Nebuzaradan had left in Mizpah. They included men, women and children. They also included women who were members of the royal court. Nebuzaradan had left them with Gedaliah, the son of Ahikam. He had also left them with the prophet Jeremiah and Baruch, the son of Neriah. Nebuzaradan was commander of the royal guard. Ahikam was the son of Shaphan.

7So the Jewish leaders disobeyed the LORD. They took everyone to Egypt. They went all the way to Tahpanhes.

8In Tahpanhes a message came to me from the LORD. He said, 9“Make sure the Jews are watching you. Then get some large stones. Go to the entrance to Pharaoh’s house in Tahpanhes. Bury the stones in the clay under the brick walkway there.

10“Then tell the Jews, ‘The LORD who rules over all is the God of Israel. He says, “I will send for my servant Nebuchadnezzar, the king of Babylonia. And I will set his throne over these stones that are buried here. He will set up his royal tent over them. 11He will come and attack Egypt. He will bring death to those I have appointed to die. He will take away as prisoners those I have appointed to be taken away. And he will kill with swords those I have appointed to be killed.

12“ ‘ “He will set the temples of the gods of Egypt on fire. He will burn their temples down. He will take the statues of their gods away. Nebuchadnezzar will be like a shepherd who wraps his coat around himself. He will wrap Egypt around himself. And he will leave there unharmed. 13At Heliopolis in Egypt he will smash the sacred pillars to pieces. And he will burn down the temples of the gods of Egypt.” ’ ”

Don’t Worship Other Gods

44 A message came to me from the LORD about all of the Jews who were living in Lower Egypt. They were living in Migdol, Tahpanhes and Memphis. It was also about all of the Jews who were living in Upper Egypt. 2The LORD who rules over all is the God of Israel. He said, “You saw all of the trouble I brought on Jerusalem. I also brought it on all of the towns in Judah. Today they lie there deserted and destroyed. 3That is because of the evil things their people did. They made me very angry. They burned incense to other gods. And they worshiped them. They and you and your people of long ago never had anything to do with those gods before.

4“Again and again I sent my servants the prophets. They said, ‘Don’t worship other gods! The LORD hates it!’

5“But the people didn’t listen. They didn’t pay any attention. They didn’t turn from their sinful ways. They didn’t stop burning incense to other gods.

6“So my burning anger was poured out. It blazed out against the towns of Judah and the streets of Jerusalem. It made them the dry and empty places they are today.”

7The LORD God who rules over all is the God of Israel. He says, “Why do you want to bring all of this trouble on yourselves? You are cutting off from Judah its men and women. You are cutting off the children and babies. Not one of you will be left. 8Why do you want to make me angry with the gods your hands have made? Why do you burn incense to the gods of Egypt, where you have come to live? You will destroy yourselves. All of the nations on earth will call down curses on you. They will bring shame on you.

9“Have you forgotten the evil things your people did long ago? The kings and queens of Judah did those same things. So did you and your wives. They were done in the land of Judah and the streets of Jerusalem.

10“To this very day the people of Judah have not made themselves low in my sight. They have not shown any respect for me. They have not obeyed my law. They have not followed the rules I gave you and your people long ago.”

11The LORD who rules over all is the God of Israel. He says, “I have decided to bring horrible trouble on you. I will destroy the whole land of Judah. 12I will destroy the people of Judah who are left. They had decided to go to Egypt and settle down there. But all of them will die in Egypt. They will die of war or hunger. All of them will die, from the least important of them to the most important. They will die of war or hunger. People will call down curses on them. They will be shocked at them. They will say bad things about them. And they will bring shame on them. [13]I will use war, hunger and plague to punish the Jews who live in Egypt. I punished Jerusalem in the same way.

[14]"None of the people of Judah who have gone to live in Egypt will escape. Not one of them will live to return to Judah. They long to return and live there. But only a few will escape from Egypt and go back."

[15]All of the Jews who were living in Lower and Upper Egypt gathered to give me their answer. A large crowd had come together. It included men who knew that their wives were burning incense to other gods. Their wives were there with them.

All of them said to me, [16]"We won't listen to the message you have spoken to us in the LORD's name! [17]We will certainly do everything we said we would. We'll burn incense to the goddess who is called the Queen of Heaven. We'll pour out drink offerings to her. We'll do just as we and our people before us did. Our kings and our officials also did it. All of us did it in the towns of Judah and the streets of Jerusalem. At that time we had plenty of food. We were well off. We didn't suffer any harm.

[18]"But then we stopped burning incense to the Queen of Heaven. We stopped pouring out drink offerings to her. And ever since that time we haven't had anything. Instead, we've been dying of war and hunger."

[19]The women added, "We burned incense to the Queen of Heaven. We poured out drink offerings to her. And our husbands knew we were making cakes that looked like her. They knew we were pouring out drink offerings to her."

[20]Then I spoke to all of the people who were answering me. I spoke to men and women alike. I said, [21]"Didn't the LORD know you were burning incense in the towns of Judah? Didn't he care that you were also doing it in the streets of Jerusalem? You and your people before you were doing it. Your kings and officials were doing it too. So were the rest of the people in the land.

[22]"The LORD couldn't put up with the evil things you were doing anymore. He hated the things you did. So people called down curses on your land. It became a dry and empty desert. No one lived there. And that's the way it still is today.

[23]"You have burned incense to other gods. You have sinned against the LORD. You haven't obeyed him or his law. You haven't followed his rules. You haven't lived up to the terms of the covenant he made with you. That's why all of this trouble has come on you. You have seen it with your own eyes."

[24]Then I spoke to all of the people. That included the women. I said, "All you people of Judah in Egypt, listen to the LORD's message. [25]The LORD who rules over all is the God of Israel. He says, 'You and your wives have done what you promised you would do. You said, "We will certainly keep the promises we made to the Queen of Heaven. We'll burn incense to her. We'll pour out drink offerings to her."'

"Go ahead then. Do what you said you would! Keep your promises! [26]But listen to the LORD's message. Listen, all you Jews living in Egypt. 'I take an oath in my own great name,' says the LORD. 'I promise that no one from Judah who lives anywhere in Egypt will ever again pray in my name. None of them will ever take an oath and say, "You can be sure that the LORD and King is alive."

[27]"'I am watching over them to do them harm and not good. The Jews in Egypt will die of war and hunger until all of them are destroyed. [28]Some will not be killed. They will return to Judah from Egypt. But they will be very few. Then all of the people of Judah who came to live in Egypt will know the truth. They will know whether what I say or what they say will come true.

[29]"'I will give you a miraculous sign that I will punish you in this place,' announces the LORD. 'Then you can be sure that my warnings of harm against you will come true.' [30]The LORD says, 'I am going to hand Pharaoh Hophra over to his enemies who want to take his life. In the same way, I handed King Zedekiah over to Nebuchadnezzar, the king of Babylonia. He was the enemy who wanted to take Zedekiah's life.'" Hophra was king of Egypt.

The LORD Speaks to Baruch

45 I, the prophet Jeremiah, talked to Baruch, the son of Neriah. It was in the fourth year that Jehoiakim, the son of Josiah, was king of Judah. But it was after Baruch had written down on a scroll the words I was telling him to write. I said, [2]"The LORD is the God of Israel. Baruch, he says to you, [3]'You have said, "How terrible it is for me! The LORD has added sorrow to my pain. I'm worn out from all of my groaning. I can't find any rest."'"

[4]The LORD said, "Tell Baruch, 'I say, "I will destroy what I have built up. I will pull up by the roots what I have planted. I will do it all through the earth. [5]So should you long for great things for yourself? Do not long for them. I will bring trouble on everyone," announces the LORD. "But no matter where you go, I will let you escape with your life."'"

The LORD's Message About the Nations

46 A message came to me from the LORD. It was about the nations.

A Message About Egypt

[2]Here is what the LORD says about Egypt.

Here is his message against the army of Pharaoh Neco. He was king of Egypt. Nebuchadnezzar, the king of Babylonia, won the battle over his

army. That happened at Carchemish on the Euphrates River. It was in the fourth year that Jehoiakim was king of Judah. He was the son of Josiah.
The message says,

3 "Egyptians, prepare your shields!
Prepare large and small shields alike!
March out for battle!
4 Get the horses and chariots ready to ride!
Take up your battle positions!
Put your helmets on!
Shine up your spears!
Put on your armor!
5 What do I see?
The Egyptians are terrified.
They are pulling back.
Their soldiers are losing.
They run away as fast as they can.
They do not look back.
There is terror on every side,"
announces the LORD.
6 "Those who run fast can't get away.
Those who are strong can't escape.
In the north by the Euphrates River
they trip and fall.
7 "Who is this that rises like the Nile River?
Who rises like rivers of rushing waters?
8 Egypt rises like the Nile River.
It rises like rivers of rushing waters.
Egypt says, 'I will rise and cover the earth.
I'll destroy cities and their people.'
9 Charge, you horses!
Drive fast, you chariot drivers!
March on, you soldiers!
March on, you men of Cush and Put who carry shields.
March on, you men of Lydia who draw bows.
10 But that day belongs to me.
I am the LORD who rules over all.
It is a day for me to pay back my enemies.
The sword will eat until it is satisfied.
It will drink until it has no more thirst for blood.
I am the Lord. I am the LORD who rules over all.
I will offer a sacrifice.
I will offer it in the land of the north
by the Euphrates River.

11 "People of Egypt,
go up to Gilead and get some healing lotion.
But no matter what you try, you will not be healed.
There isn't any healing for you.
12 The nations will hear about your shame.
Your cries of pain will fill the earth.
One soldier will trip over another.
Both of them will fall down together."

13 Nebuchadnezzar, the king of Babylonia, was coming to attack Egypt. Here is the message the LORD spoke to me about it. He said,

14 "Egyptians, here is what I want you to announce in your land.
Announce it in Migdol.
Also announce it in Memphis and Tahpanhes.
Say, 'Take up your battle positions! Get ready!
The sword eats up those who are around you.'
15 Why are your soldiers lying on the ground?
They can't stand, because I bring them down.
16 They will trip again and again.
They will fall over one another.
They will say, 'Get up. Let's go back home.
Let's return to our own people and our own lands.
Let's get away from the swords
that will bring us great harm.'
17 The Egyptian soldiers will cry out,
'Pharaoh is our king. But he's only a loud noise.
He has missed his chance to win the battle.'
18 "I am the King.
My name is The LORD Who Rules Over All.
Someone will come who is like Mount Tabor among the mountains.
He is like Mount Carmel by the Mediterranean Sea.
And that is just as sure as I am alive,"
announces the King.
19 "So pack your belongings, you who live in Egypt.
You will be taken away from your land.
Memphis will be completely destroyed.
Its buildings will be broken down.
No one will live there.

20 "Egypt is like a beautiful young cow.
But Nebuchadnezzar is coming against her from the north.
He will bite her like a fly.
21 Hired soldiers are in Egypt's army.
They are like fat calves.
All of them will turn and run away.
They will not hold their positions.
The day of trouble is coming on them.
The time for them to be punished is near.
22 The Egyptians will hiss like a snake that is trying to get away.
A powerful army will advance against them.
Their enemies will come against them with axes.
They will be like those who cut down trees.
23 Egypt is like a thick forest.
But they will chop it down,"
announces the LORD.
"There are more of them than there are locusts.
In fact, they can't even be counted.
24 The nation of Egypt will be put to shame.
It will be handed over to the people of the north."

25The LORD who rules over all is the God of Israel. He says, "I am about to punish Amon, the god
of Thebes. I will also punish Pharaoh. I will punish Egypt and its gods and kings. And I will punish those who depend on Pharaoh. 26I will hand
them over to those who are trying to kill them. I
will give them to Nebuchadnezzar, the king of
Babylonia, and his officers. But later, many people
will live in Egypt again as in times past,"
announces the LORD.

27"People of Jacob, do not be afraid.
You are my servant.
Israel, do not be terrified.
I will bring you safely out of a place far away.
I will bring your children back
from the land where they were taken.
Your people will have peace and security
again.
And no one will make them afraid.
28People of Jacob, do not be afraid.
You are my servant.
I am with you," announces the LORD.
"I will completely destroy all of the nations
among which I scatter you.
But I will not completely destroy you.
I will correct you. But I will be fair.
I will punish you in a way that is fair and
right."

A Message About the Philistines

47 A message came to me from the LORD. It was about the Philistines before Pharaoh attacked Gaza.

2The LORD said,

"The armies of Babylonia are like waters rising
in the north.
They will become a great flood.
They will flow over the land and everything
in it.
They will flow over the towns and those
who live in them.
The people will cry out.
All those who live in the land will sob.
3They will sob when they hear galloping horses.
They will sob at the noise of enemy
chariots.
They will sob at the rumble of their wheels.
Fathers will not even try to help their children.
Their hands will not be able to help them.
4The day has come
to destroy all of the Philistines.
The time has come to cut off all those
who could help Tyre and Sidon.
I am about to destroy the Philistines.
I will not leave anyone alive
who came from the coasts of Crete.
5The people of Gaza will be so sad
they will shave their heads.
And Ashkelon's people will be silent.
You who remain on the flatlands,
how long will you cut yourselves?
6"'Sword of the LORD!' you cry out.
'How long will it be until you rest?
Return to the place you came from.
Stop killing us! Be still!'
7But how can my sword rest
when I have given it a command?
I have ordered it
to attack Ashkelon and the Philistine coast."

A Message About Moab

48 Here is what the LORD says about Moab.

The LORD who rules over all is the God of Israel. He says,

"How terrible it will be for Nebo!
It will be destroyed.
Kiriathaim will be captured.
It will be put to shame.
Its fort will be broken down.
It will be put to shame.
2Moab will not be praised anymore.
In Heshbon people will plan its fall from
power.
They will say, 'Come. Let's put an end to
that nation.'
City of Madmen, you too will be silent because
you are sad.
My sword will hunt you down.
3Listen to the cries from Horonaim.
The town is being completely destroyed.
4Moab will be broken.
Her little ones will cry out.
5The people go up the road to Luhith.
They are sobbing bitterly as they go.
Loud cries are heard on the road down
to Horonaim.
People cry out because the town is being
destroyed.
6People of Moab run away! Run for your lives!
Become like a lonely bush in the desert.
7You trust in the things you can do.
You trust in your riches.
So you too will be taken away as prisoners.
Your god Chemosh will be carried away.
So will its priests and officials.
8The one who is going to destroy you
will come against every town.
Not even one of them will escape.
The valley and the high flatlands
will be destroyed.
I, the LORD, have spoken.
9Sprinkle salt all over Moab.
It will be completely destroyed.
Its towns will be a dry and empty desert.
No one will live in them.

10"May a person who is lazy when he does
my work
be under my curse!

May anyone who keeps his sword from killing
be under my curse!

11 "Moab has been at peace and rest from its
earliest days.
It is like wine that has not been shaken up.
It has not been poured from one jar to another.
Moab's people have not been taken away
from their land.
They are like wine that tastes as it always did.
Its smell has not changed at all.
12 But other days are coming,"
announces the LORD.
"At that time I will send people who pour wine
from jars.
They will pour Moab out like wine.
They will empty its jars.
They will smash its jugs.
13 Then Moab's people will be ashamed of their
god Chemosh.
They will be ashamed just as the people of
Israel were
when they trusted in their god at Bethel.

14 "How can you say, 'We are soldiers.
We are men who are brave in battle'?
15 Moab will be destroyed.
Its enemies will march into its towns.
Her finest young men will die in battle,"
announces the King.
His name is The LORD Who Rules Over All.
16 "The fall of Moab is near.
Its time of trouble will come quickly.
17 All you who live around it, sob over its people.
Be sad, you who know how famous
Moab is.
Say, 'Its powerful ruler's rod is broken!
His glorious staff is smashed.'

18 "Come down from your glorious city, you who
live in Dibon.
Come and sit on the thirsty ground.
The one who destroys your country
will come up and attack you.
Your enemies will destroy your cities
that have high walls around them.
19 Stand by the road and watch,
you who live in Aroer.
Ask the men who are running away.
Ask the women who are escaping.
Ask them, 'What has happened?'
20 Moab has been put to shame.
It has been destroyed.
Sob and cry out!
Tell everyone Moab has been destroyed.
Announce it by the Arnon River.
21 The high flatlands have been judged.
So have Holon, Jahzah and Mephaath.
22 Dibon, Nebo and Beth Diblathaim have been
judged.
23 So have Kiriathaim, Beth Gamul and Beth
Meon.
24 Kerioth and Bozrah have also been judged.
And so have all of the towns of Moab, far
and near alike.
25 Moab's power is gone.
Its strength is broken,"
announces the LORD.

26 "Moab's people think they are better
than I am.
So let their enemies make them drunk.
Let the people get sick and throw up.
Let them roll around in the mess they
have made.
Let people laugh at them.
27 Moab, you laughed at Israel, didn't you?
Were Israel's people caught among
robbers?
Is that why you shake your head at them?
Is that why you make fun of them
every time you talk about them?
28 Leave your towns,
you who live in Moab.
Go and live among the rocks.
Be like a dove that makes its nest
at the mouth of a cave.

29 "We have heard all about Moab's pride.
We have heard how very proud they are.
They think they are so much better than others.
Their pride reaches deep down inside their
hearts.
30 I know how rude they are.
But it will not get them anywhere,"
announces the LORD.
"Their bragging does not accomplish
anything.
31 So I cry out over Moab.
I cry for all of Moab's people.
I groan for the men of Kir Hareseth.
32 I sob over you as Jazer sobs,
you vines of Sibmah.
Your branches used to spread out.
They went all the way down to the
Dead Sea.
They reached as far as the sea of Jazer.
The one who destroys your country
has taken away your grapes and ripe fruit.
33 Joy has left your orchards.
Gladness is gone from your fields.
I have stopped the flow of juice from your
winepresses.
No one stomps on your grapes with shouts
of joy.
There are shouts.
But they are not shouts of joy.

34 "The sound of their cry rises from Heshbon.
It rises as far as Elealeh and Jahaz.
It rises from Zoar.
It goes all the way to Horonaim and Eglath
Shelishiyah.
Even the waters at Nimrim are dried up.

35 In Moab people sacrifice offerings on the high places.
They burn incense to their gods.
But I will put an end to those people,"
announces the LORD.
36 "Like a flute my heart sings a song of sadness for Moab.
It sings like a flute for the men of Kir Hareseth.
The wealth they had gotten is gone.
37 Every head is shaved.
Every beard is cut off.
Every hand is cut.
And every waist is covered with black cloth.
38 Sobbing is the only sound in Moab.
It is heard on all of its roofs.
It is heard in the market places.
I have broken Moab
like a jar that no one wants,"
announces the LORD.
39 "How broken Moab is! How the people sob!
They turn away from others
because they are so ashamed.
All those who are around them laugh at them.
They are shocked at them."

40 The LORD says,

"Look! Nebuchadnezzar is like an eagle diving down.
He is spreading his wings over Moab.
41 Kerioth will be captured.
Its forts will be taken.
At that time the hearts of Moab's soldiers will tremble in fear.
They will be like the heart of a woman having a baby.
42 Moab will be destroyed as a nation.
That is because its people thought
they were better than I am.
43 You people of Moab,"
announces the LORD,
"terror, a pit and a trap are waiting for you.
44 Anyone who runs away from the terror
will fall into the pit.
Anyone who climbs out of the pit
will be caught in the trap.
The time is coming
when I will punish Moab,"
announces the LORD.
45 "In the shadow of Heshbon
those who are trying to escape stand helpless.
A fire has blazed out from Heshbon.
Flames have come out from Sihon's city.
It burns the foreheads of Moab's people.
It burns the skulls of those who brag loudly.
46 How terrible it will be for you, Moab!
Those who worship Chemosh are destroyed.
Your sons are being taken to another country.
Your daughters are taken away as prisoners.
47 "But in days to come
I will bless Moab with great success again,"
announces the LORD.

That's the report about how the LORD said he would judge Moab.

A Message About Ammon

49 Here is what the LORD says about the people of Ammon.

He says,

"Doesn't Israel have any sons?
Doesn't Israel have anyone
to take over the family property?
Then why has the god Molech taken over Gad?
Why do those who worship him live in its towns?
2 But a new day is coming,"
announces the LORD.
"At that time I will sound the battle cry.
I will sound it against Rabbah in the land of Ammon.
It will become a pile of broken-down buildings.
The villages that are around it will be set on fire.
Then Israel will drive out
those who drove her out,"
says the LORD.
3 "Heshbon, sob over Ai! It is destroyed!
Cry out, you who live in Rabbah!
Put on black clothes and sob.
Run here and there inside the walls.
Your god Molech will be carried away.
So will its priests and officials.
4 Why do you brag about your valleys?
You brag that they produce so many crops.
You are an unfaithful country.
You trust in your riches. You say,
'Who will attack me?'
5 I will bring terror on you.
It will come from all those who are around you,"
announces the Lord. He is the LORD who rules over all.
"Every one of you will be driven away.
No one will bring back those who escape.
6 "But after that, I will bless the people of Ammon
with great success again,"
announces the LORD.

A Message About Edom

7 Here is what the LORD says about Edom.

The LORD who rules over all says,

"Isn't there wisdom in the town of Teman anymore?
Can't those who are wise give advice?
Has their wisdom disappeared completely?

8 Turn around and run away, you who live
in Dedan.
Hide in deep caves.
I will bring trouble on Esau's family line.
I will do it at the time I punish them.
9 Edom, suppose grape pickers came to harvest
your vines.
They would still leave a few grapes.
Suppose robbers came at night.
They would steal only as much as they
wanted.
10 But I will strip everything away from
Esau's people.
I will uncover their hiding places.
They will not be able to hide anywhere.
Their children, relatives and neighbors
will die.
Then Esau's people will be gone.
11 Leave your children whose fathers have died.
I will watch over them.
Your widows can also trust in me."

12 The LORD says, "What if those who do not
have to drink the cup must drink it anyway? Then
shouldn't you be punished? You will certainly be
punished. You must drink the cup. 13 I make a
promise with an oath in my own name. Bozrah
will be destroyed," announces the LORD. "People
will be shocked at it. They will bring shame on it.
They will call down curses on it. And all of its
towns will be destroyed forever."

14 I've heard a message from the LORD.
A messenger was sent to the nations. The
LORD told him to say,
"Gather yourselves together to attack Edom!
Prepare for battle!"
15 The LORD says to Edom, "I will make you
weak among the nations.
They will look down on you.
16 You live in the safety of the rocks.
You live on top of the hills.
But the terror you stir up has now turned
against you.
Your proud heart has tricked you.
You build your nest as high as an eagle does.
But I will bring you down from there,"
announces the LORD.
17 "People of Edom,
all those who pass by you will be shocked.
They will make fun of you
because of all of your wounds.
18 Sodom and Gomorrah were destroyed.
So were the towns that were near them,"
says the LORD.
"You will be just like them.
No one will live in your land.
No one will stay there even for a short time.

19 "I will be like a lion coming up
from the bushes by the Jordan River.
I will hunt in rich grasslands.
I will chase you from your land in an instant.
What nation will I choose to do it?
Which one will I appoint?
Is anyone like me?
Who would dare to argue with me?
What leader can stand against me?"
20 So listen to what the LORD has planned
against the people of Edom.
Hear what he has planned against those who
live in Teman.
Edom's young people will be dragged away.
The LORD will completely destroy
their grasslands because of them.
21 When the earth hears Edom fall, it will shake.
The people's cries will be heard all the way
to the Red Sea.
22 Look! An enemy is coming.
It's like an eagle diving down.
It will spread its wings over Bozrah.
At that time the hearts of Edom's soldiers
will tremble in fear.
They'll be like the heart of a woman having
a baby.

A Message About Damascus

23 Here is what the LORD says about Damascus.
He says,

"The people of Hamath and Arpad are terrified.
They have heard bad news.
They have lost all hope.
They are troubled like the rolling sea.
24 The people of Damascus have become weak.
They have turned to run away.
Panic has taken hold of them.
Suffering and pain have taken hold of them.
Their pain is like the pain of a woman
having a baby.
25 Why hasn't the famous city been deserted?
It is the town I take delight in.
26 You can be sure its young men will fall dead in
the streets.
All of its soldiers will be put to death at
that time,"
announces the LORD
who rules over all.
27 "I will set the walls of Damascus on fire.
It will burn up the strong towers of King
Ben-Hadad."

A Message About Kedar and Hazor

28 Here is what the LORD says about the land of
Kedar and the kingdoms of Hazor. Nebuchadnezzar,
the king of Babylonia, was planning to attack them.

The LORD says to the armies of Babylonia,

"Prepare for battle. Attack Kedar.
Destroy the people of the east.
29 Their tents and flocks will be taken away
from them.
Their tents will be carried off.
All of their goods and camels will be stolen.
People will shout to them,
'There is terror on every side!'

30 "Run away quickly!
You who live in Hazor, stay in deep caves,"
announces the LORD.
"Nebuchadnezzar, the king of Babylonia,
has made plans against you.
He has decided to attack you.

31 "Armies of Babylonia, prepare for battle.
Attack a nation that feels secure.
Its people do not have any worries,"
announces the LORD.
"That nation does not have gates or heavy metal bars.
Its people live all alone.
32 Their camels will be stolen.
Their large herds will be taken away.
I will scatter to the winds those who are in places far away.
I will bring trouble on them from every side,"
announces the LORD.
33 "Hazor will become a home for wild dogs.
It will be a dry and empty desert forever.
No one will live in that land.
No one will stay there even for a short time."

A Message About Elam

34 A message came to me from the LORD. It was about Elam. It came shortly after Zedekiah became king of Judah.

35 The LORD who rules over all said,

"Elam's bow is the secret of its strength.
But I will break it.
36 I will bring the four winds against Elam.
I will bring them from all four directions.
I will scatter Elam's people to the four winds.
They will be taken away
to every nation on earth.
37 I will use Elam's enemies to smash them.
Those who are trying to take their lives will kill them.
I will bring trouble on Elam's people.
My anger will burn against them,"
announces the LORD.
"I will chase them with swords.
I will hunt them down
until I have destroyed them.
38 I will set up my throne in Elam.
I will destroy its king and officials,"
announces the LORD.

39 "But in days to come I will bless Elam
with great success again,"
announces the LORD.

A Message About Babylonia

50 Here is the message the LORD spoke through me about the city of Babylon and the land of Babylonia. He said,

2 "Announce this message among the nations.
Lift up a banner.
Let the nations hear the message.
Do not keep anything back.
Say, 'Babylon will be captured.
The god Bel will be put to shame.
Marduk will be filled with terror.
Babylon's gods will be put to shame.
The gods its people made will be filled with terror.'
3 A nation from the north will attack it.
That nation will destroy Babylonia.
No one will live there.
People and animals alike will run away.

4 "A new day is coming,"
announces the LORD.
"At that time the people of Israel and Judah will gather together.
They will come in tears to me.
I am the LORD their God.
5 They will ask how to get to Zion.
Then they will turn their faces toward it.
They will come and join themselves to me.
They will enter into the covenant I make with them.
It will last forever.
It will never be forgotten.

6 "My people have been like lost sheep.
Their shepherds have led them down the wrong path.
They have caused them to wander in the mountains.
They have wandered over mountains and hills.
They have forgotten that I am their true resting place.
7 Everyone who found them destroyed them.
Their enemies said, 'We aren't guilty.
They sinned against the LORD.
He gave them everything they needed.
He has always been Israel's hope.'

8 "People of Judah, run away from Babylon.
Leave the land of Babylonia.
Be like the goats that lead the flock.
9 I will stir up great nations
that will join forces against Babylon.
I will bring them from the land of the north.
They will take up their battle positions against Babylon.
They will come from the north and capture it.
Their arrows will be like skilled soldiers.
They will not miss their mark.
10 So the riches of Babylonia will be taken away.
All those who steal from it will have more than enough,"
announces the LORD.

11 "People of Babylonia, you have stolen what belongs to me.
That has made you glad and full of joy.

You dance around like a young cow on a
threshing floor.
You neigh like stallions.
12 Because of that, you will bring great shame on
your land.
Your whole nation will be dishonored.
It will become the least important of the
nations.
It will become a dry and empty desert.
13 Because I am angry with it, no one will
live there.
It will be completely deserted.
All those who pass by it will be shocked.
They will make fun of it because of all of
its wounds.

14 "All you who draw the bow,
take up your battle positions around
Babylon.
Shoot at it! Do not spare any arrows!
Its people have sinned against me.
15 Shout against them on every side!
They are giving up.
The towers of the city are falling.
Its walls are being pulled down.
I am paying its people back.
So pay them back yourselves.
Do to them what they have done
to others.
16 Do not leave anyone in Babylonia to plant
the fields.
Do not leave anyone to harvest the
grain.
Let each of them return to his own people.
Let him run away to his own land.
If he doesn't, his enemy's sword will bring
him great harm.
17 "Israel is like a scattered flock
that lions have chased away.
The first lion that ate them up
was the king of Assyria.
The last one that broke their bones
was Nebuchadnezzar, the king of
Babylonia."

18 The LORD who rules over all is the God of Israel. He says,

"I punished the king of Assyria.
In the same way, I will punish
the king of Babylonia and his land.
19 But I will bring Israel back to their own
grasslands.
I will feed them on Mount Carmel and
in Bashan.
I will satisfy their hunger
on the hills of Ephraim and Gilead.
20 A new day is coming,"
announces the LORD.
"At that time people will search for Israel's
guilt.
But they will not find any.
They will search for Judah's sins.
But they will not find any.
That is because I will forgive the people I
have spared.

21 "Enemies of Babylonia, attack their land of
Merathaim.
Make war against those who live in Pekod.
Chase them and kill them. Destroy them
completely,"
announces the LORD.
"Do everything I have commanded you
to do.
22 The noise of battle is heard in the land.
It is the noise of a great city being
destroyed!
23 It has been broken to pieces.
It was the hammer that broke the whole
earth.
How empty Babylonia is among the nations!
24 Babylonia, I set a trap for you.
And you were caught before you knew it.
You were found and captured.
That is because you opposed me.
25 I have opened up my storeroom.
I have brought out the weapons I use when I
am angry.
I am the LORD and King who rules over all.
I have work to do in the land of the
Babylonians.
26 So come against it from far away.
Open up its storerooms.
Stack everything up like piles of grain.
Completely destroy that country.
Do not leave anyone alive there.
27 Kill all of its people.
Let them die in battle.
How terrible it will be for them!
Their time to be judged has come.
Now they will be punished.
28 Listen to those who have escaped.
Listen to those who have returned from
Babylonia.
They are announcing in Zion
how I have paid Babylonia back.
I have paid it back for destroying my
temple.

29 "Send for men who are armed with bows
and arrows.
Send them against Babylon.
Set up camp all around it.
Do not let anyone escape.
Pay it back for what its people have done.
Do to them what they have done to others.
They have dared to disobey me.
I am the Holy One of Israel.
30 You can be sure its young men will fall dead
in the streets.
All of its soldiers will be put to death at
that time,"
announces the LORD.

[31] "Proud Babylonians, I am against you,"
announces the Lord.
The Lord who rules over all says,
"Your day to be judged has come.
It is time for you to be punished.
[32] You proud people will trip and fall.
No one will help you up.
I will start a fire in your towns.
It will burn up everyone who is around you."

[33] The Lord who rules over all says,

"The people of Israel are being treated badly.
So are the people of Judah.
Those who have captured them are holding them.
They refuse to let them go.
[34] But I am strong and will save them.
My name is The Lord Who Rules Over All.
I will stand up for them.
I will bring peace and rest to their land.
But I will bring trouble to those who live in Babylonia.

[35] "A sword is coming against the Babylonians!"
announces the Lord.
"It is coming against those who live in Babylonia.
It is coming against their officials and wise men.
[36] A sword is coming against their prophets.
But they are not really prophets at all!
So they will look foolish.
A sword is coming against their soldiers!
They will be filled with terror.
[37] A sword is coming against their horses and chariots!
It is coming against all of the hired soldiers in their armies.
They will become like weak women.
A sword is coming against their treasures!
They will be stolen.
[38] There will not be any rain for their rivers.
So they will dry up.
Those things will happen because their land is full of statues of gods.
Those gods will go crazy with terror.

[39] "Desert creatures and hyenas will live in Babylon.
And so will owls.
People will never live there again.
It will not be lived in for all time to come.
[40] I destroyed Sodom and Gomorrah.
I also destroyed the towns that were near them,"
announces the Lord.
"Babylonia will be just like them.
No one will live there.
No one will stay there even for a short time.

[41] "Look! An army is coming from the north.
I am stirring up a great nation and many kings.
They are coming from a land that is very far away.
[42] Their soldiers are armed with bows and spears.
They are mean.
They do not show any mercy at all.
They come riding in on their horses.
They sound like the roaring ocean.
They are lined up for battle.
They are coming to attack you, city of Babylon.
[43] The king of Babylonia has heard reports about them.
His hands can't help him.
He is in great pain.
It is like the pain of a woman having a baby.
[44] I will be like a lion coming up from the bushes by the Jordan River.
I will hunt in rich grasslands.
I will chase the people of Babylon from their land in an instant.
What nation will I choose to do it?
Which one will I appoint?
Is anyone like me? Who would dare to argue with me?
What leader can stand against me?"
[45] So listen to what the Lord has planned against Babylon.
Hear what he has planned against the land of the Babylonians.
Their young people will be dragged away.
The Lord will completely destroy their grasslands because of them.
[46] When the earth hears that Babylonia has been captured,
it will shake.
The people's cries will be heard among the nations.

51

The Lord says,

"I will stir up the spirits of destroyers.
They will march out against Babylonia and its people.
[2] I will send other nations against it
to separate the straw from the grain.
I will send them to destroy Babylonia completely.
They will oppose it on every side.
At that time it will be destroyed.
[3] Do not let its soldiers get their bows ready to use.
Do not let them put on their armor.
Do not spare their young men.
Destroy their armies completely.
[4] They will fall down dead in Babylon.
They will receive deadly wounds in its streets.

5 The land of Israel and Judah is full of guilt.
Its people have sinned against me.
But I have not deserted them. I am their God.
I am the LORD who rules over all.
I am the Holy One of Israel.
6 "People of Judah, run away from Babylonia!
Run for your lives!
Do not be destroyed because of the sins of its people.
It is time for me to pay them back.
I will punish them for what they have done.
7 Babylon was like a gold cup in my hand.
That city made the whole earth drunk.
The nations drank its wine.
So now they have gone crazy.
8 Babylon will suddenly fall and be broken.
Sob over it!
Get healing lotion for its pain.
Perhaps it can be healed.

9 "The nations say, 'We would have healed Babylon.
But it can't be healed.
So let's leave it. Let's each go to our own land.
Babylon's sins reach all the way to the skies.
They rise up as high as the clouds.'

10 "The people of Judah say,
'The LORD has made things right for us again.
So come. Let's tell in Zion
what the LORD our God has done.'
11 "I have stirred up you kings of the Medes.
So sharpen your arrows!
Get your shields!
I plan to destroy Babylon.
I will pay the Babylonians back.
They have destroyed my temple.
12 Lift up a banner! Attack Babylon's walls!
Put more guards on duty!
Station more of them to watch over you!
Hide and wait to attack them!
I will do what I have planned.
I will do what I have decided to do
against the people of Babylon.
13 You who live by the rivers of Babylon,
your end has come.
You who are rich in treasures,
it is time for you to be destroyed.
14 I am the LORD who rules over all.
I have made a promise with an oath in my own name.
I have said, 'I will certainly fill your land with soldiers.
They will be as many as a huge number of locusts.
They will win the battle over you.
They will shout for joy.'

15 "I used my power to make the earth.
I used my wisdom to set the world in place.
I used my understanding to spread the heavens out.
16 When I thunder, the waters in the heavens roar.
I make clouds rise from one end of the earth to the other.
I send lightning with the rain.
I bring out the wind from my storerooms.

17 "No one has any sense.
No one knows anything.
Everyone who works with gold is put to shame
by his wooden gods.
His metal gods are fakes.
They can't even breathe.
18 They are worthless. People make fun of them.
When I judge them, they will be destroyed.
19 I am not like them. I am the God of Jacob.
I give my people everything they need.
I can do it because I made everything, including Israel.
It is the nation that belongs to me.
My name is The LORD Who Rules Over All.

20 "Babylonia, you are my war club.
You are my weapon for battle.
I use you to destroy nations.
I use you to wipe out kingdoms.
21 I use you to destroy horses and their riders.
I use you to destroy chariots and their drivers.
22 I use you to destroy men and women.
I use you to destroy old people and young people.
I use you to destroy young men and young women.
23 I use you to destroy shepherds and their flocks.
I use you to destroy farmers and their oxen.
I use you to destroy governors and officials.

24 "Judah, I will pay Babylon back. You will see it with your own eyes. I will pay back all those who live in Babylonia. I will pay them back for all of the wrong things they have done in Zion," announces the LORD.

25 "Babylonia, I am against you.
Your kingdom is like a destroying mountain.
You have destroyed the whole earth,"
announces the LORD.
"I will reach out my hand against you.
I will roll you off the cliffs.
I will make you like a mountain that has been burned up.
26 No rock will be taken from you to be used
as the most important stone for a building.
No stones will be taken from you
to be used for a foundation.
Your land will be empty forever,"
announces the LORD.

27 "Nations, lift up a banner in the land of
Babylonia!
Blow a trumpet among yourselves!
Prepare yourselves for battle against
Babylonia.
Send the kingdoms
of Ararat, Minni and Ashkenaz against it.
Appoint a commander against it.
Send many horses against it.
Let them be as many as a huge number of
locusts.
28 Prepare yourselves for battle against
Babylonia.
Prepare the kings of the Medes.
Prepare their governors and all of their
officials.
Prepare all of the countries they
rule over.
29 The Babylonians tremble and shake
with fear.
My plans against them stand firm.
I plan to destroy their land completely.
Then no one will live there.
30 Babylon's soldiers have stopped fighting.
They remain in their forts.
Their strength is all gone.
They have become like weak women.
Their buildings are set on fire.
The heavy metal bars on their gates
are broken.
31 One messenger after another
comes to the king of Babylonia.
All of them announce that
his entire city is captured.
32 The places where people go across the
Euphrates River have been captured.
The swamps have been set on fire.
And the soldiers are terrified."

33 The LORD who rules over all is the God of Israel. He says,

"The city of Babylon is like a threshing floor
when cattle are walking on it.
The time to destroy it will soon come."

34 The people of Jerusalem say,
"Nebuchadnezzar, the king of Babylonia,
has destroyed us.
He has thrown us into a panic.
He has emptied us out like a jar.
Like a snake he has swallowed us up.
He has filled his stomach with our
rich food.
Then he has spit us out of his mouth."
35 The people continue, "May the people of
Babylon
pay for the harmful things they have done
to us.
May those who live in Babylonia
pay for spilling the blood of our people."
That's what the people who live in Zion say.

36 So the LORD says,

"I will stand up for you.
I will pay the Babylonians back for what
they did to you.
I will dry up their water supply.
I will make their springs run dry.
37 Babylon will have all of its buildings
knocked down.
It will be a home for wild dogs.
No one will live there.
People will be shocked at it.
They will make fun of it.
38 All of its people roar like young lions.
They growl like lion cubs.
39 They are stirred up.
So I will set a big dinner in front
of them.
I will make them drunk.
And they will shout and laugh.
But then they will lie down and die.
They will never wake up,"
announces the LORD.
40 "I will lead them down like lambs to be put to
death.
They will be like rams and goats that have
been killed.

41 "Babylon will be captured!
The whole earth was very proud of it.
But it will be taken over by others!
The nations will be shocked when it falls.
42 Babylon's enemies will sweep over it like
an ocean.
Like roaring waves they will cover it.
43 The towns of Babylonia will be empty.
It will become a dry and desert land.
No one will live there.
No one will even travel through it.
44 I will punish the god Bel in Babylon.
I will make Bel spit out what it has
swallowed.
The nations will not come and worship
it anymore.
And Babylon's walls will fall down.

45 "Come out of there, my people!
Run for your lives!
Run away from my burning anger.
46 You will hear about terrible things
that are happening in Babylonia.
But do not lose hope. Do not be afraid.
You will hear one thing this year.
And you will hear something else
next year.
You will hear about awful things in the land.
You will hear about one ruler fighting
against another.
47 I will punish the gods of Babylon.
That time will certainly come.
Then the whole land will be full of shame.
Its people will lie down and die there.

48 So heaven and earth and everything in them
will shout for joy.
They will be glad because of what will
happen to Babylon.
Armies will attack it from the north.
And they will destroy it,"
announces the LORD.

49 "Babylon's people have killed my people
Israel.
They have also killed people all over
the earth.
So now Babylon itself must fall.
50 You who have not been killed in the war
against Babylon,
leave! Do not wait!
In a land far away remember me.
And think about Jerusalem."

51 The people of Judah reply, "No one honors
us anymore.
People make fun of us.
Our faces are covered with shame.
People from other lands have entered
the holy places of the LORD's house."

52 "But a new day is coming," announces the
LORD.
"At that time I will punish the gods of
Babylon.
And all through its land
wounded people will groan.
53 What if Babylon reached all the way to
the sky?
What if it made its high walls even
stronger?
I would still send destroyers against it,"
announces the LORD.

54 "The noise of people screaming comes from
Babylon.
A terrible sound comes from its land.
It is the sound of a mighty city being
destroyed.
55 I will destroy Babylon.
I will put an end to all of its noise.
Waves of enemies will sweep through it like
great waters.
The roar of their voices will fill the air.
56 A destroying army will come against
Babylon.
The soldiers in the city will be captured.
Their bows will be broken.
I am the LORD God who pays people back.
I will pay them back in full.
57 I will make Babylon's officials and wise
men drunk.
I will do the same thing to its governors,
officers and soldiers.
They will lie down and die. They will never
wake up,"
announces the King. His name is The LORD
Who Rules Over All.

58 The LORD who rules over all says,

"Babylon's thick walls will fall down flat.
Its high gates will be set on fire.
The nations wear themselves out for no reason
at all.
Their hard work will only be burned up in
the flames."

59 I gave a message to the staff officer Seraiah,
the son of Neriah. I told him to take it with him to
Babylon. He went there with Zedekiah, the king
of Judah. He left in the fourth year of Zedekiah's
rule. Neriah was the son of Mahseiah. 60 I had written about all of the trouble that would come on
Babylon. I had written it down on a scroll. It
included everything that had been recorded about
Babylon.

61 I said to Seraiah, "When you get to Babylon,
here's what I want you to do. Make sure that you
read all of these words out loud. 62 Then say,
'LORD, you have said you will destroy this place.
You have said that no people or animals will live
here. It will be empty forever.'

63 "Finish reading the scroll. Tie a stone to it.
Throw it into the Euphrates River. 64 Then say, 'In
the same way, Babylon will sink down. It will
never rise again. That is because I will bring such
horrible trouble on it. And its people will fall along
with it.'"

The words of Jeremiah end here.

Nebuchadnezzar Destroys Jerusalem

52 Zedekiah was 21 years old when he
became king. He ruled in Jerusalem for 11
years. His mother's name was Hamutal. She was
the daughter of Jeremiah. She was from Libnah.

2 Zedekiah did what was evil in the sight of the
LORD. He did just as Jehoiakim had done. 3 The
enemies of Jerusalem and Judah attacked them
because the LORD was angry. In the end he threw
them out of his land.

Zedekiah refused to obey the king of Babylonia.
4 Nebuchadnezzar was king of Babylonia. He
marched out against Jerusalem. All of his armies
went with him. It was in the ninth year of the rule
of Zedekiah. It was on the tenth day of the tenth
month. The armies set up camp outside the city.
They set up ladders and built ramps and towers all
around it. 5 It was surrounded until the 11th year of
King Zedekiah's rule.

6 By the ninth day of the fourth month, there
wasn't any food left in the city. So the people
didn't have anything to eat. 7 Then the Babylonians broke through the city wall.

Judah's whole army ran away. They left the city
at night. They went out through the gate between
the two walls that were near the king's garden.
They escaped even though the Babylonians surrounded the city. Judah's army ran toward the Arabah Valley.

8But the armies of Babylonia chased King Zedekiah. They caught up with him in the flatlands near Jericho. All of his soldiers were separated from him. They had scattered in every direction. 9The king was captured.

He was taken to the king of Babylonia at Riblah. Riblah was in the land of Hamath. That's where Nebuchadnezzar decided how he would be punished. 10At Riblah the king of Babylonia killed the sons of Zedekiah. He forced him to watch it with his own eyes. Nebuchadnezzar also killed all of the officials of Judah. 11Then he poked out Zedekiah's eyes. He put him in bronze chains. And he took him to Babylon. There he put Zedekiah in prison until the day he died.

12Nebuzaradan served the king of Babylonia. In fact, he was commander of the royal guard. He came to Jerusalem. It was in the 19th year that Nebuchadnezzar was king of Babylonia. It was on the tenth day of the fifth month.

13Nebuzaradan set the LORD's temple on fire. He also set fire to the royal palace and all of the houses in Jerusalem. He burned down every important building. 14The armies of Babylonia broke down all of the walls around Jerusalem. That's what the commander told them to do.

15Some of the poorest people still remained in the city along with the others. But the commander Nebuzaradan took them away as prisoners. He also took the rest of the skilled workers. That included the people who had joined the king of Babylonia. 16But Nebuzaradan left the rest of the poorest people of the land behind. He told them to work in the vineyards and fields.

17The armies of Babylonia destroyed the LORD's temple. They broke the bronze pillars into pieces. They broke up the bronze stands that could be moved around. And they broke up the huge bronze bowl. Then they carried all of the bronze away to Babylon.

18They also took away the pots, shovels, wick cutters, sprinkling bowls and dishes. They took away all of the bronze articles that were used for any purpose in the temple. 19The commander of the royal guard took away the bowls and the shallow cups for burning incense. He took away the sprinkling bowls, the pots, the lampstands and the dishes. He took away the bowls that were used for drink offerings. So he took away everything that was made out of pure gold or silver.

20The bronze was more than anyone could weigh. It included the bronze from the two pillars. It included the bronze from the huge bowl and the 12 bronze bulls that were under it. It also included the stands. King Solomon had made all of those things for the LORD's temple.

21Each of the pillars was 27 feet high and 18 feet around. The pillars were hollow. The metal in each of them was three inches thick. 22The bronze top of one pillar was seven and a half feet high. It was decorated with a set of bronze chains and pomegranates all around it. The other pillar was just like it. It also had pomegranates. 23There were 96 pomegranates on the sides of each of the two tops. The total number of pomegranates above the bronze chains around each top was 100.

24The commander of the guard took many prisoners. They included the chief priest Seraiah and the priest Zephaniah who was under him. They also included the three men who guarded the temple doors. 25Some people were still left in the city. The commander took as a prisoner the officer who was in charge of the fighting men. He took the seven men who gave advice to the king. He also took the secretary who was the chief officer in charge of getting the people of the land to serve in the army. And he took 60 of the secretary's men who were still in the city.

26The commander Nebuzaradan took all of them away. He brought them to the king of Babylonia at Riblah. 27There the king had them put to death. Riblah was in the land of Hamath.

So the people of Judah were taken as prisoners. They were taken far away from their own land. 28Here is the number of the people Nebuchadnezzar took to Babylon as prisoners.

In the seventh year of his rule, he took 3,023 Jews.
29 In his 18th year,
he took 832 people from Jerusalem.
30 In Nebuchadnezzar's 23rd year,
Nebuzaradan, the commander of the royal guard, took 745 Jews to Babylon.
The total number of people who were taken to Babylon was 4,600.

Jehoiachin Is Set Free

31Evil-Merodach set Jehoiachin, the king of Judah, free from prison. It was in the 37th year after Jehoiachin had been taken away to Babylon. It was also the year Evil-Merodach became king of Babylonia. It was on the 25th day of the 12th month. 32Evil-Merodach spoke kindly to Jehoiachin. He gave him a place of honor. Other kings were with Jehoiachin in Babylon. But his place was more important than theirs.

33So Jehoiachin put his prison clothes away. For the rest of Jehoiachin's life the king of Babylonia provided what he needed. 34The king did that for Jehoiachin day by day as long as he lived. He did it until the day Jehoiachin died.

Lamentations

1 The city of Jerusalem is so empty!
It used to be full of people.
But now it's like a woman whose husband
has died.
She used to be great among the nations.
She was like a queen among the kingdoms.
But now she is a slave.

2 Jerusalem sobs bitterly at night.
Tears run down her cheeks.
None of her friends comforts her.
All those who were going to help her
have turned against her.
They have become her enemies.

3 After Judah's people had suffered greatly,
they were taken away as prisoners.
Now they live among the nations.
They can't find any place to rest.
All those who were chasing them have caught
up with them.
And they can't get away.

4 The roads to Zion are empty.
No one travels to its appointed feasts.
All of the public places near its gates
are deserted.
Its priests groan.
Its young women are sad.
And Zion itself sobs bitterly.

5 Its enemies have become its masters.
They have an easy life.
The LORD has brought suffering to Jerusalem
because its people have committed so many
sins.
Its children have been taken away as prisoners.
Their enemies have forced them to leave
their homes.

6 The city of Zion used to be full of glory.
But now its glory has faded away.
Its princes are like deer.
They can't find anything to eat.
They are almost too weak to get away
from those who hunt them down.

7 Jerusalem's people are suffering and
wandering.
They remember all of the treasures
they used to have.
But they fell into the hands of their enemies.
And no one was there to help them.
Their enemies looked at them.
They laughed because Jerusalem had
been destroyed.

8 Its people have committed many sins.
They have become polluted.
All those who honored Jerusalem now look
down on it.
They look at it as if it were a naked woman.
The city groans and turns away in shame.

9 Her skirts are dirty.
She didn't think about how things might
turn out.
Her fall from power amazed everyone.
And no one was there to comfort her.
She said, "LORD, please pay attention to how
much I'm suffering.
My enemies have won the battle over me."

10 Jerusalem's enemies took away
all of its treasures.
Its people saw strangers
enter its temple.
The LORD had commanded them
not to do that.

11 All of Jerusalem's people groan
as they search for bread.
They trade their treasures for food
just to stay alive.
They say, "LORD, look at us.
Think about our condition.
Everyone looks down on us."

12 They also say, "All of you who are passing by,
don't you care about what has happened
to us?
Just look at our condition.
Has anyone suffered the way we have?
The LORD has brought all of this on us.
He has made us suffer.
His anger has burned against us.

13 "He sent fire down from heaven.
It went deep down into our very bones.
He spread a net to catch us by the feet.
He stopped us right where we were.
He made our city empty.
We are sick all the time.

14 "We must carry the heavy load of our sins.
He tied it on us with his hands.
Our sins are heavy on our necks.
The Lord has taken away our strength.
He has handed us over to our enemies.
We can't win the battle over them.

15 "The Lord has refused to accept
any of our soldiers.
He has sent for an army
to crush our young men.
We are like grapes in the Lord's winepress.
He has stomped on us,
even though we are his very own people.

16 "That's why we are sobbing.
Tears are flowing from our eyes.
No one is near to comfort us.
No one can heal our spirits.
Our children don't have anything.
Our enemies are much too strong for us."

17 Zion reaches out its hands.
But no one is there to comfort its people.
The LORD has ordered that
the neighbors of Jacob's people would
become their enemies.
Jerusalem has become polluted
among them.

18 Its people say, "The LORD always does what
is right.
But we refused to obey his commands.
Listen, all of you nations.
Pay attention to how much we're suffering.
Our young women and young men
have been taken away as prisoners.

19 "We called out to those who were going
to help us.
But they turned against us.
Our priests and elders
died in the city.
They were searching for food
just to stay alive.

20 "LORD, see how upset we are!
We are suffering deep down inside.
Our hearts are troubled.
Again and again we have refused to
obey you.
Outside the city, people are being killed
with swords.
Inside, there is nothing but death.

21 "People have heard us groan.
But no one is here to comfort us.
Our enemies have heard about all of
our troubles.
What you have done makes them happy.
So please judge them, just as you said
you would.
Let them become like us.

22 "Please pay attention to all of their sinful ways.
Punish them as you have punished us.
You judged us because we had committed
so many sins.
We groan all the time.
And our hearts are weak."

2 See how the Lord covered the city of Zion
with the cloud of his anger!
He threw Israel's glory down
from heaven to earth.
When he was angry, he turned his back
on his own city.

2 Without pity the Lord swallowed up
all of the homes of Jacob's people.
When he was angry, he tore down
the forts of the people of Judah.
He brought their kingdom and its princes
down to the ground in dishonor.

3 When he burned with anger,
he took away Israel's power.
He pulled back his powerful right hand
as the enemy approached.
His burning anger blazed out in Jacob's land.
It burned up everything that was near it.

4 Like an enemy the Lord got his bow ready
to use.
He had a sword in his right hand.
Like an enemy he destroyed
everything that used to be pleasing to him.
His anger blazed out like fire.
It burned up the homes in the city of Zion.

5 The Lord was like an enemy.
He swallowed up Israel.
He swallowed up all of its palaces.
He destroyed its forts.
He filled the people of Judah
with sorrow and sadness.

6 The LORD's temple was like a garden.
But he completely destroyed it.
He destroyed the place
where he used to meet with his people.
He made Zion's people forget
their appointed feasts and Sabbath days.
When he was very angry, he turned his
back on
king and priest alike.

7 The Lord deserted his altar.
He left his temple.
He handed the walls of Jerusalem's palaces
over to its enemies.
They shouted loudly in the house of the LORD.
You would have thought it was the day
of an appointed feast.

8 The LORD decided to tear down
the walls around the city of Zion.
He measured out what he wanted to destroy.
Then he destroyed it with his powerful
hand.
He made even its towers and walls sing songs
of sadness.
All of them fell down.

9 Its gates sank down into the ground.
He broke their metal bars and destroyed
them.
Its king and princes were taken away to
other nations.
There is no law anymore.
Jerusalem's prophets no longer receive
visions from the LORD.

10 The elders of the city of Zion
sit silently on the ground.

They have sprinkled dust on their heads.
They've put on black clothes to show how sad they are.
The young women of Jerusalem
have bowed their heads toward the ground.

11 I've cried so much I can't see very well.
I'm suffering deep down inside.
My heart is broken
because my people are destroyed.
Children and babies are fainting
in the streets of the city.

12 They say to their mothers,
"Where can we find something to eat and drink?"
They faint like wounded soldiers
in the streets of the city.
Their lives are slipping away
in their mothers' arms.

13 City of Jerusalem, what can I say about you?
What can I compare you to?
People of Zion, what are you like?
I want to comfort you.
Your wound is as deep as the ocean.
Who can heal you?

14 The visions of your prophets were lies.
They weren't worth anything.
They didn't show you the sins you had committed.
So that's why you were captured.
The messages they gave you were lies.
They led you down the wrong path.

15 All those who pass by
clap their hands and make fun of you.
They laugh at you and shake their heads
at the city of Jerusalem.
They say, "Could that be the city
that was called perfect and beautiful?
Is that the city that brought joy to everyone on earth?"

16 All of your enemies open their mouths
wide against you.
They laugh at you and grind their teeth.
They say, "We have swallowed Jerusalem's people up.
This is the day we've waited for.
And we've lived to see it."

17 The LORD has done what he planned to do.
He has made what he said come true.
He gave the command long ago.
He has destroyed you without pity.
He has let your enemies laugh at you.
He has made them stronger than you are.

18 People in the city of Zion,
cry out from your heart to the Lord.
Let your tears flow like a river
day and night.
Don't stop at all.
Don't give your eyes any rest.

19 Get up. Cry out as the night begins.
Tell the Lord all of your troubles.
Lift up your hands to him.
Pray that the lives of your children will be spared.
At every street corner they faint
because they are so hungry.

20 Jerusalem says, "LORD, look at me.
Think about my condition.
Have you ever treated anyone else like this?
Should women have to eat their babies?
Should they eat the children they've taken care of?
Should priests and prophets be killed
in your own temple?

21 "Young people and old people alike
lie dead in the dust of my streets.
My young women and young men
have been killed with swords.
You killed them when you were angry.
You put them to death without pity.

22 "You sent for terrors to come against me on every side.
It was as if you were inviting people to enjoy a feast day.
Because you were angry, no one escaped.
No one was left alive.
I took good care of my children and brought them up.
But my enemies have destroyed them."

3 I am a man who has suffered greatly.
The LORD has used the Babylonians
to punish our people.
2 He has driven me away. He has made me walk
in darkness instead of light.
3 He has turned his powerful hand against me.
He has done it again and again, all day long.

4 He has worn my body out.
He has broken my bones.
5 He has surrounded me and attacked me.
He has made me suffer bitterly.
He has made things hard for me.
6 He has made me live in darkness
like those who are dead and gone.

7 He has built walls around me. I can't escape.
He has put heavy chains on me.
8 I call out and cry for help.
But he won't listen to me when I pray.
9 He has put up a stone wall to block my way.
He has made my paths crooked.

10 He has been like a bear waiting to attack me.
He has been like a lion hiding in the bushes.
11 He has dragged me off the path.
He has torn me to pieces.
And he has left me helpless.
12 He has gotten his bow ready to use.
He has shot his arrows at me.

[13] The arrows from his bag
have gone through my heart.
[14] My people laugh at me all the time.
They sing and make fun of me all day long.
[15] The LORD has made my life bitter.
He has made me suffer bitterly.

[16] He made me chew stones that broke my teeth.
He has walked all over me in the dust.
[17] I have lost all hope of ever having any peace.
I've forgotten what good times are like.
[18] So I say, "My glory has faded away.
My hope in the LORD is gone."

[19] I remember how I suffered and wandered.
I remember how bitter my life was.
[20] I remember it very well.
My spirit is very sad deep down inside me.
[21] But here is something else I remember.
And it gives me hope.

[22] The LORD loves us very much.
So we haven't been completely destroyed.
His loving concern never fails.
[23] His great love is new every morning.
LORD, how faithful you are!
[24] I say to myself, "The LORD is everything I will ever need.
So I will put my hope in him."

[25] The LORD is good to those who put their hope in him.
He is good to those who look to him.
[26] It is good when people wait quietly
for the LORD to save them.
[27] It is good for a man to carry a heavy load of suffering
while he is young.

[28] Let him sit alone and not say anything.
The LORD has placed that load on him.
[29] Let him bury his face in the dust.
There might still be hope for him.
[30] Let him turn his cheek toward those who would slap him.
Let him be filled with shame.

[31] The Lord doesn't turn his back
on people forever.
[32] He might bring suffering.
But he will also show loving concern.
How great his faithful love is!
[33] He doesn't want to bring pain
or suffering to people.

[34] Every time people crush prisoners under their feet,
the Lord knows all about it.
[35] When people refuse to give a man his rights,
the Most High God knows it.
[36] When people don't treat a man fairly,
the Lord knows it.

[37] Suppose people order something to happen.
It won't happen unless the Lord has planned it.
[38] Troubles and good things alike come to people
because the Most High God has commanded them to come.
[39] A man who is still alive shouldn't blame God
when God punishes him for his sins.

[40] Let's take a good look at the way we're living.
Let's return to the LORD.
[41] Let's lift up our hands to God in heaven.
Let's pray to him with all our hearts.
[42] Let's say, "We have sinned.
We've refused to obey you.
And you haven't forgiven us.

[43] "You have covered yourself with the cloud of your anger.
You have chased us.
You have killed our people without pity.
[44] You have covered yourself with the cloud of your anger.
Our prayers can't get through to you.
[45] You have made us become like trash and garbage
among the nations.

[46] "All of our enemies have opened their mouths wide
to swallow us up.
[47] We are terrified and trapped.
We are broken and destroyed."
[48] Streams of tears flow from my eyes.
That's because my people are destroyed.

[49] Tears will never stop flowing from my eyes.
My eyes can't get any rest.
[50] I'll sob until the LORD looks down from heaven.
I'll cry until he notices my tears.
[51] What I see brings pain to my spirit.
All of the people in my city are suffering so much.

[52] Those who were my enemies for no reason at all
hunted me down as if I were a bird.
[53] They tried to end my life
by throwing me into a deep pit.
They threw stones down at me.
[54] The water rose and covered my head.
I thought I was going to die.

[55] LORD, I called out to you.
I called out from the bottom of the pit.
[56] I prayed, "Please don't close your ears
to my cry for help."
And you heard my appeal.
[57] You came near when I called out to you.
You said, "Do not be afraid."

[58] Lord, you stood up for me in court.
You saved my life and set me free.
[59] LORD, you have seen the wrong things
people have done to me.
Stand up for me again!

[60] You have seen how my enemies
have tried to get even with me.
You know all about their plans against me.

[61] LORD, you have heard them laugh at me.
You know all about their plans against me.
[62] You have heard my enemies
whispering among themselves.
They speak against me all day long.
[63] Just look at them sitting and standing there!
They sing and make fun of me.

[64] LORD, pay them back.
Punish them for what their hands have done.
[65] Cover their minds with a veil.
Put a curse on them!
[66] LORD, get angry with them and hunt
them down.
Wipe them off the face of the earth.

4 Look at how the gold has lost its brightness!
See how dull the fine gold has become!
The sacred jewels are scattered
at every street corner.

[2] The priceless children of Zion
were worth their weight in gold.
But now they are thought of as clay pots
made by the hands of a potter.

[3] Even wild dogs
nurse their young pups.
But my people are as mean
as ostriches in the desert.

[4] When our babies get thirsty,
their tongues stick to the roofs of their
mouths.
When our children beg for bread,
no one gives them any.

[5] Those who once ate fine food
are dying in the streets.
Those who wore fancy clothes
are now lying on piles of trash.

[6] My people have been punished
more than Sodom was.
It was destroyed in a moment.
No one offered it a helping hand.

[7] Jerusalem's princes were brighter than snow.
They were whiter than milk.
Their bodies were redder than rubies.
They looked like sapphires.

[8] But now they are blacker than coal.
No one even recognizes them in the streets.
Their skin is wrinkled on their bones.
It has become as dry as a stick.

[9] Those who have been killed with swords are
better off
than those who have to die of hunger.
Those who are hungry waste away to nothing.
They don't have any food from the fields.

[10] With their own hands, loving mothers
have had to cook even their own children.
They ate their children
when my people were destroyed.

[11] The LORD has become very angry.
He has poured out his burning anger.
He started a fire in Zion.
It burned up the very foundations.

[12] The kings of the earth couldn't believe what
was happening.
Neither could any of the world's people.
Enemies actually attacked and entered
the gates of Jerusalem.

[13] It happened because Jerusalem's prophets
had sinned.
Its priests had done evil things.
All of them spilled the blood
of those who did what was right.

[14] Now those prophets and priests
have to feel their way along the streets
like people who are blind.
The blood of those they killed has made
them "unclean."
So no one dares even to touch their clothes.

[15] "Go away! You are 'unclean'!"
people cry out to them.
"Go away! Get out of here!
Don't touch us!"
So they run away and wander around.
Then people among the nations say,
"They can't stay here anymore."

[16] The LORD himself has scattered them.
He doesn't watch over them anymore.
No one shows the priests any respect.
No one honors the elders.

[17] And that's not all. Our eyes grew tired.
We looked for help that never came.
We watched from our towers.
We kept looking for a nation that couldn't
save us.

[18] People hunted us down no matter where
we went.
We couldn't even walk in our streets.
Our end was near. We only had a few days
to live.
Our end had come.

[19] Those who were hunting us down were faster
than eagles in the sky.
They chased us over the mountains.
They hid and waited for us in the desert.

[20] Zedekiah, the LORD's anointed king, was our
last hope.
But he was caught in their traps.
We thought he would keep us safe.
We expected to continue living among
the nations.

[21] People of Edom, be joyful.
You who live in the land of Uz, be glad.
But the cup of the LORD's anger will also be passed to you.
Then you will become drunk.
Your clothes will be stripped off.

[22] People of Zion, the time for you to be punished
will come to an end.
The LORD won't keep you away from your land any longer.
But he will punish your sin, people of Edom.
He will show you the evil things you have done.

5 LORD, think about what has happened to us.
Look at the shame our enemies have brought on us.
[2] The land you gave us has been turned over to outsiders.
Our homes have been given to strangers.
[3] Our fathers have been killed.
Our mothers don't have husbands.
[4] We have to buy the water we drink.
We have to pay for the wood we use.
[5] Those who chase us are right behind us.
We're tired. We can't get any rest.
[6] We put ourselves under the control of Egypt and Assyria
just to get enough bread.
[7] Our people before us sinned.
And they are now dead.
We are being punished because of their sins.
[8] Slaves rule over us.
No one can set us free
from their powerful hands.
[9] We put our lives in danger just to get some bread to eat.
Robbers in the desert might kill us with their swords.
[10] Our skin is as hot as an oven.
We are so hungry we're burning up with fever.
[11] Our women have been raped in Zion.
Our virgins have been raped in the towns of Judah.
[12] Our princes have been hung up by their hands.
No one shows our elders any respect.
[13] Our young men are forced to grind grain at the mill.
Our boys almost fall down
as they carry heavy loads of wood.
[14] Our elders don't go to the city gate anymore.
Our young men have stopped playing their music.
[15] There isn't any joy in our hearts.
Our dancing has turned into sobbing.
[16] All of our honor is gone.
How terrible it is for us! We have sinned.
[17] So our hearts are weak.
Our eyes can't see very clearly.
[18] Mount Zion has been deserted.
Wild dogs are prowling all around on it.
[19] LORD, you rule forever.
Your throne will last for all time to come.
[20] Why do you always forget us?
Why have you deserted us for so long?
[21] LORD, please bring us back to you.
Then we can return.
Make our lives like new again.
[22] Or have you completely turned away from us?
Are you really that angry with us?

Ezekiel

The LORD Gives Ezekiel Visions of His Glory

1 I was 30 years old. I was with my people who had been taken away from their country. We were by the Kebar River in the land of Babylonia. On the fifth day of the fourth month, the heavens were opened. I saw visions of God.

[2]It was the fifth day of the month. Jehoiachin had been king of Judah. It was the fifth year since he had been brought to Babylon as a prisoner. [3]A message came to me from the LORD. I was by the Kebar River in Babylonia. The LORD put his strong hand on me there. I am Ezekiel, the son of Buzi. I'm a priest.

[4]I looked up and saw a windstorm coming from the north. I saw a huge cloud. The fire of lightning was flashing out of it. Bright light surrounded it. The center of the fire looked like glowing metal.

[5]I saw in the fire something that looked like four living creatures. They appeared to have the shape of a man. [6]But each of them had four faces and four wings. [7]Their legs were straight. Their feet looked like the feet of a calf. They were as bright as polished bronze.

[8]The creatures had a man's hands under their wings on their four sides. All four of them had faces and wings. [9]Their wings touched one another. Each of the creatures went straight ahead. They didn't change their direction as they moved.

[10]Here's what their faces looked like. Each of the four creatures had a man's face. On the right side each had the face of a lion. On the left each had the face of an ox. Each one also had an eagle's face. [11]That's what their faces looked like.

Two of their wings were spread out and lifted up. Each one touched the wing of another creature on either side. The other two wings covered their bodies. [12]All of the creatures went straight ahead. Anywhere their spirits would lead them to go, they would go. They didn't change their direction as they went.

[13]The living creatures looked like burning coals of fire or like torches. Fire moved back and forth among the creatures. It was bright. Lightning flashed out of it. [14]The creatures raced back and forth like flashes of lightning.

[15]As I looked at the living creatures, I saw wheels on the ground beside them. Each creature had four faces. [16]Here's how the wheels looked and worked. They gleamed like chrysolite. All four of them looked alike. Each one seemed to be made like a wheel inside another wheel at right angles.

[17]The wheels could go in any one of the four directions the creatures faced. The wheels didn't change their direction as the creatures moved. [18]Their rims were high and terrifying. All four rims were full of eyes all the way around them.

[19]When the creatures moved, the wheels beside them moved. When the living creatures rose from the ground, the wheels also rose. [20]Anywhere their spirits would lead them to go, they would go. And the wheels would rise along with them. That's because the spirits of the living creatures were in the wheels.

[21]When the creatures moved, the wheels also moved. When the creatures stood still, they also stood still. When the creatures rose from the ground, the wheels rose along with them. That's because the spirits of the living creatures were in the wheels.

[22]Something that looked like a huge space was spread out above the heads of the living creatures. It gleamed like ice. It was terrifying. [23]The wings of the creatures were spread out under the space. They reached out toward one another. Each creature had two wings covering its body.

[24]When the creatures moved, I heard the sound of their wings. It was like the roar of rushing waters. It sounded like the thundering voice of the Mighty One. It was like the loud noise an army makes. When the creatures stood still, they lowered their wings.

[25]Then a voice came from above the huge space over their heads. They stood with their wings lowered. [26]Above the space over their heads was something that looked like a throne made out of sapphire.

On the throne high above was a figure that appeared to be human. [27]From his waist up he looked like glowing metal that was full of fire. From his waist down he looked like fire. Bright light surrounded him. [28]The glow around him looked like a rainbow in the clouds on a rainy day.

That's what the glory of the LORD looked like. When I saw it, I fell with my face toward the ground. Then I heard the voice of someone speaking.

The LORD Chooses Ezekiel

2 He said to me, "Son of man, stand up on your feet. I will speak to you." [2]As he spoke, the Spirit of the LORD came into me. He raised me to my feet. I heard him speaking to me.

[3]He said, "Son of man, I am sending you to the people of Israel. That nation has refused to obey me. They have turned against me. They and their people before them have been against me to this very day. [4]The people I am sending you to are very stubborn. Tell them, 'Here is what the LORD and King says.'

5"They might listen, or they might not. After all,
they refuse to obey me. But whether they listen or
not, they will know that a prophet was among
them.
6"Son of man, do not be afraid of them or of
what they say. Do not be afraid, even if thorns and
bushes are all around you and you live among
scorpions. Do not be afraid of what they say. Do
not be terrified by them. They always refuse to
obey me.
7"You must give them my message. They might
listen, or they might not. After all, they refuse to
obey me. 8Son of man, listen to what I tell you. Do
not be like those who refuse to obey me. Open
your mouth. Eat what I give you."
9Then I looked up. I saw a hand reach out to me.
A scroll was in it. 10He unrolled it in front of me.
Both sides had words written on them. They spoke
about sadness, sorrow and trouble.
3 He said to me, "Son of man, eat what is in
front of you. Eat this scroll. Then go and
speak to the people of Israel." 2So I opened my
mouth. And he gave me the scroll to eat.
3Then he said to me, "Son of man, eat this scroll
I am giving you. Fill your stomach with it." So I
ate it. And it tasted as sweet as honey in my mouth.
4Then he said to me, "Son of man, go to the
people of Israel. Give them my message.
5"I am not sending you to people who speak
another language that is hard to learn. Instead, I
am sending you to the people of Israel. 6You are
not being sent to many nations whose people
speak other languages that are hard to learn. You
would not be able to understand them. Suppose I
had sent you to them. Then they certainly would
have listened to you. 7But the people of Israel do
not want to listen to you. That is because they do
not want to listen to me.
"All of the people of Israel are very stubborn.
8But I will make you just as stubborn as they are.
9I will make you very brave. So do not be afraid
of them. Do not let them terrify you, even though
they refuse to obey me."
10He continued, "Son of man, listen carefully.
Take to heart everything I tell you. 11Go now to
your own people who were brought here as prisoners. Speak to them. Tell them, 'Here is what the
LORD and King says.' Speak to them whether they
listen or not."
12Then the Spirit of the LORD lifted me up. I
heard a loud rumbling sound behind me. May the
glory of the LORD be praised in the place where he
lives! 13The sound was made by the wings of the
living creatures. They were brushing against one
another. The sound was also made by the wheels
beside them. It was a loud rumbling sound.
14Then the Spirit lifted me up and took me
away. My spirit was bitter. I was burning with
anger. The strong hand of the LORD was on me. 15I
came to my people who had been brought as prisoners to Tel Abib. It was near the Kebar River. I
went to where they were living. There I sat among
them for seven days. I was shocked by everything
that had happened.

The LORD Warns Israel

16After seven days, a message came to me from
the LORD. 17He said, "Son of man, I have appointed
you as a prophet to warn the people of Israel. So
listen to my message. Give them a warning
from me.
18"Suppose I say to a sinful person, 'You can be
sure you will die.' And you do not warn him. You
do not try to get him to change his evil ways in
order to save his life. Then he will die because he
has sinned. And I will hold you accountable for his
death.
19"But suppose you do warn that sinful person.
And he does not turn away from his sin or his evil
ways. Then he will die because he has sinned. But
you will have saved yourself.
20"Or suppose a godly person turns away from
his godliness and does what is evil. And suppose I
put something in his way that will trip him up.
Then he will die. Since you did not warn him, he
will die for his sin. The godly things he did will
not be remembered. And I will hold you accountable for his death.
21"But suppose you do warn a godly person not
to sin. And he does not sin. Then you can be sure
that he will live because he listened to your warning. And you will have saved yourself."
22The strong hand of the LORD was on me. He
said, "Get up. Go out to the flatlands. I will speak
to you there."
23So I got up and went out to the flatlands. The
glory of the LORD was standing there. It was just
like the glory I had seen by the Kebar River. So I
fell with my face toward the ground.
24Then the Spirit of the LORD came into me. He
raised me to my feet. He said to me, "Go, son of
man. Shut yourself inside your house. 25Some people will tie you up with ropes. So you will not be
able to go out among your people. 26I will make
your tongue stick to the roof of your mouth. Then
you will be silent. You will not be able to correct
them. They always refuse to obey me.
27"But later I will speak to you. I will open your
mouth. Then you will tell them, 'Here is what the
LORD and King says.' Those who listen will listen.
And those who refuse to listen will refuse. They
always refuse to obey me.

An Attack on Jerusalem Is Pictured

4 "Son of man, get a clay tablet. Put it in front
of you. Draw the city of Jerusalem on it.
2Then pretend to surround it and attack it. Make
some little models of war machines. Build a ramp
up to it. Set camps up around it. Surround it with
models of logs to be used for knocking down its
gates. 3Then get an iron pan. Put it between you
and the city. Pretend it is an iron wall. Turn your

face toward the city. It will be under attack when you begin to attack it. That will show the people of Israel what is going to happen to Jerusalem.

4“Next, lie down on your left side. Pretend that you are putting Israel’s sin on yourself. Keep their sin on you for the number of days you lie on your side. 5Let each day you lie there stand for one year of their sin. So you will keep Israel’s sin on you for 390 days.

6“After you have finished that, lie down again. This time lie on your right side. Pretend that you are putting Judah’s sin on yourself. Lie there for 40 days. That is one day for each year of their sin.

7“Next, turn your face toward the model of Jerusalem under attack. Uncover your arm as if you were a soldier ready to fight. Prophesy against the city.

8“I will tie you up with ropes. Then you will not be able to turn from one side to the other. You will stay that way until you have finished attacking Jerusalem.

9“Get some wheat and barley. Also get some beans and lentils. And get some millet and spelt. Put everything in a storage jar. Use it to make some bread for yourself. Eat it during the 390 days you are lying down on your side. 10Weigh out eight ounces of food to eat each day. Eat it at your regular mealtimes. 11Also measure out two thirds of a quart of water. Drink it at your regular mealtimes.

12“Eat your food as you would eat a barley cake. Bake it over human waste in front of the people.” 13The LORD said, “That is how the people of Israel will eat ‘unclean’ food. They will eat it in the nations where I will drive them.”

14Then I said, “No, LORD and King! I won’t do it! I’ve never eaten anything that was ‘unclean.’ From the time I was young until now, I’ve never eaten anything that was found dead. And I’ve never eaten anything that was torn apart by wild animals. ‘Unclean’ meat has never entered my mouth.”

15“All right,” he said. “I will let you bake your bread over waste from cows. You can use that instead of human waste.”

16He continued, “Son of man, I will cut off the food supply in Jerusalem. The people will be worried as they eat their tiny share of food. They will not have any hope as they drink their tiny share of water. 17There will be very little food and water. The people will be shocked as they look at one another. They will become weaker and weaker because of their sin.

5 “Son of man, get a sharp sword. Use it as a barber’s razor. Shave your head and beard with it. Then get a set of scales and weigh the hair. Separate it into three piles.

2“Burn up a third of the hair inside the city. Do it when you stop attacking the model of Jerusalem. Next, get another third of the hair. Strike it with a sword all around the city. Then scatter the last third to the winds. That is because I will chase the people with a sword that is ready to strike them down. 3But save a few of the hairs. Tuck them away in the clothes you are wearing.

4“Next, get a few more hairs. Throw them into the fire. Burn them up. The fire will spread to all of the people of Israel.”

5The LORD and King says, “This little model stands for Jerusalem. I have placed that city in the center of the nations. Countries are all around it. 6But its people are sinful. They have refused to obey my laws and rules. They have turned their backs on my laws. They have not followed my rules. Those people are worse than the nations and countries around them.”

7The LORD and King continues, “You people have been worse than the nations around you. You have not lived by my rules or kept my laws. You have not even lived up to the standards of the nations around you.”

8The LORD and King continues, “Jerusalem, I myself am against you. I will punish you in the sight of the nations. 9I will do to you what I have never done before and will never do again. That is because you worship statues of gods. I hate them. 10So parents will eat their own children inside the city. And children will eat their parents. I will punish you. And I will scatter to the winds anyone who is left alive.

11“You have made my temple ‘unclean.’ You have set up statues of all of your evil gods. You have done other things I hate. So I will not show you my favor anymore. I will not spare you or feel sorry for you. And that is just as sure as I am alive,” announces the LORD and King.

12“A third of your people will die of the plague inside your walls. Or they will die of hunger there. Another third will be killed with swords outside your walls. And I will scatter the last third of your people to the winds. I will chase them with a sword that is ready to strike them down.

13“Then I will not be angry anymore. My burning anger against them will die down. And I will be satisfied. Then they will know that I have spoken with strong feelings. And my burning anger toward them will come to an end. I am the LORD.

14“I will destroy you. I will bring shame on you in the sight of the nations that are around you. All those who pass by will see it. 15You will be put to shame. The nations will make fun of you. You will serve as a warning to others. They will be shocked when they see you. So I will punish you because my anger burns against you. You will feel the sting of my warning. I have spoken. I am the LORD.

16“I will shoot at you with my deadly, destroying arrows of hunger. I will shoot to kill. I will bring more and more hunger on you. I will cut off your food supply. 17I will send hunger and wild animals against you. They will destroy all of your children. Plague and murder will sweep over you. And I will send swords to kill you. I have spoken. I am the LORD.”

Ezekiel Prophesies Against the Mountains of Israel

6 A message came to me from the LORD. He
said, 2"Son of man, turn your attention to the
mountains of Israel. Prophesy against them. 3Say,
'Mountains of Israel, listen to the message of the
LORD and King. Here is what he says to the mountains and hills. And here is what he says to the
canyons and valleys. He tells them, "I will send
swords to kill your people. I will destroy the high
places where you worship other gods.
4" ' "Your altars will be torn down. Your incense
altars will be smashed. And I will kill your people
in front of the statues of your gods. 5I will put the
dead bodies of Israelites in front of those statues.
I will scatter your bones around your altars.
6" ' "No matter where you live, the towns will be
destroyed. The high places will be torn down. So
your altars will be completely destroyed. The statues of your gods will be smashed to pieces. Your
incense altars will be broken down. And everything you have made will be wiped out. 7Your people will fall down dead among you. Then you will
know that I am the LORD.
8" ' "But I will spare some of you. Some will
escape from being killed with swords. You will be
scattered among other lands and nations. 9You will
be taken away to those nations as prisoners. Those
of you who escape will remember me. You will
recall how much pain your unfaithful hearts gave
me. You turned away from me. Your eyes longed
to see the statues of your gods. You will hate yourselves because of all of the evil things you have
done. I hate those things too. 10You will know that
I am the LORD. I said I would bring trouble on you.
And my warning came true." ' "
11The LORD and King said to me, "Clap your
hands. Stamp your feet. Cry out, 'How sad!' Do it
because the people of Israel have done so many
evil things. I hate those things. Israel will be
destroyed by war, hunger and plague. 12Those who
are far away will die of the plague. Those who are
near will be killed with swords. Those who are left
alive and are spared will die of hunger. And my
burning anger toward them will come to an end.
13"Then they will know that I am the LORD.
Their people will lie dead among the statues of
their gods around their altars. Their bodies will lie
on every high hill and every mountaintop. They
will lie under every green tree and leafy oak tree.
They used to offer sweet-smelling incense to all of
their gods at those places. 14I will reach out my
powerful hand against them. The land will become
dry and empty. Those people will live from the
desert all the way to Diblah. They will know that
I am the LORD."

The End Has Come

7 A message came to me from the LORD. He
said, 2"Son of man, I am the LORD and King.
I say to the land of Israel, 'The end has come! It
has come on the four corners of the land. 3The end
has now come for you. I will pour out my anger
on you. I will judge you based on how you have
lived. I will pay you back for all of your evil practices. I hate them.
4" 'I will not spare you or feel sorry for you. You
can be sure that I will pay you back in keeping
with how you have lived. I will judge you for your
evil practices. I hate them. You will know that I am
the LORD.'
5"I am the LORD and King. I say, 'Horrible trouble is coming! No one has ever heard of anything
like it.
6" 'The end has come! The end has come! It has
stirred itself up against you. It is here! 7Death has
come on you who live in the land. The time for
you to be destroyed has come. The day when it
will happen is near. There is no joy on your mountains. There is nothing but panic.
8" 'I am about to pour out all of my burning
anger on you. I will judge you based on how you
have lived. I will pay you back for all of your evil
practices. I hate them.
9" 'I will not spare you or feel sorry for you. I
will pay you back based on how you have lived. I
will judge you for your evil practices. I hate them.
You will know that I am the one who strikes you
down. I am the LORD.
10" 'The day for me to punish you is here! It has
come! Death has arrived. The time is ripe for you
to be judged. Your pride has grown so much that
you will be destroyed. 11Your mean and harmful
acts have become like a rod. I will use it to punish
you for your sins. None of you will be left. No
wealth or anything of value will remain.
12" 'The time has come! The day has arrived! I
will soon pour out my burning anger on the whole
crowd of you. Do not let the buyer be happy. Do
not let the seller be sad. 13The seller will not get
back the land that was sold as long as both of them
are alive.
" 'Ezekiel, the vision I gave you about that whole
crowd will come true. They have committed many
sins. So none of them will remain alive. 14They
might blow trumpets. They might get everything
ready. But no one will go into battle. I will soon
pour out my burning anger on the whole crowd.
15" 'There is trouble everywhere. War is outside
the city. Plague and hunger are inside it. Those
who are out in the country will die in battle. Those
in the city will be destroyed by hunger and plague.
16All those who escape and are left alive will run
to the mountains. They have committed many sins.
So they will cry like sad doves in the valleys.
17" 'Their hands will be powerless to help them.
Their knees will become as weak as water. 18They
will put on black clothes. They will put on terror as
if it were their clothes. Their faces will be covered
with shame. Their heads will be shaved.
19" 'They will throw their silver into the streets.
Their gold will be like an "unclean" thing. Their

silver and gold will not be able to save them on the day I pour out my anger on them. They will not be able to satisfy their hunger. Their stomachs will not be full. Their silver and gold have tripped them up. They have made them fall into sin. 20My people were so proud of their beautiful jewelry. They used it to make statues of their evil gods. I hate those gods. So I will turn their statues into an "unclean" thing for them.

21" 'I will hand everything over to strangers. I will turn it over to sinful people in other countries. They will pollute it. 22I will turn my face away from my people. Their enemies will pollute my beautiful temple. Robbers will enter it and pollute it.

23" 'Ezekiel, get ready to put my people in chains. The land is full of murderers. They are harming one another all over Jerusalem. 24I will bring the most evil nations against them. They will take over the houses in the city. I will put an end to the pride of those who are mighty. Their holy places will be polluted.

25" 'When terror comes, they will look for peace. But there will not be any. 26Trouble after trouble will come. One report will follow another. But they will not be true. The people will try to get visions from the prophets. But there will not be any. The teaching of the law by the priests will be gone. So will advice from the elders.

27" 'The king will be filled with sadness. The princes will lose all hope. The hands of the people of the land will tremble. I will punish them based on how they have lived. I will judge them by their own standards. Then they will know that I am the LORD.' "

The People Worship Other Gods in the Temple

8 It was the sixth year since King Jehoiachin had been brought to Babylon as a prisoner. On the fifth day of the sixth month, I was sitting in my house. The elders of Judah were sitting there with me. The LORD and King put his powerful hand on me there.

2I looked up and saw a figure that appeared to be human. From his waist down he looked like fire. From his waist up he looked as bright as glowing metal. 3He reached out what appeared to be a hand. He took hold of me by the hair of my head. The Spirit of the LORD lifted me up between earth and heaven. In visions God gave me, the Spirit took me to Jerusalem. He brought me to the entrance of the north gate of the inner courtyard. The statue of a god was standing there. It made God very angry. 4There in front of me was the glory of the God of Israel. It looked just as it did in the vision I had seen on the flatlands.

5Then the LORD said to me, "Son of man, look toward the north." So I did. I saw a statue that made God angry. It was in the entrance of the gate north of the altar.

6He said to me, "Son of man, do you see what the people of Israel are doing here? They are doing things I hate very much. Those things will cause me to go far away from my temple. But you will see things I hate even more."

7Then he brought me to the entrance to the courtyard. I looked up and saw a hole in the wall. 8He said to me, "Son of man, dig into the wall." So I did. And I saw a door there.

9He continued, "Go through it. Look at the evil things they are doing here. I hate those things."

10So I went in and looked. All over the walls were pictures of all kinds of crawling things and other animals. The LORD hates it when people worship those things. There were also carvings of all of the gods of the people of Israel.

11In front of them stood 70 elders of Israel. Jaazaniah was standing there among them. He is the son of Shaphan. Each elder was holding a shallow cup. A sweet-smelling cloud of incense was rising from the cups.

12The LORD said to me, "Son of man, do you see what the elders of Israel are doing in the dark? Each of them is in his own room worshiping his own god. They say, 'The LORD doesn't see us. He has deserted the land.' " 13He continued, "You will see them doing things I hate even more."

14Then he brought me to the entrance of the north gate of the LORD's house. I saw women sitting there. They were sobbing over the god Tammuz. 15The LORD said to me, "Son of man, do you see what they are doing? You will see things I hate even more."

16Then he brought me into the inner courtyard of the LORD's house. About 25 men were there. They were at the entrance to the LORD's temple between the porch and the altar. Their backs were turned toward the temple. Their faces were turned toward the east. And they were bowing down to the sun.

17He said to me, "Son of man, have you seen all of that? The people of Judah are doing things here that I hate. This is a very serious matter. They are harming one another all through the land. They continue to make me very angry. Just look at them making fun of me! 18So I am angry with them. I will punish them. I will not spare them or feel sorry for them. They might even shout in my ears. But I will not listen to them."

The LORD Judges Those Who Worship Other Gods

9 Then I heard the LORD call out in a loud voice. He said, "Bring those who guard the city here. Make sure each of them has a weapon." 2I saw six men coming from the direction of the upper gate. It faces north. Each of them had a deadly weapon. A man who was wearing linen clothes came along with them. He was carrying a writing kit at his side. They came in and stood beside the bronze altar.

3The glory of the God of Israel had been above the cherubim. It moved from there to the doorway of the temple.

Then the LORD called to the man who was dressed in linen clothes. He had the writing kit. 4The LORD said to him, "Go all through Jerusalem. Look for those who are sad and sorry about all of the things that are being done there. I hate those things. Put a mark on the foreheads of those people."

5I heard him speak to the six men. He said, "Follow him through the city. Do not show any pity or concern. 6Kill old men and women, young men and women, and children. But do not touch anyone who has the mark. Start at my temple." So they began with the elders who were in front of the temple.

7Then he said to the men, "Make the temple 'unclean.' Fill the courtyards with dead bodies. Go!" So they went out and started killing people all through the city.

8While they were doing it, I was left alone. I fell with my face toward the ground. I cried out, "LORD and King, are you going to destroy all of the Israelites who are still left alive? Will you pour out your burning anger on all those who remain in Jerusalem?"

9He answered me, "The sin of Israel and Judah is very great. The land is full of murderers. They are not being fair to one another anywhere in Jerusalem. They say, 'The LORD has deserted the land. He doesn't see us.' 10So I will not spare them or feel sorry for them. Anything that happens to them will be their own fault."

11Then the man who was wearing linen clothes returned. He had the writing kit. He reported, "I've done what you commanded."

The Glory of the LORD Moves Out of the Temple

10 I looked up and saw something that appeared to be a throne made out of sapphire. It was above the huge space that was spread out over the heads of the cherubim. 2The LORD spoke to the man who was wearing linen clothes. He said, "Go in among the wheels beneath the cherubim. Fill your hands with burning coals from the fire that is among the cherubim. Scatter the coals over the city." As I watched, he went in.

3The cherubim were standing on the south side of the temple when the man went in. A cloud filled the inner courtyard. 4Then the glory of the LORD rose from above the cherubim. It moved to the doorway of the temple. The cloud filled the temple. And the courtyard was full of the brightness of the glory of the LORD. 5The sound the wings of the cherubim made could be heard as far away as the outer courtyard. It was like the voice of the Mighty God when he speaks.

6The LORD gave a command to the man who was dressed in linen clothes. He said, "Get some coals of fire from among the wheels. Take them from among the cherubim." So the man went in and stood beside a wheel. 7Then one of the cherubim reached out his hand. He picked up some of the burning coals that were among the wheels. He handed them to the man who was wearing linen clothes. The man took them and left. 8I saw what looked like a man's hands. They were under the wings of the cherubim.

9I looked up and saw four wheels beside the cherubim. One wheel was beside each of them. The wheels gleamed like chrysolite. 10All four of them looked alike. Each wheel appeared to be inside another wheel at right angles. 11The wheels could go in any one of the four directions the cherubim faced. The wheels didn't change their direction as the cherubim moved. The cherubim went in the direction their heads faced. They didn't change their direction as they moved.

12Their whole bodies were completely covered with eyes. That included their backs, hands and wings. Their four wheels were covered with eyes too. 13I heard someone tell the wheels to start spinning around. 14Each of the cherubim had four faces. One face was the face of a cherub. The second was a man's face. The third was the face of a lion. And the fourth was an eagle's face.

15The cherubim rose from the ground. They were the same living creatures I had seen by the Kebar River. 16When the cherubim moved, the wheels beside them moved. The cherubim spread their wings to rise from the ground. As they did, the wheels didn't leave their side. 17When the cherubim stood still, the wheels also stood still. When the cherubim rose, the wheels rose along with them. That's because the spirits of the living creatures were in the wheels.

18Then the glory of the LORD moved away from the doorway of the temple. It stopped above the cherubim. 19While I watched, they spread their wings. They rose from the ground. As they went, the wheels went along with them. They stopped at the entrance of the east gate of the LORD's house. And the glory of the God of Israel was above them.

20Those were the same living creatures I had seen by the Kebar River. I had seen them beneath the God of Israel. I realized that they were cherubim. 21Each one had four faces and four wings. Under their wings was what looked like a man's hands. 22Their faces looked the same as the ones I had seen by the Kebar River. Each of the cherubim went straight ahead.

The LORD Punishes Israel's Leaders

11 Then the Spirit of the LORD lifted me up. He brought me to the east gate of the LORD's house. There were 25 men at the entrance of the gate. I saw Jaazaniah and Pelatiah among them. They were leaders of the people. Jaazaniah is the son of Azzur. Pelatiah is the son of Benaiah.

2The LORD said to me, "Son of man, these men are making evil plans. They are giving bad advice to the city. 3They say, 'This is not the time to build houses. The city is like a cooking pot. And we are the meat.' 4So prophesy against them. Prophesy, son of man."

5Then the Spirit of the LORD came on me. He told me to tell them, "The LORD says, 'People of Israel, that is what you are saying. But I know what you are thinking. 6You have killed many people in this city. In fact, you have filled its streets with dead bodies.'

7"So the LORD and King says, 'The bodies you have thrown there are the meat. And the city is the cooking pot. But I will drive you out of it. 8You are afraid of the swords of war. But I will bring them against you,' announces the LORD and King.

9"'I will drive you out of the city. I will hand you over to strangers. And I will punish you. 10You will be killed with swords. I will judge you at the borders of Israel. Then you will know that I am the LORD.

11"'This city will not be a pot for you. And you will not be the meat in it. I will judge you at the borders of Israel. 12Then you will know that I am the LORD. You have not followed my rules. You have not kept my laws. Instead, you have lived by the standards of the nations that are around you.'"

13Pelatiah, the son of Benaiah, died as I was prophesying. Then I fell with my face toward the ground. I cried out in a loud voice. I said, "LORD and King, will you destroy all of the Israelites who are still left alive?"

14A message came to me from the LORD. He said, 15"Son of man, the people of Jerusalem have spoken about your relatives. They have also spoken about all of the other people of Israel. They have said, 'Stay far away from the LORD. This land was given to us. And it belongs to us.'

The LORD Will Bring His People Back Home

16"So tell them, 'The LORD and King says, "I sent some of my people far away among the nations. I scattered them among the countries. But for a little while I have been their temple in the countries where they have gone."'

17"Tell them, 'The LORD and King says, "I will gather you from the nations. I will bring you back from the countries where you have been scattered. I will give you back the land of Israel."'

18"They will return to it. They will remove all of its statues of evil gods. I hate those gods. 19I will give my people hearts that are completely committed to me. I will give them a new spirit that is faithful to me. I will remove their stubborn hearts from them. And I will give them hearts that obey me. 20Then they will follow my rules. They will be careful to keep my laws. They will be my people. And I will be their God.

21"But some people have hearts that are committed to worshiping the statues of their evil gods. I hate those gods. Anything that happens to those people will be their own fault," announces the LORD and King.

22Then the cherubim spread their wings. The wheels were beside them. The glory of the God of Israel was above them. 23The glory of the LORD went up from the city. It stopped above the Mount of Olives east of it.

24The Spirit of God lifted me up. He took me to those who had been brought to Babylonia as prisoners. Those are the things that happened in the visions the Spirit gave me.

Then the visions I had seen were gone. 25I told my people everything the LORD had shown me.

Many People Will Be Taken to Babylonia

12 A message came to me from the LORD. He said, 2"Son of man, you are living among people who refuse to obey me. They have eyes that can see. But they do not really see. They have ears that can hear. But they do not really hear. They refuse to obey me.

3"Son of man, pack your belongings as if you were going on a long trip. Leave in the daytime. Let the people see you. Start out from where you are. Go to another place. Perhaps they will understand the meaning of what you are doing. But they will still refuse to obey me. 4Bring out your belongings packed for a long trip. Do it during the daytime. Let the people see you. Then in the evening, pretend you are being forced to leave home. Let the people see you.

5"While the people are watching, dig through the mud bricks of your house. Then take your belongings out through the hole in the wall. 6Put them on your shoulder. Carry them out at sunset. Let the people see you. Cover your face so you can't see the land. All of that will show the people of Israel what is going to happen to them."

7So I did just as he commanded me. During the day I brought out my things as if I were going on a long trip. In the evening I dug through the wall of my house with my hands. At sunset I took my belongings out. I put them on my shoulders. The people watched what I was doing.

8In the morning a message came to me from the LORD. He said, 9"Son of man, didn't the people of Israel ask you, 'What are you doing?' They always refuse to obey me.

10"Tell them, 'The LORD and King says, "This message is about Zedekiah, the prince in Jerusalem. It is also about all of the people of Israel who still live there."' 11Tell them, 'The things I've done are a picture of what's going to happen to you. So what I've done will happen to you. You will be forced to leave home. You will be taken to Babylonia as prisoners.'

12"The prince among them will put his things on his shoulder and leave. He will do it at sunset. Someone will dig a hole in a wall for him to go through. He will cover his face so he can't see the land. 13I will spread out my net to catch him. He

will be caught in my trap. I will bring him to Babylonia. It is the land where the Chaldeans live. But
he will not see it. He will die there. 14I will scatter
to the winds all those who are around him. I will
scatter his officials and all of his troops. And I will
chase them with a sword that is ready to strike
them down.
15"They will know that I am the LORD when I
scatter them among the nations. I will send them to
other countries. 16But I will spare a few of them. I
will save them from war, hunger and plague. In
those countries they will admit they have done all
kinds of evil things. I hate those things. They will
know that I am the LORD."
17A message came to me from the LORD. He
said, 18"Son of man, tremble with fear as you eat
your food. Tremble as you drink your water.
19Speak to the people of the land. Say to them,
'Here is what the LORD and King says about those
who live in Jerusalem and Israel. He tells them,
"They will be worried as they eat their food. They
will not have any hope as they drink their water.
Their land will be stripped of everything in it
because all those who live there are harming one
another. 20The towns where people live will be
completely destroyed. The land will become a dry
and empty desert. Then you will know that I am
the LORD."' "
21A message came to me from the LORD. He
said, 22"Son of man, you have a proverb in the land
of Israel. It says, 'The days go by, and not even one
vision comes true.' 23Tell them, 'The LORD and
King says, "I am going to put an end to that proverb. They will not use that saying in Israel anymore." ' Tell them, 'The days are coming soon
when every vision will come true. 24There will be
no more false visions. People will no longer use
magic to find out whether good things are going
to happen in Israel. 25I am the LORD. So I will say
what I want to. And it will come true when I want
it to. In your days I will do everything I say I will.
But you people always refuse to obey me,'
announces the LORD and King."
26A message came to me from the LORD. He
said, 27"Son of man, the people of Israel are saying,
'The vision Ezekiel sees won't come true for many
years. He is prophesying about a time that is a long
way off.'
28"So tell them, 'The LORD and King says,
"Everything I say will come true. It will happen
when I want it to," announces the LORD and
King.' "

The LORD Punishes Those Who Pretend to Be True Prophets

13 A message came to me from the LORD. He
said, 2"Son of man, prophesy against those
who are now prophesying in Israel. What they
prophesy comes out of their own minds. Tell them,
'Listen to the LORD's message! 3The LORD and
King says, "How terrible it will be for you foolish
prophets! You say what your own minds tell you
to. Your visions did not come from me.
4" ' "Israel, your prophets are like wild dogs that
live among broken-down buildings. 5You have not
repaired the cracks in the city wall for the people
of Israel. So it will not stand firm in the battle on
the day I judge you. 6The visions of those prophets
are false. They use magic to try to find out what is
going to happen. But their magic tricks are lies.
They say, 'The LORD announces.' But I have not
sent them. In spite of that, they expect their words
to come true.
7" ' "You prophets have seen false visions. You
have used magic to try to find out what is going to
happen. But your magic tricks are lies. So you lied
when you said, 'The LORD announces.' I did not
even speak to you at all."
8" 'The LORD and King says, "I am against you
prophets. Your messages are false. Your visions do
not come true," announces the LORD and King.
9" ' "Israel, my powerful hand will be against the
prophets who see false visions. Their magic tricks
are lies. They will not be among the leaders of my
people. They will not be listed in the records of Israel. In fact, they will not even enter the land. Then
you will know that I am the LORD and King.
10" ' "They lead my people away from me. They
say, 'Peace.' But there isn't any peace. They are
like people who build a weak wall. They try to
cover up the weakness by painting the wall white.
11Tell those who do it that their wall is going to fall.
Heavy rains will come. I will send hailstones
crashing down. Powerful winds will blow. 12The
wall will fall down. Then people will ask them,
'Now where is the paint you covered it with?' "
13" 'So the LORD and King speaks. He says,
"When I am burning with anger, I will send a powerful wind. Hailstones and heavy rains will come.
They will fall with great force. 14I will tear down
the wall you prophets painted over. I will knock it
down. The only thing left will be its foundation.
When it falls, you will be destroyed along with it.
Then you will know that I am the LORD.
15" ' "So I will pour out all of my burning anger
on the wall. I will also send it against you prophets
who painted it. I will say to you, 'The wall is gone.
You who painted it will be gone too. 16You
prophets of Israel prophesied to Jerusalem. You
saw visions of peace for its people. But there
wasn't any peace,' announces the LORD and
King." '
17"Son of man, turn your attention to the daughters of your people. What they prophesy comes out
of their own minds. So prophesy against them.
18Tell them, 'The LORD and King says, "How terrible it will be for you women who sew magic
charms to put around your wrists! You make veils
of different lengths to put on your heads. You do
those things to trap people. You trap my people.
But you will also be trapped. 19You have treated
me as if I were not holy. You did it among my very

own people. You did it for a few handfuls of barley and scraps of bread. You told lies to my people. They like to listen to lies. You killed those who should have lived. And you spared those who should have died.”

20“ ‘So the LORD and King says, “I am against your magic charms. You use them to trap people as if they were birds. I will tear them off your arms. I will set free the people you trap like birds. 21I will tear your veils off your heads. I will save my people from your powerful hands. They will no longer be under your control. Then you will know that I am the LORD.

22“ ‘ “I had not made godly people sad. But when you told them lies, you made them lose all hope. You advised sinful people not to turn from their evil ways. You did not want them to save their lives. 23So you will never see false visions again. You will not use your magic tricks anymore. I will save my people from your powerful hands. Then you will know that I am the LORD.” ’ ”

The LORD Judges Those Who Worship Other Gods

14 Some of the elders of Israel came to see me. They sat down with me. 2Then a message came to me from the LORD. He said, 3“Son of man, these men have thought about nothing but other gods. They have fallen into the evil trap of worshiping them. Should I let those men ask me for any advice?

4“Speak to them. Tell them, ‘The LORD and King says, “Suppose an Israelite thinks about other gods. And he falls into the evil trap of worshiping them. Then he goes to a prophet to ask for advice. If he does, I myself will tell the prophet to answer him in keeping with his worship of many gods. 5I will win back the hearts of the people of Israel. All of them have deserted me for their other gods.” ’

6“So speak to the people of Israel. Tell them, ‘The LORD and King says, “Turn away from your sins! Also turn away from your gods. Give up all of the evil things you have done. I hate them.

7“ ‘ “Suppose an Israelite or outsider who lives in Israel separates himself from me. And he thinks about other gods. He falls into the evil trap of worshiping them. Then he goes to a prophet to ask me for advice. If he does, I myself will tell the prophet to answer him. 8I will turn against him. I will make an example out of him. People will laugh at him. I will cut him off from you. Then you will know that I am the LORD.

9“ ‘ “Suppose that prophet is stirred up to give a prophecy. Then I am the one who has stirred him up. And I will reach out my powerful hand against him. I will destroy him from among my people Israel. 10The prophet will be as much to blame as the one who asks him for advice. Both of them will be guilty. 11Then the people of Israel will no longer wander away from me. And they will not pollute themselves anymore with their many sins. They will be my people. And I will be their God,” ’ announces the LORD and King.”

The LORD Punishes All Sinners

12A message came to me from the LORD. He said, 13“Son of man, suppose the people in a certain country sin against me. And they are not faithful to me. So I reach out my powerful hand against them. I cut off their food supply. I make them very hungry. I kill them and their animals. 14And suppose Noah, Daniel and Job were in that country. Then those three men could save only themselves by doing what is right,” announces the LORD and King.

15“Or suppose I send wild animals through that country. And they kill all of its children. It becomes a dry and empty desert. No one can pass through it because of the animals. 16And suppose those three men were in that country. Then they could not save their own sons or daughters. They alone would be saved. But the land would become a dry and empty desert. And that is just as sure as I am alive,” announces the LORD and King.

17“Or suppose I send swords to kill the people in that country. And I say, ‘Let swords sweep all through the land.’ And I kill its people and their animals. 18And suppose those three men were in that country. Then they could not save their own sons or daughters. They alone would be saved. And that is just as sure as I am alive,” announces the LORD and King.

19“Or suppose I send a plague into that land. And I pour out my burning anger on it by spilling blood. I kill its people and their animals. 20And suppose Noah, Daniel and Job were in that land. Then they could not save their own sons or daughters. They could save only themselves by doing what is right. And that is just as sure as I am alive,” announces the LORD and King.

21The LORD and King says, “It will get much worse. I will punish Jerusalem in four horrible ways. There will be war, hunger, wild animals and plague. They will destroy the people and their animals.

22“But some people will be left alive. Some children will be brought out of the city. They will come to you. You will see how they act and the way they live. And you will be comforted in spite of all of the trouble I brought on Jerusalem. 23You will be comforted when you see how they act and the way they live. Then you will know that I did not do anything there without a reason,” announces the LORD and King.

Jerusalem Is Like a Useless Vine

15 A message came to me from the LORD. He said, 2“Son of man, is the wood of a vine better than the wood of any of the trees in the forest? 3Can its wood ever be made into anything useful? Can pegs be made from it to hang things on?

4“Suppose it is thrown in the fire to be burned. And the fire burns both ends and blackens the middle. Then is it useful for anything? 5It was not useful when it was whole. So how can it be made into something useful now? The fire has burned it and blackened it."

6The LORD and King says, "Instead of the wood of any tree in the forest, I have given the vine to burn in the fire. I will treat the people who live in Jerusalem the same way. 7I will turn against them. They might have come out of the fire. But the fire will destroy them anyway. I will turn against them. Then they will know that I am the LORD. 8I will make the land a dry and empty desert. My people have not been faithful to me," announces the LORD and King.

A Story That Pictures Unfaithful Jerusalem

16 A message came to me from the LORD. He said, 2"Son of man, tell the people of Jerusalem the evil things they have done. I hate those things.

3"Tell them, 'The LORD and King speaks to Jerusalem. He says, "Your history in the land of Canaan goes back a long way. Your father was an Amorite. Your mother was a Hittite. 4On the day you were born your cord was not cut. You were not washed with water to clean you up. You were not rubbed with salt. And you were not wrapped in large strips of cloth. 5No one took pity on you. No one was concerned enough to do any of those things for you. Instead, you were thrown out into an open field. You were hated on the day you were born.

6" ' "I was passing by. I saw you kicking around in your blood. As you were lying there, I said to you, 'Live!' 7I made you grow like a plant in a field. Soon you had grown up. You became the most beautiful jewel of all. Your breasts had formed. Your hair had grown. But you were naked and bare.

8" ' "Later, I was passing by again. I looked at you. I saw that you were old enough for love. So I got married to you and took good care of you. I covered your naked body. I took an oath and made a firm promise to you. I entered into a covenant with you. And you became mine," announces the LORD and King.

9" ' "I bathed you with water. I washed the blood off you. And I put lotions on you. 10I put a beautiful dress on you. I gave you leather sandals. I dressed you in fine linen. I covered you with expensive clothes. 11I decorated you with jewelry. I put bracelets on your arms. I gave you a necklace for your neck. 12I put rings on your nose and ears. And I gave you a beautiful crown for your head.

13" ' "So you were decorated with gold and silver. Your clothes were made out of fine linen. They were made of expensive and beautiful cloth. Your food was made out of fine flour, honey and olive oil. You became very beautiful. You became a queen. 14You were so beautiful that your fame spread among the nations. The glory I had given you made your beauty perfect," announces the LORD and King.

15" ' "But you trusted in your beauty. You used your fame to become a prostitute. You offered your body freely to anyone who passed by. In fact, you gave yourself to anyone who wanted you. 16You used some of your clothes to make high places colorful. That is where people worshiped other gods. You were a prostitute there. Things like that should never happen. They should never take place.

17" ' "I had given you fine jewelry. It was made out of gold and silver. You used it to make for yourself statues of male gods. You worshiped those gods. You were not faithful to me. 18You put your beautiful clothes on them. You offered my oil and incense to them. 19You also offered them the food that was made out of fine flour, olive oil and honey. I had given it to you to eat. You offered it as sweet-smelling incense to them. That is what you did," announces the LORD and King.

20" ' "Then you got your sons and daughters who belonged to me. And you sacrificed them as food to other gods. Wasn't it enough for you to be a prostitute? 21You killed my children. You sacrificed them to other gods.

22" ' "You did not remember the days when you were young. At that time you were naked and bare. You were kicking around in your blood. But now you have done evil things. I hate them. You have worshiped other gods. You have not been faithful to me.

23" ' "How terrible it will be for you!" announces the LORD and King. "How terrible for you! You continued to sin against me. 24Your people built up mounds for themselves in every market place. They put little places of worship on them. 25They set them up at every street corner. Jerusalem, you misused your beauty. You offered your body to anyone who passed by. You did it again and again.

26" ' "You committed shameful acts with the people of Egypt. They were your neighbors, and they were filled with longing for their lovers. You offered yourself to others again and again. That made me very angry. 27So I reached out my powerful hand against you. I made your territory smaller. I handed you over to your Philistine enemies. The people in their towns were shocked by your impure conduct.

28" ' "You also committed shameful acts with the people of Assyria. Nothing ever seemed to satisfy you. You could never get enough. 29Then you offered yourself to the people of Babylonia. But that did not satisfy you either. There are many traders in the land of Babylonia.

30" ' "You can't control yourself," announces the LORD and King. "Just look at all of the things you are doing! You are acting like a prostitute who has no shame at all. 31Your people built up mounds at every street corner. You put little places of worship on them in every market place. But you did not really act like a prostitute. You refused to let your lovers pay you anything.

32“ ‘You unfaithful wife! You would rather be with strangers than with your own husband! 33Every prostitute gets paid. But you give gifts to all of your lovers. You offer them money to come to you from everywhere. You want them to make love to you. You are not faithful to me. 34As a prostitute, you are the opposite of others. No one runs after you to make love to you. You are exactly the opposite. You pay them. They do not pay you.’ ”

35You prostitute, listen to the LORD’s message. 36The LORD and King says, “You poured out your wealth on your lovers. You took your clothes off and made love to them. You did it again and again. You worshiped other gods. I hate them. You even sacrificed your children to them.

37“So I am going to gather together all of the lovers you found pleasure with. They include those you loved and those you hated. I will gather them against you from everywhere. I will take your clothes off right in front of them. Then they will see you completely naked. 38I will hand down my sentence against you. You will be punished like women who commit adultery and sacrifice their children to other gods. My anger burns against you so much that I will sentence you to death for everything you have done.

39“Then I will hand you over to your lovers. They will tear down those mounds you built. They will destroy the little places of worship you put on them. They will take your clothes off. They will remove your fine jewelry. And they will leave you naked and bare.

40“They will bring a crowd against you. The crowd will put you to death by throwing stones at you. And they will chop you to pieces with their swords. 41They will burn your houses down and punish you. Many women will see it.

“I will not let you be a prostitute anymore. You will no longer pay your lovers. 42Then my burning anger against you will die down. My jealous anger will turn away from you. I will be calm. I will not be angry anymore.

43“You did not remember the days when you were young. The things you did made me very angry. So anything that happens to you will be your own fault,” announces the LORD and King. “You added impure conduct to all of the other evil things you did. I hate all of those things.

44“All those who use proverbs will use this one about you. They will say, ‘Like mother, like daughter.’ 45You are a true daughter of your mother. She hated her husband and children. And you are a true sister of your sisters. They hated their husbands and children.

“Your mother was a Hittite. Your father was an Amorite. 46Your older sister was Samaria. She lived north of you with her daughters. Your younger sister was Sodom. She lived south of you with her daughters. 47You lived exactly the way they did. You copied their evil practices. I hate those practices. Everything you did was so sinful that you soon became even worse than they were.

48“Your sister Sodom and her daughters never did what you and your daughters have done. And that is just as sure as I am alive,” announces the LORD and King.

49“Here is the sin your sister Sodom committed. She and her daughters were proud. They ate too much. They were not concerned about others. They did not help those who were poor and in need. 50They were very proud. They did many things that were evil in my sight. I hated those things. So I got rid of Sodom and her daughters, just as you have seen.

51“Samaria did not commit half the sins you did. You sinned even more than they did. I hate those sins. Compared to what you did, you made your sisters seem godly. 52So you will be dishonored. You have given your sisters an excuse for what they did. Your sins were far worse than theirs. In fact, your sisters appear to be more godly than you. So then, be ashamed. You will be dishonored. You have made them appear to be godly.

53“I will not only give you back what you had before. I will also do the same thing for Sodom and her daughters. And I will do the same for Samaria and her daughters. 54That will make you feel dishonored. You will be ashamed of everything you have done. You have made them feel better because you sinned more and were punished more than they were. 55Your sisters Sodom and Samaria and their daughters will return to what they were before. And you and your daughters will return to what you were before.

56“In the past you would not even mention your sister Sodom. You were proud at that time. 57That was before your sin was uncovered. Now the daughters of Edom make fun of you. So do all of her neighbors and the daughters of the Philistines. Everyone who lives around you looks down on you. 58You will be punished for your impure conduct. I will also punish you for the other evil things you have done. I hate all of those things,” announces the LORD.

59The LORD and King says, “I will punish you in keeping with what you have done. I sealed with an oath the covenant I made with you. You hated that oath. And you broke my covenant.

60“But I will remember my covenant with you. I made it with you when you were young. Now I will make a new covenant with you. It will last forever. 61Then you will remember how you have lived. You will be ashamed when I give you Samaria and Sodom. Samaria is your older sister. Sodom is your younger one. I will give them and their daughters to you as daughters. That can’t happen based on my old covenant with you. 62So I will make my new covenant with you. Then you will know that I am the LORD.

63“I will pay for all of the sins you have committed. Then you will remember what you have done. You will be ashamed of it. Because of your shame, you will never speak against me again,” announces the LORD and King.

Two Eagles and a Vine

17 A message came to me from the LORD. He said, 2“Son of man, tell the people of Israel a story about their kings. Let them know what will happen to them. 3Tell them, ‘The LORD and King says, “A great eagle came to the city of ‘Lebanon.’ It had powerful wings and a lot of long feathers. The feathers were colorful and beautiful. The eagle landed in the top of a cedar tree. 4It broke off the highest twig. It carried it away to Babylonia. There are many traders in that land. The eagle planted the twig in the city of Babylon.

5“ ‘ “Then it got a seed from your land. It put it in rich soil near plenty of water. It planted the seed like a willow tree. 6The seed grew into a low, spreading vine. Its branches turned toward the eagle. And its roots remained under the eagle. So the seed became a vine. It produced branches and put out leaves.

7“ ‘ “But there was another great eagle. It also had powerful wings and a lot of feathers. The vine now sent its roots out toward that eagle. It sent them out from the place where it was planted. And it reached out its branches to the eagle for water. 8The seed had been planted in good soil near plenty of water. Then it could produce branches and bear fruit. It could become a beautiful vine.” ’

9“Ezekiel, tell the Israelites, ‘The LORD and King asks, “Will the vine grow? Won’t it be pulled up by its roots? Won’t all of its fruit be stripped off? Won’t it dry up? All of its new growth will dry up. It will not take a strong arm or many people to pull it up. 10It will not grow even if it is pulled up and planted somewhere else. It will dry up completely when the east wind strikes it. It will dry up in the place where it grew.” ’ ”

11A message came to me from the LORD. He said, 12“These people refuse to obey me. Ask them, ‘Don’t you know what these things mean?’ Tell them, ‘Nebuchadnezzar went to Jerusalem. He was king of Babylonia. He carried off King Jehoiachin and the nobles. He brought them back with him to the city of Babylon.

13“ ‘Then Nebuchadnezzar made a peace treaty with Zedekiah. He was a member of Jerusalem’s royal family. Nebuchadnezzar made him take an oath and promise he would keep the treaty. He also took the leading men of the land away as prisoners. 14He did it to bring their kingdom down. It would not rise again. In fact, it would be able to last only by keeping his treaty.

15“ ‘But Zedekiah turned against him. He sent messengers to Egypt. They went there to get horses and a large army. Will he succeed? Will he who does things like that escape? Can he break the peace treaty and still escape?

16“ ‘Zedekiah will die in Babylon,’ announces the LORD and King. ‘And that is just as sure as I am alive. He will die in the land of King Nebuchadnezzar, who put him on the throne. He is the king whose oath Zedekiah hated. He also broke Nebuchadnezzar’s treaty.

17“ ‘So Nebuchadnezzar will build ramps against the walls of Jerusalem. He will set up war machines to destroy many lives. Pharaoh will not be able to help Zedekiah during the war. The huge and mighty army of Egypt will not be of any help.

18“ ‘Zedekiah hated Nebuchadnezzar’s oath and broke his treaty. He had made a firm promise to keep it. But he broke it anyway. So he will not escape.

19“ ‘The LORD and King says, “Zedekiah hated the oath he took in my name. He broke the treaty. So I will pay him back. And that is just as sure as I am alive. 20I will spread out my net to catch him. He will be caught in my trap. I will bring him to Babylon. I will judge him there because he was not faithful to me.

21“ ‘ “All of Zedekiah’s troops will be killed with swords when they try to run away. Those who are left alive will be scattered to the winds. Then you will know that I have spoken. I am the LORD.”

22“ ‘The LORD and King says, “I myself will get a twig from the very top of a cedar tree and plant it. I will break off the highest twig. I will plant it on a very high mountain. 23I will plant it on the high mountains of Israel. It will produce branches and bear fruit. It will become a beautiful cedar tree. All kinds of birds will make their nests in it. They will live in the shade of its branches. 24All of the trees in the fields will know that I bring tall trees down. I make short trees grow tall. I dry up green trees. And I make dry trees green.”

“ ‘I have spoken. I will do it. I am the LORD.’ ”

People Will Die Because of Their Own Sins

18 A message came to me from the LORD. He said, 2“You people have a proverb about the land of Israel. What do you mean by it? It says,

“ ‘The parents eat sour grapes.
But the children have a bitter taste in
their mouths.’

3“You will not use that proverb in Israel anymore,” announces the LORD and King. “And that is just as sure as I am alive. 4Everyone belongs to me. Father and son alike belong to me. People will die because of their own sins.

5“Suppose a godly man
does what is fair and right.
6And he does not eat at the mountain temples.
He does not worship the statues of Israel’s
gods.
He does not have sex with another man’s wife.
He does not make love to his own wife
during her monthly period.

7 He does not treat anyone badly.
Instead, he always gives back
what he took as security for a loan.
He does not steal.
Instead, he gives his food to hungry people.
He provides clothes for those who are naked.
8 He does not lend money and charge too
much interest.
He keeps himself from doing what is wrong.
He judges cases fairly.
9 He follows my rules.
He is faithful in keeping my laws.
He always does what is right.
You can be sure he will live,"
announces the LORD and King.

10"But suppose he has a mean son who harms
other people. The son commits murder. Or he does
some other things that are wrong. 11Suppose he
does those things even though his father never did.

"Suppose he eats at the mountain temples.
And he has sex with another man's wife.
12 He treats poor and needy people badly.
He steals.
He does not pay back what he owes.
He worships statues of gods.
He does other things I hate.
13 He lends money and charges too much
interest.

Will a man like that live? He will not! You can be
sure he will be put to death. And what happens to
him will be his own fault. He did many things I
hate.

14"But suppose that son has a son of his own.
And the son sees all of the sins his father commits.
He sees them, but he does not do them.

15 "Suppose he does not eat at the mountain
temples.
And he does not worship the statues
of Israel's gods.
He does not have sex with another
man's wife.
16 He does not treat anyone badly.
He does not make people give him
something
to prove they will pay back what they
owe him.
He does not steal.
Instead, he gives his food to hungry people.
He provides clothes for those who are naked.
17 He keeps himself from committing sins.
He does not lend money and charge too
much interest.
He keeps my laws and follows my rules.

He will not die because of his father's sin. You can
be sure he will live. 18But his father will die
because of his own sin. He got rich by cheating
others. He robbed his relatives. He also did what
was wrong among his people.

19"But you still ask, 'Is the son guilty along with
his father?' No! The son did what was fair and
right. He was careful to keep all of my rules. So
you can be sure he will live. 20People will die
because of their own sins. The son will not be
guilty because of what his father did. And the
father will not be guilty because of what his son
did. The right things a godly person does will be
added to his account. The wrong things a sinful
person does will be charged against him.

21"But suppose a sinful person turns away from
all of the sins he has committed. And he keeps all
my rules. He does what is fair and right. Then you
can be sure he will live. He will not die. 22None of
the sins he has committed will be held against him.
Because of the godly things he has done, he will
live.

23"When sinful people die, it does not give me
any joy," announces the LORD and King. "But
when they turn away from their sins and live, that
makes me very happy.

24"Suppose a godly person stops doing what is
right. And he commits sin. He does the same evil
things a sinful person does. He does things I hate.
Then he will not live. I will not remember any of
the right things he has done. He has not been faithful to me. He has also committed many other sins.
So he is guilty. He will die.

25"But you say, 'What the Lord does isn't fair.'
Listen to me, people of Israel. What I do is always
fair. What you do is not.

26"Suppose a godly person stops doing what is
right. And he commits sin. Then he will die
because of it. He will die because of the sin he has
committed.

27"But suppose a sinful person turns away from
the evil things he has done. And he does what is
fair and right. Then he will save his life. 28He
thinks about all of the evil things he has done. And
he turns away from them. So you can be sure he
will live. He will not die.

29"But the people of Israel still say, 'What the
Lord does isn't fair.' People of Israel, what I do is
always fair. What you do is not.

30"So I will judge you people. I will judge each
of you in keeping with what you have done,"
announces the LORD and King.

"Turn away from your sins! Turn away from all
of the evil things you have done. Then sin will not
bring you down. 31Get rid of all of the evil things
you have done. Let me give you a new heart and a
new spirit. Then you will be faithful to me. Why
should you die, people of Israel? 32When anyone
dies, it does not give me any joy," announces the
LORD and King. "So turn away from your sins.
Then you will live!

A Song of Sadness About Israel's Princes

19 "Sing a song of sadness about Israel's
princes. 2Say to Israel,

"'You were like a mother lion to your princes.
She lay down among the young lions.
She brought up her cubs.
3 One of them was Jehoahaz.
He became a strong lion.
He learned to tear apart what he caught.
And he ate men up.
4 The nations heard about him.
They trapped him in their pit.
They put hooks in his face.
And they led him away to Egypt.

5 "'The mother lion looked and waited.
But all of her hope was gone.
So she got another one of her cubs.
She made him into a strong lion.
6 He prowled with the lions.
He became very strong.
He learned to tear apart what he caught.
And he ate men up.
7 He broke down their forts.
He completely destroyed their towns.
The land and all those who were in it
were terrified when he roared.
8 Then nations came against him.
They came from all around him.
They spread out their net to catch him.
He was trapped in their pit.
9 They used hooks to pull him into a cage.
They brought him to the king of
Babylonia.
They put him in prison.
So his roar was not heard anymore
on the mountains of Israel.

10 "'Israel, you were like a vine in a vineyard.
It was planted near water.
It had a lot of fruit and many branches.
There was plenty of water.
11 Its branches were strong.
Each was good enough to be made into a
ruler's rod.
The vine grew high
above all of the leaves.
It stood out because it was so tall
and had so many branches.
12 But Nebuchadnezzar became angry.
He pulled it up by its roots.
He threw it to the ground.
The east wind dried it up.
Its fruit was stripped off.
Its strong branches dried up.
And fire destroyed them.
13 Now it is planted in the Babylonian desert.
It is in a dry and thirsty land.
14 One of its main branches was Zedekiah.
Fire spread from it and burned up its fruit.
None of its branches is good enough
to be made into a ruler's rod.'

"That is a song of sadness. And that is how it should be used."

Israel Refuses to Obey the LORD

20 It was the seventh year since King Jehoiachin had been brought to Babylon as a
prisoner. On the tenth day of the fifth month, some
of the elders of Israel came to ask the LORD for
advice. They sat down with me.
2 Then a message came to me from the LORD. He
said, 3 "Son of man, speak to the elders of Israel.
Tell them, 'The LORD and King says, "Have you
come to ask me for advice? I will not let you do
that," announces the LORD and King. "And that is
just as sure as I am alive."'
4 "Are you going to judge them, son of man?
Will you judge them? Tell them the evil things
their people did long ago. I hate those things. 5 Tell
them, 'The LORD and King says, "I chose Israel.
On that day I raised my hand and took an oath. I
made a promise to the members of Jacob's family
line. I made myself known to them in Egypt. I
raised my hand and told them, 'I am the LORD your
God.'
6 "'"On that day I promised I would bring them
out of Egypt. I told them I would take them to a
land I had found for them. It had plenty of milk
and honey. It was the most beautiful land of all. 7 I
said to them, 'Each of you must get rid of the statues of the evil gods you worship. Do not pollute
yourselves by worshiping the gods of Egypt. I am
the LORD your God.'
8 "'"But they refused to obey me. They would
not listen to me. They did not get rid of the evil
gods they worshiped. And they did not turn away
from Egypt's gods. So I said I would pour out all
of my burning anger on them in Egypt.
9 "'"But I wanted my name to be honored. I kept
it from being treated as if it were not holy. I did
not want that to happen in front of the nations my
people lived among. I had made myself known to
Israel in the sight of those nations. I had brought
my people out of Egypt.
10 "'"So I led them out of Egypt. I brought them
into the Desert of Sinai. 11 I gave them my rules. I
made my laws known to them. The one who obeys
them will live by them. 12 I also told them to
observe my Sabbath days. That is the sign of the
covenant I made with them. I wanted them to
know that I made them holy. I am the LORD.
13 "'"But the people of Israel refused to obey me
in the desert. They did not follow my rules. They
turned their backs on my laws. The one who obeys
them will live by them. They totally misused my
Sabbath days. So I said I would pour out my burning anger on them. I would destroy them in the
desert.
14 "'"But I wanted my name to be honored. I
kept it from being treated as if it were not holy. I
did not want that to happen in front of the nations.
They had seen me bring Israel out of Egypt.
15 "'"I also raised my hand and took an oath in
the desert. I told my people I would not bring them

into the land I had given them. It had plenty of milk and honey. It was the most beautiful land of all. 16But they turned their backs on my laws. They did not follow my rules. They misused my Sabbaths. Their hearts were committed to worshiping the statues of their gods.

17“ ‘ “Then I felt sorry for them. So I did not destroy them. I did not put an end to them in the desert. 18I spoke to their children there. I said, ‘Do not follow the rules your parents gave you. Do not obey their laws. Do not pollute yourselves by worshiping their gods. 19I am the LORD your God. So follow my rules. Be careful to obey my laws. 20Keep my Sabbath days holy. That is the sign of the covenant I made with you. You will know that I am the LORD your God.’

21“ ‘ “But their children refused to obey me. They did not follow my rules. They were not careful to keep my laws. The one who obeys them will live by them. They misused my Sabbaths. So I said I would pour out all of my burning anger on them in the desert.

22“ ‘ “But I kept myself from punishing them at that time. I wanted my name to be honored. So I kept it from being treated as if it were not holy. I did not want that to happen in front of the nations. They had seen me bring Israel out of Egypt.

23“ ‘ “I also raised my hand and took an oath in the desert. I told my people I would scatter them among the nations. I would send them to other countries. 24They had not obeyed my laws. They had turned their backs on my rules. They had misused my Sabbaths. Their eyes longed to see the statues of their parents’ gods.

25“ ‘ “I even let them follow rules that were not good. I let them have laws they could not live by. 26I let them become polluted by offering sacrifices to other gods. They even sacrificed the first male child who was born in each family. I wanted to fill them with horror. Then they would know that I am the LORD.” ’

27“Son of man, speak to the people of Israel. Tell them, ‘The LORD and King says, “Your people spoke evil things against me long ago. They deserted me. 28But I brought them into the land. I had taken an oath and promised to give the land to them. Then they offered sacrifices that made me very angry. They did it on every high hill and under every green tree. There they brought their sweet-smelling incense. And there they poured out their drink offerings. 29Then I said to them, ‘What? You are going to a high place?’ ” ’ ” That high place is called Bamah to this very day.

The LORD Judges Israel and Blesses Them

30The LORD said to me, “Speak to the people of Israel. Tell them, ‘The LORD and King says, “Are you going to pollute yourselves the way your people did? Do you long to see the statues of their evil gods? 31You pollute yourselves by offering sacrifices to other gods. You even sacrifice your children in the fire. You continue to do those things to this very day. People of Israel, should I let you ask me for advice? I will not let you do that,” announces the LORD and King. “And that is just as sure as I am alive.

32“ ‘ “You say, ‘We want to be like the other nations. We want to be like all of the other people in the world. They serve gods that are made out of wood and stone.’ But what you have in mind will never happen. 33I will rule over you by reaching out my mighty hand and powerful arm. I will pour my burning anger out on you,” announces the LORD and King. “And that is just as sure as I am alive.

34“ ‘ “I will bring you back from the nations. I will gather you together from the countries where you have been scattered. I will reach out my mighty hand and powerful arm. I will pour my burning anger out on you. 35I will send you among the nations. There I will judge you face to face. It will be as if I were judging you in the desert again. 36Long ago, I judged your people in the desert of Egypt. In the same way, I will judge you,” announces the LORD and King.

37“ ‘ “I will take note of you as you pass under my shepherd’s rod. I will separate those who obey me from those who do not. And I will give the blessings of the new covenant to those of you who obey me. 38I will get rid of those among you who turn against me and refuse to obey me. I will bring them out of the land where they are living. But they will not enter the land of Israel. Then you will know that I am the LORD.

39“ ‘ “People of Israel, the LORD and King says, ‘Go, every one of you! Serve your gods. But later you will listen to me. You will no longer treat my name as if it were not holy. You will not offer sacrifices to other gods anymore.

40“ ‘ “ ‘People of Israel, you will serve me,’ announces the LORD and King. ‘You will serve me on my high and holy mountain in Jerusalem. There I will accept you. I will require your offerings and your finest gifts. I want you to bring them along with all of your other holy sacrifices. 41I will bring you back from the nations. I will gather you together from the countries where you have been scattered. Then I will accept you as if you were sweet-smelling incense. I will show that I am holy among you. The nations will see it.

42“ ‘ “ ‘I will bring you into the land of Israel. Then you will know that I am the LORD. Long ago I raised my hand and took an oath. I promised to give that land to your people. 43There you will remember your conduct. You will think about everything you did that polluted you. And you will hate yourselves because of all of the evil things you have done.

44“ ‘ “ ‘People of Israel, I will deal with you for the honor of my name. I will not deal with you based on your evil conduct and sinful practices.

Then you will know that I am the LORD,' announces the LORD and King."'"

Ezekiel Prophesies Against the South

45 A message came to me from the LORD. He said, 46 "Son of man, turn your attention to Judah in the south. Preach against it. Prophesy against its forests. 47 Tell them, 'Listen to the LORD's message. The LORD and King says, "I am about to set you on fire. The fire will destroy all of your trees. It will burn up green trees and dry trees alike. The blazing flame will not be put out. The faces of everyone from south to north will be burned by it. 48 Everyone will see that I started the fire. It will not be put out. I am the LORD."'"

49 Then I said, "LORD and King, people are talking about me. They are saying, 'Isn't he just telling stories?'"

God Uses Babylonia to Judge Israel

21 A message came to me from the LORD. He said, 2 "Son of man, turn your attention to Jerusalem. Preach against the temple. Prophesy against the land of Israel.

3 "Tell them, 'The LORD says, "I am against you. I will pull out my sword. I will cut off from you godly people and sinful people alike. 4 Because I am going to cut them off, my sword will be ready to use. I will strike everyone down from south to north. 5 Then all people will know that I have pulled out my sword. I will not put it back. I am the LORD."'

6 "Groan, son of man! Groan in front of your people with a broken heart and bitter sorrow. 7 They will ask you, 'Why are you groaning?'

"Then you will say, 'Because of the news that is coming. The hearts of all of the people will melt away in fear. Their hands will not be able to help them. Their spirits will grow weak. And their knees will become as weak as water.'

"The news is coming! You can be sure those things will happen," announces the LORD and King.

8 A message came to me from the LORD. He said, 9 "Son of man, prophesy. Say, 'The Lord says,

"'"A sword! A sword!
A sharp and shiny sword is coming from
Babylonia!
10 It is sharpened to kill people.
It flashes like lightning."'"

The people say, "Should we take delight in the rod of the ruler of the LORD's son Judah? The sword looks down on every stick like that."

11 The LORD says,

"I have told Nebuchadnezzar to shine
his sword.
It is in his hand.
It has been sharpened and shined.
It is ready for the killer's hand.
12 Son of man, cry out and sob.
The sword is against my people.
It is against all of the princes of Israel.
It will kill them
along with the rest of my people.
So beat your chest in sorrow.

13 "You can be sure that testing will come. Why does the sword look down on the rod? Because the rod will not continue to rule," announces the LORD and King.

14 "Son of man, prophesy.
Clap your hands.
Let the sword strike twice.
Let it strike even three times.
It is a sword to kill people.
It is a sword to kill many people.
It is closing in on them from every side.
15 People's hearts will melt away in fear.
Many will be wounded or killed.
I have prepared the sword to kill people
at all of their city gates.
It flashes like lightning.
It is in the killer's hand.
16 Sword, cut to the right.
Then cut to the left.
Strike people down everywhere your blade
is turned.
17 I too will clap my hands.
My burning anger will calm down.
I have spoken. I am the LORD."

18 A message came to me from the LORD. He said, 19 "Son of man, mark out on a map two roads for the sword to take. The sword belongs to the king of Babylonia. Both roads start from the same country. Put up a sign where the road turns off to the city of Rabbah. 20 Mark out one road for the sword to take against Rabbah in Ammon. Mark out another against Judah and the walls of Jerusalem.

21 "The king of Babylonia will stop at the place where the two roads meet. He will ask his gods to tell him which way to go. He will cast lots by pulling arrows out of a bag. And he will look carefully at the liver of a sheep.

22 "His right hand will pull out the arrow for Jerusalem. There he will get huge logs ready to knock down its gates. He will give the command to kill its people. He will sound the battle cry. He will build a ramp up to the city wall. He will bring in his war machines.

23 "The decision to attack Jerusalem will seem like the wrong advice to those who made a treaty with Nebuchadnezzar. But he will remind them that they are guilty. And he will take them away as prisoners."

24 So the LORD and King says, "You people have reminded everyone of how guilty you are. You have done it by refusing to obey me or any other authority. Everything you do clearly shows how sinful you are. So you will be taken away as prisoners."

25King Zedekiah, the day for you to be punished
has finally come. You are an unholy and evil
prince in Israel. Your time is up. 26The LORD and
King says, "Take off your turban. Remove your
crown. Things will not be as they were in the past.
Those who are not important will be honored. And
those who are honored will be brought down. 27Je-
rusalem will fall. I will destroy it. It will not be
rebuilt until the true king comes. After all, the
kingdom belongs to him. I will give it to him.
28"Son of man, prophesy. Say, 'The LORD and
King speaks about the Ammonites. He also talks
about the way they laugh because of Jerusalem's
fall. He says,

"'"A sword! A sword!
    Nebuchadnezzar's sword is ready to
        kill you.
It is shined to destroy you.
    It flashes like lightning.
29 The visions of your prophets are false.
    They use magic to try to find out
    what is going to happen to you.
But their magic tricks are lies.
    The sword will strike the necks of you
        sinful people.
    You will be killed.
The day for you to be punished has finally
        come.
    Your time is up.
30 Ammon, return your sword to its place.
    In the land where you were created,
        I will judge you.
    That is where you came from.
31 I will pour out my anger on you.
    I will breathe out my burning anger
        against you.
I will hand you over to mean people.
    They are skilled at destroying others.
32 You will be burned in the fire.
    Your blood will be spilled in your land.
You will not be remembered anymore.
    I have spoken. I am the LORD."'"

Jerusalem Sins Against the LORD

22 A message came to me from the LORD. He
said, 2"Son of man, are you going to judge
Jerusalem? Will you judge this city that has so
many murderers in it? Then tell its people they
have done many evil things. I hate those things.
3Tell them, 'The LORD and King says, "Your city
brings death on itself. You spill blood inside its
walls. You pollute yourselves by making statues of
gods. 4You are guilty of spilling blood. The statues
you have made have polluted you.
"'"You have brought your days to a close. The
end of your years has come. So the nations will
make fun of you. All of the countries will laugh at
you. 5Those who are near you will tell jokes about
you. So will those who are far away. Trouble fills
the streets of your sinful city.
6"'"The princes of Israel are in your city. All of
them use their power to spill blood. 7They have
made fun of fathers and mothers alike. They have
crushed outsiders. They have treated badly the
children whose fathers have died. They have done
the same thing to widows.
8"'"You have looked down on the holy things
that were set apart to me. You have misused my
Sabbath days. 9You have spread lies about others
so you can spill someone's blood. You eat at the
mountain temples. You commit impure acts.
10"'"You bring shame on your fathers by having
sex with their wives. You have sex with women
during their monthly period. That is when they are
'unclean.' 11One of you has sex with another man's
wife. I hate that sin. Another brings shame on his
daughter-in-law by having sex with her. Still
another has sex with his sister, even though she is
his own father's daughter.
12"'"You accept money from people who want
special favors. You do it to spill someone's blood.
You charge too much interest when you lend
money. You get rich by cheating your neighbors.
And you have forgotten me," announces the LORD
and King.
13"'"I will clap my hands because I am so
angry. You got rich by cheating others. You spilled
blood inside the walls of your city. 14Will you be
brave on the day I deal with you? Will you be
strong at that time? I have spoken. I will do it. I
am the LORD.
15"'"I will scatter you among the nations. I will
send you to other countries. I will put an end to
your 'uncleanness.' 16You will be polluted in the
sight of the nations. Then you will know that I am
the LORD."'"
17A message came to me from the LORD. He
said, 18"Son of man, the people of Israel have
become like scum to me. All of them are like the
copper, tin, iron and lead that are left inside a furnace. They are only the scum that is removed from
silver."
19So the LORD and King says, "People of Israel,
all of you have become like scum. So I will gather
you together in Jerusalem. 20Men put silver, copper, iron, lead and tin into a furnace. They melt it
with a blazing fire. In the same way, I will gather
you. I will pour out my burning anger on you. I
will put you inside the city and melt you. 21I will
gather you together. My burning anger will blaze
out at you. And you will be melted inside Jerusalem. 22Silver is melted in a furnace. And you will
be melted inside the city. Then you will know that
I have poured out my burning anger on you. I am
the LORD."
23Another message came to me from the LORD.
He said, 24"Son of man, speak to the land. Tell it,
'You have not had any rain or showers. That is
because I am angry with you.'
25"Ezekiel, the princes of the land are like a roaring lion that tears its food apart. They eat people

up. They take treasures and other valuable things.
They cause many women in the land to become
widows.
26"Its priests break my law. They treat things
that are set apart to me as if they were not holy.
They treat holy and common things as if they were
the same. They teach that there is no difference
between things that are 'clean' and things that are
not. They refuse to keep my Sabbath days. So they
treat me as if I were not holy.
27"The officials in the land are like wolves that
tear their food apart. They spill blood and kill people to get rich. 28The prophets cover up those acts
for them. The visions of those prophets are false.
They use magic to try to find out what is going to
happen. But their magic tricks are lies. They say,
'The LORD and King says,' But I have not spoken
to them.
29"The people of the land get rich by cheating
others. They steal. They crush those who are poor
and in need. They treat outsiders badly. They
refuse to be fair to them.
30"I looked for a man among them who would
stand up for Jerusalem. I tried to find someone
who would pray to me for the land. Then I would
not have to destroy it. But I could not find anyone
who would pray for it. 31So I will pour out my
anger on its people. I will destroy them because
my anger burns against them. And anything that
happens to them will be their own fault,"
announces the LORD and King.

Samaria and Jerusalem Are Like Two Impure Sisters

23 A message came to me from the LORD. He
said, 2"Son of man, once there were two
women. They had the same mother. 3They became
prostitutes in Egypt. They have been unfaithful to
me since they were young. In that land they
allowed their breasts to be touched. They permitted their virgin breasts to be kissed.
4"The older sister was named Oholah. The
younger one was Oholibah. They belonged to me.
Sons and daughters were born to them. Oholah
stands for Samaria. And Oholibah stands for Jerusalem.
5"Oholah was unfaithful to me even while she
still belonged to me. She longed for her Assyrian
lovers. 6They included soldiers who wore blue uniforms. They also included governors and commanders. All of them were young and handsome.
They rode horses. 7She gave herself as a prostitute
to all of Assyria's finest warriors. She polluted herself with the statues of the gods of everyone she
longed for.
8"She started being a prostitute in Egypt. And
she never stopped. When she was young, men had
sex with her. They kissed her virgin breasts. They
used up all of their sinful longings on her.
9"So I handed her over to her Assyrian lovers.
She longed for them. 10They stripped her naked.
They took her sons and daughters away. And they
killed her with their swords. Other women laughed
when that happened. I was the one who had punished her.
11"Her sister Oholibah saw it. But her evil longing for sexual sin was worse than her sister's. 12She
too longed for the men of Assyria. They included
governors and commanders. They included soldiers who wore uniforms. They also included men
who rode horses. All of them were young and
handsome. 13I saw that she too polluted herself. So
both sisters did the same evil things.
14"But Oholibah went even further with her sexual sins. She saw pictures of men drawn on a wall.
They were figures of Babylonians drawn in red.
15They had belts around their waists. They wore
flowing turbans on their heads. All of them looked
like Babylonian chariot officers. They were from
the land of the Chaldeans.
16"As soon as she saw the pictures, she longed
for the men. So she sent messengers to them in
Babylonia. 17Then the Babylonians came to her.
They went to bed with her. They made love to her.
They polluted her when they had sex with her.
After they did it, she became sick of them. So she
turned away from them.
18"She acted like a prostitute who had no shame
at all. She openly showed her naked body. I became
sick of what she was doing. So I turned away from
her. I had also turned away from her sister.
19"But Oholibah offered her body to her lovers
again and again. She remembered the days when
she was a young prostitute in Egypt. 20There she
had longed for her lovers. Their private parts
seemed as big as those of donkeys. And their flow
of semen appeared to be as much as that of horses.
21So you wanted to return to the days when you
were young. You longed for the time when you
first became impure in Egypt. That was when you
allowed your breasts to be kissed. And you permitted your young breasts to be touched."
22So the LORD and King says, "Oholibah, I will
stir up your lovers against you. You became sick of
them. You turned away from them. But I will bring
them against you from every side. 23They include
the Babylonians and all of the Chaldeans. They
include the men from Pekod, Shoa and Koa. They
also include all of the Assyrians. They are young
and handsome. Some of them are governors and
commanders. Others are chariot officers. Still others are very high officials. All of them ride horses.
24"So a huge army will come against you with
weapons, chariots and wagons. They will take up
positions against you on every side. They will
carry large and small shields. They will wear helmets. I will turn you over to them to be punished.
They will punish you in their own way.
25"I will pour out my jealous anger on you. And
the army's anger will burn against you. They will
cut off your noses and ears. Some of you who are
left will be killed with swords. They will take your

sons and daughters away. Others of you who are
left will be burned up. 26The army will also strip
your clothes off. They will take your fine jewelry
away from you.

27"You became an impure prostitute in Egypt.
But I will put a stop to all of that. You will no
longer want to do any of it. You will not remember
Egypt anymore."

28The LORD and King says, "I am about to hand
you over to people you hate. You became sick of
them. You turned away from them. 29They will
punish you because they hate you so much. They
will take everything you have worked for away
from you. They will leave you naked and bare.
Then everyone will see that you are a prostitute
who has no shame at all. You were impure. You
offered your body to your lovers again and again.

30"That is why you will be punished. You
longed for lovers in other nations. You polluted
yourself by worshiping their gods. 31You did the
same things your sister Oholah did. So I will put
her cup in your hand. It is filled with the wine of
my anger."

32The LORD and King says to Oholibah,

"You will drink from your sister's cup.
    It is large and deep.
    It is filled with the wine of my anger.
So others will laugh at you.
    They will make fun of you.
33 You will become drunk and sad.
    The cup of my anger will completely
        destroy you.
    It is the same cup your sister Samaria
        drank from.
34 You will drink from it until it is empty.
    Then you will throw it down and break
        it in pieces.
    And you will claw at your breasts.
I have spoken," announces the LORD and King.

35So the LORD and King says, "You have forgotten me. You have pushed me behind your back.
You have been impure. You have acted like a prostitute. So I will punish you."

36The LORD said to me, "Son of man, are you
going to judge Oholah and Oholibah? Then tell
them they have done many evil things. I hate those
things. 37They have committed adultery. Their
hands are covered with the blood of the people
they have murdered. They have worshiped other
gods. They have not been faithful to me. They
have even sacrificed their children as food to other
gods. Those children belonged to me.

38"Here are some other things the sisters have
done to me. They have polluted my temple. They
have misused my Sabbath days. 39They have sacrificed their children to their gods. On that same
day they entered my temple and polluted it. That is
what they have done in my house.

40"They even sent messengers to bring men
from far away. When the men arrived, Oholibah
took a bath. She put makeup on her eyes. She put
her jewelry on. 41She sat down on a beautiful
couch. A table was in front of it. There she put the
incense and olive oil that belonged to me.

42"The noise of a carefree crowd was all around
her. Sabeans were brought from the desert. Other
men were brought along with them. They put
bracelets on the arms of the two sisters. They put
beautiful crowns on their heads.

43"Then I spoke about Oholibah. She was worn
out by adultery. I said, 'Let them use her as a prostitute. After all, that is what she is.' 44So they had
sex with her. In fact, they had sex with both of
those impure women, Oholah and Oholibah. It was
just like having sex with prostitutes.

45"But men who are right with God will sentence the sisters to be punished. They will be punished in the same way as women who commit
adultery and murder. After all, they have committed adultery. And their hands are covered with the
blood of the people they have murdered."

46The LORD and King says, "Bring an angry
crowd against the sisters. Hand them over to those
who will terrify them and steal everything they
have. 47The crowd will kill them by throwing
stones at them. They will cut them down with their
swords. They will kill their sons and daughters.
And they will burn their houses down.

48"So I will put an end to impurity in the land.
Then all of its women will be warned. They will
not want to be like the sisters. 49Those sisters will
be punished because of the impure things they
have done. They will be judged because they have
worshiped other gods. Then they will know that I
am the LORD and King."

Jerusalem Is Like a Cooking Pot

24 It was the ninth year since King Jehoiachin
had been brought to Babylon as a prisoner.
On the tenth day of the tenth month, a message
came to me from the LORD. He said, 2"Son of man,
write down today's date. The king of Babylonia
has surrounded Jerusalem and attacked it this very
day.

3"Your people refuse to obey me. So tell them a
story. Say to them, 'The LORD and King told me,

"'"Put a cooking pot on the fire.
    Pour water into it.
4 Put pieces of meat in it.
    Use all of the best pieces.
Use the leg and shoulder.
    Fill it with the best bones.
5 Pick the finest animal in the flock.
    Pile wood under the pot to cook the bones.
Bring the water to a boil.
    Cook the bones in it."'"

6The LORD and King says,

"How terrible it will be for this city!
    It has so many murderers in it.

How terrible for the pot that is coated
with scum!
The scum on it will not go away.
Take the meat and bones out of the pot piece
by piece.
Do not cast lots for them.

7 "The blood Jerusalem's people spilled is inside
its walls.
They poured it out on a bare rock.
They did not pour it on the ground.
If they had, dust would have covered it up.
8 So I put their blood on the bare rock.
I did not want it to be covered up.
I poured my burning anger out on them.
I paid them back."

9 So the LORD and King said to me,

"How terrible it will be for this city!
It has so many murderers in it.
I too will pile the wood high.
10 So pile on the wood.
Light the fire.
Cook the meat well.
Mix in the spices.
Let the bones be blackened.
11 Then set the empty pot on the coals.
Let it get hot. Let its copper glow.
Then what is not pure in it will melt.
Its scum will be burned away.
12 But it can't be cleaned up.
Its thick scum has not been removed.
Even fire can't burn it off.

13 "Jerusalem, you are really impure. I tried to
clean you up. But you would not let me make you
pure. So you will not be clean again until my burning anger against you has calmed down.

14 "I have spoken. The time has come for me to
act. I will not hold back. I will not feel sorry for
you. I will do what I said I would do. You will be
judged for your conduct and actions. I am the
LORD," announces the LORD and King.

Ezekiel's Wife Dies

15 A message came to me from the LORD. He
said, 16 "Son of man, I will take away from you the
wife you delight in. It will happen very soon. But
do not sing songs of sadness. Do not let any tears
flow from your eyes. 17 Groan quietly. Do not sob
out loud over your wife when she dies. Keep your
turban on your head. Keep your sandals on your
feet. Do not cover the lower part of your face. Do
not eat the food people eat to comfort them when
someone dies."

18 So I spoke to my people in the morning. And
in the evening my wife died. The next morning I
did what I had been commanded to do.

19 Then the people said to me, "Tell us what
these things have to do with us."

20 So I told them. I said, "A message came to me
from the LORD. He said, 21 'Speak to the people of
Israel. Tell them, "The LORD and King says, 'I am
about to pollute my temple. I will let the Babylonians burn it down. It is the beautiful building you
are so proud of. You take delight in it. You love it.
The sons and daughters you left behind will be
killed with swords.

22 " ' " 'So do what Ezekiel did. Do not cover the
lower part of your face. Do not eat the food people eat to comfort them when someone dies.
23 Keep your turbans on your heads. Keep your
sandals on your feet. Do not cry or sob. You will
waste away because you have sinned so much.
You will groan among yourselves.

24 " ' " 'What Ezekiel has done will show you
what is going to happen to you. You will do just as
he has done. Then you will know that I am the
LORD and King.' " '

25 "Son of man, I will take away their beautiful
temple. It is their joy and glory. They take delight
in it. Their hearts long for it. I will also take away
their sons and daughters. 26 On the day I destroy
everything, a man will escape. He will come and
tell you the news.

27 "At that time I will open your mouth. Then
you will no longer be silent. You will speak with
the man. That will show them what will happen to
them. And they will know that I am the LORD."

A Message About Ammon

25 A message came to me from the LORD. He
said, 2 "Son of man, turn your attention to
the Ammonites. Prophesy against them. 3 Tell
them, 'Listen to the message of the LORD and
King. He says, "You laughed when my temple was
polluted. You also laughed when the land of Israel was completely destroyed. You made fun of the
people of Judah when they were taken away as
prisoners. 4 So I am going to hand you over to the
people of the east. They will set up their tents in
your land. They will camp among you. They will
eat your fruit. They will drink your milk. 5 I will
turn the city of Rabbah into grasslands for camels.
Ammon will become a resting place for sheep.
Then you will know that I am the LORD." ' "

6 The LORD and King says, "You clapped your
hands. You stamped your feet. You hated the land
of Israel deep down inside you. You were glad
because of what happened to it. 7 So I will reach
out my powerful hand against you. I will give you
and everything you have to the nations. I will cut
you off from them. I will wipe you out. I will
destroy you. Then you will know that I am the
LORD."

A Message About Moab

8 The LORD and King says, "Moab and Edom
said, 'Look! The people of Judah have become
like all of the other nations.' 9 So I will let Moab's
enemies attack its lower hills. They will begin at
the border towns. Those towns include Beth Jeshimoth, Baal Meon and Kiriathaim. They are the

glory of that land. 10I will hand Moab over to the people of the east. I will also give the Ammonites to them. And the Ammonites will no longer be remembered among the nations. 11I will punish Moab. Then they will know that I am the LORD."

A Message About Edom

12The LORD and King says, "Edom got even with the people of Judah. That made them very guilty." 13He continues, "I will reach out my hand against Edom. I will kill its people and their animals. I will completely destroy it. They will be killed with swords from Teman all the way to Dedan. 14I will use my people Israel to pay Edom back. They will punish Edom because my anger burns against it. They will know how I pay my enemies back," announces the LORD and King.

A Message About the Philistines

15The LORD and King says, "The Philistines hated Judah deep down inside them. So they tried to get even with them. They had been Judah's enemies for many years. So they tried to destroy them." 16He continues, "I am about to reach out my hand against the Philistines. I will cut off the Kerethites. I will destroy those who remain along the coast. 17You can be sure that I will pay them back. I will punish them because my anger burns against them. When I pay them back, they will know that I am the LORD."

A Message About Tyre

26 It was the first day of a month near the end of the 11th year since King Jehoiachin had been brought to Babylon as a prisoner. A message came to me from the LORD. He said, 2"Son of man, Tyre laughed because of what happened to Jerusalem. The people of Tyre said, 'Jerusalem is the gateway to the nations. But the gate is broken. Its doors have swung open to us. Jerusalem has been destroyed. So now we will succeed.'"

3The LORD and King says, "But I am against you, Tyre. I will bring many nations against you. They will come in like the waves of the sea. 4They will destroy your walls. They will pull your towers down. I will clear away the stones of your broken-down buildings. I will turn you into nothing but a bare rock.

5"Out in the Mediterranean Sea your island city will become a place to spread fishnets. I have spoken," announces the LORD and King. "The nations will take you and everything you have. 6Your settlements on the coast will be destroyed by war. Then you will know that I am the LORD."

7The LORD and King says, "From the north I am going to bring Nebuchadnezzar against Tyre. He is king of Babylonia. He is the greatest king of all. He will come with horses and chariots. Horsemen and a great army will be brought along with him.

8"He will go to war against you. He will destroy your settlements on the coast. He will bring in war machines to attack you. A ramp will be built up to your walls. He will use his shields against you. 9He will use huge logs to knock your walls down. He will destroy your towers with his weapons.

10"He will have so many horses that they will cover you with dust. Your walls will shake because of the noise of his war horses, wagons and chariots. He will enter your gates, just as men enter a city whose walls have been broken through. 11The hoofs of his horses will pound in your streets. He will kill your people with swords. Your strong pillars will fall to the ground.

12"His men will take away from you your wealth and anything else you have. They will pull your walls down. They will completely destroy your fine houses. They will throw the stones and lumber of your broken-down buildings into the sea.

13"I will put an end to your noisy songs. No one will hear the music of your harps anymore. 14I will turn you into nothing but a bare rock. You will become a place to spread fishnets. You will never be rebuilt. I have spoken. I am the LORD," announces the LORD and King.

15The LORD and King speaks to Tyre. He says, "The lands along the coast will shake because of the sound of your fall. Wounded people will groan because so many are dying there.

16"Then all of the princes along the coast will step down from their thrones. They will put their robes away. They will take off their beautiful clothes. They will sit on the ground. They will put on terror as if it were their clothes. They will tremble with fear all the time. They will be shocked because of what has happened to you.

17"Then they will sing a song of sadness about you. They will say to you,

"'Famous city, you have been completely
destroyed!
You were filled with sea traders.
You and your citizens
were a mighty power on the seas.
You terrified everyone
who lived in you.
18 The lands along the coast trembled with fear
when you fell.
The islands in the sea
were terrified when you were destroyed.'"

19The LORD and King says to Tyre, "I will turn you into an empty city. You will be like cities where no one lives anymore. I will cause the ocean to sweep over you. Its mighty waters will cover you. 20So I will bring you down together with those who go down into the grave. The people who are there lived long ago. You will have to live in the earth below. It will be like living in buildings that were destroyed many years ago. You will go down into the grave along with others. And you will never come back. You will not take your place in this world again. 21I will bring you to a horrible end. You will be gone forever. People will look for

you. But they will never find you," announces the
LORD and King.

A Song of Sadness About Tyre

27 A message came to me from the LORD. He
said, [2]"Son of man, sing a song of sadness
about Tyre. [3]It is located at the gateway to the
Mediterranean Sea. It does business with nations
on many coasts. Say to it, 'The LORD and King
says,

"'"Tyre, you say,
'I am perfect and beautiful.'
4 You were like a ship that ruled over the
high seas.
Your builders made you perfect and
beautiful.
5 They cut all of your lumber
from pine trees on Mount Hermon.
They used a cedar tree from Lebanon
to make a mast for you.
6 They made your oars
out of oak trees from Bashan.
They made your deck out of cypress wood
from the coasts of Cyprus.
They decorated it with ivory.
7 Your sail was made out of beautiful,
Egyptian linen.
It served as your banner.
Your shades were made out of blue and
purple cloth.
They were from the coasts of Elishah.
8 Men from Sidon and Arvad manned your oars.
Tyre, your sailors were skillful.
9 Very skilled workers from Byblos were
on board.
They kept you waterproof.
All of the ships on the sea and their sailors
came up beside you.
They brought their goods to trade for yours.
10 "'"City of Tyre, men from Persia, Lydia
and Put
served as soldiers in your army.
They hung their shields and helmets on
your walls.
That brought glory to you.
11 Men from Arvad and Cilicia
guarded your walls on every side.
Men from Gammad
were in your towers.
They hung their shields around your walls.
They made you perfect and beautiful.

12 "'"Tarshish did business with you because
you had so much wealth. They traded silver, iron,
tin and lead for your goods.
13 "'"Greece, Tubal and Meshech did business
with you. They traded slaves and bronze articles
for your products.
14 "'"Men from Beth Togarmah traded work
horses, war horses and mules for your goods.
15 "'"Men from Rhodes did business with you.
Many lands along the coast bought goods from
you. They paid you with ivory tusks and ebony
wood.
16 "'"Aram did business with you because you
had so many products for sale. They traded
turquoise, purple cloth and needlework for your
goods. They also traded fine linen, coral and rubies
for them.
17 "'"Judah and Israel did business with you.
They traded wheat from Minnith, sweets, honey,
olive oil and lotion for your products.
18 "'"Damascus traded wine from Helbon and
wool from Zahar to you. They did business with
you because you had so many products and so
much wealth.
19 "'"Danites and Greeks from Uzal bought
goods from you. They traded wrought iron, cassia
and cane for your products.
20 "'"Dedan traded saddle blankets to you.
21 "'"Arabia and all of the princes of Kedar
bought goods from you. They traded you lambs,
rams and goats for them.
22 "'"Traders from Sheba and Raamah did business with you. They traded the finest spices, jewels and gold for your goods.
23 "'"Haran, Canneh and Eden did business with
you. So did traders from Sheba, Asshur and Kil-
mad. [24]In your market place they traded beautiful
clothes, blue cloth, and needlework to you. They
also traded colorful rugs that had twisted cords and
tight knots.

25 "'"The ships of Tarshish
carry your products.
You are like a ship filled with a heavy load
in the middle of the sea.
26 The sailors who man your oars take you
out to the high seas.
But the east wind will break you in pieces
in the middle of the sea.
27 You will be wrecked on that day.
Your wealth, goods and products
will sink deep into the sea.
So will your sailors, officers, carpenters,
traders and all of your soldiers.
Anyone else on board will sink too.
28 The lands along the coast will shake
when your officers cry out.
29 All those who man the oars
will desert their ships.
The sailors and all of the officers
will stand on the shore.
30 They will raise their voices.
They will cry bitterly over you.
They will sprinkle dust on their heads.
They will roll in ashes.
31 They will shave their heads because of you.
And they will put on black clothes.
They will sob over you.
Their spirits will be greatly troubled.
They will be very sad.

32 As they sob and cry over you,
they will sing a song of sadness about you.
They will say, 'Who was ever like Tyre?
It was destroyed in the sea.'
33 Your goods went out on the seas.
You supplied many nations with what
they needed.
You had so much wealth and so many
products.
You made the kings of the earth rich.
34 Now the sea has torn you apart.
You have sunk deep down into it.
Your products and all of your people
have gone down with you.
35 All those who live in the lands along the coast
are shocked because of what has happened
to you.
Their kings tremble with fear.
Their faces are twisted in horror.
36 The traders among the nations hiss at you.
You have come to a horrible end.
And you will be gone forever.""'

A Message About the King of Tyre

28 A message came to me from the LORD. He
said, 2"Son of man, speak to Ethbaal. He is
the ruler of Tyre. Tell him, 'The LORD and King
says,

"'"In your proud heart
you say, 'I am a god.
I sit on the throne of a god
in the Mediterranean Sea.'
But you are only a man. You are not a god.
In spite of that, you think you are as wise
as a god.
3 Are you wiser than Daniel?
Isn't even one secret hidden from you?
4 You are wise and understanding.
So you have become very wealthy.
You have piled up gold and silver
among your treasures.
5 You have used your great skill in trading
to increase your wealth.
You are very rich.
So your heart has become proud."'"

6The LORD and King says,

"You think you are wise.
In fact, you claim to be as wise as a god.
7 So I am going to bring strangers against you.
They will not show you any pity at all.
They will use their swords against your beauty
and wisdom.
They will strike down your shining glory.
8 They will bring you down to the grave.
You will die a horrible death
in the middle of the sea.
9 Then will you say, 'I am a god'?
Will you say that to those who kill you?
You will be only a man to those who kill you.
You will not be a god to them.
10 You will die just like those who have not been
circumcised.
Strangers will kill you.

I have spoken," announces the LORD and King.

11A message came to me from the LORD. He
said, 12"Son of man, sing a song of sadness about
the king of Tyre. Tell him, 'The LORD and King
says,

"'"You were the model of perfection.
You were full of wisdom.
You were perfect and beautiful.
13 You were in Eden.
It was my garden.
All kinds of jewels decorated you.
Here is a list of them.

ruby, topaz and emerald
chrysolite, onyx and jasper
sapphire, turquoise and beryl

Your settings and mountings were made out
of gold.
On the day you were created,
they were prepared.
14 I appointed you to be like a guardian cherub.
I anointed you for that purpose.
You were on my holy mountain.
You walked among the gleaming jewels.
15 Your conduct was without blame
from the day you were created.
But soon you began to sin.
16 You traded with many nations.
You harmed people everywhere.
And you sinned.
So I sent you away from my mountain in shame.
Guardian cherub, I drove you away
from among the gleaming jewels.
17 You thought you were so handsome
that it made your heart proud.
You thought you were so glorious
that it spoiled your wisdom.
So I threw you down to the earth.
I made an example out of you in front
of kings.
18 Your many sins and dishonest trade
polluted your temple.
So I made you go up in flames.
I turned you into nothing but ashes
on the ground.
I let everyone see it.
19 All of the nations that knew you
are shocked because of what happened
to you.
You have come to a horrible end.
And you will be gone forever."'"

A Message About Sidon

20A message came to me from the LORD. He
said, 21"Son of man, turn your attention to the city
of Sidon. Prophesy against it. 22Say, 'The LORD
and King says,

"""Sidon, I am against your people.
I will gain glory for myself inside your
city walls.
I will punish your people.
I will show that I am holy among them.
Then they will know that I am the LORD.
23 I will send a plague on them.
I will make blood flow in your streets.
Those who are killed will fall inside you.
Swords will strike your people on
every side.
Then they will know that I am the LORD.

24"""The people of Israel will no longer have
neighbors who hate them. Those neighbors will
not be like sharp and painful thorns anymore. Then
Israel will know that I am the LORD and King."'"

25The LORD and King says, "I will gather the
people of Israel together from the nations where
they have been scattered. I will show that I am
holy among them. I will let the nations see it. Then
Israel will live in their own land. I gave it to my
servant Jacob. 26My people will live there in safety.
They will build houses. They will plant vineyards.
They will live in safety. I will punish all of their
neighbors who told lies about them. Then Israel
will know that I am the LORD their God."

A Message About Egypt

29 It was the tenth year since King Jehoiachin
had been brought to Babylon as a prisoner.
On the 12th day of the tenth month, a message
came to me from the LORD. He said, 2"Son of man,
turn your attention to Pharaoh Hophra. He is king
of Egypt. Prophesy against him and the whole land
of Egypt. 3Tell him, 'The LORD and King says,

"""Pharaoh Hophra, I am against you.
King of Egypt, you are like a huge monster
lying among your streams.
You say, 'The Nile River belongs to me.
I made it for myself.'
4 But I will put hooks in your jaws.
I will make the fish in your streams
stick to your scales.
I will pull you out from among your streams.
All of the fish will stick to your scales.
5 I will leave you out in the desert.
All of the fish in your streams
will be there with you.
You will fall down in an open field.
You will not be picked up.
I will feed you to the wild animals
and to the birds of the air.

6Then everyone who lives in Egypt will know that
I am the LORD.

"""You have been like a walking stick made out
of a papyrus stem. The people of Israel tried to
lean on you. 7They took hold of you. But you
broke under their weight. You tore their shoulders
open. They leaned on you. But you snapped in
two. And their backs were broken."'"

8So the LORD and King says, "I will send Nebuchadnezzar's sword against you. He will kill your
people and their animals. 9Egypt will become a dry
and empty desert. Then your people will know that
I am the LORD.

"You said, 'The Nile River belongs to me. I
made it for myself.' 10So I am against you and your
streams. I will destroy the land of Egypt. I will turn
it into a dry and empty desert from Migdol all the
way to Aswan. I will destroy everything as far as
the border of Cush.

11"No people or animals will travel through
Egypt. No one will even live there for 40 years.
12Egypt will be more empty than any other land.
Its destroyed cities will lie empty for 40 years. I
will scatter the people of Egypt among the nations.
I will send them to other countries."

13But the LORD and King says, "At the end of
40 years I will gather the Egyptians together from
the nations where they were scattered. 14I will
bring them back from where they were taken as
prisoners. I will return them to Upper Egypt. That
is where they came from. There they will be an
unimportant kingdom.

15"Egypt will be the least important kingdom of
all. It will never place itself above the other nations
again. I will make it very weak. Then it will never
again rule over the nations. 16The people of Israel
will no longer trust in Egypt. Instead, Egypt will
remind them of how they sinned when they turned
to it for help. Then they will know that I am the
LORD and King."

17It was the 27th year since King Jehoiachin had
been brought to Babylon as a prisoner. On the first
day of the first month, a message came to me from
the LORD. He said, 18"Son of man, Nebuchadnezzar,
the king of Babylonia, drove his army in a hard military campaign against Tyre. Their helmets rubbed
their heads bare. The heavy loads they carried made
their shoulders raw. But he and his army did not gain
anything from the campaign he led against Tyre.

19"So I am going to give Egypt to Nebuchadnezzar, the king of Babylonia. He will carry off its
wealth. He will take away anything else you have.
He will give it to his army. 20I have given Egypt to
him as a reward for his efforts. After all, he and his
army attacked Egypt because I told them to,"
announces the LORD and King.

21"When Nebuchadnezzar wins the battle over
Egypt, I will make the people of Israel strong
again. Ezekiel, I will open your mouth. And you
will be able to speak to them. Then they will know
that I am the LORD."

A Song of Sadness About Egypt

30 A message came to me from the LORD. He
said, 2"Son of man, prophesy. Say, 'The
LORD and King says,

"""Cry out,
'A terrible day is coming!'

[3] The day is near.
The day of the LORD is coming.
It will be a cloudy day.
The nations have been sentenced to die.
[4] I will send Nebuchadnezzar's sword against Egypt.
Cush will suffer terribly.
Many will die in Egypt.
Then its wealth will be carried away.
Its foundations will be torn down.

[5]The people of Cush, Put, Lydia, Libya and the whole land of Arabia will be killed with swords. So will the Jews who live in Egypt. They went there from the covenant land of Israel. And the Egyptians will die too." ' "

[6]The LORD says,

"Those who were going to help Egypt will die.
The strength Egypt was so proud of will fail.
Its people will be killed with swords
from Migdol all the way to Aswan,"
announces the LORD and King.
[7] "Egypt will be more empty than any other land.
Its cities will be completely destroyed.
[8] I will set Egypt on fire.
All those who came to help it will be crushed.
Then they will know that I am the LORD.

[9]"At that time I will send messengers out in ships. They will terrify the people of Cush who are so contented. Cush will suffer greatly when Egypt falls. And you can be sure it will fall."

[10]The LORD and King says,

"I will put an end to the huge armies of Egypt.
I will use Nebuchadnezzar, the king of Babylonia, to do it.
[11] He and his armies will attack the land and destroy it.
They will not show its people any pity at all.
They will use their swords against Egypt.
They will fill the land with dead bodies.
[12] I will dry up the streams of the Nile River.
I will sell the land to evil men.
I will use the powerful hands of strangers
to destroy the land and everything in it.

"I have spoken. I am the LORD."

[13]The LORD and King says,

"I will destroy the statues of Egypt's gods.
I will put an end to the gods
the people in Memphis worship.
Egypt will not have princes anymore.
I will spread fear all through the land.
[14] I will completely destroy Upper Egypt.
I will set Zoan on fire.
I will punish Thebes.
[15] I will pour out my burning anger on Pelusium.
It is a fort in eastern Egypt.
I will cut off the huge army of Thebes.
[16] I will set Egypt on fire.
Pelusium will groan with terrible pain.
Thebes will be ripped apart.
Memphis will suffer greatly
because of everything that happens.
[17] The young men of Heliopolis and Bubastis will be killed with swords.
Their people will be taken away as prisoners.
[18] I will break Egypt's power over other lands.
That will be a dark day for Tahpanhes.
There the strength Egypt was so proud of will come to an end.
Egypt will be covered with clouds.
The people in its villages
will be taken away as prisoners.
[19] So I will punish Egypt.
Then they will know that I am the LORD."

[20]It was the 11th year since King Jehoiachin had
been brought to Babylon as a prisoner. On the seventh day of the first month, a message came to me
from the LORD. He said, [21]"Son of man, I have broken the powerful arm of Pharaoh Hophra, the king
of Egypt. No bandages have been put on his arm to
heal it. It has not been put in a cast. So his arm will
not be strong enough to use a sword. [22]I am against
Pharaoh, the king of Egypt. I will break both of his
arms. I will break his healthy arm and his broken
one. His sword will fall from his hand. [23]I will
scatter the people of Egypt among the nations. I
will send them to other countries.

[24]"I will make the arms of the king of Babylonia stronger. I will put my sword in his hand. But
I will break the arms of Pharaoh. And he will
groan in front of Nebuchadnezzar. He will cry out
like someone dying from his wounds. [25]I will make
the arms of the king of Babylonia stronger. But the
arms of Pharaoh will not be able to help Egypt. I
will put my sword in Nebuchadnezzar's hand. He
will get ready to use it against Egypt. Then they
will know that I am the LORD.

[26]"I will scatter the Egyptians among the
nations. I will send them to other countries. Then
they will know that I am the LORD."

A Cedar Tree in Lebanon

31 It was the 11th year since King Jehoiachin
had been brought to Babylon as a prisoner.
On the first day of the third month, a message
came to me from the LORD. He said, [2]"Son of man,
speak to Pharaoh Hophra, the king of Egypt. Also
speak to his huge army. Tell him,

" 'Who can be compared with your majesty?
[3] Think about what happened to Assyria.
Once it was like a cedar tree in Lebanon.
It had beautiful branches
that provided shade for the forest.

It grew very high.
Its top was above all of the leaves.
4 The waters fed it.
Deep springs made it grow tall.
Their streams flowed
all around its base.
They made their way
to all of the trees in the fields.
5 So it grew higher
than any other tree in the fields.
It grew more limbs.
Its branches grew long.
They spread because they had plenty of water.
6 All of the birds of the air
made their nests in its limbs.
All of the wild animals
had their babies under its branches.
All of the great nations
lived in its shade.
7 Its spreading branches
made it majestic and beautiful.
Its roots went down deep
to where there was plenty of water.
8 The cedar trees in my garden
were no match for it.
The pine trees
could not equal its limbs.
The plane trees
could not compare with its branches.
No tree in my garden
could match its beauty.
9 I gave it many branches.
They made it beautiful.
All of the trees in my Garden of Eden
were jealous of it.'"

10 So the LORD and King says, "The cedar tree
grew very high. Its top was above all of the leaves.
It was proud of how tall it was. 11 So I handed it
over to the Babylonian ruler of the nations. I
wanted him to punish it because it was so evil. I
decided to get rid of it.

12 "The Babylonians cut it down and left it there.
They did not show it any pity at all. Some of its
branches fell on the mountains. Others fell in all
of the valleys. They lay broken in all of the stream
beds in the land. All of the nations on earth came
out from under its shade. And they went on their
way. 13 All of the birds of the air settled on the
fallen tree. All of the wild animals moved among
its branches.

14 "So trees that receive plenty of water must
never grow so high that it makes them proud.
Their tops must never be above the rest of the
leaves. No other trees that receive a lot of water
must ever grow that high. They are appointed to
die and go down into the earth below. They will
join the other nations that go down into the grave."

15 The LORD and King says, "Assyria was like a
cedar tree. But I brought it down to the grave. On
that day I dried up the deep springs of water and
covered them. I held its streams back. I shut off its
rich supply of water. Because of that, Lebanon was
dressed in darkness as if it were clothes. All of the
trees in the fields dried up.

16 "I brought the cedar tree down to the grave. It
joined the other nations that go down there. I made
the nations on earth shake because of the sound of
its fall. Then all of the trees of Eden were comforted in the earth below. That included the finest
and best trees in Lebanon. And it included all the
trees that received plenty of water. 17 Others also
went down into the grave along with it. That
included those that lived in its shade. And it
included those nations that were going to help it.
They joined those who had been killed with
swords.

18 "Which one of the trees of Eden can be compared with you? What tree is as glorious and
majestic as you are? But you too will be brought
down to the earth below. There you will join the
trees of Eden. You will lie down with those who
have not been circumcised. You will be among
those who were killed with swords.

"That is what will happen to Pharaoh and his
huge armies," announces the LORD and King.

A Song of Sadness About Pharaoh

32 It was the 12th year since King Jehoiachin
had been brought to Babylon as a prisoner.
On the first day of the 12th month, a message
came to me from the LORD. He said, 2 "Son of man,
sing a song of sadness about Pharaoh Hophra, the
king of Egypt. Tell him,

"'You are like a lion among the nations.
You are like a monster in the sea.
You move around wildly in your rivers.
You churn the water with your feet.
You make the streams muddy.'"

3 The LORD and King says,

"I will use a large crowd of people
to throw my net over you.
They will pull you up in it.
4 Then I will throw you on the land.
I will toss you into an open field.
I will let all of the birds of the air settle on you.
I will let all of the wild animals eat you up.
5 I will scatter the parts of your body all over the mountains.
I will fill the valleys with your remains.
6 I will soak the land with your blood.
It will flow all the way to the mountains.
The valleys will be filled with the parts of your body.
7 When I wipe you out,
I will put a cover over the heavens.
I will darken the stars.
I will cover the sun with a cloud.
The moon will stop shining.

8 I will darken all of the bright lights
in the sky above you.
I will bring darkness over your land,"
announces the LORD and King.
9 "The hearts of many people will be troubled.
That is because I will destroy you among
the nations.
You had never known anything about those
lands before.
10 Many nations will be shocked
when they see what has happened to you.
Their kings will tremble with fear
when they find out about it.
I will get ready to use Nebuchadnezzar
as my sword against them.
On the day you fall from power,
each of the kings will tremble with fear.
Each will be afraid he is the next to die."

11 The LORD and King says,

"I will send against you
the sword of the king of Babylonia.
12 I will destroy your huge army.
They will be killed with the swords
of Babylonia's mighty soldiers.
The soldiers will not show them any pity.
They will bring Egypt down in all of
its pride.
Its huge armies will be thrown down.
13 I will destroy all of its cattle
from the places where they have plenty
of water.
Human feet will never stir the water up again.
The hoofs of cattle will not make it muddy
anymore.
14 I will let the waters of Egypt settle.
I will make its streams flow like olive oil,"
announces the LORD and King.
15 "I will turn Egypt into an empty land.
I will strip away everything in it.
I will strike down everyone who lives there.
Then they will know that I am the LORD.

16 "That is the song of sadness people will sing
about Egypt. Women from other nations will sing
it. They will sob over Egypt and its huge armies,"
announces the LORD and King.

17 It was the 15th day of a month near the end of
the 12th year since King Jehoiachin had been
brought to Babylon as a prisoner. A message came
to me from the LORD. He said, 18 "Son of man, sob
over the huge army of Egypt. Tell the Egyptians
they will go down into the earth below. The
women singers from the other mighty nations will
go down into the grave along with them and
others.

19 "Tell them, 'Are you any better than others?
Since you are not, go down there. Lie down with
those who have not been circumcised.'

20 "They will fall dead among those who were
killed with swords. Nebuchadnezzar is ready to
use his sword against them. Let Egypt be dragged
off together with its huge armies.

21 "The mighty leaders who are already in the
grave will talk about Egypt. They will also speak
about the nations that were going to help it. They
will say, 'They have come down here. They are
lying down with those who had not been circumcised. They are here with those who were killed
with swords.'

22 "Assyria is there with its whole army. Its king
is surrounded by the graves of all of its people who
were killed with swords. 23 Their graves are deep
down in the pit. Assyria's army lies around the
grave of its king. All those who spread terror while
they were alive are now dead. They were killed
with swords.

24 "Elam is also there. Its huge armies lie around
the grave of its king. All those who spread terror
while they were alive are now dead. They were
killed with swords. They had not been circumcised. They went down into the earth below. Their
shame is like the shame of others who go down
into the grave.

25 "A bed is made for Elam's king among the
dead. His huge armies lie around his grave. They
had not been circumcised. They were killed with
swords. They had spread terror while they were
alive. So now their shame is like the shame of others who go down into the grave. They lie down
among the dead.

26 "Meshech and Tubal are also there. Their huge
armies lie around the graves of their kings. They
had not been circumcised. They had spread their
terror while they were alive. So they were killed
with swords.

27 "They lie down with the other dead soldiers
who had not been circumcised. They and their
weapons had gone down into the grave. Their
swords had been placed under their heads. They
had spread their terror while they were alive. But
now the shame of their sin covers their bones.

28 "Pharaoh Hophra, you too will be broken. You
will lie down among those who had not been circumcised. You will be there with those who were
killed with swords.

29 "Edom is also there. So are its kings and all of
its princes. In spite of their power, they lie down
with those who were killed with swords. They lie
down with those who had not been circumcised.
They are there with others who went down into the
grave.

30 "All of the princes of the north are there too.
So are all of the people of Sidon. They went down
into the grave in dishonor. While they were alive,
they used their power to spread terror. They had
never been circumcised. But now they lie down
there with those who were killed with swords.
Their shame is like the shame of others who go
down into the grave.

31 "Pharaoh and his whole army will see all of
them. That will comfort him in spite of the fact that

his huge armies were killed with swords," announces the LORD and King. 32"I let Pharaoh spread terror while he was alive. But now he and his huge armies will be buried with those who had not been circumcised. They will lie down there with those who were killed with swords," announces the LORD and King.

The LORD Warns Israel

33 A message came to me from the LORD. He said, 2"Son of man, speak to the people of your own country. Tell them, 'Suppose I send enemies against a land. And its people choose one of their men to stand guard. 3He sees the enemies coming against the land. He blows a trumpet to warn the people.

4" 'Someone hears the trumpet. But he does not pay any attention to the warning. The enemies come and kill him. Then what happens to him will be his own fault. 5He heard the sound of the trumpet. But he did not pay any attention to the warning. So what happened to him was his own fault. If he had paid attention, he would have saved himself.

6" 'But suppose the guard sees the enemies coming. And he does not blow the trumpet to warn the people. The enemies come and kill one of them. Then his life has been taken away from him because he sinned. But I will hold the guard accountable for his death.'

7"Son of man, I have appointed you as a prophet to warn the people of Israel. So listen to my message. Give them a warning from me.

8"Suppose I say to a sinful person, 'You can be sure that you will die.' And suppose you do not try to get him to change his ways. Then he will die because he has sinned. And I will hold you accountable for his death.

9"But suppose you do warn that sinful person. You tell him to change his ways. But he does not do it. Then he will die because he has sinned. But you will have saved yourself.

10"Son of man, speak to the people of Israel. Tell them, 'You are saying, "Our sins and the wrong things we have done weigh us down. We are wasting away because we have sinned so much. So how can we live?" '

11"Tell them, 'When sinful people die, it does not give me any joy. But when they turn away from their sins and live, that makes me very happy. And that is just as sure as I am alive,' announces the LORD and King. 'So turn away from your sins! Change your evil ways! Why should you die, people of Israel?'

12"Son of man, speak to the people of your own country. Tell them, 'The right things a godly person does will not save him when he does not obey the LORD. The wrong things a sinful person does will not destroy him when he turns away from them. If a godly person sins, he will not be allowed to live just because he used to do what is right.'

13"Suppose I tell someone who is godly that he will live. And he trusts in the fact that he used to do what was right. But now he does what is evil. Then I will not remember any of the right things he has done. He will die because he has done so many evil things.

14"Suppose I say to a sinful person, 'You can be sure you will die.' And then he turns away from his sin. He does what is fair and right. 15He gives back what he took as security for a loan. He returns what he has stolen. He follows my rules that give life. He does not do what is evil. Then you can be sure he will live. He will not die. 16None of the sins he has committed will be held against him. He has done what is fair and right. So you can be sure he will live.

17"In spite of that, your people say, 'What the Lord does isn't fair.' But it is what you do that is not fair.

18"Suppose someone who is godly stops doing what is right. And he does what is evil. Then he will die because of it. 19But suppose a sinful person turns away from the evil things he has done. And he does what is fair and right. Then he will live by doing that.

20"In spite of that, you people of Israel say, 'What the Lord does isn't fair.' But I will judge each of you based on how you have lived."

The LORD Explains Why Jerusalem Fell

21It was the 12th year since we had been brought to Babylonia as prisoners. On the fifth day of the tenth month, a man who had escaped from Jerusalem came to bring me a report. He said, "The city has fallen!"

22The evening before the man arrived, the LORD put his strong hand on me. He opened my mouth before the man came to me in the morning. So my mouth was opened. I was no longer silent.

23Then a message came to me from the LORD. He said, 24"Son of man, the people who live in those broken-down buildings in Israel are saying, 'Abraham was only one man. But he owned the land. We are many people. The land must certainly belong to us.'

25"So tell them, 'The LORD and King says, "You eat meat that still has blood in it. You worship your gods. You commit murder. So should you still possess the land? 26You depend on your swords. You do things I hate. Each one of you has sex with your neighbor's wife. So should you still possess the land?" '

27"Tell them, 'The LORD and King says, "The people who are left in those broken-down buildings will be killed with swords. Wild animals will eat up those who are out in the country. Those who are in caves and other safe places will die of a plague. And that is just as sure as I am alive.

28" ' "I will turn the land into a dry and empty desert. The strength Jerusalem is so proud of will come to an end. The mountains of Israel will be deserted. No one will travel across them. 29So I will turn the land into a dry and empty desert. I will punish my people because of all of the evil things they have done. I hate those things. They will know that I am the LORD."'

30"Son of man, your people are talking about you. They are getting together by the walls of their houses and at their doors. They are saying to one another, 'Come. Listen to the LORD's message.'

31"My people come to you, just as they usually do. They sit in front of you. They listen to what you say. But they do not put it into practice. With their mouths they claim to be faithful to me. But in their hearts they want what belongs to others. They try to get rich by cheating them. 32You are nothing more to them than someone who sings love songs. They say you have a beautiful voice. They think you play an instrument well. They listen to what you say. But they do not put it into practice.

33"Everything I have told you will come true. You can be sure of it. Then the people will know that a prophet has been among them."

The LORD Is the Shepherd of His People

34 A message came to me from the LORD. He said, 2"Son of man, prophesy against the shepherds of Israel. Tell them, 'The LORD and King says, "How terrible it will be for you shepherds of Israel! You only take care of yourselves. You should take good care of your flocks. 3Instead, you eat the butter. You dress yourselves with the wool. You kill the finest animals. But you do not take care of your flocks. 4You have not made the weak ones in the flock stronger. You have not healed the sick. You have not bandaged those that are hurt. You have not brought back those that have wandered away. You have not searched for the lost. When you ruled over them, you were mean to them. You treated them badly.

5""So they were scattered because they did not have a shepherd. They became food for all of the wild animals. 6My sheep wandered all over the mountains and high hills. They were scattered over the whole earth. No one searched for them. No one looked for them."

7"'Shepherds, listen to the LORD's message. 8He says, "My flock does not have a shepherd. Many of my sheep have been stolen. They have become food for all of the wild animals. My shepherds did not care for my sheep. They did not even search for them. Instead, they only took care of themselves. And that is just as sure as I am alive," announces the LORD and King.

9"'Shepherds, listen to the LORD's message. 10The LORD and King says, "I am against the shepherds. I will hold them accountable for my flock. I will stop them from taking care of the flock. Then they will not be able to feed themselves anymore. I will save my flock from their mouths. My sheep will no longer be food for them."'"

11The LORD and King says, "I myself will search for my sheep. I will look after them. 12A shepherd looks after his scattered flock when he is with them. And I will look after my sheep. I will save them from all of the places where they were scattered on a dark and cloudy day.

13"I will bring them out from among the nations. I will gather them together from other countries. I will bring them into their own land. They will eat grass on the mountains of Israel. I will also let them eat in the valleys and in all of the places in the land where people live. 14I will take care of them in the best grasslands. They will eat grass on the high mountains of Israel. There they will lie down in the finest grasslands. They will eat grass in the best places on Israel's mountains.

15"I myself will take care of my sheep. I will let them lie down in safety," announces the LORD and King. 16"I will search for the lost. I will bring back those that have wandered away. I will bandage the ones that are hurt. I will make the weak ones stronger. But I will destroy those that are fat and strong. I will take good care of my sheep. I will treat them fairly."

17The LORD and King says, "You are my flock. I will judge between one sheep and another. I will judge between rams and goats. 18You already eat in the best grasslands. Must you also stomp all over the other fields? You already drink clear water. Must you also make the rest of the water muddy with your feet? 19Must my flock have to eat the grass you have stomped on? Must they drink the water you have made muddy?"

20So the LORD and King speaks to them. He says, "I myself will judge between the fat sheep and the skinny sheep. 21You push the other sheep around with your hips and shoulders. You use your horns to butt all of the weak sheep. Finally, you drive them away. 22But I will save my sheep. They will not be carried off anymore. I will judge between one sheep and another.

23"I will place one shepherd over them. He will belong to the family line of my servant David. He will take good care of them. He will look after them. He will be their shepherd. 24I am the LORD. I will be their God. And my servant from David's line will be prince among them. I have spoken. I am the LORD.

25"I will make a covenant with them. It promises to give them peace. I will get rid of the wild animals in the land. Then my sheep can live safely in the desert. They can sleep in the forests.

26"I will bless them. I will also bless the places surrounding my holy mountain of Zion. I will send down rain at the right time. There will be showers of blessing. 27The trees in the fields will bear their fruit. And the ground will produce its crops. The people will be secure in their land. I will break the chains that hold them. I will save them from the powerful hands of those who made them slaves. Then they will know that I am the LORD.

28“The nations will not carry them off anymore.
Wild animals will no longer eat them up. They will
live in safety. And no one will make them afraid.
29I will give them a land that is famous for its
crops. They will never be hungry there again. The
nations will not make fun of them anymore.
30“Then they will know that I am with them. I
am the LORD their God. And they will know that
they are my people Israel,” announces the LORD
and King.
31“You are the sheep belonging to my flock.
You are my people. And I am your God,”
announces the LORD and King.

A Message About Edom

35 A message came to me from the LORD. He
said, 2“Son of man, turn your attention to
Mount Seir. Prophesy against it. 3Tell it, ‘The
LORD and King says, “Mount Seir, I am against
you. I will reach out my powerful hand against
you. I will turn you into a dry and empty desert. 4I
will destroy your towns. Your land will become
empty. Then you will know that I am the LORD.
5“ ‘ “People of Edom, you have been Israel’s
enemies for a long time. You let many Israelites be
killed with swords when they were in great trouble. At that time I used Nebuchadnezzar to punish
them and destroy them completely. 6Now I will
hand you over to murderers. They will hunt you
down. You murdered others. So murderers will
chase you. And that is just as sure as I am alive,”
announces the LORD and King.
7“ ‘ “I will turn Mount Seir into a dry and empty
desert. No one will be able to go anywhere or do
anything there. 8I will fill your mountains with
dead bodies. Some of those who are killed with
swords will fall down dead on your hills. Others
will die in your valleys and in all of your canyons.
9I will make your land empty forever. No one will
live in your towns. Then you will know that I am
the LORD.
10“ ‘ “You said, ‘The nations of Israel and Judah
will belong to us. We will take them over.’ You
said that, even though I was there. I am the LORD.
11You were full of anger, jealousy and hatred
toward my people. So I will punish you. When I
judge you, they will know that I am the LORD. And
that is just as sure as I am alive,” announces the
LORD and King.
12“ ‘ “You will know that I have heard all of the
terrible things you said about those who live in the
mountains of Israel. You made fun of them. You
said, ‘They have been destroyed. They’ve been
handed over to us. Let’s wipe them out.’ 13You
bragged that you were better than I am. You spoke
against me. You did not hold anything back. But I
heard it.” ’ ”
14The LORD and King says, “The whole earth
will be glad. But I will make your land empty.
15You were happy when the land of Israel became
empty. So I will treat you in the same way. Mount
Seir, you will be empty. So will the whole land of
Edom. Then you will know that I am the LORD.”

A Message About Israel

36 “Son of man, prophesy to the mountains of
Israel. Tell them, ‘Mountains of Israel, listen to the LORD’s message. 2The LORD and King
says, “Your enemies made fun of you. They
bragged, ‘The hills you lived in for a long time
belong to us now.’ ” ’
3“Ezekiel, prophesy. Say, ‘The LORD and King
says, “Your enemies destroyed you. They hunted
you down from every side. So the rest of the
nations took over your land. People talked about
you. They told lies about you.” ’ ”
4Mountains of Israel, listen to the message of
the LORD and King. He speaks to you mountains,
hills, canyons and valleys. He speaks to you
destroyed cities and deserted towns. The rest of
the nations around you took everything of value
away from you. They made fun of you. 5So the
LORD and King says, “My anger burns against
those nations. I have spoken against them and the
whole land of Edom. They were very happy when
they took over my land. Deep down inside them
they hated Israel. They wanted to take its grasslands.
6“Ezekiel, prophesy about the land of Israel.
Speak to the mountains, hills, canyons and valleys.
Tell them, ‘The LORD and King says, “My jealous
anger burns against the nations. They have
laughed at you.” 7So the LORD and King says, “I
raise my hand and take an oath. I promise that the
nations around you will also be laughed at.
8“ ‘ “Mountains of Israel, you will produce
branches and bear fruit for my people Israel. They
will come home soon. 9I am concerned about you.
I will look on you with favor. Farmers will plow
your ground. They will plant seeds in it.
10“ ‘ “I will multiply the number of people who
live in Israel. The towns will no longer be empty.
Their broken-down houses will be rebuilt. 11I will
increase the number of your people and animals.
They will have many babies. I will settle people in
your towns, just as I did in the past. I will help you
succeed more than ever before. Then you will
know that I am the LORD.
12“ ‘ “I will let my people Israel walk there again.
They will possess you. They will receive you as
their own. You will never take their children away
from them again.” ’ ”
13The LORD and King says, “People say to you
mountains, ‘You destroy people. You let your
nation’s children be taken away.’ 14But I will not
let you destroy people anymore. I will no longer
let your nation’s children be taken away,” announces the LORD and King.
15“You will not have to listen to the nations
laughing at you anymore. People will no longer
make fun of you. You will not let your nation fall,”
announces the LORD and King.

16Another message came to me from the LORD. He said, 17"Son of man, the people of Israel used to live in their own land. But they polluted it because of how they acted and the way they lived. To me they were 'unclean' like a woman who was having her monthly period.

18"They spilled people's blood in the land. They polluted the land by worshiping other gods. So I poured out my burning anger on them. 19I scattered them among the nations. I sent them to other countries. I judged them based on how they acted and the way they lived.

20"They treated my name as if it were not holy. They did it everywhere they went among the nations. People said about them, 'They are the LORD's people. But they were forced to leave his land.' 21I was concerned about my holy name. The people of Israel treated it as if it were not holy. They did it everywhere they went among the nations.

22"But tell the people of Israel, 'The LORD and King speaks. He says, "People of Israel, I will not take action for your benefit. Instead, I will act for the honor of my holy name. You have treated it as if it were not holy. You did it everywhere you went among the nations. 23But I will show everyone how holy my great name is. You have treated it as if it were not holy. So I will use you to show the nations how holy I am. Then they will know that I am the LORD," announces the LORD and King.

24" ' "I will take you out of the nations. I will gather you together from all of the countries. I will bring you back into your own land.

25" ' "I will sprinkle pure water on you. Then you will be 'clean.' I will make you completely pure and clean. I will take all of the statues of your gods away from you. 26I will give you new hearts. I will give you a new spirit that is faithful to me. I will remove your stubborn hearts from you. I will give you hearts that obey me.

27" ' "I will put my Spirit in you. I will move you to follow my rules. I want you to be careful to keep my laws. 28You will live in the land I gave your people long ago. You will be my people. And I will be your God.

29" ' "I will save you from all of your 'uncleanness.' I will give you plenty of grain. You will have more than enough. So you will never be hungry again. 30I will multiply the fruit on your trees. I will increase the crops in your fields. Then the nations will no longer make fun of you because you are hungry.

31" ' "You will remember your evil ways and the sinful things you have done. You will hate yourselves because you have sinned so much. I also hate your evil practices. 32I want you to know that I am not doing those things for your benefit," announces the LORD and King. "People of Israel, you should be ashamed of yourselves! Your conduct has brought dishonor to you." ' "

33The LORD and King says, "I will make you pure from all of your sins. On that day I will settle you in your towns again. Your broken-down houses will be rebuilt. 34The dry and empty land will be farmed again.

"Everyone who passes through it will see that it is no longer empty. 35They will say, 'This land was completely destroyed. But now it's like the Garden of Eden. The cities were full of broken-down buildings. They were destroyed and empty. But now they have high walls around them. And people live in them.'

36"Then the nations that remain around you will know that I have rebuilt what was once destroyed. I have planted again the fields that were once empty. I have spoken. And I will do it. I am the LORD."

37The LORD and King says, "Once again I will answer the prayers of the people of Israel. Here is what I will do for them. I will multiply them as if they were sheep. 38Large flocks of animals are sacrificed at Jerusalem during the appointed feasts there. In the same way, the destroyed cities will be filled with flocks of people. Then they will know that I am the LORD."

Israel's Dry Bones Will Come to Life Again

37 The LORD put his strong hand on me. His Spirit brought me away from my home. He put me down in the middle of a valley. It was full of bones. 2He led me back and forth among them. I saw a huge number of bones in the valley. The bones were very dry.

3The LORD asked me, "Son of man, can these bones live?"

I said, "LORD and King, you are the only one who knows."

4Then he said to me, "Prophesy to these bones. Tell them, 'Dry bones, listen to the LORD's message. 5The LORD and King speaks to you. He says, "I will put breath in you. Then you will come to life again. 6I will attach tendons to you. I will put flesh on you. I will cover you with skin. So I will put breath in you. And you will come to life again. Then you will know that I am the LORD." ' "

7So I prophesied just as the LORD commanded me to. As I was prophesying, I heard a noise. It was a rattling sound. The bones came together. One bone connected itself to another. 8I saw tendons and flesh appear on them. Skin covered them. But there was no breath in them.

9Then the LORD said to me, "Prophesy to the breath. Prophesy, son of man. Tell it, 'The LORD and King says, "Breath, come from all four directions. Go into these dead bodies. Then they can live." ' "

10So I prophesied just as he commanded me to. And the breath entered them. Then they came to life again. They stood up on their feet. They were like a huge army.

11Then the LORD said to me, "Son of man, these bones stand for all of the people of Israel. The

people say, ‘Our bones are dried up. We’ve lost all
hope. We are cut off.’
12“So prophesy. Tell them, ‘The LORD and King
says, “My people, I am going to open up your
graves. I am going to bring you out of them. I will
take you back to the land of Israel. 13So I will open
up your graves and bring you out of them. Then
you will know that I am the LORD. You are my
people. 14I will put my Spirit in you. And you will
live again. I will settle you in your own land. Then
you will know that I have spoken. I have done it,”
announces the LORD.’ ”

Israel Will Be One Nation Under One King

15A message came to me from the LORD. He
said, 16“Son of man, get a stick of wood. Write on
it, ‘Belonging to the tribe of Judah and the Israelites who are connected with it.’ Then get another
stick. Write on it, ‘Ephraim’s stick. Belonging to
the tribes of Joseph and all of the Israelites connected with them.’ 17Join them together into one
stick in your hand.
18“The people of your own country will ask
you, ‘What do you mean by this?’ 19Tell them,
‘The LORD and King says, “I am going to get the
stick of Joseph and the Israelites connected with
it. That stick is in Ephraim’s hand. I am going to
join it to Judah’s stick. They will become a single
stick of wood in my hand.” ’
20“Show them the sticks you wrote on. 21Tell
them, ‘The LORD and King says, “I will take the
Israelites out of the nations where they have gone.
I will gather them together from all around. I will
bring them back to their own land. 22There I will
make them one nation. They will live on the
mountains of Israel. All of them will have one
king. They will never be two nations again. They
will never again be separated into two kingdoms.
23“ ‘ “They will no longer pollute themselves by
worshiping any of their evil gods. They will not do
wrong things anymore. They always turn away
from me. But I will save them from that sin. I will
make them pure and clean. They will be my people. And I will be their God.
24“ ‘ “A man who belongs to the family line of
my servant David will be their king. All of them
will have one shepherd. They will follow my laws.
And they will be careful to keep my rules. 25They
will live in the land I gave to my servant Jacob.
That is where your people lived long ago. They,
their children, their children’s children, and their
children after them will live there forever. And my
servant from David’s line will be their prince
forever.
26“ ‘ “I will make a covenant with them. It
promises to give them peace. The covenant will
last forever. I will make them my people. And I
will increase their numbers. I will put my temple
among them forever. 27I will live with them. I will
be their God. And they will be my people. 28My
temple will be among them forever. Then the
nations will know that I make Israel holy. I am the
LORD.” ’ ”

A Message About Gog

38 A message came to me from the LORD. He
said, 2“Son of man, turn your attention to
Gog. He is from the land of Magog. He is the chief
prince of Meshech and Tubal. Prophesy against
him.
3“Tell him, ‘The LORD and King says, “Gog, I
am against you. You are the chief prince of Meshech and Tubal. 4But I will turn you around. I will
put hooks in your jaws. I will bring you out of your
land along with your whole army. Your horses will
come with you. Your horsemen will be completely
armed. Your huge army will carry large and small
shields. All of them will be ready to use their
swords.
5“ ‘ “The men of Persia, Cush and Put will march
out with them. All of them will have shields and
helmets. 6Gomer and all of its troops will be there
too. Beth Togarmah from the far north will also
come with all of its troops. Many nations will help
you.
7“ ‘ “Get ready. Be prepared. Take command of
the huge armies that are gathered around you.
8After many years you will be called together to
fight. Later, you will march into a land that has not
had war for a while. Its people were gathered
together from many nations. They came to the
mountains of Israel. No one had lived in those
mountains for a long time. So the people had been
brought back from other nations. Now all of the
people live in safety. 9You, all of your troops and
the many nations with you will march up to attack
them. All of you will advance like a storm. You
will be like a cloud covering their land.”
10“ ‘The LORD and King says, “At that time
some ideas will come to you. You will make evil
plans. 11You will say, ‘I will march out against a
land whose villages don’t have walls around them.
I’ll attack those peaceful people. I’ll do it when
they aren’t expecting it. None of their villages has
walls or gates with heavy metal bars on them.
12“ ‘ “ ‘I will rob those people. I’ll steal everything they have. Then I’ll turn my attention to the
destroyed houses where people are living again.
They have returned there from other nations. Now
they are rich. They have plenty of livestock and all
kinds of goods. They are living in Israel. It is the
center of the earth.’
13“ ‘ “The people of Sheba and Dedan will speak
to you. So will the traders of Tarshish and all of its
villages. They will say, ‘Have you come to rob us?
Have you gathered your huge army together to
steal our silver and gold? Are you going to take our
livestock and goods away from us? Do you plan
to carry off everything we have?’ ” ’
14“Son of man, prophesy. Tell Gog, ‘The LORD
and King says, “A time is coming when my people

Israel will be living in safety. You will see that it is
a good time to attack them. [15]So you will come
from your place in the far north. Many nations will
join you. All of their men will be riding on horses.
You will have a huge and mighty army. [16]They will
advance against my people Israel. They will be
like a cloud covering their land. Gog, in days to
come I will bring you against my land. Then the
nations will know me. I will use you to show them
how holy I am."
[17]" 'The LORD and King says to Gog, "In the
past I spoke about you through my servants, the
prophets of Israel. At that time they prophesied for
years that I would bring you against them. [18]Here
is what will happen in days to come. You will
attack the land of Israel. That will stir up my hot
anger," announces the LORD and King.
[19]" ' "At that time my burning anger will blaze
out at you. There will be a great earthquake in the
land of Israel. [20]The fish in the sea, the birds of the
air and the wild animals will tremble with fear
because of what I will do. So will every creature
that moves along the ground. And so will all of the
people on earth. The mountains will come crashing down. The cliffs will break into pieces. Every
wall will fall to the ground.
[21]" ' "I will punish you on all of my mountains,"
announces the LORD and King. "Your men will use
their swords against one another. [22]I will judge
you. I will send a plague against you. A lot of
blood will be spilled. I will send heavy rain, hailstones and burning sulfur down to the earth. They
will fall on you and your troops. They will also
come down on the many nations that are helping
you. [23]That will show how great and holy I am. I
will make myself known to many nations. Then
they will know that I am the LORD." '

39 "Son of man, prophesy against Gog. Tell
him, 'The LORD and King says, "Gog, I am
against you. You are the chief prince of Meshech
and Tubal. [2]But I will turn you around. I will drag
you along. I will bring you from the far north. I
will send you against the mountains of Israel.
[3]Then I will knock your bow out of your left hand.
I will make your arrows drop from your right
hand.
[4]" ' "You will fall dead on the mountains of Israel. You and all of your troops will die there. So will
the nations that join you. I will feed you to all
kinds of birds that eat dead bodies. So they and the
wild animals will eat you up. [5]You will fall dead
in the open fields. I have spoken," announces the
LORD and King.
[6]" ' "I will send fire on the land of Magog. It will
burn up the people who live in safety on the coast.
So they will know that I am the LORD.
[7]" ' "I will make my holy name known among
my people Israel. I will no longer let them treat my
name as if it were not holy. Then the nations will
know that I am the Holy One in Israel. I am the
LORD. [8]The day I will judge you is coming. You
can be sure of it," announces the LORD and King.
"It is the day I have spoken about.
[9]" ' "At that time those who live in the towns of
Israel will go out and light a fire. They will use it
to burn up the weapons. That includes small and
large shields. It also includes bows and arrows,
war clubs and spears. It will take seven years to
burn all of them up. [10]People will not gather wood
from the fields. They will not cut the forests down.
Instead, they will burn the weapons. And they will
rob those who robbed them. They will steal from
those who stole from them," announces the LORD
and King.
[11]" ' "Gog, at that time I will bury you in a grave
in Israel. It will be in the valley where people
travel east of the Dead Sea. It will block the path
of travelers. That is because you and your huge
armies will be buried there. So it will be called The
Valley of Gog's Armies.
[12]" ' "It will take seven months for the people of
Israel to bury the bodies. They will do it to make
the land 'clean' again. [13]All of the people in the
land will bury them. That will bring glory to me.
It will be a time to remember," announces the
LORD and King.
[14]" ' "After the seven months are over, men will
be hired to finish the job of making the land
'clean' again. Some will go all through it. They
will look for any remaining human bones on the
ground. Other people will bury the bones. [15]So
some will go through the land. When they see a
bone, they will put a marker beside it. Then those
who dig the graves will take it to The Valley of
Gog's Armies. There they will bury it. [16]That is
how they will make the land 'clean' again." ' " Also
a town called Gog's Armies will be located there.
[17]The LORD and King said to me, "Son of man,
speak to every kind of bird. Call out to all of the
wild animals. Tell them, 'Gather together. Come
from everywhere. Gather around the sacrifice I am
preparing for you. It is the great sacrifice on the
mountains of Israel. There you will eat human
bodies and drink human blood.
[18]" 'You will eat the bodies of mighty men. You
will drink the blood of the princes of the earth. You
will eat their bodies and drink their blood as if they
were rams and lambs, goats and bulls. You will
enjoy it as if you were eating the fattest animals
from Bashan.
[19]" 'So I am preparing a sacrifice for you. You
will eat fat until you are completely full. You will
drink blood until you are drunk. [20]At my table you
will eat horses, riders, mighty men and soldiers
until you are full,' announces the LORD and King.
[21]" 'I will show all of the nations my glory. They
will see how I punish them when I use my powerful hand against them. [22]From that time on, the people of Israel will know that I am the LORD their God.
[23]" 'The nations will know that the people of Israel were taken away as prisoners because they
sinned against me. They were not faithful to me.

So I turned my face away from them. I handed them over to their enemies. All of them were killed with swords. 24I punished them because they were "unclean." They did many things that were wrong. So I turned my face away from them.' "

25The LORD and King says, "I will now bring the people of Jacob back home again. I will show my tender love for all of the people of Israel. I will make sure that my name is kept holy.

26"My people will forget the shameful things they have done. They will not remember all of the ways they were unfaithful to me. They used to live in safety in their land. At that time no one made them afraid.

27"So I will bring them back from the nations. I will gather them from the countries of their enemies. And I will use them to show many nations how holy I am. 28Then they will know that I am the LORD their God. I let the nations take my people away as prisoners. But now I will bring them back to their own land. I will not leave anyone behind. 29I will no longer turn my face away from the people of Israel. I will pour out my Spirit on them," announces the LORD and King.

The New Temple Area

40 It was the 14th year after Jerusalem had been captured. It was the tenth day of a month near the beginning of the 25th year since we had been brought to Babylonia as prisoners. On that very day the LORD put his strong hand on me. He took me back to my land. 2In visions God gave me, he brought me to the land of Israel. He set me on a very high mountain. Some buildings were on the south side of it. They looked like a city.

3He took me there. I saw a man who appeared to be made out of bronze. He was standing at the gate of the outer courtyard. He was holding a linen measuring tape and a measuring rod. 4The man said to me, "Son of man, look with your eyes. Listen with your ears. Pay attention to everything I show you. That is why the LORD brought you here. Tell the people of Israel everything you see."

The East Gate to the Outer Courtyard

5I saw a wall that completely surrounded the temple area. The measuring rod in the man's hand was ten and a half feet long. He measured the wall with it. The wall was as thick and as high as one measuring rod.

6Then the man went to the gate that faced east. He climbed its steps. He measured the gateway. It was one rod wide. 7The rooms where the guards stood were one rod long and one rod wide. The walls between the rooms were almost nine feet thick. The gateway next to the porch was one rod wide. The porch faced the front of the temple.

8Then the man measured the porch of the gateway. 9It was 14 feet wide. Each of its doorposts was three and a half feet thick. The porch of the gateway faced the front of the temple.

10Inside the east gate were three rooms on each side. All of the rooms were the same size. The walls on each side of the rooms had the same thickness.

11Then the man measured the entrance of the gateway. It was 17 and a half feet wide and almost 23 feet long. 12In front of each room was a wall. It was 21 inches high. The rooms measured ten and a half feet on each side.

13Then he measured the gateway from the back wall of one room to the back wall of the room across from it. It was almost 44 feet from the top of one wall to the top of the other.

14He measured along the front of the side walls that were all around the inside of the gateway. The total was 105 feet. That didn't include the porch that faced the courtyard. 15It was 87 and a half feet from the entrance of the gateway to the far end of its porch.

16The rooms and their side walls inside the gateway had narrow openings on top of them. So did the porch. All of the openings faced the inside. The front of each side wall was decorated with a palm tree.

The Outer Courtyard

17Then the man brought me into the outer courtyard. There I saw some rooms and a sidewalk. They had been built all around the courtyard. Along the sidewalk were 30 rooms. 18The sidewalk went all the way up to the sides of the gateways. It was as wide as they were long. That was the lower sidewalk.

19Then he measured from the inside of the lower gateway to the outside of the inner courtyard. The east side measured 175 feet. So did the north side.

The North Gate

20Then the man measured the gate that faced north. He wanted to show me how long and wide it was. The gate led into the outer courtyard. 21It had three rooms on each side. Their side walls and porch measured the same as the ones at the first gateway. They measured 87 and a half feet long and almost 44 feet wide. 22Its openings, porch and palm tree decorations measured the same as the ones at the east gate. Seven steps led up to the north gate. Its porch was across from them.

23The inner courtyard had a gate. It faced the gate on the north. It was just like the east gate. He measured from one gate to the one across from it. The total was 175 feet.

The South Gate

24Then the man led me to the south side of the courtyard. There I saw a gate that faced south. He measured its doorposts and porch. They measured the same as the others. 25The gateway and its porch had narrow openings all around. The openings were the same as the others had. The side walls and porch measured 87 and a half feet long and

almost 44 feet wide. 26Seven steps led up to it. Its
porch was across from them. The front of each
side wall was decorated with a palm tree.

27The inner courtyard also had a gate that faced
south. The man measured from that gate to the
outer gate on the south side. The total was 175
feet.

The Gates to the Inner Courtyard

28Then the man brought me into the inner courtyard. We went through the south gate. He measured it. It was the same size as the others. 29Its
rooms, side walls and porch measured the same as
the ones at the other gateways. The gateway and
its porch had openings all around. The side walls
and porch measured 87 and a half feet long and
almost 44 feet wide. 30The porches of the gateways
around the inner courtyard were almost 44 feet
wide and 9 feet long. 31Its porch faced the outer
courtyard. Palm trees decorated its doorposts.
Eight steps led up to it.

32Then the man brought me to the east side of
the inner courtyard. There he measured the gateway. It was the same size as the others. 33Its rooms,
side walls and porch measured the same as the
ones at the other gateways. The gateway and its
porch had openings all around. The side walls and
porch measured 87 and a half feet long and almost
44 feet wide. 34Its porch faced the outer courtyard.
Each doorpost was decorated with a palm tree.
Eight steps led up to the porch.

35Then the man brought me to the north gate.
He measured it. It was the same size as the others.
36Its rooms, side walls and porch measured the
same as the ones at the other gateways. It had
openings all around. The side walls and the porch
measured 87 and a half feet long and almost 44
feet wide. 37The porch faced the outer courtyard.
Each doorpost was decorated with a palm tree.
Eight steps led up to the porch.

The Rooms for Preparing Sacrifices

38A room with a doorway was by the porch of
each inner gateway. The burnt offerings were
washed there. 39On each side of the porch of the
gateway were two tables. The burnt offerings were
killed on them. So were the sin offerings and guilt
offerings.

40Two more tables were by the outer wall of the
gateway porch. They were near the steps at the
entrance of the north gateway. Two more tables
were on the other side of the steps. 41So there were
four tables on each side of the gateway. The total
number of tables was eight. Animals for sacrifice
were killed on all of them.

42There were also four other tables for the burnt
offerings. They were made out of blocks of stone.
Each table was two and a half feet long and two
and a half feet wide. And each was almost two feet
high. The tools for killing the burnt offerings and
other sacrifices were placed on them. 43Large
hooks hung on the walls all around. Each was
three inches long. The meat of the offerings was
placed on the tables.

The Rooms for the Priests

44Near the inner gates were two rooms. They
were in the inner courtyard. One room was next to
the north gate. It faced south. The other one was
next to the south gate. It faced north. 45The man
said to me, "The room that faces south is for the
priests who are in charge of the temple. 46The one
that faces north is for the priests who are in charge
of the altar. All of those priests are the sons of Zadok. They are the only Levites who can approach
the LORD to serve him."

47Then the man measured the courtyard. It was
square. It measured 175 feet long and 175 feet
wide. And the altar was in front of the temple.

The Temple

48The man brought me to the porch of the temple. He measured the doorposts of the porch. Each
of them was almost nine feet wide. The entrance
was 24 and a half feet wide. Each of the side walls
was a little over five feet wide. 49The porch was 35
feet wide. It was 21 feet from front to back. It was
reached by some stairs. Pillars were on each side
of the doorposts.

41 Then the man brought me to the Holy
Room in the temple. There he measured
the doorposts. Each of them was ten and a half feet
wide. 2The entrance was 17 and a half feet wide.
Each of its side walls was almost nine feet wide.
He also measured the Holy Room. It was 70 feet
long and 35 feet wide.

3Then he went into the Most Holy Room. There
he measured the doorposts at the entrance. Each
one of them was three and a half feet wide. The
entrance itself was ten and a half feet wide. Each
of its side walls was a little over 12 feet wide.

4He also measured the Most Holy Room. It was
35 feet long and 35 feet wide. He said to me, "This
is the Most Holy Room." It was beyond the back
wall of the Holy Room.

5Then the man measured the wall of the temple.
It was ten and a half feet thick. Each side room
around the temple was seven feet wide. 6The side
rooms were on three floors. There were 30 rooms
on each floor. Ledges had been built all around the
wall of the temple. So the floor beams of the side
rooms rested on the ledges. The beams didn't go
into the temple wall. 7The side rooms of the temple were wider as we went up floor by floor. A
stairway went from the lowest floor all the way up
to the top floor. It passed through the middle floor.

8I saw that the temple had a raised base all
around it. The base formed the foundation of the
side rooms. It was as long as one measuring rod.
So it was ten and a half feet long. 9The outer wall
of each side room was almost nine feet thick. The
open area between the side rooms of the temple

[10]and the priests' rooms was 35 feet wide all around the temple. [11]The side rooms had entrances from the open area. One was on the north side. Another was on the south. The base next to the open area was almost nine feet wide all around.

[12]There was a large building right behind the temple. It was on the west side of the outer courtyard. It was 122 and a half feet wide. Its wall was almost nine feet thick all around. And it was 157 and a half feet long.

[13]Then the man measured the temple. It was 175 feet long. The open area and the large building behind the temple also measured 175 feet. [14]The east side of the inner courtyard was 175 feet wide. That included the front of the temple.

[15]Then the man measured the building that was on the west side of the outer courtyard. It was behind the temple. It was 175 feet long. That included the walkways of the building on each side.

The Holy Room, the Most Holy Room and the porch that faced the inner courtyard [16]were covered with wood. So were the gateways, narrow openings and walkways around those three places. The gateways and everything beyond them were covered with wood. The floor, the wall up to the openings, and the openings themselves were also covered.

[17]The area above the outside of the entrance to the Most Holy Room was decorated. There were also decorations all around the walls of the Most Holy Room. [18]Carved cherubim and palm trees were used in the decorations. Each cherub had a palm tree next to it. And each palm tree had a cherub next to it.

Each cherub had two faces. [19]One was a man's face. It looked toward the palm tree on one side. The other was the face of a lion. It looked toward the palm tree on the other side. The decorations were carved all around the whole temple.

[20]Cherubim and palm trees decorated the wall of the Holy Room. They were carved from the floor all the way up to the area above the entrance.

[21]The Holy Room had a doorframe that was shaped like a rectangle. So did the Most Holy Room. [22]A wooden altar stood in the Holy Room. It was a little over five feet high. It was three and a half feet long and three and a half feet wide. Its corners, base and sides were made out of wood. The man said to me, "This is the table that stands in front of the LORD."

[23]The Holy Room had double doors. So did the Most Holy Room. [24]Each door had two parts that could swing back and forth. [25]Cherubim and palm trees were carved on the doors of the Holy Room. The decorations were like the ones on the walls. A wooden roof went out beyond the front of the porch. [26]The side walls of the porch had narrow openings on top of them. Palm trees were carved on each side. A wooden roof went out beyond the entrance to each side room of the temple.

The Rooms for the Priests

42 Then the man led me north into the outer courtyard of the temple. He brought me to the rooms that were across from the inner courtyard. They were across from the outer wall of the temple on the north side. [2]The rooms were in a building north of the temple. The building had a door that faced north. It was 175 feet long. It was 87 and a half feet wide.

[3]One row of rooms was next to the inner courtyard. The other row was across from the sidewalk of the outer courtyard. Each room was 35 feet long. Walkways in front of each row faced each other on all three floors. [4]Between the two rows was an inner sidewalk. It was 17 and a half feet wide and 175 feet long. Each of the rooms had a door on the north side.

[5]The rooms on the top floor were narrower than the others. The walkways took up more space from them than they did from the rooms on the other two floors. [6]The courtyards had pillars. But the rooms on the third floor didn't. So their floor space was smaller than the space in the rooms on the other floors.

[7]The building had an outer wall that was even with the outer row of rooms and with the outer courtyard. The wall continued east of the outer row for 87 and a half feet. [8]So there were two rows of rooms. The row next to the outer courtyard was 87 and a half feet long. The one closest to the temple was 175 feet long. [9]The first floor of the building had an entrance on the east side. It led to the outer courtyard.

[10]There were also two rows of rooms in a building next to the south side of the inner courtyard. The building was across from the south wall of the outer courtyard. [11]Between the two rows was an inner sidewalk. The rooms were like the ones in the north building. They were as long and wide as the rooms on the north. The doorways of the rooms on the south were like the ones on the north. [12]People entered the south rooms through the doorway at the east end of the inner sidewalk. The south wall continued east of the outer row of rooms.

[13]The man said to me, "The north and south rooms face the inner courtyard. They are the priests' rooms. That is where the priests who approach the LORD will eat the very holy offerings. They will also store them there. That includes the grain offerings, sin offerings and guilt offerings. This place is holy.

[14]"The priests who enter these holy rooms must leave behind the clothes they served in. Then they can go into the outer courtyard. The clothes they served in are holy. So they must put other clothes on. They have to do that before they go near the places where other people go."

[15]The man finished measuring what was inside the temple area. Then he led me out through the

east gate. He measured all around the area. 16He measured the east side with his measuring rod. It was 875 feet long. 17He measured the north side. It was 875 feet long. 18He measured the south side. It was 875 feet long. 19Finally, he turned and measured the west side. It was 875 feet long. 20So he measured the area on all four sides. It had a wall around it. The wall was 875 feet long and 875 feet wide. It separated what was holy from what was not.

The Glory of the LORD Returns to the Temple

43 Then the man brought me to the east gate. 2There I saw the glory of the God of Israel. He was coming from the east. His voice was like the roar of rushing waters. His glory made the land shine brightly.

3The vision I saw was like the one I had when he came to destroy the city. It was also like the visions I had seen by the Kebar River. I fell with my face toward the ground. 4The glory of the LORD entered the temple through the east gate. 5Then the Spirit lifted me up. He brought me into the inner courtyard. The glory of the LORD filled the temple.

6The man was standing beside me. I heard someone speaking to me from inside the temple. 7He said, "Son of man, this is the place where my throne is. The stool for my feet is also here. I will live here among the people of Israel forever. They will never again treat my name as if it were not holy. They and their kings will not serve other gods anymore. The people will no longer worship the lifeless gods of their kings at their high places.

8"The people of Israel placed their own doorway next to my holy doorway. They put their doorposts right beside mine. Nothing but a thin wall separated us. They treated my name as if it were not holy. I hated it when they did that. So I became angry with them and destroyed them. 9Now let them stop serving other gods. Let them quit worshiping the lifeless gods of their kings. If they obey me, I will live among them forever.

10"Son of man, tell the people of Israel about the temple. Then they will be ashamed of their sins. Let them think carefully about the plan of the temple. 11What if they are ashamed of everything they have done? Then show them all of the plans of the temple. Explain to them how it is laid out. Tell them about its exits and entrances. Show them exactly what it will look like. Give them all of its rules and laws. Write everything down so they can see it. Then they will be faithful to its plan. And they will obey all of its rules.

12"Here is the law of the temple. The whole area on top of Mount Zion will be very holy. That is the law of the temple."

The Altar

13The man said, "Here is the size of the altar. The standard measurement I am using is 21 inches. The base of the altar is 21 inches high. The base has a ledge that is 21 inches wide. It also has a rim that is nine inches wide around the edge. Here is how high the altar is. 14The lower part is three and a half feet high. It has a ledge that is 21 inches wide. The middle part is seven feet high. It has a ledge that is 21 inches wide.

15"The top part is where the sacrifices are burned. It is seven feet high. A horn sticks out from each of its upper four corners. 16The top part of the altar is square. It is 21 feet long and 21 feet wide. 17The middle part is also square. It is 24 and a half feet long. It is 24 and a half feet wide. Its rim is ten and a half inches wide. The base of the altar is 21 inches high all the way around. The steps leading up to the top of the altar face east."

18Then the man said to me, "Son of man, the LORD and King speaks. He says, 'Here are the rules for the altar when it is built. Follow them when you sacrifice burnt offerings and sprinkle blood on it. 19Give a young bull to the priests as a sin offering. They are Levites from the family of Zadok. They approach me to serve me,' announces the LORD and King. 20'Get some of the bull's blood. Put it on the four horns. Also put it on the four corners of the middle part of the altar and all around the rim. That will make the altar pure and clean. 21Use the bull for the sin offering. Burn it in the proper place outside the temple.

22" 'On the second day offer a male goat. It must not have any flaws. It is a sin offering to make the altar pure and clean. So do as you did with the bull. 23When you finish making the altar pure, offer a young bull and a ram from the flock. They must not have any flaws. 24Offer them to me. The priests must sprinkle salt on them. Then they must sacrifice them as a burnt offering to me.

25" 'Provide a male goat each day for seven days. It is a sin offering. Also provide a young bull and a ram from the flock. They must not have any flaws. 26For seven days the priests must make the altar pure and clean. That is how they will set it apart to me.

27" 'From the eighth day on, the priests must bring your burnt offerings and friendship offerings. They must sacrifice them on the altar. Then I will accept you,' announces the LORD and King."

The Prince, the Levites and the Priests

44 Then the man brought me back to the outer gate of the temple. It was the one that faced east. It was shut. 2The LORD said to me, "This gate must remain shut. It must not be opened. No one can enter through it. It must remain shut because I have entered through it. I am the God of Israel. 3The prince is the only one who can sit in the gateway. There he can eat in front of me. He must enter through the porch of the gateway. And he must go out the same way."

4Then the man brought me through the north gate. He took me to the front of the temple. I looked up and saw the glory of the LORD. It filled his temple. I fell with my face toward the ground.

5The LORD said to me, “Son of man, pay attention. Look carefully. Listen closely to everything I tell you about all of the rules concerning my temple. Pay attention to the entrance to the temple and to all of its exits.

6“Speak to the people of Israel. They refuse to obey me. Tell them, ‘The LORD and King says, “People of Israel, I have had enough of your evil practices. I hate them. 7You brought strangers into my temple. They were not circumcised. Their hearts were stubborn. You polluted my temple. But you offered me food, fat and blood anyway. When you did all of those things, you broke the covenant I made with you. I hated all of the evil things you did.

8“ ‘ “You did not do what I told you to. You did not take care of my holy things. Instead, you put other people in charge of my temple.” ’ ” 9The LORD and King says, “No stranger whose heart is stubborn can enter my temple. They have not been circumcised. Even if they live among the people of Israel they can’t enter it.

10“Some Levites wandered far away from me when Israel went down the wrong path. They worshiped the statues of their gods. So they will be punished because they have sinned. 11They might serve in my temple. They might be in charge of its gates. They might kill the burnt offerings and sacrifices for the people. And they might stand in front of the people and serve them in other ways.

12“But they served the people of Israel while they were worshiping their gods. They made the people fall into sin. So I raised my hand and took an oath. I warned them that I would punish them because of their sin,” announces the LORD and King. 13“They must not approach me to serve me as priests. They must not come near any of my holy things. They must stay away from my very holy offerings. They did many things they should have been ashamed of. I hated those things.

14“But I will still put them in charge of the temple duties. They can do all of the work that has to be done there.

15“But the priests must approach me to serve me. They are Levites from Zadok’s family line. They faithfully carried out their duties in my temple. They obeyed me when the people of Israel turned away from me. Those priests must serve me by offering sacrifices of fat and blood,” announces the LORD and King. 16“They are the only ones who can enter my temple. Only they can come near to serve me and do my work.

17“They will enter the gates of the inner courtyard. When they do, they must wear linen clothes. They will serve at the gates of the inner courtyard or inside the temple. When they do, they must not wear any clothes that are made out of wool. 18They must have linen turbans on their heads. They must wear linen underwear around their waists. They must not put anything on that makes them sweat.

19“They will go into the outer courtyard where the people are. When they do, they must take off the clothes they have been serving in. They must leave them in the sacred rooms. And they must put other clothes on. Then they will not make the people holy if the people happen to touch their clothes.

20“The priests must not shave their heads. They must not let their hair grow long. They must keep it cut short. 21No priest can drink wine when he enters the inner courtyard. 22They must not get married to widows or divorced women. They can only marry Israelite virgins or the widows of priests.

23“The priests must teach my people the difference between what is holy and what is not. They must show them how to tell the difference between what is ‘clean’ and what is not.

24“When people do not agree, the priests must serve as judges between them. They must make their decisions based on my laws. They must obey my laws and rules for all of my appointed feasts. And they must keep my Sabbath days holy.

25“A priest must not make himself ‘unclean’ by going near a dead person. But suppose the dead person was his father or mother. Or suppose it was his son or daughter or brother or unmarried sister. Then the priest can make himself ‘unclean.’ 26After he is pure and clean again, he must wait seven days. 27Then he can go to the inner courtyard to serve in the temple. But when he does, he must sacrifice a sin offering for himself,” announces the LORD and King.

28“The priests will not receive any part of the land of Israel. I myself will be their only share. 29They will eat the grain offerings, sin offerings and guilt offerings. Everything in Israel that is set apart to me in a special way will belong to them. 30The best of every first share of the people’s crops will belong to the priests. So will all of their special gifts. The people must give the priests the first share of their ground meal. Then I will bless my people’s families.

31“The priests must not eat any bird or animal that is found dead. They must not eat anything that wild animals have torn apart.

Dividing Up the Land

45 “People of Israel, you will divide up the land you will receive. When you do, give me my share of it. It will be a sacred area. It will be eight and a fourth miles long and six and a half miles wide. The entire area will be holy. 2The temple area in it will be 875 feet long and 875 feet wide. An 87-and-a-half-foot strip around it will be open land.

3“In the sacred area, measure off a large strip of land. It will be eight and a fourth miles long and three and a third miles wide. The temple will be in it. It will be the most holy place of all. 4The large strip will be the sacred share of land for the priests.

There they will serve in the temple. And they will approach me to serve me there. Their houses will be built on that land. The holy temple will also be located there.

[5]"So the Levites will serve in the temple. They will have an area eight and a fourth miles long and three and a third miles wide. The towns they live in will be located there.

[6]"Give the city an area one and two thirds miles wide and eight and a fourth miles long. It will be right next to the sacred area. It will belong to all of the people of Israel.

[7]"The prince will have land on both sides of the sacred area and the city. Its border will run east and west along the land of one of the tribes. [8]The prince will own that land in Israel. And my princes will not crush my people anymore. Instead, they will allow the people of Israel to receive their own share of land. It will be divided up based on their tribes."

[9]The LORD and King says, "Princes of Israel, you have gone far enough! Stop hurting others. Do not crush them. Do what is fair and right. Stop taking my people's land away from them," announces the LORD and King.

[10]"Use weights and measures that are honest and exact. [11]Use the same standard to measure dry and liquid products. Use a 6-bushel measure for dry products. And use a 60-gallon measure for liquids. [12]Every amount of money must be weighed out in keeping with the standard weights.

Offerings and Holy Days

[13]"You must offer a special gift. It must be 13 and a third cups out of every six bushels of grain. [14]Give two and a half quarts out of every 60 gallons of olive oil. [15]Also give one sheep from every flock of 200 sheep. Get them from the grasslands of Israel that receive plenty of water. Use them for grain offerings, burnt offerings and friendship offerings. They will be used to pay for the sin of the people," announces the LORD and King.

[16]"All of the people in the land will take part in that special gift. The prince in Israel will use it. [17]He must provide the burnt offerings, grain offerings and drink offerings. They will be for the yearly feasts, New Moon Feasts and Sabbath days. So they will be for all of the appointed feasts of the people of Israel. The prince will provide the sin offerings, grain offerings, burnt offerings and friendship offerings. They will be used to pay for the sin of the people."

[18]The LORD and King says, "Get a young bull. It must not have any flaws. Use it to make the temple pure and clean. Do it on the first day of the first month. [19]The priest must get some of the blood from the sin offering. He must put some on the doorposts of the temple. He must apply some to the four corners of the middle part of the altar. He must put the rest on the gateposts of the inner courtyard.

[20]"Do the same thing on the seventh day of the month. Do it for those who sin without meaning to. And do it for those who sin without realizing what they are doing. So you will make the temple pure and clean.

[21]"Keep the Passover Feast on the 14th day of the first month. It will last for seven days. During that time you must eat bread that is made without yeast.

[22]"The prince must provide a bull as a sin offering. It will be for him and all of the people of the land. [23]For each of the seven days of the Feast he must provide seven bulls and seven rams. They must not have any flaws. They will be a burnt offering to me. The prince must also provide a male goat for a sin offering. [24]He must bring a little over half a bushel for each bull or ram. He must also provide four quarts of olive oil for each of them.

[25]"The seven days of the Feast begin on the 15th day of the seventh month. During those days the prince must provide the same sin offerings, burnt offerings, grain offerings and olive oil."

46 The LORD and King says, "On the six working days of each week you must keep the east gate of the inner courtyard of the temple shut. But open it on Sabbath days and during New Moon Feasts. [2]The prince must enter the temple area through the porch of the gateway. He must stand by the gatepost. The priests must sacrifice his burnt offering and friendship offerings. He must worship at the entrance of the gateway. Then he must leave. But the gate will not be shut until evening.

[3]"On Sabbath days and during New Moon Feasts the people of the land must gather together at the entrance of the temple gateway. That is where they must worship me.

[4]"The prince must bring a burnt offering to me on the Sabbath. It will be six male lambs and a ram. They must not have any flaws. [5]He must offer a little over half a bushel of grain along with the ram. The grain he offers along with the lambs can be as much as he wants to give. He must also offer four quarts of olive oil for every half bushel of grain.

[6]"On the day of the New Moon Feast the prince must also offer a young bull, six lambs and a ram. They must not have any flaws. [7]He must offer a little over half a bushel of grain along with the bull or ram. The grain he offers along with the lambs can be as much as he wants to give. He must also offer four quarts of olive oil for every half bushel of grain.

[8]"When the prince enters the temple area, he must go in through the porch of the gateway. He must leave the same way.

[9]"The people of the land must worship me at the appointed feasts. Those who enter through the north gate must leave through the south gate. Those who enter through the south gate must leave

through the north gate. They must not leave through the same gate they entered. Each one must go out the opposite gate. 10The prince must be among them. He must go in when they go in. And he must leave when they leave.

11"At the yearly feasts and other appointed feasts there must be grain offerings. The prince must offer a little over half a bushel of grain along with a bull or ram. The grain he offers along with the lambs can be as much as he wants to give. He must also offer four quarts of olive oil for every half bushel of grain. 12He can also bring another offering to me because he chooses to. It might be a burnt offering or friendship offering. When he brings it, the east gate must be opened for him. He will bring his offering just as he does on the Sabbath day. Then he will leave. After he has gone out, the gate must be shut.

13"Every day you must provide a lamb that is a year old. It must not have any flaws. It is a burnt offering to me. You must provide it every morning. 14You must also offer grain along with it every morning. Bring 13 and a third cups of grain. Also bring one and a third quarts of olive oil to make the flour a little wet. So you will give the grain offering to me. That will be a law that will last for all time to come. 15Provide the lamb, grain offering and oil every morning. They will be used for a regular burnt offering."

16The LORD and King says, "Suppose the prince makes a gift from his share of land. And he gives it to one of his sons. Then the property will also belong to his sons after him. It will be handed down to them.

17"But suppose he makes a gift from his share of land to one of his servants. Then the servant can keep it until the Year of Jubilee. After that, it will be returned to the prince. His property can be handed down only to his sons. It belongs to them.

18"The prince must not take any share of land that belongs to the people. He must not drive them off their property. He must give his sons their share out of his own property. Then my people will not be separated from their property."

19The man brought me through the entrance at the side of the north building. That's where the priests' sacred rooms were located. He showed me a place west of the building. 20He said to me, "This is where the priests will cook the guilt offerings and sin offerings. They will also bake the grain offerings here. Then they will not have to bring the offerings into the outer courtyard. That will keep the people from touching the offerings and becoming holy."

21Then the man brought me to the outer courtyard. He led me around to its four corners. In each corner I saw another smaller courtyard. 22So in the four corners of the outer courtyard were walled courtyards. Each one was 70 feet long and 52 and a half feet wide. All of them were the same size. 23Around the inside of each of the four courtyards was a stone ledge. Places for fire were built all around under each ledge. 24The man said to me, "These are the kitchens. Those who serve at the temple will cook the people's sacrifices here."

A River Will Flow From the Temple

47 The man brought me back to the entrance to the temple. I saw water flowing east from under a temple gateway. The temple faced east. The water was coming down from under the south side of the temple. It was flowing south of the altar.

2Then he brought me out through the north gate of the outer courtyard. He led me around the outside to the outer gate that faced east. The water was flowing from the south side of the east gate.

3Then the man went toward the east. He had a measuring line in his hand. He measured off 1,750 feet. He led me through water that was up to my ankles. 4Then he measured off another 1,750 feet. He led me through water that was up to my knees. Then he measured off another 1,750 feet. He led me through water that was up to my waist. 5Then he measured off another 1,750 feet. But now it was a river that I could not go across. The water had risen so high that it was deep enough to swim in. 6He asked me, "Son of man, do you see this?"

Then he led me back to the bank of the river. 7When I arrived there, I saw a large number of trees. They were on both sides of the river.

8The man said to me, "This water flows toward the eastern territory. It goes down into the Arabah Valley. There it enters the Dead Sea. When it empties into it, the water there becomes fresh. 9Large numbers of creatures will live where the river flows. It will have huge numbers of fish. This water flows there and makes the salt water fresh. So where the river flows everything will live.

10"People will stand along the shore to fish. From En Gedi all the way to En Eglaim there will be places for spreading fishnets. The Dead Sea will have many kinds of fish. They will be like the fish in the Mediterranean Sea.

11"But none of the swamps will have fresh water in them. They will stay salty.

12"Fruit trees of all kinds will grow on both banks of the river. Their leaves will not dry up. The trees will always have fruit on them. Every month they will bear fruit. The water from the temple will flow to them. Their fruit will be used for food. And their leaves will be used for healing."

The Borders of the Land

13The LORD and King says, "People of Israel, here are the borders you will have after you divide up the land. Each of the 12 tribes will receive a share. But the family of Joseph will have two shares. 14Divide the land into equal parts. Long ago I raised my hand and took an oath. I promised to give the land to your people. So all of it will belong to you.

15“Here are the borders of the land.

“On the north side the border will start at the
Mediterranean Sea. It will go by the Hethlon
road past Lebo Hamath. Then it will continue
on to Zedad, 16Berothah and Sibraim. Sibraim is between Damascus and Hamath. The
border will reach all the way to Hazer Hatti-
con. It is right next to Hauran. 17The border
will go from the sea to Hazar Enan. It will run
north of Damascus and south of Hamath. That
will be the north border.
18“On the east side the border will run between
Hauran and Damascus. It will continue along
the Jordan River between Gilead and the land
of Israel. It will reach to the Dead Sea and all
the way to Tamar. That will be the east border.
19“On the south side the border will start at Tamar.
It will reach all the way to the waters of Meribah Kadesh. Then it will run along the Wadi
of Egypt. It will end at the Mediterranean Sea.
That will be the south border.
20“On the west side, the Mediterranean Sea will be
the border. It will go to a point across from
Lebo Hamath. That will be the west border.

21“You must divide up this land among yourselves. Do it based on the number of men in your
tribes. 22Each of the tribes must receive a share of
the land.

“You must also give some land to the outsiders
who have settled among you and who have children. Treat them as if they had been born in Israel. Let them have some land among your tribes.
23Outsiders can settle in any tribe. There you must
give them their share,” announces the LORD and
King.

The Land Will Be Divided Up

48 “Here are the tribes. They are listed by
their names. Dan will receive one share of
land. It will be at the northern border of Israel. The
border will follow the Hethlon road to Lebo Hamath. Hazar Enan will be part of the border. So
will the northern border of Damascus next to Hamath. Dan’s northern border will run from east to
west.

2“Asher will receive one share. It will border
the territory of Dan from east to west.

3“Naphtali will receive one share. It will border
the territory of Asher from east to west.

4“Manasseh will receive one share. It will border the territory of Naphtali from east to west.

5“Ephraim will receive one share. It will border
the territory of Manasseh from east to west.

6“Reuben will receive one share. It will border
the territory of Ephraim from east to west.

7“Judah will receive one share. It will border the
territory of Reuben from east to west.

8“You must give one share as a special gift to
me. It will border the territory of Judah from east
to west. It will be eight and a fourth miles wide. It
will be as long as the border of each of the territories of the tribes. Its border will run from east to
west. The temple will be in the center of that strip
of land.

9“Give that special share of land to me. It will
be eight and a fourth miles long and three and a
third miles wide. 10It will be the sacred share of
land for the priests. It will be eight and a fourth
miles long on the north side. It will be three and a
third miles wide on the west side. It will be three
and a third miles wide on the east side. And it will
be eight and a fourth miles long on the south side.
My temple will be in the center of it.

11“This share of land will be for the priests who
are set apart to me. They will come from the family line of Zadok. The members of that family
served me faithfully. They did not go down the
wrong path as the Levites and other Israelites did.
12Their share of land will be a special gift to them.
It will be part of the sacred share of the land. It will
be very holy. Its border will run along the territory
of the Levites.

13“The Levites will receive a share. It will be
next to the territory of the priests. The Levites’
share will be eight and a fourth miles long and
three and a third miles wide. 14They must not sell
or trade any of it. It is the best part of the land. It
must not be handed over to anyone else. It is set
apart to me.

15“The area that remains is one and two thirds
miles wide. It is eight and a fourth miles long. It
will not be holy. The people in Jerusalem can build
houses there. They can use some of it as grasslands. The city will be in the center of it. 16Each of
the four sides of the city will be one and a half
miles long. 17Each of the four sides of the city’s
grasslands will be 437 and a half feet long.

18“What remains of the area will be three and a
third miles long on the east and west sides. Its border will run along the border of the sacred share.
Its crops will supply food for the city workers.
19They will farm the area. They will come from all
of the tribes of Israel. 20The entire area will be a
square. Each of its four sides will be eight and a
fourth miles long. Set the sacred share apart as a
special gift to me. Do the same thing with the
property of the city.

21“The area that remains on both sides will
belong to the prince. So his land does not include
the sacred share and the city property. The eastern
part of his land will reach from the sacred share all
the way to the eastern border. The western part will
reach from the sacred share to the western border.
The sacred share itself is eight and a fourth miles
long on its east and west sides. Both of those areas
will be right next to the borders of the two tribes
on the north and south sides. They will belong to
the prince. The sacred share will be in the center of
them. It will have the temple in it.

22“The property of the Levites will lie in the
center of the prince’s share. So will the property

of the city. The prince's land will lie between the borders of the tribes of Judah and Benjamin.

23"Here is the land for the rest of the tribes. Benjamin will receive one share. It will reach from the eastern border to the western border.

24"Simeon will receive one share. It will border the territory of Benjamin from east to west.

25"Issachar will receive one share. It will border the territory of Simeon from east to west.

26"Zebulun will receive one share. It will border the territory of Issachar from east to west.

27"Gad will receive one share. It will border the territory of Zebulun from east to west.

28"The southern border of Gad will run south from Tamar to the waters of Meribah Kadesh. It will continue along the Wadi of Egypt. It will end at the Mediterranean Sea.

29"That is the land you must divide among the tribes of Israel. And those will be the shares they will receive," announces the LORD and King.

The Gates of the City

30"Here is a list of the gates of the city. Start with its north side. It will be a mile and a half long.
31The city gates will be named after the tribes of Israel. The north side will have three gates. They will be the gates of Reuben, Judah and Levi.

32"The east side will be a mile and a half long. It will have three gates. They will be the gates of Joseph, Benjamin and Dan.

33"The south side will be a mile and a half long. It will have three gates. They will be the gates of Simeon, Issachar and Zebulun.

34"The west side will be a mile and a half long. It will have three gates. They will be the gates of Gad, Asher and Naphtali.

35"The city will be six miles around.

"From that time on, its name will be

THE LORD IS THERE."

Daniel

Daniel Is Trained in Babylon

1 It was the third year that Jehoiakim was king of Judah. Nebuchadnezzar came to Jerusalem. His armies surrounded the city and attacked it. Nebuchadnezzar was king of Babylonia.

2The LORD handed Jehoiakim, the king of Judah, over to him. Nebuchadnezzar also took some of the articles from God's temple. He carried them off to the temple of his god in Babylonia. He put them among the treasures of his god.

3The king gave Ashpenaz an order. Ashpenaz was the chief of Nebuchadnezzar's court officials. The king told him to bring in some of the Israelites. He wanted nobles and men from the royal family. 4He was looking for young men who were healthy and handsome. They had to be able to learn anything. They had to be well educated. They had to have the ability to understand new things quickly and easily. The king wanted men who could serve in his palace. Ashpenaz was supposed to teach them the Babylonian language and writings.

5The king had his servants give them food and wine from his own table. They received a certain amount every day. The young men had to be trained for three years. After that, they could begin to serve the king.

6Some of the men were from Judah. Their names were Daniel, Hananiah, Mishael and Azariah. 7The chief official gave them new names. He gave Daniel the name Belteshazzar. He gave Hananiah the name Shadrach. He gave Mishael the name Meshach. And he gave Azariah the name Abednego.

8Daniel decided not to make himself "unclean" by eating the king's food and drinking his wine. So he asked the chief official for a favor. He wanted permission not to make himself "unclean" with the king's food and wine.

9God had caused the official to be kind and friendly to Daniel. 10But the official refused to do what Daniel asked for. He said, "I'm afraid of the king. He is my master. He has decided what you and your three friends must eat and drink. Why should he see you looking worse than the other young men who are the same age you are? When he sees how you look, he might kill me."

11So Daniel spoke to one of the guards. The chief official had appointed him over Daniel, Hananiah, Mishael and Azariah. 12Daniel said to him, "Please test us for ten days. Give us nothing but vegetables to eat. And give us only water to drink. 13Then compare us with the young men who eat the king's food. See how we look. After that, do what you want to."

14So the guard agreed. He tested them for ten days.

15After the ten days they looked healthy and well fed. In fact, they looked better than any of the young men who ate the king's food. 16So the guard didn't require Daniel and his friends to eat the special food or drink the wine. He gave them vegetables instead.

17God gave knowledge and understanding to those four young men. So they understood all kinds of writings and subjects. And Daniel could understand all kinds of visions and dreams.

18The three years the king had set for their training ended. So the chief official brought them to Nebuchadnezzar. 19The king talked with them. He didn't find anyone equal to Daniel, Hananiah, Mishael and Azariah. So they began to serve the king. 20He asked them for advice in matters that required wisdom and understanding. He always found their answers to be the best. In fact, the men were ten times better than anyone in his kingdom who claimed to get knowledge by using magic.

21Daniel served in Babylon until the first year Cyrus ruled over Babylonia. Cyrus was king of Persia.

Nebuchadnezzar Dreams About a Large Statue

2 In the second year of Nebuchadnezzar's rule, he had a dream. His mind was troubled. He couldn't sleep.

2So the king sent for those who claimed to get knowledge by using magic. He also sent for those who practiced evil magic and those who studied the heavens. He wanted them to tell him what he had dreamed. They came in and stood in front of the king. 3He said to them, "I had a dream. It troubles me. So I want to know what it means."

4Then those who studied the heavens answered the king. They spoke in Aramaic. They said, "King Nebuchadnezzar, may you live forever! Tell us what you dreamed. Then we'll explain what it means."

5The king replied to them, "I have made up my mind. You must tell me what I dreamed. And you must tell me what it means. If you don't, I'll have you cut to pieces. And I'll have your houses turned into piles of trash.

6"So tell me what I dreamed. Explain it to me. Then I'll give you gifts. I'll reward you. I'll give you great honor. So tell me the dream. And tell me what it means."

7Once more they replied, "King Nebuchadnezzar, tell us what you dreamed. Then we'll tell you what it means."

8The king answered, "I know what you are doing. You are trying to gain more time. You realize that I've made up my mind. 9You must tell me

the dream. If you don't, you will pay for it. You
have gotten together and made evil plans. You
hope things will change. So you are telling me lies.
But I want you to tell me what I dreamed. Then I'll
know that you can tell me what it means."
10 They answered the king, "There isn't a man
on earth who can do what you are asking! No king
has ever asked for anything like that. Not even a
king as great and mighty as you has asked for it.
Those who get knowledge by using magic have
never been asked to do what you are asking. And
those who study the heavens haven't been asked
to do it either. 11 What you are asking is much too
hard. No one can tell you what you dreamed
except the gods. And they don't live among human
beings."
12 That made the king very angry. He ordered
that all of the wise men in Babylon be put to death.
13 So the order was given to kill them. Men were
sent out to look for Daniel and his friends. They
were also supposed to be put to death.
14 Arioch was the commander of the king's
guard. He went out to put the wise men of Babylon to death. So Daniel spoke to him wisely and
carefully. 15 He asked the king's officer, "Why did
Nebuchadnezzar give a terrible order like that?"
Then Arioch explained to Daniel what was
going on.
16 When Daniel heard that, he went to the king.
He told him he would explain the dream to him.
But he needed more time.
17 Then Daniel returned to his house. He
explained everything to his friends Hananiah,
Mishael and Azariah. 18 He asked them to pray that
the God of heaven would give him mercy. He
wanted God to help him understand the mystery
of the king's dream. Then he and his friends
wouldn't be killed along with the other wise men
in Babylon.
19 During that night, God gave Daniel a vision.
He showed him what the mystery was all about.
Then Daniel praised the God of heaven. 20 He said,

"May God be praised for ever and ever!
He is wise and powerful.
21 He changes times and seasons.
He sets up kings.
He removes them from power.
The wisdom of those who are wise comes
from him.
He gives knowledge to those who have
understanding.
22 He explains deep and hidden things.
He knows what happens in the darkest
places.
And where he is, everything is light.
23 God of my people, I thank and praise you.
You have given me wisdom and power.
You have made known to me what we asked
you for.
You have shown us the king's dream."

Daniel Tells the King What His Dream Means

24 Then Daniel went to Arioch. The king had
appointed him to put the wise men of Babylon to
death. Daniel said to him, "Don't kill the wise men
of Babylon. Take me to the king. I'll tell him what
his dream means."
25 So Arioch took Daniel to the king at once. Arioch said, "I have found a man among those you
brought here from Judah. He can tell you what
your dream means."
26 Nebuchadnezzar spoke to Daniel, who was
also called Belteshazzar. The king asked him, "Are
you able to tell me what I saw in my dream? And
can you tell me what it means?"
27 Daniel replied, "You have asked us to explain
a mystery to you. But no wise man can do that.
And those who try to figure things out by using
magic can't do it either.
28 "But there is a God in heaven who can explain
mysteries. Nebuchadnezzar, he has shown you what
is going to happen. Here is what you dreamed. And
here are the visions that passed through your mind
while you were lying on your bed.
29 "My king, while you were still in bed your
mind thought about things that haven't happened
yet. The One who explains mysteries showed
those things to you.
30 "Now the mystery has been explained to me.
But it isn't because I have greater wisdom than
anyone else. It's because God wants you to know
what the mystery means, my king. He wants you
to understand what went through your mind.
31 "King Nebuchadnezzar, you looked up and
saw a large statue standing in front of you. It was
huge. It shone brightly. And it terrified you. 32 The
head of the statue was made out of pure gold. Its
chest and arms were made of silver. Its stomach
and thighs were bronze. 33 Its legs were made out of
iron. And its feet were partly iron and partly baked
clay.
34 "While you were watching, a rock was cut
out. But human hands didn't do it. It struck the
statue on its feet of iron and clay. It smashed them.
35 Then the iron and clay were broken to pieces. So
were the bronze, silver and gold. All of them were
broken to pieces at the same time. They became
like straw on a threshing floor at harvest time. The
wind blew them away without leaving a trace. But
the rock that struck the statue became a huge
mountain. It filled the whole earth.
36 "That was your dream. Now I will tell you
what it means. 37 Nebuchadnezzar, you are the
greatest king of all. The God of heaven has given
you authority and power. He has given you might
and glory. 38 He has put everyone under your control. He has also given you authority over the wild
animals and the birds of the air. It doesn't matter
where they live. He has made you ruler over all of
them. You are that head of gold.

39“After you, another kingdom will take over. It
won’t be as powerful as yours. Next, a third kingdom will rule over the whole earth. The bronze
part of the statue stands for that kingdom.
40“Finally, there will be a fourth kingdom. It
will be as strong as iron. Iron breaks and smashes
everything to pieces. And the fourth kingdom will
crush and break all of the others. 41You saw that
the feet and toes were made out of iron and baked
clay. And the fourth kingdom will be divided up.
But it will still be almost as strong as iron. That’s
why you saw iron mixed with clay. 42The toes were
partly iron and partly clay. And the fourth kingdom
will be partly strong and partly weak. 43You saw
the iron mixed with baked clay. And the fourth
kingdom will be made up of all kinds of people.
They won’t hold together any more than iron
mixes with clay.
44“In the time of those kings, the God of heaven
will set up a kingdom. It will never be destroyed.
And no other nation will ever take it over. It will
crush all of those other kingdoms. It will bring
them to an end. But it will last forever. 45That’s
what the vision of the rock cut out of a mountain
means. Human hands didn’t cut the rock out. It
broke the statue to pieces. It smashed the iron,
bronze, clay, silver and gold.
“The great God has shown you what will take
place in days to come. The dream is true. And you
can trust the meaning I have given you for it.”
46Then King Nebuchadnezzar bowed low in
front of Daniel. He wanted to honor him. So he
ordered that an offering and incense be offered up
to him.
47The king said to Daniel, “I’m sure your God is
the greatest God of all. He is the Lord of kings. He
explains mysteries. That’s why you were able to
explain the mystery of my dream.”
48Then the king put Daniel in a position of
authority. He gave him many gifts. He made him
ruler over the city of Babylon and the towns
around it. He put him in charge of all of its other
wise men.
49The king also did what Daniel asked him to.
He appointed Shadrach, Meshach and Abednego
to help Daniel govern Babylon and the towns
around it. Daniel himself remained at the royal
court.

Daniel’s Friends Are Thrown Into a Blazing Furnace

3 King Nebuchadnezzar made a statue that was
covered with gold. It was 90 feet tall and 9
feet wide. He set it up on the flatlands of Dura near
the city of Babylon.
2Then the king sent for the royal rulers, high
officials and governors. He sent for the advisers,
treasurers, judges and court officers. And he sent
for all of the other officials of Babylon. He asked
them to come to a special gathering to honor the
statue he had set up.
3So the royal rulers, high officials and governors
came together. So did the advisers, treasurers, judges
and court officers. All of the other officials joined
them. They came to honor the statue that King Nebuchadnezzar had set up. They stood in front of it.
4Then a messenger called out loudly, “Listen,
you people who come from every nation! Pay
attention, you who speak other languages! Here is
what the king commands you to do. 5You will soon
hear the sound of horns and flutes. You will hear
zithers, lyres, harps and pipes. In fact, you will
hear all kinds of music. When you do, you must
fall down and worship the gold statue that King
Nebuchadnezzar has set up. 6If you don’t, you will
be thrown into a blazing furnace right away.”
7All of the people heard the sound of the horns
and flutes. They heard the zithers, lyres, harps and
other musical instruments. As soon as they did,
they fell down and worshiped Nebuchadnezzar’s
gold statue. They had come from every nation and
language.
8At that time some people who studied the
heavens came forward. They spoke against the
Jews. 9They said, “King Nebuchadnezzar, may
you live forever! 10You commanded everyone to
fall down and worship the gold statue. You told
them to do it when they heard the horns, flutes,
zithers, lyres, harps, pipes and other musical
instruments. 11If they didn’t, they would be thrown
into a blazing furnace. 12But you have appointed
some Jews to help Daniel govern Babylon and the
towns around it. Their names are Shadrach, Meshach and Abednego. They don’t pay any attention
to you, King Nebuchadnezzar. They don’t serve
your gods. And they refuse to worship the gold
statue you have set up.”
13Nebuchadnezzar burned with anger. He sent
for Shadrach, Meshach and Abednego. So they
were brought to him.
14The king said to them, “Shadrach, Meshach
and Abednego, is what I heard about you true?
Don’t you serve my gods? Don’t you worship the
gold statue I set up? 15You will hear the horns,
flutes, zithers, lyres, harps, pipes and other musical instruments. When you do, fall down and worship the statue I made. If you will, that’s very
good. But if you won’t, you will be thrown at once
into a blazing furnace. Then what god will be able
to save you from my powerful hand?”
16Shadrach, Meshach and Abednego replied to
the king. They said, “King Nebuchadnezzar, we
don’t need to talk about this anymore. 17We might
be thrown into the blazing furnace. But the God
we serve is able to bring us out of it alive. He will
save us from your powerful hand.
18“But we want you to know this. Even if we
knew that our God wouldn’t save us, we still
wouldn’t serve your gods. We wouldn’t worship
the gold statue you set up.”
19Then Nebuchadnezzar’s anger burned against
Shadrach, Meshach and Abednego. The look on

his face changed. And he ordered that the furnace be heated seven times hotter than usual. 20He also gave some of the strongest soldiers in his army a command. He ordered them to tie up Shadrach, Meshach and Abednego. Then he told his men to throw them into the blazing furnace. 21So they were tied up. Then they were thrown into the furnace. They were wearing their robes, pants, turbans and other clothes.

22The king's command was carried out quickly. The furnace was so hot that its flames killed the soldiers who threw Shadrach, Meshach and Abednego into it. 23So the three men were firmly tied up. And they fell into the blazing furnace.

24Then King Nebuchadnezzar leaped to his feet. He was so amazed he asked his advisers, "Didn't we tie three men up? Didn't we throw three men into the fire?"

"Yes, we did," they replied.

25The king said, "Look! I see four men walking around in the fire. They aren't tied up. And the fire hasn't even harmed them. The fourth man looks like a son of the gods."

26Then the king approached the opening of the blazing furnace. He shouted, "Shadrach, Meshach and Abednego, come out! You who serve the Most High God, come here!"

So they came out of the fire. 27The royal rulers, high officials, governors and advisers crowded around them. They saw that the fire hadn't harmed their bodies. Not one hair on their heads was burned. Their robes weren't burned either. And they didn't even smell like smoke.

28Then Nebuchadnezzar said, "May the God of Shadrach, Meshach and Abednego be praised! He has sent his angel and saved his servants. They trusted in him. They refused to obey my command. They were willing to give up their lives. They would rather die than serve or worship any god except their own God.

29"No other god can save people that way. So I'm giving an order. No one from any nation or language can say anything against the God of Shadrach, Meshach and Abednego. If they do, they'll be cut to pieces. And their houses will be turned into piles of trash."

30Then the king honored Shadrach, Meshach and Abednego. He gave them higher positions in the city of Babylon and the towns around it.

Nebuchadnezzar Dreams About a Tree

4 I, King Nebuchadnezzar, am writing this letter.

I am sending it to you people from every nation and language in the whole world.

May you have great success!

2I am pleased to tell you what has happened. The Most High God has done miraculous signs and wonders for me.

3His miraculous signs are great.
His wonders are mighty.
His kingdom will last forever.
His rule will never end.

4I was at home in my palace. I was content and very successful. 5But I had a dream that made me afraid. I was lying on my bed. Then dreams and visions passed through my mind. They terrified me.

6So I commanded that all of the wise men in Babylon be brought to me. I wanted them to tell me what my dream meant. 7Those who try to figure things out by using magic came. So did those who study the heavens. I told all of them what I had dreamed. But they couldn't tell me what it meant.

8Finally, Daniel came to me. He is called Belteshazzar, after the name of my god. The spirit of the holy gods is in him. I told him my dream.

9I said, "Belteshazzar, you are chief of the magicians. I know that the spirit of the holy gods is in you. No mystery is too hard for you to figure out. Here is my dream. Tell me what it means.

10"Here are the visions I saw while I was lying on my bed. I looked up and saw a tree standing in the middle of the land. It was very tall. 11It had grown to be large and strong. Its top touched the sky. It could be seen anywhere on earth. 12Its leaves were beautiful. It had a lot of fruit on it. It provided enough food for people and animals. Under the tree, the wild animals found shade. The birds of the air lived in its branches. Every creature was fed from that tree.

13"While I was still lying on my bed, I looked up. In my visions, I saw a holy messenger. He was coming down from heaven. 14He called out in a loud voice. He said, 'Cut the tree down. Break off its branches. Strip its leaves off. Scatter its fruit. Let the animals that are under it run away. Let the birds that are in its branches fly off. 15But leave the stump with its roots in the ground. Let it stay in the field. Put a band of iron and bronze around it.

"'Let King Nebuchadnezzar become wet with the dew of heaven. Let him live like the animals among the plants of the earth. 16Let him no longer have the mind of a man. Instead, let him be given the mind of an animal. Let him stay that way until seven periods of time pass by.

17"'The decision is announced by holy messengers. So all who are alive will know that the Most High God is King. He rules over all of the kingdoms of men. He gives them to anyone he wants. Sometimes he puts the least important men in charge of them.'

18“That’s the dream I, King Nebuchadnezzar, had. Now tell me what it means, Belteshazzar. None of the wise men in my
kingdom can explain it to me. But you can.
After all, the spirit of the holy gods is in you.”

Daniel Explains Nebuchadnezzar’s Dream

19Daniel, who was also called Belteshazzar, was very bewildered for a while. His
thoughts terrified him. So the king said,
“Belteshazzar, don’t let the dream or its
meaning make you afraid.”
Belteshazzar answered, “My master, I
wish the dream were about your enemies! I
wish its meaning had to do with them! 20You
saw a tree. It grew to be large and strong. Its
top touched the sky. It could be seen from
anywhere on earth. 21Its leaves were beautiful. It had a lot of fruit on it. It provided
enough food for people and animals. Under
the tree, the wild animals found shade. The
birds of the air lived in its branches.
22“My king, you are that tree! You have
become great and strong. Your greatness has
grown until it reaches the sky. Your rule has
spread to all parts of the earth.
23“My king, you saw a holy messenger.
He came down from heaven. He said, ‘Cut
the tree down. Destroy it. But leave the
stump with its roots in the ground. Let it stay
in the field. Put a band of iron and bronze
around it. Let King Nebuchadnezzar become
wet with the dew of heaven. Let him live like
the wild animals. Let him stay that way until
seven periods of time pass by.’
24“My king and master, here is what your
dream means. The Most High God has given
an order against you. 25You will be driven
away from people. You will live like the wild
animals. You will eat grass just as cattle do.
You will become wet with the dew of heaven.
Seven periods of time will pass by for you.
Then you will recognize that the Most High
God rules over all of the kingdoms of men.
He gives them to anyone he wants.
26“But he gave a command to leave the
stump of the tree along with its roots. That
means your kingdom will be given back to
you. It will happen when you recognize that
the God of heaven rules.
27“So, my king, I hope you will accept my
advice. Stop being sinful. Do what is right.
Give up your evil practices. Show kindness to
those who are being treated badly. Then perhaps things will continue to go well with you.”

Nebuchadnezzar’s Dream Comes True

28All of that happened to me. 29It took
place twelve months later. I was walking on
the roof of my palace in Babylon. 30I said,
“Isn’t this the great Babylon I have built as a
place for my royal palace? I used my mighty
power to build it. It shows how glorious my
majesty is.”
31I was still speaking when a voice was
heard from heaven. It said, “King Nebuchadnezzar, here is what has been ordered concerning you. Your royal authority has been
taken from you. 32You will be driven away
from people. You will live like the wild animals. You will eat grass just as cattle do.
Seven periods of time will pass by for you.
Then you will recognize that the Most High
God rules over all of the kingdoms of men.
He gives them to anyone he wants.”
33What had been said about me came true
at once. I was driven away from people. I ate
grass just as cattle do. My body became wet
with the dew of heaven. I stayed that way until
my hair grew like the feathers of an eagle. My
nails became like the claws of a bird.

34At the end of that time I, Nebuchadnezzar, looked up toward heaven. My mind
became clear again. Then I praised the Most
High God. I gave honor and glory to the One
who lives forever.

His rule will last forever.
His kingdom will never end.
35 He considers all of the nations on earth
to be nothing.
He does as he pleases
with the powers of heaven.
He does what he wants
with the nations of the earth.
No one can hold his hand back.
No one can say to him,
“What have you done?”

36My honor and glory were returned to me
when my mind became clear again. The
glory of my kingdom was given back to me.
My advisers and nobles came to me. And I
was put back on my throne. I became even
greater than I had been before.
37Now I, Nebuchadnezzar, give praise and
honor and glory to the King of heaven.
Everything he does is right. All of his ways
are fair. He is able to bring down those who
live proudly.

A Hand Writes on the Palace Wall

5 King Belshazzar gave a big dinner. He invited
a thousand of his nobles to it. He drank wine
with them.
2While Belshazzar was drinking his wine, he
gave orders to his servants. He commanded them
to bring in some gold and silver cups. They were
the cups his father Nebuchadnezzar had taken
from the temple in Jerusalem. Belshazzar had

them brought in so everyone could drink from them. That included the king himself, his nobles, his wives and his concubines.

3So the servants brought in the gold cups that had been taken from God's temple in Jerusalem. The king and his nobles drank from them. So did his wives and concubines. 4As they drank the wine, they praised their gods. The statues of those gods were made out of gold, silver, bronze, iron, wood or stone.

5Suddenly the fingers of a human hand appeared. They wrote something on the plaster of the palace wall. It happened near the lampstand.

The king watched the hand as it wrote. 6His face turned pale. He became so afraid that his knees knocked together. His legs couldn't hold him up any longer.

7The king sent for those who try to figure things out by using magic. He also sent for those who study the heavens. All of them were wise men in Babylon. He ordered that they be brought to him. He said to them, "I want one of you to read this writing and tell me what it means. If you do, you will be dressed in purple clothes. A gold chain will be put around your neck. And you will be made the third highest ruler in the kingdom."

8Then all of the king's wise men came in. But they couldn't read the writing. They couldn't tell him what it meant. 9So King Belshazzar became even more terrified. His face grew more pale. And his nobles were bewildered.

10The queen heard the king and his nobles talking. So she came into the dining hall. "King Belshazzar, may you live forever!" she said. "Don't be afraid! Don't look so pale! 11I know a man in your kingdom who has the spirit of the holy gods in him. He has understanding and wisdom and good sense just like the gods. That was discovered when your father Nebuchadnezzar was king. Nebuchadnezzar appointed him chief of those who tried to figure things out by using magic. He also put him in charge of those who studied the heavens.

12"The man's name is Daniel. Your father called him Belteshazzar. He has a clever mind and knowledge and understanding. He is also able to tell what dreams mean. He can explain riddles and solve hard problems. Send for him. He'll tell you what the writing means."

13So Daniel was brought to the king. The king said to him, "Are you Daniel? Are you one of the prisoners my father the king brought here from Judah? 14I have heard that the spirit of the gods is in you. I've also heard that you have understanding and good sense and special wisdom.

15"The wise men and those who practice magic were brought to me. They were asked to read this writing and tell me what it means. But they couldn't.

16"I have heard that you are able to explain things and solve hard problems. I hope you can read this writing and tell me what it means. If you can, you will be dressed in purple clothes. A gold chain will be put around your neck. And you will be made the third highest ruler in the kingdom."

17Then Daniel answered the king. He said, "You can keep your gifts for yourself. You can give your rewards to someone else. But I will read the writing for you. I'll tell you what it means.

18"King Belshazzar, the Most High God was good to your father Nebuchadnezzar. He gave him authority and greatness and glory and honor. 19God gave him a high position. Then all of the people from every nation and language became afraid of the king. He put to death anyone he wanted to. He spared anyone he wanted to spare. He gave high positions to anyone he wanted to. And he brought down anyone he wanted to bring down.

20"But his heart became very stubborn and proud. So he was removed from his royal throne. His glory was stripped away from him. 21He was driven away from people. He was given the mind of an animal. He lived like the wild donkeys. He ate grass just as cattle do. His body became wet with the dew of heaven. He stayed that way until he recognized that the Most High God rules over all of the kingdoms of men. He puts anyone he wants to in charge of them.

22"But you knew all of that, Belshazzar. After all, you are Nebuchadnezzar's son. In spite of that, you are still proud. 23You have taken your stand against the Lord of heaven. You had your servants bring cups from his temple to you. You and your nobles drank wine from them. So did your wives and concubines. You praised your gods. The statues of those gods are made out of silver, gold, bronze, iron, wood or stone. They can't see or hear or understand anything. But you didn't honor the God who holds in his hand your very life and everything you do. 24So he sent the hand that wrote on the wall.

25"Here is what was written.

MENE, MENE, TEKEL, PARSIN

26"And here is what those words mean.

Mene means that God has limited the time of your rule. He has brought it to an end.

27 *Tekel* means that you have been weighed on scales. And you haven't measured up to God's standard.

28 *Peres* means that your authority over your kingdom will be taken away from you. It will be given to the Medes and Persians."

29Then Belshazzar commanded his servants to dress Daniel in purple clothes. So they did. They put a gold chain around his neck. And he was made the third highest ruler in the kingdom.

30That very night Belshazzar, the king of Babylonia, was killed. 31His kingdom was given to Darius the Mede. Darius was 62 years old.

Daniel Is Thrown Into a Den of Lions

6 It pleased Darius to appoint 120 royal rulers over his entire kingdom. 2He placed three leaders over them. One of the leaders was Daniel. The royal rulers were made accountable to the three leaders. Then the king wouldn't lose any of his wealth. 3Daniel did a better job than the other two leaders or any of the royal rulers. He was an unusually good and able man. So the king planned to put him in charge of the whole kingdom.

4But the other two leaders and the royal rulers heard about it. So they looked for a reason to bring charges against Daniel. They tried to find something wrong with the way he ran the government. But they weren't able to. They couldn't find any fault with his work. He could always be trusted. He never did anything wrong. And he always did what he was supposed to.

5Finally those men said, "It's almost impossible for us to come up with a reason to bring charges against this man Daniel. If we do, it will have to be in connection with the law of his God."

6So the two leaders and the royal rulers went as a group to the king. They said, "King Darius, may you live forever! 7All of the royal leaders, high officials, royal rulers, advisers and governors want to make a suggestion. We've agreed that you should give an order. And you should make sure it's obeyed. Here is the command you should give. King Darius, during the next 30 days don't let any of your people pray to any god or man except to you. If they do, throw them into the lions' den.

8"Now give the order. Write it down in the laws of the Medes and Persians. Then it can't be changed." 9So King Darius put the order in writing.

10Daniel found out that the king had signed the order. In spite of that, he did just as he had always done before. He went home to his upstairs room. Its windows opened toward Jerusalem. He went to his room three times a day to pray. He got down on his knees and gave thanks to his God.

11Some of the other royal officials went to where Daniel was staying. They saw him praying and asking God for help. 12So they went to the king. They spoke to him about his royal order. They said, "King Darius, didn't you sign an official order? It said that for the next 30 days none of your people could pray to any god or man except to you. If they did, they would be thrown into the lions' den."

The king answered, "The order must still be obeyed. It's one of the laws of the Medes and Persians. So it can't be changed."

13Then they spoke to the king again. They said, "Daniel is one of the prisoners from Judah. He doesn't pay any attention to you, King Darius. He doesn't obey the order you put in writing. He still prays to his God three times a day."

14When the king heard that, he was very upset. He didn't want Daniel to be harmed in any way. Until sunset, he did everything he could to save him.

15Then the men went as a group to the king. They said to him, "King Darius, remember that no order or law you make can be changed. That's what the laws of the Medes and Persians require."

16So the king gave the order. Daniel was brought out and thrown into the lions' den. The king said to him, "You always serve your God faithfully. So may he save you!"

17A stone was brought and placed over the opening of the den. The king sealed it with his own special ring. He also sealed it with the rings of his nobles. Then nothing could be done to help Daniel.

18The king returned to his palace. He didn't eat anything that night. He didn't ask for anything to be brought to him for his enjoyment. And he couldn't sleep.

19As soon as the sun began to rise, the king got up. He hurried to the lions' den. 20When he got near it, he called out to Daniel. His voice was filled with great concern. He said, "Daniel! You serve the living God. You always serve him faithfully. So has he been able to save you from the lions?"

21Daniel answered, "My king, may you live forever! 22My God sent his angel. And his angel shut the mouths of the lions. They haven't hurt me at all. That's because I haven't done anything wrong in God's sight. I've never done anything wrong to you either, my king."

23The king was filled with joy. He ordered his servants to lift Daniel out of the den. So they did. They didn't see any wounds on him. That's because he had trusted in his God.

24Then the king gave another order. The men who had said bad things about Daniel were brought in. They were thrown into the lions' den. So were their wives and children. Before they hit the bottom of the den, the lions attacked them. And the lions crushed all of their bones.

25Then King Darius wrote to the people from every nation and language in the whole world. He said,

"May you have great success!

26"I order people in every part of my kingdom to respect and honor Daniel's God.

"He is the living God.
He will live forever.
His kingdom will not be destroyed.
His rule will never end.
27 He sets people free and saves them.
He does miraculous signs and wonders.
He does them in the heavens and on the earth.
He has saved Daniel
from the power of the lions."

28So Daniel had success while Darius was king. Things went well with him during the rule of Cyrus, the Persian.

Daniel Has a Vision About Four Animals

7 It was the first year that Belshazzar was king
of Babylon. Daniel had a dream. He was lying
on his bed. In his dream, visions passed through
his mind. He wrote down what he saw.
2Daniel said, “I had a vision at night. I looked
up and saw the four winds of heaven. They were
stirring up the Mediterranean Sea. 3Four large animals came up out of the sea. Each one was different from the others.
4“The first animal was like a lion. It had the
wings of an eagle. I watched until its wings were
torn off. Then it was lifted up from the ground. It
stood on two feet like a man. And a man’s heart
was given to it.
5“I saw a second animal. It looked like a bear. It
was raised up on one of its sides. And it had three
ribs between its teeth. It was told, ‘Get up! Eat
meat until you are full!’
6“After that, I saw another animal. It looked like
a leopard. On its back were four wings like the
wings of a bird. It had four heads. And it was given
authority to rule.
7“After that, in my vision I looked up and saw
a fourth animal. It was terrifying and very powerful. It had large iron teeth. It crushed those it
attacked and ate them up. It stomped on anything
that was left. It was different from the other animals. And it had ten horns.
8“I thought about the horns. Then I saw another
horn. It was a little one. It grew up among the other
horns. Three of the first horns were pulled up by
their roots to make room for it. The little horn had
eyes like the eyes of a man. Its mouth was always
bragging.
9“As I watched,

“thrones were set in place.
    The Eternal God took his seat.
His clothes were as white as snow.
    The hair on his head was white like wool.
His throne was blazing with fire.
    And flames were all around its wheels.
10 A river of fire was flowing.
    It was coming out from in front
        of God.
Thousands and thousands of angels
        served him.
    Millions of them stood in front of him.
The court was seated.
    And the books were opened.

11“Then I continued to watch because of the
way the horn was bragging. I kept looking until the
fourth animal was killed. I watched until its body
was destroyed. It was thrown into the blazing fire.
12The authority of the other animals had been
stripped away from them. But they were allowed
to live for a period of time.
13“In my vision I saw One who looked like a
son of man. He was coming with the clouds of
heaven. He approached the Eternal God. He was
led right up to him. 14And he was given authority,
glory and a kingdom. People from every nation
and language worshiped him. His authority will
last forever. It will not pass away. His kingdom
will never be destroyed.

An Angel Tells Daniel What His Dream Means

15“My spirit was troubled. The visions that
passed through my mind upset me. 16I approached
an angel who was standing there. I asked him what
all of those things really meant.
“So he explained everything to me. He told me
what it meant. He said, 17‘The four large animals
stand for four kingdoms. The kingdoms will
appear on the earth. 18But the holy people of the
Most High God will receive the kingdom. They
will possess it forever. It will belong to them for
ever and ever.’
19“Then I wanted to know what the fourth animal stood for. It was different from the others. It
was the most terrifying of all. It had iron teeth and
bronze claws. It crushed those it attacked and ate
them up. It stomped on anything that was left.
20“I also wanted to know about the ten horns on
its head. And I wanted to know about the other
horn that grew up later. It caused three of the ten
horns to fall out. It appeared to be stronger than
the others. It had eyes. And its mouth was always
bragging.
21“I saw that the horn was at war with God’s
people. It was winning the battle over them. 22But
then the Eternal God came. He decided in favor of
his holy people. So the time came when the kingdom was given to them.
23“Here’s how the angel explained it to me. He
said, ‘The fourth animal stands for a fourth kingdom. It will appear on earth. It will be different
from the other kingdoms. It will eat up the whole
earth. It will stomp on it and crush it. 24The ten
horns stand for ten kings. They will come from the
fourth kingdom.
“ ‘After them another king will appear. He will
be different from the earlier ones. He’ll bring three
kings under his control. 25He’ll speak against the
Most High God. He’ll treat God’s people badly.
He will try to change the times and laws that were
given by God. God’s people will be handed over to
him for three and a half years.
26“ ‘But the court will open. And the power of
that king will be taken away from him. It will be
completely destroyed forever. 27Then the authority, power and greatness of all of the kingdoms on
earth will be handed over to the people of the Most
High God. His kingdom will last forever. Every
ruler will worship and obey him.’
28“That’s all I saw. My thoughts deeply troubled
me. My face turned pale. But I kept those things
to myself.”

Daniel Has a Vision About a Ram and a Goat

8 It was the third year of King Belshazzar's
rule. After the vision that had already
appeared to me, I had another one. 2In my vision I
saw myself in the city of Susa. It has high walls
around it. It is in the land of Elam. In the vision I
was beside the Ulai Waterway.

3I looked up and saw a ram that had two horns.
He was standing beside the waterway. His horns
were long. One of them was longer than the other.
But it grew up later. 4I watched the ram as he charged
toward the west. He also charged toward the north
and the south. No animal could stand up against him.
Not one of them could save anyone from his power.
He did as he pleased. And he became great.

5I was thinking about all of that. Then a goat
suddenly came from the west. He had a large horn
between his eyes. He raced across the whole earth
without even touching the ground. 6He came
toward the ram that had the two horns. It was the
ram I had seen standing beside the waterway. The
goat was burning with anger. He charged at the
ram. 7I saw him attack the ram with mighty force.
He struck the ram and broke his two horns. The
ram didn't have the power to stand up against him.
The goat knocked him to the ground and stomped
on him. No one could save the ram from his power.

8The goat became very great. But when his
power was at its greatest, his large horn was broken off. In its place four large horns grew up
toward the four winds of heaven.

9Out of one of the four horns came another
horn. It started small but became more and more
powerful. It grew to the south and to the east and
toward the beautiful land of Israel. 10It grew until
it reached the stars in the sky. It threw some of
them down to the earth. And it stomped on them.

11It set itself up to be as great as God. He is the
Prince of the heavenly army. It took the daily sacrifices away from him. And his temple in Jerusalem
was brought low. 12Because many of God's people
refused to obey him, they were handed over to the
horn. The daily sacrifices were also given over to it.
It was successful no matter what it did. And the true
worship of God was thrown down to the ground.

13Then I heard a holy angel speaking. Another
holy angel spoke to him. He asked, "How long
will it take for the vision to come true? The daily
sacrifices will be stopped. Those who refuse to
obey God will be destroyed. The temple will be
handed over to an enemy. And some of the stars
will be stomped on."

14One of the holy angels said to me, "It will take
2,300 evenings and mornings. Then the temple
will be made holy again."

Gabriel Tells Daniel What His Vision Means

15I was watching the vision. And I was trying to
understand it. Then I saw someone who looked
like a man. 16I heard a voice from the Ulai Waterway. It called out, "Gabriel, tell Daniel what his
vision means."

17Gabriel came close to where I was standing. I
was terrified and fell down flat with my face
toward the ground. He said to me, "Son of man, I
want you to understand that the vision tells about
the time of the end."

18While he was speaking to me, I was sound
asleep. I lay with my face toward the ground. Then
he touched me. He raised me to my feet.

19He said, "I am going to tell you what will happen later. It will take place when God is angry. The
vision tells about the appointed time of the end.
20You saw a ram that had two horns. It stands for
the kings of Media and Persia. 21The goat stands
for the king of Greece. The large horn between his
eyes is the first king. 22Four horns took its place
when it was broken off. They stand for four kingdoms that will come from his nation. But those
kingdoms will not be as powerful as his.

23"Toward the end of their rule, those who
refuse to obey God will become completely evil.
Then another king will appear. He will have a
mean-looking face. He will be a master at making
clever plans. 24He will become very strong. But he
will not get that way by his own power. People
will be amazed at the way he destroys everything.
He will be successful no matter what he does. He
will destroy the mighty men and the holy people.

25"He will tell lies in order to succeed. He will
think he is more important than anyone else. When
people feel safe, he will destroy many of them. He
will stand up against the greatest Prince of all.
Then he will be destroyed. But he will not be
killed by human beings.

26"The vision of the evenings and mornings that
has been given to you is true. But seal up the
vision. It tells about a time far off."

27I was worn out. I lay sick for several days.
Then I got up and returned to my work for the
king. The vision bewildered me. I couldn't understand it.

Daniel Prays to the LORD

9 It was the first year that Darius was king of
Babylonia. He was from Media and was the
son of Xerxes. 2In that year I learned from the
Scriptures that Jerusalem would remain destroyed
for 70 years. That was what the LORD had told the
prophet Jeremiah. 3So I prayed to the Lord God. I
begged him. I made many appeals to him. I didn't
eat anything. I put on black clothes. And I sat
down in ashes.

4I prayed to the LORD my God. I admitted that
we had sinned. I said,

"Lord, you are a great and wonderful
God. You keep the covenant you made with
all those who love you and obey your commands. You show them your love.

5"We have sinned and done what is
wrong. We have been evil. We have refused
to obey you. We have turned away from your
commands and laws. 6We haven't listened to
your servants the prophets. They spoke in
your name to our kings and princes. They
also brought your message to all of our people in the land.
7"Lord, you always do what is right. But
we are covered with shame today. We are the
people of Judah and Jerusalem. All of us are
Israelites, no matter where we live. We are
now living in many countries. You scattered
us among the nations because we weren't
faithful to you. 8LORD, we and our kings and
princes and people are covered with shame.
We have sinned against you.
9"You are the Lord our God. You show us
your tender love. You forgive us. But we have
turned against you. 10You are the LORD our
God. But we haven't obeyed you. We haven't
kept the laws you gave us through your servants the prophets. 11All of the people of Israel have broken your law and turned away
from it. They have refused to obey you.
"Curses and warnings are written down in
the Law of Moses. He was your servant.
Those curses have been poured out on us.
That's because we have sinned against you.
12The warnings you gave us and our rulers
have come true. You have brought great trouble on us. Nothing like what has been done
to Jerusalem has ever happened anywhere
else on earth.
13"The curses that are written in the Law
of Moses have fallen on us. We have received
nothing but trouble. You are the LORD our
God. But we haven't asked for your favor.
We haven't turned away from our sins. We've
refused to pay attention to the laws you gave
us. 14LORD, you didn't hold back from bringing this trouble on us. You always do what is
right. But we haven't obeyed you.
15"Lord our God, you used your mighty
hand to bring your people out of Egypt. You
made a name for yourself. It is still great to
this very day. But we have sinned. We've
done what is wrong. 16Lord, you saved your
people before. So turn your burning anger
away from Jerusalem again. After all, it is
your city. It's your holy mountain. All those
who live around us laugh at Jerusalem and
your people. That's because we have sinned.
Our people before us did evil things too.
17"Our God, hear my prayers. Pay attention to the appeals I make to you. Look with
favor on your temple that has been
destroyed. Do it for your own honor. 18Our
God, please listen to us. The city that belongs
to you has been destroyed. Open your eyes
and see it. We aren't asking you to answer
our prayers because we are godly. Instead,
we're asking you to do it because you love
us so much.
19"Lord, please listen! Lord, please forgive
us! Lord, hear our prayers! Take action for
your own honor. Our God, please don't wait.
Your city and your people belong to you."

Gabriel Tells Daniel About Seventy "Weeks"

20I was speaking and praying. I was admitting
that I and my people Israel had sinned. I was making my appeal to the LORD my God concerning his
holy mountain of Zion.
21While I was still praying, Gabriel came to me.
I had seen him in my earlier vision. He flew over
to me very quickly. It was about the time when the
evening sacrifice is offered. 22He helped me understand. He said, "Daniel, I have come now to give
you a good knowledge and understanding of these
things. 23You are highly respected. So as soon as
you began to pray, the LORD gave you an answer.
I have come to tell you what it is. Here is how you
must understand the vision.
24"The LORD has appointed 70 'weeks' for your
people and your holy city. During that time, acts
against God's law will be stopped. Sin will come
to an end. And the evil things people do will be
paid for. Then everyone will always do what is
right. Everything that has been made known in
visions and prophecies will come true. And the
Most Holy Room in the temple will be anointed.
25"Here is what I want you to know and understand. There will be seven 'weeks.' Then there will
be 62 'weeks.' The seven 'weeks' will begin when
an order is given to rebuild Jerusalem and make it
like new again.
"At the end of the 62 'weeks,' the Anointed
King will come. Jerusalem will have streets and a
water system when it is rebuilt. But that will be
done in times of trouble. 26After the 62 'weeks,'
the Anointed King will be cut off. His followers
will desert him. And everything he has will be
taken away from him. The army of the ruler who
will come will destroy the city and the temple. The
end will come like a flood. War will continue until
the end. The LORD has ordered that many places
be destroyed.
27"A covenant will be put into effect with many
people for one 'week.' In the middle of the 'week'
sacrifices and offerings will come to an end. In one
part of the temple a hated thing that destroys will
be set up. It will remain until the LORD brings the
end he has ordered."

Daniel Has a Vision About What Will Happen to Israel

10 It was the third year that Cyrus, the king of
Persia, ruled over Babylonia. At that time I
was living in Babylon. There the people called me
Belteshazzar. A message came to me from God. It

was true. It was about a great war. I had a vision
that showed me what it meant.
2At that time I was very sad for three weeks. 3I
didn't eat any rich food. No meat or wine touched
my lips. I didn't use any lotions at all until the
three weeks were over.
4I was standing on the bank of the great Tigris
River. It was the 24th day of the first month. 5I
looked up and saw a man who was dressed in linen
clothes. A belt that was made out of the finest gold
was around his waist. 6His body gleamed like
chrysolite. His face shone like lightning. His eyes
were like flaming torches. His arms and legs were
as bright as polished bronze. And his voice was
like the sound of a large crowd.
7I was the only one who saw the vision. The
men who were there with me didn't see it. But they
were so terrified that they ran and hid. 8So I was
left alone as I was watching that great vision. I felt
very weak. My face turned as pale as death. And I
was helpless.
9Then I heard the man speak. As I listened to
him, I fell sound asleep. My face was toward the
ground.
10A hand touched me. It pulled me up on my
hands and knees. I began to tremble with fear.
11The man said, "Daniel, you are highly respected.
Think carefully about what I am going to say to
you. And stand up. God has sent me to you." When
he said that, I trembled as I stood up.
12He continued, "Do not be afraid, Daniel. You
decided to get more understanding. You went
without food as you worshiped your God. Since
the first day you did those things, your words were
heard. I have come to give you an answer. 13But
the prince of Persia opposed me for 21 days. Then
Michael came to help me. He is one of the leaders
of the angels. He helped me win the battle over the
king of Persia.
14"Now I have come to explain the vision to
you. I will tell you what will happen to your people. The vision shows what will take place in days
to come."
15While he was telling me those things, I bowed
with my face toward the ground. I wasn't able to
speak. 16Then someone who looked like a man
touched my lips. I opened my mouth. I began to
speak to the one who was standing in front of me.
I said, "My master, I'm greatly troubled because
of the vision I've seen. And I'm helpless. 17How
can I talk with you? I feel very weak. In fact, I can
hardly breathe."
18The one who looked like a man touched me
again. He gave me strength. 19"Do not be afraid,"
he said. "You are highly respected. May peace be
with you! Be strong now. Be strong."
When he spoke to me, I became stronger. I said,
"Speak, my master. You have given me strength."
20So he said, "Do you know why I have come
to you? Soon I will return to fight against the
prince of Persia. When I go, the prince of Greece
will come. 21But first I will tell you what is written
in the Book of Truth. No one gives me any help
against those princes except Michael. He is your
11 leader. 1I stepped forward to help him and
keep him safe. It was the first year that Darius, the Mede, was king.

The Kings of Egypt and Syria

2"Now then, what I'm about to tell you is true.
Three more kings will appear in Persia. Then a
fourth one will rule. He will be much richer than
all of the others. He will use his wealth to gain
power. And he will stir up everyone against the
kingdom of Greece.
3"After him, a mighty king will appear. He will
rule with great power. He will do as he pleases.
4Not long after his rule ends, his kingdom will be
broken up. It will be divided up into four parts. His
children will not receive it when he dies. And it will
not be as strong as his kingdom. It will be pulled
up by the roots. And it will be given to others.
5"The king of Egypt will become strong. But
one of his commanders will become even stronger.
He will rule over his own kingdom with great
power. 6After many years, the two kingdoms will
join forces. The daughter of the next king of Egypt
will go to the king of Syria. She will join forces
with him. But she will not hold on to her power.
And he and his power will not last either. In those
days she and her attendants will be put to death.
Her father will die. So will the one who helped her.
7"Someone from her family line will take her
place. He will attack the army of the next king of
Syria. Then he will enter his fort. He will fight
against that army and win. 8He will take the metal
statues of their gods. He will also take away their
priceless articles of silver and gold. He will carry
everything off to Egypt. For many years he will
leave the king of Syria alone.
9"That king will march into territory that was
controlled by Egypt. Then he will return to his
own country. 10His sons will prepare for war. They
will gather a huge army. It will sweep along like a
mighty flood. It will fight its way as far as one of
the Egyptian forts.
11"Another king of Egypt will march out with
mighty force. He will fight against the next king
of Syria. That king will gather a huge army. But it
will lose the battle. 12His soldiers will be carried
off. Then the king of Egypt will be filled with
pride. He will kill many thousands of soldiers. But
his success will not last.
13"The king of Syria will bring another army
together. It will be larger than the first one. After
several years, he will march out with a huge army.
It will have everything it needs for battle.
14"In those times many people will rise up
against the next king of Egypt. Lawless men in
your own nation will refuse to obey him. That is
what you saw in your vision. But they will not
succeed.

[15]"Then the king of Syria will go to a certain city that has high walls around it. He will build ramps against them. And he will capture that city. The forces of Egypt will not have the power to stop him. Even their best troops will not be strong enough to stand up against him. [16]He will do anything he wants to. No one will be able to stand up against him. He will take over the beautiful land of Israel. And he will have the power to destroy it.

[17]"He will decide to come with the might of his entire kingdom. He will join forces with the king of Egypt. And he will give him his daughter to become his wife. He will do it in order to take control of Egypt. But his plans will not succeed. They will not help him.

[18]"Then he will turn his attention to the lands along the Mediterranean coast. He will take over many of them. But a commander will put an end to his proud actions. He will turn his pride back on him.

[19]"After that, the king of Syria will return to the forts in his own country. But he will trip and fall. And he will never be seen again.

[20]"The next king after him will send someone out to collect taxes. The taxes will help maintain the glory of his kingdom. But in a few years the king will be destroyed. It will not happen because someone becomes angry with him or kills him in battle.

[21]"Another king will take his place. Many people will hate him. He will not be honored as a king should be. He will lead an army into the kingdom when its people feel secure. He will make clever plans to capture it. [22]Then he will sweep away a huge army. The army and a prince of the covenant will be destroyed.

[23]"The king of Syria will make an agreement with that prince. But then he will not keep his word. He will rise to power with the help of only a few people. [24]When the people in the richest areas feel secure, he will attack them. He will do what the kings before him could not do. And he will reward his followers with the goods and wealth he takes. He will make clever plans to take over the forts. But that will last for only a short time.

[25]"He will stir up his strength and courage. With a large army he will go to war against the next king of Egypt. That king will fight against him with a huge and very powerful army. But he will not be able to stand up against him. So the plans of the king of Syria will succeed. [26]The trusted advisers of the king of Egypt will try to destroy him. His army will be swept away. Many of his soldiers will be wounded or killed.

[27]"The kings of Syria and Egypt will sit at the same table. But in their hearts they will plan to do what is evil. And they will tell lies to each other. But it will not do them any good. God will put an end to their plans at his appointed time.

[28]"The king of Syria will return to his own country. He will go back there with great wealth. But he will make evil plans against the holy temple in Jerusalem. He will do a lot of harm to the temple and the people who worship there. Then he will return to his own country.

[29]"At God's appointed time, the king of Syria will march south again. But this time things will turn out differently. [30]Roman ships will oppose him. He will lose hope. Then he will turn back. He will take out his anger against the holy temple. And he will show favor to the Jews who desert it.

[31]"His army will come and make the temple area 'unclean.' They will put a stop to the daily sacrifices. Then they will set up a hated thing that destroys. [32]He will pretend to praise those who have broken the covenant. He will lead them to do what is evil. But the people who know their God will firmly oppose him.

[33]"Those who are wise will teach many others. But for a while, some of the wise will be killed with swords. Others will be burned to death. Still others will be made prisoners. Or they will be robbed of everything they have. [34]When that happens, they will receive a little help. Many who are not honest will join them.

[35]"So some of the wise people will suffer. They will be made pure in the fire. They will be made spotless until the time of the end. It will still come at God's appointed time.

A King Will Honor Himself

[36]"A certain king will do as he pleases. He will honor himself. He will put himself above every god. He will say things that have never been heard before against the greatest God of all. He will have success until God is not angry anymore. What God has decided to do must take place.

[37]"The king will not show any respect for the gods his people have always worshiped. He will not respect the one women long for. He will not have respect for any god. Instead, he will put himself above all of them. [38]In place of them, he will worship a god of war. He will honor a god his people have not had anything to do with before. He will give gold and silver to that god. He will bring jewels and expensive gifts to it.

[39]"He will attack the strongest forts. A new god will help him do it. He will greatly honor those who recognize him as their leader. He will make them rulers over many people. And he will give them land as a reward.

[40]"A king in the south will go to war against him. It will happen at the time of the end. The king who will honor himself will rush out against him. He will come with chariots and horsemen. He will attack with a lot of ships. He will lead his army into many countries. He will sweep through them like a flood.

[41]"He will also march into the beautiful land of Israel. Many countries will fall. But Edom, Moab and the leaders of Ammon will be saved from his mighty hand. [42]His power will reach out into many countries. Even Egypt will not escape. [43]He will

gain control of all of Egypt’s riches. He will take
their gold and silver treasures. The people of Libya and Cush will be under his control.
44 “But reports from the east and the north will
terrify him. He will burn with anger and march out
to destroy many people and wipe them out. 45 He
will set up his royal tents. He will put them
between the Mediterranean Sea and the beautiful
holy mountain of Zion. But his end will come. And
no one will help him.

The Time of the End

12 “At that time Michael will appear. He is the
great leader of the angels who guards your
people. There will be a time of terrible suffering.
Things will be worse than at any time since nations
began. But at that time of suffering your people
will be saved. Their names are written in the Book
of Life.
2 “Huge numbers of people who lie dead in their
graves will wake up. Some will rise up to life that
will never end. Others will rise up to shame that
will never end. 3 Those who are wise will shine like
the brightness of the sky. Those who lead many
others to do what is right will be like the stars for
ever and ever.
4 “But I want you to roll up the scroll, Daniel.
Seal it until the time of the end. Many people will
go here and there to increase their knowledge.”

5 Then I looked up and saw two other angels.
One was on this side of the Tigris River. And one
was on the other side. 6 The man who was dressed
in linen was above the waters of the river. One of
the angels said to him, “How long will it be before
these amazing things come true?”
7 The man raised both hands toward heaven. I
heard him take an oath in the name of the One who
lives forever. He answered me, “Three and a half
years. Then the power of the holy people will be
broken at last. And all of those things will come
true.”
8 I heard what he said. But I didn’t understand
it. So I asked, “My master, what will come of all
of this?”
9 He answered, “Go on your way, Daniel. The
scroll is rolled up. It is sealed until the time of the
end. 10 Many people will be made pure in the fire.
They will be made spotless. But sinful people will
continue to be evil. Not one sinful person will
understand. But those who are wise will.
11 “The daily sacrifices will be stopped. And the
hated thing that destroys will be set up. After that,
there will be 1,290 days. 12 Blessed are those who
wait for the 1,335 days and reach the end of them.
13 “Daniel, go on your way until the end. Your
body will rest in the grave. Then at the end of the
days you will rise from the dead. And you will
receive what God has appointed for you.”

Hosea

1 A message came to Hosea from the LORD. He was the son of Beeri. The message came while Uzziah, Jotham, Ahaz and Hezekiah were kings of Judah. It also came while Jeroboam was king of Israel. He was the son of Jehoash. Here is what Hosea said.

Hosea's Wife and Children

2 The LORD began to speak through me. He said to me, "Go. Get married to a woman who will commit adultery. Take as your own the children who will be born as a result of her adultery. Marry her because the people of the land are guilty of the worst kind of adultery. They have not been faithful to me."
3 So I married Gomer. She was the daughter of Diblaim. Gomer became pregnant. And she had a son by me.

4 Then the LORD said to me, "Name him Jezreel. That is because I will soon punish Jehu's royal family. He killed many people at the city of Jezreel. So I will put an end to the kingdom of Israel.
5 At that time I will break their military power. It will happen in the Valley of Jezreel."

6 Gomer became pregnant again. She had a daughter. Then the LORD said to me, "Name her Lo-Ruhamah. That is because I will no longer show love to the people of Israel. I will not forgive them anymore.
7 But I will show love to the people of Judah. And I will save them. I will not use bows or swords or other weapons of war to do it. I will not save them by using horses and horsemen either. Instead, I will use my own power to save them. I am the LORD their God."

8 Later, Gomer stopped nursing Lo-Ruhamah. After that, she had another son.
9 Then the LORD said, "Name him Lo-Ammi. That is because Israel is no longer my people. And I am no longer their God.

10 "But the time will come when the people of Israel will be like the sand on the seashore. It can't be measured or counted. Now it is said about them, 'You are not my people.' But at that time they will be called 'children of the living God.'
11 The people of Judah and Israel will be brought together again. They will appoint one leader. They will increase their numbers in the land. And Jezreel's day will be great. That is because I will plant Israel in the land again.

2 "People of Israel, call your brothers My People. And call your sisters My Loved Ones."

Israel Is Punished and Brought Back to the LORD

2 I said to my children,

"Talk things over with your mother.
Talk to her.
She isn't acting like a wife to me anymore.
She no longer treats me as her husband.
Tell her to stop looking and acting like a prostitute.
Tell her not to let her lovers
lie on her breasts anymore.
3 If she doesn't stop it, I will strip her naked.
I'll make her as bare as she was on the day she was born.
I'll make her like a desert.
She will become like dry land.
And I'll let her die of thirst."

4 I won't show my love to Gomer's children.
They are the children of other men.
5 Their mother hasn't been faithful to me.
She who became pregnant with them
has brought shame on herself.
She said, "I will chase after my lovers.
They give me my food and water.
They provide me with wool and linen.
They give me olive oil and wine."
6 So I will block her path with bushes that have thorns.
I'll build a wall around her.
Then she can't go to her lovers.
7 She will still chase after her lovers.
But she won't catch them.
She'll look for them.
But she won't find them.
Then she'll say,
"I'll go back to my husband.
That's where I was at first.
I was better off then than I am now."
8 She wouldn't admit that I was the one
who gave her everything she had.
I provided her with grain, olive oil and fresh wine.
I gave her plenty of silver and gold.
But she used it to make statues of Baal.

9 So I will take away my grain when it gets ripe.
I'll take my fresh wine when it's ready.
I'll take back my wool and my linen.
I gave them to her to cover her naked body.
10 So now I'll uncover her body.
All of her lovers will see it.
No one can stop me from punishing her.
11 I will put a stop to the special times she celebrates.
I'll bring an end to the feasts she celebrates each year.
I'll stop her New Moon Feasts and her Sabbath days.
I'll bring all of her appointed feasts to an end.

[12] I will destroy her vines and her fig trees.
She said they were her pay from her lovers.
I'll make them like clumps of bushes
and weeds.
Wild animals will eat them up.

[13] The LORD announces,

"Israel burned incense to the gods
that were named after Baal.
I will punish her
for all of the times she did that.
She decorated herself with rings and jewelry.
Then she went after her lovers.
But she forgot all about me.

[14] "So now I am going to draw her back to me.
I will lead her into the desert.
There I will speak tenderly to her.
[15] I will give her back her vineyards.
I will make the Valley of Achor a door of
hope for her.
Then she will love me, as she did when she
was young.
She will love me just as she did
when she came up out of Egypt.

[16] "A new day is coming," announces the LORD.
"Israel will call me My Husband.
She will no longer call me My Master.
[17] She will no longer speak about the gods
that are named after Baal.
She will not pray to them for help anymore.
[18] At that time I will make a covenant
for the good of my people.
I will make it with the wild animals
and the birds of the air.
It will also be made with the creatures
that move on the ground.
I will remove bows and swords
and other weapons of war from the land.
Then my people can lie down in safety.
[19] I will make Israel my own.
She will belong to me forever.
I will do to her what is right and fair.
I will love her tenderly.
[20] I will be faithful to her.
And she will recognize me as the LORD.

[21] "So at that time I will answer her,"
announces the LORD.
"I will command the skies
to send rain on the earth.
[22] Then the earth will produce grain, olive oil
and fresh wine.
And Israel will be called Jezreel.
That is because I will answer her prayers.
[23] I will plant her in the land for myself.
I will show my love to the one I called Not
My Loved One.
I will say, 'You are my people'
to those who were called Not My People.
And they will say, 'You are my God.'"

Hosea Brings His Wife Back to Himself

3 The LORD said to me, "Go. Show your love to
your wife again. She is loved by another man.
And she has committed adultery. But I want you
to love her just as I love the people of Israel. They
turn to other gods. And they love to offer raisin
cakes to Baal and eat them. In spite of that, I love
my people."
[2] So I bought Gomer for six ounces of silver and
about ten bushels of barley. [3] Then I told her, "You
must wait for me for a long time. You must not be
a prostitute. You must not have sex with any man.
And I will wait for you."
[4] So the people of Israel will live for a long time
without a king or prince. They won't have sacrifices or sacred stones. They won't have sacred
linen aprons or statues of family gods. [5] After that,
the people of Israel will return to the LORD their
God. They will look to him and to a king from the
family line of David. In the last days, they will
tremble with fear as they come to the LORD. And
they will receive his full blessing.

The LORD Brings Charges Against Israel

4 People of Israel, listen to the LORD's
message.
He is bringing charges
against you who live in Israel.
He says, "There is no faithfulness
or love in the land.
No one recognizes me as God.
[2] People call down curses on others.
They tell lies and commit murder.
They steal and commit adultery.
They break all of my laws.
They keep on spilling the blood of others.
[3] That is why the land is drying up.
All those who live in it
are getting weaker and weaker.
The wild animals and the birds of the air are
dying.
So are the fish in the ocean.

[4] "But you priests should not blame the people.
You should not find fault with one another.
After all, your people
could also bring charges against you.
[5] You trip and fall day and night.
And the prophets fall down along with you.
So I will destroy your nation.
She is the one who gave birth to you.
[6] My people are destroyed
because they do not know me.

"You priests have refused to obey me.
So I will refuse to accept you as my priests.
You have not paid any attention to my law.
So I will not let your children be my priests.
[7] The more priests there are,
the more they sin against me.
They have traded their glorious God for that
shameful god Baal.

[8] They live off the sins of my people.
And they want them to keep on sinning.
[9] So here is what I will do.
I will punish people and priests alike.
I will judge them because of their sinful lives.
I will pay them back
for the evil things they have done.

[10] "My people will eat.
But they will not have enough.
They will have sex with prostitutes.
But they will not have any children.
That is because they have deserted me.
[11] They have sex with prostitutes.
They drink old wine and fresh wine.
When they do those things,
it destroys their ability to understand.
[12] They ask a wooden statue of a god for advice.
They expect to get answers from a stick
of wood.
They act like prostitutes.
That leads them down the wrong path.
I am their God.
But they are not faithful to me.
[13] They offer sacrifices on the mountaintops.
They burn offerings on the hills.
They worship under oak, poplar and
terebinth trees.
The trees provide plenty of shade.
So your daughters become prostitutes.
And your daughters-in-law commit adultery.

[14] "I will not punish your daughters
when they become prostitutes.
I will not judge your daughters-in-law
when they commit adultery.
After all, the men themselves have sex with
sinful women.
They offer sacrifices where temple
prostitutes earn their living.
People who can't understand will be
destroyed!

[15] "Israel, you are not faithful to me.
But I do not want Judah to become
guilty too.

"My people, do not go to Gilgal to offer
sacrifices.
Do not go up to Bethel to worship
other gods.
Do not take an oath and say,
'You can be sure that the LORD is alive.'
[16] The people of Israel are stubborn.
They are as stubborn as a young cow.
So how can I take care of them
like lambs in a meadow?
[17] The people of Ephraim have joined themselves
to other gods.
And nothing can be done to help them.
[18] They continue to be unfaithful to me
even when their drinks are gone.
And their rulers love to do shameful things.
[19] A windstorm will blow all of them away.
And their sacrifices will bring shame on
them.

The LORD Judges Israel

5 "Listen to me, you priests!
Pay attention, people of Israel!
Listen, you members of the royal family!
Here is my decision against you.
You have been like a trap at Mizpah.
You have been like a net spread out on
Mount Tabor.
[2] You refuse to obey me.
You offer sacrifices to other gods.
So I will punish all of you.
[3] People of Ephraim, I know all about you.
What you are doing is not hidden
from me.
Now you have joined yourselves to
other gods.
You have made yourselves 'unclean.'
[4] "You can't return to me
because you have done so many evil things.
In your hearts you long to act like prostitutes.
You do not recognize me as the LORD.
[5] Israel, your pride witnesses that you are guilty.
People of Ephraim, you trip and fall because
you have sinned.
Judah, you fall down along with them.
[6] Israel, you will come to worship me.
You will bring your animals to offer as
sacrifices.
But you will not find me.
I have turned away from you.
[7] You are not faithful to me.
Your children do not belong to me.
The way you act at your New Moon Feasts
will destroy you and your fields.
[8] "My people, blow trumpets in Gibeah!
Blow horns in Ramah!
Shout the battle cry in Bethel!
Say to Benjamin, 'The Assyrian army
is coming!'
[9] People of Ephraim, you will be completely
destroyed
when it is time for me to punish you.
You can be sure it will happen.
I am announcing it among your tribes.
[10] Judah, your leaders have stolen some land.
They have moved their borders farther
north.
So I will pour out my anger on you
like a flood of water.
[11] Ephraim, you will soon be crushed.
The Assyrians will stomp all over you.
It will happen because you have made up
your minds
to chase after other gods.
[12] Ephraim, I will be like a moth to you.
Judah, I will cause you to rot away.

13 "Ephraim, you saw how sick you were.
Judah, you saw that you were wounded.
Ephraim, you turned to Assyria for help.
You sent gifts to the great King
Tiglath-Pileser.
But he is not able to make you well.
He can't heal your wounds.
14 Ephraim, I will be like a lion to you.
Judah, I will attack you like a
powerful lion.
I will tear you to pieces.
I will drag you off.
Then I will leave you.
No one will be able to save you.
15 I will go back to my home in heaven.
I will stay there until you admit you
have sinned.
Then you will turn to me.
You will suffer so much
that you will really want me to help you."

Israel Refuses to Turn Away From Their Sins

6 The people say, "Come.
Let us return to the LORD.
He has torn us to pieces.
But he will heal us.
He has wounded us.
But he'll bandage our wounds.
2 After two days he will give us new life.
On the third day he'll make us like
new again.
Then we will enjoy his blessing.
3 Let's recognize him as the LORD.
Let's keep trying to really know him.
You can be sure the sun will rise.
And you can be just as sure the LORD
will appear.
He will come to renew us like the
winter rains.
He will be like the spring rains that
water the earth."

4 The LORD says, "Ephraim, what can I do
with you?
And what can I do with you, Judah?
Your love for me vanishes like the
morning mist.
It soon disappears like the early dew.
5 So I used the words of my prophets to cut
you in pieces.
I used my words to put you to death.
When I judged you, I struck you like
lightning.
6 I want mercy and not sacrifice.
I want you to recognize me as God
instead of bringing me burnt offerings.
7 Just as Adam disobeyed me,
you have broken the covenant I made
with you.
You were not faithful to me in the land
I gave you.
8 Ramoth Gilead is a city where sinful
people live.
It is stained with footprints of blood.
9 On the road to Shechem, groups of priests act
like robbers.
They hide and wait to attack people.
They murder them
and commit other shameful crimes.
10 People of Israel, I have seen
a horrible thing in your land.
People of Ephraim, you have joined yourselves
to other gods.
You have made yourselves 'unclean.'

11 "People of Judah, I have appointed a time
for you to be destroyed.

"My people, I would like to bless you
with great success again."

7 The LORD says,

"I would like to heal Israel.
But when I try to, Ephraim's sins
are brought out into the open.
The crimes of Samaria
are made known to everyone.
The people tell lies.
They break into houses and steal.
They rob others in the streets.
2 But they do not realize
that I remember all of the evil things
they do.
Their sins pile up and cover them.
I am always aware of those sins.

3 "Their evil conduct even makes the king glad.
Their lies make the princes happy.
4 But all of the people are unfaithful to the king.
Their anger against him burns
like the coals in an oven.
The baker does not even need to stir up
the fire
until the dough is ready."

5 On special days to honor our king,
the princes get drunk with wine.
And the king enjoys the party.
He joins hands with those
who pretend to be faithful to him.
6 Their hearts are as hot as an oven.
They make evil plans to get rid of him.
Their anger burns like a slow fire all night.
In the morning it blazes out like a
flaming fire.
7 All of them are as hot as an oven.
They destroy their rulers.
All of their kings fall from power.
But none of them calls on the LORD
for help.

8 The people of Ephraim mix with the nations.
They are like a flat cake
that is baked on only one side.

[9]People from other lands make them weaker
and weaker.
But they don't realize it.
Their hair is becoming gray.
But they don't even notice it.
[10]The pride of Israel witnesses that they
are guilty.
But in spite of everything,
they don't return to the LORD their God.
They don't go to him for help.

[11]The LORD says,

"The people of Ephraim are like a dove.
They are easily tricked.
They do not have any sense at all.
First they call out to Egypt for help.
Then they turn to Assyria.
[12]When they send for help,
I will throw my net over them.
I will capture them like birds of the air.
I will punish them,
just as I warned them I would.
[13]How terrible it will be for them!
They have wandered away from me.
So they will be destroyed.
They have refused to obey me.
I long to save them.
But they tell lies about me.
[14]They do not cry out to me from their hearts.
Instead, they just lie on their beds and sob.
They cut themselves when they pray
to Baal
for grain and fresh wine.
So they turn away from me.
[15]I brought them up and made them strong.
But they make evil plans against me.
[16]I am the Most High God. But they do not
turn to me.
They are like a bow that does not
shoot straight.
Their leaders will be killed with swords.
They will die because they have spoken
too proudly.
The people of Egypt
will make fun of them."

Israel Will Harvest a Windstorm

8 The LORD said to me,

"Put a trumpet to your lips!
Give a warning to my people!
Assyria is like an eagle.
It is ready to attack my land.
My people have broken the covenant I made
with them.
They have refused to obey my law.
[2]Israel shouts to me,
'We recognize you as our God!'
[3]But they have turned away from what
is good.
So an enemy will chase them.
[4]My people appoint kings I do not want.
They choose princes without my
permission.
They use their silver and gold
to make statues of gods.
That is how they destroy themselves."
[5]The LORD says, "People of Samaria,
throw out your god that looks like a calf!
My anger burns against you.
How long will it be until you are able
to remain faithful to me?
[6]Your calf is not God.
A skilled worker from Israel made it.
But it will be broken to pieces."

[7]The LORD says,

"Worshiping other gods is like worshiping
the wind.
It is like planting worthless seeds.
Assyria is like a windstorm.
That is all my people will harvest.
There are no heads of grain
on the stems that will come up.
So they will not produce any flour.
Even if they did produce grain,
the Assyrians would eat all of it up.
[8]So the people of Israel are swallowed up.
Now they are like a worthless pot to me
among the nations.
[9]They have gone up to Assyria for help.
They are like a wild donkey
that wanders around by itself.
Ephraim's people have sold themselves
to their Assyrian lovers.
[10]They have sold themselves to the nations
to get their help.
But now I will gather them together.
They will get weaker and weaker.
The mighty kings of Assyria will crush
them.

[11]"Ephraim built many altars where they
sacrificed
sin offerings to other gods.
So their altars have become
places where they commit sin.
[12]I wrote down many things in my law for
their good.
But they considered my laws as something
strange.
[13]They offer sacrifices to me.
They eat the meat of the animals they bring.
But I am not pleased with any of that.
I will remember the evil things they have done.
I will punish them for their sins.
And they will return to Egypt.
[14]Israel has forgotten the One who made them.
They have built palaces for themselves.
Judah has built forts in many towns.
But I will send fire down on their cities.
It will burn up their forts."

Israel Will Be Punished

9 Israel, don't be joyful.
Don't be glad as the other nations are.
You haven't been faithful to your God.
You love to get paid for being a prostitute.
Your pay is the grain at every threshing floor.
2 But soon there won't be any grain or wine to feed you.
There won't even be any fresh wine.
3 You won't remain in the LORD's land.
Ephraim, you will return to Egypt.
You will eat "unclean" food in Assyria.
4 You won't pour out wine offerings to the LORD.
Your sacrifices won't please him.
They'll be like the bread people eat when someone dies.
Everyone who eats those sacrifices will be "unclean."
They themselves will have to eat that kind of food.
They can't bring it into the LORD's temple.

5 What will you do when your appointed feasts come?
What will you do on the LORD's special days?
6 Some of you will escape without being destroyed.
But you will die in Egypt.
Your bodies will be buried at Memphis.
Weeds will cover your treasures of silver.
Thorns will grow up in your tents.
7 The time when God will punish you is coming.
The day when he will judge you is near.
I want you to know that.
You have committed many sins.
And you hate me very much.
That's why you think I'm foolish.
You think I'm crazy.
But the LORD speaks through me.
8 People of Ephraim, I'm a true prophet.
My God is warning you through me.
But you set traps for me everywhere I go.
You hate me so much
you even wait for me in God's house.
9 You have sunk very deep into sin,
just as our people did at Gibeah long ago.
God will remember the evil things you have done.
He will punish you for your sins.

10 The LORD says,

"When I first found Israel,
it was like finding grapes in the desert.
When I saw your people long ago,
it was like seeing the early fruit on a fig tree.
But then they went to Baal Peor.
There they gave themselves to that shameful god Baal.
They became as evil as the god they loved.
11 Ephraim's greatness and glory will be gone.
It will fly away like a bird.
Women will no longer have children.
They will not be able to get pregnant.
12 But suppose they do have children.
Then I will kill every one of them.
How terrible it will be for them
when I turn away from them!"

13 Tyre is planted in a pleasant place.
And so is Ephraim.
But the Assyrians will kill
Ephraim's children.
14 LORD, what should you do to Ephraim's people?
Give them women whose babies die before they are born.
Give them women whose breasts don't have any milk.

15 The LORD says,

"My people did many evil things in Gilgal.
That is why I hated them there.
They committed many sins.
So I will drive them out of my land.
I will not love them anymore.
All of their leaders refuse to obey me.
16 Ephraim is like a worthless plant.
Its roots are dried up.
It does not produce any fruit.
Suppose Ephraim's people have children.
Then I will kill the children they love so much."

17 My God will turn his back on his people.
They have not obeyed him.
So they will wander among other nations.

10 Israel was like a spreading vine.
They produced fruit for themselves.
As they grew more fruit,
they built more altars.
As their land became richer,
they made the sacred stones they worshiped more beautiful.
2 Their hearts are dishonest.
So now they must pay for their sins.
The LORD will tear their altars down.
He'll destroy their sacred stones.

3 Then they'll say, "We don't have a king.
That's because we didn't have
any respect for the LORD.
But suppose we did have a king.
What could he do for us?"
4 They make a lot of promises.
They make agreements among themselves.
They take oaths they don't mean to keep.
So court cases spring up
like poisonous weeds in a plowed field.

5 The people who live in Samaria are filled
with fear.
They are afraid their god that looks like
a calf
will be carried off from Bethel.
They will sob over it.
So will the priests who lead them to
worship it.
The priests were full of joy
because their statue was so glorious.
But it will be captured
and taken far away from them.
6 It will be carried off to Assyria.
The people of Ephraim will be forced
to give it to the great king.
They will be dishonored.
Israel will be ashamed
that all they have left to worship is a
wooden god.
7 Samaria's king will be carried off.
He will be like a twig floating away in
a river.
8 The high places where Israel worshiped
other gods
will be destroyed.
That's where they sinned against the LORD.
Thorns and weeds will grow up there.
They will cover the altars.
Then the people will say to the mountains,
"Cover us!"
They'll say to the hills, "Fall on us!"

9 The LORD says,

"Israel, you have done evil things
ever since your people sinned at Gibeah
long ago.
And you are still doing what is evil.
War caught up
with those who sinned at Gibeah.
10 So I will punish you when I want to.
Nations will gather together to fight
against you.
They will put you in chains
because you have committed so
many sins.
11 Ephraim, you were like a well-trained
young cow.
It loved to thresh grain.
I spared its pretty neck
from pulling heavy loads.
But now I will make you do hard work.
Judah also must plow.
So all of the people of Jacob
must break up the ground.
12 Your hearts are as hard as a field
that has not been plowed.
If you change your ways,
you will produce good crops.
So plant the seeds of doing what is right.
Then you will harvest the fruit of your
faithful love.
It is time to turn to me.
When you do, I will come
and shower my blessings on you.
13 But you have planted the seeds of doing
what is wrong.
So you have harvested the fruit of your
evil conduct.
You have had to eat the fruit of your lies.
You have trusted in your own strength.
You have depended on your many
soldiers.
14 But the roar of battle will come against you.
All of your forts will be completely
destroyed.
It will happen just as Shalman
destroyed Beth Arbel in a battle.
Mothers and their children
were smashed on the ground.
15 People of Bethel, that will happen to you.
You have committed far too many sins.
When the time for me to punish you comes,
your king will be completely destroyed."

The LORD Loves Israel

11 The LORD continues,

"When Israel was a young nation, I loved
them.
I chose to bring my son out of Egypt.
2 But the more I called out to Israel,
the further they went away from me.
They brought sacrifices to the statues of
the gods
that were named after Baal.
And they burned incense to them.
3 I taught Israel to walk.
I took them up in my arms.
But they did not realize
I was the one who took care of them.
4 I led them with kindness and love.
I did not lead them with ropes.
I lifted the heavy loads from their shoulders.
I bent down and fed them.
5 "But they refuse to turn away from their sins.
So they will return to Egypt.
And Assyria will rule over them.
6 Swords will flash in their cities.
The heavy metal bars on their gates will
be destroyed.
Their plans will come to an end.
7 My people have made up their minds
to turn away from me.
Even if they call out to me,
I will certainly not honor them.
I am the Most High God."

8 The LORD continues,

"People of Ephraim, how can I give you up?
Israel, how can I hand you over to your
enemies?

Can I destroy you as I did the town of Admah?
Can I treat you like Zeboiim?
My heart is stirred inside me.
It is filled with pity for you.
9 My anger will not burn against you anymore.
I will not completely destroy you.
After all, I am God.
I am not a mere man.
I am the Holy One among you.
My burning anger will not come against you.
10 I will roar like a lion against my enemies.
You will follow me.
When I roar, my children will come home trembling with fear.
You will return from the west.
11 You will come trembling like birds from Egypt.
You will return like doves from Assyria.
I will settle you again in your homes,"
announces the LORD.

Israel Has Sinned

12 The people of Ephraim tell nothing but lies.
Israel has not been honest with me.
And Judah continues to wander away from God.
They have deserted the faithful Holy One.

12 1 The people of Ephraim look to others for help.
It's like chasing the wind.
The wind they keep chasing
is hot and dry.
They tell more and more lies.
They are always hurting others.
They make a peace treaty with Assyria.
They send olive oil to Egypt to get help.
2 The LORD is bringing charges against Judah.
He will punish Jacob's people
because of how they act.
He'll pay them back
for the evil things they've done.
3 Even before Jacob was born,
he was holding on to his brother's heel.
When he became a man,
he struggled with God.
4 At Peniel he struggled with the angel and won.
He sobbed and begged for his blessing.
God also met with him at Bethel.
He talked with him there.
5 He is the LORD God who rules over all.
He wants us to remember
that his name is The LORD.
6 People of Jacob, you must return to your God.
You must hold on to love and do what is fair.
You must trust in your God always.

7 You are like a trader who uses dishonest scales.
You love to cheat others.
8 People of Ephraim, you brag,
"We are very rich.
We've become wealthy.
And no one can prove we sinned
to gain all of this wealth."

9 The LORD says,

"I am the LORD your God.
I brought you out of Egypt.
But I will make you live in tents again.
That is what you did when you celebrated
the Feast of Booths in the desert.
10 I spoke to the prophets.
They saw many visions.
I gave you warnings through them."
11 The people of Gilead are evil!
They aren't worth anything!
Gilgal's people sacrifice bulls to other gods.
Their altars will become like piles of stones
on a plowed field.
12 Jacob ran away to the country of Aram.
There Israel served Laban to get a wife.
He took care of sheep to pay for her.
13 The prophet Moses brought Israel up from Egypt.
The LORD used him to take care of them.
14 But Ephraim's people have made the LORD very angry.
Their Lord will hold them accountable for the blood they've spilled.
He'll pay them back for the shameful things they've done.

The LORD Is Angry With Israel

13 When the tribe of Ephraim spoke,
the other tribes trembled with fear.
Ephraim was honored in Israel.
But its people sinned by worshiping Baal.
So they were as good as dead.
2 Now they sin more and more.
They use their silver
to make statues of gods for themselves.
The statues come from their own clever ideas.
Skilled workers make all of them.
The people pray to those gods.
They offer human sacrifices to them.
They kiss the gods that look like calves.
3 So those people will vanish like the morning mist.
They will soon disappear like the early dew.
They will be like straw
that the wind blows around on a threshing floor.
They will be like smoke
that escapes through a window.

4 The LORD says,

"People of Israel, I am the LORD your God.
I brought you out of Egypt.
You must not recognize any God but me.
You must not have any Savior except me.

5 I took care of you in the desert.
It was a land of burning heat.
6 I fed you until you were satisfied.
Then you became proud.
You forgot all about me.
7 So I will leap on you like a lion.
I will hide and wait
beside the road like a leopard.
8 I will attack you like a bear
that is robbed of her cubs.
I will rip you wide open.
Like a lion I will eat you up.
Like a wild animal I will tear
you apart.

9 "Israel, you will be destroyed.
I helped you. But you turned against me.
10 Where is your king?
Wasn't he supposed to save you?
Where are the rulers in all of your towns?
You said, 'Give us a king and princes.'
11 So I became angry and gave you a king.
Then I took him away from you.
12 Ephraim, your guilt is piling up.
I am keeping a record of all of your sins.
13 You will suffer pain like a woman having
a baby.
You are like a foolish child.
It is time for you to be born.
But you refuse to come out of your
mother's body.

14 "I will set you free from the power of
the grave.
I will save you from death.
Death, where are your plagues?
Grave, where is your power to destroy?

"Ephraim, I will no longer pity you.
15 Even though you are doing well among the
other tribes,
trouble will come to you.
I will send a hot and dry wind from the east.
It will blow in from the desert.
Your springs will not have any water.
Your wells will dry up.
All of your treasures
will be taken out of your storerooms.
16 People of Samaria, you must pay for
your sins.
You have refused to obey me.
You will be killed with swords.
Your little children will be smashed on
the ground.
Your pregnant women will be ripped
wide open."

The LORD Blesses Those Who Turn Away From Sin

14 Israel, return to the LORD your God.
Your sins have destroyed you!
2 Tell the LORD you are turning away from
your sins.
Return to him.
Say to him,
"Forgive us for all of our sins.
Please be kind to us.
Welcome us back to you.
Then our lips will offer you our praise.
3 Assyria can't save us.
We won't trust in our war horses.
Our own hands have made statues of gods.
But we will never call them our gods again.
We are like children whose fathers have died.
But you show us your tender love."

4 Then the LORD will answer,

"My people always wander away from me.
But I will put an end to that.
My anger has turned away from them.
Now I will love them freely.
5 I will be like the dew to Israel.
They will bloom like a lily.
They will send their roots down deep
like a cedar tree in Lebanon.
6 They will spread out like new branches.
They will be as beautiful as an olive tree.
They will smell as sweet as the cedar trees
in Lebanon.
7 Once again my people will live
in the safety of my shade.
They will grow like grain.
They will bloom like vines.
And they will be as famous
as wine from Lebanon.
8 Ephraim will have nothing more to do with
other gods.
I will answer the prayers of my people.
I will take good care of them.
I will be like a green pine tree to them.
All of the fruit they bear will come
from me."

9 If you are wise, you will realize
that what I've said is true.
If you have understanding,
you will know what it means.
The ways of the LORD are right.
People who are right with God live the way
he wants them to.
But those who refuse to obey him trip
and fall.

Joel

1 A message came to Joel from the LORD. He was the son of Pethuel. Here is what Joel said.

Locusts Attack the Land

2 Elders, listen to me.
Pay attention, all you who live in the land.
Has anything like this ever happened in your whole life?
Did it ever happen to your people
who lived long ago?
3 Tell your children about it.
Let them tell their children.
And let their children tell it
to those who live after them.
4 The giant locusts have eaten
what the common locusts have left.
The young locusts have eaten
what the giant locusts have left.
And other locusts have eaten
what the young locusts have left.

5 Get up and sob, you people who drink too much!
Cry, all you who drink wine!
Cry because the fresh wine
has been taken away from you.
6 The locusts are like an army
that has marched into our land.
There are so many of them
they can't even be counted.
Their teeth are as sharp as a lion's teeth.
They are like the fangs of a female lion.
7 The locusts have completely destroyed our vines.
They have wiped out our fig trees.
They've stripped off the bark and thrown it away.
They've left the branches bare.

8 My people, sob like a virgin
who is dressed in black clothes.
She is sad because she has lost
the young man she was going to marry.
9 No one brings grain offerings and drink offerings
to the LORD's house anymore.
So the priests who serve the LORD
are filled with sorrow.
10 Our fields are wiped out.
The ground is dried up.
The grain is destroyed.
The fresh wine is gone.
And there isn't any more olive oil.
11 Farmers, be sad.
Cry, you who grow vines.
Sob because the wheat and barley are gone.
The crops in the fields are destroyed.
12 The vines and fig trees are dried up.
The pomegranate, palm and apple trees
don't have any fruit on them.
In fact, all of the trees in the fields are dried up.
And my people's joy has faded away.

Turn Away From Sin

13 Priests, put on black clothes and sob.
Cry, you who serve at the altar.
Come, you who serve my God in the temple.
Spend the night dressed in black clothes.
Sob because no one brings grain offerings and drink offerings
to the house of your God anymore.
14 Announce a holy fast.
Tell the people not to eat anything.
Gather them together for a special service.
Send for all of the elders
who live in the land.
Have them come to the house of the LORD your God.
And pray to him.
15 The day of the LORD is near.
How sad it will be on that day!
The Mighty One is coming to destroy you.

16 Our food has been taken away
right in front of our eyes.
There isn't any joy or gladness
in the house of our God.
17 The seeds have dried up in the ground.
The grain is also gone.
The storerooms have been destroyed.
The barns are broken down.
18 Listen to the cattle groan!
The herds wander around.
They don't have any grass to eat.
The flocks of sheep are also suffering.

19 LORD, I call out to you.
Fire has burned up the grasslands.
Flames have destroyed all of the trees in the fields.
20 Even the wild animals cry out to you for help.
The streams of water have dried up.
Fire has burned up the grasslands.

The LORD Sends an Army of Locusts

2 Priests, blow the trumpets in Zion.
Give a warning on my holy mountain.
Let everyone who lives in the land tremble with fear.
The day of the LORD is coming.
It is very near.
2 That day will be dark and sad.
It will be black and cloudy.

A huge army of locusts is coming.
They will spread across the mountains
like the sun when it rises.
There has never been an army like it.
And there will never be another
for all time to come.
3 Like fire they eat up everything in their path.
Behind them it looks as if flames have
burned the land.
In front of them the land is like the Garden
of Eden.
Behind them it is a dry and empty desert.
Nothing escapes them.
4 They look like horses.
Like war horses they charge ahead.
5 They sound like chariots as they leap over the
mountaintops.
They crackle like fire burning up
dry weeds.
They are like a mighty army
that is ready for battle.
6 When people see them, they tremble with fear.
All of their faces turn pale.
7 The locusts charge ahead like warriors.
They climb over walls like soldiers.
All of them march in line.
They don't turn to the right or the left.
8 They don't bump into one another.
Each of them marches straight ahead.
They charge through everything that tries to
stop them.
But they still stay in line.
9 They attack a city.
They run along its wall.
They climb into houses.
They enter through windows like
robbers.
10 As they march forward, the earth shakes.
The sky trembles as they approach.
The sun and moon grow dark.
And the stars stop shining.
11 The LORD thunders with his mighty voice
as he leads his army.
He has so many forces they can't even
be counted.
Those who obey his commands are great
in number.
The day of the LORD is great and terrifying.
Who can live through it?

Let Your Hearts Be Broken

12 The Lord announces to his people,

"Return to me with all your heart.
There is still time.
Do not eat any food.
Sob and cry."

13 Don't just tear your clothes to show how
sad you are.
Let your hearts be broken.
Return to the LORD your God.
He is gracious.
He is tender and kind.
He is slow to get angry.
He is full of love.
He takes pity on you.
He won't destroy you.
14 Who knows? He might turn toward you
and have pity on you.
He might even give you his blessing.
Then you can bring grain offerings and drink
offerings
to the LORD your God.

15 Priests, blow the trumpets in Zion.
Announce a holy fast.
Tell the people not to eat anything.
Gather them together for a special service.
16 Bring them together.
Set all of them apart to me.
Bring together the elders.
Gather the children and the babies
who are still nursing.
Let the groom leave his bedroom.
Let the bride leave their marriage bed.
17 Let the priests who serve the LORD sob.
Let them cry between the temple porch and
the altar.
Let them say, "LORD, spare your people.
Don't let others make fun of them.
Don't let the nations laugh at them.
Don't let them tease your people and say,
'Where is their God?'"

The LORD Answers the Prayer of His People

18 Then the LORD will show concern for his land.
He will take pity on his people.

19 He will reply,

"I will send you grain, olive oil and fresh wine.
It will be enough to satisfy you completely.
I will never allow other nations
to make fun of you again.

20 "I will drive far away from you
the army that comes from the north.
I will send some of its forces
into a dry and empty land.
Those in front will be pushed into the
Dead Sea.
The ones in back will be driven into the
Mediterranean Sea.
Their dead bodies will give off a
bad smell."

The LORD has done great things.
21 Land, don't be afraid.
Be glad and full of joy.
The LORD has done great things.
22 Wild animals, don't be afraid.
The grasslands are turning green again.

The trees are bearing their fruit.
The vines and fig trees are producing rich crops.
23 People of Zion, be glad.
Be joyful because of what the LORD your God has done.
He has given you the right amount of rain in the fall.
He has sent you plenty of showers.
He has sent fall and spring rains alike,
just as he did before.
24 Your threshing floors will be covered with grain.
Olive oil and fresh wine will spill over
from the places where they are stored.

25 The LORD says,

"I sent a great army of locusts to attack you.
They included common locusts, giant locusts,
young locusts and other locusts.
I will make up for the years
they ate your crops.
26 You will have plenty to eat.
It will satisfy you completely.
Then you will praise me.
I am the LORD your God.
I have done wonderful miracles for you.
My people will never be put to shame again.
27 You will know that I am with you in Israel.
I am the LORD your God.
There is no other God.
So my people will never be put to shame again.

The Day of the LORD Is Coming

28 "After that, I will pour out my Spirit on all people.
Your sons and daughters will prophesy.
Your old men will have dreams.
Your young men will have visions.
29 In those days I will pour out my Spirit
on those who serve me, men and women alike.
30 I will show wonders in the heavens and on the earth.
There will be blood and fire and clouds of smoke.
31 The sun will become dark.
The moon will turn red like blood.
It will happen before the great and terrible day of the LORD comes.
32 Everyone who calls out to me will be saved.
On Mount Zion and in Jerusalem
some of my people will be left alive.
I have chosen them.
That is what I have promised.

The LORD Judges the Nations

3 "At that time I will bless Judah and Jerusalem
with great success again.
2 I will gather all of the nations together.
I will bring them down to the Valley of Jehoshaphat.
There I will judge them.
I will punish them for what they have done
to my people Israel.
They scattered them among the nations.
They divided up my land among themselves.
3 They cast lots for my people.
They sold boys into slavery to get prostitutes.
They sold girls to buy some wine to drink.

4 "Tyre and Sidon, why are you doing things like
that to me? And why are you doing them, all of
you people in Philistia? Are you trying to get even
with me for something I have done? If you are, I
will pay you back for it in a quick and speedy way.
5 You took my silver and gold. You carried off my
finest treasures to your temples. 6 You sold the people of Judah and Jerusalem to the Greeks. You
wanted to send them far away from their own
country.

7 "But now I will stir them up into action. I will
bring them back from the places you sold them to.
And I will do to you what you did to them. 8 I will
sell your sons and daughters to the people of Judah. And they will sell them to the Sabeans far
away." The LORD has spoken.

9 Announce this among the nations.
Tell them to prepare for battle.
Nations, get your soldiers ready!
Bring all of your fighting men together
and march out to attack.
10 Hammer your plows into swords.
Hammer your pruning tools into spears.
Let those who are weak say,
"We are soldiers!"
11 Come quickly, all of you surrounding nations.
Gather together in the Valley of Jehoshaphat.

LORD, send your soldiers
down from heaven!

12 The LORD says,

"Stir up the nations into action!
Let them march into the valley
where I will judge them.
I will take my seat in court.
I will judge all of the surrounding nations.
13 My soldiers, swing your sickles.
The nations are ripe for harvest.
Come. Stomp on them as if they were grapes.
Crush them until the winepress of my anger is full.
Do it until the wine spills over
from the places where it is stored.
The nations have committed far too many sins!"

[14] Huge numbers of soldiers are gathered in
the valley
where the LORD will hand down his
sentence.
The day of the LORD is near in that valley.
[15] The sun and moon will become dark.
The stars won't shine anymore.
[16] The LORD will roar like a lion from Jerusalem.
His voice will sound like thunder
from Zion.
The earth and sky will tremble.
But the LORD will keep the people of
Israel safe.
He will be a place of safety for them.

The LORD Blesses His People

[17] The LORD says,
"You will know that I am the LORD your God.
I live in Zion.
It is my holy mountain.
Jerusalem will be my holy city.
People from other lands
will never attack it again.
[18] "At that time fresh wine will drip from the
mountains.
Milk will flow down from the hills.
Water will run through all of Judah's
valleys.
A fountain will flow out of my temple.
It will water the places where acacia
trees grow.
[19] But Egypt will be deserted.
Edom will become a dry and empty desert.
They did terrible harm to the people of Judah.
My people were not guilty of doing
anything wrong.
But Egypt and Edom spilled their
blood anyway.
[20] My people will live in Judah and Jerusalem
forever.
The land will be their home for all time
to come.
[21] Egypt and Edom have spilled my people's
blood.
I will punish them for it."

The LORD lives in Zion!

Amos

1 These are the words of Amos. He was a shepherd from the town of Tekoa. Here is the
vision he saw concerning Israel. It came to him
two years before the earthquake. At that time Uzziah was king of Judah. Jeroboam was king of Israel. He was the son of Jehoash. Here are the
words of Amos.
2 I said,

"The LORD roars like a lion from Jerusalem.
His voice sounds like thunder from Zion.
The grasslands of the shepherds turn brown.
The top of Mount Carmel dries up."

The LORD Punishes Israel's Neighbors

3 The LORD says,

"The people of Damascus have sinned again
and again.
So I will punish them.
They used threshing sleds with iron teeth
to crush Gilead's people.
4 So I will send fire to destroy the palace of
King Hazael.
It will burn up the forts of his son
Ben-Hadad.
5 I will break down the city gate of Damascus.
I will cut off the king
who lives in the Valley of Aven.
He holds the ruler's rod in Beth Eden.
The people of Aram will be taken away to
Kir as prisoners,"
says the LORD.

6 The LORD says,

"The people of Gaza have sinned again
and again.
So I will punish them.
They captured whole communities.
They sold them to Edom.
7 So I will send fire to destroy the walls
of Gaza.
It will burn up its forts.
8 I will cut off the king of Ashdod.
He holds the ruler's rod in Ashkelon.
I will use my powerful hand against Ekron.
Every single Philistine will die,"
says the LORD and King.

9 The LORD says,

"The people of Tyre have sinned again and
again.
So I will punish them.
They captured whole communities.
They sold them to Edom.
They did not honor the treaty
of friendship they had made.
10 So I will send fire to destroy the walls
of Tyre.
It will burn up its forts."

11 The LORD says,

"The people of Edom have sinned again
and again.
So I will punish them.
They chased Israel with swords
that were ready to strike them down.
They did not show them any pity.
They were angry all the time.
Their anger blazed out.
It could not be stopped.
12 So I will send fire to destroy the city
of Teman.
It will burn up Bozrah's forts."

13 The LORD says,

"The people of Ammon have sinned again
and again.
So I will punish them.
They ripped open the pregnant women in
Gilead.
They wanted to add land to their territory.
14 So I will set fire to destroy the walls
of Rabbah.
It will burn up its forts.
War cries will be heard on that day of battle.
Strong winds will blow on that stormy day.
15 Ammon's god Molech will be carried away.
So will its officials,"
says the LORD.

2 The LORD says,

"The people of Moab have sinned again
and again.
So I will punish them.
They burned the bones
of Edom's king to ashes.
2 So I will send fire to destroy Moab.
It will burn up Kerioth's forts.
Moab will come crashing down with a
loud noise.
War cries will be heard.
So will the blast of trumpets.
3 I will cut off Moab's ruler.
I will also kill all of its officials,"
says the LORD.

4 The LORD says,

"The people of Judah have sinned again
and again.
So I will punish them.
They have refused to obey my law.
They have not kept my rules.

Other gods have led them down the
wrong path.
Their people before them
worshiped those gods.
5 So I will send fire to destroy Judah.
It will burn up Jerusalem's forts."

The LORD Punishes Israel

6 The LORD says,

"The people of Israel have sinned again
and again.
So I will punish them.
They sell into slavery those who do what
is right.
They trade needy people
for a mere pair of sandals.
7 They grind the heads of the poor
into the dust of the ground.
They refuse to be fair to those who
are crushed.
A father and his son have sex with the
same girl.
They treat my name as if it were not holy.
8 They lie down beside every altar
on clothes they had taken
until the owner paid back what was owed.
In the house of their God
they drink wine that was taken as fines.

9 "I destroyed the Amorites to make room
for my people in the land.
The Amorites were as tall as cedar trees.
They were as strong as oak trees.
But I cut off their fruit above the ground
and their roots below it.
10 "People of Israel, I brought you up out
of Egypt.
I led you in the desert for 40 years.
I gave you the land of the Amorites.
11 I raised up prophets from among your children.
I also set some of your young people apart
to me as Nazirites.
Isn't that true, people of Israel?"
announces the LORD.
12 "But you made the Nazirites drink wine.
You commanded the prophets not to
prophesy.
13 "A cart that is loaded with grain
crushes anything it runs over.
In the same way, I will crush you.
14 Your fastest runners will not escape.
The strongest people will not get away.
Even soldiers will not be able
to save their own lives.
15 Men who are armed with bows will lose
the battle.
Soldiers who are quick on their feet
will not escape.
Horsemen will not be able
to save their own lives.
16 Even your bravest soldiers
will run away naked on that day,"
announces the LORD.

The LORD Judges His Chosen People

3 People of Israel, listen to the LORD's message.
It is against you. It is against the whole family he brought up out of Egypt. He says,

2 "Out of all of the families on earth
I have chosen only you.
So I will punish you
because you have committed so
many sins."

3 Do two people walk together
unless they've agreed to do so?
4 Does a lion roar in the bushes
when it doesn't have any food?
Does it growl in its den
when it hasn't caught anything?
5 Does a bird fall into a trap on the ground
where no one has set a trap for it?
Does a net spring up from the earth
when there isn't anything for it to catch?
6 When someone blows a trumpet in a city,
don't the people tremble with fear?
When trouble comes to a city,
hasn't the LORD caused it?
7 The LORD and King never does anything
without telling his servants the prophets
about it.
8 A lion has roared.
Who isn't afraid?
The LORD and King has spoken.
Who can do anything but prophesy?

9 Speak to the people in the forts of Ashdod
and Egypt.
Tell them, "Gather together
on the mountains of Samaria.
Look at the great trouble in that city.
Its people are committing many crimes."
10 "They do not know how to do what is right,"
announces the LORD.
"They pile up stolen goods in their forts."

11 So the LORD and King says,

"Enemies will take over your land.
They will pull down your places of safety.
They will rob your forts."

12 The LORD says,

"Suppose a shepherd saves only two leg bones
from a lion's mouth.
Or he might save only a piece of an ear.
That is how the Israelites will be saved.
They sit in Samaria
on the edge of their beds.
They lie down in Damascus
on their couches."

13 "Listen to me," announces the LORD. "Witness against the people of Jacob," says the LORD God who rules over all.
14 "I will punish Israel for their sins.
When I do, I will destroy their altars
at Bethel.
The horns that stick out from the upper corners
of their main altar will be cut off.
They will fall to the ground.
15 I will tear their winter houses down.
I will also pull down their summer houses.
The houses they have decorated with ivory will
be destroyed.
And their princely houses will be torn
down,"
announces the LORD.

Israel Has Not Returned to the LORD

4 Listen to the LORD's message,
you women who live on the hill
of Samaria.
You treat poor people badly.
You crush those who are in need.
You say to your husbands,
"Bring us some drinks!"
But you are already as fat
as the cows in Bashan.
2 The LORD and King has taken an oath
in his own holy name.
He says, "You can be sure
that the time will come
when your enemies will put hooks in
your faces.
They will lead every one of you away
with fishhooks.
3 Each of you will go straight out
through a gap in the wall.
You will be thrown out of the city
on the hill where you crush others,"
announces the LORD.
4 "People of Samaria, go to Bethel and sin!
Go to Gilgal! Sin there even more!
Bring your sacrifices every morning.
Every third year, bring a tenth
of everything you produce.
5 Bake some bread with yeast.
Burn it as a thank offering.
Brag about the offerings you freely give.
That is what you Israelites love to do,"
announces the LORD and King.

6 "I made sure your stomachs were empty in
every city.
You did not have enough bread in any of
your towns.
In spite of that, you still have not returned
to me,"
announces the LORD.

7 "I also held rain back from you.
The time to harvest crops
was still three months away.
I sent rain on one town.
But I held it back from another.
One field had rain.
Another did not. So it dried up.
8 People wandered from town to town to look
for water.
But they did not get enough to drink.
In spite of that, you still have not returned
to me,"
announces the LORD.

9 "Many times I struck your gardens and
vineyards.
I sent hot winds to dry them up completely.
Locusts ate up your fig and olive trees.
In spite of that, you still have not returned
to me,"
announces the LORD.

10 "I sent plagues on you,
just as I did on Egypt.
I killed your young men with swords.
I also let the horses you had captured
be killed.
I filled your noses with the bad smell of your
camps.
In spite of that, you still have not returned
to me,"
announces the LORD.

11 "I destroyed some of you,
just as I did Sodom and Gomorrah.
You were like a burning stick that was pulled
out of the fire.
In spite of that, you still have not returned
to me,"
announces the LORD.

12 "People of Israel, I will punish you.
Because I will do that to you,
prepare to meet your God!"
13 The LORD forms the mountains.
He creates the wind.
He makes his thoughts known to human
beings.
He turns sunrise into darkness.
He rules over the highest places on earth.
His name is The LORD God Who Rules
Over All.

Look to the LORD and Live

5 People of Israel, listen to the LORD's message.
Hear my song of sadness about you. I say,

2 "The people of Israel have fallen.
They will never get up again.
They are deserted in their own land.
No one can lift them up."

3 The LORD and King says,

"A thousand soldiers will march out from a
city in Israel.
But only a hundred will return.

A hundred soldiers will march out from a town.
But only ten will come back."

4 The LORD speaks to the people of Israel. He says,

"Look to me and live.
5 Do not look to Bethel.
Do not go to Gilgal.
Do not travel to Beersheba.
The people of Gilgal will be taken away as prisoners.
Nothing will be left of Bethel."

6 Israel, look to the LORD and live.
If you don't, he will sweep through
the people of Joseph like a fire.
It will burn everything up.
And Bethel won't have anyone to put it out.

7 You turn what is fair into something bitter.
What is right you throw down to the ground.
8 The LORD made the Pleiades and Orion.
He turns darkness into sunrise.
He makes the day fade into night.
He sends for the waters in the clouds.
Then he pours them out on the surface of the land.
His name is The LORD.
9 He destroys places of safety.
He tears down cities
that have high walls around them.
10 Israel, you hate those who do what is right in court.
You can't stand those who tell the truth.
11 You walk all over poor people.
You make them give you grain.
You have built stone houses.
But you won't live in them.
You have planted fruitful vineyards.
But you won't drink the wine they produce.
12 I know how many crimes you have committed.
You have sinned far too much.

You crush those who do what is right.
You accept money from people who want special favors.
You take away the rights of poor people in the courts.
13 So those who are wise keep quiet in times like these.
That's because the times are evil.

14 Look to what is good, not to what is evil.
Then you will live.
And the LORD God who rules over all
will be with you,
just as you say he is.
15 Hate what is evil. Love what is good.
Do what is fair in the courts.
Perhaps the LORD God who rules over all
will show you his favor.
After all, you are the only ones left
in the family line of Joseph.

16 The LORD God rules over all. The Lord says,
"People will sob in all of the streets.
They will be very sad in every market place.
Even farmers will be told to cry loudly.
People will sob over the dead.
17 Workers will cry in all of the vineyards.
That is because I will punish you,"
says the LORD.

The Day of the LORD Is Coming

18 How terrible it will be for you
who long for the day of the LORD!
Why do you want it to come?
That day will be dark, not light.
19 It will be like a man running away from a lion
only to meet a bear.
He enters his house and rests his hand on a wall
only to be bitten by a snake.
20 The day of the LORD will be dark, not light.
It will be very black.
There won't be a ray of sunlight anywhere.

21 The LORD says,

"I hate your holy feasts.
I can't stand them.
I hate it when you gather together.
22 You bring me burnt offerings and grain offerings.
But I will not accept them.
You bring your best friendship offerings.
But I will not even look at them.
23 Take the noise of your songs away!
I will not listen to the music of your harps.
24 I want you to treat others fairly.
So let fair treatment roll on
just as a river does!
Always do what is right.
Let right living flow along
like a stream that never runs dry!

25 "People of Israel, did you bring me sacrifices and offerings
for 40 years in the desert?
26 Yes. But you have honored the place
where your king worshiped other gods.
You have carried the stands
the statues of your gods were on.
You have lifted up the banners
of the stars you worship as gods.
You made all of those things for yourselves.
27 So I will send you away
as prisoners beyond Damascus,"
says the LORD.
His name is God Who Rules Over All.

The LORD Judges Israel's Pride

6 How terrible it will be for you men
who are so contented on Mount Zion!
How terrible for you who feel secure
on the hill of Samaria!

You are famous men from the greatest nation.
The people of Israel come to you
for help and advice.
2 Go to the city of Calneh. Look at it.
Go from there to the great city of Hamath.
Then go down to Gath in Philistia.
Are those places better off than your two kingdoms?
Is their land larger than yours?
3 You are trying to avoid the time
when trouble will come.
But you are only bringing closer
the Assyrian rule of terror.
4 You lie down on beds
that are decorated with ivory.
You rest on your couches.
You eat the best lambs
and the fattest calves.
5 You pluck away on your harps as David did.
You play new songs on musical instruments.
6 You drink wine by the bowlful.
You use the finest lotions.
But Joseph's people will soon be destroyed.
And you aren't even sad about it.
7 So you will be among the first
to be taken away as prisoners.
You won't be able to enjoy good food.
You won't lie around on couches anymore.

8 The LORD and King has taken an oath in his own name. He is the LORD God who rules over all. He announces,

"I hate the pride of Jacob's people.
I can't stand their forts.
I will hand the city of Samaria
and everything in it over to their enemies."

9 Ten men might be left in one house. If they are,
they will die there. 10 Relatives might come to burn
the dead bodies. If they do, they'll have to carry
them out of the house first. They might ask someone still hiding there, "Is anyone here with you?"
If the answer is no, the relatives will say, "Be
quiet! We must not pray in the LORD's name."

11 The LORD has already given an order.
He will smash large houses to pieces.
He will crush small houses to bits.

12 Horses don't run on rocky ground.
People don't plow there with oxen.
But you have turned fair treatment into poison.
You have turned the fruit of right living into bitterness.
13 You are happy because you captured the town of Lo Debar.
You say, "We were strong enough to take Karnaim too."

14 But the LORD God rules over all. He announces, "People of Israel,
I will stir up a nation against you.
They will crush you from Lebo Hamath
all the way down to the Arabah Valley."

The LORD Gives Amos Three Visions

7 The LORD and King gave me a vision. He was
bringing large numbers of locusts on the land.
The king's share of the first crop had already been
harvested. Now the second crop was coming up.
2 The locusts stripped the land clean. Then I cried
out, "LORD and King, forgive Israel! How can Jacob's people continue? They are such a weak
nation!"

3 So the LORD had pity on them.

"I will let them continue for now," he said.

4 The LORD and King gave me a second vision.
He was using fire to punish his people. It dried up
the deep waters. It burned the land up. 5 Then I
cried out, "LORD and King, please stop! How can
Jacob's people continue? They are such a weak
nation!"

6 So the LORD had pity on them.

"I will let them continue for now," the LORD and King said.

7 Then the Lord gave me a third vision. He was
standing by a wall. It had been built very straight,
all the way up and down. He was holding a plumb
line. 8 The LORD asked me, "What do you see,
Amos?"

"A plumb line," I replied.

Then the Lord said, "Look at what I am doing. I am hanging a plumb line next to my people Israel. It will show how crooked they are. I will no longer spare them.

9 "The high places where Isaac's people worship other gods will be destroyed.
The other places of worship in Israel will also be torn down.
I will use my sword
to attack Jeroboam's royal family."

Amaziah Tells Amos to Stop Prophesying

10 Amaziah was priest of Bethel. He sent a message to Jeroboam, the king of Israel. He said,
"Amos is making evil plans against you right here
in Israel. The people in the land can't stand to listen to what he's saying. 11 Amos is telling them,

" 'Jeroboam will be killed with a sword.
The people of Israel will be taken away as prisoners.
They will be carried off from their own land.' "

12 Then Amaziah said to Amos, "Get out of Israel, you prophet! Go back to the land of Judah.
Earn your living there. Do your prophesying there.
13 Don't prophesy here at Bethel anymore. This is
where the king worships. The main temple in the
kingdom is located here."

14 Amos answered Amaziah, "I was not a
prophet. I wasn't even a prophet's son. I was a
shepherd. I also took care of sycamore-fig trees.
15 But the LORD took me away from taking care of

the flock. He said to me, 'Go. Prophesy to my people Israel.' 16Now then, listen to the LORD's message. You say,

"'Don't prophesy against Israel.
Stop preaching against the people of Isaac.'

17"But the LORD says,

"'Your wife will become a prostitute
in the city of Bethel.
Your sons and daughters will be killed
with swords.
Your land will be measured and divided up.
And you yourself will die in another
country.
The people of Israel will be taken away
as prisoners.
They will be carried off from their
own land.'"

The LORD Gives Amos Another Vision

8 The LORD and King gave me a vision. He showed me a basket of ripe fruit. 2"What do you see, Amos?" he asked.

"A basket of ripe fruit," I replied.

Then the LORD said to me, "The time is ripe for my people Israel. I will no longer spare them.

3"The time is coming when the songs in the temple will turn to crying," announces the LORD and King. "Many, many bodies will be thrown everywhere! So be quiet!"

4 Listen to me, you who walk all over needy
people.
You crush those who are poor in the land.

5You say,

"When will the New Moon Feast be over?
Then we can sell our grain.
When will the Sabbath day come to an end?
Then people can buy our wheat."
But you don't measure out the right amount.
You raise your prices.
You cheat others by using dishonest scales.
6 You buy poor people to make slaves out
of them.
You buy those who are in need for a mere
pair of sandals.
You even sell the worthless parts of
your wheat.

7People of Jacob, you are proud that the LORD is your God. But he has taken an oath in his own name. He says, "I will never forget anything Israel has done.

8 "The land will tremble because of what
will happen.
Everyone who lives in it will sob.
So the whole land will rise like the Nile River.
It will be stirred up.
Then it will settle back down again
like that river in Egypt."

9The LORD and King announces,

"At that time I will make the sun go down
at noon.
The earth will become dark in the middle
of the day.
10 I will turn your holy feasts into times for
sobbing.
I will turn all of your songs into crying.
You will have to wear black clothes.
You will shave your heads.
I will make you sob as if your only son
had died.
The end of that time will be like a
bitter day."

11The LORD and King announces,

"The days are coming
when I will send hunger through the land.
But people will not be hungry for food.
They will not be thirsty for water.
Instead, they will be hungry
to hear a message from me.
12 People will wander from the Dead Sea to the
Mediterranean.
They will travel from north to east.
They will look for a message from me.
But they will not find it.

13"At that time

"the lovely young women and strong
young men
will faint because they are so thirsty.
14 Some people take oaths in the name
of Samaria's shameful god.
Others say, 'People of Dan, you can be sure
that your god is alive.'
Still others say, 'You can be sure
that Beersheba's god is alive.'
But all of those people will fall dead.
They will never get up again."

The LORD Gives Amos a Final Vision

9 I saw the Lord standing next to the altar in the temple. He said to me,

"Strike the tops of the temple pillars.
Then the heavy stones at the base of the
entrance will shake.
Bring everything down on the heads of
everyone there.
I will kill with my swords
those who are left alive.
Not one of them will escape.
None will get away.
2 They might dig down to the deepest parts
of the grave.
But my powerful hand will take them
out of there.
They might climb up to the heavens.
But I will bring them down from there.

3 They might hide on top of Mount Carmel.
But I will hunt them down
and grab hold of them.
They might hide from me at the bottom of
the ocean.
But I will command the serpent to
bite them.
4 Their enemies might take them away
as prisoners to another country.
But I will command their enemies
to kill them with their swords.
I will turn my eyes toward them to
harm them.
I will not help them."

5 The LORD rules over all.
The Lord touches the earth, and
it melts.
Everyone who lives in it sobs.
The whole land rises like the Nile River.
Then it settles back down again
like that river in Egypt.
6 The LORD builds his palace high in the
heavens.
He lays its foundation on the earth.
He sends for the waters in the clouds.
Then he pours them out on the surface
of the land.
His name is The LORD.

7 "You Israelites are just like
the people of Cush to me,"
announces the LORD.
"I brought Israel up from Egypt.
I also brought the Philistines from
Crete
and the Arameans from Kir.

8 "I am the LORD and King.
My eyes are watching the sinful
kingdom of Israel.
I will wipe it off the face of the earth.
But I will not totally destroy the people
of Jacob,"
announces the LORD.

9 "I will give an order.
I will shake the people of Israel
among all of the nations.
They will be like grain that is shaken through
a screen.
Not a pebble will fall to the ground.
10 All of the sinners among my people
will be killed with swords.
They say, 'Nothing bad will ever happen
to us.'

Israel Will Be Made Like New Again

11 "The time will come when I will rebuild
David's fallen tent.
I will repair its broken places.
I will rebuild what was destroyed.
I will make it what it used to be.
12 Then my people will take control of those
who are left alive in Edom.
They will also possess all of the nations
that belong to me,"
announces the LORD.
He will do all of those things.

13 "A new day is coming," announces the LORD.

"At that time those who plow the land
will catch up with those who harvest
the crops.
Those who stomp on grapes
will catch up with those who plant the vines.
Fresh wine will drip from the mountains.
It will flow down from all of the hills.
14 I will bring my people Israel back home.
I will bless them with great success again.
They will rebuild the destroyed cities and
live in them.
They will plant vineyards and drink the wine
they produce.
They will make gardens and eat their fruit.
15 I will plant Israel in their own land.
They will never again be removed
from the land I have given them,"
says the LORD your God.

Obadiah

1 This is the vision about Edom that Obadiah had. Here is what he said.

We've heard a message from the LORD
and King.
A messenger was sent to the nations.
The LORD told him to say,
"Get up! Let us go and make war against
Edom."
2 The LORD says to Edom,
"I will make you weak among the nations.
They will look down on you.
3 You live in the safety of the rocks.
You make your home high up in the
mountains.
But your proud heart has tricked you.
So you say to yourself,
'No one can bring me down to
the ground.'
4 You have built your home as high as an
eagle does.
You have made your nest among the stars.
But I will bring you down from there,"
announces the LORD.
5 "Edom, suppose robbers came to you
at night.
They would steal only as much as
they wanted.
Suppose grape pickers came to harvest your
vines.
They would still leave a few grapes.
But you are facing horrible trouble!
6 People of Esau, everything will be taken
away from you.
Your hidden treasures will be stolen.
7 All those who are helping you
will force you to leave your country.
Your friends will trick you and overpower
you.
Those who eat bread with you
will set a trap for you.
But you will not see it."

8 The LORD announces, "At that time
I will destroy the wise men of Edom.
I will wipe out the men of understanding
in the mountains of Esau.
9 People of Teman, your soldiers will be
terrified.
Everyone in Esau's mountains
will be cut down with swords.
10 You did harmful things to your brothers,
the people of Jacob.
So you will be covered with shame.
You will be destroyed forever.
11 Strangers entered the gates of Jerusalem.
They cast lots to see what each one
would get.
They carried off its wealth.
When that happened, you just stood there
and did nothing.
You were like one of them.
12 That was a time of trouble for your brothers.
So you should not have looked down
on them.
The people of Judah were destroyed.
So you should not have been happy about it.
You should not have laughed at them so much
when they were in trouble.
13 You should not have marched
through the gates of my people's city
when they were having so much trouble.
You should not have looked down on them.
You should not have stolen their wealth.
14 You waited where the roads cross.
You wanted to cut down those who were
running away.
You should not have done that.
You handed over to their enemies
those who were still left alive.
You should not have done that.
They were in trouble.

15 "The day of the LORD is near
for all of the nations.
Others will do to you
what you have done to them.
You will be paid back
for what you have done.
16 You Edomites polluted my holy mountain
of Zion
by drinking and celebrating there.
So all of the nations will drink
from the cup of my anger.
And they will keep on drinking from it.
They will vanish.
It will be as if they had never existed.
17 But on Mount Zion some of my people will be
left alive.
I will save them.
Zion will be my holy mountain once again.
And the people of Jacob
will again receive the land as their own.
18 They will be like a fire.
Joseph's people will be like a flame.
The nation of Esau will be like straw.
Jacob's people will set Edom on fire and
burn it up.
No one will be left alive
among Esau's people."
The LORD has spoken.

[19] Israelites from the Negev Desert
will take over Esau's mountains.
Israelites from the western hills
will possess Philistia.
They'll take over the territories
of Ephraim and Samaria.
Israelites from the tribe of Benjamin
will possess the land of Gilead.
[20] Some Israelites were forced to leave
their homes.
They'll come back to Canaan and possess
it all the way to the town of Zarephath.
Some people from Jerusalem were taken
to the city of Sepharad.
They'll return and possess
the towns of the Negev Desert.
[21] Leaders from Mount Zion will go
and rule over the mountains of Esau.
And the kingdom will belong to
the LORD.

Jonah

Jonah Runs Away From the LORD

1 A message from the LORD came to Jonah. He
was the son of Amittai. The LORD said, 2“Go
to the great city of Nineveh. Preach against it. The
sins of its people have come to my attention.”
3But Jonah ran away from the LORD. He headed
for Tarshish. So he went down to the port of Joppa. There he found a ship that was going to Tarshish. He paid the fare and went on board. Then
he sailed for Tarshish. He was running away from
the LORD.
4But the LORD sent a strong wind over the
Mediterranean Sea. A wild storm came up. It was
so wild that the ship was in danger of breaking
apart. 5All of the sailors were afraid. Each one
cried out to his own god for help. They threw the
ship’s contents into the sea. They were trying to
make the ship lighter.
But Jonah had gone below deck. There he lay
down and fell into a deep sleep. 6The captain went
down to him and said, “How can you sleep? Get
up and call out to your god for help! Maybe he’ll
pay attention to what’s happening to us. Then we
won’t die.”
7The sailors said to one another, “Come. Let’s
cast lots to find out who is to blame for getting us
into all of this trouble.” So they did. And Jonah
was picked.
8They asked him, “What terrible thing have you
done to bring all of this trouble on us? Tell us.
What do you do for a living? Where do you come
from? What is your country? What people do you
belong to?”
9He answered, “I’m a Hebrew. I worship the
LORD. He is the God of heaven. He made the sea
and the land.”
10They found out he was running away from the
LORD. That’s because he had told them. Then they
became terrified. So they asked him, “How could
you do a thing like that?”
11The sea was getting rougher and rougher. So
they asked him, “What should we do to you to
make the sea calm down?”
12“Pick me up and throw me into the sea,” he
replied. “Then it will become calm. I know it’s my
fault that this terrible storm has come on you.”
13Instead of doing what he said, the men did
their best to row back to land. But they couldn’t.
The sea got even rougher than before.
14Then they cried out to the LORD. They prayed,
“LORD, please don’t let us die for taking this man’s
life. After all, he might not be guilty of doing anything wrong. So don’t hold us accountable for
killing him. LORD, you always do what you want
to.” 15Then they took Jonah and threw him overboard. And the stormy sea became calm.
16When the men saw what had happened, they
began to have great respect for the LORD. They
offered a sacrifice to him. And they made promises
to him.
17But the LORD sent a huge fish to swallow Jonah. And Jonah was inside the fish for three days
and three nights.

Jonah Prays to the LORD

2 From inside the fish Jonah prayed to the LORD
his God. 2He said,

“When I was in trouble, I called out to you.
  And you answered me.
When I had almost drowned,
  I called out for help.
  And you listened to my cry.
3 You threw me into the Mediterranean Sea.
  I was in the middle of its waters.
  They were all around me.
All of your rolling waves
  were sweeping over me.
4 I said, ‘I have been driven away from you.
  But I will look again
  toward your holy temple in Jerusalem.’
5 I had almost drowned in the waves.
  The deep waters were all around me.
  Seaweed was wrapped around my head.
6 I sank down to the bottom of the mountains.
  I thought I had died
  and gone down into the grave forever.
But you brought my life up
  from the very edge of the pit.
  You are the LORD my God.

7 “When my life was nearly over,
  I remembered you, LORD.
My prayer rose up to you.
  It reached you in your holy temple
    in heaven.

8 “Some people worship the worthless statues of
    their gods.
  They turn away from the grace
  you want to give them.
9 But I will sacrifice a thank offering to you.
  And I will sing a song of thanks.
I will do what I have promised.
  LORD, you are the one who saves.”

10The LORD gave the fish a command. And it
spit Jonah up onto dry land.

Jonah Goes to Nineveh

3 A message came to Jonah from the LORD a
second time. He said, 2“Go to the great city of
Nineveh. Announce to its people the message I
give you.”

3 Jonah obeyed the LORD. He went to Nineveh. It was a very important city. In fact, it took about three days to see all of it. 4 On the first day, Jonah started into the city. He announced, "In 40 days Nineveh will be destroyed."

5 The people of Nineveh believed God's warning. They decided not to eat any food for a while. All of them put on black clothes. That's what everyone from the least important of them to the most important did.

6 The news reached the king of Nineveh. He got up from his throne. He took his royal robes off and dressed himself in black clothes. He sat down in the dust. 7 Then he sent out a message to the people of Nineveh. He said,

"I and my nobles give this order.

"Don't let any person or animal taste anything. That includes your herds and flocks. People and animals must not eat or drink anything. 8 Let people and animals alike be covered with black cloth. All of you must call out to God with all your hearts. Stop doing what is evil. Don't harm others. 9 Who knows? God might take pity on us. He might turn away from his burning anger. Then we won't die."

10 God saw what they did. They stopped doing what was evil. So he took pity on them. He didn't destroy them as he had said he would.

The LORD Shows Concern for Nineveh

4 But Jonah was very upset. He became angry. 2 He prayed to the LORD and said, "LORD, isn't this exactly what I thought would happen when I was still at home? That's why I was so quick to run away to Tarshish. I knew that you are gracious. You are tender and kind. You are slow to get angry. You are full of love. You are a God who takes pity on people. You don't want to destroy them. 3 LORD, take away my life. I'd rather die than live."

4 But the LORD replied, "Do you have any right to be angry?"

5 Jonah left the city. He sat down at a place east of it. There he put some branches over his head. He sat in their shade. He waited to see what would happen to the city.

6 Then the LORD God sent a vine and made it grow up over Jonah. It gave him more shade for his head. It made him more comfortable. Jonah was very happy he had the vine. 7 But before sunrise the next day, God sent a worm. It chewed the vine so much that it dried up.

8 When the sun rose, God sent a burning east wind. The sun beat down on Jonah's head. It made him very weak. He wanted to die. So he said, "I'd rather die than live."

9 But God said to Jonah, "Do you have any right to be angry about what happened to the vine?"

"I do," he said. "In fact, I'm angry enough to die."

10 But the LORD said, "You have been concerned about this vine. But you did not take care of it. You did not make it grow. It grew up in one night and died the next. 11 Nineveh has more than 120,000 people. They can't tell right from wrong. Nineveh also has a lot of cattle. So shouldn't I show concern for that great city?"

Micah

1 A message came to Micah from the LORD. He was from the town of Moresheth. The message came while Jotham, Ahaz and Hezekiah were kings of Judah. This is the vision Micah saw concerning Samaria and Jerusalem. Here is what he said.

2 Listen to me, all of you nations!
Earth and everyone who lives in it,
pay attention!
The LORD and King will be a witness
against you.
The Lord will speak from his holy temple
in heaven.

The LORD Will Judge Samaria and Jerusalem

3 The LORD is about to come down
from his home in heaven.
He rules over the highest places on earth.
4 The mountains will melt under him
like wax near a fire.
The valleys will be broken apart
by water rushing down a slope.
5 All of that will happen because
Jacob's people have done what is wrong.
The people of Israel
have committed many sins.
Who is to blame
for the wrong things Jacob has done?
Samaria!
Who is to blame for the high places
where Judah's people worship other gods?
Jerusalem!

6 So the LORD says,

"I will turn Samaria into a pile of trash.
It will become a place for planting
vineyards.
I will dump its stones down into the valley.
And I will destroy it
down to its very foundations.
7 All of the statues of Samaria's gods
will be broken to pieces.
All of the gifts its people gave to temple
prostitutes
will be burned with fire.
I will destroy all of the statues of its gods.
Samaria collected gifts that were paid to
temple prostitutes.
So the Assyrians will use the gifts
to pay their own temple prostitutes."

Micah Sobs Over His People

8 I will sob and cry because Samaria will
be destroyed.
I'll walk around barefoot.
I won't have anything on but my underwear.
I'll bark like a wild dog.
I'll hoot like an owl.
9 Samaria's wounds can't be healed.
The LORD will also judge Judah.
Enemies will march up to the very gate of
my people.
They will reach Jerusalem itself.
10 Don't tell the people of Gath about it.
Don't let them see you sob.
People in Beth Ophrah, roll in the dust.
11 You who live in the town of Shaphir,
leave in shame and without your clothes.
Those who live in Zaanan
won't come out to help you.
The people in Beth Ezel will sob.
They won't be able to help keep you safe.
12 Those who live in Maroth will groan
with pain
as they wait for help.
That's because the LORD will bring trouble
on them.
It will reach the very gate of Jerusalem.
13 You who live in Lachish,
get your horses ready to pull their chariots.
You trust in military power.
That was the beginning of sin
for the people of Zion.
The wrong things Israel did
were also done by you.
14 People of Judah, you might as well say
good-by
to Moresheth near Gath.
The town of Aczib won't give any help
to the kings of Israel.
15 An enemy will attack
you who live in Mareshah.
Israel's glorious leaders will have to
run away
and hide in the cave of Adullam.
16 The children you enjoy so much
will be taken away as prisoners.
So shave your heads and sob.
Make them as bare as the head of
a vulture.

People's Plans and God's Plans

2 How terrible it will be for those
who plan to harm others!
How terrible for those who make evil plans
before they even get out of bed!
As soon as daylight comes,
they carry them out.
That's because they have the power to do it.
2 If they want fields or houses,
they take them.
They cheat men out of
their homes and property.

3 So the LORD says to them,

"I am planning to send trouble on you.
You will not be able to save yourselves from it.
You will not live so proudly anymore.
It will be a time of trouble.
4 At that time people will make fun of you.
They will tease you by singing a song of sadness.
They will pretend to be you and say,
'We are totally destroyed.
Our enemies have divided up our land.
The LORD has taken it away from us!
He has given our fields to those
who turned against us.'"

5 So you won't even have anyone left
in the LORD's community
who can divide up the land for you.

Some Prophets Aren't Really Prophets at All

6 "Don't prophesy," the people's prophets say.
"Don't prophesy about bad things.
Nothing shameful is going to happen to us."
7 People of Jacob, should others say,
"The LORD isn't angry with us.
He doesn't do things like that"?

The LORD replies, "What I promise brings good things
to those who lead honest lives.
8 But lately my people have attacked one another
as if they were enemies.
You strip the rich robes off
those who happen to pass by.
They thought they were as safe as men
returning from a battle they had won.
9 You drive the women among my people
out of their pleasant homes.
You take my blessing away
from their children forever.
10 Get up! Leave this land!
It is no longer your resting place.
You have made it 'unclean.'
You have completely destroyed it.
11 Suppose a prophet goes around telling lies.
And he prophesies that you will have
plenty of wine and beer.
Then that kind of prophet would be
just right for this nation!

The LORD Promises He Will Save His People

12 "People of Jacob, I will gather all of you.
I will bring together
you who are still left alive in Israel.
I will gather you together like sheep in a pen.
You will be like a flock in its grasslands.
Your country will be filled with people.
13 I will open the way for you to return.
I will march in front of you.
You will break through the city gates and go free.
I am your King. I will pass through the gates
in front of you.
I will lead the way."

The LORD Warns Israel's Leaders and Prophets

3 Then I said,

"Listen, you leaders of Jacob's people!
Pay attention, you rulers of Israel!
You should know how to judge others fairly.
2 But you hate what is good.
And you love what is evil.
You are like someone
who tears the skin off my people.
You pull the meat off their bones.
3 You eat my people's bodies.
You strip their skin off.
You break their bones in pieces.
You chop them up like meat.
You put them in a cooking pot."

4 The time will come when Israel
will cry out to the LORD.
But he won't answer them.
In fact, he'll turn his face away from them.
They have done what is evil.

5 The LORD says,

"You prophets are leading my people
down the wrong path.
If they feed you,
you promise them peace.
If they do not,
you prepare to go to war against them.
6 So night will come on you.
But you will not have any visions.
Darkness will cover you.
But you will not be able
to figure out what is going to happen.
The sun will set on you prophets.
The day will become dark for you.
7 You who see visions will be put to shame.
You who try to figure out what is going to happen
will be dishonored.
All of you will cover your faces.
I will not answer you."

8 The Spirit of the LORD
has filled me with power.
He helps me do what is fair.
He makes me brave.
Now I'm prepared to tell Jacob's people
what they've done wrong.
I'm ready to tell Israel they've sinned.
9 Listen to me, you leaders of Jacob's people!
Pay attention, you rulers of Israel!

You hate to do what is fair.
You twist everything that is right.
10 You build up Zion by spilling the blood of others.
You build Jerusalem by doing what is evil.
11 Your judges take money from people who want special favors.
Your priests teach only if they get paid for it.
Your prophets won't tell fortunes unless they receive money.
But you still claim to depend on the LORD.
You say, "The LORD is with us.
No trouble will come on us."
12 So because of what you have done,
Zion will be plowed up like a field.
Jerusalem will be turned into a pile of trash.
The temple hill will be covered with bushes and weeds.

People From Many Nations Will Worship at Mount Zion

4 In the last days
the mountain where the LORD's temple is located will be famous.
It will be the most important mountain of all.
It will stand out above the hills.
And nations will go to it.

2 People from many nations will go there. They will say,

"Come, let us go up to the LORD's mountain.
Let's go to the house of Jacob's God.
He will teach us how we should live.
Then we will live the way he wants us to."
The law of the LORD will be taught at Zion.
His message will go out from Jerusalem.
3 He will judge between people from many nations.
He'll settle problems among strong nations everywhere.
They will hammer their swords into plows.
They'll hammer their spears into pruning tools.
Nations will not go to war against one another.
They won't even train to fight anymore.
4 Every man will have
his own vine and fig tree.
And no one will make them afraid.
That's what the LORD who rules over all has promised.
5 Other nations worship and trust in their gods.
But we will worship and obey the LORD.
He will be our God for ever and ever.

The LORD's Kingdom Will Come

6 "The time is coming
when I will gather those who are disabled,"
announces the LORD.
"I will bring together those
who were taken away as prisoners.
I will gather those I have allowed to suffer.
7 I will make the disabled my faithful people.
I will make those who were driven away from their homes a strong nation.
I will rule over them on Mount Zion.
I will be their King from that time on and forever.
8 Jerusalem, you used to be
like a guard tower for my flock.
City of Zion, you used to be
a place of safety for my people.
The glorious kingdom you had before
will be given back to you.
Once again a king will rule over your people."

9 Why are you crying out so loudly now?
Don't you have a king?
Have your advisers died?
Is that why pain comes on you
like the pain of a woman having a baby?
10 People of Zion, groan with pain.
Cry out like a woman having a baby.
Soon you must leave your city.
You must camp in the open fields.
You will have to go to Babylonia.
But that's where the LORD will save you.
There he will set you free
from the powerful hand of your enemies.

11 But now many nations
have gathered together to attack you.
They say, "Let Jerusalem be polluted.
We want to see others laugh when Zion suffers!"
12 But those nations don't know
what the LORD has in mind.
They don't understand his plan.
He will gather them up like bundles of grain.
He will take them to his threshing floor.

13 The LORD says,

"People of Zion, get up
and crush your enemies.
I will make you like a threshing ox.
I will give you iron horns and bronze hoofs.
So you will crush many nations."

They got their money in the wrong way.
But you will set it apart to the LORD.
You will give their wealth
to the Lord of the whole earth.

A Ruler Will Come From Bethlehem

5 Jerusalem, you are being attacked.
So bring your troops together.
Our enemies have surrounded us.
They want to slap the face of Israel's ruler.

2 The LORD says,

"Bethlehem, you might not be
an important town in the nation of Judah.
But out of you will come
a ruler over Israel for me.
His family line goes back
to the early years of your nation.
It goes all the way back
to days of long ago."
Bethlehem was also called Ephrathah.

3 The LORD will hand his people over to
their enemies.
That will last until the promised ruler
is born.
Then his relatives in Judah
will return to their land.
The LORD will rule over them
and the people of Israel.

4 The promised ruler will stand firm
and take care of his flock.
The LORD will give him the strength to do it.
The LORD his God will give him
the authority to rule.
His people will live safely.
His greatness will reach
from one end of the earth to the other.
5 And he will bring them peace.

The LORD Will Save His People From Their Enemies

The Assyrians will attack our land.
Enemies will march through our forts.
But we will raise up many shepherds
against them.
We'll send out against them
as many leaders as we need to.
6 They will use their swords to rule over Assyria.
They'll rule the land of Nimrod
with swords that are ready to strike.
The Assyrians will march across our borders
and attack our land.
But the promised ruler will save us
from them.

7 Jacob's people who are still left alive
will be scattered among many nations.
They will be like dew the LORD has sent.
It doesn't wait for a man's command.
They will be like rain that falls on the grass.
Rain doesn't wait for someone to give
it orders.
8 So Jacob's people will be scattered
among many nations.
They will be like a lion
among the animals in the forest.
They'll be like a young lion
among flocks of sheep.
Lions attack and tear as they move along.
No one can keep them
from killing what they want.

9 LORD, your powerful hand will win the battle
over your enemies.
All of them will be destroyed.

10 "At that time I will destroy
your war horses," announces the LORD.
"I will smash your chariots.
11 I will destroy the cities in your land.
I will tear down all of your forts.
12 I will destroy your worship of evil powers.
You will no longer be able
to put a spell on anyone.
13 I will destroy the statues of your gods.
I will take your sacred stones away
from you.
You will no longer bow down
to the gods your hands have made.
14 I will pull down the poles you used
to worship the goddess Asherah.
And I will destroy your cities completely.
15 I will pay back the nations
that have not obeyed me.
My anger will burn against them."

The LORD Brings Charges Against Israel

6 Israel, listen to the LORD's message. He says
to me,

"Stand up in court.
Let the mountains serve as witnesses.
Let the hills hear what you have to say."

2 Hear the LORD's case, you mountains.
Listen, you age-old foundations of the earth.
The LORD has a case against his people Israel.
He is bringing charges against them.

3 The LORD says,

"My people, what have I done to you?
Have I made things too hard for you?
Answer me.
4 I brought your people up out of Egypt.
I set them free from the land
where they were slaves.
I sent Moses to lead them.
Aaron and Miriam helped him.
5 Remember how Balak, the king of Moab,
planned to put a curse on your people.
But Balaam, the son of Beor,
gave them a blessing instead.
Remember their journey from Shittim
to Gilgal.
I want you to know
that I always do what is right."

6 The people of Israel say,

"What should we bring with us
when we go to worship the LORD?
What should we offer the God of heaven
when we bow down to him?
Should we take burnt offerings to him?
Should we sacrifice calves
that are a year old?

7 Will the LORD be pleased with thousands
of rams?
Will he take delight in 10,000 rivers of
olive oil?
Should we offer our oldest sons
for the wrong things we've done?
Should we sacrifice our own children
to pay for our sins?"

8 The LORD has shown you what is good.
He has told you what he requires of you.
You must treat people fairly.
You must love others faithfully.
And you must be very careful to live
the way your God wants you to.

The LORD Will Punish His People

9 The LORD is calling out to Jerusalem.
And it would be wise to pay attention to him.
He says, "Listen, tribe of Judah
and you people who are gathered in the city.
10 You sinful people, should I forget
that you got your treasures by stealing
them?
You use dishonest measures to cheat others.
I have placed a curse on that practice.
11 Should I forgive you who use dishonest scales?
You use weights that weigh things heavier
or lighter than they really are.
12 The rich people among you harm others.
You are always telling lies.
You try to fool others by what you say.
13 So I will strike you down.
I will destroy you
because you have sinned so much.
14 You will eat. But you will not be satisfied.
Your stomachs will still be empty.
You will try to save what you can.
But you will not be able to.
If you do save something,
it will be destroyed in battle.
15 You will plant seeds.
But you will not harvest any crops.
You will press olives.
But you will not use the oil for yourselves.
You will crush grapes.
But you will not drink the wine
that is made from them.
16 You have followed the evil practices
of King Omri of Israel.
You have done what the family
of King Ahab did.
You have followed their bad example.
So I will let you be destroyed.
Others will make fun of you.
The nations will laugh at you."

Micah Is Sad Because Israel Has Sinned

7 I'm suffering very much!
I'm like someone who gathers summer fruit
in a vineyard
after the good fruit has already been picked.
No grapes are left to eat.
None of the early figs I long for remain.
2 Faithful people have disappeared from
the land.
Those who are honest are gone.
All men hide and wait
to spill the blood of others.
They use nets to try and trap one another.
3 They are very good at doing what is evil.
Rulers require gifts.
Judges accept money from people
who want special favors.
Those who are powerful
always get what they want.
All of them make evil plans together.
4 The best of them are as harmful as thorns.
The most honest of them are even worse.
The time your prophets warned you about
has come.
God is about to punish you.
Panic has taken hold of you.
5 Don't trust your neighbors.
Don't put your faith in your friends.
Be careful of what you say
even to your own wife.
6 Sons don't honor their fathers.
Daughters refuse to obey their mothers.
Daughters-in-law are against their
mothers-in-law.
A man's enemies are the members of his
own family.

7 So I will look to the LORD.
I'll put my trust in God my Savior.
He will hear me.

Jerusalem Will Be Rebuilt

8 The people of Jerusalem say,

"Don't laugh when we suffer,
you enemies of ours!
We have fallen.
But we'll get up.
Even though we sit in the dark,
the LORD will give us light.
9 We've sinned against the LORD.
So he is angry with us.
That will continue until he takes up our case.
Then he'll do what is right for us.
He'll bring us out into the light.
Then we'll see him save us.
10 The people of Nineveh will see it too.
And they will be put to shame.
After all, they said to us,
'Where is the LORD your God?'
But we will see them destroyed.
Soon they will be stomped on
like mud in the streets."

11 People of Jerusalem, the time will come
when your walls will be rebuilt.
Land will be added to your territory.

Jesus Dies

After Jesus cried out again in a loud voice, he died.
—Matthew 27:50

Jesus Rises

The angel said to the women, "Don't be afraid. I know that you are looking for Jesus, who was crucified. He is not here! He has risen!"
—Matthew 28:5–6

[12] At that time your people will come back
to you.
They'll return from Assyria
and the cities of Egypt.
They'll come from the countries
between Egypt and the Euphrates River.
They'll return from the lands
between the seas.
They'll come back from the countries
between the mountains.
[13] But the rest of the earth will be deserted.
The people who live in it
have done many evil things.

Prayer and Praise

[14] LORD, be like a shepherd to your people.
Take good care of them.
They are your flock.
They live by themselves
in the safety of a forest.
Rich grasslands are all around them.
Let them eat grass in Bashan and Gilead
just as they did long ago.

[15] The LORD says to his people,

"I showed your people my wonders
when they came out of Egypt long ago.
In the same way, I will show them to you."

[16] When the nations see those wonders,
they will be put to shame.
All of their power will be taken away
from them.
They will be so amazed
that they won't be able to speak or hear.
[17] They'll be forced to eat dust like a snake.
They'll be like creatures
that have to crawl on the ground.
They'll come out of their dens
trembling with fear.
They'll show respect for the LORD our God.
They will also have respect for his people.
[18] LORD, who is a God like you?
You forgive sin.
You forgive your people
when they do what is wrong.
You don't stay angry forever.
Instead, you take delight in showing
your faithful love to them.
[19] Once again you will show loving concern
for us.
You will completely wipe out
the evil things we've done.
You will throw all of our sins
into the bottom of the sea.
[20] You will be true to Jacob's people.
You will show your faithful love
to Abraham's children.
You will do what you promised to do for
our people
when you took an oath long ago.

Nahum

1 Here is a message the LORD gave Nahum in a vision about Nineveh. It is written on a scroll. Nahum was from the town of Elkosh. Here is what he said.

The LORD Is Angry With Nineveh

2 The LORD is a jealous God who punishes
people.
He pays them back for the evil things
they do.
His anger burns against them.
The LORD punishes his enemies.
He holds his anger back
until the right time to use it.
3 The LORD is slow to get angry.
He is very powerful.
The LORD will not let guilty people go
without punishing them.
When he marches out, he stirs up winds
and storms.
Clouds are the dust kicked up by his feet.
4 He controls the seas. He dries them up.
He makes all of the rivers run dry.
Bashan and Mount Carmel dry up.
The flowers in Lebanon fade.
5 He causes the mountains to shake.
The hills melt away.
The earth trembles because he is there.
So do the world and all those who live
in it.
6 Who can stand firm when his anger
burns?
Who can live when he is angry?
His anger blazes out like fire.
He smashes the rocks to pieces.

7 The LORD is good.
When people are in trouble,
they can go to him for safety.
He takes good care of those
who trust in him.
8 But he will destroy Nineveh
with a powerful flood.
He will chase his enemies
into the darkness of punishment.

9 The LORD will put an end
to anything they plan against him.
He won't allow Assyria to win the battle
over his people a second time.
10 His enemies will be tangled up among
thorns.
Their wine will make them drunk.
They'll be burned up like dry straw.
11 Nineveh, a king has marched out from you.
He makes evil plans against the LORD.
He gives harmful advice.

12 The LORD says,

"His army has many soldiers.
Other nations are helping them.
But they will be cut off and pass away.
Judah, I punished you.
But I will not do it anymore.
13 Now I will break Assyria's yoke off your neck.
I will tear off the ropes that hold you."

14 Nineveh, the LORD has given an order
concerning you.
He has said, "You will not have any children
to carry on your name.
I will destroy the wooden and metal statues
that are in the temple of your gods.
I will get your grave ready for you.
You are worthless."

15 Look at the mountains of Judah!
I see a messenger running to bring
good news!
He's telling us that peace has come!
People of Judah, celebrate your feasts.
Carry out your promises.
The evil Assyrians won't attack you again.
They'll be completely destroyed.

The LORD Will Destroy Nineveh

2 Nineveh, armies are coming to attack you.
Guard the forts!
Watch the roads!
Get ready!
Gather all of your strength!

2 Assyria once took everything of value from
God's people.
Its army destroyed all of their vines.
But the LORD will bring back
the glory of Jacob's people.
He'll make Israel glorious again.

3 The shields of the soldiers attacking Nineveh
are red.
The armies are dressed in bright red
uniforms.
The metal on their chariots flashes
when they are prepared for war.
Their spears are ready to use.
4 The chariots race through the main streets.
They rush back and forth through them.
They look like flaming torches.
They dart around like lightning.

5 The commander of the attackers
sends for his special troops.
But they trip and fall on their way.
They run toward the city wall.
They keep their shield in front of them.

[6]They open the gates that hold back
the waters of the river.
And the palace falls down.
[7]The attackers order that the city's people
be taken away as prisoners.
The female slaves cry like sad doves.
They beat their chests.
[8]Nineveh is like a pool.
Its water is draining away.
"Stop running away!" someone cries out.
But no one turns back.
[9]"Steal the silver!" the attackers shout.
"Grab the gold!"
The supply is endless.
There is plenty of wealth
among all of the city's treasures.
[10]Nineveh is destroyed, robbed and stripped!
Hearts melt away in fear.
Knees give way.
Bodies tremble with fear.
Everyone's face turns pale.

[11]Assyria is like a lion.
Where is the lions' den now?
Where did they feed their cubs?
Where did all of the lions go?
In their den they had nothing to fear.
[12]The lion killed enough for his cubs to eat.
He choked what he caught for his mate.
He filled his home with what he had killed.
He brought to his dens what he
had caught.

[13]"Nineveh, I am against you,"
announces the LORD who rules over all.
"I will burn up your chariots with fire.
Your young lions will be killed with swords.
I will leave you nothing on earth to catch.
The voices of your messengers
will no longer be heard."

The LORD Will Judge Nineveh

3 How terrible it will be for Nineveh!
It is a city of murderers!
It is full of liars!
It's filled with stolen goods!
The killing never stops!
[2]Whips crack!
Wheels clack!
Horses charge!
Chariots rumble!
[3]Horsemen attack!
Swords flash!
Spears gleam!
Many people die.
Dead bodies pile up.
They can't even be counted.
People trip over them.
[4]All of that was caused by the evil longings
of the prostitute Nineveh.
That woman who practiced evil magic
was very beautiful.
She used her sinful charms
to make slaves out of the nations.
She worshiped evil powers
in order to trap others.

[5]"Nineveh, I am against you,"
announces the LORD who rules over all.
"I will pull your skirts up over your face.
I will show the nations your naked body.
Kingdoms will make fun of your shame.
[6]I will throw garbage at you.
I will look down on you.
I will make an example out of you.
[7]All those who see you will run away from you.
They will say, 'Nineveh is destroyed.
Who will sob over it?'
Where can I find someone
to comfort your people?"

[8]Nineveh, are you better than Thebes
on the Nile River?
There was water all around that city.
The river helped to keep it safe.
The waters were like a wall around it.
[9]Cush and Egypt gave it all of the strength
it needed.
Put and Libya also helped it.
[10]But Thebes was captured anyway.
Its people were taken away as prisoners.
Its babies were smashed to pieces
at every street corner.
The Assyrian soldiers cast lots
for all of its great leaders.
They put them in chains
and made slaves out of them.
[11]People of Nineveh, you too will get drunk.
You will try to hide from your enemies.
You will look for a place of safety.

[12]All of your forts are like fig trees
that have their first ripe fruit on them.
When the trees are shaken,
the figs fall into the mouths
of those who eat them.
[13]Look at your troops.
All of them are weak.
The gates of your forts
are wide open to your enemies.
Fire has destroyed their heavy metal bars.

[14]Prepare for the attack by storing up water!
Make your walls as strong as you can!
Make some bricks out of clay!
Mix the mud to hold them together!
Use them to repair the walls!
[15]In spite of all of your hard work,
fire will burn you up inside your city.
Your enemies will cut you down with
their swords.
They will destroy you
just as grasshoppers eat up crops.
Multiply like grasshoppers!
Increase your numbers like locusts!

16 You have more traders
than the number of stars in the sky.
But like locusts they strip the land.
Then they fly away.
17 Your guards are like grasshoppers.
Your officials are like large numbers
of locusts.
They settle in the walls on a cold day.
But when the sun appears, they
fly away.
And no one knows where they go.

18 King of Assyria, your leaders are asleep.
Your nobles lie down to rest.
Your people are scattered on the mountains.
No one is left to gather them together.
19 Nothing can heal your wounds.
You will die of them.
All those who hear the news about you clap
their hands
because you have fallen from power.
All of them suffered
because you never showed them any pity.

Habakkuk

1 This is a vision the prophet Habakkuk received from the LORD. Here is what Habakkuk said.

Habakkuk Asks the LORD a Question

2 LORD, how long do I have to call out for help?
Why don't you listen to me?
How long must I keep telling you
that things are terrible?
Why don't you save us?
3 Why do you make me watch while
people treat others so unfairly?
Why do you put up with the wrong things
they are doing?
I have to look at death.
People are harming others.
They are arguing and fighting all the time.
4 The law can't do what it's supposed to do.
Fairness never comes out on top.
Sinful people surround those
who do what is right.
So people are never treated fairly.

The LORD Gives His Answer

5 The LORD replies,

"Look at the nations. Watch them.
Be totally amazed at what you see.
I am going to do something in your days
that you would never believe.
You would not believe it
even if someone told you about it.
6 I am going to send the armies of Babylonia to attack you.
They are very mean. They move quickly.
They sweep across the whole earth.
They take over places
that do not belong to them.
7 They terrify others.
They do not recognize any laws but their own.
That is how proud they are.
8 Their horses are faster than leopards.
They are meaner than wolves in the dark.
Their horsemen charge straight into battle.
They ride in from far away.
They come down like an eagle
diving for its food.
9 All of them are ready to destroy others.
Their huge armies advance like a wind out of the desert.
They gather prisoners like sand.
10 They laugh at kings
and make fun of rulers.
They laugh at all of the cities
that have high walls around them.
They build dirt ramps against the walls
and capture the cities.
11 They sweep past like the wind.
Then they go on their way.
They are guilty.
They worship their own strength."

Habakkuk Asks the LORD Another Question

12 LORD, haven't you existed forever?
You are my holy God.
So we won't die, will we?
LORD, you have appointed the Babylonians
to punish your people.
My Rock, you have chosen them to judge us.
13 Your eyes are too pure to look at what is evil.
You can't put up with the wrong things people do.
So why do you put up
with those who can't be trusted?
The evil Babylonians swallow up
those who are more godly than themselves.
So why are you silent?
14 You have made men as if they were only fish in the sea.
They are like sea creatures that don't have a ruler.
15 The evil Babylonians pull all of them up with hooks.
They catch them in their nets.
They gather them up.
So they celebrate.
They are glad.
16 They offer sacrifices to their nets.
They burn incense to them.
Their nets allow them to live in great comfort.
They enjoy the finest food.
17 Are you going to let them
keep on emptying their nets?
Will they go on destroying nations
without showing them any mercy?

2 I will go up to the lookout tower.
I'll station myself on the city wall.
I'll wait to see how the LORD will reply to me.
Then I'll try to figure out how to answer him.

The LORD Gives His Answer

2 The LORD replies,

"Write down the message I am showing you in a vision.
Write it clearly on the tablets you use.
Then a messenger can read it
and run to announce it.

3 The message I give you
waits for the time I have appointed.
It speaks about what is going to happen.
And all of it will come true.
It might take a while.
But wait for it.
You can be sure it will come.
It will happen when I want it to.

4 "The Babylonians are very proud.
What they want is not good.

"But the one who is right with God
will live by faith.

5 "Wine makes the Babylonians do foolish things.
They are proud. They never rest.
Like the grave, they are always hungry for more.
Like death, they are never satisfied.
They gather all of the nations to themselves.
They take their people away as prisoners.

6 "Won't those people laugh at the Babylonians?
Won't they make fun of them? They will say to them,

" 'How terrible it will be for you
who pile up stolen goods!
You get rich by cheating others.
How long will that go on?
7 Those who owe you money will suddenly rise up.
You charge them too much interest.
So they will wake up
and make you tremble with fear.
Then they will take away
everything you have.
8 You have robbed many nations.
So the nations that are left will rob you.
You have spilled man's blood.
You have destroyed lands and cities
and everyone in them.'

9 "How terrible it will be for the Babylonians!
They build their kingdom with money
they gained by cheating others.
They have tried to make the kingdom
as secure as possible.
After all, they did not want to be destroyed.
10 They have planned to wipe out many nations.
But they have brought shame on their own kingdom.
So they must pay with their own lives.
11 The stones in the walls of their homes will cry out.
And the wooden beams will echo that cry.

12 "How terrible it will be for the Babylonians!
They build cities by spilling the blood of others.
They establish towns by committing crimes.
13 I am the LORD who rules over all.
Human effort is no better than wood that feeds a fire.
So the nations wear themselves out for nothing.
14 The oceans are full of water.
In the same way, the earth will be filled
with the knowledge of my glory.

15 "How terrible it will be for the Babylonians!
They give drinks to their neighbors.
They pour the drinks from wineskins
until their neighbors are drunk.
They want to look at their naked bodies.
16 But the Babylonians will be filled
with shame instead of glory.
So now it is their turn to drink
and be stripped of their clothes.
The cup of anger in my powerful right hand
is going to punish them.
They will be covered with shame instead of glory.
17 The harm they have done to Lebanon
will bring them down.
Because they have killed so many animals,
animals will terrify them.
They have spilled man's blood.
They have destroyed lands and cities
and everyone in them.

18 "If someone carves a statue of a god, what is it worth?
What value is there in a god
that teaches lies?
The one who trusts in another god
worships his own creation.
He makes statues of gods that can't speak.
19 How terrible it will be for the Babylonians!
They say to a wooden god, 'Come to life!'
They say to a stone god, 'Wake up!'
Can those gods give advice?
They are covered with gold and silver.
They can't even breathe.
20 But I am in my holy temple.
Let the whole earth be silent in front of me."

Habakkuk Prays to the LORD

3 This is a prayer of the prophet Habakkuk. It is on *shigionoth*. Here is what he said.

2 LORD, I know how famous you are.
I have great respect for you
because of your mighty acts.
Do them again for us.
Make them known in our time.
When you are angry,
please show us your tender love.

3 God, you came from Teman.
You, the Holy One, came from
Mount Paran. *Selah*
Your glory covered the heavens.
Your praise filled the earth.

[4] Your glory was like the sunrise.
Rays of light flashed from your mighty hand.
Your power was hidden there.
[5] You sent plagues ahead of you.
Sickness followed behind you.
[6] When you stood up, the earth shook.
When you looked at the nations,
they trembled with fear.
The age-old mountains crumbled.
The ancient hills fell down.
Your mighty acts will last forever.
[7] I saw the tents of Cushan in trouble.
The people of Midian were suffering greatly.
[8] LORD, did your anger burn against the rivers?
Were you angry with the streams?
Were you angry with the Red Sea?
You rode your horses and chariots to overcome it.
[9] You got your bow ready to use.
You asked for many arrows. *Selah*
You broke up the surface of the earth with rivers.
[10] The mountains saw you and shook.
Floods of water swept by.
The sea roared.
It lifted its waves high.
[11] The sun and moon stood still in the sky.
They stopped because your flying arrows flashed by.
Your gleaming spear shone like lightning.
[12] When you were angry, you marched across the earth.
Because of your anger you destroyed the nations.
[13] You came out to set your people free.
You saved your chosen ones.
You crushed Pharaoh, the leader of that evil land of Egypt.
You stripped him from head to foot. *Selah*
[14] His soldiers rushed out to scatter us.
They were laughing at us.
They thought they would easily destroy us.
They saw us as weak people who were trying to hide.
So you wounded Pharaoh's head with his own spear.
[15] Your horses charged into the Red Sea.
They stirred up the great waters.
[16] I listened and my heart pounded.
My lips trembled at the sound.
My bones seemed to rot.
And my legs shook.
But I will be patient.
I'll wait for the day of trouble to come on Babylonia.
It's the nation that is attacking us.
[17] The fig trees might not bud.
The vines might not produce any grapes.
The olive crop might fail.
The fields might not produce any food.
There might not be any sheep in the pens.
There might not be any cattle in the barns.
[18] But I will still be glad
because of what the LORD has done.
God my Savior fills me with joy.

[19] The LORD and King gives me strength.
He makes my feet like the feet of a deer.
He helps me walk on the highest places.

This prayer is for the director of music. It should be sung while being accompanied by stringed instruments.

Zephaniah

1 A message came to Zephaniah from the LORD. He was the son of Cushi. Cushi was the son of Gedaliah. Gedaliah was the son of Amariah. Amariah was the son of King Hezekiah. The LORD spoke to Zephaniah during the rule of Josiah. He was king of Judah and the son of Amon.

The LORD Will Judge the World

2 "I will sweep away everything
from the face of the earth,"
announces the LORD.
3 "I will destroy people and animals alike.
I will wipe out the birds of the air
and the fish in the waters.
I will destroy sinful people along with
their gods.
I will wipe man off the face of the earth,"
announces the LORD.

The LORD Warns Judah

4 "I will reach out my powerful hand
against Judah.
I will punish all those who live
in Jerusalem.
I will cut off from that place
what is left of Baal worship.
The officials and priests who serve
other gods
will be removed.
5 I will wipe out those who bow down on
their roofs
to worship all of the stars.
I will destroy those who take oaths
not only in my name but also in the name
of Molech.
6 I will cut off those who stop following me.
They no longer look to me or ask me
for advice.
7 Be silent in front of me.
I am the LORD and King.
The day of the LORD is near.
I have prepared a sacrifice.
I have set apart for myself
the people I invited.
8 When my sacrifice is ready to be offered,
I will punish the princes and the king's sons.
I will also judge all those who follow
the practices of other nations.
9 At that time I will punish
all those who worship other gods.
They fill the temples of their gods
with lies and other harmful things.

10 "At that time people at the Fish Gate in
Jerusalem
will cry out," announces the LORD.
"So will those at the New Quarter.
The buildings on the hills will come
crashing down
with a loud noise.
11 Cry out, you who live in the market places.
All of your merchants will be wiped out.
Those who trade in silver will be destroyed.
12 At that time I will search Jerusalem
with lamps.
I will punish those who are so contented.
They are like wine that has not been
shaken up.
They think, 'The LORD won't do anything.
It doesn't matter whether it's good or bad.'
13 Their wealth will be stolen.
Their houses will be destroyed.
They will build houses.
But they will not live in them.
They will plant vineyards.
But they will not drink the wine they
produce.

The Day of the LORD Is Coming

14 "The great day of the LORD is near.
In fact, it is coming quickly.
Listen! The cries on that day will be bitter.
Even soldiers will cry out in fear.
15 At that time I will pour out my anger.
There will be great suffering and pain.
It will be a day of horrible trouble.
It will be a time of darkness and gloom.
It will be filled with the blackest clouds.
16 Trumpet blasts and battle cries will be heard.
Soldiers will attack cities
that have forts and corner towers.
17 I will bring trouble on the people.
They will trip and fall as if they were blind.
They have sinned against me.
Their blood will be poured out like dust.
Their bodies will lie rotting on the
ground.
18 Their silver and gold
will not be able to save them
on the day I pour out my anger.
The whole world will be burned up
when my jealous anger blazes out.
Everyone who lives on earth
will come to a sudden end."

2 Gather your people together,
you shameful nation of Judah!
Gather them together!
2 Come together before the appointed time
arrives.
The day of the LORD will sweep in
like straw blown by the wind.

Soon the LORD's anger will burn against you.
The day of his anger will come on you.
3 So look to him, all of you people in the land
who worship him faithfully.
You always do what he commands
you to do.
Continue to do what is right.
Don't be proud.
Then perhaps the LORD will keep you safe
on the day he pours out his anger on
the world.

A Message About Philistia

4 Gaza will be deserted.
Ashkelon will be destroyed.
Ashdod will be emptied out at noon.
Ekron will be pulled up by its roots.
5 How terrible it will be for you Kerethites
who live by the Mediterranean Sea!
Philistia, the LORD has spoken against you.
What happened to Canaan will happen
to you.

The LORD says, "I will destroy you.
No one will be left."

6 The Kerethites live in the land by the sea.
It will become a place for shepherds and
sheep pens.
7 It will belong to those who are still left alive
among the people of Judah.
They will find grasslands there.
They will take over
the houses in Ashkelon and live in them.
The LORD their God will take care of them.
He will bless them with great success again.

A Message About Moab and Ammon

8 The LORD says,

"I have heard Moab make fun of my people.
The Ammonites also laughed at them.
They told them that bad things
would happen to their land.
9 So Moab will become like Sodom,"
announces the LORD who rules over all.
"Ammon will be like Gomorrah.
Weeds and salt pits will cover those countries.
They will be dry and empty deserts forever.
Those who are still left alive among my people
will take all of their valuable things.
So they will receive those lands as
their own.
And that is just as sure as I am alive."
The LORD is the God of Israel.

10 Moab and Ammon will be judged
because they are so proud.
They made fun of the LORD's people.
They laughed at them.
11 The LORD who rules over all will terrify
Moab and Ammon.
He will destroy all of the gods on earth.
Then the nations on every shore will
worship him.
All of them will serve him in their
own lands.

A Message About Cush

12 The LORD says, "People of Cush,
you too will be killed with my sword."

A Message About Assyria

13 The LORD will reach out his powerful hand
against the north.
He will destroy Assyria.
He'll leave Nineveh totally empty.
It will be as dry as a desert.
14 Flocks and herds will lie down there.
So will creatures of every kind.
Desert owls and screech owls
will rest on its pillars.
Their cries will echo through the windows.
The doorways will be full of trash.
The cedar beams will be showing.
15 Nineveh is a carefree city.
It lived in safety.
It said to itself,
"I am like a god.
No one is greater than I am."
But it has been destroyed.
Wild animals make their home there.
All those who pass by laugh
and shake their fists at it.

The LORD Will Save Jerusalem

3 How terrible it will be for Jerusalem!
Its people crush others.
They refuse to obey the LORD.
They are "unclean."
2 They don't obey anyone.
They don't accept the LORD's warnings.
They don't trust in him.
They don't ask their God for his help.
3 Their officials are like roaring lions.
Their rulers are like wolves that hunt
in the evening.
They don't leave anything to eat in
the morning.
4 Their prophets are proud.
They can't be trusted.
Their priests pollute the temple.
They break the law they teach others
to obey.
5 In spite of that, the LORD is good to Jerusalem.
He never does anything that is wrong.
Every morning he does what is fair.
Each new day he does the right thing.
But those who do what is wrong
aren't even ashamed of it.

6 The LORD says to his people,

"I have cut off other nations.
I have wiped out their forts.

I have left their streets deserted.
No one walks along them.
Their cities are destroyed.
Not even one person is left.
7 I said to you people of Jerusalem,
'Because I cut off other nations,
you will have respect for me.
Now you will accept my warning.'
I wish you had returned to me.
Then your homes would not have been torn down.
And I would not have had to punish you so much.
But you still wanted to go on sinning
in every way you could.
8 So wait for me to come as judge,"
announces the LORD.
"Wait for the day I will stand up
to witness against all sinners.
I have decided to gather the nations.
I will bring the kingdoms together.
And I will pour out all of my burning anger on them.
The fire of my jealous anger
will burn the whole world up.

9 "But then I will purify what all of the nations say.
And they will use their words to worship me.
They will serve me together.
10 My scattered people, you will come to me
from beyond the rivers of Cush.
You will worship me.
You will bring me offerings.
11 You have done many wrong things to me.
But at that time you will not be put to shame anymore.
Then I will remove from this city
those who take delight in their pride.
You will never be proud again
on my holy mountain of Zion.
12 But inside your city I will leave
those who are not proud at all.
They trust in me.
13 Those who are still left alive in Israel
will not do anything wrong.
They will not tell any lies.
They will not say anything to fool others.
They will eat and lie down in peace.
And no one will make them afraid."

14 People of Zion, sing!
Israel, shout loudly!
People of Jerusalem, be glad!
Let your hearts be full of joy.
15 The LORD has stopped punishing you.
He has made your enemies turn away from you.
The LORD is the King of Israel.
He is with you.
You will never again be afraid
that others will harm you.
16 The time is coming when people will say to Jerusalem,
"Zion, don't be afraid.
Don't give up.
17 The LORD your God is with you.
He is mighty enough to save you.
He will take great delight in you.
The quietness of his love will calm you down.
He will sing with joy because of you."

18 The LORD says to his people,

"You used to celebrate my appointed feasts in Jerusalem.
You are sad because you can't do that anymore.
So others make fun of those feasts.
That was a heavy load for you to carry.
But I will bring you back to your city.
19 At that time I will punish
all those who crushed you.
I will save those among you who are disabled.
I will gather those who have been scattered.
I will give you praise and honor
in every land where you were put to shame.
20 At that time I will gather you together.
And I will bring you home.
I will give you honor and praise
among all of the nations on earth.
I will bless you with great success again,"
says the LORD.

Haggai

Haggai Tells His People to Rebuild the LORD's Temple

1 A message came to the prophet Haggai from the LORD. Haggai gave it to Zerubbabel and Jeshua. It came on the first day of the sixth month of the second year that Darius was king of Persia. Zerubbabel was governor of Judah and the son of Shealtiel. Jeshua was high priest and the son of Jehozadak. Here is what Haggai said.

2The LORD who rules over all says, "The people of Judah are saying, 'The time hasn't come yet for the LORD's temple to be rebuilt.' "

3So the message came to me from the LORD. He said, 4"My temple is still destroyed. In spite of that, you are living in your houses that have beautiful wooden walls."

5The LORD who rules over all says, "Think carefully about how you are living. 6You have planted many seeds. But the crops you have gathered are small. So you eat. But you never have enough. You drink. But you are never full. You put your clothes on. But you are not warm. You earn your pay. But it will not buy everything you need."

7He continues, "Think carefully about how you are living. 8Go up into the mountains. Bring logs down. Use them to rebuild my house. Then I will enjoy it. And you will honor me," says the LORD.

9"You expected a lot. But you can see what a small amount it turned out to be," announces the LORD who rules over all. "I blew away what you brought home. Why? Because my temple is still destroyed. In spite of that, each one of you is busy with your own house.

10"So because of what you have done, the heavens have held back the dew. And the earth has not produced its crops. 11I ordered the rain not to fall on the fields and mountains. Then the ground did not produce any grain. There were not enough grapes to make fresh wine. The trees did not bear enough olives to make oil. People and cattle suffered. All of your hard work failed."

12Then Zerubbabel, the son of Shealtiel, and the high priest Jeshua, the son of Jehozadak, obeyed the LORD their God. So did all of the LORD's people who were still left alive. He had given his message to them through me. He had sent me to speak to them. And the people had respect for him.

13I was the LORD's messenger. So I gave his message to the people. I told them, "The LORD announces, 'I am with you.' "

14So the LORD stirred up the spirits of Zerubbabel, the governor of Judah, and the high priest Jeshua. He also stirred up the rest of the people to help them. Then everyone began to work on the temple of the LORD who rules over all. He is their God. 15It was the 24th day of the sixth month of the second year that Darius was king.

The New Temple Will Be Beautiful

2 A second message came to me from the LORD. It came on the 21st day of the seventh month. The LORD said, 2"Speak to Zerubbabel, the governor of Judah and the son of Shealtiel. Also speak to the high priest Jeshua, the son of Jehozadak. And speak to all of my people who are still left alive. Ask them, 3'Did any of you who are here see how beautiful this temple used to be? How does it look to you now? It doesn't look so good, does it?

4" 'But be strong, Zerubbabel,' announces the LORD. 'Be strong, Jeshua. Be strong, all of you people in the land,' announces the LORD. 'Start rebuilding. I am with you,' announces the LORD who rules over all. 5'That is what I promised you when you came out of Egypt. My Spirit continues to be with you. So do not be afraid.' "

6The LORD says, "In a little while I will shake the heavens and the earth once more. I will also shake the ocean and the dry land. 7I will shake all of the nations. Then what they consider to be priceless will come to my temple. And I will fill the temple with glory," says the LORD who rules over all.

8"The silver belongs to me. So does the gold," announces the LORD. 9"The new temple will be more beautiful than the first one was," says the LORD. "And in this place I will give peace to my people," announces the LORD who rules over all.

The LORD Will Make His People Pure and Clean

10A third message came to me from the LORD. It came on the 24th day of the ninth month of the second year that Darius was king. 11The LORD who rules over all speaks. He says, "Ask the priests what the law says. 12Suppose someone carries holy meat in the clothes he is wearing. And the clothes touch some bread or stew. Or they touch some wine, olive oil or other food. Then do those things also become holy?"

The priests answered, "No."

13So I said, "Suppose someone is made 'unclean' by touching a dead body. And then he touches one of those things. Does it become 'unclean' too?"

"Yes," the priests replied. "It does."

14Then I said, "The LORD announces, 'That is how I look at these people and this nation. Anything they do and anything they sacrifice on the altar is "unclean."

15" 'Now think carefully about the time before

one stone was laid on top of another in my temple.
[16]People went to get 20 measures of grain. But they could find only 10. They went to where the wine was stored to get 50 measures. But only 20 were there.
[17]You worked very hard to produce all of those things. But I struck them with rot, mold and hail. And you still did not turn to me,' announces the LORD.

[18]"'It is the 24th day of the ninth month. From this day on, think carefully about the day when the foundation of my temple was laid. Think about it carefully.
[19]Are any seeds still left in your barns? Until now, your vines and fig trees have not produced any fruit. Your pomegranate and olive trees have not produced any either.

"'But from this day on I will bless you.'"

The LORD Compares Zerubbabel to His Royal Ring

[20]A final message came to me from the LORD. It also came on the 24th day of the ninth month. He said,
[21]"Speak to Zerubbabel, the governor of Judah. Tell him I will shake the heavens and the earth.
[22]I will throw down royal thrones. I will smash the power of other kingdoms. I will destroy chariots and their drivers. Horses and their riders will fall. They will be killed with the swords of their relatives.

[23]"'Zerubbabel, at that time I will pick you,' announces the LORD. 'You are my servant,' announces the LORD. 'You will be like a ring that has my royal seal on it. I have chosen you,' announces the LORD who rules over all."

Zechariah

The LORD Wants His People to Return to Him

1 A message came to the prophet Zechariah from the LORD. It was the eighth month of the second year that Darius was king of Persia. Zechariah was the son of Berekiah. Berekiah was the son of Iddo. Here is what Zechariah said.

2The LORD who rules over all was very angry with our people years ago. 3And now he says to us, "Return to me. Then I will return to you," announces the LORD. 4"Do not be like your people years ago. The earlier prophets gave them my message. I said, 'Stop doing what is evil. Turn away from your sinful practices.' But they would not listen to me. They would not pay any attention," announces the LORD.

5"Where are those people now? And what about my prophets? Do they live forever? 6I commanded my servants the prophets what to say. I told them what I planned to do. But your people refused to obey me. So I had to punish them.

"Then they had a change of heart. They said, 'The LORD who rules over all has punished us because of how we have lived. He was fair and right to do that. He has done to us just what he decided to do.'"

A Vision of a Horseman Among Some Myrtle Trees

7During the second year that Darius was king, a message came to me from the LORD. It was the 24th day of the 11th month. That's the month of Shebat.

8I had a vision at night. I saw a man riding a red horse. He was standing among the myrtle trees in a valley. Behind him were red, brown and white horses.

9An angel was talking with me. I asked him, "Sir, what are these?"

He answered, "I will show you what they are."

10Then the man who was standing among the myrtle trees said, "They are the messengers the LORD has sent out. He told them to go all through the earth."

11They brought a report to the angel of the LORD. He was standing among the myrtle trees. They said to him, "We have gone all through the earth. We've found the whole world enjoying peace and rest."

12Then the angel of the LORD spoke up. He said, "LORD, you rule over all. How long will you keep from showing your tender love to Jerusalem? How long will you keep it from the towns of Judah? You have been angry with them for 70 years."

13So the LORD replied with kind and comforting words. He spoke them to the angel who talked with me.

14Then the angel said, "Announce this message. Say, 'The LORD who rules over all says, "I am very jealous for my people in Jerusalem and Zion. 15But I am very angry with the nations that feel secure. I was only a little angry with my people. But the nations went too far and tried to wipe them out."

16"'So the LORD says, "I will return to Jerusalem. I will show its people my tender love. My temple will be rebuilt there. Workers will use a measuring line when they rebuild Jerusalem," announces the LORD.

17"'He says, "My towns will be filled with good things once more. I will comfort Zion. And I will choose Jerusalem again."'"

A Vision of Four Horns and Four Skilled Workers

18Then I looked up and saw four animal horns. 19I spoke to the angel who was talking with me. "What are these horns?" I asked.

He said, "They are the powerful nations that scattered Judah, Israel and Jerusalem."

20Then the LORD showed me four skilled workers. 21I asked, "What are they coming to do?"

He answered, "They are the powerful nations that scattered the people of Judah. That made them helpless. But the workers have come to terrify the horns. They will destroy the power of those nations. They had used their power to scatter Judah's people."

A Vision of a Man Holding a Measuring Line

2 Then I looked up and saw a man. He was holding a measuring line. 2"Where are you going?" I asked.

"To measure Jerusalem," he answered. "I want to find out how wide and how long it is."

3Then the angel who was talking with me left. Another angel came over to him. 4He said to him, "Run! Tell that young man Zechariah, 'Jerusalem will be like a city that does not have any walls around it. It will have huge numbers of people and animals in it. 5And I myself will be like a wall of fire around it,' announces the LORD. 'I will be the city's glory.'"

6"Israel, I have scattered you in all four directions," announces the LORD. "Come quickly! Run away from the land of the north," announces the LORD.

7"Come, people of Zion who are in Babylonia! Escape, you who live in the city of Babylon!" 8The LORD rules over all. His angel says to Israel, "The LORD has sent me to honor him. He wants me to punish the nations that have robbed you of everything. After all, anyone who hurts you hurts those the LORD loves and guards. 9So I will raise my powerful hand to strike your enemies down. Their own slaves will rob them of everything. Then you will know that the LORD who rules over all has sent me.

10"'People of Zion, shout and be glad! I am coming to live among you,' announces the LORD. 11'At that time many nations will join themselves to me. And they will become my people. I will live among you.' says the LORD. Then you will know that the LORD who rules over all has sent me to you.

12"He will receive Judah as his share in the holy land. And he will choose Jerusalem again.

13"All you people of the world, be still because the LORD is coming. He is getting ready to come down from his holy temple in heaven."

A Vision of the High Priest Dressed in Fine Clothes

3 Then the LORD showed me the high priest Jeshua. He was standing in front of the angel of the LORD. Satan was standing to the right of Jeshua. He was there to bring charges against the high priest. 2The LORD said to Satan, "May the LORD correct you! He has chosen Jerusalem. So may he correct you! Isn't this man Jeshua like a burning stick pulled out of the fire?"

3Jeshua stood in front of the angel. He was wearing clothes that were very dirty. 4The angel spoke to those who were standing near him. He said, "Take his dirty clothes off."

He said to Jeshua, "I have taken your sin away. I will put fine clothes on you."

5I added, "Put a clean turban on his head." So they did. And they dressed him while the angel of the LORD stood by.

6Then the angel spoke to Jeshua. He said, 7"The LORD who rules over all says, 'You must live the way I want you to. And you must do what I want you to do. Then you will rule in my temple. You will be in charge of my courtyards. And I will give you a place among these who are standing here.

8"'High priest Jeshua, pay attention! I want you other priests who are sitting with Jeshua to listen also. All of you men are signs of things to come. I am going to bring my servant the Branch. 9Look at the stone I have put in front of Jeshua! There are seven eyes on that one stone. I will carve a message on it,' says the LORD who rules over all. 'And I will remove the sin of this land in one day.

10"'At that time each of you will invite your neighbors to visit you. They will sit under your vines and fig trees,' announces the LORD."

A Vision of the Gold Lampstand and Two Olive Trees

4 Then the angel who was talking with me returned. He woke me up. It was as if I had been asleep. 2"What do you see?" he asked me.

"I see a solid gold lampstand," I answered. "It has a bowl on top of it. There are seven lamps on it. Seven tubes lead to each of them. 3There are two olive trees by the lampstand. One is on its right side. The other is on its left."

4I asked the angel who was talking with me, "Sir, what are these?"

5He answered, "Don't you know what they are?"

"No, sir," I replied.

6So he said to me, "A message came to Zerubbabel from the LORD. He said, 'Your strength will not get my temple rebuilt. Your power will not do it either. Only the power of my Spirit will do it,' says the LORD who rules over all.

7"So nothing can stop Zerubbabel from completing the temple. Even a mountain of problems will be smoothed out by him. When the temple is finished, he will put its most important stone in place. Then the people will shout, 'God bless it! God bless it!'"

8A message came to me from the LORD. His angel said, 9"The hands of Zerubbabel have laid the foundation of this temple. His hands will also complete it. Then you will know that the LORD who rules over all has sent me to you.

10"Do not look down on the small amount of work done on the temple so far. People will be filled with joy when they see Zerubbabel holding the most important stone.

"The seven eyes on the stone are the eyes of the LORD himself. He looks out over the whole earth."

11Then I said to the angel, "I see two olive trees. One is on the right side of the lampstand. The other is on the left. What are those trees?"

12I continued, "I also see two olive branches. They are next to the two gold pipes that pour out golden olive oil. What are those branches?"

13He answered, "Don't you know what they are?"

"No, sir," I said.

14So he told me, "They are Zerubbabel and Jeshua. The Lord of the whole earth has anointed them to serve him."

A Vision of a Flying Scroll

5 I looked up again and saw a flying scroll. 2"What do you see?" the angel asked me.

"A flying scroll," I replied. "It's 30 feet long and 15 feet wide."

3He said to me, "A curse sent by the LORD is written on it. It is going out over the whole land. Every thief will be driven out of the land. That is what it says on one side of the scroll. Everyone who lies when taking an oath to tell the truth will also be driven out. That is what it says on the other side. 4The LORD who rules over all announces, 'I will send the curse out. It will enter the house of the thief. It will also enter the house of anyone who lies when taking an oath in my name. It will remain in that house and destroy it. It will pull down its beams and stones.'"

A Vision of a Woman in a Basket

5Then the angel who was talking with me came forward. He said to me, "Look at what is coming."

6"What is it?" I asked.

"A measuring basket," he replied. "The sins of the people all through the land are in it."

7 Then the basket's cover was lifted up. It was made out of lead. A woman was sitting in the basket! 8 The angel said, "She stands for everything that is evil." Then he pushed her down into the basket. He put the lead cover back over its opening.

9 I looked up and saw two other women. They had wings like the wings of a stork. A wind sent by the LORD carried them along. They lifted the basket up between heaven and earth.

10 "Where are they taking the basket?" I asked the angel.

11 He replied, "To the country of Babylonia. A temple will be built for it. When the temple is ready, the basket will be set there in its place."

A Vision of Four Chariots

6 I looked up again and saw four chariots. They were coming out from between two mountains. The mountains were made out of bronze.

2 The first chariot was pulled by red horses. The second one had black horses. 3 The third had white horses. And the fourth had spotted horses. All of the horses were powerful.

4 I asked the angel who was talking with me, "Sir, what are these?"

5 The angel answered, "The four spirits of heaven. They are going out to serve the Lord of the whole world. 6 The chariot pulled by the black horses is going toward the north country. The one with the white horses is going toward the west. And the one with the spotted horses is going toward the south."

7 The powerful horses went out. They were in a hurry to go all over the earth. The angel said, "Go all through the earth!" So they did.

8 Then the LORD called out to me, "Look! The horses going toward the north have given my Spirit rest in the north country."

A Crown Is Given to Jeshua

9 A message came to me from the LORD. His angel said, 10 "Get some silver and gold from Heldai, Tobijah and Jedaiah. They have just come back from Babylonia. On that same day go to Josiah's house. He is the son of Zephaniah. 11 Use the silver and gold to make a crown. Set it on the head of the high priest Jeshua. He is the son of Jehozadak.

12 "Give Jeshua a message from the LORD who rules over all. He says, 'Here is the man whose name is The Branch. He will branch out and build my temple. 13 That is what he will do. He will be dressed in majesty as if it were his royal robe. He will sit as king on his throne. He will also be a priest there. So he will combine the positions of king and priest in himself.'

14 "The crown will be given to Heldai, Tobijah, Jedaiah and Zephaniah's son Hen. The crown will be kept in the LORD's temple. It will remind everyone that the LORD's promises will come true.

15 "Those who are far away will come to Jerusalem. They will help build the LORD's temple. Then his people will know that the LORD who rules over all has sent me to them. It will happen if they are careful to obey the LORD their God."

Treat Everyone Fairly

7 During the fourth year that Darius was king, a message came to me from the LORD. It was the fourth day of the ninth month. That's the month of Kislev.

2 The people of Bethel wanted to ask the LORD to show them his favor. So they sent Sharezer and Regem-Melech and their men. 3 They went to the prophets and priests at the LORD's temple. They asked them, "Should we sob and go without eating in the fifth month? That's what we've done for many years."

4 Then the message came to me from the LORD who rules over all. He said, 5 "Ask the priests and all of the people in the land a question for me. Say to them, 'You sobbed and fasted in the fifth and seventh months. You did it for the past 70 years. But did you really do it for me? 6 And when you were eating and drinking, weren't you just enjoying good food for yourselves?

7 "'Didn't I tell you the same thing through the earlier prophets? That was when Jerusalem and the towns around it were at rest and enjoyed success. People lived in the Negev Desert and the western hills at that time.'"

8 Another message came to me from the LORD. 9 He rules over all. He says to his people, "Treat everyone fairly. Show faithful love and tender concern to one another. 10 Do not take advantage of widows. Do not mistreat children whose fathers have died. Do not crush strangers or poor people. Do not make evil plans against one another."

11 But they refused to pay attention to the LORD. They were stubborn. They turned their backs and covered up their ears. 12 They made their hearts as hard as the hardest stone. They wouldn't listen to the law. They wouldn't pay attention to the LORD's messages.

So the LORD who rules over all was very angry. After all, his Spirit had spoken to his people through the earlier prophets.

13 "When I called, they did not listen," says the LORD. "So when they called, I would not listen. 14 I used a windstorm to scatter them among all of the nations. They were strangers there. The land they left behind became dry and empty. No one could even travel through it. That is how they turned the pleasant land into a dry and empty desert."

The LORD Promises to Bless Jerusalem

8 Another message came to me from the LORD who rules over all. He said, 2 "I am very jealous for my people in Zion. In fact, I am burning with jealousy for them."

3 He continued, "I will return to Zion. I will live among my people in Jerusalem. Then Jerusalem

will be called The City of Truth. And my mountain will be called The Holy Mountain."
4He continued, "Once again old men and
women will sit in the streets of Jerusalem. All of
them will be using canes because they are old.
5The city streets will be filled with boys and girls.
They will be playing there."
6He continued, "All of that might seem wonderful to the people who are living at that time. But
it will not seem wonderful to me."
7He continued, "I will save my people. I will
gather them from the countries of the east and the
west. 8I will bring them back to live in Jerusalem.
They will be my people. I will be their faithful
God. I will keep my promises to them."
9The LORD who rules over all says to his people, "Listen to the words that were spoken by the
prophets Haggai and Zechariah. They spoke to you
when the work on my temple started up again. Let
your hands be strong so that you can rebuild the
temple.
10"Before the work was started again, there was
no pay for the people or food for the animals. People could not go about their business safely
because of their enemies. I had turned all of them
against one another. 11But now I will not punish
you who are living at this time. I will not treat you
as I treated your people before you," announces
the LORD who rules over all.
12"Your seeds will grow well. Your vines will
bear fruit. The ground will produce crops for you.
And the heavens will drop their dew on your land.
I will give all of those things to those who are still
left alive here.
13"Judah and Israel, in the past the nations called
down curses on you. But now I will save you. You
will be a blessing to others. Do not be afraid. Let
your hands be strong so that you can do my work."
14The LORD who rules over all says, "Years ago
your people made me angry. So I decided to bring
trouble on them. I did not show them any pity.
15But now I plan to do good things to Jerusalem
and Judah again. So do not be afraid.
16"Here is what you must do. Speak the truth to
one another. Make true and wise decisions in your
courts. 17Do not make evil plans against your
neighbors. When you take an oath to tell the truth,
do not lie. Many people love to do that. But I hate
all of those things," announces the LORD.
18Another message came to me from the LORD
who rules over all. He said, 19"You have established
special times to go without eating. They are your
fasts in the fourth, fifth, seventh and tenth months.
They will become days of joy. They will be happy
times for Judah. It will happen if you take delight
in telling the truth and bringing about peace."
20He continued, "Many nations will still come
to you. And those who live in many cities will also
come. 21The people who live in one city will go to
another city. They will say, 'Let's go right away to
ask the LORD to show us his favor. Let's look to
him as our God. We ourselves are going.' 22Large
numbers of people and nations will come to Jerusalem. They will look to me. They will ask me to
show them my favor."
23He continued, "At that time many men from
all nations and languages will take hold of one
Jew. They will grab hold of the hem of his robe.
And they will say, 'We want to go to Jerusalem
with you. We've heard that God is with you.'"

The LORD Destroys Israel's Enemies

9 This is the LORD's message
against the land of Hadrach.
He will judge Damascus.
That's because all of the tribes of Israel look
to him.
So do other people.
2 The LORD will judge Hamath too.
It's next to Damascus.
He will also punish Tyre and Sidon
even though they are very clever.
3 Tyre's people have built a fort for themselves.
They've piled up silver like dust.
They have as much gold as the dirt in
the streets.
4 But the Lord will take away everything
they have.
He'll destroy their power on the
Mediterranean Sea.
And Tyre will be completely burned up.
5 Ashkelon will see it and become afraid.
Gaza will groan with pain.
So will Ekron. Its hope will vanish.
Gaza will no longer have a king.
Ashkelon will be deserted.
6 Strangers will take over Ashdod.
The LORD says, "I will take away everything
the Philistines are so proud of.
7 They will no longer drink the blood of their
animal sacrifices.
I will remove the 'unclean' food from
between their teeth.
The Philistines who are left will belong to
our God.
They will become leaders in Judah.
And Ekron will be like the Jebusites.
So the Philistines will become part of Israel.
8 But I will guard my temple
against enemy armies.
No one will ever crush my people again.
I will make sure it does not happen.

A King Comes to Zion

9 "City of Zion, be full of joy!
People of Jerusalem, shout!
See, your king comes to you.
He always does what is right.
He has the power to save.
He is gentle and riding on a donkey.
He is sitting on a donkey's colt.
10 I will take the chariots away from Ephraim.

I will remove the war horses from
Jerusalem.
I will break the bows that are used in battle.
Your king will announce peace to the nations.
He will rule from ocean to ocean.
His kingdom will reach from the Euphrates
River
to the ends of the earth.
11 I will set your prisoners free
from where their enemies are keeping them.
I will do it because of the blood
that put my covenant with you into effect.
12 Return to your place of safety,
you prisoners who still have hope.
Even now I announce that I will give you back
much more than you had before.
13 I will bend Judah as I bend my bow.
I will make Ephraim's people my arrows.
Zion, I will stir up your sons.
Greece, they will attack your sons.
My people, I will use you as my sword."

The LORD Will Appear

14 Then the LORD will appear over his people.
His arrows will flash like lightning.
The LORD and King will blow the trumpet of
his thunder.
He'll march out like a storm in the south.
15 The LORD who rules over all
will be like a shield to his people.
They will destroy their enemies.
They'll use slings to throw stones at them.
They'll drink the blood of their enemies
as if it were wine.
They'll be full like the bowl that is used
for sprinkling the corners of the altar.
16 The LORD their God will save his people
on that day.
They will be like sheep that belong to
his flock.
They will gleam in his land
like jewels in a crown.
17 How very beautiful they will be!
Grain and fresh wine
will make the young men and women
strong.

The LORD Will Take Care of Judah

10 People of Judah, ask the LORD
to send rain in the spring.
He is the one who makes the storm clouds.
He sends down showers of rain on all people.
He gives everyone the plants in the fields.
2 Other gods tell lies.
Those who practice magic
see visions that aren't true.
They tell dreams that fool people.
They give comfort that doesn't do any good.
So the people wander around like sheep.
They are crushed because they don't have a
shepherd.

3 The LORD who rules over all says,
"My anger burns against the shepherds.
I will punish the leaders.
I will take care of my flock.
They are the people of Judah.
I will make them like a proud horse
in battle.
4 The most important building stone
will come from the tribe of Judah.
The tent stake will also come from it.
And the bow that is used in battle will
come from it.
In fact, every ruler will come from it.
5 Together they will be like soldiers in battle.
They will fight their way
through the muddy streets.
I will be with them.
So they will fight against the horsemen
and destroy them.

6 "I will make the family of Judah strong.
I will save the people of Joseph.
I will bring them back
because I have tender love for them.
It will be as if
I had not sent them away.
I am the LORD their God.
I will help them.
7 The people of Ephraim will become like
mighty men.
Their hearts will be glad
as if they were drinking wine.
Their children will see it
and be filled with joy.
I will make their hearts glad.
8 I will whistle for my people
and gather them in.
I will set them free.
There will be as many of them as before.
9 I have scattered them among the nations.
But in lands far away they will remember me.
They and their children will be kept alive.
And they will return.
10 I will bring them back from Egypt.
I will gather them from Assyria.
I will bring them to Gilead and Lebanon.
There will not be enough room for them.
11 They will pass through a sea of trouble.
The stormy sea will calm down.
All of the deep places in the Nile River
will dry up.
Assyria's pride will be brought down.
Egypt's right to rule will disappear.
12 I will make my people strong.
They will worship and obey me,"
announces the LORD.

11 Lebanon, open your doors!
Then fire can burn up your cedar trees.
2 Pine trees, cry out!
The cedar trees have fallen down.
The majestic trees are destroyed.

Cry out, you oak trees of Bashan!
The thick forest has been cut down.
3 Listen to the shepherds cry out!
Their rich grasslands are destroyed.
Listen to the lions roar!
The trees and bushes along the Jordan River
are gone.

The Two Shepherds

4The LORD my God says, "Take care of the sheep that are set apart to be sacrificed. 5Those who buy them kill them. And they are not punished for it. Those who sell them say, 'Praise the LORD! We're rich!' And their own shepherds do not spare them.

6"I will no longer have pity on the people in the land," announces the LORD. "I will hand all of them over to their neighbors and their king. They will crush the people in the land. And I will not save them from their powerful hands."

7So I took care of the sheep set apart to be sacrificed. I took special care of those that had been crushed. Then I got two shepherd's staffs. I called one of them Favor. I called the other one Union. And I took care of the flock. 8In one month I got rid of three worthless shepherds.

The sheep hated me. And I got tired of them. 9So I said, "I won't be your shepherd anymore. Let those of you who are dying die. Let those who are passing away pass away. Let those who are left eat one another up."

10Then I got my staff called Favor. I broke it. That meant the covenant the LORD had made with all of the nations was broken. 11It happened that very day. The sheep that had been crushed were watching me. They knew it was the LORD's message.

12I told them, "If you think it is best, give me my pay. But if you don't think so, you keep it." So they paid me 30 silver coins.

13The LORD said to me, "Throw the coins to the potter." What a good price they had set for me! So I threw the 30 silver coins to the potter in the LORD's temple.

14Then I broke my second staff called Union. That broke the union between Judah and Israel.

15The LORD said to me, "Now pretend to be a foolish shepherd. Get the things you need. 16I am going to raise up a shepherd over the land. He will not take care of those that are wounded. He will not look for the young ones. He will not heal those that are hurt. He will not feed the healthy ones. Instead, he will eat the best sheep. He will even tear their hoofs off.

17 "How terrible it will be for that worthless
shepherd!
He deserts the flock.
May a sword strike his arm and his right eye!
May his powerful arm become weak!
May his right eye be totally blinded!"

The LORD Will Destroy Jerusalem's Enemies

12 This is the LORD's message about Israel. The LORD spread out the heavens. He laid the foundation of the earth. He created the spirits of all men. He says, 2"Jerusalem will be like a cup in my hand. It will make all of the surrounding nations drunk from the wine of my anger. Judah will be attacked by its enemies. So will Jerusalem.

3"At that time all of the nations on earth will gather together against Jerusalem. Then it will become like a rock that can't be moved. All of the nations that try to move it will only hurt themselves. 4On that day I will fill every horse with panic. I will make every rider crazy," announces the LORD. "I will watch over the people of Judah. But I will make all of the horses of the nations blind.

5"Then the leaders of Judah will say in their hearts, 'The people of Jerusalem are strong. That's because the LORD who rules over all is their God.'

6"At that time Judah's leaders will be like a fire pot in a pile of wood. They will be like a burning torch among bundles of grain. They will destroy all of the surrounding nations on every side. But Jerusalem will remain unharmed in its place.

7"I will save the houses in Judah first. The honor of David's family line is great. So is the honor of those who live in Jerusalem. But their honor will not be greater than the honor of the rest of Judah.

8"At that time I will be like a shield to those who live in Jerusalem. Then even the weakest among them will be great warriors like David. And David's family line will be like the Angel of the LORD who leads them. 9On that day I will begin to destroy all of the nations that attack Jerusalem.

Israel's People Will Sob Over the One They Pierced

10"I will pour out a spirit of grace and prayer on David's family line. I will also send it on those who live in Jerusalem. They will look to me. I am the one they have pierced. They will sob over me as someone sobs over an only child who has died. They will be full of sorrow over me, just like someone who is full of sorrow over an oldest son.

11"At that time there will be a lot of crying in Jerusalem. It will sound like the sobs of the people at Hadad Rimmon over Josiah's death in the Valley of Megiddo. 12Everyone in the land will sob. Each family will cry by themselves and their wives by themselves. That will include the family lines of David, Nathan, 13Levi, Shimei and 14all of the others.

The LORD Makes Israel Pure and Clean

13 "At that time a fountain will be opened for the benefit of David's family line. It will also bless the others who live in Jerusalem. It will wash away their sins. It will make them pure and clean.

2“On that day I will remove the names of other
gods from the land. They will not even be remembered anymore,” announces the LORD who rules
over all. “I will drive the evil prophets out of the
land. I will get rid of the spirit that put lies in their
mouths. 3Some people might still prophesy. But
their own fathers and mothers will speak to them.
They will tell them, ‘You must die. You have told
lies in the LORD’s name.’ When they prophesy,
their own parents will stab them.
4“At that time every prophet will be ashamed of
his vision. He will no longer pretend to be a true
prophet. He will not put on clothes that are made
out of hair in order to trick people. 5In fact, he will
say, ‘I’m not really a prophet. I’m a farmer. I’ve
farmed the land since I was young.’ 6Suppose
someone asks him, ‘What are those wounds on
your body?’ Then he will answer, ‘I was given
these wounds at the house of my friends.’

The Good Shepherd Is Killed and the Sheep Are Scattered

7“My sword, wake up! Attack my shepherd!
Attack the man who is close to me,”
announces the LORD who rules over all.
“Strike the shepherd down.
Then the sheep will be scattered.
And I will turn my hand against their
little ones.
8Here is what will happen in the whole land,”
announces the LORD.
“Two-thirds of the people will be struck down
and die.
But one-third will be left.
9I will put that third in the fire.
I will make them as pure as silver.
I will test them like gold.
They will call out to me.
And I will answer them.
I will say, ‘They are my people.’
And they will say, ‘The LORD is our God.’”

The LORD Will Be King Over the Whole Earth

14 The day of the LORD is coming. At that
time Jerusalem’s enemies will steal everything its people have. They will divide it up right
in front of them.
2The LORD will gather all of the nations
together. They will fight against Jerusalem.
They’ll capture the city. Its houses will be robbed.
Its women will be raped. Half of the people will
be taken away as prisoners. But the rest of them
won’t be taken.
3Then the LORD will march out and fight against
those nations. He will go to war against them.
4On that day he will stand on the Mount of
Olives. It’s east of Jerusalem. It will be split in two
from east to west. Half of the mountain will move
north. The other half will move south. A large valley will be formed. 5The people will run away
through that mountain valley. It will reach all the
way to Azel. They’ll run away just as they ran
from the earthquake when Uzziah was king of Judah. Then the LORD my God will come. All of the
holy ones will come with him.
6There won’t be any light on that day. The sun,
moon and stars will not shine. 7It will be a day
unlike any other. It won’t be separated into day and
night. It will be a day known only to the LORD.
After that day is over, there will be light again.
8At that time water that gives life will flow out
from Jerusalem. Half of it will run into the Dead
Sea. The other half will go to the Mediterranean
Sea. The water will flow in summer and winter.
9The LORD will be king over the whole earth.
On that day there will be one LORD. His name will
be the only name.
10The whole land south of Jerusalem will be
changed. From Geba to Rimmon it will become
like the Arabah Valley. But Jerusalem will be
raised up. It will remain in its place. From the Benjamin Gate to the First Gate to the Corner Gate
nothing will be changed. From the Tower of Hananel to the royal winepress the city will remain the
same. 11People will live in it. Jerusalem will never
be destroyed again. It will be secure.
12The LORD will punish all of the nations that
fought against Jerusalem. He’ll strike them with a
plague. It will make their bodies rot while they are
still standing on their feet. Their eyes will rot in
their heads. Their tongues will rot in their mouths.
13On that day the LORD will fill people with great
panic. They will grab one another by the hand.
And they’ll attack each other.
14Judah will also fight at Jerusalem. The wealth
of all of the surrounding nations will be collected.
Huge amounts of gold, silver and clothes will be
gathered up. 15The same kind of plague will strike
the horses, mules, camels and donkeys. In fact, it
will strike all of the animals in the army camps.
16But some people from all of the nations that
have attacked Jerusalem will still be left alive. All
of them will go up there to worship the King. He
is the LORD who rules over all. Year after year they
will celebrate the Feast of Booths.
17Some nations might not go up to Jerusalem to
worship the King. If they don’t, they won’t have
any rain. 18The people of Egypt might not go up
there to take part. Then they won’t have any rain
either. That’s the plague the LORD will send on the
nations that don’t go to celebrate the Feast of
Booths. 19Egypt will be punished. So will all of the
other nations that don’t celebrate the Feast.
20On that day HOLY TO THE LORD will be carved
on the bells of the horses. The cooking pots in the
LORD’s temple will be just like the sacred bowls in
front of the altar for burnt offerings. 21Every pot in
Jerusalem and Judah will be set apart to the LORD.
All those who come to offer sacrifices will get
some of the pots and cook in them. At that time
there won’t be any Canaanites in the LORD’s temple. He is the LORD who rules over all.

Malachi

1 This is the LORD's message to Israel through Malachi.

The LORD Chooses Jacob Instead of Esau

2"Israel, I have loved you," says the LORD.

"But you ask, 'How have you loved us?'

"Wasn't Esau Jacob's brother?" says the LORD. "But I chose Jacob 3instead of Esau. I turned Esau's mountains into a dry and empty land. I left that land of Edom to the wild dogs in the desert."

4Edom might say, "We have been crushed. But we'll rebuild our cities."

The LORD who rules over all says, "They might rebuild their cities. But I will destroy them. They will be called The Evil Land. My anger will always remain on them. 5You will see it with your own eyes. You will say, 'The LORD is great! He rules even beyond the borders of Israel!'

Give Your Best to the LORD

6"A son honors his father. A servant honors his master. If I am a father, where is the honor I should have? If I am a master, where is the respect you should give me?" says the LORD who rules over all. "You priests look down on me.

"But you ask, 'How have we looked down on you?'

7"You put 'unclean' food on my altar.

"But you ask, 'How have we made you "unclean?"'

"You do it by looking down on my altar. 8You sacrifice blind animals to me. Isn't that wrong? You sacrifice disabled or sick animals. Isn't that wrong? Try offering them to your governor! Would he be pleased with you? Would he accept you?" says the LORD who rules over all.

9"Now you dare to ask me to show you my favor! But as long as you give offerings like those, how can I accept you?" says the LORD.

10"You might as well shut the temple doors! Then you would not light useless fires on my altar. I am not pleased with you," says the LORD. "I will not accept any of the offerings you bring.

11"My name will be great among the nations. They will worship me from where the sun rises in the east to where it sets in the west. In every place, incense and pure offerings will be brought to me. That is because my name will be great among the nations," says the LORD.

12"But you treat my name as if it were not holy. You say my altar is 'unclean.' And you look down on its food. 13You say, 'What a heavy load our work is!' And you turn your nose up as if you hate working for me," says the LORD who rules over all.

"You bring animals that have been hurt. Or you bring disabled or sick animals. Then you dare to offer them to me as sacrifices! Should I accept them from you?" says the LORD.

14"Suppose you have a male sheep or goat that does not have any flaws. And you promise to offer it to me. But then you sacrifice an animal that has flaws. When you do that, you cheat me. And anyone who cheats me is under my curse. After all, I am a great king," says the LORD who rules over all. "The other nations have respect for my name. So why don't you respect it?

The LORD Warns the Priests

2 "Now I am giving a warning to you priests. 2Listen to it. Honor me with all your heart," says the LORD who rules over all. "If you do not, I will send a curse on you. I will turn your blessings into curses. In fact, I have already done that because you have not honored me with all your heart.

3"Because of what you have done, I will punish your children. I will smear the guts from your sacrifices on your faces. And you will be carried off to the dump along with them. 4You will know that I have given you a warning. I have warned you so that my covenant with Levi will continue," says the LORD who rules over all.

5"My covenant promised Levi life and peace. So I gave them to him. I required him to respect me. And he had great respect for my name. 6True teaching came from his mouth. Nothing but the truth came from his lips. He walked with me in peace. He did what was right. He turned many people away from their sins.

7"The lips of a priest should guard knowledge. People should look for true teaching from his mouth. After all, he is my messenger. 8But you have turned away from the right path. Your teaching has caused many people to trip and fall. You have broken my covenant with Levi," says the LORD who rules over all. 9"So I have caused all of the people to hate you. They have lost respect for you. You have not done what I told you to do. Instead, you have favored one person over another in matters of the law."

Judah Is Not Faithful to the LORD

10People of Judah, all of us have one Father. One God created us. So why do we break the covenant the LORD made with our people long ago? We don't even keep our promises to one another.

11You have broken your promises. A hateful thing has been done in Israel and Jerusalem. The LORD loves his temple. But you have polluted it. You men have married women who worship other gods.

12 May the LORD punish you who do that. It doesn't matter who you are. May the LORD who rules over all cut you off from the tents of Jacob's people. May he remove you even if you bring offerings to him.

13 Here's something else you do. You flood the LORD's altar with your tears. You sob and cry because he doesn't pay attention to your offerings anymore. He doesn't accept them from your hands with pleasure.

14 You ask, "Why?" It's because the LORD is holding you accountable. He watches how you treat the wife you married when you were young. You have broken your promise to her. You did it even though she's your partner. You promised to stay married to her. And the LORD was a witness to it.

15 Hasn't he made the two of you one? Both of you belong to him in body and spirit. And why has he made you one? Because he was looking for godly children. So guard yourself in your spirit. Don't break your promise to the wife you married when you were young.

16 "I hate divorce," says the LORD God of Israel. "I hate it when people do anything that harms others," says the LORD who rules over all.

So guard yourself in your spirit. And don't break your promises.

The LORD Will Judge His People

17 You have worn the LORD out by what you keep saying.

"How have we worn him out?" you ask.

You have done it by saying, "All those who do evil things are good in the LORD's sight. And he is pleased with them." Or you ask, "Is God really fair?"

3 The LORD who rules over all says, "I will send my messenger. He will prepare my way for me. Then suddenly the Lord you are looking for will come to his temple. The messenger of the covenant will come. He is the one you long for."

2 But who can live through the day when he comes? Who will be left standing when he appears? He will be like a fire that makes things pure. He will be like soap that makes things clean. 3 He will act like one who makes silver pure. And he will purify the Levites, just as gold and silver are purified with fire.

Then the LORD's people will bring proper offerings. 4 And the offerings of Judah and Jerusalem will be acceptable to him. It will be as it was in days and years gone by.

5 "So I will come and judge you. I will be quick to bring charges against all of you," says the LORD who rules over all. "I will bring charges against you sinful people who do not have any respect for me. That includes those who practice evil magic. It includes those who commit adultery and those who tell lies in court. It includes those who cheat workers out of their pay. It includes those who crush widows. It also includes those who mistreat children whose fathers have died. And it includes those who take away the rights of outsiders in the courts.

Do Not Steal From God

6 "I am the LORD. I do not change. That is why I have not destroyed you members of Jacob's family. 7 You have turned away from my rules. You have not obeyed them. You have lived that way ever since the days of your people long ago. Return to me. Then I will return to you," says the LORD who rules over all.

"But you ask, 'How can we return?'

8 "Will a man dare to steal from me? But you rob me!

"You ask, 'How do we rob you?'

"By holding back your offerings. You also steal from me when you do not bring me a tenth of everything you produce. 9 So you are under my curse. In fact, your whole nation is under it. That is because you are robbing me.

10 "Bring the entire tenth to the storerooms in my temple. Then there will be plenty of food. Put me to the test," says the LORD. "Then you will see that I will throw open the windows of heaven. I will pour out so many blessings that you will not have enough room for them. 11 I will keep bugs from eating up your crops. And your grapes will not drop from the vines before they are ripe," says the LORD.

12 "Then all of the nations will call you blessed. Your land will be delightful," says the LORD who rules over all.

13 "You have spoken bad things against me," says the LORD.

"But you ask, 'What have we spoken against you?'

14 "You have said, 'It is useless to serve God. What did we gain by obeying his laws? And what did we get by pretending to be sad in front of the LORD? 15 But now we call proud people blessed. Things go well with those who do what is evil. And God doesn't even punish those who argue with him.'"

16 Those who had respect for the LORD talked with one another. They cheered each other up. And the LORD heard them. A list of people and what they did was written on a scroll in front of him. It included the names of those who respected the LORD and honored him.

17 "They will belong to me," says the LORD who rules over all. "They will be my special treasure. I will spare them just as a loving father spares his son who serves him. 18 Then once again you will see the difference between godly people and sinful people. And you will see the difference between those who serve me and those who do not.

The Day of the LORD Is Coming

4 "You can be sure the day of the LORD is coming. My anger will burn like a furnace. All those who are proud will be like straw. So will all

those who do what is evil. The day that is coming
will set them on fire," says the LORD who rules over
all. "Not even a root or a branch will be left to them.
2"But here is what will happen for you who
have respect for me. The sun that brings life will
rise. Its rays will bring healing to my people. You
will go out and leap like calves that have just been
let out of the barn.
3"Then you will stomp on sinful people. They
will be like ashes under your feet. That will happen
on the day I act," says the LORD.

4"Remember the law my servant Moses gave
you. Remember the rules and laws I gave him at
Mount Horeb. They were for the whole nation of
Israel.
5"I will send you the prophet Elijah. He will
come before the day of the LORD arrives. It will be
a great and terrifying day. 6Elijah will teach parents how to love their children. He will also teach
children how to honor their parents. If that does
not happen, I will come. And I will put a curse on
the land."

New Testament

Matthew

The Family Line of Jesus

1 This is a record of the family line of Jesus
Christ. He is the son of David. He is also the
son of Abraham.

2 Abraham was the father of Isaac.
Isaac was the father of Jacob.
Jacob was the father of Judah and his brothers.
3 Judah was the father of Perez and Zerah. Tamar was their mother.
Perez was the father of Hezron.
Hezron was the father of Ram.
4 Ram was the father of Amminadab.
Amminadab was the father of Nahshon.
Nahshon was the father of Salmon.
5 Salmon was the father of Boaz. Rahab was Boaz's mother.
Boaz was the father of Obed. Ruth was Obed's mother.
Obed was the father of Jesse.
6 And Jesse was the father of King David.

David was the father of Solomon. Solomon's mother had been Uriah's wife.
7 Solomon was the father of Rehoboam.
Rehoboam was the father of Abijah.
Abijah was the father of Asa.
8 Asa was the father of Jehoshaphat.
Jehoshaphat was the father of Jehoram.
Jehoram was the father of Uzziah.
9 Uzziah was the father of Jotham.
Jotham was the father of Ahaz.
Ahaz was the father of Hezekiah.
10 Hezekiah was the father of Manasseh.
Manasseh was the father of Amon.
Amon was the father of Josiah.
11 And Josiah was the father of Jeconiah and his brothers. At that time, the Jewish people were forced to go away to Babylon.

12 After this, the family line continued.
Jeconiah was the father of Shealtiel.
Shealtiel was the father of Zerubbabel.
13 Zerubbabel was the father of Abiud.
Abiud was the father of Eliakim.
Eliakim was the father of Azor.
14 Azor was the father of Zadok.
Zadok was the father of Akim.
Akim was the father of Eliud.
15 Eliud was the father of Eleazar.
Eleazar was the father of Matthan.
Matthan was the father of Jacob.
16 Jacob was the father of Joseph. Joseph was the husband of Mary. And Mary gave birth to Jesus, who is called Christ.

17 So there were 14 generations from Abraham
to David. There were 14 from David until the Jewish people were forced to go away to Babylon.
And there were 14 from that time to the Christ.

Jesus Christ Is Born

18 This is how the birth of Jesus Christ came
about. His mother Mary and Joseph had promised
to get married. But before they started to live
together, it became clear that she was going to
have a baby. She became pregnant by the power
of the Holy Spirit. 19 Her husband Joseph was a
godly man. He did not want to put her to shame in
public. So he planned to divorce her quietly.
20 But as Joseph was thinking about this, an
angel of the Lord appeared to him in a dream. The
angel said, "Joseph, son of David, don't be afraid
to take Mary home as your wife. The baby inside
her is from the Holy Spirit. 21 She is going to have
a son. You must give him the name Jesus. That is
because he will save his people from their sins."
22 All of this took place to bring about what the
Lord had said would happen. He had said through
the prophet, 23 "The virgin is going to have a baby.
She will give birth to a son. And he will be called
Immanuel." *(Isaiah 7:14)* The name Immanuel
means "God with us."
24 Joseph woke up. He did what the angel of the
Lord commanded him to do. He took Mary home
as his wife. 25 But he did not make love to her until
after she gave birth to a son. And Joseph gave him
the name Jesus.

The Wise Men Visit Jesus

2 Jesus was born in Bethlehem in Judea. This
happened while Herod was king of Judea.
After Jesus' birth, Wise Men from the east came
to Jerusalem. 2 They asked, "Where is the child
who has been born to be king of the Jews? When
we were in the east, we saw his star. Now we have
come to worship him."
3 When King Herod heard about it, he was very
upset. Everyone in Jerusalem was troubled too. 4 So
Herod called together all the chief priests of the
people. He also called the teachers of the law. He
asked them where the Christ was going to be born.
5 "In Bethlehem in Judea," they replied. "This is
what the prophet has written. He said,

6 " 'But you, Bethlehem, in the land of Judah,
are certainly not the least important among
the towns of Judah.
A ruler will come out of you.
He will be the shepherd of my people
Israel.' " *(Micah 5:2)*

7 Then Herod called for the Wise Men secretly.
He found out from them exactly when the star had
appeared. 8 He sent them to Bethlehem. He said,

"Go! Make a careful search for the child. As soon as you find him, bring me a report. Then I can go and worship him too."

9 After the Wise Men had listened to the king, they went on their way. The star they had seen when they were in the east went ahead of them. It finally stopped over the place where the child was. 10 When they saw the star, they were filled with joy.

11 The Wise Men went to the house. There they saw the child with his mother Mary. They bowed down and worshiped him. Then they opened their treasures. They gave him gold, incense and myrrh. 12 But God warned them in a dream not to go back to Herod. So they returned to their country on a different road.

Jesus' Family Escapes to Egypt

13 When the Wise Men had left, Joseph had a dream. In the dream an angel of the Lord appeared to him. "Get up!" the angel said. "Take the child and his mother and escape to Egypt. Stay there until I tell you to come back. Herod is going to search for the child. He wants to kill him."

14 Joseph got up. During the night, he left for Egypt with the child and his mother Mary. 15 They stayed there until King Herod died. So the words the Lord had spoken through the prophet came true. He had said, "I chose to bring my son out of Egypt." *(Hosea 11:1)*

16 Herod realized that the Wise Men had tricked him. So he became very angry. He gave orders concerning Bethlehem and the area around it. All the boys two years old and under were to be killed. This agreed with the time when the Wise Men had seen the star.

17 In this way, the words the prophet Jeremiah spoke came true. He had said,

18 "A voice is heard in Ramah.
  It's the sound of crying and deep sadness.
Rachel is crying over her children.
  She refuses to be comforted,
because they are gone." *(Jeremiah 31:15)*

Jesus' Family Returns to Nazareth

19 After Herod died, Joseph had a dream while he was still in Egypt. In the dream an angel of the Lord appeared to him. 20 The angel said, "Get up! Take the child and his mother. Go to the land of Israel. Those who were trying to kill the child are dead."

21 So Joseph got up. He took the child and his mother Mary back to the land of Israel. 22 But then he heard that Archelaus was king of Judea. Archelaus was ruling in place of his father Herod. This made Joseph afraid to go there.

Warned in a dream, Joseph went back to the land of Galilee instead. 23 There he lived in a town called Nazareth. So what the prophets had said about Jesus came true. They had said, "He will be called a Nazarene."

John the Baptist Prepares the Way

3 In those days John the Baptist came and preached in the Desert of Judea. 2 He said, "Turn away from your sins! The kingdom of heaven is near."

3 John is the one the prophet Isaiah had spoken about. He had said,

"A messenger is calling out in the desert,
'Prepare the way for the Lord.
  Make straight paths for him.'" *(Isaiah 40:3)*

4 John's clothes were made out of camel's hair. He had a leather belt around his waist. His food was locusts and wild honey. 5 People went out to him from Jerusalem and all of Judea. They also came from the whole area around the Jordan River. 6 When they admitted they had sinned, John baptized them in the Jordan.

7 John saw many Pharisees and Sadducees coming to where he was baptizing. He said to them, "You are like a nest of poisonous snakes! Who warned you to escape the coming of God's anger? 8 Produce fruit that shows you have turned away from your sins. 9 Don't think you can say to yourselves, 'Abraham is our father.' I tell you, God can raise up children for Abraham even from these stones. 10 The ax is already lying at the roots of the trees. All the trees that don't produce good fruit will be cut down. They will be thrown into the fire.

11 "I baptize you with water, calling you to turn away from your sins. But after me, one will come who is more powerful than I am. And I'm not fit to carry his sandals. He will baptize you with the Holy Spirit and with fire. 12 His pitchfork is in his hand to clear the straw from his threshing floor. He will gather his wheat into the storeroom. But he will burn up the husks with fire that can't be put out."

Jesus Is Baptized

13 Jesus came from Galilee to the Jordan River. He wanted to be baptized by John. 14 But John tried to stop him. He told Jesus, "I need to be baptized by you. So why do you come to me?"

15 Jesus replied, "Let it be this way for now. It is right for us to do this. It carries out God's holy plan." Then John agreed.

16 As soon as Jesus was baptized, he came up out of the water. At that moment heaven was opened. Jesus saw the Spirit of God coming down on him like a dove.

17 A voice from heaven said, "This is my Son, and I love him. I am very pleased with him."

Jesus Is Tempted

4 The Holy Spirit led Jesus into the desert. There the devil tempted him. 2 After 40 days and 40 nights of going without eating, Jesus was hungry.

3 The tempter came to him. He said, "If you are the Son of God, tell these stones to become bread."

4 Jesus answered, "It is written, 'Man doesn't
live only on bread. He also lives on every word that
comes from the mouth of God.'" *(Deuteronomy 8:3)*
5 Then the devil took Jesus to the holy city. He
had him stand on the highest point of the temple.
6 "If you are the Son of God," he said, "throw yourself down. It is written,

"'The Lord will command his angels to take
good care of you.
They will lift you up in their hands.
Then you won't trip over a stone.'"
(Psalm 91:11,12)

7 Jesus answered him, "It is also written, 'Do
not put the Lord your God to the test.'" *(Deuteronomy 6:16)*
8 Finally, the devil took Jesus to a very high
mountain. He showed him all the kingdoms of the
world and their glory. 9 "If you bow down and worship me," he said, "I will give you all of this."
10 Jesus said to him, "Get away from me, Satan!
It is written, 'Worship the Lord your God. He is
the only one you should serve.'" *(Deuteronomy 6:13)*
11 Then the devil left Jesus. Angels came and
took care of him.

Jesus Begins to Preach

12 John had been put in prison. When Jesus heard
about this, he returned to Galilee.
13 Jesus left Nazareth. He went to live in the city
of Capernaum. It was by the lake in the area of
Zebulun and Naphtali. 14 In that way, what the
prophet Isaiah had said came true. He had said,

15 "Land of Zebulun! Land of Naphtali!
Galilee, where non-Jewish people live!
Land along the Mediterranean Sea! Territory
east of the Jordan River!
16 The people who are now living in darkness
will see a great light.
They are now living in a very dark land.
But a light will shine on them." *(Isaiah 9:1,2)*

17 From that time on Jesus began to preach.
"Turn away from your sins!" he said. "The kingdom of heaven is near."

Jesus Chooses the First Disciples

18 One day Jesus was walking beside the Sea of
Galilee. There he saw two brothers. They were Simon Peter and his brother Andrew. They were
throwing a net into the lake. They were fishermen.
19 "Come. Follow me," Jesus said. "I will make you
fishers of people."
20 At once they left their nets and followed him.
21 Going on from there, he saw two other brothers. They were James, son of Zebedee, and his
brother John. They were in a boat with their father
Zebedee. As they were preparing their nets, Jesus
called out to them.
22 Right away they left the boat and their father
and followed Jesus.

Jesus Heals Sick People

23 Jesus went all over Galilee. There he taught in
the synagogues. He preached the good news of
God's kingdom. He healed every illness and sickness the people had.
24 News about him spread all over Syria. People
brought to him all who were ill with different
kinds of sicknesses. Some were suffering great
pain. Others were controlled by demons. Some
were shaking wildly. Others couldn't move at all.
And Jesus healed all of them.
25 Large crowds followed him. Some people
came from Galilee, from the area known as the
Ten Cities, and from Jerusalem and Judea. Others
came from the area across the Jordan River.

Jesus Gives Blessings

5 Jesus saw the crowds. So he went up on a
mountainside and sat down. His disciples
came to him. 2 Then he began to teach them.
He said,

3 "Blessed are those who are spiritually needy.
The kingdom of heaven belongs to them.
4 Blessed are those who are sad.
They will be comforted.
5 Blessed are those who are free of pride.
They will be given the earth.
6 Blessed are those who are hungry and thirsty
for what is right.
They will be filled.
7 Blessed are those who show mercy.
They will be shown mercy.
8 Blessed are those whose hearts are pure.
They will see God.
9 Blessed are those who make peace.
They will be called sons of God.
10 Blessed are those who suffer for doing what
is right.
The kingdom of heaven belongs to them.

11 "Blessed are you when people make fun of
you and hurt you because of me. You are also
blessed when they tell all kinds of evil lies about
you because of me. 12 Be joyful and glad. Your
reward in heaven is great. In the same way, people hurt the prophets who lived long ago.

Salt and Light

13 "You are the salt of the earth. But suppose the
salt loses its saltiness. How can it be made salty
again? It is no longer good for anything. It will be
thrown out. People will walk all over it.
14 "You are the light of the world. A city on a hill
can't be hidden. 15 Also, people do not light a lamp
and put it under a bowl. Instead, they put it on its
stand. Then it gives light to everyone in the house.
16 "In the same way, let your light shine in front
of others. Then they will see the good things you
do. And they will praise your Father who is in
heaven.

Jesus Gives Full Meaning to the Law

17“Do not think I have come to get rid of what is written in the Law or in the Prophets. I have not come to do that. Instead, I have come to give full meaning to what is written. 18What I'm about to tell you is true. Heaven and earth will disappear before the smallest letter disappears from the Law. Not even the smallest stroke of a pen will disappear from the Law until everything is completed.

19“Do not break even one of the least important commandments. And do not teach others to break them. If you do, you will be called the least important person in the kingdom of heaven. Instead, practice and teach these commands. Then you will be called important in the kingdom of heaven.

20“Here is what I tell you. You must be more godly than the Pharisees and the teachers of the law. If you are not, you will certainly not enter the kingdom of heaven.

Murder

21“You have heard what was said to people who lived long ago. They were told, ‘Do not commit murder. *(Exodus 20:13)* Anyone who murders will be judged for it.’ 22But here is what I tell you. Do not be angry with your brother. Anyone who is angry with his brother will be judged. Again, anyone who says to his brother, ‘Raca,’ must stand trial in the Sanhedrin. But anyone who says, ‘You fool!’ will be in danger of the fire in hell.

23“Suppose you are offering your gift at the altar. And you remember that your brother has something against you. 24Leave your gift in front of the altar. First go and make peace with your brother. Then come back and offer your gift.

25“Suppose someone has a claim against you and is taking you to court. Settle the matter quickly. Do it while you are still with him on your way. If you don't, he may hand you over to the judge. The judge may hand you over to the officer. And you may be thrown into prison. 26What I'm about to tell you is true. You will not get out until you have paid the very last penny!

Adultery

27“You have heard that it was said, ‘Do not commit adultery.’ *(Exodus 20:14)* 28But here is what I tell you. Do not even look at a woman in the wrong way. Anyone who does has already committed adultery with her in his heart.

29“If your right eye causes you to sin, poke it out and throw it away. Your eye is only one part of your body. It is better to lose it than for your whole body to be thrown into hell.

30“If your right hand causes you to sin, cut it off and throw it away. Your hand is only one part of your body. It is better to lose it than for your whole body to go into hell.

Divorce

31“It has been said, ‘Suppose a man divorces his wife. If he does, he must give her a letter of divorce.’ *(Deuteronomy 24:1)* 32But here is what I tell you. Anyone who divorces his wife causes her to commit adultery. And anyone who gets married to the divorced woman commits adultery. A man may divorce his wife only if she has not been faithful to him.

Oaths

33“Again, you have heard what was said to your people long ago. They were told, ‘Do not break the promises you make to the Lord. Keep the oaths you have made to him.’ 34But here is what I tell you. Do not make any promises like that at all. Do not make them in the name of heaven. That is God's throne. 35Do not make them in the name of the earth. That is the stool for God's feet. Do not make them in the name of Jerusalem. That is the city of the Great King. 36And do not take an oath in the name of your head. You can't make even one hair white or black.

37“Just let your ‘Yes’ mean ‘Yes.’ Let your ‘No’ mean ‘No.’ Anything more than this comes from the evil one.

Be Kind to Others

38“You have heard that it was said, ‘An eye must be put out for an eye. A tooth must be knocked out for a tooth.’ *(Exodus 21:24; Leviticus 24:20; Deuteronomy 19:21)* 39But here is what I tell you. Do not fight against an evil person.

“Suppose someone hits you on your right cheek. Turn your other cheek to him also. 40Suppose someone takes you to court to get your shirt. Let him have your coat also. 41Suppose someone forces you to go one mile. Go two miles with him.

42“Give to the one who asks you for something. Don't turn away from the one who wants to borrow something from you.

Love Your Enemies

43“You have heard that it was said, ‘Love your neighbor. *(Leviticus 19:18)* Hate your enemy.’ 44But here is what I tell you. Love your enemies. Pray for those who hurt you. 45Then you will be sons of your Father who is in heaven.

“He causes his sun to shine on evil people and good people. He sends rain on those who do right and those who don't.

46“If you love those who love you, what reward will you get? Even the tax collectors do that. 47If you greet only your own people, what more are you doing than others? Even people who are ungodly do that. 48So be perfect, just as your Father in heaven is perfect.

Giving to Needy People

6 “Be careful not to do ‘good works’ in front of others. Don't do them to be seen by others. If you do, your Father in heaven will not reward you.

2“When you give to needy people, do not announce it by having trumpets blown. Do not be like those who only pretend to be holy. They announce what they do in the synagogues and on the streets. They want to be honored by others. What I'm about to tell you is true. They have received their complete reward.

3"When you give to the needy, don't let your left hand know what your right hand is doing. 4Then your giving will be done secretly. Your Father will reward you. He sees what you do secretly.

Prayer

5"When you pray, do not be like those who only pretend to be holy. They love to stand and pray in the synagogues and on the street corners. They want to be seen by others. What I'm about to tell you is true. They have received their complete reward.

6"When you pray, go into your room. Close the door and pray to your Father, who can't be seen. He will reward you. Your Father sees what is done secretly.

7"When you pray, do not keep talking on and on the way ungodly people do. They think they will be heard because they talk a lot. 8Do not be like them. Your Father knows what you need even before you ask him.

9"This is how you should pray.

"'Our Father in heaven,
may your name be honored.
10 May your kingdom come.
May what you want to happen be done
on earth as it is done in heaven.
11 Give us today our daily bread.
12 Forgive us our sins,
just as we also have forgiven those who
sin against us.
13 Keep us from falling into sin when we are
tempted.
Save us from the evil one.'

14"Forgive people when they sin against you. If you do, your Father who is in heaven will also forgive you. 15But if you do not forgive people their sins, your Father will not forgive your sins.

Fasting

16"When you go without eating, do not look gloomy like those who only pretend to be holy. They make their faces very sad. They want to show people they are fasting. What I'm about to tell you is true. They have received their complete reward.

17"But when you go without eating, put olive oil on your head. Wash your face. 18Then others will not know that you are fasting. Only your Father, who can't be seen, will know it. He will reward you. Your Father sees what is done secretly.

Put Away Riches in Heaven

19"Do not put away riches for yourselves on earth. Moths and rust can destroy them. Thieves can break in and steal them. 20Instead, put away riches for yourselves in heaven. There, moths and rust do not destroy them. There, thieves do not break in and steal them. 21Your heart will be where your riches are.

22"The eye is like a lamp for the body. Suppose your eyes are good. Then your whole body will be full of light. 23But suppose your eyes are bad. Then your whole body will be full of darkness. If the light inside you is darkness, then it is very dark!

24"No one can serve two masters at the same time. He will hate one of them and love the other. Or he will be faithful to one and dislike the other. You can't serve God and Money at the same time.

Do Not Worry

25"I tell you, do not worry. Don't worry about your life and what you will eat or drink. And don't worry about your body and what you will wear. Isn't there more to life than eating? Aren't there more important things for the body than clothes?

26"Look at the birds of the air. They don't plant or gather crops. They don't put away crops in storerooms. But your Father who is in heaven feeds them. Aren't you worth much more than they are? 27"Can you add even one hour to your life by worrying?

28"And why do you worry about clothes? See how the wild flowers grow. They don't work or make clothing. 29But here is what I tell you. Not even Solomon in all of his glory was dressed like one of those flowers.

30"If that is how God dresses the wild grass, won't he dress you even better? After all, the grass is here only today. Tomorrow it is thrown into the fire. Your faith is so small!

31"So don't worry. Don't say, 'What will we eat?' Or, 'What will we drink?' Or, 'What will we wear?' 32People who are ungodly run after all of those things. Your Father who is in heaven knows that you need them.

33"But put God's kingdom first. Do what he wants you to do. Then all of those things will also be given to you.

34"So don't worry about tomorrow. Tomorrow will worry about itself. Each day has enough trouble of its own.

Be Fair When You Judge Others

7 "Do not judge others. Then you will not be judged. 2You will be judged in the same way you judge others. You will be measured in the same way you measure others.

3"You look at the bit of sawdust in your friend's eye. But you pay no attention to the piece of wood in your own eye. 4How can you say to your friend, 'Let me take the bit of sawdust out of your eye'? How can you say this while there is a piece of wood in your own eye?

5"You pretender! First take the piece of wood out of your own eye. Then you will be able to see

clearly to take the bit of sawdust out of your
friend's eye.
6"Do not give holy things to dogs. Do not throw
your pearls to pigs. If you do, they might walk all
over them. Then they might turn around and tear
you to pieces.

Ask, Search, Knock

7"Ask, and it will be given to you. Search, and
you will find. Knock, and the door will be opened
to you. 8Everyone who asks will receive. He who
searches will find. The door will be opened to the
one who knocks.
9"Suppose your son asks for bread. Which of
you will give him a stone? 10Or suppose he asks
for a fish. Which of you will give him a snake?
11Even though you are evil, you know how to give
good gifts to your children. How much more will
your Father who is in heaven give good gifts to
those who ask him!
12"In everything, do to others what you would
want them to do to you. This is what is written in
the Law and in the Prophets.

The Large and Small Gates

13"Enter God's kingdom through the narrow
gate. The gate is large and the road is wide that
lead to death and hell. Many people go that way.
14But the gate is small and the road is narrow that
lead to life. Only a few people find it.

A Tree and Its Fruit

15"Watch out for false prophets. They come to
you pretending to be sheep. But on the inside they
are hungry wolves. 16You can tell what they really
are by what they do.
"Do people pick grapes from bushes? Do they
pick figs from thorns? 17In the same way, every
good tree bears good fruit. But a bad tree bears bad
fruit. 18A good tree can't bear bad fruit. And a bad
tree can't bear good fruit. 19Every tree that does not
bear good fruit is cut down. It is thrown into the
fire. 20You can tell each tree by its fruit.
21"Not everyone who says to me, 'Lord, Lord,'
will enter the kingdom of heaven. Only those who
do what my Father in heaven wants will enter.
22"Many will say to me on that day, 'Lord!
Lord! Didn't we prophesy in your name? Didn't
we drive out demons in your name? Didn't we do
many miracles in your name?' 23Then I will tell
them clearly, 'I never knew you. Get away from
me, you who do evil!'

The Wise and Foolish Builders

24"So then, everyone who hears my words and
puts them into practice is like a wise man. He
builds his house on the rock. 25The rain comes
down. The water rises. The winds blow and beat
against that house. But it does not fall. It is built
on the rock.
26"But everyone who hears my words and does
not put them into practice is like a foolish man. He
builds his house on sand. 27The rain comes down.
The water rises. The winds blow and beat against
that house. And it falls with a loud crash."
28Jesus finished saying all these things. The
crowds were amazed at his teaching. 29He taught
like one who had authority. He did not speak like
their teachers of the law.

Jesus Heals a Man Who Had a Skin Disease

8 Jesus came down from the mountainside.
Large crowds followed him.
2A man who had a skin disease came and got
down on his knees in front of Jesus. He said,
"Lord, if you are willing to make me 'clean,' you
can do it."
3Jesus reached out his hand and touched the
man. "I am willing to do it," he said. "Be 'clean'!"
Right away the man was healed of his skin
disease.
4Then Jesus said to him, "Don't tell anyone. Go
and show yourself to the priest. Offer the gift Moses commanded. It will be a witness to them."

A Roman Commander Has Faith

5When Jesus entered Capernaum, a Roman
commander came to him. He asked Jesus for help.
6"Lord," he said, "my servant lies at home and
can't move. He is suffering terribly."
7Jesus said, "I will go and heal him."
8The commander replied, "Lord, I am not good
enough to have you come into my house. But just
say the word, and my servant will be healed. 9I
myself am a man under authority. And I have soldiers who obey my orders. I tell this one, 'Go,' and
he goes. I tell that one, 'Come,' and he comes. I
say to my servant, 'Do this,' and he does it."
10When Jesus heard this, he was amazed. He
said to those following him, "What I'm about to
tell you is true. In Israel I have not found anyone
whose faith is so strong.
11"I say to you that many will come from the
east and the west. They will take their places at the
feast in the kingdom of heaven. They will sit with
Abraham, Isaac and Jacob. 12But those who think
they belong to the kingdom will be thrown outside,
into the darkness. There they will sob and grind
their teeth."
13Then Jesus said to the Roman commander,
"Go! It will be done just as you believed it would."
And his servant was healed at that very hour.

Jesus Heals Many People

14When Jesus came into Peter's house, he saw
Peter's mother-in-law. She was lying in bed. She
had a fever.
15Jesus touched her hand, and the fever left her.
She got up and began to wait on him.
16When evening came, many people controlled
by demons were brought to Jesus. He drove out the
spirits with a word. He healed all who were sick.

17He did it to make what the prophet Isaiah had said come true. He had said,

"He suffered the things we should have
suffered.
He took on himself the sicknesses that
should have been ours." *(Isaiah 53:4)*

It Costs to Follow Jesus

18Jesus saw the crowd around him. So he gave his disciples orders to go to the other side of the Sea of Galilee.

19Then a teacher of the law came to him. He said, "Teacher, I will follow you no matter where you go."

20Jesus replied, "Foxes have holes. Birds of the air have nests. But the Son of Man has no place to lay his head."

21Another follower said to him, "Lord, first let me go and bury my father."

22But Jesus told him, "Follow me. Let the dead bury their own dead."

Jesus Calms the Storm

23Jesus got into a boat. His disciples followed him. 24Suddenly a terrible storm came up on the lake. The waves crashed over the boat. But Jesus was sleeping.

25The disciples went and woke him up. They said, "Lord! Save us! We're going to drown!"

26He replied, "Your faith is so small! Why are you so afraid?"

Then Jesus got up and ordered the winds and the waves to stop. It became completely calm.

27The disciples were amazed. They asked, "What kind of man is this? Even the winds and the waves obey him!"

Jesus Heals Two Men Controlled by Demons

28Jesus arrived at the other side of the lake in the area of the Gadarenes. Two men controlled by demons met him. They came from the tombs. The men were so wild that no one could pass that way.

29"Son of God, what do you want with us?" they shouted. "Have you come here to punish us before the time for us to be judged?"

30Not very far away, a large herd of pigs was feeding. 31The demons begged Jesus, "If you drive us out, send us into the herd of pigs."

32Jesus said to them, "Go!"

So the demons came out of the men and went into the pigs. The whole herd rushed down the steep bank. They ran into the lake and drowned in the water.

33Those who were tending the pigs ran off. They went into the town and reported all this. They told the people what had happened to the men who had been controlled by demons.

34Then the whole town went out to meet Jesus. When they saw him, they begged him to leave their area.

Jesus Heals a Man Who Could Not Walk

9 Jesus stepped into a boat. He went over to the other side of the lake and came to his own town. 2Some men brought to him a man who could not walk. He was lying on a mat. Jesus saw that they had faith. So he said to the man, "Don't lose hope, son. Your sins are forgiven."

3Then some teachers of the law said to themselves, "This fellow is saying a very evil thing!"

4Jesus knew what they were thinking. So he said, "Why do you have evil thoughts in your hearts? 5Is it easier to say, 'Your sins are forgiven'? Or to say, 'Get up and walk'? 6I want you to know that the Son of Man has authority on earth to forgive sins."

Then he spoke to the man who could not walk. "Get up," he said. "Take your mat and go home." 7The man got up and went home.

8When the crowd saw this, they were filled with wonder. They praised God for giving that kind of authority to men.

Jesus Chooses Matthew

9As Jesus went on from there, he saw a man named Matthew. He was sitting at the tax collector's booth.

"Follow me," Jesus told him. Matthew got up and followed him.

10Later Jesus was having dinner at Matthew's house. Many tax collectors and "sinners" came. They ate with Jesus and his disciples.

11The Pharisees saw this. So they asked the disciples, "Why does your teacher eat with tax collectors and 'sinners'?"

12Jesus heard that. So he said, "Those who are healthy don't need a doctor. Sick people do. 13Go and learn what this means, 'I want mercy and not sacrifice.' *(Hosea 6:6)* I have not come to get those who think they are right with God to follow me. I have come to get sinners to follow me."

Jesus Is Asked About Fasting

14One day John's disciples came. They said to Jesus, "We and the Pharisees go without eating. Why don't your disciples go without eating?"

15Jesus answered, "How can the guests of the groom be sad while he is with them? The time will come when the groom will be taken away from them. Then they will fast.

16"People don't sew a patch of new cloth on old clothes. The new piece will pull away from the old. That will make the tear worse.

17"People don't pour new wine into old wineskins. If they do, the skins will burst. The wine will run out, and the wineskins will be destroyed. No, everyone pours new wine into new wineskins. Then both are saved."

A Dead Girl and a Suffering Woman

18While Jesus was saying this, a ruler came. He got down on his knees in front of Jesus. He said,

"My daughter has just died. But come and place your hand on her. Then she will live again."

19Jesus got up and went with him. So did his disciples.

20Just then a woman came up behind Jesus. She had a sickness that made her bleed. It had lasted for 12 years. She touched the edge of his clothes. 21She thought, "I only need to touch his clothes. Then I will be healed."

22Jesus turned and saw her. "Dear woman, don't give up hope," he said. "Your faith has healed you." The woman was healed at that very moment.

23When Jesus entered the ruler's house, he saw the flute players there. And he saw the noisy crowd. 24He said, "Go away. The girl is not dead. She is sleeping." But they laughed at him.

25After the crowd had been sent outside, Jesus went in. He took the girl by the hand, and she got up. 26News about what Jesus had done spread all over that area.

Jesus Heals Two Blind Men

27As Jesus went on from there, two blind men followed him. They called out, "Have mercy on us, Son of David!"

28When Jesus went indoors, the blind men came to him. He asked them, "Do you believe that I can do this?"

"Yes, Lord," they replied.

29Then he touched their eyes. He said, "It will happen to you just as you believed." 30They could now see again. Jesus strongly warned them, "Be sure that no one knows about this." 31But they went out and spread the news. They talked about him all over that area.

32While they were going out, another man was brought to Jesus. A demon controlled him, and he could not speak. 33When the demon was driven out, the man spoke.

The crowd was amazed. They said, "Nothing like this has ever been seen in Israel." 34But the Pharisees said, "He drives out demons by the power of the prince of demons."

There Are Only a Few Workers

35Jesus went through all the towns and villages. He taught in their synagogues. He preached the good news of the kingdom. And he healed every illness and sickness. 36When he saw the crowds, he felt deep concern for them. They were beaten down and helpless, like sheep without a shepherd.

37Then Jesus said to his disciples, "The harvest is huge. But there are only a few workers. 38So ask the Lord of the harvest to send workers out into his harvest field."

Jesus Sends Out the Twelve Disciples

10 Jesus called for his 12 disciples to come to him. He gave them authority to drive out evil spirits and to heal every illness and sickness.

2Here are the names of the 12 apostles. First are Simon Peter and his brother Andrew. Then come James, son of Zebedee, and his brother John. 3Next are Philip and Bartholomew, and also Thomas and Matthew the tax collector. Two more are James, son of Alphaeus, and Thaddaeus. 4The last are Simon the Zealot and Judas Iscariot. Judas is the one who was later going to hand Jesus over to his enemies.

5Jesus sent these 12 out with the following orders. "Do not go among those who aren't Jews," he said. "Do not enter any town of the Samaritans. 6Instead, go to the people of Israel. They are like sheep that have become lost. 7As you go, preach this message, 'The kingdom of heaven is near.' 8Heal those who are sick. Bring those who are dead back to life. Make those who have skin diseases 'clean' again. Drive out demons. You have received freely, so give freely.

9"Do not take along any gold, silver or copper in your belts. 10Do not take a bag for the journey. Do not take extra clothes or sandals or walking sticks. A worker should be given what he needs.

11"When you enter a town or village, look for someone who is willing to welcome you. Stay at that person's house until you leave. 12As you enter the home, greet those who live there. 13If that home welcomes you, give it your blessing of peace. If it does not, don't bless it.

14"Some people may not welcome you or listen to your words. If they don't, shake the dust off your feet when you leave that home or town. 15What I'm about to tell you is true. On judgment day it will be easier for Sodom and Gomorrah than for that town.

16"I am sending you out like sheep among wolves. So be as wise as snakes and as harmless as doves.

17"Watch out! Men will hand you over to the local courts. They will whip you in their synagogues. 18You will be brought to governors and kings because of me. You will be witnesses to them and to those who aren't Jews.

19"But when they arrest you, don't worry about what you will say or how you will say it. At that time you will be given the right words to say. 20It will not be you speaking. The Spirit of your Father will be speaking through you.

21"Brothers will hand over brothers to be killed. Fathers will hand over their children. Children will rise up against their parents and have them put to death. 22Everyone will hate you because of me. But anyone who stands firm to the end will be saved.

23"When people attack you in one place, escape to another. What I'm about to tell you is true. You will not finish going through the cities of Israel before the Son of Man comes.

24"A student is not better than his teacher. A servant is not better than his master. 25It is enough for the student to be like his teacher. And it is enough for the servant to be like his master. If the head of

the house has been called Beelzebub, what can the
others who live there expect?
26“So don’t be afraid of your enemies. Everything that is secret will be brought out into the
open. Everything that is hidden will be uncovered.
27What I tell you in the dark, speak in the daylight.
What is whispered in your ear, shout from the
rooftops. 28Do not be afraid of those who kill the
body but can’t kill the soul. Instead, be afraid of
the One who can destroy both soul and body in
hell.
29“Aren’t two sparrows sold for only a penny?
But not one of them falls to the ground without
your Father knowing it. 30He even counts every
hair on your head! 31So don’t be afraid. You are
worth more than many sparrows.
32“What about someone who says in front of
others that he knows me? I will also say in front
of my Father who is in heaven that I know him.
33But what about someone who says in front of
others that he doesn’t know me? I will say in front
of my Father who is in heaven that I don’t know
him.
34“Do not think that I came to bring peace to the
earth. I didn’t come to bring peace. I came to bring
a sword. 35I have come to turn

“‘sons against their fathers.
Daughters will refuse to obey their mothers.
Daughters-in-law will be against their
mothers-in-law.
36 A man’s enemies will be the members of
his own family.’ *(Micah 7:6)*

37“Anyone who loves his father or mother more
than me is not worthy of me. Anyone who loves
his son or daughter more than me is not worthy of
me. 38And anyone who does not pick up his cross
and follow me is not worthy of me. 39If anyone
finds his life, he will lose it. If anyone loses his life
because of me, he will find it.
40“Anyone who welcomes you welcomes me.
And anyone who welcomes me welcomes the One
who sent me. 41Suppose someone welcomes a
prophet as a prophet. That one will receive a
prophet’s reward. And suppose someone welcomes a godly person as a godly person. That one
will receive a godly person’s reward. 42Suppose
someone gives even a cup of cold water to a little
one who follows me. What I’m about to tell you is
true. That one will certainly be rewarded.”

Jesus and John the Baptist

11 Jesus finished teaching his 12 disciples.
Then he went on to teach and preach in the
towns of Galilee.
2John was in prison. When he heard what Christ
was doing, he sent his disciples to him. 3They
asked Jesus, “Are you the one who was supposed
to come? Or should we look for someone else?”
4Jesus replied, “Go back to John. Report to him
what you hear and see. 5Blind people receive sight.
Disabled people walk. Those who have skin diseases are healed. Deaf people hear. Those who are
dead are raised to life. And the good news is
preached to those who are poor. 6Blessed are those
who do not give up their faith because of me.”
7As John’s disciples were leaving, Jesus began
to speak to the crowd about John. He said, “What
did you go out into the desert to see? Tall grass
waving in the wind? 8If not, what did you go out to
see? A man dressed in fine clothes? No. People
who wear fine clothes are in kings’ palaces. 9Then
what did you go out to see? A prophet? Yes, I tell
you, and more than a prophet. 10He is the one written about in Scripture. It says,

“‘I will send my messenger ahead of you.
He will prepare your way for you.’
(Malachi 3:1)

11“What I’m about to tell you is true. No one
more important than John the Baptist has ever
been born. But the least important person in the
kingdom of heaven is more important than he is.
12Since the days of John the Baptist, the kingdom
of heaven has been advancing with force. And
forceful people are taking hold of it. 13All the
Prophets and the Law prophesied until John came.
14If you are willing to accept it, John is the Elijah
who was supposed to come. 15Those who have
ears should listen.
16“What can I compare today’s people to? They
are like children sitting in the market places and
calling out to others. They say,

17 “‘We played the flute for you.
But you didn’t dance.
We sang a funeral song.
But you didn’t become sad.’

18When John came, he didn’t eat or drink as you
do. And people say, ‘He has a demon.’ 19But when
the Son of Man came, he ate and drank as you do.
And people say, ‘This fellow is always eating and
drinking far too much. He’s a friend of tax collectors and “sinners.”’ Those who act wisely prove
that wisdom is right.”

Cities That Do Not Turn Away From Sin

20Jesus began to speak against the cities where
he had done most of his miracles. The people there
had not turned away from their sins. So he said,
21“How terrible it will be for you, Korazin! How
terrible for you, Bethsaida! Suppose the miracles
done in you had been done in Tyre and Sidon.
They would have turned away from their sins long
ago. They would have put on black clothes. They
would have sat down in ashes. 22But I tell you this.
On judgment day it will be easier for Tyre and Sidon than for you.
23“And what about you, Capernaum? Will you
be lifted up to heaven? No! You will go down to
the place of the dead. Suppose the miracles done in
you had been done in Sodom. It would still be here

today. 24But I tell you this. On judgment day it will be easier for Sodom than for you."

Rest for All Who Are Tired

25At that time Jesus said, "I praise you, Father. You are Lord of heaven and earth. You have hidden these things from the wise and educated. But you have shown them to little children. 26Yes, Father. This is what you wanted.

27"My Father has given all things to me. The Father is the only one who knows the Son. And the only ones who know the Father are the Son and those to whom the Son chooses to make him known.

28"Come to me, all of you who are tired and are carrying heavy loads. I will give you rest. 29Become my servants and learn from me. I am gentle and free of pride. You will find rest for your souls. 30Serving me is easy, and my load is light."

Jesus Is Lord of the Sabbath Day

12 One Sabbath day Jesus walked through the grainfields. His disciples were hungry. So they began to break off some heads of grain and eat them. 2The Pharisees saw this. They said to Jesus, "Look! It is against the Law to do this on the Sabbath. But your disciples are doing it anyway!"

3Jesus answered, "Haven't you read about what David did? He and his men were hungry. 4So he entered the house of God. He and his men ate the holy bread. Only priests were allowed to eat it. 5Haven't you read the Law? It tells how every Sabbath day the priests in the temple have to do their work on that day. But they are not considered guilty.

6"I tell you that one who is more important than the temple is here. 7Scripture says, 'I want mercy and not sacrifice.' *(Hosea 6:6)* You don't know what those words mean. If you did, you would not bring charges against those who are not guilty. 8The Son of Man is Lord of the Sabbath day."

9Going on from that place, Jesus went into their synagogue. 10A man with a weak and twisted hand was there. The Pharisees were trying to find fault with Jesus. So they asked him, "Does the Law allow us to heal on the Sabbath day?"

11He said to them, "What if one of your sheep falls into a pit on the Sabbath? Won't you take hold of it and lift it out? 12A man is worth more than sheep! So the Law allows us to do good on the Sabbath day."

13Then Jesus said to the man, "Stretch out your hand." So he stretched it out. It was as good as new, just as good as the other hand. 14But the Pharisees went out and planned how to kill Jesus.

God's Chosen Servant

15Jesus knew all about the Pharisees' plans. So he left that place. Many followed him, and he healed all their sick people. 16But he warned them not to tell who he was. 17This was to make what was spoken through the prophet Isaiah come true. It says,

18"Here is my servant. I have chosen him.
He is the one I love. I am very pleased
with him.
I will put my Spirit on him.
He will announce to the nations that
everything will be made right.
19He will not argue or cry out.
No one will hear his voice in the streets.
20He will not break a bent twig.
He will not put out a dimly burning flame.
He will make everything right.
21 The nations will put their hope in him."
(Isaiah 42:1–4)

Jesus and Beelzebub

22A man controlled by demons was brought to Jesus. The man was blind and could not speak. Jesus healed him. Then the man could speak and see. 23All the people were amazed. They said, "Could this be the Son of David?"

24The Pharisees heard this. So they said, "This fellow drives out demons by the power of Beelzebub, the prince of demons."

25Jesus knew what they were thinking. So he said to them, "Every kingdom that fights against itself will be destroyed. Every city or family that is divided against itself will not stand. 26If Satan drives out Satan, he fights against himself. Then how can his kingdom stand? 27You say I drive out demons by the power of Beelzebub. Then by whose power do your people drive them out? So then, they will be your judges. 28But suppose I drive out demons by the Spirit of God. Then God's kingdom has come to you.

29"Or think about this. How can you enter a strong man's house and just take what the man owns? You must first tie him up. Then you can rob his house.

30"Anyone who is not with me is against me. Anyone who does not gather sheep with me scatters them. 31So here is what I tell you. Every sin and every evil word spoken against God will be forgiven. But speaking evil things against the Holy Spirit will not be forgiven. 32Anyone who speaks a word against the Son of Man will be forgiven. But anyone who speaks against the Holy Spirit will not be forgiven. A person like that won't be forgiven either now or in days to come.

33"If you make a tree good, its fruit will be good. If you make a tree bad, its fruit will be bad. You can tell a tree by its fruit.

34"You nest of poisonous snakes! How can you who are evil say anything good? Your mouths say everything that is in your hearts. 35A good man says good things. These come from the good that is put away inside him. An evil man says evil things. These come from the evil that is put away

inside him. 36But here is what I tell you. On judgment day, people will have to account for every
careless word they have spoken. 37By your words
you will be found guilty or not guilty."

The Miraculous Sign of Jonah

38Some of the Pharisees and the teachers of the
law came to Jesus. They said, "Teacher, we want
to see a miraculous sign from you."
39He answered, "Evil and unfaithful people ask
for a miraculous sign! But none will be given
except the sign of the prophet Jonah. 40Jonah was
in the stomach of a huge fish for three days and
three nights. Something like that will happen to the
Son of Man. He will spend three days and three
nights in the grave.
41"The men of Nineveh will stand up on judgment day with the people now living. And the Nin-
evites will prove that those people are guilty. The
men of Nineveh turned away from their sins when
Jonah preached to them. And now one who is
more important than Jonah is here.
42"The Queen of the South will stand up on
judgment day with the people now living. And she
will prove that they are guilty. She came from very
far away to listen to Solomon's wisdom. And now
one who is more important than Solomon is here.
43"What happens when an evil spirit comes out
of a man? It goes through dry areas looking for a
place to rest. But it doesn't find it. 44Then it says,
'I will return to the house I left.' When it arrives
there, it finds the house empty. The house has been
swept clean and put in order. 45Then the evil spirit
goes and takes with it seven other spirits more evil
than itself. They go in and live there. That man is
worse off than before. That is how it will be with
the evil people of today."

Jesus' Mother and Brothers

46While Jesus was still talking to the crowd, his
mother and brothers stood outside. They wanted
to speak to him. 47Someone told him, "Your
mother and brothers are standing outside. They
want to speak to you."
48Jesus replied to him, "Who is my mother?
And who are my brothers?" 49Jesus pointed to his
disciples. He said, "Here is my mother! Here are
my brothers! 50Anyone who does what my Father
in heaven wants is my brother or sister or mother."

The Story of the Farmer

13 That same day Jesus left the house and sat
by the Sea of Galilee. 2Large crowds gathered around him. So he got into a boat. He sat
down in it. All the people stood on the shore.
3Then he told them many things by using stories.
He said, "A farmer went out to plant his seed.
4He scattered the seed on the ground. Some fell on
a path. Birds came and ate it up. 5Some seed fell on
rocky places, where there wasn't much soil. The
plants came up quickly, because the soil wasn't
deep. 6When the sun came up, it burned the plants.
They dried up because they had no roots. 7Other
seed fell among thorns. The thorns grew up and
crowded out the plants. 8Still other seed fell on
good soil. It produced a crop 100, 60 or 30 times
more than what was planted. 9Those who have ears
should listen."
10The disciples came to him. They asked, "Why
do you use stories when you speak to the people?"
11He replied, "You have been given the chance
to understand the secrets of the kingdom of
heaven. It has not been given to outsiders. 12Every-
one who has that kind of knowledge will be given
more. In fact, they will have very much. If anyone
doesn't have that kind of knowledge, even what
little he has will be taken away from him. 13Here is
why I use stories when I speak to the people. I say,

"They look, but they don't really see.
They listen, but they don't really hear or
understand.

14"In them the words of the prophet Isaiah come
true. He said,

"'You will hear but never understand.
You will see but never know what you
are seeing.
15The hearts of these people have become
stubborn.
They can barely hear with their ears.
They have closed their eyes.
Otherwise they might see with their eyes.
They might hear with their ears.
They might understand with their hearts.
They might turn to the Lord, and then he
would heal them.' *(Isaiah 6:9,10)*

16"But blessed are your eyes because they see.
And blessed are your ears because they hear.
17What I'm about to tell you is true. Many prophets
and godly people wanted to see what you see. But
they didn't see it. They wanted to hear what you
hear. But they didn't hear it.
18"Listen! Here is the meaning of the story of
the farmer. 19People hear the message about the
kingdom but do not understand it. Then the evil
one comes. He steals what was planted in their
hearts. Those people are like the seed planted on a
path. 20Others received the seed that fell on rocky
places. They are those who hear the message and
at once receive it with joy. 21But they have no
roots. So they last only a short time. They quickly
fall away from the faith when trouble or suffering
comes because of the message. 22Others received
the seed that fell among the thorns. They are those
who hear the message. But then the worries of this
life and the false promises of wealth crowd it out.
They keep it from producing fruit. 23But still others received the seed that fell on good soil. They
are those who hear the message and understand it.
They produce a crop 100, 60 or 30 times more than
the farmer planted."

The Story of the Weeds

24Jesus told the crowd another story. "Here is
what the kingdom of heaven is like," he said. "A
man planted good seed in his field. 25But while
everyone was sleeping, his enemy came. The
enemy planted weeds among the wheat and then
went away. 26The wheat began to grow and form
grain. At the same time, weeds appeared.
27"The owner's servants came to him. They
said, 'Sir, didn't you plant good seed in your field?
Then where did the weeds come from?'
28" 'An enemy did this,' he replied.
"The servants asked him, 'Do you want us to
go and pull the weeds up?'
29" 'No,' the owner answered. 'While you are
pulling up the weeds, you might pull up the wheat
with them. 30Let both grow together until the harvest. At that time I will tell the workers what to do.
Here is what I will say to them. First collect the
weeds. Tie them in bundles to be burned. Then
gather the wheat. Bring it into my storeroom.' "

The Stories of the Mustard Seed and the Yeast

31Jesus told the crowd another story. He said,
"The kingdom of heaven is like a mustard seed.
Someone took the seed and planted it in a field. 32It
is the smallest of all your seeds. But when it grows,
it is the largest of all garden plants. It becomes a
tree. Birds come and rest in its branches."
33Jesus told them still another story. "The kingdom of heaven is like yeast," he said. "A woman
mixed it into a large amount of flour. The yeast
worked its way all through the dough."
34Jesus spoke all these things to the crowd by
using stories. He did not say anything to them
without telling a story. 35So the words spoken by
the prophet came true. He had said,

"I will open my mouth and tell stories.
I will speak about things that were hidden
since the world was made." *(Psalm 78:2)*

Jesus Explains the Story of the Weeds

36Then Jesus left the crowd and went into the
house. His disciples came to him. They said,
"Explain to us the story of the weeds in the field."
37He answered, "The one who planted the good
seed is the Son of Man. 38The field is the world.
The good seed stands for the people who belong
to the kingdom. The weeds are the people who
belong to the evil one. 39The enemy who plants
them is the devil. The harvest is judgment day.
And the workers are angels.
40"The weeds are pulled up and burned in the
fire. That is how it will be on judgment day. 41The
Son of Man will send out his angels. They will
weed out of his kingdom everything that causes sin.
They will also get rid of all who do evil. 42They will
throw them into the blazing furnace. There people
will sob and grind their teeth. 43Then God's people
will shine like the sun in their Father's kingdom.
Those who have ears should listen.

The Stories of the Hidden Treasure and the Pearl

44"The kingdom of heaven is like treasure that
was hidden in a field. When a man found it, he hid
it again. He was very happy. So he went and sold
everything he had. And he bought that field.
45"Again, the kingdom of heaven is like a trader
who was looking for fine pearls. 46He found one
that was very valuable. So he went away and sold
everything he had. And he bought that pearl.

The Story of the Net

47"Again, the kingdom of heaven is like a net. It
was let down into the lake. It caught all kinds of
fish. 48When it was full, the fishermen pulled it up
on the shore. Then they sat down and gathered the
good fish into baskets. But they threw the bad fish
away. 49This is how it will be on judgment day.
The angels will come. They will separate the people who did what is wrong from those who did
what is right. 50They will throw the evil people into
the blazing furnace. There the evil ones will sob
and grind their teeth.
51"Do you understand all these things?" Jesus
asked.
"Yes," they replied.
52He said to them, "Every teacher of the law
who has been taught about the kingdom of heaven
is like the owner of a house. He brings new treasures out of his storeroom as well as old ones."

A Prophet Without Honor

53Jesus finished telling these stories. Then he
moved on from there. 54He came to his hometown
of Nazareth. There he began teaching the people
in their synagogue. They were amazed.
"Where did this man get this wisdom? Where
did he get this power to do miracles?" they asked.
55"Isn't this the carpenter's son? Isn't his mother's
name Mary? Aren't his brothers James, Joseph, Simon and Judas? 56Aren't all his sisters with us?
Then where did this man get all these things?"
57They were not pleased with him at all.
But Jesus said to them, "A prophet is not honored in his hometown. He doesn't receive any
honor in his own home."
58He did only a few miracles there because they
had no faith.

John the Baptist's Head Is Cut Off

14 At that time Herod, the ruler of Galilee and
Perea, heard reports about Jesus. 2He said
to his attendants, "This is John the Baptist. He has
risen from the dead! That is why he has the power
to do miracles."
3Herod had arrested John. He had tied him up
and put him in prison because of Herodias. She
was the wife of Herod's brother Philip. 4John had

been saying to Herod, "It is against the Law for you to have her." [5]Herod wanted to kill John. But he was afraid of the people, because they thought John was a prophet.

[6]On Herod's birthday the daughter of Herodias danced for Herod and his guests. She pleased Herod very much. [7]So he promised with an oath to give her anything she asked for. [8]Her mother told her what to say. So the girl said to Herod, "Give me the head of John the Baptist on a big plate."

[9]The king was very upset. But he thought of his promise and his dinner guests. So he told one of his men to give her what she asked for. [10]Herod had John's head cut off in the prison. [11]His head was brought in on a big plate and given to the girl. She then carried it to her mother.

[12]John's disciples came and took his body and buried it. Then they went and told Jesus.

Jesus Feeds the Five Thousand

[13]Jesus heard what had happened to John. He wanted to be alone. So he went in a boat to a quiet place. The crowds heard about this. They followed him on foot from the towns. [14]When Jesus came ashore, he saw a large crowd. He felt deep concern for them. He healed their sick people.

[15]When it was almost evening, the disciples came to him. "There is nothing here," they said. "It's already getting late. Send the crowds away. They can go and buy some food in the villages."

[16]Jesus replied, "They don't need to go away. You give them something to eat."

[17]"We have only five loaves of bread and two fish," they answered.

[18]"Bring them here to me," he said. [19]Then Jesus directed the people to sit down on the grass. He took the five loaves and the two fish. He looked up to heaven and gave thanks. He broke the loaves into pieces. Then he gave them to the disciples. And the disciples gave them to the people.

[20]All of them ate and were satisfied. The disciples picked up 12 baskets of leftover pieces. [21]The number of men who ate was about 5,000. Women and children also ate.

Jesus Walks on the Water

[22]Right away Jesus made the disciples get into the boat. He had them go on ahead of him to the other side of the Sea of Galilee. Then he sent the crowd away. [23]After he had sent them away, he went up on a mountainside by himself to pray. When evening came, he was there alone. [24]The boat was already a long way from land. It was being pounded by the waves because the wind was blowing against it.

[25]Early in the morning, Jesus went out to the disciples. He walked on the lake. [26]They saw him walking on the lake and were terrified. "It's a ghost!" they said. And they cried out in fear.

[27]Right away Jesus called out to them, "Be brave! It is I. Don't be afraid."

[28]"Lord, is it you?" Peter asked. "If it is, tell me to come to you on the water."

[29]"Come," Jesus said.

So Peter got out of the boat. He walked on the water toward Jesus. [30]But when Peter saw the wind, he was afraid. He began to sink. He cried out, "Lord! Save me!"

[31]Right away Jesus reached out his hand and caught him. "Your faith is so small!" he said. "Why did you doubt me?"

[32]When they climbed into the boat, the wind died down. [33]Then those in the boat worshiped Jesus. They said, "You really are the Son of God!"

[34]They crossed over the lake and landed at Gennesaret. [35]The men who lived there recognized Jesus. So they sent a message all over the nearby countryside. People brought all their sick to Jesus. [36]They begged him to let those who were sick just touch the edge of his clothes. And all who touched him were healed.

What Makes People "Unclean"?

15 Some Pharisees and some teachers of the law came from Jerusalem to see Jesus. They asked, [2]"Why don't your disciples obey what the elders teach? Your disciples don't wash their hands before they eat!"

[3]Jesus replied, "And why don't you obey God's command? You would rather follow your own teachings! [4]God said, 'Honor your father and mother.' *(Exodus 20:12; Deuteronomy 5:16)* He also said, 'If anyone calls down a curse on his father or mother, he will be put to death.' *(Exodus 21:17; Leviticus 20:9)* [5]But you allow people to say to their parents, 'Any help you might have received from us is a gift set apart for God.' [6]So they do not need to honor their parents with their gift. You make the word of God useless in order to follow your own teachings.

[7]"You pretenders! Isaiah was right when he prophesied about you. He said,

[8]" 'These people honor me by what they say.
 But their hearts are far away from me.
[9]Their worship doesn't mean anything to me.
 They teach nothing but human rules.' "
(Isaiah 29:13)

[10]Jesus called the crowd to him. He said, "Listen and understand. [11]What goes into your mouth does not make you 'unclean.' It's what comes out of your mouth that makes you 'unclean.' "

[12]Then the disciples came to him. They asked, "Do you know that the Pharisees were angry when they heard this?"

[13]Jesus replied, "There are plants that my Father in heaven has not planted. They will be pulled up by the roots. [14]Leave them. The Pharisees are blind guides. If a blind person leads another who is blind, both of them will fall into a pit."

[15]Peter said, "Explain this to us."

16"Don't you understand yet?" Jesus asked them. 17"Don't you see? Everything that enters the mouth goes into the stomach. Then it goes out of the body. 18But the things that come out of the mouth come from the heart. Those are the things that make you 'unclean.' 19Evil thoughts come out of the heart. So do murder, adultery, and other sexual sins. And so do stealing, false witness, and telling lies about others. 20Those are the things that make you 'unclean.' But eating without washing your hands does not make you 'unclean.'"

The Faith of a Woman From Canaan

21Jesus left Galilee and went to the area of Tyre and Sidon. 22A woman from Canaan lived near Tyre and Sidon. She came to him and cried out, "Lord! Son of David! Have mercy on me! A demon controls my daughter. She is suffering terribly."

23Jesus did not say a word. So his disciples came to him. They begged him, "Send her away. She keeps crying out after us."

24Jesus answered, "I was sent only to the people of Israel. They are like lost sheep."

25Then the woman fell to her knees in front of him. "Lord! Help me!" she said.

26He replied, "It is not right to take the children's bread and throw it to their dogs."

27"Yes, Lord," she said. "But even the dogs eat the crumbs that fall from their owners' table."

28Then Jesus answered, "Woman, you have great faith! You will be given what you are asking for." And her daughter was healed at that very moment.

Jesus Feeds the Four Thousand

29Jesus left there. He walked along the Sea of Galilee. Then he went up on a mountainside and sat down. 30Large crowds came to him. They brought blind people and those who could not walk. They also brought disabled people, those who could not speak, and many others. They laid them at his feet, and he healed them.

31The people were amazed. Those who could not speak were speaking. The disabled were made well. Those not able to walk were walking. Those who were blind could see. So the people praised the God of Israel.

32Then Jesus called for his disciples to come to him. He said, "I feel deep concern for these people. They have already been with me three days. They don't have anything to eat. I don't want to send them away hungry. If I do, they will become too weak on their way home."

33His disciples answered him. "There is nothing here," they said. "Where could we get enough bread to feed this large crowd?"

34"How many loaves do you have?" Jesus asked.

"Seven," they replied, "and a few small fish."

35Jesus told the crowd to sit down on the ground. 36He took the seven loaves and the fish and gave thanks. Then he broke them and gave them to the disciples. And the disciples passed them out to the people. 37All of them ate and were satisfied. After that, the disciples picked up seven baskets of leftover pieces. 38The number of men who ate was 4,000. Women and children also ate.

39After Jesus had sent the crowd away, he got into the boat. He went to the area near Magadan.

Jesus Is Asked for a Miraculous Sign

16 The Pharisees and Sadducees came to put Jesus to the test. They asked him to show them a miraculous sign from heaven.

2He replied, "In the evening you look at the sky. You say, 'It will be good weather. The sky is red.' 3And in the morning you say, 'Today it will be stormy. The sky is red and cloudy.' You know the meaning of what you see in the sky. But you can't understand the signs of what is happening right now. 4An evil and unfaithful people look for a miraculous sign. But none will be given to them except the sign of Jonah."

Then Jesus left them and went away.

The Yeast of the Pharisees and Sadducees

5The disciples crossed over to the other side of the lake. They had forgotten to take bread. 6"Be careful," Jesus said to them. "Watch out for the yeast of the Pharisees and Sadducees."

7The disciples talked about this among themselves. They said, "He must be saying this because we didn't bring any bread."

8Jesus knew what they were saying. So he said, "Your faith is so small! Why are you talking to each other about having no bread? 9Don't you understand yet? Don't you remember the five loaves for the 5,000? Don't you remember how many baskets of pieces you gathered? 10Don't you remember the seven loaves for the 4,000? Don't you remember how many baskets of pieces you gathered? 11How can you possibly not understand? I wasn't talking to you about bread. But watch out for the yeast of the Pharisees and Sadducees."

12Then the disciples understood that Jesus was not telling them to watch out for the yeast used in bread. He was warning them against what the Pharisees and Sadducees taught.

Peter Says That Jesus Is the Christ

13Jesus went to the area of Caesarea Philippi. There he asked his disciples, "Who do people say the Son of Man is?"

14They replied, "Some say John the Baptist. Others say Elijah. Still others say Jeremiah, or one of the prophets."

15"But what about you?" he asked. "Who do you say I am?"

16Simon Peter answered, "You are the Christ. You are the Son of the living God."

17 Jesus replied, "Blessed are you, Simon, son of Jonah! No mere man showed this to you. My Father in heaven showed it to you. 18 Here is what I tell you. You are Peter. On this rock I will build my church. The gates of hell will not be strong enough to destroy it. 19 I will give you the keys to the kingdom of heaven. What you lock on earth will be locked in heaven. What you unlock on earth will be unlocked in heaven."

20 Then Jesus warned his disciples not to tell anyone that he was the Christ.

Jesus Tells About His Coming Death

21 From that time on Jesus began to explain to his disciples what would happen to him. He told them he must go to Jerusalem. There he must suffer many things from the elders, the chief priests and the teachers of the law. He must be killed and on the third day rise to life again.

22 Peter took Jesus to one side and began to scold him. "Never, Lord!" he said. "This will never happen to you!"

23 Jesus turned and said to Peter, "Get behind me, Satan! You are standing in my way. You do not have in mind the things of God. Instead, you are thinking about human things."

24 Then Jesus spoke to his disciples. He said, "If anyone wants to follow me, he must say no to himself. He must pick up his cross and follow me. 25 If he wants to save his life, he will lose it. But if he loses his life for me, he will find it.

26 "What good is it if someone gains the whole world but loses his soul? Or what can anyone trade for his soul? 27 The Son of Man is going to come in his Father's glory. His angels will come with him. And he will reward everyone in keeping with what they have done.

28 "What I'm about to tell you is true. Some who are standing here will not die before they see the Son of Man coming in his kingdom."

Jesus' Appearance Is Changed

17 After six days Jesus took Peter, James, and John the brother of James with him. He led them up a high mountain. They were all alone. 2 There in front of them his appearance was changed. His face shone like the sun. His clothes became as white as the light. 3 Just then Moses and Elijah appeared in front of them. Moses and Elijah were talking with Jesus.

4 Peter said to Jesus, "Lord, it is good for us to be here. If you wish, I will put up three shelters. One will be for you, one for Moses, and one for Elijah."

5 While Peter was still speaking, a bright cloud surrounded them. A voice from the cloud said, "This is my Son, and I love him. I am very pleased with him. Listen to him!"

6 When the disciples heard this, they were terrified. They fell with their faces to the ground. 7 But Jesus came and touched them. "Get up," he said. "Don't be afraid." 8 When they looked up, they saw no one except Jesus.

9 They came down the mountain. On the way down, Jesus told them what to do. "Don't tell anyone what you have seen," he said. "Wait until the Son of Man has been raised from the dead."

10 The disciples asked him, "Why do the teachers of the law say that Elijah has to come first?"

11 Jesus replied, "That's right. Elijah is supposed to come and make all things new again. 12 But I tell you, Elijah has already come. People didn't recognize him. They have done to him everything they wanted to do. In the same way, they are going to make the Son of Man suffer."

13 Then the disciples understood that Jesus was talking to them about John the Baptist.

Jesus Heals a Boy Who Had a Demon

14 When they came near the crowd, a man approached Jesus. He got on his knees in front of him. 15 "Lord," he said, "have mercy on my son. He shakes wildly and suffers a great deal. He often falls into the fire or into the water. 16 I brought him to your disciples. But they couldn't heal him."

17 "You unbelieving and evil people!" Jesus replied. "How long do I have to stay with you? How long do I have to put up with you? Bring the boy here to me."

18 Jesus ordered the demon to leave the boy, and it came out of him. He was healed at that very moment.

19 Then the disciples came to Jesus in private. They asked, "Why couldn't we drive out the demon?"

20/21 He replied, "Because your faith is much too small. What I'm about to tell you is true. If you have faith as small as a mustard seed, it is enough. You can say to this mountain, 'Move from here to there.' And it will move. Nothing will be impossible for you."

22 They came together in Galilee. Then Jesus said to them, "The Son of Man is going to be handed over to men. 23 They will kill him. On the third day he will rise from the dead."

Then the disciples were filled with deep sadness.

Jesus Pays the Temple Tax

24 Jesus and his disciples arrived in Capernaum. There the tax collectors came to Peter. They asked him, "Doesn't your teacher pay the temple tax?"

25 "Yes, he does," he replied.

When Peter came into the house, Jesus spoke first. "What do you think, Simon?" he asked. "Who do the kings of the earth collect taxes and fees from? Do they collect from their own sons or from others?"

26 "From others," Peter answered.

"Then the sons don't have to pay," Jesus said to him. 27 "But we don't want to make them angry. So go to the lake and throw out your fishing line. Take the first fish you catch. Open its mouth. There you will find the exact coin you need. Take it and give it to them for my tax and yours."

Who Is the Most Important Person in the Kingdom?

18 At that time the disciples came to Jesus. They asked him, "Who is the most important person in the kingdom of heaven?"

[2]Jesus called a little child over to him. He had the child stand among them. [3]Jesus said, "What I'm about to tell you is true. You need to change and become like little children. If you don't, you will never enter the kingdom of heaven. [4]Anyone who becomes as free of pride as this child is the most important in the kingdom of heaven.

[5]"Anyone who welcomes a little child like this in my name welcomes me.

[6]"But what if someone leads one of these little ones who believe in me to sin? If he does, it would be better for him to have a large millstone hung around his neck and be drowned at the bottom of the sea.

[7]"How terrible it will be for the world because of the things that lead people to sin! Things like that must come. But how terrible for those who cause them!

[8]"If your hand or foot causes you to sin, cut it off and throw it away. It would be better for you to enter the kingdom of heaven with only one hand or one foot than to go into hell with two hands and two feet. In hell the fire burns forever. [9]If your eye causes you to sin, poke it out and throw it away. It would be better for you to enter the kingdom of heaven with one eye than to have two eyes and be thrown into the fire of hell.

The Story of the Lost Sheep

[10/11]"See that you don't look down on one of these little ones. Here is what I tell you. Their angels in heaven can go at any time to see my Father who is in heaven.

[12]"What do you think? Suppose a man owns 100 sheep and one of them wanders away. Won't he leave the 99 sheep on the hills? Won't he go and look for the one that wandered off? [13]What I'm about to tell you is true. If he finds that sheep, he is happier about the one than about the 99 that didn't wander off. [14]It is the same with your Father in heaven. He does not want any of these little ones to be lost.

When Someone Sins Against You

[15]"If your brother sins against you, go to him. Tell him what he did wrong. Keep it between the two of you. If he listens to you, you have won him back.

[16]"But what if he won't listen to you? Then take one or two others with you. Scripture says, 'Every matter must be proved by the words of two or three witnesses.' *(Deuteronomy 19:15)* [17]But what if he also refuses to listen to the witnesses? Then tell it to the church. And what if he refuses to listen even to the church? Then don't treat him as your brother. Treat him as you would treat an ungodly person or a tax collector.

[18]"What I'm about to tell you is true. What you lock on earth will be locked in heaven. What you unlock on earth will be unlocked in heaven.

[19]"Again, here is what I tell you. Suppose two of you on earth agree about anything you ask for. My Father in heaven will do it for you. [20]Where two or three people meet together in my name, I am there with them."

The Servant Who Had No Mercy

[21]Peter came to Jesus. He asked, "Lord, how many times should I forgive my brother when he sins against me? Up to seven times?"

[22]Jesus answered, "I tell you, not seven times, but 77 times.

[23]"The kingdom of heaven is like a king who wanted to collect all the money his servants owed him. [24]As the king began to do it, a man who owed him millions of dollars was brought to him. [25]The man was not able to pay. So his master gave an order. The man, his wife, his children, and all he owned had to be sold to pay back what he owed.

[26]"The servant fell on his knees in front of him. 'Give me time,' he begged. 'I'll pay everything back.'

[27]"His master felt sorry for him. He forgave him what he owed and let him go.

[28]"But then that servant went out and found one of the other servants who owed him a few dollars. He grabbed him and began to choke him. 'Pay back what you owe me!' he said.

[29]"The other servant fell on his knees. 'Give me time,' he begged him. 'I'll pay you back.'

[30]"But the first servant refused. Instead, he went and had the man thrown into prison. The man would be held there until he could pay back what he owed. [31]The other servants saw what had happened. It troubled them greatly. They went and told their master everything that had happened.

[32]"Then the master called the first servant in. 'You evil servant,' he said. 'I forgave all that you owed me because you begged me to. [33]Shouldn't you have had mercy on the other servant just as I had mercy on you?' [34]In anger his master turned him over to the jailers. He would be punished until he paid back everything he owed.

[35]"This is how my Father in heaven will treat each of you unless you forgive your brother from your heart."

Jesus Teaches About Divorce

19 When Jesus finished saying these things, he left Galilee. He went into the area of Judea on the other side of the Jordan River. [2]Large crowds followed him. He healed them there.

[3]Some Pharisees came to put him to the test. They asked, "Does the Law allow a man to divorce his wife for any reason at all?"

4Jesus replied, "Haven't you read that in the beginning the Creator 'made them male and female'? *(Genesis 1:27)* 5He said, 'That's why a man will leave his father and mother and be joined to his wife. The two will become one.' *(Genesis 2:24)* 6They are no longer two, but one. So a man must not separate what God has joined together."

7They asked, "Then why did Moses command that a man can give his wife a letter of divorce and send her away?"

8Jesus replied, "Moses let you divorce your wives because you were stubborn. But it was not this way from the beginning. 9Here is what I tell you. Anyone who divorces his wife and gets married to another woman commits adultery. A man may divorce his wife only if she has not been faithful to him."

10The disciples said to him, "If that's the way it is between a husband and wife, it is better not to get married."

11Jesus replied, "Not everyone can accept the idea of staying single. Only those who have been helped to live without getting married can accept it. 12Some men are not able to have children because they were born that way. Some have been made that way by other people. Others have made themselves that way in order to serve the kingdom of heaven. The one who can accept living that way should do it."

Little Children Are Brought to Jesus

13Some people brought little children to Jesus. They wanted him to place his hands on the children and pray for them. But the disciples told the people to stop.

14Jesus said, "Let the little children come to me. Don't keep them away. The kingdom of heaven belongs to people like them." 15Jesus placed his hands on them. Then he went on from there.

Jesus and the Rich Young Man

16A man came up to Jesus. He asked, "Teacher, what good thing must I do to receive eternal life?"

17"Why do you ask me about what is good?" Jesus replied. "There is only One who is good. If you want to enter the kingdom, obey the commandments."

18"Which ones?" the man asked.

Jesus said, " 'Do not commit murder. Do not commit adultery. Do not steal. Do not give false witness. 19Honor your father and mother.' *(Exodus 20:12–16; Deuteronomy 5:16–20)* And 'love your neighbor as you love yourself.' " *(Leviticus 19:18)*

20"I have obeyed all those commandments," the young man said. "What else do I need to do?"

21Jesus answered, "If you want to be perfect, go and sell everything you have. Give the money to those who are poor. You will have treasure in heaven. Then come and follow me."

22When the young man heard this, he went away sad. He was very rich.

23Then Jesus said to his disciples, "What I'm about to tell you is true. It is hard for rich people to enter the kingdom of heaven. 24Again I tell you, it is hard for a camel to go through the eye of a needle. But it is even harder for the rich to enter God's kingdom."

25When the disciples heard this, they were really amazed. They asked, "Then who can be saved?"

26Jesus looked at them and said, "With man, that is impossible. But with God, all things are possible."

27Peter answered him, "We have left everything to follow you! What reward will be given to us?"

28"What I'm about to tell you is true," Jesus said to them. "When all things are made new, the Son of Man will sit on his glorious throne. Then you who have followed me will also sit on 12 thrones. You will judge the 12 tribes of Israel. 29Everyone who has left houses or families or fields because of me will receive 100 times as much. They will also receive eternal life. 30But many who are first will be last. And many who are last will be first.

The Story of the Workers in the Vineyard

20 "The kingdom of heaven is like a man who owned land. He went out early in the morning to hire people to work in his vineyard. 2He agreed to give them the usual pay for a day's work. Then he sent them into his vineyard.

3"About nine o'clock in the morning he went out again. He saw others standing in the market place doing nothing. 4He told them, 'You also go and work in my vineyard. I'll pay you what is right.' 5So they went.

"He went out again about noon and at three o'clock and did the same thing. 6About five o'clock he went out and found still others standing around. He asked them, 'Why have you been standing here all day long doing nothing?'

7" 'Because no one has hired us,' they answered.

"He said to them, 'You also go and work in my vineyard.'

8"When evening came, the owner of the vineyard spoke to the person who was in charge of the workers. He said, 'Call the workers and give them their pay. Begin with the last ones I hired. Then go on to the first ones.'

9"The workers who were hired about five o'clock came. Each received the usual day's pay. 10So when those who were hired first came, they expected to receive more. But each of them also received the usual day's pay.

11"When they received it, they began to complain about the owner. 12'These people who were hired last worked only one hour,' they said. 'You have paid them the same as us. We have done most of the work and have been in the hot sun all day.'

13"The owner answered one of them. 'Friend,' he said, 'I'm being fair to you. Didn't you agree to work for the usual day's pay? 14Take your money and go. I want to give the ones I hired last the same pay I gave you. 15Don't I have the right to do what I want with my own money? Do you feel cheated because I gave so freely to the others?'

16"So those who are last will be first. And those who are first will be last."

Jesus Again Tells About His Coming Death

17Jesus was going up to Jerusalem. On the way, he took the 12 disciples to one side to talk to them. 18"We are going up to Jerusalem," he said. "The Son of Man will be handed over to the chief priests and the teachers of the law. They will sentence him to death. 19Then they will turn him over to people who are not Jews. The people will make fun of him and whip him. They will nail him to a cross. On the third day, he will rise from the dead!"

A Mother Asks a Favor of Jesus

20The mother of Zebedee's sons came to Jesus. Her sons came with her. Getting on her knees, she asked a favor of him.

21"What do you want?" Jesus asked.

She said, "Promise me that one of my two sons may sit at your right hand in your kingdom. Promise that the other one may sit at your left hand."

22"You don't know what you're asking for," Jesus said to them. "Can you drink the cup of suffering I am going to drink?"

"We can," they answered.

23Jesus said to them, "You will certainly drink from my cup. But it is not for me to say who will sit at my right or left hand. These places belong to those my Father has prepared them for."

24The other ten disciples heard about this. They became angry at the two brothers.

25Jesus called them together. He said, "You know about the rulers of the nations. They hold power over their people. Their high officials order them around. 26Don't be like that. Instead, anyone who wants to be important among you must be your servant. 27And anyone who wants to be first must be your slave.

28"Be like the Son of Man. He did not come to be served. Instead, he came to serve others. He came to give his life as the price for setting many people free."

Two Blind Men Receive Their Sight

29Jesus and his disciples were leaving Jericho. A large crowd followed him. 30Two blind men were sitting by the side of the road. They heard that Jesus was going by. So they shouted, "Lord! Son of David! Have mercy on us!"

31The crowd commanded them to stop. They told them to be quiet. But the two men shouted even louder, "Lord! Son of David! Have mercy on us!"

32Jesus stopped and called out to them. "What do you want me to do for you?" he asked.

33"Lord," they answered, "we want to be able to see."

34Jesus felt deep concern for them. He touched their eyes. Right away they could see. And they followed him.

Jesus Enters Jerusalem

21 As they all approached Jerusalem, they came to Bethphage. It was on the Mount of Olives. Jesus sent out two disciples. 2He said to them, "Go to the village ahead of you. As soon as you get there, you will find a donkey tied up. Her colt will be with her. Untie them and bring them to me. 3If anyone says anything to you, say that the Lord needs them. The owner will send them right away."

4This took place so that what was spoken through the prophet would come true. It says,

5"Say to the city of Zion,
'See, your king comes to you.
He is gentle and riding on a donkey.
He is riding on a donkey's colt.'"
(Zechariah 9:9)

6The disciples went and did what Jesus told them to do. 7They brought the donkey and the colt. They placed their coats on them. Then Jesus sat on the coats. 8A very large crowd spread their coats on the road. Others cut branches from the trees and spread them on the road. 9Some of the people went ahead of him, and some followed. They all shouted,

"Hosanna to the Son of David!"

"Blessed is the one who comes in the
name of the Lord!" *(Psalm 118:26)*

"Hosanna in the highest heaven!"

10When Jesus entered Jerusalem, the whole city was stirred up. The people asked, "Who is this?"

11The crowds answered, "This is Jesus. He is the prophet from Nazareth in Galilee."

Jesus Clears Out the Temple

12Jesus entered the temple area. He began chasing out all those who were buying and selling there. He turned over the tables of the people who were exchanging money. He also turned over the benches of those who were selling doves. 13He said to them, "It is written that the Lord said, 'My house will be called a house where people can pray.' *(Isaiah 56:7)* But you are making it a 'den for robbers.'" *(Jeremiah 7:11)*

14Blind people and those who were disabled came to Jesus at the temple. There he healed them. 15The chief priests and the teachers of the law saw the wonderful things he did. They also saw the children in the temple area shouting, "Hosanna to the Son of David!" But when they saw all of this, they became angry.

16"Do you hear what these children are saying?" they asked him.

"Yes," replied Jesus. "Haven't you ever read about it in Scripture? It says,

"'You have made sure that children and infants
praise you.'" *(Psalm 8:2)*

17Then Jesus left the people and went out of the city to Bethany. He spent the night there.

The Fig Tree Dries Up

18Early in the morning, Jesus was on his way back to Jerusalem. He was hungry. 19He saw a fig tree by the road. He went up to it but found nothing on it except leaves. Then he said to it, "May you never bear fruit again!" Right away the tree dried up.

20When the disciples saw this, they were amazed. "How did the fig tree dry up so quickly?" they asked.

21Jesus replied, "What I'm about to tell you is true. You must have faith and not doubt. Then you can do what was done to the fig tree. And you can say to this mountain, 'Go and throw yourself into the sea.' It will be done. 22If you believe, you will receive what you ask for when you pray."

The Authority of Jesus Is Questioned

23Jesus entered the temple courtyard. While he was teaching there, the chief priests and the elders of the people came to him. "By what authority are you doing these things?" they asked. "Who gave you this authority?"

24Jesus replied, "I will also ask you one question. If you answer me, I will tell you by what authority I am doing these things. 25Where did John's baptism come from? Was it from heaven? Or did it come from men?"

They talked to each other about it. They said, "If we say, 'From heaven,' he will ask, 'Then why didn't you believe him?' 26But what if we say, 'From men'? We are afraid of the people. Everyone believes that John was a prophet."

27So they answered Jesus, "We don't know."

Jesus said, "Then I won't tell you by what authority I am doing these things either.

The Story of the Two Sons

28"What do you think about this? A man had two sons. He went to the first and said, 'Son, go and work today in the vineyard.'

29"'I will not,' the son answered. But later he changed his mind and went.

30"Then the father went to the other son. He said the same thing. The son answered, 'I will, sir.' But he did not go.

31"Which of the two sons did what his father wanted?"

"The first," they answered.

Jesus said to them, "What I'm about to tell you is true. Tax collectors and prostitutes will enter the kingdom of God ahead of you. 32John came to show you the right way to live. And you did not believe him. But the tax collectors and the prostitutes did. You saw this. But even then you did not turn away from your sins and believe him.

The Story of the Renters

33"Listen to another story. A man who owned some land planted a vineyard. He put a wall around it. He dug a pit for a winepress in it. He also built a lookout tower. He rented the vineyard out to some farmers. Then he went away on a journey. 34When harvest time approached, he sent his servants to the renters. He told the servants to collect his share of the fruit.

35"But the renters grabbed his servants. They beat one of them. They killed another. They threw stones at the third to kill him. 36Then the man sent other servants to the renters. He sent more than he did the first time. The renters treated them the same way.

37"Last of all, he sent his son to them. 'They will respect my son,' he said.

38"But the renters saw the son coming. They said to each other, 'This is the one who will receive all the owner's property someday. Come, let's kill him. Then everything will be ours.' 39So they took him and threw him out of the vineyard. Then they killed him.

40"When the owner of the vineyard comes back, what will he do to those renters?"

41"He will destroy those evil people," they replied. "Then he will rent the vineyard out to other renters. They will give him his share of the crop at harvest time."

42Jesus said to them, "Haven't you ever read what the Scriptures say,

"'The stone the builders didn't accept
has become the most important stone of all.
The Lord has done it.
It is wonderful in our eyes'? *(Psalm 118:22,23)*

43"So here is what I tell you. The kingdom of God will be taken away from you. It will be given to people who will produce its fruit. 44Everyone who falls on that stone will be broken to pieces. But the stone will crush anyone it falls on."

45The chief priests and the Pharisees heard Jesus' stories. They knew he was talking about them. 46So they looked for a way to arrest him. But they were afraid of the crowd. The people believed that Jesus was a prophet.

The Story of the Wedding Dinner

22 Jesus told them more stories. He said, 2"Here is what the kingdom of heaven is like. A king prepared a wedding dinner for his son. 3He sent his servants to those who had been invited to the dinner. The servants told them to come. But they refused.

4"Then he sent some more servants. He said, 'Tell those who were invited that I have prepared my dinner. I have killed my oxen and my fattest cattle. Everything is ready. Come to the wedding dinner.'

5“But the people paid no attention. One went away to his field. Another went away to his business. 6The rest grabbed his servants. They treated them badly and then killed them.

7“The king became very angry. He sent his army to destroy them. They killed those murderers and burned their city.

8“Then the king said to his servants, ‘The wedding dinner is ready. But those I invited were not fit to come. 9Go to the street corners. Invite to the dinner anyone you can find.’ 10So the servants went out into the streets. They gathered all the people they could find, both good and bad. Soon the wedding hall was filled with guests.

11“The king came in to see the guests. He noticed a man there who was not wearing wedding clothes. 12‘Friend,’ he asked, ‘how did you get in here without wedding clothes?’ The man couldn’t think of anything to say.

13“Then the king told his servants, ‘Tie up his hands and feet. Throw him outside into the darkness. Out there people will sob and grind their teeth.’

14“Many are invited, but few are chosen.”

Is It Right to Pay Taxes to Caesar?

15The Pharisees went out. They made plans to trap Jesus with his own words. 16They sent their followers to him. They sent the Herodians with them.

“Teacher,” they said, “we know you are a man of honor. You teach the way of God truthfully. You don’t let others tell you what to do or say. You don’t care how important they are. 17Tell us then, what do you think? Is it right to pay taxes to Caesar or not?”

18But Jesus knew their evil plans. He said, “You pretenders! Why are you trying to trap me? 19Show me the coin people use for paying the tax.”

They brought him a silver coin.

20He asked them, “Whose picture is this? And whose words?”

21“Caesar’s,” they replied.

Then he said to them, “Give to Caesar what belongs to Caesar. And give to God what belongs to God.”

22When they heard this, they were amazed. So they left him and went away.

Marriage When the Dead Rise

23That same day the Sadducees came to Jesus with a question. They do not believe that people rise from the dead.

24“Teacher,” they said, “here is what Moses told us. If a man dies without having children, his brother must get married to the widow. He must have children to carry on his brother’s name. 25There were seven brothers among us. The first one got married and died. Since he had no children, he left his wife to his brother. 26The same thing happened to the second and third brothers. It happened right on down to the seventh brother. 27Finally, the woman died. 28Now then, when the dead rise, whose wife will she be? All seven of them were married to her.”

29Jesus replied, “You are mistaken, because you do not know the Scriptures. And you do not know the power of God. 30When the dead rise, they won’t get married. And their parents won’t give them to be married. They will be like the angels in heaven.

31“What about the dead rising? Haven’t you read what God said to you? 32He said, ‘I am the God of Abraham. I am the God of Isaac. And I am the God of Jacob.’ *(Exodus 3:6)* He is not the God of the dead. He is the God of the living.”

33When the crowds heard this, they were amazed by what he taught.

The Most Important Commandment

34The Pharisees heard that the Sadducees weren’t able to answer Jesus. So the Pharisees got together. 35One of them was an authority on the law. So he tested Jesus with a question. 36“Teacher,” he asked, “which is the most important commandment in the Law?”

37Jesus replied, “ ‘Love the Lord your God with all your heart and with all your soul. Love him with all your mind.’ *(Deuteronomy 6:5)* 38This is the first and most important commandment. 39And the second is like it. ‘Love your neighbor as you love yourself.’ *(Leviticus 19:18)* 40Everything that is written in the Law and the Prophets is based on these two commandments.”

Whose Son Is the Christ?

41The Pharisees were gathered together. Jesus asked them, 42“What do you think about the Christ? Whose son is he?”

“The son of David,” they replied.

43He said to them, “Then why does David call him ‘Lord’? The Holy Spirit spoke through David himself. David said,

44“ ‘The Lord said to my Lord,
“Sit at my right hand
until I put your enemies
under your control.” ’ *(Psalm 110:1)*

45So if David calls him ‘Lord,’ how can he be David’s son?”

46No one could answer him with a single word. From that day on, no one dared to ask him any more questions.

Jesus Judges the Pharisees and the Teachers of the Law

23 Jesus spoke to the crowds and to his disciples. 2“The teachers of the law and the Pharisees sit in Moses’ seat,” he said. 3“So you must obey them. Do everything they tell you. But don’t do what they do. They don’t practice what they preach. 4They tie up heavy loads and put them on other people’s shoulders. But they themselves aren’t willing to lift a finger to move them.

5“Everything they do is done for others to see. On their foreheads and arms they wear little boxes that hold Scripture verses. They make the boxes very wide. And they make the tassels on their coats very long.

6“They love to sit down in the place of honor at dinners. They also love to have the most important seats in the synagogues. 7They love to be greeted in the market places. They love it when people call them ‘Rabbi.’

8“But you shouldn’t be called ‘Rabbi.’ You have only one Master, and you are all brothers. 9Do not call anyone on earth ‘father.’ You have one Father, and he is in heaven. 10You shouldn’t be called ‘teacher.’ You have one Teacher, and he is the Christ. 11The most important person among you will be your servant. 12Anyone who lifts himself up will be brought down. And anyone who is brought down will be lifted up.

13/14“How terrible it will be for you, teachers of the law and Pharisees! You pretenders! You shut the kingdom of heaven in people’s faces. You yourselves do not enter. And you will not let those enter who are trying to.

15“How terrible for you, teachers of the law and Pharisees! You pretenders! You travel everywhere to win one person to your faith. Then you make him twice as much a son of hell as you are.

16“How terrible for you, blind guides! You say, ‘If anyone takes an oath in the name of the temple, it means nothing. But anyone who takes an oath in the name of the gold of the temple must keep the oath.’ 17You are blind and foolish! Which is more important? Is it the gold? Or is it the temple that makes the gold holy?

18“You also say, ‘If anyone takes an oath in the name of the altar, it means nothing. But anyone who takes an oath in the name of the gift on it must keep the oath.’ 19You blind men! Which is more important? Is it the gift? Or is it the altar that makes the gift holy?

20“So anyone who takes an oath in the name of the altar takes an oath in the name of it and of everything on it. 21And anyone who takes an oath in the name of the temple takes an oath in the name of it and of the One who lives in it. 22And anyone who takes an oath in the name of heaven takes an oath in the name of God’s throne and of the One who sits on it.

23“How terrible for you, teachers of the law and Pharisees! You pretenders! You give God a tenth of your spices, like mint, dill and cummin. But you have not practiced the more important things of the law, like fairness, mercy and faithfulness. You should have practiced the last things without failing to do the first. 24You blind guides! You remove the smallest insect from your food. But you swallow a whole camel!

25“How terrible for you, teachers of the law and Pharisees! You pretenders! You clean the outside of the cup and dish. But on the inside you are full of greed. You only want to satisfy yourselves. 26Blind Pharisee! First clean the inside of the cup and dish. Then the outside will also be clean.

27“How terrible for you, teachers of the law and Pharisees! You pretenders! You are like tombs that are painted white. They look beautiful on the outside. But on the inside they are full of the bones of the dead. They are also full of other things that are not pure and clean. 28It is the same with you. On the outside you seem to be doing what is right. But on the inside you are full of what is wrong. You pretend to be what you are not.

29“How terrible for you, teachers of the law and Pharisees! You pretenders! You build tombs for the prophets. You decorate the graves of the godly. 30And you say, ‘If we had lived in the days of those who lived before us, we wouldn’t have done what they did. We wouldn’t have helped to kill the prophets.’ 31So you give witness against yourselves. You admit that you are the children of those who murdered the prophets. 32So finish the sins that those who lived before you started!

33“You nest of poisonous snakes! How will you escape from being sentenced to hell? 34So I am sending you prophets, wise men, and teachers. You will kill some of them. You will nail some to a cross. Others you will whip in your synagogues. You will chase them from town to town.

35“So you will pay for all the godly people’s blood spilled on earth. I mean from the blood of godly Abel to the blood of Zechariah, the son of Berekiah. Zechariah was the one you murdered between the temple and the altar. 36What I’m about to tell you is true. All this will happen to those who are now living.

37“Jerusalem! Jerusalem! You kill the prophets and throw stones in order to kill those who are sent to you. Many times I have wanted to gather your people together. I have wanted to be like a hen who gathers her chicks under her wings. But you would not let me! 38Look, your house is left empty. 39I tell you, you will not see me again until you say, ‘Blessed is the one who comes in the name of the Lord.’” *(Psalm 118:26)*

Signs of the End

24 Jesus left the temple. He was walking away when his disciples came up to him. They wanted to call his attention to the temple buildings.

2“Do you see all these things?” Jesus asked. “What I’m about to tell you is true. Not one stone here will be left on top of another. Every stone will be thrown down.”

3Jesus was sitting on the Mount of Olives. There the disciples came to him in private. “Tell us,” they said. “When will this happen? And what will be the sign of your coming? What will be the sign of the end?”

4Jesus answered, “Keep watch! Be careful that no one fools you. 5Many will come in my name.

They will claim, 'I am the Christ!' They will fool many people.

6"You will hear about wars. You will also hear people talking about future wars. Don't be alarmed. Those things must happen. But the end still isn't here. 7Nation will fight against nation. Kingdom will fight against kingdom. People will go hungry. There will be earthquakes in many places. 8All these are the beginning of birth pains.

9"Then people will hand you over to be treated badly and killed. All nations will hate you because of me. 10At that time, many will turn away from their faith. They will hate each other. They will hand each other over to their enemies. 11Many false prophets will appear. They will fool many people. 12Because evil will grow, most people's love will grow cold. 13But the one who stands firm to the end will be saved. 14This good news of the kingdom will be preached in the whole world. It will be a witness to all nations. Then the end will come.

15"The prophet Daniel spoke about 'the hated thing that destroys.' *(Daniel 9:27; 11:31; 12:11)* Someday you will see it standing in the holy place. The reader should understand this. 16Then those who are in Judea should escape to the mountains. 17No one on the roof should go down into his house to take anything out. 18No one in the field should go back to get his coat. 19How awful it will be in those days for pregnant women! How awful for nursing mothers! 20Pray that you will not have to escape in winter or on the Sabbath day. 21There will be terrible suffering in those days. It will be worse than any other from the beginning of the world until now. And there will never be anything like it again. 22If the time had not been cut short, no one would live. But because of God's chosen people, it will be shortened.

23"At that time someone may say to you, 'Look! Here is the Christ!' Or, 'There he is!' Do not believe it. 24False Christs and false prophets will appear. They will do great signs and miracles. They will try to fool God's chosen people if possible. 25See, I have told you ahead of time.

26"So if anyone tells you, 'He is far out in the desert,' do not go out there. Or if anyone says, 'He is deep inside the house,' do not believe it. 27Lightning that comes from the east can be seen in the west. It will be the same when the Son of Man comes. 28The vultures will gather wherever there is a dead body.

29"Right after the terrible suffering of those days,

"'The sun will be darkened.
The moon will not shine.
The stars will fall from the sky.
The heavenly bodies will be shaken.'
(Isaiah 13:10; 34:4)

30"At that time the sign of the Son of Man will appear in the sky. All the nations on earth will be sad. They will see the Son of Man coming on the clouds of the sky. He will come with power and great glory. 31He will send his angels with a loud trumpet call. They will gather his chosen people from all four directions. They will bring them from one end of the heavens to the other.

32"Learn a lesson from the fig tree. As soon as its twigs get tender and its leaves come out, you know that summer is near. 33In the same way, when you see all those things happening, you know that the end is near. It is right at the door. 34What I'm about to tell you is true. The people living at that time will certainly not pass away until all those things have happened. 35Heaven and earth will pass away. But my words will never pass away.

The Day and Hour Are Not Known

36"No one knows about that day or hour. Not even the angels in heaven know. The Son does not know. Only the Father knows.

37"Remember how it was in the days of Noah. It will be the same when the Son of Man comes.

38"In the days before the flood, people were eating and drinking. They were getting married. They were giving their daughters to be married. They did all those things right up to the day Noah entered the ark. 39They knew nothing about what would happen until the flood came and took them all away. That is how it will be when the Son of Man comes.

40"Two men will be in the field. One will be taken and the other left. 41Two women will be grinding with a hand mill. One will be taken and the other left.

42"So keep watch. You do not know on what day your Lord will come. 43You must understand something. Suppose the owner of the house knew what time of night the robber was coming. Then he would have kept watch. He would not have let his house be broken into. 44So you also must be ready. The Son of Man will come at an hour when you don't expect him.

45"Suppose a master puts one of his servants in charge of the other servants in his house. The servant's job is to give them their food at the right time. The master wants a faithful and wise servant for this. 46It will be good for the servant if the master finds him doing his job when the master returns. 47What I'm about to tell you is true. The master will put that servant in charge of everything he owns.

48"But suppose that servant is evil. Suppose he says to himself, 'My master is staying away a long time.' 49Suppose he begins to beat the other servants. And suppose he eats and drinks with those who drink too much. 50The master of that servant will come back on a day the servant doesn't expect him. He will return at an hour the servant does not know. 51Then the master will cut him to pieces. He will send him to the place where pretenders go. There people will sob and grind their teeth.

The Story of Ten Bridesmaids

25 "Here is what the kingdom of heaven will be like at that time. Ten bridesmaids took their lamps and went out to meet the groom. 2Five

of them were foolish. Five were wise. 3The foolish ones took their lamps but didn't take any olive oil with them. 4The wise ones took oil in jars along with their lamps. 5The groom did not come for a long time. So the bridesmaids all grew tired and fell asleep.

6"At midnight someone cried out, 'Here's the groom! Come out to meet him!'

7"Then all the bridesmaids woke up and got their lamps ready. 8The foolish ones said to the wise ones, 'Give us some of your oil. Our lamps are going out.'

9"'No,' they replied. 'There may not be enough for all of us. Instead, go to those who sell oil. Buy some for yourselves.'

10"So they went to buy the oil. But while they were on their way, the groom arrived. The bridesmaids who were ready went in with him to the wedding dinner. Then the door was shut.

11"Later, the other bridesmaids also came. 'Sir! Sir!' they said. 'Open the door for us!'

12"But he replied, 'What I'm about to tell you is true. I don't know you.'

13"So keep watch. You do not know the day or the hour that the groom will come.

The Story of Three Servants

14"Again, here is what the kingdom of heaven will be like. A man was going on a journey. He sent for his servants and put them in charge of his property. 15He gave $10,000 to one. He gave $4,000 to another. And he gave $2,000 to the third. The man gave each servant the amount of money he knew the servant could take care of. Then he went on his journey.

16"The servant who had received the $10,000 went at once and put his money to work. He earned $10,000 more. 17The one with the $4,000 earned $4,000 more. 18But the man who had received $2,000 went and dug a hole in the ground. He hid his master's money in it.

19"After a long time the master of those servants returned. He wanted to collect all the money they had earned. 20The man who had received $10,000 brought the other $10,000. 'Master,' he said, 'you trusted me with $10,000. See, I have earned $10,000 more.'

21"His master replied, 'You have done well, good and faithful servant! You have been faithful with a few things. I will put you in charge of many things. Come and share your master's happiness!'

22"The man with $4,000 also came. 'Master,' he said, 'you trusted me with $4,000. See, I have earned $4,000 more.'

23"His master replied, 'You have done well, good and faithful servant! You have been faithful with a few things. I will put you in charge of many things. Come and share your master's happiness!'

24"Then the man who had received $2,000 came. 'Master,' he said, 'I knew that you are a hard man. You harvest where you have not planted. You gather crops where you have not scattered seed. 25So I was afraid. I went out and hid your $2,000 in the ground. See, here is what belongs to you.'

26"His master replied, 'You evil, lazy servant! So you knew that I harvest where I have not planted? You knew that I gather crops where I have not scattered seed? 27Well then, you should have put my money in the bank. When I returned, I would have received it back with interest.'

28"Then his master commanded the other servants, 'Take the $2,000 from him. Give it to the one who has $20,000. 29Everyone who has will be given more. He will have more than enough. And what about anyone who doesn't have? Even what he has will be taken away from him. 30Throw that worthless servant outside. There in the darkness, people will sob and grind their teeth.'

The Sheep and the Goats

31"The Son of Man will come in all his glory. All the angels will come with him. Then he will sit on his throne in the glory of heaven. 32All the nations will be gathered in front of him. He will separate the people into two groups. He will be like a shepherd who separates the sheep from the goats. 33He will put the sheep to his right and the goats to his left.

34"Then the King will speak to those on his right. He will say, 'My Father has blessed you. Come and take what is yours. It is the kingdom prepared for you since the world was created. 35I was hungry. And you gave me something to eat. I was thirsty. And you gave me something to drink. I was a stranger. And you invited me in. 36I needed clothes. And you gave them to me. I was sick. And you took care of me. I was in prison. And you came to visit me.'

37"Then the people who have done what is right will answer him. 'Lord,' they will ask, 'when did we see you hungry and feed you? When did we see you thirsty and give you something to drink? 38When did we see you as a stranger and invite you in? When did we see you needing clothes and give them to you? 39When did we see you sick or in prison and go to visit you?'

40"The King will reply, 'What I'm about to tell you is true. Anything you did for one of the least important of these brothers of mine, you did for me.'

41"Then he will say to those on his left, 'You are cursed! Go away from me into the fire that burns forever. It has been prepared for the devil and his angels. 42I was hungry. But you gave me nothing to eat. I was thirsty. But you gave me nothing to drink. 43I was a stranger. But you did not invite me in. I needed clothes. But you did not give me any. I was sick and in prison. But you did not take care of me.'

44"They also will answer, 'Lord, when did we see you hungry or thirsty and not help you? When did we see you as a stranger or needing clothes or sick or in prison and not help you?'

45“He will reply, ‘What I’m about to tell you is true. Anything you didn’t do for one of the least important of these, you didn’t do for me.’

46“Then they will go away to be punished forever. But those who have done what is right will receive eternal life.”

The Plan to Kill Jesus

26 Jesus finished saying all these things. Then he said to his disciples, 2“As you know, the Passover Feast is two days away. The Son of Man will be handed over to be nailed to a cross.”

3Then the chief priests met with the elders of the people. They met in the palace of Caiaphas, the high priest. 4They made plans to arrest Jesus in a clever way. They wanted to kill him. 5“But not during the Feast,” they said. “The people may stir up trouble.”

A Woman Pours Perfume on Jesus

6Jesus was in Bethany. He was in the home of a man named Simon, who had a skin disease. 7A woman came to Jesus with a special sealed jar of very expensive perfume. She poured the perfume on his head while he was at the table.

8When the disciples saw this, they became angry. “Why this waste?” they asked. 9“The perfume could have been sold at a high price. The money could have been given to poor people.”

10Jesus was aware of this. So he said to them, “Why are you bothering this woman? She has done a beautiful thing to me. 11You will always have poor people with you. But you will not always have me. 12She poured the perfume on my body to prepare me to be buried. 13What I’m about to tell you is true. What she has done will be told anywhere this good news is preached all over the world. It will be told in memory of her.”

Judas Agrees to Hand Jesus Over

14One of the Twelve went to the chief priests. His name was Judas Iscariot. 15He asked, “What will you give me if I hand Jesus over to you?” So they counted out 30 silver coins for him. 16From then on, Judas watched for the right time to hand Jesus over to them.

The Lord’s Supper

17It was the first day of the Feast of Unleavened Bread. The disciples came to Jesus. They asked, “Where do you want us to prepare for you to eat the Passover meal?”

18He replied, “Go into the city to a certain man. Tell him, ‘The Teacher says, “My time is near. I am going to celebrate the Passover at your house with my disciples.” ’ ”

19So the disciples did what Jesus had told them to do. They prepared the Passover meal.

20When evening came, Jesus was at the table with the Twelve. 21While they were eating, he said, “What I’m about to tell you is true. One of you will hand me over to my enemies.”

22The disciples became very sad. One after the other, they began to say to him, “It’s not I, Lord, is it?”

23Jesus replied, “The one who has dipped his hand into the bowl with me will hand me over. 24The Son of Man will go just as it is written about him. But how terrible it will be for the one who hands over the Son of Man! It would be better for him if he had not been born.”

25Judas was the one who was going to hand him over. He said, “It’s not I, Rabbi, is it?”

Jesus answered, “Yes. It is you.”

26While they were eating, Jesus took bread. He gave thanks and broke it. He handed it to his disciples and said, “Take this and eat it. This is my body.”

27Then he took the cup. He gave thanks and handed it to them. He said, “All of you drink from it. 28This is my blood of the new covenant. It is poured out to forgive the sins of many. 29Here is what I tell you. From now on, I won’t drink wine with you again until the day I drink it with you in my Father’s kingdom.”

30Then they sang a hymn and went out to the Mount of Olives.

Jesus Says That Peter Will Fail

31Jesus told them, “This very night you will all turn away because of me. It is written that the Lord said,

“ ‘I will strike the shepherd down.
Then the sheep of the flock will be scattered.’ *(Zechariah 13:7)*

32But after I rise from the dead, I will go ahead of you into Galilee.”

33Peter replied, “All the others may turn away because of you. But I never will.”

34“What I’m about to tell you is true,” Jesus answered. “It will happen this very night. Before the rooster crows, you will say three times that you don’t know me.”

35But Peter said, “I may have to die with you. But I will never say I don’t know you.” And all the other disciples said the same thing.

Jesus Prays in Gethsemane

36Then Jesus went with his disciples to a place called Gethsemane. He said to them, “Sit here while I go over there and pray.”

37He took Peter and the two sons of Zebedee along with him. He began to be sad and troubled. 38Then he said to them, “My soul is very sad. I feel close to death. Stay here. Keep watch with me.”

39He went a little farther. Then he fell with his face to the ground. He prayed, “My Father, if it is possible, take this cup of suffering away from me. But let what you want be done, not what I want.”

40Then he returned to his disciples and found them sleeping. “Couldn’t you men keep watch with me for one hour?” he asked Peter. 41“Watch

and pray. Then you won't fall into sin when you
are tempted. The spirit is willing. But the body is
weak."
42Jesus went away a second time. He prayed,
"My Father, is it possible for this cup to be taken
away? But if I must drink it, may what you want
be done."
43Then he came back. Again he found them
sleeping. They couldn't keep their eyes open. 44So
he left them and went away once more. For the
third time he prayed the same thing.
45Then he returned to the disciples. He said to
them, "Are you still sleeping and resting? Look!
The hour is near. The Son of Man is about to be
handed over to sinners. 46Get up! Let us go! Here
comes the one who is handing me over to them!"

Jesus Is Arrested

47While Jesus was still speaking, Judas arrived.
He was one of the Twelve. A large crowd was with
him. They were carrying swords and clubs. The
chief priests and the elders of the people had sent
them.
48Judas, who was going to hand Jesus over, had
arranged a signal with them. "The one I kiss is the
man," he said. "Arrest him."
49So Judas went to Jesus at once. He said,
"Greetings, Rabbi!" And he kissed him.
50Jesus replied, "Friend, do what you came
to do."
Then the men stepped forward. They grabbed
Jesus and arrested him. 51At that moment, one of
Jesus' companions reached for his sword. He
pulled it out and struck the servant of the high
priest with it. He cut off the servant's ear.
52"Put your sword back in its place," Jesus said
to him. "All who use the sword will die by the
sword. 53Do you think I can't ask my Father for
help? He would send an army of more than 70,000
angels right away. 54But then how would the Scriptures come true? They say it must happen in this
way."
55At that time Jesus spoke to the crowd. "Am I
leading a band of armed men against you?" he
asked. "Do you have to come out with swords and
clubs to capture me? Every day I sat in the temple
courtyard teaching. And you didn't arrest me.
56But all this has happened so that the words of the
prophets would come true."
Then all the disciples left him and ran away.

Jesus Is Taken to the Sanhedrin

57Those who had arrested Jesus took him to Caiaphas, the high priest. The teachers of the law and
the elders had come together there. 58Not too far
away, Peter followed Jesus. He went right up to
the courtyard of the high priest. He entered and sat
down with the guards to see what would happen.
59The chief priests and the whole Sanhedrin
were looking for something to use against Jesus.
They wanted to put him to death. 60But they did
not find any proof, even though many false witnesses came forward.
Finally, two other witnesses came forward.
61They said, "This fellow claimed, 'I am able to
destroy the temple of God. I can build it again in
three days.'"
62Then the high priest stood up. He asked Jesus,
"Aren't you going to answer? What are these
charges that these men are bringing against you?"
63But Jesus remained silent.
The high priest said to him, "I command you
under oath by the living God. Tell us if you are the
Christ, the Son of God."
64"Yes. It is just as you say," Jesus replied. "But
here is what I say to all of you. In days to come,
you will see the Son of Man sitting at the right
hand of the Mighty One. You will see the Son of
Man coming on the clouds of heaven."
65Then the high priest tore his clothes. He said,
"He has spoken a very evil thing against God!
Why do we need any more witnesses? You have
heard him say this evil thing. 66What do you
think?"
"He must die!" they answered.
67Then they spit in his face. They hit him with
their fists. Others slapped him. 68They said,
"Prophesy to us, Christ! Who hit you?"

Peter Says He Does Not Know Jesus

69Peter was sitting out in the courtyard. A
female servant came to him. "You also were with
Jesus of Galilee," she said.
70But in front of all of them, Peter said he was
not. "I don't know what you're talking about," he
said.
71Then he went out to the gate leading into the
courtyard. There another woman saw him. She
said to the people, "This fellow was with Jesus of
Nazareth."
72Again he said he was not. With an oath he
said, "I don't know the man!"
73After a little while, those standing there went
up to Peter. "You must be one of them," they said.
"The way you talk gives you away."
74Then Peter began to call down curses on himself. He took an oath and said to them, "I don't
know the man!"
Right away a rooster crowed. 75Then Peter
remembered what Jesus had said. "The rooster will
crow," Jesus had told him. "Before it does, you
will say three times that you don't know me." Peter went outside. He broke down and sobbed.

Judas Hangs Himself

27 It was early in the morning. All the chief
priests and the elders of the people decided
to put Jesus to death. 2They tied him up and led
him away. Then they handed him over to Pilate,
who was the governor.
3Judas, who had handed him over, saw that
Jesus had been sentenced to die. He felt deep

shame and sadness for what he had done. So he
returned the 30 silver coins to the chief priests and
the elders. 4"I have sinned," he said. "I handed
over a man who is not guilty."
"What do we care?" they replied. "That's your
problem."
5So Judas threw the money into the temple and
left. Then he went away and hanged himself.
6The chief priests picked up the coins. They
said, "It's against the law to put this money into
the temple fund. It is blood money. It has paid for
a man's death." 7So they decided to use the money
to buy a potter's field. People from other countries
would be buried there. 8That is why it has been
called The Field of Blood to this very day. 9Then
the words spoken by Jeremiah the prophet came
true. He had said, "They took the 30 silver coins.
That price was set for him by the people of Israel.
10They used the coins to buy a potter's field, just as
the Lord commanded me." *(Zechariah 11:12,13; Jeremiah 19:1–13; 32:6–9)*

Jesus Is Brought to Pilate

11Jesus was standing in front of the governor.
The governor asked him, "Are you the king of the
Jews?"
"Yes. It is just as you say," Jesus replied.
12But when the chief priests and the elders
brought charges against him, he did not answer.
13Then Pilate asked him, "Don't you hear the
charges they are bringing against you?"
14But Jesus made no reply, not even to a single
charge. The governor was really amazed.
15It was the governor's practice at the Passover
Feast to let one prisoner go free. The people could
choose the one they wanted. 16At that time they
had a well-known prisoner named Barabbas. 17So
when the crowd gathered, Pilate asked them,
"Which one do you want me to set free? Barabbas? Or Jesus who is called Christ?" 18Pilate knew
that the leaders were jealous. He knew this was
why they had handed Jesus over to him.
19While Pilate was sitting on the judge's seat,
his wife sent him a message. It said, "Don't have
anything to do with that man. He is not guilty. I
have suffered a great deal in a dream today
because of him."
20But the chief priests and the elders talked the
crowd into asking for Barabbas and having Jesus
put to death.
21"Which of the two do you want me to set
free?" asked the governor.
"Barabbas," they answered.
22"Then what should I do with Jesus who is
called Christ?" Pilate asked.
They all answered, "Crucify him!"
23"Why? What wrong has he done?" asked Pilate.
But they shouted even louder, "Crucify him!"
24Pilate saw that he wasn't getting anywhere.
Instead, the crowd was starting to get angry. So he
took water and washed his hands in front of them.
"I am not guilty of this man's death," he said. "You
are accountable for that!"
25All the people answered, "We and our children will accept the guilt for his death!"
26Pilate let Barabbas go free. But he had Jesus
whipped. Then he handed him over to be nailed to
a cross.

The Soldiers Make Fun of Jesus

27The governor's soldiers took Jesus into the
palace, which was called the Praetorium. All the rest
of the soldiers gathered around him. 28They took off
his clothes and put a purple robe on him. 29Then
they twisted thorns together to make a crown. They
placed it on his head. They put a stick in his right
hand. Then they fell on their knees in front of him
and made fun of him. "We honor you, king of the
Jews!" they said. 30They spit on him. They hit him
on the head with the stick again and again.
31After they had made fun of him, they took off
the robe. They put his own clothes back on him.
Then they led him away to nail him to a cross.

Jesus Is Nailed to a Cross

32On their way out of the city, they met a man
from Cyrene. His name was Simon. They forced
him to carry the cross.
33They came to a place called Golgotha. The
word Golgotha means The Place of the Skull.
34There they mixed wine with bitter spices and
gave it to Jesus to drink. After tasting it, he refused
to drink it.
35When they had nailed him to the cross, they
divided up his clothes by casting lots. 36They sat
down and kept watch over him there.
37Above his head they placed the written charge
against him. It read, THIS IS JESUS, THE KING OF THE
JEWS.
38Two robbers were crucified with him. One
was on his right and one was on his left.
39Those who passed by shouted at Jesus and
made fun of him. They shook their heads 40and
said, "So you are going to destroy the temple and
build it again in three days? Then save yourself!
Come down from the cross, if you are the Son of
God!"
41In the same way the chief priests, the teachers
of the law and the elders made fun of him. 42"He
saved others," they said. "But he can't save himself! He's the King of Israel! Let him come down
now from the cross! Then we will believe in him.
43He trusts in God. Let God rescue him now if he
wants him. He's the one who said, 'I am the Son of
God.'"
44In the same way the robbers who were being
crucified with Jesus also made fun of him.

Jesus Dies

45From noon until three o'clock, the whole land
was covered with darkness. 46About three o'clock,

Jesus cried out in a loud voice. He said, *"Eloi,*
Eloi, lama sabachthani?" This means "My God,
my God, why have you deserted me?" *(Psalm 22:1)*
47 Some of those standing there heard Jesus cry
out. They said, "He's calling for Elijah."
48 Right away one of them ran and got a sponge.
He filled it with wine vinegar and put it on a stick.
He offered it to Jesus to drink. 49 The rest said,
"Leave him alone. Let's see if Elijah comes to save
him."
50 After Jesus cried out again in a loud voice, he
died.
51 At that moment the temple curtain was torn in
two from top to bottom. The earth shook. The
rocks split. 52 Tombs broke open. The bodies of
many holy people who had died were raised to life.
53 They came out of the tombs. After Jesus was
raised to life, they went into the holy city. There
they appeared to many people.
54 The Roman commander and those guarding
Jesus saw the earthquake and all that had happened. They were terrified. They exclaimed, "He
was surely the Son of God!"
55 Not very far away, many women were watching. They had followed Jesus from Galilee to take
care of his needs. 56 Mary Magdalene was among
them. Mary, the mother of James and Joses, was
also there. So was the mother of Zebedee's sons.

Jesus Is Buried

57 As evening approached, a rich man came from
the town of Arimathea. His name was Joseph. He
had become a follower of Jesus. 58 He went to Pilate and asked for Jesus' body. Pilate ordered that
it be given to him.
59 Joseph took the body and wrapped it in a clean
linen cloth. 60 He placed it in his own new tomb
that he had cut out of the rock. He rolled a big
stone in front of the entrance to the tomb. Then he
went away.
61 Mary Magdalene and the other Mary were sitting there across from the tomb.

The Guards at the Tomb

62 The next day was the day after Preparation
Day. The chief priests and the Pharisees went to
Pilate. 63 "Sir," they said, "we remember something
that liar said while he was still alive. He claimed,
'After three days I will rise again.' 64 So give the
order to make the tomb secure until the third day.
If you don't, his disciples might come and steal the
body. Then they will tell the people that Jesus has
been raised from the dead. This last lie will be
worse than the first."
65 "Take some guards with you," Pilate
answered. "Go. Make the tomb as secure as you
can." 66 So they went and made the tomb secure.
They put a seal on the stone and placed some
guards on duty.

Jesus Rises From the Dead

28 The Sabbath day was now over. It was
dawn on the first day of the week. Mary
Magdalene and the other Mary went to look at the
tomb.
2 There was a powerful earthquake. An angel of
the Lord came down from heaven. The angel went
to the tomb. He rolled back the stone and sat on it.
3 His body shone like lightning. His clothes were
as white as snow. 4 The guards were so afraid of
him that they shook and became like dead men.
5 The angel said to the women, "Don't be afraid.
I know that you are looking for Jesus, who was
crucified. 6 He is not here! He has risen, just as he
said he would! Come and see the place where he
was lying. 7 Go quickly! Tell his disciples, 'He has
risen from the dead. He is going ahead of you into
Galilee. There you will see him.' Now I have told
you."
8 So the women hurried away from the tomb.
They were afraid, but they were filled with joy.
They ran to tell the disciples.
9 Suddenly Jesus met them. "Greetings!" he
said.
They came to him, took hold of his feet and
worshiped him.
10 Then Jesus said to them, "Don't be afraid. Go
and tell my brothers to go to Galilee. There they
will see me."

The Guards Report to the Chief Priests

11 While the women were on their way, some of
the guards went into the city. They reported to the
chief priests all that had happened.
12 When the chief priests met with the elders,
they came up with a plan. They gave the soldiers
a large amount of money. 13 They told the soldiers,
"We want you to say, 'His disciples came during
the night. They stole his body while we were
sleeping.' 14 If the governor hears this report, we
will pay him off. That will keep you out of
trouble."
15 So the soldiers took the money and did as they
were told. This story has spread all around among
the Jews to this very day.

Jesus' Final Orders to His Disciples

16 Then the 11 disciples went to Galilee. They
went to the mountain where Jesus had told them
to go. 17 When they saw him, they worshiped him.
But some still had their doubts.
18 Then Jesus came to them. He said, "All
authority in heaven and on earth has been given to
me. 19 So you must go and make disciples of all
nations. Baptize them in the name of the Father
and of the Son and of the Holy Spirit. 20 Teach them
to obey everything I have commanded you. And
you can be sure that I am always with you, to the
very end."

Mark

John the Baptist Prepares the Way

1 This is the beginning of the good news about
Jesus Christ, the Son of God.
[2]Long ago Isaiah the prophet wrote,

"I will send my messenger ahead of you.
He will prepare your way." *(Malachi 3:1)*
[3]"A messenger is calling out in the desert,
'Prepare the way for the Lord.
Make straight paths for him.'" *(Isaiah 40:3)*

[4]And so John came. He baptized people in the
desert. He also preached that people should be
baptized and turn away from their sins. Then God
would forgive them. [5]All the people from the
countryside of Judea went out to him. All the people from Jerusalem went too. When they admitted
they had sinned, John baptized them in the Jordan
River. [6]John wore clothes made out of camel's
hair. He had a leather belt around his waist. And
he ate locusts and wild honey.
[7]Here is what John was preaching. "After me,
one will come who is more powerful than I am.
I'm not good enough to bend down and untie his
sandals. [8]I baptize you with water. But he will baptize you with the Holy Spirit."

Jesus Is Baptized and Tempted

[9]At that time Jesus came from Nazareth in Galilee. John baptized him in the Jordan River. [10]Jesus
was coming up out of the water. Just then he saw
heaven being torn open. He saw the Holy Spirit
coming down on him like a dove. [11]A voice spoke
to him from heaven. It said, "You are my Son, and
I love you. I am very pleased with you."
[12]At once the Holy Spirit sent Jesus out into the
desert. [13]He was in the desert 40 days. There Satan tempted him. The wild animals didn't harm
Jesus. Angels took care of him.

Jesus Chooses the First Disciples

[14]After John was put in prison, Jesus went into
Galilee. He preached God's good news. [15]"The
time has come," he said. "The kingdom of God is
near. Turn away from your sins and believe the
good news!"
[16]One day Jesus was walking beside the Sea of
Galilee. There he saw Simon and his brother Andrew. They were throwing a net into the lake. They
were fishermen. [17]"Come. Follow me," Jesus said.
"I will make you fishers of people."
[18]At once they left their nets and followed him.
[19]Then Jesus walked a little farther. As he did,
he saw James, son of Zebedee, and his brother
John. They were in a boat preparing their nets.
[20]Right away he called out to them. They left their
father Zebedee in the boat with the hired men.
Then they followed Jesus.

Jesus Drives Out an Evil Spirit

[21]Jesus and those with him went to Capernaum.
When the Sabbath day came, he went into the synagogue. There he began to teach. [22]The people
were amazed at his teaching. He taught them like
one who had authority. He did not talk like the
teachers of the law.
[23]Just then a man in their synagogue cried out.
He was controlled by an evil spirit. He said,
[24]"What do you want with us, Jesus of Nazareth?
Have you come to destroy us? I know who you
are. You are the Holy One of God!"
[25]"Be quiet!" said Jesus firmly. "Come out of
him!"
[26]The evil spirit shook the man wildly. Then it
came out of him with a scream.
[27]All the people were amazed. So they asked
each other, "What is this? A new teaching! And
with so much authority! He even gives orders to
evil spirits, and they obey him." [28]News about
Jesus spread quickly all over Galilee.

Jesus Heals Many People

[29]Jesus and those with him left the synagogue.
Right away they went with James and John to the
home of Simon and Andrew. [30]Simon's mother-in-
law was lying in bed. She had a fever. They told
Jesus about her. [31]So he went to her. He took her
hand and helped her up. The fever left her. Then
she began to serve them.
[32]That evening after sunset, the people brought
to Jesus all who were sick. They also brought all
who were controlled by demons. [33]All the people
in town gathered at the door. [34]Jesus healed many
of them. They had all kinds of sicknesses. He also
drove out many demons. But he would not let the
demons speak, because they knew who he was.

Jesus Prays in a Quiet Place

[35]It was very early in the morning and still dark.
Jesus got up and left the house. He went to a place
where he could be alone. There he prayed. [36]Simon
and his friends went to look for Jesus. [37]When they
found him, they called out, "Everyone is looking
for you!"
[38]Jesus replied, "Let's go somewhere else. I
want to go to the nearby towns. I must preach there
also. That is why I have come." [39]So he traveled
all around Galilee. He preached in their synagogues. He also drove out demons.

Jesus Heals a Man Who Had a Skin Disease

[40]A man who had a skin disease came to Jesus.
On his knees he begged Jesus. He said, "If you are
willing to make me 'clean,' you can do it."
[41]Jesus was filled with deep concern. He
reached out his hand and touched the man. "I am

willing to do it," he said. "Be 'clean'!" 42Right away the disease left him. He was healed.

43Jesus sent him away at once. He gave the man a strong warning. 44"Don't tell this to anyone," he said. "Go and show yourself to the priest. Offer the sacrifices that Moses commanded. It will be a witness to the priest and the people that you are 'clean.'"

45But the man went out and started talking right away. He spread the news to everyone. So Jesus could no longer enter a town openly. He stayed outside in lonely places. But people still came to him from everywhere.

Jesus Heals a Man Who Could Not Walk

2 A few days later, Jesus entered Capernaum again. The people heard that he had come home. 2So many people gathered that there was no room left. There was not even room outside the door. And Jesus preached the word to them.

3Four of those who came were carrying a man who could not walk. 4But they could not get him close to Jesus because of the crowd. So they made a hole in the roof above Jesus. Then they lowered the man through it on a mat.

5Jesus saw their faith. So he said to the man, "Son, your sins are forgiven."

6Some teachers of the law were sitting there. They were thinking, 7"Why is this fellow talking like that? He's saying a very evil thing! Only God can forgive sins!"

8Right away Jesus knew what they were thinking. So he said to them, "Why are you thinking these things? 9Is it easier to say to this man, 'Your sins are forgiven'? Or to say, 'Get up, take your mat and walk'? 10I want you to know that the Son of Man has authority on earth to forgive sins."

Then Jesus spoke to the man who could not walk. 11"I tell you," he said, "get up. Take your mat and go home."

12The man got up and took his mat. Then he walked away while everyone watched. All the people were amazed. They praised God and said, "We have never seen anything like this!"

Jesus Chooses Levi

13Once again Jesus went out beside the Sea of Galilee. A large crowd came to him. He began to teach them. 14As he walked along he saw Levi, son of Alphaeus. Levi was sitting at the tax collector's booth. "Follow me," Jesus told him. Levi got up and followed him.

15Later Jesus was having dinner at Levi's house. Many tax collectors and "sinners" were eating with him and his disciples. They were part of the large crowd following Jesus.

16Some teachers of the law who were Pharisees were there. They saw Jesus eating with "sinners" and tax collectors. So they asked his disciples, "Why does he eat with tax collectors and 'sinners'?"

17Jesus heard that. So he said to them, "Those who are healthy don't need a doctor. Sick people do. I have not come to get those who think they are right with God to follow me. I have come to get sinners to follow me."

Jesus Is Asked About Fasting

18John's disciples and the Pharisees were going without eating. Some people came to Jesus. They said to him, "John's disciples are fasting. The disciples of the Pharisees are also fasting. But your disciples are not. Why aren't they?"

19Jesus answered, "How can the guests of the groom go without eating while he is with them? They will not fast as long as he is with them. 20But the time will come when the groom will be taken away from them. On that day they will go without eating.

21"People don't sew a patch of new cloth on old clothes. If they do, the new piece will pull away from the old. That will make the tear worse. 22People don't pour new wine into old wineskins. If they do, the wine will burst the skins. Then the wine and the wineskins will both be destroyed. No, everyone pours new wine into new wineskins."

Jesus Is Lord of the Sabbath Day

23One Sabbath day Jesus was walking with his disciples through the grainfields. The disciples began to break off some heads of grain. 24The Pharisees said to Jesus, "Look! It is against the Law to do this on the Sabbath. Why are your disciples doing it?"

25He answered, "Haven't you ever read about what David did? He and his men were hungry. They needed food. 26It was when Abiathar was high priest. David entered the house of God and ate the holy bread. Only priests were allowed to eat it. David also gave some to his men."

27Then Jesus said to them, "The Sabbath day was made for man. Man was not made for the Sabbath day. 28So the Son of Man is Lord even of the Sabbath day."

3 Another time Jesus went into the synagogue. A man with a weak and twisted hand was there. 2Some Pharisees were trying to find fault with Jesus. They watched him closely. They wanted to see if he would heal the man on the Sabbath day.

3Jesus spoke to the man with the weak and twisted hand. "Stand up in front of everyone," he said.

4Then Jesus asked them, "What does the Law say we should do on the Sabbath day? Should we do good? Or should we do evil? Should we save life? Or should we kill?" But no one answered.

5Jesus looked around at them in anger. He was very upset because their hearts were stubborn. Then he said to the man, "Stretch out your hand." He stretched it out, and his hand was as good as new.

6Then the Pharisees went out and began to make plans with the Herodians. They wanted to kill Jesus.

Crowds Follow Jesus

7Jesus went off to the Sea of Galilee with his
disciples. A large crowd from Galilee followed.
8People heard about all that Jesus was doing. And
many came to him. They came from Judea, Jerusalem, and Idumea. They came from the lands east
of the Jordan River. And they came from the area
around Tyre and Sidon.

9Because of the crowd, Jesus told his disciples
to get a small boat ready for him. This would keep
the people from crowding him. 10Jesus had healed
many people. So those who were sick were pushing forward to touch him.

11When people with evil spirits saw him, they
fell down in front of him. The spirits shouted,
"You are the Son of God!" 12But Jesus ordered
them not to tell who he was.

Jesus Appoints the Twelve Apostles

13Jesus went up on a mountainside. He called
for certain people to come to him, and they came.
14He appointed 12 of them and called them apostles. From that time on they would be with him.
He would also send them out to preach. 15They
would have authority to drive out demons.

16So Jesus appointed the Twelve. Simon was
one of them. Jesus gave him the name Peter.
17There were James, son of Zebedee, and his
brother John. Jesus gave them the name Boanerges. Boanerges means Sons of Thunder. 18There
were also Andrew, Philip, Bartholomew, Matthew,
Thomas, and James, son of Alphaeus. And there
were Thaddaeus and Simon the Zealot. 19Judas Iscariot was one of them too. He was the one who
was later going to hand Jesus over to his enemies.

Jesus and Beelzebub

20Jesus entered a house. Again a crowd gathered. It was so large that Jesus and his disciples
were not even able to eat. 21His family heard about
this. So they went to take charge of him. They said,
"He is out of his mind."

22Some teachers of the law were there. They had
come down from Jerusalem. They said, "He is
controlled by Beelzebub! He is driving out
demons by the power of the prince of demons."

23So Jesus called them over and spoke to them
by using stories. He said, "How can Satan drive
out Satan? 24If a kingdom fights against itself, it
can't stand. 25If a family is divided, it can't stand.
26And if Satan fights against himself, and his
helpers are divided, he can't stand. That is the end
of him. 27In fact, none of you can enter a strong
man's house and just take what the man owns. You
must first tie him up. Then you can rob his house.

28"What I'm about to tell you is true. Everyone's sins and evil words against God will be forgiven. 29But anyone who speaks evil things against
the Holy Spirit will never be forgiven. His guilt
will last forever."

30Jesus said this because the teachers of the law
were saying, "He has an evil spirit."

Jesus' Mother and Brothers

31Jesus' mother and brothers came and stood
outside. They sent someone in to get him. 32A
crowd was sitting around Jesus. They told him,
"Your mother and your brothers are outside. They
are looking for you."

33"Who is my mother? Who are my brothers?"
he asked.

34Then Jesus looked at the people sitting in a
circle around him. He said, "Here is my mother!
Here are my brothers! 35Anyone who does what
God wants is my brother or sister or mother."

The Story of the Farmer

4 Again Jesus began to teach by the Sea of Galilee. The crowd that gathered around him was
very large. So he got into a boat. He sat down in it
out on the lake. All the people were along the
shore at the water's edge. 2He taught them many
things by using stories.

In his teaching he said, 3"Listen! A farmer went
out to plant his seed. 4He scattered the seed on the
ground. Some fell on a path. Birds came and ate it
up. 5Some seed fell on rocky places, where there
wasn't much soil. The plants came up quickly,
because the soil wasn't deep. 6When the sun came
up, it burned the plants. They dried up because they
had no roots. 7Other seed fell among thorns. The
thorns grew up and crowded out the plants. So the
plants did not bear grain. 8Still other seed fell on
good soil. It grew up and produced a crop 30, 60,
or even 100 times more than the farmer planted."

9Then Jesus said, "Those who have ears should
listen."

10Later Jesus was alone. The Twelve asked him
about the stories. So did the others around him.
11He told them, "The secret of God's kingdom has
been given to you. But to outsiders everything is
told by using stories. 12In that way,

"'They will see but never know what they
are seeing.
They will hear but never understand.
Otherwise they might turn and be forgiven!'"
(Isaiah 6:9,10)

13Then Jesus said to them, "Don't you understand this story? Then how will you understand
any stories of this kind? 14The seed the farmer
plants is God's message. 15What is seed scattered
on a path like? The message is planted. The people hear the message. Then Satan comes. He takes
away the message that was planted in them. 16And
what is seed scattered on rocky places like? The
people hear the message. At once they receive it
with joy. 17But they have no roots. So they last
only a short time. They quickly fall away from the
faith when trouble or suffering comes because of
the message. 18And what is seed scattered among

thorns like? The people hear the message. 19But
then the worries of this life come to them. Wealth
comes with its false promises. The people also
long for other things. All of those are the kinds of
things that crowd out the message. They keep it
from producing fruit. 20And what is seed scattered
on good soil like? The people hear the message.
They accept it. They produce a good crop 30, 60,
or even 100 times more than the farmer planted."

A Lamp on a Stand

21Jesus said to them, "Do you bring in a lamp to
put it under a large bowl or a bed? Don't you put
it on its stand? 22What is hidden is meant to be
seen. And what is put out of sight is meant to be
brought out into the open. 23Everyone who has ears
should listen."

24"Think carefully about what you hear," he
said. "As you give, so you will receive. In fact, you
will receive even more. 25If you have something,
you will be given more. If you have nothing, even
what you have will be taken away from you."

The Story of the Growing Seed

26Jesus also said, "Here is what God's kingdom
is like. A farmer scatters seed on the ground.
27Night and day the seed comes up and grows. It
happens whether the farmer sleeps or gets up. He
doesn't know how it happens. 28All by itself the
soil produces grain. First the stalk comes up. Then
the head appears. Finally, the full grain appears in
the head. 29Before long the grain ripens. So the
farmer cuts it down, because the harvest is ready."

The Story of the Mustard Seed

30Again Jesus said, "What can we say God's
kingdom is like? What story can we use to explain
it? 31It is like a mustard seed, which is the smallest
seed planted in the ground. 32But when you plant
the seed, it grows. It becomes the largest of all garden plants. Its branches are so big that birds can
rest in its shade."

33Using many stories like those, Jesus spoke the
word to them. He told them as much as they could
understand. 34He did not say anything to them
without using a story. But when he was alone with
his disciples, he explained everything.

Jesus Calms the Storm

35When evening came, Jesus said to his disciples, "Let's go over to the other side of the lake."
36They left the crowd behind. And they took him
along in a boat, just as he was. There were also
other boats with him.

37A wild storm came up. Waves crashed over the
boat. It was about to sink. 38Jesus was in the back,
sleeping on a cushion. The disciples woke him up.
They said, "Teacher! Don't you care if we drown?"

39He got up and ordered the wind to stop. He
said to the waves, "Quiet! Be still!" Then the wind
died down. And it was completely calm.

40He said to his disciples, "Why are you so
afraid? Don't you have any faith at all yet?"

41They were terrified. They asked each other,
"Who is this? Even the wind and the waves obey
him!"

Jesus Heals a Man Controlled by Demons

5 They went across the Sea of Galilee to the
area of the Gerasenes. 2Jesus got out of the
boat. A man with an evil spirit came from the
tombs to meet him. 3The man lived in the tombs.
No one could keep him tied up anymore. Not even
a chain could hold him. 4His hands and feet had
often been chained. But he tore the chains apart.
And he broke the iron cuffs on his ankles. No one
was strong enough to control him. 5Night and day
he screamed among the tombs and in the hills. He
cut himself with stones.

6When he saw Jesus a long way off, he ran to
him. He fell on his knees in front of him. 7He
shouted at the top of his voice, "Jesus, Son of the
Most High God, what do you want with me?
Promise before God that you won't hurt me!"
8This was because Jesus had said to him, "Come
out of this man, you evil spirit!"

9Then Jesus asked the demon, "What is your
name?"

"My name is Legion," he replied. "There are
many of us." 10And he begged Jesus again and
again not to send them out of the area.

11A large herd of pigs was feeding on the nearby
hillside. 12The demons begged Jesus, "Send us
among the pigs. Let us go into them." 13Jesus
allowed it. The evil spirits came out of the man and
went into the pigs. There were about 2,000 pigs in
the herd. The whole herd rushed down the steep
bank. They ran into the lake and drowned.

14Those who were tending the pigs ran off. They
told the people in the town and countryside what
had happened. The people went out to see for
themselves.

15Then they came to Jesus. They saw the man
who had been controlled by many demons. He was
sitting there. He was now dressed and thinking
clearly. All this made the people afraid. 16Those
who had seen it told them what had happened to
the man. They told about the pigs as well. 17Then
the people began to beg Jesus to leave their area.

18Jesus was getting into the boat. The man who
had been controlled by demons begged to go with
him. 19Jesus did not let him. He said, "Go home to
your family. Tell them how much the Lord has done
for you. Tell them how kind he has been to you."

20So the man went away. In the area known as
the Ten Cities, he began to tell how much Jesus
had done for him. And all the people were amazed.

A Dying Girl and a Suffering Woman

21Jesus went across the Sea of Galilee in a boat.
It landed at the other side. There a large crowd

gathered around him. [22]Then a man named Jairus came. He was a synagogue ruler. Seeing Jesus, he fell at his feet. [23]He begged Jesus, "Please come. My little daughter is dying. Place your hands on her to heal her. Then she will live." [24]So Jesus went with him.

A large group of people followed. They crowded around him. [25]A woman was there who had a sickness that made her bleed. It had lasted for 12 years. [26]She had suffered a great deal, even though she had gone to many doctors. She had spent all the money she had. But she was getting worse, not better. [27]Then she heard about Jesus. She came up behind him in the crowd and touched his clothes. [28]She thought, "I just need to touch his clothes. Then I will be healed." [29]Right away her bleeding stopped. She felt in her body that her suffering was over.

[30]At once Jesus knew that power had gone out from him. He turned around in the crowd. He asked, "Who touched my clothes?"

[31]"You see the people," his disciples answered. "They are crowding against you. And you still ask, 'Who touched me?'"

[32]But Jesus kept looking around. He wanted to see who had touched him.

[33]Then the woman came and fell at his feet. She knew what had happened to her. She was shaking with fear. But she told him the whole truth.

[34]He said to her, "Dear woman, your faith has healed you. Go in peace. You are free from your suffering."

[35]While Jesus was still speaking, some people came from the house of Jairus. He was the synagogue ruler. "Your daughter is dead," they said. "Why bother the teacher anymore?"

[36]But Jesus didn't listen to them. He told the synagogue ruler, "Don't be afraid. Just believe."

[37]He let only Peter, James, and John, the brother of James, follow him. [38]They came to the home of the synagogue ruler. There Jesus saw a lot of confusion. People were crying and sobbing loudly. [39]He went inside. Then he said to them, "Why all this confusion and sobbing? The child is not dead. She is only sleeping." [40]But they laughed at him.

He made them all go outside. He took only the child's father and mother and the disciples who were with him. And he went in where the child was. [41]He took her by the hand. Then he said to her, *"Talitha koum!"* This means, "Little girl, I say to you, get up!" [42]The girl was 12 years old. Right away she stood up and walked around. They were totally amazed at this. [43]Jesus gave strict orders not to let anyone know what had happened. And he told them to give her something to eat.

A Prophet Without Honor

6 Jesus left there and went to his hometown of Nazareth. His disciples went with him. [2]When the Sabbath day came, he began to teach in the synagogue. Many who heard him were amazed.

"Where did this man get these things?" they asked. "What's this wisdom that has been given to him? He even does miracles! [3]Isn't this the carpenter? Isn't this Mary's son? Isn't this the brother of James, Joseph, Judas and Simon? Aren't his sisters here with us?" They were not pleased with him at all.

[4]Jesus said to them, "A prophet is not honored in his hometown. He doesn't receive any honor among his relatives. And he doesn't receive any in his own home."

[5]Jesus laid his hands on a few sick people and healed them. But he could not do any other miracles there. [6]He was amazed because they had no faith.

Jesus Sends Out the Twelve Disciples

Jesus went around teaching from village to village. [7]He called the Twelve to him. Then he sent them out two by two. He gave them authority to drive out evil spirits.

[8]Here were his orders. "Take only a walking stick for your trip. Do not take bread or a bag. Take no money in your belts. [9]Wear sandals. But do not take extra clothes. [10]When you are invited into a house, stay there until you leave town. [11]Some places may not welcome you or listen to you. If they don't, shake the dust off your feet when you leave. That will be a witness against the people living there."

[12]They went out. And they preached that people should turn away from their sins. [13]They drove out many demons. They poured olive oil on many sick people and healed them.

John the Baptist's Head Is Cut Off

[14]King Herod heard about this. Jesus' name had become well known. Some were saying, "John the Baptist has been raised from the dead! That is why he has the power to do miracles."

[15]Others said, "He is Elijah."

Still others claimed, "He is a prophet. He is like one of the prophets of long ago."

[16]But when Herod heard this, he said, "I had John's head cut off. And now he has been raised from the dead!"

[17]In fact, it was Herod himself who had given orders to arrest John. He had him tied up and put in prison. He did this because of Herodias. She was the wife of Herod's brother Philip. But now Herod was married to her. [18]John had been saying to Herod, "It is against the Law for you to have your brother's wife." [19]Herodias held that against John. She wanted to kill him. But she could not, [20]because Herod was afraid of John. So he kept John safe. Herod knew John was a holy man who did what was right. When Herod heard him, he was very puzzled. But he liked to listen to him.

[21]Finally the right time came. Herod gave a big dinner on his birthday. He invited his high officials and military leaders. He also invited the most

important men in Galilee. 22 Then the daughter of Herodias came in and danced. She pleased Herod and his dinner guests.

The king said to the girl, "Ask me for anything you want. I'll give it to you." 23 And he promised her with an oath, "Anything you ask for I will give you. I'll give you up to half of my kingdom."

24 She went out and said to her mother, "What should I ask for?"

"The head of John the Baptist," she answered.

25 At once the girl hurried to ask the king. She said, "I want you to give me the head of John the Baptist on a big plate right now."

26 The king was very upset. But he thought of his promise and his dinner guests. So he did not want to say no to the girl. 27 He sent a man right away to bring John's head. The man went to the prison and cut off John's head. 28 He brought it back on a big plate. He gave it to the girl, and she gave it to her mother.

29 John's disciples heard about this. So they came and took his body. Then they placed it in a tomb.

Jesus Feeds the Five Thousand

30 The apostles gathered around Jesus. They told him all they had done and taught. 31 But many people were coming and going. So they did not even have a chance to eat.

Then Jesus said to his apostles, "Come with me by yourselves to a quiet place. You need to get some rest." 32 So they went away by themselves in a boat to a quiet place.

33 But many people who saw them leaving recognized them. They ran from all the towns and got there ahead of them. 34 When Jesus came ashore, he saw a large crowd. He felt deep concern for them. They were like sheep without a shepherd. So he began teaching them many things.

35 By that time it was late in the day. His disciples came to him. "There is nothing here," they said. "It's already very late. 36 Send the people away. They can go and buy something to eat in the nearby countryside and villages."

37 But Jesus answered, "You give them something to eat."

They said to him, "That would take eight months of a person's pay! Should we go and spend that much on bread? Are we supposed to feed them?"

38 "How many loaves do you have?" Jesus asked. "Go and see."

When they found out, they said, "Five loaves and two fish."

39 Then Jesus directed them to have all the people sit down in groups on the green grass. 40 So they sat down in groups of 100s and 50s.

41 Jesus took the five loaves and the two fish. He looked up to heaven and gave thanks. He broke the loaves into pieces. Then he gave them to his disciples to set in front of the people. He also divided the two fish among them all.

42 All of them ate and were satisfied. 43 The disciples picked up 12 baskets of broken pieces of bread and fish. 44 The number of men who had eaten was 5,000.

Jesus Walks on the Water

45 Right away Jesus made his disciples get into the boat. He had them go on ahead of him to Bethsaida. Then he sent the crowd away. 46 After leaving them, he went up on a mountainside to pray.

47 When evening came, the boat was in the middle of the Sea of Galilee. Jesus was alone on land. 48 He saw the disciples pulling hard on the oars. The wind was blowing against them.

Early in the morning, he went out to them. He walked on the lake. When he was about to pass by them, 49 they saw him walking on the lake. They thought he was a ghost. They cried out. 50 They all saw him and were terrified.

Right away he said to them, "Be brave! It is I. Don't be afraid."

51 Then he climbed into the boat with them. The wind died down. And they were completely amazed. 52 They had not understood about the loaves. They were stubborn.

53 They crossed over the lake and landed at Gennesaret. There they tied up the boat. 54 As soon as Jesus and his disciples got out, people recognized him. 55 They ran through that whole area to bring to him those who were sick. They carried them on mats to where they heard he was.

56 He went into the villages, the towns and the countryside. Everywhere he went, the people brought the sick to the market places. Those who were sick begged him to let them touch just the edge of his clothes. And all who touched him were healed.

What Makes People "Unclean"?

7 The Pharisees gathered around Jesus. So did some of the teachers of the law. All of them had come from Jerusalem. 2 They saw some of his disciples eating food with "unclean" hands. That means they were not washed.

3 The Pharisees and all the Jews do not eat unless they wash their hands to make them pure. That's what the elders teach. 4 When they come from the market place, they do not eat unless they wash. And they follow many other teachings. For example, they wash cups, pitchers, and kettles in a special way.

5 So the Pharisees and the teachers of the law questioned Jesus. "Why don't your disciples live by what the elders teach?" they asked. "Why do they eat their food with 'unclean' hands?"

6 He replied, "Isaiah was right. He prophesied about you people who pretend to be good. He said,

" 'These people honor me by what they say.
But their hearts are far away from me.
7 Their worship doesn't mean anything to me.
They teach nothing but human rules.'
(Isaiah 29:13)

8You have let go of God's commands. And you are holding on to the teachings that men have made up."

9Jesus then said to them, "You have a fine way of setting aside God's commands! You do this so you can follow your own teachings. 10Moses said, 'Honor your father and mother.' *(Exodus 20:12; Deuteronomy 5:16)* He also said, 'If anyone calls down a curse on his father or mother, he will be put to death.' *(Exodus 21:17; Leviticus 20:9)* 11But you allow people to say to their parents, 'Any help you might have received from us is Corban.' (Corban means 'a gift set apart for God.') 12So you no longer let them do anything for their parents. 13You make the word of God useless by putting your own teachings in its place. And you do many things like that."

14Again Jesus called the crowd to him. He said, "Listen to me, everyone. Understand this. 15/16Nothing outside of you can make you 'unclean' by going into you. It is what comes out of you that makes you 'unclean.'"

17Then he left the crowd and entered the house. His disciples asked him about this teaching.

18"Don't you understand?" Jesus asked. "Don't you see? Nothing that enters people from the outside can make them 'unclean.' 19It doesn't go into the heart. It goes into the stomach. Then it goes out of the body." In saying this, Jesus was calling all foods "clean."

20He went on to say, "What comes out of people makes them 'unclean.' 21Evil thoughts come from the inside, from people's hearts. So do sexual sins, stealing and murder. Adultery, 22greed, hate and cheating come from people's hearts too. So do desires that are not pure, and wanting what belongs to others. And so do telling lies about others and being proud and being foolish. 23All those evil things come from inside a person. They make him 'unclean.'"

The Faith of a Greek Woman

24Jesus went from there to a place near Tyre. He entered a house. He did not want anyone to know where he was. But he could not keep it a secret. 25Soon a woman heard about him. An evil spirit controlled her little daughter. The woman came to Jesus and fell at his feet. 26She was a Greek, born in Syrian Phoenicia. She begged Jesus to drive the demon out of her daughter.

27"First let the children eat all they want," he told her. "It is not right to take the children's bread and throw it to their dogs."

28"Yes, Lord," she replied. "But even the dogs under the table eat the children's crumbs."

29Then he told her, "That was a good reply. You may go. The demon has left your daughter."

30So she went home and found her child lying on the bed. And the demon was gone.

Jesus Heals a Man Who Could Not Hear or Speak

31Then Jesus left the area of Tyre and went through Sidon. He went down to the Sea of Galilee and into the area known as the Ten Cities. 32There some people brought a man to him. The man was deaf and could hardly speak. They begged Jesus to place his hand on him.

33Jesus took the man to one side, away from the crowd. He put his fingers into the man's ears. Then he spit and touched the man's tongue. 34Jesus looked up to heaven. With a deep sigh, he said to the man, *"Ephphatha!"* That means "Be opened!" 35The man's ears were opened. His tongue was freed up, and he began to speak clearly.

36Jesus ordered the people not to tell anyone. But the more he did so, the more they kept talking about it.

37People were really amazed. "He has done everything well," they said. "He even makes deaf people able to hear. And he makes those who can't speak able to talk."

Jesus Feeds the Four Thousand

8 During those days another large crowd gathered. They had nothing to eat. So Jesus called for his disciples to come to him. He said, 2"I feel deep concern for these people. They have already been with me three days. They don't have anything to eat. 3If I send them away hungry, they will become too weak on their way home. Some of them have come from far away."

4His disciples answered him. "There is nothing here," they said. "Where can anyone get enough bread to feed them?"

5"How many loaves do you have?" Jesus asked.

"Seven," they replied.

6He told the crowd to sit down on the ground. He took the seven loaves and gave thanks to God. Then he broke them and gave them to his disciples. They set the loaves down in front of the people. 7The disciples also had a few small fish. Jesus gave thanks for them too. He told the disciples to pass them around. 8The people ate and were satisfied.

After that, the disciples picked up seven baskets of leftover pieces. 9About 4,000 men were there. Jesus sent them away. 10Then he got into a boat with his disciples. He went to the area of Dalmanutha.

11The Pharisees came and began to ask Jesus questions. They wanted to put him to the test. So they asked him for a miraculous sign from heaven. 12He sighed deeply. He said, "Why do you people ask for a sign? What I'm about to tell you is true. No sign will be given to you."

13Then he left them. He got back into the boat and crossed to the other side of the lake.

The Yeast of the Pharisees and Herod

14The disciples had forgotten to bring bread. They had only one loaf with them in the boat.

15"Be careful," Jesus warned them. "Watch out for the yeast of the Pharisees. And watch out for the yeast of Herod."

16They talked about this with each other. They said, "He must be saying this because we don't have any bread."

[17]Jesus knew what they were saying. So he asked them, "Why are you talking about having no bread? Why can't you see or understand? Are you stubborn? [18]Do you have eyes and still don't see? Do you have ears and still don't hear? And don't you remember? [19]Earlier I broke five loaves for the 5,000. How many baskets of pieces did you pick up?"

"Twelve," they replied.

[20]"Later I broke seven loaves for the 4,000. How many baskets of pieces did you pick up?"

"Seven," they answered.

[21]He said to them, "Can't you understand yet?"

Jesus Heals a Blind Man

[22]Jesus and his disciples came to Bethsaida. Some people brought a blind man. They begged Jesus to touch him.

[23]He took the blind man by the hand. Then he led him outside the village. He spit on the man's eyes and put his hands on him.

"Do you see anything?" Jesus asked.

[24]The man looked up. He said, "I see people. They look like trees walking around."

[25]Once more Jesus put his hands on the man's eyes. Then his eyes were opened so that he could see again. He saw everything clearly.

[26]Jesus sent him home. He told him, "Don't go into the village."

Peter Says That Jesus Is the Christ

[27]Jesus and his disciples went on to the villages around Caesarea Philippi. On the way he asked them, "Who do people say I am?"

[28]They replied, "Some say John the Baptist. Others say Elijah. Still others say one of the prophets."

[29]"But what about you?" he asked. "Who do you say I am?"

Peter answered, "You are the Christ."

[30]Jesus warned them not to tell anyone about him.

Jesus Tells About His Coming Death

[31]Jesus then began to teach his disciples. He taught them that the Son of Man must suffer many things. He taught them that the elders would not accept him. The chief priests and the teachers of the law would not accept him either. He must be killed and after three days rise again. [32]He spoke clearly about this.

Peter took Jesus to one side and began to scold him.

[33]Jesus turned and looked at his disciples. He scolded Peter. "Get behind me, Satan!" he said. "You are not thinking about the things of God. Instead, you are thinking about human things."

[34]Jesus called the crowd to him along with his disciples. He said, "If anyone wants to come after me, he must say no to himself. He must pick up his cross and follow me. [35]If he wants to save his life, he will lose it. But if he loses his life for me and for the good news, he will save it. [36]What good is it if someone gains the whole world but loses his soul? [37]Or what can anyone trade for his soul?

[38]"Suppose you are ashamed of me and my words among these adulterous and sinful people. Then the Son of Man will be ashamed of you when he comes in his Father's glory with the holy angels."

9 Jesus said to them, "What I'm about to tell you is true. Some who are standing here will not die before they see God's kingdom coming with power."

Jesus' Appearance Is Changed

[2]After six days Jesus took Peter, James and John with him. He led them up a high mountain. They were all alone. There in front of them his appearance was changed. [3]His clothes became so white they shone. They were whiter than anyone in the world could bleach them. [4]Elijah and Moses appeared in front of Jesus and his disciples. The two of them were talking with Jesus.

[5]Peter said to Jesus, "Rabbi, it is good for us to be here. Let us put up three shelters. One will be for you, one for Moses, and one for Elijah." [6]Peter didn't really know what to say, because they were so afraid.

[7]Then a cloud appeared and surrounded them. A voice came from the cloud. It said, "This is my Son, and I love him. Listen to him!"

[8]They looked around. Suddenly they no longer saw anyone with them except Jesus.

[9]They came down the mountain. On the way down, Jesus ordered them not to tell anyone what they had seen. He told them to wait until the Son of Man had risen from the dead. [10]So they kept the matter to themselves. But they asked each other what "rising from the dead" meant.

[11]Then they asked Jesus, "Why do the teachers of the law say that Elijah has to come first?"

[12]Jesus replied, "That's right. Elijah does come first. He makes all things new again. So why is it written that the Son of Man must suffer much and not be accepted? [13]I tell you, Elijah has come. They have done to him everything they wanted to do. They did it just as it is written about him."

Jesus Heals a Boy Who Had an Evil Spirit

[14]When Jesus and those who were with him came to the other disciples, they saw a large crowd around them. The teachers of the law were arguing with them. [15]When all the people saw Jesus, they were filled with wonder. And they ran to greet him.

[16]"What are you arguing with them about?" Jesus asked.

[17]A man in the crowd answered. "Teacher," he said, "I brought you my son. He is controlled by a spirit. Because of this, my son can't speak anymore. [18]When the spirit takes hold of him, it

throws him to the ground. He foams at the mouth. He grinds his teeth. And his body becomes stiff. I asked your disciples to drive out the spirit. But they couldn't do it."

19"You unbelieving people!" Jesus replied. "How long do I have to stay with you? How long do I have to put up with you? Bring the boy to me."

20So they brought him. As soon as the spirit saw Jesus, it threw the boy into a fit. He fell to the ground. He rolled around and foamed at the mouth.

21Jesus asked the boy's father, "How long has he been like this?"

"Since he was a child," he answered. 22"The spirit has often thrown him into fire or water to kill him. But if you can do anything, take pity on us. Please help us."

23" 'If you can'?" said Jesus. "Everything is possible for the one who believes."

24Right away the boy's father cried out, "I do believe! Help me overcome my unbelief!"

25Jesus saw that a crowd was running over to see what was happening. Then he ordered the evil spirit to leave the boy. "You spirit that makes him unable to hear and speak!" he said. "I command you, come out of him. Never enter him again."

26The spirit screamed. It shook the boy wildly. Then it came out of him. The boy looked so lifeless that many people said, "He's dead." 27But Jesus took him by the hand. He lifted the boy to his feet, and the boy stood up.

28Jesus went indoors. Then his disciples asked him in private, "Why couldn't we drive out the evil spirit?"

29He replied, "This kind can come out only by prayer."

30They left that place and passed through Galilee. Jesus did not want anyone to know where they were. 31That was because he was teaching his disciples.

He said to them, "The Son of Man is going to be handed over to men. They will kill him. After three days he will rise from the dead." 32But they didn't understand what he meant. And they were afraid to ask him about it.

Who Is the Most Important Person?

33Jesus and his disciples came to a house in Capernaum. There he asked them, "What were you arguing about on the road?" 34But they kept quiet. On the way, they had argued about which one of them was the most important person.

35Jesus sat down and called for the Twelve to come to him. Then he said, "If you want to be first, you must be the very last. You must be the servant of everyone."

36Jesus took a little child and had the child stand among them. Then he took the child in his arms. He said to them, 37"Anyone who welcomes one of these little children in my name welcomes me. And anyone who welcomes me doesn't welcome only me but also the One who sent me."

Anyone Who Is Not Against Us Is for Us

38"Teacher," said John, "we saw a man driving out demons in your name. We told him to stop, because he was not one of us."

39"Do not stop him," Jesus said. "No one who does a miracle in my name can in the next moment say anything bad about me. 40Anyone who is not against us is for us.

41"What I'm about to tell you is true. Suppose someone gives you a cup of water in my name because you belong to me. That one will certainly not go without a reward.

Leading People to Sin

42"What if someone leads one of these little ones who believe in me to sin? If he does, it would be better for him to be thrown into the sea with a large millstone tied around his neck.

43/44"If your hand causes you to sin, cut it off. It would be better for you to enter God's kingdom with only one hand than to go into hell with two hands. In hell the fire never goes out.

45/46"If your foot causes you to sin, cut it off. It would be better for you to enter God's kingdom with only one foot than to have two feet and be thrown into hell.

47"If your eye causes you to sin, poke it out. It would be better for you to enter God's kingdom with only one eye than to have two eyes and be thrown into hell. 48In hell,

" 'The worms do not die.
The fire is not put out.' *(Isaiah 66:24)*

49Everyone will be salted with fire.

50"Salt is good. But suppose it loses its saltiness. How can you make it salty again? Have salt in yourselves. And be at peace with each other."

Jesus Teaches About Divorce

10 Jesus left that place and went into the area of Judea and across the Jordan River. Again crowds of people came to him. As usual, he taught them.

2Some Pharisees came to put him to the test. They asked, "Does the Law allow a man to divorce his wife?"

3"What did Moses command you?" he replied.

4They said, "Moses allowed a man to write a letter of divorce and send her away."

5"You were stubborn. That's why Moses wrote you this law," Jesus replied. 6"But at the beginning of creation, God 'made them male and female.' *(Genesis 1:27)* 7'That's why a man will leave his father and mother and be joined to his wife. 8The two of them will become one.' *(Genesis 2:24)* They are no longer two, but one. 9So a man must not separate what God has joined together."

10When they were in the house again, the disciples asked Jesus about this.

11He answered, "What if a man divorces his wife and gets married to another woman? He commits adultery against her. 12And what if she divorces her husband and gets married to another man? She commits adultery."

Little Children Are Brought to Jesus

13People were bringing little children to Jesus. They wanted him to touch them. But the disciples told the people to stop.

14When Jesus saw this, he was angry. He said to his disciples, "Let the little children come to me. Don't keep them away. God's kingdom belongs to people like them. 15What I'm about to tell you is true. Anyone who will not receive God's kingdom like a little child will never enter it."

16Then he took the children in his arms. He put his hands on them and blessed them.

Jesus and the Rich Young Man

17As Jesus started on his way, a man ran up to him. He fell on his knees before Jesus. "Good teacher," he said, "what must I do to receive eternal life?"

18"Why do you call me good?" Jesus answered. "No one is good except God. 19You know what the commandments say. 'Do not commit murder. Do not commit adultery. Do not steal. Do not give false witness. Do not cheat. Honor your father and mother.'" *(Exodus 20:12–16; Deuteronomy 5:16–20)*

20"Teacher," he said, "I have obeyed all those commandments since I was a boy."

21Jesus looked at him and loved him. "You are missing one thing," he said. "Go and sell everything you have. Give the money to those who are poor. You will have treasure in heaven. Then come and follow me."

22The man's face fell. He went away sad, because he was very rich.

23Jesus looked around. He said to his disciples, "How hard it is for rich people to enter God's kingdom!"

24The disciples were amazed at his words. But Jesus said again, "Children, how hard it is to enter God's kingdom! 25Is it hard for a camel to go through the eye of a needle? It is even harder for the rich to enter God's kingdom!"

26The disciples were even more amazed. They said to each other, "Then who can be saved?"

27Jesus looked at them and said, "With man, that is impossible. But not with God. All things are possible with God."

28Peter said to him, "We have left everything to follow you!"

29"What I'm about to tell you is true," Jesus replied. "Has anyone left home or family or fields for me and the good news? 30They will receive 100 times as much in this world. They will have homes and families and fields. But they will also be treated badly by others. In the world to come they will live forever. 31But many who are first will be last. And the last will be first."

Jesus Again Tells About His Coming Death

32They were on their way up to Jerusalem. Jesus was leading the way. The disciples were amazed. Those who followed were afraid.

Again Jesus took the Twelve to one side. He told them what was going to happen to him. 33"We are going up to Jerusalem," he said. "The Son of Man will be handed over to the chief priests and the teachers of the law. They will sentence him to death. Then they will hand him over to people who are not Jews. 34The people will make fun of him and spit on him. They will whip him and kill him. Three days later he will rise from the dead!"

James and John Ask a Favor of Jesus

35James and John came to Jesus. They were the sons of Zebedee. "Teacher," they said, "we would like to ask a favor of you."

36"What do you want me to do for you?" he asked.

37They replied, "Let one of us sit at your right hand in your glorious kingdom. Let the other one sit at your left hand."

38"You don't know what you're asking for," Jesus said. "Can you drink the cup of suffering I drink? Or can you go through the baptism of suffering I must go through?"

39"We can," they answered.

Jesus said to them, "You will drink the cup I drink. And you will go through the baptism I go through. 40But it is not for me to say who will sit at my right or left hand. These places belong to those they are prepared for."

41The other ten disciples heard about it. They became angry at James and John.

42Jesus called them together. He said, "You know about those who are rulers of the nations. They hold power over their people. Their high officials order them around. 43Don't be like that. Instead, anyone who wants to be important among you must be your servant. 44And anyone who wants to be first must be the slave of everyone. 45Even the Son of Man did not come to be served. Instead, he came to serve others. He came to give his life as the price for setting many people free."

Blind Bartimaeus Receives His Sight

46Jesus and his disciples came to Jericho. They were leaving the city. A large crowd was with them.

A blind man was sitting by the side of the road begging. His name was Bartimaeus. Bartimaeus means Son of Timaeus. 47He heard that Jesus of Nazareth was passing by. So he began to shout, "Jesus! Son of David! Have mercy on me!"

48Many people commanded him to stop. They told him to be quiet. But he shouted even louder, "Son of David! Have mercy on me!"

49Jesus stopped and said, "Call for him."

So they called out to the blind man, "Cheer up! Get up on your feet! Jesus is calling for you."

50He threw his coat to one side. Then he jumped to his feet and came to Jesus.

51"What do you want me to do for you?" Jesus asked him.

The blind man said, "Rabbi, I want to be able to see."

52"Go," said Jesus. "Your faith has healed you."

Right away he could see. And he followed Jesus along the road.

Jesus Enters Jerusalem

11 As they all approached Jerusalem, they came to Bethphage and Bethany at the Mount of Olives. Jesus sent out two of his disciples. 2He said to them, "Go to the village ahead of you. Just as you enter it, you will find a donkey's colt tied there. No one has ever ridden it. Untie it and bring it here. 3Someone may ask you, 'Why are you doing this?' If so, say, 'The Lord needs it. But he will send it back here soon.' "

4So they left. They found a colt out in the street. It was tied at a doorway. They untied it. 5Some people standing there asked, "What are you doing? Why are you untying that colt?" 6They answered as Jesus had told them to. So the people let them go.

7They brought the colt to Jesus. They threw their coats over it. Then he sat on it.

8Many people spread their coats on the road. Others spread branches they had cut in the fields. 9Those in front and those in back shouted,

"Hosanna!"

"Blessed is the one who comes in the name
of the Lord!" *(Psalm 118:25,26)*

10"Blessed is the coming kingdom of
our father David!"

"Hosanna in the highest heaven!"

11Jesus entered Jerusalem and went to the temple. He looked around at everything. But it was already late. So he went out to Bethany with the Twelve.

Jesus Clears the Temple

12The next day as Jesus and his disciples were leaving Bethany, they were hungry. 13Not too far away, he saw a fig tree. It was covered with leaves. He went to find out if it had any fruit. When he reached it, he found nothing but leaves. It was not the season for figs.

14Then Jesus said to the tree, "May no one ever eat fruit from you again!" And his disciples heard him say it.

15When Jesus reached Jerusalem, he entered the temple area. He began chasing out those who were buying and selling there. He turned over the tables of the people who were exchanging money. He also turned over the benches of those who were selling doves. 16He would not allow anyone to carry items for sale through the temple courtyards. 17Then he taught them. He told them, "It is written that the Lord said,

" 'My house will be called
a house where people from all nations
can pray.' *(Isaiah 56:7)*

But you have made it a 'den for robbers.' " *(Jeremiah 7:11)*

18The chief priests and the teachers of the law heard about this. They began looking for a way to kill Jesus. They were afraid of him, because the whole crowd was amazed at his teaching.

19When evening came, Jesus and his disciples left the city.

The Dried-up Fig Tree

20In the morning as Jesus and his disciples walked along, they saw the fig tree. It was dried up all the way down to the roots.

21Peter remembered. He said to Jesus, "Rabbi, look! The fig tree you put a curse on has dried up!"

22"Have faith in God," Jesus said. 23"What I'm about to tell you is true. Suppose one of you says to this mountain, 'Go and throw yourself into the sea.' You must not doubt in your heart. You must believe that what you say will happen. Then it will be done for you.

24"So I tell you, when you pray for something, believe that you have already received it. Then it will be yours. 25/26And when you stand praying, forgive anyone you have anything against. Then your Father in heaven will forgive your sins."

The Authority of Jesus Is Questioned

27Jesus and his disciples arrived again in Jerusalem. He was walking in the temple courtyards. Then the chief priests came to him. The teachers of the law and the elders came too.

28"By what authority are you doing these things?" they asked. "Who gave you authority to do this?"

29Jesus replied, "I will ask you one question. Answer me, and I will tell you by what authority I am doing these things. 30Was John's baptism from heaven? Or did it come from men? Tell me!"

31They talked to each other about it. They said, "If we say, 'From heaven,' he will ask, 'Then why didn't you believe him?' 32But what if we say, 'From men'?" They were afraid of the people. Everyone believed that John really was a prophet.

33So they answered Jesus, "We don't know."

Jesus said, "Then I won't tell you by what authority I am doing these things either."

The Story of the Renters

12 Jesus began to speak to the people by using stories. He said, "A man planted a vineyard. He put a wall around it. He dug a pit for a winepress. He also built a lookout tower. He rented

the vineyard out to some farmers. Then he went
away on a journey.
2“At harvest time he sent a servant to the
renters. He told the servant to collect from them
some of the fruit of the vineyard. 3But they
grabbed the servant and beat him up. Then they
sent him away with nothing. 4So the man sent
another servant to the renters. They hit this one on
the head and treated him badly. 5The man sent still
another servant. The renters killed him. The man
sent many others. The renters beat up some of
them. They killed the others.
6“The man had one person left to send. It was
his son, and he loved him. He sent him last of all.
He said, ‘They will respect my son.’
7“But the renters said to each other, ‘This is the
one who will receive all the owner’s property
someday. Come, let’s kill him. Then everything
will be ours.’ 8So they took him and killed him.
They threw him out of the vineyard.
9“What will the owner of the vineyard do then?
He will come and kill those renters. He will give
the vineyard to others.
10“Haven’t you read what Scripture says,

“ ‘The stone the builders didn’t accept
has become the most important stone of all.
11 The Lord has done it.
It is wonderful in our eyes’?”
(Psalm 118:22,23)

12Then the religious leaders looked for a way to
arrest Jesus. They knew he had told the story
against them. But they were afraid of the crowd.
So they left him and went away.

Is It Right to Pay Taxes to Caesar?

13Later the religious leaders sent some of the
Pharisees and Herodians to Jesus. They wanted to
trap him with his own words.
14They came to him and said, “Teacher, we
know you are a man of honor. You don’t let others
tell you what to do or say. You don’t care how
important they are. But you teach the way of God
truthfully. Is it right to pay taxes to Caesar or not?
15Should we pay or shouldn’t we?”
But Jesus knew what they were trying to do. So
he asked, “Why are you trying to trap me? Bring
me a silver coin. Let me look at it.”
16They brought the coin.
He asked them, “Whose picture is this? And
whose words?”
“Caesar’s,” they replied.
17Then Jesus said to them, “Give to Caesar what
belongs to Caesar. And give to God what belongs
to God.”
They were amazed at him.

Marriage When the Dead Rise

18The Sadducees came to Jesus with a question.
They do not believe that people rise from the dead.
19“Teacher,” they said, “Moses wrote for us about
a man who died and didn’t have any children. But
he did leave a wife behind. That man’s brother
must get married to the widow. He must have children to carry on his dead brother’s name.
20“There were seven brothers. The first one got
married. He died without leaving any children.
21The second one got married to the widow. He
also died and left no child. It was the same with
the third one. 22In fact, none of the seven left any
children. Last of all, the woman died too. 23When
the dead rise, whose wife will she be? All seven of
them were married to her.”
24Jesus replied, “You are mistaken because you
do not know the Scriptures. And you do not know
the power of God. 25When the dead rise, they won’t
get married. And their parents won’t give them to
be married. They will be like the angels in heaven.
26“What about the dead rising? Haven’t you read
in the scroll of Moses the story of the bush? God
said to Moses, ‘I am the God of Abraham. I am the
God of Isaac. And I am the God of Jacob.’ *(Exodus
3:6)* 27He is not the God of the dead. He is the God
of the living. You have made a big mistake!”

The Most Important Commandment

28One of the teachers of the law came and heard
the Sadducees arguing. He noticed that Jesus had
given the Sadducees a good answer. So he asked
him, “Which is the most important of all the
commandments?”
29Jesus answered, “Here is the most important
one. Moses said, ‘Israel, listen to me. The Lord is
our God. The Lord is one. 30Love the Lord your
God with all your heart and with all your soul.
Love him with all your mind and with all your
strength.’ *(Deuteronomy 6:4,5)* 31And here is the second one. ‘Love your neighbor as you love yourself.’ *(Leviticus 19:18)* There is no commandment
more important than these.”
32“You have spoken well, teacher,” the man
replied. “You are right in saying that God is one.
There is no other God but him. 33To love God with
all your heart and mind and strength is very important. So is loving your neighbor as you love yourself. These things are more important than all burnt
offerings and sacrifices.”
34Jesus saw that the man had answered wisely.
He said to him, “You are not far from God’s
kingdom.”
From then on, no one dared to ask Jesus any
more questions.

Whose Son Is the Christ?

35Jesus was teaching in the temple courtyard.
He asked, “Why do the teachers of the law say that
the Christ is the son of David? 36The Holy Spirit
spoke through David himself. David said,

“ ‘The Lord said to my Lord,
“Sit at my right hand
until I put your enemies
under your control.” ’
(Psalm 110:1)

37David himself calls him 'Lord.' So how can he
be David's son?"
The large crowd listened to Jesus with delight.
38As he taught, he said, "Watch out for the
teachers of the law. They like to walk around in
long robes. They like to be greeted in the market
places. 39They love to have the most important
seats in the synagogues. They also love to have the
places of honor at dinners. 40They take over the
houses of widows. They say long prayers to show
off. God will punish those men very much."

The Widow's Offering

41Jesus sat down across from the place where
people put their temple offerings. He watched the
crowd putting their money into the offering boxes.
Many rich people threw large amounts into them.
42But a poor widow came and put in two very
small copper coins. They were worth much less
than a penny.
43Jesus asked his disciples to come to him. He
said, "What I'm about to tell you is true. That poor
widow has put more into the offering box than all
the others. 44They all gave a lot because they are
rich. But she gave even though she is poor. She put
in everything she had. She gave all she had to
live on."

Signs of the End

13 Jesus was leaving the temple. One of his
disciples said to him, "Look, Teacher!
What huge stones! What wonderful buildings!"
2"Do you see these huge buildings?" Jesus
asked. "Not one stone here will be left on top of
another. Every stone will be thrown down."
3Jesus was sitting on the Mount of Olives,
across from the temple. Peter, James, John and Andrew asked him a question in private. 4"Tell us,"
they said. "When will these things happen? And
what will be the sign that they are all about to
come true?"
5Jesus said to them, "Keep watch! Be careful
that no one fools you. 6Many will come in my
name. They will claim, 'I am he.' They will fool
many people.
7"You will hear about wars. You will also hear
people talking about future wars. Don't be
alarmed. Those things must happen. But the end
still isn't here. 8Nation will fight against nation.
Kingdom will fight against kingdom. There will
be earthquakes in many places. People will go
hungry. All of those things are the beginning of
birth pains.
9"Watch out! You will be handed over to the
local courts. You will be whipped in the synagogues. You will stand in front of governors and
kings because of me. In that way you will be witnesses to them. 10The good news has to be
preached to all nations before the end comes.
11You will be arrested and brought to trial. But
don't worry ahead of time about what you will say.
Just say what God brings to your mind at the time.
It is not you speaking, but the Holy Spirit.
12"Brothers will hand over brothers to be killed.
Fathers will hand over their children. Children will
rise up against their parents and have them put to
death. 13Everyone will hate you because of me. But
the one who stands firm to the end will be saved.
14"You will see 'the hated thing that destroys.'
(Daniel 9:27; 11:31; 12:11) It will stand where it does
not belong. The reader should understand this.
Then those who are in Judea should escape to the
mountains. 15No one on the roof should go down
into his house to take anything out. 16No one in the
field should go back to get his coat. 17How awful
it will be in those days for pregnant women! How
awful for nursing mothers! 18Pray that this will not
happen in winter.
19"Those days will be worse than any others
from the time God created the world until now.
And there will never be any like them again. 20If
the Lord had not cut the time short, no one would
live. But because of God's chosen people, he has
shortened it.
21"At that time someone may say to you, 'Look!
Here is the Christ!' Or, 'Look! There he is!' Do not
believe it. 22False Christs and false prophets will
appear. They will do signs and miracles. They will
try to fool God's chosen people if possible. 23Keep
watch! I have told you everything ahead of time.
24"So in those days there will be terrible suffering. After that, Scripture says,

"'The sun will be darkened.
The moon will not shine.
25The stars will fall from the sky.
The heavenly bodies will be shaken.'
(Isaiah 13:10; 34:4)

26"At that time people will see the Son of Man
coming in clouds. He will come with great power
and glory. 27He will send his angels. He will gather
his chosen people from all four directions. He will
bring them from the ends of the earth to the ends
of the heavens.
28"Learn a lesson from the fig tree. As soon as
its twigs get tender and its leaves come out, you
know that summer is near. 29In the same way, when
you see those things happening, you know that the
end is near. It is right at the door. 30What I'm about
to tell you is true. The people living at that time
will certainly not pass away until all those things
have happened. 31Heaven and earth will pass away.
But my words will never pass away.

The Day and Hour Are Not Known

32"No one knows about that day or hour. Not
even the angels in heaven know. The Son does not
know. Only the Father knows.
33"Keep watch! Stay awake! You do not know
when that time will come. 34It's like a man going
away. He leaves his house and puts his servants in
charge. Each one is given a task to do. He tells the
one at the door to keep watch.

35“So keep watch! You do not know when the
owner of the house will come back. It may be in
the evening or at midnight. It may be when the
rooster crows or at dawn. 36He may come suddenly. So do not let him find you sleeping.
37“What I say to you, I say to everyone. ‘Watch!’”

A Woman Pours Perfume on Jesus

14 The Passover and the Feast of Unleavened
Bread were only two days away. The chief
priests and the teachers of the law were looking for
a clever way to arrest Jesus. They wanted to kill
him. 2“But not during the Feast,” they said. “The
people may stir up trouble.”

3Jesus was in Bethany. He was at the table in the
home of a man named Simon, who had a skin disease. A woman came with a special sealed jar of
very expensive perfume. It was made out of pure
nard. She broke the jar open and poured the perfume on Jesus’ head.

4Some of the people there became angry. They
said to one another, “Why waste this perfume? 5It
could have been sold for more than a year’s pay.
The money could have been given to poor people.”
So they found fault with the woman.

6“Leave her alone,” Jesus said. “Why are you
bothering her? She has done a beautiful thing to
me. 7You will always have poor people with you.
You can help them any time you want to. But you
will not always have me. 8She did what she could.
She poured perfume on my body to prepare me to
be buried. 9What I’m about to tell you is true. What
she has done will be told anywhere the good news
is preached all over the world. It will be told in
memory of her.”

10Judas Iscariot was one of the Twelve. He went
to the chief priests to hand Jesus over to them.
11They were delighted to hear that he would do this.
They promised to give Judas money. So he watched
for the right time to hand Jesus over to them.

The Lord’s Supper

12It was the first day of the Feast of Unleavened
Bread. That was the time to sacrifice the Passover
lamb.

Jesus’ disciples asked him, “Where do you want
us to go and prepare for you to eat the Passover
meal?”

13So he sent out two of his disciples. He told
them, “Go into the city. A man carrying a jar of
water will meet you. Follow him. 14He will enter a
house. Say to its owner, ‘The Teacher asks,
“Where is my guest room? Where can I eat the
Passover meal with my disciples?”’ 15He will show
you a large upstairs room. It will have furniture
and will be ready. Prepare for us to eat there.”

16The disciples left and went into the city. They
found things just as Jesus had told them. So they
prepared the Passover meal.

17When evening came, Jesus arrived with the
Twelve. 18While they were at the table eating,
Jesus said, “What I’m about to tell you is true. One
of you who is eating with me will hand me over to
my enemies.”

19The disciples became sad. One by one they
said to him, “It’s not I, is it?”

20“It is one of the Twelve,” Jesus replied. “It is
the one who dips bread into the bowl with me.
21The Son of Man will go just as it is written about
him. But how terrible it will be for the one who
hands over the Son of Man! It would be better for
him if he had not been born.”

22While they were eating, Jesus took bread. He
gave thanks and broke it. He handed it to his disciples and said, “Take it. This is my body.”

23Then he took the cup. He gave thanks and
handed it to them. All of them drank from it.

24“This is my blood of the new covenant,” he
said to them. “It is poured out for many. 25What
I’m about to tell you is true. I won’t drink wine
with you again until the day I drink it in God’s
kingdom.”

26Then they sang a hymn and went out to the
Mount of Olives.

Jesus Says That Peter Will Fail

27“You will all turn away,” Jesus told the disciples. “It is written,

“‘I will strike the shepherd down.
Then the sheep will be scattered.’
(Zechariah 13:7)

28But after I rise from the dead, I will go ahead of
you into Galilee.”

29Peter said, “All the others may turn away. But
I will not.”

30“What I’m about to tell you is true,” Jesus
answered. “It will happen today, this very night.
Before the rooster crows twice, you yourself will
say three times that you don’t know me.”

31But Peter would not give in. He said, “I may
have to die with you. But I will never say I don’t
know you.” And all the others said the same thing.

Jesus Prays in Gethsemane

32Jesus and his disciples went to a place called
Gethsemane. Jesus said to them, “Sit here while I
pray.”

33He took Peter, James and John along with
him. He began to be very upset and troubled.
34“My soul is very sad. I feel close to death,” he
said to them. “Stay here. Keep watch.”

35He went a little farther. Then he fell to the
ground. He prayed that, if possible, the hour might
pass by him. 36“*Abba*,” he said, “everything is possible for you. Take this cup of suffering away from
me. But let what you want be done, not what I
want.” *Abba* means Father.

37Then he returned to his disciples and found
them sleeping. “Simon,” he said to Peter, “are you
asleep? Couldn’t you keep watch for one hour?
38Watch and pray. Then you won’t fall into sin

when you are tempted. The spirit is willing. But the body is weak."

39Once more Jesus went away and prayed the same thing. 40Then he came back. Again he found them sleeping. They couldn't keep their eyes open. They did not know what to say to him.

41Jesus returned the third time. He said to them, "Are you still sleeping and resting? Enough! The hour has come. Look! The Son of Man is about to be handed over to sinners. 42Get up! Let us go! Here comes the one who is handing me over to them!"

Jesus Is Arrested

43Just as Jesus was speaking, Judas appeared. He was one of the Twelve. A crowd was with him. They were carrying swords and clubs. The chief priests, the teachers of the law, and the elders had sent them.

44Judas, who was going to hand Jesus over, had arranged a signal with them. "The one I kiss is the man," he said. "Arrest him and have the guards lead him away."

45So Judas went to Jesus at once. He said, "Rabbi!" And he kissed him.

46The men grabbed Jesus and arrested him.

47Then one of those standing nearby pulled his sword out. He struck the servant of the high priest and cut off his ear.

48"Am I leading a band of armed men against you?" asked Jesus. "Do you have to come out with swords and clubs to capture me? 49Every day I was with you. I taught in the temple courtyard, and you didn't arrest me. But the Scriptures must come true."

50Then everyone left him and ran away.

51A young man was following Jesus. The man was wearing nothing but a piece of linen cloth. When the crowd grabbed him, 52he ran away naked. He left his clothing behind.

Jesus Is Taken to the Sanhedrin

53The crowd took Jesus to the high priest. All of the chief priests, the elders, and the teachers of the law came together.

54Not too far away, Peter followed Jesus. He went right into the courtyard of the high priest. There he sat with the guards. He warmed himself at the fire.

55The chief priests and the whole Sanhedrin were looking for something to use against Jesus. They wanted to put him to death. But they did not find any proof. 56Many witnesses lied about him. But their stories did not agree.

57Then some stood up. They gave false witness about him. 58"We heard him say, 'I will destroy this temple made by human hands. In three days I will build another temple, not made by human hands.'" 59But what they said did not agree.

60Then the high priest stood up in front of them. He asked Jesus, "Aren't you going to answer? What are these charges these men are bringing against you?"

61But Jesus remained silent. He gave no answer. Again the high priest asked him, "Are you the Christ? Are you the Son of the Blessed One?"

62"I am," said Jesus. "And you will see the Son of Man sitting at the right hand of the Mighty One. You will see the Son of Man coming on the clouds of heaven."

63The high priest tore his clothes. "Why do we need any more witnesses?" he asked. 64"You have heard him say a very evil thing against God. What do you think?"

They all found him guilty and said he must die.

65Then some began to spit at him. They blindfolded him. They hit him with their fists. They said, "Prophesy!" And the guards took him and beat him.

Peter Says He Does Not Know Jesus

66Peter was below in the courtyard. One of the high priest's female servants came by. 67When she saw Peter warming himself, she looked closely at him.

"You also were with Jesus, that Nazarene," she said.

68But Peter said he had not been with him. "I don't know or understand what you're talking about," he said. He went out to the entrance to the courtyard.

69The servant saw him there. She said again to those standing around, "This fellow is one of them."

70Again he said he was not.

After a little while, those standing nearby said to Peter, "You must be one of them. You are from Galilee."

71He began to call down curses on himself. He took an oath and said to them, "I don't know this man you're talking about!"

72Right away the rooster crowed the second time. Then Peter remembered what Jesus had spoken to him. "The rooster will crow twice," he had said. "Before it does, you will say three times that you don't know me." Peter broke down and sobbed.

Jesus Is Brought to Pilate

15 It was very early in the morning. The chief priests, with the elders, the teachers of the law, and the whole Sanhedrin, made a decision. They tied Jesus up and led him away. Then they handed him over to Pilate.

2"Are you the king of the Jews?" asked Pilate.

"Yes. It is just as you say," Jesus replied.

3The chief priests brought many charges against him. 4So Pilate asked him again, "Aren't you going to answer? See how many things they charge you with."

5But Jesus still did not reply. Pilate was amazed.

6It was the usual practice at the Passover Feast to let one prisoner go free. The people could choose the one they wanted. 7A man named Barabbas was in prison. He was there with some other people who had fought against the country's rulers. They had committed murder while they were fighting against the rulers. 8 The crowd came up and asked Pilate to do for them what he usually did.

9 "Do you want me to let the king of the Jews go free?" asked Pilate. 10 He knew that the chief priests had handed Jesus over to him because they were jealous. 11 But the chief priests stirred up the crowd. So the crowd asked Pilate to let Barabbas go free instead.

12 "Then what should I do with the one you call the king of the Jews?" Pilate asked them.

13 "Crucify him!" the crowd shouted.

14 "Why? What wrong has he done?" asked Pilate. But they shouted even louder, "Crucify him!"

15 Pilate wanted to satisfy the crowd. So he let Barabbas go free. He ordered that Jesus be whipped. Then he handed him over to be nailed to a cross.

The Soldiers Make Fun of Jesus

16 The soldiers led Jesus away into the palace. It was called the Praetorium. They called together the whole company of soldiers.

17 The soldiers put a purple robe on Jesus. Then they twisted thorns together to make a crown. They placed it on his head. 18 They began to call out to him, "We honor you, king of the Jews!" 19 Again and again they hit him on the head with a stick. They spit on him. They fell on their knees and pretended to honor him.

20 After they had made fun of him, they took off the purple robe. They put his own clothes back on him. Then they led him out to nail him to a cross.

Jesus Is Nailed to a Cross

21 A man named Simon from Cyrene was passing by. He was the father of Alexander and Rufus. Simon was on his way in from the country. The soldiers forced him to carry the cross.

22 They brought Jesus to the place called Golgotha. The word Golgotha means The Place of the Skull. 23 Then they gave him wine mixed with spices. But he did not take it.

24 They nailed him to the cross. Then they divided up his clothes. They cast lots to see what each of them would get.

25 It was nine o'clock in the morning when they crucified him. 26 They wrote out the charge against him. It read, THE KING OF THE JEWS.

27/28 They crucified two robbers with him. One was on his right and one was on his left.

29 Those who passed by shouted at Jesus and made fun of him. They shook their heads and said, "So you are going to destroy the temple and build it again in three days? 30 Then come down from the cross! Save yourself!"

31 In the same way the chief priests and the teachers of the law made fun of him among themselves. "He saved others," they said. "But he can't save himself! 32 Let this Christ, this King of Israel, come down now from the cross! When we see that, we will believe."

Those who were being crucified with Jesus also made fun of him.

Jesus Dies

33 At noon, darkness covered the whole land. It lasted three hours. 34 At three o'clock Jesus cried out in a loud voice, *"Eloi, Eloi, lama sabachthani?"* This means "My God, my God, why have you deserted me?" *(Psalm 22:1)*

35 Some of those standing nearby heard Jesus cry out. They said, "Listen! He's calling for Elijah."

36 One of them ran and filled a sponge with wine vinegar. He put it on a stick. He offered it to Jesus to drink. "Leave him alone," he said. "Let's see if Elijah comes to take him down."

37 With a loud cry, Jesus took his last breath.

38 The temple curtain was torn in two from top to bottom.

39 A Roman commander was standing there in front of Jesus. He heard his cry and saw how Jesus died. Then he said, "This man was surely the Son of God!"

40 Not very far away, some women were watching. Mary Magdalene was among them. Mary, the mother of the younger James and of Joses, was also there. So was Salome. 41 In Galilee those women had followed Jesus. They had taken care of his needs.

Many other women were also there. They had come up with him to Jerusalem.

Jesus Is Buried

42 It was the day before the Sabbath. That day was called Preparation Day. As evening approached, 43 Joseph went boldly to Pilate and asked for Jesus' body. Joseph was from the town of Arimathea. He was a leading member of the Jewish Council. He was waiting for God's kingdom.

44 Pilate was surprised to hear that Jesus was already dead. So he called for the Roman commander. He asked him if Jesus had already died. 45 The commander said it was true. So Pilate gave the body to Joseph.

46 Then Joseph bought some linen cloth. He took the body down and wrapped it in the linen. He put it in a tomb cut out of rock. Then he rolled a stone against the entrance to the tomb.

47 Mary Magdalene and Mary the mother of Joses saw where Jesus' body had been placed.

Jesus Rises From the Dead

16 The Sabbath day ended. Mary Magdalene, Mary the mother of James, and Salome bought spices. They were going to apply them to Jesus' body.

2 Very early on the first day of the week, they were on their way to the tomb. It was just after

sunrise. [3]They asked each other, "Who will roll the stone away from the entrance to the tomb?"

[4]Then they looked up and saw that the stone had been rolled away. The stone was very large.

[5]They entered the tomb. As they did, they saw a young man dressed in a white robe. He was sitting on the right side. They were alarmed.

[6]"Don't be alarmed," he said. "You are looking for Jesus the Nazarene, who was crucified. But he has risen! He is not here! See the place where they had put him. [7]Go! Tell his disciples and Peter, 'He is going ahead of you into Galilee. There you will see him. It will be just as he told you.'"

[8]The women were shaking and confused. They went out and ran away from the tomb. They said nothing to anyone, because they were afraid.

---

[9]Jesus rose from the dead early on the first day of the week. He appeared first to Mary Magdalene. He had driven seven demons out of her. [10]She went and told those who had been with him. She found them crying. They were very sad. [11]They heard that Jesus was alive and that she had seen him. But they did not believe it.

[12]After that, Jesus appeared in a different form to two of them. This happened while they were walking out in the country. [13]The two returned and told the others about it. But the others did not believe them either.

[14]Later Jesus appeared to the Eleven as they were eating. He spoke firmly to them because they had no faith. They would not believe those who had seen him after he rose from the dead.

[15]He said to them, "Go into all the world. Preach the good news to everyone. [16]Anyone who believes and is baptized will be saved. But anyone who does not believe will be punished. [17]Here are the miraculous signs that those who believe will do. In my name they will drive out demons. They will speak in languages they had not known before. [18]They will pick up snakes with their hands. And when they drink deadly poison, it will not hurt them at all. They will place their hands on sick people. And the people will get well."

[19]When the Lord Jesus finished speaking to them, he was taken up into heaven. He sat down at the right hand of God.

[20]Then the disciples went out and preached everywhere. The Lord worked with them. And he backed up his word by the signs that went with it.

Luke

Luke Writes an Orderly Report

1 Many people have attempted to write about
the things that have taken place among us.
2Reports of these things were handed down to us.
There were people who saw these things for themselves from the beginning and then passed the
word on.
3I myself have carefully looked into everything
from the beginning. So it seemed good also to me
to write down an orderly report of exactly what
happened. I am doing this for you, most excellent
Theophilus. 4I want you to know that the things
you have been taught are true.

The Coming Birth of John the Baptist

5Herod was king of Judea. During the time he
was ruling, there was a priest named Zechariah.
He belonged to a group of priests named after Abijah. His wife Elizabeth also came from the family
line of Aaron. 6Both of them did what was right in
God's eyes. They obeyed all the Lord's commandments and rules faithfully. 7But they had no
children, because Elizabeth was not able to have
any. And they were both very old.
8One day Zechariah's group was on duty. He
was serving as a priest in God's temple. 9He happened to be chosen, in the usual way, to go into the
temple of the Lord. There he was supposed to burn
incense. 10The time came for this to be done. All
who had gathered to worship were praying
outside.
11Then an angel of the Lord appeared to Zechariah. The angel was standing at the right side of
the incense altar. 12When Zechariah saw him, he
was amazed and terrified.
13But the angel said to him, "Do not be afraid,
Zechariah. Your prayer has been heard. Your wife
Elizabeth will have a child. It will be a boy, and you
must name him John. 14He will be a joy and delight
to you. His birth will make many people very glad.
15He will be important in the Lord's eyes.
"He must never use wine or other such drinks.
He will be filled with the Holy Spirit from the time
he is born. 16He will bring many of Israel's people
back to the Lord their God. 17And he will prepare
the way for the Lord. He will have the same spirit
and power that Elijah had. He will teach parents
how to love their children. He will also teach people who don't obey to be wise and do what is right.
In this way, he will prepare a people who are ready
for the Lord."
18Zechariah asked the angel, "How can I be sure
of this? I am an old man, and my wife is old too."
19The angel answered, "I am Gabriel. I serve
God. I have been sent to speak to you and to tell
you this good news. 20And now you will have to be
silent. You will not be able to speak until after John
is born. That's because you did not believe my
words. They will come true when the time is right."
21During that time, the people were waiting for
Zechariah to come out. They wondered why he
stayed in the temple so long. 22When he came out,
he could not speak to them. They realized he had
seen a vision in the temple. They knew this
because he kept motioning to them. He still could
not speak.
23When his time of service was over, he
returned home. 24After that, his wife Elizabeth
became pregnant. She stayed at home for five
months. 25"The Lord has done this for me," she
said. "In these days, he has been kind to me. He
has taken away my shame among the people."

The Coming Birth of Jesus

26In the sixth month after Elizabeth had become
pregnant, God sent the angel Gabriel to Nazareth,
a town in Galilee. 27He was sent to a virgin. The
girl was engaged to a man named Joseph. He came
from the family line of David. The virgin's name
was Mary. 28The angel greeted her and said, "The
Lord has given you special favor. He is with you."
29Mary was very upset because of his words.
She wondered what kind of greeting this could be.
30But the angel said to her, "Do not be afraid,
Mary. God is very pleased with you. 31You will
become pregnant and give birth to a son. You must
name him Jesus. 32He will be great and will be
called the Son of the Most High God. The Lord
God will make him a king like his father David of
long ago. 33He will rule forever over his people,
who came from Jacob's family. His kingdom will
never end."
34"How can this happen?" Mary asked the
angel. "I am a virgin."
35The angel answered, "The Holy Spirit will
come to you. The power of the Most High God
will cover you. So the holy one that is born will be
called the Son of God. 36Your relative Elizabeth is
old. And even she is going to have a child. People
thought she could not have children. But she has
been pregnant for six months now. 37Nothing is
impossible with God."
38"I serve the Lord," Mary answered. "May it
happen to me just as you said it would." Then the
angel left her.

Mary Visits Elizabeth

39At that time Mary got ready and hurried to a
town in Judea's hill country. 40There she entered
Zechariah's home and greeted Elizabeth. 41When
Elizabeth heard Mary's greeting, the baby inside
her jumped. And Elizabeth was filled with the Holy

Spirit. 42In a loud voice she called out, "God has blessed you more than other women. And blessed is the child you will have! 43But why is God so kind to me? Why has the mother of my Lord come to me? 44As soon as I heard the sound of your voice, the baby inside me jumped for joy. 45You are a woman God has blessed. You have believed that what the Lord has said to you will be done!"

Mary's Song

46Mary said,

"My soul gives glory to the Lord.
47 My spirit delights in God my Savior.
48 He has taken note of me
even though I am not important.
From now on all people will call me blessed.
49 The Mighty One has done great things
for me.
His name is holy.
50 He shows his mercy to those who have respect
for him,
from parent to child down through the years.
51 He has done mighty things with his arm.
He has scattered those who are proud in
their deepest thoughts.
52 He has brought down rulers from their thrones.
But he has lifted up people who are not
important.
53 He has filled those who are hungry with
good things.
But he has sent those who are rich
away empty.
54 He has helped the people of Israel, who
serve him.
He has always remembered to be kind
55 to Abraham and his children down through
the years.
He has done it just as he said to our people
of long ago."

56Mary stayed with Elizabeth about three months. Then she returned home.

John the Baptist Is Born

57The time came for Elizabeth to have her baby. She gave birth to a son. 58Her neighbors and relatives heard that the Lord had been very kind to her. They shared her joy.

59On the eighth day, they came to have the child circumcised. They were going to name him Zechariah, like his father. 60But his mother spoke up. "No!" she said. "He must be called John."

61They said to her, "No one among your relatives has that name."

62Then they motioned to his father. They wanted to find out what he would like to name the child. 63He asked for something to write on. Then he wrote, "His name is John." Everyone was amazed. 64Right away Zechariah could speak again. His first words gave praise to God. 65The neighbors were all filled with fear and wonder. All through Judea's hill country, people were talking about all these things. 66Everyone who heard this wondered about it. And because the Lord was with John, they asked, "What is this child going to be?"

Zechariah's Song

67His father Zechariah was filled with the Holy Spirit. He prophesied,

68 "Give praise to the Lord, the God of Israel!
He has come and set his people free.
69 He has acted with great power and has
saved us.
He did it for those who are from the family
line of his servant David.
70 Long ago holy prophets said he would do it.
71 He has saved us from our enemies.
We are rescued from all who hate us.
72 He has been kind to our people.
He has remembered his holy covenant.
73 He made an oath to our father Abraham.
74 He promised to save us from our enemies,
so that we could serve him without fear.
75 He wants us to be holy and godly as long
as we live.

76 "And you, my child, will be called a prophet of
the Most High God.
You will go ahead of the Lord to prepare the
way for him.
77 You will tell his people how they can be saved.
You will tell them that their sins can be
forgiven.
78 All of that will happen because our God is
tender and caring.
His kindness will bring the rising sun to us
from heaven.
79 It will shine on those living in darkness
and in the shadow of death.
It will guide our feet on the path of peace."

80The child grew up, and his spirit became strong. He lived in the desert until he appeared openly to Israel.

Jesus Is Born

2 In those days, Caesar Augustus made a law. It required that a list be made of everyone in the whole Roman world. 2It was the first time a list was made of the people while Quirinius was governor of Syria. 3All went to their own towns to be listed.

4So Joseph went also. He went from the town of Nazareth in Galilee to Judea. That is where Bethlehem, the town of David, was. Joseph went there because he belonged to the family line of David. 5He went there with Mary to be listed. Mary was engaged to him. She was expecting a baby.

6While Joseph and Mary were there, the time came for the child to be born. 7She gave birth to her first baby. It was a boy. She wrapped him in large strips of cloth. Then she placed him in a manger. There was no room for them in the inn.

Angels Appear to the Shepherds

8There were shepherds living out in the fields
nearby. It was night, and they were looking after
their sheep. 9An angel of the Lord appeared to
them. And the glory of the Lord shone around
them. They were terrified.
10But the angel said to them, "Do not be afraid.
I bring you good news of great joy. It is for all the
people. 11Today in the town of David a Savior has
been born to you. He is Christ the Lord. 12Here is
how you will know I am telling you the truth. You
will find a baby wrapped in strips of cloth and
lying in a manger."
13Suddenly a large group of angels from heaven
also appeared. They were praising God. They said,

14 "May glory be given to God in the highest
heaven!
And may peace be given to those he is
pleased with on earth!"

15The angels left and went into heaven. Then the
shepherds said to one another, "Let's go to Bethlehem. Let's see this thing that has happened,
which the Lord has told us about."
16So they hurried off and found Mary and Joseph and the baby. The baby was lying in the
manger. 17After the shepherds had seen him, they
told everyone. They reported what the angel had
said about this child. 18All who heard it were
amazed at what the shepherds said to them.
19But Mary kept all these things like a secret
treasure in her heart. She thought about them over
and over.
20The shepherds returned. They gave glory and
praise to God. Everything they had seen and heard
was just as they had been told.

Joseph and Mary Take Jesus to the Temple

21When the child was eight days old, he was circumcised. At the same time he was named Jesus.
This was the name the angel had given him before
his mother became pregnant.
22The time for making them pure came as it is
written in the Law of Moses. So Joseph and Mary
took Jesus to Jerusalem. There they presented him
to the Lord. 23In the Law of the Lord it says, "The
first boy born in every family must be set apart for
the Lord." *(Exodus 13:2,12)* 24They also offered a
sacrifice. They did it in keeping with the Law,
which says, "a pair of doves or two young
pigeons." *(Leviticus 12:8)*
25In Jerusalem there was a man named Simeon.
He was a good and godly man. He was waiting for
God's promise to Israel to happen. The Holy Spirit
was with him. 26The Spirit had told Simeon that he
would not die before he had seen the Lord's Christ.
27The Spirit led him into the temple courtyard.
Then Jesus' parents brought the child in. They
came to do for him what the Law required.
28Simeon took Jesus in his arms and praised
God. He said,

29 "Lord, you are the King over all.
Now let me, your servant, go in peace.
That is what you promised.
30 My eyes have seen your salvation.
31 You have prepared it in the sight of
all people.
32 It is a light to be given to those who
aren't Jews.
It will bring glory to your people Israel."

33The child's father and mother were amazed at
what was said about him. 34Then Simeon blessed
them. He said to Mary, Jesus' mother, "This child
is going to cause many people in Israel to fall and
to rise. God has sent him. But many will speak
against him. 35The thoughts of many hearts will be
known. A sword will wound your own soul too."
36There was also a prophet named Anna. She
was the daughter of Penuel from the tribe of Asher. Anna was very old. After getting married, she
lived with her husband seven years. 37Then she
was a widow until she was 84. She never left the
temple. She worshiped night and day, praying and
going without eating.
38Anna came up to Jesus' family at that very
moment. She gave thanks to God. And she spoke
about the child to all who were looking forward to
the time when Jerusalem would be set free.
39Joseph and Mary did everything the Law of
the Lord required. Then they returned to Galilee.
They went to their own town of Nazareth. 40And
the child grew and became strong. He was very
wise. He was blessed by God's grace.

The Boy Jesus at the Temple

41Every year Jesus' parents went to Jerusalem
for the Passover Feast. 42When he was 12 years
old, they went up to the Feast as usual.
43After the Feast was over, his parents left to go
back home. The boy Jesus stayed behind in Jerusalem. But they were not aware of it. 44They
thought he was somewhere in their group. So they
traveled on for a day.
Then they began to look for him among their
relatives and friends. 45They did not find him. So
they went back to Jerusalem to look for him.
46After three days they found him in the temple
courtyard. He was sitting with the teachers. He
was listening to them and asking them questions.
47Everyone who heard him was amazed at how
much he understood. They also were amazed at his
answers.
48When his parents saw him, they were amazed.
His mother said to him, "Son, why have you
treated us like this? Your father and I have been
worried about you. We have been looking for you
everywhere."
49"Why were you looking for me?" he asked.
"Didn't you know I had to be in my Father's

house?" 50But they did not understand what he
meant by that.

51Then he went back to Nazareth with them, and
he obeyed them. But his mother kept all these
things like a secret treasure in her heart. 52Jesus
became wiser and stronger. He also became more
and more pleasing to God and to people.

John the Baptist Prepares the Way

3 Tiberius Caesar had been ruling for 15 years.
Pontius Pilate was governor of Judea. Herod
was the ruler of Galilee. His brother Philip was the
ruler of Iturea and Traconitis. Lysanias was ruler of
Abilene. 2Annas and Caiaphas were high priests.
At that time God's word came to John, son of
Zechariah, in the desert. 3He went into all the
countryside around the Jordan River. There he
preached that people should be baptized and turn
away from their sins. Then God would forgive
them.

4Here is what is written in the scroll of the
prophet Isaiah. It says,

"A messenger is calling out in the desert,
'Prepare the way for the Lord.
Make straight paths for him.
5Every valley will be filled in.
Every mountain and hill will be made level.
The crooked roads will become straight.
The rough ways will become smooth.
6And everyone will see God's salvation.' "
(Isaiah 40:3–5)

7John spoke to the crowds coming to be baptized by him. He said, "You are like a nest of poisonous snakes! Who warned you to escape the
coming of God's anger? 8Produce fruit that shows
you have turned away from your sins. And don't
start saying to yourselves, 'Abraham is our father.'
I tell you, God can raise up children for Abraham
even from these stones. 9The ax is already lying at
the roots of the trees. All the trees that don't produce good fruit will be cut down. They will be
thrown into the fire."

10"Then what should we do?" the crowd asked.

11John answered, "If you have extra clothes,
you should share with those who have none. And
if you have extra food, you should do the same."

12Tax collectors also came to be baptized.
"Teacher," they asked, "what should we do?"

13"Don't collect any more than you are required
to," John told them.

14Then some soldiers asked him, "And what
should we do?"

John replied, "Don't force people to give you
money. Don't bring false charges against people.
Be happy with your pay."

15The people were waiting. They were expecting something. They were all wondering in their
hearts if John might be the Christ.

16John answered them all, "I baptize you with
water. But One who is more powerful than I am will
come. I'm not good enough to untie the straps of his
sandals. He will baptize you with the Holy Spirit
and with fire. 17His pitchfork is in his hand to toss
the straw away from his threshing floor. He will
gather the wheat into his storeroom. But he will
burn up the husks with fire that can't be put out."

18John said many other things to warn the people. He also preached the good news to them.

19But John found fault with Herod, the ruler of
Galilee, because of Herodias. She was the wife of
Herod's brother. John also spoke strongly to Her-
od about all the other evil things he had done. 20So
Herod locked him up in prison. He added this sin
to all his others.

The Baptism and Family Line of Jesus

21When all the people were being baptized,
Jesus was baptized too. And as he was praying,
heaven was opened. 22The Holy Spirit came down
on him in the form of a dove. A voice came from
heaven. It said, "You are my Son, and I love you.
I am very pleased with you."

23Jesus was about 30 years old when he began
his special work for God and others. It was thought
that he was the son of Joseph.

Joseph was the son of Heli.
24Heli was the son of Matthat.
Matthat was the son of Levi.
Levi was the son of Melki.
Melki was the son of Jannai.
Jannai was the son of Joseph.
25Joseph was the son of Mattathias.
Mattathias was the son of Amos.
Amos was the son of Nahum.
Nahum was the son of Esli.
Esli was the son of Naggai.
26Naggai was the son of Maath.
Maath was the son of Mattathias.
Mattathias was the son of Semein.
Semein was the son of Josech.
Josech was the son of Joda.
27Joda was the son of Joanan.
Joanan was the son of Rhesa.
Rhesa was the son of Zerubbabel.
Zerubbabel was the son of Shealtiel.
Shealtiel was the son of Neri.
28Neri was the son of Melki.
Melki was the son of Addi.
Addi was the son of Cosam.
Cosam was the son of Elmadam.
Elmadam was the son of Er.
29Er was the son of Joshua.
Joshua was the son of Eliezer.
Eliezer was the son of Jorim.
Jorim was the son of Matthat.
Matthat was the son of Levi.
30Levi was the son of Simeon.
Simeon was the son of Judah.
Judah was the son of Joseph.
Joseph was the son of Jonam.
Jonam was the son of Eliakim.

31 Eliakim was the son of Melea.
Melea was the son of Menna.
Menna was the son of Mattatha.
Mattatha was the son of Nathan.
Nathan was the son of David.
32 David was the son of Jesse.
Jesse was the son of Obed.
Obed was the son of Boaz.
Boaz was the son of Salmon.
Salmon was the son of Nahshon.
33 Nahshon was the son of Amminadab.
Amminadab was the son of Ram.
Ram was the son of Hezron.
Hezron was the son of Perez.
Perez was the son of Judah.
34 Judah was the son of Jacob.
Jacob was the son of Isaac.
Isaac was the son of Abraham.
Abraham was the son of Terah.
Terah was the son of Nahor.
35 Nahor was the son of Serug.
Serug was the son of Reu.
Reu was the son of Peleg.
Peleg was the son of Eber.
Eber was the son of Shelah.
36 Shelah was the son of Cainan.
Cainan was the son of Arphaxad.
Arphaxad was the son of Shem.
Shem was the son of Noah.
Noah was the son of Lamech.
37 Lamech was the son of Methuselah.
Methuselah was the son of Enoch.
Enoch was the son of Jared.
Jared was the son of Mahalalel.
Mahalalel was the son of Kenan.
38 Kenan was the son of Enosh.
Enosh was the son of Seth.
Seth was the son of Adam.
Adam was the son of God.

Jesus Is Tempted

4 Jesus, full of the Holy Spirit, returned from
the Jordan River. The Spirit led him into the
desert. 2There the devil tempted him for 40 days.
Jesus ate nothing during that time. At the end of
the 40 days, he was hungry.
3The devil said to him, "If you are the Son of
God, tell this stone to become bread."
4Jesus answered, "It is written, 'Man doesn't
live only on bread.'" *(Deuteronomy 8:3)*
5Then the devil led Jesus up to a high place. In
an instant, he showed Jesus all the kingdoms of the
world. 6He said to him, "I will give you all their
authority and glory. It has been given to me, and I
can give it to anyone I want to. 7So if you worship
me, it will all be yours."
8Jesus answered, "It is written, 'Worship the
Lord your God. He is the only one you should
serve.'" *(Deuteronomy 6:13)*
9Then the devil led Jesus to Jerusalem. He had
him stand on the highest point of the temple. "If
you are the Son of God," he said, "throw yourself
down from here. 10It is written,

"'The Lord will command his angels to take
good care of you.
11 They will lift you up in their hands.
Then you won't trip over a stone.'"
(Psalm 91:11,12)

12Jesus answered, "Scripture says, 'Do not put
the Lord your God to the test.'" *(Deuteronomy 6:16)*
13When the devil finished all this tempting, he
left Jesus until a better time.

Jesus Is Not Accepted in Nazareth

14Jesus returned to Galilee in the power of the
Holy Spirit. News about him spread through the
whole countryside. 15He taught in their synagogues, and everyone praised him.
16Jesus went to Nazareth, where he had been
brought up. On the Sabbath day he went into the
synagogue as he usually did. And he stood up to
read.
17The scroll of the prophet Isaiah was handed to
him. He unrolled it and found the right place.
There it is written,

18 "The Spirit of the Lord is on me.
He has anointed me
to tell the good news to poor people.
He has sent me to announce freedom for
prisoners.
He has sent me so that the blind will
see again.
He wants me to free those who are
beaten down.
19 And he has sent me to announce the year
when he will set his people free."
(Isaiah 61:1,2)

20Then Jesus rolled up the scroll. He gave it
back to the attendant and sat down. The eyes of
everyone in the synagogue were staring at him.
21He began by saying to them, "Today this pas-
sage of Scripture is coming true as you listen."
22Everyone said good things about him. They
were amazed at the gracious words they heard
from his lips. "Isn't this Joseph's son?" they asked.
23Jesus said, "Here is a saying you will certainly
apply to me. 'Doctor, heal yourself! Do the things
here in your hometown that we heard you did in
Capernaum.'"
24"What I'm about to tell you is true," he continued. "A prophet is not accepted in his hometown.
25I tell you for sure that there were many widows in
Israel in the days of Elijah. And there had been no
rain for three and a half years. There wasn't enough
food to eat anywhere in the land. 26But Elijah was
not sent to any of those widows. Instead, he was
sent to a widow in Zarephath near Sidon. 27And
there were many in Israel who had skin diseases in
the days of Elisha the prophet. But not one of them
was healed except Naaman the Syrian."

[28]All the people in the synagogue were very angry when they heard that. [29]They got up and ran Jesus out of town. They took him to the edge of the hill on which the town was built. They planned to throw him down the cliff. [30]But Jesus walked right through the crowd and went on his way.

Jesus Drives Out an Evil Spirit

[31]Then Jesus went to Capernaum, a town in Galilee. On the Sabbath day he began to teach the people. [32]They were amazed at his teaching, because his message had authority.

[33]In the synagogue there was a man controlled by a demon, an evil spirit. He cried out at the top of his voice. [34]"Ha!" he said. "What do you want with us, Jesus of Nazareth? Have you come to destroy us? I know who you are. You are the Holy One of God!"

[35]"Be quiet!" Jesus said firmly. "Come out of him!"

Then the demon threw the man down in front of everybody. And it came out without hurting him.

[36]All the people were amazed. They said to each other, "What is this teaching? With authority and power he gives orders to evil spirits. And they come out!"

[37]The news about Jesus spread throughout the whole area.

Jesus Heals Many People

[38]Jesus left the synagogue and went to the home of Simon. At that time, Simon's mother-in-law was suffering from a high fever. So they asked Jesus to help her. [39]He bent over her and commanded the fever to leave, and it left her. She got up at once and began to serve them.

[40]At sunset, people brought to Jesus all who were sick. He placed his hands on each one and healed them. [41]Also, demons came out of many people. The demons shouted, "You are the Son of God!" But he commanded them to be quiet. He would not allow them to speak, because they knew he was the Christ.

[42]At dawn, Jesus went out to a place where he could be by himself. The people went to look for him. When they found him, they tried to keep him from leaving them. [43]But he said, "I must announce the good news of God's kingdom to the other towns also. That is why I was sent." [44]And he kept on preaching in the synagogues of Judea.

Jesus Chooses the First Disciples

5 One day Jesus was standing by the Sea of Galilee. The people crowded around him and listened to the word of God. [2]Jesus saw two boats at the edge of the water. They had been left there by the fishermen, who were washing their nets. [3]He got into the boat that belonged to Simon. Jesus asked him to go out a little way from shore. Then he sat down in the boat and taught the people.

[4]When he finished speaking, he turned to Simon. He said, "Go out into deep water. Let the nets down so you can catch some fish."

[5]Simon answered, "Master, we've worked hard all night and haven't caught anything. But because you say so, I will let down the nets."

[6]When they had done so, they caught a large number of fish. There were so many that their nets began to break. [7]So they motioned to their partners in the other boat to come and help them. They came and filled both boats so full that they began to sink.

[8]When Simon Peter saw this, he fell at Jesus' knees. "Go away from me, Lord!" he said. "I am a sinful man!"

[9]He and everyone with him were amazed at the number of fish they had caught. [10]So were James and John, the sons of Zebedee, who worked with Simon.

Then Jesus said to Simon, "Don't be afraid. From now on you will catch people."

[11]So they pulled their boats up on shore. Then they left everything and followed him.

Jesus Heals a Man With a Skin Disease

[12]While Jesus was in one of the towns, a man came along. He had a skin disease all over his body. When he saw Jesus, he fell with his face to the ground. He begged him, "Lord, if you are willing to make me 'clean,' you can do it."

[13]Jesus reached out his hand and touched the man. "I am willing to do it," he said. "Be 'clean'!" Right away the disease left him.

[14]Then Jesus ordered him, "Don't tell anyone. Go and show yourself to the priest. Offer the sacrifices that Moses commanded. It will be a witness to the priest and the people that you are 'clean.'"

[15]But the news about Jesus spread even more. So crowds of people came to hear him. They also came to be healed of their sicknesses. [16]But Jesus often went away to be by himself and pray.

Jesus Heals a Man Who Could Not Walk

[17]One day Jesus was teaching. Pharisees and teachers of the law were sitting there. They had come from every village of Galilee and from Judea and Jerusalem. They heard that the Lord had given Jesus the power to heal the sick.

[18]Some men came carrying a man who could not walk. He was lying on a mat. They tried to take him into the house to place him in front of Jesus. [19]They could not find a way to do this because of the crowd. So they went up on the roof. Then they lowered the man on his mat through the opening in the roof tiles. They lowered him into the middle of the crowd, right in front of Jesus.

[20]When Jesus saw that they had faith, he said, "Friend, your sins are forgiven."

[21]The Pharisees and the teachers of the law began to think, "Who is this fellow who says such an evil thing? Who can forgive sins but God alone?"

22 Jesus knew what they were thinking. So he
asked, "Why are you thinking these things in your
hearts? 23 Is it easier to say, 'Your sins are forgiven'? Or to say, 'Get up and walk'? 24 I want you
to know that the Son of Man has authority on earth
to forgive sins." So he spoke to the man who could
not walk. "I tell you," he said, "get up. Take your
mat and go home."

25 Right away, the man stood up in front of them.
He took his mat and went home praising God.
26 Everyone was amazed and gave praise to God.
They were filled with wonder. They said, "We
have seen unusual things today."

Jesus Chooses Levi

27 After this, Jesus left the house. He saw a tax
collector sitting at the tax booth. The man's name
was Levi.

"Follow me," Jesus said to him.

28 Levi got up, left everything and followed him.

29 Then Levi gave a huge dinner for Jesus at his
house. A large crowd of tax collectors and others
were eating with them. 30 But the Pharisees and
their teachers of the law complained to Jesus' disciples. They said, "Why do you eat and drink with
tax collectors and 'sinners'?"

31 Jesus answered them, "Those who are healthy
don't need a doctor. Sick people do. 32 I have not
come to get those who think they are right with
God to follow me. I have come to get sinners to
turn away from their sins."

Jesus Is Asked About Fasting

33 Some of the people who were there said to
Jesus, "John's disciples often pray and go without
eating. So do the disciples of the Pharisees. But
yours go on eating and drinking."

34 Jesus answered, "Can you make the guests of
the groom go without eating while he is with them?
35 But the time will come when the groom will be
taken away from them. In those days they will fast."

36 Then Jesus gave them an example. He said,
"People don't tear a patch from new clothes and
sew it on old clothes. If they do, they will tear the
new clothes. Also, the patch from the new clothes
will not match the old clothes. 37 People don't pour
new wine into old wineskins. If they do, the new
wine will burst the skins. The wine will run out,
and the wineskins will be destroyed. 38 No, new
wine must be poured into new wineskins. 39 After
people drink old wine, they don't want the new.
They say, 'The old wine is better.'"

Jesus Is Lord of the Sabbath Day

6 One Sabbath day Jesus was walking through
the grainfields. His disciples began to break
off some heads of grain. They rubbed them in their
hands and ate them.

2 Some of the Pharisees said, "It is against the
Law to do this on the Sabbath. Why are you
doing it?"

3 Jesus answered them, "Haven't you ever read
about what David did? He and his men were hungry. 4 He entered the house of God and took the
holy bread. He ate the bread that only priests were
allowed to eat. David also gave some to his men."

5 Then Jesus said to them, "The Son of Man is
Lord of the Sabbath day."

6 On another Sabbath day, Jesus went into the
synagogue and was teaching. A man whose right
hand was weak and twisted was there. 7 The Pharisees and the teachers of the law were trying to find
fault with Jesus. So they watched him closely. They
wanted to see if he would heal on the Sabbath.

8 But Jesus knew what they were thinking. He
spoke to the man who had the weak and twisted
hand. "Get up and stand in front of everyone," he
said. So the man got up and stood there.

9 Then Jesus said to them, "What does the Law
say we should do on the Sabbath day? Should we
do good? Or should we do evil? Should we save
life? Or should we destroy it?"

10 He looked around at all of them.

Then he said to the man, "Stretch out your
hand."

He did, and his hand was as good as new.

11 But the Pharisees and the teachers of the law
were very angry. They began to talk to each other
about what they might do to Jesus.

Jesus Chooses the Twelve Apostles

12 On one of those days, Jesus went out to a
mountainside to pray. He spent the night praying
to God. 13 When morning came, he called for his
disciples to come to him. He chose 12 of them and
made them apostles.

14 Simon was one of them. Jesus gave him the
name Peter. There were also Simon's brother Andrew, James, John, Philip and Bartholomew. 15 And
there were Matthew, Thomas, and James, son of
Alphaeus. There were also Simon who was called
the Zealot 16 and Judas, son of James. Judas Iscariot was one of them too. He was the one who
would later hand Jesus over to his enemies.

Jesus Gives Blessings and Warnings

17 Jesus went down the mountain with them and
stood on a level place. A large crowd of his disciples was there. A large number of other people
were there too. They came from all over Judea,
including Jerusalem. They also came from the
coast of Tyre and Sidon.

18 They had all come to hear Jesus and to be
healed of their sicknesses. People who were troubled by evil spirits were made well. 19 Everyone
tried to touch Jesus. Power was coming from him
and healing them all.

20 Jesus looked at his disciples. He said to them,

"Blessed are you who are needy.
God's kingdom belongs to you.
21 Blessed are you who are hungry now.
You will be satisfied.

Blessed are you who are sad now.
You will laugh.
22 Blessed are you when people hate you,
when they have nothing to do with you
and say bad things about you,
and when they treat your name as something evil.
They do all this because you are followers of the Son of Man.

23 "Their people treated the prophets the same way long ago. When these things happen to you, be glad and jump for joy. You will receive many blessings in heaven.

24 "But how terrible it will be for you who are rich!
You have already had your easy life.
25 How terrible for you who are well fed now!
You will go hungry.
How terrible for you who laugh now!
You will cry and be sad.
26 How terrible for you when everyone says good things about you!
Their people treated the false prophets the same way long ago.

Love Your Enemies

27 "But here is what I tell you who hear me.
Love your enemies. Do good to those who hate
you. 28 Bless those who call down curses on you.
And pray for those who treat you badly.
29 "Suppose someone hits you on one cheek.
Turn your other cheek to him also. Suppose someone takes your coat. Don't stop him from taking
your shirt.
30 "Give to everyone who asks you. And if anyone takes what belongs to you, don't ask to get it
back. 31 Do to others as you want them to do to you.
32 "Suppose you love those who love you.
Should anyone praise you for that? Even 'sinners'
love those who love them. 33 And suppose you do
good to those who are good to you. Should anyone praise you for that? Even 'sinners' do that.
34 And suppose you lend money to those who can
pay you back. Should anyone praise you for that?
Even a 'sinner' lends to 'sinners,' expecting them
to pay everything back.
35 "But love your enemies. Do good to them.
Lend to them without expecting to get anything
back. Then you will receive a lot in return. And
you will be sons of the Most High God. He is kind
to people who are evil and are not thankful. 36 So
have mercy, just as your Father has mercy.

Be Fair When You Judge Others

37 "If you do not judge others, then you will not
be judged. If you do not find others guilty, then
you will not be found guilty. Forgive, and you will
be forgiven. 38 Give, and it will be given to you. A
good amount will be poured into your lap. It will
be pressed down, shaken together, and running
over. The same amount you give will be measured
out to you."
39 Jesus also gave them another example. He
asked, "Can a blind person lead another blind person? Won't they both fall into a pit? 40 Students are
not better than their teachers. But everyone who is
completely trained will be like his teacher.
41 "You look at the bit of sawdust in your
friend's eye. But you pay no attention to the piece
of wood in your own eye. 42 How can you say to
your friend, 'Let me take the bit of sawdust out of
your eye'? How can you say this while there is a
piece of wood in your own eye? You pretender!
First take the piece of wood out of your own eye.
Then you will be able to see clearly to take the bit
of sawdust out of your friend's eye.

A Tree and Its Fruit

43 "A good tree doesn't bear bad fruit. And a bad
tree doesn't bear good fruit. 44 You can tell each
tree by the kind of fruit it bears. People do not pick
figs from thorns. And they don't pick grapes from
bushes.
45 "A good man says good things. These come
from the good that is put away in his heart. An evil
man says evil things. These come from the evil
that is put away in his heart. Their mouths say
everything that is in their hearts.

The Wise and Foolish Builders

46 "Why do you call me, 'Lord, Lord,' and still
don't do what I say? 47 Some people come to me
and listen to me and do what I say. I will show you
what they are like. 48 They are like someone who
builds a house. He digs down deep and sets it on
solid rock. When a flood comes, the river rushes
against the house. But the water can't shake it. The
house is well built.
49 "But here is what happens when people listen
to my words and do not obey them. They are like
someone who builds a house on soft ground
instead of solid rock. The moment the river rushes
against that house, it falls down. It is completely
destroyed."

A Roman Commander Has Faith

7 Jesus finished saying all those things to the
people. Then he entered Capernaum.
2 There the servant of a Roman commander was
sick and about to die. His master thought highly of
him. 3 The commander heard about Jesus. So he
sent some elders of the Jews to him. He told them
to ask Jesus to come and heal his servant.
4 They came to Jesus and begged him, "This
man deserves to have you do this. 5 He loves our
nation and has built our synagogue." 6 So Jesus
went with them.

When Jesus came near the house, the Roman
commander sent friends to him. He told them to
say, "Lord, don't trouble yourself. I am not good
enough to have you come into my house. 7 That is

why I did not even think I was fit to come to you. But just say the word, and my servant will be healed. [8]I myself am a man who is under authority. And I have soldiers who obey my orders. I tell this one, 'Go,' and he goes. I tell that one, 'Come,' and he comes. I say to my servant, 'Do this,' and he does it."

[9]When Jesus heard this, he was amazed at him. He turned to the crowd that was following him. He said, "I tell you, even in Israel I have not found anyone whose faith is so strong."

[10]Then the men who had been sent to Jesus returned to the house. They found that the servant was healed.

Jesus Raises a Widow's Son From the Dead

[11]Some time later, Jesus went to a town called Nain. His disciples and a large crowd went along with him. [12]He approached the town gate. Just then, a dead person was being carried out. He was the only son of his mother. She was a widow. A large crowd from the town was with her.

[13]When the Lord saw her, he felt sorry for her. So he said, "Don't cry."

[14]Then he went up and touched the coffin. Those carrying it stood still.

Jesus said, "Young man, I say to you, get up!"

[15]The dead man sat up and began to talk. Then Jesus gave him back to his mother.

[16]The people were all filled with wonder and praised God. "A great prophet has appeared among us," they said. "God has come to help his people." [17]This news about Jesus spread all through Judea and the whole country.

Jesus and John the Baptist

[18]John's disciples told him about all these things. So he chose two of them. [19]He sent them to the Lord. They were to ask Jesus, "Are you the one who was supposed to come? Or should we look for someone else?"

[20]The men came to Jesus. They said, "John the Baptist sent us to ask you, 'Are you the one who was supposed to come? Or should we look for someone else?' "

[21]At that very time Jesus healed many people. They had illnesses, sicknesses and evil spirits. He also gave sight to many who were blind. [22]So Jesus replied to the messengers, "Go back to John. Tell him what you have seen and heard. Blind people receive sight. Disabled people walk. Those who have skin diseases are healed. Deaf people hear. Those who are dead are raised to life. And the good news is preached to those who are poor. [23]Blessed are those who do not give up their faith because of me."

[24]So John's messengers left. Then Jesus began to speak to the crowd about John. He said, "What did you go out into the desert to see? Tall grass waving in the wind? [25]If not, what did you go out to see? A man dressed in fine clothes? No. Those who wear fine clothes and have many expensive things are in palaces. [26]Then what did you go out to see? A prophet? Yes, I tell you, and more than a prophet.

[27]"He is the one written about in Scripture. It says,

" 'I will send my messenger ahead of you.
He will prepare your way for you.'
(Malachi 3:1)

[28]I tell you, no one more important than John has ever been born. But the least important person in God's kingdom is more important than he is."

[29]All the people who heard Jesus' words agreed that God's way was right. Even the tax collectors agreed. These people had all been baptized by John. [30]But the Pharisees and the authorities on the law did not accept God's purpose for themselves. They had not been baptized by John.

[31]"What can I compare today's people to?" Jesus asked. "What are they like? [32]They are like children sitting in the market place and calling out to each other. They say,

" 'We played a flute for you.
But you didn't dance.
We sang a funeral song.
But you didn't cry.'

[33]"That is how it has been with John the Baptist. When he came to you, he didn't eat bread or drink wine. And you say, 'He has a demon.' [34]But when the Son of Man came, he ate and drank as you do. And you say, 'This fellow is always eating and drinking far too much. He's a friend of tax collectors and "sinners." ' [35]All who follow wisdom prove that wisdom is right."

A Sinful Woman Pours Perfume on Jesus

[36]One of the Pharisees invited Jesus to have dinner with him. So he went to the Pharisee's house. He took his place at the table.

[37]There was a woman in that town who had lived a sinful life. She learned that Jesus was eating at the Pharisee's house. So she came with a special sealed jar of perfume. [38]She stood behind Jesus and cried at his feet. She began to wet his feet with her tears. Then she wiped them with her hair. She kissed them and poured perfume on them.

[39]The Pharisee who had invited Jesus saw this. He said to himself, "If this man were a prophet, he would know who is touching him. He would know what kind of woman she is. She is a sinner!"

[40]Jesus answered him, "Simon, I have something to tell you."

"Tell me, teacher," he said.

[41]"Two people owed money to a certain lender. One owed him 500 silver coins. The other owed him 50 silver coins. [42]Neither of them had the money to pay him back. So he let them go without paying. Which of them will love him more?"

43Simon replied, "I suppose the one who owed
the most money."
"You are right," Jesus said.
44Then he turned toward the woman. He said to
Simon, "Do you see this woman? I came into your
house. You did not give me any water to wash my
feet. But she wet my feet with her tears and wiped
them with her hair. 45You did not give me a kiss.
But this woman has not stopped kissing my feet
since I came in. 46You did not put any olive oil on
my head. But she has poured perfume on my feet.
47So I tell you this. Her many sins have been forgiven. She has loved a lot. But the one who has
been forgiven little loves only a little."
48Then Jesus said to her, "Your sins are forgiven."
49The other guests began to talk about this
among themselves. They said, "Who is this who
even forgives sins?"
50Jesus said to the woman, "Your faith has
saved you. Go in peace."

The Story of the Farmer

8 After this, Jesus traveled around from one
town and village to another. He announced the
good news of God's kingdom. The Twelve were
with him. 2So were some women who had been
healed of evil spirits and sicknesses. One was
Mary Magdalene. Seven demons had come out of
her. 3Another was Joanna, the wife of Cuza. He
was the manager of Herod's household. Susanna
and many others were there also. These women
were helping to support Jesus and the Twelve with
their own money.
4A large crowd gathered together. People came
to Jesus from town after town. As they did, he told
a story. He said, 5"A farmer went out to plant his
seed. He scattered the seed on the ground. Some
fell on a path. People walked on it, and the birds of
the air ate it up. 6Some seed fell on rocky places.
When it grew, the plants dried up because they had
no water. 7Other seed fell among thorns. The
thorns grew up with it and crowded out the plants.
8Still other seed fell on good soil. It grew up and
produced a crop 100 times more than the farmer
planted."
When Jesus said this, he called out, "Those who
have ears should listen."
9His disciples asked him what the story meant.
10He said, "You have been given the chance to
understand the secrets of God's kingdom. But to
outsiders I speak by using stories. In that way,

"'They see, but they will not know what they
are seeing.
They hear, but they will not understand what
they are hearing.' *(Isaiah 6:9)*

11"Here is what the story means. The seed is
God's message. 12People on the path are those who
hear. But then the devil comes. He takes away the
message from their hearts. He does it so they
won't believe. Then they can't be saved. 13Those
on the rock are the ones who hear the message and
receive it with joy. But they have no roots. They
believe for a while. But when they are put to the
test, they fall away from the faith. 14The seed that
fell among thorns stands for those who hear the
message. But as they go on their way, they are
choked by life's worries, riches and pleasures. So
they do not reach full growth.
15"But the seed on good soil stands for those
with an honest and good heart. They hear the message. They keep it in their hearts. They remain
faithful and produce a good crop.

A Lamp on a Stand

16"People do not light a lamp and then hide it in
a jar or put it under a bed. Instead, they put it on a
stand. Then those who come in can see its light.
17What is hidden will be seen. And what is out of
sight will be brought into the open and made
known.
18"So be careful how you listen. If you have
something, you will be given more. If you have
nothing, even what you think you have will be
taken away from you."

Jesus' Mother and Brothers

19Jesus' mother and brothers came to see him.
But they could not get near him because of the
crowd. 20Someone told him, "Your mother and
brothers are standing outside. They want to see
you."
21He replied, "My mother and brothers are those
who hear God's word and do what it says."

Jesus Calms the Storm

22One day Jesus said to his disciples, "Let's go
over to the other side of the lake." So they got into
a boat and left.
23As they sailed, Jesus fell asleep. A storm came
down on the lake. It was so bad that the boat was
about to sink. They were in great danger.
24The disciples went and woke Jesus up. They
said, "Master! Master! We're going to drown!"
He got up and ordered the wind and the huge
waves to stop. The storm quieted down. It was
completely calm.
25"Where is your faith?" he asked his disciples.
They were amazed and full of fear. They asked
one another, "Who is this? He commands even the
winds and the waves, and they obey him."

Jesus Heals a Man Controlled by Demons

26Jesus and his disciples sailed to the area of the
Gerasenes across the lake from Galilee. 27When
Jesus stepped on shore, he was met by a man from
the town. The man was controlled by demons. For
a long time he had not worn clothes or lived in a
house. He lived in the tombs.
28When he saw Jesus, he cried out and fell at his
feet. He shouted at the top of his voice, "Jesus, Son

of the Most High God, what do you want with me? I beg you, don't hurt me!"

29This was because Jesus had commanded the evil spirit to come out of the man. Many times the spirit had taken hold of him. His hands and feet were chained, and he was kept under guard. But he had broken his chains. And then the demon had forced him to go out into lonely places in the countryside.

30Jesus asked him, "What is your name?"

"Legion," he replied, because many demons had gone into him. 31And they begged Jesus again and again not to order them to go into the Abyss.

32A large herd of pigs was feeding there on the hillside. The demons begged Jesus to let them go into the pigs. And he allowed it.

33When the demons came out of the man, they went into the pigs. Then the herd rushed down the steep bank. They ran into the lake and drowned.

34Those who were tending the pigs saw what had happened. They ran off and reported it in the town and countryside. 35The people went out to see what had happened.

Then they came to Jesus. They found the man who was now free of the demons. He was sitting at Jesus' feet. He was dressed and thinking clearly. All this made the people afraid.

36Those who had seen it told the others how the man who had been controlled by demons was now healed. 37Then all the people who lived in the area of the Gerasenes asked Jesus to leave them. They were filled with fear. So he got into the boat and left.

38The man who was now free of the demons begged to go with him. But Jesus sent him away. He said to him, 39"Return home and tell how much God has done for you."

So the man went away. He told people all over town how much Jesus had done for him.

A Dying Girl and a Suffering Woman

40When Jesus returned, a crowd welcomed him. They were all expecting him.

41Then a man named Jairus came. He was a synagogue ruler. He fell at Jesus' feet. He begged Jesus to come to his house. 42His only daughter was dying. She was about 12 years old.

As Jesus was on his way, the crowds almost crushed him.

43A woman was there who had a sickness that made her bleed. Her sickness had lasted for 12 years. No one could heal her. 44She came up behind Jesus and touched the edge of his clothes. Right away her bleeding stopped.

45"Who touched me?" Jesus asked.

They all said they didn't do it. Then Peter said, "Master, the people are crowding and pushing against you."

46But Jesus said, "Someone touched me. I know that power has gone out from me."

47The woman realized that people would notice her. Shaking with fear, she came and fell at his feet. In front of everyone, she told why she had touched him. She also told how she had been healed in an instant.

48Then he said to her, "Dear woman, your faith has healed you. Go in peace."

49While Jesus was still speaking, someone came from the house of Jairus. Jairus was the synagogue ruler. "Your daughter is dead," the messenger said. "Don't bother the teacher anymore."

50Hearing this, Jesus said to Jairus, "Don't be afraid. Just believe. She will be healed."

51When he arrived at the house of Jairus, he did not let everyone go in with him. He took only Peter, John and James, and the child's father and mother. 52During this time, all the people were crying and sobbing loudly over the child. "Stop crying!" Jesus said. "She is not dead. She is sleeping."

53They laughed at him. They knew she was dead.

54But he took her by the hand and said, "My child, get up!"

55Her spirit returned, and right away she stood up. Then Jesus told them to give her something to eat. 56Her parents were amazed. But Jesus ordered them not to tell anyone what had happened.

Jesus Sends Out the Twelve Disciples

9 Jesus called the Twelve together. He gave them power and authority to drive out all demons and to heal sicknesses. 2Then he sent them out to preach about God's kingdom and to heal those who were sick.

3He told them, "Don't take anything for the journey. Do not take a walking stick or a bag. Do not take any bread, money or extra clothes. 4When you are invited into a house, stay there until you leave town. 5Some people may not welcome you. If they don't, shake the dust off your feet when you leave their town. This will be a witness against the people living there."

6So the Twelve left. They went from village to village. They preached the good news and healed people everywhere.

7Now Herod, the ruler of Galilee, heard about everything that was going on. He was bewildered, because some were saying that John the Baptist had been raised from the dead. 8Others were saying that Elijah had appeared. Still others were saying that a prophet of long ago had come back to life. 9But Herod said, "I had John's head cut off. So who is it that I hear such things about?" And he tried to see Jesus.

Jesus Feeds the Five Thousand

10The apostles returned. They told Jesus what they had done. Then he took them with him. They went off by themselves to a town called Bethsaida. 11But the crowds learned about it and followed Jesus. He welcomed them and spoke to them about God's kingdom. He also healed those who needed to be healed.

[12]Late in the afternoon the Twelve came to him. They said, "Send the crowd away. They can go to the nearby villages and countryside. There they can find food and a place to stay. There is nothing here."

[13]Jesus replied, "You give them something to eat."

The disciples answered, "We have only five loaves of bread and two fish. We would have to go and buy food for all this crowd." [14]About 5,000 men were there.

But Jesus said to his disciples, "Have them sit down in groups of about 50 each." [15]The disciples did so, and everyone sat down.

[16]Jesus took the five loaves and the two fish. He looked up to heaven and gave thanks. He broke them into pieces. Then he gave them to the disciples to set in front of the people. [17]All of them ate and were satisfied. The disciples picked up 12 baskets of leftover pieces.

Peter Says That Jesus Is the Christ

[18]One day Jesus was praying alone. Only his disciples were with him. He asked them, "Who do the crowds say I am?"

[19]They replied, "Some say John the Baptist. Others say Elijah. Still others say that one of the prophets of long ago has come back to life."

[20]"But what about you?" he asked. "Who do you say I am?"

Peter answered, "The Christ of God."

[21]Jesus strongly warned them not to tell this to anyone. [22]He said, "The Son of Man must suffer many things. The elders will not accept him. The chief priests and teachers of the law will not accept him either. He must be killed and on the third day rise from the dead."

[23]Then he said to all of them, "If anyone wants to follow me, he must say no to himself. He must pick up his cross every day and follow me. [24]If he wants to save his life, he will lose it. But if he loses his life for me, he will save it. [25]What good is it if someone gains the whole world but loses or gives up his very self?

[26]"Suppose you are ashamed of me and my words. The Son of Man will come in his glory and in the glory of the Father and the holy angels. Then he will be ashamed of you.

[27]"What I'm about to tell you is true. Some who are standing here will not die before they see God's kingdom."

Jesus' Appearance Is Changed

[28]About eight days after Jesus said this, he went up on a mountain to pray. He took Peter, John and James with him.

[29]As he was praying, the appearance of his face changed. His clothes became as bright as a flash of lightning. [30]Two men, Moses and Elijah, [31]appeared in shining glory. Jesus and the two of them talked together. They spoke about his coming death. He was going to die soon in Jerusalem.

[32]Peter and his companions had been very sleepy. But then they became completely awake. They saw Jesus' glory and the two men standing with him.

[33]As the men were leaving Jesus, Peter spoke up. "Master," he said to him, "it is good for us to be here. Let us put up three shelters. One will be for you, one for Moses, and one for Elijah." He didn't really know what he was saying.

[34]While Jesus was speaking, a cloud appeared. It surrounded them. The disciples were afraid as they entered the cloud. [35]A voice came from the cloud. It said, "This is my Son, and I have chosen him. Listen to him." [36]When the voice had spoken, they found that Jesus was alone.

The disciples kept quiet about this. They didn't tell anyone at that time what they had seen.

Jesus Heals a Boy Who Had an Evil Spirit

[37]The next day Jesus and those who were with him came down from the mountain. A large crowd met Jesus.

[38]A man in the crowd called out. "Teacher," he said, "I beg you to look at my son. He is my only child. [39]A spirit takes hold of him, and he suddenly screams. It throws him into fits so that he foams at the mouth. It hardly ever leaves him. It is destroying him. [40]I begged your disciples to drive it out. But they couldn't do it."

[41]"You unbelieving and evil people!" Jesus replied. "How long do I have to stay with you? How long do I have to put up with you?"

Then he said to the man, "Bring your son here."

[42]Even while the boy was coming, the demon threw him into a fit. The boy fell to the ground. But Jesus ordered the evil spirit to leave the boy. Then Jesus healed him and gave him back to his father. [43]They were all amazed at God's greatness.

Everyone was wondering about all that Jesus did. Then Jesus said to his disciples, [44]"Listen carefully to what I am about to tell you. The Son of Man is going to be handed over to men." [45]But they didn't understand what this meant. That was because it was hidden from them. And they were afraid to ask Jesus about it.

Who Is the Most Important Person?

[46]The disciples began to argue about which one of them would be the most important person. [47]Jesus knew what they were thinking. So he took a little child and had the child stand beside him.

[48]Then he spoke to them. "Anyone who welcomes this little child in my name welcomes me," he said. "And anyone who welcomes me welcomes the One who sent me. The least important person among all of you is the most important."

[49]"Master," said John, "we saw a man driving out demons in your name. We tried to stop him, because he is not one of us."

[50]"Do not stop him," Jesus said. "Anyone who is not against you is for you."

The Samaritans Do Not Welcome Jesus

51 The time grew near for Jesus to be taken up to heaven. So he made up his mind to go to Jerusalem. 52 He sent messengers on ahead. They went into a Samaritan village to get things ready for him. 53 But the people there did not welcome Jesus. That was because he was heading for Jerusalem.

54 The disciples James and John saw this. They asked, "Lord, do you want us to call down fire from heaven to destroy them?"

55 But Jesus turned and commanded them not to do it. 56 They went on to another village.

It Costs to Follow Jesus

57 Once Jesus and those who were with him were walking along the road. A man said to Jesus, "I will follow you no matter where you go."

58 Jesus replied, "Foxes have holes. Birds of the air have nests. But the Son of Man has no place to lay his head."

59 He said to another man, "Follow me."

But the man replied, "Lord, first let me go and bury my father."

60 Jesus said to him, "Let dead people bury their own dead. You go and tell others about God's kingdom."

61 Still another man said, "I will follow you, Lord. But first let me go back and say good-by to my family."

62 Jesus replied, "Suppose you start to plow and then look back. If you do, you are not fit for service in God's kingdom."

Jesus Sends Out the Seventy-two

10 After this the Lord appointed 72 others. He sent them out two by two ahead of him. They went to every town and place where he was about to go.

2 He told them, "The harvest is huge, but the workers are few. So ask the Lord of the harvest to send out workers into his harvest field.

3 "Go! I am sending you out like lambs among wolves. 4 Do not take a purse or bag or sandals. And don't greet anyone on the road.

5 "When you enter a house, first say, 'May this house be blessed with peace.' 6 If someone there loves peace, your blessing of peace will rest on him. If not, it will return to you. 7 Stay in that house. Eat and drink anything they give you. Workers are worthy of their pay. Do not move around from house to house.

8 "When you enter a town and are welcomed, eat what is set down in front of you. 9 Heal the sick people who are there. Tell them, 'God's kingdom is near you.'

10 "But what if you enter a town and are not welcomed? Then go into its streets and say, 11 'We wipe off even the dust of your town that sticks to our feet. We do it to show that God isn't pleased with you. But here is what you can be sure of. God's kingdom is near.'

12 "I tell you this. On judgment day it will be easier for Sodom than for that town.

13 "How terrible it will be for you, Korazin! How terrible for you, Bethsaida! Suppose the miracles done in you had been done in Tyre and Sidon. They would have turned away from their sins long ago. They would have put on black clothes. They would have sat down in ashes. 14 On judgment day it will be easier for Tyre and Sidon than for you.

15 "And what about you, Capernaum? Will you be lifted up to heaven? No! You will go down to the place of the dead.

16 "Anyone who listens to you listens to me. Anyone who does not accept you does not accept me. And anyone who does not accept me does not accept the One who sent me."

17 The 72 returned with joy. They said, "Lord, even the demons obey us when we speak in your name."

18 Jesus replied, "I saw Satan fall like lightning from heaven. 19 I have given you authority to walk all over snakes and scorpions. You will be able to destroy all the power of the enemy. Nothing will harm you. 20 But do not be glad when the evil spirits obey you. Instead, be glad that your names are written in heaven."

21 At that time Jesus was full of joy through the Holy Spirit. He said, "I praise you, Father. You are Lord of heaven and earth. You have hidden these things from the wise and educated. But you have shown them to little children. Yes, Father. This is what you wanted.

22 "My Father has given all things to me. The Father is the only one who knows who the Son is. And the only ones who know the Father are the Son and those to whom the Son chooses to make the Father known."

23 Then Jesus turned to his disciples. He said to them in private, "Blessed are the eyes that see what you see. 24 I tell you, many prophets and kings wanted to see what you see. But they didn't see it. They wanted to hear what you hear. But they didn't hear it."

The Story of the Good Samaritan

25 One day an authority on the law stood up to put Jesus to the test. "Teacher," he asked, "what must I do to receive eternal life?"

26 "What is written in the Law?" Jesus replied. "How do you understand it?"

27 He answered, " 'Love the Lord your God with all your heart and with all your soul. Love him with all your strength and with all your mind.' *(Deuteronomy 6:5)* And, 'Love your neighbor as you love yourself.' " *(Leviticus 19:18)*

28 "You have answered correctly," Jesus replied. "Do that, and you will live."

29 But the man wanted to make himself look good. So he asked Jesus, "And who is my neighbor?"

30Jesus replied, "A man was going down from Jerusalem to Jericho. Robbers attacked him. They stripped off his clothes and beat him. Then they went away, leaving him almost dead. 31A priest happened to be going down that same road. When he saw the man, he passed by on the other side. 32A Levite also came by. When he saw the man, he passed by on the other side too.

33But a Samaritan came to the place where the man was. When he saw the man, he felt sorry for him. 34He went to him, poured olive oil and wine on his wounds and bandaged them. Then he put the man on his own donkey. He took him to an inn and took care of him. 35The next day he took out two silver coins. He gave them to the owner of the inn. 'Take care of him,' he said. 'When I return, I will pay you back for any extra expense you may have.'

36"Which of the three do you think was a neighbor to the man who was attacked by robbers?"

37The authority on the law replied, "The one who felt sorry for him."

Jesus told him, "Go and do as he did."

Jesus at the Home of Martha and Mary

38Jesus and his disciples went on their way. Jesus came to a village where a woman named Martha lived. She welcomed him into her home. 39She had a sister named Mary.

Mary sat at the Lord's feet listening to what he said. 40But Martha was busy with all the things that had to be done. She came to Jesus and said, "Lord, my sister has left me to do the work by myself. Don't you care? Tell her to help me!"

41"Martha, Martha," the Lord answered. "You are worried and upset about many things. 42But only one thing is needed. Mary has chosen what is better. And it will not be taken away from her."

Jesus Teaches About Prayer

11 One day Jesus was praying in a certain place. When he finished, one of his disciples spoke to him. "Lord," he said, "teach us to pray, just as John taught his disciples."

2Jesus said to them, "When you pray, this is what you should say.

"'Father,
may your name be honored.
May your kingdom come.
3Give us each day our daily bread.
4Forgive us our sins,
as we also forgive everyone who sins
against us.
Keep us from falling into sin when we
are tempted.'"

5Then Jesus said to them, "Suppose someone has a friend. He goes to him at midnight. He says, 'Friend, lend me three loaves of bread. 6A friend of mine on a journey has come to stay with me. I have nothing for him to eat.'

7"Then the one inside answers, 'Don't bother me. The door is already locked. My children are with me in bed. I can't get up and give you anything.'

8"I tell you, that person will not get up. And he won't give the man bread just because he is his friend. But because the man keeps on asking, he will get up. He will give him as much as he needs.

9"So here is what I say to you. Ask, and it will be given to you. Search, and you will find. Knock, and the door will be opened to you. 10Everyone who asks will receive. He who searches will find. And the door will be opened to the one who knocks.

11"Fathers, suppose your son asks for a fish. Which of you will give him a snake instead? 12Or suppose he asks for an egg. Which of you will give him a scorpion? 13Even though you are evil, you know how to give good gifts to your children. How much more will your Father who is in heaven give the Holy Spirit to those who ask him!"

Jesus and Beelzebub

14Jesus was driving out a demon. The man who had the demon could not speak. When the demon left, the man began to speak. The crowd was amazed.

15But some of them said, "Jesus is driving out demons by the power of Beelzebub, the prince of demons." 16Others put Jesus to the test by asking for a miraculous sign from heaven.

17Jesus knew what they were thinking. So he said to them, "Any kingdom that fights against itself will be destroyed. A family that is divided against itself will fall. 18If Satan fights against himself, how can his kingdom stand?

"I say this because of what you claim. You say I drive out demons by the power of Beelzebub. 19Suppose I do drive out demons with Beelzebub's help. With whose help do your followers drive them out? So then, they will be your judges. 20But suppose I drive out demons with the help of God's powerful finger. Then God's kingdom has come to you.

21"When a strong man is completely armed and guards his house, what he owns is safe. 22But when someone stronger attacks, he is overpowered. The attacker takes away the armor the man had trusted in. Then he divides up what he has stolen.

23"Anyone who is not with me is against me. Anyone who does not gather sheep with me scatters them.

24"What happens when an evil spirit comes out of a man? It goes through dry areas looking for a place to rest. But it doesn't find it. Then it says, 'I will return to the house I left.' 25When it arrives there, it finds the house swept clean and put in order. 26Then the evil spirit goes and takes seven other spirits more evil than itself. They go in and live there. That man is worse off than before."

27As Jesus was saying these things, a woman in the crowd called out. She shouted, "Blessed is the mother who gave you birth and nursed you."

28He replied, "Instead, blessed are those who
hear God's word and obey it."

The Miraculous Sign of Jonah

29As the crowds grew larger, Jesus spoke to
them. "The people of today are evil," he said.
"They ask for a miraculous sign from God. But
none will be given except the sign of Jonah. 30He
was a sign from God to the people of Nineveh. In
the same way, the Son of Man will be a sign from
God to the people of today.

31"The Queen of the South will stand up on
judgment day with the men now living. And she
will prove that they are guilty. She came from very
far away to listen to Solomon's wisdom. And now
one who is more important than Solomon is here.
32"The men of Nineveh will stand up on judgment day with the people now living. And the Nin-
evites will prove that those people are guilty. The
men of Nineveh turned away from their sins when
Jonah preached to them. And now one who is
more important than Jonah is here.

The Eye Is the Lamp of the Body

33"No one lights a lamp and hides it. No one puts
it under a bowl. Instead, people put a lamp on its
stand. Then those who come in can see the light.
34"Your eye is like a lamp for your body. Suppose your eyes are good. Then your whole body
also is full of light. But suppose your eyes are bad.
Then your body also is full of darkness. 35So make
sure that the light inside you is not darkness.

36"Suppose your whole body is full of light.
And suppose no part of it is dark. Then your body
will be completely lit up. It will be as when the
light of a lamp shines on you."

Six Warnings

37Jesus finished speaking. Then a Pharisee
invited him to eat with him. So Jesus went in and
took his place at the table. 38But the Pharisee
noticed that Jesus did not wash before the meal.
He was surprised.

39Then the Lord spoke to him. "You Pharisees
clean the outside of the cup and dish," he said.
"But inside you are full of greed and evil. 40You
foolish people! Didn't the one who made the outside make the inside also? 41Give to poor people
what is inside the dish. Then everything will be
clean for you.

42"How terrible it will be for you Pharisees! You
give God a tenth of your garden plants, such as
mint and rue. But you have forgotten to be fair and
to love God. You should have practiced the last
things without failing to do the first.

43"How terrible for you Pharisees! You love the
most important seats in the synagogues. You love
having people greet you in the market places.

44"How terrible for you! You are like graves that
are not marked. People walk over them without
knowing it."

45An authority on the law spoke to Jesus. He
said, "Teacher, when you say things like that, you
say bad things about us too."

46Jesus replied, "How terrible for you authorities on the law! You put such heavy loads on people that they can hardly carry them. But you
yourselves will not lift one finger to help them.

47"How terrible for you! You build tombs for
the prophets. It was your people of long ago who
killed them. 48So you give witness that you agree
with what your people did long ago. They killed
the prophets, and now you build the prophets'
tombs.

49"So God in his wisdom said, 'I will send
prophets and apostles to them. They will kill some.
And they will try to hurt others.' 50So the people
of today will be punished. They will pay for all the
prophets' blood spilled since the world began. 51I
mean from the blood of Abel to the blood of Zechariah, who was killed between the altar and the
temple. Yes, I tell you, the people of today will be
punished for all these things.

52"How terrible for you authorities on the law!
You have taken away the key to the door of knowledge. You yourselves have not entered. And you
have stood in the way of those who were entering."
53When Jesus left there, the Pharisees and the
teachers of the law strongly opposed him. They
threw a lot of questions at him. 54They set traps for
him. They wanted to catch him in something he
might say.

Jesus Gives Words of Warning and Hope

12 During that time a crowd of many thousands had gathered. There were so many
people that they were stepping on one another.

Jesus spoke first to his disciples. "Be on your
guard against the yeast of the Pharisees," he said.
"They just pretend to be godly. 2Everything that is
secret will be brought out into the open. Everything that is hidden will be uncovered. 3What you
have said in the dark will be heard in the daylight.
What you have whispered to someone behind
closed doors will be shouted from the rooftops.

4"My friends, listen to me. Don't be afraid of
those who kill the body but can't do any more than
that. 5I will show you whom you should be afraid
of. Be afraid of the One who can kill the body and
also has the power to throw you into hell. Yes, I
tell you, be afraid of him.

6"Aren't five sparrows sold for two pennies? But
God does not forget even one of them. 7In fact, he
even counts every hair on your head! So don't be
afraid. You are worth more than many sparrows.

8"What about someone who says in front of others that he knows me? I tell you, the Son of Man
will say that he knows that person in front of God's
angels. 9But what about someone who says in front
of others that he doesn't know me? I, the Son of
Man, will say that I don't know him in front of
God's angels.

10“Everyone who speaks a word against the Son of Man will be forgiven. But anyone who speaks evil things against the Holy Spirit will not be forgiven.

11“You will be brought before synagogues, rulers and authorities. But do not worry about how to stand up for yourselves or what to say. 12The Holy Spirit will teach you at that time what you should say.”

The Story of the Rich Man

13Someone in the crowd spoke to Jesus. “Teacher,” he said, “tell my brother to divide the family property with me.”

14Jesus replied, “Friend, who made me a judge or umpire between you?”

15Then he said to them, “Watch out! Be on your guard against wanting to have more and more things. Life is not made up of how much a person has.”

16Then Jesus told them a story. He said, “A certain rich man’s land produced a good crop. 17He thought to himself, ‘What should I do? I don’t have any place to store my crops.’

18“Then he said, ‘This is what I’ll do. I will tear down my storerooms and build bigger ones. I will store all my grain and my other things in them. 19I’ll say to myself, “You have plenty of good things stored away for many years. Take life easy. Eat, drink and have a good time.”’

20“But God said to him, ‘You foolish man! This very night I will take your life away from you. Then who will get what you have prepared for yourself?’

21“That is how it will be for anyone who stores things away for himself but is not rich in God’s eyes.”

Do Not Worry

22Then Jesus spoke to his disciples. He said, “I tell you, do not worry. Don’t worry about your life and what you will eat. And don’t worry about your body and what you will wear. 23There is more to life than eating. There are more important things for the body than clothes.

24“Think about the ravens. They don’t plant or gather crops. They don’t have any storerooms at all. But God feeds them. You are worth much more than birds!

25“Can you add even one hour to your life by worrying? 26You can’t do that very little thing. So why worry about the rest?

27“Think about how the lilies grow. They don’t work or make clothing. But here is what I tell you. Not even Solomon in all of his glory was dressed like one of those flowers. 28If that is how God dresses the wild grass, how much better will he dress you! After all, the grass is here only today. Tomorrow it is thrown into the fire. Your faith is so small!

29“Don’t spend time thinking about what you will eat or drink. Don’t worry about it. 30People who are ungodly run after all of those things. Your Father knows that you need them.

31“But put God’s kingdom first. Then those other things will also be given to you.

32“Little flock, do not be afraid. Your Father has been pleased to give you the kingdom. 33Sell what you own. Give to those who are poor. Provide purses for yourselves that will not wear out. Put away riches in heaven that will not be used up. There, no thief can come near it. There, no moth can destroy it. 34Your heart will be where your riches are.

Be Ready

35“Be dressed and ready to serve. Keep your lamps burning. 36Be like servants waiting for their master to return from a wedding dinner. When he comes and knocks, they can open the door for him at once.

37“It will be good for those servants whose master finds them ready when he comes. What I’m about to tell you is true. The master will then dress himself so he can serve them. He will have them take their places at the table. And he will come and wait on them. 38It will be good for those servants whose master finds them ready. It will even be good if he comes very late at night.

39“But here is what you must understand. Suppose the owner of the house knew at what hour the robber was coming. He would not have let his house be broken into. 40You also must be ready. The Son of Man will come at an hour when you don’t expect him.”

41Peter asked, “Lord, are you telling this story to us, or to everyone?”

42The Lord answered, “Suppose a master puts one of his servants in charge of his other servants. The servant’s job is to give them the food they are to receive at the right time. The master wants a faithful and wise manager for this. 43It will be good for the servant if the master finds him doing his job when the master returns. 44What I’m about to tell you is true. The master will put that servant in charge of everything he owns.

45“But suppose the servant says to himself, ‘My master is taking a long time to come back.’ Suppose he begins to beat the other servants. Suppose he feeds himself. And suppose he drinks until he gets drunk. 46The master of that servant will come back on a day the servant doesn’t expect him. He will return at an hour the servant doesn’t know. Then the master will cut him to pieces. He will send him to the place where unbelievers go.

47“Suppose a servant knows his master’s wishes. But he doesn’t get ready. And he doesn’t do what his master wants. That servant will be beaten with many blows.

48“But suppose the servant does not know his master’s wishes. And suppose he does things for which he should be punished. He will be beaten with only a few blows.

"Much will be required of everyone who has been given much. Even more will be asked of the person who is supposed to take care of much.

Jesus Will Separate People From One Another

49"I have come to bring fire on the earth. How I wish the fire had already started! 50But I have a baptism of suffering to go through. And I will be very troubled until it is completed.

51"Do you think I came to bring peace on earth? No, I tell you. I have come to separate people. 52From now on there will be five members in a family, each one against the other. There will be three against two and two against three. 53They will be separated. Father will turn against son and son against father. Mother will turn against daughter and daughter against mother. Mother-in-law will turn against daughter-in-law and daughter-in-law against mother-in-law."

Understanding What Is Happening

54Jesus spoke to the crowd. He said, "You see a cloud rising in the west. Right away you say, 'It's going to rain.' And it does. 55The south wind blows. So you say, 'It's going to be hot.' And it is. 56You pretenders! You know how to understand the appearance of the earth and the sky. Why can't you understand the meaning of what is happening right now?

57"Why don't you judge for yourselves what is right? 58Suppose someone has a claim against you, and you are on your way to court. Try hard to settle the matter on the way. If you don't, that person may drag you off to the judge. The judge may turn you over to the officer. And the officer may throw you into prison. 59I tell you, you will not get out until you have paid the very last penny!"

Jesus Gives a Warning

13 Some people who were there at that time told Jesus about certain Galileans. Pilate had mixed their blood with their sacrifices.

2Jesus said, "These people from Galilee suffered greatly. Do you think they were worse sinners than all the other Galileans? 3I tell you, no! But unless you turn away from your sins, you will all die too. 4Or what about the 18 people in Siloam? They died when the tower fell on them. Do you think they were more guilty than all the others living in Jerusalem? 5I tell you, no! But unless you turn away from your sins, you will all die too."

6Then Jesus told a story. "A man had a fig tree," he said. "It had been planted in his vineyard. When he went to look for fruit on it, he didn't find any. 7So he went to the man who took care of the vineyard. He said, 'For three years now I've been coming to look for fruit on this fig tree. But I haven't found any. Cut it down! Why should it use up the soil?'

8"'Sir,' the man replied, 'leave it alone for one more year. I'll dig around it and feed it. 9If it bears fruit next year, fine! If not, then cut it down.'"

Jesus Heals a Disabled Woman on the Sabbath Day

10Jesus was teaching in one of the synagogues on a Sabbath day. 11A woman there had been disabled by an evil spirit for 18 years. She was bent over and could not stand up straight.

12Jesus saw her. He asked her to come to him. He said to her, "Woman, you will no longer be disabled. I am about to set you free." 13Then he put his hands on her.

Right away she stood up straight and praised God.

14Jesus had healed the woman on the Sabbath day. This made the synagogue ruler angry. He told the people, "There are six days for work. So come and be healed on those days. But do not come on the Sabbath."

15The Lord answered him, "You pretenders! Doesn't each of you go to the barn and untie his ox or donkey on the Sabbath day? Then don't you lead it out to give it water? 16This woman is a member of Abraham's family line. But Satan has kept her disabled for 18 long years. Shouldn't she be set free on the Sabbath day from what was keeping her disabled?"

17When Jesus said this, all those who opposed him were put to shame. But the people were delighted. They loved all the wonderful things he was doing.

The Stories of the Mustard Seed and the Yeast

18Then Jesus asked, "What is God's kingdom like? What can I compare it to? 19It is like a mustard seed. Someone took the seed and planted it in a garden. It grew and became a tree. The birds sat in its branches."

20Again he asked, "What can I compare God's kingdom to? 21It is like yeast that a woman used. She mixed it into a large amount of flour. The yeast worked its way all through the dough."

The Narrow Door

22Then Jesus went through the towns and villages, teaching the people. He was on his way to Jerusalem. 23Someone asked him, "Lord, are only a few people going to be saved?"

He said to them, 24"Try very hard to enter through the narrow door. I tell you, many will try to enter and will not be able to. 25The owner of the house will get up and close the door. Then you will stand outside knocking and begging. You will say, 'Sir, open the door for us.'

"But he will answer, 'I don't know you. And I don't know where you come from.'

26"Then you will say, 'We ate and drank with you. You taught in our streets.'

27"But he will reply, 'I don't know you. And I don't know where you come from. Get away from me, all you who do evil!'

28“You will sob and grind your teeth when you see those who are in God’s kingdom. You will see Abraham, Isaac and Jacob and all the prophets there. But you yourselves will be thrown out. 29People will come from east and west and north and south. They will take their places at the feast in God’s kingdom. 30Then the last will be first. And the first will be last.”

Jesus’ Sadness Over Jerusalem

31At that time some Pharisees came to Jesus. They said to him, “Leave this place. Go somewhere else. Herod wants to kill you.”

32He replied, “Go and tell that fox, ‘I will drive out demons. I will heal people today and tomorrow. And on the third day I will reach my goal.’ 33In any case, I must keep going today and tomorrow and the next day. Certainly no prophet can die outside Jerusalem!

34“Jerusalem! Jerusalem! You kill the prophets and throw stones in order to kill those who are sent to you. Many times I have wanted to gather your people together. I have wanted to be like a hen who gathers her chicks under her wings. But you would not let me!

35“Look, your house is left empty. I tell you, you will not see me again until you say, ‘Blessed is the one who comes in the name of the Lord.’” ***(Psalm 118:26)***

Jesus Eats at a Pharisee’s House

14 One Sabbath day, Jesus went to eat in the house of a well-known Pharisee. While he was there, he was being carefully watched. 2In front of him was a man whose body was badly swollen.

3Jesus turned to the Pharisees and the authorities on the law. He asked them, “Is it breaking the Law to heal on the Sabbath?”

4But they remained silent.

So Jesus took hold of the man and healed him. Then he sent him away.

5He asked them another question. He said, “Suppose one of you has a son or an ox that falls into a well on the Sabbath day. Wouldn’t you pull him out right away?” 6And they had nothing to say.

7Jesus noticed how the guests picked the places of honor at the table. So he told them a story. 8He said, “Suppose someone invites you to a wedding feast. Do not take the place of honor. A person more important than you may have been invited. 9If so, the host who invited both of you will come to you. He will say, ‘Give this person your seat.’ Then you will be filled with shame. You will have to take the least important place.

10“But when you are invited, take the lowest place. Then your host will come over to you. He will say, ‘Friend, move up to a better place.’ Then you will be honored in front of all the other guests. 11Anyone who lifts himself up will be brought down. And anyone who is brought down will be lifted up.”

12Then Jesus spoke to his host. “Suppose you give a lunch or a dinner,” he said. “Do not invite your friends, your brothers or sisters, or your relatives, or your rich neighbors. If you do, they may invite you to eat with them. So you will be paid back.

13“But when you give a big dinner, invite those who are poor. Also invite those who can’t walk, the disabled and the blind. 14Then you will be blessed. Your guests can’t pay you back. But you will be paid back when those who are right with God rise from the dead.”

The Story of the Big Dinner

15One of the people at the table with Jesus heard him say those things. So he said to Jesus, “Blessed is the one who will eat at the feast in God’s kingdom.”

16Jesus replied, “A certain man was preparing a big dinner. He invited many guests. 17Then the day of the dinner arrived. He sent his servant to those who had been invited. The servant told them, ‘Come. Everything is ready now.’

18“But they all had the same idea. They began to make excuses. The first one said, ‘I have just bought a field. I have to go and see it. Please excuse me.’

19“Another said, ‘I have just bought five pairs of oxen. I’m on my way to try them out. Please excuse me.’

20“Still another said, ‘I just got married, so I can’t come.’

21“The servant came back and reported this to his master.

“Then the owner of the house became angry. He ordered his servant, ‘Go out quickly into the streets and lanes of the town. Bring in those who are poor. Also bring those who can’t walk, the blind and the disabled.’

22“ ‘Sir,’ the servant said, ‘what you ordered has been done. But there is still room.’

23“Then the master told his servant, ‘Go out to the roads. Go out to the country lanes. Make the people come in. I want my house to be full. 24I tell you, not one of those men who were invited will get a taste of my dinner.’ ”

It Costs to Be a Disciple

25Large crowds were traveling with Jesus. He turned and spoke to them. He said, 26“Anyone who comes to me must hate his father and mother. He must hate his wife and children. He must hate his brothers and sisters. And he must hate even his own life. Unless he does, he can’t be my disciple. 27Anyone who doesn’t carry his cross and follow me can’t be my disciple.

28“Suppose someone wants to build a tower. Won’t he sit down first and figure out how much it will cost? Then he will see whether he has enough money to finish it. 29Suppose he starts building and is not able to finish. Then everyone who sees what he has done will laugh at him. 30They will say, 'This fellow started to build. But he wasn't able to finish.'

31"Or suppose a king is about to go to war against another king. And suppose he has 10,000 men, while the other has 20,000 coming against him. Won't he first sit down and think about whether he can win?

32"And suppose he decides he can't win. Then he will send some men to ask how peace can be made. He will do this while the other king is still far away.

33"In the same way, you must give up everything you have. If you don't, you can't be my disciple.

34"Salt is good. But suppose it loses its saltiness. How can it be made salty again? 35It is not good for the soil. And it is not good for the trash pile. It will be thrown out.

"Those who have ears should listen."

The Story of the Lost Sheep

15 The tax collectors and "sinners" were all gathering around to hear Jesus. 2But the Pharisees and the teachers of the law were whispering among themselves. They said, "This man welcomes sinners and eats with them."

3Then Jesus told them a story. 4He said, "Suppose one of you has 100 sheep and loses one of them. Won't he leave the 99 in the open country? Won't he go and look for the one lost sheep until he finds it? 5When he finds it, he will joyfully put it on his shoulders 6and go home. Then he will call his friends and neighbors together. He will say, 'Be joyful with me. I have found my lost sheep.'

7"I tell you, it will be the same in heaven. There will be great joy when one sinner turns away from sin. Yes, there will be more joy than for 99 godly people who do not need to turn away from their sins.

The Story of the Lost Coin

8"Or suppose a woman has ten silver coins and loses one. She will light a lamp and sweep the house. She will search carefully until she finds the coin. 9And when she finds it, she will call her friends and neighbors together. She will say, 'Be joyful with me. I have found my lost coin.'

10"I tell you, it is the same in heaven. There is joy in heaven over one sinner who turns away from sin."

The Story of the Lost Son

11Jesus continued, "There was a man who had two sons. 12The younger son spoke to his father. He said, 'Father, give me my share of the family property.' So the father divided his property between his two sons.

13"Not long after that, the younger son packed up all he had. Then he left for a country far away. There he wasted his money on wild living. 14He spent everything he had.

"Then the whole country ran low on food. So the son didn't have what he needed. 15He went to work for someone who lived in that country, who sent him to the fields to feed the pigs. 16The son wanted to fill his stomach with the food the pigs were eating. But no one gave him anything.

17"Then he began to think clearly again. He said, 'How many of my father's hired workers have more than enough food! But here I am dying from hunger! 18I will get up and go back to my father. I will say to him, "Father, I have sinned against heaven. And I have sinned against you. 19I am no longer fit to be called your son. Make me like one of your hired workers."' 20So he got up and went to his father.

"While the son was still a long way off, his father saw him. He was filled with tender love for his son. He ran to him. He threw his arms around him and kissed him.

21"The son said to him, 'Father, I have sinned against heaven and against you. I am no longer fit to be called your son.'

22"But the father said to his servants, 'Quick! Bring the best robe and put it on him. Put a ring on his finger and sandals on his feet. 23Bring the fattest calf and kill it. Let's have a big dinner and celebrate. 24This son of mine was dead. And now he is alive again. He was lost. And now he is found.'

"So they began to celebrate.

25"The older son was in the field. When he came near the house, he heard music and dancing. 26So he called one of the servants. He asked him what was going on.

27"'Your brother has come home,' the servant replied. 'Your father has killed the fattest calf. He has done this because your brother is back safe and sound.'

28"The older brother became angry. He refused to go in. So his father went out and begged him.

29"But he answered his father, 'Look! All these years I've worked like a slave for you. I have always obeyed your orders. You never gave me even a young goat so I could celebrate with my friends. 30But this son of yours wasted your money with some prostitutes. Now he comes home. And for him you kill the fattest calf!'

31"'My son,' the father said, 'you are always with me. Everything I have is yours. 32But we had to celebrate and be glad. This brother of yours was dead. And now he is alive again. He was lost. And now he is found.'"

The Story of the Clever Manager

16 Jesus told his disciples another story. He said, "There was a rich man who had a manager. Some said that the manager was wasting what the rich man owned. 2So the rich man told him to come in. He asked him, 'What is this I hear about you? Tell me exactly how you have handled what I own. You can't be my manager any longer.'

3"The manager said to himself, 'What will I do now? My master is taking away my job. I'm not

strong enough to dig. And I'm too ashamed to beg.
4I know what I'm going to do. I'll do something
so that when I lose my job here, people will welcome me into their houses.'
5"So he called in each person who owed his
master something. He asked the first one, 'How
much do you owe my master?'
6"'I owe 800 gallons of olive oil,' he replied.
"The manager told him, 'Take your bill. Sit
down quickly and change it to 400 gallons.'
7"Then he asked the second one, 'And how
much do you owe?'
"'I owe 1,000 bushels of wheat,' he replied.
"The manager told him, 'Take your bill and
change it to 800 bushels.'
8"The manager had not been honest. But the
master praised him for being clever. The people of
this world are clever in dealing with those who are
like themselves. They are more clever than God's
people.
9"I tell you, use the riches of this world to help
others. In that way, you will make friends for yourselves. Then when your riches are gone, you will
be welcomed into your eternal home in heaven.
10"Suppose you can be trusted with very little.
Then you can be trusted with a lot. But suppose
you are not honest with very little. Then you will
not be honest with a lot.
11"Suppose you have not been worthy of trust in
handling worldly wealth. Then who will trust you
with true riches? 12Suppose you have not been worthy of trust in handling someone else's property.
Then who will give you property of your own?
13"No servant can serve two masters at the same
time. He will hate one of them and love the other.
Or he will be faithful to one and dislike the other.
You can't serve God and Money at the same time."
14The Pharisees loved money. They heard all
that Jesus said and made fun of him. 15Jesus said to
them, "You try to make yourselves look good in
the eyes of other people. But God knows your
hearts. What is worth a great deal among people is
hated by God.

More Teachings

16"The teachings of the Law and the Prophets
were preached until John came. Since then, the
good news of God's kingdom is being preached.
And everyone is trying very hard to enter it. 17It is
easier for heaven and earth to disappear than for
the smallest part of a letter to drop out of the Law.
18"Anyone who divorces his wife and gets married to another woman commits adultery. Also, the
man who gets married to a divorced woman commits adultery.

The Rich Man and Lazarus

19"Once there was a rich man. He was dressed
in purple cloth and fine linen. He lived an easy life
every day. 20A man named Lazarus was placed at
his gate. Lazarus was a beggar. His body was covered with sores. 21Even dogs came and licked his
sores. All he wanted was to eat what fell from the
rich man's table.
22"The time came when the beggar died. The
angels carried him to Abraham's side. The rich
man also died and was buried. 23In hell, the rich
man was suffering terribly. He looked up and saw
Abraham far away. Lazarus was by his side. 24So
the rich man called out, 'Father Abraham! Have
pity on me! Send Lazarus to dip the tip of his finger in water. Then he can cool my tongue with it.
I am in terrible pain in this fire.'
25"But Abraham replied, 'Son, remember what
happened in your lifetime. You received your good
things. Lazarus received bad things. Now he is comforted here, and you are in terrible pain. 26Besides,
a wide space has been placed between us and you.
So those who want to go from here to you can't go.
And no one can cross over from there to us.'
27"The rich man answered, 'Then I beg you,
father. Send Lazarus to my family. 28I have five
brothers. Let Lazarus warn them. Then they will
not come to this place of terrible suffering.'
29"Abraham replied, 'They have the teachings
of Moses and the Prophets. Let your brothers listen to them.'
30"'No, father Abraham,' he said. 'But if someone from the dead goes to them, they will turn
away from their sins.'
31"Abraham said to him, 'They do not listen to
Moses and the Prophets. So they will not be convinced even if someone rises from the dead.'"

Sin, Faith and Duty

17 Jesus spoke to his disciples. "Things that
make people sin are sure to come," he said.
"But how terrible it will be for the person who
brings them! 2Suppose people lead one of these little ones to sin. It would be better for those people
to be thrown into the sea with a millstone tied
around their neck. 3So watch what you do.
"If your brother sins, tell him he is wrong. Then
if he turns away from his sins, forgive him. 4Sup-
pose he sins against you seven times in one day.
And suppose he comes back to you each time and
says, 'I'm sorry.' Forgive him."
5The apostles said to the Lord, "Give us more
faith!"
6He replied, "Suppose you have faith as small
as a mustard seed. Then you can say to this mul-
berry tree, 'Be pulled up. Be planted in the sea.'
And it will obey you.
7"Suppose one of you had a servant plowing or
looking after the sheep. And suppose the servant
came in from the field. Would you say to him,
'Come along now and sit down to eat'? 8No.
Instead, you would say, 'Prepare my supper. Get
yourself ready. Wait on me while I eat and drink.
Then after that you can eat and drink.' 9Would you
thank the servant because he did what he was told
to do?

10“It’s the same with you. Suppose you have done everything you were told to do. Then you should say, ‘We are not worthy to serve you. We have only done our duty.’ ”

Jesus Heals Ten Men

11Jesus was on his way to Jerusalem. He traveled along the border between Samaria and Galilee. 12As he was going into a village, ten men met him. They had a skin disease. They were standing close by. 13And they called out in a loud voice, “Jesus! Master! Have pity on us!”

14Jesus saw them and said, “Go. Show yourselves to the priests.” While they were on the way, they were healed.

15When one of them saw that he was healed, he came back. He praised God in a loud voice. 16He threw himself at Jesus’ feet and thanked him. The man was a Samaritan.

17Jesus asked, “Weren’t all ten healed? Where are the other nine? 18Didn’t anyone else return and give praise to God except this outsider?”

19Then Jesus said to him, “Get up and go. Your faith has healed you.”

The Coming of God’s Kingdom

20Once the Pharisees asked Jesus when God’s kingdom would come. He replied, “The coming of God’s kingdom is not something you can see just by watching for it carefully. 21People will not say, ‘Here it is.’ Or, ‘There it is.’ God’s kingdom is among you.”

22Then Jesus spoke to his disciples. “The time is coming,” he said, “when you will long to see one of the days of the Son of Man. But you won’t see it. 23People will tell you, ‘There he is!’ Or, ‘Here he is!’ Don’t go running off after them.

24“When the Son of Man comes, he will be like the lightning. It flashes and lights up the sky from one end to the other. 25But first the Son of Man must suffer many things. He will not be accepted by the people of today.

26“Remember how it was in the days of Noah. It will be the same when the Son of Man comes. 27People were eating and drinking. They were getting married. They were giving their daughters to be married. They did all those things right up to the day Noah entered the ark. Then the flood came and destroyed them all.

28“It was the same in the days of Lot. People were eating and drinking. They were buying and selling. They were planting and building. 29But on the day Lot left Sodom, fire and sulfur rained down from heaven. And all the people were destroyed.

30“It will be just like that on the day the Son of Man is shown to the world. 31Suppose someone is on the roof of his house on that day. And suppose his goods are inside the house. He should not go down to get them. No one in the field should go back for anything either. 32Remember Lot’s wife! 33Anyone who tries to keep his life will lose it. Anyone who loses his life will keep it.

34“I tell you, on that night two people will be in one bed. One person will be taken and the other left. 35/36Two women will be grinding grain together. One will be taken and the other left.”

37“Where, Lord?” his disciples asked.

He replied, “The vultures will gather where there is a dead body.”

The Story of the Widow Who Would Not Give Up

18 Jesus told his disciples a story. He wanted to show them that they should always pray and not give up. 2He said, “In a certain town there was a judge. He didn’t have any respect for God or care about people. 3A widow lived in that town. She came to the judge again and again. She kept begging him, ‘Make things right for me. Someone is doing me wrong.’

4“For some time the judge refused. But finally he said to himself, ‘I don’t have any respect for God. I don’t care about people. 5But this widow keeps bothering me. So I will see that things are made right for her. If I don’t, she will wear me out by coming again and again!’ ”

6The Lord said, “Listen to what the unfair judge says.

7“God’s chosen people cry out to him day and night. Won’t he make things right for them? Will he keep putting them off? 8I tell you, God will see that things are made right for them. He will make sure it happens quickly.

“But when the Son of Man comes, will he find people on earth who have faith?”

The Story of the Pharisee and the Tax Collector

9Jesus told a story to some people who were sure they were right with God. They looked down on everybody else. 10He said to them, “Two men went up to the temple to pray. One was a Pharisee. The other was a tax collector.

11“The Pharisee stood up and prayed about himself. ‘God, I thank you that I am not like other people,’ he said. ‘I am not like robbers or those who do other evil things. I am not like those who commit adultery. I am not even like this tax collector. 12I fast twice a week. And I give a tenth of all I get.’

13“But the tax collector stood not very far away. He would not even look up to heaven. He beat his chest and said, ‘God, have mercy on me. I am a sinner.’

14“I tell you, the tax collector went home accepted by God. But not the Pharisee. Everyone who lifts himself up will be brought down. And anyone who is brought down will be lifted up.”

Little Children Are Brought to Jesus

15People were also bringing babies to Jesus. They wanted him to touch them. When the disciples saw this, they told the people to stop.

16But Jesus asked the children to come to him. “Let the little children come to me,” he said.

"Don't keep them away. God's kingdom belongs to people like them. 17What I'm about to tell you is true. Anyone who will not receive God's kingdom like a little child will never enter it."

Jesus and the Rich Ruler

18A certain ruler asked Jesus a question. "Good teacher," he said, "what must I do to receive eternal life?"

19"Why do you call me good?" Jesus answered. "No one is good except God. 20You know what the commandments say. 'Do not commit adultery. Do not commit murder. Do not steal. Do not give false witness. Honor your father and mother.'" *(Exodus 20:12–16; Deuteronomy 5:16–20)*

21"I have obeyed all those commandments since I was a boy," the ruler said.

22When Jesus heard this, he said to him, "You are still missing one thing. Sell everything you have. Give the money to those who are poor. You will have treasure in heaven. Then come and follow me."

23When the ruler heard this, he became very sad. He was very rich.

24Jesus looked at him. Then he said, "How hard it is for rich people to enter God's kingdom! 25Is it hard for a camel to go through the eye of a needle? It is even harder for the rich to enter God's kingdom!"

26Those who heard this asked, "Then who can be saved?"

27Jesus replied, "Things that are impossible with people are possible with God."

28Peter said to him, "We have left everything we had in order to follow you!"

29"What I'm about to tell you is true," Jesus said to them. "Has anyone left home or family for God's kingdom? 30They will receive many times as much in this world. In the world to come they will live forever."

Jesus Again Tells About His Coming Death

31Jesus took the Twelve to one side. He told them, "We are going up to Jerusalem. Everything that the prophets wrote about the Son of Man will come true. 32He will be handed over to people who are not Jews. They will make fun of him. They will laugh at him and spit on him. They will whip him and kill him. 33On the third day, he will rise from the dead!"

34The disciples did not understand any of this. Its meaning was hidden from them. So they didn't know what Jesus was talking about.

A Blind Beggar Receives His Sight

35Jesus was approaching Jericho. A blind man was sitting by the side of the road begging. 36The blind man heard the crowd going by. He asked what was happening. 37They told him, "Jesus of Nazareth is passing by."

38So the blind man called out, "Jesus! Son of David! Have mercy on me!"

39Those who led the way commanded him to stop. They told him to be quiet. But he shouted even louder, "Son of David! Have mercy on me!"

40Jesus stopped and ordered the man to be brought to him. When the man came near, Jesus spoke to him. 41"What do you want me to do for you?" Jesus asked.

"Lord, I want to be able to see," the blind man replied.

42Jesus said to him, "Receive your sight. Your faith has healed you."

43Right away he could see. He followed Jesus, praising God. When all the people saw it, they also praised God.

Zacchaeus the Tax Collector

19 Jesus entered Jericho and was passing through. 2A man named Zacchaeus lived there. He was a chief tax collector and was very rich.

3Zacchaeus wanted to see who Jesus was. But he was a short man. He could not see Jesus because of the crowd. 4So he ran ahead and climbed a sycamore-fig tree. He wanted to see Jesus, who was coming that way.

5Jesus reached the spot where Zacchaeus was. He looked up and said, "Zacchaeus, come down at once. I must stay at your house today." 6So Zacchaeus came down at once and welcomed him gladly.

7All the people saw this. They began to whisper among themselves. They said, "Jesus has gone to be the guest of a 'sinner.'"

8But Zacchaeus stood up. He said, "Look, Lord! Here and now I give half of what I own to those who are poor. And if I have cheated anybody out of anything, I will pay it back. I will pay back four times the amount I took."

9Jesus said to Zacchaeus, "Today salvation has come to your house. You are a member of Abraham's family line. 10The Son of Man came to look for the lost and save them."

The Story of Three Servants

11While the people were listening to these things, Jesus told them a story. He was near Jerusalem. The people thought that God's kingdom was going to appear right away.

12Jesus said, "A man from an important family went to a country far away. He went there to be made king and then return home. 13So he sent for ten of his servants. He gave them each about three months' pay. 'Put this money to work until I come back,' he said.

14"But those he ruled over hated him. They sent some messengers after him. They were sent to say, 'We don't want this man to be our king.'

15"But he was made king and returned home. Then he sent for the servants he had given the money to. He wanted to find out what they had earned with it.

16“The first one came to him. He said, ‘Sir, your money has earned ten times as much.’

17“ ‘You have done well, my good servant!’ his master replied. ‘You have been faithful in a very small matter. So I will put you in charge of ten towns.’

18“The second servant came to his master. He said, ‘Sir, your money has earned five times as much.’

19“His master answered, ‘I will put you in charge of five towns.’

20“Then another servant came. He said, ‘Sir, here is your money. I have kept it hidden in a piece of cloth. 21I was afraid of you. You are a hard man. You take out what you did not put in. You harvest what you did not plant.’

22“His master replied, ‘I will judge you by your own words, you evil servant! So you knew that I am a hard man? You knew that I take out what I did not put in? You knew that I harvest what I did not plant? 23Then why didn’t you put my money in the bank? When I came back, I could have collected it with interest.’

24“Then he said to those standing by, ‘Take his money away from him. Give it to the one who has ten times as much.’

25“ ‘Sir,’ they said, ‘he already has ten times as much!’

26“He replied, ‘I tell you that everyone who has will be given more. But here is what will happen to anyone who has nothing. Even what he has will be taken away from him. 27And what about my enemies who did not want me to be king over them? Bring them here! Kill them in front of me!’ ”

Jesus Enters Jerusalem

28After Jesus had said this, he went on ahead. He was going up to Jerusalem.

29He approached Bethphage and Bethany. The hill there was called the Mount of Olives. Jesus sent out two of his disciples. He said to them, 30“Go to the village ahead of you. As soon as you get there, you will find a donkey’s colt tied up. No one has ever ridden it. Untie it and bring it here. 31Someone may ask you, ‘Why are you untying it?’ If so, say, ‘The Lord needs it.’ ”

32Those who were sent ahead went and found the young donkey. It was there just as Jesus had told them. 33They were untying the colt when its owners came. The owners asked them, “Why are you untying the colt?”

34They replied, “The Lord needs it.”

35Then the disciples brought the colt to Jesus. They threw their coats on the young donkey and put Jesus on it. 36As he went along, people spread their coats on the road.

37Jesus came near the place where the road goes down the Mount of Olives. There the whole crowd of disciples began to praise God with joy. In loud voices they praised him for all the miracles they had seen. They shouted,

38“Blessed is the king who comes in the
name of the Lord!” *(Psalm 118:26)*

“May there be peace and glory in the
highest heaven!”

39Some of the Pharisees in the crowd spoke to Jesus. “Teacher,” they said, “tell your disciples to stop!”

40“I tell you,” he replied, “if they keep quiet, the stones will cry out.”

41He approached Jerusalem. When he saw the city, he began to sob. 42He said, “I wish you had known today what would bring you peace! But now it is hidden from your eyes.

43“The days will come when your enemies will arrive. They will build a wall of dirt up against your city. They will surround you and close you in on every side. 44You didn’t recognize the time when God came to you. So your enemies will smash you to the ground. They will destroy you and all the people inside your walls. They will not leave one stone on top of another.”

Jesus Clears Out the Temple

45Then Jesus entered the temple area. He began chasing out those who were selling there. 46He told them, “It is written that the Lord said, ‘My house will be a house where people can pray.’ *(Isaiah 56:7)* But you have made it a ‘den for robbers.’ ” *(Jeremiah 7:11)*

47Every day Jesus was teaching at the temple. But the chief priests and the teachers of the law were trying to kill him. So were the leaders among the people. 48But they couldn’t find any way to do it. All the people were paying close attention to his words.

The Authority of Jesus Is Questioned

20 One day Jesus was teaching the people in the temple courtyard. He was preaching the good news to them.

The chief priests and the teachers of the law came up to him. The elders came with them. 2“Tell us by what authority you are doing these things,” they all said. “Who gave you this authority?”

3Jesus replied, “I will also ask you a question. Tell me, 4was John’s baptism from heaven? Or did it come from men?”

5They talked to each other about it. They said, “If we say, ‘From heaven,’ he will ask, ‘Why didn’t you believe him?’ 6But if we say, ‘From men,’ all the people will throw stones at us and kill us. They believe that John was a prophet.”

7So they answered Jesus, “We don’t know where John’s baptism came from.”

8Jesus said, “Then I won’t tell you by what authority I am doing these things either.”

The Story of the Renters

9 Jesus went on to tell the people a story. "A man planted a vineyard," he said. "He rented it out to some farmers. Then he went away for a long time. 10 "At harvest time he sent a servant to the renters. They were supposed to give him some of the fruit of the vineyard. But the renters beat the servant. Then they sent him away with nothing. 11 So the man sent another servant. They beat that one and treated him badly. They also sent him away with nothing. 12 The man sent a third servant. The renters wounded him and threw him out.

13 "Then the owner of the vineyard said, 'What should I do? I have a son, and I love him. I will send him. Maybe they will respect him.'

14 "But when the renters saw the son, they talked the matter over. 'This is the one who will receive all the owner's property someday,' they said. 'Let's kill him. Then everything will be ours.' 15 So they threw him out of the vineyard. And they killed him.

"What will the owner of the vineyard do to the renters? 16 He will come and kill them. He will give the vineyard to others."

When the people heard this, they said, "We hope this never happens!"

17 Jesus looked right at them and said, "Here is something I want you to explain the meaning of. It is written,

"'The stone the builders didn't accept
has become the most important stone of all.'
(Psalm 118:22)

18 Everyone who falls on that stone will be broken to pieces. But the stone will crush anyone it falls on."

19 The teachers of the law and the chief priests looked for a way to arrest Jesus at once. They knew he had told that story against them. But they were afraid of the people.

Is It Right to Pay Taxes to Caesar?

20 The religious leaders sent spies to keep a close watch on Jesus. The spies pretended to be honest. They hoped they could trap Jesus with something he would say. Then they could hand him over to the power and authority of the governor.

21 So the spies questioned Jesus. "Teacher," they said, "we know that you speak and teach what is right. We know you don't favor one person over another. You teach the way of God truthfully. 22 Is it right for us to pay taxes to Caesar or not?"

23 Jesus saw they were trying to trick him. So he said to them, 24 "Show me a silver coin. Whose picture and words are on it?"

25 "Caesar's," they replied.

He said to them, "Then give to Caesar what belongs to Caesar. And give to God what belongs to God."

26 They were not able to trap him with what he had said there in front of all the people. Amazed by his answer, they became silent.

Marriage When the Dead Rise

27 The Sadducees do not believe that people rise from the dead. Some of them came to Jesus with a question. 28 "Teacher," they said, "Moses wrote for us about a man's brother who dies. Suppose the brother leaves a wife but has no children. Then the man must get married to the widow. He must have children to carry on his dead brother's name.

29 "There were seven brothers. The first one got married to a woman. He died without leaving any children. 30 The second one got married to her. 31 And then the third one got married to her. One after another, the seven brothers got married to her. They all died. None left any children. 32 Finally, the woman died too. 33 Now then, when the dead rise, whose wife will she be? All seven brothers were married to her."

34 Jesus replied, "People in this world get married. And their parents give them to get married. 35 But it will not be like that when the dead rise. Those who are considered worthy to take part in what happens at that time won't get married. And their parents won't give them to be married. 36 They can't die anymore. They are like the angels. They are God's children. They will be given a new form of life when the dead rise.

37 "Remember the story of Moses and the bush. Even Moses showed that the dead rise. The Lord said to him, 'I am the God of Abraham. I am the God of Isaac. And I am the God of Jacob.' *(Exodus 3:6)* 38 He is not the God of the dead. He is the God of the living. In his eyes, everyone is alive."

39 Some of the teachers of the law replied, "You have spoken well, teacher!" 40 And no one dared to ask him any more questions.

Whose Son Is the Christ?

41 Jesus said to them, "Why do people say that the Christ is the Son of David? 42 David himself says in the Book of Psalms,

"'The Lord said to my Lord,
"Sit at my right hand
43 until I put your enemies
under your control."'
(Psalm 110:1)

44 David calls him 'Lord.' So how can he be David's son?"

45 All the people were listening. Jesus said to his disciples, 46 "Watch out for the teachers of the law. They like to walk around in long robes. They love to be greeted in the market places. They love to have the most important seats in the synagogues. They also love to have the places of honor at dinners. 47 They take over the houses of widows. They say long prayers to show off. God will punish those men very much."

The Widow's Offering

21 As Jesus looked up, he saw rich people putting their gifts into the temple offering boxes. 2 He also saw a poor widow put in two very small copper coins.

3"What I'm about to tell you is true," Jesus said. "That poor widow has put in more than all the others. 4All of those other people gave a lot because they are rich. But even though she is poor, she put in everything. She had nothing left to live on."

Signs of the End

5Some of Jesus' disciples were talking about the temple. They spoke about how it was decorated with beautiful stones and with gifts that honored God. But Jesus asked, 6"Do you see all this? The time will come when not one stone will be left on top of another. Every stone will be thrown down."

7"Teacher," they asked, "when will these things happen? And what will be the sign that they are about to take place?"

8Jesus replied, "Keep watch! Be careful that you are not fooled. Many will come in my name. They will claim, 'I am he!' And they will say, 'The time is near!' Do not follow them. 9Do not be afraid when you hear about wars and about fighting against rulers. Those things must happen first. But the end will not come right away."

10Then Jesus said to them, "Nation will fight against nation. Kingdom will fight against kingdom. 11In many places there will be powerful earthquakes. People will go hungry. There will be terrible sicknesses. Things will happen that will make people afraid. There will be great and miraculous signs from heaven.

12"But before all this, people will arrest you and treat you badly. They will hand you over to synagogues and prisons. You will be brought to kings and governors. All this will happen to you because of my name. 13In that way you will be witnesses to them. 14But make up your mind not to worry ahead of time about how to stand up for yourselves. 15I will give you words of wisdom. None of your enemies will be able to withstand them or oppose them.

16"Even your parents, brothers, sisters, relatives and friends will hand you over to the authorities. They will put some of you to death. 17Everyone will hate you because of me. 18But not a hair on your head will be harmed. 19If you stand firm, you will gain life.

20"A time is coming when you will see armies surround Jerusalem. Then you will know that it will soon be destroyed. 21Those who are in Judea should then escape to the mountains. Those in the city should get out. Those in the country should not enter the city. 22This is the time when God will punish Jerusalem. Everything will come true, just as it has been written.

23"How awful it will be in those days for pregnant women! How awful for nursing mothers! There will be terrible suffering in the land. There will be great anger against those people. 24Some will be killed by the sword. Others will be taken as prisoners to all the nations. Jerusalem will be overrun by those who aren't Jews until the times of the non-Jews come to an end.

25"There will be miraculous signs in the sun, moon and stars. The nations of the earth will be in terrible pain. They will be puzzled by the roaring and tossing of the sea. 26Terror will make people faint. They will be worried about what is happening in the world. The sun, moon and stars will be shaken from their places.

27"At that time people will see the Son of Man coming in a cloud. He will come with power and great glory. 28When these things begin to take place, stand up. Hold your head up with joy and hope. The time when you will be set free will be very close."

29Jesus told them a story. "Look at the fig tree and all the trees," he said. 30"When you see leaves appear on the branches, you know that summer is near. 31In the same way, when you see these things happening, you will know that God's kingdom is near.

32"What I'm about to tell you is true. The people living at that time will certainly not pass away until all these things have happened. 33Heaven and earth will pass away. But my words will never pass away.

34"Be careful. If you aren't, your hearts will be loaded down with wasteful living, drunkenness and the worries of life. Then the day the Son of Man returns will close on you like a trap. You will not be expecting it. 35That day will come upon every person who lives on the whole earth.

36"Always keep watching. Pray that you will be able to escape all that is about to happen. Also, pray that you will not be judged guilty when the Son of Man comes."

37Each day Jesus taught at the temple. And each evening he went to spend the night on the hill called the Mount of Olives. 38All the people came to the temple early in the morning. They wanted to hear Jesus speak.

Judas Agrees to Hand Jesus Over

22 The Feast of Unleavened Bread, called the Passover, was near. 2The chief priests and the teachers of the law were looking for a way to get rid of Jesus. They were afraid of the people.

3Then Satan entered Judas, who was called Iscariot. Judas was one of the Twelve. 4He went to the chief priests and the officers of the temple guard. He talked with them about how he could hand Jesus over to them. 5They were delighted and agreed to give him money.

6Judas accepted their offer. He watched for the right time to hand Jesus over to them. He wanted to do it when no crowd was around.

The Last Supper

7Then the day of Unleavened Bread came. That was the time the Passover lamb had to be sacrificed. 8Jesus sent Peter and John on ahead. "Go," he told them. "Prepare for us to eat the Passover meal."

9"Where do you want us to prepare for it?" they asked.

10Jesus replied, "When you enter the city, a man carrying a jar of water will meet you. Follow him to the house he enters. 11Then say to the owner of the house, 'The Teacher asks, "Where is the guest room? Where can I eat the Passover meal with my disciples?"' 12He will show you a large upstairs room with furniture in it. Prepare for us to eat there."

13Peter and John left. They found things just as Jesus had told them. So they prepared the Passover meal.

14When the hour came, Jesus and his apostles took their places at the table. 15He said to them, "I have really looked forward to eating this Passover meal with you. I wanted to do this before I suffer. 16I tell you, I will not eat the Passover meal again until it is celebrated in God's kingdom."

17After Jesus took the cup, he gave thanks. He said, "Take this cup and share it among yourselves. 18I tell you, I will not drink wine with you again until God's kingdom comes."

19Then Jesus took bread. He gave thanks and broke it. He handed it to them and said, "This is my body. It is given for you. Every time you eat it, do it in memory of me."

20In the same way, after the supper he took the cup. He said, "This cup is the new covenant in my blood. It is poured out for you. 21But someone here is going to hand me over to my enemies. His hand is with mine on the table. 22The Son of Man will go to his death, just as God has already decided. But how terrible it will be for the one who hands him over!"

23The apostles began to ask each other about this. They wondered which one of them would do it.

24They also started to argue. They disagreed about which of them was thought to be the most important person.

25Jesus said to them, "The kings of the nations hold power over their people. And those who order them around call themselves Protectors. 26But you must not be like that. Instead, the most important among you should be like the youngest. The one who rules should be like the one who serves.

27"Who is more important? Is it the one at the table, or the one who serves? Isn't it the one who is at the table? But I am among you as one who serves. 28You have stood by me during my troubles. 29And I give you a kingdom, just as my Father gave me a kingdom. 30Then you will eat and drink at my table in my kingdom. And you will sit on thrones, judging the 12 tribes of Israel.

31"Simon, Simon! Satan has asked to sift you disciples like wheat. 32But I have prayed for you, Simon. I have prayed that your faith will not fail. When you have turned back, help your brothers to be strong."

33But Simon replied, "Lord, I am ready to go with you to prison and to death."

34Jesus answered, "I tell you, Peter, you will say three times that you don't know me. And you will do it before the rooster crows today."

35Then Jesus asked the disciples, "Did you need anything when I sent you without a purse, bag or sandals?"

"Nothing," they answered.

36He said to them, "But now if you have a purse, take it. And also take a bag. If you don't have a sword, sell your coat and buy one. 37It is written, 'He was counted among those who had committed crimes.' *(Isaiah 53:12)* I tell you that what is written about me must come true. Yes, it is already coming true."

38The disciples said, "See, Lord, here are two swords."

"That is enough," he replied.

Jesus Prays on the Mount of Olives

39Jesus went out as usual to the Mount of Olives. His disciples followed him. 40When they reached the place, Jesus spoke. "Pray that you won't fall into sin when you are tempted," he said to them.

41Then he went a short distance away from them. There he got down on his knees and prayed. 42He said, "Father, if you are willing, take this cup of suffering away from me. But do what you want, not what I want."

43An angel from heaven appeared to Jesus and gave him strength. 44Because he was very sad and troubled, he prayed even harder. His sweat was like drops of blood falling to the ground.

45After that, he got up from prayer and went back to the disciples. He found them sleeping. They were worn out because they were very sad. 46"Why are you sleeping?" he asked them. "Get up! Pray that you won't fall into sin when you are tempted."

Jesus Is Arrested

47While Jesus was still speaking, a crowd came up. The man named Judas was leading them. He was one of the Twelve. Judas approached Jesus to kiss him.

48But Jesus asked him, "Judas, are you handing over the Son of Man with a kiss?"

49Jesus' followers saw what was going to happen. So they said, "Lord, should we use our swords against them?" 50One of them struck the servant of the high priest and cut off his right ear.

51But Jesus answered, "Stop this!" And he touched the man's ear and healed him.

52Then Jesus spoke to the chief priests, the officers of the temple guard, and the elders. They had all come for him. "Am I leading a band of armed men against you?" he asked. "Do you have to come with swords and clubs? 53Every day I was with you in the temple courtyard. And you didn't lay a hand on me. But this is your hour. This is when darkness rules."

Peter Says He Does Not Know Jesus

54 Then the men arrested Jesus and led him away. They took him into the high priest's house. Peter followed from far away. 55 They started a fire in the middle of the courtyard. Then they sat down together. Peter sat down with them.

56 A female servant saw him sitting there in the firelight. She looked closely at him. Then she said, "This man was with Jesus."

57 But Peter said he had not been with him. "Woman, I don't know him," he said.

58 A little later someone else saw Peter. "You also are one of them," he said.

"No," Peter replied. "I'm not!"

59 About an hour later, another person spoke up. "This fellow must have been with Jesus," he said. "He is from Galilee."

60 Peter replied, "Man, I don't know what you're talking about!"

Just as he was speaking, the rooster crowed. 61 The Lord turned and looked right at Peter. Then Peter remembered what the Lord had spoken to him. "The rooster will crow today," Jesus had said. "Before it does, you will say three times that you don't know me." 62 Peter went outside. He broke down and sobbed.

The Guards Make Fun of Jesus

63 There were men guarding Jesus. They began laughing at him and beating him. 64 They blindfolded him. They said, "Prophesy! Who hit you?" 65 They also said many other things to make fun of him.

Jesus Is Brought to Pilate and Herod

66 At dawn the elders of the people met together. These included the chief priests and the teachers of the law. Jesus was led to them. 67 "If you are the Christ," they said, "tell us."

Jesus answered, "If I tell you, you will not believe me. 68 And if I asked you, you would not answer. 69 But from now on, the Son of Man will be seated at the right hand of the mighty God."

70 They all asked, "Are you the Son of God then?"

He replied, "You are right in saying that I am."

71 Then they said, "Why do we need any more witnesses? We have heard it from his own lips."

23 Then the whole group got up and led Jesus off to Pilate. 2 They began to bring charges against Jesus. They said, "We have found this man misleading our people. He is against paying taxes to Caesar. And he claims to be Christ, a king."

3 So Pilate asked Jesus, "Are you the king of the Jews?"

"Yes. It is just as you say," Jesus replied.

4 Then Pilate spoke to the chief priests and the crowd. He announced, "I find no basis for a charge against this man."

5 But they kept it up. They said, "His teaching stirs up the people all over Judea. He started in Galilee and has come all the way here."

6 When Pilate heard this, he asked if the man was from Galilee. 7 He learned that Jesus was from Herod's area of authority. So Pilate sent Jesus to Herod. At that time Herod was also in Jerusalem.

8 When Herod saw Jesus, he was very pleased. He had been wanting to see Jesus for a long time. He had heard much about him. He hoped to see Jesus do a miracle.

9 Herod asked him many questions, but Jesus gave him no answer. 10 The chief priests and the teachers of the law were standing there. With loud shouts they brought charges against him.

11 Herod and his soldiers laughed at him and made fun of him. They dressed him in a beautiful robe. Then they sent him back to Pilate. 12 That day Herod and Pilate became friends. Before this time they had been enemies.

13 Pilate called together the chief priests, the rulers and the people. 14 He said to them, "You brought me this man. You said he was turning the people against the authorities. I have questioned him in front of you. I have found no basis for your charges against him. 15 Herod hasn't either. So he sent Jesus back to us. As you can see, Jesus has done nothing that is worthy of death. 16/17 So I will just have him whipped and let him go."

18 With one voice the crowd cried out, "Kill this man! Give Barabbas to us!" 19 Barabbas had been thrown into prison. He had taken part in a struggle in the city against the authorities. He had also committed murder.

20 Pilate wanted to let Jesus go. So he made an appeal to the crowd again. 21 But they kept shouting, "Crucify him! Crucify him!"

22 Pilate spoke to them for the third time. "Why?" he asked. "What wrong has this man done? I have found no reason to have him put to death. So I will just have him whipped and let him go."

23 But with loud shouts they kept calling for Jesus to be crucified. The people's shouts won out. 24 So Pilate decided to give them what they wanted. 25 He set free the man they asked for. The man had been thrown in prison for murder and for fighting against the authorities. Pilate gave Jesus over to them so they could carry out their plans.

Jesus Is Nailed to a Cross

26 As they led Jesus away, they took hold of Simon. Simon was from Cyrene. He was on his way in from the country. They put a wooden cross on his shoulders. Then they made him carry it behind Jesus.

27 A large number of people followed Jesus. Some were women whose hearts were filled with sorrow. They cried loudly because of him.

28 Jesus turned and said to them, "Daughters of Jerusalem, do not cry for me. Cry for yourselves and for your children. 29 The time will come when you will say, 'Blessed are the women who can't have children! Blessed are those who never gave birth or nursed babies!' 30 It is written,

"'The people will say to the mountains,
"Fall on us!"
They'll say to the hills, "Cover us!"'
(Hosea 10:8)

31People do these things when trees are green. So what will happen when trees are dry?"

32Two other men were also led out with Jesus to be killed. Both of them had broken the law. 33The soldiers brought them to the place called The Skull. There they nailed Jesus to the cross. He hung between the two criminals. One was on his right and one was on his left.

34Jesus said, "Father, forgive them. They don't know what they are doing." The soldiers divided up his clothes by casting lots.

35The people stood there watching. The rulers even made fun of Jesus. They said, "He saved others. Let him save himself if he is the Christ of God, the Chosen One."

36The soldiers also came up and poked fun at him. They offered him wine vinegar. 37They said, "If you are the king of the Jews, save yourself."

38A written sign had been placed above him. It read, THIS IS THE KING OF THE JEWS.

39One of the criminals hanging there made fun of Jesus. He said, "Aren't you the Christ? Save yourself! Save us!"

40But the other criminal scolded him. "Don't you have any respect for God?" he said. "Remember, you are under the same sentence of death. 41We are being punished fairly. We are getting just what our actions call for. But this man hasn't done anything wrong."

42Then he said, "Jesus, remember me when you come into your kingdom."

43Jesus answered him, "What I'm about to tell you is true. Today you will be with me in paradise."

Jesus Dies

44It was now about noon. The whole land was covered with darkness until three o'clock. 45The sun had stopped shining. The temple curtain was torn in two. 46Jesus called out in a loud voice, "Father, into your hands I commit my very life." After he said this, he took his last breath.

47The Roman commander saw what had happened. He praised God and said, "Jesus was surely a man who did what was right."

48The people had gathered to watch that sight. When they saw what happened, they beat their chests and went away. 49But all those who knew Jesus stood not very far away, watching those things. They included the women who had followed him from Galilee.

Jesus Is Buried

50A man named Joseph was a member of the Jewish Council. He was a good and honest man. 51He had not agreed with what the leaders had decided and done. He was from Arimathea, a town in Judea. He was waiting for God's kingdom.

52Joseph went to Pilate and asked for Jesus' body. 53He took it down and wrapped it in linen cloth. Then he put it in a tomb cut in the rock. No one had ever been buried there. 54It was Preparation Day. The Sabbath was about to begin.

55The women who had come with Jesus from Galilee followed Joseph. They saw the tomb and how Jesus' body was placed in it. 56Then they went home. There they prepared spices and perfumes. But they rested on the Sabbath day in order to obey the Law.

Jesus Rises From the Dead

24 It was very early in the morning on the first day of the week. The women took the spices they had prepared. Then they went to the tomb. 2They found the stone rolled away from it. 3When they entered the tomb, they did not find the body of the Lord Jesus. 4They were wondering about this.

Suddenly two men in clothes as bright as lightning stood beside them. 5The women were terrified. They bowed down with their faces to the ground.

Then the men said to them, "Why do you look for the living among the dead? 6Jesus is not here! He has risen! Remember how he told you he would rise. It was while he was still with you in Galilee. 7He said, 'The Son of Man must be handed over to sinful people. He must be nailed to a cross. On the third day he will rise from the dead.'"

8Then the women remembered Jesus' words.

9They came back from the tomb. They told all these things to the Eleven and to all the others. 10Mary Magdalene, Joanna, Mary the mother of James, and the others with them were the ones who told the apostles. 11But the apostles did not believe the women. Their words didn't make any sense to them.

12But Peter got up and ran to the tomb. He bent over and saw the strips of linen lying by themselves. Then he went away, wondering what had happened.

On the Road to Emmaus

13That same day two of Jesus' followers were going to a village called Emmaus. It was about seven miles from Jerusalem. 14They were talking with each other about everything that had happened.

15As they talked about those things, Jesus himself came up and walked along with them. 16But God kept them from recognizing him.

17Jesus asked them, "What are you talking about as you walk along?"

They stood still, and their faces were sad. 18One of them was named Cleopas. He said to Jesus, "You must be a visitor to Jerusalem. If you lived there, you would know the things that have happened there in the last few days."

19"What things?" Jesus asked.

"About Jesus of Nazareth," they replied. "He was a prophet. He was powerful in what he said and did in the eyes of God and all of the people. 20The chief priests and our rulers handed Jesus over to be sentenced to death. They nailed him to a cross. 21But we had hoped that he was the one who was going to set Israel free. Also, it is the third day since all this happened.

22"Some of our women amazed us too. Early this morning they went to the tomb. 23But they didn't find his body. So they came and told us what they had seen. They saw angels, who said Jesus was alive. 24Then some of our friends went to the tomb. They saw it was empty, just as the women had said. They didn't see Jesus' body there."

25Jesus said to them, "How foolish you are! How long it takes you to believe all that the prophets said! 26Didn't the Christ have to suffer these things and then receive his glory?"

27Jesus explained to them what was said about himself in all the Scriptures. He began with Moses and all the Prophets.

28The two men approached the village where they were going. Jesus acted as if he were going farther. 29But they tried hard to keep him from leaving. They said, "Stay with us. It is nearly evening. The day is almost over." So he went in to stay with them.

30He joined them at the table. Then he took bread and gave thanks. He broke it and began to give it to them. 31Their eyes were opened, and they recognized him. But then he disappeared from their sight.

32They said to each other, "He talked with us on the road. He opened the Scriptures to us. Weren't our hearts burning inside us during that time?"

33They got up and returned at once to Jerusalem. There they found the Eleven and those with them. They were all gathered together. 34They were saying, "It's true! The Lord has risen! He has appeared to Simon!"

35Then the two of them told what had happened to them on the way. They told how they had recognized Jesus when he broke the bread.

Jesus Appears to the Disciples

36The disciples were still talking about this when Jesus himself suddenly stood among them. He said, "May peace be with you!"

37They were surprised and terrified. They thought they were seeing a ghost.

38Jesus said to them, "Why are you troubled? Why do you have doubts in your minds? 39Look at my hands and my feet. It is really I! Touch me and see. A ghost does not have a body or bones. But you can see that I do."

40After he said that, he showed them his hands and feet. 41But they still did not believe it. They were amazed and filled with joy.

So Jesus asked them, "Do you have anything here to eat?"

42They gave him a piece of cooked fish. 43He took it and ate it in front of them.

44Jesus said to them, "This is what I told you while I was still with you. Everything written about me must happen. Everything written about me in the Law of Moses, the Prophets and the Psalms must come true."

45Then he opened their minds so they could understand the Scriptures. 46He told them, "This is what is written. The Christ will suffer. He will rise from the dead on the third day. 47His followers will preach in his name. They will tell others to turn away from their sins and be forgiven. People from every nation will hear it, beginning at Jerusalem. 48You have seen these things with your own eyes.

49"I am going to send you what my Father has promised. But for now, stay in the city. Stay there until you have received power from heaven."

Jesus Is Taken Up Into Heaven

50Jesus led his disciples out to the area near Bethany. Then he lifted up his hands and blessed them. 51While he was blessing them, he left them. He was taken up into heaven.

52Then they worshiped him. With great joy, they returned to Jerusalem. 53Every day they went to the temple, praising God.

John

The Word Became Human

1 In the beginning, the Word was already there. The Word was with God, and the Word was God. 2He was with God in the beginning.

3All things were made through him. Nothing that has been made was made without him. 4Life was in him, and that life was the light for all people. 5The light shines in the darkness. But the darkness has not understood it.

6A man came who was sent from God. His name was John. 7He came to give witness about that light. He gave witness so that all people could believe.

8John himself was not the light. He came only as a witness to the light. 9The true light that gives light to every man was coming into the world.

10The Word was in the world that was made through him. But the world did not recognize him. 11He came to what was his own. But his own people did not accept him.

12Some people did accept him. They believed in his name. He gave them the right to become children of God. 13To be a child of God has nothing to do with human parents. Children of God are not born because of human choice or because a husband wants them to be born. They are born because of what God does.

14The Word became a human being. He made his home with us. We have seen his glory. It is the glory of the one and only Son.

He came from the Father. And he was full of grace and truth.

15John gives witness about him. He cries out and says, "This was the one I was talking about. I said, 'He who comes after me is more important than I am. He is more important because he existed before I was born.'"

16We have all received one blessing after another. God's grace is not limited. 17Moses gave us the law. Jesus Christ has given us grace and truth.

18No one has ever seen God. But God, the one and only Son, is at the Father's side. He has shown us what God is like.

John the Baptist Is Not the Christ

19The Jews of Jerusalem sent priests and Levites to ask John who he was. John gave witness to them. 20He did not try to hide the truth. He spoke to them openly. He said, "I am not the Christ."

21They asked him, "Then who are you? Are you Elijah?"

He said, "I am not."

"Are you the Prophet we've been expecting?" they asked.

"No," he answered.

22They asked one last time, "Who are you? Give us an answer to take back to those who sent us. What do you say about yourself?"

23John replied, using the words of Isaiah the prophet. John said, "I'm the messenger who is calling out in the desert, 'Make the way for the Lord straight.'" *(Isaiah 40:3)*

24Some Pharisees who had been sent 25asked him, "If you are not the Christ, why are you baptizing people? Why are you doing that if you aren't Elijah or the Prophet we've been expecting?"

26"I baptize people with water," John replied. "But One is standing among you whom you do not know. 27He is the One who comes after me. I am not good enough to untie his sandals."

28This all happened at Bethany on the other side of the Jordan River. That was where John was baptizing.

Jesus Is the Lamb of God

29The next day John saw Jesus coming toward him. John said, "Look! The Lamb of God! He takes away the sin of the world! 30This is the One I was talking about. I said, 'A man who comes after me is more important than I am. That's because he existed before I was born.' 31I did not know him. But God wants to make it clear to Israel who this person is. That's the reason I came baptizing with water."

32Then John told them, "I saw the Holy Spirit come down from heaven like a dove. The Spirit remained on Jesus. 33I would not have known him. But the One who sent me to baptize with water told me, 'You will see the Spirit come down and remain on someone. He is the One who will baptize with the Holy Spirit.' 34I have seen it happen. I give witness that this is the Son of God."

Jesus Chooses the First Disciples

35The next day John was again with two of his disciples. 36He saw Jesus walking by. John said, "Look! The Lamb of God!"

37The two disciples heard him say this. So they followed Jesus.

38Then Jesus turned around and saw them following. He asked, "What do you want?"

They said, "Rabbi, where are you staying?" *Rabbi* means Teacher.

39"Come," he replied. "You will see."

So they went and saw where he was staying. They spent the rest of the day with him. It was about four o'clock in the afternoon.

40Andrew was Simon Peter's brother. Andrew was one of the two disciples who heard what John had said. He had also followed Jesus. 41The first thing Andrew did was to find his brother Simon. He told him, "We have found the Messiah." Messiah means Christ. 42And he brought Simon to Jesus.

Jesus looked at him and said, "You are Simon, son of John. You will be called Cephas." Cephas means Peter (or rock).

Jesus Chooses Philip and Nathanael

43The next day Jesus decided to leave for Galilee. He found Philip and said to him, "Follow me."

44Philip was from the town of Bethsaida. So were Andrew and Peter. 45Philip found Nathanael and told him, "We have found the One that Moses wrote about in the Law. The prophets also wrote about him. He is Jesus of Nazareth, the son of Joseph."

46"Nazareth! Can anything good come from there?" Nathanael asked.

"Come and see," said Philip.

47Jesus saw Nathanael approaching. Here is what Jesus said about him. "He is a true Israelite. There is nothing false in him."

48"How do you know me?" Nathanael asked.

Jesus answered, "I saw you while you were still under the fig tree. I saw you there before Philip called you."

49Nathanael replied, "Rabbi, you are the Son of God. You are the King of Israel."

50Jesus said, "You believe because I told you I saw you under the fig tree. You will see greater things than that."

51Then he said to the disciples, "What I'm about to tell you is true. You will see heaven open. You will see the angels of God going up and coming down on the Son of Man."

Jesus Changes Water Into Wine

2 On the third day there was a wedding. It took place at Cana in Galilee. Jesus' mother was there. 2Jesus and his disciples had also been invited to the wedding. 3When the wine was gone, Jesus' mother said to him, "They have no more wine."

4"Dear woman, why do you bring me into this?" Jesus replied. "My time has not yet come."

5His mother said to the servants, "Do what he tells you."

6Six stone water jars stood nearby. The Jews used water from that kind of jar for special washings to make themselves pure. Each jar could hold 20 to 30 gallons.

7Jesus said to the servants, "Fill the jars with water." So they filled them to the top.

8Then he told them, "Now dip some out. Take it to the person in charge of the dinner."

They did what he said. 9The person in charge tasted the water that had been turned into wine. He didn't realize where it had come from. But the servants who had brought the water knew.

Then the person in charge called the groom to one side. 10He said to him, "Everyone brings out the best wine first. They bring out the cheaper wine after the guests have had too much to drink. But you have saved the best until now."

11That was the first of Jesus' miraculous signs. He did it at Cana in Galilee. Jesus showed his glory by doing it. And his disciples put their faith in him.

Jesus Clears Out the Temple

12After this, Jesus went down to Capernaum. His mother and brothers and disciples went with him. They all stayed there for a few days.

13It was almost time for the Jewish Passover Feast. So Jesus went up to Jerusalem. 14In the temple courtyard he found people who were selling cattle, sheep and doves. Others were sitting at tables exchanging money.

15So Jesus made a whip out of ropes. He chased all the sheep and cattle from the temple area. He scattered the coins of the people exchanging money. And he turned over their tables. 16He told those who were selling doves, "Get these out of here! How dare you turn my Father's house into a market!"

17His disciples remembered what had been written. It says, "My great love for your house will destroy me." *(Psalm 69:9)*

18Then the Jews asked him, "What miraculous sign can you show us? Can you prove your authority to do all of this?"

19Jesus answered them, "Destroy this temple. I will raise it up again in three days."

20The Jews replied, "It has taken 46 years to build this temple. Are you going to raise it up in three days?"

21But the temple Jesus had spoken about was his body.

22His disciples later remembered what he had said. That was after he had been raised from the dead. Then they believed the Scriptures. They also believed the words that Jesus had spoken.

23Meanwhile, he was in Jerusalem at the Passover Feast. Many people saw the miraculous signs he was doing. And they believed in his name. 24But Jesus did not fully trust them. He knew what people are like. 25He didn't need others to tell him what people are like. He already knew what was in the human heart.

Jesus Teaches Nicodemus

3 There was a Pharisee named Nicodemus. He was one of the Jewish rulers. 2He came to Jesus at night and said, "Rabbi, we know you are a teacher who has come from God. We know that God is with you. If he weren't, you couldn't do the miraculous signs you are doing."

3Jesus replied, "What I'm about to tell you is true. No one can see God's kingdom without being born again."

4"How can I be born when I am old?" Nicodemus asked. "I can't go back inside my mother! I can't be born a second time!"

5Jesus answered, "What I'm about to tell you is true. No one can enter God's kingdom without being born through water and the Holy Spirit. 6People give birth to people. But the Spirit gives birth to spirit. 7You should not be surprised when I say, 'You must all be born again.'

8"The wind blows where it wants to. You hear the sound it makes. But you can't tell where it comes from or where it is going. It is the same with everyone who is born through the Spirit."

9"How can this be?" Nicodemus asked.

10"You are Israel's teacher," said Jesus. "Don't you understand these things?

11"What I'm about to tell you is true. We speak about what we know. We give witness to what we have seen. But still you people do not accept our witness. 12I have spoken to you about earthly things, and you do not believe. So how will you believe if I speak about heavenly things?

13"No one has ever gone into heaven except the One who came from heaven. He is the Son of Man. 14Moses lifted up the snake in the desert. The Son of Man must be lifted up also. 15Then everyone who believes in him can live with God forever.

16"God loved the world so much that he gave his one and only Son. Anyone who believes in him will not die but will have eternal life.

17"God did not send his Son into the world to judge the world. He sent his Son to save the world through him. 18Anyone who believes in him is not judged. But anyone who does not believe is judged already. He has not believed in the name of God's one and only Son.

19"Here is the judgment. Light has come into the world, but people loved darkness instead of light. They loved darkness because what they did was evil.

20"Everyone who does evil things hates the light. They will not come into the light. They are afraid that what they do will be seen. 21But anyone who lives by the truth comes into the light. He does this so that it will be easy to see that what he has done is with God's help."

John the Baptist Gives Witness About Jesus

22After this, Jesus and his disciples went out into the countryside of Judea. There he spent some time with them. And he baptized people there.

23John was also baptizing. He was at Aenon near Salim, where there was plenty of water. People were coming all the time to be baptized. 24That was before John was put in prison.

25Some of John's disciples and a certain Jew began to argue. They argued about special washings to make people "clean." 26They came to John and said to him, "Rabbi, that man who was with you on the other side of the Jordan River is baptizing people. He is the one you gave witness about. Everyone is going to him."

27John replied, "A person can receive only what God gives him from heaven. 28You yourselves are witnesses that I said, 'I am not the Christ. I was sent ahead of him.' 29The bride belongs to the groom. The friend who helps the groom waits and listens for him. He is full of joy when he hears the groom's voice. That joy is mine, and it is now complete. 30He must become more important. I must become less important.

31"The One who comes from above is above everything. The one who is from the earth belongs to the earth and speaks like someone from the earth. The One who comes from heaven is above everything. 32He gives witness to what he has seen and heard. But no one accepts what he says. 33Anyone who has accepted it has said, 'Yes. God is truthful.' 34The One whom God has sent speaks God's words. God gives the Holy Spirit without limit.

35"The Father loves the Son and has put everything into his hands. 36Anyone who believes in the Son has eternal life. Anyone who says no to the Son will not have life. God's anger remains on him."

Jesus Talks With a Woman From Samaria

4 The Pharisees heard that Jesus was winning and baptizing more disciples than John. 2But in fact Jesus was not baptizing. His disciples were. 3When the Lord found out about all this, he left Judea. He went back to Galilee again.

4Jesus had to go through Samaria. 5He came to a town in Samaria called Sychar. It was near the piece of land Jacob had given his son Joseph. 6Jacob's well was there. Jesus was tired from the journey. So he sat down by the well. It was about noon.

7A woman from Samaria came to get some water. Jesus said to her, "Will you give me a drink?" 8His disciples had gone into the town to buy food.

9The Samaritan woman said to him, "You are a Jew. I am a Samaritan woman. How can you ask me for a drink?" She said this because Jews don't have anything to do with Samaritans.

10Jesus answered her, "You do not know what God's gift is. And you do not know who is asking you for a drink. If you did, you would have asked him. He would have given you living water."

11"Sir," the woman said, "you don't have anything to get water with. The well is deep. Where can you get this living water?

12"Our father Jacob gave us the well. He drank from it himself. So did his sons and his flocks and herds. Are you more important than he is?"

13Jesus answered, "All who drink this water will be thirsty again. 14But anyone who drinks the water I give him will never be thirsty. In fact, the water I give him will become a spring of water in him. It will flow up into eternal life."

15The woman said to him, "Sir, give me this water. Then I will never be thirsty. And I won't have to keep coming here to get water."

16He told her, "Go. Get your husband and come back."

17“I have no husband,” she replied.
Jesus said to her, “You are right when you say
you have no husband. 18The fact is, you have had
five husbands. And the man you have now is not
your husband. What you have just said is very
true.”
19“Sir,” the woman said, “I can see that you are
a prophet. 20Our people have worshiped on this
mountain for a long time. But you Jews claim that
the place where we must worship is in Jerusalem.”
21Jesus said, “Believe me, woman. A time is
coming when you will not worship the Father on
this mountain or in Jerusalem. 22You Samaritans
worship what you do not know. We worship what
we do know. Salvation comes from the Jews.
23“But a new time is coming. In fact, it is
already here. True worshipers will worship the
Father in spirit and in truth. They are the kind of
worshipers the Father is looking for.
24“God is spirit. His worshipers must worship
him in spirit and in truth.”
25The woman said, “I know that Messiah is
coming.” (He is called Christ.) “When he comes,
he will explain everything to us.”
26Then Jesus said, “I, the one speaking to you,
am he.”

The Disciples Join Jesus Again

27Just then Jesus’ disciples returned. They were
surprised to find him talking with a woman. But
no one asked, “What do you want from her?” No
one asked, “Why are you talking with her?”
28The woman left her water jar and went back to
the town. She said to the people, 29“Come. See a
man who told me everything I’ve ever done. Could
this be the Christ?”
30The people came out of the town and made
their way toward Jesus.
31His disciples were saying to him, “Rabbi, eat
something!”
32But he said to them, “I have food to eat that
you know nothing about.”
33Then his disciples asked each other, “Did
someone bring him food?”
34Jesus said, “My food is to do what my Father
sent me to do. My food is to finish his work.
35“You say, ‘Four months more, and then it will
be harvest time.’ But I tell you, open your eyes!
Look at the fields! They are ripe for harvest right
now. 36Those who gather the crop are already getting paid. They are already harvesting the crop for
eternal life. So those who plant and those who
gather can now be glad together.
37“Here is a true saying. ‘One plants and another
gathers.’ 38I sent you to gather what you have not
worked for. Others have done the hard work. You
have gathered the benefits of their work.”

Many Samaritans Believe in Jesus

39Many of the Samaritans from the town of Sychar believed in Jesus. They believed because of
the woman’s witness. She said, “He told me everything I’ve ever done.”
40Then the Samaritans came to him and tried to
get him to stay with them. So he stayed two days.
41Because of his words, many more people became
believers.
42They said to the woman, “We no longer
believe just because of what you said. We have
now heard for ourselves. We know that this man
really is the Savior of the world.”

Jesus Heals the Official’s Son

43After the two days, Jesus left for Galilee. 44He
himself had pointed out that a prophet is not
respected in his own country. 45When he arrived in
Galilee, the people living there welcomed him.
They had seen everything he had done in Jerusalem at the Passover Feast. That was because they
had also been there.
46Once more, Jesus visited Cana in Galilee.
Cana is where he had turned the water into wine.
A royal official was there. His son was sick in bed
at Capernaum. 47The official heard that Jesus had
arrived in Galilee from Judea. So he went to Jesus
and begged him to come and heal his son. The boy
was close to death.
48Jesus told him, “You people will never believe
unless you see miraculous signs and wonders.”
49The royal official said, “Sir, come down
before my child dies.”
50Jesus replied, “You may go. Your son will live.”
The man believed what Jesus said, and so he
left. 51While he was still on his way home, his servants met him. They gave him the news that his
boy was living. 52He asked what time his son got
better. They said to him, “The fever left him yesterday afternoon at one o’clock.”
53Then the father realized what had happened.
That was the exact time Jesus had said to him,
“Your son will live.” So he and all his family
became believers.
54This was the second miraculous sign that
Jesus did after coming from Judea to Galilee.

Jesus Heals a Disabled Man

5 Some time later, Jesus went up to Jerusalem
for a Jewish feast. 2In Jerusalem near the Sheep
Gate is a pool. In the Aramaic language it is called
Bethesda. It is surrounded by five rows of columns
with a roof over them. 3/4Here a great number of
disabled people used to lie down. Among them
were those who were blind, those who could not
walk, and those who could hardly move.
5One person who was there had been disabled
for 38 years. 6Jesus saw him lying there. He knew
that the man had been in that condition for a long
time. So he asked him, “Do you want to get well?”
7“Sir,” the disabled man replied, “I have no one
to help me into the pool when an angel stirs the
water up. I try to get in, but someone else always
goes down ahead of me.”

8Then Jesus said to him, "Get up! Pick up your mat and walk."

9At once the man was healed. He picked up his mat and walked.

The day this happened was a Sabbath. 10So the Jews said to the man who had been healed, "It is the Sabbath. The law does not allow you to carry your mat."

11But he replied, "The one who made me well said to me, 'Pick up your mat and walk.'"

12They asked him, "Who is this fellow? Who told you to pick it up and walk?"

13The one who was healed had no idea who it was. Jesus had slipped away into the crowd that was there.

14Later Jesus found him at the temple. Jesus said to him, "See, you are well again. Stop sinning, or something worse may happen to you." 15The man went away. He told the Jews it was Jesus who had made him well.

Life Because of the Son

16Jesus was doing these things on the Sabbath day. So the Jews began to oppose him.

17Jesus said to them, "My Father is always doing his work. He is working right up to this very day. I am working too."

18For this reason the Jews tried even harder to kill him. Jesus was not only breaking the Sabbath. He was even calling God his own Father. He was making himself equal with God.

19Jesus answered, "What I'm about to tell you is true. The Son can do nothing by himself. He can do only what he sees his Father doing. What the Father does, the Son also does. 20This is because the Father loves the Son. He shows him everything he does. Yes, you will be amazed! The Father will show him even greater things than these.

21"The Father raises the dead and gives them life. In the same way, the Son gives life to anyone he wants to.

22"Also, the Father does not judge anyone. He has given the Son the task of judging. 23Then all people will honor the Son just as they honor the Father. Those who do not honor the Son do not honor the Father, who sent him.

24"What I'm about to tell you is true. Anyone who hears my word and believes him who sent me has eternal life. He will not be found guilty. He has crossed over from death to life.

25"What I'm about to tell you is true. A time is coming for me to give life. In fact, it has already begun. The dead will hear the voice of the Son of God. Those who hear it will live.

26"The Father has life in himself. He has also allowed the Son to have life in himself. 27And the Father has given him the authority to judge. This is because he is the Son of Man.

28"Do not be amazed at this. A time is coming when all who are in the grave will hear his voice. 29They will all come out of their graves. Those who have done good will rise and live again. Those who have done evil will rise and be found guilty.

30"I can do nothing by myself. I judge only as I hear. And my judging is fair. I do not try to please myself. I try only to please the One who sent me.

Giving Witness About Jesus

31"If I give witness about myself, it doesn't count. 32There is someone else who gives witness in my favor. And I know that his witness about me counts.

33"You have sent people to John. He has given witness to the truth. 34I do not accept human witness. I only talk about it so you can be saved. 35John was like a lamp that burned and gave light. For a while you chose to enjoy his light.

36"The witness I have is more important than John's. I am doing the very work the Father gave me to finish. It gives witness that the Father has sent me.

37"The Father who sent me has himself given witness about me. You have never heard his voice. You have never seen what he really looks like. 38And his word does not live in you. This is because you do not believe the One he sent.

39"You study the Scriptures carefully. You study them because you think they will give you eternal life. The Scriptures you study give witness about me. 40But you refuse to come to me and receive life.

41"I do not accept praise from people. 42But I know you. I know that you do not have love for God in your hearts. 43I have come in my Father's name, and you do not accept me. But if someone else comes in his own name, you will accept him.

44"You accept praise from one another. But you make no effort to receive the praise that comes from the only God. So how can you believe?

45"Do not think I will bring charges against you in front of the Father. Moses is the one who does that. And he is the one you build your hopes on.

46"Do you believe Moses? Then you should believe me. He wrote about me. 47But you do not believe what he wrote. So how are you going to believe what I say?"

Jesus Feeds the Five Thousand

6 Some time after this, Jesus crossed over to the other side of the Sea of Galilee. It is also called the Sea of Tiberias. 2A large crowd of people followed him. They had seen the miraculous signs he had done on those who were sick.

3Then Jesus went up on a mountainside. There he sat down with his disciples. 4The Jewish Passover Feast was near.

5Jesus looked up and saw a large crowd coming toward him. So he said to Philip, "Where can we buy bread for these people to eat?" 6He asked this only to put Philip to the test. He already knew what he was going to do.

7Philip answered him, "Eight months' pay would not buy enough bread for each one to have a bite!"

8Another of his disciples spoke up. It was Andrew, Simon Peter's brother. 9He said, "Here is a
boy with five small loaves of barley bread. He also
has two small fish. But how far will that go in such
a large crowd?"
10Jesus said, "Have the people sit down." There
was plenty of grass in that place, and they sat
down. The number of men among them was about
5,000.
11Then Jesus took the loaves and gave thanks.
He handed out the bread to those who were seated.
He gave them as much as they wanted. And he did
the same with the fish.
12When all of them had enough to eat, Jesus
spoke to his disciples. "Gather the leftover pieces,"
he said. "Don't waste anything."
13So they gathered what was left over from the
five barley loaves. They filled 12 baskets with the
pieces left by those who had eaten.
14The people saw the miraculous sign that Jesus
did. Then they began to say, "This must be the
Prophet who is supposed to come into the world."
15But Jesus knew that they planned to come and
force him to be their king. So he went away again
to a mountain by himself.

Jesus Walks on the Water

16When evening came, Jesus' disciples went
down to the Sea of Galilee. 17There they got into a
boat and headed across the lake toward Capernaum. By now it was dark. Jesus had not yet joined
them.
18A strong wind was blowing, and the water
became rough. 19They rowed three or three and a
half miles. Then they saw Jesus coming toward the
boat. He was walking on the water. They were
terrified.
20But he said to them, "It is I. Don't be afraid."
21Then they agreed to take him into the boat.
Right away the boat reached the shore where they
were heading.
22The next day the crowd that had stayed on the
other side of the lake realized something. They
saw that only one boat had been there. They knew
that Jesus had not gotten into it with his disciples.
And they knew that the disciples had gone away
alone.
23Then some boats from Tiberias landed. It was
near the place where the people had eaten the
bread after the Lord gave thanks. 24The crowd realized that Jesus and his disciples were not there. So
they got into boats and went to Capernaum to look
for Jesus.

Jesus Is the Bread of Life

25They found him on the other side of the lake.
They asked him, "Rabbi, when did you get here?"
26Jesus answered, "What I'm about to tell you is
true. You are not looking for me because you saw
miraculous signs. You are looking for me because
you ate the loaves until you were full. 27Do not
work for food that spoils. Work for food that lasts
forever. That is the food the Son of Man will give
you. God the Father has put his seal of approval
on him."
28Then they asked him, "What does God want
from us? What works does he want us to do?"
29Jesus answered, "God's work is to believe in
the One he has sent."
30So they asked him, "What miraculous sign
will you give us? What will you do so we can see
it and believe you? 31Long ago our people ate the
manna in the desert. It is written in Scripture, 'The
Lord gave them bread from heaven to eat.'" *(Exodus 16:4; Nehemiah 9:15; Psalm 78:24,25)*
32Jesus said to them, "What I'm about to tell
you is true. It is not Moses who has given you the
bread from heaven. It is my Father who gives you
the true bread from heaven. 33The bread of God is
the One who comes down from heaven. He gives
life to the world."
34"Sir," they said, "give us this bread from
now on."
35Then Jesus said, "I am the bread of life. No
one who comes to me will ever go hungry. And no
one who believes in me will ever be thirsty.
36"But it is just as I told you. You have seen me,
and you still do not believe. 37Everyone the Father
gives me will come to me. I will never send away
anyone who comes to me.
38"I have not come down from heaven to do
what I want to do. I have come to do what the One
who sent me wants me to do. 39The One who sent
me doesn't want me to lose anyone he has given
me. He wants me to raise them up on the last day.
40My Father wants all who look to the Son and
believe in him to have eternal life. I will raise them
up on the last day."
41Then the Jews began to complain about Jesus.
That was because he said, "I am the bread that
came down from heaven." 42They said, "Isn't this
Jesus, the son of Joseph? Don't we know his father
and mother? How can he now say, 'I came down
from heaven'?"
43"Stop complaining among yourselves," Jesus
answered. 44"No one can come to me unless the
Father who sent me brings him. Then I will raise
him up on the last day.
45"It is written in the Prophets, 'God will teach
all of them.' *(Isaiah 54:13)* Everyone who listens to
the Father and learns from him comes to me.
46"No one has seen the Father except the One
who has come from God. Only he has seen the
Father. 47What I'm about to tell you is true. Everyone who believes has life forever.
48"I am the bread of life. 49Long ago your people
ate the manna in the desert, and they still died. 50But
here is the bread that comes down from heaven. A
person can eat it and not die. 51I am the living bread
that came down from heaven. Everyone who eats
some of this bread will live forever. The bread is
my body. I will give it for the life of the world."

52Then the Jews began to argue sharply among themselves. They said, "How can this man give us his body to eat?"

53Jesus said to them, "What I'm about to tell you is true. You must eat the Son of Man's body and drink his blood. If you don't, you have no life in you. 54Anyone who eats my body and drinks my blood has eternal life. I will raise him up on the last day.

55"My body is real food. My blood is real drink. 56Anyone who eats my body and drinks my blood remains in me. And I remain in him.

57"The living Father sent me, and I live because of him. In the same way, those who feed on me will live because of me. 58This is the bread that came down from heaven. Long ago your people ate manna and died. But those who feed on this bread will live forever."

59He said this while he was teaching in the synagogue in Capernaum.

Many Disciples Leave Jesus

60Jesus' disciples heard this. Many of them said, "This is a hard teaching. Who can accept it?"

61Jesus was aware that his disciples were complaining about his teaching. So he said to them, "Does this upset you? 62What if you see the Son of Man go up to where he was before? 63The Holy Spirit gives life. The body means nothing at all. The words I have spoken to you are from the Spirit. They give life. 64But there are some of you who do not believe."

Jesus had known from the beginning which of them did not believe. And he had known who was going to hand him over to his enemies. 65So he continued speaking. He said, "This is why I told you that no one can come to me unless the Father helps him."

66From this time on, many of his disciples turned back. They no longer followed him.

67"You don't want to leave also, do you?" Jesus asked the Twelve.

68Simon Peter answered him, "Lord, who can we go to? You have the words of eternal life. 69We believe and know that you are the Holy One of God."

70Then Jesus replied, "Didn't I choose you, the 12 disciples? But one of you is a devil!" 71He meant Judas, the son of Simon Iscariot. Judas was one of the Twelve. But later he was going to hand Jesus over to his enemies.

Jesus Goes to the Feast of Booths

7 After this, Jesus went around in Galilee. He stayed away from Judea on purpose. He knew that the Jews there were waiting to kill him.

2The Jewish Feast of Booths was near. 3Jesus' brothers said to him, "You should leave here and go to Judea. Then your disciples will see the kinds of things you do. 4No one who wants to be well known does things in secret. Since you are doing these things, show yourself to the world." 5Even Jesus' own brothers did not believe in him.

6So Jesus told them, "The right time has not yet come for me. For you, any time is right. 7The people of the world can't hate you. But they hate me. This is because I give witness that what they do is evil.

8"You go to the Feast. I am not yet going up to this Feast. For me, the right time has not yet come."

9After he said this, he stayed in Galilee.

10When his brothers had left for the Feast, he went also. But he went secretly, not openly. 11At the Feast the Jews were watching for him. They were asking, "Where is he?"

12Many people in the crowd were whispering about him. Some said, "He is a good man."

Others replied, "No. He fools the people."

13But no one would say anything about him openly. They were afraid of the Jews.

Jesus Teaches at the Feast

14Jesus did nothing until halfway through the Feast. Then he went up to the temple courtyard and began to teach. 15The Jews were amazed. They asked, "How did this man learn so much without studying?"

16Jesus answered, "What I teach is not my own. It comes from the One who sent me. 17Anyone who chooses to do what God wants him to do will find out whether my teaching comes from God or from me. 18Someone who speaks on his own does it to get honor for himself. But someone who works for the honor of the One who sent him is truthful. There is nothing false about him.

19"Didn't Moses give you the law? But not one of you keeps the law. Why are you trying to kill me?"

20"You are controlled by demons," the crowd answered. "Who is trying to kill you?"

21Jesus said to them, "I did one miracle, and you are all amazed. 22Moses gave you circumcision, and so you circumcise a child on the Sabbath day. But circumcision did not really come from Moses. It came from Abraham. 23You circumcise a child on the Sabbath day. You think that if you do, you won't break the law of Moses. Then why are you angry with me? I healed a whole man on the Sabbath!

24"Stop judging only by what you see. Judge correctly."

Is Jesus the Christ?

25Then some of the people of Jerusalem began asking questions. They said, "Isn't this the man some people are trying to kill? 26Here he is! He is speaking openly. They aren't saying a word to him. Have the authorities really decided that he is the Christ? 27But we know where this man is from. When the Christ comes, no one will know where he is from."

28Jesus was still teaching in the temple courtyard. He cried out, "Yes, you know me. And you know where I am from. I am not here on my own.

The One who sent me is true. You do not know
him. 29But I know him. I am from him, and he
sent me."
30When he said this, they tried to arrest him. But
no one laid a hand on him. His time had not yet
come.
31Still, many people in the crowd put their faith
in him. They said, "How will it be when the Christ
comes? Will he do more miraculous signs than this
man?"
32The Pharisees heard the crowd whispering
things like this about him. Then the chief priests
and the Pharisees sent temple guards to arrest him.
33Jesus said, "I am with you for only a short
time. Then I will go to the One who sent me. 34You
will look for me, but you won't find me. You can't
come where I am going."
35The Jews said to one another, "Where does
this man plan to go? Does he think we can't find
him? Will he go where our people live scattered
among the Greeks? Will he go there to teach the
Greeks? 36What did he mean when he said, 'You
will look for me, but you won't find me'? And,
'You can't come where I am going'?"
37It was the last and most important day of the
Feast. Jesus stood up and spoke in a loud voice.
He said, "Let anyone who is thirsty come to me
and drink. 38Does anyone believe in me? Then, just
as Scripture says, streams of living water will flow
from inside him."
39When he said this, he meant the Holy Spirit.
Those who believed in Jesus would receive the
Spirit later. Up to that time, the Spirit had not been
given. This was because Jesus had not yet received
glory.
40When some of the people heard his words,
they said, "This man must be the Prophet we've
been expecting."
41Others said, "He is the Christ."
Still others asked, "How can the Christ come
from Galilee? 42Doesn't Scripture say that the
Christ will come from David's family? Doesn't it
say that he will come from Bethlehem, the town
where David lived?"
43So the people did not agree about who Jesus
was. 44Some wanted to arrest him. But no one laid
a hand on him.

The Jewish Leaders Do Not Believe

45Finally the temple guards went back to the
chief priests and the Pharisees. They asked the
guards, "Why didn't you bring him in?"
46"No one ever spoke the way this man does,"
the guards replied.
47"You mean he has fooled you also?" the Pharisees asked. 48"Have any of the rulers or Pharisees
believed in him? 49No! But this mob knows nothing about the law. There is a curse on them."
50Then Nicodemus, a Pharisee, spoke. He was
the one who had gone to Jesus earlier. He asked,
51"Does our law find someone guilty without hearing him first? Doesn't it want to find out what he
is doing?"
52They replied, "Are you from Galilee too?
Look into it. You will find that a prophet does not
come out of Galilee."

53Then each of them went home.
8 But Jesus went to the Mount of Olives. 2At
sunrise he arrived in the temple courtyard
again. All the people gathered around him there.
He sat down to teach them.
3The teachers of the law and the Pharisees
brought in a woman. She had been caught in adultery. They made her stand in front of the group.
4They said to Jesus, "Teacher, this woman was
caught having sex with a man who was not her
husband. 5In the Law, Moses commanded us to kill
such women by throwing stones at them. Now
what do you say?" 6They were trying to trap Jesus
with that question. They wanted to have a reason
to bring charges against him.
But Jesus bent down and started to write on the
ground with his finger.
7They kept asking him questions. So he stood
up and said to them, "Has any one of you not
sinned? Then you be the first to throw a stone at
her."
8He bent down again and wrote on the ground.
9Those who heard what he had said began to go
away. They left one at a time, the older ones first.
Soon only Jesus was left. The woman was still
standing there.
10Jesus stood up and asked her, "Woman, where
are they? Hasn't anyone found you guilty?"
11"No one, sir," she said.
"Then I don't find you guilty either," Jesus said.
"Go now and leave your life of sin."

Jesus' Witness Is True

12Jesus spoke to the people again. He said, "I
am the light of the world. Those who follow me
will never walk in darkness. They will have the
light that leads to life."
13The Pharisees argued with him. "Here you
are," they said, "appearing as your own witness.
But your witness does not count."
14Jesus answered, "Even if I give witness about
myself, my witness does count. I know where I
came from. And I know where I am going. But you
have no idea where I come from or where I am
going. 15You judge by human standards. I don't
judge anyone.
16"But if I do judge, what I decide is right. This
is because I am not alone. I stand with the Father,
who sent me. 17Your own Law says that the witness of two is what counts. 18I give witness about
myself. My other witness is the Father, who
sent me."

19Then they asked him, "Where is your father?"

"You do not know me or my Father," Jesus replied. "If you knew me, you would know my Father also."

20He spoke these words while he was teaching in the temple area. He was near the place where the offerings were put. But no one arrested him. His time had not yet come.

21Once more Jesus spoke to them. "I am going away," he said. "You will look for me, and you will die in your sin. You can't come where I am going."

22This made the Jews ask, "Will he kill himself? Is that why he says, 'You can't come where I am going'?"

23But Jesus said, "You are from below. I am from heaven. You are from this world. I am not from this world. 24I told you that you would die in your sins. Do you believe that I am the one I claim to be? If you don't, you will certainly die in your sins."

25"Who are you?" they asked.

"Just what I have been claiming all along," Jesus replied. 26"I have a lot to say that will judge you. But the One who sent me can be trusted. And I tell the world what I have heard from him."

27They did not understand that Jesus was telling them about his Father. 28So Jesus said, "You will lift up the Son of Man. Then you will know that I am the one I claim to be. You will also know that I do nothing on my own. I speak just what the Father has taught me. 29The One who sent me is with me. He has not left me alone, because I always do what pleases him."

30Even while Jesus was speaking, many people put their faith in him.

The Children of Abraham

31Jesus spoke to the Jews who had believed him. "If you obey my teaching," he said, "you are really my disciples. 32Then you will know the truth. And the truth will set you free."

33They answered him, "We are Abraham's children. We have never been slaves of anyone. So how can you say that we will be set free?"

34Jesus replied, "What I'm about to tell you is true. Everyone who sins is a slave of sin. 35A slave has no lasting place in the family. But a son belongs to the family forever. 36So if the Son of Man sets you free, you will really be free.

37"I know you are Abraham's children. But you are ready to kill me. You have no room for my word. 38I am telling you what I saw when I was with my Father. You do what you have heard from your father."

39"Abraham is our father," they answered.

Jesus said, "Are you really Abraham's children? If you are, you will do the things Abraham did. 40But you have decided to kill me. I am a man who has told you the truth I heard from God. Abraham didn't do the things you want to do. 41You are doing the things your own father does."

"We are not children of people who weren't married to each other," they objected. "The only Father we have is God himself."

The Children of the Devil

42Jesus said to them, "If God were your Father, you would love me. I came from God, and now I am here. I have not come on my own. He sent me. 43"Why aren't my words clear to you? Because you can't really hear what I say. 44You belong to your father, the devil. You want to obey your father's wishes.

"From the beginning, the devil was a murderer. He has never obeyed the truth. There is no truth in him. When he lies, he speaks his natural language. He does this because he is a liar. He is the father of lies.

45"But because I tell the truth, you don't believe me! 46Can any of you prove I am guilty of sinning? Am I not telling the truth? Then why don't you believe me?

47"Everyone who belongs to God hears what God says. The reason you don't hear is that you don't belong to God."

Jesus Makes Claims About Himself

48The Jews answered Jesus, "Aren't we right when we say you are a Samaritan? Aren't you controlled by a demon?"

49"I am not controlled by a demon," said Jesus. "I honor my Father. You do not honor me. 50I am not seeking glory for myself. But there is One who brings glory to me. He is the judge. 51What I'm about to tell you is true. Anyone who obeys my word will never die."

52Then the Jews cried out, "Now we know you are controlled by a demon! Abraham died. So did the prophets. But you say that anyone who obeys your word will never die. 53Are you greater than our father Abraham? He died. So did the prophets. Who do you think you are?"

54Jesus replied, "If I bring glory to myself, my glory means nothing. You claim that my Father is your God. He is the one who brings glory to me. 55You do not know him. But I know him. If I said I did not, I would be a liar like you. But I do know him. And I obey his word.

56"Your father Abraham was filled with joy at the thought of seeing my day. He saw it and was glad."

57"You are not even 50 years old," the Jews said to Jesus. "And you have seen Abraham?"

58"What I'm about to tell you is true," Jesus answered. "Before Abraham was born, I am!"

59When he said this, they picked up stones to kill him. But Jesus hid himself. He slipped away from the temple area.

Jesus Heals a Man Born Blind

9 As Jesus went along, he saw a man who was blind. He had been blind since he was born. 2Jesus' disciples asked him, "Rabbi, who sinned?

Was this man born blind because he sinned? Or did his parents sin?"

[3]"It isn't because this man sinned," said Jesus. "It isn't because his parents sinned. This happened so that God's work could be shown in his life. [4]While it is still day, we must do the work of the One who sent me. Night is coming. Then no one can work. [5]While I am in the world, I am the light of the world."

[6]After he said this, he spit on the ground. He made some mud with the spit. Then he put the mud on the man's eyes.

[7]"Go," he told him. "Wash in the Pool of Siloam." Siloam means Sent.

So the man went and washed. And he came home able to see.

[8]His neighbors and those who had earlier seen him begging asked questions. "Isn't this the same man who used to sit and beg?" they asked.

[9]Some claimed that he was.

Others said, "No. He only looks like him."

But the man who had been blind kept saying, "I am the man."

[10]"Then how were your eyes opened?" they asked.

[11]He replied, "The man they call Jesus made some mud and put it on my eyes. He told me to go to Siloam and wash. So I went and washed. Then I could see."

[12]"Where is this man?" they asked him.

"I don't know," he said.

The Pharisees Want to Know What Happened

[13]They brought to the Pharisees the man who had been blind. [14]The day Jesus made the mud and opened the man's eyes was a Sabbath. [15]So the Pharisees also asked him how he was able to see.

"He put mud on my eyes," the man replied. "Then I washed. And now I can see."

[16]Some of the Pharisees said, "Jesus has not come from God. He does not keep the Sabbath day."

But others asked, "How can a sinner do such miraculous signs?"

So the Pharisees did not agree with each other.

[17]Finally they turned again to the blind man. "What do you have to say about him?" they asked. "It was your eyes he opened."

The man replied, "He is a prophet."

[18]The Jews still did not believe that the man had been blind and now could see. So they sent for his parents. [19]"Is this your son?" they asked. "Is this the one you say was born blind? How is it that now he can see?"

[20]"We know he is our son," the parents answered. "And we know he was born blind. [21]But we don't know how he can now see. And we don't know who opened his eyes. Ask him. He is an adult. He can speak for himself."

[22]His parents said this because they were afraid of the Jews. The Jews had already decided that anyone who said Jesus was the Christ would be put out of the synagogue. [23]That was why the man's parents said, "He is an adult. Ask him."

[24]Again they called the man who had been blind to come to them. "Give glory to God by telling the truth!" they said. "We know that the man who healed you is a sinner."

[25]He replied, "I don't know if he is a sinner or not. I do know one thing. I was blind, but now I can see!"

[26]Then they asked him, "What did he do to you? How did he open your eyes?"

[27]He answered, "I have already told you. But you didn't listen. Why do you want to hear it again? Do you want to become his disciples too?"

[28]Then they began to attack him with their words. "You are this fellow's disciple!" they said. "We are disciples of Moses! [29]We know that God spoke to Moses. But we don't even know where this fellow comes from."

[30]The man answered, "That is really surprising! You don't know where he comes from, and yet he opened my eyes. [31]We know that God does not listen to sinners. He listens to godly people who do what he wants them to do. [32]Nobody has ever heard of anyone opening the eyes of a person born blind. [33]If this man had not come from God, he could do nothing."

[34]Then the Pharisees replied, "When you were born, you were already deep in sin. How dare you talk like that to us!" And they threw him out of the synagogue.

The Blind Will See

[35]Jesus heard that the Pharisees had thrown the man out. When he found him, he said, "Do you believe in the Son of Man?"

[36]"Who is he, sir?" the man asked. "Tell me, so I can believe in him."

[37]Jesus said, "You have now seen him. In fact, he is the one speaking with you."

[38]Then the man said, "Lord, I believe." And he worshiped him.

[39]Jesus said, "I have come into this world to judge it. I have come so that the blind will see and those who see will become blind."

[40]Some Pharisees who were with him heard him say this. They asked, "What? Are we blind too?"

[41]Jesus said, "If you were blind, you would not be guilty of sin. But since you claim you can see, you remain guilty.

The Shepherd and the Flock

10 "What I'm about to tell you is true. What if someone does not enter the sheep pen through the gate but climbs in another way? That person is a thief and a robber. [2]The one who enters through the gate is the shepherd of the sheep. [3]The gatekeeper opens the gate for him. The sheep listen to his voice. He calls his own sheep by name and leads them out. [4]When he has brought all of his own sheep out, he goes on ahead of them. His sheep follow him because they know his voice. 5But they will never follow a stranger. In fact, they will run away from him. They don't recognize a stranger's voice."

6Jesus used this story. But the Jews who were there didn't understand what he was telling them.

7So Jesus said again, "What I'm about to tell you is true. I am like a gate for the sheep. 8All those who ever came before me were thieves and robbers. But the sheep did not listen to them. 9I'm like a gate. Anyone who enters through me will be saved. He will come in and go out. And he will find plenty of food. 10The thief comes only to steal and kill and destroy. I have come so they can have life. I want them to have it in the fullest possible way.

11"I am the good shepherd. The good shepherd gives his life for the sheep. 12The hired man is not the shepherd who owns the sheep. So when the hired man sees the wolf coming, he leaves the sheep and runs away. Then the wolf attacks the flock and scatters it. 13The man runs away because he is a hired man. He does not care about the sheep.

14"I am the good shepherd. I know my sheep, and my sheep know me. 15They know me just as the Father knows me and I know the Father. And I give my life for the sheep.

16"I have other sheep that do not belong to this sheep pen. I must bring them in too. They also will listen to my voice. Then there will be one flock and one shepherd.

17"The reason my Father loves me is that I give up my life. But I will take it back again. 18No one takes it from me. I give it up myself. I have the authority to give it up. And I have the authority to take it back again. I received this command from my Father."

19After Jesus spoke these words, the Jews again could not agree with each other. 20Many of them said, "He is controlled by a demon. He has gone crazy! Why should we listen to him?"

21But others said, "A person controlled by a demon does not say things like this. Can a demon open the eyes of someone who is blind?"

The Jews Do Not Believe

22Then came the Feast of Hanukkah at Jerusalem. It was winter. 23Jesus was in the temple area walking in Solomon's Porch. 24The Jews gathered around him. They said, "How long will you keep us waiting? If you are the Christ, tell us plainly."

25Jesus answered, "I did tell you. But you do not believe. The kinds of things I do in my Father's name speak for me. 26But you do not believe, because you are not my sheep.

27"My sheep listen to my voice. I know them, and they follow me. 28I give them eternal life, and they will never die. No one can steal them out of my hand. 29My Father, who has given them to me, is greater than anyone. No one can steal them out of my Father's hand. 30I and the Father are one."

31Again the Jews picked up stones to kill him. 32But Jesus said to them, "I have shown you many miracles from the Father. Which one of these are you throwing stones at me for?"

33"We are not throwing stones at you for any of these," replied the Jews. "We are stoning you for saying a very evil thing. You are only a man. But you claim to be God."

34Jesus answered them, "Didn't God say in your Law, 'I have said you are gods'? *(Psalm 82:6)* 35We know that Scripture is always true. God spoke to some people and called them 'gods.' 36If that is true, what about the One the Father set apart as his very own and sent into the world? Why do you charge me with saying a very evil thing? Is it because I said, 'I am God's Son'?

37"Don't believe me unless I do what my Father does. 38But what if I do it? Even if you don't believe me, believe the miracles. Then you will know and understand that the Father is in me and I am in the Father."

39Again they tried to arrest him. But he escaped from them.

40Then Jesus went back across the Jordan River. He went to the place where John had been baptizing in the early days. There he stayed. 41Many people came to him. They said, "John never did a miraculous sign. But everything he said about this man was true." 42And in that place many believed in Jesus.

Lazarus Dies

11 A man named Lazarus was sick. He was from Bethany, the village where Mary and her sister Martha lived. 2Mary would later pour perfume on the Lord. She would also wipe his feet with her hair. Her brother Lazarus was sick in bed. 3So the sisters sent a message to Jesus. "Lord," they told him, "the one you love is sick."

4When Jesus heard this, he said, "This sickness will not end in death. No, it is for God's glory. God's Son will receive glory because of it."

5Jesus loved Martha and her sister and Lazarus. 6But after he heard Lazarus was sick, he stayed where he was for two more days.

7Then he said to his disciples, "Let us go back to Judea."

8"But Rabbi," they said, "a short time ago the Jews tried to kill you with stones. Are you still going back there?"

9Jesus answered, "Aren't there 12 hours of daylight? A person who walks during the day won't trip and fall. He can see because of this world's light. 10But when he walks at night, he'll trip and fall. He has no light."

11After he said this, Jesus went on speaking to them. "Our friend Lazarus has fallen asleep," he said. "But I am going there to wake him up."

12His disciples replied, "Lord, if he's sleeping, he will get better."

13Jesus had been speaking about the death of Lazarus. But his disciples thought he meant natural sleep.

14 So then he told them plainly, "Lazarus is dead.
15 For your benefit, I am glad I was not there. Now
you will believe. But let us go to him."
16 Then Thomas, who was called Didymus,
spoke to the rest of the disciples. "Let us go also,"
he said. "Then we can die with Jesus."

Jesus Comforts the Sisters

17 When Jesus arrived, he found out that Lazarus had already been in the tomb for four days.
18 Bethany was less than two miles from Jerusalem.
19 Many Jews had come to Martha and Mary. They
had come to comfort them because their brother
was dead.
20 When Martha heard that Jesus was coming,
she went out to meet him. But Mary stayed at
home.
21 "Lord," Martha said to Jesus, "I wish you had
been here! Then my brother would not have died.
22 But I know that even now God will give you anything you ask for."
23 Jesus said to her, "Your brother will rise
again."
24 Martha answered, "I know he will rise again.
This will happen when people are raised from the
dead on the last day."
25 Jesus said to her, "I am the resurrection and
the life. Anyone who believes in me will live, even
if he dies. 26 And those who live and believe in me
will never die. Do you believe this?"
27 "Yes, Lord," she told him. "I believe that you
are the Christ, the Son of God. I believe that you
are the One who was supposed to come into the
world."
28 After she said this, she went back home. She
called her sister Mary to one side to talk to her.
"The Teacher is here," Martha said. "He is asking
for you."
29 When Mary heard this, she got up quickly and
went to him. 30 Jesus had not yet entered the village. He was still at the place where Martha had
met him. 31 Some Jews had been comforting Mary
in the house. They noticed how quickly she got up
and went out. So they followed her. They thought
she was going to the tomb to cry there.
32 Mary reached the place where Jesus was.
When she saw him, she fell at his feet. She said,
"Lord, I wish you had been here! Then my brother
would not have died."
33 Jesus saw her crying. He saw that the Jews
who had come along with her were crying also.
His spirit became very sad, and he was troubled.
34 "Where have you put him?" he asked.
"Come and see, Lord," they replied.
35 Jesus sobbed.
36 Then the Jews said, "See how much he loved
him!"
37 But some of them said, "He opened the eyes
of the blind man. Couldn't he have kept this man
from dying?"

Jesus Raises Lazarus From the Dead

38 Once more Jesus felt very sad. He came to the
tomb. It was a cave with a stone in front of the
entrance.
39 "Take away the stone," he said.
"But, Lord," said Martha, the sister of the dead
man, "by this time there is a bad smell. Lazarus
has been in the tomb for four days."
40 Then Jesus said, "Didn't I tell you that if you
believed, you would see God's glory?"
41 So they took away the stone.
Then Jesus looked up. He said, "Father, I thank
you for hearing me. 42 I know that you always hear
me. But I said this for the benefit of the people
standing here. I said it so they will believe that you
sent me."
43 Then Jesus called in a loud voice. He said,
"Lazarus, come out!"
44 The dead man came out. His hands and feet
were wrapped with strips of linen. A cloth was
around his face.
Jesus said to them, "Take off the clothes he was
buried in and let him go."

The Plan to Kill Jesus

45 Many of the Jews who had come to visit Mary
saw what Jesus did. So they put their faith in him.
46 But some of them went to the Pharisees. They
told the Pharisees what Jesus had done. 47 Then the
chief priests and the Pharisees called a meeting of
the Sanhedrin.
"What can we do?" they asked. "This man is
doing many miraculous signs. 48 If we let him keep
on doing this, everyone will believe in him. Then
the Romans will come. They will take away our
temple and our nation."
49 One of them spoke up. His name was Caiaphas. He was high priest at that time. He said, "You
don't know anything at all! 50 You don't realize
what is good for you. It is better if one man dies for
the people than if the whole nation is destroyed."
51 He did not say this on his own. But he was
high priest at that time. So he told ahead of time
that Jesus would die for the Jewish nation. 52 He
also prophesied that Jesus would die for God's
children scattered everywhere. He would die to
bring them together and make them one.
53 So from that day on, the Jewish rulers planned
to kill Jesus.
54 Jesus no longer moved around openly among
the Jews. Instead, he went away to an area near the
desert. He went to a village called Ephraim. There
he stayed with his disciples.
55 It was almost time for the Jewish Passover
Feast. Many people went up from the country to
Jerusalem. They went there for the special washing that would make them pure before the Passover Feast. 56 They kept looking for Jesus as they
stood in the temple area. They asked one another,
"What do you think? Isn't he coming to the Feast
at all?"

57But the chief priests and the Pharisees had
given orders. They had commanded anyone who
found out where Jesus was staying to report it.
Then they could arrest him.

Mary Pours Perfume on Jesus

12 It was six days before the Passover Feast.
Jesus arrived at Bethany, where Lazarus
lived. Lazarus was the one Jesus had raised from
the dead. 2A dinner was given at Bethany to honor
Jesus. Martha served the food. Lazarus was among
those at the table with Jesus.

3Then Mary took about a pint of pure nard. It
was an expensive perfume. She poured it on Jesus'
feet and wiped them with her hair. The house was
filled with the sweet smell of the perfume.

4But Judas Iscariot didn't like what Mary did.
He was one of Jesus' disciples. Later he was going
to hand Jesus over to his enemies. Judas said,
5"Why wasn't this perfume sold? Why wasn't the
money given to poor people? It was worth a year's
pay."

6He didn't say this because he cared about the
poor. He said it because he was a thief. Judas was
in charge of the money bag. He used to help himself to what was in it.

7"Leave her alone," Jesus replied. "The perfume was meant for the day I am buried. 8You will
always have the poor among you. But you won't
always have me."

9Meanwhile a large crowd of Jews found out
that Jesus was there, so they came. But they did
not come only because of Jesus. They also came
to see Lazarus. After all, Jesus had raised him from
the dead.

10So the chief priests made plans to kill Lazarus
too. 11Because of Lazarus, many of the Jews were
starting to follow Jesus. They were putting their
faith in him.

Jesus Enters Jerusalem

12The next day the large crowd that had come
for the Feast heard that Jesus was on his way to Jerusalem. 13So they took branches from palm trees
and went out to meet him. They shouted,

"Hosanna!"

"Blessed is the one who comes in the name
of the Lord!" *(Psalm 118:25,26)*

"Blessed is the King of Israel!"

14Jesus found a young donkey and sat on it. This
is just as it is written in Scripture. It says,

15"City of Zion, do not be afraid.
See, your king is coming.
He is sitting on a donkey's colt."
(Zechariah 9:9)

16At first, Jesus' disciples did not understand all
this. They realized it only after he had received
glory. Then they realized that these things had
been written about him. They realized that the people had done these things to him.

17A crowd had been with Jesus when he called
Lazarus from the tomb and raised him from the
dead. So they continued to tell everyone about
what had happened. 18Many people went out to
meet him. They had heard that he had done this
miraculous sign.

19So the Pharisees said to one another, "This
isn't getting us anywhere. Look how the whole
world is following him!"

Jesus Tells About His Coming Death

20There were some Greeks among the people
who went up to worship during the Feast. 21They
came to ask Philip for a favor. Philip was from
Bethsaida in Galilee.

"Sir," they said, "we would like to see Jesus."

22Philip went to tell Andrew. Then Andrew and
Philip told Jesus.

23Jesus replied, "The hour has come for the Son
of Man to receive glory. 24What I'm about to tell
you is true. Unless a grain of wheat falls to the
ground and dies, it remains only one seed. But if it
dies, it produces many seeds.

25"Anyone who loves his life will lose it. But
anyone who hates his life in this world will keep it
and have eternal life. 26Anyone who serves me
must follow me. And where I am, my servant will
also be. My Father will honor the one who
serves me.

27"My heart is troubled. What should I say?
'Father, save me from this hour'? No. This is the
very reason I came to this hour. 28Father, bring
glory to your name!"

Then a voice came from heaven. It said, "I have
brought glory to my name. I will bring glory to it
again."

29The crowd there heard the voice. Some said it
was thunder. Others said an angel had spoken to
Jesus.

30Jesus said, "This voice was for your benefit,
not mine. 31Now it is time for the world to be
judged. Now the prince of this world will be
thrown out. 32But I am going to be lifted up from
the earth. When I am, I will bring all people to
myself." 33He said this to show them how he was
going to die.

34The crowd spoke up. "The Law tells us that
the Christ will remain forever," they said. "So how
can you say, 'The Son of Man must be lifted up'?
Who is this 'Son of Man'?"

35Then Jesus told them, "You are going to have
the light just a little while longer. Walk while you
have the light. Do this before darkness catches up
with you. Anyone who walks in the dark does not
know where he is going. 36While you have the
light, put your trust in it. Then you can become
sons of light."

When Jesus had finished speaking, he left and
hid from them.

The Jews Still Do Not Believe

37Jesus had done all these miraculous signs in
front of them. But they still would not believe in
him. 38This happened as Isaiah the prophet had
said it would. He had said,

"Lord, who has believed what we've
been saying?
Who has seen the Lord's saving power?"
(Isaiah 53:1)

39For this reason, they could not believe. As Isaiah says in another place,

40"The Lord has blinded their eyes.
He has closed their minds.
So they can't see with their eyes.
They can't understand with their minds.
They can't turn to the Lord. If they could,
he would heal them." *(Isaiah 6:10)*

41Isaiah said this because he saw Jesus' glory and
spoke about him.
42At the same time that Jesus did those miracles,
many of the leaders believed in him. But because
of the Pharisees, they would not admit they
believed. They were afraid they would be thrown
out of the synagogue. 43They loved praise from
people more than praise from God.
44Then Jesus cried out, "Anyone who believes
in me does not believe in me only. He also believes
in the One who sent me. 45When he looks at me,
he sees the One who sent me.
46"I have come into the world to be a light. No
one who believes in me will stay in darkness.
47"I don't judge a person who hears my words
but does not obey them. I didn't come to judge the
world. I came to save it. 48But there is a judge for
anyone who does not accept me and my words.
The very words I have spoken will judge him on
the last day.
49"I did not speak on my own. The Father who
sent me commanded me what to say. He also told
me how to say it. 50I know that his command leads
to eternal life. So everything I say is just what the
Father has told me to say."

Jesus Washes His Disciples' Feet

13 It was just before the Passover Feast. Jesus
knew that the time had come for him to
leave this world. It was time for him to go to the
Father. Jesus loved his disciples who were in the
world. So he now showed them how much he
really loved them.
2The evening meal was being served. The devil
had already tempted Judas Iscariot, son of Simon.
He had told Judas to hand Jesus over to his enemies. 3Jesus knew that the Father had put everything under his power. He also knew he had come
from God and was returning to God.
4So he got up from the meal and took off his
outer clothes. He wrapped a towel around his
waist. 5After that, he poured water into a large
bowl. Then he began to wash his disciples' feet.
He dried them with the towel that was wrapped
around him.
6He came to Simon Peter.
"Lord," Peter said to him, "are you going to
wash my feet?"
7Jesus replied, "You don't realize now what I
am doing. But later you will understand."
8"No," said Peter. "You will never wash my
feet."
Jesus answered, "Unless I wash you, you can't
share life with me."
9"Lord," Simon Peter replied, "not just my feet!
Wash my hands and my head too!"
10Jesus answered, "A person who has had a bath
needs to wash only his feet. The rest of his body is
clean. And you are clean. But not all of you are."
11Jesus knew who was going to hand him over
to his enemies. That was why he said not every
one was clean.
12When Jesus finished washing their feet, he put
on his clothes. Then he returned to his place.
"Do you understand what I have done for you?"
he asked them. 13"You call me 'Teacher' and 'Lord.'
You are right. That is what I am. 14I, your Lord and
Teacher, have washed your feet. So you also should
wash one another's feet. 15I have given you an
example. You should do as I have done for you.
16"What I'm about to tell you is true. A servant
is not more important than his master. And a messenger is not more important than the one who
sends him. 17Now you know these things. So you
will be blessed if you do them.

Jesus Tells What Judas Will Do

18"I am not talking about all of you. I know
those I have chosen. But this will happen so that
Scripture will come true. It says, 'The one who
shares my bread has deserted me.' *(Psalm 41:9)*
19"I am telling you now, before it happens. When
it does happen, you will believe that I am he.
20What I'm about to tell you is true. Anyone who
accepts someone I send accepts me. And anyone
who accepts me accepts the One who sent me."
21After he had said this, Jesus' spirit was troubled. Here is the witness he gave. "What I'm about
to tell you is true," he said. "One of you is going
to hand me over to my enemies."
22His disciples stared at one another. They had
no idea which one of them he meant. 23The disciple Jesus loved was next to him at the table. 24Si-
mon Peter motioned to that disciple. He said, "Ask
Jesus which one he means."
25The disciple was leaning back against Jesus.
He asked him, "Lord, who is it?"
26Jesus answered, "It is the one I will give this
piece of bread to. I will give it to him after I have
dipped it in the dish."
He dipped the piece of bread. Then he gave it
to Judas Iscariot, son of Simon. 27As soon as Judas took the bread, Satan entered into him.

“Do quickly what you are going to do,” Jesus
told him.
28But no one at the meal understood why Jesus
said this to him. 29Judas was in charge of the
money. So some of the disciples thought Jesus was
telling him to buy what was needed for the Feast.
Others thought Jesus was talking about giving
something to poor people.
30As soon as Judas had taken the bread, he went
out. And it was night.

Jesus Says That Peter Will Fail

31After Judas was gone, Jesus spoke. He said,
“Now the Son of Man receives glory. And he
brings glory to God. 32If the Son brings glory to
God, God himself will bring glory to the Son. God
will do it at once.
33“My children, I will be with you only a little
longer. You will look for me. Just as I told the
Jews, so I am telling you now. You can’t come
where I am going.
34“I give you a new command. Love one
another. You must love one another, just as I have
loved you. 35If you love one another, everyone will
know you are my disciples.”
36Simon Peter asked him, “Lord, where are you
going?”
Jesus replied, “Where I am going you can’t follow now. But you will follow me later.”
37“Lord,” Peter asked, “why can’t I follow you
now? I will give my life for you.”
38Then Jesus answered, “Will you really give
your life for me? What I’m about to tell you is true.
Before the rooster crows, you will say three times
that you don’t know me!

Jesus Comforts His Disciples

14 “Do not let your hearts be troubled. Trust
in God. Trust in me also.
2“There are many rooms in my Father’s house.
If this were not true, I would have told you. I am
going there to prepare a place for you. 3If I go and
do that, I will come back. And I will take you to
be with me. Then you will also be where I am.
4“You know the way to the place where I am
going.”

Jesus Is the Way to the Father

5Thomas said to him, “Lord, we don’t know
where you are going. So how can we know the
way?”
6Jesus answered, “I am the way and the truth
and the life. No one comes to the Father except
through me. 7If you really knew me, you would
know my Father also. From now on, you do know
him. And you have seen him.”
8Philip said, “Lord, show us the Father. That
will be enough for us.”
9Jesus answered, “Don’t you know me, Philip?
I have been among you such a long time! Anyone
who has seen me has seen the Father. So how can
you say, ‘Show us the Father’?
10“Don’t you believe that I am in the Father?
Don’t you believe that the Father is in me? The
words I say to you are not just my own. The Father
lives in me. He is the One who is doing his work.
11Believe me when I say I am in the Father. Also
believe that the Father is in me. Or at least believe
what the miracles show about me.
12“What I’m about to tell you is true. Anyone
who has faith in me will do what I have been
doing. In fact, he will do even greater things. That
is because I am going to the Father.
13“And I will do anything you ask in my name.
Then the Son will bring glory to the Father. 14You
may ask me for anything in my name. I will do it.

The Father Will Send the Holy Spirit

15“If you love me, you will obey what I command. 16I will ask the Father. And he will give you
another Friend to help you and to be with you forever. 17The Friend is the Spirit of truth. The world
can’t accept him. That is because the world does
not see him or know him. But you know him. He
lives with you, and he will be in you.
18“I will not leave you like children who don’t
have parents. I will come to you.
19“Before long, the world will not see me anymore. But you will see me. Because I live, you will
live also. 20On that day you will realize that I am in
my Father. You will know that you are in me, and
I am in you.
21“Anyone who has my commands and obeys
them loves me. My Father will love the one who
loves me. I too will love him. And I will show
myself to him.”
22Then Judas spoke. “Lord,” he said, “why do
you plan to show yourself only to us? Why not
also to the world?” The Judas who spoke those
words was not Judas Iscariot.
23Jesus replied, “Anyone who loves me will
obey my teaching. My Father will love him. We
will come to him and make our home with him.
24Anyone who does not love me will not obey my
teaching. The words you hear me say are not my
own. They belong to the Father who sent me.
25“I have spoken all these things while I am still
with you. 26But the Father will send the Friend in
my name to help you. The Friend is the Holy
Spirit. He will teach you all things. He will remind
you of everything I have said to you.
27“I leave my peace with you. I give my peace
to you. I do not give it to you as the world does.
Do not let your hearts be troubled. And do not be
afraid.
28“You heard me say, ‘I am going away. And I
am coming back to you.’ If you loved me, you
would be glad I am going to the Father. The Father
is greater than I am. 29I have told you now before
it happens. Then when it does happen, you will
believe.
30“I will not speak with you much longer. The
prince of this world is coming. He has no power

over me. 31But the world must learn that I love the
Father. They must also learn that I do exactly what
my Father has commanded me to do.
"Come now. Let us leave.

The Vine and the Branches

15 "I am the true vine. My Father is the gardener. 2He cuts off every branch joined to
me that does not bear fruit. He trims every branch
that does bear fruit. Then it will bear even more
fruit.
3"You are already clean because of the word I
have spoken to you. 4Remain joined to me, and I
will remain joined to you. No branch can bear fruit
by itself. It must remain joined to the vine. In the
same way, you can't bear fruit unless you remain
joined to me.
5"I am the vine. You are the branches. If anyone
remains joined to me, and I to him, he will bear a
lot of fruit. You can't do anything without me. 6If
anyone does not remain joined to me, he is like a
branch that is thrown away and dries up. Branches
like those are picked up. They are thrown into the
fire and burned.
7"If you remain joined to me and my words
remain in you, ask for anything you wish. And it
will be given to you. 8When you bear a lot of fruit,
it brings glory to my Father. It shows that you are
my disciples.
9"Just as the Father has loved me, I have loved
you. Now remain in my love. 10If you obey my
commands, you will remain in my love. In the
same way, I have obeyed my Father's commands
and remain in his love. 11I have told you this so that
my joy will be in you. I also want your joy to be
complete.
12"Here is my command. Love each other, just
as I have loved you. 13No one has greater love than
the one who gives his life for his friends. 14You are
my friends if you do what I command.
15"I do not call you servants anymore. Servants
do not know their master's business. Instead, I
have called you friends. I have told you everything
I learned from my Father.
16"You did not choose me. Instead, I chose you.
I appointed you to go and bear fruit. It is fruit that
will last. Then the Father will give you anything
you ask for in my name.
17"Here is my command. Love each other.

The World Hates the Disciples

18"Does the world hate you? Remember that it
hated me first. 19If you belonged to the world, it
would love you like one of its own. But you do not
belong to the world. I have chosen you out of the
world. That is why the world hates you.
20"Remember the words I spoke to you. I said,
'A servant is not more important than his master.'
(John 13:16) If people hated me and tried to hurt
me, they will do the same to you. If they obeyed
my teaching, they will obey yours also. 21They will
treat you like that because of my name. They do
not know the One who sent me.
22"If I had not come and spoken to them, they
would not be guilty of sin. But now they have no
excuse for their sin. 23Those who hate me hate my
Father also.
24"I did miracles among them that no one else
did. If I hadn't, they would not be guilty of sin. But
now they have seen those miracles. And still they
have hated both me and my Father. 25This has happened so that what is written in their Law would
come true. It says, 'They hated me without any
reason.' *(Psalms 35:19; 69:4)*
26"I will send the Friend to you from the Father.
He is the Spirit of truth, who comes out from the
Father. When the Friend comes to help you, he will
give witness about me.
27"You also must give witness. This is because
you have been with me from the beginning.
16 "I have told you all of this so that you will
not go down the wrong path. 2You will be
thrown out of the synagogue. In fact, a time is
coming when those who kill you will think they
are doing God a favor. 3They will do things like
that because they do not know the Father or me.
4"Why have I told you this? So that when the
time comes, you will remember that I warned you.
I didn't tell you this at first because I was with you.

What the Holy Spirit Will Do

5"Now I am going to the One who sent me. But
none of you asks me, 'Where are you going?'
6Because I have said these things, you are filled
with sadness.
7"But what I'm about to tell you is true. It is for
your good that I am going away. Unless I go away,
the Friend will not come to help you. But if I go, I
will send him to you. 8When he comes, he will
prove that the world's people are guilty. He will
prove their guilt concerning sin and godliness and
judgment.
9"The world is guilty as far as sin is concerned.
That is because people do not believe in me. 10The
world is guilty as far as godliness is concerned.
That is because I am going to the Father, where you
can't see me anymore. 11The world is guilty as far
as judgment is concerned. That is because the devil,
the prince of this world, has already been judged.
12"I have much more to say to you. It is more
than you can handle right now. 13But when the
Spirit of truth comes, he will guide you into all
truth. He will not speak on his own. He will speak
only what he hears. And he will tell you what is
still going to happen.
14"He will bring me glory by receiving something from me and showing it to you. 15Everything
that belongs to the Father is mine. That is why I
said the Holy Spirit will receive something from
me and show it to you.
16"In a little while, you will no longer see me.
Then after a little while, you will see me."

The Disciples' Sadness Will Turn Into Joy

17Some of his disciples spoke to one another.
They said, "What does he mean by saying, 'In a little while, you will no longer see me. Then after a
little while, you will see me'? And what does he
mean by saying, 'I am going to the Father'?"
18They kept asking, "What does he mean by 'a little while'? We don't understand what he is saying."
19Jesus saw that they wanted to ask him about
those things. So he said to them, "Are you asking
one another what I meant? Didn't you understand
when I said, 'In a little while, you will no longer
see me. Then after a little while, you will see me'?
20What I'm about to tell you is true. You will cry
and be full of sorrow while the world is full of joy.
You will be sad, but your sadness will turn into joy.
21"A woman giving birth to a baby has pain.
This is because her time to give birth has come.
But when her baby is born, she forgets the pain.
She forgets because she is so happy that a baby has
been born into the world.
22"That's the way it is with you. Now it's your
time to be sad. But I will see you again. Then you
will be full of joy. And no one will take your joy
away.
23"When that day comes, you will no longer ask
me for anything. What I'm about to tell you is true.
My Father will give you anything you ask for in
my name. 24Until now you have not asked for anything in my name. Ask, and you will receive what
you ask for. Then your joy will be complete.
25"I have not been speaking to you plainly. But
a time is coming when I will speak clearly. Then I
will tell you plainly about my Father. 26When that
day comes, you will ask for things in my name. I
am not saying I will ask the Father instead of you
asking him. 27No, the Father himself loves you
because you have loved me. He also loves you
because you have believed that I came from God.
28"I came from the Father and entered the
world. Now I am leaving the world and going back
to the Father."
29Then Jesus' disciples said, "Now you are
speaking plainly. You are using examples that are
clear. 30Now we can see that you know everything.
You don't even need anyone to ask you questions.
This makes us believe that you came from God."
31"At last you believe!" Jesus said. 32"But a time
is coming when you will be scattered and go to
your own homes. In fact, that time is already here.
You will leave me all alone. But I am not really
alone. My Father is with me.
33"I have told you these things, so that you can
have peace because of me. In this world you will
have trouble. But cheer up! I have won the battle
over the world."

Jesus Prays for Himself

17 After Jesus said this, he looked toward
heaven and prayed. He said,
"Father, the time has come. Bring glory to
your Son. Then your Son will bring glory to
you. 2You gave him authority over all people. He gives eternal life to all those you
have given him.
3"And what is eternal life? It is knowing
you, the only true God, and Jesus Christ,
whom you have sent. 4I have brought you
glory on earth. I have finished the work you
gave me to do. 5So now, Father, give glory
to me in heaven where your throne is. Give
me the glory I had with you before the world
began.

Jesus Prays for His Disciples

6"I have shown you to the disciples you
gave me out of the world. They were yours.
You gave them to me. And they have obeyed
your word. 7Now they know that everything
you have given me comes from you. 8I gave
them the words you gave me. And they
accepted them. They knew for certain that I
came from you. They believed that you
sent me.
9"I pray for them. I am not praying for the
world. I am praying for those you have given
me, because they are yours. 10All I have is
yours, and all you have is mine. Glory has
come to me because of my disciples.
11"I will not remain in the world any
longer. But they are still in the world, and I
am coming to you. Holy Father, keep them
safe by the power of your name. It is the
name you gave me. Keep them safe so they
can be one, just as you and I are one.
12"While I was with them, I guarded them.
I kept them safe through the name you gave
me. None of them has been lost, except the
one who was sentenced to be destroyed. It
happened so that Scripture would come true.
13"I am coming to you now. But I say
these things while I am still in the world. I
say them so that those you gave me can have
all my joy inside them. 14I have given them
your word. The world has hated them. This is
because they are not part of the world any
more than I am. 15I do not pray that you will
take them out of the world. I pray that you
will keep them safe from the evil one.
16"They do not belong to the world, just
as I do not belong to it. 17Use the truth to
make them holy. Your word is truth. 18You
sent me into the world. In the same way, I
have sent them into the world. 19I make
myself holy for them so that they too can be
made holy in a true sense.

Jesus Prays for All Believers

20"I do not pray only for them. I pray also
for those who will believe in me because of
their message. 21Father, I pray that all of

them will be one, just as you are in me and I
am in you. I want them also to be in us. Then
the world will believe that you have sent me.
22"I have given them the glory you gave
me. I did this so they would be one, just as
we are one. 23I will be in them, just as you
are in me. I want them to be brought together
perfectly as one. This will let the world know
that you sent me. It will also show the world
that you have loved those you gave me, just
as you have loved me.
24"Father, I want those you have given me
to be with me where I am. I want them to see
my glory, the glory you have given me. You
gave it to me because you loved me before
the world was created.
25"Father, you are holy. The world does not
know you, but I know you. Those you have
given me know you have sent me. 26I have
shown you to them. And I will continue to
show you to them. Then the love you have for
me will be in them. I myself will be in them."

Jesus Is Arrested

18 When Jesus had finished praying, he left
with his disciples. They crossed the Kidron
Valley. On the other side there was a grove of olive
trees. Jesus and his disciples went into it.
2Judas knew the place. He was going to hand
Jesus over to his enemies. Jesus had often met in
that place with his disciples. 3So Judas came to the
grove. He was guiding a group of soldiers and
some officials. The chief priests and the Pharisees
had sent them. They were carrying torches,
lanterns and weapons.
4Jesus knew everything that was going to happen to him. So he went out and asked them, "Who
is it that you want?"
5"Jesus of Nazareth," they replied.
"I am he," Jesus said.
Judas, who was going to hand Jesus over, was
standing there with them. 6When Jesus said, "I am
he," they moved back. Then they fell to the ground.
7He asked them again, "Who is it that you
want?"
They said, "Jesus of Nazareth."
8"I told you I am he," Jesus answered. "If you
are looking for me, then let these men go." 9This
happened so that the words Jesus had spoken
would come true. He had said, "I have not lost
anyone God has given me." *(John 6:39)*
10Simon Peter had a sword and pulled it out. He
struck the high priest's servant and cut off his right
ear. The servant's name was Malchus.
11Jesus commanded Peter, "Put your sword
away! Shouldn't I drink the cup of suffering the
Father has given me?"

Jesus Is Taken to Annas

12Then the group of soldiers, their leader and the
Jewish officials arrested Jesus. They tied him up
13and brought him first to Annas. He was the
father-in-law of Caiaphas, the high priest at that
time. 14Caiaphas had advised the Jews that it
would be good if one man died for the people.

Peter Says He Is Not Jesus' Disciple

15Simon Peter and another disciple were following Jesus. The high priest knew the other disciple. So that disciple went with Jesus into the high
priest's courtyard. 16But Peter had to wait outside
by the door.
The other disciple came back. He was the one
the high priest knew. He spoke to the woman who
was on duty there. Then he brought Peter in.
17The woman at the door spoke to Peter. "You are
not one of Jesus' disciples, are you?" she asked him.
"I am not," he replied.
18It was cold. The servants and officials stood
around a fire. They had made it to keep warm. Peter was also standing with them. He was warming
himself.

The High Priest Questions Jesus

19Meanwhile, the high priest questioned Jesus.
He asked him about his disciples and his teaching.
20"I have spoken openly to the world," Jesus
replied. "I always taught in synagogues or at the
temple, where all the Jews come together. I didn't
say anything in secret. 21Why question me? Ask
the people who heard me. They certainly know
what I said."
22When Jesus said that, one of the officials
nearby hit him in the face. "Is this any way to
answer the high priest?" he asked.
23"Have I said something wrong?" Jesus
replied. "If I have, give witness to it. But if I spoke
the truth, why did you hit me?"
24While Jesus was still tied up, Annas sent him
to Caiaphas, the high priest.

Peter Again Says He Is Not Jesus' Disciple

25Simon Peter stood there. He was warming
himself. Then someone asked him, "You aren't
one of Jesus' disciples, are you?"
He said, "I am not."
26One of the high priest's servants was a relative of the man whose ear Peter had cut off. He
said to Peter, "Didn't I see you with Jesus in the
olive grove?"
27Again Peter said no.
At that very moment a rooster began to crow.

Jesus Is Brought to Pilate

28Then the Jews led Jesus from Caiaphas to the
palace of the Roman governor. By now it was
early morning. The Jews did not want to be made
"unclean." They wanted to be able to eat the Passover meal. So they did not enter the palace.
29Pilate came out to them. He asked, "What
charges are you bringing against this man?"

30 “He has committed crimes,” they replied. “If
he hadn’t, we would not have handed him over to
you.”
31 Pilate said, “Take him yourselves. Judge him
by your own law.”
“But we don’t have the right to put anyone to
death,” the Jews complained. 32 This happened so
that the words Jesus had spoken about how he was
going to die would come true.
33 Then Pilate went back inside the palace. He
ordered Jesus to be brought to him. Pilate asked
him, “Are you the king of the Jews?”
34 “Is that your own idea?” Jesus asked. “Or did
others talk to you about me?”
35 “Am I a Jew?” Pilate replied. “It was your
people and your chief priests who handed you over
to me. What have you done?”
36 Jesus said, “My kingdom is not part of this
world. If it were, those who serve me would fight.
They would try to keep the Jews from arresting
me. My kingdom is from another place.”
37 “So you are a king, then!” said Pilate.
Jesus answered, “You are right to say I am a
king. In fact, that’s the reason I was born. I came
into the world to give witness to the truth. Everyone who is on the side of truth listens to me.”
38 “What is truth?” Pilate asked.
Then Pilate went out again to the Jews. He said,
“I find no basis for any charge against him. 39 But
it is your practice for me to set one prisoner free
for you at Passover time. Do you want me to set
‘the king of the Jews’ free?”
40 They shouted back, “No! Not him! Give us
Barabbas!” Barabbas had taken part in an armed
struggle against the country’s rulers.

Jesus Is Sentenced to Be Crucified

19 Then Pilate took Jesus and had him
whipped. 2 The soldiers twisted thorns
together to make a crown. They put it on Jesus’
head. Then they put a purple robe on him. 3 They
went up to him again and again. They kept saying,
“We honor you, king of the Jews!” And they hit
him in the face.
4 Once more Pilate came out. He said to the
Jews, “Look, I am bringing Jesus out to you. I
want to let you know that I find no basis for a
charge against him.”
5 Jesus came out wearing the crown of thorns
and the purple robe. Then Pilate said to them,
“Here is the man!”
6 As soon as the chief priests and their officials
saw him, they shouted, “Crucify him! Crucify him!”
But Pilate answered, “You take him and crucify
him. I myself find no basis for a charge against
him.”
7 The Jews replied, “We have a law. That law says
he must die. He claimed to be the Son of God.”
8 When Pilate heard that, he was even more
afraid. 9 He went back inside the palace. “Where
do you come from?” he asked Jesus.
But Jesus did not answer him.
10 “Do you refuse to speak to me?” Pilate said.
“Don’t you understand? I have the power to set
you free or to nail you to a cross.”
11 Jesus answered, “You were given power from
heaven. If you weren’t, you would have no power
over me. So the one who handed me over to you is
guilty of a greater sin.”
12 From then on, Pilate tried to set Jesus free. But
the Jews kept shouting, “If you let this man go,
you are not Caesar’s friend! Anyone who claims
to be a king is against Caesar!”
13 When Pilate heard that, he brought Jesus out.
Pilate sat down on the judge’s seat. It was at a
place called The Stone Walkway. In the Aramaic
language it was called Gabbatha. 14 It was about
noon on Preparation Day in Passover Week.
“Here is your king,” Pilate said to the Jews.
15 But they shouted, “Kill him! Kill him! Crucify him!”
“Should I crucify your king?” Pilate asked.
“We have no king but Caesar,” the chief priests
answered.
16 Finally, Pilate handed Jesus over to them to be
nailed to a cross.

Jesus Is Nailed to a Cross

So the soldiers took charge of Jesus. 17 He had to
carry his own cross. He went out to a place called
The Skull. In the Aramaic language it was called
Golgotha. 18 There they nailed Jesus to the cross.
Two other men were crucified with him. One was
on each side of him. Jesus was in the middle.
19 Pilate had a notice prepared. It was fastened
to the cross. It read, JESUS OF NAZARETH, THE KING
OF THE JEWS. 20 Many of the Jews read the sign. The
place where Jesus was crucified was near the city.
The sign was written in the Aramaic, Latin and
Greek languages.
21 The chief priests of the Jews argued with Pilate.
They said, “Do not write ‘The King of the Jews.’
Write that this man claimed to be king of the Jews.”
22 Pilate answered, “I have written what I have
written.”
23 When the soldiers crucified Jesus, they took
his clothes. They divided them into four parts.
Each soldier got one part. Jesus’ long, inner robe
was left. It did not have any seams. It was made
out of one piece of cloth from top to bottom.
24 “Let’s not tear it,” they said to one another.
“Let’s cast lots to see who will get it.”
This happened so that Scripture would come
true. It says,

“They divided up my clothes among them.
They cast lots for what I was wearing.”
(Psalm 22:18)

So that is what the soldiers did.
25 Jesus’ mother stood near his cross. So did his
mother’s sister, Mary the wife of Clopas, and Mary
Magdalene.

26 Jesus saw his mother there. He also saw the
disciple he loved standing nearby. Jesus said to his
mother, "Dear woman, here is your son." 27 He said
to the disciple, "Here is your mother." From that
time on, the disciple took her into his home.

Jesus Dies

28 Later Jesus said, "I am thirsty." He knew that
everything was now finished. He knew that what
Scripture said must come true. 29 A jar of wine
vinegar was there. So they soaked a sponge in it.
They put the sponge on a stem of the hyssop plant.
Then they lifted it up to Jesus' lips.

30 After Jesus drank he said, "It is finished."
Then he bowed his head and died.

31 It was Preparation Day. The next day would be
a special Sabbath. The Jews did not want the bodies left on the crosses during the Sabbath. So they
asked Pilate to have the legs broken and the bodies
taken down. 32 The soldiers came and broke the legs
of the first man who had been crucified with Jesus.
Then they broke the legs of the other man.

33 But when they came to Jesus, they saw that he
was already dead. So they did not break his legs.
34 Instead, one of the soldiers stuck his spear into
Jesus' side. Right away, blood and water flowed
out. 35 The man who saw it has given witness. And
his witness is true. He knows that he tells the truth.
He gives witness so that you also can believe.

36 These things happened in order that Scripture
would come true. It says, "Not one of his bones
will be broken." *(Exodus 12:46; Numbers 9:12; Psalm
34:20)* 37 Scripture also says, "They will look to the
one they have pierced." *(Zechariah 12:10)*

Jesus Is Buried

38 Later Joseph asked Pilate for Jesus' body. Joseph
was from the town of Arimathea. He was a follower
of Jesus. But he followed Jesus secretly because he
was afraid of the Jews. After Pilate gave him permission, Joseph came and took the body away.

39 Nicodemus went with Joseph. He was the man
who had earlier visited Jesus at night. Nicodemus
brought some mixed spices, about 75 pounds.
40 The two men took Jesus' body. They wrapped it
in strips of linen cloth, along with the spices. That
was the way the Jews buried people's bodies.

41 At the place where Jesus was crucified, there
was a garden. A new tomb was there. No one had
ever been put in it before. 42 That day was the Jewish Preparation Day, and the tomb was nearby. So
they placed Jesus there.

The Tomb Is Empty

20 Early on the first day of the week, Mary
Magdalene went to the tomb. It was still
dark. She saw that the stone had been moved away
from the entrance. 2 So she ran to Simon Peter and
another disciple, the one Jesus loved. She said,
"They have taken the Lord out of the tomb! We
don't know where they have put him!"

3 So Peter and the other disciple started out for
the tomb. 4 Both of them were running. The other
disciple ran faster than Peter. He reached the tomb
first. 5 He bent over and looked in at the strips of
linen lying there. But he did not go in.

6 Then Simon Peter, who was behind him,
arrived. He went into the tomb. He saw the strips
of linen lying there. 7 He also saw the burial cloth
that had been around Jesus' head. The cloth was
folded up by itself. It was separate from the linen.

8 The disciple who had reached the tomb first
also went inside. He saw and believed. 9 They still
did not understand from Scripture that Jesus had
to rise from the dead.

Jesus Appears to Mary Magdalene

10 Then the disciples went back to their homes.
11 But Mary stood outside the tomb crying. As she
cried, she bent over to look into the tomb. 12 She saw
two angels dressed in white. They were seated where
Jesus' body had been. One of them was where Jesus'
head had been laid. The other sat where his feet had
been placed.

13 They asked her, "Woman, why are you
crying?"

"They have taken my Lord away," she said. "I
don't know where they have put him."

14 Then she turned around and saw Jesus standing there. But she didn't realize that it was Jesus.

15 "Woman," he said, "why are you crying? Who
are you looking for?"

She thought he was the gardener. So she said,
"Sir, did you carry him away? Tell me where you
put him. Then I will go and get him."

16 Jesus said to her, "Mary."

She turned toward him. Then she cried out in
the Aramaic language, "Rabboni!" Rabboni means
Teacher.

17 Jesus said, "Do not hold on to me. I have not
yet returned to the Father. Instead, go to those who
believe in me. Tell them, 'I am returning to my
Father and your Father, to my God and your
God.'"

18 Mary Magdalene went to the disciples with
the news. She said, "I have seen the Lord!" And
she told them that he had said these things to her.

Jesus Appears to His Disciples

19 On the evening of that first day of the week,
the disciples were together. They had locked the
doors because they were afraid of the Jews.

Jesus came in and stood among them. He said,
"May peace be with you!" 20 Then he showed them
his hands and his side. The disciples were very
happy when they saw the Lord.

21 Again Jesus said, "May peace be with you!
The Father has sent me. So now I am sending
you." 22 He then breathed on them. He said,
"Receive the Holy Spirit. 23 If you forgive anyone's
sins, they are forgiven. If you do not forgive them,
they are not forgiven."

Jesus Appears to Thomas

24 Thomas was one of the Twelve. He was called Didymus. He was not with the other disciples when Jesus came. 25 So they told him, "We have seen the Lord!"

But he said to them, "First I must see the nail marks in his hands. I must put my finger where the nails were. I must put my hand into his side. Only then will I believe what you say."

26 A week later, Jesus' disciples were in the house again. Thomas was with them. Even though the doors were locked, Jesus came in and stood among them.

He said, "May peace be with you!" 27 Then he said to Thomas, "Put your finger here. See my hands. Reach out your hand and put it into my side. Stop doubting and believe."

28 Thomas said to him, "My Lord and my God!"

29 Then Jesus told him, "Because you have seen me, you have believed. Blessed are those who have not seen me but still have believed."

30 Jesus did many other miraculous signs in front of his disciples. They are not written down in this book. 31 But these are written down so that you may believe that Jesus is the Christ, the Son of God. If you believe this, you will have life because you belong to him.

Jesus Does a Miracle at the Sea

21 After this, Jesus appeared to his disciples again. It was by the Sea of Galilee. Here is what happened.

2 Simon Peter and Thomas, who was called Didymus, were there together. Nathanael from Cana in Galilee and the sons of Zebedee were with them. So were two other disciples.

3 "I'm going out to fish," Simon Peter told them. They said, "We'll go with you." So they went out and got into the boat. That night they didn't catch anything.

4 Early in the morning, Jesus stood on the shore. But the disciples did not realize that it was Jesus.

5 He called out to them, "Friends, don't you have any fish?"

"No," they answered.

6 He said, "Throw your net on the right side of the boat. There you will find some fish."

When they did, they could not pull the net into the boat. There were too many fish in it.

7 Then the disciple Jesus loved said to Simon Peter, "It is the Lord!"

As soon as Peter heard that, he put his coat on. He had taken it off earlier. Then he jumped into the water.

8 The other disciples followed in the boat. They were towing the net full of fish. The shore was only about 100 yards away. 9 When they landed, they saw a fire of burning coals. There were fish on it. There was also some bread.

10 Jesus said to them, "Bring some of the fish you have just caught."

11 Simon Peter climbed into the boat. He dragged the net to shore. It was full of large fish. There were 153 of them. But even with that many fish the net was not torn.

12 Jesus said to them, "Come and have breakfast."

None of the disciples dared to ask him, "Who are you?" They knew it was the Lord.

13 Jesus came, took the bread and gave it to them. He did the same thing with the fish. 14 This was the third time Jesus appeared to his disciples after he was raised from the dead.

Jesus Takes Peter Back

15 When Jesus and the disciples had finished eating, Jesus spoke to Simon Peter. He asked, "Simon, son of John, do you really love me more than these others do?"

"Yes, Lord," he answered. "You know that I love you."

Jesus said, "Feed my lambs."

16 Again Jesus asked, "Simon, son of John, do you really love me?"

He answered, "Yes, Lord. You know that I love you."

Jesus said, "Take care of my sheep."

17 Jesus spoke to him a third time. He asked, "Simon, son of John, do you love me?"

Peter felt bad because Jesus asked him the third time, "Do you love me?" He answered, "Lord, you know all things. You know that I love you."

Jesus said, "Feed my sheep. 18 What I'm about to tell you is true. When you were younger, you dressed yourself. You went wherever you wanted to go. But when you are old, you will stretch out your hands. Someone else will dress you. Someone else will lead you where you do not want to go."

19 Jesus said this to point out how Peter would die. His death would bring glory to God.

Then Jesus said to him, "Follow me!"

20 Peter turned around. He saw that the disciple Jesus loved was following them. He was the one who had leaned back against Jesus at the supper. He had said, "Lord, who is going to hand you over to your enemies?" 21 When Peter saw that disciple, he asked, "Lord, what will happen to him?"

22 Jesus answered, "Suppose I want him to remain alive until I return. What does that matter to you? You must follow me."

23 Because of what Jesus said, a false report spread among the believers. The story was told that the disciple Jesus loved wouldn't die. But Jesus did not say he would not die. He only said, "Suppose I want him to remain alive until I return. What does that matter to you?"

24 This is the disciple who gives witness to these things. He also wrote them down. We know that his witness is true.

25 Jesus also did many other things. What if every one of them were written down? I suppose that even the whole world would not have room for the books that would be written.

Acts

Jesus Is Taken Up Into Heaven

1 Theophilus, I wrote about Jesus in my earlier book. I wrote about all he did and taught [2]until the day he was taken up to heaven. Before Jesus left, he gave orders to the apostles he had chosen. He did this through the Holy Spirit. [3]After his suffering and death, he appeared to them. In many ways he proved that he was alive. He appeared to them over a period of 40 days. During that time he spoke about God's kingdom.

[4]One day Jesus was eating with them. He gave them a command. "Do not leave Jerusalem," he said. "Wait for the gift my Father promised. You have heard me talk about it. [5]John baptized with water. But in a few days you will be baptized with the Holy Spirit."

[6]When the apostles met together, they asked Jesus a question. "Lord," they said, "are you going to give the kingdom back to Israel now?"

[7]He said to them, "You should not be concerned about times or dates. The Father has set them by his own authority. [8]But you will receive power when the Holy Spirit comes on you. Then you will be my witnesses in Jerusalem. You will be my witnesses in all Judea and Samaria. And you will be my witnesses from one end of the earth to the other."

[9]After Jesus said this, he was taken up to heaven. They watched until a cloud hid him from their sight.

[10]While he was going up, they kept on looking at the sky. Suddenly two men dressed in white clothing stood beside them. [11]"Men of Galilee," they said, "why do you stand here looking at the sky? Jesus has been taken away from you into heaven. But he will come back in the same way you saw him go."

Matthias Is Chosen to Take the Place of Judas

[12]The apostles returned to Jerusalem from the Mount of Olives. It is almost a mile from the city. [13]When they arrived, they went upstairs to the room where they were staying. Peter, John, James and Andrew were there. Philip, Thomas, Bartholomew and Matthew were there too. So were James, son of Alphaeus, Simon the Zealot, and Judas, son of James. [14]They all came together regularly to pray. The women joined them too. So did Jesus' mother Mary and his brothers.

[15]In those days Peter stood up among the believers. About 120 of them were there. [16]Peter said, "Brothers, a long time ago the Holy Spirit spoke through David's mouth about Judas. What he said in Scripture had to come true. Judas was the guide for the men who arrested Jesus. [17]But Judas was one of us. He shared with us in our work for God."

[18]Judas bought a field with the reward he got for the evil thing he had done. He fell down headfirst in the field. His body burst open. All his insides spilled out. [19]Everyone in Jerusalem heard about this. So they called that field Akeldama. In their language, Akeldama means The Field of Blood.

[20]Peter said, "Here is what is written in the book of Psalms. It says,

"'May his home be deserted.
May no one live in it.' *(Psalm 69:25)*

The Psalms also say,

"'Let someone else take his place as leader.' *(Psalm 109:8)*

[21]So we need to choose someone to take his place. It will have to be a man who was with us the whole time the Lord Jesus lived among us. [22]That time began when John was baptizing. It ended when Jesus was taken up from us. The one we choose must join us in giving witness that Jesus rose from the dead."

[23]So they suggested two men. One was Joseph, who was called Barsabbas. He was also called Justus. The other man was Matthias. [24]Then they prayed. "Lord," they said, "you know everyone's heart. Show us which of these two you have chosen. [25]Show us who should take the place of Judas as an apostle. He gave up being an apostle to go where he belongs." [26]Then they cast lots. Matthias was chosen. So he was added to the 11 apostles.

The Holy Spirit Comes at Pentecost

2 The day of Pentecost came. The believers all gathered in one place. [2]Suddenly a sound came from heaven. It was like a strong wind blowing. It filled the whole house where they were sitting. [3]They saw something that looked like tongues of fire. The flames separated and settled on each of them. [4]All of them were filled with the Holy Spirit. They began to speak in languages they had not known before. The Spirit gave them the ability to do this.

[5]Godly Jews from every country in the world were staying in Jerusalem. [6]A crowd came together when they heard the sound. They were bewildered because they each heard the believers speaking in their own language. [7]The crowd was really amazed. They asked, "Aren't all these people from Galilee? [8]Why, then, do we each hear them speaking in our own native language? [9]We are Parthians, Medes and Elamites. We live in Mesopotamia, Judea and Cappadocia. We are from Pontus, Asia, [10]Phrygia and Pamphylia. Others of us are from Egypt and the parts of Libya near Cyrene. Still others are visitors from Rome. [11]Some

of the visitors are Jews. Others have accepted the Jewish faith. Also, Cretans and Arabs are here. We hear all these people speaking about God's wonders in our own languages!" 12They were amazed and bewildered. They asked one another, "What does this mean?"

13But some people in the crowd made fun of the believers. "They've had too much wine!" they said.

Peter Speaks to the Crowd

14Then Peter stood up with the Eleven. In a loud voice he spoke to the crowd. "My Jewish friends," he said, "let me explain this to you. All of you who live in Jerusalem, listen carefully to what I say. 15You think these people are drunk. But they aren't. It's only nine o'clock in the morning! 16No, here is what the prophet Joel meant. 17He said,

"'In the last days, God says,
I will pour out my Holy Spirit on all people.
Your sons and daughters will prophesy.
Your young men will see visions.
Your old men will have dreams.
18 In those days I will pour out my Spirit
even on those who serve me, both men and women.
When I do, they will prophesy.
19 I will show wonders in the heavens above.
I will show miraculous signs on the earth below.
There will be blood and fire and clouds of smoke.
20 The sun will become dark.
The moon will turn red like blood.
This will happen before the coming of the great and glorious day of the Lord.
21 Everyone who calls
on the name of the Lord will be saved.'
(Joel 2:28–32)

22"Men of Israel, listen to this! Jesus of Nazareth was a man who had God's approval. God did miracles, wonders and signs among you through Jesus. You yourselves know this. 23Long ago God planned that Jesus would be handed over to you. With the help of evil people, you put Jesus to death. You nailed him to the cross. 24But God raised him from the dead. He set him free from the suffering of death. It wasn't possible for death to keep its hold on Jesus. 25David spoke about him. He said,

"'I know that the Lord is always with me.
He is at my right hand.
I will always be secure.
26 So my heart is glad. Joy is on my tongue.
My body also will be full of hope.
27 You will not leave me in the grave.
You will not let your Holy One rot away.
28 You always show me the path that leads to life.
You will fill me with joy when I am with you.'
(Psalm 16:8–11)

29"Brothers, you can be sure that King David died. He was buried. His tomb is still here today. 30But David was a prophet. He knew that God had made a promise to him. He had taken an oath that someone in David's family line would be king after him. 31David saw what was ahead. So he spoke about the Christ rising from the dead. He said that the Christ would not be left in the grave. His body wouldn't rot in the ground. 32God has raised this same Jesus back to life. We are all witnesses of this. 33Jesus has been given a place of honor at the right hand of God. He has received the Holy Spirit from the Father. This is what God had promised. It is Jesus who has poured out what you now see and hear. 34David did not go up to heaven. But he said,

"'The Lord said to my Lord,
"Sit at my right hand.
35 I will put your enemies
under your control."'
(Psalm 110:1)

36"So be sure of this, all you people of Israel. You nailed Jesus to the cross. But God has made him both Lord and Christ."

37When the people heard this, their hearts were filled with shame. They said to Peter and the other apostles, "Brothers, what should we do?"

38Peter replied, "All of you must turn away from your sins and be baptized in the name of Jesus Christ. Then your sins will be forgiven. You will receive the gift of the Holy Spirit. 39The promise is for you and your children. It is also for all who are far away. It is for all whom the Lord our God will choose."

40Peter said many other things to warn them. He begged them, "Save yourselves from these evil people." 41Those who accepted his message were baptized. About 3,000 people joined the believers that day.

The Believers Share Life Together

42The believers studied what the apostles taught. They shared life together. They broke bread and ate together. And they prayed. 43Everyone felt that God was near. The apostles did many wonders and miraculous signs. 44All the believers were together. They shared everything they had. 45They sold what they owned. They gave each other everything they needed. 46Every day they met together in the temple courtyard. In their homes they broke bread and ate together. Their hearts were glad and honest and true. 47They praised God. They were respected by all the people. Every day the Lord added to their group those who were being saved.

Peter Heals the Disabled Beggar

3 One day Peter and John were going up to the temple. It was three o'clock in the afternoon. It was the time for prayer. 2A man unable to walk was being carried to the temple gate called Beautiful. He had been that way since he was born.

Every day someone put him near the gate. There he would beg from people going into the temple courtyards.

3He saw that Peter and John were about to enter. So he asked them for money. 4Peter looked straight at him, and so did John. Then Peter said, "Look at us!" 5So the man watched them closely. He expected to get something from them.

6Peter said, "I don't have any silver or gold. But I'll give you what I have. In the name of Jesus Christ of Nazareth, get up and walk." 7Then Peter took him by the right hand and helped him up. At once the man's feet and ankles became strong. 8He jumped to his feet and began to walk. He went with Peter and John into the temple courtyards. He walked and jumped and praised God. 9All the people saw him walking and praising God. 10They recognized him as the same man who used to sit and beg at the temple gate called Beautiful. They were filled with wonder. They were amazed at what had happened to him.

Peter Speaks to the Jews

11The beggar was holding on to Peter and John. All the people were amazed. They came running to them at Solomon's Porch. 12When Peter saw this, he said, "Men of Israel, why does this surprise you? Why do you stare at us? We haven't made this man walk by our own power or godliness. 13The God of our fathers, Abraham, Isaac and Jacob, has done this. He has brought glory to Jesus, who serves him. But you handed Jesus over to be killed. Pilate had decided to let him go. But you spoke against Jesus when he was in Pilate's court. 14You spoke against the Holy and Blameless One. You asked for a murderer to be set free instead. 15You killed the one who gives life. But God raised him from the dead. We are witnesses of this. 16This man whom you see and know was made strong because of faith in Jesus' name. Faith in Jesus has healed him completely. You can see it with your own eyes.

17"My friends, I know you didn't realize what you were doing. Neither did your leaders. 18But God had given a promise through all the prophets. And this is how he has made his promise come true. He said that his Christ would suffer. 19So turn away from your sins. Turn to God. Then your sins will be wiped away. The time will come when the Lord will make everything new. 20He will send the Christ. Jesus has been appointed as the Christ for you. 21He must remain in heaven until the time when God makes everything new. He promised this long ago through his holy prophets. 22Moses said, 'The Lord your God will raise up for you a prophet like me. He will be one of your own people. You must listen to everything he tells you. 23Those who do not listen to him will be completely cut off from their people.' *(Deuteronomy 18:15,18,19)*

24"Samuel and all the prophets after him spoke about this. They said these days would come. 25What the prophets said was meant for you. The covenant God made with your people long ago is yours also. He said to Abraham, 'All nations on earth will be blessed through your children.' *(Genesis 22:18; 26:4)* 26God raised up Jesus, who serves him. God sent him first to you. He did it to bless you. He wanted to turn each of you from your evil ways."

Peter and John Are Taken to the Sanhedrin

4 Peter and John were speaking to the people. The priests, the captain of the temple guard, and the Sadducees came up to the apostles. 2They were very upset by what the apostles were teaching the people. The apostles were saying that because Jesus rose from the dead, people can be raised from the dead. 3So the temple authorities arrested Peter and John. It was already evening, so they put them in prison until the next day. 4But many who heard the message believed. The number of men who believed grew to about 5,000.

5The next day the rulers, the elders and the teachers of the law met in Jerusalem. 6Annas, the high priest, was there. So were Caiaphas, John, Alexander and others in the high priest's family. 7They had Peter and John brought to them. They wanted to question them. "By what power did you do this?" they asked. "And through whose name?"

8Peter was filled with the Holy Spirit. He said to them, "Rulers and elders of the people! 9Are you asking us to explain our actions today? Do you want to know why we were kind to a disabled man? Are you asking how he was healed? 10Then listen to this, you and all the people of Israel! You nailed Jesus Christ of Nazareth to the cross. But God raised him from the dead. It is through Jesus' name that this man stands healed in front of you. 11Scripture says that Jesus is

"'the stone you builders did not accept.
But it has become the most important stone
of all.' *(Psalm 118:22)*

12You can't be saved by believing in anyone else. God has given us no other name under heaven that will save us."

13The leaders saw how bold Peter and John were. They also realized that Peter and John were ordinary men with no training. This surprised the leaders. They realized that these men had been with Jesus. 14The leaders could see the man who had been healed standing there with them. So there was nothing they could say. 15They ordered Peter and John to leave the Sanhedrin. Then they talked things over. 16"What can we do with these men?" they asked. "Everybody in Jerusalem knows they have done an outstanding miracle. We can't say it didn't happen. 17We have to stop this thing. It must not spread any further among the people. We have to warn these men. They must never speak to anyone in Jesus' name again."

18Once again the leaders called in Peter and John. They commanded them not to speak or teach at all in Jesus' name. 19But Peter and John replied, "Judge for yourselves. Which is right from God's point of view? Should we obey you? Or God? 20There's nothing else we can do. We have to speak about the things we've seen and heard."

21The leaders warned them again. Then they let them go. They couldn't decide how to punish Peter and John. They knew that all the people were praising God for what had happened. 22The man who had been healed by the miracle was over 40 years old.

The Believers Pray

23Peter and John were allowed to leave. They went back to their own people. They reported everything the chief priests and the elders had said to them. 24When the believers heard this, they raised their voices together in prayer to God. "Lord and King," they said, "you made the heavens, the earth and the sea. You made everything in them. 25Long ago you spoke by the Holy Spirit through the mouth of our father David, who served you. You said,

"'Why are the nations angry?
Why do the people make useless plans?
26The kings of the earth take their stand against
the Lord.
The rulers of the earth gather together
against his Anointed King.' *(Psalm 2:1,2)*

27"In fact, Herod and Pontius Pilate met together in this city with those who weren't Jews. They also met with the people of Israel. All of them made plans against your holy servant Jesus. He is the one you anointed. 28They did what your power and purpose had already decided should happen. 29Now, Lord, consider the bad things they say they are going to do. Help us to be very bold when we speak your word. 30Stretch out your hand to heal. Do miraculous signs and wonders through the name of your holy servant Jesus."

31After they prayed, the place where they were meeting was shaken. They were all filled with the Holy Spirit. They were bold when they spoke God's word.

The Believers Share What They Own

32All the believers were agreed in heart and mind. They didn't claim that anything they had was their own. They shared everything they owned. 33With great power the apostles continued their teaching. They gave witness that the Lord Jesus had risen from the dead. And they were greatly blessed by God.

34There were no needy persons among them. From time to time, those who owned land or houses sold them. They brought the money from the sales. 35They put it down at the apostles' feet. It was then given out to anyone who needed it.

36Joseph was a Levite from Cyprus. The apostles called him Barnabas. The name Barnabas means Son of Help. 37Barnabas sold a field he owned. He brought the money from the sale. He put it down at the apostles' feet.

Ananias and Sapphira

5 A man named Ananias and his wife, Sapphira, also sold some land. 2He kept part of the money for himself. Sapphira knew he had kept it. He brought the rest of it and put it down at the apostles' feet.

3Then Peter said, "Ananias, why did you let Satan fill your heart? He made you lie to the Holy Spirit. You have kept some of the money you received for the land. 4Didn't the land belong to you before it was sold? After it was sold, you could have used the money as you wished. What made you think of doing such a thing? You haven't lied to just anyone. You've lied to God."

5When Ananias heard this, he fell down and died. All who heard what had happened were filled with fear. 6Some young men came and wrapped up his body. They carried him out and buried him.

7About three hours later, the wife of Ananias came in. She didn't know what had happened. 8Peter asked her, "Tell me. Is this the price you and Ananias sold the land for?"

"Yes," she said. "That's the price."

9Peter asked her, "How could you agree to test the Spirit of the Lord? Listen! You can hear the steps of the men who buried your husband. They are at the door. They will carry you out also."

10At that very moment she fell down at his feet and died. Then the young men came in. They saw that Sapphira was dead. So they carried her out and buried her beside her husband. 11The whole church and all who heard about these things were filled with fear.

The Apostles Heal Many People

12The apostles did many miraculous signs and wonders among the people. All the believers used to meet together at Solomon's Porch. 13No outsider dared to join them. But the people thought highly of them. 14More and more men and women believed in the Lord. They joined the other believers. 15So people brought those who were sick into the streets. They placed them on beds and mats. They hoped that at least Peter's shadow might fall on some of them as he walked by. 16Crowds even gathered from the towns around Jerusalem. They brought their sick. They also brought those who were suffering because of evil spirits. All of them were healed.

An Angel Opens the Prison Doors

17The high priest and all his companions were Sadducees. They were very jealous of the apostles. 18So they arrested them and put them in the public prison. 19But during the night an angel of the Lord

came. He opened the prison doors and brought the
apostles out. 20“Go! Stand in the temple courtyard,” the angel said. “Tell the people all about this
new life.”
21Early the next day they did as they had been
told. They entered the temple courtyard. There
they began to teach the people.
The high priest and his companions arrived.
They called the Sanhedrin together. The Sanhedrin
was a gathering of all the elders of Israel. They sent
for the apostles who were in prison. 22The officers
arrived at the prison. But they didn’t find the apostles there. So they went back and reported it. 23“We
found the prison locked up tight,” they said. “The
guards were standing at the doors. But when we
opened the doors, we didn’t find anyone inside.”
24When the captain of the temple guard and the
chief priests heard this report, they were bewildered. They wondered what would happen next.
25Then someone came and said, “Look! The
men you put in prison are standing in the temple
courtyard. They are teaching the people.” 26So the
captain went with his officers and brought the
apostles back. But they didn’t use force. They
were afraid the people would kill them by throwing stones at them.
27They brought the apostles to be judged by the
Sanhedrin. The high priest questioned them. 28“We
gave you clear orders not to teach in Jesus’ name,”
he said. “But you have filled Jerusalem with your
teaching. You want to make us guilty of this man’s
death.”
29Peter and the other apostles replied, “We must
obey God instead of people! 30You had Jesus killed
by nailing him to a cross. But the God of our people raised Jesus from the dead. 31Now Jesus is
Prince and Savior. God has proved this by giving
him a place of honor at his own right hand. He did
it so that he could turn Israel away from their sins
and forgive them. 32We are witnesses of these
things. And so is the Holy Spirit. God has given
the Spirit to those who obey him.”
33When the leaders heard this, they became very
angry. They wanted to put the apostles to death.
34But a Pharisee named Gamaliel stood up in the
Sanhedrin. He was a teacher of the law. He was
honored by all the people. He ordered the men to be
taken outside for a little while. 35Then he spoke to
the Sanhedrin. “Men of Israel,” he said, “think carefully about what you plan to do to these men.
36Some time ago Theudas appeared. He claimed he
was really somebody. About 400 people followed
him. But he was killed. All his followers were scattered. So they accomplished nothing. 37After this,
Judas from Galilee came along. This was in the
days when the Romans made a list of all the people. Judas led a gang of men against the Romans.
He too was killed. All his followers were scattered.
38So let me give you some advice. Leave these men
alone! Let them go! If their plans and actions are
only human, they will fail. 39But if their plans come
from God, you won’t be able to stop these men. You
will only find yourselves fighting against God.”
40His speech won the leaders over. They called
the apostles in and had them whipped. The leaders ordered them not to speak in Jesus’ name. Then
they let the apostles go.
41The apostles were full of joy as they left the
Sanhedrin. They considered it an honor to suffer
shame for the name of Jesus. 42Day after day, they
kept teaching in the temple courtyards and from
house to house. They never stopped telling the
good news that Jesus is the Christ.

Seven Leaders Are Chosen

6 In those days the number of believers was
growing. The Jews who followed Greek practices complained against the Jews who followed
only Jewish practices. They said that the widows
of men who followed Greek practices were not
being taken care of. They weren’t getting their fair
share of food each day. 2So the Twelve gathered
all the believers together. They said, “It wouldn’t
be right for us to give up teaching God’s word in
order to wait on tables. 3Brothers, choose seven of
your men. They must be known as men who are
wise and full of the Holy Spirit. We will turn this
important work over to them. 4Then we can give
our attention to prayer and to teaching the word.”
5This plan pleased the whole group. They chose
Stephen. He was full of faith and of the Holy Spirit.
Philip, Procorus, Nicanor, Timon and Parmenas
were chosen too. The group also chose Nicolas
from Antioch. He had accepted the Jewish faith.
6The group brought them to the apostles. Then the
apostles prayed and placed their hands on them.
7So God’s word spread. The number of believers in Jerusalem grew quickly. Also, a large number of priests began to obey Jesus’ teachings.

Stephen Is Arrested

8Stephen was full of God’s grace and power. He
did great wonders and miraculous signs among the
people. 9But members of the group called the Synagogue of the Freedmen began to oppose him.
Some of them were Jews from Cyrene and Alexandria. Others were Jews from Cilicia and Asia
Minor. They all began to argue with Stephen. 10But
he was too wise for them. They couldn’t stand up
against the Holy Spirit who spoke through him.
11Then in secret they talked some men into
lying about Stephen. They said, “We heard Stephen speak evil things against Moses. He also
spoke evil things against God.”
12So the people were stirred up. The elders and
the teachers of the law were stirred up too. They
arrested Stephen and brought him to the Sanhedrin. 13They found people who were willing to tell
lies. The false witnesses said, “This fellow never
stops speaking against this holy place. He also
speaks against the law. 14We have heard him say
that this Jesus of Nazareth will destroy this place.

He says Jesus will change the practices that Moses handed down to us."
15 All who were sitting in the Sanhedrin looked
right at Stephen. They saw that his face was like
the face of an angel.

Stephen Speaks to the Sanhedrin

7 Then the high priest questioned Stephen. "Is
what these people are saying true?" he asked.
2 "Brothers and fathers, listen to me!" Stephen
replied. "The God of glory appeared to our father
Abraham. At that time Abraham was still in Mesopotamia. He had not yet begun living in Haran.
3 'Leave your country and your people,' God said.
'Go to the land I will show you.' *(Genesis 12:1)*
4 "So Abraham left the land of Babylonia. He settled in Haran. After his father died, God sent Abraham to this land where you are now living. 5 God
didn't give him any property here. He didn't give
him even a foot of land. But God made a promise
to him and to all his family after him. He said they
would possess the land. The promise was made
even though at that time Abraham had no child.
6 "Here is what God said to him. 'Your family
after you will be strangers in a country that is not
their own. They will be slaves and will be treated
badly for 400 years. 7 But I will punish the nation
that makes them slaves,' God said. 'After that, they
will leave that country and worship me here.'
(Genesis 15:13,14)
8 "Then God made a covenant with Abraham.
God told him that circumcision would show who
the members of the covenant were. Abraham
became Isaac's father. He circumcised Isaac eight
days after he was born. Later, Isaac became Jacob's father. Jacob had 12 sons. They became the
founders of the 12 tribes of Israel.
9 "Jacob's sons were jealous of their brother Joseph. So they sold him as a slave. He was taken to
Egypt. But God was with him. 10 He saved Joseph
from all his troubles. God made Joseph wise. He
helped him to become the friend of Pharaoh, the
king of Egypt. So Pharaoh made Joseph ruler over
Egypt and his whole palace.
11 "There was not enough food for all Egypt and
Canaan. This brought great suffering. Jacob and
his sons couldn't find food. 12 But Jacob heard that
there was grain in Egypt. So he sent his sons on
their first visit. 13 On their second visit, Joseph told
his brothers who he was. Pharaoh learned about
Joseph's family.
14 "After this, Joseph sent for his father Jacob
and his whole family. The total number of people
was 75. 15 Then Jacob went down to Egypt. There
he and his family died. 16 Some of their bodies were
brought back to Shechem. They were placed in a
tomb Abraham had bought. He had purchased it
from Hamor's sons at Shechem for a certain
amount of money.
17 "In Egypt the number of our people grew and
grew. It was nearly time for God to make his
promise to Abraham come true. 18 Another king
became ruler of Egypt. He knew nothing about Joseph. 19 He was very evil and dishonest with our
people. He beat them down. He forced them to
throw out their newborn babies to die.
20 "At that time Moses was born. He was not an
ordinary child. For three months he was taken care
of by his family. 21 Then he was placed outside. But
Pharaoh's daughter took him home. She brought
him up as her own son. 22 Moses was taught all the
knowledge of the people of Egypt. He became a
powerful speaker and a man of action.
23 "When Moses was 40 years old, he decided to
visit the people of Israel. They were his own people. 24 He saw one of them being treated badly by
a man of Egypt. So he went to help him. He got
even by killing the man. 25 Moses thought his own
people would realize that God was using him to
save them. But they didn't.
26 "The next day Moses saw two men of Israel
fighting. He tried to make peace between them.
'Men, you are both of Israel,' he said. 'Why do
you want to hurt each other?'
27 "But the man who was treating the other one
badly pushed Moses to one side. He said, 'Who
made you ruler and judge over us? 28 Do you want
to kill me as you killed the Egyptian yesterday?'
(Exodus 2:14) 29 When Moses heard this, he escaped
to Midian. He lived there as a stranger. He became
the father of two sons there.
30 "Forty years passed. Then an angel appeared
to Moses in the flames of a burning bush. This
happened in the desert near Mount Sinai. 31 When
Moses saw the bush, he was amazed. He went over
for a closer look. There he heard the Lord's voice.
32 'I am the God of your fathers,' the Lord said. 'I
am the God of Abraham, Isaac and Jacob.' *(Exodus
3:6)* Moses shook with fear. He didn't dare to look.
33 "Then the Lord said to him, 'Take off your
sandals. The place you are standing on is holy
ground. 34 I have seen my people beaten down in
Egypt. I have heard their groans. I have come
down to set them free. Now come. I will send you
back to Egypt.' *(Exodus 3:5,7,8,10)*
35 "This is the same Moses the two men of Israel would not accept. They had said, 'Who made
you ruler and judge?' But God himself sent Moses
to rule the people of Israel and set them free. He
spoke to Moses through the angel who had
appeared to him in the bush. 36 So Moses led them
out of Egypt. He did wonders and miraculous
signs in Egypt, at the Red Sea, and for 40 years in
the desert.
37 "This is the same Moses who spoke to the
people of Israel. 'God will send you a prophet,' he
said. 'He will be like me. He will come from your
own people.' *(Deuteronomy 18:15)* 38 Moses was with
the Israelites in the desert. He was with the angel
who spoke to him on Mount Sinai. Moses was
with our people of long ago. He received living
words to pass on to us.

[39]“But our people refused to obey Moses. They
would not accept him. In their hearts, they wished
they were back in Egypt. [40]They told Aaron,
‘Make us a god who will lead us. This fellow Moses led us out of Egypt. But we don’t know what
has happened to him!’ *(Exodus 32:1)* [41]That was the
time they made a statue to be their god. It looked
like a calf. They brought sacrifices to it. They were
glad because of what they had made with their
own hands. [42]But God turned away from them. He
left them to worship the sun, moon and stars. This
agrees with what is written in the book of the
prophets. There it says,

“ ‘People of Israel, did you bring me sacrifices
and offerings
for 40 years in the desert?
[43] You lifted up the place where Molech was
worshiped.
You lifted up the star of your god Rephan.
You made statues of them to worship.
So I will send you away from your country.’
(Amos 5:25–27)
God sent them to Babylon and even farther.

[44]“Long ago our people had with them in the
desert the holy tent where the tablets of the
covenant were kept. Moses had made the holy tent
as God had commanded him. It was made like the
pattern he had seen. [45]Our people received the tent
from God. They brought it with them when they
took the land of Canaan. God drove out the nations
that were in their way. At that time Joshua was Israel’s leader.

“The tent remained in the land until David’s
time. [46]David was blessed by God. So David asked
if he could build a house for the God of Jacob.
[47]Instead, it was Solomon who built it for him.

[48]“But the Most High God does not live in
houses made by human hands. As God says
through the prophet,

[49] “ ‘Heaven is my throne.
The earth is under my control.
What kind of house will you build for me?
says the Lord.
Where will my resting place be?
[50] Didn’t my hand make all these things?’
(Isaiah 66:1,2)

[51]“You people! You won’t obey! You are stubborn! You won’t listen! You are just like your people of long ago! You always oppose the Holy
Spirit! [52]Was there ever a prophet your people
didn’t try to hurt? They even killed those who told
about the coming of the Blameless One. And now
you have handed him over to his enemies. You
have murdered him. [53]The law you received was
brought by angels. But you haven’t obeyed it.”

Stephen Is Killed

[54]When the Sanhedrin heard this, they became
very angry. They ground their teeth at Stephen.
[55]But he was full of the Holy Spirit. He looked up
to heaven and saw God’s glory. He saw Jesus
standing at God’s right hand. [56]“Look!” he said. “I
see heaven open. The Son of Man is standing at
God’s right hand.”

[57]When the Sanhedrin heard this, they covered
their ears. They yelled at the top of their voices.
They all rushed at him. [58]They dragged him out of
the city. They began to throw stones at him to kill
him. The witnesses took off their coats. They
placed them at the feet of a young man named
Saul.

[59]While the members of the Sanhedrin were
throwing stones at Stephen, he prayed. “Lord
Jesus, receive my spirit,” he said. [60]Then he fell on
his knees. He cried out, “Lord! Don’t hold this sin
against them!” When he had said this, he died.

8 Saul was there. He had agreed that Stephen
should die.

The Church Is Scattered

On that day the church in Jerusalem began to
be attacked and treated badly. All except the apostles were scattered throughout Judea and Samaria.
[2]Godly Jews buried Stephen. They sobbed and
sobbed over him.

[3]But Saul began to destroy the church. He went
from house to house. He dragged men and women
away and put them in prison.

Philip Goes to Samaria

[4]The believers who had been scattered preached
the word everywhere they went. [5]Philip went
down to a city in Samaria. There he preached
about the Christ. [6]The crowds listened to Philip.
They saw the miraculous signs he did. They all
paid close attention to what he said. [7]Evil spirits
screamed and came out of many people. Many
who were disabled or who couldn’t walk were
healed. [8]So there was great joy in that city.

Simon the Evil Magician

[9]A man named Simon lived in the city. For quite
a while he had practiced evil magic there. He
amazed all the people of Samaria. He claimed to
be someone great. [10]All of the people listened to
him, from the least important of them to the most
important. They exclaimed, “This man is known
as the Great Power of God!” [11]He had amazed
them for a long time with his magic. So they followed him.

[12]But Philip preached the good news of God’s
kingdom. He preached the name of Jesus Christ.
So men and women believed and were baptized.
[13]Simon himself believed and was baptized. He
followed Philip everywhere. He was amazed by
the great signs and miracles he saw.

[14]The apostles in Jerusalem heard that people in
Samaria had accepted God’s word. So they sent
Peter and John to them. [15]When they arrived there,
they prayed that the believers would receive the

Holy Spirit. 16The Holy Spirit had not yet come on
any of them. They had only been baptized in the
name of the Lord Jesus. 17Then Peter and John
placed their hands on them. And they received the
Holy Spirit.
18Simon watched as the apostles placed their
hands on them. He saw that the Spirit was given to
them. So he offered money to Peter and John. 19He
said, "Give me this power too. Then everyone I
place my hands on will receive the Holy Spirit."
20Peter answered, "May your money be
destroyed with you! Do you think you can buy
God's gift with money? 21You have no part or
share in this holy work. Your heart is not right with
God. 22Turn away from this evil sin of yours. Pray
to the Lord. Perhaps he will forgive you for having
such a thought in your heart. 23I see that you are
very bitter. You are a prisoner of sin."
24Then Simon answered, "Pray to the Lord for
me. Pray that nothing you have said will happen
to me."
25Peter and John gave witness and preached the
Lord's word. Then they returned to Jerusalem. On
the way they preached the good news in many villages in Samaria.

Philip and the Man From Ethiopia

26An angel of the Lord spoke to Philip. "Go
south to the desert road," he said. "It's the road that
goes down from Jerusalem to Gaza." 27So Philip
started out. On his way he met an Ethiopian official. The man had an important position. He was in
charge of all the wealth of Candace. She was the
queen of Ethiopia. He had gone to Jerusalem to
worship. 28On his way home he was sitting in his
chariot. He was reading the book of Isaiah the
prophet. 29The Holy Spirit told Philip, "Go to that
chariot. Stay near it."
30So Philip ran up to the chariot. He heard the
man reading Isaiah the prophet. "Do you understand what you're reading?" Philip asked.
31"How can I?" he said. "I need someone to
explain it to me." So he invited Philip to come up
and sit with him.
32Here is the part of Scripture the official was
reading. It says,

"He was led like a sheep to be killed.
Just as lambs are silent while their wool is
being cut off,
he did not open his mouth.
33 When he was treated badly, he was refused
a fair trial.
Who can say anything about his children?
His life was cut off from the earth."
(Isaiah 53:7,8)

34The official said to Philip, "Tell me, please.
Who is the prophet talking about? Himself, or
someone else?" 35Then Philip began with that
same part of Scripture. He told him the good news
about Jesus.
36/37As they traveled along the road, they came
to some water. The official said, "Look! Here is
water! Why shouldn't I be baptized?" 38He gave
orders to stop the chariot. Then both Philip and the
official went down into the water. Philip baptized
him. 39When they came up out of the water, the
Spirit of the Lord suddenly took Philip away. The
official did not see him again. He went on his way
full of joy. 40Philip was seen next at Azotus. From
there he traveled all around. He preached the good
news in all the towns. Finally he arrived in Caesarea.

Saul Becomes a Believer

9 Meanwhile, Saul continued to oppose the
Lord's followers. He said they would be put
to death. He went to the high priest. 2He asked the
priest for letters to the synagogues in Damascus.
He wanted to find men and women who belonged
to the Way of Jesus. The letters would allow him
to take them as prisoners to Jerusalem.
3On his journey, Saul approached Damascus.
Suddenly a light from heaven flashed around him.
4He fell to the ground. He heard a voice speak to
him. "Saul! Saul!" the voice said. "Why are you
opposing me?"
5"Who are you, Lord?" Saul asked.
"I am Jesus," he replied. "I am the one you are
opposing. 6Now get up and go into the city. There
you will be told what you must do."
7The men traveling with Saul stood there. They
weren't able to speak. They had heard the sound.
But they didn't see anyone. 8Saul got up from the
ground. He opened his eyes, but he couldn't see.
So they led him by the hand into Damascus. 9For
three days he was blind. He didn't eat or drink
anything.
10In Damascus there was a believer named Ananias. The Lord called out to him in a vision. "Ananias!" he said.
"Yes, Lord," he answered.
11The Lord told him, "Go to the house of Judas
on Straight Street. Ask for a man from Tarsus
named Saul. He is praying. 12In a vision he has
seen a man named Ananias. The man has come
and placed his hands on him. Now he will be able
to see again."
13"Lord," Ananias answered, "I've heard many
reports about this man. They say he has done great
harm to God's people in Jerusalem. 14Now he has
come here to arrest all those who worship you. The
chief priests have given him authority to do this."
15But the Lord said to Ananias, "Go! I have chosen this man to work for me. He will carry my
name to those who aren't Jews and to their kings.
He will bring my name to the people of Israel. 16I
will show him how much he must suffer for me."
17Then Ananias went to the house and entered
it. He placed his hands on Saul. "Brother Saul," he
said, "you saw the Lord Jesus. He appeared to you
on the road as you were coming here. He has sent

me so that you will be able to see again. You will be filled with the Holy Spirit."

18Right away something like scales fell from Saul's eyes. And he could see again. He got up and was baptized. 19After eating some food, he got his strength back.

Saul in Damascus and Jerusalem

Saul spent several days with the believers in Damascus. 20At once he began to preach in the synagogues. He taught that Jesus is the Son of God. 21All who heard him were amazed. They asked, "Isn't he the man who caused great trouble in Jerusalem for those who worship Jesus? Hasn't he come here to take them as prisoners to the chief priests?" 22But Saul grew more and more powerful. The Jews living in Damascus couldn't believe what was happening. Saul proved to them that Jesus is the Christ.

23After many days, the Jews had a meeting. They planned to kill Saul. 24But he learned about their plan. Day and night they watched the city gates closely in order to kill him. 25But his followers helped him escape by night. They lowered him in a basket through an opening in the wall.

26When Saul came to Jerusalem, he tried to join the believers. But they were all afraid of him. They didn't believe he was really one of Jesus' followers. 27But Barnabas took him to the apostles. He told them about Saul's journey. He said that Saul had seen the Lord. He told how the Lord had spoken to Saul. Barnabas also said that Saul had preached without fear in Jesus' name in Damascus.

28So Saul stayed with the believers. He moved about freely in Jerusalem. He spoke boldly in the Lord's name. 29He talked and argued with Jews who followed Greek practices. But they tried to kill him. 30The other believers heard about this. They took Saul down to Caesarea. From there they sent him off to Tarsus.

31Then the church throughout Judea, Galilee and Samaria enjoyed a time of peace. The Holy Spirit gave the church strength and boldness. So they grew in numbers. And they worshiped the Lord.

Peter Goes to Lydda and Joppa

32As Peter traveled around the country, he went to visit God's people in Lydda. 33There he found a disabled man named Aeneas. For eight years the man had spent most of his time in bed. 34"Aeneas," Peter said to him, "Jesus Christ heals you. Get up! Take care of your mat!" So Aeneas got up right away. 35Everyone who lived in Lydda and Sharon saw him. They turned to the Lord.

36In Joppa there was a believer named Tabitha. Her name in the Greek language was Dorcas. She was always doing good and helping poor people. 37About that time she became sick and died. Her body was washed and placed in a room upstairs. 38Lydda was near Joppa. The believers heard that Peter was in Lydda. So they sent two men to him. They begged him, "Please come at once!"

39Peter went with them. When he arrived, he was taken upstairs to the room. All the widows stood around him crying. They showed him the robes and other clothes Dorcas had made while she was still alive.

40Peter sent them all out of the room. Then he got down on his knees and prayed. He turned toward the dead woman. He said, "Tabitha, get up." She opened her eyes. When she saw Peter, she sat up. 41He took her by the hand and helped her to her feet. Then he called the believers and the widows. He brought her to them. They saw that she was alive. 42This became known all over Joppa. Many people believed in the Lord. 43Peter stayed in Joppa for some time. He stayed with Simon, a man who worked with leather.

Cornelius Calls for Peter

10 A man named Cornelius lived in Caesarea. He was a Roman commander in the Italian Regiment. 2Cornelius and all his family were faithful and worshiped God. He gave freely to people who were in need. He prayed to God regularly. 3One day about three o'clock in the afternoon he had a vision. He saw an angel of God clearly. The angel came to him and said, "Cornelius!"

4Cornelius was afraid. He stared at the angel. "What is it, Lord?" he asked.

The angel answered, "Your prayers and gifts to poor people have come up like an offering to God. So he has remembered you. 5Now send men to Joppa. Have them bring back a man named Simon. He is also called Peter. 6He is staying with another Simon, a man who works with leather. His house is by the sea."

7The angel who spoke to him left. Then Cornelius called two of his servants. He also called a godly soldier who was one of his attendants. 8He told them everything that had happened. Then he sent them to Joppa.

Peter Has a Vision

9It was about noon the next day. The men were on their journey and were approaching the city. Peter went up on the roof to pray. 10He became hungry. He wanted something to eat. While the meal was being prepared, Peter had a vision. 11He saw heaven open up. There he saw something that looked like a large sheet. It was being let down to earth by its four corners. 12It had all kinds of four-footed animals in it. It also had reptiles of the earth and birds of the air. 13Then a voice told him, "Get up, Peter. Kill and eat."

14"No, Lord! I will not!" Peter replied. "I have never eaten anything that is not pure and 'clean.'"

15The voice spoke to him a second time. "Do not say anything is not pure that God has made 'clean,'" it said.

16This happened three times. Right away the sheet was taken back up to heaven.

17 Peter was wondering what the vision meant.
At that very moment the men sent by Cornelius
found Simon's house. They stopped at the gate
18 and called out. They asked if Simon Peter was
staying there.
19 Peter was still thinking about the vision. The
Holy Spirit spoke to him. "Simon," he said, "three
men are looking for you. 20 Get up and go down-
stairs. Don't let anything keep you from going
with them. I have sent them."
21 Peter went down and spoke to the men. "I'm
the one you're looking for," he said. "Why have
you come?"
22 The men replied, "We have come from Cornelius, the Roman commander. He is a good man
who worships God. All the Jewish people respect
him. A holy angel told him to invite you to his
house. Cornelius wants to hear what you have to
say." 23 Then Peter invited the men into the house
to be his guests.

Peter Goes to the House of Cornelius

The next day Peter went with the three men.
Some of the believers from Joppa went along.
24 The following day he arrived in Caesarea. Cornelius was expecting them. He had called together
his relatives and close friends.
25 When Peter entered the house, Cornelius met
him. As a sign of respect, he fell at Peter's feet.
26 But Peter made him get up. "Stand up," he said.
"I am only a man myself."
27 Talking with Cornelius, Peter went inside.
There he found a large group of people. 28 He said
to them, "You know that it is against our law for a
Jew to have anything to do with those who aren't
Jews. But God has shown me that I should not say
anyone is not pure and 'clean.' 29 So when you sent
for me, I came without asking any questions. May
I ask why you sent for me?"
30 Cornelius answered, "Four days ago at this
very hour I was in my house praying. It was three
o'clock in the afternoon. Suddenly a man in shining clothes stood in front of me. 31 He said, 'Cornelius, God has heard your prayer. He has
remembered your gifts to poor people. 32 Send
someone to Joppa to get Simon Peter. He is a guest
in the home of another Simon, who works with
leather. He lives by the sea.' 33 So I sent for you
right away. It was good of you to come. Now we
are all here. And God is here with us. We are ready
to listen to everything the Lord has commanded
you to tell us."
34 Then Peter began to speak. "I now realize how
true it is that God treats everyone the same," he said.
35 "He accepts people from every nation. He accepts
all who have respect for him and do what is right.
36 "You know the message God sent to the people of Israel. It is the good news of peace through
Jesus Christ. He is Lord of all. 37 You know what
has happened all through Judea. It started in Galilee after John preached about baptism. 38 You know
how God anointed Jesus of Nazareth with the Holy
Spirit and with power. Jesus went around doing
good. He healed all who were under the devil's
power. God was with him.
39 "We are witnesses of everything he did in the
land of the Jews and in Jerusalem. They killed him
by nailing him to a cross. 40 But on the third day
God raised him from the dead. God allowed Jesus
to be seen. 41 But he wasn't seen by all the people.
He was seen only by us. We are witnesses whom
God had already chosen. We ate and drank with
him after he rose from the dead.
42 "He commanded us to preach to the people.
He told us to give witness that he is the one
appointed by God to judge the living and the dead.
43 All the prophets give witness about him. They
say that all who believe in him have their sins forgiven through his name."
44 While Peter was still saying these things, the
Holy Spirit came on all who heard the message.
45 Some Jewish believers had come with Peter.
They were amazed because the gift of the Holy
Spirit had been poured out even on those who
weren't Jews. 46 They heard them speaking in languages they had not known before. They also
heard them praising God.
Then Peter said, 47 "Can anyone keep these people from being baptized with water? They have
received the Holy Spirit just as we have." 48 So he
ordered that they be baptized in the name of Jesus
Christ. Then they asked Peter to stay with them for
a few days.

Peter Explains His Actions

11 The apostles and the believers all through
Judea heard that people who were not Jews
had also received God's word. 2 Peter went up to
Jerusalem. There the Jewish believers found fault
with him. 3 They said, "You went into the house of
those who aren't Jews. You ate with them."
4 Peter explained everything to them. He told
them exactly what had happened. 5 "I was in the
city of Joppa praying," he said. "There I had a
vision. I saw something that looked like a large
sheet. It was being let down from heaven by its
four corners. It came down to where I was. 6 I
looked into it and saw four-footed animals of the
earth. There were also wild animals, reptiles and
birds. 7 Then I heard a voice speaking to me. 'Get
up, Peter,' the voice said. 'Kill and eat.'
8 "I replied, 'No, Lord! I will not! Nothing that is
not pure and "clean" has ever entered my mouth.'
9 "A second time the voice spoke from heaven.
'Do not say anything is not pure that God has made
"clean,"' the voice said. 10 This happened three
times. Then the sheet was pulled up into heaven.
11 "Just then three men stopped at the house
where I was staying. They had been sent to me
from Caesarea. 12 The Holy Spirit told me not to let
anything keep me from going with them. These six
brothers here went with me. We entered the man's

Peter

Peter said, "I don't have any silver or gold. But I'll give you what I have. In the name of Jesus Christ of Nazareth, get up and walk."

—Acts 3:6

Jesus Is Coming Back

"Look! I am coming soon! I will reward each person for what he has done. I am the First and the Last. I am the Beginning and the End."

—Revelation 22:12–13

house. [13]He told us how he had seen an angel appear in his house. The angel said, 'Send to Joppa for Simon Peter. [14]He has a message to bring to you. You and your whole family will be saved through it.'

[15]"As I began to speak, the Holy Spirit came on them. He came just as he had come on us at the beginning. [16]Then I remembered the Lord's words. 'John baptized with water,' he had said. 'But you will be baptized with the Holy Spirit.' [17]God gave them the same gift he gave those of us who believed in the Lord Jesus Christ. So who was I to think that I could oppose God?"

[18]When they heard this, they didn't object anymore. They praised God. They said, "So then, God has allowed even those who aren't Jews to turn away from their sins and live."

Believers Are Called Christians for the First Time

[19]Some believers had been scattered by the suffering that came to them after Stephen's death. They traveled as far as Phoenicia, Cyprus and Antioch. But they told the message only to Jews. [20]Some believers from Cyprus and Cyrene went to Antioch. There they began to speak to Greeks also. They told them the good news about the Lord Jesus. [21]The Lord's power was with them. Large numbers of people believed and turned to the Lord.

[22]The church in Jerusalem heard about this. So they sent Barnabas to Antioch. [23]When he arrived and saw what the grace of God had done, he was glad. He told them all to remain true to the Lord with all their hearts. [24]Barnabas was a good man. He was full of the Holy Spirit and of faith. Large numbers of people came to know the Lord.

[25]Then Barnabas went to Tarsus to look for Saul. [26]He found him there. Then he brought him to Antioch. For a whole year Barnabas and Saul met with the church. They taught large numbers of people. At Antioch the believers were called Christians for the first time.

[27]In those days some prophets came down from Jerusalem to Antioch. [28]One of them was named Agabus. He stood up and spoke through the Spirit. He said there would not be nearly enough food anywhere in the Roman world. This happened while Claudius was the emperor. [29]The believers decided to provide help for the brothers and sisters living in Judea. All of them helped as much as they could. [30]They sent their gift to the elders through Barnabas and Saul.

An Angel Helps Peter Escape From Prison

12 About this time, King Herod arrested some people who belonged to the church. He planned to make them suffer greatly. [2]He had James killed with a sword. James was John's brother. [3]Herod saw that the death of James pleased the Jews. So he arrested Peter also. This happened during the Feast of Unleavened Bread. [4]After Herod arrested Peter, he put him in prison. Peter was placed under guard. He was watched by four groups of four soldiers each. Herod planned to put Peter on public trial. It would take place after the Passover Feast.

[5]So Peter was kept in prison. But the church prayed hard to God for him.

[6]It was the night before Herod was going to bring him to trial. Peter was sleeping between two soldiers. Two chains held him there. Lookouts stood guard at the entrance. [7]Suddenly an angel of the Lord appeared. A light shone in the prison cell. The angel struck Peter on his side. Peter woke up. "Quick!" the angel said. "Get up!" The chains fell off Peter's wrists.

[8]Then the angel said to him, "Put on your clothes and sandals." Peter did so. "Put on your coat," the angel told him. "Follow me." [9]Peter followed him out of the prison. But he had no idea that what the angel was doing was really happening. He thought he was seeing a vision. [10]They passed the first and second guards. Then they came to the iron gate leading to the city. It opened for them by itself. They went through it. They walked the length of one street. Suddenly the angel left Peter.

[11]Then Peter realized what had happened. He said, "Now I know for sure that the Lord sent his angel. He set me free from Herod's power. He saved me from everything the Jewish people were hoping for."

[12]When Peter understood what had happened, he went to Mary's house. Mary was the mother of John Mark. Many people had gathered in her home. They were praying there. [13]Peter knocked at the outer entrance. A servant named Rhoda came to answer the door. [14]She recognized Peter's voice. She was so excited that she ran back without opening the door. "Peter is at the door!" she exclaimed.

[15]"You're out of your mind," they said to her. But she kept telling them it was true. So they said, "It must be his angel."

[16]Peter kept on knocking. When they opened the door and saw him, they were amazed. [17]Peter motioned with his hand for them to be quiet. He explained how the Lord had brought him out of prison. "Tell James and the others about this," he said. Then he went to another place.

[18]In the morning the soldiers were bewildered. They couldn't figure out what had happened to Peter. [19]So Herod had them look everywhere for Peter. But they didn't find him. Then Herod questioned the guards closely. He ordered that they be put to death.

Herod Dies

Herod went from Judea to Caesarea. He stayed there awhile. [20]He had been quarreling with the people of Tyre and Sidon. So they got together and asked for a meeting with him. This was because they depended on the king's country to supply them with food. They gained the support of Blastus and asked for peace. Blastus was a trusted personal servant of the king.

21The appointed day came. Herod was seated on his throne. He was wearing his royal robes. He made a speech to the people. 22Then they shouted, "This is the voice of a god. It's not the voice of a man." 23Right away an angel of the Lord struck Herod down. Herod had not given praise to God. So he was eaten by worms and died.

24But God's word continued to increase and spread.

25Barnabas and Saul finished their task. Then they returned from Jerusalem. They took John Mark with them.

Barnabas and Saul Are Sent Off

13 In the church at Antioch there were prophets and teachers. Among them were Barnabas, Simeon, and Lucius from Cyrene. Simeon was also called Niger. Another was Manaen. He had been brought up with Herod, the ruler of Galilee. Saul was among them too. 2While they were worshiping the Lord and fasting, the Holy Spirit spoke. "Set apart Barnabas and Saul for me," he said. "I have appointed them to do special work." 3The prophets and teachers fasted and prayed. They placed their hands on Barnabas and Saul. Then they sent them off.

Events on Cyprus

4Barnabas and Saul were sent on their way by the Holy Spirit. They went down to Seleucia. From there they sailed to Cyprus. 5They arrived at Salamis. There they preached God's word in the Jewish synagogues. John was with them as their helper.

6They traveled all across the island until they came to Paphos. There they met a Jew named Bar-Jesus. He was an evil magician and a false prophet. 7He was an attendant of Sergius Paulus, the governor. Paulus was a man of understanding. He sent for Barnabas and Saul. He wanted to hear God's word. 8But Elymas, the evil magician, opposed them. The name Elymas means "magician." He tried to keep the governor from becoming a believer. 9Saul was also known as Paul. He was filled with the Holy Spirit. He looked straight at Elymas. He said to him, 10"You are a child of the devil! You are an enemy of everything that is right! You cheat people. You use all kinds of tricks. Won't you ever stop twisting the right ways of the Lord? 11Now the Lord's hand is against you. You are going to go blind. You won't be able to see the light of the sun for a while."

Right away mist and darkness came over him. He tried to feel his way around. He wanted to find someone to lead him by the hand. 12When the governor saw what had happened, he believed. He was amazed at what Paul was teaching about the Lord.

Paul Preaches in Pisidian Antioch

13From Paphos, Paul and his companions sailed to Perga in Pamphylia. There John left them and returned to Jerusalem. 14From Perga they went on to Pisidian Antioch. On the Sabbath day they entered the synagogue and sat down. 15The Law and the Prophets were read aloud. Then the synagogue rulers sent word to Paul and his companions. They said, "Brothers, do you have a message of hope for the people? If you do, please speak."

16Paul stood up and motioned with his hand. Then he said, "Men of Israel, and you non-Jews who worship God, listen to me! 17The God of Israel chose our people who lived long ago. He blessed them greatly while they were in Egypt. With his mighty power he led them out of that country. 18He put up with them for about 40 years in the desert. 19He destroyed seven nations in Canaan. Then he gave the land to his people as their rightful share. 20All of this took about 450 years.

"After this, God gave them judges until the time of Samuel the prophet. 21Then the people asked for a king. He gave them Saul, son of Kish. Saul was from the tribe of Benjamin. He ruled for 40 years. 22God removed him and made David their king. Here is God's witness about him. 'David, son of Jesse, is a man dear to my heart,' he said. 'He will do everything I want him to do.'

23"From this man's family line God has brought to Israel the Savior Jesus. This is what he had promised. 24Before Jesus came, John preached that we should turn away from our sins and be baptized. He preached this to all Israel. 25John was coming to the end of his work. 'Who do you think I am?' he said. 'I am not the one you are looking for. No, he is coming after me. I am not good enough to untie his sandals.'

26"Listen, brothers, you children of Abraham! Listen, you non-Jews who worship God! This message of salvation has been sent to us. 27The people of Jerusalem and their rulers did not recognize Jesus. By finding him guilty, they made the prophets' words come true. These are read every Sabbath day. 28The people and their rulers had no reason at all for sentencing Jesus to death. But they asked Pilate to have him killed. 29They did everything that had been written about Jesus. Then they took him down from the cross. They laid him in a tomb. 30But God raised him from the dead. 31For many days he was seen by those who had traveled with him from Galilee to Jerusalem. Now they are his witnesses to our people.

32"We are telling you the good news. What God promised our people long ago 33he has done for us, their children. He has raised up Jesus. This is what is written in the second Psalm. It says,

"'You are my Son.
Today I have become your Father.'
(Psalm 2:7)

[34]God raised Jesus from the dead. He will never rot in the grave. This is what is written in Scripture. It says,

"'Holy and sure blessings were promised
to David.
I will give them to you.' *(Isaiah 55:3)*

[35]In another place it says,

"'You will not let your Holy One rot away.'
(Psalm 16:10)

[36]"David carried out God's purpose while he lived. Then he died. He was buried with his people. His body rotted away. [37]But the One whom God raised from the dead did not rot away.

[38]"My brothers, here is what I want you to know. I announce to you that your sins can be forgiven because of what Jesus has done. [39]Through him everyone who believes is made right with God. Moses' law could not make you right in God's eyes. [40]Be careful! Don't let what the prophets spoke about happen to you. They said,

[41]"'Look, you who make fun of the truth!
Wonder and die!
I am going to do something in your days
that you would never believe.
You wouldn't believe it even if someone
told you.'" *(Habakkuk 1:5)*

[42]Paul and Barnabas started to leave the synagogue. The people invited them to say more about these things on the next Sabbath day. [43]The people were told they could leave the service. Many Jews followed Paul and Barnabas. Many non-Jews who faithfully worshiped the God of the Jews did the same. Paul and Barnabas talked with them. They tried to get them to keep living in God's grace.

[44]On the next Sabbath day, almost the whole city gathered to hear the word of the Lord. [45]When the Jews saw the crowds, they became very jealous. They said evil things against what Paul was saying.

[46]Then Paul and Barnabas answered them boldly. "We had to speak God's word to you first," they said. "But you don't accept it. You don't think you are good enough for eternal life. So now we are turning to those who aren't Jews. [47]This is what the Lord has commanded us to do. He said,

"'I have made you a light for those who
aren't Jews.
You will bring salvation to the
whole earth.'" *(Isaiah 49:6)*

[48]When the non-Jews heard this, they were glad. They honored the word of the Lord. All who were appointed for eternal life believed.

[49]The word of the Lord spread through the whole area. [50]But the Jews stirred up the important women who worshiped God. They also stirred up the men who were leaders in the city. They tried to get them to attack Paul and Barnabas. They threw them out of that area. [51]Paul and Barnabas didn't like this. So they shook the dust from their feet. They went on to Iconium. [52]The believers were filled with joy and with the Holy Spirit.

Paul and Barnabas Preach in Iconium

14 At Iconium, Paul and Barnabas went into the Jewish synagogue as usual. They spoke there with great power. Large numbers of Jews and non-Jews became believers. [2]But the Jews who refused to believe stirred up those who weren't Jews. They poisoned their minds against the two men and the new believers. [3]So Paul and Barnabas spent a lot of time there. They spoke boldly for the Lord. He gave them the ability to do miraculous signs and wonders. In this way the Lord showed that they were telling the truth about his grace.

[4]The people of the city did not agree with each other. Some were on the side of the Jews. Others were on the side of the apostles. [5]Jews and non-Jews alike planned to treat Paul and Barnabas badly. Their leaders agreed. They planned to kill them by throwing stones at them. [6]But Paul and Barnabas found out about the plan. They escaped to the Lycaonian cities of Lystra and Derbe and to the surrounding area. [7]There they continued to preach the good news.

Paul Preaches in Lystra

[8]In Lystra there sat a man who couldn't walk. He hadn't been able to use his feet since the day he was born. [9]He listened as Paul spoke. Paul looked right at him. He saw that the man had faith to be healed. [10]So he called out, "Stand up on your feet!" Then the man jumped up and began to walk.

[11]The crowd saw what Paul had done. They shouted in the Lycaonian language. "The gods have come down to us in human form!" they exclaimed. [12]They called Barnabas Zeus. Paul was the main speaker. So they called him Hermes. [13]Just outside the city was the temple of the god Zeus. The priest of Zeus brought bulls and wreaths to the city gates. He and the crowd wanted to offer sacrifices to Paul and Barnabas.

[14]But the apostles Barnabas and Paul heard about this. So they tore their clothes. They rushed out into the crowd. They shouted, [15]"Why are you men doing this? We are only human, just like you. We are bringing you good news. Turn away from these worthless things. Turn to the living God. He is the one who made the heavens and the earth and the sea. He made everything in them. [16]In the past, he let all nations go their own way. [17]But he has given proof of what he is like. He has shown kindness by giving you rain from heaven. He gives you crops in their seasons. He provides you with plenty of food. He fills your hearts with joy." [18]Paul and Barnabas told them all these things. But they had trouble keeping the crowd from offering sacrifices to them.

[19]Then some Jews came from Antioch and Iconium. They won the crowd over to their side. They threw stones at Paul. They thought he was dead,

so they dragged him out of the city. 20The believers gathered around Paul. Then he got up and went
back into the city. The next day he and Barnabas
left for Derbe.

Paul and Barnabas Return to Antioch

21Paul and Barnabas preached the good news in
the city of Derbe. They won large numbers of followers. Then they returned to Lystra, Iconium and
Antioch. 22There they helped the believers gain
strength. They told them to remain true to what
they had been taught. "We must go through many
hard times to enter God's kingdom," they said.
23Paul and Barnabas appointed elders for them in
each church. The elders had trusted in the Lord.
Paul and Barnabas prayed and fasted. They placed
the elders in the Lord's care.

24After going through Pisidia, Paul and Barnabas came into Pamphylia. 25They preached the
word in Perga. Then they went down to Attalia.

26From Attalia they sailed back to Antioch. That
was where they had been committed to God's
grace. They had now completed the work God had
given them to do. 27When they arrived at Antioch,
they gathered the church together. They reported
all that God had done through them. They told
how he had opened the way for non-Jews to
believe. 28And they stayed there a long time with
the believers.

Church Leaders Meet in Jerusalem

15 Certain people came down from Judea to
Antioch. Here is what they were teaching
the believers. "Moses commanded you to be circumcised," they said. "If you aren't, you can't be
saved." 2But Paul and Barnabas didn't agree with
this. They argued strongly with them. So Paul and
Barnabas were appointed to go up to Jerusalem.
Some other believers were chosen to go with them.
They were supposed to see the apostles and elders
about this question.

3The church sent them on their way. As they
traveled through Phoenicia and Samaria, they told
how those who weren't Jews had turned to God.
This news made all the believers very glad.

4When they arrived in Jerusalem, the church
welcomed them. The apostles and elders welcomed them too. Then Paul and Barnabas reported
everything God had done through them.

5Some of the believers were Pharisees. They
stood up and said, "Those who aren't Jews must be
circumcised. They must obey the law of Moses."

6The apostles and elders met to consider this
question. 7After they had talked it over, Peter got
up and spoke to them.

"Brothers," he said, "you know that some time
ago God chose me to take the good news to those
who aren't Jews. He wanted them to hear the good
news and believe. 8God knows the human heart.
By giving the Holy Spirit to non-Jews, he showed
that he accepted them. He did the same for them
as he had done for us. 9He showed that there is no
difference between us and them. He made their
hearts pure because of their faith.

10"Now then, why are you trying to test God? You
test him when you put a heavy load on the believers' shoulders. Our people of long ago couldn't carry
that load. We can't either. 11No! We believe we are
saved through the grace of our Lord Jesus. Those
who aren't Jews are saved in the same way."

12Everyone became quiet as they listened to
Barnabas and Paul. They were telling about the
miraculous signs and wonders God had done
through them among non-Jews.

13When they finished, James spoke up. "Brothers," he said, "listen to me. 14Simon Peter has
explained to us how God first showed his concern
for those who aren't Jews. He chose some of them
to be his very own people.

15The prophets' words agree with that. They say,

16"'After this I will return
  and rebuild David's fallen tent.
I will rebuild what was destroyed.
  I will make it what it used to be.
17 Then the rest of the people can look
    to the Lord.
  This means all the non-Jews who belong
    to me.
The Lord says this. He is the one who does
    these things.' *(Amos 9:11,12)*
18 The Lord does things that have been known
    for a long time.

19"Now here is my opinion. We should not
make it hard for the non-Jews who are turning to
God. 20Here is what we should write to them. They
must not eat food polluted by being offered to statues of gods. They must not commit sexual sins.
They must not eat the meat of animals that have
been choked to death. And they must not drink
blood. 21These laws of Moses have been preached
in every city from the earliest times. They are read
out loud in the synagogues every Sabbath day."

A Letter Is Written to Non-Jewish Believers

22Then the apostles, the elders and the whole
church decided what to do. They would choose
some of their own men. They would send them to
Antioch with Paul and Barnabas. So they chose
two leaders among the believers. Their names
were Judas Barsabbas and Silas. 23Here is the letter they sent with them.

The apostles and elders, your brothers, are
writing this letter.

We are sending it to the non-Jewish believers in Antioch, Syria and Cilicia.

Greetings.

24We have heard that some of our people
came to you and caused trouble. You were

upset by what they said. But we had given
them no authority to go. 25So we all agreed
to send our dear friends Barnabas and Paul
to you. We chose some others to go with
them. 26Barnabas and Paul have put their
lives in danger for the name of our Lord
Jesus Christ. 27So we are sending Judas and
Silas with them. What they say will agree
with this letter.
28It seemed good to the Holy Spirit and to
us not to give you a load that is too heavy.
So here are a few basic rules. 29Don't eat
food that has been offered to statues of gods.
Don't drink blood. Don't eat the meat of animals that have been choked to death. And
don't commit sexual sins. You will do well
to keep away from these things.

Farewell.

30The men were sent down to Antioch. There
they gathered the church together. They gave the
letter to them. 31The people read it. They were glad
for its message of hope. 32Judas and Silas were
prophets. They said many things to give strength
and hope to the believers. 33/34Judas and Silas
stayed there for some time. Then the believers sent
them away with the blessing of peace. They sent
them back to those who had sent them out.
35Paul and Barnabas remained in Antioch.
There they and many others taught and preached
the word of the Lord.

Paul and Barnabas Do Not Agree

36Some time later Paul spoke to Barnabas.
"Let's go back to all the towns where we preached
the word of the Lord," he said. "Let's visit the
believers and see how they are doing." 37Barnabas
wanted to take John Mark with them. 38But Paul
didn't think it was wise to take him. Mark had
deserted them in Pamphylia. He hadn't continued
with them in their work. 39Barnabas and Paul
strongly disagreed with each other. So they went
their separate ways. Barnabas took Mark and
sailed for Cyprus. 40But Paul chose Silas. The
believers asked the Lord to give his grace to Paul
and Silas as they went. 41Paul traveled through
Syria and Cilicia. He gave strength to the churches
there.

Timothy Joins Paul and Silas

16 Paul came to Derbe. Then he went on to
Lystra. A believer named Timothy lived
there. His mother was Jewish and a believer. His
father was a Greek. 2The believers at Lystra and
Iconium said good things about Timothy. 3Paul
wanted to take him along on the journey. So he circumcised Timothy because of the Jews who lived
in that area. They all knew that Timothy's father
was a Greek. 4Paul and his companions traveled
from town to town. They reported what the apostles and elders in Jerusalem had decided. The people were supposed to obey what was in the report.
5So the churches were made strong in the faith.
The number of believers grew every day.

Paul's Vision of the Man From Macedonia

6Paul and his companions traveled all through
the area of Phrygia and Galatia. The Holy Spirit
had kept them from preaching the word in Asia
Minor. 7They came to the border of Mysia. From
there they tried to enter Bithynia. But the Spirit of
Jesus would not let them. 8So they passed by Mysia. Then they went down to Troas.
9During the night Paul had a vision. He saw a
man from Macedonia standing and begging him.
"Come over to Macedonia!" the man said. "Help
us!" 10After Paul had seen the vision, we got ready
at once to leave for Macedonia. We decided that
God had called us to preach the good news there.

Lydia Becomes a Believer

11At Troas we got into a boat. We sailed straight
for Samothrace. The next day we went on to Ne-
apolis. 12From there we traveled to Philippi, a Roman colony. It is an important city in that part of
Macedonia. We stayed there several days.
13On the Sabbath day we went outside the city
gate. We walked down to the river. There we
expected to find a place of prayer. We sat down
and began to speak to the women who had gathered together. 14One of those listening was a
woman named Lydia. She was from the city of
Thyatira. Her business was selling purple cloth.
She was a worshiper of God. The Lord opened her
heart to accept Paul's message. 15She and her family were baptized. Then she invited us to her home.
"Do you consider me a believer in the Lord?" she
asked. "If you do, come and stay at my house."
She succeeded in getting us to go home with her.

Paul and Silas Are Thrown Into Prison

16One day we were going to the place of prayer.
On the way we were met by a female slave. She
had a spirit that helped her to tell ahead of time
what was going to happen. She earned a lot of
money for her owners by telling fortunes. 17The
woman followed Paul and the rest of us around.
She shouted, "These men serve the Most High
God. They are telling you how to be saved." 18She
kept this up for many days. Finally Paul became
upset. Turning around, he spoke to the spirit. "In
the name of Jesus Christ," he said, "I command
you to come out of her!" At that very moment the
spirit left her.
19The female slave's owners realized that their
hope of making money was gone. So they grabbed
Paul and Silas. They dragged them into the market place to face the authorities. 20They brought
them to the judges. "These men are Jews," her
owners said. "They are making trouble in our city.
21They are suggesting practices that are against

Roman law. These are practices we can't accept or take part in."

22The crowd joined the attack against Paul and Silas. The judges ordered that Paul and Silas be stripped and beaten. 23They were whipped without mercy. Then they were thrown into prison. The jailer was commanded to guard them carefully. 24When he received his orders, he put Paul and Silas deep inside the prison. He fastened their feet so they couldn't get away.

25About midnight Paul and Silas were praying. They were also singing hymns to God. The other prisoners were listening to them. 26Suddenly there was a powerful earthquake. It shook the prison from top to bottom. All at once the prison doors flew open. Everybody's chains came loose.

27The jailer woke up. He saw that the prison doors were open. He pulled out his sword and was going to kill himself. He thought the prisoners had escaped. 28"Don't harm yourself!" Paul shouted. "We are all here!"

29The jailer called out for some lights. He rushed in, shaking with fear. He fell down in front of Paul and Silas. 30Then he brought them out. He asked, "Sirs, what must I do to be saved?"

31They replied, "Believe in the Lord Jesus. Then you and your family will be saved." 32They spoke the word of the Lord to him. They also spoke to all the others in his house.

33At that hour of the night, the jailer took Paul and Silas and washed their wounds. Right away he and his whole family were baptized. 34The jailer brought them into his house. He set a meal in front of them. He and his whole family were filled with joy. They had become believers in God.

35Early in the morning the judges sent their officers to the jailer. They ordered him, "Let those men go." 36The jailer told Paul, "The judges have ordered me to set you and Silas free. You can leave now. Go in peace."

37But Paul replied to the officers. "They beat us in public," he said. "We weren't given a trial. And we are Roman citizens! They threw us into prison. And now do they want to get rid of us quietly? No! Let them come themselves and personally lead us out."

38The officers reported this to the judges. When the judges heard that Paul and Silas were Roman citizens, they became afraid. 39So they came and said they were sorry. They led them out of the prison. Then they asked them to leave the city. 40After Paul and Silas came out of the prison, they went to Lydia's house. There they met with the believers. They told them to be brave. Then they left.

Paul and Silas Arrive in Thessalonica

17 Paul and Silas passed through Amphipolis and Apollonia. They came to Thessalonica. A Jewish synagogue was there. 2Paul went into the synagogue as he usually did. For three Sabbath days in a row he talked about the Scriptures with the Jews. 3He explained and proved that the Christ had to suffer and rise from the dead. "This Jesus I am telling you about is the Christ!" he said. 4His words won some of the Jews over. They joined Paul and Silas. A large number of Greeks who worshiped God joined them too. So did quite a few important women.

5But the Jews were jealous. So they rounded up some evil fellows from the market place. Forming a crowd, they started all kinds of trouble in the city. The Jews rushed to Jason's house. They were looking for Paul and Silas. They wanted to bring them out to the crowd. 6But they couldn't find them. So they dragged Jason and some other believers to the city officials. "These men have caused trouble all over the world," they shouted. "Now they have come here. 7Jason has welcomed them into his house. They are all disobeying Caesar's commands. They say there is another king. He is called Jesus."

8When the crowd and the city officials heard this, they became very upset. 9They made Jason and the others give them money. They wanted to make sure they would return to the court. Then they let them go.

Paul and Silas Are Sent to Berea

10As soon as it was night, the believers sent Paul and Silas away to Berea. When they arrived, they went to the Jewish synagogue.

11The Bereans were very glad to receive Paul's message. They studied the Scriptures carefully every day. They wanted to see if what Paul said was true. So they were more noble than the Thessalonians. 12Many of the Jews believed. A number of important Greek women also became believers. And so did many Greek men.

13The Jews in Thessalonica found out that Paul was preaching God's word in Berea. So they went there too. They stirred up the crowds and got them all worked up.

14Right away the believers sent Paul to the coast. But Silas and Timothy stayed in Berea. 15The men who went with Paul took him to Athens. Then they returned with orders that Silas and Timothy were supposed to join him as soon as they could.

Paul Preaches in Athens

16Paul was waiting for Silas and Timothy in Athens. He was very upset to see that the city was full of statues of gods. 17So he went to the synagogue. There he talked with Jews and with Greeks who worshiped God. Each day he spoke with anyone who happened to be in the market place.

18A group of Epicurean and Stoic thinkers began to argue with him. Some of them asked, "What is this fellow chattering about?" Others said, "He seems to be telling us about gods we've never heard of." They said this because Paul was preaching the good news about Jesus. He was telling them that Jesus had risen from the dead.

19They took him to a meeting of the Areopagus. There they said to him, "What is this new teaching you're giving us? 20You have some strange ideas. We've never heard them before. We want to know what they mean."

21All the people of Athens spent their time talking about and listening to the latest ideas. People from other lands who lived there did the same.

22Then Paul stood up in the meeting of the Areopagus. He said, "Men of Athens! I see that you are very religious in every way. 23As I walked around, I looked carefully at the things you worship. I even found an altar with TO AN UNKNOWN GOD written on it. Now I am going to tell you about this 'unknown god' that you worship.

24"He is the God who made the world. He also made everything in it. He is the Lord of heaven and earth. He doesn't live in temples built by hands. 25He is not served by human hands. He doesn't need anything. He himself gives life and breath to all people. He also gives them everything else they have. 26From one man he made all the people of the world. Now they live all over the earth. He decided exactly when they should live. And he decided exactly where they should live. 27God did this so that people would seek him. Then perhaps they would reach out for him and find him. They would find him even though he is not far from any of us. 28'In him we live and move and exist.' As some of your own poets have also said, 'We are his children.'

29"Yes, we are God's children. So we shouldn't think that God is made out of gold or silver or stone. He isn't a statue planned and made by clever people. 30In the past, God didn't judge people for what they didn't know. But now he commands all people everywhere to turn away from their sins. 31He has set a day when he will judge the world fairly. He has appointed a man to be its judge. God has proved this to all people by raising that man from the dead."

32When they heard Paul talk about the dead rising, some of them made fun of it. But others said, "We want to hear you speak about this again." 33So Paul left the meeting of the Areopagus. 34A few men became followers of Paul and believed in Jesus. Dionysius was one of them. He was a member of the Areopagus. A woman named Damaris also became a believer. And so did some others.

Paul Goes to Corinth

18 After this, Paul left Athens and went to Corinth. 2There he met a Jew named Aquila, who was a native of Pontus. Aquila had recently come from Italy with his wife Priscilla. The emperor Claudius had ordered all the Jews to leave Rome. Paul went to see Aquila and Priscilla. 3They were tentmakers, just as he was. So he stayed and worked with them. 4Every Sabbath day he went to the synagogue. He was trying to get both Jews and Greeks to believe in the Lord.

5Silas and Timothy came from Macedonia. Then Paul spent all his time preaching. He gave witness to the Jews that Jesus was the Christ. 6But the Jews opposed Paul. They treated him badly. He didn't like this. So he shook out his clothes. Then he said to them, "Anything that happens to you will be your own fault! Don't blame me for it! From now on I will go to people who are not Jews."

7Then Paul left the synagogue. He went next door to the house of Titius Justus, a man who worshiped God. 8Crispus was the synagogue ruler. He and his whole family came to believe in the Lord. Many others who lived in Corinth heard Paul. They too believed and were baptized.

9One night the Lord spoke to Paul in a vision. "Don't be afraid," he said. "Keep on speaking. Don't be silent. 10I am with you. No one will attack you and harm you. I have many people in this city." 11So Paul stayed there for a year and a half. He taught them God's word.

12At that time Gallio was governor of Achaia. The Jews got together and attacked Paul. They brought him into court. 13"This man," they charged, "is trying to talk people into worshiping God in ways that are against the law."

14Paul was about to speak up for himself. But just then Gallio spoke to the Jews. "You Jews are not claiming that Paul has committed a crime, whether large or small," he said. "If you were, it would make sense for me to listen to you. 15But this is about your own law. It is a question of words and names. Settle the matter yourselves. I will not be a judge of such things." 16So he had them thrown out of the court. 17Then all the Jews turned against Sosthenes. He was the synagogue ruler. They beat him up in front of the court. But Gallio didn't care at all.

Priscilla and Aquila Teach Apollos

18Paul stayed in Corinth for some time. Then he left the believers and sailed for Syria. Priscilla and Aquila went with him. Before he sailed, he had his hair cut off at Cenchrea. He did this because he had made a promise to God. 19They arrived at Ephesus. There Paul said good-by to Priscilla and Aquila. He himself went into the synagogue and talked with the Jews. 20The Jews asked him to spend more time with them. But he said no. 21As he left, he made them a promise. "If God wants me to," he said, "I will come back." Then he sailed from Ephesus. 22When he landed at Caesarea, he went up to Jerusalem. There he greeted the church. He then went down to Antioch.

23Paul spent some time in Antioch. Then he left and traveled all over Galatia and Phrygia. He gave strength to all the believers there.

24At that time a Jew named Apollos came to Ephesus. He was an educated man from Alexandria. He knew the Scriptures very well. 25Apollos had been taught the way of the Lord. He spoke with great power. He taught the truth about Jesus. But he only knew about John's baptism. 26He began to speak boldly in the synagogue. Priscilla and Aquila heard him. So they invited him to their home. There they gave him a better understanding of the way of God.

27Apollos wanted to go to Achaia. The brothers agreed with him. They wrote to the believers there. They asked them to welcome him. When he arrived, he was a great help to those who had become believers by God's grace. 28He argued strongly against the Jews in public meetings. He proved from the Scriptures that Jesus was the Christ.

Paul Goes to Ephesus

19 While Apollos was at Corinth, Paul took the road to Ephesus. When he arrived, he found some believers there. 2He asked them, "Did you receive the Holy Spirit when you became believers?"

"No," they answered. "We haven't even heard that there is a Holy Spirit."

3So Paul asked, "Then what baptism did you receive?"

"John's baptism," they replied.

4Paul said, "John baptized people, calling them to turn away from their sins. He told them to believe in the one who was coming after him. Jesus is that one." 5After hearing this, they were baptized in the name of the Lord Jesus. 6Paul placed his hands on them. Then the Holy Spirit came on them. They spoke in languages they had not known before. They also prophesied. 7There were about 12 of them in all.

8Paul entered the synagogue. There he spoke boldly for three months. He tried to talk the people into accepting his teaching about God's kingdom. 9But some of them wouldn't listen. They refused to believe. In public they said evil things about the Way of Jesus. So Paul left them. He took the believers with him. Each day he talked with people in the lecture hall of Tyrannus. 10This went on for two years. So all the Jews and Greeks who lived in Asia Minor heard the word of the Lord.

11God did amazing miracles through Paul. 12Even handkerchiefs and aprons that had touched him were taken to those who were sick. When this happened, their sicknesses were healed and evil spirits left them.

13Some Jews went around driving out evil spirits. They tried to use the name of the Lord Jesus to set free those who were controlled by demons. They said, "In Jesus' name I command you to come out. He is the Jesus that Paul is preaching about." 14Seven sons of Sceva were doing this. Sceva was a Jewish chief priest. 15One day the evil spirit answered them, "I know Jesus. And I know about Paul. But who are you?" 16Then the man who had the evil spirit jumped on Sceva's sons. He overpowered them all. He gave them a terrible beating. They ran out of the house naked and bleeding.

17The Jews and Greeks living in Ephesus heard about this. They were all overcome with fear. They held the name of the Lord Jesus in high honor. 18Many who believed now came and openly admitted the evil they had done. 19A number of those who had practiced evil magic brought their scrolls together. They set them on fire out in the open. They added up the value of the scrolls. They found that it would take more than two lifetimes to earn what the scrolls were worth.

20The word of the Lord spread everywhere. It became more and more powerful.

21After all this had happened, Paul decided to go to Jerusalem. He went through Macedonia and Achaia. "After I have been to Jerusalem," he said, "I must visit Rome also." 22He sent Timothy and Erastus, two of his helpers, to Macedonia. But he stayed a little longer in Asia Minor.

Trouble in Ephesus

23At that time many people became very upset about the Way of Jesus. 24There was a man named Demetrius who made things out of silver. He made silver models of the temple of the goddess Artemis. He brought in a lot of business for the other skilled workers. 25One day he called them together. He also called others who were in the same kind of business. "Men," he said, "you know that we make good money from our work. 26You have seen and heard what this fellow Paul is doing. He has talked to large numbers of people here in Ephesus. Almost everywhere in Asia Minor he has led people away from our gods. He says that the gods we make are not gods at all. 27Our work is in danger of losing its good name. People's faith in the temple of the great goddess Artemis will be weakened. Now she is worshiped through all of Asia Minor and the whole world. But soon she will be robbed of her greatness."

28When they heard this, they became very angry. They began shouting, "Great is Artemis of the Ephesians!" 29Soon people were making trouble in the whole city. They all rushed into the theater. They dragged Gaius and Aristarchus along with them. These two men had come with Paul from Macedonia. 30Paul wanted to appear in front of the crowd. But the believers wouldn't let him. 31Some of the officials in Asia Minor were friends of Paul. They sent him a message, begging him not to go into the theater.

32The crowd didn't know what was going on. Some were shouting one thing and some another. Most of the people didn't even know why they were there. 33The Jews pushed Alexander to the front. Some of the crowd tried to tell him what to say. But he motioned for them to be quiet. He wanted to speak up for himself in front of the people. 34But then they realized that he was a Jew. So they all shouted the same thing for about two hours. "Great is Artemis of the Ephesians!" they yelled.

35 The city clerk quieted the crowd down. "Men of Ephesus!" he said. "The whole world knows that the city of Ephesus guards the temple of the great Artemis. They know that Ephesus guards her statue, which fell from heaven. 36 These facts can't be questioned. So calm down. Don't do anything foolish.

37 "These men haven't robbed any temples. They haven't said evil things against our goddess. But you have brought them here anyhow. 38 Demetrius and the other skilled workers may feel they have been wronged by someone. Let them bring charges. The courts are open. We have our governors. 39 Is there anything else you want to bring up? Settle it in a court of law. 40 As it is, today we are in danger of being charged with causing all this trouble. But there is no reason for it. We wouldn't be able to explain what has happened." 41 After he said this, he sent the people away.

Paul Travels Through Macedonia and Greece

20 All the trouble came to an end. Then Paul sent for the believers. After cheering them up, he said good-by. He then left for Macedonia. 2 He traveled through that area, speaking many words of hope to the people. Finally he arrived in Greece. 3 There he stayed for three months. He was just about to sail for Syria. But the Jews were making plans against him. So he decided to go back through Macedonia. 4 Sopater, son of Pyrrhus, from Berea went with him. Aristarchus and Secundus from Thessalonica, Gaius from Derbe, and Timothy went too. Tychicus and Trophimus from Asia Minor also went with him. 5 These men went on ahead. They waited for us at Troas. 6 But we sailed from Philippi after the Feast of Unleavened Bread. Five days later we joined the others at Troas. We stayed there for seven days.

Eutychus Is Raised From the Dead

7 On the first day of the week we met to break bread and eat together. Paul spoke to the people. He kept on talking until midnight because he planned to leave the next day. 8 There were many lamps in the room upstairs where we were meeting. 9 A young man named Eutychus was sitting in a window. He sank into a deep sleep as Paul talked on and on. Sound asleep, Eutychus fell from the third floor. When they picked him up from the ground, he was dead.

10 Paul went down and threw himself on the young man. He put his arms around him. "Don't be alarmed," he told them. "He's alive!" 11 Then Paul went upstairs again. He broke bread and ate with them. He kept on talking until daylight. Then he left. 12 The people took the young man home. They were greatly comforted because he was alive.

Paul Says Good-by to the Ephesian Elders

13 We went on ahead to the ship. We sailed for Assos. There we were going to take Paul on board. He had planned it this way because he wanted to go there by land. 14 So he met us at Assos. We took him on board and went on to Mitylene.

15 The next day we sailed from there. We arrived near Kios. The day after that we crossed over to Samos. We arrived at Miletus the next day. 16 Paul had decided to sail past Ephesus. He didn't want to spend time in Asia Minor. He was in a hurry to get to Jerusalem. If he could, he wanted to be there by the day of Pentecost.

17 From Miletus, Paul sent for the elders of the church at Ephesus. 18 When they arrived, he spoke to them. "You know how I lived the whole time I was with you," he said. "From the first day I came into Asia Minor, 19 I was free of pride. I served the Lord with tears. I served him even though I was greatly tested by the evil plans of the Jews. 20 You know I haven't let anyone keep me from preaching anything that would be helpful to you. I have taught you in public and from house to house. 21 I have told both Jews and Greeks that they must turn away from their sins to God. They must have faith in our Lord Jesus.

22 "Now I am going to Jerusalem. The Holy Spirit compels me. I don't know what will happen to me there. 23 I only know that in every city the Spirit warns me. He tells me that I will face prison and suffering. 24 But my life means nothing to me. I only want to finish the race. I want to complete the work the Lord Jesus has given me. He wants me to give witness to others about the good news of God's grace.

25 "I have spent time with you preaching about the kingdom. I know that none of you will ever see me again. 26 So I tell you today that I am not guilty if anyone has not believed. 27 I haven't let anyone keep me from telling you everything God wants you to do.

28 "Keep watch over yourselves. Keep watch over all the believers. The Holy Spirit has made you leaders over them. Be shepherds of God's church. He bought it with his own blood.

29 "I know that after I leave, wild wolves will come in among you. They won't spare any of the sheep. 30 Even men from your own people will rise up and twist the truth. They want to get the believers to follow them. 31 So be on your guard! Remember that for three years I never stopped warning you. Night and day I warned each of you with tears.

32 "Now I commit you to God's care. I commit you to the word of his grace. It can build you up. Then you will share in what God plans to give all his people. 33 I haven't longed for anyone's silver or gold or clothing. 34 You yourselves know that I have used my own hands to meet my needs. I have

also met the needs of my companions. 35In everything I did, I showed you that we must work hard and help the weak. We must remember the words of the Lord Jesus. He said, 'It is more blessed to give than to receive.'"

36When Paul had said this, he got down on his knees with all of them and prayed. 37They all cried as they hugged and kissed him. 38What hurt them the most was that he had said they would never see his face again. Then they went with him to the ship.

Paul Continues His Journey

21 After we had torn ourselves away from the Ephesian elders, we headed out to sea. We sailed straight to Cos. The next day we went to Rhodes. From there we continued on to Patara. 2We found a ship crossing over to Phoenicia. So we went on board and headed out to sea. 3We came near Cyprus and passed to the south of it. Then we sailed on to Syria. We landed at Tyre. There our ship was supposed to unload. 4We found the believers there and stayed with them for seven days. Led by the Holy Spirit, they tried to get Paul not to go on to Jerusalem. 5But when it was time to leave, we continued on our way. All the believers and their families went with us out of the city. There on the beach we got down on our knees to pray. 6We said good-by to each other. Then we went on board the ship. And they returned home.

7Continuing on from Tyre, we landed at Ptolemais. There we greeted the brothers and sisters. We stayed with them for a day. 8The next day we left and arrived at Caesarea. We stayed at the house of Philip the evangelist. He was one of the seven deacons. 9He had four unmarried daughters who prophesied.

10We stayed there several days. Then a prophet named Agabus came down from Judea. 11He came over to us. Then he took Paul's belt and tied his own hands and feet with it. He said, "The Holy Spirit says, 'This is how the Jews of Jerusalem will tie up the owner of this belt. They will hand him over to people who are not Jews.'"

12When we heard this, we all begged Paul not to go up to Jerusalem. 13He asked, "Why are you crying? Why are you breaking my heart? I'm ready to be put in prison. In fact, I'm ready to die in Jerusalem for the Lord Jesus." 14We couldn't change his mind. So we gave up. We said, "May what the Lord wants to happen be done."

15After this, we got ready and went up to Jerusalem. 16Some of the believers from Caesarea went with us. They brought us to Mnason's home. We were supposed to stay there. Mnason was from Cyprus. He was one of the first believers.

Paul Arrives in Jerusalem

17When we arrived in Jerusalem, the brothers and sisters gave us a warm welcome. 18The next day Paul and the rest of us went to see James. All the elders were there. 19Paul greeted them. Then he reported everything God had done among the non-Jews through his work.

20When they heard this, they praised God. Then they spoke to Paul. "Brother," they said, "you see that thousands of Jews have become believers. All of them try very hard to obey the law. 21They have been told that you teach all the Jews who live among the non-Jews to turn away from Moses. They think that you teach them not to circumcise their children. They think that you teach them to give up our Jewish ways.

22"What should we do? They will certainly hear that you have come. 23So do what we tell you. There are four men with us who have made a promise to God. 24Take them with you. Join them in the Jewish practice that makes people pure and clean. Pay their expenses so they can have their heads shaved. Then everybody will know that these reports about you are not true in any way. They will know that you yourself obey the law.

25"We have already given written directions to the believers who are not Jews. They must not eat food that has been offered to statues of gods. They must not drink blood. They must not eat the meat of animals that have been choked to death. And they must not commit sexual sins."

26The next day Paul took the men with him. They all made themselves pure and clean in the usual way. Then Paul went to the temple. There he reported the date when the days of cleansing would end. At that time the proper offering would be made for each of them.

Paul Is Arrested

27The seven days of cleansing were almost over. Some Jews from Asia Minor saw Paul at the temple. They stirred up the whole crowd. They arrested Paul. 28"Men of Israel, help us!" they shouted. "This is the man who teaches everyone in all places against our people. He speaks against our law and against this holy place. Besides, he has brought Greeks into the temple area. He has made this holy place unclean." 29They said this because they had seen Trophimus the Ephesian in the city with Paul. They thought Paul had brought him into the temple area.

30The whole city was stirred up. People came running from all directions. They grabbed Paul and dragged him out of the temple. Right away the temple gates were shut. 31The people were trying to kill Paul. But news reached the commander of the Roman troops. He heard that people were making trouble in the whole city of Jerusalem. 32At once he took some officers and soldiers with him. They ran down to the crowd. The people causing the trouble saw the commander and his soldiers. So they stopped beating Paul.

33The commander came up and arrested Paul. He ordered him to be held with two chains. Then he asked who Paul was and what he had done. 34Some in the crowd shouted one thing, some another. But the commander couldn't get the facts

because of all the noise. So he ordered that Paul
be taken into the fort. 35Paul reached the steps. But
then the mob became so wild that he had to be carried by the soldiers. 36The crowd that followed
kept shouting, "Kill him!"

Paul Speaks to the Crowd

37The soldiers were about to take Paul into the
fort. Then he asked the commander, "May I say
something to you?"
"Do you speak Greek?" he replied. 38"Aren't
you the Egyptian who turned some of our people
against their leaders? Didn't you lead 4,000 ter-
rorists out into the desert some time ago?"
39Paul answered, "I am a Jew from Tarsus in Cilicia. I am a citizen of an important city. Please let
me speak to the people."
40The commander told him he could. So Paul
stood on the steps and motioned to the crowd.
When all of them were quiet, he spoke to them in
22 the Aramaic language. 1"Brothers and
fathers," Paul began, "listen to me now. I
want to speak up for myself."
2When they heard that he was speaking to them
in Aramaic, they became very quiet.
Then Paul said, 3"I am a Jew. I was born in Tarsus in Cilicia. But I grew up here in Jerusalem. I
was well trained by Gamaliel in the law of our
people. I wanted to serve God as much as any of
you do today. 4I hurt the followers of the Way of
Jesus. I sent many of them to their death. I arrested
men and women. I threw them into prison. 5The
high priest and the whole Council can give witness
to this. I even had some official letters they had
written to their friends in Damascus. So I went
there to bring these people as prisoners to Jerusalem to be punished.
6"I had almost reached Damascus. About noon
a bright light from heaven suddenly flashed
around me. 7I fell to the ground and heard a voice
speak to me. 'Saul! Saul!' it said. 'Why are you
opposing me?'
8" 'Who are you, Lord?' I asked.
" 'I am Jesus of Nazareth,' he replied. 'I am the
one you are opposing.'
9"The light was seen by my companions. But
they didn't understand the voice of the one speaking to me.
10" 'What should I do, Lord?' I asked.
" 'Get up,' the Lord said. 'Go into Damascus.
There you will be told everything you have been
given to do.' 11The brightness of the light had
blinded me. So my companions led me by the
hand into Damascus.
12"A man named Ananias came to see me. He
was a godly Jew who obeyed the law. All the Jews
living there respected him very much. 13He stood
beside me and said, 'Brother Saul, receive your
sight!' At that very moment I was able to see him.
14"Then he said, 'The God of our people has
chosen you. He wanted to tell you his plans for
you. You have seen the Blameless One. You have
heard words from his mouth. 15Now you will give
witness to all people about what you have seen and
heard. 16So what are you waiting for? Get up and
call on his name. Be baptized. Have your sins
washed away.'
17"I returned to Jerusalem and was praying at
the temple. Then it seemed to me that I was dreaming. 18I saw the Lord speaking to me. 'Quick!' he
said. 'Leave Jerusalem at once. These people will
not accept your witness about me.'
19" 'Lord,' I replied, 'these people know what I
used to do. I went from one synagogue to another
and put believers in prison. I also beat them. 20Ste-
phen was a man who gave witness to others about
you. I stood there when he was killed. I had agreed
that he should die. I even guarded the coats of
those who were killing him.'
21"Then the Lord said to me, 'Go. I will send
you far away to people who are not Jews.' "

Paul the Roman Citizen

22The crowd listened to Paul until he said this.
Then they shouted, "Kill him! He isn't fit to live!"
23They shouted and threw off their coats. They
threw dust into the air. 24So the commanding officer ordered Paul to be taken into the fort. He gave
orders for Paul to be whipped and questioned. He
wanted to find out why the people were shouting
at him like this.
25A commander was standing there as they
stretched Paul out to be whipped. Paul said to him,
"Does the law allow you to whip a Roman citizen
who hasn't even been found guilty?"
26When the commander heard this, he went to
the commanding officer and reported it. "What are
you going to do?" the commander asked. "This
man is a Roman citizen."
27So the commanding officer went to Paul. "Tell
me," he asked. "Are you a Roman citizen?"
"Yes, I am," Paul answered.
28Then the officer said, "I had to pay a lot of
money to become a citizen."
"But I was born a citizen," Paul replied.
29Right away those who were about to question
him left. Even the officer was alarmed. He realized
that he had put Paul, a Roman citizen, in chains.

Paul Is Taken to the Sanhedrin

30The commanding officer wanted to find out
exactly what the Jews had against Paul. So the next
day he let Paul out of prison. He ordered a meeting
of the chief priests and all the Sanhedrin. Then he
brought Paul and had him stand in front of them.
23 Paul looked straight at the Sanhedrin. "My
brothers," he said, "I have always done my
duty to God. To this very day I feel that I have
done nothing wrong."
2Ananias the high priest heard this. So he
ordered the men standing near Paul to hit him on
the mouth.

3 Then Paul said to him, "You pretender! God will hit you! You sit there and judge me by the law. But you yourself broke the law when you commanded them to hit me!"

4 Those who were standing near Paul said, "How dare you talk like that to God's high priest!"

5 Paul replied, "Brothers, I didn't realize he was the high priest. It is written, 'Do not speak evil about the ruler of your people.'" *(Exodus 22:28)*

6 Paul knew that some of them were Sadducees and the others Pharisees. So he called out in the Sanhedrin. "My brothers," he said, "I am a Pharisee. I am the son of a Pharisee. I believe that people will rise from the dead. That's why I am on trial."

7 When he said this, the Pharisees and the Sadducees started to argue. They began to take sides. 8 The Sadducees say that people will not rise from the dead. They don't believe there are angels or spirits either. But the Pharisees believe all these things.

9 People were causing trouble and making a lot of noise. Some of the teachers of the law who were Pharisees stood up. They argued strongly. "We find nothing wrong with this man," they said. "What if a spirit or an angel has spoken to him?" 10 The arguing got out of hand. The commanding officer was afraid that Paul would be torn to pieces by those who were arguing. So he ordered the soldiers to go down and take him away from them by force. They were supposed to bring him into the fort.

11 The next night the Lord stood near Paul. He said, "Be brave! You have given witness about me in Jerusalem. You must do the same in Rome."

The Plan to Kill Paul

12 The next morning the Jews gathered secretly to make plans against Paul. They took an oath that they would not eat or drink anything until they had killed him. 13 More than 40 men took part in this plan. 14 They went to the chief priests and the elders. They said, "We have taken a strong oath. We have made a special promise to God. We will not eat anything until we have killed Paul. 15 Now then, you and the Sanhedrin must make an appeal to the commanding officer. Ask him to bring Paul to you. Pretend you want more facts about his case. We are ready to kill him before he gets here."

16 But Paul's nephew heard about this plan. So he went into the fort and told Paul.

17 Then Paul called one of the commanders. He said to him, "Take this young man to the commanding officer. He has something to tell him." 18 So the commander took Paul's nephew to the officer.

The commander said, "Paul, the prisoner, sent for me. He asked me to bring this young man to you. The young man has something to tell you."

19 The commanding officer took the young man by the hand. He spoke to him in private. "What do you want to tell me?" the officer asked.

20 He said, "The Jews have agreed to ask you to bring Paul to the Sanhedrin tomorrow. They will pretend they want more facts about him. 21 Don't give in to them. More than 40 of them are waiting in hiding to attack him. They have taken an oath that they will not eat or drink anything until they have killed him. They are ready now. All they need is for you to bring Paul to the Sanhedrin."

22 The commanding officer let the young man go. But he gave him a warning. "Don't tell anyone you have reported this to me," he said.

Paul Is Taken to Caesarea

23 Then the commanding officer called for two of his commanders. He ordered them, "Gather a company of 200 soldiers, 70 horsemen and 200 men armed with spears. Get them ready to go to Caesarea at nine o'clock tonight. 24 Provide horses for Paul so that he may be taken safely to Governor Felix."

25 Here is the letter the officer wrote.

> 26 I, Claudius Lysias, am writing this letter.
>
> I am sending it to His Excellency, Governor Felix.
>
> Greetings.
>
> 27 The Jews grabbed Paul. They were about to kill him. But I came with my soldiers and saved him. I had learned that he is a Roman citizen. 28 I wanted to know why they were bringing charges against him. So I brought him to their Sanhedrin. 29 I found out that the charge against him was based on questions about their law. But there was no charge against him worthy of death or prison. 30 Then I was told about a plan against the man. So I sent him to you at once. I also ordered those bringing charges against him to tell you their case.

31 The soldiers followed their orders. During the night they took Paul with them. They brought him as far as Antipatris. 32 The next day they let the horsemen go on with him. The soldiers returned to the fort. 33 The horsemen arrived in Caesarea. They gave the letter to the governor. Then they handed Paul over to him. 34 The governor read the letter. He asked Paul where he was from. He learned that Paul was from Cilicia. 35 So he said, "I will hear your case when those bringing charges against you get here." Then he ordered that Paul be kept under guard in Herod's palace.

Paul's Trial in Front of Felix

24 Five days later Ananias the high priest went down to Caesarea. Some elders and a lawyer named Tertullus went with him. They brought their charges against Paul to the governor. 2 So Paul was called in. Tertullus began to bring the

charges against Paul. He said to Felix, "We have enjoyed a long time of peace while you have been ruling. You are a wise leader. You have made this a better nation. [3]Most excellent Felix, we gladly admit this everywhere and in every way. And we are very thankful. [4]I don't want to bother you. But would you be kind enough to listen to us for a short time?

[5]"We have found that Paul is a troublemaker. He stirs up trouble among Jews all over the world. He is a leader of those who follow Jesus of Nazareth. [6/7]He even tried to pollute our temple. So we arrested him. [8]Question him yourself. Then you will learn the truth about all these charges we are bringing against him."

[9]The Jews said the same thing. They agreed that the charges were true.

[10]The governor motioned for Paul to speak. Paul said, "I know that you have been a judge over this nation for quite a few years. So I am glad to stand up for myself. [11]About 12 days ago I went up to Jerusalem to worship. You can easily check on this. [12]Those bringing charges against me did not find me arguing with anyone at the temple. I wasn't stirring up a crowd in the synagogues or anywhere else in the city. [13]They can't prove to you any of the charges they are making against me.

[14]"It is true that I worship the God of our people. I am a follower of the Way of Jesus. Those bringing charges against me call it a cult. I believe everything that agrees with the Law. I believe everything written in the Prophets. [15]I have the same hope in God that these men have. I believe that both the godly and the ungodly will rise from the dead. [16]So I always try not to do anything wrong in the eyes of God and man.

[17]"I was away for several years. Then I came to Jerusalem to bring my people gifts for those who were poor. I also came to offer sacrifices. [18]They found me doing this in the temple courtyard. I had already been made pure and clean in the usual way. There was no crowd with me. I didn't stir up any trouble.

[19]"But there are some other Jews who should be here in front of you. They are from Asia Minor. They should bring charges if they have anything against me. [20]Let the Jews who are here tell you what crime I am guilty of. After all, I was put on trial by the Sanhedrin. [21]Perhaps they blame me for what I said when I was on trial. I shouted, 'I believe that people will rise from the dead. That is why I am on trial here today.'"

[22]Felix knew all about the Way of Jesus. So he put off the trial for the time being. "Lysias the commanding officer will come," he said. "Then I will decide your case." [23]He ordered the commander to keep Paul under guard. He told him to give Paul some freedom. He also told him to allow Paul's friends to take care of his needs.

[24]Several days later Felix came with his wife Drusilla. She was a Jew. Felix sent for Paul and listened to him speak about faith in Christ Jesus. [25]Paul talked about how to live right. He talked about how people should control themselves. He also talked about the time when God will judge everyone. Then Felix became afraid. "That's enough for now!" he said. "You may leave. When I find the time, I will send for you." [26]He was hoping that Paul would offer him some money to let him go. So he often sent for Paul and talked with him.

[27]Two years passed. Porcius Festus took the place of Felix. But Felix wanted to do the Jews a favor. So he left Paul in prison.

Paul's Trial in Front of Festus

25 Three days after Festus arrived, he went up from Caesarea to Jerusalem. [2]There the chief priests and Jewish leaders came to him and brought their charges against Paul. [3]They tried to get Festus to have Paul taken to Jerusalem. They asked for this as a favor. They were planning to hide and attack Paul along the way. They wanted to kill him. [4]Festus answered, "Paul is being held at Caesarea. Soon I'll be going there myself. [5]Let some of your leaders come with me. If the man has done anything wrong, they can bring charges against him there."

[6]Festus spent eight or ten days in Jerusalem with them. Then he went down to Caesarea. The next day he called the court together. He ordered Paul to be brought to him. [7]When Paul arrived, the Jews who had come down from Jerusalem stood around him. They brought many strong charges against him. But they couldn't prove them.

[8]Then Paul spoke up for himself. He said, "I've done nothing wrong against the law of the Jews or against the temple. I've done nothing wrong against Caesar."

[9]But Festus wanted to do the Jews a favor. So he said to Paul, "Are you willing to go up to Jerusalem? Are you willing to go on trial there? Are you willing to face these charges in my court?"

[10]Paul answered, "I'm already standing in Caesar's court. This is where I should go on trial. I haven't done anything wrong to the Jews. You yourself know that very well. [11]If I am guilty of anything worthy of death, I'm willing to die. But the charges brought against me by these Jews are not true. No one has the right to hand me over to them. I make my appeal to Caesar!"

[12]Festus talked it over with the members of his court. Then he said, "You have made an appeal to Caesar. To Caesar you will go!"

Festus Talks With King Agrippa

[13]A few days later King Agrippa and Bernice arrived in Caesarea. They came to pay a visit to Festus. [14]They were spending many days there. So Festus talked with the king about Paul's case. He said, "There's a man here that Felix left as a prisoner. [15]When I went to Jerusalem, the Jewish chief

priests and the elders brought charges against the man. They wanted him to be found guilty.

16“I told them that this is not the way Romans do things. We don’t judge people before they have faced those bringing charges against them. They must have a chance to speak up for themselves. 17When the Jews came back with me, I didn’t waste any time. I called the court together the next day. I ordered the man to be brought in. 18Those bringing charges against him got up to speak. But they didn’t charge him with any of the crimes I had expected. 19Instead, they argued with him about their own beliefs. They didn’t agree about a dead man named Jesus. Paul claimed Jesus was alive.

20“I had no idea how to look into such matters. So I asked Paul if he would be willing to go to Jerusalem. There he could be tried on these charges. 21But Paul made an appeal to have the Emperor decide his case. So I ordered him to be held until I could send him to Caesar.”

22Then Agrippa said to Festus, “I would like to hear this man myself.”

Festus replied, “Tomorrow you will hear him.”

Paul Speaks to Agrippa

23The next day Agrippa and Bernice arrived. They acted like very important people. They entered the courtroom. The most important officers and the leading men of the city came with them. When Festus gave the command, Paul was brought in. 24Festus said, “King Agrippa, and all who are here with us, take a good look at this man! Both in Jerusalem and here in Caesarea a large number of Jews have come to me about him. They keep shouting that he shouldn’t live any longer. 25I have found that he hasn’t done anything worthy of death. But he made his appeal to the Emperor. So I decided to send him to Rome.

26“I don’t have anything certain to write about him to His Majesty. So I have brought him here today. Now all of you will be able to hear him. King Agrippa, it will also be very good for you to hear him. As a result of this hearing, I will have something to write. 27It doesn’t make sense to send a prisoner to Rome without listing the charges against him.”

26 Agrippa said to Paul, “You may now speak for yourself.”

So Paul motioned with his hand. Then he began to stand up for himself. 2“King Agrippa,” he said, “I am happy to be able to stand here today. I will speak up for myself against all the charges brought by the Jews. 3I am very pleased that you are familiar with Jewish ways. You know the kinds of things they argue about. So I beg you to be patient as you listen to me.

4“The Jews all know how I have lived ever since I was a child. They know all about me from the beginning of my life. They know how I lived in my own country and in Jerusalem. 5They have known me for a long time. So if they wanted to, they could give witness that I lived by the rules of the Pharisees. Those rules are harder to obey than the rules of any other group in the Jewish faith.

6“Today I am on trial because of the hope I have. I believe in what God promised our people long ago. 7It is the promise that our 12 tribes are hoping to see come true. Because of this hope they serve God with a true and honest heart day and night. King Agrippa, it is also because of this hope that the Jews are bringing charges against me. 8Why should any of you think it is impossible for God to raise the dead?

9“I myself believed that I should do everything I could to oppose the name of Jesus of Nazareth. 10That’s just what I was doing in Jerusalem. On the authority of the chief priests, I put many of God’s people in prison. I agreed that they should die. 11I often went from one synagogue to another to have them punished. I tried to force them to speak evil things against Jesus. I hated them so much that I even went to cities in other lands to hurt them.

12“On one of these journeys I was on my way to Damascus. I had the authority and commission of the chief priests. 13About noon, King Agrippa, I was on the road. I saw a light coming from heaven. It was brighter than the sun. It was shining around me and my companions. 14We all fell to the ground. I heard a voice speak to me in the Aramaic language. ‘Saul! Saul!’ it said. ‘Why are you opposing me? It is hard for you to go against what you know is right.’

15“Then I asked, ‘Who are you, Lord?’

“‘I am Jesus,’ the Lord replied. ‘I am the one you are opposing. 16Now get up. Stand on your feet. I have appeared to you to appoint you to serve me and be my witness. You will tell others that you have seen me today. You will also tell them that I will show myself to you again.

17“‘I will save you from your own people and from those who aren’t Jews. I am sending you to them 18to open their eyes. I want you to turn them from darkness to light. I want you to turn them from Satan’s power to God. I want their sins to be forgiven. They will be forgiven when they believe in me. They will have their place among God’s people.’

19“So then, King Agrippa, I obeyed the vision that appeared from heaven. 20First I preached to people in Damascus. Then I preached in Jerusalem and in all Judea. I preached also to people who are not Jews. I told them to turn away from their sins to God. The way they live must prove that they have turned away from their sins. 21That’s why the Jews grabbed me in the temple courtyard and tried to kill me.

22“But God has helped me to this very day. So I stand here and give witness to both small and great. I have been saying nothing different from what the prophets and Moses said would happen. 23They said the Christ would suffer. He would be the first to rise from the dead. He would announce the light of life to his own people and to those who aren't Jews."

24While Paul was still speaking up for himself, Festus interrupted. "You are out of your mind, Paul!" he shouted. "Your great learning is driving you crazy!"

25"I am not crazy, most excellent Festus," Paul replied. "What I am saying is true and reasonable. 26The king is familiar with these things. So I can speak openly to him. I am certain he knows everything that has been going on. After all, it was not done in secret. 27King Agrippa, do you believe the prophets? I know you do."

28Then Agrippa spoke to Paul. "Are you trying to talk me into becoming a Christian?" he said. "Do you think you can do that in such a short time?"

29Paul replied, "I don't care if it takes a short time or a long time. I pray to God for you and all who are listening to me today. I pray that you may become like me, except for these chains."

30The king stood up. The governor and Bernice and those sitting with them stood up too. 31They left the room and began to talk with one another. "Why should this man die or be put in prison?" they said. "He has done nothing worthy of that!"

32Agrippa said to Festus, "This man could have been set free. But he has made an appeal to Caesar."

Paul Sails for Rome

27 It was decided that we would sail for Italy. Paul and some other prisoners were handed over to a Roman commander named Julius. He belonged to the Imperial Guard. 2We boarded a ship from Adramyttium. It was about to sail for ports along the coast of Asia Minor. We headed out to sea. Aristarchus was with us. He was a Macedonian from Thessalonica.

3The next day we landed at Sidon. There Julius was kind to Paul. He let Paul visit his friends so they could give him what he needed. 4From there we headed out to sea again. We passed the calmer side of Cyprus because the winds were against us.

5We sailed across the open sea off the coast of Cilicia and Pamphylia. Then we landed at Myra in Lycia. 6There the commander found a ship from Alexandria sailing for Italy. He put us on board. 7We moved along slowly for many days. We had trouble getting to Cnidus. The wind did not let us stay on course. So we passed the calmer side of Crete, opposite Salmone. 8It was not easy to sail along the coast. Then we came to a place called Fair Havens. It was near the town of Lasea.

9A lot of time had passed. Sailing had already become dangerous. By now it was after the Day of Atonement, a day of fasting. So Paul gave them a warning. 10"Men," he said, "I can see that our trip is going to be dangerous. The ship and everything in it will be lost. Our own lives will be in danger also."

11But the commander didn't listen to what Paul said. Instead, he followed the advice of the pilot and the ship's owner. 12The harbor wasn't a good place for ships to stay during winter. So most of the people decided we should sail on. They hoped we would reach Phoenix. They wanted to spend the winter there. Phoenix was a harbor in Crete. It faced both southwest and northwest.

The Storm

13A gentle south wind began to blow. They thought that this was what they had been waiting for. So they pulled up the anchor and sailed along the shore of Crete. 14Before very long, a wind blew down from the island. It had the force of a hurricane. It was called a "northeaster."

15The ship was caught by the storm. We could not keep it sailing into the wind. So we gave up and were driven along. 16We passed the calmer side of a small island called Cauda. We almost lost the lifeboat. 17So the men lifted it on board. Then they tied ropes under the ship itself to hold it together. They were afraid it would get stuck on the sandbars of Syrtis. They lowered the sea anchor and let the ship be driven along.

18We took a very bad beating from the storm. The next day the crew began to throw the ship's contents overboard. 19On the third day, they even threw the ship's gear overboard with their own hands. 20The sun and stars didn't appear for many days. The storm was terrible. So we gave up all hope of being saved.

21The men had not eaten for a long time. Paul stood up in front of them. "Men," he said, "you should have taken my advice not to sail from Crete. Then you would have avoided this harm and loss.

22"Now I beg you to be brave. Not one of you will die. Only the ship will be destroyed. 23I belong to God and serve him. Last night his angel stood beside me. 24The angel said, 'Do not be afraid, Paul. You must go on trial in front of Caesar. God has shown his grace by sparing the lives of all those sailing with you.'

25"Men, continue to be brave. I have faith in God. It will happen just as he told me. 26But we must run the ship onto the beach of some island."

The Ship Is Destroyed

27On the 14th night we were still being driven across the Sea of Adria. About midnight the sailors had a feeling that they were approaching land. 28They measured how deep the water was. They found that it was 120 feet deep. A short time later they measured the water again. This time it was 90 feet deep. 29They were afraid we would crash against the rocks. So they dropped four anchors from the back of the ship. They prayed that daylight would come.

30The sailors wanted to escape from the ship. So they let the lifeboat down into the sea. They pretended they were going to lower some anchors from the front of the ship. 31But Paul spoke to the

commander and the soldiers. "These men must
stay with the ship," he said. "If they don't, you
can't be saved." 32So the soldiers cut the ropes that
held the lifeboat. They let it drift away.
33Just before dawn Paul tried to get them all to
eat. "For the last 14 days," he said, "you have
wondered what would happen. You have gone
without food. You haven't eaten anything. 34Now
I am asking you to eat some food. You need it to
live. Not one of you will lose a single hair from
your head."
35After Paul said this, he took some bread and
gave thanks to God. He did this where they all
could see him. Then he broke it and began to eat.
36All of them were filled with hope. So they ate
some food. 37There were 276 of us on board.
38They ate as much as they wanted. They needed to
make the ship lighter. So they threw the rest of the
grain into the sea.
39When daylight came, they saw a bay with a
sandy beach. They didn't recognize the place. But
they decided to run the ship onto the beach if they
could. 40So they cut the anchors loose and left
them in the sea. At the same time, they untied the
ropes that held the rudders. They lifted the sail at
the front of the ship to the wind. Then they headed
for the beach. 41But the ship hit a sandbar. So the
front of it got stuck and wouldn't move. The back
of the ship was broken to pieces by the pounding
of the waves.
42The soldiers planned to kill the prisoners.
They wanted to keep them from swimming away
and escaping. 43But the commander wanted to save
Paul's life. So he kept the soldiers from carrying
out their plan. He ordered those who could swim
to jump overboard first and swim to land. 44The
rest were supposed to get there on boards or other
pieces of the ship. That is how everyone reached
land safely.

On Shore at Malta

28 When we were safe on shore, we found out
that the island was called Malta. 2The people of the island were unusually kind. It was raining and cold. So they built a fire and welcomed all
of us.
3Paul gathered some sticks and put them on the
fire. A poisonous snake was driven out by the heat.
It fastened itself on Paul's hand. 4The people of the
island saw the snake hanging from his hand. They
said to each other, "This man must be a murderer.
He escaped from the sea. But Justice won't let him
live." Justice was the name of a goddess.
5Paul shook the snake off into the fire. He was
not harmed. 6The people expected him to swell up.
They thought he would suddenly fall dead. They
waited for a long time. But they didn't see anything unusual happen to him. So they changed
their minds. They said he was a god.
7Publius owned property nearby. He was the
chief official on the island. He welcomed us to his
home. For three days he took care of us. He treated
us with kindness. 8His father was sick in bed. The
man suffered from fever and dysentery. So Paul
went in to see him. Paul prayed for him. He placed
his hands on him and healed him.
9Then the rest of the sick people on the island
came. They too were healed. 10The people of the
island honored us in many ways. When we were
ready to sail, they gave us the supplies we needed.

Paul Arrives in Rome

11After three months we headed out to sea. We
sailed in a ship that had stayed at the island during
the winter. It was a ship from Alexandria. On the
front of it the figures of twin gods were carved.
Their names were Castor and Pollux. 12We landed
at Syracuse and stayed there for three days.
13From there we sailed to Rhegium. The next
day the south wind came up. The day after that, we
reached Puteoli. 14There we found some believers.
They invited us to spend a week with them.
At last we came to Rome. 15The brothers and
sisters there had heard we were coming. They traveled as far as the Forum of Appius and the Three
Taverns to meet us. When Paul saw these people,
he thanked God and was cheered up. 16When we
got to Rome, Paul was allowed to live by himself.
But a soldier guarded him.

Paul Preaches in Rome

17Three days later Paul called a meeting of the
Jewish leaders. So they came. Paul said to them,
"My brothers, I have done nothing against our
people. I have also done nothing against what our
people of long ago practiced. But I was arrested in
Jerusalem. I was handed over to the Romans.
18"They questioned me. And they wanted to let
me go. They saw I wasn't guilty of any crime worthy of death. 19But the Jews objected. So I had to
make an appeal to Caesar.
"It wasn't that I had anything against my own
people. 20I share Israel's hope. That is why I am
held with this chain. So I have asked to see you
and talk with you."
21They replied, "We have not received any letters from Judea about you. None of our companions who came from there has reported or said
anything bad about you. 22But we want to hear
what your ideas are. We know that people everywhere are talking against those who believe as
you do."
23They decided to meet Paul on a certain day. At
that time even more people came to the place
where he was staying. From morning until evening,
he told them about God's kingdom and explained
it to them. Using the Law of Moses and the
Prophets, he tried to get them to believe in Jesus.
24Some believed what he said. Others did not.
25They didn't agree with each other. They began to
leave after Paul had made a final statement. He
said, "The Holy Spirit was right when he spoke to

your people long ago. Through Isaiah the prophet
the Spirit said,

26"'Go to your people. Say to them,
"You will hear but never understand.
You will see but never know what you are
seeing."
27These people's hearts have become stubborn.
They can barely hear with their ears.
They have closed their eyes.
Otherwise they might see with their eyes.
They might hear with their ears.
They might understand with their hearts.
They might turn, and then I would heal them.'
(Isaiah 6:9,10)

28/29"Here is what I want you to know. God has
sent his salvation to people who are not Jews. And
they will listen!"

30For two whole years Paul stayed there in a
house he rented. He welcomed all who came to see
him. 31He preached boldly about God's kingdom.
No one could keep him from teaching people
about the Lord Jesus Christ.

Romans

1 I, Paul, am writing this letter. I serve Christ Jesus. I have been appointed to be an apostle. God set me apart to tell others his good news. 2He promised the good news long ago. He announced it through his prophets in the Holy Scriptures.

3The good news is about God's Son. As a human being, the Son of God belonged to King David's family line. 4By the power of the Holy Spirit, he was appointed to be the mighty Son of God because he rose from the dead. He is Jesus Christ our Lord.

5I received God's grace because of what Jesus did so that I could bring glory to him. He made me an apostle to all those who aren't Jews. I must invite them to have faith in God and obey him. 6You also are among those who are appointed to belong to Jesus Christ.

7I am sending this letter to all of you in Rome who are loved by God and appointed to be his people.

May God our Father and the Lord Jesus Christ give you grace and peace.

Paul Longs to Visit Rome

8First, I thank my God through Jesus Christ for all of you. People all over the world are talking about your faith. 9I serve God with my whole heart. I preach the good news about his Son. God knows that I always remember you 10in my prayers. I pray that now at last it may be God's plan to open the way for me to visit you.

11I long to see you. I want to make you strong by giving you a gift from the Holy Spirit. 12I want us to cheer each other up by sharing our faith.

13Brothers and sisters, I want you to know that I planned many times to visit you. But until now I have been kept from coming. My work has produced results among others who are not Jews. In the same way, I want to see results among you.

14I have a duty both to Greeks and to non-Greeks. I have a duty both to wise people and to foolish people. 15So I really want to preach the good news also to you who live in Rome.

16I am not ashamed of the good news. It is God's power. And it will save everyone who believes. It is meant first for the Jews. It is meant also for those who aren't Jews.

17The good news shows how God makes people right with himself. From beginning to end, becoming right with God depends on a person's faith. It is written, "Those who are right with God will live by faith." *(Habakkuk 2:4)*

God's Anger Against Sinners

18God shows his anger from heaven. It is against all the godless and evil things people do. They are so evil that they say no to the truth. 19The truth about God is plain to them. God has made it plain.

20Ever since the world was created it has been possible to see the qualities of God that are not seen. I'm talking about his eternal power and about the fact that he is God. Those things can be seen in what he has made. So people have no excuse for what they do.

21They knew God. But they didn't honor him as God. They didn't thank him. Their thinking became worthless. Their foolish hearts became dark. 22They claimed to be wise. But they made fools of themselves. 23They would rather have statues of gods than the glorious God who lives forever. Their statues of gods are made to look like people, birds, animals and reptiles.

24So God let them go. He allowed them to do what their sinful hearts wanted to. He let them commit sexual sins. They polluted one another's bodies by what they did.

25They chose a lie instead of God's truth. They worshiped and served created things. They didn't worship the Creator. But he must be praised forever. Amen.

26So God let them go. They were filled with shameful longings. Their women committed sexual acts that were not natural. 27In the same way, the men turned away from their natural love for women. They burned with sexual longing for each other. Men did shameful things with other men. They suffered in their bodies for all the twisted things they did.

28They didn't think it was important to know God. So God let them go. He allowed them to have dirty minds. They did things they shouldn't do.

29They are full of every kind of sin, evil and ungodliness. They want more than they need. They commit murder. They want what belongs to other people. They fight and cheat. They hate others. They say mean things about other people. 30They tell lies about them. They hate God. They are rude and proud. They brag. They think of new ways to do evil. They don't obey their parents. 31They are foolish. They can't be trusted. They are not loving and kind.

32They know that God's commands are right. They know that those who do evil things should die. But they continue to do those very things. They also approve of others who do them.

God Judges Fairly

2 If you judge someone else, you have no excuse for it. When you judge another person, you are judging yourself. You do the same things you blame others for doing.

2We know that when God judges those who do evil things, he judges fairly. 3Though you are only a human being, you judge others. But you yourself do the same things. So how do you think you will escape when God judges you?

4Do you make fun of God's great kindness and favor? Do you make fun of God when he is patient with you? Don't you realize that God's kindness is meant to turn you away from your sins?

5But you are stubborn. In your heart you are not sorry for your sins. You are storing up anger against yourself. The day of God's anger is coming. Then his way of judging fairly will be shown. 6God "will give to each person in keeping with what he has done." *(Psalm 62:12; Proverbs 24:12)*

7God will give eternal life to those who keep on doing good. They want glory, honor, and life that never ends. 8But there are others who only look out for themselves. They don't accept the truth. They go down an evil path. God will pour out his burning anger on them. 9There will be trouble and suffering for everyone who does evil. That is meant first for the Jews. It is also meant for the non-Jews. 10But there will be glory, honor and peace for everyone who does good. That is meant first for the Jews. It is also meant for the non-Jews. 11God treats everyone the same.

12Some people do not know God's law when they sin. They will not be judged by the law when they die. Others do know God's law when they sin. They will be judged by the law. 13Hearing the law does not make a person right with God. People are considered to be right with God only when they obey the law.

14Those who aren't Jews do not have the law. Sometimes they just naturally do what the law requires. They are a law for themselves. This is true even though they don't have the law. 15They show that what the law requires is written on their hearts. The way their minds judge them gives witness to that fact. Sometimes their thoughts find them guilty. At other times their thoughts find them not guilty.

16People will be judged on the day God appoints Jesus Christ to judge their secret thoughts. That's part of my good news.

The Jews and the Law

17Suppose you call yourself a Jew. You trust in the law. You brag that you are close to God. 18You know what God wants. You agree with what is best because the law teaches you. 19You are sure you can lead people who are blind. You are sure you are a light for those who are in the dark. 20You claim to be able to teach foolish people. You can even teach babies. You think that in the law you have all knowledge and truth.

21You teach others. But you don't teach yourself! You preach against stealing. But you steal! 22You say that people should not commit adultery. But you commit adultery! You hate statues of gods. But you rob temples! 23You brag about the law. But when you break it, you rob God of his honor! 24It is written, "Those who aren't Jews say evil things against God's name because of you." *(Isaiah 52:5; Ezekiel 36:22)*

25Circumcision has value if you obey the law. But if you break the law, it is just as if you hadn't been circumcised.

26Sometimes those who aren't circumcised do what the law requires. Won't God accept them as if they had been circumcised? 27Many are not circumcised physically, but they obey the law. They will prove that you are guilty. You are breaking the law, even though you have the written law and are circumcised.

28A man is not a Jew if he is a Jew only on the outside. And circumcision is more than just something done to the outside of a man's body.

29No, a man is a Jew only if he is a Jew on the inside. And true circumcision means that the heart has been circumcised. It is done by the Holy Spirit. It is more than just obeying the written Law. Then a man's praise will not come from others. It will come from God.

God Is Faithful

3 Is there any advantage in being a Jew? Is there any value in being circumcised?

2There is great value in every way! First of all, the Jews have been given the very words of God.

3What if some Jews did not believe? Will the fact that they don't have faith keep God from being faithful? 4Not at all! God is true, even though every human being is a liar. It is written,

"You are right when you sentence me.
 You are fair when you judge me."
(Psalm 51:4)

5Doesn't the fact that we are wrong prove more clearly that God is right? Then what can we say? Can we say that God is not fair when he brings his anger down on us? As you can tell, I am just using human ways of thinking. 6God is certainly fair! If he weren't, how could he judge the world?

7Someone might argue, "When I lie, it becomes clearer that God is truthful. It makes his glory shine more brightly. Why then does he find me guilty of sin?"

8Why not say, "Let's do evil things so that good things will happen"? Some people actually lie by reporting that this is what we say. They are the ones who should be found guilty.

No One Is Right With God

9What should we say then? Are we Jews any better? Not at all! We have already claimed that Jews are sinners. The same is true of those who aren't Jews.

10It is written,

"No one is right with God, no one at all.
11 No one understands.
 No one trusts in God.

12 All of them have turned away.
They have all become worthless.
No one does anything good,
no one at all."
(Psalms 14:1–3; 53:1–3; Ecclesiastes 7:20)
13 "Their throats are like open graves.
With their tongues they tell lies." *(Psalm 5:9)*
"The words from their lips are like the poison
of a snake." *(Psalm 140:3)*
14 "Their mouths are full of curses and
bitterness." *(Psalm 10:7)*
15 "They run quickly to commit murder.
16 They leave a trail of failure and pain.
17 They do not know the way of peace."
(Isaiah 59:7,8)
18 "They don't have any respect for God."
(Psalm 36:1)

19 What the law says, it says to those who are
ruled by the law. Its purpose is to shut every mouth
and make the whole world accountable to God.
20 So it can't be said that anyone will be made right
with God by obeying the law. Not at all! The law
makes us more aware of our sin.

Becoming Right With God

21 But now God has shown us how to become
right with him. The Law and the Prophets give witness to this. It has nothing to do with obeying the
law. 22 We are made right with God by putting our
faith in Jesus Christ. That happens to all who believe.

It is no different for the Jews than for anyone
else. 23 Everyone has sinned. No one measures up
to God's glory. 24 The free gift of God's grace
makes all of us right with him. Christ Jesus paid
the price to set us free. 25 God gave him as a sacrifice to pay for sins. So he forgives the sins of those
who have faith in his blood.

God did all of that to prove that he is fair.
Because of his mercy he did not punish people for
the sins they had committed before Jesus died for
them. 26 God did that to prove in our own time that
he is fair. He proved that he is right. He also made
right with himself those who believe in Jesus.

27 So who can brag? No one! Are people saved
by obeying the law? Not at all! They are saved
because of their faith. 28 We firmly believe that people are made right with God because of their faith.
They are not saved by obeying the law.

29 Is God the God of Jews only? Isn't he also the
God of those who aren't Jews? Yes, he is their God
too. 30 There is only one God. When those who are
circumcised believe in him, he makes them right
with himself. When those who are not circumcised
believe in him, he also makes them right with himself. 31 Does faith make the law useless? Not at all!
We agree with the law.

Abraham's Faith Made Him Right With God

4 What should we say about those things? What
did our father Abraham discover about being
right with God? 2 Did he become right with God
because of something he did? If so, he could brag
about it. But he couldn't brag to God. 3 What do we
find in Scripture? It says, "Abraham believed God.
God accepted Abraham's faith, and so his faith
made him right with God." *(Genesis 15:6)*

4 When a man works, his pay is not considered
a gift. It is owed to him. 5 But things are different
with God. He makes evil people right with himself. If people trust in him, their faith is accepted
even though they do not work. Their faith makes
them right with God.

6 King David says the same thing. He tells us
how blessed some people are. God makes those
people right with himself. But they don't have to
do anything in return. David says,

7 "Blessed are those
whose lawless acts are forgiven.
Blessed are those
whose sins are taken away.
8 Blessed is the man
whose sin the Lord never counts
against him." *(Psalm 32:1,2)*

9 Is that blessing only for those who are circumcised? Or is it also for those who are not circumcised? We have been saying that God accepted
Abraham's faith, and so his faith made him right
with God. 10 When did it happen? Was it after Abraham was circumcised, or before? It was before he
was circumcised, not after! 11 He was circumcised
as a sign of the covenant God had made with him.
It showed that his faith had made him right with
God before he was circumcised.

So Abraham is the father of all believers who
have not been circumcised. God accepts their faith.
So their faith makes them right with him. 12 Abraham is also the father of the circumcised who
believe. So just being circumcised is not enough.
Those who are circumcised must also follow the
steps of our father Abraham. He had faith before
he was circumcised.

13 Abraham and his family received a promise.
God promised that Abraham would receive the
world. It would not come to him because he
obeyed the law. It would come because of his faith,
which made him right with God.

14 Do those who obey the law receive the
promise? If they do, faith would have no value.
God's promise would be worthless. 15 The law
brings God's anger. Where there is no law, the law
can't be broken.

16 The promise is based on God's grace. The
promise comes by faith. All of Abraham's children
will certainly receive the promise. And it is not
only for those who are ruled by the law. Those
who have the same faith that Abraham had are also
included. He is the father of us all.

17 It is written, "I have made you a father of many
nations." *(Genesis 17:5)* God considers Abraham to
be our father. The God that Abraham believed in
gives life to the dead. Abraham's God also speaks
of things that do not exist as if they do exist.

[18]When there was no reason for hope, Abraham believed because he had hope. He became the father of many nations, exactly as God had promised. God said, "That is how many children you will have." *(Genesis 15:5)*

[19]Without becoming weak in his faith, Abraham accepted the fact that he was past the time when he could have children. At that time he was about 100 years old. He also realized that Sarah was too old to have children.

[20]But he kept believing in God's promise. He became strong in his faith. He gave glory to God. [21]He was absolutely sure that God had the power to do what he had promised. [22]That's why "God accepted Abraham because he believed. So his faith made him right with God."

[23]The words "God accepted Abraham's faith" were written not only for Abraham. [24]They were written also for us. We believe in the God who raised Jesus our Lord from the dead. So God will accept our faith and make us right with himself.

[25]Jesus was handed over to die for our sins. He was raised to life in order to make us right with God.

Peace and Joy

5 We have been made right with God because of our faith. Now we have peace with him because of our Lord Jesus Christ. [2]Through faith in Jesus we have received God's grace. In that grace we stand. We are full of joy because we expect to share in God's glory.

[3]And that's not all. We are full of joy even when we suffer. We know that our suffering gives us the strength to go on. [4]The strength to go on produces character. Character produces hope. [5]And hope will never let us down. God has poured his love into our hearts. He did it through the Holy Spirit, whom he has given to us.

[6]At just the right time Christ died for ungodly people. He died for us when we had no power of our own. [7]It is unusual for anyone to die for a godly person. Maybe someone would be willing to die for a good person. [8]But here is how God has shown his love for us. While we were still sinners, Christ died for us.

[9]The blood of Christ has made us right with God. So we are even more sure that Jesus will save us from God's anger. [10]Once we were God's enemies. But we have been brought back to him because his Son has died for us. Now that God has brought us back, we are even more secure. We know that we will be saved because Christ lives.

[11]And that is not all. We are full of joy in God because of our Lord Jesus Christ. Because of him, God has brought us back to himself.

Death Through Adam, Life Through Christ

[12]Sin entered the world because one man sinned. And death came because of sin. Everyone sinned, so death came to all people.

[13]Before the law was given, sin was in the world. But sin is not judged when there is no law. [14]Death ruled from the time of Adam to the time of Moses. Death ruled even over those who did not sin as Adam did. He broke God's command. But he also became a pattern of the One who was going to come.

[15]God's gift is different from Adam's sin. Many people died because of the sin of that one man. But it was even more sure that God's grace would also come through one man. That man is Jesus Christ. God's gift of grace was more than enough for the whole world.

[16]The result of God's gift is different from the result of Adam's sin. God judged one sin. That brought guilt. But after many sins, God's gift made people right with him.

[17]One man sinned, and death ruled because of his sin. But we are even more sure of what will happen because of what the one man, Jesus Christ, has done. Those who receive the rich supply of God's grace will rule with Christ in his kingdom. They have received God's gift and have been made right with him.

[18]One man's sin brought guilt to all people. So also one right act made all people right with God. And all who are right with God will live. [19]Many people were made sinners because one man did not obey. But one man did obey. That is why many people will be made right with God.

[20]The law was given so that sin would increase. But where sin increased, God's grace increased even more. [21]Sin ruled because of death. So also grace rules in the lives of those who are right with God. The grace of God brings eternal life because of what Jesus Christ our Lord has done.

Living a New Life

6 What should we say then? Should we keep on sinning so that God's grace can increase? [2]Not at all! As far as sin is concerned, we are dead. So how can we keep on sinning? [3]All of us were baptized into Christ Jesus. Don't you know that we were baptized into his death? [4]By being baptized, we were buried with Christ into his death. Christ has been raised from the dead by the Father's glory. And like Christ we also can live a new life.

[5]By being baptized, we have been joined with him in his death. We will certainly also be joined with him in his resurrection. [6]We know that what we used to be was nailed to the cross with him. That happened so our sinful bodies would lose their power. We are no longer slaves of sin. [7]Those who have died have been set free from sin.

[8]We died with Christ. So we believe that we will also live with him. [9]We know that Christ was raised from the dead and will never die again. Death doesn't control him anymore. [10]When he died, he died once and for all time as far as sin is concerned. Now that he lives, he lives as far as God is concerned.

11In the same way, consider yourselves to be dead as far as sin is concerned. Now that you believe in Christ Jesus, consider yourselves to be alive as far as God is concerned.

12So don't let sin rule your body, which is going to die. Don't obey its evil longings. 13Don't give the parts of your body to serve sin. Don't let them be used to do evil. Instead, give yourselves to God. You have been brought from death to life. Give the parts of your body to him to do what is right.

14Sin will not be your master. Law does not rule you. God's grace has set you free.

Slaves to Right Living

15What should we say then? Should we sin because we are not ruled by law but by God's grace? Not at all!

16Don't you know that when you give yourselves to obey someone you become that person's slave? You can be slaves of sin. Then you will die. Or you can be slaves who obey God. Then you will live a godly life. 17You used to be slaves of sin. But thank God that with your whole heart you obeyed the teachings you were given! 18You have been set free from sin. You have become slaves to right living.

19Because you are human, you find this hard to understand. So I have said it in a way that will help you understand it. You used to give the parts of your body to be slaves to unclean living. You were becoming more and more evil. Now give your bodies to be slaves to right living. Then you will become holy.

20Once you were slaves of sin. At that time right living did not control you. 21What benefit did you gain from doing the things you are now ashamed of? Those things lead to death!

22You have been set free from sin. God has made you his slaves. The benefit you gain leads to holy living. And the end result is eternal life. 23When you sin, the pay you get is death. But God gives you the gift of eternal life because of what Christ Jesus our Lord has done.

An Example From Marriage

7 Brothers and sisters, I am speaking to you who know the law. Don't you know that the law has authority over us only as long as we are alive? 2For example, by law a married woman is joined to her husband as long as he is living. But suppose her husband dies. Then the marriage law no longer applies to her. 3But suppose that married woman gets married again while her husband is still alive. Then she is called a woman who commits adultery. But suppose her husband dies. Then she is free from that law. She is not guilty of adultery even if she marries another man.

4My brothers and sisters, when Christ died you also died as far as the law is concerned. Then it became possible for you to belong to him. He was raised from the dead. Now our lives can be useful to God. 5Our sinful nature used to control us. The law stirred up sinful longings in our bodies. So the things we did resulted in death.

6But now we have died to what used to control us. We have been set free from the law. Now we serve in the new way of the Holy Spirit. We no longer serve in the old way of the written law.

Struggling With Sin

7What should we say then? That the law is sin? Not at all! I wouldn't have known what sin was unless the law had told me. The law said, "Do not want what belongs to other people." *(Exodus 20:17; Deuteronomy 5:21)* If the law hadn't said that, I would not have known what it was like to want what belonged to others. 8But the commandment gave sin an opportunity. Sin caused me to want all kinds of things that belonged to others. No one can break a law that doesn't exist.

9Before I knew about the law, I was alive. But then the commandment came. Sin came to life, and I died. 10I found that the commandment that was supposed to bring life actually brought death. 11When the commandment gave sin the opportunity, sin tricked me. It used the commandment to put me to death. 12So the law is holy. The commandment also is holy and right and good.

13Did what is good cause me to die? Not at all! Sin had to be recognized for what it really is. So it produced death in me through what was good. Because of the commandment, sin became totally sinful.

14We know that the law is holy. But I am not. I have been sold to be a slave of sin. 15I don't understand what I do. I don't do what I want to do. Instead, I do what I hate to do. 16I do what I don't want to do. So I agree that the law is good. 17As it is, I am no longer the one who does these things. It is sin living in me that does them.

18I know there is nothing good in my sinful nature. I want to do what is good, but I can't. 19I don't do the good things I want to do. I keep on doing the evil things I don't want to do. 20I do what I don't want to do. But I am not really the one who is doing it. It is sin living in me.

21Here is the law I find working in me. When I want to do good, evil is right there with me. 22Deep inside me I find joy in God's law. 23But I see another law working in the parts of my body. It fights against the law of my mind. It makes me a prisoner of the law of sin. That law controls the parts of my body.

24What a terrible failure I am! Who will save me from this sin that brings death to my body? 25I give thanks to God. He will do it through Jesus Christ our Lord.

So in my mind I am a slave to God's law. But in my sinful nature I am a slave to the law of sin.

The Holy Spirit Gives Life

8 Those who belong to Christ Jesus are no longer under God's sentence. 2I am now con-

trolled by the law of the Holy Spirit. That law gives me life because of what Christ Jesus has done. It has set me free from the law of sin that brings death.

[3]The written law was made weak by our sinful nature. But God did what the written law could not do. He made his Son to be like those who have a sinful nature. He sent him to be an offering for sin. In that way, he judged sin in his Son's human body. [4]Now we can do everything the law requires. Our sinful nature no longer controls the way we live. The Holy Spirit now controls the way we live.

[5]Don't live under the control of your sinful nature. If you do, you will think about what your sinful nature wants. Live under the control of the Holy Spirit. If you do, you will think about what the Spirit wants.

[6]The way a sinful person thinks leads to death. But the mind controlled by the Spirit brings life and peace. [7]The sinful mind is at war with God. It does not obey God's law. It can't. [8]Those who are controlled by their sinful nature can't please God.

[9]But your sinful nature does not control you. The Holy Spirit controls you. The Spirit of God lives in you. Anyone who does not have the Spirit of Christ does not belong to Christ.

[10]Christ lives in you. So your body is dead because of sin. But your spirit is alive because you have been made right with God. [11]The Spirit of the One who raised Jesus from the dead is living in you. So the God who raised Christ from the dead will also give life to your bodies, which are going to die. He will do this by the power of his Spirit, who lives in you.

[12]Brothers and sisters, we have a duty. Our duty is not to live under the control of our sinful nature. [13]If you live under the control of your sinful nature, you will die. But by the power of the Holy Spirit you can put to death the sins your body commits. Then you will live.

[14]Those who are led by the Spirit of God are children of God. [15]You didn't receive a spirit that makes you a slave to fear once again. Instead you received the Holy Spirit, who makes you God's child. By the Spirit's power we call God *"Abba." Abba* means Father. [16]The Spirit himself joins with our spirits. Together they give witness that we are God's children.

[17]As his children, we will receive all that he has for us. We will share what Christ receives. But we must share in his sufferings if we want to share in his glory.

The Hope of Future Glory

[18]What we are suffering now is nothing compared with the glory that will be shown in us. [19]Everything God created looks forward to the time when his children will appear in their full and final glory. [20]The created world was bound to fail. But that was not the result of its own choice. It was planned that way by the One who made it. God planned [21]to set the created world free. He didn't want it to rot away completely. Instead, he wanted it to have the same glorious freedom that his children have.

[22]We know that all that God created has been groaning. It is in pain as if it were giving birth to a child. The created world continues to groan even now. [23]And that's not all. We have the Holy Spirit as the promise of future blessing. But we also groan inside ourselves as we look forward to the time when God will adopt us as full members of his family. Then he will give us everything he has for us. He will raise our bodies and give glory to them.

[24]That's the hope we had when we were saved. But hope that can be seen is no hope at all. Who hopes for what he already has? [25]We hope for what we don't have yet. So we are patient as we wait for it.

[26]In the same way, the Holy Spirit helps us when we are weak. We don't know what we should pray for. But the Spirit himself prays for us. He prays with groans too deep for words. [27]God, who looks into our hearts, knows the mind of the Spirit. And the Spirit prays for God's people just as God wants him to pray.

We Will Win

[28]We know that in all things God works for the good of those who love him. He appointed them to be saved in keeping with his purpose.

[29]God planned that those he had chosen would become like his Son. In that way, Christ will be the first and most honored among many brothers. [30]And those God has planned for, he has also appointed to be saved. Those he has appointed, he has made right with himself. To those he has made right with himself, he has given his glory.

[31]What should we say then? Since God is on our side, who can be against us? [32]God did not spare his own Son. He gave him up for us all. Then won't he also freely give us everything else?

[33]Who can bring any charge against God's chosen ones? God makes us right with himself. [34]Who can sentence us to death? Christ Jesus is at the right hand of God and is also praying for us. He died. More than that, he was raised to life.

[35]Who can separate us from Christ's love? Can trouble or hard times or harm or hunger? Can nakedness or danger or war? [36]It is written,

"Because of you, we face death all day long.
We are considered as sheep to be killed."
(Psalm 44:22)

[37]No! In all these things we will do even more than win! We owe it all to Christ, who has loved us.

[38]I am absolutely sure that not even death or life can separate us from God's love. Not even angels or demons, the present or the future, or any powers can do that. [39]Not even the highest places or the lowest, or anything else in all creation can do that.

Nothing at all can ever separate us from God's love
because of what Christ Jesus our Lord has done.

God's Free Choice

9 I speak the truth in Christ. I am not lying. My
mind tells me that what I say is true. It is
guided by the Holy Spirit. 2My heart is full of sorrow. My sadness never ends. 3I am so concerned
about my people, who are members of my own
race. I am ready to be cursed, if that would help
them. I am even willing to be separated from
Christ.
4They are the people of Israel. They have been
adopted as God's children. God's glory belongs to
them. So do the covenants. They received the law.
They were taught to worship in the temple. They
were given the promises. 5The founders of our
nation belong to them. Christ comes from their
family line. He is God over all. May he always be
praised! Amen.
6Their condition does not mean that God's word
has failed. Not everyone in the family line of Israel really belongs to Israel. 7Not everyone in Abraham's family line is really his child. Not at all!
Scripture says, "Your family line will continue
through Isaac." *(Genesis 21:12)*
8In other words, God's children are not just
Abraham's natural children. Instead, they are the
children God promised to him. They are the ones
considered to be Abraham's children. 9God
promised, "I will return at the appointed time. Sarah will have a son." *(Genesis 18:10,14)*
10And that's not all. Rebekah's children had the
same father. He was our father Isaac.
11Here is what happened. Rebekah's twins had
not even been born. They hadn't done anything
good or bad yet. So they show that God's purpose
is based firmly on his free choice. 12It was not
because of anything they did but because of God's
choice. So Rebekah was told, "The older son will
serve the younger one." *(Genesis 25:23)* 13It is written, "I chose Jacob instead of Esau." *(Malachi 1:2,3)*
14What should we say then? Is God unfair? Not
at all! 15He said to Moses,

"I will have mercy on whom I have mercy.
I will show love to those I love."
(Exodus 33:19)

16So it doesn't depend on what we want or do.
It depends on God's mercy.
17In Scripture, God says to Pharaoh, "I had a
special reason for making you king. I decided to
use you to show my power. I wanted my name to
become known everywhere on earth." *(Exodus
9:16)* 18So God does what he wants to do. He shows
mercy to one person and makes another stubborn.
19One of you will say to me, "Then why does
God still blame us? Who can oppose what he
wants to do?" 20But you are a mere man. So who
are you to talk back to God? Scripture says, "Can
what is made say to the one who made it, 'Why
did you make me like this?'" *(Isaiah 29:16; 45:9)*
21Isn't the potter free to make different kinds of
pots out of the same lump of clay? Some are for
special purposes. Others are for ordinary use.
22What if God chose to show his great anger?
What if he chose to make his power known? That
is why he put up with people he was angry with.
They had been made to be destroyed. 23What if he
did that to show the riches of his glory to others?
Those are the people he shows his mercy to. He
had prepared them to receive his glory. 24We are
those people. He has chosen us. We do not come
only from the Jewish race. Many of us are not
Jews. 25God says in Hosea,

"I will call those who are not my people
'my people.'
I will call the one who is not my loved one
'my loved one.'" *(Hosea 2:23)*

26He also says,

"Once it was said to them,
'You are not my people.'
In that very place they will be called 'children
of the living God.'" *(Hosea 1:10)*

27Isaiah cries out concerning Israel. He says,

"The number of people from Israel may be like
the sand by the sea.
But only a few of them will be saved.
28 The Lord will carry out his sentence.
He will be quick to carry it out on earth,
once and for all." *(Isaiah 10:22,23)*

29Earlier Isaiah had said,

"The Lord who rules over all
left us children and grandchildren.
If he hadn't, we would have become
like Sodom.
We would have been like Gomorrah."
(Isaiah 1:9)

Israel Does Not Believe

30What should we say then? Those who aren't
Jews did not look for a way to be right with God.
But they found it by having faith. 31Israel did look
for a law that could make them right with God. But
they didn't find it.
32Why not? Because they didn't look for it by
faith. They tried to get it by working for it. They
tripped over the stone that causes people to trip
and fall. 33It is written,

"Look! In Zion I am laying a stone that causes
people to trip.
It is a rock that makes them fall.
The one who trusts in him will never be put
to shame." *(Isaiah 8:14; 28:16)*

10 Brothers and sisters, with all my heart I
long for the people of Israel to be saved. I
pray to God for them. 2I can give witness about
them that they really want to serve God. But how

they are trying to do it is not based on what they know.

3They didn't know how God makes people right with himself. They tried to get right with God in their own way. They didn't do it in God's way.

4Christ has completed the law. So now everyone who believes can be right with God.

5Moses explained how the law could help a person do what God requires. He said, "The one who does those things will live by them." *(Leviticus 18:5)*

6But the way to do what God requires must begin by having faith in him. Scripture says, "Do not say in your heart, 'Who will go up into heaven?'" *(Deuteronomy 30:12)* That means to go up into heaven and bring Christ down. 7"And do not say, 'Who will go down into the grave?'" *(Deuteronomy 30:13)* That means to bring Christ up from the dead.

8But what does it say? "The word is near you. It's in your mouth and in your heart." *(Deuteronomy 30:14)* That means the word we are preaching. You must put your faith in it.

9Say with your mouth, "Jesus is Lord." Believe in your heart that God raised him from the dead. Then you will be saved. 10With your heart you believe and are made right with God. With your mouth you say that Jesus is Lord. And so you are saved. 11Scripture says, "The one who trusts in him will never be put to shame." *(Isaiah 28:16)*

12There is no difference between those who are Jews and those who are not. The same Lord is Lord of all. He richly blesses everyone who calls on him. 13Scripture says, "Everyone who calls on the name of the Lord will be saved." *(Joel 2:32)*

14How can they call on him unless they believe in him? How can they believe in him unless they hear about him? How can they hear about him unless someone preaches to them? 15And how can anyone preach without being sent? It is written, "How beautiful are the feet of those who bring good news!" *(Isaiah 52:7)*

16But not all the people of Israel accepted the good news. Isaiah says, "Lord, who has believed our message?" *(Isaiah 53:1)* 17So faith comes from hearing the message. And the message that is heard is the word of Christ.

18But I ask, "Didn't the people of Israel hear?" Of course they did. It is written,

"Their voice has gone out into the whole earth.
 Their words have gone out from one end of the world to the other." *(Psalm 19:4)*

19Again I ask, "Didn't Israel understand?" First, Moses says,

"I will use people who are not a nation to make you jealous.
 I will use a nation that has no understanding to make you angry." *(Deuteronomy 32:21)*

20Then Isaiah boldly speaks about what God says. God said,

"I was found by those who were not trying to find me.
 I made myself known to those who were not asking for me." *(Isaiah 65:1)*

21But Isaiah also speaks about what God says concerning Israel. God said,

"All day long I have held out my hands.
 I have held them out to a stubborn people who do not obey me." *(Isaiah 65:2)*

God's Faithful People in Israel

11 So here is what I ask. Did God turn his back on his people? Not at all! I myself belong to Israel. I am one of Abraham's children. I am from the tribe of Benjamin. 2God didn't turn his back on his people. After all, he chose them.

Don't you know what Scripture says about Elijah? He complained to God about Israel. 3He said, "Lord, they have killed your prophets. They have torn down your altars. I'm the only one left. And they are trying to kill me." *(1 Kings 19:10,14)*

4How did God answer him? God said, "I have kept 7,000 people for myself. They have not bowed down to Baal." *(1 Kings 19:18)*

5Some are also faithful today. They have been chosen by God's grace. 6And if they are chosen by grace, it is no longer a matter of working for it. If it were, grace wouldn't be grace anymore.

7What should we say then? Israel did not receive what they wanted so badly. But those who were chosen did. God made the rest of them stubborn. 8It is written,

"God made it hard for them to understand.
 He gave them eyes that could not see.
 He gave them ears that could not hear.
And they are still like that today."
(Deuteronomy 29:4; Isaiah 29:10)

9David says,

"Let their feast be a trap and a snare.
 Let it make Israel trip and fall. Let Israel get what's coming to them.
10Let their eyes grow dark so they can't see.
 Let their backs be bent forever." *(Psalm 69:22,23)*

Two Kinds of Olive Branches

11Again, here is what I ask. They didn't trip and fall once and for all time, did they? Not at all! Because Israel sinned, those who aren't Jews can be saved. That will make Israel jealous of them. 12Israel's sin brought riches to the world. Their loss brought riches to the non-Jews. What greater riches will come when all Israel turns to God!

13I am talking to you who are not Jews. I am the apostle to the non-Jews. So I think the work I do for God and others is very important.

14I hope somehow to stir up my own people to want what you have. Perhaps I can save some of them. 15When they were not accepted, it became possible for the whole world to be brought back to God. So what will happen when they are accepted? It will be like life from the dead.

16The first handful of dough that is offered is holy. This makes all of the dough holy.

If the root is holy, so are the branches.

17Some of the natural branches have been broken off. You are a wild olive branch. But you have been joined to the tree with the other branches. Now you enjoy the life-giving sap of the olive tree root. 18So don't think you are better than the other branches. Remember, you don't give life to the root. The root gives life to you.

19You will say, "Some branches were broken off so that I could be joined to the tree." 20That's true. But they were broken off because they didn't believe. You stand only because you do believe. So don't be proud. Be afraid. 21God didn't spare the natural branches. He won't spare you either.

22Think about how kind God is! Also think about how firm he is! He was hard on those who stopped following him. But he is kind to you. So you must continue to live in his kindness. If you don't, you also will be cut off.

23If the people of Israel do not continue in their unbelief, they will again be joined to the tree. God is able to join them to the tree again.

24After all, weren't you cut from a wild olive tree? Weren't you joined to an olive tree that was taken care of? And wasn't that the opposite of how things should be done? How much more easily will the natural branches be joined to their own olive tree!

All Israel Will Be Saved

25Brothers and sisters, here is a mystery I want you to understand. It will keep you from being proud. Part of Israel has refused to obey God. That will continue until the full number of non-Jews has entered God's kingdom. 26And so all Israel will be saved. It is written,

"The One who saves will come from
Mount Zion.
He will remove sin from Jacob.
27Here is my covenant with them.
I will take away their sins."
(Isaiah 59:20,21; 27:9; Jeremiah 31:33,34)

28As far as the good news is concerned, the people of Israel are enemies. That is for your good. But as far as God's choice is concerned, the people of Israel are loved. That is because of God's promises to the founders of our nation. 29God does not take back his gifts. He does not change his mind about those he has chosen.

30At one time you did not obey God. But now you have received mercy because Israel did not obey. 31In the same way, Israel has not been obeying God. But now they receive mercy because of God's mercy to you. 32God has found everyone guilty of not obeying him. So now he can have mercy on everyone.

Praise to God

33How very rich are God's wisdom and
knowledge!
How he judges is more than we
can understand!
The way he deals with people is more than
we can know!
34"Who can ever know what is in the
Lord's mind?
Or who can ever give him advice?"
(Isaiah 40:13)
35"Has anyone ever given anything to God,
so that God has to pay him back?" *(Job 41:11)*
36All things come from him.
All things are directed by him.
All things are for his good.
May God be given the glory forever! Amen.

Living for God

12 Brothers and sisters, God has shown you his mercy. So I am asking you to offer up your bodies to him while you are still alive. Your bodies are a holy sacrifice that is pleasing to God. When you offer your bodies to God, you are worshiping him. 2Don't live any longer the way this world lives. Let your way of thinking be completely changed. Then you will be able to test what God wants for you. And you will agree that what he wants is right. His plan is good and pleasing and perfect.

3God's grace has been given to me. So here is what I say to every one of you. Don't think of yourself more highly than you should. Be reasonable when you think about yourself. Keep in mind the amount of faith God has given you.

4Each of us has one body with many parts. And the parts do not all have the same purpose. 5So also we are many persons. But in Christ we are one body. And each part of the body belongs to all the other parts.

6We all have gifts. They differ in keeping with the grace that God has given each of us. Do you have the gift of prophecy? Then use it in keeping with the faith you have. 7Is it your gift to serve? Then serve. Is it teaching? Then teach. 8Is it telling others how they should live? Then tell them. Is it giving to those who are in need? Then give freely. Is it being a leader? Then work hard at it. Is it showing mercy? Then do it cheerfully.

Love

9Love must be honest and true. Hate what is evil. Hold on to what is good. 10Love each other deeply. Honor others more than yourselves. 11Never let the fire in your heart go out. Keep it alive. Serve the Lord.

12When you hope, be joyful. When you suffer, be patient. When you pray, be faithful. 13Share with God's people who are in need. Welcome others into your homes.

14 Bless those who hurt you. Bless them, and do not call down curses on them. 15 Be joyful with those who are joyful. Be sad with those who are sad. 16 Agree with each other. Don't be proud. Be willing to be a friend of people who aren't considered important. Don't think that you are better than others.

17 Don't pay back evil with evil. Be careful to do what everyone thinks is right. 18 If possible, live in peace with everyone. Do that as much as you can.

19 My friends, don't try to get even. Leave room for God to show his anger. It is written, "I am the One who judges people. I will pay them back," *(Deuteronomy 32:35)* says the Lord. 20 Do just the opposite. Scripture says,

"If your enemies are hungry, give them food
to eat.
If they are thirsty, give them something
to drink.
By doing those things, you will pile up burning
coals on their heads."

(Proverbs 25:21,22)

21 Don't let evil overcome you. Overcome evil by doing good.

Obey Those in Authority

13 All of you must be willing to obey completely those who rule over you. There are no authorities except the ones God has chosen. Those who now rule have been chosen by God. 2 So when you oppose the authorities, you are opposing those whom God has appointed. Those who do that will be judged.

3 If you do what is right, you won't need to be afraid of your rulers. But watch out if you do what is wrong! You don't want to be afraid of those in authority, do you? Then do what is right. The one in authority will praise you. 4 He serves God and will do you good. But if you do wrong, watch out! The ruler doesn't carry a sword for no reason at all. He serves God. And God is carrying out his anger through him. The ruler punishes anyone who does wrong.

5 You must obey the authorities. Then you will not be punished. You must also obey them because you know it is right.

6 That's also why you pay taxes. The authorities serve God. Ruling takes up all their time. 7 Give to everyone what you owe. Do you owe taxes? Then pay them. Do you owe anything else to the government? Then pay it. Do you owe respect? Then give it. Do you owe honor? Then show it.

Love, Because the Day Is Near

8 Pay everything you owe. But you can never pay back all the love you owe each other. Those who love others have done everything the law requires. 9 Here are some commandments to think about. "Do not commit adultery." "Do not commit murder." "Do not steal." "Do not want what belongs to others." *(Exodus 20:13–15,17; Deuteronomy 5:17–19,21)* These and other commandments are all included in one rule. Here's what it is. "Love your neighbor as you love yourself." *(Leviticus 19:18)* 10 Love does not harm its neighbor. So love does everything the law requires.

11 When you do those things, keep in mind the times we are living in. The hour has come for you to wake up from your sleep. Our full salvation is closer now than it was when we first believed in Christ. 12 The dark night of evil is nearly over. The day of Christ's return is almost here. So let us get rid of the works of darkness. Let us put on the armor of light.

13 Let us act as we should, like people living in the daytime. Have nothing to do with wild parties. Don't get drunk. Don't take part in sexual sins or evil conduct. Don't fight with each other. Don't be jealous of anyone. 14 Instead, put on the Lord Jesus Christ as your clothing. Don't think about how to satisfy what your sinful nature wants.

The Weak and the Strong

14 Accept those whose faith is weak. Don't judge them where you have differences of opinion.

2 The faith of some people allows them to eat anything. But others eat only vegetables because their faith is weak. 3 People who eat everything must not look down on those who do not. And people who don't eat everything must not judge those who do. God has accepted them.

4 Who are you to judge someone else's servants? Whether they are faithful or not is their own master's concern. They will be faithful, because the Lord has the power to make them faithful.

5 Some people consider one day to be more holy than another. Others think all days are the same. Each person should be absolutely sure in his own mind. 6 Those who think one day is special do it to honor the Lord. Those who eat meat do it to honor the Lord. They give thanks to God. Those who don't eat meat do it to honor the Lord. They also give thanks to God.

7 We don't live for ourselves alone. And we don't die all by ourselves. 8 If we live, we live to honor the Lord. If we die, we die to honor the Lord. So whether we live or die, we belong to the Lord.

9 Christ died and came back to life. He did this to become the Lord of both the dead and the living.

10 Now then, who are you to judge your brother or sister? Why do you look down on them? We will all stand in God's courtroom to be judged. 11 It is written,

"'You can be sure that I live,' says the Lord.
'And you can be just as sure that every knee
will bow down in front of me.
Every tongue will tell the truth to God.'"

(Isaiah 45:23)

12So we will all have to explain to God the things
we have done.
13Let us stop judging one another. Instead, make
up your mind not to put anything in your brother's
way that would make him trip and fall.
14I am absolutely sure that no food is "unclean"
in itself. I say this as one who belongs to the Lord
Jesus. But some people may consider a thing to be
"unclean." If they do, it is "unclean" for them. 15Your
brothers and sisters may be upset by what you eat. If
they are, you are no longer acting as though you love
them. So don't destroy them by what you eat. Christ
died for them. 16Don't let something you consider
good be spoken of as if it were evil.
17God's kingdom has nothing to do with eating
or drinking. It is a matter of being right with God.
It brings the peace and joy the Holy Spirit gives.
18Those who serve Christ in this way are pleasing to God. They are pleasing to people too.
19So let us do all we can to live in peace. And
let us work hard to build each other up.
20Don't destroy the work of God because of
food. All food is "clean." But it is wrong for you
to eat anything that causes someone else to trip and
fall. 21Don't eat meat if it will cause your brothers
and sisters to fall. Don't drink wine or do anything
else that will make them fall.
22No matter what you think about those things,
keep it between yourself and God. Blessed are those
who do not have to feel guilty for what they allow.
23But those who have doubts are guilty if they
eat. Their eating is not based on faith. Everything
that is not based on faith is sin.

15 We who have strong faith should help the
weak with their problems. We should not
please only ourselves. 2We should all please our
neighbors. Let us do what is good for them. Let us
build them up.
3Even Christ did not please himself. It is written, "Those who make fun of you have made fun
of me also." *(Psalm 69:9)* 4Everything that was written in the past was written to teach us. The Scriptures give us strength to go on. They cheer us up
and give us hope.
5Our God is a God who strengthens you and
cheers you up. May he help you agree with each
other as you follow Christ Jesus. 6Then you can
give glory to God with one heart and voice. He is
the God and Father of our Lord Jesus Christ.
7Christ has accepted you. So accept one another
in order to bring praise to God.
8I tell you that Christ has become a servant of
the Jews. He teaches us that God is true. He shows
us that God will keep the promises he made to the
founders of our nation. 9Jesus became a servant of
the Jews so that people who are not Jews could
give glory to God for his mercy. It is written,

"I will praise you among those who
aren't Jews.
I will sing praises to you."
(2 Samuel 22:50; Psalm 18:49)

10Again it says,

"You non-Jews, be full of joy.
Be joyful together with God's people."
(Deuteronomy 32:43)

11And again it says,

"All you non-Jews, praise the Lord.
All you nations, sing praises to him."
(Psalm 117:1)

12And Isaiah says,

"The Root of Jesse will grow up quickly.
He will rule over the nations.
Those who aren't Jews will put their hope
in him."
(Isaiah 11:10)

13May the God who gives hope fill you with
great joy. May you have perfect peace as you trust
in him. May the power of the Holy Spirit fill you
with hope.

Paul Serves the Non-Jews

14My brothers and sisters, I am sure that you are
full of goodness. What you know is complete. You
are able to teach one another.
15I have written to you very boldly about some
things. I wanted you to think about them again.
The grace of God has allowed me 16to serve Christ
Jesus among those who aren't Jews. My duty as a
priest is to preach God's good news. Then the non-
Jews will become an offering that pleases God.
The Holy Spirit will make the offering holy.
17Because I belong to Christ Jesus, I can take
pride in my work for God. 18I will not try to speak
of anything except what Christ has done through
me. He has been leading those who aren't Jews to
obey God. He has been doing this by what I have
said and done.
19He has given me power to do signs and miracles. He has given me the power of the Holy Spirit.
From Jerusalem all the way around to Illyricum
I have finished preaching the good news about
Christ. 20I have always wanted to preach the good
news where Christ was not known. I don't want to
build on what someone else has started. 21It is
written,

"Those who were not told about him will
understand.
Those who have not heard will know what
it all means."
(Isaiah 52:15)

22That's why I have often been kept from coming
to you.

Paul Plans to Visit Rome

23Now there is no more place for me to work in
those areas. For many years I have been longing
to see you. 24So I plan to see you when I go to
Spain. I hope to visit you while I am passing
through. And I hope you will help me on my journey there. But first I want to enjoy being with you
for a while.

25 Now I am on my way to Jerusalem to serve
God's people there. 26 The believers in Macedonia
and Achaia were pleased to take an offering for those
who were poor among God's people in Jerusalem.
27 They were happy to do it. And of course they owe
it to them. Those who aren't Jews have shared from
the Jews' spiritual blessings. So the non-Jews should
share their earthly blessings with the Jews.

28 I want to finish my task. I want to make sure
that the poor in Jerusalem have received the offering. Then I will go to Spain. On my way I will visit
you. 29 I know that when I come to you, I will come
with the full blessing of Christ.

30 Brothers and sisters, I am asking you through
the authority of our Lord Jesus Christ to join me
in my struggle by praying to God for me. Pray for
me with the love the Holy Spirit provides. 31 Pray
that I will be saved from those in Judea who do not
believe. Pray that my work in Jerusalem will be
accepted by God's people there. 32 Then, as God
has planned, I will come to you with joy. Together
we will be renewed.

33 May the God who gives peace be with you all.
Amen.

Personal Greetings

16 I would like you to welcome our sister
Phoebe. She serves the church in Cen-
chrea. 2 I ask you to receive her as one who belongs
to the Lord. Receive her in the way God's people
should. Give her any help she may need from you.
She has been a great help to many people, including me.

3 Greet Priscilla and Aquila. They work together
with me in serving Christ Jesus. 4 They have
put their lives in danger for me. I am thankful
for them. So are all the non-Jewish churches.

5 Greet also the church that meets in the house of
Priscilla and Aquila.

Greet my dear friend Epenetus. He was the first
person in Asia Minor to become a believer in
Christ.

6 Greet Mary. She worked very hard for you.

7 Greet Andronicus and Junias, my relatives. They
have been in prison with me. They are leaders
among the apostles. They became believers in
Christ before I did.

8 Greet Ampliatus. I love him as a brother in the
Lord.

9 Greet Urbanus. He works together with me in serving Christ. And greet my dear friend Stachys.

10 Greet Apelles. Even though he was put to the
test, he remained faithful as one who
belonged to Christ.

Greet those who live in the house of Aristobulus.

11 Greet Herodion, my relative.

Greet the believers who live in the house of Nar-
cissus.

12 Greet Tryphena and Tryphosa. Those women
work hard for the Lord.

Greet my dear friend Persis. She is another
woman who has worked very hard for the
Lord.

13 Greet Rufus. He is a choice believer in the Lord.
And greet his mother. She has been like a
mother to me too.

14 Greet Asyncritus, Phlegon and Hermes. Greet
Patrobas, Hermas and the believers with
them.

15 Greet Philologus, Julia, Nereus and his sister.
Greet Olympas and all of God's people with
them.

16 Greet one another with a holy kiss.

All the churches of Christ send their greetings.

17 I am warning you, brothers and sisters, to
watch out for those who try to keep you from staying together. They want to trip you up. They teach
you things opposite to what you have learned. Stay
away from them. 18 People like that are not serving
Christ our Lord. They are serving only themselves.
With smooth talk and with words they don't mean
they fool people who don't know any better.

19 Everyone has heard that you obey God. So
you have filled me with joy. I want you to be wise
about what is good. And I want you to have nothing to do with what is evil.

20 The God who gives peace will soon crush Satan under your feet.

May the grace of our Lord Jesus be with you.

21 Timothy works together with me. He sends his
greetings to you. So do Lucius, Jason and Sosipa-
ter, my relatives.

22 I, Tertius, wrote down this letter. I greet you
as a believer in the Lord.

23/24 Gaius sends you his greetings. He has welcomed me and the whole church here into his
house.

Erastus is the director of public works here in
the city. He sends you his greetings. Our brother
Quartus also greets you.

25 May God receive glory. He is able to
strengthen your faith because of the good news I
preach. It is the message about Jesus Christ. It is in
keeping with the mystery that was hidden for a
very long time. 26 The mystery has now been made
known through the writings of the prophets. The
eternal God commanded that it be made known.
He wanted all nations to believe and obey him.
27 May the only wise God receive glory forever
through Jesus Christ. Amen.

1 Corinthians

1 I, Paul, am writing this letter. I have been chosen to be an apostle of Christ Jesus just as God
planned. Our brother Sosthenes joins me in
writing.

2 We are sending this letter to you, the members
of God's church in Corinth. You have been made
holy because you belong to Christ Jesus. God has
chosen you to be his holy people. He has done the
same for all those everywhere who pray to our
Lord Jesus Christ. Jesus is their Lord and ours.

3 May God our Father and the Lord Jesus Christ
give you grace and peace.

Paul Gives Thanks

4 I always thank God for you. I thank him
because of the grace he has given to you who
belong to Christ Jesus. 5 You have been blessed in
every way because of him. All your teaching of the
truth is better. Your understanding of it is more
complete. 6 Our witness about Christ has been
proved to be true in you.
7 There is no gift of the Holy Spirit that you
don't have. You are full of hope as you wait for our
Lord Jesus Christ to come again. 8 God will keep
you strong to the very end. Then you will be without blame on the day our Lord Jesus Christ returns.
9 God is faithful. He has chosen you to share life
with his Son, Jesus Christ our Lord.

Taking Sides in the Church

10 Brothers and sisters, I ask all of you to agree
with one another. I make my appeal in the name
of our Lord Jesus Christ. Then you won't take
sides. You will be in complete agreement in all that
you think.
11 My brothers and sisters, some people who live
in Chloe's house have told me you are arguing
with each other. 12 Here is what I mean. One of you
says, "I follow Paul." Another says, "I follow
Apollos." Another says, "I follow Peter." And still
another says, "I follow Christ."
13 Does Christ take sides? Did Paul die on the
cross for you? Were you baptized in the name of
Paul? 14 I'm thankful that I didn't baptize any of
you except Crispus and Gaius. 15 No one can say
that you were baptized in my name.
16 It's true that I also baptized those who live in
the house of Stephanas. Besides that, I don't
remember if I baptized anyone else.
17 Christ did not send me to baptize. He sent me
to preach the good news. He commanded me not
to use the kind of wisdom that people commonly
use. That would take all the power away from the
cross of Christ.

Christ Is God's Power and Wisdom

18 The message of the cross seems foolish to
those who are lost and dying. But it is God's power
to us who are being saved. 19 It is written,

"I will destroy the wisdom of those who
are wise.
I will do away with the cleverness of those
who think they are so smart."
(Isaiah 29:14)

20 Where is the wise person? Where is the educated person? Where are the great thinkers of this
world? Hasn't God made the wisdom of the world
foolish? 21 God wisely planned that the world
would not know him through its own wisdom. It
pleased God to use the foolish things we preach to
save those who believe.
22 Jews require miraculous signs. Greeks look
for wisdom. 23 But we preach about Christ and his
death on the cross. That is very hard for Jews to
accept. And everyone else thinks it's foolish.
24 But there are those God has chosen, both Jews
and others. To them Christ is God's power and
God's wisdom. 25 The foolish things of God are
wiser than human wisdom. The weakness of God
is stronger than human strength.
26 Brothers and sisters, think of what you were
when God chose you. Not many of you were considered wise by human standards. Not many of
you were powerful. Not many of you belonged to
important families.
27 But God chose the foolish things of the world
to shame the wise. He chose the weak things of the
world to shame the strong. 28 God chose the things
of this world that are common and looked down
on. He chose what is not considered to be important to do away with what is considered to be
important. 29 So no one can brag to God.
30 Because of what God has done, you belong to
Christ Jesus. He has become God's wisdom for us.
He makes us right with God. He makes us holy
and sets us free. 31 It is written, "The one who brags
should brag about what the Lord has done." *(Jeremiah 9:24)*

2 Brothers and sisters, when I came to you I
didn't come with fancy words or great wisdom. I preached to you the truth about God's love.
2 I made up my mind to pay attention to only one
thing while I was with you. That one thing was
Jesus Christ and his death on the cross.
3 When I came to you, I was weak and afraid and
trembling all over. 4 I didn't preach my message
with clever and compelling words. As I preached,
the Holy Spirit showed his power. 5 That was so
you would believe not because of human wisdom
but because of God's power.

Wisdom From the Holy Spirit

6 The words we speak to those who have grown
in the faith are wise. Our words are different from
the words of the wise people or rulers of this
world. People like that aren't going anywhere.
7 No, we speak about God's secret wisdom. His
wisdom has been hidden. But before time began,
God planned that his wisdom would bring us heavenly glory.
8 None of the rulers of this world understood
God's wisdom. If they had, they would not have
nailed the Lord of glory to the cross. 9 It is written,

"No eye has seen,
   no ear has heard,
no mind has known
   what God has prepared for those who
      love him." *(Isaiah 64:4)*

10 But God has shown it to us through his Spirit.
The Spirit understands all things. He understands even the deep things of God. 11 Who can
know the thoughts of another person? Only a person's own spirit can know them. In the same way,
only the Spirit of God knows God's thoughts.
12 We have not received the spirit of the world.
We have received the Spirit who is from God. The
Spirit helps us understand what God has freely
given us.
13 That is what we speak about. We don't use
words taught to us by people. We use words taught
to us by the Holy Spirit. We use the words of the
Spirit to teach the truths of the Spirit.
14 Some people don't have the Holy Spirit. They
don't accept the things that come from the Spirit
of God. Things like that are foolish to them. They
can't understand them. In fact, such things can't
be understood without the Spirit's help.
15 Everyone who has the Spirit can judge all
things. But no one can judge those who have the
Spirit. It is written,

16 "Who can ever know what is in the
      Lord's mind?
   Can anyone ever teach him?" *(Isaiah 40:13)*

But we have the mind of Christ.

Taking Sides in the Church

3 Brothers and sisters, I couldn't speak to you
as if you were guided by the Holy Spirit. I had
to speak to you as if you were following the ways
of the world. You aren't growing as Christ wants
you to. You are still like babies. 2 The words I
spoke to you were like milk, not like solid food.
You weren't ready for solid food yet. And you still
aren't ready for it.
3 You are still following the ways of the world.
Some of you are jealous. Some of you argue. So
aren't you following the ways of the world? Aren't
you acting like ordinary human beings? 4 One of you
says, "I follow Paul." Another says, "I follow Apollos." Aren't you acting like ordinary human beings?
5 After all, what is Apollos? And what is Paul?
We are only people who serve. We helped you to
believe. The Lord has given each of us our own
work to do. 6 I planted the seed. Apollos watered it.
But God made it grow.
7 So the one who plants is not important. The one
who waters is not important. It is God who makes
things grow. He is the One who is important. 8 The
one who plants and the one who waters have the
same purpose. The Lord will give each of us a
reward for our work. 9 We work together with God.
You are like God's field. You are like his building.
10 God has given me the grace to lay a foundation as a master builder. Now someone else is
building on it. But each one should build carefully.
11 No one can lay any other foundation than the one
that has already been laid. That foundation is Jesus
Christ.
12 A person may build on it using gold, silver,
jewels, wood, hay or straw. 13 But each person's
work will be shown for what it is. On judgment
day it will be brought to light. It will be put
through fire. The fire will test how good everyone's work is. 14 If the building doesn't burn up,
God will give the builder a reward for his work.
15 If the building burns up, the builder will lose
everything. The builder will be saved, but only like
one escaping through the flames.
16 Don't you know that you yourselves are God's
temple? God's Spirit lives in you. 17 If anyone
destroys God's temple, God will destroy him.
God's temple is holy. And you are that temple.
18 Don't fool yourselves. Suppose some of you
think you are wise by the standards of the world.
Then you should become a "fool" so that you can
become wise.
19 The wisdom of this world is foolish in God's
eyes. It is written, "God catches wise people in
their own tricks." *(Job 5:13)* 20 It is also written,
"The Lord knows that the thoughts of the wise
don't amount to anything." *(Psalm 94:11)*
21 So no more bragging about human beings! All
things are yours. 22 That means Paul or Apollos or
Peter or the world or life or death or the present or
the future. All are yours. 23 You are joined to Christ
and belong to him. And Christ is joined to God.

Apostles of Christ

4 Here is how you should think of us. We serve
Christ. We are trusted with God's secret truth.
2 Those who have been given a trust must prove
that they are faithful.
3 I care very little if I am judged by you or by
any human court. I don't even judge myself. 4 I
don't feel I have done anything wrong. But that
doesn't mean I'm not guilty. The Lord judges me.
5 So don't judge anything before the appointed
time. Wait until the Lord returns. He will bring to
light what is hidden in the dark. He will show the
real reasons why people do what they do. At that
time each person will receive praise from God.

6Brothers and sisters, I have used myself and
Apollos as examples to help you. You can learn
from us the meaning of the saying, "Don't go
beyond what is written." Then you won't be proud
that you follow one person instead of another.
7Who makes you different from anyone else?
What do you have that you did not receive? And if
you did receive it, why do you brag as though you
did not?
8You already have everything you want, don't
you? Have you already become rich? Have you
begun to rule as kings? And did you do that without us? I wish that you really had begun to rule.
Then we could rule with you!
9It seems to me that God has put us apostles on
display at the end of a parade. We are like men
sentenced to die in front of a crowd. We have been
made a show for the whole creation to see. Angels
and people are staring at us.
10We are fools for Christ. But you are so wise
in Christ! We are weak. But you are so strong! You
are honored. But we are looked down on! 11Up to
this very hour we are hungry and thirsty. We are
dressed in rags. We are being treated badly. We
have no homes. 12We work hard with our own
hands. When others call down a curse on us, we
bless them. When we are attacked, we put up with
it. 13When others say bad things about us, we
answer kindly. Up to this moment we have become
the world's garbage. We are everybody's trash.
14I am not writing this to shame you. You are
my dear children, and I want to warn you. 15You
may have 10,000 believers in Christ watching over
you. But you don't have many fathers. I became
your father by serving Christ Jesus and telling you
the good news. 16So I'm asking you to follow my
example.
17That's the reason I'm sending Timothy to you.
He is like a son to me, and I love him. He is faithful in serving the Lord. He will remind you of my
way of life in serving Christ Jesus. And that agrees
with what I teach everywhere in every church.
18Some of you have become proud. You act as
if I weren't coming to you. 19But I will come very
soon, if that's what the Lord wants. Then I will
find out how those proud people are talking. I will
also find out what power they have. 20The kingdom of God is not a matter of talk. It is a matter of
power.
21Which do you want? Should I come to you
with a whip? Or should I come in love and with a
gentle spirit?

Throw the Evil Person Out!

5 It is actually reported that there is sexual sin
among you. I'm told that a man is living with
his father's wife and is having sex with her. Even
people who do not know God don't commit that
sin. 2And you are proud! Shouldn't you be filled
with sadness instead? Shouldn't you have put the
man who did that out of your church?
3Even though I am not right there with you, I
am with you in spirit. And I have already judged
the one who did that, just as if I were there.
4When you come together in the name of our
Lord Jesus, I will be with you in spirit. The power
of our Lord Jesus will also be with you. 5When
you come together like that, hand that man over to
Satan. Then his sinful nature will be destroyed. His
spirit will be saved on the day the Lord returns.
6Your bragging is not good. It is like yeast.
Don't you know that just a little yeast works its
way through the whole batch of dough? 7Get rid
of the old yeast. Be like a new batch of dough
without yeast. That is what you really are, because
Christ has been offered up for us. He is our Passover lamb.
8So let us keep the Feast, but not with the old
yeast. I'm talking about yeast that is full of hatred
and evil. Let us keep the Feast with bread made
without yeast. Let us do it with bread that is honest and true.
9I wrote a letter to you to tell you to stay away
from people who commit sexual sins. 10I didn't
mean the people of this world who sin that way or
who always want more and more. I didn't mean
those who cheat or who worship statues of gods. In
that case you would have to leave this world!
11But here is what I am writing to you. You must
stay away from anyone who claims to be a
believer but who does those things. Stay away
from anyone who commits sexual sins or who
always wants more and more things. Stay away
from a person who worships statues of gods or
who tells lies about others. Stay away from anyone who gets drunk or who cheats. Don't even eat
with a person like that.
12Is it my business to judge those outside the
church? Aren't you supposed to judge those inside
the church? 13God will judge those outside. Scripture says, "Get rid of that evil person!" *(Deuteronomy 17:7; 19:19; 21:21; 22:21,24; 24:7)*

Do Not Take Believers to Court

6 Suppose one of you wants to bring a charge
against another believer. Should you take it to
the ungodly to be judged? Why not take it to God's
people?
2Don't you know that God's people will judge
the world? And if you are going to judge the world,
aren't you able to judge small cases? 3Don't you
know that we will judge angels? Then we should
be able to judge the things of this life even more!
4So if you want to press charges in matters like
that, appoint as judges members of the church who
aren't very important! 5I say this to shame you. Is
it possible that no one among you is wise enough
to judge matters between believers? 6Instead, one
believer goes to court against another. And this
happens in front of unbelievers!
7The very fact that you take another believer to
court means you have lost the battle already. Why

not be treated wrongly? Why not be cheated? [8]Instead, you yourselves cheat and do wrong. And you do it to your brothers and sisters.

[9]Don't you know that evil people will not receive God's kingdom? Don't be fooled. Those who commit sexual sins will not receive the kingdom. Neither will those who worship statues of gods or commit adultery. Neither will men who are prostitutes or who commit homosexual acts. [10]Neither will thieves or those who always want more and more. Neither will those who are often drunk or tell lies or cheat. People who live like that will not receive God's kingdom.

[11]Some of you used to do those things. But your sins were washed away. You were made holy. You were made right with God. All of that was done in the name of the Lord Jesus Christ and by the Spirit of our God.

Sexual Sins

[12]Some of you say, "Everything is permitted for me." But not everything is good for me. Again some of you say, "Everything is permitted for me." But I will not be controlled by anything. [13]Some of you say, "Food is for the stomach. And the stomach is for food." But God will destroy both of them.

The body is not meant for sexual sins. The body is meant for the Lord. And the Lord is meant for the body. [14]By his power God raised the Lord from the dead. He will also raise us up.

[15]Don't you know that your bodies belong to the body of Christ? Should I take what belongs to Christ and join it to a prostitute? Never! [16]Don't you know that when you join yourself to a prostitute, you become one with her in body? Scripture says, "The two will become one." *(Genesis 2:24)* [17]But anyone who is joined to the Lord becomes one with him in spirit.

[18]Keep far away from sexual sins. All the other sins a person commits are outside his body. But sexual sins are sins against one's own body.

[19]Don't you know that your bodies are temples of the Holy Spirit? The Spirit is in you. You have received him from God. You do not belong to yourselves. [20]Christ has paid the price for you. So use your bodies in a way that honors God.

Marriage

7 Now I want to deal with the things you wrote me about.

Some of you say, "It is good for a man not to have sex with a woman." [2]But since there is so much sexual sin, each man should have his own wife. And each woman should have her own husband. [3]A husband should satisfy his wife's sexual needs. And a wife should satisfy her husband's sexual needs.

[4]The wife's body does not belong only to her. It also belongs to her husband. In the same way, the husband's body does not belong only to him. It also belongs to his wife. [5]You shouldn't stop giving yourselves to each other except when you both agree to do so. And that should be only to give yourselves time to pray for a while. Then you should come together again. In that way, Satan will not tempt you when you can't control yourselves.

[6]I say those things to you as my advice, not as a command. [7]I wish all of you were like me. But you each have your own gift from God. One has this gift. Another has that.

[8]I speak to those who are not married. I also speak to widows. It is good for you to stay single like me. [9]But if you can't control yourselves, you should get married. It is better to get married than to burn with sexual longing.

[10]I give a command to those who are married. It is a direct command from the Lord, not from me. A wife must not leave her husband. [11]But if she does, she must not get married again. Or she can go back to her husband. And a husband must not divorce his wife.

[12]I also have something to say to everyone else. It is from me, not a direct command from the Lord. Suppose a brother has a wife who is not a believer. If she is willing to live with him, he must not divorce her. [13]And suppose a woman has a husband who is not a believer. If he is willing to live with her, she must not divorce him. [14]The unbelieving husband has been made holy through his wife. The unbelieving wife has been made holy through her believing husband. If that were not the case, your children would not be pure and clean. But as it is, they are holy.

[15]If the unbeliever leaves, let that person go. In that case, a believing man or woman does not have to stay married. God wants us to live in peace. [16]Wife, how do you know if you can save your husband? Husband, how do you know if you can save your wife?

[17]But each of you should remain in the place in life that the Lord has given you. Stay as you were when God chose you. That's the rule all the churches must follow.

[18]Was a man already circumcised when God chose him? Then he should not become uncircumcised. Was he uncircumcised when God chose him? Then he should not be circumcised. [19]Being circumcised means nothing. Being uncircumcised means nothing. Doing what God commands is what counts.

[20]Each of you should stay as you were when God chose you.

[21]Were you a slave when God chose you? Don't let it trouble you. But if you can get your master to set you free, do it. [22]Those who were slaves when the Lord chose them are now the Lord's free people. Those who were free when God chose them are now slaves of Christ. [23]Christ has paid the price for you. Don't become slaves of human beings.

[24]Brothers and sisters, you are accountable to God. So all of you should stay as you were when God chose you.

25Now I want to say something about virgins. I have no direct command from the Lord. But I give my opinion. Because of the Lord's mercy, I give it as one who can be trusted.

26Times are hard for you right now. So I think it's good for you to stay as you are. 27Are you married? Then don't get a divorce. Are you single? Then don't look for a wife. 28But if you get married, you have not sinned. And if a virgin gets married, she has not sinned. But those who get married will have many troubles in this life. I want to save you from that.

29Brothers and sisters, what I mean is that the time is short. From now on, those who have a husband or wife should live as if they did not. 30Those who are sad should live as if they were not. Those who are happy should live as if they were not. Those who buy something should live as if it were not theirs to keep. 31Those who use the things of the world should not become all wrapped up in them. The world as it now exists is passing away.

32I don't want you to have anything to worry about. A single man is concerned about the Lord's matters. He wants to know how he can please the Lord. 33But a married man is concerned about the matters of this world. He wants to know how he can please his wife. 34His concerns pull him in two directions.

A single woman or a virgin is concerned about the Lord's matters. She wants to serve the Lord with both body and spirit. But a married woman is concerned about the matters of this world. She wants to know how she can please her husband.

35I'm saying those things for your own good. I'm not trying to hold you back. I want you to be free to live in a way that is right. I want you to give yourselves completely to the Lord.

36Suppose a man thinks he is not acting properly toward the virgin he has promised to marry. Suppose she is getting old, and he feels that he should marry her. He should do as he wants. He is not sinning. They should get married.

37But suppose the man has decided not to marry the virgin. And suppose he has no compelling need to get married and can control himself. If he has made up his mind not to get married, he also does the right thing.

38So then, the man who marries the virgin does the right thing. But the man who doesn't marry her does an even better thing.

39A woman has to stay married to her husband as long as he lives. If he dies, she is free to marry anyone she wants to. But the one she marries must belong to the Lord. 40In my opinion, she is happier if she stays single. And I also think that I am led by the Spirit of God in saying that.

Food Offered to Statues of Gods

8 Now I want to deal with food offered to statues of gods.

We know that we all have knowledge. Knowledge makes people proud. But love builds them up. 2Those who think they know something still don't know as they should. 3But those who love God are known by God.

4So then, here is what I say about eating food that is offered to statues of gods. We know that a god made by human hands is really nothing at all in the world. We know there is only one God. 5There may be so-called gods either in heaven or on earth. In fact, there are many "gods" and many "lords." 6But for us there is only one God. He is the Father. All things came from him, and we live for him. And there is only one Lord. He is Jesus Christ. All things came because of him, and we live because of him.

7But not everyone knows that. Some people still think that statues of gods are real gods. When they eat food that was offered to statues of gods, they think of it as food that was offered to real gods. And because they have a weak sense of what is right and wrong, they feel guilty. 8But food doesn't bring us close to God. We are no worse if we don't eat. We are no better if we do eat.

9But be careful how you use your freedom. Be sure it doesn't trip up someone who is weaker than you.

10Suppose you who have that knowledge are eating in a temple of one of those gods. And suppose someone who has a weak sense of what is right and wrong sees you. Won't that person become bold and eat what has been offered to statues of gods? 11If so, then your knowledge destroys that weak brother or sister for whom Christ died.

12When you sin against other believers in that way, you harm their weak sense of what is right and wrong. By doing that you sin against Christ.

13So what should I do if what I eat causes my brother or sister to fall into sin? I will never eat meat again. In that way, I will not cause them to fall.

The Rights of an Apostle

9 Am I not free? Am I not an apostle? Haven't I seen Jesus our Lord? Aren't you the result of my work for the Lord? 2Even though others may not think of me as an apostle, I am certainly one to you! You are the proof that I am the Lord's apostle. 3That is what I say to stand up for myself when people judge me.

4Don't we have the right to eat and drink? 5Don't we have the right to take a believing wife with us when we travel? The other apostles do. The Lord's brothers do. Peter does. 6Or are Barnabas and I the only ones who have to work for a living?

7Who serves as a soldier but doesn't get paid? Who plants a vineyard but doesn't eat any of its grapes? Who takes care of a flock but doesn't drink any of the milk? 8Do I say that from only a human point of view? The Law says the same thing.

9Here is what is written in the Law of Moses. "Do not stop an ox from eating while it helps separate the grain from the straw." *(Deuteronomy 25:4)*

Is it oxen that God is concerned about? 10Doesn't
he say that for us? Yes, it was written for us. When
a farmer plows and separates the grain, he does it
because he hopes to share in the crop.
11We have planted spiritual seed among you. Is
it too much to ask that we receive from you some
of the things we need? 12Others have the right to
receive help from you. Don't we have even more
right to do so?

But we didn't use that right. No, we have put
up with everything. We didn't want to keep the
good news of Christ from spreading.
13Don't you know that those who work in the
temple get their food from the temple? Don't you
know that those who serve at the altar eat from
what is offered on the altar? 14In the same way,
those who preach the good news should receive
their living from their work. That is what the Lord
has commanded.
15But I haven't used any of those rights. And
I'm not writing because I hope you will do things
like that for me. I would rather die than have anyone take away my pride in my work. 16But when I
preach the good news, I can't brag. I have to
preach it. How terrible it will be for me if I do not
preach the good news!
17If I preach because I want to, I get a reward. If
I preach because I have to, I'm only doing my
duty. 18Then what reward do I get? Here is what it
is. I am able to preach the good news free of
charge. And I can do it without making use of my
rights when I preach it.
19I am free. I don't belong to anyone. But I
make myself a slave to everyone. I do it to win as
many as I can to Christ.
20To the Jews I became like a Jew. That was to
win the Jews. To those under the law I became like
one who was under the law, even though I myself
am not under the law. That was to win those under
the law. 21To those who don't have the law I
became like one who doesn't have the law. I am
not free from God's law. I am under Christ's law.
Now I can win those who don't have the law. 22To
those who are weak I became weak. That was to
win the weak.

I have become all things to all people so that in
all possible ways I might save some. 23I do all of
that because of the good news. And I want to share
in its blessings.
24In a race all the runners run. But only one gets
the prize. You know that, don't you? So run in a
way that will get you the prize. 25All who take part
in the games train hard. They do it to get a crown
that will not last. But we do it to get a crown that
will last forever.
26So I do not run like someone who doesn't run
toward the finish line. I do not fight like a boxer
who hits nothing but air. 27No, I train my body and
bring it under control. Then after I have preached
to others, I myself will not break the rules and fail
to win the prize.

Warnings From Israel's History

10 Brothers and sisters, here is what I want
you to know about our people who lived
long ago. They were all led by the cloud. They all
walked through the Red Sea. 2They were all baptized into Moses in the cloud and in the sea. 3They
all ate the same supernatural food. 4They all drank
the same supernatural water. They drank from the
supernatural rock that went with them. That rock
was Christ.
5But God was not pleased with most of them.
Their bodies were scattered all over the desert.
6Now those things happened as examples for us.
They are supposed to keep us from longing for evil
things, as the people of Israel did.
7So don't worship statues of gods, as some of
them did. It is written, "The people sat down to eat
and drink. Then they got up to dance wildly in
front of their god." *(Exodus 32:6)* 8We should not
commit sexual sins, as some of them did. In one
day 23,000 of them died. 9We should not put the
Lord to the test, as some of them did. They were
killed by snakes. 10Don't tell your leaders how
unhappy you are with them. That's what some of
the people of Israel did. And they were killed by
the destroying angel.
11Those things happened to them as examples
for us. They were written down to warn us who are
living at the time when God's work is being completed. 12So be careful. When you think you are
standing firm, you might fall.
13You are tempted in the same way all other
human beings are. God is faithful. He will not let
you be tempted any more than you can take. But
when you are tempted, God will give you a way
out so that you can stand up under it.

Sharing in the Body and Blood of Christ

14My dear friends, run away from statues of
gods. Don't worship them. 15I'm talking to people
who are reasonable. Judge for yourselves what I
say.
16When we give thanks for the cup at the Lord's
Supper, aren't we sharing in the blood of Christ?
When we break the bread, aren't we sharing in the
body of Christ? 17Just as there is one loaf, so we
who are many are one body. We all eat from the
one loaf.
18Think about the people of Israel. Don't those
who eat the offerings share in the altar? 19Do I
mean that what is offered to a statue of a god is
anything? Do I mean that a statue of a god is anything? 20No! But what is offered by those who
worship statues of gods is really offered to
demons. It is not offered to God. I don't want you
to be sharing with demons.
21You can't drink the cup of the Lord and the
cup of demons too. You can't have a part in both
the Lord's table and the table of demons. 22Are we
trying to make the Lord jealous? Are we stronger
than he is?

The Believer's Freedom

23You say, "Everything is permitted." But not
everything is good for us. Again you say, "Everything is permitted." But not everything builds us
up. 24We should not look out for our own interests.
Instead, we should look out for the interests of
others.

25Eat anything that is sold in the meat market.
Don't ask if it's right or wrong. 26Scripture says,
"The earth belongs to the Lord. And so does every-
thing in it." *(Psalm 24:1)*

27Suppose an unbeliever invites you to a meal
and you want to go. Then eat anything that is put
in front of you. Don't ask if it's right or wrong.

28But suppose someone says to you, "This food
has been offered to a statue of a god." Then don't
eat it. Keep in mind the good of the one who told
you. And don't eat because of a sense of what is
right and wrong. 29I'm talking about the other person's sense of what is right and wrong, not yours.

Why should my freedom be judged by what
someone else thinks? 30Suppose I give thanks
when I eat. Then why should I be blamed for eating food I thank God for?

31So eat and drink and do everything else for the
glory of God. 32Don't do anything that causes
another person to trip and fall. It doesn't matter if
that person is a Jew or a Greek or a member of
God's church.

33Follow my example. I try to please everyone
in every way. I'm not looking out for what is good
for me. I'm looking out for the interests of others.
I do it so that they might be saved.

11 Follow my example, just as I follow the
example of Christ.

Proper Worship

2I praise you for being faithful in remembering
me. I also praise you for staying true to all my
teachings, just as I gave them to you.

3Now I want you to know that the head of every
man is Christ. The head of the woman is the man.
And the head of Christ is God. 4Every man who
prays or prophesies with his head covered brings
shame on his head. 5And every woman who prays
or prophesies with her head uncovered brings
shame on her head. It is just as if her head were
shaved.

6What if a woman does not cover her head? She
should have her hair cut off. But it is shameful for
her to cut her hair or shave it off. So she should
cover her head.

7A man should not cover his head. He is the
likeness and glory of God. But the woman is the
glory of the man. 8The man did not come from the
woman. The woman came from the man.

9Also, the man was not created for the woman.
The woman was created for the man. 10That's why
a woman should have her head covered. It shows
that she is under authority. She should also cover
her head because of the angels.

11But here is how things are for those who
belong to the Lord. The woman is not independent
of the man. And the man is not independent of the
woman. 12The woman came from the man, and the
man is born from the woman. But everything
comes from God.

13You be the judge. Is it proper for a woman to
pray to God without covering her head? 14Suppose
a man has long hair. Doesn't the very nature of
things teach you that it is shameful? 15And suppose
a woman has long hair. Doesn't the very nature of
things teach you that it is her glory? Long hair is
given to her as a covering.

16If anyone wants to argue about that, we don't
have any other practice. And God's churches don't
either.

The Lord's Supper

17In the following matters, I don't praise you.
Your meetings do more harm than good.

18First, here is what people are telling me. When
you come together as a church, you take sides.
And in some ways I believe it. 19No doubt you
need to take sides in order to show which of you
God agrees with!

20When you come together, it is not the Lord's
Supper you eat. 21As you eat, each of you goes
ahead without waiting for anyone else. One
remains hungry and another gets drunk. 22Don't
you have homes to eat and drink in? Or do you
think so little of God's church that you shame
those in it who have nothing? What should I say
to you? Should I praise you for that? Certainly not!

23I passed on to you what I received from the
Lord. On the night the Lord Jesus was handed over
to his enemies, he took bread. 24When he had given
thanks, he broke it. He said, "This is my body. It is
given for you. Every time you eat it, do it in memory of me." 25In the same way, after supper he took
the cup. He said, "This cup is the new covenant in
my blood. Every time you drink it, do it in memory of me."

26When you eat the bread and drink the cup, you
are announcing the Lord's death until he comes
again.

27So do not eat the bread or drink the cup of the
Lord in a way that isn't worthy of him. If you do,
you will be guilty of sinning against the body and
blood of the Lord.

28A person should take a careful look at himself
before he eats the bread and drinks from the cup.
29Anyone who eats and drinks must recognize the
body of the Lord. If he doesn't, God will judge
him for it. 30That is why many of you are weak and
sick. That is why a number of you have died.

31We should judge ourselves. Then we would
not be found guilty. 32When the Lord judges us, he
corrects us. Then we will not be judged along with
the rest of the world.

33My brothers and sisters, when you come
together to eat, wait for each other. 34Those who

are hungry should eat at home. Then when you come together, you will not be judged.

When I come, I will give you more directions.

Gifts of the Holy Spirit

12 Brothers and sisters, I want you to know about the gifts of the Holy Spirit.

2 You know that at one time you were unbelievers. You were somehow drawn away to worship statues of gods that couldn't even speak. 3 So I tell you that no one who is speaking with the help of God's Spirit says, "May Jesus be cursed." And without the help of the Holy Spirit no one can say, "Jesus is Lord."

4 There are different kinds of gifts. But they are all given by the same Spirit. 5 There are different ways to serve. But they all come from the same Lord. 6 There are different ways to work. But the same God makes it possible for all of us to have all those different things.

7 The Holy Spirit is given to each of us in a special way. That is for the good of all. 8 To some people the Spirit gives the message of wisdom. To others the same Spirit gives the message of knowledge. 9 To others the same Spirit gives faith. To others that one Spirit gives gifts of healing. 10 To others he gives the power to do miracles. To others he gives the ability to prophesy. To others he gives the ability to tell the spirits apart. To others he gives the ability to speak in different kinds of languages they had not known before. And to still others he gives the ability to explain what was said in those languages.

11 All of the gifts are produced by one and the same Spirit. He gives them to each person, just as he decides.

One Body but Many Parts

12 There is one body. But it has many parts. Even though it has many parts, they make up one body. It is the same with Christ. 13 We were all baptized by one Holy Spirit into one body. It didn't matter whether we were Jews or Greeks, slaves or free people. We were all given the same Spirit to drink. 14 The body is not made up of just one part. It has many parts. 15 Suppose the foot says, "I am not a hand. So I don't belong to the body." It is still part of the body. 16 And suppose the ear says, "I am not an eye. So I don't belong to the body." It is still part of the body.

17 If the whole body were an eye, how could it hear? If the whole body were an ear, how could it smell? 18 God has placed each part in the body just as he wanted it to be. 19 If all the parts were the same, how could there be a body? 20 As it is, there are many parts. But there is only one body.

21 The eye can't say to the hand, "I don't need you!" The head can't say to the feet, "I don't need you!" 22 In fact, it is just the opposite. The parts of the body that seem to be weaker are the ones we can't do without. 23 The parts that we think are less important we treat with special honor. The private parts aren't shown. But they are treated with special care. 24 The parts that can be shown don't need special care.

But God has joined together all the parts of the body. And he has given more honor to the parts that didn't have any. 25 In that way, the parts of the body will not take sides. All of them will take care of each other. 26 If one part suffers, every part suffers with it. If one part is honored, every part shares in its joy.

27 You are the body of Christ. Each one of you is a part of it. 28 First, God has appointed apostles in the church. Second, he has appointed prophets. Third, he has appointed teachers. Then he has appointed people who do miracles and those who have gifts of healing. He also appointed those able to help others, those able to direct things, and those who can speak in different kinds of languages they had not known before.

29 Is everyone an apostle? Is everyone a prophet? Is everyone a teacher? Do all work miracles? 30 Do all have gifts of healing? Do all speak in languages they had not known before? Do all explain what is said in those languages? 31 But above all, you should want the more important gifts.

Love

And now I will show you the best way of all.

13 Suppose I speak in the languages of human beings and of angels. If I don't have love, I am only a loud gong or a noisy cymbal. 2 Suppose I have the gift of prophecy. Suppose I can understand all the secret things of God and know everything about him. And suppose I have enough faith to move mountains. If I don't have love, I am nothing at all. 3 Suppose I give everything I have to poor people. And suppose I give my body to be burned. If I don't have love, I get nothing at all.

4 Love is patient. Love is kind. It does not want what belongs to others. It does not brag. It is not proud. 5 It is not rude. It does not look out for its own interests. It does not easily become angry. It does not keep track of other people's wrongs.

6 Love is not happy with evil. But it is full of joy when the truth is spoken. 7 It always protects. It always trusts. It always hopes. It never gives up.

8 Love never fails. But prophecy will pass away. Speaking in languages that had not been known before will end. And knowledge will pass away.

9 What we know now is not complete. What we prophesy now is not perfect. 10 But when what is perfect comes, the things that are not perfect will pass away.

11 When I was a child, I talked like a child. I thought like a child. I had the understanding of a child. When I became a man, I put childish ways behind me.

12 Now we see only a dim likeness of things. It is as if we were seeing them in a mirror. But someday we will see clearly. We will see face to face.

What I know now is not complete. But someday I
will know completely, just as God knows me
completely.
13The three most important things to have are
faith, hope and love. But the greatest of them is
love.

The Gifts the Holy Spirit Gives

14 Follow the way of love. You should also
want the gifts the Holy Spirit gives. Most
of all, you should want the gift of prophecy.
2Anyone who speaks in a language he had not
known before doesn't speak to people. He speaks
only to God. In fact, no one understands that person. What he says with his spirit remains a mystery. 3But anyone who prophesies speaks to
people. He says things to make them stronger, to
give them hope and to comfort them. 4Those who
speak in other languages build themselves up. But
those who prophesy build up the church.
5I would like all of you to speak in other languages. But I would rather have you prophesy.
Those who prophesy are more helpful than those
who speak in other languages. But that is not the
case if those who speak in other languages explain
what they have said. Then the whole church can
be built up.
6Brothers and sisters, suppose I were to come
to you and speak in other languages. What good
would I be to you? None! I would need to come
with new truth or knowledge, or a prophecy or a
teaching.
7Here are some examples. Certain objects make
sounds. Take a flute or a harp. No one will know
what the tune is unless different notes are played.
8Also, if the trumpet call isn't clear, who will get
ready for battle?
9It's the same with you. You must speak words
that people understand. If you don't, no one will
know what you are saying. You will just be speaking into the air.
10It is true that there are all kinds of languages
in the world. And they all have meaning. 11But if I
don't understand what someone is saying, I am a
stranger to that person. And that person is a
stranger to me.
12It's the same with you. You want to have gifts
of the Spirit. So try to do your best in using gifts
that build up the church.
13For that reason, those who speak in languages
they had not known before should pray that they
can explain what they say. 14If I pray in another
language, my spirit prays. But my mind does not
pray. 15So what should I do? I will pray with my
spirit. But I will also pray with my mind. I will
sing with my spirit. But I will also sing with my
mind.
16Suppose you are praising God with your
spirit. And suppose there are visitors among you
who don't understand what's going on. How can
they say "Amen" when you give thanks? They
don't know what you are saying. 17You might be
giving thanks well enough. But the others are not
being built up.
18I thank God that I speak in other languages
more than all of you do. 19But in the church I
would rather speak five words that people can
understand than 10,000 words in another language. Then I would be teaching others.
20Brothers and sisters, stop thinking like children. Be like babies as far as evil is concerned. But
be grown up in your thinking. 21In the Law it is
written,

"Through people who speak unfamiliar
languages
and through the lips of strangers
I will speak to these people.
But even then they will not listen to me."
(Isaiah 28:11,12)

That is what the Lord says.
22So speaking in other languages is a sign for
those who don't believe. It is not a sign for those
who do believe. But prophecy is for believers. It
is not for those who don't believe.
23Suppose the whole church comes together and
everyone speaks in other languages. And suppose
visitors or unbelievers come in. Won't they say
you are out of your minds? 24But suppose unbelievers or visitors come in while everyone is
prophesying. Then they will be shown by all who
speak that they are sinners. They will be judged by
all. 25The secrets of their hearts will be brought out
into the open. They will fall down and worship
God. They will exclaim, "God is really here
among you!"

Proper Worship

26Brothers and sisters, what should we say then?
When you come together, every one of you brings
something. You bring a hymn or a teaching or a
word from God. You bring a message in another
language or explain what was said. All of those
things must be done to make the church strong.
27No more than two or three people should
speak in another language. And they should speak
one at a time. Then someone must explain what
was said. 28If there is no one to explain, the speak-
ers should keep quiet in the church. They can
speak to themselves and to God.
29Only two or three prophets are supposed to
speak. Others should decide if what is being said
is true. 30What if a message from God comes to
someone else who is sitting there? Then the one
who is speaking should stop.
31Those who prophesy can all take turns. In that
way, everyone can be taught and be given hope.
32Those who prophesy should control their speaking. 33God is not a God of disorder. He is a God of
peace.
As in all the churches of God's people,
34women should remain silent in the meetings.

They are not allowed to speak. They must follow the lead of those who are in authority, as the Law says. 35If they have a question about something, they should ask their own husbands at home. It is shameful for women to speak in church meetings.

36Did the word of God begin with you? Or are you the only people it has reached? 37Suppose some think they are prophets or have gifts of the Holy Spirit. They should agree that what I am writing to you is the Lord's command. 38Anyone who does not recognize that will not be recognized.

39Brothers and sisters, you should want to prophesy. And don't stop people from speaking in languages they had not known before. 40But everything should be done in a proper and orderly way.

Paul Explains the Good News

15 Brothers and sisters, I want to remind you of the good news I preached to you. You received it and have put your faith in it. 2Because you believed the good news, you are saved. But you must hold firmly to the message I preached to you. If you don't, you have believed it for nothing.

3What I received I passed on to you. And it is the most important of all. Here is what it is. Christ died for our sins, just as Scripture said he would. 4He was buried. He was raised from the dead on the third day, just as Scripture said he would be. 5He appeared to Peter.

Then he appeared to the Twelve. 6After that, he appeared to more than 500 believers at the same time. Most of them are still living. But some have died. 7He appeared to James. Then he appeared to all the apostles. 8Last of all, he also appeared to me. I was like someone who wasn't born at the right time or in a normal way.

9I am the least important of the apostles. I'm not even fit to be called an apostle. I tried to destroy God's church. 10But because of God's grace I am what I am. And his grace was not wasted on me. No, I have worked harder than all the other apostles. But I didn't do the work. God's grace was with me.

11So whether it was I or the other apostles who preached to you, that is what we preach. And that is what you believed.

Believers Will Rise From the Dead

12We have preached that Christ has been raised from the dead. So how can some of you say that no one rises from the dead? 13If no one rises from the dead, then not even Christ has been raised. 14And if Christ has not been raised, what we preach doesn't mean anything. Your faith doesn't mean anything either. 15More than that, we would be lying about God. We have given witness that God raised Christ from the dead. But he did not raise him if the dead are not raised.

16If the dead are not raised, then Christ has not been raised either. 17And if Christ has not been raised, your faith doesn't mean anything. Your sins have not been forgiven. 18Those who have died believing in Christ are also lost.

19Do we have hope in Christ only for this life? Then people should pity us more than anyone else.

20But Christ really has been raised from the dead. He is the first of all those who will rise.

21Death came because of what a man did. Rising from the dead also comes because of what a man did. 22Because of Adam, all people die. So because of Christ, all will be made alive.

23But here is the order of events. Christ is the first of those who rise from the dead. When he comes back, those who belong to him will be raised. 24Then the end will come. Christ will destroy all rule, authority and power. He will hand over the kingdom to God the Father.

25Christ must rule until he has put all his enemies under his control. 26The last enemy that will be destroyed is death. 27Scripture says that God "has put everything under his control." *(Psalm 8:6)* It says that "everything" has been put under him. But it is clear that this does not include God himself, who puts everything under Christ. 28When he has done that, the Son also will be under God's rule. God puts everything under the Son. In that way, God will be all in all.

29Suppose no one rises from the dead. Then what will people do who are baptized for the dead? Suppose the dead are not raised at all. Then why are people baptized for them? 30And why would we put ourselves in danger every hour?

31I die every day. I really mean that, brothers and sisters. Here is something you can be sure of. I take pride in what Christ Jesus our Lord has done for you through my work. 32Did I fight wild animals in Ephesus for only human reasons? Then what have I gotten for it? If the dead are not raised,

"Let us eat and drink,
because tomorrow we will die." *(Isaiah 22:13)*

33Don't let anyone fool you. "Bad companions make a good person bad." 34You should come back to your senses and stop sinning. Some of you don't know anything about God. I say this to make you ashamed.

The Body That Rises From the Dead

35But someone might ask, "How are the dead raised? What kind of body will they have?" 36How foolish! What you plant doesn't come to life unless it dies. 37When you plant something, it isn't a completely grown plant that you put in the ground. You only plant a seed. Maybe it's wheat or something else. 38But God gives the seed a body just as he has planned. And to each kind of seed he gives its own body.

39All earthly creatures are not the same. People have one kind of body. Animals have another. Birds have another kind. Fish have still another.

40There are also heavenly bodies as well as earthly bodies. Heavenly bodies have one kind of glory. Earthly bodies have another. [41]The sun has one kind of glory. The moon has another kind. The stars have still another. And one star's glory is different from that of another star.

[42]It will be like that with bodies that are raised from the dead. The body that is planted does not last forever. The body that is raised from the dead lasts forever. [43]It is planted without honor. But it is raised in glory. It is planted in weakness. But it is raised in power. [44]It is planted as an earthly body. But it is raised as a spiritual body.

Just as there is an earthly body, there is also a spiritual body. [45]It is written, "The first man Adam became a living person." *(Genesis 2:7)* The last Adam became a spirit that gives life. [46]What is spiritual did not come first. What is earthly came first. What is spiritual came after that. [47]The first man came from the dust of the earth. The second man came from heaven.

[48]Those who belong to the earth are like the one who came from the earth. And those who are spiritual are like the one who came from heaven. [49]We are like the earthly man. And we will be like the man from heaven.

[50]Brothers and sisters, here is what I'm telling you. Bodies made of flesh and blood can't share in the kingdom of God. And what dies can't share in what never dies.

[51]Listen! I am telling you a mystery. We will not all die. But we will all be changed. [52]That will happen in a flash, as quickly as you can wink an eye. It will happen when the last trumpet sounds. The trumpet will sound, and the dead will be raised to live forever. And we will be changed.

[53]Our natural bodies don't last forever. They must be dressed with what does last forever. What dies must be dressed with what does not die. [54]In fact, that is going to happen. What does not last will be dressed with what lasts forever. What dies will be dressed with what does not die. Then what is written will come true. It says, "Death has been swallowed up. It has lost the battle." *(Isaiah 25:8)*

[55]"Death, where is the battle you thought you
were winning?
Death, where is your sting?" *(Hosea 13:14)*

[56]The sting of death is sin. And the power of sin is the law. [57]But let us give thanks to God! He wins the battle for us because of what our Lord Jesus Christ has done.

[58]My dear brothers and sisters, stand firm. Don't let anything move you. Always give yourselves completely to the work of the Lord. Because you belong to the Lord, you know that your work is not worthless.

The Offering for God's People

16 Now I want to deal with the offering of money for God's people.

Do what I told the churches in Galatia to do. [2]On the first day of every week, each of you should put some money away. The amount should be in keeping with how much money you make. Save the money so that you won't have to take up an offering when I come. [3]When I arrive, I will send some people with your gift to Jerusalem. They will be people you consider to be good. And I will give them letters that explain who they are. [4]If it seems good for me to go also, they will go with me.

What Paul Asks for Himself

[5]After I go through Macedonia, I will come to you. I will only be passing through Macedonia. [6]But I might stay with you for a while. I might even spend the winter. Then you can help me on my journey everywhere I go.

[7]I don't want to see you now while I am just passing through. I hope to spend some time with you, if the Lord allows it. [8]But I will stay at Ephesus until the day of Pentecost. [9]A door has opened wide for me to do some good work here. There are many people who oppose me.

[10]Timothy might come to you. Make sure he has nothing to worry about while he is with you. He is doing the work of the Lord, just as I am. [11]No one should refuse to accept him. Send him safely on his way so he can return to me. I'm expecting him to come back along with the others.

[12]I want to say something about our brother Apollos. I tried my best to get him to go to you with the others. But he didn't want to go right now. He will go when he can.

[13]Be on your guard. Stand firm in the faith. Be brave. Be strong. [14]Be loving in everything you do.

[15]You know that the first believers in Achaia were from the family of Stephanas. They have spent all their time serving God's people. Brothers and sisters, I am asking you [16]to follow the lead of people like them. Follow everyone who joins in the task and works hard at it.

[17]I was glad when Stephanas, Fortunatus and Achaicus arrived. They have supplied me with what you couldn't give me. [18]They renewed my spirit, and yours also. People like that are worthy of honor.

Final Greetings

[19]The churches in Asia Minor send you greetings. Aquila and Priscilla greet you warmly because of the Lord's love. So does the church that meets in their house. [20]All the brothers and sisters here send you greetings. Greet one another with a holy kiss.

[21]I, Paul, am writing this greeting with my own hand.

[22]If anyone does not love the Lord, let a curse be on that person! Come, Lord!

[23]May the grace of the Lord Jesus be with you.

[24]I give my love to all of you who belong to Christ Jesus. Amen.

2 Corinthians

1 I, Paul, am writing this letter. I am an apostle of Christ Jesus just as God planned. Timothy our brother joins me in writing.

We are sending this letter to you, the members of God's church in Corinth. It is also for all of God's people everywhere in Achaia.

2May God our Father and the Lord Jesus Christ give you grace and peace.

God Gives Comfort

3Give praise to the God and Father of our Lord Jesus Christ! He is the Father who gives tender love. All comfort comes from him. 4He comforts us in all our troubles. Now we can comfort others when they are in trouble. We ourselves have received comfort from God. 5We share the sufferings of Christ. We also share his comfort.

6If we are having trouble, it is so that you will be comforted and renewed. If we are comforted, it is so that you will be comforted. Then you will be able to put up with the same suffering we have gone through. 7Our hope for you remains firm. We know that you suffer just as we do. In the same way, God comforts you just as he comforts us.

8Brothers and sisters, we want you to know about the hard times we suffered in Asia Minor. We were having a lot of trouble. It was far more than we could stand. We even thought we were going to die. 9In fact, in our hearts we felt as if we were under the sentence of death.

But that happened so that we would not depend on ourselves but on God. He raises the dead to life. 10God has saved us from deadly dangers. And he will continue to do it. We have put our hope in him. He will continue to save us.

11You must help us by praying for us. Then many people will give thanks because of what will happen to us. They will thank God for his kindness to us in answer to the prayers of many.

Paul Changes His Plans

12Here is what we take pride in. Our sense of what is right and wrong gives witness that we have acted in God's holy and honest ways. That is how we live in the world. We live that way most of all when we are dealing with you. Our way of living is not wise in the eyes of the world. But it is in keeping with God's grace.

13We are writing only what you can read and understand. And here is what I hope. 14Up to this point you have understood some of the things we have said. But now I hope that someday you will be able to take pride in us, just as we will take pride in you on the day the Lord Jesus returns. When you are able to do that, you will understand us completely.

15I was sure of those things. So I planned to visit you first. Here is how I thought you would be helped twice. 16I planned to visit you on my way to Macedonia. I would have come back to you from there. Then you would have sent me on my way to Judea.

17When I planned all of that, did I do it without much thought? No. I don't make my plans the way the world makes theirs. In the same breath the world says, "Yes! Yes!" and "No! No!"

18But just as sure as God is faithful, our message to you is not "Yes" and "No." 19Silas, Timothy and I preached to you about the Son of God, Jesus Christ. Our message did not say "Yes" and "No" at the same time. The message of Christ has always been "Yes."

20God has made a great many promises. They are all "Yes" because of what Christ has done. So through Christ we say "Amen." We want God to receive glory.

21He makes both us and you stand firm because we belong to Christ. He anointed us. 22He put his Spirit in our hearts and marked us as his own. We can now be sure that he will give us everything he promised us.

23I call God as my witness. I wanted to spare you. So I didn't return to Corinth. 24Your faith is not under our control. You stand firm in your own faith. But we work together with you for your joy.

2 So I made up my mind that I would not make another painful visit to you. 2If I make you sad, who is going to make me glad? Only you, the one I made sad.

3I wrote what I did for a special reason. When I came, I didn't want to be troubled by those who should make me glad. I was sure that all of you would share my joy. 4I was very troubled when I wrote to you. My heart was sad. My eyes were full of tears. I didn't want to make you sad. I wanted to let you know that I love you very deeply.

Forgive Those Who Make You Sad

5Suppose someone has made us sad. In some ways, he hasn't made me sad so much as he has made all of you sad. But I don't want to put this too strongly. 6He has been punished because most of you decided he should be. That is enough for him.

7Now you should forgive him and comfort him. Then he won't be sad more than he can stand. 8So I'm asking you to tell him again that you still love him.

9I wrote to you for a special reason. I wanted to see if you could stand the test. I wanted to see if you could obey everything that was asked of you.

10Anyone you forgive I also forgive. Was there anything to forgive? If so, I have forgiven it for your benefit, knowing that Christ is watching. 11We don't want Satan to outsmart us. We know how he does his evil work.

Serving Under the New Covenant

12I went to Troas to preach the good news about Christ. There I found that the Lord had opened a door of opportunity for me. 13But I still had no peace of mind. I couldn't find my brother Titus there. So I said good-by to the believers at Troas and went on to Macedonia.

14Give thanks to God! He always leads us in the winners' parade because we belong to Christ. Through us, God spreads the knowledge of Christ everywhere like perfume. 15God considers us to be the sweet smell that Christ is spreading among people who are being saved and people who are dying. 16To the one, we are the smell of death. To the other, we are the perfume of life. Who is able to do that work?

17Unlike many people, we aren't selling God's word to make money. In fact, it is just the opposite. Because of Christ we speak honestly before God. We speak like people God has sent.

3 Are we beginning to praise ourselves again? Some people need letters that speak well of them. Do we need those kinds of letters, either to you or from you?

2You yourselves are our letter. You are written on our hearts. Everyone knows you and reads you. 3You make it clear that you are a letter from Christ. You are the result of our work for God. You are a letter written not with ink but with the Spirit of the living God. You are a letter written not on tablets made out of stone but on human hearts.

4Through Christ, we can be sure of this because of our faith in God's power. 5In ourselves we are not able to claim anything for ourselves. The power to do what we do comes from God. 6He has given us the power to serve under a new covenant. The covenant is not based on the written Law of Moses. It comes from the Holy Spirit. The written Law kills, but the Spirit gives life.

The Glory of the New Covenant

7The Law was written in letters on stone. Even though it was a way of serving God, it led to death. But even that way of serving God came with glory. And even though the glory was fading, the people of Israel couldn't look at Moses' face very long.

8Since all of that is true, won't the work of the Holy Spirit be even more glorious? 9The Law that sentences people to death is glorious. How much more glorious is the work of the Spirit! His work makes people right with God.

10The glory of the old covenant is nothing compared with the far greater glory of the new. 11The glory of the old is fading away. How much greater is the glory of the new! It will last forever.

12Since we have that kind of hope, we are very bold. 13We are not like Moses. He used to cover his face with a veil. That was to keep the people of Israel from looking at his face while the brightness was fading away.

14But their minds were made stubborn. To this very day, the same veil remains when the old covenant is read. The veil has not been removed. Only faith in Christ can take it away. 15To this very day, when the Law of Moses is read, a veil covers the minds of those who hear it.

16But when anyone turns to the Lord, the veil is taken away. 17Now the Lord is the Holy Spirit. And where the Spirit of the Lord is, freedom is also there.

18Our faces are not covered with a veil. We all display the Lord's glory. We are being changed to become more like him so that we have more and more glory. And the glory comes from the Lord, who is the Holy Spirit.

A Treasure in Clay Jars

4 So because of God's mercy, we have work to do. He has given it to us. And we don't give up. 2Instead, we have given up doing secret and shameful things. We don't twist God's word. In fact, we do just the opposite. We present the truth plainly. In the sight of God, we make our appeal to everyone's sense of what is right and wrong.

3Suppose our good news is covered with a veil. Then it is veiled to those who are dying. 4The god of this world has blinded the minds of those who don't believe. They can't see the light of the good news of Christ's glory. He is the likeness of God. 5We do not preach about ourselves. We preach about Jesus Christ. We say that he is Lord. And we serve you because of him.

6God said, "Let light shine out of darkness." *(Genesis 1:3)* He made his light shine in our hearts. It shows us the light of God's glory in the face of Christ.

7Treasure is kept in clay jars. In the same way, we have the treasure of the good news in these earthly bodies of ours. That shows that the mighty power of the good news comes from God. It doesn't come from us.

8We are pushed hard from all sides. But we are not beaten down. We are bewildered. But that doesn't make us lose hope. 9Others make us suffer. But God does not desert us. We are knocked down. But we are not knocked out. 10We always carry around the death of Jesus in our bodies. In that way, the life of Jesus can be shown in our bodies.

11We who are alive are always in danger of death because we are serving Jesus. So his life can be shown in our earthly bodies. 12Death is at work in us. But life is at work in you.

13It is written, "I believed, and so I have spoken." *(Psalm 116:10)* With that same spirit of faith we also believe. And we also speak.

14We know that God raised the Lord Jesus from the dead. And he will also raise us up with Jesus.

He will bring us with you to God in heaven. 15All of that is for your benefit. God's grace is reaching more and more people. So they will become more and more thankful. They will give glory to God.

16We don't give up. Our bodies are becoming weaker and weaker. But our spirits are being renewed day by day. 17Our troubles are small. They last only for a short time. But they are earning for us a glory that will last forever. It is greater than all our troubles.

18So we don't spend all our time looking at what we can see. Instead, we look at what we can't see. What can be seen lasts only a short time. But what can't be seen will last forever.

Our Home in Heaven

5 We know that the earthly tent we live in will be destroyed. But we have a building made by God. It is a house in heaven that lasts forever. Human hands did not build it.

2During our time on earth we groan. We long to put on our house in heaven as if it were clothing. 3Then we will not be naked.

4While we live in this tent of ours, we groan under our heavy load. We don't want to be naked. We want to be dressed with our house in heaven. What must die will be swallowed up by life.

5God has made us for that very purpose. He has given us the Holy Spirit as a down payment. The Spirit makes us sure of what is still to come.

6So here is what we can always be certain about. As long as we are at home in our bodies, we are away from the Lord. 7We live by believing, not by seeing. 8We are certain about that. We would rather be away from our bodies and at home with the Lord. 9So we try our best to please him. We want to please him whether we are at home in our bodies or away from them.

10We must all stand in front of Christ to be judged. Each one of us will be judged for the good things and the bad things we do while we are in our bodies. Then each of us will receive what we are supposed to get.

Christ Brings Us Back to God

11We know what it means to have respect for the Lord. So we try to help other people to understand it.

What we are is plain to God. I hope it is also plain to your way of thinking. 12We are not trying to make an appeal to you again. But we are giving you a chance to take pride in us. Then you can answer those who take pride in how people look rather than in what is really in their hearts.

13Are we out of our minds? That is because we want to serve God. Does what we say make sense? That is because we want to serve you.

14Christ's love controls us. We are sure that one person died for everyone. And so everyone died.

15Christ died for everyone. He died so that those who live should not live for themselves anymore. They should live for Christ. He died for them and was raised again.

16So from now on we don't look at anyone the way the world does. At one time we looked at Christ in that way. But we don't anymore.

17Anyone who believes in Christ is a new creation. The old is gone! The new has come! 18It is all from God. He brought us back to himself through Christ's death on the cross. And he has given us the task of bringing others back to him through Christ.

19God was bringing the world back to himself through Christ. He did not hold people's sins against them. God has trusted us with the message that people may be brought back to him. 20So we are Christ's official messengers. It is as if God were making his appeal through us. Here is what Christ wants us to beg you to do. Come back to God!

21Christ didn't have any sin. But God made him become sin for us. So we can be made right with God because of what Christ has done for us.

6 We work together with God. So we are asking you not to receive God's grace and then do nothing with it. 2He says,

> "When I showed you my favor, I heard you.
> On the day I saved you, I helped you."
> *(Isaiah 49:8)*

I tell you, now is the time God shows his favor. Now is the day he saves.

Paul's Sufferings

3We don't put anything in anyone's way. So no one can find fault with our work for God. 4Instead, we make it clear that we serve God in every way. We serve him by holding steady. We stand firm in all kinds of trouble, hard times and suffering.

5We don't give up when we are beaten or put in prison. When people stir up trouble in the streets, we continue to serve God. We work hard for him. We go without sleep and food. 6We remain pure. We understand completely what it means to serve God. We are patient and kind. We serve him in the power of the Holy Spirit. We serve him with true love. 7We speak the truth. We serve in the power of God. We hold the weapons of godliness in the right hand and in the left. 8We serve God in times of glory and shame. We serve him whether the news about us is bad or good. We are true to our calling.

But people treat us as if we were pretenders. 9We are known, but people treat us as if we were unknown. We are dying, but we continue to live. We are beaten, but we are not killed. 10We are sad, but we are always full of joy. We are poor, but we make many people rich. We have nothing, but we own everything.

11Believers at Corinth, we have spoken freely to you. We have opened our hearts wide to you. 12We are not holding back our love from you. But you are holding back your love from us. 13I speak to

you as if you were my children. It is only fair that
you open your hearts wide to us also.

Do Not Be Joined to Unbelievers

14Do not be joined to unbelievers. What do right
and wrong have in common? Can light and darkness be friends? 15How can Christ and Satan
agree? What does a believer have in common with
an unbeliever? 16How can the temple of the true
God and the statues of other gods agree?

We are the temple of the living God. God has
said, "I will live with them. I will walk among
them. I will be their God. And they will be my people." *(Leviticus 26:12; Jeremiah 32:38; Ezekiel 37:27)*

17"So come out from among them
and be separate,
says the Lord.
Do not touch anything that is not pure
and clean.
Then I will receive you."
(Isaiah 52:11; Ezekiel 20:34,41)
18"I will be your Father.
You will be my sons and daughters,
says the Lord who rules over all."
(2 Samuel 7:14; 7:8)

7 Dear friends, we have these promises from
God. So let us make ourselves pure from
everything that pollutes our bodies and spirits. Let
us be completely holy. We want to honor God.

Paul's Joy

2Make room for us in your hearts. We haven't
done anything wrong to anyone. We haven't
caused anyone to sin. We haven't taken advantage
of anyone.

3I don't say this to judge you. I have told you
before that you have an important place in our
hearts. We would live or die with you. 4I have great
faith in you. I am very proud of you. I am very
happy. Even with all our troubles, my joy has no
limit.

5When I came to Macedonia, my body wasn't
able to rest. I was attacked no matter where I went.
I had battles on the outside and fears on the inside.

6But God comforts those who are sad. He comforted me when Titus came. 7I was comforted not
only when he came but also by the comfort you had
given him. He told me how much you longed for
me. He told me about your deep sadness and concern for me. That made my joy greater than ever.

8Even if my letter made you sad, I'm not sorry I
sent it. At first I was sorry. I see that my letter hurt
you, but only for a little while. 9Now I am happy.
I'm not happy because you were made sad. I'm
happy because your sadness led you to turn away
from your sins. You became sad just as God wanted
you to. So you were not hurt in any way by us.

10Godly sadness causes us to turn away from
our sins and be saved. And we are certainly not
sorry about that! But worldly sadness brings death.

11Look at what that godly sadness has produced
in you. You are working hard to clear yourselves.
You are angry and alarmed. You are longing to see
me. You are concerned. You are ready to make
sure that the right thing is done. In every way you
have proved that you are not guilty in that matter.

12So even though I wrote to you, it wasn't
because of the one who did the wrong. It wasn't
because of the one who was hurt. Instead, I wrote
you so that in the sight of God you could see for
yourselves how faithful you are to us. 13All of that
cheers us up.

We were also very glad to see how happy Titus
was. You have all renewed his spirit. 14I had
bragged about you to him. And you have not let
me down. Everything we said to you was true. In
the same way, our bragging about you to Titus has
also turned out to be true. 15His love for you is
even greater when he remembers that you all
obeyed his teaching. You received him with fear
and trembling. 16I am glad I can have complete
faith in you.

Giving Freely to Others

8 Brothers and sisters, we want you to know
about the grace that God has given to the
churches in Macedonia. 2They have suffered a
great deal. But their joy was more than full. Even
though they were very poor, they gave very freely.

3I give witness that they gave as much as they
could. In fact, they gave even more than they could.
Completely on their own, 4they begged us for the
chance to share in serving God's people in that
way. 5They did more than we expected. First they
gave themselves to the Lord. Then they gave themselves to us in keeping with what God wanted.

6Titus had already started collecting money
from you. So we asked him to get you to finish
making your kind gift.

7You do well in everything else. You do well in
faith and in speaking. You do well in knowledge
and in complete commitment. And you do well in
your love for us. So make sure that you also do
well in the grace of giving to others.

8I am not commanding you to do it. But I want
to put you to the test. I want to find out if you
really love God. I want to compare your love with
that of others.

9You know the grace shown by our Lord Jesus
Christ. Even though he was rich, he became poor
to help you. Because he became poor, you can
become rich.

10Here is my advice about what is best for you
in that matter. Last year you were the first to give.
You were also the first to want to give. 11So finish
the work. Then your longing to do it will be
matched by your finishing it. Give on the basis of
what you have.

12Do you really want to give? Then the gift is
received in keeping with what you have, not with
what you don't have.

13We don't want others to have it easy at your expense. We want things to be equal. 14Right now you have plenty in order to take care of what they need. Then they will have plenty to take care of what you need. That will make things equal. 15It is written, "Those who gathered a lot didn't have too much. And those who gathered a little had enough." *(Exodus 16:18)*

Paul Sends Titus to Corinth

16God put into the heart of Titus the same concern I have for you. I am thankful to God for this. 17Titus welcomed our appeal. He is also excited about coming to you. It was his own idea.

18Along with Titus, we are sending another brother. All the churches praise him for his service in telling the good news. 19He was also chosen by the churches to go with us as we bring the offering. We are in charge of it. We want to honor the Lord himself. We want to show how ready we are to help.

20We want to keep anyone from blaming us for how we take care of that large gift. 21We are trying hard to do what is right in the Lord's eyes and in the eyes of people.

22We are also sending another one of our brothers with them. He has often proved to us in many ways that he is very committed. He is now even more committed because he has great faith in you.

23Titus is my helper. He and I work together among you. Our brothers are messengers from the churches. They honor Christ. 24So show them that you really love them. Show them why we are proud of you. Then the churches can see it.

9 I don't need to write to you about giving to God's people. 2I know how much you want to help. I have been bragging about it to the people in Macedonia. I have been telling them that since last year you who live in Achaia were ready to give. You are so excited that it has stirred up most of them to take action.

3But I am sending the brothers. Then our bragging about you in this matter will have a good reason. You will be ready, just as I said you would be.

4Suppose people from Macedonia come with me and find out that you are not prepared. Then we, as well as you, would be ashamed of being so certain.

5So I thought I should try to get the brothers to visit you ahead of time. They will finish the plans for the large gift you had promised. Then it will be ready as a gift that is freely given. It will not be given by force.

Planting Many Seeds

6Here is something to remember. The one who plants only a little will gather only a little. And the one who plants a lot will gather a lot. 7You should each give what you have decided in your heart to give. You shouldn't give if you don't want to. You shouldn't give because you are forced to. God loves a cheerful giver.

8And God is able to shower all kinds of blessings on you. In all things and at all times you will have everything you need. You will do more and more good works. 9It is written,

"They have spread their gifts around to
poor people.
Their good works continue forever."
(Psalm 112:9)

10God supplies seed to the planter. He supplies bread for food. God will also supply and increase the amount of your seed. He will increase the results of your good works. 11You will be made rich in every way. Then you can always give freely. We will take your many gifts to the people who need them. And they will give thanks to God.

12Your gifts meet the needs of God's people. And that's not all. Your gifts also cause many people to thank God.

13You have shown yourselves to be worthy by what you have given. So people will praise God because you obey him. That proves that you really believe the good news about Christ. They will also praise God because you share freely with them and with everyone else. 14Their hearts will be filled with longing for you when they pray for you. God has given you grace that is better than anything.

15Let us give thanks to God for his gift. It is so great that no one can tell how wonderful it really is!

Paul Speaks Up for Himself

10 Christ is gentle and free of pride. So I make my appeal to you. I, Paul, am the one you call shy when I am face to face with you. But when I am away from you, you call me bold. 2I beg you that when I come I won't have to be as bold as I expect to be toward some people. They think that I live the way the people of this world live.

3I do live in the world. But I don't fight my battles the way the people of the world do. 4The weapons I fight with are not the weapons the world uses. In fact, it is just the opposite. My weapons have the power of God to destroy the camps of the enemy.

5I destroy every claim and every reason that keeps people from knowing God. I keep every thought under control in order to make it obey Christ. 6Until you have obeyed completely, I will be ready to punish you every time you don't obey.

7You are looking only at what appears on the surface of things. Suppose you are sure you belong to Christ. Then you should consider again that I belong to Christ just as much as you do.

8Do I brag too much about the authority the Lord gave me? If I do, it's because I want to build you up, not pull you down. And I'm not ashamed of that kind of bragging.

9Don't think that I'm trying to scare you with my letters. 10Some say, "His letters sound important. They are powerful. But in person he doesn't seem like much. And what he says doesn't amount to anything." 11People like that have a lot to learn. What I say in my letters when I'm away from you, I will do in my actions when I'm with you.

12I don't dare to compare myself with those who praise themselves. I'm not that kind of person. They measure themselves by themselves. They compare themselves with themselves. When they do that, they are not wise.

13But I won't brag more than I should. Instead, I will brag only about what I have done in the area God has given me. It is an area that reaches all the way to you. 14I am not going too far in my bragging. I would be going too far if I hadn't come to where you live. But I did get there with the good news about Christ.

15And I won't brag about work done by others. If I did, I would be bragging more than I should. As your faith continues to grow, I hope that my work among you will greatly increase. 16Then I will be able to preach the good news in the areas beyond you. I don't want to brag about work already done in someone else's territory.

17But, "The one who brags should brag about what the Lord has done." *(Jeremiah 9:24)* 18Those who praise themselves are not accepted. Those the Lord praises are accepted.

Paul and Those Who Pretend to Be Apostles

11 I hope you will put up with a little of my foolish bragging. But you are already doing that. 2My jealousy for you comes from God himself. I promised to give you to only one husband. That husband is Christ. I wanted to be able to give you to him as if you were a pure virgin. 3But Eve was tricked by the snake's clever lies. And I'm afraid that in the same way your minds will somehow be led down the wrong path. They will be led away from your true and pure love for Christ.

4Suppose someone comes to you and preaches about a Jesus different from the Jesus we preached about. Or suppose you receive a spirit different from the one you received before. Or suppose you receive a message of good news different from the one you accepted earlier. You put up with those kinds of things easily enough.

5But I don't think I'm in any way less important than those "super-apostles." 6I may not be a trained speaker. But I do have knowledge. I've made that very clear to you in every way.

7When I preached God's good news to you free of charge, I put myself down in order to lift you up. Was that a sin? 8Did I rob other churches when I received help from them so that I could serve you? 9When I was with you and needed something, I didn't cause you any expense. The believers who came from Macedonia gave me what I needed. I haven't caused you any expense at all. And I won't ever do it.

10I'm sure that the truth of Christ is in me. And I'm just as sure that nobody in Achaia will keep me from bragging. 11Why? Because I don't love you? No! God knows I do! 12And I will keep on doing what I'm doing. That will stop those who claim they have things to brag about. They think they have a chance to be considered equal with us. 13People like that are false apostles. They work hard to trick others. They only pretend to be apostles of Christ.

14That comes as no surprise. Even Satan himself pretends to be an angel of light. 15So it doesn't surprise us that those who serve Satan pretend to be serving God. They will finally get exactly what they should.

Paul Brags About His Sufferings

16I will say it again. Don't let anyone think I'm a fool. But if you do, receive me just as you would receive a fool. Then I can do a little bragging.

17When I brag about myself like this, I'm not talking the way the Lord would. I'm talking like a fool. 18Many are bragging the way the people of the world do. So I will brag like that too.

19You are so wise! You gladly put up with fools! 20In fact, you even put up with anyone who makes you a slave or uses you. You put up with those who take advantage of you. You put up with those who claim to be better than you. You put up with those who slap you in the face.

21I'm ashamed to have to say that I was too weak for that!

What anyone else dares to brag about, I also dare to brag about. I'm speaking like a fool! 22Are they Hebrews? So am I. Do they belong to the people of Israel? So do I. Are they Abraham's children? So am I. 23Are they serving Christ? I am serving him even more. I'm out of my mind to talk like this!

I have worked much harder. I have been in prison more often. I have suffered terrible beatings. Again and again I almost died. 24Five times the Jews gave me 39 strokes with a whip. 25Three times I was beaten with sticks. Once they tried to kill me by throwing stones at me. Three times I was shipwrecked. I spent a night and a day in the open sea.

26I have had to keep on the move. I have been in danger from rivers. I have been in danger from robbers. I have been in danger from people from my own country. I have been in danger from those who aren't Jews. I have been in danger in the city, in the country, and at sea. I have been in danger from people who pretended they were believers.

27I have worked very hard. Often I have gone without sleep. I have been hungry and thirsty. Often I have gone without food. I have been cold and naked.

28Besides everything else, every day I am concerned about all the churches. It is a very heavy load. 29If anyone is weak, I feel weak. If anyone is led into sin, I burn on the inside.

30If I have to brag, I will brag about the things that show how weak I am. 31I am not lying. The God and Father of the Lord Jesus knows this. May God be praised forever. 32In Damascus the governor who served under King Aretas had their city guarded. He wanted to arrest me. 33But I was lowered in a basket from a window in the wall. So I slipped through the governor's hands.

Paul's Vision and His Painful Problem

12 We can't gain anything by bragging. But I have to do it anyway. I am going to tell you what I've seen. I want to talk about what the Lord has shown me.

2I know a believer in Christ who was taken up to the third heaven 14 years ago. I don't know if his body was taken up or not. Only God knows. 3I don't know if that man was in his body or out of it. Only God knows. But I do know that 4he was taken up to paradise. He heard things that couldn't be put into words. They were things that people aren't allowed to talk about.

5I will brag about a man like that. But I won't brag about myself. I will brag only about how weak I am.

6Suppose I decide to brag. That would not make me a fool, because I would be telling the truth. But I don't do it. Then no one will think more of me than he should because of what I do or say.

7I could have become proud of myself because of the amazing and wonderful things God has shown me. So I was given a problem that caused pain in my body. It is a messenger from Satan to make me suffer. 8Three times I begged the Lord to take it away from me. 9But he said to me, "My grace is all you need. My power is strongest when you are weak."

So I am very happy to brag about how weak I am. Then Christ's power can rest on me. 10Because of how I suffered for Christ, I'm glad that I am weak. I am glad in hard times. I am glad when people say mean things about me. I am glad when things are difficult. And I am glad when people make me suffer. When I am weak, I am strong.

Paul's Concern for the People of Corinth

11I have made a fool of myself. But you made me do it. You should have praised me. Even though I am nothing, I am in no way less important than the "super-apostles." 12You can recognize apostles by the signs, wonders and miracles they do. Those things were faithfully done among you no matter what happened.

13How were you less important than the other churches? The only difference was that I didn't cause you any expense. Forgive me for that wrong!

14Now I am ready to visit you for the third time. I won't cause you any expense. I don't want what you have. What I really want is you. After all, children shouldn't have to save up for their parents. Parents should save up for their children. 15So I will be very happy to spend everything I have for you. I will even spend myself. If I love you more, will you love me less?

16In any case, I haven't caused you any expense. But I'm such a tricky fellow! I have caught you by tricking you!

17Did I take advantage of you through any of the men I sent to you? 18I asked Titus to go to you. And I sent our brother with him. Titus didn't take advantage of you, did he? Didn't I act in the same spirit? Didn't I follow the same path?

19All this time, have you been thinking that I've been speaking up for myself? No, I've been speaking with God as my witness. I've been speaking like a believer in Christ. Dear friends, everything I do is to help you become stronger.

20I'm afraid that when I come I won't find you as I want you to be. I'm afraid that you won't find me as you want me to be. I'm afraid there will be arguing, jealousy and fits of anger. I'm afraid you will separate into your own little groups. Then you will tell lies about each other. You will talk about each other. I'm afraid you will be proud and cause trouble.

21I'm afraid that when I come again my God will put me to shame in front of you. Then I will be sad about many who sinned earlier and have not turned away from it. They have not turned away from uncleanness, sexual sins and wild living. They have done all those things.

Final Warnings

13 This will be my third visit to you. Scripture says, "Every matter must be proved by the words of two or three witnesses." *(Deuteronomy 19:15)* 2I already warned you during my second visit. I now say it again while I'm away. When I return, I won't spare those who sinned earlier. I won't spare any of the others either.

3You are asking me to prove that Christ is speaking through me. He is not weak in dealing with you. He is powerful among you. 4It is true that Christ was nailed to the cross because he was weak. But he lives by God's power. In the same way, I share his weakness. But by God's power I will live with him to serve you.

5Take a good look at yourselves to see if you are really believers. Test yourselves. Don't you realize that Christ Jesus is in you? Unless, of course, you fail the test! 6I hope you will discover that I haven't failed the test.

7I pray to God that you won't do anything wrong. I don't pray so that people will see that I have passed the test. Instead, I pray so that you will do what is right, even if it seems I have failed. 8I can't do anything to stop the truth. I can only work for the truth.

9I'm glad when I am weak but you are strong. I pray that you will become perfect. 10That's why I write these things before I come to you. Then when I do come, I won't have to be hard on you when I use my authority.

The Lord gave me the authority to build you up. He didn't give it to me to tear you down.

Final Greetings

11Finally, brothers and sisters, good-by. Try to be perfect. Pay attention to what I'm saying. Agree with one another. Live in peace. And the God who gives love and peace will be with you.

12Greet one another with a holy kiss. 13All of God's people send their greetings.

14May the grace shown by the Lord Jesus Christ, and the love that God has given us, and the sharing of life brought about by the Holy Spirit be with you all.

Galatians

1 I, Paul, am writing this letter. I am an apostle.
People have not sent me. No human authority
has sent me. I have been sent by Jesus Christ and by
God the Father. God raised Jesus from the dead. [2]All
the brothers who are with me join me in writing.

We are sending this letter to you, the members
of the churches in Galatia.

[3]May God our Father and the Lord Jesus Christ
give you grace and peace. [4]Jesus gave his life for
our sins. He set us free from this evil world. That
was what our God and Father wanted. [5]Give glory
to God for ever and ever. Amen.

There Is No Other Good News

[6]I am amazed. You are so quickly deserting the
One who chose you because of the grace that
Christ has provided. You are turning to a different
"good news." [7]What you are accepting is really not
the good news at all.

It seems that some people have gotten you all
mixed up. They are trying to twist the good news
about Christ.

[8]But suppose even we should preach a different
"good news." Suppose even an angel from heaven
should preach it. I'm talking about a different one
than the good news we gave you. Let anyone who
does that be judged by God forever. [9]I have already
said it. Now I will say it again. Anyone who
preaches a "good news" that is different from the
one you accepted should be judged by God
forever.

[10]Am I now trying to get people to think well of
me? Or do I want God to think well of me? Am I
trying to please people? If I were, I would not be
serving Christ.

Paul Was Appointed by God

[11]Brothers and sisters, here is what I want you to
know. The good news I preached is not something
a human being made up. [12]No one gave it to me.
No one taught it to me. Instead, I received it from
Jesus Christ. He showed it to me.

[13]You have heard of my earlier way of life as a
Jew. With all my strength I attacked the church of
God. I tried to destroy it. [14]I was moving ahead in
my Jewish way of life. I went beyond many Jews
who were my own age. I held firmly to the teachings passed down by my people.

[15]But God set me apart from the time I was born.
He showed me his grace by appointing me. He was
pleased [16]to show his Son in my life. He wanted me
to preach about Jesus among those who aren't Jews.

When God appointed me, I didn't talk to anyone. [17]I didn't go up to Jerusalem to see those who
were apostles before I was. Instead, I went at once
into Arabia. Later I returned to Damascus.

[18]Then after three years I went up to Jerusalem.
I went there to get to know Peter. I stayed with him
for 15 days. [19]I didn't see any of the other apostles.
I only saw James, the Lord's brother. [20]Here is
what you can be sure of. And God gives witness
to it. What I am writing you is not a lie.

[21]Later I went to Syria and Cilicia. [22]The members of Christ's churches in Judea did not know me
in a personal way. [23]They only heard others say,
"The man who used to attack us has changed. He
is now preaching the faith he once tried to
destroy." [24]And they praised God because of me.

Paul Is Accepted by the Apostles

2 Fourteen years later I went up again to Jerusalem. This time I went with Barnabas. I took
Titus along also. [2]I went because God showed me
what he wanted me to do. I told the people there
the good news that I preach among those who
aren't Jews. But I spoke in private to those who
seemed to be leaders. I was afraid that I was running or had run my race for nothing.

[3]Titus was with me. He was a Greek. But even
he was not forced to be circumcised.

[4]That matter came up because some who pretended to be believers had slipped in among us.
They wanted to find out about the freedom we
have because we belong to Christ Jesus. They
wanted to make us slaves again.

[5]We didn't give in to them for a moment. We
wanted the truth of the good news to remain with
you.

[6]Some people in Jerusalem seemed to be impor-
tant. It makes no difference to me what they were.
God does not judge by what he sees on the outside.
Those people added nothing to my message.

[7]In fact, it was just the opposite. They saw that
I had been trusted with the task of preaching the
good news just as Peter had been. My task was to
preach to the non-Jews. Peter's task was to preach
to the Jews. [8]God was working through Peter as an
apostle to the Jews. He was also working through
me as an apostle to the non-Jews.

[9]James, Peter and John are considered to be pillars in the church. They recognized the special
grace that was given to me. So they shook my
hand and the hand of Barnabas. They wanted to
show they accepted us. They agreed that we
should go to the non-Jews. They would go to the
Jews. [10]They asked only one thing. They wanted
us to continue to remember poor people. That was
what I really wanted to do anyway.

Paul Opposes Peter

[11]When Peter came to Antioch, I told him to his
face that I was against what he was doing. He was
clearly wrong. [12]He used to eat with those who

weren't Jews. But certain men came from the group that was led by James. When they arrived, Peter began to draw back. He separated himself from the non-Jews. He was afraid of the circumcision group.

[13]Peter's actions were not honest. The other Jews joined him. Even Barnabas was led down the wrong path.

[14]I saw what they were doing. It was not in line with the truth of the good news. So I spoke to Peter in front of them all. "You are a Jew," I said. "But you live like one who is not. So why do you force non-Jews to follow Jewish ways?"

God's Grace and Our Faith

[15]We are Jews by birth. We are not "non-Jewish sinners." [16]We know that no one is made right with God by obeying the law. It is by believing in Jesus Christ. So we too have put our faith in Christ Jesus. That is so we can be made right with God by believing in Christ, not by obeying the law. No one can be made right with God by obeying the law.

[17]We are trying to be made right with God through Christ. But it is clear that we are sinners. So does that mean that Christ causes us to sin? Certainly not! [18]Suppose I build again what I had destroyed. Then I prove that I break the Law.

[19]Because of the law, I died as far as the law is concerned. I died so that I might live for God. [20]I have been crucified with Christ. I don't live any longer. Christ lives in me. My faith in the Son of God helps me to live my life in my body. He loved me. He gave himself for me.

[21]I do not get rid of the grace of God. What if a person could become right with God by obeying the law? Then Christ died for nothing!

Faith or Obeying the Law

3 You foolish people of Galatia! Who has put you under an evil spell? When I preached, I clearly showed you that Jesus Christ had been nailed to the cross.

[2]I would like to learn just one thing from you. Did you receive the Holy Spirit by obeying the law? Or did you receive the Spirit by believing what you heard? [3]Are you so foolish? You began with the Holy Spirit. Are you now trying to complete God's work in you by your own strength?

[4]Have you suffered so much for nothing? And was it really for nothing? [5]Why does God give you his Spirit? Why does he work miracles among you? Is it because you do what the law says? Or is it because you believe what you have heard?

[6]Think about Abraham. Scripture says, "Abraham believed God. God accepted Abraham because he believed. So his faith made him right with God." *(Genesis 15:6)* [7]So you see, those who have faith are children of Abraham.

[8]Long ago, Scripture knew that God would make non-Jews right with himself by believing in him. He announced the good news ahead of time to Abraham. He said, "All nations will be blessed because of you." *(Genesis 12:3; 18:18; 22:18)* [9]So those who have faith are blessed along with Abraham. He was the man of faith.

[10]All who depend on obeying the law are under a curse. It is written, "May everyone who doesn't continue to do everything that is written in the Book of the Law be under God's curse." *(Deuteronomy 27:26)* [11]We know that no one is made right with God by keeping the law. Scripture says, "Those who are right with God will live by faith." *(Habakkuk 2:4)*

[12]The law is not based on faith. In fact, it is just the opposite. It teaches that "the one who does those things will live by them." *(Leviticus 18:5)*

[13]Christ set us free from the curse of the law. He did it by becoming a curse for us. It is written, "Everyone who is hung on a pole is under God's curse." *(Deuteronomy 21:23)* [14]Christ Jesus set us free so that the blessing given to Abraham would come to non-Jews through Christ. He did it so that we might receive the promise of the Holy Spirit by believing in Christ.

The Law and the Promise

[15]Brothers and sisters, let me give you an example from everyday life. No one can get rid of an official agreement between people. No one can add to it. It can't be changed after it has been made. It is the same with God's covenant. [16]The promises were given to Abraham. They were also given to his seed. Scripture does not say, "and to seeds." That means many people. It says, "and to your seed." *(Genesis 12:7; 13:15; 24:7)* That means one person. And that one person is Christ.

[17]Here is what I mean. The law came 430 years after the promise. But the law does not get rid of God's covenant and promise. The covenant had already been made by God. So the law does not do away with the promise.

[18]The great gift that God has for us does not depend on the law. If it did, it would no longer depend on a promise. But God gave it to Abraham as a free gift through a promise.

[19]Then what was the purpose of the law? It was added because of human sin. And it was supposed to control us until the promised Seed had come. The law was put into effect through angels by a go-between. [20]A go-between does not take sides. God didn't use a go-between when he made his promise to Abraham. But the same God was at work in both the law and the promise.

[21]So is the law opposed to God's promises? Certainly not! What if a law had been given that could give life? Then people could become right with God by obeying the law. [22]But Scripture announces that the whole world is a prisoner because of sin. It does so in order that what was promised might be given to those who believe. The promise comes through faith in Jesus Christ.

[23]Before faith in Christ came, we were held prisoners by the law. We were locked up until faith

was made known. 24So the law was put in charge until Christ came. He came so that we might be made right with God by believing in Christ.

25But now faith in Christ has come. So we are no longer under the control of the law.

Children of God

26You are all children of God by believing in Christ Jesus. 27All of you who were baptized into Christ have put on Christ as if he were your clothes. 28There is no Jew or Greek. There is no slave or free person. There is no male or female. Because you belong to Christ Jesus, you are all one.

29You who belong to Christ are Abraham's seed. You will receive what God has promised.

4 Here is what I have been saying. As long as your own children are young, they are no different from slaves in your house. They are no different, even though they own all of the property. 2They are under the care of guardians and those who manage the property. They are under their care until the time when their fathers give them the property. 3It is the same with us. When we were children, we were slaves to the basic things the people of the world believe.

4But then the right time came. God sent his Son. A woman gave birth to him. He was born under the authority of the law. 5He came to set free those who were under the law. He wanted us to be adopted as children with all the rights children have.

6Because you are his children, God sent the Spirit of his Son into our hearts. He is the Holy Spirit. By his power we call God "*Abba.*" *Abba* means Father.

7So you aren't slaves any longer. You are God's children. Because you are his children, he gives you what he promised to give his people.

Paul's Concern for the Believers in Galatia

8At one time you didn't know God. You were slaves to gods that are really not gods at all. 9But now you know God. Even better, God knows you. So why are you turning back to those weak and worthless beliefs? Do you want to be slaves to them all over again?

10You are observing special days and months and seasons and years! 11I am afraid for you. I am afraid that somehow I have wasted my efforts on you.

Paul's Appeal to the Believers

12I make my appeal to you, brothers and sisters. I'm asking you to become like me. After all, I became like you. You didn't do anything wrong to me.

13As you know, it was because I was sick that I first preached the good news to you. 14My sickness was hard on you. But you didn't put me off. You didn't make fun of me. Instead, you welcomed me as if I were an angel of God. You welcomed me as if I were Christ Jesus himself.

15What has happened to all of your joy? If you could have torn out your own eyes and given them to me, you would have. I can give witness to that. 16Have I become your enemy now by telling you the truth?

17Those people are trying hard to win you over. But it is not for your good. They want to take you away from us. They want you to commit yourselves to them. 18It is fine to be committed to something, if the purpose is good. And you shouldn't be committed only when I am with you. You should always be committed.

19My dear children, I am in pain for you. Once again I have pain like a woman giving birth. And my pain will continue until Christ makes you like himself.

20I wish I could be with you now. I wish I could change my tone of voice. As it is, you bewilder me.

Hagar and Sarah

21You who want to be under the authority of the law, tell me something. Don't you know what the law says? 22It is written that Abraham had two sons. The slave woman gave birth to one of them. The free woman gave birth to the other one. 23Abraham's son by the slave woman was born in the usual way. But his son by the free woman was born because of God's promise.

24Those things can be taken as examples. The two women stand for two covenants. One covenant comes from Mount Sinai. It gives birth to children who are going to be slaves. It is Hagar. 25Hagar stands for Mount Sinai in Arabia. She stands for the present city of Jerusalem. That's because she and her children are slaves.

26But the Jerusalem that is above is free. She is our mother. 27It is written,

"Be glad, woman,
  you who have no children.
Start shouting,
  you who have no labor pains.
The woman who is all alone has more children
  than the woman who has a husband."

(Isaiah 54:1)

28Brothers and sisters, you are children because of God's promise just as Isaac was. 29At that time, the son born in the usual way tried to hurt the son born by the power of the Holy Spirit. It is the same now. 30But what does Scripture say? "Get rid of the slave woman. Get rid of her son. The slave woman's son will never have a share of the family's property with the free woman's son." *(Genesis 21:10)*

31Brothers and sisters, we are not the slave woman's children. We are the free woman's children.

Christ Sets Us Free

5 Christ has set us free. He wants us to enjoy freedom. So stand firm. Don't let the chains of slavery hold you again.

2Here is what I, Paul, say to you. Don't let yourselves be circumcised. If you do, Christ won't be of any value to you. 3I say it again. Every man who lets himself be circumcised must obey the whole law.

4Some of you are trying to be made right with God by obeying the law. You have been separated from Christ. You have fallen away from God's grace.

5But we expect to be made completely holy because of our faith in Christ. Through the Holy Spirit we wait in hope. 6Circumcision and uncircumcision aren't worth anything to those who believe in Christ Jesus. The only thing that really counts is faith that shows itself through love.

7You were running a good race. Who cut in on you and kept you from obeying the truth? 8The One who chooses you does not keep you from obeying the truth. 9You should know that "just a little yeast works its way through the whole batch of dough."

10The Lord makes me certain that you will not think in any other way. The one who has gotten you all mixed up will pay the price. It doesn't matter who that may be.

11Brothers and sisters, I am not still preaching that people must be circumcised. If I were, why am I still being opposed? If that were what I preach, then the cross wouldn't upset anyone.

12So then, what about troublemakers who try to get others to be circumcised? I wish they would go the whole way! I wish they would cut off everything that marks them as men!

Chosen to Be Free

13My brothers and sisters, you were chosen to be free. But don't use your freedom as an excuse to live in sin. Instead, serve one another in love. 14The whole law can be found in a single command. "Love your neighbor as you love yourself." *(Leviticus 19:18)*

15You must not keep on biting each other. You must not keep eating each other up. Watch out! You might destroy each other.

Living by the Holy Spirit's Power

16So I say, live by the Holy Spirit's power. Then you will not do what your sinful nature wants you to do.

17The sinful nature does not want what the Spirit delights in. And the Spirit does not want what the sinful nature delights in. The two are at war with each other. That's what makes you do what you don't want to do. 18But if you are led by the Spirit, you are not under the authority of the law.

19What the sinful nature does is clear. It enjoys sexual sins, impure acts and wild living. 20It worships statues of gods. It also worships evil powers. It is full of hatred and fighting. It is full of jealousy and fits of anger. It is interested only in getting ahead. It stirs up trouble. It separates people into their own little groups. 21It wants what others have. It gets drunk and takes part in wild parties. It does many things of that kind. I warn you now as I did before. People who live like that will not receive God's kingdom.

22But the fruit the Holy Spirit produces is love, joy and peace. It is being patient, kind and good. It is being faithful 23and gentle and having control of oneself. There is no law against things of that kind.

24Those who belong to Christ Jesus have nailed their sinful nature to his cross. They don't want what their sinful nature loves and longs for.

25Since we live by the Spirit, let us march in step with the Spirit. 26Let us not become proud. Let us not make each other angry. Let us not want what belongs to others.

Do Good to Everyone

6
Brothers and sisters, what if someone is caught in a sin? Then you who are guided by the Spirit should correct that person. Do it in a gentle way. But be careful. You could be tempted too. 2Carry each other's heavy loads. If you do, you will give the law of Christ its full meaning.

3If you think you are somebody when you are nobody, you are fooling yourselves. 4Each of you should put your own actions to the test. Then you can take pride in yourself. You won't be comparing yourself to somebody else. 5Each of you should carry your own load.

6Those who are taught the word must share all good things with their teacher.

7Don't be fooled. You can't outsmart God. A man gathers a crop from what he plants. 8Some people plant to please their sinful nature. From that nature they will harvest death. Others plant to please the Holy Spirit. From the Spirit they will harvest eternal life.

9Let us not become tired of doing good. At the right time we will gather a crop if we don't give up. 10So when we can do good to everyone, let us do it. Let us make a special point of doing good to those who belong to the family of believers.

The Creation of a New Nature

11Look at the big letters I'm using as I write to you with my own hand!

12Some people want others to think well of them. They are trying to force you to be circumcised. They do it for only one reason. They don't want to suffer by being connected with the cross of Christ. 13Even those who are circumcised don't obey the law. But they want you to be circumcised. Then they can brag about what has been done to your body.

14I never want to brag about anything except the cross of our Lord Jesus Christ. Through that cross the ways of the world have been crucified as far as I am concerned. And I have been crucified as far as the ways of the world are concerned.

15Circumcision and uncircumcision don't mean anything. What really counts is the creation of a new nature.

16May peace and mercy be given to all who follow this rule. May peace and mercy be given to the Israel that belongs to God.

17Finally, let no one cause trouble for me. My body has marks that show I belong to Jesus.

18Brothers and sisters, may the grace of our Lord Jesus Christ be with your spirit. Amen.

Ephesians

1 I, Paul, am writing this letter. I am an apostle of Christ Jesus just as God planned.

I am sending this letter to you, God's people in Ephesus. Because you belong to Christ Jesus, you are faithful.

[2]May God our Father and the Lord Jesus Christ give you grace and peace.

God Gives Spiritual Blessings

[3]Give praise to the God and Father of our Lord Jesus Christ. He has blessed us with every spiritual blessing. Those blessings come from the heavenly world. They belong to us because we belong to Christ.

[4]God chose us to belong to Christ before the world was created. He chose us to be holy and without blame in his eyes. He loved us. [5]So he decided long ago to adopt us as his children. He did it because of what Jesus Christ has done. It pleased God to do it. [6]All those things bring praise to his glorious grace. God freely gave us his grace because of the One he loves.

[7]We have been set free because of what Christ has done. Through his blood our sins have been forgiven. We have been set free because God's grace is so rich. [8]He poured his grace on us by giving us great wisdom and understanding.

[9]He showed us the mystery of his plan. It was in keeping with what he wanted to do. It was what he had planned through Christ. [10]It will all come about when history has been completed. God will then bring together all things in heaven and on earth under one ruler. The ruler is Christ.

[11]We were also chosen to belong to him. God decided to choose us long ago in keeping with his plan. He works out everything to fit his plan and purpose. [12]We were the first to put our hope in Christ. We were chosen to bring praise to his glory.

[13]You also became believers in Christ. That happened when you heard the message of truth. It was the good news about how you could be saved. When you believed, he marked you with a seal. The seal is the Holy Spirit that he promised.

[14]The Spirit marks us as God's own. We can now be sure that someday we will receive all that God has promised. That will happen after God sets all of his people completely free. All of those things will bring praise to his glory.

Paul Prays and Gives Thanks

[15]I have heard about your faith in the Lord Jesus. I have also heard about your love for all of God's people. That is why [16]I have not stopped thanking God for you. I always remember you in my prayers.

[17]I pray to the God of our Lord Jesus Christ. God is the glorious Father. I keep asking him to give you the wisdom and understanding that come from the Holy Spirit. I want you to know God better.

[18]I also pray that your mind might see more clearly. Then you will know the hope God has chosen you to receive. You will know that the things God's people will receive are rich and glorious. [19]And you will know his great power. It can't be compared with anything else. It is at work for us who believe. It is like the mighty strength [20]God showed when he raised Christ from the dead.

He seated him at his right hand in his heavenly kingdom. [21]There Christ sits far above all who rule and have authority. He also sits far above all powers and kings. He is above every title that can be given in this world and in the world to come.

[22]God placed all things under Christ's rule. He appointed him to be ruler over everything for the church. [23]The church is Christ's body. It is filled by Christ. He fills everything in every way.

God Has Given Us New Life Through Christ

2 You were living in your sins and lawless ways. But in fact you were dead. [2]You used to live as sinners when you followed the ways of this world. You served the one who rules over the spiritual forces of evil. He is the spirit who is now at work in those who don't obey God.

[3]At one time we all lived among them. We tried to satisfy what our sinful nature wanted to do. We followed its longings and thoughts. God was angry with us and everyone else because of the kind of people we were.

[4]But God loves us deeply. He is full of mercy. [5]So he gave us new life because of what Christ has done. He gave us life even when we were dead in sin. God's grace has saved you.

[6]God raised us up with Christ. He has seated us with him in his heavenly kingdom because we belong to Christ Jesus. [7]He has done it to show the riches of his grace for all time to come. His grace can't be compared with anything else. He has shown it by being kind to us because of what Christ Jesus has done.

[8]God's grace has saved you because of your faith in Christ. Your salvation doesn't come from anything you do. It is God's gift. [9]It is not based on anything you have done. No one can brag about earning it.

[10]God made us. He created us to belong to Christ Jesus. Now we can do good things. Long ago God prepared them for us to do.

God's New Family

11You who are not Jews by birth, here is what I want you to remember. You are called "uncircumcised" by those who call themselves "circumcised." But they have only been circumcised in their bodies by human hands.

12Before you believed in Christ, you were separated from him. You were not considered to be citizens of Israel. You were not included in what the covenants promised. You were without hope and without God in the world. 13At one time you were far away from God. But now you belong to Christ Jesus. He spilled his blood for you. That has brought you near to God.

14Christ himself is our peace. He has made Jews and non-Jews into one group of people. He has destroyed the hatred that was like a wall between us. 15Through his body on the cross, Christ put an end to the law with all its commands and rules. He wanted to create one new group of people out of the two. He wanted to make peace between them. 16He planned to bring both of them as one body back to God because of the cross. Christ put their hatred to death on that cross.

17He came and preached peace to you who were far away. He also preached peace to those who were near. 18Through Christ we both come to the Father by the power of one Holy Spirit.

19So you are no longer strangers and outsiders. You are citizens together with God's people. You are members of God's family.

20You are a building that is built on the apostles and prophets. They are the foundation. Christ Jesus himself is the most important stone in the building. 21The whole building is held together by him. It rises to become a holy temple because it belongs to the Lord.

22And because you belong to him, you too are being built together. You are being made into a house where God lives through his Spirit.

Paul Is the Messenger to Non-Jews

3 I, Paul, am a prisoner because of Christ Jesus. I am in prison because of my work among you who are not Jews.

2I am sure you have heard that God appointed me to share his grace with you. 3I'm talking about the mystery God showed me. I have already written a little about it. 4By reading it you will be able to understand what I know about the mystery of Christ.

5The mystery was not made known to people of other times. But now the Holy Spirit has made it known to God's holy apostles and prophets.

6Here is the mystery. Because of the good news, God's promises are for non-Jews as well as for Jews. Both groups are parts of one body. They share in the promise. It belongs to them because they belong to Christ Jesus.

7I now serve the good news because God gave me his grace. His power is at work in me. 8I am by far the least important of all of God's people. But he gave me the grace to preach to the non-Jews about the wonderful riches that Christ gives.

9God told me to make clear to everyone how the mystery came about. In times past it was kept hidden in the mind of God, who created all things. 10He wanted the rulers and authorities in the heavenly world to come to know his great wisdom. The church would make it known to them.

11That was God's plan from the beginning. He has worked it out through Christ Jesus our Lord. 12Through him and through faith in him we can approach God. We can come to him freely. We can come without fear.

13So here is what I'm asking you to do. Don't lose hope because I am suffering for you. It will lead to the time when God will give you his glory.

Paul Prays for God's People

14I bow in prayer to the Father because of my work among you. 15From the Father his whole family in heaven and on earth gets its name.

16I pray that he will use his glorious riches to make you strong. May his Holy Spirit give you his power deep down inside you. 17Then Christ will live in your hearts because you believe in him.

And I pray that your love will have deep roots. I pray that it will have a strong foundation. 18May you have power with all God's people to understand Christ's love. May you know how wide and long and high and deep it is. 19And may you know his love, even though it can't be known completely. Then you will be filled with everything God has for you.

20God is able to do far more than we could ever ask for or imagine. He does everything by his power that is working in us. 21Give him glory in the church and in Christ Jesus. Give him glory through all time and for ever and ever. Amen.

The Body of Christ Is One

4 I am a prisoner because of the Lord. So I am asking you to live a life worthy of what God chose you for.

2Don't be proud at all. Be completely gentle. Be patient. Put up with one another in love. 3The Holy Spirit makes you one in every way. So try your best to remain as one. Let peace keep you together.

4There is one body. There is one Spirit. You were appointed to one hope when you were chosen. 5There is one Lord. There is one faith and one baptism. 6There is one God and Father of all. He is over everything. He is through everything. He is in everything.

7But each one of us has received a gift of grace, just as Christ wanted us to have it. 8That is why Scripture says,

"When he went up to his place on high,
he led a line of prisoners.
He gave gifts to people." *(Psalm 68:18)*

9What does "he went up" mean? It can only mean that he also came down to the lower, earthly places. 10The One who came down is the same as the One who went up higher than all the heavens. He did it in order to fill all of creation. 11He is the One who gave some the gift to be apostles. He gave some the gift to be prophets. He gave some the gift of preaching the good news. And he gave some the gift to be pastors and teachers. 12He did it so that they might prepare God's people to serve. If they do, the body of Christ will be built up.

13That will continue until we all become one in the faith and in the knowledge of God's Son. Then we will be grown up in the faith. We will receive everything that Christ has for us.

14We will no longer be babies in the faith. We won't be like ships tossed around by the waves. We won't be blown here and there by every new teaching. We won't be blown around by the cleverness and tricks of people who try to hide their evil plans. 15Instead, we will speak the truth in love. We will grow up into Christ in every way.

He is the Head. 16He makes the whole body grow and build itself up in love. Under the control of Christ, each part of the body does its work. It supports the other parts. In that way, the body is joined and held together.

Living as Children of Light

17Here is what I'm telling you. I am speaking for the Lord as I warn you. You must no longer live like those who aren't Jews. Their thoughts don't have any purpose. 18They can't understand the truth. They are separated from the life of God. That is because they don't know him. And they don't know him because their hearts are stubborn.

19They have lost all feeling for what is right. They have given themselves over to the evil pleasures of their bodies. They take part in every kind of unclean act. And they always long for more.

20But that is not what you have learned about Christ. 21I'm sure you heard of him. I'm sure you were taught by him. What you learned was the truth about Jesus.

22You were taught not to live the way you used to. You must get rid of your old way of life. That's because it is polluted by longing for things that lead you down the wrong path.

23You were taught to be made new in your thinking. 24You were taught to start living a new life. It is created to be truly good and holy, just as God is.

25So each of you must get rid of your lying. Speak the truth to your neighbor. We are all parts of one body.

26Scripture says, "When you are angry, do not sin." *(Psalm 4:4)* Do not let the sun go down while you are still angry. 27Don't give the devil a chance.

28Those who have been stealing must never steal again. Instead, they must work. They must do something useful with their own hands. Then they will have something to give to people in need.

29Don't let any evil talk come out of your mouths. Say only what will help to build others up and meet their needs. Then what you say will help those who listen.

30Do not make God's Holy Spirit sad. He marked you with a seal for the day when God will set you completely free.

31Get rid of all hard feelings, anger and rage. Stop all fighting and lying. Put away every form of hatred. 32Be kind and tender to one another. Forgive each other, just as God forgave you because of what Christ has done.

5 You are the children that God dearly loves. So be just like him. 2Lead a life of love, just as Christ did. He loved us. He gave himself up for us. He was a sweet-smelling offering and sacrifice to God.

3There should not be even a hint of sexual sin among you. Don't do anything unclean. And do not always want more and more. Things like that are not what God's holy people should do.

4There must not be any unclean speech or foolish talk or dirty jokes. All of them are out of place. Instead, you should give thanks.

5Here is what you can be sure of. Those who give themselves over to sexual sins are lost. So are people whose lives are not pure. The same is true of those who always want more and more. People who do those things might as well worship statues of gods. No one who does them will receive a share in the kingdom of Christ and of God.

6Don't let anyone fool you with words that don't mean anything. Because of things like that, God is angry with those who don't obey. 7So don't go along with people like that.

8At one time you were in the dark. But now you are in the light because of what the Lord has done. Live like children of the light. 9The light produces what is completely good, right and true. 10Find out what pleases the Lord.

11Have nothing to do with the acts of darkness. They don't produce anything good. Show what they are really like. 12It is shameful even to talk about what people who don't obey do in secret.

13But everything the light shines on can be seen. 14Light makes everything clear. That is why it is said,

"Wake up, sleeper.
  Rise from the dead.
Then Christ will shine on you."

15So be very careful how you live. Do not live like people who aren't wise. Live like people who are wise. 16Make the most of every opportunity. The days are evil. 17So don't be foolish. Instead, understand what the Lord wants.

18Don't fill yourself up with wine. Getting drunk will lead to wild living. Instead, be filled with the Holy Spirit.

19Speak to each other with psalms, hymns and spiritual songs. Sing and make music in your heart to the Lord. [20]Always give thanks to God the Father for everything. Give thanks to him in the name of our Lord Jesus Christ.

[21]Follow the lead of one another because of your respect for Christ.

Wives and Husbands

[22]Wives, follow the lead of your husbands as you follow the Lord. [23]The husband is the head of the wife, just as Christ is the head of the church. The church is Christ's body. He is its Savior. [24]The church follows the lead of Christ. In the same way, wives should follow the lead of their husbands in everything.

[25]Husbands, love your wives. Love them just as Christ loved the church. He gave himself up for her. [26]He did it to make her holy. He made her clean by washing her with water and the word. [27]He did it to bring her to himself as a brightly shining church. He wants a church that has no stain or wrinkle or any other flaw. He wants a church that is holy and without blame.

[28]In the same way, husbands should love their wives. They should love them as they love their own bodies. Any man who loves his wife loves himself. [29]After all, people have never hated their own bodies. Instead, they feed and care for their bodies. And that is what Christ does for the church. [30]We are parts of his body.

[31]Scripture says, "That's why a man will leave his father and mother and be joined to his wife. The two will become one." *(Genesis 2:24)* [32]That is a deep mystery. But I'm talking about Christ and the church.

[33]A husband also must love his wife. He must love her just as he loves himself. And a wife must respect her husband.

Children and Parents

6 Children, obey your parents as believers in the Lord. Obey them because it's the right thing to do. [2]Scripture says, "Honor your father and mother." That is the first commandment that has a promise. [3]"Then things will go well with you. You will live a long time on the earth." *(Deuteronomy 5:16)*

[4]Fathers, don't make your children angry. Instead, train them and teach them the ways of the Lord as you raise them.

Slaves and Masters

[5]Slaves, obey your masters here on earth. Respect them and honor them with a heart that is true. Obey them just as you would obey Christ. [6]Don't obey them only to please them when they are watching. Do it because you are slaves of Christ. Be sure your heart does what God wants.

[7]Serve your masters with all your heart. Work as if you were not serving people but the Lord. [8]You know that the Lord will give you a reward. He will give to each of you in keeping with the good you do. It doesn't matter whether you are slaves or free.

[9]Masters, treat your slaves in the same way. When you warn them, don't be too hard on them. You know that the One who is their Master and yours is in heaven. And he treats everyone the same.

God's Armor

[10]Finally, let the Lord make you strong. Depend on his mighty power. [11]Put on all of God's armor. Then you can stand firm against the devil's evil plans. [12]Our fight is not against human beings. It is against the rulers, the authorities and the powers of this dark world. It is against the spiritual forces of evil in the heavenly world.

[13]So put on all of God's armor. Evil days will come. But you will be able to stand up to anything. And after you have done everything you can, you will still be standing.

[14]So stand firm. Put the belt of truth around your waist. Put the armor of godliness on your chest. [15]Wear on your feet what will prepare you to tell the good news of peace. [16]Also, pick up the shield of faith. With it you can put out all of the flaming arrows of the evil one. [17]Put on the helmet of salvation. And take the sword of the Holy Spirit. The sword is God's word.

[18]At all times, pray by the power of the Spirit. Pray all kinds of prayers. Be watchful, so that you can pray. Always keep on praying for all of God's people.

[19]Pray also for me. Pray that when I open my mouth, the right words will be given to me. Then I can be bold as I tell the mystery of the good news. [20]Because of the good news, I am being held by chains as the Lord's messenger. So pray that I will be bold as I preach the good news. That's what I should do.

Final Greetings

[21]Tychicus is a dear brother. He is faithful in serving the Lord. He will tell you everything about me. Then you will know how I am and what I am doing. [22]That's why I am sending him to you. I want you to know how we are. And I want him to cheer you up.

[23]May God the Father and the Lord Jesus Christ give peace to the brothers and sisters. May they also give them love and faith.

[24]May grace be given to everyone who loves our Lord Jesus Christ with a love that will never die.

Philippians

1 We, Paul and Timothy, are writing this letter. We serve Christ Jesus.

We are sending this letter to you, all of God's people in Philippi. You belong to Christ Jesus. We are also sending this letter to your leaders and deacons.

2May God our Father and the Lord Jesus Christ give you grace and peace.

Paul Prays and Gives Thanks

3I thank my God every time I remember you. 4In all my prayers for all of you, I always pray with joy. 5I am happy because you have joined me in spreading the good news. You have done so from the first day until now.

6I am sure that the One who began a good work in you will carry it on until it is completed. That will be on the day Christ Jesus returns.

7It is right for me to feel this way about all of you. I love you with all my heart. I may be held by chains, or I may be standing up for the truth of the good news. Either way, all of you share in God's grace together with me. 8God can give witness that I long for all of you. I love you with the love that Christ Jesus gives.

9I pray that your love will grow more and more. And let it be based on knowledge and understanding. 10Then you will be able to know what is best. You will be pure and without blame until the day Christ returns. 11You will be filled with the fruit of right living produced by Jesus Christ. All of those things bring glory and praise to God.

Paul Honors Christ in Prison

12Brothers and sisters, here is what I want you to know. What has happened to me has really helped to spread the good news. 13One thing has become clear. I am being held by chains because of my stand for Christ. All of the palace guards and everyone else know it.

14Because I am being held by chains, most of the believers in the Lord have become bolder. They now speak God's word more boldly and without fear.

15It's true that some preach about Christ because they are jealous. But others preach about Christ to help me in my work. 16The last group acts out of love. They know I have been put here to stand up for the good news. 17But the others preach about Christ only to get ahead. They are not honest and true. They think they can stir up trouble for me while I am being held by chains.

18But what does it matter? Here is the important thing. Whether for reasons that are right or wrong, Christ is being preached about. That makes me very glad.

And I will continue to be glad. 19I know that you are praying for me. I also know that the Spirit of Jesus Christ will help me. So no matter what happens, I'm sure I will still be saved.

20I completely expect and hope that I won't be ashamed in any way. I'm sure I will be brave enough. Now as always Christ will be lifted high through my body. He will be lifted up whether I live or die.

21For me, life finds all of its meaning in Christ. Death also has its benefits.

22Suppose I go on living in my body. Then I will be able to carry on my work. It will bear a lot of fruit. But what should I choose? I don't know. 23I can't decide between the two. I long to leave this world and be with Christ. That is better by far.

24But it is more important for you that I stay alive. 25I'm sure of that. So I know I will remain with you. And I will continue with all of you to help you grow and be joyful in what you have been taught. 26I'm sure I will be with you again. Then your joy in Christ Jesus will be greater than ever because of me.

27No matter what happens, live in a way that brings honor to the good news about Christ. Then I will know that you stand firm with one purpose. I may come and see you or only hear about you. But I will know that you work together as one person. And I will know that you work to spread the teachings of the good news.

28So don't be afraid in any way of those who oppose you. That will show them that they will be destroyed and that you will be saved. That's what God will do.

29Here is what he has given you to do for Christ. You must not only believe in him. You must also suffer for him.

30You are going through the same struggle you saw me go through. As you have heard, I am still struggling.

Thinking Like Christ

2 Are you cheerful because you belong to Christ? Does his love comfort you? Is the Holy Spirit your companion? Has Christ been gentle and loving toward you? 2Then make my joy complete by agreeing with each other. Have the same love. Be one in spirit and purpose.

3Don't do anything only to get ahead. Don't do it because you are proud. Instead, be free of pride. Think of others as better than yourselves.

4None of you should look out just for your own good. You should also look out for the good of others.

5You should think in the same way Christ Jesus does.

6 In his very nature he was God.
But he did not think that being equal with God was something he should hold on to.
7 Instead, he made himself nothing.
He took on the very nature of a servant.
He was made in human form.
8 He appeared as a man.
He came down to the lowest level.
He obeyed God completely, even though it led to his death.
In fact, he died on a cross.
9 So God lifted him up to the highest place.
He gave him the name that is above every name.
10 When the name of Jesus is spoken, everyone's knee will bow to worship him.
Every knee in heaven and on earth and under the earth will bow to worship him.
11 Everyone's mouth will say that Jesus Christ is Lord.
And God the Father will receive the glory.

Living Like Christ

12 My dear friends, you have always obeyed God. You obeyed while I was with you. And you have obeyed even more while I am not with you. So continue to work out your own salvation. Do it with fear and trembling. 13 God is working in you. He wants your plans and your acts to be in keeping with his good purpose.

14 Do everything without finding fault or arguing. 15 Then you will be pure and without blame. You will be children of God without fault in a sinful and evil world. Among the people of the world you shine like stars in the heavens. 16 You shine as you hold out to them the word of life. So I can brag about you on the day Christ returns. I can be happy that I didn't run or work for nothing.

17 But my life might even be poured out like a drink offering on your sacrifices. I'm talking about the way you serve because you believe. Even so, I am glad. I am joyful with all of you. 18 So you too should be glad and joyful with me.

Timothy and Epaphroditus

19 I hope to send Timothy to you soon if the Lord Jesus allows it. Then I will be cheered up when I receive news about you. 20 I have no one else like Timothy. He truly cares about how you are doing. 21 All the others are looking out for their own interests. They are not looking out for the interests of Jesus Christ. 22 But you know that Timothy has proved himself. He has served with me like a son with his father in spreading the good news. 23 So I hope to send him as soon as I see how things go with me. 24 And I'm sure I myself will come soon if the Lord allows it.

25 But I think it's necessary to send Epaphroditus back to you. He is my brother in the Lord. He is a worker and a soldier of Christ together with me. He is also your messenger. You sent him to take care of my needs. 26 He longs for all of you. He is troubled because you heard he was sick. 27 He was very sick. In fact, he almost died. But God had mercy on him. He also had mercy on me. God spared me sadness after sadness. 28 So I want even more to send him to you. Then when you see him again, you will be glad. And I won't worry so much. 29 Welcome him as a brother in the Lord with great joy. Honor people like him. 30 He almost died for the work of Christ. He put his life in danger to make up for the help you couldn't give me.

Do Not Trust Human Nature

3 Finally, my brothers and sisters, be joyful because you belong to the Lord. It is no trouble for me to write about some important matters to you again. If you know about them, you will have a safe path to follow.

2 Watch out for those dogs. They do evil things. When they circumcise, it is nothing more than a useless cutting of the body. 3 But we have been truly circumcised. We worship God by the power of his Spirit. We brag about what Christ Jesus has done. We don't put our trust in our weak human nature.

4 I have many reasons to trust in my human nature. Others may think they have reasons to trust in theirs. But I have even more. 5 I was circumcised on the eighth day. I am part of the people of Israel. I am from the tribe of Benjamin. I am a pure Hebrew. As far as the law is concerned, I am a Pharisee. 6 As far as being committed is concerned, I opposed and attacked the church. As far as keeping the Law is concerned, I kept it perfectly.

7 I thought things like that were for my benefit. But now I consider them to be nothing because of Christ. 8 Even more, I consider everything to be nothing compared to knowing Christ Jesus my Lord. To know him is the best thing of all. Because of him I have lost everything. But I consider all of it to be garbage so I can get to know Christ. 9 I want to be joined to him.

For me, being right with God does not come from the law. It comes because I believe in Christ. It comes from God. It is received by faith.

10 I want to know Christ better. I want to know the power that raised him from the dead. I want to share in his sufferings. I want to become like him by sharing in his death. 11 Then by God's grace I will rise from the dead.

Moving on Toward the Goal

12 I have not yet received all of those things. I have not yet been made perfect. But I move on to take hold of what Christ Jesus took hold of me for. 13 Brothers and sisters, I don't consider that I have taken hold of it yet. But here is the one thing I do. I forget what is behind me. I push hard

toward what is ahead of me. 14I move on toward the goal to win the prize. God has appointed me to win it. The heavenly prize is Christ Jesus himself.

15All of us who are grown up in the faith should see things that way. Maybe you think differently about something. But God will make it clear to you. 16Only let us live up to what we have already reached.

17Brothers and sisters, join with others in following my example. Pay close attention to those who live in keeping with the pattern we gave you.

18I have told you those things many times before. Now I say it again with tears in my eyes. Many people live like enemies of the cross of Christ. 19The only thing they have coming to them is death. Their stomach is their god. They brag about what they should be ashamed of. They think only about earthly things.

20But we are citizens of heaven. And we can hardly wait for a Savior from there. He is the Lord Jesus Christ. 21He has the power to bring every thing under his control. By his power he will change our earthly bodies. They will become like his glorious body.

4 My brothers and sisters, that is how you should stand firm in the Lord's strength. I love you and long for you. Dear friends, you are my joy and my crown.

Do What Is Best

2Here is what I'm asking Euodia and Syntyche to do. I want them to agree with each other because they belong to the Lord.

3My true companion, here is what I ask you to do. Help those women. They have served at my side. They have helped me spread the good news. So have Clement and the rest of those who have worked together with me. Their names are all written in the Book of Life.

4Always be joyful because you belong to the Lord. I will say it again. Be joyful. 5Let everyone know how gentle you are. The Lord is coming soon.

6Don't worry about anything. Instead, tell God about everything. Ask and pray. Give thanks to him. 7Then God's peace will watch over your hearts and your minds because you belong to Christ Jesus. God's peace can never be completely understood.

8Finally, my brothers and sisters, always think about what is true. Think about what is noble, right and pure. Think about what is lovely and worthy of respect. If anything is excellent or worthy of praise, think about those kinds of things. 9Do what you have learned or received or heard from me. Follow my example.

The God who gives peace will be with you.

Paul Gives Thanks for Help Received

10At last you are concerned about me again. That makes me very happy. We belong to the Lord. I know that you have been concerned. But you had no chance to show it.

11I'm not saying that because I need anything. I have learned to be content no matter what happens to me. 12I know what it's like not to have what I need. I also know what it's like to have more than I need. I have learned the secret of being content no matter what happens. I am content whether I am well fed or hungry. I am content whether I have more than enough or not enough. 13I can do everything by the power of Christ. He gives me strength.

14But it was good of you to share in my troubles. 15And you believers at Philippi know what happened when I left Macedonia. Not one church helped me in the matter of giving and receiving. You were the only one that did. That was in the early days when you first heard the good news. 16Even when I was in Thessalonica, you sent me help when I needed it. You did it again and again.

17I'm not looking for a gift. I'm looking for what is best for you. 18I have received my full pay, and even more than that. I have everything I need. That's because Epaphroditus brought me the gifts you sent. They are a sweet-smelling offering. They are a gift that God accepts. He is pleased with it.

19My God will meet all your needs. He will meet them in keeping with his wonderful riches that come to you because you belong to Christ Jesus.

20Give glory to our God and Father for ever and ever. Amen.

Final Greetings

21Greet all of God's people. They belong to Christ Jesus. The brothers who are with me send greetings. 22All of God's people here send you greetings. Most of all, those who live in the palace of Caesar send you greetings.

23May the grace of the Lord Jesus Christ be with your spirit. Amen.

Colossians

1 I, Paul, am writing this letter. I am an apostle
of Christ Jesus just as God planned. Our
brother Timothy joins me in writing.

2We are sending this letter to you, our brothers
and sisters in Colosse. You belong to Christ. You
are holy and faithful.

May God our Father give you grace and peace.

Paul Prays and Gives Thanks

3We always thank God, the Father of our Lord
Jesus Christ, when we pray for you. 4We thank him
because we have heard about your faith in Christ
Jesus. We have also heard that you love all of
God's people.

5Your faith and love are based on the hope you
have. What you hope for is stored up for you in
heaven. You have already heard about it. You were
told about it when the message of truth was given
to you. I'm talking about the good news 6that has
come to you.

All over the world the good news is bearing
fruit and growing. It has been doing that among
you since the day you heard it. That is when you
understood God's grace in all its truth.

7You learned the good news from Epaphras. He
is dear to us. He serves Christ together with us. He
faithfully works for Christ and for us among you.
8He also told us about your love that comes from
the Holy Spirit.

9That's why we have not stopped praying for
you. We have been praying for you since the day
we heard about you. We have been asking God to
fill you with the knowledge of what he wants. We
pray that he will give you spiritual wisdom and
understanding.

10We pray that you will lead a life that is worthy
of the Lord. We pray that you will please him in
every way. So we want you to bear fruit in every
good thing you do. We want you to grow to know
God better. 11We want you to be very strong, in
keeping with his glorious power. We want you to
be patient. Never give up. Be joyful 12as you give
thanks to the Father.

He has made you fit to share with all his people.
You will all receive a share in the kingdom of
light.

13He has saved us from the kingdom of darkness. He has brought us into the kingdom of the
Son he loves. 14Because of what the Son has done,
we have been set free. Because of him, all of our
sins have been forgiven.

Christ Is Far Above Everything

15Christ is the exact likeness of God, who can't
be seen. He is first, and he is over all of creation.
16All things were created by him. He created
everything in heaven and on earth. He created
everything that can be seen and everything that
can't be seen. He created kings, powers, rulers and
authorities. Everything was created by him and
for him. 17Before anything was created, he was
already there. He holds everything together.

18And he is the head of the body, which is the
church. He is the beginning. He is the first to be
raised from the dead. That happened so that he
would be far above everything. 19God was pleased
to have his whole nature living in Christ. 20God was
pleased to bring all things back to himself because
of what Christ has done. That includes all things on
earth and in heaven. God made peace through
Christ's blood, through his death on the cross.

21At one time you were separated from God.
You were enemies in your minds because of your
evil ways. 22But because Christ died, God has
brought you back to himself. Christ's death has
made you holy in God's sight. So now you don't
have any flaw. You are free from blame.

23But you must keep your faith steady and firm.
Don't move away from the hope that the good
news holds out to you. It is the good news that you
heard. It has been preached to every creature under
heaven. I, Paul, now serve the good news.

Paul's Work for the Church

24I am happy because of what was suffered for
you. And in my body I fill up my share in Christ's
sufferings. I do it for his body, which is the church.
25I serve the church. God appointed me to bring all
of his word to you.

26That word contains the mystery that has been
hidden for many ages. But now it has been made
known to God's people. 27God has chosen to make
known to them the glorious riches of that mystery.
He has made it known among those who aren't
Jews. And here is what it is. Christ is in you. He is
your hope of glory.

28We preach about him. With all the wisdom we
have, we warn and teach everyone. When we bring
them to God, we want them to be perfect as people who belong to Christ.

29That's what I'm working for. I work hard with
all of Christ's strength. His strength works power-
fully in me.

2 I want you to know how hard I am working
for you. I'm concerned for those who are in
Laodicea. I'm also concerned for everyone who
has not met me in person. 2I want their hearts to be
made cheerful and strong. I want them to be joined
together in love. Then their understanding will be
rich and complete. They will know the mystery of
God. That mystery is Christ.

3All the treasures of wisdom and knowledge are
hidden in him.
4But I don't want anyone to fool you with fast
talk that only sounds good. 5So even though I am
away from you in body, I am with you in spirit. I
am glad to see that you are doing everything in
good order. And I am happy that your faith in
Christ is so strong.

Freedom From Human Rules

6You received Christ Jesus as Lord. So keep on
living in him. 7Have your roots in him. Build yourselves up in him. Grow strong in what you believe,
just as you were taught. Be more thankful than
ever before.
8Make sure no one captures you. They will try
to capture you by using false reasoning that has no
meaning. Their ideas depend on human teachings.
They also depend on the basic things the people of
this world believe. They don't depend on Christ.
9God's whole nature is living in Christ in
human form. 10Because you belong to Christ, you
have everything you need. He is the ruler over
every power and authority.
11When you received Christ, you were also circumcised by putting away your sinful nature.
Human hands didn't circumcise you. Christ did.
12When you were baptized, you were buried
together with him. You were raised to life together
with him by believing in God's power. God raised
Jesus from the dead.
13At one time you were dead in your sins. Your
sinful nature was not circumcised. But God gave
you new life together with Christ. He forgave us
all of our sins.
14He wiped out the written Law with its rules.
The Law was against us. It opposed us. He took it
away and nailed it to the cross. 15He took away the
weapons of the powers and authorities. He made a
public show of them. He won the battle over them
by dying on the cross.
16So don't let anyone judge you because of what
you eat or drink. Don't let anyone judge you about
holy days. I'm talking about special feasts and
New Moons and Sabbath days. 17They are only a
shadow of the things that were going to come. But
what is real is found in Christ.
18Some people enjoy pretending they aren't
proud. They worship angels. But don't let people
like that hold you back from winning the prize.
They tell you every little thing about what they
have seen. Their minds are not guided by the Holy
Spirit. So they are proud of their useless ideas.
19They aren't connected to the Head. But the
whole body grows from the Head. The muscles
and tendons hold the body together. And God
causes it to grow.
20The people of the world believe certain basic
things. You died with Christ as far as things like
that are concerned. So why do you act as if you
still belong to the world? Here are the rules you
follow. 21"Do not handle! Do not taste! Do not
touch!" 22Rules like that are all going to die out as
time goes by. They are only based on human rules
and teachings.
23It is true that those rules seem wise. Because
of them, people give themselves over to their own
kind of worship. They pretend they aren't proud.
They treat their bodies very badly. But rules like
that don't help. They don't stop people from chasing after sinful pleasures.

Rules for Holy Living

3 You have been raised up with Christ. So think
about things that are in heaven. That is where
Christ is. He is sitting at God's right hand. 2Think
about things that are in heaven. Don't think about
things that are on earth.
3You died. Now your life is hidden with Christ
in God. 4Christ is your life. When he appears
again, you also will appear with him in heaven's
glory.
5So put to death anything that belongs to your
earthly nature. Get rid of your sexual sins and
unclean acts. Don't let your feelings get out of
control. Remove from your life all evil longings.
Stop always wanting more and more. You might
as well be worshiping statues of gods. 6God's
anger is going to come because of those things.
7That's the way you lived at one time in your life.
8But now here are the kinds of things you must
get rid of. You must put away anger, rage, hate and
lies. Let no dirty words come out of your mouths.
9Don't lie to each other.
You have gotten rid of your old way of life and
its habits. 10You have started living a new life. It is
being made new so that what you know has the
Creator's likeness.
11Here there is no Greek or Jew. There is no difference between those who are circumcised and
those who are not. There is no rude outsider, or
even a Scythian. There is no slave or free person.
But Christ is everything. And he is in everything.
12You are God's chosen people. You are holy
and dearly loved. So put on tender mercy and
kindness as if they were your clothes. Don't be
proud. Be gentle and patient. 13Put up with each
other. Forgive the things you are holding against
one another. Forgive, just as the Lord forgave you.
14And over all of those good things put on love.
Love holds them all together perfectly as if they
were one.
15Let the peace that Christ gives rule in your
hearts. As parts of one body, you were appointed
to live in peace. And be thankful.
16Let Christ's word live in you like a rich treasure. Teach and correct each other wisely. Sing
psalms, hymns and spiritual songs. Sing with
thanks in your hearts to God. 17Do everything you
say or do in the name of the Lord Jesus. Always
give thanks to God the Father through Christ.

Rules for Christian Families

18 Wives, follow the lead of your husbands.
That's what the Lord wants you to do.

19 Husbands, love your wives. Don't be mean to
them.

20 Children, obey your parents in everything.
That pleases the Lord.

21 Fathers, don't make your children bitter. If
you do, they will lose hope.

22 Slaves, obey your earthly masters in everything. Don't do it just to please them when they
are watching you. Obey them with an honest heart.
Do it out of respect for the Lord.

23 Work at everything you do with all your heart.
Work as if you were working for the Lord, not for
human masters. 24 Work because you know that you
will finally receive as a reward what the Lord
wants you to have. You are serving the Lord Christ.

25 Anyone who does wrong will be paid back for
what he does. God treats everyone the same.

4 Masters, give your slaves what is right and
fair. Do it because you know that you also
have a Master in heaven.

More Directions

2 Spend a lot of time in prayer. Always be watchful and thankful.

3 Pray for us too. Pray that God will open a door
for our message. Then we can preach the mystery
of Christ. Because I preached it, I am being held by
chains. 4 Pray that I will preach it clearly, as I should.

5 Be wise in the way you act toward outsiders.
Make the most of every opportunity. 6 Let the words
you speak always be full of grace. Season them with
salt. Then you will know how to answer everyone.

Final Greetings

7 Tychicus will tell you all the news about me.
He is a dear brother. He is a faithful worker. He
serves the Lord together with us. 8 I am sending
him to you for one reason. I want you to know
what is happening here. I want him to cheer you
up and make your hearts strong.

9 He is coming with Onesimus, our faithful and
dear brother. He is one of you. They will tell you
everything that is happening here.

10 Aristarchus is in prison with me. He sends you
his greetings. So does Mark, the cousin of Barnabas. You have been given directions about him. If
he comes to you, welcome him. 11 Jesus, who is
called Justus, also sends greetings. They are the
only Jews who work together with me for God's
kingdom. They have been a comfort to me.

12 Epaphras sends greetings. He is one of you.
He serves Christ Jesus. He is always praying hard
for you. He prays that you will stand firm in holding to all that God has in mind for us. He prays that
you will continue to grow in your knowledge of
what God wants you to do. He also prays that you
will be completely sure about it. 13 I am happy to
tell you that he is working very hard for you. He is
also working hard for everyone in Laodicea and
Hierapolis.

14 Our dear friend Luke, the doctor, sends greetings. So does Demas.

15 Give my greetings to the brothers and sisters
in Laodicea. Also give my greetings to Nympha
and the church that meets in her house.

16 After this letter has been read to you, send it
on. Be sure that it is also read to the church in Laodicea. And be sure that you read the letter from
Laodicea.

17 Tell Archippus, "Be sure that you complete
the work the Lord gave you to do."

18 I, Paul, am writing this greeting with my own
hand. Remember that I am being held by chains.
May grace be with you.

1 Thessalonians

1 I, Paul, am writing this letter. Silas and Timothy join me in writing.

We are sending this letter to you, the members of the church in Thessalonica. You belong to God the Father and the Lord Jesus Christ.

May grace and peace be given to you.

Paul Gives Thanks

2We always thank God for all of you. We pray for you. 3We never forget you when we pray to our God and Father. Your work is produced by your faith. Your service is the result of your love. Your strength to continue comes from your hope in our Lord Jesus Christ.

4Brothers and sisters, you are loved by God. We know that he has chosen you. 5Our good news didn't come to you only in words. It came with power. It came with the Holy Spirit's help. He gave us complete faith in what we were preaching. You know how we lived among you for your good.

6We and the Lord were your examples. You followed us. You suffered terribly. Even so, you welcomed our message with the joy the Holy Spirit gives. 7So you became a model to all the believers in the lands of Macedonia and Achaia.

8The Lord's message rang out from you. That was true not only in Macedonia and Achaia. Your faith in God has also become known everywhere. So we don't have to say anything about it. 9The believers themselves report the kind of welcome you gave us. They tell about how you turned away from statues of gods to serve the living and true God. 10They tell about how you are waiting for his Son to come from heaven.

God raised him from the dead. He is Jesus. He saves us from God's anger, and his anger is sure to come.

Paul's Work for God in Thessalonica

2 Brothers and sisters, you know that our visit to you was not a failure. 2You know what happened earlier in the city of Philippi. We suffered, and people treated us badly there. But God gave us the boldness to tell you his good news. We preached to you even though people opposed us strongly.

3The appeal we make is based on truth. It comes from a pure heart. We are not trying to trick you. 4In fact, it is just the opposite. God has accepted us to preach. He has trusted us with the good news. We aren't trying to please people. We want to please God. He puts our hearts to the test.

5As you know, we never praised you if we didn't mean it. We didn't put on a mask to cover up any sinful longing. God is our witness that this is true. 6We were not expecting people to praise us. We were not looking for praise from you or anyone else.

As Christ's apostles, we could have caused you some expense. 7But we were gentle among you. We were like a mother caring for her little children. 8We loved you so much that we were happy to share with you God's good news. We were also happy to share our lives with you. You had become very special to us.

9Brothers and sisters, I am sure you remember how hard we worked. We labored night and day while we preached to you God's good news. We didn't want to cause you any expense.

10You are witnesses of how we lived among you believers. God is also a witness that we were holy and godly and without blame. 11You know that we treated each of you as a father treats his own children.

12We gave you hope and strength. We comforted you. We really wanted you to live in a way that is worthy of God. He chooses you to enter his glorious kingdom.

13We never stop thanking God for the way you received his word. You heard it from us. But you didn't accept it as a human word. You accepted it for what it really is. It is God's word. It is at work in you who believe.

14Brothers and sisters, you became like the members of God's churches in Judea. They are believers in Christ Jesus, just as you are. People in your own country made you suffer. You went through the same things the church members in Judea suffered from the Jews.

15The Jews who killed the Lord Jesus and the prophets also forced us to leave. They do not please God. They are enemies of everyone. 16They try to keep us from speaking to those who aren't Jews. The Jews don't want them to be saved. In that way, the Jews always increase their sins to the limit. God's anger has come on them at last.

Paul Longs to See the Believers in Thessalonica

17Brothers and sisters, we were torn away from you for a short time. We were no longer with you in person, but we kept you in our thoughts. We really longed to see you. So we tried very hard to do so. 18We wanted to come to you. Again and again I, Paul, wanted to come. But Satan stopped us.

19What is our hope? What is our joy? When our Lord Jesus returns, what is the crown we will delight in? Isn't it you? 20Yes, you are our glory and our joy.

3 We couldn't wait any longer. So we thought it was best to be left by ourselves in Athens. 2We sent our brother Timothy to give you strength

and hope in your faith. He works together with God in spreading the good news about Christ. 3We sent him so that no one would be upset by times of testing.

You know very well that we have to go through them. 4In fact, when we were with you, we kept telling you that our enemies would make us suffer. As you know very well, it has turned out that way.

5That's the reason I sent someone to find out about your faith. I couldn't wait any longer. I was afraid that Satan might have tempted you in some way. Then our efforts would have been useless.

Timothy Brings a Good Report

6But Timothy has come to us from you just now. He has brought good news about your faith and love. He has told us that you always have happy memories of us. He has also said that you long to see us, just as we long to see you.

7Brothers and sisters, in all our trouble and suffering your faith cheered us up. 8Now we really live, because you are standing firm in the Lord.

9How can we thank God enough for you because of all the joy that comes only from our God? 10Night and day we pray very hard that we will see you again. We want to give you what is missing in your faith.

11Now may our God and Father himself and our Lord Jesus open up a way for us to come to you. 12May the Lord make your love grow. May it be like a rising flood. May your love for one another increase. May it also increase for everyone else. May it be just like our love for you. 13May the Lord give you strength in your hearts. Then you will be holy and without blame in the sight of our God and Father. May that be true when our Lord Jesus comes with all his holy ones.

Living in a Way That Pleases God

4 Finally, brothers and sisters, we taught you how to live in a way that pleases God. In fact, that is how you are living. In the name of the Lord Jesus we ask and beg you to do it more and more.

2You know the directions we gave you. They were given by the authority of the Lord Jesus.

3God wants you to be made holy. He wants you to stay away from sexual sins. 4He wants all of you to learn to control your own bodies. You must live in a way that is holy. You must live with honor. 5Don't long to commit sexual sins like those who don't know God. 6None of you should sin against your brother by doing that. You should not take advantage of him. The Lord will punish everyone who commits those kinds of sins. We have already told you and warned you about that. 7God chose us to live pure lives. He wants us to be holy.

8So if you refuse to accept my teaching, you turn your back on God, not on people. God gives you his Holy Spirit.

9We don't need to write to you about love among believers. God himself has taught you to love each other. 10In fact, you do love all the brothers and sisters all around Macedonia. But we are asking you to love each other more and more.

11Do everything you can to live a quiet life. Mind your own business. Work with your hands, just as we told you to. 12Then unbelievers will have respect for your everyday life. And you won't have to depend on anyone.

The Lord Is Coming

13Brothers and sisters, we want you to know what happens to those who die. We don't want you to be sad, as other people are. They don't have any hope.

14We believe that Jesus died and rose again. When he returns, many who believe in him will have died already. We believe that God will bring them back with Jesus.

15That agrees with what the Lord has said. When the Lord comes, many of us will still be alive. We tell you that we will certainly not go up before those who have died.

16The Lord himself will come down from heaven. We will hear a loud command. We will hear the voice of the leader of the angels. We will hear a blast from God's trumpet. Many who believe in Christ will have died already. They will rise first. 17After that, we who are still alive and are left will be caught up together with them. We will be taken up in the clouds. We will meet the Lord in the air. And we will be with him forever.

18So cheer each other up with these words of comfort.

5 Brothers and sisters, we don't have to write to you about times and dates. 2You know very well that the day of the Lord will come like a thief in the night. 3People will be saying that everything is peaceful and safe. Then suddenly they will be destroyed. It will happen like birth pains coming on a pregnant woman. None of the people will escape.

4Brothers and sisters, you are not in darkness. So that day should not surprise you as a thief would. 5All of you are children of the light. You are children of the day. We don't belong to the night. We don't belong to the darkness.

6So let us not be like the others. They are asleep. Instead, let us be wide awake and in full control of ourselves.

7Those who sleep, sleep at night. Those who get drunk, get drunk at night. 8But we belong to the day. So let us control ourselves. Let us put the armor of faith and love on our chest. Let us put on the hope of salvation like a helmet.

9God didn't choose us to receive his anger. He chose us to receive salvation because of what our Lord Jesus Christ has done.

10Jesus died for us. Some will be alive when he comes. Others will be dead. Either way, we will live together with him. 11So cheer each other up with the hope you have. Build each other up. In fact, that's what you are doing.

Final Directions

[12]Brothers and sisters, we ask you to have respect for the godly leaders who work hard among you. They have authority over you. They correct you. [13]Have a lot of respect for them. Love them because of what they do. Live in peace with each other.

[14]Brothers and sisters, we are asking you to warn those who don't want to work. Cheer up those who are shy. Help those who are weak. Put up with everyone. [15]Make sure that nobody pays back one wrong act with another. Always try to be kind to each other and to everyone else.

[16]Always be joyful. [17]Never stop praying. [18]Give thanks no matter what happens. God wants you to thank him because you believe in Christ Jesus.

[19]Don't put out the Holy Spirit's fire. [20]Don't treat prophecies as if they amount to nothing. [21]Put everything to the test. Hold on to what is good. [22]Stay away from every kind of evil.

[23]God is the God who gives peace. May he make you holy through and through. May your whole spirit, soul and body be kept free from blame. May you be without blame from now until our Lord Jesus Christ comes. [24]The One who has chosen you is faithful. He will do all these things.

[25]Brothers and sisters, pray for us. [26]Greet all the believers with a holy kiss. [27]While the Lord is watching, here is what I command you. Have this letter read to all the believers.

[28]May the grace of our Lord Jesus Christ be with you.

2 Thessalonians

1 I, Paul, am writing this letter. Silas and Timothy join me in writing.

We are sending this letter to you, the members of the church in Thessalonica. You belong to God our Father and the Lord Jesus Christ.

2May God the Father and the Lord Jesus Christ give you grace and peace.

Paul Prays and Gives Thanks

3Brothers and sisters, we should always thank God for you. That is only right, because your faith is growing more and more. The love you all have for each other is increasing. 4So among God's churches we brag about the fact that you don't give up easily. We brag about your faith in all the suffering and testing you are going through.

5All of this proves that when God judges, he is fair. So you will be considered worthy to enter God's kingdom. You are suffering for his kingdom.

6God is fair. He will pay back trouble to those who give you trouble. 7He will help you who are troubled. And he will also help us.

All of those things will happen when the Lord Jesus appears from heaven. He will come in blazing fire. He will come with the angels who are given the power to do what God wants. 8He will punish those who don't know God. He will punish those who don't obey the good news about our Lord Jesus. 9They will be destroyed forever. They will be shut out of heaven. They will never see the glory of the Lord's power.

10All of those things will happen when he comes. On that day his glory will be seen in his holy people. Everyone who has believed will be amazed when they see him. That includes you, because you believed the witness we gave you.

11Keeping this in mind, we never stop praying for you. Our God has chosen you. We pray that he will consider you worthy of his choice. We pray that by his power he will make every good thing you have planned come true. We pray that he will make perfect all that you have done by faith. 12We pray this so that the name of our Lord Jesus will receive glory through what you have done. We also pray that you will receive glory through what he has done. We pray all these things in keeping with the grace of our God and the Lord Jesus Christ.

The Man of Sin

2 Brothers and sisters, we want to ask you something. It has to do with the coming of our Lord Jesus Christ. It concerns the time when we will go to be with him.

2What if you receive a prophecy, report or letter that is supposed to have come from us? What if it says that the day of the Lord has already come? If it does, we ask you not to become easily upset or alarmed.

3Don't let anyone trick you in any way. That day will not come until people rise up against God. It will not come until the man of sin appears. He is a marked man. He is sentenced to be destroyed. 4He will oppose everything that is called God. He will oppose everything that is worshiped. He will give himself power over everything. He will set himself up in God's temple. He will announce that he himself is God.

5Don't you remember? When I was with you, I used to tell you those things.

6Now you know what is holding the man of sin back. He is held back so that he can make his appearance at the right time. 7The secret power of sin is already at work. But the one who now holds that power back will keep doing it until he is taken out of the way.

8Then the man of sin will appear. The Lord Jesus will overthrow him with the breath of his mouth. The glorious brightness of Jesus' coming will destroy the man of sin.

9The coming of the man of sin will be Satan's work. His work will be seen in all kinds of fake miracles, signs and wonders. 10It will be seen in every kind of evil that fools people who are dying. They are dying because they refuse to love the truth. The truth would save them.

11So God will fool them completely. Then they will believe the lie. 12Many will not believe the truth. They will take pleasure in evil. They will be judged.

Stand Firm

13Brothers and sisters, we should always thank God for you. The Lord loves you. God chose you from the beginning. He wanted you to be saved. Salvation comes through the Holy Spirit's work. He makes people holy. It also comes through believing the truth. 14He chose you to be saved by accepting the good news that we preach. And you will share in the glory of our Lord Jesus Christ.

15Brothers and sisters, stand firm. Hold on to what we taught you. We passed our teachings on to you by what we preached and wrote.

16Our Lord Jesus Christ and God our Father loved us. By his grace God gave us comfort that will last forever. The hope he gave us is good.

May our Lord Jesus Christ and God our Father 17comfort your hearts. May they make you strong in every good thing you do and say.

Paul Asks for Prayer

3 Finally, brothers and sisters, pray for us. Pray that the Lord's message will spread quickly.

Pray that others will honor it just as you did. [2]And
pray that we will be saved from sinful and evil
people. Not everyone is a believer.
[3]But the Lord is faithful. He will strengthen
you. He will guard you from the evil one.
[4]We trust in the Lord. So we are sure that you
are doing the things we tell you to do. And we are
sure that you will keep on doing them.
[5]May the Lord fill your hearts with God's love.
May Christ give you the strength to go on.

Paul Warns Those Who Do Not Want to Work

[6]Brothers and sisters, here is a command we
give you in the name of the Lord Jesus Christ.
Keep away from every believer who doesn't want
to work. Keep away from anyone who doesn't live
up to the teaching you received from us.
[7]You know how you should follow our example. We worked when we were with you. [8]We
didn't eat anyone's food without paying for it. In
fact, it was just the opposite. We worked night and
day. We worked very hard so that we wouldn't
cause any expense to any of you.
[9]We worked, even though we have the right to
receive help from you. We did it in order to be a
model for you to follow. [10]Even when we were
with you, we gave you a rule. We said, "Anyone
who will not work will not eat."
[11]We hear that some people among you don't
want to work. They aren't really busy. Instead,
they are bothering others. [12]We belong to the Lord
Jesus Christ. So we strongly command people like
that to settle down. They have to earn the food
they eat.
[13]Brothers and sisters, don't ever get tired of
doing the right thing.
[14]Keep an eye on anyone who doesn't obey the
directions in our letter. Watch that person closely.
Have nothing to do with him. Then he will feel
ashamed. [15]But don't think of him as an enemy.
Instead, warn him as a brother or sister.

Final Greetings

[16]May the Lord who gives peace give you peace
at all times and in every way. May the Lord be
with all of you.
[17]I, Paul, write this greeting in my own hand-
writing. That's how I prove that I am the author of
all my letters. I always do it that way.
[18]May the grace of our Lord Jesus Christ be
with you all.

1 Timothy

1 I, Paul, am writing this letter. I am an apostle
of Christ Jesus, just as God our Savior commanded. Christ Jesus also commanded it. We have
put our hope in him.

2Timothy, I am sending you this letter. You are
my true son in the faith.

May God the Father and Christ Jesus our Lord
give you grace, mercy and peace.

Paul Warns Against Certain Teachers of the Law

3Stay there in Ephesus. That is what I told you
to do when I went into Macedonia. I want you to
command certain people not to teach things that
aren't true. 4Command them not to spend their
time on stories that aren't completely true. They
must not waste time on family histories that never
end. Things like that cause people to argue instead
of doing God's work. His work is done by faith.
5Love is the purpose of my command. Love
comes from a pure heart. It comes from a good
sense of what is right and wrong. It comes from
faith that is honest and true.
6Some have wandered away from those teachings. They would rather talk about things that have
no meaning. 7They want to be teachers of the law.
And they are very sure about that law. But they
don't know what they are talking about.
8We know that the law is good if it is used properly. 9We also know that the law isn't made for
godly people. It is made for those who break the
law. It is for those who refuse to obey. It is for
ungodly and sinful people. It is for those who aren't
holy and who don't believe. It is for those who kill
their fathers or mothers. It is for murderers.
10It is for those who commit adultery. It is for
those who have a twisted view of sex. It is for people who buy and sell slaves. It is for liars. It is for
those who give witness to things that aren't true.
And it is for anything else that is the opposite of
true teaching.
11True teaching agrees with the glorious good
news of the blessed God. He trusted me with that
good news.

The Lord Pours Out His Grace on Paul

12I am thankful to Christ Jesus our Lord. He has
given me strength. I thank him that he considered
me faithful. And I thank him for appointing me to
serve him.
13I used to speak evil things against Jesus. I tried
to hurt his followers. I really pushed them around.
But God showed me mercy anyway. I did those
things without knowing any better. I wasn't a
believer.
14Our Lord poured out more and more of his
grace on me. Along with it came faith and love
from Christ Jesus.
15Here is a saying that you can trust. It should
be accepted completely. Christ Jesus came into the
world to save sinners.
And I am the worst sinner of all. 16But for that
very reason, God showed me mercy. And I am the
worst of sinners. He showed me mercy so that
Christ Jesus could show that he is very patient. I
was an example for those who would come to
believe in him. Then they would receive eternal life.
17The eternal King will never die. He can't be
seen. He is the only God. Give him honor and
glory for ever and ever. Amen.
18My son Timothy, I give you these teachings.
They are in keeping with the prophecies that were
once made about you. By following them, you can
fight the good fight. 19Then you will hold on to
faith. You will hold on to a good sense of what is
right and wrong.
Some have not accepted these teachings. By
doing that, they have destroyed their faith. They
are like a ship that has sunk. 20Hymenaeus and Alexander are among them. I have handed them over
to Satan. That will teach them not to speak evil
things against God.

Directions for Worship

2 First, I want all of you to pray for everyone.
Ask God to bless them. Give thanks for them.
2Pray for kings. Pray for all who are in authority. Pray that we will live peaceful and quiet lives.
And pray that we will be godly and holy.
3That is good. It pleases God our Savior. 4He
wants everyone to be saved. He wants them to
come to know the truth.
5There is only one God. And there is only one
go-between for God and human beings. He is the
man Christ Jesus. 6He gave himself to pay for the
sins of everyone. That was a witness given by God
at just the right time.
7I was appointed to be a messenger and an apostle to preach the good news. I am telling the truth.
I'm not lying. God appointed me to be a teacher
of the true faith to those who aren't Jews.
8I want men everywhere to pray. I want them to
lift up holy hands. I don't want them to be angry
when they pray. I don't want them to argue.
9I also want women to dress simply. They
should wear clothes that are right and proper. They
shouldn't braid their hair. They shouldn't wear
gold or pearls. They shouldn't spend too much on
clothes. 10Instead, they should put on good works
as if they were their clothes. That is proper for
women who claim to worship God.

11When a woman is learning, she should be quiet. She should follow the leaders in every way. 12I do not let women teach. I do not let them have authority over men. They must be quiet.

13Adam was made first. Then Eve was made. 14Adam was not the one who was tricked. The woman was tricked and became a sinner. 15Will women be saved by having children? Only if they keep on believing, loving, and leading a holy life in a proper way.

Leaders and Deacons

3 Here is a saying you can trust. If anyone wants to be a leader in the church, he wants to do a good work for God and people.

2A leader must be free from blame. He must be faithful to his wife. In anything he does, he must not go too far. He must control himself. He must be worthy of respect. He must welcome people into his home. He must be able to teach. 3He must not get drunk. He must not push people around. He must be gentle. He must not be a person who likes to argue. He must not love money.

4He must manage his own family well. He must make sure that his children obey him and show him proper respect. 5Suppose someone doesn't know how to manage his own family. Then how can he take care of God's church?

6The leader must not be a new believer. If he is, he might become proud. Then he would be judged just like the devil.

7The leader must also be respected by those who are outside the church. Then he will not be put to shame. He will not fall into the devil's trap.

8Deacons also must be worthy of respect. They must be honest and true. They must not drink too much wine. They must not try to get money by cheating people. 9They must hold on to the deep truths of the faith. Even their own minds tell them to do that. 10First they must be tested. Then let them serve as deacons if there is nothing against them.

11In the same way, their wives must be worthy of respect. They must not say things that harm others. In anything they do, they must not go too far. They must be worthy of trust in everything.

12A deacon must be faithful to his wife. He must manage his children and family well. 13Those who have served well earn the full respect of others. They also become more sure of their faith in Christ Jesus.

14I hope I can come to you soon. But now I am writing these directions to you. 15Then if I have to put off my visit, you will know how you should act in God's family. The family of God is the church of the living God. It is the pillar and foundation of the truth.

16There is no doubt that godliness is a great mystery.

Jesus appeared in a body.
The Holy Spirit proved that he was the
Son of God.
He was seen by angels.
He was preached among the nations.
People in the world believed in him.
He was taken up to heaven in glory.

Directions for Timothy

4 The Holy Spirit clearly says that in the last days some people will leave the faith. They will follow spirits that will fool them. They will believe things that demons will teach them.

2Teachings like those come from liars who pretend to be what they are not. Their sense of what is right and wrong has been burned as if with a hot iron. 3They do not allow people to get married. They order them not to eat certain foods. But God created those foods. So people who believe and know the truth should receive them and give thanks for them.

4Everything God created is good. You shouldn't turn anything down. Instead, you should thank God for it. 5The word of God and prayer make it holy.

6Point these things out to the brothers and sisters. Then you will serve Christ Jesus well. You were brought up in the truths of the faith. You received good teaching. You followed it.

7Don't have anything to do with godless stories and silly tales. Instead, train yourself to be godly. 8Training the body has some value. But being godly has value in every way. It promises help for the life you are now living and the life to come.

9Here is a saying you can trust. You can accept it completely. 10We work hard for it. Here is the saying. We have put our hope in the living God. He is the Savior of all people. Most of all he is the Savior of those who believe.

11Command those things. Teach them. 12Don't let anyone look down on you because you are young. Set an example for the believers in what you say and in how you live. Also set an example in how you love and in what you believe. Show the believers how to be pure.

13Until I come, spend your time reading Scripture out loud to one another. Spend your time preaching and teaching. 14Don't fail to use the gift the Holy Spirit gave you. He gave it to you through a message from God. It was given when the elders placed their hands on you.

15Keep on doing those things. Give them your complete attention. Then everyone will see how you are coming along. 16Be careful of how you live and what you believe. Never give up. Then you will save yourself and those who hear you.

Advice About Widows, Elders and Slaves

5 Don't tell an older man off. Make an appeal to him as if he were your father. Treat younger men as if they were your brothers. 2Treat older women as if they were your mothers. Treat younger women as if they were your sisters. Be completely pure in the way you treat them.

3Take care of the widows who really need help. 4But suppose a widow has children or grandchildren. They should first learn to put their faith into practice. They should care for their own family. In that way they will pay back their parents and grandparents. That pleases God.

5The widow who really needs help and is left all alone puts her hope in God. Night and day she keeps on praying. Night and day she asks God for help. 6But the widow who lives for pleasure is dead even while she is still living.

7Give those directions to the people also. Then no one can be blamed. 8Everyone should provide for his own relatives. Most of all, everyone should take care of his own family. If he doesn't, he has left the faith. He is worse than someone who doesn't believe.

9No widow should be put on the list of widows unless she is more than 60 years old. She must also have been faithful to her husband. 10She must be well known for the good things she does. That includes bringing up children. It includes inviting guests into her home. It includes washing the feet of God's people. It includes helping those who are in trouble. A widow should spend her time doing all kinds of good things.

11Don't put younger widows on that kind of list. They might want pleasure more than they want Christ. Then they would want to get married again. 12If they do that, they will be judged. They have broken their first promise.

13Besides, they get into the habit of having nothing to do. They go around from house to house. They waste time. They talk about others. They bother people. They say things they shouldn't say. 14So here is the advice I give to younger widows. Get married. Have children. Take care of your own homes. Don't give the enemy the chance to tell lies about you. 15In fact, some have already turned away to follow Satan.

16Suppose a woman is a believer and has widows in her family. She should help them. She shouldn't let the church pay the expenses. Then the church can help the widows who really need it.

17The elders who do the church's work well are worth twice as much honor. That is true in a special way of elders who preach and teach. 18Scripture says, "Do not stop the ox from eating while it helps separate the grain from the straw." *(Deuteronomy 25:4)* Scripture also says, "Workers are worthy of their pay." *(Luke 10:7)*

19Don't believe a charge against an elder unless two or three witnesses bring it. 20Elders who sin should be corrected in front of the other believers. That will be a warning to the others.

21I command you to follow those directions. I command you in the sight of God and Christ Jesus and the chosen angels. Treat everyone the same. Don't favor one person over another.

22Don't be too quick to place your hands on others to set them apart to serve God. Don't take part in the sins of others. Keep yourself pure.

23Stop drinking only water. If your stomach is upset, drink a little wine. It can also help the other sicknesses you often have.

24The sins of some people are easy to see. They are already being judged. Others will be judged later. 25In the same way, good works are easy to see. But even good works that are hard to see can't stay hidden.

6 All who are forced to serve as slaves should consider their masters worthy of full respect. Then people will not speak evil things against God's name and against what we teach.

2Some slaves have masters who are believers. They shouldn't show less respect for their masters just because they are believers. Instead, they should serve them even better. That's because those who benefit from their service are believers. They are loved by them.

Teach the slaves those things. Try hard to get them to do them.

Love for Money

3Suppose someone teaches ideas that are false. He doesn't agree with the true teaching of our Lord Jesus Christ. He doesn't agree with godly teaching. 4People like that are proud. They don't understand anything. They like to argue more than they should. They can't agree about what words mean.

All of that results in wanting what others have. It causes fighting, harmful talk, and evil distrust. 5It stirs up trouble all the time among people whose minds are twisted by sin. The truth they once had has been taken away from them. They think they can get rich by being godly.

6You gain a lot when you live a godly life. But you must be happy with what you have. 7We didn't bring anything into the world. We can't take anything out of it. 8If we have food and clothing, we will be happy with that.

9People who want to get rich are tempted. They fall into a trap. They are tripped up by wanting many foolish and harmful things. Those who live like that are dragged down by what they do. They are destroyed and die.

10Love for money causes all kinds of evil. Some people want to get rich. They have wandered away from the faith. They have wounded themselves with many sorrows.

Paul Gives a Command to Timothy

11But you are a man of God. Run away from all of those things. Try hard to do what is right and godly. Have faith, love and gentleness. Hold on to what you believe. 12Fight the good fight along with all other believers. Take hold of eternal life. You were chosen for it when you openly told others what you believe. Many witnesses heard you.

13God gives life to everything. Christ Jesus told the truth when he gave witness to Pontius Pilate. In the sight of God and Christ, I give you a command. [14]Obey it until our Lord Jesus Christ appears. Obey it completely. Then no one can find fault with it or you.

[15]God will bring Jesus back at a time that pleases him. God is the blessed and only Ruler. He is the greatest King of all. He is the most powerful Lord of all. [16]God is the only one who can't die. He lives in light that no one can get close to. No one has seen him. No one can see him.

Give honor and power to him forever. Amen.

[17]Command people who are rich in this world not to be proud. Tell them not to put their hope in riches. Wealth is so uncertain. Command those who are rich to put their hope in God. He richly provides us with everything to enjoy.

[18]Command the rich to do what is good. Tell them to be rich in doing good things. They must give freely. They must be willing to share. [19]In that way they will put riches away for themselves. It will provide a firm basis for the next life. Then they will take hold of the life that really is life.

[20]Timothy, guard what God has trusted you with. Turn away from godless chatter. Stay away from opposing ideas that are falsely called knowledge. [21]Some people believe them. By doing that they have wandered away from the faith.

May God's grace be with you.

2 Timothy

1 I, Paul, am writing this letter. I am an apostle
of Christ Jesus just as God planned. He sent
me to tell about the promise of life that is found in
Christ Jesus.

[2]Timothy, I am sending you this letter. You are
my dear son.

May God the Father and Christ Jesus our Lord
give you grace, mercy and peace.

Paul Tells Timothy to Be Faithful

[3]I serve God, knowing that what I have done is
right. That is how our people served him long ago.
Night and day I thank God for you. Night and day
I always remember you in my prayers.

[4]I remember your tears. I long to see you so that
I can be filled with joy. [5]I remember your honest
and true faith. It was alive first in your grandmother Lois and in your mother Eunice. And I am
certain that it is now alive in you also.

[6]That is why I remind you to help God's gift
grow, just as a small spark grows into a fire. God
put his gift in you when I placed my hands on you.

[7]God didn't give us a spirit that makes us weak
and fearful. He gave us a spirit that gives us power
and love. It helps us control ourselves.

[8]So don't be ashamed to give witness about our
Lord. And don't be ashamed of me, his prisoner.
Instead, join with me as I suffer for the good news.
God's power will help us do that.

[9]God has saved us. He has chosen us to live a
holy life. It wasn't because of anything we have
done. It was because of his own purpose and grace.
Through Christ Jesus, God gave us that grace even
before time began. [10]It has now been made known
through the coming of our Savior, Christ Jesus. He
has destroyed death. Because of the good news, he
has brought life out into the light. That life never
dies.

[11]I was appointed to announce the good news. I
was appointed to be an apostle and a teacher.
[12]That's why I'm suffering the way I am. But I'm
not ashamed. I know the One I have believed in. I
am sure he is able to take care of what I have given
him. I can trust him with it until the day he returns
as judge.

[13]Follow what you heard from me as the pattern
of true teaching. Follow it with faith and love
because you belong to Christ Jesus. [14]Guard the truth
of the good news that you were trusted with. Guard
it with the help of the Holy Spirit who lives in us.

[15]You know that all the believers in Asia Minor
have deserted me. They include Phygelus and Her-
mogenes.

[16]May the Lord show mercy to all who live in
the house of Onesiphorus. He often cheered me
up. He was not ashamed that I was being held by
chains. [17]In fact, it was just the opposite. When he
was in Rome, he looked everywhere for me. At
last he found me.

[18]May Onesiphorus find mercy from the Lord
on the day Jesus returns as judge. You know very
well how many ways Onesiphorus helped me in
Ephesus.

2 My son, be strong in the grace that is found in
Christ Jesus. [2]You have heard me teach in
front of many witnesses. Pass on to men you can
trust the things you've heard me say. Then they
will be able to teach others also. [3]Like a good soldier of Christ Jesus, share in the hard times
with us.

[4]A soldier does not take part in things that don't
have anything to do with the army. He wants to
please his commanding officer. [5]In the same way,
anyone who takes part in a sport doesn't receive
the winner's crown unless he plays by the rules.
[6]The farmer who works hard should be the first to
receive a share of the crops.

[7]Think about what I'm saying. The Lord will
help you understand what all of it means.

[8]Remember Jesus Christ. He came from David's family line. He was raised from the dead.
That is my good news. [9]I am suffering for it. I have
even been put in chains like someone who has
committed a crime. But God's word is not held
back by chains.

[10]So I put up with everything for the good of
God's chosen people. Then they also can be saved.
Christ Jesus saves them. He gives them glory that
will last forever.

[11]Here is a saying you can trust.

If we died with him,
    we will also live with him.
[12]If we don't give up,
    we will also rule with him.
If we say we don't know him,
    he will also say he doesn't know us.
[13]Even if we are not faithful,
    he will remain faithful.
    He must be true to himself.

A Worker Who Pleases God

[14]Keep reminding the believers of those things.
While God is watching, warn them not to argue
about words. That doesn't have any value. It only
destroys those who listen.

[15]Do your best to please God. Be a worker who
doesn't need to be ashamed. Teach the message of
truth correctly.

[16]Stay away from godless chatter. Those who
take part in it will become more and more ungodly.
[17]Their teaching will spread like a deadly sickness.

Hymenaeus and Philetus are two of those teachers. 18They have wandered away from the truth. They say that the time when people will rise from the dead has already come. They destroy the faith of some people.

19But God's solid foundation stands firm. Here is the message written on it. "The Lord knows who his own people are." *(Numbers 16:5)* Also, "All who say they believe in the Lord must turn away from evil."

20In a large house there are things made out of gold and silver. But there are also things made out of wood and clay. Some have honorable purposes. Others do not. 21Suppose someone stays away from what is not honorable. Then the Master will be able to use him for honorable purposes. He will be made holy. He will be ready to do any good work.

22Run away from the evil things that young people long for. Try hard to do what is right. Have faith, love and peace. Do these things together with those who call on the Lord from a pure heart. 23Don't have anything to do with arguing. It is dumb and foolish. You know it only leads to fights.

24Anyone who serves the Lord must not fight. Instead, he must be kind to everyone. He must be able to teach. He must not hold anything against anyone. 25He must gently teach those who oppose him.

Maybe God will give a change of heart to those who are against you. That will lead them to know the truth. 26Maybe they will come to their senses. Maybe they will escape the devil's trap. He has taken them prisoner to do what he wanted.

Terrible Times in the Last Days

3 Here is what I want you to know. There will be terrible times in the last days. 2People will love themselves. They will love money. They will brag and be proud. They will tear others down. They will not obey their parents. They won't be thankful or holy. 3They won't love others. They won't forgive others. They will tell lies about people. They will be out of control. They will be wild. They will hate what is good.

4They will turn against their friends. They will act without thinking. They will think they are better than others. They will love what pleases them instead of loving God. 5They will act as if they were serving God. But what they do will show that they have turned their backs on God's power. Have nothing to do with those people.

6They are the kind who worm their way into the homes of silly women. They get control over them. Women like that are loaded down with sins. They give in to all kinds of evil longings. 7They are always learning. But they never come to know the truth.

8Jannes and Jambres opposed Moses. In the same way, the teachers I'm talking about oppose the truth. Their minds are twisted. As far as the faith is concerned, God doesn't accept them. 9They won't get very far. Just like Jannes and Jambres, their foolish ways will be clear to everyone.

Paul Gives a Command to Timothy

10But you know all about my teaching. You know how I live and what I live for. You know about my faith and love. You know how patient I am. You know I haven't given up. 11You know that I was treated badly. You know that I suffered greatly. You know what kinds of things happened to me in Antioch, Iconium and Lystra. You know how badly I have been treated. But the Lord saved me from all of my troubles.

12In fact, everyone who wants to live a godly life in Christ Jesus will be treated badly. 13Evil people and pretenders will go from bad to worse. They will fool others, and others will fool them.

14But I want you to continue to follow what you have learned. Don't give up what you are sure of. You know the people you learned it from. 15You have known the Holy Scriptures ever since you were a little child. They are able to teach you how to be saved by believing in Christ Jesus.

16God has breathed life into all of Scripture. It is useful for teaching us what is true. It is useful for correcting our mistakes. It is useful for making our lives whole again. It is useful for training us to do what is right. 17By using Scripture, a man of God can be completely prepared to do every good thing.

4 I give you a command in the sight of God and Christ Jesus. Christ will judge the living and the dead. Because he and his kingdom are coming, here is the command I give you. 2Preach the word. Be ready to serve God in good times and bad. Correct people's mistakes. Warn them. Cheer them up with words of hope. Be very patient as you do these things. Teach them carefully.

3The time will come when people won't put up with true teaching. Instead, they will try to satisfy their own longings. They will gather a large number of teachers around them. The teachers will say what the people want to hear. 4The people will turn their ears away from the truth. They will turn to stories that aren't completely true.

5But I want you to keep your head no matter what happens. Don't give up when times are hard. Work to spread the good news. Do everything God has given you to do.

6I am already being poured out like a drink offering. The time has come for me to leave.

7I have fought the good fight. I have finished the race. I have kept the faith. 8Now there is a crown waiting for me. It is given to those who are right with God. The Lord, who judges fairly, will give it to me on the day he returns. He will not give it only to me. He will also give it to all those who are longing for him to return.

Personal Words

9Do your best to come to me quickly.

10Demas has deserted me. He has gone to Thessalonica. He left me because he loved this world. Crescens has gone to Galatia. Titus has gone to

Dalmatia. 11Only Luke is with me. Get Mark and
bring him with you. He helps me in my work for
the Lord. 12I sent Tychicus to Ephesus.
13When you come, bring my coat. I left it with
Carpus at Troas. Also bring my scrolls. Most of all,
bring the ones made out of animal skins.
14Remember Alexander, the one who works
with metal? He did me a great deal of harm. The
Lord will pay him back for what he has done.
15You too should watch out for him. He strongly
opposed our message.
16The first time I was put on trial, no one came
to help me. Everyone deserted me. I hope they will
be forgiven for it.
17The Lord stood at my side. He gave me the
strength to preach the whole message. Then all
those who weren't Jews heard it. I was saved from
the lion's mouth. 18The Lord will save me from
every evil attack. He will bring me safely to his
heavenly kingdom.
Give him glory for ever and ever. Amen.

Final Greetings

19Greet Priscilla and Aquila. Greet those who
live in the house of Onesiphorus.
20Erastus stayed in Corinth. I left Trophimus
sick in Miletus.
21Do your best to get here before winter.
Eubulus greets you. So do Pudens, Linus, Claudia and all the brothers.
22May the Lord be with your spirit. May God's
grace be with you.

Titus

1 I, Paul, am writing this letter. I serve God. I
am an apostle of Jesus Christ. God sent me to
help his chosen people believe in Christ. I have
been sent to help them understand the truth that
leads to godly living. 2 Faith and understanding rest
on the hope of eternal life. Before time began, God
promised to give that life. And he does not lie. 3 At
just the right time he made his word plain. He did
it through the preaching that he trusted me with.
God our Savior has commanded all those things.

4 Titus, I am sending you this letter. You are my
true son in the faith we share.

May God the Father and Christ Jesus our Savior give you grace and peace.

The Work of Titus on Crete

5 I left you on the island of Crete. There were
some things that hadn't been finished. You needed
to sort them out. You also had to appoint elders in
every town. I told you how to do it.

6 An elder must be without blame. He must be
faithful to his wife. His children must be believers. They must not give anyone a reason to say that
they are wild and don't obey.

7 A church leader is trusted with God's work.
That's why he must be without blame. He must not
look after only his own interests. He must not get
angry easily. He must not get drunk. He must not
push people around. He must not try to get money
by cheating people.

8 Instead, he must welcome people into his
home. He must love what is good. He must control his mind and feelings. He must do what is
right. He must be holy. He must control what his
body longs for. 9 The message as it has been taught
can be trusted. He must hold firmly to it. Then he
will be able to use true teaching to comfort others
and build them up. He will be able to prove that
people who oppose it are wrong.

10 Many people refuse to obey God. All they do
is talk a lot. They try to fool others. No one does
these things more than the circumcision group.
11 They must be stopped. They are destroying entire
families. They are teaching things they shouldn't.
They do it to get money by cheating people.

12 Even one of their own prophets has said, "People from Crete are always liars. They are evil beasts.
They don't want to work. They live only to eat."
13 What I have just said is true. So give them a strong
warning. Then they will understand the faith correctly. 14 They will pay no attention to Jewish stories
that aren't completely true. They won't listen to the
commands of those who turn away from the truth.

15 To people who are pure, all things are pure. But
to those who have twisted minds and don't believe,
nothing is pure. In fact, their minds and their sense
of what is right and wrong are twisted. 16 They claim
to know God. But their actions show they don't
know him. They are hated by God. They refuse to
obey him. They aren't fit to do anything good.

Teaching God's People

2 What you teach must agree with true teaching.
2 Tell the older men that in anything they do,
they must not go too far. They must be worthy of
respect. They must control themselves. They must
have true faith. They must love others. They must
not give up.

3 In the same way, teach the older women to lead
a holy life. They must not tell lies about others. They
must not let wine control them. Instead, they must
teach what is good. 4 Then they can train the younger
women to love their husbands and children.

5 The younger women must control themselves.
They must be pure. They must take good care of
their homes. They must be kind. They must follow
the lead of their husbands. Then no one will be
able to speak evil things against God's word.

6 In the same way, help the young men to control
themselves. 7 Do what is good. Set an example for
them in everything. When you teach, be honest
and serious. 8 No one can question the truth. So
teach what is true. Then those who oppose you
will be ashamed. That's because they will have
nothing bad to say about us.

9 Teach slaves to obey their masters in everything
they do. Tell them to try to please their masters. They
must not talk back to them. 10 They must not steal
from them. Instead, they must show that they can be
trusted completely. Then they will make the teaching
about God our Savior appealing in every way.

11 God's saving grace has appeared to all people.
12 It teaches us to say no to godless ways and sinful longings. We must control ourselves. We must
do what is right. We must lead godly lives in
today's world. 13 That's how we should live as we
wait for the blessed hope God has given us.

We are waiting for Jesus Christ to appear in all
his glory. He is our great God and Savior. 14 He
gave himself for us. By doing that, he set us free
from all evil. He wanted to make us pure. He
wanted us to be his very own people. He wanted us
to long to do what is good.

15 Those are the things you should teach. Cheer
people up and give them hope. Correct them with
full authority. Don't let anyone look down on you.

Do What Is Good

3 Remind God's people to obey rulers and
authorities. Remind them to be ready to do
what is good. 2 Tell them not to speak evil things

against anyone. Remind them to live in peace. They must consider the needs of others. They must be kind and gentle toward all people.

3At one time we too acted like fools. We didn't obey God. We were tricked. We were controlled by all kinds of longings and pleasures. We were full of evil. We wanted what belongs to others. People hated us, and we hated one another.

4But the kindness and love of God our Savior appeared. 5He saved us. It wasn't because of the good things we had done. It was because of his mercy. He saved us by washing away our sins. We were born again. The Holy Spirit gave us new life. 6God poured out the Spirit on us freely because of what Jesus Christ our Savior has done. 7His grace made us right with God. So now we have received the hope of eternal life as God's children.

8You can trust that saying. Those things are important. Treat them that way. Then those who have trusted in God will be careful to commit themselves to doing what is good. Those things are excellent. They are for the good of everyone.

9But keep away from foolish disagreements. Don't argue about family histories. Don't make trouble. Don't fight about what the law teaches. Don't argue about things like that. It doesn't do any good. It doesn't help anyone.

10Warn anyone who tries to get believers to take sides and separate into their own little groups. Warn him more than once. After that, have nothing to do with him. 11You can be sure that someone like that is twisted and sinful. His own actions judge him.

Final Words

12I will send Artemas or Tychicus to you. Then do your best to come to me at Nicopolis. I've decided to spend the winter there.

13Do everything you can to help Zenas the lawyer and Apollos. Send them on their way. See that they have everything they need.

14Our people must learn to commit themselves to doing what is good. Then they will be able to provide for the daily needs of others. If they do that, their lives won't turn out to be useless.

15Everyone who is with me sends you greetings. Greet those who love us in the faith.

May God's grace be with you all.

Philemon

[1]I, Paul, am writing this letter. I am a prisoner
because of Christ Jesus. Our brother Timothy joins
me in writing.

Philemon, we are sending you this letter. You
are our dear friend. You work together with us.
[2]We are also sending it to our sister Apphia and to
Archippus. He is a soldier of Christ together with
us. And we are sending it to the church that meets
in your home.

[3]May God our Father and the Lord Jesus Christ
give you grace and peace.

Paul Prays and Gives Thanks

[4]I always thank my God when I remember you
in my prayers. [5]That's because I hear about your
faith in the Lord Jesus. I hear about your love for
all of God's people. [6]I pray that you will be active
in sharing what you believe. Then you will completely understand every good thing we have in
Christ.

[7]Your love has given me great joy. It has
cheered me up. My brother, you have renewed the
hearts of God's people.

Paul Makes an Appeal for Onesimus

[8]Because of the authority Christ has given me,
I could be bold. I could order you to do what you
should do anyway. [9]But I make my appeal to you
on the basis of our love for each other.

I, Paul, am an old man. I am now also a prisoner because of Christ Jesus. [10]I make an appeal to
you for my son Onesimus. He became a son to me
while I was being held by chains. [11]Before that, he
was useless to you. But now he has become useful
to you and to me.

[12]I'm sending Onesimus back to you. My very
heart goes with him. [13]I would have liked to keep
him with me. Then he could have taken your place
in helping me while I'm being held by chains
because of the good news. [14]But I didn't want to
do anything unless you agreed. Any favor you do
must be done because you want to do it, not
because you have to.

[15]Onesimus was separated from you for a little
while. Maybe that was so you could have him back
for good. [16]You could have him back not as a
slave. Instead, he would be better than a slave. He
would be a dear brother. He is very dear to me. But
he is even more dear to you, both as a man and as
a brother in the Lord.

[17]Do you think of me as a believer who works
together with you? Then welcome Onesimus as
you would welcome me. [18]Has he done anything
wrong to you? Does he owe you anything? Then
charge it to me. [19]I'll pay it back. I, Paul, am writing this with my own hand. I won't even mention
that you owe me your very life.

[20]My brother, I wish I could receive some benefit from you because we both belong to the Lord.
Renew my heart. We know that Christ is the one
who really renews it. [21]I'm sure you will obey. So
I'm writing to you. I know you will do even more
than I ask.

[22]There is one more thing. Have a guest room
ready for me. I hope I can return to all of you in
answer to your prayers.

[23]Epaphras sends you greetings. Together with
me, he is a prisoner because of Christ Jesus.
[24]Mark, Aristarchus, Demas and Luke work
together with me. They also send you greetings.

[25]May the grace of the Lord Jesus Christ be with
your spirit.

Hebrews

The Son Is Greater Than the Angels

1 In the past, God spoke to our people through
the prophets. He spoke at many times. He
spoke in different ways. 2But in these last days, he
has spoken to us through his Son. He is the one
whom God appointed to receive all things. God
made everything through him. 3The Son is the
gleaming brightness of God's glory. He is the exact
likeness of God's being. He uses his powerful word
to hold all things together. He provided the way for
people to be made pure from sin. Then he sat down
at the right hand of the King, the Majesty in
heaven. 4So he became higher than the angels. The
name he received is more excellent than theirs.
5God never said to any of the angels,

"You are my Son.
Today I have become your Father."
(Psalm 2:7)

Or,

"I will be his Father.
And he will be my Son."
(2 Samuel 7:14; 1 Chronicles 17:13)

6God's first and only Son is over all things.
When God brings him into the world, he says,

"Let all of God's angels worship him."
(Deuteronomy 32:43)

7Here is something else God says about the
angels.

"God makes his angels to be like winds.
He makes those who serve him to be like
flashes of lightning." *(Psalm 104:4)*

8But here is what he says about the Son.

"You are God. Your throne will last for ever
and ever.
Your kingdom will be ruled by what is right.
9 You have loved what is right and hated what
is evil.
So your God has placed you above your
companions.
He has filled you with joy by pouring the
sacred oil on your head." *(Psalm 45:6,7)*

10He also says,

"Lord, in the beginning you made the earth
secure. You placed it on its
foundations.
The heavens are the work of your hands.
11 They will pass away. But you remain.
They will all wear out like a piece of
clothing.
12 You will roll them up like a robe.
They will be changed as a person changes
clothes.
But you remain the same.
Your years will never end." *(Psalm 102:25–27)*

13God never said to an angel,

"Sit at my right hand
until I put your enemies
under your control." *(Psalm 110:1)*

14All angels are spirits who serve. God sends them
to serve those who will receive salvation.

A Warning to Pay Attention

2 So we must pay more careful attention to
what we have heard. Then we will not drift
away from it. 2Even the message God spoke
through angels had to be obeyed. Every time people broke the Law, they were punished. Every time
they didn't obey, they were punished. 3Then how
will we escape if we don't pay attention to God's
great salvation?

The Lord first announced that salvation. Those
who heard him gave us the message about it. 4God
gave witness to it through signs and wonders. He
gave witness through different kinds of miracles.
He also gave witness through the gifts of the Holy
Spirit. He gave them out as it pleased him.

Jesus Was Made Like His Brothers

5God has not put angels in charge of the world
that is going to come. We are talking about that
world. 6There is a place where someone has given
witness to it. He said,

"What is a human being that you think
about him?
What is the son of man that you take care
of him?
7 You made him a little lower than the angels.
You placed on him a crown of glory
and honor.
8 You have put everything under his control."
(Psalm 8:4–6)

So God has put everything under him. Everything
is under his control.

We do not now see everything under his control. 9But we do see Jesus already given a crown
of glory and honor. He was made a little lower
than the angels. He suffered death. By the grace of
God, he tasted death for everyone. That is why he
was given his crown.

10God has made everything. He has acted in
exactly the right way. He is bringing his many sons
and daughters to share in his glory. To do so, he
has made the One who saved them perfect because
of his sufferings.

11The One who makes people holy and the people he makes holy belong to the same family. So

Jesus is not ashamed to call them his brothers and
sisters. 12He says,

"I will announce your name to my brothers
and sisters.
I will sing your praises among those who
worship you." *(Psalm 22:22)*

13Again he says,

"I will put my trust in him." *(Isaiah 8:17)*

And again he says,

"Here I am. Here are the children God has
given me." *(Isaiah 8:18)*

14Those children have bodies made out of flesh
and blood. So Jesus became human like them in
order to die for them. By doing that, he could
destroy the one who rules over the kingdom of
death. I'm talking about the devil. 15Jesus could set
people free who were afraid of death. All their
lives they were held as slaves by that fear.

16It is certainly Abraham's children that he
helps. He doesn't help angels. 17So he had to be
made like his brothers in every way. Then he could
serve God as a kind and faithful high priest. And
then he could pay for the sins of the people by
dying for them.

18He himself suffered when he was tempted. Now
he is able to help others who are being tempted.

Jesus Is Greater Than Moses

3 Holy brothers and sisters, God chose you to
be his people. So keep thinking about Jesus.
He is our apostle. He is our high priest. We believe
in him.

2Moses was faithful in everything he did in the
house of God. In the same way, Jesus was faithful
to the One who appointed him.

3The person who builds a house has greater
honor than the house itself. In the same way, Jesus
has been found worthy of greater honor than Moses. 4Every house is built by someone. But God is
the builder of everything.

5Moses was faithful as one who serves in the
house of God. He gave witness to what God would
say in days to come. 6But Christ is faithful as a son
over God's house. We are his house if we continue
to come boldly to God. We must also hold on to
the hope we take pride in.

A Warning Against Unbelief

7The Holy Spirit says,

"Listen to his voice today.
8 If you hear it, don't be stubborn.
You were stubborn when you opposed me.
You did that when you were put to the test
in the desert.
9 There your people of long ago put me to
the test.
For 40 years they saw what I did.
10 That is why I was angry with them.
I said, 'Their hearts are always going down
the wrong path.
They have not known my ways.'
11 So in my anger I took an oath.
I said, 'They will never enjoy the rest I
planned for them.'" *(Psalm 95:7–11)*

12Brothers and sisters, make sure that none of
you has a sinful heart. Do not let an unbelieving
heart turn you away from the living God. 13But
build one another up every day. Do it as long as
there is still time. Then none of you will become
stubborn. You won't be fooled by sin's tricks.

14We belong to Christ if we hold firmly to the
faith we had at first. But we must hold to it until
the end. 15It has just been said,

"Listen to his voice today.
If you hear it, don't be stubborn.
You were stubborn when you opposed me."
(Psalm 95:7,8)

16Who were those who heard and refused to
obey? Weren't they all the people Moses led out of
Egypt? 17Who was God angry with for 40 years?
Wasn't it with those who sinned? They died in the
desert. 18What people did God promise with an
oath that they would never enjoy the rest he
planned for them? Wasn't it those who didn't obey?

19So we see that they weren't able to enter.
That's because they didn't believe.

God's People Enter His Sabbath Rest

4 God's promise of enjoying his rest still stands.
So be careful that none of you fails to receive it.

2The good news was preached to our people
long ago. It has also been preached to us. The message they heard didn't have any value for them.
They didn't combine it with faith. 3Now we who
have believed enjoy that rest. God said,

"When I was angry I took an oath.
I said, 'They will never enjoy the rest I
planned for them.'" *(Psalm 95:11)*

Ever since God created the world, his work has
been finished.

4Somewhere he spoke about the seventh day.
He said, "On the seventh day God rested from all
his work." *(Genesis 2:2)* 5In the part of Scripture I
talked about earlier God said, "They will never
enjoy the rest I planned for them." *(Psalm 95:11)*

6It is still true that some will enjoy that rest. But
those who had the good news preached to them earlier didn't go in. That was because they didn't obey.

7So God again chose a certain day. He named it
Today. He did that when he spoke through David
a long time later. As it was said earlier,

"Listen to his voice today.
If you hear it, don't be stubborn."
(Psalm 95:7,8)

8Suppose Joshua had given them rest. If he had,
God would not have spoken later about another day.
9So there is still a Sabbath rest for God's people.

10 God rested from his work. Those who enjoy God's rest also rest from their work. 11 So let us make every effort to enjoy that rest. Then no one will fall into sin by following the example of those who didn't obey God.

12 The word of God is living and active. It is sharper than any sword that has two edges. It cuts deep enough to separate soul from spirit. It can separate joints from bones. It judges the thoughts and purposes of the heart. 13 Nothing God created is hidden from him. His eyes see everything. He will hold us accountable for everything we do.

Jesus Is the Great High Priest

14 We have a great high priest. He has gone up into the heavens. He is Jesus the Son of God. So let us hold firmly to what we say we believe.

15 We have a high priest who can feel it when we are weak and hurting. We have a high priest who has been tempted in every way, just as we are. But he did not sin. 16 So let us boldly approach the throne of grace. Then we will receive mercy. We will find grace to help us when we need it.

5 Every high priest is chosen from among men. He is appointed to act for them in everything that has to do with God. He offers gifts and sacrifices for their sins. 2 He is able to deal gently with those who have gone down the wrong path without knowing it. He can do that because he himself is weak. 3 That's why he has to offer sacrifices for his own sins. He must also do it for the sins of the people.

4 No one can take that honor for himself. He must be appointed by God, just as Aaron was.

5 Even Christ did not take the glory of becoming a high priest for himself. God said to him,

"You are my Son.
  Today I have become your Father."
(Psalm 2:7)

6 In another place he said,

"You are a priest forever,
  just like Melchizedek." *(Psalm 110:4)*

7 Jesus prayed while he lived on earth. He made his appeal with loud cries and tears. He prayed to the One who could save him from death. God heard him because he truly honored God.

8 Jesus was God's Son. But by suffering he learned what it means to obey. 9 In that way he was made perfect. Eternal salvation comes from him. He saves all those who obey him.

10 God appointed him to be the high priest, just like Melchizedek.

A Warning Against Falling Away

11 We have a lot to say about that. But it is hard to explain it to you. You learn too slowly. 12 By this time you should be teachers. But in fact, you need someone to teach you all over again. You need even the simple truths of God's word. You need milk, not solid food. 13 Anyone who lives on milk is still a baby. That person does not want to learn about living a godly life. 14 Solid food is for those who are grown up. They have trained themselves with a lot of practice. They can tell the difference between good and evil.

6 So let us leave the simple teachings about Christ. Let us grow up as believers. Let us not start all over again with the basic teachings. They taught us that we need to turn away from doing things that lead to death. They taught us that we must have faith in God. 2 They taught us about different kinds of baptism. They taught us about placing hands on people. They taught us that people will rise from the dead. They taught us that God will judge everyone. And they taught us that what he decides will last forever.

3 If God permits, we will go beyond those teachings and grow up.

4 What if some people fall away from the faith? It won't be possible to bring them back. It is true that they have seen the light. They have tasted the heavenly gift. They have shared in the Holy Spirit. 5 They have tasted the good things of God's word. They have tasted the powers of the age to come. 6 But they have fallen away from the faith. So it won't be possible to bring them back. They won't be able to turn away from their sins. They are losing everything. That's because they are nailing the Son of God to the cross all over again. They are bringing shame on him in front of everyone.

7 Some land drinks the rain that falls on it. It produces a crop that is useful to those who farm the land. That land receives God's blessing. 8 But other land produces only thorns and weeds. That land isn't worth anything. It is in danger of coming under God's curse. In the end, it will be burned.

9 Dear friends, we have to say these things. But we are sure of better things in your case. We are talking about the things that go along with being saved.

10 God is fair. He will not forget what you have done. He will remember the love you have shown him. You showed it when you helped his people. And you show it when you keep on helping them.

11 We want each of you to be faithful to the very end. We want you to be sure of what you hope for. 12 We don't want you to slow down. Instead, be like those who have faith and are patient. They will receive what God promised.

God Keeps His Promise

13 When God made his promise to Abraham, he took an oath to keep it. But there was no one greater than himself to take an oath by. So he took his oath by making an appeal to himself.

14 He said, "I will certainly bless you. I will give you many children." *(Genesis 22:17)* 15 Abraham was patient while he waited. Then he received what God promised him.

16 People take oaths by someone greater than themselves. An oath makes a promise certain. It puts an end to all arguing. 17 So God took an oath

when he made his promise. He wanted to make it
very clear that his purpose does not change. He
wanted those who would receive what was promised to know that.
18God took an oath so we would have good reason not to give up. We have run away from everything else to take hold of the hope offered to us in
God's promise. So God gave his promise and his
oath. Those two things can't change. He couldn't
lie about them.
19Our hope is certain. It is something for the
soul to hold on to. It is strong and secure. It goes
all the way into the Most Holy Room behind the
curtain. 20That is where Jesus has gone. He went
there to open the way ahead of us. He has become
a high priest forever, just like Melchizedek.

Melchizedek the Priest

7 Melchizedek was the king of Salem. He was
the priest of God Most High. He met Abraham, who was returning from winning a battle
over some kings. Melchizedek blessed him. 2Abra-
ham gave him a tenth of everything.
First, the name Melchizedek means "king of
what is right." Also, "king of Salem" means "king
of peace." 3Melchizedek has no father or mother.
He has no family line. His days have no beginning.
His life has no end. He remains a priest forever,
just like the Son of God.
4Think how great Melchizedek was. Even our
father Abraham gave him a tenth of what he had captured. 5Now the law lays down a rule for the sons of
Levi who become priests. They must collect a tenth
from the people. They must collect it even from
those who belong to the family line of Abraham.
6Melchizedek did not trace his family line from
Levi. But he collected a tenth from Abraham. Melchizedek blessed the one who had received the
promises. 7Without a doubt, the more important
person blesses the less important one. 8In the one
case, the tenth is collected by men who die. But in
the other case, it is collected by the one who is said
to be living.
9Levi collects the tenth. But we might say that
Levi paid the tenth through Abraham. 10That's
because when Melchizedek met Abraham, Levi
was still in Abraham's body.

Jesus Is Like Melchizedek

11Suppose the Levites who were priests could
have made people perfect. The law was given to the
people so they could become perfect through the
priests. Then why was there still a need for another
priest to come? And why did he need to be like Melchizedek? Why wasn't he from Aaron's family line?
12A change of priests requires a change of law.
13Those things are said about one who is from a
different tribe. No one from that tribe has ever
served at the altar. 14It is clear that our Lord came
from the family line of Judah. Moses said nothing
about priests who were from that tribe.
15But suppose another priest like Melchizedek
appears. Then what we have said is even more
clear. 16He has not become a priest because of a
rule about his family line. He has become a priest
because of his powerful life. His life can never be
destroyed. 17Scripture says,

"You are a priest forever,
just like Melchizedek." *(Psalm 110:4)*

18The old rule is done away with. It was weak
and useless. 19The law didn't make anything perfect. Now a better hope has been given to us. That
hope brings us near to God.
20The change of priests was made with an oath.
Others became priests without any oath. 21But Jesus
became a priest with an oath. God said to him,

"The Lord has taken an oath and made
a promise.
He will not change his mind. He has said,
'You are a priest forever.'" *(Psalm 110:4)*

22Because of that oath, Jesus makes the promise of
a better covenant certain.
23There were many priests in Levi's family line.
Death kept them from continuing in office. 24But
Jesus lives forever. So he always holds the office
of priest. 25People now come to God through him.
And he is able to save them completely and for all
time. Jesus lives forever. He prays for them.
26A high priest like that meets our need. He is
holy, pure and without blame. He isn't like other
people. He does not sin. He is lifted high above the
heavens.
27He isn't like the other high priests. They need
to offer sacrifices day after day. First they bring
offerings for their own sins. Then they do it for the
sins of the people. But Jesus gave one sacrifice for
the sins of the people. He gave it once and for all
time. He did it by offering himself.
28The law appoints men who are weak to be
high priests. But God's oath came after the law.
The oath appointed the Son. He has been made
perfect forever.

The High Priest of a New Covenant

8 Here is the point of what we are saying. We
have a high priest like that. He sat down at the
right hand of the throne of the King, the Majesty in
heaven. 2He serves in the sacred tent. The Lord set
up the true holy tent. A mere man did not set it up.
3Every high priest is appointed to offer gifts and
sacrifices. So that priest also had to have something to offer.
4What if he were on earth? Then he would not
be a priest. There are already priests who offer the
gifts required by the law. 5They serve at a sacred
tent. But it is only a copy and shadow of what is in
heaven. That's why God warned Moses when he
was about to build the holy tent. God said, "Be
sure to make everything just like the pattern I
showed you on the mountain." *(Exodus 25:40)*

6 Jesus has been given a greater work to do for
God. He is the go-between for the new covenant.
That covenant is better than the old one. It is based
on better promises.

7 Suppose nothing had been wrong with that first
covenant. Then no one would have looked for
another covenant. 8 But God found fault with the
people. He said,

"A new day is coming, says the Lord.
I will make a new covenant
with the people of Israel.
I will also make it with the people of Judah.
9 It will not be like the covenant
I made with their people of long ago.
That was when I took them by the hand.
I led them out of Egypt.
My new covenant will be different because
they didn't remain faithful to my old
covenant.
So I turned away from them,
says the Lord.
10 This is the covenant I will make with Israel
after that time, says the Lord.
I will put my laws in their minds.
I will write them on their hearts.
I will be their God.
And they will be my people.
11 A man will not teach his neighbor anymore.
And he will not teach his friend anymore.
He will not say, 'Know the Lord.'
Everyone will know me.
From the least important of them to the most
important,
all of them will know me.
12 I will forgive their evil ways.
I will not remember their sins anymore."
(Jeremiah 31:31–34)

13 God called that covenant "new." So he has
made the first one out of date. And what is out of
date and getting older will soon disappear.

Worship in the Holy Tent on Earth

9 The first covenant had rules for worship. It
also had a sacred tent on earth.

2 A holy tent was set up. The lampstand was in
the first room. So were the table and the holy
bread. That was called the Holy Room. 3 Behind
the second curtain was a room called the Most
Holy Room. 4 It had the golden altar for incense. It
also had the wooden chest called the ark of the
covenant. The ark was covered with gold. It held
the gold jar of manna. It held Aaron's wooden staff
that had budded. It also held the stone tablets. The
words of the covenant were written on them.

5 The cherubim were above the ark. God showed
his glory there. The cherubim spread their wings
over the place where sin was paid for. But we can't
deal with those things more completely now.

6 That's how everything was arranged in the
holy tent. The priests entered it at regular times.
They went into the outer room to do their work for
God and others. 7 But only the high priest went into
the inner room. He went in only once a year. He
never entered without taking blood with him. He
offered the blood for himself. He also offered it for
the sins the people had committed because they
didn't know any better.

8 Here is what the Holy Spirit was showing us.
He was telling us that God had not yet clearly
shown the way into the Most Holy Room. It would
not be clearly shown as long as the first holy tent
was still standing.

9 That's an example for the present time. It
shows us that the gifts and sacrifices they offered
were not enough. They were not able to remove
the worshiper's feelings of guilt. 10 They deal only
with food and drink and different kinds of special
washings. They are rules that deal with things outside our bodies. People had to obey them only
until the new covenant came.

The Blood of Christ

11 Christ came to be the high priest of the good
things that are already here. When he came, he
went through the greater and more perfect holy
tent. The tent was not made by people. In other
words, it is not a part of this creation.

12 He did not enter by spilling the blood of goats
and calves. He entered the Most Holy Room by
spilling his own blood. He did it once and for all
time. He paid the price to set us free from sin
forever.

13 The blood of goats and bulls is sprinkled on
people. So are the ashes of a young cow. They are
sprinkled on people the Law called unclean. The
people are sprinkled to make them holy. That
makes them clean on the outside.

14 But Christ offered himself to God without any
flaw. He did this through the power of the eternal
Holy Spirit. So how much more will his blood
wash from our minds our feelings of guilt for committing sin! Sin always leads to death. But now we
can serve the living God.

15 That's why Christ is the go-between of a new
covenant. Now those God calls to himself will
receive the eternal gift he promised. They will
receive it now that Christ has died to save them.
He died to set them free from the sins they committed under the first covenant.

16 What happens in the case of a will? It is necessary to prove that the person who made the will has
died. 17 A will is in effect only when somebody has
died. It never takes effect while the one who made
it is still living. 18 That's why even the first covenant
was not put into effect without the spilling of blood.

19 Moses first announced every commandment of
the law to all the people. Then he took the blood of
calves. He also took water, bright red wool and
branches of a hyssop plant. He sprinkled the scroll.
He also sprinkled all of the people. 20 He said, "This
is the blood of the covenant God has commanded

you to keep." *(Exodus 24:8)* 21 In the same way, he
sprinkled the holy tent with blood. He also sprinkled everything that was used in worship there.
22 In fact, the law requires that nearly everything
be made clean with blood. Without the spilling of
blood, no one can be forgiven.
23 So the copies of the heavenly things had to be
made pure with those sacrifices. But the heavenly
things themselves had to be made pure with better
sacrifices.
24 Christ did not enter a sacred tent made by people. That tent was only a copy of the true one. He
entered heaven itself. He did it to stand in front of
God for us. He is there right now.
25 The high priest enters the Most Holy Room
every year. He enters with blood that is not his own.
But Christ did not enter heaven to offer himself
again and again. 26 If he had, he would have had to
suffer many times since the world was created. But
now he has appeared once and for all time. He has
come at the end of the ages to do away with sin. He
has done that by offering himself.
27 People have to die once. After that, God will
judge them. 28 In the same way, Christ was offered
up once. He took away the sins of many people.

He will also come a second time. At that time
he will not suffer for sin. Instead, he will come to
bring salvation to those who are waiting for him.

Christ's Sacrifice Is Once and for All Time

10 The law is only a shadow of the good
things that are coming. It is not the real
things themselves. The same sacrifices have to be
offered over and over again. They must be offered
year after year. That's why the law can never make
perfect those who come near to worship. 2 If it
could, wouldn't the sacrifices have stopped being
offered? The worshipers would have been made
clean once and for all time. They would not have
felt guilty for their sins anymore.
3 But those offerings remind people of their sins
every year. 4 It isn't possible for the blood of bulls
and goats to take away sins.
5 So when Christ came into the world, he said,

"You didn't want sacrifices and offerings.
Instead, you prepared a body for me.
6 You weren't pleased
with burnt offerings and sin offerings.
7 Then I said, 'Here I am. It is written about me
in the scroll.
God, I have come to do what you want.'"
(Psalm 40:6–8)

8 First Christ said, "You didn't want sacrifices
and offerings. You didn't want burnt offerings and
sin offerings. You weren't pleased with them." He
said that even though the law required people to
bring them. 9 Then he said, "Here I am. I have
come to do what you want." He did away with the
first. He did it to put the second in place.

10 We have been made holy by what God
wanted. We have been made holy because Jesus
Christ offered his body once and for all time.
11 Day after day every priest stands and does his
special duties. He offers the same sacrifices again
and again. But they can never take away sins.
12 Jesus our priest offered one sacrifice for sins
for all time. Then he sat down at the right hand of
God. 13 Since that time, he waits for his enemies to
be put under his control. 14 By that one sacrifice he
has made perfect forever those who are being
made holy.
15 The Holy Spirit also gives witness to us about
this. First he says,

16 "This is the covenant I will make with them
after that time, says the Lord.
I will put my laws in their hearts.
I will write my laws on their minds."
(Jeremiah 31:33)

17 Then he adds,

"I will not remember their sins anymore.
I will not remember the evil things they
have done." *(Jeremiah 31:34)*

18 Where those have been forgiven, there is no
longer any offering for sin.

A Warning to Remain Faithful

19 Brothers and sisters, we are not afraid to enter
the Most Holy Room. We enter boldly because of
the blood of Jesus. 20 His way is new because he
lives. It has been opened for us through the curtain. I'm talking about his body.
21 We also have a great priest over the house of
God. 22 So let us come near to God with an honest
and true heart. Let us come near with a faith that is
sure and strong. Our hearts have been sprinkled.
Our minds have been cleansed from a sense of guilt.
Our bodies have been washed with pure water.
23 Let us hold firmly to the hope we claim to
have. The One who promised is faithful.
24 Let us consider how we can stir up one
another to love. Let us help one another to do good
works. 25 Let us not give up meeting together.
Some are in the habit of doing this. Instead, let us
cheer each other up with words of hope. Let us do
it all the more as you see the day coming when
Christ will return.
26 What if we keep sinning on purpose? What if
we do it even after we know the truth? Then there
is no offering for our sins. 27 All we can do is to
wait in fear for God to judge. His blazing fire will
burn up his enemies.
28 Anyone who did not obey the law of Moses
died without mercy if there were two or three witnesses. 29 What should be done to anyone who has
hated the Son of God or has said no to him? What
should be done to a person who treated as an
unholy thing the blood of the covenant that makes
him holy? What should be done to someone who
has made fun of the Holy Spirit who brings God's

grace? Don't you think people like that should be punished more than anyone else?

30We know the One who said, "I am the One who judges people. I will pay them back." *(Deuteronomy 32:35)* Scripture also says, "The Lord will judge his people." *(Deuteronomy 32:36; Psalm 135:14)*

31It is a terrible thing to fall into the hands of the living God.

32Remember those earlier days after you received the light. At that time you stood firm in a great struggle. You did it even in the face of suffering.

33Sometimes you were made fun of in front of others. You were treated badly. At other times you stood side by side with people who were being treated like that. 34You suffered together with people in prison. When your property was taken from you, you accepted it with joy. You knew that God had given you better and more lasting things.

35So don't throw away your bold faith. It will bring you rich rewards. 36You need to be faithful. Then you will do what God wants. You will receive what he has promised. 37In just a very little while,

"The one who is coming will come. He will
not wait.
38 The one who is in the right will live
by faith.
If he pulls back,
I will not be pleased with him."
(Habakkuk 2:3,4)

39But we aren't people who pull back and are destroyed. We are people who believe and are saved.

Living by Faith

11 Faith is being sure of what we hope for. It is being certain of what we do not see. 2That is what the people of long ago were praised for.

3We have faith. So we understand that everything was made when God commanded it. That's why we believe that what we see was not made out of what could be seen.

4Abel had faith. So he offered to God a better sacrifice than Cain did. Because of his faith Abel was praised as a godly man. God said good things about his offerings. Because of his faith Abel still speaks. He speaks even though he is dead.

5Enoch had faith. So he was taken from this life. He didn't die. He just couldn't be found. God had taken him away. Before God took him, Enoch was praised as one who pleased God.

6Without faith it isn't possible to please God. Those who come to God must believe that he exists. And they must believe that he rewards those who look to him.

7Noah had faith. So he built an ark to save his family. He built it because of his great respect for God. God had warned him about things that could not yet be seen. Because of his faith he showed the world that it was guilty. Because of his faith he was considered right with God.

8Abraham had faith. So he obeyed God. God called him to go to a place he would later receive as his own. So he went. He did it even though he didn't know where he was going. 9Because of his faith he made his home in the land God had promised him. He was like an outsider in a strange country. He lived there in tents. So did Isaac and Jacob. They received the same promise he did. 10Abraham was looking forward to the city that has foundations. He was waiting for the city that God planned and built.

11Abraham had faith. So God made it possible for him to become a father. He became a father even though he was too old. Sarah also was too old to have children. But Abraham believed that the One who made the promise was faithful. 12Abraham was past the time when he could have children. But many children came from that one man. They were as many as the stars in the sky. They were as many as the sand on the seashore. No one could count them.

13All those people were still living by faith when they died. They didn't receive the things God had promised. They only saw them and welcomed them from a long way off. They openly said that they were outsiders and strangers on earth.

14People who say things like that show that they are looking for a country of their own. 15What if they had been thinking of the country they had left? Then they could have returned to it. 16Instead, they longed for a better country. They wanted one in heaven.

So God is pleased when they call him their God. In fact, he has prepared a city for them.

17Abraham had faith. So he offered Isaac as a sacrifice. That happened when God put him to the test. Abraham had received the promises. But he was about to offer his one and only son. 18God had said to him, "Your family line will continue through Isaac." *(Genesis 21:12)* Even so, Abraham was going to offer him up. 19Abraham believed that God could raise the dead. In a way, he did receive Isaac back from death.

20Isaac had faith. So he blessed Jacob and Esau. He told them what was ahead for them.

21Jacob had faith. So he blessed each of Joseph's sons. He blessed them when he was dying. Because of his faith he worshiped God as he leaned on the top of his wooden staff.

22Joseph had faith. So he spoke to the people of Israel about their leaving Egypt. He gave directions about his bones. He did that toward the end of his life.

23Moses' parents had faith. So they hid him for three months after he was born. They saw he was a special child. They were not afraid of the king's command.

24Moses had faith. So he refused to be called the son of Pharaoh's daughter. That happened after he had grown up. 25He chose to be treated badly together with the people of God. He chose that instead of enjoying sin's pleasures for a short time. 26 He suffered shame because of Christ. He thought it had great value. He considered it better than the riches of Egypt. He was looking ahead to God's reward.

27 Because of his faith he left Egypt. It wasn't because he was afraid of the king's anger. He didn't let anything stop him. He saw the One who can't be seen.

28 Because of his faith he was the first to keep the Passover Feast. He commanded the people of Israel to sprinkle blood on their doorways. He did it so that the destroying angel would not touch their oldest sons.

29 The people had faith. So they passed through the Red Sea. They went through it as if it were dry land. The Egyptians tried to do it also. But they drowned.

30 The people had faith. So the walls of Jericho fell down. It happened after they had marched around the city for seven days.

31 Rahab, the prostitute, had faith. So she welcomed the spies. That's why she wasn't killed with those who didn't obey God.

32 What more can I say? I don't have time to tell about all the others. I don't have time to talk about Gideon, Barak, Samson and Jephthah. I don't have time to tell about David, Samuel and the prophets. 33 Because of their faith they took over kingdoms. They ruled fairly. They received the blessings God had promised. They shut the mouths of lions. 34 They put out great fires. They escaped being killed by the sword. Their weakness was turned to strength. They became powerful in battle. They beat back armies from other countries.

35 Women received their dead back. The dead were raised to life again. Others were made to suffer greatly. But they refused to be set free. They did that so that after death they would be raised to a better life.

36 Some were laughed at. Some were whipped. Still others were held by chains. They were put in prison. 37 Some were killed with stones. They were sawed in two. They were put to death by the sword. They went around wearing the skins of sheep and goats. They were poor. They were attacked. They were treated badly. 38 The world was not worthy of them. They wandered in deserts and mountains. They lived in caves. They lived in holes in the ground.

39 All of those people were praised because they had faith. But none of them received what God had promised. 40 God had planned something better for us. So they would only be made perfect together with us.

12 A huge cloud of witnesses is all around us. So let us throw off everything that stands in our way. Let us throw off any sin that holds on to us so tightly. Let us keep on running the race marked out for us.

2 Let us keep looking to Jesus. He is the author of faith. He also makes it perfect. He paid no attention to the shame of the cross. He suffered there because of the joy he was looking forward to. Then he sat down at the right hand of the throne of God.

3 He put up with attacks from sinners. So think about him. Then you won't get tired. You won't lose hope.

God Trains His Children

4 You struggle against sin. But you have not yet fought to the point of spilling your blood. 5 You have forgotten that word of hope. It speaks to you as children. It says,

"My son, think of the Lord's training as
important.
Do not lose hope when he corrects you.
6 The Lord trains those he loves.
He punishes everyone he accepts as a son."
(Proverbs 3:11,12)

7 Put up with hard times. God uses them to train you. He is treating you as children. What children are not trained by their parents? 8 God trains all of his children. But what if he doesn't train you? Then you are like children of people who weren't married to each other. You are not truly God's children.

9 Besides, we have all had human parents who trained us. We respected them for it. How much more should we be trained by the Father of our spirits and live!

10 Our parents trained us for a little while. They did what they thought was best. But God trains us for our good. He wants us to share in his holiness.

11 No training seems pleasant at the time. In fact, it seems painful. But later on it produces a harvest of godliness and peace. It does that for those who have been trained by it.

12 So lift your sagging arms. Strengthen your weak knees. 13 "Make level paths for your feet to walk on." *(Proverbs 4:26)* Then those who have trouble walking won't be disabled. Instead, they will be healed.

A Warning Against Saying No to God

14 Try your best to live in peace with everyone. Try to be holy. Without holiness no one will see the Lord.

15 Be sure that no one misses God's grace. See to it that a bitter plant doesn't grow up. If it does, it will cause trouble. And it will pollute many people. 16 See to it that no one commits sexual sins.

See to it that no one is godless like Esau. He sold the rights to what he would receive as the oldest son. He sold them for a single meal. 17 As you know, after that he wanted to receive his father's blessing. But he was turned away. With tears he tried to get the blessing. But he couldn't get his father to change his mind.

18 You haven't come to a mountain that can be touched. You haven't come to a mountain that is

burning with fire. You haven't come to darkness, gloom and storm. 19You haven't come to a blast from God's trumpet. You haven't come to a voice speaking to you. When people heard that voice long ago, they begged it not to say anything more to them. 20What God commanded was too much for them. He said, "If even an animal touches the mountain, it must be killed with stones." *(Exodus 19:12,13)* 21The sight was terrifying. Moses said, "I am trembling with fear." *(Deuteronomy 9:19)*

22But you have come to Mount Zion. You have come to the Jerusalem in heaven. It is the city of the living God. You have come to a joyful gathering of angels. There are thousands and thousands of them. 23You have come to the church of God's people. God's first and only Son is over all things. God's people share in what belongs to his Son. Their names are written in heaven. You have come to God. He is the judge of all people.

You have come to the spirits of godly people who have been made perfect. 24You have come to Jesus. He is the go-between of a new covenant. You have come to the sprinkled blood. It promises better things than the blood of Abel.

25Be sure that you don't say no to the One who speaks. People did not escape when they said no to the One who warned them on earth. And what if we turn away from the One who warns us from heaven? How much less will we escape!

26At that time his voice shook the earth. But now he has promised, "Once more I will shake the earth. I will also shake the heavens." *(Haggai 2:6)* 27The words "once more" point out that what can be shaken can be taken away. I'm talking about created things. Then what can't be shaken will remain.

28We are receiving a kingdom that can't be shaken. So let us be thankful. Then we can worship God in a way that pleases him. We will worship him with deep respect and wonder. 29Our "God is like a fire that burns everything up." *(Deuteronomy 4:24)*

Final Words

13 Keep on loving each other as brothers and sisters. 2Don't forget to welcome strangers. By doing that, some people have welcomed angels without knowing it.

3Remember those in prison as if you were in prison with them. And remember those who are treated badly as if you yourselves were suffering.

4All of you should honor marriage. You should keep the marriage bed pure. God will judge the person who commits adultery. He will judge everyone who commits sexual sins.

5Don't be controlled by love for money. Be happy with what you have. God has said,

"I will never leave you.
I will never desert you." *(Deuteronomy 31:6)*

6So we can say boldly,

"The Lord helps me. I will not be afraid.
What can a mere man do to me?"
(Psalm 118:6,7)

7Remember your leaders. They spoke God's word to you. Think about the results of their way of life. Copy their faith.

8Jesus Christ is the same yesterday and today and forever.

9Don't be carried away by all kinds of strange teachings. It is good that God's grace makes our hearts strong. Don't depend on foods the Law requires. They have no value for the people who eat them. 10Some worship at the holy tent. But we have an altar that they have no right to eat from.

11The high priest carries the blood of animals into the Most Holy Room. He brings their blood as a sin offering. But the bodies are burned outside the camp. 12Jesus also suffered outside the city gate. He suffered to make the people holy by spilling his own blood.

13So let us go to him outside the camp. Let us be willing to suffer the shame he suffered. 14Here we do not have a city that lasts. But we are looking for the city that is going to come.

15So let us never stop offering to God our praise through Jesus. Let us offer it as the fruit of lips that say they believe in him.

16Don't forget to do good. Don't forget to share with others. God is pleased with those kinds of offerings.

17Obey your leaders. Put yourselves under their authority. They keep watch over you. They know they are accountable to God for everything they do. Obey them so that their work will be a joy. If you make their work a heavy load, it won't do you any good.

18Pray for us. We feel sure we have done what is right. We long to live as we should in every way. 19I beg you to pray that I may return to you soon.

20Our Lord Jesus is the great Shepherd of the sheep. The God who gives peace brought him back from the dead. He did it because of the blood of the eternal covenant. May God 21supply you with everything good. Then you can do what he wants. May he do in us what is pleasing to him. We can do it only with the help of Jesus Christ. Give him glory for ever and ever. Amen.

22Brothers and sisters, I beg you to accept my word. It tells you to be faithful. I have written you only a short letter.

23I want you to know that our brother Timothy has been set free. If he arrives soon, I will come with him to see you.

24Greet all of your leaders. Greet all of God's people. The believers from Italy send you their greetings.

25May grace be with you all.

James

1 I, James, am writing this letter. I serve God
and the Lord Jesus Christ.
I am sending this letter to you, the 12 tribes that
are scattered among the nations.
Greetings.

Facing All Kinds of Trouble

2 My brothers and sisters, you will face all kinds
of trouble. When you do, think of it as pure joy.
3 Your faith will be put to the test. You know that
when that happens it will produce in you the strength
to continue. 4 The strength to keep going must be
allowed to finish its work. Then you will be all you
should be. You will have everything you need.
5 If any of you need wisdom, ask God for it. He
will give it to you. God gives freely to everyone.
He doesn't find fault.
6 But when you ask, you must believe. You must
not doubt. People who doubt are like waves of the
sea. The wind blows and tosses them around. 7 A
man like that shouldn't expect to receive anything
from the Lord. 8 He can't make up his mind. He can
never decide what to do.
9 A believer who finds himself in a low position
in life should be proud that God has given him a
high position. 10 But someone who is rich should
take pride in his low position. That's because he
will fade away like a wild flower.
11 The sun rises. Its burning heat dries up the
plants. Their blossoms fall. Their beauty is destroyed. In the same way, a rich person will fade
away even as he goes about his business.
12 Blessed is the man who keeps on going when
times are hard. After he has come through them,
he will receive a crown. The crown is life itself.
God has promised it to those who love him.
13 When you are tempted, you shouldn't say,
"God is tempting me." God can't be tempted by
evil. And he doesn't tempt anyone.
14 But your own evil longings tempt you. They
lead you on and drag you away. 15 When they are
allowed to grow, they give birth to sin. When sin
has grown up, it gives birth to death.
16 My dear brothers and sisters, don't let anyone
fool you. 17 Every good and perfect gift is from
God. It comes down from the Father. He created
the heavenly lights. He does not change like shadows that move.
18 God chose to give us new birth through the
message of truth. He wanted us to be the first and
best of everything he created.

Listen to the Word and Do What It Says

19 My dear brothers and sisters, pay attention to
what I say. Everyone should be quick to listen. But
they should be slow to speak. They should be slow
to get angry. 20 A man's anger doesn't produce the
kind of life God wants.
21 So get rid of everything that is dirty and sinful. Get rid of the evil that is all around us. Don't
be too proud to accept the word that is planted in
you. It can save you.
22 Don't just listen to the word. You fool yourselves if you do that. You must do what it says.
23 Suppose you listen to the word but don't do
what it says. Then you are like a man who looks at
his face in a mirror. 24 After looking at himself, he
leaves. Right away he forgets what he looks like.
25 But suppose you take a good look at the perfect law that gives freedom. You keep looking at it.
You don't forget what you've heard, but you do
what the law says. Then you will be blessed in
what you do.
26 Suppose you think your beliefs are right
because of how you live. But you don't control
what you say. Then you are fooling yourselves.
Your beliefs are not worth anything at all.
27 Here are the kinds of beliefs that God our
Father accepts as pure and without fault. When
widows and children who have no parents are in
trouble, take care of them. And keep yourselves
from being polluted by the world.

Treat Everyone the Same

2 My brothers and sisters, you are believers in
our glorious Lord Jesus Christ. So treat everyone the same.
2 Suppose a man comes into your meeting wearing a gold ring and fine clothes. And suppose a
poor man in worn-out clothes also comes in.
3 Would you show special attention to the one who
is wearing fine clothes? Would you say, "Here's a
good seat for you"? Would you say to the poor person, "You stand there"? Or "Sit on the floor by my
feet"? 4 If you would, aren't you treating some people better than others? Aren't you like judges who
have evil thoughts?
5 My dear brothers and sisters, listen to me.
Hasn't God chosen those who are poor in the
world's eyes to be rich in faith? Hasn't he chosen
them to receive the kingdom? Hasn't he promised
it to those who love him?
6 But you have put poor people down. Aren't
rich people taking advantage of you? Aren't they
dragging you into court? 7 Aren't they speaking
evil things against the worthy name of Jesus?
Remember, you belong to him.
8 The royal law is found in Scripture. It says,
"Love your neighbor as you love yourself."
(Leviticus 19:18) If you really keep that law, you are
doing what is right. 9 But you sin if you don't treat

everyone the same. The law judges you because you have broken it.

10 Suppose you keep the whole law but trip over just one part of it. Then you are guilty of breaking all of it. 11 God said, "Do not commit adultery." *(Exodus 20:14; Deuteronomy 5:18)* He also said, "Do not commit murder." *(Exodus 20:13; Deuteronomy 5:17)* Suppose you don't commit adultery but do commit murder. Then you have broken the Law.

12 Speak and act like people who are going to be judged by the law that gives freedom. 13 Those who have not shown mercy will not receive mercy when they are judged. To show mercy is better than to judge.

Show Your Faith by What You Do

14 My brothers and sisters, what good is it if people claim they have faith but don't act like it? Can that kind of faith save them?

15 Suppose a brother or sister has no clothes or food. 16 Suppose one of you says to them, "Go. I hope everything turns out fine for you. Keep warm. Eat well." And you do nothing about what they really need. Then what good have you done?

17 It is the same with faith. If it doesn't cause us to do something, it's dead.

18 But someone will say, "You have faith. I do good works."

Show me your faith that doesn't do good works. And I will show you my faith by what I do. 19 You believe there is one God. Good! Even the demons believe that. And they tremble!

20 You foolish man! Do you want proof that faith without good works is useless? 21 Our father Abraham offered his son Isaac on the altar. Wasn't he considered to be right with God because of what he did? 22 So you see that what he believed and what he did were working together. What he did made his faith complete.

23 That is what Scripture means where it says, "Abraham believed God. God accepted Abraham because he believed. So his faith made him right with God." *(Genesis 15:6)* And that's not all. God called Abraham his friend. 24 So you see that a person is made right with God by what he does. It doesn't happen only because of what he believes.

25 Didn't God make even Rahab the prostitute right with him? That's because of what she did. She gave the spies a place to stay. Then she sent them off in a different direction.

26 The body without the spirit is dead. In the same way, faith without good works is dead.

Control What You Say

3

My brothers and sisters, most of you shouldn't want to be teachers. You know that those of us who teach will be held more accountable.

2 All of us get tripped up in many ways. Suppose someone is never wrong in what he says. Then he is a perfect man. He is able to keep his whole body under control.

3 We put a bit in the mouth of a horse to make it obey us. We can control the whole animal with it. 4 And how about ships? They are very big. They are driven along by strong winds. But they are steered by a very small rudder. It makes them go where the captain wants to go.

5 In the same way, the tongue is a small part of the body. But it brags a lot. Think about how a small spark can set a big forest on fire.

6 The tongue also is a fire. The tongue is the most evil part of the body. It pollutes the whole person. It sets a person's whole way of life on fire. And the tongue is set on fire by hell.

7 People have controlled all kinds of animals, birds, reptiles and creatures of the sea. They still control them. 8 But no one can control the tongue. It is an evil thing that never rests. It is full of deadly poison.

9 With our tongues we praise our Lord and Father. With our tongues we call down curses on people. We do it even though they have been created to be like God. 10 Praise and cursing come out of the same mouth. My brothers and sisters, it shouldn't be that way.

11 Can fresh water and salt water flow out of the same spring? 12 My brothers and sisters, can a fig tree bear olives? Can a grapevine bear figs? Of course not. And a saltwater spring can't produce fresh water either.

Two Kinds of Wisdom

13 Are any of you wise and understanding? You should show it by living a good life. Wise people aren't proud when they do good works.

14 But suppose your hearts are jealous and bitter. Suppose you are concerned only about getting ahead. Don't brag about it. Don't say no to the truth. 15 Wisdom like that doesn't come down from heaven. It belongs to the earth. It doesn't come from the Holy Spirit. It comes from the devil.

16 Are you jealous? Are you concerned only about getting ahead? Then your life will be a mess. You will be doing all kinds of evil things.

17 But the wisdom that comes from heaven is pure. That's the most important thing about it. And that's not all. It also loves peace. It thinks about others. It obeys. It is full of mercy and good fruit. It is fair. It doesn't pretend to be what it is not.

18 Those who make peace should plant peace like a seed. If they do, it will produce a crop of right living.

Obey God

4

Why do you fight and argue among yourselves? Isn't it because of your sinful longings? They fight inside you.

2 You want something, but you can't get it. You kill and want what others have. But you can't have what you want. You argue and fight. You don't have what you want, because you don't ask God. 3 When you do ask for something, you don't

receive it. Why? Because you ask for the wrong reason. You want to spend your money on your sinful pleasures.

4You are not faithful to God. Don't you know that to be a friend of the world is to hate God? Anyone who chooses to be a friend of the world becomes an enemy of God. 5Don't you know what Scripture says? The spirit that God caused to live in us wants us to belong only to God. Don't you think Scripture has a reason for saying that? 6God continues to give us more grace. That's why Scripture says,

"God opposes those who are proud.
But he gives grace to those who are not."
(Proverbs 3:34)

7So obey God. Stand up to the devil. He will run away from you. 8Come near to God, and he will come near to you. Wash your hands, you sinners. Make your hearts pure, you who can't make up your minds.

9Be full of sorrow. Cry and sob. Change your laughter to crying. Change your joy to sadness. 10Bow down to the Lord. He will lift you up.

11My brothers and sisters, don't speak against one another. Anyone who speaks against another believer speaks against the law. And anyone who judges another believer judges the law. When you judge the law, you are not keeping it. Instead, you are acting as if you were its judge.

12There is only one Lawgiver and Judge. He is the One who is able to save life or destroy it. But who are you to judge your neighbor?

Bragging About Tomorrow

13Now listen, you who say, "Today or tomorrow we will go to this or that city. We will spend a year there. We will buy and sell and make money." 14You don't even know what will happen tomorrow. What is your life? It is a mist that appears for a little while. Then it disappears. 15Instead, you should say, "If it pleases the Lord, we will live and do this or that."

16As it is, you are proud. You brag about it. That kind of bragging is evil. 17So when you know the good things you should do and don't do them, you sin.

A Warning to Rich People

5 You rich people, listen to me. Cry and sob, because you will soon be suffering.

2Your riches have rotted. Moths have eaten your clothes. 3Your gold and silver have lost their brightness. Their dullness will give witness against you. Your wanting more and more will eat your body like fire. You have stored up riches in these last days.

4You have even failed to pay the workers who mowed your fields. Their pay is crying out against you. The cries of those who gathered the harvest have reached the ears of the Lord who rules over all.

5You have lived an easy life on earth. You have given yourselves everything you wanted. You have made yourselves fat like cattle that will soon be butchered. 6You have judged and murdered people who aren't guilty. And they weren't even opposing you.

Be Patient When You Suffer

7Brothers and sisters, be patient until the Lord comes. See how the farmer waits for the land to produce its rich crop. See how patient he is for the fall and spring rains. 8You too must be patient. You must stand firm. The Lord will soon come back.

9Brothers and sisters, don't find fault with one another. If you do, you will be judged. And the Judge is standing at the door!

10Brothers and sisters, think about the prophets who spoke in the name of the Lord. They are an example of how to be patient when you suffer. 11As you know, we think that people who don't give up are blessed. You have heard that Job was patient. And you have seen what the Lord finally did for him. The Lord is full of tender mercy and loving concern.

12My brothers and sisters, don't take an oath when you make a promise. Don't call on heaven or earth or anything else to back up what you say. Let your "Yes" be yes. And let your "No" be no. If you don't, you will be judged.

The Prayer of Faith

13Are any of you in trouble? Then you should pray. Are any of you happy? Then sing songs of praise.

14Are any of you sick? Then send for the elders of the church to pray over you. Ask them to anoint you with oil in the name of the Lord. 15The prayer offered by those who have faith will make you well. The Lord will heal you. If you have sinned, you will be forgiven.

16So admit to one another that you have sinned. Pray for one another so that you might be healed. The prayer of a godly person is powerful. It makes things happen.

17Elijah was just like us. He prayed hard that it wouldn't rain. And it didn't rain on the land for three and a half years. 18Then he prayed again. That time it rained. And the earth produced its crops.

19My brothers and sisters, suppose one of you wanders away from the truth and someone brings you back. 20Then here is what I want everyone to remember. Anyone who turns a sinner from going down the wrong path will save him from death. God will erase many sins by forgiving him.

1 Peter

1 I, Peter, am writing this letter. I am an apostle of Jesus Christ.

I am sending this letter to you, God's chosen people. You are strangers in the world. You are scattered all over Pontus, Galatia, Cappadocia, Asia and Bithynia. [2]You have been chosen in keeping with what God the Father had planned. That happened through the Spirit's work to make you pure and holy. God chose you so that you might obey Jesus Christ. He wanted you to be made clean by the blood of Christ.

May more and more grace and peace be given to you.

Peter Praises God for a Hope That Is Alive

[3]Give praise to the God and Father of our Lord Jesus Christ. In his great mercy he has given us a new birth and a hope that is alive. It is alive because Jesus Christ rose from the dead. [4]He has given us new birth so that we might share in what belongs to him. It is a gift that can never be destroyed. It can never spoil or even fade away. It is kept in heaven for you. [5]Through faith you are kept safe by God's power. Your salvation is going to be completed. It is ready to be shown to you in the last days.

[6]Because you know this, you have great joy. You have joy even though you may have had to suffer for a little while. You may have had to suffer sadness in all kinds of trouble.

[7]Your troubles have come in order to prove that your faith is real. It is worth more than gold. Gold can pass away even though fire has made it pure. Your faith is meant to bring praise, honor and glory to God. That will happen when Jesus Christ returns.

[8]Even though you have not seen him, you love him. Though you do not see him now, you believe in him. You are filled with a glorious joy that can't be put into words. [9]You are receiving the salvation of your souls. It is the result of your faith.

[10]The prophets searched very hard and with great care to find out about that salvation. They spoke about the grace that was going to come to you. [11]They wanted to find out when that salvation would come. The Spirit of Christ in them was telling them about the sufferings of Christ that were going to come. He was also telling them about the glory that would follow.

[12]It was made known to the prophets that they were not serving themselves. Instead, they were serving you when they spoke about the things that you have now heard. Those who have preached the good news to you have told you those things. They have done it with the help of the Holy Spirit sent from heaven. Even angels long to look into those things.

Be Holy

[13]So prepare your minds for action. Control yourselves. Put your hope completely in the grace that will be given to you when Jesus Christ returns.

[14]You should obey. You shouldn't give in to evil longings. They controlled your life when you didn't know any better. [15]The one who chose you is holy. So you should be holy in all that you do. [16]It is written, "Be holy, because I am holy." *(Leviticus 11:44,45; 19:2)*

[17]You call on a Father who judges each person's work without favoring one over another. So live your lives as strangers here. Have the highest respect for God.

[18]The blood of Christ set you free from an empty way of life. That way of life was handed down to you by your own people long ago. You know that you were not bought with things that can pass away, like silver or gold. [19]Instead, you were bought by the priceless blood of Christ. He is a perfect lamb. He doesn't have any flaws at all. [20]He was chosen before God created the world. But he came into the world in these last days for you.

[21]Because of what Christ has done, you believe in God. It was God who raised him from the dead. And it was God who gave him glory. So your faith and hope are in God.

[22]You have made yourselves pure by obeying the truth. So you have an honest and true love for your brothers and sisters. Love each other deeply, from the heart.

[23]You have been born again by means of the living word of God. His word lasts forever. You were not born again from a seed that will die. You were born from a seed that can't die. [24]It is written,

"All people are like grass.
All of their glory is like the flowers
in the field.
The grass dries up. The flowers fall
to the ground.
25 But the word of the Lord stands forever."
(Isaiah 40:6–8)

And that word was preached to you.

2 So get rid of every kind of evil. Stop telling lies. Don't pretend to be something you are not. Stop wanting what others have. Don't speak against each other.

[2]Like babies that were just born, you should long for the pure milk of God's word. It will help you grow up as believers. [3]You can do it now that you have tasted how good the Lord is.

The Living Stone and a Chosen People

4Christ is the living Stone. People did not accept him. But God chose him. God places the highest value on him.

5You also are like living stones. As you come to him you are being built into a house for worship. There you will be holy priests. You will offer spiritual sacrifices. God will accept them because of what Jesus Christ has done.

6In Scripture it says,

"Look! I am placing a stone in Zion.
It is a chosen and very valuable stone.
It is the most important stone in the building.
The one who trusts in him
will never be put to shame." *(Isaiah 28:16)*

7The stone is very valuable to you who believe. But to people who do not believe,

"The stone the builders did not accept
has become the most important stone of all." *(Psalm 118:22)*

8And,

"It is a stone that causes people to trip.
It is a rock that makes them fall." *(Isaiah 8:14)*

They trip and fall because they do not obey the message. That is also what God planned for them.

9But God chose you to be his people. You are royal priests. You are a holy nation. You are a people who belong to God. All of this is so that you can sing his praises. He brought you out of darkness into his wonderful light. 10Once you were not a people. But now you are the people of God. Once you had not received mercy. But now you have received mercy.

11Dear friends, you are outsiders and strangers in this world. So I'm asking you not to give in to your sinful longings. They fight against your soul. 12People who don't believe might say you are doing wrong. But lead good lives among them. Then they will see your good works. And they will give glory to God on the day he comes to judge.

Obey Your Rulers and Masters

13Follow the lead of every human authority. Do it because the Lord wants you to. Obey the king. He is the highest authority. 14Obey the governors. The king sends them to punish those who do wrong. He also sends them to praise those who do right. 15By doing good you will put a stop to the talk of foolish people. They don't know what they are saying. God wants you to stop them.

16Live like free people. But don't use your freedom to cover up evil. Live like people who serve God. 17Show proper respect to everyone. Love the community of believers. Have respect for God. Honor the king.

18Slaves, obey your masters with all the respect you should give them. Obey not only those who are good and kind. Obey also those who are not kind. 19Suppose a person suffers pain unfairly because he wants to obey God. That is worthy of praise. 20But suppose you receive a beating for doing wrong, and you put up with it. Will anyone honor you for that? Of course not. But suppose you suffer for doing good, and you put up with it. God will praise you for that.

21Christ suffered for you. He left you an example. He expects you to follow in his steps. You too were chosen to suffer. 22Scripture says,

"He didn't commit any sin.
No lies ever came out of his mouth." *(Isaiah 53:9)*

23People shouted at him and made fun of him. But he didn't do the same back to them. He suffered. But he didn't say that bad things would happen to them. Instead, he trusted in the One who judges fairly.

24He himself carried our sins in his body on the cross. He did it so that we would die as far as sins are concerned. Then we would lead godly lives. His wounds have made you whole.

25You were like sheep who were wandering away. But now you have returned to the Shepherd. He is the Leader of your souls.

Wives and Husbands

3 Wives, follow the lead of your husbands. Suppose some of them don't believe God's word. Then let them be won to Christ without words by seeing how their wives behave. 2Let them see how pure you are. Let them see that your lives are full of respect for God.

3Braiding your hair doesn't make you beautiful. Wearing gold jewelry or fine clothes doesn't make you beautiful. 4Instead, your beauty comes from inside you. It is the beauty of a gentle and quiet spirit. Beauty like that doesn't fade away. God places great value on it.

5This is how the holy women of the past used to make themselves beautiful. They put their hope in God. And they followed the lead of their own husbands.

6Sarah was like that. She obeyed Abraham. She called him her master. Do you want to be like her? Then do what is right. And don't give in to fear.

7Husbands, take good care of your wives. They are weaker than you. So treat them with respect. Honor them as those who will share with you the gracious gift of life. Then nothing will stand in the way of your prayers.

Suffering for Doing Good

8Finally, I want all of you to live together in peace. Be understanding. Love one another like members of the same family. Be kind and tender. Don't be proud. 9Don't pay back evil with evil.

Don't pay back unkind words with unkind words.
Instead, pay them back with kind words. That's
what you have been chosen to do. You can receive
a blessing by doing it.
10 Scripture says,

"Do you want to love life
and see good days?
Then keep your tongues from speaking evil.
Keep your lips from telling lies.
11 Turn away from evil, and do good.
Look for peace, and go after it.
12 The Lord's eyes look with favor on those who
are godly.
His ears are open to their prayers.
But the Lord doesn't look with favor on those
who do evil." *(Psalm 34:12–16)*

13 Who is going to hurt you if you really want to
do good? 14 But suppose you suffer for doing what
is right. Then you will be blessed. Scripture also
says, "Don't fear what others fear. Don't be
afraid." *(Isaiah 8:12)*
15 But make sure in your hearts that Christ is
Lord. Always be ready to give an answer to anyone who asks you about the hope you have. Be
ready to give the reason for it. But do it gently and
with respect.
16 Live so that you don't have to feel you've
done anything wrong. Some people may say evil
things about your good conduct as believers in
Christ. If they do, they will be put to shame for
speaking like that about you. 17 It is better to suffer
for doing good than for doing evil if that's what
God wants.
18 Christ died for sins once and for all time. The
One who did what is right died for those who don't
do right. He died to bring you to God. His body
was put to death. But the Holy Spirit brought him
back to life.
19 By means of the Spirit, Christ went and
preached to the spirits in prison. 20 Long ago they
did not obey. God was patient while Noah was
building the ark. He waited, but only a few people
went into the ark. A total of eight were saved by
means of water.
21 The water of the flood is a picture of the baptism that now saves you also. The baptism I'm
talking about has nothing to do with removing dirt
from your body. Instead, it promises God that you
will keep a clear sense of what is right and wrong.
Jesus Christ has saved you by rising from the
dead. 22 He has gone into heaven. He is at God's
right hand. Angels, authorities and powers are
under his control.

Living for God

4 Christ suffered in his body. So get ready as a
soldier does. Prepare yourselves to think in
the same way Christ did. Do it because those who
have suffered in their bodies are finished with sin.
2 As a result, they don't live the rest of their lives on
earth controlled by evil human longings. Instead,
they live to do what God wants.
3 You have spent enough time in the past doing
what ungodly people choose to do. You lived a
wild life. You longed for evil things. You got
drunk. You went to wild parties. You worshiped
statues of gods. The Lord hates that.
4 Ungodly people think that it's strange when
you no longer join them in what they do. They
want you to rush into the same flood of wasteful
living. So they say bad things about you.
5 But they will have to explain their actions to
God. He is ready to judge the living and the dead.
6 That's why the good news was preached even to
people who are now dead. Human judges said they
were guilty as far as their bodies were concerned.
But God set their spirits free to live as he wanted
them to.
7 The end of all things is near. So keep a clear
mind. Control yourselves. Then you can pray.
8 Most of all, love one another deeply. Love erases
many sins by forgiving them. 9 Welcome others
into your homes without complaining.
10 God's gifts of grace come in many forms.
Each of you has received a gift in order to serve
others. You should use it faithfully. 11 If you speak,
you should do it like one speaking God's very
words. If you serve, you should do it with the
strength God provides. Then in all things God will
be praised through Jesus Christ.
Give him the glory and the power for ever and
ever. Amen.

Suffering for Being a Christian

12 Dear friends, don't be surprised by the painful
suffering you are going through. Don't feel as if
something strange were happening to you. 13 Be
joyful that you are taking part in Christ's sufferings. Then you will be filled with joy when Christ
returns in glory.
14 Suppose people make fun of you because you
believe in Christ. Then you are blessed, because
God's Spirit rests on you. He is the Spirit of glory.
15 Suppose you suffer. Then it shouldn't be because
you are a murderer or a thief. It shouldn't be
because you do evil things. It shouldn't be because
you poke your nose into other people's business.
16 But suppose you suffer for being a Christian.
Then don't be ashamed. Instead, praise God
because you are known by that name.
17 It is time for people to be judged. It will begin
with the family of God. And since it begins with
us, what will happen to people who don't obey
God's good news? 18 Scripture says,

"Suppose it is hard for godly people
to be saved.
Then what will happen to ungodly people
and sinners?" *(Proverbs 11:31)*

19 Some people will suffer because God has
planned it that way. They should commit them-

selves to their faithful Creator. And they should
continue to do good.

To Elders and Young Men

5 I'm speaking to the elders among you. I was
a witness of Christ's sufferings. And I will
also share in the glory that is going to come. I'm
making my appeal to you as one who is an elder
together with you. 2Be shepherds of God's flock,
the believers who are under your care. Serve as
their leaders. Don't serve them because you have
to. Instead, do it because you want to. That's what
God wants you to do. Don't do it because you
want to get more and more money. Do it because
you really want to serve.

3Don't act as if you were a ruler over those who
are under your care. Instead, be examples to the
flock. 4The Chief Shepherd will come again. Then
you will receive the crown of glory. It is a crown
that will never fade away.

5Young men, follow the lead of those who are
older. All of you, put on a spirit that is free of pride
toward each other as if it were your clothes. Scripture says,

"God opposes those who are proud.
But he gives grace to those who are not."
(Proverbs 3:34)

6So don't be proud. Put yourselves under God's
mighty hand. Then he will honor you at the right
time. 7Turn all your worries over to him. He cares
about you.

8Control yourselves. Be on your guard. Your
enemy the devil is like a roaring lion. He prowls
around looking for someone to chew up and swallow. 9Stand up to him. Stand firm in what you
believe. All over the world you know that your
brothers and sisters are going through the same
kind of suffering.

10God always gives you all the grace you need.
So you will only have to suffer for a little while.
Then God himself will build you up again. He will
make you strong and steady. And he has chosen
you to share in his eternal glory because you
belong to Christ.

11Give him the power for ever and ever. Amen.

Final Greetings

12I consider Silas to be a faithful brother. With
his help I have written you this short letter. I have
written it to cheer you up. And I have written to
give witness about the true grace of God. Stand
firm in it.

13The members of the church in Babylon send
you their greetings. They were chosen together
with you. Mark, my son in the faith, also sends you
his greetings. 14Greet each other with a friendly
kiss.

May God give peace to all of you who believe
in Christ.

2 Peter

1 I, Simon Peter, am writing this letter. I serve Jesus Christ. I am his apostle.

I am sending this letter to you who have received a faith as valuable as ours. You received it because our God and Savior Jesus Christ does what is right and fair for everyone.

2May more and more grace and peace be given to you. May they come to you as you learn more about God and about Jesus our Lord.

Be Sure That God Has Chosen You

3God's power has given us everything we need to lead a godly life. All of that has come to us because we know the One who chose us. He chose us because of his own glory and goodness.

4He has also given us his very great and valuable promises. He did it so you could share in his nature. He also did it so you could escape from the evil in the world. That evil is caused by sinful longings.

5So you should try very hard to add goodness to your faith. To goodness, add knowledge. 6To knowledge, add the ability to control yourselves. To the ability to control yourselves, add the strength to keep going. To the strength to keep going, add godliness. 7To godliness, add kindness to believers. And to kindness to believers, add love.

8You should possess more and more of those good points. They will make you useful and fruitful as you get to know our Lord Jesus Christ better.

9But what if some of you do not have those good points? Then you can't see very well. You are blind. You have forgotten that your past sins have been washed away.

10My brothers and sisters, be very sure that God has appointed you to be saved. Be sure that he has chosen you. If you do everything I have just said, you will never trip and fall. 11You will receive a rich welcome into the kingdom that lasts forever. It is the kingdom of our Lord and Savior Jesus Christ.

Prophecy Comes From God

12So I will always remind you of these things. I'll do it even though you know them. I'll do it even though you now have deep roots in the truth. 13I think it is right for me to remind you. It is right as long as I live in this tent. I'm talking about my body.

14I know my tent will soon be removed. Our Lord Jesus Christ has made that clear to me. 15I hope that you will always be able to remember these things after I'm gone. I will try very hard to see that you do.

16We told you about the time our Lord Jesus Christ came with power. But we didn't make up stories when we told you about it. With our own eyes we saw him in all his majesty. 17God the Father gave him honor and glory. The voice of the Majestic Glory came to him. It said, "This is my Son, and I love him. I am very pleased with him." *(Matthew 17:5; Mark 9:7; Luke9:35)* 18We ourselves heard the voice that came from heaven. We were with him on the sacred mountain.

19The word of the prophets is made more certain. We have that word. You must pay attention to it. It is like a light shining in a dark place. It will shine until the day Jesus comes. Then the Morning Star will rise in your hearts.

20Above all, here is what you must understand. No prophecy in Scripture ever came from a prophet's own understanding. 21It never came simply because a prophet wanted it to. Instead, the Holy Spirit guided the prophets as they spoke. So prophecy comes from God.

False Teachers Will Be Destroyed

2 But there were also false prophets among the people. In the same way there will be false teachers among you. In secret they will bring in teachings that will destroy you. They will even turn against the Lord and Master who died to save them. His death paid for their sins. They will quickly destroy themselves. 2Many people will follow their shameful ways. They will give the way of truth a bad name.

3Those teachers are never satisfied. They want to get something out of you. So they make up stories to take advantage of you. They have been under a sentence of death for a long time. The One who will destroy them has not been sleeping.

4God did not spare angels when they sinned. Instead, he sent them to hell. He put them in dark prisons. He will keep them there until he judges them. 5God did not spare the world's ungodly people long ago. He brought the flood on them. But Noah preached about the right way to live. God kept him safe. He also saved seven others. 6God judged the cities of Sodom and Gomorrah. He burned them to ashes. He made them an example of what is going to happen to ungodly people.

7God saved Lot. He was a man who did what was right. He was shocked by the dirty, sinful lives of people who didn't obey God's laws. 8That good man lived among them day after day. He saw and heard the evil things they were doing. They were breaking God's laws. And his godly spirit was deeply troubled.

9So the Lord knows how to keep godly people safe in times of testing. He also knows how to keep ungodly people under guard until the day they will be judged. In the meantime, he continues to punish them. 10Most of all, this is true of people who follow the evil longings of their sinful natures. They hate to be under authority.

Those false prophets are bold and proud. They
aren't afraid to speak evil things against heavenly
beings. [11]Angels are stronger and more powerful
than those people. But even angels don't bring to
the Lord evil charges against heavenly beings.

[12]Those people speak evil about things they
don't understand. They are like wild animals. They
do what comes naturally to them. They are born
only to be caught and destroyed. Just like animals,
they too will die.

[13]They will be paid back with harm for the harm
they have done. Their idea of pleasure is to have
wild parties in the middle of the day. They are like
spots and stains. They enjoy their sinful pleasures
while they eat with you. [14]They stare at women
who are not their wives. They want to have sex
with them. They never stop sinning. They trap
those who are not firm in their faith. They have
mastered the art of getting what they want. God
has placed them under his curse.

[15]They have left God's way. They have wandered off. They follow the way of Balaam, son of
Beor. He loved to get paid for doing his evil work.
[16]But a donkey corrected him for the wrong he did.
Animals don't speak. But the donkey spoke with a
human voice. It tried to stop the prophet from
doing a very dumb thing.

[17]Those false prophets are like springs without
water. They are like mists driven by a storm. The
blackest darkness is reserved for them.

[18]They speak empty, bragging words. They make
their appeal to the earthly longings of people's sinful nature. They tempt new believers who are just
escaping from the company of sinful people. [19]They
promise to give freedom to the new believers. But
they themselves are slaves to sinful living. A person
is a slave to anything that controls him.

[20]They may have escaped the sin of the world.
They may have come to know our Lord and Savior Jesus Christ. But what if they are once again
caught up in sin? And what if it has become their
master? Then they are worse off at the end than
they were at the beginning.

[21]What if they had not known the way of godliness? That would have been better than to have
known it and then to have turned their backs on it.
The way of godliness is the sacred command that
was passed on to them.

[22]What the proverbs say about them is true. "A
dog returns to where it has thrown up." *(Proverbs
26:11)* And, "A pig that is washed goes back to
rolling in the mud."

The Day of the Lord

3 Dear friends, this is now my second letter to
you. I have written both of them as reminders.
I want to stir you up to think in a way that is pure.
[2]I want you to remember the words the holy
prophets spoke in the past. Remember the command
our Lord and Savior gave through your apostles.

[3]First of all, here is what you must understand.
In the last days people will make fun of the truth.
They will laugh at it. They will follow their own
evil longings. [4]They will say, "Where is this
'return' he promised? Everything goes on in the
same way it has since our people of long ago died.
In fact, it has continued that way since God first
created everything."

[5]Long ago, God's word brought the heavens
into being. His word separated the earth from the
waters. And the waters surrounded it. But those
people forget things like that on purpose. [6]The
waters also flooded the world of that time. It was
destroyed.

[7]By God's word the heavens and earth of today
are being reserved for fire. They are being kept for
the day when God will judge. Then ungodly people will be destroyed.

[8]Dear friends, here is one thing you must not
forget. With the Lord a day is like a thousand
years. And a thousand years are like a day. [9]The
Lord is not slow to keep his promise. He is not
slow in the way some people understand it. He is
patient with you. He doesn't want anyone to be
destroyed. Instead, he wants all people to turn
away from their sins.

[10]But the day of the Lord will come like a thief.
The heavens will disappear with a roar. Fire will
destroy everything in them. God will judge the
earth and everything in it.

[11]So everything will be destroyed. And what
kind of people should you be? You should lead
holy and godly lives. [12]Live like that as you look
forward to the day of God. It will make the day
come more quickly. On that day fire will destroy
the heavens. Its heat will melt everything in them.

[13]But we are looking forward to a new heaven
and a new earth. Godliness will make its home
there. All of this is in keeping with God's promise.

[14]Dear friends, I know you are looking forward
to that. So try your best to be found pure and without blame. Be at peace with God. [15]Remember that
while our Lord is waiting patiently to return, people are being saved.

Our dear brother Paul also wrote to you about
that. God made him wise to write as he did. [16]He
writes the same way in all his letters. He speaks
about what I have just told you. His letters include
some things that are hard to understand. People
who don't know better and aren't firm in the faith
twist what he says. They twist the other Scriptures
too. So they will be destroyed.

[17]Dear friends, you already know that. So be on
your guard. Then you won't be led down the
wrong path by the mistakes of people who don't
obey the law. You won't fall from your safe
position.

[18]Grow in the grace of our Lord and Savior
Jesus Christ. Get to know him better.

Give him glory both now and forever. Amen.

1 John

The Word of Life

1 Here is what we announce to everyone about
the Word of life. He was already here from the
beginning. We have heard him. We have seen him
with our eyes. We have looked at him. Our hands
have touched him. 2That life has appeared. We
have seen him. We give witness about him. And
we announce to you that same eternal life. He was
already with the Father. He has appeared to us.

3We announce to you what we have seen and
heard. We do it so you can share life together with
us. And we share life with the Father and with his
Son, Jesus Christ. 4We are writing this to make our
joy complete.

Walking in the Light

5Here is the message we have heard from him
and announce to you. God is light. There is no
darkness in him at all.

6Suppose we say that we share life with God but
still walk in the darkness. Then we are lying. We
are not living by the truth. 7But suppose we walk
in the light, just as he is in the light. Then we share
life with one another. And the blood of Jesus, his
Son, makes us pure from all sin.

8Suppose we claim we are without sin. Then we
are fooling ourselves. The truth is not in us. 9But
God is faithful and fair. If we admit that we have
sinned, he will forgive us our sins. He will forgive
every wrong thing we have done. He will make us
pure. 10If we say we have not sinned, we are calling God a liar. His word has no place in our lives.

2 My dear children, I'm writing this to you so
that you will not sin. But suppose someone
does sin. Then we have one who speaks to the
Father for us. He stands up for us. He is Jesus
Christ, the Blameless One. 2He gave his life to pay
for our sins. But he not only paid for our sins. He
also paid for the sins of the whole world.

3We know that we have come to know God if
we obey his commands.

4Suppose someone says, "I know him." But suppose that person does not do what God commands.
Then that person is a liar and is not telling the truth.
5But if anyone obeys God's word, then God's love
is truly made complete in that person. Here is how
we know we belong to him. 6Those who claim to
belong to him must live just as Jesus did.

7Dear friends, I'm not writing you a new command. Instead, I'm writing one you have heard
before. You have had it since the beginning.

8But I am writing what amounts to a new command. Its truth was shown in how Jesus lived. It is
also shown in how you live. The darkness is passing away. The true light is already shining.

9Suppose someone claims to be in the light but
hates his brother or sister. Then he is still in the
darkness.

10Those who love their brothers and sisters are
living in the light. There is nothing in them to
make them fall into sin. 11But those who hate a
brother or sister are in the darkness. They walk
around in the darkness. They don't know where
they are going. The darkness has made them blind.

12Dear children, I'm writing to you
because your sins have been forgiven.
They have been forgiven because of what
Jesus has done.
13Fathers, I'm writing to you
because you have known the One who is
from the beginning.
Young people, I'm writing to you
because you have won the battle over
the evil one.

Dear children, I'm writing to you
because you have known the Father.
14Fathers, I'm writing to you
because you have known the One who is
from the beginning.
Young people, I'm writing to you
because you are strong.
God's word lives in you.
You have won the battle over the evil one.

Do Not Love the World

15Do not love the world or anything in it. If you
love the world, love for the Father is not in you.

16Here is what people who belong to this world
do. They try to satisfy what their sinful natures
want to do. They long for what their sinful eyes
look at. They brag about what they have and what
they do. All of this comes from the world. It
doesn't come from the Father.

17The world and its evil longings are passing
away. But those who do what God wants them to
do live forever.

A Warning About the Enemies of Christ

18Dear children, we are living in the last days.
You have heard that the great enemy of Christ is
coming. But even now many enemies of Christ
have already come. That's how we know that these
are the last days.

19The enemies left our group. They didn't really
belong to us. If they had belonged to us, they
would have remained with us. But by leaving they
showed that none of them belonged to us.

20You have received the Spirit from the Holy
One. And all of you know the truth. 21I'm not writing to you because you don't know the truth but

because you do know it. I'm writing to you because no lie comes from the truth.

22 Who is the liar? The person who says that Jesus is not the Christ. People who say that are the enemies of Christ. They say no to the Father and the Son. 23 Those who say no to the Son don't belong to the Father. But anyone who says yes to the Son belongs to the Father also.

24 Make sure that you don't forget what you have heard from the beginning. Then you will remain joined to the Son and to the Father. 25 That's what God has promised us. We have eternal life.

26 I'm writing these things to warn you about those who are trying to lead you down the wrong path.

27 But you have received the Holy Spirit from God. He continues to live in you. So you don't need anyone to teach you. God's Spirit teaches you about everything. What he says is true. He doesn't lie. Remain joined to Christ, just as you have been taught by the Spirit.

Children of God

28 Dear children, remain joined to Christ. Then when he comes, we can be bold. We will not be ashamed to meet him when he comes.

29 You know that God is right and always does what is right. And you know that everyone who does what is right has been born again because of what God has done.

3 How great is the love the Father has given us so freely! Now we can be called children of God. And that's what we really are! The world doesn't know us because it didn't know him.

2 Dear friends, now we are children of God. He still hasn't let us know what we will be. But we know that when Christ appears, we will be like him. We will see him as he really is. 3 He is pure. All who hope to be like him make themselves pure.

4 Everyone who sins breaks the law. In fact, breaking the law is sin. 5 But you know that Christ came to take our sins away. And there is no sin in him. 6 No one who remains joined to him keeps on sinning. No one who keeps on sinning has seen him or known him.

7 Dear children, don't let anyone lead you down the wrong path. Those who do what is right are holy, just as Christ is holy. 8 Those who do what is sinful belong to the devil. They are just like him. He has been sinning from the beginning. But the Son of God came to destroy the devil's work.

9 Those who are born again because of what God has done will not keep on sinning. God's very nature remains in them. They can't go on sinning. They have been born again because of what God has done.

10 Here is how you can tell the difference between the children of God and the children of the devil. Those who don't do what is right do not belong to God. Those who don't love their brothers and sisters do not belong to him either.

Love One Another

11 From the beginning we have heard that we should love one another. 12 Don't be like Cain. He belonged to the evil one. He murdered his brother. And why did he murder him? Because the things Cain had done were wrong. But the things his brother had done were right.

13 My brothers and sisters, don't be surprised if the world hates you. 14 We know that we have left our old dead condition and entered into new life. We know it because we love one another. Those who do not are still living in their old condition.

15 Those who hate their brothers and sisters are murderers. And you know that murderers do not have eternal life in their hearts.

16 We know what love is because Jesus Christ gave his life for us. So we should give our lives for our brothers and sisters.

17 Suppose someone sees a brother or sister in need and is able to help them. If he doesn't take pity on them, how can the love of God be in him?

18 Dear children, don't just talk about love. Put your love into action. Then it will truly be love. 19 That's how we know that we hold to the truth. And that's how we put our hearts at rest, knowing that God is watching. 20 Our hearts may judge us. But God is greater than our hearts. He knows everything.

21 Dear friends, if our hearts do not judge us, we can be bold with God. 22 And he will give us anything we ask. That's because we obey his commands. We do what pleases him.

23 God has commanded us to believe in the name of his Son, Jesus Christ. He has also commanded us to love one another. 24 Those who obey his commands remain joined to him. And he remains joined to them.

How do we know that God lives in us? We know it because of the Holy Spirit he gave us.

Put the Spirits to the Test

4 Dear friends, do not believe every spirit. Put the spirits to the test to see if they belong to God. Many false prophets have gone out into the world.

2 How can you recognize the Spirit of God? Every spirit that agrees that Jesus Christ came in a human body belongs to God. 3 But every spirit that doesn't agree with this does not belong to God. It is the spirit of the great enemy of Christ. You have heard that the enemy is coming. Even now he is already in the world.

4 Dear children, you belong to God. You have not accepted the teachings of the false prophets. That's because the One who is in you is more powerful than the one who is in the world.

5 False prophets belong to the world. So they speak from the world's point of view. The world listens to them. 6 We belong to God. And those who know God listen to us. But those who don't belong

to God don't listen to us. That's how we can tell the difference between the Spirit of truth and the spirit of lies.

We Love Because God Loved Us

7 Dear friends, let us love one another, because love comes from God. Everyone who loves has been born again because of what God has done. That person knows God. 8 Anyone who does not love does not know God, because God is love.

9 How did God show his love for us? He sent his one and only Son into the world. He sent him so we could receive life through him.

10 What is love? It is not that we loved God. It is that he loved us and sent his Son to give his life to pay for our sins.

11 Dear friends, since God loved us that much, we should also love one another. 12 No one has ever seen God. But if we love one another, God lives in us. His love is made complete in us.

13 We know that we belong to him and he belongs to us. He has given us his Holy Spirit.

14 The Father has sent his Son to be the Savior of the world. We have seen it. We give witness to it. 15 God lives in anyone who agrees that Jesus is the Son of God. That kind of person remains joined to God. 16 So we know that God loves us. We depend on it.

God is love. Anyone who leads a life of love shows that he is joined to God. And God is joined to him.

17 So love is made complete among us. We will be bold on the day God judges us. That's because in this world we love as Jesus did.

18 There is no fear in love. Instead, perfect love drives fear away. Fear has to do with being punished. The one who fears does not have perfect love.

19 We love because he loved us first. 20 Anyone who says he loves God but in fact hates his brother or sister is a liar. He doesn't love his brother or sister, whom he has seen. So he can't love God, whom he has not seen.

21 Here is the command God has given us. Anyone who loves God must also love his brothers and sisters.

Faith in the Son of God

5 Everyone who believes that Jesus is the Christ is born again because of what God has done. And everyone who loves the Father loves his children as well.

2 How do we know that we love God's children? We know it when we love God and obey his commands. 3 Here is what it means to love God. It means that we obey his commands. And his commands are not hard to obey. 4 That's because everyone who is a child of God has won the battle over the world. Our faith has won the battle for us.

5 Who is it that has won the battle over the world? Only the person who believes that Jesus is the Son of God.

6 Jesus Christ is the one who was baptized in water and died on the cross. He wasn't just baptized in water. He also died on the cross. The Holy Spirit has given a truthful witness about him. That's because the Spirit is the truth.

7 There are three that give witness about Jesus. 8 They are the Holy Spirit, the baptism of Jesus and his death. And the three of them agree.

9 We accept the witness of people. But the witness of God is more important because it is God who gives it. He has given witness about his Son. 10 Those who believe in the Son of God have accepted that witness in their hearts. Those who do not believe God's witness are calling him a liar. That's because they have not believed his witness about his Son.

11 Here is God's witness. He has given us eternal life. That life is found in his Son. 12 Those who belong to the Son have life. Those who do not belong to the Son of God do not have life.

Final Words

13 I'm writing these things to you who believe in the name of the Son of God. I'm doing it so you will know that you have eternal life.

14 There is one thing we can be sure of when we come to God in prayer. If we ask anything in keeping with what he wants, he hears us. 15 If we know that God hears what we ask for, we know that we have it.

16 Suppose you see your brother or sister commit a sin. But that sin is not the kind that leads to death. Then you should pray for them. And God will give life to them. I'm talking about someone whose sin does not lead to death. But there is a sin that does lead to death. I'm not saying that you should pray about that. 17 Every wrong thing we do is sin. But there are sins that do not lead to death.

18 We know that those who are children of God do not keep on sinning. The Son of God keeps them safe. The evil one can't harm them. 19 We know that we are children of God. We know that the whole world is under the control of the evil one.

20 We also know that the Son of God has come. He has given us understanding. Now we can know the One who is true. And we belong to the One who is true. We also belong to his Son, Jesus Christ. He is the true God. He is eternal life.

21 Dear children, keep away from statues of gods.

2 John

1I, the elder, am writing this letter.

I am sending it to the chosen lady and her children. I love all of you because of the truth. I'm not
the only one who loves you. So does everyone
who knows the truth. 2I love you because of the
truth that is alive in us. That truth will be with us
forever.

3God the Father and Jesus Christ his Son will
give you grace, mercy and peace. Those blessings
will be with us because we love the truth.

4It has given me great joy to find some of your
children living by the truth. That's just what the
Father commanded us to do.
5Dear lady, I'm not writing you a new command. I'm writing a command we've had from the
beginning. I'm asking that we love one another.
6The way we show our love is to obey God's commands. He commands you to lead a life of love.
That's what you have heard from the beginning.

7Many people who try to fool others have gone
out into the world. They don't agree that Jesus
Christ came in a human body. People like that try
to trick others. They are enemies of Christ. 8Watch
out that you don't lose what you have worked for.
Make sure that you get your complete reward.
9Some people run ahead of others. They don't
follow the teaching of Christ. People like that don't
belong to God. But those who follow the teaching
of Christ belong to the Father and the Son.
10Suppose someone comes to you and doesn't
teach these truths. Then don't take him into your
house. Don't welcome him. 11Anyone who welcomes him shares in his evil work.
12I have a lot to write to you. But I don't want
to use paper and ink. Instead, I hope I can visit
you. Then I can talk with you face to face. That
will make our joy complete.

13The children of your chosen sister send their
greetings.

3 John

1I, the elder, am writing this letter.

I am sending it to you, my dear friend Gaius. I
love you because of the truth.

2Dear friend, I know that your spiritual life is
going well. I pray that you also may enjoy good
health. And I pray that everything else may go well
with you.
3Some believers came to me and told me that
you are faithful to the truth. They told me that you
continue to live by it. That gave me great joy. 4I
have no greater joy than to hear that my children
are living by the truth.
5Dear friend, you are faithful in what you are
doing for the believers. You are faithful even
though they are strangers to you. 6They have told
the church about your love. Please help them by
sending them on their way in a manner that honors
God.
7They started on their journey to serve Jesus
Christ. They didn't receive any help from those
who aren't believers. 8So we should welcome people like them. We should work together with them
for the truth.
9I wrote to the church. But Diotrephes won't have
anything to do with us. He loves to be the first in
everything. 10So if I come, I will point out what he is
doing. He is saying evil things about us to others.
Even that doesn't satisfy him. He refuses to welcome
other believers. He also keeps others from welcom-
ing them. In fact, he throws them out of the church.
11Dear friend, don't be like those who do evil.
Be like those who do good. Anyone who does
what is good belongs to God. Anyone who does
what is evil hasn't really seen or known God.
12Everyone says good things about Demetrius.
He lives in keeping with the truth. We also say
good things about him. And you know that our
witness is true.
13I have a lot to write to you. But I don't want
to write with pen and ink. 14I hope I can see you
soon. Then we can talk face to face.

May you have peace. The friends here send
their greetings. Greet the friends there by name.

Jude

1 I, Jude, am writing this letter. I serve Jesus
Christ. I am a brother of James.

I am sending this letter to you who have been
chosen by God. You are loved by God the Father.
You are kept safe by Jesus Christ.

2 May more and more mercy, peace, and love be
given to you.

A Warning Against Ungodly Teachers

3 Dear friends, I really wanted to write to you
about the salvation we share. But now I feel I
should write and ask you to stand up for the faith.
God's people were trusted with it once and for all
time.

4 Certain people have slipped in among you in
secret. Long ago it was written that they would be
judged. They are godless people. They use the
grace of our God as an excuse for sexual sins.
They say no to Jesus Christ. He is our only Lord
and King.

5 I want to remind you about some things you
already know. The Lord saved his people. He
brought them out of Egypt. But later he destroyed
those who did not believe. 6 Some of the angels
didn't stay where they belonged. They didn't keep
their positions of authority. The Lord has kept those
angels in darkness. They are held by chains that last
forever. On judgment day, God will judge them.

7 The people of Sodom and Gomorrah and the
towns around them also did evil things. They gave
themselves over to sexual sins. They committed
sins of the worst possible kind. They are an example of those who are punished with fire. The fire
never goes out.

8 In the very same way, those dreamers pollute
their own bodies. They don't accept authority.
They speak evil things against heavenly beings.
9 But not even Michael did that. He was the leader
of the angels. He argued with the devil about the
body of Moses. But he didn't dare to speak evil
things against the devil. Instead, he said, "May the
Lord stop you!"

10 But those people speak evil things against
what they don't understand. They are like wild animals. They can't think for themselves. They do
what comes naturally to them. Those are the very
things that destroy them.

11 How terrible it will be for them! They followed the way of Cain. They rushed ahead and
made the same mistake as Balaam did. They did it
because they loved money. They are like Korah.
He turned against his leaders. Those people will
certainly be destroyed, just as Korah was.

12 They are like stains at the meals you share.
They eat too much. They have no shame. They are
shepherds who feed only themselves. They are like
clouds without rain. They are blown along by the
wind. They are like trees in the fall. Since they
have no fruit, they are pulled up. So they die twice.

13 They are like wild waves of the sea. Their
shame rises up like foam. They are like falling
stars. God has reserved a place of very black darkness for them. He will keep them there forever.

14 Enoch was the seventh man in the family line
of Adam. He gave a prophecy about those people.
He said, "Look! The Lord is coming with thousands and thousands of his holy ones. 15 He is coming to judge everyone. He is coming to sentence
all ungodly people. He will judge them for all the
ungodly acts they have done. They have done
them in ungodly ways. He will sentence ungodly
sinners for all the bad things they have said about
him."

16 Those people complain. They find fault with
others. They follow their own evil longings. They
brag about themselves. They praise others to help
themselves.

Remain in God's Love

17 Dear friends, remember what the apostles of
our Lord Jesus Christ said was going to happen.
18 They told you, "In the last days, some people will
make fun of the truth. They will follow their own
ungodly longings." 19 They are the people who separate you from one another. They do only what
comes naturally. They are not led by the Holy
Spirit.

20 Dear friends, build yourselves up in your most
holy faith. Let the Holy Spirit guide and help you
when you pray. 21 The mercy of our Lord Jesus
Christ will bring you eternal life. As you wait for
his mercy, remain in God's love.

22 Show mercy to those who doubt. 23 Pull others
out of the fire. Save them. To others, show mercy
mixed with fear. Hate even the clothes that are
stained by the sins of those who wear them.

Praise to God

24 Give praise to the One who is able to keep you
from falling into sin. He will bring you into his
heavenly glory without any fault. He will bring
you there with great joy. 25 Give praise to the only
God. He is our Savior. Glory, majesty, power and
authority belong to him. Give praise to him
through Jesus Christ our Lord. Give praise to the
One who was before all time, who now is, and
who will be forever. Amen.

Revelation

1 This is the revelation that God gave to Jesus Christ. Jesus shows those who serve God what will happen soon. God made it known by sending his angel to his servant John. 2 John gives witness to everything he saw. The things he gives witness to are God's word and what Jesus Christ has said.

3 Blessed is the one who reads the words of this prophecy. Blessed are those who hear it and think everything it says is important. The time when these things will come true is near.

Greetings

4 I, John, am writing this letter.

I am sending it to the seven churches in Asia Minor.

May grace and peace come to you from the One who is, and who was, and who will come. May grace and peace come to you from the seven spirits who are in front of God's throne. 5 May grace and peace come to you from Jesus Christ. What Jesus gives witness to can always be trusted. He was the first to rise from the dead. He rules over the kings of the earth.

Give glory and power to the One who loves us! He has set us free from our sins by pouring out his blood for us. 6 He has made us members of his royal family. He has made us priests who serve his God and Father. Give him glory and power for ever and ever! Amen.

7 Look! He is coming with the clouds!
Every eye will see him.
Even those who pierced him will see him.
All the nations of the earth will be sad
because of him.
This will really happen! Amen.

8 "I am the Alpha and the Omega, the First and the Last," says the Lord God. "I am the One who is, and who was, and who will come. I am the Mighty One."

One Who Looks Like a Son of Man

9 I, John, am a believer like you. I am a friend who suffers like you. As members of Jesus' royal family, we can put up with anything that happens to us.

I was on the island of Patmos because I taught God's word and what Jesus said. 10 The Holy Spirit took complete control of me on the Lord's Day. I heard a loud voice behind me that sounded like a trumpet. 11 The voice said, "Write on a scroll what you see. Send it to the seven churches in Asia Minor. They are Ephesus, Smyrna, Pergamum, Thyatira, Sardis, Philadelphia and Laodicea."

12 I turned around to see who was speaking to me. When I turned, I saw seven golden lampstands. 13 In the middle of them was someone who looked "like a son of man." *(Daniel 7:13)*

He was dressed in a long robe with a gold strip of cloth around his chest. 14 The hair on his head was white like wool, as white as snow. His eyes were like a blazing fire. 15 His feet were like bronze metal glowing in a furnace. His voice sounded like rushing waters. 16 He held seven stars in his right hand. Out of his mouth came a sharp sword that had two edges. His face was like the sun shining in all of its brightness.

17 When I saw him, I fell at his feet as if I were dead.

Then he put his right hand on me and said, "Do not be afraid. I am the First and the Last. 18 I am the Living One. I was dead. But look! I am alive for ever and ever! And I hold the keys to Death and Hell.

19 "So write down what you have seen. Write about what is happening now and what will happen later. 20 Here is what the mystery of the seven stars you saw in my right hand means. They are the angels of the seven churches. And the seven golden lampstands you saw stand for the seven churches.

The Letter to the Church in Ephesus

2 "Here is what I command you to write to the church in Ephesus.

Here are the words of the One who holds the seven stars in his right hand. He also walks among the seven golden lampstands. He says,

2 'I know what you are doing. You work long and hard. I know you can't put up with those who are evil. You have tested those who claim to be apostles but are not. You have found out that they are liars. 3 You have been faithful and have put up with a lot of trouble because of me. You have not given up.

4 'But here is something I hold against you. You don't have as much love as you had at first. 5 Remember how far you have fallen! Turn away from your sins. Do the things you did at first. If you don't, I will come to you and remove your lampstand from its place.

6 'But you do have this in your favor. You hate the way the Nicolaitans act. I hate it too.

7 'Those who have ears should listen to what the Holy Spirit says to the churches. I will allow those who overcome to eat from the tree of life in God's paradise.'

The Letter to the Church in Smyrna

8 "Here is what I command you to write to the church in Smyrna.

Here are the words of the One who is the First and the Last. He is the One who died and came to life again. He says, 9'I know that you suffer and are poor. But you are rich! Some people say they are Jews but are not. I know that their words are evil. Their worship is satanic.

10'Don't be afraid of what you are going to suffer. I tell you, the devil will put some of you in prison to test you. You will be treated badly for ten days. Be faithful, even if it means you must die. Then I will give you a crown. The crown is life itself.

11'Those who have ears should listen to what the Holy Spirit says to the churches. Those who overcome will not be hurt at all by the second death.'

The Letter to the Church in Pergamum

12"Here is what I command you to write to the church in Pergamum.

Here are the words of the One with the sharp sword that has two edges. He says, 13'I know that you live where Satan has his throne. But you remain true to me. You did not give up your faith in me, even in the days of Antipas, my faithful witness. He was put to death in your city, where Satan lives.

14'But I have a few things against you. You have people there who follow the teaching of Balaam. He taught Balak to lead the people of Israel into sin. So they ate food that had been offered to statues of gods. And they committed sexual sins. 15You also have people who follow the teaching of the Nicolaitans.

16'So turn away from your sins! If you don't, I will come to you soon. I will fight against those people with the sword that comes out of my mouth.

17'Those who have ears should listen to what the Holy Spirit says to the churches. I will give hidden manna to those who overcome. I will also give each of them a white stone with a new name written on it. Only the one who receives that name will know what it is.'

The Letter to the Church in Thyatira

18"Here is what I command you to write to the church in Thyatira.

Here are the words of the Son of God. He is the One whose eyes are like blazing fire. His feet are like polished bronze. He says, 19'I know what you are doing. I know your love and your faith. I know how well you have served. I know you don't give up easily. In fact, you are doing more now than you did at first.

20'But here is what I have against you. You put up with that woman Jezebel. She calls herself a prophet. With her teaching, she has led my servants into sexual sin. She has tricked them into eating food offered to statues of gods.

21'I've given her time to turn away from her sinful ways. But she doesn't want to. 22She sinned on a bed. So I will make her suffer on a bed. And those who commit adultery with her will suffer greatly. Their only way out is to turn away from what she taught them to do. 23I will strike her children dead. Then all the churches will know that I am the One who searches hearts and minds. I will pay each of you back for what you have done.

24'I won't bother the rest of you in Thyatira. You don't follow the teaching of Jezebel. You haven't learned what some people call Satan's deep secrets. 25Just hold on to what you have until I come.

26'I'll give authority over the nations to all who overcome and who carry out my plans to the end. 27It is written,

'"He will rule them with an iron rod.
He will break them to pieces like
clay pots." *(Psalm 2:9)*

I have received this authority from my Father. 28I will also give the morning star to all who overcome.

29'Those who have ears should listen to what the Holy Spirit says to the churches.'

The Letter to the Church in Sardis

3 "Here is what I command you to write to the church in Sardis.

Here are the words of the One who holds the seven spirits of God. He has the seven stars in his hand. He says, 'I know what you are doing. People think you are alive, but you are dead. 2Wake up! Strengthen what is left, or it will die. You have not done all that my God wants you to do.

3'So remember what you have been taught and have heard. Obey it. Turn away from your sins. If you don't wake up, I will come like a thief. You won't know when I will come to you.

4'But you have a few people in Sardis who have kept their clothes clean. They will walk with me, dressed in white, because they are worthy. 5Those who overcome will also be dressed in white. I will never erase their names from the Book of Life. I will speak of them by name to my Father and his angels.

6'Those who have ears should listen to what the Holy Spirit says to the churches.'

The Letter to the Church in Philadelphia

7"Here is what I command you to write to the church in Philadelphia.

Here are the words of the One who is holy and true. He holds the key of David. No one can shut what he opens. And no one can open what he shuts. He says, 8'I know what you are doing. Look! I have put an open door in front of you. No one can shut it. I know that you don't have much strength. But you have obeyed my word. You have not said no to me.

9'Some people claim they are Jews but are not. They are liars. Their worship is from Satan. I will make them come and fall down at your feet. I will make them say in public that I love you.

10'You have kept my command to put up with anything that happens. So I will keep you from the time of suffering that is going to come to the whole world. It will test those who live on the earth.

11'I am coming soon. Hold on to what you have. Then no one will take away your crown.

12'I'll see to it that those who overcome will be pillars in the temple of my God. They will never leave it again. I will write the name of my God on them. I will write the name of the city of my God on them. This is the new Jerusalem, which is coming down out of heaven from my God. I will also write my new name on them.

13'Those who have ears should listen to what the Holy Spirit says to the churches.'

The Letter to the Church in Laodicea

14"Here is what I command you to write to the church in Laodicea.

Here are the words of the One who is the Amen. What he gives witness to is faithful and true. He rules over what God has created. He says, 15'I know what you are doing. I know you aren't cold or hot. I wish you were either one or the other! 16But you are lukewarm. You aren't hot or cold. So I am going to spit you out of my mouth.

17'You say, "I am rich. I've become wealthy and don't need anything." But you don't realize how pitiful and miserable you have become. You are poor, blind and naked.

18'So here's my advice. Buy from me gold made pure by fire. Then you will become rich. Buy from me white clothes to wear. Then you will be able to cover your shameful nakedness. And buy from me healing lotion to put on your eyes. Then you will be able to see.

19'I correct and train those I love. So be sincere, and turn away from your sins.

20'Here I am! I stand at the door and knock. If any of you hears my voice and opens the door, I will come in and eat with you. And you will eat with me.

21'I'll give those who overcome the right to sit with me on my throne. In the same way, I overcame. Then I sat down with my Father on his throne.

22'Those who have ears should listen to what the Holy Spirit says to the churches.'"

The Throne in Heaven

4 After this I looked, and there in front of me was a door standing open in heaven. I heard the voice I had heard before. It sounded like a trumpet. The voice said, "Come up here. I will show you what must happen after this."

2At once the Holy Spirit took complete control of me. There in front of me was a throne in heaven with someone sitting on it. 3The One who sat there shone like jewels. Around the throne was a rainbow that looked like an emerald.

4Twenty-four other thrones surrounded that throne. Twenty-four elders were sitting on them. The elders were dressed in white. They had gold crowns on their heads.

5From the throne came flashes of lightning, rumblings and thunder. Seven lamps were blazing in front of the throne. These stand for the seven spirits of God. 6There was something that looked like a sea of glass in front of the throne. It was as clear as crystal.

In the inner circle, around the throne, were four living creatures. They were covered with eyes, in front and in back. 7The first creature looked like a lion. The second looked like an ox. The third had a man's face. The fourth looked like a flying eagle. 8Each of the four living creatures had six wings. Each creature was covered all over with eyes, even under the wings. Day and night, they never stop saying,

"Holy, holy, holy
is the Lord God who rules over all.
He was, and he is, and he will come."

9The living creatures give glory, honor and thanks to the One who sits on the throne and who lives for ever and ever. 10At the same time, the 24 elders fall down and worship the One who sits on the throne and who lives for ever and ever. They lay their crowns in front of the throne. They say,

11"You are worthy, our Lord and God!
You are worthy to receive glory and honor
and power.
You are worthy because you created all things.
They were created and they exist.
That is the way you planned it."

The Scroll and the Lamb

5 Then I saw a scroll in the right hand of the One sitting on the throne. The scroll had writing on both sides. It was sealed with seven seals.

2I saw a mighty angel calling out in a loud voice, "Who is worthy to break the seals and open the scroll?" 3But no one in heaven or on earth or

under the earth could open the scroll. No one could
even look inside it.
4 I cried and cried because no one was found
who was worthy to open the scroll or look inside.
5 Then one of the elders said to me, "Do not cry!
The Lion of the tribe of Judah has won the battle.
He is the Root of David. He is able to break the
seven seals and open the scroll."
6 Then I saw a Lamb that looked as if he had
been put to death. He stood in the center of the area
around the throne. The Lamb was surrounded by
the four living creatures and the elders. He had
seven horns and seven eyes. The eyes stand for the
seven spirits of God, which are sent out into all the
earth.
7 The Lamb came and took the scroll from the
right hand of the One sitting on the throne. 8 Then
the four living creatures and the 24 elders fell
down in front of the Lamb. Each one had a harp.
They were holding golden bowls full of incense,
which stand for the prayers of God's people.
9 Here is the new song they sang.

"You are worthy to take the scroll
and break open its seals.
You are worthy because you were put to death.
With your blood you bought people for God.
They come from every tribe, language,
people and nation.
10 You have made them members of a
royal family.
You have made them priests to serve
our God.
They will rule on the earth."

11 Then I looked and heard the voice of millions
and millions of angels. They surrounded the
throne. They surrounded the living creatures and
the elders. 12 In a loud voice they sang,

"The Lamb, who was put to death, is worthy!
He is worthy to receive power and wealth and
wisdom and strength!
He is worthy to receive honor and glory
and praise!"

13 All creatures in heaven, on earth, under the
earth, and on the sea, and all that is in them, were
singing. I heard them say,

"May praise and honor for ever and ever
be given to the One who sits on the throne
and to the Lamb!
Give them glory and power
for ever and ever!"

14 The four living creatures said, "Amen." And
the elders fell down and worshiped.

The Seals

6 I watched as the Lamb broke open the first of
the seven seals. Then I heard one of the four
living creatures say in a voice that sounded like
thunder, "Come!" 2 I looked, and there in front of
me was a white horse! Its rider held a bow in his
hands. He was given a crown. He rode out like a
hero on his way to victory.
3 The Lamb broke open the second seal. Then I
heard the second living creature say, "Come!"
4 Another horse came out. It was flaming red. Its
rider was given power to take peace from the earth
and to make people kill each other. He was given
a large sword.
5 The Lamb broke open the third seal. Then I
heard the third living creature say, "Come!" I
looked, and there in front of me was a black horse!
Its rider was holding a pair of scales in his hand.
6 Next, I heard what sounded like a voice coming
from among the four living creatures. It said, "A
quart of wheat for a day's pay. And three quarts of
barley for a day's pay. But don't spoil the olive oil
and the wine!"
7 The Lamb broke open the fourth seal. Then I
heard the voice of the fourth living creature say,
"Come!" 8 I looked, and there in front of me was a
pale horse! Its rider's name was Death. Following
close behind him was Hell. They were given
power over a fourth of the earth. They were given
power to kill people with the sword, hunger and
sickness. They could also use the earth's wild animals to kill.
9 He broke open the fifth seal. I saw souls under
the altar. They were the souls of people who were
killed because of God's word and their faithful
witness. 10 They called out in a loud voice. "How
long, Lord and King, holy and true?" they asked.
"How long will you wait to judge those who live
on the earth? How long will it be until you pay
them back for killing us?"
11 Then each of them was given a white robe.
"Wait a little longer," they were told. "There are
still more of your believing brothers and sisters
who must be killed."
12 I watched as he broke open the sixth seal. There
was a powerful earthquake. The sun turned black
like black clothes that were made from the hair of a
goat. The whole moon turned as red as blood. 13 The
stars in the sky fell to earth. They dropped like ripe
figs from a tree shaken by a strong wind. 14 The sky
rolled back like a scroll. Every mountain and island
was moved out of its place.
15 Everyone hid in caves and among the rocks of
the mountains. This included the kings of the
earth, the princes and the generals, rich people and
powerful people. It also included every slave and
everyone who was free. 16 They called out to the
mountains and rocks, "Fall on us! Hide us from the
face of the One who sits on the throne! Hide us
from the anger of the Lamb! 17 The great day of
their anger has come. Who can live through it?"

144,000 Are Sealed

7 After this I saw four angels. They were standing at the four corners of the earth. They were
holding back the four winds of the earth. This kept

the winds from blowing on the land or on the sea
or on any tree.
2Then I saw another angel coming up from the
east. He had the seal of the living God. He called
out in a loud voice to the four angels who had been
allowed to harm the land and the sea. 3"Do not
harm the land or the sea or the trees," he said.
"Wait until we mark with a seal the foreheads of
those who serve our God."
4Then I heard how many people were sealed.
There were 144,000 from all the tribes of Israel.

5 From the tribe of Judah, 12,000
were sealed.
From the tribe of Reuben, 12,000.
From the tribe of Gad, 12,000.
6 From the tribe of Asher, 12,000.
From the tribe of Naphtali, 12,000.
From the tribe of Manasseh, 12,000.
7 From the tribe of Simeon, 12,000.
From the tribe of Levi, 12,000.
From the tribe of Issachar, 12,000.
8 From the tribe of Zebulun, 12,000.
From the tribe of Joseph, 12,000.
From the tribe of Benjamin, 12,000.

The Huge Crowd Wearing White Robes

9After this I looked, and there in front of me
was a huge crowd of people. They stood in front of
the throne and in front of the Lamb. There were so
many that no one could count them. They came
from every nation, tribe, people and language.
They were wearing white robes. In their hands
they were holding palm branches. 10They cried out
in a loud voice,

"Salvation belongs to our God,
who sits on the throne.
Salvation also belongs to the Lamb."

11All the angels were standing around the throne.
They were standing around the elders and the four
living creatures. They fell down on their faces in
front of the throne and worshiped God. 12They said,

"Amen!
May praise and glory
and wisdom be given to our God for ever
and ever.
Give him thanks and honor and power
and strength.
Amen!"

13Then one of the elders spoke to me. "Who are
these people dressed in white robes?" he asked.
"Where did they come from?"
14I answered, "Sir, you know."
He said, "They are the ones who have come out
of the time of terrible suffering. They have washed
their robes and made them white in the blood of
the Lamb. 15So

"they are in front of the throne of God.
They serve him day and night in his temple.
The One who sits on the throne will spread
his tent over them.
16 Never again will they be hungry.
Never again will they be thirsty.
The sun will not beat down on them.
The heat of the desert will not harm them.
17 The Lamb, who is at the center of the area
around the throne, will be their
shepherd.
He will lead them to springs of living water.
And God will wipe away every tear from their
eyes."

The Seventh Seal and the Gold Cup

8 The Lamb opened the seventh seal. Then there
was silence in heaven for about half an hour.
2I saw the seven angels who stand in front of
God. Seven trumpets were given to them.
3Another angel came and stood at the altar. He
had a shallow gold cup for burning incense. He
was given a lot of incense to offer on the golden
altar in front of the throne. With the incense he
offered the prayers of all God's people. 4The
smoke of the incense together with the prayers of
God's people rose up from the angel's hand. It
went up in front of God.
5Then the angel took the cup and filled it with
fire from the altar. He threw it down on the earth.
There were rumblings and thunder, flashes of
lightning, and an earthquake.

The Trumpets

6Then the seven angels who had the seven trumpets got ready to blow them.
7The first angel blew his trumpet. Hail and fire
mixed with blood were thrown down on the earth.
A third of the earth was burned up. A third of the
trees were burned up. All the green grass was
burned up.
8The second angel blew his trumpet. Something
that looked like a huge mountain on fire was
thrown into the sea. A third of the sea turned into
blood. 9A third of the living creatures in the sea
died. A third of the ships were destroyed.
10The third angel blew his trumpet. Then a great
star fell from the sky. It looked like a blazing torch.
It fell on a third of the rivers and on the springs of
water. 11The name of the star is Wormwood. A
third of the water turned bitter. Many people died
from it.
12The fourth angel blew his trumpet. Then a
third of the sun was struck. A third of the moon
was struck. A third of the stars were struck. So a
third of each of them turned dark. Then a third of
the day had no light. The same thing happened to
a third of the night.
13As I watched, I heard an eagle that was flying
high in the air. It called out in a loud voice, "How
terrible! How terrible it will be for those living on
the earth! How terrible! They will suffer as soon
as the next three angels blow their trumpets!"

9 The fifth angel blew his trumpet. Then I saw a star that had fallen from the sky to the earth. The star was given the key to the tunnel leading down into the Abyss. 2When the star opened the Abyss, smoke rose up from it like the smoke from a huge furnace. The sun and sky were darkened by the smoke from the Abyss.

3Out of the smoke came locusts. They settled down on the earth. They were given power like the power of scorpions of the earth. 4They were told not to harm the grass of the earth or any plant or tree. They were supposed to harm only the people who didn't have God's seal on their foreheads. 5They were not allowed to kill them. But they could hurt them over and over for five months. The pain the people suffered was like the sting of a scorpion when it strikes a man.

6In those days, people will look for a way to die but won't find it. They will want to die, but death will escape them.

7The locusts looked like horses ready for battle. On their heads they wore something like crowns of gold. Their faces looked like human faces. 8Their hair was like women's hair. Their teeth were like lions' teeth. 9Their chests were covered with something that looked like armor made out of iron. The sound of their wings was like the thundering of many horses and chariots rushing into battle. 10They had tails and stings like scorpions. And in their tails they had power to hurt people over and over for five months.

11Their king was the angel of the Abyss. In the Hebrew language his name is Abaddon. In Greek it is Apollyon.

12The first terrible judgment is past. Two others are still coming.

13The sixth angel blew his trumpet. Then I heard a voice coming from the corners of the golden altar that stands in front of God. 14The voice spoke to the sixth angel who had the trumpet. It said, "Set the four angels free who are held at the great river Euphrates."

15The four angels had been ready for this very hour and day and month and year. They were set free to kill a third of all people. 16The number of troops on horseback was 200,000,000. I heard how many there were.

17The horses and riders I saw in my vision had armor on their chests. It was flaming red, dark blue, and yellow like sulfur. The heads of the horses looked like lions' heads. Out of their mouths came fire, smoke and sulfur. 18A third of all people were killed by the three plagues of fire, smoke and sulfur that came out of the horses' mouths. 19The power of the horses was in their mouths and in their tails. The tails were like snakes whose heads could bite.

20The people who were not killed by these plagues still did not turn away from what they had been doing. They did not stop worshiping demons. They kept worshiping statues of gods made out of gold, silver, bronze, stone and wood, which can't see or hear or walk. 21The people also did not turn away from their murders, witchcraft, sexual sins and stealing.

The Angel and the Little Scroll

10 Then I saw another mighty angel coming down from heaven. He was wearing a cloud like a robe. There was a rainbow above his head. His face was like the sun. His legs were like pillars of fire.

2He was holding a little scroll. It was lying open in his hand. The angel put his right foot on the sea and his left foot on the land. 3Then he gave a loud shout like the roar of a lion. When he shouted, the voices of the seven thunders spoke.

4When they had spoken, I was getting ready to write. But I heard a voice from heaven say, "Seal up what the seven thunders have said. Do not write it down."

5Then the angel I had seen standing on the sea and on the land raised his right hand to heaven. 6He made a promise in the name of the One who lives for ever and ever. He took an oath in the name of the One who created the sky, earth and sea and all that is in them. He said, "There will be no more waiting! 7But in the days when the seventh angel is ready to blow his trumpet, the last part of God's plan will be carried out. God told all this to the prophets who served him long ago."

8Then the voice I had heard from heaven spoke to me again. It said, "Go and take the scroll from the angel standing on the sea and on the land. It is lying open in his hand."

9So I went to the angel and asked him to give me the little scroll. He said to me, "Take it and eat it. It will become sour in your stomach. But in your mouth it will taste as sweet as honey." 10I took the little scroll from the angel's hand and ate it. In my mouth it tasted as sweet as honey. But when I had eaten it, it became sour in my stomach. 11Then I was told, "You must prophesy again about many peoples, nations, languages and kings."

The Two Witnesses

11 I was given a long stick that looked like a measuring rod. I was told, "Go and measure the temple of God and the altar. Count the worshipers who are there. 2But do not measure the outer courtyard. It has been given to those who aren't Jews. They will overrun the holy city for 42 months.

3"I will give power to my two witnesses. They will prophesy for 1,260 days. They will be dressed in black clothes to show how sad they are."

4The witnesses are the two olive trees and the two lampstands that stand in front of the Lord of the earth. 5If anyone tries to harm them, fire comes from their mouths and eats up their enemies. This is how anyone who wants to harm them must die.

6These witnesses have power to close up the sky. Then it will not rain while they are prophesying.

They also have power to turn the waters into blood.
And they can strike the earth with every kind of
plague as often as they want to.
7When they have finished giving their witness,
the beast that comes up from the Abyss will attack
them. He will overpower them and kill them.
8Their bodies will lie in the street of the great city
where their Lord was nailed to the cross. The city
is sometimes pictured as Sodom, or as Egypt.
9For three and a half days, people from every
tribe, language and nation will stare at their bodies.
They will refuse to bury them. 10Those who live
on the earth will be happy about this and will celebrate. They will send each other gifts, because
these two prophets had made them suffer.
11But after the three and a half days, a breath of
life from God entered the two witnesses. They
stood up. Terror struck those who saw them.
12Then the two witnesses heard a loud voice
from heaven. It said to them, "Come up here."
They went up to heaven in a cloud. Their enemies
watched it happen.
13At that very hour there was a powerful earthquake. A tenth of the city crumbled and fell. In the
earthquake, 7,000 people were killed. Those who
lived through it were terrified. They gave glory to
the God of heaven.
14The second terrible judgment has passed. The
third is coming soon.

The Seventh Trumpet

15The seventh angel blew his trumpet. There
were loud voices in heaven. They said,

"The kingdom of the world has become the
kingdom of our Lord and of his Christ.
He will rule for ever and ever."

16The 24 elders were sitting on their thrones in
front of God. They fell on their faces and worshiped God. 17They said,

"Lord God who rules over all, we give thanks
to you.
You are the One who is and who was.
We give you thanks because you have taken
your great power
and have begun to rule.
18 The nations were angry,
and the time for your anger has come.
The time has come to judge the dead.
It is time to reward your servants the prophets
and your own people and those who
honor you.
There is a reward for all your people,
both great and small.
It is time to destroy
those who destroy the earth."

19Then God's temple in heaven was opened.
Inside it the wooden chest called the ark of his
covenant could be seen. There were flashes of
lightning, rumblings and thunder, an earthquake
and a great hailstorm.

The Woman and the Dragon

12 A great and miraculous sign appeared in
heaven. It was a woman wearing the sun
like clothes. The moon was under her feet. On her
head she wore a crown of 12 stars. 2She was pregnant. She cried out in pain because she was about
to have a baby.
3Then another sign appeared in heaven. It was
a huge red dragon. He had seven heads and ten
horns. On his seven heads he wore seven crowns.
4His tail swept a third of the stars out of the sky. It
threw them down to earth.
The dragon stood in front of the woman who
was about to have a baby. He wanted to eat her
child the moment it was born.
5She gave birth to a son. He will rule all the
nations with an iron rod. Her child was taken up
to God and to his throne.
6The woman escaped into the desert where God
had a place prepared for her. There she would be
taken care of for 1,260 days.
7There was war in heaven. Michael and his angels
fought against the dragon. And the dragon and his
angels fought back. 8But the dragon wasn't strong
enough. He and his angels lost their place in heaven.
9The great dragon was thrown down to the
earth, and his angels with him. The dragon is that
old serpent called the devil, or Satan. He leads the
whole world down the wrong path.
10Then I heard a loud voice in heaven. It said,

"Now the salvation and the power and the
kingdom of our God have come.
The authority of his Christ has come.
Satan, who brings charges against our brothers
and sisters,
has been thrown down.
He brings charges against them before our
God day and night.
11 They overcame him
because the Lamb gave his life's blood
for them.
They overcame him
by giving witness about Jesus to others.
They were willing to risk their lives,
even if it led to death.
12 So be joyful, you heavens!
Be glad, all you who live there!
But how terrible it will be for the earth and
the sea!
The devil has come down to you.
He is very angry.
He knows his time is short."

13The dragon saw that he had been thrown
down to the earth. So he chased the woman who
had given birth to the boy.
14The woman was given the two wings of a
great eagle so that she could fly away. She could
fly to the place prepared for her in the desert.
There she would be taken care of for three and a
half years. She would be out of the serpent's reach.

15Then the serpent spit water like a river out of his mouth. He wanted to catch her and sweep her away in the flood. 16But the earth helped the woman. It opened its mouth and swallowed the river that the dragon had spit out.

17The dragon was very angry with the woman. He went off to make war against the rest of her children. They obey God's commands and hold

13 firmly to what Jesus has said. 1The dragon stood on the seashore.

The Beast out of the Sea

I saw a beast coming out of the sea. He had ten horns and seven heads. There were ten crowns on his horns. On each head was an evil name that was displeasing to God.

2The beast I saw looked like a leopard. But he had feet like a bear and a mouth like a lion. The dragon gave the beast his power, his throne, and great authority. 3One of the beast's heads seemed to have had a deadly wound. But the wound had been healed. The whole world was amazed and followed the beast.

4People worshiped the dragon, because he had given authority to the beast. They also worshiped the beast. They asked, "Who is like the beast? Who can make war against him?"

5The beast was given a mouth to brag and speak evil things against God. The beast was allowed to use his authority for 42 months. 6He opened his mouth to speak evil things against God. He told lies about God's character and about the place where God lives and about those who live in heaven with him. 7He was allowed to make war against God's people and to overcome them. He was given authority over every tribe, people, language and nation.

8All who live on earth whose names have not been written in the Book of Life will worship the beast. The Book of Life belongs to the Lamb whose death was planned before the world was created.

9Everyone who has ears should listen.

10Everyone who is supposed to be captured
 will be captured.
Everyone who is supposed to be killed with
 a sword
 will be killed with a sword.

So God's people must be patient and faithful.

The Beast out of the Earth

11Then I saw another beast. This one came out of the earth. He had two horns like a lamb. But he spoke like a dragon. 12He had all the authority of the first beast. He did what that beast wanted. He made the earth and all who live on it worship the first beast. The first beast was the one whose deadly wound had been healed.

13The second beast did great and miraculous signs. He even made fire come from heaven. It came down to earth where everyone could see it. 14He did the signs the first beast wanted him to do. In that way the second beast tricked those who live on the earth. He ordered them to set up a statue to honor the first beast.

The first beast was the one who had been wounded by the sword and still lived.

15The second beast was allowed to give breath to the statue so it could speak. He was allowed to kill all who refused to worship the statue. 16He also forced everyone to receive a mark on the right hand or on the forehead. People great or small, rich or poor, free or slave had to receive the mark. 17They could not buy or sell anything unless they had the mark. The mark is the name of the beast or the number of his name.

18Here is a problem that you have to be wise to figure out. If you can, figure out what the beast's number means. It is man's number. His number is 666.

The Lamb and the 144,000

14 I looked, and there in front of me was the Lamb. He was standing on Mount Zion. With him were 144,000 people. Written on their foreheads were his name and his Father's name.

2I heard a sound from heaven. It was like the roar of rushing waters and loud thunder. The sound I heard was like the music of harps being played.

3Then everyone sang a new song in front of the throne. They sang it in front of the four living creatures and the elders. No one could learn the song except the 144,000. They had been set free from the evil of the earth.

4They had not committed sexual sins with women. They had kept themselves pure. They follow the Lamb wherever he goes. They were purchased from among people as a first offering to God and the Lamb. 5Their mouths told no lies. They are without blame.

The Three Angels

6I saw another angel. He was flying high in the air. He came to tell everyone on earth the good news that will always be true. He told it to every nation, tribe, language and people. 7In a loud voice he said, "Have respect for God. Give him glory. The hour has come for God to judge. Worship him who made the heavens and the earth. Worship him who made the sea and the springs of water."

8A second angel followed him. He said, "Fallen! Babylon the Great has fallen! The city of Babylon made all the nations drink the strong wine of her terrible sins."

9A third angel followed them. He said in a loud voice, "Watch out, all you who worship the beast and his statue! Watch out, all you who have his mark on your forehead or your hand! 10You, too, will drink the wine of God's great anger. His wine has been poured full strength into the cup of his anger. You will be burned with flaming sulfur. The holy angels and the Lamb will see it happen. 11The smoke of your terrible suffering will rise for ever and ever. Day and night, there is no rest for you who worship the beast and his statue. There is no rest for you who receive the mark of his name."

12God's people need to be very patient. They are the ones who obey God's commands. They remain faithful to Jesus.

13Then I heard a voice from heaven. "Write this," it said. "Blessed are the dead who die as believers in the Lord from now on."

"Yes," says the Holy Spirit. "They will rest from their labor. What they have done will not be forgotten."

The Harvest of the Earth

14I looked, and there in front of me was a white cloud. Sitting on the cloud was One who looked "like a son of man." *(Daniel 7:13)* He wore a gold crown on his head. In his hand was a sharp, curved blade for cutting grain.

15Then another angel came out of the temple. He called in a loud voice to the one sitting on the cloud. "Take your blade," he said. "Cut the grain. The time has come. The earth is ready to be harvested."

16So the one sitting on the cloud swung his blade over the earth. And the earth was harvested.

17Another angel came out of the temple in heaven. He too had a sharp, curved blade. 18Still another angel came from the altar. He was in charge of the fire on the altar. He called out in a loud voice to the angel who had the sharp blade. "Take your blade," he said, "and gather the bunches of grapes from the earth's vine. Its grapes are ripe."

19So the angel swung his blade over the earth. He gathered its grapes. Then he threw them into a huge winepress. The winepress stands for God's anger.

20In the winepress outside the city, the grapes were stomped on. Blood flowed out of the pit. It spread over the land for about 180 miles. It rose as high as the horses' heads.

Seven Angels With Seven Plagues

15 I saw in heaven another great and miraculous sign. Seven angels were about to bring the seven last plagues. The plagues would complete God's anger.

2Then I saw something that looked like a sea of glass mixed with fire. Standing beside the sea were those who had won the battle over the beast. They had also overcome his statue and the number of his name. They held harps given to them by God.

3They sang the song of Moses, who served God, and the song of the Lamb. They sang,

"Lord God who rules over all,
  everything you do is great and wonderful.
King of the ages,
  your ways are true and fair.
4Lord, who will not have respect for you?
  Who will not bring glory to your name?
You alone are holy.
All nations will come
  and worship you.
They see that the things you do are right."

5After this I looked, and the temple was opened in heaven. The temple is the holy tent where the tablets of the covenant were kept.

6Out of the temple came the seven angels who were bringing the seven plagues. They were dressed in clean, shining linen. They wore gold strips of cloth around their chests.

7Then one of the four living creatures gave seven golden bowls to the seven angels. The bowls were filled with the anger of God, who lives for ever and ever. 8The temple was filled with smoke that came from the glory and power of God. No one could enter the temple until the seven plagues of the seven angels were completed.

The Seven Bowls of God's Anger

16 Then I heard a loud voice from the temple speaking to the seven angels. "Go," it said. "Pour out the seven bowls of God's anger on the earth."

2The first angel went and poured out his bowl on the land. Ugly and painful sores broke out on the people who had the mark of the beast and worshiped his statue.

3The second angel poured out his bowl on the sea. It turned into blood like the blood of a dead person. Every living thing in the sea died.

4The third angel poured out his bowl on the rivers and on the springs of water. They became blood.

5Then I heard the angel who was in charge of the waters. He said,

"The way you judge is fair.
  You are the Holy One.
  You are the One who is and who was.
6The beast's worshipers have poured out the
    life's blood of your people and your
    prophets.
  So you have given those worshipers blood
    to drink.
  That's exactly what they should get."

7Then I heard the altar reply,

"Lord God who rules over all,
  the way you judge is true and fair."

8The fourth angel poured out his bowl on the sun. The sun was allowed to burn people with fire. 9They were burned by the blazing heat. So they spoke evil things against the name of God, who controlled these plagues. But they refused to turn away from their sins. They did not give glory to God.

10The fifth angel poured out his bowl on the throne of the beast. The kingdom of the beast became very dark. People bit their tongues because they were suffering so much. 11They spoke evil things against the God of heaven because of their pains and their sores. But they refused to turn away from the sins they had committed.

12The sixth angel poured out his bowl on the great river Euphrates. Its water dried up to prepare the way for the kings from the East.

13Then I saw three evil spirits that looked like frogs. They came out of the mouths of the dragon, the beast and the false prophet. 14They are spirits of demons performing miraculous signs. They go out to gather the kings of the whole world for battle. That battle will take place on the great day of the God who rules over all.

15"Look! I am coming like a thief! Blessed are those who stay awake and keep their clothes with them. They will not be caught naked. They will not be put to shame."

16Then the evil spirits gathered the kings together. The place where the kings met is called Armageddon in the Hebrew language.

17The seventh angel poured out his bowl into the air. Out of the temple came a loud voice from the throne. It said, "It is done!"

18Then there came flashes of lightning, rumblings, thunder and a powerful earthquake. There has never been an earthquake as terrible as this since man has lived on earth. 19The great city split into three parts. The cities of the nations crumbled and fell. God remembered Babylon the Great. He gave her the cup filled with the wine of his terrible anger.

20Every island ran away. The mountains could not be found. 21Huge hailstones of about 100 pounds each fell from the sky. The hail crushed people. They spoke evil things against God because the plague of hail was so terrible.

The Woman and the Beast

17 One of the seven angels who had the seven bowls came to me. He said, "Come. I will show you how the great prostitute will be punished. She is the one who sits on many waters. 2The kings of the earth took part in her evil ways. The people living on earth were drunk with the wine of her terrible sins."

3Then the angel carried me away in a vision. The Holy Spirit took me into a desert. There I saw a woman sitting on a bright red beast. It was covered with names that say evil things that are displeasing to God. It had seven heads and ten horns.

4The woman was dressed in purple and bright red. She was gleaming with gold, jewels and pearls. In her hand she held a golden cup filled with things that God hates. It was filled with her terrible, dirty sins. 5Here is the name that was written on her forehead.

MYSTERY
THE GREAT CITY OF BABYLON
THE MOTHER OF PROSTITUTES
THE MOTHER OF EVERYTHING ON EARTH
THAT GOD HATES

6I saw that the woman was drunk with the blood of God's people. They are the ones who gave witness to Jesus.

When I saw her, I was very amazed.

7Then the angel said to me, "Why are you amazed? I will explain to you the mystery of the woman and of the beast she rides on. The beast is the one who has the seven heads and ten horns. 8The beast that you saw used to exist. But now he does not. He will come up out of the Abyss. He will be destroyed. Some of the people who live on the earth will be amazed when they see the beast. Their names have not been written in the Book of Life from the time the world was created. They will be amazed because even though the beast used to exist and now does not, he will come again.

9"Here is a problem that you have to be wise to understand. The seven heads are seven hills that the woman sits on. 10They are also seven kings. Five have fallen, one is ruling, and the other has still not come. When he does come, he must remain for a little while.

11"The beast who used to exist, and now does not, is an eighth king. He belongs to the other seven. He will be destroyed.

12"The ten horns you saw are ten kings. They have not yet received a kingdom. But for one hour they will receive authority to rule together with the beast. 13They have only one purpose. So they give their power and authority to the beast. 14They will make war against the Lamb. But the Lamb will overcome them because he is the most powerful Lord of all and the greatest King of all. His appointed, chosen and faithful followers will be with him."

15Then the angel spoke to me. "You saw the waters the prostitute sits on," he said. "They stand for all the nations of the world, no matter what their race or language is. 16The beast and the ten horns you saw will hate the prostitute. They will destroy her and leave her naked. They will eat her flesh and burn her with fire. 17God has put it into their hearts to carry out his purpose. So they agreed to give the beast their power to rule. They will give him that power until God's words come true.

18"The woman you saw stands for the great city that rules over the kings of the earth."

Babylon Falls

18 After these things I saw another angel coming down from heaven. He had great authority. His glory filled the earth with light. 2With a mighty voice he shouted,

"Fallen! Babylon the Great has fallen!
She has become a place where demons live.
She has become a den for every evil spirit.
She has become a nest for every 'unclean'
and hated bird.

3 All the nations have drunk
the strong wine of her terrible sins.
The kings of the earth took part in her
evil ways.
The traders of the world grew rich from her
great wealth."

4Then I heard another voice from heaven. It said,

"Come out of her, my people.
Then you will not take part in her sins.
You will not suffer from any of her plagues.
5 Her sins are piled up to heaven.
God has remembered her crimes.
6 Do to her as she has done to others.
Pay her back double for what she has done.
Mix her a double dose of what she has
mixed for others.
7 Give her as much pain and suffering
as the glory and wealth she gave herself.
She brags to herself,
'I rule like a queen. I am not a widow.
I will never be sad.'
8 But she will be plagued by death, sadness
and hunger.
In a single day they will all catch up
with her.
She will be burned up by fire.
The Lord God who judges her is mighty.

9"The kings of the earth who committed terrible sins with her will sob. They will be sad because
they used to share her riches. They will see the
smoke rising as she burns. 10They will be terrified
by her suffering. Standing far away, they will
exclaim,

"'How terrible! How terrible it is for you,
great city!
How terrible for you, Babylon, city
of power!
In just one hour you have been destroyed!'

11"The traders of the world will cry and be sad
over her. No one buys what they sell anymore.
12Here is what they had for sale.

Gold, silver, jewels, pearls.
Fine linen, purple, silk, bright red cloth.
Every kind of expensive wood.
All sorts of articles made out of ivory,
valuable wood, bronze, iron and marble.
13 Cinnamon, spice, incense, myrrh, frankin-
cense.
Wine, olive oil, fine flour, wheat.
Cattle, sheep, horses, carriages, human
slaves.

14"The merchants will say, 'The pleasure you
longed for has left you. All your riches and glory
have disappeared forever.' 15The traders who sold
these things and became rich because of her will
stand far away. Her suffering will terrify them.
They will cry and be sad. 16They will cry out,

"'How terrible! How terrible it is for you,
great city,
dressed in fine linen, purple and bright red!
How terrible for you, great city, gleaming
with gold, jewels and pearls!
17 In just one hour your great wealth has been
destroyed!'

"Every sea captain and all who travel by ship
will stand far away. So will the sailors and all who
earn their living from the sea. 18They will see the
smoke rising as Babylon burns. They will ask,
'Was there ever a city like this great city?' 19They
will throw dust on their heads. They will cry and
be sad. They will cry out,

"'How terrible! How terrible it is for you,
great city!
All who had ships on the sea
became rich because of her wealth!
In just one hour she has been destroyed!'
20 Heaven, be glad for this!
God's people, be glad! Apostles and
prophets, be glad!
God has judged her for the way she
treated you.'"

21Then a mighty angel picked up a huge rock. It
was the size of a large millstone. He threw it into
the sea. Then he said,

"That is how
the great city of Babylon will be
thrown down.
Never again will it be found.
22 The songs of musicians will never be heard in
you again.
Gone will be the music of harp, flute
and trumpet.
No worker of any kind
will ever be found in you again.
The sound of a millstone
will never be heard in you again.
23 The light of a lamp
will never shine in you again.
The voices of brides and grooms
will never be heard in you again.
Your traders were among the world's most
important people.
By your magic spell all the nations were led
down the wrong path.
24 You were guilty of the murder of prophets and
God's people.
You were guilty of the blood of all who
have been killed on the earth."

Hallelujah!

19 After these things I heard a roar in heaven.
It sounded like a huge crowd shouting,

"Hallelujah!
Salvation and glory and power belong to
our God.

2 The way he judges is true and fair.
He has judged the great prostitute.
She polluted the earth with her terrible sins.
God has paid her back for killing those who
served him."

3Again they shouted,

"Hallelujah!
The smoke from her fire goes up for ever
and ever."

4The 24 elders and the four living creatures
bowed down. They worshiped God, who was sitting on the throne. They cried out,

"Amen! Hallelujah!"

5Then a voice came from the throne. It said,

"Praise our God,
all you who serve him!
Praise God, all you who have respect for him,
both great and small!"

6Then I heard the noise of a huge crowd. It
sounded like the roar of rushing waters and like
loud thunder. The people were shouting,

"Hallelujah!
Our Lord God is the King who rules
over all.
7 Let us be joyful and glad!
Let us give him glory!
It is time for the Lamb's wedding.
His bride has made herself ready.
8 Fine linen, bright and clean,
was given to her to wear."

Fine linen stands for the right things that God's
people do.

9Here is what the angel told me to write.
"Blessed are those who are invited to the wedding
supper of the Lamb!" Then he added, "These are
the true words of God."

10When I heard this, I fell at his feet to worship
him.

But he said to me, "Don't do that! I serve God,
just as you do. I am God's servant, just like other
believers who hold firmly to what Jesus has
taught. Worship God! What Jesus taught is the
very heart of prophecy."

The Rider on the White Horse

11I saw heaven standing open. There in front of
me was a white horse. Its rider is called Faithful
and True. When he judges or makes war, he is
always fair. 12His eyes are like blazing fire. On his
head are many crowns. A name is written on him
that only he knows. 13He is dressed in a robe
dipped in blood. His name is The Word of God.

14The armies of heaven were following him,
riding on white horses. They were dressed in fine
linen, white and clean.

15Out of the rider's mouth comes a sharp sword.
He will strike down the nations with it. Scripture
says, "He will rule them with an iron rod." *(Psalm
2:9)* He stomps on the grapes of God's winepress.
The winepress stands for the terrible anger of the
God who rules over all.

16Here is the name that is written on the rider's
robe and on his thigh.

THE GREATEST KING OF ALL
AND THE MOST POWERFUL LORD OF ALL

17I saw an angel standing in the sun. He cried in
a loud voice to all the birds flying high in the air,
"Come! Gather together for the great supper of
God. 18Come and eat the dead bodies of kings,
generals, and other mighty people. Eat the bodies
of horses and their riders. Eat the bodies of all people, free and slave, great and small."

19Then I saw the beast and the kings of the earth
with their armies. They had gathered together to
make war against the rider on the horse and his army.

20But the beast and the false prophet were captured. The false prophet had done miraculous signs
for the beast. In this way the false prophet had
tricked those who had received the mark of the beast
and had worshiped his statue. The beast and the false
prophet were thrown alive into the lake of fire that
burns with sulfur. 21The rest of them were killed with
the sword that came out of the rider's mouth. All the
birds stuffed themselves with the dead bodies.

The Thousand Years

20 I saw an angel coming down out of
heaven. He had the key to the Abyss. In his
hand he held a heavy chain.

2He grabbed the dragon, that old serpent. The
serpent is also called the devil, or Satan. The angel
put him in chains for 1,000 years. 3Then he threw
him into the Abyss. He locked it and sealed him
in. This was to keep Satan from fooling the nations
anymore until the 1,000 years were ended. After
that, he must be set free for a short time.

4I saw thrones. Those who had been given
authority to judge were sitting on them. I also saw
the souls of those whose heads had been cut off
because they had given witness for Jesus and
because of God's word. They had not worshiped
the beast or his statue. They had not received his
mark on their foreheads or hands. They came to
life and ruled with Christ for 1,000 years.

5This is the first resurrection. The rest of the
dead did not come to life until the 1,000 years
were ended.

6Blessed and holy are those who take part in the
first resurrection. The second death has no power
over them. They will be priests of God and of
Christ. They will rule with him for 1,000 years.

Satan Is Judged

7When the 1,000 years are over, Satan will be
set free from his prison. 8He will go out to fool the

nations. He will gather them from the four corners of the earth. He will bring Gog and Magog together for battle.

Their troops are as many as the grains of sand on the seashore. [9]They marched across the whole earth. They surrounded the place where God's people were camped. It was the city he loves. But fire came down from heaven and burned them up.

[10]The devil, who fooled them, was thrown into the lake of burning sulfur. That is where the beast and the false prophet had been thrown. They will all suffer day and night for ever and ever.

The Dead Are Judged

[11]I saw a great white throne and the One who was sitting on it. When the earth and sky saw his face, they ran away. There was no place for them.

[12]I saw the dead, great and small, standing in front of the throne. Books were opened. Then another book was opened. It was the Book of Life. The dead were judged by what they had done. The things they had done were written in the books. [13]The sea gave up the dead that were in it. And Death and Hell gave up their dead. Each of the dead was judged by what he had done.

[14]Then Death and Hell were thrown into the lake of fire. The lake of fire is the second death. [15]Anyone whose name was not written in the Book of Life was thrown into the lake of fire.

The New Jerusalem

21 I saw a new heaven and a new earth. The first heaven and the first earth were completely gone. There was no longer any sea.

[2]I saw the Holy City, the new Jerusalem. It was coming down out of heaven from God. It was prepared like a bride beautifully dressed for her husband.

[3]I heard a loud voice from the throne. It said, "Now God makes his home with people. He will live with them. They will be his people. And God himself will be with them and be their God. [4]He will wipe away every tear from their eyes. There will be no more death or sadness. There will be no more crying or pain. Things are no longer the way they used to be."

[5]He who was sitting on the throne said, "I am making everything new!" Then he said, "Write this down. You can trust these words. They are true."

[6]He said to me, "It is done. I am the Alpha and the Omega, the First and the Last. I am the Beginning and the End. Anyone who is thirsty may drink from the spring of the water of life. It doesn't cost anything! [7]Anyone who overcomes will receive all this from me. I will be his God, and he will be my child.

[8]"But others will have their place in the lake of fire that burns with sulfur. Those who are afraid and those who do not believe will be there. Murderers and those who pollute themselves will join them. Those who commit sexual sins and those who practice witchcraft will go there. Those who worship statues of gods and all who tell lies will be there too. It is the second death."

[9]One of the seven angels who had the seven bowls came and spoke to me. The bowls were filled with the seven last plagues. The angel said, "Come. I will show you the bride, the wife of the Lamb."

[10]Then he carried me away in a vision. The Spirit took me to a huge, high mountain. He showed me Jerusalem, the Holy City. It was coming down out of heaven from God. [11]It shone with the glory of God. It gleamed like a very valuable jewel. It was like a jasper, as clear as crystal.

[12]The city had a huge, high wall with 12 gates. Twelve angels were at the gates, one at each of them. On the gates were written the names of the 12 tribes of Israel. [13]There were three gates on the east and three on the north. There were three gates on the south and three on the west. [14]The wall of the city had 12 foundations. Written on them were the names of the 12 apostles of the Lamb.

[15]The angel who talked with me had a gold measuring rod. He used it to measure the city, its gates and its walls.

[16]The city was laid out like a square. It was as long as it was wide. The angel measured the city with the rod. It was 1,400 miles long. It was as wide and high as it was long.

[17]He measured the wall of the city. It was 200 feet thick. The angel did the measuring as a man would. [18]The wall was made out of jasper. The city was made out of pure gold, as pure as glass.

[19]The foundations of the city walls were decorated with every kind of jewel. The first foundation was made out of jasper. The second was made out of sapphire. The third was made out of chalcedony. The fourth was made out of emerald. [20]The fifth was made out of sardonyx. The sixth was made out of carnelian. The seventh was made out of chrysolite. The eighth was made out of beryl. The ninth was made out of topaz. The tenth was made out of chrysoprase. The eleventh was made out of jacinth. The twelfth was made out of amethyst.

[21]The 12 gates were made from 12 pearls. Each gate was made out of a single pearl. The main street of the city was made out of pure gold, as clear as glass.

[22]I didn't see a temple in the city. This was because the Lamb and the Lord God who rules over all are its temple. [23]The city does not need the sun or moon to shine on it. God's glory is its light, and the Lamb is its lamp.

[24]The nations will walk by the light of the city. The kings of the world will bring their glory into it. [25]Its gates will never be shut, because there will be no night there. [26]The glory and honor of the nations will be brought into it.

[27]Only what is pure will enter it. No one who fools others or does shameful things will enter it.

Only those whose names are written in the Lamb's
Book of Life will enter the city.

The River of Life

22 Then the angel showed me the river of the
water of life. It was as clear as crystal. It
flowed from the throne of God and of the Lamb. 2It
flowed down the middle of the city's main street.

On each side of the river stood the tree of life,
bearing 12 crops of fruit. Its fruit was ripe every
month. The leaves of the tree bring healing to the
nations.

3There will no longer be any curse. The throne
of God and of the Lamb will be in the city. God's
servants will serve him. 4They will see his face.
His name will be on their foreheads.

5There will be no more night. They will not
need the light of a lamp or the light of the sun. The
Lord God will give them light. They will rule for
ever and ever.

6The angel said to me, "You can trust these words.
They are true. The Lord is the God of the spirits of
the prophets. He sent his angel to show those who
serve him the things that must soon take place."

Jesus Is Coming

7"Look! I am coming soon! Blessed are those
who obey the words of the prophecy in this book."

8I, John, am the one who heard and saw these
things.

After I had heard and seen them, I fell down to
worship at the feet of the angel. He is the one who
had been showing me these things.

9But he said to me, "Don't do that! I serve God,
just as you do. I am God's servant, just like the
other prophets and all who obey the words of this
book. Worship God!"

10Then he told me, "Do not seal up the words of
the prophecy in this book. These things are about
to happen. 11Let those who do wrong keep on
doing wrong. Let those who are evil continue to
be evil. Let those who do what is right keep on
doing what is right. And let those who are holy
continue to be holy."

12"Look! I am coming soon! I bring my rewards
with me. I will reward each person for what he has
done. 13I am the Alpha and the Omega. I am the
First and the Last. I am the Beginning and the End.

14"Blessed are those who wash their robes. They
will have the right to come to the tree of life. They
will be allowed to go through the gates into the city.

15"Outside the city are the dogs and those who
practice witchcraft. Outside are also those who
commit sexual sins and murder. Those who worship statues of gods, and everyone who loves and
does what is false, are outside too.

16"I, Jesus, have sent my angel to give you this
witness for the churches. I am the Root and the
Son of David. I am the bright Morning Star."

17The Holy Spirit and the bride say, "Come!"
Let those who hear say, "Come!" Anyone who is
thirsty should come. Anyone who wants to take the
free gift of the water of life should do so.

18I am warning everyone who hears the words
of the prophecy of this book. If you add anything
to them, God will add to you the plagues told
about in this book. 19If you take any words away
from this book of prophecy, God will take away
from you your share in the tree of life. He will also
take away your place in the Holy City. This book
tells about these things.

20He who gives witness to these things says,
"Yes. I am coming soon."

Amen. Come, Lord Jesus!

21May the grace of the Lord Jesus be with God's
people. Amen.

Dictionary

A

abyss
A deep pit where evil spirits live. Satan will be held there in chains.

altar
A table or raised place on which a gift, or sacrifice, was offered to God.

amen
A word that means "it is true" or "let it be true."

angel
A spirit who is God's helper. A spirit who tells people God's words. See also cherubim.

anoint
1. To pour olive oil on people or things. This sets them apart for God. 2. To pour oil on people as part of praying for their healing.

anointed
To be set apart as God's special servant.

apostle
One of the twelve men who spent about three years with Jesus. They taught others about Jesus, too. See also disciple.

Aramaic
A language spoken by many people during Bible times. The Jews in Jesus' time most often spoke this language.

ark of the covenant
A large gold box that held the stone tablets of the Ten Commandments. The ark was God's throne on earth.

armor
A special outer covering like clothes made of metal. People wore it to help keep them safe in battle.

Asherah
A false god. People thought she was the Canaanite mother goddess and goddess of the sea.

B

Baal
The name of the most popular false god of Canaan.

Babel
A city where people tried to build a tower up to the sky.

Babylon
1. The capital city of the empire of Babylonia. 2. Any powerful, sinful city.

baptize
To sprinkle, pour on or cover a person with water. It is a sign that the person belongs to Jesus.

Beelzebub
Another name for the devil. Satan.

believe
To accept as true. To trust. See also faith.

blessed
1. Made joyful. 2. Helped by God.

C

cast lots
Something done to find out what God wants. It is like drawing straws to see who will go first.

chariot
A cart with two wheels pulled by horses. People, especially soldiers, rode in them.

cherubim
1. Spirits like angels who have large wings. They were and are a sign that God is sitting on his throne. 2. Spirits who serve God.

chief priest
See high priest.

Christ
A Greek word that means "the Anointed One." It is one of the names given to Jesus. It means the same thing as the Hebrew word Messiah. See also Jesus.

clean
1. Something that God accepts. 2. Something that doesn't have sin.

clean animals
Animals that God said were acceptable to eat or to give as offerings.

commandment
A law or rule that God gives. See also law.

concubine
A woman who belonged to a man but was not his legal wife.

Council
See Sanhedrin.

covenant
1. A treaty, or promise, between two persons or groups. In the Bible it is a promise made between God and the people. 2. Promises from God for salvation.

cross
A wooden post with a bar near the top that extends to the right and left. A cross looks like the letter "T." The Romans killed people by nailing them to crosses.

crucify
To kill people by nailing them to crosses.

curse
1. A call for God to punish someone. 2. A command of God that punishment will come on someone or something.

D

deacon
A church leader who helps people in Jesus' name.

dedicate
To set apart for a special purpose, often for God's use.

demon
An evil spirit.

devil
The one who tempts people to sin. See also Satan.

disciple
A person who follows a teacher. This person does what their teacher says to do. See also apostle. See also Twelve, the.

divorce
The end of a husband and wife's marriage.

E

Eden
The place where God made a garden for Adam and Eve.

elder
The leader of a church, town or nation. This person makes important decisions.

eternal
Forever. Without beginning or end.

evangelist
A person who tells others the Good News of Jesus.

evil
Bad. Wicked. Doing things that do not please God.

evil spirit
A demon. One of the devil's helpers.

F

faith
Trust and belief in God. Knowing that God is real, even though we can't see him. See also believe.

famine
A time when there is not enough food to eat.

fast
Going without food and/or drink for a special reason.

Feast of Booths
A celebration or festival when the Israelites thanked God for the harvest of their crops. During the feast they lived in little tents for seven days to help remember when they traveled to Canaan.

Feast of Hanukkah
A celebration praising God that the Israelites and Jews today have to remember the cleaning and rededication of the temple. The temple had been made "unclean" by an enemy.

Feast of Weeks
A festival or celebration day at the beginning of the wheat harvest when the Israelites gave thanks to God. See also Pentecost.

Feast of Passover
See Passover.

Feast of Unleavened Bread
A week for remembering when God set the Israelites free from Egypt. It began the day after the Feast of Passover. During this time the people ate bread made without yeast, like they did when they left Egypt in a hurry.

fig
A sweet fruit that grows on trees in warm countries like Israel.

G

glory
1. God's greatness. 2. Praise and honor.

God
The maker and ruler of the world and all people.

grace
The kindness and forgiveness God gives to people. This is a gift. It cannot be earned.

H

hallelujah
A Hebrew word that means "praise the LORD."

Hanukkah
See Feast of Hanukkah.

harvest
Picking a crop when it is ripe.

heaven
1. God's home. 2. The sky. 3. Where Christians go after they die.

Hebrew
1. Another name for an Israelite. 2. The language spoken by the Israelites. The Old Testament is written in this language.

hell
A place of punishment for people who don't follow Jesus. They go there after they die.

Herod
The first name of five rulers from the same family. They ruled over Israel during the time of the New Testament.

high places
Places where people worshiped false gods. These places were found on top of hills.

high priest
A person from the family line of Aaron. He was in charge of everything in the holy tent or in the temple. He was in charge of everyone who came there to work and worship, too.

holy
Set apart for God. Belonging to God. Pure.

holy bread
Twelve loaves of bread placed in the Holy Room of the holy tent each week. They were a gift to God.

Holy Spirit
God's Spirit who creates life. He helps people do God's work. He helps people to believe in Jesus, to love him and to live like him.

holy tent
Also called the Tent of Meeting. A place where the Israelites worshiped God. They used this tent

after they left Egypt and while they were in the desert for 40 years. Years later Solomon built the first temple. Then the people worshiped God there and not in the tent.

honor
To show respect to. To give credit to.

hosanna
A Hebrew word used to praise God.

hymn
A song of praise to God.

hyssop
A plant that smelled like mint. Its branches were used to shake water or blood on something to make it pure.

I

Immanuel
A name for Jesus that means "God with us."

incense
Spices that give a pleasing smell when they are burned. It was placed on the altar in the holy tent.

Israel
1. The new name God gave to Abraham's grandson Jacob. 2. The nation that came from the family line of Jacob. 3. The northern tribes that broke away from Judah to serve their own king.

Israelites
People from the nation of Israel. God's chosen people.

J

jealous
1. How God feels when people worship other things. 2. How we feel when someone else has something we want.

Jesus
The Greek form of the Hebrew name Joshua. It means "the LORD saves." See also Christ. See also Immanuel. See also Savior.

Jews
Another name for the people of Israel. This name was used after 600 B.C.

Jubilee
See Year of Jubilee.

judge
1. To decide if something is right or wrong. 2. A person who decides what is right or wrong in legal matters.

K

kingdom
An area or group of people ruled by a king.

L

law
Rules about what is right and wrong that God gave the people of Israel. See also law, the.

Law, the
The first five books of the Bible.

Levites
Men from the tribe of Levi. They took care of the holy tent and the temple.

locust
A type of insect similar to a grasshopper. A huge number of them sometimes eats and destroys crops.

Lord
A personal name for God or Christ. It shows respect to him as our master and ruler.

M

manger
A food box for animals.

manna
Special food sent from heaven. It tasted like wafers, or crackers, sweetened with honey. God gave it to the Israelites in the desert, after they left Egypt.

mercy
More kindness and forgiveness than people deserve to get.

Messiah
A Hebrew word that means, "The Anointed One." It means the same thing as the Greek word *Christ*. See also Jesus.

miracle
An amazing thing that happens that only God can do. This includes such things as calming a storm or bringing someone back to life.

miraculous signs
Amazing things that God does to point us to him. These things cannot be explained by the laws of nature.

myrrh
A spice with a sweet smell. It came from plants and was made into perfume, incense and medicine.

N

nard
A costly oil made from a plant grown in India. It was used as a perfume to make skin smell good.

Nazarene
A person who came from the town of Nazareth. Jesus was called a Nazarene.

Nazirite
A person who was set apart to God in a special way. Or, a person who promised to do something special for God.

O

oath
A promise made before God.

obey
To do what you are told to do. To carry out God's commands.

offering
Something people give to God. It was and is a part of their worship. See also sacrifice.

P

papyrus
A tall, grassy plant that grows in shallow water. People made boats with these plants and paper from their stems.

Passover
A feast that happened every year. It reminded the people of the time when God "passed over" their homes in Egypt. Since the people put blood on the doorways, God did not hurt them.

paradise
A perfect place. Another name used for heaven.

Pentecost
1. A Jewish celebration held 50 days after Passover. 2. The day the Holy Spirit came in a special way to live in Christians.

Pharaoh
The title of the ruler of Egypt in Bible times.

Pharisees
A group of Jews who carefully followed God's laws and their own rules about God's laws. Some Pharisees were also known as "teachers of the law."

Philistines
Strong enemies of Israel, especially during Saul and David's time.

pillar
1. A tall, upright post that helped to hold up a building. 2. A pillar could also mark a special place.

pillar of cloud
A cloud God used to lead the people of Israel. They could see it all day long when they were in the desert.

pillar of fire
A column of fire God used to lead the people of Israel. They could see it all night long when they were in the desert.

plague
1. A sickness that kills many people. 2. Anything that brings a lot of suffering or loss.

plumb line
A string that has a weight tied to the end of it. It is used to tell whether a wall is straight or not.

pomegranate
A round fruit with a tough skin, many seeds and a juicy red center.

praise
To give glory or honor to someone. To say good things about someone or something.

Preparation Day
The day before the Sabbath day. A day to get all work done so that a person could rest on the Sabbath.

priest
A person who worked in the holy tent or the temple. He was responsible to give his own as well as other people's gifts and prayers to God.

prophecy
Important words or messages that God gives to his people. God gives these words through a special person called a prophet.

prophesy
1. To give a message from God. 2. To tell what the future will be.

prophet
A person who hears messages from God and tells them to others.

proverb
A wise saying.

psalm
A poem of praise, prayer or teaching. The book of Psalms is full of these poems.

Purim
A feast in which the Israelites remembered when God helped Queen Esther save the Jews.

R

Rabbi
The title of a teacher of Jewish law.

resurrection
Coming back to life in a whole new way and never dying again.

right hand
A place of honor and power. Jesus is at the right hand of God.

Rome
1. The empire that controlled a lot of the world when Jesus lived here on the earth. 2. The capital city of that empire. It is in Italy.

S

Sabbath
The seventh day of the week. On that day the Israelites rested from their work and turned their thoughts toward God.

sacred
Set apart for God. Holy.

sacrifice
1. To give something to God as a gift. 2. Something that is given to God as a gift of worship. See also offering.

Sadducees
A group of Jewish leaders. They followed only the first five books of the Bible. They did not believe that people rise from the dead.

salvation
Free from the guilt of sin. Jesus died for our sins and rose up from the dead. With this sacrifice, he paid for our sin. He has saved us if we believe in him.

Sanhedrin
A group of 71 Jewish leaders. They were led by the high priest. They were the most important Jewish court of law in Jesus' time.

Satan
God's most powerful enemy in the spirit world. Also called the devil.

saved
Set free from danger or sin.

Savior
The One who sets us free from our sins. A name belonging to Jesus Christ. See also Jesus.

Scripture
God's written Word to us. We also call this the Bible.

scroll
A long strip of paper or animal skin to write on. It was rolled up on two sticks to make it easy to use and store.

seal
1. A tool or a ring with a drawing or pattern cut into it. 2. A mark made by pressing this tool into clay, wax or paper.

seer
A person who can tell the future with God's help. See also prophet.

shepherd
A person who takes care of sheep or goats.

sin
To disobey or displease God.

Sodom and Gomorrah
Two cities that God destroyed. The people who lived there were very evil.

Son of Man
A name Jesus gave to himself. It shows he is the Messiah. See also Messiah.

soul
A person's true inner self.

spiritual
Having to do with the things of God or the Bible.

staff
A stick a shepherd uses to take care of sheep or goats.

synagogue
A Jewish place of worship and teaching.

T

tassels
Hanging groups of thread that are tied together at one end. God told the Israelites to sew tassels onto their clothing to remind them of God's commands.

temple
1. Any place of worship. 2. The building where the people of Israel worshiped God and brought their sacrifices. God was present there in a special way.

tempt
To try to get someone to do bad things.

Tent of Meeting
See holy tent.

threshing floor
A place where heads, or tops, of grain are beaten or stepped on. This is done to knock the seeds of grain from the stems.

tomb
A place to put dead bodies. It was often a cave with a big, stone door.

treaty
An agreement between two people or groups or nations.

Twelve, the
The men who Jesus chose to be his special followers. See also disciples.

U

unclean
Something that God does not accept. Not pure. Not pleasing to God.

Urim and Thummim
Objects that were worn on the high priest's vest. They were used by the high priest to get a message from God.

V

vineyard
A place where grapes grow and are picked.

vision
A dream from God. The person who saw it was usually awake. God gave these kinds of dreams to people to show them what he was going to do.

W

wafer
A thin, crisp cracker. Wafers were one kind of offering the Israelites brought to the Lord.

widow
A woman whose husband has died.

winepress
A place where juice is pressed out of grapes to make wine.

wisdom
Understanding that comes from God. Wise thinking.

worship
To give praise, honor and glory to God.

Y

Year of Jubilee
A special year that was to happen every 50 years in Israel. No crops could be planted. Any money that was owed was forgiven. Slaves were set free. Property was given back to its first owner.

yoke
1. A strong piece of wood. It fit on the necks of two oxen so that they could pull carts or plows. 2. A piece of wood put on the neck of a slave or a prisoner.

Z

Zealot
A Jew who was willing to fight to get rid of the Roman rulers. Simon may have been part of this group before becoming one of Jesus' twelve disciples.

Zion
1. The city of Jerusalem. 2. The hill on which King David's house and the temple once stood. 3. Another name sometimes used for heaven.

About the Bible

What Is the Bible?

The word *Bible* means "book." The book we call the Bible was given this name because it is the most important book in the world. The Bible is also called *Scripture*. *Scripture* means "something written." The Bible is like a library of books. In fact, the Bible has 66 books. But the Bible is more than a collection of books. The Bible is the Word of God. The Bible gives God's message to us. It tells us about God. The Bible shows us God's mighty acts in the lives of his people. It tells us how the people responded to God. From the Bible we can learn what God is like and what he expects us to do.

How the Bible Was Written

It took a long time to write the Bible. It took about 1500 years. The first book, Genesis, was written at the time of Moses. John wrote the last book, Revelation. He wrote it about 65 years after Christ's death. Many different people wrote the Bible. They lived at different times. They wrote in different places. But none of their words contradict each other. God guided them when they wrote. The writers used their own words to say what God wanted them to say. This makes the Bible a completely dependable book. We can trust and believe everything it says.

The Old Testament

The Bible has two major parts. The first part is called the Old Testament. The second part is called the New Testament. The Old Testament has 39 books. Jews and Christians accept these books as Scripture. The Old Testament starts with the story of creation. It tells about the beginning of the world. It tells about the start of the human race too. Then it gives the history of God's chosen people. It tells about Abraham, Isaac and Jacob. It tells how God made their children into the nation of Israel. In the Old Testament God begins to show his plan to save us from sin. God gives lots of promises in the Old Testament too. He promises many times to send the Messiah to save us from our sins.

The New Testament

The New Testament is made up of 27 books. Christians accept these books as Scripture. The New Testament tells about Jesus Christ, the Messiah. It tells about his life and death. And it tells how God brought Jesus back to life too. It explains why Jesus died. It teaches us how to be saved from sin. The New Testament tells about the start of the Christian church too.

How the Bible Came to Us

When the Bible was written, it was written by hand. The only way someone could have a Bible was if they copied it completely by hand. Men who copied the Bible were called scribes. They worked day by day copying the Bible. They carefully copied it letter by letter. This took a long time. And very few people owned a copy of the Bible.

The Old Testament was written in many languages. It was first written in Hebrew and Aramaic. About 250 years before Jesus' birth, it was copied into Greek. The New Testament was written in Greek too. About 350 years after Jesus' death, people spoke a new language. That language was Latin. Jerome was a leader in the early church. He copied the Bible into Latin. His copy of the Bible was called the Vulgate. This Bible was used in Europe for more than 1,000 years.

As time passed, no one spoke Latin anymore. Many people spoke English. John Wycliffe lived in the late 1300s. He was a Bible teacher. He wanted people to read the Bible in their own language. He and his friends copied the Bible into English. The printing press had not been invented yet. John and his friends copied their Bibles by hand. They made only a few copies. About 140 years later William Tyndale copied the New Testament from Greek into English. This was the first English Bible made on a printing press.

The king of England wanted a new Bible too. Bible teachers wrote it in 1611. It is the best-known English Bible. It is the King James Version. In the last 100 years many new English Bibles have been written. The people who wrote these Bibles were very careful. They did not want to make any mistakes. They wanted people to learn about God. They wanted people to understand God's Word.

The New International Version of the Bible is a new English Bible. It was finished in 1978. The people who wrote it were very careful too. They checked the Hebrew Old Testament. They checked the Greek New Testament. They looked at every word. They wanted to know just what the writers of the Bible said. Then they wrote their English Bible. They wanted to use the same words we use today when we talk to each other. They wanted us to understand God's Word. They wanted us to know God's plan for our lives.

The Bible you hold in your hand is very special. It has been put together very carefully. It is the true Word of God. Yet it is easy to understand. It uses short sentences. It uses short words. It explains words that may be hard to understand. We hope you will put your faith in Jesus after reading this Bible. We hope you will become a strong believer after studying it. And if that happens, we will give God all of the glory.

Life in New Testament Times

Many years ago there were trails that came into the land of Israel. They came from the east and from the north. Other trails came from Egypt in the south.

Traders used these trails to travel from one place to another. They traveled mostly by camel. They bought and sold goods along the way. The trails went through Israel. But they also met in Israel. It was almost like Israel was the center of the world.

In a way, Israel was the center of the world. Jesus was born there. All of the things that happened in Bible times seemed to say, "Israel is a special land."

Places of Worship

The beautiful temple stood in the city of Jerusalem. It was the center of worship for the Jews. Herod rebuilt the temple not long before Jesus was born. The temple was on a hill. Its shining white marble walls could be seen all over the city. Large stone gates opened on all four sides. Jesus called this temple his Father's house (John 2:16).

Each Jewish town also had a smaller meeting place. These were called "synagogues." The leader of the synogogue studied the Old Testament and the Jewish laws. He then could teach the people.

On the inside synagogues looked much like some of our churches. The people sat on benches. The leader stood on a stage. A special box held the scrolls of the books of the Bible.

On the Sabbath day the people came to the synagogue to worship. The leader read a verse to call the people to worship. Then there were readings of thanksgiving and praise. Someone would lead in prayer. After that, the leader might ask someone to read from the Bible. Any member who was able to teach could give the sermon. The service was closed with a blessing.

The Laws of God

God gave the Jews the Ten Commandments and many other laws at Mount Sinai. Many Jews thought that trying to keep the law was the only way to please God. They began to add many of their own laws to God's laws. They began to see themselves as very good people.

Jesus told the Jews that they were going in the wrong direction. They were so busy doing many little things that they were forgetting big things that were more important. They were forgetting to love others. They were forgetting to take care of the poor. They were forgetting to love God.

The Sabbath Day

God gave the people of Israel the Sabbath as a day of rest. On the seventh day of every week they rested from their work. They offered special sacrifices.

The scribes and Pharisees later added hundreds of laws about how people should keep the Sabbath day holy. Then the people forgot that God gave the Sabbath day to be a special day. Instead they just worried about obeying all the rules.

On the Sabbath day people could not travel very far. They could not carry anything from one place to another. They were not supposed to spit on the ground. If they did they might be plowing a little row in the dirt. And that would be work! If a hen laid an egg on the Sabbath, they were not supposed to eat that egg. The hen had worked on the Sabbath to lay it.

When Jesus and his disciples picked some grain and ate it on the Sabbath, the Pharisees said they were working. When Jesus healed sick people on the Sabbath, the Pharisees said he was breaking the law. They got angry and wanted to kill him.

Religious Groups

The most important religious groups in New Testament times were the Pharisees and the Sadducees. The Sadducees were rich and powerful men. The high priest, the chief priests and rich businessmen all belonged to the Sadducees. The Sadducees were against any new group that tried to change Jewish life. That's why they were against Jesus and his disciples. The Sadducees also turned away from many of the teachings of the Pharisees. They did not believe that people would rise from the dead. They did not believe in angels or demons. They did not keep all the laws of the Pharisees. They only kept the law of Moses.

The Pharisees added hundreds of laws to the law God gave Moses. They were mostly interested in keeping all these laws. Many of the Pharisees forgot God's other laws. They were proud of how good they were, but they did not love other people. However, there were also Pharisees who truly loved God and others and tried to do what was right.

Seventy of the most important Pharisees and Sadducees made up the Jewish high court. This court was called the Sanhedrin. The high priest led the court. The Romans let this court decide what to do when someone had broken a Jewish law. But this court did not have the power to put anyone to death. If the Sanhedrin thought someone should die, they had to bring the person to the Roman courts.

The Roman Empire

Rome had begun to grow larger and stronger before Christ was born. Wars were fought and many new lands were added to the Roman Empire. This empire was very large. It included Spain and Germany, North Africa, Asia Minor, Syria and Israel.

Many good things happened because of Roman rule. There was peace among all of the different countries in the empire. The Romans also set up good government everywhere. They built roads for safe and easy travel. Many of the people were able to speak and understand the same language—Greek.

The Romans did not know that all these things would make it easier for the gospel to spread to many lands. They did not know that God had prepared the way for Jesus and the spread of the good news. Later Jesus' disciples traveled more easily to far-away lands because there was peace and because there were good roads. They could bring the gospel in the Greek language to many people in many areas.

Tax Collectors

The Jews hated the Romans. They believed the Romans had no right to rule over them. They believed the Romans had no right to take their money for taxes. They didn't like the soldiers who lived in their country. The Jews also hated the Romans because they tried to change the Jewish way of life. The Romans wanted everyone to act like Romans. The Jews were looking for the Messiah. They thought he would become their king and would free them from the Romans.

The Jews hated tax collectors even more than Romans. Many tax collectors were Jews who were working for Rome. Many tax collectors were not honest. They took more money than they were supposed to take. They were cheating their own people to help the enemy.

Jesus often talked and ate with tax collectors. Matthew was a tax collector. So was Zacchaeus. Both became followers of Jesus.

Everyday Life

Life in New Testament times was much different from life today. It was a simple life. Most people did not have any extras. In fact, they often had just enough to live. The people worked hard, and children had to share in the work.

The people built their houses of mud bricks that were hardened by laying them out in the sun. Sometimes the front part of the house had no roof over it. This part was like a small yard. Behind it was a living room with small bedrooms at the back. The floor of the house was of hard and smooth clay. Builders made the roof of heavy wooden beams with boards laid across them. They covered the boards with a mixture of mud and straw. This flat roof was a good place to work or to sit. Sometimes people slept on the roof on hot nights. Usually a ladder or sometimes steps led up to the roof.

Most people had very little furniture–just some wooden stools, a low wooden table and some sleeping mats. There was a place for fire and sometimes a small clay oven for baking bread. There was no chimney, so the smoke had to find its way out of the small, high window openings. Some houses had wooden doors. Others had doorways covered with grass mats or cloth.

Food

The people ate foods like milk and cheese, grapes, figs, olives, honey and barley cakes, eggs, chicken, fish, goat meat, beans, cucumbers and onions.

The first meal of the day was usually bread and cheese. Sometimes a family would eat a light meal at noon. Again, bread was the main part. The people had their large meal of the day in the evening. They usually ate bread and fish, fruit and vegetables. The common people often ate meat only on very special days.

Clothing

The clothing of New Testament times was simple. Besides underclothing, the people wore robes with a belt tied around the waist. Over the robe they often wore a cape. Children usually had shorter, knee-length clothing. They sometimes wore a kind of pull-over shirt. Women decorated their clothing with brightly colored weaving and sewing.

The people wore sandals without socks. Their feet were often dusty from walking on their dirt streets and roads. They washed their feet often.

Work

The people did many different kinds of work. Some were farmers and builders and makers of pottery. Others were bakers and doctors and teachers. There were watchmen who guarded the cities. There were workers in leather and workers in metal. Jesus' father was a carpenter. Jesus also knew about herding sheep. Peter and James and John were fishermen. Matthew was a tax collector. There were scribes who wrote letters and copied the laws and the books of the Bible.

Women had to work hard in their homes. The first thing they would do in the morning was make the bread for the day. They would grind the grain into flour, then make dough into loaves of bread and bake them. The women also had to carry water from the well and get wood for the fire. They made all the clothes for the family, spinning and weaving their own cloth out of flax and wool.

Parents expected their children to help with the work. Girls helped their mothers with all the household work. Boys helped their fathers in their work and were expected to follow the same trade as their fathers.

Schools

Parents taught their children Bible verses when they were still very young. They learned verses from the law and stories from the Old Testament.

When boys were five or six years old, they went to school. The leader of the synagogue taught them. For the first four years, they studied mostly the first five books of the Bible. By then they knew the laws of God very well. They also learned how to read and write Hebrew. For the next several years they studied other books of the Bible and other Jewish writings.

When a Jewish boy reached the age of twelve or thirteen, he was considered to be a man. The boy and his family and friends celebrated with a special ceremony and often a party. Most boys left school at this age.

Conclusion

The time of the New Testament was the best time for Jesus to come. The people were looking and waiting for him. The safe roads made it much easier for early Christians to travel to spread the good news of the Savior. The common language made it much easier for them to tell others about Jesus. People were eager to hear about him. God had everything planned and ready.

The ABCs of Salvation

A

All people are sinners.

Romans 3:23

Everyone has sinned. No one measures up to God's glory.

B

The **Bible** is God's word of love and salvation.

John 20:31

But these are written down so that you may believe that Jesus is the Christ, the Son of God. If you believe this, you will have life because you belong to him.

C

The **condition** of sinners is serious.

2 Thessalonians 2:12

Many will not believe the truth. They will take pleasure in evil. They will be judged.

D

Christ **died** to save sinners.

Romans 5:8

While we were still sinners, Christ died for us.

E

Everyone who believes will have **eternal** life.

John 3:16

Anyone who believes in [Jesus] will not die but will have eternal life.

F

You are saved through **faith.**

Romans 1:17

The good news shows how God makes people right with himself. From beginning to end, becoming right with God depends on a person's faith.

G

Good works will not save you.

Ephesians 2:8–9

God's grace has saved you because of your faith in Christ. Your salvation doesn't come from anything you do. It is God's gift. It is not based on anything you have done.

H

Hell and punishment are waiting for those who don't believe.

2 Thessalonians 1:8–9

He will punish those who don't know God. He will punish those who don't obey the good news about our Lord Jesus. They will be destroyed forever. They will be shut out of heaven. They will never see the glory of the Lord's power.

I

Nothing is **impossible** for God.

Luke 1:37

Nothing is impossible with God.

J

There is **joy** in heaven over one sinner who repents.

Luke 15:10

There is joy in heaven over one sinner who turns away from sin.

K

If you trust God, he will **keep** you from sin.

Jude 24

Give praise to the One who is able to keep you from falling into sin.

L

God **loves** sinners and wants to save them.

John 3:16

God loved the world so much that he gave his one and only Son. Anyone who believes in him will not die but will have eternal life.

M

God has **mercy** on unbelievers.

Romans 11:32

God has found everyone guilty of not obeying him. So now he can have mercy on everyone.

N

Jesus is the only **name** by which you can be saved.

Acts 4:12

You can't be saved by believing in anyone else. God has given us no other name under heaven that will save us.

O

You show God you love him by **obeying** his commandments.

1 John 5:3

Here is what it means to love God. It means that we obey his commands. And his commands are not hard to obey.

P

God is **patient** with unbelievers.

2 Peter 3:9

The Lord is not slow to keep his promise. He is not slow in the way some people understand it. He is patient with you. He doesn't want anyone to be destroyed. Instead, he wants all people to turn away from their sins.

Q

Those who don't believe should **quickly** decide to follow Jesus.

2 Corinthians 6:2

I tell you, now is the time God shows his favor. Now is the day he saves.

R

Christians have a reason to **rejoice.**

Luke 10:20

Be glad that your names are written in heaven.

S

The Bible, the **Scriptures,** can teach you how to be saved.

2 Timothy 3:15

You have known the Holy Scriptures ever since you were a little child. They are able to teach you how to be saved by believing in Christ Jesus.

T

You should give **thanks** to God for the wonderful gift of salvation.

2 Corinthians 9:15

Let us give thanks to God for his gift. It is so great that no one can tell how wonderful it really is!

U

The Holy Spirit helps us **understand** God's Word.

1 Corinthians 2:12

We have not received the spirit of the world. We have received the Spirit who is from God. The Spirit helps us understand what God has freely given us.

V

Jesus has gained **victory** over death for you.

1 Corinthians 15:54

What does not last will be dressed with what lasts forever. What dies will be dressed with what does not die. Then what is written will come true. It says, "Death has been swallowed up. It has lost the battle."

W

Whoever calls on Jesus will be saved.

Acts 2:21

Everyone who calls on the name of the Lord will be saved.

Y

God loves **you** so much he calls you his child.

1 John 3:1

How great is the love the Father has given us so freely! Now we can be called children of God. And that's what we really are!

NIrV Children's Bible
Beginner's Bible edition

Project Management and Editorial:
Catherine DeVries and Donna Huisjen
Interior Design and Typesetting:
Sherri Hoffman and Nancy Wilson,
Zondervan Composition, Grand Rapids, MI
Interior Proofreading: Peachtree Editorial and
Proofreading Service, Peachtree City, GA
Printing: RR Donnelley & Sons Company, Crawfordsville, IN

Guarantee

Zondervan's manufacturer's warranty provides coverage for defective bindings on hardcover, softcover, Leather-Look™ and Italian Duo-Tone™ Bibles for four years, and on bonded and top-grain leather Bibles for six years. This warranty does not apply to normal wear. A lifetime warranty applies to defects within the Bible – for example: missing or misplaced pages, chapters or books. Please return defective Bibles to the original place of purchase for replacement or refund. If this is not possible, please go to www.zondervan.com and click on "Contact Us."

Care

We suggest loosening the binding of your new Bible by gently pressing on a small section of pages at a time from the center. To ensure against breakage of the spine, it is best not to bend the cover backward around the spine or to carry study notes, church bulletins, pens, and the like, inside the cover. Because a felt-tipped marker will "bleed" through the pages, we recommend use of a ball-point pen or pencil to underline favorite passages. Your Bible should not be exposed to excessive heat, cold or humidity. Protecting the gold or silver edges of the paper from moisture will avoid spotting, streaking or fading.